TABLE OF CONTENTS-Contin

GENERAL SERVICE

GEN —TAB 3

Page No.

BUICK

CADILLAC

CHEVROLET

OLDSMOBILE

PONTIAC

ERVICE

AUTO REPAIR MANUAL

DAIMLERCHRYSLER CORPORATION, FORD MOTOR COMPANY AND GENERAL MOTORS CORPORATION

65th Edition, Volume 1

First Printing

MOTOR
INFORMATION SYSTEMS

MOTOR is a trademark of Hearst Business Publishing, Inc.

Published by Motor Information Systems, a division of Hearst Business Publishing, Inc. A Unit Of The Hearst Corporation

5600 Crooks Road, Troy, MI 48098
Printed in the U.S.A.

ISBN 1-58251-087-3

VEHICLE IDENTIFICATION

INDEX

1st POSITION
COUNTRY
1 = United States
2 = Canada
3 = Mexico
4 = United States

2nd POSITION
MAKE
B = Dodge
C = Chrysler
E = Eagle
P = Plymouth

3rd POSITION
VEHICLE TYPE
3 = Passenger Car
4 = Multipurpose Vehicle
7 = Truck

4th POSITION
RESTRAINT/G.V.W.R.
RESTRAINT
A = Dual Air Bags
A = Air Bag
A = Auto Belts & Driver Air Bag
A = Manual Belts & Dual Air Bags
B = Automatic Belts
B = Manual Belts
C = Automatic Belts
C = Manual Belts
D = W/O Air Bags
E = Active Dual Air Bags
E = Active, Passenger Air Bag
E = Manual Belts & Dual Air Bags
F = Manual Belts (Mexico)
H = HYBRID Air Bag
H = Active Dual AirBag
X = Air Bag, Passenger Manual
Y = Air Bag, Passenger Automatic
G.V.W.R.
D = 1-3000 LB
E = 3001-4000 LB
F = 4001-5000 LB
G = 5001-6000 LB
H = 6001-7000 LB

5th POSITION
CARLINE
A = LeBaron LE/Landau
A = Spirit/Spirit LE
A = Acclaim
C = New Yorker
C = Chrysler "LHS"
C = New Yorker Salon
C = Dynasty/Dynasty LE
C = Town & Country
D = Concorde LX/LXI
D = Intrepid
D = Vision
D = New Yorker
D = Chrysler "LHS"
D = Caravan/Grand Caravan
E = Chrysler Vision
E = 300M
F = Laser/Talon (FWD)
G = Laser/Talon (AWD)
H = Minivan (FWD)
H = Intrepid
J = Stratus
J = Cirrus LX / LXI / Breeze
K = Minivan (AWD)
K = Talon / Talon ESI/ TSI (FWD)
L = Concorde
L = Sebring Convertible
L = Talon / Talon TSI(AWD)
L = Sebring (JX) (JXi)
M = Lebaren

5th POSITION (Cont'd)
CARLINE
P = Shadow/Shadow ES
P = Sundance/Duster
P = Minivan (FWD)
R = Viper, RT/10 & "GTS" Coupe
R = Durango 2WD
S = Laser/Talon (FWD)
S = Neon/Neon Sport
S = Durango 4WD
T = Laser/Talon (AWD)
T = Minivan (AWD)
U = LeBaron/LeBaron LS
U = LeBaron GTC/Convertible
U = Sebring/Avenger
V = Imperial
V = New Yorker Fifth Ave
W = Daytona/Daytona ES
W = Daytona IROC
W = Daytona IROC R/T
W = Prowler (RWD) Roadster
7 = R/T

6th POSITION
SERIES
1 = Economy (E)
2 = Low Line (L)
2 = Caravan / Grand Caravan
2 = Voyager / Grand Voyager
2 = Talon
2 = Durango & Durango SLT
3 = Medium Line (M)
4 = High Line (H)
4 = Talon ESI
4 = Avenger / Avenger ES
4 = Sebring LX
4 = SE Minivan
4 = Concorde/Intrepid
5 = Premium (P)
5 = Avenger ES
5 = Talon TSI (FWD)
5 = Talon Tsi Turbo FWD & AWD
5 = Sebring LXI
5 = Caravan / Grand Caravan LE /ES
5 = Voyager LE / SE & Grand Voyager LE / SE.
5 = Intrepid ES/LHS
6 = Special/Sport (S)
6 = Sebring LX
6 = Town & country LXI
7 = Performance / Image (X)
7 = Sport Utility (2WD)
8 = Talon TSI (AWD)
8 = Avenger ES
8 = Sport Utility (4WD)

7th POSITION
BODY STYLE
PASSENGER CAR
1 = 2 Door Coupe/Sedan
2 = 2 Door Pillared H.T.
4 = 2 Door Hatchback
4 = 3 Door Hatchback
4 = NS
5 = 2 Door Convertible
5 = NS
5 = Convertible - Open Body
6 = 4 Door Sedan
7 = 4 Door Pillared H.T.
8 = 4 Door Hatchback
9 = 4 Door Wagon
9 = 2 Door Specialty Coupe
TRUCK
1 = Van
4 = Extended Wagon/Van
5 = Wagon
8 = Sport Utility 4 Door

8th POSITION
ENGINE CODE
A = 2.2-L4, 16V Turbo III
A = 1.8-L4
B = 2.5-L4, TBI
B = 1.8-L4, MFI
B = 2.4-L4, 16V DOHC MPI
B = 2.0-L4, DOHC MPI
C = 2.0-L4, 16V SOHC
C = 2.2-L4, Turbo
D = 2.2-L4, TBI
E = 8.0-V10, MPI
E = 8.0-V10, SFI
E = 2.0-L4, MFI
E = 2.0-L4, MPI Turbo
F = 3.5-V6, 24V MPI
F = 2.0-L4, MFI Turbo
F = 2.0 DOHC_MPI Turbo
F = 2.0L-L4 Turbo T/C
G = 2.4-V6, MPI
G = 3.5-V6, SOHC 24 Valve
H = 2.5-L4, SPI
H = 2.5-V6, SOHC
J = 2.5-L4, Turbo
J = 3.3-V6, CNG
J = 3.2-V6, SOHC 24 Valve
K = 2.5-L4, TBI
L = 3.8-V6, MPI
L = 3.8-V6, SFI
M = 2.5-L4, Eurostar Diesel
N = 2.0-L4, SFI-SOHC
N = 2.5-V6, 24 Valve
N = 2.5 SOHC, MPI
P = 2.5-L4, SFI Turbo II
R = 3.3-V6, MPI
R = 2.0-L4, MPI
R = 2.7-V6, DOHC 24 Valve
S = 2.4-L4, DOHC Turbo
T = 1.8-L4, MPI
T = 3.3-V6, MPI
U = 2.0-L4, MPI Turbo
U = 3.3-V6, Flex Fuel MPI
V = 2.5-L4, Flex Fuel TBI
W = 2.5-L4, TBI
X = 2.4-L4, 16V DOHC
X = 3.9-V6
Y = 5.2-V8
Y = 2.0-L4, SFI-DOHC
Y = 2.0-L4, MPI
Z = 5.9-V8
2 = 2.5-L4, SFI Turbo
3 = 3.0-V6, MPI
9 = 54-KW, Electric

9th POSITION
CHECK DIGIT

10th POSITION
MODEL YEAR
N = 1992
P = 1993
R = 1994
S = 1995
T = 1996
V = 1997
W = 1998
X = 1999

11th POSITION
ASSEMBLY PLANT

12th Thru 17th POSITION
PRODUCTION SEQUENCE NUMBER

CR1130200945010X

Fig. 1 VIN Identification (Part 1 of 2). DaimlerChrysler

1st POSITION
COUNTRY
1 = United States
2 = Canada
3 = Mexico
4 = United States

2nd POSITION
MAKE
B = Dodge
C = Chrysler
E = Eagle
P = Plymouth

3rd POSITION
VEHICLE TYPE
3 = Passenger Car
4 = Multipurpose Vehicle
7 = Truck
8 = MPV w/Side Air Bags
A = PT Cruiser w/Side Air Bags

4th POSITION
RESTRAINT/G.V.W.R.
RESTRAINT
A = Active Front & Side Air Bags
A = Manual Belts & Dual Air Bags
B = Manual/Active Uni-Belt
C = Front Manual Belts
D = W/O Air Bag
E = Front Manual Belts
E = Active Belts & Dual Air Bags
E = Dual Air Bags
H = Active Front Air Bags (CGW)
G.V.W.R.
D = 1-3000 LB
E = 3001-4000 LB
F = 4001-5000 LB
G = 5001-6000 LB
H = 6001-7000 LB

5th POSITION
CARLINE
C = LHS
D = Concorde LX/LXI
D = Intrepid
E = 300M
G = Stratus
G = Sebring
H = Intrepid
H = Caravan/Grand Caravan
H = Voyager/Grand Voyager
J = Breeze
J = Cirrus LX/LXI
J = Stratus
J = Sebring LX/LXi
J = Voyager
L = Stratus
L = Sebring JX/JXI & Convertible
L = Caravan
L = Voyager/Grand Voyager
M = Stratus
P = Town & Country, FWD
P = Voyager/Grand Voyager, FWD
P = Grand Caravan, FWD
P = Caravan, FWD
R = Durango 2WD
R = Viper RT/10
R = GTS Coupe
S = Town & Country
S = Neon
S = Durango 4WD

5th POSITION (Cont'd)
CARLINE
T = AWD, Grand Caravan, Voyager, Town & Country
W = Prowler (RWD) Roadster
Y = PT Cruiser
2 = Stratus (Mexico Built)
7 = Viper, R/T or GTS

6th POSITION
SERIES
1 = Economy (E)
2 = Low Line (L)
2 = Durango & Durango SLT
2 = Grand/Caravan, Grand/Voyager
3 = Medium Line (M)
4 = High Line (H)
4 = Concorde/Intrepid
4 = PT Cruiser
4 = Stratus, ES, Sebring LX
4 = Grand/Caravan SE Sport, Grand/Voyager SE/Rallye
5 = Premium Line
5 = Intrepid ES/LHS
5 = Stratus ES, Sebring Lxi
5 = Grand/Caravan LE / ES, Grand/Voyager LE, Town & Country LX
6 = X Series
6 = Special/Sport
6 = 300M
6 = Town & Country LXI
7 = X Series

7th POSITION
BODY STYLE
PASSENGER CAR
1 = 2 Door
2 = 2 Door Pillared Hardtop
4 = NS
4 = 3Door Hatchback
5 = 2 Door Convertible
5 = NS
5 = Convertible - Open Body
6 = 4 Door Sedan
7 = 4 Door Pillared Hardtop
8 = Sport Utility
9 = 2 Door Specialty Coupe
B = Hatch Back
TRUCK
1 = Van
4 = Extended Wagon/Van
5 = Wagon
8 = Sport Utility 4 Door

8th POSITION
ENGINE CODE
B = 2.4-L4, 16 valve
B = 2.0-16 valve
C = 2.0-L4, 16 valve
E = 8.0-V10
F = 2.0L- 4Cyl, SOHC
F = 3.5-V6, 24 valve
G = 3.5-V6, 24 valve
G = 2.4L
H = 2.5-L4, V6
H = 3.0L
J = 3.5-V6, DOHC
J = 3.2-24 valve

8th POSITION (Cont'd)
ENGINE CODE
J = 3.3-CNG
L = 3.8-V6
N = 4.7- V8
P = 1.6L- 4Cyl, SOHC
R = 2.7-V6 DOHC
R = 3.3-V6
S = 2.4- L4, 16 valve, Turbo
U = 2.7L-V6, 24 valve
V = 3.5L- 6Cyl, 24 valve
X = 2.4-L4, 16 valve
X = 3.9-V6
Y = 5.2-V8
Y = 2.0-16 valve
Z = 5.9-V8
3 = 3.0-V6

9th POSITION
CHECK DIGIT

10th POSITION
MODEL YEAR
Y = 2000
1 = 2001
2 = 2002

11th POSITION
ASSEMBLY PLANT

12th Thru 17th POSITION
PRODUCTION SEQUENCE NUMBER

CR1130200945020X

Fig. 1 VIN Identification (Part 2 of 2). DaimlerChrysler

1st POSITION
COUNTRY
1 = United States
2 = Canada
3 = Mexico
4 = United States
5 = United States
9 = Brazil
J = Japan
K = Korea
L = Taiwan

2nd POSITION
MAKE
B = Ford
C = Ford
F = Ford
F = Mazda
F = Mercury
L = Lincoln
M = Mercury
N = Continental
N = Ford
N = Nissan
Z = Ford
Z = mercury

3rd POSITION
TYPE
A = Passenger Car
A = Imported Mercury Tracer
B = Bus
C = Basic, Stripped Chassis
D = Incomplete Vehicle
E = Passenger Car
E = Incomplete Vehicle
F = Equiped Without Power Train
F = Imported, Incomplete Truck
H = Incomplete Vehicle
I = Passenger Car
J = Incomplete Vehicle
J = Passenger Car
J = Imported Car, Aspire
M = Multi Purpose Vehicle
N = Passenger Car
P = Passenger Car, Imported
T = Basic, Complete
T = Truck, Complete
V = Passenger Car
W = Passenger Car
1 = Limousine
2 = Truck, Complete, Imported
2 = Multi Purpose Vehicle
3 = Incomplete Vehicle
4 = Truck, Complete
4 = Incomplete Vehicle, Imported
8 = Bus Chassis, Incomplete

4th POSITION
RESTRAINT SYSTEM
A = Active Driver, Passive Passenger
A = Active Rear & Driver Air Bag
B = Active Belts
C = Air Bags & Active Belts
D = Active Belts
F = Active Belts, Second Generation Air Bags
H = Active Belts, Second Generation Air Bags
K = Active Belts, Second Generation Air Bags
L = Air Bags & Active Belts
P = Passive & Active Belts
R = Passive, Active & Driver Air Bag
S = Passive, Active & Dual Air Bags

5th POSITION
IDENTIFICATION
M = Lincoln/Mercury Make
P = Ford Make
T = Imported & Non-Ford Built

6th & 7th POSITION
BODY SERIES NUMBER
See The Body Series Pages

8th POSITION
ENGINE CODE
A = 2.0-L4, MFI, Mazda
A = 3.9-V8, MFI, DOHC
B = 2.5-V6, MFI, Mazda
C = 5.8-V8, MFI
D = 5.0-V8, MFI
G = 2.5L-V6, DOHC
H = 1.3-L4, MFI, Mazda
H = 5.4-V8, MFI
J = 1.9-L4, CVH SEFI
K = 1.9-L4, HO-CVH-SEFI
L = 2.5-V6, MFI, EFI
N = 3.4-V8, MFI, SHO-DOHC
P = 3.2-V6, SHO DOHC
P = 2.0-L4, SOHC, MFI, EFI-SPI
R = 3.8-V6, SUPERCHARGED
R = 4.6-DOHC, Ram Air
S = 3.0-V6, MFI, DOHC, EFI
T = 5.0-V8, MFI, OHV
U = 3.0-V6, MFI, EFI
V = 4.6-V8, MFI, DOHC, EFI
W = 4.6-V8, MFI, SOHC, EFI
X = 4.6 EFI, SOHC
X = 2.3-L4, MFI, OHV
Y = 3.0-V6, MFI, Yamaha
Y = 4.6-DOHC SC
Z = 1.6-L4, MFI, Mazda
1 = 76kW Electric 300Volts
1 = 3.0-V6, MFI Flex Fuel
2 = 3.0 EFI-FFV
3 = 2.0-L4, MFI-ZETA
3 = 2.0 EFI, ZETEC DOHC
4 = 3.8-V6, MFI-SEFI / EFI
5 = 2.0-EFI-ZETEC SVT
5 = 5kW General Elec. 72 Volts

8th POSITION (Cont'd)
ENGINE CODE
6 = 1.6-L4, MFI/TC, Mazda
7 = 71kW Electric 312Volts
8 = 1.8-L4, MFI, Mazda
9 = 4.6-V8, Natural Gas

9th POSITION
CHECK DIGIT

10th POSITION
MODEL YEAR
S = 1995
T = 1996
V = 1997
W = 1998
X = 1999
Y = 2000
1 = 2001
2 = 2002

11th POSITION
ASSEMBLY PLANT
A = Atlanta, GA
F = Dearborn, MI
G = Chicago, IL
H = Lorain, OH
K = Kansas City, MO
M = Cuautitlan
R = Hermosillo, Mexico
S = Allen Park, MI
W = Wayne, MI
X = St. Thomas, Canada
Y = Wixom, MI
5 = Flat Rock, MI
6 = Kia, Korea
8 = Broadmeadows, Australia

12th Thru 17th POSITION
PRODUCTION SEQUENCE NUMBER

FM1130201023000X

Fig. 2 VIN Identification. Ford Motor Co.

1st POSITION
COUNTRY
1 = United States
2 = Canada
3 = Mexico
4 = United States
J = Japan
W = Germany

2nd POSITION
MANUFACTURER
G = General Motors
G = Genasys L.C.
C = CAMI
O = Opel
Y = Nummi
8 = Isuzu

3rd POSITION
DIVISION
4 = Buick
7 = GM of Canada

4th POSITION
CARLINE CODE
A = Century
B = Estate Wagon (RWD)
B = Coachbuilder Wagon
B = Roadmaster
C = Park Avenue (FWD)
E = Riviera
G = Riviera
H = LeSabre (FWD)
N = Somerset/Skylark
W = Regal
W = Century (1997-02)
W = Century

5th POSITION
CARLINE SERIES
B = Regal Custom
B = Regal Gran Sport (2D)
B = Regal LS Sedan
B = Regal LS
B = Coachbuilder Wagon
D = Regal Limited
D = Riviera
F = Regal Gran Sport (4D)
G = Century Spl & Wagon
H = Century Custom/Wagon
J = Skylark
K = Regal Limited
L = Century Limited Wagon
L = Century Custom
M = Skylark Gran Sport
N = Roadmaster
P = LeSabre Custom
R = LeSabre Limited
R = Roadmaster Est Wagon
S = Century Custom (1997-02)
S = Century Custom
T = Roadmaster Limited
U = Park Avenue - Ultra
V = Somerset
V = Skylark Custom
V = Skylark LTD/Gran Sport
W = Park Avenue
Y = Century Limited (1997-02)
Y = Century Limited
Z = Riviera

6th POSITION
BODY TYPE
1 = 2 Door Coupe
2 = 2 Door
2 = 2 Door Sedan
3 = 2 Door Convertible
4 = 2 Door Wagon
5 = 4 Door Sedan
6 = 4 Door
8 = 4 Door Wagon

7th POSITION
RESTRAINT SYSTEM
1 = Manual Belts
2 = Manual Belts (Dual Air Bags)
3 = Manual Belts (Driver Air Bag)
4 = Automatic Belts
4 = Manual Belts (Dual & Side Air Bags)
5 = Automatic Belts (Driver Air Bag)
5 = Manual Belts (Dual Front & Side Air Bags)
6 = Automatic Belts (Dual Air Bags)
6 = Manual Belts (Dual Front & Side Air Bags & Auto Occupant Sensor)
7 = Manual Driver Belt, Automatic Passenger Belt, (Dual Air Bags)
7 = Manual Belts (Dual Air Bags & Front & Rear Side Air Bags)

8th POSITION
ENGINE CODE
D = 2.3-L4, MFI
J = 3.1L-V6,SFI
K = 3.8-V6, MFI
L = 3.8-V6, MFI
M = 3.1-V6, MFI
N = 3.3-V6, MFI
P = 5.7-V8, MFI
R = 2.5-L4, TBI
T = 3.1-V6, MFI (1993)
T = 2.4-L4, MFI (1996)
T = 2.4L-L4,MFI
1 = 3.8-V6, MFI
3 = 2.3-L4, MFI
4 = 2.2-L4, MFI
7 = 5.7-V8, TBI

9th POSITION
CHECK DIGIT

10th POSITION
MODEL YEAR
P = 1993
R = 1994
S = 1995
T = 1996
V = 1997
W = 1998
X = 1999
Y = 2000
1 = 2001
2 = 2002

11th POSITION
ASSEMBLY PLANT

12th Thru 17th POSITION
PRODUCTION SEQUENCE NUMBER

GC1130201148000X

Fig. 3 VIN Identification. Buick

1st POSITION
COUNTRY
1 = United States
2 = Canada
3 = Mexico Built
4 = United States
J = Japan Built
W = Germany

2nd POSITION
MANUFACTURER
G = General Motors
G = Genasys
C = CAMI
O = Opel
Y = NUMMI
8 = Isuzu

3rd POSITION
DIVISION
6 = Cadillac
7 = GM of Canada

4th POSITION
CARLINE CODE
C = Fleetwood/DeVille (FWD)
C = Commercial Chassis
C = Sixty Special
C = DeVille/DeVille Touring
D = Fleetwood/DeVille (RWD)
D = Brougham
D = Commercial Chassis (RWD)
E = Eldorado
E = Eldorado Touring
J = Cimarron
K = Concours
K = DeVille
K = Seville
K = Seville Touring
V = Allante'
V = Catera

5th POSITION
CARLINE SERIES
B = Fleetwood (FWD)
B = Sixty Special
D = DeVille / (FWD)
E = Deville D'Elegance
F = Concours
F = Fleetwood Limo
F = Deville Touring
G = Cimarron
G = Fleetwood 60 Special
H = Fleetwood Limo
H = Commercial Chassis (RWD)
H = Hearse
J = Limousine
L = Eldorado
M = Deville (RWD)
R = Allante' Conv. & HT
R = Catera
S = Seville
S = SLS
S = Allante' Convertible
S = Fleetwood 60 Special
T = Eldorado Touring
T = DeVille Touring

5th POSITION (Cont'd)
CARLINE SERIES
W = Fleetwood Brougham
Y = Seville Touring Sedan
Z = Commercial Chassis

6th & 7th POSITION, 1985-86
BODY TYPE
19 = 4 Door Sedan
27 = 2 Door Coupe
35 = 4 Door Wagon
37 = 2 Door Coupe
47 = 2 Door Coupe
57 = 2 Door Coupe
67 = 2 Door Convertable
69 = 4 Door Sedan
77 = 2 Door Hatchback
87 = 2 Door Coupe

6th POSITION, 1987-02
BODY TYPE
1 = 2 Door Coupe
2 = 2 Door
2 = 2 Door Sedan
3 = 2 Door Convertible
5 = 4 Door Sedan
6 = 4 Door
8 = 4 Door Station Wagon

7th POSITION, 1987-02
RESTRAINT SYSTEM
1 = Manual Belts
2 = Manual Belts (Built in Saftey)
2 = Manual Belts (Dual Air Bags)
3 = Manual Belts (Driver Air Bag)
4 = Automatic Belts
4 = Manual Belts (Dual & Side Air Bags)
5 = Automatic Belts (Dual Air Bag)
5 = Manual Belts (Dual Front & Side Air Bags)
6 = Automatic Belts (Dual Air Bags)
6 = Manual Belts (Dual Front & Side Air Bags & Auto Occupant Sensor)
7 = Manual Driver Belt, Automatic Passenger Belt (Dual Air Bags)
7 = Manual Belts (Dual Front & Side Air Bags & Rear Side Air Bags)

8th POSITION
ENGINE CODE
B = 4.9-V8, MFI
E = 5.0-V8, TBI
K = 3.8-V6, MFI
N = 5.7-V8, Diesel
P = 2.0-L4, EFI
P = 5.7-V8, MFI
R = 3.0-V6, MFI
W = 2.8-V6, MFI
Y = 5.0-V8, 4 Barrel
Y = 4.6-V8, MFI

8th POSITION (Cont'd)
ENGINE CODE
3 = 4.5-V8, MFI
5 = 4.5-V8, Fuel Injected
6 = 4.5-V8, Fuel Injected
7 = 4.1-V8, Fuel Injected
7 = 5.7-V8, TBI
8 = 4.1-V8, DFI
8 = 4.5-V8, MFI
9 = 5.0-V8, 4 Barrel
9 = 4.6-V8, MFI

9th POSITION
CHECK DIGIT

10th POSITION
MODEL YEAR
F = 1985
G = 1986
H = 1987
J = 1988
K = 1989
L = 1990
M = 1991
N = 1992
P = 1993
R = 1994
S = 1995
T = 1996
V = 1997
W = 1998
X = 1999
Y = 2000
1 = 2001
2 = 2002

11th POSITION
ASSEMBLY PLANT

12th Thru 17th POSITION
PRODUCTION SEQUENCE NUMBER

GC1130201144000X

Fig. 4 VIN Identification. Cadillac

1st POSITION
COUNTRY
1 = United States
2 = Canada
3 = Mexico
4 = United States
J = Japan
W = Germany

2nd POSITION
MANUFACTURER
C = CAMI
G = General Motors, Genasys L.C.
O = Opel
Y = N.U.M.M.I.
8 = Isuzu

3rd POSITION
DIVISION
1 = Chevrolet
7 = GM of Canada

4th POSITION
CARLINE CODE
B = Impala
B = Caprice
F = Camaro
J = Cavalier
J = Toyota
L = Corsica, Beretta
M = Geo Metro & Metro LSI
N = Malibu
N = Alero
S = Geo Prizm
L = Lumina
W = Lumina
W = Monte Carlo
W = Impala
Y = Corvette

5th POSITION
CARLINE SERIES
C = Cavalier
D = Corsica
D = Malibu, Malibu LX
E = Malibu LS
F = Cavalier Convertible
F = Cavalier Z24 & LS
F = Impala
G = Toyota (Sedan & Coupe)
H = Toyota (Coupe & Sedan)
H = Impala LS
L = Impala SS
L = Caprice/Caprice Wagon
L = Lumina Sedan
L = Lumina, Lumina LS
L = Export Only
K = Geo Prizm LSi
N = Lumina LS
N = Lumina LTZ
P = Camaro Sport Coupe & Conv.
R = Geo Metro & Metro LSI
V = Beretta
W = Beretta Z26
W = Monte Carlo SS
W = Monte Carlo LS

5th POSITION (Cont'd)
CARLINE SERIES
X = Monte Carlo Z34
X = Monte Carlo SS
Y = Corvette & Convertible
Z = Corvette ZR1

6th POSITION
BODY TYPE
1 = 2 Door Coupe
2 = 2 Door
2 = 2 Door Sedan
3 = 2 Door Convertible
4 = 2 Door Wagon
5 = 4 Door Sedan
6 = 4 Door Sedan
6 = 4 Door Hatchback
7 = 4 Door Liftback
8 = 4 Door Wagon

7th POSITION
RESTRAINT SYSTEM
1 = Manual Belts
2 = Manual Belts (Dual Air Bags)
3 = Manual Belts (Driver Air Bag)
4 = Manual Belts (Dual & Side Air Bags)
4 = Automatic Belts
5 = Automatic Belts (Driver Air Bags)
5 = Manual Belts (Dual Air Bag/Dual Side Air Bag)
6 = Automatic Belts (Dual Air Bags)
6 = Manual Belts (Dual & Side Air Bags), Occupant Sensor
7 = Manual Belts (Dual & Side Air Bags)
7 = Manual Driver Belt, Automatic Passenger Belt, Dual Air Bags
7 = Manual Belts (Dual & Side Air Bags), Rear Side Air Bags

8th POSITION
ENGINE CODE
D = 2.3-L4, MFI
F = 2.2-L4, MFI
G = 5.7-V8, MFI (1997-02)
J = 5.7-V8, MFI
J = 3.1-V6, SFI
K = 3.8-V6, MFI
M = 3.1-V6, MFI
P = 5.7-V8, MFI
S = 3.4-V6, MFI
S = 5.7-V8, SFI
T = 2.4-L4, MFI (96-01)
T = 3.1-V6,MFI
W = 4.3-V8, MFI
X = 3.4-V6, MFI
2 = 1.3-L4, MFI
4 = 2.2-L4, MFI
4 = 2.2-L3, SFI
5 = 5.7-V8, MFI

8th POSITION (Cont'd)
ENGINE CODE
6 = 1.0-L3, TBI
6 = 1.6-L4, MFI
8 = 1.8-L4, MFI
9 = 1.3-L4, TBI

9th POSITION
CHECK DIGIT

10th POSITION
MODEL YEAR
S = 1995
T = 1996
V = 1997
W = 1998
X = 1999
Y = 2000
1 = 2001
2 = 2002

11th POSITION
ASSEMBLY PLANT

12th Thru 17th POSITION
PRODUCTION SEQUENCE NUMBER

GC1130201145000X

Fig. 5 VIN Identification. Chevrolet

1st POSITION
COUNTRY
1 = United States
2 = Canada
3 = Mexico
4 = United States
J = Japan
W = Germany

2nd POSITION
MANUFACTURER
C = CAMI
G = General Motors
G = Genasys, L.C.
O = Opel
Y = Nummi
8 = Isuzu

3rd POSITION
DIVISION
3 = Oldsmobile
7 = GM of Canada

4th POSITION
CARLINE CODE
A = Cutlass Ciera/Cruiser
B = 88 Custom Cruiser (RWD)
C = 98 Touring Sedan
C = 98 Regency/Elite
E = Toronado
E = Toronado Trofe'o
G = Aurora
H = 88 Royale/LS (FWD)
H = Regency
H = LSS
N = Achieva
N = Ciera
N = Cutlass
N = Alero
W = Cutlass
W = Intrigue

5th POSITION
CARLINE SERIES
B = Ciera
B = Cutlass
B = Cutlass GL
C = Regency
F = Achieva SL & SC
F = Alero GLS
G = Cutlass
G = Cutlass Ciera S
G = Cutlass GLS
H = Intrigue
H = Cutlass Supreme SL
H = Cutlass Supreme S
J = Cutlass S/SL & Wagon
K = Alero GX
L = Cutlass Ciera S
L = Achieva SL & SC
L = Achieva S
L = Alero GL
M = Cutlass Ciera SL
M = Cutlass Cruiser SL Wagon
N = 88 LS

5th POSITION (Cont'd)
CARLINE SERIES
N = 88 Royale
P = Custom Cruiser
R = Cutlass Supreme Int'l
R = Aurora
S = Intrigue GL
T = Cutlass Convertible
V = Toranado Trofe'o
V = 98 Touring Sedan
W = 98 Regency Elite
X = 98 Regency (FWD)
X = 98 Regency Elite
X = Intrigue GLS
Y = LSS
Y = 88 Royale LS
Z = Toronado

6th POSITION
BODY TYPE
1 = 2 Door Coupe
2 = 2 Door
3 = 2 Door Convertible
4 = 2 Door Wagon
5 = 4 Door Sedan
6 = 4 Door Sedan
8 = 4 Door Wagon

7th POSITION
RESTRAINT SYSTEM
1 = Manual Belts
2 = Manual Belts (Dual Air Bags)
3 = Manual Belts (Driver Air Bag)
4 = Manual Belts (Dual & Side Air Bag)
4 = Automatic Belts
5 = Automatic Belts (Driver Air Bag)
5 = Manual belts (Dual Front & Side Air Bags)
6 = Automatic Belts (Dual Air Bag)
6 = Manual Belts (Dual Front & Side Air Bag & Occupant Sensor)
7 = Manual Driver Belt, Automatic Passenger Belt, (Dual Air Bags)
7 = Manual Belts (Front Dual & Side Air Bags & Rear Side Air Bags)

8th POSITION
ENGINE CODE
A = 2.3-L4, MFI
C = 4.0-V8, MFI
D = 2.3-L4, MFI
E = 3.4-V6, MFI
E = 5.0-V8, TBI
H = 3.5-V6, MFI
K = 3.8-V6, MFI
L = 3.8-V6, MFI
M = 3.1-V6, MFI
N = 3.3-V6, MFI
R = 2.5-L4, TBI

8th POSITION (Cont'd)
ENGINE CODE
T = 2.4-L4, MFI (96-00)
T = 3.1-V6, MFI (1993)
X = 3.4-V6, MFI
1 = 3.8-V6, MFI
3 = 2.3-L4, MFI
4 = 2.2-L4, MFI
7 = 5.7-V8, TBI

9th POSITION
CHECK DIGIT

10th POSITION
MODEL YEAR
P = 1993
R = 1994
S = 1995
T = 1996
V = 1997
W = 1998
X = 1999
Y = 2000

11th POSITION
ASSEMBLY PLANT
B = Lansing, MI
B = Baltimore, MD
C = Lansing, MI
C = Charlotte, MI
D = Doraville, GA
E = Linden, NJ
F = Flint, MI
F = Fairfax II, KS
G = Framingham, MA
H = Flint, MI
J = Janesville, WI
K = Leeds, MO
K = Linden, NJ
M = Lansing, MI
R = Arlington, TX
T = Shreveport, LA
U = Hamtramck, MI
W = Willow Run, MI
X = Fairfax, KS
Y = Wilmington, DE
Z = Spring Hill, TN
Z = Fremont, CA
Z = Fort Wayne, IN
1 = Wentzville, MO
1 = Oshawa #2, Canada
2 = Ste. Therese, Canada
2 = Moraine, OH
3 = Detroit, MI
4 = Orion, MI
5 = Bowling Green, KY
6 = Ingersoll, Canada
6 = Oklahoma, OK
7 = Lordstown, OH
8 = Shreveport, LA
9 = Oshawa #1, Canada

12th Thru 17th POSITION
PRODUCTION SEQUENCE NUMBER

GC1130201146010X

Fig. 6 VIN Identification (Part 1 of 2). Oldsmobile

1st POSITION
COUNTRY

1 = United States
2 = Canada

2nd POSITION
MANUFACTURER

G = General Motors

3rd POSITION
DIVISION

3 = Oldsmobile

4th POSITION
CARLINE CODE

G = Aurora
N = Alero
W = Intrigue

5th POSITION
CARLINE SERIES

F = Alero GLS
H = Intrigue GX
K = Alero GX
L = Alero GL
R = Aurora
S = Intrigue GL
S = Aurora
X = Intrigue GLS

6th POSITION
BODY TYPE

1 = 2 Door Coupe
2 = 2 Door Coupe
2 = 2 Door Sedan
3 = 2 Door Convertible
5 = 4 Door Sedan
6 = 4 Door Sedan
8 = 4 Door Wagon

7th POSITION
RESTRAINT SYSTEM

1 = Manual Belts
2 = Manual Belts (Dual Air Bags)
4 = Manual Belts (Dual & Side Air Bag)
5 = Manual belts (Dual Front & Side Air Bags)
6 = Manual Belts (Dual Front & Side Air Bag & Occupant Sensor)
7 = Manual Belts (Front Dual & Side Air Bags & Rear Side Air Bags)

8th POSITION
ENGINE CODE

C = 4.0-V8, SFI
E = 3.4-V6, MFI
F = 2.2-L4, MFI
H = 3.5-V6, MFI
J = 3.1-V6, SFI
T = 2.4-L4, MFI

9th POSITION
CHECK DIGIT

10th POSITION
MODEL YEAR

1 = 2001
2 = 2002

11th POSITION
ASSEMBLY PLANT

B = Lansing, MI
C = Lansing, MI
F = Fairfax II, KS
H = Flint, MI
M = Lansing, MI
U = Hamtramck, MI
Y = Wilmington, DE
Z = Spring Hill, TN
0 = Lansing, MI
4 = Orion, MI
5 = Bowling Green, KY
6 = Oklahoma, OK
7 = Lordstown, OH

12th Thru 17th POSITION
PRODUCTION SEQUENCE NUMBER

GC1130201146020X

Fig. 6 VIN Identification (Part 2 of 2). Oldsmobile

1st POSITION
COUNTRY

1 = United States
2 = Canada
3 = Mexico
4 = United States
J = Japan Built
W = Germany

2nd POSITION
MANUFACTURER

C = CAMI
G = General Motors
G = General Motors, Genasys L.C.
O = Opel
Y = Nummi
8 = Isuzu

3rd POSITION
DIVISION

1 = Chevrolet
2 = Pontiac
3 = Oldsmobile
3 = Toyota (4G3)
4 = Buick
5 = Electric Vehicle
6 = Cadillac
7 = GM of Canada
8 = Saturn

4th POSITION
CARLINE CODE

F = Firebird / Formula / Trans AM
H = Bonneville
J = Sunbird & Convertible
J = Sunfire
M = Firefly
N = Grand Am
W = Grand Prix

5th POSITION
CARLINE SERIES

B = Sunbird SE & Convertible
B = Sunfire/ SE & Convertible
D = Sunfire, Sunfire GT
E = Grand Am SE
F = Grand Am SE1
G = Grand Am SE2
J = Grand Prix SE
K = Grand Prix SE1
L = Sunbird SE
M = Grand Prix
P = Grand Prix, Gand Prix GT
R = Grand Prix GTP
R = Firefly
S = Firebird & Convertible
V = Formula & Convertible
V = Trans Am
V = Grand Am GT1
W = Grand Am GT
X = Bonneville SE
Y = Bonneville SLE
Z = Bonneville SSE / SSEI

6th POSITION
BODY TYPE

1 = 2 Door Coupe
2 = 2 Door Coupe
2 = 2 Door Sedan
3 = 2 Door Convertible
4 = 2 Door Wagon
5 = 2 Door Sedan
5 = 4 Door Sedan
6 = 4 Door Sedan
8 = 4 Door Wagon

7th POSITION
RESTRAINT SYSTEM

1 = Manual Belts
2 = Manual Belts (Dual Air Bags)
3 = Manual Belts (Driver Air Bags)
4 = Manual Belts (Dual & Side Air Bags)
4 = Automatic Belts
5 = Automatic Belts (Driver Air Bags)
5 = Manual Belts (Dual & Side Air Bags)
6 = Manual Belts (Dual & Side Air Bags), Occupant Sensor
6 = Automatic Belts (Dual Air Bags)
7 = Manual Driver Belt, Automatic Passenger Belt, (Dual Air Bags)
7 = Manual Belts (Dual & Side Air Bags, Front & Rear)

8th POSITION
ENGINE CODE

A = 2.3-L4, MFI
B = 3.8-V6, MFI
D = 2.3-L4, MFI
E = 3.4-V6, MFI
F = 2.2-L4, MFI
G = 5.7-V8, MFI
H = 2.0-L4, MFI
J = 3.1L-V6,SFI
K = 3.8-V6, MFI
L = 3.8-V6, MFI
M = 3.1-V6, MFI
P = 5.7-V8, MFI
S = 3.4-V6, MFI
T = 3.1-V6, MFI (93-94)
T = 2.4-L4, MFI (96-02)
X = 3.4-V6, MFI
1 = 3.8-V6, MFI
3 = 2.3-L4, MFI
4 = 2.2-L4, MFI

9th POSITION
CHECK DIGIT

10th POSITION
MODEL YEAR

R = 1994
S = 1995
T = 1996
V = 1997
W = 1998
X = 1999
Y = 2000
1 = 2001
2 = 2002

11th POSITION
ASSEMBLY PLANT

12th Thru 17th POSITION
PRODUCTION SEQUENCE NUMBER

GC1130201147000X

Fig. 7 VIN Identification. Pontiac

1st POSITION
COUNTRY
1 = United States
W = Germany

2nd POSITION
MANUFACTURER
G = General Motors
O = Opel

3rd POSITION
DIVISION
8 = Saturn

4th POSITION
CARLINE CODE
J = LS,LS1,LS2
Z = SL, SL1&2, SC
Z = SC1&2, SW1&2

5th POSITION
CARLINE SERIES
B = SC2 Coupe, SW1 Wagon
B = SL Sedan, SL1 Sedan
C = SC1 Coupe
D = SL2 Sedan, SW2 Wagon
E = SC1 Coupe, Manual
F = SC1 Coupe, Auto
F = SL Sedan, Manual
G = SL1 Sedan, SC
G = SC2 Sedan, SW1 Wagon
G = Manual, SL1
H = SL1 Sedan, SC
H = SC2 Coupe, SW1 Wagon
H = Auto, SL1
J = SL2 Sedan, SW2 Wagon
J = Manual, SW2, SL2
K = SL2 Sedan, SW2 Wagon
K = SL2 AUTO
M = Auto RHD
M = SW1
N = SC1 Manual, SW2 Auto
P = Auto, SC1
R = Manual, SC2, LS
S = Auto, LS
T = Manual, LS1
U = Auto, LW1, LS1
W = LW2, LS2
Y = Auto, SC2

6th POSITION
BODY TYPE
1 = 2 Door Coupe
1 = 3 Door Coupe
2 = 2 Door
2 = 2 Door Sedan
3 = 2 Door Convertible
4 = 2 Door Wagon
5 = 4 Door Sedan
6 = 4 Door
8 = 5 Door Wagon
8 = 4 Door Wagon

7th POSITION
RESTRAINT SYSTEM
1 = Manual Belts
2 = Manual Belts (Dual Air Bags)
3 = Manual Belts (Driver Air Bag)
4 = Manual Belts (Dual & Side Air Bag)
4 = Automatic Belts
5 = Automatic Belts (Driver Air Bag)
5 = Manual Belts (Dual & Side Air Bag)
6 = Automatic Belts (Dual Air Bags)
6 = Manual Belt (Dual & Side Air Bag & Auto Occupant Sensor)
7 = Manual Driver Belt, Automatic Passenger Belt, (Dual Air Bags)
7 = Manual Belts (Dual & Front/Rear Side Air Bags)

8th POSITION
ENGINE CODE
5 = AC EV (Electri Vehcle)
7 = 1.9-L4, MFI
7 = 1.9-L4,SFI
8 = 1.9-L4, MFI
8 = 1.9-L4,SFI
9 = 1.9-L4, TBI
F = 2.2L-L4,MFI
R = 3.0L-V6,MFI

9th POSITION
CHECK DIGIT

10th POSITION
MODEL YEAR
M = 1991
N = 1992
P = 1993
R = 1994
S = 1995
T = 1996
V =1997
W = 1998
X = 1999
Y = 2000
1 = 2001
2 = 2002

11th POSITION
ASSEMBLY PLANT
Y = Wilmington, DE
Z = Spring Hill, TN

12th Thru 17th POSITION
PRODUCTION SEQUENCE NUMBER

G31130200044000X

Fig. 8 VIN Identification. Saturn

AIR BAG SYSTEM PRECAUTIONS

INDEX

DAIMLERCHRYSLER

DISARMING

It may be necessary to access and record all Diagnostic Trouble Codes (DTCs) prior to disarming the air bag system.

1. Place ignition switch in Lock position.
2. **On Avenger, Breeze, Cirrus, Neon, Sebring, Stratus and Talon models,** disconnect and isolate battery ground cable.
3. **On Concorde, Intrepid, LHS and 300M models,** disconnect and isolate battery negative cable remote terminal at remote battery post, **Fig. 1.**
4. **On all models except Sebring and Stratus Coupe, wait at least two minutes after disconnection before doing any further work on vehicle. The air bag system is designed to retain enough voltage to deploy air bags for a short time even after battery has been disconnected.**
5. **On Sebring and Stratus Coupe, wait at least sixty seconds after disconnection before doing any further work on vehicle. The air bag system is designed to retain enough voltage to deploy air bags for a short time even after battery has been disconnected.**

ARMING

1. **Ensure no one is inside vehicle and ignition switch is in Lock position.**
2. Connect battery ground or negative remote cable or terminal.
3. Turn ignition On **from a safe position below or at the sides of the air bag modules.**
4. The SRS lamp should light for seven to ten seconds, then remain off for at least 45 seconds to indicate SRS is functioning properly.
5. If SRS indicator does not perform as specified, refer to "Diagnosis & Testing."

FORD MOTOR CO.

DISARMING

CONTINENTAL

1998–99

1. Disconnect battery ground cable.
2. Wait one minute for battery back-up power supply to deplete.

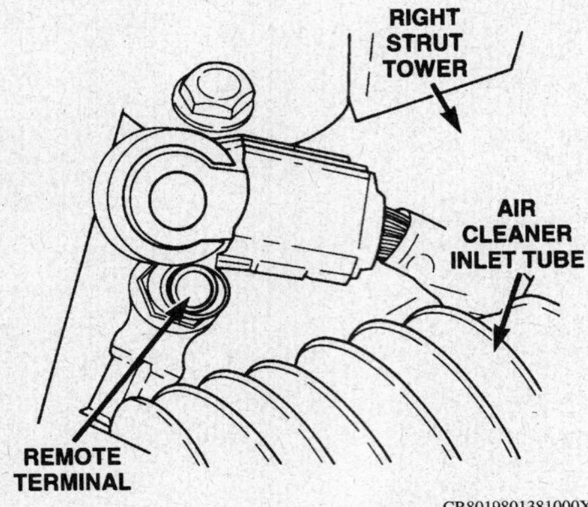

Fig. 1 Battery negative remote terminal. Concorde, Intrepid, LHS & 300M

3. Remove two air bag retaining bolt hole covers from steering wheel spokes.
4. Remove two air bag module retaining bolts, then carefully lift air bag module from steering wheel.
5. Disconnect drivers air bag module connector.
6. Attach Rotunda air bag simulator tool, or equivalent, to air bag terminals on clockspring assembly to simulate air bag.
7. Open glove compartment and rotate downward past stops.
8. Disconnect passenger air bag module electrical connector.
9. Remove three bolts retaining lower passenger's air bag module mounting bracket to instrument panel through glove compartment opening.
10. Remove passengers air bag module by pushing module outward from inside instrument panel. Do not grab edges of deployment doors.
11. Attach Rotunda air bag simulator tool to air bag terminals on wiring harness side of passenger's air bag module connector.
12. **On 1999 models,** disconnect side air bag module electrical connectors located beneath driver's and passenger's seats, then attach Rotunda air bag simulator tools, or equivalent, to side air bag connectors on vehicle wiring harness side.
13. **On all models,** connect battery ground cable.

2000–02

1. Disconnect and isolate battery ground cable.
2. **On models equipped with auxiliary batteries and power supplies,** disconnect and isolate these items.
3. **On all models,** wait one minute for back-up power supply to deplete.
4. Remove driver's air bag module as follows:
   a. Remove two steering wheel spoke bolt covers, if equipped.
   b. Remove two air bag module to steering wheel attaching bolts.
   c. Carefully lift air bag module away from steering wheel, then disconnect air bag module and horn to clockspring electrical connectors. **When carrying a live air bag module, ensure bag and trim cover are pointed away from your body. To prevent injury by accidental deployment, place module on a bench with trim cover facing upward.**
   d. Remove air bag module.
5. Attach Rotunda air bag simulator tool No. 105-R0012, or equivalent, to vehicle harness connector at top of steering column.
6. Open glove compartment, then push tabs in and rotate door downward past stops.
7. Disconnect passenger's air bag module electrical connector.
8. Attach Rotunda air bag simulator tool No. 105-R0012, or equivalent, to passenger's air bag module electrical connector on vehicle wiring harness side.
9. Disconnect side air bag module electrical connector located beneath driver's seat.
10. Attach Rotunda air bag simulator tool No. 105-R0012, or equivalent, to side air bag connector under driver's seat on vehicle wiring harness side
11. Disconnect side air bag module electrical connector located beneath passenger's seat.
12. Attach Rotunda air bag simulator tool No. 105-R0012, or equivalent, to side air bag connector under passenger's seat on vehicle wiring harness side
13. If side air bag diagnosis or service is to be performed, remove front seats as follows:
   a. Move front seat all the way rearward, then remove seat track front bolt covers and bolts.

b. Move front seat all the way forward, then remove seat track rear bolt covers and bolts.
c. Disconnect front seat electrical connectors, then remove front seats from vehicle.

14. Connect battery ground cable.

CONTOUR & MYSTIQUE

1998

1. Disconnect and isolate battery ground cable, then the positive cable. Allow at least one minute for back-up power supply to deplete.
2. Rotate steering wheel as necessary to access and remove air bag retaining bolts.
3. Disconnect driver's air bag module connector, then carefully remove module from vehicle. Place module on a bench with trim cover facing upward.
4. Connect Rotunda air bag simulator tool No. 105-R0012, or equivalent, to vehicle harness at top of steering column.
5. Open glove compartment, then lower compartment to floor by pressing inward on sides.
6. Remove four glove compartment upper panel screws, then disconnect glove compartment lamp.
7. Remove glove compartment upper panel.
8. Remove A/C evaporator register duct.
9. Disconnect passenger's air bag module electrical connector.
10. Remove two bolts from rear of passenger's air bag module.
11. Remove two nuts from front of passenger's air bag module, then carefully lift module from vehicle. **To prevent injury by accidental deployment, place module on a bench with trim cover facing upward.**
12. Connect second Rotunda air bag simulator tool No. 105-R0012, or equivalent, to wiring harness in place of passenger's air bag.
13. Connect battery positive battery cable, then the ground cable.

1999–2000

1. Disconnect and isolate battery ground cable.
2. Allow at least one minute for back-up power supply to deplete.
3. Remove driver's air bag module as follows:
   a. Remove two driver's air bag module Torx retaining screws at rear of steering wheel.
   b. Lift driver's air bag module upward, then disconnect air bag module electrical connector.
   c. Remove the air bag module. **When carrying a live air bag module, ensure bag and trim cover are pointed away from your body. To prevent injury by accidental deployment, place module on a bench with trim cover facing upward.**
4. Connect Rotunda air bag simulator tool No. 105-R0012, or equivalent, to vehicle harness at top of steering column.
5. Open glove compartment, then lower compartment to floor by pressing inward on sides.
6. Remove four glove compartment upper panel screws, then disconnect glove compartment lamp.
7. Remove glove compartment upper panel.
8. Remove passenger's air vent duct.
9. Disconnect passenger's air bag module electrical connector.
10. Connect second Rotunda air bag simulator tool No. 105-R0012, or equivalent, to wiring harness in place of passenger's air bag.
11. Connect battery ground cable.

COUGAR

Prior to disconnecting battery, record preset radio frequencies.

1. Disconnect and isolate battery ground cable, then the positive cable
2. **On models equipped with auxiliary batteries and power supplies,** disconnect and isolate these items.
3. **On all models,** allow at least one minute for back-up power supply to deplete.
4. Remove driver's air bag module as follows:
   a. Remove two driver's air bag module Torx retaining screws at rear of steering wheel.
   b. Lift driver's air bag module upward, then disconnect air bag module electrical connector.
   c. Remove the air bag module. **When carrying a live air bag module, ensure bag and trim cover are pointed away from your body. To prevent injury by accidental deployment, place module on a bench with trim cover facing upward.**
5. Connect Rotunda air bag simulator tool No. 105-R0012, or equivalent, to vehicle harness at top of steering column.
6. Remove passenger's air bag module as follows:
   a. Remove three glove compartment Torx retaining screws.
   b. Open glove compartment, then depress side stops to detach sides.
   c. Remove four Torx screws, then the glove compartment finish panel.
   d. Remove passenger's air register duct.
   e. Disconnect passenger's air bag module electrical connector.
   f. Remove two bolts retaining passenger's air bag module to cross beam.
   g. Lower front edge of passenger's air bag module, roll air bag module around cross beam. Lower the air bag module to the passenger's foot well and remove from vehicle. **When carrying a live air bag module, ensure bag and trim cover are pointed away from your body. To prevent injury by accidental deployment, place module on a bench with trim cover facing upward.**
7. Connect second Rotunda air bag simulator tool No. 105-R0012, or equivalent, to wiring harness in place of passenger's air bag.
8. **On models equipped with side air bags,** proceed as follows:
   a. From driver's and passenger's seats, remove seat back rest, cover and pad.
   b. Depress retaining tang at each side and disconnect side air bag module electrical connector at driver's and passenger's seats.
   c. Remove side air bag module retaining nuts from driver's and passenger's seats.
9. **On all models,** connect battery ground cable.

CROWN VICTORIA & GRAND MARQUIS

1998–2000

1. Disconnect and isolate battery ground cable, then wait one minute for back-up power supply to deplete.
2. **On models equipped with auxiliary batteries and power supplies,** disconnect and isolate these items also.
3. **On all models,** wait one minute for back-up power supply to deplete.
4. Remove driver's air bag module, as follows:
   a. Remove two bolts retaining air bag assembly to steering wheel.
   b. Carefully lift air bag module from steering wheel, then disconnect air bag module and horn switch electrical connectors. **When carrying a live air bag module, ensure bag and trim cover are pointed away from your body. To prevent injury by accidental deployment, place module on a bench with trim cover facing upward.**
5. Connect Rotunda air bag simulator tool No. 105-00012, or equivalent, to vehicle air bag wiring harness at top of steering column.
6. Remove passenger's air bag as follows:
   a. Open glove compartment, then disconnect glove compartment locator.
   b. Push inward on glove compartment door tabs and position door downward.
   c. **On 1999 models,** detach trim panel located below air bag module from instrument panel by pulling straight out to release clips, then disconnect clock electrical connector and remove trim panel.
   d. **On all models,** disconnect passenger's air bag module electrical connector.
   e. Remove two air bag module retaining bolts and screws.
   f. Place one hand in glove compartment opening, then push air bag module from instrument panel. **When carrying a live air bag module, ensure bag and trim cover are pointed away from your body. To prevent injury by**

accidental deployment, place module on a bench with trim cover facing upward.

7. Attach Rotunda air bag simulator tool No. 105-00012, or equivalent, to harness side of passenger's air bag module connector.
8. Connect battery ground cable.

2001-02

1. Disconnect battery ground cable.
2. Wait at least one minute for back-up power supply in restraints control module (RCM) to deplete its' stored energy.
3. Remove two steering wheel back cover plugs, then the two air bag module bolts.
4. Release two air bag retaining tabs. Label driver air bag squib number on air bag module connector before disconnecting.
5. Remove wire harness from holder.
6. Disconnect horn switch electrical connector.
7. Remove air bag module from vehicle.
8. Attach restraint system diagnostic tools 418-F395, or equivalent, to the clockspring side of driver air bag module electrical connectors.
9. Disconnect rear window defroster switch, clock and air bag deactivation lamp electrical connectors, then remove trim panel.
10. Open glove compartment and disconnect glove compartment isolator.
11. While pushing in on two glove compartment door tabs, lower glove compartment door.
12. Remove air bag module bolts through glove compartment opening,
13. Place one hand in glove compartment opening and push air bag module out from instrument panel. **Do not handle passenger air bag module by grabbing the edges of deployment doors.**
14. Attach restraint system diagnostic tools 418-F395, or equivalent, to vehicle harness side of passenger air bag module electrical connectors.
15. Remove front seats.
16. Access passenger safety belt retractor and pretensioner located behind passenger side B-pillar.
17. Disconnect passenger safety belt retractor and pretensioner electrical connector.
18. Attach restraint system diagnostic tool 418-F088, or equivalent, to passenger safety belt retractor and pretensioner electrical connector.
19. Access driver safety belt retractor and pretensioner located behind driver side B-pillar.
20. Disconnect driver safety belt retractor and pretensioner electrical connector.
21. Attach restraint system diagnostic tool 418-F088, or equivalent, to driver safety belt retractor and pretensioner electrical connector.
22. Reconnect battery ground cable.

ESCORT, TRACER & ZX2

1. Disconnect and isolate battery ground cable. Allow at least one minute for back-up power supply to deplete.
2. **On models equipped with auxiliary batteries and power supplies,** disconnect and isolate these items also.
3. **On all models,** remove two bolts retaining air bag module to steering wheel, then disconnect air bag and horn electrical connectors.
4. Carefully remove driver's air bag module from steering wheel. **When carrying a live air bag module, ensure bag and trim cover are pointed away from your body. To prevent injury by accidental deployment, place module on a bench with trim cover facing upward.**
5. Connect air bag simulator tool No. 105–00012, or equivalent, to vehicle air bag wiring harness at top steering column.
6. Open glove compartment, push in on two door tabs, then roll door downward.
7. Remove four passenger's air bag module attaching bolts.
8. Carefully pull passenger's air bag module from instrument panel, then disconnect electrical connector. **When carrying a live air bag module, ensure bag and trim cover are pointed away from your body. To prevent injury by accidental deployment, place module on a bench with trim cover facing upward.**
9. Connect Rotunda air bag simulator tool No. 105-R00010, or equivalent, to wiring harness in place of passenger's air bag module.
10. Connect battery ground cable.

FOCUS

1. Disconnect and isolate battery ground cable.
2. **On models equipped with auxiliary batteries and power supplies,** disconnect and isolate these items also.
3. **On all models,** wait one minute for back-up power supply to deplete.
4. Remove two bolts retaining air bag module to steering wheel, then disconnect air bag and horn electrical connectors.
5. Carefully remove driver's air bag module from steering wheel. **When carrying a live air bag module, ensure bag and trim cover are pointed away from your body. To prevent injury by accidental deployment, place module on a bench with trim cover facing upward.**
6. Connect air bag simulator tool No. 418–037, or equivalent, to vehicle air bag wiring harness at top steering column.
7. Remove glove compartment retaining screws, then the glove compartment.
8. Disconnect passenger's air bag module electrical connector.
9. Connect Rotunda air bag simulator tool 418–138, or equivalent, to wiring harness in place of passenger's air bag module.
10. From beneath driver's seat, disconnect side air bag module electrical connector. Connect Rotunda air bag simulator tool 418–139, or equivalent, to connector on wiring harness side of side air bag harness.
11. From beneath passenger's seat, disconnect side air bag module electrical connector. Connect Rotunda air bag simulator tool 418–139, or equivalent, to connector on wiring harness side of side air bag harness.
12. Disconnect driver's seat belt pretensioner electrical connector. Connect Rotunda air bag simulator tool 418–139, or equivalent, to connector on wiring harness side of seat belt pretensioner harness.
13. Disconnect passenger's seat belt pretensioner electrical connector. Connect Rotunda air bag simulator tool 418–139, or equivalent, to connector on wiring harness side of seat belt pretensioner harness.
14. Connect battery ground cable.

LS

1. Disconnect and isolate battery ground cable.
2. **On models equipped with auxiliary batteries and power supplies,** disconnect and isolate these items.
3. **On all models,** wait one minute for back-up power supply to deplete.
4. Remove two rear cover plugs from steering wheel in order to access air bag module screws.
5. Remove driver's air bag module bolts, then disconnect electrical connector and carefully remove air bag module from vehicle. **When carrying a live air bag module, ensure bag and trim cover are pointed away from your body. To prevent injury by accidental deployment, place module on a bench with trim cover facing upward.**
6. Connect Rotunda air bag simulator tool No. 418-F395, or equivalent, to vehicle air bag wiring harness at top steering column.
7. Remove glove compartment.
8. Reaching over cross car beam, slide passenger's air bag connector lock downward. Squeeze connector lock tabs, then pull connector from air bag.
9. Connect Rotunda air bag simulator tool No. 418-F395, or equivalent, to vehicle side of passenger's air bag wiring harness connector.
10. From beneath driver's seat, disconnect side air bag module electrical connector. Connect Rotunda air bag simulator tool 418–133, or equivalent, to connector on wiring harness side of side air bag harness.
11. From beneath passenger's seat, disconnect side air bag module electrical connector. Connect Rotunda air bag simulator tool 418–133, or equivalent, to connector on wiring harness side of side air bag harness.
12. Remove driver's side B-pillar pillar trim.
13. Access and disconnect driver's side seat belt pretensioner electrical connector. Connect Rotunda seat belt pretensioner simulator tool 105–R0012, or equivalent, to seat belt pretensioner electrical connector.

14. Remove passenger's side B-pillar pillar trim.
15. Access and disconnect passenger's side seat belt pretensioner electrical connector. Connect Rotunda seat belt pretensioner simulator tool 105–R0012, or equivalent, to seat belt pretensioner electrical connector.
16. Connect battery ground cable.

MARK VIII

1. Disconnect and isolate battery ground cable and any auxiliary batteries and power supplies.
2. Wait one minute for back-up power supply to discharge.
3. Remove air bag module screw covers from rear of steering wheel.
4. Remove driver's air bag module to steering wheel retaining screws and washers.
5. Disconnect driver's air bag module electrical connector.
6. Connect Rotunda air bag simulator tool No. 105-00012, or equivalent, to vehicle harness at top of steering column.
7. Move tilt steering column to its lowest position.
8. Remove lower instrument panel steering column cover retaining screws, then the column cover.
9. Disconnect all steering column electrical connectors.
10. Remove steering column to instrument panel reinforcing bar nuts and lower steering column onto reinforcing bar.
11. Remove steering column upper cover to instrument panel attaching screws, then the column cover.
12. Remove headlamp switch knob and shaft assembly by firmly gripping knob and pulling straight back.
13. Unsnap lefthand instrument panel finish panel from instrument panel finish panel.
14. Detach bulb and socket from finish panel, then remove finish panel.
15. Release instrument panel dimmer switch retaining clips, then disconnect electrical connector and remove switch.
16. Remove righthand finish panel to instrument panel attaching screws, then the finish panel.
17. Open glove compartment, press insides of compartment inward and lower glove compartment to floor.
18. Remove two A/C evaporator register duct attaching screws, then the duct.
19. Remove four air bag module retaining bolts.
20. While removing air bag module, disconnect electrical connector from lefthand side of air bag.
21. Install Rotunda air bag simulator tool No. 105-00010, or equivalent, on vehicle air bag harness connector in place of air bag.
22. Connect battery ground cable.

MUSTANG

1. Disconnect battery ground cable.
2. Allow at least one minute for back-up power supply to deplete.
3. **On models equipped with auxiliary batteries and power supplies,** disconnect and isolate these items also.
4. **On all models,** remove two rear cover plugs from steering wheel in order to access air bag module screws.
5. Remove driver's air bag module screws and washers, then disconnect electrical connector and carefully remove air bag module from vehicle. **To prevent injury by accidental deployment, place module on a bench with trim cover facing upward.**
6. Connect Rotunda air bag simulator tool, or equivalent, to vehicle air bag wiring at top of steering column.
7. Open glove compartment, press sides inward to release it from instrument panel and lower glove compartment to floor.
8. Remove righthand A/C duct, then remove passenger's air bag retaining bolts from instrument panel steel reinforcement.
9. Disconnect electrical connector at lower lefthand corner of passenger's air bag module, then remove connector from instrument panel reinforcement.
10. Gently pull upon each corner of air bag cover to disengage from instrument panel, then push air bag module out from behind instrument panel. **To prevent injury by accidental deployment, place module on a bench with trim cover facing upward.**
11. Install second air bag simulator Rotunda air bag simulator tool, or equivalent, on passenger's air bag harness.
12. Connect battery ground cable.

SABLE & TAURUS

1998–99

1. Disconnect battery ground cable.
2. Allow at least one minute for back-up power supply to deplete.
3. Remove two air bag retaining screw covers from rear of steering wheel.
4. Remove two screw and washer assemblies retaining driver's air bag module to steering wheel.
5. Attach Rotunda air bag simulator tool, or equivalent, to air bag terminals on clockspring assembly to simulate air bag.
6. Unsnap passenger's air bag trim cover tabs.
7. Open glove compartment and press sides inward, then lower glove compartment to floor.
8. Working through glove compartment opening, remove two air bag module retaining screws.
9. Disconnect two air bag module electrical connectors, then remove air bag module.
10. Connect Rotunda air bag simulator tool, or equivalent, to wiring harness in place of passenger's air bag module. Connect tool to wiring harness having LB/O and PK/BK wires.
11. Connect battery ground cable.

2000–02

1. Move front seat to full rear and highest position.
2. Disconnect and isolate battery ground cable.
3. **On models equipped with auxiliary batteries and power supplies,** disconnect and isolate these items also.
4. **On all models,** wait one minute for back-up power supply to deplete.
5. Remove retaining screws and pull out release clips, then remove lower steering column cover with reinforcement.
6. Disconnect driver's air bag sliding contact electrical connect at base of steering column.
7. Connect driver's air bag restraint system diagnostic tool 418–F403, or equivalent, to vehicle side of driver's air bag sliding contact 4-pin electrical connector.
8. Open glove compartment, then push in on tabs and release glove compartment.
9. Through glove compartment opening, remove two passenger's air bag module attaching bolts.
10. Pull lefthand corner of passenger's air bag trim cover away from instrument panel.
11. From left to right, slide across seam between instrument panel and trim cover to release trim cover retaining clips.
12. Pull passenger's air bag module and trim cover away from instrument panel.
13. Disconnect passenger's air bag module electrical connector, then remove harness retainer from air bag module.
14. Remove passenger's air bag module. **When carrying a live air bag module, ensure bag and trim cover are pointed away from your body. To prevent injury by accidental deployment, place module on a bench with trim cover facing upward.**
15. Connect passenger's air bag restraint system diagnostic tool 418–F403, or equivalent, to vehicle side of passenger's air bag electrical connector.
16. **On models equipped with side air bags,** disconnect passenger's seat air bag electrical connector, then attach side air bag restraint system diagnostic tool 418–133, or equivalent, to side air bag floor electrical connector on passenger's side.
17. **On all models,** disconnect passenger's seat belt pretensioner electrical connector.
18. Attach passenger's seat belt pretensioner restraint system diagnostic tool 418–F407, or equivalent, to floor electrical connector.
19. **On models equipped with side air bags,** disconnect driver's seat air bag electrical connector, then attach side air bag restraint system diagnostic tool 418–133, or equivalent, to side air bag floor electrical connector on driver's side.
20. **On all models,** disconnect driver's seat belt pretensioner electrical connector.
21. Attach driver's seat belt pretensioner restraint system diagnostic tool 418–F405, or equivalent, to floor electrical connector.
22. Connect battery ground cable.

AIR BAG SYSTEM PRECAUTIONS

THUNDERBIRD

1. Disconnect battery ground cable and wait at least one minute for back-up power supply to deplete.
2. Remove two pin-type retainers from lower steering column opening finish panel, then pull out on finish panel far enough to access and disconnect electrical connectors.
3. Remove lower steering column finish panel.
4. Remove two pin-type retainers from driver side lower insulator panel.
5. Remove light socket from insulator panel, then the panel from instrument panel.
6. Remove hood latch assembly to steering column reinforcement attaching screws, then separate hood latch assembly from reinforcement.
7. Remove heater duct attaching screw, then the heater duct.
8. Position carpet aside, then loosen two driver side instrument panel tunnel brace bolts
9. Remove lower steering column reinforcement attaching screws, then the reinforcement from instrument panel.
10. Disconnect clockspring electrical connector located at the base of the steering column.
11. Attach restraint system diagnostic tool No. 418-F088, or equivalent, to clockspring electrical connector.
12. Remove glove compartment and door.
13. Locate passenger air bag module electrical connector by reaching through the glove compartment opening towards center of instrument panel and above the cross-car beam. **The passenger air bag module connector is not visible due to its mounting position in the instrument panel.**
14. Disconnect passenger air bag module electrical connector.
15. Attach restraint system diagnostic tool No. 418-F395, or equivalent, to vehicle harness side of passenger air bag electrical connector.
16. Connect battery ground cable and move front seats to their highest and most forward positions.
17. Disconnect battery ground cable and wait at least one minute for back-up power supply to deplete.
18. Disconnect passenger seat side air bag electrical connector located under passenger seat.
19. Attach restraint system diagnostic tool No. 418-F133, or equivalent, to passenger seat side air bag electrical connector.
20. Remove passenger side door scuff plate and weatherstripping.
21. Remove safety belt from passenger seat guide.
22. Remove speaker grille from passenger side rear trim panel.
23. Remove snap screws, then the passenger side rear trim panel.
24. Disconnect passenger safety belt retractor pretensioner electrical connector.
25. Attach restraint system diagnostic tool No. 418-F395, or equivalent, to passenger safety belt retractor pretensioner electrical connector.
26. Disconnect driver seat side air bag electrical connector located under driver seat.
27. Attach restraint system diagnostic tool No. 418-F133, or equivalent, to driver seat side air bag electrical connector.
28. Remove driver side door scuff plate and weatherstripping.
29. Remove safety belt from driver seat guide.
30. Remove speaker grille from driver side rear trim panel.
31. Remove snap screws, then the driver side rear trim panel.
32. Disconnect driver safety belt retractor pretensioner electrical connector.
33. Attach restraint system diagnostic tool No. 418-F395, or equivalent, to driver safety belt retractor pretensioner electrical connector.
34. Connect battery ground cable.

TOWN CAR

1998

1. Disconnect and isolate battery ground cable, then allow at least one minute for back-up power supply to deplete.
2. Remove air bag retaining screw covers from rear of steering wheel, then the two air bag module retaining screws.
3. Disconnect driver's air bag module and horn switch connectors.
4. Connect Rotunda air bag simulator tool No. 105-00012, or equivalent, to vehicle air bag wiring harness at top steering column.
5. Open glove compartment and disconnect its compartment isolator.
6. Working through glove compartment opening, disconnect passenger's air bag module electrical connector.
7. Remove two passenger's air bag module retaining bolts, then the air bag module.
8. Connect second Rotunda air bag simulator tool No. 105-00012, or equivalent, to wiring harness in place of passenger's air bag module.
9. Connect battery ground cable.

1999

1. Disconnect and isolate battery ground cable, then allow at least one minute for back-up power supply to deplete.
2. Remove driver's air bag module as follows:
   a. Remove two air bag module retaining screws.
   b. Disconnect driver's air bag module and horn switch connectors. **When carrying a live air bag module, ensure bag and trim cover are pointed away from your body. To prevent injury by accidental deployment, place module on a bench with trim cover facing upward.**
3. Connect Rotunda air bag simulator tool No. 105-00012, or equivalent, to vehicle air bag wiring harness at top steering column.
4. Open glove compartment and disconnect glove compartment isolator.
5. Push in on glove compartment door tabs and position downward.
6. Disconnect passenger's air bag module electrical connector.
7. Connect second Rotunda air bag simulator tool No. 105-00012, or equivalent, to wiring harness in place of passenger's air bag module.
8. Disconnect side air bag module electrical connector located beneath driver's seat.
9. Attach Rotunda air bag simulator tool No. 105-00012, or equivalent, to side air bag connector under driver's seat on vehicle wiring harness side
10. Disconnect side air bag module electrical connector located beneath passenger's seat.
11. Attach Rotunda air bag simulator tool No. 105-00012, or equivalent, to side air bag connector under passenger's seat on vehicle wiring harness side
12. Connect battery ground cable.

2000

1. Disconnect and isolate battery ground cable.
2. **On models equipped with auxiliary batteries and power supplies,** disconnect and isolate these items, too.
3. **On all models,** wait one minute for back-up power supply to deplete.
4. Remove two steering wheel spoke bolt covers, if equipped.
5. Remove two air bag module to steering wheel attaching bolts.
6. Carefully lift air bag module away from steering wheel, then disconnect air bag module and horn to clockspring electrical connectors. **When carrying a live air bag module, ensure bag and trim cover are pointed away from your body. To prevent injury by accidental deployment, place module on a bench with trim cover facing upward.**
7. Remove air bag module and Attach Rotunda air bag simulator tool No. 105-R0012, or equivalent, to vehicle harness connector at top of steering column.
8. Open glove compartment, then push tabs in and rotate door downward past stops.
9. Disconnect passenger's air bag module electrical connector.
10. Attach Rotunda air bag simulator tool No. 105-R0012, or equivalent, to passenger's air bag module electrical connector on vehicle wiring harness side.
11. Disconnect side air bag module electrical connector located beneath driver's seat.
12. Attach Rotunda air bag simulator tool No. 105-R0012, or equivalent, to side air bag connector under driver's seat on vehicle wiring harness side
13. Disconnect side air bag module electrical connector located beneath passenger's seat.
14. Attach Rotunda air bag simulator tool No. 105-R0012, or equivalent, to side air bag connector under passenger's

seat on vehicle wiring harness side

15. If side air bag diagnosis or service is to be performed, remove front seats as follows:
    a. Move front seat all the way rearward, then remove seat track front bolt covers and bolts.
    b. Move front seat all the way forward, then remove seat track rear bolt covers and bolts.
    c. Disconnect front seat electrical connectors, then remove front seats from vehicle.
16. Connect battery ground cable.

2001-02

1. Disconnect and isolate battery ground cable.
2. **On models equipped with auxiliary batteries and power supplies,** disconnect and isolate these items, too.
3. **On all models,** wait one minute for back-up power supply to deplete.
4. Remove steering column opening lower finish panel by removing parking brake release assembly then pulling out at top of panel to release retaining clips.
5. Remove attaching bolts, then the steering column lower reinforcement.
6. Remove lefthand lower instrument panel insulator.
7. Pushing in on release tab, disconnect clockspring electrical connector at base of steering column.
8. Attach restraint system diagnostic tool No. 418–F403, or equivalent to vehicle harness side of clockspring electrical connector.
9. Remove audio unit.
10. Remove instrument panel cluster finish panel from instrument panel.
11. Open glove compartment and disconnect glove compartment isolator.
12. While pushing in on two glove compartment door tabs, position glove compartment downward.
13. Through glove compartment opening, remove passenger air bag module wire harness pin type fasteners from instrument panel.
14. Through glove box opening, remove passenger air bag module bolts.
15. Placing one hand in glove compartment opening, push passenger air bag module out from instrument panel. **Do not handle air bag module by grabbing edges of deployment doors.**
16. Disconnect passenger air bag module electrical connector, then remove air bag module from vehicle.
17. Attach restraint system diagnostic tool No. 418–F403, or equivalent, to vehicle harness side of passenger side air bag module electrical connector.
18. Connect battery ground cable.
19. Move and tilt front seats to their highest and most forward position.
20. Disconnect battery ground cable an wait at least one minute for back-up power supply to deplete.
21. **On models less side air bags,** proceed as follows:
    a. **Do not deactivate side air bags module circuit by removing the side air bag bridge resistor from the side air bag floor electrical connector.**
    b. If side air bag bridge resistor is removed, an open circuit fault will be generated by restraints control module (RCM)
    c. If a restraint system diagnostic tool is installed at the side air bag floor electrical connector, a low resistance fault will be generated by RCM.
22. **On models equipped with side air bags,** proceed as follows:
    a. From under front passenger seat, release tab and disconnect passenger seat side air bag electrical connector.
    b. Attach restraint system diagnostic tool No. 418–F088, or equivalent, to vehicle harness side of passenger seat side air bag electrical connector.
23. **On all models,** remove passenger side B-pillar lower trim panel.
24. Push in on release tab and disconnect passenger safety belt retractor pretensioner electrical connector.
25. Attach restraint system diagnostic tool No. 418–F088, or equivalent, to vehicle harness side of passenger safety belt retractor pretensioner electrical connector
26. **On models equipped with side air bags,** proceed as follows:
    a. From under driver seat, release tab and disconnect driver seat side air bag electrical connector.
    b. Attach restraint system diagnostic tool No. 418–F088, or equivalent, to vehicle harness side of driver seat air bag electrical connector.
27. **On all models,** remove driver side b-pillar lower trim panel.
28. Push in on release tab, then disconnect driver safety belt retractor pretensioner electrical connector.
29. Attach restraint system diagnostic tool to vehicle harness side of driver side safety belt retractor pretensioner electrical connector.
30. Connect battery ground cable.
31. With restraint system diagnostic tools installed on all deployable devices, prove out supplemental restraint system as follows:
    a. Turn ignition switch from Off to Run position and visually monitor air bag indicator with air bag modules and pretensioners or restraint system diagnostic tools installed.
    b. Air bag lamp will illuminate for approximately six seconds, then turn off.
    c. If an air bag supplemental restraint system fault is present, air bag indicator will either fail to illuminate, remain illuminate continuously or flash.
32. Disconnect battery ground cable and wait for at least one minute for back-up power supply to deplete.

ARMING

CONTINENTAL

1998-99

1. Disconnect battery ground cable. Allow at least one minute for back-up power supply to deplete.
2. Remove air bag simulator from clockspring connector at top of steering column.
3. Connect driver's air bag electrical connector.
4. Install driver's air bag module to steering wheel.
5. **On 1998 models, torque** air bag module attaching bolts/nuts to 90–121 inch lbs., then install bolt covers.
6. **On 1999 models, torque** air bag module attaching bolts/nuts to 108 inch lbs., then install bolt covers.
7. **On all models,** remove air bag simulator tool at passenger's air bag connector.
8. Position passenger's air bag module to instrument panel.
9. Though glove compartment opening, install three passenger's air bag module lower mounting bracket to instrument panel bolts. Install two forward bolts, then the center bolt.
10. **On 1998 models, torque** air bag module attaching bolts/nuts to 62–97 inch lbs.
11. **On 1999 models, torque** air bag module attaching bolts/nuts to 80 inch lbs
12. **On all models,** connect passenger's air bag electrical connector, then close glove compartment.
13. **On 1999 models,** remove air bag simulator tool from side air bag connectors located beneath driver's and passenger's seat, then connect side air bag electrical connectors.
14. **On all models,** connect battery ground cable.
15. Place ignition switch in Run position and note air bag warning lamp operation. Indicator lamp should illuminate for approximately six seconds, then turn off.

2000-02

1. Disconnect and isolate battery ground cable.
2. **On models equipped with auxiliary batteries and power supplies,** disconnect and isolate these items, too.
3. **On all models,** wait one minute for back-up power supply to deplete.
4. Remove air bag simulator from vehicle harness connector at top of steering column.
5. Install driver's air bag module as follows:
    a. **When carrying a live air bag module, ensure bag and trim cover are pointed away from your body. To prevent injury by accidental deployment, place module on a bench with trim cover facing upward.**
    b. Connect driver's air bag module

and horn to clockspring electrical connectors.

c. Position driver's air bag module to steering wheel.
d. Install two driver's air bag module to steering wheel retaining bolts. Torque retaining bolts to specifications.
e. **Torque** retaining bolts to 108 inch lbs.
f. Install two steering wheel spoke bolt covers, if equipped.

6. Remove air bag simulator at passenger's air bag connector.
7. Connect passenger's air bag electrical connector, then close glove compartment.
8. Remove air bag simulator from side air bag connector located beneath driver's seat, then connect the side air bag electrical connector.
9. Remove air bag simulator from side air bag connector located beneath passenger's seat, then connect the side air bag electrical connector.
10. If front seats were removed, install as follows:
    a. Disconnect side air simulator tools from side air bag module floor connectors at driver's and passenger's sides.
    b. Position front seat in vehicle.
    c. Move front seat all the way forward, then install seat track rear bolts and covers.
    d. Move front seat all the way rearward, then install seat track front bolts and covers.
    e. Disconnect side air simulator tools from side air bag module floor connectors at driver's and passenger's sides.
    f. Connect driver's and passenger's front seat electrical connectors.
11. Connect battery ground cable.
12. Place ignition switch in Run position **from a safe location at side or below air bag modules** and note air bag warning lamp operation. Indicator lamp should light for approximately six seconds, then turn off.

CONTOUR & MYSTIQUE

1998

1. Disconnect and isolate battery ground cable, then the positive cable. Allow at least one minute for back-up power supply to deplete.
2. Remove air bag simulator tool from driver's air bag sliding contact connector.
3. Connect driver's air bag connect, then install air bag module to steering wheel.
4. **Torque** mounting bolts/nuts to 44 inch lbs.
5. Remove air bag simulator tool from passenger's air bag wiring harness, then position air bag module into instrument panel.
6. Install retaining bolts and nuts, then **torque** to 12 ft. lbs.
7. Install A/C evaporator register duct and glove compartment upper cover, then connect glove compartment lamp and install screws.
8. Install glove compartment assembly into instrument panel.
9. Connect battery positive cable, then the ground cable.
10. Place ignition switch in Run position **from a safe location at sides or below air bag modules** and note air bag warning lamp operation. Indicator lamp should light for approximately six seconds, then turn off.

1999–2000

1. Disconnect and isolate battery ground cable.
2. Allow at least one minute for back-up power supply to deplete.
3. Remove air bag simulator tool from driver's air bag sliding contact connector.
4. Install driver's air bag module as follows:
    a. Connect driver's air bag module electrical connector.
    b. Position driver's air bag module to steering wheel.
    c. Install two air bag module bolt and washer assemblies at rear or sides of steering wheel.
    d. **Torque** mounting bolts/nuts to 44 inch lbs.
5. Remove air bag simulator tool from passenger's air bag wiring harness.
6. Connect passenger's air bag module electrical connector.
7. Install passenger's air vent duct and glove compartment upper cover, then connect glove compartment lamp and install screws.
8. Install glove compartment assembly in instrument panel.
9. Connect battery ground cable.
10. Place ignition switch in Run position **from a safe location at sides or below air bag modules** and note air bag warning lamp operation. Indicator lamp should light for approximately six seconds, then turn off.

COUGAR

1. Disconnect and isolate battery ground cable.
2. Allow at least one minute for back-up power supply to deplete.
3. Remove air bag simulator tool from driver's air bag sliding contact connector.
4. Connect driver's air bag module electrical connector.
5. Position driver's air bag module to steering wheel.
6. Install driver's air bag module Torx retaining screws.
7. **Torque** mounting screws to 44 inch lbs.
8. Remove air bag simulator tool from passenger's air bag wiring harness.
9. From passenger's foot well, roll passenger's air bag module around cross beam.
10. After positioning air bag module, install two air bag module to cross beam retaining bolts.
11. **Torque** mounting bolts/nuts to 12 ft. lbs.
12. Connect passenger's air bag module electrical connector.
13. Install passenger's air register duct.
14. Install glove compartment finish panel and secure with four Torx retaining screws.
15. Depress side stops to attach glove compartment sides, then close glove compartment.
16. Install three glove compartment Torx retaining screws.
17. **On models equipped with side air bags,** proceed as follows:
    a. Install side air bag module.
    b. **Torque** side air bag module retaining bolts/nuts to 12 ft. lbs.
    c. Connect side air bag module electrical connector at driver's and passenger's seats.
    d. Install seat pads, covers and back rests.
18. **On all models,** connect battery ground cable.
19. Place ignition switch in Run position **from a safe location at sides or below air bag modules** and note air bag warning lamp operation. Indicator lamp should light for approximately three seconds, then turn off.

CROWN VICTORIA & GRAND MARQUIS

1998–2000

1. Disconnect and isolate battery ground cable, then wait one minute for back-up power supply to deplete.
2. Remove air bag simulator from harness on top of steering column.
3. Connect driver's air bag and horn electrical connectors.
4. Position driver's air bag on steering wheel and secure with two retaining bolts.
5. **Torque** driver's air bag module retaining bolts/nuts to 108 inch lbs.
6. **On all models,** remove air bag simulator from passenger side air bag harness connector.
7. Position air bag module in instrument panel.
8. Install two passengers air bag module retaining screws and bolts.
9. **On 1998 models, torque** passenger air nag module lower screws to 68–92 inch lbs., and upper screws to 19–25 inch lbs.
10. **On 1999–2000 models, torque** passenger air bag module retaining bolts/nuts to 80 inch lbs.
11. **On all models,** connect passenger's air bag module electrical connector.
12. **On 1999 models,** connect clock electrical connector, then position the trim panel to instrument panel. Attach trim panel by pulling inward to seat clips.
13. **On all models,** push inward on glove compartment door tabs then position door upward
14. Install glove compartment locator.
15. Connect battery ground cable.
16. Place ignition switch in Run position **from a safe location at sides of or below air bag modules** and note air bag warning lamp operation. Indicator lamp should light for approximately six seconds, then turn off.

17. Reset radio stations and the clock.

2001–02

1. Disconnect battery ground cable.
2. Wait at least one minute for back-up power supply to deplete.
3. Remove restraint system diagnostic tool from driver safety belt retractor and pretensioner electrical connector.
4. Connect driver safety belt retractor and pretensioner electrical connectors.
5. Remove restraint system diagnostic tool from passenger safety belt retractor and pretensioner electrical connectors.
6. Connect passenger safety belt retractor and pretensioner electrical connectors.
7. Install front seats.
8. Remove restraint system diagnostic tools from passenger air bag module electrical connectors.
9. Install passenger air bag module electrical connector.
10. Remove restraint system diagnostic tools from driver air bag module electrical connectors.
11. Install driver air bag module electrical connector.
12. Reconnect battery ground cable.
13. Prove out system as follows:
    a. Turn the ignition switch from the OFF to the RUN position and visually monitor the air bag indicator with the air bag modules and safety belt pretensioners or restraint system diagnostic tools installed.
    b. The air bag indicator will light continuously for approximately six seconds and then turn off.
    c. If an air bag supplemental restraint system (SRS) fault is present, the air bag indicator will either fail to light, remain lit continuously, or flash.
    d. The flashing might not occur until approximately 30 seconds after the ignition switch has been turned from the OFF to the RUN position. This is the time required for the restraints control module (RCM) to complete the testing of the SRS.
    e. If the air bag indicator is inoperative and an SRS fault exists, a chime will sound in a pattern of five sets of five beeps. If this occurs, the air bag indicator will need to be repaired before diagnosis can continue.

ESCORT, TRACER & ZX2

1. Disconnect battery ground cable. Allow one minute for back-up power supply to deplete.
2. **On models equipped with auxiliary batteries and power supplies,** disconnect and isolate these items also.
3. **On all models,** remove air bag simulator from harness on top of steering column.
4. Connect driver's air bag connector.
5. Position driver's air bag on steering wheel and secure with two bolts.
6. **Torque** mounting bolts to 70–86 inch lbs.
7. Remove air bag simulator from passenger's air bag harness connector.
8. Connect air bag module electrical connector, then position module in instrument panel.
9. Install four air bag module bolts.
10. **Torque** air bag module retaining bolts to 72–103 inch lbs.
11. Push glove compartment door back into instrument panel.
12. Connect battery ground cable.
13. Place ignition switch in Run position **from a safe location at side of or below air bag modules** and note air bag warning lamp operation, which should light for approximately six seconds, then turn off. If air bag indicator is inoperative and an SRS fault exists, a chime will sound in a pattern of five sets of beeps. If this occurs, air bag indicator will need to be repaired before diagnosis can continue
14. Reset radio stations and the clock.

FOCUS

1. Disconnect and isolate battery ground cable.
2. **On models equipped with auxiliary batteries and power supplies,** disconnect and isolate these items, too.
3. **On all models,** wait one minute for back-up power supply to deplete.
4. Remove air bag simulator from harness on top of steering column.
5. Connect driver's air bag connector.
6. Position driver's air bag on steering wheel and secure with two bolts. **When carrying a live air bag module, ensure bag and trim cover are pointed away from your body. To prevent injury by accidental deployment, place module on a bench with trim cover facing upward.**
7. **Torque** mounting screws to 44 inch lbs.
8. Remove air bag simulator from passenger's air bag harness connector.
9. Connect passenger's air bag module electrical connector.
10. Remove air bag simulator from driver's side seat belt pretensioner connector.
11. Connect driver's side seat belt pretensioner electrical connector.
12. Remove air bag simulator from driver's side air bag connector.
13. Connect driver's side air bag electrical connector.
14. Remove air bag simulator from passenger's side seat belt pretensioner connector.
15. Connect passenger's side seat belt pretensioner electrical connector.
16. Remove air bag simulator from passenger's side air bag connector.
17. Connect passenger's side air bag electrical connector.
18. Install glove compartment.
19. Connect battery ground cable.
20. Place ignition switch in Run position **from a safe location at side of or below air bag modules** and note air bag warning lamp operation, which should light for approximately six seconds, then turn off.
21. Reset radio stations and the clock.

LS

1. Disconnect and isolate battery ground cable.
2. **On models equipped with auxiliary batteries and power supplies,** disconnect and isolate these items also.
3. **On all models,** wait one minute for back-up power supply to deplete.
4. Remove seat belt pretensioner simulator tool from passenger's seat belt pretensioner harness connector.
5. Connect passenger's seat belt pretensioner electrical connector.
6. Install passenger side B-pillar pillar trim.
7. Remove seat belt pretensioner simulator tool from driver's seat belt pretensioner harness connector.
8. Connect driver's seat belt pretensioner electrical connector.
9. Install driver side B-pillar pillar trim.
10. Remove air bag simulator tool from harness connector at top of steering column.
11. Connect driver's air bag electrical connector.
12. Position driver's air bag on steering wheel and secure with its bolts. **When carrying a live air bag module, ensure bag and trim cover are pointed away from your body. To prevent injury by accidental deployment, place module on a bench with trim cover facing upward.**
13. **Torque** mounting bolts to 108 inch lbs.
14. Remove air bag simulator from passenger's air bag harness connector.
15. Connect passenger's air bag module electrical connector.
16. Install glove compartment.
17. Remove air bag simulator from passenger's side air bag connector.
18. Connect passenger's side air bag electrical connector.
19. Remove air bag simulator from driver's side air bag connector.
20. Connect driver's side air bag electrical connector.
21. Connect battery ground cable.
22. Place ignition switch in Run position **from a safe location at side or below air bag modules** and note air bag warning lamp operation. Indicator lamp should light for approximately six seconds, then turn off.
23. Reset radio stations and the clock.

MARK VIII

1. Disconnect battery ground cable.
2. Allow at least one minute for back-up power supply to deplete.
3. Remove air bag simulator from clockspring connector at top of steering column.
4. Connect driver's air bag electrical connector.
5. Position driver's air bag on steering wheel and secure with two screw and washer assemblies.
6. **Torque** mounting bolts to 90–122 inch lbs.
7. Remove air bag simulator from passenger harness connector.
8. Connect electrical connector to air bag module and position air bag module in

instrument panel.
9. Install air bag module retaining bolts and screws.
10. **Torque** passenger's air bag module upper retaining bolts to 9–17 inch lbs. and lower retaining screws to 62–97 inch lbs.
11. Install side defroster duct screws.
12. Reverse removal procedure to install glove compartment, instrument trim covers and steering column covers.
13. Connect battery ground cable.
14. Place ignition switch in Run position **from a safe location at side or below air bag modules** and note air bag warning lamp operation. Indicator lamp should light for approximately six seconds, then turn off.
15. Reset radio stations and the clock.

MUSTANG

1. Disconnect battery ground cable.
2. **On models equipped with auxiliary batteries and power supplies,** disconnect and isolate these items also.
3. **On all models,** allow at least one minute for back-up power supply to deplete.
4. Remove air bag simulator tool from harness connector at top of steering column.
5. Connect driver's air bag connector.
6. Position driver's air bag on steering wheel and secure with four nut and bolt assemblies.
7. **On 1998 models, torque** driver's air bag module retaining bolts/nuts to 90–122 inch lbs.
8. **On 1999–2002 models, torque** driver's air bag module retaining bolts/nuts to 80 inch lbs.
9. **On all models,** remove air bag simulator tool from passenger's air bag module harness then position module in instrument panel.
10. Attach connector to instrument panel reinforcement, then connect to wiring harness.
11. Install passenger's air bag retaining bolt.
12. **Torque** passenger's air bag module retaining bolts to 80 inch lbs.
13. Press gently on air bag module corners to engage with instrument panel trim, then install righthand side A/C duct.
14. Press sides of glove compartment assembly together and lift into position in instrument panel. Close glove compartment door.
15. Connect battery ground cable.
16. Place ignition switch in Run position and note air bag warning lamp operation. Warning lamp should illuminate for approximately six seconds, then turn off.

SABLE & TAURUS

1998–99

Prior to disconnecting battery, record user 1 and user 2 pre-set radio frequencies.

1. Disconnect battery ground cable.
2. Wait one minute for back-up power supply to deplete.
3. Remove air bag simulator tool from clockspring connector.
4. Position driver's air bag on steering wheel and secure with screw and washer assemblies.
5. **Torque** mounting screws to 90–122 inch lbs.
6. Remove air bag simulator from air bag module wiring harness connector.
7. Connect electrical connectors to passenger's air bag module in instrument panel.
8. Install passenger's air bag module retaining bolts.
9. **Torque** mounting bolts to 68–92 inch lbs.
10. Return glove compartment to upright position.
11. Connect battery ground cable.
12. Install air bag trim panel
13. Place ignition switch in Run position and note air bag warning lamp operation. Indicator lamp should illuminate for approximately six seconds, then turn off.

2000–02

1. Disconnect and isolate battery ground cable.
2. **On models equipped with auxiliary batteries and power supplies,** disconnect and isolate these items also.
3. **On all models,** wait one minute for back-up power supply to deplete.
4. Disconnect driver's air bag restraint system diagnostic tool from vehicle side of driver's air bag sliding contact electrical connector.
5. Connect driver's air bag sliding contact electrical connector.
6. Install steering column lower cover and reinforcement.
7. Disconnect passenger's air bag restraint system diagnostic tool from vehicle side of passenger's air bag electrical connector.
8. Check position of passenger's air bag module J-nuts.
9. Position air bag module and trim cover to instrument panel. **When carrying a live air bag module, ensure bag and trim cover are pointed away from your body. To prevent injury by accidental deployment, place module on a bench with trim cover facing upward..**
10. Install wiring harness pin retaining to air bag module.
11. Connect passenger's air bag module electrical connector.
12. Align air bag module channels with instrument panel rails.
13. Starting at lefthand side of air bag module trim cover, install upper and lower alignment pins into instrument panel.
14. Working from left to right, install trim cover alignment pins and retainers into instrument panel. When all channels and rails are aligned, gap around the perimeter of the air bag module trim cover will be even.
15. Through glove compartment opening, install passengers air bag module attaching bolts.
16. **Torque** attaching bolts to 71 inch lbs.
17. Close glove compartment.
18. Disconnect passenger's seat belt pretensioner restraint system diagnostic tool from 10 pin floor electrical connector.
19. Connect passenger's seat belt pretensioner electrical connector.
20. **On models equipped with side air bags,** disconnect side air bag restraint system diagnostic tool from side air bag floor electrical connector on passenger's side. Connect side air bag electrical connector on passenger's side.
21. **On all models,** disconnect driver's seat belt pretensioner restraint system diagnostic tool from 10 pin floor electrical connector.
22. Connect driver's seat belt pretensioner electrical connector.
23. **On models equipped with side air bags,** disconnect side air bag restraint system diagnostic tool from side air bag floor electrical connector on driver's side.
24. **On models equipped with side air bags,** connect side air bag electrical connector on driver's side.
25. **On all models,** connect battery ground cable.
26. From a safe location at side or below air bag modules, place ignition switch in Run position and note air bag warning lamp operation. Indicator lamp should light for approximately six seconds, then turn off.

THUNDERBIRD

1. Disconnect battery ground cable and wait at least one minute for back-up power supply to deplete.
2. Remove diagnostic tool No. 418-F395, or equivalent, from driver side safety belt retractor pretensioner electrical connector.
3. Connect driver side safety belt retractor pretensioner electrical connector.
4. Install driver side rear trim panel and speaker grille.
5. Position safety belt back into driver seat guide, then install driver side door weatherstripping and scuff plate.
6. Remove diagnostic tool No. 418-F133, or equivalent, from driver seat side air bag module electrical connector located under driver seat.
7. Connect driver seat side air bag module electrical connector.
8. Remove diagnostic tool No. 418-F395, or equivalent, from passenger side safety belt retractor pretensioner electrical connector.
9. Connect passenger side safety belt retractor pretensioner electrical connector.
10. Install passenger side rear trim panel and speaker grille.
11. Position safety belt back into passenger seat guide, then install passenger side door weatherstripping and scuff plate.
12. Remove diagnostic tool No. 418-F133, or equivalent, from passenger seat side air bag module electrical connector located under passenger seat.
13. Connect passenger seat side air bag module electrical connector.

14. Connect battery ground cable and move seats as far rearward as possible.
15. Disconnect battery ground cable and wait at least one minute for back-up power supply to deplete.
16. Reach through glove compartment opening and remove diagnostic tool No. 418-F395, or equivalent, from passenger air bag module electrical connector located behind center of instrument panel, above the cross car brace.
17. Connect passenger air bag module electrical connector, then install glove compartment and door.
18. Remove diagnostic tool No. 418-F088, or equivalent, from clockspring electrical connector located at base of steering column.
19. Connect clocksrping electrical connector, then install steering column reinforcement.
20. Tighten two driver side instrument panel tunnel brace bolts, then position carpet back in place.
21. Install heater duct and hood latch assembly.
22. Install driver side insulator panel and light socket.
23. Connect electrical connectors, then install lower steering column opening finish panel.
24. Connect battery ground cable.
25. Place ignition switch in the RUN position, then **from a safe location at side or below air bag modules,** note air bag warning lamp operation. Indicator lamp should light for approximately six seconds, then turn off.

TOWN CAR

1998

1. Disconnect and isolate battery ground cable, then wait one minute for back-up power supply to deplete.
2. Remove air bag simulator tool from harness connector at top of steering column.
3. Connect air bag module electrical connector.
4. Position driver's air bag module on steering wheel and secure with two retaining screws. Install the two retaining screw covers to rear of steering wheel.
5. **Torque** driver's air bag module retaining bolts/screws to 90–122 inch lbs., then install bolt covers.
6. Remove air bag simulator from passenger's harness connector.
7. Install two passenger's air bag module retaining bolts, **torque** to 67–92 inch lbs.
8. Connect electrical connector to air bag module in instrument panel.
9. Return glove compartment to proper position.
10. Connect battery ground cable.
11. Place ignition switch in Run position **from a safe location at side or below air bag modules** and note air bag warning lamp operation. Indicator lamp should light for approximately six seconds, then turn off.
12. Reset radio stations and the clock.

1999

1. Disconnect and isolate battery ground cable, then wait one minute for back-up power supply to deplete.
2. Remove air bag simulator tool from harness connector at top of steering column.
3. Connect air bag module electrical connector.
4. Position driver's air bag module on steering wheel and secure with two retaining screws.
5. **Torque** driver's air bag module retaining screws to 108 inch lbs.
6. Remove air bag simulator from passenger's harness connector.
7. Install two passenger air bag module retaining bolts, **torque** to 80 inch lbs.
8. Connect electrical connector to air bag module in instrument panel.
9. Return glove compartment to proper position.
10. Remove air bag simulator from side air bag connector located beneath driver's seat, then connect the side air bag electrical connector.
11. Remove air bag simulator from side air bag connector located beneath passenger's seat, then connect the side air bag electrical connector.
12. Connect battery ground cable.
13. Place ignition switch in Run position **from a safe location at side or below air bag modules** and note air bag warning lamp operation. Indicator lamp should light for approximately six seconds, then turn off.
14. Reset radio stations and the clock.

2000

1. Disconnect and isolate battery ground cable.
2. **On models equipped with auxiliary batteries and power supplies,** disconnect and isolate these items also.
3. **On all models,** wait one minute for back-up power supply to deplete.
4. Remove air bag simulator from vehicle harness connector at top of steering column.
5. Connect driver's air bag module and horn to clockspring electrical connectors. **When carrying a live air bag module, ensure bag and trim cover are pointed away from your body. To prevent injury by accidental deployment, place module on a bench with trim cover facing upward.**
6. Position driver's air bag module to steering wheel.
7. Install two driver's air bag module to steering wheel retaining bolts.
8. **Torque** driver's air bag module retaining bolts/nuts to 108 inch lbs.
9. Install two steering wheel spoke bolt covers, if equipped.
10. Remove air bag simulator at passenger's air bag connector.
11. Connect passenger's air bag electrical connector, then close glove compartment.
12. Remove air bag simulator from side air bag connector located beneath driver's seat, then connect the side air bag electrical connector.
13. Remove air bag simulator from side air bag connector located beneath passenger's seat, then connect the side air bag electrical connector.
14. If front seats were removed, install as follows:
    a. Position front seat in vehicle.
    b. Move front seat all the way forward, then install seat track rear bolts and covers.
    c. Move front seat all the way rearward, then install seat track front bolts and covers.
    d. Disconnect side air simulator tools from side air bag module floor connectors at driver's and passenger's sides.
    e. Connect driver's and passenger's front seat electrical connectors.
15. Connect battery ground cable.
16. Place ignition switch in Run position **from a safe location at side or below air bag modules** and note air bag warning lamp operation. Indicator lamp should light for approximately six seconds, then turn off.

2001–02

1. Disconnect and isolate battery ground cable.
2. **On models equipped with auxiliary batteries and power supplies,** disconnect and isolate these items also.
3. **On all models,** wait one minute for back-up power supply to deplete.
4. Remove air bag simulator from vehicle harness connector at top of steering column.
5. Connect driver's air bag module and horn to clockspring electrical connectors. **When carrying a live air bag module, ensure bag and trim cover are pointed away from your body. To prevent injury by accidental deployment, place module on a bench with trim cover facing upward.**
6. Position driver's air bag module to steering wheel.
7. Install two driver's air bag module to steering wheel retaining bolts, **torque** to 108 inch lbs.
8. Install two steering wheel spoke bolt covers, if equipped.
9. Remove air bag simulator at passenger's air bag connector.
10. Connect passenger's air bag electrical connector, then close glove compartment.
11. Remove air bag simulator from side air bag connector located beneath driver's seat, then connect the side air bag electrical connector.
12. Remove air bag simulator from side air bag connector located beneath passenger's seat, then connect the side air bag electrical connector.
13. If front seats were removed, install as follows:
    a. Position front seat in vehicle.
    b. Move front seat all the way forward, then install seat track rear bolts and covers.
    c. Move front seat all the way rearward, then install seat track front bolts and covers.
    d. Disconnect side air simulator tools

from side air bag module floor connectors at driver's and passenger's sides.
   e. Connect driver's and passenger's front seat electrical connectors.
14. Connect battery ground cable.
15. Place ignition switch in Run position **from a safe location at side or below air bag modules** and note air bag warning lamp operation. Indicator lamp should light for approximately six seconds, then turn off.

GENERAL MOTORS

On Buick, Cadillac, Chevrolet, Oldsmobile, Pontiac, Metro and Prizm models, the Diagnostic Energy Reserve Module or Sensing and Diagnostic Module (DERM/SDM) can maintain enough voltage to cause air bag deployment for up to ten minutes after the ignition is turned Off and the battery is disconnected. Servicing the SIR system during this period may result in accidental deployment and personal injury.

DISARMING

ACHIEVA & SKYLARK

1. Ensure front wheels are pointed straight-ahead.
2. Turn ignition to Lock position and remove key.
3. Remove AIR BAG fuse from fuse block.
4. Remove lefthand sound insulator.
5. Disconnect Connector Position Assurance (CPA) and driver's air bag module yellow two-way connector at base of steering column.
6. Remove righthand sound insulator.
7. **On models equipped with passenger's air bag module,** remove righthand sound insulator and disconnect CPA and yellow two-way connector from passenger's air bag module pigtail.

ALERO, CUTLASS & MALIBU

1. Ensure front wheels are pointed straight-ahead.
2. Ensure ignition switch is in Off or Lock position. Remove key.
3. Remove lefthand instrument panel wiring harness junction block access panel.
4. Remove AIR BAG fuse from lefthand instrument panel fuse junction block.
5. Disconnect Connector Position Assurance (CPA) located above lefthand instrument panel wiring harness junction block.
6. Disconnect steering wheel module coil connector.
7. Remove righthand instrument panel wiring harness junction block access panel.
8. Disconnect CPA located above righthand instrument panel wiring harness junction block.
9. Disconnect passenger's air bag module connector.

AURORA

1998-99

Refer to "Achieva & Skylark" for disarming procedure.

2001-02

1. Ensure front wheels are pointing straight ahead.
2. Turn ignition switch to Off position and remove key.
3. Remove SIR fuse from rear fuse block located under rear seat.
4. Remove instrument panel lefthand side sound insulator.
5. Remove Connector Position Assurance (CPA) from driver's air bag module yellow connector located next to steering column.
6. Disconnect driver's air bag module yellow connector from vehicle harness yellow connector.
7. Remove instrument panel righthand side sound insulator.
8. Remove CPA from passenger's air bag module yellow connector located above instrument panel righthand side sound insulator.
9. Disconnect passenger's air bag module yellow connector from vehicle harness yellow connector.
10. Remove CPA from lefthand side impact air bag module yellow connector located under driver's seat.
11. Disconnect lefthand side impact air bag module yellow connector from vehicle harness yellow connector.
12. Remove CPA from righthand side impact air bag module yellow connector located under righthand front seat.
13. Disconnect righthand side impact air bag module yellow connector from vehicle harness yellow connector.

BONNEVILLE, EIGHTY-EIGHT, LESABRE, LSS & REGENCY

1998-99

Refer to "Achieva & Skylark" for disarming procedure.

2000-02

1. Ensure front wheels are pointed straight-ahead.
2. Turn ignition switch to Off position and remove key.
3. Remove SIR fuse from rear fuse block located under rear seat.
4. Remove instrument panel lefthand sound insulator.
5. Disconnect Connector Position Assurance (CPA) from driver's air bag module yellow two-way connector at base of steering column.
6. Disconnect driver's air bag module yellow two-way connector from vehicle harness yellow connector.
7. Remove righthand sound insulator.
8. Disconnect CPA and yellow two-way connector from passenger's air bag module yellow connector located above righthand sound insulator.
9. Disconnect passenger's air bag module yellow connector from vehicle harness yellow connector.
10. Disconnect CPA from lefthand side impact air bag module yellow electrical connector located under driver's seat.
11. Disconnect lefthand side impact air bag module yellow electrical connector from vehicle harness yellow connector.
12. Remove CPA from righthand side impact air bag module electrical connector located under righthand front seat.
13. Disconnect righthand side impact air bag module yellow electrical connector from vehicle harness yellow connector.

CAMARO & FIREBIRD

1. Ensure front wheels are pointed straight-ahead.
2. Turn ignition switch to Off position and remove key.
3. Remove instrument panel fuse block access door.
4. Remove AIR BAG fuse from instrument panel fuse box.
5. Remove lefthand instrument panel insulator.
6. Disconnect Connector Position Assurance (CPA) from inflatable restraint steering wheel module coil connector located at base of steering column.
7. Disconnect steering wheel module coil connector located at base of steering column.
8. Remove righthand instrument panel insulator.
9. Disconnect CPA from passenger's air bag module connector located behind instrument panel compartment door.
10. Disconnect yellow two-way connector from passenger's air bag module located behind glove compartment.

CATERA

1998

1. Turn steering wheel to straight-ahead position.
2. Turn ignition switch to Lock position and remove key.
3. Wait one minute until energy reserve capacitors in SIR system have discharged.

1999-2001

1. Turn steering wheel to straight-ahead position.
2. Turn ignition switch to Off position and remove key.
3. Remove steering column upper and lower covers.
4. Disconnect inflatable restraint steering wheel module coil connector from inflatable restraint steering wheel module coil.
5. Remove passenger's air bag module cover.
6. Disconnect Connector Position Assurance (CPA) from passenger's air bag module electrical connector.
7. Disconnect passenger's air bag module electrical connector.
8. Remove driver's outer seat track cover.
9. Disconnect driver's seat belt pretensioner two-way electrical connector from inline connector C315.

10. Disconnect CPA from lefthand side impact air bag module electrical connector.
11. Disconnect lefthand side impact air bag module electrical connector.
12. Remove righthand front outer seat track cover.
13. Disconnect passenger's seat belt pretensioner two-way electrical connector from inline connector C316.
14. Remove CPA from righthand side impact air bag module electrical connector.
15. Disconnect righthand side impact air bag module electrical connector.

CAVALIER & SUNFIRE

1998-99

1. Ensure front wheels are pointed straight-ahead.
2. Turn ignition switch to Lock position and remove key.
3. **On 1998 models,** remove AIR BG 1 fuse from instrument panel fuse block.
4. **On 1999 models,** remove AIR BAG fuse from instrument panel fuse block.
5. **On all models,** remove lefthand lower trim panel.
6. Disconnect Connector Position Assurance (CPA) and both yellow two-way SIR electrical connectors at base of steering column.
7. Wait at least two minutes before proceeding with diagnosis or service.

2000-02

1. Ensure front wheels are pointed straight-ahead.
2. Turn ignition switch to Off position and remove key.
3. Remove lefthand instrument panel junction block access panel.
4. Remove SIR or AIR BAG fuse from lefthand instrument panel fuse block.
5. Disconnect Connector Position Assurance (CPA) from driver's air bag module coil connector located above lefthand instrument panel wiring harness junction block.
6. Disconnect steering wheel module coil connector.
7. Remove righthand instrument panel wiring harness junction block access panel.
8. Disconnect CPA from passenger's air bag module connector located above righthand instrument panel wiring harness junction block.
9. Disconnect passenger's air bag module connector.

CENTURY & REGAL

1998-99

1. Ensure front wheels are pointed straight-ahead.
2. Turn ignition switch to Lock position and remove ignition key.
3. Remove AIR BAG or SIR system fuse from instrument panel fuse block.
4. Remove lefthand underdash trim panel.
5. Disconnect Connector Position Assurance (CPA) and yellow air bag module connectors at base of steering column.
6. Disconnect passenger's air bag module CPA and yellow air bag module connectors located to right of steering column.

2000-02

1. Ensure front wheels are pointed straight-ahead.
2. Turn ignition to Off position and remove ignition key.
3. Remove instrument panel fuse block access door.
4. Remove AIR BAG fuse from instrument panel fuse block.
5. Remove lefthand underdash trim panel.
6. Disconnect Connector Position Assurance (CPA) from driver's air bag module coil connector located at base of steering column.
7. Disconnect driver's air bag module coil connector.
8. Disconnect passenger's air bag module CPA located to right of steering column.
9. Disconnect passenger's air bag module yellow air bag module connector.
10. **On models equipped with side impact air bag modules,** proceed as follows:
    a. Remove CPA from lefthand side impact air bag module impact module.
    b. Disconnect lefthand side impact air bag module.

CORVETTE

1. Place front wheels in straight-ahead position.
2. Turn ignition switch to Off position and remove key.
3. Remove front floor kick-up panel.
4. Remove SDM fuse from instrument panel fuse block.
5. Remove lefthand sound insulator.
6. Disconnect Connector Position Assurance (CPA) from driver's air bag module coil connector located at base of steering column.
7. Disconnect driver's air bag module coil yellow two-way SIR electrical connector at base of steering column.
8. Disconnect CPA from passenger's air bag module coil connector located at base of steering column.
9. Disconnect passenger's air bag module coil yellow two-way SIR electrical connector at base of steering column.

DEVILLE

1998-99

1. Place front wheels in straight-ahead position.
2. Turn ignition switch to Lock position and remove key.
3. Remove SIR fuse from trunk compartment fuse block.
4. Remove instrument panel lefthand sound insulator.
5. Disconnect Connector Position Assurance (CPA) and both yellow two-way SIR electrical connectors at base of steering column.
6. Remove glove compartment.
7. Disconnect CPA and yellow two-way connector from passenger's air bag module pigtail behind instrument panel.
8. Remove left and righthand front door panels.
9. Disconnect CPA and yellow two-way connectors located near side impact air bag module sensing module.

2000-02

1. Place front wheels in straight-ahead position.
2. Turn ignition to Off position and remove key.
3. Remove rear seat cushion.
4. Remove SIR fuse from fuse block under rear seat.
5. Remove instrument panel lefthand sound insulator.
6. Disconnect Connector Position Assurance (CPA) from driver's air bag module yellow connector located next to steering column.
7. Disconnect driver's air bag module connector from vehicle harness yellow connector.
8. Remove instrument panel righthand sound insulator.
9. Disconnect CPA from passenger's air bag module yellow connector located above righthand sound insulator.
10. Disconnect passenger's air bag module yellow connector from vehicle harness yellow connector.
11. Remove both CPAs locks from lefthand side impact air bag module and pretensioner yellow electrical connectors located under seat.
12. Disconnect lefthand side impact air bag module and pretensioner yellow electrical connectors from the vehicle harness yellow connector.
13. Disconnect both CPAs from righthand side impact air bag module and pretensioner yellow electrical connectors located under seat.
14. Disconnect righthand side impact air bag module and pretensioner yellow electrical connectors.
15. **On models equipped with rear side impact air bag modules,** proceed as follows:
    a. Remove rear seatback.
    b. Disconnect CPA from righthand rear side impact air bag module yellow electrical connector.
    c. Disconnect righthand rear side impact air bag module yellow electrical connector.
    d. Disconnect CPA from lefthand rear side impact air bag module yellow electrical connector.
    e. Disconnect lefthand rear side impact air bag module yellow electrical connector.

ELDORADO

1. Place front wheels in straight-ahead position.
2. Turn ignition to Lock position and remove key.
3. Remove SIR fuse from trunk compartment fuse block.
4. Remove instrument panel lefthand sound insulator.
5. Disconnect CPA and both yellow two-way SIR electrical connectors at base

of steering column.
6. Remove glove compartment.
7. Disconnect CPA and yellow two-way connector from passenger's air bag module pigtail behind instrument panel.

GRAND AM

1998

Refer to "Achieva & Skylark" for disarming procedure

1999–2002

Refer to "Alero, Cutlass & Malibu" for disarming procedure.

GRAND PRIX & INTRIGUE

Refer to "Century & Regal," "1998–99" for disarming procedure.

IMPALA

1. Ensure front wheels are pointed straight-ahead.
2. Turn ignition switch to Off position and remove ignition key.
3. Remove lefthand instrument panel fuse access cover.
4. Remove SRS fuse from fuse block.
5. Disconnect Connector Position Assurance (CPA) from driver's air bag module coil connector, located at lefthand side of instrument panel.
6. Disconnect driver's air bag module coil connector.
7. Remove instrument panel righthand access hole cover.
8. Unclip driver's and passenger's air bag modules' yellow four-way electrical connector from metal rail.
9. Disconnect CPA from passenger's air bag module connector, located at righthand side if instrument panel.
10. Disconnect passenger's air bag module connector.
11. Disconnect CPA from side impact air bag module, located under driver's seat.
12. Disconnect the side impact module.

LUMINA

1998

1. Ensure front wheels are pointed straight-ahead.
2. Turn ignition switch to Lock position and remove ignition key.
3. Remove AIR BAG system fuse from fuse block.
4. Remove lefthand underdash trim panel.
5. Disconnect Connector Position Assurance (CPA) and yellow air bag module connectors at base of steering column.
6. Flip down instrument panel compartment door to access connectors.
7. Disconnect passenger's air bag module CPA and yellow air bag module connectors, found behind and above instrument panel compartment.

1999–2001

1. Ensure front wheels are pointed straight-ahead.
2. Turn ignition to Lock position and remove ignition key.
3. Remove instrument panel fuse block door.
4. Remove Fuse 21 from fuse block.
5. Remove instrument panel lefthand sound insulator.
6. Disconnect CPA and yellow air bag module electrical connectors at base of steering column.
7. Remove instrument panel righthand sound insulator.
8. Open glove compartment door.
9. Disconnect passenger's air bag module CPA and yellow electrical connector.

METRO

1. Ensure front wheels are pointed straight-ahead.
2. Turn ignition to Lock position.
3. Remove AIR BAG fuse from fuse block near steering wheel base.
4. Remove steering wheel side cap.
5. Remove Connector Position Assurance (CPA) and disconnect yellow two-way electrical connector for driver's air bag module.
6. Pull glove compartment out while pushing inward on left and righthand stoppers.
7. Remove CPA and disconnect passenger's air bag module electrical connector.

MONTE CARLO

1998–99

Refer to "Lumina" for disarming procedure.

2000–02

Refer to "Impala" for disarming procedure.

PARK AVENUE

1998

Refer to "Bonneville & LeSabre" for disarming procedure.

2000–02

1. Ensure front wheels are pointed straight-ahead.
2. Turn ignition to Lock position and remove key.
3. Remove SIR fuse from underhood fuse block.
4. Remove lefthand sound insulator.
5. Disconnect Connector Position Assurance (CPA) and driver's air bag module yellow two-way connector at base of steering column.
6. Remove righthand sound insulator.
7. Disconnect CPA and yellow two-way connector from passenger's air bag module wiring.
8. Disconnect CPA and yellow two-way connector from righthand side impact air bag module electrical connector under front seat.

PRIZM

1998

1. Ensure front wheels are pointed straight-ahead.
2. Turn ignition switch to Lock position.
3. Remove IGN and CIG-RADIO fuses from junction block No. 1.
4. Remove Connector Position Assurance (CPA) and disconnect yellow two-way electrical connector at base of steering column.
5. **On models equipped with passenger's air bag module,** proceed as follows:
   a. Remove glove compartment from instrument panel.
   b. Remove CPA and disconnect yellow two-way connector from passenger's air bag module.

1999–2002

1. Ensure front wheels are pointed straight-ahead.
2. Turn ignition to Lock position.
3. Remove IGN and CIG fuses from junction block No. 1 near base of steering column.
4. Remove steering column lower trim cover.
5. Remove Connector Position Assurance (CPA) and disconnect yellow two-way electrical connector at base of steering column.
6. Remove glove compartment from instrument panel.
7. Remove CPA and disconnect yellow two-way connector from passenger's air bag module.
8. Release, unlock and disconnect side impact air bag modules' electrical connectors.

RIVIERA

Refer to "Aurora" for disarming procedure.

SEVILLE

Refer to "DeVille," "2000–02" for disarming procedure.

ARMING

ACHIEVA & SKYLARK

1. Turn steering wheel to straight-ahead position and turn ignition switch to Lock position.
2. Connect yellow two-way connector to passenger's air bag module pigtail and install CPA.
3. Install righthand sound insulator.
4. Connect yellow two-way SIR electrical connector at base of steering column and install CPA.
5. Install lefthand sound insulator.
6. Install AIR BAG fuse into fuse block.
7. Staying well away from both air bag modules, place ignition switch in the On position.
8. Ensure SIR lamp flashes 7–9 times and turns off.

ALERO, CUTLASS & MALIBU

1. Ensure front wheel are in straight ahead position.
2. Place ignition in Lock position, then remove ignition key.
3. Connect yellow two-way connector to passenger's air bag module pigtail and install CPA.
4. Connect yellow two-way SIR electrical connector and install CPA.

5. Install AIR BAG fuse into fuse block.
6. From a safe position at sides of or below air bag modules, turn ignition On.
7. Ensure SIR lamp flashes seven times and turns off.

AURORA

1998-99

Refer to "Achieva & Skylark" for arming procedure.

2001-02

1. Remove key from ignition switch.
2. Connect righthand side impact air bag module yellow connector to vehicle harness yellow connector located under righthand front seat.
3. Install connector position assurance (CPA) to righthand side impact air bag module yellow connector.
4. Connect lefthand side impact air bag module yellow connector to vehicle harness yellow connector located under driver's seat.
5. Install CPA to lefthand side impact air bag module yellow connector.
6. Connect passenger's air bag module yellow connector to vehicle harness yellow connector located above righthand sound insulator.
7. Install CPA to passenger's air bag module yellow connector.
8. Install instrument panel righthand side sound insulator.
9. Connect driver's air bag module yellow connector to vehicle harness yellow connector located next to steering column.
10. Install CPA to driver's air bag module yellow connector.
11. Install instrument panel lefthand side sound insulator.
12. Install SIR fuse to rear fuse block located under rear seat.
13. Staying well away from all air bag modules, turn ignition switch to ON position.
14. AIR BAG warning lamp will flash seven times, then turn OFF.

BONNEVILLE, EIGHTY-EIGHT, LESABRE, LSS, NINETY-EIGHT & REGENCY

1998-99

Refer to "Achieva & Skylark" for arming procedure.

2000-02

1. Turn steering wheel to straight-ahead position.
2. Turn ignition to Lock position, then remove key.
3. Connect yellow two-way connector and CPA at righthand side impact air bag module electrical connector under front seat.
4. Connect yellow two-way connector and CPA at lefthand side impact air bag module electrical connector under front seat.
5. Connect yellow two-way connector to passenger's air bag module wiring and install CPA.
6. Install righthand sound insulator.
7. Connect yellow two-way SIR electrical connector at base of steering column and install CPA.
8. Install lefthand sound insulator.
9. Install SIR fuse into rear fuse block.
10. From a safe position at sides of or below air bag modules, turn ignition On.
11. Ensure SIR lamp flashes seven times, then turns off.

CAMARO & FIREBIRD

1. Turn ignition key to Lock and remove key.
2. Connect yellow two-way connector to passenger's air bag module, then install CPA.
3. Install righthand instrument panel insulator.
4. Connect driver's air bag module yellow two-way SIR electrical connector.
5. Install CPA near base of steering column.
6. Install lefthand sound insulator.
7. Install AIR BAG fuse.
8. From a safe position at sides of or below air bag modules, turn ignition On.
9. Ensure SIR lamp flashes seven times, then turns off.

CATERA

1998

1. Turn steering wheel to straight-ahead position.
2. Turn ignition switch to Lock position.
3. Connect SDM, if necessary.
4. Turn ignition switch to Run position while staying well away from air bag modules.
5. Verify that AIR BAG warning lamp illuminates for 3–4 seconds and then turns off.

1999-2001

1. Turn steering wheel to straight-ahead position.
2. Turn ignition to Lock position.
3. Connect SDM electrical connectors if required.
4. Connect righthand side impact air bag module electrical connector and install CPA.
5. Connect righthand front seat belt pretensioner electrical connector.
6. Install rightand front seat track trim cover.
7. Connect lefthand side impact air bag module electrical connector and install CPA.
8. Connect driver's seat belt pretensioner electrical connector.
9. Install driver's front seat track trim cover.
10. Connect passenger's front air bag module electrical connector and install CPA.
11. Install passenger's front air bag module cover.
12. Connect driver's air bag module electrical connector to SRS coil assembly (clockspring).
13. Install steering column lower and upper covers.
14. From a safe position at sides of or below air bag modules, turn ignition On.
15. Ensure AIR BAG warning lamp flashes seven times, then turns off.

CAVALIER & SUNFIRE

1998-99

1. Turn ignition switch to Lock position and remove key.
2. Connect both yellow SIR connectors at base of steering column.
3. Install CPA, then lefthand lower trim panel.
4. Install AIR BAG fuse into fuse block.
5. Install instrument panel lefthand end cap.
6. Staying well away from both air bag modules, turn ignition On.
7. Ensure AIR BAG warning lamp flashes seven times, then turns off.

2000-02

1. Turn ignition to Lock position and remove key.
2. Connect both yellow SIR connectors at base of steering column.
3. Install CPAs, then lefthand lower trim panel.
4. Install SIR AIR BAG fuse into fuse block.
5. Install instrument panel lefthand end cap.
6. From a safe position at sides of or below air bag modules, turn ignition On.
7. Ensure AIR BAG warning lamp flashes seven times, then turns off.

CENTURY & REGAL

1998-99

1. Ensure front wheels are in straight-ahead position and key is removed from ignition switch.
2. Connect passenger's air bag module CPA and air bag module yellow connectors located to the right of steering column.
3. Connect driver's air bag module CPA and yellow air bag module connectors at base of steering column.
4. Install AIR BAG or SIR fuse into fuse block.
5. Staying well away from both air bag modules, turn ignition On.
6. Ensure AIR BAG warning lamp lights and flashes seven times, then turns off.

2000-02

1. Ensure front wheels are in straight-ahead position and key is removed from ignition.
2. Connect side impact air bag module connector located under driver's seat.
3. Install Connector Position Assurance (CPA) to side impact module.
4. Connect passenger's air bag module CPA and air bag module yellow connectors located to right of steering column.
5. Connect driver's air bag module CPA and yellow air bag module connectors at base of steering column.

6. Install AIR BAG or SIR fuse into fuse block.
7. From a safe position at sides of or below air bag modules, turn ignition On.
8. Ensure AIR BAG warning lamp lights and flashes seven times, then turns off.

CORVETTE

1. Turn ignition to Lock position and remove key.
2. Connect both yellow SIR connectors and install CPA.
3. Insert courtesy lamp through panel and install lefthand sound insulation panel.
4. Install push-on nut to steering column bracket stud and twist rivets clockwise to secure.
5. Align courtesy lamp and push into place.
6. Install SDM fuse into instrument panel fuse block.
7. Install front floor kick-up panel.
8. From a safe position at sides of or below air bag modules, turn ignition On.
9. Ensure AIR BAG warning lamp flashes seven times and turns off.

DEVILLE

1998–99

1. Turn ignition switch to Lock position, then remove key.
2. Connect side impact yellow two-way connectors, then install both front door panels.
3. Connect yellow two-way connector to passenger's air bag module pigtail and install CPA.
4. Install glove compartment.
5. Connect yellow two-way SIR electrical connectors at base of steering column and install CPA.
6. Install lefthand sound insulator.
7. Install SIR fuse into fuse block.
8. Staying well away from air bag modules, turn ignition On.
9. Ensure SIR lamp flashes seven times, then turns off.

2000–02

1. Turn ignition to Lock, then remove key.
2. **On models equipped with rear side impact air bag modules (AW9),** proceed as follows:
   a. Connect lefthand rear side impact air bag module yellow electrical connector.
   b. Install CPA for lefthand rear side impact air bag module yellow electrical connector.
   c. Connect righthand rear side impact air bag module yellow electrical connector.
   d. Install CPA for righthand rear side impact air bag module yellow electrical connector.
   e. Install rear seatback.
3. **On all models,** connect yellow two-way connector to passenger's air bag module pigtail and install CPA.
4. Connect yellow two-way connector to driver's air bag module pigtail and install CPA.
5. Connect yellow two-way SIR electrical connector at base of steering column and install CPA.
6. Install lefthand sound insulator.
7. Install SIR fuse into fuse block.
8. From safe position at sides of or below air bag modules, turn ignition On.
9. Ensure SIR lamp flashes seven times, then turns off.

ELDORADO

1. Turn ignition to Lock position, then remove key.
2. Connect yellow two-way connector to passenger's air bag module pigtail and install CPA.
3. Install glove compartment.
4. Connect yellow two-way SIR electrical connectors at base of steering column and install CPA.
5. Install lefthand sound insulator.
6. Install SIR fuse into fuse block.
7. From a safe position at sides of or below air bag modules, turn ignition On.
8. Ensure SIR lamp flashes seven times, then turns off.

GRAND AM

1998

Refer to "Achieva & Skylark" for arming procedure.

1999–2002

Refer to "Alero, Cutlass & Malibu" for arming procedure.

GRAND PRIX & INTRIGUE

Refer to "Century & Regal" "1998–99," for arming procedure.

IMPALA

1. Ensure front wheels are in straight-ahead position and key is removed from ignition.
2. **On models equipped with lefthand side impact air bag module,** connect yellow electrical connector under driver's seat and install CPA.
3. **On all models,** connect driver's air bag module CPA and yellow air bag module connector.
4. Install instrument panel righthand access hole cover.
5. Install SDM fuse into fuse block.
6. Install instrument panel fuse access cover.
7. From a safe position at sides of or below air bag modules, turn ignition On.
8. Ensure AIR BAG warning lamp lights and flashes seven times, then turns off.

LUMINA

1998

1. Ensure wheels are in straight-ahead position and key is removed from ignition switch.
2. Connect passenger's air bag module CPA and yellow air bag module connector and close instrument panel compartment door.
3. Connect driver's air bag module CPA and yellow air bag module connectors at base of steering column.
4. Install AIR BAG fuse into fuse block.
5. Turn ignition to Run position.
6. Ensure AIR BAG warning lamp lights and flashes 7–9 times, then turns off.

1999–2001

1. Ensure front wheels are in straight-ahead position and key is removed from ignition.
2. Connect passenger's air bag module CPA and yellow air bag module connector, then close glove compartment door.
3. Install righthand sound insulator.
4. Connect CPA and yellow air bag module connectors at base of steering column.
5. Install lefthand sound insulator.
6. Install Fuse 21 into fuse block.
7. Install instrument panel fuse block door.
8. From a safe position at sides of or below air bag modules, turn ignition On.
9. Ensure AIR BAG warning lamp lights and flashes seven times, then turns off.

METRO

1. Turn ignition key to Lock position, then remove key.
2. Connect passenger's air bag module yellow electrical connector.
3. Install passenger's air bag module CPA and close glove compartment.
4. Connect yellow two-way electrical connector inside steering wheel air bag module housing.
5. Install driver's air bag module CPA, then the steering wheel side cap.
6. Install AIR BAG fuse into Air Bag fuse block.
7. From a safe position at sides of or below air bag modules, turn ignition On.
8. Ensure AIR BAG lamp flashes seven times and turns off.

MONTE CARLO

1998–99

1. Turn ignition to Lock and remove key.
2. Open glove compartment door and connect yellow 2-way connector and Connector Position Assurance (CPA).
3. Connect yellow 2-way connector at base of steering column, then install Connector Position Assurance (CPA).
4. Install trim panel under steering column.
5. Install AIR BAG fuse into instrument panel fuse block.
6. Turn ignition to Run and ensure AIR BAG/INFLATABLE RESTRAINT warning lamp flashes seven times, then turns off. If lamp does not operate as specified, refer to **MOTOR's "Air Bag Manual."**

2000–02

1. Ensure front wheels are in straight-ahead position and key is removed from ignition.
2. **On models equipped with driver's side air bag module,** connect yellow electrical connector under driver's seat

and install CPA.
3. **On all models,** connect frontal air bag module CPA and yellow air bag connector.
4. Install instrument panel Passenger's access hole cover.
5. Install SDM fuse into fuse block.
6. Install instrument panel fuse access cover.
7. From a safe position at sides of or below air bag modules, turn ignition On.
8. Ensure AIR BAG warning lamp lights and flashes seven times, then turns off.

PARK AVENUE

1998

Refer to "Bonneville & LeSabre" for arming procedure.

2000–02

1. Turn steering wheel to straight-ahead position.
2. Turn ignition switch to Lock position, then remove key.
3. Connect yellow two-way connector to passenger's air bag module wiring and install CPA.
4. Install righthand sound insulator.
5. Connect yellow two-way SIR electrical connector at base of steering column and install CPA.
6. Install lefthand sound insulator.
7. Install SIR fuse into under hood bussed electrical center.
8. Staying well away from both air bag modules, turn ignition On.
9. Ensure SIR lamp flashes seven times, then turns off.

PRIZM

1998

1. Turn ignition switch to Lock position, then remove key.
2. Connect passenger's air bag module yellow two-way connector and secure with CPA.
3. Install glove compartment.
4. Connect yellow two-way connector on lower steering column and secure with CPA.
5. Install AIR BAG fuse.
6. Staying well away from both air bag modules, place ignition switch in the On position.
7. Ensure AIR BAG lamp lights for approximately six seconds and then turns off.

1999–2002

1. Turn ignition to Lock position, then remove key.
2. Connect side impact air bag modules electrical connectors.
3. Connect passenger's air bag module yellow two-way connector and secure with CPA.
4. Install glove compartment.
5. Connect yellow two-way connector on lower steering column and secure with CPA.
6. Install steering column lower trim cover.
7. Install CIG and IGN fuses in junction block.
8. From a safe position at sides of or below air bag modules, turn ignition On.
9. Ensure AIR BAG lamp lights for approximately six seconds, then turns off.

RIVIERA

Refer to "Aurora" for arming procedure.

SEVILLE

Refer to "DeVille" "2000–02," for arming procedure.

SATURN

DISARMING

L-SERIES

1. Place front wheels in straight-ahead position.
2. Turn ignition to Lock position and remove key.
3. Remove IGN1 mini-fuse from underhood fuse block.
4. Remove instrument panel lefthand lower close-out panel.
5. Push out clips securing yellow two-way SIR connectors to instrument panel brace.
6. Disconnect SIR connectors.

S-SERIES

1998–99

1. Place front wheels in straight-ahead position.
2. Turn ignition to Lock position and remove key.
3. Remove AIR BAG fuse from instrument panel junction block.
4. Remove Connector Position Assurance (CPA) from yellow two-way SIR connector at base of steering column and disconnect connector.
5. Remove upper trim panel extension located on top righthand side of instrument panel.
6. Remove upper instrument panel screw caps, located on top center of instrument panel, then the upper trim panel mounting screws.
7. Lift upper trim panel off of instrument panel and remove upper trim panel insulator.
8. Remove CPA from yellow two-way Supplemental Inflatable Restraint (SIR) connector, located on pigtail from passenger's air bag module.
9. Disconnect air bag module connector.

2000–02

1. Place front wheels in straight-ahead position.
2. Turn ignition to Lock position and remove key.
3. Remove AIR BAG fuse from instrument panel fuse block.
4. Disconnect driver's air bag module two-way yellow electrical connector clipped to steering column brace.
5. Reach under instrument panel on righthand side and detach clip which retains yellow two-way SIR electrical connector to metal brace near HVAC fan.
6. Disconnect passenger's air bag module connector.

ARMING

L-SERIES

1. Turn ignition to Lock position and remove key.
2. Connect SIR connectors.
3. Push in clips securing yellow two-way SIR connectors to instrument panel brace.
4. Install instrument panel lefthand lower close-out panel.
5. Install IGN1 mini-fuse in underhood fuse block.
6. From a safe position at sides of or below air bag modules, turn ignition On.
7. Ensure air bag lamp flashes seven times, then turns and remains off.

S-SERIES

1998–99

1. Turn ignition key to Lock position and remove key.
2. Connect yellow two-way SIR connector at base of steering column and install CPA.
3. Connect yellow two-way SIR connector at pigtail of passenger's air bag module and install CPA.
4. Install upper trim panel insulator. **Ensure all flaps are tucked in.**
5. Ensure upper trim panel seal is place, then Install upper trim panel into clips at base of windshield.
6. Lower panel and push down at clip locations.
7. Install upper trim panel mounting screws, then the screw caps.
8. Install AIR BAG fuse.
9. From a position well away from air bag modules, turn ignition to Run position.
10. Ensure air bag lamp flashes seven times, then turns and remains off.

2000–02

1. Turn ignition to Lock position and remove key.
2. Connect passenger's air bag module connector.
3. Reach under instrument panel on righthand side and install clip which retains yellow two-way SIR electrical connector to metal brace near HVAC fan.
4. Connect driver's air bag module two-way yellow electrical connector clipped to steering column brace.
5. Install AIR BAG fuse into instrument panel fuse block.
6. From a safe position at sides of or below air bag modules, turn ignition On.
7. Ensure air bag lamp flashes seven times, then turns and remains off.

COMPUTER RELEARN PROCEDURE

INDEX

DAIMLERCHRYSLER

Powertrain Control Module (PCM)

1998

If battery cable has been disconnected, the PCM must relearn a new operating strategy. Connect battery cable and run engine until operating temperature is reached. After engine warm-up, drive vehicle under various operating conditions until PCM has relearned new strategy.

1999-2002

Anytime the PCM is replaced the VIN and vehicle mileage must be programmed into the new PCM. If the PCM is not programmed, Diagnostic Trouble Codes (DTCs) will set. To program the PCM, connect a DRB or suitably programmed scan tool to the Data Link Connector (DLC) and follow scan tool manufacturers' instructions. On models equipped with the Sentry Key Immobilizer System (SKIS), refer to "Sentry Key Immobilizer System (SKIS)" to program secret key into the PCM.

Sentry Key Immobilizer System (SKIS)

When replacing the PCM on these models, it will be necessary to program the SKIS I.D. code into the new PCM. The new PCM will not allow the engine to operate unless it receives the correct I.D. code from the Sentry Key Immobilizer Module (SKIM). Use the following procedure to program the secret key into the PCM.

1. Obtain vehicle's four digit PIN number.
2. Ensure transmission or transaxle is in Park or Neutral, then turn ignition to the On position.
3. Connect a DRB or suitably programmed scan tool to Data Link Connector (DLC).
4. Select THEFT ALARM, SKIM, MISCELLANEOUS, then PCM REPLACED from scan tool menu.
5. Enter secured access mode by entering the vehicle's four digit PIN number.
6. Press ENTER to transfer secret key code to PCM.
7. **If incorrect code is entered three times, secured access mode will be locked out for one hour. To exit this lockout mode, turn the ignition key to the RUN position for one hour, then enter the correct PIN (ensure all accessories are turned off and monitor state of battery charge, connect a battery charger if necessary).**

FORD MOTOR CO.

Powertrain Control Module (PCM)

1998

Disconnect negative battery cable for a minimum of five minutes. After clearing memory, it is required to drive vehicle a minimum of 10 miles to allow PCM time to relearn operating strategy.

1999-2002

Automatic Data Transfer

1. Prior to removing old PCM, connect a suitably programmed scan tool to Data Link Connector (DLC).
2. Follow scan tool manufacturers' instructions to download data from old PCM.

3. Install new PCM and connect scan tool to DLC.
4. Follow scan tool manufacturers' instructions to download data from scan tool to replacement PCM.

Manual Data Entry

1. Install new PCM.
2. Connect a suitably programmed scan tool to Data Link Connector (DLC).
3. Follow scan tool manufacturers' instructions to manually program VID block data to PCM. If instructed by the scan tool to contact "AS BUILT" data center, proceed as follows.
   a. Contact Fed World website at "fedworld.gov."
   b. Select auto service information and search for "Calibrations" or "Vehicle Calibrations."
   c. Specify vehicle manufacturer, model name and model year as required.

GENERAL MOTORS

Body Control Module (BCM)

ALERO & GRAND AM

This procedure must be performed if the BCM, Passlock sensor or PCM is replaced. If BCM is not properly programmed, it will not control all the features properly.

1. Ensure battery is fully charged and ignition switch is in the ON position.
2. Connect a suitably programmed Tech II, or equivalent, scan tool to Data Link Connector (DLC).
3. Access scan tool "Special Functions" menu and follow scan tool instructions to program BCM.
4. If BCM fails to accept the program, inspect all BCM connections and ensure scan tool is equipped with latest software.

AURORA

Refer to "Dash Integration Module (DIM)," "Instrument Panel Integration Module (IPM)" and "Rear Integration Module (RIM)" for programming procedures.

BONNEVILLE

Refer to "Dash Integration Module (DIM)," "Instrument Panel Integration Module (IPM)" and "Rear Integration Module (RIM)" for programming procedures.

CAMARO & FIREBIRD

This customer key learn procedure must be performed anytime the BCM is replaced.

1. Insert customer key into the ignition cylinder and turn to the ON position.
2. Start engine to verify system operation.
3. Observe SECURITY indicator lamp for the following:
   a. If indicator lamp lights for approximately five seconds and then goes out, BCM is properly programmed.
   b. If indicator lamp flashes at a rate of one flash per second, BCM is not properly programmed, check BCM wiring and connectors for a fault.

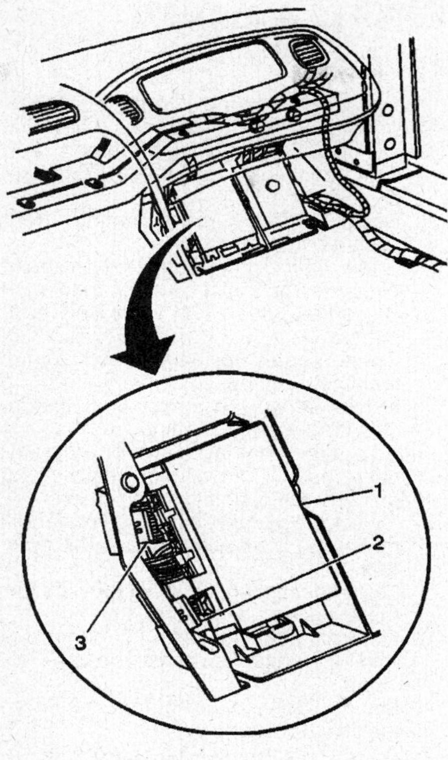

Fig. 1 Splice pack/star connectors. 1998-2000 Corvette

CATERA

Anytime battery power is disconnected the following accessory programing procedure must be performed.

1. To program the Electronic Throttle Control (ETC), proceed as follows:
   a. Turn ignition switch to the RUN position, but do not start engine.
   b. Leave ignition switch in the RUN position for approximately three minutes to allow ETC to cycle and relearn its home position.
   c. Turn ignition switch off, then start engine and allow to run for 30 seconds.
2. To program the power sunroof, proceed as follows:
   a. Turn ignition switch to the RUN position.
   b. Turn power sunroof switch to the CLOSED position.
   c. After sunroof fully closes and motor stops, press and hold switch in the CLOSED position for three seconds.
   d. Turn power sunroof switch to the TILT position.
   e. After sunroof reaches tilt position and motor stops, press and hold switch in the TILT position for three seconds.
   f. Turn power sunroof switch to the FULL OPEN position.
   g. After sunroof reaches full open position and motor stops, press and hold switch in the FULL OPEN position for three seconds.
   h. Turn power sunroof switch to the CLOSED position.
   i. After sunroof fully closes and motor stops, press and hold switch in the CLOSED position for three seconds.
3. To program the power windows, proceed as follows:
   a. Turn ignition switch to the RUN position.
   b. Press power window switch to the DOWN position.
   c. After window reaches full down position, press and hold switch in the DOWN position for three seconds.
   d. Press power window switch to the UP position.
   e. After window reaches full up position, press and hold switch in the UP position for three seconds.
   f. Repeat steps a through e for each window.
4. To program the heat and A/C control head, proceed as follows:
   a. Turn ignition switch to the RUN position.
   b. Simultaneously press and hold the AUTO and OFF buttons for at least five seconds.
   c. Stepper motors should cycle from one stop to another while calibrating.
   d. Ensure heater and A/C head operates correctly.

CAVALIER & SUNFIRE

2000-02

This procedure must be performed if the BCM Is replaced. If BCM is not properly programmed with the proper RPO configurations, it will not control all the features properly.

1. Ensure battery is fully charged.
2. Connect a suitably programmed Tech II, or equivalent, scan tool to the Data Link Connector (DLC).
3. Turn ignition switch to the ON position.
4. Access "SPECIAL FUNCTIONS" from scan tool menu, then select "NEW BCM SETUP" and follow scan tool instructions to program new BCM.
5. If BCM fails to accept the program, inspect all BCM connections and ensure scan tool is equipped with latest software.
6. Anytime the BCM is replaced, it will necessary for the PCM to learn the new fuel continue password. Use the following procedure to learn the fuel continue password:
   a. Turn ignition switch to the ON position.
   b. Attempt to start engine, then release key to ON (vehicle will not start).
   c. Observe "SECURITY" telltale

lamp, after approximately 10 minutes the lamp will turn off.
  d. Turn off ignition switch and wait 5 seconds.
  e. Repeat steps a through c two more times for a total of 3 cycles/30 minutes.
  f. Turn ignition switch to the OFF position.
  g. Start engine, vehicle has now learned Passlock sensor data password.

CENTURY

2001-02

The following procedure must be performed anytime the BCM is replaced. After performing the BCM programming procedure, program the theft deterrent system as outlined under "Theft Deterrent Systems."

1. Connect a suitably programmed Tech II, or equivalent, scan tool to the Data Link Connector (DLC).
2. Turn ignition switch to the ON position.
3. Select "Diagnostics" from scan tool menu and enter vehicle data when prompted by scan tool.
4. Select "Body," then "Body Control Module" from scan tool menu.
5. Select "Special Functions" and "New VIN" from scan tool menu, then follow scan tool instructions to input all required data.
6. Exit back to "Special Functions" menu and select "BCM Reprogramming."
7. Scan tool should inquire "Do you want to setup a Body Control Module?"
8. At the prompt, select "Setup BCM" on the scan tool.
9. Scan tool will display "Now setting up the new Body Control Module."
10. When successful programming is complete, scan tool will display "Body Control Module setup is complete."
11. Program theft deterrent system as outlined under "Theft Deterrent Systems."

CORVETTE

1. Ensure battery is fully charged.
2. Connect a suitably programmed Tech II, or equivalent, scan tool to Data Link Connector (DLC).
3. Select NEW BCM SETUP and program BCM with proper RPO configuration.
4. Turn ignition On and leave on for 11 minutes.
5. Turn ignition Off position for 30 seconds.
6. Turn ignition On for 11 minutes or until DTC P1630 sets.
7. Turn ignition Off for 30 seconds.
8. Turn ignition On for 30 seconds, then start engine.
9. If engine starts, proceed as follows:
   a. Clear DTCs, then turn ignition Off for 30 seconds.
   b. Ensure engine starts and runs.
10. If engine cranks but will not start, refer to **MOTOR's Domestic Engine Performance & Driveability Manual.**

CUTLASS & MALIBU

1998-99

Access to a General Motors' techline terminal is required to program this BCM.

1. Connect a suitably programmed Tech II, or equivalent, scan tool to Data Link Connector (DLC).
2. Select "Service Programming" from scan tool menu.
3. Enter vehicle information and choose "Request Inf." soft key on scan tool.
4. Disconnect scan tool from DLC connector.
5. Connect scan tool to a General Motors' techline terminal.
6. Select Service Programming System (SPS) at techline terminal.
7. Select terminal to scan tool programming method, then follow instructions on communications setup screen.
8. Select program BCM, the terminal will download the information to the scan tool.
9. Disconnect scan tool from techline terminal.
10. Connect scan tool to DLC connector and turn ignition switch to the RUN position.
11. Select "Service Programming" from the scan tool menu.
12. Answer prompts from scan tool regarding model year and vehicle type.
13. Press BCM soft key on scan tool, BCM will now be programmed with configuration file stored on scan tool.
14. Perform Password learn procedure as follows:
    a. Attempt to start vehicle, vehicle will stall.
    b. Leave ignition in the ON position approximately 10 minutes until Theft System telltale lamp turns off.
    c. Turn ignition switch off and attempt to start vehicle.
    d. Vehicle should start, indicating password has been learned.
15. Program PCM as outlined under "Powertrain Control Module."
16. Ensure all body systems are working properly.

2000-02

This procedure must be performed if the BCM, Passlock sensor or PCM is replaced. If BCM is not properly programmed, it will not control all the features properly.

1. Ensure battery is fully charged and ignition switch is in the ON position.
2. Connect a Tech II, or equivalent, scan tool to Data Link Connector (DLC).
3. Access scan tool "Special Functions" menu and follow scan tool instructions to program BCM.
4. If BCM fails to accept the program, inspect all BCM connections and ensure scan tool is equipped with latest software.

DEVILLE

Refer to "Dash Integration Module (DIM)," "Instrument Panel Integration Module (IPM)" and "Rear Integration Module (RIM)" for programming procedures.

GRAND PRIX & REGAL

1998-2000

The following procedure must be performed anytime the BCM is replaced.

1. Connect a suitably programmed Tech II, or equivalent, scan tool to the Data Link Connector (DLC).
2. Input all required data when prompted by scan tool.
3. Turn ignition switch to the RUN position.
4. Select "SPECIAL FUNCTIONS" from "MAIN MENU" screen.
5. Select "NEW VIN" and input all required data.
6. Exit back to "SPECIAL FUNCTION" menu and select "BCM REPROGRAMMING."
7. Scan tool will display "DO YOU WANT TO SETUP A BODY CONTROL MODULE?" Select "SETUP BCM" hotspot on scan tool.
8. Scan tool will display "NOW SETTING UP THE BODY CONTROL MODULE."
9. When BCM has been setup successfully, scan tool will display "BODY CONTROL MODULE SETUP IS COMPLETE."
10. After performing the BCM programming procedure, program the theft deterrent system as outlined under "Theft Deterrent Systems."

2001-02

The following procedure must be performed anytime the BCM is replaced. After performing the BCM programming procedure, program the theft deterrent system as outlined under "Theft Deterrent Systems."

1. Connect a suitably programmed Tech II, or equivalent, scan tool to the Data Link Connector (DLC).
2. Turn ignition switch to the ON position.
3. Select "Diagnostics" from scan tool menu and enter vehicle data when prompted by scan tool.
4. Select "Body," then "Body Control Module" from scan tool menu.
5. Select "Special Functions" and "New VIN" from scan tool menu, then follow scan tool instructions to input all required data.
6. Exit back to "Special Functions" menu and select "BCM Reprogramming."
7. Scan tool should inquire "Do you want to setup a Body Control Module?"
8. At the prompt, select "Setup BCM" on the scan tool.
9. Scan tool will display "Now setting up the new Body Control Module."
10. When successful programming is complete, scan tool will display "Body Control Module setup is complete."
11. Program theft deterrent system as outlined under "Theft Deterrent Systems."

IMPALA & MONTE CARLO

The following procedure must be performed anytime the BCM is replaced. After performing the BCM programming procedure, program the theft deterrent system as outlined under "Theft Deterrent Systems."

1. Connect a suitably programmed Tech II, or equivalent, scan tool to the Data

Link Connector (DLC).
2. Turn ignition switch to the ON position.
3. Select "Diagnostics" from scan tool menu and enter vehicle data when prompted by scan tool.
4. Select "Body Control Module" from scan tool menu.
5. Select "Special Functions" and "New VIN" from scan tool menu, then follow scan tool instructions to input all required data.
6. Exit back to "Special Functions" menu and select "BCM Reprogramming."
7. Scan tool should inquire "Do You Want To Setup A Body Control Module?"
8. At the prompt, select "Setup BCM" on the scan tool.
9. Scan tool will display "Now Setting Up The New Body Control Module."
10. When successful programming is complete, scan tool will display "Body Control Module Setup Is Complete."
11. Exit back to "Special Functions" menu and select "Set Options."
12. Select "Point Of Sale" and input all required data when prompted by scan tool.
13. Exit back to "Set Options" menu and select "Option Configuration."
14. Input all required data when prompted by scan tool.
15. After BCM, VIN, Point Of Sale and Option Configuration have been entered, program theft deterrent system as outlined under "Theft Deterrent Systems."

INTRIGUE

1998-99

The following procedure must be performed anytime the BCM is replaced.

1. Connect a suitably programmed Tech II, or equivalent, scan tool to the Data Link Connector (DLC).
2. Input all required data when prompted by scan tool.
3. Turn ignition switch to the RUN position.
4. Select "SPECIAL FUNCTIONS" from "MAIN MENU" screen.
5. Select "NEW VIN" and input all required data.
6. Exit back to "SPECIAL FUNCTION" menu and select "BCM REPROGRAMMING."
7. Scan tool will display "DO YOU WANT TO SETUP A BODY CONTROL MODULE?" Select "SETUP BCM" hotspot on scan tool.
8. Scan tool will display "NOW SETTING UP THE BODY CONTROL MODULE."
9. When BCM has been setup successfully, scan tool will display "BODY CONTROL MODULE SETUP IS COMPLETE."
10. After performing the BCM programming procedure, program the theft deterrent system as outlined under "Theft Deterrent Systems."

2000-02

The following procedure must be performed anytime the BCM is replaced. After performing the BCM programming procedure, program the theft deterrent system as outlined under "Theft Deterrent Systems."

1. Connect a suitably programmed Tech II, or equivalent, scan tool to the Data Link Connector (DLC).
2. Turn ignition switch to the ON position.
3. Select "Diagnostics" from scan tool menu and enter vehicle data when prompted by scan tool.
4. Select "Body," then "Body Control Module" from scan tool menu.
5. Select "Special Functions" and "New VIN" from scan tool menu, then follow scan tool instructions to input all required data.
6. Exit back to "Special Functions" menu and select "BCM Reprogramming."
7. Scan tool should inquire "Do you want to setup a Body Control Module?"
8. At the prompt, select "Setup BCM" on the scan tool.
9. Scan tool will display "Now setting up the new Body Control Module."
10. When successful programming is complete, scan tool will display "Body Control Module setup is complete."
11. Program theft deterrent system as outlined under "Theft Deterrent Systems."

LESABRE

Refer to "Dash Integration Module (DIM)," "Instrument Panel Integration Module (IPM)" and "Rear Integration Module (RIM)" for programming procedures.

PARK AVENUE

1998-99

The following procedure must be performed anytime the Body Control Module (SBM) is replaced. If the SBM is not properly programmed, the vehicle will exhibit a no crank condition. If the SBM is not properly configured, the SBM may set default values for some systems, which may cause malfunctions in other systems.

1. Connect a suitably programmed Tech II, or equivalent, scan tool to the Data Link Connector (DLC).
2. Input all required data when prompted by scan tool.
3. Program SBM to identify the following items:
   a. Real Time Damping (RTD).
   b. Memory options.
   c. Tire Pressure Monitor (TPM).
   d. HVAC.
   e. Dual zone HVAC.
   f. Country of sale.

2000-02

The following procedure must be performed anytime the BCM is replaced.

1. Connect a suitably programmed Tech II, or equivalent, scan tool to the Data Link Connector (DLC).
2. Turn ignition switch to the ON position.
3. Select "Body Control Module" from scan tool menu.
4. Select "Special Functions," then "Setup SDM Serial Number In BCM," follow scan tool instructions to input all required data.
5. Exit back to "Special Functions" menu and select "Setup BCM."
6. Scan tool should inquire "Do You Want To Setup A Body Control Module?"
7. At the prompt, select "Setup BCM" on the scan tool.
8. Scan tool will display "Now Setting Up The New Body Control Module."
9. When successful programming is complete, scan tool will display "Body Control Module Setup Is Complete."
10. Exit back to "Special Functions" menu and select "Set Options."
11. Select "Point Of Sale" and input all required data when prompted by scan tool.
12. Exit back to "Set Options" menu and select "Load Management Option."
13. Input all required data when prompted by scan tool.
14. Exit back to "Special Functions."

SEVILLE

Refer to "Dash Integration Module (DIM)," "Instrument Panel Integration Module (IPM)" and "Rear Integration Module (RIM)" for programming procedures.

Dash Integration Module (DIM)

AURORA, BONNEVILLE, DEVILLE, LESABRE & SEVILLE

1. Ensure battery is fully charged and all modules on serial data line are connected.
2. Connect a suitably programmed Tech II, or equivalent, scan tool to the Data Link Connector (DLC).
3. Turn ignition switch to the ON position.
4. Access DIM menu on scan tool, then select "Special Functions."
5. Select "New VIN" from special functions menu and follow scan tool instructions.
6. Select "Setup SDM Serial Number In DIM," scan tool should ask "Do you want to set up a Dash Integration Module?" Answer yes to set up module.
7. When scan tool displays "Module Initialized," DIM module is setup.
8. To program vehicle options, access "Special Functions" menu, then select "Set Options" and proceed as follows:
   a. Select "Automatic/Manual HVAC" and follow scan tool instructions to select RPO configuration.
   b. Select "Options" and follow scan tool instructions to Select Headlamp Type option configuration.
   c. Select "LH Drvr. Personalization" and follow scan tool instructions to select LH Drvr. Personalization option configuration.
   d. Select "Magna Steer Option" and follow scan tool instructions to select RPO configuration.
   e. Select "Miscellaneous Options No. 1" and follow scan tool instructions to select RPO configuration.
   f. Select "Miscellaneous Options No. 2" and follow scan tool instructions to select RPO configuration.
   g. Select "Universal Theft Deterrent" and follow scan tool instructions to select RPO configuration.

9. Exit back to "Special Functions" menu.

Engine Control Module (ECM)

CATERA

This procedure should only be performed when the ECM is replaced, when requested by the ECM or when informed by a service bulletin. In order to perform this programming procedure, access to a General Motors' Techline Information System 2000 PC Techline Terminal will be necessary.

1. Turn ignition switch off.
2. Select "Service Programming System" from Techline Terminal.
3. Select "Programming Process" and "Vehicle" for ECU location.
4. Turn ignition switch to the ON position.
5. Connect Tech II, or equivalent, scan tool to Data Link Connector (DLC).
6. Connect cable tool No. RS-232, between Techline Terminal and scan tool.
7. Turn scan tool on and wait for start screen.
8. Ensure VIN displayed on Techline Terminal matches vehicle VIN.
9. Select type of module to be programmed and type of programming necessary.
10. Select appropriate calibration file and verify current calibration with selected calibration.
11. Select "Next" to initiate download of calibration files.
12. After download is complete, turn ignition switch off for at least 30 seconds, then activate theft deterrent system immobilizer as follows:
    a. Select "Special Functions" from scan tool "Immobilizer" menu.
    b. Select "Program Immobilizer," then follow scan tool instructions to activate immobilizer.
13. After activating immobilizer, select "EXIT" service programming.

Instrument Panel Integration Module (IPM)

AURORA, BONNEVILLE, DEVILLE, LESABRE & SEVILLE

1. Connect a suitably programmed Tech II, or equivalent, scan tool to the Data Link Connector (DLC).
2. Turn ignition switch to the ON position.
3. Select "Instrument Panel Module," then "Special Functions" from scan tool menu.
4. Select "Miscellaneous Test" and "IPM Recalibration."
5. After scan tool recalibrates IPM, verify latest version has been installed by selecting "Data Display" and "Module Information", then view calibration ID number. ID number must match version loaded on scan tool.

Powertrain Control Module (PCM)

ACHIEVA, ALERO, GRAND AM & SKYLARK

The following procedure must be performed anytime the PCM is replaced or Diagnostic Trouble Code (DTC) P0601 is set. Code P0601 indicates that EEPROM programming has malfunctioned.

1. Ensure battery is fully charged.
2. Connect a suitably programmed Tech II, or equivalent, scan tool to Data Link Connector (DLC).
3. Follow scan tool instructions to program EEPROM.
4. If PCM will not program properly, replace PCM.
5. Perform CKP system variation learn procedure as outlined under "Crankshaft Position System Variation Learn."
6. **On 1999 models,** perform password learn procedure as outlined under "Passkey Theft Deterrent System Password Learn."
7. **On 2000–02 models,** program theft deterrent system as outlined under "Theft Deterrent System Programming."

AURORA

1998-2000

The following procedure must be performed anytime the PCM is replaced or Diagnostic Trouble Code (DTC) P0602 is set. Code P0602 indicates that the EEPROM is not programmed or has malfunctioned.

1. Ensure battery is fully charged.
2. Connect a suitably programmed Tech II, or equivalent, scan tool to Data Link Connector (DLC).
3. Follow scan tool instructions to program EEPROM.
4. If PCM will not program properly, replace PCM.

2001-02

This procedure should only be performed when the PCM is replaced, when requested by the PCM or when informed by a service bulletin. In order to perform this programming procedure, access to a General Motors' Techline Information System 2000 PC Techline Terminal will be necessary.

1. Turn ignition switch to the OFF position.
2. Connect a suitably programmed Tech II, or equivalent, scan tool to Data Link Connector (DLC).
3. Turn ignition switch to the ON position and turn all accessories off.
4. Select "Service Programming" from scan tool menu.
5. Input vehicle information requested by scan tool.
6. Select type of module to be programmed and type of programming to be performed.
7. Compare VIN displayed on scan tool with vehicle VIN. If VIN does not match, write down actual VIN and correct at Techline terminal.
8. Exit "Service Programming" and turn off scan tool.
9. Disconnect scan tool from DLC connector and turn off ignition switch.
10. Connect scan tool to Techline Terminal and select "Service Programming."
11. Select type of scan tool and type of programming to be performed.
12. Verify displayed VIN with vehicle VIN, correct as necessary.
13. Select type of module to be programmed, then identify type of programming to be performed as follows:
    a. Normal: This type of programming is for updating an existing calibration or programming a new controller.
    b. Vehicle Configuration Index (VCI): This selection is used if the vehicle VIN is unavailable or is not recognized by Techline Terminal. The Techline Customer Support center will have to be contacted to use this option.
    c. Reconfigure: This type of programming is used to reconfigure a vehicle, such as tire size or axle ration changes.
14. Select appropriate calibration file and verify all connections are secure.
15. Select "Reprog" to initiate download of new calibration to scan tool.
16. After download is complete, turn off scan tool and disconnect from Techline Terminal.
17. Connect scan tool to DLC.
18. Turn scan tool on, then the ignition switch to the ON position.
19. Select "Service Programming" and "Select Program."
20. After download is complete, exit "Service Programming."
21. Turn ignition switch off for 30 seconds.
22. Turn scan tool off.
23. If control module was replaced, perform the following service procedures:
    a. CKP system variation learn.
    b. GM Oil Life System reseting.
    c. Program theft deterrent system.

BONNEVILLE, EIGHTY EIGHT, LESABRE, LSS & PARK AVENUE

Refer to "Aurora" for PCM programming.

CAMARO & FIREBIRD

Refer to "Aurora" for PCM programming.

CENTURY, GRAND PRIX, IMPALA, INTRIGUE, LUMINA, MONTE CARLO & REGAL

Refer to "Aurora" for PCM programming.

CORVETTE

1998-2000

The following procedure must be performed anytime the PCM is replaced, when requested by the PCM or when informed by a service bulletin.

1. Ensure battery is fully charged.

2. Connect a Tech II, or equivalent, scan tool to Data Link Connector (DLC).
3. Turn ignition switch off and remove passenger side floor access panel.
4. Remove splice pack/star connector shorting bars from both splice pack/star connectors, **Fig. 1.** It may be necessary to remove splice pack/star connectors from mounting positions.
5. Connect Star connector cable No. 1 of Serial Data Link Tester tool No. J 42236-A, or equivalent, to 12-pin splice pack connector No. 3 (8 or 9 wires).
6. Connect Star connector cable No. 2 of Serial Data Link Tester tool No. J 42236-A, or equivalent, to 12-pin splice pack connector No. 2 (4 wires).
7. Select Star connector No. 1 on Serial Data Link Tester tool toggle switch.
8. Select position "B" on Serial Data Link Tester.
9. Turn ignition switch to the ON position.
10. Program PCM using latest software matching the vehicle.
11. Perform theft deterrent password incorrect procedure as follows:
    a. Enter "Service Programming System (SPS)" with scan tool.
    b. Enter vehicle information requested.
    c. Choose "Request Info" soft key on scan tool and select "Done."
    d. Follow instructions on scan tool vehicle set-up screen.
    e. Disconnect scan tool from DLC and connect scan tool to Techline Terminal.
    f. Select "Service Programming System" at Techline Terminal.
    g. Select terminal to Tech II programming method.
    h. Select "Done," then follow remaining instructions from Techline Terminal.
    i. Select "Vehicle Theft Re-Learn" option.
    j. Select "Program" at summary screen, Techline Terminal will download information to Tech II.
    k. Return scan tool to vehicle and connect to DLC.
    l. Select "Service Programming" from scan tool main menu.
    m. Answer prompts regarding model year and vehicle type.
    n. Press "Theft Re-Learn" soft key on scan tool and follow instructions.
    o. BCM and PCM will be prepared for relearn, a security timer will be on for approximately 11 minutes or until DTC code P1630 sets. **It is important to keep the scan tool connected to the DLC during the 11 minute wait.**
    p. After 11 minute wait, turn ignition switch off for 30 seconds, then start the engine.
12. **On models equipped with automatic transmission,** perform idle learn procedure as follows:
    a. Turn off ignition switch and restore PCM battery feed.
    b. Turn off A/C controls, set parking brake and block drive wheels.
    c. Start and run engine until it reaches operating temperature of 176°F.
    d. Shift transmission into Drive and allow engine to idle for approximately five minutes.
    e. Shift transmission into Park and allow engine to idle for approximately five minutes.
    f. Turn off engine for 30 seconds.
13. **On models equipped with manual transmissions,** perform idle learn procedure as follows:
    a. Turn off ignition switch and restore PCM battery feed.
    b. Turn off A/C controls, set parking brake and block drive wheels.
    c. Place transmission in Neutral.
    d. Start and run engine until it reaches operating temperature of 176°F.
    e. Allow engine to idle for approximately five minutes.
    f. Turn off engine for 30 seconds.

2001-02

Refer to "2001–02" under "Aurora" for PCM programming.

CUTLASS & MALIBU

1998-2000

Refer to "Achieva, Alero, Grand Am & Skylark" for PCM EEPROM programming.

2001-02

Refer to "2001–02" under "Aurora" for PCM programming.

DEVILLE, ELDORADO & SEVILLE

Refer to "Aurora" for PCM programming.

RIVIERA

Refer to "Aurora" for PCM programming.

Crankshaft Position System Variation Learn

2.2L & 2.4L ENGINES

The following procedure must be performed when any of the following procedures are performed; PCM is replaced, engine is replaced, crankshaft is replaced, crankshaft position sensor is replaced, or any engine repair that disturbs the crankshaft/harmonic balancer to the crankshaft position sensor relationship.

1. Ensure battery is fully charged, parking brake is applied and vehicle wheels are blocked.
2. Place transaxle in the Park or Neutral position.
3. Turn all accessories off and connect Tech II, or equivalent, scan tool to Data Link Connector (DLC).
4. Start and run engine until it reaches operating temperature of at least 185°F.
5. With engine running, enable "Crankshaft Position System Variation Learning" procedure with scan tool.
6. Press and hold brake pedal firmly and raise engine speed to 3,920 RPM, release throttle as soon as engine cuts out.
7. With scan tool, verify crankshaft variation has been learned.
8. Perform this procedure up to 10 times. If PCM will not learn variation, a DTC 1336 should set. Refer to **Motors' "Domestic Engine Performance & Driveability Manual"** for DTC P1336 diagnosis.

3.1L, 3.4L, 3800, 4.0L & 4.6L ENGINES

The crankshaft position system values are stored within PCM memory after a learn procedure is performed. If crankshaft position system variation is not within value stored in PCM memory, DTC P0300 may be set.

The crankshaft variation learn procedure must be performed under the following conditions: DTC P1336, PCM replacement, PCM reprogramming, engine replacement, crankshaft replacement, crankshaft damper replacement and crankshaft position sensor replacement.

When performing this procedure, ensure vehicle is at operating temperature, no DTCs other than P1336 are present and that no camshaft position sensor faults are present. Proceed as follows for CKP learn procedure:

1. Set parking brake and block drive wheels.
2. Start and run engine until it reaches operating temperature.
3. Turn engine off and turn ignition key to the ON position.
4. Connect a Tech II, or equivalent, scan tool to Data Link Connector (DLC), then select "CKP Variation Learn Procedure" from scan tool function list.
5. Start engine and when instructed by the scan tool, apply brake pedal firmly.
6. Ensure transaxle is in PARK, then increase pedal position until CKP system variation learn fuel cut-off is reached at 5150 RPM.
7. Release accelerator pedal after second fuel cut-off is reached.
8. CKP system variation compensating values are learned when RPM decreases back to idle.
9. Monitor scan tool for DTC P1336. If scan tool indicates DTC P1336 ran and passed, learn procedure is complete. If scan tool indicates DTC P1336 failed or did not run, inspect for DTCs. If no DTCs other than P1336 exist, repeat learn procedure.

3.5L ENGINE

The crankshaft position system values are stored within PCM memory after a learn procedure is performed. If crankshaft position system variation is not within value stored in PCM memory, DTC P0300 may be set.

The crankshaft variation learn procedure must be performed under the following conditions: DTC P1336, PCM replacement, PCM reprogramming, engine replacement, crankshaft replacement, crankshaft damper replacement and crankshaft position sensor replacement.

When performing this procedure, ensure vehicle is at operating temperature, no DTCs other than P1336 are present and that no camshaft position sensor faults are present. Proceed as follows for CKP learn procedure:

1. Set parking brake and block drive wheels.
2. Start and run engine until it reaches operating temperature.
3. Turn engine off and turn ignition key to the ON position.
4. Connect a Tech II, or equivalent, scan tool to Data Link Connector (DLC), then select "CKP Variation Learn Procedure" from scan tool function list.
5. Start engine and when instructed by the scan tool, apply brake pedal firmly.
6. Ensure transaxle is in PARK.
7. **On 1999–2000 models,** increase pedal position until CKP system variation learn fuel cut-off is reached at 4300 RPM.
8. **On 2001–02 models,** increase pedal position until CKP system variation learn fuel cut-off is reached at 4050 RPM.
9. **On all models,** release accelerator pedal after second fuel cut-off is reached.
10. CKP system variation compensating values are learned when RPM decreases back to idle.
11. Monitor scan tool for DTC P1336. If scan tool indicates DTC P1336 ran and passed, learn procedure is complete. If scan tool indicates DTC P1336 failed or did not run, inspect for DTCs. If no DTCs other than P1336 exist, repeat learn procedure.

5.7L ENGINE

Camaro & Firebird

1. Connect a suitably programmed Tech II, or equivalent, scan tool to Data Link Connector (DLC).
2. Apply parking brake, block drive wheels and close hood.
3. **On models equipped with automatic transmission,** place selector lever in the PARK position.
4. **On models equipped with manual transmission,** place shift lever in the NEUTRAL position.
5. **On all models,** start and run engine until coolant temperature is at least 150°F.
6. Turn off all accessories and apply brakes.
7. Enable "Crankshaft Variation Learn Procedure" with scan tool.
8. Slowly raise engine speed to 4000 RPM, then immediately release throttle when engine speed decreases.
9. Turn ignition off for 15 seconds after learn procedure is completed.

Corvette

Refer to "3.1L, 3.4L, 3800, 4.0L & 4.6L Engines" for CKP variation learn procedures on this engine.

Rear Integration Module

AURORA, BONNEVILLE, DEVILLE, LESABRE & SEVILLE

1. Connect a suitably programmed Tech II, or equivalent, scan tool to the Data Link Connector (DLC).
2. Turn ignition switch to the ON position.
3. Access "Chassis Main" menu and select "Rear Integration Module."
4. Select "Recalibration" and follow scan tool instructions to recalibrate the automatic level control.

Theft Deterrent System Programming

ACHIEVA, CAVALIER, SKYLARK & SUNFIRE

In order for a theft deterrent vehicle to run, a password is communicated between the PCM and Instrument Panel Cluster (IPC). If the PCM is replaced, the new PCM needs to learn the correct password for the vehicle. When the new PCM is installed, the EEPROM calibration is flashed into the PCM and the vehicle will learn its' new password upon initial ignition ON. If the IPC is replaced, the PCM needs to learn the new password from the IPC. Use the following procedure to learn the new password.

1. Attempt to start vehicle, then leave ignition on.
2. Telltale "THEFT SYSTEM" lamp will flash for approximately 10 minutes.
3. When lamp stops flashing, start vehicle.
4. When vehicle is running, password is learned.

ALERO & MALIBU

The following procedure must be performed anytime the BCM, PCM or Passlock sensor is replaced.

1. Ensure battery is fully charged and there are no Diagnostic Trouble Codes (DTCs) present.
2. Turn ignition switch from the OFF position to the CRANK position attempting to start the vehicle. Vehicle should start and then stall.
3. After vehicle stalls, leave ignition in the ON position and observe security indicator on instrument cluster.
4. When security indicator turns off, turn ignition switch off and wait 10 seconds.
5. Repeat steps 2 through 4 two more times (3 times total).
6. BCM and PCM will learn the new code on the next start attempt.

AURORA, BONNEVILLE, GRAND PRIX, LESABRE & PARK AVENUE

2000–02

The following procedure must be performed when any of the following components are replaced; ignition keys, theft deterrent control module or PCM.

1. If replacing theft deterrent control module, proceed as follows:
   a. Connect a suitably programmed Tech II, or equivalent, scan tool to Data Link Connector (DLC).
   b. Turn ignition switch to the ON position.
   c. Select "Setup New VTD Module" from scan tool special functions menu.
   d. Follow scan tool instructions to setup theft deterrent control module.
2. Turn ignition switch to the ON position, using a master Passkey III key.
3. Observe instrument cluster security lamp, after approximately 10 minutes, lamp should turn off.
4. After lamp turns off, turn ignition switch to the OFF position and wait five seconds.
5. Repeat steps 2 through 4 two more times (3 times total).
6. With a master Passkey III key, start the vehicle.
7. Vehicle has now learned key transponder information and PCM has now learned fuel continue password.
8. Clear any Diagnostic Trouble Codes (DTCs) with scan tool.

CATERA

1999–2001

The following procedure must be performed anytime the theft deterrent control module is replaced.

Programming a new theft control module means the consecutive programming of the security code, engine type, key cylinder number, VIN number and ECM to learn the new frequency code. The engine type, VIN number and key cylinder number may also be programmed individually.

The security code and key cylinder number can be obtained by contacting GM TRACS 2000, phone number 1-800-433-6961.

1. Program security code as follows:
   a. Connect a suitably programmed Tech II, or equivalent, scan tool to Data Link Connector (DLC).
   b. Access theft deterrent system on scan tool menu.
   c. Use arrow keys on scan tool to enter security code obtained from General Motors. **The security code is a four alpha numeric character combination and can only be programmed once. After it is entered, the combination can not be altered or erased. However, the security code is always entered twice for a cross check. Scan tool will compare entered codes and evaluate results. If a mismatch occurs, security code input must be repeated.**
   d. If a mistake is made when entering security code (more than two times), the module will internally activate a security wait time. After first

and second attempts, a waiting time of 10 seconds each will occur. After third attempt, a waiting time of approximately 10 minutes occurs. Each attempt after that will double the wait time. Any attempt to enter security code during wait time will fail.
   e. Security wait time can be viewed through scan tool menu.
2. Access engine type on scan tool and follow scan tool instructions to program engine type.
3. Enter key cylinder number obtained from General Motors.
4. Program VIN number with scan tool.
5. New ECMs are delivered with the immobilizer function deactivated, to activate the immobilizer, proceed as follows:
   a. Select "Special Functions" from scan tool "Immobilizer" menu.
   b. Select "Program Immobilizer," then follow scan tool instructions to activate immobilizer.

CENTURY, IMPALA, INTRIGUE, MONTE CARLO & REGAL

The following procedure must be performed anytime the BCM or PCM is replaced.

1. Ensure battery is fully charged and there are no Diagnostic Trouble Codes (DTCs) present.
2. Turn ignition switch from the OFF position to the CRANK position attempting to start the vehicle. Vehicle should start and then stall.
3. After vehicle stalls, leave ignition in the ON position and observe security indicator on instrument cluster.
4. When security indicator turns off, turn ignition switch off and wait 5 seconds.
5. Repeat steps 2 through 4 two more times (3 times total).
6. Start engine, BCM and PCM have now learned new code.
7. Clear any Diagnostic Trouble Codes (DTCs) present.

CORVETTE

1998-2000

The following procedure must be performed anytime the BCM or ignition key is replaced.

1. Connect a suitably programmed Tech II, or equivalent, scan tool to Data Link Connector (DLC).
2. Program BCM as outlined under "Body Control Module (BCM)."
3. Turn ignition switch to the ON position for 11 minutes, then turn ignition switch off for 30 seconds.
4. Turn ignition switch to the ON position for 11 minutes, then turn ignition switch off for 30 seconds.
5. Turn ignition switch to the ON position for 11 minutes or until DTC P1630 sets, then turn ignition switch off for 30 seconds.
6. Turn ignition switch to the ON position for 30 seconds, then attempt to start engine.
7. Engine should start, indicating password has been learned.
8. If engine still will not start, diagnose engine control system as outlined in **MOTORS' "Domestic Engine Performance & Driveability Manual."**
9. Clear Diagnostic Trouble Codes (DTCs).

2001-02

To program the theft deterrent system on these models, refer to "Century, Impala, Intrigue, Monte Carlo & Regal."

DEVILLE

1998-99

The following procedure must be performed anytime the Instrument Panel Cluster (IPC) or PCM is replaced.

1. Turn ignition switch to the ON position.
2. Attempt to start engine, then release key to the ON position.
3. Observe SECURITY telltale lamp, after approximately 10 minutes lamp should turn off.
4. After lamp turns off, turn ignition switch off and wait five seconds.
5. Repeat steps 2 through 4 two more times (total of three).
6. Start engine, vehicle has now learned password.
7. Clear any Diagnostic Trouble Codes (DTCs) with a suitably programmed scan tool.

2000-02

To program the theft deterrent system on these models, refer to "Aurora, Bonneville, Grand Prix, LeSabre & Park Avenue."

ELDORADO

To program the theft deterrent system on these models, refer to "1998–99" under "DeVille."

GRAND AM

1998-99

To program this theft deterrent system, refer to "Achieva, Cavalier, Skylark & Sunfire."

2000-02

To program this theft deterrent system, refer to "Alero & Malibu."

SEVILLE

To program the theft deterrent system on these models, refer to "Aurora, Bonneville, Grand Prix, LeSabre & Park Avenue."

SATURN

CRANKSHAFT LEARN PROCEDURE

The PCM uses crankshaft velocity calculations to determine engine misfire and to run misfire self-diagnostics. The PCM must know precisely the variability in crankshaft notches for this function. The PCM has a notch learn process that learns the variability between notches which must be reset if the crankshaft has been replaced. Using a suitable scan tool, the "Crankshaft Learn Procedure" can be set to "Relearn."

CRANKSHAFT RELEARN PROCEDURE

Any time a PCM or crankshaft position sensor is replaced the PCM must relearn the crankshaft notches. Using a suitable scan tool, select Crankshaft Position Variation Learn under the SPECIAL FUNCTIONS menu and follow the on screen prompts. This procedure will not be initiated if a misfire has been detected. If misfire DTCs are present, diagnose and repair before proceeding with crankshaft relearn procedure.

PCM/ECM LEARNING PROCEDURE

If the battery is disconnected or if the PCM is replaced, the PCM must go through the learning process. To allow the PCM to relearn, the following steps must be performed:

1. Start vehicle and run until engine reaches normal operating temperature.
2. Drive vehicle at part throttle, with moderate acceleration and idle conditions until normal performance returns.
3. Park vehicle and engage parking brake with engine running.
4. **On models equipped with automatic transaxle,** place transaxle in Drive position.
5. **On models equipped with manual transaxle,** place transaxle in Neutral position.
6. **On all models,** allow vehicle to idle for approximately two minutes until engine idle stabilizes. Ensure engine is at normal operating temperature.

PASSLOCK THEFT DETERRENT RELEARN PROCEDURE

There are two methods used to reprogram the Passlock security system, the Seed and Key method and the Auto Learn method. If no components were replaced or the Passlock sensor was the only component replaced, the Auto Learn technique may be used to program the security system. If the BCM or PCM were replaced then the "Seed & Key" method must be used.

SEED & KEY METHOD

1. Turn ignition On.
2. Using a suitable scan tool, inspect for body control module (BCM) or powertrain control module (PCM) diagnostic trouble codes (DTCs).
3. Record and repair DTCs.
4. Turn ignition Off.
5. Using Saturn Programming System, or equivalent, reprogramming tool, select "Passlock Relearn" option.
6. Wait for ten minutes, then observe security telltale changing from Flashing to On to Off.
7. If ignition is turned Off before telltale

changes state, relearn procedure must be performed again.
8. Turn ignition Off.
9. Vehicle should start on next ignition switch cycle.

AUTO LEARN METHOD

1. Turn ignition On.
2. Momentarily rotate ignition to Crank position, but do not start vehicle.
3. Wait for ten minutes.
4. Observe SECURITY telltale changing from Flashing to On to Off.
5. If ignition is turned Off before telltale changes state, procedure will have to be performed again.
6. Turn Ignition Off.
7. Repeat procedure two more times.
8. If vehicle does not start on next ignition switch cycle, repeat procedure.

REMOTE KEYLESS ENTRY SYNCHRONIZATION

The remote keyless entry system does not send the same signal twice. The body control module (BCM) will not execute a signal if it has been sent previously. To synchronize a transmitter with the BCM, simultaneously press and hold the Lock and Unlock buttons on the transmitter for approximately ten seconds near the vehicle. The doors locks will cycle to confirm synchronization.

SERVICE REMINDER & WARNING LAMP RESET PROCEDURES

TABLE OF CONTENTS

DaimlerChrysler Corp.

INDEX

AIR BAG WARNING LAMP

If the Air Bag warning lamp lights and stays on, diagnosis and repair of the air bag system will be necessary to reset the lamp.

ANTI-LOCK BRAKE SYSTEM WARNING LAMP

This lamp should light when the ignition is turned On. The lamp may light for as long as 30 seconds as a bulb and system inspection. If the lamp remains lit or lights while operating the vehicle, a fault condition in the anti-lock brake system is indicated. When the lamp is lit, turn ignition Off, then start the engine again. If the lamp still remains lit, the anti-lock brake system should be serviced. The brake system will remain functional, but without the anti-lock function. After servicing the anti-lock brake system, the lamp will automatically reset. **On some models,** it may be necessary to operate the vehicle at a speed over 18 mph and make several hard brake applications from 40 mph to reset the lamp.

CHECK ENGINE LAMP

CHRYSLER, DODGE & PLYMOUTH

The Check Engine lamp should light for approximately 3 seconds after the ignition has been turned On as a bulb inspection. If improper or no signals are received by the Single Board Engine Controller (SBEC) from various sensors or if the PCM enters its Limp-In mode, the SBEC will light the Check Engine lamp. After diagnosing and servicing the fuel injection system or emission related systems, the SBEC memory will be cleared after approximately 40 to 100 ignition key On-Off cycles.

On 1998 and newer models, the Check Engine lamp may light if the fuel filler cap has not been completely tightened. The lamp should turn off after the cap has been properly tightened and the vehicle has successfully completed a predetermined number of trip cycles.

MONACO & PREMIER

This lamp should light during engine starting as a bulb inspection. Once the engine has started, the lamp should go off. If the lamp remains lit, the fuel injection and emission control system diagnosis should be performed using tester DRB II. During the diagnosis and repair procedure with tester DRB II, the Check Engine lamp will be reset.

CHECK ENGINE OR MALFUNCTION INDICATOR LAMP

CHRYSLER, DODGE & PLYMOUTH EXCEPT COLT & SUMMIT

The powertrain control module monitors a variety of sensors in the fuel injection, ignition, emission and engines systems. Each time the ignition is turned On, the instrument panel MIL should light for approximately two seconds and then go out. If the PCM senses a fault condition with a monitored circuit often enough to indicate an actual fault condition or if it enters its Limp-In mode, it stores a Diagnostic Trouble Code (DTC) in the PCM's memory. If the code applies to a non-emissions related components or system and the fault condition is repaired or ceases to exist, the PCM cancels the code after 40 warm-up cycles. DTCs that affect vehicle emissions light the MIL. Use a suitable scan tool to retrieve and erase DTC's and to reset the MIL.

On 1998 and newer models, the Check Engine lamp may light if the fuel filler cap

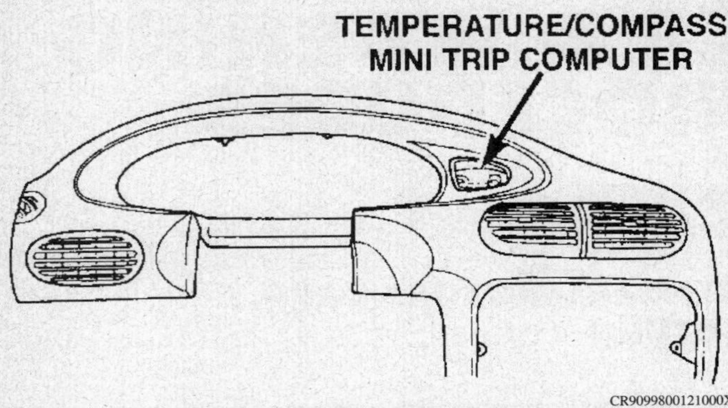

Fig. 1 Compass/temperature mini trip computer. Concorde, Intrepid, LHS, Vision, 300M & 1994–96 New Yorker

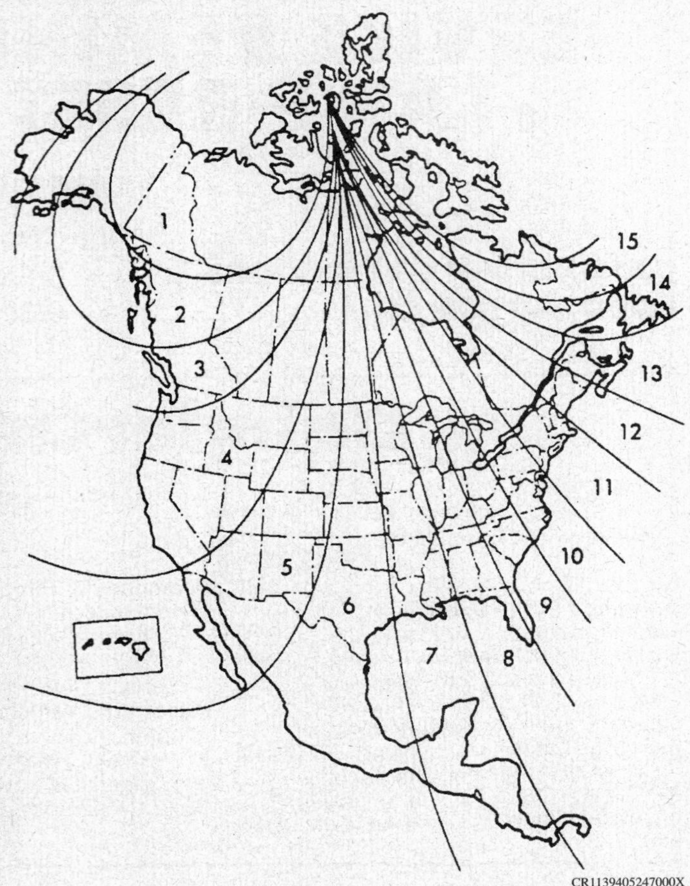

Fig. 2 Variance zone map. Concorde, Intrepid, LHS, Vision, 300M & 1994–96 New Yorker

has not been completely tightened. The lamp should turn off after the cap has been properly tightened and the vehicle has successfully completed a predetermined number of trip cycles.

COLT & SUMMIT

This lamp is used to monitor fuel injection and emission control system components for malfunctions. When the ignition is turned On, the lamp will light for 2 to 3 seconds as a bulb inspection. If the lamp remains on, a malfunction in the fuel injection or emission control system is indicated. If malfunction is intermittent, the lamp will go off when the Electronic Control Unit (ECU) receives a normal signal from the malfunctioning component. If the ECU receives an improper signal from a malfunctioning component for a time longer than that programmed into the ECU, a code will be stored in the ECU memory and the Malfunction Indicator Lamp should light. After servicing the indicated component, the Malfunction Indicator Lamp can be reset by clearing the ECU memory. The ECU memory is cleared by using a suitable scan tool or disconnecting the battery ground cable for approximately 10 seconds.

COMPASS & TEMPERATURE MINI TRIP COMPUTER

CONCORDE, INTREPID, LHS, VISION, 300M & 1994-96 NEW YORKER

1. Set mini trip computer to Compass/Temperature mode, **Fig. 1.**
2. Press US/M and STEP buttons simultaneously until VAR and current variance zone number is displayed.
3. Press STEP until proper variance zone number is displayed, **Fig. 2.**
4. After 5 seconds of inactivity, displayed zone will be set automatically. Ensure accuracy of compass by pointing vehicle in N, S, E and W directions.

SEBRING CONVERTIBLE

If the CAL indicator lights, the compass will need to be calibrated. This should be done on a level surface free of large metal objects such as other vehicles, bridges, buildings, railroads and underground cables. Proceed as follows:

1. Drive in complete circles, keeping steering wheel in a fixed position, at speeds of 7–10 mph until CAL indicator turns Off. This may require two to six turns.
2. When CAL indicator turns Off, compass has been calibrated and should now display proper headings.
3. Inspect for proper calibrations by selecting North, South, East and West.
4. If compass does not appear to be reading accurately, the calibration procedure should be repeated in another area.

ELECTRONIC VEHICLE INFORMATION CENTER

1992-93 DYNASTY, FIFTH AVENUE, IMPERIAL & NEW YORKER

The Electronic Vehicle Information Center is a computer controlled warning system which monitors various sensors used on the vehicle. The system supplements the warning indicators in the instrument cluster. When a warning message has been activated, a tone will sound to attract the driver's attention. The warning message will then be displayed on the overhead console, **Fig. 3,** until the condition has been corrected or a new display function is called up. A tone will announce each new warning condition. The "Service Reminder" warning message will be indicated at 7,500 mile or 12 month intervals to indicate that required service is to be performed. After performing the required service, the Service Reminder message can be reset by using a DRB II diagnostic readout tool.

OVERHEAD TRAVEL INFORMATION SYSTEM (OTIS)

CONCORDE, INTREPID, LHS, VISION, 300M & 1994-96 NEW YORKER

Overhead Travel Information System (OTIS) is a module with six informational displays and four buttons, **Fig. 4.** When the ignition is turned ON, OTIS blanks the display for one second, then returns to the display active when the vehicle was last turned OFF.

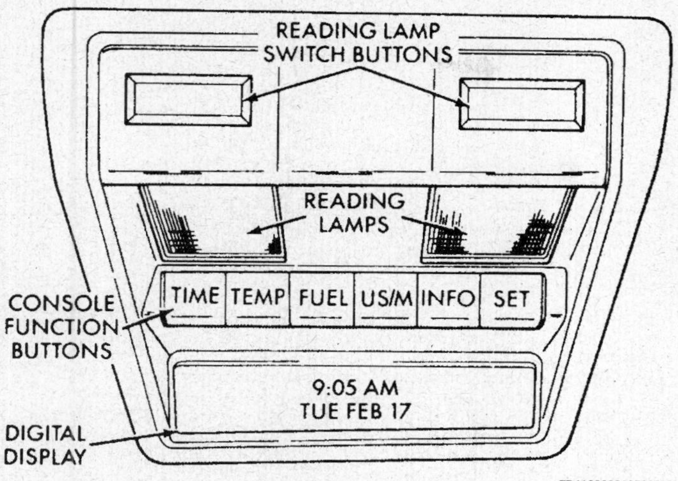

Fig. 3 Electronic Vehicle Information Center display console. 1992–93 Dynasty, Fifth Avenue, Imperial & New Yorker

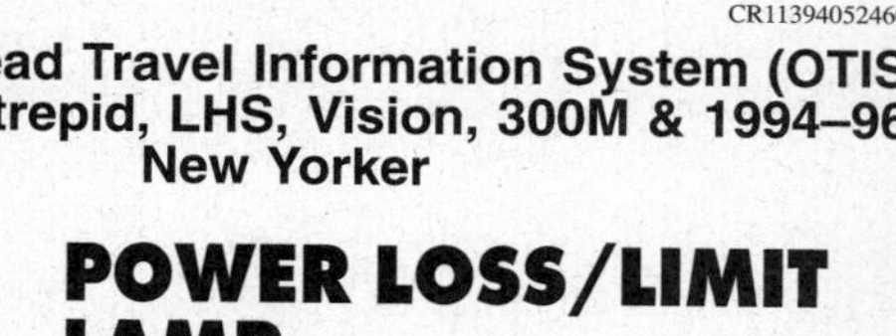

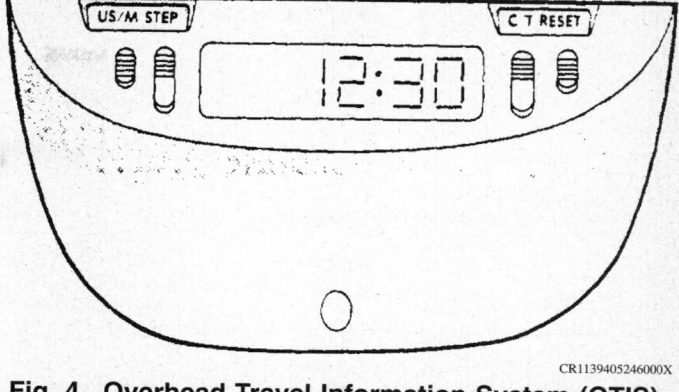

Fig. 4 Overhead Travel Information System (OTIS). Concorde, Intrepid, LHS, Vision, 300M & 1994–96 New Yorker

LOW OIL PRESSURE—This message will be displayed when a low engine oil pressure condition exists. If message is encountered with vehicle operating at idle speed, increase engine RPM. If message remains or if message is encountered while operating vehicle, the engine lubricating system should be inspected and serviced immediately. After engine lubricating system has been serviced, the message will be automatically cancelled.

SERVICE REMINDER—This message will be indicated at 7,500 mile or 12 month intervals to indicate that required service is to be performed. After performing the required service, with the Service Reminder message displayed, depress the Vehicle Electronic Information Center Reset button.

TURN SIGNAL ON—This message will be indicated when the turn signal is on and the vehicle has traveled a distance over ½ mile at a speed above 15 mph. The message will be reset when the turn signal lever has been returned to Off.

VOLTAGE IMPROPER—When this message is displayed, a fault condition in the charging or electrical system exists. After servicing, the message will be reset after the ignition has been cycled to the OFF position.

WASHER FLUID LOW—When this message is displayed, bring washer fluid to proper level. This message will be reset after the ignition has been cycled to the OFF position.

The six informational displays on the OTIS are as follows:

1. Compass/temperature.
2. Average fuel economy.
3. Distance to empty.
4. Instantaneous fuel economy.
5. Trip odometer.
6. Elapsed time.

The four buttons on the OTIS are as follows:

1. STEP—Depress this button to select display modes except Compass/temperature.
2. C/T—Depress this button to display compass (vehicle direction) and temperature.
3. U/SM—Switches display information between English and Metric readings.
4. RESET—Depress this button to reset the current display (for displays that can be reset.)

COMPASS CALIBRATION

Do not attempt to set compass calibration near large metal objects, such as other vehicles, buildings or bridges.

1. Remove all magnetic devices from roof panel.
2. Turn ignition On.
3. Press C/T button to select Compass/temperature display.
4. Depress and hold RESET button for about 5 seconds. The VAR symbol will light during this time.
5. Continue to hold RESET button for about 10 seconds until CAL symbol lights.
6. Drive vehicle through three complete 360° turns in no less than 48 seconds. The compass will be calibrated when the CAL symbol is extinguished.
7. Reset compass variance as follows:
   a. Press and hold RESET button for about 5 seconds until VAR symbol is lit.
   b. The OTIS will display variance zone and VAR.
   c. Press STEP button to display variance zone, **Fig. 2.**
   d. Press RESET button to set new variance zone and resume normal operation.

LOW COOLANT WARNING LAMP

1992 LASER & TALON

The Low Coolant warning lamp should light whenever coolant level in the coolant reservoir is below a predetermined level. Add coolant to bring reservoir to proper level to turn lamp off.

POWER LOSS/LIMIT LAMP

CHRYSLER, DODGE & PLYMOUTH

The Power Loss/Limit lamp should light for approximately 3 seconds after the ignition has been turned On as a bulb inspection. If improper or no signals are received by the logic module from various sensors, the logic module will light the Power Loss/Limit lamp. After diagnosing and servicing the fuel injection system or EGR system (California models with EGR sensor), the logic module memory can be cleared by disconnecting and reconnecting the battery quick-disconnect.

VEHICLE MAINTENANCE MONITOR (VMM) SYSTEM

MONACO & PREMIER

This system, **Fig. 5,** monitors regular service and maintenance intervals, engine oil level, engine coolant level, windshield washer fluid level, brake and tail lamps, door ajar and oil, coolant and washer sensors.

When the vehicle is started and no faults are present, the display will indicate "MONITOR." If the monitor detects a fault, it will be noted on the display. If more than one fault is noted, the fault of the highest priority will be displayed first. The display will then note all existing faults and return to the fault of highest priority. The VMM fault messages are as follows:

DOOR—Door Ajar—Close door indicated on vehicle outline display to reset monitor.

LAMP—Brake or Tail Lamp Outage—The display should light when brake is applied or headlamp switch is in the On position and a burned out lamp bulb is present. To reset monitor, replace burned out bulb.

COOLANT—Low Engine Coolant Level—Bringing coolant to proper level will reset monitor.

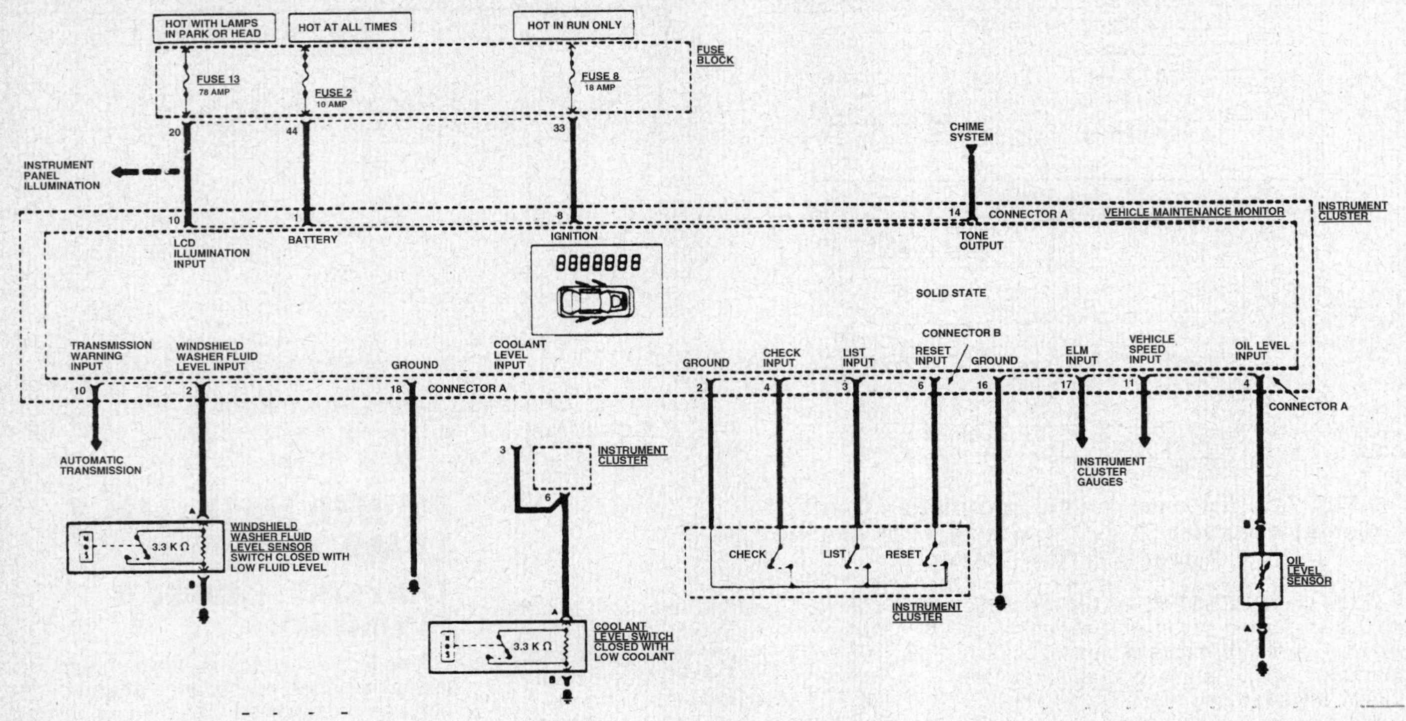

Fig. 5 Vehicle Maintenance Monitor (VMM) System wiring schematic (Part 1 of 2). Monaco & Premier

OIL—Low Engine Oil Level—The system will inspect engine oil level approximately 12 minutes after the ignition has been turned Off. A low oil level condition must be indicated three consecutive times before the monitor will display "Oil." To reset monitor, add oil to bring to proper level. Then, while display is indicating the "Oil" message, depress RESET select switch until a beep is noted. Even if RESET select switch is not depressed, the system will automatically reset monitor after three proper oil level readings have been obtained.

WASHER—Low Washer Fluid Level—Bringing washer fluid to proper level will reset monitor.

SERVICE—Perform Required Service and Maintenance—This message will be indicated at 7,500 mile intervals to indicate that required service is to be performed. After performing required service, depress the Reset select switch until a beep is noted.

SENSOR—This message will be indicated when a defect in the oil, coolant or washer sensor circuit is noted. Refer to "Self Diagnosis."

MILES (KMS)—Mile to next scheduled service interval.

SELF DIAGNOSIS

To diagnose, depress and hold the Check and List select switches, then turn ignition On. With the instrument cluster switch in the English mode, all diagnosis will be performed automatically in sequence. With the instrument cluster in the Metric mode, the Check select switch will have to be depressed to proceed to the next test. The display will indicate which components are faulty or satisfactory. Refer to **Fig. 6.** After completing diagnosis, depress Check and List select switches to exit diagnosis mode.

TROUBLESHOOTING

1. If a condition of no display or improper information exists, start engine and inspect the following:
   a. **On models less passive restraint,** inspect fuses 8 and 19 in fuse panel. **On models with passive restraint,** inspect fuses 2 and 8 in fuse panel. Replace any blown fuses.
   b. Using a suitable voltmeter, inspect terminal Nos. 1 and 5 of connector A, **Fig. 5.** Voltmeter should indicate battery voltage. If not, inspect for open circuit to fuse panel.
   c. Connect a suitable ohmmeter between terminal Nos. 15 and 18 of connector A, **Fig. 5.** Ohmmeter should indicate zero ohms. If a no display condition is present, replace monitor. If an improper information condition is present, refer to "Self Diagnosis." If reading is other than zero ohms, inspect for open circuit.
   d. With all doors closed, connect an ohmmeter between terminal Nos. 6, 7, 8 and 9 of connector A, **Fig. 5.** Ohmmeter should indicate an infinite reading. If reading is other than infinite, inspect for short circuit to ground.
2. If monitor fails to change modes, disconnect electrical connector B, **Fig. 5,** and proceed as follows:
   a. With Check select switch depressed, connect ohmmeter between terminal Nos. 2 and 4 of connector B. If ohmmeter reading is zero ohms, proceed to step b. If ohmmeter reading is other than zero ohms, replace mode select switches.
   b. With List select switch depressed, connect ohmmeter between terminal Nos. 2 and 3 of connector B. If ohmmeter reading is zero ohms, proceed to step c. If ohmmeter reading is other than zero ohms, replace mode select switches.
   c. With Reset select switch depressed, connect ohmmeter between terminal Nos. 2 and 5 of connector B. Ohmmeter reading should be zero ohms. If ohmmeter reading is other than zero ohms, replace mode select switches.

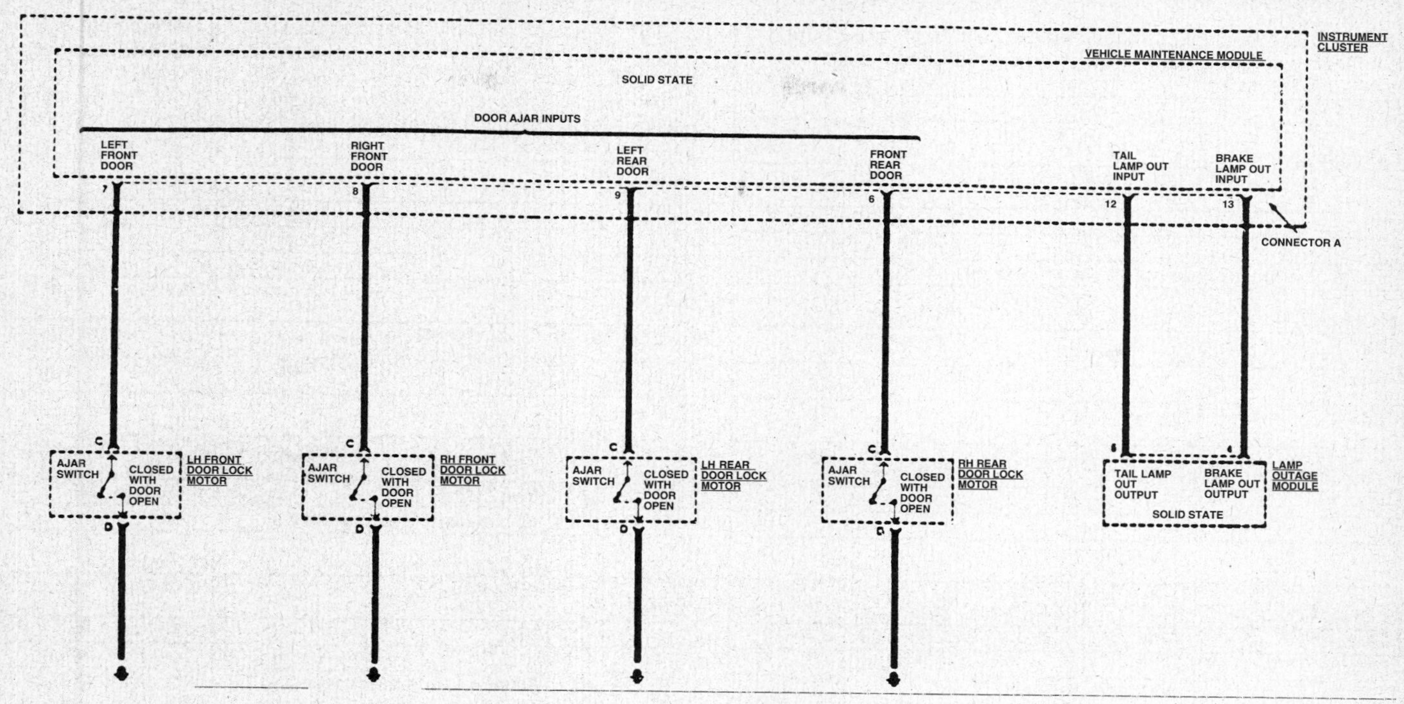

Fig. 5 Vehicle Maintenance Monitor (VMM) System wiring schematic (Part 2 of 2). Monaco & Premier

TEST 1 Initially, a number will be displayed on the monitors screen. The number indicates the version of the maintenance module installed in the vehicle.

TEST 2

In Display	Meaning
"CAL O"	Monitor Bad
"CAL 1–7"	Monitor OK
"CAL F"	Monitor Bad

TEST 3 The module internal memory is tested

In Display	Meaning
"RAM P"	Monitor OK
"RAM F"	Monitor Bad

TEST 4 The module program is tested

In Display	Meaning
"ROM P"	Monitor OK
"ROM F"	Monitor Bad

TEST 5 The monitor's clocks are tested

In Display	Meaning
"TIME P"	Monitor OK
"TIME F"	Monitor Bad

TEST 6 The monitor's storage capability is tested

In Display	Meaning
"NVM P"	Monitor OK
"NVM F"	Monitor Bad

TEST 7 The monitor's internal synchronization is tested

In Display	Meaning
"PAR 0"	Monitor OK
"PAR N"	Monitor Bad

TEST 8 The monitor's display screen is tested

In Display	Meaning
All segments ON	Monitor OK
All segments OFF	Monitor OK
"0"	Monitor OK
"1"	Monitor OK
"10"	Monitor OK
"100"	Monitor OK
"1000"	Monitor OK
"10000"	Monitor OK
"100000"	Monitor OK
"111111"	Monitor OK
"122222"	Monitor OK
"133333"	Monitor OK
"144444"	Monitor OK
"155555"	Monitor OK
"166666"	Monitor OK
"177777"	Monitor OK
"188888"	Monitor OK
"199999"	Monitor OK

The graphics segments will light one at a time, in the following order, the engine symbol, the car outline, right front door, rear tail lamps, left front door, and left front door. Any deviation from the above patterns signifies a bad monitor. Should any of the segments fail to light, the monitor is bad.

TEST 9 The test can only be performed while the test program is in manual mode. OIL will flash. Release CHECK button and press and hold LIST button until OIL flashes three times, then release LIST button and OIL will stop flashing. There will be a 30–45 second delay while system is testing. Oil level faults are displayed at this time. The engine oil level is tested.

In Display	Meaning
"OIL H"	Monitor OK, Oil Level Normal
"OIL L"	Monitor OK, But Oil Level Is Low
"OIL O"	Monitor OK, Oil Level Normal
OIL S"	Monitor OK, Oil Level Normal

TEST 10 The oil level probe is tested. The intermittent fault can be cleared in diagnostic program by pressing RESET switch while message is displayed

In Display	Meaning
"OIL IF"	Intermittent Fault With Oil Sensor
NO MESSAGE	Monitor OK, Sensor OK

TEST 11 The washer fluid level is tested

In Display	Meaning
"WASH H"	Washer Fluid Level Normal
"WASH L"	Washer Fluid Level Low
"WASH O"	Washer Fluid Level Probe Open

TEST 12 The washer level sensor is tested. The intermittent fault can be cleared in diagnostic program by pressing RESET switch while message is displayed

In Display	Meaning
"WASHER IF"	Intermittent Fault With Washer Fluid Sensor
NO MESSAGE	Monitor OK, Sensor OK

TEST 13 The coolant fluid level is tested

In Display	Meaning
"COOL H"	Coolant Fluid Level Normal
"COOL L"	Coolant Fluid Level Low
"COOL O"	Coolant Fluid Level Probe Open

TEST 14 The coolant fluid level sensor is tested. The intermittent fault can be cleared in diagnostic program by pressing reset switch while message is displayed

In Display	Meaning
"COOL IF"	Intermittent Fault With Coolant Level Sensor
NO MESSAGE	Monitor OK, Sensor OK

TEST 15 The tail lamp circuit is tested

In Display	Meaning
"TLO P"	Tail Lamp Circuit OK
"TLO F"	Tail Lamp Circuit Open

TEST 16 The brake lamp circuit is tested

In Display	Meaning
"BLO P"	Brake Lamp Circuit OK
"BLO F"	Brake Lamp Circuit Open

TEST 17 The status of the transmission diagnostic modules is tested

In Display	Meaning
"TRANS P"	Transmission Module OK
"TRANS F"	Transmission Module Fault

TEST 18 The frequency of the road speed sensor is displayed. When in manual mode, continuous monitoring is possible

In Display	Meaning
"SPD XXX" *	Frequency of Vehicle Speed Sensor

* Note XXX will vary from 0 and increase on vehicle speed increases

Fig. 6 Vehicle Maintenance Monitor (VMM) System self diagnosis test chart. Monaco & Premier

Ford Motor Co.

INDEX

AIR BAG WARNING LAMP

If the Air Bag warning lamp lights and stays on, diagnosis and repair of the air bag system will be necessary to reset the lamp.

ANTI-LOCK BRAKE WARNING LAMP

This lamp should light when the ignition is turned On. It may light for as long as 30 seconds as a bulb and system inspect. If the lamp remains lit or lights while operating the vehicle, a fault condition in the anti-lock brake system is indicated. When the lamp is lit, turn ignition Off, then start engine again. If the lamp still remains lit, the anti-lock brake system should be serviced. The brake system will remain functional, but without the anti-lock function. After servicing the anti-lock brake system, the lamp will automatically reset when the vehicle is operated at a speed over 25 mph.

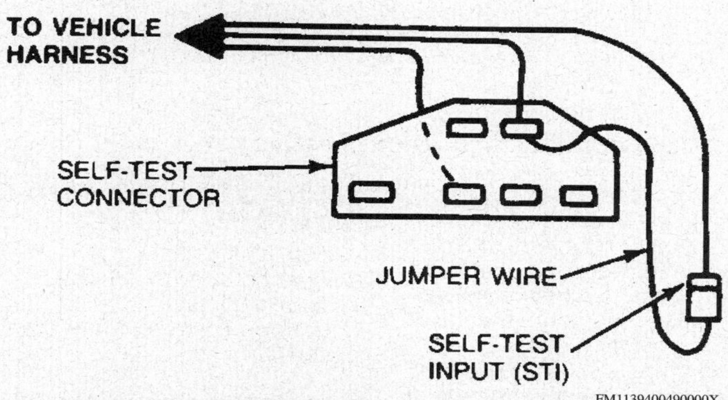

Fig. 1 Jumper wire connections for resetting Check Engine lamp. EEC-IV Except Festiva, Probe w/2.2L Engine & Escort & Tracer w/1.8L Engine

CHECK ENGINE LAMP

1992–93 MODELS w/ EEC-IV

EXCEPT FESTIVA, PROBE w/ 2.2L ENGINE & ESCORT & TRACER W/1.8L ENGINE

This lamp should light when the ignition is turned On. After the engine is started, the lamp should go off, unless a fault condition is detected by the EEC-IV system. Following diagnosis and repair, the Check Engine/MIL lamp will automatically reset when the stored codes are cleared from the EEC-IV system memory. After diagnosis and repair, the EEC-IV memory may be cleared of stored codes as follows:

1. With ignition turned Off, connect a jumper wire between Self Test and Self Test Input (STI) connectors, **Fig. 1. On Crown Victoria, Grand Marquis and Town Car models,** the Self Test and STI connectors are gray in color and are located on the front of the lefthand fender apron, near the Electronic Engine Control (EEC) relay. **On Mustang models,** the Self Test and STI connectors are gray in color and are located on the lefthand fender apron. **On Tempo and Topaz models,** the Self Test connector is gray in color and the STI connector is black in color and they are both located on the righthand fender apron, near the front of the strut tower. **On Taurus and Sable models,** the Self Test and STI connectors are gray in color and are located on the righthand fender apron, near the front of the engine in the area of the AIR pump and alternator. **On 1992–93 Thunderbird and Cougar models,** the Self Test and STI connectors are gray in color and are located on the righthand fender apron, near the strut tower.
2. **On all models,** turn ignition On, then disconnect jumper wire from test connector terminals. Disconnect jumper as soon as Check Engine lamp starts flashing.

FESTIVA

The Check Engine Indicator lamp should light when the ignition is in the RUN position with the engine not operating. When the engine is started, the Check Engine lamp should go off. If the lamp remains on, a service code has been stored in the EEC-IV self test system memory. After diagnosis and repair, the self test memory may be cleared of stored codes as follows:

1. With ignition turned Off, connect a jumper wire between Self Test Input (STI) connector terminal and ground. The STI connector is located in rear lefthand side of engine compartment, **Fig. 2.**
2. Turn ignition On, then disconnect and reconnect jumper wire connected between STI connector and ground.
3. Disconnect jumper from STI connector as soon as Check Engine lamp stops flashing.
4. Disconnect battery ground cable and depress brake pedal for approximately 5 to 10 seconds.
5. Connect battery ground cable.

PROBE w/2.2L ENGINE & ESCORT & TRACER W/1.8L ENGINE

This lamp should light when the ignition is turned On. After engine is started, the

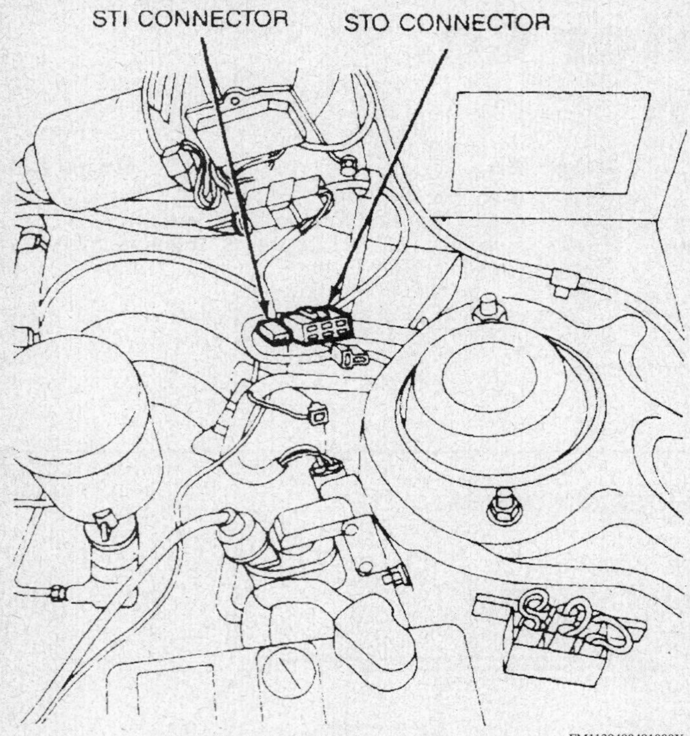

Fig. 2 STI connector location. Festiva

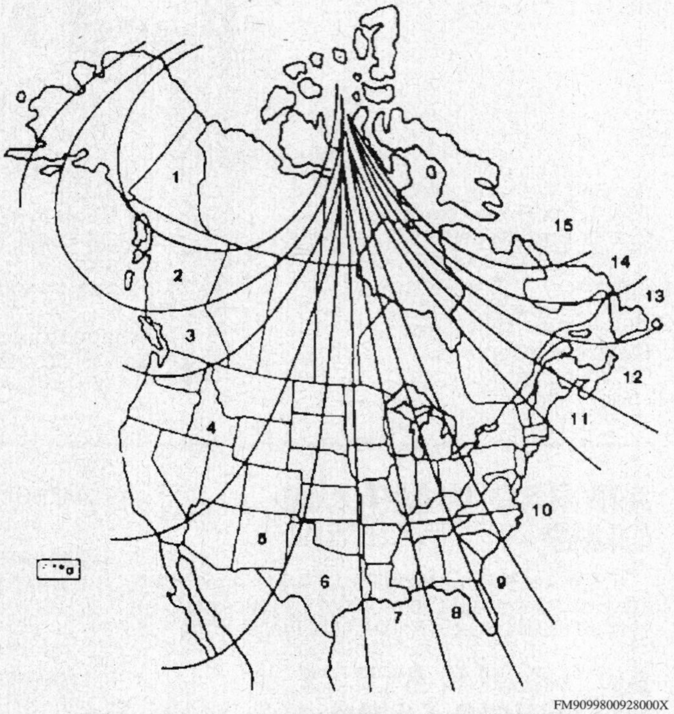

FM9099800928000X

Fig. 3 Magnetic zone map. Continental. Mark VIII & Town Car

lamp should go off, unless a fault condition is detected by the system. After diagnosis and repair, the Check Engine lamp will automatically reset when stored codes are cleared from the system memory. After diagnosis and repair, memory may be cleared of stored codes as follows:

1. Disconnect battery ground cable, then depress brake pedal for approximately 5 to 10 seconds.
2. Connect battery ground cable again.

1995–97 MODELS w/EEC-IV

This lamp should light when the ignition is turned On. After engine starts, the lamp should go off, unless a fault condition is detected by the EEC-IV system. A diagnostic trouble code is stored in the PCM. Following diagnosis and repair, the Check Engine/MIL lamp will automatically reset when stored diagnostic trouble codes are cleared from PCM memory. The PCM reset procedure allows the scan tool to command the PCM to clear all diagnostic trouble codes.

PCM RESET USING STAR TESTER

1. Turn ignition Off.
2. Perform required vehicle preparation and visual inspection.
3. Connect Star tester, then select vehicle model and year.
4. Follow operating instructions on tester screen. Select Generic OBD II Functions.
5. Press CONT button if all OBD II monitors are not complete.
6. Turn ignition On.
7. Select Clear Diagnostic Codes and press Start key.

PCM RESET USING GENERIC SCAN TOOL

1. Turn ignition Off.
2. Connect scan tool to DLC.
3. Turn ignition On.
4. Perform scan tool reset, then turn ignition Off.

KEEP ALIVE MEMORY (KAM) RESET & PCM RESET LESS ELECTRONIC TESTER

To clear KAM, disconnect battery ground cable for at least 5 minutes. This will also result in PCM reset.

MODELS w/EEC-V

1. Turn ignition Off.
2. Connect scan tool to DLC.
3. Turn ignition On.
4. Perform scan tool reset, then turn ignition Off.
5. **On 1998 and newer models,** the Check Engine lamp may light if fuel filler cap has not been completely tightened. Lamp should turn off after cap has been properly tightened and vehicle has successfully completed a predetermined number of trip cycles.

CHECK FUEL CAP LAMP

The Check Fuel Cap Lamp will illuminate momentarily when the ignition switch is placed in the On position as a bulb check. If the lamp remains On, check fuel cap for proper installation. After properly installing the fuel cap the lamp should go off after a normal period of driving.

ELECTRONIC COMPASS

CONTINENTAL

1. Determine magnetic zone, **Fig. 3.**
2. Insert a suitable rod into compass module, **Fig. 4,** and press internal switch until ZONE and current zone setting are displayed.
3. Turn ignition On, then release switch.
4. Press internal switch until proper zone number is displayed, then release to exit zone setting mode and lock in zone.

MARK VIII

1. Press and hold COMPASS button, then the RESET button until ECO-ZONE and RSETCAL is displayed.
2. Press FUEL ECONOMY button to enter the zone set mode.
3. Refer to **Fig. 3** for proper compass zone selection.
4. Press RESET until correct zone is selected.
5. Press COMPASS button to end zone adjustment.

TOWN CAR

The compass module is located at the back of the rearview mirror.

1. Select compass magnetic zone, **Fig. 3.**
2. Press and hold reset button on top of compass module until message center display reads current magnetic zone setting.
3. Press calibration button on compass module to select proper zone setting.
4. To exit zone setting mode, do not press any buttons for 10 seconds.

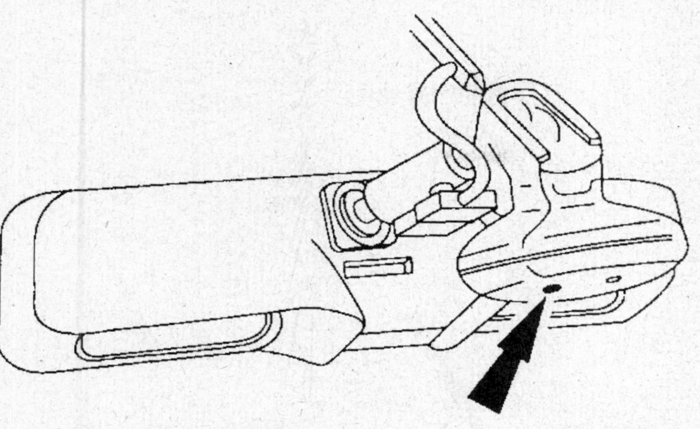

Fig. 4 Compass module location. Continental

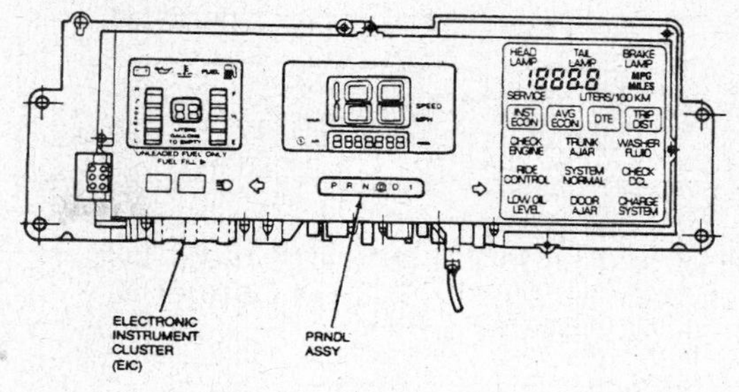

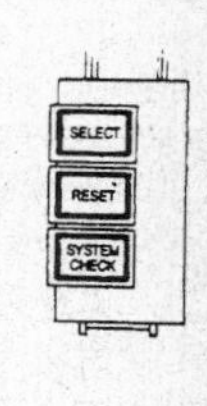

Fig. 5 Instrument cluster & message center. Continental

LOW COOLANT WARNING SYSTEM

The low coolant warning lamp should light whenever the coolant level in the coolant recovery bottle is ¼ to ¾ inch or more below the cold full mark. Raise coolant level in recovery bottle to the cold full mark to turn lamp off.

On models equipped with GEM module and low coolant level warning system, the low coolant level indicator lights for two seconds during engine startup or when ignition is turned to RUN. If coolant level falls below specification for more than 15 seconds, the GEM module generates a single one second tone. Raise coolant level in recovery bottle to specified level to turn lamp off.

LOW OIL LEVEL WARNING INDICATOR

This system is used to indicate when the engine oil level is 1½ quarts or more below the specified level. The lamp should light during engine starting. If the oil level is sufficient, the lamp will go off when the engine is operating. If the oil level is low, the lamp will remain on until engine oil is added and the ignition is turned Off. The module will take approximately 5 minutes to reset. If the engine is started during this period, the last recorded reading will be displayed.

MALFUNCTION INDICATOR LAMP (MIL)

Refer to "Check Engine Lamp" for lamp reset procedure.

MESSAGE CENTER

CROWN VICTORIA, GRAND MARQUIS & TOWN CAR

The message center may be located to the right of the instrument cluster, or it may be a part of the cluster itself. It consists of three buttons: Select, E/M and Reset. The E/M button switches the display between English and Metric. The Reset button set data to zero of instantaneous information. The Select button cycles the message display through the following selections:

1. Average speed.
2. Fuel remaining.
3. Average fuel economy and instantaneous fuel economy.
4. Distance to empty.
5. Trip distance.

MARK VIII

AIR RIDE SWITCH OFF

This warning message is displayed when the air suspension service switch, located in the luggage compartment, is turned Off.

CHECK AIR RIDE SYSTEM

This warning message is displayed when an air suspension system diagnostic trouble code is detected by the air suspension/EVO control module.

CHECK CHARGING SYSTEM

This warning message is displayed when the electrical system is not maintaining a proper voltage at the message center.

CHECK ENGINE TEMP

This warning message is displayed when the coolant is overheating.

LOW ENGINE COOLANT

This warning message is displayed when the engine coolant level is below the cold line of the coolant recovery reservoir.

CHECK EXTERIOR LAMPS

This warning message is displayed when one of the following lamps is turned on and at least one is burned out: stop lamp, rear parking lamp or low beam headlamp.

CHANGE OIL SOON OR OIL CHANGE REQUIRED

The oil life functions include oil life, change oil soon and oil change required. The oil life is determined by three functions: Smart Tach pulses, miles driven and time elapsed.

When the oil life drops down to the range of 1–5%, the "Change Oil Soon" message will appear. When oil life is 0%, the "Oil Change Required" message will appear.

Depressing the oil change reset button will reset the oil life to 100%.

SERVICE INTERVAL REMINDER

CONTINENTAL

After performing the required interval service, the service interval reminder mileage display on the instrument cluster can be reset as follows:

1. Depress System Check button on instrument panel. Service interval reminder mileage should be displayed on fuel computer display, **Fig. 5.**
2. Depress Reset button. Service interval reminder mileage should start flashing.
3. Depress Reset and System Check buttons at the same time to reset mileage.

1992–93 COUGAR & THUNDERBIRD

At approximately 7,500 miles, for models less super charged engine, the engine oil change indicator on the Vehicle Maintenance Monitor will indicate an oil change is needed. On models with super charged engine, the need for engine oil change will be indicated at 5,000 miles. After completing the required service, the oil change indicate can be reset by depressing the reset switch, **Fig. 6.**

1999 COUGAR

Some of these models are equipped with an optional overhead warning lamp system which includes a Service Interval reminder. This will light after approximately 358 days or 4800 miles to indicate that routine service is needed.

After service has been performed, the lamp can be reset by holding the trip computer SELECT and UNITS buttons for 5 seconds. The Service Interval lamp will light, then turn off after approximately four seconds.

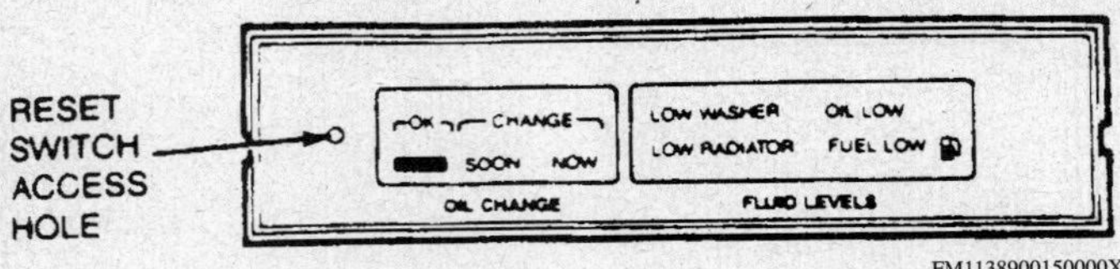

Fig. 6 Oil change interval indicator reset switch access hole location. 1992–93 Cougar & Thunderbird

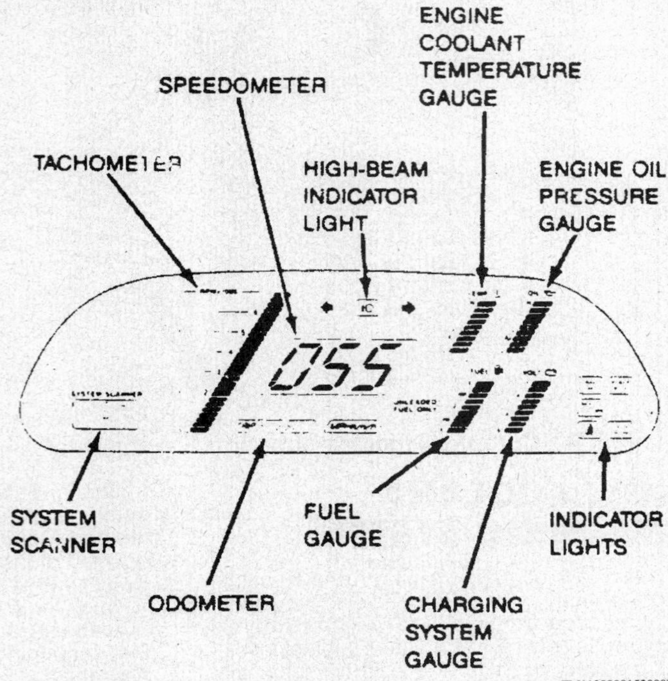

Fig. 7 Electronic instrument cluster. Probe

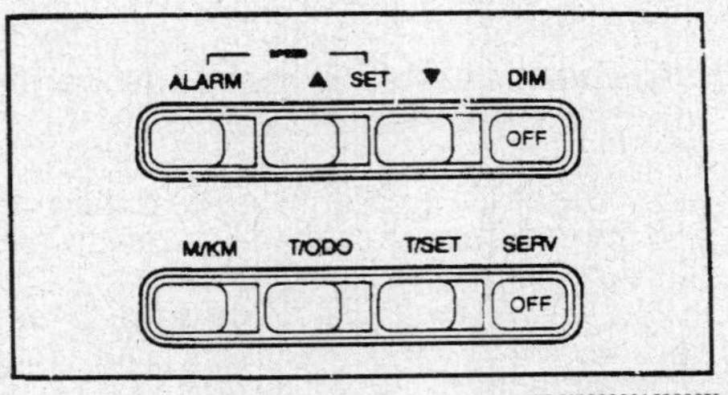

Fig. 8 Speed alarm keyboard. Probe

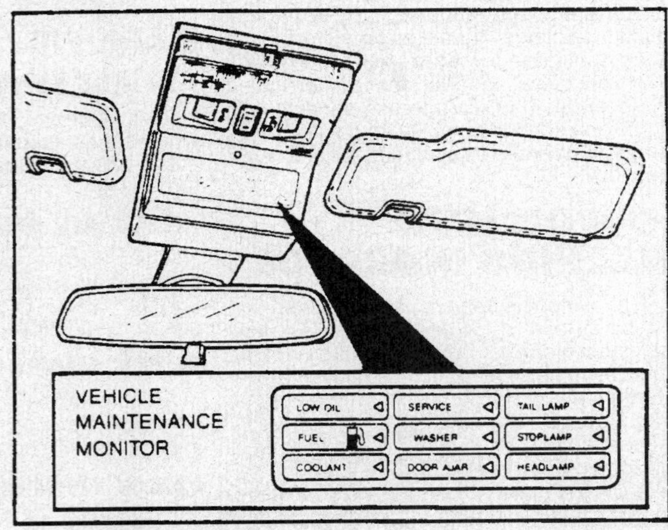

Fig. 9 Vehicle maintenance monitor. Probe

2000-02 COUGAR

The maintenance interval warning indicator is controlled by the HEC. The HEC illuminates the indicator advising a scheduled maintenance (which is dependant on time of distance). The indicator is reset by placing the ignition switch in position II and depressing SELECT & UNITS buttons simultaneously for 5 seconds until maintenance light extinguishes.

LINCOLN LS

CHANGE OIL SOON OR OIL CHANGE REQUIRED

The oil life functions include “Oil Life OK, Change Oil Soon” and “Oil Change Required.” The oil life is determined by the engine oil level and temperature sensors, ABS control module, odometer data and PCM RPM data.

When the oil life reaches the range of 1–5%, the “Change Oil Soon” message will appear. When oil life is 0%, the “Oil Change Required” message will appear.

Depressing the oil change RESET button will reset the oil life to 100%.

MARK VIII

CHANGE OIL SOON OR OIL CHANGE REQUIRED

The oil life functions include “Oil Life OK, Change Oil Soon” and “Oil Change Required.” The oil life is determined by the engine oil level and temperature sensors, ABS control module, odometer data and PCM RPM data.

When the oil life reaches the range of 1–5%, the “Change Oil Soon” message will appear. When oil life is 0%, the “Oil Change Required” message will appear.

Depressing the oil change RESET button will reset the oil life to 100%.

PROBE

ELECTRONIC INSTRUMENT CLUSTER

At 7,500 mile intervals, a Service Check message will be displayed under the System Scanner nomenclature on the instrument cluster for 3 minutes after engine starts, **Fig. 7.** After performing the required interval service, reset the service interval by depressing and holding the Service reset button, located on the speed alarm keyboard, until three tones have sounded, **Fig. 8.**

VEHICLE MAINTENANCE MONITOR

At 7,500 mile intervals a Service lamp, located on the overhead map lamp console, should light for 3 minutes after engine start, **Fig. 9.** After performing the required interval service, reset the service interval. **On models equipped with speed alarm keypad,** depress and hold the Service reset button, until three tones have sounded. **On models less speed alarm keypad,** locate reset hole in overhead console, then use a suitable tool to depress the reset button located behind the hole.

General Motors Corp.

INDEX

AIR BAG WARNING LAMP

If the air bag warning lamp lights and stays on, diagnosis and repair of the air bag system will be necessary to reset the lamp.

ANTI-LOCK WARNING LAMP

This lamp should light when the ignition is turned On. The lamp may light for as long as 30 seconds as a bulb and system inspection. If lamp remains lit or lights while operating the vehicle, a fault condition in the anti-lock brake system is indicated. When lamp is lit, turn ignition Off, then restart engine. If lamp still remains lit, the anti-lock brake system should be serviced. The brake system will remain functional, but without the anti-lock function. After servicing the anti-lock brake system the lamp will automatically reset. **On some models,** it may be necessary to operate vehicle at a speed over 18 mph to reset lamp.

CHANGE AUTOMATIC TRANSMISSION/ TRANSAXLE FLUID INDICATOR

2000 ELDORADO & 2000–02 DEVILLE & SEVILLE

1. Turn the ignition switch to the On position.
2. Press the Info button on the Driver Information Center (DIC) button to display Trans Fluid Life.
3. Press and hold the Info Reset button on the DIC until the display reads 100% Trans Fluid Life. The transaxle fluid life index should now be reset.
4. Place the ignition switch in the Off position

2001–02 ELDORADO

1. Turn the ignition switch to the On position.
2. Press and hold the Off and Rear Defog buttons on the climate control until Trans fluid Life Reset appears on the DIC
3. The transaxle fluid life index should now be reset.
4. Place the ignition switch in the Off position

CHANGE ENGINE OIL MESSAGE

BUICK

1997 CENTURY & REGAL

The Driver Information Center (DIC) engine oil life monitor indicates when to change oil. The "Change Oil" or "Change Oil Soon" messages might appear before 2,000 miles when operating under severe conditions.

To reset the oil change indicator after an oil change, proceed as follows:

1. Turn ignition On.
2. Fully depress and release accelerator pedal three times in 5 seconds.
3. If "Change Oil" or "Change Oil Soon" message flashes twice, indicator has properly reset.
4. If "Change Oil" or "Change Oil Soon" message stays on for 5 seconds, indicator has not properly reset and must be reset again.
5. **On models equipped with Oil Life Monitor,** press and hold RESET button for more than 5 seconds while oil monitor is being displayed or until oil life percentage reaches 100%.

1998–99 CENTURY & REGAL

The Engine Oil Life monitor indicates when an oil and filter change are needed, usually from 3000 to 10,000 miles since the last change. The CHANGE OIL SOON indicator may light even before 3000 miles if the vehicle has been operated under severe service.

The monitor will not detect dust in the oil. If operating in dusty conditions be sure to change the oil and filter every 3000 miles or sooner if the CHANGE OIL SOON lamp lights.

To reset the Engine Oil Life monitor proceed as follows:

1. Turn ignition On, but do not start engine.
2. Fully depress and release accelerator pedal three times within 5 seconds.
3. If CHANGE OIL SOON lamp flashes twice, this means system is properly reset.
4. If CHANGE OIL SOON lamp lights and stays lit for 5 seconds, system did not reset. Repeat reset procedure.

2000–02 CENTURY & REGAL

To reset the Engine Oil Life monitor proceed as follows:

1. Turn ignition On, but do not start engine.
2. Fully depress and release accelerator pedal three times within 5 seconds. The oil life indicator will begin to flash indicating the system is resetting.
3. Place ignition switch in Off position, then start engine.
4. The engine oil change light should illuminate as a bulb check and then go Off.
5. If oil change light remains On, repeat reset procedure.

1992–95 LESABRE & PARK AVENUE

After the engine oil has been changed, the "Change Oil Soon" lamp must be reset. With ignition On, use a pencil to depress the RESET button, located under the right-hand side of the instrument panel, for 5 seconds. The lamp should flash four times to indicate the Oil Life Monitor System has been reset.

1996–97 LESABRE & PARK AVENUE

After the engine oil has been changed, display the oil life index on the DIC, then hold the RESET button for 5 seconds. When a DIC message of RESET is displayed and the oil life index equals 100%, the reset is complete.

1997–98 RIVIERA & 1998 LESABRE & PARK AVENUE

1. Turn ignition to Run.
2. Press TRIP button on driver information center until OIL LIFE REMAINING is displayed.
3. Press and hold RESET for 6 seconds, then turn ignition off.

1999 LESABRE & PARK AVENUE

1. Turn ignition On, then press TRIP button on driver information center (DIC) switch to view various menu choices and stop on OIL LIFE REMAINING. A message will display percentage of oil life remaining.
2. Press and hold RESET button on DIC switch for at least two seconds. A message will display the percentage of oil life remaining as 99%. The engine oil life monitor is now reset.
3. Turn ignition Off.

2000–02 LESABRE & PARK AVENUE

1. Turn ignition switch to On position.
2. While Oil Life Index is being displayed, press and hold DIS RESET button for more than 5 seconds until display reads 100%.
3. Turn ignition Off.

1999 RIVIERA

1. Turn ignition to On, then press TRIP button on driver information center (DIC) switch to view various menu choices and stop on OIL LIFE REMAINING. A message will display percentage of oil life remaining.
2. Press and hold RESET button on DIC switch for at least two seconds. A message will display percentage of oil life remaining as 99%. The engine oil life monitor is now reset.
3. Turn ignition Off.

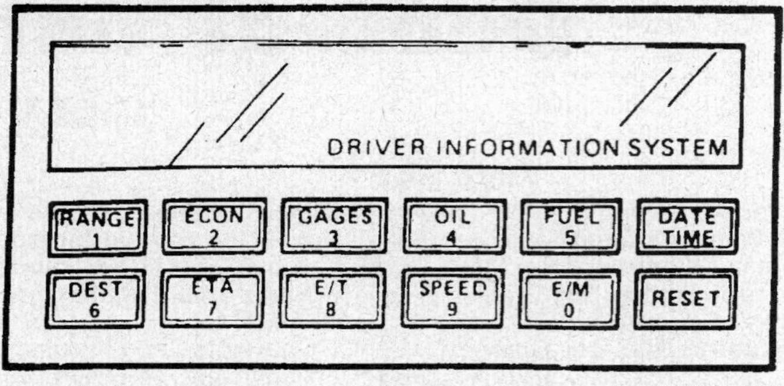

GC1138800168000X

Fig. 1 Driver Information Center. Oldsmobile except Alero, Aurora, Intrigue, LSS, Toronado & 1992–98 Eighty Eight & Ninety-Eight

1994 ROADMASTER

After engine oil has been changed, the Change Oil lamp must be reset. Remove the instrument panel fuse box cover. With ignition On, depress the OIL RESET button for 5 seconds. The Change Oil lamp should go off.

1995–96 ROADMASTER

1. Turn ignition On, without starting engine.
2. Within 5 seconds, depress accelerator pedal to wide open position and release three times.
3. When lamp goes out, engine oil life monitor is reset. PCM will acknowledge if reset was successful by flashing Change Oil lamp twice, then will turn lamp off. If lamp does not reset, turn ignition Off and repeat procedure.

CADILLAC

When the engine oil life index has reached zero, the Change Engine Oil message will be indicated on the Driver Information Display. After performing the engine oil change, the engine Oil Life Index may be reset as follows:

ALLANTE

Press RANGE button until oil index appears, then simultaneously press and hold the AVG SPD and RANGE buttons for a minimum of 5 seconds.

1992 DEVILLE & FLEETWOOD FWD

Press RANGE and FUEL USED buttons simultaneously to display oil life index, then press the RANGE and RESET buttons until "Change Oil Soon" light flashes (approximately 5 seconds). The oil life index will not remain displayed.

1992 ELDORADO & SEVILLE

Press and hold the ENG DATA and RANGE buttons for a minimum of 5 seconds.

1993 DEVILLE & SIXTY SPECIAL

Reset the Engine Oil Life Index (EOLI) after each oil change by pressing the RANGE and RESET keys on the Fuel Data Center for 5–50 seconds. The "Change Oil Soon" lamp will flash four times to indicate that the index has been reset.

1993 ELDORADO & SEVILLE

Press the INFORMATION button until oil life index is displayed, then press STORE/RECALL until oil life index resets to 100 (approximately 5 seconds).

1994–98 DEVILLE, ELDORADO & SEVILLE

Press the INFORMATION button until Oil Life Index is displayed, then press and hold RESET button until Oil Life Index resets to 100 (approximately 5 seconds).

1999 DEVILLE, ELDORADO & SEVILLE

1. Turn ignition On, then press TRIP button on driver information center (DIC) switch to view various menu choices and stop on OIL LIFE REMAINING. A message will display percentage of oil life remaining.
2. Press and hold RESET button on DIC switch for at least two seconds. A message will display the percentage of oil life remaining as 99%. The engine oil life monitor is now reset.
3. Turn ignition Off.

2000–02 DEVILLE, ELDORADO & SEVILLE

1. Turn ignition On, then press Gauge Info button on driver information center (DIC) switch to view various menu choices and stop on OIL LIFE REMAINING. A message will display percentage of oil life remaining.
2. Press and hold RESET button on DIC switch until display reads Oil Life Index 100% Normal.
3. Turn ignition Off.

FLEETWOOD (RWD)

1. Turn ignition On, without starting engine.
2. Press accelerator pedal to wide open throttle (WOT) position and release

three times within 5 seconds.
3. If "Change Oil" warning indicator goes out, system has been reset.
4. If "Change Oil" warning indicator does not reset, turn ignition Off and repeat procedure.

CHEVROLET

1999–2002 CAMARO

1. Turn ignition to Run, engine Off.
2. Press TRIP/OIL RESET button on instrument panel for 12 seconds. The OIL CHANGE lamp will start to flash to confirm that the system is reset. When reset is complete the lamp will go out.
3. Turn ignition Off.

1994 CAPRICE & IMPALA SS

After engine oil has been changed, the "Change Oil" lamp must be reset. Remove the instrument panel fuse box cover. With ignition On, depress the OIL RESET button for 5 seconds. The lamp should go off.

1995–96 CAPRICE & IMPALA SS

1. Turn ignition On, without starting engine.
2. Within 5 seconds, depress accelerator pedal to wide open position and release three times.
3. When lamp goes out, engine oil life monitor is reset. PCM will acknowledge if reset was successful by flashing "Change Oil" lamp twice, then will turn lamp off. If lamp does not reset, turn ignition Off and repeat procedure.

1992–96 CORVETTE

1. Turn ignition key to On position, without starting engine.
2. Press ENG MET button on the trip monitor and release, then press and release again within 5 seconds.
3. Within 5 seconds of previous step, press and hold GAUGES button on trip monitor. "Change Oil" lamp will flash.
4. Hold GAUGES button until "Change Oil" lamp stops flashing and goes out.
5. When lamp goes out, engine oil life monitor is reset. If it does not reset, turn ignition Off and repeat procedure.

1997 CORVETTE

1. Turn ignition to Run.
2. Press TRIP button on the Driver Information Center (DIC) switch to view menu. Stop at OIL LIFE REMAINING. A message will display percentage of oil life remaining.
3. Press and hold the DIC switch RESET button for at least two seconds. A message will display the percentage of oil life remaining as 100%. Oil life monitor has been reset.
4. Turn ignition Off.

1998–2002 CORVETTE

The Driver Information Center (DIC) engine oil life monitor indicates when to change oil, usually between 3000 to 7500 miles, although the "Change Oil" message might appear before 3000 miles when operating under severe conditions.

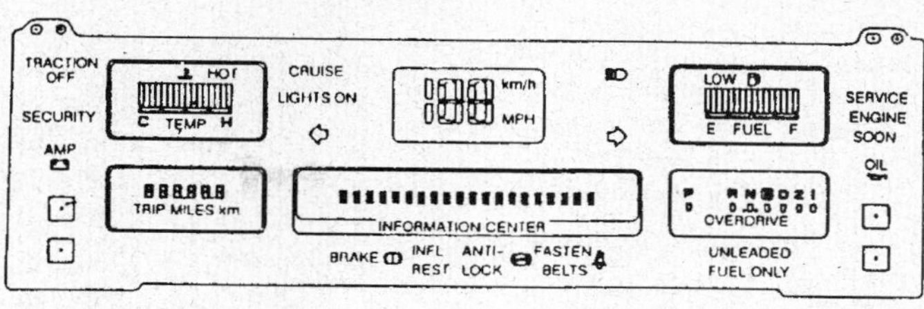

Fig. 2 Driver information center. 1992–93 Eighty-Eight & Ninety-Eight

To reset the oil life monitor after an oil change, proceed as follows:

1. Turn ignition On.
2. Press TRIP button on DIC to view menu choices, then stop on "Oil Life Remaining."
3. Press and hold RESET button for more than two seconds. When remaining oil life percentage changes to 99% for 1998–2000 models, 100% for 2001 models, the monitor has been properly reset.
4. Turn ignition Off.

1998–2001 LUMINA

The Engine Oil Life monitor indicates when an oil and filter change are needed, usually from 3000 to 10,000 miles since the last change. The CHANGE OIL SOON indicator may light even before 3000 miles if the vehicle has been operated under severe service.

The monitor will not detect dust in the oil. If operating in dusty conditions be sure to change the oil and filter every 3000 miles or sooner if the CHANGE OIL SOON lamp lights.

To reset the Engine Oil Life monitor proceed as follows:

1. Turn ignition On, but do not start engine.
2. Fully depress and release accelerator pedal three times within 5 seconds.
3. If CHANGE OIL SOON lamp flashes twice, this means system is properly reset.
4. If CHANGE OIL SOON lamp lights and stays lit for 5 seconds, system did not reset. Repeat reset procedure.

IMPALA & MONTE CARLO

Less DE Series Radio

Refer to "1998–2001 Lumina" for lamp reset procedure.

With DE Series Radio

1. Place ignition switch in On position with radio Off.
2. Press and hold the Disp button on the radio for at least 5 seconds until Settings is displayed.
3. Press the Seek up or down arrow to scroll though the main menu.
4. Scroll until Oil Life appears on the display.
5. Press the Prev or Next button to enter the sub-menu. Reset will be displayed.
6. Press the Disp button to reset. A chime will be heard to verify the new setting and Done will be displayed for one second.
7. Once the message has been reset, scroll until Exit appears on the display.
8. Press the Disp button to exit programming. A chime will be heard to verify the exit.

OLDSMOBILE

EXCEPT ALERO, AURORA, INTRIGUE, LSS, TORONADO & 1992–98 EIGHTY EIGHT & NINETY-EIGHT

When the engine oil life index has reached 10 or less, the Driver Information System display will indicate distance to oil change and sound a beep when ignition is turned to Run or Accessory for the first time each day. When the engine oil life index has reached 0, the Driver Information System display will indicate Change Oil Now and sound a beep when ignition is turned to Run or Accessory for the first time each day. After engine oil change has been performed, the oil life index may be reset by depressing and holding the Oil and Reset buttons for approximately 5 seconds, **Fig. 1.**

ALERO

The Engine Oil Life monitor indicates when an oil and filter change are needed, usually from 3000 to 7500 miles since the last change. The indicator may light even before 3000 miles if the vehicle has been operated under severe service.

The monitor will not detect dust in the oil. If operating in dusty conditions be sure to change the oil and filter every 3000 miles or sooner if the CHANGE OIL SOON lamp lights.

To reset the Engine Oil Life monitor proceed as follows:

1. Turn ignition On, but do not start engine.
2. Press and release RESET button. CHANGE OIL indicator will begin flashing.
3. Press and release RESET button again.
4. The reset is complete when the light goes out and the chime sounds.

1992–95 EIGHTY EIGHT & NINETY-EIGHT & 1995 AURORA

When the engine oil life index has reached 10 or less, the Driver Information System display will indicate distance to oil change and sound a beep when the ignition is placed in the RUN or ACC position for the first time each day. When the engine oil life index has reached zero, the Driver Information System display will indicate "Change Oil Now" and sound a beep, when ignition is turned to RUN or ACC for the first time each day. After engine oil change has been performed, the oil life index may be reset as follows:

1. **On 1992–93 Eighty Eight and Ninety-Eight and 1995 Aurora,** depress the TEST button and release.
2. Depress OIL button and release.
3. **On 1994–95 Eighty-Eight and Ninety Eight,** select OIL menu by depressing MODE button.
4. **On all models,** depress and hold the RESET button for 5 to 7 seconds.

1996 NINETY-EIGHT, 1996–97 EIGHTY-EIGHT, LSS, 1997 REGENCY & 1996–99 AURORA

After the engine oil has been changed, display the oil life index on the DIC, then hold the RESET button for 5 seconds. When a DIC message of RESET is displayed and the oil life index equals 100%, the reset is complete.

1998–99 EIGHTY-EIGHT, LSS & REGENCY

The Driver Information Center (DIC) engine oil life monitor indicates when to change oil, usually between 3000 to 7500 miles, although the "Change Oil" message might appear before 3000 miles when operating under severe conditions.

To reset the oil life monitor after an oil change, proceed as follows:

1. Turn ignition On.
2. Press TRIP button on DIC to view menu choices, then stop on "Oil Life Remaining."
3. Press and hold RESET button for more than 5 seconds. Monitor has been properly reset when remaining oil life percentage changes to 100%.
4. Turn ignition Off.

2001–02 AURORA

1. Place ignition switch in On position.
2. Press the Select button until the Oil Life % is displayed.
3. Press and hold the Reset button until the display indicates Oil Life 100%.
4. Engine oil life monitor is reset.

INTRIGUE

The "Change Oil" lamp will light when the engine oil's useful life is close to its expiration. This lighting may appear earlier than described in the owner's manual, depending on driving patterns.

To reset the oil life monitor after an oil change, proceed as follows:

1. Turn ignition On.
2. Fully depress and release accelerator pedal three times in 5 seconds.
3. If "Change Oil" message flashes, monitor has properly reset.
4. If "Change Oil" message stays on for 5 seconds, monitor has not properly reset and must be reset again.
5. **On models equipped with U20 option,** reset the oil life low indicator as follows:
   a. Press and hold MODE button until light appears next to OIL LIFE.
   b. Press and hold trip RESET button until oil life percentage changes to 99%.

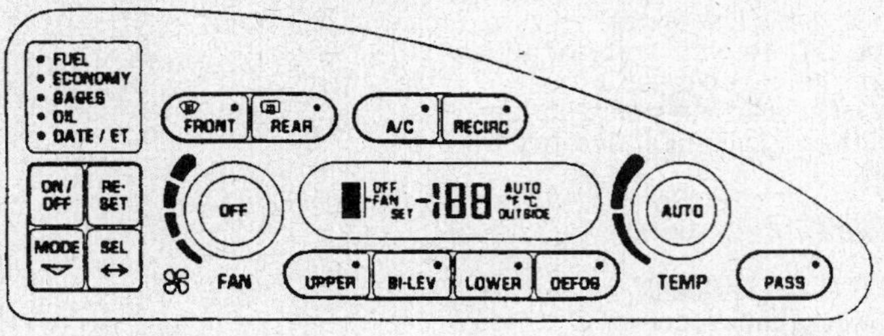

Fig. 3 Driver information center. LSS, 1994–96 Eighty-Eight & Ninety-Eight

1992 TORONADO

On vehicles less CRT Driver Information Display option, oil life is displayed by pressing the ENG DATA button on the Driver Information System (DIS) keypad several times. To reset the oil life index, press and hold the RESET/ENTER key for 5 seconds while the oil life is displayed.

On vehicles equipped with Driver Information Display option U68, oil life may be displayed by pressing the INFO button and then selecting the OIL LIFE option. Oil life is reset is reset by pressing RESET on the oil life display and then pressing YES on the confirmation screen. This will reset the oil life index and OIL LIFE INDEX 100. The Change Oil message will remain off until the next oil change is needed.

PONTIAC

1992–95 BONNEVILLE

After changing engine oil and filter, if required, reset service interval indicator by depressing and releasing the service reminder button until the desired item is displayed. When the desired item is displayed, do not release service reminder button. After button has been depressed for approximately 10 seconds, the service interval mileage display will begin to count down in 500 mile intervals. When desired service interval mileage is reached, release button. The service interval reminder indicates miles to service, not miles from last service.

1996–97 BONNEVILLE

After the engine oil has been changed, display the oil life index on the DIC, then hold the RESET button for 5 seconds. When a DIC message of RESET is displayed and the oil life index equals 99% or 100%, the reset is complete.

1998 BONNEVILLE

1. Turn ignition switch to RUN position.
2. Press TRIP button on driver information center (DIC) switch to view menu choices.
3. Select OIL LIFE REMAINING.
4. Press and hold RESET button on DIC for more than 5 seconds until oil life changes to 100%.
5. Turn ignition switch to OFF position.

1999 BONNEVILLE

1. Turn ignition switch to RUN position.
2. Press and hold reset button in glove compartment for at least 5 seconds but not more than 60 seconds.
3. After 5 seconds, observe the CHANGE OIL SOON light flash four times before light turns OFF.
4. Engine oil life monitor has been reset.

2000–02 BONNEVILLE

1. Turn ignition switch to On position.
2. Press MODE button on driver information center (DIC) until VIEW DATA is visible.
3. Press SELECT button until OIL LIFE % is visible.
4. Press and hold RESET button on DIC until display reads OIL LIFE 100% NORMAL.
5. Engine oil life monitor is now reset.

1999–2002 FIREBIRD

1. Turn ignition to Run, engine Off.
2. Press TRIP/OIL RESET button on instrument panel for 12 seconds. The OIL CHANGE lamp will start to flash to confirm that the system is reset. When reset is complete the lamp will go out.
3. Turn ignition Off.

1999–2002 GRAND AM

The Engine Oil Life monitor indicates when an oil and filter change are needed. Usually from 3000 to 7500 miles for 1999–2000 models, from 3000 to 12,500 miles for 2001 models, since the last change. The indicator may light even before 3000 miles if the vehicle has been operated under severe service.

The monitor will not detect dust in the oil. If operating in dusty conditions be sure to change the oil and filter every 3000 miles or sooner if the CHANGE OIL SOON lamp lights.

To reset the Engine Oil Life monitor proceed as follows:

1. Turn ignition On, but do not start engine.
2. Press and release RESET button. CHANGE OIL indicator will begin flashing.
3. Press and release RESET button again.

1992–96 GRAND PRIX

Ensure oil life indicator is displayed by pressing Driver Information System SYSTEMS CHECK button. Press and hold the

RESET button until oil life display is returned to 100%.

1997-99 GRAND PRIX

Change Oil Soon Indicator

1. To reset "Change Oil Soon" indicator, turn ignition On, but do not start engine.
2. Fully depress and release accelerator three times within 5 seconds. Opening hood and manually operating throttle linkage may be required.
3. If "Change Oil Soon" lamp flashes this means system is resetting.
4. Turn ignition Off, then start engine.
5. If "Change Oil Soon" lamp lights, repeat reset procedure. Using Tech 2 or an equivalent scan tool to reset lamp may be required.

1997-98 GRAND PRIX

Oil Life Monitor

To reset Oil Life Monitor, press trip calculator MODE button until light appears next to "Oil Life," then press and hold RESET button until oil life percentage reaches 100%.

2000-02 GRAND PRIX

To reset the Engine Oil Life monitor proceed as follows:

1. To reset Engine Oil Life monitor on models equipped with DIC proceed as follows:
   a. Turn ignition On, but do not start engine.
   b. Fully depress and release accelerator pedal three times within 5 seconds. The oil life indicator will begin to flash indicating the system is resetting.
   c. Place ignition switch in Off position, then start engine.
   d. The engine oil change light should illuminate as a bulb check and then go Off.
   e. If oil change light remains On, repeat reset procedure.
2. To reset Engine Oil Life monitor on models equipped with Trip Computer proceed as follows:
   a. Depress Mode button until light appears next to Oil Life.
   b. Depress Trip Reset button until oil life percentage reads 99%.

SATURN

CHANGE OIL SOON TELLTALE LAMP

The PCM has the ability to calculate when the engine oil needs to be changed based on vehicle mileage, engine revolutions and engine coolant temperature. The PCM bases the engine oil change interval within a window of 3000–6000 miles regardless of engine revolutions and engine coolant temperature. To reset the PCM oil life monitor, proceed as follows:

1. Remove cover from the underhood fuse relay center.
2. Place the ignition switch in the On position.
3. Press the red Oil Reset Button and hold for 5 seconds.
4. If the Change Engine Oil Soon lamp is flashing, the system is reset. The lamp will flash for 30 seconds or until the ignition switch is placed in the Off position.
5. If the lamp comes On and remains On for 30 seconds at the next ignition On cycle, the lamp did not reset. The reset procedure must be performed again.

CHECK ENGINE LAMP

On 1998 and newer models, the Check Engine lamp may light if the fuel filler cap has not been completely tightened. This lamp should turn off after the cap has been properly tightened and the vehicle has successfully completed a predetermined number of trip cycles.

CHECK ENGINE OR SERVICE NOW/SOON ENGINE INDICATOR LAMPS (GASOLINE ENGINES w/ELECTRONIC ENGINE CONTROLS OR EFI)

EXCEPT CHEVROLET/GEO METRO, PRIZM & STORM & PONTIAC LEMANS

The Check Engine lamp should light when the ignition is turned On. When the engine is started, the lamp should go off. If the lamp remains On for 10 seconds or constantly after the engine is started, the self diagnosis system has detected a fault condition and has stored a code in the system Electronic Control Module (ECM) or Powertrain Control Module (PCM). After diagnosis and repair, the ECM memory can be cleared of codes as follows:

On models except Cadillac with DEFI, remove the ECM/PCM fuse or disconnect the battery ground cable for approximately 30 seconds, with ignition turned Off. It should be noted, if battery ground cable is disconnected to clear codes, components such as clocks, electronically tuned radios etc., will have to be reset.

On vehicles that are equipped as such, the ECM/PCM power feed is connected by a pigtail, inline fuse holder, at the positive battery terminal. To clear codes within the ECM/PCM system and protect the components that need resetting, disconnect the inline fuse.

On Cadillac Eldorado and Seville and Oldsmobile Toronado/Trofeo models, the stored codes are cleared during the self-diagnostic procedure.

On 1998 and newer models, the Check Engine lamp may light if the fuel filler cap has not been completely tightened. This lamp should turn off after the cap has been properly tightened and the vehicle has successfully completed a predetermined number of trip cycles.

CHEVROLET/GEO METRO

The Check Engine lamp should light when the ignition is turned On with engine not operating. When engine is started, the Check Engine lamp should go off. If lamp remains on, a code has been stored by the Electronic Control Module (ECM) memory. After diagnosis and repair, turn ignition Off, then clear codes stored in the ECM memory by disconnecting the battery ground cable, for approximately 20 seconds.

On 1998 and newer models, the Check Engine lamp may light if the fuel filler cap has not been completely tightened. This lamp should turn off after the cap has been properly tightened and the vehicle has successfully completed a predetermined number of trip cycles.

CHEVROLET/GEO PRIZM

The Check Engine lamp should light when the ignition is in the On position with engine not operating. When engine is started, the Check Engine lamp should go off. If lamp remains on, a code has been stored by the Electronic Control Unit (ECU) memory. After diagnosis and repair, turn ignition Off, then clear codes stored in the ECU memory by removing the Stop Fuse. The Stop fuse is located in a fuse panel, in the passenger compartment, on driver's side, behind kick panel. The fuse must be removed for 10 seconds or longer, depending on ambient temperature. The lower the ambient temperature, the longer the fuse will have to be removed.

GEO STORM

The Check Engine lamp should light when the ignition is in the On position with engine not operating. When engine is started, the Check Engine lamp should go off. If lamp remains on, a code has been stored by the Electronic Control Module (ECM) memory. After diagnosis and repair, turn ignition Off, then clear codes stored in the ECM memory by disconnecting the battery ground cable for approximately 30 seconds.

PONTIAC LEMANS

The Check Engine lamp should light when the ignition is turned On. When the engine is started, them should go off. If the lamp remains On for 10 seconds or constantly after the engine is started, the self diagnosis system has detected a fault condition and has stored a code in the system Electronic Control Module (ECM). After diagnosis and repair, the ECM memory can be cleared of codes, by disconnecting battery ground cable for 10 seconds, with ignition turned Off.

CHECK FUEL CAP LAMP

The Check Fuel Cap Lamp will illuminate momentarily when the ignition switch is placed in the On position as a bulb check. If the lamp remains On, check fuel cap for proper installation. After properly installing the fuel cap the lamp should go off.

CHECK GAUGE WARNING LAMP

The Check Gauge warning lamp will light to warn the driver to inspect the oil pressure gauge, engine coolant temperature gauge and the voltmeter. When lit, the "Check Gauge" lamp indicates that one of these gauges is operating in an abnormal range.

CHECK INFO CENTER WARNING LAMP

1992 CADILLAC ELDORADO & SEVILLE

This lamp will light for a few seconds when the ignition is turned On as a bulb inspection. If lamp remains lit, a message is stored in the Driver Information Center. Refer to "Driver Information Center."

DRIVER INFORMATION CENTER

CADILLAC

1992 Eldorado & Seville

This system incorporates a warning lamp, located on the instrument cluster, that is lit when the ignition is in the On position. After a few seconds the lamp should go off, unless a message in The Driver Information System is present. The driver information center will display the following messages:

A/C Overheated—A/C Compressor Off—This message is displayed when excessive pressure in the refrigerant system is encountered. When this condition is encountered, the A/C Compressor clutch will be de-energized and cool air will not be delivered to the vehicle interior. The message will continue to appear and the A/C compressor clutch will continue to be de-energized until the system pressure returns to normal range. If this message frequently appears, the A/C system should be serviced.

A/C Sensor Fault—This message will be displayed when the sensor controlling A/C compressor clutch cycling has failed. When this sensor has failed, the A/C compressor will not operate and the A/C system will emit warmer air. After servicing system and replacing sensor, the display message will be cancelled.

Battery Volts High—This message will appear when the charging system is overcharging the battery. After completing charging system diagnosis and repair, the message will be cancelled when battery voltage returns to 11.5 to 15.5 volts with engine operating. Battery voltage can be displayed on the Drive Information Center Display by depressing the Eng-Data button three times.

Battery Volts Low—If this message is displayed while driving the vehicle or after vehicle has been started, a fault condition in the charging system is present or battery has been drained. After diagnosing charging system or electrical system for cause of battery drain, the message will be cancelled when engine is operating and battery voltage is between 11.5 to 15.5 volts. Battery voltage can be displayed on the Drive Information Center Display by depressing the Eng-Data button three times.

Change Engine Oil—When the engine oil life index has reached 0, the Change Engine Oil message will be indicated. After performing the engine oil change, the engine Oil Life Index may be reset by depressing and holding the Engine Data and Range buttons for at least 5 seconds

Cooling Fan Fault—This message will appear when the engine cooling fan system inoperative. After repairing cooling fan system the message will be automatically cancelled.

Engine Hot—A/C Compressor Off—This message will appear when A/C system is Auto or Defrost and engine coolant temperature is excessive. The A/C compressor clutch will be automatically de-energized when excessive engine coolant temperatures are encountered. When engine coolant temperature returns to normal, the A/C compressor clutch will be energized and the message on the display will be cancelled.

Front Or Rear Door Ajar—This message will appear when the transmission selector lever is moved out of the Park position and a door is not properly closed. The message can be cancelled by properly closing the indicated door.

Fuel Level Very Low—When low fuel level conditions are encountered this message will appear. To cancel message, add fuel.

Gear Select Problem—This message will appear if a fault condition in the transaxle gear select system is encountered while operating vehicle. After performing required service, the message will automatically be cancelled.

Headlamps Or Parking Lamps On—This message will be displayed when the headlamp switch is On, vehicle is moving and the sensed level of outside light indicates that headlamps should not be lit. This message may be cancelled by turning the headlamp switch Off.

Headlamps Suggested—This message will be displayed when the Twilight Sentinel is in the Off position, vehicle is moving and the sensed level of outside light indicates that headlamps should be lit. This message may be cancelled by activating the Twilight Sentinel System.

Low A/C Refrigerant—A/C Compressor Off—This message will be displayed when the A/C system detects a refrigerant charge low enough to cause compressor damage. When this condition is encountered, the A/C compressor clutch is de-energized and the A/C system is switched from AUTO to ECON. The system will remain in ECON until required repairs are made and system is recharged. After completing required repairs and recharging the system, A/C system operation will return to normal and the message on the display will be cancelled.

Low A/C Refrigerant—Service A/C Soon—This message will be displayed when the A/C system detects that refrigerant charge is low enough to cause a reduction in cooling capacity. This message will be displayed until system has been recharged.

Low Washer Fluid—This message will appear when windshield washer fluid level is low. To cancel message, refill windshield washer fluid reservoir.

Oil Life Index—The oil life index is a series of numerals ranging from 0–100. The 100 is indicated when engine oil has been drained and replacement engine oil has been installed. The 0 is an indication that the engine oil should be changed. The oil life index is accessed by depressing the Engine Data button four times.

Service Electrical System—This message will appear when a fault condition in the charging system is present. After repairing charging system, the message will be automatically cancelled.

Set Timing Mode—This message will appear if ignition timing is improperly set. After performing required service, the message will be automatically cancelled.

Starting Disabled/Due to Theft System/Remove Ignition Key—This message is an indication of a fault condition in the vehicle security system that may prohibit the vehicle from being restarted after the ignition has been turned Off. After servicing the vehicle security system the message will be automatically cancelled.

System Satisfactory—This message will be displayed for approximately 5 seconds after ignition has been turned On, unless a fault condition in the system has been detected. After approximately 5 seconds the display will return to the last display function selected.

System Problem—Service Car Soon—This message will be displayed when one or more of the vehicle computers supplying information to the Driver Information Center become faulty. After diagnosis and repair of the faulty computer, the message will be automatically cancelled.

Theft System Problem/Car May Not Start—This message will appear when the vehicle security system senses an improper ignition key has been placed in the ignition. After removing key from ignition, the Driver Information Center display will indicate "Wait 3 Minutes," "Wait 2 Minutes," Wait 1 Minute and then "Start Car." When the "Start Car" message appears, insert ignition key and attempt to start vehicle. If message appears again, inspect ignition key for damage and replace as required. If key appears to be satisfactory, clean pellet contacts with a soft cloth and attempt to restart vehicle.

Trunk Open—This message will appear when the ignition is the Run position and the trunk is not properly closed. The message can be cancelled by properly closing the trunk.

OLDSMOBILE

1992–93 EIGHTY-EIGHT & NINETY-EIGHT & 1995–99 AURORA

The Driver Information Center Display, **Fig. 2,** is located on the instrument panel (Eighty-Eight and Ninety-Eight models with digital cluster or touring sedan gauge cluster). It provides traveling and performance information on the following:

1. Date and Time—This information is displayed for 5 seconds when the ignition is turned On. The DT/TM button may be depressed at any time to display current date and time.
2. Fuel Economy—The ECON button displays average fuel economy.
3. Remaining Fuel/Fuel Used—Depressing FUEL button displays amount of fuel used since reset button was last pressed. Depressing FUEL button a second time displays amount of fuel remaining.
4. Fuel Range—Depress RANGE to display distance that may be driven before refueling. To display amount of fuel used from a specific starting point, depress FUEL then RESET.
5. Average Speed—Depress SPEED to display average speed. To reset average speed, depress SPEED then RESET.
6. Remaining Oil Life and Oil Change Information—The OIL button displays information on oil life. Refer to "Change Oil Or Change Oil Now Message" for reset procedure.
7. Engine Coolant Temperature, Oil Pressure, Battery Voltage and Tachometer—Depressing GAGES once displays coolant temperature. Pressing GAGES a second time displays oil pressure. Pressing GAGES a third time displays battery voltage. Pressing GAGES a fourth time displays tachometer RPM.
8. Distance To Destination—Depress DEST then RESET and enter length of trip. Display will then count backwards to zero distance remaining. When the display reaches zero, "TRIP COMPLETE" is displayed. This message will clear when the TEST button is depressed or the ignition is turned Off.
9. Estimated Time of Arrival—After entering distance to destination, Press ETA button to display time remaining to destination (based on average speed).
10. Elapsed Time—Depressing the E/T button activates a stopwatch that records up to 100 hours.

LSS, 1994-96 EIGHTY-EIGHT & NINETY-EIGHT

The Driver Information Center Display, **Fig. 3,** is located on the instrument panel. When the ignition is turned On, the display will go through a system inspection while the message "Monitored Systems OK" is displayed. If no fault conditions are detected, the screen returns to the mode displayed before the ignition was turned Off.

There are four buttons that control the functions of the driver information center:

1. The MODE button, when pressed, cycles through a series of displays in the following order:
   a. ECON—Average fuel economy and instantaneous fuel economy.
   b. FUEL—Amount of fuel used since last fuel-used reset, and fuel remaining.
   c. RANGE—Fuel range and low fuel range.
   d. OIL—Oil life index and next required oil change.
   e. GAGES—Oil pressure, tachometer and battery voltage information.
   f. ET—Elapsed time since last reset.
   g. DT/TM—Date and time.
2. The ON/OFF button is used to input numbers and to blank out the display.
3. The RESET button is used with other buttons to reset the system. Depressing this button once enters the reset mode. Pressing this button again aborts the reset.
4. The SEL button is used to select different displays within a specific mode. For example, when the SEL button is depressed while in the GAGES mode, the display will cycle from oil pressure to battery voltage to tachometer.

PONTIAC

BONNEVILLE

The Driver Information Center Display is located on the instrument panel. When the ignition is turned On, the display will go through a bulb inspection in which the vehicle graph and message title will be displayed in sequence. After the sequence has been completed, all messages and vehicle graph will remain lit for approximately two seconds. After approximately two seconds, if all monitored systems are functioning properly, the message titles should go off and only the vehicle outline should be lit. If a fault condition in any of the monitored systems is present, the particular title for the monitored system should light and its approximate location on the vehicle graphic display should light. The following messages will be displayed:

1. **Function Monitor**—The coolant level, fuel level and windshield washer levels are monitored when ignition is turned On.
   a. Coolant Level—This message will be indicated when engine coolant level in the radiator drops below a predetermined level. To cancel message, inspect cooling system, then add coolant to bring system to proper level.
   b. Fuel Level—This message will be indicated when fuel level is 5 gallons or less. To cancel message add fuel to fuel tank.
   c. Washer Fluid—This message will be indicated when windshield washer fluid is at about 40% of capacity. To cancel message, add washer fluid to reservoir.
2. **Lamp Check**—The headlamps, tail lamps, brake lamps and turn signal lamps will be inspected whenever the lamp system is activated. To cancel this message, replace bulb or inspect and repair electrical system as required for lamp system indicated.
3. **Security**—Door, Hood Or Trunk Ajar are monitored. This message will appear when the indicated component is open or improperly closed. To cancel message, properly close indicated component.
4. **Service Reminder**—Oil change, oil filter change, engine tune-up and tire rotation intervals are monitored.
   a. After the bulb inspection sequence has been completed, the service interval can be inspected by depressing the service reminder button. Depressing the button once will display the Change Oil indication and mileage remaining to service interval. Depressing the button a second time, will display the Change Oil Filter indication and mileage remaining to service interval. Depressing the button a third time will display the Rotate Tires and mileage to service interval. Depressing the button a fourth time will display Tune-Up indication and mileage to service interval.
   b. After completing the required service, reset service interval indicator by depressing and releasing the service reminder button until the desired item is displayed. When the desired item is displayed, do not release service reminder button. After button has been depressed for approximately 10 seconds, the service interval mileage display will begin to count down in 500 mile intervals. When desired service interval mileage is reached, release button. The service interval reminder indicates miles to service, not miles from last service.

ENGINE COOLANT TEMPERATURE TELLTALE LAMP

SATURN

If the engine coolant temperature exceeds 244°F, or if the transaxle fluid temperature exceeds 284°F, the coolant temperature telltale lamp will light. The PCM will turn the cooling fan on if an ECT DTC is active.

LOW COOLANT LAMP

This lamp should light when engine coolant level in the radiator drops below a predetermined level. To turn lamp off, inspect cooling system, then add coolant to bring system to proper level.

LOW OIL LEVEL INDICATOR

The Low Oil indicator ground is controlled by the PCM. To inspect for a low oil condition, the PCM inspects the low oil level sensor after the ignition has been turned to the Off or Lock position. The PCM inspects for a low oil condition 32 minutes after the ignition is turned Off if the previous ignition cycle was less than 12 minutes. The PCM inspects for a low oil condition 3 minutes after the ignition is turned off if the previous ignition cycle was less than 12 minutes.

LOW OIL PRESSURE TELLTALE LAMP

SATURN

The engine oil pressure switch is normally closed and open when engine oil pressure is 1.4–5.8 psi. If the lamp is lit with engine running, inspect wiring for oil pressure switch circuit and the engine lubrication system for proper oil pump output pressure.

LOW WASHER FLUID INDICATOR

The windshield washer solvent tank has a switch that closes when the washer solvent level becomes low, illuminating the "Low Washer Fluid" indicator.

MALFUNCTION INDICATOR LAMP (MIL)

SATURN

As a bulb and system check, the lamp will light with the ignition On and the engine not running. When the engine is started, the lamp will turn off. If the lamp remains On, the self diagnostic system has detected a malfunction. If the malfunction is intermittent or the system is repaired, the lamp will go Off after three trips but a diagnostic trouble code (DTC) will be stored in the PCM. Use a suitable scan tool to retrieve and erase any DTCs using the "Clear DTC Information" option. If the lamp remains lit while the engine is running or when a malfunction is suspected due to a driveability problem, perform an OBD system inspection. Scan the serial data stream using a suitable scan tool.

PASSLOCK TELLTALE LAMP

2000-02 SATURN

The instrument panel cluster contains the security telltale lamp. The security telltale has three modes of operation: Off, Flashing & On. The security telltale will be off if ignition is in the Off position or if the ignition is in the Run, Start or Acc position and the security system diagnostics have all passed. The security telltale will be on if the body control module (BCM) is performing a bulb test at vehicle start up, the security system diagnostics have not yet completed at vehicle start up or if a security system diagnostic trouble code (DTC) is set in the BCM or PCM. The security telltale will be flashing if the tamper hall effect has been triggered, there was improper Passlock sensor data to the BCM for more than 5 seconds during vehicle start, there was no Passlock sensor data to the BCM for more than 5 seconds during vehicle start or there was improper password from the BCM to the PCM after 5 seconds during vehicle start. Repair or replace components as required, and retrieve and clear any associated DTCs to reset the telltale lamp.

SERVICE AIR COND LAMP

CADILLAC

This lamp should light when the A/C system detects a low refrigerant charge. The lamp should light for approximately two seconds after ignition has been turned On as a bulb inspection.

If while operating vehicle, the lamp lights for approximately 60 seconds and then goes off, the refrigerant level is low enough to cause reduced cooling capacity. At this point the blower motor will increase speed to try to offset the loss in cooling capacity. The lamp will be automatically reset after system has been inspected and refrigerant charge has been brought to proper level.

If lamp is lit for approximately 60 seconds after engine start up, the refrigerant charge may be low enough to cause A/C compressor damage. When this condition is encountered, the A/C compressor clutch is de-energized and the A/C system is switched from Auto to Econ. The system will remain in ECON until required repairs are made and system is recharged. After completing required repairs and recharging the system, A/C system operation will return to normal and the lamp will be automatically reset.

SERVICE ELECTRICAL SYSTEM LAMP

CADILLAC

This lamp should light when a fault condition in the charging system is present. The lamp should light during engine starting as a bulb inspection. If lamp is lit while engine is operating, the charging system should be inspected. After repairing charging system, the lamp will be automatically reset.

SERVICE TELLTALE LAMP

SATURN

The service telltale lamp is used for non-emissions related failures which without being serviced could lead to component damage to other sub systems. As a bulb check, the lamp will light for 2 to 3 seconds and then turn off. If the lamp remains lit, the system has detected a fault condition. If the condition is intermittent or the system is repaired, the lamp will turn off 3 seconds after the PCM diagnostic test passes. Any DTCs will be stored in the freeze frame/failure records. Use a suitable scan tool to retrieve and erase any DTCs using the "Clear DTC Information" option.

VEHICLE LIFT POINTS

TABLE OF CONTENTS

DaimlerChrysler

INDEX

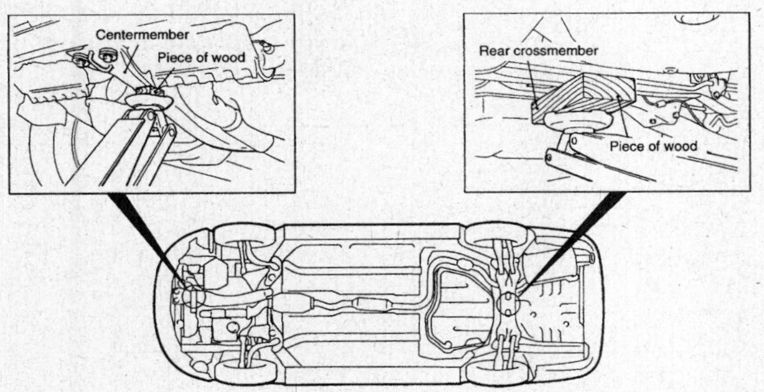

Fig. 1 Vehicle Lift Points (Floor Jack). Avenger, Sebring Coupe & 2001–02 Stratus Coupe

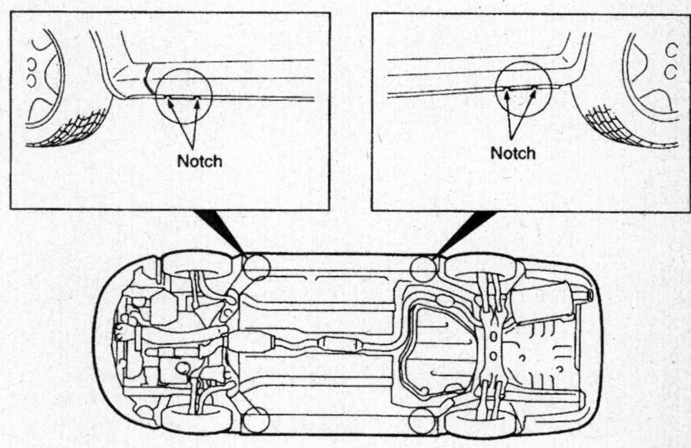

Fig. 2 Vehicle Lift Points (Post Type Hoist). Avenger, Sebring Coupe & 2001–02 Stratus Coupe

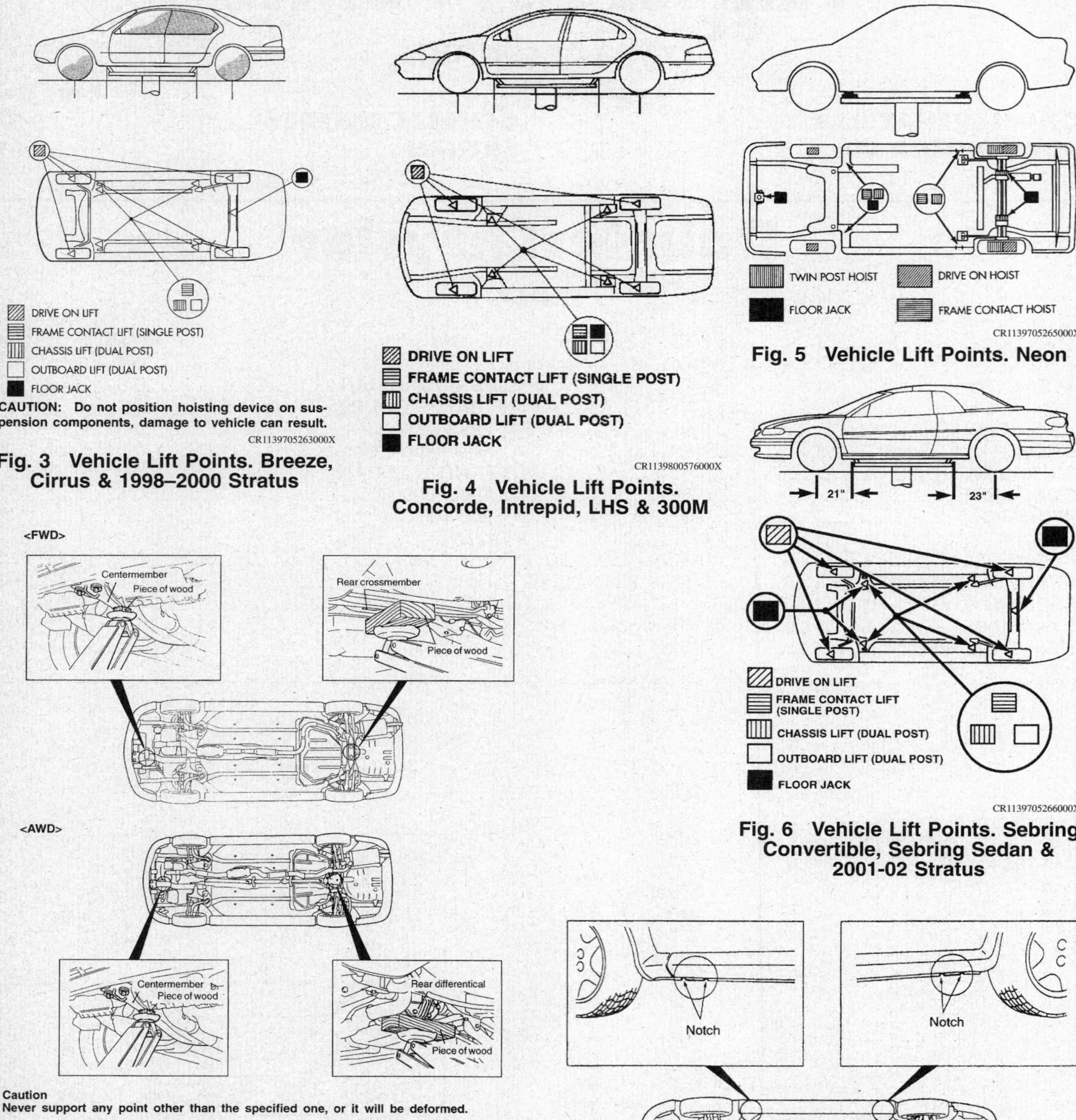

Fig. 3 Vehicle Lift Points. Breeze, Cirrus & 1998–2000 Stratus

Fig. 4 Vehicle Lift Points. Concorde, Intrepid, LHS & 300M

Fig. 5 Vehicle Lift Points. Neon

Fig. 6 Vehicle Lift Points. Sebring Convertible, Sebring Sedan & 2001-02 Stratus

Fig. 7 Vehicle Lift Points (Floor Jack). Talon

CR113970526800BX

Fig. 8 Vehicle Lift Points (Post Type Hoist). Talon

Ford Motor Co.

INDEX

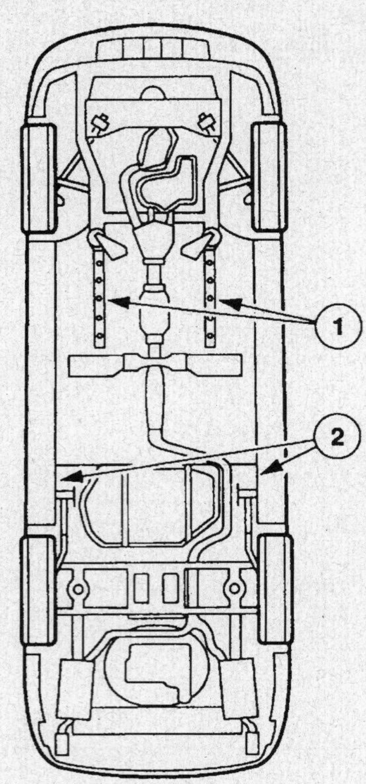

1 Front frame lift points.

2 Rear pinch point notches.

FM1139800564000X

Fig. 1 Vehicle Lift Points. Continental

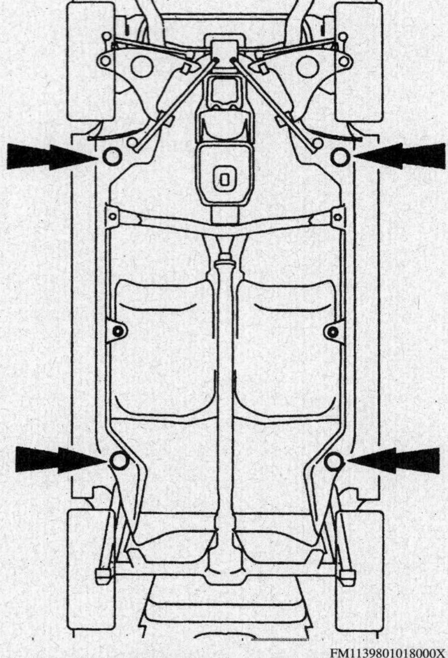

FM1139801018000X

Fig. 4 Vehicle Lift Points (Single Post Hoist). Town Car & 1999–2002 Crown Victoria & Grand Marquis

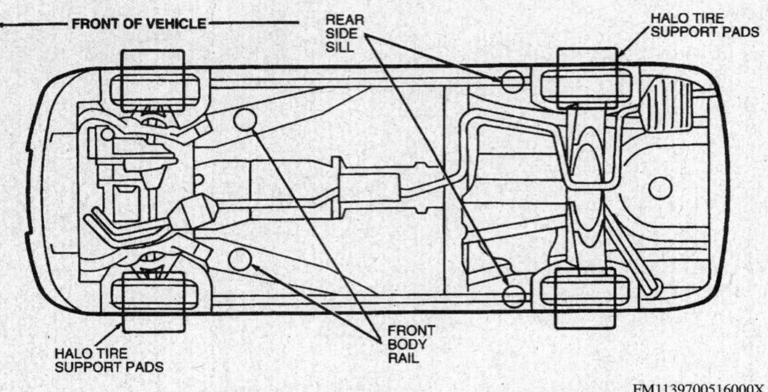

FM1139700516000X

Fig. 2 Vehicle Lift Points. Contour, Cougar & Mystique

On frame contact hoists, adapters are necessary to lift the vehicle. The adapters must be placed at four contact points. Position the adapters so they are centered on the adapter contact area.

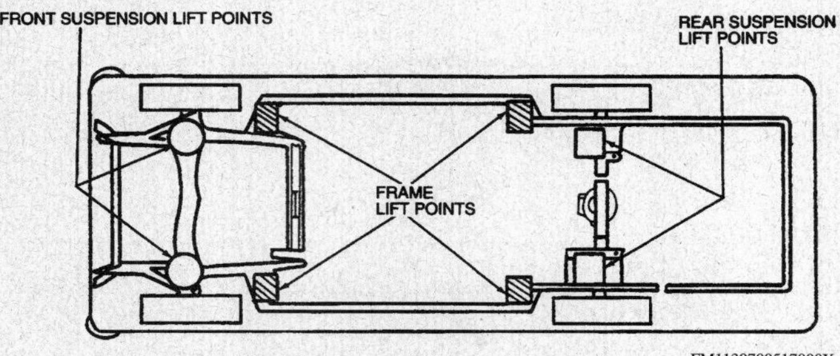

FM1139700517000X

Fig. 3 Vehicle Lift Points. 1998 Crown Victoria & Grand Marquis

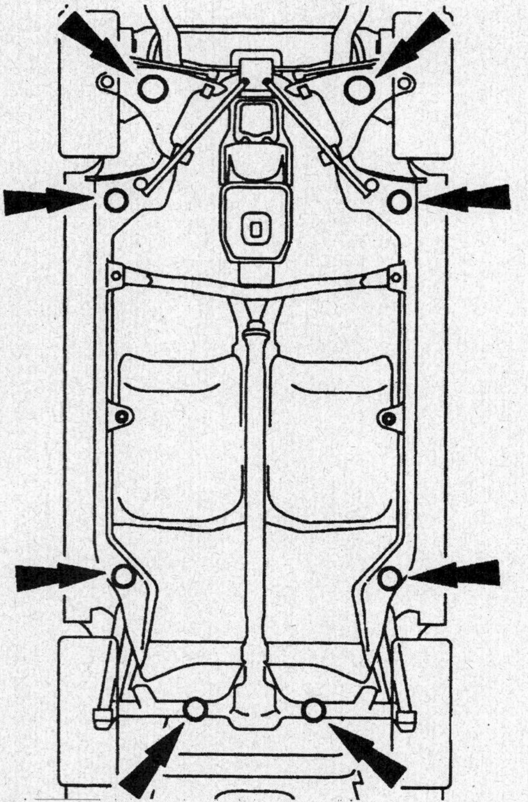

FM1139801019000X

Fig. 5 Vehicle Lift Points (Two Post Hoist). Town Car & 1999–2002 Crown Victoria & Grand Marquis

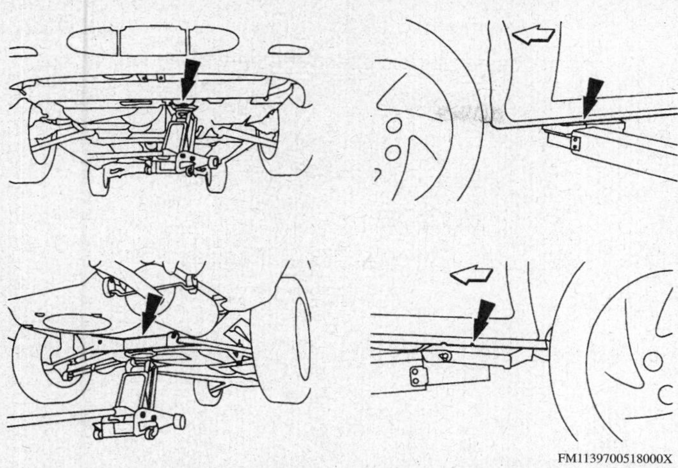

Fig. 6 Vehicle Lift Points. Escort, Tracer & ZX2

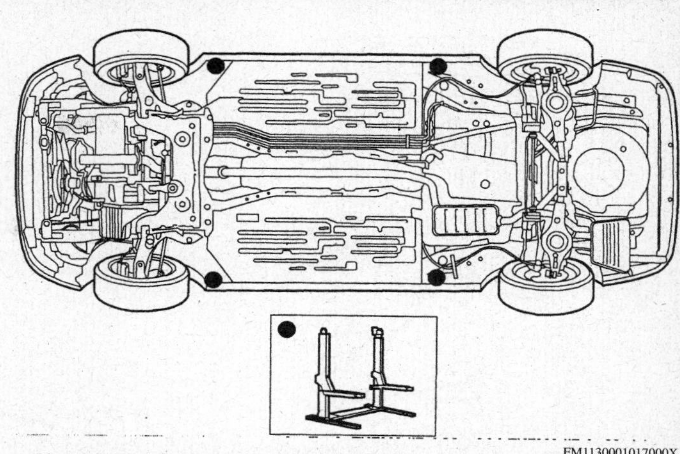

Fig. 7 Vehicle Lift Points. Focus

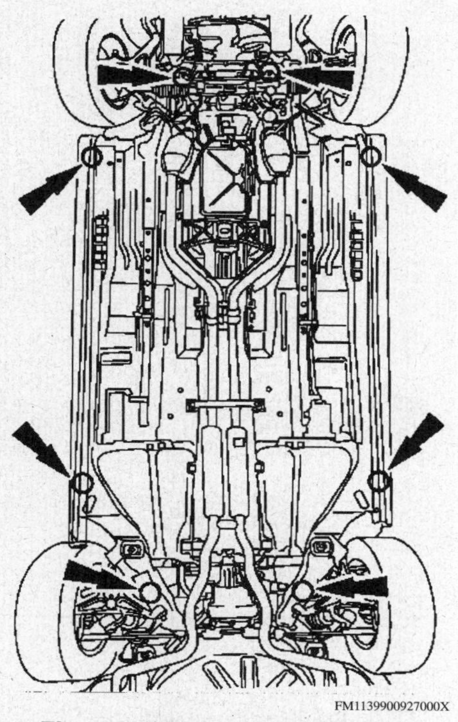

Fig. 8 Vehicle Lift Points. LS

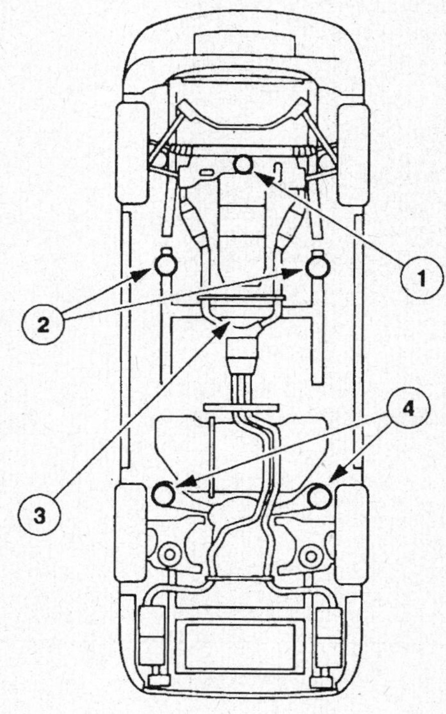

1 Front suspension lift point.
2 Front frame lift points.
3 No. 3 crossmember.
4 Rear frame lift points.

FM1139700519000A

Fig. 9 Vehicle Lift Points. Mark VIII

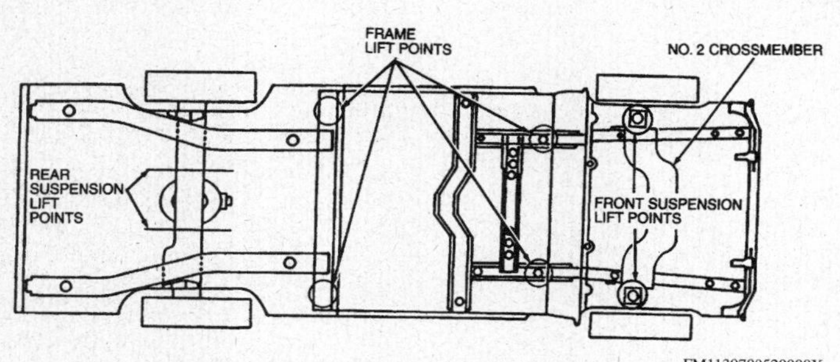

Fig. 10 Vehicle Lift Points. 1998 Mustang

VEHICLE LIFT POINTS

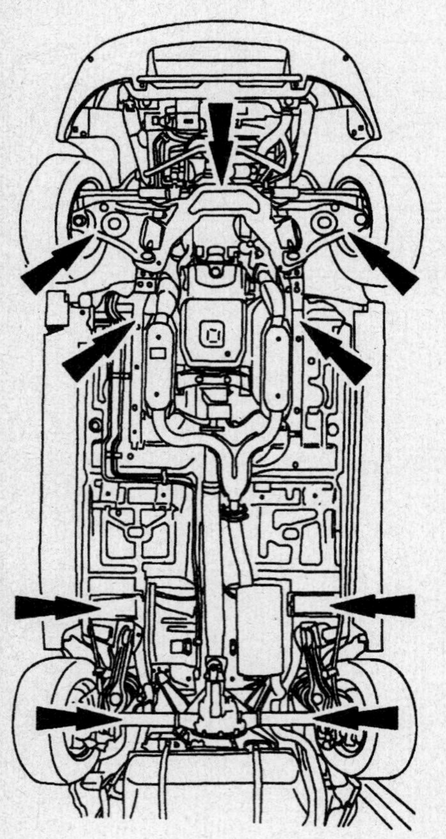

Fig. 11 Vehicle lift points. 1999–2002 Mustang

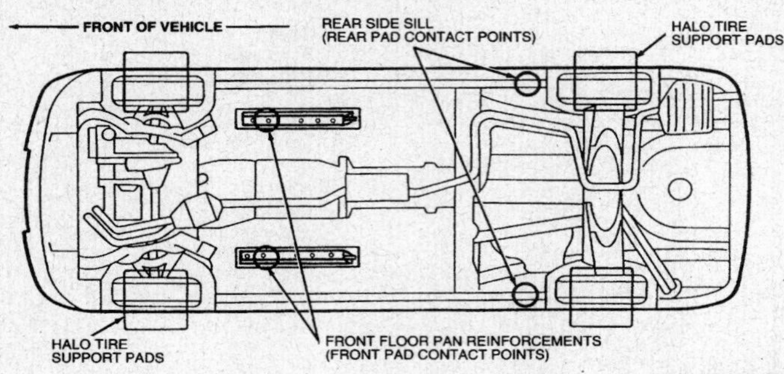

Fig. 12 Vehicle Lift Points. 1998–99 Sable & Taurus

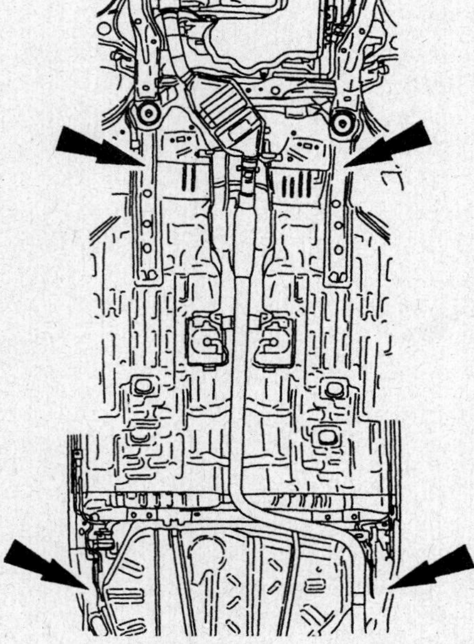

Fig. 13 Vehicle Lift Points. 2000–02 Sable & Taurus

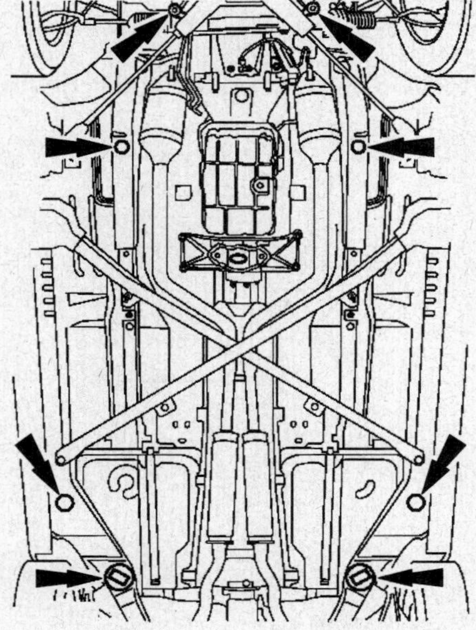

Fig. 14 Vehicle Lift Points. Thunderbird

General Motors

INDEX

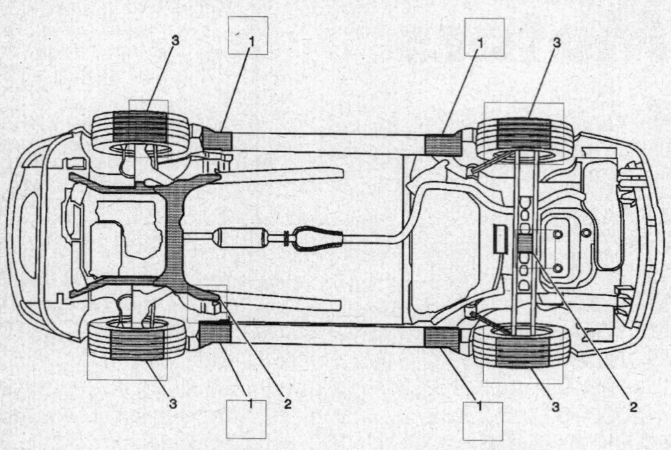

Fig. 1 Vehicle Lift Points. Achieva, Alero, Cutlass, Grand Am, Malibu & Skylark

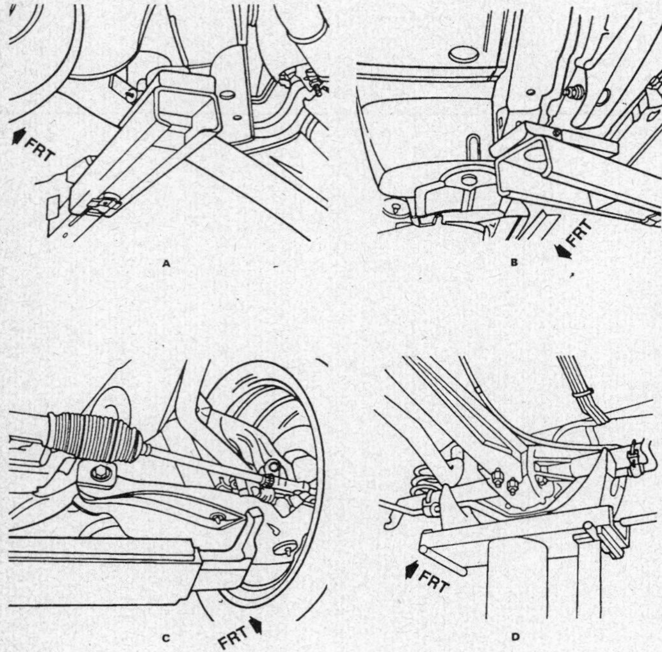

Fig. 3 Vehicle Lift Points. Camaro & Firebird

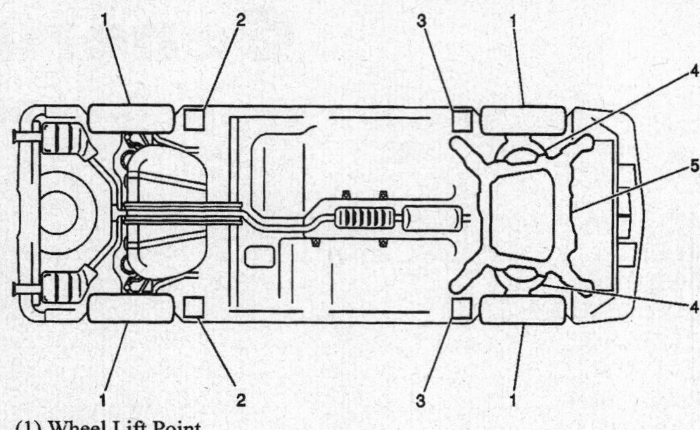

Fig. 2 Vehicle Lift Points. Aurora, Bonneville, DeVille, Eighty-Eight, LeSabre, LSS, Park Avenue, Regency, Riviera & Seville

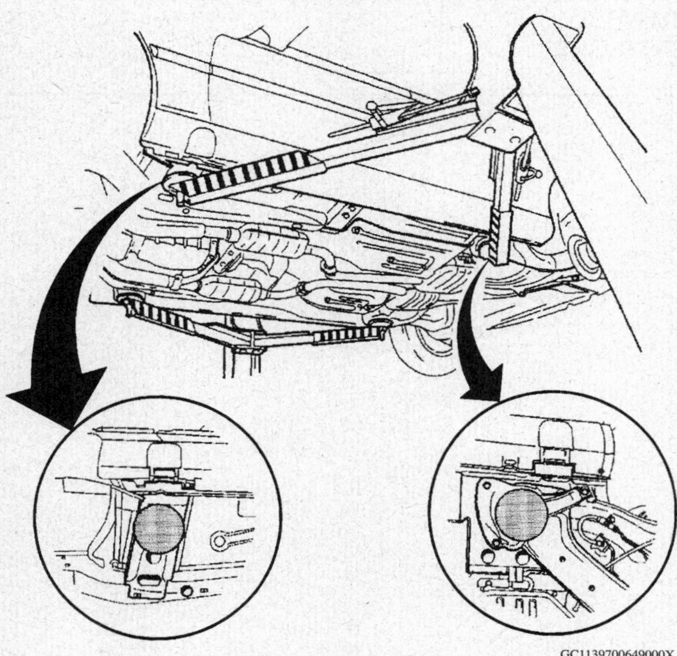

Fig. 4 Vehicle Lift Points. Catera

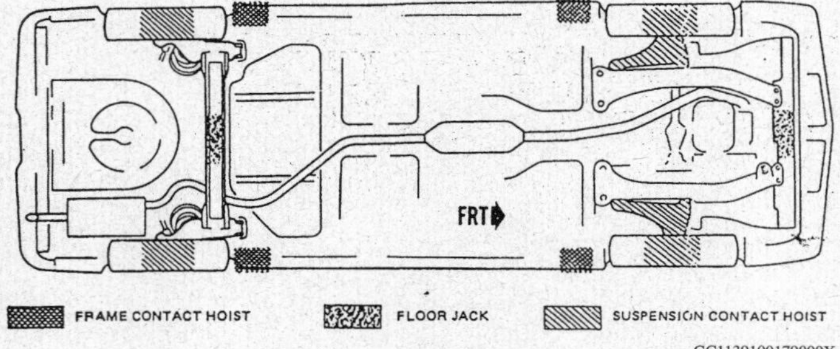

Fig. 5 Vehicle Lift Points. Cavalier & Sunfire

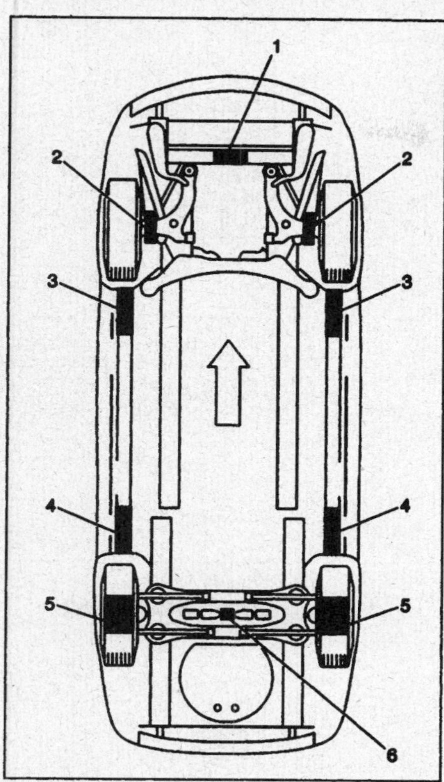

Legend

(1) Front Floor Jacking Location
(2) Front Suspension Contact to Suspension Automotive Lift Location
(3) Front Frame Contact Automotive Lift Location
(4) Rear Frame Contact Automotive Lift Location
(5) Rear Suspension Contact to Suspension Automotive Lift Location
(6) Rear Floor Jacking Location

GC1139700648000X

Fig. 6 Vehicle Lift Points. Century, Grand Prix, Impala, Intrigue, Regal & 2000–02 Monte Carlo

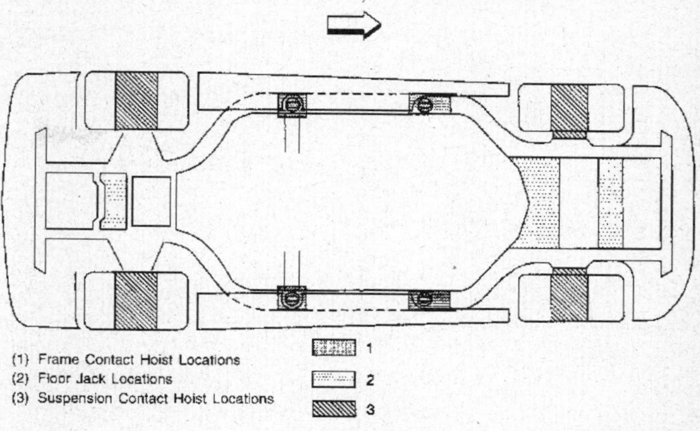

GC1139700674000X

Fig. 7 Vehicle Lift Points. Corvette

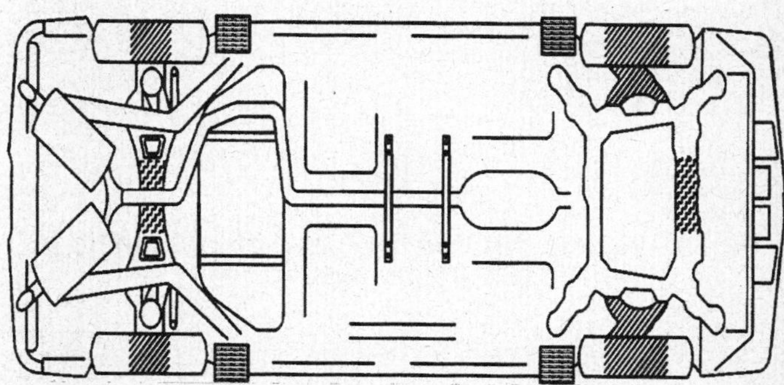

GC1139901139000X

Fig. 8 Vehicle Lift Points. Eldorado

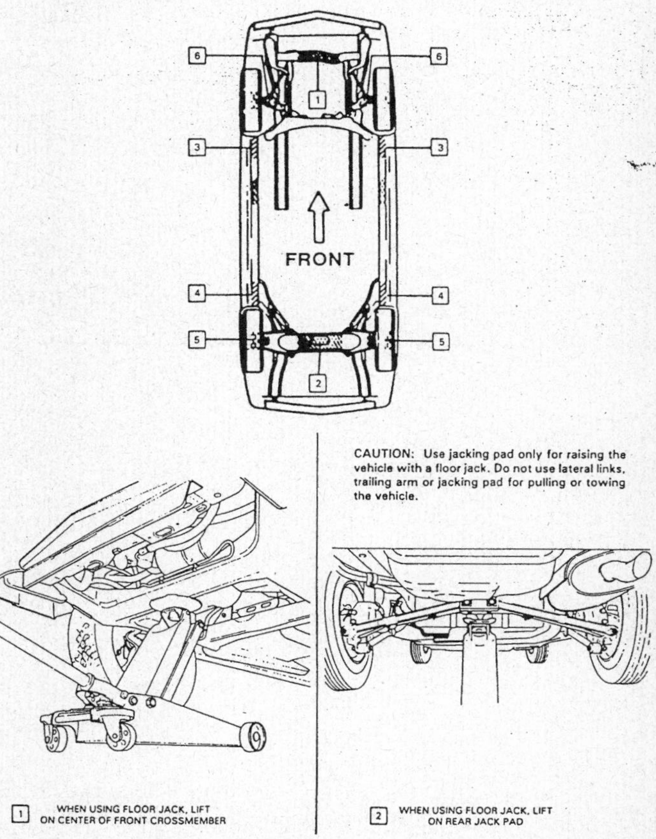

GC1139100178010X

Fig. 9 Vehicle Lift Points (Part 1 of 2). Lumina & 1998–99 Monte Carlo

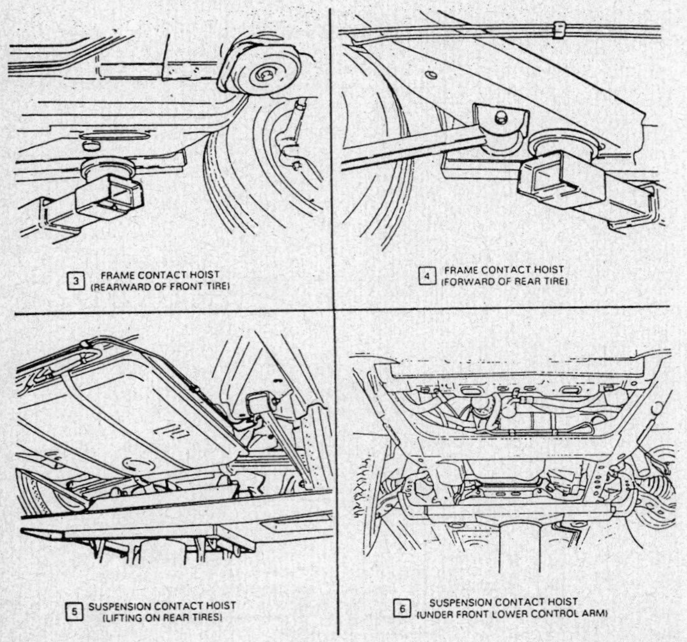

Fig. 9 Vehicle Lift Points (Part 2 of 2). Lumina & 1998–99 Monte Carlo

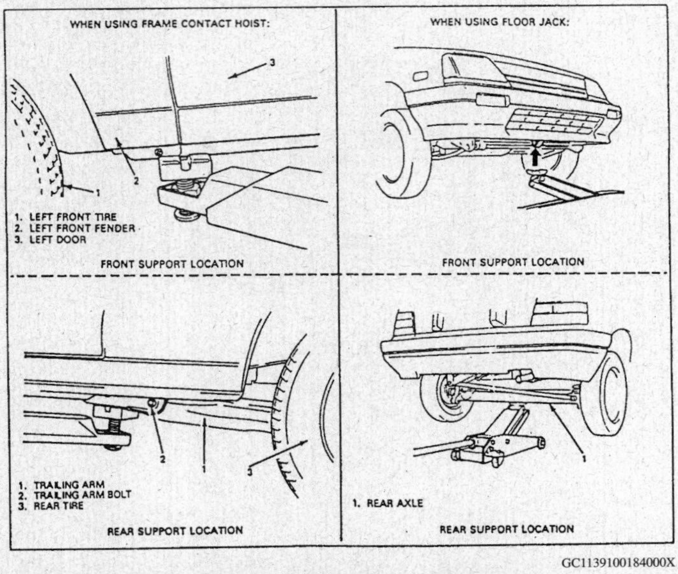

WHEN USING FRAME CONTACT HOIST:

1. LEFT FRONT TIRE
2. LEFT FRONT FENDER
3. LEFT DOOR

FRONT SUPPORT LOCATION

1. TRAILING ARM
2. TRAILING ARM BOLT
3. REAR TIRE

REAR SUPPORT LOCATION

WHEN USING FLOOR JACK:

FRONT SUPPORT LOCATION

1. REAR AXLE

REAR SUPPORT LOCATION

GC1139100184000X

Fig. 10 Vehicle Lift Points. Metro

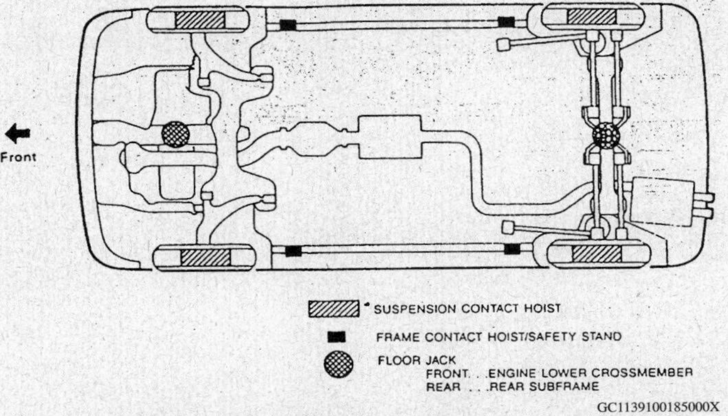

Fig. 11 Vehicle Lift Points. Prizm

Saturn

INDEX

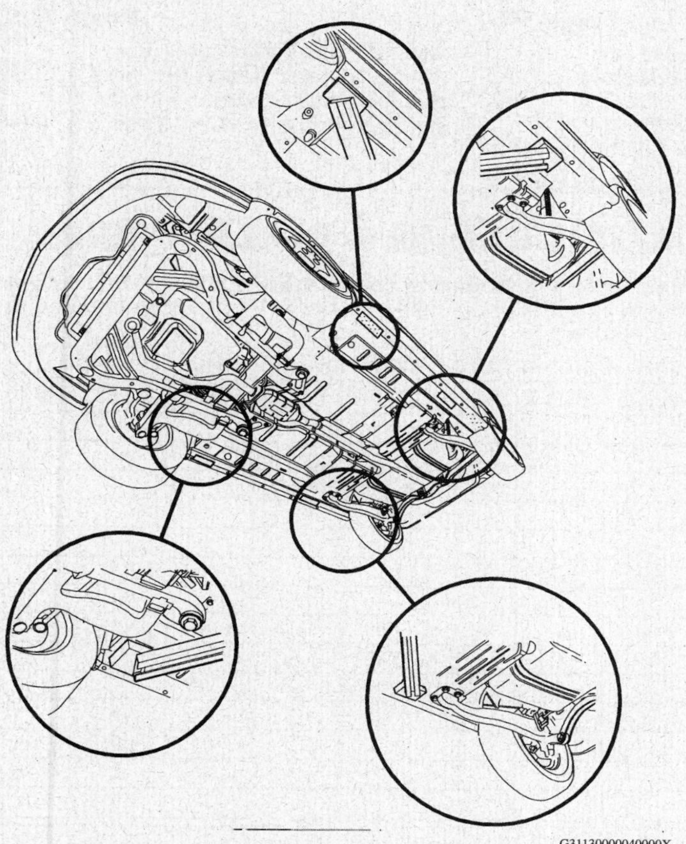

Fig. 1 Vehicle Lift Points. L Series

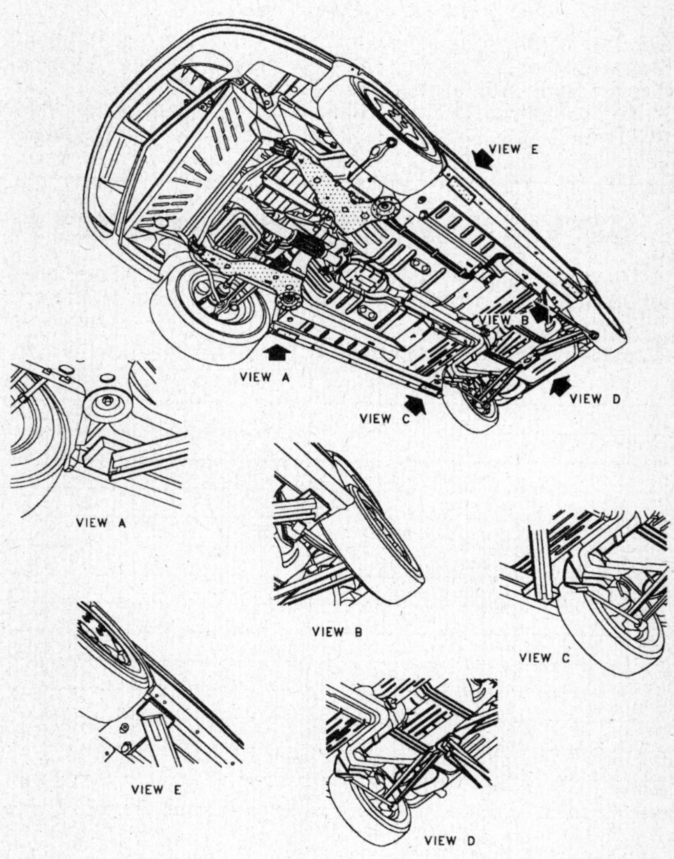

Fig. 2 Vehicle Lift Points. S Series

NON-STANDARD TIRE & WHEEL SIZE ADJUSTMENT TO RIDE HEIGHT SPECIFICATIONS & TIRE SIZE ADJUSTMENT CHARTS

INDEX

SECTION WIDTH ADJUSTMENT FOR METRIC RADIAL & BIAS PLY TIRES

The specifications listed below are approximate and are only intended for use in making approximate ride height checks and adjustments on models with non-standard tires. These specifications should not be used in place of those recommended by the vehicle manufacturer.

Standard Tire	Optional Tire, Tire Section Width Change Adjustment To Ride Height Specification, Inch													
	P145	P155	P165	P175	P185	P195	P205	P215	P225	P235	P245	P255	P265	P275
P145	0	+.25	+.50											
P155	–.25	0	+.25	+.50										
P165	–.50	–.25	0	+.25	+.50									
P175		–.50	–.25	0	+.25	+.50								
P185			–.50	–.25	0	+.25	+.50							
P195				–.50	–.25	0	+.25	+.50						
P205					–.50	–.25	0	+.25	+.50					
P215						–.50	–.25	0	+.25	+.50				
P225							–.50	–.25	0	+.25	+.50			
P235								–.50	–.25	0	+.25	+.50		
P245									–.50	–.25	0	+.25	+.50	
P255										–.50	–.25	0	+.25	+.50
P265											–.50	–.25	0	+.25
P275												–.50	–.25	0

ASPECT RATIO ADJUSTMENT FOR P145-215 METRIC RADIAL & BIAS PLY TIRES

The specifications listed below are approximate and are only intended for use in making approximate ride height checks and adjustments on models with non-standard tires. These specifications should not be used in place of those recommended by the vehicle manufacturer.

Standard Tire	Optional Tire, Tire Aspect Ratio Change to Ride Height Specification, Inch				
	60	65	70	75	80
60	0	+.38	+.75		
65	–.38	0	+.38	+.75	
70	–.75	–.38	0	+.38	+.75
75		–.75	–.38	0	+.38
80			–.75	–.38	0

ASPECT RATIO ADJUSTMENT FOR P225-275 METRIC RADIAL & BIAS PLY TIRES

The specifications listed below are approximate and are only intended for use in making approximate ride height checks and adjustments on models with non-standard tires. These specifications should not be used in place of those recommended by the vehicle manufacturer.

Standard Tire	Optional Tire, Tire Aspect Ratio Change to Ride Height Specification, Inch				
	60	65	70	75	80
60	0	+.50	+1.00		
65	–.50	0	+.50	+1.00	
70	–1.00	–.50	0	+.50	+1.00
75		–.75	–.50	0	+.50
80			–1.00	–.50	0

NON-STANDARD TIRE & WHEEL SIZE ADJUSTMENT TO RIDE HEIGHT SPECIFICATIONS & TIRE SIZE ADJUSTMENT CHARTS

SECTION WIDTH ADJUSTMENT FOR ALPHA-NUMERIC RADIAL PLY TIRES

The specifications listed below are approximate and are only intended for use in making approximate ride height checks and adjustments on models with non-standard tires. These specifications should not be used in place of those recommended by the vehicle manufacturer.

Standard Tire	Optional Tire, Tire Section Width Change Adjustment To Ride Height Specification, Inch						
	DR	ER	FR	GR	HR	JR	LR
DR	0	+.19	+.44				
ER	–.19	0	+.25	+.50			
FR	–.44	–.25	0	+.25	+.63		
GR		–.50	–.25	0	+.31	+.50	
HR			–.63	–.31	0	+.19	+.44
JR				–.50	–.19	0	+.25
LR					–.44	–.25	0

ASPECT RATIO ADJUSTMENT FOR ALPHA-NUMERIC RADIAL PLY TIRES

The specifications listed below are approximate and are only intended for use in making approximate ride height checks and adjustments on models with non-standard tires. These specifications should not be used in place of those recommended by the vehicle manufacturer.

Standard Tire	Optional Tire, Change Adjustment to Ride Height Specification, Inch		
	60	70	78
60	0	+.50	+.62
70	–.50	0	+.13
78	–.62	–.13	0

SECTION WIDTH ADJUSTMENT FOR ALPHA-NUMERIC BIAS PLY TIRES

The specifications listed below are approximate and are only intended for use in making approximate ride height checks and adjustments on models with non-standard tires. These specifications should not be used in place of those recommended by the vehicle manufacturer.

Standard Tire	Optional Tire, Change Adjustment To Ride Height Specifications, Inch							
	A	B	C	D	E	F	G	H
A	0	+.25	+.50					
B	–.25	0	+.25	+.38				
C	–.50	–.25	0	+.13	+.37			
D		–.37	–.13	0	+.25	+.50		
E			–.38	–.25	0	+.25	+.50	
F				–.50	–.25	0	+.25	+.56
G					–.50	–.25	0	+.31
H						–.56	–.31	0

ELECTRICAL SYMBOL & WIRE COLOR CODE IDENTIFICATION

TABLE OF CONTENTS

Electrical Symbol Identification

INDEX

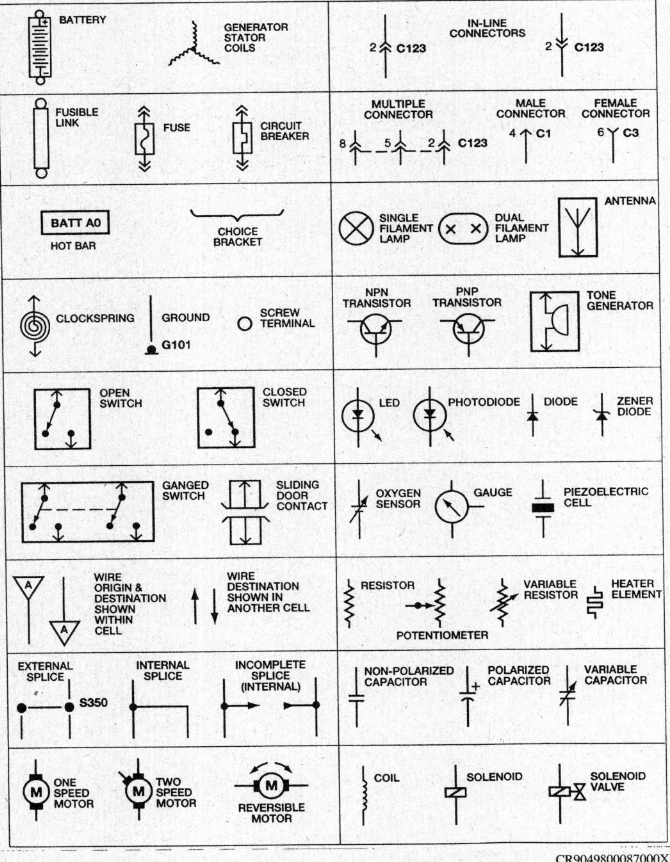

Fig. 1 Symbol Identification. DaimlerChrysler

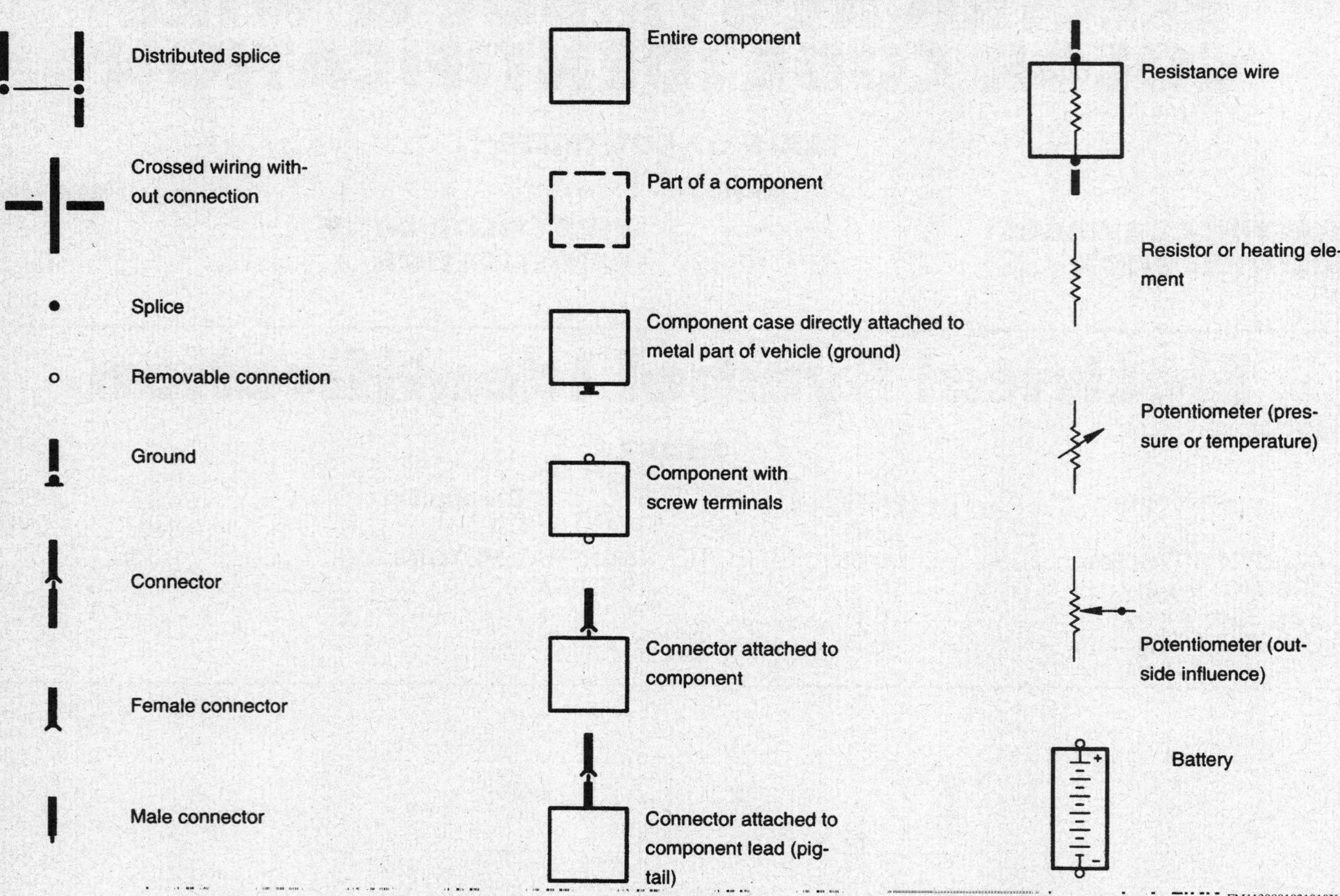

Fig. 2 Symbol Identification (Part 1 of 6). Ford Motor Co. w/New Style Wiring

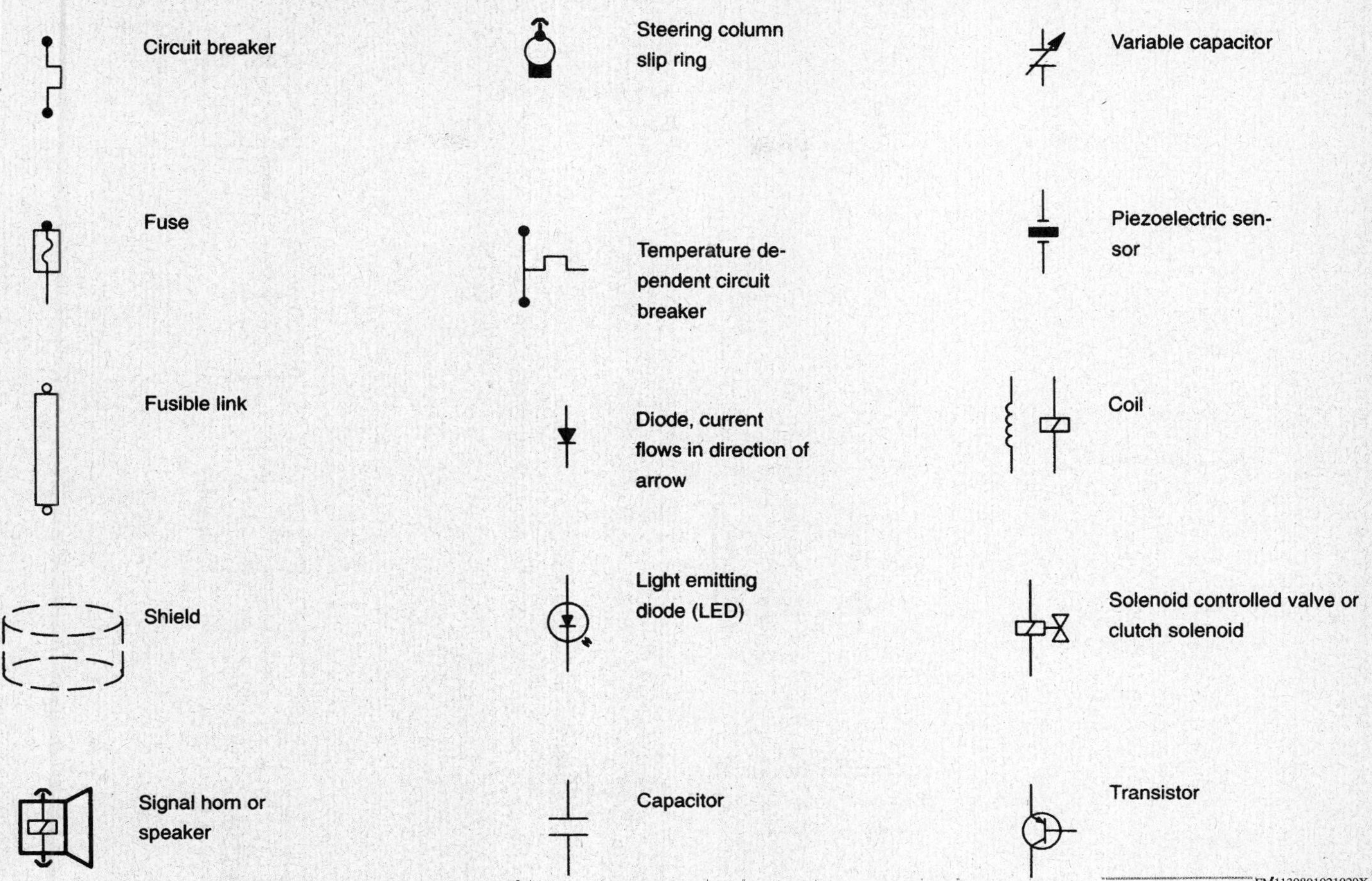

Fig. 2 Symbol Identification (Part 2 of 6). Ford Motor Co. w/New Style Wiring

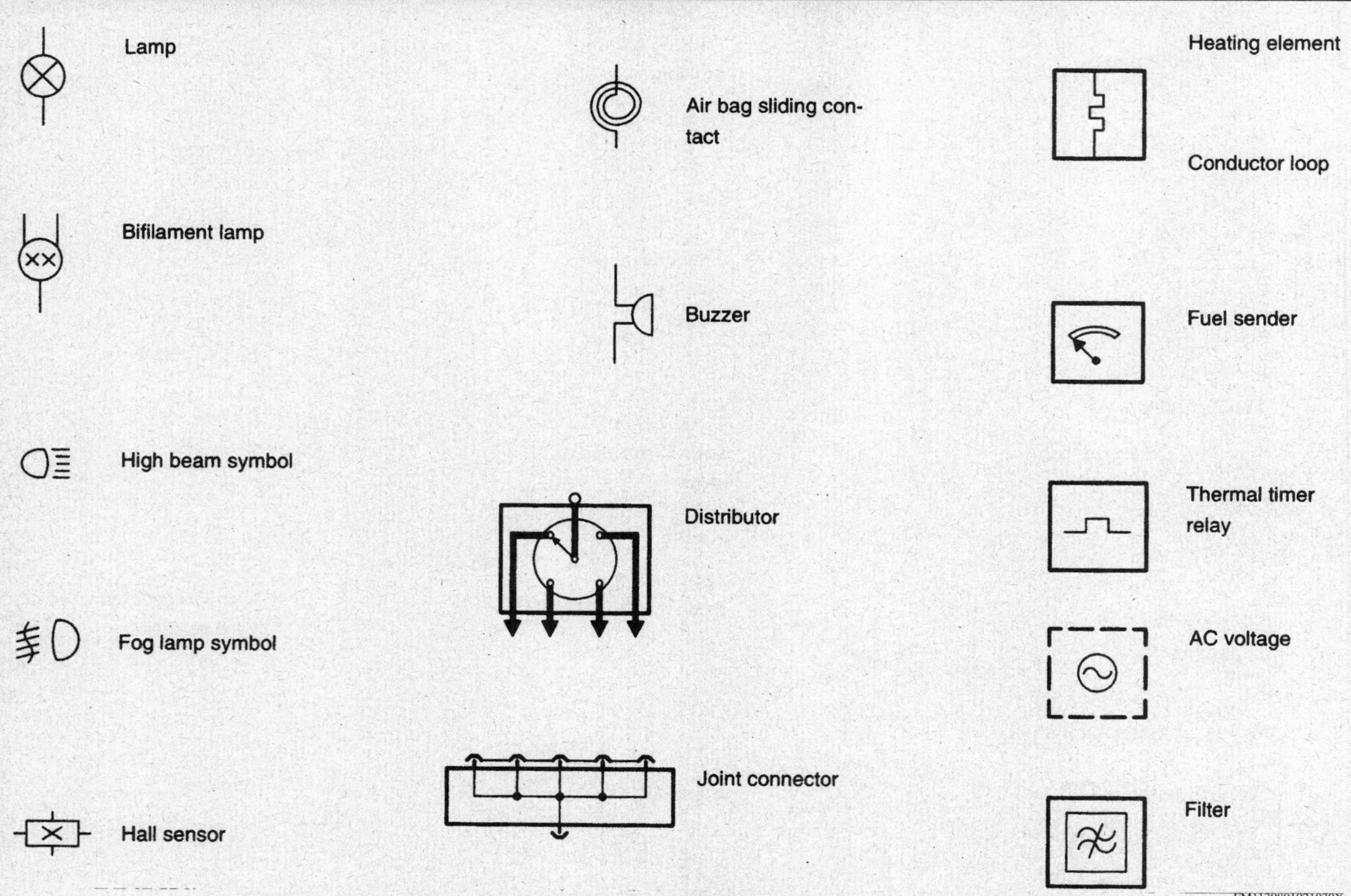

Fig. 2 Symbol Identification (Part 3 of 6). Ford Motor Co. w/New Style Wiring

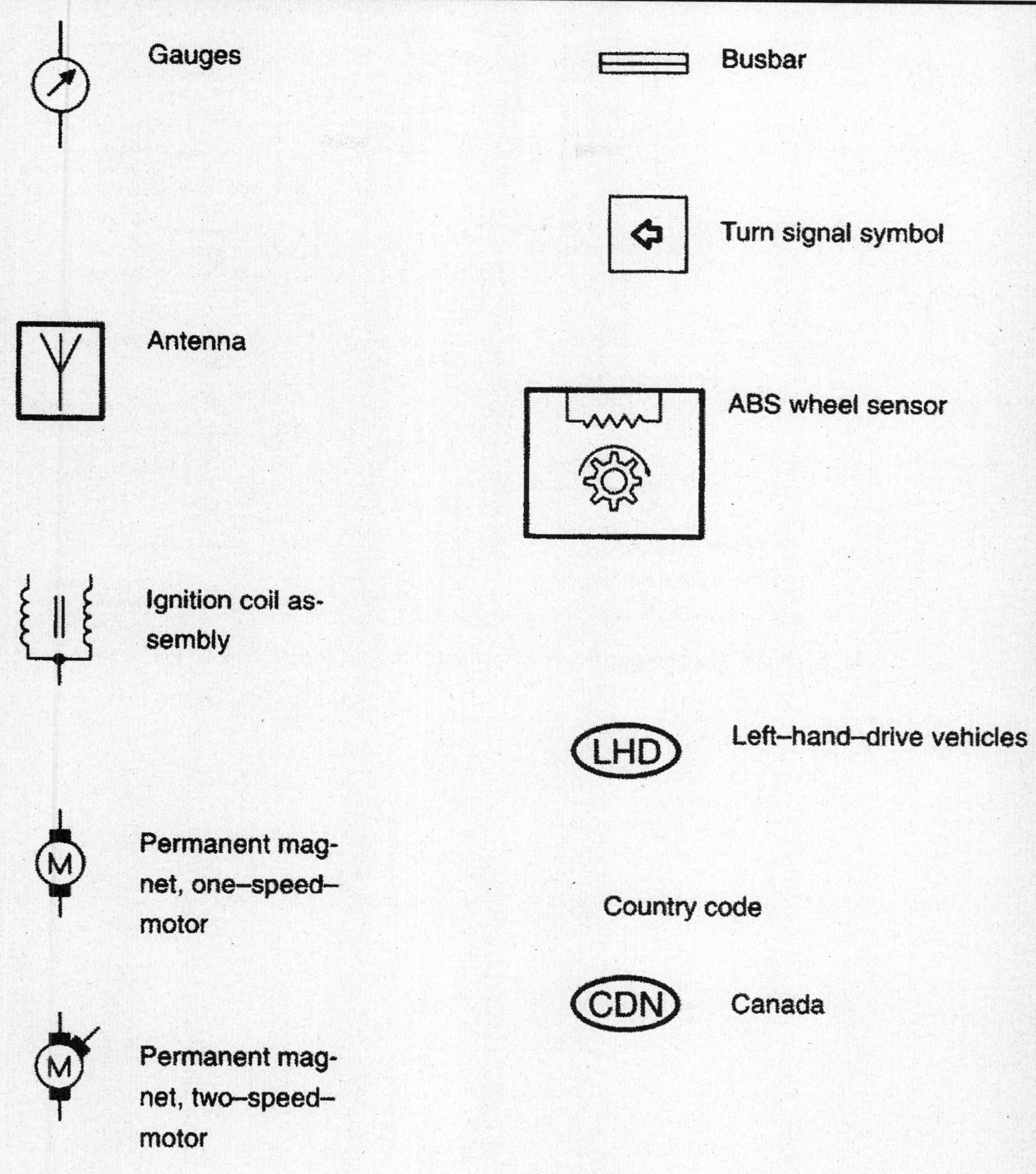

Fig. 2 Symbol Identification (Part 4 of 6). Ford Motor Co. w/New Style Wiring

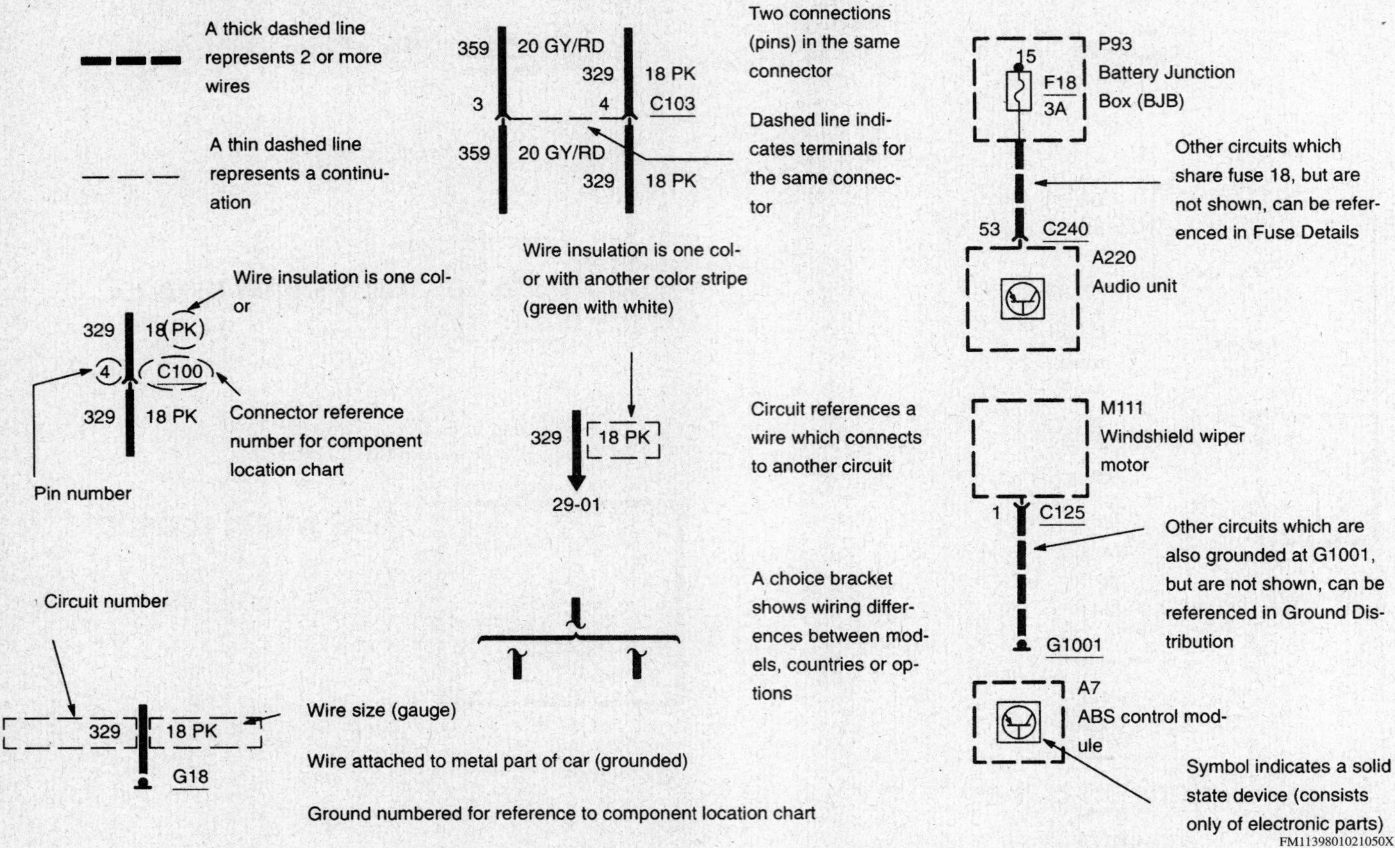

Fig. 2 Symbol Identification (Part 5 of 6). Ford Motor Co. w/New Style Wiring

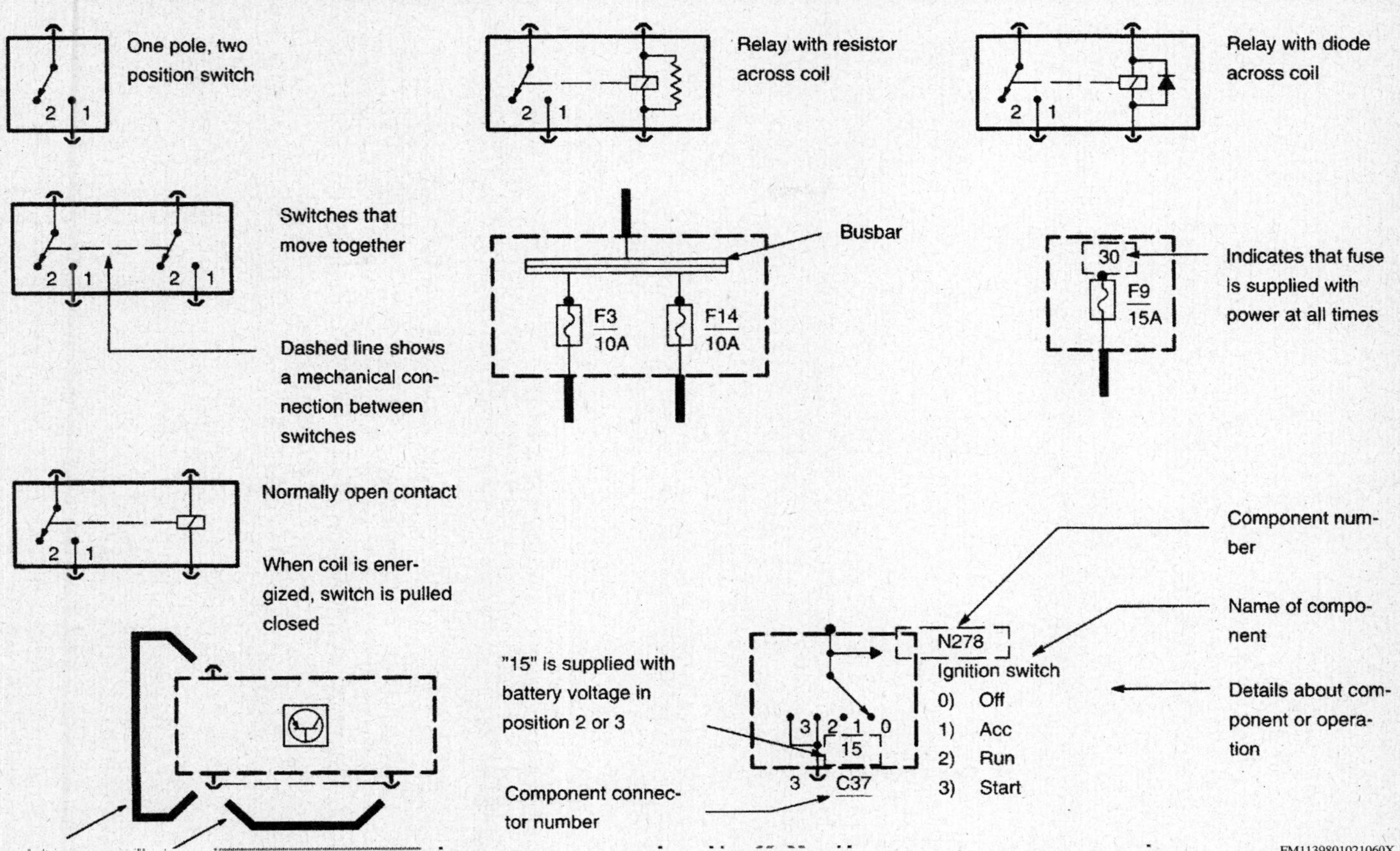

Fig. 2 Symbol Identification (Part 6 of 6). Ford Motor Co. w/New Style Wiring

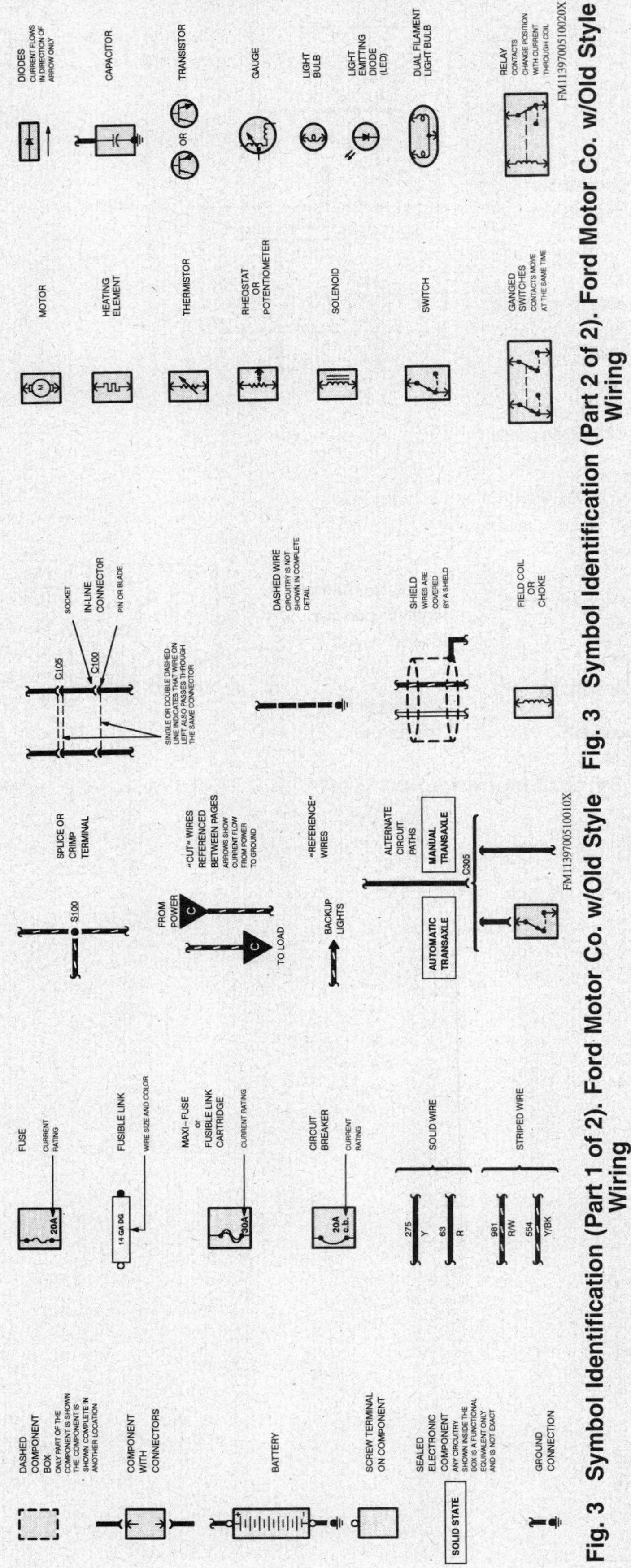

Fig. 3 Symbol Identification (Part 1 of 2). Ford Motor Co. w/Old Style Wiring

Fig. 3 Symbol Identification (Part 2 of 2). Ford Motor Co. w/Old Style Wiring

Symbol	Description
	Supplemental Inflatable Restraint (SIR) or Supplemental Restraint System (SRS) Icon This icon is used to alert the technician that the system contains SIR/SRS components that require certain precautions before servicing.
OBD II	On-Board Diagnostic (OBD II) Icon This icon is used to alert the technician that the circuit is essential for proper OBD II emission controls circuit operation. Any circuit which, if it fails, causes the malfunction indicator lamp (MIL) to turn on, is identified as an OBD II circuit.
	Important Icon This icon is used to alert the technician that there is additional information that will aid in servicing a system.
Hot At All Times Hot In Run Hot In Start Hot In Acc And Run Hot In Run And Start Hot In Run, Bulb Test And Start Hot With Headlamp Switch In Park Or Head Hot In Retained Accessory Power (RAP)	Voltage Indicator Boxes These boxes are used on schematics to indicate when voltage is present at a fuse.
	Partial Component When a component is represented in a dashed box, the component or its wiring is not shown in its entirety.

Symbol	Description
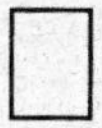	Entire Component When a component is represented in a solid box the component or its wiring is shown in its entirety.
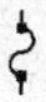	Fuse
	Circuit Breaker
	Fusible Link
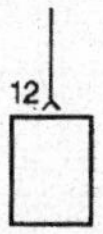 12	Connector Attached to Component

GC1139801141010X

Fig. 4 Symbol Identification (Part 1 of 4). General Motors

Symbol	Description
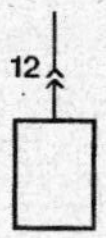 12	Pigtail Connector
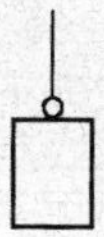	Bolt On or Screw On Eyelet Terminal
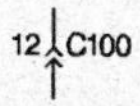 12 C100	Inline Harness Connector
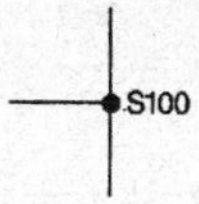 S100	Splice
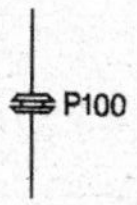 P100	Pass Through the Grommet

Symbol	Description
 G100	Chassis Ground
	Case Ground
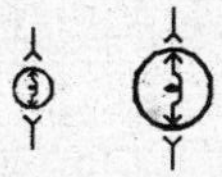	Single Filament Light Bulbs
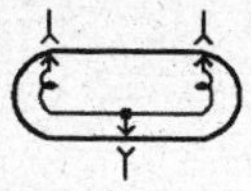	Double Filament Light Bulb
	Light Emitting Diodes

GC1139801141020X

Fig. 4 Symbol Identification (Part 2 of 4). General Motors

Symbol	Description
	Capacitor
	Battery
	Variable Battery
	Resistor
	Variable Resistor

Symbol	Description
	Position Sensor
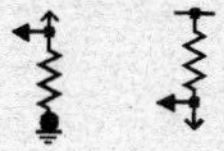	I/O Resistors
	I/O Switches
	Diode
	Crystal

GC113980114103OX

Fig. 4 Symbol Identification (Part 3 of 4). General Motors

Symbol	Description
	Heating Elements
	Motor
	Solenoid
	Coil
	Antenna

Symbol	Description
	Shield
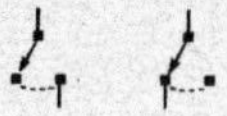	Switches
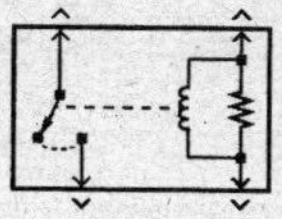	Single Pole Single Throw Relay
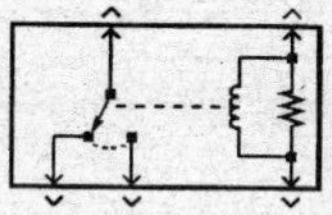	Single Pole Double Throw Relay

GC113980114104OX

Fig. 4 Symbol Identification (Part 4 of 4). General Motors

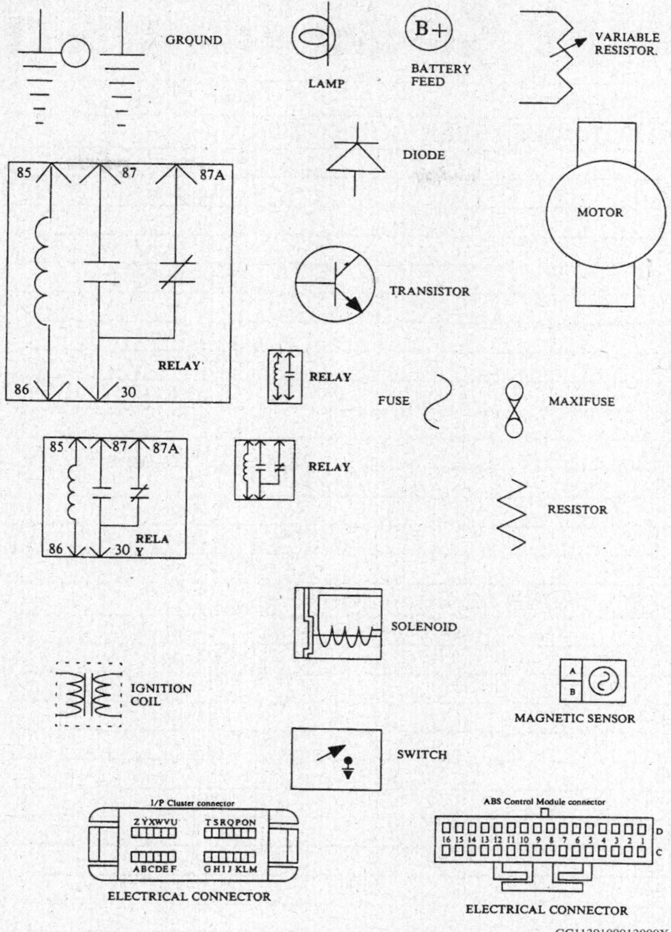

Fig. 5 Symbol Identification. Saturn

Wire Color Code Identification

Abbreviation	Wire Color
DAIMLERCHRYSLER DOMESTIC	
BL	Blue
BK	Black
BR	Brown
DB	Dark Blue
DG	Dark Green
GY	Gray
LB	Light Blue
LG	Light Green
OR	Orange
PK	Pink
RD	Red
TN	Tan
VT	Violet
WT	White
YL	Yellow
DAIMLERCHRYSLER IMPORTS	
B	Black
BR	Brown
G	Green
GR	Gray
L	Blue
LG	Light Green
O	Orange
P	Pink
R	Red
SB	Sky Blue
V	Violet
W	White
Y	Yellow
FORD MOTOR CO. w/NEW STYLE WIRING	
BK	Black
BN	Brown
BR	Brown
BU	Blue
GN	Green
GY	Gray
LG	Light Green
NA	Natural
OG	Orange
PK	Pink
P	Purple
RD	Red
SR	Silver
VT	Violet
WH	White
YE	Yellow
FORD MOTOR CO. w/OLD STYLE WIRING	
BL	Blue
BK	Black
BN	Brown
BR	Brown
DB	Dark Blue
DG	Dark Green
GN	Green
GY	Gray

Continued

Abbreviation	Wire Color
FORD MOTOR CO. w/OLD STYLE WIRING	
LB	Light Blue
LG	Light Green
N	Natural
O	Orange
PK	Pink
P	Purple
R	Red
T	Tan
W	White
Y	Yellow
GENERAL MOTORS & SATURN	
Black	BLK
Blue	BLU
Brown	BRN
Dark Blue	DK BLU
Dark Green	DK GRN
Gray	GRA/GRY
Green	GRN
Light Blue	LT BLU
Light Green	LT GRN
Light Gray	LT GRAY
Orange	ORN
Pink	PNK
Purple	PPL
Red	RED
Tan	TAN
White	WHT
Yellow	YEL

VEHICLE MAINTENANCE SCHEDULES

TABLE OF CONTENTS

DaimlerChrysler Cirrus & Sebring Convertible, Dodge Neon & Stratus & Plymouth Breeze & Neon

Recommended Service & Intervals (Months)	Service Interval In Miles①																																						
	3000	6000	7500	9000	12000	15000	18000	21000	22500	24000	27000	30000	33000	36000	37500	39000	42000	45000	48000	51000	52500	54000	57000	60000	63000	66000	67500	69000	72000	75000	78000	81000	82500	84000	87000	90000	93000	96000	97500	99000
BODY																																								
Inspect Supplemental Restraint System												X												X												X				
BRAKES																																								
Inspect Brake Connections, Hoses & Lines	Normal Service Every 6 Months Or 7,500 Miles, Severe Service Every 3,000 Miles																																							
Inspect Brake Drums & Rotors (Normal Service Every 18 Mos.)					S				N	S				S				N		S				S			N		S					S		N		S		
Inspect Brake Pads, Linings & Wheel Bearings (Normal Service Every 18 Mos.), 1998–99					S				N	S				S				N		S				S			N		S					S		N		S		
Inspect Brake Pads, Linings & Wheel Bearings, 2000	Normal Service Every 22,500 Miles; Severe Every 12,000 Miles																																							
Inspect Brake, Linings & Wheel Bearings, 2001–02	Normal Service Every 2 Years Or 30,000 Miles																																							
Inspect Brake Hoses & Pads, 2001–02	Normal Service Every 12 Months Or 15,000 Miles																																							
CLUTCH & TRANSMISSION																																								
Change Automatic Transaxle Filter, Fluid & Adjust Bands, Neon & 1998–99 Sebring Convertible, Breeze, Cirrus & Stratus	Normal Service Every 30,000 Miles; Severe Service Every 15,000 Miles																																							
Change Automatic Transaxle Filter, Fluid & Adjust Bands, 2000 Stratus & 2000–02 Breeze, Cirrus & Sebring Convertible	Normal Service Every 100,000 Miles; Severe Service Every 48,000 Miles																																							
Change Automatic Transaxle Filter, Fluid & Adjust Bands, 2001–02 Stratus	Normal Service Inspect Every 15,000 Miles; Severe Service Replace Every 30,000 Miles																																							
DRIVESHAFT																																								
Inspect CV Joints	S	S	X	S	S	X	S	S	X	S	S	X	S	S	X	S	S	X	S	S	X	S	S	X	S	S	X	S	S	X	S	S	X	S	S	X	S	S	X	S

Recommended Service & Intervals (Months)	Service Interval In Miles①																																							
	3000	6000	7500	9000	12000	15000	18000	21000	22500	24000	27000	30000	33000	36000	37500	39000	42000	45000	48000	51000	52500	54000	57000	60000	63000	66000	67500	69000	72000	75000	78000	81000	82500	84000	87000	90000	93000	96000	97500	99000
ENGINE																																								
Change Engine Coolant, 1998	At 36 Months Or 45,000 Miles, Then At 60 Months Or 75,000 Miles																																							
Change Engine Coolant, 1999–2000	At 36 Months Or 45,000 Miles, Then Every 30,000 Miles Thereafter																																							
Change Engine Coolant, 2001–02	At 48 Months Or 60,000 Miles, Then Every 30,000 Miles Thereafter																																							
Change Engine Oil (Normal Service Every 6 Mos.)	S	S	N	S	S	X	S	S	N	S	S	X	S	S	N	S	S	X	S	S	N	S	S	X	S	S	N	S	S	X	S	S	N	S	S	X	S	S	N	S
Change Engine Oil Filter (Normal Service Every 12 Mos.), 1998		S			S	N	S			S		X		S			S	N	S			S		X		S			S	N	S			S		X		S		
Change Engine Oil Filter, 1999	2.4L Normal Service Every 7500 Miles; Severe Service Every 3000 Miles; V6 Normal Service Every 15,000 Miles;Severe Service Every 6000 Miles																																							
Change Engine Oil Filter, 2000–02	Normal Service Every 7500 Miles; Severe Service Every 3000 Miles																																							
Inspect Air Filter②						S						X						S						X						S						X				
Inspect Coolant Level	At Every Engine Oil Change																																							
Inspect EVAP & Fuel Systems Filler Pipe, Hoses, Lines, Tank & Cap												X												X												X				
Inspect Exhaust System	S	S	N	S	S	X	S	S	N	S	S	X	S	S	N	S	S	X	S	S	N	S	S	X	S	S	N	S	S	X	S	S	N	S	S	X	S	S	N	S
Inspect PCV Valve (Normal Service Every 48 Mos.), 1997–99												S												X												S				
Inspect PCV Valve (Normal Service Every 48 Mos.), 2000②	Normal Service Every 60,000 Miles; Severe Service Every 30,000 Miles																																							
Inspect & Adjust Drive Belts,						X						X						X						X						X						X				
Replace Drive Belts	Every 60,000 Miles																																							
Replace Spark Plugs, 2.0L & 2.4L												X												X												X				
Replace Spark Plugs, 1998–2000 2.5L	Normal Service Every 100,000 Miles; Severe Service Every 75,000 Miles																																							
Replace Spark Plugs, Platinum, 2001–02, 3.0L Stratus & Sebring	Normal Service Every 100,000 Miles; Severe Service Every 15,000 Miles																																							
Replace Spark Plugs, Except Platinum, 2001–02, 3.0L Stratus & Sebring	Normal Service Every 60,000 Miles; Severe Service Every 15,000 Miles																																							
Replace Spark Plugs, Except Platinum, 2001–02	Normal Service Every 30,000 Miles; Severe Service Every 15,000 Miles																																							
Replace Timing Belt	At 105,000 Miles																																							

Recommended Service & Intervals (Months)	Service Interval In Miles①																																							
	3000	6000	7500	9000	12000	15000	18000	21000	22500	24000	27000	30000	33000	36000	37500	39000	42000	45000	48000	51000	52500	54000	57000	60000	63000	66000	67500	69000	72000	75000	78000	81000	82500	84000	87000	90000	93000	96000	97500	99000
STEERING, SUSPENSION & TIRES																																								
Inspect Ball Joints												X												X												X				
Lubricate Suspension & Steering Linkage												X												X												X				
Rotate Tires & Adjust Pressure, 1998–99			X			X			X			X			X			X			X			X			X			X			X			X			X	
Rotate Tires & Adjust Pressure, 2000–02	Inspect And Rotate Tires Normal Service Every 7500 Miles; Severe Service Every 6000 Miles																																							

Mos. — Months
N — Normal Service
S — Severe Service
X — Normal Or Severe Service
① — After vehicles passes 99,000 mile mark return to beginning of mileage table & start cycle over again.
② — This maintenance is recommended by DaimlerChrysler Corporation to the owner but is not required to maintain the emissions warranty.

DaimlerChrysler Concorde, LHS & 300M & Dodge Intrepid

Recommended Service & Intervals (Months)	Service Interval In Miles①																																							
	3000	6000	7500	9000	12000	15000	18000	21000	22500	24000	27000	30000	33000	36000	37500	39000	42000	45000	48000	51000	52500	54000	57000	60000	63000	66000	67500	69000	72000	75000	78000	81000	82500	84000	87000	90000	93000	96000	97500	99000
BODY																																								
Inspect Supplemental Restraint System												X												X												X				
BRAKES																																								
Inspect Brake Connections, Hoses & Lines	Normal Service Every 6 Mos. Or 7,500 Miles; Severe Service Every 3,000 Miles																																							
Inspect Brake Drums & Rotors					S				N	S				S				N	S					S			N		S					S		N		S		
Inspect Brake Pads, Linings					S				N	S				S				N	S					S			N		S					S		N		S		
CLUTCH & TRANSMISSION																																								
Change Automatic Transaxle Fluid & Filter, 1998						S						S						S						S						S						S				
Change Automatic Transaxle Fluid & Filter, 1999																									S															
Change Automatic Transaxle Fluid & Filter, 2000	Normal Service At 100,000 Miles; Severe Service Every 48,000 Miles																																							
Change Automatic Transaxle Fluid & Filter, 2001–02	Severe Service Every 48,000 Miles																																							
DRIVESHAFT & CV JOINTS																																								
Inspect CV Joints	S	S	N	S	S	X	S	S	N	S	S	X	S	S	N	S	S	X	S	S	N	S	S	X	S	S	N	S	S	X	S	S	N	S	S	X	S	S	N	S
ENGINE																																								
Change Engine Coolant	Every 60 Months Or 100,000 Miles																																							
Change Engine Oil (Normal Service Every 6 Mos.)	S	S	N	S	S	X	S	S	N	S	S	X	S	S	N	S	S	X	S	S	N	S	S	X	S	S	N	S	S	X	S	S	N	S	S	X	S	S	N	S
Change Engine Oil Filter (Normal Service Every 12 Mos.), 1998		S			S	N	S			S		X		S			S	N	S			S		X		S			S	N	S			S		X		S		
Change Engine Oil Filter (Normal Service Every 12 Mos.), 1999	Normal Service Every 15,000 Miles; Severe Service Every 3000 Miles																																							
Change Engine Oil Filter (Normal Service Every 6 Mos.), 2000–02	Normal Service Every 7500 Miles; Severe Service Every 3000 Miles																																							
Inspect Air Filter						S						X						S						X						S						X				

Recommended Service & Intervals (Months)	Service Interval In Miles①																																							
	3000	6000	7500	9000	12000	15000	18000	21000	22500	24000	27000	30000	33000	36000	37500	39000	42000	45000	48000	51000	52500	54000	57000	60000	63000	66000	67500	69000	72000	75000	78000	81000	82500	84000	87000	90000	93000	96000	97500	99000
ENGINE																																								
Inspect EVAP & Fuel Systems Filler Pipe, Hoses, Lines, Tank & Cap												X												X												X				
Inspect Exhaust System	S	S	N	S	S	X	S	S	N	S	S	X	S	S	N	S	S	X	S	S	N	S	S	X	S	S	N	S	S	X	S	S	N	S	S	X	S	S	N	S
Inspect PCV Valve, 1998–99												S												S												X				
Inspect PCV Valve, 2000–02	Normal Service Replace at 60,000 Miles & Inspect Every 30,000 Thereafter; Severe Service Replace Every 30,000 Miles																																							
Inspect & Adjust Drive Belts						X						X						X						X						X						X				
Replace Drive Belts																								S																
Replace Spark Plugs, 1998	Normal Service Every 84 Months Or 105,000 Miles; Severe Service Every 102,000 Miles																																							
Replace Spark Plugs, 1999–2002	Every 100,000 Miles																																							
Replace Timing Belt, 3.2L & 3.5L, 1998	At 105,000 Miles																																							
Replace Timing Belt, 3.2L & 3.5L, 1999–2002②	At 100,000 Miles																																							
Replace Timing Belt, 3.2L & 3.5L, 1999–2002③	At 105,000 Miles																																							
STEERING, SUSPENSION & TIRES																																								
Inspect Ball Joints		S	N		S	N	S		N	S		X		S	N		S	N	S		N	S		X		S	N		S	N	S		N	S		X		S	N	
Lubricate Suspension & Steering Linkage						S						S						S						X						S						S				
Rotate Tires & Adjust Pressure		S	N		S	N	S		N	S		X		S	N		S.	N	S		N	S		X		S	N		S	N	S		N	S		X		S	N	

Mos. — Months
N — Normal Service
S — Severe Service
X — Normal Or Severe Service
① — After vehicles passes 99,000 mile mark return to beginning of mileage table & start cycle over again.
② — Federal emissions.
③ — California emissions.

DaimlerChrysler Sebring Coupe & Dodge Avenger

Recommended Service & Intervals (Months)	Service Interval In Miles①																																							
	3000	6000	7500	9000	12000	15000	18000	21000	22500	24000	27000	30000	33000	36000	37500	39000	42000	45000	48000	51000	52500	54000	57000	60000	63000	66000	67500	69000	72000	75000	78000	81000	82500	84000	87000	90000	93000	96000	97500	99000
BODY																																								
Inspect Supplemental Restraint System Components	Every 10 Years From Vehicle Build Date																																							
BRAKES																																								
Inspect Brake Connections, Hoses & Lines	Every 12 Months Or 15,000 Miles																																							
Inspect Disc Brake Pads (Every 12 Mos.)	Normal Service Check for Wear Every 15,000 Miles; Severe Service Every 6000 Miles																																							
Inspect Drum Brake Shoes (Every 24 Mos.)	Normal Service Check For Wear Every 30,000 Miles; Severe Service Every 15,000 Miles																																							
CLUTCH & TRANSMISSION																																								
Change Or Inspect Automatic Transaxle Fluid & Filter	Normal Service, Inspect Every 15,000 Miles; Severe Service, Change Fluid Every 15,000 Miles, Change Filter Every 30,000 Miles.																																							
Change Manual Transaxle Lubricant												S												S												S				
DRIVESHAFT & CV JOINTS																																								
Inspect CV Joint Boots (Every 12 Mos.)						X						X						X						X						X						X				
ENGINE																																								
Change Engine Coolant	Every 24 Months Or 30,000 Miles																																							
Change Engine Oil (Normal Service Every 6 Mos./Severe Service Every 3 Mos.)	S	S	N	S	S	X	S	S	N	S	S	X	S	S	N	S	S	X	S	S	N	S	S	X	S	S	N	S	S	X	S	S	N	S	S	X	S	S	N	S
Change Engine Oil & Filter		S			S	N	S			S		X		S			S	N	S			S		X		S			S	N	S			S		X		S		
Inspect Air Filter						S						X						S						X						S						X				
Inspect Coolant Level	At Every Engine Oil Change																																							
Inspect Distributor Cap & Rotor																								X																
Inspect EVAP System																								X																
Inspect Exhaust System & Heat Shields	S	S	N	S	S	X	S	S	N	S	S	X	S	S	N	S	S	X	S	S	N	S	S	X	S	S	N	S	S	X	S	S	N	S	S	X	S	S	N	S
Inspect Fuel Filler Cap																								X																
Inspect Fuel Hoses, Lines & Connections																								X																
Inspect Fuel Tank																								X																
Inspect & Adjust Drive Belts						X						X						X						X						X						X				
Replace Spark Plugs, DOHC						S						X						S						X						S						X				
Replace Spark Plugs, SOHC	Normal Service Every 100,000 Miles; Severe Service Every 15,000 Miles																																							

Recommended Service & Intervals (Months)	Service Interval In Miles①																																							
	3000	6000	7500	9000	12000	15000	18000	21000	22500	24000	27000	30000	33000	36000	37500	39000	42000	45000	48000	51000	52500	54000	57000	60000	63000	66000	67500	69000	72000	75000	78000	81000	82500	84000	87000	90000	93000	96000	97500	99000
ENGINE																																								
Replace Timing Belt																								X																
STEERING, SUSPENSION & TIRES																																								
Inspect Ball Joints & Steering Linkage Grease Seals (Every 24 Mos.)												X												X												X				
Lubricate Suspension & Steering Linkage (Every 24 Mos.)												X												X												X				
Rotate Tires & Adjust Pressure (Every 6 Mos.)			X			X			X			X			X			X			X			X			X			X			X			X			X	

Mos. — Months
N — Normal Service
S — Severe Service
X — Normal Or Severe Service
① — After vehicles passes 99,000 mile mark return to beginning of mileage table & start cycle over again.

Ford Contour & Mercury Mystique

Recommended Service	Service Interval In Miles①																														
	3000	5000	6000	7500	9000	10000	12000	15000	18000	20000	21000	22500	24000	25000	27000	30000	33000	35000	36000	37500	39000	40000	42000	45000	48000	50000	51000	52500	54000	55000	57000	60000
BODY																																
Inspect A/C Refrigerant Charge & System Operation	Every 12 Months Or 15,000 Miles, Before Warm Season Arrives																															
Inspect Instrument Panel Warning Lamps & Gauges	At Every Engine Oil Change																															
Lubricate Body Hardware & Hinges								X								X								X								X
Lubricate Hood Latch Pivot Points & All Contact Areas				X				X				X				X				X				X				X				X
Replace Passenger Compartment Pollen Filter								X								X								X								X
BRAKES																																
Inspect Brake Drums, Linings, Pads, Rotors, Lubricate Caliper Slide Rails, 1998					S	N			S	N					S	N			S			N		S		N			S			N
Inspect Brake Drums, Linings, Pads, Rotors, Lubricate Caliper Slide Rails, 1999–2000	Normal Service Every 15,000 Miles; Severe Service Every 5000 Miles																															
Inspect Parking Brake System Operation								X								X								X								X
CLUTCH & TRANSMISSION																																
Change Automatic Transmission Fluid & Filter, 1998																S																S
Change Automatic Transmission Fluid & Filter, 1999–2000	Normal Service Inspect Every 15,000 Miles; Severe Service Change Every 30,000 Miles.																															
Lubricate Transmission Control Linkage								X								X								X								X
DRIVESHAFT																																
Inspect CV Joint Boots (Every 6 Mos.)								X								X								X								X
ENGINE																																
Change Engine Coolant, 1998	At 48 Months Or 50,000 Miles, Then Every 36 Months Or 30,000 Miles Thereafter																															
Change Engine Coolant, 1999–2000	Replace Green Coolant If Equipped, Every 45,000 Miles, Then Every 30,000 Miles Thereafter; Replace Orange Coolant If Equipped, Every 150,000 Miles																															
Change Engine Oil & Filter	S	N	S		S	N	S	X	S	N	S		S	N	S	X	S	N	S		S	N	S	X	S	N	S		S	N	S	X
Inspect Cooling & Protection Level	Annually Or Every 15,000 Miles																															
Inspect Drive Belts, 1998																X																X
Inspect Drive Belts, 1999–2000	Every 100,000 Miles																															
Inspect Exhaust Heat System																X																X
Inspect Fluid & Lubricant Levels	At Every Engine Oil Change																															
Inspect Fuel System Connections, Hoses & Lines								X								X								X								X
Replace Fuel Filter, 1999–2000②	Every 30,000 Miles																															
Replace Air Filter																X																X
Replace PCV Valve, 1998	Every 100,000 Miles																															
Replace PCV Valve, 1999–2000	4 Cylinder Every 60,000 Miles; 6 Cylinder Every 100,000 Miles																															
Replace Spark Plugs, 2.5L	Normal Service Every 100,000 Miles; Severe Service Every 60,000 Miles																															
Replace Spark Plugs, 2.0L	Every 100,000 Miles																															

Recommended Service	Service Interval In Miles① 3000	5000	6000	7500	9000	10000	12000	15000	18000	20000	21000	22500	24000	25000	27000	30000	33000	35000	36000	37500	39000	40000	42000	45000	48000	50000	51000	52500	54000	55000	57000	60000
STEERING, SUSPENSION & TIRES																																
Rotate Tires, 1998		N	S					X					S	N			S	N					S	N			S			N		S
Rotate Tires, 1999–2000	Inspect For Wear And Rotate Every 5000 Miles																															

Mos. — Months
N — Normal Service
S — Severe Service
X — Normal Or Severe Service
① — After vehicle has passed 60,000 mile mark return to beginning of mileage table & start cycle over again.
② — On vehicles equipped with California emissions.

Ford Crown Victoria & Mercury Grand Marquis

Recommended Service	Service Interval In Miles① 3000	5000	6000	7500	9000	10000	12000	15000	18000	20000	21000	22500	24000	25000	27000	30000	33000	35000	36000	37500	39000	40000	42000	45000	48000	50000	51000	52500	54000	55000	57000	60000
BODY																																
Inspect A/C Refrigerant Charge & System Operation	Every 12 Months Or 15,000 Miles																															
Inspect Instrument Panel Warning Lamps & Gauges	At Every Engine Oil Change																															
Lubricate Body Hardware & Hinges								X								X								X								X
Lubricate Hood Latch Pivot Points & All Contact Areas				X				X				X				X				X				X				X				X
BRAKES																																
Inspect Brake Drums, Linings, Pads, Rotors, Lubricate Caliper Slide Rails, 1998	Normal Service Every 15,000 Miles; Severe Service Every 12,000 Miles																															
Inspect Brake Drums, Linings, Pads, Rotors, Lubricate Caliper Slide Rails, 1999–2002	Normal Service Every 15,000 Miles; Severe Service Every 5000 Miles																															
Inspect Parking Brake System Operation								X								X								X								X
CLUTCH & TRANSMISSION																																
Change Automatic Transmission Fluid & Filter, 1998											S					N							S									N
Change Automatic Transmission Fluid & Filter, 1999–2002	Normal Service Inspect Every 15,000 Miles; Change Every 30,000 Miles																															
Lubricate Transmission Control Linkage								X								X								X								X
DRIVE AXLE & DRIVESHAFT																																
Change Differential Lubricant	②																															
Lubricate Driveshaft								X								X								X								X

Recommended Service	Service Interval In Miles①																															
	3000	5000	6000	7500	9000	10000	12000	15000	18000	20000	21000	22500	24000	25000	27000	30000	33000	35000	36000	37500	39000	40000	42000	45000	48000	50000	51000	52500	54000	55000	57000	60000
ENGINE																																
Change Engine Coolant, 1998	At 48 Months Or 50,000 Miles, Then Every 36 Months Or 30,000 Miles Thereafter																															
Change Engine Coolant, 1999–2002	Replace Green, If Equipped, Every 45,000 Miles, Then Every 30,000 Miles Thereafter. Replace Orange, If Equipped, Every 150,000 Miles.																															
Change Engine Oil & Filter	S		S	N	S		S	X	S		S	N	S		S	X	S		S	N	S		S	X	S		S	N	S		S	X
Inspect Cooling System & Protection Level	Annually Or Every 15,000 Miles																															
Inspect Drive Belts, 1998																																X
Inspect Drive Belts, 1999–2002	Every 100,000 Miles																															
Inspect Exhaust System																X																X
Inspect Fluid & Lubricant Levels	At Every Engine Oil Change																															
Inspect Fuel System Connections, Hoses & Lines								X								X								X								X
Inspect & Clean Choke Linkage, 5.8L																X																X
Inspect & Replace Engine Air Filter								S								X								S								X
Replace Engine Air Filter	Every 30,000 Miles																															
Replace Fuel Filter Element & Housing O-Ring Seal, Drain Coalescent Filter Bowl, 1998–2001 NGV	Every 120,000 Miles																															
Replace PCV Valve, 1998																																X
Replace PCV Valve, 1999–2002	Every 100,000 Miles																															
Replace Spark Plugs, NGV,																																X
Replace Spark Plugs, Except NGV	Normal Service Every 100,000 Miles; Severe Service Every 60,000 Miles																															
STEERING, SUSPENSION & TIRES																																
Inspect & Repack Front Wheel Bearings																X																X
Lubricate Steering & Suspension Components								X								X								X								X
Rotate Tires, 1998		N	S					X					S	N			S	N					S	N			S			N		S
Rotate Tires, 1999–2002	Normal Service Inspect for Wear & Rotate Every 5,000 Miles.																															

N — Normal Service
NGV — Natural Gas Vehicle
S — Severe Service
X — Normal Or Severe Service
① — After vehicle has passed 60,000 mile mark return to beginning of mileage table & start cycle over again.
② — Normal Vehicle Axle Maintenance: Rear axle units containing synthetic lubricant are lubricated for life. These lubricants are not to be checked or changed unless a leak is suspected, service is required or the axle assembly has been submerged in water. The axle lubricant should be changed anytime the axle has been submerged in water. Non-synthetic rear axle lubricants should be replaced every 3000 miles or 3 months, whichever occurs first, during extended trailer tow operation above (70°F) ambient and wide open throttle for extended periods above 45 mph. The 3000 mile lube change interval may be waived if the axle was filled with 75W140 synthetic gear lubricant meeting Ford specification WSL-M2C192–A. Add four ounces of additive friction modifier C8AZ-19B546–A or equivalent for complete refill of Traction-Lok rear axles. The rear axle lubricant should be changed anytime the axle has been submerged in water.

Ford Escort & ZX2 & Mercury Tracer

Recommended Service	Service Interval In Miles①																														
	3000	5000	6000	7500	9000	10000	12000	15000	18000	20000	21000	22500	24000	25000	27000	30000	33000	35000	36000	37500	39000	40000	42000	45000	48000	50000	51000	52500	54000	55000	57000	60000
BODY																																
Inspect A/C Refrigerant Charge & System Operation	Every 12 Months Or 15,000 Miles																															
Inspect Instrument Panel Warning Lamps & Gauges	At Every Engine Oil Change																															
Lubricate Body Hardware & Hinges								X								X								X								X
Lubricate Hood Latch Pivot Points & All Contact Areas				X				X				X				X				X				X				X				X
Tighten Body Fasteners								S								X								S								X
BRAKES																																
Inspect Brake Drums, Linings, Pads, Rotors, Lubricate Caliper Slide Rails, 1998	Normal Service Every 30,000 Miles; More Frequently In Severe Service																															
Inspect Brake Drums, Linings, Pads, Rotors, Lubricate Caliper Slide Rails, 1999–2002	Normal Service Every 15,000 Miles; Severe Service Every 5000 Miles																															
Inspect Parking Brake System Operation								X								X								X								X
CLUTCH & TRANSMISSION																																
Change Automatic Transmission Fluid & Filter, 1998–99	Normal Service Inspect Every 15,000 Miles; Severe Service Change Every 30,000 Miles.																															
Change Automatic Transmission Fluid & Filter, 2000–02	Normal Service Inspect Every 15,000 Miles; Severe Service Change Every 30,000 Miles.																															
Inspect Clutch Pedal Operation																X																X
Lubricate Transmission Control Linkage								X								X								X								X
DRIVESHAFT																																
Inspect CV Joint Boots								X								X								X								X
ENGINE																																
Change Engine Coolant, 1998	At 48 Months Or 50,000 Miles, Then Every 36 Months Or 30,000 Miles Thereafter																															
Change Engine Coolant, 1999–2002	Replace Green Coolant, If Equipped, Every 45,000 Miles, Then Every 30,000 Miles Thereafter. Replace Orange Coolant, If Equipped, Every 150,000 Miles																															
Change Engine Oil & Filter, 1998	S	N	S		S	N	S	X	S	N	S		S	N	S	X	S	N	S		S	N	S	X	S	N	S		S	N	S	X
Change Engine Oil & Filter, 1999–2002	Normal Service Every 5000 Miles; Severe Service Every 3000 Miles																															
Inspect Cooling System & Protection Level	Annually Or Every 15,000 Miles																															
Inspect Drive Belts, 1998								S								X								S								X
Inspect Drive Belts, 1999–2002	Every 100,000 Miles																															
Inspect Exhaust System																X																X
Inspect Fuel System Connections, Hoses & Lines								X								X								X								X
Inspect & Replace Engine Air Filter																X																X
Replace Fuel Filter, 1998–2000	Every 30,000 Miles																															
Replace Fuel Filter, 2001–02	Normal Service Every 30,000 Miles; Severe Service Every 15,000 Miles																															
Replace PCV Valve																																X
Replace Spark Plugs	Every 100,000 Miles																															

Recommended Service	Service Interval In Miles①																															
	3000	5000	6000	7500	9000	10000	12000	15000	18000	20000	21000	22500	24000	25000	27000	30000	33000	35000	36000	37500	39000	40000	42000	45000	48000	50000	51000	52500	54000	55000	57000	60000
ENGINE																																
Replace Timing Belt, 1999–2002 2.0L	Every 120,000 Miles																															
STEERING, SUSPENSION & TIRES																																
Inspect & Repack Rear Wheel Bearings																X																X
Lubricate Steering & Suspension Components								X								X								X								X
Rotate Tires, 1998		N	S					X					S	N			S	N					S	N			S			N		S
Rotate Tires, 1999–2002	Normal Service Inspect For Wear And Rotate Every 5000 Miles																															
Tighten Chassis Fasteners								S								X								S								X

FFV — Flexible Fuel Vehicle
N — Normal Service
NGV — Natural Gas Vehicle
S — Severe Service
X — Normal Or Severe Service
① — After vehicle has passed 60,000 mile mark return to beginning of mileage table & start cycle over again.

Ford Focus

Recommended Service	Service Interval In Miles①																															
	3000	5000	6000	7500	9000	10000	12000	15000	18000	20000	21000	22500	24000	25000	27000	30000	33000	35000	36000	37500	39000	40000	42000	45000	48000	50000	51000	52500	54000	55000	57000	60000
BODY																																
Inspect A/C Refrigerant Charge & System Operation	Every 12 Months Or 15,000 Miles																															
Inspect Instrument Panel Warning Lamps & Gauges	At Every Engine Oil Change																															
Lubricate Body Hardware & Hinges								X								X								X								X
Lubricate Hood Latch Pivot Points & All Contact Areas				X				X				X				X				X				X				X				X
Tighten Body Fasteners								S								X								S								X
BRAKES																																
Inspect Brake Drums, Linings, Pads, Rotors, Lubricate Caliper Slide Rails	Normal Service Every 15,000 Miles; Severe Service Every 5000 Miles																															
Inspect Parking Brake System Operation								X								X								X								X
CLUTCH & TRANSMISSION																																
Change Automatic Transmission Fluid & Filter	Inspect Every 15,000 Miles; Change Every 30,000 Miles.																															
Inspect Clutch Pedal Operation																X																X
Lubricate Transmission Control Linkage								X								X								X								X
DRIVESHAFT																																
Inspect CV Joint Boots								X								X								X								X
ENGINE																																
Change Engine Coolant	Replace Green Coolant, If Equipped, Every 45,000 Miles, Then Every 30,000 Miles Thereafter. Replace Orange Coolant, If Equipped, Every 150,000 Miles																															
Change Engine Oil & Filter	Normal Service Every 5000 Miles; Severe Service Every 3000 Miles																															
Inspect Cooling System & Protection Level	Annually Or Every 15,000 Miles																															
Replace Accessory Drive Belts	Every 60,000 Miles																															
Inspect Exhaust System																X																X
Inspect Fuel System Connections, Hoses & Lines								X								X								X								X
Inspect & Replace Engine Air Filter																X																X
Replace Fuel Filter	Normal Service Every 30,000 Miles; Severe Service Every 15,000 Miles																															
Replace PCV Valve	Every 60,000 Miles																															
Replace Spark Plugs	Every 100,000 Miles																															
Replace Timing Belt	Every 120,000 Miles																															
STEERING, SUSPENSION & TIRES																																
Inspect & Repack Rear Wheel Bearings																X																X
Lubricate Steering & Suspension Components								X								X								X								X
Rotate Tires	Normal Service Inspect For Wear And Rotate Every 5000 Miles																															
Tighten Chassis Fasteners								S								X								S								X

FFV — Flexible Fuel Vehicle
N — Normal Service
NGV — Natural Gas Vehicle
S — Severe Service
X — Normal Or Severe Service
① — After vehicle has passed 60,000 mile mark return to beginning of mileage table & start cycle over again.

Ford Mustang

Recommended Service	Service Interval In Miles①																														
	3000	5000	6000	7500	9000	10000	12000	15000	18000	20000	21000	22500	24000	25000	27000	30000	33000	35000	36000	37500	39000	40000	42000	45000	48000	50000	51000	52500	54000	55000	57000	60000
BODY																																
Inspect A/C Refrigerant Charge & System Operation	Every 12 Months Or 15,000 Miles																															
Inspect Instrument Panel Warning Lamps & Gauges	At Every Engine Oil Change																															
Lubricate Body Hardware & Hinges								X								X								X								X
Lubricate Hood Latch Pivot Points & All Contact Areas				X				X				X				X				X				X				X				X
BRAKES																																
Inspect Brake Drums, Linings, Pads, Rotors, Lubricate Caliper Slide Rails, 1998	Normal Service Every 30,000 Miles; Severe Service Every 12,000 Miles																															
Inspect Brake Drums, Linings, Pads, Rotors, Lubricate Caliper Slide Rails, 1999–2002	Normal Service Every 15,000 Miles; Severe Service Every 5,000 Miles																															
Inspect Parking Brake System Operation								X								X								X								X
CLUTCH & TRANSMISSION																																
Adjust Clutch Pedal, 1998	S	N	S		S	N	S	X	S	N	S		S	N	S	X	S	N	S		S	N	S	X	S	N	S		S	N	S	X
Change Automatic Transmission Fluid & Filter, 1998											S					N							S									N
Change Automatic Transmission Fluid & Filter, 1999–2002	Inspect Every 15,000 Miles; Change Every 30,000 Miles.																															
Lubricate Transmission Control Linkage								X								X								X								X
DRIVE AXLE & DRIVESHAFT																																
Change Differential Lubricant	③																															
Lubricate Driveshaft								X								X								X								X
ENGINE																																
Change Engine Coolant, 1998	At 48 Months Or 50,000 Miles, Then Every 36 Months Or 30,000 Miles Thereafter																															
Change Engine Coolant, 1999–2002	Replace Green Coolant, If Equipped, Every 45,000 Miles, Then Every 30,000 Miles Thereafter. Replace Orange Coolant, If Equipped, Every 150,000 Miles.																															
Change Engine Oil & Filter	S	N	S		S	N	S	X	S	N	S		S	N	S	X	S	N	S		S	N	S	X	S	N	S		S	N	S	X
Inspect Cooling System & Protection Level	Annually Or Every 15,000 Miles																															
Inspect Drive Belts, 1998																																X
Inspect Drive Belts, 1999–2002	Every 100,000 Miles																															
Inspect Exhaust System																X																X
Inspect Fluid & Lubricant Levels	At Every Engine Oil Change																															
Inspect Fuel System Connections, Hoses & Lines								X								X								X								X
Inspect Timing Belt, 2.3L SOHC																																X
Inspect & Replace Engine Air Filter								S								X								S								X
Replace Engine Air Filter	Every 30,000 Miles																															
Replace Fuel Filter, ②	Every 30,000 Miles																															
Replace PCV Valve, 1998																																X

Recommended Service	Service Interval In Miles①																															
	3000	5000	6000	7500	9000	10000	12000	15000	18000	20000	21000	22500	24000	25000	27000	30000	33000	35000	36000	37500	39000	40000	42000	45000	48000	50000	51000	52500	54000	55000	57000	60000
ENGINE																																
Replace PCV Valve, 1999–2002	Every 100,000 Miles																															
Replace Spark Plugs	Normal Service Every 100,000 Miles; Severe Service Every 60,000 Miles																															
STEERING, SUSPENSION & TIRES																																
Inspect & Repack Front Wheel Bearings																X																X
Lubricate Steering & Suspension Components								X								X								X								X
Rotate Tires, 1998		N	S					X					S	N			S	N					S	N			S			N		S
Rotate Tires, 1999–2002	Normal Service Inspect For Wear And Rotate Every 5,000 Miles.																															

N — Normal Service
NGV — Natural Gas Vehicle
S — Severe Service
X — Normal Or Severe Service
① — After vehicle has passed 60,000 mile mark return to beginning of mileage table & start cycle over again.
② — On All vehicles equipped with California emissions.
③ — Normal Vehicle Axle Maintenance: Rear axle units containing synthetic lubricant are lubricated for life. These lubricants are not to be checked or changed unless a leak is suspected, service is required or the axle assembly has been submerged in water. The axle lubricant should be changed anytime the axle has been submerged in water. Non-synthetic rear axle lubricants should be replaced every 3000 miles or 3 months, whichever occurs first, during extended trailer tow operation above (70°F) ambient and wide open throttle for extended periods above 45 mph. The 3000 mile lube change interval may be waived if the axle was filled with 75W140 synthetic gear lubricant meeting Ford specification WSL-M2C192–A. Add four ounces of additive friction modifier C8AZ-19B546–A or equivalent for complete refill of Traction-Lok rear axles. The rear axle lubricant should be changed anytime the axle has been submerged in water.

Police and Taxi Vehicle Axle Maintenance: Replace rear axle lubricant every 160,000km (100,000 miles). Rear axle lubricant change may be waived if the axle was filled with 75W140 synthetic gear lubricant meeting Ford specification WSL-M2C192–A. Add four ounces of additive friction modifier C8AZ-19B546–A or equivalent for complete refill of Traction-Lok rear axles. The rear axle lubricant should be changed anytime the axle has been submerged in water.

Ford Taurus & Mercury Sable

Recommended Service	Service Interval In Miles①																														
	3000	5000	6000	7500	9000	10000	12000	15000	18000	20000	21000	22500	24000	25000	27000	30000	33000	35000	36000	37500	39000	40000	42000	45000	48000	50000	51000	52500	54000	55000	57000	60000
BODY																																
Inspect A/C Refrigerant Charge & System Operation	Every 12 Months Or 15,000 Miles, Before Warm Season Arrives																															
Inspect Instrument Panel Warning Lamps & Gauges	At Every Engine Oil Change																															
Lubricate Body Hardware & Hinges								X								X								X								X
Lubricate Hood Latch Pivot Points & All Contact Areas				X				X				X				X				X				X				X				X
Replace Passenger Compartment Pollen Filter								X								X								X								X
BRAKES																																
Inspect Brake Drums, Linings, Pads, Rotors, Lubricate Caliper Slide Rails, 1998							S						S			N			S						S							X
Inspect Brake Drums, Linings, Pads, Rotors, Lubricate Caliper Slide Rails, 1999–2002	Normal Service Every 15,000 Miles; Severe Service Every 5000 Miles																															
Inspect Brake Lines & Hoses							S						S			N			S						S							X
Inspect Parking Brake System Operation								X								X								X								X
CLUTCH & TRANSMISSION																																
Change Automatic Transmission Fluid & Filter, 1998											S					N							S									N
Change Automatic Transmission Fluid & Filter, 1999–2002	Inspect Every 15,000 Miles; Change Every 30,000 Miles.																															
Lubricate Transmission Control Linkage								X								X								X								X
DRIVESHAFT																																
Inspect CV Joint Boots								X								X								X								X
ENGINE																																
Change Engine Coolant, 1998	At 48 Months Or 50,000 Miles, Then Every 36 Months Or 30,000 Miles Thereafter																															
Change Engine Coolant, 1999–2002	Replace Green Coolant, If Equipped, Every 45,000 Miles, Then Every 30,000 Miles Thereafter. Replace Orange Coolant, If Equipped, Every 150,000 Miles.																															
Change Engine Oil & Filter	S	N	S		S	N	S	X	S	N	S		S	N	S	X	S	N	S		S	N	S	X	S	N	S		S	N	S	X
Inspect Cooling System & Protection Level	Annually Or Every 15,000 Miles																															
Inspect Drive Belts 1998																X																X
Inspect Drive Belts 1999–2002	Inspect Accessory Drive Belts Every 100,000 Miles.																															
Inspect Exhaust System																X																X
Inspect Fluid & Lubricant Levels	At Every Engine Oil Change																															
Inspect Fuel System Connections, Hoses & Lines								X								X								X								X
Inspect & Adjust Engine Valve Clearance, 1998 Taurus SHO	Every 100,000 Miles																															
Inspect & Replace Engine Air Filter																X																X
Replace Crankcase Emission Filter Or PCV Filter Element, 2.5L	Normal Service Every 30,000 Miles; More Frequently In Severe Service																															
Replace Fuel Filter, 1999–2000	Every 30,000 Miles																															
Replace Fuel Filter, 2001–02	Normal Service Every 30,000 Miles; Severe Service Every 15,000 Miles																															

Recommended Service	Service Interval In Miles①																															
	3000	5000	6000	7500	9000	10000	12000	15000	18000	20000	21000	22500	24000	25000	27000	30000	33000	35000	36000	37500	39000	40000	42000	45000	48000	50000	51000	52500	54000	55000	57000	60000
ENGINE																																
Replace PCV Valve, 1998	Normal Service Every 100,000 Miles; Severe Service Every 90,000 Miles																															
Replace PCV Valve, 1999–2002	Every 100,000 Miles																															
Replace Spark Plugs	Normal Service Every 100,000 Miles; Severe Service Every 60,000 Miles																															
STEERING, SUSPENSION & TIRES																																
Lubricate Steering & Suspension Components								X								X								X								X
Rotate Tires, 1998		N	S					X					S	N			S	N					S	N			S			N		S
Rotate Tires, 1999–2002	Normal Service Inspect For Wear And Rotate Every 5000 Miles																															

N — Normal Service
S — Severe Service
X — Normal Or Severe Service
① — After vehicle has passed 60,000 mile mark return to beginning of mileage table & start cycle over again.

Lincoln

Recommended Service	Service Interval In Miles①																															
	3000	5000	6000	7500	9000	10000	12000	15000	18000	20000	21000	22500	24000	25000	27000	30000	33000	35000	36000	37500	39000	40000	42000	45000	48000	50000	51000	52500	54000	55000	57000	60000
BODY																																
Inspect A/C Refrigerant Charge & System Operation	Every 12 Months Or 15,000 Miles, Before Warm Season Arrives																															
Inspect Instrument Panel Warning Lamps & Gauges	At Every Engine Oil Change																															
Lubricate Body Hardware & Hinges								X								X								X								X
Lubricate Hood Latch Pivot Points & All Contact Areas				X				X				X				X				X				X				X				X
Replace Passenger Compartment Pollen Filter, 1998					S			N	S						S	N			S					X					S			N
Replace Passenger Compartment Pollen Filter, 1999–2002	Normal Service Every 15,000 Miles; Severe Service Inspect Every 3000 Miles And Change As Necessary																															
BRAKES																																
Inspect Brake Drums, Linings, Pads, Rotors, Lubricate Caliper Slide Rails, 1998	Normal Service Every 30,000 Miles; Severe Service Every 12,000 Miles																															
Inspect Brake Drums, Linings, Pads, Rotors, Lubricate Caliper Slide Rails, 1999–2002	Normal Service Every 15,000 Miles; Severe Service Every 5000 Miles																															
Inspect Brake Lines & Hoses	Normal Service Every 30,000 Miles; Severe Service Every 12,000 Miles																															
Inspect Parking Brake System Operation								X								X								X								X
CLUTCH & TRANSMISSION																																
Change Automatic Transmission Fluid & Filter, 1998											S					N							S									N
Change Automatic Transmission Fluid & Filter, 1999–2002	Inspect Every 15,000 Miles; Change Every 30,000 Miles.																															
Change Manual Transmission Fluid, LS	Every 60,000 Miles.																															
Lubricate Transmission Control Linkage								X								X								X								X
DRIVE AXLE & DRIVESHAFT																																
Change Differential Lubricant, Rear Wheel Drive Models	②																															
Inspect CV Joint Boots								X								X								X								X
Lubricate Driveshaft								X								X								X								X
ENGINE																																
Change Engine Coolant, 1998	At 48 Months Or 50,000 Miles, Then Every 36 Months Or 30,000 Miles																															
Change Engine Coolant, 1999–2002	Replace Green Coolant, If Equipped, Every 45,000 Miles, Then Every 30,000 Miles Thereafter. Replace Orange Coolant, If Equipped, Every 150,000 Miles.																															
Change Engine Oil & Filter, 1998 Town Car	S		S	N	S		S	X	S		S	N	S		S	X	S		S	N	S		S	X	S		S	N	S		S	X
Change Engine Oil & Filter, Except 1998 Town Car	S	N	S		S	N	S	X	S	N	S		S	N	S	X	S	N	S		S	N	S	X	S	N	S		S	N	S	X
Inspect Cooling System & Protection Level	Annually Or Every 15,000 Miles																															
Inspect Drive Belts, 1998																X																X
Inspect Drive Belts, 1999–2002	Every 100,000 Miles																															
Inspect Exhaust System																X																X
Inspect Fuel System Connections, Hoses & Lines								X								X								X								X
Inspect & Replace Engine Air Filter																X																X

Recommended Service	Service Interval In Miles①																															
	3000	5000	6000	7500	9000	10000	12000	15000	18000	20000	21000	22500	24000	25000	27000	30000	33000	35000	36000	37500	39000	40000	42000	45000	48000	50000	51000	52500	54000	55000	57000	60000
ENGINE																																
Replace PCV Valve, 1998 Town Car																																X
Replace PCV Valve, 1998 Continental	Normal Service Every 100,000 Miles; Severe Service Every 90,000 Miles																															
Replace PCV Valve, 1999–2002	Every 100,000 Miles																															
Replace Fuel Filter	Normal Service Every 60,000 Miles; Severe Service Every 15,000 Miles																															
Replace Spark Plugs	Normal Service Every 100,000 Miles; Severe Service Every 60,000 Miles																															
STEERING, SUSPENSION & TIRES																																
Inspect & Repack Front Wheel Bearings																X																X
Lubricate Steering & Suspension Components								X								X								X								X
Rotate Tires, 1998		N	S					X					S	N			S	N					S	N			S			N		S
Rotate Tires, 1999–2002	Normal Service Inspect for Wear And Rotate Every 5000 Miles																															

N — Normal Service
S — Severe Service
X — Normal Or Severe Service
① — After vehicle has passed 60,000 mile mark return to beginning of mileage table & start cycle over again.
② — Normal Vehicle Axle Maintenance: Rear axle units containing synthetic lubricant are lubricated for life. These lubricants are not to be checked or changed unless a leak is suspected, service is required or the axle assembly has been submerged in water. The axle lubricant should be changed anytime the axle has been submerged in water. Non-synthetic rear axle lubricants should be replaced every 3000 miles or 3 months, whichever occurs first, during extended trailer tow operation above (70°F) ambient and wide open throttle for extended periods above 45 mph. The 3000 mile lube change interval may be waived if the axle was filled with 75W140 synthetic gear lubricant meeting Ford specification WSL-M2C192–A. Add four ounces of additive friction modifier C8AZ-19B546–A or equivalent for complete refill of Traction-Lok rear axles. The rear axle lubricant should be changed anytime the axle has been submerged in water.

Police and Taxi Vehicle Axle Maintenance: Replace rear axle lubricant every 160,000km (100,000 miles). Rear axle lubricant change may be waived if the axle was filled with 75W140 synthetic gear lubricant meeting Ford specification WSL-M2C192–A. Add four ounces of additive friction modifier C8AZ-19B546–A or equivalent for complete refill of Traction-Lok rear axles. The rear axle lubricant should be changed anytime the axle has been submerged in water.

Mercury Cougar

Recommended Service	Service Interval In Miles①																															
	3000	5000	6000	7500	9000	10000	12000	15000	18000	20000	21000	22500	24000	25000	27000	30000	33000	35000	36000	37500	39000	40000	42000	45000	48000	50000	51000	52500	54000	55000	57000	60000
BODY																																
Inspect A/C Refrigerant Charge & System Operation	Every 12 Months Or 15,000 Miles																															
Inspect Instrument Panel Warning Lamps & Gauges	At Every Engine Oil Change																															
Lubricate Body Hardware & Hinges								X								X								X								X
Lubricate Hood Latch Pivot Points & All Contact Areas				X				X				X				X				X				X				X				X
BRAKES																																
Inspect Brake Drums, Linings, Pads, Rotors, Lubricate Caliper Slide Rails	Normal Service Every 15,000 Miles; Severe Service Every 5000 Miles																															
Inspect Parking Brake System Operation								X								X								X								X
CLUTCH & TRANSMISSION																																
Change Automatic Transmission Fluid & Filter	Normal Service Inspect Every 15,000 Miles; Severe Service Every 30,000 Miles.																															
Lubricate Transmission Control Linkage								X								X								X								X
Change Transfer Case Fluid																																S
DRIVE AXLE & DRIVESHAFT																																
Lubricate Driveshaft								X								X								X								X
ENGINE																																
Change Engine Coolant	Replace Green Coolant, If Equipped, Every 45,000 Miles, Then Every 30,000 Miles Thereafter. Replace Orange Coolant, If Equipped, Every 150,000 Miles.																															
Change Engine Oil & Filter	S	N	S		S	N	S	X	S	N	S		S	N	S	X	S	N	S		S	N	S	X	S	N	S		S	N	S	X
Inspect Cooling System & Protection Level	Annually Or Every 15,000 Miles																															
Inspect Drive Belts	Every 100,000 Miles																															
Inspect Exhaust System																X																X
Inspect Fluid & Lubricant Levels	At Every Engine Oil Change																															
Inspect Fuel System Connections, Hoses & Lines								X								X								X								X
Inspect & Replace Engine Air Filter								S								X								S								X
Replace Engine Air Filter	Every 30,000 Miles																															
Replace Fuel Filter, 1999–2000②	Every 30,000 Miles																															
Replace Fuel Filter, 2001–02	Normal Service Every 30,000 Miles; Severe Service Every 15,000 Miles																															
Replace PCV Valve	4 Cylinder Every 60,000 Miles; V6 Every 100,000 Miles																															
Replace Spark Plugs	Normal Service Every 100,000 Miles; Severe Service Every 60,000 Miles																															
Replace Timing Belt, 2.0L	Every 120,000 Miles																															
STEERING, SUSPENSION & TIRES																																
Lubricate Steering & Suspension Components								X								X								X								X
Rotate Tires	Normal Service Inspect For Wear And Rotate Every 5000 Miles																															

N — Normal Service
NGV — Natural Gas Vehicle
S — Severe Service
X — Normal Or Severe Service
① — After vehicle has passed 60,000 mile mark return to beginning of mileage table & start cycle over again.
② — California emissions.

Buick Century & Regal, Chevrolet Impala, Lumina & Monte Carlo, Oldsmobile Intrigue, Pontiac Grand Prix

Recommended Service	Service Interval In Miles①																																							
	3000	6000	7500	9000	12000	15000	18000	21000	22500	24000	27000	30000	33000	36000	37500	39000	42000	45000	48000	51000	52500	54000	57000	60000	63000	66000	67500	69000	72000	75000	78000	81000	82500	84000	87000	90000	93000	96000	97500	99000
BODY																																								
Inspect Lamps, Seat Belts & Warning Devices	At Least Once Every 6 Months																																							
Lubricate Hinges, Latches, Lock Cylinders & Strikers	At Engine Oil Changes Or At Least Every 12 Months																																							
Replace Passenger Compartment Air Filter						X						X						X						X						X						X				
BRAKES																																								
Inspect Brake System,	Every 6 Months																																							
Inspect Disc Brake Pads, Rotors, Shoes & Drums	At 7,500 Miles, Then Every 15,000 Miles																																							
Inspect Parking Brake Operation	At Least Once Every 12 Months																																							
Lubricate Parking Brake Cable Guides		S	N		S	N	S		N	S		X		S	N		S	N	S		N	S		X		S	N		S	N	S		N	S		X		S	N	
CLUTCH & TRANSAXLE																																								
Change Automatic Transmission Fluid & Filter	Normal Service Every 100,000 Miles; Severe Service Every 50,000 Miles																																							
Inspect Neutral Safety & BTSI & Lubricate Shift Linkage		S	N		S	N	S		N	S		X		S	N		S	N	S		N	S		X		S	N		S	N	S		N	S		X		S	N	
DRIVE AXLE & DRIVESHAFT																																								
Inspect CV Joint Boots	At Tire Rotations																																							

Recommended Service	Service Interval In Miles①																																							
	3000	6000	7500	9000	12000	15000	18000	21000	22500	24000	27000	30000	33000	36000	37500	39000	42000	45000	48000	51000	52500	54000	57000	60000	63000	66000	67500	69000	72000	75000	78000	81000	82500	84000	87000	90000	93000	96000	97500	99000
ENGINE																																								
Change Engine Coolant	Every 60 Months Or 150,000 Miles																																							
Change Engine Oil & Filter, Less Turbo②	S	S	N	S	S	X	S	S	N	S	S	X	S	S	N	S	S	X	S	S	N	S	S	X	S	S	N	S	S	X	S	S	N	S	S	X	S	S	N	S
Change Engine Oil & Filter, w/Turbo②	X	X		X	X	X	X	X		X	X	X	X	X		X	X	X	X	X		X	X	X	X	X		X	X	X	X	X		X	X	X	X	X		X
Inspect Drive Belts & EGR System, 1998												X												X												X				
Inspect Drive Belts & EGR System, 1999–2002	Inspect Every 60,000 Miles																																							
Inspect Exhaust System	At Engine Oil Changes																																							
Inspect Fuel Filler System & PCV												X												X												X				
Inspect Spark Plug Wires	At Spark Plug Changes																																							
Inspect TBI Unit Mounting Fastener Security		S	N																																					
Inspect Throttle Linkage Operation	At Air Cleaner Element Changes																																							
Replace Air Filter & PCV Filter						S						X						S						X						S						X				
Replace Spark Plugs	Every 100,000 Miles																																							
STEERING, SUSPENSION & TIRES																																								
Inspect Steering & Suspension System	At Tire Rotations																																							
Lubricate Chassis & Suspension		S	N		S	N	S		N	S		X		S	N		S	N	S		N	S		X		S	N		S	N	S		N	S		X		S	N	
Rotate Tires, 1998		S	N				S		N			S			N		S				N	S					X					S	N				S		N	
Rotate Tires, 1999–2002	Inspect For Wear And Rotate Every 7,500 Miles																																							

N — Normal Service
S — Severe Service
X — Normal Or Severe Service
BTSI — Brake Transmission Shift Interlock
IAC — Idle Air Control
ISC — Idle Speed Control System
① — After vehicle passes 99,000 mile mark return to beginning of mileage table & start cycle over again.
② — If equipped, the engine oil life monitor will indicate when to change engine oil, usually 3000–10,000 miles. Under severe driving conditions, engine oil may need to be changed before 3000 miles. If vehicle is driven in a dusty area, change engine oil every 3000 miles.

Buick LeSabre & Park Avenue, Oldsmobile Eighty-Eight, LSS & Regency & Pontiac Bonneville

	Service Interval In Miles①																																							
Recommended Service	3000	6000	7500	9000	12000	15000	18000	21000	22500	24000	27000	30000	33000	36000	37500	39000	42000	45000	48000	51000	52500	54000	57000	60000	63000	66000	67500	69000	72000	75000	78000	81000	82500	84000	87000	90000	93000	96000	97500	99000
BODY																																								
Clean Power Antenna Mast		S	N		S	N	S		N	S		X		S	N		S	N	S		N	S		X		S	N		S	N	S		N	S		X		S	N	
Flush Vehicle Underside, Inspect Drain Holes	At Least Every 12 Months																																							
Inspect Lamps & Seat Belts & Warning Devices	At Least Once Every 6 Months																																							
Lubricate Hinges, Latches, Lock Cylinders & Strikers	At Engine Oil Changes Or At Least Every 12 Months																																							
Replace Passenger Compartment Air Filter						X						X						X						X						X						X				
BRAKES																																								
Inspect Brake Fluid Level	Every 6 Months																																							
Inspect Brake System 1998	At 7,500 Miles, Then Every 15,000 Miles																																							
Inspect Brake System 1999–2002	Normal Service AT 7,500 Miles, Then Every 10,000 Miles Thereafter; Severe Service Every 7,500 Miles																																							
Inspect Parking Brake Operation	Once Every 12 Months																																							
Lubricate Parking Brake Cable Guides		S	N		S	N	S		N	S		X		S	N		S	N	S		N	S		X		S	N		S	N	S		N	S		X		S	N	
CLUTCH & TRANSAXLE																																								
Inspect Neutral Safety & BTSI & Lubricate Shift Linkage		S	N		S	N	S		N	S		X		S	N		S	N	S		N	S		X		S	N		S	N	S		N	S		X		S	N	
DRIVESHAFT																																								
Inspect CV Joint Boots	At Engine Oil Changes & Tire Rotations																																							
ENGINE																																								
Change Engine Coolant③	Every 60 Months Or 150,000 Miles																																							
Change Engine Oil & Filter②	S	S	N	S	S	X	S	S	N	S	S	X	S	S	N	S	S	X	S	S	N	S	S	X	S	S	N	S	S	X	S	S	N	S	S	X	S	S	N	S
Inspect Drive Belts & EGR System												X												X												X				
Inspect Exhaust System	At Engine Oil Changes																																							
Inspect Fuel System & PCV Valve & Supercharger Lubricant Level③												X												X												X				

Recommended Service	Service Interval In Miles①																																						
	3000	6000	7500	9000	12000	15000	18000	21000	22500	24000	27000	30000	33000	36000	37500	39000	42000	45000	48000	51000	52500	54000	57000	60000	63000	66000	67500	69000	72000	75000	78000	81000	82500	84000	87000	90000	93000	96000	97500	99000
ENGINE																																								
Inspect TBI Unit Mounting Fastener Security		S	N																																					
Inspect Thermostatically Controlled Air Cleaner Operation												X												X												X				
Inspect Throttle Linkage Operation	At Engine Oil Or Air Cleaner Element Changes																																							
Replace Air Filter & PCV Filter, 1998						S						X						S						X						S						X				
Replace Air Filter & PCV Filter, 1999–2002③	Every 30,000 Miles																																							
Replace Spark Plugs ③	Every 100,000 Miles																																							
STEERING, SUSPENSION & TIRES																																								
Inspect Power Steering Fluid Level & Suspension System	At Engine Oil Changes & Tire Rotations																																							
Lubricate Chassis & Suspension		S	N		S	N	S		N	S		X		S	N		S	N	S		N	S		X		S	N		S	N	S		N	S		X		S	N	
Rotate Tires, 1998		S	N				S		N			S			N		S				N	S					X					S	N				S		N	
Rotate Tires, 1999–2002	Normal Service Inspect For Wear & Rotate Every 7,500 Miles; Severe Service Every 6000 Miles																																							

N — Normal Service
S — Severe Service
X — Normal Or Severe Service
BTSI — Brake Transmission Shift Interlock
IAC — Idle Air Control
ISC — Idle Speed Control System

① — After vehicle passes 99,000 mile mark return to beginning of mileage table & start cycle over again.

② — If equipped, the engine oil life monitor will indicate when to change engine oil, usually 3,000–10,000 miles. Under severe driving conditions, engine oil may need to be changed before 3000 miles. If vehicle is driven in a dusty area, change engine oil every 3000 miles.

③ — The U.S. Environmental Protection Agency or the California Air Resources Board has determined the failure to perform this maintenance item will not nullify the emission warranty or limit recall liability prior to the completion of the vehicle's useful life. We, however, urge that all recommended maintenance services be performed at the indicated intervals and the maintenance be recorded.

Oldsmobile Aurora & Buick Riviera

Recommended Service	Service Interval In Miles① 3000	6000	7500	9000	12000	15000	18000	21000	22500	24000	27000	30000	33000	36000	37500	39000	42000	45000	48000	51000	52500	54000	57000	60000	63000	66000	67500	69000	72000	75000	78000	81000	82500	84000	87000	90000	93000	96000	97500	99000
BODY																																								
Clean Power Antenna Mast		S	N		S	N	S		N	S		X		S	N		S	N	S		N	S		X		S	N		S	N	S		N	S		X		S	N	
Inspect Lamps, Seat Belts & Warning Devices	At Least Every 6 Months																																							
Lubricate Hinges, Latches, Lock Cylinders & Strikers	At Engine Oil Changes Or At Least Every 12 Months																																							
Replace Passenger Compartment Air Filter						X						X						X						X						X						X				
BRAKES																																								
Inspect Brake System, 1998②	At 7,500 Miles, Then Every 15,000 Miles																																							
Inspect Brake System, 1999–2002②	At 7,500 Miles, Then Every 10,000 Miles Thereafter; Severe Service Every 7,500 Miles																																							
Inspect Parking Brake Operation	At Least Once Every 12 Months																																							
Lubricate Parking Brake Cable Guides		S	N		S	N	S		N	S		X		S	N		S	N	S		N	S		X		S	N		S	N	S		N	S		X		S	N	
CLUTCH & TRANSAXLE																																								
Change Automatic Transmission Fluid & Filter	No Normal Service Required; Severe Service Every 50,000 Miles																																							
Inspect Neutral Safety & BTSI Operation		S	N		S	N	S		N	S		X		S	N		S	N	S		N	S		X		S	N		S	N	S		N	S		X		S	N	
Lubricate Transmission Shift Linkage		S	N		S	N	S		N	S		X		S	N		S	N	S		N	S		X		S	N		S	N	S		N	S		X		S	N	
DRIVESHAFT																																								
Inspect CV Joint Boots	At Tire Rotations																																							
ENGINE																																								
Change Engine Coolant	Every 150,000 Miles																																							
Change Engine Oil & Filter	S	S	N	S	S	X	S	S	N	S	S	X	S	S	N	S	S	X	S	S	N	S	S	X	S	S	N	S	S	X	S	S	N	S	S	X	S	S	N	S
Inspect Drive Belts												X												X												X				
Inspect EGR System												X												X												X				
Inspect Exhaust System	At Engine Oil Changes																																							
Inspect Fuel Filler Cap												X												X												X				
Inspect Fuel System Hoses, Lines & Connections												X												X												X				
Inspect PCV Valve												X												X												X				
Inspect Spark Plug Wires	At Spark Plug Changes																																							

Recommended Service	Service Interval In Miles①																																						
	3000	6000	7500	9000	12000	15000	18000	21000	22500	24000	27000	30000	33000	36000	37500	39000	42000	45000	48000	51000	52500	54000	57000	60000	63000	66000	67500	69000	72000	75000	78000	81000	82500	84000	87000	90000	93000	96000	97500	99000
ENGINE																																								
Inspect Supercharger Lubricant Level												X												X												X				
Inspect Throttle Body Bores & Plates, Remove Any Deposits, 4.0L						X												X												X										
Inspect Throttle Linkage Operation	At Air Cleaner Element Changes																																							
Replace Air Filter & PCV Filter						S						X						S						X						S						X				
Replace Spark Plugs	Every 100,000 Miles																																							
STEERING, SUSPENSION & TIRES																																								
Inspect Steering & Suspension System	At Tire Rotations																																							
Lubricate Chassis & Suspension		S	N		S	N	S		N	S		X		S	N		S	N	S		N	S		X		S	N		S	N	S		N	S		X		S	N	
Rotate Tires, 1997–98		S	N				S		N			S			N		S				N	S					X					S	N				S		N	
Rotate Tires, 1999–2002	Normal Service Inspect for Wear & Rotate Every 7,500 Miles; Severe Service Every 6,000 Miles																																							

N — Normal Service
S — Severe Service
X — Normal Or Severe Service
BTSI — Brake Transmission Shift Interlock
IAC — Idle Air Control
ISC — Idle Speed Control System
① — After vehicle passes 99,000 mile mark return to beginning of mileage table & start cycle over again.
② — Inspect brakes every time wheels are removed.

Buick Skylark, Chevrolet Malibu, Oldsmobile Achieva, Alero & Cutlass & Pontiac Grand Am

Recommended Service	Service Interval In Miles①																																							
	3000	6000	7500	9000	12000	15000	18000	21000	22500	24000	27000	30000	33000	36000	37500	39000	42000	45000	48000	51000	52500	54000	57000	60000	63000	66000	67500	69000	72000	75000	78000	81000	82500	84000	87000	90000	93000	96000	97500	99000
BODY																																								
Clean Power Antenna Mast		S	N		S	N	S		N	S		X		S	N		S	N	S		N	S		X		S	N		S	N	S		N	S		X		S	N	
Inspect Lamps, Seat Belts & Warning Devices	At Least Once Every 6 Months																																							
Lubricate Hinges, Latches, Lock Cylinders & Strikers	At Engine Oil Changes Or At Least Every 12 Months																																							
Replace Passenger Compartment Air Filter						X						X						X						X						X						X				
BRAKES																																								
Inspect Brake System, 1998	At 7,500 Miles, Then Every 15,000 Miles																																							
Inspect Brake System, 1999–2002	Every 7500 Miles																																							
Inspect Parking Brake Operation	At Least Once Every 12 Months																																							
Lubricate Parking Brake Cable Guides		S	N		S	N	S		N	S		X		S	N		S	N	S		N	S		X		S	N		S	N	S		N	S		X		S	N	
CLUTCH & TRANSAXLE																																								
Change Automatic Transmission Fluid & Filter, 1997–99	No Normal Service Required; Severe Service Every 50,000 Miles																																							
Change Automatic Transmission Fluid & Filter, 2000–02	Normal Service Every 100,000 Miles; Severe Service Every 50,000 Miles																																							
Inspect Neutral Safety & BTSI Operation & Lubricate Shift Linkage		S	N		S	N	S		N	S		X		S	N		S	N	S		N	S		X		S	N		S	N	S		N	S		X		S	N	
DRIVESHAFT																																								
Inspect CV Joint Boots	At Engine Oil Changes & Tire Rotations																																							
ENGINE																																								
Change Engine Coolant	Every 150,000 Miles																																							
Change Engine Oil & Filter, Less Turbo②	S	S	N	S	S	X	S	S	N	S	S	X	S	S	N	S	S	X	S	S	N	S	S	X	S	S	N	S	S	X	S	S	N	S	S	X	S	S	N	S
Change Engine Oil & Filter, w/Turbo②	X	X		X	X	X	X	X		X	X	X	X	X		X	X	X	X	X		X	X	X	X	X		X	X	X	X	X		X	X	X	X	X		X

Service Interval In Miles①

Recommended Service	3000	6000	7500	9000	12000	15000	18000	21000	22500	24000	27000	30000	33000	36000	37500	39000	42000	45000	48000
ENGINE																			
Inspect Drive Belts & EGR System, 1998												X							
Inspect Drive Belts & EGR System, 1999–2002	Every 60,000 Miles																		
Inspect Exhaust System	At Engine Oil Changes																		
Inspect Spark Plug Wires	At Spark Plug Changes																		
Inspect Thermostatically Controlled Air Cleaner Operation & Fuel & PCV System												X							
Inspect Throttle Linkage Operation	At Air Cleaner Element Changes																		
Replace Air Filter & PCV Filter, 1998						S						X						S	
Replace Air Filter & PCV Filter, 1999–2002③	Every 30,000 Miles																		
Replace Spark Plugs③	Every 100,000 Miles																		
Replace Timing Belt																			
STEERING, SUSPENSION & TIRES																			
Inspect Steering & Suspension System	At Tire Rotations																		
Lubricate Chassis & Suspension		S	N		S	N	S		N	S		X		S	N		S	N	S
Rotate Tires, 1998		S	N				S		N			S			N		S		
Rotate Tires, 1999–2002	Inspect for Wear and Rotate Every 7500 Miles																		

Recommended Service	51000	52500	54000	57000	60000	63000	66000	67500	69000	72000	75000	78000	81000	82500	84000	87000	90000	93000	96000	97500	99000
ENGINE																					
Inspect Drive Belts & EGR System, 1998					X												X				
Inspect Thermostatically Controlled Air Cleaner Operation & Fuel & PCV System					X												X				
Replace Air Filter & PCV Filter, 1998					X						S						X				
Replace Timing Belt					X																
STEERING, SUSPENSION & TIRES																					
Lubricate Chassis & Suspension		N	S		X		S	N		S	N	S		N	S		X		S	N	
Rotate Tires, 1998		N	S					X					S	N				S		N	

N — Normal Service
S — Severe Service
X — Normal Or Severe Service
BTSI — Brake Transmission Shift Interlock
IAC — Idle Air Control
ISC — Idle Speed Control System

① — After vehicle passes 99,000 mile mark return to beginning of mileage table & start cycle over again.

② — If equipped, the engine oil life monitor will indicate when to change engine oil, usually 3,000–10,000 miles. Under severe driving conditions, engine oil may need to be changed before 3000 miles. If vehicle is driven in a dusty area, change engine oil every 3000 miles.

③ — The U.S. Environmental Protection Agency or the California air Resources Board has determined the failure to perform this maintenance item will not nullify the emission warranty or limit recall liability prior to the completion of the vehicle's useful life. We, however, urge that all recommended maintenance services be performed at the indicated intervals and the maintenance be recorded.

Cadillac Catera

Recommended Service	Service Interval In Miles① 3000	6000	7500	9000	12000	15000	18000	21000	22500	24000	27000	30000	33000	36000	37500	39000	42000	45000	48000	51000	52500	54000	57000	60000	63000	66000	67500	69000	72000	75000	78000	81000	82500	84000	87000	90000	93000	96000	97500	99000
BODY																																								
Flush Vehicle Underside, Inspect Drain Holes	At Least Every 12 Months, Especially In Winter & Springtime																																						
Inspect Lamps, Seat Belts & Warning Devices	At Least Once Every 6 Months																																						
Lubricate Hinges, Latches, Lock Cylinders & Strikers	At Engine Oil Changes Or At Least Every 12 Months																																						
Replace Passenger Compartment Air Filter						X						X						X						X						X						X				
BRAKES																																								
Inspect Brake System, 1998	At 7,500 Miles, Then Every 15,000 Miles																																						
Inspect Brake System, 1999–2001	Every 5000 Miles																																						
Inspect Parking Brake Operation	At Least Once Every 12 Months																																						
Lubricate Parking Brake Cable Guides		S	N		S	N	S		N	S		X		S	N		S	N	S		N	S		X		S	N		S	N	S		N	S		X		S	N	
CLUTCH & TRANSAXLE																																								
Change Automatic Transmission Fluid & Filter②	Every 50,000 Miles																																						
Inspect Neutral Safety & BTSI Operation		S	N		S	N	S		N	S		X		S	N		S	N	S		N	S		X		S	N		S	N	S		N	S		X		S	N	
Lubricate Transmission Shift Linkage		S	N		S	N	S		N	S		X		S	N		S	N	S		N	S		X		S	N		S	N	S		N	S		X		S	N	
ENGINE																																								
Change Engine Coolant	Every 60 Months Or 150,000 Miles																																						
Change Engine Oil & Filter	Normal Service Initially At 5000 Miles, Then Every 10,000 Miles Thereafter; Severe Service Every 5000 Miles																																						
Inspect Air Cleaner Element						X												X												X						X				
Inspect Drive Belts, 1998												X												X												X				
Inspect Drive Belts, 1999–2001	Every 60,000 Miles																																						
Inspect EGR System												X												X												X				
Inspect Exhaust System	At Engine Oil Changes																																						
Inspect Fuel Filler Cap												X												X												X				
Inspect Fuel System Hoses, Lines & Connections												X												X												X				
Inspect PCV Valve												X												X												X				
Inspect Spark Plug Wires	At Spark Plug Changes																																						

Recommended Service	3000	6000	7500	9000	12000	15000	18000	21000	22500	24000	27000	30000	33000	36000	37500	39000	42000	45000	48000	51000	52500	54000	57000	60000	63000	66000	67500	69000	72000	75000	78000	81000	82500	84000	87000	90000	93000	96000	97500	99000
ENGINE																																								
Replace Air Filter & PCV Filter, 1998						S						X						S						X						S						X				
Replace Air Filter & PCV Filter, 1999–2001	Every 30,000 Miles																																							
Replace Fuel Filter	Every 100,000 Miles																																							
Replace Spark Plugs	Every 100,000 Miles																																							
Replace Timing Belt	Replace Every 100,000 Miles Under Normal Operating Conditions; Replace Every 60,000 Miles If Driven Without An Engine Coolant Heater At Ambient Temperatures Of −20°F Or Less, Then Inspect At 15,000 Mile Intervals.																																							
STEERING, SUSPENSION & TIRES																																								
Inspect Steering & Suspension System	At Tire Rotations																																							
Lubricate Chassis & Suspension		S	N		S	N	S		N	S		X		S	N		S	N	S		N	S		X		S	N		S	N	S		N	S		X		S	N	
Rotate Tires	Initial Service At 5000 Miles, Then Every 10,000 Miles Thereafter																																							

(Column headings: Service Interval In Miles①)

N — Normal Service
S — Severe Service
X — Normal Or Severe Service
BTSI — Brake Transmission Shift Interlock
IAC — Idle Air Control
ISC — Idle Speed Control System
① — After vehicle passes 99,000 mile mark return to beginning of mileage table & start cycle over again.
② — If driven in heavy city traffic where temperature reaches 90° F, in hilly or mountainous terrain, frequent towing of a trailer or any high performance operation.

Chevrolet Cavalier & Pontiac Sunfire

Recommended Service	Service Interval In Miles①																																							
	3000	6000	7500	9000	12000	15000	18000	21000	22500	24000	27000	30000	33000	36000	37500	39000	42000	45000	48000	51000	52500	54000	57000	60000	63000	66000	67500	69000	72000	75000	78000	81000	82500	84000	87000	90000	93000	96000	97500	99000
BODY																																								
Inspect Lamps, Seat Belt & Warning Devices	At Least Once Every 6 Months																																							
Lubricate Hinges, Latches, Lock Cylinders & Strikers	At Engine Oil Changes Or At Least Every 12 Months																																							
Replace Passenger Compartment Air Filter						X						X						X												X						X				
BRAKES																																								
Inspect Brake System, 1998	At 7,500 Miles, Then Every 15,000 Miles																																							
Inspect Brake System, 1999–2002	Normal Service At 7,500 Miles, Then Every 10,000 Miles Thereafter; Severe Service Every 7,500 Miles																																							
Inspect Parking Brake Operation	At Least Once Every 12 Months																																							
Lubricate Parking Brake Cable Guides		S	N		S	N	S		N	S		X		S	N		S	N	S		N	S				S	N		S	N	S		N	S		X		S	N	
CLUTCH & TRANSAXLE																																								
Change Automatic Transmission Fluid & Filter	No Normal Service Required; Severe Service Every 50,000 Miles																																							
Inspect Neutral Safety & BTSI Operation & Lubricate Shift Linkage		S	N		S	N	S		N	S		X		S	N		S	N	S		N	S				S	N		S	N	S		N	S		X		S	N	
DRIVESHAFT																																								
Inspect CV Joint Boots	At Tire Rotations																																							
ENGINE																																								
Change Engine Coolant	Every 60 Months Or 150,000 Miles																																							
Change Engine Oil & Filter, Less Turbo	S	S	N	S	S	X	S	S	N	S	S	X	S	S	N	S	S	X	S	S	N	S	S		S	S	N	S	S	X	S	S	N	S	S	X	S	S	N	S
Change Engine Oil & Filter, w/Turbo	X	X		X	X	X	X	X		X	X	X	X	X		X	X	X	X	X		X	X		X	X		X	X	X	X	X		X	X	X	X	X		X
Inspect Drive Belts & EGR System & Fuel & PCV System												X																								X				
Inspect Exhaust System	At Engine Oil Changes																																							
Inspect Spark Plug Wires	At Spark Plug Changes																																							
Inspect Thermostatically Controlled Air Cleaner Operation												X																								X				

Recommended Service	Service Interval In Miles① 3000	6000	7500	9000	12000	15000	18000	21000	22500	24000	27000	30000	33000	36000	37500	39000	42000	45000	48000	51000	52500	54000	57000	60000	63000	66000	67500	69000	72000	75000	78000	81000	82500	84000	87000	90000	93000	96000	97500	99000
ENGINE																																								
Inspect Throttle Linkage Operation	At Engine Oil Or Air Cleaner Element Changes																																							
Replace Air Filter & PCV Filter						S						X						S												S						X				
Replace Spark Plugs	Every 100,000 Miles																																							
STEERING, SUSPENSION & TIRES																																								
Inspect Steering & Suspension System	At Tire Rotations																																							
Lubricate Chassis & Suspension		S	N		S	N	S		N	S		X		S	N		S	N	S		N	S				S	N		S	N	S		N	S		X		S	N	
Rotate Tires, 1998		S	N				S		N			S			N		S				N	S					X					S	N				S		N	
Rotate Tires, 1999–2002	Normal Service Inspect For Wear & Rotate Every 7,500 Miles; Severe Service Every 6,000 Miles																																							

N — Normal Service
S — Severe Service
X — Normal Or Severe Service
BTSI — Brake Transmission Shift Interlock
IAC — Idle Air Control
ISC — Idle Speed Control System
① — After vehicle passes 99,000 mile mark return to beginning of mileage table & start cycle over again.

Chevrolet Camaro & Pontiac Firebird

Recommended Service	Service Interval In Miles① 3000	6000	7500	9000	12000	15000	18000	21000	22500	24000	27000	30000	33000	36000	37500	39000	42000	45000	48000	51000	52500	54000	57000	60000	63000	66000	67500	69000	72000	75000	78000	81000	82500	84000	87000	90000	93000	96000	97500	99000
BODY																																								
Clean Power Antenna Mast		S	N		S	N	S		N	S		X		S	N		S	N	S		N	S		X		S	N		S	N	S		N	S		X		S	N	
Flush Vehicle Underside, Inspect Drain Holes	At Least Every 12 Months																																							
Inspect Lamps, Seat Belts & Warning Devices	At Least Once Every 6 Months																																							
Lubricate Hinges, Latches, Lock Cylinders & Strikers	At Engine Oil Changes Or At Least Every 12 Months																																							
Replace Passenger Compartment Air Filter						X						X						X						X						X						X				

Recommended Service	Service Interval In Miles①																																							
	3000	6000	7500	9000	12000	15000	18000	21000	22500	24000	27000	30000	33000	36000	37500	39000	42000	45000	48000	51000	52500	54000	57000	60000	63000	66000	67500	69000	72000	75000	78000	81000	82500	84000	87000	90000	93000	96000	97500	99000
BRAKES																																								
Inspect Brake System, 1998	At 7,500 Miles, Then Every 15,000 Miles																																							
Inspect Brake System, 1999–2002	Normal Service At 7,500 Miles, Then Every 10,000 Miles Thereafter; Severe Service Every 7,500 Miles																																							
Inspect Parking Brake Operation	At Least Once Every 12 Months																																							
Lubricate Parking Brake Cable Guides		S	N		S	N	S		N	S		X		S	N		S	N	S		N	S		X		S	N		S	N	S		N	S		X		S	N	
CLUTCH & TRANSAXLE																																								
Change Automatic Transmission Fluid & Filter	Normal Service Every 100,000 Miles; Severe Service Every 50,000 Miles																																							
Inspect Neutral Safety & BTSI Operation		S	N		S	N	S		N	S		X		S	N		S	N	S		N	S		X		S	N		S	N	S		N	S		X		S	N	
Lubricate Transmission Shift Linkage		S	N		S	N	S		N	S		X		S	N		S	N	S		N	S		X		S	N		S	N	S		N	S		X		S	N	
ENGINE																																								
Change Engine Coolant	Every 60 Months Or 150,000 Miles																																							
Change Engine Oil & Filter	S	S	N	S	S	X	S	S	N	S	S	X	S	S	N	S	S	X	S	S	N	S	S	X	S	S	N	S	S	X	S	S	N	S	S	X	S	S	N	S
Inspect Drive Belts												X												X												X				
Inspect EGR System												X												X												X				
Inspect Exhaust System	At Engine Oil Changes																																							
Inspect Fuel Filler Cap												X												X												X				
Inspect Fuel System Hoses, Lines & Connections												X												X												X				
Inspect PCV Valve												X												X												X				
Inspect Spark Plug Wires	At Spark Plug Changes																																							
Inspect TBI Unit Mounting Fastener Security		S	N																																					
Inspect Thermostatically Controlled Air Cleaner Operation												X												X												X				
Inspect Throttle Linkage Operation	At Air Cleaner Element Changes																																							
Replace Air Filter & PCV Filter, 1998	Normal Service Every 36 Months Or 30,000 Miles; More Frequently In Severe Service Or Dusty Conditions																																							
Replace Air Filter & PCV Filter, 1999–2002②	Inspect and Replace If Necessary Every 10,000 Miles.																																							
Replace Spark Plugs	Every 100,000 Miles																																							

Recommended Service	Service Interval In Miles①																																							
	3000	6000	7500	9000	12000	15000	18000	21000	22500	24000	27000	30000	33000	36000	37500	39000	42000	45000	48000	51000	52500	54000	57000	60000	63000	66000	67500	69000	72000	75000	78000	81000	82500	84000	87000	90000	93000	96000	97500	99000
STEERING, SUSPENSION & TIRES																																								
Inspect Steering & Suspension System	At Tire Rotations																																							
Lubricate Chassis & Suspension		S	N		S	N	S		N	S		X		S	N		S	N	S		N	S		X		S	N		S	N	S		N	S		X		S	N	
Rotate Tires, 1998		S	N				S		N			S			N		S				N	S					X					S	N				S		N	
Rotate Tires, 1999–2002	Normal Service Inspect For Wear & Rotate Every 7,500 Miles; Severe Service Every 6,000 Miles																																							

N — Normal Service
S — Severe Service
X — Normal Or Severe Service
BTSI — Brake Transmission Shift Interlock
IAC — Idle Air Control
ISC — Idle Speed Control System
① — After vehicle passes 99,000 mile mark return to beginning of mileage table & start cycle over again.
② — The U.S. environmental Protection Agency or the California Air Resources Board has determined the failure to perform this maintenance item will not nullify the emission warranty or limit recall liability prior to the completion of the vehicle's useful life. We, however, urge that all recommended maintenance services be performed at the indicated intervals and the maintenance be recorded.

Chevrolet Corvette

Recommended Service	Service Interval In Miles①																																							
	3000	6000	7500	9000	12000	15000	18000	21000	22500	24000	27000	30000	33000	36000	37500	39000	42000	45000	48000	51000	52500	54000	57000	60000	63000	66000	67500	69000	72000	75000	78000	81000	82500	84000	87000	90000	93000	96000	97500	99000
BODY																																								
Clean Power Antenna Mast		S	N		S	N	S		N	S		X		S	N		S	N	S		N	S		X		S	N		S	N	S		N	S		X		S	N	
Inspect Lamps, Seat Belts & Warning Devices	At Least Once Every 6 Months																																							
Lubricate Hinges, Latches, Lock Cylinders & Strikers	At Engine Oil Changes Or At Least Every 12 Months																																							
Replace Passenger Compartment Air Filter						X						X						X						X						X						X				
BRAKES																																								
Inspect Brake System, 1998	At 7,500 Miles, Then Every 15,000 Miles																																							
Inspect Brake System, 1999–2002	Normal Service At 7,500 Miles, Then Every 10,000 Miles Thereafter; Severe Service Every 7,500 Miles																																							

Recommended Service	Service Interval In Miles①																																						
	3000	6000	7500	9000	12000	15000	18000	21000	22500	24000	27000	30000	33000	36000	37500	39000	42000	45000	48000	51000	52500	54000	57000	60000	63000	66000	67500	69000	72000	75000	78000	81000	82500	84000	87000	90000	93000	96000	97500	99000
BRAKES																																								
Inspect Parking Brake Operation	At Least Once Every 12 Months																																							
Lubricate Parking Brake Cable Guides		S	N		S	N	S		N	S		X		S	N		S	N	S		N	S		X		S	N		S	N	S		N	S		X		S	N	
CLUTCH & TRANSAXLE																																								
Change Automatic Transmission Fluid & Filter	No Normal Service Required; Severe Service Every 50,000 Miles																																							
Inspect Neutral Safety & BTSI Operation & Lubricate Shift Linkage		S	N		S	N	S		N	S		X		S	N		S	N	S		N	S		X		S	N		S	N	S		N	S		X		S	N	
ENGINE																																								
Change Engine Coolant	Every 60 Months Or 150,000 Miles																																							
Change Engine Oil & Filter②	Normal Service Every 12 Months Or 10,000 Miles; Severe Service Every 3000 Miles																																							
Inspect Air Cleaner Element, 1998	Every 10,000 Miles, Replace Every 30,000 Miles																																							
Inspect Air Cleaner Element, 1999–2002②	Inspect At 15,000 Miles, Replace Every 30,000 Miles																																							
Inspect Drive Belts, EGR, Fuel & PCV System												X												X												X				
Inspect Exhaust System	At Engine Oil Changes																																							
Inspect Spark Plug Wires	At Spark Plug Changes																																							
Inspect TBI Unit Mounting Fastener Security		S	N																																					
Inspect Thermostatically Controlled Air Cleaner Operation												X												X												X				
Inspect Throttle Linkage Operation	At Air Cleaner Element Changes																																							
Replace Air Filter & PCV Filter, 1998						S						X						S						X						S						X				
Replace Spark Plugs	Every 100,000 Miles																																							
STEERING, SUSPENSION & TIRES																																								
Inspect Steering & Suspension System	At Tire Rotations																																							
Lubricate Chassis & Suspension		S	N		S	N	S		N	S		X		S	N		S	N	S		N	S		X		S	N		S	N	S		N	S		X		S	N	

N — Normal Service

S — Severe Service

X — Normal Or Severe Service

BTSI — Brake Transmission Shift Interlock
IAC — Idle Air Control
ISC — Idle Speed Control System
① — After vehicle passes 99,000 mile mark return to beginning of mileage table & start cycle over again.
② — The U.S. Environmental Protection Agency or the California air Resources Board has determined the failure to perform this maintenance item will no nullify the emissions warranty or limit recall liability prior to the completion of the vehicle's useful life. We, however, urge that all recommended maintenance services be performed at the indicated intervals and the maintenance be recorded.

Chevrolet Metro

Recommended Service	Service Interval In Miles①																																							
	3000	6000	7500	9000	12000	15000	18000	21000	22500	24000	27000	30000	33000	36000	37500	39000	42000	45000	48000	51000	52500	54000	57000	60000	63000	66000	67500	69000	72000	75000	78000	81000	82500	84000	87000	90000	93000	96000	97500	99000
BODY																																								
Inspect Seat Belts & Related Components & Lubricate Lock Cylinders	At Least Once Every 12 Months																																							
Inspect Supplemental Restraint System	10 Years From Vehicle Build Date																																							
Inspect Warning Lamps & Devices	S	S	N	S	S	X	S	S	N	S	S	X	S	S	N	S	S	X	S	S	N	S	S	X	S	S	N	S	S	X	S	S	N	S	S	X	S	S	N	S
Lubricate Door Hinges	At Every Engine Oil Change																																							
BRAKES																																								
Change Brake Fluid																								X																
Inspect Brake System		S	N		S				N	S				S	N				S		N			S			N		S				N	S				S	N	
CLUTCH & TRANSAXLE																																								
Change Automatic Transaxle Fluid & Filter	No Normal Service Interval Recommended By Manufacturer; Severe Service Every 50,000 Miles																																							
Change Manual Transaxle Lubricant					S					S		N		S					S					X					S					S		N		S		
Inspect Clutch Pedal Freeplay		S	N		S	N	S		N	S		X		S	N		S	N	S		N	S		X		S	N		S	N	S		N	S		X		S	N	
Inspect Neutral Safety & Shift Interlock Switch Operation	At Least Once Every 12 Months																																							
Inspect Transaxle Fluid & Shift Control Operation	At Every Engine Oil Change																																							
Replace Automatic Transaxle Fluid Cooler Hoses																		X																		X				
DRIVESHAFT																																								
Inspect CV Joint Boots		S	N		S	N	S		N	S		X			N		S	N	S		N	S		X		S	N		S	N	S		N	S		X		S	N	
ENGINE																																								
Change Engine Coolant & Inspect Ignition Coils												X												X												X				

Recommended Service	Service Interval In Miles①																																							
	3000	6000	7500	9000	12000	15000	18000	21000	22500	24000	27000	30000	33000	36000	37500	39000	42000	45000	48000	51000	52500	54000	57000	60000	63000	66000	67500	69000	72000	75000	78000	81000	82500	84000	87000	90000	93000	96000	97500	99000
ENGINE																																								
Change Engine Oil & Filter	S	S	N	S	S	X	S	S	N	S	S	X	S		N	S	S	X	S	S	N	S	S	X	S	S	N	S	S	X	S	S	N	S	S	X	S	S	N	S
Inspect Air Filter Element	S	S		S	S	S	S	S		S	S	S	S			S	S	S	S	S		S	S	S	S	S		S	S	S	S	S		S	S	S	S	S		S
Inspect Distributor Cap & Rotor & Drive Belts & PCV valve						S						S						S						X						S						S				
Inspect Engine Valve Clearance						X						X						X						X						X						X				
Inspect Exhaust, Fuel & EVAP System & Coolant						X						X						X						X						X						X				
Inspect Spark Plug Wires						S						S						S												S						S				
Inspect Warning Lamps	S	S	N	S	S	X	S	S	N	S	S	X	S		N	S	S	X	S	S	N	S	S	X	S	S	N	S	S	X	S	S	N	S	S	X	S	S	N	S
Replace Engine Air Filter Element & PCV Filter	Normal Service Every 30,000 Miles; More Frequently In Severe Service Or Dusty Conditions																																							
Replace EVAP Canister Filter	Every 10 Years Or 120,000 Miles																																							
Replace Fuel Filter, 1998	Every 10 Years Or 120,000 Miles																																							
Replace Fuel Filter, 1999–2002	Every 100,000 Miles																																							
Replace Spark Plugs												X												X												X				
Replace Spark Plug Wires																								X																
STEERING, SUSPENSION & TIRES																																								
Inspect Power Steering, Steering & Suspension & Wheel Bearings		S	N		S	N	S		N	S		X			N		S	N	S		N	S		X		S	N		S	N	S		N	S		X		S	N	
Lubricate Chassis & Suspension	At Every Engine Oil Change																																							
Rotate Tires, 1998		S	N		S	N	S		N	S		X			N		S	N	S		N	S		X		S	N		S	N	S		N	S		X		S	N	
Rotate Tires, 1999–2002	Inspect For Wear & Rotate Every 6000 Miles																																							

N — Normal Service
S — Severe Service
X — Normal Or Severe Service
① — After vehicle passes 99,000 mile mark return to beginning of mileage table & start cycle over again.

Chevrolet Prizm

Recommended Service	Service Interval In Miles①																																							
	3000	6000	7500	9000	12000	15000	18000	21000	22500	24000	27000	30000	33000	36000	37500	39000	42000	45000	48000	51000	52500	54000	57000	60000	63000	66000	67500	69000	72000	75000	78000	81000	82500	84000	87000	90000	93000	96000	97500	99000
BODY																																								
Inspect Body Fastener Security	Severe Service Every 5000 Miles																																							
Inspect Seat Belts & Related Components	At Least Once Every 12 Months																																							
Supplemental Restraint System	10 Years From Vehicle Build Date, Then Every 24 Months Thereafter																																							
Inspect Lamps & Warning Devices	S	S	N	S	S	X	S	S	N	S	S	X	S	S	N	S	S	X	S	S	N	S	S	X	S	S	N	S	S	X	S	S	N	S	S	X	S	S	N	S
Lubricate Lock Cylinders	At Least Once Every 12 Months																																							
BRAKES																																								
Inspect Brake System Hoses, Lines & Connections	Normal Service Every 15,000 Miles; Severe Service Every 5000 Miles																																							
CLUTCH & TRANSAXLE																																								
Change Automatic Transmission Fluid & Filter						X						X						X						X						X						X				
Change Differential & Manual Transaxle Lubricant						S						S						S						S						S						S				
Inspect Neutral Safety & Shift Interlock Switch Operation	At Least Once Every 12 Months																																							
Inspect Transaxle Lubricant Level	At Every Engine Oil Change																																							
DRIVESHAFT																																								
Inspect CV Joint Boots & Tighten Driveshaft Flange	Normal Service Every 15,000 Miles; Severe Service Every 5000 Miles																																							
ENGINE																																								
Change Engine Coolant②	Every 24 Months Or 30,000 Miles																																							
Change Engine Oil & Filter	Normal Service Every 7500 Miles; Severe Service Every 3 Months or 3000 Miles																																							
Inspect Cooling System & Drive Belts						X						X						X						X						X						X				
Inspect Engine Valve Clearance																								X																
Inspect EVAP Charcoal Canister	Every 72 Months Or 60,000 Miles																																							
Inspect EVAP & Fuel System						X						X						X						X						X						X				
Inspect Exhaust System					X						X						X						X						X						X					
Inspect Thermostatic Air Cleaner System Operation												X												X												X				

Recommended Service	Service Interval In Miles①																																						
	3000	6000	7500	9000	12000	15000	18000	21000	22500	24000	27000	30000	33000	36000	37500	39000	42000	45000	48000	51000	52500	54000	57000	60000	63000	66000	67500	69000	72000	75000	78000	81000	82500	84000	87000	90000	93000	96000	97500	99000
ENGINE																																								
Replace Air Filter Element & PCV Filter	Normal Service Every 30,000 Miles; More Frequently In Severe Service Or Dusty Conditions																																							
Replace Spark Plugs (Standard Type)												X												X												X				
Replace Spark Plugs (Platinum Tip Type)																								X																
STEERING, SUSPENSION & TIRES																																								
Inspect Chassis Fastener Security	Severe Service Every 5000 Miles																																							
Inspect Steering & Suspension			S			X			S			X			S			X			S			X			S			X			S			X			S	
Lubricate Chassis & Suspension & Rotate Tires	At Every Engine Oil Change																																							
Lubricate Chassis & Suspension & Rotate Tires	Every 6000 Miles																																							

N — Normal Service
S — Severe Service
X — Normal Or Severe Service
① — After vehicle passes 99,000 mile mark return to beginning of mileage table & start cycle over again.
② — The U. S. Environmental Protection Agency or the California Air Resources Board has determined that the failure to perform this maintenance item will not nullify the emission warranty or limit recall liability prior to the completion of the vehicle's useful life. We, however, urge that all recommended maintenance services be performed at the indicated intervals and the maintenance be recorded.

Saturn

Service Interval In Miles①

Recommended Service	3000	6000	7500	9000	12000	15000	18000	21000	22500	24000	27000	30000	33000	36000	37500	39000	42000	45000	48000	51000	52500	54000	57000	60000	63000	66000	67500	69000	72000	75000	78000	81000	82500	84000	87000	90000	93000	96000	97500	99000
BODY																																								
Inspect Seat Belts & Restraint Systems	At Least Once Every 6 Months																																							
Inspect Wiper Blades & Inserts	At Least Once Every 6 Months																																							
Lubricate Door Check Straps & Hinges		X		X		X		X		X		X		X		X		X		X		X		X		X		X		X		X		X		X		X		X
Lubricate Hood Latch		X		X		X		X		X		X		X		X		X		X		X		X		X		X		X		X		X		X		X		X
Lubricate Headlamp Doors		X		X		X		X		X		X		X		X		X		X		X		X		X		X		X		X		X		X		X		X
Lubricate Sunroof		X		X		X		X		X		X		X		X		X		X		X		X		X		X		X		X		X		X		X		X
BRAKES																																								
Inspect Disc Brake Calipers For Freedom Of Movement (Lubricate If Required)		X				X				X				X				X				X				X				X				X				X		
Inspect Disc Brake Pads & Rotors		X				X				X				X				X				X				X				X				X				X		
Inspect Brake Drums & Shoes		X				X				X				X				X				X				X				X				X				X		
Inspect Brake Hoses, Lines & Connections		X				X				X				X				X				X				X				X				X				X		
CLUTCH & TRANSAXLE																																								
Change Automatic Transaxle Fluid & Filter										X										X										X										X
Change Manual Transaxle Lubricant	Once Only At 6000 Miles																																							
DRIVESHAFT																																								
Inspect CV Joint Boots		X		X		X		X		X		X		X		X		X		X		X		X		X		X		X		X		X		X		X		X
ENGINE																																								
Change Engine Coolant & Inspect Pressure Cap	Every 60 Months Or 100,000 Miles																																							
Change Engine Oil & Filter	S	X	S	X	S	X	S	X	S	X	S	X	S	X	S	X	S	X	S	X	S	X	S	X	S	X	S	X	S	X	S	X	S	X	S	X	S	X	S	X
Inspect Cooling System & Protection Level						X						X						X						X						X						X				
Inspect Drive Belts						X						X						X						X						X						X				
Inspect Emission Hoses, Lines & Connections										X										X										X										X
Inspect Exhaust System		X		X		X		X		X		X		X		X		X		X		X		X		X		X		X		X		X		X		X		X
Inspect Fuel Hoses, Lines & Connections										X										X										X										X

Recommended Service	Service Interval In Miles①																																							
	3000	6000	7500	9000	12000	15000	18000	21000	22500	24000	27000	30000	33000	36000	37500	39000	42000	45000	48000	51000	52500	54000	57000	60000	63000	66000	67500	69000	72000	75000	78000	81000	82500	84000	87000	90000	93000	96000	97500	99000
ENGINE																																								
Inspect Fuel Tank Filler Cap										X										X										X										X
Replace Air Filter	Normal Service Every 30,000 Miles; More Frequently In Severe Service Or Dusty Conditions																																							
Replace Fuel Filter, 1998																				X																				X
Replace Fuel Filter, 1999–2002	Every 100,000 Miles																																							
Replace Spark Plugs										X										X										X										X
STEERING, SUSPENSION & TIRES																																								
Inspect Ball Joint Seals		X		X		X		X		X		X		X		X		X		X		X		X		X		X		X		X		X		X		X		X
Inspect Suspension		X		X		X		X		X		X		X		X		X		X		X		X		X		X		X		X		X		X		X		X
Rotate Tires		X				X				X				X				X				X				X				X				X				X		

N — Normal Service
S — Severe Service
X — Normal Or Severe Service
BTSI — Brake Transaxle Shift Interlock
① — After vehicle passes 120,000 mile mark return to beginning of mileage table & start cycle over again.

DAIMLERCHRYSLER CORP.

DAIMLERCHRYSLER CORP.

AVENGER, SEBRING COUPE & 2001–02 STRATUS COUPE

NOTE: Refer To The Rear Of This Manual For Vehicle Manufacturers Special Service Tool Suppliers.

INDEX OF SERVICE OPERATIONS

Specifications

GENERAL ENGINE SPECIFICATIONS

Year	Engine		Fuel System	Bore x Stroke, Inches	Comp. Ratio	Net HP @ RPM	Maximum Torque, Ft. Lbs. @ RPM	Normal Oil Pressure @ Idle, psi
	Liter	VIN Code①						
1998–1999	2.0L	Y	SMFI	3.44 x 3.27	9.6	140 @ 6000	130 @ 4800	4.0
1998–2000	2.5L	N	SMFI	3.29 x 2.99	9.5	163 @ 5500	170 @ 4400	11.4
2001–02	2.4L	G	MFI	3.41 x 3.94	9.0	②	158 @ 4000	11.4
	3.0L	H	MFI	3.59 x 2.99	9.0	200 @ 5500	205 @ 4500	11.6

MFI — Multi-Port Fuel Injection
SMFI — Sequential Multi-Port Fuel Injection

① — Eighth digit of Vehicle Identification Number (VIN) denotes engine code.

② — Manual transmission, 147 bhp @ 5500 RPM; automatic transmission, 150 bhp @ 5500 RPM.

TUNE UP SPECIFICATIONS

Engine Liter	Spark Plug Gap, Inch	Firing Order④	Ignition Timing °BTDC			Curb Idle Speed①		Fuel Pump Pressure, psi.③	Valve Lash, Inch
			Man. Trans.	Auto. Trans.	Mark Fig.	Man. Trans.	Auto. Trans.		
2.0L	.048–.053	A	12②	12②	⑤	800⑥	800⑥	47–50	⑦
2.4L	.039–.043	1-3-4-2	10	10	⑤	700⑥	700⑥	47–50	⑦
2.5L	.039–.043	B	—	10②	⑤	750⑥	750⑥	47–50	⑦
3.0L	.039–.043	1-2-3-4-5-6	15	15	⑤	700⑥	700⑥	47–50	⑦

BTDC — Before Top Dead Center.

① — When adjusting idle speed, set parking brake & chock drive wheels.

② — Direct (Distributorless) Ignition System (DIS), not adjustable.

③ — Remove rear seat cushion, then the protector. Disconnect fuel pump connector. Start engine & let run until it stops naturally, then turn ignition to Off. Connect fuel pump connector, install protector & rear seat cushion. Remove cover from service valve on fuel rail. Connect suitable fuel pressure test gauge to service valve. Switch ignition in Run position, then use scan tool to activate fuel pump & pressurize system.

④ — Before disconnecting wires from coil unit, determine location of ignition wires in coil towers, as position may have been altered from that shown.

⑤ — Equipped w/crankshaft position sensor.

⑥ — Non-adjustable.

⑦ — Equipped w/hydraulic lash adjusters.

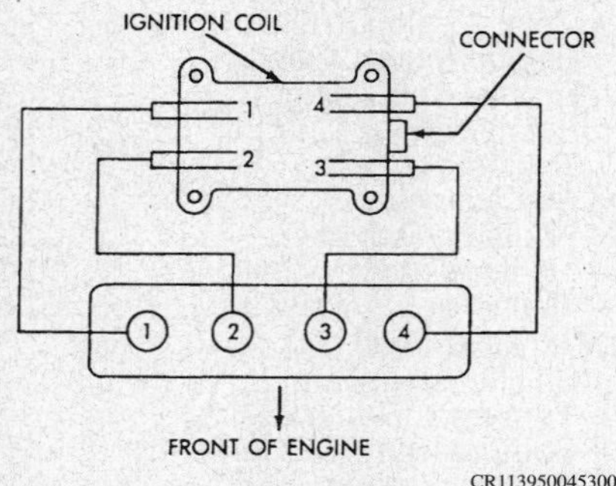

Fig. A

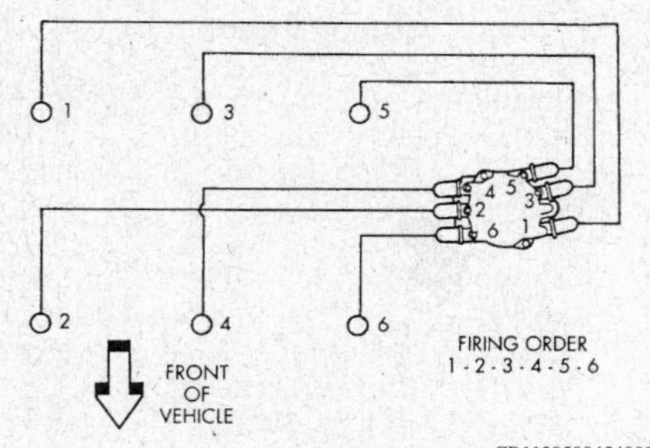

Fig. B

FRONT WHEEL ALIGNMENT SPECIFICATIONS

Year	Camber Angle, Degrees ①		Toe, Inch③		Caster, Degrees		Ball Joint Wear
	Limits	Desired	Limits	Desired	Limits	Desired	
1998–2000	-.5 to +.05	0	-.12 to +.12	0	+2.83 to +5.83	4.33	②
2001–02	-.5 to +.05	0	-.12 to +.12	0	+2.50 to +3.50	3	②

① — Not adjustable.
② — Refer to "Ball Joint Inspection" under "Front Suspension & Steering."
③ — Toe in (+); toe out (-).

REAR WHEEL ALIGNMENT SPECIFICATIONS

Year	Camber, Degrees			Total Toe, Inch①	
	Limits	Desired	Max. LH/RH Deviation	Limits	Desired
1998–2002	-1.83 to -.83	-1.33	.5	0 to +.24	+.12

① — Toe in (+); toe out (-).

VEHICLE RIDE HEIGHT SPECIFICATIONS

Model	Year	Body Style	Manu-facturer's Original Tire Size	Measurement Points & Specifications③					
				Front			Rear		
				Dim.	Specification Inches	Specification mm	Dim.	Specification Inches	Specification mm
Avenger	1998–2000	2.0L	①	G	6.13-6.63	156-168	H	5.63-6.13	143-156
		2.5L	①	G	6.50-7.00	165-178	H	6.00-6.50	152-165
Sebring Coupe	1998–2000	All	①	G	6.13-6.63	156-168	H	5.63-6.13	143-156
Stratus	1998–2000	All	①	A	27.31②	694	B	27.25②	692
Sebring/ Stratus Coupe	2001–02	All	①	G	5.9	150	H	5.9	150

A Dim — Ground to Lower Edge of Front Wheel Well
B Dim — Ground to Lower Edge of Rear Wheel Well
G Dim — Ground to Front Rocker Panel
H Dim — Ground to Rear Rocker Panel
① — See door sticker or inside of glove box for manufacturer's original tire size specifications.
② — ±.25″ (6.35 mm).
③ — Measurement is w/fuel, radiator coolant & engine oil full, spare tire, jack, hand tools & mats in designated positions & tires properly inflated.

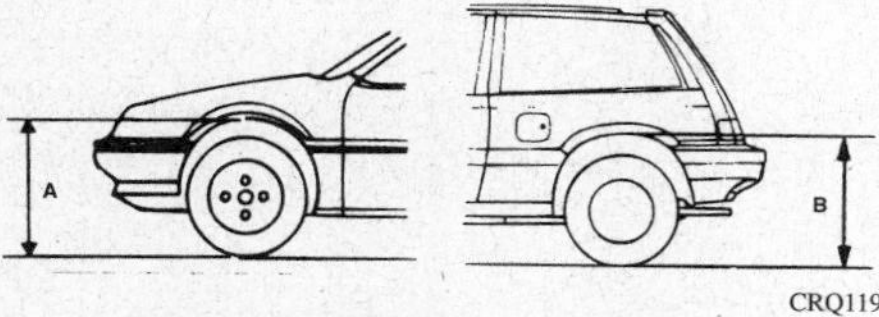

Dimensions A & B

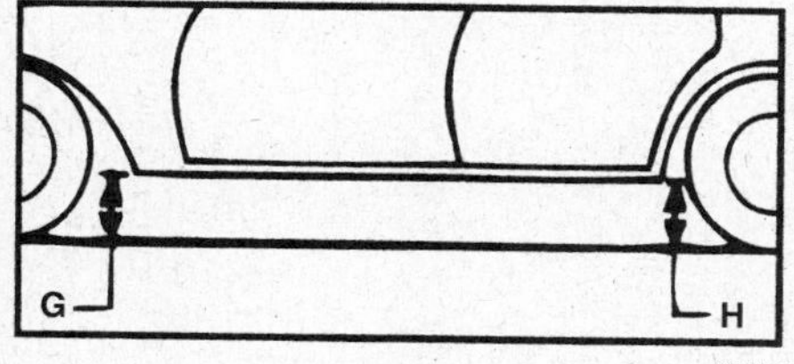

Dimensions G & H

FLUID CAPACITIES & COOLING SYSTEM DATA

Year	Engine	Coolant Capacity, Qts.	Coolant Type	Radiator Cap Relief Pressure, Lbs.	Thermo. Opening Temp. °F	Fuel Tank Capacity, Gals.	Engine Oil Refill, Qts.①	Transaxle Oil, Qts.	
								Manual	Auto.
1998–2002	2.0L	7.4	Ethylene Glycol	16	195	16.9	4	2.1	9.1
	2.4L	7.4	Ethylene Glycol	11–15	190	16.4	4.2	2.3	8.1
	2.5L	7.4	Ethylene Glycol	11–15	180	16.9	4	—	9.1
	3.0L	8.5	Ethylene Glycol	11–15	190	16.4	4.2	3	8.5

① — Capacity without oil filter. Add additional 1/2 quart when changing filter.

LUBRICANT DATA

Year	Lubricant Type①			Brake System
	Transaxle		Power Steering	
	Manual	Automatic		
1998–2000	Mopar Type M.S. 9417	Mopar ATF Type 7176	Dexron II ATF	DOT 3 or 4
2001–02	API GL-4	Diamond ATF SP-III or SP-IIM	Dexron II ATF	DOT 3 or 4

① — Automatic Transaxle Fluid.

Electrical

NOTE: On Air Bag Equipped Models, Refer To "Air Bag System Precautions" Located In The Front Of This Manual For System Disarming & Arming Procedures.

NOTE: Refer To "Computer Relearn Procedures" Located In The Front Of This Manual When Battery Power To The Computer Has Been Interrupted.

INDEX

PRECAUTIONS

AIR BAG SYSTEMS

Refer to "Air Bag System Precautions" in the front of this manual for system disarming and arming procedures.

BATTERY GROUND CABLE

Prior to service, disconnect battery ground cable and isolate as required.

FUSE PANEL & FLASHER LOCATION

1998–2000

The fuse panel is located behind the lower lefthand side of the instrument panel. The turn signal and hazard flasher unit is located behind the center of the instrument panel, near the A/C and heater control panel.

2001–02

The engine compartment fuse panel is located on the lefthand side of the engine compartment. The interior fuse panel is located on the lefthand side of the instrument panel. The turn signal and hazard flasher are incorporated into the ETACS-ECU.

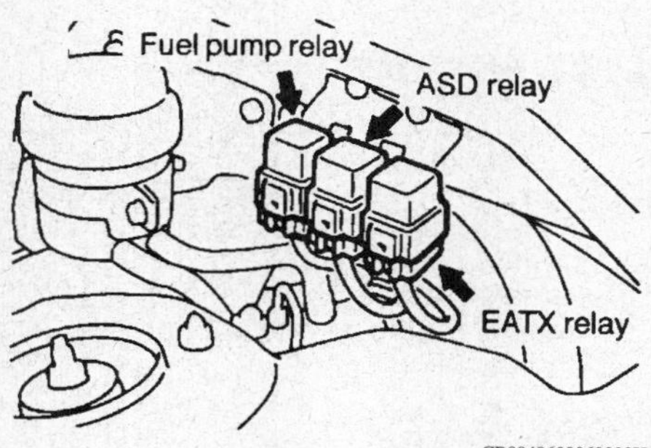

Fig. 1 Fuel pump relay location. 1998–2000

FUEL PUMP RELAY LOCATION

1998–2001

The fuel pump relay is located in the rear lefthand corner of the engine compartment, behind the left shock tower, **Figs. 1 and 2.**

2002

The fuel pump relay are located on the lefthand side of the instrument panel, left of steering column **Fig. 3**.

STARTER

REPLACE

1. Disconnect starter terminal and electrical connector.
2. Remove starter from vehicle.
3. Reverse procedure to install, noting the following:
   a. **On models equipped with 2.0L engine, torque** starter mounting bolts to 40 ft. lbs.
   b. **On models equipped with 2.4L, 2.5L and 3.0L engines, torque** starter mounting bolts to 20–25 ft. lbs.

ALTERNATOR

REPLACE

2.0L ENGINE

1. Remove alternator drive belt, **Fig. 4.**
2. Disconnect alternator electrical connector.
3. Remove alternator bracket, then the alternator and brace.
4. Reverse procedure to install. **Torque** alternator mounting bolt to 45 ft. lbs.

2.4L ENGINE

1. Remove oil pressure hose and tube assembly clamp bolts, **Fig. 5.**

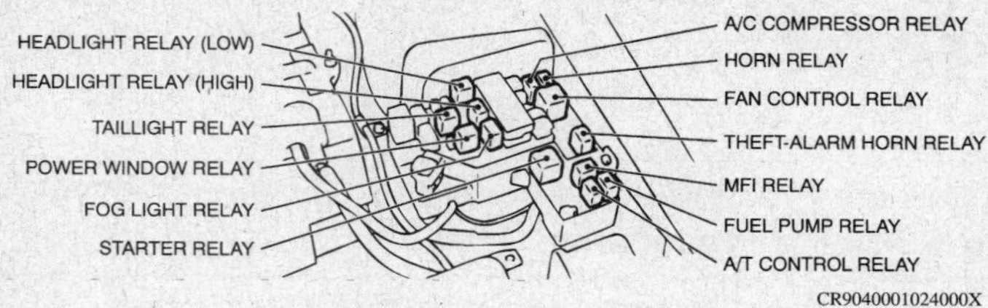

Fig. 2 Fuel pump relay location. 2001

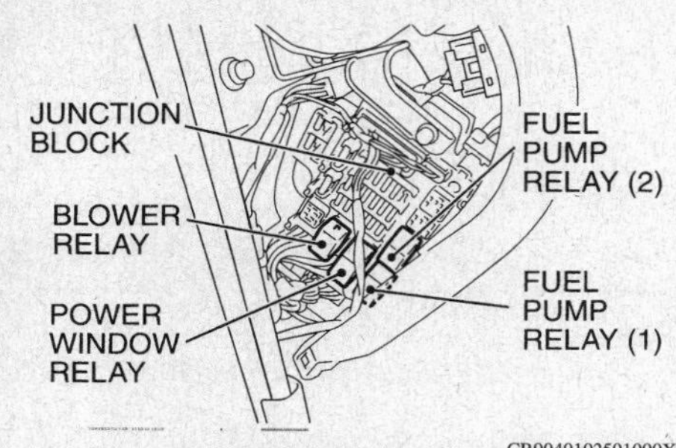

Fig. 3 Fuel pump relay location. 2002

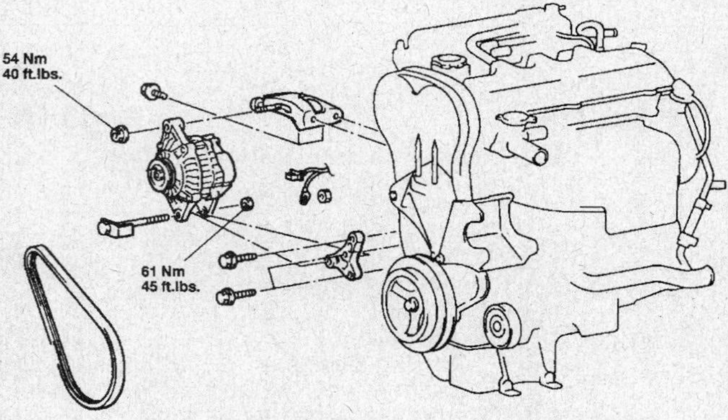

Fig. 4 Alternator replacement. 2.0L engine

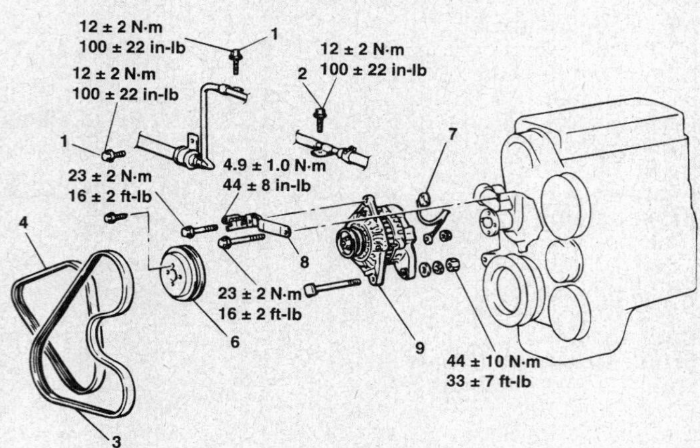

Fig. 5 Alternator replacement. 2.4L engine

2. Remove oil return tube assembly clamp bolt.
3. Remove drive belts, then the water pump pulley.
4. Remove oil level gauge unit.
5. Disconnect alternator electrical connector.
6. Remove alternator brace, then the alternator.
7. Reverse procedure to install. **Torque** alternator mounting bolts to 26–40 ft. lbs.

2.5L ENGINE

1. Remove pump cover and A/C compressor drive belt, **Fig. 6.**
2. Remove power steering pump and alternator drive belt.
3. Remove intake manifold plenum.
4. Remove alternator bracket.
5. Remove intake manifold plenum stay.
6. Disconnect alternator electrical connector.
7. Remove alternator.
8. Remove tensioner pulley, then bracket.
9. Remove alternator bracket.
10. Reverse procedure to install.

3.0L ENGINE

1. Remove drive belt, then the oil level gauge unit **Fig. 7.**
2. Disconnect alternator electrical connector.
3. Remove alternator.
4. Reverse procedure to install. **Torque** alternator mounting bolt to 26–40 ft. lbs.

DISTRIBUTOR

REPLACE

2.5L ENGINE

1. Remove spark plug wires.
2. Remove distributor mounting bolts, then distributor.
3. Remove distributor O-ring.
4. Reverse procedure to install.

3.0L ENGINE

1. Disconnect distributor electrical connection, then the spark plug wires.
2. Remove intake plenum as outlined under "Intake Manifold, Replace."
3. Remove distributor.
4. Reverse procedure to install aligning mating marks on distributor housing and coupling.

COIL PACK

REPLACE

2.0L & 2.4L ENGINES

1. Remove spark plug wires.
2. Remove coil pack mounting bolts, then coil pack.
3. Reverse procedure to install, noting the following:
   a. **On 2.0L engines, torque** mounting bolts to 108 inch lbs.
   b. **On 2.4L engines, torque** mounting bolts to 70–104 inch lbs.

IGNITION LOCK

REPLACE

1998–2000

1. Remove steering wheel as outlined under "Steering Wheel, Replace."
2. Remove lower instrument panel plug, **Fig. 8.**
3. Remove hood lock release handle.
4. Remove instrument panel under cover.
5. Remove steering column lower and upper covers.
6. Remove clockspring.
7. Remove column multi-function switch.
8. Remove ignition key illumination ring or ring cover.
9. Insert key in steering lock cylinder and turn to ACC position.
10. Using screwdriver or suitable pointed tool, push lock pin of steering lock cylinder inward, then pull lock cylinder outward to remove.
11. Reverse procedure to install. Refer to "Supplemental Restraint Systems" for clockspring installation procedure.

2001–02

Refer to "Ignition Switch, Replace" for ignition lock replacement.

IGNITION SWITCH

REPLACE

1998–2000

1. Remove steering wheel as described under "Steering Wheel, Replace."
2. Remove lower instrument panel plug, **Fig. 8.**
3. Remove hood lock release handle.

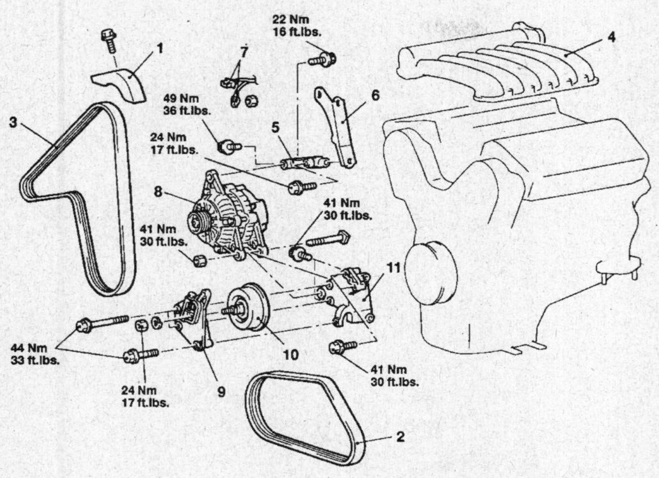

1. Pump cover
2. Drive belt (A/C compressor)
3. Drive belt (Power steering oil pump and generator)
4. Intake manifold plenum
5. Generator bracket
6. Intake manifold plenum stay
7. Generator harness connector
8. Generator
9. Tensioner pulley bracket
10. Tensioner pulley
11. Generator bracket

CR1049600014000X

Fig. 6 Alternator replacement. 2.5L engine

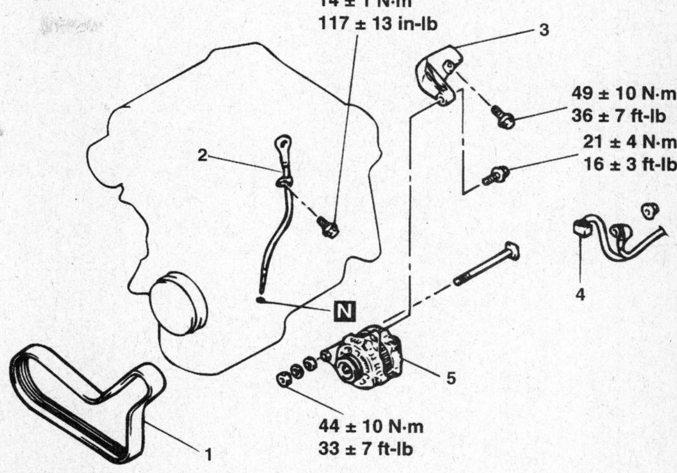

1- DRIVE BELT
2- OIL LEVEL GAUGE
3- ALTERNATOR BRACKET
4- ALTERNATOR HARNESS
5- ALTERNATOR

CR1040000032000X

Fig. 7 Alternator replacement. 3.0L engine

4. Remove instrument panel under cover.
5. Remove steering column lower and upper covers.
6. Remove clockspring.
7. Locate ignition switch attached to ignition lock cylinder.
8. Disconnect ignition switch electrical connector, then remove switch.
9. Reverse procedure to install. Refer to "Supplemental Restraint Systems" for clockspring installation procedure.

2001-02

1. Remove steering column upper and lower covers, **Fig. 9**.
2. Remove key ring antenna and key reminder switch.
3. Insert key into cylinder lock and turn to ACC position. Using a suitable Phillips head screwdriver, remove cylinder.
4. Remove ignition switch.
5. Reverse procedure to install noting the following:
   a. If a new ignition key is to be used it must be registered using scan tool No. MB9911502 or equivalent. Follow scan tool manufactures instructions for key registration.

NEUTRAL SAFETY SWITCH

REPLACE

1998-2000

The neutral safety switch is located at the lower left side of the transaxle housing, under the air cleaner assembly, **Fig. 10.**

1. Disconnect neutral safety switch electrical connector.
2. Remove switch from transaxle case.
3. Reverse procedure to install.

MULTI-FUNCTION SWITCH

REPLACE

1998-2000

1. Remove steering wheel as described under "Steering Wheel, Replace."
2. Remove lower instrument panel plug, **Fig. 8.**
3. Remove hood lock release handle.
4. Remove instrument panel under cover.
5. Remove steering column lower and upper covers.
6. Remove clockspring.
7. Remove column multi-function switch.
8. Reverse procedure to install. Refer to "Passive Restraint Systems" for clockspring installation procedure.

2001-02

1. Remove steering wheel as outlined under "Steering Wheel, Replace."
2. Remove instrument panel lower cover.
3. Remove upper and lower steering column cover.
4. Remove multi-function switch.
5. Reverse procedure to install. Refer to "Passive Restraint Systems" for clockspring installation procedure.

STEERING WHEEL

REPLACE

1998-2000

1. Remove air bag module mounting nut from back side of steering wheel.
2. Remove air bag module from steering wheel, **Fig. 11.**
3. Turn air bag module over and press air bag lock toward outer side to spread it open, then use a flat-tipped screwdriver to gently pry apart clockspring connector, **Fig. 12.**
4. Remove steering wheel nut and steering wheel using suitable steering wheel puller tool. **Do not use hammer to remove steering wheel as this may damage the collapsible shaft.**
5. Reverse procedure to install. **Torque** steering wheel nut to 30 ft. lbs.

2001-02

1. Remove air bag module.
2. Remove steering wheel using suitable puller.
3. Reverse procedure to install. **Torque** steering wheel nut to 26–36 ft. lbs.

INSTRUMENT CLUSTER

REPLACE

1998-2000

1. Remove steering wheel as outlined under "Steering Wheel, Replace."
2. Remove two screws from under top of instrument cluster bezel.
3. Remove instrument cluster bezel. It may be necessary to remove the steering column upper shroud.
4. Remove instrument cluster retaining screws at top of cluster.
5. Pull instrument cluster forward slightly, then disconnect electrical connectors from back of cluster.

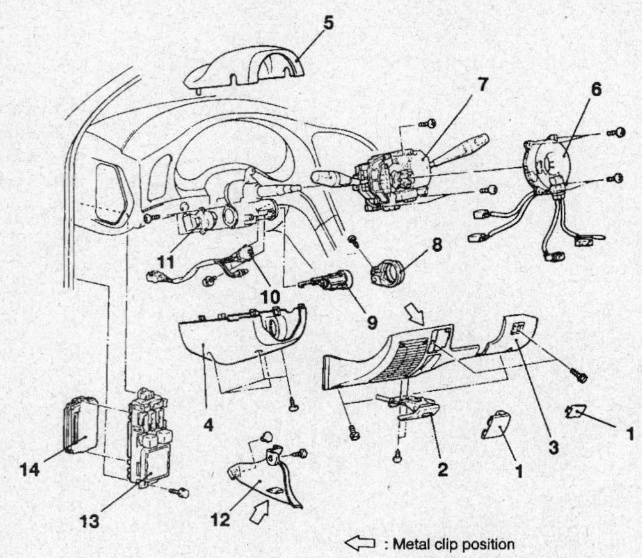

- Steering wheel

1. Plug
2. Hood lock release handle
3. Instrument under cover
4. Column cover lower
5. Column cover upper
6. Clock spring
7. Column switch
8. Ignition key illumination ring or ring cover
9. Steering lock cylinder

CR1049600015000X

Fig. 8 Ignition lock/switch & multi-function switch replacement. 1998–2000

SECTION A - A

SECTION B - B

CLAW

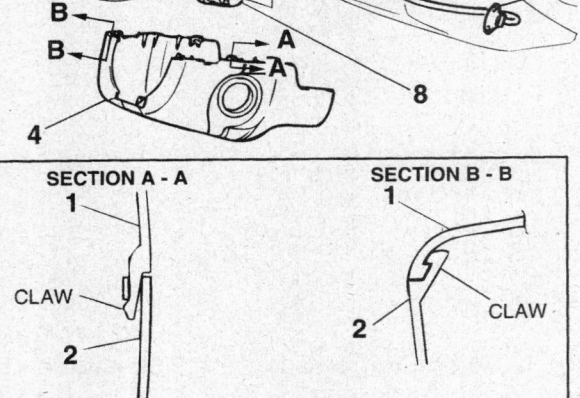

1. ETACS-ECU
2. IMMOBILIZER-ECU
3. COLUMN COVER UPPER
4. COLUMN COVER LOWER
5. KEY RING ANTENNA
6. KEY REMINDER SWITCH
7. STEERING LOCK CYLINDER
8. IGNITION SWITCH

CR1040100034000X

Fig. 9 Ignition switch replacement. 2001–02

6. Remove instrument cluster from instrument panel.
7. Reverse procedure to install.

2001-02

1. Remove instrument cluster bezel.
2. Remove instrument cluster.
3. Reverse procedure to install.

RADIO

REPLACE

1998-2000

1. Remove instrument panel center panel, **Fig. 13.**
2. Remove radio and tape player or CD player. Disconnect electrical connectors.
3. Remove floor console assembly installer screws.
4. Pull upper part of floor bracket back slightly and remove radio bracket.
5. Reverse procedure to install.

2001-02

1. Remove center panel assembly.
2. Remove radio and tape or CD player.
3. Remove radio bracket.
4. Reverse procedure to install.

WIPER MOTOR

REPLACE

1. Remove wiper arm and blade assembly.
2. Remove front deck garnish/cowl screen.
3. Remove wiper motor and link assembly and disconnect motor electrical connector.
4. Reverse procedure to install.

BLOWER MOTOR

REPLACE

1998-2000

1. Remove glove compartment.
2. **On models equipped with A/C,** remove automatic compressor ECM mounted under blower motor.
3. **On all models,** disconnect blower motor electrical connector.
4. Remove blower motor and fan assembly mounting screws and lower motor/fan assembly from blower unit.
5. Reverse procedure to install.

2001-02

1. Remove glove compartment.
2. Remove air purifier assembly.
3. Remove joint duct, then the resistor.
4. Remove blower motor assembly.
5. Reverse procedure to install.

HEATER CORE

REPLACE

1998-2000

1. Recover as much coolant from cooling system as possible to prevent spillage when heater hoses are disconnected, then remove center console in numbered sequence shown in **Fig. 14.**
2. Remove steering wheel and column covers, **Fig. 15,** then the instrument panel as outlined under "Dash Panel Service."
3. Remove heater unit and core in numbered sequence shown in **Fig. 16,** noting the following:
   a. **On models equipped with manual transaxle,** ensure vehicle speed

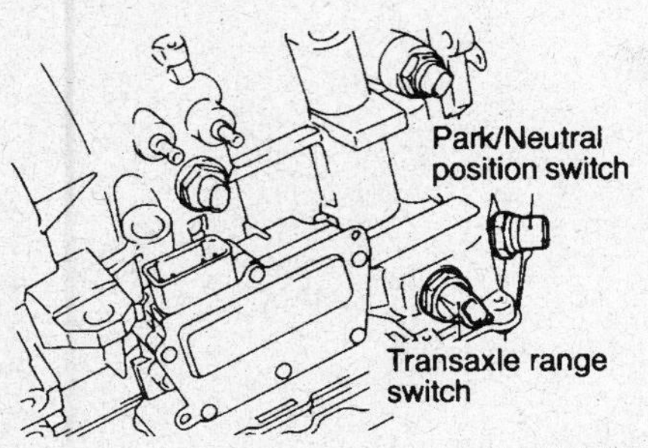

Fig. 10 Neutral safety switch. 1998–2000

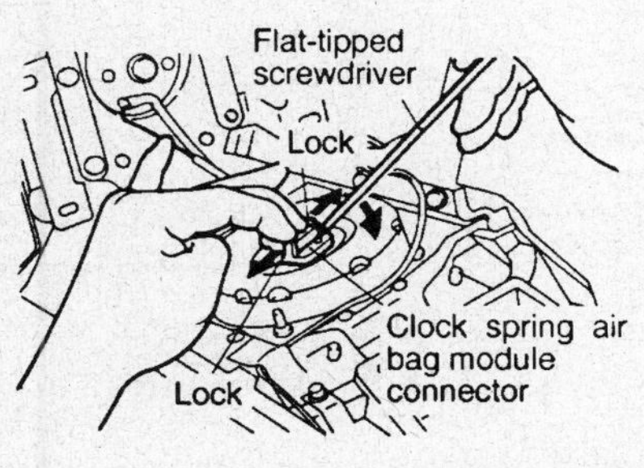

Fig. 12 Air bag module clockspring connector. 1998–2000

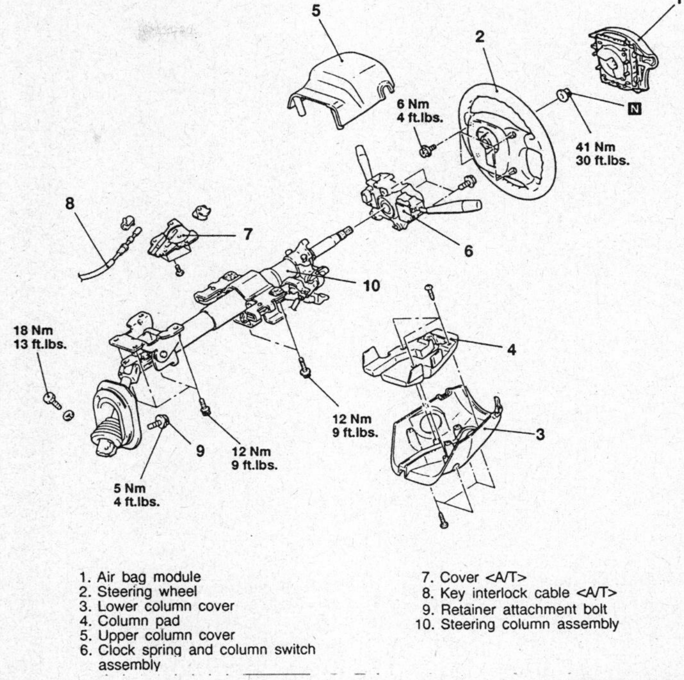

Fig. 11 Steering wheel replacement. 1998–2000

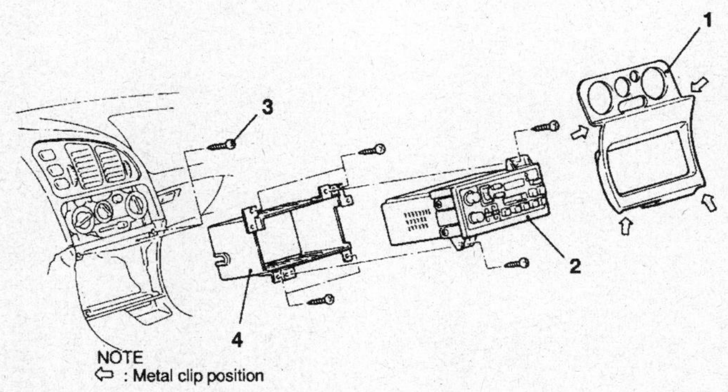

Fig. 13 Radio removal. 1998–2000

sensor is protected from coolant spillage when heater hoses are disconnected.
   b. **On all models,** use a suitable Philips head screwdriver to remove duct clips by pressing center of each clip inward approximately .08 inch while pulling outward. **Do not push pins in farther than necessary, grommet may be damaged or pins may fall through grommet holes.**
   c. It may be necessary to slide cooling unit outward slightly before removing heater unit.
4. Reverse to install noting the following:
   a. Install in numbered sequence shown in **Fig. 16.**
   b. Refer to **Fig. 15** when installing steering wheel and column covers.
   c. Install center console by reversing numbered sequence shown in **Fig. 14.**
   d. Refill cooling system and check for leaks.

2001-02

1. **On models equipped with A/C,** proceed as follows:
   a. Remove automatic compressor controller.
   b. Recover refrigerant as outlined in "Air Conditioning" section.
   c. Remove A/C pipe, expansion valve, then the evaporator core.
   d. Remove drain hose.
2. **On all models,** drain coolant into suitable container.
3. Remove heater hoses.
4. Remove radio as outlined under "Radio, Replace."
5. Remove heater control assembly.
6. Remove steering wheel as outlined under "Steering Wheel, Replace."
7. Remove floor console in numbered sequence shown in **Fig. 17.**
8. Remove instrument panel as outlined under "Dash Panel Service."
9. Remove front deck crossmember, then the foot duct.
10. Remove heater/cooler unit, then the heater core.
11. Reverse procedure to install.

EVAPORATOR CASE

REPLACE

1998-2000

1. Recover refrigerant as outlined in "Air Conditioning" section.
2. Disconnect A/C drain hose, **Fig. 18.**
3. Disconnect suction pipe and liquid pipe.
4. Remove glove compartment and instrument panel corner panel.
5. Remove glove compartment frame.
6. Remove righthand center console side cover.
7. Remove ABS-ECU cover and bracket.
8. Remove cooling unit retaining pin by pushing center of pin into grommet with a suitable screwdriver. Push pin inward to a depth of about .08 inch, then pull outward to remove.
9. Remove cooling unit from vehicle.
10. Reverse procedure to install.

2001-02

Refer to "Heater Core, Replace" for evaporator case replacement.

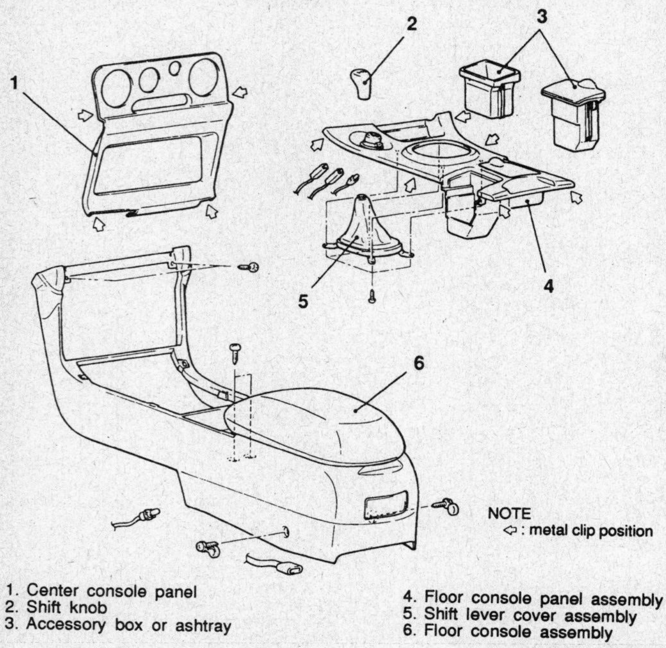

Fig. 14 Center console replacement. 1998–2000

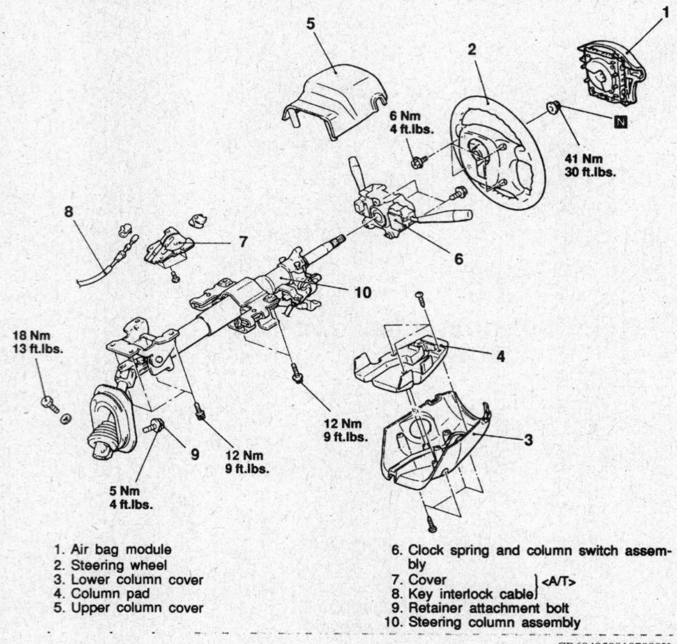

Fig. 15 Exploded view of steering column & wheel assembly. 1998–2000

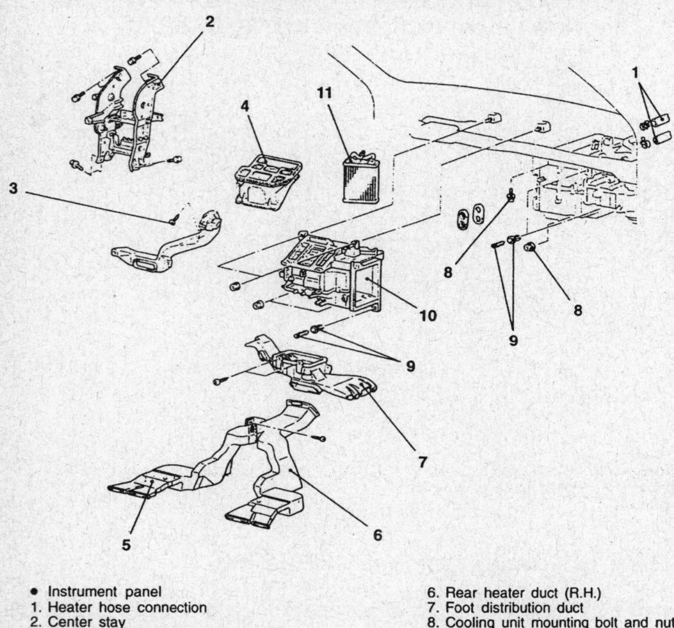

Fig. 16 Heater unit & core replacement. 1998–2000

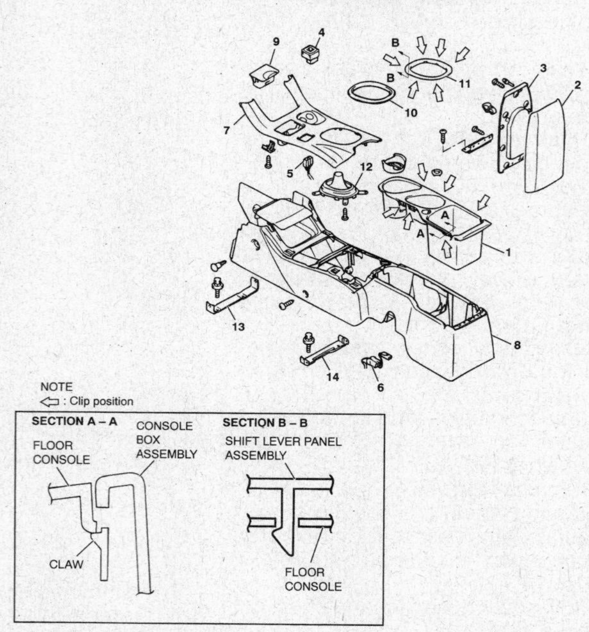

1. CONSOLE BOX ASSEMBLY
2. CONSOLE LID
3. CONSOLE LID COVER
4. DOOR MIRROR CONTROL SWITCH
5. DOOR MIRROR CONTROL SWITCH HARNESS
6. ACCCESSARY SOCKET HARNESS
7. FLOOR CONSOLE INDICATOR PANEL
8. FLOOR CONSOLE
9. ASHTRAY
10. SHIFT LEVER PANEL ASSEMBLY <M/T>
11. GARNISH <A/T>
12. SHIFT LEVER BOOT <M/T>
13. FLOOR CONSOLE BRACKET A
14. FLOOR CONSOLE BRACKET B

CR9140000071000X

Fig. 17 Floor console removal. 2001–02

EVAPORATOR CORE

REPLACE

1998–2000

1. Recover refrigerant as outlined under "Air Conditioning."
2. Remove evaporator case in numbered sequence shown in **Fig. 19.**
3. Use a suitable Phillips head screwdriver to remove evaporator case clips by pressing center of each clip inward approximately .08 inch while pulling outward.
4. Disassemble evaporator case in numbered sequence shown in **Fig. 20.**
5. Install evaporator and evaporator case by reversing numbered sequences shown in **Figs. 19 and 20.**

2001–02

Refer to "Heater Core, Replace" for evaporator core replacement.

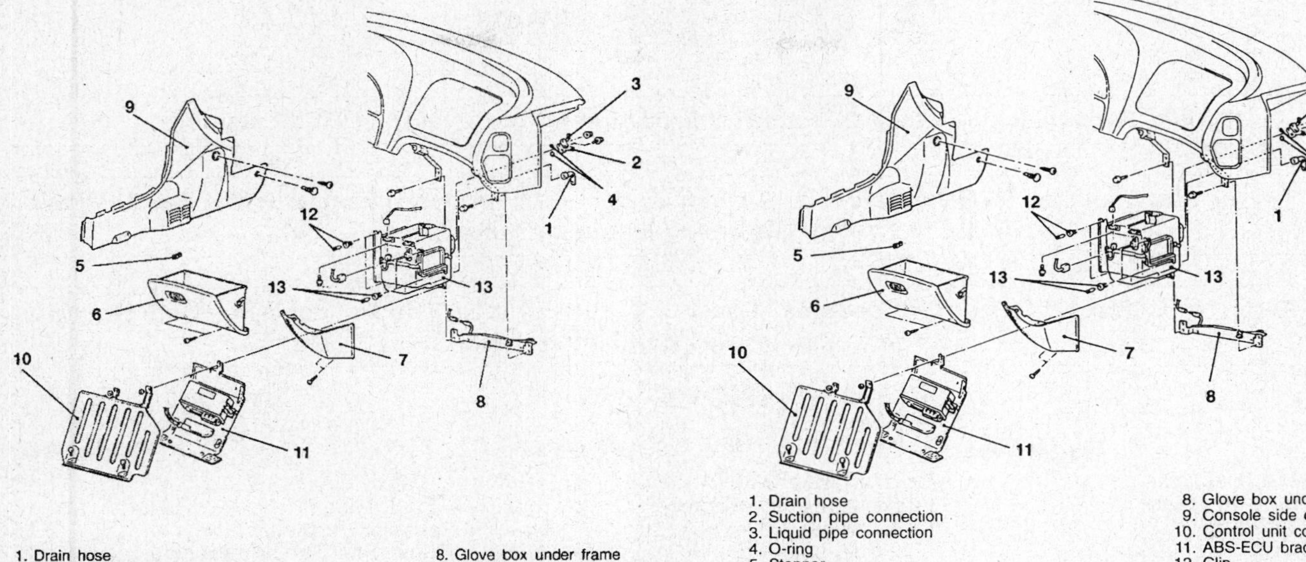

1. Drain hose
2. Suction pipe connection
3. Liquid pipe connection
4. O-ring
5. Stopper
6. Glove box
7. Corner panel
8. Glove box under frame
9. Console side cover <R.H.>
10. Control unit cover
11. ABS-ECU bracket
12. Clip
13. Cooling unit

CR7029600268000X

Fig. 18 Evaporator case removal. 1998–2000

1. Drain hose
2. Suction pipe connection
3. Liquid pipe connection
4. O-ring
5. Stopper
6. Glove box
7. Corner panel
8. Glove box under frame
9. Console side cover <R.H.>
10. Control unit cover
11. ABS-ECU bracket
12. Clip
13. Cooling unit

CR7029500232000X

Fig. 19 Evaporator case replacement. 1998–2000

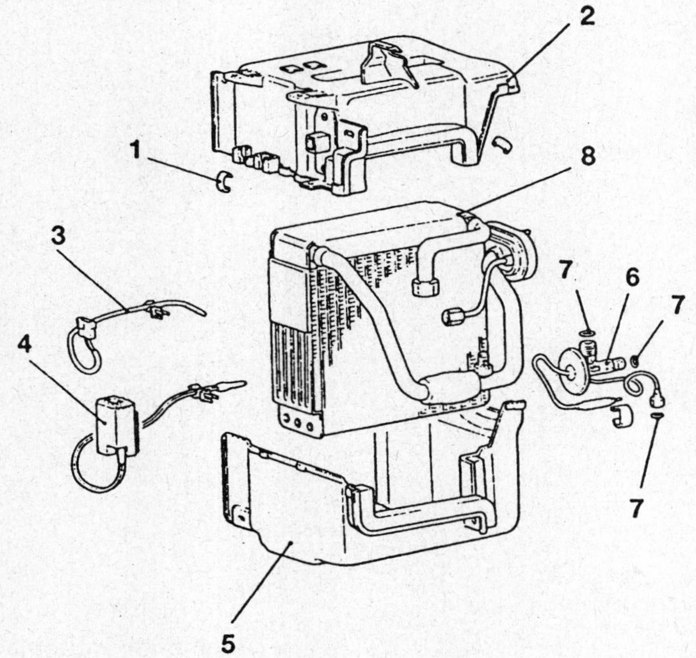

1. Clip
2. Evaporator case (upper)
3. Fin thermo sensor <DOHC>
4. Automatic compressor-ECM and fin thermo sensor assembly <SOHC>
5. Evaporator case (lower)
6. Expansion valve
7. O-ring
8. Evaporator

CR7029500233000X

Fig. 20 Evaporator case disassembly. 1998–2000

2.0L Engine

NOTE: Refer To The "Talon" Chapter For Procedures Not Covered In This Section.

NOTE: On Air Bag Equipped Models, Refer To "Air Bag System Precautions" Located In The Front Of This Manual For System Disarming & Arming Procedures.

NOTE: Refer To "Computer Relearn Procedures" Located In The Front Of This Manual When Battery Power To The Computer Has Been Interrupted.

INDEX

PRECAUTIONS

AIR BAG SYSTEMS

Refer to "Air Bag System Precautions" in the front of this manual for system disarming and arming procedures.

BATTERY GROUND CABLE

Prior to service, disconnect battery ground cable and isolate as required.

FUEL SYSTEM PRESSURE RELIEF

1. Remove rear seat cushion.
2. Remove protector to disconnect fuel pump connector.
3. Start engine and run until it stops naturally, then turn ignition switch off.
4. Connect fuel pump connector and install protector.
5. Install rear cushion.

COMPRESSION PRESSURE

Perform compression test with engine at normal operating temperature, spark plugs removed and throttle wide open. Standard compression pressure is 170–225 psi. The minimum compression pressure is 100 psi with a maximum variation between highest and lowest cylinders of 25 percent.

ENGINE MOUNT

REPLACE

1. Remove radiator coolant reserve tank.
2. Raise and support engine so there is no weight on the engine mount bracket insulator.
3. Remove engine mount insulator mounting bolt, **Fig. 1.**
4. Remove engine mount bracket and stopper.
5. Reverse procedure to install.

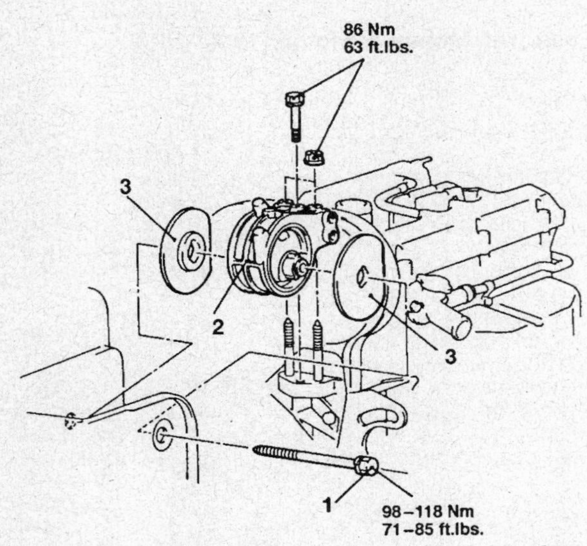

Fig. 1 Engine mount replacement

ENGINE

REPLACE

1. Relieve fuel system pressure as described under "Precautions."
2. Drain engine coolant into a suitable container.
3. Mark and remove hood.
4. **On models equipped with manual transaxle,** remove transaxle assembly as outlined in "Clutch & Manual Transaxle" section.
5. **On models equipped with automatic transaxle,** remove transaxle as outlined in "Automatic Transmissions/ Transaxles" chapter.
6. **On all models,** remove engine under cover.
7. Disconnect the following electrical harness connectors:
   a. A/C compressor connector, **Fig. 2.**
   b. Power steering pressure switch connector.
   c. Heated oxygen sensor connector.
   d. Engine coolant temperature gauge unit connector.

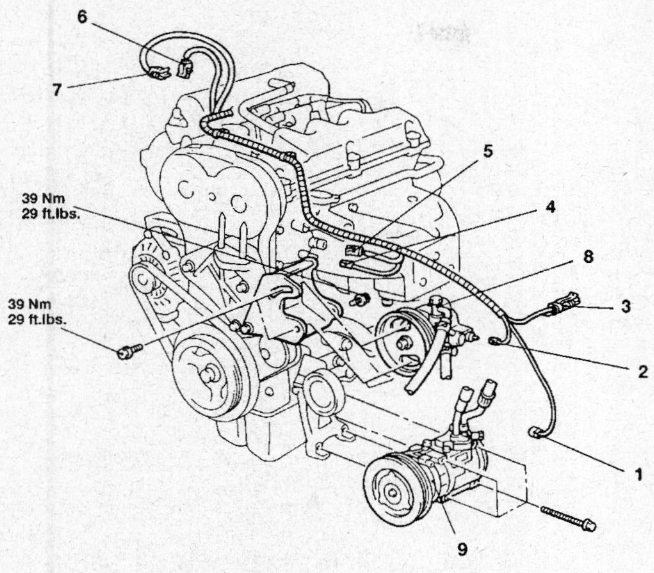

1. A/C compressor connector
2. Power steering pressure switch connector
3. Heated oxygen sensor connector
4. Engine coolant temperature gauge unit connector
5. Engine coolant temperature sensor connector
6. MAP sensor connector
7. Intake air temperature sensor connector
8. Power steering pump connection
9. A/C compressor connection

CR1069600642010X

Fig. 2 Engine removal (Part 1 of 3)

4.9 Nm
3.6 ft.lbs.

Fuel rail

O-ring

Engine oil

2.5 Nm
1.8 ft.lbs.

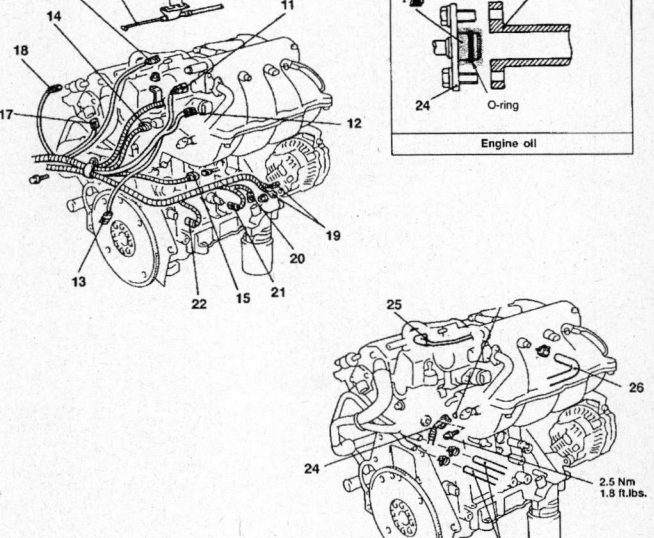

10. Accelerator cable connection
11. Throttle position sensor connector
12. Idle air control motor connector
13. Vehicle speed sensor connector <M/T>
14. Injector harness connector
15. Generator harness connector
16. Ignition coil connector
17. Camshaft position sensor connector
18. EGR solenoid valve connector
19. Generator connector
20. Crankshaft position sensor connector
21. Knock sensor connector
22. Oil pressure switch connector
23. Heater hose connection
24. High pressure fuel hose connection
25. Purge air hose connection
26. Brake booster vacuum hose connection

CR1069600642020X

Fig. 2 Engine removal (Part 2 of 3)

e. Engine coolant temperature sensor connector.
f. Manifold Absolute Pressure (MAP) sensor connector.
g. Intake air temperature sensor connector.
h. Throttle position sensor connector.
i. Idle air control connector.
j. Vehicle speed sensor connector.
k. Injector harness connector.
l. Alternator harness connector.
m. Ignition coil connector.
n. Camshaft position sensor connector.
o. Crankshaft position sensor connector.
p. Knock sensor connector.
q. EGR solenoid valve connector.

8. Remove power steering pump from bracket with hose attached.
9. Remove A/C compressor from bracket with hose attached.
10. Disconnect accelerator cable.
11. Disconnect oil pressure switch connector.
12. Disconnect heater hose connection.
13. Disconnect high pressure fuel hose.
14. Disconnect purge air hose.
15. Disconnect brake booster vacuum hose and vapor hose.
16. Disconnect front exhaust pipe connection.
17. Support engine with suitable jack.
18. Hold engine assembly with chain block or similar tool.
19. Place jack against engine oil pan with a piece of wood in between, then raise engine so the weight of the engine is no longer being applied to mounting bracket.
20. Remove mounting bracket.
21. Ensure all cables, hoses and harness connectors have been remove from engine, then lift chain block to remove engine from engine compartment.
22. Reverse procedure to install, noting the following:
    a. When connecting high pressure fuel hose to fuel rail, apply clean engine oil to hose union.
    b. Tighten all fasteners to specifications.

INTAKE MANIFOLD

REPLACE

1. Release fuel system pressure as described under "Precautions."
2. Drain engine coolant.
3. Disconnect air intake hose and breather hose, **Fig. 3.**
4. Disconnect accelerator cable and remove cable retaining clips.
5. Disconnect Manifold Absolute Pressure (MAP) sensor connector.
6. Disconnect intake air temperature sensor connector.
7. Disconnect vacuum hose connection.
8. Disconnect Throttle Position Sensor (TPS) connector.
9. Disconnect idle air control motor connector.
10. Remove control wiring harness.
11. Disconnect alternator wiring harness.
12. Remove Positive Crankcase Ventilation (PCV) hose assembly.
13. Disconnect vacuum hose.
14. Disconnect brake booster vacuum hose.
15. Disconnect EGR pipe.
16. Disconnect high pressure fuel hose.
17. Remove intake manifold stay and engine hanger.
18. Disconnect injector connector.
19. Remove throttle body.
20. Remove intake manifold plenum and gasket.
21. Remove fuel rail/injector/pressure regulator assembly.
22. Remove injector O-rings.
23. Remove intake manifold and gasket.
24. Reverse procedure to install. Tighten to specifications.

EXHAUST MANIFOLD

REPLACE

1. Drain engine coolant.
2. Remove air intake hose, **Fig. 4.**
3. Disconnect radiator upper hose connection.
4. Disconnect air hose and control wiring harness.
5. Remove water pipe assembly.
6. Remove engine oil dipstick.
7. Remove heat protector and engine hanger.
8. Disconnect front exhaust pipe.
9. Remove heat protector.
10. Remove exhaust manifold and gasket.
11. Reverse procedure to install. Tighten to specifications.

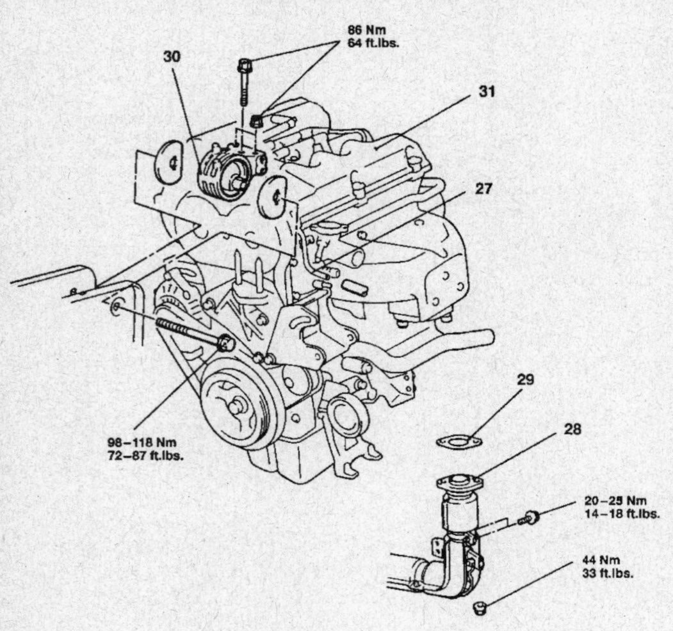

27. Vapor hose connection
28. Front exhaust pipe connection
29. Gasket
30. Engine mount bracket
31. Engine assembly

CR1069600642030X

Fig. 2 Engine removal (Part 3 of 3)

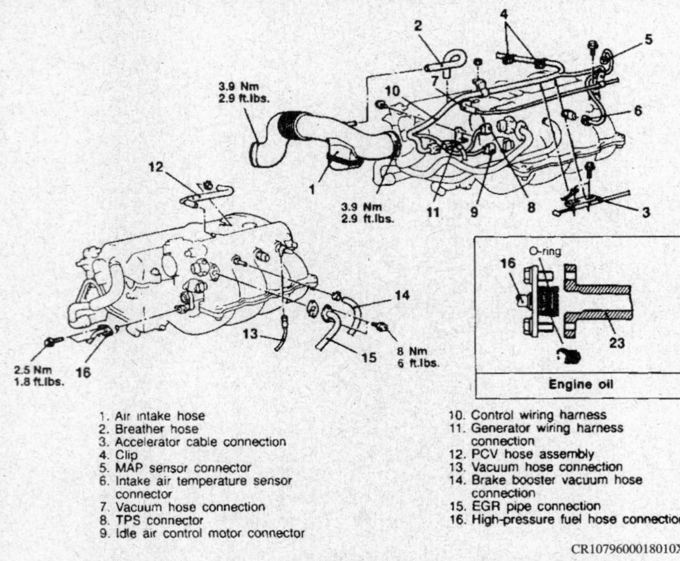

1. Air intake hose
2. Breather hose
3. Accelerator cable connection
4. Clip
5. MAP sensor connector
6. Intake air temperature sensor connector
7. Vacuum hose connection
8. TPS connector
9. Idle air control motor connector
10. Control wiring harness
11. Generator wiring harness connection
12. PCV hose assembly
13. Vacuum hose connection
14. Brake booster vacuum hose connection
15. EGR pipe connection
16. High-pressure fuel hose connection

CR1079600018010X

Fig. 3 Intake manifold removal (Part 1 of 2)

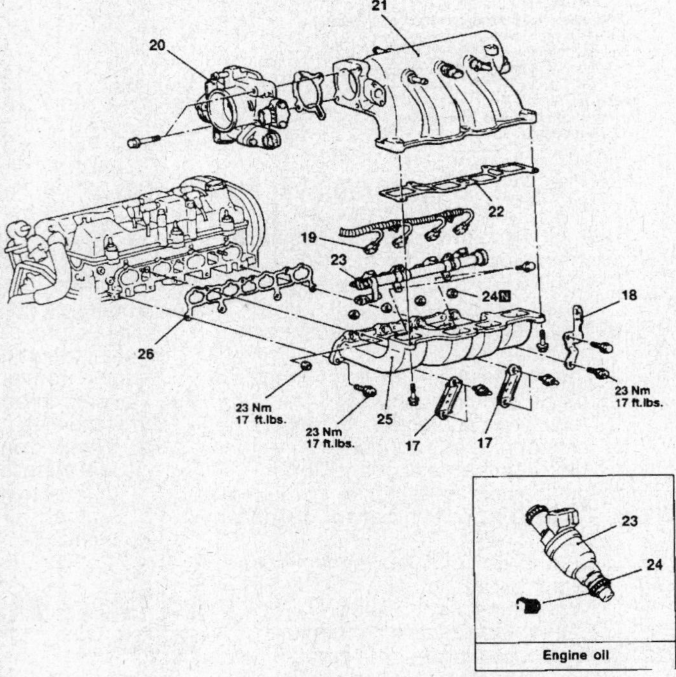

17. Intake manifold stay
18. Engine hanger
19. Injector connector
20. Throttle body
21. Intake manifold plenum
22. Intake manifold plenum gasket
23. Fuel rail, injector and pressure regulator assembly
24. O-ring
25. Intake manifold
26. Intake manifold gasket

CR1079600018020X

Fig. 3 Intake manifold removal (Part 2 of 2)

RADIATOR

REPLACE

1. Drain radiator.
2. Disconnect overflow hose, then remove reserve tank and bracket, **Fig. 5.**
3. Disconnect radiator upper hose and lower hose.
4. **On models equipped with automatic transaxle,** disconnect transaxle fluid cooler hose.
5. **On all models,** remove upper insulator.
6. Remove radiator assembly, then the lower insulator.
7. **On models equipped with A/C,** remove condenser fan motor assembly.
8. **On all models,** remove radiator fan motor assembly.
9. Remove fan, fan motor and shroud.
10. Reverse procedure to install.

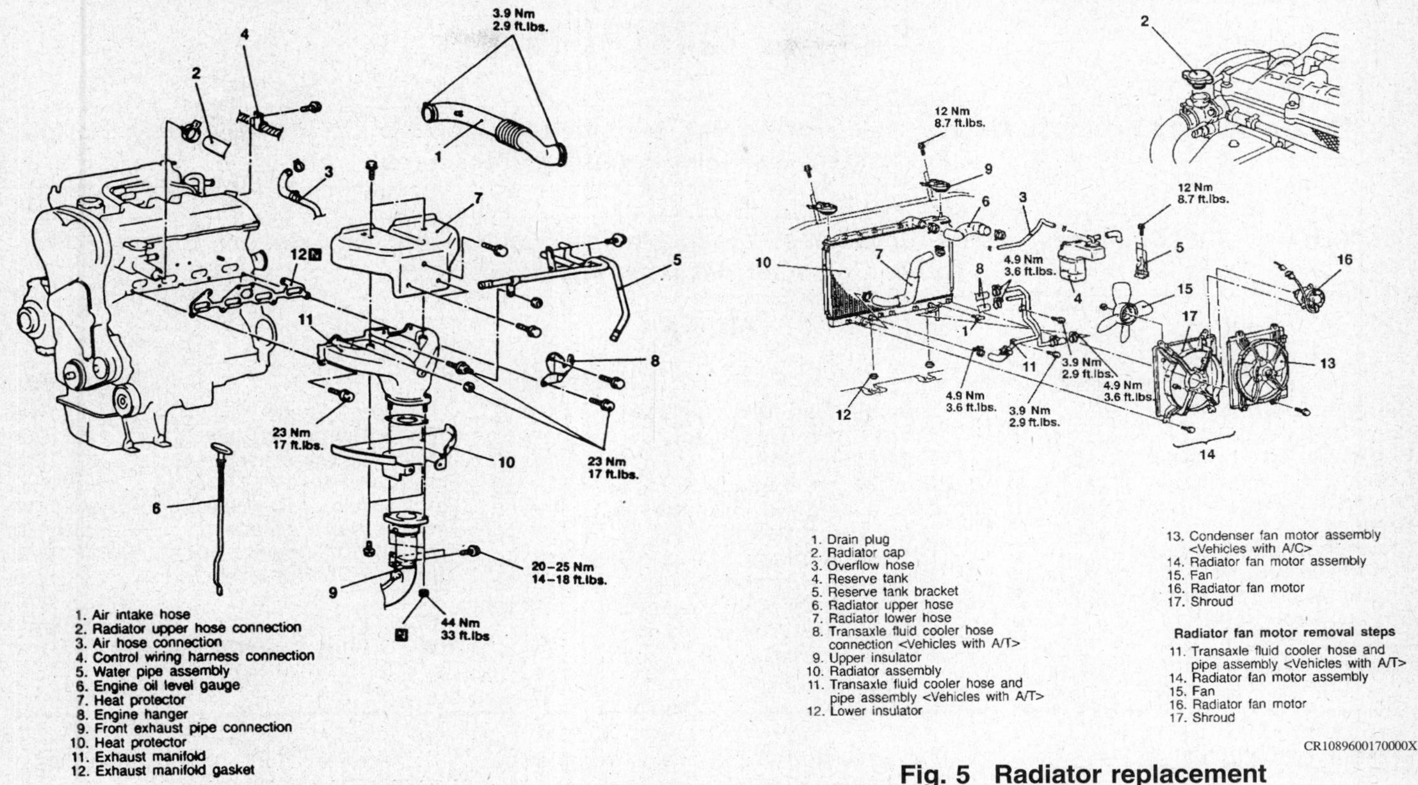

Fig. 4 Exhaust manifold replacement

Fig. 5 Radiator replacement

TIGHTENING SPECIFICATIONS

Year	Component	Torque/Ft. Lbs.
1998-99	Coolant Reserve Tank Bracket Bolt	108①
	Engine Mount Bracket Bolts	63
	Engine Mount Insulator Mounting Bolt	71–85
	Front Exhaust Pipe Connection Bolt	14–18
	Power Steering Pump Retaining Bolts	29
	Radiator Upper Insulator Mounting Bolts	108①

① — Inch lbs.

2.4L Engine

NOTE: On Air Bag Equipped Models, Refer To "Air Bag System Precautions" Located In The Front Of This Manual For System Disarming & Arming Procedures.

NOTE: Refer To "Computer Relearn Procedures" Located In The Front Of This Manual When Battery Power To The Computer Has Been Interrupted.

INDEX

PRECAUTIONS

AIR BAG SYSTEMS

Refer to "Air Bag System Precautions" in the front of this manual for system disarming and arming procedures.

BATTERY GROUND CABLE

Prior to service, disconnect battery ground cable and isolate as required.

FUEL SYSTEM PRESSURE RELIEF

1. Remove fuel pump relay.
2. Start engine and let it run until it stops, then turn ignition switch off.
3. Reconnect fuel pump relay.

COMPRESSION PRESSURE

Perform compression test with engine at normal operating temperature, spark plugs removed, crankshaft position sensor disconnected and throttle wide open. Standard compression pressure at cranking speed is 185 psi. The minimum compression pressure is 139 psi with a maximum variation between cylinders of 14 psi.

ENGINE MOUNT

REPLACE

1. Hold engine with a chain block or similar tool.
2. Raise engine so there is no weight on engine mount bracket using a suitable floor jack and piece of wood placed under oil pan.
3. Remove engine mount.
4. Reverse procedure to install tightening to specifications.

ENGINE

REPLACE

1. Release fuel pressure as outlined under "Precautions."
2. Mark and remove hood.
3. Remove strut tower bar.
4. Remove radiator as outlined under "Radiator, Replace."
5. Remove air cleaner, then the front exhaust pipe.
6. Disconnect accelerator cable, then the purge hose.
7. Disconnect vacuum hose connections.
8. Disconnect the following electrical connections:
   a. Ignition coil.
   b. Fuel injectors.
   c. Ignition failure sensor.
   d. Manifold differential pressure sensor.
   e. Throttle position sensor.
   f. Heated oxygen sensor.
   g. Capacitor.
   h. Engine coolant temperature sensor.
   i. Camshaft position sensor.
   j. Knock sensor.
   k. Engine coolant temperature gauge unit.
   l. Idle air control motor.
   m. Evaporative emission purge solenoid valve.
   n. EGR solenoid valve.
   o. Alternator.
   p. Oil pressure switch.
   q. Crankshaft position sensor.
   r. Power steering pressure switch.
9. Disconnect high pressure fuel hose, then the fuel return hose.
10. Remove oil dipstick and guide.
11. Remove pressure hose, then the heater hose.
12. Remove drive belts.
13. Remove power steering pump with hoses attached and position aside.
14. Remove A/C compressor with lines attached and position aside.
15. Remove transaxle as outlined under "Transaxle, Replace."
16. Support engine with jack and hold engine with chain block or similar support tool.
17. Place jack under engine oil pan with piece of wood in between, then raise engine so that weight of engine is no longer on engine mount bracket.
18. Remove engine mount stopper, then the engine.
19. Reverse procedure to install. Tighten all fasteners to specifications.

INTAKE MANIFOLD

REPLACE

1. Release fuel pressure as outlined under "Precautions."
2. Drain engine coolant into suitable container, then remove air cleaner assembly.
3. Disconnect accelerator cable.
4. Disconnect throttle position sensor, then the idle air control motor electrical connections.
5. Remove throttle body assembly.
6. Disconnect purge hose, then the brake booster vacuum hose.
7. Disconnect ignition coil, then the fuel injector electrical connections.
8. Disconnect ignition failure sensor, then

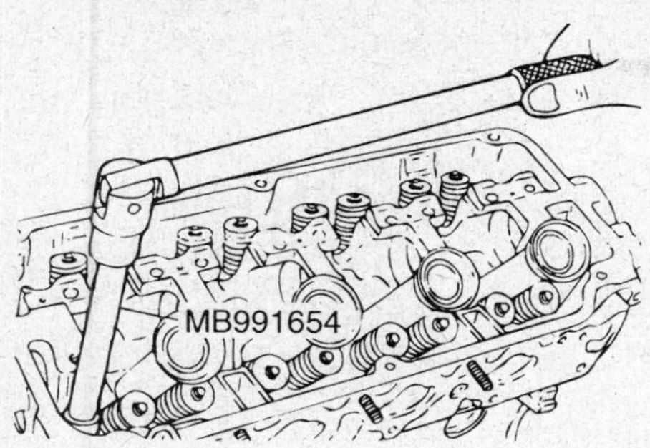

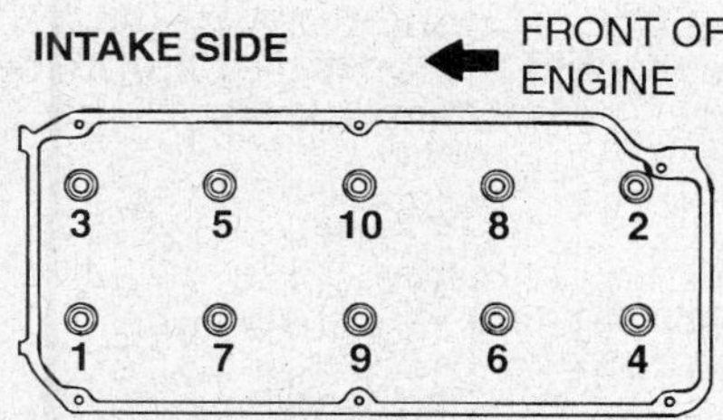

Fig. 1 Cylinder head bolt removal

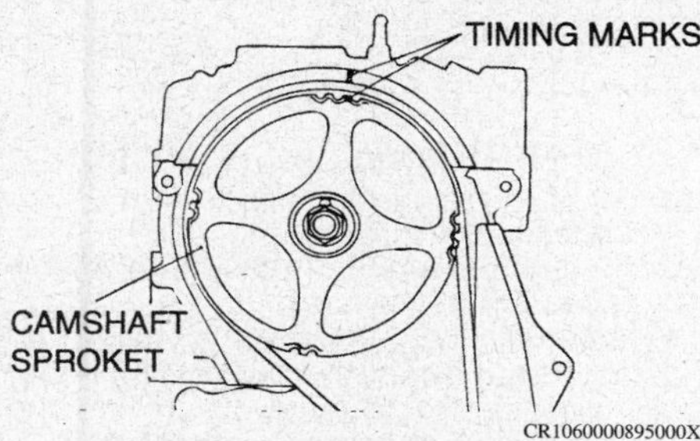

Fig. 4 Camshaft sprocket timing marks

the manifold differential pressure sensor electrical connections.
9. Disconnect evaporative emission purge solenoid valve connector.
10. Disconnect EGR solenoid valve connector.
11. Disconnect high pressure and return fuel hoses.
12. Remove oil dipstick and guide.
13. Remove PCV hose, then the fuel return pipe.
14. Remove fuel hose.
15. Remove fuel rail, injector and fuel pressure regulator.
16. Remove insulator, then the vacuum pipe.
17. Remove EGR valve.
18. Remove intake manifold.
19. Reverse procedure to install tightening to specifications.

EXHAUST MANIFOLD

REPLACE

1. Remove front heated oxygen sensor.
2. Remove heat protector, then the engine hanger.
3. Remove exhaust manifold and bracket.
4. Reverse procedure to install tightening to specifications.

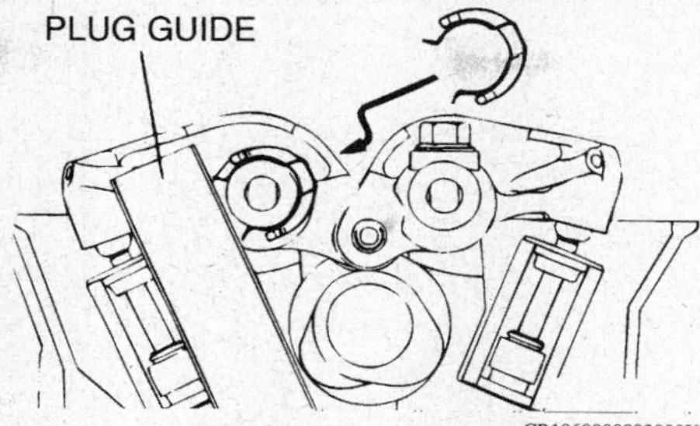

Fig. 2 Rocker arm shaft spring installation

CYLINDER HEAD

REPLACE

1. Release fuel pressure as outlined under "Precautions," then drain cooling system.
2. Remove strut tower brace, then the air cleaner assembly.
3. Remove thermostat case assembly.
4. Remove front exhaust pipe.
5. Disconnect accelerator cable.
6. Disconnect purge hose, then the brake booster vacuum hose connections.
7. Disconnect the following electrical connections:
   a. Ignition coil and injectors.
   b. Manifold differential pressure sensor.
   c. Throttle position sensor.
   d. Heated oxygen sensor.
   e. Capacitor.
   f. Engine coolant temperature sensor.
   g. Camshaft position sensor.
   h. Idle air control motor.
   i. Evaporative emission purge solenoid valve.
   j. EGR solenoid.
8. Disconnect fuel high pressure and return hoses.
9. Remove oil dipstick and guide.
10. Remove spark plug wires, then the ignition coil.
11. Remove upper radiator hose.
12. Disconnect PCV hose.
13. Remove rocker cover, then the spark plug guide oil seal.
14. Remove timing belt as outlined under "Timing Belt, Replace."
15. Remove power steering pressure switch.
16. Remove power steering pump with hose attached and position aside.
17. Remove exhaust manifold bracket.
18. Using cylinder head bolt removal tool No. MB991654, or equivalent, loosen bolts in two or three steps in sequence shown in **Fig. 1**.
19. Remove cylinder head ensuring not to damage plug guides when removing bolts.
20. Reverse procedure to install noting the following:
   a. Match shapes of cylinder head holes with holes in cylinder head gasket.
   b. Replace cylinder head bolts if length below head of bolt is longer than 3.91 inches.
   c. Using reverse order of removal,

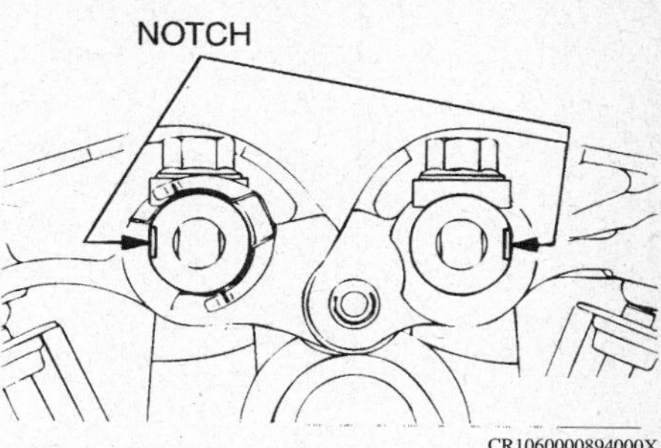

Fig. 3 Rocker arm shaft notch direction

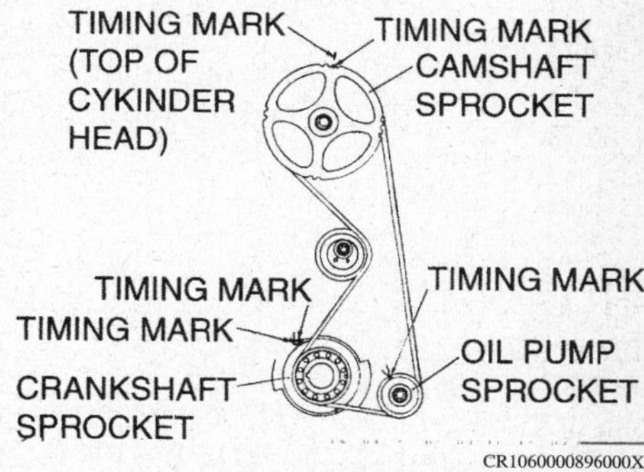

Fig. 5 Timing marks

tighten cylinder head bolts in five steps. First step **torque** bolts to 55–61 ft. lbs.; second step fully loosen bolts in sequence, **Fig. 1;** third step **torque** bolts to 14–16 ft. lbs.; fourth step tighten an additional 90°; fifth step tighten an additional 90°.

ROCKER ARMS

REPLACE

1. Remove breather hose, then the PCV valve.
2. Remove valve cover.
3. Using lash adjuster holding tool No. MD998443, or equivalent, to hold lash adjuster in place remove rocker arm shafts.
4. Remove rocker arm shaft springs, then the rocker arms.
5. Remove lash adjusters.
6. Reverse procedure to install noting the following:
   a. Install exhaust side rocker arm shaft assembly.
   b. Install intake side rocker arm shaft assembly.
   c. Install rocker arm shaft spring to intake side rocker arm shaft, **Fig. 2.**
   d. Ensure notch in end of rocker arm shaft is facing direction shown in **Fig. 3.**

FRONT COVER

REPLACE

1. Remove drive belts.
2. Remove water pump pulley, then the crankshaft pulley.
3. Remove timing belt upper cover, then the lower cover.
4. Reverse procedure to install.

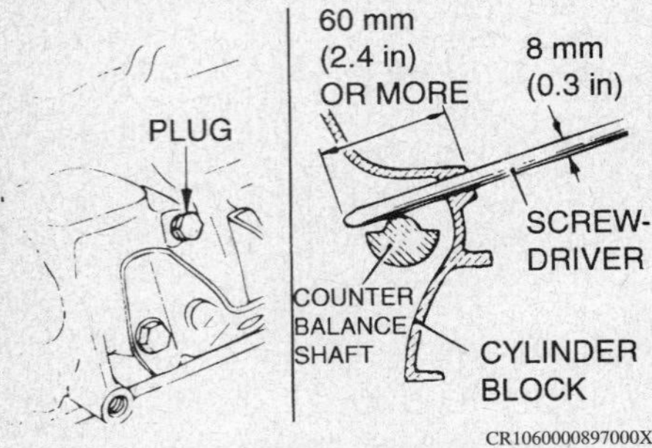

Fig. 6 Cylinder block plug location

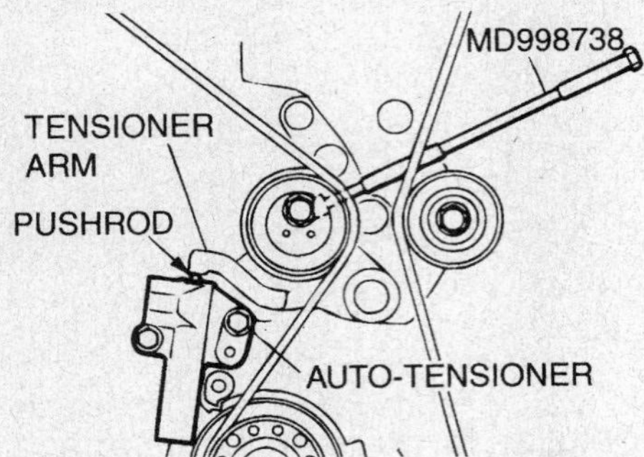

Fig. 7 Adjusting screw tool installation

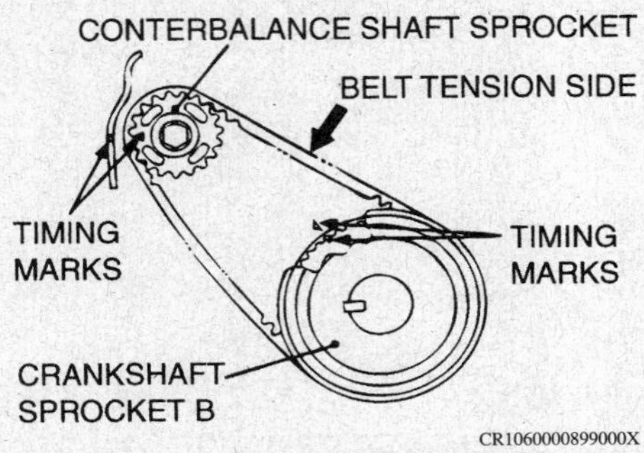

Fig. 8 Counterbalance shaft sprocket & crankshaft sprocket timing marks

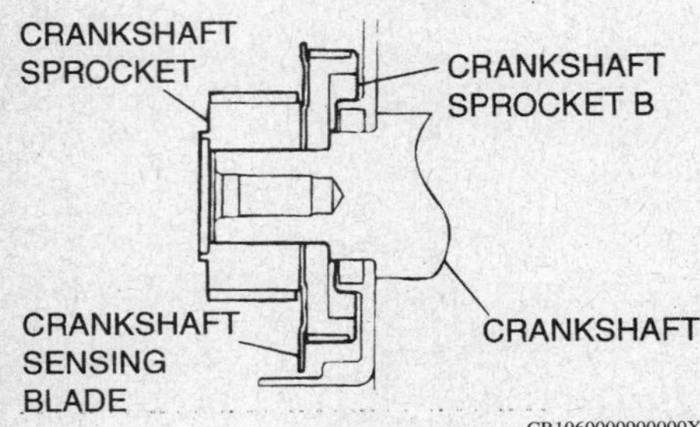

Fig. 9 Crankshaft sensing blade installation

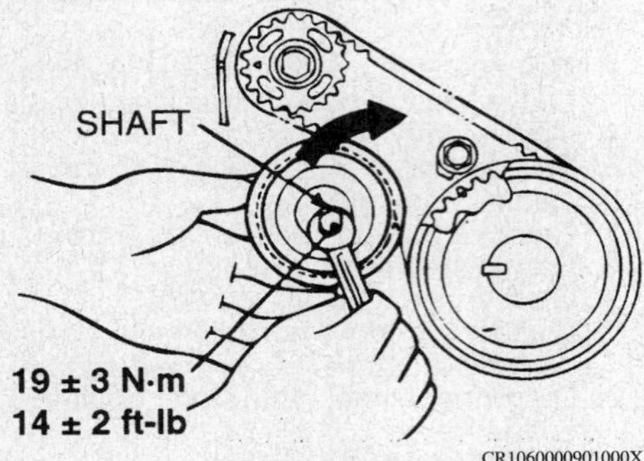

Fig. 10 Timing belt tensioner adjustment

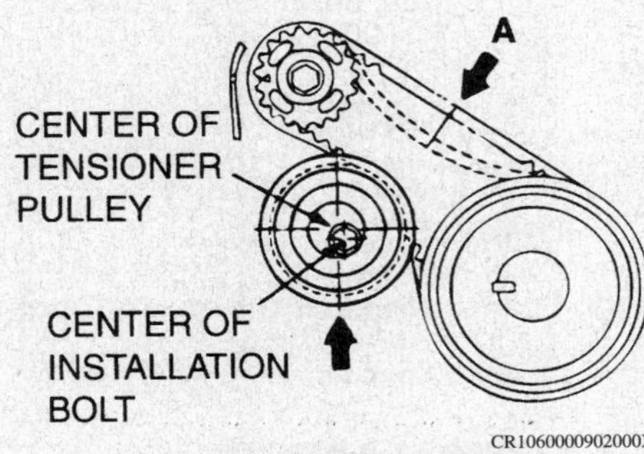

Fig. 11 Timing belt deflection

TIMING BELT

REPLACE

FRONT

Removal

1. Remove front cover as outlined under "Front Cover, Replace."
2. Turn crankshaft clockwise to align camshaft sprocket timing marks, **Fig. 4.**
3. Loosen timing belt tensioner bolt.
4. If timing belt is to be re-used, mark flat side of belt with an arrow to indicate clockwise rotating direction.
5. Move tensioner pulley toward water pump side, then remove timing belt.

Installation

1. Align timing marks on camshaft sprocket, crankshaft sprocket and oil pump sprocket **Fig. 5.**
2. Remove cylinder block plug and insert a suitable .3 inch Phillips head screw driver **Fig. 6.**
3. Ensure screwdriver goes in 2.4 inches or more. If screwdriver will only go in 1.0 inch, turn sprocket one revolution and insert screw driver again. **Do not remove screw driver until timing belt is installed.**
4. Install timing belt to crankshaft sprocket, oil pump sprocket and camshaft sprocket in that order so there is no slack in belt tension.
5. Set tension pulley so that pin holes are at bottom, then press lightly against timing belt. Temporarily tighten bolt.
6. Adjust timing belt tension as follows:
   a. Remove rubber plug from rear of timing belt cover, then screw in adjusting screw tool No. MD998738, or equivalent, by hand until tensioner arm is touching auto-tensioner pushrod **Fig. 7.**
   b. Turn crankshaft ¼ turn counterclockwise, then turn clockwise until timing marks are aligned.
   c. Loosen tensioner pulley bolt, then use tensioner pulley socket tool No. MD998767, or equivalent, to **torque** bolt to 32–40 ft. lbs. while applying 31 inch lbs. of tension to belt.
   d. Turn crankshaft two revolutions clockwise so that timing marks are aligned.
   e. After leaving auto-tensioner for 15 minutes, measure protrusion of pushrod. Pushrod should protrude .15–.18 inch. In not repeat steps a through d.
7. Check again that timing marks on each sprocket are aligned.
8. Install front cover.

REAR

Removal

1. Remove front timing belt as outlined under "Timing Belt, Replace."
2. Using crankshaft holding tool No. MB991367, or equivalent, remove crankshaft sprocket.
3. Remove crankshaft sensing blade.
4. Remove rear timing belt tensioner, then the rear timing belt.

Installation

1. Install rear timing belt crankshaft sprocket ensuring timing marks are aligned **Fig. 8.**
2. Install rear timing belt ensuring there is no slack in belt.
3. Install crankshaft sensing blade so it faces as shown in **Fig. 9.**
4. Adjust timing belt tension as follows:
   a. Temporarily fix timing belt tensioner so center of pulley is to left and above center of mounting bolt.
   b. Holding timing belt tensioner up in direction of arrow **Fig. 10,** apply pressure on timing belt so belt is taut. **Torque** bolt to 12–16 ft. lbs.
   c. Ensure timing belt deflection at point (A) is 0.2–0.3 inch, **Fig. 11.**

CAMSHAFT

REPLACE

1. Remove air cleaner assembly.
2. Remove rocker arms as outlined under "Rocker Arms, Replace."
3. Remove camshaft position sensor support.
4. Remove camshaft position sensing cylinder, then the camshaft sprocket.
5. Remove spark plug guide oil seal.
6. Using end yoke holder tool No. MB990767 and crankshaft pulley holding tool No. MD998719, or equivalents, remove camshaft sprocket.
7. Remove camshaft oil seal, then the camshaft.
8. Reverse procedure to install noting the following:
   a. Using oil seal installer tool No. MD998713, or equivalent, install camshaft oil seal.

PISTON & ROD ASSEMBLY

The front mark on piston must face toward timing belt side of engine. Connecting

CRANKSHAFT JOURNAL OUTSIDE DIAMETER		CYLINDER BLOCK BEARING BORE	CRANKSHAFT BEARING	CRANKSHAFT BEARING FOR NO.3
IDENTIFICATION COLOR	SIZE mm (in)	IDENTIFICATION MARK	IDENTIFICATION MARK OR COLOR	IDENTIFICATION MARK OR COLOR
Yellow	56.994 - 57.000 (2.2439 - 2.2441)	0	1 or Green	0 or Black
		1	2 or Yellow	1 or Green
		2	3 or None	2 or Yellow
None	56.988 - 56.994 (2.2436 - 2.2439)	0	2 or Yellow	1 or Green
		1	3 or None	2 or Yellow
		2	4 or Blue	3 or None
White	56.982 - 56.988 (2.2438 - 2.2436)	0	3 or None	2 or Yellow
		1	4 or Blue	3 or None
		2	5 or Red	4 or Blue

CR1060000905000X

Fig. 12 Main bearing selection chart

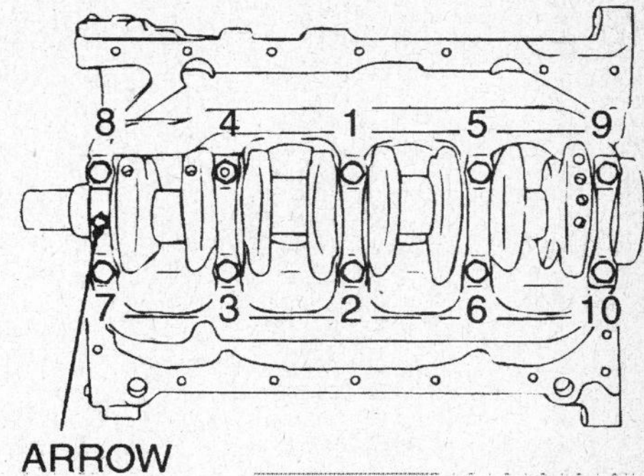

Fig. 13 Main bearing tightening sequence

rods and caps must be installed in original positions. **Torque** bolts to 13–15 ft. lbs, then an additional 90–94°.

MAIN & ROD BEARINGS

If bearing replacement is required, measure crankshaft journal diameter and select appropriate bearing from the chart **Fig. 12. Torque** bolts to 17–19 ft. lbs. in sequence shown **Fig. 13,** then an additional 90°.

CRANKSHAFT SEAL

REPLACE

1. Remove front timing belt as outlined under "Timing Belt, Replace."
2. Remove crankshaft position sensor.
3. Using crankshaft spanner tool No. MB991367, or equivalent, remove crankshaft sprocket.
4. Remove crankshaft sensing blade.
5. Remove rear timing belt as outlined under "Timing Belt, Replace."
6. Remove rear timing belt crankshaft sprocket.
7. Remove key, then the crankshaft front oil seal.
8. Reverse procedure to install noting the following:
   a. Apply engine oil to entire inside diameter of oil seal lip.
   b. Using crankshaft oil seal installer tool No. MD998375, or equivalent, press in oil seal until it is flush with front case.
   c. Install crankshaft sensing blade as shown in **Fig. 9.**

CRANKSHAFT REAR OIL SEAL

REPLACE

1. Remove oil pan as outlined under "Oil Pan, Replace."
2. Remove transaxle as outlined under "Transaxle, Replace."
3. **On models with manual transaxles,** remove clutch disc, flywheel and adapter plate.
4. **On models with automatic transaxles,** remove drive plate.
5. **On all models,** remove crankshaft bushing.
6. Remove crankshaft rear oil seal.
7. Reverse procedure to install noting the following:
   a. Apply a small amount of engine oil to entire inside diameter of oil seal lip.
   b. Using oil seal installer tool Nos. MB990938 and MD998776, or equivalents, tap in oil seal as shown **Fig. 14.**

OIL PAN

REPLACE

1. Drain engine oil, then remove dipstick.
2. Remove front exhaust pipe, then the bell housing cover.
3. Using oil pan removal tool No. MD998727, or equivalent, remove oil pan.
4. Reverse procedure to install noting the following:
   a. Apply sealant part No. MD970389, or equivalent, around gasket surface of oil pan.
   b. Install oil pan within 15 minutes after applying sealant.
   c. Wait at least one hour before starting engine after installing oil pan.

OIL PUMP

REPLACE

1. Remove oil filter, then the oil pressure switch.
2. Remove oil pan as outlined under "Oil Pan, Replace."
3. Remove oil screen then the oil screen gasket.
4. Using plug wrench tool No. MD998162 and plug wrench retainer tool No. MD998783, or equivalents, remove plug on front case.
5. Remove plug on side of cylinder block, then insert a suitable screw driver to lock counterbalance shaft. Remove flange bolt.
6. Remove relief plug, then the gasket.
7. Remove relief spring, then the plunger.
8. Remove oil filter bracket, then the gasket.
9. Remove oil pump front case assembly.
10. Remove oil pump cover.
11. Remove oil pump driven gear, then the drive gear.
12. Remove crankshaft front oil seal.
13. Remove oil pump oil seal.
14. Remove counterbalance shaft oil seal, then the front case.
15. Remove right and left counterbalance shafts.
16. Using bearing puller tool No. MD998371, or equivalent, remove counterbalance shaft front bearing.
17. Remove right and left rear counterbalance shaft bearings.
18. Reverse procedure to install noting the following:
    a. Using bearing installer tool No. MD998705, or equivalent, install right rear counterbalance shaft bearing ensuring oil holes are aligned.
    b. Using bearing installer stopper tool No. MB991603, or equivalent installed on cylinder block, install left rear counterbalance shaft bearing.
    c. Using bearing installer tool No. MD998705, or equivalent, install front counterbalance shaft bearing ensuring oil holes are aligned.
    d. Using oil seal installer tool No. MD998375, or equivalent, install crankshaft front oil seal.
    e. Install oil pump gears ensuring to align alignment marks, **Fig. 15.**
    f. Using crankshaft front oil seal guide tool No. MD998285, or equivalent set on front end of crankshaft, install oil pump case assembly.

OIL PUMP SERVICE

1. Ensure oil pump gears rotate smoothly with no looseness.
2. Check for ridge wear on contact surface between front case and gear surface of oil pump cover.
3. Check gear side clearance. Clearance should be .004–.006 inch for drive gear and .003–.004 inch for driven gear.

BELT TENSION DATA

Apply 22 lbs. of force to middle of belt between generator pulley and water pump pulley. Deflection should be .26–.35 inch.

COOLING SYSTEM BLEED

Start engine and bring to operating temperature. Rev engine repeatedly to 3000 RPM. After engine has cooled down remove radiator cap and fill to top of radiator.

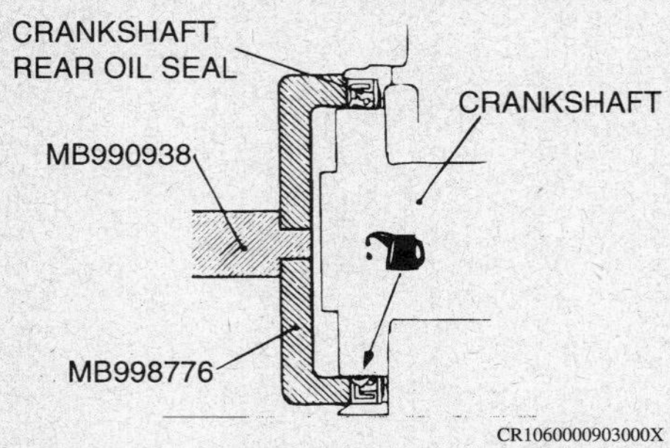

Fig. 14 Crankshaft rear oil seal installation

THERMOSTAT

REPLACE

1. Drain coolant into suitable container.
2. Remove air cleaner assembly.
3. Disconnect lower radiator hose, then the water inlet fitting.
4. Remove thermostat.
5. Reverse procedure to install noting the following:
   a. Install thermostat with jiggle valve facing straight up.

WATER PUMP

REPLACE

1. Drain coolant into suitable container.
2. Remove timing belt tensioner as outlined under "Timing Belt, Replace."
3. Remove alternator brace.
4. Remove water pump assembly.
5. Reverse procedure to install.

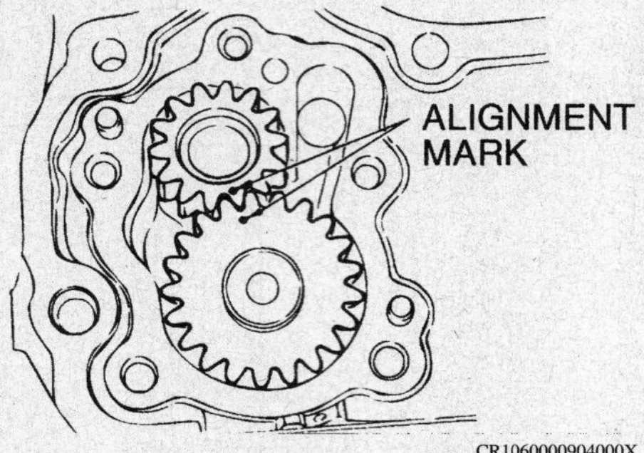

Fig. 15 Oil pump gear alignment marks

RADIATOR

REPLACE

1. Drain coolant into suitable container, then disconnect radiator hoses.
2. Remove reserve tank assembly.
3. **On models with automatic transaxles,** disconnect transaxle cooler lines.
4. **On all models,** remove radiator supports, then the radiator.
5. Remove radiator fan motor assembly.
6. Reverse procedure to install.

FUEL PUMP

REPLACE

1. Remove rear seat cushion, then the access plate.
2. Relieve fuel pressure as outlined under "Precautions"
3. Disconnect fuel hose and electrical connector.

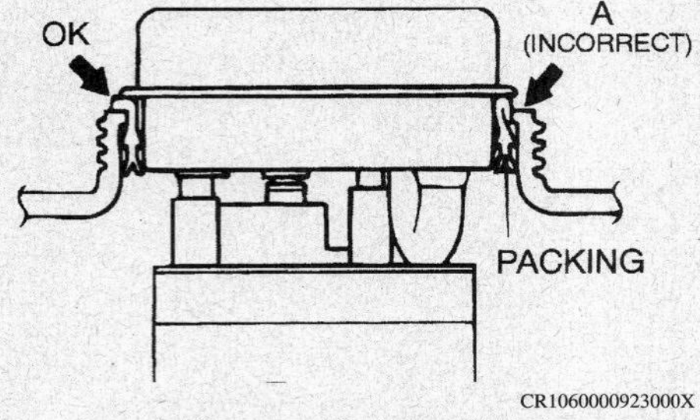

Fig. 16 Fuel pump packing installation

4. Using tank cap wrench tool No. MB991480, or equivalent, remove fuel pump module.
5. Reverse procedure to install noting the following:
   a. Install packing to fuel tank **Fig. 16,** then install fuel pump module.
   b. Align mating mark on fuel pump module with mark on fuel tank.

FUEL FILTER

REPLACE

1. Remove fuel pump as outlined under "Fuel Pump, Replace."
2. Remove thermistor case, then the fuel gage unit.
3. Remove packing, then the reservoir cup.
4. Remove pump support assembly.
5. Remove electrical harness, then the lock bracket.
6. Remove fuel pump, then the fuel filter.

TIGHTENING SPECIFICATIONS

Year	Component	Torque Ft. Lbs.
2001–02	Auto-Tensioner Attaching Bolt	14–20
	Camshaft Sprocket	58–72
	Camshaft Position Sensor	104–130①
	Connecting Rod Bearing Cap	③
	Crankshaft Pulley	14–22
	Crankshaft Sprocket	80–94
	Cylinder Head	②
	Drive Plate	94–102
	Engine Mount (M12x74)	56–74
	Engine Mount (M12x108)	51–69
	Engine Mount Bracket	56–72
	Exhaust Manifold	20–24
	Exhaust Manifold Bracket	22–30
	Flywheel (Manual Trans.)	95–101
	Front Case	15–19
	Ignition Coil Bolt	70–104①
	Intake Manifold Bolt	44–52①
	Intake Manifold Nut	12–16
	Intake Manifold Stay	21–23
	Main Bearing Cap	④
	Oil Filter Bracket	12–16
	Oil Pan	53–69①
	Oil Pan Drain Plug	25–33
	Oil Pump Cover	11–13
	Power Steering Pump	29–43
	Rocker Arm Shaft	21–25
	Rocker Cover	27–35
	Timing Belt Lower Cover	88–104①
	Timing Belt Tensioner	12–16
	Timing Belt Upper Cover	114–120①
	Water Pump Pulley	69–77

① — Inch lbs.
② — Refer to "Cylinder Head Replace" for tightening procedures & specifications.
③ — Refer to "Piston & Rod Assembly" for tightening procedure & specifications.
④ — Refer to "Main & Rod Bearings" for tightening procedure & specifications.

2.5L Engine

NOTE: Refer To The "Breeze, Cirrus, 1998–2000 Sebring Convertible & Stratus & 2001–02 Sebring & Stratus Sedan"Chapter For Procedures Not Covered In This Section.

NOTE: On Air Bag Equipped Models, Refer To "Air Bag System Precautions" Located In The Front Of This Manual For System Disarming & Arming Procedures.

NOTE: Refer To "Computer Relearn Procedures" Located In The Front Of This Manual When Battery Power To The Computer Has Been Interrupted.

INDEX

PRECAUTIONS

AIR BAG SYSTEMS

Refer to "Air Bag System Precautions" in the front of this manual for system disarming and arming procedures.

BATTERY GROUND CABLE

Prior to service, disconnect battery ground cable and isolate as required.

FUEL SYSTEM PRESSURE RELIEF

1. Remove rear seat cushion.
2. Remove protector to disconnect fuel pump connector.
3. Start engine and run until it stops naturally, then turn ignition switch off.
4. Connect fuel pump connector and install protector.
5. Install rear cushion.

COMPRESSION PRESSURE

Perform compression test with engine at normal operating temperature, spark plugs removed and throttle wide open. Standard compression pressure at cranking speed is 185 psi. The minimum compression pressure is 139 psi with a maximum variation between cylinders of 14 psi.

ENGINE MOUNT

REPLACE

1. Remove radiator coolant reserve tank.
2. Raise and support engine so there is no weight on the engine mount bracket insulator.
3. Remove engine mount insulator mounting bolt, **Fig. 1.**
4. Remove engine mount bracket.
5. Remove engine mount stopper.

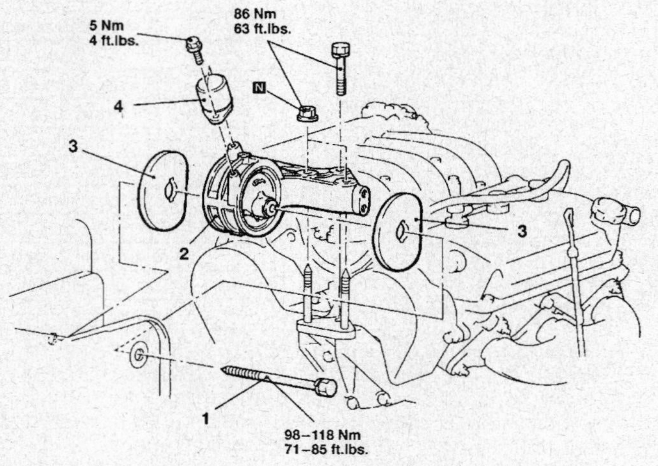

Fig. 1 Engine mount replacement

6. Remove dynamic damper.
7. Reverse procedure to install. Tighten to specifications.

ENGINE

REPLACE

1. Release fuel pressure as described under "Precautions."
2. Mark and remove hood.
3. Remove radiator as described under "Radiator, Replace."
4. Remove front exhaust pipe.
5. Remove transaxle as outlined in "Automatic Transmissions/Transaxles" chapter.
6. Disconnect the following electrical connectors:
   a. Power steering pressure switch, **Fig. 2.**
   b. Intake air temperature sensor.
   c. Oxygen sensors.
   d. A/C compressor.
   e. Injectors.
   f. Engine coolant temperature gauge unit.
   g. Engine coolant temperature sensor.
   h. Ignition coil.
   i. Idle air control motor.
   j. Crankshaft position sensor.
   k. Alternator wiring harness.
   l. Throttle position sensor.
   m. Relay box.

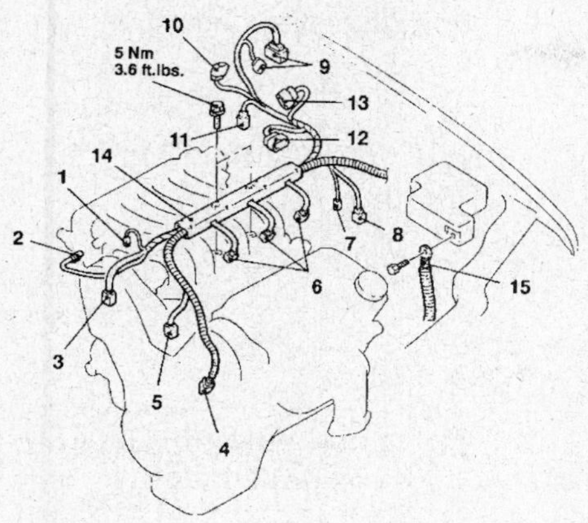

1. Power steering pressure switch connector
2. Intake air temperature sensor connector
3. Heated oxygen sensor connector
4. A/C compressor connector
5. Heated oxygen sensor connector
6. Injector connector
7. Engine coolant temperature gauge unit connector
8. Engine coolant temperature sensor connector
9. Ignition coil connector
10. Idle air control motor connector
11. Crankshaft position sensor connector
12. Generator wiring harness connector
13. TPS connector
14. Control wiring harness
15. Relay box and generator wiring harness connection

CR1069600644010X

Fig. 2 Engine replacement (Part 1 of 2)

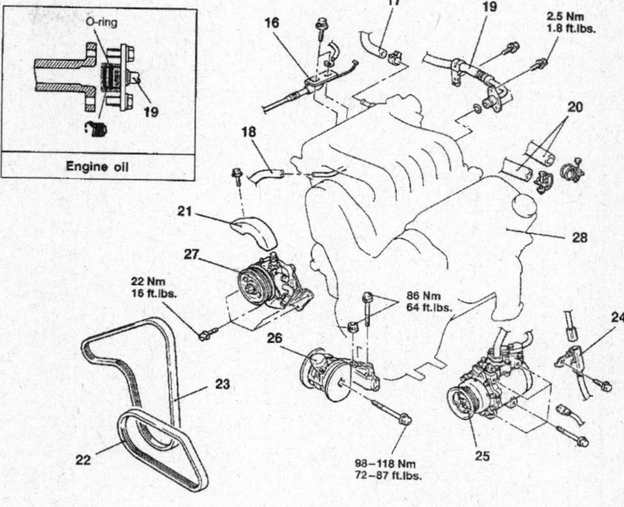

16. Accelerator cable connection
17. Brake booster vacuum hose connection
18. Purge hose connection
19. High-pressure fuel hose connection
20. Heater hose connection
21. Pump cover
22. Drive belt (A/C compressor)
23. Drive belt (Power steering oil pump and generator)
24. Heated oxygen sensor connection
25. A/C compressor
26. Engine mount bracket
27. Power steering oil pump and bracket assembly
28. Engine assembly

CR1069600644020X

Fig. 2 Engine replacement (Part 2 of 2)

7. Disconnect accelerator cable.
8. Disconnect brake booster vacuum hose.
9. Disconnect purge hose.
10. Disconnect high pressure fuel hose.
11. Disconnect heater hose.
12. Remove power steering pump cover.
13. Remove accessory drive belts.
14. Remove A/C compressor with hose attached.
15. Support engine with jack and hold engine with chain block or similar support tool.
16. Place jack under engine oil pan with piece of wood in between, then raise engine so the weight of the engine is no longer being applied to mounting bracket.
17. Remove engine mount bracket.
18. Remove power steering pump with hoses attached. Suspend pump with wire.
19. Ensure all cables, connectors and hoses have been disconnected, then raise engine slowly from engine compartment.
20. Reverse procedure to install. Tighten all fasteners to specifications.

TIMING BELT

REPLACE

With the timing belt removed, avoid turning the camshaft or crankshaft. If movement is required, exercise extreme caution to avoid valve damage caused by piston contact.

1. Remove cooling system reserve tank.
2. Remove A/C compressor drive belt, then the alternator and power steering pump drive belt.
3. Remove alternator bracket.
4. Remove front center undercover.
5. Support engine by positioning a suitable jack and wooden block under oil pan.
6. Using pulling tool Nos. MB998754 and MB990767, or equivalents, remove the crankshaft pulley, **Fig. 3.**
7. Disconnect oxygen sensor electrical connector.
8. Remove engine mount bracket and support bracket, **Fig. 3. Spray upper engine support bracket (reamer) bolt with lubricant and use care when removing, as bolt may be heat seized, Fig. 4.**
9. Remove power steering pump and bracket, then position aside with hoses attached.
10. Remove timing belt upper and lower covers.
11. Rotate crankshaft to align camshaft and crankshaft sprocket timing marks, **Fig. 5.**
12. Loosen timing belt tensioner pulley center bolt, then remove timing belt.
13. Remove timing belt tensioner attaching bolts, then the tensioner.
14. Inspect timing belt tensioner for leaks and tensioner push rod for cracks. Replace tensioner if leaks or cracks are present.
15. Position timing belt tensioner in a soft jawed vise.
16. Carefully press push rod into tensioner body. Press push rod into pump body until pin holes are aligned, **Fig. 6.**
17. Insert a .06 inch pin through tensioner body and push rod pin holes, **Fig. 7. Do not remove pin until after timing belt has been installed.**
18. Ensure camshaft and crankshaft sprocket timing marks are aligned, **Fig. 5.**
19. Position timing belt over crankshaft sprocket, idler pulley, front bank camshaft sprocket, water pump pulley, rear bank camshaft sprocket, then the timing belt tensioner pulley. **Do not to allow timing belt to slack during installation.** Use binder clips to hold timing belt in place during installation. After timing belt has been installed, remove binder clips.
20. Apply force in counterclockwise direction to rear bank camshaft sprocket until timing belt tension side is taut, **Fig. 8.** Ensure the camshaft and crankshaft sprocket timing marks are aligned, **Fig. 5.**
21. Carefully raise tensioner pulley so that timing belt does not sag, then tighten tensioner pulley center bolt, **Fig. 8.**
22. Rotate crankshaft ¼ turn counterclockwise, then turn crankshaft clockwise until camshaft and crankshaft timing marks are aligned, **Fig. 5.**
23. Loosen timing belt tensioner pulley center bolt.
24. Using holding tool No. MD998776, or equivalent, and a suitable torque wrench, apply 3.3 ft. lbs. of tension to the timing belt, **Fig. 9.** While applying tension to timing belt, torque tensioner pulley center bolt to 35 ft. lbs. **When tightening tensioner pulley center bolt, do not allow tensioner pulley to rotate.**
25. Remove .06 inch pin from tensioner push rod and tensioner body pin holes.
26. Rotate crankshaft two turns in clockwise direction.
27. Wait approximately five minutes, then check if .06 inch pin can be easily inserted through tensioner body and push rod pin holes. If pin cannot be easily inserted, check tensioner push rod projection, **Fig. 10.** Tensioner push

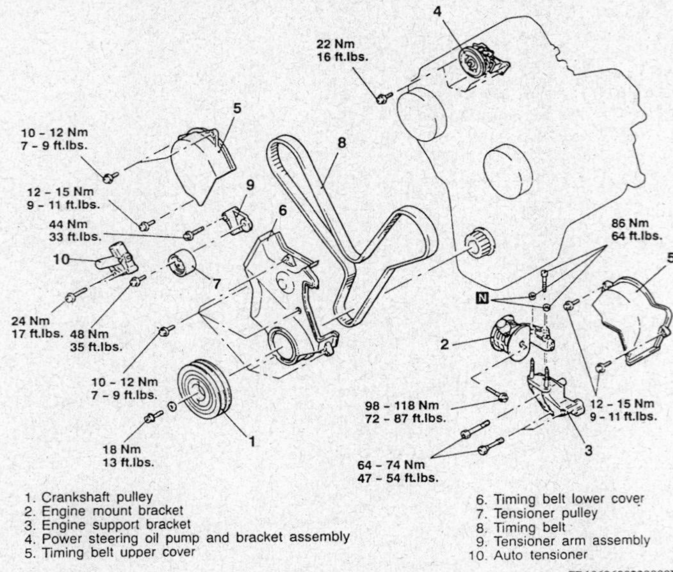

Fig. 3 Timing belt & components

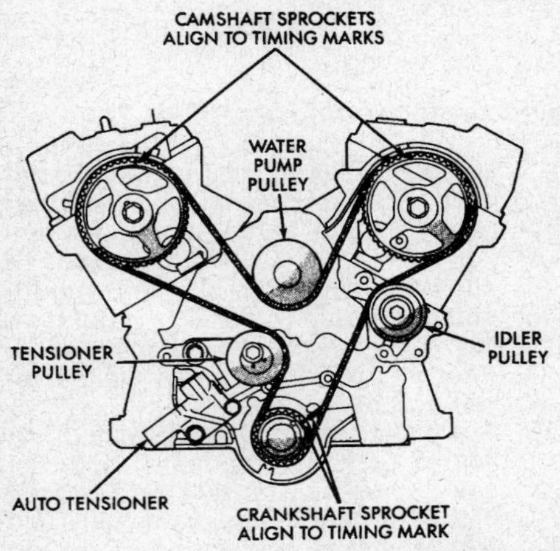

Fig. 5 Camshaft & crankshaft timing marks

rod projection should be .149–.177 inch. If projection is not within limits, repeat previous six steps.

28. Ensure camshaft and crankshaft sprocket timing marks are aligned, **Fig. 5.**
29. Install timing belt lower and upper covers.
30. Install power steering pump and bracket.
31. Install engine mount bracket and support bracket, **Fig. 3. Spray upper engine support bracket bolt with lubricant and use care when installing. When installing engine mount bracket, ensure arrow on engine mount stopper is facing toward engine, Fig. 11.**

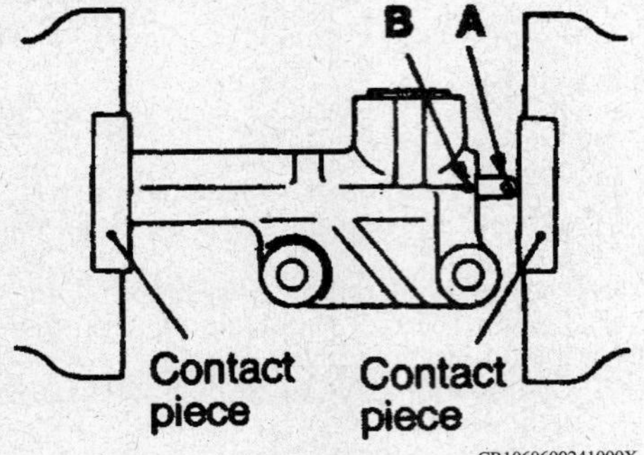

Fig. 6 Pressing tensioner push rod into tensioner housing

32. Using holding tool No. MB990767, or equivalent and a suitable torque wrench, install crankshaft pulley bolt. Tighten crankshaft pulley bolt to specifications.
33. Connect oxygen sensor electrical connector.
34. Remove jack and wooden block from under oil pan.
35. Install alternator bracket.
36. Install front center undercover.
37. Install alternator and power steering pump drive belt, then the A/C compressor drive belt.
38. Install cooling system reserve tank.
39. Check and adjust ignition timing as necessary.

RADIATOR

REPLACE

1. Remove radiator drain plug and drain

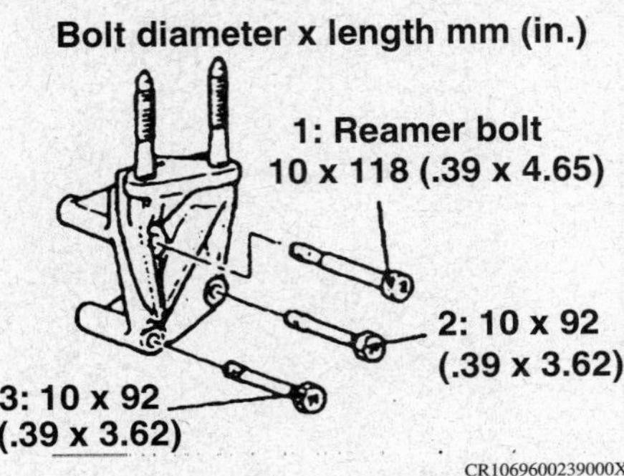

Fig. 4 Engine support bolt identification

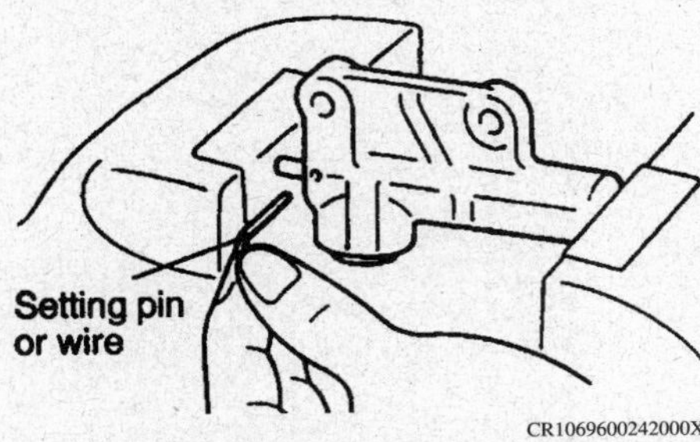

Fig. 7 Tensioner push rod pin installation

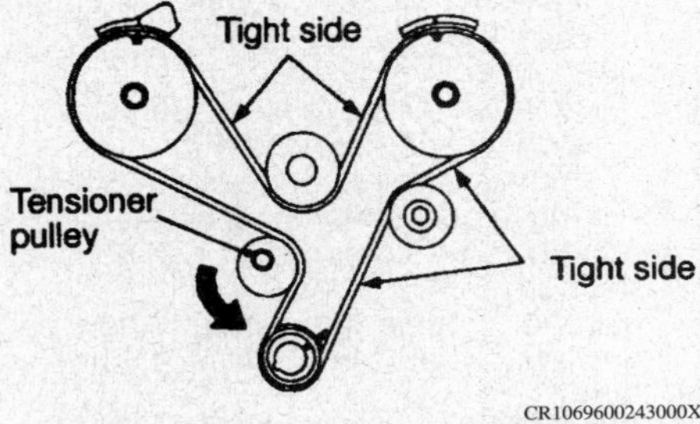

Fig. 8 Timing belt removal

engine coolant into a suitable container.

2. Remove radiator cap.
3. Disconnect overflow hose and remove coolant reserve tank.
4. Remove reserve tank bracket.
5. After making mating marks on radiator hoses and hose clamps, remove upper and lower radiator hoses.
6. Disconnect transaxle fluid cooler hose and pipe assembly. Plug radiator port to prevent foreign material from entering.
7. Remove upper insulator, then the radiator.
8. Remove lower insulator.
9. Remove condenser fan motor and fan.
10. Remove radiator fan motor and fan.
11. Remove radiator fan shroud.
12. Reverse procedure to install. Tighten to specifications.

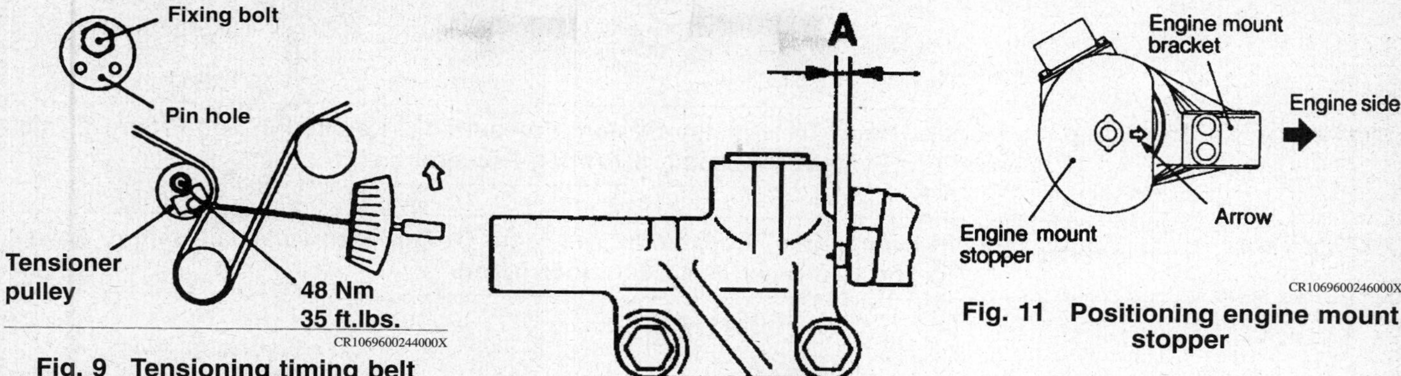

Fig. 9 Tensioning timing belt

Fig. 10 Tensioner push rod protrusion inspection

Fig. 11 Positioning engine mount stopper

TIGHTENING SPECIFICATIONS

Year	Component	Torque/ Ft. Lbs.
1998–2000	Coolant Reserve Tank Bracket Bolts	108①
	Crankshaft Pulley Bolt	134
	Dynamic Damper Bolt	48①
	Engine Mount Bracket Bolt & Nut	63
	Engine Mount Bracket/Stopper Through Bolt	71–85
	Power Steering Pump Mounting Bolt	16
	Upper Radiator Insulator Bolts	108①

① — Inch lbs.

3.0L Engine

NOTE: On Air Bag Equipped Models, Refer To "Air Bag System Precautions" Located In The Front Of This Manual For System Disarming & Arming Procedures.

NOTE: Refer To "Computer Relearn Procedures" Located In The Front Of This Manual When Battery Power To The Computer Has Been Interrupted.

INDEX

PRECAUTIONS

AIR BAG SYSTEMS

Refer to "Air Bag System Precautions" in the front of this manual for system disarming and arming procedures.

BATTERY GROUND CABLE

Prior to service, disconnect battery ground cable and isolate as required.

FUEL SYSTEM PRESSURE RELIEF

1. Remove fuel pump relay.
2. Start engine and let it run until it stops naturally, then turn ignition to off position.
3. Reconnect fuel pump relay.

COMPRESSION PRESSURE

Perform compression pressure check with throttle valve wide open and crankshaft position sensor disconnected. Standard compression pressure is 119 psi at cranking speed. The minimum pressure is 83 psi with a maximum variance between cylinders of 14 psi.

ENGINE MOUNT

REPLACE

1. Place a suitable jack under engine so there is no weight on engine mount.
2. Remove coolant reserve tank, then the suction hose.

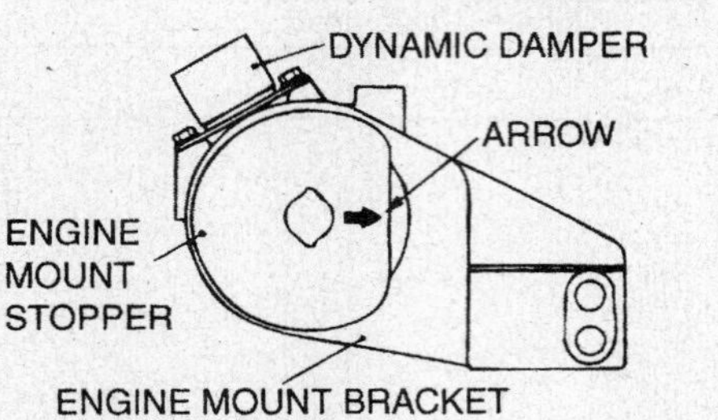

Fig. 1 Engine mount stopper installation

3. Remove insulator mounting bolt, then the mount bracket.
4. Remove engine mount stopper, then the dynamic damper.
5. Reverse procedure to install noting the following:
   a. Install engine mount stopper as shown in **Fig. 1.**
   b. Tighten bolts to specifications.

ENGINE

REPLACE

1. Remove hood, then drain coolant into suitable container.
2. Release fuel pressure as outlined under "Precautions."
3. Remove strut tower brace, then the air cleaner assembly.
4. Remove radiator reserve tank, then the front exhaust pipe.
5. Disconnect accelerator cable.
6. Disconnect engine wiring harness electrical connections.
7. Disconnect high-pressure fuel hose, then the return hose.
8. Disconnect heater hoses.
9. Remove drive belts.
10. Remove A/C compressor with lines attached, then position aside.
11. Remove power steering pump with hose attached, then position aside.
12. Remove engine mount stay.
13. Remove transaxle as outlined under "Transaxle, Replace."
14. Remove engine mount bracket, then the stopper.
15. Remove engine assembly.
16. Reverse procedure to install.

INTAKE MANIFOLD

REPLACE

1. Release fuel pressure as outlined under "Precautions."
2. Drain engine coolant into suitable container.
3. Remove air cleaner assembly, then the throttle body.
4. Remove strut tower brace.
5. Disconnect engine wiring harness electrical connections.
6. Disconnect brake booster vacuum hose connection.
7. Remove EGR valve, then the pipe connection.
8. Remove power steering pump drive belt.
9. Remove power steering pump bracket stay.
10. Remove front and rear intake manifold plenum stay.
11. Remove intake manifold plenum.
12. Disconnect high-pressure fuel hose, then the return hose.

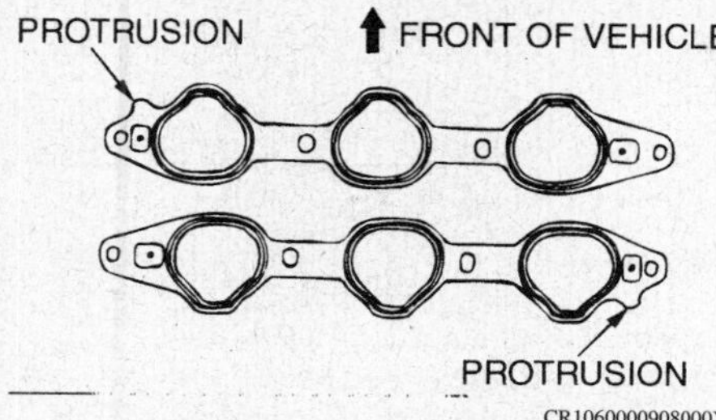

Fig. 2 Intake manifold gasket installation

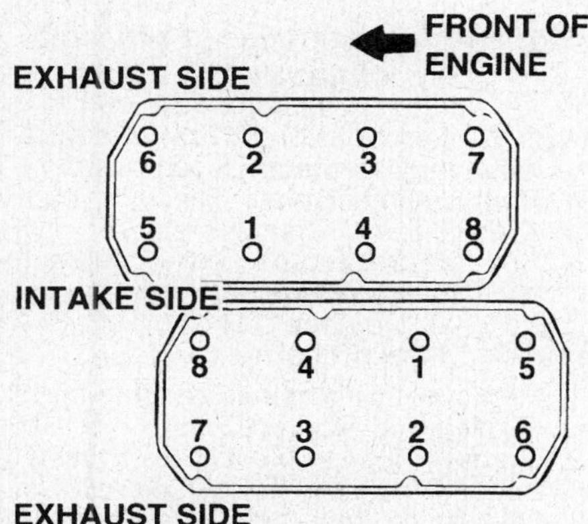

Fig. 5 Cylinder head bolt tightening sequence

13. Remove fuel rail, then the fuel pressure regulator.
14. Remove timing belt left and right upper covers.
15. Remove intake manifold.
16. Reverse procedure to install noting the following:
    a. Install intake gasket as shown in **Fig. 2.**
    b. Tighten intake bolts as shown in **Fig. 3.**

EXHAUST MANIFOLD

REPLACE

1. Remove front exhaust pipe.
2. Remove air cleaner assembly, then the battery and battery tray.
3. Remove engine oil dipstick guide, then the strut tower brace.
4. Remove left bank manifold upper and lower heat shields.
5. Remove left exhaust manifold, then the EGR pipe.
6. Remove right bank manifold upper and lower heat shields
7. Remove right exhaust manifold.
8. Reverse procedure to install tightening to specifications.

CYLINDER HEAD

REPLACE

1. Drain engine coolant into suitable container.
2. Remove timing belt as outlined under "Timing Belt, Replace."
3. Remove alternator, then the intake manifold as outlined under "Intake Manifold, Replace."

ORDER	MOUNTING NUTS	TIGHTENING TORQUE
1st	Right-bank nuts	6.4 ± 1.4 N·m (56 ± 13 in-lb)
2nd	Left-bank nuts	22 ± 1 N·m (16 ± 1 ft-lb)
3rd	Right-bank nuts	22 ± 1 N·m (16 ± 1 ft-lb)
4th	Left-bank nuts	22 ± 1 N·m (16 ± 1 ft-lb)
5th	Right-bank nuts	22 ± 1 N·m (16 ± 1 ft-lb)

CR1060000909000X

Fig. 3 Intake manifold tightening sequence

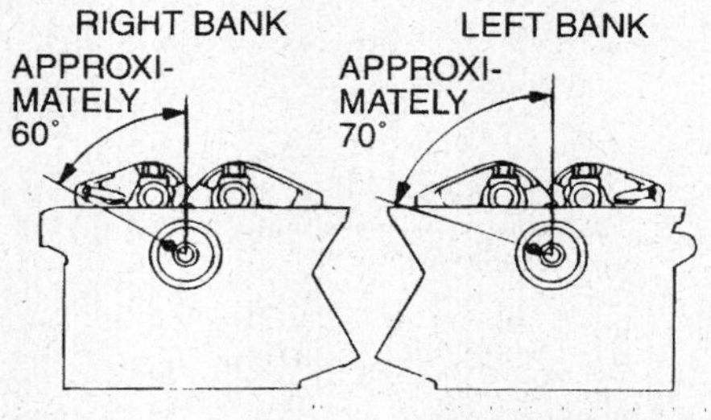

Fig. 6 Camshaft alignment

4. Remove exhaust manifold as outlined under "Exhaust Manifold, Replace."
5. Remove water inlet pipe.
6. Remove valve cover blow by hose, then the breather hose.
7. Remove PCV hose, then the spark plug wires.
8. Remove valve covers, then the timing belt rear cover.
9. Using cylinder head bolt wrench tool No. MD998051, or equivalent, loosen cylinder head bolts in two or three steps in sequence **Fig. 4.**
10. Reverse procedure to install noting the following:
    a. Install cylinder head bolt washers with rounded shoulder facing up.
    b. **Torque** cylinder head bolts to 77–83 ft. lbs. in two or three steps in sequence shown in **Fig. 5,** then loosen bolts in reverse order.
    c. **Torque** cylinder head bolts again progressively to 77–83 ft. lbs. in sequence.

ROCKER ARMS

REPLACE

1. Remove intake manifold as outlined under "Intake Manifold, Replace."
2. Remove breather hose, then the PCV valve from valve cover.
3. Remove valve cover.
4. Remove rocker arm shaft cap.
5. Install lash adjuster holder tool No. MD998713, or equivalent, to prevent lash adjuster from coming free.
6. Remove rocker arms and shaft.
7. Reverse procedure to install noting the following:
    a. Rotate camshaft until dowel pin on front end is located as shown in **Fig. 6.**

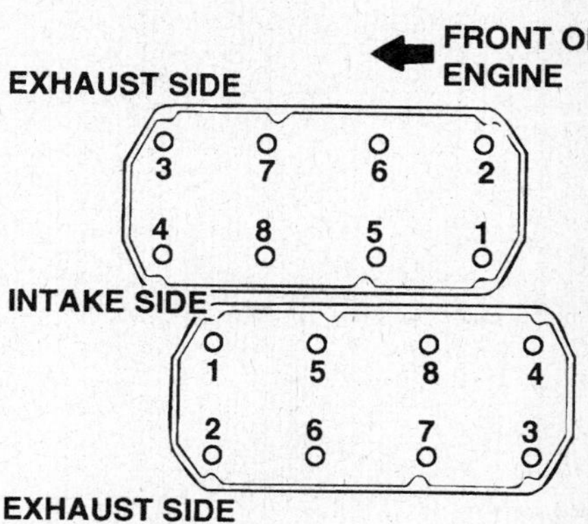

Fig. 4 Cylinder head bolt loosening sequence

Fig. 7 Rocker arm shaft notch position

    b. Ensure notch in end of rocker arm shaft is facing as shown in **Fig. 7.**
    c. Tighten bolts to specifications.

FRONT COVER

REPLACE

1. Remove power steering pump drive belt.
2. Using end yoke holder tool No. MB990767 and crankshaft pulley holder pin tool No. MD998715, or equivalents, remove crankshaft pulley,
3. Remove power steering pump tensioner pulley.
4. Remove right and left timing belt upper covers.
5. Remove timing belt lower cover.
6. Reverse procedure to install tightening bolts to specifications.

TIMING BELT

REPLACE

REMOVAL

1. Remove alternator, then the engine mount as outlined under "Engine Mount, Replace."
2. Remove timing belt cover as outlined under "Front Cover, Replace."
3. Remove right side engine support bracket.
4. Turn crankshaft clockwise to align each timing mark and set No. 1 cylinder at TDC on compression stroke, **Fig. 8.**

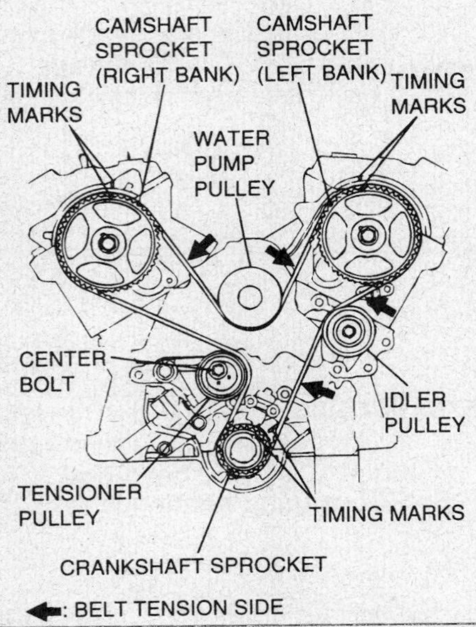

Fig. 8 Timing belt alignment marks

5. If reusing timing belt, chalk an arrow on flat side of belt to indicate clockwise direction.
6. Loosen center bolt of tensioner pulley, then remove timing belt.
7. Remove auto tensioner.

INSTALLATION

1. Align timing marks on camshaft sprockets with marks on rocker covers and timing mark on crankshaft with mark on engine block, **Fig. 8.**
2. Install timing belt in the following order:
   a. Crankshaft sprocket.
   b. Idler pulley.
   c. Left bank camshaft sprocket.
   d. Water pump pulley.
   e. Right bank camshaft sprocket.
   f. Tensioner pulley.
3. Turn right bank camshaft sprocket counterclockwise until tension side of timing belt is firmly stretched, then recheck timing marks.
4. Using tensioner wrench tool No. MD998767, or equivalent, push tensioner pulley into timing belt and temporarily tighten center bolt.
5. Using crankshaft pulley spacer tool No. MD998769, or equivalent, turn crankshaft ¼ turn counterclockwise, then turn it again clockwise until timing marks are aligned.
6. Loosen center bolt of tensioner pulley.
7. Using tensioner wrench tool No. MD998767, or equivalent and suitable torque wrench, apply 39 inch lbs. of tension torque to timing belt **Fig. 9.** Tighten center bolt to specifications.
8. Place two wooden blocks in a suitable vise, then place auto-tensioner perpendicular between blocks. If there is a plug at base of tensioner, insert a washer to protect plug.
9. Slowly compress pushrod of auto-tensioner until pin hole (A) in pushrod is aligned with pin hole (B) in cylinder

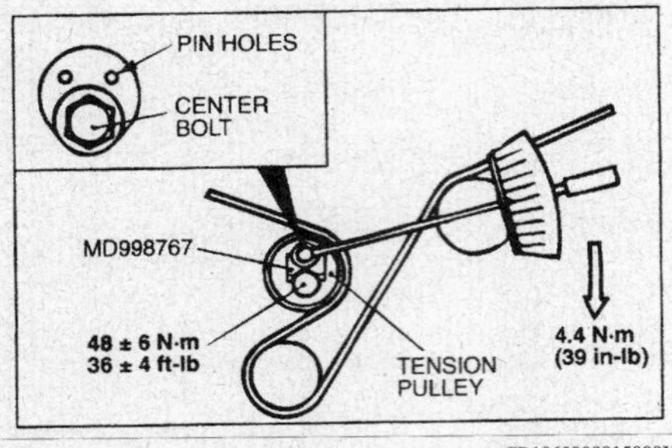

Fig. 9 Timing belt tension torque

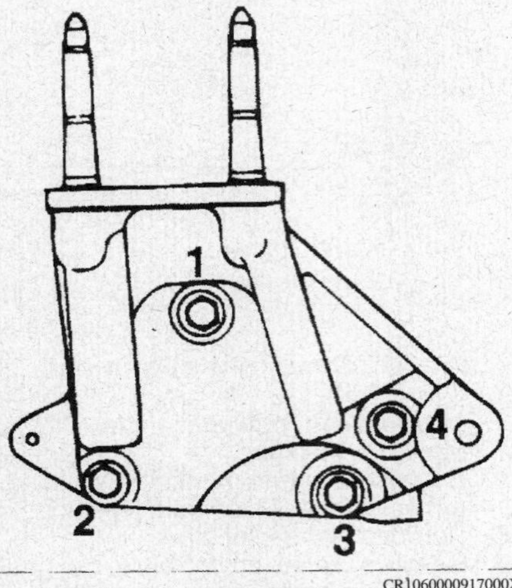

Fig. 11 Engine support bracket tightening sequence

Fig. 10, then insert a suitable pin into holes once they are aligned.

10. Install auto-tensioner on engine, then remove pin.
11. Turn crankshaft clockwise twice to align timing marks.
12. Wait at least five minutes, then check that auto-tensioner push rod extends .15–.20 inch. If not repeat steps 5 through 12.
13. Install engine support bracket, tighten bolts in sequence **Fig. 11** to specifications.
14. Install timing belt cover as outlined under "Front Cover, Replace."

CAMSHAFT

REPLACE

LEFT BANK

1. Remove timing belt as outlined under "Timing Belt, Replace."
2. Remove thermostat housing assembly.
3. Disconnect blow by hose, then the PCV hose from valve cover.
4. Remove spark plug wires, then the valve cover.
5. Remove rocker arm and shaft assembly as outlined under "Rocker Arms, Replace."
6. Using end yoke holder tool No. MB990767 and crankshaft pulley holder pin tool No. MD998715, or equivalents, remove camshaft sprocket.

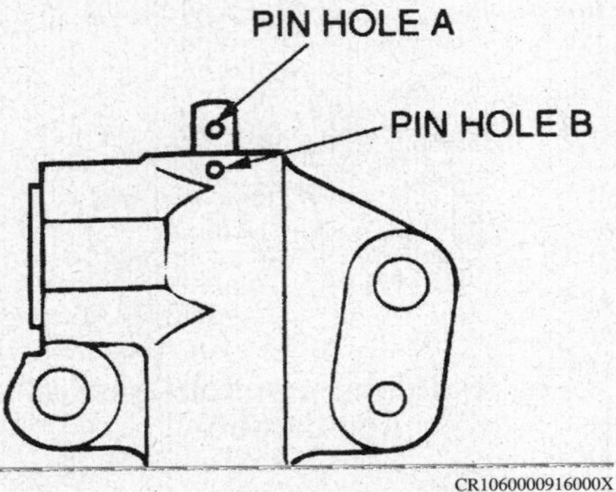

Fig. 10 Auto-tensioner pin hole alignment

7. Remove thrust plate, then the camshaft.
8. Reverse procedure to install tightening bolts to specifications.

RIGHT BANK

1. Remove timing belt as outlined under "Timing Belt, Replace."
2. Remove intake plenum as outlined under "Intake Manifold, Replace."
3. Disconnect breather hose, then the blow by hose from valve cover.
4. Remove spark plug wires, then the valve cover.
5. Remove rocker arms and shaft assembly as outlined under "Rocker Arms, Replace."
6. Remove distributor assembly.
7. Using end yoke holder tool No. MB990767 and crankshaft pulley holder pin tool No. MD998715, or equivalents, remove camshaft sprocket.
8. Remove camshaft.
9. Reverse procedure to install noting the following:
   a. Align timing mark on camshaft sprocket with mark on cylinder head.
   b. Align mating marks on distributor housing and coupling, then install on engine.
   c. Tighten bolts to specifications.

CRANKSHAFT

REPLACE

1. Remove engine as outlined under "Engine, Replace."
2. Remove oil pan as outlined under "Oil Pan, Replace."
3. **On models equipped with manual transaxle,** remove flywheel.
4. **On models equipped with automatic transaxle,** remove drive plate.
5. **On all models,** remove rear plate.
6. Remove rear oil seal as outlined under "Crankshaft Rear Oil Seal, Replace," then the seal case.
7. Remove bearing cap bolts, then the bearing cap.
8. Remove thrust washers, then the crankshaft.
9. Reverse procedure to install noting the following:

CRANKSHAFT JOURNAL OUTSIDE DIAMETER		CYLINDER BLOCK BEARING BORE	CRANK-SHAFT BEARING
ID COLOR	SIZE mm (inch)	ID MARK	ID COLOR
Yellow	59.990 - 59.996 (2.3618 - 2.3620)	I	Pink
		II	Red
		III	Green
None	59.984 - 59.990 (2.3616 - 2.3618)	I	Red
		II	Green
		III	Black
White	59.978 - 59.984 (2.3613 - 2.3616)	I	Green
		II	Black
		III	Brown

CR1060000925000X

Fig. 12 Crankshaft bearing selection chart

CR1060000918000X

Fig. 15 Upper oil pan removal

a. If bearing replacement is required, measure crankshaft journal diameter and select correct bearing from chart **Fig. 12.**
b. Cylinder block bearing bore diameter identification marks are stamped on block, **Fig. 13.**
c. Install thrust bearing with groove facing crankshaft web.
d. Install bearing cap with arrow facing timing belt side, then **torque** bolts is sequence **Fig. 14** to 65–73 ft. lbs.

CRANKSHAFT SEAL

REPLACE

1. Remove timing belt as outlined under "Timing Belt, Replace."
2. Remove crankshaft position sensor, then the sensing blade.
3. Remove crankshaft spacer and key.
4. Remove crankshaft front oil seal.
5. Reverse procedure to install noting the following:
   a. Apply a small amount of engine oil to seal lip before installing.
   b. Using crankshaft front oil seal installer tool No. MD998717, or equivalent, tap oil seal into front case.

CRANKSHAFT REAR OIL SEAL

REPLACE

1. Remove transaxle as outlined under "Transaxle, Replace."
2. **On models equipped with manual transaxle,** remove clutch as outlined under "Clutch, Replace."

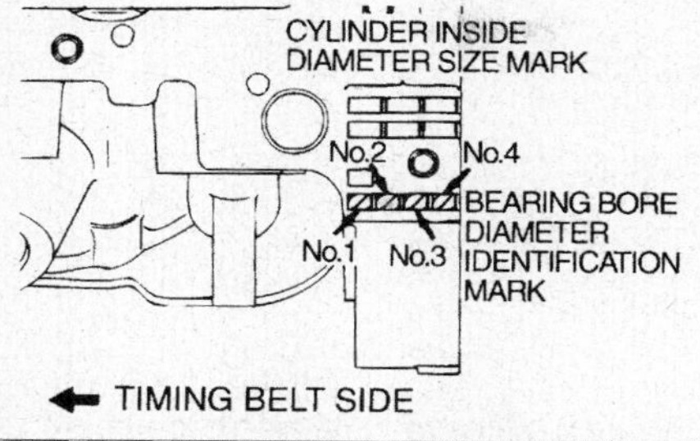

CR1060000926000X

Fig. 13 Block bearing bore identification location

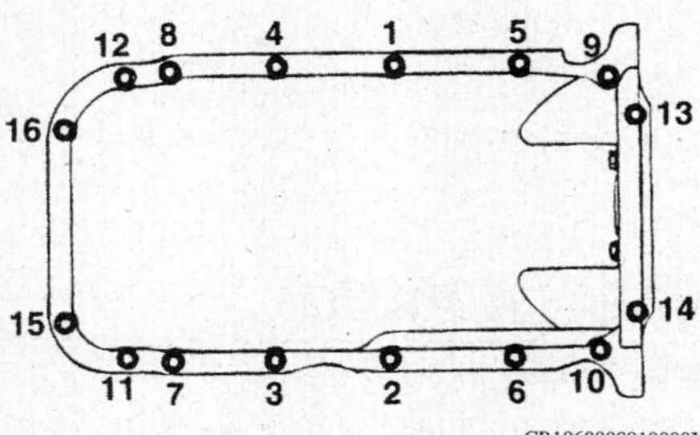

CR1060000919000X

Fig. 16 Upper oil pan tightening sequence

3. **On models equipped with manual transaxle,** using flywheel stopper tool No. MB998781, or equivalent, remove flywheel adapter plate, then the flywheel.
4. **On models equipped with automatic transaxle,** remove drive plate using flywheel stopper tool No. MB998781, or equivalent.
5. **On all models,** remove rear oil seal.
6. Reverse procedure to install noting the following:
   a. Apply a small amount of engine oil to seal lip before installing.
   b. Using crankshaft rear seal installer tool No. MD998718, or equivalent, tap in rear oil seal.

OIL PAN

REPLACE

1. Drain engine oil into suitable container, then remove front exhaust pipe.
2. Remove lower oil pan bolts, then the lower oil pan.
3. Disconnect starter motor connector, then remove starter motor.
4. Remove oil dipstick, then the dipstick guide.
5. Remove upper oil pan bolts, then screw two M10 bolts in bolts holes shown in **Fig. 15** and remove upper oil pan.
6. Reverse procedure to install noting the following:
   a. Tighten upper oil pan bolts in sequence **Fig. 16** to specifications.
   b. Tighten lower oil pan bolts in sequence **Fig. 17** to specifications.

OIL PUMP

REPLACE

1. Remove oil pressure switch.

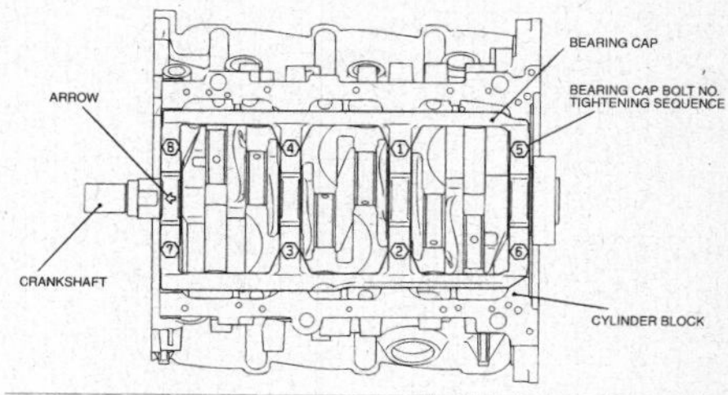

CR1060000927000X

Fig. 14 Bearing cap bolt tightening sequence

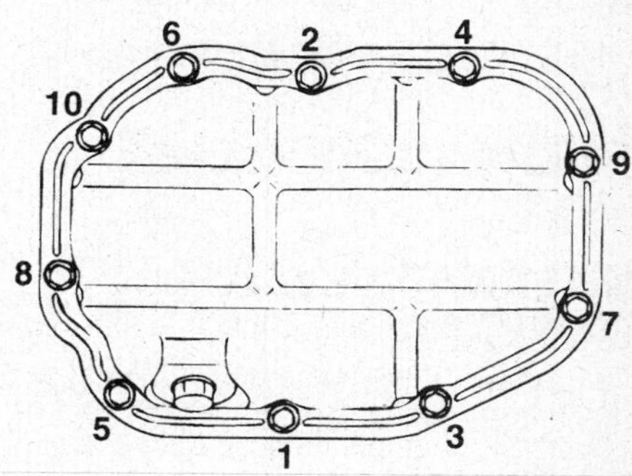

CR1060000920000X

Fig. 17 Lower oil pan tightening sequence

2. Remove oil filter, then the oil filter bracket.
3. Remove oil pan as outlined under "Oil Pan, Replace."
4. Remove lower baffle plate, then the oil screen
5. Remove upper baffle plate, then the plug.
6. Remove relief spring, then the relief plunger.
7. Remove crankshaft front oil seal as outlined under "Crankshaft Oil Seal, Replace."
8. Remove oil pump case assembly.
9. Reverse procedure to install tightening to specifications.

OIL PUMP SERVICE

DISASSEMBLE

1. Remove oil pump cover.
2. Make alignment marks on outer and inner rotors for reference during assembly.
3. Remove outer and inner rotors.

INSPECTION

1. Measure rotor tip clearance. Clearance should be .003–.007 inch.
2. Measure rotor side clearance. Clearance should be .002–.003 inch.
3. Measure body clearance. Clearance should be .004–.007 inch.

ASSEMBLE

1. Apply engine oil to rotors.
2. Install rotors ensuring alignment marks made during disassembly are aligned.

ITEMS	DURING ADJUSTMENT	DURING REPLACEMENT
Vibration frequency Hz	141 - 153	170 - 190
Tension N (lb)	539 - 637 (121 - 143)	785 - 981 (176 - 221)
Deflection (Reference value) mm (in)	9.0 - 10.1 (0.35 - 0.40)	6.2 - 7.6 (0.24 - 0.30)

CR1060000921000X

Fig. 18 Alternator & A/C compressor belt tension chart

BELT TENSION DATA

Refer **Figs. 18 and 19** to for belt tension data.

SERPENTINE DRIVE BELT

ALTERNATOR & A/C COMPRESSOR BELT

1. Loosen tensioner pulley fixing nut.
2. **Torque** fixing bolt temporarily to 11 ft. lbs., then adjust belt tension using adjusting bolt.
3. Tighten tension pulley bolt to specifications.

POWER STEERING PUMP BELT

1. Loosen tensioner pulley nut behind tension pulley.
2. Adjust belt tension using adjusting bolt.
3. Tighten tensioner pulley nut to specifications.

COOLING SYSTEM BLEED

Start engine and bring to operating temperature. Rev engine repeatedly to 3000 RPM. After engine has cooled down remove radiator cap and fill to top of radiator.

THERMOSTAT

REPLACE

1. Drain engine coolant into suitable container.

ITEMS	WHEN CHECKED	DURING ADJUSTMENT	DURING REPLACEMENT
Vibration frequency Hz	125 - 154	133 - 148	160 - 183
Tension N (lb)	373 - 569 (84 - 128)	422 - 520 (95 - 117)	608 - 804 (137 - 181)
Deflection (Reference value) mm (in)	11.0 - 14.2 (0.43 - 0.56)	11.7 - 13.4 (0.46 - 0.53)	8.4 - 9.3 (0.33 - 0.37)

CR1060000922000X

Fig. 19 Power steering pump belt tension chart

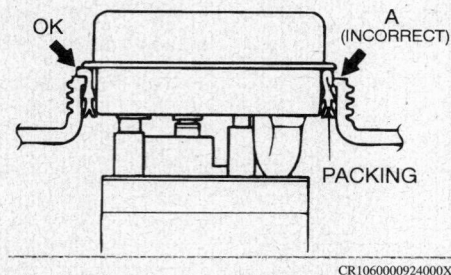

2. Remove air cleaner assembly, then the lower radiator hose.
3. Remove thermostat housing, then the thermostat.
4. Reverse procedure to install ensuring jiggle valve on thermostat is facing up.

WATER PUMP

REPLACE

1. Drain engine coolant into suitable container.
2. Remove timing belt as outlined under "Timing Belt, Replace."
3. Remove thermostat as outlined under "Thermostat, Replace."
4. Remove water pump assembly.
5. Reverse procedure to install tightening bolts to specifications.

RADIATOR

REPLACE

1. Drain engine coolant into suitable container.
2. Disconnect reserve tank hose, then remove reserve tank.
3. Remove upper and lower radiator hoses.
4. **On models equipped with automatic transaxle,** disconnect oil cooler lines.

CR1060000924000X

Fig. 20 Fuel pump packing installation

5. **On all models,** remove radiator supports.
6. Remove radiator, then the fan motor assembly.
7. Reverse procedure to install.

FUEL PUMP

REPLACE

1. Remove rear seat cushion, then the access plate.
2. Relieve fuel pressure as outlined under "Precautions"
3. Disconnect fuel hose and electrical connector.
4. Using tank cap wrench tool No. MB991480, or equivalent, remove fuel pump module.
5. Reverse procedure to install noting the following:
   a. Install packing to fuel tank **Fig. 20,** then install fuel pump module.
   b. Align mating mark on fuel pump module with mark on fuel tank.

FUEL FILTER

REPLACE

1. Remove fuel pump as outlined under "Fuel Pump, Replace."
2. Remove thermistor case, then the fuel gage unit.
3. Remove packing, then the reservoir cup.
4. Remove pump support assembly.
5. Remove electrical harness, then the lock bracket.
6. Remove fuel pump, then the fuel filter.

TIGHTENING SPECIFICATIONS

Year	Component	Torque Ft. Lbs.
2001–02	Alternator & A/C Compressor Belt Tensioner	29–43
	Camshaft Sprocket	58–73
	Connecting Rod Bearing Cap	37–39
	Crankshaft Bearing Cap	③
	Crankshaft Pulley	131–137
	Cylinder Head	②
	Engine Mount Bracket	58–72
	Engine Mount	51–69
	Engine Support Bracket	30–36
	Exhaust Manifold	30–36
	Oil Pan (Lower)	88–104①
	Oil Pan (Upper)	43–51①
	Oil Pump Case (M8 Bolt)	113–130①
	Oil Pump Case (M10 Bolt)	24–36
	Power Steering Pump Belt Tensioner	26–40
	Rocker Arm Shaft	21–25
	Thermostat Housing	100–130①
	Timing Belt Cover	88–104①
	Timing Belt Tensioner Pulley	32–40
	Valve Cover	27–35①
	Water Pump	14–20

①— Inch Lbs.
②— Refer to "Cylinder Head, Replace" for tightening procedures & specifications.
③— Refer to "Crankshaft, Replace" for tightening procedures & specifications.

Clutch & Manual Transaxle

NOTE: On Air Bag Equipped Models, Refer To "Air Bag System Precautions" Located In The Front Of This Manual For System Disarming & Arming Procedures.

NOTE: Refer To "Computer Relearn Procedures" Located In The Front Of This Manual When Battery Power To The Computer Has Been Interrupted.

INDEX

ADJUSTMENTS

CLUTCH PEDAL

1. Turn up carpet under clutch pedal.
2. Measure clutch pedal height and clutch pedal clevis pin play, **Fig. 1.** Pedal height (A) should be 7.0–7.1 inches. Clevis pin play (B) should be .04–.12 inch.
3. If pedal height is outside standard limits, loosen locknut and adjust pedal height using adjusting bolt, **Figs. 2 and 3.**
4. If clutch pedal play is outside standard limits, adjust with push rod.
5. After completing adjustments, confirm pedal freeplay and distance between clutch pedal and firewall with clutch disengaged are within specifications. Referring to **Fig. 4,** freeplay (C) should be .24–.51 inch. Distance between clutch pedal and firewall (D) should be at least 2.76 inches on 1998–2000 models and 3.5 inches on 2001–02 models.
6. If these measurements are not within specifications, it may be the result of air trapped in the hydraulic system or a faulty master cylinder and/or clutch.

INTERLOCK SWITCH

Ensure the interlock switch is as shown in **Fig. 5** when the clutch pedal is depressed at its full stroke. If necessary, loosen locknut to adjust switch.

HYDRAULIC SYSTEM SERVICE

CLUTCH SYSTEM BLEED

1. Connect a clear plastic hose to slave cylinder bleeder screw valve and submerge other end of hose in a clear container of clean DOT 3 or 4 brake fluid.
2. With parking brake applied, pump clutch pedal several times, then fully release.
3. Open bleeder valve, then depress clutch pedal to floor and hold.

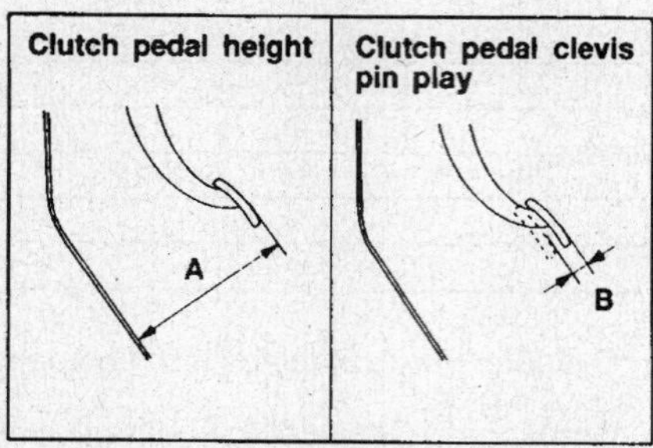

Fig. 1 Clutch pedal height measurement

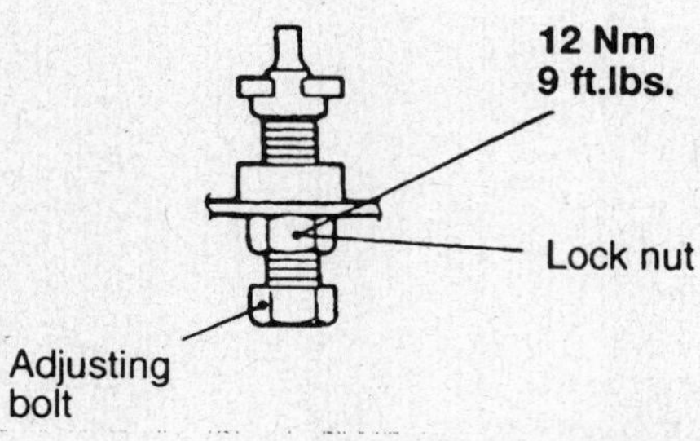

Fig. 2 Pedal height adjusting bolt. 1998–2000

4. Close bleeder valve, then release pedal.
5. Repeat procedure until bubbles can no longer be seen emerging from bleeder valve. **Keep clutch master cylinder full of clean DOT 3 or 4 brake fluid.**
6. Ensure bleeder valve is closed, then inspect clutch operation.

COMPONENT REPLACEMENT

Master Cylinder, Slave Cylinder & Hydraulic Lines

1. Drain clutch hydraulic fluid into a suitable container.
2. Remove master cylinder, slave cylinder and/or hydraulic lines in numbered sequences shown, **Figs. 6 and 7.**
3. Reverse procedure to install, noting the following:
   a. Fill and bleed clutch hydraulic system as outlined under "Clutch System Bleed" in this section.
   b. Adjust clutch pedal as outlined under "Adjustments."
   c. Tighten all fasteners to specifications.

CLUTCH

REPLACE

The modular clutch assembly is comprised of a single, dry clutch disc, diaphragm style cover and flywheel. These components are not independently serviceable; the entire clutch module must be replaced as an assembly.

1. Drain clutch hydraulic fluid and transaxle fluid into suitable containers.
2. Remove transaxle as outlined under "Transaxle, Replace."
3. Remove clutch assembly in numbered sequence, **Figs. 8 through 10.**
4. Reverse procedure to install, noting the following:
   a. Apply Mitsubishi grease part No. 0101011, or equivalent, to contact points at ends of clutch release lever and to clutch disc splines. Use a suitable brush to force grease into splines.

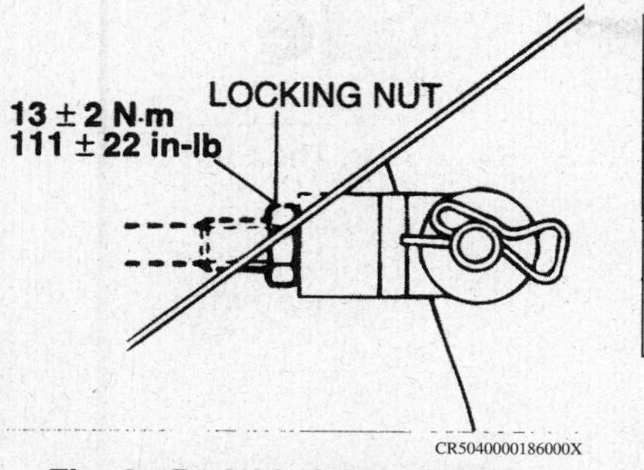

Fig. 3 Pedal height adjusting bolt. 2001–02

Clutch pedal free play | Distance between the clutch pedal and the firewall when the clutch is disengaged

CR5049600093000X

Fig. 4 Clutch pedal freeplay adjustment

Lock nut
Interlock switch
3.5 mm (.14in.)
Clutch pedal

CR5049600094000X

Fig. 5 Interlock switch adjustment

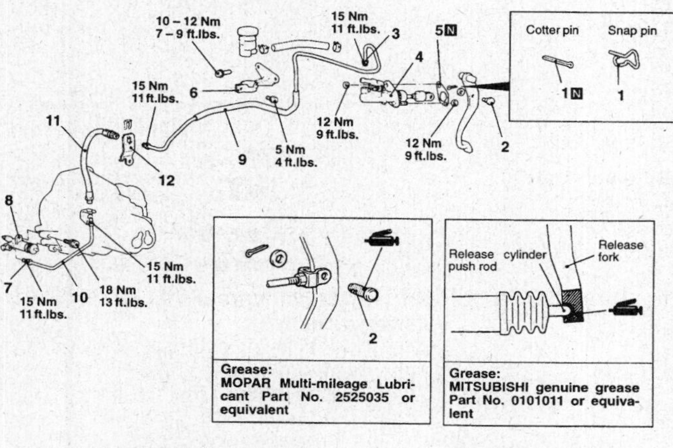

Clutch master cylinder removal steps

1. Cotter pin or snap pin
2. Clevis pin
3. Clutch pipe connection
4. Clutch master cylinder
5. Sealer
6. Reservoir bracket

Clutch release cylinder removal steps

7. Clutch pipe connection
8. Clutch release cylinder

Clutch line removal steps

9. Clutch pipe
10. Clutch pipe
11. Clutch hose
12. Clutch hose bracket

CR5049500172000X

Fig. 6 Clutch hydraulic system component replacement. 1998–2000

15 ± 2 N·m
12 ± 1 ft-lb
11 ± 1 N·m
96 ± 8 in-lb
5.0 ± 1.0 N·m
44 ± 9 in-lb
(GREASE: MOPAR® MULTI-MILEAGE LUBRICANT PART NO. 2525035 OR EQUIVALENT)
13 ± 2 N·m
111 ± 22 in-lb
<2.4L ENGINE>
19 ± 3 N·m
14 ± 2 ft-lb
<3.0L ENGINE>
RELEASE CYLINDER PUSH ROD
RELEASE FORK
GREASE: MITSUBISHI GENUINE GREASE PART NO. 0101011 OR EQUIVALENT

CLUTCH MASTER CYLINDER REMOVAL STEPS

1. CLEVIS PIN
2. CLUTCH TUBE CONNECTION
3. RESERVOIR HOSE CONNECTION
4. CLUTCH MASTER CYLINDER

CLUTCH RESERVOIR TANK REMOVAL STEPS

5. RESERVOIR HOSE
6. RESERVOIR CAP
7. RESERVOIR TANK
8. RESERVOIR BRACKET

CLUTCH RELEASE CYLINDER REMOVAL STEPS

9. CLUTCH TUBE CONNECTION
10. CLUTCH RELEASE CYLINDER

CLUTCH LINE REMOVAL STEPS

11. CLUTCH TUBE
12. BRACKET
13. CLUTCH HOSE

CR5040000187000X

Fig. 7 Clutch hydraulic system component replacement. 2001–02

b. Fill and bleed clutch hydraulic system as outlined under "Hydraulic System Service."
c. Fill transaxle with correct type of lubricant.

TRANSAXLE

REPLACE

1998–2000

1. Drain transaxle fluid into a suitable container, then remove battery.
2. Remove lower engine cover.
3. Remove air cleaner cover and air hose assembly, **Fig. 11.**
4. Remove air cleaner element, then the battery tray and stay.
5. Disconnect shift cable.
6. Disconnect back-up lamp switch and vehicle speed sensor connectors.
7. Remove starter motor.
8. Remove rear roll stopper bracket mounting bolts.
9. Raise transaxle with jack, then remove transaxle mounting bracket nuts.
10. Install engine support tool No. C-4852, or equivalent.
11. Raise and support vehicle, then loosen tie rod end nut.
12. Disconnect stabilizer link and remove damper fork.
13. Loosen end nuts on lateral lower arm and compression lower arm connections.
14. Insert pry bar between transaxle case and driveshaft, then remove driveshaft. Do not remove hub and knuckle from driveshaft.
15. Suspend driveshaft with wire so there are no sharp bends in any of the joints.
16. Remove center member assembly.
17. Remove clutch release cylinder without disconnecting oil lines.
18. Remove front plate and rear plate.
19. Remove transaxle lower case, then support transaxle with suitable jack
20. Remove flex plate bolts while turning crankshaft.
21. Chalk mating marks on flex plate and clutch pressure plate for installation, **Fig. 12.**
22. Press clutch pressure plate into transaxle for easier removal.
23. Remove transaxle assembly mounting bolts and lower transaxle.
24. Reverse procedure to install. Tighten fasteners to specifications.

2001–02

1. Drain transaxle fluid into suitable container, then remove battery and tray.
2. Remove air cleaner assembly.
3. Disconnect shift and select cables, **Figs. 13 and 14.**
4. Disconnect back-up light switch, then the vehicle speed sensor.
5. Remove starter motor with harness still connected and position aside

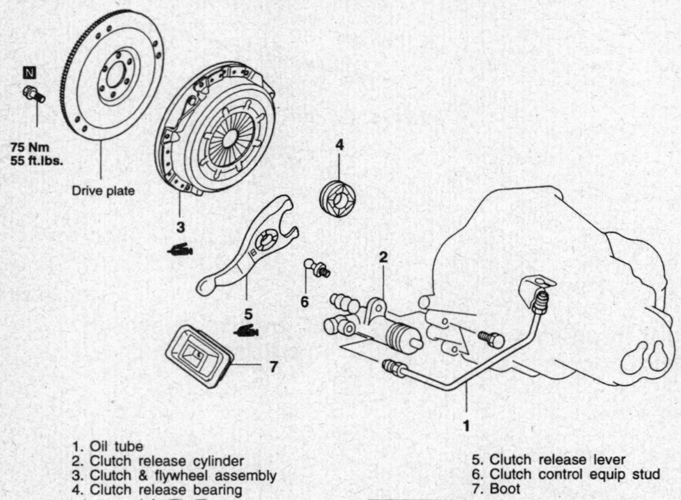

Fig. 8 Modular clutch replacement. 1998–2000

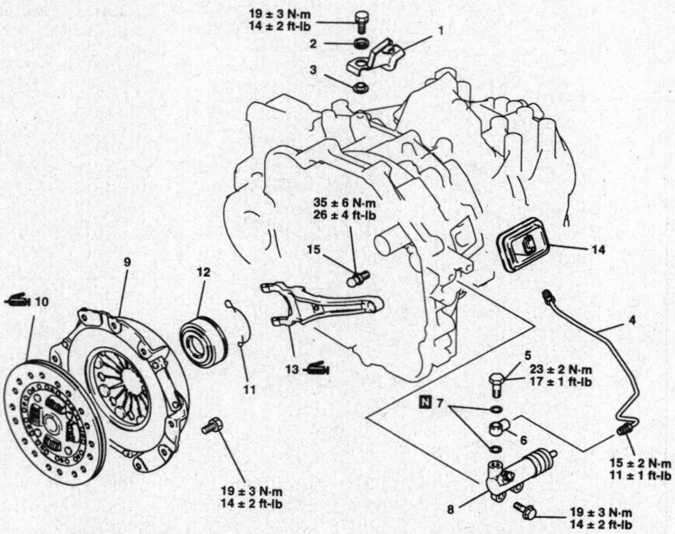

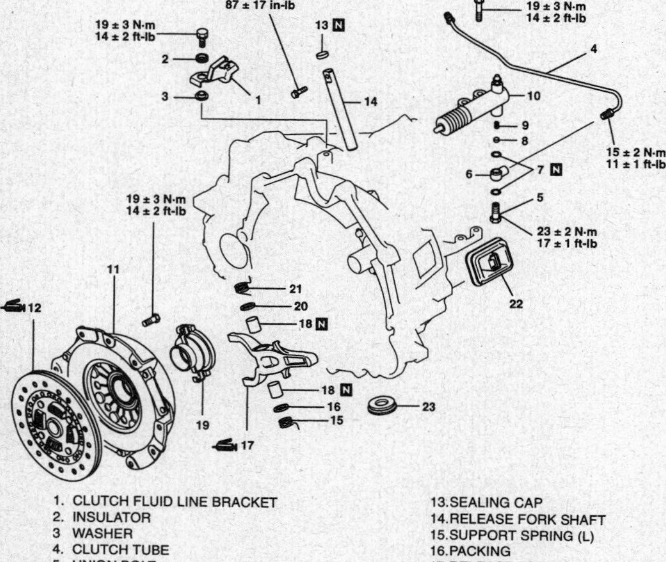

Fig. 10 Modular clutch replacement. 2001–02 w/3.0L engine

6. Remove clutch release cylinder with oil line still connected and position aside.
7. Remove transaxle upper coupling bolts.
8. Using engine hanger and lifter tool Nos. MB991453 and MZ203827, or equivalents, support engine and remove centermember assembly.
9. Remove rear roll stopper.
10. Remove transaxle mount bracket and stopper.
11. Disconnect strut side stabilizer links.
12. Disconnect wheel speed sensor, then the brake hose clamp.

19 ± 3 N-m
14 ± 2 ft-lb
35 ± 6 N-m
26 ± 4 ft-lb
23 ± 2 N-m
17 ± 1 ft-lb
15 ± 2 N-m
11 ± 1 ft-lb

1. CLUTCH FLUID LINE BRACKET
2. INSULATOR
3 WASHER
4. CLUTCH TUBE
5. UNION BOLT
6. UNION
7. GASKET
8. CLUTCH RELEASE CYLINDER
9. CLUTCH COVER
10.CLUTCH DISC
11.RETURN CLIP
12.CLUTCH RELEASE BEARING
13.RELEASE FORK
14.RELEASE FORK BOOT
15.FULCRUM

CR5040000188000X

Fig. 9 Modular clutch replacement. 2001–02 w/2.4L engine

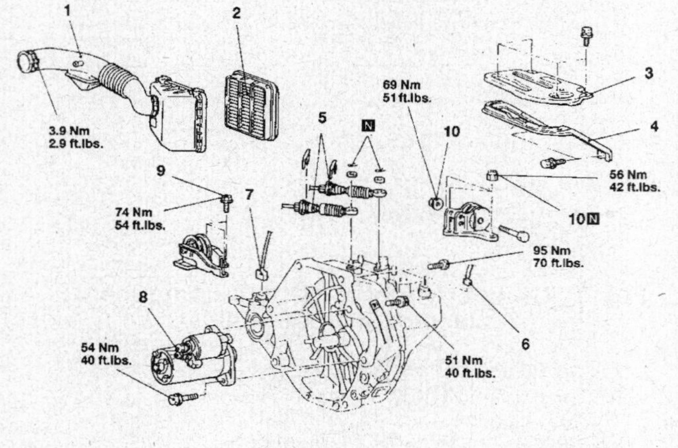

1. Air cleaner cover and air intake hose assembly
2. Air cleaner element
3. Battery tray
4. Battery tray stay
5. Shift cable and select cable connection
6. Backup light switch connector
7. Vehicle speed sensor connector
8. Starter motor
9. Rear roll stopper bracket mounting bolts
10. Transaxle mounting bracket mounting nuts

CR5039601006010X

Fig. 11 Transaxle removal (Part 1 of 2). 1998–2000

13. Using steering linkage puller tool No. MB991113, or equivalent, loosen but do not remove tie rod end.
14. Insert a suitable pry bar between transaxle case and driveshaft, then remove drive shaft.
15. **On models with 2.4L engine,** remove bell housing cover.
16. **On models with 3.0L engine,** remove upper oil pan connecting bolt.
17. **On all models,** remove lower transaxle coupling bolts, then lower transaxle.
18. Reverse procedure to install noting the following:
    a. Install transaxle mount stopper as shown in **Fig. 15.**

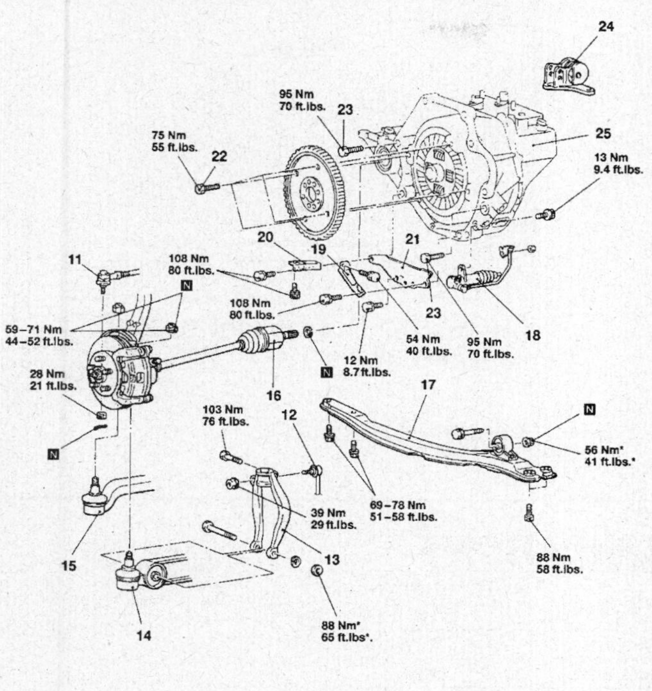

11. Tie rod end connection
12. Stabilizer link connection
13. Damper fork
14. Lateral lower arm connection
15. Compression lower arm connection
16. Drive shaft connection
17. Center member assembly
18. Clutch release cylinder connection
19. Front plate
20. Rear plate
21. Transaxle case lower cover
22. Flex plate connecting bolts
23. Transaxle assembly mounting bolts
24. Transaxle mounting
25. Transaxle assembly

Caution
*: Indicates parts which should be temporarily tightened, and then fully tightened with the vehicle on the ground in the unladen condition.

CR5039601006020X

Fig. 11 Transaxle removal (Part 2 of 2). 1998–2000

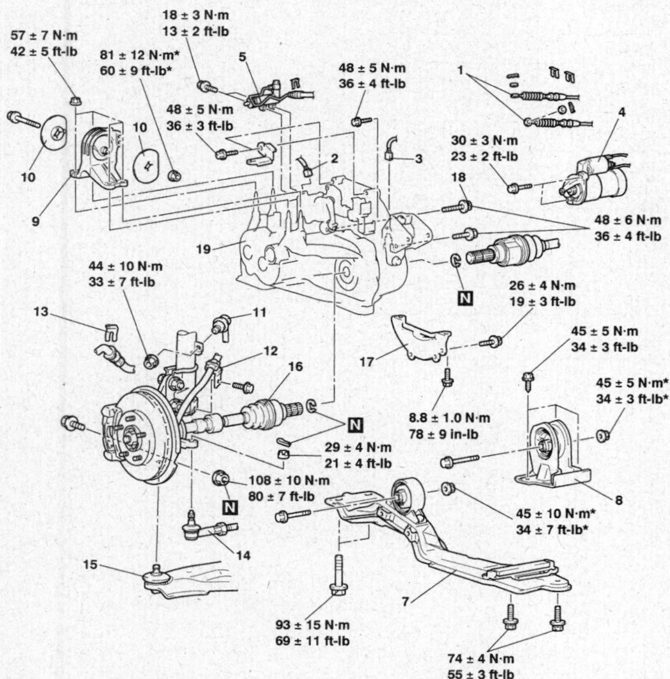

CR5030001086010X

Fig. 13 Transaxle removal (Part 1 of 2). 2001–02 w/2.4L engine

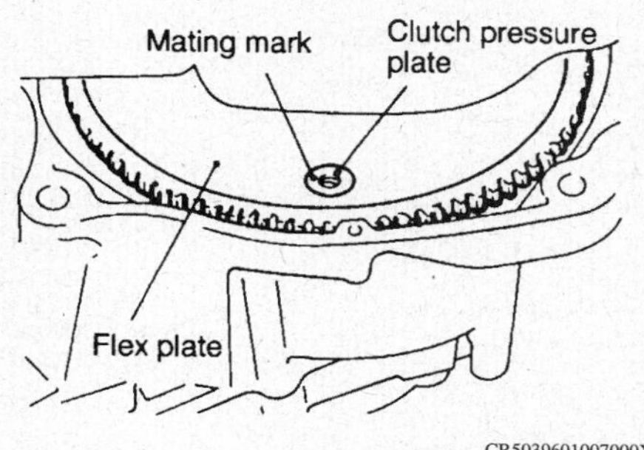

CR5039601007000X

Fig. 12 Flex plate match marks

1. SHIFT CABLE AND SELECT CABLE CONNECTION
2. BACKUP LIGHT SWITCH CONNECTOR
3. VEHICLE SPEED SENSOR CONNECTOR
4. STARTER MOTOR
5. CLUTCH RELEASE CYLINDER CONNECTION
6. TRANSAXLE ASSEMBLY UPPER PART COUPLING BOLTS
7. CENTERMEMBER ASSEMBLY
8. REAR ROLL STOPPER
9. TRANSAXLE MOUNT BRACKET
10. TRANSAXLE MOUNT STOPPER
11. STABILIZER LINK CONNECTION <STRUT SIDE>
12. WHEEL SPEED SENSOR CABLE CONNECTION <VEHICLES WITH ABS>
13. BRAKE HOSE CLAMP
14. TIE ROD END CONNECTION
15. LOWER ARM CONNECTION
16. DRIVESHAFT CONNECTION
17. BELL HOUSING COVER
18. TRANSAXLE ASSEMBLY LOWER PART COUPLING BOLTS
19. TRANSAXLE ASSEMBLY

CR5030001086020X

Fig. 13 Transaxle removal (Part 2 of 2). 2001–02 w/2.4L engine

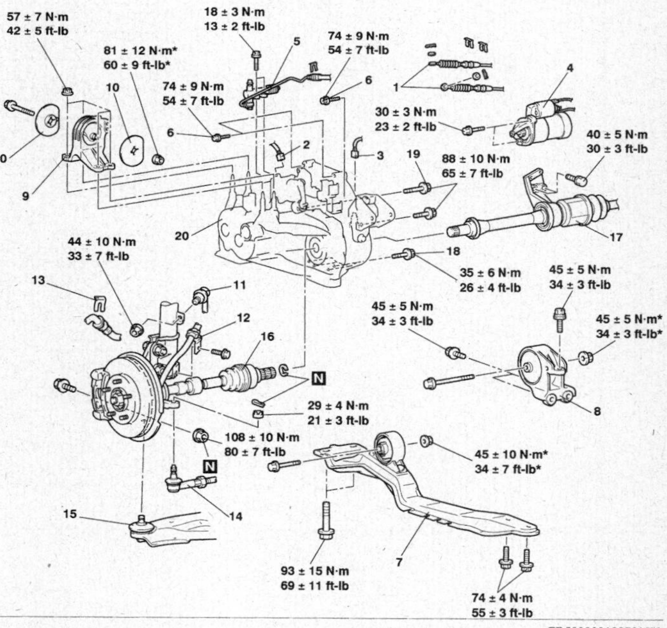

CR5030001087010X

Fig. 14 Transaxle removal (Part 1 of 2). 2001–02 w/3.0L engine

1. SHIFT CABLE AND SELECT CABLE CONNECTION
2. BACKUP LIGHT SWITCH CONNECTOR
3. VEHICLE SPEED SENSOR CONNECTOR
4. STARTER MOTOR
5. CLUTCH RELEASE CYLINDER CONNECTION
6. TRANSAXLE ASSEMBLY UPPER PART COUPLING BOLTS
7. CENTERMEMBER ASSEMBLY
8. REAR ROLL STOPPER
9. TRANSAXLE MOUNT BRACKET
10. TRANSAXLE MOUNT STOPPER
11. STABILIZER LINK CONNECTION <STRUT SIDE>
12. WHEEL SPEED SENSOR CABLE CONNECTION <VEHICLES WITH ABS>
13. BRAKE HOSE CLAMP
14. TIE ROD END CONNECTION
15. LOWER ARM CONNECTION
- CLUTCH RELEASE BEARING ENGAGEMENT
16. DRIVESHAFT CONNECTION
17. DRIVESHAFT AND INNER SHAFT CONNECTION
18. UPPER OIL PAN CONNECTING BOLT
19. TRANSAXLE ASSEMBLY LOWER PART COUPLING BOLTS
20. TRANSAXLE ASSEMBLY

CR5030001087020X

Fig. 14 Transaxle removal (Part 2 of 2). 2001–02 w/3.0L engine

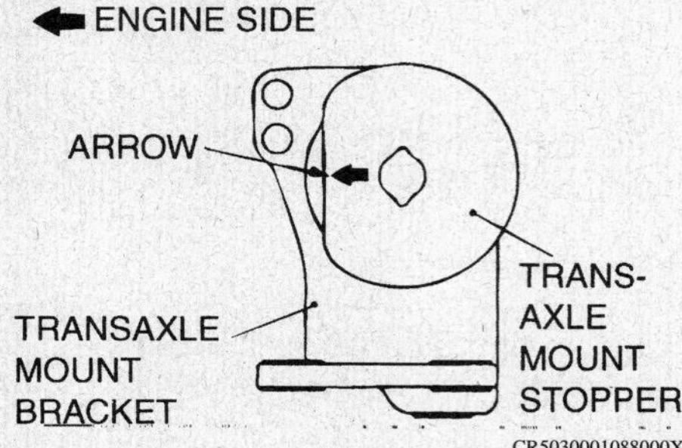

Fig. 15 Transaxle mount stopper installation. 2001–02

TIGHTENING SPECIFICATIONS

Year	Component	Torque/Ft. Lbs.
1998-2000	Clutch Fluid Pipe Fittings	11
	Clutch Master Cylinder Bolts	108①
	Clutch Release Cylinder Bolts	13
	Damper Fork	65
	Flex Plate Bolts	55
	Reservoir Bracket Bolts	84–108①
	Stabilizer Link Nut	29
	Transaxle Mounting Bolts	70
2001–02	Clutch Cover Bolts	12–16
	Clutch Master Cylinder Bolt	89–133①
	Clutch Release Cylinder Bolt	12–16
	Reservoir Bracket Bolt	35–53①
	Stabilizer Link Nut	26–40
	Transaxle Lower Coupling Bolt (2.4L)	32–40
	Transaxle Lower Coupling Bolt (3.0L)	58–72
	Transaxle Mount Bracket Nut	38–47
	Transaxle Mount Stopper Nut	51–69
	Transaxle Upper Coupling Bolt (2.4L)	33–39
	Transaxle Upper Coupling Bolt (3.0L, Bolt, Flange)	47–61
	Transaxle Upper Coupling Bolt (3.0L, Bolt, Washer Assembly)	58–72

① — Inch lbs.

Rear Suspension

NOTE: On Air Bag Equipped Models, Refer To "Air Bag System Precautions" Located In The Front Of This Manual For System Disarming & Arming Procedures.

NOTE: Refer To "Computer Relearn Procedures" Located In The Front Of This Manual When Battery Power To The Computer Has Been Interrupted.

NOTE: Prior To Performing Any Service Operations Listed In This Section, Consult The "Technical Service Bulletins" Section For Related Information.

INDEX

DESCRIPTION

The rear suspension is a modified double-wishbone design with coil springs and direct acting shock absorbers, **Fig. 1.** The rear axle consists of a knuckle, rear hub, unit bearing and axle shaft. The unit bearing is press-fitted to the rear axle shaft and bolted to the knuckle. On models equipped with ABS, a rotor for detecting vehicle speed is located on the axle shaft and a speed sensor is located on the knuckle.

HUB & BEARING

REPLACE

1. Raise and support vehicle.
2. **On models equipped with ABS,** remove rear speed sensor.
3. **On models equipped with rear disc brakes,** remove and suspend brake caliper assembly, **Fig. 2.**
4. **On all models,** remove brake drum or disc.
5. Remove clip mounting bolt.
6. Remove brake shoe and lining assembly.
7. Remove rear hub and ABS rotor.
8. Reverse procedure to install. Tighten to specifications.

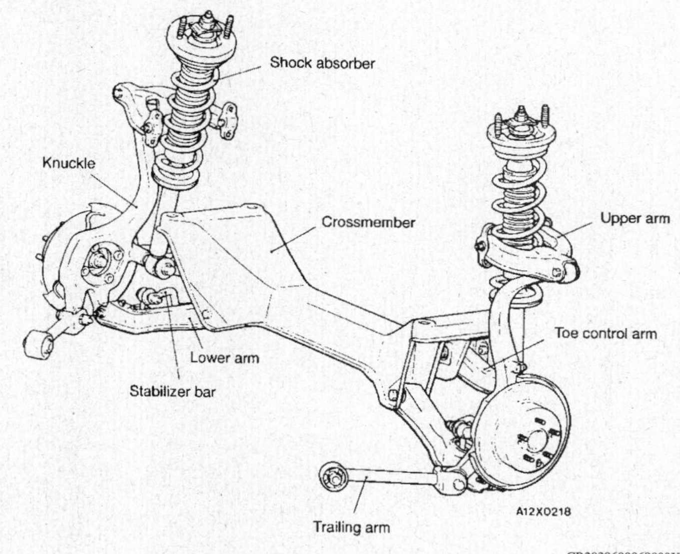

Fig. 1 Rear suspension

SHOCK ABSORBER

REPLACE

1. Remove shock absorber cap.
2. Remove flange nuts under cap.
3. Remove shock absorber lower bolt and the shock absorber.
4. Reverse procedure to install. Tighten to specifications.

COIL SPRING

REPLACE

Remove shock absorber and coil spring assembly and disassemble as shown, **Fig. 3,** to replace coil spring. Compress coil spring using compressor tool Nos. MB991237 and MB991239, or equivalents.

CONTROL ARM

REPLACE

UPPER

1. Raise and support vehicle.
2. Remove upper arm and knuckle connecting bolt. **Fig. 4.**
3. Remove upper arm mounting bolt.
4. Remove upper arm assembly.
5. Remove upper arm bracket.
6. Reverse procedure to install. Tighten to specifications.

LOWER

1. Raise and support vehicle.
2. Remove stabilizer link, **Fig. 5.**
3. **On models equipped with ABS,** remove wheel speed sensor clamp bolts.
4. **On all models,** remove lower arm assembly and knuckle connecting bolt.
5. Remove lower arm mounting bolt.
6. Disconnect toe control arm ball joint from knuckle.
7. Remove toe control arm mounting bolt.
8. Remove toe control arm assembly.
9. Reverse procedure to install. Tighten to specifications.

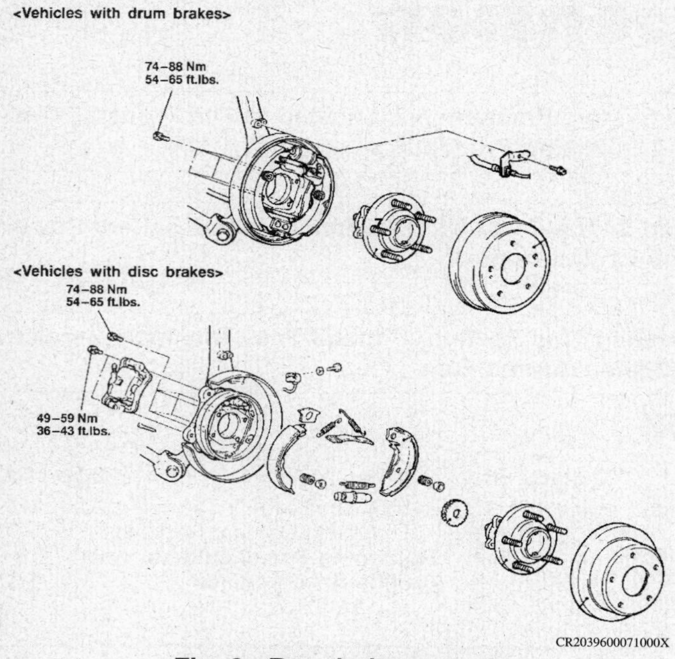

Fig. 2 Rear hub removal

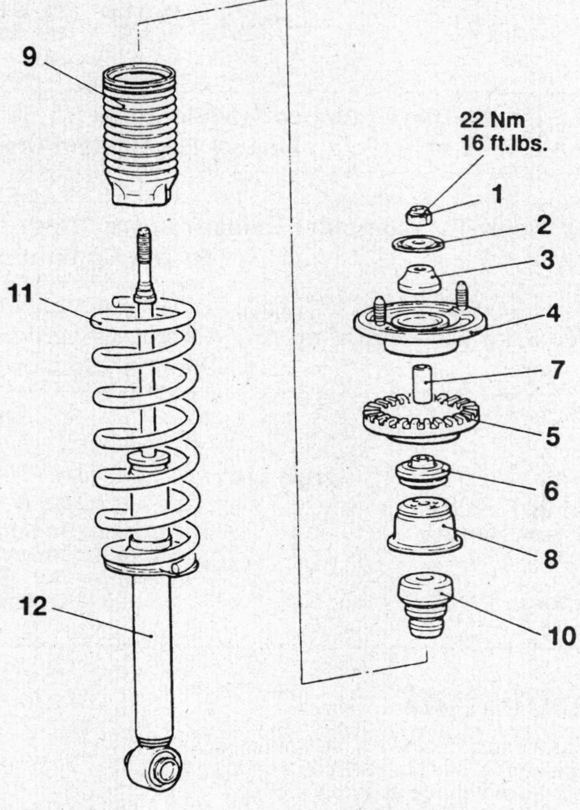

1. Self-locking nut
2. Washer
3. Upper bushing A
4. Bracket
5. Spring pad
6. Upper bushing B
7. Collar
8. Cup
9. Dust cover
10. Bump rubber
11. Coil spring
12. Shock absorber assembly

CR2039600073000X

Fig. 3 Coil spring replacement

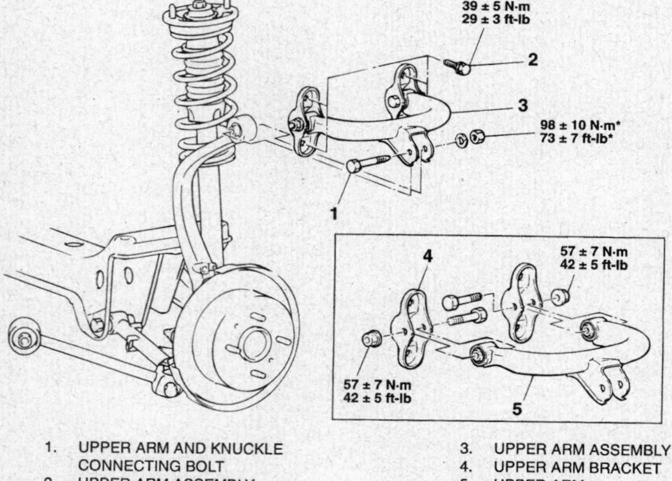

1. UPPER ARM AND KNUCKLE CONNECTING BOLT
2. UPPER ARM ASSEMBLY MOUNTING BOLTS
3. UPPER ARM ASSEMBLY
4. UPPER ARM BRACKET
5. UPPER ARM

CR2030100108000X

Fig. 4 Upper control arm replacement

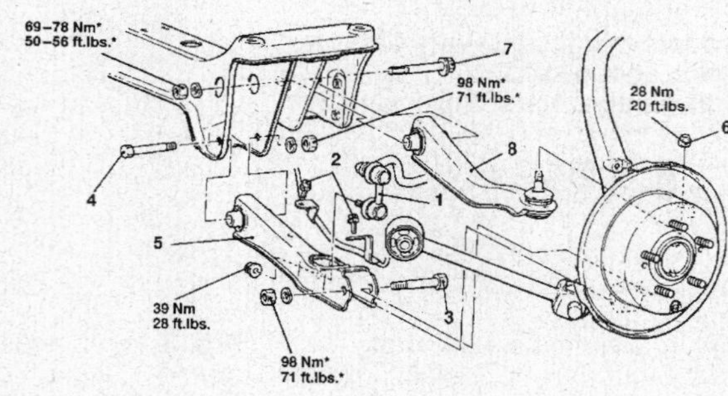

1. Stabilizer link
2. ABS wheel-speed sensor clamp bolts <Vehicles with ABS>
3. Lower arm assembly and knuckle connecting bolt
4. Lower arm assembly mounting bolt
5. Lower arm assembly
6. Toe control arm ball joint and knuckle connection
7. Toe control arm assembly mounting bolt
8. Toe control arm assembly

Caution
*** : Indicates parts which should be temporarily tightened, and then fully tightened with the vehicles on the ground in the unladen condition.**

CR2039600074000X

Fig. 5 Lower arm & toe control arm removal

KNUCKLE

REPLACE

1. Raise and support vehicle.
2. Remove rear hub as described under "Hub & Bearing, Replace."
3. Disconnect trailing arm, **Fig. 6.**
4. Disconnect lower arm.
5. Disconnect toe control arm. Loosen nut but do not remove.
6. Disconnect shock absorber.
7. Disconnect upper arm.
8. Remove knuckle.
9. **On models less ABS,** remove hub cap.
10. **On all models,** reverse procedure to install. Tighten to specifications.

TRAILING ARM

REPLACE

1. Raise and support vehicle.
2. Disconnect knuckle and trailing arm assembly connecting bolt.
3. Remove grommet.
4. Remove trailing arm assembly mounting bolt.
5. Remove stopper.

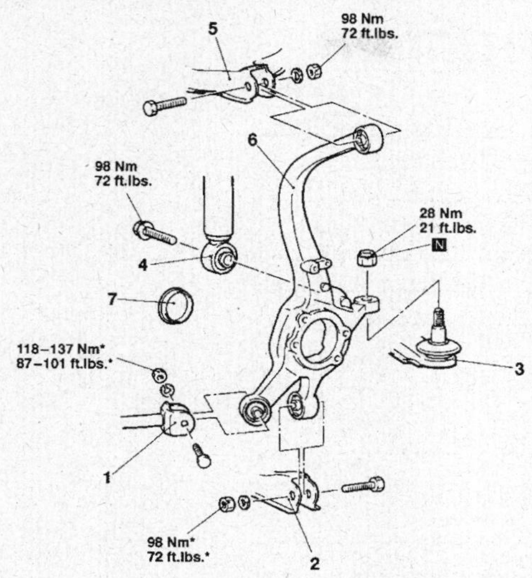

1. Trailing arm connection
2. Lower arm connection
3. Toe control arm connection
4. Shock absorber connection
5. Upper arm connection
6. Knuckle
7. Hub cap <Vehicles without ABS>

Caution
***: Indicates parts which should be temporarily tightened, and then fully tightened with the vehicle on the ground in the unladen condition.**

CR2039600072000X

Fig. 6 Knuckle replacement

6. Remove trailing arm.
7. Reverse procedure to install. Tighten to specifications.

STABILIZER BAR

REPLACE

1. Raise and support vehicle.
2. Remove stabilizer link mounting nuts.
3. Remove stabilizer link.
4. Remove stabilizer bar brackets.
5. Remove stabilizer bar bracket bushings.
6. Remove stabilizer bar.
7. Reverse procedure to install. Tighten to specifications.

TECHNICAL SERVICE BULLETINS

SQUEAKING OR HARD RUBBING

1998

On these models there may be a squeaking or hard rubbing noise on bumps.

This condition may be caused by trailing arm bushing stoppers. To correct this condition, replace one piece trailing arm bushing stoppers with upgraded, two-piece parts (outside part No. MR316383, inside part No. MR316384).

2001

On these models there may be a squeaking or hard rubbing noise on bumps.

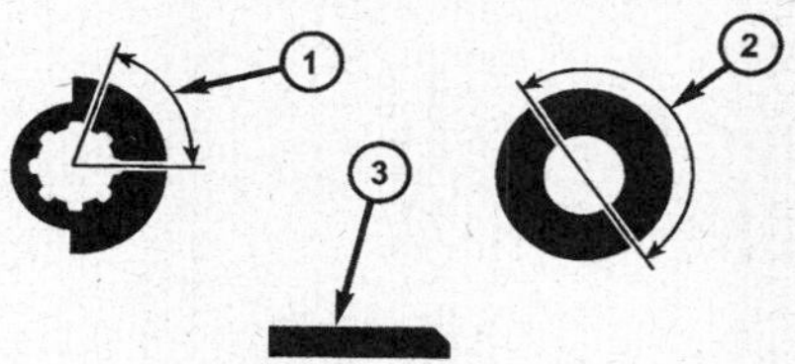

1 - Bevel Edge Of Outer Stopper - 1 to 3 O'clock Position
2 - Bevel Edge Of Inner Stopper - 11 to 5 O'clock Position
3 - Bevel Outer Edge (Away From Trailing Arm)

CR2030100109000X

Fig. 7 Trailing arm stopper trim angles. 2001

This condition may be caused by low lubricant in stopper bushings or the bushings rubbing against the body bracket. To correct this condition proceed as follows:

1. Remove trailing arm as outlined under "Trailing Arm, Replace."
2. Place trailing arm on bench, mark original position of stoppers for reassembly.
3. Remove stopper and trim surface, **Fig. 7.**
4. Reverse procedure to install noting the following:
   a. Lubricate all surfaces of stoppers using Dielectric grease part No. J8126688, or equivalent.
   b. Tighten attaching bolts and nuts to specification.

LIGHT KNOCKING OR TAPPING

1998

On these models there may be a light knocking or tapping from rear shock area on bumps.

This condition may be caused by rear shock bracket assembly. To correct this condition, replace rear shock bracket assembly with redesigned insulator (part No. MR311114).

TIGHTENING SPECIFICATIONS

Year	Component	Torque/Ft. Lbs.
1998-2002	Brake Hose Connection	11
	Caliper Mounting Bolts	36–43
	Crossmember Mounting Self-Locking Nuts	64
	Lower Arm & Knuckle Connecting Nut	71
	Lower Arm Mounting Nuts	71
	Shock Absorber Lower Bolt	72
	Shock Absorber Upper Flange Bolts	32
	Shock Tower Self-Locking Nut	16
	Stabilizer Bar Bracket Bolts	7–10
	Stabilizer Link Mounting Nuts	28
	Toe Control Arm Ball Joint & Knuckle Connecting Nut	20
	Trailing Arm Connecting Nut	87–101
	Trailing Arm Mounting Bolt	99–114
	Upper Arm Assembly Mounting Bolt	28
	Upper Arm Bracket Nuts	41
	Upper Arm & Knuckle Connecting Bolt	72
	Wheel Lug Nuts	87–101

Front Suspension & Steering

NOTE: On Air Bag Equipped Models, Refer To "Air Bag System Precautions" Located In The Front Of This Manual For System Disarming & Arming Procedures.

NOTE: Refer To "Computer Relearn Procedures" Located In The Front Of This Manual When Battery Power To The Computer Has Been Interrupted.

NOTE: Prior To Performing Any Service Operations Listed In This Section, Consult The "Technical Service Bulletins" Section For Related Information.

INDEX

PRECAUTIONS

AIR BAG SYSTEMS

Refer to "Air Bag System Precautions" in the front of this manual for system disarming and arming procedures.

BATTERY GROUND CABLE

Prior to service, disconnect battery ground cable and isolate as required.

HUB & BEARING

REPLACE

1. Raise and support vehicle, then remove tire.
2. **On models equipped with ABS,** remove front speed sensor.
3. **On all models,** remove brake caliper assembly and suspend with wire.
4. Remove brake disc.
5. Remove driveshaft nut cotter pin.
6. Remove driveshaft end nut.
7. Remove tie rod and stabilizer link.
8. Disconnect lower arm from steering knuckle.
9. Remove hub assembly.
10. Reverse procedure to install. Tighten to specifications.

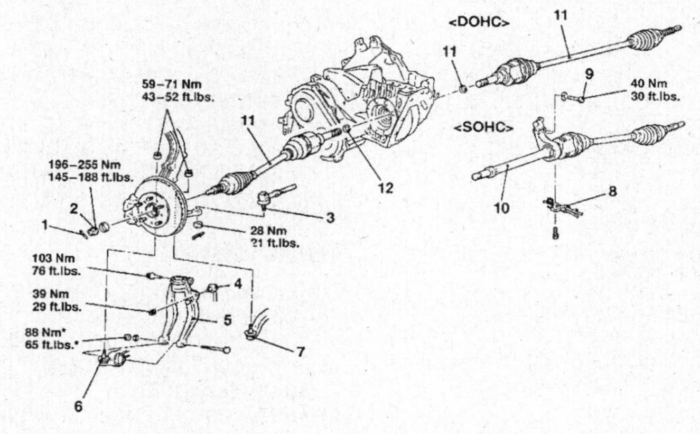

1. Cotter pin
2. Drive shaft nut
3. Tie rod end connection
4. Stabilizer link connection
5. Damper fork
6. Lateral lower arm connection
7. Compression lower arm connection
8. Harness clip
9. Bolt
10. Drive shaft and inner shaft (RH) <SOHC>
11. Drive shaft
12. Circlip

Caution
* : Indicates parts which should be temporarily tightened, and then fully tightened with the vehicle on the ground in the unladen condition.

CR2029600121000X

Fig. 1 Driveshaft removal. 1998–2000

DRIVESHAFT

REPLACE

1998–2000

1. Raise and support vehicle.
2. Remove tire and wheel assembly.
3. Remove driveshaft nut, **Fig. 1.**
4. Disconnect tie rod end.
5. Disconnect stabilizer link.
6. Remove damper fork.
7. Disconnect lateral lower arm.
8. Disconnect compression lower arm.
9. Remove harness clip.
10. Remove driveshaft to transaxle bolt.
11. Tap center bearing bracket lightly with plastic hammer to remove drive shaft and inner shaft from transaxle.
12. Insert pry bar between transaxle case and driveshaft, then pry driveshaft from transaxle.
13. Reverse procedure to install. Tighten to specifications.

2001–02

1. **On models equipped with ABS,** disconnect front speed sensor.
2. **On all models,** remove brake hose clip and cotter pin.
3. Remove drive shaft nut, **Fig. 2.**

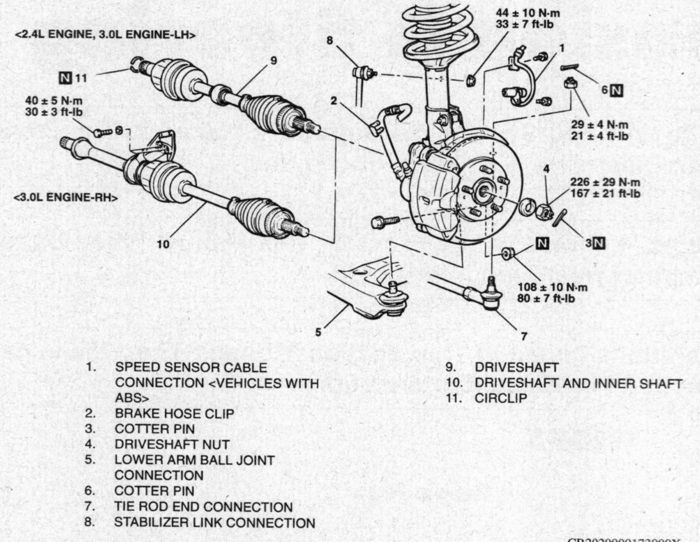

Fig. 2 Driveshaft replacement. 2001–02

4. Using steering linkage puller tool No. MB991113, or equivalent, loosen but do not remove ball joint nut.
5. Using steering linkage puller tool No. MB991113, or equivalent, loosen but do not remove tie rod end.
6. Disconnect stabilizer link.
7. Using puller body tool No. MB991354, puller bar tool No. MB990242 and yoke holder tool No. MB990767, or equivalents, push driveshaft out from hub.
8. Insert a suitable pry bar between transaxle case and driveshaft, then remove driveshaft.
9. Reverse procedure to install.

BALL JOINT INSPECTION

Use torque wrench tool No. MB990326, or equivalent, to measure ball joint breakaway torque. Breakaway torque should be as specified in **Fig. 3 and 4.**

COIL SPRING

REPLACE

Remove shock absorber as described under "Shock Absorber, Replace," then disassemble shock/coil spring unit as shown in **Figs. 5 and 6.**

SHOCK ABSORBER

REPLACE

1. Remove stabilizer link mounting nut.
2. From engine compartment, remove shock absorber upper mounting nuts.
3. Raise and support vehicle.
4. Remove shock absorber lower mounting bolt.
5. Remove damper fork mounting bolt and damper fork.
6. Remove shock absorber from vehicle.
7. Reverse procedure to install. Tighten to specifications.

CONTROL ARM

REPLACE

UPPER

1. Raise and support vehicle.
2. Disconnect upper arm ball joint from knuckle, **Fig. 7.**
3. At engine compartment shock tower, remove self-locking nut for upper arm installation.
4. Remove upper arm assembly.
5. Remove dust cover.
6. Reverse procedure to install. Install upper arm shaft at angle shown in **Fig. 8,** and tighten to specifications.

LOWER

1998–2000

1. Raise and support vehicle.
2. Disconnect compression lower arm ball joint from knuckle, **Fig. 9.**
3. Remove compression lower arm mounting bolt.
4. Remove compression lower arm dust cover.
5. Remove lateral lower arm stay.
6. Remove shock absorber lower bolt and nut.
7. Disconnect lateral lower arm ball joint from knuckle.
8. Remove lateral lower arm mounting bolt and nut.
9. Remove lateral lower arm assembly.
10. Remove dust cover.
11. Reverse procedure to install. Tighten to specifications.

2001–02

1. Raise and support vehicle.
2. Disconnect lower ball joint from steering knuckle using ball joint remover/installer tool No. MB990799, or equivalent, **Fig. 10.**
3. Remove lower arm mounting bolt.
4. **On models equipped with 2.4L engine,** remove lower arm clamp, **Fig. 10.**
5. **On all models,** remove lower arm

Ball Joint	Breakaway Torque, Inch Lbs.
Compression Lower Arm	4–22
Lateral Lower Arm	9–13
Stabilizer Link	4–13
Upper Arm	3–13

Fig. 3 Ball joint specifications. 1998–2000

Ball Joint	Breakaway Torque, Inch Lbs.
Lower Ball Joint	22–54
Stabilizer Link	30–80

Fig. 4 Ball joint specifications. 2001–02

6. Reverse procedure to install.

STEERING KNUCKLE

REPLACE

1. Raise and support vehicle.
2. Remove front wheel and tire assembly.
3. **On models equipped with ABS,** remove front wheel speed sensor.
4. **On all models,** remove hub assembly as described under "Hub & Bearing, Replace."
5. Refer to **Fig. 11 and 12** for removal of steering knuckle.
6. Reverse procedure to install. Tighten to specifications.

STABILIZER BAR

REPLACE

1. Raise and support vehicle.
2. Remove stabilizer link mounting nut.
3. Remove stabilizer link.
4. Remove stabilizer bar bracket and bushing.
5. Remove stabilizer bar.
6. Reverse procedure to install. Tighten to specifications.

CROSSMEMBER

REPLACE

1998–2000

1. Raise and support vehicle.
2. Drain power steering fluid and remove steering gear as described under "Power Steering Gear, Replace."
3. Remove front exhaust pipe.
4. Remove stabilizer bar as described under "Stabilizer Bar, Replace."
5. Refer to **Fig. 13** to remove crossmember.
6. Reverse procedure to install. Tighten to specifications.

2001–02

1. Drain power steering fluid, then remove center member.
2. Remove front exhaust pipe.

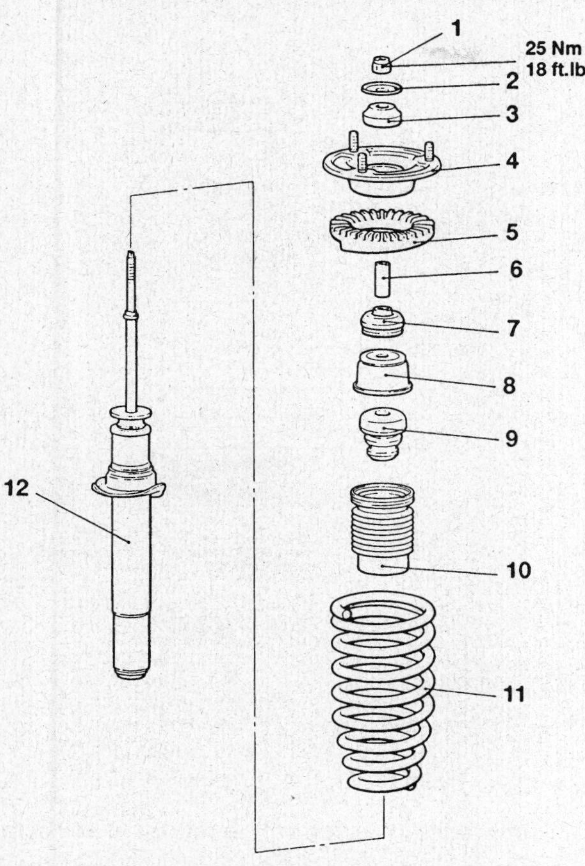

1. Self-locking nut
2. Washer
3. Upper bushing A
4. Upper bracket assembly
5. Upper spring pad
6. Collar
7. Upper bushing B
8. Cup assembly
9. Bump rubber
10. Dust cover
11. Coil spring
12. Shock absorber assembly

CR2029600115000X

Fig. 5 Coil spring replacement. 1998–2000

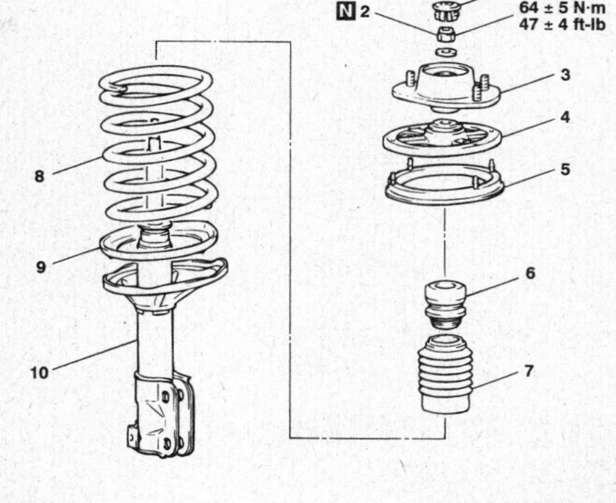

1. DUST COVER
2. JAM NUT
3. STRUT INSULATOR
4. SPRING SEAT, UPPER
5. SPRING PAD, UPPER
6. BUMP RUBBER
7. DUST COVER
8. COIL SPRING
9. SPRING PAD, LOWER
10. STRUT ASSEMBLY

CR2020000174000X

Fig. 6 Coil spring replacement. 2001–02

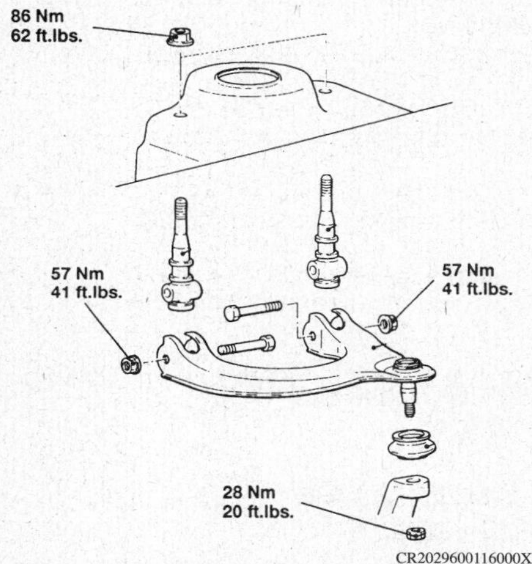

Fig. 7 Upper arm removal

3. Remove stabilizer bar as outlined under "Stabilizer Bar, Replace."
4. Remove lower arm, then the clamp.
5. Remove crossmember mounting nuts, then the crossmember.
6. Reverse procedure to install.

POWER STEERING GEAR

REPLACE

1998-2000

1. Drain power steering fluid.
2. Remove stabilizer bar as described under "Stabilizer Bar, Replace."
3. Remove windshield washer reservoir.
4. Remove steering gear, **Fig. 14.**
5. Reverse procedure to install, noting the following:
   a. Tighten bolts to specifications.
   b. Add power steering fluid and bleed system as described under "Power Steering System Bleed."

2001-02

1. Drain power steering fluid.
2. Remove transaxle and front roll stopper bolt, then the center member.
3. Remove front exhaust pipe.
4. Remove stabilizer bar as outlined under "Stabilizer Bar, Replace."
5. Remove steering shaft assembly connecting bolt.
6. Using steering linkage puller tool No. MB991113, or equivalent, disconnect tie rod ends.
7. Disconnect return hose , then the pressure tube.
8. Remove cylinder clamp, then the steering gear.
9. Reverse procedure to install noting the following:
   a. Tighten bolts to specifications.
   b. Add power steering fluid and bleed as outlined under "Power Steering System Bleed."

POWER STEERING PUMP

REPLACE

1. Drain power steering fluid into a suitable container.
2. Remove power steering pump drive belt.
3. Disconnect suction hose.
4. Disconnect pressure hose from pump.
5. Remove gasket or O-ring, if equipped.
6. Disconnect pressure switch electrical connector, if equipped.
7. Remove oil pump and bracket.
8. Reverse procedure to install and tighten to specifications. Add power steering fluid and bleed system as described under "Power Steering System Bleed."

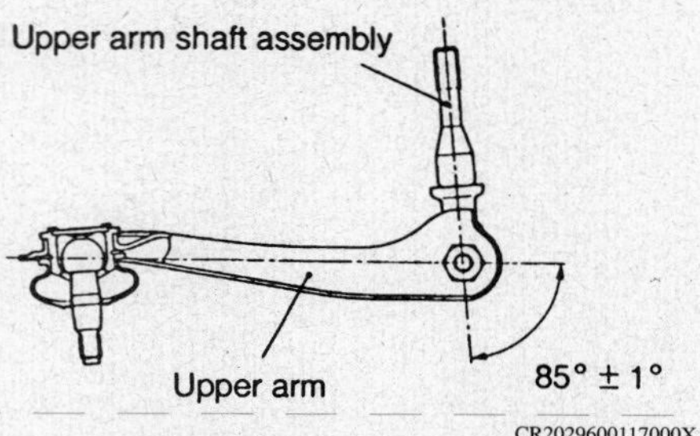

Fig. 8 Upper arm shaft installation

POWER STEERING SYSTEM BLEED

1. Raise and support front wheels.
2. **On 1998–2000 models,** manually turn oil pump pulley a few turns.
3. **On 1998–2000 models,** turn steering wheel to full left and full right five or six times.
4. **On all models,** disconnect high tension ignition cable, then while operating starter motor intermittently, turn steering wheel full left and full right five or six times.
5. Connect ignition cable, then start engine and run at idle.
6. Turn steering wheel to left and right until there are no bubbles in the reservoir.
7. Confirm fluid is not milky and that fluid level is up to specified position on dipstick.
8. Confirm there is very little change in fluid level when steering wheel is turned to left or right.

TECHNICAL SERVICE BULLETINS

FRONT STABILIZER BUSHING NOISE

2001

On some of these models a creaking, popping or metallic clang sound may be heard from the front end. The sound may occur at low speed while braking hard or when accelerating briskly. This may be caused by the stabilizer bar moving in the mounting bushing.

To correct this condition replace stabilizer bushings using part No. MR589815 for models equipped with a 2.4L engine and part No. MR589817 for models equipped with a 3.0L engine.

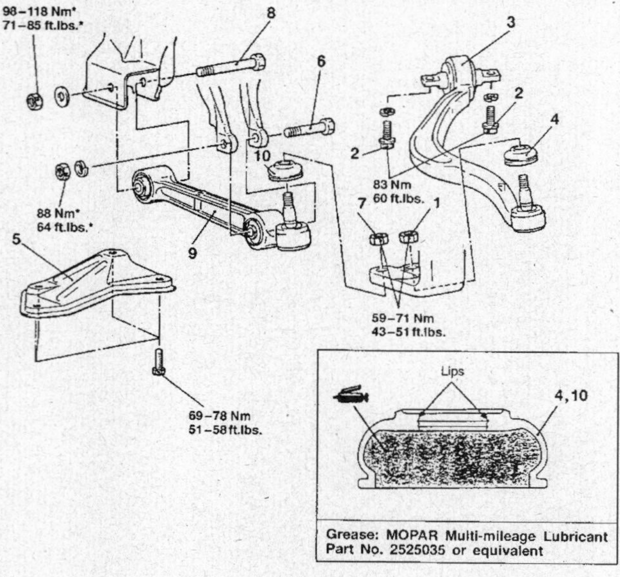

1. Compression lower arm ball joint and knuckle connection
2. Compression lower arm mounting bolt
3. Compression lower arm assembly
4. Dust cover
5. Stay
6. Shock absorber lower mounting bolt and nut
7. Lateral lower arm ball joint and knuckle connection
8. Lateral lower arm mounting bolt and nut
9. Lateral lower arm assembly
10. Dust cover

CR2029600118000X

Fig. 9 Compression lower arm & lateral lower arm. 1998–2000

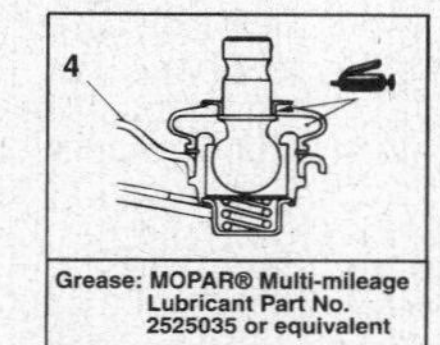

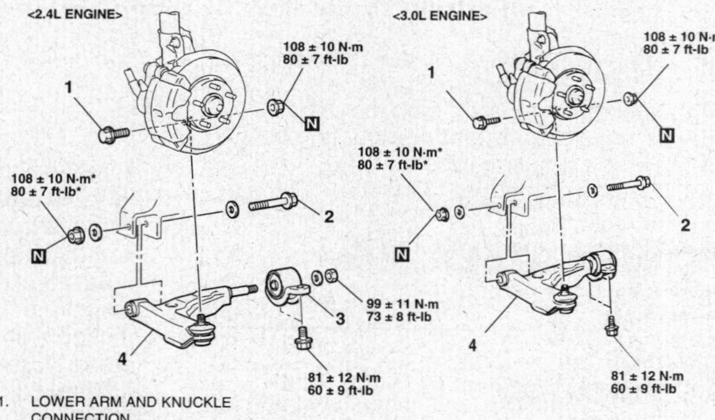

1. LOWER ARM AND KNUCKLE CONNECTION
2. LOWER ARM MOUNTING BOLT
3. LOWER ARM CLAMP <2.4L ENGINE>
4. LOWER ARM

CR2020100178000X

Fig. 10 Lower control arm replacement. 2001–02

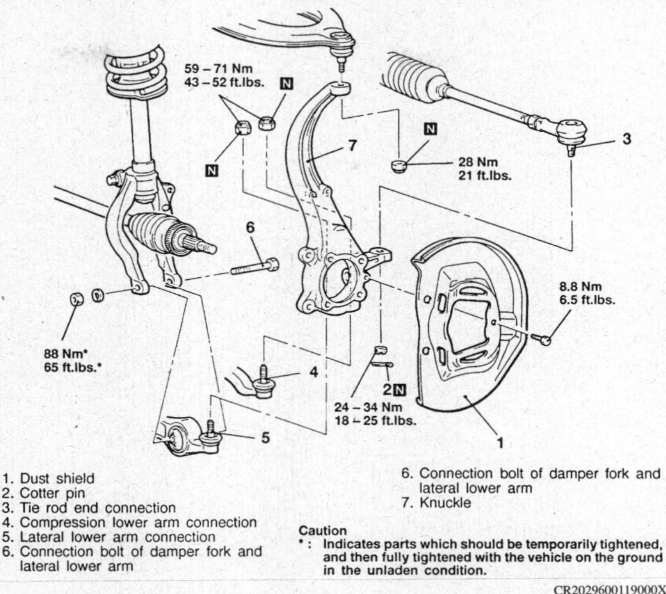

1. Dust shield
2. Cotter pin
3. Tie rod end connection
4. Compression lower arm connection
5. Lateral lower arm connection
6. Connection bolt of damper fork and lateral lower arm
7. Knuckle

Caution
*: Indicates parts which should be temporarily tightened, and then fully tightened with the vehicle on the ground in the unladen condition.

CR2029600119000X

Fig. 11 Steering knuckle removal. 1998–2000

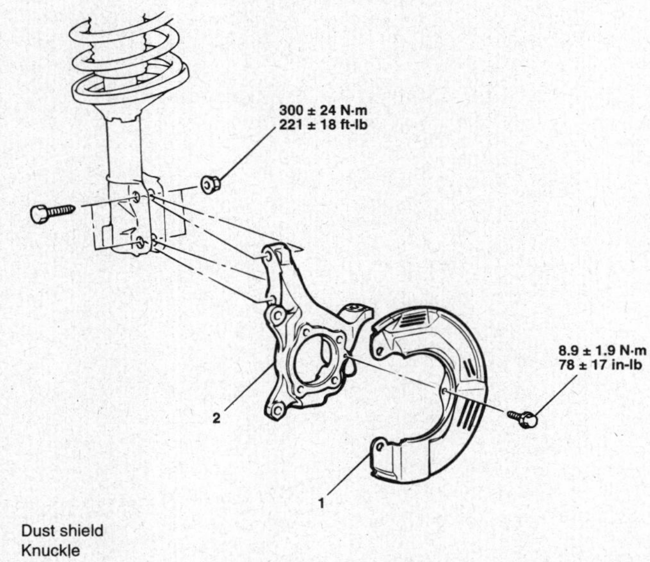

1. Dust shield
2. Knuckle

CR2020000175000X

Fig. 12 Steering knuckle replacement. 2001–02

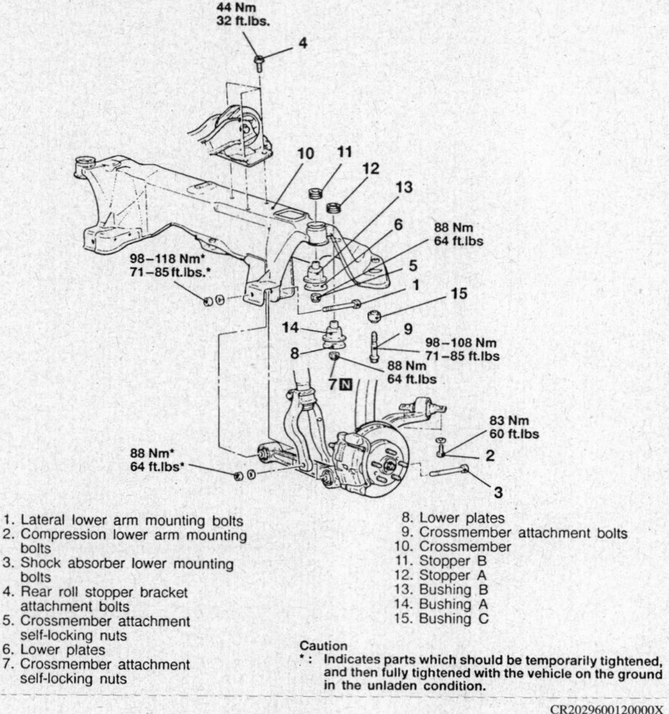
44 Nm
32 ft.lbs.
4
10
11
12
13
6
88 Nm
64 ft.lbs
5
1
15
98–118 Nm*
71–85 ft.lbs.*
14
9
8
98–108 Nm
71–85 ft.lbs
88 Nm
64 ft.lbs
7 N
83 Nm
60 ft.lbs
2
3
88 Nm*
64 ft.lbs*
1. Lateral lower arm mounting bolts
2. Compression lower arm mounting bolts
3. Shock absorber lower mounting bolts
4. Rear roll stopper bracket attachment bolts
5. Crossmember attachment self-locking nuts
6. Lower plates
7. Crossmember attachment self-locking nuts
8. Lower plates
9. Crossmember attachment bolts
10. Crossmember
11. Stopper B
12. Stopper A
13. Bushing B
14. Bushing A
15. Bushing C
Caution
* : Indicates parts which should be temporarily tightened, and then fully tightened with the vehicle on the ground in the unladen condition.
CR2029600120000X

Fig. 13 Crossmember removal

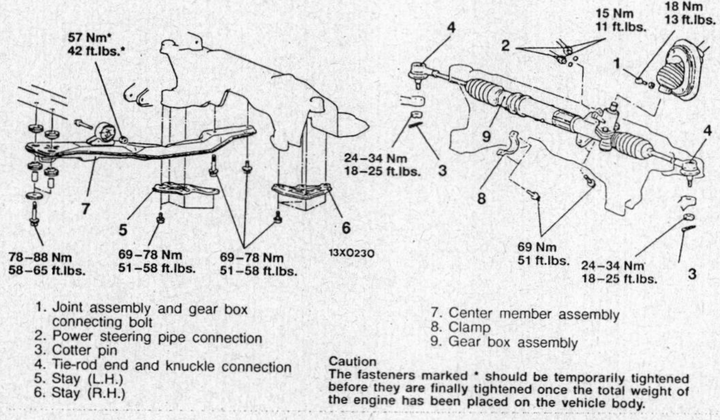
57 Nm*
42 ft.lbs.*
7
5
6
78–88 Nm
58–65 ft.lbs.
69–78 Nm
51–58 ft.lbs.
69–78 Nm
51–58 ft.lbs.
13XO23O
4
15 Nm
11 ft.lbs.
18 Nm
13 ft.lbs.
2
1
9
4
24–34 Nm
18–25 ft.lbs.
3
8
69 Nm
51 ft.lbs.
24–34 Nm
18–25 ft.lbs.
3
1. Joint assembly and gear box connecting bolt
2. Power steering pipe connection
3. Cotter pin
4. Tie-rod end and knuckle connection
5. Stay (L.H.)
6. Stay (R.H.)
7. Center member assembly
8. Clamp
9. Gear box assembly
Caution
The fasteners marked * should be temporarily tightened before they are finally tightened once the total weight of the engine has been placed on the vehicle body.
CR2029600122000X

Fig. 14 Center member & power steering gear replacement. 1998–2000

TIGHTENING SPECIFICATIONS

Year	Component	Torque/Ft. Lbs.
1998–2002	Axle Nut	145–188
	Centermember Rear Assembly Bolts	64
	Centermember To Bracket Bolts	32
	Centermember To Crossmember Bolts	51–58
	Compression Lower Arm Ball Joint To Knuckle	43–51
	Compression Lower Arm Mounting Bolt	60
	Crossmember Lower Plate Bolts	71–85
	Crossmember To Rear Roll Bracket Bolts	32
	Damper Fork Mounting Bolt	75
	Damper Fork To Lateral Lower Arm Through Bolt	65
	Driveshaft Nut	145–188
	Driveshaft To Transaxle Bolt	30
	Hub Nut	145–188
	Joint Assembly & Steering Gear Connection	13
	Lateral Lower Arm Mounting Bolt & Nut	71–85
	Lateral Lower Arm To Knuckle Nuts	43–52
	Power Steering Gear Clamp Bolts	51
	Power Steering Pipe Connection	11
	Power Steering Pump Bracket Bolts (2.0L)	29
	Power Steering Pump Bracket Bolt (2.4L - M8)	18–24
	Power Steering Pump Bracket Bolt (2.4L - M10)	29–43
	Power Steering Pump Bracket Bolts (2.5L)	16
	Power Steering Pump Bracket Bolts (3.0L - M8)	14–20
	Power Steering Pump Bracket Bolts (3.0L - M10)	26–40
	Power Steering Pump Mounting Bolt (2.0L)	42
	Shock Absorber Lower Mounting Bolt	64
	Shock Absorber Upper Mounting Nut	32
	Stabilizer Bar Bracket	28
	Stabilizer Link Mounting Nut	28
	Tie Rod End To Steering Knuckle	18–25
	Upper Arm Self-Locking Nut	62
	Upper Arm Shaft To Control Arm	41

Wheel Alignment

INDEX

DESCRIPTION

Caster and camber are preset at the factory and cannot be adjusted. If camber is not within specifications, inspect and replace bent or damaged parts.

PRELIMINARY INSPECTION

Wheel alignment should be measured with alignment equipment on a level surface. The suspension, steering system and wheels should be serviced to normal condition prior to measurement of wheel alignment. Inspect wheel runout as follows:

1. Raise and support vehicle.
2. While slowly turning wheel, measure runout with dial indicator.
3. Radial and lateral runout should be .05 inch or less for steel wheel, and .04 inch or less for aluminum wheel.
4. If wheel runout exceeds limit, replace wheel.

FRONT WHEEL ALIGNMENT

CASTER

Caster is preset from the factory and cannot be adjusted.

CAMBER

1998-2000

Camber is preset at the factory and cannot be adjusted.

2001-02

1. Measure camber, use table, **Fig. 1** to select proper camber adjusting bolt.
2. Replace upper and lower knuckle to strut attaching bolt with new bolts, **Fig. 2.**
3. Loosely tighten bolts, push or pull on front axle to adjust camber, **Fig. 3.**
4. **Torque** upper and lower knuckle to strut attaching bolt to 203–240 ft. lbs.

TOE-IN

If toe measurement is not within specifications, adjust as follows:

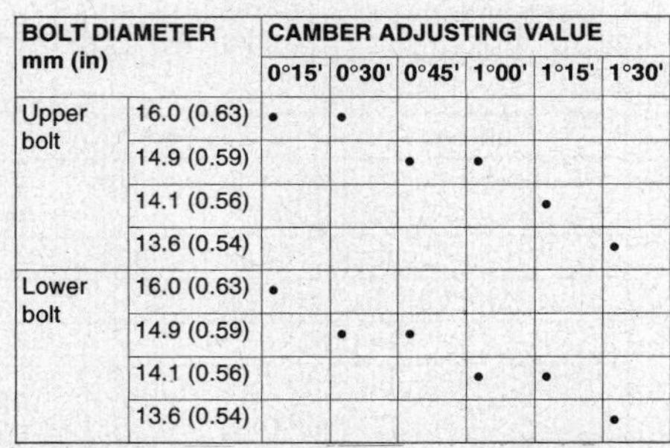

BOLT DIAMETER mm (in)		CAMBER ADJUSTING VALUE					
		0°15'	0°30'	0°45'	1°00'	1°15'	1°30'
Upper bolt	16.0 (0.63)	•	•				
	14.9 (0.59)			•	•		
	14.1 (0.56)					•	
	13.6 (0.54)						•
Lower bolt	16.0 (0.63)	•					
	14.9 (0.59)		•	•			
	14.1 (0.56)				•	•	
	13.6 (0.54)						•

CR2040100062000X

Fig. 1 Camber adjusting bolt selection table. 2001–02

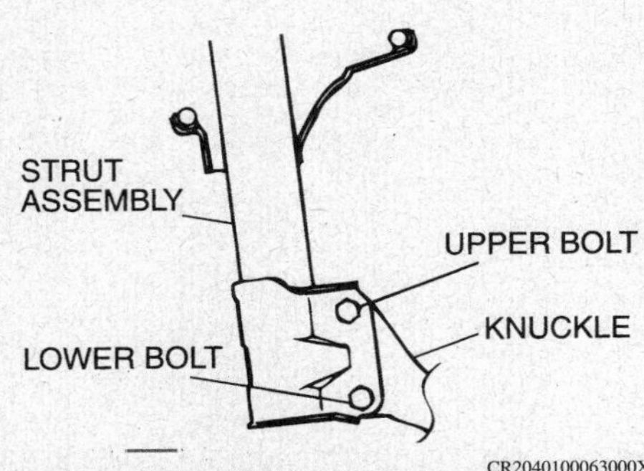

Fig. 2 Camber adjusting bolts. 2001–02

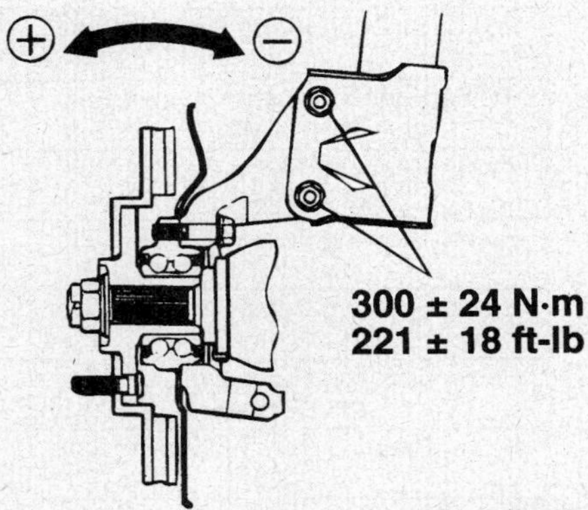

Fig. 3 Camber adjustment. 2001–02

1. Undo clips and turn left and right tie rod turnbuckles by the same amount in opposite directions, **Fig. 4.**
2. Toe will move out as left turnbuckle is turned toward front of vehicle and right turnbuckle is turned toward rear of vehicle.

REAR WHEEL ALIGNMENT

Toe is adjusted by turning the toe control arm mounting bolt to the left or right in equal amounts, **Fig. 5.** Turning the lefthand bolt clockwise adjusts in the toe-out direction. Turning the righthand bolt clockwise adjusts in the toe-in direction. Toe adjustments are made in graduations of .05 inch.

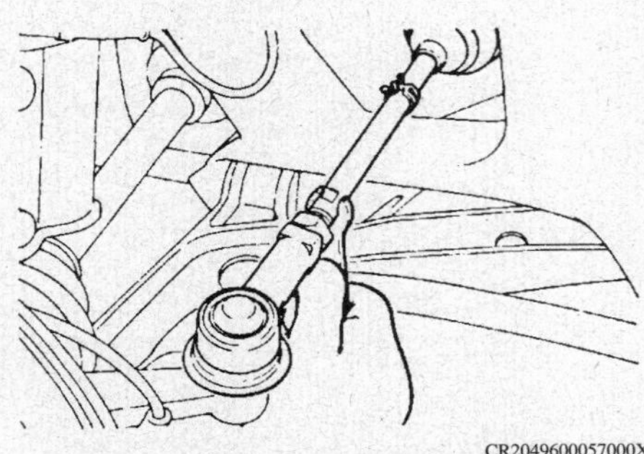

Fig. 4 Front toe adjustment

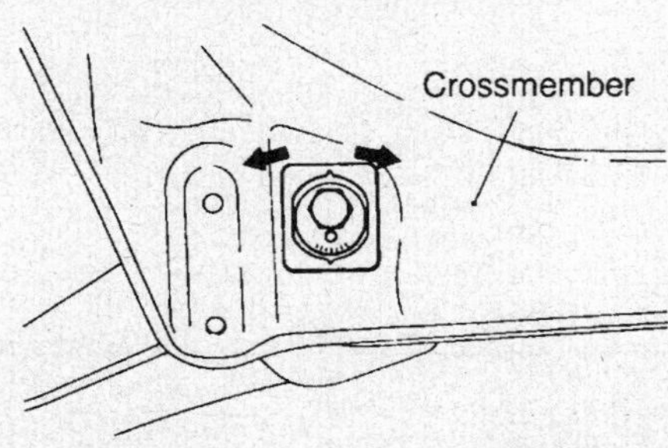

Fig. 5 Rear toe adjustment

BREEZE, CIRRUS & SEBRING CONVERTIBLE & 1998-2000 STRATUS & 2001-02 SEBRING & STRATUS SEDAN

NOTE: Refer To The Rear Of This Manual For Manufacturer's Special Service Tool Supplies.

INDEX OF SERVICE OPERATIONS

Specifications

GENERAL ENGINE SPECIFICATIONS

Year	Engine		Fuel System	Bore & Stroke, Inches	Comp. Ratio	Net HP @ RPM	Maximum Torque, Ft. Lbs. @ RPM	Normal Oil Pressure, psi @ 3000 RPM
	Liter	VIN Code①						
1998–2000	2.0L	C	SMPI	3.45 x 3.27	9.8	132 @ 6000	129 @ 5000	25–80
	2.4L	X	SMPI	3.44 x 3.98	9.4	150 @ 5200	167 @ 4000	25–80
	2.5L	H	SMPI	3.29 x 2.99	9.4	168 @ 5800	170 @ 4350	35–75
2001–02	2.4L	X	SMPI	3.44 x 3.98	9.5	150 @ 5200	167 @ 4000	25–80
	2.7L	U	SMPI	3.386 x 3.091	9.7	200 @ 5800	190 @ 4850	45–105

SMPI — Sequential Multi-Port Injection

① — Eighth digit of Vehicle Identification Number (VIN) denotes engine code.

TUNE UP SPECIFICATIONS

Year & Engine	Spark Plug Gap, Inch	Ignition Timing			Minimum Air Flow Idle Speed, RPM②	Fuel Pump Pressure, psi	Valve Clearance
		Firing Order	Firing Order Fig.	°BTDC			
1998–2000							
2.0L	.035	1-3-4-2	A	②	600–1300	49④	①
2.4L	.050	1-3-4-2	A	②	600–1300	49④	①
2.5L	.041	1-2-3-4-5-6	B	②	500–1100	47–51③	①
2001–02							
2.4L	.050	1-3-4-2	A	②	600–1300	58	①
2.7L	.048–.053	1-2-3-4-5-6	C	②	350–700	58	①

BTDC — Before Top Dead Center

① — Equipped w/hydraulic valve adjusters. No adjustment is necessary.

② — Controlled by PCM; not adjustable.

③ — Disconnect fuel rail wiring harness. Connect a jumper wire between 12 volt power source & A142 circuit terminal of fuel rail wiring harness connector. Connect one end of a jumper wire to ground, then connect other end of jumper wire to each injector terminal in harness. Disconnect fuel line from fuel rail & connect a suitable fuel pressure test gauge between fuel line & fuel rail. Connect DRB scan tool, or equivalent. Place ignition switch in On position, the use scan tool to activate ADSD fuel system test.

④ — Remove cap from fuel pressure test port on fuel rail. Connect a suitable fuel pressure test gauge to fuel rail test port. Connect DRB scan tool, or equivalent. Place ignition switch in On position, then use scan tool to activate ADSD fuel system test.

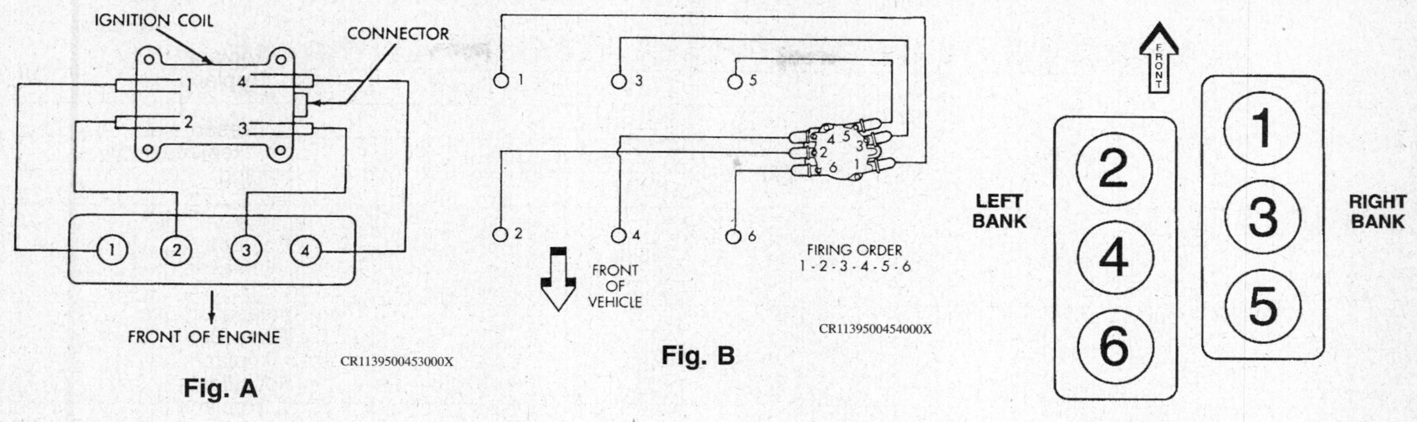

Fig. A

Fig. B

FIRING ORDER 1-2-3-4-5-6

CR1139800545000X

Fig. C

FRONT WHEEL ALIGNMENT SPECIFICATIONS

Year	Model	Camber Angle, Degrees		Toe, Degrees③		Caster, Degrees①	Ball Joint Wear
		Limits	Desired	Individual	Total		
1998–2000	Breeze, Cirrus & Stratus	-.6 to +.6	0	+.05	+.1	+3.3	②
	Sebring Convertible	-.5 to +.7	+.1	+.05	+.1	+3.1	②
2001	Sebring & Stratus Sedan & Sebring Convertible	-.5 to +.7	+.1	+.05	+.1	+3.1	②
2002	Sebring & Stratus Sedan & Sebring Convertible	-.9 to +.3	-.3	+.12	+.24	+3.3	②

① — Not adjustable.

② — Refer to "Ball Joint Inspection" in "Front Suspension & Steering" section.

③ — Toe in (+); toe out (-).

REAR WHEEL ALIGNMENT SPECIFICATIONS

Year	Model	Camber Angle, Degrees		Toe, Degrees①		Thrust Angle, Degrees	
		Limits	Desired	Individual	Total	Limits	Desired
1998–2000	Breeze, Cirrus & Stratus	-.6 to +.2	-.2	+.05	+.1	-.15 to +.15	0
	Sebring Convertible	-.5 to +.3	-.1	+.05	+.1	-.15 to +.15	0
2001	Sebring & Stratus Sedan & Sebring Convertible	-.5 to +.3	-.1	+.05	+.1	-.15 to +.15	0
2002	Sebring & Stratus Sedan & Sebring Convertible	-.9 to -.1	-.5	+.05	+.1	-.15 to +.15	0

① — Toe in (+); toe out (-).

VEHICLE RIDE HEIGHT SPECIFICATIONS

Model	Year	Body Style	Manufacturer's Original Tire Size	Measurement Points & Specifications②					
				Front			Rear		
				Dim.	Specification		Dim.	Specification	
					Inches	mm		Inches	mm
Breeze	1998–2000	All	①	A	27.31	694	B	27.25	692
Cirrus		All	①	A	27.31	694	B	27.25	693
Sebring Convertible		All	①	A	27.31	694	B	27.25	692
Stratus		All	①	A	27.31	694	B	27.25	692

Continued

VEHICLE RIDE HEIGHT SPECIFICATIONS—Continued

Model	Year	Body Style	Manufacturer's Original Tire Size	Measurement Points & Specifications②					
				Front			Rear		
				Dim.	Specification		Dim.	Specification	
					Inches	mm		Inches	mm
Sebring & Stratus Sedan & Sebring Convertible	2001	All	①	A	28.00	710	B	28.00	710
Sebring & Stratus Sedan & Sebring Convertible	2002	All	①	A	27.75	705	B	28.00	710

A Dim — Ground to lower edge of front wheelwell
B Dim — Ground to lower edge of rear wheelwell
① — See door sticker or inside of glove box for manufacturers original tire size specifications. If tires on vehicle do not match manufacturer's original tire size & measurement is not within limits, it will be necessary to refer to the "Non-Standard Tire & Wheel Size Adjustment To Ride Height Specification & Tire Size Adjustment Charts" in the front of this manual for approximate changes in ride height specifications.
② — Measurement is w/fuel, radiator coolant, engine oil full, jack, hand tools & mats in designated positions and tires properly inflated.

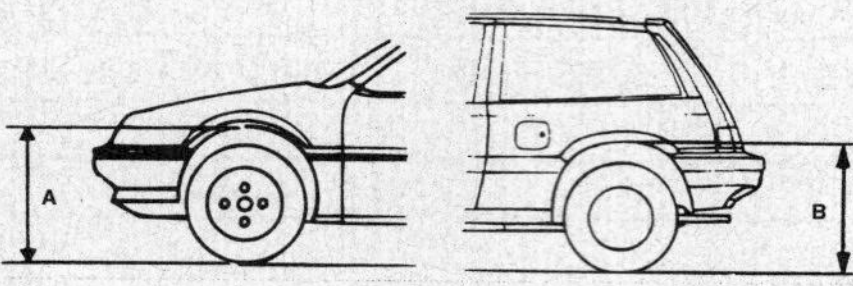

Dimensions A & B

FLUID CAPACITIES & COOLING SYSTEM DATA

Year	Engine	Coolant Capacity, Qts.	Coolant Type	Radiator Cap Relief Pressure, Lbs.	Thermo. Opening Temp., °F	Fuel Tank Capacity, Gals.	Engine Oil Refill, Qts.①	Transaxle Oil, Qts.	
								Manual Trans.	Auto. Trans.
1998–2000	2.0L	8.5	Ethylene Glycol	14–18	192–199	16	4.5	4.4	②
	2.4L	9.0	Ethylene Glycol	14–18	192–199	16	5.0	4.4	②
	2.5L	10.5	Ethylene Glycol	14–18	192–199	16	4.5	4.4	②
2001–02	2.4L	10.5	Ethylene Glycol	14–18	192–199	16	5.0	—	②
	2.7L	9.5	Ethylene Glycol	14–18	192–199	16	5.0	—	②

① — Includes filter change.
② — Service fill, 4.0 qts.; overhaul fill w/torque converter, 9.1 qts.

LUBRICANT DATA

Year	Lubricant Type			
	Transaxle		Power Steering	Brake System
	Manual	Automatic		
1998–2000	Mopar Type M.S. 9417	Mopar ATF Type 7176	Mopar Part No. 4549617	DOT 3
2001–02	Mopar ATF+4 Type 9602	Mopar ATF+4 Type 9602	Mopar ATF+4 Type 9602	DOT 3

Electrical

NOTE: On Air Bag Equipped Models, Refer To "Air Bag System Precautions" Located In The Front Of This Manual For System Disarming & Arming Procedures.

NOTE: Refer To "Computer Relearn Procedures" Located In The Front Of This Manual When Battery Power To The Computer Has Been Interrupted.

INDEX

PRECAUTIONS

AIR BAG SYSTEMS

Refer to Air Bag System Precautions in the front of this manual for system disarming and arming procedures.

BATTERY GROUND CABLE

Prior to service, disconnect battery ground cable and isolate as required.

FUSE PANEL LOCATION

The interior accessory fuse panel is located between the instrument panel and the driver's side door. The door must be open to access the fuse panel. The fuse panel contains the headland relay, horn relay, rear window defogger relay, circuit breakers, and several fuses.

FUEL PUMP RELAY LOCATION

The fuel pump relay is located in the Power Distribution Center (PDC), which is near the battery on the leftward side of the engine compartment.

RELAY CENTER LOCATION

The engine compartment relays are located in the Power Distribution Center (PDC) next to the battery. The PDC contains the starter relay, radiator fan relay, A/C compressor clutch relay, auto shutdown relay, wiper relay, back-up lamp relay, transaxle control relay, fuel pump relay and several fuses.

STARTER

REPLACE

2.0L ENGINE

Automatic Transaxle

Refer to the "2.4L Engine" starter replacement procedure.

Manual Transaxle

1. Remove air cleaner resonator.
2. Remove battery positive cable nut from starter, then remove the battery positive cable and alternator output wire from starter.
3. Disconnect push on solenoid connector.
4. Remove two bolts attaching starter to transaxle housing and remove starter from vehicle.
5. Reverse procedure to install. Clean corrosion from wire terminals before installation.

2.4L ENGINE

1998-2000

1. Remove air cleaner resonator.
2. Remove three Transaxle Control Module (TCM) mounting screws. Move TCM to provide access to top starter mounting bolt. **Do not disconnect TCM wiring.**
3. Remove bolt attaching starter to transaxle housing, then raise and support vehicle.
4. Remove battery cable nut from starter and remove cable.
5. Disconnect push on solenoid connector.
6. Remove top bolt attaching starter to transaxle housing, then the starter from vehicle.
7. Reverse procedure to install, noting the following:

a. **Torque** starter mounting bolts to 40 ft. lbs.
b. Clean corrosion from wire terminals before connecting wiring to solenoid.

2001-02

1. Remove air cleaner box.
2. Remove lower and upper bolt, then ground wire.
3. Remove starter, then wires from starter.
4. Reverse procedure to install. **Torque** starter bolts to 40 ft. lbs.

2.5L ENGINE

1. Raise and support vehicle.
2. Remove oil filter.
3. Remove battery positive cable nut from starter and remove cable.
4. Disconnect push-on solenoid connector.
5. Remove three bolts attaching starter to transaxle housing and remove starter from vehicle.
6. Reverse procedure to install. Clean corrosion from wire terminals before installation.
7. Reverse procedure to install. **Torque** starter motor bolts to 40–45 ft. lbs.

2.7L ENGINE

1. Raise and support vehicle.
2. Disconnect O2 sensor electrical connector, then remove O2 sensor.
3. Remove front mount bracket from engine block.
4. Disconnect battery cable from starter.
5. Remove lower starter bolt, then the starter.
6. Reverse procedure to install noting the following:
   a. **Torque** upper and lower attaching bolts to 40 ft. lbs
   b. **Torque** front mount through bolt to 45 ft. lbs.

ALTERNATOR

REPLACE

2.0L ENGINES

1. Unplug field circuit from alternator.
2. Remove B+ terminal cover by spreading the cover with a small flat blade tool.
3. Remove B+ terminal nut and wire.
4. Loosen adjusting bolt, but do not remove.
5. Loosen pivot bolt, but do not remove.
6. Loosen adjusting bolt to allow removal of the alternator drive belt.
7. Remove adjusting bolt.
8. Remove pivot bolt, do not drop spacer.
9. **On models equipped with 2.0L engine,** proceed as follows:
   a. Release alternator from mounting bracket and move it toward passenger headlamp bucket.
   b. Remove alternator from head lamp bucket area.
10. **On models equipped with 2.4L engine,** proceed as follows:
    a. Remove ABS braking unit by removing the two lower plate mounting bolts.
    b. Remove coolant overflow bottle.
    c. Remove by sliding alternator under air conditioning lines towards passenger side of vehicle.
11. **On all models,** reverse procedure to install.

2.4L ENGINE

1998-2000

Refer to "2.0L Engine" for alternator replacement procedure.

2001-02

1. Remove drive belt cover.
2. Unplug field circuit from alternator.
3. Remove B+ terminal cover by spreading cover using a suitable small flat blade tool.
4. Remove B+ terminal nut and wire.
5. Raise and support vehicle.
6. Remove serpentine drive belt.
7. Lower vehicle, then remove MAP sensor from intake manifold.
8. Remove alternator bolts, then the alternator.
9. Reverse procedure to install.

2.5L ENGINE

1. Unplug field circuit from alternator.
2. Remove B+ terminal nut and wire.
3. Loosen top mounting ear bolt.
4. Loosen pivot bolt, but do not remove.
5. Loosen adjusting bolt on idler to allow removal of alternator drive belt.
6. Remove pivot bolt. Do not drop spacer.
7. Remove top mounting ear bolt.
8. Remove upper alternator bracket, then the alternator.
9. Reverse procedure to install.

2.7L ENGINE

1. Raise and support vehicle.
2. Remove serpentine drive belt splash shield, then loosen serpentine drive belt.
3. Remove lower mounting bolt, then lower vehicle.
4. Disconnect A/C pressure switch and clutch electrical connectors.
5. Remove engine oil dip stick.
6. Remove two upper mounting bolts, then the alternator.
7. Reverse procedure to install.

DISTRIBUTOR

REPLACE

2.5L ENGINE

Removal

1. Remove bolt holding air inlet resonator to intake manifold.
2. Loosen clamps holding air cleaner cover to air cleaner housing.
3. Remove PCV air hose from air inlet tube.
4. Loosen hose clamp at throttle body.
5. Remove air inlet tube, resonator and air cleaner cover.
6. Remove EGR tube.
7. Remove spark plug cables from distributor cap.
8. Loosen distributor cap hold-down screws and remove cap.
9. Mark rotor position for installation reference, then remove rotor.
10. Remove two harness connectors from distributor.
11. Remove two sets of distributor hold-down nuts and washers from studs.
12. Remove bolt and spark plug cable mounting bracket from top of distributor housing.
13. Remove bolt and transaxle dipstick tube.
14. Carefully remove distributor from engine.

Installation

1. Install rotor on shaft.
2. Position distributor in engine and ensure O-ring is properly seated on distributor. Replace O-ring if it is cracked or nicked.
3. Carefully engage distributor drive with slotted end of camshaft. When the distributor is installed properly, the rotor will be in line with previously marked line on air intake plenum.
4. If engine was cranked while distributor was removed, establish proper relationship between distributor shaft and No. 1 piston position as follows:
   a. Rotate crankshaft until number one piston is at top of compression stroke.
   b. Rotate rotor to No. 1 rotor terminal.
   c. Lower distributor into opening, engaging distributor drive with drive on camshaft. With distributor fully seated on engine, rotor should be under No. 1 terminal.
5. Install distributor hold-down washers and nuts. **Torque** to 108 inch lbs.
6. Install spark plug cable bracket.
7. Install two harness connectors to distributor.
8. Install distributor cap.
9. Install transaxle dipstick tube.
10. Install EGR tube to intake manifold. **Torque** bolts to 96 inch lbs.

COIL PACK

REPLACE

2.0L, 2.4L & 2.7L ENGINES

1. Disconnect coil pack electrical connector.
2. Remove mounting nuts, then the coil pack.
3. Reverse procedure to install. If a new coil pack is to be installed, transfer spark plug cables to corresponding towers on new unit.

IGNITION LOCK

REPLACE

1. Remove upper steering column shroud.
2. Pull lower shroud down far enough to access lock cylinder retaining tab.
3. Place key cylinder in Run position. Depress retaining tab and remove key cylinder.

4. Reverse procedure to install.

IGNITION SWITCH

REPLACE

1. Remove fuse panel cover from left end of instrument panel. Remove screw holding end of instrument panel top cover.
2. Pull center bezel off.
3. Remove screws holding instrument panel top cover to center of instrument panel.
4. Pull instrument panel top cover up enough to gain access to knee bolster screws.
5. Remove lower knee bolster screws and knee bolster.
6. Remove screws from lower steering column shroud.
7. Pull lower shroud to clear ignition cylinder and key release, if equipped.
8. Hold tilt wheel lever down and slide lower shroud forward to remove it from column.
9. Tilt wheel to full down position and remove upper steering column shroud.
10. Remove screws holding multiplication switch to lock housing.
11. Place key cylinder in Run position. Depress lock cylinder retaining tab and remove key cylinder.
12. Disconnect electrical connectors from ignition switch.
13. Remove ignition switch mounting screw with a suitable Torx bit.
14. Depress retaining tabs and pull ignition switch from steering column.
15. Reverse procedure to install.

MULTI-FUNCTION SWITCH

REPLACE

1. Remove upper steering column cover.
2. Remove multiplication switch mounting screws.
3. Disconnect wire connectors. Lift switch straight up to remove.
4. Reverse procedure to install.

STEERING WHEEL

REPLACE

BREEZE & CIRRUS

1. Place front wheels in straight ahead position.
2. Remove air bag as outlined in "Passive Restraint Systems" section.
3. Remove speed control switch screws from back of steering wheel. Pull switch pods out and disconnect wires.
4. Disconnect horn wire from the air bag module mounting bracket. Remove speed control wires from under the bracket and from wire guides.
5. Remove steering wheel retaining nut.
6. Remove steering wheel with wheel a suitable fuller tool. Feed all wires through steering wheel armature to avoid damaging wires.
7. Reverse procedure to install, noting the following:
   a. **Torque** steering wheel retaining nut to 45 ft. lbs.
   b. **Torque** air bag module bolts to 84 inch. lbs.

SEBRING CONVERTIBLE

1998–2000

1. Place front wheels in straight ahead position, then rotate steering wheel 180° clockwise.
2. Lock steering column with ignition lock.
3. Remove and disconnect speed control switches, then air bag module as outlined in "Passive Restraint Systems" section.
4. Disconnect horn electrical connectors.
5. Remove steering wheel retaining nut, then use a suitable fuller to remove wheel, noting the following:
   a. **Do not hammer on end of steering shaft during removal.**
   b. Carefully feed wires through holes in clocking armature.
6. Reverse procedure to install, noting the following:
   a. **Torque** steering wheel retaining nut to 45 ft. lbs.
   b. **Torque** air bag module bolts to 96 inch. lbs.

2001–02

1. Adjust wheels to straight ahead position.
2. Remove speed control switches, then air bag attaching screws from steering wheel.
3. Disconnect horn wire from air bag mounting bracket, then remove speed control wires from under bracket.
4. Loosen steering wheel bolt, then loosen steering wheel using suitable puller.
5. Remove steering wheel bolt, then steering wheel.
6. Reverse procedure to install noting the following:
   a. Install clockspring. Refer to "Passive Restraint Systems" for clockspring installation procedure.
   b. **Torque** steering wheel bolt to 40 ft. lbs.
   c. Install air bag bolts. **Torque** air bag bolts to 75–95 inch lbs. Tighten left side bolt first.

SEBRING SEDAN

2001–02

Refer to "2001–02" under "Sebring Convertible" for steering wheel replacement procedure.

STRATUS

Refer to "Breeze & Cirrus" for steering wheel replacement procedure.

STRATUS SEDAN

2001–02

Refer to"2001–02" under "Sebring Convertible" for steering wheel replacement procedure.

INSTRUMENT CLUSTER

REPLACE

BREEZE & CIRRUS

1. Remove instrument panel left end cap.
2. Tilt steering column down to its lowest position.
3. Remove instrument panel center bezel by disengaging four clips.
4. Remove instrument cluster hood by doing the following:
   a. Remove two screws adjacent radio.
   b. Remove screw below HVAC control in center.
   c. Remove screw at left end of panel.
   d. Pull on hood to disengage eight clips.
5. Remove instrument cluster from panel. Pull cluster rearward to disconnect wire connectors from base panel.
6. Reverse procedure to install.

SEBRING CONVERTIBLE

1998–2000

Refer to "Breeze & Cirrus" for instrument cluster replacement procedure.

2001–02

1. Remove left end cap.
2. Using trim stick tool No. C-4755, or equivalent, pry up and remove power mirror switch.
3. Using trim stick, gently pry up on instrument panel center trim bezel.
4. Disconnect HVAC control connector.
5. Remove one screw from passenger side trim bezel, then remove trim by unsnapping clips.
6. Remove four screws to left lower instrument panel trim.
7. Remove five screws to cluster bezel, then pry out using trim stick.
8. If equipped with Mini-Trip Computer (CMTC/Traveler), disconnect module, then remove the cluster bezel.
9. Tilt steering column to its lowest position, then depress hazard switch.
10. Remove cluster attaching screws.
11. Pull cluster rearward to disconnect 26-way electrical connector, then tilt cluster downward slightly and slide sideways to remove.
12. Reverse procedure to install.

SEBRING SEDAN

2001–02

Refer to "2001–02" under "Sebring Convertible" for instrument cluster replacement procedure.

STRATUS

1998–2000

Refer to "Breeze & Cirrus" for instrument cluster replacement procedure.

STRATUS SEDAN

2001–02

Refer to "2001–02" under "Sebring Convertible" for instrument cluster replacement procedure.

RADIO

REPLACE

1. Remove center bezel and two radio retaining screws.
2. Pull radio straight out and disconnect both electrical connectors, antenna cable and radio ground strap, then remove radio from vehicle.
3. Reverse procedure to install.

WIPER MOTOR

REPLACE

1. Remove wiper arms and blades.
2. Remove cowl screen.
3. Remove wiper motor mounting screws, then lift assembly to access harness clip.
4. Disconnect harness clip at forward mounting leg, then disconnect motor electrical connector.
5. Disconnect drive linkage at motor output crank, then use a suitable ball joint separator tool to separate ball cap from ball.
6. Remove motor.
7. Reverse procedure to install. **Torque** mounting screws to 96–108 inch. lbs.

BLOWER MOTOR

REPLACE

BREEZE & CIRRUS

1. Remove lower right under panel silencer duct.
2. Remove blower motor connector from resistor block.
3. Remove blower motor retaining screws.
4. Lower blower motor from housing and remove fan scroll from motor shaft.
5. Remove motor from case.
6. Reverse procedure to install.

SEBRING CONVERTIBLE

1998–2000

Refer to "Breeze & Cirrus" for blower motor replacement procedure.

2001–02

1. Remove lower right silencer panel.
2. Remove right sill plate and kick panel.
3. Fold back right upper corner of carpet, then disconnect blower motor electrical connector.
4. Remove three blower motor mounting screws, then the blower motor from housing.
5. Reverse procedure to install.

SEBRING SEDAN

2001–02

Refer to "2001–02" under "Sebring Convertible" for blower motor replacement procedure.

STRATUS

1998–2000

Refer to "Breeze & Cirrus" for blower motor replacement procedure.

STRATUS SEDAN

2001–02

Refer to "2001–02" under "Sebring Convertible" for blower motor replacement procedure.

HEATER CORE

REPLACE

BREEZE & CIRRUS

1. Remove radio and climate control bezel, then the right instrument panel side trim.
2. Remove two screws at lower right side support beam.
3. Remove bolt for instrument panel support at A-pillar.
4. Remove left instrument panel side trim.
5. Remove upper instrument panel bezel.
6. Remove lower knee bolster.
7. Remove console screws at instrument panel.
8. Remove gearshift knob and shifter bezel.
9. Remove console screws at rear, then the rear half of console.
10. Remove front console screws, then the front half of console.
11. Remove right side instrument panel support strut.
12. Drain coolant.
13. Remove heater hoses at cowl.
14. Remove heater core cover screws and cover.
15. Remove heater core.
16. Reverse procedure to install.

SEBRING CONVERTIBLE

1998–2000

Refer to "Breeze & Cirrus" for heater core replacement procedure.

2001–02

1. Remove HVAC housing as outlined under "Evaporator Case, Replace."
2. Disconnect electrical connector from recirculation motor.
3. Remove wiring harness connector from top of housing.
4. Remove seal around evaporator core inlet/outlet.
5. Remove retaining screw from top of housing.
6. Separate upper housing from lower housing, then lift heater core out of lower housing.
7. Reverse procedure to install.

SEBRING SEDAN

2001–02

Refer to "2001–02" under "Sebring Convertible" for heater core replacement procedure.

STRATUS

1998–2000

Refer to "Breeze & Cirrus" for heater core replacement procedure.

STRATUS SEDAN

2001–02

Refer to "2001–02" under "Sebring Convertible" for heater core replacement procedure.

EVAPORATOR CASE

REPLACE

BREEZE & CIRRUS

1. Recover A/C system as outlined under "Air Conditioning."
2. Remove air cleaner hose and air distribution duct from the engine.
3. Drain engine coolant into a suitable container.
4. Disconnect heater hoses at dash panel, then plug the heater core inlet and outlet tubes.
5. Remove both A/C lines from expansion valve using special disconnect tool No. 7193, or equivalent, to disconnect connectors on A/C lines.
6. Cap expansion valve openings and the A/C hose openings to prevent dirt or moisture from entering refrigerant system during servicing.
7. Remove trim bezel around radio and climate control module.
8. Remove cluster hood bezel retaining screws in the trim bezel opening.
9. Pry up cluster hood bezel a few inches to expose the cubby bin bezel and wiring.
10. Remove cubby bin bezel and wiring.
11. Remove control module retaining screws.
12. Drop the A/C control module into cubby bin bezel opening, then disconnect wiring on rear of control module.
13. Release cable clips from top of control module. Retain clips for installation.
14. Disconnect temperature control and recirculation control cables.
15. Remove control module.
16. Remove upper instrument panel bezel.
17. Remove right and left instrument panel end caps.
18. Remove left lower knee bolster. Disconnect mode door motor wiring.
19. Remove right and left interior door post kick panel.
20. Remove front and rear halves of floor console.
21. Remove radio as outlined under "Radio, Replace."
22. Remove right side lower silencer/duct.
23. Remove glove compartment assembly.
24. Remove right side vertical support strut brace.
25. Remove left side vertical support strut brace.
26. Remove center lower distribution housing.
27. Remove bolts securing heater-A/C housing to instrument panel metal frame.
28. Remove upper instrument panel cowl trim cover.
29. Disconnect steering column from instrument panel. Lower steering column.

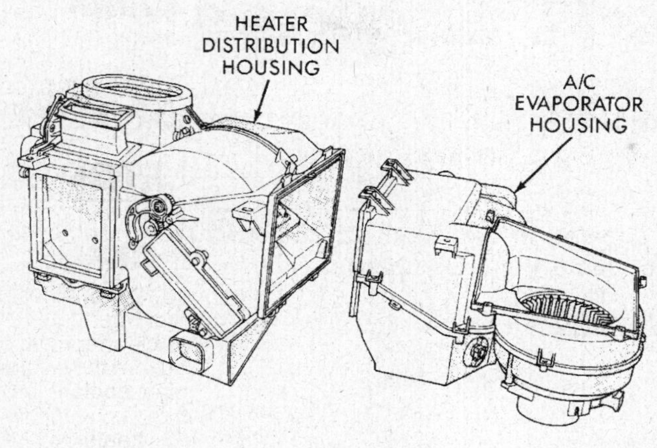

Fig. 1 A/C & Heater housing unit

30. Remove instrument panel bolts at cowl fence.
31. Remove bolts at lower A-posts.
32. Remove instrument frame and wiring.
33. Remove bolts securing Heater-A/C housing to cowl.
34. Reverse procedure to install. Verify cables are properly adjusted and control module is seated properly.

SEBRING CONVERTIBLE

1998–2000

Refer to "Breeze & Cirrus" for evaporator case replacement procedures.

2001–02

1. Recover A/C system as outlined under "Air Conditioning."
2. Drain engine coolant, then disconnect heater hoses from heater core.
3. Remove quick connect clips from A/C lines at expansion valve.
4. Remove A/C lines from expansion valve using quick connectors tool kit No. 7193 or equivalent.
5. Remove expansion valve, then cap A/C lines to prevent moisture from entering refrigerant system.
6. Remove floor console as follows:
   a. Remove shifter boot.
   b. Remove screws attaching front of console to shifter bracket.
   c. Remove screws attaching rear of console to floor bracket.
   d. Engage parking brake, then pull console up off floor bracket.
   e. Disconnect electrical connectors, then remove floor console.
7. Remove rear heat ducts.
8. Remove nuts securing HVAC housing to dash panel under hood.
9. Remove instrument panel as outlined under "Dash Panel Service" section.
10. Disconnect electrical connector from left side of housing, then remove HVAC housing from instrument panel.

SEBRING SEDAN

2001–02

Refer to "2001–02" under "Sebring Convertible" for evaporator case replacement procedure.

STRATUS

1998–2000

Refer to "Breeze & Cirrus" for evaporator case replacement procedures.

STRATUS SEDAN

2001–02

Refer to "2001–02" under "Sebring Convertible" for evaporator case replacement procedure.

EVAPORATOR CORE

REPLACE

BREEZE & CIRRUS

1. Remove evaporator case as described under "Evaporator Case, Replace."
2. Remove recirculation door inlet cover.
3. Remove evaporator temperature probe.
4. Remove clips retaining evaporator housing to heater/distribution housing.
5. Separate evaporator housing from heater/distribution housing, **Fig. 1.**
6. Remove seal around evaporator tube inlet.
7. Remove evaporator housing upper cover.
8. Lift evaporator out of lower housing.
9. Remove foam seal around evaporator.
10. Transfer evaporator sensor. Place the evaporator sensor in the same location as on the previous evaporator.
11. Reverse procedure to install.

SEBRING CONVERTIBLE

1998–2000

Refer to "Breeze & Cirrus" for evaporator core replacement procedure.

2001–02

1. Remove HVAC housing as outlined under "Evaporator Case, Replace."
2. Disconnect electrical connector from recirculation motor.
3. Remove wiring harness connector from top of housing.
4. Remove seal around evaporator core inlet/outlet.
5. Remove retaining screw from top of housing.
6. Separate upper housing from lower housing.
7. Remove evaporator temperature sensor.
8. Lift evaporator out of bottom housing, then remove styrofoam seal around evaporator.

SEBRING SEDAN

2001–02

Refer to "2001–02" under "Sebring Convertible" for evaporator core replacement procedure.

STRATUS

1998–2000

Refer to "Breeze & Cirrus" for evaporator core replacement procedure.

STRATUS SEDAN

2001–02

Refer to "2001–02" under "Sebring Convertible" for evaporator core replacement procedure.

2.0L & 2.4L Engines

NOTE: On Air Bag Equipped Models, Refer To "Air Bag System Precautions" Located In The Front Of This Manual For System Disarming & Arming Procedures.

NOTE: Refer To "Computer Relearn Procedures" Located In The Front Of This Manual When Battery Power To The Computer Has Been Interrupted.

INDEX

PRECAUTIONS

AIR BAG SYSTEMS

Refer to "Air Bag System Precautions" in the front of this manual for system disarming and arming procedures.

BATTERY GROUND CABLE

Prior to service, disconnect battery ground cable and isolate as required.

FUEL SYSTEM PRESSURE RELIEF

1998–2000

1. Disconnect ground cable from auxiliary jumper terminal.
2. Remove fuel filler cap.
3. Remove protective cap from fuel pressure test port on fuel rail, **Fig. 1.**
4. Place open end of fuel pressure release hose tool No. C-4799-1, or equivalent, into a suitable gasoline container, then connect other hose end to fuel pressure test port. Fuel pressure should bleed off through hose into container.

2001–02

1. Remove fuel pump relay from power distribution center.
2. Start and run engine until it stalls.
3. Attempt to restart engine until it will no longer run, then turn ignition key to Off.
4. Install fuel pump relay, then erase any DTC's that may have been stored due to removing fuel pump relay.

COMPRESSION PRESSURE

Compression pressure should be 170–225 psi with no more than a 25% variation in pressure between cylinders.

ENGINE MOUNT

REPLACE

RIGHT SIDE MOUNT

1. Raise and support vehicle, then remove the inner splash.
2. Remove right engine support assembly attaching bolts from frame rail, **Fig. 2.**
3. Lower vehicle and support engine assembly with floor jack to remove pressure on motor mounts.
4. Remove three engine support to engine bracket attaching bolts.
5. Reverse procedure to install. Tighten attaching nuts and bolts to specifications shown in **Fig. 2.**

ENGINE CRADLE (SUPPORT MODULE)

Breeze, Cirrus & 1998–2000 Sebring Convertible & Stratus

1. Raise and support vehicle, then remove rear mount through bolt and bolts securing cradle to crossover, **Fig. 3.**
2. Remove rear support strut bracket upper bolt and bolts securing cradle to lower radiator support.
3. With cooling module supported, remove lower radiator support.
4. Remove front through bolt, then the cradle.
5. Reverse procedure to install, noting the following:
   a. Do not tighten front through bolt until rear through bolt is installed and tightened.

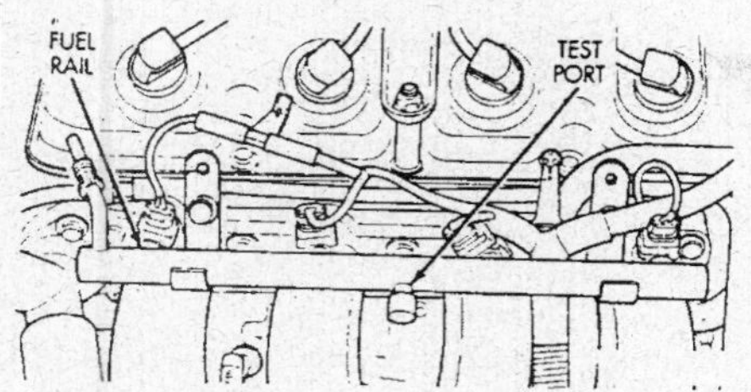

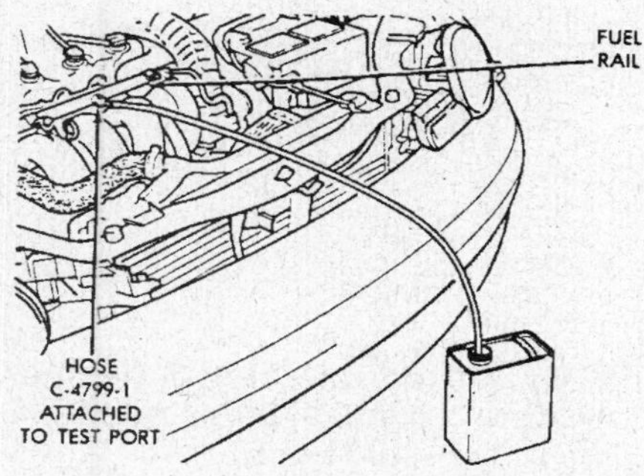

Fig. 1 Fuel system test port location & pressure relief equipment. 1998–2000

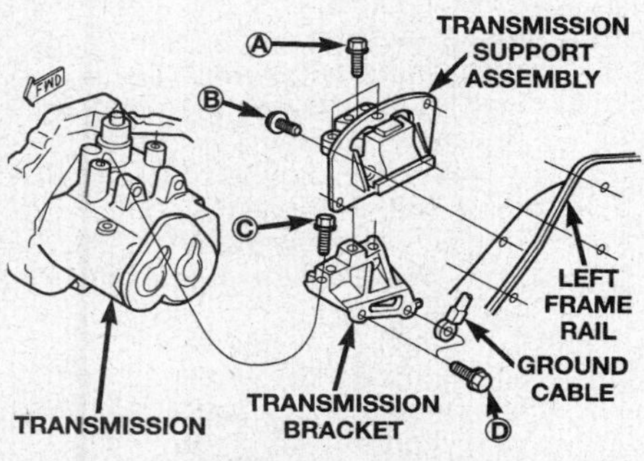

ITEM	DESCRIPTION	TORQUE
A	Bolt	61 N·m (45 ft. lbs.)
B	Bolt	33 N·m (24 ft. lbs.)
C	Bolt	61 N·m (45 ft. lbs.)
D	Bolt	61 N·m (45 ft. lbs.)

CR1069500597000X

Fig. 4 Left engine mount replacement. 2.0L engine

b. Tighten bolts to specifications.

LEFT SIDE MOUNT

1. Support transaxle with suitable jack.
2. Remove three engine mount to transaxle attaching bolts, **Figs. 4 and 5.**
3. Remove transaxle mount attaching bolts, then the mount.
4. Reverse procedure to install. Tighten attaching nuts and bolts to specifications shown in **Figs. 4 and 5.**

REAR MOUNT

1. Raise and support vehicle, then remove left front wheel.
2. Support transaxle with transaxle jack.
3. Remove mount and rear suspension crossover insulator attaching bolt, **Figs. 6 and 7.**
4. Remove four transaxle mount attaching bolts, then the mount.
5. Reverse procedure to install. Tighten attaching nuts and bolts to specifications shown in **Figs. 6 and 7.**

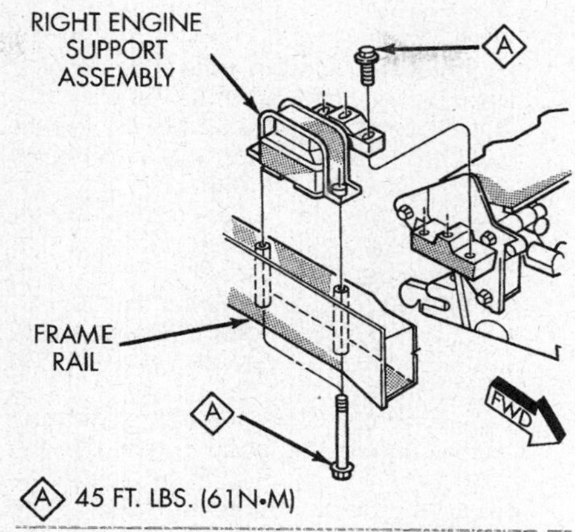

Fig. 2 Right side engine mount replacement

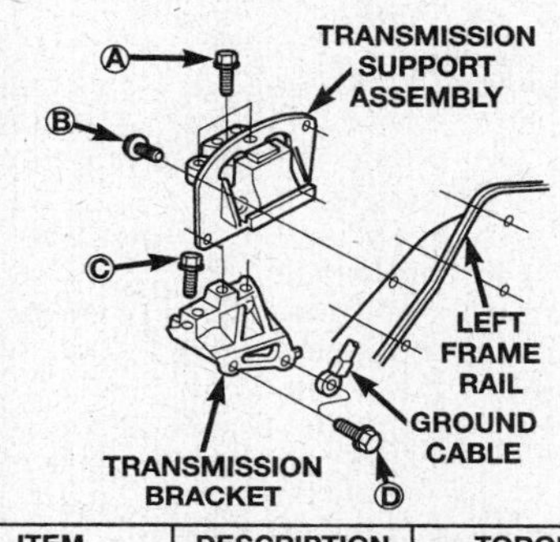

ITEM	DESCRIPTION	TORQUE
A	Bolt	61 N·m (45 ft. lbs.)
B	Bolt	33 N·m (24 ft. lbs.)
C	Bolt	61 N·m (45 ft. lbs.)
D	Bolt	61 N·m (45 ft. lbs.)

CR1069500598000X

Fig. 5 Left engine mount replacement. 2.4L engine

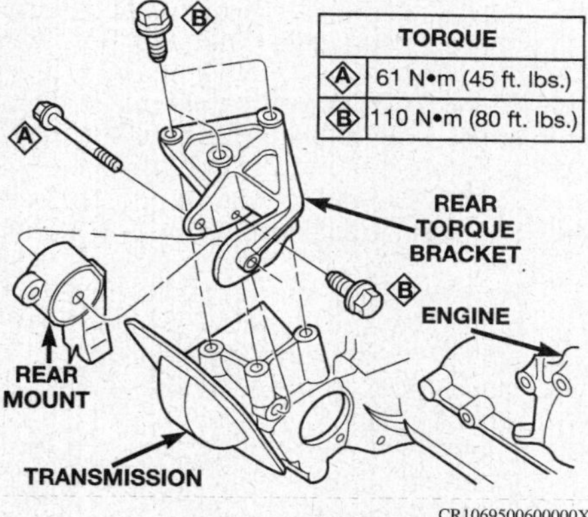

TORQUE	
A	61 N•m (45 ft. lbs.)
B	110 N•m (80 ft. lbs.)

CR1069500600000X

Fig. 7 Rear engine mount replacement. 2.4L engine

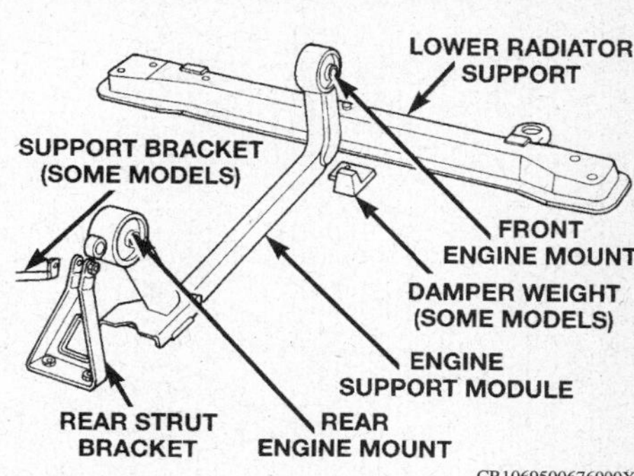

Fig. 3 Engine cradle (support module)

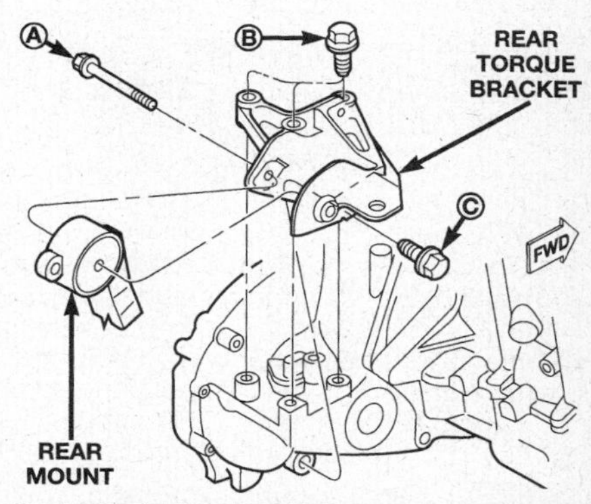

ITEM	DESCRIPTION	TORQUE
A	Bolt	61 N·m (45 ft. lbs.)
B & C	Bolt—w/Auto. Transaxle	110 N·m (80 ft. lbs.)
	Bolt—w/Manual Transaxle	61 N·m (45 ft. lbs.)

CR1069500599000X

Fig. 6 Rear engine mount replacement. 2.0L engine

FRONT MOUNT

2001–02 Sebring & Stratus Sedan & Sebring Convertible

1. Raise and support vehicle.
2. Remove front mount to bracket horizontal through bolt, **Fig. 8.**
3. Remove front mount vertical bolts, then mount.
4. Reverse procedure to install, tighten mounting bolts to specifications.

ENGINE

REPLACE

1998–2000

1. Relieve fuel system pressure as outlined under "Precautions."
2. Disconnect and remove battery and tray, then disconnect Pertain Control Module (PCM) electrical connector and position aside.
3. Drain coolant into a suitable container.
4. Remove upper radiator hose, fan module and radiator as outlined under "Radiator, Replace."
5. Remove lower radiator hose.

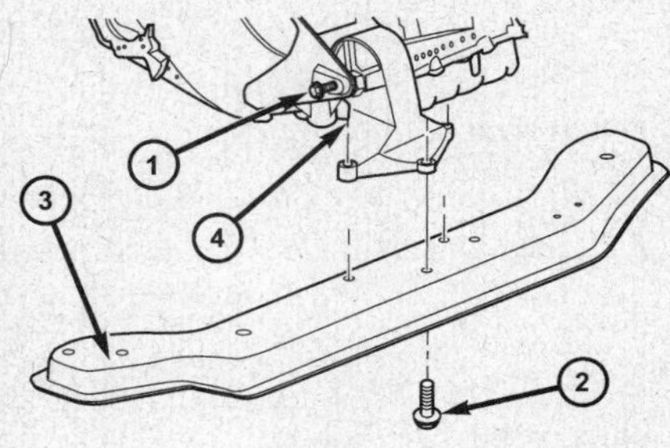

Fig. 8 Front engine mount replacement. 2001–02 Sebring & Stratus Sedan & Sebring Convertible

6. **On models equipped with manual transaxle,** disconnect clutch cable and shift linkage.
7. **On models equipped with automatic transaxle,** disconnect and plug transaxle cooler line.
8. **On all models,** disconnect throttle body linkage.
9. Disconnect engine wiring harness electrical connectors.
10. Disconnect heater hoses.
11. Recover A/C refrigerant as outlined in "Air Conditioning" section.
12. Raise and support vehicle, then remove the right inner splash shield.
13. Remove accessory drive belts.
14. Remove axle shafts.
15. Disconnect exhaust pipe from manifold.
16. Remove front and rear engine mount bracket from the body.
17. Lower vehicle, then remove the air cleaner assembly.
18. Remove power steering pump and reservoir.
19. Remove A/C compressor.
20. Remove ground straps to body.
21. Raise and support vehicle to install engine dolly and cradle tool Nos. 6135 and 6710, or equivalents.
22. **On models equipped with 2.4L engine,** install post tool No. 6848, or equivalent.
23. **On all models,** loosen engine cradle mounts to position engine locating holes in belated, then lower the vehicle until engine rests on cradle mounts and tighten mounts to cradle frame to prevent mount movement.
24. Lower vehicle so weight of engine and transaxle is only on cradle.
25. Remove engine and transaxle mount attaching bolts.
26. Slowly raise and support vehicle, move engine and transaxle assembly on cradle to allow for removal around body flanges as required.
27. Reverse procedure to install.

2001-02

1. Relieve fuel system pressure as outlined under "Precautions."
2. Drain coolant into a suitable container.
3. Evacuate A/C system as outlined under "Air Conditioning."
4. Remove throttle body air inlet hose, then the air cleaner assembly.
5. Remove upper radiator crossmember, then upper and lower radiator hoses.
6. Cut transaxle oil cooler lines flush with fittings using a suitable hose cutter. Plug lines and fittings.
7. Disconnect A/C lines from condenser, then remove the cooling module assembly.
8. Disconnect electrical harness from transaxle, then the shift cable.
9. Disconnect engine electrical harness from PCM and bulkhead connector.
10. Raise and support vehicle.
11. Remove front wheels, then both splash shields.
12. Remove both drive axles as outlined under "Front Wheel Drive Axles."
13. Drain engine oil, then remove accessory drive belts.
14. Remove power steering pump from bracket and place aside.
15. Disconnect heater return hose from pipe connection, then A/C compressor electrical connector.
16. Remove exhaust pipe from manifold.
17. Remove front and rear engine mount through bolts.
18. Remove rear mount bracket from transmission.
19. Remove structural collar and torque reaction bracket, **Fig. 9.**
20. Mark flex plate to torque converter position, then remove torque converter bolts.
21. Lower vehicle, then disconnect battery positive cable from PCM.
22. Disconnect throttle and speed control cables, then coolant recovery overflow hose.
23. Remove heater hose from thermostat housing, then all engine ground straps.
24. Disconnect brake booster and vapor purge hoses, then fuel line from fuel rail.
25. Remove intake manifold as outlined under "Intake Manifold, Replace."
26. Remove alternator.
27. Remove A/C suction line at compressor, then compressor. Plug port and line.
28. Raise and support vehicle to install engine dolly and cradle tool Nos. 6135 and 6710, or equivalents.
29. Install post tool No. 6848, or equivalent.
30. Loosen engine cradle mounts to position engine locating holes in bedplate, then lower the vehicle until engine rests on cradle mounts and tighten mounts to cradle frame to prevent mount movement.
31. Lower vehicle so weight of engine and transaxle is only on cradle.
32. Remove right and left side vertical mount attaching bolts.
33. Slowly raise and support vehicle, move engine and transaxle assembly on cradle to allow for removal around body flanges as required.
34. Reverse procedure to install noting the following:
    a. Place structural collar into position between transaxle and oil pan, install transaxle bolt (1) hand tight, **Fig. 9.**
    b. Install collar to oil pan bolts (4) and (5), hand tighten.
    c. Position torque reaction bracket in place, install bolts (2) and (3), hand tighten.
    d. **Torque** bolts 1–3 to 75 ft. lbs.
    e. Install bolts (6) and (7) through torque reduction bracket into block, hand tighten.
    f. **Torque** bolts 4 and 5 to 35 ft. lbs.
    g. **Torque** bolts 6 and 7 to 45 ft. lbs.
    h. Install front engine mount through bolt, **torque** to 45 ft. lbs.
    i. Tighten nuts and bolts to specifications.

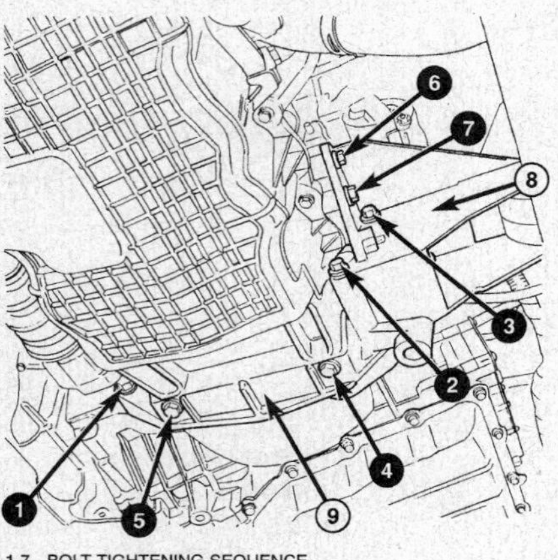

Fig. 9 Structural collar & torque reaction bracket replacement. 2001–02

INTAKE MANIFOLD

REPLACE

1998-2000

1. Relieve fuel system pressure as outlined under "Precautions."
2. Remove air inlet resonator.
3. Disconnect fuel supply line quick connect from fuel tube assembly.
4. Remove fuel rail assembly attaching screws, then the fuel rail assembly cover injector holes.
5. Remove accelerator and speed control cables from throttle lever and bracket.
6. Disconnect Idle Air Control (IAC) motor and Throttle Position Sensor (TPS) electrical connectors.
7. Disconnect vacuum hoses from throttle body.
8. Disconnect Manifold Absolute Pressure (MAP) intake air temperature electrical connectors.

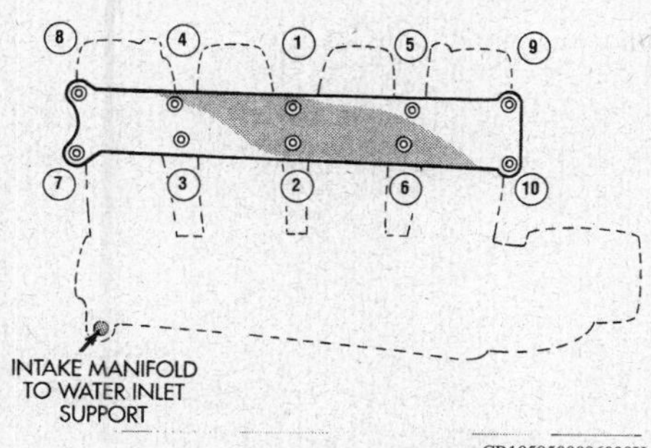

Fig. 10 Intake manifold bolt tightening sequence. Breeze, Cirrus & Stratus w/2.0L engine

9. Disconnect vapor and brake booster hoses.
10. Disconnect knock sensor electrical connector and harness from tab located on intake manifold .
11. Remove transaxle to throttle body support bracket bolts at throttle body and loosen bolt at transaxle.
12. Remove EGR tube attaching bolts, then the tube.
13. Remove intake manifold to inlet water tube support bolt and manifold support bracket, if required.
14. Remove ten intake manifold attaching bolts and washers, then the intake manifold.
15. Reverse procedure to install, noting the following:
    a. Clean all mating surfaces, then check for cracked or distorted manifold and torn or missing Rings.
    b. **On models equipped with 2.0L engine,** replace all seals, bolts and washers.
    c. **On all models,** tighten intake manifold attaching bolts in sequence, **Figs. 10 and 11,** to specifications.
    d. Tighten attaching nuts and bolts to specifications.

2001-02 SEBRING & STRATUS SEDAN & SEBRING CONVERTIBLE

1. Relieve fuel system pressure as outlined under "Precautions," then drain engine coolant.
2. Remove throttle body air inlet hose and air cleaner housing assembly.
3. Remove throttle and speed control cables from throttle lever and bracket.
4. Remove EGR tube, then the oil dipstick tube.
5. Disconnect vacuum hoses from intake manifold.
6. Disconnect fuel supply line at fuel rail.
7. Remove fastener holding fuel rail bracket to side of cylinder head.
8. Disconnect the following electrical connectors:
    a. Fuel injectors.
    b. Knock sensor.
    c. ECT sensor.
    d. IAC.
    e. TPS.
    f. MAP sensor.
    g. A/C pressure sensor.
    h. A/C compressor clutch.
    i. Alternator.
9. Position wiring harness aside, then remove fuel rail.
10. Remove coolant outlet connector.
11. Remove intake manifold bolts, then the intake manifold.
12. Reverse procedure to install noting the following:
    a. Clean all mating surfaces, then install new gasket.
    b. Tighten intake manifold bolts gradually in sequence, **Fig. 12,** to specifications.

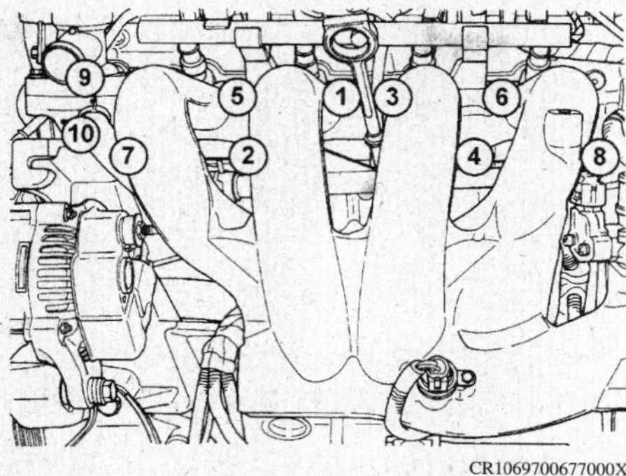

Fig. 11 Intake manifold bolt tightening sequence. Breeze, Cirrus & 1998–2000 Sebring Convertible & Stratus w/2.4L engine

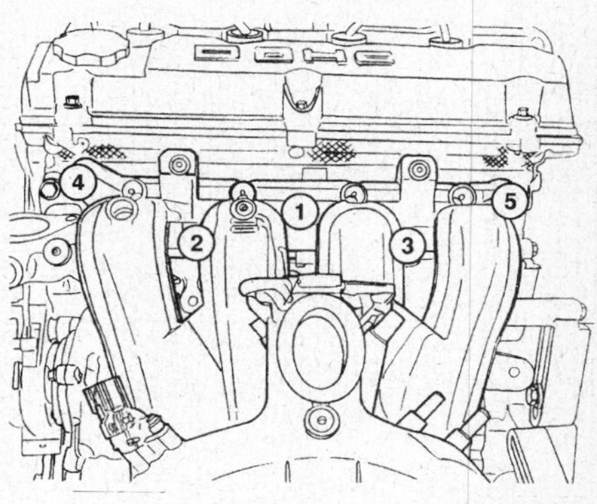

Fig. 12 Intake manifold tightening sequence. 2001–02

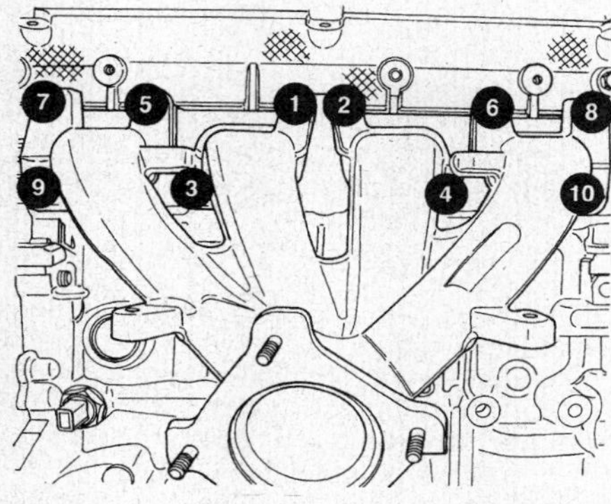

Fig. 13 Exhaust manifold tightening sequence. 2001–02

EXHAUST MANIFOLD

REPLACE

1998-2000

1. Raise and support vehicle.
2. Remove exhaust pipe from manifold. It may be necessary to remove entire exhaust system.
3. Remove exhaust manifold heat shield attaching bolts and heat shield.
4. Remove eight exhaust manifold attaching bolts and exhaust manifold.
5. Reverse procedure to install, noting the following:
    a. Install new manifold gasket.
    b. Tighten exhaust manifold and exhaust pipe attaching bolts to specifications.

2001-02

1. Raise and support vehicle.
2. Remove complete exhaust system.
3. Remove rear engine mount and transaxle bracket as outlined under "Engine Mount, Replace."
4. Remove exhaust manifold heat shield.
5. Disconnect oxygen sensor electrical connector.
6. Remove exhaust manifold bolts, then the exhaust manifold.
7. Reverse procedure to install noting the following:
    a. Install new gasket.
    b. **Torque** bolts in sequence **Fig. 13** to specifications.

CYLINDER HEAD

REPLACE

1998-2000

1. Relieve fuel system pressure as outlined under "Precautions," then drain cooling system.
2. Remove air cleaner and disconnect all vacuum lines, electrical harnesses and fuel lines from throttle body.
3. Remove throttle linkage.
4. Remove accessory drive belts.
5. Remove intake manifold power brake vacuum connection.
6. Raise and support vehicle, then remove exhaust pipe from manifold.
7. Remove and set aside power steering pump assembly.
8. Disconnect coil pack electrical connector and remove coil pack and bracket.
9. Remove cam sensor and fuel injector electrical connectors.
10. Remove timing belt and camshaft sprocket.
11. Remove valve cover.
12. Remove rocker arm shaft assemblies.
13. Remove cylinder head bolts.
14. Reverse procedure to install, noting the following:
    a. Apply oil to bolts before installing.
    b. Install four short bolts in positions 7, 8, 9 and 10, **Figs. 14 and 15.**
    c. Using sequence shown in **Figs. 14 and 15,** tighten cylinder head bolts in four steps. First step, **torque** bolts to 25 ft. lbs.; second step,

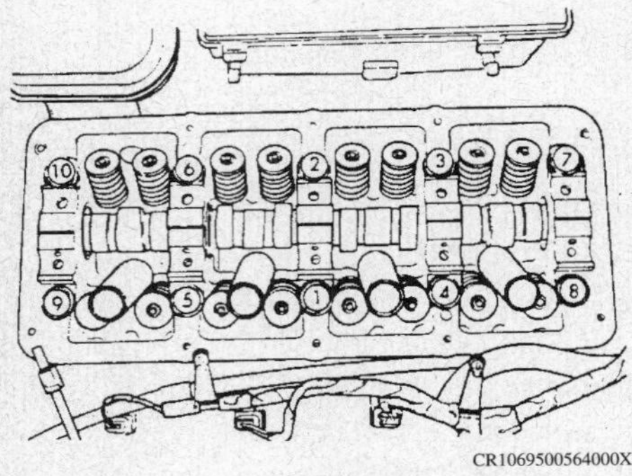

Fig. 14 Cylinder head bolt tightening sequence. 2.0L engine

torque bolts to 50 ft. lbs.; third step, **torque** bolts to 50 ft. lbs.; fourth step, tighten bolts an additional ¼ turn without using a torque wrench.

2001-02

1. Relieve fuel system pressure as outlined under "Precautions," then drain cooling system.
2. Remove throttle body air inlet hose and air cleaner housing assembly.
3. Remove intake manifold as outlined under "Intake Manifold, Replace."
4. Disconnect heater hose from thermostat housing.
5. Remove heater tube support bracket from cylinder head.
6. Disconnect camshaft position sensor, then the EGR solenoid electrical connectors.
7. Raise and support vehicle, then disconnect exhaust pipe from exhaust manifold.
8. Remove accessory drive belts, then the crankshaft damper.
9. Remove upper and lower timing belt covers as outlined under "Front Cover, Replace."
10. Remove timing belt as outlined under "Timing Belt, Replace."
11. Remove camshaft sprockets.
12. Remove timing belt idler pulley, then the rear timing belt cover.
13. Remove valve cover as outlined under "Valve Cover, Replace."
14. Remove camshafts, then the rocker arms.
15. Remove cylinder head bolts, then the cylinder head.
16. Reverse procedure to install noting the following:
    a. Apply oil to head bolts before installing.
    b. Using sequence shown in **Fig. 15** tighten cylinder head bolts in four steps. First step, **torque** bolts to 25 ft. lbs.; second step, **torque** bolts to 50 ft. lbs.; third step, **torque** bolts to 50 ft. lbs.; fourth step, tighten bolts an additional ¼ turn without using a torque wrench.

VALVE COVER

REPLACE

2.0L ENGINE

1. Remove air cleaner inlet duct.

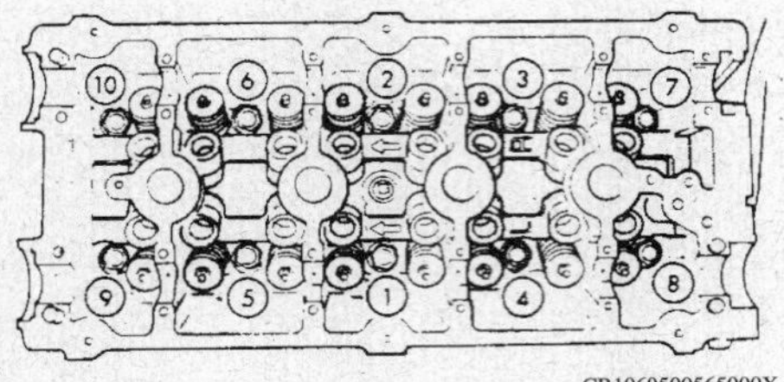

Fig. 15 Cylinder head bolt tightening sequence. 2.4L engine

2. Remove coil pack as outlined in "Electrical" section, then remove valve cover bolts.
3. Remove valve cover bolts, then the cover from engine.
4. Reverse procedure to install, noting the following:
    a. Install a new valve cover gasket.
    b. Tighten valve cover bolts to specifications.

2.4L ENGINE

1. Disconnect engine ground strap, then remove ignition coil pack as outlined in "Electrical" section.
2. Remove valve cover fasteners, then the cover.
3. Reverse procedure to install, noting the following:
    a. Install new valve cover gaskets and spark plug seals. **Do not allow oil or solvents to contact timing belt.**
    b. Apply silicone rubber adhesive sealant to camshaft cap corners and at top edge of half-round seal.
    c. **Torque** valve cover fasteners in three steps: first to 40 inch lbs., then to 80 inch lbs. and, finally, to 105 inch lbs.

VALVE ARRANGEMENT

Intake valves are located on intake manifold side of engine and exhaust valves are located on exhaust manifold side of engine.

CAMSHAFT LOBE LIFT SPECIFICATIONS

Engine	Lift, Inch	
	Intake	Exhaust
2.0L	.283	.277
2.4L	.324	.256

VALVE CLEARANCE SPECIFICATIONS

These engines are equipped with hydraulic lash adjusters designed to maintain zero lash at all times.

ROCKER ARMS

REPLACE

2.0L ENGINE

1. Remove valve cover as outlined under "Valve Cover, Replace."

Fig. 16 Rocker arm shaft notch alignment. 2.0L engine

2. Identify rocker are shaft assemblies, then remove attaching bolts and rocker arm shaft assemblies.
3. Reverse procedure to install, noting the following:
    a. Install rocker arm and shaft assemblies with notches on shafts facing up and toward timing belt side of engine, **Fig. 16.**
    b. Tighten bolts to specifications in sequence shown, **Fig. 17.**

2.4L ENGINE

1. Remove valve cover as outlined under "Valve Cover, Replace," then the spark plugs.
2. Rotate engine until camshaft lobe on rocker being removed is positioned on its base circle. Piston should be a minimum of .25 inch below TDC.
3. Using valve spring compressor tool Nos. 8215-A and 8436 or equivalents, depress valve assembly until rocker arms can be removed.
4. Reverse procedure to install.

FRONT COVER

REPLACE

2.0L ENGINE

1. Remove accessory drive belts.
2. Raise and support vehicle on a hoist and remove right inner splash shield.
3. Remove crankshaft damper bolt, then remove damper using fuller tool No. 1023 and insert tool No. C-4685-C2, or equivalents.
4. Lower vehicle and place jack under engine.
5. Remove purge duty solenoid and wiring harness from right engine mount.
6. Remove right engine mount and bracket.
7. Remove upper timing belt cover attaching bolts, then the upper timing belt cover.
8. Remove lower timing belt cover attaching bolts, then the lower timing belt cover.
9. Reverse procedure to install.

2.4L ENGINE

1. Remove upper cover bolts, then cover, **Fig. 18.**
2. Raise and support vehicle.
3. Remove right front wheel, then belt splash shield.
4. Remove accessory drive belts.
5. Remove crankshaft damper bolt, then

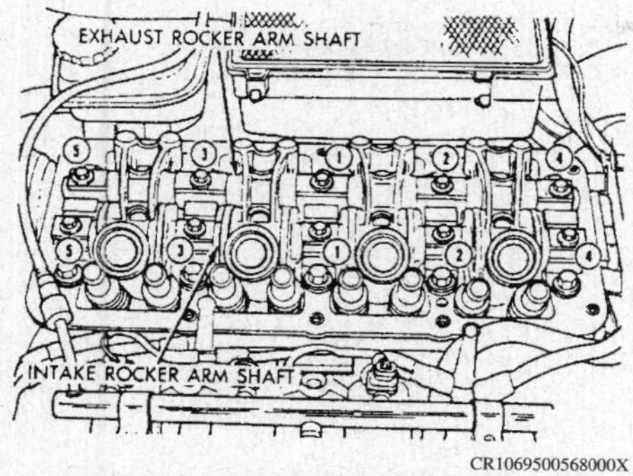

CR1069500568000X

Fig. 17 Rocker arm shaft tightening sequence. 2.0L engine

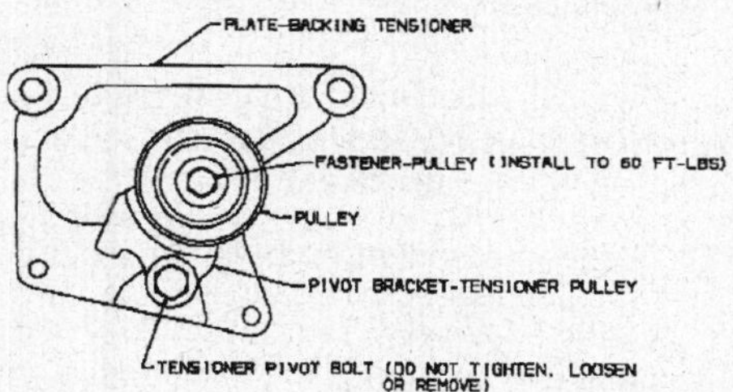

CR1069500679000X

Fig. 20 Tensioner pivot bracket. 2.0L engine

remove damper using fuller tool No. 1026 and insert tool No. 6827, or equivalents.

6. Remove A/C alternator belt tensioner, then lower vehicle.
7. Remove alternator and bracket, the raise vehicle.
8. Remove lower cover attaching bolts, **Fig. 18,** then the cover.
9. Reverse procedure to install. Tighten bolts to specifications.

TIMING BELT

REPLACE

2.0L ENGINE

The following procedure has been revised by a Technical Service Bulletin.

Removal

1. Remove timing belt front cover as described under "Front Cover, Replace."
2. Align crankshaft and camshaft sprocket marks, **Fig. 19,** then loosen timing belt tensioner attaching bolts.
3. Remove timing belt. If belt is to be reused, mark running direction on belt for installation reference.
4. Remove timing belt tensioner. **tensioner pivot bolt, Fig. 20, should never be tightened, loosened or removed, as factory locking compound is not reusable. If pivot bolt is disturbed, entire pivot bracket assembly must be replaced (part No. 4777346).**
5. Inspect timing belt for cracks, missing teeth, rubber hardening and abnormal wear and replace as necessary.

Installation

1. Position timing belt tensioner in a soft

1 - UPPER TIMING BELT COVER FASTENERS
2 - ENGINE SUPPORT BRACKET FASTENERS
3 - LOWER TIMING BELT COVER FASTENERS

CR1060100966000X

Fig. 18 Front cover replacement. 2.4L engine

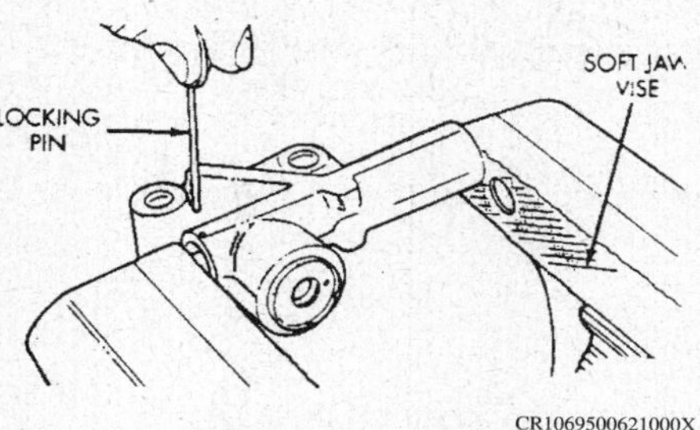

CR1069500621000X

Fig. 21 Timing belt tensioner locking pin installation. 2.0L engine

jawed vise, then slowly compress tensioner plunger into tensioner body.

2. With tensioner plunger compressed into body, insert a 5/64 inch hex wrench or other suitable locking pin through holes in tensioner body, **Fig. 21.** This will hold plunger in position until after tensioner has been installed on engine.
3. Align mark on crankshaft sprocket with arrow mark on oil pump housing, then back off to three sprocket teeth before Top Dead Center (TDC), **Fig. 22.**
4. Align camshaft sprocket mark with arrow mark on timing belt rear cover, **Fig. 19.**
5. Position crankshaft sprocket at ½ tooth before TDC, **Fig. 23.**
6. Position timing belt over crankshaft sprocket, around water pump sprocket, over camshaft sprocket, then around tensioner pulley.
7. Place crankshaft sprocket in TDC position to take up slack in timing belt.
8. Position timing belt tensioner on engine block, then loosely install attaching bolts. **tensioner pivot bolt, Fig. 20, should never be tightened, loosened or removed, as factory locking compound is not reusable. If pivot bolt is disturbed, entire pivot bracket assembly must be replaced (part No. 4777346).**

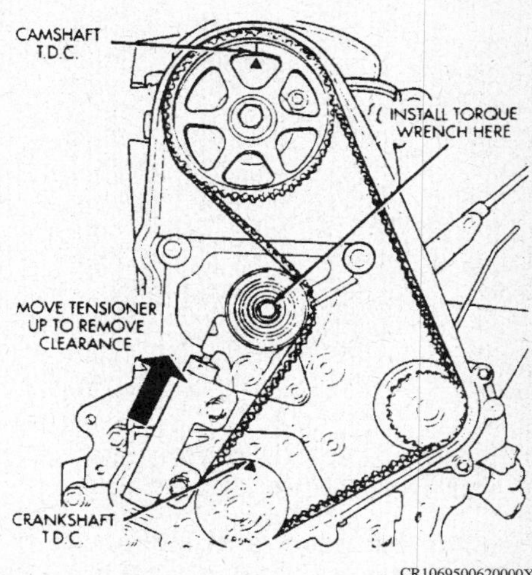

CR1069500620000X

Fig. 19 Crankshaft & camshaft timing mark alignment. 2.0L engine

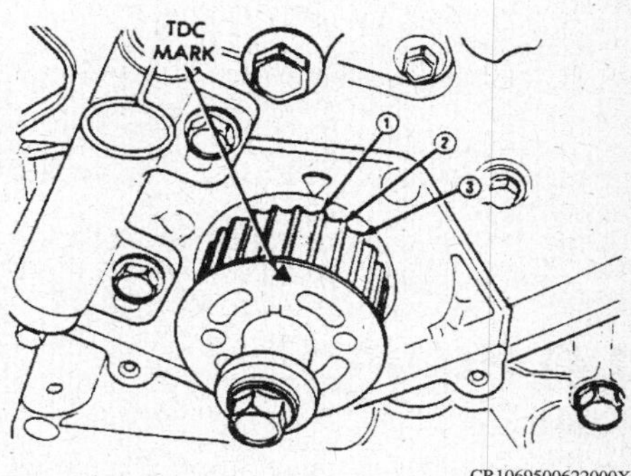

CR1069500622000X

Fig. 22 Crankshaft sprocket & oil pump housing alignment marks. 2.0L engine

9. Using a suitable torque wrench, apply a force of 20–21 ft. lbs. to timing belt tensioner pulley, **Fig. 19.**
10. While applying tension on tensioner pulley, move timing belt tensioner up against tensioner pulley bracket, then tighten tensioner attaching bolts to specifications.
11. Remove hex wrench or locking pin retaining tensioner plunger in body. Timing belt pretension is correct when wrench or pin can be freely removed from and installed in tensioner body holes.
12. Rotate crankshaft two revolutions in normal direction of rotation, then check crankshaft and camshaft sprocket timing mark alignment, **Fig. 19.** If timing marks are not properly aligned, repeat belt installation procedure.
13. Install front cover as described under "Front Cover, Replace."
14. **After completing installation, perform camshaft and crankshaft alignment relearn procedure using**

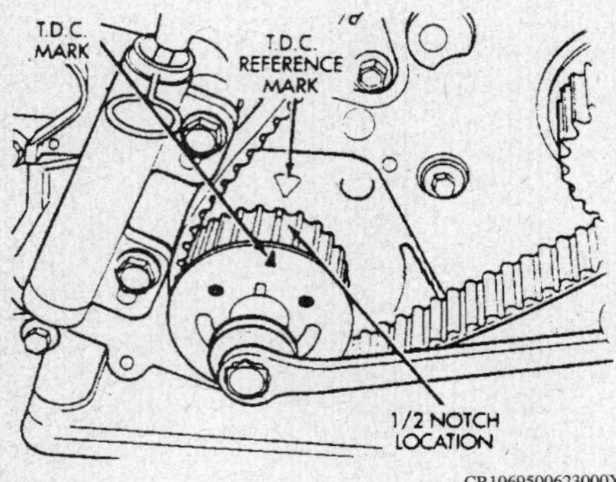

Fig. 23 Crankshaft sprocket ½ tooth rotation. 2.0L engine

DRB scan tool and attendant instructions. Failure to perform relearn will set Diagnostic Trouble Code P1390 and illuminate Check Engine lamp.

15. Inspect valve timing as follows:
    a. Remove No. 1 spark plug from cylinder head.
    b. Using a suitable dial indicator, set No. 1 cylinder at TDC on its compression stroke.
    c. Remove access plug from timing belt front cover.
    d. Timing mark on camshaft sprocket should be aligned with arrow mark on timing belt rear cover, **Fig. 19.**

2.4L ENGINE

Removal

1. Remove timing belt front covers as outlined under "Front Cover, Replace."
2. Align crankshaft and camshaft sprocket timing marks, **Fig. 24.**
3. Position a 6mm hex head wrench to timing belt tensioner pulley and insert a 3mm hex head wrench into tensioner pulley pin hole, **Fig. 25.**
4. With 6mm hex head wrench, rotate tensioner pulley counterclockwise until 3mm hex head wrench can be inserted into locking hole on cylinder block.
5. Remove timing belt.

Installation

1. Ensure crankshaft sprocket timing mark is aligned.
2. Position camshaft sprockets so the exhaust sprocket is ½ notch below intake sprocket, **Fig. 26.**
3. Install timing belt over crankshaft sprocket, around water pump sprocket, idler pulley, camshaft sprockets and tensioner pulley.
4. Move exhaust camshaft sprocket counterclockwise and align timing marks, to remove slack from belt.
5. Remove 3 mm hex head wrench from cylinder block and tensioner.
6. Rotate crankshaft sprocket two revolutions in normal direction of engine rotation.
7. Ensure all timing marks are aligned, then install front covers as outlined under "Front Cover, Replace."

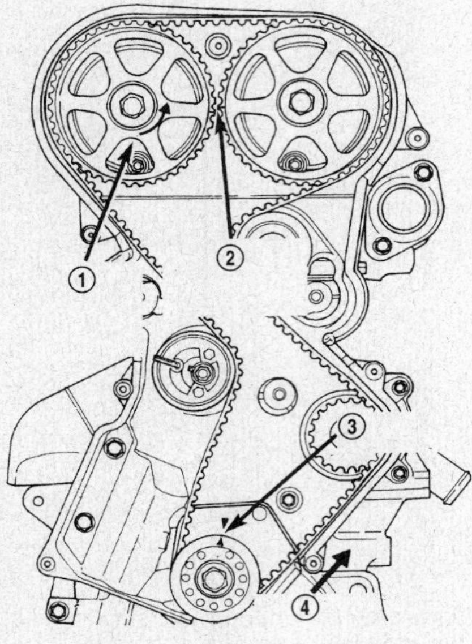

Fig. 24 Crankshaft & camshaft sprocket timing mark alignment. 2.4L engine

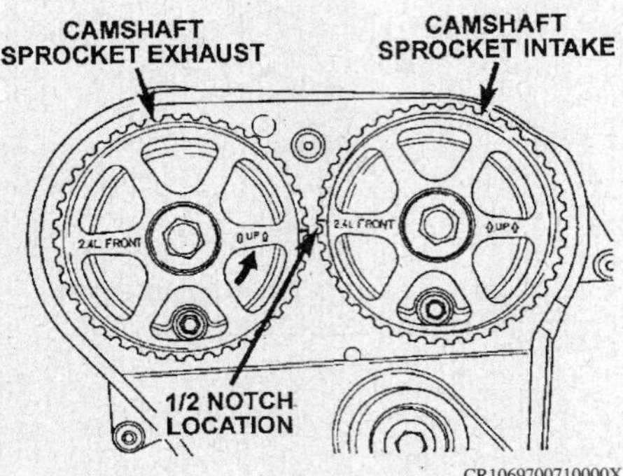

Fig. 26 Camshaft sprocket alignment. 2.4L engine

CAMSHAFT

REPLACE

2.0L ENGINE

1. Relieve fuel system pressure as outlined under "Precautions."
2. Remove valve cover, then mark rocker arm shaft assemblies so that they can be installed in their original positions.
3. Remove rocker shaft bolts, then the timing belt front cover and belt as outlined under "Timing Belt, Replace."
4. Remove rear timing belt cover, then the cylinder head as outlined under "Cylinder Head, Replace."
5. Remove camshaft sensor and camshaft target magnet, then the camshaft sprocket bolt.

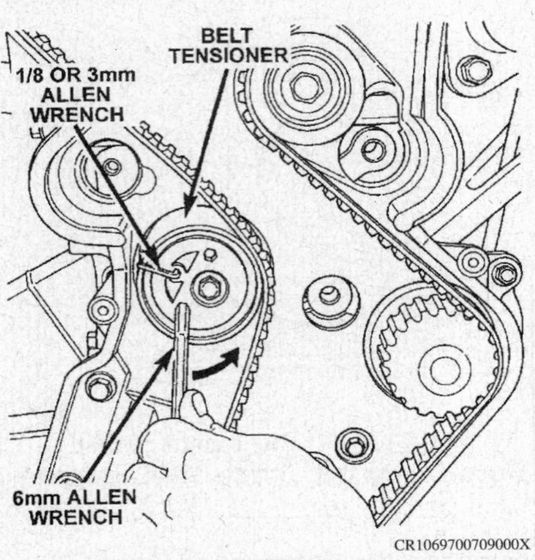

Fig. 25 Locking timing belt tensioner in release position. 2.4L engine

6. Remove sprocket from camshaft with modified sprocket removal tool No. C-4687-1, or equivalent, **Fig. 27.** Hold camshaft sprocket with modified tool while removing bolt.
7. Remove camshaft seal using camshaft seal remover tool No. C-4679, or equivalent.
8. Remove camshaft from rear of cylinder head.
9. Reverse procedure to install, noting the following:
    a. Install new camshaft seal with seal insertion tool No. MD998306, or equivalent.
    b. Install camshaft sprocket retaining bolt. Hold camshaft sprocket with tool No. C-4687 and adapter tool No. C-4687-1, or equivalents, and tighten to specifications.

2.4L ENGINE

1. Remove valve cover as outlined under "Valve Cover, Replace."
2. Remove timing belt, sprockets and covers as outlined under "Timing Belt, Replace."
3. Bearing caps are identified for location. Remove outside bearing caps L1, R1, L6 and R6 first.
4. Loosen camshaft bearing cap attaching bolts in sequence, **Fig. 28,** one camshaft at a time.
5. Identify camshafts before removing from head. Camshafts are not interchangeable.
6. Reverse procedure to install, noting the following:
    a. Install right and left inside camshaft bearing caps , and R6 outside camshaft bearing cap. **Tighten** caps in sequence, **Fig. 29,** to specifications, one camshaft at a time. **Outside camshaft bearing cap R6, is to be tightened as an inside bearing cap.**
    b. Install outside camshaft bearing caps L1, R1 and L6, tighten to specifications.

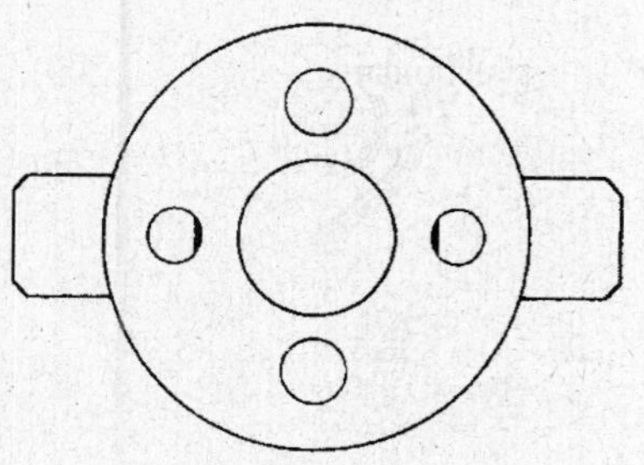

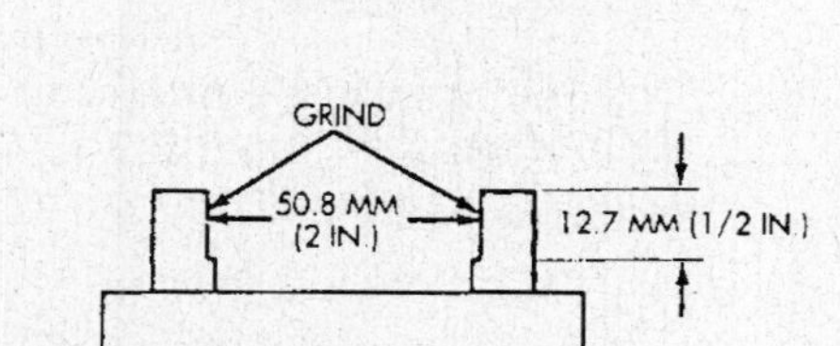

Fig. 27 Sprocket removal tool modification. 2.0L engine

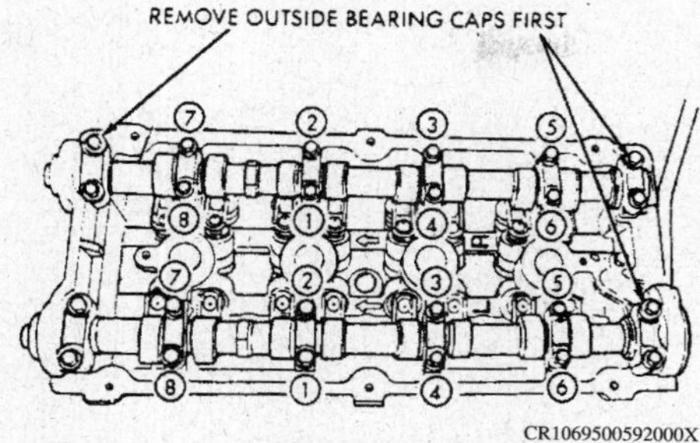

Fig. 28 Camshaft bearing cap removal. 2.4L engine

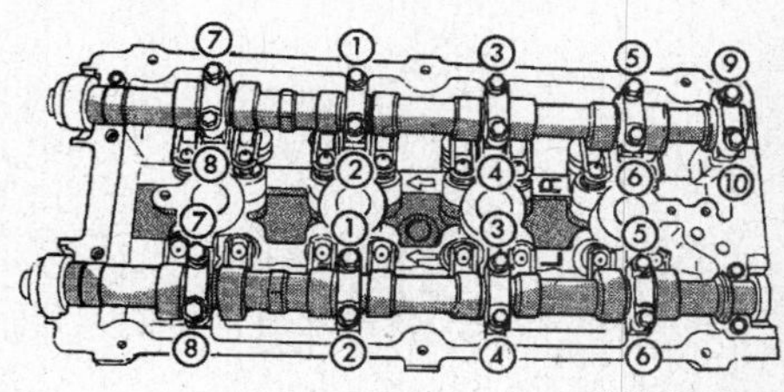

Fig. 29 Camshaft bearing cap tightening sequence. 2.4L engine

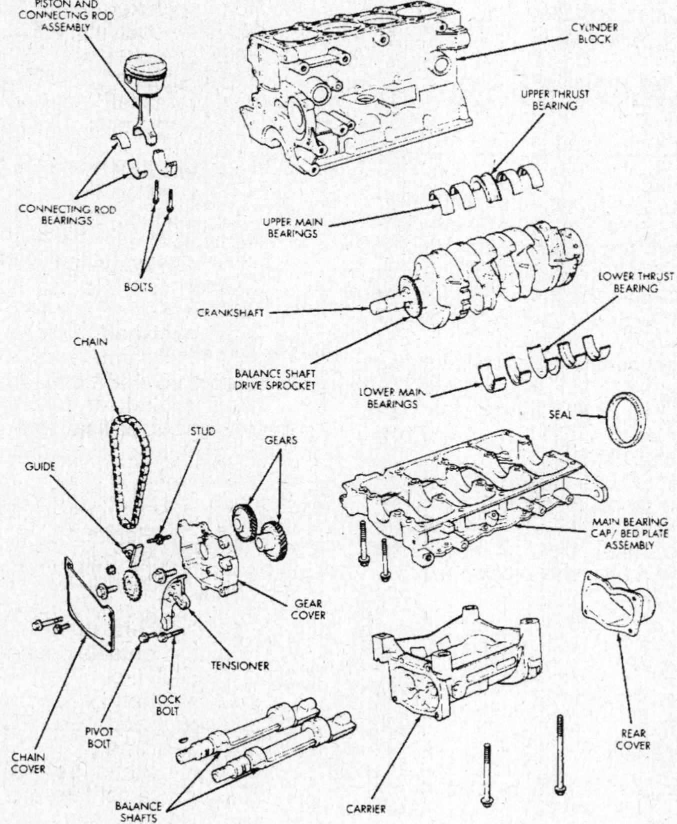

Fig. 30 Exploded view of cylinder block, balance shafts, crankshaft, piston & connecting rod assembly. 2.4L engine

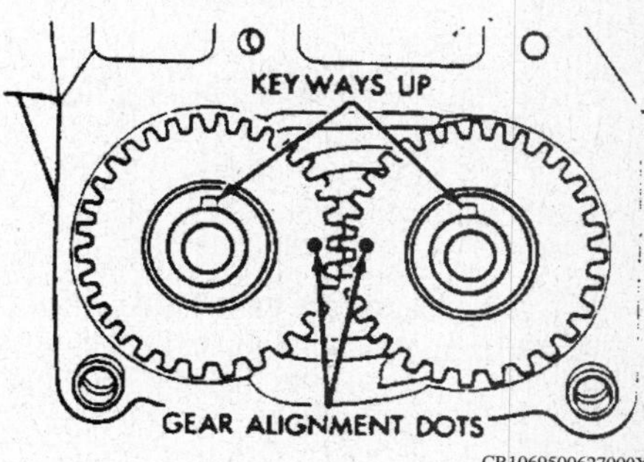

Fig. 31 Balance shaft gear alignment. 2.4L engine

BALANCE SHAFT

REPLACE

2.4L ENGINE

1. Remove timing belt front cover as outlined under "Front Cover, Replace."
2. Remove gear cover double ended retaining stud, gear and chain covers and gears, **Fig. 30.**
3. Remove balance shaft gear and chain sprocket retaining bolts and crankshaft chain sprocket. To remove chain and sprocket assembly, use two pry bars to work sprocket back and forth.
4. Remove carrier rear cover and balance shafts.
5. Remove four carrier to crankcase attaching bolts to separate carrier.
6. Reverse procedure to install, noting the following:
   a. Dot marks on balance shaft gears must be aligned and balance shaft keys must face upward, **Fig. 31.**
   b. Balance shaft timing chain and gear timing marks must be aligned as shown in **Fig. 32.**
   c. When adjusting balance shaft timing chain tension, position a shim .039 inch thick by 2.75 inches long between tensioner and chain. Push tensioner and shim against timing chain with a force of 5.5–6.6 lbs., **Fig. 33.** With force applied to timing chain, tighten top tensioner bolt, then bottom tensioner bolt to specifications.

PISTON & ROD ASSEMBLY

The L or H stamping on the front portion of the piston must face toward the front of the engine. The connecting rod and cap are stamped on the side with a cylinder number identification. The numbered side of the connecting rod cap must be installed on the same side as the numbered side of the rod. When installing cap bolts, **torque** to 20 ft. lbs., then tighten an additional ¼ turn.

MAIN & ROD BEARINGS

2.0L ENGINE

Main and rod bearings are available in the standard size and in undersides of .025 mm and .250 mm. **Torque** main bearing M8 cap bolts to 22–25 ft. lbs. and M11 bolts to 60 ft. lbs.

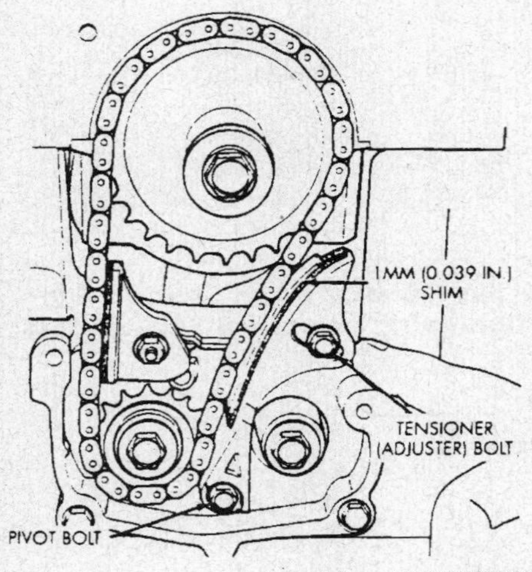

Fig. 32 Balance shaft timing chain & gears. 2.4L engine

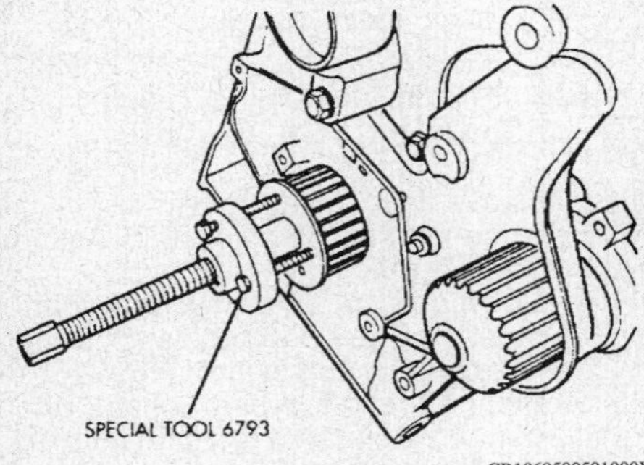

Fig. 35 Crankshaft sprocket removal

2.4L ENGINE

Main and rod bearings are available in the standard size and in undersides of .001, .002, .010, .011 and .012 inch. **Torque** main bearing M8 cap bolts to 20–21 ft. lbs. and M11 bolts to 30 ft. lbs. plus an additional ¼ turn, in sequence, **Fig. 34.**

CRANKSHAFT SEAL

REPLACE

1. Remove components to access crankshaft sprocket as outlined under "Timing Belt, Replace."
2. Remove crankshaft sprocket using sprocket remover tool No. 6793 and insert tool No. C-4685-C2, or equivalents, **Fig. 35.**
3. Remove seal using oil seal remover tool No. 6771, or equivalent, to remove front crankshaft oil seal, **Fig. 36.**
4. Reverse procedure to install, noting the following:
   a. Install new seal using seal installation tool No. 6780-1, or equivalent.
   b. Install crankshaft sprocket using tool No. 6792, or equivalent.

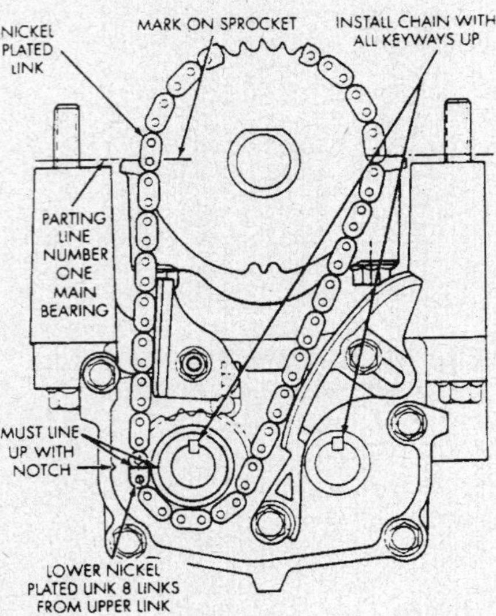

Fig. 33 Balance shaft timing chain tension adjustment. 2.4L engine

CRANKSHAFT REAR OIL SEAL

REPLACE

1. Remove transaxle, then flex plate.
2. Insert a 3⁄16 screwdriver between dust lip and metal case of seal seat. Pry out seal.
3. Inspect shaft seal surface for nicks or dirt. Polish with 400 grit sandpaper if necessary.
4. Reverse procedure to install, noting the following:
   a. Seal should be installed dry, with "THIS SIDE OUT" mark facing away from block.
   b. Use pilot tool No. 6926-1, seal installation tool No. 6926-2 and handle tool No. C-4171, or equivalents, to install seal. **Do not drive seal beyond flush with block surface.**

OIL PAN

REPLACE

2.0L ENGINE

1. Drain engine oil into a suitable container.
2. Remove front engine mount bracket, then the pertain bending strut.
3. Remove structural collar from oil pan to transaxle, then the transaxle dust cover.
4. **On models equipped with A/C,** remove oil filter and adapter.
5. **On all models,** remove oil pan attaching bolts and the pan.
6. Clean oil pan and all gasket surfaces.
7. Reverse procedure to install, noting the following:
   a. Apply Molar silicone rubber adhesive sealant, or equivalent, at oil pump to engine block parting line and on oil pan gasket to hold gasket in place.
   b. Tighten pan bolts to specifications.

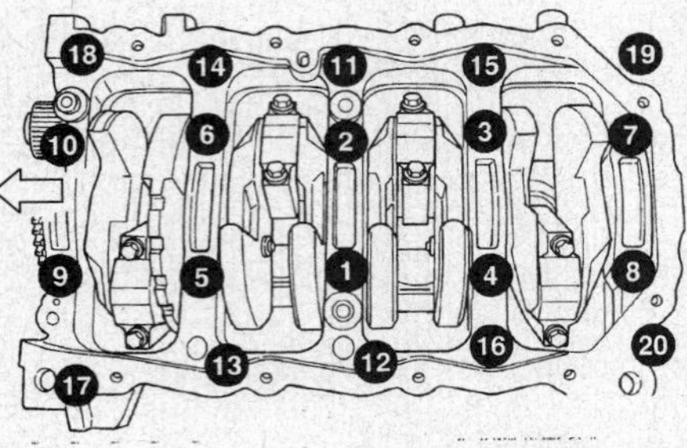

Fig. 34 Main bearing tightening sequence. 2.4L engine

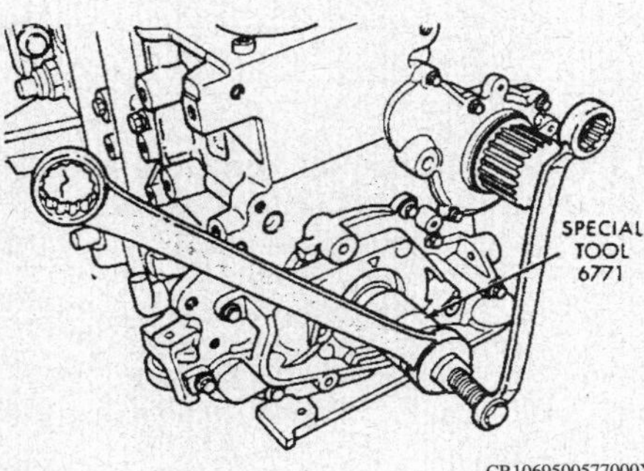

Fig. 36 Front crankshaft oil seal removal

2.4L ENGINE

1. Drain engine oil into a suitable container.
2. Remove front engine torque bracket from bending strut and insulator mount.
3. Remove collar and bending strut attaching bolts, then the strut and collar from engine, oil pan and transaxle.
4. Remove oil pan attaching bolts, then the oil pan.
5. Clean oil pan and cylinder block gasket surfaces.
6. Reverse procedure to install, noting the following:
   a. Apply Molar silicone rubber adhesive sealant, or equivalent, at oil pump to engine block parting line and on oil pan gasket to hold gasket in place.
   b. Tighten pan bolts to specifications.

OIL PUMP

REPLACE

1. Remove components to access oil pump as outlined under "Timing Belt, Replace."
2. Remove oil pick-up tube.
3. Remove oil pump attaching bolts, then the pump.
4. Reverse procedure to install. Tighten attaching bolts to specifications.

Accessory Drive Belts	Gauge
2.0/2.4/2.5L Engines	
Air Conditioning Compressor & Generator	NEW BELT: 150 LB.
Power Steering Pump	USED BELT: 90 LB.

CR1089800195000X

Fig. 37 Belt tension chart

OIL PUMP SERVICE

DISASSEMBLE

1. Remove relief valve plug and gasket, then the spring and relief valve.
2. Remove oil pump attaching bolts and cover.
3. Remove pump rotors.

INSPECTION

1. Clean all parts thoroughly in a suitable solvent. Mating surface of oil pump should be smooth. Replace pump cover if scratched or grooved.
2. Lay a straightedge across pump cover surface. If .001 inch feeler gauge can be inserted between cover and straightedge, replace cover.
3. Measure thickness and diameter of outer rotor. If outer rotor thickness measures .301 inch or less, or if diameter is 3.148 inches or less, replace outer rotor.
4. If inner rotor measures .301 inch or less, replace inner rotor.
5. Place outer rotor into pump housing and press to one side. Measure clearance between rotor and housing. If measurement is .015 inch or more, replace housing.
6. Install inner rotor into pump housing. If clearance between inner and outer rotors is .008 or more, replace rotors.
7. Place a straightedge across face of pump housing, between bolt holes. If a feeler gauge of .004 inch or more can be inserted between rotors and straightedge, replace pump assembly, only if rotors are in specification.
8. Inspect oil pressure relief valve plunger for scoring and free operation in its bore. Small marks may be removed with 400 grit wet/dry sandpaper.
9. Oil pump relief valve spring is approximately 2.39 inches in length and should indicate 18–19 lbs. resistance when compressed to 1.6 inches. Replace spring if it fails to meet specification.

ASSEMBLE

1. Assemble pump using new parts as required. Install inner rotor with chamfer facing cast iron oil pump cover.
2. Apply Molar gasket maker lightly to cover mounting surface on pump body. Attach cover and tighten to specifications.
3. Install relief valve, spring, gasket and cap and tighten to specifications.
4. Prime oil pump before installation by filling rotor cavity with clean engine oil.
5. Apply Molar gasket maker to oil pump. Install oil-ring into counter bore on oil pump body discharge passage.
6. Install oil pump slowly onto crankshaft until seated to engine block. Tighten attaching bolts to specifications.

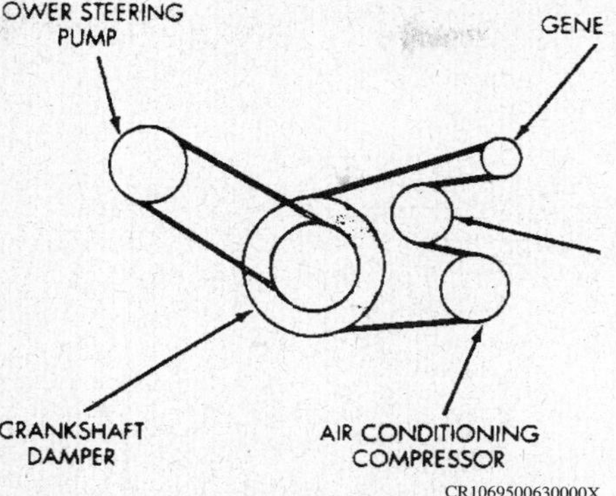

Fig. 38 Serpentine drive belt routing. 1998–2000

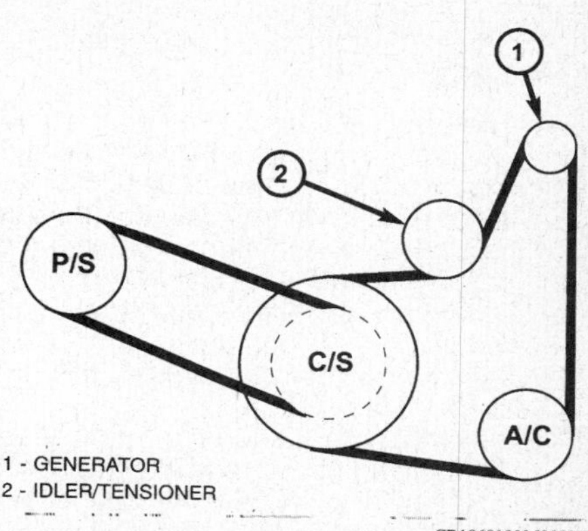

Fig. 39 Serpentine drive belt routing. 2001–02

BELT TENSION DATA

Refer to **Fig. 37** for belt tension data.

SERPENTINE DRIVE BELT

1. Loosen bolt locking nut and pivot bolt to replace Polyp Belt and/or adjust belt tension, **Figs . 38 and 39.**
2. Tighten adjusting bolt to adjust belt tension to specification shown in belt tension chart, **Fig. 37.**
3. Tighten bolt locking nut and pivot bolt to specifications.

COOLING SYSTEM BLEED

The air bleed valve is located on the front of the engine in the thermostat housing to engine outlet connector. There is a relief in the cylinder head for locating the air bleed. To bleed, open valve while engine is running until all has bled from cooling system.

THERMOSTAT

REPLACE

1. Drain coolant into a suitable container until below thermostat level.
2. Remove coolant recovery system hose and thermostat to engine outlet connector bolts.
3. Remove thermostat assembly, and clean sealing surfaces.
4. Reverse procedure to install. Fill and bleed cooling system as necessary.

WATER PUMP

REPLACE

1. Raise and support vehicle and remove right inner splash shield.
2. Remove accessory drive belts and power steering pump.
3. Drain coolant into a suitable container.
4. Support engine from bottom and remove right engine mount.
5. Remove power steering pump bracket attaching bolts and set pump and bracket assembly aside. Power steering lines do not need to be disconnected.
6. Remove right engine mount bracket.
7. Remove timing belt as outlined under "Timing Belt, Replace."
8. Remove inner timing belt cover.
9. Remove water pump attaching bolts, then the water pump.
10. Reverse procedure to install, noting the following:
    a. Install new O-ring gasket in water pump body O-ring groove.
    b. Tighten water pump mounting bolts to specifications.
    c. Fill and bleed cooling system as necessary.

RADIATOR

REPLACE

1998-2000

1. Remove air inlet resonator, then drain coolant into a suitable container.
2. Remove upper radiator crossover.
3. Remove hose clamps and hoses from radiator.
4. Disconnect engine block heater electrical wire, if equipped.
5. Disconnect and plug automatic transaxle hoses at cooler.
6. Disconnect fan electrical connector.
7. Remove air conditioning condenser attaching screws located at front of radiator, if equipped.
8. Remove radiator from engine compartment by lifting upward.
9. Reverse procedure to install.

2001-02

1. Drain coolant into suitable container, then remove upper radiator crossmember.
2. Disconnect radiator fan electrical connector, then remove radiator fan.
3. Disconnect hoses from radiator.
4. Remove screw holding support bracket for transmission cooler tubes to left side of radiator.
5. Remove A/C lines support bracket.
6. Carefully lift out radiator.
7. Reverse procedure to install.

FUEL PUMP

REPLACE

The electric fuel pump is not serviceable. If the fuel pump requires service, the entire fuel pump module must be replaced.

1. Relieve fuel system pressure as outlined under "Precautions."
2. Drain and remove fuel tank.
3. Disconnect fuel filter lines at fuel pump module.
4. Clean top of tank to remove dirt and debris.
5. Remove lockout securing pump module with fuel pump module ring spanner tool No. 6856, or equivalent, **Fig. 40.**
6. Remove fuel pump module and O-ring from tank, then discard O-ring.
7. Reverse procedure to install, noting the following:
   a. Install new pump module Oaring.
   b. Tighten fuel pump module lock ring to specifications.

FUEL FILTER

REPLACE

1998–2000

1. Release fuel system pressure as outlined under "Precautions."
2. From inside trunk, disconnect fuel pump module wiring jumper from main body harness. Connector is located under leftward side of trunk mat, near base of shock tower.
3. Locate body grommet for jumper near base of rear seat and push grommet out, then feed jumper through hole in body.

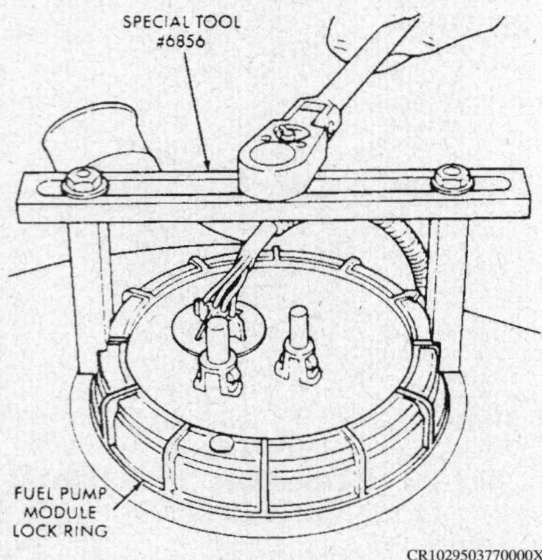

Fig. 40 Fuel pump module lockout

4. Raise and support vehicle.
5. Position a suitable fuel container with a capacity of at least 16 gallons, under drain plug located on bottom left edge of tank.
6. Remove drain plug and allow fuel to drain.
7. When tank stops draining, install drain plug and tighten to specifications.
8. Remove driver's side fuel tank strap and loosen, but do not remove, passenger's side fuel tank strap, allowing fuel tank fill neck to touch rear suspension crossover.
9. Disconnect fuel lines from fuel pump module. These are quick connect fittings located on top of tank.
10. Disconnect fuel supply line from fuel brake module.
11. Remove fuel filter.
12. Reverse procedure to install.

2001–02

The fuel filter is part of the fuel pressure regulator and is located on top of the fuel pump module.

1. Relief fuel pressure as outlined under "Precautions."
2. Drain fuel tank into holding tank or properly labeled gasoline safety container.
3. Raise and support vehicle.
4. Remove fuel tank as follows:
   a. Use suitable transmission jack to support fuel tank.
   b. Remove fuel tank strap bolts, then lower tank slightly.
   c. Disconnect fuel filler vent tube, fuel line, then vapor line.
   d. Disconnect vacuum line from the LDP.
   e. Loosen clamp, then remove fuel filler tube.
   f. Unlock fuel pump module electrical connector, then disconnect.
   g. Lower fuel tank.
5. Disconnect fuel supply line at filter/regulator nipple.
6. Depress locking spring tab on side of fuel regulator, rotate 90° counterclockwise and remove.
7. Reverse procedure to install.

TIGHTENING SPECIFICATIONS

Year	Component	Torque/ Ft. Lbs.
1998–2002	Balance Shaft Timing Chain Tensioner (2.4L)	96–108⑤
	Camshaft Bearing Cap (M6)	105⑤
	Camshaft Bearing Cap (M8)	21
	Camshaft Sprocket Bolt (2.0L)	85
	Camshaft Sprocket Bolt (2.4L)	75
	Connecting Rod Cap Bolt	②
	Coolant Outlet To Cylinder Head	108⑤
	Crankshaft Damper Bolt (2.0L)	105
	Crankshaft Pulley Bolt (2.4L)	100
	Cylinder Head	①
	EGR Tube	84–96⑤
	Engine Cradle Through Bolts	45
	Engine Mount Bracket	30
	Engine Mounts	③
	Exhaust Flange	20–21
	Exhaust Manifold Heat Shield	96–108⑤
	Exhaust Manifold To Cylinder Head (1998–2000)	16–17
	Exhaust Manifold To Cylinder Head (2001–02)	17
	Fuel Pump Module Lock Ring	40
	Fuel Rail To Intake Manifold	16–17

Continued

TIGHTENING SPECIFICATIONS—Continued

Year	Component	Torque/ Ft. Lbs.
1998–2002	Fuel Tank Drain Plug	32⑤
	Inside Camshaft Bearing Caps (2.4L)	10
	Intake Manifold (2.0L)	96–108⑤
	Intake Manifold (2.4L)	20
	Main Bearing Cap Bolts	④
	Oil Filter	15
	Oil Filter Adapter To Engine	40
	Oil Pan Drain Plug	25
	Oil Pan To Engine Block	105⑤
	Oil Pump Cover	96–108⑤
	Oil Pump Mounting Bolts	20
	Oil Pump Pickup Tube Screw	20
	Oil Pump Relief Valve Retaining Cap (2.0L)	30
	Oil Pump Relief Valve Retaining Cap (2.4L)	40
	Outside Camshaft Bearing Caps (2.4L)	21
	Rocker Arm And Shaft Assembly (2.0L)	20–21
	Serpentine Belt bolt	40
	Spark Plugs	20
	Thermostat Housing Bolts	16–17
	Throttle Body Support Bracket	96–108⑤
	Throttle Body To Intake	15–16
	Timing Belt Tensioner (2.0L)	23
	Timing Belt Tensioner (2.4L)	20
	Timing Belt Tensioner Pulley (2.4L)	30
	Timing Cover Bolts	80⑤
	Valve Cover (2.0L)	96–108⑤
	Valve Cover (2.4L)	⑥
	Water Pump	105⑤

①— Refer to "Cylinder Head, Replace" for tightening procedure & specifications.
②— Refer to "Piston & Rod Assembly" for tightening procedure & specifications.
③— Refer to "Engine Mount, Replace" illustrations for tightening specifications.
④— Refer to "Main & Rod Bearings" for tightening procedure & specifications.
⑤— Inch lbs.
⑥— Refer to "Valve Cover, Replace" for tightening procedure & specifications.

2.5L Engine

NOTE: On Air Bag Equipped Models, Refer To "Air Bag System Precautions" Located In The Front Of This Manual For System Disarming & Arming Procedures.

NOTE: Refer To "Computer Relearn Procedures" Located In The Front Of This Manual When Battery Power To The Computer Has Been Interrupted.

INDEX

PRECAUTIONS

AIR BAG SYSTEMS

Refer to "Air Bag System Precautions" in the front of this manual for system disarming and arming procedures.

BATTERY GROUND CABLE

Prior to service, disconnect battery ground cable and isolate as required.

FUEL SYSTEM PRESSURE RELIEF

1. Disconnect fuel rail electrical harness from engine harness.
2. Connect suitable jumper wire between fuel rail harness connector terminal A142 and 12 volt power source.
3. Connect another suitable jumper wire to ground source, then momentarily ground one injector harness connector terminal, to release fuel system pressure.
4. Repeat procedure for two to three injectors.

COMPRESSION PRESSURE

Compression pressure should be 178 psi at 250 RPM with no more than a 14 psi variation in pressure between cylinders.

ENGINE MOUNT

REPLACE

RIGHT SIDE MOUNT

1. Raise and support vehicle, then remove the inner splash.
2. Remove right engine support assembly attaching bolts from frame rail, **Fig. 1.**
3. Lower vehicle and support engine assembly with floor jack to remove pressure on motor mounts.
4. Remove three engine support to engine bracket attaching bolts.
5. Reverse procedure to install. Tighten attaching nuts and bolts to specifications shown in **Fig. 1.**

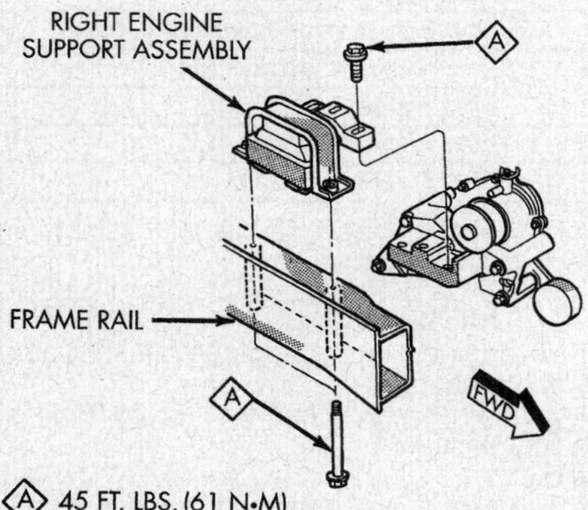

Fig. 1 Right side engine mount replacement

ENGINE CRADLE (SUPPORT MODULE)

1. Raise and support vehicle, then remove rear mount through bolt and bolts securing cradle to crossover.
2. Remove rear support strut bracket upper bolt and bolts securing cradle to lower radiator support.
3. With cooling module supported, remove lower radiator support.
4. Remove front through bolt, then the cradle.
5. Reverse procedure to install, noting the following:
   a. Do not tighten front through bolt until rear through bolt is installed and tightened.
   b. Tighten bolts to specifications.

ENGINE

REPLACE

1. Relieve fuel system pressure as outlined under "Precautions."
2. Disconnect and remove battery and tray, then disconnect Pertain Control Module (PCM) electrical connector and position aside.
3. Drain coolant into a suitable container.
4. Remove upper radiator hose, fan module and radiator as outlined under "Radiator, Replace."
5. Remove lower radiator hose.
6. **On models equipped with manual transaxle,** disconnect clutch cable and shift linkage.
7. **On models equipped with automatic transaxle,** disconnect and plug transaxle cooler line.
8. **On all models,** disconnect throttle body linkage.
9. Disconnect engine wiring harness electrical connectors.
10. Disconnect heater hoses.
11. Recover A/C refrigerant as outlined in "Air Conditioning" section.

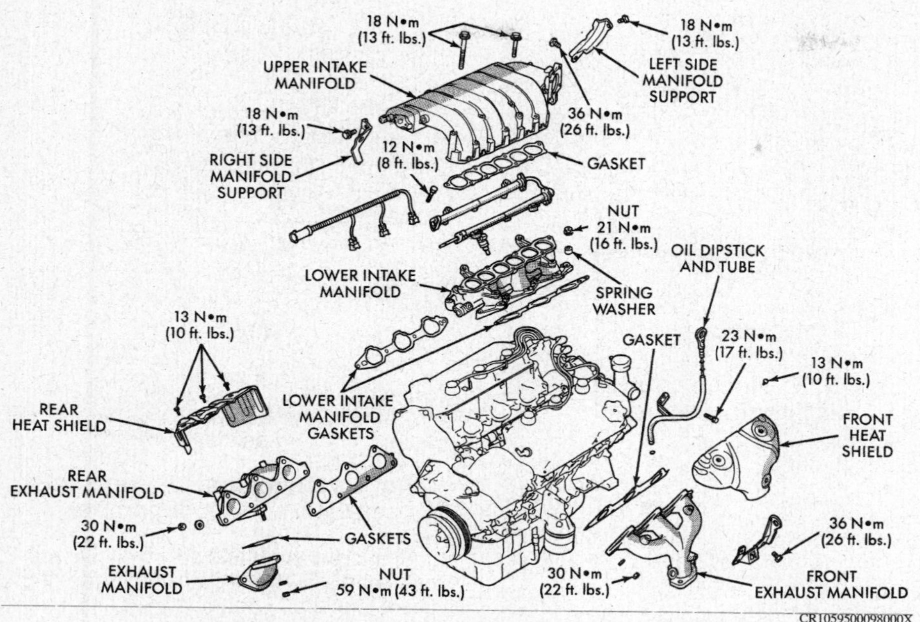

Fig. 2 Exploded view of intake & exhaust manifolds

12. Raise and support vehicle, then remove the right inner splash shield.
13. Remove accessory drive belts.
14. Remove axle shafts.
15. Disconnect exhaust pipe from manifold.
16. Remove front and rear engine mount bracket from the body.
17. Lower vehicle, then remove the air cleaner assembly.
18. Remove power steering pump and reservoir.
19. Remove A/C compressor.
20. Remove ground straps to body.
21. Raise and support vehicle to install engine dolly and cradle tool Nos. 6135 and 6710, or equivalents.
22. Loosen engine cradle mounts to position engine locating holes in belated, then lower the vehicle until engine rests on cradle mounts and tighten mounts to cradle frame to prevent mount movement.
23. Lower vehicle so weight of engine and transaxle is only on cradle.
24. Remove engine and transaxle mount attaching bolts.
25. Slowly raise and support vehicle, move engine and transaxle assembly on cradle to allow for removal around body flanges as required.
26. Reverse procedure to install.

INTAKE MANIFOLD

REPLACE

1. Relieve fuel system pressure as outlined under "Precautions."
2. Disconnect fuel supply tube from rail, using a towel to catch any gasoline spillage.
3. Disconnect Manifold Absolute Pressure (MAP) and Intake Air Temperature (IAT) sensor electrical connectors.
4. Remove plenum support bracket bolt, located rearward of MAP sensor, **Fig. 2.**
5. Remove air inlet resonator to intake manifold bolt.
6. Loosen throttle body air inlet hose clamp, release snaps holding air cleaner housing cover to housing, then remove the air cleaner cover and inlet hoses.
7. Disconnect Throttle Position Sensor (TPS) and Idle Air Control (IAC) motor electrical connectors.
8. Depress throttle cable retainer tab and pull cable rearward out of bracket, then repeat for speed control cable, if equipped.
9. Remove EGR tube from intake manifold.
10. Remove plenum support bracket bolt, rearward of EGR tube.
11. Remove upper intake plenum attaching bolts, then the plenum.
12. Disconnect fuel injector electrical connectors.
13. Remove four fuel rail attaching bolts and spacers, then the fuel rail.
14. Remove lower intake manifold attaching bolts, then the intake manifold.
15. Reverse procedure to install, noting the following:
    a. Clean all mating surfaces, then inspect for cracked or distorted manifold and torn or missing Rings.
    b. Install intake manifold with new gaskets and install intake manifold onto cylinder head tightening to specifications in sequence shown in **Fig. 3.**
    c. Tighten attaching nuts and bolts to specifications.

EXHAUST MANIFOLD

REPLACE

1. Raise and support vehicle.
2. Disconnect exhaust pipe from rear exhaust manifold at flex joint. It may be necessary to remove entire exhaust system.

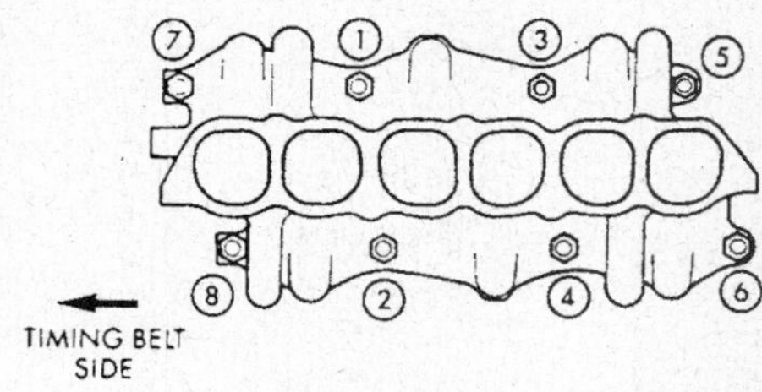

Fig. 3 Intake manifold bolt tightening sequence

3. Remove crossover pipe to manifold attaching bolts, then remove assembly.
4. Remove power steering pump bracket.
5. Remove rear manifold to cylinder head attaching nuts, then the manifold.
6. Lower vehicle, then remove front heat shield to manifold attaching screws.
7. Remove front manifold attaching nuts, then the manifold.
8. Reverse procedure to install, noting the following:
    a. Install new manifold gaskets.
    b. Tighten all attaching bolts and nuts to specifications.

CYLINDER HEAD

REPLACE

1. Relieve fuel system pressure as outlined under "Precautions," then drain cooling system.
2. Remove camshaft sprockets as outlined under "Timing Belt, Replace."
3. Remove rocker arms as outlined under "Rocker Arms, Replace."
4. Remove upper intake manifold assembly as outlined under "Intake Manifold, Replace."
5. Remove distributor as outlined in "Electrical" section.
6. Remove exhaust manifolds and crossover pipe as outlined under "Exhaust Manifold, Replace."
7. Remove cylinder head bolts and cylinder head.
8. Reverse procedure to install. Using sequence shown in **Fig. 4, torque** cylinder head bolts gradually in two or three steps to 80 ft. lbs.

VALVE COVER

REPLACE

1. Remove intake plenum as outlined under "Intake Manifold, Replace."
2. Cover lower intake manifold, then disconnect spark plug wires and position aside.
3. Remove bolts, then the valve cover.
4. Reverse procedure to install, noting the following:
    a. Install a new valve cover gasket.
    b. Tighten bolts to specifications.

VALVE ARRANGEMENT

Intake valves are located on upper sides of cylinder heads and exhaust valves are on lower sides of cylinder heads.

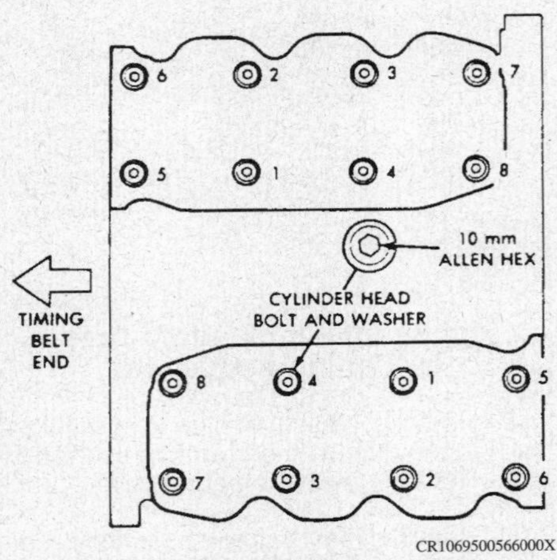

Fig. 4 Cylinder head bolt tightening sequence

Fig. 5 Rocker arm shaft tightening sequence

Fig. 6 Crankshaft & camshaft sprocket mark alignment

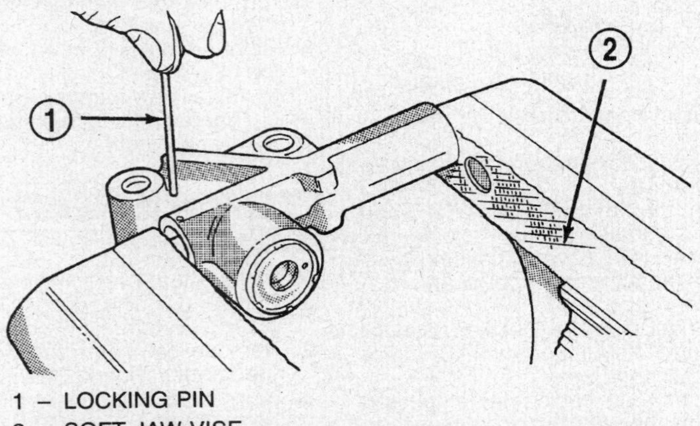

Fig. 7 Timing belt tensioner locking pin installation

VALVE CLEARANCE SPECIFICATIONS

These engines are equipped with hydraulic lash adjusters designed to maintain zero lash at all times.

ROCKER ARMS

REPLACE

1. Remove valve covers as outlined under "Valve Cover, Replace."
2. Identify rocker arm shaft assemblies before removal.
3. Install auto lash adjuster retainer tool No. MD998443, or equivalent. These retainers hold lash adjuster into position when rocker arms are serviced.
4. Remove rocker arm bolts and shaft assemblies.
5. Reverse procedure to install, noting the following:
   a. Install rocker arm and shaft assemblies with flat spot in rocker arm shafts facing toward timing belt side of engine for right cylinder head. For left cylinder head, install rocker arm and shaft assemblies with flat spot in rocker arm shafts facing toward transaxle side of engine. Install retainers and spring clips in their original positions on exhaust and intake shafts.
   b. Tighten bolts to specifications in sequence shown, **Fig. 5.**
   c. Remove lash adjuster retainers from rocker arms.

FRONT COVER

REPLACE

1. Remove radiator as outlined under "Radiator, Replace."
2. Remove right inner splash shield.
3. Remove accessory drive belts.
4. Remove right engine mount as outlined under "Engine Mount, Replace."
5. Remove crankshaft damper.
6. Remove engine mount bracket.
7. Remove timing belt upper left cover, then upper right cover and, finally, lower cover.
8. Reverse procedure to install.

TIMING BELT

REPLACE

REMOVAL

1. Remove timing belt front cover as outlined under "Front Cover, Replace."
2. Align crankshaft and camshaft sprocket marks, **Fig. 6,** then loosen timing belt tensioner attaching bolts.
3. Remove timing belt and tensioner. If timing belt is to be reused, mark running direction for installation reference.
4. Inspect timing belt for cracks, missing teeth, hardened rubber and abnormal wear.

INSTALLATION

1. Position timing belt tensioner in a soft jawed vise, then slowly compress tensioner plunger into tensioner body.
2. With tensioner plunger compressed into body, insert a suitable locking pin through holes in tensioner body, **Fig. 7.** This will hold plunger in position until after tensioner has been installed on engine.
3. Align mark on crankshaft sprocket with arrow mark on oil pump housing, then back off to three sprocket teeth before Top Dead Center (TDC), **Fig. 8.**
4. Align camshaft sprocket marks with marks on valve covers, **Fig. 6.**
5. Install timing belt as follows:
   a. Position timing belt over rear camshaft sprocket. Use a binder clip to secure timing belt to camshaft sprocket.
   b. With timing belt held taut, install belt under water pump pulley, then over front camshaft sprocket. Use a binder clip to secure timing belt to camshaft sprocket.
   c. Align crankshaft sprocket TDC mark with mark on oil pump cover, **Fig. 6.**
   d. Install timing belt over idler pulley, crankshaft sprocket and tensioner pulley.
6. Apply rotating force in clockwise direction to crankshaft sprocket to remove timing belt slack. Ensure timing marks are aligned, **Fig. 6.**
7. Using a suitable torque wrench and torque wrench tool No. MD998767, or equivalent, apply a force of 39 inch lbs. to timing belt tensioner pulley, then

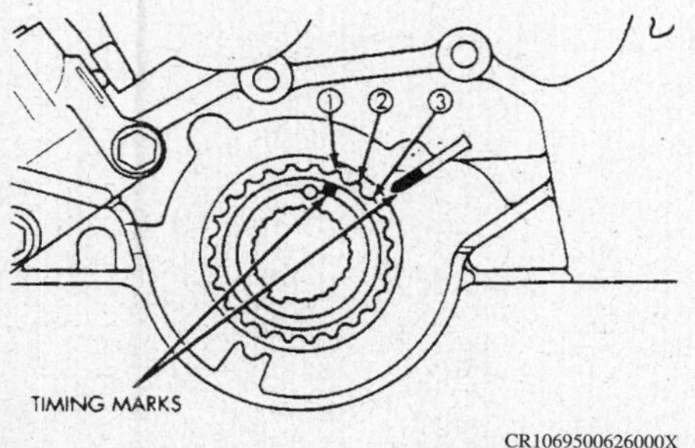

Fig. 8 Crankshaft sprocket teeth & mark location

torque tensioner pulley bolt to 35 ft. lbs.

8. With force still upon tensioner pulley, install timing belt tensioner to tensioner pulley bracket. **Torque** attaching bolts to 23 ft. lbs.
9. Remove locking pin retaining tensioner plunger in body.
10. Rotate crankshaft two revolutions in clockwise direction, then check camshaft and crankshaft sprocket mark alignment, **Fig. 6,** and ensure locking pin slides freely through tensioner body holes. If camshaft and crankshaft sprocket marks are not properly aligned and/or locking pin cannot slide freely through tensioner holes, repeat procedure.
11. Install front cover as outlined under "Front Cover, Replace."

CAMSHAFT

REPLACE

1. Remove timing belt, sprockets and covers as outlined under "Timing Belt, Replace."
2. Remove valve covers as outlined under "Valve Cover, Replace."
3. Attach auto lash adjuster retainer tool No. MD998443, or equivalent.
4. Mark rocker arm shaft assemblies for installation reference.
5. Remove rocker arm shaft bolts as outlined under "Rocker Arms, Replace."
6. Remove cylinder head as outlined under "Cylinder Head, Replace."
7. Remove thrust case from left head assembly and camshaft from rear of head.
8. Remove distributor from right head assembly and camshaft from rear of head.
9. Reverse procedure to install. Tighten thrust case and camshaft sprocket to specifications.

PISTON & ROD ASSEMBLY

The pistons are stamped with a letter and an arrow. Pistons stamped "R" are installed in cylinders 1, 3 and 5; pistons stamped "L" are installed in cylinders 2, 4 and 6. When a piston is installed in the engine, its arrow mark must face the front of the engine. The connecting rod and cap are stamped on the side with a cylinder number identification. The numbered side of the connecting rod cap must be installed on the same side as the numbered side of the rod.

MAIN JOURNAL

SIZE	NEW	CURRENT
59.543 to 59.695 mm (2.344 to 2.350 in.)	2	WHITE ENAMEL
59.695 to 59.848 mm (2.350 to 2.356 in.)	1	NONE
59.848 to 60.000 mm (2.356 to 2.362 in.)	0	YELLOW ENAMEL

CONNECTING ROD JOURNAL

SIZE	NEW	CURRENT
49.492 to 49.619 mm (1.949 to 1.954 in.)	III	WHITE ENAMEL
49.619 to 49.873 mm (1.954 to 1.964 in.)	II	NONE
49.873 to 50.000 mm (1.964 to 1.969 in.)	I	YELLOW ENAMEL

CR1069500678000X

Fig. 9 Crankshaft journal markings

MAIN & ROD BEARINGS

Service replacement parts carry identification marks, but factory parts are unmarked. The crankshaft journal markings, **Fig. 9,** may aid in the selection of bearings.

CRANKSHAFT SEAL

REPLACE

1. Remove components necessary to access crankshaft sprocket as outlined under "Timing Belt, Replace."
2. Remove crankshaft sprocket and key.
3. Pry out front oil seal with a flat tip screwdriver. **Cover the end of the screwdriver with a shop towel.**
4. Reverse procedure to install.

CRANKSHAFT REAR OIL SEAL

REPLACE

After the crankshaft rear oil seal housing and old seal have been removed, a new rear oil seal can be installed with seal installation tool No. MD998718, or equivalent, **Fig. 10.** Apply Molar silicon rubber adhesive sealant, or equivalent, to the oil seal housing and a light coating of engine oil to the entire circumference of the oil seal lip. Tighten bolts to specifications.

OIL PAN

REPLACE

1. Disconnect ground cable from remote battery jumper terminal.
2. Drain engine oil into a suitable container.
3. Remove dipstick tube, then the starter as outlined in "Electrical" section.

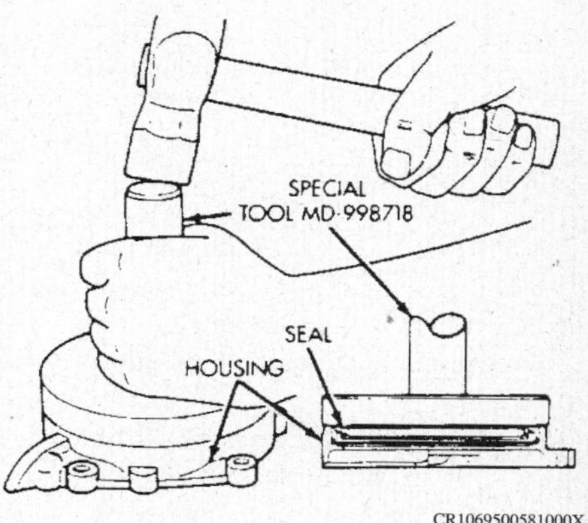

Fig. 10 Rear oil seal installation

4. Remove engine to transaxle struts, then the transaxle inspection cover.
5. Remove oil pan attaching bolts, then the oil pan.
6. Clean oil pan and cylinder block gasket surfaces.
7. Reverse procedure to install, noting the following:
   a. Apply Molar silicone rubber adhesive sealant, or equivalent, as shown, **Fig. 11.**
   b. Tighten pan bolts to specifications.

OIL PUMP

REPLACE

1. Remove components to access oil pump as outlined under "Timing Belt, Replace."
2. Remove oil pump attaching bolts, then the pump.
3. Reverse procedure to install. Tighten attaching bolts to specifications.

OIL PUMP SERVICE

DISASSEMBLE & INSPECTION

1. Inspect oil pump case for damage and remove rear cover.
2. Remove pump rotors and inspect case for excessive wear.
3. Insert rotor into oil pump case and measure clearance, **Figs. 12 and 13.**
4. Replace if out of specifications.

ASSEMBLE

1. Clean block and pump surfaces.
2. Assemble pump using new parts as required; lubricate with clean oil. Align marks on inner and outer rotors when assembling.
3. Install cover and tighten to specifications.
4. Install relief valve, spring, gasket and cap and tighten to specifications.
5. Prime oil pump before installation by filling rotor cavity with clean engine oil.

BELT TENSION DATA

Refer to **Fig. 14** for belt tension data.

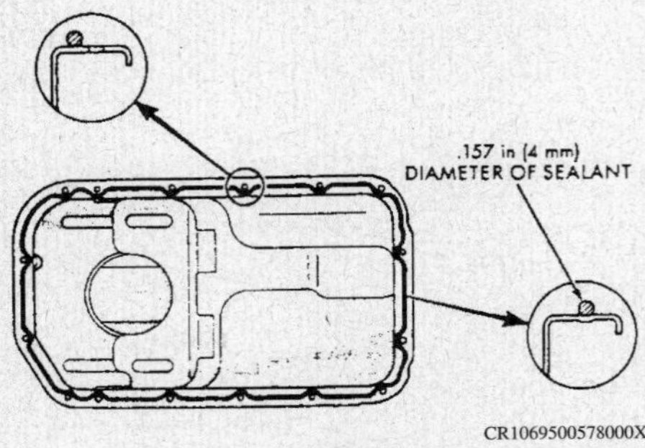

Fig. 11 Oil pan sealant application

SERPENTINE DRIVE BELT

Refer to "2.0L & 2.4L Engines" section for serpentine drive belt.

COOLING SYSTEM BLEED

Refer to "2.0L & 2.4L Engines" section for cooling system bleed procedure.

THERMOSTAT

REPLACE

Refer to "2.0L & 2.4L Engines" section for thermostat replacement procedure.

WATER PUMP

REPLACE

1. Remove timing belt as outlined under "Timing Belt, Replace."
2. Drain coolant into a suitable container.
3. Remove mounting bolts.
4. Separate pump from water inlet pipe and remove water pump.
5. Reverse procedure to install, noting the following:

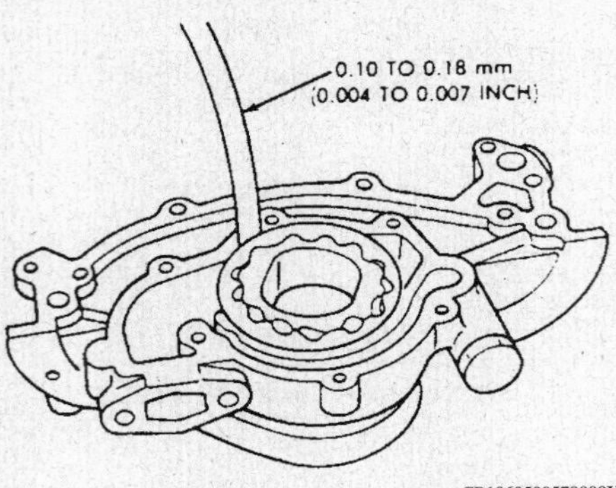

Fig. 12 Outer rotor & case clearance inspection

Accessory Drive Belts	Gauge
2.0/2.4/2.5L Engines	
Air Conditioning Compressor & Generator	NEW BELT: 150 LB.
Power Steering Pump	USED BELT: 90 LB.

CR1080100335000X

Fig. 14 Belt tension chart

a. Inspect pump for cracks or leaks and replace if necessary.
b. Install new water pipe Oaring and pump gasket.
c. Tighten water pump mounting bolts to specifications.
d. Fill and bleed cooling system as necessary.

RADIATOR

REPLACE

1. Remove air inlet resonator, then drain coolant into a suitable container.
2. Remove upper radiator crossover.
3. Remove hose clamps and hoses from radiator.

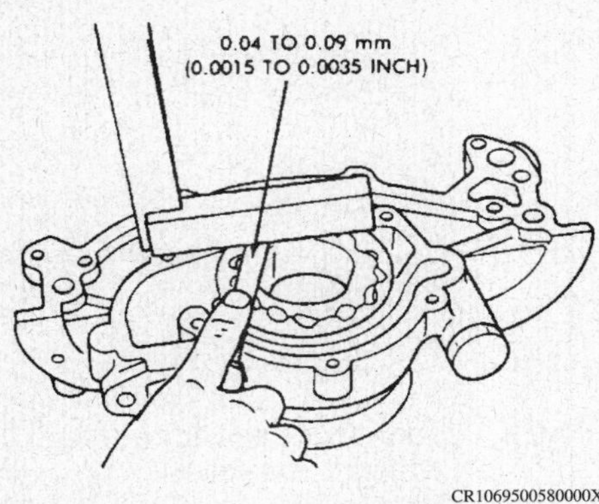

Fig. 13 Rotor end clearance inspection

4. Disconnect engine block heater electrical wire, if equipped.
5. Disconnect and plug automatic transaxle hoses at cooler.
6. Disconnect fan electrical connector.
7. Remove air conditioning condenser attaching screws located at front of radiator, if equipped.
8. Remove radiator from engine compartment by lifting upward.
9. Reverse procedure to install.

FUEL PUMP

REPLACE

The electric fuel pump is not serviceable. If the fuel pump requires service, the entire fuel pump module must be replaced.

Refer to "2.0L & 2.4L Engines" section for fuel pump replacement procedure.

FUEL FILTER

REPLACE

Refer to "2.0L & 2.4L Engines" section for fuel filter replacement procedure.

TIGHTENING SPECIFICATIONS

Year	Component	Torque/Ft. Lbs.
1998–2000	Air Intake Plenum	12–13
	Auto Tensioner Bolt	17
	Band Clamp	60
	Camshaft Sprocket	65
	Connecting Rod Cap Nut	37
	Coolant Inlet Elbow	96–108②
	Crankshaft Bolt	134
	Crankshaft Rear Oil Seal Retainer	96–108②
	Crossover	22
	Cylinder Head	①
	Engine Cradle Through Bolts	45
	Engine Support Bracket	33
	Exhaust Manifold	22
	Front Engine Mount Bolts	45
	Fuel Pump Module Lock Ring	40
	Fuel Tank Drain Plug	32②
	Heater Pipe Assembly	13
	Idler Pulley Bolt	33
	Intake Manifold	16
	Main Bearing Cap Bolts	69
	Oil Filter	10
	Oil Pan	48②
	Oil Pan Drain Plug	25
	Oil Pump Cover	84②
	Oil Pump Relief Valve Cap	30
	Oil Pump To Engine Block	17–19
	Oil Screen	13
	Rocker Arm And Shaft Assembly	16–17
	Serpentine Belt bolt	40
	Spark Plugs	18
	Tensioner Arm Assembly	33
	Tensioner Pulley Bolt	35
	Thermostat Housing	13
	Thrust Case	85
	Valve Cover	96–108②
	Water Inlet Pipe	10
	Water Pump	17

①— Refer to "Cylinder Head, Replace" for tightening procedure & specifications.
②— Inch lbs.

2.7L Engine

NOTE: Refer to "2.7L Engine" in "Concorde, Intrepid, LHS, Vision & 300M" Chapter For Procedures Not Covered In This Section.

NOTE: On Air Bag Equipped Models, Refer To "Air Bag System Precautions" Located In The Front Of This Manual For System Disarming & Arming Procedures.

NOTE: Refer To "Computer Relearn Procedures" Located In The Front Of This Manual When Battery Power To The Computer Has Been Interrupted.

INDEX

PRECAUTIONS

AIR BAG SYSTEMS

Refer to "Air Bag System Precautions" in the front of this manual for system disarming and arming procedures.

BATTERY GROUND CABLE

Prior to service, disconnect battery ground cable and isolate as required.

FUEL SYSTEM PRESSURE RELIEF

1. Remove fuel pump relay from power distribution center.
2. Start and run engine until it stalls.
3. Attempt to restart engine until it will no longer run, then turn ignition key to Off.
4. Install fuel pump relay, then erase any DTC's that may have been stored due to removing fuel pump relay.

COMPRESSION PRESSURE

The minimum compression pressure should be no less than 100 psi and the maximum variation between cylinders should be no more than 25%.

ENGINE MOUNT

REPLACE

LEFT SIDE MOUNT

1. Remove throttle body air inlet hose, then the air cleaner housing assembly.
2. Remove two nuts securing speed control servo bracket to left shock tower, then position servo aside.

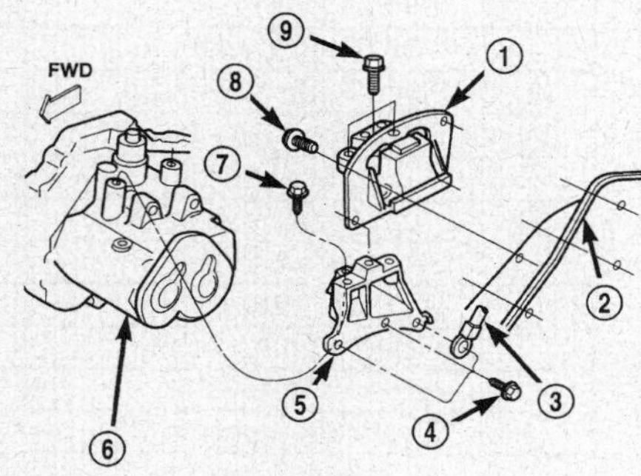

1 - TRANSMISSION SUPPORT ASSEMBLY
2 - LEFT FRAME RAIL
3 - GROUND CABLE
4 - BOLT (D)
5 - TRANSMISSION BRACKET
6 - TRANSMISSION
7 - BOLT (C)
8 - BOLT (B)
9 - BOLT (A)

CR1060000930000X

Fig. 1 Left side engine mount replacement

3. Support transaxle with floor jack and wooden block.
4. Remove three vertical bolts from mount to transaxle bracket, **Fig. 1.**
5. Slightly lower transaxle with floor jack.
6. Remove mount to frame rail bolts, then the mount.
7. Reverse procedure to install tightening bolts to specifications.

REAR MOUNT

1. Remove throttle body air inlet hose, then the air cleaner housing assembly.
2. Remove three vertical bolts attaching rear mount bracket to transaxle case, **Fig. 2.**
3. Raise and support vehicle, then remove rear mount bracket through bolt.
4. Remove horizontal bolt attaching rear mount bracket to transaxle case.
5. Remove mount bracket.
6. Remove rear mount to suspension crossmember attaching bolts, then the rear mount.
7. Reverse procedure to install tightening bolts to specifications.

RIGHT SIDE MOUNT

1. Remove engine coolant overflow container, then the heater tube attaching screw.
2. Raise and support vehicle, then remove inner splash shield.
3. Remove heater tube rear attaching screw.
4. Remove right engine support assembly vertical bolts from frame rail, **Fig. 3.**
5. Lower vehicle, then support load of engine using a floor jack and block of wood placed under oil pan.
6. Remove bolts attaching engine support assembly to engine bracket, then remove right engine mount.
7. Reverse procedure to install tightening bolts to specifications.

FRONT MOUNT

1. Raise and support vehicle, then remove front mount to bracket horizontal through bolt, **Fig. 4.**
2. Remove front mount vertical bolts, then the front mount.
3. Reverse procedure to install tightening bolts to specifications.

ENGINE

REPLACE

1. Relieve fuel pressure as outlined

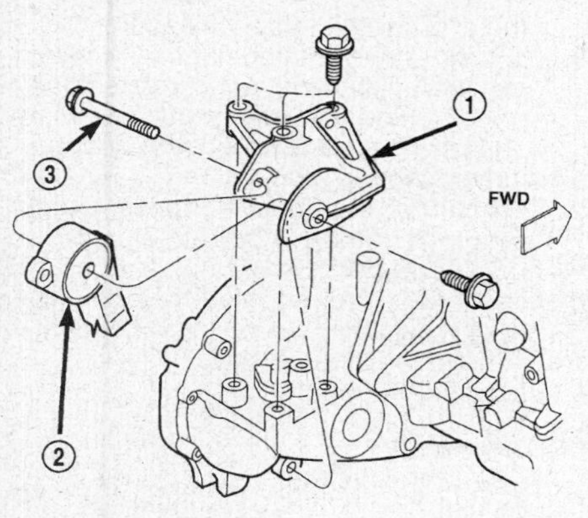

Fig. 2 Rear engine mount replacement

under "Precautions," then drain cooling system.

2. Recover A/C refrigerant as outlined in "Air Conditioning" section.
3. Remove throttle body air inlet hose, then the air cleaner housing assembly.
4. Raise and support vehicle, then remove both front wheels.
5. Remove left and right splash shields, then the fasteners attaching lower front fascia to crossmember.
6. Remove fasteners attaching lower air shield to crossmember.
7. Remove front bumper fascia, then lower vehicle.
8. Remove upper radiator crossmember, then disconnect upper and lower radiator hoses at radiator.
9. Disconnect transaxle oil cooler lines at transaxle, then plug openings.
10. Disconnect A/C lines at condenser, then remove cooling fan module.
11. Disconnect transaxle electrical connectors, then the shift cable.
12. Disconnect engine electrical harness from PCM and bulkhead connectors.
13. Remove ABS brake module and position aside.
14. Disconnect brake line from retaining clips, then raise and support vehicle.
15. Remove both axle shafts.
16. Remove front engine mount through bolt, then the mount from lower radiator crossmember.
17. Remove lower radiator crossmember, then the accessory drive belts.
18. Remove power steering pump and bracket assembly with lines attached, then position aside.
19. Disconnect heater return from pipe connection at right front frame rail area.
20. Disconnect A/C compressor electrical connector, then remove compressor and position aside.
21. Remove structural collar, then the exhaust cross-under pipe.
22. Remove rear engine mount and transaxle bracket, then drain engine oil into suitable container.
23. Remove transaxle torque converter

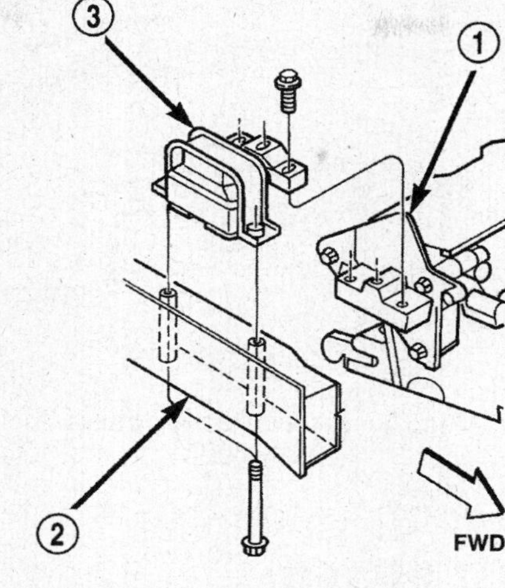

Fig. 3 Right side mount replacement

housing cover.

24. Mark flex plate to torque converter position, then remove torque converter bolts.
25. Lower vehicle, then disconnect positive cable from battery and PDC.
26. Disconnect ground cable from left side transaxle mount bracket.
27. Disconnect throttle and speed control cables.
28. Disconnect coolant pressure bottle hose from engine outlet connector.
29. Disconnect heater hose from engine outlet connector.
30. Disconnect ground strap at right shock tower, then the fuel line.
31. Disconnect brake booster and vapor purge vacuum hoses.
32. Disconnect all ground straps attached to engine.
33. Lower vehicle enough to install engine dolly tool No. 6135 and cradle tool No. 6710 with posts tool No. 6848 or equivalents.
34. Loosen cradle engine mounts to allow movement for positioning onto engine locating holes on engine block, compressor mount bracket and oil pan rail.
35. Lower vehicle and position cradle until engine is resting on posts, then tighten post mounts to cradle frame.
36. Lower vehicle so only weight of engine is on cradle.
37. Remove right and left side engine mount bolts.
38. Slowly raise vehicle to remove engine.
39. Reverse procedure to install tightening all bolts to specifications.

SERPENTINE DRIVE BELT

A/C COMPRESSOR/ ALTERNATOR BELT

1. Raise and support vehicle, then re-

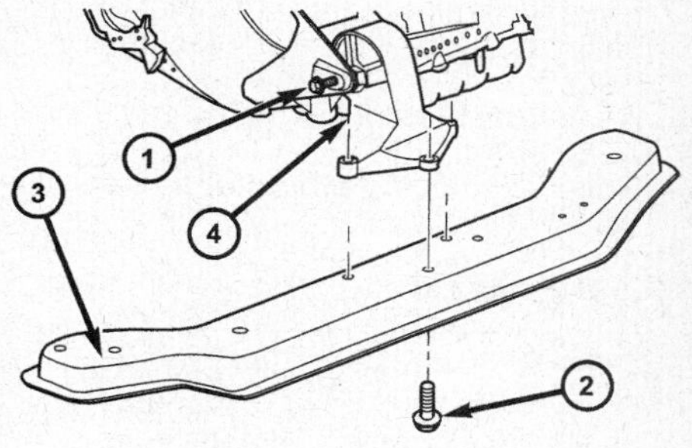

Fig. 4 Front engine mount replacement

move right front wheel and splash shield.

2. Loosen tensioner locking bolt and pivot bolt.
3. Rotate tensioner clockwise to allow slack, then remove belt.
4. Reverse procedure to install.

POWER STEERING PUMP BELT

1. Raise and support vehicle, then remove right front wheel and splash shield.
2. Remove A/C compressor/alternator belt as previously described.
3. Loosen belt adjusting bolt, then pivot power steering pump and remove belt.
4. Reverse procedure to install.

THERMOSTAT

REPLACE

1. Drain cooling system, then raise and support vehicle.
2. Remove right front wheel and belt splash shield.
3. Remove accessory drive belts, then the lower generator mounting bolt.
4. Lower vehicle, disconnect alternator electrical connectors.
5. Disconnect A/C clutch and pressure sensor electrical connectors.
6. Remove oil dipstick and tube, then plug hole.
7. Remove alternator, then disconnect hoses at thermostat housing.
8. Remove thermostat housing bolts, then the thermostat housing.
9. Reverse procedure to install noting the following:
   a. Install thermostat with bleed valve located at 12 o'clock position.
   b. Tighten bolts to specifications.

WATER PUMP

REPLACE

1. Drain cooling system, then remove timing chain cover as outlined under "Front Cover, Replace."

2. Remove timing chain and guides as outlined under "Timing Chain, Replace."
3. Remove water pump bolts, then the water pump.
4. Reverse procedure to install tightening bolts to specifications.

RADIATOR

REPLACE

1. Drain cooling system, then remove upper radiator crossmember.
2. Disconnect radiator fan electrical connector, then remove fan.
3. Disconnect radiator hoses.
4. Remove screw holding support bracket for transaxle cooler tubes at left side of radiator.
5. Remove A/C lines support bracket from right side of radiator.
6. Remove A/C condenser attaching screw, then the condenser from radiator.
7. Carefully lift radiator from vehicle.
8. Reverse procedure to install.

FUEL PUMP

REPLACE

1. Relieve fuel pressure as outlined under "Precautions," then remove fuel tank.
2. Disconnect fuel line from fuel pump module by depressing quick connect retainers.
3. Disconnect fuel pump electrical connector by pushing down on retainer and pulling connector off.
4. Using spanner wrench tool No. 6856 or equivalent, remove fuel pump module lock nut.
5. Remove fuel pump and O-ring seal from tank, then discard old seal.

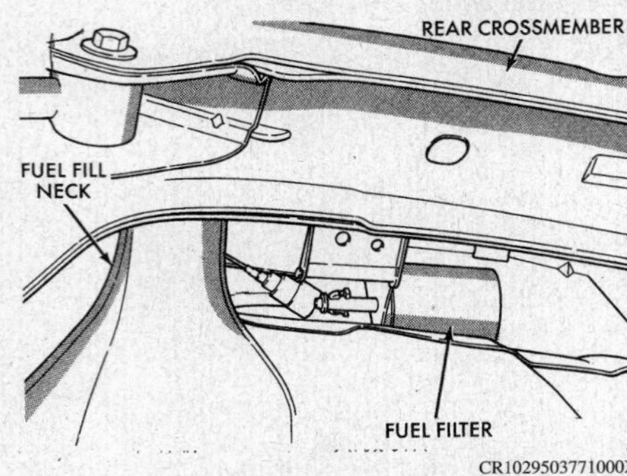

Fig. 5 Fuel filter location. 1998–2000

6. Reverse procedure to install.

FUEL FILTER

REPLACE

1998-2000

1. Release fuel system pressure as outlined under "Precautions."
2. From inside trunk, disconnect fuel pump module wiring jumper from main body harness. Connector is located under leftward side of trunk mat, near base of shock tower.
3. Locate body grommet for jumper near base of rear seat and push grommet out, then feed jumper through hole in body.
4. Raise and support vehicle.
5. Position a suitable fuel container with a capacity of at least 16 gallons, under drain plug located on bottom left edge of tank.
6. Remove drain plug and allow fuel to drain.
7. When tank stops draining, install drain plug and tighten to specifications.
8. Remove driver's side fuel tank strap and loosen, but do not remove, passenger's side fuel tank strap, allowing fuel tank fill neck to touch rear suspension crossover.
9. Disconnect fuel lines from fuel pump module. These are quick connect fittings located on top of tank.
10. Disconnect fuel supply line from fuel brake module.
11. Remove fuel filter, **Fig. 5.**
12. Reverse procedure to install.

2001-02

The fuel filter is part of the fuel pressure regulator and is located on top of the fuel pump module.

1. Relief fuel pressure as outlined under "Precautions."
2. Drain fuel tank into holding tank or properly labeled gasoline safety container.
3. Raise and support vehicle.
4. Remove fuel tank as follows:
   a. Use suitable transmission jack to support fuel tank.
   b. Remove fuel tank strap bolts, then lower tank slightly.
   c. Disconnect fuel filler vent tube, fuel line, then vapor line.
   d. Disconnect vacuum line from the LDP.
   e. Loosen clamp then remove fuel filler tube.
   f. Unlock fuel pump module electrical connector, then disconnect.
   g. Lower fuel tank.
5. Disconnect fuel supply line at filter/regulator nipple.
6. Depress locking spring tab on side of fuel regulator, rotate 90° counterclockwise and remove.
7. Reverse procedure to install.

TIGHTENING SPECIFICATIONS

Year	Component	Torque Ft. Lbs.
2001–02	A/C Compressor To Engine	21
	Alternator Bracket	30
	Front Engine Mount	45
	Left Engine Mount To Frame Rail	24
	Left Engine Mount To Transaxle Bracket	45
	Rear Engine Mount Bracket To Transaxle	80
	Rear Engine Mount To Bracket	45
	Rear Engine Mount To Crossmember	45
	Right Engine Mount To Frame Rail	45
	Right Engine Mount To Support Bracket	45
	Thermostat Housing	105①
	Water Pump	105①

① — Inch lbs.

Clutch & Manual Transaxle

NOTE: On Air Bag Equipped Models, Refer To "Air Bag System Precautions" Located In The Front Of This Manual For System Disarming & Arming Procedures.

NOTE: Refer To "Computer Relearn Procedures" Located In The Front Of This Manual When Battery Power To The Computer Has Been Interrupted.

INDEX

PRECAUTIONS

AIR BAG SYSTEMS

Refer to "Air Bag System Precautions" in the front of this manual for system disarming and arming procedures.

BATTERY GROUND CABLE

Prior to service, disconnect battery ground cable and isolate as required.

ADJUSTMENTS

The clutch cable has a self-adjusting mechanism built into the cable which compensates for clutch disc wear. The cable requires no maintenance or lubrication and is not adjustable.

HYDRAULIC SYSTEM SERVICE

CLUTCH SYSTEM BLEED

The clutch hydraulic system must be bled whenever the system has been opened for any reason or when performance is not satisfactory.

1. Connect a clear plastic hose to slave cylinder bleeder screw valve and submerge other end of hose in a clear container of clean DOT 3 brake fluid.
2. With parking brake applied, pump clutch pedal several times, then fully release.
3. Open bleeder valve, then depress clutch pedal to floor and hold.
4. Close bleeder valve, then release pedal.
5. Repeat procedure until bubbles can no longer be seen emerging from bleeder valve. **Keep clutch master cylinder full of clean DOT 3 brake fluid.**
6. Ensure bleeder valve is closed, then inspect clutch operation.

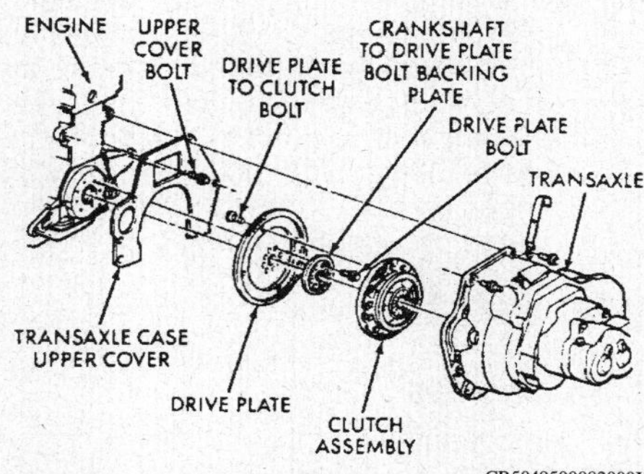

Fig. 1 Exploded view of clutch assembly

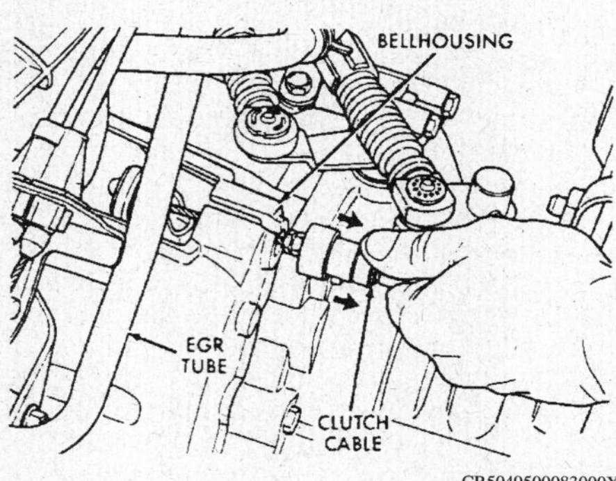

Fig. 2 Clutch cable removal

CLUTCH

REPLACE

The modular clutch assembly used in these models consists of a single dry-type clutch disc and a diaphragm style clutch cover. The clutch assembly is serviced as a unit and cannot be disassembled.

1. Raise and support vehicle.
2. Remove starter wiring, then the starter assembly.
3. Remove transaxle as outlined under "Transaxle, Replace."
4. Remove modular clutch assembly from transaxle input shaft, **Fig. 1. Handle carefully to avoid contaminating friction surfaces.**
5. Reverse procedure to install, noting the following:
   a. Install drive plate mounting bolts in a crisscross pattern until all bolts are seated.
   b. Tighten bolts to specifications using same crisscross pattern.

SHIFT CABLE

REPLACE

1. Pull up and remove Power Distribution Center (PDC).
2. Remove air cleaner assembly, then the clutch cable inspection cover.
3. Pull back on clutch cable housing and disengage cable from housing, **Fig. 2.**
4. Disconnect clutch cable up-stop/spacer with cable strand, **Fig. 3.** Depressing the clutch pedal provides access to clutch cable strand.
5. Disconnect cable up-stop/spacer from pedal pivot by wedging a suitable flat blade pry tool between pin and retaining tab.
6. Hold tab slightly away from pin, then pull the up-stop/spacer off pedal.
7. Remove cable end from up-stop/spacer.
8. Reverse procedure to install.

CLUTCH SLAVE CYLINDER

2.7L ENGINE

1. Raise and support vehicle.
2. Disconnect hydraulic clutch circuit quick connect fitting using tool No. 6638A, or equivalent.
3. Remove clutch slave cylinder by lifting nylon tab using a suitable screwdriver by depressing cylinder inward towards case and rotating cylinder 60° counterclockwise, **Fig. 4.**
4. Reverse procedure to install.

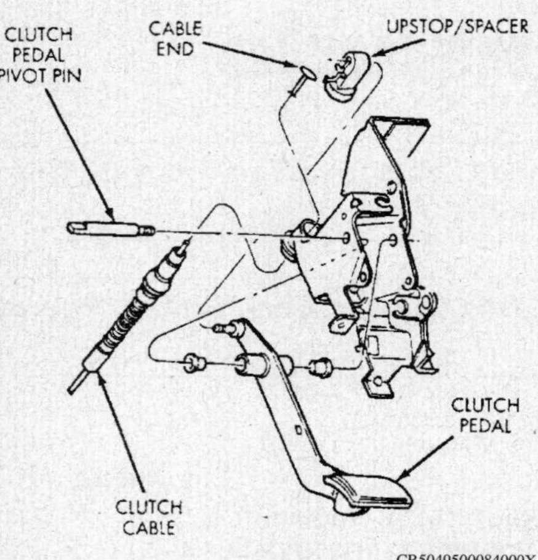

Fig. 3 Clutch cable end separation from pedal assembly

CLUTCH MASTER CYLINDER

2.7L ENGINE

1. Remove fuse box access cover, then instrument panel lower close-out panel.
2. Disconnect clutch cylinder pushrod from clutch pedal pin.
3. Remove air cleaner assembly, then clutch master cylinder reservoir from speed control servo.
4. Remove purge solenoid from mounting bracket and place aside.
5. Remove speed control servo bracket from strut tower and place aside.
6. Raise vehicle on hoist, disconnect clutch hydraulic quick connect fitting using tool No. 6638, or equivalent.
7. Lower vehicle, then rotate master cylinder ¼ turn counterclockwise and remove from clutch pedal bracket.
8. Reverse procedure to install.

TRANSAXLE

REPLACE

1998-2000

1. Remove the air cleaner at throttle body inlet.
2. Remove clutch housing vent cap, exposing clutch cable end and release lever, then disconnect clutch cable at transaxle.
3. Remove selector cable lever at transaxle.
4. Remove crossover lever cable, then the shift cable mounting bracket.
5. Disconnect accelerator cables ends and bracket from throttle body.
6. Remove upper starter bolt and upper bellowing stud nut, then the throttle body support bracket.
7. Remove upper transaxle mounting bolts, then the upper bellhousing bolts.
8. Remove Vehicle Speed Sensor (VSS), then disconnect back-up lamp wiring at transaxle.
9. Install suitable engine bridge fixture and support engine.
10. Raise and support vehicle, then remove front wheels.
11. Drain transaxle fluid.
12. Remove both front driveshafts.
13. Remove left lower splash shield/battery cover.
14. Remove left transaxle mount lower bracket bolts.
15. Remove engine lower crossbar retaining bolts.
16. Remove front engine steel mount bracket, then the bolts on front engine aluminum mount bracket.
17. Remove lower starter bolt, then the rear transaxle mount bracket.
18. Remove transaxle to rear lateral bending strut from engine and transaxle.
19. Remove lower dust shield screw.
20. Using suitable transaxle support jack, support transaxle.
21. Rotate engine crankshaft clockwise to gain access to driveplate clutch bolts, then remove driveplate clutch bolts.
22. Remove lower transaxle to engine bellhousing bolts, then the transaxle.
23. Reverse procedure to install.

2001-02

2.4L Engine

1. Remove air cleaner assembly.
2. Disconnect back-up lamp/vehicle speed sensor switch harness connector.
3. Remove clutch release access cap, then disconnect release cable.
4. Disconnect crossover and selector cables from transaxle.
5. Remove gearshift cable and place aside.
6. Remove starter, then three rear mount bracket to transaxle bolts.
7. Raise and support vehicle, then remove half shafts.
8. Remove rear mount bracket to transaxle horizontal bolts.
9. Remove rear mount through bolts, then rear mount to crossmember bolts.
10. Remove rear mount and bracket.
11. Remove front mount through bolt, front pencil strut brace, then the front mount.
12. Remove structural collar, then the bellhousing dust cover.
13. Remove left wheel opening splash shield, then the modular clutch to drive plate bolts.
14. Support oil pan using suitable jack and block of wood.
15. Remove upper mount through bolt, then lower engine/transaxle assembly.
16. Remove upper mount, transaxle to engine bolts, then transaxle.
17. Reverse procedure to install.

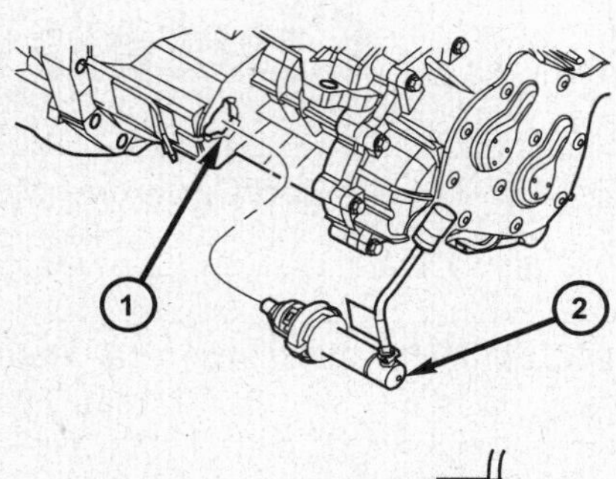

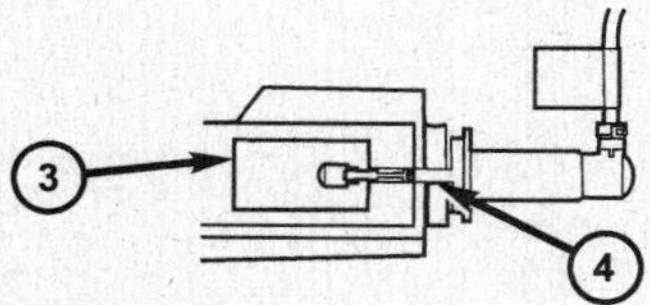

1 - MOUNTING HOLE
2 - SLAVE CYLINDER
3 - ACCESS HOLE
4 - NYLON ANTI-ROTATION TAB

CR5040100190000X

Fig. 4 Slave cylinder replacement. 2.7L engine

2.7L Engine

1. Remove air cleaner assembly
2. Disconnect gearshift cable at transaxle, then remove retaining clips at mount bracket and place aside.
3. Remove three vertical rear mount bolts.
4. Remove crankshaft position sensor from transaxle case.
5. Remove throttle body support bracket, then upper mount to case vertical bolt.
6. Remove front mount bracket/starter upper bolt, then the starter heat shield bolts.
7. Disconnect oxygen sensor, then raise and support vehicle.
8. Remove structural collar, then clutch/drive plate inspection cover.
9. Remove modular clutch to drive plate bolts, then front mount and bracket.
10. Remove starter.
11. Remove hydraulic clutch quick connect fitting using tool No. 6638A, or equivalent.
12. Remove clutch slave cylinder by lifting nylon tab using suitable screwdriver and depressing cylinder inward toward case and rotating 60° counterclockwise.
13. Disconnect back-up lamp switch connector.
14. Place suitable jack and block of wood under oil pan, then remove upper mount bolts.
15. Lower engine/transaxle assembly enough to gain access to bellhousing bolts. Loosen bolts but do not remove.
16. Secure a suitable transmission jack to transmission, then remove bellhousing bolts.
17. Remove transaxle from vehicle.
18. Reverse procedure to install.

TIGHTENING SPECIFICATIONS

Year	Component	Torque/Ft. Lbs.
1998–2002	Back-Up Lamp Switch	18
	Clutch Pedal Pivot Shaft Nut (1998–2000)	30
	Clutch Pedal Pivot Shaft Nut (2001–02)	25
	Drive Plate To Crankshaft Bolts	70
	Drive Plate To Modular Clutch Bolts (1998–2000)	55
	Drive Plate To Modular Clutch Bolts (2001–02)	65
	End Plate Cover Bolts	21
	Front Engine Mount To Transaxle	80
	Front Transaxle Mount Through Bolt	45
	Front Transaxle Mount To Engine Bolt	40
	Lateral Bending Strut To Engine	40
	Lateral Bending Strut To Transaxle	40
	Rear Mount Bolts (2.4L)	80
	Rear Mount Bolts (2.7)	40
	Left Transaxle Mount Through Bolt	80
	Transaxle To Engine Bolts	70
	Transaxle To Engine Intake Bracket Stud	70
	Upper Mount Bracket Bolt	48

Rear Suspension

NOTE: On Air Bag Equipped Models, Refer To "Air Bag System Precautions" Located In The Front Of This Manual For System Disarming & Arming Procedures.

NOTE: Refer To "Computer Relearn Procedures" Located In The Front Of This Manual When Battery Power To The Computer Has Been Interrupted.

INDEX

DESCRIPTION

The rear suspension, **Fig. 1,** is a fully independent short and long arm style suspension. An upper control arm bolts to the top of each rear cast knuckle to the rear suspension crossmember. The movement of the rear knuckle is controlled laterally by two lower lateral links going from the front and rear of the knuckle to the rear crossmember and upper control arm. Fore and aft movement of the knuckle is controlled by a trailing arm.

HUB & BEARING

REPLACE

All models are equipped with permanently lubricated, sealed-for-life wheel bearings. There is no periodic lubrication or maintenance recommended for these units. If servicing is required, proceed as follows:

1. Raise and support vehicle, then remove rear wheel and tire assembly.
2. Remove brake drum.
3. Remove dust cap from hub/bearing assembly to spindle retaining nut.
4. Remove hub/bearing retainer assembly from spindle by pulling straight on spindle by hand.
5. Reverse procedure to install. Tighten hub/bearing assembly retaining nut to specifications.

SHOCK ABSORBER

REPLACE

1. Roll back carpeting on top of rear shock tower to access shock mounting

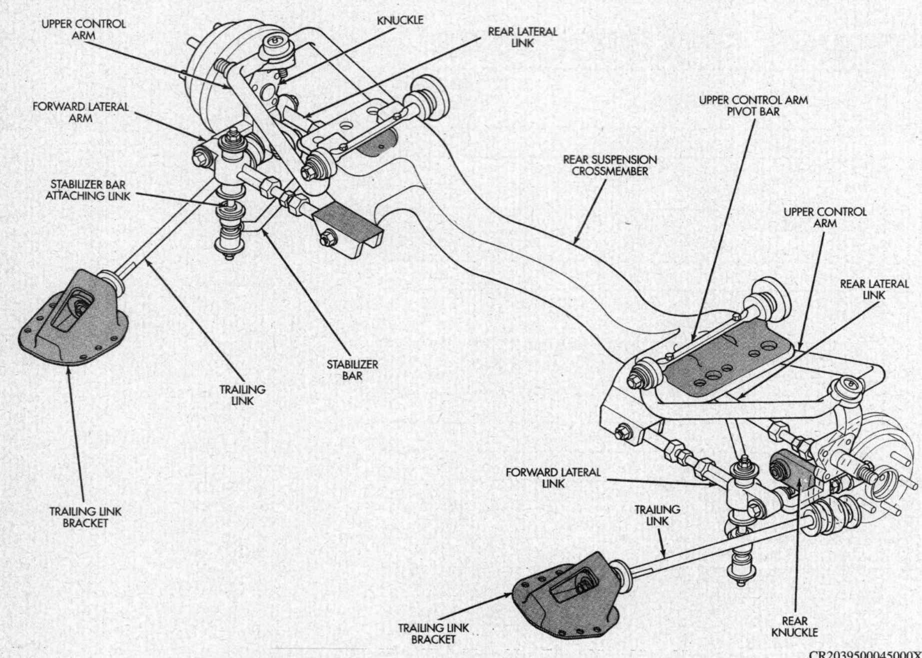

Fig. 1 Rear suspension components

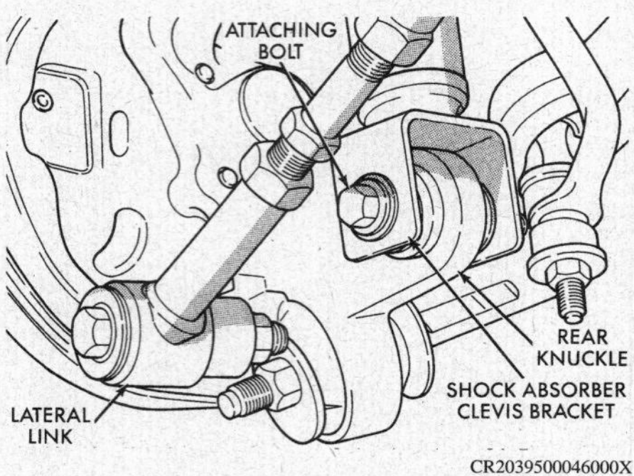

Fig. 2 Shock & knuckle location

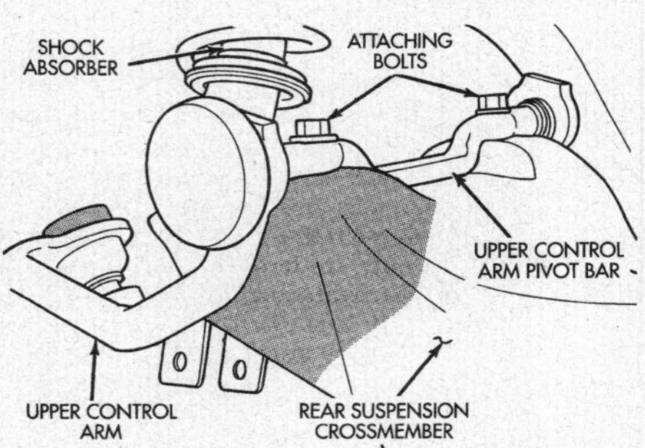

Fig. 5 Upper control arm & crossmember

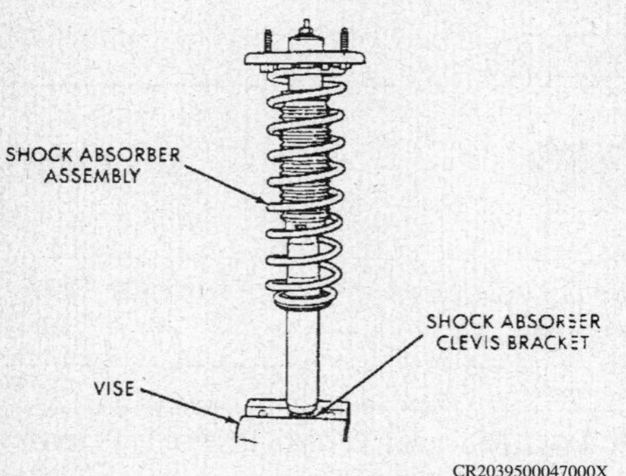

Fig. 3 Coil spring removal

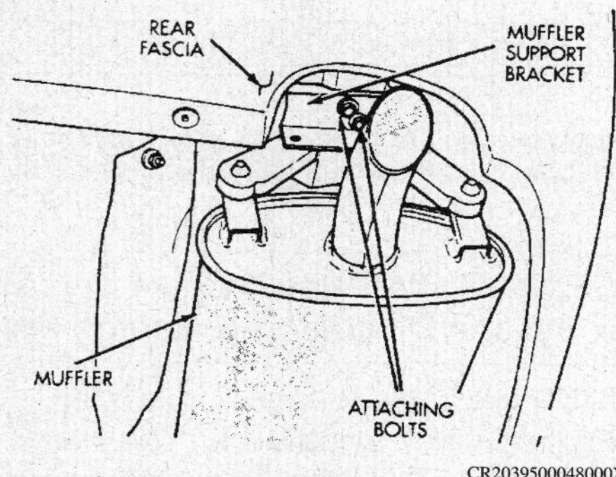

Fig. 4 Muffler support bracket

bolts, then remove shock tower cover.
2. Remove two attaching nuts.
3. Raise and support vehicle.
4. Remove rear wheel and tire assembly, then the bolt attaching clevis bracket on shock to knuckle, **Fig. 2.**
5. Remove shock absorber clevis bracket from knuckle by pushing down on suspension.
6. Move shock absorber downward and tilt top of shock outward.
7. Remove shock from vehicle through top of wheelwell opening.
8. Reverse procedure to install.

COIL SPRING

REPLACE

1. Remove shock absorber as outlined under "Shock Absorber, Replace."
2. Position shock assembly in a vise, **Fig. 3,** clamping by clevis bracket at bottom of shock.
3. Mark coil spring and strut assembly right or left as needed.
4. Using coil spring compressor tool No. GP-2020-S2.5, or equivalent, compress coil spring.
5. Using a suitable tool, keep shock shaft rod from turning and remove shock shaft nut.
6. Remove washer, shock mounting bracket, washer on top of dust shield, then the dust shield.
7. Remove coil spring and spring compressor as an assembly.
8. Reverse procedure to install. Tighten mounting nuts to specifications.

CONTROL ARM

REPLACE

1. Raise and support vehicle, then remove both rear wheel and tire assemblies.
2. Remove shock absorber clevis bracket as outlined under "Shock Absorber, Replace" on both sides of vehicle.
3. Remove muffler support bracket from rear frame, **Fig. 4.**
4. Remove rear exhaust pipe hanger bracket from rear suspension crossmember and move exhaust down far as possible.
5. Remove cotter pin and castle nut from ball joint.
6. **On models equipped with ABS,** remove speed sensor heads from knuckle.
7. **On all models,** side of vehicle requiring control arm removal, separate control arm ball joint from rear knuckle using puller tool No. CT-1106, or equivalent. **Reinstall castle nut on ball joint stud to protect threads.**
8. Position a suitable floor jack and block of wood under center of rear suspension crossmember to support and lower crossmember during removal. **Do not put strain on brake flex hoses or damage may occur.**
9. Remove routing clips for wheel speed sensor cable from brackets on both upper control arms.
10. Remove four bolts securing rear suspension crossmember to rear frame rails.
11. Lower rear suspension crossmember far enough to access upper control arm pivot bar to crossmember attaching bolts, then the two bolts attaching upper control arm to crossmember, **Fig. 5.**
12. Remove control arm from vehicle.
13. Reverse procedure to install, noting the following:
    a. Align upper control arm pivot bar with mounting holes in rear suspension crossmember.
    b. Install the two pivot bar nuts to crossmember attaching bolts. Tighten to specifications.
    c. Using suitable jackstand, raise rear suspension crossmember up to frame rails and loosely install the

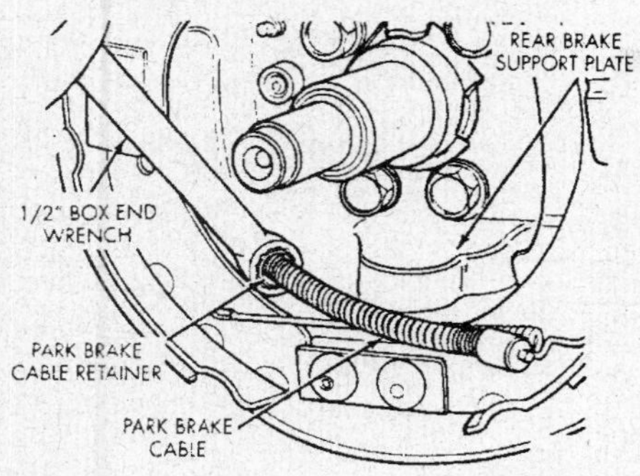

Fig. 6 Parking brake cable removal

four attaching nuts.

d. Position appropriate size drift into position hole in each side of rear suspension crossmember and crossmember locating holes in frame rails, then tighten frame rail attaching bolts to specifications.
e. Install upper ball joint stud in knuckle, then the ball join castle nut and tighten to specifications.

KNUCKLE

REPLACE

1. Raise and support vehicle, then remove rear wheel and tire assembly.
2. Remove brake drum or disc brake.
3. Remove rear wheel speed sensor.
4. **On models equipped with ABS,** remove rear wheel speed sensor from brake support plate.
5. **On all models,** remove parking brake cable from brake actuator lever.
6. Remove parking brake cable as follows:
   a. Position a ½ inch box end wrench over cable retainer, **Fig. 6,** to collapse retaining tabs.
   b. Pull brake cable from brake support plate.
7. Remove rear hub/bearing assembly retaining nut, then the washer and hub/bearing assembly from knuckle.
8. Remove four attaching bolts from rear support plate and knuckle.
9. Remove brake support plate, brake shoes and wheel cylinder as an assembly from knuckle.
10. Remove attaching nuts and bolts holding forward and rear lateral links to knuckle.
11. Disconnect ball joint stud from knuckle following procedure outlined under "Control Arm, Replace."
12. Remove knuckle.
13. Reverse procedure to install.

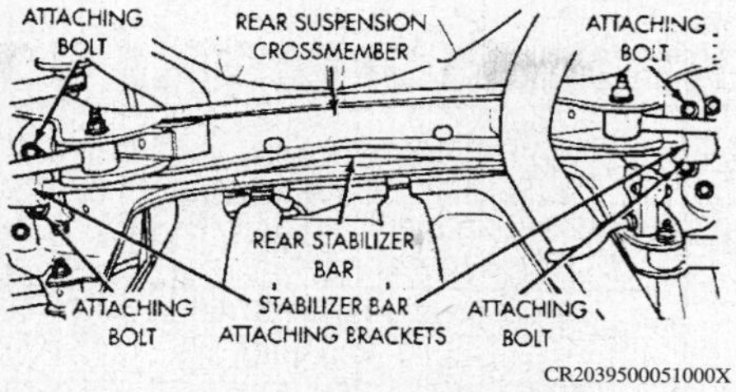

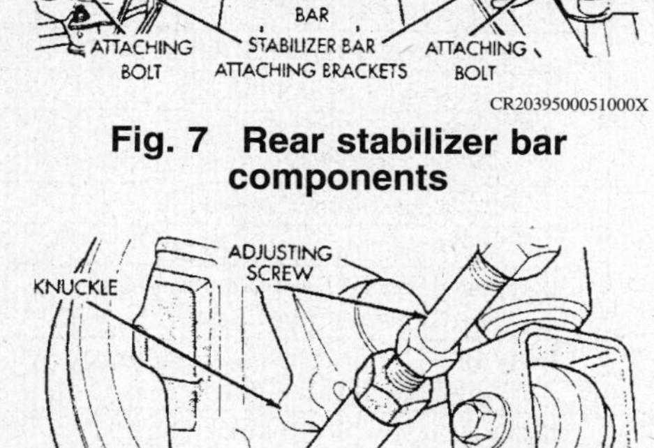

Fig. 7 Rear stabilizer bar components

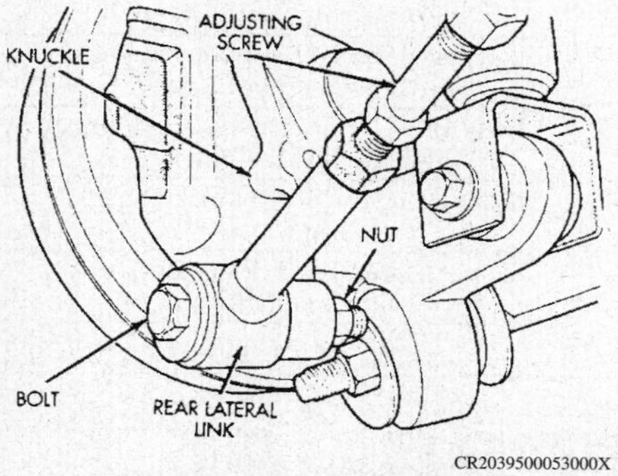

Fig. 9 Rear lateral link

STABILIZER BAR

REPLACE

1. Raise and support vehicle, then remove both rear wheel and tire assemblies.
2. Using a suitable wrench to keep stabilizer links from rotating, remove nuts attaching stabilizer link isolator bushings to stabilizer links.
3. Remove four bolts attaching stabilizer bar bushing clamps to rear suspension crossmember, **Fig. 7.**
4. Remove rear stabilizer bar to crossmember bushing clamps and bushings from stabilizer bar.
5. Remove stabilizer bar between exhaust pipe and rear suspension crossmember.
6. Reverse procedure to install.

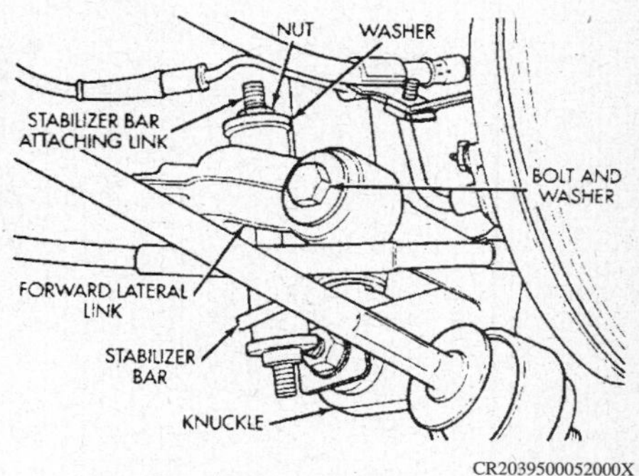

Fig. 8 Forward lateral link

LATERAL LINK

REPLACE

FORWARD

1. Raise and support vehicle, then remove rear wheel and tire assembly from side of car being serviced.
2. Remove rear stabilizer bar attaching link from forward lateral link to knuckle, **Fig. 8.**
3. Remove nut, bolt and washer attaching lateral link to knuckle.
4. Remove nut and bolt attaching lateral link to rear suspension crossmember, then the lateral link.
5. Reverse procedure to install.

REAR

1. Raise and support vehicle, then remove rear wheel and tire assembly from side of car being serviced.
2. Remove nut, bolt and washer attaching lateral link to knuckle, **Fig. 9.**
3. Remove nut and bolt attaching lateral link to rear suspension crossmember, then the lateral link.
4. Reverse procedure to install.

TIGHTENING SPECIFICATIONS

Year	Component	Torque/Ft. Lbs.
1998–2002	Brake Support Plate To Knuckle Mounting Bolts	45
	Hub & Bearing Assembly	184–185
	Lateral Link Attaching Nut	70
	Shock Assembly Clevis Bracket To Knuckle	70
	Shock Assembly Shaft Nut	40
	Shock Assembly To Body	25
	Sway Bar Isolator Bushing Retainer To Crossmember Bolt	20
	Sway Bar To Forward Lateral Link Attaching Link Nut	24
	Upper Ball Joint To Knuckle Castle Nut	63
	Upper Control Arm Pivot Bar To Crossmember	79
	Wheel Lug Nuts	100

Front Suspension & Steering

NOTE: On Air Bag Equipped Models, Refer To "Air Bag System Precautions" Located In The Front Of This Manual For System Disarming & Arming Procedures.

NOTE: Refer To "Computer Relearn Procedures" Located In The Front Of This Manual When Battery Power To The Computer Has Been Interrupted.

INDEX

WHEEL BEARING

ADJUST

These models are equipped with permanently–sealed front wheel bearings. There is no periodic lubrication or maintenance recommended.

HUB & BEARING

REPLACE

1. Raise and support vehicle.
2. Remove cotter pin, lock nut and spring washer from front stub axle.
3. Lower vehicle, then loosen hub nut while vehicle is on the ground and brakes are applied.
4. Raise and support vehicle, then remove from wheel and tire assembly.
5. Remove front disc brake caliper and brake disc assembly and support aside from steering knuckle.

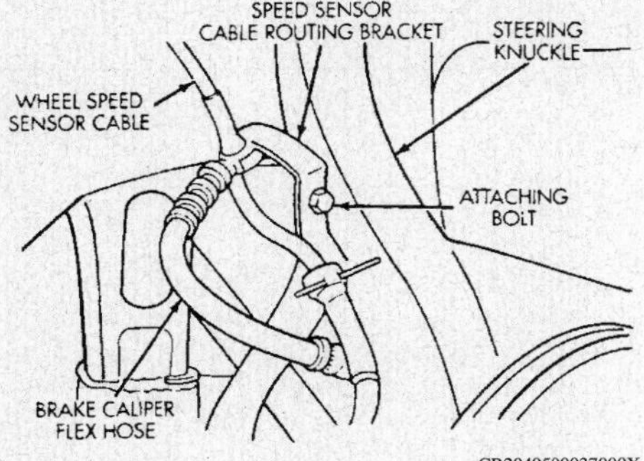

Fig. 1 Speed sensor cable routing bracket

6. Remove attaching outer tie rod end to steering knuckle.
7. Using remover tool No. MB-991113, or equivalent, remove tie rod end from steering knuckle.
8. Remove speed sensor cable routing bracket, **Fig. 1.**
9. Remove cotter pin and castle nut from stud of lower ball joint at steering knuckle.
10. Turn steering knuckle so front of steering knuckle is facing as far outboard in wheelwell as possible. Lightly tap boss on steering knuckle to separate from stud of lower ball joint. **Do not hit lower control arm or ball joint grease seal.**
11. Lift up on steering knuckle and separate from ball joint stud. **Support driveshaft so it does not hang by inner Constant Velocity (CV) joint.**
12. Separate steering knuckle from outer CV joint by pulling away, **Fig. 2.**
13. Remove cotter pin and nut from upper ball joint to steering knuckle attachment.

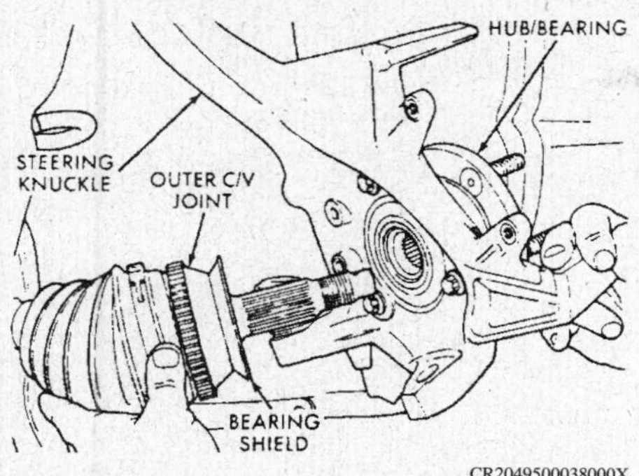

Fig. 2 Steering knuckle & outer CV joint

14. Remove upper ball joint stud using puller tool No. C3894-A, or equivalent, then the steering knuckle.
15. Mount steering knuckle securely in a vise, then remove three bolts attaching hub/bearing assembly to steering knuckle.
16. Remove hub/bearing assembly from steering knuckle. **If bearing does not come out, tap lightly using a rubber mallet.**
17. Before installing hub/bearing assembly, clean all mounting surfaces thoroughly.
18. Install hub/bearing assembly in steering knuckle aligning bolts in bearing flange with hole in steering knuckle.
19. Reverse remaining procedure to install.

DRIVESHAFT

REPLACE

1. Loosen, but do not remove, stub axle to hub/bearing retaining nut while vehicle is on floor and brakes applied, then raise and support vehicle and remove front wheel and tire assembly.
2. Remove brake caliper and support aside, then the brake disc.
3. Remove tie rod end attaching nut, then the tie rod end stud from steering knuckle using remover tool No. MB-991113, or equivalent.
4. Remove vehicle speed sensor cable routing bracket.
5. Remove cotter pin and castle nut from stud of lower ball joint at steering knuckle.
6. Turn steering knuckle so front of knuckle is facing as far outboard in wheelwell as possible. Lightly tap boss on steering knuckle to separate from stud of lower ball joint.
7. Pull steering knuckle assembly out and away from outer CV joint.
8. Support outer end of driveshaft assembly, then insert a pry bar between tripod joint and transaxle case side gear, **Fig. 3,** as far as possible by hand.
9. Hold inner tripod joint and interconnecting shaft of driveshaft assembly.
10. Remove inner tripod joint from transaxle by pulling it straight out of transaxle side gear.
11. Reverse procedure to install. Tighten all nuts and bolts to specifications.

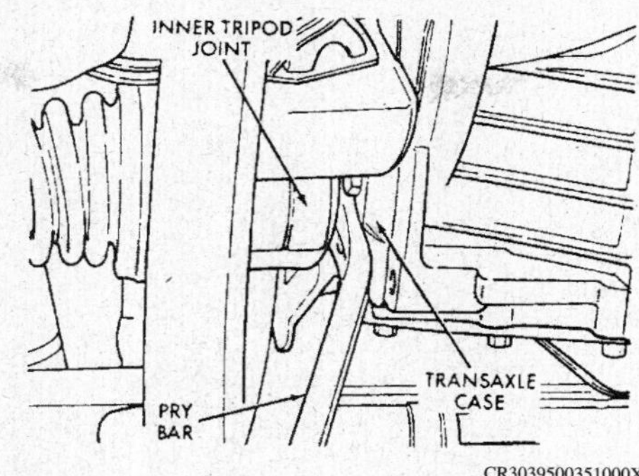

Fig. 3 Inner tripod joint removal

BALL JOINT INSPECTION

LOWER

1. Raise and support vehicle.
2. Install dial indicator so it contacts top surface of steering knuckle near lower ball joint stud castle nut.
3. Grasp wheel and tire assembly and push it up and down firmly.
4. Record amount of up and down movement of steering knuckle from dial indicator.
5. Replace lower control arm if movement exceeds .059 inch.

UPPER

With the weight of the vehicle resting on its wheels, attempt to move the grease fitting with no mechanical assistance. If any movement of the grease fitting is detected, the ball joint is worn.

BALL JOINT

REPLACE

The ball joints are not a replaceable component of the control arms. If determined to be defective, the entire control arm will have to be replaced as outlined under "Control Arm, Replace."

SHOCK ABSORBER

REPLACE

1. Raise and support vehicle, then remove the front wheel and tire assembly.
2. Remove vehicle speed sensor cable routing bracket.
3. Remove cotter pin and castle nut from upper ball joint stud to steering knuckle attachment.
4. Remove upper ball joint stud from steering knuckle using pull tool No. C-3894-A, or equivalent, then position steering outward toward rear of wheelwell.
5. Remove pinch bolt attaching shock clevis to shock.
6. Remove through bolt attaching shock to lower control arm.
7. Remove clevis from shock by carefully tapping clevis with soft brass drift off shock fluid reservoir.

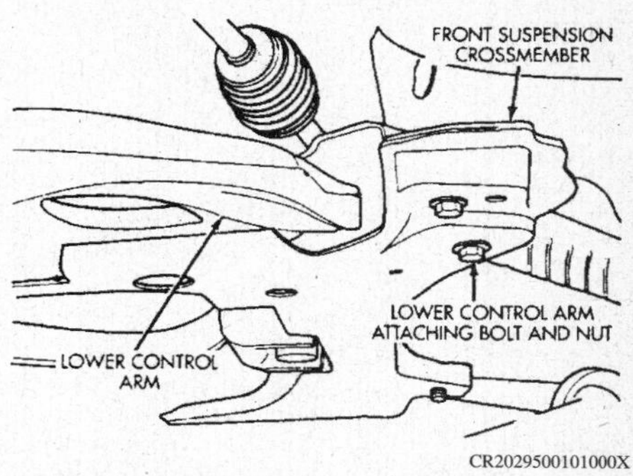

Fig. 4 Lower control arm removal

8. Remove four bolts attaching shock/upper control arm mounting bracket to shock tower.
9. Remove shock and upper control arm mounting bracket as an assembly through front area of wheelwell.
10. Reverse procedure to install. Tighten all nuts and bolts to specifications.

CONTROL ARM

REPLACE

LOWER

1. Raise and support vehicle, then remove the front wheel and tire assembly.
2. Remove lower ball joint heat shield.
3. Remove disc brake caliper and support aside, then the brake disc.
4. Disconnect ball joint from steering knuckle, then turn steering knuckle so front of knuckle is facing as far outboard as possible.
5. Separate steering knuckle from lower ball joint by lightly tapping with a rubber mallet.
6. Remove shock absorber clevis from lower control.
7. Using an Allen wrench to prevent stabilizer bar link from rotating, remove nut attaching stabilizer bar link assembly to lower control arm.
8. Remove attaching bolts of stabilizer bar bushing to front suspension crossmember and body of vehicle.
9. Lower one side of stabilizer bar away from lower control arm.
10. Remove nut and bolt attaching rear isolator bushing of lower control arm, **Fig. 4,** then the nut and bolt attaching front isolator bushing of lower control arm.
11. Remove front isolator bushing of lower control arm to front suspension crossmember.
12. To remove lower control arm, proceed as follows:
    a. Remove front of lower control arm from front suspension crossmember first.
    b. Remove rear of lower control arm from between the top and bottom half of front suspension crossmember, keeping lower control arm as level as possible.
13. Reverse procedure to install.

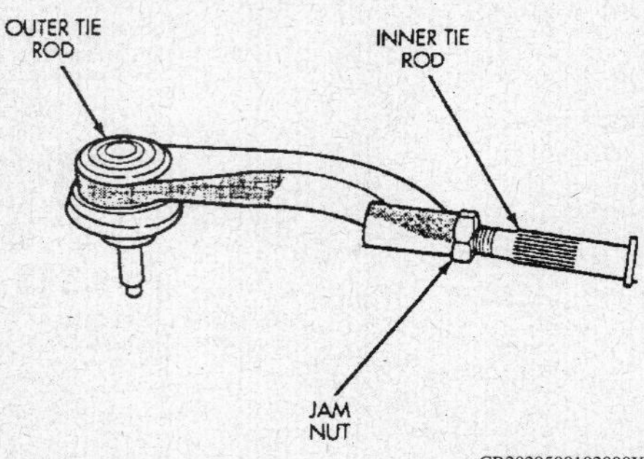

Fig. 5 Tie rod replacement

UPPER

1. Raise and support vehicle, then remove the front wheel and tire assembly.
2. Remove vehicle speed sensor cable routing bracket.
3. Remove cotter pin and castle nut from upper ball joint stud to steering knuckle attachment.
4. Remove upper ball joint stud from steering knuckle using puller tool No. C-3894-A, or equivalent, then position the steering outward toward rear of wheelwell.
5. Remove pinch bolt attaching shock clevis to shock.
6. Remove through bolt attaching shock to lower control arm.
7. Remove clevis from shock by carefully tapping clevis with soft brass drift off shock fluid reservoir.
8. Remove four bolts attaching upper control arm/shock absorber mounting bracket to shock tower.
9. Remove shock absorber and upper control arm mounting bracket as an assembly.
10. Reverse procedure to install.

STEERING KNUCKLE

REPLACE

Refer to "Hub & Bearing, Replace" for knuckle replacement procedures.

STABILIZER BAR

REPLACE

1. Raise and support vehicle.
2. Using a suitable hex wrench to prevent stabilizer bar link from rotating, remove nut attaching stabilizer bar link assembly to lower control arm.
3. Remove attaching bolts of stabilizer bar bushing to front suspension crossmember and body of vehicle.
4. Remove bushings, bushing retainers, and attaching links, then the stabilizer bar.
5. Reverse procedure to install.

TIE ROD

REPLACE

1. Raise and support vehicle, then remove the front wheel and tire assembly.

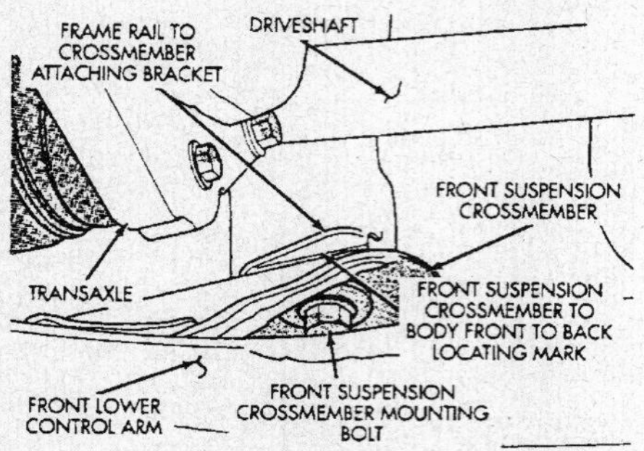

Fig. 6 Front suspension crossmember front to back locating mark (Part 1 of 2)

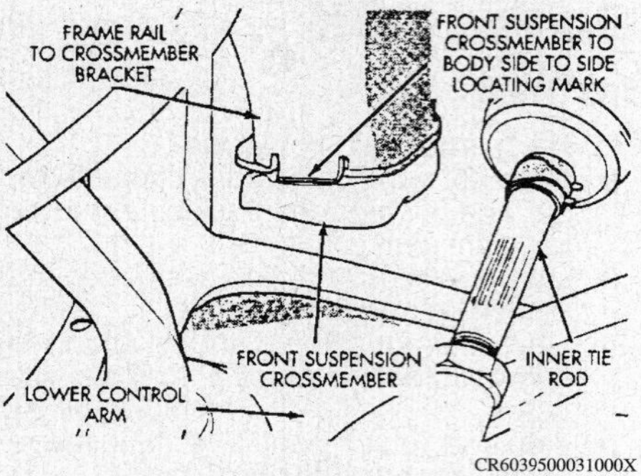

Fig. 7 Front suspension crossmember side to side locating mark

2. Remove nuts attaching both outer tie rod ends to steering knuckle.
3. Using remover tool No. MB-991113, or equivalent, remove both tie rod end studs from steering knuckles.
4. Loosen inner to outer tie rod jam nut, **Fig. 5,** then remove the outer tie rod from inner tie rod.
5. Remove jam nut, then using pliers, expand tie rod boot, to inner tie rod clamp and remove from steering gear.
6. Reverse procedure to install.

POWER STEERING GEAR

REPLACE

1. Siphon power steering fluid from remote power steering reservoir
2. From interior of vehicle, remove retaining pin from intermediate shaft coupler pinch bolt, then the pinch bolt from intermediate shaft coupler.
3. Separate intermediate shaft coupler from gear shaft.
4. Raise and support vehicle, then remove both front wheel and tire assemblies.
5. Remove nuts attaching both outer tie rod ends to steering knuckles.
6. Using remover tool No. MB-991113, or equivalent, remove both tie rod end studs from steering knuckles.
7. Using an awl, scribe a line on body, **Fig. 6,** marking the front to back installed location where front suspension crossmember is mounted on each side of vehicle.

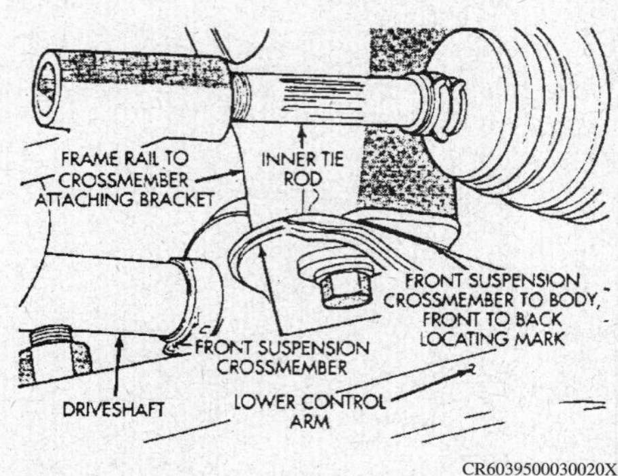

Fig. 6 Front suspension crossmember front to back locating mark (Part 2 of 2)

8. Using an awl, scribe a line on front suspension crossmember, **Fig. 7,** marking side to side installed location where front suspension crossmember is mounted against body on both sides of vehicle.
9. Remove stabilizer bar bushing clamp to body attaching bolts only.
10. Remove three ABS control unit bolts, then secure unit to body for suspension crossmember removal. **Do not let unit hang by brake tubes.**
11. Remove bolts attaching shock absorber clevis to lefthand and righthand lower control arms.
12. Remove two bolt attaching engine support bracket to front suspension crossmember.
13. Position a suitable jackstand under center of front suspension crossmember.
14. Remove from both sides of vehicle front two bolts attaching front suspension crossmember to frame rail of vehicle, then the rear attaching bolts.
15. Using jackstand, lower front suspension crossmember enough to allow steering gear to be removed from crossmember. **Ensure crossmember is supported by jackstand to avoid damage.**
16. Drain power steering fluid, pressure and return hoses from power steering gear assembly.
17. Disconnect power steering harness connector from fluid reservoir switch.
18. Remove two bolts at isolators, **Figs. 8 and 9,** attaching steering gear assembly to front suspension crossmember, then the two bolts attaching steering gear saddle bracket to front suspension crossmember, **Fig. 10.**
19. Remove steering gear assembly.
20. Reverse procedure to install.

POWER STEERING PUMP

REPLACE

2.0L & 2.4L ENGINES

1. Siphon power steering fluid out of remote power steering fluid reservoir.

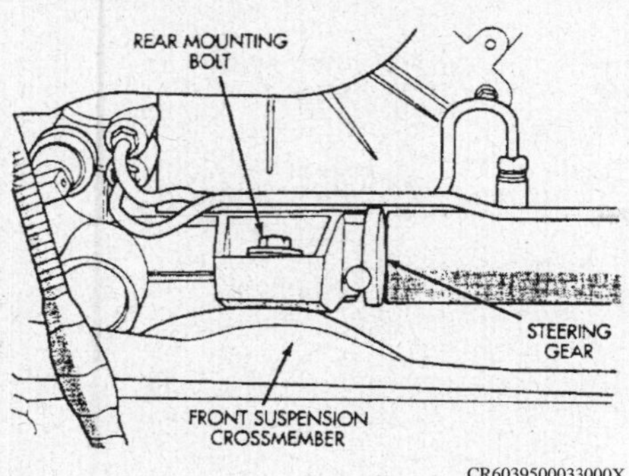

Fig. 8 Steering gear rear mounting isolator bolts

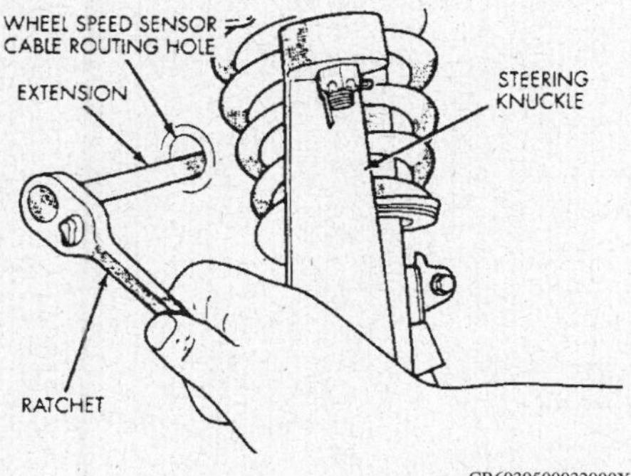

Fig. 11 Top bolt for power steering pump mounting bracket. 2.0L & 2.4L engines

2. Raise and support vehicle, then remove righthand wheel and tire assembly.
3. Remove accessory drive splash shield from righthand front wheelwell.
4. Disconnect power steering fluid pressure hose from pressure fitting on power steering pump, then drain remaining power steering fluid.
5. Remove attaching hose clamp from power steering suction fitting, then the power steering supply hose.
6. Remove power steering pump adjusting nut, then the bolt attaching power steering pump to aluminum mounting bracket.
7. Remove ABS hydraulic control unit heat shield.
8. Remove speed sensor cable sealing grommet from inner fender, then disconnect the wheel speed sensor cable from wiring harness and secure aside.

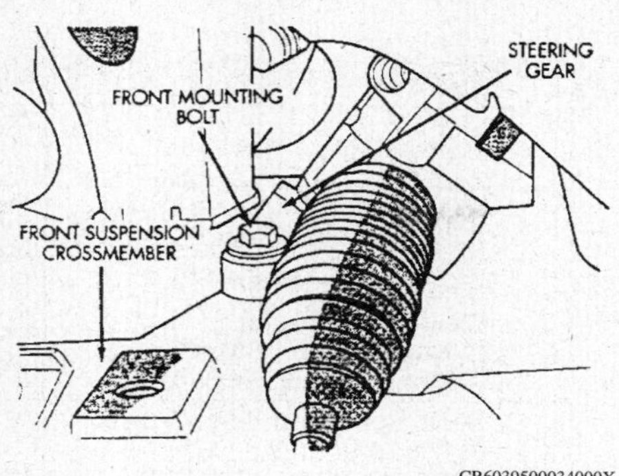

Fig. 9 Steering gear front mounting isolator bolts

Pull through hole in inner fender and unclip wiring harness trough from frame rail.

9. Remove ABS sealing plug from hole in firewall.
10. Remove bolt attaching top of power steering pump front bracket to mounting bracket, **Fig. 11.**
11. Remove power steering pump drive belt.
12. Remove power steering pump and bracket as an assembly.
13. Reverse procedure to install.

2.5L ENGINE

1. Siphon power steering fluid out of remote power steering fluid reservoir.
2. Raise and support vehicle, then remove the righthand wheel and tire assembly.
3. Remove accessory drive splash shield from righthand front wheelwell.
4. Disconnect power steering fluid pressure hose from pressure fitting on power steering pump, then drain remaining power steering fluid.
5. Remove power steering pressure hose from fitting on pump.
6. Remove ABS hydraulic control unit heat shield.
7. Remove adjusting bolt in accessory drive mounting bracket.
8. Remove bolt at adjusting slot, **Fig. 12,** then the bolt from at top of power steering pump front mounting brackets.
9. Remove power steering drive belt.
10. Remove power steering pump.
11. Reverse procedure to install.

2.7L ENGINE

1. Siphon power steering fluid out of re-

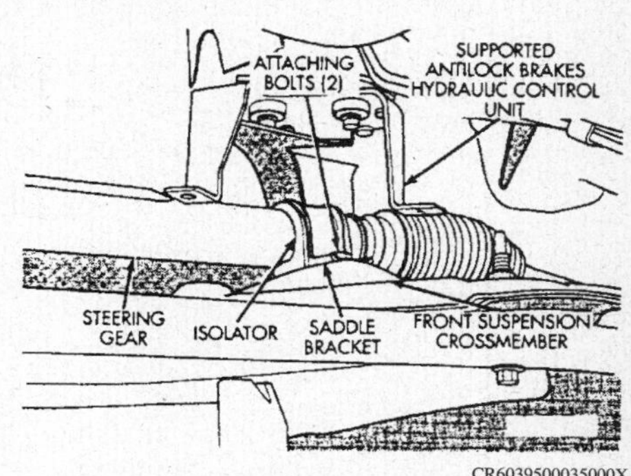

Fig. 10 Steering gear saddle bracket mounting bolts

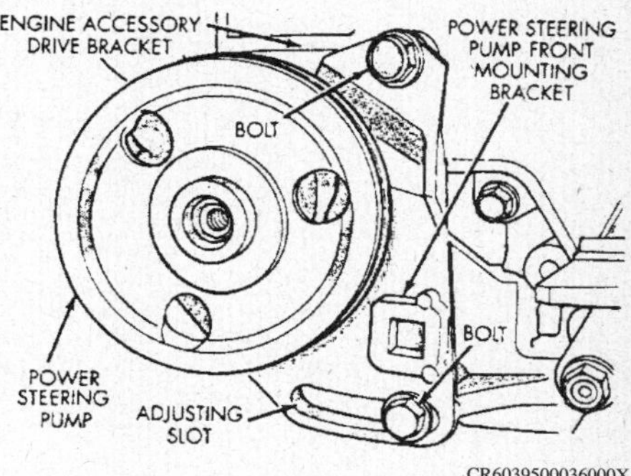

Fig. 12 Power steering pump front bracket. 2.5L engine

mote power steering fluid reservoir.

2. Remove power steering fluid supply hose from power steering pump supply fitting.
3. Raise and support vehicle, then remove drive belt splash shield.
4. Remove power steering fluid pressure hose from fitting on power steering pump.
5. Remove oxygen sensor harness and clip from edge of pump heat shield.
6. Remove bolt as slot in stamped pump adjuster bracket and remove power steering drive belt.
7. Pivot pump out past full-adjust position, then remove three bolts attaching power steering pump bracket to engine.
8. Remove power steering pump through opening between frame rail and right driveshaft.
9. Reverse procedure to install.

TIGHTENING SPECIFICATIONS

Year	Component	Torque/Ft. Lbs.
1998–2002	Ball Joint Stud To Shock Tower Attaching Bolts	23
	Ball Joint Stud To Steering Gear Castle Nut	70
	Disc Brake Caliper Assembly To Steering Knuckle Bolts	16
	Front Crossmember Assembly To Body Mounting Nuts	120
	Front Stub Axle To Hub/Bearing Assembly	180
	Lower Control Arm To Crossmember Pivot Bolt	120
	Outer Tie Rod To Inner Tie Rod Lock Nut	55
	Power Steering Bracket To Engine Mounting Bolt	40
	Power Steering Pump Mounting To Front Bracket	40
	Power Steering & Return Hose	21–23
	Pressure Hose To Return Hose (2.0L & 2.4L)	84①
	Pressure Hose To Return Hose (2.5L)	40
	Shock Absorber Shaft Nut	40
	Shock Assembly Clevis Bracket To Lower Control Arm Nut	68
	Stabilizer Bar Bushing Retainer To Crossmember Bolts	45
	Stabilizer Bar To Control Arm Attaching Link Nut	75
	Steering Gear To Crossmember Bolts	50
	Tie Rod End To Steering Knuckle Attaching Nut	45
	Wheel Lug Nuts	100

① — Inch lbs.

Wheel Alignment

INDEX

PRECAUTIONS

Vehicle hoisting equipment used must be frame contact type only. Use of equipment designed to lift vehicles by the rear axle cannot be used, as damage to rear suspension components will occur. Do not attempt to modify any suspension or steering components by heating or bending of the component.

DESCRIPTION

This vehicle is equipped with a non-adjustable front caster and camber suspension. Front caster and camber settings are determined at the time of design and require no adjustment during alignment. Though not adjustable, front caster and camber must be checked and components replaced when outside of vehicle specification. Inspect all components for damage or signs of bending and replace as required.

Prior to checking or adjusting front or rear suspension alignment, inspect suspension components and wheel bearings for damage or excessive wear and replace as needed. Ensure tire pressure is properly adjusted, then raise and release front or rear bumper several times to allow vehicle to assume ride height.

Toe, measured in degrees or inches, is the amount of difference in distance between the front and rear tire edges, **Fig. 1.**

Thrust angle is the average of the toe setting on each rear wheel, **Fig. 1.**

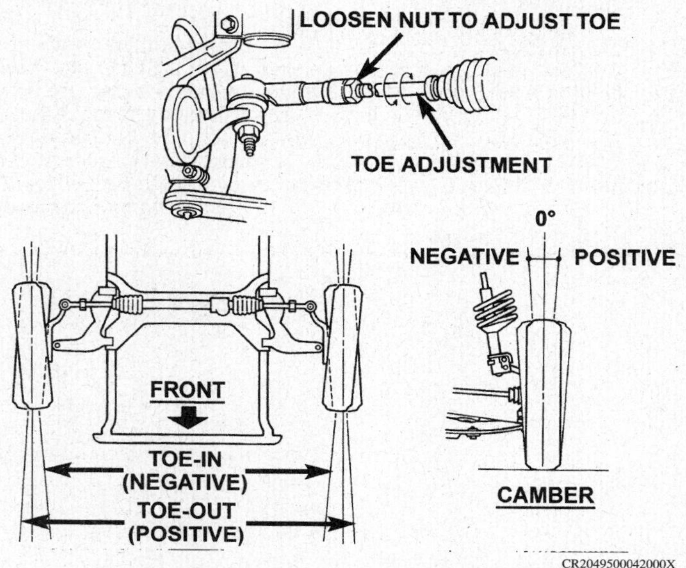

Fig. 1 Toe & camber angle adjustment

PRELIMINARY INSPECTION

1. Ensure gas tank is full.
2. Inspect tire pressure and inflate specification. Ensure tires are of same size and tread.
3. Inspect front wheel and tire radial runout.
4. Ensure all suspension fasteners are tightened properly.
5. Inspect ball joints and steering linkage for wear, looseness or damage.
6. Inspect all suspension component rubber bushings for wear or deterioration.

FRONT WHEEL ALIGNMENT

CAMBER

Camber adjustment is not normally required. Inspect all front suspension components for damage or wear, then check rear alignment setting prior to adjusting camber setting.

1. Mark position of all shock assembly mounting bolts on shock tower of side to be adjusted.
2. Raise and support vehicle by frame until front tires and suspension are not supporting vehicle.
3. Loosen shock mounting bolts on side to be adjusted. Only loosen far enough to allow removal of plastic locating pins that align upper mounting bracket with shock tower.
4. Remove both plastic retaining pins using suitable punch or pliers.
5. Position shock assembly inboard or outboard as required to adjust camber. Ensure fore and aft position is same as marked and that rearward and forward bolts are moved an equal length.
6. **Do not enlarge any existing holes to increase adjustment range.**
7. **Torque** upper shock assembly mounting bolts to 68 ft. lbs.
8. Lower vehicle, then bounce front and rear of vehicle an equal amount of times.
9. Recheck camber setting and readjust as necessary.

TOE

Prior to performing front alignment, check rear alignment.

1. **Perform rear wheel alignment as outlined under "Rear Wheel Alignment."**
2. Loosen front inner and outer tie rod jam nuts and rotate inner tie rod end, **Fig. 2,** at steering gear to set front toe.

REAR WHEEL ALIGNMENT

1. Center steering wheel and lock using a suitable steering wheel clamp.
2. Loosen adjusting screw jam nuts on four of the lateral arms and adjusting screws. Note each adjusting screw has one right-handed and one left-handed nut, **Fig. 3.** When setting rear camber and toe, the maximum lateral link lengths, **Fig. 4,** must not be exceeded. If exceeded, inadequate retention of adjustment link to inner and outer link may result.
3. Adjust rear lateral link adjusting screw, **Fig. 3,** to obtain approximate rear camber setting, then adjust forward

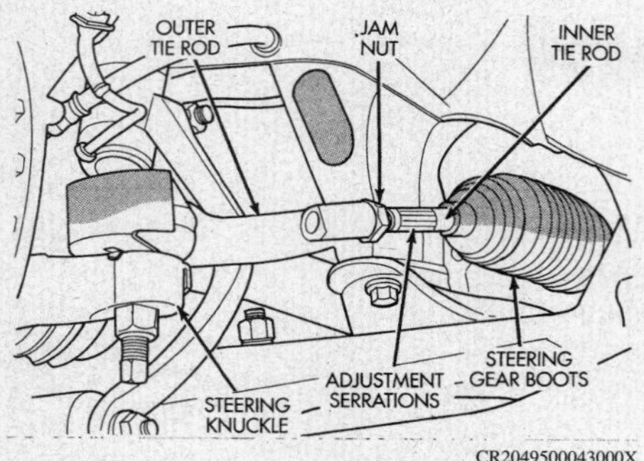

Fig. 2 Inner & outer tie rod adjustment

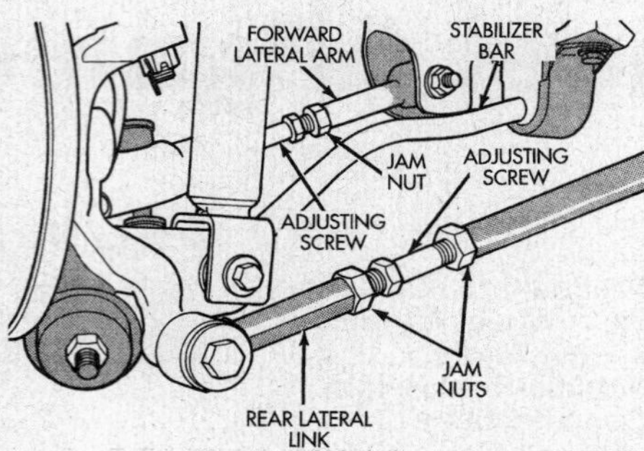

Fig. 3 Rear lateral arm adjustment

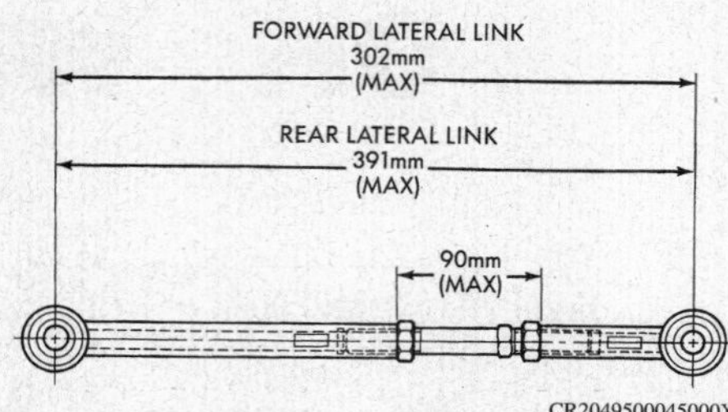

Fig. 4 Lateral link maximum length

lateral link adjusting screw in combination with rear lateral link to reach preferred specification.

4. Adjust forward lateral link adjusting screw, **Fig. 3,** to set preferred rear toe specification.
5. **Toe adjustment will cause a slight change in the camber setting. Should camber setting change during toe adjustment, continue to adjust camber and toe until both are at preferred specifications.**
6. Using crow foot and torque wrench, **torque** lateral link adjusting screw jam nuts to 48 ft. lbs., while holding adjustment screws from turning.

THRUST ANGLE

The thrust angle is the average of the toe settings on each rear wheel. If measurement is not within specifications, readjust rear wheel toe to provide each wheel with ½ of the total toe measurement. When readjusting, do not exceed the total toe specification.

CONCORDE, INTREPID, LHS & 300M

NOTE: Refer To Rear Of This Manual For Vehicle Manufacturer's Special Service Tool Suppliers.

INDEX OF SERVICE OPERATIONS

Specifications

GENERAL ENGINE SPECIFICATIONS

Engine	Engine Code①	Fuel System	Bore & Stroke, Inch	Comp. Ratio	Brake HP @ RPM	Maximum Torque, Ft. Lbs. @ RPM	Normal Oil Pressure, psi	
							Idle	3000 RPM
1998								
2.7L	R	SMPI	3.386 x 3.091	9.7	200 @ 5800	190 @ 4850	5	30–80
3.2L	J	SMPI	3.622 x 3.189	9.5	225 @ 6300	225 @ 3800	5	30–80
1999								
2.7L	R	SMPI	3.386 x 3.091	9.7	200 @ 5800	190 @ 4850	5	30–80
3.2L	J	SMPI	3.622 x 3.189	9.5	225 @ 6300	225 @ 4000	5	30–80
3.5L	G	SMPI	3.780 x 3.189	9.9	253 @ 6400	255 @ 3950	5	30–80
2000								
2.7L	R	SMPI	3.386 x 3.091	9.7	200 @ 5800	190 @ 4850	5	25–105
3.2L	J	SMPI	3.622 x 3.189	9.5	225 @ 6300	225 @ 3800	5	25–105
3.5L	G	SMPI	3.780 x 3.189	9.9	253 @ 6400	255 @ 3950	5	25–105
2001								
2.7L	R/U	SMPI	3.386 x 3.091	9.7	200 @ 5800	190 @ 4850	5	45–105
3.2L	J	SMPI	3.622 x 3.189	9.5	222 @ 6400	222 @ 3950	5	45–105
3.5L	G/V	SMPI	3.780 x 3.189	9.9	250 @ 6400	250 @ 3900	5	45–105
2002								
2.7L	R	SMPI	3.386 x 3.091	9.7	200 @ 5800	190 @ 4850	5	45–105
3.5L	G/V	SMPI	3.780 x 3.189	9.9	250 @ 6400	250 @ 3900	5	45–105

SMPI: Sequential Multi-Port Fuel Injection.

① — Eighth digit of VIN denotes engine code.

TUNE UP SPECIFICATIONS

Engine	Spark Plug Gap, Inch	Firing Order Fig.④	Ignition Timing		Idle Speed, RPM	Fuel Pump Pressure, psi⑥	Valve Clearance, Inch
			°BTDC	Mark			
1998							
2.7L	.048–.058	B	②	⑤	350–700⑦	49	③
3.2L	.048–.053	B	②	⑤	350–700⑦	49	③
1999							
2.7L	.048–.058	B	②	⑤	350–700⑦	49	③
3.2L	.048–.053	B	②	⑤	350–700⑦	49	③
3.5L	.048–.053	B	②	⑤	350–700⑦	49	③
2000							
2.7L	.048–.058	B	②	⑤	350–700⑦	49	③
3.2L	.048–.053	B	②	⑤	350–700⑦	49	③
3.5L	.048–.053	B	②	⑤	350–700⑦	49	③
2001							
2.7L	.048–.058	B	②	⑤	①	58	③
3.2L	.048–.053	B	②	⑤	①	58	③

Continued

TUNE UP SPECIFICATIONS—Continued

Engine	Spark Plug Gap, Inch	Firing Order Fig.④	Ignition Timing		Idle Speed, RPM	Fuel Pump Pressure, psi⑥	Valve Clearance, Inch
			°BTDC	Mark			
2001							
3.5L	.048–.053	B	②	⑤	①	58	③
2002							
2.7L	.048–.058	B	②	⑤	①	58	③
3.5L	.048–.053	B	②	⑤	①	58	③

BTDC — Before Top Dead Center

N — Neutral

① — Controlled by PCM.

② — Direct (Distributorless) Ignition System (DIS); not adjustable.

③ — Equipped w/hydraulic lash adjusters, no adjustment is necessary.

④ — Before disconnecting wires from coil unit, determine location of No. 1 wire, as position may have been altered from that shown in Fig. A.

⑤ — Equipped w/crankshaft position sensor.

⑥ — Remove cover from service valve on fuel rail. Connect suitable fuel pressure test gauge to service valve. With ignition switch in Run position, use Diagnostic Read-Out Box to activate fuel pump & pressurize system.

⑦ — Minimum air flow idle RPM.

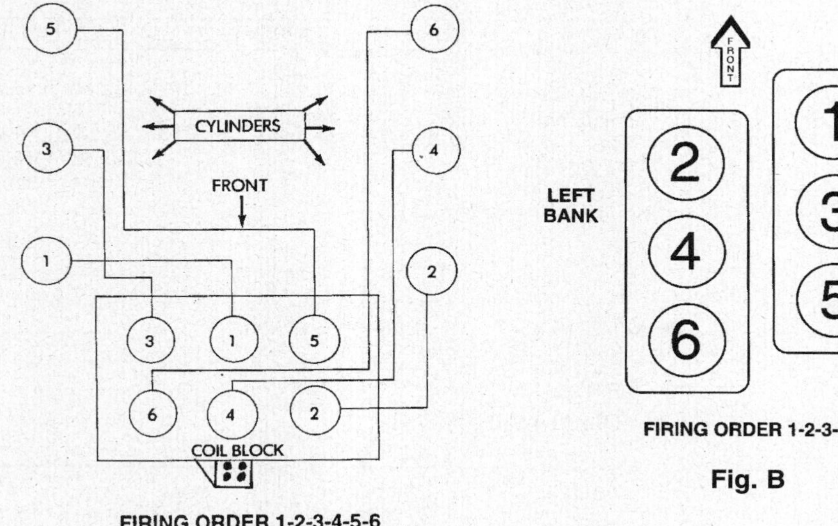

Fig. A

Fig. B

FRONT WHEEL ALIGNMENT SPECIFICATIONS

Year	Camber Angle, Degrees①		Caster Angle, Degrees①		Toe In, Degrees		Ball Joint Wear
	Limits	Desired	Limits	Desired	Limits	Desired	
1998–99	–.6 to +.6②	0	+2 to +4③	+3	+.3 to -.1	+.1	④
2000–02	–.6 to +.6②	0	+2 to +4③	+3	+.2 to -.2	0	④

① — Reference angle only; not adjustable.

② — Side to side differential not to exceed .7.°

③ — Side to side differential not to exceed 1.°

④ — Refer to "Ball Joint Inspection" in "Front Suspension & Steering."

REAR WHEEL ALIGNMENT SPECIFICATIONS

Year	Camber Angle, Degrees①		Toe In, Degrees		Thrust Angle①
	Limits	Desired	Limits	Desired	
1998	–.6 to +.4	–.1	-.2 to +.4	+.1	–.15 to +.15
1999–2002	–.7 to +.3	–.2	-.2 to +.4	+.1	–.15 to +.15

① — Reference angle only; not adjustable.

VEHICLE RIDE HEIGHT SPECIFICATIONS

Model	Year	Body Style	Manufacturer's Original Tire Size	Measurement Points & Specifications					
				Front			Rear		
				Dim.	Specification①		Dim.	Specification①	
					Inches	mm		Inches	mm
Concorde	1998–2002	All	②	A	29.09	739	B	29.68	754
Intrepid	1998–2002	All	②	A	28.70	729	B	28.93	735
LHS	1998–2002	All	②	A	29.09	739	B	29.68	754
300M	1998–2002	All	②	A	29.09	739	B	29.68	754

A Dim. — Ground to Lower Edge of Front Wheel Well
B Dim. — Ground to Lower Edge of Rear Wheel Well
① — ± 0.79 Inches (20 mm).
② — See door sticker or inside of glove box for manufacturers original tire size specifications. If tires on vehicle do not match manufacturers original tire size & measurement is not within limits, it will be necessary to refer to the "Non-Standard Tire & Wheel Size Adjustment To Ride Height Specification & Tire Size Adjustment Charts" in the front of this manual for approximate changes in ride height specifications..

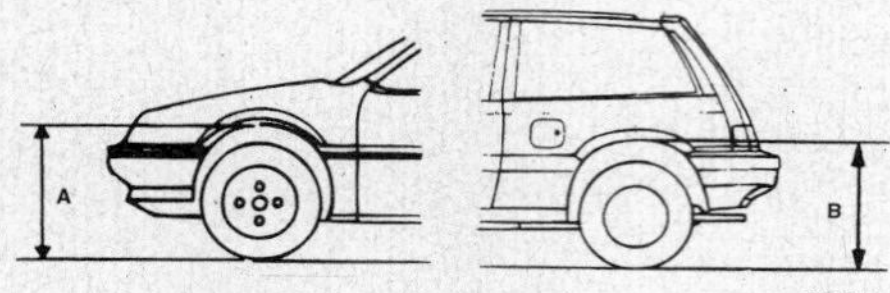

Dimensions A & B

FLUID CAPACITIES & COOLING SYSTEM DATA

Engine	Coolant Capacity, Qts.	Recom-mended Engine Coolant Type	Radiator Cap Relief Pressure, Lbs.③	Thermo-stat. Opening Temp., °F	Fuel Tank, Gals.	Engine Oil Refill, Qts.①	Transaxle Oil, Qts.②	Differential Oil, Qts.
1998–99								
2.7L	11	Ethylene Glycol	18	215–220	17	5.0	9.9	1.0
3.2L	12	Ethylene Glycol	18	215–220	17	5.0	9.9	1.0
3.5L	12	Ethylene Glycol	18	215–220	17	5.5	9.9	1.0
2000								
2.7L	9.4	Ethylene Glycol	18	203–220	18	5.0	9.9	1.0
3.2L	9.4	Ethylene Glycol	18	203–220	18	5.0	9.9	1.0
3.5L	9.4	Ethylene Glycol	18	203–220	18	5.0	9.9	1.0
2001								
2.7L	9.4	Ethylene Glycol	16	203–220	18	5.0	9.3	.78
3.2L	9.4	Ethylene Glycol	16	203–220	18	5.0	9.3	.78
3.5L	9.4	Ethylene Glycol	16	203–220	18	5.0	9.3	.78
2002								
2.7L	9.4	Ethylene Glycol	16	203–220	17	5.0	9.3	.78
3.5L	9.4	Ethylene Glycol	16	203–220	17	5.0	9.3	.78

① — Includes oil filter.

② — Approximate; make final check w/dipstick. Includes torque converter sump.

③ — ± 2 psi.

LUBRICANT DATA

Year	Lubricant Type			
	Transaxle	Differential	Power Steering	Brake System
1998–01	Mopar ATF 3 Type 9933①	Mopar 75W-90 Hypoid Gear Lubricant	Mopar P/N 4318055	DOT 3
2001–02	Mopar ATF+ 4 Type 9602 ②	Mopar 75W-90 Hypoid Gear Lubricant	Mopar P/N 5013457AA	DOT 3

① — Built before June 05–2001.

② — Built after June 05–2001.

Electrical

NOTE: On Air Bag Equipped Models, Refer To "Air Bag System Precautions" Located In The Front Of This Manual For System Disarming & Arming Procedures.

NOTE: Refer To "Computer Relearn Procedures" Located In The Front Of This Manual When Battery Power To The Computer Has Been Interrupted.

NOTE: Prior To Performing Any Service Operations Listed In This Section, Consult The "Technical Service Bulletins" Section For Related Information.

INDEX

PRECAUTIONS

AIR BAG SYSTEMS

Refer to "Air Bag System Precautions" in the front of this manual for system disarming and arming procedures.

BATTERY GROUND CABLE

Prior to service, disconnect battery ground cable and isolate as required.

FUSE PANEL & FLASHER LOCATION

The fuse panel/junction block is located under the lefthand side of the instrument panel. The hazard flasher unit is located under the lefthand side of the instrument panel between the junction block and the brake pedal.

FUEL PUMP RELAY LOCATION

The fuel pump relay is located in the power distribution center. The power distribution center is located in the engine compartment in front coolant reservoir bottle.

STARTER

REPLACE

1998-2000

2.7L Engine

1. Raise and support vehicle.
2. Remove catalyst support bracket mounting nuts, then battery feed and posi-lock wiring harness connectors.
3. Remove starter heat shield mounting bolts and nuts, then starter mounting bolts.
4. Remove starter from transaxle housing, then rotate starter solenoid toward engine and slide starter motor rear between catalyst and engine mount.
5. Reverse procedure install. **Torque** starter mounting bolts to 40 ft. lbs. and solenoid battery nut to 90 inch lbs.

3.2L & 3.5L Engines

1. Raise and support vehicle.
2. Remove catalyst support bracket mounting nuts, then battery feed wire.
3. Remove starter mounting bolts.
4. Remove starter solenoid from transaxle housing, then position starter to access posi-lock wiring connector.
5. Using suitable jack stand beneath engine, slightly lift engine to relieve lefthand engine mount pressure.
6. Remove lefthand engine mount mounting bolts.
7. Using suitable jack, raise engine slightly for starter maneuver room.
8. Slide starter motor rear between catalyst and engine mount, disconnect posi-lock starter solenoid connector and remove starter.
9. Reverse procedure install. **Torque** starter mounting bolts to 40 ft. lbs. and solenoid battery nut to 90 inch lbs.

2001-02

1. Raise and support vehicle.
2. Remove bolts mounting starter to transaxle.
3. Remove battery feed wire from starter.
4. Remove starter solenoid assembly from transaxle housing, then position starter to access Connector Positive Assurance (CPA) wiring connector.
5. Using suitable jack stand beneath engine, slightly lift engine to relieve lefthand engine mount pressure.
6. Remove lefthand engine mount mounting bolts.
7. Using suitable jack, raise engine slightly to allow for clearance for starter removal.
8. Slide starter motor out between catalyst and engine mount, disconnect posi-lock starter solenoid connector and remove starter.

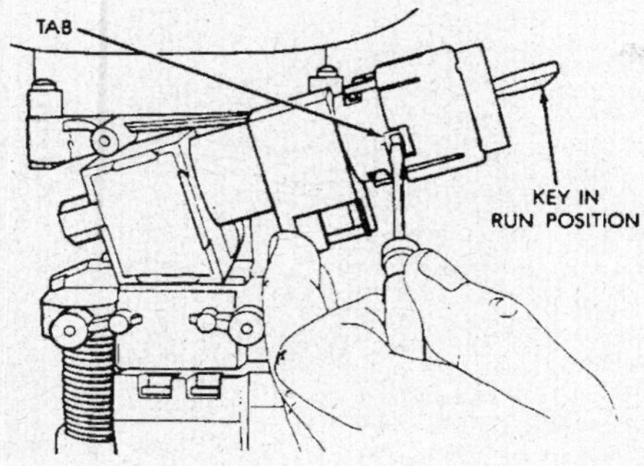

Fig. 1 Lock cylinder replacement

9. Reverse procedure install. **Torque** starter mounting bolts to 40 ft. lbs. and solenoid battery nut to 90 inch lbs.

COIL PACK

REPLACE

These engines are equipped with a coil on plug ignition system. Each cylinder has a dedicated coil sitting atop each plug. No secondary wires are required and connection from the coil to plug is made with a boot that is attached to the coil.

1. Clean area around coil and spark plug with compressed air spray.
2. Remove electrical connector from ignition coil.
3. **On models equipped with 3.2L and 3.5L engines,** alternately loosen screws back and forth. **Do not lose spacers under coil.**
4. **On all models,** remove fasteners and ignition coil.
5. Reverse procedure to install, noting following:
   a. **On models equipped with 2.7L engines, torque** mounting screws to 55 inch lbs.
   b. **On models equipped with 3.2L and 3.5L engines, torque** mounting screws to 60 inch lbs.

IGNITION LOCK

REPLACE

CYLINDER

1. Remove tilt lever.
2. Remove upper and lower column covers.
3. Turn ignition key to Run position, then depress lock cylinder mounting tab and slide cylinder out of housing as shown in **Fig. 1.**
4. Reverse procedure to install.

HOUSING

1. Remove upper and lower column covers.
2. Remove tilt lever.
3. Remove ignition switch as outlined under "Ignition Switch, Replace."
4. Center punch tamper proof screws as shown in **Fig. 2.**
5. Using a ¼ inch drill bit, drill out screw heads.
6. Remove lock cylinder housing from steering column.

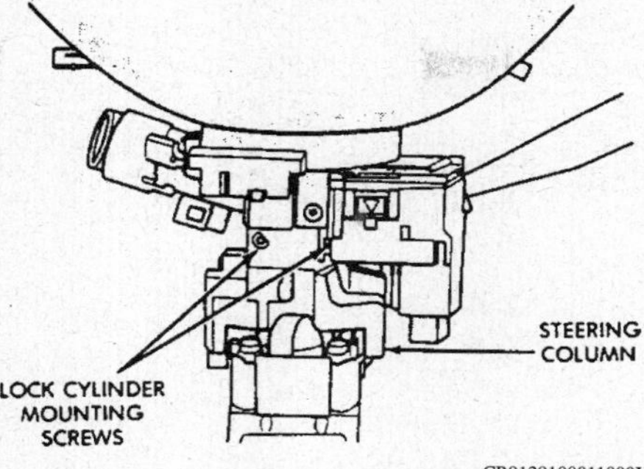

Fig. 2 Lock cylinder housing replacement

7. Use suitable pliers to remove bolts from steering column.
8. Reverse procedure to install. Tighten new tamper proof screws until heads twist off.

IGNITION SWITCH

REPLACE

1. Remove tilt lever, then upper and lower column covers.
2. Remove Sentry Key Immobilizer Module (SKIM), if equipped.
3. Remove multi-function switch.
4. Disconnect electrical connector from ignition switch.
5. Remove ignition switch mounting screws and ignition switch as shown in **Fig. 3.**
6. Reverse procedure to install. Align tab on ignition switch with slot on lock housing.

HEADLAMP SWITCH

REPLACE

1. Open front door and remove lefthand end cover.
2. Remove screw from lefthand end of instrument panel and pull headlight bezel rearward to disengage clips.
3. Remove headlight switch screws and pull switch out to disconnect electrical connectors.
4. Remove headlight switch.
5. Reverse procedure to install.

STOP LIGHT SWITCH

REPLACE

REMOVAL

1. Press and hold brake pedal.
2. Rotate switch 30° counterclockwise, pull rearward and remove from bracket.
3. Disconnect wiring harness connector.

INSTALLATION

1. Hold stop lamp switch firmly in one hand, then using other hand, pull plunger outward until it ratchets to its fully extended position.
2. Connect wiring harness connector.
3. Press brake pedal as far down as possible, then install switch in bracket by aligning switch index key with mounting bracket square hole slot.
4. When fully installed, rotate switch 30° clockwise to lock.
5. Gently pull brake pedal back until pedal stops moving and switch plunger ratchets to correct position.

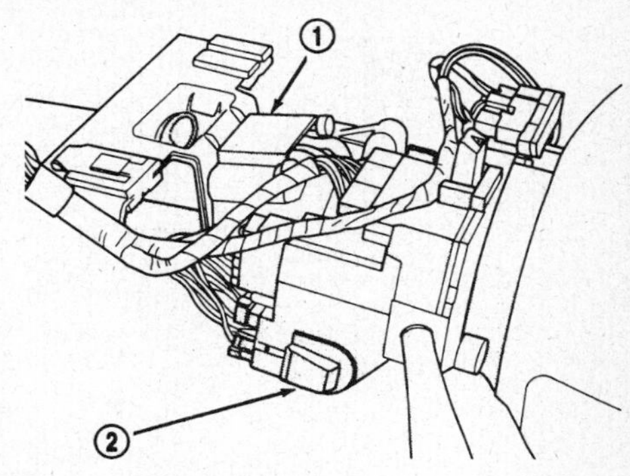

Fig. 3 Ignition switch replacement

MULTI-FUNCTION SWITCH

REPLACE

1. Remove tilt lever, then upper and lower steering column covers.
2. Remove multi-function switch to column mounting screws.
3. Disconnect multi-function switch electrical connections.
4. Reverse procedure to install. **Torque** multi-function switch to column screws to 17 inch lbs.

TURN SIGNAL SWITCH

REPLACE

Refer to "Multi-Function Switch, Replace" for turn signal switch replacement.

DIMMER SWITCH

REPLACE

Refer to "Multi-Function Switch, Replace" for dimmer switch replacement.

STEERING WHEEL

REPLACE

REMOVAL

1. Lock steering column by turning steering wheel ½ turn (180°) clockwise from straight ahead position.
2. Place ignition in Off/Lock position and remove ignition key. This will ensure no damage occurs to clockspring.
3. Remove drivers air bag as outlined in "Passive Restraint Systems."
4. Remove steering wheel mounting nut from steering column shaft.
5. Remove steering wheel using steering wheel puller tool No. C-3428B, or equivalent.

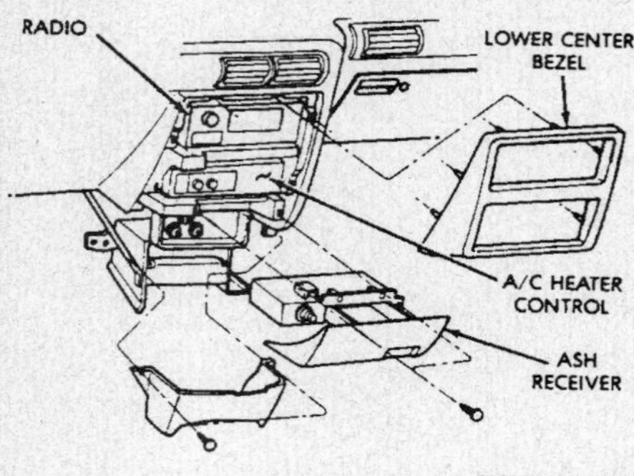

Fig. 4 Radio replacement

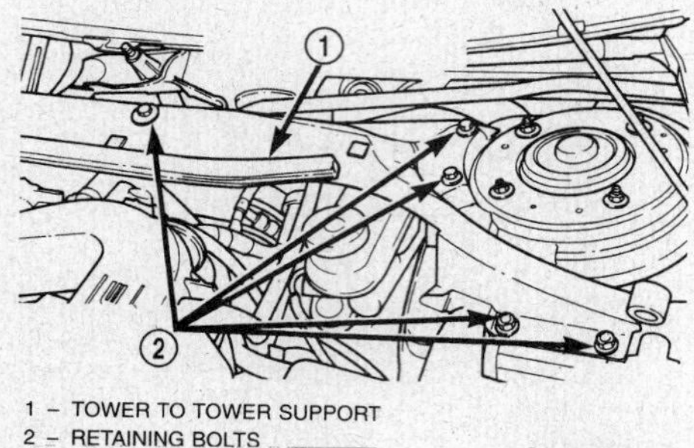

Fig. 5 Tower to tower support removal

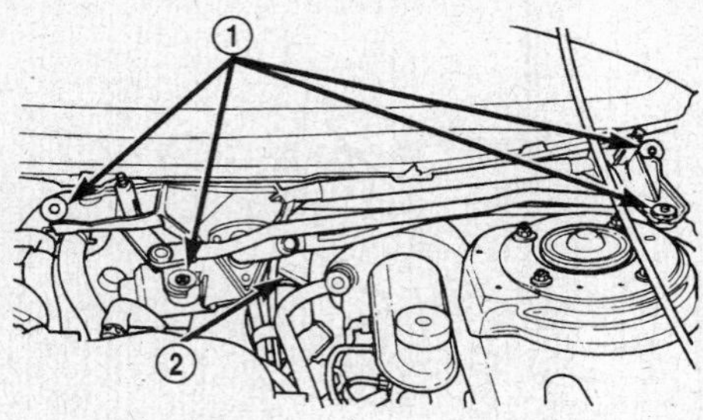

Fig. 6 Wiper module retaining bolt removal

INSTALLATION

1. Confirm that steering wheel position is a half turn (180°) to right.
2. Lock column into position with ignition cylinder lock.
3. Ensure turn signal stalk is in neutral, then pull all wires through larger opening of hub area on wheel.
4. Install steering wheel ensuring flats on hub align with clockspring.
5. Install steering wheel mounting nut and tighten nut to draw steering wheel onto column. **Torque** steering column shaft nut to 45 ft. lbs.
6. Connect wiring harness on air bag module.
7. Install drivers air bag module into steering wheel as outlined in "Passive Restraint Systems."

INSTRUMENT CLUSTER

REPLACE

1. Remove instrument panel lefthand end cap.
2. Remove steering column shroud cover, then tilt steering wheel down.
3. **On LHS and 300M models,** remove one screw from cluster bezel.
4. **On all models,** remove all items to expose bezel mounting screws.
5. Remove two screws over upper cluster bezel in instrument panel brow and all remaining screws.
6. Remove instrument panel cluster bezel using a trim stick tool No. C-4755 or equivalent.
7. Remove instrument cluster screws and disengage upper latch.
8. Remove instrument cluster from panel. **Instrument panel wiring harness connectors are mounted directly to rear panel. A force of approximately 20–30 lbs. will be required to disengage cluster from connectors.**
9. Reverse procedure to install.

RADIO

REPLACE

1. Remove lower center bezel, radio mounting screws, then remove radio as shown in **Fig. 4.**
2. Pull radio straight out and disconnect electrical and antenna connections.
3. Remove radio ground strap, then radio.

4. Reverse procedure to install.

WIPER MOTOR

REPLACE

1. Remove wiper arms.
2. Remove cowl screen panel.
3. Remove wiper module mounting bolt from top of tower to tower beam.
4. Remove bolts to tower to tower support as shown in **Fig. 5.**
5. Remove retaining bolts to wiper module as shown in **Fig. 6.**
6. Remove wiper module, disconnect electrical connector.
7. Disconnect wiper module master link from motor crank with ball and socket wedge. Do not damage ball, socket or seal when removing.
8. Remove nut to crank arm as shown in **Fig. 7.**
9. Remove wiper motor from wiper module.
10. Reverse procedure to install.

WIPER SWITCH

REPLACE

Refer to "Multi-Function Switch, Replace" for wiper switch replacement.

BLOWER MOTOR

REPLACE

1. Remove lower righthand under panel duct.
2. Disconnect blower motor connector from resistor block/power module.
3. Squeeze blower motor wiring grommet, push grommet through blower motor housing cover.
4. Remove blower motor housing cover.
5. Remove blower motor mounting screws, lower blower motor from housing.
6. Reverse procedure to install.

HEATER CORE

REPLACE

1. Remove heater and A/C housing as outlined under "Evaporator Case, Replace."
2. Pull back heater core mounting clips, then pull heater core out of housing.
3. Install new heater core.
4. Place mounting brackets over heater core and fasten with screws provided with new heater core as shown in **Fig. 8.**
5. Install heater housing into vehicle as outlined under "Evaporator Case, Replace."

EVAPORATOR CASE

REPLACE

1. Remove instrument panel as outlined under "Dash Panel Service."
2. Recover refrigerant as outlined under "Air Conditioning."
3. Drain engine coolant into suitable container.
4. Remove air cleaner hose and distribution duct from engine.
5. Remove fasteners from heater hoses at dash panel and remove hoses from heater core.
6. Plug heater core inlet and outlet tubes to block coolant from entering interior.
7. Remove one nut at expansion valve retaining both A/C lines to expansion valve.
8. Cap expansion valve and A/C openings.
9. Remove three retaining nuts from studs from dash panel into engine compartment.
10. Remove two screws from defrost duct and remove duct.
11. Remove two nuts, two screws attaching housing to dash panel.
12. Remove four nuts retaining rear seat heat duct and remove duct.
13. Remove rear seat heat duct elbow push pin fastener.
14. Disconnect harness connector.
15. Gently pull unit housing rearward from dash panel.
16. Reverse procedures to install.

EVAPORATOR CORE

REPLACE

1. Remove heater and A/C housing as outlined under "Evaporator Case, Replace."
2. Remove recirculation door actuator.
3. Remove recirculation door and housing.
4. Remove upper housing mounting screws, then upper half of heater housing.
5. Lift evaporator out of lower housing.

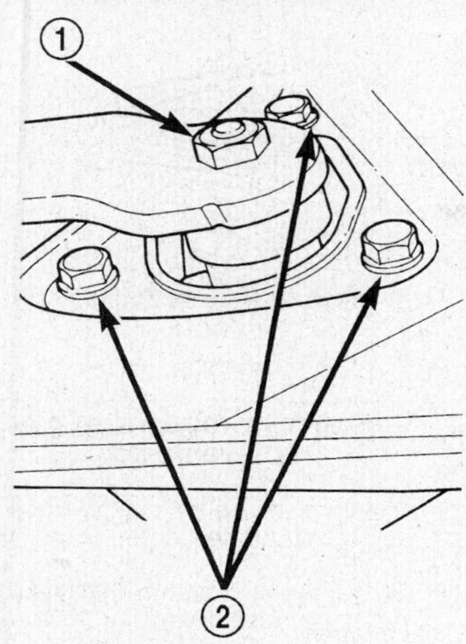

Fig. 7 Wiper motor crank and retaining bolts

6. Transfer expansion valve onto new evaporator using new gaskets.
7. Reverse procedure to install.

TECHNICAL SERVICE BULLETINS

POOR HEATER PERFORMANCE

1998

2.7L Engine

On these models, heater performance may be poor.

This condition may be caused by heater outlet duct location or the engine thermostat. To correct this condition, proceed as follows:

1. Inspect and correct engine coolant level.
2. Ensure lefthand heater outlet duct faces down toward foot area. Remove and orient as necessary.
3. Fully warm engine at 1500–2000 RPM for 15–20 minutes.
4. Using suitable scan tool, ensure coolant temperature is above 180°F.
5. If coolant temperature is not above 180°F, remove thermostat.
6. Replace thermostat that is propped or stuck open.
7. If coolant temperature is above 180°F, but heater performance is still poor, conduct HVAC diagnosis as outlined in **MOTOR's "Air Conditioner & Heater Manual."**

3.2L Engine

On these models, heater performance may be poor.

This condition may be caused by heater outlet duct location, core sand contamination or the engine thermostat. To correct this condition, proceed as follows:

1. Inspect and correct engine coolant level.
2. Ensure lefthand heater outlet duct faces down toward foot area. Remove and orient as necessary.
3. Fully warm engine at 1500–2000 RPM for 15–20 minutes.
4. Using suitable scan tool, ensure coolant temperature is above 180°F.
5. If coolant temperature is above 180°F, but heater performance is still poor, conduct HVAC diagnosis as outlined in **MOTOR's "Air Conditioner & Heater Manual."**
6. Shine suitable flashlight into plastic coolant hot bottle next to filler cap and view bottle bottom with adjustable mirror.
7. If there is a dark shadow larger than a quarter, there may be excessive core sand accumulation. Proceed to next step. If core sand accumulation is not excessive (all vehicles may show core sand accumulation), proceed as follows:
   a. If coolant temperature is not above 180°F, remove thermostat.
   b. Replace thermostat that is propped or stuck open.
8. At 65 mph shift transmission to low or 2nd gear and drive approximately ½ mile between 4500–6500 RPM. Engine temperature should drop. **This test is best performed at low ambient temperatures.**
9. Shift transmission into overdrive and maintain 65 mph for at least three miles.
10. If coolant temperature does not return 180°F, but continues to drop, thermostat has been held open by core sand. Proceed as follows:
    a. Replace thermostat.
    b. Flush cooling system.
    c. Clean coolant hot bottle.
11. If coolant temperature does return to 180°F, repeat 65 mph procedure three times.

FLAG SPEAKER BUZZ

1998

Infinity Audio System

On these models, a buzz noise may come from door flag speaker, most noticeably with deep male voices on talk radio.

This condition may be caused by flag speaker seal/gasket. To correct this condition, install revised front door flag speaker seal/gasket P/N 05014669AA.

COURTESY LAMPS FLICKER

1999

On these models built between July 20,

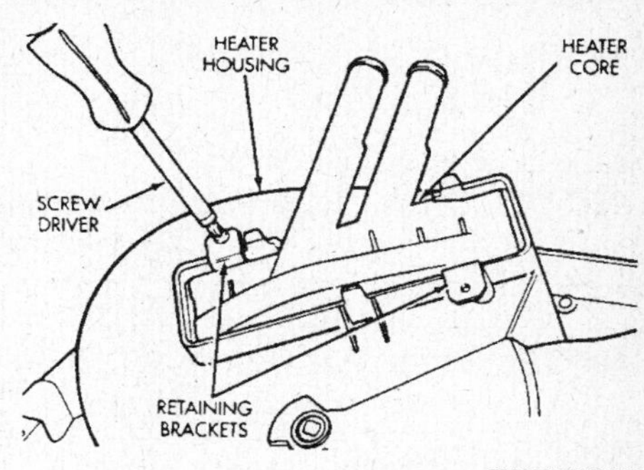

Fig. 8 Heater core replacement

1998 and October 23, 1998, the headliner mounted courtesy lamps may intermittently flicker when they would normally be "ON."

This condition may be caused by faulty wiring from the M-1 circuit and C-11 connector. To correct this condition proceed as follows:

1. Disconnect negative battery cable remote terminal.
2. Remove C-11 connector from fuse panel.
3. Lift locking wedge tab up 2 mm, remove pink M-1 circuit from connector using tool No. 6680–2, or equivalent.
4. Cut off existing terminal at base of terminal.
5. Strip off insulation from wire to expose ⅛ inch copper.
6. Carefully attach terminal P/N 56019990 into wire using Crimping tool No. PWC46, or equivalent.
7. Install pink M-1 wire/terminal into connector, reset locking wedge.
8. Install C-11 connector and verify lamp operation.

AM/FM RADIO RECEPTION

1998-99

AM/FM reception performance can be poor. These conditions can be caused by car phone antennas and rear window glass tint.

Car phone antennas mounted on the rear window glass, particularly at the top of the glass where AM grid resides. The grid design varies between models, but all provide adequate mounting area near the top of the glass to mount a car phone antenna base to the glass. Care must be exercised to avoid the car phone antenna mounting base from coming into contact with any of the antenna grid lines.

Conductive window tint film containing titanium applied to the rear window glass has the effect of grounding the AM antenna and altering the FM antenna signal. Customers who wish to have rear window glass film, should use only non-conductive tint film.

2.7L Engine

NOTE: On Air Bag Equipped Models, Refer To "Air Bag System Precautions" Located In The Front Of This Manual For System Disarming & Arming Procedures.

NOTE: Refer To "Computer Relearn Procedures" Located In The Front Of This Manual When Battery Power To The Computer Has Been Interrupted.

NOTE: Prior To Performing Any Service Operations Listed In This Section, Consult The "Technical Service Bulletins" Section For Related Information.

INDEX

PRECAUTIONS

AIR BAG SYSTEMS

Refer to "Air Bag System Precautions" in the front of this manual for system disarming and arming procedures.

BATTERY GROUND CABLE

Prior to service, disconnect battery ground cable and isolate as required.

FUEL SYSTEM PRESSURE RELIEF

1. Remove fuel pump relay for power distribution center.
2. Start and run engine until it stalls.
3. Attempt to start engine until it no longer runs.
4. Turn ignition switch to Off position.
5. Place rag or towel under fuel line quick-connector fitting at fuel rail.
6. Install fuel pump relay.
7. One or more Diagnostic Trouble Codes (DTCs) may have been stored because of removing fuel pump relay. Clear these DTCs with suitably programmed scan tool.

COMPRESSION PRESSURE

The minimum compression pressure should be no less than 100 psi and the maximum variation between cylinders should be no more than 25%.

ENGINE MOUNT

REPLACE

LEFTHAND & RIGHTHAND

1. Raise and support vehicle.
2. Remove isolator mounting nuts from top of mounting bracket.
3. Support engine with suitable jack and wood block across full width of oil pan.
4. Remove lower mounting nuts from frame.
5. Raise engine carefully, then remove isolator with heat shield.
6. Reverse procedure to install.

REAR

1. Raise and support vehicle.
2. Support transaxle with suitable jack.
3. Remove mounting nuts, then the crossmember bolts and mount.
4. Reverse procedure to install.

STRUCTURAL COLLAR

REPLACE

1. Raise and support vehicle.
2. Remove mounting bolts, then the structural collar from oil pan and transaxle housing.
3. Reverse procedure to install. Bolts must be installed and tightened in following sequence:
   a. Install vertical collar oil pan bolts and **torque** to10 inch lbs.
   b. Install collar to transaxle bolts and **torque** to 40 ft. lbs.

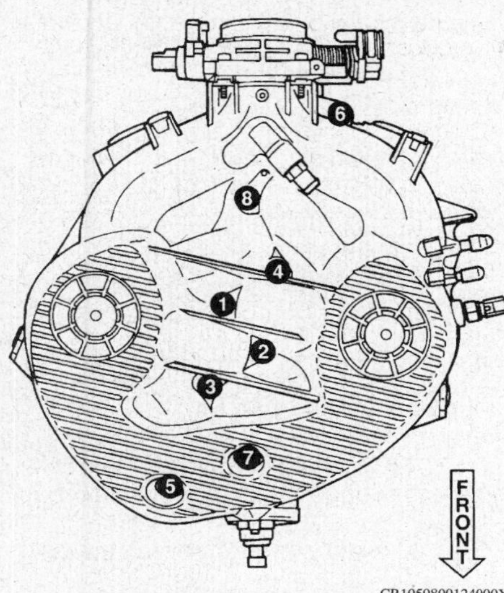

Fig. 1 Upper intake manifold tightening sequence

c. Starting with center vertical bolt and working outward, **torque** mounting bolts to 40 ft. lbs.

ENGINE

REPLACE

1. Relieve fuel pressure as described under "Precautions."
2. Mark hood position at hinges and remove, then drain cooling system into suitable container.
3. Remove wiper arms, right and lefthand cowl screens (covers), then cowl support as outlined under "Wiper Motor, Replace."
4. Remove air cleaner assembly and air inlet hose, then upper radiator crossmember.
5. Disconnect hood release cable from latch, then remove cooling fan module.
6. Disconnect upper radiator hose from engine and lower hose from radiator, then transaxle cooler lines from radiator.
7. Remove A/C condenser to radiator fasteners, then transaxle cooler lines support bracket and mounting screw on radiator lefthand side.
8. Remove radiator, then accessory drive belts.
9. Remove mounting bolts and set power steering pump aside.
10. Disconnect electrical connector, remove mounting bolts and set A/C compressor aside.
11. Remove exhaust manifold V-band clamps, then disconnect throttle and speed control cables.
12. Disconnect coolant pressure bottle hoses, then heater hoses.
13. Disconnect fuel line, then vacuum lines, electrical connectors and engine ground straps.
14. Raise and support vehicle, then drain engine oil into suitable container.
15. Remove catalytic converter down pipe front and rear fasteners.
16. Remove mounting bolts and structural collar.
17. Mark flexplate to torque converter position and remove converter mounting bolts.
18. Disconnect transaxle cooler line brackets from engine, then remove starter.
19. Remove crankshaft position sensor and lower transaxle to block bolts.
20. Lower vehicle, then remove fuel line and electrical harness throttle body mounting screws.
21. Remove electrical harness attaching bracket and transaxle shift cable attaching bracket.
22. Remove throttle body support bracket fasteners from transaxle to block double-ended bolts.
23. Remove upper transaxle to block bolts, then right and lefthand engine mount isolator to engine mount bracket mounting fasteners.
24. Remove cam sensor from lefthand cylinder head.
25. Attach suitable lifting device to engine, support transaxle with suitable floor jack, and remove engine.
26. Reverse procedure to install, noting following:
    a. Tighten all fasteners to specifications.
    b. Do not tighten transaxle case to engine block bolts until all bolts have been started and mating surface are completely joined.

INTAKE MANIFOLD

REPLACE

UPPER

1. Remove air inlet resonator and inlet tube.
2. Remove throttle and speed control cables from throttle arm and bracket, then bracket.
3. Disconnect Manifold Absolute Pressure (MAP), Intake Air Temperature (IAT), Throttle Position (TPS) sensors, Manifold Tune Valve (MTV) and Idle Air Control (IAC) motor electrical connectors.
4. Disconnect vapor purge, brake booster, speed control servo and Positive Crankcase Ventilation (PCV) hoses.
5. Remove Exhaust Gas Recirculation (EGR) tube.
6. Loosen throttle body support bracket upper fastener, then support brackets upper fasteners at right and lefthand sides of upper manifold.
7. Apply upward pressure to release retaining clip and remove engine name cover.
8. Remove mounting bolts and upper manifold.
9. Reverse procedure to install, noting following:
    a. Ensure fuel injectors and wiring harnesses are positioned to not interfere with installation.
    b. Tighten manifold to specifications using sequence as shown in **Fig. 1.**
    c. Tighten throttle body support bracket fasteners to specifications.

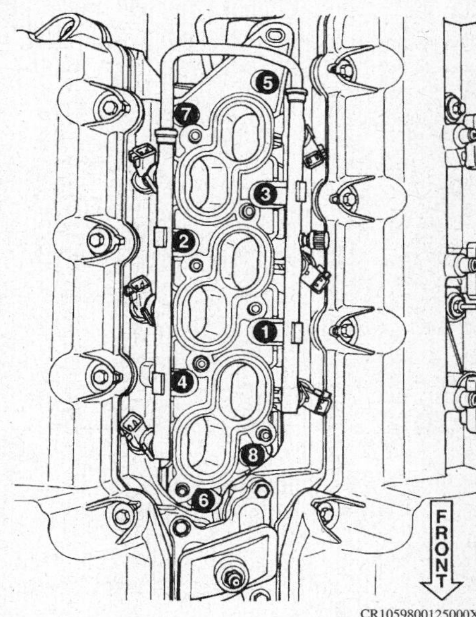

Fig. 2 Lower intake manifold tightening sequence

LOWER

1. Relieve fuel pressure as described under "Precautions."
2. Remove upper intake manifold as outlined under "Intake Manifold, Replace."
3. Remove fuel rail fuel supply hose, then screw mounting fuel rail support bracket to throttle body support bracket.
4. Remove mounting bolts, then fuel rail and injectors as an assembly.
5. Remove mounting bolts and lower intake manifold.
6. Reverse procedure to install, noting following:
    a. To properly position manifold, install bolt 2–3 turns in rearmost attaching hole.
    b. Tighten mounting bolts to specifications using sequence shown in **Fig. 2.**
    c. Ensure fuel injectors are located in correct positions.

EXHAUST MANIFOLD

REPLACE

RIGHTHAND

1. Remove air intake plenum and air filter housing.
2. Remove battery cable housing tube to transmission housing mounting bolt.
3. Remove EGR tube to exhaust manifold and EGR valve mounting bolts.
4. Disconnect electrical connector, then remove exhaust manifold oxygen sensor.
5. Remove manifold to catalytic converter V-band clamp.
6. Remove mounting screws and heat shields.
7. Remove mounting bolts and exhaust manifold.
8. Reverse procedure to install, noting following:

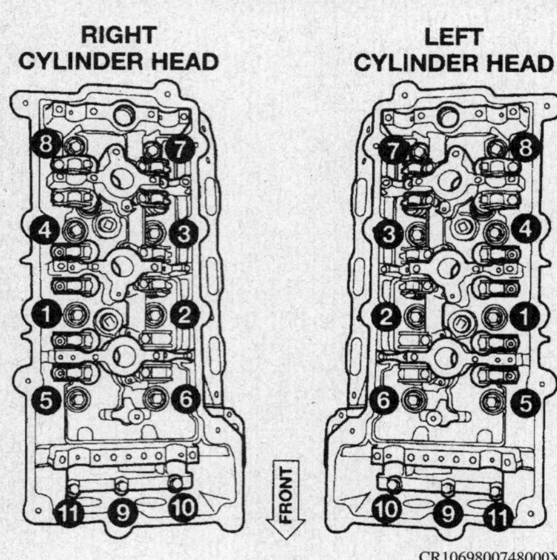

Fig. 3 Cylinder head bolt tightening sequence

a. Tighten exhaust manifold mounting bolts to specifications from center outwards.
b. Tighten heat shield mounting screws to specifications.
c. Use new V-band clamp and tighten to specifications.
d. Use new gasket and tighten EGR tube mounting screws to specifications.

LEFTHAND

1. Raise and support vehicle.
2. Remove exhaust system, then lefthand catalytic converter.
3. Remove transmission dipstick tube mounting bolt, then rotate housing away from engine.
4. Lower vehicle.
5. Disconnect electrical connectors and remove harness mounting screws from support bracket, then engine wiring harness support bracket from cylinder head.
6. Disconnect connector and remove exhaust manifold oxygen sensor.
7. Remove engine oil dipstick tube.
8. Remove mounting screws and heat shield.
9. Remove mounting bolts and exhaust manifold.
10. Reverse procedure to install, noting following:
    a. Tighten exhaust manifold mounting bolts to specifications from center working outward.
    b. Tighten heat shield mounting screws to specifications.
    c. Install new engine oil dipstick O-ring.
    d. Use new V-band clamp and tighten to specifications.

CYLINDER HEAD

REPLACE

1. Relieve fuel pressure as described under "Precautions."
2. Drain cooling system into suitable container and remove accessory drive belts.
3. Remove crankshaft damper as outlined under "Crankshaft Damper, Replace."
4. Remove upper and lower intake manifolds as outlined under "Intake Manifold, Replace."
5. Remove cylinder head cover as outline under "Valve Cover, Replace" and timing chain cover as outlined under "Front Cover, Replace."
6. Remove water outlet connector.
7. Rotate crankshaft until crankshaft sprocket timing mark aligns with oil pump housing timing mark, then remove timing chain.
8. Remove camshafts as described under "Camshaft, Replace."
9. Remove catalytic converter pipe V-band clamps at exhaust manifold.
10. Remove cylinder head mounting bolts in reverse of tightening sequence as shown in **Fig. 3,** then cylinder heads.
11. Reverse procedure to install, noting following:
    a. Because cylinder head bolts are tightened using torque plus angle procedure, bolts with stretched threads must be replaced.
    b. Use new cylinder head gasket.
    c. Ensure head is properly positioned over locating dowels.
    d. Lubricate bolt threads with clean engine oil.
    e. **Torque** cylinder head bolt Nos. 1–8 to 35 ft. lbs. in sequence, **Fig. 3.**
    f. **Torque** bolt Nos. 1–8 to 55 ft. lbs.
    g. Bolts 1–8 to +90° turn. **Do not use torque wrench for this step.**
    h. **Torque** cylinder head bolt Nos. 9–11 to 21 ft. lbs.
    i. Use new V-band clamp and tighten to specifications.

VALVE COVER

REPLACE

1. Remove upper intake manifold as outlined under "Intake Manifold, Replace."
2. Remove ignition coil electrical connectors.
3. Remove righthand cylinder head ground strap, then disconnect electrical and vacuum harness retaining clips from studs.
4. Remove ignition coil capacitor fasteners, then right and lefthand upper intake manifold support brackets.
5. Loosen mounting bolts and remove cylinder head covers. Mounting bolts are captured in cover.
6. Reverse procedure to install, noting following:
    a. Replace gaskets as necessary.
    b. Ensure double-ended studs are in correct locations as shown in **Fig. 4.**
    c. Tighten mounting bolts to specifications.

VALVE ADJUSTMENT

Rocker arms are equipped with hydraulic lash adjusters. No adjustment is necessary.

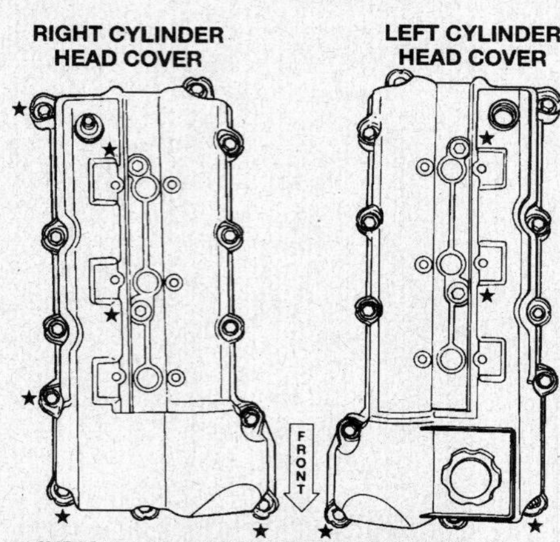

Fig. 4 Valve cover replacement

ROCKER ARMS

REPLACE

REMOVAL

1. Remove valve covers as outlined under "Valve Cover, Replace."
2. Turn crankshaft to rotate engine until cam lobe is on base circle (heel) of rocker arm being removed.
3. Using Valve Spring Compressor tool No. 8215 and Adapter tool No. 8216, or equivalent, depress valve spring only enough to release tension and remove rocker arm.
4. Identify rocker arm position.
5. Repeat procedure for each rocker arm being removed.

INSTALLATION

1. Lubricate rocker arm(s) with clean engine oil.
2. Turn crankshaft to rotate engine until cam lobe is on base circle (heel) of rocker arm being removed.
3. Using Valve Spring Compressor tool No. 8215 and Adapter tool No. 8216, or equivalent, depress valve spring only enough to release tension.
4. Install rocker arm in original position and release valve spring tension.
5. Repeat procedure for each rocker arm to be installed.
6. Install valve cover(s) as outlined under "Valve Cover, Replace."

VALVE SPRINGS

REPLACE

IN-VEHICLE

Ensure piston is at TDC on cylinder from which valve spring(s) is being removed.

1. Relieve fuel pressure as described under "Precautions."
2. Remove air cleaner housing cover and inlet hose.
3. Remove upper intake manifold as outlined under "Intake Manifold, Replace."
4. Remove valve covers as outlined under "Valve Cover, Replace."

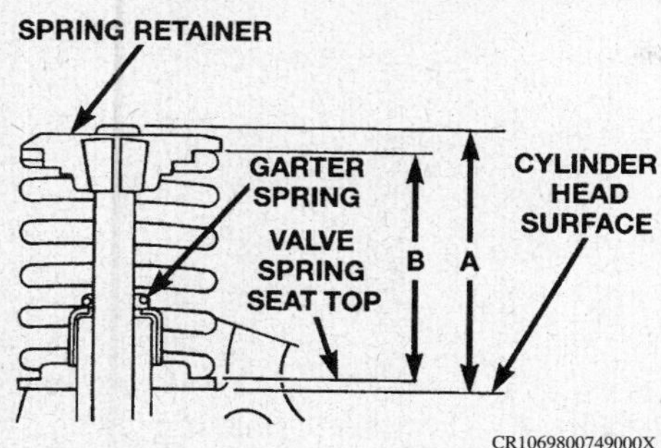

Fig. 5 Valve tip & spring installed heights inspection

5. Remove crankshaft damper as outlined under "Crankshaft Damper, Replace."
6. Remove timing chain as outlined under "Timing Chain, Replace."
7. Remove camshaft(s) as outlined under "Camshaft, Replace."
8. Install suitable spark plug adapter into cylinder being serviced, then apply 90–100 psi air pressure to hold valves in place.
9. Using Valve Spring Compressor tool No. MD-998772A with Adapter tool No. 6779, or equivalent, compress valve spring, then remove valve locks, retainer and spring.
10. Using suitable valve seal tool, remove valve stem seals.
11. Reverse procedure to install, noting following:
    a. Push valve steam seal/seat firmly and squarely over valve guide with stem as guide.
    b. Do not force seal against guide top.
    c. When install retainer locks, compress spring only enough to install locks.

HEAD REMOVED

Removal

1. Using Valve Spring Compressor tool No. C-3422-B, or equivalent, compress valve spring.
2. Remove valve retaining locks, valve spring retainers, valve springs and valve springs seat/stem seal assembly.
3. Identify valves for installation, then remove valve stem lock groove burrs.
4. Remove valves.

Installation

1. Coat with clean engine oil and install valve stems.
2. If valves and/or seats have been ground, proceed as follows:
    a. Measure valve tip height (A) from cylinder head surface to valve stem top as shown in **Fig. 5.**
    b. If intake valve tip height is more than 1.8737 inches, grind tip to specifications.
    c. If exhaust valve tip height is more than 1.9347 inches, grind tip to specifications.
3. Install seal/spring seat assembly over valve guides.
4. Ensure garter spring is intact around rubber seal top, then install valve springs and retainers.
5. Compress valve springs with suitable valve spring compressor, then install locks and release tool.
6. If valves and/or seats have been ground, proceed as follows:
    a. Measure springs installed height (B) from spring seal to spring retainer bottom surface as shown in **Fig. 5.**
    b. If height is more than 1.5256 inches, install .030 inch spacer in head counterbore under valve spring seat.

HYDRAULIC LIFTERS

REPLACE

1. Remove rocker arm as outlined under "Rocker Arm, Replace."
2. Mark position for assembly.
3. Remove hydraulic lash adjuster.
4. Reverse procedure to install, ensure adjuster is at least partially full of oil.

CRANKSHAFT DAMPER

REPLACE

1. Remove upper radiator crossmember, then fan module.
2. Remove accessory and air conditioning belts.
3. Using Crankshaft Damper Holder tool No. 8191, or equivalent, and Three-Jaw Puller tool No. 1023, or equivalent, remove damper.
4. Reverse procedure to install. Tighten center bolt to specifications.

FRONT COVER

REPLACE

1. Remove upper radiator support crossmember, then fan module and accessory drive belts.
2. Remove crankshaft damper as outlined under "Crankshaft Damper, Replace."
3. Remove power steering pump from mounting bracket, then accessory drive belt tensioner pulley and bracket.
4. Remove mounting bolts and timing chain cover.
5. Reverse procedure to install, noting following:
    a. If front crankshaft seal was bench installed, place Crankshaft Seal Protection tool No. 6780-2, or equivalent, over nose.
    b. Apply 1/8 inch bead of suitable silicone rubber adhesive sealant to parting lines between oil pan and cylinder block.
    c. Tighten mounting bolts to specifications.
    d. If front crankshaft seal was not installed, use Crankshaft Seal Installer and Sleeve tool No. 6780-2, or equivalent, to install seal.

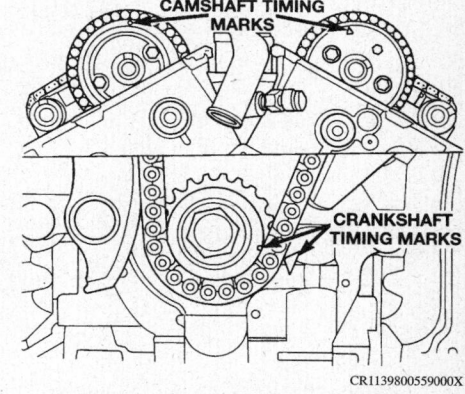

CR1139800559000X

Fig. 6 Timing chain mark alignment

TIMING CHAIN

REPLACE

With the timing chain removed, avoid turning the camshaft or crankshaft. If movement is required, exercise caution to avoid valve damage caused by piston contact.

REMOVAL

1. Remove upper intake manifold as outlined under "Upper Intake Manifold, Replace."
2. Remove valve covers as outlined under "Valve Cover, Replace."
3. Remove crankshaft damper as outlined under "Crankshaft Damper, Replace."
4. Remove front cover as outlined under "Front Cover, Replace."
5. Rotate crankshaft to align crankshaft sprocket timing with oil pump housing marks. Cylinder No. 1 should be at 60° ATDC.
6. Remove primary timing chain tensioner from righthand cylinder head.
7. Remove camshaft position sensor from lefthand cylinder head, then chain guide access plug.
8. Remove righthand camshaft sprocket mounting bolts, then damper and sprocket.
9. Remove mounting bolts and lefthand camshaft sprocket.
10. Remove lower chain guide, then tensioner arm.
11. Remove primary timing chain.

INSTALLATION

1. Align crankshaft sprocket and oil pump housing timing marks as shown in **Fig. 6.**
2. Place lefthand side primary chain sprocket on chain so that timing mark is between two plated links.
3. Lower primary chain with lefthand side sprocket through lefthand cylinder head opening.
4. Loosely position lefthand side camshaft sprocket over camshaft hub.
5. Align plated link to crankshaft sprocket timing mark as shown in **Fig. 7.**
6. Position primary chain onto water pump drive sprocket.

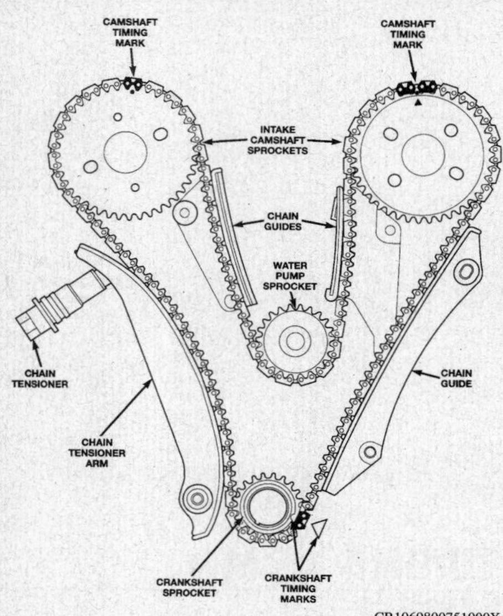

Fig. 7 Primary timing chain alignment marks

7. Align righthand camshaft sprocket timing mark to timing chain plated link and loosely position over camshaft hub.
8. Ensure all plated links are properly aligned to sprockets' timing marks.
9. Install lefthand lower chain guide and tensioner arm, then tighten to specifications.
10. Install chain guide access plug to lefthand cylinder head and tighten to specifications.
11. Remove tensioner from housing and place check ball end into shallow end of Timing Chain Tensioner Resetting Gauge tool No. 8186, or equivalent.
12. Using hand pressure, slowly depress tensioner until oil is purged from cylinder, then install into housing.
13. Position cylinder plunger into deeper end of Timing Chain Tensioner Resetting Gauge tool No. 8186, or equivalent, then apply downward force until tensioner bottoms against top edge of tool.
14. Install chain tensioner into righthand cylinder head.
15. Insert suitable 3/8 inch square drive extension with breaker bar into righthand cylinder bank intake camshaft drive hub, then rotate until camshaft hub aligns with camshaft sprocket and damper attaching holes.
16. Install sprocket mounting bolts and tighten to specifications.
17. Insert suitable 3/8 inch square drive extension with breaker bar into lefthand cylinder bank intake camshaft drive hub, then rotate until camshaft hub aligns with camshaft sprocket and damper attaching holes.
18. Install sprocket mounting bolts and tighten to specifications.
19. Rotate engine slightly clockwise to remove timing chain slack.
20. Using suitable flat bladed pry tool, gently pry tensioner arm toward tensioner slightly, then release tensioner arm and ensure tensioner extends and arms.
21. Install front cover, crankshaft damper, cylinder heads, camshaft position sensor, electrical connector and upper intake manifold.

TIMING CHAIN TENSIONER

REPLACE

Refer to "Timing Chain, Replace" for tensioner replacement.

TIMING CHAIN TENSIONER BLEED

Refer to "Timing Chain, Replace" for tensioner bleed.

CAMSHAFT

REPLACE

With the timing chain removed, avoid turning the camshaft or crankshaft. If movement is required, exercise caution to avoid valve damage caused by piston contact.

REMOVAL

1. Remove primary timing chain as outlined under "Timing Chain, Replace," then secondary chain tensioner mounting bolts.
2. Loosen camshaft bearing cap bolts in reverse order of installation as shown in **Fig. 8,** then remove bearing caps.
3. Remove camshafts, secondary chain and tensioner as an assembly.
4. Remove tensioner and chain from camshaft.

INSTALLATION

1. Assemble camshaft chain on cams with plated links facing front and aligned with camshaft sprocket dots as shown in **Fig. 9.**
2. **On models equipped with early build tensioners that separate into subcomponents,** separate cylinder from tensioner housing.
3. Carefully drain housing oil without removing internal components.
4. Assemble plunger to housing.
5. Compress tensioner with hand pressure and lock with fabricated lock pin.
6. **On models equipped with late build tensioners that do not separate into subcomponents,** place tensioner into suitable soft jaw vise, slowly compress tensioner and install fabricated lock pin.
7. **On all models,** remove compressed and locked tensioner from vise.
8. Iinstall compressed and locked camshaft chain tensioner between camshafts and chain.
9. Rotate cams so plated links and sprocket dots are at 12 o'clock position, then install to cylinder head. Ensure rocker arms are correctly seated and in proper positions.

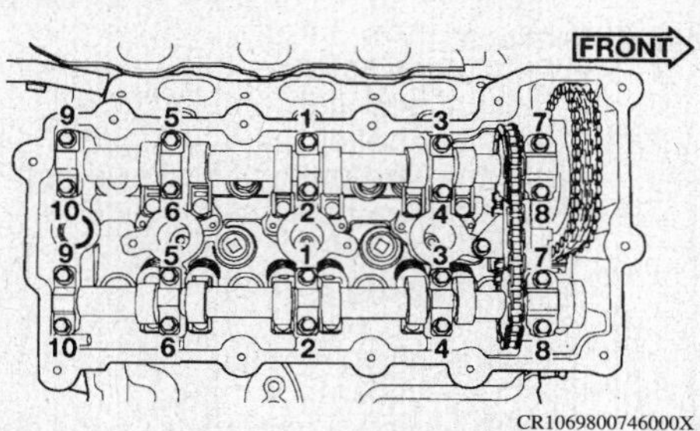

Fig. 8 Camshaft bearing cap tightening sequence

10. Install camshaft bearing caps in same position as removed.
11. **Torque** bearing caps gradually to 108 inch lbs. in sequence as shown in **Fig. 8.**
12. Install secondary chain tensioner mounting bolts and tighten to supplications.
13. Measure camshaft endplay.
14. Install primary timing chain as outlined under "Timing Chain, Replace."

PISTON & ROD ASSEMBLY

REMOVAL

1. Remove cylinder bores top ridge with suitable ridge reamer before removing pistons.
2. Rotate crankshaft so connecting rod is centered in cylinder bore.
3. Mark connecting rod and bearing caps with permanent ink marker or suitable scribe tool for assembly. Do not use stamp or punch to mark connecting rods.
4. Remove connecting rod cap.
5. Install Connecting Rod Guide tools No. 8189, or equivalent, into connecting rod, then remove piston and rod assembly from top of cylinder block.
6. Install bearing cap on mating rod.

INSTALLATION

1. Install oil ring expander.
2. Place one end of upper side rail between piston ring groove and expander, then hold end firmly and press down portion to be installed until side rail is in position. **Do not use piston ring expander.**
3. Place one end of lower side rail between piston ring groove and expander, then hold end firmly and press down portion to be installed until side rail is in position. **Do not use piston ring expander.**
4. Install No. 2 intermediate piston ring. Ensure manufacturers I.D. dot mark faces up, towards top of piston as shown in **Fig. 10.**
5. Install piston ring No. 1.
6. Position piston ring end gaps as shown in **Fig. 11.**
7. Ensure compression ring gaps are staggered so neither is in line with oil ring rail gap.
8. Ensure oil ring expander ends are butted and rail gaps properly located before installing ring compressor.

9. Immerse piston head and rings in clean engine oil, slide ring compressor over piston and tighten. Ensure ring position does not change.
10. Position bearing onto connecting rod. Ensure bearing half hole aligns with connecting rod hole.
11. Lubricate bearing surface with engine oil.
12. Install Connecting Rod Guide tools No. 8189, or equivalent.
13. Pistons are marked on top with arrow and F above pin boss. These marks must point toward front of engine in both cylinder banks.
14. Connecting rod oil squirt hole faces major thrust (righthand) side of block.
15. Rotate crankshaft so connecting rod journal is centered in cylinder bore, then insert rod and piston into bore and guide rod over crankshaft journal.
16. Using suitable hammer handle, tap piston down cylinder bore and guide connecting rod onto connecting rod journal.
17. Lubricate rod bolts and bearing surfaces with engine oil.
18. Install connecting rod cap and bearing. Tighten to specifications.

CRANKSHAFT

REPLACE

REMOVAL

1. Remove engine as outlined under "Engine, Replace."
2. Drain engine oil into suitable container and remove oil filter.
3. Remove oil pan as outlined under "Oil Pan, Replace" and oil pickup tube.
4. Remove accessory drive idler pulley bracket.
5. Remove upper intake manifold as outlined under "Upper Intake Manifold, Replace."
6. Remove valve covers as outlined under "Valve Cover, Replace."
7. Remove front cover as outlined under "Front Cover, Replace."
8. Remove timing chain as outlined under "Timing Chain, Replace."
9. Remove crankshaft sprocket as outlined under "Crankshaft Sprocket, Replace."
10. Remove oil pump as outlined under "Oil Pump, Replace."
11. Remove crankshaft rear oil seal retainer as outlined under "Crankshaft Rear Oil Seal, Replace."
12. Remove structural windage tray.
13. Using permanent ink marker or suitable scribe tool, mark connecting rod cap position for assembly. Do not use punch or stamp to mark connecting rods.
14. Remove connecting rod bearing caps.
15. Remove main bearing cap and tie bolts, then main bearing caps.
16. Remove crankshaft.

INSTALLATION

Upper and lower bearing halves are not interchangeable.

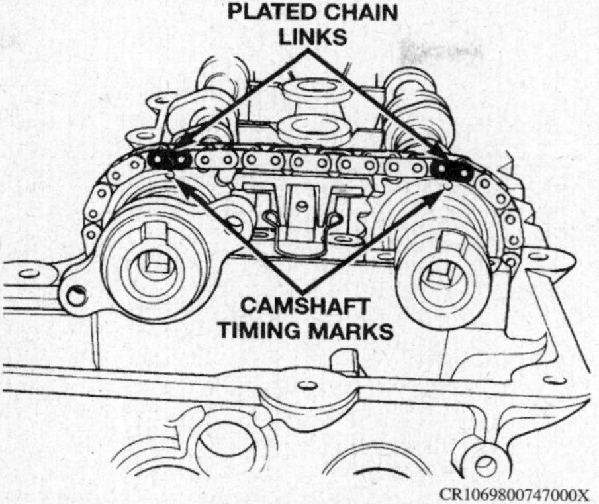

Fig. 9 Camshaft chain timing

1. Lubricate upper main bearing halves with engine oil.
2. Push crankshaft forward.
3. Roll lubricate front thrust washer onto machined shelf between No. 3 upper main bulk head and crankshaft thrust surface. Ensure crankshaft thrust washer coated and oil groove side faces crankshaft thrust surface.
4. Move crankshaft rearward.
5. Roll lubricate rear thrust washer onto machined shelf between No. 3 upper main bulk head and crankshaft thrust surface. Ensure crankshaft thrust washer coated and oil groove side faces crankshaft thrust surface.
6. Lubricate lower main bearings with engine oil, then install main bearings and caps.
7. Install inside main bearing cap bolts, then **torque** to 15 ft. lbs. and finally tighten an addition 1/4 turn.
8. Measure crankshaft endplay.
9. Install connecting rods and measure side clearance.
10. Install windage tray.
11. Lubricate windage tray mounting bolts with engine oil, then **torque** to 20 ft. lbs., and finally tighten an addition 1/4 turn.
12. Install main cap tie bolts and tighten to specifications.
13. Install rear crankshaft oil seal retainer and oil seal.
14. Install oil pump, crankshaft sprocket, timing chain, front cover and valve covers.
15. Install accessory drive idler pulley bracket, then oil pickup tube and O-ring.
16. Install oil pan and filter, then oil dipstick tube.
17. Install engine and fill crankcase with suitable oil.

CRANKSHAFT SPROCKET

REPLACE

With the timing chain removed, avoid turning the camshaft or crankshaft. If movement is required, exercise caution to avoid valve damage caused by piston contact.

REMOVAL

1. Remove timing chain as outlined under "Timing Chain, Replace."
2. Using crankshaft damper bolt and suitable puller, remove sprocket.

INSTALLATION

1. Using Crankshaft Seal and Sprocket Installer tool No. 6780-1 and Crankshaft Damper Installer Screw tool No. 8179, or equivalent, install sprocket until it bottoms against crankshaft step flange.
2. Measure from sprocket outer face to end of crankshaft. Ensure measurement is 1.5174–1.5574 inches.
3. Install primary timing chain.

MAIN & ROD BEARINGS

Refer to "Crankshaft, Replace" for main and rod bearings service.

CRANKSHAFT SEAL

REPLACE

1. Remove crankshaft damper.
2. Insert Crankshaft Damper Remover Insert tool No. 8194, or equivalent, into crankshaft nose.
3. Using Crankshaft Seal Remover tool No. 6771, or equivalent, remove seal.
4. Reverse procedure to install using Crankshaft Seal Protector tool No. 6780-2, Crankshaft Seal and Sprocket Installer tool 6780-1 and Crankshaft Damper Installer Screw tool No. 8179, or equivalent.

CRANKSHAFT REAR OIL SEAL

REPLACE

SEAL

Removal

1. Remove transaxle and drive plate.
2. Insert suitable 3/16 inch wide flat bladed screwdriver between lip and seal metal case.
3. Angle screwdriver through dust lip against metal case and pry out seal. **Do not allow screwdriver blade to contact seal surface.**

Installation

1. Place magnetic base, Crankshaft Rear Seal Pilot Guide tool No. 6926-1, or equivalent on crankshaft.
2. Place seal over pilot tool and ensure seal lip faces towards crankshaft.
3. Using Crankshaft Rear Seal Installer tool No. 6926-2 and Handle Tool No. C-4171, or equivalent, drive seal into retainer housing until seal is flush with surface.
4. Install drive plate and transaxle.

RETAINER

Removal

1. Remove rear oil seal as outlined under "Crankshaft Rear Oil Seal, Replace."
2. Remove oil pan as outlined under "Oil Pan, Replace."
3. Remove mounting screws, retainer and gasket.

Installation

1. Install gasket and loosen assemble seal retainer.
2. Attach Crankshaft Real Seal Retainer Alignment Fixture tools No. 8225, or equivalent, to pan rail using oil pan fasteners. Ensure 2.7L stamped is facing cylinder block with flat side of tools against pan rail.
3. While applying firm pressure to seal with alignment fixture tools, tighten retainer screws to specifications.
4. Install oil pan and crankshaft rear oil seal.

OIL PAN

REPLACE

REMOVAL

1. Remove dipstick and tube, then raise and support vehicle.
2. Drain engine oil into suitable container, then remove oil filter.
3. Disconnect suspension stabilizer bar, reposition for oil pan clearance.
4. Remove structural collar as outlined under "Structural Collar, Replace"
5. Remove mounting bolts, oil pan and gasket. Ensure timing cover to oil pan bolts are removed, before removing pan.

INSTALLATION

1. Apply 1/8 inch bead of suitable silicone rubber adhesive sealant to front T-joints as shown in **Fig. 12.**
2. Install gasket to block.
3. Install oil pan, then finger tighten bolts and nuts until gasket's rubber seal is compressed.
4. Install timing chain cover and **torque** mounting bolts (4) to 105 inch lbs.
5. **Torque** mounting bolts (2) to 21 ft. lbs.
6. **Torque** mounting nuts (1 and 3) to 105 inch lbs.
7. Install structural collar as outlined under "Structural Collar, Replace."
8. Install oil filter and drain plug, then lower vehicle and install dipstick and tube.
9. Connect stabilizer bar.
10. Fill crankcase with suitable oil.

OIL PUMP

REPLACE

1. Remove crankshaft damper as outlined under "Crankshaft, Replace."
2. Remove front cover as outlined under "Front Cover, Replace."
3. Remove timing chain as outlined under "Timing Chain, Replace."

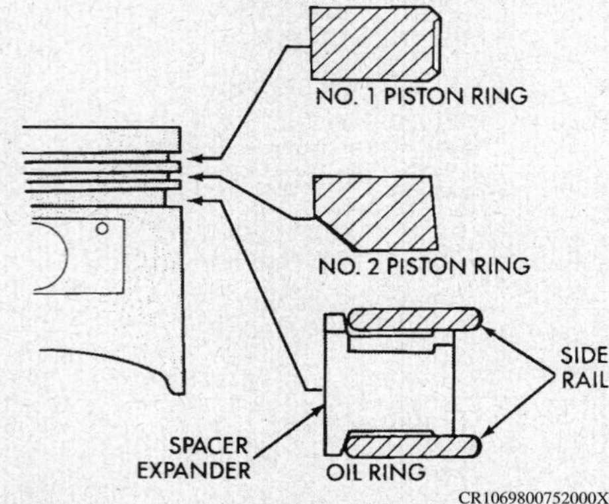

Fig. 10 Piston ring installation

4. Remove crankshaft sprocket as outlined under "Crankshaft, Replace."
5. Remove oil pan as outlined under "Oil Pan, Replace."
6. Remove oil pickup tube and O-ring.
7. Ensure crankshaft sprocket and oil pump marks align, with crankshaft position at cylinder No. 1 at 60° ATDC.
8. Remove mounting bolts, then oil pump.
9. Reverse procedure to install, noting following:
   a. Ensure pump is primed with oil before installation.
   b. Ensure crankshaft sprocket and oil pump marks align, with crankshaft position at cylinder No. 1 at 60° ATDC.
   c. Tighten mounting bolts to specifications.

OIL PUMP SERVICE

1. Remove retaining cap, spring and pressure relief valve.
2. Remove mounting screws and lift cover plate off.
3. Remove pump rotors.
4. Wash parts in suitable solvent, then inspect for damage or wear.
5. Lay straightedge across pump cover surface. If .001 inch feeler gauge can be inserted between cover and straight edge, replace cover.
6. Measure thickness and diameter of rotors.
7. If outer rotor thickness is less than .373 inch or diameter less than 3.5108 inches, replace rotor.
8. If inner rotor thickness is less than .373 inch, replace rotor.
9. Slide outer rotor into body, press to one side with fingers and measure clearance between rotor and body. If clearance is more than .015 inch, replace body.
10. Install inner rotor and measure clearance between rotors. If clearance is more than .003 inch, replace pump assembly.
11. Inspect oil pressure relief valve plunger for scoring and free operation in bore. Small marks may be removed with 400-grit wet or dry sandpaper.
12. Relief valve spring free length should be approximately 1.95 inches. Compress spring with 23–25 lbs. If length is not 1.34 inches, replace spring.
13. Reverse procedure to assemble. Tighten screws and retaining cap to specifications

BELT TENSION DATA

Belt	Belt Tension, Lbs.	
	New	Used
Accessory①	180–200	120
A/C②	150–170	120

① — Poly-V Belt.
② — V-Belt.

SERPENTINE DRIVE BELT

1. Loosen tensioner pulley locking nut.
2. Loosen belt adjusting bolt.
3. Remove accessory drive belt.
4. Reverse procedure to install.

SEPARATED ACCESSORY DRIVE SYSTEM

AIR CONDITIONING

Removal

1. Remove alternator/power steering serpentine drive belt.
2. Loosen tensioner locking and pivot bolts. Do not remove.
3. Insert suitable 1/2 inch drive breaker bar into belt tensioner square opening, rotate tensioner counterclockwise until belt can be removed from pulleys.
4. Slowly rotate tensioner clockwise to relieve spring load.

Installation

1. Insert suitable 1/2 inch drive breaker bar into tensioner square opening, then hold counterclockwise pressure on tensioner while removing locking bolt.
2. Carefully release tensioner torsion spring load.
3. Remove pivot bolt, tensioner and spring from front timing cover.
4. Insert spring arm into appropriate New or Used tensioner belt position.
5. Install torsion spring, tensioner and pivot bolt. Tighten pivot bolt to specifications.
6. Using 1/2 inch drive breaker bar, apply counterclockwise pressure on tensioner until locking bolt can be installed.
7. Rotate tensioner counterclockwise until belt can be installed on pulleys.
8. Release tensioner and remove socket wrench, then tighten tensioner locking bolt to specifications.
9. Install accessory drive belt.

COOLING SYSTEM BLEED

1. Close radiator drain hand tight.

2. Attach approximately 48 inches of .250 inch I.D. clear hose to bleed valve.
3. Route hose away from accessory drive belt, drive pulleys and electrical cooling fan to clean container.
4. Open cooling system bleed valve, then attach Filling Aid Funnel tool No. 8195, or equivalent, to pressure bottle filler neck.
5. Pinch overflow hose between coolant bottle chambers.
6. Pour 50/50 mix of suitable coolant and distilled water into large section of filling funnel.
7. Slowly fill until steady stream of coolant flows from bleed valve hose.
8. Close bleed valve and continue filling system to top of funnel.
9. Remove overflow hose clip and allow funnel to drain into overflow chamber.
10. Remove funnel and install coolant pressure bottle cap.
11. Remove bleed valve hose, then start and run engine until operating temperature is reached.
12. Shut off engine and allow to cool.
13. With engine cold, ensure pressure chamber level is between MIN and MAX marks. Adjust as necessary.

THERMOSTAT

REPLACE

1998–99

1. Drain cooling system into suitable container.
2. Remove accessory drive belt, then raise and support vehicle.
3. Remove alternator mounting bolts, then position alternator aside.
4. Remove lower radiator and heater hoses from thermostat housing.
5. Remove mounting bolts, housing and thermostat.
6. Reverse procedure to install, noting following:
   a. Install thermostat with bleed valve at 12 o'clock position.
   b. Tighten mounting bolts to specifications.

2000–02

1. Drain cooling system into suitable container.
2. Remove oil dipstick tube and cover tube opening to prevent coolant from entering the engine.
3. Raise and support vehicle.
4. Remove left engine mount as outlined under "Motor Mount, Replace."
5. Remove alternator support strut, then electrical connector.
6. Remove transaxle dipstick tube bracket mounting bolt.
7. Remove lower heater hose and lower radiator hose from thermostat housing.
8. Remove thermostat housing mounting bolts, then the thermostat and housing.

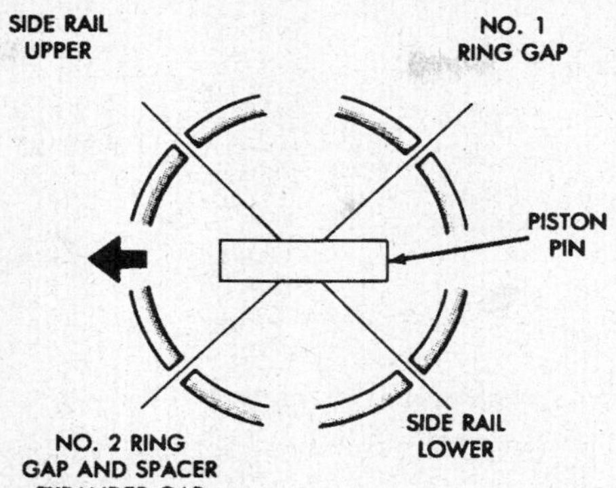

Fig. 11 Piston ring end gap positions

9. Reverse procedure to install, noting following:
   a. Install thermostat with bleed valve at 12 o'clock position.
   b. Tighten mounting bolts to specifications.

WATER PUMP

REPLACE

1. Drain cooling system into suitable container.
2. Remove upper radiator crossmember.
3. Remove radiator fan assembly.
4. Remove accessory and air conditioning drive belts.
5. Remove timing chain and all chain guides as outlined under "Timing Chain, Replace."
6. Remove water pump mounting bolts, then the water pump and gasket.
7. Clean all sealing surfaces, install new water pump gasket.
8. Reverse procedure to install.

RADIATOR

REPLACE

1. Drain cooling system into suitable container.
2. Remove upper radiator crossmember, then clamps and hoses from radiator.
3. Disconnect transmission hoses from cooler and plug.
4. Disconnect engine oil cooler lines.
5. Disconnect radiator fan electrical connector, then remove mounting bolts and fan module.
6. Remove air conditioning condenser mounting screws and transmission cooler line bracket.
7. Lift condenser up enough to clear upper mounting clips, then rest condenser on lower radiator crossmember.
8. Remove radiator.
9. Reverse procedure to install. Tighten bolts and screws to specifications.

FUEL PUMP

REPLACE

1. Relieve fuel pressure as outlined under "Precautions."
2. Remove rear seat, then disconnect fuel pump electrical connector.
3. Raise and support vehicle, then drain fuel tank into suitable container.
4. Loosen brackets from body and swing rear stabilizer bar toward rear.
5. Remove fuel filler tube from tank, then disconnect fuel and EVAP lines.
6. Position suitable transmission jack under fuel tank, then remove fuel tank strap bolts, passenger side first.
7. Lower fuel tank, then remove purge and vent lines.
8. Depress quick connector retainers and disconnect fuel line from pump.
9. Slide fuel pump module electrical connector lock to unlock, then push connector retainer down and pull off module.
10. Using Fuel Pump Removal/Installation tool No. 6856, or equivalent, remove fuel pump module locknut.
11. Remove fuel pump and O-ring seal.
12. Reverse procedure to install.

FUEL FILTER

REPLACE

A combination fuel filter/pressure regulator is located on top of fuel pump module. A separate frame mount filter is not used.

1. Relieve fuel pressure as outlined under "Precautions."
2. Lower fuel tank as outlined under "Fuel Pump, Replace."
3. Remove fuel tank purge and vent lines.
4. Disconnect pressure regulator fuel line, then push locking tab in from locking slot and turn pressure regulator to unlock.
5. Pull regulator straight up and remove.
6. Reverse procedure to install.

TECHNICAL SERVICE BULLETINS

EXHAUST DRONE

1998

On these models, there may be an exhaust drone between 1600–2000 RPM.

This condition may be caused by lefthand exhaust pipe. If exhaust system is free and not grounded by body or suspension, proceed as follows:

1. Replace lefthand front exhaust pipe/catalytic converter (Federal emissions part No. 04581705AF; California emission part No. 04581707AF).
2. Use new V-band exhaust manifold clamp (part No. 04581013AC).
3. Remove and discard righthand front exhaust piper support bracket.

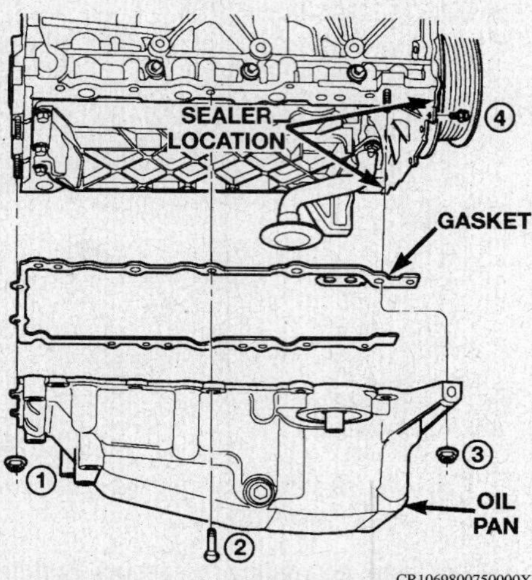

Fig. 12 Oil pan replacement

TIGHTENING SPECIFICATIONS

Year	Component	Torque, Ft. Lbs.
1998–2002	A/C Belt Tensioner	21
	A/C Compressor	21
	A/C Condenser To Radiator	45①
	Alternator	30
	Alternator/Power Steering Belt Tensioner	40
	Camshaft Bearing Cap	⑦
	Camshaft Chain Tensioner	105①
	Camshaft Sprocket	21
	Condenser Inlet Tube	45①
	Connecting Rod Cap	③
	Cooling System Bleed	110①
	Crankshaft Damper	125
	Crankshaft Main Bearing Cap	②
	Crankshaft Main Bearing Cap, Tie	21
	Cylinder Head	④
	Cylinder Head Cover	105①
	Engine Mount (Left & Right)	45
	Engine Mount (Rear) Isolator To Crossmember	21
	Engine Mount (Rear) Upper Isolator Nuts	45
	Engine Oil Cooler Lines	13
	Exhaust Manifold Heat Shield	105①
	Exhaust Manifold To Catalytic Converter	96①
	Exhaust Manifold To Cylinder Head	21
	Fan Blade	45①
	Fan Module	45①
	Fan Motor	25①
	Front Cover, M10	40
	Front Cover, M6	105①
	Fuel Pump Locking Ring	40

Continued

TIGHTENING SPECIFICATIONS—Continued

Year	Component	Torque, Ft. Lbs.
1998–2002	Fuel Pump Module	40
	Fuel Rail	16
	Fuel Tank Straps	44
	Intake Manifold	105①⑤
	Oil Pan	⑧
	Oil Pan Drain Plug	25
	Oil Pan Filter	15
	Oil Pump	21
	Oil Pump Cover	105①
	Oil Pump Pickup Tube	21
	Oil Pump Pressure Relief Valve Cap	105①
	PCV Valve	60①
	Rear Crankshaft Seal Retainer	108①
	Spark Plug	15
	Starter	30
	Structural Collar	⑥
	Thermostat Housing	105①
	Throttle Body	105①
	Throttle Body Support Bracket, Lower	50①
	Throttle Body Support Bracket, Upper	105①
	Timing Chain Cover, M6	105①
	Timing Chain Cover, M10	40
	Timing Chain Guide	21
	Timing Chain Guide Access Plug	15
	Timing Chain Tensioner	40
	Water Pump	105①
	Water Outlet Housing	105①
	Water Outlet Housing Bleed	105①

① — Inch lbs.
② — Refer to "Crankshaft, Replace" for tightening specifications and sequence.
③ — Torque to 20 ft. lbs., then tighten an additional ¼ turn.
④ — Refer to "Cylinder Head, Replace" for tightening specifications and sequence.
⑤ — Refer to "Intake Manifold, Replace" for tightening sequence.
⑥ — Refer to "Structural Collar, Replace" for tightening specifications and sequence.
⑦ — Refer to "Camshaft, Replace" for tightening specifications and sequence.
⑧ — Refer to "Oil Pan, Replace" for tightening specifications and sequence.

3.2L & 3.5L Engines

NOTE: On Air Bag Equipped Models, Refer To "Air Bag System Precautions" Located In The Front Of This Manual For System Disarming & Arming Procedures.

NOTE: Refer To "Computer Relearn Procedures" Located In The Front Of This Manual When Battery Power To The Computer Has Been Interrupted.

NOTE: Prior To Performing Any Service Operations Listed In This Section, Consult The "Technical Service Bulletins" Section For Related Information.

INDEX

PRECAUTIONS

AIR BAG SYSTEMS

Refer to "Air Bag System Precautions" in the front of this manual for system disarming and arming procedures.

BATTERY GROUND CABLE

Prior to service, disconnect battery ground cable and isolate as required.

FUEL SYSTEM PRESSURE RELIEF

1. Remove fuel pump relay for power distribution center.
2. Start and run engine until it stalls.
3. Attempt to start engine until it no longer runs.
4. Turn ignition switch to Off position.
5. Place rag or towel under fuel line quick-connector fitting at fuel rail.
6. Install fuel pump relay.
7. One or more Diagnostic Trouble Codes (DTCs) may have been stored because of removing fuel pump relay. Clear these DTCs with suitably programmed scan tool.

COMPRESSION PRESSURE

The minimum compression pressure should be no less than 100 psi and the maximum variation between cylinders should be no more than 25%.

ENGINE MOUNT

REPLACE

Refer to "2.7L Engine" for engine mount replacement.

STRUCTURAL COLLAR

REPLACE

Refer to "2.7L Engine" for structural collar replacement.

ENGINE

REPLACE

1. Relieve fuel pressure as described under "Precautions."
2. Mark hood position at hinges and remove, then drain cooling system into suitable container.
3. Remove wiper arms, right and lefthand cowl covers, then cowl support.
4. **On 2000–02 models** Remove wiper arms, right and lefthand cowl screens, then strut tower brace.
5. **On all models** remove air cleaner assembly and air inlet hose, then upper radiator crossmember.
6. Disconnect hood release cable from latch, then remove radiator fan assembly and accessory drive belts.
7. Drain coolant into suitable container.
8. Disconnect upper radiator hose at engine and lower hose at radiator, then engine oil and transaxle cooler lines at radiator.
9. Remove power steering line bracket at lefthand side of radiator, then A/C condenser to radiator fasteners.
10. Remove radiator, then accessory drive belts.
11. Remove alternator, then power steering pump mounting bolts and set pump aside.
12. Remove mounting bolts and set A/C compressor aside.
13. Remove righthand exhaust manifold

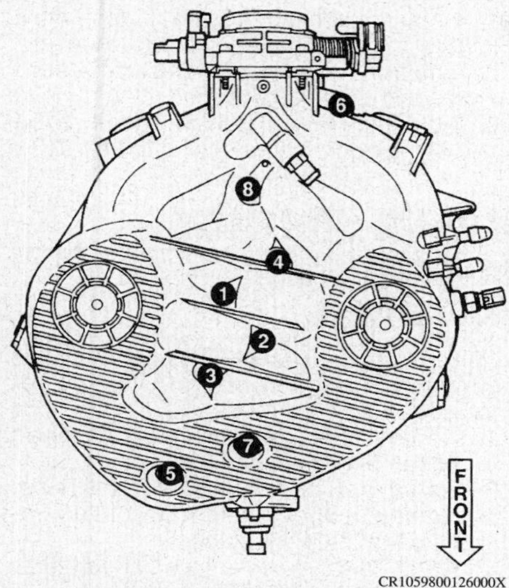

Fig. 1 Upper intake manifold tightening sequence. 1998

V-band clamps, then righthand side catalytic converter down pipe front and rear support bracket fasteners.

14. Relieve fuel pressure as outlined under "Precautions," then disconnect fuel line.
15. Disconnect throttle and speed control cables, then coolant bottle hoses.
16. Disconnect vacuum lines and engine ground straps at both cylinder heads.
17. Remove upper intake manifold as described under "Intake Manifold, Replace."
18. Disconnect heater hoses, then remove rear throttle body support bracket.
19. Remove water piper fastener at transmission to block bolt, then four upper transmission to block bolts.
20. Disconnect electrical connections, then raise and support vehicle.
21. Drain engine oil into suitable container, then remove mounting bolts and structural collar.
22. Mark flexplate to torque converter position and remove converter mounting bolts.
23. Disconnect transaxle cooler line brackets from engine.
24. Remove lefthand exhaust manifold V-band clamp, then starter.
25. Remove left and righthand engine mount bolts.
26. Remove crankshaft position sensor and lower transaxle to block bolts.
27. Lower vehicle and attach suitable lifting device to engine.
28. Support transaxle with suitable floor jack and small block of wood, then remove engine.
29. Reverse procedure to install, noting following:
    a. Tighten all fasteners to specifications.
    b. Do not tighten transaxle case to engine block bolts until all bolts have been started and mating surface are completely joined.

INTAKE MANIFOLD

REPLACE

UPPER

1. Remove air cleaner housing and inlet hose.
2. Remove throttle and speed control cables from throttle arm and bracket.
3. Disconnect Secondary Runner Valve (SRV), Manifold Tuning Valve (MTV), Throttle Position Sensor (TPS), Idle Air Control (IAC) and Intake Air Temperature/Manifold Absolute Pressure (TMAP) electrical connectors.
4. Disconnect SRV reservoir, speed control reservoir and Positive Crankcase Ventilation (PCV) vacuum hoses.
5. Remove right and left side intake manifold supports, then support brackets at intake manifold front corners and MTV.
6. Remove EGR tubes mounting clips.
7. Remove mounting bolts and upper manifold.
8. Reverse procedure to install, noting following:
    a. Hand start all intake manifold mounting bolts.
    b. Tighten manifold mounting bolts to specifications using sequence as shown in **Figs. 1 and 2.**

LOWER

1. Relieve fuel pressure as described under "Precautions," then drain cooling system into suitable container.
2. Remove upper intake manifold as outlined under "Intake Manifold, Replace."
3. Disconnect fuel injectors and coolant temperature sensor electrical connectors, then heater hose quick connect tee from heater tube.
4. Disconnect fuel rail fuel supply hose from fuel rail, then remove screw mounting fuel rail support bracket to throttle body support bracket.
5. Remove mounting bolts, then fuel rail and injectors as an assembly.
6. Remove mounting bolts and lower intake manifold.
7. Reverse procedure to install. Gradually **torque** mounting bolts to 21 ft. lbs. in sequence as shown in **Fig. 3.**

EXHAUST MANIFOLD

REPLACE

RIGHTHAND

1. Raise and support vehicle, then remove exhaust system.
2. Loosen converter pipe support mounting bolt at transaxle mount.
3. Loosen A/C drive belt, then lower vehicle.
4. Remove air cleaner housing and air inlet tube.
5. Remove manifold V-band clamp.
6. Remove mounting bolts and set A/C compressor aside.
7. Remove engine oil dipstick tube, then A/C compressor bracket.

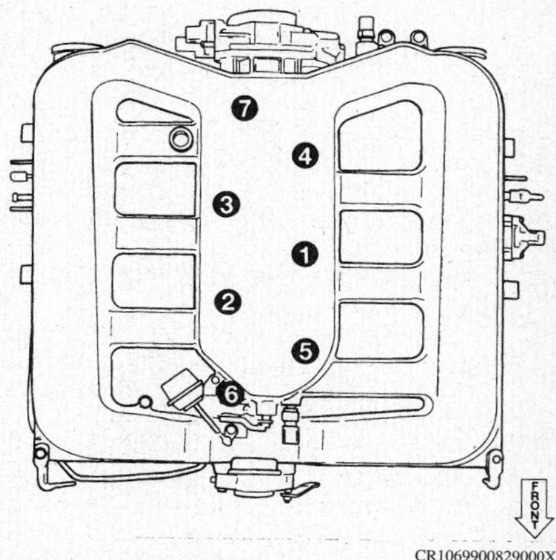

Fig. 2 Upper intake manifold tightening sequence. 1999–2002

8. Disconnect electrical connector and remove oxygen sensor.
9. Remove mounting screws and heat shields.
10. Remove mounting bolts and exhaust manifold.
11. Reverse procedure to install, noting following:
    a. Tighten exhaust manifold mounting bolts to specifications from center outwards.
    b. Tighten heat shield mounting screws to specifications.
    c. Use new V-band clamp and tighten to specifications.

LEFTHAND

1. Raise and support vehicle.
2. Remove exhaust system, then loosen converter pipe support mounting bolt at transaxle.
3. Lower vehicle and remove exhaust manifold connector V-band clamp.
4. Disconnect connector and remove exhaust manifold oxygen sensor.
5. Remove mounting screws and heat shield.
6. Remove mounting bolts and exhaust manifold.
7. Reverse procedure to install, noting following:
    a. Tighten exhaust manifold mounting bolts to specifications from center working outward.
    b. Tighten heat shield mounting screws to specifications.
    c. Use new V-band clamp and tighten to specifications.

CYLINDER HEAD

REPLACE

1. Remove crankshaft damper as outlined under "Crankshaft Damper, Replace."
2. Remove timing belt covers as outlined under "Front Cover, Replace."
3. Remove camshaft sprockets as outlined under "Camshaft Sprocket, Replace."

4. Remove upper and lower intake manifolds as "Intake Manifold, Replace."
5. Remove exhaust manifold to catalytic converter pipe connection V-band clamps.
6. Remove rear timing belt cover to cylinder head fasteners and rear covers.
7. Remove mounting bolts and cylinder heads.
8. Reverse procedure to install, noting following:
   a. Cylinder head bolts are tightened using a torque plus angle procedure. **Bolts with stretched threads must be replaced.**
   b. Use new cylinder head gasket. Gaskets for 3.5L engine have perfectly round combustion sealing rings, for 3.2L engine, combustion sealing rings are not perfectly round.
   c. Ensure head is properly positioned over locating dowels.
   d. Lubricate bolt threads with clean engine oil.
   e. **Torque** cylinder head bolts to 45 ft. lbs. in sequence as shown in **Fig. 4.**
   f. **Torque** bolts to 65 ft. lbs.
   g. **Torque** bolts again to 65 ft. lbs.
   h. Tighten bolts an additional 90.° **Do not use torque wrench.**
   i. Final cylinder head bolt torque should be 90 ft. lbs. If not, replace bolts.
   j. Install new O-ring seal in righthand rear timing belt cover.
   k. Use new V-band clamp and tighten to specifications.

VALVE COVER

REPLACE

1. Remove air cleaner assembly, then upper intake manifold plenum as outlined under "Intake Manifold, Replace."
2. Cover lower intake manifold.
3. Disconnect electrical connectors and remove ignition coils.
4. Remove mounting bolts and cylinder head cover.
5. Reverse procedure to install, noting following:
   a. Using suitable pry tool, remove spark plug tube seals.
   b. Position new seal with part number facing cylinder head cover and install with Installer tool No. MB-998306, or equivalent.
   c. Tighten cylinder head cover mounting bolts to specifications.

SPARK PLUG TUBES

REPLACE

1. Remove cylinder head cover as outlined under "Cylinder Head, Replace."
2. Using suitable locking pliers, remove tube from cylinder head.
3. Apply suitable stud and bearing mount to new tube approximately .039 inch from tube end, in .118 inch wide area.
4. Install seater end of tube into cylinder head, then carefully install tube using suitable hardwood block and mallet until seated into bore bottom.
5. Install cylinder head cover.

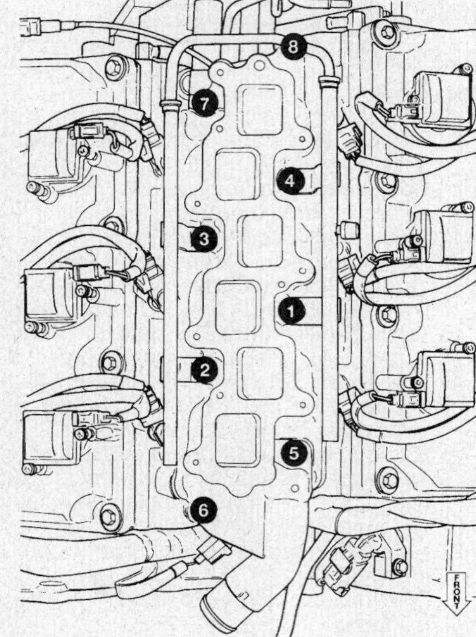

Fig. 3 Lower intake manifold tightening sequence

VALVE ADJUSTMENT

Rocker arms are equipped with hydraulic lash adjusters. No adjustment is necessary.

ROCKER ARMS

REPLACE

REMOVAL

1. Remove cylinder heads as outlined under "Cylinder Head, Replace."
2. Identify rocker arm assembly and rocker arm for installation.
3. Remove mounting bolts and rocker arm assembly.
4. To prevent air ingestion into lash adjusters, avoid turning rocker arm assembly upside down.
5. Do not rest rocker arm assembly on lash adjusters.
6. Install screw, nut, spacer and washer into pin, tighten screw into pin, then loosen nut and pull out shaft support dowel as shown in **Fig. 5.**
7. Remove rocker arms and pedestals in order.

INSTALLATION

1. Install rocker arms and pedestals into shaft. Rocker shaft notches face up. Righthand cylinder bank notches face toward rear and lefthand notches face toward front.
2. Press new dowel pins until they bottom against shaft in pedestal. Pins pass through pedestal into exhaust rocker shafts.
3. Rotate camshafts until lobes are in neutral position as shown in **Fig. 6.**
4. Install rocker arm and shaft assembly. Ensure identification marks face engine front on lefthand head and toward rear on righthand head.
5. Tighten mounting bolts to specification using sequence as shown in **Fig. 7.**

VALVE SPRINGS

REPLACE

IN-VEHICLE

Ensure piston is at TDC on cylinder from which valve spring(s) is being removed.

1. Relieve fuel pressure as described under "Precautions."
2. Remove air cleaner housing and hose.
3. Remove upper intake manifold as "Intake Manifold, Replace."
4. Remove valve cover as outlined under "Valve Cover, Replace."
5. Remove rocker arm and shaft assembly as outlined under "Rocker Arm, Replace."
6. Rotate crankshaft clockwise until piston No. 1 is at TDC.
7. Install suitable spark plug adapter into cylinder being serviced, then apply 90–100 psi air pressure to hold valves in place.
8. Using Valve Spring Compressor tool No. MD-998772-A with Adapter tool No. 6527, or equivalent, compress valve spring, then remove valve locks, retainer and spring.
9. Using suitable valve seal tool, remove valve stem seals.
10. Repeat procedure in firing sequence 1-2-3-4-5-6. **Ensure piston is at TDC on cylinder from which valve spring(s) is being removed.**
11. Reverse procedure to install, noting following:
    a. Push valve steam seal/seat firmly and squarely over valve guide with stem as guide.
    b. Do not force seal against guide top.
    c. When install retainer locks, compress spring only enough to install locks.

HEAD REMOVED

Removal

1. Using Valve Spring Compressor tool No. C-3422-B, or equivalent, compress valve spring.
2. Remove valve retaining locks, valve spring retainers, valve springs and valve springs seat/stem seal assembly.
3. Identify valves for installation, then remove valve stem lock groove burrs.
4. Remove valves.

Installation

1. Coat with clean engine oil and install valve stems.
2. If valves and/or seats have been ground, proceed as follows:
   a. Measure valve tip height (A) form cylinder head surface to valve stem top as shown in **Fig. 8.**
   b. If intake valve tip height is more

than 1.7185 inches, grind tip to specifications.

c. If exhaust valve tip height is more than 1.8102 inches, grind tip to specifications.

3. Install seal/spring seat assembly over valve guides.
4. Ensure garter spring is intact around rubber seal top, then install valve springs and retainers.
5. Compress valve springs with suitable valve spring compressor, then install locks and release tool.
6. If valves and/or seats have been ground, proceed as follows:
   a. Measure springs installed height (B) from spring seal to spring retainer bottom surface as shown in **Fig. 5.**
   b. If height is more than 1.5256 inches, install .030 inch spacer in head counterbore under valve spring seat.

CRANKSHAFT DAMPER

REPLACE

1. Remove upper radiator crossmember, then fan module.
2. Remove accessory drive belts.
3. Hold crankshaft damper with Holder tool No. 8191, or equivalent, then remove center bolt.
4. Using Three-Jaw Puller tool No. 1023 and Crankshaft Damper Remover Insert tool No. C-4685-C2, or equivalent to remove damper.
5. Reverse procedure to install. Tighten center bolt to specifications.

FRONT COVER

REPLACE

1. Remove upper radiator crossmember, then cooling fan module and accessory drive belts.
2. Remove crankshaft damper as outlined under "Crankshaft, Replace."
3. Remove lower belt cover, stamped steel cover and lefthand cast cover.
4. Do not remove cover sealer. If some sealer is missing, replace with suitable silicone rubber adhesive sealant.
5. Reverse procedure to install.

TIMING BELT

REPLACE

With the timing belt removed, avoid turning the camshaft or crankshaft. If movement is required, exercise caution to avoid valve damage caused by piston contact.

This procedure can only be used when camshaft sprockets have not been loosened or removed. If camshaft sprockets have been loosened or removed, refer to "Camshaft Timing, Adjust" for proper procedure.

REMOVAL

1. Remove upper radiator crossmember, then disconnect radiator fan electrical connector.

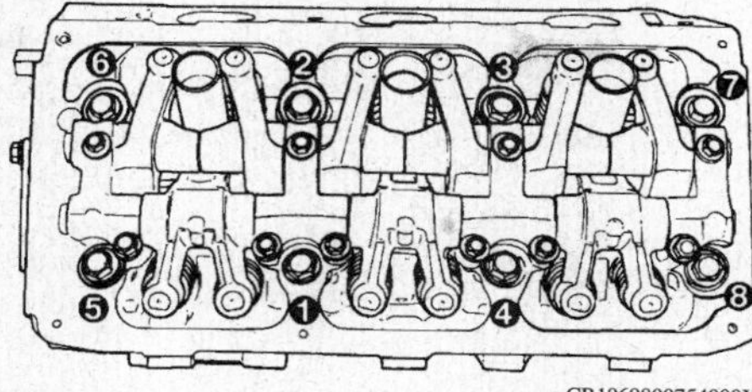

Fig. 4 Cylinder head tightening sequence

2. Remove fan module and accessory drive belts.
3. Remove crankshaft damper and front cover as outlined under "Front Cover, Replace."
4. If reusing timing belt, mark rotational direction on belt.
5. Turn crankshaft clockwise until crankshaft mark aligns with oil pump housing TDC mark and camshaft sprocket timing marks are between rear cover marks as shown in **Fig. 9.**
6. Using ink or paint, mark camshaft sprocket timing mark position to two rear timing cover timing marks.
7. Remove timing belt tensioner and store with plunger facing up.
8. Remove timing belt.

INSTALLATION

1. Place crankshaft sprocket with oil pump housing TDC mark as shown in **Fig. 9.**
2. Align camshaft sprockets to reference marks between rear cover marks.
3. Slowly preload tensioner with suitable vise and install locking pin. Store pin with plunger facing up until ready to install.
4. Install timing belt starting at crankshaft sprocket and going in counterclockwise direction. Maintain tension on belt when positioned around tensioner pulley.
5. Ensure camshaft sprockets mark still fall between cover marks.
6. Hold tensioner pulley against belt, install tensioner and tighten to specifications.
7. Pull retaining pin and allow tensioner to extend to pulley bracket.
8. Ensure camshaft sprocket marks are still aligned.
9. Rotate crankshaft sprocket two revolutions and ensure timing marks align.
10. Install front covers and crankshaft damper, then accessory drive belts and cooling fan module.
11. Install upper radiator crossmember.

CAMSHAFT SPROCKET

REPLACE

With the timing belt removed, avoid turning the camshaft or crankshaft. If movement is required, exercise caution to avoid valve damage caused by piston contact.

1. Hold camshaft sprocket with suitable box wrench, then remove bolt and washer. If engine is in vehicle, it may be necessary to lift engine side.
2. Remove camshaft sprocket.
3. Camshaft sprockets are not interchangeable. Lefthand sprocket has DIS pickup slots while righthand sprocket does not.
4. For installation, refer to "Camshaft Timing, Adjust."

CAMSHAFT

REPLACE

With the timing belt removed, avoid turning the camshaft or crankshaft. If movement is required, exercise caution to avoid valve damage caused by piston contact.

1. Remove camshaft sprocket(s) as outlined under "Camshaft Sprocket, Replace."
2. Remove cylinder head(s) as outlined under "Cylinder Head, Replace."
3. Mark rocker arm and shaft assembly for installation, then remove.
4. Remove rear camshaft cover and O-ring.
5. Carefully remove camshaft from cylinder head rear.
6. Reverse procedure to install. Lubricate camshaft journals and cam with clean engine oil before installation.

CAMSHAFT OIL SEAL

REPLACE

1. Remove camshaft sprocket(s) as outlined under "Camshaft Sprocket, Replace."
2. Using Camshaft Seal Remover tool No. C-3981B, or equivalent, remove oil seal.
3. Reverse procedure to install, noting following:
   a. Lightly coat oil seal lip with clean engine oil.
   b. Use Seal Protector Sleeve tool No. 6788 and Seal Installer tool No. 6052, or equivalent, to install oil seal.

CAMSHAFT TIMING

ADJUST

With the timing belt removed, avoid turning the camshaft or crankshaft. If movement is required, exercise caution to avoid valve damage caused by piston contact.

1. Place crankshaft sprocket with oil pump housing TDC mark as shown in **Fig. 9.**
2. Install dial indicator in cylinder No. 1 and rotate crankshaft until piston is at exactly TDC.
3. Install Camshaft Alignment tools No. 6642, or equivalent, on each cylinder head rear.
4. Slowly preload tensioner with suitable vise and install locking pin. Store pin with plunger facing up until ready to install.
5. Install camshaft sprockets with timing mark between cover timing marks.
6. Install new mounting bolts. Lefthand

mounting bolt is 10 inches long, right-hand 8⅜ inches. Do not tighten at this time.
7. Install timing belt starting at crankshaft sprocket and going in counterclockwise direction. Maintain tension on belt when positioned around tensioner pulley.
8. Ensure camshaft sprockets mark still fall between cover marks.
9. Hold tensioner pulley against belt, install tensioner and tighten to specifications.
10. Pull retaining pin and allow tensioner to extend to pulley bracket.
11. Ensure No. 1 piston is at TDC, then hold camshaft sprocket hex with suitable wrench and tighten camshaft bolts to specifications.
12. Remove dial indicator and install spark plug.

TIMING BELT TENSIONER BLEED

Operate engine at 1600–2000 RPM for 10–15 minutes. This will purge air from tensioner and noise will dissipate.

PISTON & ROD ASSEMBLY

Refer to "2.7L Engine" for piston and rod assembly service.

CRANKSHAFT

REPLACE

REMOVAL

1. Remove engine as outlined under "Engine, Replace."
2. Remove oil pan as described under "Oil Pan, Replace," then oil pickup tube.
3. Remove crankshaft damper as outlined under "Crankshaft Damper, Replace."
4. Remove accessory drive belt idler pulley.
5. Remove front covers as outlined under "Front Cover, Replace."
6. Remove timing belt and tensioner as outlined under "Timing Chain, Replace."
7. Remove crankshaft sprocket as outlined under "Crankshaft Seal, Replace."
8. Tap crankshaft dowel pin out, then remove oil pump assembly.
9. Remove rear oil seal retainer.
10. Mark connecting rod bearing caps for assembly, then remove.
11. Mark main bearing caps for assembly, then remove.
12. Remove crankshaft.

INSTALLATION

Upper and lower bearing halves are not interchangeable.

1. Lubricate upper main bearing halves with engine oil.
2. Push crankshaft forward.
3. Roll lubricate front thrust washer onto machined shelf between No. 2 upper main bulk head and crankshaft thrust surface.
4. Move crankshaft rearward.
5. Roll lubricate rear thrust washer onto machined shelf between No. 2 upper main bulk head and crankshaft thrust surface.
6. Lubricate lower main bearings with engine oil, then install main bearings and caps.
7. Install inside main bearing cap bolts and **torque** to 15 ft. lbs., then tighten an additional ¼ turn.
8. Measure crankshaft end play.
9. Install connecting rods and measure side clearance.
10. Install windage tray.
11. Lubricate windage tray mounting bolts with engine oil and **torque** to 20 ft. lbs., then tighten an additional ¼ turn.
12. Install main cap tie bolts and tighten to specifications.
13. Install rear crankshaft oil seal retainer and oil seal.
14. Install oil pump, crankshaft dowel pin, crankshaft sprocket, timing belt, covers and crankshaft damper.
15. Install accessory drive idler pulley, then oil pickup tube and pan.
16. Install engine and fill crankcase with suitable oil.

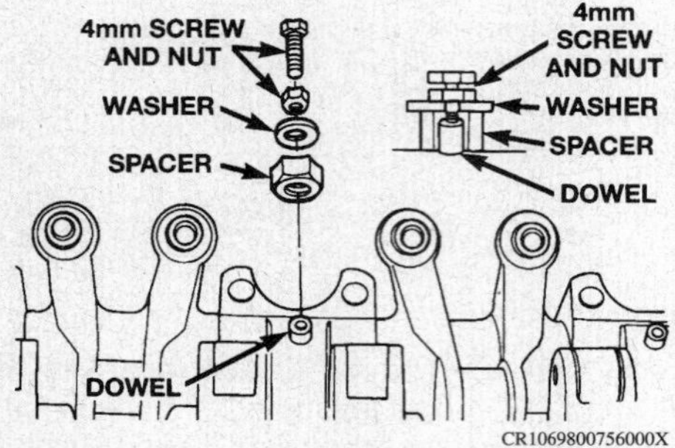

Fig. 5 Rocker arm dowel removal

MAIN & ROD BEARINGS

REMOVAL

1. Remove oil pan as outlined under "Oil Pan, Replace," then oil pickup tube and windage tray.
2. Mark bearing caps for assembly.
3. Remove bearing caps one at a time.
4. Insert Main Bearing tool No. C-3059, or equivalent, into crankshaft oil hole, rotate crankshaft clockwise and force bearing shell upper half out.

INSTALLATION

When installing new upper bearing shells, slightly chamfer sharp edges from plain side.

1. Lubricate main bearing with clean engine oil.
2. Start bearing in place and insert Main Bearing tool No. C-3059, or equivalent, into crankshaft oil hole.
3. Slowly rotate crankshaft counterclockwise, sliding bearing into place, then remove tool.
4. Lubricate and install lower bearing half.
5. Lubricate main bearing cap bolts and finger tighten.
6. Move crankshaft to forward travel limit.
7. Roll lubricate front thrust washer onto machined shelf between No. 2 upper main bulk head and crankshaft thrust surface.
8. Move crankshaft rearward.
9. Roll lubricate rear thrust washer onto machined shelf between No. 2 upper main bulk head and crankshaft thrust surface.
10. Install main bearing cap and tighten inner bolts finger tight.
11. **Torque** inside main bearing cap bolts to 15 ft. lbs., then an additional ¼ turn.
12. Measure crankshaft end play.
13. Install windage tray.
14. Lubricate windage tray mounting bolts with engine oil and **torque** to 20 ft. lbs., then an additional ¼ turn.
15. Install main cap tie bolts and tighten to specifications.
16. Install oil pump, pickup tube and oil pan.
17. Install engine and fill crankcase with suitable oil.

CRANKSHAFT SEAL

REPLACE

REMOVAL

1. Remove timing belt as outlined under "Timing Belt, Replace."
2. Using Crankshaft Sprocket Puller tool No. L-4407-A, or equivalent, remove crankshaft sprocket.
3. Tape dowel pin out of crankshaft.
4. Using Crankshaft Seal Remover tool No. 6341A, or equivalent, remove seal.

INSTALLATION

1. Using Crankshaft Seal Installer tool No. 6342, or equivalent, install crankshaft seal.
2. Install crankshaft dowel pin to .047 inch protrusion.
3. Using Crankshaft Sprocket Installer tool No. 6641 or Crankshaft Damper Installer Bolt tool No. C-4685-C1, or equivalent, install crankshaft sprocket.
4. Install timing belt.

CRANKSHAFT REAR OIL SEAL

REPLACE

Refer to "2.7L Engine" for crankshaft rear oil seal and retainer replacement.

OIL PAN

REPLACE

1. Remove dipstick and tube, then raise and support vehicle.
2. Drain engine oil into suitable container.
3. Remove structural collar as outlined under "Structural Collar, Replace."
4. Remove engine oil cooler line, then transmission oil cooler line clips.

5. Remove mounting bolts, oil pan and gasket.
6. Reverse procedure to install, noting following:
   a. Apply ⅛ inch bead of suitable silicone rubber adhesive sealant to parting line of oil pump housing and rear seal retainer.

OIL PUMP

REPLACE

1. Drain cooling system into suitable container, then remove fan module and accessory drive belts.
2. Remove crankshaft damper and front cover as outlined under "Crankshaft Damper, Replace" and "Front Cover, Replace."
3. Remove crankshaft sprocket as outline under "Crankshaft Seal, Replace."
4. Remove oil pan as outlined under "Oil Pan, Replace," then oil pickup tube.
5. Remove mounting bolts, then oil pump and gasket.
6. Reverse procedure to install, noting following:
   a. Prime oil pump before installing.
   b. Tighten mounting bolts to specifications.
   c. Install new O-ring with oil pickup tube.

OIL PUMP SERVICE

1. Remove cotter pin and drill ⅛ inch hole into relief valve retainer cap, then insert self-threading sheet metal screw into cap.
2. Clamp screw into suitable vise, support oil pump body and remove cap by tapping on body with suitable soft hammer.
3. Discard cap, then remove spring and pressure relief valve.
4. Remove mounting screws and lift cover plate off.
5. Remove pump rotors.
6. Wash parts in suitable solvent, then inspect for damage or wear.
7. Lay straightedge across pump cover surface. If .001 inch feeler gauge can be inserted between cover and straight edge, replace cover.
8. Measure thickness and diameter of rotors.
9. If outer rotor thickness is less than .563 inch or diameter less than 3.141 inches, replace rotor.
10. If inner rotor thickness is less than .563 inch, replace rotor.
11. Slide outer rotor into body, press to one side with fingers and measure clearance between rotor and body. If clearance is more than .015 inch, replace body.
12. Install inner rotor and measure clearance between rotors. If clearance is more than .008 inch, replace pump assembly.
13. Place straightedge across body face between bolt holes. If clearance between rotors and straightedge is more than .003 inch replace pump assembly.
14. Inspect oil pressure relief valve plunger for scoring and free operation in bore. Small marks may be removed with 400-grit wet or dry sandpaper.
15. Relief valve spring free length should be approximately 1.95 inches. Compress spring with 23–25 lbs. If length is not 1.34 inches, replace spring.
16. Reverse procedure to assembly. Tighten screws and retaining cap to specifications

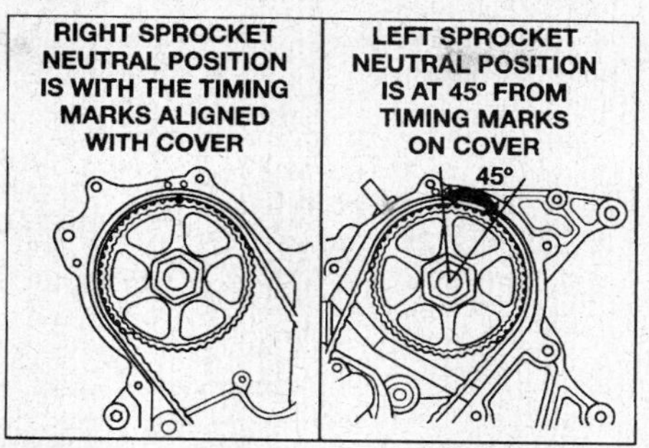

Fig. 6 Camshaft sprockets neutral position

BELT TENSION DATA

Belt	Tension, Lbs.	
	New	Used
Accessory①	180–200	120
A/C②	150–170	120

① — Poly-V Belt.
② — V-Belt.

SERPENTINE DRIVE BELT

1. Remove tensioner pulley locking nut.
2. Raise and support vehicle.
3. Remove push clips attaching lower air shield to engine cradle, then air shield.
4. Loosen tensioner adjusting bolt until belt can be removed.
5. Reverse procedure to install. Tighten belt to specifications.

SEPARATED ACCESSORY DRIVE SYSTEM

AIR CONDITIONING

1. Remove accessory drive belt as outlined under "Serpentine Drive Belt."
2. Loosen tensioner pulley lock nut, then tensioner pulley adjusting screw until belt can be removed.
3. Reverse procedure to install, tighten tensioner nut to specification.

COOLING SYSTEM BLEED

Refer to procedure under "2.7L Engine" for cooling system bleed procedure.

THERMOSTAT

REPLACE

1. Drain cooling system into suitable container, then raise and support vehicle.
2. Disconnect engine oil pressure and power steering pressure switch electrical connectors.
3. Disconnect radiator and heater hoses from thermostat.
4. Remove mounting bolts, housing, thermostat and gasket.
5. Reverse procedure to install. Tighten mounting bolts to specifications.

WATER PUMP

REPLACE

1. Drain cooling system into suitable container.
2. Remove accessory drive belts.
3. Remove timing belt components necessary to access water pump as outlined under "Timing Belt, Replace."
4. Remove mount bolt and water pump.
5. Reverse procedure to install, noting following:
   a. Apply suitable dielectric grease to O-ring.
   b. Tighten mounting bolts to specifications.

RADIATOR

REPLACE

Refer to procedure under "2.7L Engine" for radiator replacement.

FUEL PUMP

REPLACE

Refer to "2.7L Engine" for fuel pump replacement.

FUEL FILTER

REPLACE

Refer to "2.7L Engine" for fuel filter replacement.

TECHNICAL SERVICE BULLETINS

EXHAUST DRONE

1998

On some of these models, there may be an exhaust drone between 1600–2000 RPM.

This condition may be caused by left-hand exhaust pipe. If exhaust system is free and not grounded by body or suspension, proceed as follows:

1. Replace lefthand front exhaust pipe/catalytic converter (Federal emissions part No. 04581701AF; California emission part No. 04581703AF).
2. Use new V-band exhaust manifold clamp (part No. 04581013AC).
3. Remove and discard righthand front exhaust piper support bracket.

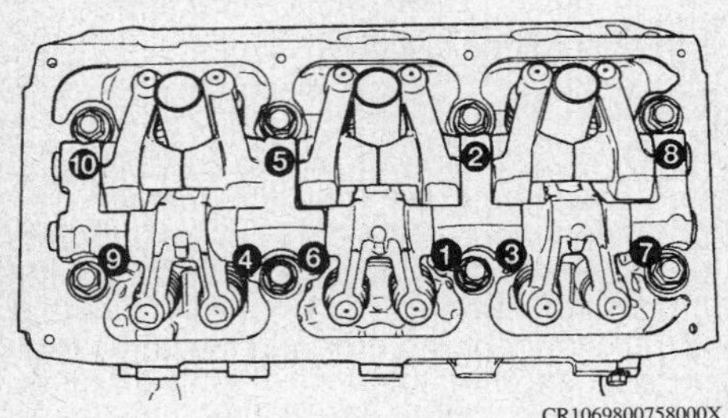

Fig. 7 Rocker arm & shaft assembly tightening sequence

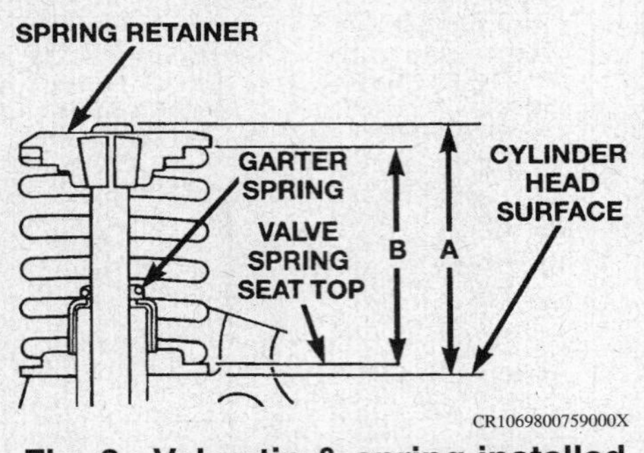

Fig. 8 Valve tip & spring installed heights inspection

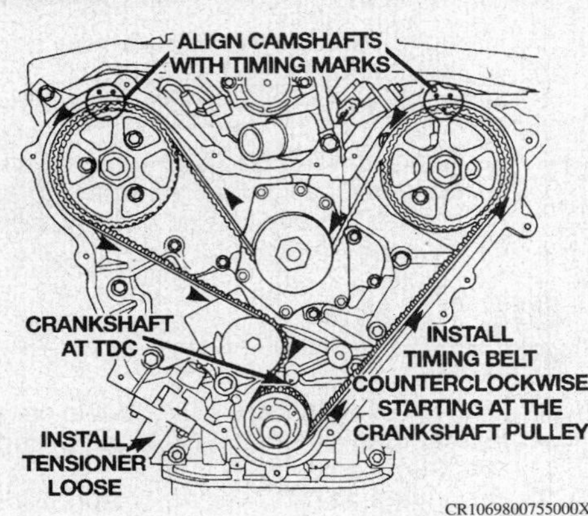

Fig. 9 Camshaft sprocket timing mark alignment

TIGHTENING SPECIFICATIONS

Year	Component	Torque, Ft. Lbs.
1998–2002	A/C Belt Tensioner	40
	A/C Compressor To Bracket	21
	A/C Compressor To Engine Block	40
	A/C Condenser	45①
	A/C Condenser Inlet Tube Bracket	45①
	Alternator	40
	Camshaft Sprocket	②
	Camshaft Thrust Plate	21
	Cooling System Bleed	72①
	Connecting Rod Cap	③
	Crankshaft Damper	70
	Crankshaft Main Bearing Cap	③
	Crankshaft Main Bearing Cap, Tie Bolts	21
	Cylinder Head	⑥
	Cylinder Head Cover	105①
	Engine Mount Bracket	45
	Engine Mount Isolator	40
	Exhaust Manifold Heat Shield	105①
	Exhaust Manifold To Cylinder Head	17
	Exhaust Pipe Flange	25
	Fan Blade	45①
	Fan Module	45①
	Fan Motor	25①
	Fuel Pump Module	40
	Fuel Rail, 3.2L	16
	Fuel Rail, 3.5L	96①
	Fuel Tank Straps	40
	Intake Manifold, Lower	21④
	Intake Manifold, Upper	105④
	Oil Pan	105①
	Oil Pan Drain Plug	20
	Oil Pan Filter	15
	Oil Pump Cover	105①
	Oil Pump Pick-Up Tube	21
	PCV Valve	60①
	Rear Crankshaft Seal Retainer	105①
	Rocker Arm & Shaft	23⑥
	Spark Plug	20

Continued

TIGHTENING SPECIFICATIONS—Continued

Year	Component	Torque, Ft. Lbs.
1998–2002	Spark Plug Tube	45
	Structural Collar	⑤
	Thermostat Housing	105①
	Throttle Body	105①
	Timing Belt Cover, M6	105①
	Timing Belt Cover, M8	21
	Timing Belt Cover, M10	40
	Timing Belt Tensioner	21
	Timing Belt Tensioner Pulley	45
	Water Pump	105①
	Water Outlet Housing	72①

①— Inch Lbs.
②— Righthand side, 75 ft. lbs., then an additional 1/4 turn; lefthand side, 85 ft. lbs., then an additional 1/4.
③— Refer to "Crankcase, Replace" for tightening specifications and sequence.
④— Refer to "Intake Manifold, Replace" for tightening procedure.
⑤— Refer to "Structural Collar, Replace" for tightening specifications and sequence.
⑥— Refer to "Rocker Arm, Replace" for tightening sequence.

Rear Axle & Suspension

NOTE: On Air Bag Equipped Models, Refer To "Air Bag System Precautions" Located In The Front Of This Manual For System Disarming & Arming Procedures.

NOTE: Refer To "Computer Relearn Procedures" Located In The Front Of This Manual When Battery Power To The Computer Has Been Interrupted.

INDEX

REAR WHEEL SPINDLE

REPLACE

1. Raise and support vehicle, then remove rear tire and wheel assemblies.
2. Remove rear caliper assembly and suspend from frame using suitable wire.
3. Remove rear disc brake rotor.
4. Remove rear hub and bearing assembly.
5. Remove speed sensor head from rear disc brake adapter, **Fig. 1.**
6. Remove speed sensor cable routing tube from trailing arm.
7. Remove disc brake adapter, disc shield, park brake shoes and park brake cable as an assembly, **Fig. 2.**
8. Disconnect trailing arm from trailing arm bracket, **Fig. 3.**
9. Disconnect lateral rod from spindle, **Fig. 4.**
10. Loosen and remove rear spindle to strut assembly pinch bolt.
11. Tap suitable center punch into hole on spindle until punch is jammed into hole, **Fig. 5. Do not punch hole in strut with center punch.**
12. Using suitable hammer, tap on top surface of spindle, driving it down and off strut assembly, **Fig. 6.**
13. Remove spindle from vehicle.
14. Reverse procedure to install, noting following:
    a. Push or tap spindle assembly onto strut until notch in spindle is tightly seated against locating tab on strut assembly.
    b. Check rear toe as outlined under "Wheel Alignment."

STRUT

REPLACE

1. Remove rear seat cushion and back assembly.
2. Remove upper and lower quarter trim panels.
3. Remove rear parcel shelf trim panel.
4. Remove rear speakers and mounting plates, then disconnect speaker wiring.
5. Raise and support vehicle, then remove rear wheel and tire assembly.
6. Remove rear caliper assembly and suspend from frame using suitable wire.
7. Remove rear disc brake rotor.
8. Remove speed sensor cable routing tube on trailing arm bracket to spindle.
9. Remove bolt attaching lateral link to rear spindle assembly, **Fig. 7.**
10. Remove rear strut assembly to stabilizer bar attaching link at stabilizer bar.
11. Loosen and remove rear spindle to strut assembly pinch bolt.
12. Tap suitable center punch into hole on spindle until punch is jammed into hole, **Fig. 5. Do not punch hole in strut with center punch.**
13. Using suitable hammer, tap on top surface of spindle, driving it down and off strut assembly, **Fig. 6.**
14. Let rear spindle and assembled components hang from trailing arm while strut is out of vehicle.
15. Lower vehicle.
16. Remove rear upper strut mount from vehicle by accessing upper strut mount tower and removing three attaching nuts from luggage compartment of vehicle.
17. Remove strut from vehicle.
18. Reverse procedure to install, noting following:
    a. Push or tap spindle assembly onto strut until notch in spindle is tightly seated against locating tab on strut assembly.
    b. Check rear toe as outlined under "Wheel Alignment."

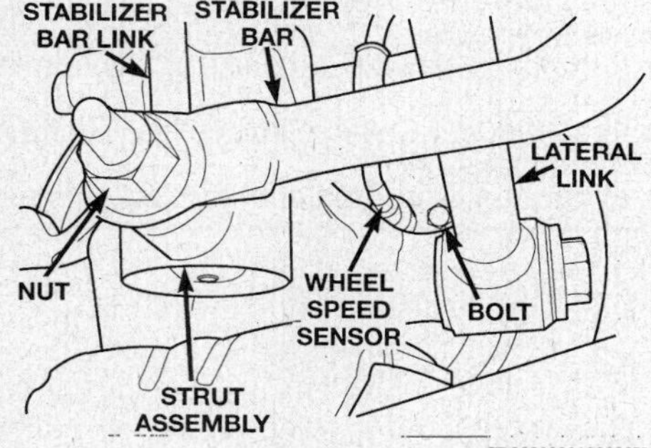

Fig. 1 Speed sensor head

STRUT SERVICE

1. Remove strut assembly from vehicle as outlined under "Strut, Replace."
2. Position strut assembly in suitable vise.
3. Mark strut assembly lower spring isolator, spring and upper strut mount for indexing.
4. Position Spring Compressor tool No. 7520, or equivalent, on strut assembly spring and compress coil spring until all load is removed from upper strut mount assembly.
5. Install Strut Rod Ratchet Socket tool No. 6864, or equivalent, on strut nut.
6. Insert an 8 mm Allen wrench into end of strut shaft and remove shaft nut from shaft.
7. Remove upper strut mount assembly from strut shaft.
8. Remove coil spring, plate, spring compressor, dust shield, jounce bumper and lower spring isolator.
9. Inspect all components for signs of abnormal wear or failure, replacing any component as required.
10. Reverse procedure to install. Align marks made during disassembly.

REAR CROSSMEMBER

REPLACE

REMOVAL

1. Open fuel filler door and remove filler neck mounting screws and cap.
2. Raise and support vehicle, then remove rear tire and wheel assemblies.
3. Remove lateral links mounting bolts and nuts. Lefthand front lateral link bolt cannot be removed until crossmember is lowered.
4. Remove brake tubes mounting screws

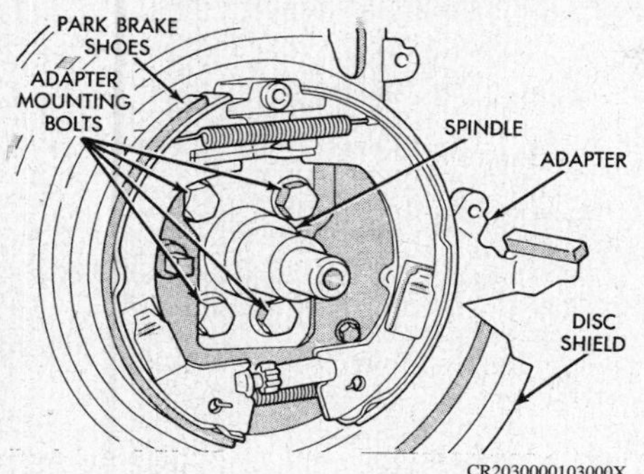

Fig. 2 Disc brake adapter mounting

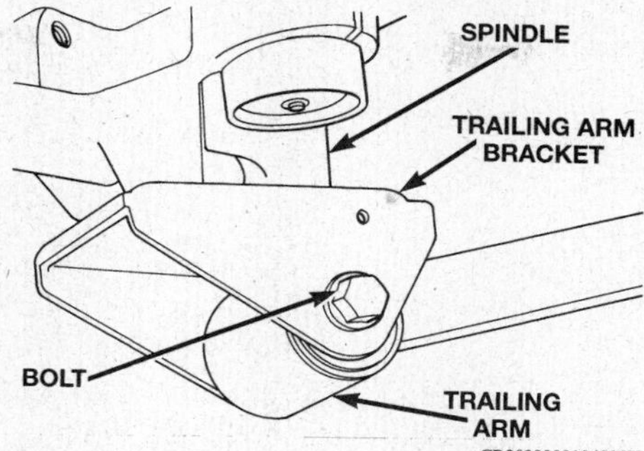

Fig. 3 Trailing arm to bracket bolt

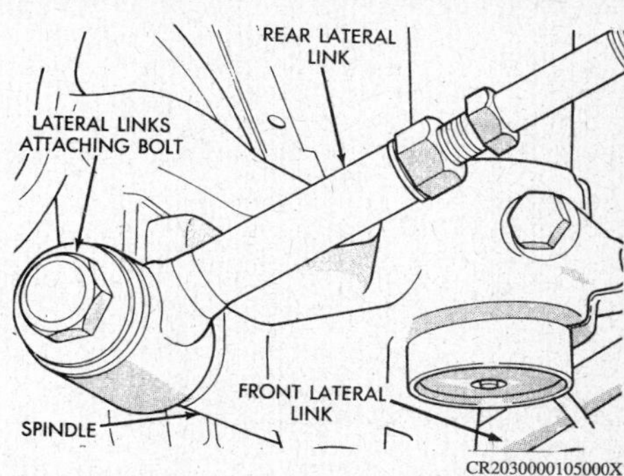

Fig. 4 Lateral links to spindle attaching bolts

from lefthand stabilizer bar isolator bushing retainer.

5. Remove stabilizer bar isolation bushing retaining frame rail mounting bolts and allow bar to hang down.
6. Remove tensioner from intermediate parking brake cable, then from lefthand rear parking brake cable.
7. Remove righthand rear parking brake cable from intermediate parking brake cable.
8. Remove retainer clips and rear parking brake cables from crossmember.
9. Remove brake proportioning valve mounting nuts.
10. Position suitable transmission jack under muffler.
11. Disconnect exhaust resonator hanger from rear frame rail, then muffler hangers on each side of muffler.
12. Lower jack and muffler enough to access crossmember.
13. Remove fuel filler neck lefthand frame rail mounting screw.
14. Remove crossmember rear corner mounting bolts, then lower crossmember as low as possible to access lateral link mounting bolt at lefthand front corner.
15. Remove mounting bolt and link, then crossmember.

INSTALLATION

1. Install rear suspension crossmember above muffler. Ensure brake tubes are properly routed as crossmember is installed.
2. Install rear proportioning valve mounting brackets and nuts, then intermediate parking brake cable routing clip.
3. Attach lefthand front lateral link to crossmember, then install mounting bolt through front of crossmember. Do not install nut at this time.
4. Raise crossmember against frame rails and install, but do not tighten two rear mounting bolts at this time.
5. Raise exhaust into place, then install hangers.
6. Install mounting screw and attach fuel filler neck to lefthand frame rail.
7. Position rear parking brake cables into crossmember alignment holes, then install retaining clips.
8. Connect righthand rear parking brake cable to intermediate parking brake cable, then install parking brake cable tensioner.
9. Install stabilizer bar isolator bushing retainer mounting bolts and tighten to specifications.
10. Tighten rear suspension crossmember rear mounting bolts to specifications.
11. Install brake tubes mounting screws.
12. Install remaining lateral links and mounting bolts. Forward mounting bolts must point towards rear and rear mounting bolts should point towards front.
13. Install lateral link mounting nuts but do not tighten now. **Tighten mounting bolts when vehicle is at curb riding height.**
14. Install tire and wheel assemblies. Tighten wheel mounting stud nuts to half specification, then to specifications.
15. Lower vehicle, then install filler neck mounting screws and fuel filler cap.
16. Tighten lateral arm to crossmember mounting bolts to specifications.
17. Inspect and set rear wheel toe to specifications.

STABILIZER BAR

REPLACE

1. Raise and support vehicle.
2. Using suitable thin wrench to keep attaching link stud from turning, remove stabilizer bar to strut attaching link stud nuts.
3. Remove links from stabilizer bar.
4. Remove stabilizer bar isolator bushing retainers mounting bolts, then stabilizer bar.
5. Mount bar in suitable soft jawed vise, then carefully pry back upper bushing retainer wider end tabs from lower half.
6. Using suitable hammer and brass drift punch, tap bushing retainer upper half forward, then off of lower half and bushing.
7. Remove bushing retainer lower half, then bushing.
8. Remove bar from vise and repeat procedure to remove other bushing.
9. Reverse procedure to install, noting following:
   a. Bushing slit points toward front of vehicle.
   b. Tighten mounting bolts to specifications.

LATERAL LINK

REPLACE

LEFTHAND FRONT

1. Raise and support vehicle, then remove lefthand rear tire and wheel assembly.
2. Remove lateral link to spindle mounting nut and bolt.
3. Remove link to rear crossmember mounting nut. Bolt cannot be removed now.
4. Remove brake tubes to lefthand stabilizer bar isolator bushing retainer mounting screws.
5. Remove stabilizer bar isolator bushing retainers mounting bolts.
6. Remove fuel filler neck to frame rail mounting screw, then position suitable transmission jack under fuel tank.
7. Remove righthand, then lefthand fuel tank mounting strap mounting bolts, allow straps to hang.
8. Lower fuel tank enough to remove lateral link to crossmember mounting bolt, then lefthand front lateral link.
9. Reverse procedure to install, noting following:
   a. Do not tighten lateral link mounting bolt until vehicle is at curb riding height.
   b. Tighten mounting screws and bolts to specifications.
   c. Inspect and correct rear wheel toe.

LEFTHAND REAR & RIGHTHAND FRONT & REAR

1. Raise and support vehicle, then remove tire and wheel assemblies.
2. Remove lateral link to rear crossmember mounting nuts and bolts.
3. Remove lateral links.
4. Reverse procedure to install, noting following:
   a. Do not tighten lateral link mounting bolt until vehicle is at curb riding height.
   b. Tighten mounting screws and bolts to specifications.
   c. Inspect and correct rear wheel toe.

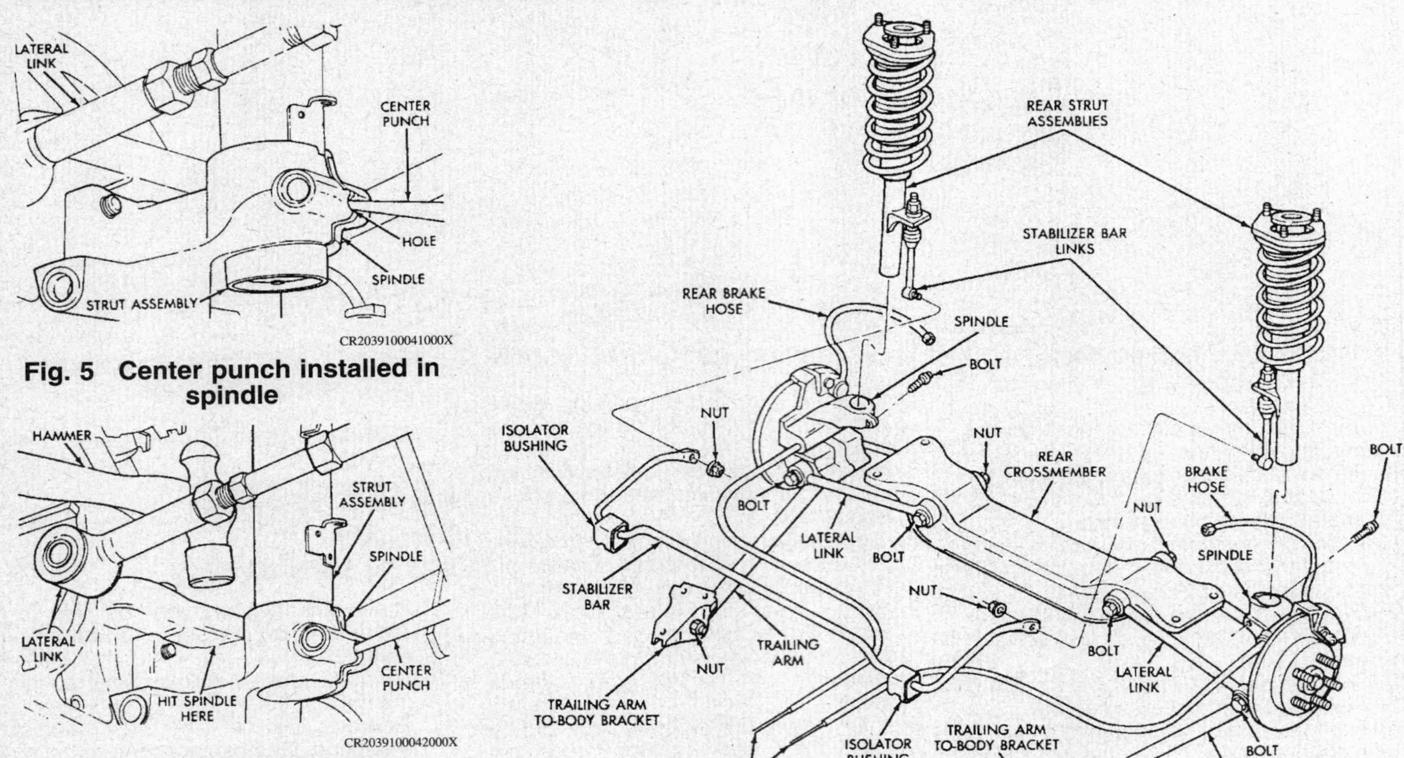

Fig. 5 Center punch installed in spindle

Fig. 6 Spindle removal

Fig. 7 Exploded view of rear suspension

TIGHTENING SPECIFICATIONS

Year	Component	Torque/Ft. Lbs.
1998–2002	Brake Hose	35
	Brake Hose Bracket	17
	Brake Support Plate	80
	Caliper Adapter To Spindle	85
	Caliper To Adapter	16
	Crossmember To Body	75
	Hub & Bearing Assembly To Spindle	124
	Lateral Link Jam Nut	65
	Lateral Link To Spindle	100
	Lateral Link To Suspension Crossmember	70
	Spindle Mounting Bolts	80
	Stabilizer Bar Isolator Bushing Retainer	30
	Stabilizer Bar To Strut Link	70
	Strut Shaft To Upper Mount	55
	Strut To Body	19
	Strut To Spindle Pinch Bolt	40
	Strut To Stabilizer Bar Link	17
	Trailing Arm	75
	Trailing Arm Bracket	80
	Trailing Arm Bracket To Body	45
	Wheel Lug Nut	100

Front Suspension & Steering

NOTE: On Air Bag Equipped Models, Refer To "Air Bag System Precautions" Located In The Front Of This Manual For System Disarming & Arming Procedures.

NOTE: Refer To "Computer Relearn Procedures" Located In The Front Of This Manual When Battery Power To The Computer Has Been Interrupted.

NOTE: Prior To Performing Any Service Operations Listed In This Section, Consult The "Technical Service Bulletins" Section For Related Information.

INDEX

PRECAUTIONS

AIR BAG SYSTEMS

Refer to "Air Bag System Precautions" in the front of this manual for system disarming and arming procedures.

BATTERY GROUND CABLE

Prior to service, disconnect battery ground cable and isolate as required.

HUB & BEARING

REPLACE

1. Raise and support vehicle, then remove tire and wheel.
2. Remove front caliper assembly and rotor from steering knuckle as outlined under "Disc Brakes."
3. Remove hub and bearing retaining nut.
4. Remove hub bolts, then hub and bearing assembly from steering knuckle by sliding it straight off end of hub axle. **CAUTION: When removing hub and bearing assembly from steering knuckle, be careful not to damage flinger disc on hub and bearing assembly. If flinger disc becomes damaged, hub and bearing assembly must be replaced with a new hub and bearing assembly as shown in Fig. 1.**
5. If hub and bearing will not slide out of knuckle, insert suitable pry bar between hub and steering knuckle as shown in **Fig. 2.**
6. Reverse procedure to install, noting following:
   a. Use new hub and bearing retaining nut when installing.

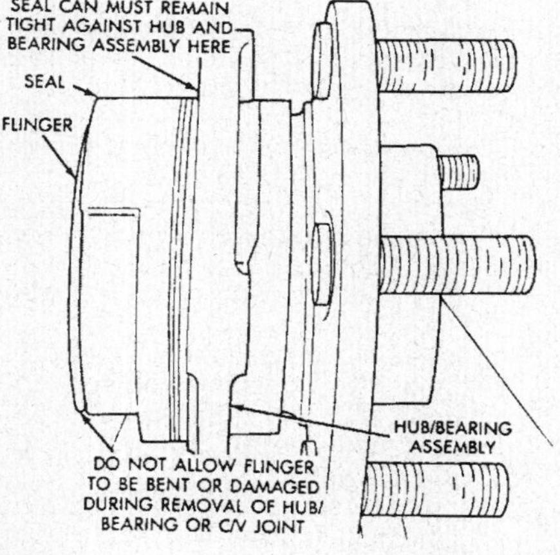

SEAL CAN MUST REMAIN TIGHT AGAINST HUB AND BEARING ASSEMBLY HERE
SEAL
FLINGER
HUB/BEARING ASSEMBLY
DO NOT ALLOW FLINGER TO BE BENT OR DAMAGED DURING REMOVAL OF HUB/ BEARING OR C/V JOINT
CR3039100346000X

Fig. 1 Hub & bearing assembly

   b. Install tire and wheel assembly tightening mounting nuts in sequence, **Fig. 3** until all nuts are torqued to half specification, then repeat tightening sequence to full specification.
   c. Lower vehicle, with brakes applied, tighten hub and braining retaining nut to specifications.

BALL JOINT INSPECTION

The lower ball joint is serviced with the lower control arm.

1. Raise and support front of vehicle.
2. Grasp tire at top and bottom then apply in and out force on wheel and tire assembly.
3. While applying force to tire, look for movement between lower ball joint and lower control arm.
4. If there is any movement, replace lower control arm.

CONTROL ARM

REPLACE

LOWER

1. Raise and support vehicle, then remove tire and wheel assembly.
2. Remove ball joint stud to steering knuckle clamp nut and bolt as shown in **Fig. 4.**
3. Insert suitable pry bar between lower control arm and steering knuckle to separate ball joint stud from steering knuckle as shown in **Fig. 5. Pulling steering knuckle out away from vehicle after releasing from ball joint can separate inner tripod joint.**
4. Remove and discard tension strut to cradle nut and washer from end of tension strut as shown in **Fig. 6. Never reuse tension strut nut.**
5. Loosen and remove lower control arm pivot bushing bolt.
6. Separate lower control arm and tension strut from cradle as an assembly by first removing pivot bushing from cradle and then sliding tension strut out of isolator bushing as shown in **Fig. 7.**
7. Reverse procedure to install, tightening lower control arm pivot bushing to cradle bracket attaching bolt with full weight of vehicle on suspension.

STEERING KNUCKLE

REPLACE

1. Raise and support vehicle, then remove tire and wheel assembly.

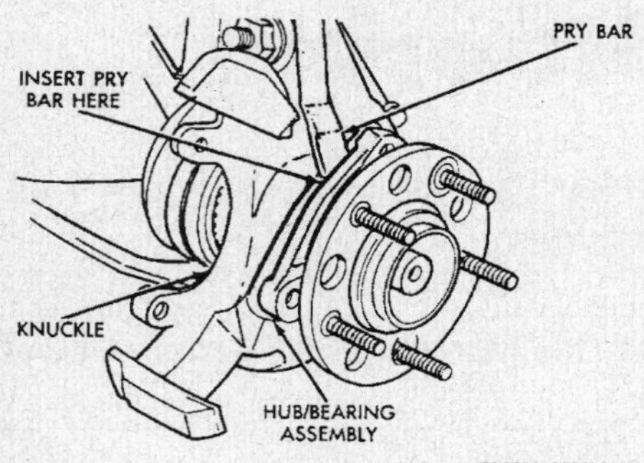

Fig. 2 Hub & bearing removal

2. Remove brake caliper and rotor as outlined under "Caliper, Replace" in "Disc Brakes."
3. Remove ABS speed sensor screw.
4. Carefully remove speed sensor head from knuckle. If sensor has seized due to corrosion use a hammer and a punch to tap edge of sensor ear, rocking sensor until free as shown in **Fig. 8. Do not use pliers on sensor head.**
5. Remove hub and bearing as outlined under "Hub & Bearing, Replace."
6. Remove ball joint stud to steering knuckle clamp nut and bolt as shown in **Fig. 4.**
7. Insert suitable pry bar between lower control arm and steering knuckle to separate ball joint stud from steering knuckle as shown in **Fig. 5. Do not pull steering knuckle out away from vehicle after releasing from ball joint as this can separate inner tripod joint.**
8. Remove strut assembly to steering knuckle attaching bolts. **Strut bolts have a serrated shaft for a tight fit into steering knuckle. Turn nut on bolts only, do not turn bolts.**
9. Remove steering knuckle from vehicle.
10. Reverse procedure, noting following:
    a. **Strut bolts have a serrated shaft so do not turn bolts in steering knuckle. Turn nut on bolts do not turn bolts.**
    b. Coat speed sensor head with high temperature multi-purpose EP grease before installing.
    c. Lower vehicle and with brake applied, tighten new hub and bearing retaining nut to specifications.

STABILIZER BAR

REPLACE

1. Remove righthand upper mount to strut tower mounting nut and washer.
2. Raise and support vehicle, then remove righthand front tire and wheel assembly.
3. Remove mounting nut and righthand stabilizer bar attaching link at strut.
4. Remove mounting nut and lefthand stabilizer bar attaching link at strut.
5. Loosen but do not remove righthand outer tie rod end to strut arm mounting nut.

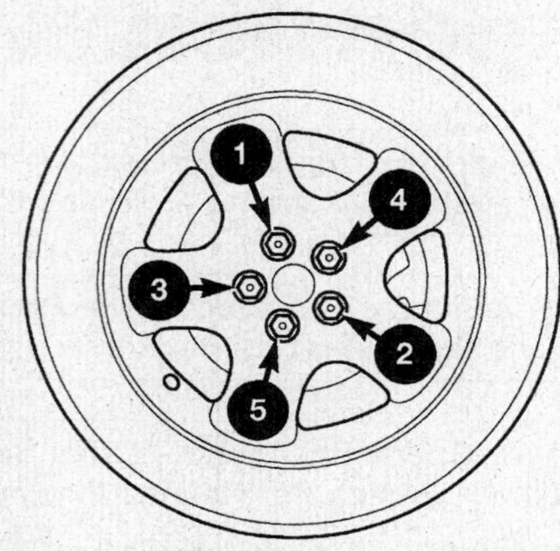

Fig. 3 Tire & wheel tightening sequence

6. Using puller tool No. C-3894A, or equivalent, release righthand outer tie rod end from strut steering arm, then remove nut and tire rod.
7. **On models equipped with ABS,** remove speed sensor cable routing bracket.
8. **On all models,** remove strut to steering knuckle mounting bolts, then righthand front strut.
9. Remove structural collar to engine oil pan mounting bolts, then stabilizer bushing retainers to cradle mounting bolts.
10. Remove stabilizer bar isolator bushing retainers and bushings.
11. Position suitable transmission jack under engine oil pan with a wood block buffer between jack and oil pan.
12. Carefully raise jack until motor mounts clear cradle.
13. Rotate stabilizer bar and remove out righthand wheel opening, routing it in front righthand half-staff than between knuckle. **Be careful to not pull knuckle outward.**
14. Reverse procedure to install. Tighten mounting bolts to specifications.

STRUT DAMPNER

REPLACE

Refer to **Fig. 9** when performing this procedure.

1. Raise and support vehicle, then remove tire and wheel assembly.
2. Remove stabilizer bar link at strut assembly as shown in **Fig. 10.**
3. Loosen, but do not remove, outer tie rod end nut, then remove outer tie rod end using suspension component puller tool No. C-3894A, or equivalent.
4. Remove speed sensor cable routing bracket from strut assembly.
5. Remove brake caliper and brake rotor as outlined under "Disc Brakes." Suspend caliper from frame using suitable wire.
6. Disconnect lower strut from steering knuckle. **Strut bolts have a serrated shaft for a tight fit into steering knuckle. Turn nut on bolts only, do not turn bolts.**
7. Disconnect upper strut from shock tower and remove strut assembly from vehicle.
8. If damper is to be serviced, proceed as follows:
    a. Position strut assembly in suitable vise by clamping strut by steering arm.
    b. Mark strut unit, lower spring isolator, spring and upper strut mount for indexing of parts during assembly.
    c. Install Spring Compressor tool No. 7520 or equivalent, **Fig. 11** on coil spring and compress coil spring to release all load from upper strut mount assembly.
    d. Install Strut Rod Socket tool No. 6864 or equivalent, **Fig. 12** on strut shaft nut; then, using a 10 mm socket on strut shaft end, remove strut shaft nut.
    e. Remove upper strut mount, jounce bumper, seat/bearing, dust shield, coil spring and lower spring mount from strut.
    f. Reverse procedure to assemble, aligning marks made during disassembly.
9. Reverse procedure to install. **Strut bolts have a serrated shaft; do not turn bolts in steering knuckle. Turn nut on bolts instead of turning bolts.**

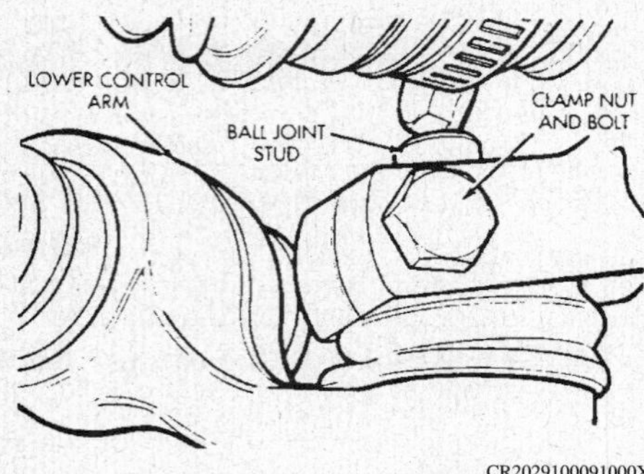

Fig. 4 Ball joint stud to steering knuckle clamp nut & bolt removal

TENSION STRUT

REPLACE

1. Remove lower control arm as outlined under "Lower Control Arm, Replace."
2. Separate tension strut from lower control arm.
3. Install replacement tension strut into lower control arm. Position tension strut with word Front stamped in strut positioned away from control arm as shown in **Fig. 13.**
4. Install lower control arm and tension strut into vehicle.
5. Install washer and new nut on tension strut.

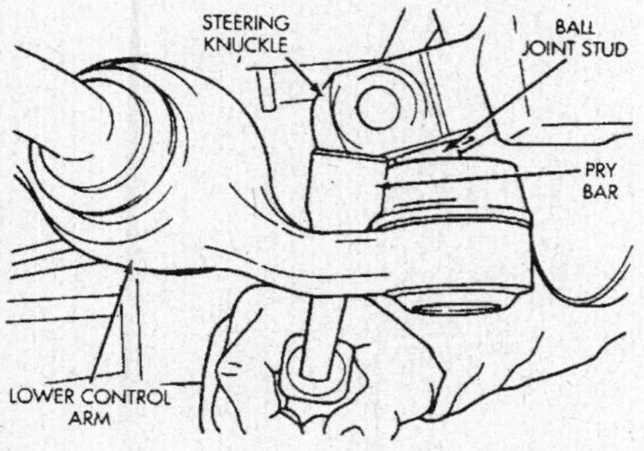

Fig. 5 Ball joint separation from steering knuckle

6. Install tire and wheel assembly.
7. Tighten lower control arm pivot bushing to cradle bracket attaching bolt with full weight of vehicle on suspension.

TIE ROD END

REPLACE

OUTER

1. Raise and support vehicle.
2. Remove tire and wheel assembly.
3. Loosen pinch bolt on tie rod sleeve, then remove tie rod to steering arm mounting nut.
4. Remove tie rod from steering arm using suspension component puller tool No. C-3894A, or equivalent.
5. Remove tie rod from sleeve.
6. Reverse procedure to install noting the following:
   a. Do not tighten adjustment pinch bolt at this time, tie rod to steering arm bolt must be tightened to specifications.
   b. Adjust toe as outlined under "Wheel Alignment."

INNER

1. Position wheels straight ahead.
2. Remove caps, mounting nuts and wiper arms, then the wiper module and cowl covers.
3. Remove mounting bolts, then reinforcement.
4. Remove inline resonator and inlet hose from throttle body, then the air inlet hose from air cleaner housing.
5. Raise and support vehicle until wheels are just off the ground.
6. Remove wheel assembly.
7. Turn steering wheel to full right position.
8. Remove tie rod end to steering arm mounting nut, then remove tie rod using suspension component puller tool No. C-3894A or equivalent.
9. Bend back tie rod to steering gear mounting bolt mounting plate retaining tabs.
10. Remove mounting bolts, mounting plate and washers. **Do not lose washer behind tie rod.**
11. Rotate loose end of mounting plate for clearance.
12. Remove tie rod assembly through wheel opening.

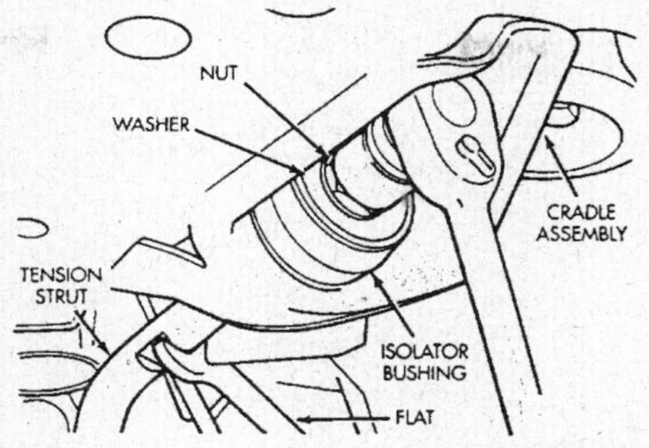

Fig. 6 Tension strut to cradle mounting

13. Loosen pinch bolt at inner to outer tie rod adjusting sleeve.
14. Remove tie rod from inner adjuster sleeve.
15. Reverse procedure to install noting the following:
    a. Adjust toe as outlined under "Wheel Alignment."
    b. Tighten all mounting bolts to specifications.

POWER STEERING GEAR

REPLACE

1. Position wheels straight ahead.
2. Remove caps, mounting nuts and wiper arms, then the wiper module and cowl covers.
3. Remove mounting bolts, then the reinforcement.
4. Remove inline resonator and inlet hose from throttle body, then the air inlet hose from air cleaner housing.
5. Raise and support vehicle until wheels are just off the ground.
6. Using suitable clamp, lock steering wheel from rotating, **to avoid damaging clock spring.**
7. Remove steering column coupler retaining pin and bolt, then separate intermediate steering shaft from column coupler.
8. Bend back tie rod to steering gear mounting bolt mounting plate retaining tabs.
9. Remove mounting bolts, mounting plate and washers, then lay tie rods on top of transaxle bell housing, **Fig. 14.**
10. Using suitable siphon pump, remove as much power steering fluid as possible from reservoir.
11. Remove power steering fluid pressure and return hoses from steering gear.
12. **On models equipped with speed proportional steering gear,** remove solenoid wiring harness connector.
13. **On all models,** remove mounting nuts, then the master cylinder with brake tubes connected from vacuum booster. Carefully position master cylinder upright on lefthand side valve cover.
14. Remove steering gear to crossmember lefthand, then righthand side mounting bolts. Loosen righthand

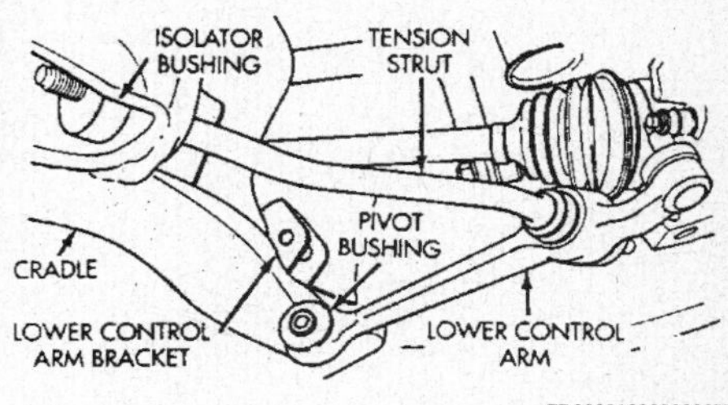

Fig. 7 Lower control arm removal

mounting bracket mounting bolts to clear air conditioning lines, if necessary.

15. Slide steering gear and intermediate shaft into engine compartment to access intermediate shaft flex coupler roll pin, **Fig. 15.**
16. Remove roll pin and separate intermediate steering shaft from steering gear, using roll pin remover tool No. 6831-A, or equivalent.
17. Raise and support vehicle, then remove righthand front tire and wheel assembly.
18. Remove tie rod end to steering arm mounting nut, using suspension puller tool No. C-3894-A, or equivalent, then remove tie rod.
19. **On models equipped with 2.7L engine,** turn front of lefthand front tire and wheel assembly as far outward as possible, for required clearance to remove steering gear.
20. **On all models,** slide steering gear end through righthand side inner fender tie rod hole until approximately half gear is through hole.
21. Lift lefthand end of gear up between engine and cowl, then pull gear out.
22. Reverse procedure to install, noting following:
    a. Ensure tie rod spacer block inside steering gear bellows is aligned with steering gear and gear bellow holes.
    b. Adjust toe as outlined under "Wheel Alignment."

POWER STEERING PUMP

REPLACE

1. Using suitable siphon pump, remove as much power steering fluid as possible from power steering reservoir.
2. Remove power steering fluid return hose from reservoir, then let fluid drain from reservoir and pump into suitable container.
3. Cap power steering fluid reservoir open nipple.
4. Remove pressure hose from power steering pump and let remaining fluid drain from pump into container.
5. **On models equipped with 3.2 and 3.5L engines,** remove power steering pressure switch wiring harness connector.
6. **On all models,** loosen serpentine drive belt tensioner locknut, then,

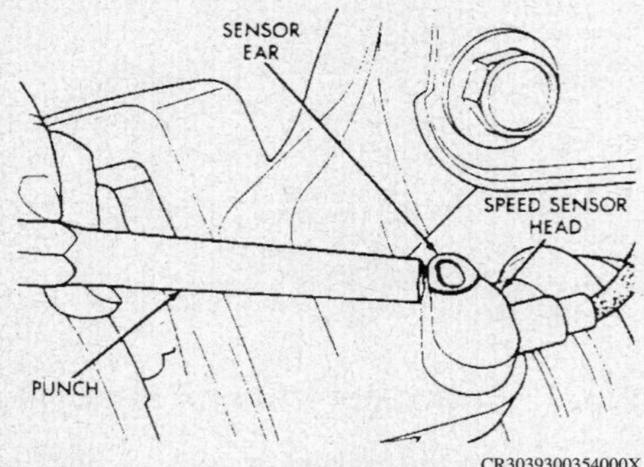

Fig. 8 Speed sensor removal

using adjustment bolt, remove power steering pump drive belt tension.
7. Remove drive belt from power steering pump pulley.
8. Remove pump mounting bolts through pulley face holes.
9. Insert suitable screwdriver between pump and tensioner bracket sleeve, then push sleeve forward in tensioner bracket until it is flush with tensioner bracket back.
10. Remove pump and pulley as an assembly. On 2.7L engines, reservoir is part of pump.
11. Reverse procedure to install, noting following:
    a. Long mounting bolt is install in tensioner bracket sleeve.
    b. Ensure return hose clamp is installed past nipple upset bead.
    c. Tighten mounting bolts to specifications.

POWER STEERING SYSTEM BLEED

During bleeding procedure, keep fluid in reservoir at correct level.

1. Raise and support front of vehicle.
2. Manually turn oil pump pulley a few times.
3. Turn steering wheel from stop to stop five or six times.
4. Disconnect high tension cable then operate starter motor intermittently while turning steering wheel from stop to stop five or six times.
5. Connect high tension cable and start engine.
6. Turn steering wheel from stop to stop until no bubbles appear in reservoir.
7. Ensure fluid is not milky and that at proper level.
8. Confirm there is little or no change in fluid level when steering wheel is turned from stop to stop.
9. Ensure difference in fluid level is no more than .2 inch with engine running and when it is stopped.
10. If fluid level is not as specified, system is not completely bled. Repeat procedure.

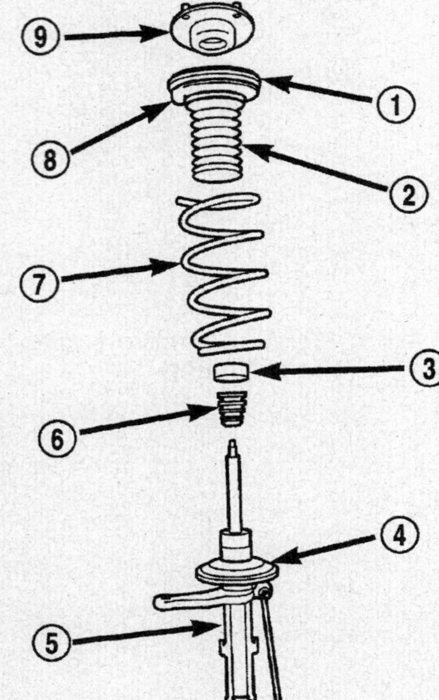

Fig. 9 Exploded view of strut assembly

TECHNICAL SERVICE BULLETINS

LOOSE FEEL OR CLUNK IN STEERING WHEEL

1998–2001

On these models loose feel or clunk in steering wheel as wheel is moved from side to side.

This condition can be caused by inner tie rod bushings.

Replacement of both tie rod bushings and all mounting hardware is recommended.

To correct this condition, install inner tie rod bushing kit P/N 05072586AA as follows:

1. Remove inner tie rods as outlined under "Tie Rod End, Replace."
2. Replace inner tie rod bushings using receiver tool No. 8438-1, 8438-3, 8438-4 and bushing sizer tool No. 8438-2.
3. Refer to **Figs. 16 and 17** to assemble receiver tool for bushing removal.
4. Mount receiver tool into suitable vise.
5. Place inner tie rod bushing end into receiver.
6. Place remover/installer tool No. 8438–4, or equivalent, small end down on top of bushing.
7. Insert screw tool No. 8438–3, or equivalent, through remover/installer tool and tie rod bushing until it threads into bottom of receiver.
8. To remove bushing hand tighten screw until it bottoms out.
9. Remove screw, receiver, tie rod end, then bushing from receiver.
10. Use Mopar silicone spray P/N 04318070, or equivalent, spray bushing, inner tie rod end, then inside bushing sizer.
11. **Inner tie rod bushing is symmetrical. There is no designated top or bottom.**
12. Place new bushing in bore of sizer tool, slide bushing to bottom of sizer bore.
13. Mount receiver into suitable vise, then place inner tie rod end into receiver.
14. Place sizer with bushing on top of tie rod bushing bore with tapered end facing downward.
15. Place Installer tool No. 8438-4, or equivalent, small end down on top of bushing.
16. Insert screw tool No. 8438-3, or equivalent, through installer bushing with sizer, then tie rod end until threads bottom in receiver.
17. Slowly tighten screw, pushing bushing out of sizer into tie rod end bore until it bottoms out.
18. Disassemble receiver and sizer tools, then remove tie rod from receiver.
19. Bushing will appear slightly off center in tie rod, this is a normal condition.
20. Install tie rod end as outlined under "Tie Rod End, Replace."

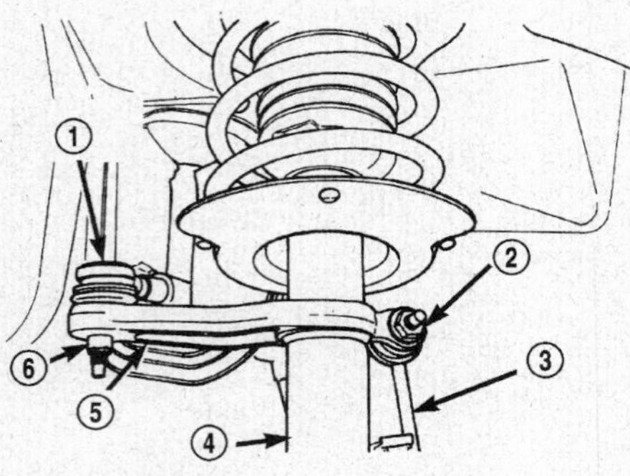

Fig. 10 Stabilizer bar link at strut

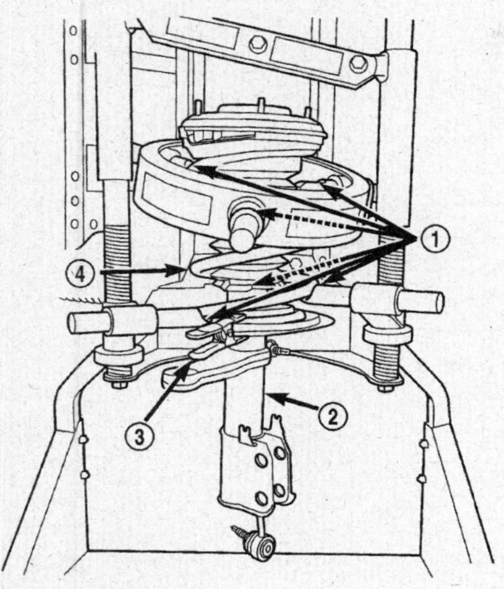

1 - HOOKS
2 - STRUT ASSEMBLY
3 - CLAMP
4 - COIL SPRING

CR2020100181000X

Fig. 11 Strut assembly in compressor

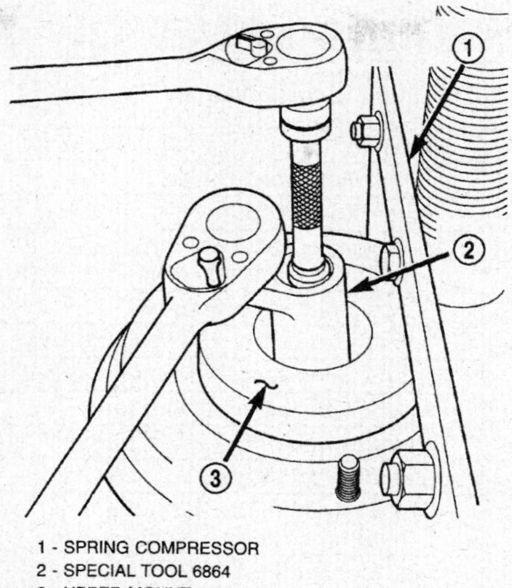

1 - SPRING COMPRESSOR
2 - SPECIAL TOOL 6864
3 - UPPER MOUNT

CR2020100182000X

Fig. 12 Strut shaft removal

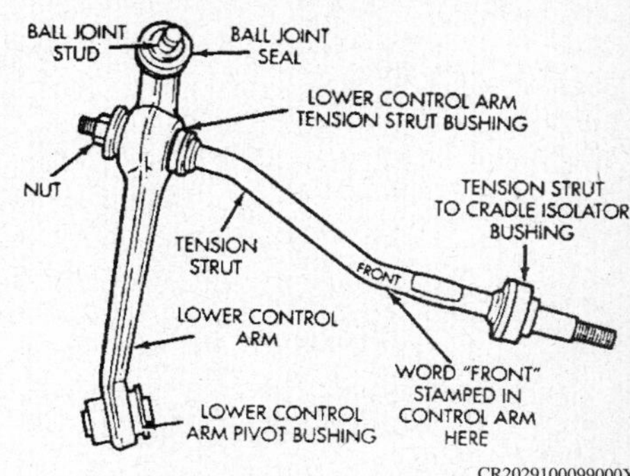

CR2029100099000X

Fig. 13 Tension strut removal from control arm

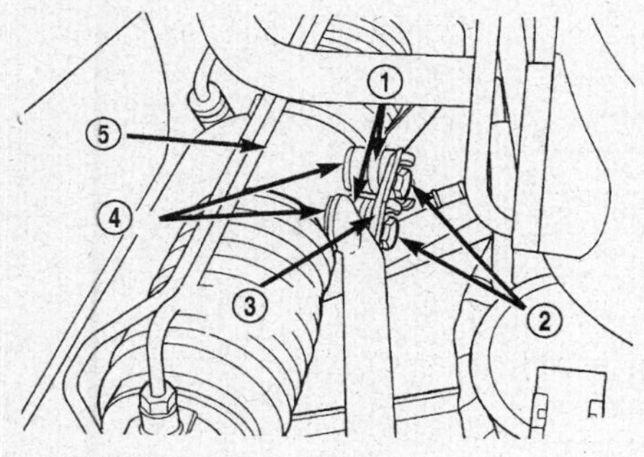

1 - TIE RODS
2 - BOLTS
3 - MOUNTING PLATE
4 - WASHERS
5 - STEERING GEAR

CR6030100231000X

Fig. 14 Tie rod to steering gear attaching bolts

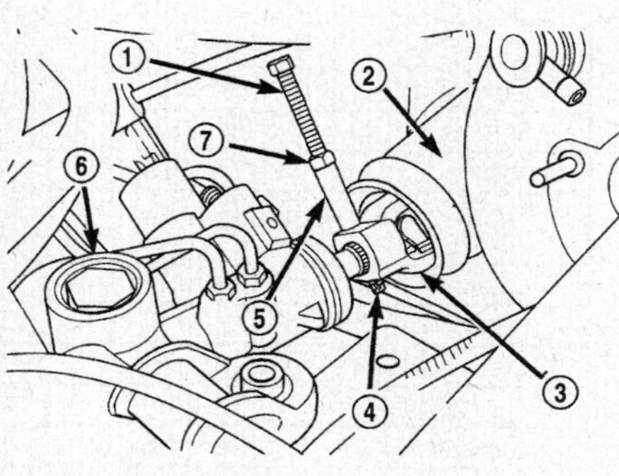

1 - SPECIAL TOOL 6831–A
2 - DASH PANEL SEAL & BOOT
3 - FLEX JOINT
4 - KNURLED NUT
5 - SLEEVE
6 - STEERING GEAR
7 - NUT

CR6030100232000X

Fig. 15 Steering gear roll pin removal

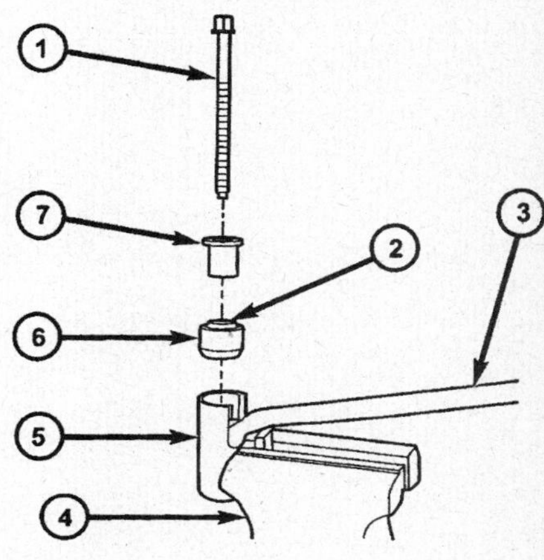

1 - 8438-3 SCREW
2 - BUSHING
3 - INNER TIE ROD END
4 - VISE
5 - 8438-1 (RECEIVER)
6 - 8438-2 (SIZER)
7 - 8438-4 (REMOVER/INSTALLER)

CR2020100185000X

Fig. 16 Receiver tool & tie rod end. 1998–2001

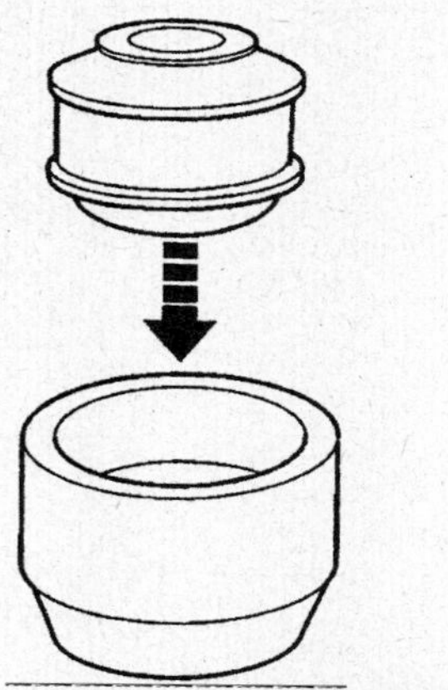

CR2020100186000X

Fig. 17 Bushing sizer tool & bushing. 1998–2001

TIGHTENING SPECIFICATIONS

Year	Component	Torque/Ft. Lbs.
1998–2002	Ball Joint Stud To Steering Knuckle	40
	Disc Brake Caliper	16
	Front Cradle Assembly To Body	120
	Hub & Bearing Assembly To Steering Knuckle	80
	Hub & Bearing Axle Nut	105
	Inner Tie Rod To Steering Gear	74
	Lower Control Arm To Cradle Pivot	105
	Master Cylinder Mounting Nuts	21
	Outer Tie Rod Adjuster Pinch Bolt	28
	Outer Tie Rod To Steering Arm Nut	27
	Power Steering Fluid Pressure Hose To Discharge Fitting	62
	Power Steering Pressure Hose Tube	35
	Power Steering Pressure Switch	15
	Power Steering Pump To Bracket Bolts	21
	Power Steering Return Tube	23
	Reservoir Mounting Bolts 2.7L Pulley Side	10
	Reservoir Mounting Bolts 2.7L Rear	18
	Reservoir Mounting Screws 3.2L/3.5L	①105
	Stabilizer Bar Attaching Link To Strut	17
	Stabilizer Bar Bushing Retainer To Cradle	45
	Stabilizer Bar Link Lower Nut	65
	Stabilizer Bar Link Upper Nut	70
	Steering Gear To Crossmember	43
	Strut Assembly Shaft	70
	Strut Assembly To Shock Tower	28
	Strut Assembly To Steering Knuckle	150②
	Sway Bar To Strut Link	70
	Tension Strut	95
	Wheel Lug Nut	100③

① — Inch lbs.
② — Strut bolts have a serrated shaft so do not turn bolts in steering knuckle. Turn nuts on bolts. Do not turn bolts.
③ — Refer to “Hub & Bearing, Replace” for tightening sequence.

Wheel Alignment

NOTE: Prior To Performing Any Service Operations Listed In This Section, Consult The "Technical Service Bulletins" Section For Related Information.

INDEX

PRELIMINARY INSPECTION

Before any attempt is made to change or correct front wheel alignment, the following inspections and necessary corrections must be made.

1. Ensure tire pressure is at recommended pressure, all tires should be same size and in good condition and have approximately same wear.
2. Check front wheels and tire assembly for radial runout.
3. Inspect lower ball joint and steering linkage for looseness.
4. Check for broken or damaged front and rear springs.
5. **Just prior to each alignment reading, then vehicle should be jounced (rear first, then front) by grasping bumper at center and jouncing each end of vehicle an equal number of times. Always release bumpers at bottom of down cycle.**

FRONT WHEEL ALIGNMENT

CAMBER

1998

If front camber is not within specifications, and strut and steering knuckles are not bent or damaged, use following procedure to modify strut clevis bracket to adjust camber.

1. Raise and support front of vehicle, then remove tire and wheel assemblies.
2. Remove stabilizer bar link from strut, then loosen, but do not remove outer tie rod end nut.
3. Using Puller tool No. C-3894-A, or equivalent, remove tie rod end from steering arm.
4. Remove ABS wheel speed sensor routing bracket from strut.
5. Remove mounting bolts, then separate strut from steering knuckle and position knuckle out of way.
6. Using suitable grinder and cutting tool, elongate bottom strut bracket mounting hole .0789 inch left and right.
7. Install steering knuckle and loosely install bolts attaching strut to knuckle.
8. Install speed sensor bracket.
9. Install outer tie rod and tighten nut to specifications.
10. Install stabilizer bar attaching link and tighten nut to specifications.
11. Install tire and wheel assemblies.
12. Lower vehicle, then jounce front and rear of vehicle equal number of times.
13. Adjust front camber to preferred specifications by pushing in or pulling out on top of tire and wheel assembly.
14. Tighten upper and lower mounting bolts enough to not allow steering knuckle to move, then jounce front and rear of vehicle equal number of times.
15. Ensure camber is with specifications, then tighten mounting bolts to specifications.
16. Inspect and correct toe as necessary.

1999–2002

If front camber is not within specifications, strut and steering knuckles are not bent or damaged there are special undersize camber adjustment bolts and nuts are available to allow adjustment. This involves replacing the original clevis to knuckle bolts using the following procedure.

1. Raise and support front of vehicle, then remove tire and wheel assemblies.
2. Remove strut assembly to steering knuckle attaching bolts. **Strut bolts have a serrated shaft for a tight fit into steering knuckle. Turn nut on bolts only, do not turn bolts.**
3. Loosely install special undersize camber bolts so nuts are toward front of vehicle.
4. Install wheels lower vehicle, then jounce front and rear of vehicle.
5. Adjust front camber to preferred specifications by pulling in or pushing outward on top of wheel assembly, tighten bolts to specifications.
6. Inspect and correct toe as necessary.

TOE

1. Prepare vehicle as outlined under "Preliminary Inspection."
2. Center steering wheel and hold with steering wheel clamp.
3. Loosen tie rod adjustment sleeve jam nuts. Rotate adjustment sleeve to align toe to specifications.
4. **When setting toe, maximum threads exposed on inner and outer tie rod can not exceed 20 mm, Fig. 1.**
5. When tightening adjustment pinch bolt use following procedure.
   a. Using a tie rod adjustment tool, **Fig. 2** on neck area of outer tie rod to maintain correct perpendicular orientation of tie rod stud within tie rod end.
   b. **Torque** tie rod adjustment pinch nut to 28 ft. lbs.
   c. Remove steering wheel clamp.

REAR WHEEL ALIGNMENT

TOE

1. Prepare vehicle as outlined under "Preliminary Inspection."
2. Loosen lateral link adjustment link jam nuts.
3. Rotate adjustment link as required to set rear wheel toe to specification.
4. **Do not exceed maximum length dimension of lateral links as shown in Fig. 3. Both dimensions must be checked.**
5. **Torque** lateral links locknuts to 65ft. lbs.

TECHNICAL SERVICE BULLETINS

LEADS OR PULLS ON FLAT NON-CROWNED ROADS

On these models from 1993–99, the vehicle leads or pulls on a flat non-crowned road.

This condition may be caused by caster bias. To correct this condition, proceed as follows:

1. Loosen engine cradle to frame bolts.
2. **If vehicle leads left,** rotate cradle to increase lefthand caster .8° and reduce righthand caster .8°.
3. **If vehicle leads right,** rotate cradle to increase righthand caster .8° and reduce lefthand caster .8°.

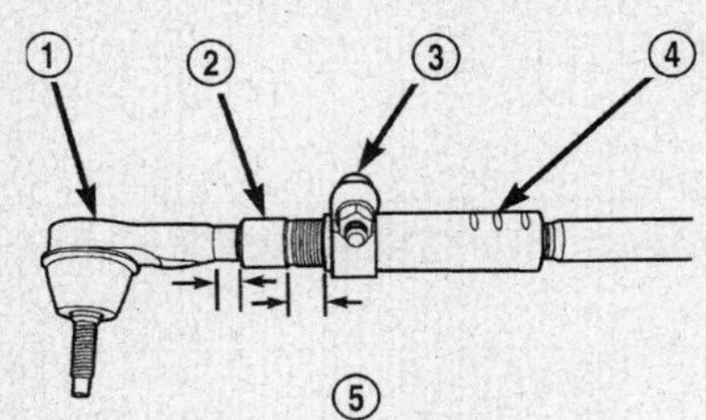

Fig. 1 Front tie rod adjustment dimensions

4. **On all models, torque** engine cradle to frame bolts to 129 ft. lbs.
5. Center steering wheel and set toe. If condition still exists, proceed to next step.
6. raise and support vehicle, then remove tire and wheel assemblies.

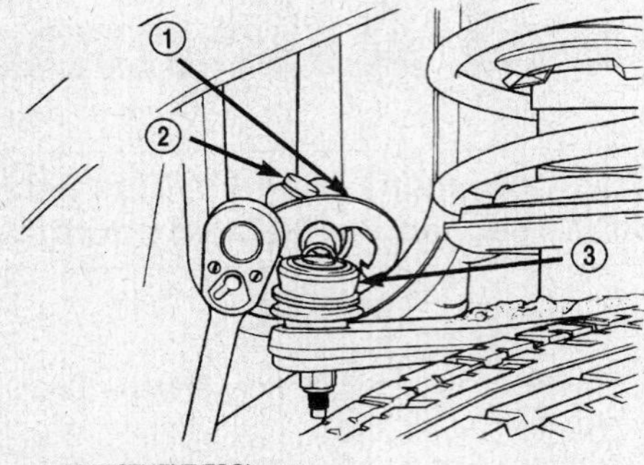

Fig. 2 Front wheel toe adjustment location

7. Remove strut clevis to knuckle bolts and nuts.
8. Loosely assembly new clevis to knuckle bolts (part No. 06505363AA) and nuts (part No. 06505363AA).

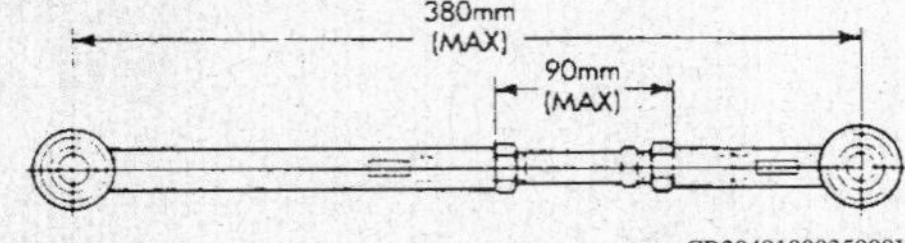

Fig. 3 Rear tie rod adjustment dimensions

9. Install tire and wheel assemblies, then lower vehicle.
10. Adjust front camber to preferred setting by physically pushing or pulling on top of tire.
11. When camber is correct, **torque** upper then lower strut clevis bolt to 160 ft. lbs.
12. Set front toe to specifications.
13. Road test vehicle.
14. If vehicle still drifts or leads, repeat camber adjustment procedure but bias cross camber setting opposite lead tendency. If vehicle leads left, set front lefthand camber to minus .3° and front righthand camber to plus .6°.

NEON

NOTE: Refer To The Rear Of This Manual For Manufacturer's Special Service Tool Supplies.

INDEX OF SERVICE OPERATIONS

Specifications

GENERAL ENGINE SPECIFICATIONS

Engine	Engine VIN Code①	Fuel System	Bore & Stroke, Inches	Compres-sion Ratio	Net HP @ RPM	Maximum Torque, Ft. Lbs. @ RPM	Normal Oil Pressure, psi	
							Curb Idle	3000 RPM
1998–99								
2.0L	Y	SMPI	3.45 X 3.27	9.6	150 @ 6500	133 @ 5500	4	25–80
2.0L	C	SMPI	3.45 X 3.27	9.8	132 @ 6000	129 @ 5000	4	25–80
2000–02								
2.0L	C	SMPI	3.45 X 3.27	9.8	132 @ 5600	130 @ 4600	4	25–80
2.0L	F	SMPI	3.45 X 3.27	9.8	150 @ 6500	135 @ 4400	4	25–80

DOHC — Dual Overhead Cam
SMPI — Sequential Multi-Port Fuel Injection
SOHC — Single Overhead Cam
① — Eighth digit of VIN denotes engine code.

TUNE UP SPECIFICATIONS

Engine	Spark Plug Gap, Inch	Ignition Timing		Curb Idle Speed	Fuel Pump Pressure, psi	Valve Clearance, Inch
		Firing Order ④	°BTDC			
1998–99						
2.0L	.035	1-3-4-2	①	③	48②	⑤
2000–02						
2.0L	.035	1-3-4-2	①	550–1300	48.7–49.7	⑤

BTDC — Before Top Dead Center
① — Direct Ignition System (DIS); not adjustable.
② — Less vacuum applied to pressure regulator.
③ — Less than 1000 miles, 550–1300 RPM. More than 1000 miles, 600–1300 RPM.
④ — Refer to **Fig. A** for spark plug wire connections.
⑤ — Equipped w/non-adjustable hydraulic lash adjusters.

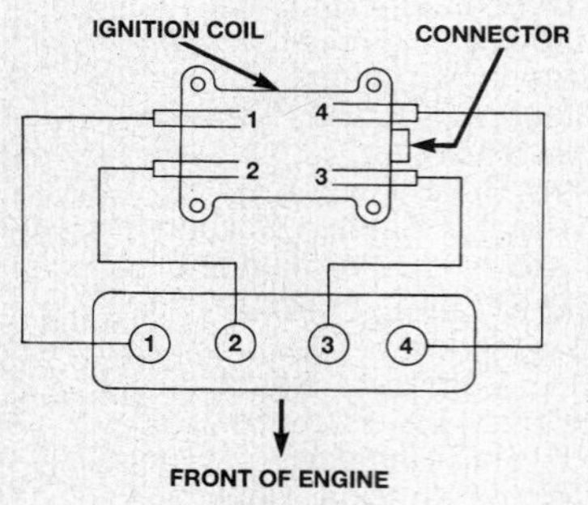

Fig. A

FRONT WHEEL ALIGNMENT SPECIFICATIONS

Year	Camber, Degrees①		Caster, Degrees①		Toe In, Degrees		Ball Joint Wear
	Limits	Desired	Limits	Desired	Limits	Desired	
1998–99	−0.4 to +0.4	0	+1.8 to +3.8②	+2.8	−0.1 to +0.3	+0.1	③
2000–02	−0.4 to +0.4	0	+1.6 to +3.6②	+2.6	−0.1 to +0.3	+0.1	③

① — Reference angle only; not adjustable.

② — Side to side differential not to exceed 0.1°.

③ — Refer to "Ball Joint Inspection" under "Front Suspension & Steering."

REAR WHEEL ALIGNMENT SPECIFICATIONS

Year	Camber Angle, Degrees①		Total Toe, Degrees①		Thrust Angle, Degrees①
	Limits	Desired	Limits	Desired	
1998–99	–.75 to +.25	–.25	–.1 to +.3	+.1	–.1 to +.1
2000–02	–.65 to +.15	–.25	–.1 to +.5	+.3	–.1 to +.1

① — Reference angle only. Non-adjustable.

VEHICLE RIDE HEIGHT SPECIFICATIONS

Year	Body Style	Manufacturer's Original Tire Size	Measurement Points & Specifications①					
			Front			Rear		
			Dim.	Specification		Dim.	Specification	
				Inches	mm		Inches	mm
1998-99	2 door	①	G	7.75②	197	H	8.62②	219
	4 door	①	G	6.50②;	165	H	7.50②	190
2000	All	①	A	26.43②	672	B	26.75②	679
2001–02	All	①	A	26.46③	672	B	26.73③	679

A Dim. — Ground to Lower Edge of Front Wheel Well
B Dim. — Ground to Lower Edge of Rear Wheel Well
G Dim. — Ground to Front Rocker Panel
H Dim. — Ground to Rear Rocker Panel
① — See door sticker or inside of glove box for manufacturer's original tire size specifications. If tires on vehicle do not match manufacturer's original tire size & measurement is not within limits, it will be necessary to refer to the "Non-Standard Tire & Wheel Size Adjustment To Ride Height Specification & Tire Size Adjustment Charts" in the front of this manual for approximate changes in ride height specifications.
② — ±.25″ (6.35 mm).
③ — ±.32″ (8 mm).

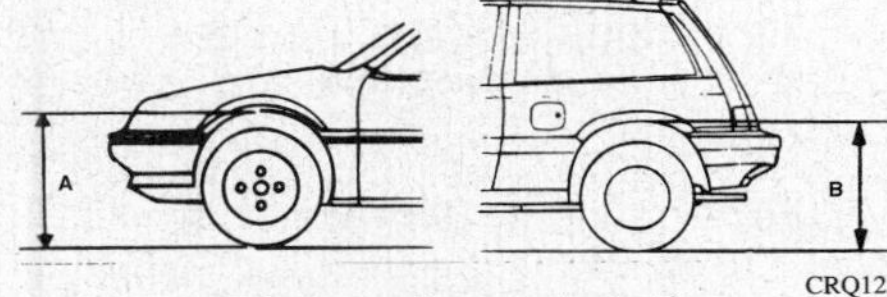

Dimensions A & B

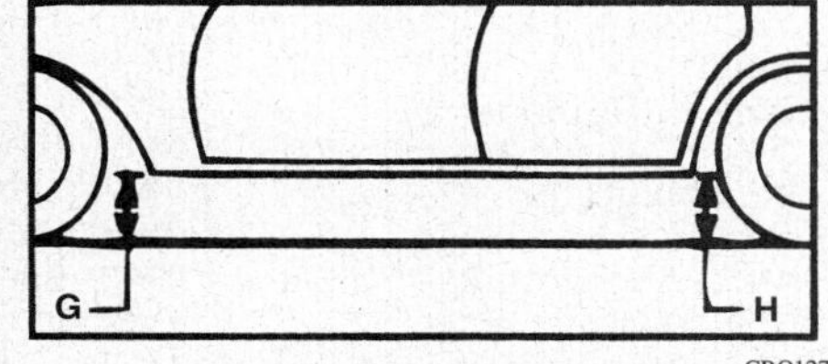

Dimensions G & H

FLUID CAPACITIES & COOLING SYSTEM DATA

Year	Coolant Capacity, Qts.	Coolant Type	Radiator Cap Relief Pressure, Lbs.	Thermo. Opening Temp., °F	Fuel Tank, Gals.	Engine Oil Refill, Qts.③	Auto. Transaxle Oil, Qts.②	Man. Transaxle Oil, Pts.
1998–99	7.4	Ethylene Glycol	16	195	12.5	4.5	①	4.0–4.6
2000–02	6.5	Ethylene Glycol	14–18	192–199	12.5	4	④	4.0–4.6

① — Fluid change only, 4.0 qts. After overhaul: except fleet models, 8.9 qts.; fleet models, 9.2 qts.
② — Approximate. Make final inspection w/dipstick.
③ — Includes oil filter.
④ — Fluid change only, 4.0 qts. After overhaul, 8.6 qts.

LUBRICANT DATA

Year	Transaxle		Power Steering	Brake System
	Automatic	Manual		
1998	Mopar ATF Type 7176	Mopar Type MS 9417	Mopar No. 4318055	DOT 3
1999	Mopar ATF Type 7176	Mopar Type MS 9417	Mopar No. 5010304AA	DOT 3
2000–01	Mopar ATF+4 Type 9602	Mopar Type MS 9417	Mopar No. 5010304AA	DOT 3
2002	Mopar ATF+4 Type 9602	Mopar ATF+4 Type 9602	Mopar ATF+4 Type 9602	DOT 3

Electrical

NOTE: On Air Bag Equipped Models, Refer To "Air Bag System Precautions" Located In The Front Of This Manual For System Disarming & Arming Procedures.

NOTE: Refer To "Computer Relearn Procedures" Located In The Front Of This Manual When Battery Power To The Computer Has Been Interrupted.

INDEX

PRECAUTIONS

AIR BAG SYSTEMS

Refer to "Air Bag System Precautions" in the front of this manual for system disarming and arming procedures.

BATTERY GROUND CABLE

Prior to service, disconnect battery ground cable and isolate as required.

FUSE PANEL LOCATION

On 1998–99 models, the fuse panel is located behind the lefthand side of the instrument panel, to the left of the steering column.

On 2000–02 models, the fuse block is positioned on a mounting bracket up and under the lefthand side of the instrument panel, secured by two screws. It can be accessed by removing the instrument panel end cap.

FUEL PUMP RELAY LOCATION

The fuel pump relay is located in the Power Distribution Center (PDC), at the lefthand side of the engine compartment near the battery.

RELAY CENTER LOCATION

The relay center is located on the lefthand side of the engine compartment, next to the battery.

STARTER

REPLACE

1. Raise and support vehicle.
2. **On 1998–99 models equipped with A/C,** proceed as follows:
   a. Support engine and transaxle so it will not rotate using suitable floor jack or jack stand.
   b. Remove front engine mount insulator through bolt and front crossmember mounting bracket.
   c. Lower engine to rotate assembly forward to access starter.
3. **On models equipped with VIN F engine,** disconnect inlet hose from intake manifold and reposition air cleaner box.
4. **On all models,** remove starter to transaxle housing mounting bolts.
5. Remove starter transaxle to access electrical connectors.
6. Remove starter and solenoid connectors, as required. Record wiring and electrical locations for installation.
7. **On 1998–99 models,** position starter vertically with flange pointed downward and position air conditioning lines for clearance.
8. **On all models,** remove starter.
9. Reverse procedure to install, noting the following:
   a. **Torque** starter mounting bolts to 40 ft. lbs.
   b. **Torque** front engine mount through bolt to 40 ft. lbs.

ALTERNATOR

REPLACE

1. Loosen alternator adjustment nut.
2. **On 1998–99 models,** turn front wheels fully to right.
3. **On all models,** raise and support vehicle.
4. Remove lower splash shield.
5. Disconnect alternator wiring.
6. Loosen alternator pivot bolt.
7. Remove alternator drive belt.
8. Remove pivot bracket mounting bolts.
9. Remove pivot nut from T-bolt while supporting alternator.
10. Lower alternator and remove through wheelwell.
11. Reverse procedure to install, noting the following:
    a. **Torque** alternator mounting bolts to 40 ft. lbs.
    b. **Torque** alternator feed terminal nut to 72 inch lbs.

COIL PACK

REPLACE

1. Disconnect coil pack electrical connector and remove mounting bolts.
2. Remove coil pack from valve cover.
3. Reverse procedure to install, noting the following:
    a. **On 1998–99 models, torque** coil pack to valve cover bolts to 17 ft. lbs.
    b. **On 2000–02 models, torque** coil pack to valve cover bolts to 106 inch lbs.
    c. **On all models,** transfer spark plug wires to corresponding coil pack towers.

IGNITION LOCK

REPLACE

Refer to "Ignition Switch, Replace" for ignition lock replacement procedure.

IGNITION SWITCH

REPLACE

1. Turn ignition to Run position.
2. Using suitable tool, depress lock cylinder retaining tab through hole in lower column shroud and remove lock cylinder.
3. Remove steering column upper and lower shrouds as required.
4. Disconnect ignition switch electrical connectors.
5. Remove ignition switch mounting screw.
6. Depress retaining tabs and pull ignition switch from steering column.
7. Reverse procedure to install, ensuring ignition switch and actuator rod in lock housing are both in Run position.

CLUTCH START SWITCH

REPLACE

1998–99

1. Disconnect electrical connector.

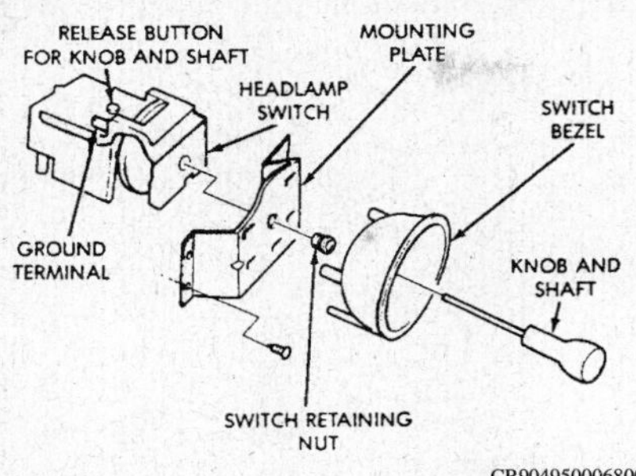

Fig. 1 Headlamp switch replacement. 1998–99

2. Depress switch tabs and push through mounting bracket.
3. Reverse procedure to install.

2000

1. Remove instrument panel as outlined in "Dash Panel Service" chapter.
2. **Record clutch interlock/upstop switch wiring routing to avoid interference with pedals.**
3. Disconnect clutch interlock/upstop switch electrical connector.
4. Depress plastic wing tabs and remove switch.
5. Reverse procedure to install, noting the following:
    a. **On models equipped with tilt steering,** do not release tilt lever from locked position until after steering column has been securely installed on instrument panel.
    b. **On all models, torque** two steering column lower and upper mounting nuts to 12 ft. lbs.
    c. **Torque** column pinch bolt to 21 ft. lbs.
    d. **Torque** steering wheel mounting nut to 45 ft. lbs.
    e. **Torque** driver's air bag module to steering wheel bolts to 90 inch lbs.

2001–02

1. Remove left lower instrument panel bezel.
2. Disconnect clutch master cylinder rod from clutch pedal pin. **Inspect plastic retainer upon removal, it must be replaced if damaged.**
3. Remove brake booster push rod retaining clip from brake pedal, then disengage rod from pedal.
4. Remove pedal assembly bracket to instrument panel nuts, then brake booster/pedal bracket to cowl nuts.
5. From under hood, pull brake master cylinder/booster forward enough to obtain pedal to bracket stud clearance.
6. Remove pedal bracket assembly, then the pedal pivot shaft and brake/clutch pedals.
7. Remove interlock/upstop switch assembly from brake/clutch pedal bracket assembly by depressing four plastic wing tabs on each switch.
8. Reverse procedure to install noting the following:
    a. **Torque** pivot shaft nut, brake booster mounting nuts and pedal bracket to instrument panel nuts to 25 ft. lbs.
    b. **Torque** adjustment screw to 70 inch lbs.

HEADLAMP SWITCH

REPLACE

1998–99

1. Remove steering column cover and liner.
2. Remove three screws securing headlamp switch mounting plate to instrument panel.
3. Pull headlamp switch rearward from instrument panel opening.
4. Disconnect electrical connectors.
5. Depress button on bottom of switch and pull control knob out of switch, **Fig. 1.**
6. Unsnap headlamp switch bezel from mounting plate for access to mounting nut.
7. Remove mounting nut and mounting plate.
8. Reverse procedure to install.

2000–02

Refer to "Combination Switch, Replace" for procedures.

STOP LIGHT SWITCH

REPLACE

1. Depress brake pedal and rotate switch counterclockwise approximately 30°.
2. Pull switch rearward and remove from mounting bracket.
3. Disconnect electrical connector.
4. Pull switch plunger head out until ratchet sound stops.
5. Reverse procedure to install.

COMBINATION SWITCH

REPLACE

1. Remove steering column upper and lower shrouds.
2. Disconnect all combination switch electrical connectors.
3. Remove mounting screws and combination switch.
4. Reverse procedure to install. Transfer any components from old to new switch, as required.

TURN SIGNAL SWITCH

REPLACE

Refer to "Combination Switch, Replace" for procedure.

DIMMER SWITCH

REPLACE

Refer to "Combination Switch, Replace" for procedure.

STEERING WHEEL

REPLACE

1. Place front wheels in straight ahead position.

2. Rotate steering wheel 180° clockwise.
3. Lock steering with column lock cylinder.
4. Remove speed control switch and connector.
5. Remove air bag as outlined in "Passive Restraint Systems" section.
6. Remove steering wheel mounting nut and vibration damper, if equipped.
7. Using appropriate puller tool, remove steering wheel while avoiding damage to clockspring wiring.
8. Reverse procedure to install, noting the following:
   a. Install steering wheel ensuring flats on hub align with clockspring.
   b. **On 1998–2000 models, torque** steering wheel mounting nut to 45 ft. lbs.
   c. **On 2001–02 models, torque** steering wheel mounting nut to 40 ft. lbs.

INSTRUMENT CLUSTER

REPLACE

1. **On 2000–02 models,** using trim stick tool No. C-4755, or equivalent, remove A-pillar moldings.
2. **On all models,** remove instrument panel top cover and cluster bezel.
3. Remove cluster housing to base panel mounting screws.
4. Pull cluster rearward to disconnect from base panel.
5. Remove cluster assembly.
6. Reverse procedure to install.

RADIO

REPLACE

1. Remove instrument panel center module bezel.
2. Remove radio mounting screws and pull radio out of instrument panel.
3. Disconnect radio electrical connectors, ground wire and antenna lead.
4. Reverse procedure to install.

WIPER MOTOR

REPLACE

1998–99

1. Remove wiper arms and blades.
2. Remove rear hood seal and cowl screen.
3. Remove electrical connector at wiper motor.
4. Remove wiper mounting screws.
5. Disconnect wiper motor wiper bellcrank linkage.
6. Reverse procedure to install.

2000–02

1. Remove wiper arms and blades.
2. Remove cowl cover to cowl screws at base of windshield opening.
3. Remove hood to cowl seal at leading edge of cowl cover. Pull seal toward front of vehicle.
4. Remove cowl cover.
5. Disconnect electrical connectors at wiper motor.
6. Remove windshield wiper module.

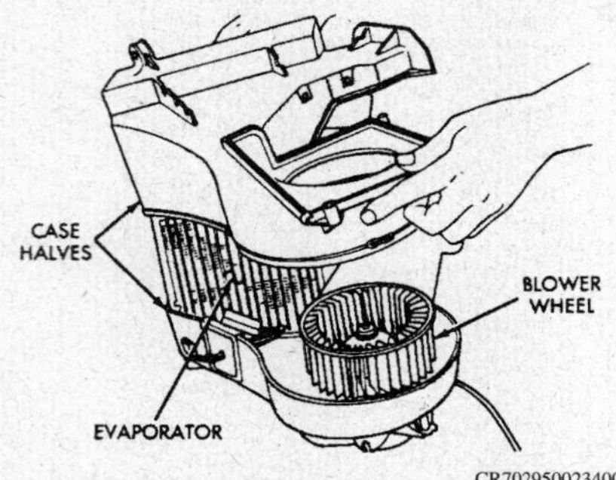

Fig. 2 Typical evaporator case separation

7. Remove motor crank linkage by inserting suitable screwdriver between crank and linkage, then twisting and lifting straight up.
8. Remove mounting screws and separate windshield wiper motor from linkage.
9. Reverse procedure to install, noting the following:
   a. Add suitable unilube grease to socket.
   b. **Torque** motor mounting screws to 45–55 inch lbs.
   c. **Torque** drive link nut to 98–106 inch lbs.

WIPER SWITCH

REPLACE

1998–99

1. Remove mounting screws and steering column shroud upper half.
2. Remove mounting screws on switch and remove switch.
3. Disconnect electrical connector.
4. Reverse procedure to install.

2000–02

Refer to "Combination Switch, Replace" for procedures.

BLOWER MOTOR

REPLACE

1. **On models less air conditioning,** disconnect electrical connector and remove blower motor by turning approximately ⅛ turn counterclockwise while pulling down locking tab.
2. **On models equipped with air conditioning,** remove righthand side scuff plate and pull back carpet.
3. **On 1998–99 models,** cut wheel housing silencer in line with blower motor wiring.
4. **On all models,** disconnect blower motor wiring connector.
5. Remove mounting screws and lower blower motor from housing.
6. Reverse procedure to install, taping silencer in position.

HEATER CORE

REPLACE

1998–99

1. Drain coolant into suitable container.
2. Remove instrument panel as outlined in "Dash Panel Service" chapter.
3. Disconnect heater hoses at dash panel.
4. Plug heater core outlets to prevent coolant spillage during housing removal.
5. **On models equipped with A/C,** evacuate and recover A/C refrigerant.
6. **On all models,** remove suction line at expansion valve. Plug refrigerant lines to prevent contamination of system.
7. Remove expansion valve and drain hose.
8. Remove engine compartment firewall mounting nuts.
9. Remove righthand heater case mounting screw.
10. Disconnect blue five-way connector from plenum.
11. Remove heater case.
12. Remove clips and screws to separate air distribution and evaporator/blower modules.
13. Remove panel opening, demister opening and heater core tube foam seals.
14. Remove clips and screws holding housing halves together.
15. Turn unit upside down, separate module halves and lift heater core out of case.
16. Reverse procedure to install.

2000–02

1. Drain coolant into suitable container.
2. Remove instrument panel as outlined in "Dash Panel Service" chapter.
3. Disconnect heater hoses at dash panel.
4. Plug heater core outlets to prevent coolant spillage during housing removal.
5. **On models equipped with A/C,** evacuate and recover A/C refrigerant.
6. **On all models,** remove coolant reservoir fasteners and position reservoir aside.
7. Remove suction line at expansion valve. Plug refrigerant lines to prevent contamination of system.
8. Remove expansion valve. Plug all fittings.
9. Remove rubber drain tube extension from evaporator drain.
10. Disconnect vacuum harness at brake booster.
11. Unsnap and remove defroster duct.
12. Remove engine side of firewall housing mounting nuts.
13. Remove righthand side mounting screw.
14. Remove one remaining nut located on dash panel stud.
15. Disconnect electrical connectors as required.
16. Remove unit housing.
17. Separate air distribution outlet foam seals at case halves.
18. Remove foam seals at evaporator and heater core tubes.
19. Remove retaining clips and screws holding halves together.
20. Separate housing halves.
21. Lift heater core out of housing.
22. Reverse procedure to install.

EVAPORATOR CORE

REPLACE

1. Remove unit housing as outlined under "Heater Core, Replace."
2. Remove clips and screws to separate evaporator/blower case.
3. Remove evaporator case foam seal.
4. Remove mounting screws and air duct with recirculation door assembly.
5. Disconnect fin sensing switch.
6. Remove upper and lower clips and screws, then separate case halves, **Fig. 2.**
7. Remove evaporator.
8. Reverse procedure to install.

2.0L Engine

NOTE: On Models Equipped With Dual Overhead Cam (DOHC) Engine, Refer To The "2.0L Engine" Chapter In The "Talon" Section Of This Manual For Any Procedures Not Covered In This Section.

NOTE: On Models Equipped With Single Overhead Cam (SOHC) Engine, Refer To The "2.0L Engine" Section In The "Breeze, Cirrus, Sebring Convertible & 1998–2000 Stratus & 2001-02 Sebring & Stratus Sedan" Chapter Of This Manual For Any Procedures Not Covered In This Section.

NOTE: On Air Bag Equipped Models, Refer To "Air Bag System Precautions" Located In The Front Of This Manual For System Disarming & Arming Procedures.

NOTE: Refer To "Computer Relearn Procedures" Located In The Front Of This Manual When Battery Power To The Computer Has Been Interrupted.

NOTE: Prior To Performing Any Service Operations Listed In This Section, Consult The "Technical Service Bulletins" For Related Information.

INDEX

PRECAUTIONS

AIR BAG SYSTEMS

Refer to "Air Bag System Precautions" in the front of this manual for system disarming and arming procedures.

BATTERY GROUND CABLE

Prior to service, disconnect battery ground cable and isolate as required.

FUEL SYSTEM PRESSURE RELIEF

1998–99

1. Disconnect ground cable from auxiliary jumper terminal.
2. Remove fuel filler cap.
3. Remove protective cap from fuel rail fuel pressure test port.
4. Place open end of fuel pressure release hose tool No. C-4799-1, or equivalent, into suitable gasoline container.
5. Connect other hose end to fuel pressure test port. Fuel pressure should bleed off through hose into container.

2000–02

1. Remove fuel pump relay from Power Distribution Center (PDC).
2. Start engine and allow it to run until it stalls from lack of fuel.
3. Attempt to start engine until it will not start.
4. Turn ignition Off.

COMPRESSION PRESSURE

Proper compression pressure is 170–225 psi and should not vary more than 25% from cylinder to cylinder.

ENGINE MOUNT

REPLACE

FRONT

1. Raise and support vehicle, then support engine and transaxle with suitable floor jack.
2. Remove front engine mount through bolt from insulator and crossmember mounting bracket.
3. Remove mass damper, front mounting nuts and insulator.
4. Remove front mounting bracket
5. Reverse procedure to install.

LEFT

1998–99

1. Raise and support vehicle, then remove lefthand front tire.
2. Remove power distribution center and place aside.

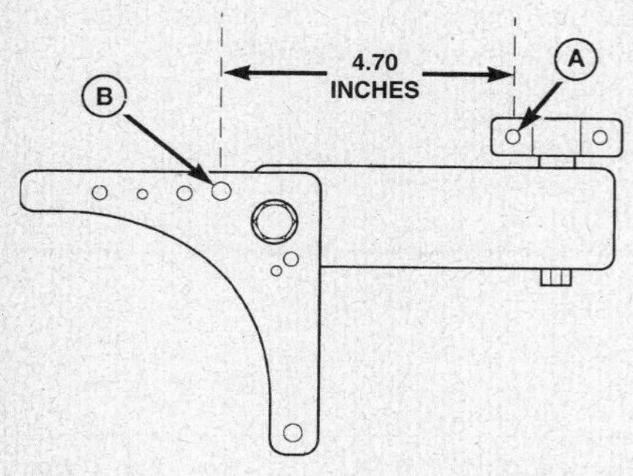

Fig. 1 Engine mount bracket stud alignment.

3. Support transaxle with suitable jack and remove insulator through bolt.
4. Remove mounting bolts and transaxle mount.
5. Reverse procedure to install.

2000-02

Removal

1. Remove air cleaner.
2. Remove battery and tray.
3. Loosen lefthand front wheel lugnuts.
4. Raise and support vehicle approximately one foot on suitable hoist.
5. Support transaxle with suitable jack.
6. Remove lefthand front wheel.
7. Remove lefthand front splash shield.
8. Remove through bolt access plug at lefthand side outer frame rail.
9. Remove mount through bolt.
10. Disconnect transaxle shift cable from lefthand mount and transaxle linkage.
11. Remove lefthand mount bracket to body frame rail fasteners.
12. Remove mounting bolts and mount.

Installation

1. Install mount and fasteners. Tighten to specifications.
2. Install engine mount to body frame rail fasteners. Tighten to specifications.
3. Position engine and transaxle for through bolt installation. Tighten to specifications.
4. Remove jack.
5. Install through bolt access plug.
6. Install lefthand splash shield and wheel.
7. Connect transaxle shift linkage.
8. Lower vehicle.
9. Tighten lugnuts in order to half specification. Repeat procedure and tighten to full specification.
10. Install battery and tray.
11. Install air cleaner.

RIGHT

1998-99

1. Remove purge duty solenoid from engine mount bracket.
2. Remove righthand engine mount insulator vertical fasteners.
3. Support engine/transaxle assembly to relieve pressure on mount.
4. Remove through bolt and insulator.
5. Reverse procedure to install.

2000-02

Removal

1. Remove engine accessory drive belts.
2. Remove righthand splash shield.
3. Using three-jaw puller tool No. 1026 and insert No. 6827-A, or equivalents, remove crankshaft damper.
4. Remove upper and lower engine torque struts.
5. Support engine using suitable jack.
6. Remove access cover and righthand engine mount bolt.
7. Mark position of engine mount to body frame rail.
8. Remove mount to body mounting bolts.
9. Remove mount between engine and body frame rail. This might require lowering or raising engine to provide clearance.

Installation

1. Position mount in its original location on body frame rail.
2. If mount location was not marked before removal or if frame rail has been replaced, proceed as follows:
   a. Insert new mount loosely in frame rail.
   b. Align mount's four holes with mating holes in rail so they are concentric and centered.
   c. Mark position of engine mount to body frame rail.
3. Ensure mount stays put in its original location. Tighten bolts to specifications.
4. Install engine mount bracket. Tighten bolts to specifications.
5. Install crankshaft damper using washer, thrust bearing and nut from tool No. 6792 and suitable M12 × 1.75 × 150 mm bolt.
6. Install damper bolt while holding crankshaft damper in place with holder tool No. 6847, or equivalent. Tighten bolt to specifications.
7. Install righthand splash shield.
8. Install engine accessory drive belts.

TORQUE STRUTS

REPLACEMENT

Lower

1. Raise and support vehicle on hoist.
2. Remove righthand splash shield.
3. Remove lower strut to crossmember and strut bracket bolts.
4. Remove lower torque strut.
5. Reverse procedure to install. Refer to "Adjustment" for adjustment procedure.

Upper

1. Remove upper torque strut mounting bolts.
2. Remove upper torque strut.
3. Reverse procedure to install. Refer to "Adjustment" for adjustment procedure.

ADJUSTMENT

The lower and upper torque struts re-

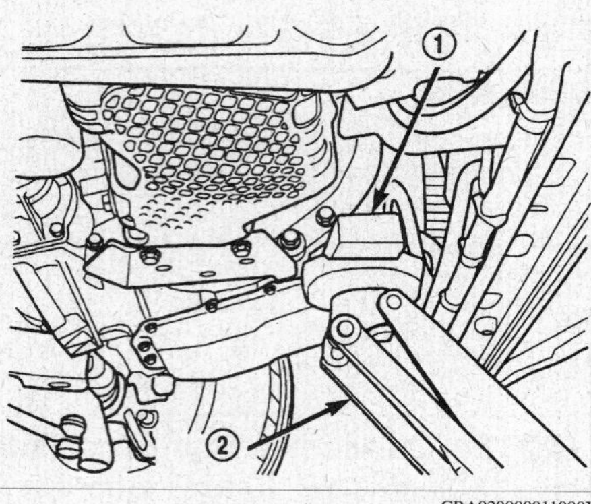

Fig. 2 Engine support. 2000–01

quire adjustment together whenever a mounting bolt has been loosened. Proceed as follows:

1. Loosen upper and lower torque strut mounting bolt at suspension crossmember and strut tower bracket.
2. Position suitable floor jack and wood block under forward edge of transaxle bellhousing.
3. Carefully exert upward force, allowing upper engine to rotate rearward until distance between center of rearmost engine mount bracket mounting stud, point "A," **Fig. 1,** and center of strut tower bracket washer hose clip hole, point B is 4.70 inches.
4. Hold engine in this position and tighten torque strut bolts to specifications.
5. Remove floor jack.

ENGINE

REPLACE

1998-99

1. Relieve fuel system pressure as outlined under "Precautions."
2. Remove battery and tray.
3. Disconnect Powertrain Control Module (PCM) electrical connector and position aside.
4. Drain coolant into suitable container.
5. Remove upper radiator hose and radiator fan module.
6. Remove lower radiator hose.
7. **On models equipped with automatic transaxle,** disconnect oil cooler lines.
8. **On models equipped with manual transaxle,** disconnect clutch cable, transaxle and throttle body linkage.
9. **On all models,** disconnect engine wiring harness electrical connectors.
10. Disconnect heater hoses.
11. Recover A/C refrigerant as outlined in "Air Conditioning" section.
12. Raise and support vehicle, then remove righthand inner splash shield.
13. Remove accessory drive belts.
14. Remove axle shafts.
15. Disconnect exhaust pipe from manifold.
16. Remove front and rear engine mount bracket.
17. Lower vehicle and remove air cleaner.
18. Remove power steering pump and reservoir.

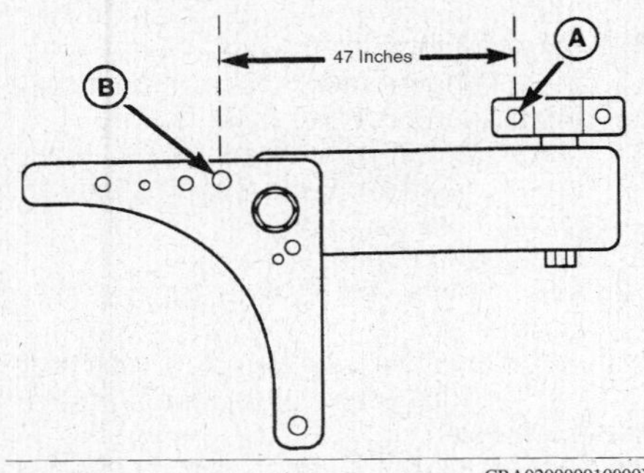

Fig. 3 Lower torque strut measurement. 2000–01

19. Remove A/C compressor.
20. Remove ground straps to body.
21. Raise and support vehicle to install engine dolly and cradle tool Nos. 6135, 6710 and 6810, or equivalents.
22. Loosen cradle engine mounts, to position engine locating holes to bed plate, then lower vehicle until engine rests on cradle mounts.
23. Tighten mounts to cradle frame to prevent mount movement.
24. Lower vehicle so weight of engine and transaxle is only on cradle.
25. Remove engine and transaxle mount mounting bolts.
26. Slowly raise and support vehicle, move engine and transaxle assembly on cradle to allow for removal around body flanges as required.
27. Reverse procedure to install.

2000-02

1. Relieve fuel system pressure as outlined under "Precautions."
2. Drain coolant into suitable container.
3. Remove battery and tray.
4. Recover A/C refrigerant as outlined in "Air Conditioning" section.
5. Disconnect air intake duct at intake manifold.
6. Disconnect throttle cables.
7. Disconnect electrical connectors at throttle body and air cleaner housing.
8. Remove air cleaner housing.
9. Remove upper radiator hose.
10. Remove fan module.
11. Remove lower radiator hose.
12. **On models equipped with automatic transaxle,** disconnect and plug fluid cooler lines.
13. **On models equipped with manual transaxle,** proceed as follows:
    a. Disconnect shift linkage.
    b. Disconnect transaxle electrical connectors.
    c. Disconnect clutch cable.
14. **On all models,** disconnect engine wiring harness.
15. Disconnect positive cable from PDC and ground wire from vehicle body.
16. Disconnect heater hoses.
17. Disconnect brake booster vacuum hose.
18. Disconnect coolant reserve and recovery hose.
19. Remove engine accessory drive belts.
20. Remove power steering pump and reservoir. Position them aside with hoses intact.
21. Loosen front wheel lugnuts.
22. Raise and support vehicle on hoist.
23. Drain engine oil into suitable container.
24. Remove righthand inner splash shield.
25. Remove front wheels.
26. Remove axle shafts.
27. Disconnect exhaust system at exhaust manifold.
28. Disconnect downstream HO2S sensor electrical connector.
29. Remove engine lower torque strut.
30. Lower vehicle and remove air conditioning compressor.
31. Raise vehicle just enough, then install engine dolly tool No. 6135 and cradle tool No. 6710, or equivalents, under vehicle.
32. Loosen engine support posts to allow movement for positioning onto engine locating holes and flange on engine bedplate.
33. Lower vehicle and position cradle until engine is resting on support posts. Tighten mounts to cradle frame.
34. Install safety straps around engine to cradle. Tighten straps and lock into position. **Safety straps must be used.**
35. Raise vehicle enough to ensure straps are tight enough to hold cradle to engine.
36. Lower vehicle so engine and transaxle's weight only is on cradle.
37. Remove engine upper torque strut.
38. Remove righthand and lefthand engine and transaxle through bolts.
39. Raise vehicle slowly until body is approximately six inches above normal engine mounting locations.
40. Remove alternator, its lower bracket and mounting bolt.
41. Continue slowly raising vehicle until powertrain clears engine compartment. Movement of powertrain might be required to steer it clear of body flanges.
42. Reverse procedure to install.

RADIATOR

REPLACE

1998-99

1. Drain cooling system into suitable container and remove radiator hose clamps.
2. Disconnect automatic transaxle hoses from cooler and plug.
3. Remove radiator to battery strut and fan module by disconnecting fan motor electrical connector.
4. Remove fan shroud to mounting screws.
5. Lift shroud up and out of bottom clips.
6. **On models equipped with dual cooling fans,** remove lefthand and righthand fan modules.
7. **On all models,** remove upper radiator isolator bracket mounting screws and engine block heater, if equipped.
8. Remove air conditioning condenser mounting screws located at front of radiator, if equipped. Do not discharge air conditioning system.
9. Remove radiator by lifting upward.

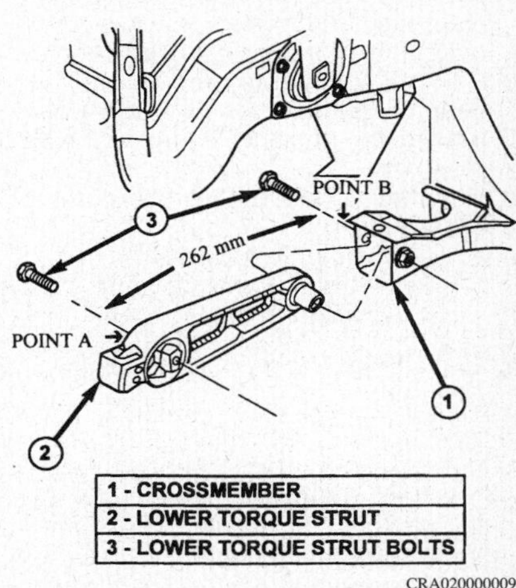

Fig. 4 Upper torque strut measurement. 2000–01

10. Reverse procedure to install.

2000-02

1. Drain coolant into suitable container.
2. Disconnect upper hose at radiator.
3. **On models equipped with automatic transaxle,** disconnect and cap fluid cooler lines.
4. **On all models,** disconnect cooling fan motor electrical connector.
5. Remove cooling fan module mounting screws on shroud top.
6. Lift shroud up and out of lower shroud clips.
7. Remove lower radiator hose.
8. Remove upper radiator isolator bracket mounting screws.
9. **On models equipped with engine block heater,** disconnect block heater wiring.
10. **On all models,** remove A/C condenser mounting screws at front of radiator, allowing condenser to lean forward. **Discharging and recovering refrigerant is not required.**
11. Lift and remove radiator.
12. Reverse procedure to install, noting the following:
    a. Radiator requires approximately .20–.31 inch upward clearance after installation.
    b. Align hoses and clamps to prevent them from interfering with engine components or hood movement.
    c. Close radiator petcock, fill cooling system and inspect for leaks.

FUEL PUMP

REPLACE

1998-99

1. Drain fuel from tank into suitable container.
2. Disconnect fuel pump module fuel line quick connect fitting and disengage electrical connector lock.
3. Disconnect electrical connector and support fuel tank using suitable transmission jack.
4. Remove fuel tank strap bolts and lower tank slightly.

5. Remove fuel pump module locknut using tool No. 6856, or equivalent.
6. Remove fuel pump module and O-ring seal. **Residual fuel may spill out of fuel pump module reservoir during removal.**
7. Reverse procedure to install, noting the following:
   a. Install new O-ring seal.
   b. Tighten fuel pump module locknut to specifications.

2000-02

1. Relieve fuel system pressure as outlined under "Precautions."
2. Raise and support vehicle on hoist.
3. Disconnect EVAP canister tube vapor line.
4. Remove EVAP canister.
5. Remove port cap and drain fuel into suitable container. **Replace cap after fuel has drained.**
6. Disconnect fuel pump module electrical connector and ground wire.
7. Disconnect fuel filter and regulator fuel tube.
8. Disconnect fuel filler tube and filler vent tube.
9. Support tank with suitable transmission jack.
10. Loosen tank mounting straps and slightly lower tank.
11. Remove mounting straps and tank.
12. Remove fuel pump module locknut using locknut wrench tool No. 6856, or equivalent.
13. Remove fuel pump and O-ring.
14. Reverse procedure to install, noting the following:
   a. Ensure tank's O-ring surface is clean.
   b. Install new O-ring.
   c. Position fuel pump in tank, ensuring alignment on pump's underside flange sits in fuel tank notch.
   d. Tighten locknut using locknut wrench tool to specifications. **Do not overtighten.**
   e. Ensure tank mounting straps do not twist or bend.

TECHNICAL SERVICE BULLETINS

STEERING WHEEL OR SEAT SHAKE AT IDLE

2000-01

On some these models there may be a shake in the steering wheel or seat at idle.

This condition may be caused by the righthand engine mount and location of two radiator upper mounting brackets.

To correct this condition, proceed as follows:

1. Remove accessory drive belts.
2. Raise and support vehicle, then remove righthand side splash shield.
3. Remove crankshaft damper.
4. Remove mounting bolts and lower torque strut.
5. Lower vehicle.
6. Remove mounting bolts and upper torque strut.
7. Disconnect ground strap and power steering hose support clip from engine mount bracket.
8. Remove power steering power and position aside.
9. Support engine with suitable jack and raise engine slightly.
10. Remove access cover, mounting bolt and righthand engine mount bracket.
11. Mark engine mount position on frame rail.
12. Remove mounting bolts and engine mount. Raise or lower engine as required.
13. Position revised elastic material engine mount in original marked position and **torque** mounting bolts to 21 ft. lbs.
14. Install engine mount bracket and **torque** mounting bolts to 45 ft. lbs.
15. Install engine mount to bracket mounting bolt and **torque** to 87 ft. lbs.
16. Remove support, then install power steering pump, hose support clip and ground strap.
17. Raise and support vehicle.
18. Install lower torque strut and mounting bolts.
19. Install crankshaft damper, alternator belt and righthand side splash shield.
20. Lower vehicle.
21. Install upper torque strut and mounting bolts. **Do not tighten mounting bolts now.**
22. Loosen upper and lower torque strut mounting bolts at suspension crossmember and shock tower bracket.
23. Support engine with suitable jack positioned on transaxle bell housing forward edge, **Fig. 2.**
24. Raise jack and rotate upper engine rearward until distance between engine mount bracket rearmost mounting stud center (A) and shock tower bracket washer hose clip center (B) is 4.7 inches, **Fig. 3.**
25. **Torque** upper strut mounting bolts to 87 ft. lbs.
26. Adjust lower torque strut distance between torque strut bracket center point (A) and crossmember bolt center (B) to 10.3 inches, **Fig. 4.**
27. Install accessory drive belts.
28. Attempt to move radiator in upper radiator mounting brackets. If radiator moves freely, no further adjustments are required. If radiator does not move freely or binds, proceed as follows:
   a. Remove left and righthand upper radiator mounting bracket bolts.
   b. Position brackets perpendicular to upper radiator crossmember.
   c. **Torque** mounting bolts to 110 in lbs.
   d. Ensure radiator has free movement in both mounting brackets.

TIGHTENING SPECIFICATIONS

Year	Component	Torque/Ft. Lbs.
1998–99	Engine Mount Bracket	45
	Fuel Pump Module Locknut	40–41
	Oil Drain Plug	20
	Radiator Isolator Mounting Bracket	72①
	Water Pump Mounting	105①
	Wheel Lug nuts	95
2000–02	Crankshaft Damper	100
	Engine Mount Bracket To Body Frame Rail	21
	Engine Mount, Lefthand	50
	Engine Mount Bracket, Righthand	45
	Engine Mount Through Bolt	87
	Engine Mount Torque Strut	87
	Fuel Pump Module Locknut	40–41
	Fuel Tank Strap	17
	Oil Drain Plug	20
	Oil Pan	105①
	Radiator Isolator Mounting Bracket	90①
	Wheel Lug nuts	100

① — Inch lbs.

Clutch & Manual Transaxle

NOTE: On Air Bag Equipped Models, Refer To "Air Bag System Precautions" Located In The Front Of This Manual For System Disarming & Arming Procedures.

NOTE: Refer To "Computer Relearn Procedures" Located In The Front Of This Manual When Battery Power To The Computer Has Been Interrupted.

INDEX

PRECAUTIONS

AIR BAG SYSTEMS

Refer to "Air Bag System Precautions" in the front of this manual for system disarming and arming procedures.

BATTERY GROUND CABLE

Prior to service, disconnect battery ground cable and isolate as required.

ADJUSTMENTS

CLUTCH

The clutch cable used on these vehicles incorporates a self adjusting mechanism within the cable outer housing at the pedal end of the cable. A preload spring is used to take up slack in the cable and to keep the release bearing tensional against the fingers of the clutch pressure plate.

GEARSHIFT

The gearshift selector cable is not adjustable. If adjustment is required, only the crossover cable may be adjusted.

1. Remove gearshift console.
2. Loosen crossover cable adjustment screw, **Fig. 1.**
3. Pin crossover cable lever to transaxle using ¼ inch drill bit, or suitable equivalent, **Fig. 2.** Ensure drill bit engages through crossover lever into transaxle case at least ½ inch.
4. Ensure shift lever is in spring loaded neutral position. If necessary, move lever forward and back, then allow lever to fall into its natural neutral position.
5. Without allowing movement in either cable or lever, hand tighten crossover cable adjustment screw. Tighten screw to specifications.
6. Remove pin from transaxle crossover lever and inspect transaxle shift functions.
7. Install gearshift console.

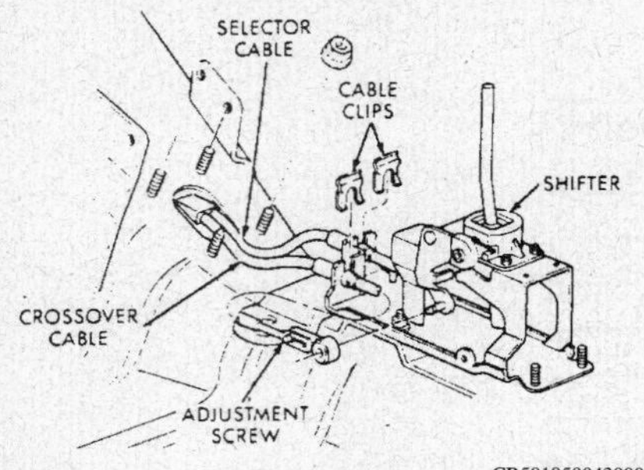

Fig. 1 Gearshift crossover cable adjustment

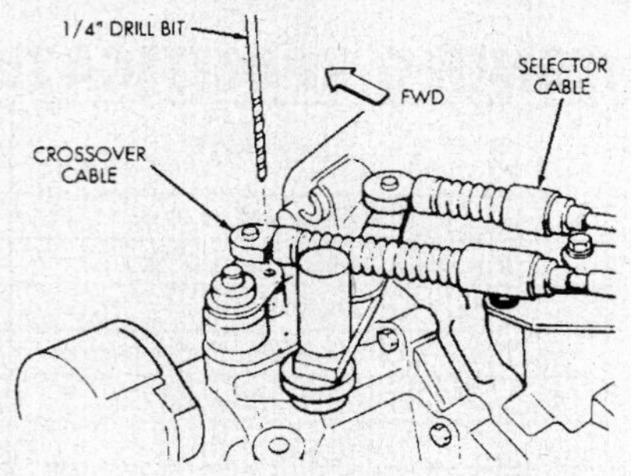

Fig. 2 Crossover lever attachment to transaxle

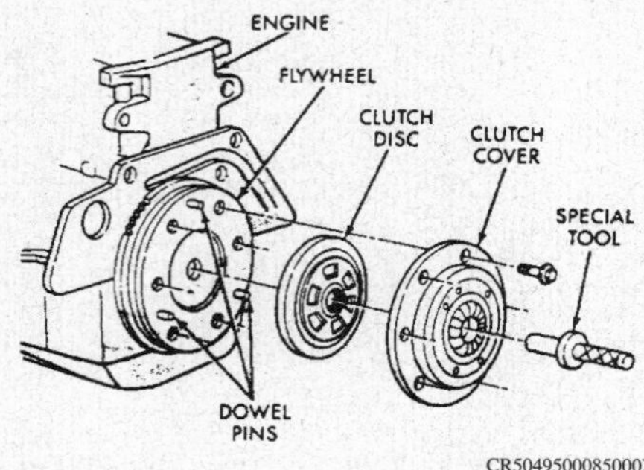

Fig. 3 Conventional clutch assembly

HYDRAULIC SYSTEM SERVICE

HYDRAULIC CLUTCH SYSTEM BLEED

Whenever any component of the hydraulic clutch system has been removed, bleeding must be performed.

Ensure clutch hydraulic cylinder is full, have helper depress clutch pedal and hold, open bleeder screw on hydraulic cylinder, then close bleeder screw. Repeat procedure until all air is bled from system.

CLUTCH

REPLACE

Two types of clutches are used on these vehicles. A single, conventional dry disc with a diaphragm cover is used on 1998–99 models produced at the Toluca assembly plant. On 1998–99 models produced at the Belvedere plant and all 2000 –02 models, a modular clutch assembly is used. The modular clutch assembly can only be serviced as a unit. The two types of clutches can be identified by the 11th digit of the Vehicle Identification Number (VIN). The Belvedere plant is identified by the letter "D." The Toluca plant is identified by the letter "T."

CONVENTIONAL

1. Remove transaxle as outlined under "Transaxle, Replace."
2. Mark clutch cover for installation reference.
3. Support clutch disc with clutch pilot tool No. 6724, or equivalent, during removal to prevent damage.
4. Loosen clutch cover bolts in cross pattern, two turns at time to prevent clutch cover damage.
5. Remove clutch cover and clutch plate, **Fig. 3.**
6. Reverse procedure to install, noting the following:
   a. Flywheel is manufactured with slightly tapered surface and clutch cover may have concave taper of zero–.0039 inch.
   b. All surfaces must be clean and free of oil or corrosion.
   c. Align clutch disc to flywheel using clutch pilot tool No. 6724, or equivalent.
   d. Tighten clutch cover bolts to specifications in alternating pattern, about two turns at a time, to prevent clutch cover damage.

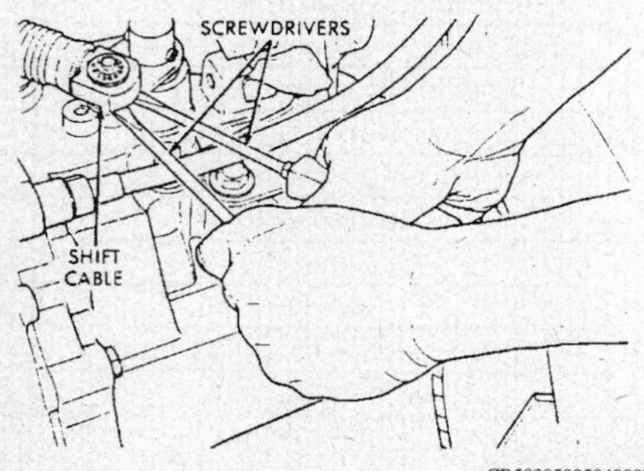

Fig. 4 Shift cable disconnection. 1998–99

MODULAR

1998-99

1. Remove starter as outlined in "Electrical" section.
2. Remove front and rear transaxle support brackets.
3. Remove modular clutch mounting bolts and transaxle as outlined under "Transaxle, Replace." **Transaxle and clutch are removed as an assembly.**
4. Remove modular clutch assembly from transaxle input shaft. **Do not allow friction surfaces to become contaminated.**
5. Reverse procedure to install, noting the following:
   a. Inspect engine rear main and transaxle input shaft seals for leakage. Correct any leaks prior to installing new clutch assembly.
   b. Install new clutch to flywheel bolts and tighten to specifications in alternating pattern.

2000-02

1. Remove transaxle as outlined under "Transaxle, Replace."
2. Remove clutch from transaxle input shaft.
3. Reverse procedure to install, noting the following:
   a. Install new flywheel to clutch bolts and tighten in criss-cross pattern until clutch is evenly seated. Tighten to specifications.
   b. Raise engine and transaxle with screw jack until upper mount through bolt hole aligns with hole in mount bracket. Tighten to specifications.
   c. When installing structural collar, position collar and install all bolts finger tight. **Torque** collar to oil pan bolts to 30 inch lbs. **Torque** collar to transaxle bolts to 80 ft. lbs. **Torque** collar to oil pan bolts to 40 ft. lbs.

SLAVE CYLINDER, REPLACE

Replacement slave cylinders come prefilled with fluid. No fluid service should be required, unless excessive air has been introduced to system.

1. Raise and support vehicle
2. Disconnect clutch hydraulic quick connect Using clutch line disconnect tool 6638A, or equivalent.
3. Remove left lateral bending brace.
4. Remove damper bracket.
5. Remove slave cylinder retaining bolts then the slave cylinder.
6. Reverse procedure to install, noting the following:
   a. Tighten to specifications.
   b. Verify clutch master cylinder is full.
   c. Actuate clutch pedal ten times to allow any air ingested into the system to vent to master cylinder reservoir.
   d. If excessive air is injested into system bleed hydraulic clutch system as outlined under "Hydraulic Clutch System Bleed."

TRANSAXLE

REPLACE

1998-99

The transaxle may be removed without removing the engine.

1. Pull power distribution center up and out of its holding bracket, then position aside.
2. Remove battery heat shield, battery and battery tray.
3. **On models equipped with cruise control,** disconnect cruise control.
4. **On all models,** disconnect back-up lamp switch and speed sensor wiring connectors.
5. Using two suitable pry bars and applying equal pressure to each side of shift

cable end and crossover cable end, pry cable ends from transaxle shift levers, **Fig. 4.**

6. Remove clutch housing cap to expose clutch cable and release lever.
7. Pull clutch cable outer housing back to unseat cable from transaxle and disconnect cable from release lever.
8. Remove shift cable mounting bracket, intake manifold support bracket and upper starter bolt.
9. Remove upper bellhousing bolts.
10. Install suitable engine support bridge fixture.
11. Adjust support bridge to relieve engine and transaxle mounts' tension.
12. Raise and support vehicle, then remove front wheels.
13. Drain transaxle oil into suitable container.
14. Remove both front drive axles as outlined under "Driveshaft, Replace" in "Front Wheel Drive Axles" chapter.
15. Remove engine damper and bracket.
16. Disconnect starter wiring, then remove lower starter mounting bolt and starter.
17. Remove engine to transaxle braces.
18. Remove lower bellhousing dust shield bolts.
19. Support transaxle with suitable jack.
20. Remove through bolt and front motor mount bolts.
21. Remove through bolt and lefthand transaxle mount.
22. Lower and remove transaxle.
23. Reverse procedure to install, noting the following:
    a. Tighten bolts to specifications.
    b. Fill transaxle to bottom of filler plug hole.
    c. Use new driveshaft retaining clips.

2000–02

1. Remove battery and tray.
2. Remove air cleaner and throttle body unit.
3. Disconnect back-up lamp switch electrical connector.
4. Remove bellhousing cap.
5. Disconnect clutch cable from release lever and remove cable from transaxle.
6. Remove shift cable to bracket clips.
7. Disconnect shift selector and crossover cable from levers.
8. Remove shift selector and crossover cables, then position aside.
9. Disconnect vehicle speed sensor electrical connector.
10. Raise and support vehicle on hoist.
11. Remove transaxle lubricant drain plug and allow lubricant to drain into suitable container.
12. Remove lefthand and righthand axle shafts.
13. Remove bellhousing lower structural collar.
14. Remove lefthand engine to transaxle lateral bending brace.
15. Remove bellhousing inspection cover.
16. Remove righthand engine to transaxle lateral bending brace.
17. Remove starter as outlined under "Starter, Replace" in "Electrical" section.
18. Remove flywheel to clutch module bolts.
19. Support engine at oil pan with suitable screw jack and wooden block.
20. Remove transaxle upper mount through bolt. This is accessed through driver's side wheelhouse.
21. Lower engine and transaxle on screw jack until sufficient clearance is obtained.
22. Have assistant hold transaxle in place, then remove transaxle to engine mounting bolts.
23. Remove transaxle.
24. Reverse procedure to install, noting the following:
    a. Fill transaxle with suitable amount of Mopar ATF+4 or equivalent.
    b. Road test vehicle and check for leaks.

TIGHTENING SPECIFICATIONS

Year	Component	Torque/Ft. Lbs.
1998–99	Clutch Cover (Conventional)	20–21
	Clutch Pedal Pivot Shaft	30
	Clutch To Flywheel (Modular)	55
	Crossover Cable Adjustment Screw	72①
	Flywheel To Crankshaft (Conventional)	70
	Flywheel To Crankshaft (Modular)	70
	Front Engine Mount To Transaxle	80
	Transaxle Drain Plug	22
	Transaxle Mount, Lefthand	40
	Transaxle To Engine	70
	Wheel Lugnuts	95
2000–02	Clutch To Flywheel	65
	Crossover Cable Adjustment Screw	72①
	Flywheel To Crankshaft	70
	Lateral Bending Brace, Righthand	60
	Slave Cylinder	14
	Transaxle Drain Plug	21
	Transaxle To Engine	70
	Wheel Lugnuts	100

① — Inch lbs.

Rear Suspension

NOTE: On Air Bag Equipped Models, Refer To "Air Bag System Precautions" Located In The Front Of This Manual For System Disarming & Arming Procedures.

NOTE: Refer To "Computer Relearn Procedures" Located In The Front Of This Manual When Battery Power To The Computer Has Been Interrupted.

INDEX

DESCRIPTION

Because the construction of this type of suspension, only frame contact or wheel lift type hoisting equipment should be used to raise vehicle.

Rear suspension components which become damaged must be replaced. No attempt should be made to repair these components.

The rear suspension is a fully independent strut type, **Figs. 1 and 2.** A forged spindle knuckle is bolted to the strut assembly. Lateral links and tension struts are used to control position and movement of the rear suspension.

HUB & BEARING

REPLACE

The rear hub and bearing are serviced as an assembly.

1. Raise and support vehicle, then remove wheel and tire.
2. **On models equipped with rear disc brakes,** remove caliper and disc as outlined in "Disc Brakes" chapter.
3. **On models equipped with rear drum brakes,** remove drum as outlined in "Drum Brakes" chapter of this manual.
4. **On all models,** remove mounting nut, hub and bearing assembly.
5. Reverse procedure to install. Tighten new mounting nuts and bolts to specifications.

SPINDLE KNUCKLE

REPLACE

1998–99

1. Remove rear hub and bearing as outlined under "Hub & Bearing, Replace."
2. **On models equipped with ABS,** remove mounting bolt and speed sensor, **Figs. 3 and 4.** If speed sensor is seized, do not use pliers to remove. Gently tap on mounting ear with suitable punch and hammer to loosen sensor.
3. **On models equipped with rear drum brakes,** remove brake support plate mounting bolts, then, without disconnecting brake fluid hose, position and support assembly aside. **Do not allow assembly to hang from brake fluid hose.**
4. **On models equipped with rear disc brakes,** remove disc brake adapter plate mounting bolts, then, without disconnecting brake fluid hose, position and support assembly aside. **Do not allow assembly to hang from brake fluid hose.**
5. **On all models,** loosen but do not remove spindle knuckle to strut clevis nuts. **Spindle knuckle to strut clevis bolts are serrated for tight fit into knuckle. Do not turn bolt when loosening. Turn nut only.**
6. Remove lateral link to knuckle bolt.
7. Remove tension strut nut, washer and bushing using suitable adjustable wrench to prevent tension strut from turning, **Fig. 5.**
8. Remove spindle knuckle to strut clevis bolts, pull spindle knuckle straight out of strut and rotate off tension strut.
9. Reverse procedure to install, noting the following:
   a. Tighten bolts and nuts to specifications.
   b. When tightening spindle knuckle to strut clevis bolts, do not turn bolts. Tighten by turning nuts only.

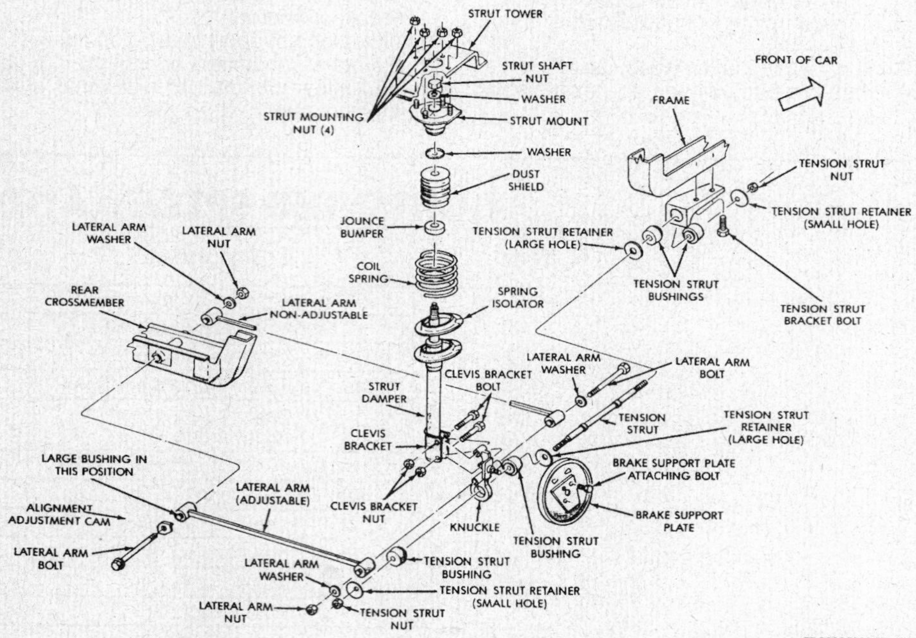

Fig. 1 Exploded view of rear suspension. 1998–99

c. **Lateral link to spindle knuckle bolt must be installed with head of bolt towards front of vehicle.**
d. Lateral link bolts must be tightened to specifications with suspension supporting vehicle weight.
e. Refer to **Fig. 6** when installing tension strut mounter washers and bushings.
f. Inspect and adjust rear wheel alignment as outlined under "Wheel Alignment."

2000-02

Removal

1. Remove rear hub and bearing as outlined under "Hub & Bearing, Replace."
2. **On models equipped with ABS,** remove sensor bracket to strut screw.
3. **On models equipped with rear drum brakes,** proceed as follows:
   a. Remove four brake support plate to knuckle bolts.
   b. Remove brake support plate, brake shoes and wheel cylinder as an assembly from knuckle. Leave brake hose intact.
   c. Tie assembly aside with suitable cord or string. **Avoid overextending brake hose.**
4. **On models equipped with rear disc brakes,** proceed as follows:
   a. Remove four brake adapter to knuckle bolts.
   b. Remove adapter, rotor shield, parking brake shoes and cable as an assembly.
   c. Tie assembly aside with suitable cord or string.
5. **On all models,** loosen, but do not completely remove, two knuckle to strut nuts and bolts. **These bolts are serrated and must not be turned during removal. Hold bolts in place in knuckle while removing nuts and tap bolts out using suitable pin punch.**
6. Remove rear knuckle to lateral arm nuts and bolt.
7. Remove tension strut rear nut using suitable wrench on strut's flat to prevent tension strut from turning.
8. Remove tension strut retainer.
9. Remove rear tension strut bayonet bushing from strut.
10. Remove rear knuckle to strut mounting nuts and bolts. Tap out bolts using suitable pin punch.
11. Remove knuckle.

Installation

1. Align hole in lower end of rear knuckle with forward bayonet bushing on tension strut. Ensure bushing's stepped area seats squarely into knuckle's hole.
2. Rotate knuckle until its upper mounting holes align with holes in strut's clevis bracket.
3. Install strut to rear knuckle mounting bolts from front side. Install nuts on bolts. Tighten to specifications.
4. Align lateral arms with hole in center of knuckle. Install arm to knuckle bolts. Start bolt from front side. Install nut, but do not tighten completely.
5. Install rear bayonet bushing onto tension strut. Ensure stepped area seats squarely into hole in knuckle.
6. Install rear tension strut retainer and nut. Tighten to nut specifications while holding strut in place with suitable wrench on flat area.
7. Install brake support plate or adapter onto knuckle. Tighten fasteners to specifications.
8. **On models equipped with ABS,** install sensor bracket to strut screw. Tighten to specifications.
9. **On all models,** install tire and wheel. Tighten lugnuts in proper sequence to half specification. Repeat sequence again to full specification.
10. Lower vehicle to ground and rock to bring to curb height.
11. Tighten lateral arm to knuckle mounting bolt to specifications.
12. Inspect and adjust rear toe. Refer to "Rear Wheel Alignment Specifications" in "Specifications" section.

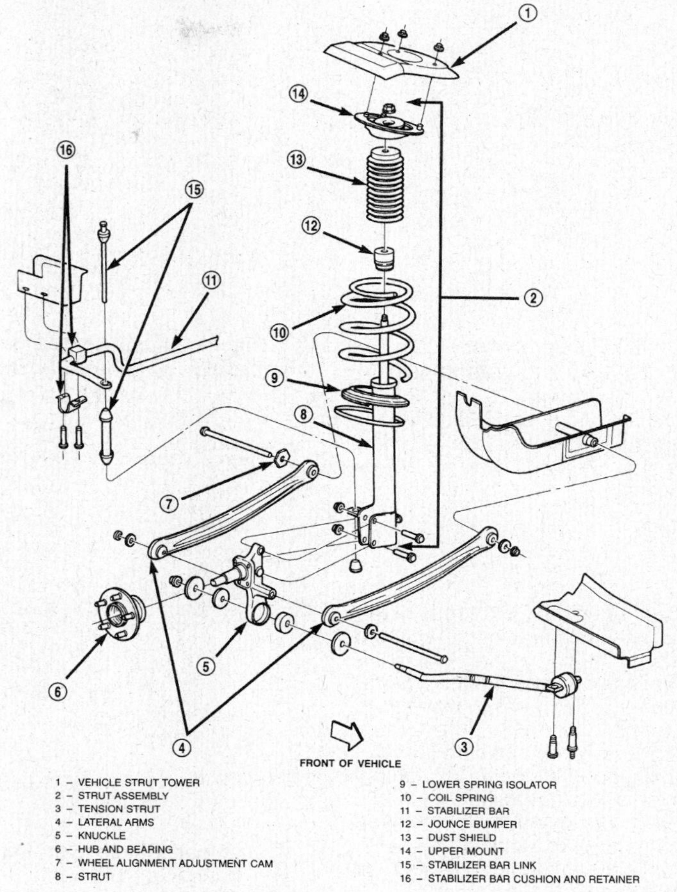

Fig. 2 Exploded view of rear suspension. 2000–02

STRUT

REPLACE

1998-99

1. Raise and support vehicle, then remove wheel.
2. Remove brake fluid hose support bracket from strut.
3. **On models equipped with ABS,** remove speed sensor cable and routing clip from strut.
4. **On all models,** loosen but do not remove spindle knuckle to strut clevis bolts. **Spindle knuckle to strut clevis bolts are serrated for tight fit into knuckle. Do not turn bolt when loosening. Turn nut only.**
5. Lower vehicle. Removing carpeting and dust shield as required.
6. Loosen but do not remove upper strut to tower mounting nuts.
7. Support suspension using suitable device. **Do not allow suspension components to hang after removing strut. Do not place support under lateral links or tension strut.**
8. Remove previously loosened upper strut mounting nuts and strut to spindle knuckle bolts.
9. Slide strut straight back off spindle knuckle and lower strut.
10. Reverse procedure to install, noting the following:
    a. Tighten bolts and nuts to specifications.
    b. **Do not turn bolts when tightening spindle knuckle to strut clevis bolts. Tighten by turning nuts only.**

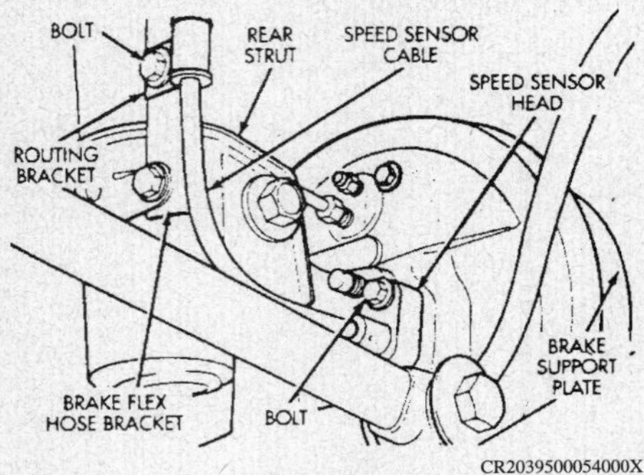

Fig. 3 ABS speed sensor location. 1998–99 w/rear drum brakes

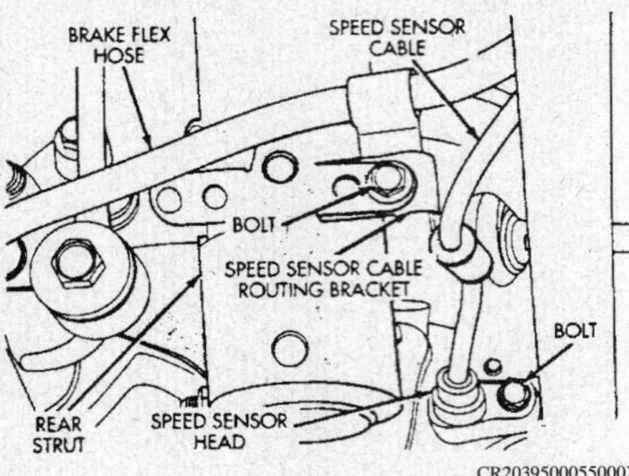

Fig. 4 ABS speed sensor location. 1998–99 w/rear disc brakes

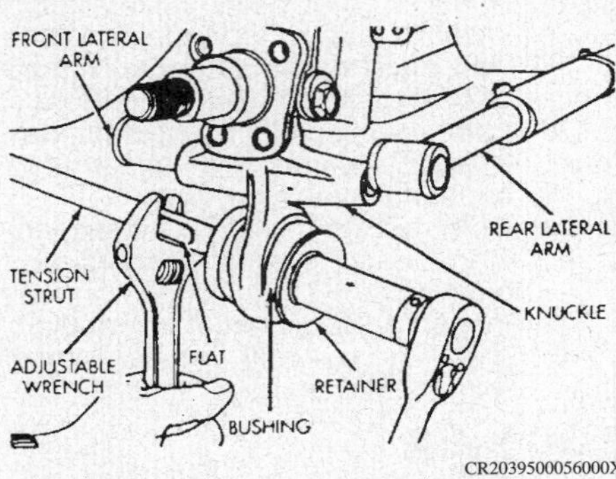

Fig. 5 Tension strut removal. 1998–99

c. Inspect and adjust rear wheel alignment as outlined under "Wheel Alignment."

2000-02

1. Raise and support vehicle.
2. Remove wheel and tire.
3. **On models equipped with rear drum brakes,** remove brake hose bracket to strut screw.
4. **On models equipped with ABS,** remove wheel speed sensor bracket to strut screw.
5. **On all models,** remove nut from end of rear stabilizer bar link bolt. Pull bolt out through top and remove link.
6. **On models equipped with rear disc brakes,** proceed as follows:
   a. Remove four brake adapter to knuckle bolts.
   b. Remove adapter, rotor shield, parking brake shoes and cable as an assembly.
   c. Tie assembly aside with suitable cord or string.
7. **On all models,** remove two knuckle to strut nuts and bolts. **These bolts are serrated and must not be turned during removal. Hold bolts in place in knuckle while removing nuts and tap bolts out using suitable pin punch.**
8. Lower vehicle only enough to climb into luggage compartment without tires reaching ground.
9. Remove carpeting from top of strut tower inside luggage compartment.
10. Loosen, but do not completely remove, three strut to tower nuts.
11. Hold strut firmly in place and remove mounting nuts.
12. Remove strut from knuckle by sliding it away from knuckle, lowering it between lateral arms, then angling top outward and out through wheelwell opening.
13. Reverse procedure to install, noting the following:
   a. Tighten three tower nuts to specifications.
   b. Align holes in strut clevis bracket on strut's lower end with knuckle's mounting holes.
   c. Install tire and wheel. Tighten lugnuts in proper sequence to half specification. Repeat sequence again to full specification.

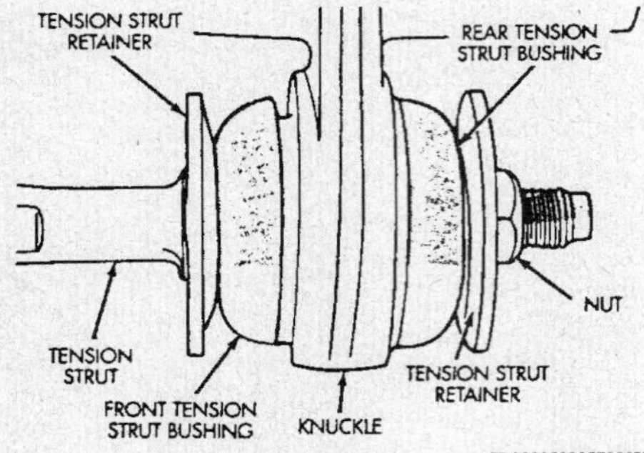

Fig. 6 Tension strut bushings. 1998–99

d. Lower vehicle to ground and rock to bring to curb height.
e. Tighten stabilizer bar link nut to specifications.
f. Inspect and adjust rear toe. Refer to "Rear Wheel Alignment Specifications" in "Specifications" section.

STRUT SERVICE

Coil springs on these models are available in different load rates. Spring rates may be different on each side of the vehicle depending on how the vehicle is equipped. Ensure proper spring rates are chosen during assembly.

The gas-charged strut damper cannot be rebuilt and is serviced as a unit.

1998-99

1. Remove strut as previously described.
2. Place match marks on strut components to aid alignment.
3. Place strut into suitable vise, **Fig. 7. Do not clamp body of strut into vise.**
4. Compress spring until tension is removed from upper strut mount using coil spring compressor tool No. C-4838, or equivalent,
5. Remove strut shaft nut using strut nut wrench tool No. L-4558A, or equivalent, socket and breaker bar to hold strut shaft, **Fig. 8.**
6. Remove outer washer, upper strut mount, coil spring, inner washer, dust shield, jounce bumper and spring isolator from strut **Fig. 1.**
7. Reverse procedure to install, noting the following:
   a. Tighten nuts to specifications.
   b. Install inner strut shaft washer with raised edge up and outer strut shaft washer with raised edge down.
   c. Transfer alignment marks to any replaced component. Ensure alignment of all components during assembly.

2000-02

1. Remove strut as previously described.
2. Record orientation of all markings, letters and assembly tips before proceeding.
3. Place match marks on components to aid alignment.
4. Position strut in compressor tool No. PSE W-7200, or equivalent, following tool manufacturer's instructions.
5. Compress coil spring until all spring tension is off upper mount.
6. Install strut nut socket tool No. 6864, or equivalent, on strut shaft mounting nut.
7. Install socket on shaft's end hex.
8. Remove shaft nut while preventing strut shaft from turning.
9. Remove upper mount from strut shaft.
10. Remove clamp from bottom of spring.
11. Pull strut through bottom of spring.
12. Remove dust shield and jounce bumper by pulling them straight up.
13. Remove lower spring isolator from strut's lower spring seat.
14. If coil spring is being replaced, proceed as follows:
   a. Record spring's position in compressor tool for easier assembly.
   b. Back off compressor drive completely to release spring tension.
   c. Push hooks back and remove spring.
15. Reverse procedure to install, noting the following:
   a. Mount coil spring into original position.
   b. Inspect upper mount before installation. Ensure proper mount is being installed. Righthand mounts are marked R, while lefthand has L marking.
   c. Tighten all fasteners to specifications.

TENSION STRUT

REPLACE

1. Remove wheel and tire as required.

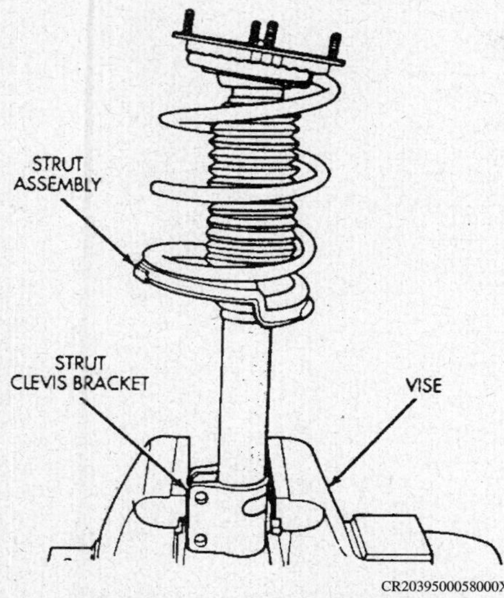

Fig. 7 Strut assembly mounted in vise. 1998–99

2. Remove nuts from both ends of tension strut using suitable wrench on flat to prevent tension strut from turning.
3. Record orientation of tension strut bushings and washers.
4. Remove bushings, washers and tension strut.
5. Reverse procedure to install, noting the following:
   a. Tighten nuts to specifications.
   b. **On 1998–99 models,** refer to **Fig. 6** when installing tension strut bushings and washers.
   c. **On all models,** inspect and adjust rear wheel alignment as outlined under "Wheel Alignment."

ROLL BAR

REPLACE

1. Raise and support vehicle, then remove both rear wheels.
2. Disconnect roll bar from mounting links at each side and swing bar down to clear links.
3. Remove mounting bracket and roll bar. **Record bushing orientation.**
4. Reverse procedure to install, noting the following:
   a. Tighten nuts and bolts to specifications.
   b. Ensure bushings are installed in original positions.

LATERAL LINK

REPLACE

1998–99

Rear suspension lateral link bushings are not replaceable. They are serviced as a unit.

The lateral links are not interchangeable. The forward link is non-adjustable and both bushing sleeves are the same size. The rearward link is adjustable. The small bushing sleeve must be placed at the spindle knuckle to allow for toe adjustments.

1. Raise and support vehicle, then remove rear wheels.
2. Remove spindle knuckle lateral link mounting bolt and washers.
3. Remove cross member mounting bolt, washers, adjustment cams and lateral links.
4. Reverse procedure to install, noting the following:
   a. Tighten nuts and bolts to specifications.
   b. Forward lateral links have same size bushing sleeves at each end.
   c. Rearward lateral links have two different size bushing sleeves, **small bushing sleeve must be installed at spindle knuckle end.**
   d. Short mounting bolt is used at spindle knuckle end, **and must be installed with head of bolt towards front of vehicle.**
   e. Long mounting bolt is used at crossmember end, **and must be installed with head of bolt towards rear of vehicle.**
   f. Lateral link bolts must be tightened to specifications with suspension supporting vehicle weight.
   g. Inspect and adjust rear wheel alignment as outlined under "Wheel Alignment."

2000–02

Removal

1. Raise and support vehicle.
2. Remove tire and wheel.
3. Remove lateral link to knuckle nut, bolt and washers.
4. Remove nut, washer, bolt and wheel alignment cam mounting lateral arms to rear crossmember.
5. Remove lateral arms.

Installation

The lateral arms have a specific installation orientation. The arm with identical size bushing sleeves on both ends must be mounted on the forward side of the crossmember and knuckle with the trimmed outer edge facing rearward. This front arm also displays the word FORWARD facing forward.

The arm with differing size bushing sleeves mounts on the rearward side of the crossmember and knuckle. Position the smaller sleeve end at the knuckle and the larger end at the rear crossmember. **If the rear arm will be mounted on the righthand side,** the trimmed outer edge must face rearward. **If the rear arm will be mounted on the lefthand side,** the trimmed outer edge must face forward.

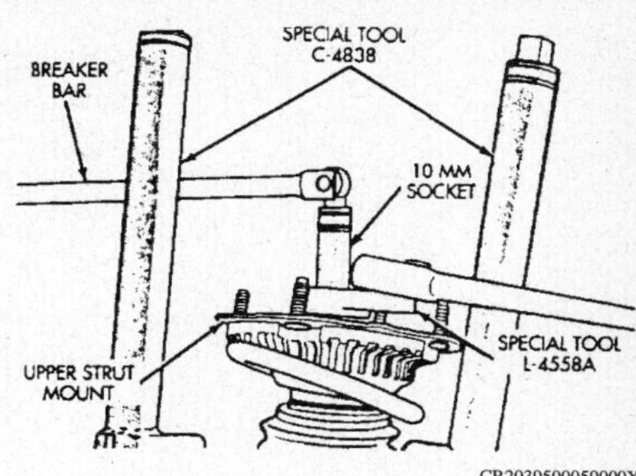

Fig. 8 Strut shaft nut replacement. 1998–99

1. Place forward lateral arm against leading edge of knuckle.
2. Install short lateral arm mounting bolt with washer through lateral arm and knuckle and out trailing end of knuckle.
3. Install small sleeved end of rear lateral arm onto end of bolt previously installed.
4. Install washer and nut onto end of mounting bolt, but do not tighten completely.
5. Install alignment cam on long arm mounting bolt.
6. Hold rear lateral arm up against crossmember and install long mounting bolt with adjustment cam through lateral arm bushing and rear crossmember. Ensure bolt is installed with alignment cam's notch pointing straight up.
7. Position forward lateral arm against rear crossmember hole.
8. Route long mounting bolt through lateral arm bushing sleeve.
9. Install washer and nut onto end of mounting bolt at rear crossmember, but do not tighten completely, noting the following:
   a. When properly installed, each lateral arm will have bow in its length facing downward.
   b. Both righthand side arms will have trimmed outer edges facing rear of vehicle.
   c. Lefthand side arms will have trimmed outer edges facing each other.
   d. Mounting bolt at knuckle will have nut at rear, while mounting bolt at crossmember will have nut at front.
10. Install tire and wheel. Tighten lugnuts in proper sequence to half specification. Repeat sequence again to full specification.
11. Lower vehicle to ground and rock to bring to curb height.
12. Tighten lateral arm mounting bolt nut at knuckle to specifications.
13. Tighten lateral arm mounting bolt nut at crossmember to specifications.
14. Inspect and adjust rear toe. Refer to "Rear Wheel Alignment Specifications" in "Specifications" section.

TIGHTENING SPECIFICATIONS

Year	Component	Torque/Ft. lbs.
1998–99	Brake Hose	35
	Brake Hose Bracket	17
	Brake Plate To Spindle Knuckle	50
	Caliper To Disc Brake Adapter	16
	Disc Brake Adapter To Spindle Knuckle	50
	Hub And Bearing To Spindle Knuckle	124
	Lateral Link	70
	Roll Bar Isolator Bracket To Frame	25
	Roll Bar To Rear Strut Link	25
	Strut Assembly Shaft	55
	Strut Assembly To Spindle Knuckle Clevis	70
	Strut Assembly To Tower	25
	Tension Strut Shaft	70
	Tension Strut To Body Mounting Bracket	70
	Wheel Lugnuts	95
2000–02	Brake Hose Bracket	23
	Brake Support Plate	55
	Disc Brake Adapter	55
	Hub & Bearing To Knuckle	160
	Knuckle	65
	Lateral Arm Nut At Crossmember	65
	Lateral Arm Nut At Knuckle	70
	Parking Brake Cable	21
	Roll Bar Cushion Retainer	25
	Roll Bar Link	17
	Strut Assembly Shaft	55
	Tension Strut Frame Rail	70
	Tension Strut Rear	70
	Tower	25
	Wheel Lugnuts	100①

① — Tighten lugnuts in proper sequence to half specification. Repeat sequence again to full specification.

Front Suspension & Steering

NOTE: On Air Bag Equipped Models, Refer To "Air Bag System Precautions" Located In The Front Of This Manual For System Disarming & Arming Procedures.

NOTE: Refer To "Computer Relearn Procedures" Located In The Front Of This Manual When Battery Power To The Computer Has Been Interrupted.

NOTE: Prior To Performing Any Service Operations Listed In This Section, Consult The "Technical Service Bulletins" For Related Information.

INDEX

DESCRIPTION

This suspension is a gas pressurized strut system used in place of front suspension upper ball joint and upper control arm. The bottom of the strut is attached directly to the steering knuckle using two mounting bolts and nuts going through the clevis bracket and steering knuckle, **Figs. 1 and 2.**

A cast lower arm assembly is attached to the front suspension crossmember using two rubber isolator bushings and to the steering knuckle by means of a ball joint.

A sealed for life front hub and bearing assembly is attached to the front steering knuckle. The outer CV joint assembly is splined to the front hub and bearing assembly.

HUB & BEARING

REPLACE

1998–99

1. Remove cotter pin, castle nut and hub nut while vehicle is still on floor with brakes applied.
2. Raise and support vehicle, then remove front tire and wheel assembly.
3. Remove front disc brake caliper and place aside. **Do not let caliper assembly hang by hose.**
4. Remove front disc brake and disconnect tie rod from steering knuckle using removal tool No. MB990635, or equivalent.

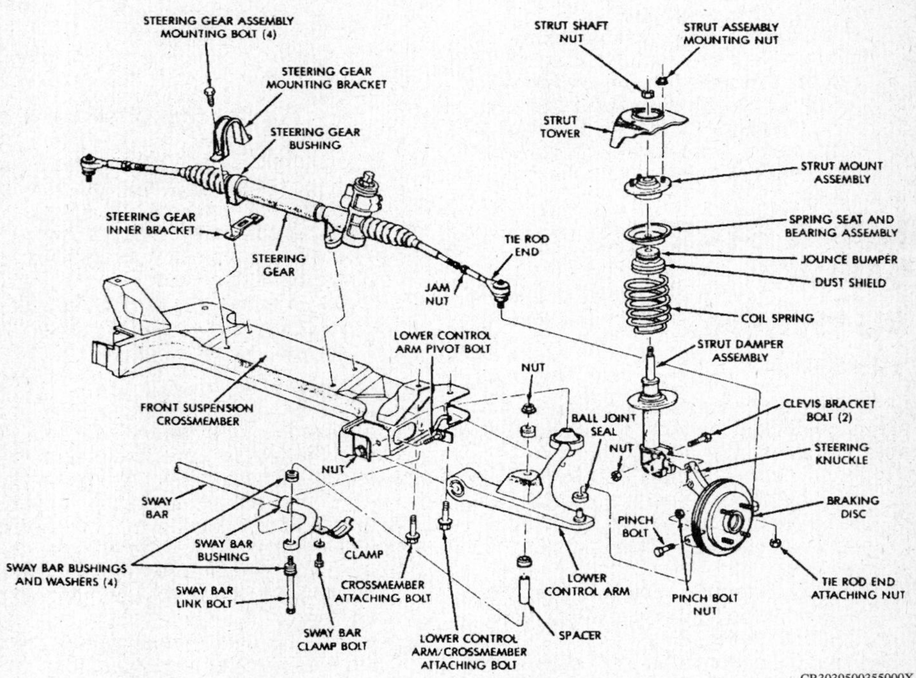

Fig. 1 Exploded view of front suspension. 1998–99

5. Separate ball joint stud from steering knuckle by prying down on lower control arm. **Ensure ball joint seal is not damaged.**
6. Pull steering knuckle assembly out and away from outer CV joint of driveshaft assembly.
7. Remove mounting bolts, steering knuckle and hub/bearing assembly.
8. Reverse procedure to install. **Torque**

clamp bolt to 70 ft. lbs.

2000-02

The cartridge type front wheel bearing on these models is not transferable to a new knuckle. If a new knuckle does not arrive with a new bearing, a new bearing must be installed. This must be done before the knuckle is installed on the vehicle.

1. Apply and hold brakes.
2. Raise and support vehicle.
3. Remove tire and wheel.
4. Keep brakes applied, loosen and remove hub nut on end of driveshaft.
5. Remove caliper to knuckle guide pin bolts.
6. Remove caliper from knuckle and position aside with suitable cord or wire. **Do not let caliper hang by brake hose.**
7. Remove any clips from wheel studs.
8. Remove rotor from hub.
9. Remove outer tie rod to knuckle nut.
10. Remove tie rod end from knuckle using tie rod remover tool No. MB991113, or equivalent.
11. Remove tie rod heat shield.
12. Remove ball joint stud to knuckle nut and pinch bolt.
13. Remove two strut to knuckle bolts. **These bolts are serrated and must not be turned during removal. Hold bolts in place in knuckle while removing nuts and tap bolts out using suitable pin punch.**
14. Separate ball joint from knuckle by prying down on lower control arm and up against ball joint knuckle boss. **Do not cutting or tearing seal.**
15. Pull knuckle off driveshaft outer CV joint splines and remove knuckle. **Do not let driveshaft hang by inner CV joint. Support it with suitable cord.**
16. Refer to "Hub & Bearing Service" for continuation of bearing replacement procedure.

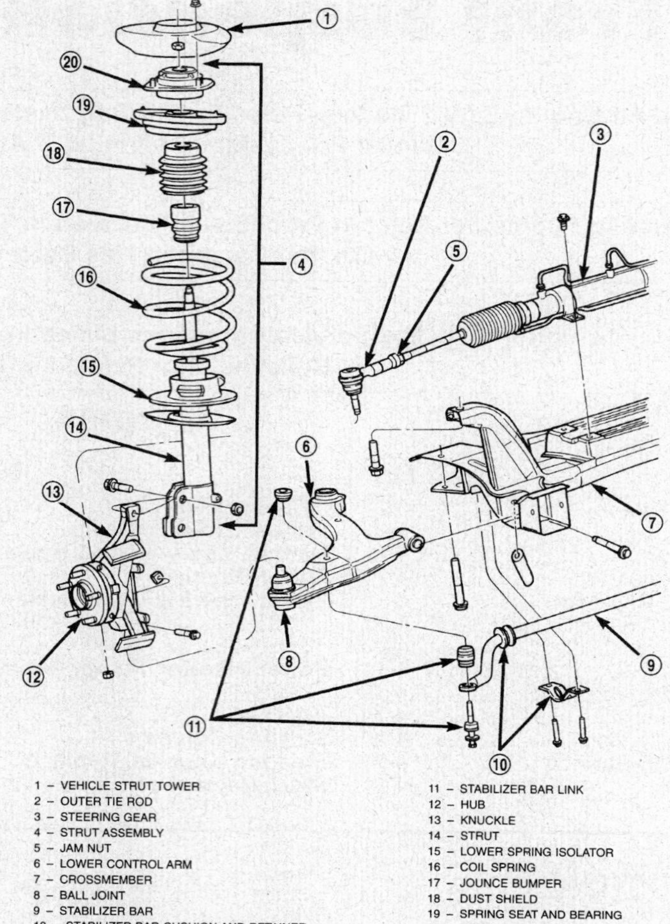

Fig. 2 Exploded view of front suspension. 2000–02

HUB & BEARING SERVICE

DISASSEMBLE

1998-99

All steps of the hub bearing removal from steering knuckle must be done using a suitable hydraulic arbor press.

1. Install bearing splitter tool No. P334, or equivalent, on steering knuckle and hub/bearing assembly to support steering knuckle when pressing out bearing.
2. Position steering knuckle and hub/bearing assembly in vise supported by splitter tool, **Fig. 3.**
3. Press hub from bearing using driver tool No. 6644-2, or equivalent, on small end of hub. One bearing race may come out with hub
4. Remove bearing splitter from steering knuckle and place steering knuckle in press supported by press blocks, **Fig. 4.**
5. Place bearing driver tool No. MB990799, or equivalent, on outer race of hub bearing and press hub bearing completely out of steering knuckle.
6. Install bearing splitter tool on hub so it is between flange of hub and bearing race remaining on hub.
7. Install assembly into press, place driver tool on end of hub and press hub out of hub bearing race, **Fig. 5.**

2000-02

The cartridge type front wheel bearing on these models is not transferable to a new knuckle. If a new knuckle does not arrive with a new bearing, a new bearing must also be installed. This must be done before the knuckle is installed on the vehicle.

1. Using stud remover tool No. 4150A, or equivalent, press one wheel stud out of hub flange.
2. Rotate hub until removed stud aligns with bearing retainer plate notch.
3. Remove stud from hub.
4. Rotate hub until open stud hole faces away from caliper lower rail on knuckle.
5. Install one half of bearing splitter tool No. 1130, or equivalent between hub and bearing plate.
6. Align threaded hole in first half of bearing splitter with caliper rail on knuckle.
7. Install remaining portions of splitter. Hand tighten nuts to hold splitter in place on knuckle.
8. Ensure retainer plate to knuckle bolts are contacting splitter. **Retainer plate should not support knuckle or contact splitter.**
9. Mount knuckle in suitable arbor press supported by bearing splitter, **Fig. 3.**
10. Position driver tool No. 6644-2, or equivalent on hub's small end.
11. Remove hub from wheel bearing using arbor press. Outer race normally comes out of bearing when hub is pressed.
12. Remove bearing splitter tool from knuckle.
13. Remove mounting bolts and bearing retainer plate.
14. Mount knuckle in arbor press again, supported by press blocks, **Fig. 4.** Ensure press blocks do not obstruct knuckle bore or bearing will not slide out.
15. Place bearing driver tool No. MB990799, or equivalent on bearing's outer race.
16. Press bearing out of knuckle.
17. Install bearing splitter tool on hub between hub flange and outer bearing race.

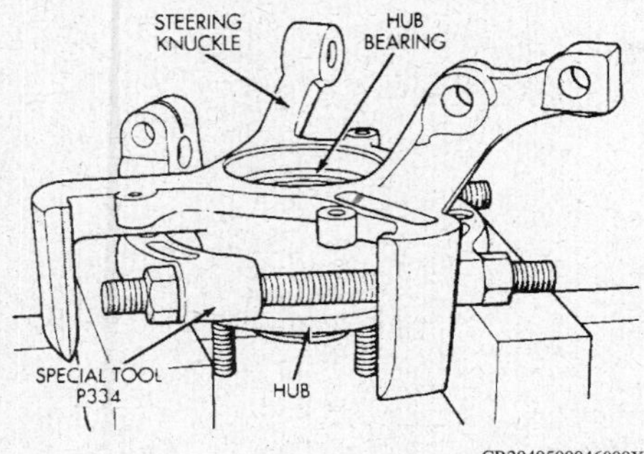

Fig. 3 Hub, bearing & steering knuckle supported for hub removal

18. Place hub, race and splitter in arbor press.
19. Place driver tool on end of hub.
20. Press hub out of bearing race.

ASSEMBLE

1998-99

1. Install new bearing into bore of steering knuckle so it is square with bore.
2. Place steering knuckle in press with receiver tool No. C-4698-2, or equivalent, supporting steering knuckle.
3. Press hub bearing into steering knuckle until it is fully bottom in bearing bore of steering knuckle using driver tool No. 5052, or equivalent, on outer race of hub.
4. Install hub bearing retaining snap ring into groove in hub bearing bore of steering knuckle. **Ensure snap ring is fully seated.**
5. Place steering knuckle with hub bearing installed in press with receiver tool No. MB990799, or equivalent, supporting inner race of hub bearing, **Fig. 6.**
6. Place hub into hub bearing ensuring it is square with bearing.
7. Press hub into bearing until it bottoms in hub bearing using driver tool No. 6522, or equivalent, on front face of hub.

2000-02

The cartridge type front wheel bearing on these models is not transferable to a new knuckle. If a new knuckle does not arrive with a new bearing, a new bearing must also be installed. This must be done before the knuckle is installed on the vehicle.

1. Wipe knuckle bore clean with clean, dry lint free towel. Ensure no dirt or grease remains.
2. Place new bearing into knuckle bore, perfectly square.
3. Place knuckle in arbor press with receiver tool No. C-4698-2, or equivalent supporting knuckle.
4. Place driver tool 5052, or equivalent, on bearing outer race.
5. Press bearing into knuckle until it has fully bottomed. Remove knuckle from press.
6. Install bearing retainer plate onto knuckle with three original or exact replacement bolts. **Do not use substitutions.** Tighten mounting bolts to specifications.
7. Place previously removed wheel stud back into hub flange.
8. Place hub in arbor press supported by tool No. C-4698-1, or equivalent.
9. Press stud into hub flange until it seats fully against flange's rear side. Remove hub from press.
10. Place knuckle with its newly installed bearing back into arbor press with receiver tool No. MB990799, or equivalent, supporting bearing inner race.
11. Place hub in bearing, ensuring it is square with inner race.
12. Press hub into bearing until it fully bottoms in bearing.
13. Remove knuckle from press.

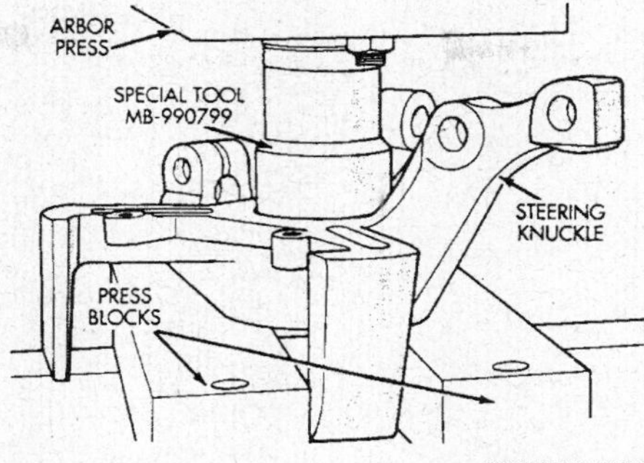

Fig. 4 Hub bearing removal

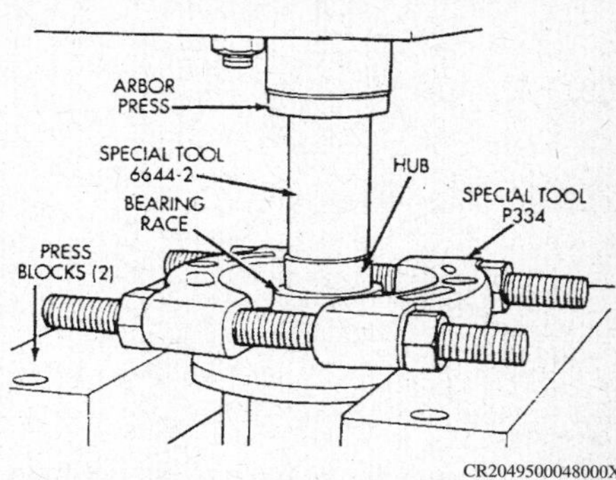

Fig. 5 Hub bearing race removal

BALL JOINT INSPECTION

With weight of vehicle resting on wheels, grasp grease fitting and, with no mechanical assistance or added force, attempt to move grease fitting, **Fig. 7.**

If the ball joint is worn the grease fitting will move easily. If there is movement replace ball joint as required.

BALL JOINT

REPLACE

1998-99

1. Remove lower control arm following procedure outlined under "Control Arm, Replace."
2. Pry ball joint seal boot off joint using suitable screwdriver .
3. Position receiving cup tool No. 6758, or equivalent, to support lower control arm while receiving ball joint.
4. Install receiver/installer tool No. 6804, or equivalent, in top of ball joint,
5. Press ball joint assembly completely out of control arm using suitable press.
6. Reverse procedure to install.

2000-02

Removal

1. Remove lower control arm following procedure outlined under "Control Arm, Replace."
2. Pry ball joint seal boot off ball joint using suitable screwdriver.
3. Position receiver tool No. 6908-2, or equivalent, on hydraulic press to support lower control arm while receiving ball joint.
4. Place control arm on top of receiver tool so bottom of ball joint sits in receiver cup.
5. Place larger end of adapter tool No. 6804, or equivalent, on top of ball joint.
6. Press ball joint completely out of control arm use hydraulic press.
7. Remove arm and all tools from press.

Installation

1. Position new ball joint by hand into its control arm bore, with notch in stud facing control arm front isolator bushing, to ease assembly. Ensure it moves in straight and square.
2. Position installer tool No. 6758, or equivalent on hydraulic press to support control arm. Place control arm on top of installer in upside-down position, aligning ball joint stud squarely with installer cup.
3. Place larger end of adapter tool No. 6804, or equivalent on top of ball joint.
4. Use hydraulic press to press ball joint into control arm until joint's shoulder bottoms in its bore. **Do not apply excessive pressure after joint has bottomed.**
5. Remove all tools and control arm from press.
6. Install new ball joint seal over stud. Position upward lip on outside perimeter of seal boot outward away from control arm once installed. Start installation by hand.
7. Position installer tool No. 6758, or equivalent over boot's outer diameter. Use hand pressure on top of tool until boot is pressed squarely down against top surface of control arm.
8. Install lower control arm following procedure outlined under "Control Arm, Replace."

STRUT

REPLACE

1998-99

1. Loosen wheel lugnuts, then raise and support vehicle.
2. Remove wheel and tire assembly, then disconnect hydraulic brake hose routing bracket from strut bracket.
3. **On models equipped with ABS,**

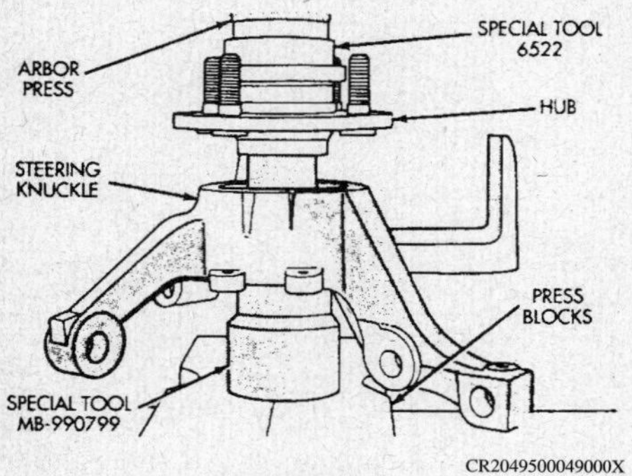

Fig. 6 Hub bearing installation. 1998–99

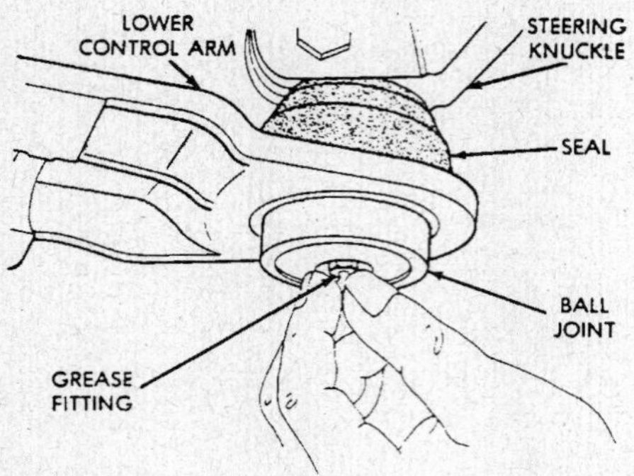

Fig. 7 Ball joint wear inspection

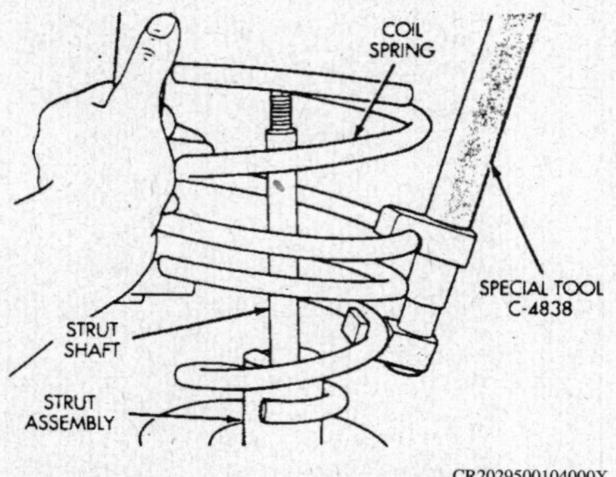

Fig. 8 Coil spring removal. 1998–99

speed sensor is combined with hydraulic hose routing bracket.

4. **On all models,** remove strut clevis bracket to steering knuckle mounting bolts.
5. Remove upper mount to strut tower mounting nuts and strut.
6. Reverse procedure to install.

2000-02

Removal

1. Raise and support vehicle on hoist.
2. Remove tire and wheel.
3. Mark strut assemblies if both lefthand and righthand units will be replaced.
4. Remove ground wire screw at rear of strut.
5. **On models equipped with ABS,** remove ABS sensor bracket screw at rear of strut.
6. **On all models,** remove two strut to knuckle bolts. Hold bolts in place in knuckle while removing nuts and tap bolts out using suitable pin punch. **These bolts are serrated and must not be turned during removal.**
7. Lower vehicle enough to open hood, but do not let tires reach ground.
8. Remove three strut to tower mounting nuts.
9. Remove strut.

Installation

1. Install new strut into tower. Ensure three studs align with tower holes. Tighten nuts to specifications.
2. Close hood.
3. Position lower end of strut in line with upper end of knuckle and align mounting holes.
4. Install strut to knuckle bolts with nuts facing front of vehicle.
5. Tighten mounting nuts to specifications, then final tighten an additional 90°. **These bolts are serrated and must not be turned during removal. Hold bolts in place in knuckle while installing nuts.**
6. **On models equipped with ABS,** mount wheel speed sensor to rear ear of strut. Tighten to specifications.
7. **On all models,** attach ground wire to rear of strut. Tighten to specifications.
8. Install tire and wheel. Tighten lugnuts in proper sequence to half specification. Repeat sequence again to full specification.

STRUT SERVICE

1998-99

1. Clamp strut by clevis bracket into suitable vise.
2. Scribe coil spring and strut as righthand or lefthand side.
3. Compress coil spring using compressor tool No. C-4838, or equivalent, **Fig. 8.**
4. Install socket strut nut tool No. L4558A, or equivalent, on strut shaft mounting nut.
5. Install 10 mm socket on hex head of strut shaft and remove nut while holding strut to keep from rotating.
6. Remove upper spring seat, pivot bearing and dust shield as an assembly.
7. Remove coil spring.
8. Reverse procedure to install.

2000-02

Removal

1. Remove strut as previously described.
2. Position strut into coil spring compressor tool No. PSE W-7200, or equivalent, following manufacturer's instructions. Set lower and upper hooks.
3. Place clamp on lower end of spring to hold strut in place when shaft nut is removed. **Do not remove strut shaft nut until after spring has been compressed.**
4. Compress spring until all tension is gone from upper mount.
5. When spring has been sufficiently compressed, install strut nut socket tool No. 6864, or equivalent on nut.
6. Install suitable socket on strut shaft hex end, then hold shaft in place and remove nut.
7. Remove upper spring seat and bearing with upper spring isolator as a unit from top of coil spring by pulling straight up. Isolator can be separated after removal.
8. Remove dust shield and jounce bumper by pulling straight up.
9. If coil spring is being replaced, release spring tension by completely backing off compressor drive. Push hooks back and remove spring.

Installation

1. Place coil spring into compressor tool following manufacturer's instructions.
2. Rotate spring so end of top coil is directly in rear.
3. Slowly compress spring until strut can be assembled.
4. Install lower spring isolator on strut's lower spring seat.
5. Install strut through bottom of spring until clevis bracket is positioned straight outward away from compressor.
6. Install clamp on lower end of spring and strut so strut stays in place.
7. Install jounce bumper on strut shaft, with smaller end pointing downward toward lower seat.
8. Install dust shield on strut shaft. Shield's bottom will snap past retainer on top of strut housing.
9. Install upper spring isolator on upper spring seat and bearing.
10. Install upper spring seat and bearing on top of spring. Position notch in upper edge of seat straight out away from compressor.
11. Install strut upper mount over strut shaft, onto top of upper spring seat and bearing.
12. Loosely install strut shaft mounting nut.
13. Install strut nut socket tool No. 6864, or equivalent, on strut shaft mounting nut.
14. Install suitable socket on hex end of strut shaft, hold shaft in place and tighten nut to specifications.
15. Slowly release coil spring tension by completely backing off tensioner drive. Ensure upper mount, seat and bearing properly align, and upper mount does not bind.
16. Remove clamp from lower end of spring and strut. Push hooks back and remove strut from compressor.
17. Install strut as previously described.

CONTROL ARM

REPLACE

1998-99

1. Raise and support vehicle, then remove wheel and tire assembly.
2. Remove attaching links connecting sway bar to lower control arm.
3. Loosen, but do not remove, sway bar retainers to front suspension crossmember mounting bolts.

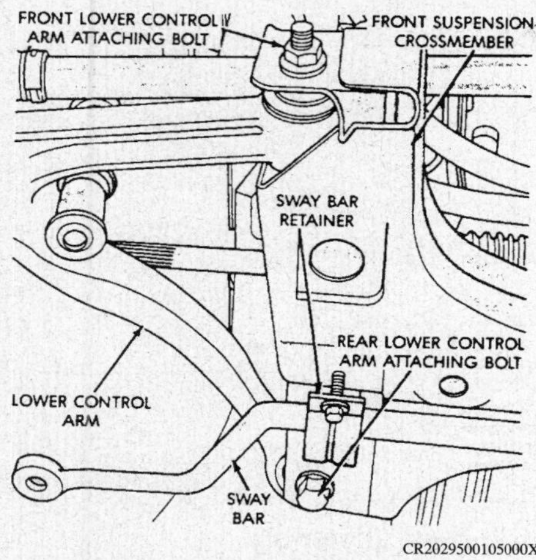

Fig. 9 Lower control arm removal. 1998–99

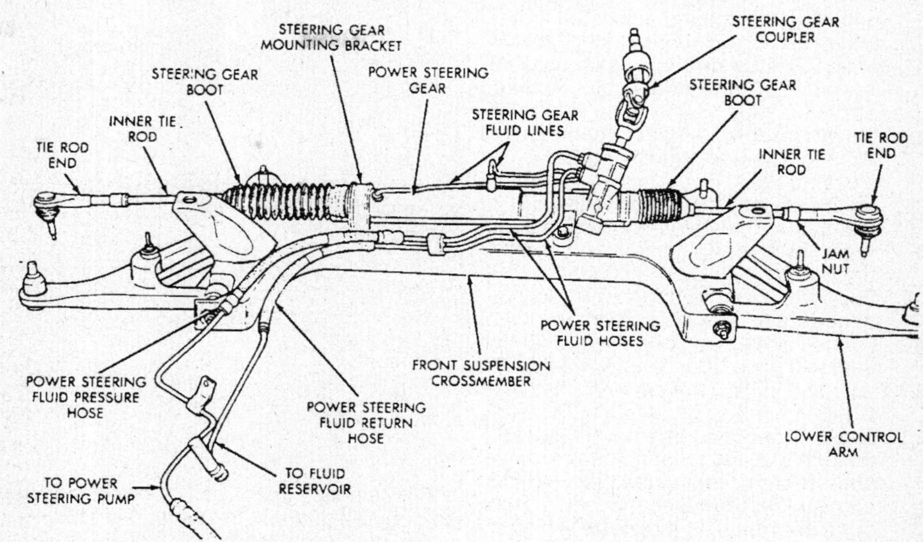

Fig. 10 Power steering gear assembly. 1998–99

4. Rotate sway bar away from lower control arm.
5. Separate steering knuckle from ball joint stud using suitable pry bar.
6. Remove front lower control arm bushing to crossmember mounting nut and bolt.
7. Remove crossmember and frame mounting bolt and rear lower control arm, **Fig. 9.**
8. Reverse procedure to install.

2000–02

This procedure has been revised by a Technical Service Bulletin.

1. Raise and support vehicle.
2. Remove tires and wheels.
3. Remove stabilizer links.
4. Rotate forward ends of stabilizer bar downward. Loosen bar cushion retainers if required.
5. Remove ball joint stud nut and pinch bolt at knuckle. **Do not pull outward on knuckle. This might separate inner CV joint on driveshaft.**
6. Separate ball joint stud from knuckle, avoiding seal cuts and tears. Pry downward on control arm and up against knuckle's ball joint boss.
7. On righthand control arm, remove mounting bolts and engine torque strut.
8. Remove control arm front pivot bolt at crossmember.
9. Remove control arm rear pivot bolt at crossmember and frame rail.
10. Remove control arm from crossmember.
11. Reverse procedure to install, noting the following:
    a. Position control arm into crossmember.
    b. Install rear pivot bolt at crossmember and frame rail, but do not fully tighten at this time.
    c. Install control arm front pivot bolt at crossmember.
    d. Tighten control arm rear and front pivot bolt to specifications.
    e. If righthand control arm was replaced, install engine torque strut and adjust as outlined under "Adjustment" in "Engine Mount, Replace" section.
    f. Install new ball joint pinch bolt and tighten to specifications.
    g. Lower vehicle to ground and rock to bring to curb height.
    h. If original stabilizer link bolts are being installed, clean all grease, oil and loose material, then apply two drops of Mopar Lock And Seal part No. 4318031, or equivalent, to last ½ inch of each bolt's threads.
    i. Tighten stabilizer link bolts to specifications.

STEERING KNUCKLE

REPLACE

Refer to "Hub & Bearing, Replace" for procedure.

POWER STEERING GEAR

REPLACE

1998–99

1. Disconnect steering gear coupler from steering column shaft coupler, **Fig. 10.**
2. Raise and support vehicle, then remove both front wheel and tire assemblies.
3. Remove engine/transaxle dampener.
4. Remove mounting nuts from both tie rod ends.
5. Remove both tie rod end studs from steering knuckle using remover tool No. MB990635, or equivalent.
6. Disconnect wiring harness connector from power steering fluid pressure switch.
7. Remove power steering pressure and return hose routing bracket from front suspension crossmember.
8. Remove power steering fluid, pressure and return hoses from power steering gear.
9. Scribe line marking location where front suspension crossmember is mounted against body.
10. Position suitable transaxle jack under front suspension center and remove front suspension crossmember to frame rails mounting bolts.
11. Loosen both rear bolts and lower control arm to body of vehicle.
12. Using transaxle jack lower front suspension crossmember enough to allow steering gear to be removed.
13. Remove mounting bolts and steering gear.
14. Reverse procedure to install.

2000–02

1. Ensure front wheels are in straight ahead position and lock it using steering wheel holder tool.
2. Remove steering column coupler retainer pin inside passenger compartment.
3. Back nut off and remove coupling pinch bolt .
4. Separate steering column upper and lower couplings.
5. Raise and support vehicle.
6. Remove both front tires and wheels.
7. Remove both outer tie rod to knuckle nuts. Hold tie rods stationary while removing nuts.
8. Remove outer tie rods from knuckles using tie rod remover tool No. MB991113, or equivalent.
9. Remove tie rod heat shield.
10. Release locking tab and disconnect power steering fluid pressure switch wiring electrical connector.
11. Back out tube nut securing power steering fluid pressure hose to gear.
12. **On models less power steering fluid cooler,** disconnect fluid return hose from gear and remove hose from C-clamps on outside of two routing clips on gear's front side.
13. **On models equipped with power steering fluid cooler,** disconnect cooler hose from steering gear.
14. **On all models,** remove pressure hose

from front of steering gear.
15. **On models equipped with power steering fluid cooler,** remove mounting screws and allow cooler to hang aside.
16. **On all models,** remove engine torque strut to righthand forward corner of crossmember.
17. Scribe alignment marks to ease crossmember to body installation and avoid losing front wheel caster and camber settings.
18. Support crossmember with suitable transmission jack under center.
19. Loosen and completely remove two front crossmember to frame rail bolts.
20. Loosen, but do not remove, two rear crossmember to frame rail bolts.
21. Lower front crossmember with jack enough to allow steering gear removal from rear of crossmember. **Do not allow crossmember to hang from control arms. Let jack take weight.**
22. Remove roll pin where steering column lower coupling meets pinion shaft using suitable punch. Push lower coupling up and off pinion shaft.
23. Release pinion shaft firewall cover seal from tabs cast into steering gear housing and remove seal from gear.
24. Loosen and remove four steering gear to crossmember bolts.
25. Remove steering gear from front crossmember.
26. Reverse procedure to install, noting the following:
    a. Start rear crossmember mounting bolts into tapping plates on body.
    b. Install front crossmember to frame rail mounting bolts.
    c. Temporarily tighten mounting bolts to 20 inch lbs.
    d. Tap crossmember back into alignment with scribe marks made during removal using suitable soft-faced hammer.
    e. When properly position, tighten rear bolts, rear control arm bolts and front crossmember bolts to specifications.
    f. Ensure grease is present on dash to coupling seal lip where it meets coupling's plastic collar.
    g. Fill and bleed power steering fluid system.
    h. Inspect and adjust front toe setting as outlined under "Wheel Alignment."

POWER STEERING PUMP

REPLACE

1998–99

1. Disconnect pressure hose from power steering pump.
2. Remove fitting and power steering fluid supply hose.
3. Remove power steering pump to cast bracket mounting and adjusting bolts.
4. Loosen front power steering pump to front engine mount mounting bracket mounting bolt far enough to slide bracket from behind bolt.
5. Remove drive belt, power steering pump and bracket as an assembly.
6. Reverse procedure to install.

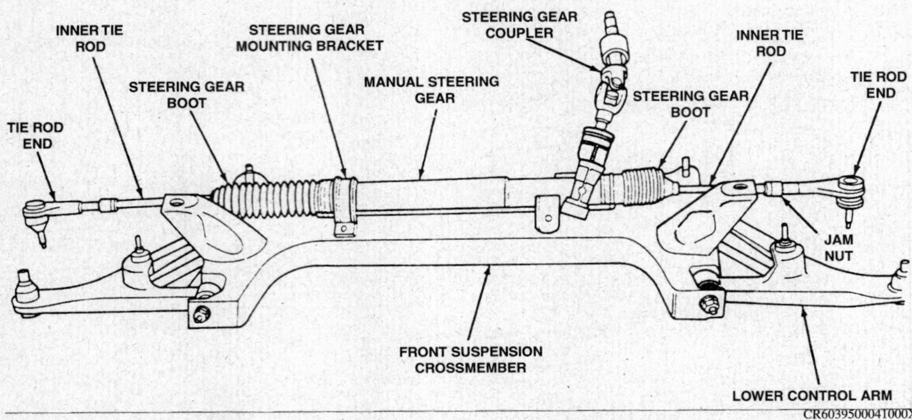

Fig. 11 Manual steering gear assembly

2000–02

1. Siphon all possible power steering fluid from pump reservoir.
2. Remove steering pump drive belt.
3. Disconnect fluid return hose from reservoir.
4. Disconnect fluid pressure hose from steering pump.
5. Remove steering pump to rear support bracket bolt.
6. Loosen two support bracket to engine block bolts.
7. Working through pump pulley holes, remove three pump to cast bracket bolts.
8. Remove power steering pump with reservoir.
9. Reverse procedure to install, noting the following:
    a. Tighten all fasteners to specifications.
    b. Fill and bleed power steering fluid system.
    c. Inspect for and correct any leaks.

MANUAL STEERING GEAR

REPLACE

Refer to "Power Steering Gear, Replace" and **Fig. 11** for service procedures.

TECHNICAL SERVICE BULLETINS

SMOOTH ROAD VIBRATION

1998–99

On some of these models, there may be a smooth rod oscillation/vibration back and forth at approximately 72 mph.

This condition may be caused by the front suspension lower control arm bushing.

To correct this condition, replace the front lower control arm rear isolation bushing.

SNAPPING NOISE

2000–01

On some of these models there may be a snapping noise from front suspension.

This condition may be caused by front crossmember tightening.

To correct this condition, proceed as follows:

1. Raise and support vehicle.
2. **Torque** front crossmember rear mounting bolts to 175 ft. lbs.

POWER STEERING MOAN

2000–01

On some of these models there may be a power steering moan at low engine speeds during slow turns and parking.

This condition may be caused by low, aerated fluid level.

To correct this condition, proceed as follows:

1. **Do not start vehicle.**
2. Remove power steering fluid cap.
3. Raise and support front wheels enough to allow wheels to be turned side to side.
4. Cycle steering wheel lock to lock three times.
5. Inspect fluid level and adjust as required.
6. Apply 15–20 in Hg vacuum to power steering system at reservoir neck for five minutes.
7. Remove vacuum.
8. Start engine and slow turn steering wheel lock to lock 10 times while maintaining approximately 1850–2150 RPM. **Do not hold steering against lock.**
9. Allow engine to idle three minutes.
10. Turn ignition switch to Off position and lower vehicle.
11. Inspect fluid level and adjust as required.

POPPING NOISE OVER BUMPS

1998

On some of these models there may be a front end popping noise while traveling over bumps. This noise may be more apparent when suspension is wet.

This condition may be caused by the front coil spring.

To correct this condition, proceed as follows:

1. Remove strut.
2. Clean spring and strut spring seat. Use smooth scuff pad to remove rust.
3. Install spring sleever (part No. 5273399) to spring.
4. Assemble strut.

COLD POWER STEERING NOISE

1998

On some of these models the power steering may make noise when ambient temperatures are 10°F, or below, and may less than one minute.

This condition may be cause by the power steering fluid.

To correct this condition replace original power steering fluid with improved version (part No. MS9933).

POPPING CREAKING NOISE

1998

On some of these models built before Aug. 30, 1997, there may be a popping or creaking noise when going in reverse or forward with steering wheel tuned completely in one direction, when shifting from drive to reverse or reverse to drive, when pulling in or out of driveway, or on large dips or bumps such as speed bumps.

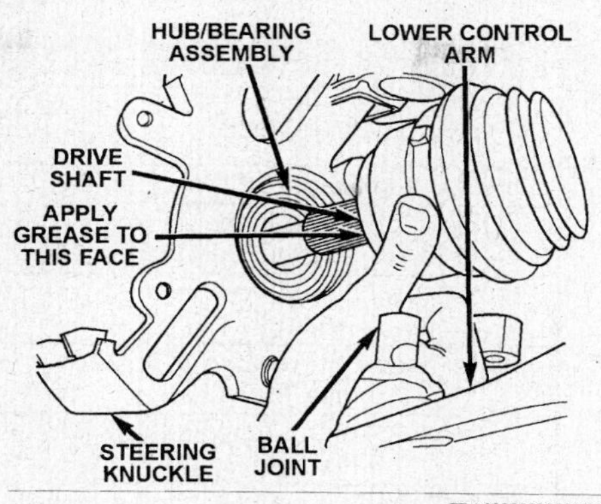

Fig. 12 Lubricating driveshaft face. 1998

This condition may be caused by front wheel bearings, steering knuckles, front upper strut mounts, engine mounts or driveshafts.

To correct this condition, proceed as follows:

1. Remove left and righthand front knuckle/bearing/hub assemblies.
2. Press hub out of front knuckle/bearing/hub assemblies.
3. Press hub into new front knuckle/bearing/hub assemblies:
   a. **On models with five-stud hub,** lefthand part No. 04897662AA and righthand 04897663AA.
   b. **On models with four-stud hub,** lefthand part No. 04897928AA and righthand 04897929AA.
4. **On all models,** lubricate entire driveshaft face were it contacts hub bearing assembly with wheel bearing lub No. 04318064, or equivalent, **Fig. 12.**
5. Install left and righthand front knuckle/bearing/hub assemblies.
6. Replace upper strut mount (part No. 0426100AB).
7. **Torque** new mounting nuts to 45 ft. lbs.
8. Remove and replace righthand engine mount (part No. 04668200).
9. Fill gap between mount snubber and engine bracket with silicone spray No. 04318070, or equivalent non-petrolium based grease.
10. Inspect and tighten suspension components to specifications.

TIGHTENING SPECIFICATIONS

Year	Component	Torque/Ft. Lbs.
1998–99	Lower Control Arm To Crossmember	120
	Outer Tie Rod To Inner Tie Rod Locknut	45
	Power Steering Pressure Hose Banjo Fitting	25
	Power Steering Pressure & Return Hose Tube	23
	Power Steering Pump To Rear Bracket	40
	Stabilizer Bar To Crossmember	21
	Steering Gear To Crossmember	50
	Strut Shaft	55
	Strut To Shock Tower	25
	Tie Rod End To Steering Knuckle	45
	Tie Rod To Steering Knuckle	45
	Wheel Lugnuts	95
2000–02	ABS Wheel Speed Sensor	10
	Ball Joint Pinch Bolt	70
	Brake Caliper Guide Bolts	16
	Control Arm Front Pivot Bolt	120
	Control Arm Rear Pivot Bolt	150
	Driveshaft Hub	180
	Front Crossmember, Front	105
	Front Crossmember, Rear	150
	Ground Wire To Strut	10
	Hub Bearing Retainer Plate	21
	Power Steering Cooler	90①
	Power Steering Fluid Pressure Switch	70①
	Power Steering Hose Tube	25
	Power Steering Pump	21
	Power Steering Pump Pressure Fitting	65
	Power Steering Pump Pressure Hose Tube	25
	Power Steering Pump Rear Support Bracket To Engine	40
	Stabilizer Bar Cushion	21
	Stabilizer Link	22
	Steering Column Lower Coupling Pinch Bolt	21
	Strut Shaft	55
	Strut To Knuckle	40②
	Strut To Tower	25
	Wheel Lugnuts	100③

① — Inch lbs.

② — Final tighten an additional 90°.

③ — Tighten lugnuts in proper sequence to half specification. Repeat sequence again to full specification.

Wheel Alignment

INDEX

PRELIMINARY INSPECTION

Ensure vehicle has a full tank of gas when wheel alignment specifications are inspected or adjusted. If tank is not full, this change in weight will affect curb height of vehicle and alignment specifications. Inspect and adjust tire pressure. Ensure all tires are the same size. Inspect all suspension components for looseness or damage. Components showing signs of wear or damage should be replaced before alignment.

FRONT WHEEL ALIGNMENT

Caster and camber settings are determined by the location of vehicle's suspension components, **Fig. 1.** No adjustment of caster and camber is possible after vehicle is built or when servicing suspension components. Caster and camber are not normally considered an adjustable specification when performing an alignment on these models.

CASTER

If caster is not within specifications, inspect for damaged suspension components or body damage causing component locations to change. No adjustment is possible for caster.

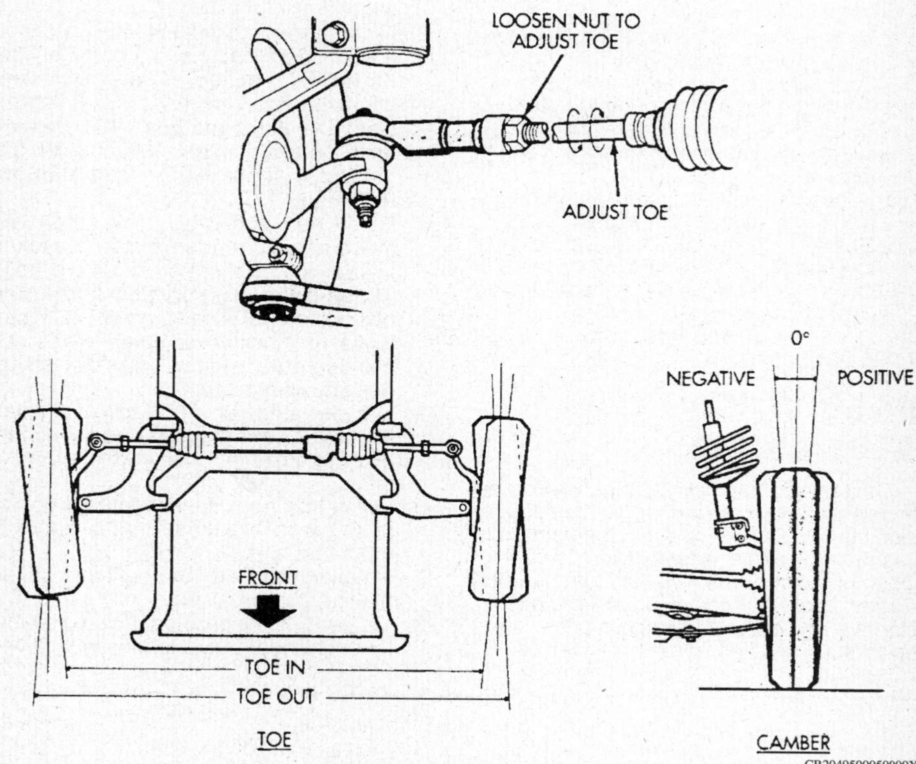

Fig. 1 Camber & toe alignment

CAMBER

1. Properly position vehicle on alignment rack and install all required equipment per alignment equipment specifications.
2. Center steering wheel and lock in place using steering wheel clamp.
3. Jounce vehicle, read front alignment settings and compare to specifications.
4. If camber readings obtained are not within specifications, Mopar Service Kit will be required. Different kits are designed for front and rear suspension. **On 2000 models, this procedure should only be used on vehicles less ACR Competition Package.**
5. Raise and support vehicle, then remove original front strut clevis bracket to steering knuckle upper mounting bolt. **These bolts are serrated and must not be turned during removal. Hold bolts in place in knuckle while removing nuts and tap bolts out using suitable pin punch.**
6. Loosen strut clevis bracket to steering knuckle mounting lower bolt enough to allow knuckle to move in clevis bracket.
7. Install bolt from service kit into upper strut clevis bracket to steering knuckle mounting hole.
8. Install nut provided by service kit on replacement bolt.
9. Tighten upper bolt and nut from service kit until snug, but still allowing movement between strut clevis bracket and knuckle.
10. Remove original lower bolt and install bolt from service kit into lower strut clevis bracket hole. Install nut and tighten until snug.
11. Lower vehicle until full weight is supported by suspension.
12. Jounce front and rear of vehicle equal number of times.
13. Adjust camber to preferred setting by pushing or pulling top of tire.
14. Tighten upper and lower strut clevis bracket bolts.
15. Jounce vehicle equal number of times and ensure rear camber setting. When vehicle is at proper setting, **torque** both front strut clevis brackets to 40 ft. lbs. plus additional ¼ turn.

TOE

Rear wheel toe must be set prior to setting front wheel toe. Proceed as follows:

1. Center steering wheel and lock in place using steering wheel clamp.
2. Loosen lefthand and righthand lateral links to rear crossmember mounting bolts' nuts, **Fig. 2.**
3. Rotate lateral link adjustment cams until preferred rear toe specification is obtained, **Fig. 3.**
4. Tighten righthand and lefthand lateral links to rear crossmember mounting

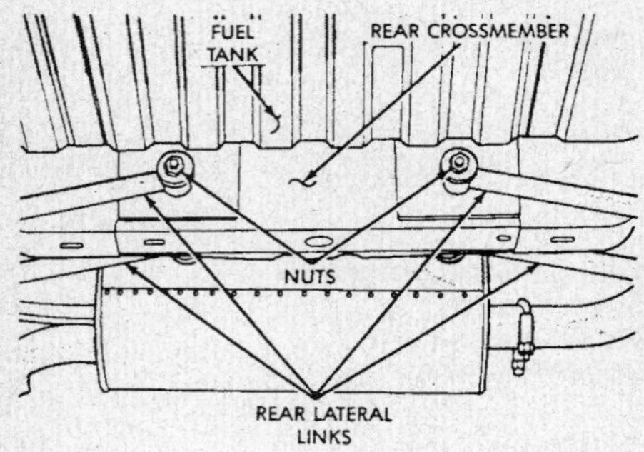

Fig. 2 Rear lateral link toe setting

bolt nuts while holding toe adjustment cams from turning. This will securely hold adjustment cams in position.

5. **Torque** lateral link mounting bolt to 70 ft. lbs. while prevent lateral link mounting bolt and adjustment cam from turning.
6. Loosen front inner tie rod end jam nuts and grasp inner tie rods at serration.
7. Rotate inner tie rods of steering gear and set front toe specifications.
8. **On 1998–99 models, torque** tie rod locknuts to 45 ft. lbs.
9. **On 2000–02 models, torque** tie rod locknuts to 55 ft. lbs.

REAR WHEEL ALIGNMENT

Caster and camber settings are determined by the location of vehicle's suspension components, **Fig. 1**. No adjustment of caster is possible after vehicle is built or when servicing suspension components. Caster and camber are not normally considered an adjustable specification when performing an alignment on this vehicle.

CASTER

If caster is not within specifications, inspect for damaged suspension components or body damage causing component locations to change. No adjustment is possible for caster.

CAMBER

1. Properly position vehicle on alignment rack and install all required equipment, per alignment equipment specifications.
2. Jounce vehicle and read rear alignment settings and compare to specifications.
3. If camber readings obtained are not within specifications, Mopar Service Kit will be required. Different kits are designed for front and rear suspension. **On 2000 models, this procedure should only be used on vehicles less ACR Competition Package.**
4. Raise and support vehicle, then remove original rear strut clevis bracket to rear knuckle upper mounting bolt. **These bolts are serrated and must not be turned during removal. Hold bolts in place in knuckle while removing nuts and tap bolts out using suitable pin punch.**
5. Loosen strut clevis bracket to rear knuckle lower mounting bolt enough to allow knuckle to move in clevis bracket.
6. Install bolt from service kit into upper strut clevis bracket to rear knuckle mounting hole.
7. Install nut provided by service kit on replacement bolt.
8. Tighten upper bolt and nut from service kit until snug, but still allowing movement between strut clevis bracket and knuckle.

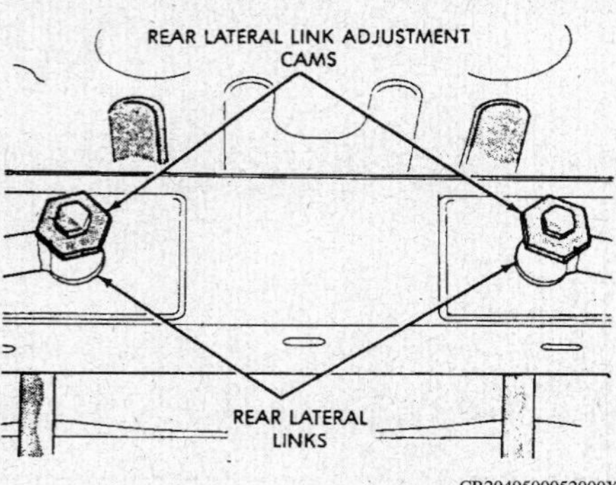

Fig. 3 Rear wheel toe adjustment cams

9. Remove original lower bolt and install bolt from service kit into lower strut clevis bracket hole. Install nut and tighten until snug.
10. Lower vehicle until full weight is supported by suspension.
11. Jounce front and rear of vehicle equal number of times.
12. Adjust camber to preferred setting by pushing or pulling top of tire.
13. Tighten upper and lower strut clevis bracket bolts.
14. Jounce vehicle equal number of times and ensure rear camber setting. When vehicle is at proper setting, **torque** rear strut clevis brackets to 70 ft. lbs.

TOE

Rear wheel toe must be set prior to setting front wheel toe. Refer to "Front Wheel Alignment" in this section for front and rear wheel toe setting procedures.

TALON

NOTE: Refer To The Rear Of This Manual For Manufacturer's Special Service Tool Supplies.

INDEX OF SERVICE OPERATIONS

Specifications

GENERAL ENGINE SPECIFICATIONS

Year	Engine		Fuel System	Bore and Stroke, Inch	Compression Ratio	Net HP @ RPM ②	Maximum Torque, Ft. Lbs. @ RPM	Minimum Oil Pressure, psi @ RPM
	Liter	VIN①						
1998	2.0L④	Y	MFI③	3.44 x 3.27	9.6	140 @ 6000	130 @ 4800	4.0 @ 800
	2.0L⑤	F	MFI③	3.35 x 3.46	8.5	⑥	⑦	11.4 @ 750

① — Eighth digit of VIN denotes engine code.
② — Ratings are net as installed in vehicle.
③ — Multi-Port Fuel Injection.
④ — Non-turbocharged.
⑤ — Turbocharged.
⑥ — 210 @ 6000 w/manual transaxle; 205 @ 6000 w/automatic transaxle.
⑦ — 214 @ 3000 w/manual transaxle; 220 @ 3000 w/automatic transaxle.

TUNE UP SPECIFICATIONS

Year & Engine (VIN Code)①	Spark Plug Gap	Ignition Timing °BTDC				Curb Idle Speed, RPM		Fast Idle Speed, RPM		Fuel Pump Pressure, psi.	Valve Clearance, inch
		Firing Order Fig.④	Man. Trans.	Auto. Trans.	Mark Fig.	Man. Trans.	Auto Trans.	Man. Trans.	Auto. Trans.		
1998											
2.0L (Y)⑧	.050	B	⑥	⑥	A	800②	800②	②	②	47–50③	⑦
2.0L (F)⑤	.030	C	⑥	⑥	A	750②	750②	②	②	42–45⑨	⑦

BTDC — Before Top Dead Center
N — Neutral
① — The eighth digit of the Vehicle Identification Number (VIN) denotes engine code.
② — Controlled by the idle air control motor.
③ — Disconnect fuel pump electrical connector, located at fuel tank. Start engine & operate until it stalls. Disconnect battery ground cable, then connect fuel pump electrical connector. Install suitable fuel pressure gauge to fuel pressure test port on fuel rail. Connect battery, then place ignition switch in the On position & use scan tool to perform fuel system pressure test. Note fuel pressure reading.
④ — Before disconnecting wires from distributor cap, determine location of No. 1 wire in cap, as distributor position may have been altered from that shown at the end of this chart.
⑤ — Turbocharged.
⑥ — Ignition timing is electronically controlled, and is not adjustable.
⑦ — Equipped w/hydraulic lash adjusters. No periodic adjustment is needed.
⑧ — Non-turbocharged.
⑨ — Disconnect fuel pump electrical connector, located at fuel tank. Start engine & operate until it stalls. Disconnect battery ground cable, then reconnect fuel pump electrical connector. Place shop towels around fuel high pressure hose at fuel delivery pipe side, then disconnect hose. Install suitable fuel pressure gauge between fuel delivery pipe & high pressure hose. Disconnect & plug vacuum hose from fuel pressure regulator. Connect battery ground cable & inspect fuel pressure w/engine idling.

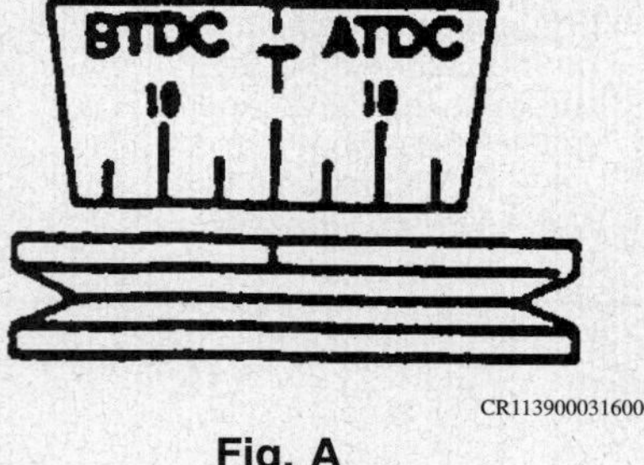

Fig. A

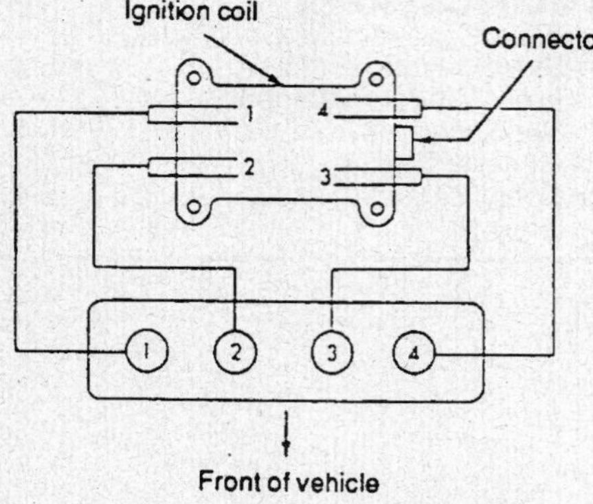

Fig. B

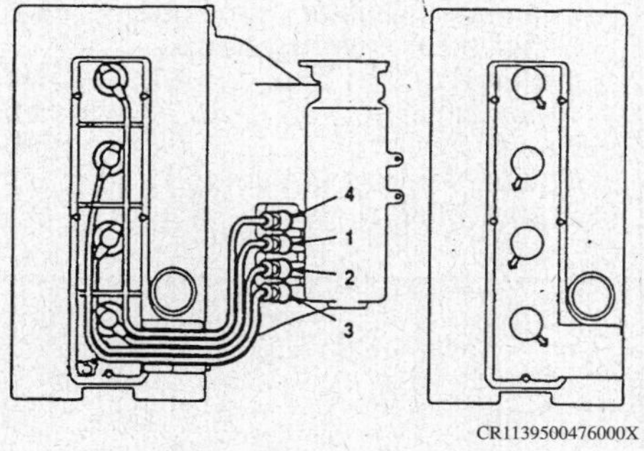

Fig. C

FRONT WHEEL ALIGNMENT SPECIFICATIONS

Year	Model	Camber Angle, Degrees②		Caster Angle, Degrees②		Toe In, Inch	Ball Joint Wear
		Limits	Desired	Limits	Desired		
1998	③	-5/6 to +1/6	-1/3	+3 1/6 to +6 1/6	+4 2/3	0④	①
	⑤	-7/12 to +5/12	-1/12	+3 1/6 to +6 1/6	+4 2/3	0④	①

① — Ball joint breakaway torque for the compression lower arm ball joint should be 4–22 inch lbs. Ball joint breakaway torque for the lateral lower arm ball joint should be 9–30 inch lbs. when under a load of 838 lbs.

② — Reference angle only. Non adjustable.

③ — FWD models & models w/16 inch wheels.

④ — Plus or minus .12 inch.

⑤ — AWD models & models w/14 inch wheels.

REAR WHEEL ALIGNMENT SPECIFICATIONS

Year	Model	Camber Angle, Degrees		Toe In, Inch	Ball Joint Wear
		Limits	Desired		
1998	②	-1 5/6 to -5/6①	-1 1/3①	.12⑤	③
	④	-2 1/6 to -1 1/6	-1 2/3①	.12⑤	③

① — Reference angle only. Non adjustable.

② — FWD models w/14 inch wheels & AWD models.

③ — Ball joint breakaway torque for the lower arm and toe control ball joints should be 1–23 inch lbs. Ball joint breakaway torque for the stabilizer link ball joint should be 4–13 inch lbs.

④ — FWD models w/16 inch wheels.

⑤ — Plus or minus .12 inch.

VEHICLE RIDE HEIGHT SPECIFICATIONS

Model	Year	Body Style	Manufacturer's Original Tire Size	Measurement Points & Specifications②					
				Front			Rear		
				Dim.	Specification		Dim.	Specification	
					Inches	mm		Inches	mm
Talon	1998	FWD	①	A	6.12	155	B	5.5	139.7
		AWD	①	A	6.75	171.4	B	6.18	157

Dim. — Dimension
FWD — Front Wheel Drive
AWD — All Wheel Drive
A Dim. — Ground to Front Rocker Panel
B Dim. — Ground to Rocker Panel

① — See door sticker or inside of glove box for manufacturer's original tire size specifications

② — Measurement is w/fuel, radiator coolant & engine oil full, spare tire, jack, hand tools & mats in designated positions & tires properly inflated.

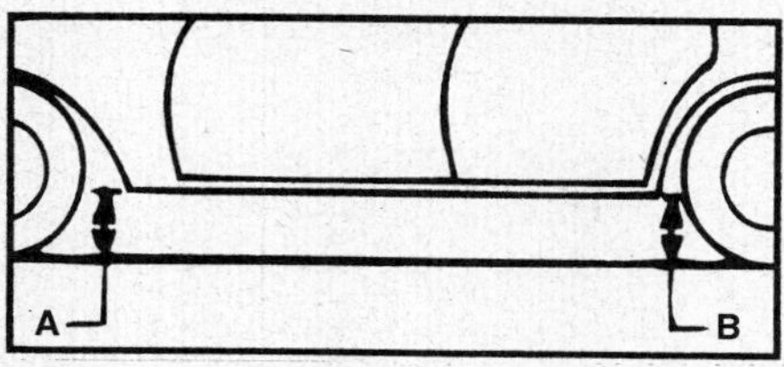

Fig. A Dimensions A & B

FLUID CAPACITIES & COOLING SYSTEM DATA

Year	Liter	VIN Code	Coolant Capacity, Qts.	Radiator Cap Relief Pressure, Lbs.	Thermo. Opening Temp., °F	Fuel Tank, Gals.	Engine Oil Refill, Qts.	Transaxle Oil		Rear Axle, Pts.
								5 Speed, Pts.	Auto. Trans., Qts.①	
1998	2.0L⑤	Y	7.4	16	195	15.9	4.0③	4.2	9.1	—
	2.0L②	F	7.4	13	180	15.9	4.2④	4.6⑥	7.1⑥	1.8

① — Approximate. Make final inspection w/dipstick.
② — Turbocharged engine.
③ — With filter change add .5 qt.
④ — With filter change add .5 qt. Oil cooler capacity, .5 qt.
⑤ — Non-turbocharged engine.
⑥ — Transfer, .63 qts.

LUBRICANT DATA

Year	Model	Lubricant Type					
		Transaxle		Transfer Case	Rear Axle	Power Steering	Brake System
		Manual	Automatic				
1998	All	③	①	75W–90 API GL-4	80W–90 API GL-5	②	DOT 3 or 4

① — Mopar ATF type 7176, Dia. ATF SP or equivalent.
② — Mopar ATF type 7176, Dia. ATF SP, Dexron or Dexron II.
③ — Non-turbocharged, Mopar MS9417 MTX fluid, or equivalent; turbocharged, 75W-90 GL-4, or 75W–85W GL-4.

Electrical

NOTE: On Air Bag Equipped Models, Refer To "Air Bag System Precautions" Located In The Front Of This Manual For System Disarming & Arming Procedures.

NOTE: Refer To "Computer Relearn Procedures" Located In The Front Of This Manual When Battery Power To The Computer Has Been Interrupted.

INDEX

PRECAUTIONS

AIR BAG SYSTEMS

Refer to "Air Bag System Precautions" in the front of this manual for system disarming and arming procedures.

BATTERY GROUND CABLE

Prior to service, disconnect battery ground cable and isolate as required.

FUSE PANEL & FLASHER LOCATION

The multi-purpose fuse panel and dedicated fuse panel are located under the driver's side instrument panel.

The hazard and turn signal flasher are located behind the center console.

On non-turbocharged models, the No. 1–12 dedicated fuse panel/power distribution block is located in the front lefthand side of the engine compartment.

On turbocharged models, the No. 1–12 dedicated fuse panel/power distribution block is located in the righthand side of the engine compartment.

On all models, the No. 13 dedicated fuse is located in the interior relay box under the driver's side instrument panel.

FUEL PUMP RELAY LOCATION

NON-TURBOCHARGED ENGINE

The fuel pump relay is located in the lefthand rear corner of the engine compartment.

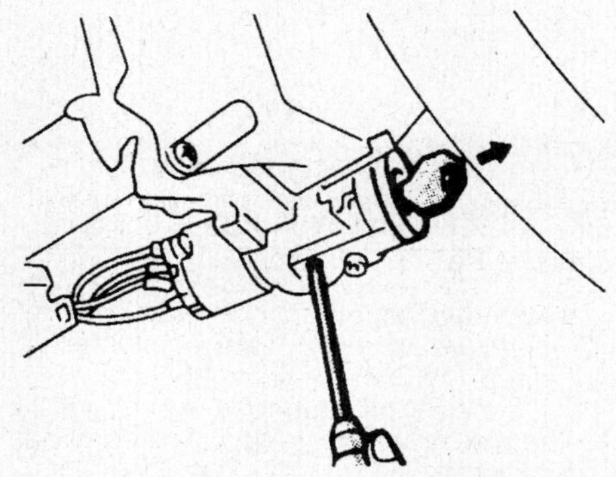

Fig. 1 Ignition lock release

TURBOCHARGED ENGINE

The fuel pump relay is located behind the center dash panel.

STARTER

REPLACE

1. Raise and support vehicle.
2. **On non-turbocharged models with manual transmission,** remove aspirator assembly.
3. **On turbocharged models,** remove air hose.
4. **On all models,** remove starter terminal and connector.
5. Remove starter.
6. Reverse procedure to install.

DISTRIBUTOR

REPLACE

This engine uses a direct ignition system (DIS), with a coil pack rather than a distributor. Refer to "Coil Pack Replace" for replacement procedure.

COIL PACK

REPLACE

1. **On turbocharged models,** remove center cover.
2. **On all models,** disconnect spark plug cables from ignition coil. **Label cables for installation reference.**
3. Remove coil pack mounting screws, then the coil pack.
4. Reverse procedure to install.

IGNITION LOCK

REPLACE

1. Remove upper and lower steering column covers.
2. Insert key in steering lock cylinder, then turn to Accessory position.
3. Using suitable screwdriver, push lockpin, **Fig. 1,** of steering lock cylinder inward and pull lock cylinder out of housing.
4. Reverse procedure to install.

IGNITION SWITCH

REPLACE

1. Remove instrument panel undercover, **Fig. 2.**
2. Remove upper and lower column covers.
3. Disconnect ignition switch wiring connector.
4. Remove ignition switch.
5. Reverse procedure to install.

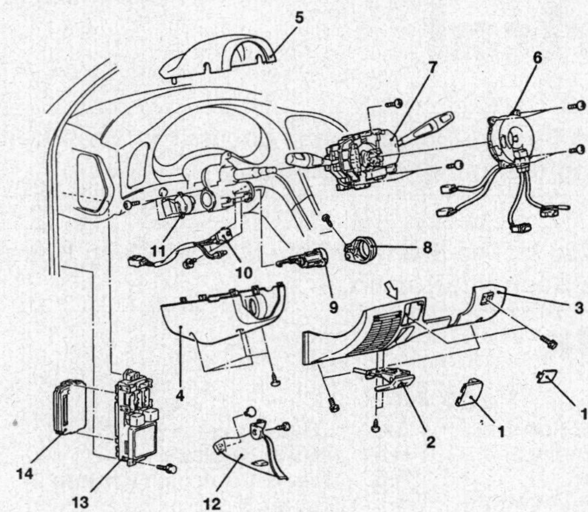

Steering lock cylinder removal steps
1. Plug
2. Hood lock release handle
3. Instrument under cover
4. Column cover lower
5. Column cover upper
6. Clock spring
7. Column switch
8. Ignition key illumination ring or ring cover
9. Steering lock cylinder

Key reminder switch segment or key hole illumination light removal steps
4. Column cover lower
5. Column cover upper
10. Key reminder switch segment or key hole illumination light

Ignition switch segment removal steps
4. Column cover lower
5. Column cover upper
11. Ignition switch segment

ETACS-ECU removal steps
12. Cowl side trim (L.H.)
13. Junction block
14. ETACS-ECU

CR9049500067000X

Fig. 2 Ignition switch removal

HEADLAMP SWITCH

REPLACE

Refer to "Combination Switch, Replace" for procedure.

COMBINATION SWITCH

REPLACE

1. Remove air bag module as described under "Air Bag System."
2. Remove steering wheel as described under "Steering Wheel, Replace."
3. Remove column switch in numbered sequence, **Fig. 2.**
4. Reverse procedure to install.

DIMMER SWITCH

REPLACE

Refer to "Combination Switch, Replace" for procedure.

STEERING WHEEL

REPLACE

1. Remove air bag module as described under "Air Bag System."
2. Remove steering wheel attaching bolt, **Fig. 3.**
3. Remove steering wheel using suitable wheel puller. **Do not use hammer as this may damage the collapsible mechanism.**
4. Reverse procedure to install.

INSTRUMENT CLUSTER

REPLACE

1. Remove instrument cluster bezel.
2. Remove screws holding cluster to dash.
3. Gently pull cluster outward enough to remove connectors and clips from rear of cluster, allowing it to be removed.
4. Reverse procedure to install.

RADIO

REPLACE

1. Use suitable plastic trim tool to pry lower part of radio panel out of console.
2. Remove floor console assembly.
3. Remove radio bracket.
4. Gently pull outward on radio assembly enough to remove connectors from rear of unit.
5. Reverse procedure to install.

WIPER MOTOR

REPLACE

FRONT

Remove front windshield wiper motor and transmission in numbered sequence, **Fig. 4,** noting the following:
1. Mark position of wiper arms before removal.
2. Reverse procedure to install.

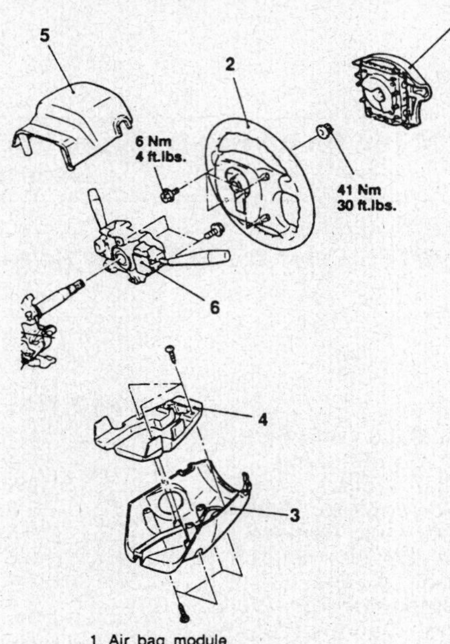

1. Air bag module
2. Steering wheel
3. Lower column cover
4. Column pad
5. Upper column cover
6. Clock spring and column switch assembly

CR6049500104000X

Fig. 3 Steering wheel removal

REAR

Remove rear windshield wiper motor and transmission in numbered sequence, **Fig. 5,** noting the following:
1. Mark position of wiper arm before removal.
2. Reverse procedure to install

WIPER TRANSMISSION

REPLACE

Refer to "Wiper Motor, Replace" for procedure.

BLOWER MOTOR

REPLACE

Remove blower motor in numbered sequence, **Fig. 6,** noting the following:
1. Clean blower case before installation.
2. Reverse procedure to install.

HEATER CORE

REPLACE

Remove heater unit in numbered sequence, **Fig. 7,** noting the following:
1. Drain engine coolant.
2. Remove instrument panel as outlined in the "Dash Panel Service" section.
3. Reverse procedure to install. Fill up engine coolant.

EVAPORATOR CORE

REPLACE

Remove evaporator unit in numbered sequence, **Figs. 8 and 9,** noting the following:
1. Properly recover refrigerant from A/C

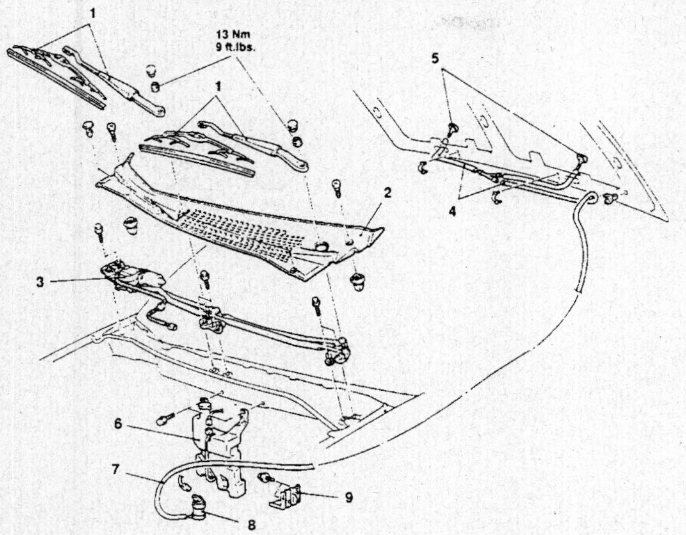

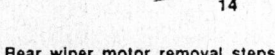

Motor and link assembly removal steps
1. Wiper arm and blade assembly
2. Front deck garnish
3. Motor and link assembly

Washer nozzle removal steps
4. Washer hose connection
5. Washer nozzle

Washer tank removal steps
6. Windshield washer tank
7. Washer hose
8. Washer motor
9. Washer tank bracket

CR9029500132000X

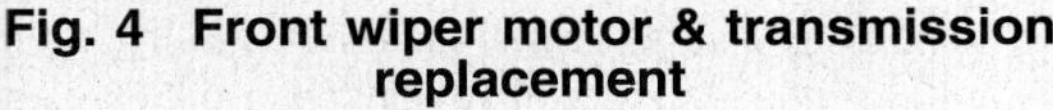

Fig. 4 Front wiper motor & transmission replacement

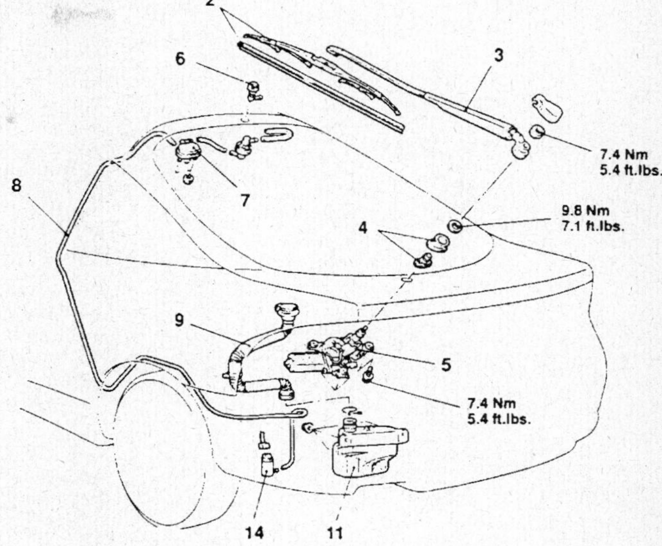

Rear wiper motor removal steps
2. Wiper blade
3. Wiper arm
4. Spacer assembly
- Liftgate lower trim

5. Rear wiper motor

Rear washer tank and hose removal steps
- Quarter upper trim (LH)
- Quarter lower trim (LH)
- Rear end trim
- Rear side trim
- Liftgate upper trim

6. Washer nozzle
7. Joint assembly
8. Tube assembly
9. Hose assembly
11. Rear washer tank
14. Rear washer motor

CR9029500133000X

Fig. 5 Rear wiper motor & transmission replacement

system as described in the "Air Conditioning" section.

2. Plug refrigerant lines to prevent air from mixing when disconnecting them.
3. **On non-turbocharged models,** refill evaporator with 1.35 fl. oz. ND-OIL 8 compressor oil, or equivalent, before replacing evaporator.
4. **On turbocharged models,** refill evaporator with 2.03 fl. oz. SUN PAG 56 compressor oil, or equivalent, before replacing evaporator.
5. **On all models,** reverse procedure to install. Be sure A/C system is properly charged as described in the "Air Conditioning" section.

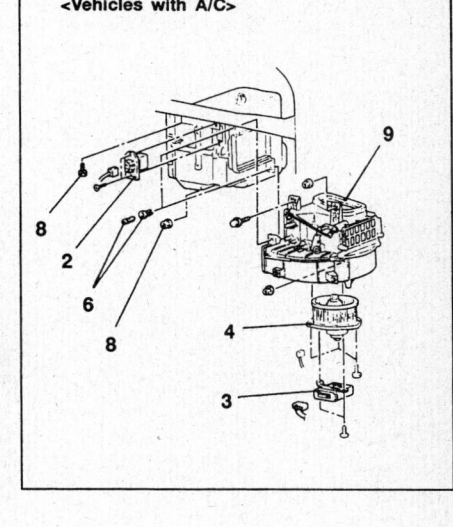

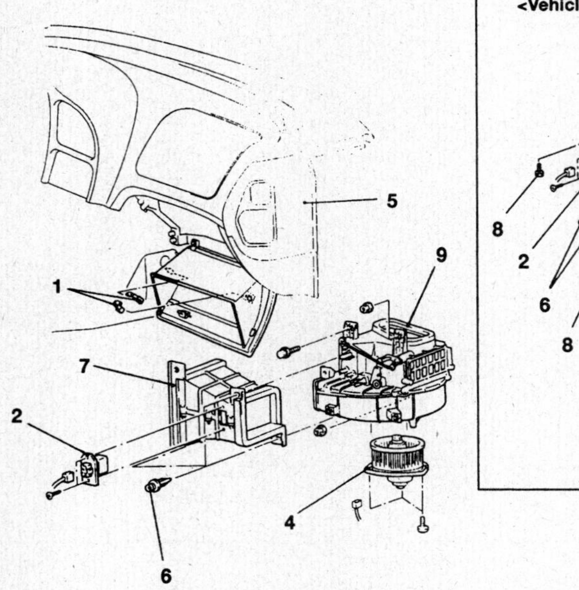

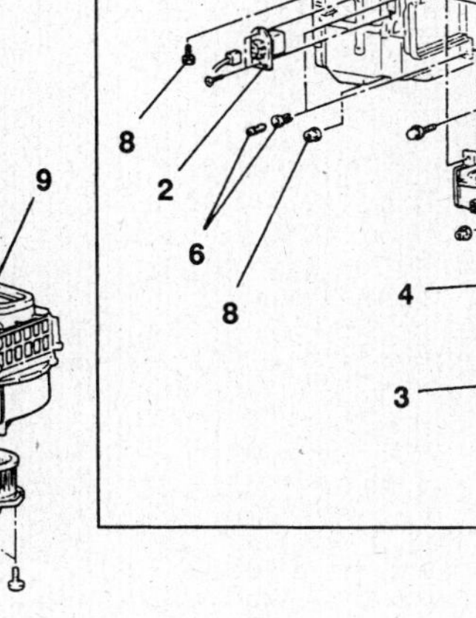

Resistor removal steps
1. Stopper
2. Resistor

Blower fan and motor removal steps

3. Automatic compressor – ECM <Vehicles with A/C for non-turbo>
4. Blower fan and motor

Blower unit removal steps

5. Instrument panel
6. Clip
7. Joint duct <Vehicles without A/C>
8. Cooling unit installation bolts and nuts <Vehicles with A/C>
9. Blower unit assembly

CR7029500230000X

Fig. 6 Blower motor replacement

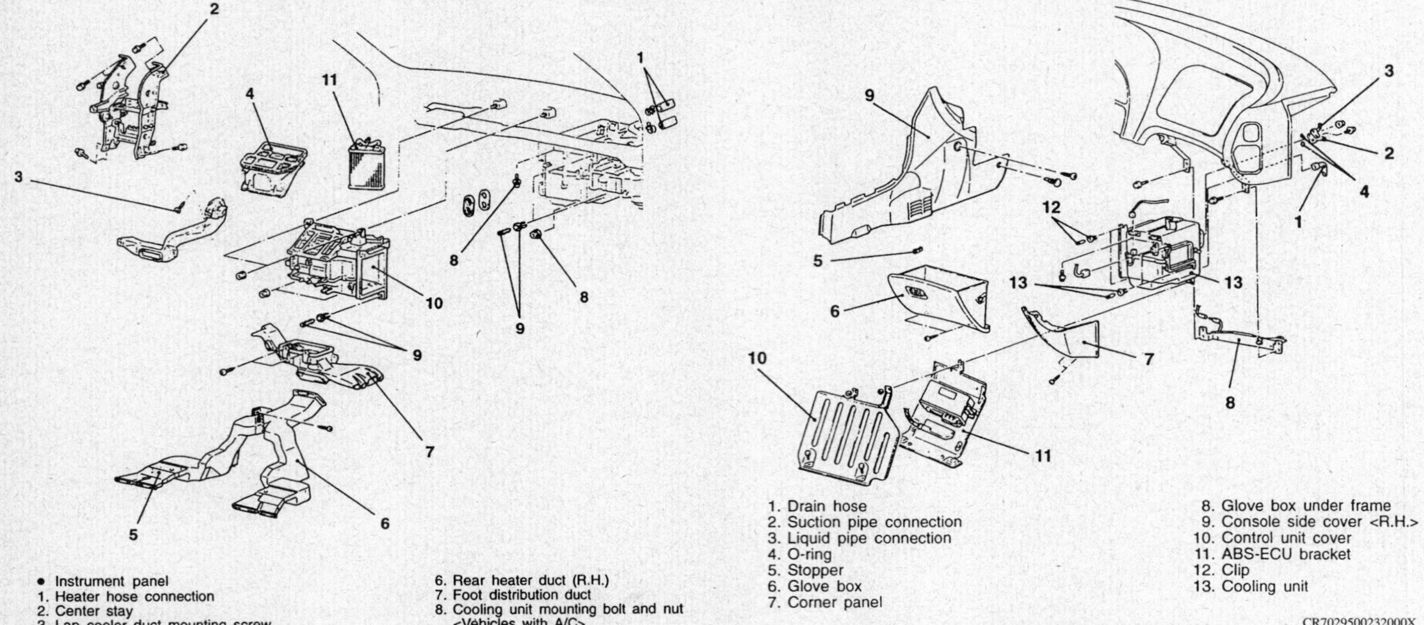

- Instrument panel
1. Heater hose connection
2. Center stay
3. Lap cooler duct mounting screw
4. Center duct
5. Rear heater duct (L.H.)
6. Rear heater duct (R.H.)
7. Foot distribution duct
8. Cooling unit mounting bolt and nut <Vehicles with A/C>
9. Clip
10. Heater unit
11. Heater core

CR7029500231000X

Fig. 7 Heater unit removal

1. Drain hose
2. Suction pipe connection
3. Liquid pipe connection
4. O-ring
5. Stopper
6. Glove box
7. Corner panel
8. Glove box under frame
9. Console side cover <R.H.>
10. Control unit cover
11. ABS-ECU bracket
12. Clip
13. Cooling unit

CR7029500232000X

Fig. 8 Evaporator replacement

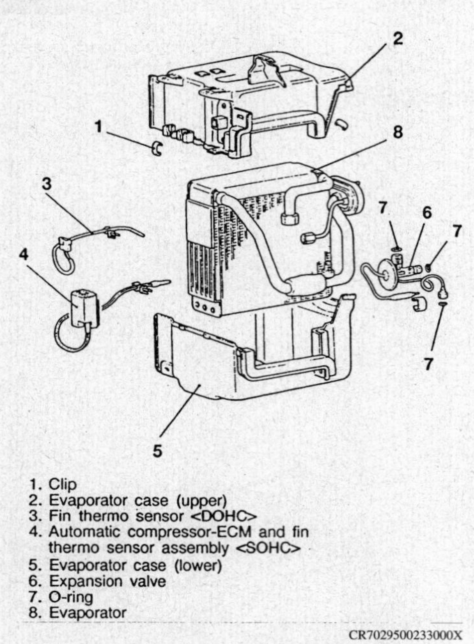

1. Clip
2. Evaporator case (upper)
3. Fin thermo sensor <DOHC>
4. Automatic compressor-ECM and fin thermo sensor assembly <SOHC>
5. Evaporator case (lower)
6. Expansion valve
7. O-ring
8. Evaporator

CR7029500233000X

Fig. 9 Evaporator unit disassemble

2.0L Engine

NOTE: On Air Bag Equipped Models, Refer To "Air Bag System Precautions" Located In The Front Of This Manual For System Disarming & Arming Procedures.

NOTE: Refer To "Computer Relearn Procedures" Located In The Front Of This Manual When Battery Power To The Computer Has Been Interrupted.

INDEX

PRECAUTIONS

FUEL SYSTEM PRESSURE RELIEF

1. Disconnect fuel pump harness connector at fuel tank.
2. Start engine and let it run until it stalls, then turn ignition switch to off.
3. Reconnect fuel pump harness connector.

BATTERY GROUND CABLE

Prior to service, disconnect battery ground cable and isolate as required.

COMPRESSION PRESSURE

Refer to **Fig. 1** for compression pressure data.

Year	Engine	Compression Pressure, psi①	Minimum Pressure, psi	Max. Variation Between Cylinders, psi
1998	2.0L②	170-225	100	④
	2.0L③	178	133	14

① — At 250–400 psi.
② — Non-turbocharged engine.
③ — Turbocharged engine.
④ — 25 aximum variation between cylinders.

Fig. 1 Compression pressure data

ENGINE MOUNT

REPLACE

UPPER MOUNT

Remove engine mount in numbered sequence, **Fig. 2,** noting the following:

1. Slightly raise and support engine, removing weight of engine from mount.
2. Inspect insulators for damage or cracks and replace as necessary.
3. Inspect brackets and replace if deformed or damaged.
4. When installing mounting stoppers, ensure arrow on stopper faces center of engine, **Fig. 3.**
5. Reverse procedure to install. Tighten to specifications.

ENGINE ROLL STOPPER

Remove engine roll stoppers in numbered sequence, **Fig. 4,** noting the following:

1. Slightly raise and support engine, removing weight of engine from mount.
2. Inspect insulators for damage or cracks and replace as necessary.
3. Inspect brackets and replace if deformed or damaged.
4. Inspect front roll stopper bracket assembly. If the dimension shown in **Fig. 5** is not 1.57–1.81 inches when the weight of the engine is on the body, replace the front roll stopper assembly.
5. When installing mounting stoppers, ensure arrow on stopper faces center of engine, **Fig. 3.**
6. Reverse procedure to install. Tighten to specifications.

ENGINE

REPLACE

1. Relieve fuel pressure as outlined under "Precautions."
2. Remove hood.
3. Drain coolant into a suitable container as follows:
   a. Place instrument panel temperature control lever in Hot position.
   b. Carefully remove radiator cap.
   c. Remove radiator drain plug.
4. Remove transaxle assembly.
5. Remove radiator as outlined under "Radiator, Replace."
6. Remove engine in numbered sequence, **Figs. 6 and 7,** noting the following:
   a. Remove power steering pump from bracket with hoses attached, then

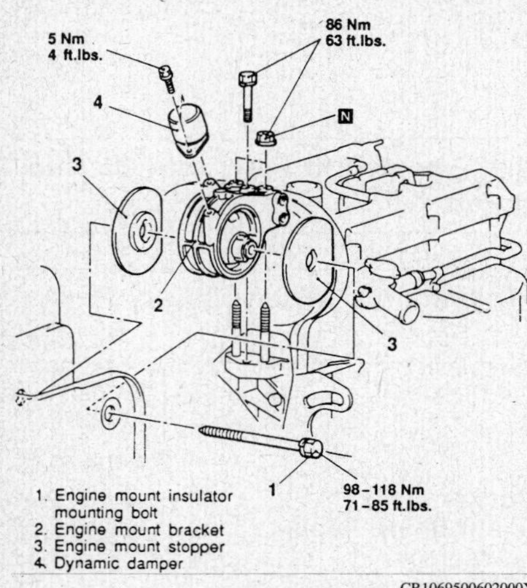

CR1069500602000X

Fig. 2 Engine upper mount replacement

secure pump out of the way with a piece of wire.
b. Remove air conditioner compressor from bracket with hoses attached, then secure compressor out of the way with a piece of wire.
c. Using a suitable engine hoist, slightly raise engine, then remove engine mount bracket.
7. Reverse procedure to install.

INTAKE MANIFOLD

REPLACE

REMOVAL

Remove intake manifold in numbered sequence, **Fig. 8,** noting the following:

1. Drain coolant into a suitable container as follows:
   a. Place instrument panel temperature control lever in Hot position.
   b. Carefully remove radiator cap.
   c. Remove radiator drain plug.
2. Before disconnecting high pressure fuel line, release fuel pressure as outlined under "Precautions."
3. Remove delivery pipe, fuel injector and regulator as an assembly.

INSPECTION

Inspect intake manifold and air intake plenum (if equipped) as follows:

1. Inspect for damage, cracks or defects.
2. Ensure coolant and jet air passages are clear.
3. Inspect installation surfaces with a straightedge. Replace if deflection exceeds .012 inch.

INSTALLATION

Reverse removal procedure to install. When installing throttle body, refer to bolt length chart, **Fig. 9.**

EXHAUST MANIFOLD

REPLACE

Remove exhaust manifold in numbered sequence, referring to **Figs. 10 and 11,** noting the following:

1. **On turbocharged models,** drain engine oil and coolant prior to removing exhaust manifold. To drain coolant into a suitable container, proceed as follows:
   a. Place instrument panel temperature control lever in Hot position.
   b. Carefully remove radiator cap.
   c. Remove radiator drain plug.
2. **On all models,** use oxygen sensor socket tool No. MD998703, or equivalent, to remove oxygen sensor.
3. **On turbocharged models,** leave power steering hoses attached when disconnecting power steering pump. Position pump out of the way and secure with a piece of wire.
4. **On all models,** reverse procedure to install. On turbocharged engine, apply machine oil to inner surface pipe flare prior to installing water pipe (18), **Fig. 11.**

CYLINDER HEAD

REPLACE

TURBOCHARGED ENGINE

Removal

Remove cylinder head in numbered sequence, **Fig. 12,** noting the following:

1. Before disconnecting high pressure fuel line, release fuel pressure as outlined under "Precautions."
2. Before removing upper radiator hose, mark hose clamp in relation to hose for assembly reference, then drain coolant into a suitable container as follows:
   a. Place instrument panel temperature control lever in Hot position.
   b. Carefully remove radiator cap.
   c. Remove radiator drain plug.
3. Remove timing belt as described under "Timing Belt, Replace."
4. Using cylinder head bolt wrench tool No. MD998051, or MB991654, or equivalent, remove cylinder head bolts in sequence as shown in **Fig. 13.**

Installation

Reverse removal procedure to install, noting the following:

1. Install cylinder head gasket as follows:
   a. Using a suitable scraper, remove old gasket material from cylinder block, using care not to allow old gasket material to fall into cylinder or passages.
   b. Clean head and block surfaces that come in contact with head gasket.
   c. Place head gasket on block with identification mark at top front. **Do not apply sealant to head gasket.**
2. When installing cylinder head, install head bolt washers, then tighten head bolts as follows:
   a. Inspect shank length of each bolt before installation. If shank length exceeds 3.91 inch, then replace the bolt.
   b. **Torque** bolts to 58 ft. lbs. in order shown in **Fig. 14.**
   c. Fully loosen bolts in order shown in **Fig. 13.**
   d. **Torque** bolts to 14–15 ft. lbs. in

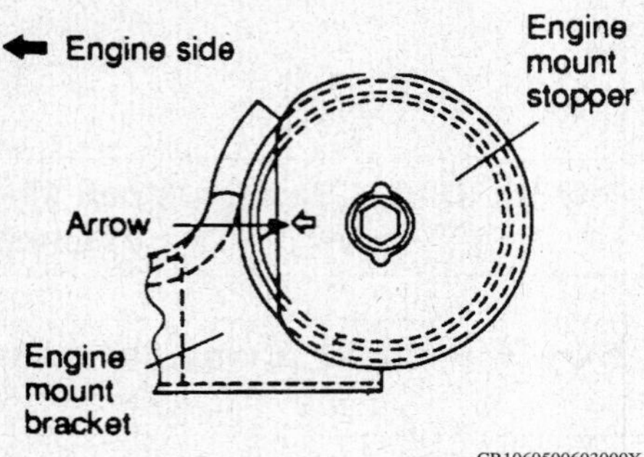

CR1069500603000X

Fig. 3 Engine mount stopper installation

order shown in **Fig. 14,** then tighten in sequence an additional 180° in 90° increments.
3. When installing semi-circular packing, apply liberal amount of gasket sealant onto circumference of packing.
4. When installing rocker cover, apply gasket sealant to area as shown in **Fig. 15.**
5. Install timing belt as described under "Timing Belt, Replace."
6. When installing high pressure fuel line (5), apply small amount of gasoline to hose union. Use care to avoid damaging O-ring.

NON-TURBOCHARGED ENGINE

1. Relieve fuel system pressure as described under "Precautions."
2. Drain engine coolant, then drain crankcase.
3. Disconnect electrical connectors from A/C compressor clutch, power steering pump switch, oxygen sensor, engine coolant temperature switch and sensor, MAP sensor and intake air temperature sensor.
4. Disconnect accelerator cable.
5. Disconnect TPS, IAC motor and injector harness electrical connectors.
6. Disconnect ignition coil, camshaft position sensor and EGR solenoid electrical connectors.
7. Disconnect heater hose, upper radiator hose, overflow tube and water hose connection. **Mark relationship between radiator hose and clamp for installation reference.**
8. Disconnect fuel high pressure and return hoses.
9. Disconnect purge air hose.
10. Disconnect power brake booster vacuum hose connection.
11. Remove intake manifold stay.
12. Remove intake and exhaust camshafts as described under "Camshaft, Replace."
13. Disconnect exhaust pipe from exhaust manifold.
14. Remove cylinder head attaching bolts, then remove cylinder head and gasket. After cylinder head removal, remove intake and exhaust manifold as necessary.
15. Reverse procedure to install, noting the following:
   a. Prior to installation, inspect cylinder

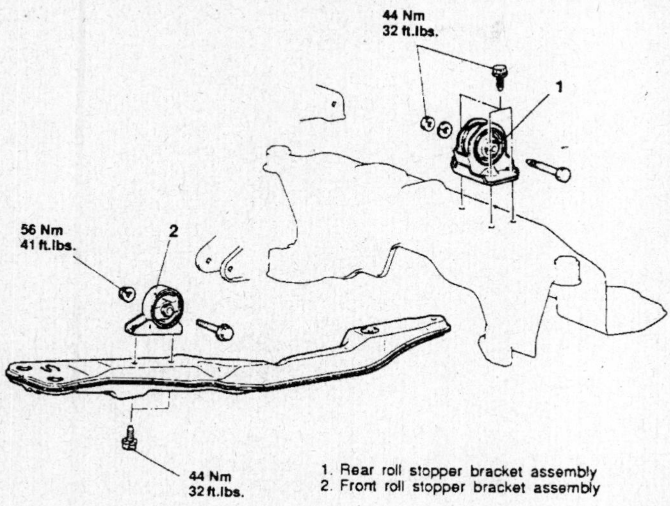

CR1069500604000X

Fig. 4 Engine roll stopper replacement

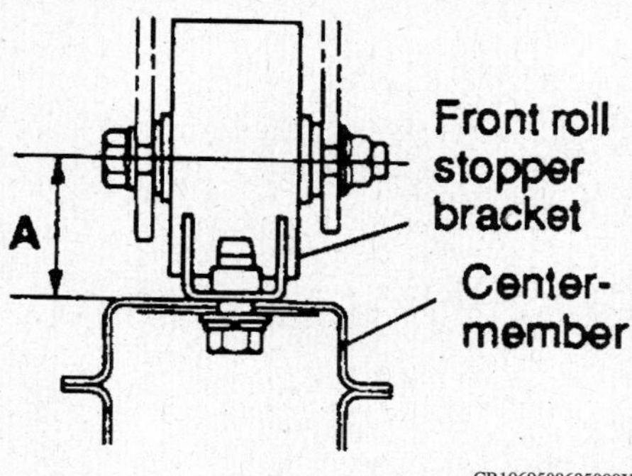

CR1069500605000X

Fig. 5 Front roll stopper clearance

head bolts for stretching by placing a straightedge against bolt threads. If all threads do not contact straightedge, replace bolt.

b. Clean bolt threads and lubricate with clean engine oil.

c. Tighten cylinder head bolts in sequence shown in **Fig. 16. Torque** bolts 1 through 6 to 25 ft. lbs., and bolts 7 through 10 to 20 ft. lbs. Next, **torque** bolts 1 through 6 to 50 ft. lbs. and bolts 7 through 10 to 20 ft. lbs. Again, **torque** bolts 1 through 6 to 50 ft. lbs., then bolts 7 through 10 to 20 ft. lbs. Finally, tighten all bolts an additional 90.°

d. When installing radiator hoses, align marks on clamps and respective hoses.

VALVE ARRANGEMENT

Intake valves are on the righthand side of the engine. The exhaust valves are on the lefthand side of the engine.

VALVE ADJUSTMENT

Hydraulic lash adjusters are used. No periodic adjustment is necessary.

ROCKER ARMS

Refer to "Camshaft, Replace" for rocker arm and rocker arm shaft replacement procedures.

TIMING BELT

REPLACE

NON-TURBOCHARGED ENGINE

With the timing belt removed, avoid turning the camshaft or crankshaft. If movement is required, exercise extreme caution to avoid valve damage caused by piston contact.

1. Remove the cooling system reserve tank.
2. Remove the under cover.
3. Remove the A/C compressor and power steering pump drive belt.
4. Remove the alternator drive belt.
5. Remove the crankshaft pulley.
6. Remove the power steering pump from the bracket with the hoses attached and position out of way.
7. Support engine by positioning a suitable jack and wooden block under the engine oil pan.
8. Remove the engine mount bracket assembly, **Fig.17**
9. Remove the timing belt front cover.
10. Align the camshaft and crankshaft sprocket timing marks, **Fig. 18.**
11. Loosen the timing belt tensioner, then remove the timing belt.
12. Remove the timing belt tensioner.
13. Position the timing belt tensioner in a soft jawed vise, then carefully compress the plunger. After the plunger has been compressed, insert a pin through the tensioner body to hold the plunger in place, **Fig. 19.**
14. Ensure the crankshaft sprocket mark is aligned with mark on oil pump housing and the camshaft timing marks are aligned, **Fig. 18.**
15. Move the crankshaft sprocket to 1/2 notch before TDC, **Fig. 20.**
16. Install the timing belt over the crankshaft sprocket, water pump sprocket, idler pulley, camshaft sprockets and

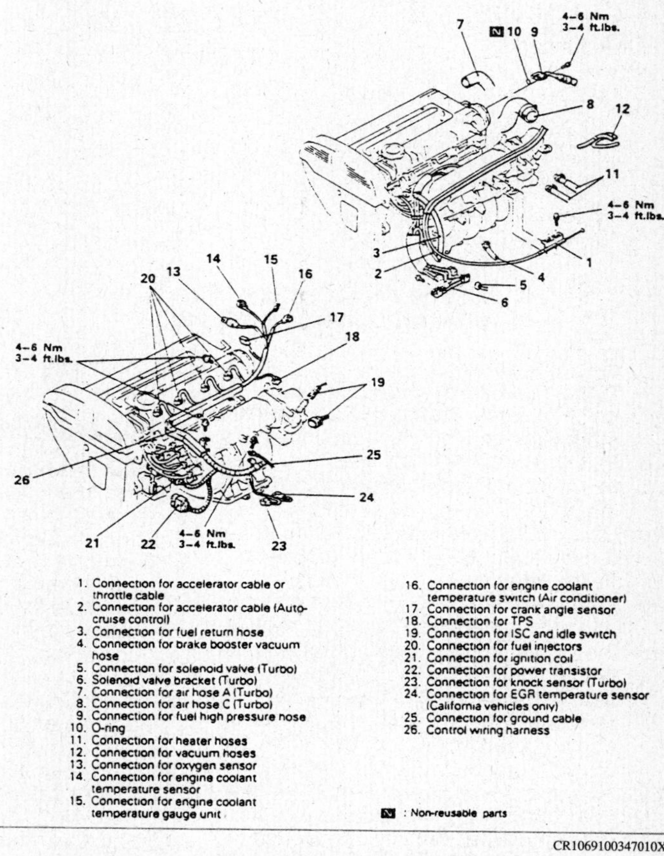

CR1069100347010X

Fig. 6 Engine replacement (Part 1 of 2). Non-turbocharged engine

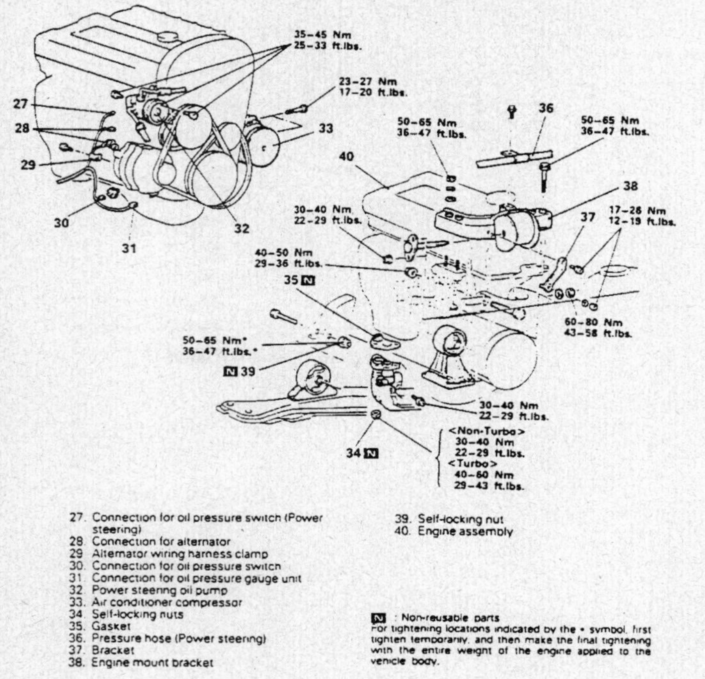

Fig. 6 Engine replacement (Part 2 of 2). Non-turbocharged engine

1. Power steering pressure switch connector
2. Generator connectors
3. Oil pressure switch connector
4. Oil pressure gauge unit connector
5. Generator
6. Power steering pump connection
7. A/C compressor connection

CR1069500606010X

Fig. 7 Engine replacement (Part 1 of 2). Turbocharged engine

tensioner pulley.

17. Move the crankshaft sprocket 1/2 notch, aligning the crankshaft sprocket mark with mark on oil pump housing.
18. Install the timing belt tensioner onto the engine. Do not tighten the attaching bolts.
19. Using a suitable torque wrench, apply a torque of 21 ft. lbs. to the tensioner pulley, **Fig. 21.**
20. While applying torque to the tensioner pulley, move the tensioner up against the pulley bracket and tighten the attaching bolts, **Fig. 21. Torque** the tensioner attaching bolts to 23 ft. lbs.
21. Remove the pin from the tensioner body. Pretension is correct when the pin can be removed and installed.
22. Rotate crankshaft two turn in the normal direction of rotation. Check if crankshaft and camshaft timing marks are aligned, **Fig. 18.** If marks are not aligned, the timing belt must be removed and re-installed.
23. Install the timing belt front cover.
24. Install the engine mount bracket assembly, **Fig. 17.**
25. Remove jack and wooden block from under the engine oil pan.
26. Install the power steering pump to the bracket.
27. Install the crankshaft pulley. **Torque** the crankshaft pulley bolt to 105 ft. lbs.
28. Install the alternator drive belt. **Refer to "Belt Tension Data" in this section for proper belt tension.**
29. Install the A/C compressor and power steering pump drive belt. **Refer to "Belt Tension Data" in this section for proper belt tension.**
30. Install the undercover.
31. Install the cooling system reserve tank.

Add engine coolant to system as necessary

TURBOCHARGED ENGINE

With the timing belt removed, avoid turning the camshaft or crankshaft. If movement is required, exercise extreme caution to avoid valve damage caused by piston contact.

1. Remove the undercover.
2. Remove the clamp securing the power steering pressure hose and the air conditioner high pressure hose to the body.
3. Using a wood block and a jack, place the wood block under the engine oil pan and raise the engine only enough to relieve tension on the top engine mount, then remove the mount and the bracket.
4. Remove the accessory drive belts. **Prior to removing the water pump drive belt, loosen the water pump pulley bolts.**
5. Remove the tensioner pulley and the bracket.
6. Remove the crankshaft pulley, then the water pump pulley.
7. Remove the upper and lower timing covers.
8. Rotate the crankshaft clockwise to bring No. 1 cylinder to top dead center of the compression stroke. **Rotate the crankshaft only in the clockwise direction.** The No. 1 cylinder is at top dead center of the compression stroke when the timing marks on the camshaft sprockets are aligned with the upper surface of the cylinder head and the dowel pins on the camshaft sprockets are facing up as shown, **Fig. 22.**
9. Remove the auto-tensioner.
10. Remove the timing belt.
11. Remove the tensioner pulley and arm, then the idler pulley.
12. Remove the crankshaft sprocket bolt, special washer, sprocket and the flange.
13. Remove the tensioner "B," then the timing belt "B."
14. Ensure the timing marks of the balance shaft sprocket and the crankshaft sprocket "B" are aligned, **Fig. 23,** then install the timing belt "B" over both sprockets and ensure the belt has no slack.
15. Adjust the timing belt "B" tension as follows:
    a. Temporarily install the timing belt "B" tensioner so that the center of the tensioner pulley is to the left and above the center of the installation bolt, then temporarily attach the tensioner pulley so that the flange is toward the front of engine, **Fig. 24.**
    b. Hold the timing belt "B" tensioner up in the direction shown by the arrow in, **Fig. 25,** then place pressure on the timing belt so that the tension side of the belt is taut.
    c. **Torque** the tensioner "B"' bolt to 11-16 ft. lbs. **When torquing the bolt, do not allow the tensioner pulley shaft to rotate.**
    d. To check belt tension, depress the belt at point (A), **Fig. 26.** The belt deflection should be .20-.28 inch . If not, readjust the belt tension.
16. Install the crankshaft sprocket flange, sprocket and special washer. **Torque** the crankshaft sprocket bolt to 80-94 ft. lbs. **Ensure the flange and sprocket are correctly installed as shown Fig. 27.**

17. Install the auto-tensioner. If the tensioner rod is fully extended, proceed as follows:
    a. Position the auto-tensioner level in a soft jawed vise. If the plug at the bottom of the tensioner protrudes, apply a plain washer to prevent the plug from direct contact with the vise.
    b. Slowly push the tensioner rod in, using the vise, until the set hole (A) is aligned with the hole (B) in the tensioner cylinder, **Fig. 28.**
    c. Insert a .055 inch wire into the set holes, then remove the auto-tensioner from the vise.
    d. Install the auto-tensioner, then **torque** the retaining bolt to 14-20 ft. lbs. **Leave the wire installed in the auto-tensioner.**
18. Install the tensioner pulley onto the tensioner arm, position the hole in pulley shaft to the left of the center bolt, then tighten the center bolt finger tight.
19. Ensure the camshaft sprockets dowel pins are located on top, then ensure the timing marks are facing each other and are aligned with the top surface of cylinder head, **Fig. 29.** When the exhaust camshaft is released, it will rotate one tooth in the counterclockwise direction. This should be taken into account when installing the timing belt on the sprockets. **The camshaft sprockets are interchangeable and have two sets of timing marks. When the sprocket is mounted on the exhaust camshaft, use the timing mark on the right with dowel pin hole on top. For the intake sprocket, use the mark on the left with dowel pin hole on top, Fig. 30.**
20. Ensure the crankshaft sprocket and the oil pump sprocket timing marks align as shown, **Fig. 31.**
21. With the oil pump sprocket timing marks aligned, remove the plug from the lefthand side of cylinder block and insert a screwdriver with a shaft diameter of .3 inch, **Fig. 32.** If the screwdriver can be inserted 2.4 inches or more, alignment is correct. If the screwdriver can be inserted only 1 inch, rotate the oil pump sprocket one revolution and realign the timing marks. Ensure the screwdriver can be inserted 2.4 inches or more. This check is performed to ensure the balance shaft and the oil pump sprocket are properly positioned. Leave the screwdriver inserted in the hole until after the timing belt has been installed.
22. Install the timing belt as follows:
    a. Install the timing belt around the tensioner pulley and the crankshaft sprocket. Hold the timing belt on the tensioner pulley with your left hand.
    b. Pulling the timing belt with your right hand, install the belt around the oil pump sprocket.
    c. Install the timing belt around the idler pulley, then around the intake camshaft sprocket.
    d. Rotate the exhaust camshaft sprocket one tooth clockwise to align the timing mark with cylinder head top surface, then pulling the belt with both hands, install around the exhaust camshaft sprocket.
    e. Gently raise the tensioner pulley in the direction shown by the arrow in **Fig. 33** so the belt does not sag, then temporarily tighten the center bolt.
23. Adjust the timing belt tension as follows:
    a. Remove the screwdriver from hole in lefthand side of cylinder block and install the plug.
    b. Rotate the crankshaft 1/4 turn counterclockwise, then rotate clockwise to move No. 1 cylinder to TDC.
    c. Loosen the tensioner pulley center bolt. Use Chrysler wrench tool No. MD998767, or equivalent, and a torque wrench, apply a torque of 30 inch lbs. to the tensioner pulley, **Fig. 34.** Use a torque wrench capable of measuring within a range of 0-30 inch lbs. If the vehicle body interferes with the torque wrench, use a suitable jack to slightly raise the engine.
    d. While holding the tensioner pulley with the tool, **torque** the pulley center bolt to 31-40 ft. lbs.
    e. Screw Chrysler set screw tool No. MD998738, or equivalent, into the left engine support bracket until the end of tool makes contact with the tensioner arm, **Fig. 35.** Turn the tool enough to relieve the tension on the auto-tensioner rod, then remove the set wire previously installed in the auto-tensioner.
    f. Remove the set screw tool.
    g. Rotate the crankshaft clockwise two complete turns, then let sit for 15 minutes.
    h. Measure clearance (A) between the tensioner arm and the auto-tensioner body, **Fig. 36.** If clearance is not .15-.18 inch, repeat steps a to g until the clearance is correct.
    i. If clearance (A) can not be measured with the engine in the vehicle, screw in Chrysler set screw No. MD998738 or equivalent, until the end of tool makes contact with the tensioner arm.
    j. Starting in this position, count the number of turns of the tool required to bring the tensioner arm in contact with the auto-tensioner body. Ensure contact is made within 2.5–3 turns, then remove the tool.
    k. Install the rubber plug into the timing belt rear cover.
24. Install the upper and lower timing covers.
25. Install the crankshaft pulley and the water pump pulley.
26. Install the tensioner pulley and the bracket.
27. Install the accessory drive belts. **Refer to "Belt tension Data" in this section for proper belt tension.**
28. Install the engine mount and the bracket.
29. Remove the jack and wooden block

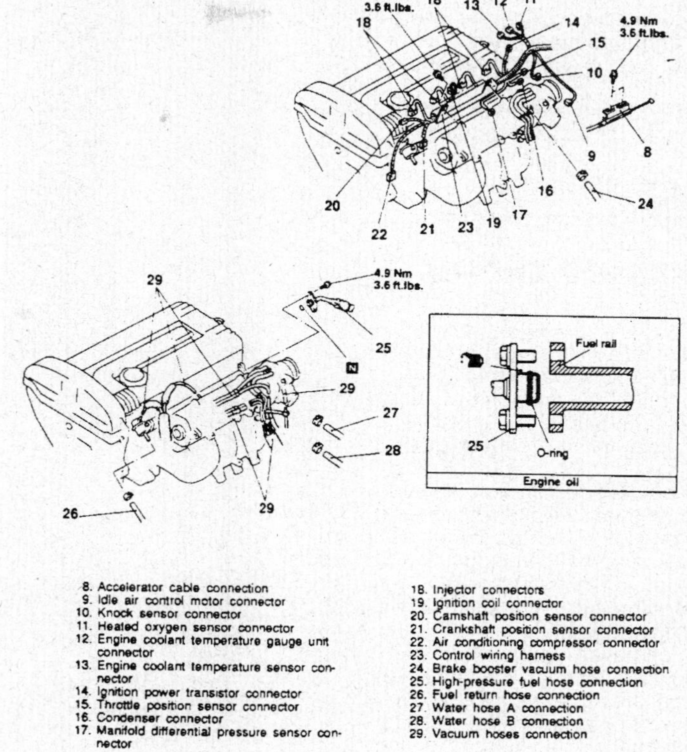

Fig. 7 Engine replacement (Part 2 of 2). Turbocharged engine

positioned under the oil pan.
30. Install the clamp securing the power steering pressure hose and the air conditioner high pressure hose to the body.
31. Install the undercover. Check and adjust the ignition timing as necessary.

CAMSHAFT

REPLACE

TURBOCHARGED ENGINE

Removal

Remove camshaft in numbered sequence, **Fig. 37,** noting the following:

1. Remove timing belt as outlined under "Timing Belt, Replace."
2. Remove camshaft sprockets as follows:
   a. While holding camshaft in position with a crescent wrench at hexagon between No. 2 and No. 3 journals, remove camshaft sprocket bolt.
   b. Remove camshaft sprockets.
3. Remove camshaft oil seals using a suitable screwdriver.
4. Remove camshaft bearing caps by loosening installation bolts in two or three steps. If bearing cap is difficult to remove, gently tap on the rear portion of the camshaft with a plastic hammer.

Installation

Reverse removal procedure to install, noting the following:

1. Install the camshafts on the cylinder head. **Ensure intake side camshaft is installed on intake side and exhaust side camshaft is installed on exhaust side.** Intake side camshaft has a slot machined in the back end to drive the crank angle sensor. Once installed, the camshaft dowel pins should be in the positions as shown in **Fig. 38.**
2. When installing camshaft bearing caps, tighten evenly, in two or three steps.
3. When installing camshaft oil seal, use oil seal guide tool No. MD998307 and oil seal installation tool No. MD998306, or equivalents, as shown, **Fig. 39.**
4. Install crank angle sensor as follows:
   a. Ensure mating mark on housing of crank angle sensor is aligned with notch in plate.
   b. Ensure crank angle sensor does not move when tightening attaching nut.
5. When installing semi-circular packing, apply liberal amount of gasket sealant onto circumference of packing.
6. When installing rocker cover, apply gasket sealant to area as shown in **Fig. 15.**

NON-TURBOCHARGED ENGINE

Removal

Remove camshaft in numbered sequence, **Fig. 40,** noting the following:

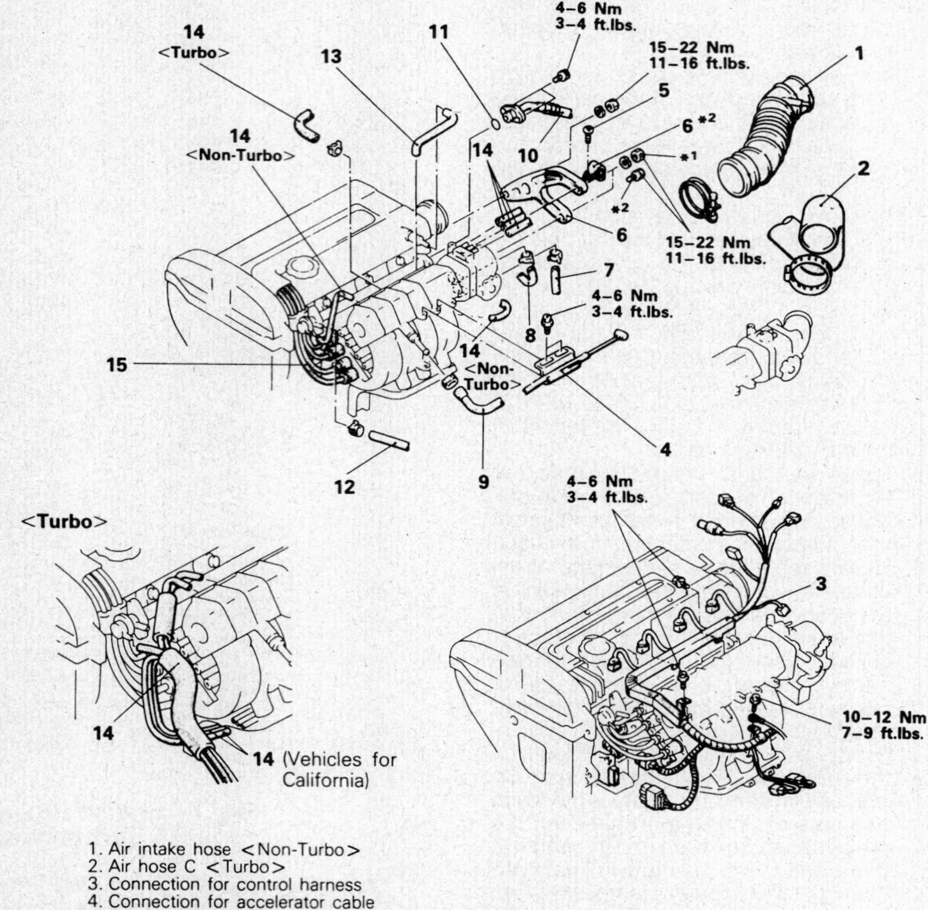

1. Air intake hose <Non-Turbo>
2. Air hose C <Turbo>
3. Connection for control harness
4. Connection for accelerator cable
5. Ground plate installation screw
6. Throttle body stay and ground plate
7. Connection for water by-pass hose
8. Connection for water hose
9. Connection for brake booster vacuum hose
10. Connection for fuel high pressure hose
11. O-ring
12. Connection for fuel return hose
13. Connection for PCV hose
14. Connection for vacuum hoses
15. Connection for spark plug cable

(4) *1: <Non-Turbo>
(5) *2: <Turbo>

CR1059100061010X

Fig. 8 Intake manifold replacement (Part 1 of 2)

1. Use camshaft sprocket holder and adapter tools No. C-4687 and C-4687–1, or equivalent, to ensure camshaft sprockets do not turn during removal.
2. Mark and identify intake camshaft and exhaust camshaft before removal as they are not interchangeable.
3. Loosen camshaft bearing cap attaching bolts in sequence shown in **Fig. 41,** one camshaft at a time.
4. Remove camshaft oil seals using suitable screwdriver to pry seal out.

Installation

1. Install new camshaft oil seals using special oil seal seating tools No. MB991554 and MB998713, or equivalents, **Fig. 42.**
2. **Ensure piston is not at top dead center when installing camshaft.**
3. Install camshaft bearing cap attaching bolts in sequence shown in **Fig. 41,** one camshaft at a time. Tighten to specifications.
4. Use camshaft sprocket holder and adapter tools No. C-4687 and C-4687–1, or equivalents, to ensure camshaft sprockets do not turn during installation.
5. Install cylinder head cover assembly to head and tighten in sequence shown in **Fig. 43. Torque** in three steps; first to 3.3 ft. lbs., then to 6.6 ft. lbs., finally to 8.9 ft. lbs.

SILENT SHAFT

REPLACE

DISASSEMBLE

Disassemble front case, oil pump and silent shaft in numbered sequence, **Fig. 44,** noting the following:

1. Use oil pressure switch socket tool No. MD998054, or equivalent, to remove oil pressure switch.
2. Remove oil pan as outlined under "Oil Pan & Oil Screen, Replace."

3. Use plug cap socket No. tool No. MD998162, or equivalent, to remove front case plug cap (17).
4. When removing oil pump driven gear bolt, insert a Phillips screwdriver into plug hole, **Fig. 45,** to block the silent shaft.
5. Using silent shaft bearing puller tool No. MD998371, or equivalent, remove silent shaft front bearing as shown, **Fig. 46.**
6. Using silent shaft bearing puller tool No. MD998372, or equivalent, remove righthand silent shaft rear bearing as shown, **Fig. 47.**
7. Using silent shaft bearing puller tool No. MD998374, or equivalent, remove lefthand silent shaft rear bearing as shown, **Fig. 48.**

INSPECTION

1. Inspect front case for the following:
   a. Clogged oil passages.
   b. Damaged or seized lefthand silent shaft front bearing section.
   c. Cracks or other signs of damage on case.
2. Inspect oil seal lip for wear or damage, replacing as necessary.
3. Inspect oil switch as follows:
   a. Connect an ohmmeter between switch terminal and switch body.
   b. If ohmmeter reads no continuity, replace switch. If ohmmeter reads continuity, proceed to following step.
   c. Insert a fine wedge into oil switch hole. Ohmmeter should read no continuity when wedge is slightly pressed into hole. If ohmmeter reads continuity, replace switch.
4. **On turbocharged models,** inspect oil cooler bypass valve as follows:
   a. Ensure valves move smoothly.
   b. Measure dimension L on bypass valve, **Fig. 49.** At room temperature, dimension L should be 1.358 inches.
   c. Dip valve in engine oil heated to 212°F. Dimension L should now be at least 1.570 inches.
5. **On all models,** inspect oil pump as follows:
   a. Install oil pump gears in front case and rotate gears. Ensure smooth rotation without excessive looseness.
   b. Inspect for ridge wear on surface of oil pump cover.
   c. Inspect drive gear and driven gear tip clearance.
   d. Inspect side clearance of gears.
6. Inspect silent shaft for the following:
   a. Clogged oil passages.
   b. Seized or damaged journal.
   c. Ensure oil clearance is within specifications. Clearance should be as follows: righthand front, .0008–.0024 inch; righthand rear, .0008–.0021 inch; lefthand front, .0002–.0036 inch; lefthand rear, .0017–.0033 inch.
7. Inspect oil jet and check valve for clogging or damage.

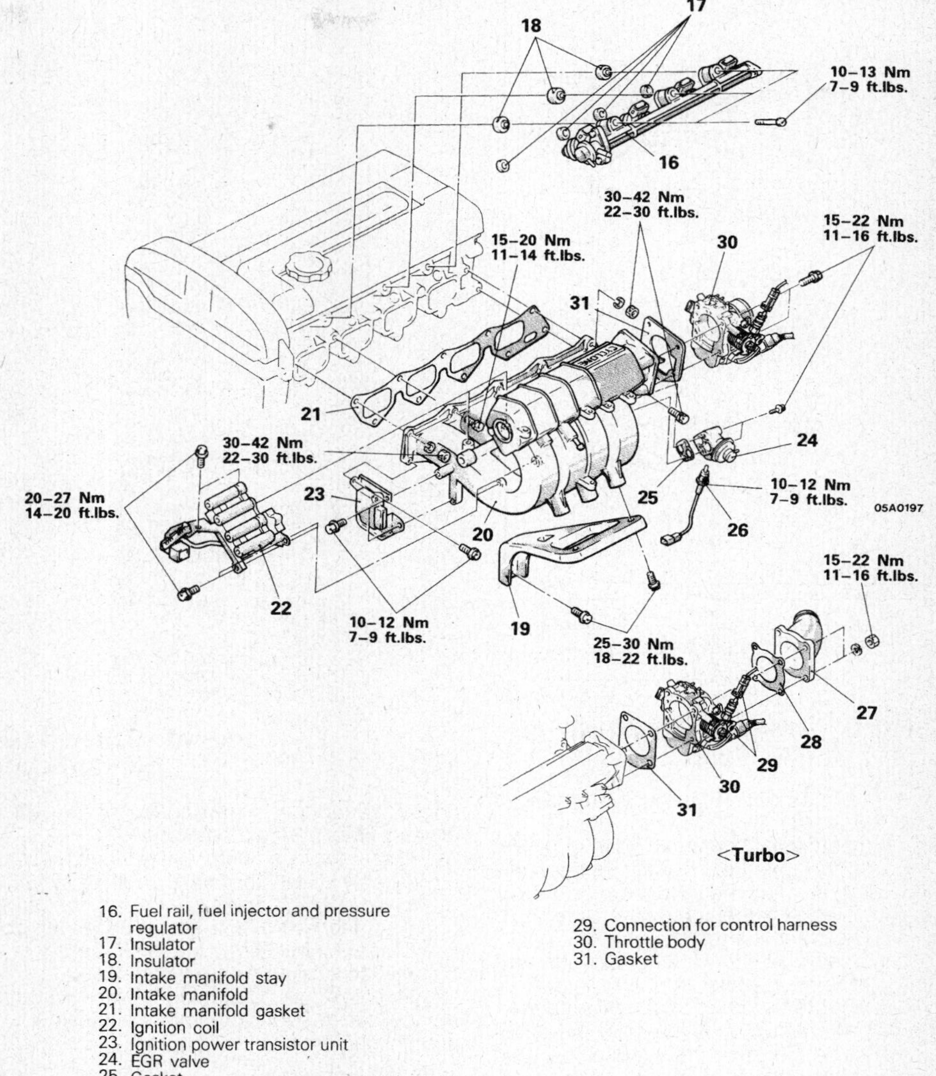

Fig. 8 Intake manifold replacement (Part 2 of 2)

ASSEMBLE

Reverse removal procedure to install, noting the following:

1. When installing oil jet, ensure nozzle is installed toward the piston.
2. When installing lefthand silent shaft rear bearing, apply clean engine oil to engine block bearing hole and to outer circumference of bearing. Using bearing installation tool No. MD998374, or equivalent, **Fig. 50,** install bearing into cylinder block.
3. When installing righthand silent shaft rear bearing, apply clean engine oil to engine block bearing hole and to outer circumference of bearing. Using bearing installation tool No. MD998373 or equivalent, **Fig. 51,** install bearing into cylinder block. **Ensure oil hole in bearing is aligned with oil hole in cylinder block.**
4. When installing silent shaft front bearing, apply clean engine oil to engine block bearing hole and to outer circumference of bearing. Using bearing installation tool No. MD998373, or equivalent, **Fig. 52,** install bearing into cylinder block. **Ensure oil hole in bearing is aligned with oil hole in cylinder block.**
5. When installing oil pump gears, coat gears with clean engine oil, then align mark on drive gear notch with mark on driven gear tooth.
6. Install crankshaft oil seal using oil seal installation tool No. MD998375, or equivalent.
7. Install oil seal (22) and silent shaft oil seal (23) by placing a socket over the top of the seal and pressing it into the case.
8. Install front case as follows:
   a. Place crankshaft front oil seal guide No. MD998285, or equivalent, over front end of crankshaft, then apply

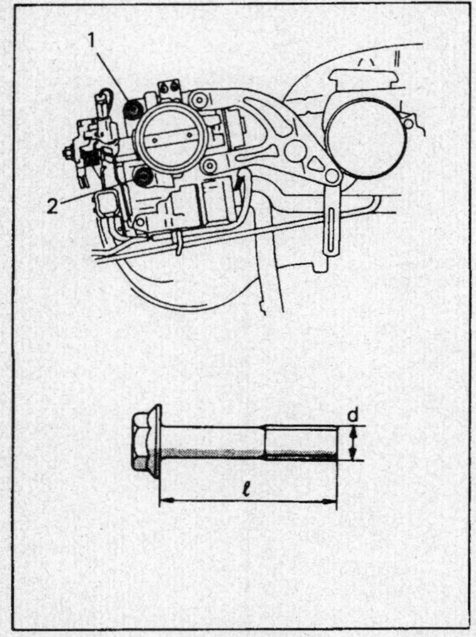

No.	d × ℓ mm (in.)
1	8 × 30 (.31 × 1.18)
2	8 × 55 (.31 × 2.16)

CR1059100062000X

Fig. 9 Throttle body attaching bolts

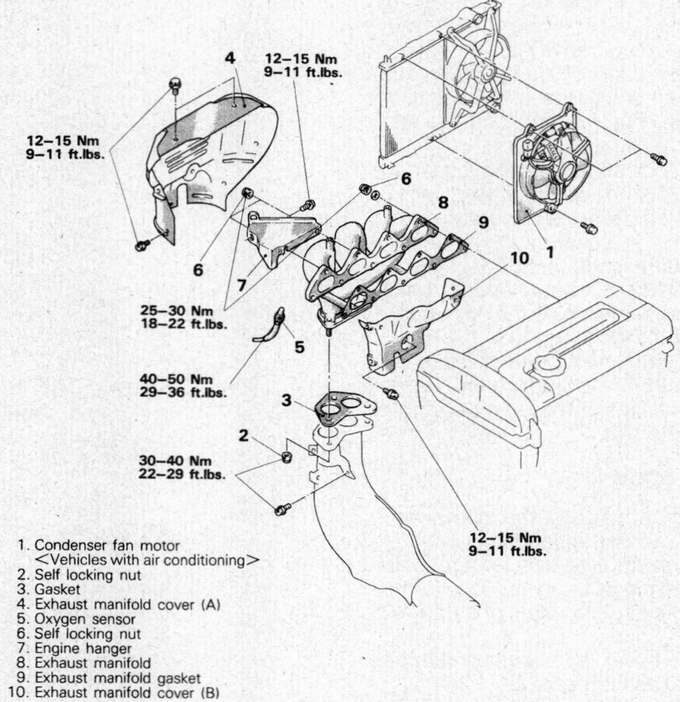

Fig. 10 Exhaust manifold replacement. Non-turbocharged engine

engine oil to outer circumference of guide.

b. Install front case over top of guide, onto cylinder block. Temporarily tighten all bolts except the filter bracket attaching bolts, referring to bolt length chart, **Fig. 53.**
c. Install oil filter bracket and the four attaching bolts.
d. Tighten all bolts to specifications.

9. When installing driven gear bolt (19), insert a Phillips screwdriver into plug hole on lefthand side of cylinder block, **Fig. 45,** to block the silent shaft.
10. When installing plug cap, place a new O-ring into groove of case, then use plug cap socket No. MD998162 or equivalent to tighten cap.
11. Install oil pan as outlined under "Oil Pan, Replace."
12. When installing oil pressure switch, coat threads of switch with gasket adhesive. **Do not allow hole in end of switch to be covered with adhesive.** Install switch using oil pressure switch socket tool No. MD998054, or equivalent.

PISTON & ROD ASSEMBLY

When installing piston and rod assembly, arrow on top of piston must face toward timing belt side of engine, **Fig. 54.**

OIL PAN

REPLACE

REMOVAL

Remove oil pan and oil screen in numbered sequence, referring to **Figs. 55 through 57** , noting the following:

1. Once all oil pan bolts are removed, use oil pan separator tool No. MD998727, or equivalent, and a hammer to loosen pan. **Do not use a screwdriver or a chisel to perform this task, as damage to oil pan flange may result.**
2. Remove pan by placing a brass bar at corner of separator tool and striking it with a hammer.

INSPECTION

Replace the oil pan if damaged or cracked. Ensure screen is not clogged, cracked or damage.

INSTALLATION

Reverse removal procedure to install. When installing oil pan, ensure mating surfaces are clean, then apply gasket adhesive into groove in oil pan flange. Do not allow adhesive to cover bolt holes.

OIL PUMP

REPLACE

Refer to "Silent Shaft, Replace" for procedure.

BELT TENSION DATA

Refer to **Fig. 58** for belt tension data.

COOLING SYSTEM BLEED

These engines do not require a specified bleed procedure. After filling cooling system, run engine to operating temperature with radiator/pressure cap off. Air will then be automatically bled through cap opening.

THERMOSTAT

REPLACE

Do not remove pressure cap while engine is hot or under pressure.

Remove thermostat in numbered sequence, **Fig. 59,** noting the following:

1. Drain coolant to below level of thermostat housing.
2. Mark and note the position of the hose clamps before removal.
3. Clean mating surfaces.
4. Reverse procedure to install, noting the following:
   a. Install retaining bolts and tighten to specifications.
   b. Align hose clamps in position as marked.
   c. Ensure drain is closed, then fill up coolant. Replace cap, start engine until warm. Inspect for leaks, then inspect coolant and fill if necessary.

WATER PUMP

REPLACE

NON-TURBOCHARGED ENGINE

Remove water pump in numbered sequence, **Fig. 60,** noting the following:

1. Drain engine coolant into a suitable container as follows:
   a. Place instrument panel temperature control lever in Hot position.
   b. Carefully remove radiator cap.

c. Remove radiator drain plug.
2. Remove timing belt rear cover as described under "Timing Belt, Replace."
3. Reverse procedure to install. Coat O-ring with water or coolant to ease installation.

TURBOCHARGED ENGINE

Remove water pump in numbered sequence, **Fig. 61,** noting the following:

1. Drain engine coolant into a suitable container as follows:
   a. Place instrument panel temperature control lever in Hot position.
   b. Carefully remove radiator cap.
   c. Remove radiator drain plug.
2. Remove timing belt rear cover as described under "Timing Belt, Replace."
3. Reverse procedure to install, noting the following:
   a. Coat O-ring with water or coolant to ease installation.
   b. Refer to bolt inset, **Fig. 61,** when installing water pump attaching bolts.

RADIATOR

REPLACE

Remove radiator in numbered sequence, **Figs. 62 and 63,** noting the following:

1. Drain engine coolant into a suitable container as follows:
   a. Place instrument panel temperature control lever in Hot position.
   b. Carefully remove radiator cap.
   c. Remove radiator drain plug.
2. Mark and note the position of the hose clamps before removal.
3. **On turbocharged models,** remove air cleaner bracket.
4. **On models equipped with automatic transaxle,** plug or cover nipples and hoses for cooling lines to ensure dust, dirt or other contaminants do not enter lines.
5. **On all models,** reverse procedure to install, noting the following:
   a. Align hose clamps in position as marked.
   b. **On turbocharged models,** install air cleaner bracket
   c. **On models equipped with automatic transaxle,** install cooling lines.
   d. **On all models,** ensure drain is closed, then fill up coolant. Replace cap, then run engine until warm. Inspect for leaks, then inspect coolant level and fill if necessary.

FUEL PUMP

REPLACE

FWD MODELS

Removal

Remove fuel pump in numbered sequence, **Fig. 64.**

1. Relieve fuel pressure as outlined under "Precautions."
2. Remove fuel from fuel tank into a suitable container.
3. When disconnecting high pressure fuel line, cover fuel line connection with rags to prevent spraying of fuel.
4. Remove rear seat cushion and floor plate for access to fuel pump.
5. Disconnect hoses and connectors to remove fuel pump

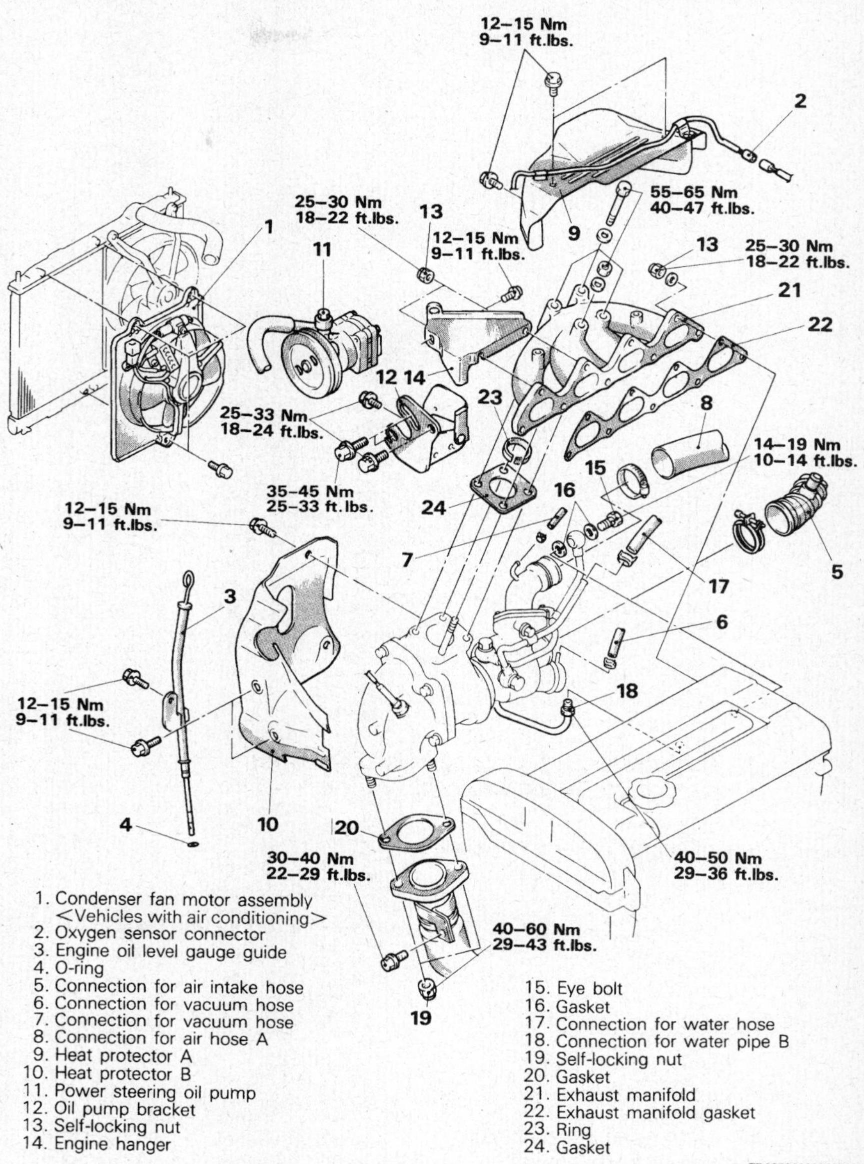

Fig. 11 Exhaust manifold replacement. Turbocharged engine

Installation

Reverse removal procedure to install, noting the following:

1. Align packing position projections with holes in fuel pump assembly.
2. Ensure fuel pump assembly and hoses are not leaking.
3. Before installing hole cover plate, apply suitable sealant to rear floor pan.

AWD MODELS

Removal

Relieve fuel pressure as outlined under "Precautions."

Remove fuel pump in numbered sequence, **Fig. 65.**

1. Remove fuel from fuel tank into a suitable container.
2. When disconnecting high pressure fuel line, cover fuel line connection with rags to prevent spraying of fuel.
3. Remove rear seat cushion and floor plate for access to fuel pump.
4. Disconnect hoses and connectors to remove fuel pump

Installation

Reverse removal procedure to install, noting the following:

1. Ensure packing seal is not damaged or deformed.
2. Apply soapy water to fuel tank threads, then install fuel pump and cap.
3. Using special cap tightening tool No. MB991480, or equivalent, **Fig. 66, torque** cap to 36 ft. lbs.
4. Ensure fuel pump assembly and hoses

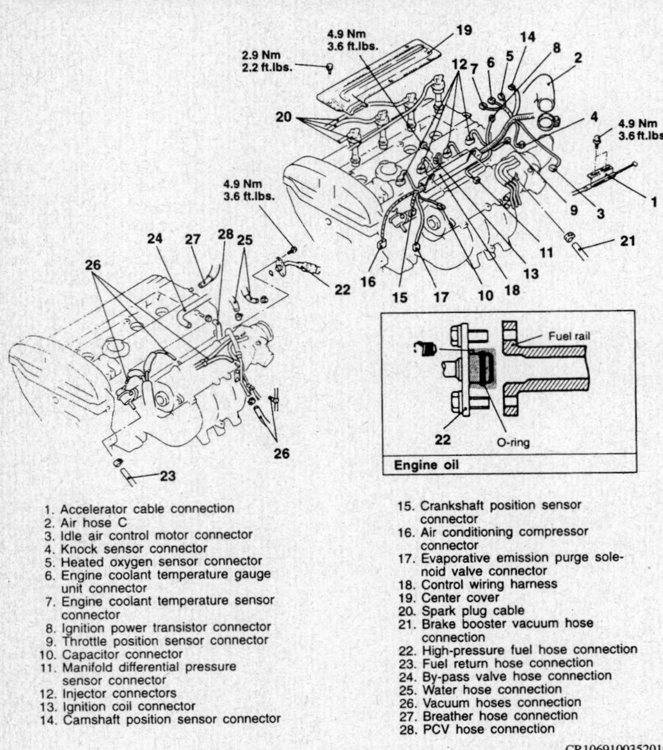

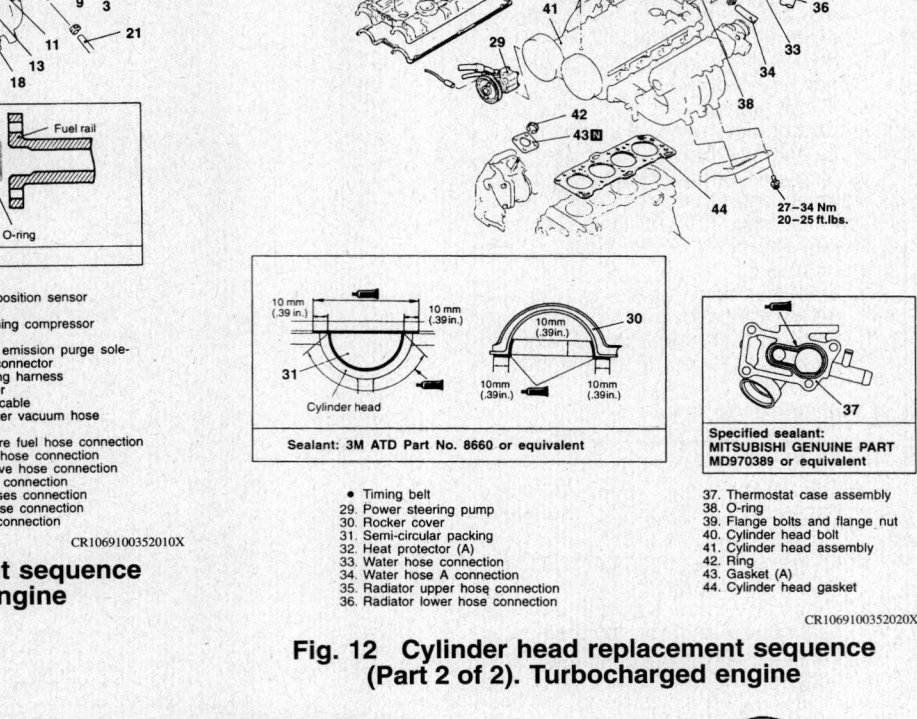

1. Accelerator cable connection
2. Air hose C
3. Idle air control motor connector
4. Knock sensor connector
5. Heated oxygen sensor connector
6. Engine coolant temperature gauge unit connector
7. Engine coolant temperature sensor connector
8. Ignition power transistor connector
9. Throttle position sensor connector
10. Capacitor connector
11. Manifold differential pressure sensor connector
12. Injector connectors
13. Ignition coil connector
14. Camshaft position sensor connector
15. Crankshaft position sensor connector
16. Air conditioning compressor connector
17. Evaporative emission purge solenoid valve connector
18. Control wiring harness
19. Center cover
20. Spark plug cable
21. Brake booster vacuum hose connection
22. High-pressure fuel hose connection
23. Fuel return hose connection
24. By-pass valve hose connection
25. Water hose connection
26. Vacuum hoses connection
27. Breather hose connection
28. PCV hose connection

CR1069100352010X

Fig. 12 Cylinder head replacement sequence (Part 1 of 2). Turbocharged engine

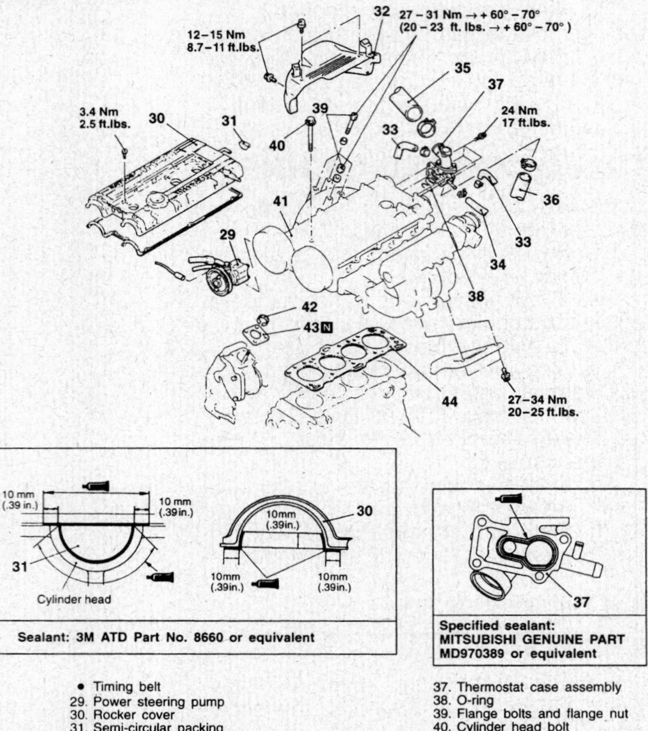

• Timing belt
29. Power steering pump
30. Rocker cover
31. Semi-circular packing
32. Heat protector (A)
33. Water hose connection
34. Water hose A connection
35. Radiator upper hose connection
36. Radiator lower hose connection
37. Thermostat case assembly
38. O-ring
39. Flange bolts and flange nut
40. Cylinder head bolt
41. Cylinder head assembly
42. Ring
43. Gasket (A)
44. Cylinder head gasket

CR1069100352020X

Fig. 12 Cylinder head replacement sequence (Part 2 of 2). Turbocharged engine

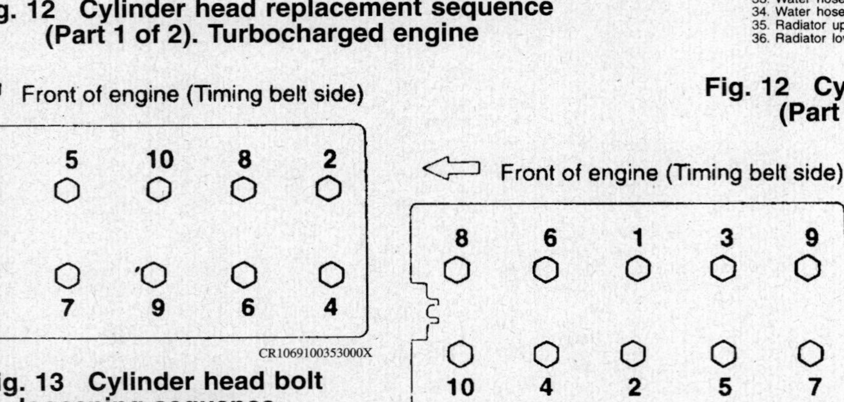

CR1069100353000X

Fig. 13 Cylinder head bolt loosening sequence. Turbocharged engine

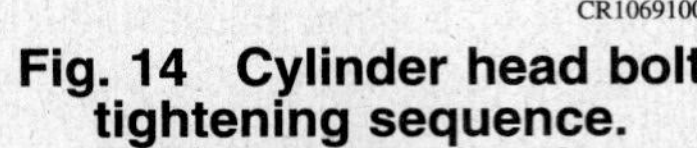

CR1069100354000X

Fig. 14 Cylinder head bolt tightening sequence. Turbocharged engine

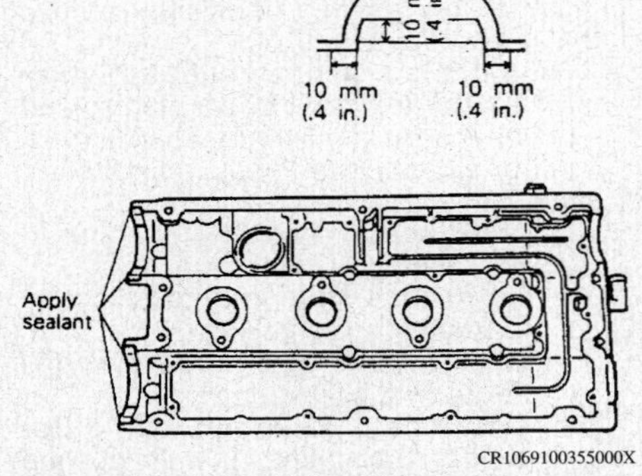

CR1069100355000X

Fig. 15 Rocker cover installation. Turbocharged engine

are not leaking.

FUEL FILTER

REPLACE

Relieve fuel pressure as outlined under "Precautions."

1. When replacing fuel filter, refer to **Fig. 67** for removal and installation procedure.
2. **On turbocharged models,** remove battery and air intake hose to access fuel filter.
3. **On all models,** reverse procedure to install.

TURBOCHARGER

REPLACE

Remove turbocharger in numbered sequence, **Fig. 68,** noting the following:

1. Drain engine cooling system into a suitable container as follows:
   a. Place temperature control lever in hot position.
   b. Carefully remove radiator cap.
   c. Remove radiator drain plug.
2. Drain engine oil.
3. Disconnect oxygen sensor electrical connector, then using oxygen sensor socket tool No. MD998748, or equivalent, and an offset box-end wrench, remove oxygen sensor.
4. Remove power steering pump from bracket with hoses attached, then secure pump aside with a piece of wire.
5. Remove turbocharger assembly with water pipes A and B and oil pipe attached. **After disconnecting oil pipe, ensure foreign material does not enter oil passage hole of turbocharger.**
6. Reverse procedure to install, noting the following:
   a. Prior to installing turbocharger assembly, pour a small quantity of clean engine oil into oil supply pipe fitting hole in turbocharger.
   b. Clean alignment surfaces of turbocharger. **Use caution not to allow gasket or other foreign material to enter oil passage hole.**
   c. Use new gaskets, locknuts and O-rings.
   d. Install oxygen sensor using oxygen sensor socket tool No. MD998748, or equivalent, and an offset box-end wrench, then connect oxygen sensor electrical connector.

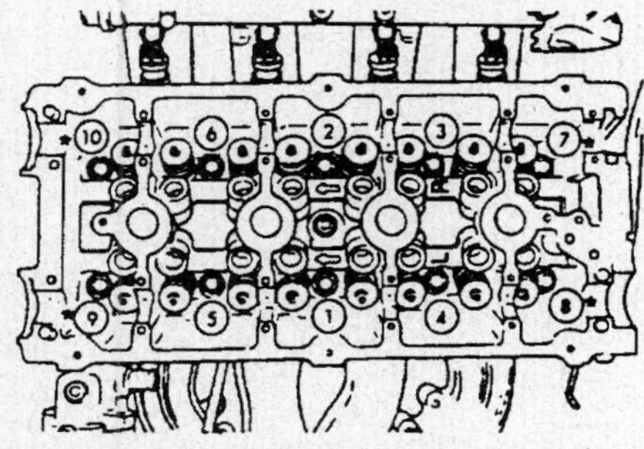

*Location of 110 mm (4.330 in.) short bolts.

CR1069500631000X

Fig. 16 Cylinder head bolt tightening sequence. Non-turbocharged engine

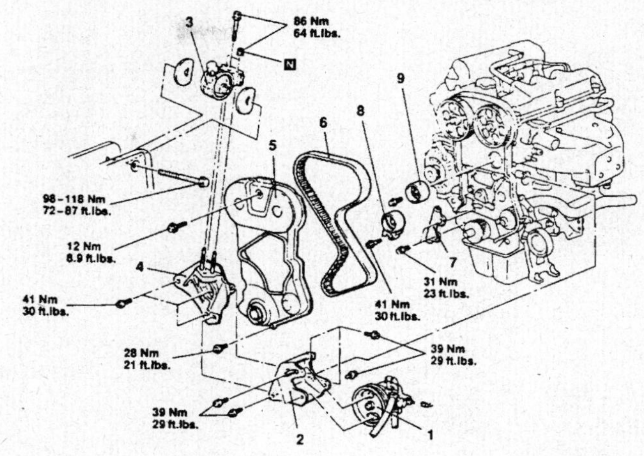

1. Power steering oil pump connection
2. Power steering oil pump bracket
3. Engine mount bracket assembly
4. Engine mount bracket
5. Front timing belt cover
6. Timing belt
7. Timing belt tensioner
8. Tensioner pulley
9. Idle pulley

CR1069500160000X

Fig. 17 Timing belt & components. Non-turbocharged engine

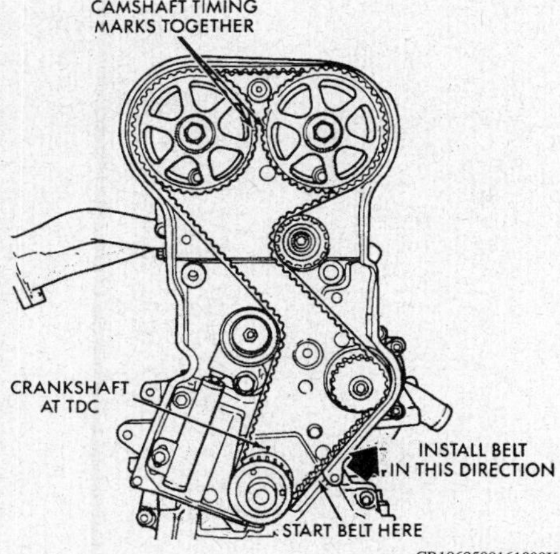

CR1069500161000X

Fig. 18 Camshaft & crankshaft sprocket timing marks. Non-turbocharged engine

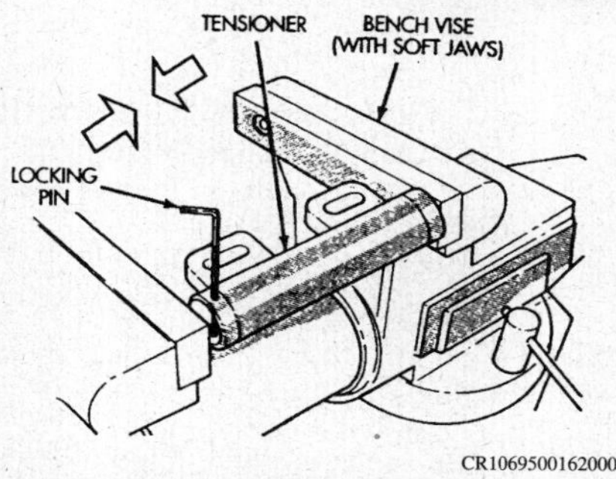

CR1069500162000X

Fig. 19 Compressing timing belt tensioner rod. Non-turbocharged engine

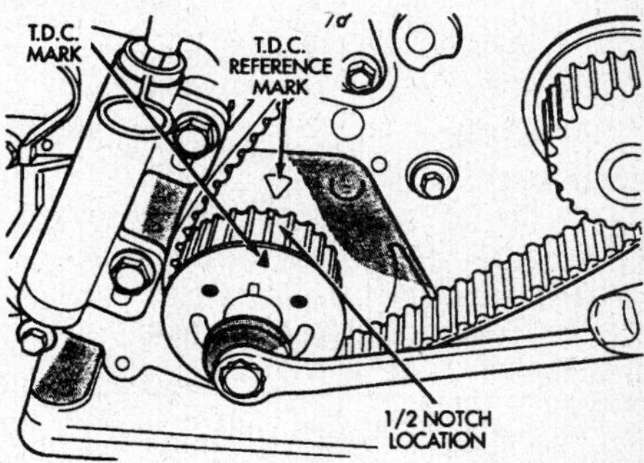

CR1069500163000X

Fig. 20 Positioning crankshaft sprocket 1/2 notch from TDC. Non-turbocharged engine

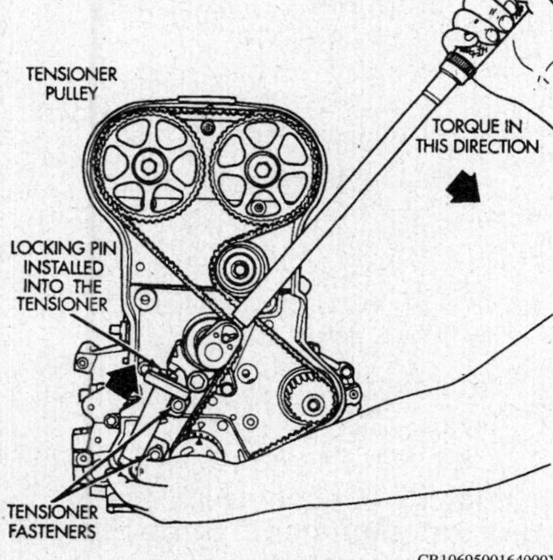

CR1069500164000X

Fig. 21 Adjusting timing belt tension. Non-turbocharged engine

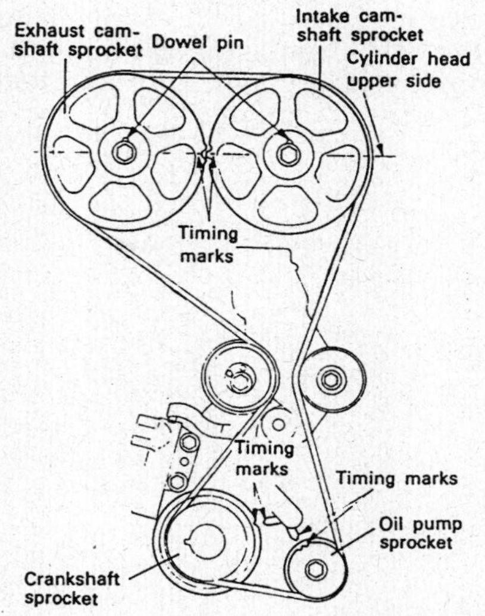

CR1069000165000X

Fig. 22 Camshaft, crankshaft & oil pump sprocket timing mark alignment. Turbocharged engine

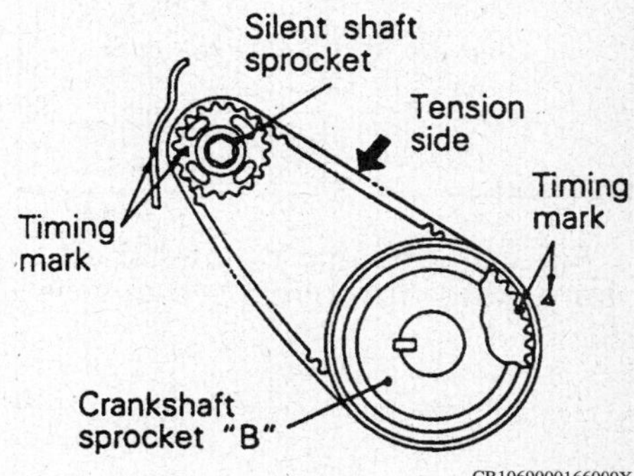

CR1069000166000X

Fig. 23 Timing belt "B" installation. Turbocharged engine

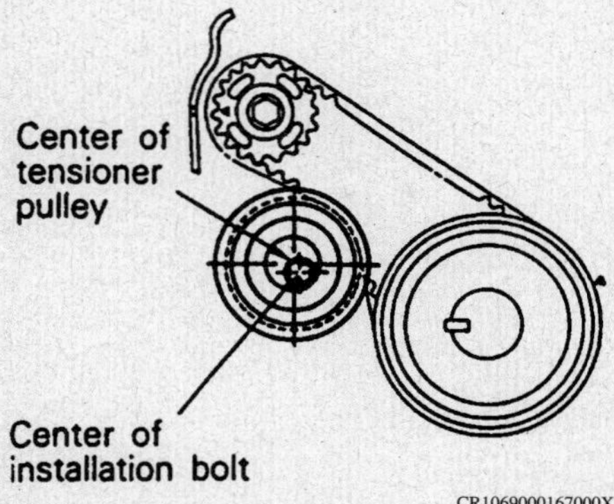

Fig. 24 Timing belt "B" tensioner pulley installation. Turbocharged engine

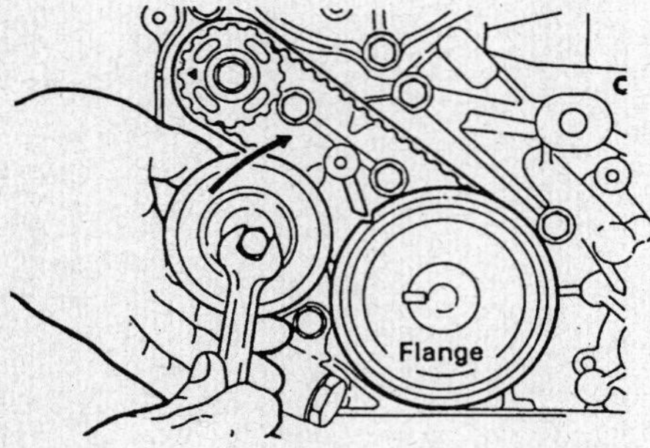

Fig. 25 Tensioning timing belt "B." Turbocharged engine

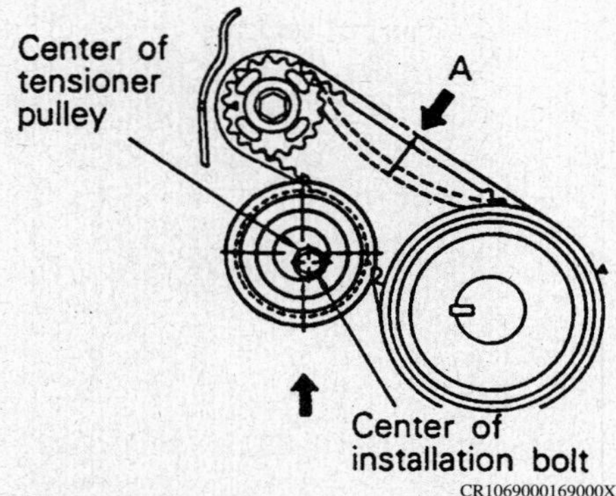

Fig. 26 Checking timing belt "B" tension. Turbocharged engine

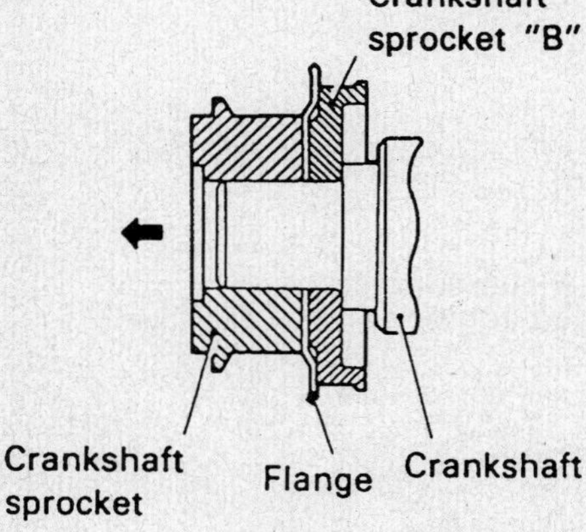

Fig. 27 Flange & crankshaft sprocket installation. Turbocharged engine

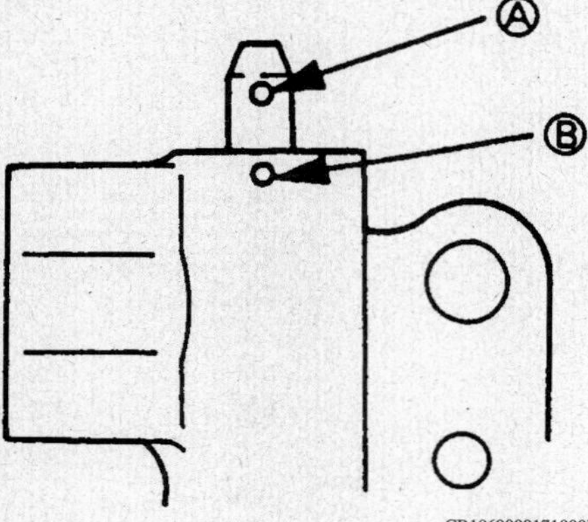

Fig. 28 Tensioner rod alignment. Turbocharged engine

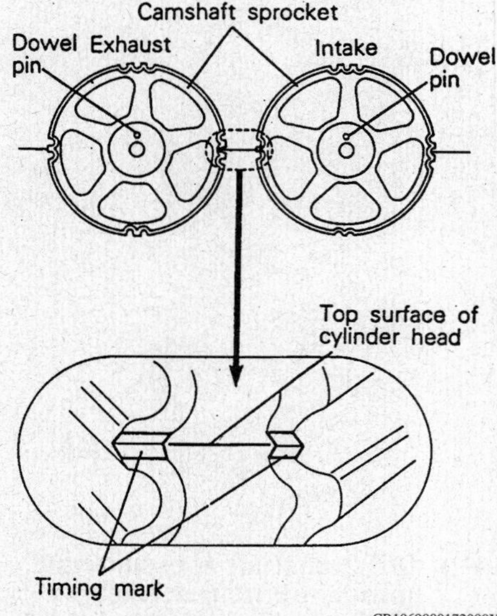

Fig. 29 Camshaft sprocket timing mark alignment. Turbocharged engine

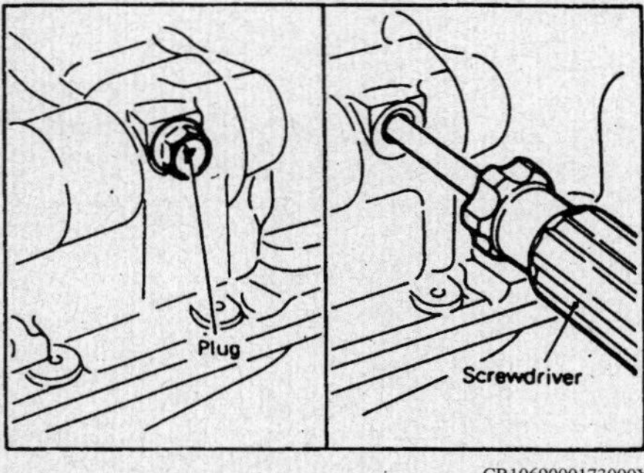

Fig. 30 Positioning camshaft sprockets. Turbocharged engine

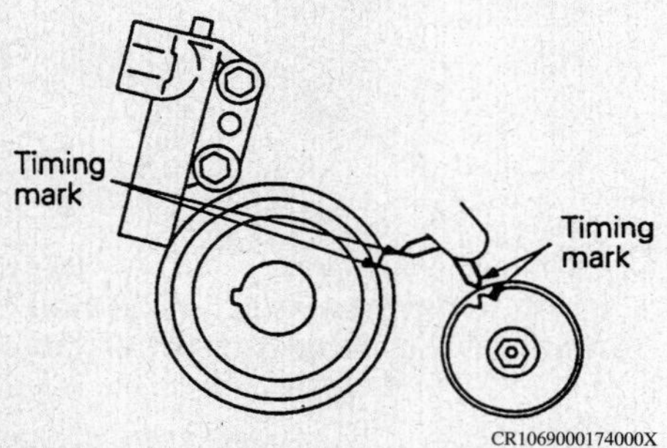

Fig. 31 Crankshaft & oil pump sprocket alignment. Turbocharged engine

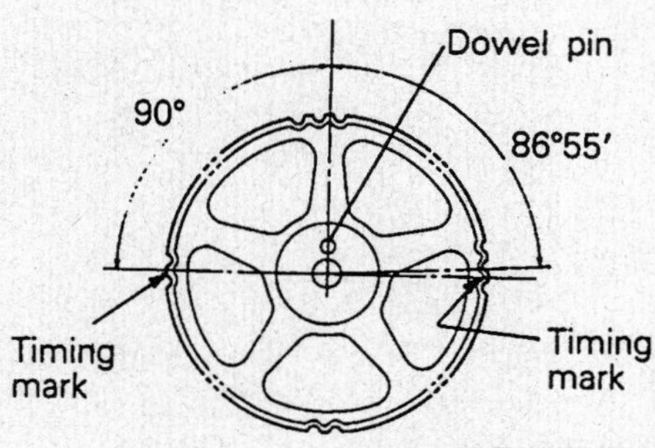

Fig. 32 Checking oil pump sprocket alignment. Turbocharged engine

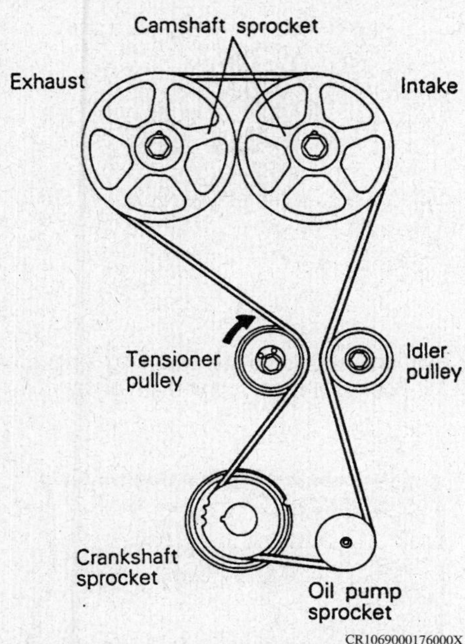

Fig. 33 Timing belt installation. Turbocharged engine

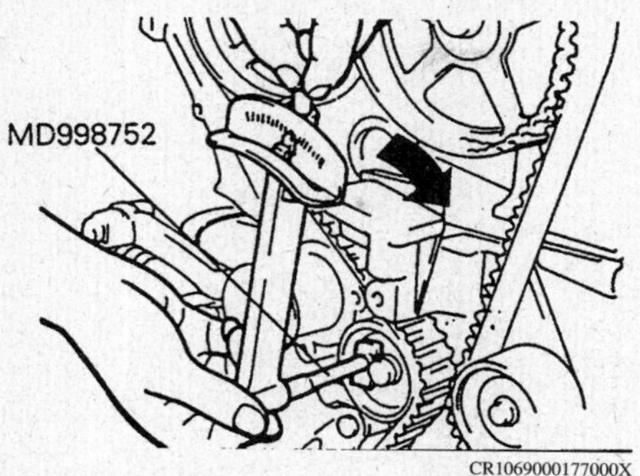

Fig. 34 Tightening tensioner pulley center bolt. Turbocharged engine

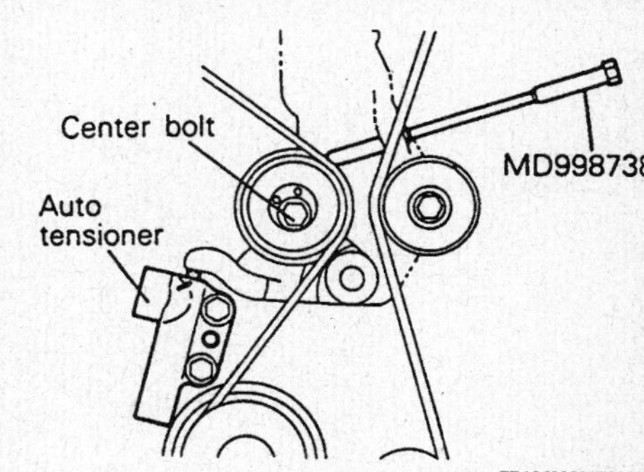

Fig. 35 Set screw tool installation. Turbocharged engine

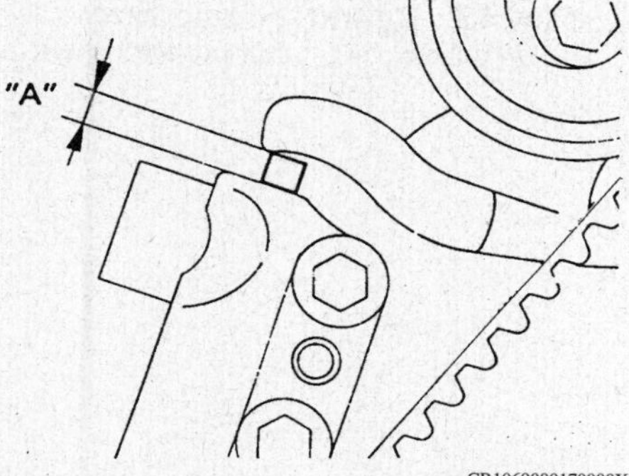

Fig. 36 Auto-tensioner protrusion measurement. Turbocharged engine

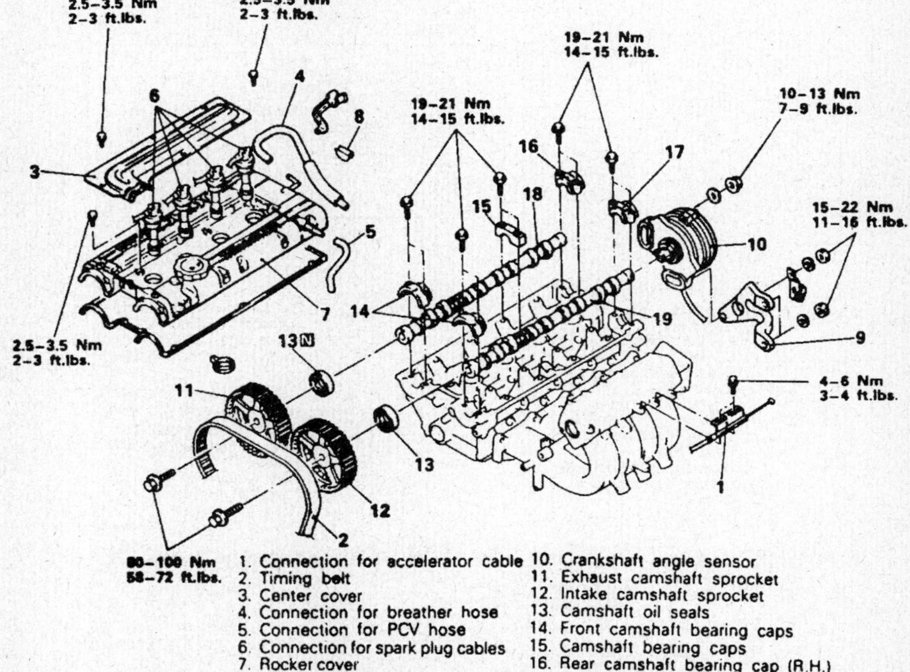

Fig. 37 Camshaft replacement. Turbocharged engine

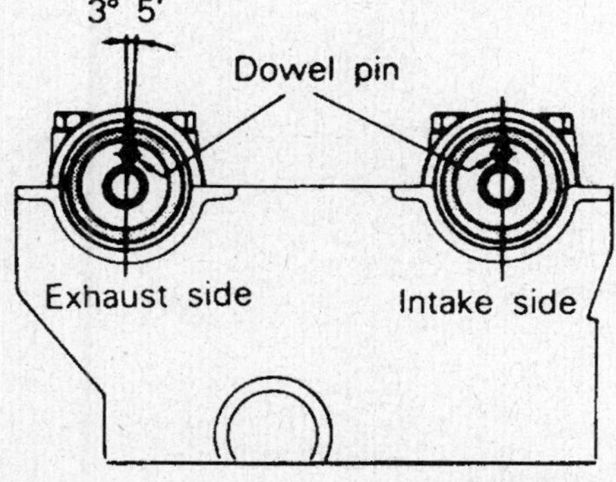

Fig. 38 Camshaft installation. Turbocharged engine

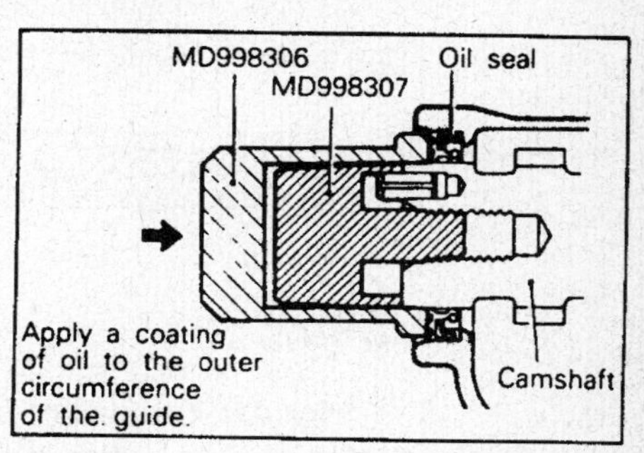

Fig. 39 Camshaft oil seal installation. Turbocharged engine

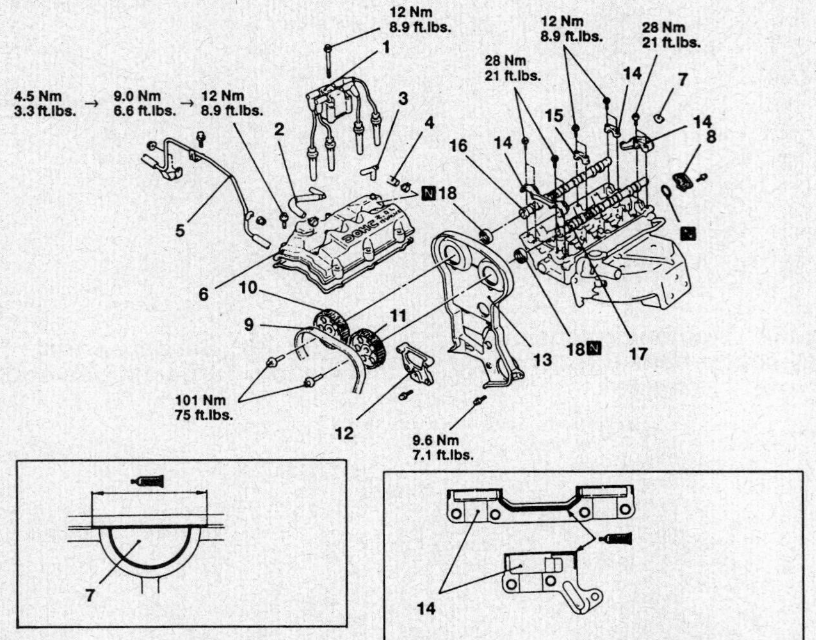

Camshaft removal steps

1. Ignition coil pack
2. PCV hose
3. Breather hose
4. Air hose
5. Vapor hose and pipe assembly connection
6. Cylinder head cover
7. Semi–circular packing
8. Camshaft position sensor
9. Timing belt
10. Intake camshaft sprocket
11. Exhaust camshaft sprocket
12. Bracket
13. Rear timing belt cover
14. Outside camshaft bearing cap
15. Camshaft bearing cap
16. Intake camshaft
17. Exhaust camshaft

Camshaft oil seal removal steps

9. Timing belt
10. Intake camshaft sprocket
11. Exhaust camshaft sprocket
12. Bracket
13. Rear timing belt cover
18. Camshaft oil seal

CR1069500614000X

Fig. 40 Camshaft replacement. Non-turbocharged engine

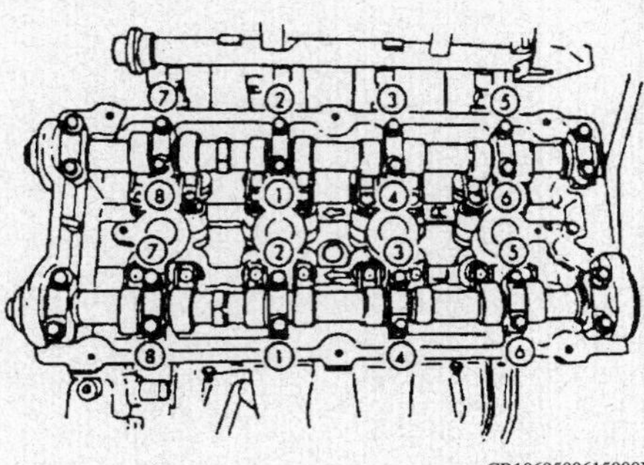

CR1069500615000X

Fig. 41 Camshaft bearing caps. Non-turbocharged engine

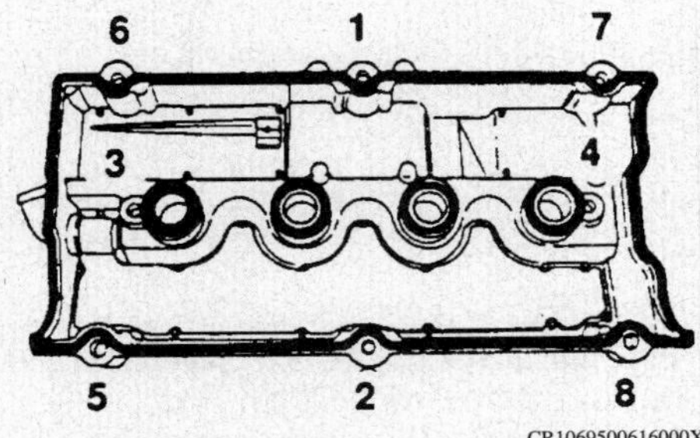

CR1069500616000X

Fig. 43 Cylinder head cover installation. Non-turbocharged engine

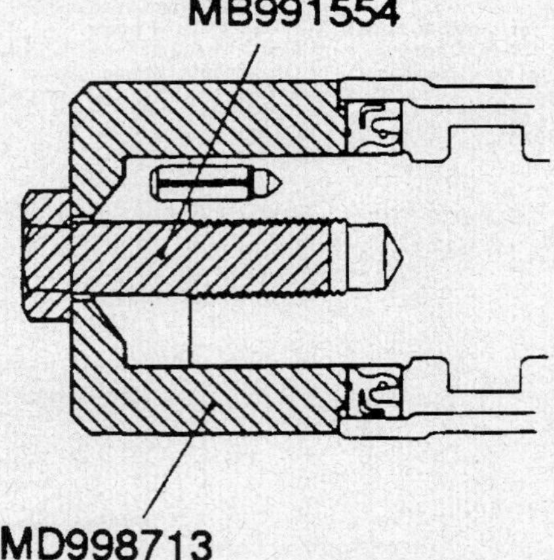

CR1069500617000X

Fig. 42 Camshaft oil seal installation. Non-turbocharged engine

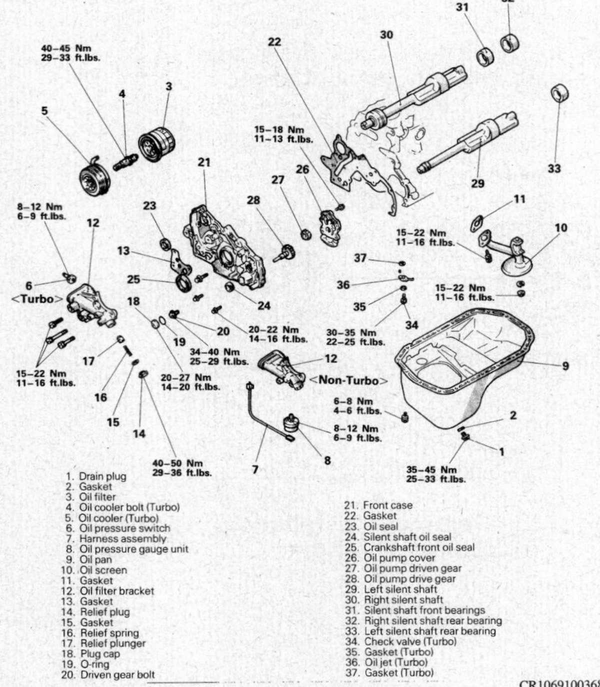

CR1069100368000X

Fig. 44 Front case, oil pump & silent shaft assembly

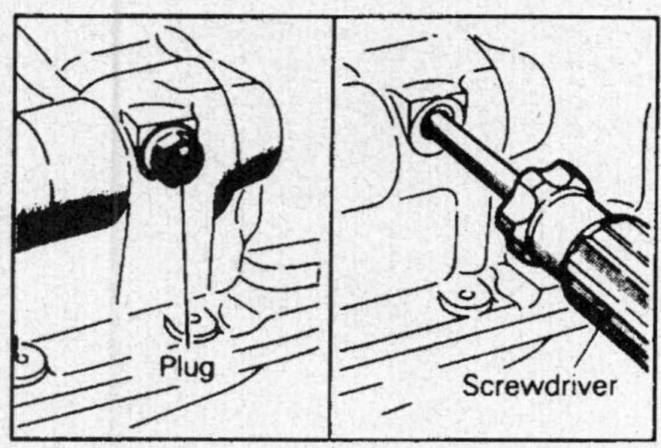

Fig. 45 Blocking silent shaft for oil pump sprocket removal

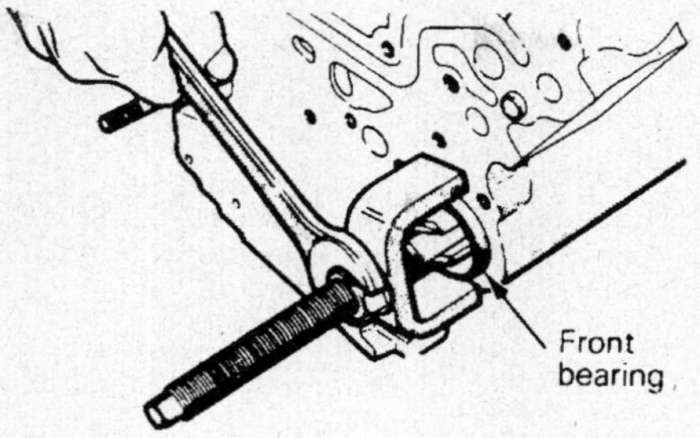

Fig. 46 Silent shaft front bearing removal

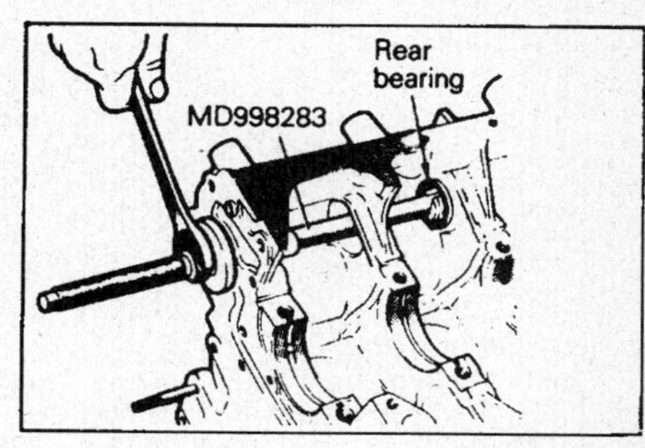

Fig. 47 Righthand silent shaft rear bearing removal

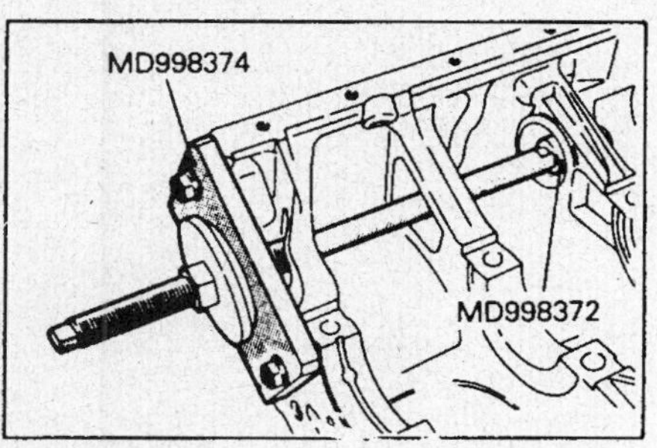

Fig. 48 Lefthand silent shaft rear bearing removal

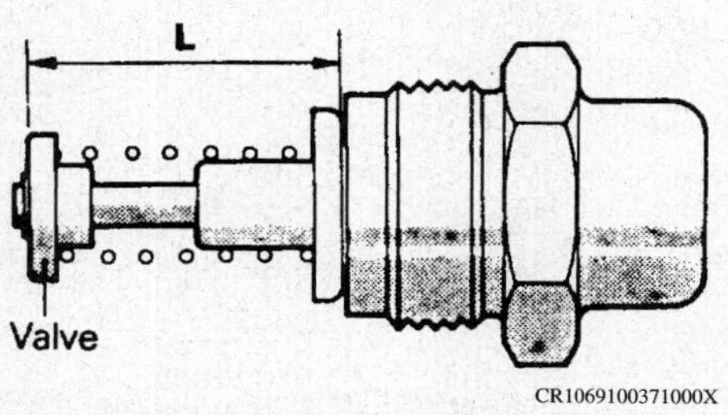

Fig. 49 Oil cooler bypass valve

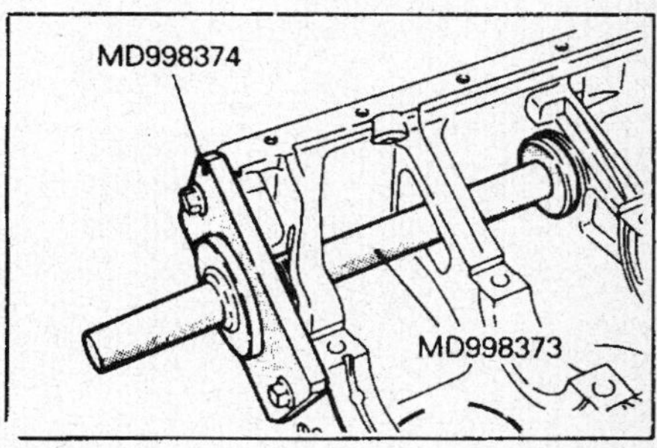

Fig. 50 Lefthand silent shaft rear bearing installation

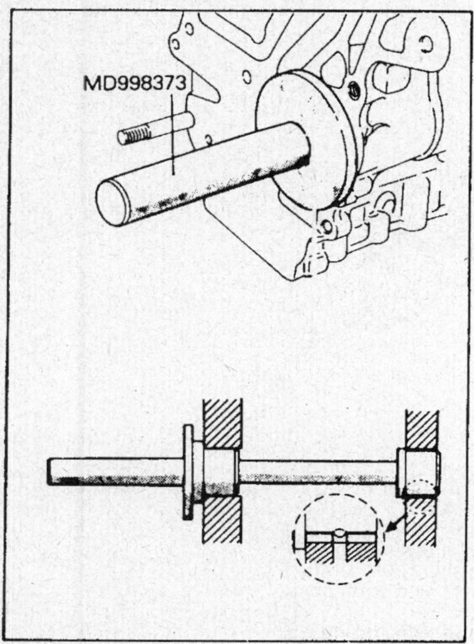

Fig. 51 Righthand silent shaft rear bearing installation

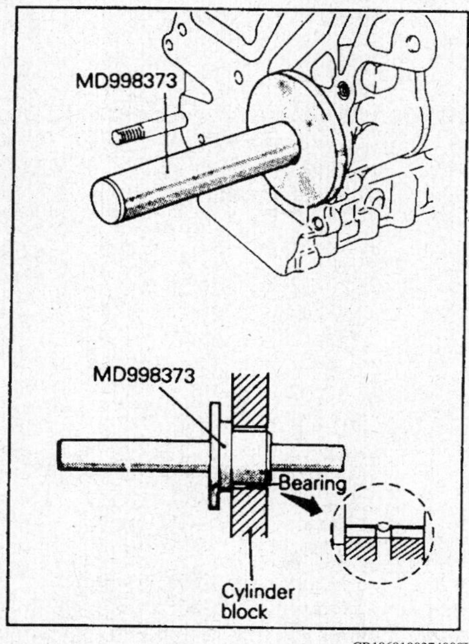

Fig. 52 Silent shaft front bearing installation

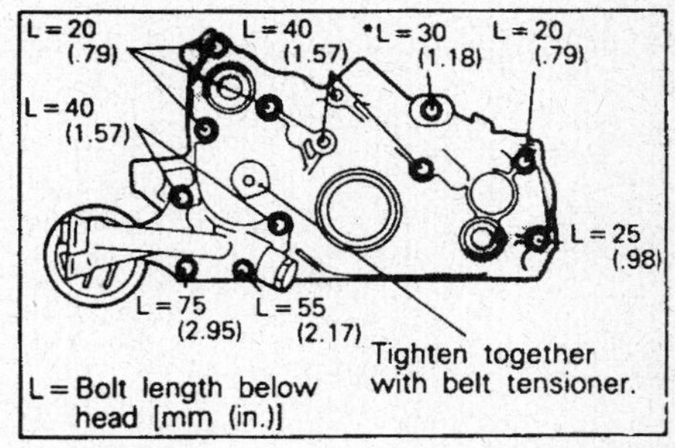

Fig. 53 Front case attaching bolts

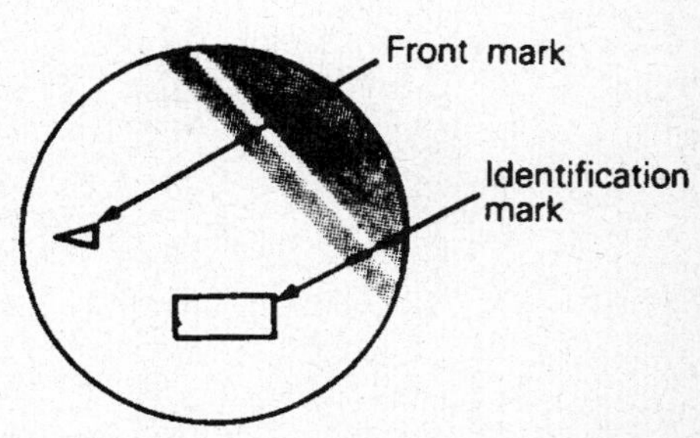

Fig. 54 Top view of piston

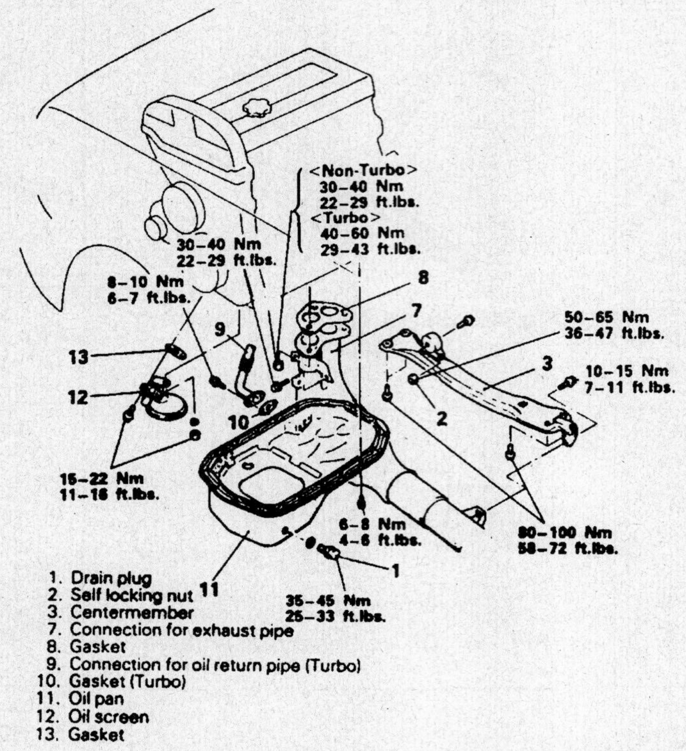

Fig. 55 Oil pan & screen replacement. Turbo FWD models

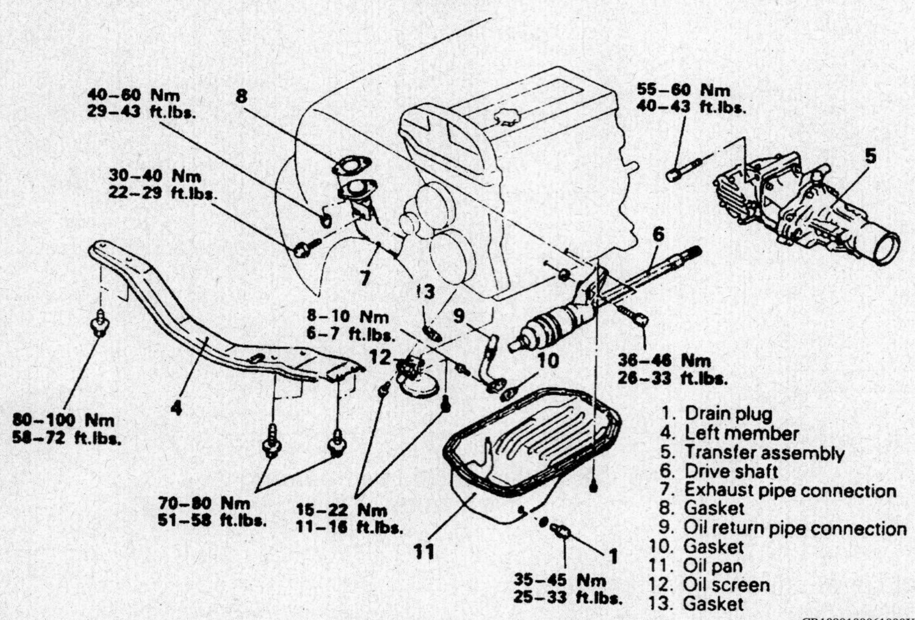

Fig. 56 Oil pan & screen replacement. Turbo AWD models

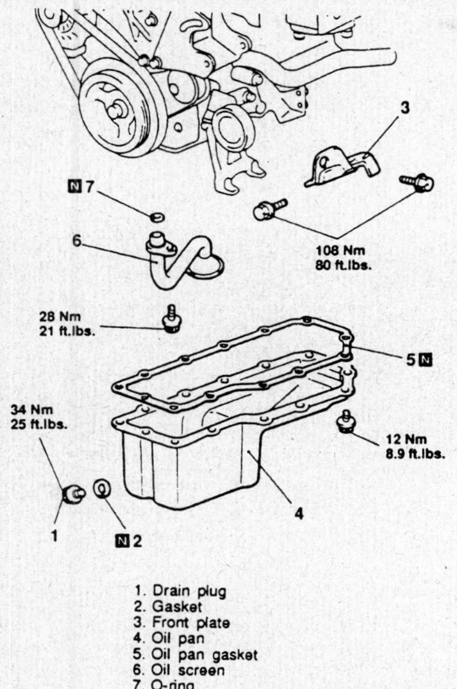

Fig. 57 Oil pan & screen replacement. Non-turbocharged engine

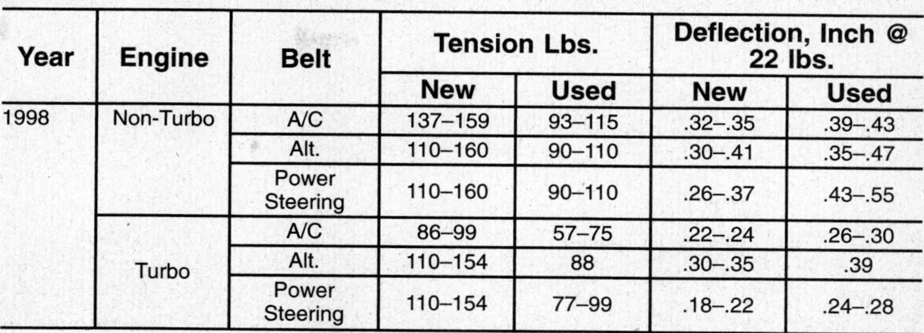

Year	Engine	Belt	Tension Lbs.		Deflection, Inch @ 22 lbs.	
			New	Used	New	Used
1998	Non-Turbo	A/C	137–159	93–115	.32–.35	.39–.43
		Alt.	110–160	90–110	.30–.41	.35–.47
		Power Steering	110–160	90–110	.26–.37	.43–.55
	Turbo	A/C	86–99	57–75	.22–.24	.26–.30
		Alt.	110–154	88	.30–.35	.39
		Power Steering	110–154	77–99	.18–.22	.24–.28

Fig. 58 Belt tension data

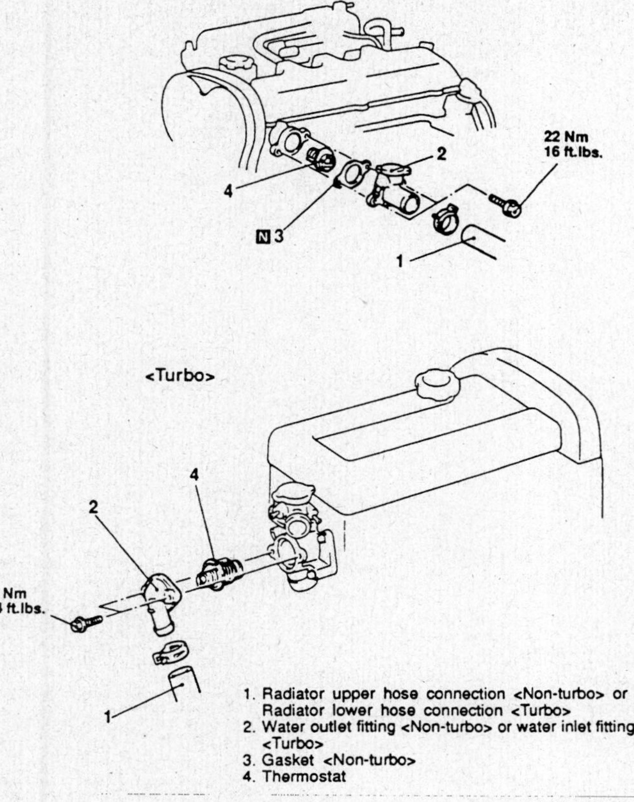

Fig. 59 Thermostat replacement

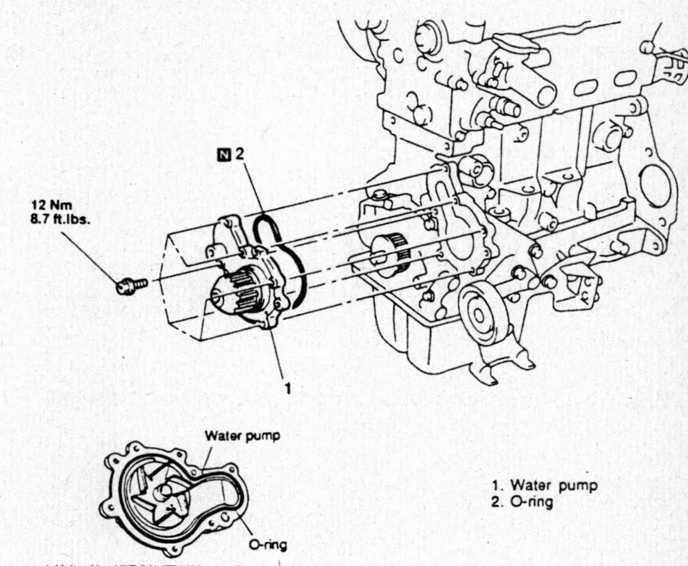

Fig. 60 Water pump removal. Non-turbocharged engine

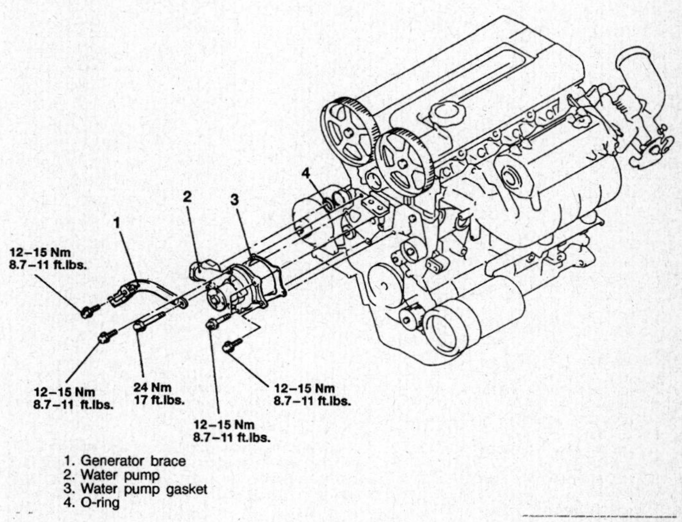

Fig. 61 Water pump removal. Turbocharged engine

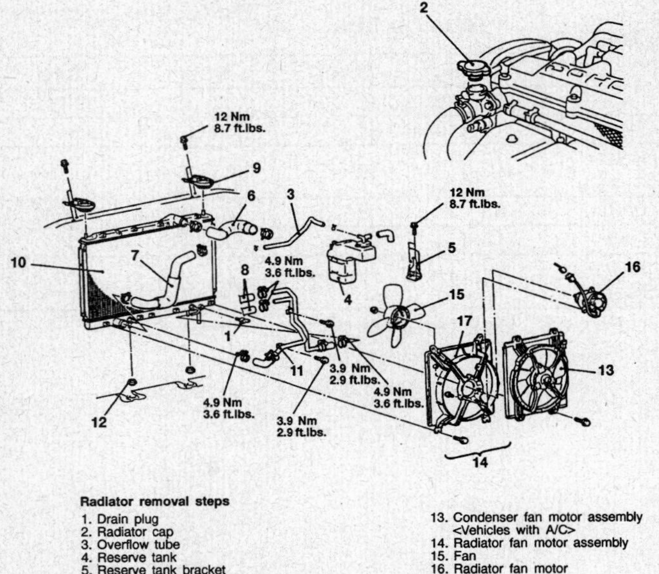

Radiator removal steps

1. Drain plug
2. Radiator cap
3. Overflow tube
4. Reserve tank
5. Reserve tank bracket
6. Radiator upper hose
7. Radiator lower hose
8. Transaxle fluid cooler hose connection <Vehicles with A/T>
9. Upper insulator
10. Radiator assembly
11. Transaxle fluid cooler hose and pipe assembly <Vehicles with A/T>
12. Lower insulator
13. Condenser fan motor assembly <Vehicles with A/C>
14. Radiator fan motor assembly
15. Fan
16. Radiator fan motor
17. Shroud

Radiator fan motor removal steps

11. Transaxle fluid cooler hose and pipe assembly <Vehicles with A/T>
14. Radiator fan motor assembly
15. Fan
16. Radiator fan motor
17. Shroud

CR1089500149000X

Fig. 62 Radiator replacement. Non-turbocharged engine

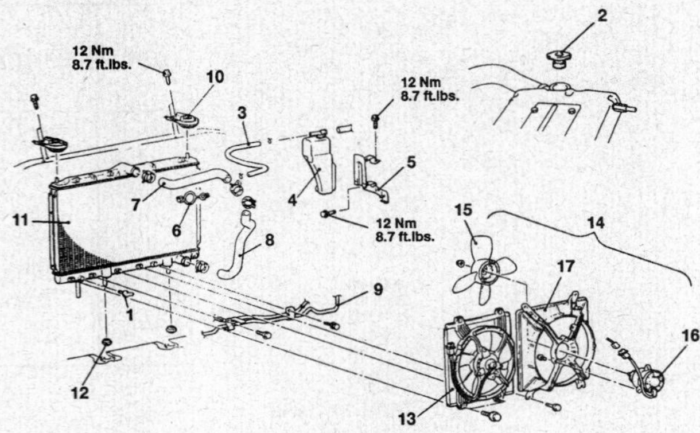

Radiator removal steps

1. Drain plug
2. Radiator cap
3. Overflow tube
4. Reserve tank
5. Reserve tank bracket
6. Clip
7. Radiator upper hose
8. Radiator lower hose
9. Transaxle fluid cooler hose and pipe assembly <Vehicles with A/T>
10. Upper insulator
11. Radiator assembly
12. Lower insulator
13. Condenser fan motor assembly <Vehicles with A/C>
14. Radiator fan motor assembly
15. Fan
16. Radiator fan motor
17. Shroud

Radiator fan motor removal steps

4. Reserve tank
9. Transaxle fluid cooler hose and pipe assembly <Vehicles with A/T>
14. Radiator fan motor assembly
15. Fan
16. Radiator fan motor
17. Shroud

CR1089500150000X

Fig. 63 Radiator replacement. Turbocharged engine

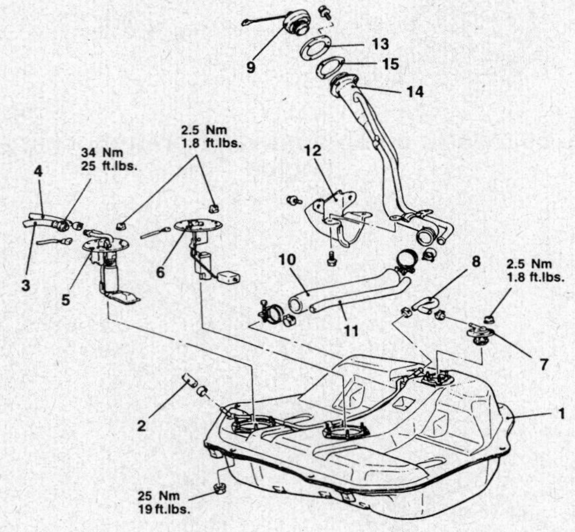

1. Fuel tank
2. Vapor hose
3. High-pressure fuel hose
4. Return hose
5. Fuel pump assembly
6. Fuel gauge unit
7. Fuel cut-off valve assembly
8. Vapor hose
9. Fuel tank filler tube cap
10. Filler hose
11. Vapor hose
12. Fuel tank filler tube protector
13. Reinforcement
14. Fuel tank filler tube assembly
15. Packing

NOTE
When replacing the fuel pump assembly or the fuel gauge unit only, it is possible to work from the service holes underneath the rear seat cushion without having to remove the fuel tank.

CR1029503772000X

Fig. 64 Fuel pump removal. FWD models

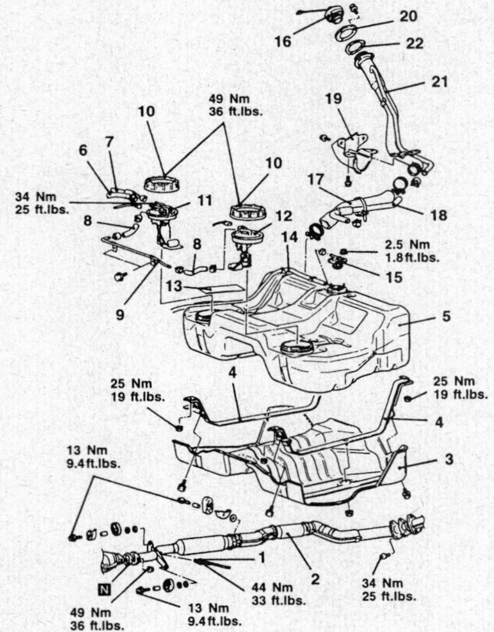

1. Heated oxygen sensor connection
2. Center exhaust pipe
3. Protector
4. Band
5. Fuel tank
6. High-pressure fuel hose
7. Return hose
8. Suction hose
9. Pipe
10. Cap
11. Fuel gauge unit and pump assembly
12. Fuel gauge unit and pipe assembly
13. Tape
14. Vapor hose
15. Fuel cut-off valve assembly
16. Fuel tank filler tube cap
17. Filler hose
18. Vapor hose
19. Fuel tank filler tube protector
20. Reinforcement
21. Fuel tank filler tube assembly
22. Packing

NOTE
When replacing the fuel gauge unit and pump assembly or the fuel gauge unit and pipe assembly only, it is possible to work from the service holes underneath the rear seat cushion without having to remove the fuel tank.

CR1029503773000X

Fig. 65 Fuel pump removal. AWD models

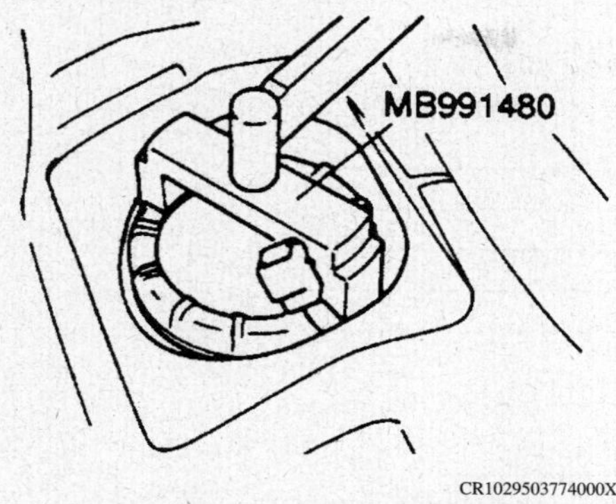

CR1029503774000X

Fig. 66 Fuel pump cap installation. AWD models

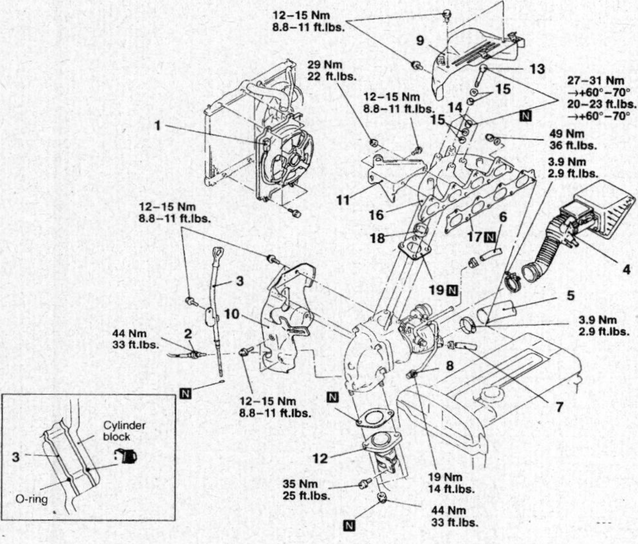

1. Condenser fan motor assembly <Vehicles with air conditioning>
2. Heated oxygen sensor <front>
3. Engine oil level gauge guide
4. Air cleaner and air intake hose assembly
5. Air hose (A) connection
6. Water hose connection
7. Water hose connection
8. Oil pipe (A) connection
9. Heat protector (A)
10. Heat protector (B)
11. Engine hanger
12. Front exhaust pipe connection
13. Flange bolts
14. Flange nut
15. Coned disc spring
16. Exhaust manifold
17. Exhaust manifold gasket
18. Ring
19. Gasket (A)

CR1059600119010X

Fig. 68 Turbocharger removal (Part 1 of 2)

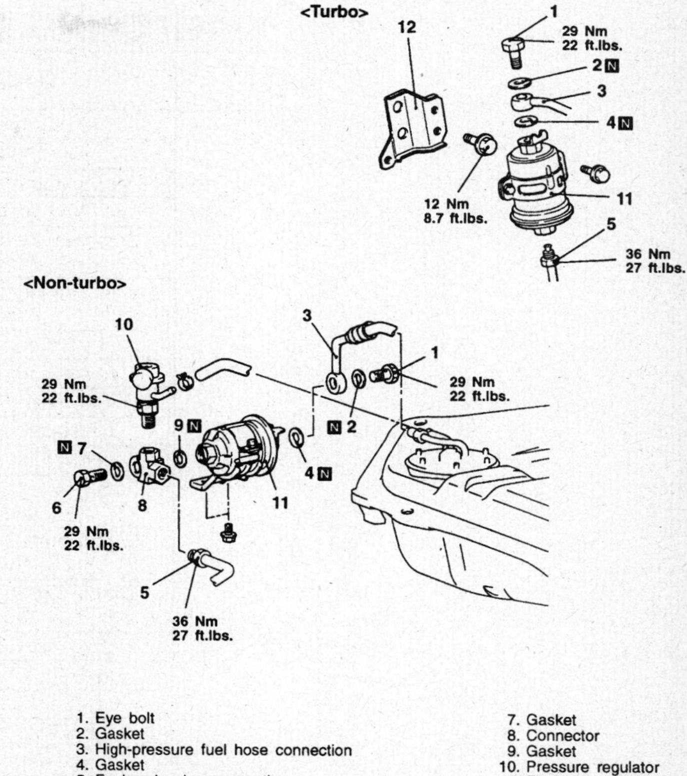

1. Eye bolt
2. Gasket
3. High-pressure fuel hose connection
4. Gasket
5. Fuel main pipe connection
6. Eye bolt
7. Gasket
8. Connector
9. Gasket
10. Pressure regulator
11. Fuel filter
12. Fuel filter bracket

CR1029607304000X

Fig. 67 Fuel filter replacement

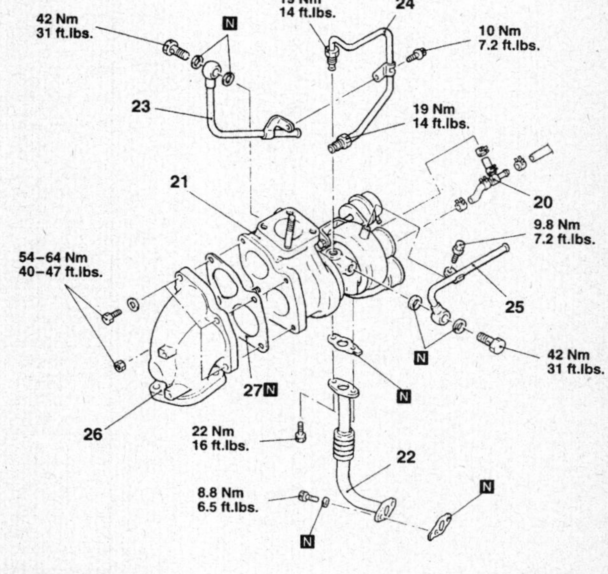

20. Vacuum hose assembly
21. Turbocharger assembly
22. Oil return pipe
23. Water pipe assembly (B)
24. Oil pipe assembly
25. Water pipe assembly (A)
26. Exhaust manifold fitting
27. Gasket

CR1059600119020X

Fig. 68 Turbocharger removal (Part 2 of 2)

TIGHTENING SPECIFICATIONS

Year	Component	Torque/Ft. Lbs.
1998	A/C Compressor Bracket	17–20
	Air CleanerTo-Body	72–84⑤
	Auto Tensioner (Non-Turbo)	23
	Auto Tensioner (Turbo)	17
	Camshaft Bearing Cap Bolt-Main (Non-Turbo)	21
	Camshaft Bearing Cap Bolt-Small (Non-Turbo)	108⑤
	Camshaft Bearing Cap Bolt (Turbo)	14–15
	Camshaft Sprocket (Non-Turbo)	75
	Camshaft Sprocket (Turbo)	65
	Center Cover (Turbo)	26⑤
	Connecting Rod Bearing Caps (Turbo)	15③
	Connecting Rod Bearing Caps (Non-Turbo)	20⑥
	Crankshaft Bearing Caps Inner (Non-Turbo)	55
	Crankshaft Bearing Caps- Outer (Non-Turbo)	20
	Crankshaft Bearing Cap (Turbo)	18③
	Crankshaft Pulley (Non-Turbo)	105
	Crankshaft Pulley (Turbo)	18
	Crankshaft Sprocket (Turbo)	80–94
	Cylinder Head Bolt	①
	EGR Valve	16
	Electric Fuel Pump (Bolt)	22⑤
	Engine Coolant Temperature Sensor	60⑤
	Engine Mount Insulator Mounting Bolt	49
	Engine Mount Stopper Bolt	71–85
	Engine Oil Cooler Mounting Bolt (Turbo)	29–33
	Engine Roller Stopper (Front)	41
	Engine Roller Stopper (Rear)	32
	Exhaust Manifold To Engine (Non-Turbo)	17
	Exhaust Manifold To Engine (Turbo)	22
	Exhaust Manifold To Turbocharger (Turbo)	②
	Exhaust Pipe Clamp Bolt	113⑤
	Exhaust Pipe To Hanger	113⑤
	Exhaust Pipe To Manifold (Non-Turbo)	33
	Exhaust Pipe To Manifold (Turbo)	33–36
	Flywheel	94–101
	Fuel Gauge Unit (AWD)	36
	Fuel Gauge Unit (FWD)	22⑤
	Heat Shield To Exhaust Manifold (Turbo)	9–11
	Intake Manifold To Engine (Non-Turbo)	17
	Intake Manifold To Engine (Turbo)	14
	Oil Filter Bracket (Turbo)	11–16
	Oil Pan (Non-Turbo)	108⑤
	Oil Pan (Turbo)	60⑤
	Oil Pan Drain Plug (Non-Turbo)	25
	Oil Pan Drain Plug (Turbo)	29
	Oil Pressure Gauge Unit (Turbo)	84⑤
	Oil Pressure Switch (Turbo)	84⑤
	Oil Pump Cover (Non-Turbo)	17

Continued

TIGHTENING SPECIFICATIONS—Continued

Year	Component	Torque/Ft. Lbs.
1998	Oil Pump Cover (Turbo)	9–12
	Oil Pump Driven Gear (Turbo)	84⑤
	Oil Return Pipe To Oil Pan (Turbo)	78
	Oil Screen (Non-Turbo)	21
	Oil Screen (Turbo)	14
	Oxygen Sensor	22
	Tensioner Pulley Bracket (Turbo)	17–20
	Throttle Body	11–16
	Timing Belt B Tensioner Bolt (Turbo)	14
	Timing Belt Front Cover, Bottom (Non-Turbo)	21
	Timing Belt Front Cover, Top (Non-Turbo)	108⑤
	Timing Belt Front Cover (Turbo)	④
	Timing Belt Tensioner (Turbo)	17–20
	Timing Belt Tensioner Pulley (Non-Turbo)	30
	Water Pump (Non-Turbo)	104⑤
	Water Pump (Turbo)	9–11

①— Refer to “Cylinder Head, Replace” for procedure.
②— Refer to “Exhaust Manifold, Replace” for procedure.
③— Tighten an additional 90–100.°
④— Refer to “Timing Belt, Replace” for procedure.
⑤— Inch lbs.
⑥— Tighten an additional 90.°

Clutch & Manual Transaxle

NOTE: On Air Bag Equipped Models, Refer To "Air Bag System Precautions" Located In The Front Of This Manual For System Disarming & Arming Procedures.

NOTE: Refer To "Computer Relearn Procedures" Located In The Front Of This Manual When Battery Power To The Computer Has Been Interrupted.

INDEX

ADJUSTMENTS

CLUTCH PEDAL

1. Measure clutch pedal height or clevis pin play as shown, **Fig. 1.**
2. If height is higher than 7.0–7.1 inches, refer to **Fig. 2** for adjustment.
3. If pedal height is lower than 7.0–7.1 inches, proceed as follows:
   a. Loosen bolt or clutch switch and turn pushrod until pedal height is proper, **Fig. 3. Do not move pushrod toward master cylinder.**
   b. After adjustment, tighten bolt or clutch switch to reach pedal stopper, then lock with locknut.
4. If clevis pin play is not .04–.12 inch, turn pushrod until clevis pin play is proper.
5. Ensure interlock switch is as shown, **Fig. 4,** when clutch pedal is fully depressed, and if necessary, adjust.
6. Confirm clutch pedal freeplay, **Fig. 5,** is .24 –.51 inches.
7. Confirm distance between clutch pedal and firewall, when clutch is disengaged, **Fig. 5,** is 2.7 inches or more. If distance is not as specified, problem may be the result of air in hydraulic system or faulty master cylinder or clutch.

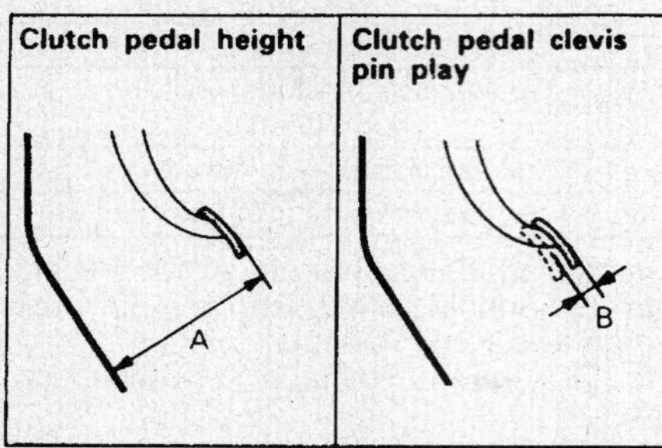

Fig. 1 Clutch pedal inspection

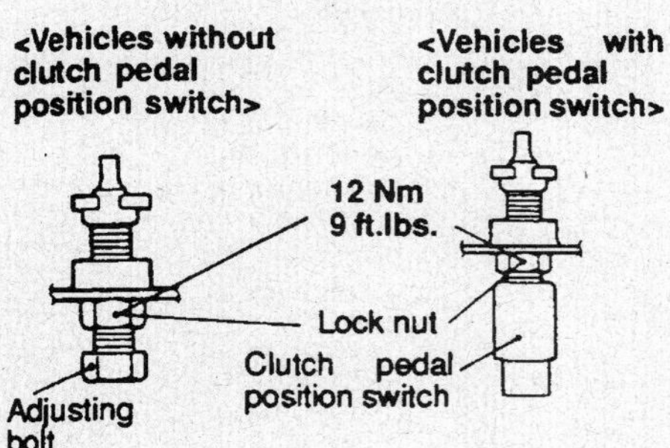

Fig. 2 Clutch pedal adjustment

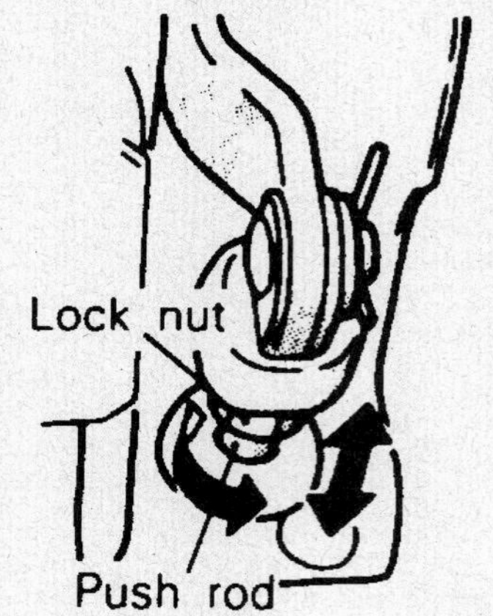

Fig. 3 Pushrod adjustment

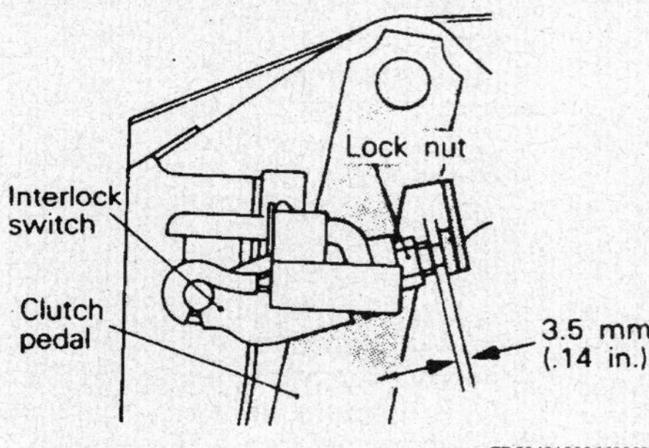

Fig. 4 Interlock switch adjustment

HYDRAULIC SYSTEM SERVICE

HYDRAULIC CLUTCH SYSTEM BLEED

Whenever the any component of the hydraulic clutch system has been removed, bleeding must be performed.

Ensure clutch hydraulic cylinder is full, have helper depress clutch pedal and hold, open bleeder screw on hydraulic cylinder, then close bleeder screw. Repeat procedure until all air is bled from system.

CLUTCH SLAVE CYLINDER, REPLACE

1. Drain clutch fluid into a suitable container.
2. Disconnect clutch slave cylinder tube connections.
3. Remove slave cylinder retaining bolts then the slave cylinder.
4. Reverse procedure to install, noting the following:
   a. Apply multi-purpose grease to slave cylinder pushrod where it contacts the release fork.
   b. Bleed hydraulic clutch system as outlined under "Hydraulic Clutch System Bleeding."

CLUTCH

REPLACE

Replace clutch in numbered sequence **Fig. 6,** noting the following:

1. Remove transaxle as outlined under "Transaxle, Replace."
2. Diagonally loosen clutch cover bolts in two or three steps.
3. Support clutch cover and remove cover bolts, lowering clutch and clutch cover.
4. Slide release fork in direction of arrow as shown in **Fig. 7** and disengage fulcrum from clip to release fork. **Do not push the release fork in direction other than arrow or remove with force as clip may be damaged.**

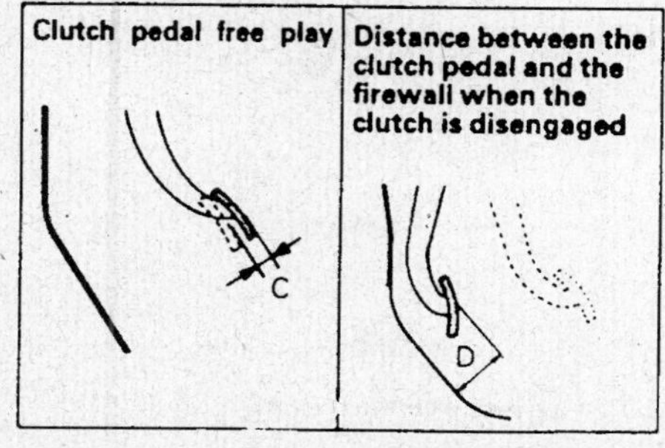

Fig. 5 Clutch pedal operation inspection

5. Reverse procedure to install. Use special clutch positioning tool No. MD998126, or equivalent, to install clutch disc on flywheel, **Fig. 8.**

TRANSAXLE

REPLACE

Remove transaxle in numbered sequence, **Fig. 9** for non-turbocharged models, **Fig. 10** for turbocharged models with Front Wheel Drive (FWD), and **Fig. 11** for turbocharged models with All Wheel Drive (AWD), noting the following:

1. Remove battery.
2. Raise and support vehicle.
3. Drain transaxle oil.
4. Remove undercover.
5. **On AWD models,** remove transfer case.
6. **On all models,** using a suitable jack, slightly raise transaxle, then remove mounting bracket nuts. **Do not tilt transaxle assembly.**
7. Use special engine support tool No. MZ203827, or equivalent, to support engine assembly, **Fig. 12.**
8. Using special tool No. MB991113, or equivalent, remove tie rod ends, lateral lower arms, and compression lower arms, **Figs. 13 through 15. Loosen but do not remove nuts. Suspend special tool by cord to hold in place.**
9. **On AWD models,** remove driveshaft nut using special tool No. MB990767, or equivalent, **Fig. 16.**
10. **On all models,** disconnect driveshaft as follows:
    a. Insert pry bar between transaxle case and driveshaft, **Fig. 17,** then pry driveshaft from transaxle. **Do not pull on driveshaft, as doing so will damage inboard joint. Do not insert pry bar so deep as to damage oil seal.** Suspend driveshaft with suitable wire.
11. **On AWD models,** lightly tap center bearing bracket using a suitable plastic hammer to remove inner shaft from transaxle, **Fig. 18.**
12. **On all models,** remove clutch release cylinder without disconnecting fluid line and suspend it nearby with suitable wire.
13. **On FWD models,** remove flexplate connecting bolts and transaxle assembly mounting bolts, ensuring the following:
    a. Transaxle must be solidly supported by suitable jack.
    b. Chalk mating marks on the flex plate and clutch pressure plate for easier installation, **Fig. 19.**
    c. Press clutch pressure plate into the transaxle for easier removal.
14. **On all models,** reverse procedure to install noting;
    a. Inspect front roll stopper. If dimension shown in **Fig. 20** is not 1.57–1.81 inches, replace roll stopper bracket assembly.
    b. Ensure serrated part of driveshaft does not damage oil seal lip.
    c. **On AWD models,** install driveshaft nut washer as shown in **Fig. 21.** Using special tool No. MB990767, or equivalent, tighten driveshaft nut as specified in **Fig. 21.** Ensure there is no load on wheel bearings.

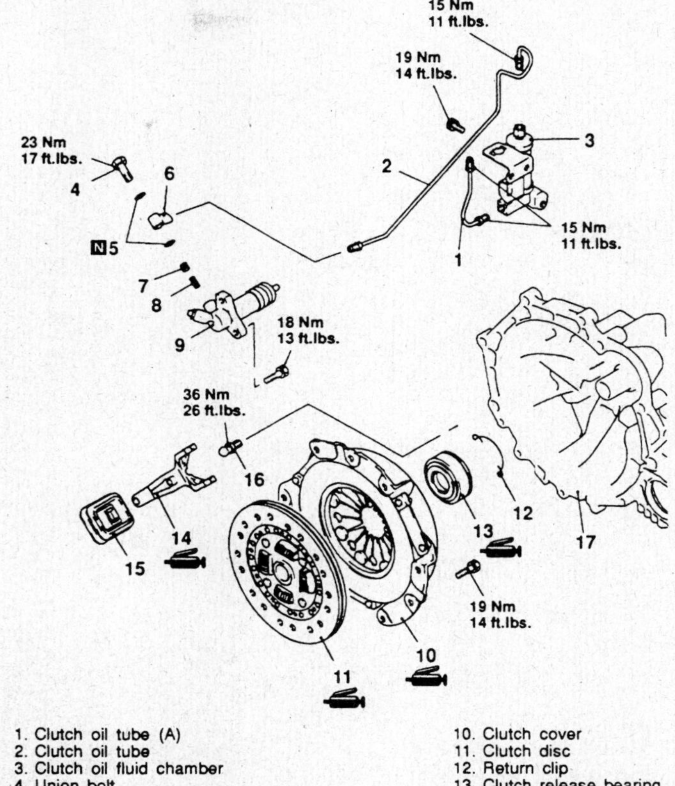

Fig. 6 Clutch assembly replacement

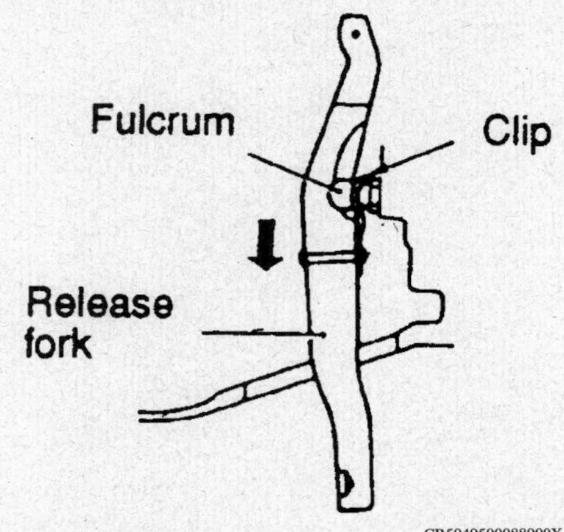

Fig. 7 Release fork removal

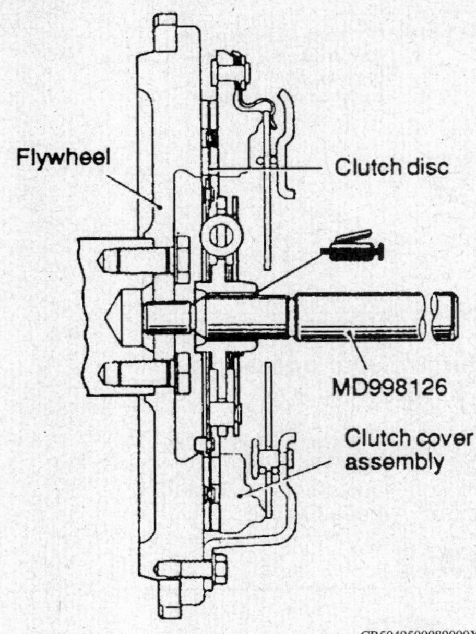

Fig. 8 Clutch disc installation

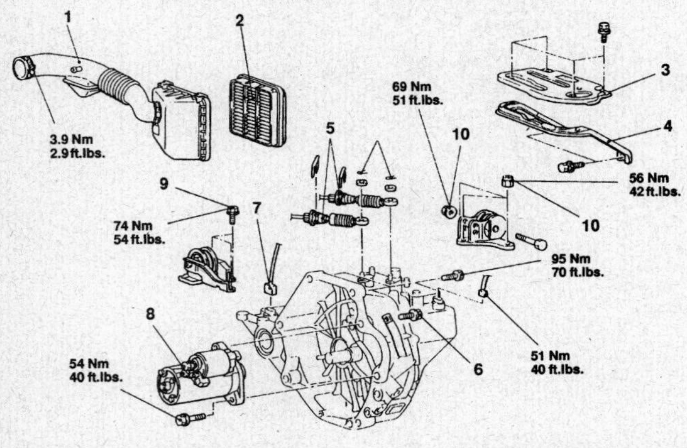

1. Air cleaner cover and air intake hose assembly
2. Air cleaner element
3. Battery tray
4. Battery tray stay
5. Shift cable and select cable connection
6. Backup light switch connector
7. Vehicle speed sensor connector
8. Starter motor
9. Rear roll stopper bracket mounting bolts
10. Transaxle mounting bracket mounting nuts

CR5039500925010X

Fig. 9 Transaxle replacement (Part 1 of 2) Non-turbocharged engine

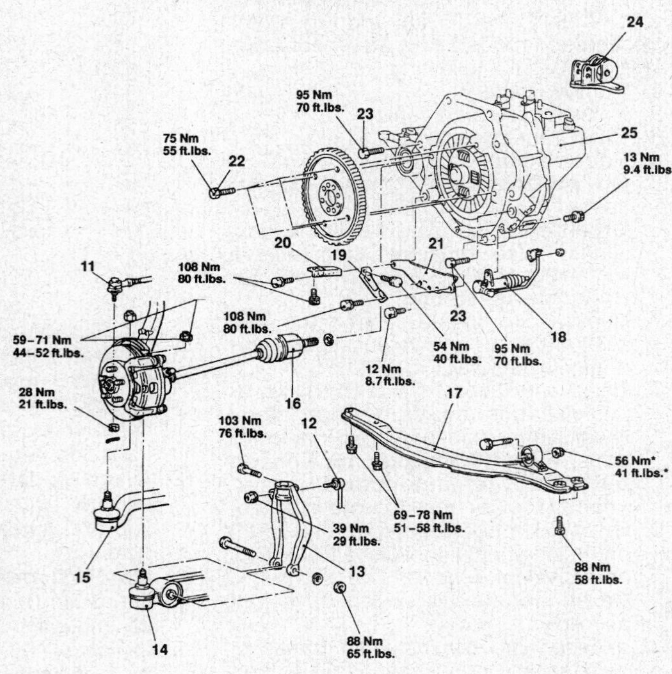

Lifting up of the vehicle

11. Tie rod end connection
12. Stabilizer link connection
13. Damper fork
14. Lateral lower arm connection
15. Compression lower arm connection
16. Drive shaft connection
17. Center member assembly
18. Clutch release cylinder connection
19. Front plate
20. Rear plate
21. Transaxle case lower cover
22. Flex plate connecting bolts
23. Transaxle assembly mounting bolts
24. Transaxle mounting
25. Transaxle assembly

CR5039500925020X

Fig. 9 Transaxle replacement (Part 2 of 2). Non-turbocharged engine

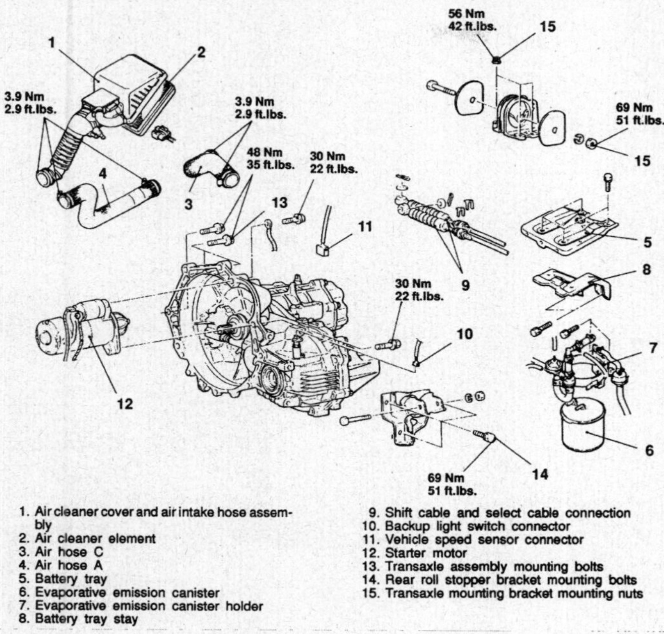

Fig. 10 Transaxle replacement (Part 1 of 2). Turbocharged FWD models

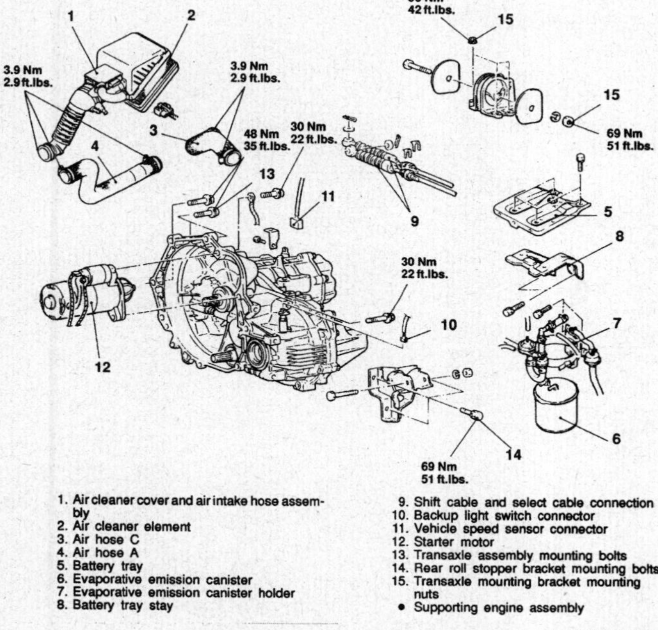

Fig. 11 Transaxle replacement (Part 1 of 2). Turbocharged AWD models

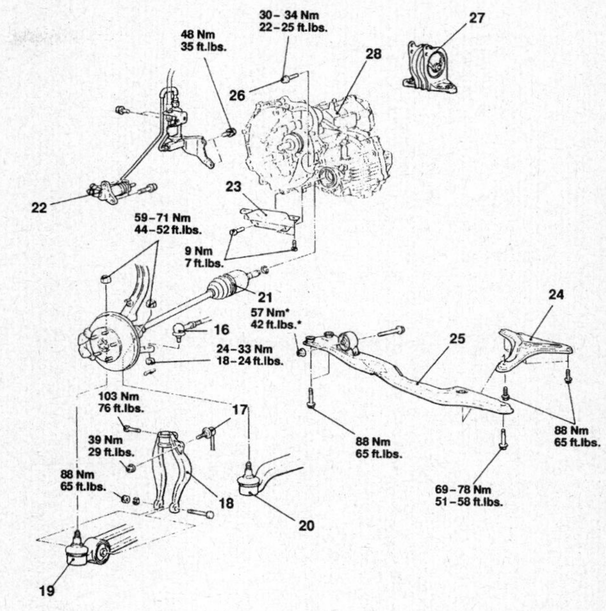

Fig. 10 Transaxle replacement (Part 2 of 2). Turbocharged FWD models

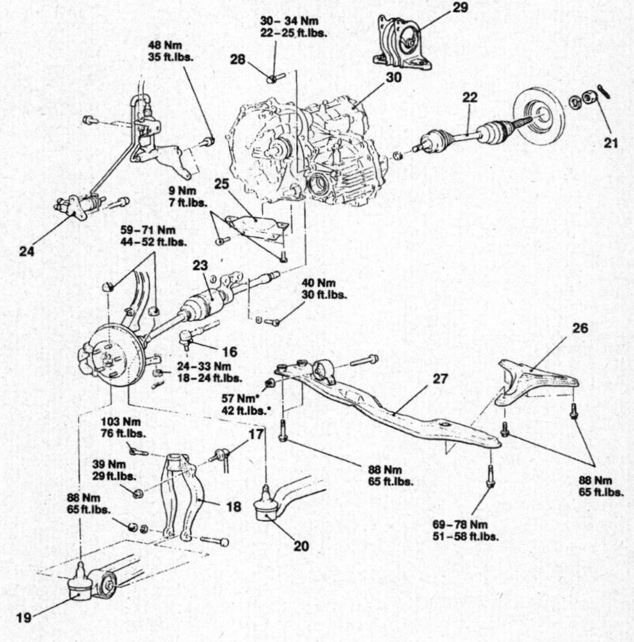

Fig. 11 Transaxle replacement (Part 2 of 2). Turbocharged AWD models

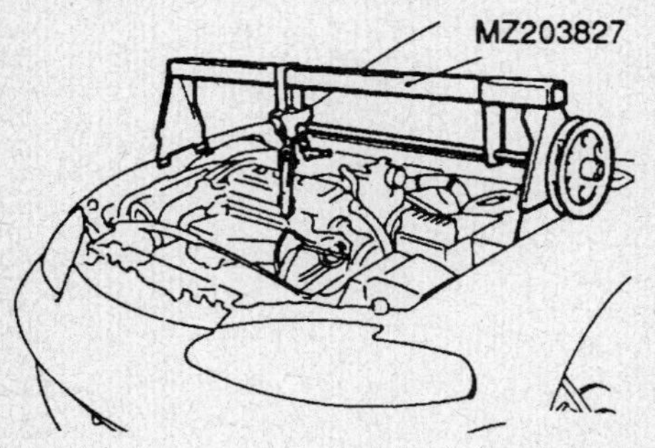

Fig. 12 Engine assembly support

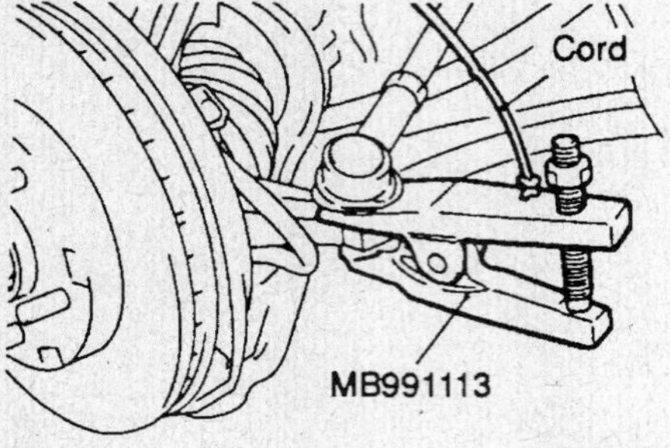

Fig. 13 Tie rod end removal

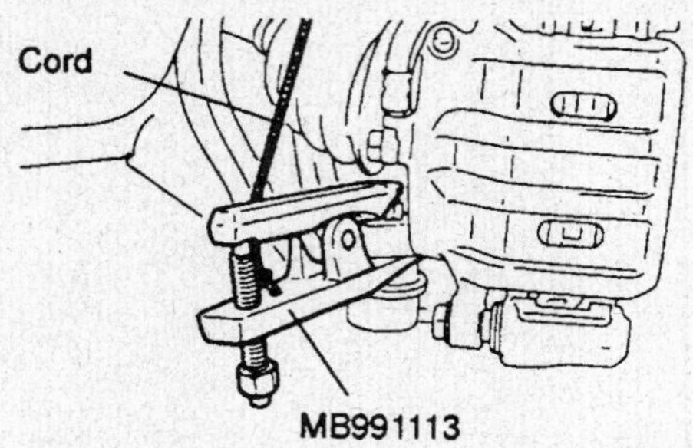

Fig. 14 Lateral lower arm removal

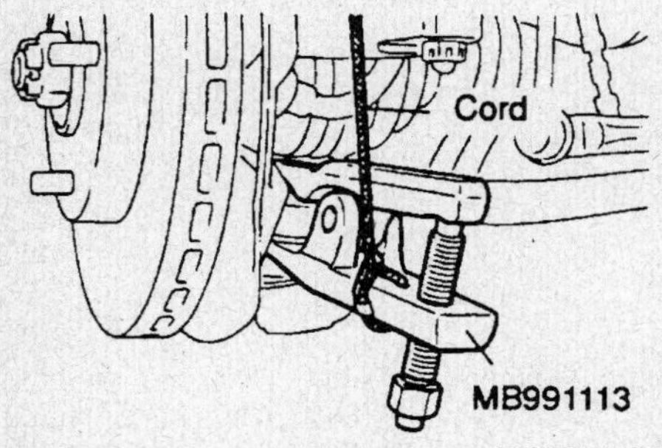

Fig. 15 Compression lower arm removal

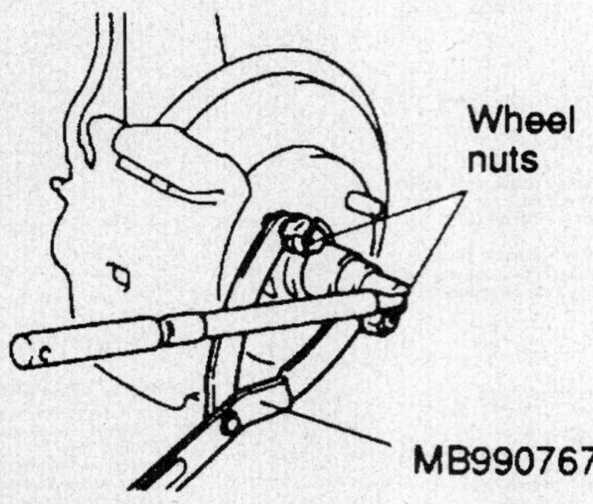

Fig. 16 Driveshaft nut removal. AWD models

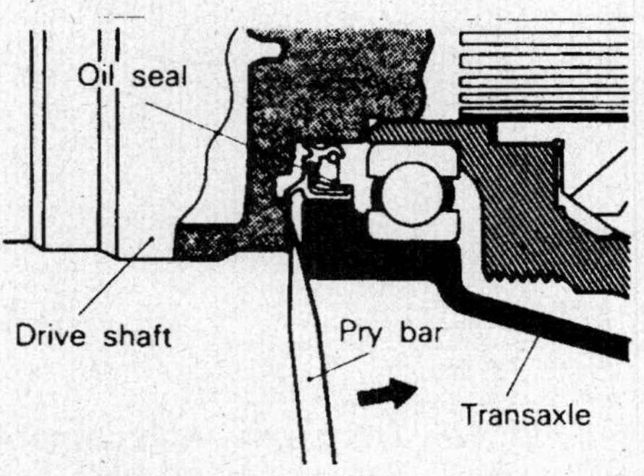

Fig. 17 Driveshaft removal

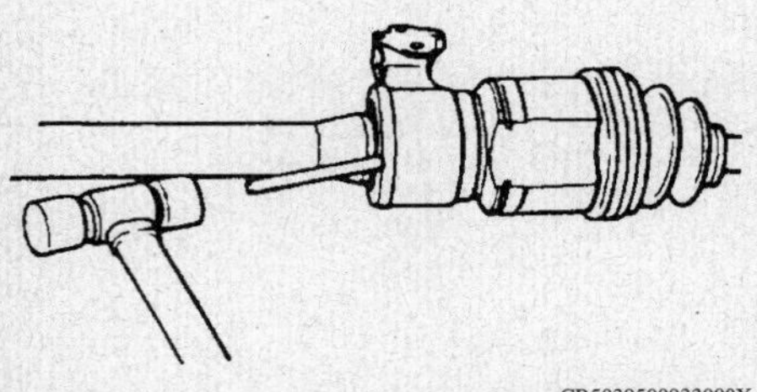

Fig. 18 Inner shaft removal. AWD models

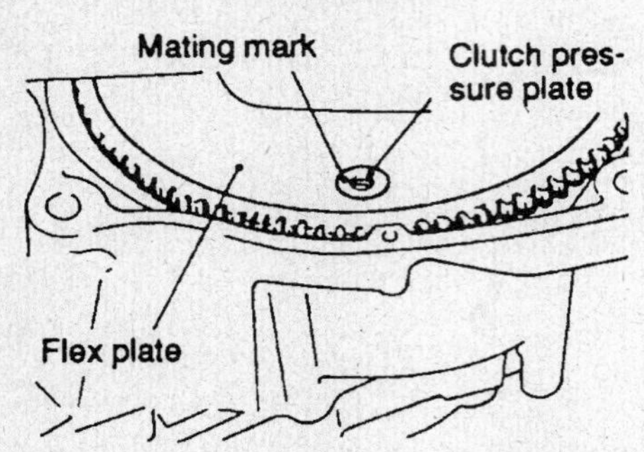
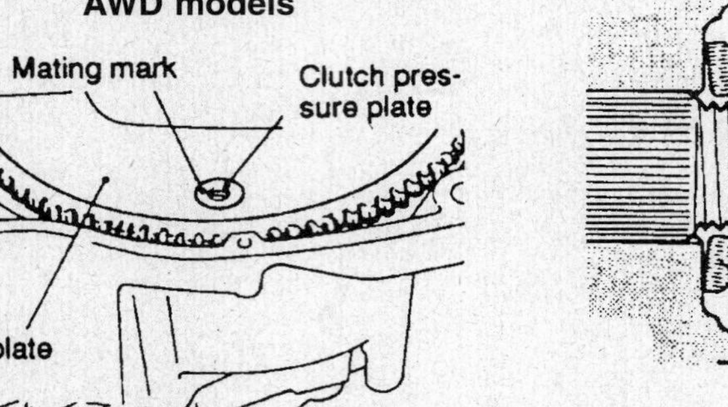

Fig. 19 Flex plate mating marks. FWD models

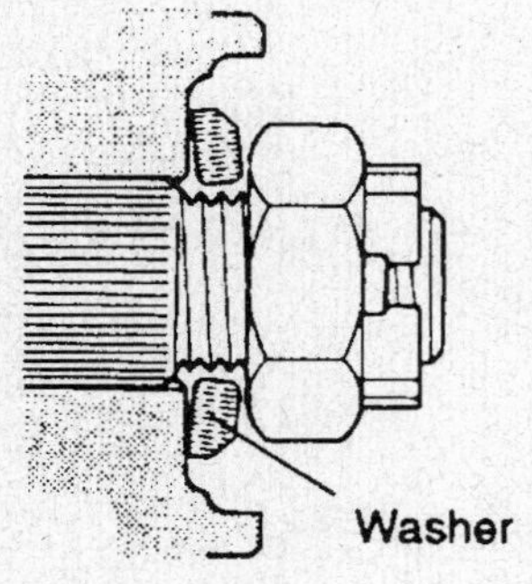

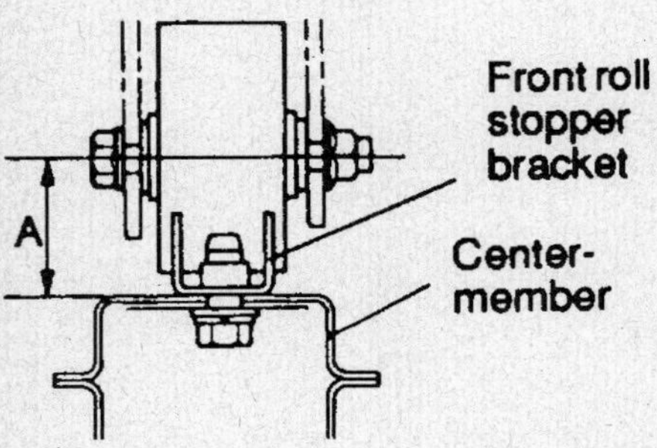

Fig. 20 Front roll stopper inspection

196-255 Nm
145-188 ft.lbs.
MB990767
CR5039500936000X

Fig. 21 Driveshaft nut installation. AWD models

TIGHTENING SPECIFICATIONS

Year	Component	Torque/Ft. Lbs.
1998	Back-Up Lamp Switch	22
	Bearing Retainer Bolt	14
	Clutch Cover Assembly	11–16
	Clutch Pedal Bracket	72–108①
	Clutch Pedal Support Bracket	72–108①
	Clutch Pedal To Support Bracket	14–18
	Clutch Release Cylinder	11–16
	Compression Lower Arm	44–52
	Flywheel Bolts	55
	Lower Arm Ball Joint To Knuckle	44–52
	Poppet Plug	27
	Rear Housing Cover Bolt	14
	Rear Roll Stopper Bracket	51
	Restrict Ball Assembly	24
	Shift & Select Cable To Transaxle	11–16
	Speedometer Sleeve Bolt	36①
	Starter Motor Mounting Bolt	40
	Stop Lamp Switch	24
	Tie Rod End To Knuckle	18–24
	Transaxle Case Tightening Bolt	29
	Transaxle Mounting Bolt	35
	Transfer Assembly Mounting Bolt	40–44
	Wheel Lug Nut	88–108

① — Inch lbs.

Rear Axle & Suspension

NOTE: On Air Bag Equipped Models, Refer To "Air Bag System Precautions" Located In The Front Of This Manual For System Disarming & Arming Procedures.

NOTE: Refer To "Computer Relearn Procedures" Located In The Front Of This Manual When Battery Power To The Computer Has Been Interrupted.

INDEX

REAR AXLE SHAFT

REPLACE

Remove rear driveshaft in numbered sequence, **Fig. 1** noting the following:

1. Remove driveshaft nut using removal tool No. MB990767, or equivalent.
2. Remove driveshaft by pushing the lower part of the knuckle to the outside of the vehicle, then separate the driveshaft from the differential carrier. At this time, use a suitable tire lever or similar tool to separate the driveshaft connection.
3. Reverse procedure to install, noting the following:
   a. Ensure proper driveshaft placement. The righthand driveshaft has an orange boot band, while the lefthand driveshaft has a green boot band.
   b. Ensure differential carrier oil seal is not damaged by driveshaft spline.
   c. Using special tool No. MB990767, or equivalent, tighten driveshaft nut to specifications. Ensure there is no load on wheel bearings.

DIFFERENTIAL CARRIER

REPLACE

Replace differential carrier in numbered sequence shown in **Fig. 2,** noting the following:

1. Remove rear axle shaft as described under "Rear Axle Shaft, Replace."
2. Mark with mating marks, then disconnect propeller shaft assembly.
3. Suspend propeller shaft out of the way.
4. Support differential carrier with suitable jack for removal.
5. Reverse procedure to install.

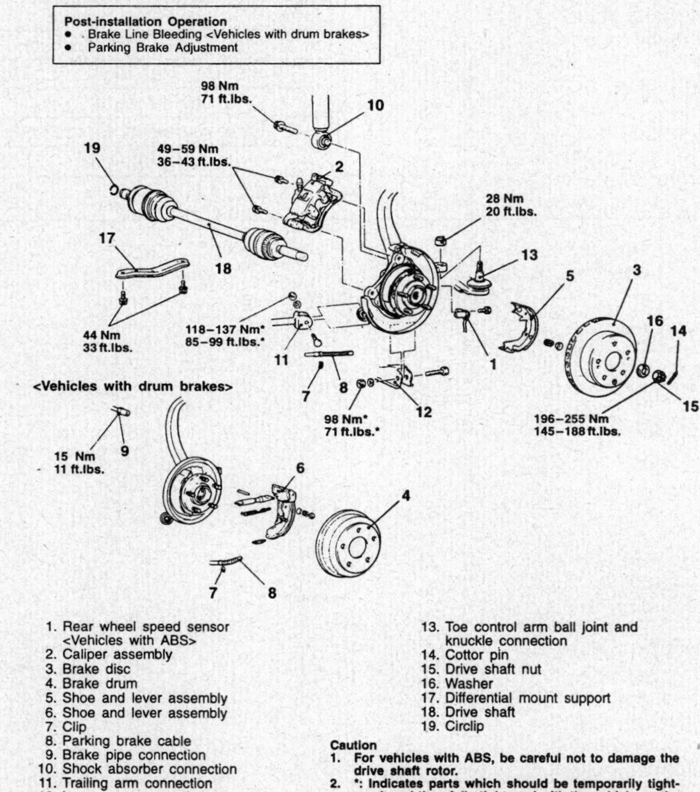

Fig. 1 Driveshaft replacement

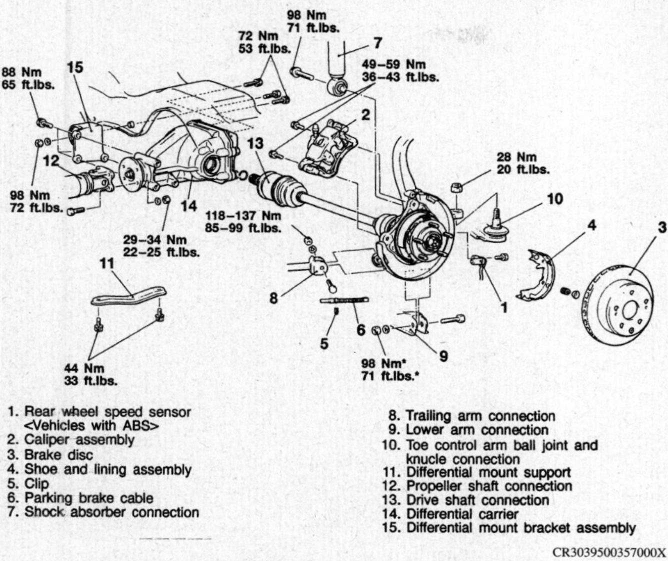

Fig. 2 Differential carrier assembly

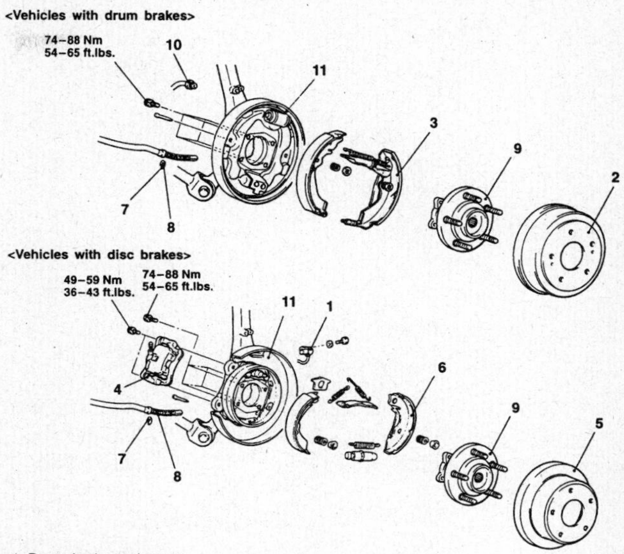

<Vehicles with drum brakes>

74–88 Nm 54–65 ft.lbs.

<Vehicles with disc brakes>

49–59 Nm 36–43 ft.lbs.

74–88 Nm 54–65 ft.lbs.

1. Rear wheel speed sensor <Vehicles with ABS>
2. Brake drum
3. Shoe and lever assembly
4. Caliper assembly
5. Brake disc
6. Shoe and lining assembly
7. Clip
8. Parking brake cable
9. Rear hub assembly
10. Brake pipe connection
11. Dust seal

Caution
The rear hub assembly should not be disassembled.

CR3039500358000A

Fig. 3 Rear axle hub replacement. FWD models

HUB & BEARING

REPLACE

FWD MODELS

Remove rear axle hub in numbered sequence, **Fig. 3,** noting the following:

1. Remove rear speed sensor.
2. Remove and suspend caliper assembly with a piece of wire. **Do not hang caliper by brake hose.**
3. Reverse procedure to install.

BALL JOINT INSPECTION

AWD MODELS

Inspect ball joint for proper starting torque as follows:

1. Move ball joint stud from side to side several times.
2. Mount two nuts on ball joint, then using a suitable torque wrench measure starting torque. Starting torque should be within 17–78 inch lbs. for lower arm and upper arm ball joints, and 15–28 inch lbs. for stabilizer link ball joint.
3. If starting torque exceeds upper limit, replace lower arm assembly.
4. If starting torque is below lower limit, the ball joint may still be reused unless it has drag or excessive play.

WHEEL BEARING

ADJUST

1. To inspect bearing endplay, proceed as follows:
   a. Place hub in suitable vise, protected by wood blocks, **Fig. 4.**
   b. Place dial gauge against hub surface, then move hub in axial direction.
   c. If endplay exceeds .002 inch, use special wheel bearing installer tool No. MB990998, or equivalent, to tighten bearing. **Torque** special tool to 145–188 ft. lbs.
2. Replace hub bearing unit if adjustment cannot be made to within limit.

STRUT

REPLACE

FWD MODELS

Remove strut assembly in numbered sequence, **Fig. 5,** noting the following:

1. Jack up torsion axle and arm assembly in order to release tension. Place jack at center of axle beam. Ensure jack does not contact lateral rod
2. Reverse procedure to install.

AWD MODELS

Remove shock absorber assembly in numbered sequence, **Fig. 5,** noting the following:

1. Jack up torsion axle and arm assembly in order to release tension. Place jack at center of axle beam. Ensure jack does not contact lateral rod.
2. Reverse procedure to install.

STRUT SERVICE

Disassemble strut assembly in numbered sequence shown in **Fig. 6,** noting the following:

1. Compress spring using spring compression tools No. MB991237 and MB991239, or equivalents, to ease in disassembly and assembly.
2. Ensure spring is properly seated in upper and lower spring seat when installing.
3. Install strut upper bracket as shown in **Fig. 7,** then tighten strut rod nut to specifications.

CONTROL ARM

REPLACE

AWD MODELS

Remove upper and lower arm in numbered sequences, **Figs. 8 and 9,** noting the following:

1. Loosen, but do not remove self-locking nut.
2. Inspect all bushings and bolts for wear and damage.
3. Reverse procedures to install.

TRAILING ARM

REPLACE

AWD MODELS

Remove trailing arm in numbered sequence, **Fig. 10,** noting the following:

1. Inspect bushings and bolts for wear or damage.
2. Inspect trailing arm for bends or damage.
3. Reverse procedure to install.

STABILIZER BAR

REPLACE

AWD MODELS

Remove stabilizer bar in numbered sequence, **Fig. 11,** noting the following:

1. Reverse procedure to install, noting the following:
   a. Set stabilizer bar so identification mark is at the left.
   b. Install the bushing, ensure the dimension is as shown in **Fig. 12.**

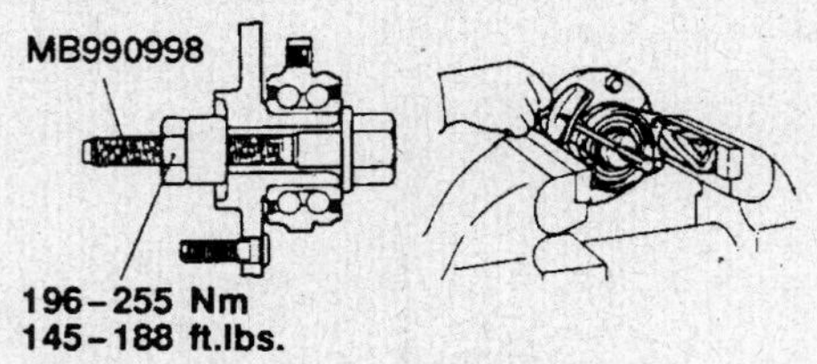

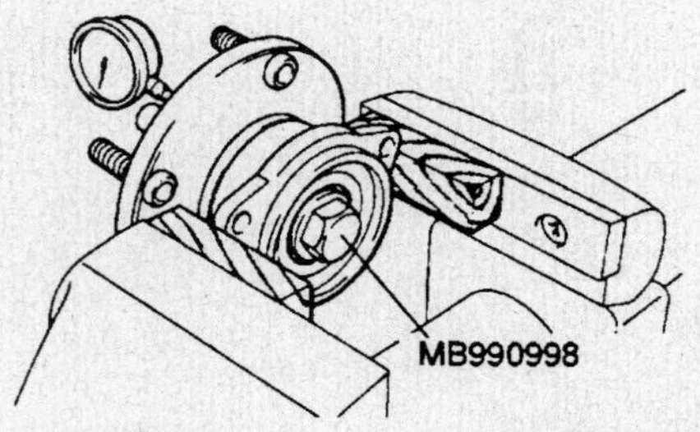

CR3039500359000X

Fig. 4 Hub endplay adjustment

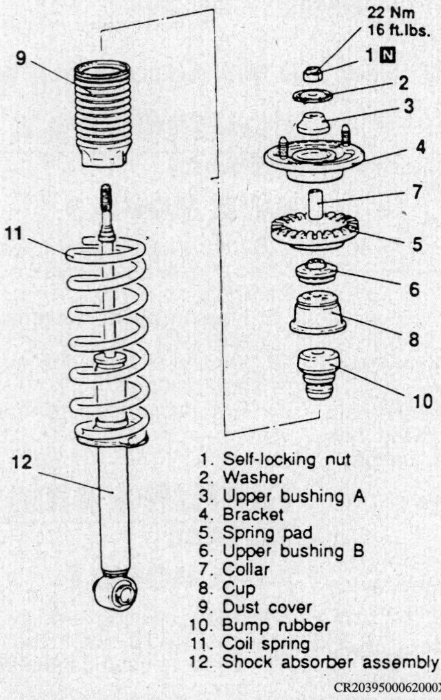

1. Self-locking nut
2. Washer
3. Upper bushing A
4. Bracket
5. Spring pad
6. Upper bushing B
7. Collar
8. Cup
9. Dust cover
10. Bump rubber
11. Coil spring
12. Shock absorber assembly

CR2039500062000X

Fig. 6 Exploded view of strut assembly

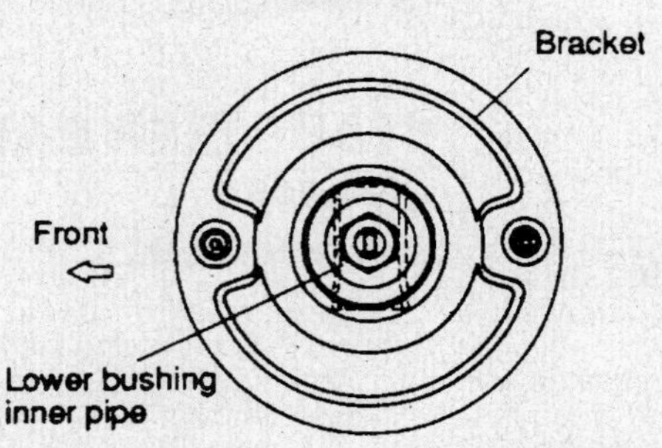

CR2039500063000X

Fig. 7 Upper spring mount installation

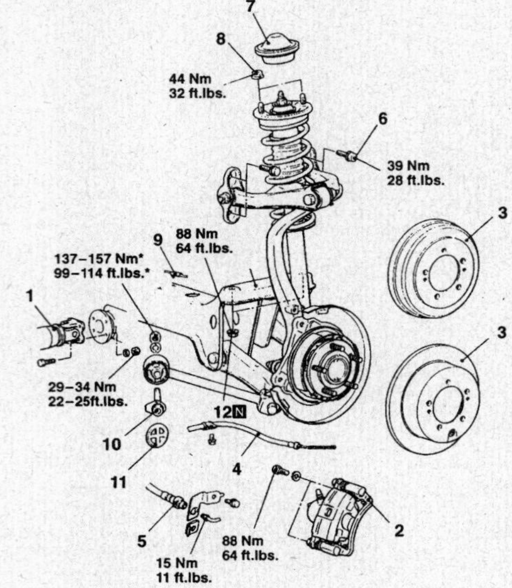

1. Propeller shaft connection <AWD>
2. Brake caliper assembly
3. Brake disc <Vehicles with disc brakes> or brake drum <Vehicles with drum brakes>
4. Parking brake cable end
5. Brake hose connection <Vehicles with drum brakes>
6. Upper arm bracket mounting bolts
7. Cap
8. Shock absorber mounting nuts
9. Rear wheel-speed sensor connector <Vehicles with ABS>
10. Grommet
11. Trailing arm mounting bolt
12. Crossmember mounting self-locking nuts
13. Rear suspension assembly

Caution
*** : indicates parts which should be temporarily tightened, and then fully tightened with the vehicles on the ground in the unladen condition.**

CR2039500061000A

Fig. 5 Strut assembly removal

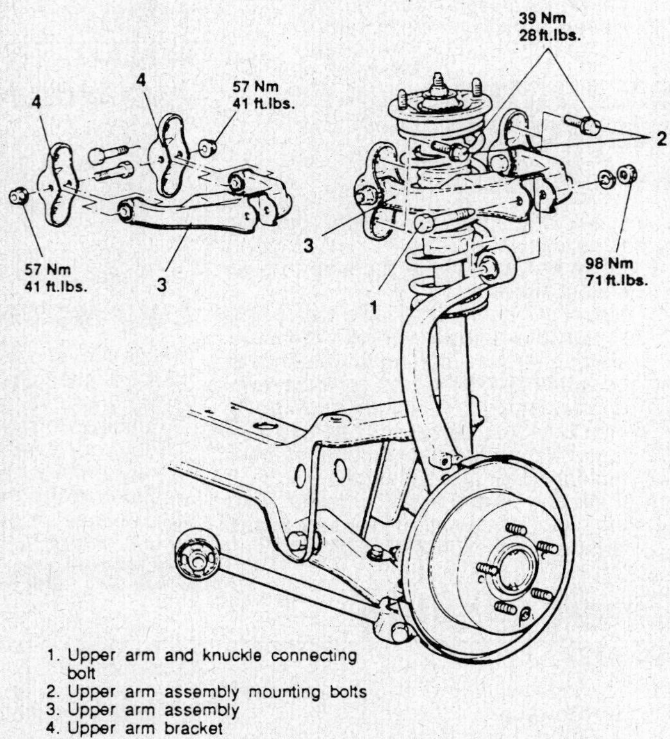

1. Upper arm and knuckle connecting bolt
2. Upper arm assembly mounting bolts
3. Upper arm assembly
4. Upper arm bracket

CR2039500064000X

Fig. 8 Upper arm replacement. AWD models

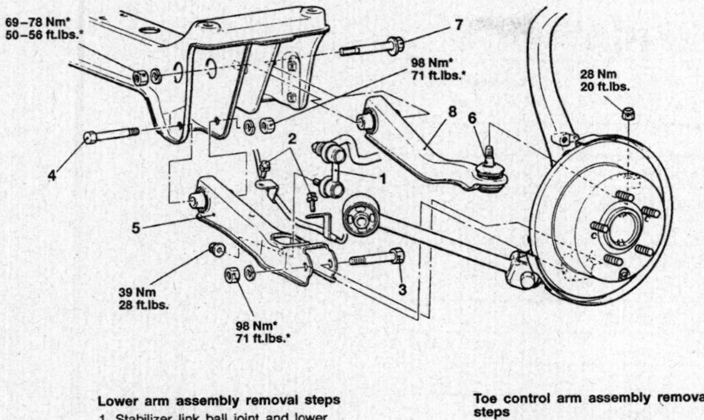

Lower arm assembly removal steps

1. Stabilizer link ball joint and lower arm connection
2. ABS wheel-speed sensor clamp bolts <Vehicles with ABS>
3. Lower arm assembly and knuckle connecting bolt
4. Lower arm assembly mounting bolt
5. Lower arm assembly

Toe control arm assembly removal steps

6. Toe control arm ball joint and knuckle connection
7. Toe control arm assembly mounting bolt
8. Toe control arm assembly

CR2039500065000X

Fig. 9 Lower arm replacement. AWD models

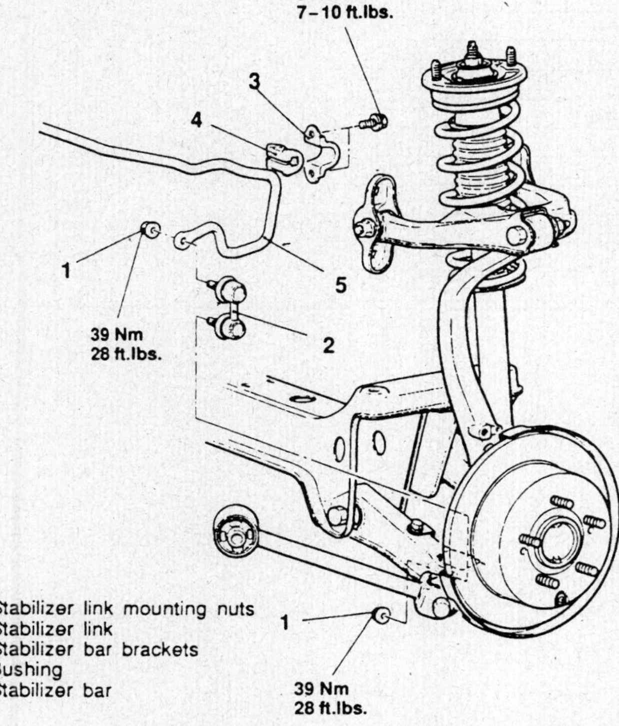

1. Stabilizer link mounting nuts
2. Stabilizer link
3. Stabilizer bar brackets
4. Bushing
5. Stabilizer bar

CR2039500067000X

Fig. 11 Stabilizer bar replacement. AWD models

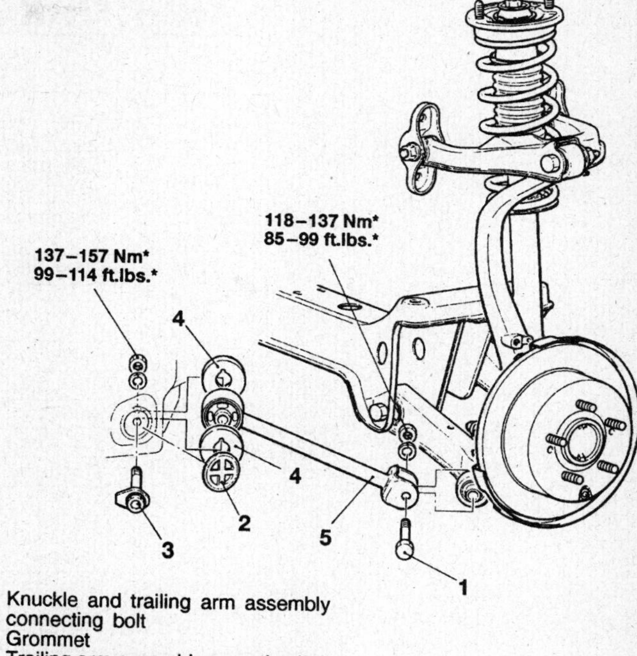

1. Knuckle and trailing arm assembly connecting bolt
2. Grommet
3. Trailing arm assembly mounting bolt
4. Stopper
5. Trailing arm assembly

CR2039500066000X

Fig. 10 Trailing arm assembly. AWD models

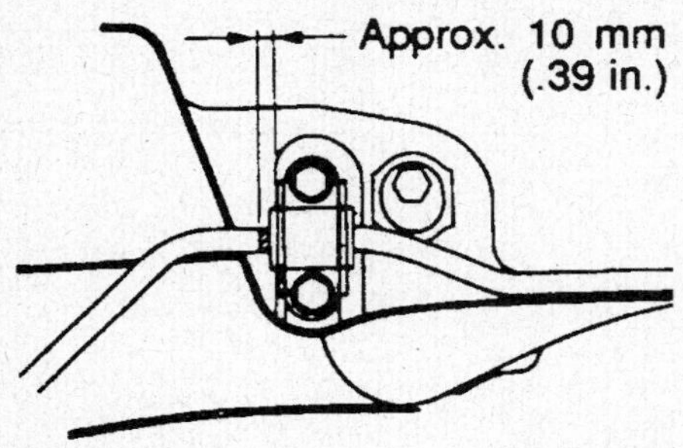

CR2039500068000X

Fig. 12 Stabilizer bar bushing alignment. AWD models

TIGHTENING SPECIFICATIONS

Year	Component	Torque/Ft. Lbs.
1998	Axle Nut	145–188
	Brake Caliper Assembly	36–43
	Differential Mounting Bracket To Crossmember	72
	Differential Mounting Bracket To Differential	65
	Differential Mount Support Bolts	33
	Driveshaft Nut	145-188
	Hub Nut	145–188
	Lower Arm To Crossmember	71
	Lower Arm To Knuckle	71–72
	Lower Shock Absorber Mounting Bolt	71–72
	Piston Rod Tightening Nut	16
	Propeller Shaft To Differential	22–25
	Rear Hub To Knuckle	54–65
	Stabilizer Bar Mounting Bracket	7–10
	Stabilizer Link To Lower Arm	28
	Stabilizer Link To Stabilizer Bar	28
	Toe Control Arm To Crossmember	50–56
	Toe Control Arm To Knuckle	20–21
	Trailing Arm To Body	99–114
	Trailing Arm To Knuckle	85–101
	Upper Arm Bracket To Body	28
	Upper Arm Bracket To Upper Arm	41
	Upper Arm To Knuckle	71
	Upper Shock Absorber Mounting Nut	32
	Wheel Lug Nut	88-108

Front Suspension & Steering

NOTE: On Air Bag Equipped Models, Refer To "Air Bag System Precautions" Located In The Front Of This Manual For System Disarming & Arming Procedures.

NOTE: Refer To "Computer Relearn Procedures" Located In The Front Of This Manual When Battery Power To The Computer Has Been Interrupted.

INDEX

WHEEL HUB & STEERING KNUCKLE

REPLACE

REMOVAL

Remove knuckle and hub assembly in numbered sequence, **Fig. 1,** noting the following:

1. Loosen driveshaft nut with vehicle on floor and brakes applied.
2. Loosen, but do not remove tie rod end nut.
3. Remove and suspend caliper assembly out of the way using a piece of wire.
4. Shift the knuckle to the outside in order to maintain the clearance between the front hub assembly mounting bolts and the driveshaft. **Do not damage the ball joint boot.**
5. **On models with ABS,** ensure to not damage rotor.

DISASSEMBLE & ASSEMBLE

The front hub assembly should not be disassembled. If required by damage or wear, it should be replaced.

Disassemble knuckle assembly in numbered sequence, **Fig. 2,** noting the following:

1. Loosen, but do not remove tie rod end nut.
2. Loosen, but do not remove compression lower arm nut.
3. Loosen, but do not remove lateral lower arm nut.

INSTALLATION

Reverse removal procedure to install, noting the following:

1. Ensure to install driveshaft washer as shown, **Fig. 3.**
2. After installing wheel, lower vehicle to ground, then final-tighten driveshaft nut.
3. If cotter pin holes do not line up, **torque** nut up to 188 ft. lbs.

BALL JOINT INSPECTION

Inspect ball joint for proper starting torque as follows:

1. Move ball joint stud from side to side several times.
2. Mount two nuts on ball joint, then using a suitable torque wrench measure starting torque.
3. Starting torque should be within 3–13 inch lbs. for upper arm ball joint, and 4–13 inch lbs. for stabilizer link ball joint.
4. If starting torque exceeds upper limit, replace lower arm assembly.
5. If starting torque is below lower limit, the ball joint may still be reused unless it has drag or excessive play.

STRUT

REPLACE

REMOVAL

Remove strut assembly in numbered sequence, **Fig. 4.**

DISASSEMBLE & ASSEMBLE

Disassemble strut in numbered sequence, **Fig. 5** noting the following:

1. Compress spring using spring compression tools No. MB991237 and MB991239, or equivalents, to ease in disassembly and assembly.

INSTALLATION

Reverse removal procedure to install, noting the following:

1. Ensure spring is properly seated in upper and lower spring seat when installing.
2. Install strut upper bracket as shown in **Fig. 6,** then tighten strut rod nut to specifications.

CONTROL ARM

REPLACE

LOWER

Remove compression and lateral lower control arms in numbered sequence, **Fig. 7,** noting the following:

1. Loosen but do not remove compression lower arm ball joint.
2. Inspect compression lower arm ball joint breakaway torque. This should be 4–22 inch lbs. If reading exceeds specified amount, replace lower arm assembly.
3. Loosen but do not remove knuckle/lateral lower arm ball joint.
4. Inspect lateral lower arm ball joint breakaway torque. This should be 9–30 inch lbs. If reading exceeds specified amount, replace lower arm assembly.

UPPER

Remove upper control arm in numbered sequence, **Fig. 8,** noting the following:

1. Use ball joint separator tool No. MB991113, or equivalent, to loosen, **but not remove,** tie rod end mounting nut.
2. Inspect ball joint as follows:
   a. Inspect ball joint starting torque, which should be within 3–22 inch lbs. Replace ball joint if torque exceeds specifications.
   b. Inspect ball joint dust cover, and replace control arm assembly if any cracks or tears are found.
   c. Install upper arm shaft assembly at angle shown, **Fig. 9.**
   d. When upper arm shaft is installed as shown, **Fig. 9,** inspect upper arm for bends or other damage, **Fig. 10.** Replace arm if needed.

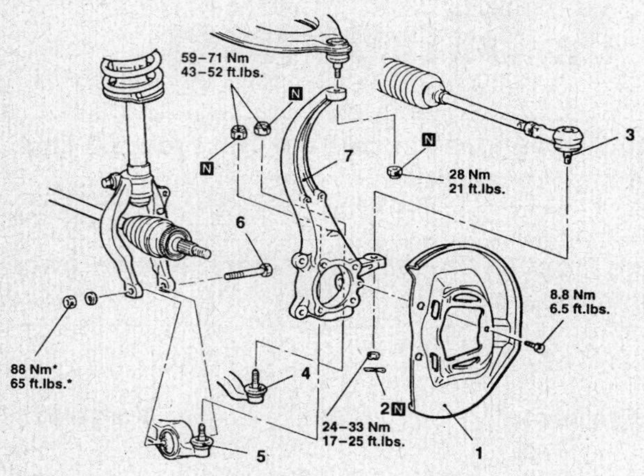

1. Dust shield
2. Cotter pin
3. Tie rod end ball joint and knuckle connection
4. Compression lower arm ball joint and knuckle connection
5. Lateral lower arm ball joint and knuckle connection
6. Connecting bolt of damper fork and lateral lower arm
7. Knuckle

Caution
*** : Indicates parts which should be temporarily tightened, and then fully tightened with the vehicles on the ground in the unladen condition.**

CR3039500360000A

Fig. 1 Hub & knuckle assembly removal

1. Cotter pin
2. Drive shaft nut
3. Tie rod end ball joint and knuckle connection
4. Stabilizer link ball joint and damper fork connection
5. Damper fork
6. Lateral lower arm ball joint and knuckle connection
7. Compression lower arm ball joint and knuckle connection
8. Drive shaft
9. Circlip

Caution
***: Indicates parts which should be temporarily tightened, and then fully tightened with the vehicles on the ground in the unladen condition.**

CR3039500361000A

Fig. 2 Knuckle assembly

3. Reverse procedure to install.

STABILIZER BAR

REPLACE

FWD MODELS

Remove stabilizer bar in numbered sequence, **Fig. 11,** noting the following:

1. Reverse procedure to install, noting the following:
   a. Set stabilizer bar so identification mark is at the left.
   b. Install bushing, ensure the dimension is as shown in **Fig. 12.**

AWD MODELS

1. Remove stabilizer bar in numbered sequence, **Fig. 11.**
2. Reverse procedure to install. Ensure stabilizer bar is set so identification mark is at the left. Install bushing, ensure the dimension is as shown in **Fig. 12.**

POWER STEERING GEAR

REPLACE

Remove rack and pinion in numbered sequence, **Fig.13,** noting the following:

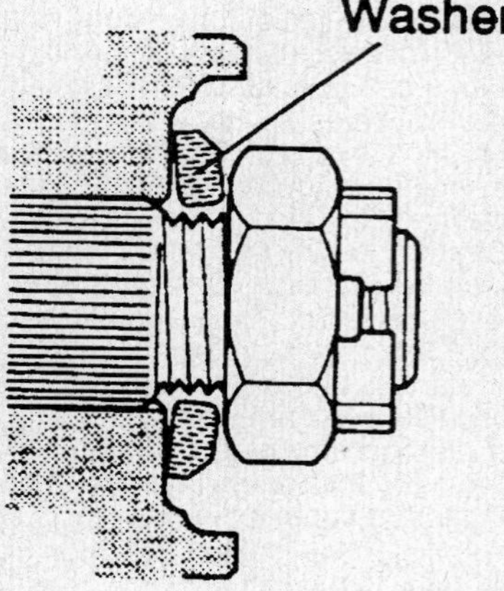

CR3039500362000X

Fig. 3 Driveshaft washer installation

1. Turn rack completely to righthand, the disconnect gearbox from crossmember.
2. While tilting gearbox downward, remove from lefthand side.
3. Reverse procedure to install.

POWER STEERING PUMP

REPLACE

Remove steering pump in numbered sequence, **Figs. 14 and 15** noting the following:

1. Remove reservoir cap and disconnect return hose to drain fluid.
2. Raise and support vehicle.
3. Cover alternator (located under oil pump) if any hoses are removed
4. Reverse procedure to install. Ensure oil pump is installed in position toward front of bracket. Adjust belt tension using air conditioning tension pulley.

MANUAL STEERING GEAR

REPLACE

Remove rack and pinion in numbered sequence, **Fig. 16,** noting the following:

1. Turn rack completely to right, the disconnect gearbox from crossmember.
2. While tilting gearbox downward, remove from lefthand side.
3. Reverse procedure to install.

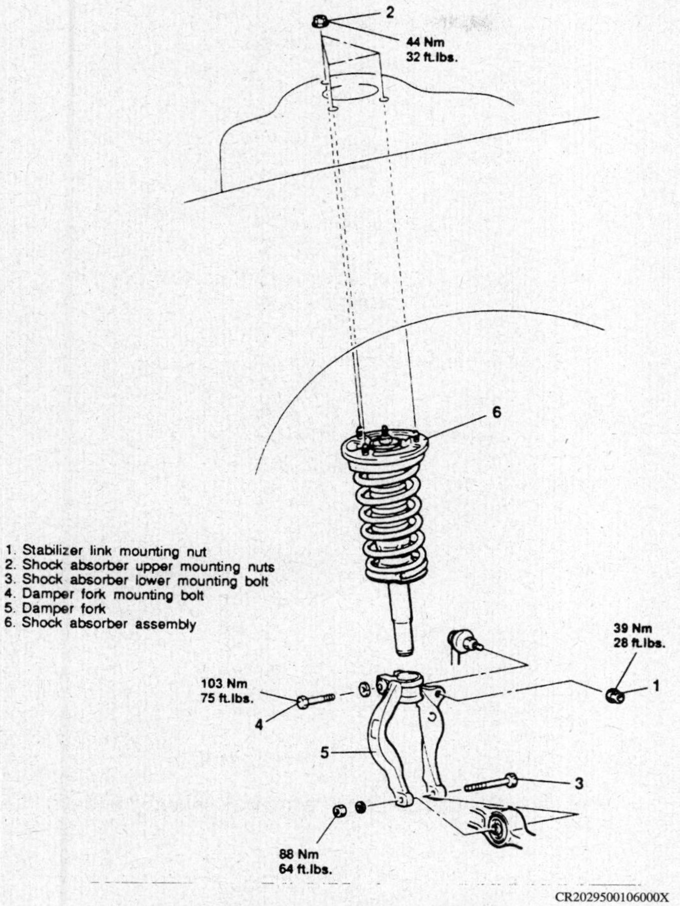

1. Stabilizer link mounting nut
2. Shock absorber upper mounting nuts
3. Shock absorber lower mounting bolt
4. Damper fork mounting bolt
5. Damper fork
6. Shock absorber assembly

CR2029500106000X

Fig. 4 Strut assembly removal

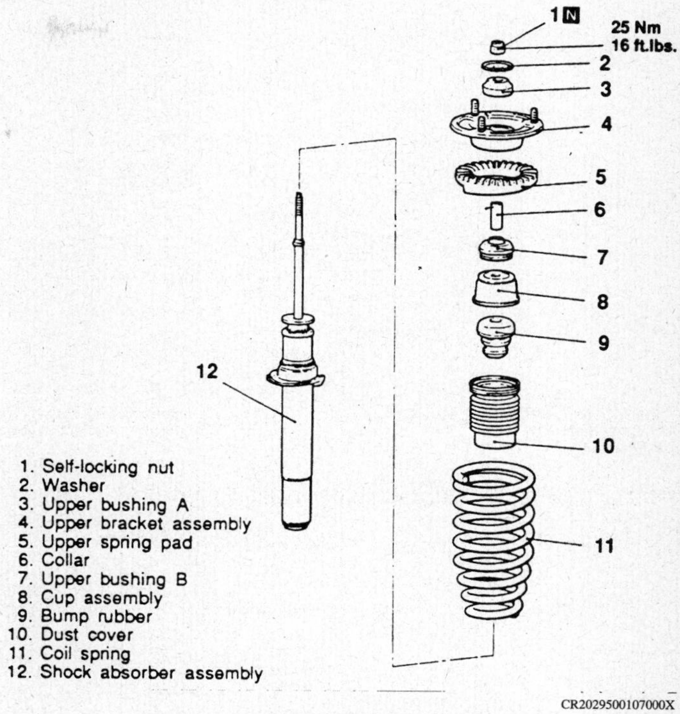

1. Self-locking nut
2. Washer
3. Upper bushing A
4. Upper bracket assembly
5. Upper spring pad
6. Collar
7. Upper bushing B
8. Cup assembly
9. Bump rubber
10. Dust cover
11. Coil spring
12. Shock absorber assembly

CR2029500107000X

Fig. 5 Strut disassembly

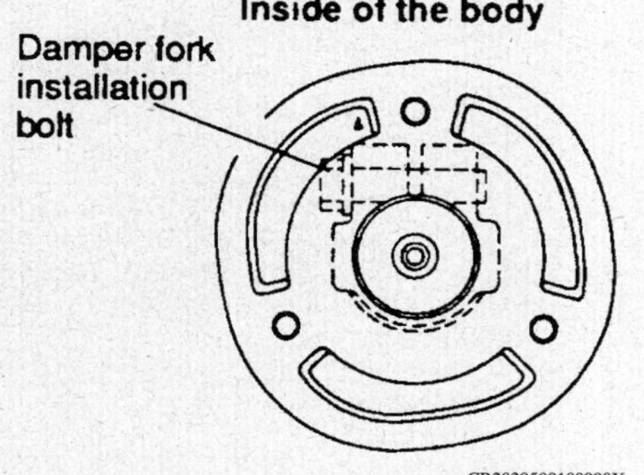

CR2029500108000X

Fig. 6 Upper bracket installation

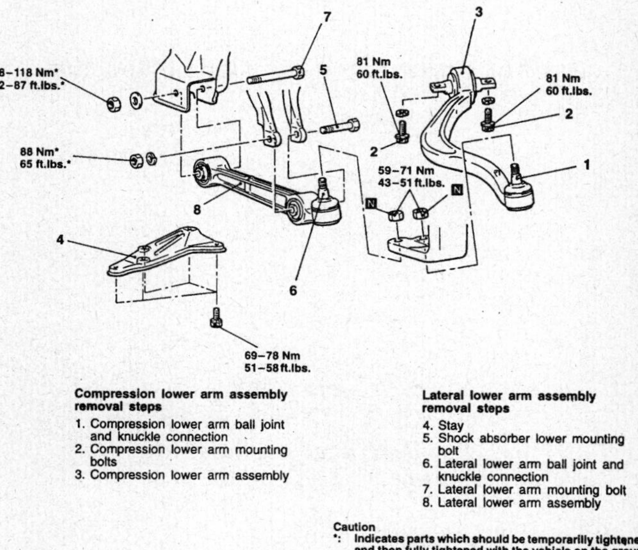

CR2029500109000A

Fig. 7 Compression & lateral lower arm assemblies

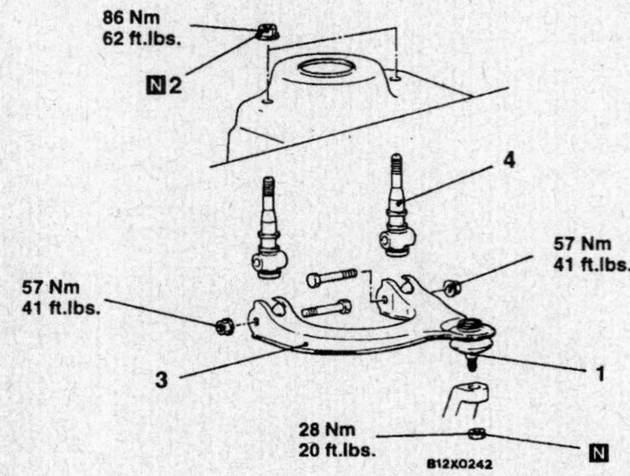

1. Upper arm ball joint and knuckle connection
2. Upper arm self-locking nut
3. Upper arm assembly
4. Upper arm shaft assembly

CR2029500144000X

Fig. 8 Upper control arm removal

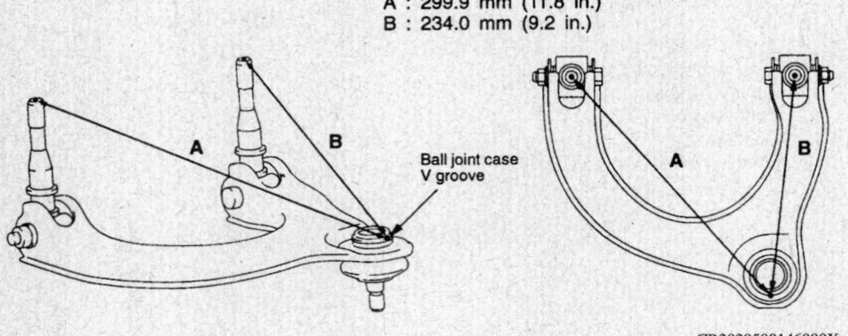

CR2029500146000X

Fig. 10 Upper arm dimensions inspection

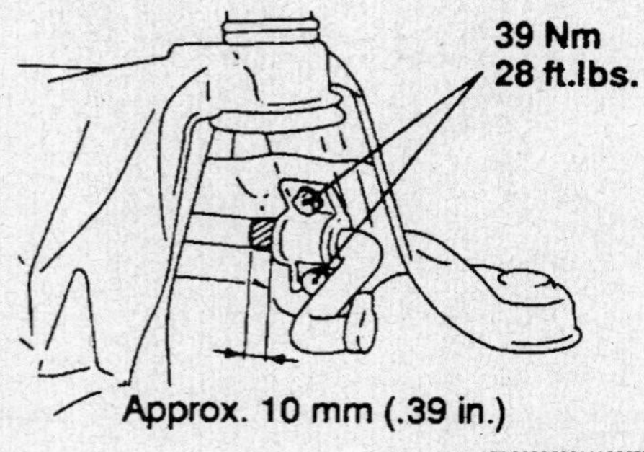

CR2029500111000X

Fig. 12 Stabilizer bar bushing alignment. FWD models

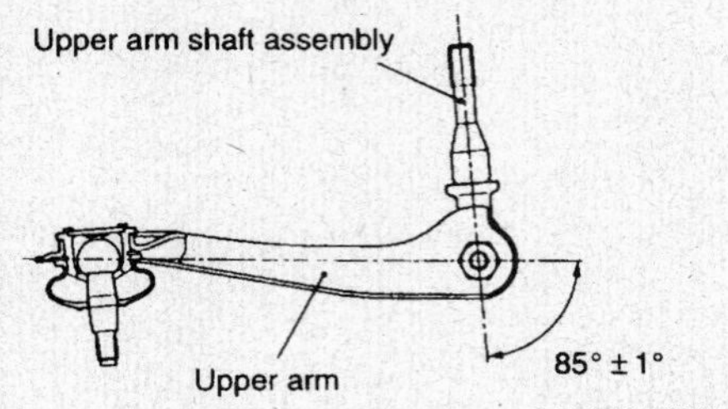

CR2029500145000X

Fig. 9 Upper arm shaft assembly installation

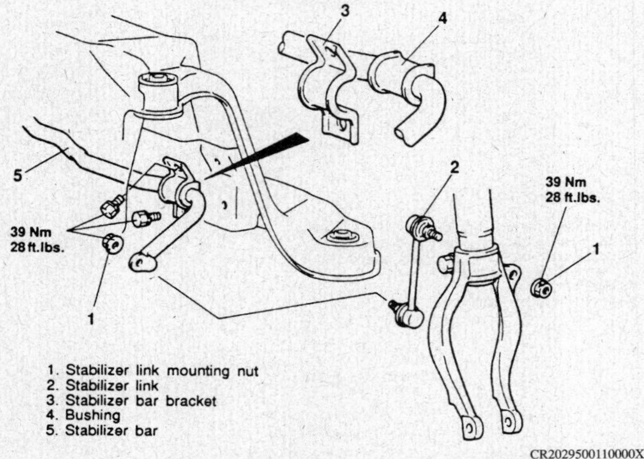

1. Stabilizer link mounting nut
2. Stabilizer link
3. Stabilizer bar bracket
4. Bushing
5. Stabilizer bar

CR2029500110000X

Fig. 11 Stabilizer bar removal. FWD models

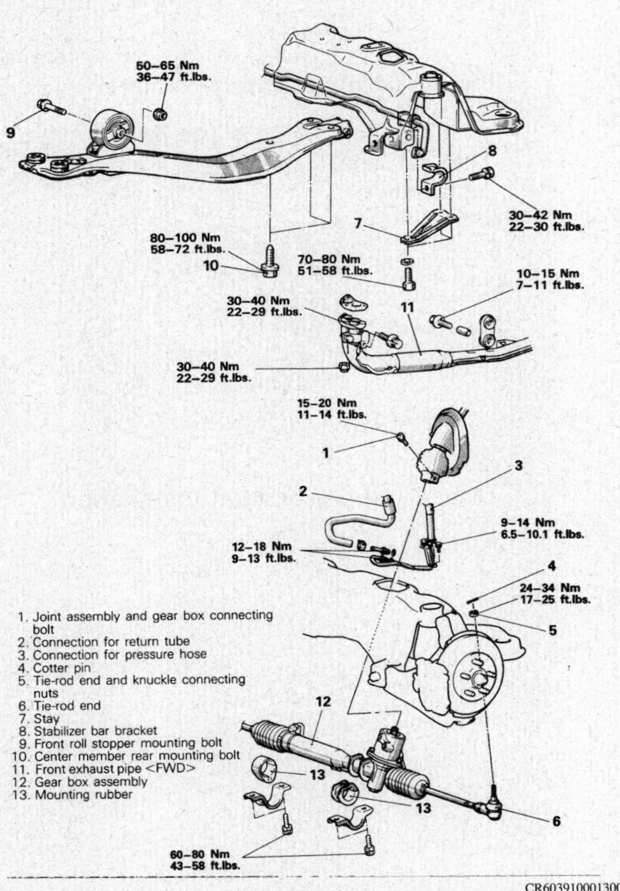

1. Joint assembly and gear box connecting bolt
2. Connection for return tube
3. Connection for pressure hose
4. Cotter pin
5. Tie-rod end and knuckle connecting nuts
6. Tie-rod end
7. Stay
8. Stabilizer bar bracket
9. Front roll stopper mounting bolt
10. Center member rear mounting bolt
11. Front exhaust pipe <FWD>
12. Gear box assembly
13. Mounting rubber

CR6039100013000X

Fig. 13 Power steering rack & pinion removal

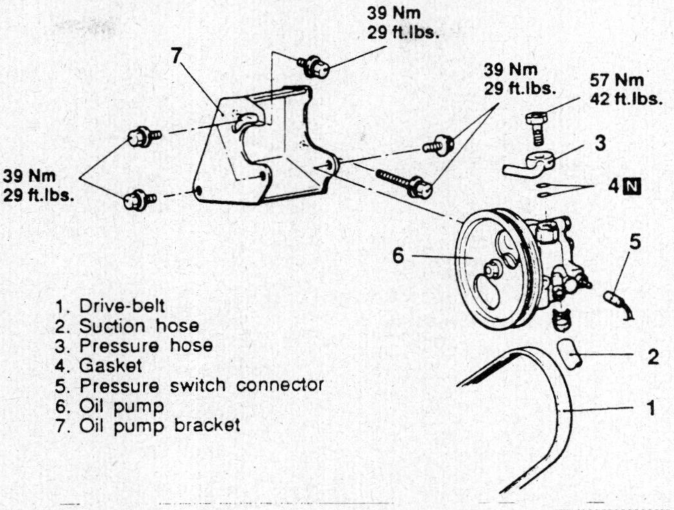

Fig. 14 Power steering pump removal. Non-turbocharged engine

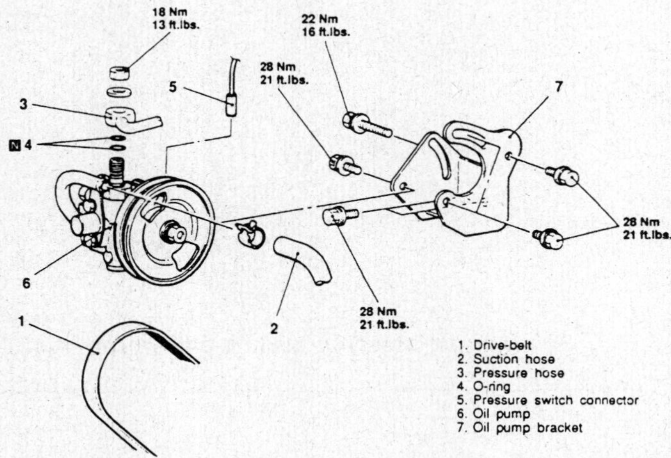

Fig. 15 Power steering pump removal. Turbocharged engine

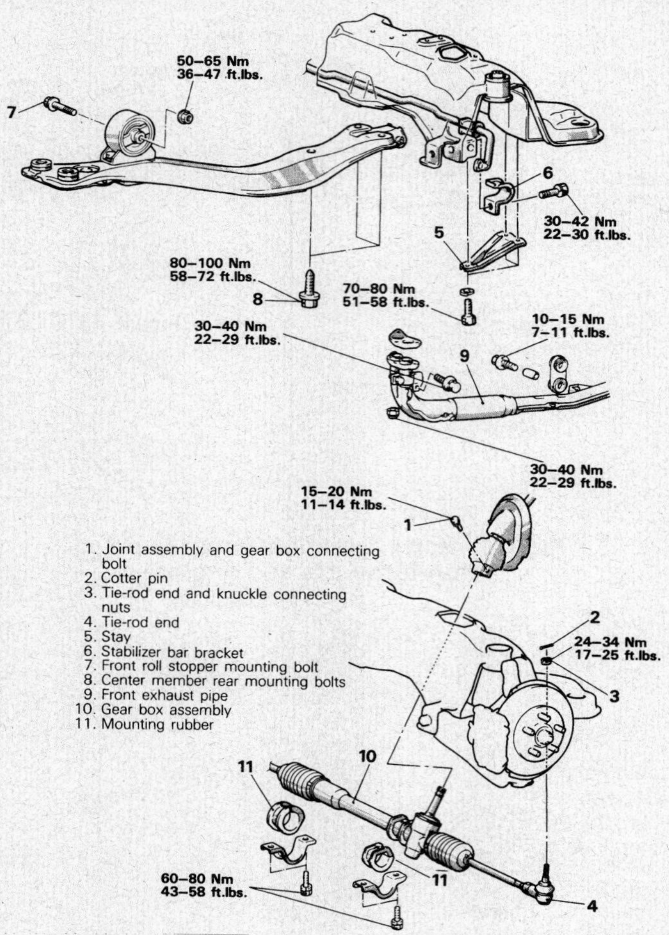
50–65 Nm
36–47 ft.lbs.
7
6
30–42 Nm
22–30 ft.lbs.
5
80–100 Nm
58–72 ft.lbs.
8
70–80 Nm
51–58 ft.lbs.
30–40 Nm
22–29 ft.lbs.
10–15 Nm
7–11 ft.lbs.
9
30–40 Nm
22–29 ft.lbs.
15–20 Nm
11–14 ft.lbs.
1
1. Joint assembly and gear box connecting bolt
2. Cotter pin
3. Tie-rod end and knuckle connecting nuts
4. Tie-rod end
5. Stay
6. Stabilizer bar bracket
7. Front roll stopper mounting bolt
8. Center member rear mounting bolts
9. Front exhaust pipe
10. Gear box assembly
11. Mounting rubber
2
24–34 Nm
17–25 ft.lbs.
3
11
10
60–80 Nm
43–58 ft.lbs.
11
4
CR6039100012000X

Fig. 16 Manual steering rack & pinion removal

TIGHTENING SPECIFICATIONS

Year	Component	Torque/Ft. Lbs.
1998	Axle Nut	145–188
	Caliper Assembly Mounting Bolt	65
	Center Member To Body	58–65
	Compression Lower Arm To Crossmember	60
	Compression Lower Arm To Knuckle	43–52
	Driveshaft Nut	145–188
	Dust Shield To Knuckle	78①
	Hub Assembly To Knuckle	65
	Hub Nut	145–188
	Joint Assembly & Gear Box Bolt	13
	Knuckle To Compression Lower Arm	43–52
	Knuckle Upper Mounting	21
	Lateral Lower Arm To Crossmember	71–85
	Lateral Lower Arm To Damper Fork	65
	Lateral Lower Arm To Knuckle	43–52
	Power Steering Brackets To Crossmember	51
	Power Steering Oil Pump To Bracket	21–29
	Power Steering Pipe Connections	11
	Power Steering Pressure Hose To Pump (Non-Turbo)	42
	Power Steering Pressure Hose To Pump (Turbo)	13
	Stabilizer Bar Bracket	28
	Stabilizer Link To Dampener Fork	28
	Stabilizer Link To Stabilizer Bar	28
	Stay To Crossmember	51–58
	Strut Lower Mounting	75
	Strut Top End Nut	16
	Strut Upper Mounting Nut	32
	Tie Rod End To Knuckle	17–25
	Upper Arm To Knuckle	17–25
	Wheel Lug Nuts	88–108

① — Inch lbs.

Wheel Alignment

INDEX

PRELIMINARY INSPECTION

1. Prior to wheel alignment, ensure tires are at recommended pressure, are of equal size and have approximately the same wear pattern.
2. Inspect front wheel and tire assembly for radial runout and inspect lower ball joints and steering linkage for looseness
3. Inspect front and rear springs for sagging or damage.
4. Front suspension inspections should be performed on a level floor or alignment rack with fuel tank at capacity and vehicle free of luggage and passenger compartment load. The vehicle should be bounced an equal number of times from the center of the bumper alternately, first from the rear, then the front, releasing at the bottom of down cycle.

FRONT WHEEL ALIGNMENT

CASTER & CAMBER

Caster and camber are preset at the factory and cannot be adjusted. If caster or camber are not within specifications, replace bent or damaged components.

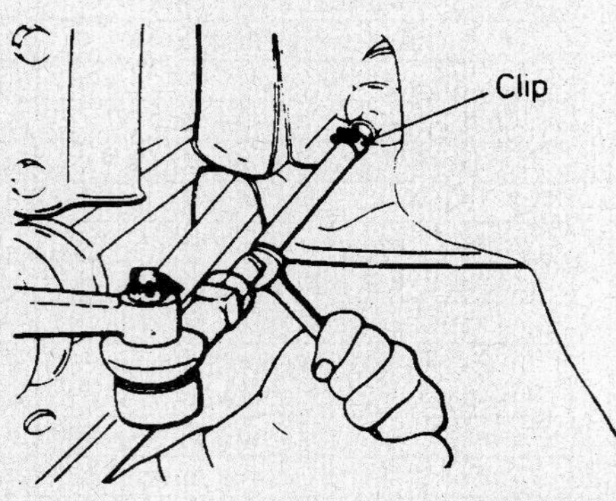

Fig. 1 Toe-in adjustment

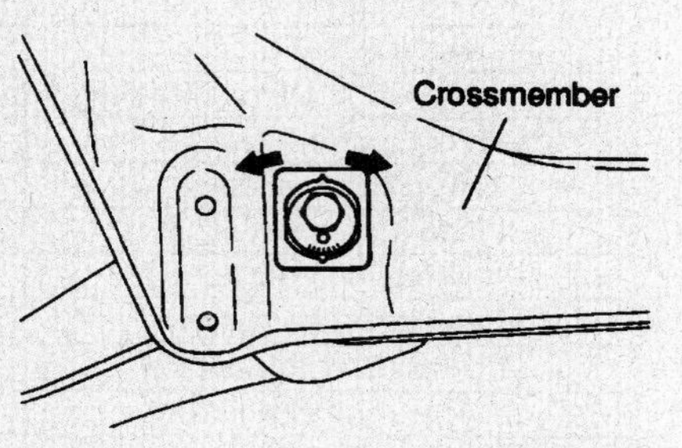

Fig. 2 Rear wheel toe-in adjustment

TOE-IN

Adjust toe-in by undoing clips and turning each tie rod turnbuckle an equal amount in opposite directions, **Fig. 1.** Toe will move out as the lefthand turnbuckle is turned toward front of vehicle and the righthand turnbuckle is turned toward rear of vehicle. For each half turn, toe-in will increase or decrease .24 inch.

REAR WHEEL ALIGNMENT

CAMBER

Camber is preset at the factory and cannot be adjusted. If camber is not within specifications, replace bent or damaged components.

TOE-IN

1. Measure toe-in using a toe-in gauge.
2. If toe-in is not within specifications, adjust by turning toe control arm mounting bolt on crossmember to left or right by equal amounts, **Fig. 2.**
3. Toe adjustments can be made at graduations of .05 inch.

AIR CONDITIONING

TABLE OF CONTENTS

System Testing

NOTE: On Air Bag Equipped Models, Refer To "Air Bag System Precautions" Located In The Front Of This Manual For System Disarming & Arming Procedures.

NOTE: Refer To "Computer Relearn Procedures" Located In The Front Of This Manual When Battery Power To The Computer Has Been Interrupted.

INDEX

PRECAUTIONS

BATTERY GROUND CABLE

Prior to service, disconnect battery ground cable and isolate as required.

R-134A SYSTEMS

R-134a refrigerant is a non-toxic, non-flammable, clear, colorless, odorless liquefied gas.

R-134a refrigerant is not compatible with R-12 refrigerant. Even small amounts of R-12 in an R-134a system will cause lubricant contamination, compressor failure, or improper A/C performance. Never add R-12 to an R-134a system.

New service ports have been added to the compressor to prevent charging the system with R-12 refrigerant. **R-134a systems require a special compressor lubricant. Use PAG compressor oil when servicing system.**

Avoid breathing A/C R-134a refrigerant and lubricant vapor or mist. Exposure may irritate eyes, nose and throat. Use only approved service equipment to discharge R-134a systems.

Always wear eye protection when servicing the air conditioning system. Serious injury may result from eye contact with refrigerant. If this happens, seek prompt medical attention.

EXERCISE SYSTEM

A/C units must be used periodically. Manufacturers caution that when the air conditioner is not used regularly, particularly during cold months, it should be turned on for a few minutes once every two or three weeks while the engine is running. This keeps the system in good operating condition.

Inspecting the system for effects of infrequent usage before the onset of summer is one of the most important aspects of A/C servicing.

First, clean out the condenser core, in all cases in front of the radiator. All obstructions such as leaves, bugs and dirt must be removed, as they will reduce heat transfer and impair the efficiency of the system. Ensure the space between the condenser and the radiator is also free of foreign matter.

Ensure evaporator water drain is open. The evaporator cools and dehumidifies the air before it enters the passenger compartment. At that point, the refrigerant is changed from a liquid to a vapor. As the core cools the air, moisture condenses on it but is prevented from collecting in the evaporator by the water drain.

PERFORMANCE TEST

Vehicle should not be in direct sunlight when performing this test.

AVENGER, SEBRING COUPE & 2001-02 SEBRING & STRATUS SEDAN

1. Connect manifold gauge set to vehicle, then start engine.
2. Set A/C controls as follows:
   a. A/C switch to MAX A/C.
   b. Mode selection to face position.
   c. Air to recirculation position.
   d. Temperature control to maximum cool.
   e. Blower on High.
3. Adjust idle to 1000 RPM with A/C clutch engaged. Engine should be at normal operating temperature. Doors and windows should be closed.
4. Insert thermometer in left center A/C outlet and operate the engine for 20 minutes.
5. **On models with 2.0L and 2.5L engines,** have A/C clutch engaged, compare discharge air temperature to A/C performance temperature charts as shown in **Figs. 1 and 2.**
6. **On 2001–02 Sebring and Stratus Sedan models,** evaporator inlet line

temperature should be no more than 10°F cooler than discharged air temperature.

7. **On all models,** if discharge air temperature fails to meet specifications, further diagnosis of air conditioning system should be performed.

TALON

1. Connect a suitable manifold gauge set and tachometer.
2. Set controls of air conditioner as follows:
   a. Air conditioning switch to A/C On position.
   b. Place mode selection lever in Face position.
   c. Place temperature control lever in Max. cooling position.
   d. Place air selection lever in Recirculation position.
   e. Place blower switch to high position.
3. Start engine, then adjust idle to 1000 RPM with compressor clutch engaged.
4. Vehicle doors should be closed, windows up and engine should be at normal operating temperature.
5. Insert a thermometer in the left center vent and allow engine to run for 20 minutes.
6. Note discharge temperature and compare with chart as shown in **Fig. 3. Reading should be taken with compressor clutch engaged.**

CONCORDE, INTREPID, LHS & 300M

1. Connect a suitable manifold gauge set and tachometer.
2. Start engine and hold at a steady 1000 RPM.
3. **On models with manual air conditioning,** set air conditioner controls as follows:
   a. Air conditioning switch to A/C On position.
   b. Place air selection lever in Panel-Recirculation position.
   c. Place temperature control lever in Max. cooling position.
   d. Place blower switch to High position.
4. **On models with automatic temperature control,** set controls of air conditioner as follows:
   a. Air conditioning switch to A/C On position.
   b. Rotate blower knob to High, full clockwise position.
   c. Rotate temperature control knob to full cool, counterclockwise position.
   d. Push panel mode button.
   e. Push Recirculation button. A/C and REC buttons should now be lit.
5. **On all models,** close all vehicle windows and doors, then allow engine to reach operating temperature.
6. Insert a thermometer in the lefthand center vent and allow engine to run for five minutes. The A/C clutch may cycle depending on ambient conditions.
7. Note discharge temperature and compare with chart as shown in **Figs. 4** .Reading should be taken with compressor clutch engaged.

Garage ambient temperature °C (°F)	20 (68)	25 (77)	35 (95)	40 (104)
Discharge air temperature °C (°F)	2.0–7.0 (36–45)	3.0–7.0 (37–45)	6.0 (43)	12 (54)
Compressor high pressure kPa (psi)	1,089–1,304 (158.0–189.2)	1,422–1,579 (206.3–229.1)	1,863 (270.3)	2,167 (314.4)
Compressor low pressure kPa (psi)	177–304 (25.7–44.1)	206–226 (29.9–32.8)	265 (38.4)	343 (49.8)

CR7029500259000X

Fig. 1 Performance temperature chart. Avenger & 1998–2000 Sebring Coupe w/2.0L engine

Garage ambient temperature °C (°F)	20 (68)	25 (77)	35 (95)	40 (104)
Discharge air temperature °C (°F)	2.5–5.0 (37–41)	3.0–6.0 (37–43)	3.5–7.5 (38–46)	4.0–8.0 (39–46)
Compressor high pressure kPa (psi)	892 (129.4)	892 (129.4)	1,422 (206.3)	1,824 (264.6)
Compressor low pressure kPa (psi)	186 (27.0)	186 (27.0)	206 (29.9)	275 (39.9)

CR7029500260000X

Fig. 2 Performance temperature chart. Avenger & 1998–2000 Sebring Coupe w/2.5L engine

Garage ambient temperature °C (°F)	20 (68)	25 (77)	35 (95)	40 (104)
Discharge air temperature °C (°F)	2.5–5.0 (37–41)	3.0–6.0 (37–43)	3.5–7.5 (38–46)	4.0–8.0 (39–46)
Compressor high pressure kPa (psi)	700–900 (101.6–130.6)	740–1,100 (107.4–159.6)	750–1,350 (108.8–195.4)	960–1,570 (139.3–227.8)
Compressor low pressure kPa (psi)	140 (20.3)	140–210 (20.3–30.5)	140–220 (20.3–31.9)	150–230 (21.8–33.4)

CR7029500261000X

Fig. 3 Performance temperature chart. Talon

BREEZE, CIRRUS, NEON & 1998–2000 SEBRING CONVERTIBLE & STRATUS

1. Connect a suitable manifold gauge set and tachometer.
2. Attach a suitable thermocouple to evaporator inlet line.
3. Set controls to PANEL, FULL COOL, RECIRC, HIGH BLOWER with A/C on.
4. Start engine, then adjust idle to 1000 RPM with compressor clutch engaged.
5. Vehicle doors should be closed, windows up and engine should be at normal operating temperature.
6. Insert a thermometer in the lefthand center vent and allow engine to run for five minutes. The A/C clutch may cycle depending on ambient conditions.
7. **On Breeze, Cirrus, Sebring Convertible and Stratus models,** compare discharge air temperature to evaporator inlet line temperature. The inlet line reading should not be more than 10°F cooler than discharge temperature.
8. **On Neon models,** note discharge temperature and compare with chart as shown in **Fig. 5. Reading should be taken with compressor clutch engaged.**

2001–02 SEBRING & STRATUS COUPE

1. Connect a suitable manifold gauge set and tachometer.
2. Start engine, then set A/C control as follows:
   a. A/C switch: A/C to ON position.
   b. Mode selection: FACE position.
   c. Temperature control: MAXIMUM COOLING position.
   d. Air selection: RECIRCULATION position.
   e. Blower switch.
3. Adjust engine speed to 1500 RPM with A/C clutch engaged.
4. Engine idle to normal operating temperature with doors and windows closed.
5. Insert thermometer in center air outlet and operate engine for 20 minutes.
6. Note discharge of air temperature. **If clutch cycles, take reading before clutch disengages,** as shown in **Fig. 6.**

LEAK TEST

Do not pressure test R-134a systems with compressed air. Some mixtures of air and R-134a have been shown to be combustible at higher pressures.

A leak detector designed for R-12 will not detect leaks in an R-134a system.

Park vehicle in a wind-free work area, then proceed as follows:

1. Inspect charge level as described under "Performance Test" in this section.
2. When performing this test with original discharge pressure less than 30 psi, reclaim remaining refrigerant, then

AMBIENT TEMPERATURE	21°C (70°F)	26.5°C (80°F)	32.5°C (90°F)	37°C (100°F)	43°C (110°F)
MAXIMUM ALLOWABLE AIR TEMPERATURE AT CENTER LEFT PANEL OUTLET	6°C (42°F)	7°C (45°F)	10°C (50°F)	12°C (54°F)	15°C (59°F)
COMPRESSOR DISCHARGE PRESSURE	1379–1585 kPa (200–230 psi)	1448–1723 kPa (210–250 psi)	1654–1930 kPa (240–280 psi)	1930–2206 kPa (280–320 psi)	2206–2516 kPa (320–365 psi)
COMPRESSOR SUCTION PRESSURE	103–172 kPa (15–25 psi)	139–208 kPa (20–30 psi)	172–241 kPa (25–35 psi)	208–276 kPa (30–40 psi)	241–310 kPa (35–45 psi)

CR7029900528000X

Fig. 4 Performance temperature chart. 1998–2002 Concorde, Intrepid, LHS & 300M

Ambient Temperature	21°C (70°F)	26.5°C (80°F)	32°C (90°F)	37°C (100°F)	43°C (110°F)
Air Temperature at Left Center Panel Outlet	1-8°C (34-46°F)	3-9°C (37-49°F)	4-10°C (39-50°F)	6-11°C (43-52°F)	7-18°C (45-65°F)
Compressor Discharge Pressure After the Filter Drier	1034-1724 kPa (150-250 PSI)	1517-2275 kPa (220-330 PSI	1999-2620 kPa (290-380 PSI)	2068-2965 kPa (300-430 PSI)	2275-3421 kPa (330-496 PSI)
Evaporator Suction Pressure	103-207 kPa (15-30 PSI)	117-221 kPa (17-32 PSI)	138-241 kpa (20-35 PSI)	172-269 kpa (25-39 PSI)	207-345 kPa (30-50 PSI)

CR7020000584000X

Fig. 5 Performance temperature chart. Neon

GARAGE AMBIENT TEMPERATURE °C (°F)	20 (68)	25 (77)	35 (95)	40 (104)
Discharge air temperature °C (°F)	5.0 - 10.0 (42 - 50)	6.0 - 10.5 (43 - 51)	7.5 - 12.0 (46 - 54)	7.5 - 12.5 (46 - 55)
Compressor high pressure kPa (psi)	1,540 - 1,935 (224 - 281)	1,618 - 2,000 (235 - 290)	2,070 - 2,205 (301 - 320)	2,140 - 2,620 (311 - 380)
Compressor low pressure kPa (psi)	125 - 155 (18 - 23)	125 - 155 (18 - 23)	150 - 180 (22 - 26)	145 - 190 (21 - 28)

CR7020000626000X

Fig. 6 Performance temperature chart. 2001–02 Sebring & Stratus Coupe

connect suitable vacuum pump and evacuate system to lowest vacuum possible.

3. Ensure system holds vacuum reading for at least 15 minutes. If system holds vacuum for 15 minutes a leak is probably not present. If vacuum did not hold for 15 minutes proceed as follows:
   a. Ensure transaxle is in Park.
   b. Run engine for five minutes, then ensure engine is idling at 700 RPM.
   c. Charge system with 10 ounces of R-134a refrigerant.
   d. Set A/C control to 100% outside air.
   e. Set panel mode to full cool.
   f. Set blower to high speed.
   g. Place A/C button in ON position.
   h. Open vehicle windows.
4. Turn engine Off, wait approximately 5 minutes, then use a suitable electronic leak detector designed for R-134a refrigerant systems and inspect system for leakage. If a leak is found repair as required. If no leak was found fill system as outlined under "Performance Test" in this section.

DISCHARGING SYSTEM

The use of refrigerant recovery and recycling stations allows the recovery and reuse of refrigerant after contaminants and moisture have been removed.

When using a recovery or recycling station, follow the manufacturer's operating instructions, noting the following:

1. **Use extreme caution and observe all safety and service precautions related to use of refrigerants.**
2. Connect refrigerant recycling station hose(s) to vehicle A/C service port(s) and recovery station inlet fitting. Hoses used should have shutoff devices or check valve within 12 inches of hose ends to minimize introduction of air into recycling station and to minimize amount of refrigerant released when hose(s) is disconnected.
3. Turn recycling station On to start recovery process. Allow recycling station to pump refrigerant from A/C system until station pressure gauge indicates vacuum. Vacuum gauge should read 26 inches for at least 45 minutes.
4. After vehicle A/C system has been evacuated, close station inlet valve, if equipped.
5. Turn station Off. With some stations, pump will automatically be turned Off by a low pressure switch.
6. Allow vehicle A/C system to remain closed for approximately two minutes. Observe vacuum level indicated on gauge. If pressure does not rise, disconnect recycling station hose(s).
7. If system pressure rises, repeat steps 3 through 6 until vacuum level remains stable for two minutes.
8. Service A/C system as required, then evacuate and recharge A/C system.

SYSTEM EVACUATION

USING VACUUM PUMP

Vacuum pumps suitable for removing air and moisture from A/C systems are commercially available. A specification for system pump-down used here is 26–29½ inches of vacuum. This reading can be attained at or near sea level only. For each 1000 feet of altitude this operation is being performed, the vacuum reading will be 1 inch lower. As an example, at 5000 feet elevation, only 21–24½ inches of vacuum can be obtained.

The system must be completely discharged before it can be evacuated. Damage to vacuum pump may result if pressurized refrigerant is allowed to enter.

1. With gauges connected into system, remove cap from vacuum hose connector. Install center hose from gauge manifold to vacuum pump connector. Mid-position the high and low side compressor service valves (if used). Open high and low side gauge manifold hand valves.
2. Operate vacuum pump a minimum of 30 minutes for air and moisture removal. Watch compound gauge that system pumps down into a vacuum. System will reach 26–29½ inches vacuum in 5 minutes or less. If system does not pump down, inspect all connections and leak-test if required.
3. Close gauge manifold hand valves and shutoff vacuum pump.
4. Inspect ability of system to hold vacuum. Watch compound gauge to ensure gauge does not rise at a faster rate than 1 inch of vacuum every 4 or 5 minutes. If compound gauge rises at too rapid a rate, install partial charge and leak-test, then evacuate system as outlined above.
5. If system holds vacuum, charge system with refrigerant.

USING CHARGING STATION

On systems using R-134a refrigerant use a charging station designed for R-134a refrigerant systems.

A vacuum pump is built into the charging station and is constructed to withstand repeated and prolonged use without damage. Complete moisture removal from the system is possible only with a vacuum pump constructed for the purpose.

The system must be completely discharged before it can be evacuated. Damage to the vacuum pump may result if pressurized refrigerant is allowed to enter.

1. Connect hose to vacuum pump if system was discharged through charging station.
2. Open high and low side gauge valves of charging station.
3. Connect station to proper electrical outlet.
4. Engage "Off-On" switch to vacuum pump according to directions of specific station being used.
5. System should pump down into a 28–29½ inches vacuum in 5 minutes or less. If system fails to meet this specification, repair as required.
6. Operate pump a minimum of 30 minutes to remove all air and moisture.
7. Close high and low side gauge valves. Open switch to turn off pump.
8. Inspect ability of system to hold vacuum by watching compound gauge to ensure it does not rise at a rate higher than 1 inch of vacuum every 4 or 5 minutes. If rise rate is not within specifications, repair system as required. If rise rate is within specifications, charge system with refrigerant.

CHARGING SYSTEM

AVENGER, TALON & 1998–2000 SEBRING COUPE

Never use cans to charge into high pressure side of system (compressor

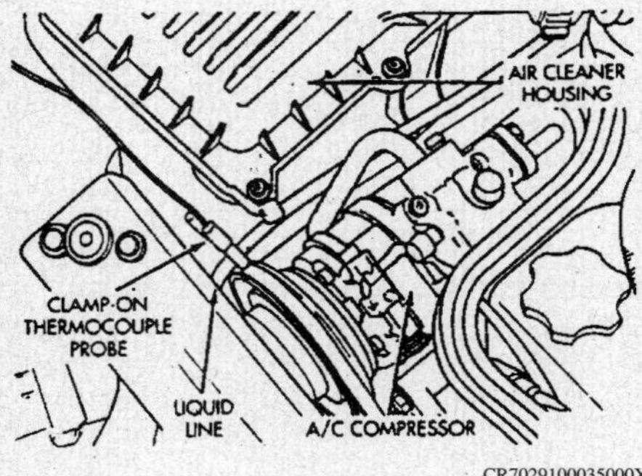

Fig. 7 Thermocouple clamp attachment to liquid line. Concorde, Intrepid, LHS & 300M

discharge port) or into system at high temperature, as high system pressure transferred into charging can may cause it to explode.

1. Attach center hose from manifold gauge set to refrigerant dispensing manifold. Turn refrigerant manifold valves completely counterclockwise to open fully, and remove protective caps from refrigerant manifold.
2. Screw refrigerant cans into manifold. Ensure gasket is in place and in good condition. **Torque** can and manifold nuts to 72–96 inch lbs.
3. Turn refrigerant manifold valves clockwise to puncture cans and close manifold valves.
4. Loosen charging hose at gauge set manifold and turn a refrigerant valve counterclockwise to release refrigerant and purge air from charging hose. When refrigerant gas escapes from loose connection, tighten hose again.
5. Fully open all refrigerant manifold valves being used and place refrigerant cans into pan of hot water at 125°F to aid transfer of refrigerant gas. **Do not heat refrigerant cans over 125°F as they may explode. Place water pan and refrigerant cans on scale and note weight.**
6. Start engine and turn A/C On, then index blower switch to low position.
7. Low pressure cutout switch will prevent clutch from engaging until refrigerant is added to system. If clutch does engage, replace switch before continuing.
8. Charge through suction side of system by slowly opening suction manifold valve. Adjust valve so charging pressure does not exceed 50 psi.
9. Adjust engine speed to fast idle of 1400–1550 RPM.
10. After specified refrigerant charge has entered system, close gauge set manifold valves and refrigerant manifold valves, then connect wiring.

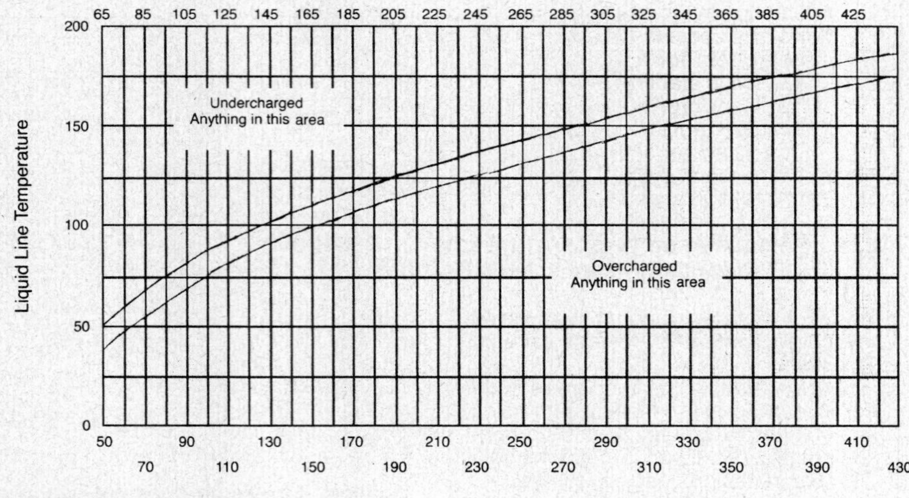

Fig. 8 Charge determination chart. 1998–2001 Concorde, Intrepid, LHS & 300M

CONCORDE, INTREPID, LHS & 300M

1. Connect suitable pressure gauge to discharge side of compressor, then attach clamp on thermocouple part No. PSE 66-324-0014, 80PK-1A, or equivalent, to liquid line as shown in **Fig. 7.** It must be attached as close to condenser as possible to read liquid line temperature.
2. With transaxle in Park and engine idling at 700 RPM, set air conditioning controls as follows:
   a. A/C control set to outside air.
   b. Set panel mode to full cool.
   c. Blower to high speed.
   d. A/C button in On position.
   e. **On models equipped with ATC,** turn Recirc button Off.
3. **On all models,** open all vehicle windows, operate system and allow to stabilize, then set system pressure to 260 psi by placing a piece of cardboard over part of condenser to obtain specified gauge reading.
4. Observe discharge pressure and liquid line temperature, then refer to charge determination graph as shown in **Fig. 8,** to determine system charge.
5. If charge is not within specification, add or reclaim two ounces of refrigerant at a time, then read gauge pressure and liquid line temperature. Continue procedure until proper charge area on chart determination graph is obtained as shown in **Fig. 8.**

BREEZE, CIRRUS & 1998–2000 SEBRING CONVERTIBLE & STRATUS

This test can be accomplished using a manifold gauge set or a DRB scan tool.

1. Connect a manifold gauge set to discharge side of compressor or connect a DRB, or equivalent, scan tool, to Diagnostic Link Connector (DLC) and set scan tool to "Partial Charge Test."
2. Attach a clamp on thermocouple part No. PSE 66-324-0014, or equivalent, onto liquid line as close to condenser outlet as possible, to observe liquid line temperature.
3. With transaxle in Park, engine idling at 700 RPM and windows open, set air conditioning controls as follows:
   a. Controls set to "Outside Air."
   b. Panel mode to full cool.
   c. Blower on high.
   d. A/C button in ON position.
4. Operate system for a couple of minutes to allow system to stabilize.
5. Set system pressure to about 260 psi, by blocking off airflow to front grille area. This will maintain a constant pressure and stop the cooling fans from alternating between high and low speeds.
6. **When using a manifold gauge set,** proceed as follows:
   a. Observe discharge pressure and liquid line temperature, using graph as shown in **Fig. 9,** to determine where the system is currently operating.
   b. If system is in undercharged region of graph, add two ounces of refrigerant to system and inspect readings again.
   c. If system is in overcharged region of graph, drain two ounces of refrigerant from system and inspect readings again.
   d. Repeat steps "b" and "c" until readings are within proper operating range.
7. **When using a DRB, or equivalent, scan tool,** it is not necessary to use a graph. Scan tool will calculate proper liquid line temperature automatically.

NEON

1. Connect suitable pressure gauge to discharge side of compressor, then attach thermocouple part No. PSE 66-324-0014, or equivalent, to liquid line as close to filter-dryer as possible.
2. With transaxle in Park and engine idling, set air conditioning controls as follows:
   a. A/C control set to outside air.
   b. Set panel mode to full cool.
   c. Blower to high speed.

d. A/C button in On position, with windows and doors closed.
3. Operate system for a few minutes to allow system to stabilize.
4. Observe filter-dryer pressure and liquid line temperature.
5. Using the chart as shown in **Fig. 10,** determine where system is currently operating. If the system is not in the proper range, reclaim all the refrigerant and recharge per A/C label, using suitable refrigerant recovery and charging equipment.

2001-02 SEBRING & STRATUS

Coupe

Use the refrigerant recovery station to discharge and charge the refrigerant gas from system, following instruction manual for operation of station.

Sedan

This A/C system does not have or use a sight glass to check or charge system. After system has been tested for leaks and evacuated, a charge can be injected into system.

1. If using a separate vacuum pump, close all valves before disconnecting pump. Connect manifold gauge set to A/C service ports.
2. Verify refrigerant capacities, refer to equipment instructions to proceed.
3. Ensure engine is shut off. Open suction and discharge valves.
4. Open charge valve to allow refrigerant into system, when refrigerant has stopped, close suction and discharge valves.
5. If all of charge did not transfer from dispensing device, place vehicle controls as follows:
   a. Automatic transaxle in park or manual transmission in neutral.
   b. Engine idling at 700 RPM.
   c. A/C control set in 100% outside air.
   d. Panel mode.
   e. Blower motor ON high speed.
   f. Vehicle windows closed.
6. If A/C compressor does not engage, test compressor clutch control circuit and correct ant failure.
7. Open suction valve to allow remaining refrigerant to transfer into system. **Do not open discharge (high-pressure) valve at this time.**
8. Close all valves and test A/C system.
9. Disconnect charging station or manifold gauge, install service port caps.

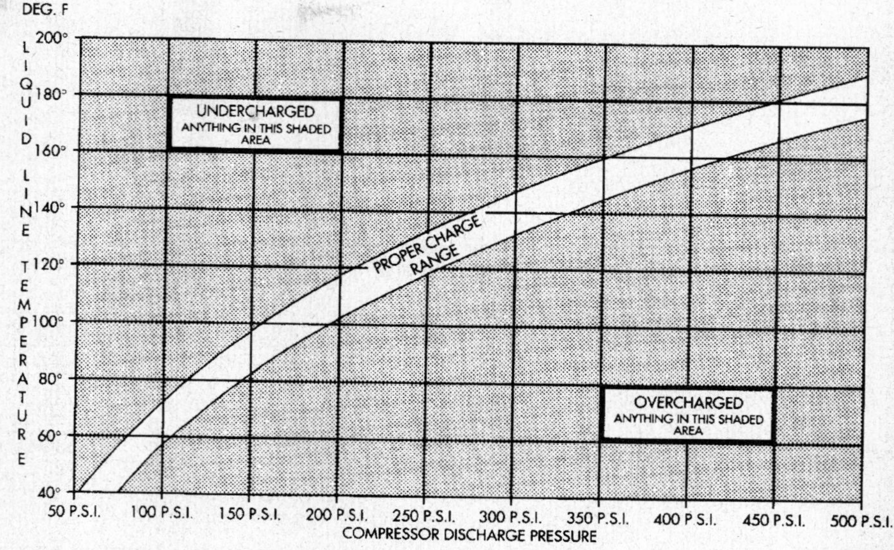

Fig. 9 Charge determination chart. Breeze, Cirrus, Stratus & 1998–99 Sebring Convertible

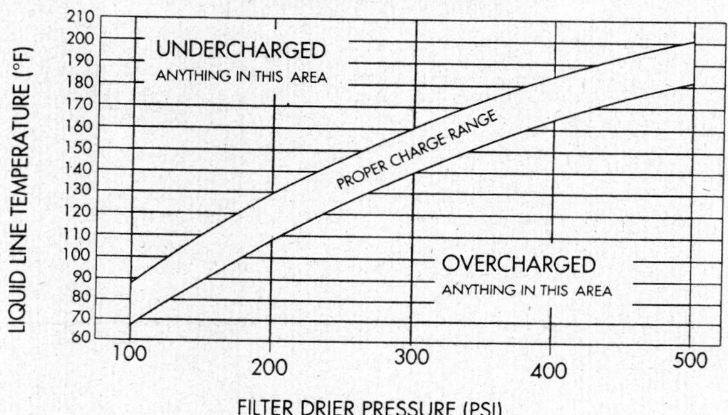

Fig. 10 Charge determination chart. Neon

System Service

INDEX

OIL CHARGE

Model	Year	Compressor	Component	Oil①④
Avenger & Sebring Coupe	1998	10PA17C⑤	Condenser	1.35
			Evaporator	1.35
			Lines	.34
			Receiver-Dryer	.34
	1998–2000	MSC105CVS⑥	Condenser	.51
			Evaporator	2.03
			Lines	.34
			Receiver-Dryer	.34
Breeze, Cirrus & Stratus	1998–2000	TRS90	Condenser	1.0
			Evaporator	2.0
			Line	1.5
			Receiver-Dryer	1.0
Sebring & Stratus Coupe	2001–02	Scroll Type MSC90C	Condenser	.5
			Evaporator	2.0
			Lines	.3
			Receiver	.3
Sebring & Stratus Sedan	2001–02	Sanden TRS-090 Scroll Type	Condenser	1.0
			Evaporator	2.0
			Filter/Drier	1.0
			Lines	1.5
Sebring Convertible	1998–2002	Sanden TRS-090 Scroll Type	Condenser	1.0
			Evaporator	2.0
			Filter/Drier	1.0
			Lines	1.5
Concorde, Intrepid, LHS & 300M②	1998–2002	10PA17–R134a③	Condenser	1.0
			Evaporator	2.0
			Lines	1.5
			Receiver-Dryer	1.0
Neon	1998–99	10PA17-R-134a③	Condenser	1.0
			Evaporator	2.0
			Lines	1.5
			Receiver-Dryer	1.0
	2000–01	Nippondenso 10S17	Condenser	1.0
			Evaporator	2.0
			Lines	1.5
			Receiver-Dryer	1.0
	2002	Nippondenso 10S15	Condenser	1.0
			Evaporator	2.0
			Lines	1.5
			Receiver-Dryer	1.0

Continued

OIL CHARGE—Continued

Model	Year	Compressor	Component	Oil①④
Talon	1998	10PA17C⑦	Condenser	1.35
			Evaporator	1.35
			Lines	.34
			Receiver-Dryer	.34
		MSC105CVS⑧	Condenser	.51
			Evaporator	2.03
			Lines	.34
			Receiver-Dryer	.34

① — Ounces.
② — When components of an A/C system utilizing R-134a refrigerant are replaced, use only ND8 PSG compressor oil No. 82300101, or equivalent.
③ — The 10PA17–R12 compressor looks the same & has the same bolt pattern as the 10PA17–R134a compressor. Ensure proper compressor is used when replacement is required.
④ — Refer to A/C Specifications for refrigerant oil type.
⑤ — 2.0L engine.
⑥ — 2.5L engine.
⑦ — Less turbocharged engine.
⑧ — Turbocharged engine.

OIL LEVEL CHECK

The oil level of these compressors should be inspected whenever refrigerant has been lost due to leakage or through normal system servicing.

Specifications

INDEX

A/C SPECIFICATIONS

Year	Model	Refrigerant		Viscosity	Total System Capacity, Ounces	Compressor Oil Check	Compressor Clutch Air Gap, Inch
		Capacity, Lbs.	Type				
1998	Avenger DOHC	1.54–1.63	R-134a	ND8 PAG	2.7	①	.016–.024
	Avenger SOHC	1.54–1.63	R-134a	SUN PAG 56	5.7	①	.016–.024
	Breeze	1.63	R-134a	ND8 PAG	5.0	①	.013–.025
	Cirrus	1.63	R-134a	ND8 PAG	5.0	①	.013–.025
	Concorde	1.56	R-134a	ND8 PAG	5.0	①	.014–.026
	Intrepid	1.56	R-134a	ND8 PAG	5.0	①	.014–.026
	Neon	1.57	R-134a	ND8 PAG	6.8	①	.014–.026
	Sebring Coupe DOHC	1.54–1.63	R-134a	ND8 PAG	2.7	①	.016–.024
	Sebring Coupe SOHC	1.54–1.63	R-134a	SUN PAG 56	5.7	①	.016–.024
	Sebring Convertible	1.75	R-134a	ND8 PAG	5.0	①	.013–.025
	Stratus	1.63	R-134a	ND8 PAG	5.0	①	.013–.025
	Talon Non-Turbocharged Engine	1.54–1.63	R-134a	ND8 PAG	2.7	①	.014–.026
	Talon w/Turbocharged Engine	1.54–1.63	R-134a	SUN PAG 56	5.7	①	.016–.026
1999	Avenger DOHC	1.54–1.63	R-134a	ND8 PAG	2.7	①	.016–.024
	Avenger SOHC	1.54–1.63	R-134a	SUN PAG 56	5.7	①	.016–.024
	Breeze	1.25	R-134a	ND8 PAG	5.0	①	.013–.025
	Cirrus	1.25	R-134a	ND8 PAG	5.0	①	.013–.025
	Concorde	1.56	R-134a	ND8 PAG	5.0	①	.014–.026
	Intrepid	1.56	R-134a	ND8 PAG	5.0	①	.014–.026
	LHS	1.56	R-134a	ND8 PAG	5.0	①	.014–.026
	Neon	1.57	R-134a	ND8 PAG	6.8	①	.014–.026
	Sebring Convertible	1.75	R-134a	ND8 PAG	5.0	①	.013–.025
	Sebring Coupe DOHC	1.54–1.63	R-134a	ND8 PAG	2.7	①	.016–.024
	Sebring Coupe SOHC	1.54–1.63	R-143a	SUN PAG 56	5.7	①	.016–.024
	Stratus	1.25	R-134a	ND8 PAG	5.0	①	.013–.025
	300M	1.56	R-134a	ND8 PAG	5.0	①	.014–.026

Continued

A/C SPECIFICATIONS—Continued

Year	Model	Refrigerant Capacity, Lbs.	Refrigerant Type	Viscosity	Total System Capacity, Ounces	Compressor Oil Check	Compressor Clutch Air Gap, Inch
2000	Avenger SOHC	1.54–1.63	R-134a	SUN PAG 56	5.7	①	.016–.024
	Breeze	1.19	R-134a	SP-15 PAG	5.0	①	.016–.031
	Cirrus	1.19	R-134a	SP-15 PAG	5.0	①	.016–.031
	Concorde	1.56	R-134a	ND8 PAG	5.0	①	.014–.026
	Intrepid	1.56	R-134a	ND8 PAG	5.0	①	.014–.026
	LHS	1.56	R-134a	ND8 PAG	5.0	①	.014–.026
	Neon	1.69	R-134a	ND8 PAG	6.1	①	.014–.026
	Sebring Convertible	1.75	R-134a	ND8 PAG	5.0	①	.013–.025
	Sebring Coupe SOHC	1.54–1.63	R-134a	SUN PAG 56	5.7	①	.016–.024
	Stratus	1.19	R-134a	SP-15 PAG	5.0	①	.016–.031
	300M	1.56	R-134a	ND8 PAG	5.0	①	.014–.026
2001–02	Concorde	1.56	R-134a	ND8 PAG	5.0	①	.014–.026
	Intrepid	1.56	R-134a	ND8 PAG	5.0	①	.014–.026
	LHS	1.56	R-134a	ND8 PAG	5.0	①	.014–.026
	Neon	1.69	R-134a	ND8 PAG	6.1	①	.014–.026
	Sebring Convertible	③	R134a	SP-15 PAG	5.0	②	.016–.031
	Sebring/Stratus Coupe	1.54–1.63	R-134a	SUN PAG 56	5.1	①	②
	Sebring/Stratus Sedan	1.69	R-134a	SP-15 PAG	5.0	①	.013–.025
	300M	1.56	R-134a	ND8 PAG	5.0	①	.014–.026

① — Oil Level cannot be inspected. Refer to total capacity in ounces.

② — 2.4L engine, 0.012–0.020 inch; 3.0L engine, 0.016–0.024.

③ — Refer to inderhood label for refrigerant capacity.

CHARGING VALVE LOCATION

AVENGER, BREEZE, CIRRUS, SEBRING CONVERTIBLE, SEBRING COUPE, STRATUS & 2001-02 SEBRING & STRATUS COUPE

The low side valve is located on the suction line. The high side valve is located on the high pressure line.

CONCORDE, INTREPID, LHS & 300M

On models equipped with 2.7L engines, the high pressure gauge port is located on the liquid line and the low pressure gauge port is located on the suction line. On models equipped with 3.2L and 3.5L engines, the high and low side pressure connectors are located on the A/C compressor.

NEON

The low side valve is located on the suction line. The high side valve is located on the filter-dryer.

TALON

The low side valve is located on the suction line. The high side valve is located on the high pressure line.

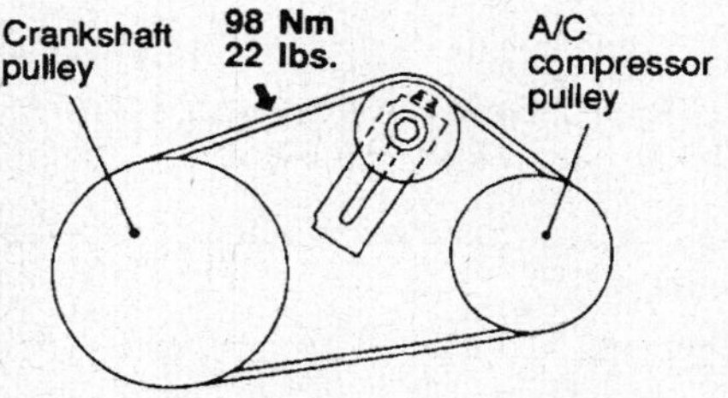

Fig. 1 Belt tension inspection. Avenger & Sebring Coupe w/2.0L engine

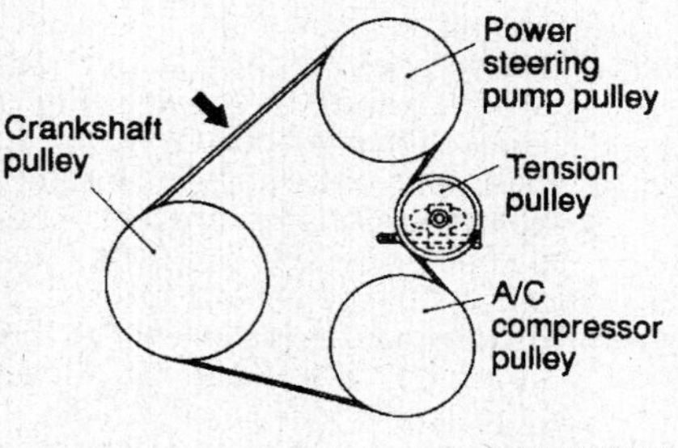

Fig. 2 Belt tension inspection. Avenger & Sebring Coupe w/2.5L engine

2001-02 SEBRING & STRATUS SEDAN

The high side valve is located on the discharge line near the front of the engine compartment. The low side service valve is located on the suction line.

BELT TENSION

AVENGER & SEBRING COUPE

2.0L Engine

1. Install a suitable belt tension gauge in middle of belt span as shown in **Fig. 1.**
2. Proper belt tension is 93–114 lbs.
3. Adjust belt tension as follows:
   a. Loosen tension pulley nut.
   b. Adjust tension using adjusting bolt.
   c. Adjust new belt to 137–158 lbs., and used belt to 93–114 lbs.
   d. Tighten pulley nut.

2.5L Engine

1. Install a suitable belt tension gauge in middle of belt span as shown in **Fig. 2.**
2. Proper belt tension is 66–86 lbs.
3. Adjust belt tension as follows:
   a. Loosen tension pulley nut.
   b. Adjust tension using adjusting bolt.
   c. Adjust new belt to 110–132 lbs., and used belt to 66–86 lbs.
   d. Tighten pulley nut.

BREEZE, CIRRUS, SEBRING CONVERTIBLE & STRATUS

1. Install a suitable belt tension gauge in middle of belt span.
2. Proper belt tension is 66–86 lbs.
3. Adjust belt tension as follows:

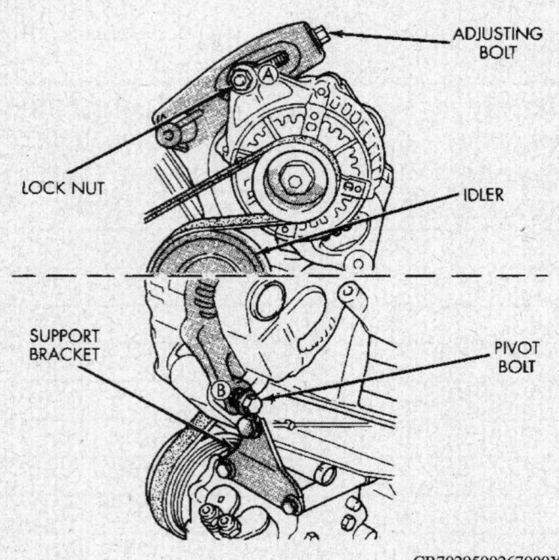

Fig. 3 Belt tension adjustment. Breeze, Cirrus, Sebring Convertible & Stratus

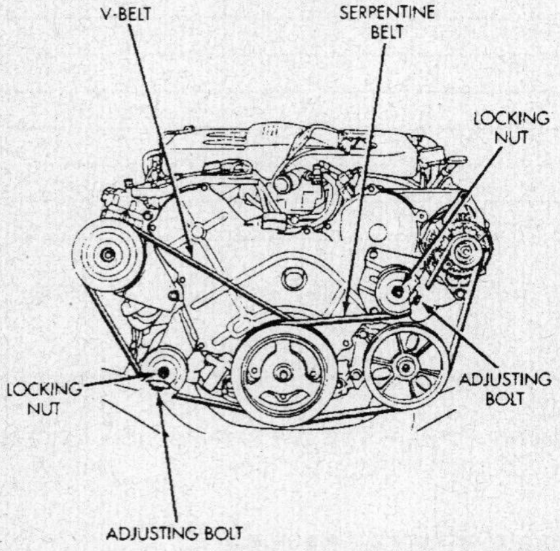

Fig. 6 Belt tension inspection. Concorde, Intrepid, LHS & 300M w/3.2L & 3.5L engines

a. Loosen locking nut and pivot bolt as shown in **Fig. 3.**
b. Adjust tension by tightening adjusting bolt.
c. Adjust new belt to 150 lbs. and used belt to 80 lbs.
d. **Torque** locking nut and pivot bolt to 40 ft. lbs.

CONCORDE, INTREPID, LHS & 300M

1. Use belt tensioning tool No. C-7198, or equivalent, to measure A/C compressor belt tension.
2. With new belts, tension should be 140–160 lbs.
3. With used belts, tension should be 120 lbs.
4. If not within specification, tighten belt as follows:
   a. Loosen tensioner pulley locking nut as shown in **Figs. 4 through 6.**
   b. Adjust tension to specification with adjusting bolt, 140–160 lbs. for a new belt and 120 lbs. for a used belt.
   c. **Torque** locking nut to 40 ft. lbs.

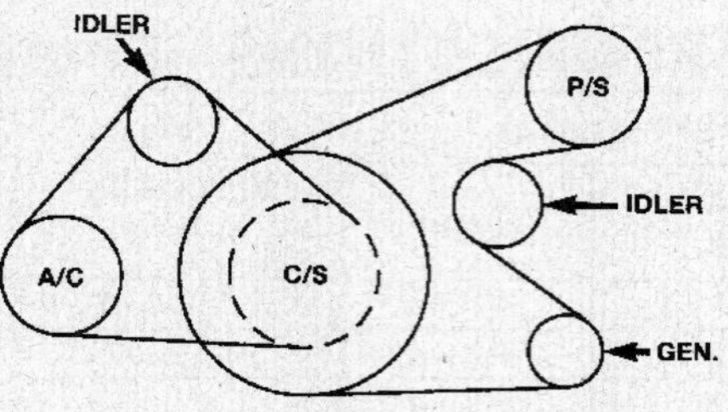

Fig. 4 Belt tension inspection. Concorde, Intrepid, LHS & 300M w/2.7L engine

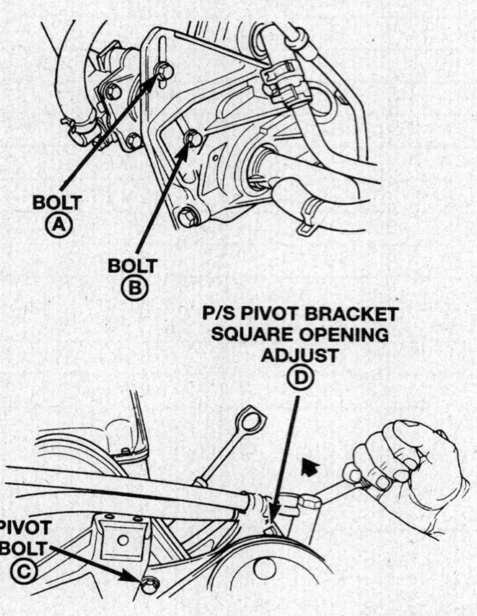

Fig. 7 Belt tension inspection. 1998–99 Neon

5. Inspect belt tension after driving vehicle.

NEON

1998–99

1. Using belt tensioning tool No. C-4162, or equivalent, ensure belt tension is 100 lbs. If not within specification, tighten belt as follows:
   a. Loosen power steering pump locking bolts A and B as shown in **Fig. 7,** then loosen pivot bolt C.
   b. Adjust tension by applying torque to square hole on idler bracket. A new belt should be set to 135 lbs. Used belts should be set to 100 lbs.
   c. **Torque** in order, locking bolt A, then locking bolt B to 20 ft. lbs. Finally, **torque** pivot bolt C to 40 ft. lbs.
2. Inspect belt tension after driving vehicle.

2000–02

On these models an automatic belt tensioning device is incorporated with the engine mount bracket assembly as shown in **Fig. 8.** The tensioner pulley is a serviceable component.

Slight tensioner arm axial movement is normal. Ensure the arm moves freely and can maintain 50–70 lbs. of tension on the belt.

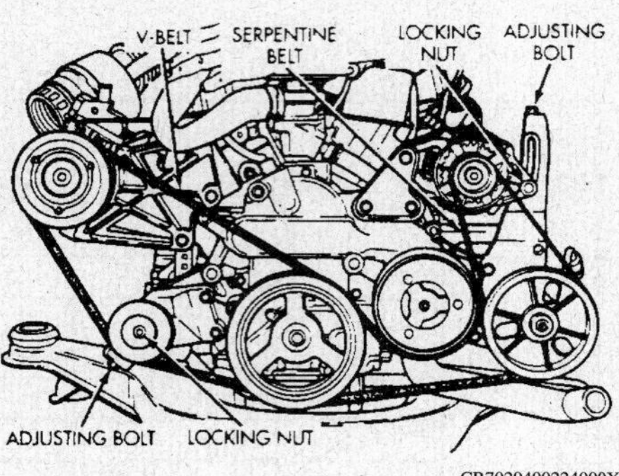

Fig. 5 Belt tension inspection. Concorde, Intrepid & LHS w/3.3L engine

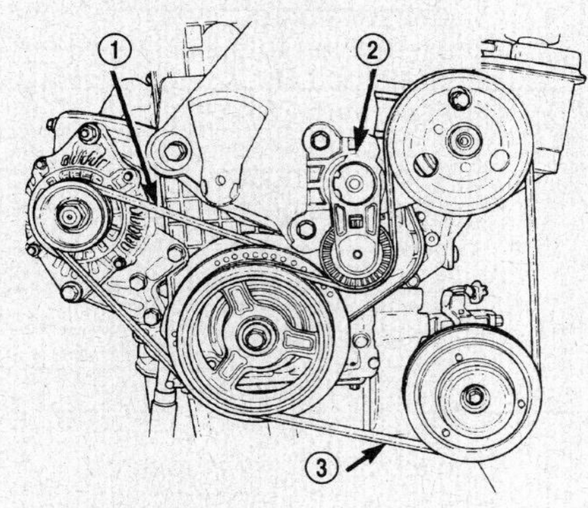

Fig. 8 Belt tensioning system. 2000–02 Neon

TALON

Non-Turbocharged Engine

1. Using a suitable belt tension gauge, measure drive belt deflection by pulling or pushing at midpoint of the belt between pulleys as shown in **Fig. 9,** with a force of 22 lbs.
2. Deflection should be .39–.43 inch. If deflection is not within specifications, tighten belt as follows:
   a. Loosen tension pulley securing nut.
   b. Adjust tension to specification with adjusting bolt, .32–.35 inch for a new belt and .39–.43 inch for used belt.
   c. Tighten securing nut.
3. Inspect belt tension after driving vehicle.

Turbocharged Engine

1. Using a suitable belt tension gauge, measure drive belt deflection by pulling or pushing at midpoint of the belt between pulleys as shown in **Fig. 10,** with a force of 22 lbs.
2. Deflection should be .26–.30 inch. If deflection is not within specifications, tighten belt as follows:

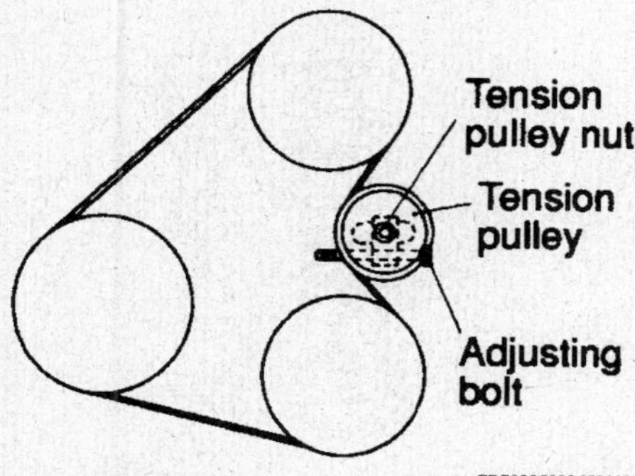

Fig. 9 Belt tension inspection. Talon less turbocharged engine

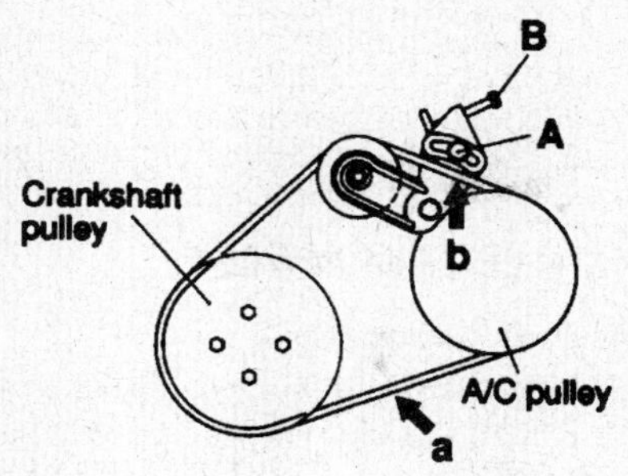

Fig. 10 Belt tension inspection. Talon w/turbocharged engine

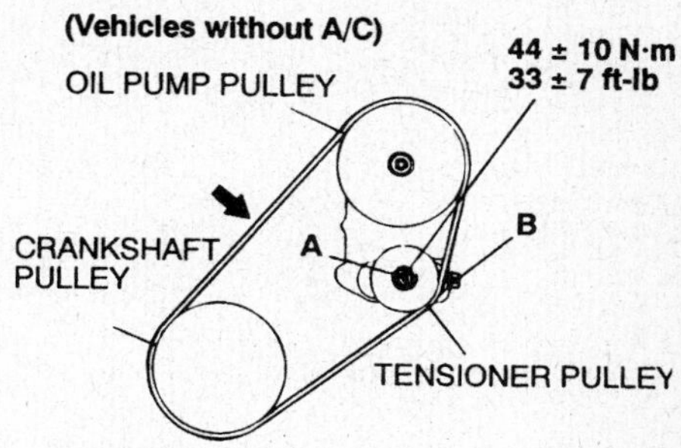

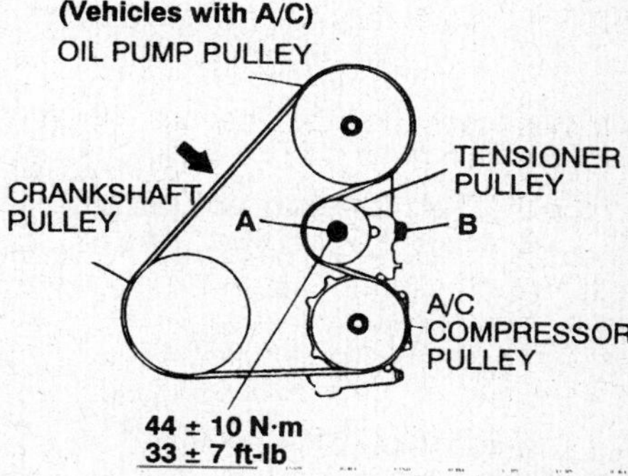

Fig. 11 Belt tension inspection. 2001–02 Sebring & Stratus Coupe w/2.4L engine

a. Loosen tension pulley fixing bolt A.
b. Adjust tension to specification with adjusting bolt B, .22–.24 inch for a new belt and .26–.30 inch for used belt.
c. **Torque** fixing nut to 17–20 ft. lbs.

3. Inspect belt tension after driving vehicle.

2001–2002 SEBRING & STRATUS COUPE

1. Loosen tension pulley fixing nut “A” behind tension pulley as shown in **Figs. 11 and 12.**
2. Adjust belt tension amount using adjusting bolt “B.”
3. Torque fixing nut to 33 ft. lbs.
4. Check belt tension and readjust as required.

2001–2002 SEBRING & STRATUS SEDAN

1. Raise and support vehicle.
2. Remove right front wheel.
3. Remove belt splash shield.
4. **On models with 2.0 and 2.4L engines,** rotate belt tensioner clockwise until belt can be removed from pulleys.
5. **On models with 2.7L engine,** loosen tensioner locking and pivot bolt, then rotate tensioner clockwise to remove belt.
6. **On all models,** reverse procedure to install, noting following:
   a. **On models with 2.7L engine,** insert ½ inch drive breaker bar into square opening in tensioner.
   b. Hold clockwise pressure on tensioner and tighten locking and pivot bolt.

TECHNICAL SERVICE BULLETINS

A/C COMPRESSOR LOCK-UP AT LOW MILEAGE

1998–2000 Neon

On these models the A/C compressor may lock-up, leading to a drive belt slip and squeal condition. The temporary lock-up does not always indicate the compressor has failed.

This condition may be caused by the normal refrigerant movement within the A/C system caused by temperature differences between the various components. This washes the refrigerant oil out of the compressor.

The A/C system should be operated for a minimum of five minutes in the Fresh Air A/C High Blower Mode, with the engine idling, prior to taking a vehicle out of operation or storing it for more than two weeks. This ensures adequate oil flow-back to the compressor.

To determine the extent of this condition, start and operate the engine at idle. Turn the A/C system On and listen for the squealing drive belt. **If the belt squeal starts, immediately turn the A/C system Off.** If the squealing stops, proceed as follows:

1. Using an oil filter strap wrench, grasp outer diameter of A/C clutch hub that houses rubber donut. While facing compressor, attempt to rotate hub clockwise, then counterclockwise. If hub will not rotate, replace compressor. If hub rotates, proceed to next step.
2. Turn hub clockwise 5 complete revolutions, then remove strap wrench.
3. Start and operate engine at idle, then turn A/C system On.
4. Observe A/C system and compressor for proper operation for cool-down and noise levels.
5. If A/C operation is within specifications, allow system to operate at idle for 5 minutes.
6. If A/C system operates acceptably for 5 minutes, compressor is still serviceable. Inspect drive belt for damage and replace if required.
7. If A/C system does not operate acceptably, or if compressor is internally damaged, replace compressor.

A/C COMPRESSOR MOAN AT 2000 RPM

1998–99 Concorde, Intrepid, LHS & 300M

On these models, equipped with 3.2L or 3.5L engines, this condition may occur with the compressor clutch engaged and the engine running at 2000 RPM.

To determine the proper procedure to correct this condition, remove compressor mounting bolt “A,” as shown in **Fig. 13.** If the moan is greatly reduced or eliminated, perform the repair procedure. If the moan is still present, install bolt “A” and **torque** to 16.7–25 ft. lbs. Remove bolt “B” and listen for the moaning again. If the moan is greatly reduced or eliminated, perform repair procedure as follows:

1. Remove A/C compressor drive belt.
2. Remove air cleaner housing and frame rail air cleaner housing mounting stud.
3. Remove compressor mounting bolts, then position compressor aside with hoses intact.
4. Remove compressor bracket from engine block.
5. File 2 mm off A/C bracket boss “B,” then remove threads in bracket with a ⅜ inch drill bit.
6. Install bracket back onto block. **Torque** bolts to 30–50 ft. lbs.
7. Install compressor onto bracket, but do not use bolt “B.” **Torque** remaining three bolts to 16.7–25 ft. lbs.
8. Install compressor drive belt. Adjust tension as outlined under “Belt Tension.”

A/C HONK OR FOG HORN SOUND

2001–02 Sebring Convertible, Sebring Sedan & Stratus Sedan

Vehicles may exhibit a “Honk” or “Fog Horn” sound coming from the A/C expansion valve within a few seconds of A/C clutch engagement, or immediately after A/C clutch engagement. This sound lasts anywhere from one to three seconds and can be confused with the sound that a vehicle braking system makes when the vehicle

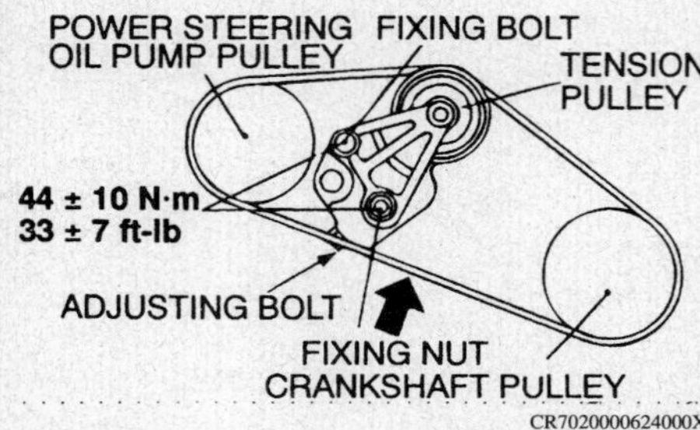

Fig. 12 Belt tension inspection. 2001–02 Sebring & Stratus Coupe w/3.0L engine

is allowed to creep forward at curb idle. Vibration from this condition may be felt in the passenger compartment especially in the steering wheel and seats. An updated A/C expansion valve is available to address this concern. (Replacing the A/C expansion valve will not improve any vehicle noise conditions that last longer than three seconds).

A/C KNOCKING WHEN A/C COMPRESSOR CYCLES

1998 Avenger & Sebring

A knocking noise may be heard coming from the front of the engine when the A/C compressor cycles. This may be caused by insufficient clearance between the A/C bracket and the oil pump. Damage to the oil pump may also occur.

Inspect for interference between the A/C bracket and the oil pump case. If interference is noted, operate A/C system and listen for knocking noise coming from front of engine. If oil pump damage is noted, inspect oil pump case, seals and sealing surface. If interference is found along with any resulting damage, replace A/C compressor bracket with updated part No. MR298598, and repair or replace oil pump assembly as necessary.

A/C PERFORMANCE COMPLAINTS AND/OR A/C COMPRESSOR FAILURE

1998-99 Breeze, Cirrus, Sebring Convertible & Stratus

These vehicles may exhibit A/C performance complaints and/or A/C compressor failures at high ambient temperatures (90°F and above). This condition can be agravated by start and stop city driving and/or extended periods of idling with A/C running.

If the A/C compressor has failed, replace compressor and update PCM software with the latest revision. If A/C performance at high ambient temperature is unsatisfactory, update PCM software with the latest revisions.

A/C SYSTEM NOISE

2000-01 Neon

On vehicles built prior to December 22, 2000, if vehicle is shut off with the air conditioning compressor engaged and allowed to sit overnight, an audible "clunk" type sound may be heard from engine compartment at initial engine start up. This condition is most noticeable in moderate to warm ambient temperatures and is not detrimental to the operation of the compressor.

On all 2000–01 Neon models, a "honk" sound may be noticed coming from the expansion valve when the ambient temperature is around 80°F and the humidity is approximately 40%, with vehicle engine warmed up. The sound may be heard after the engine speed is raised to 3500–4000 RPM for one minute and then allowed to return to idle. The "honk" noise will occur within 30 seconds.

An updated expansion valve is available to address both of these concerns.

HISSING SOUND FROM A/C SYSTEM WHEN A/C CYCLES

1998-99 Concorde, Intrepid, LHS & 300M

A hissing sound may be heard from the inside of vehicle every time the air conditioning clutch cycles from Off to On. The hissing noise is caused by the turbulent flow of R134a refrigerant through the inlet tube to the evaporator core. If the hissing noise can be heard when A/C clutch cycles On and Off, install evaporator inlet flow straightener, part number 04885585AA, or equivalent.

POOR A/C PERFORMANCE/ EXPANSION VALVE NOISE

2001 Neon Built Before June 11, 2001

Under high ambient conditions (above 100°F), the A/C compressor may cycle On and Off repeatedly producing poor A/C performance immediately after a hot engine restart or during city driving. Under similar

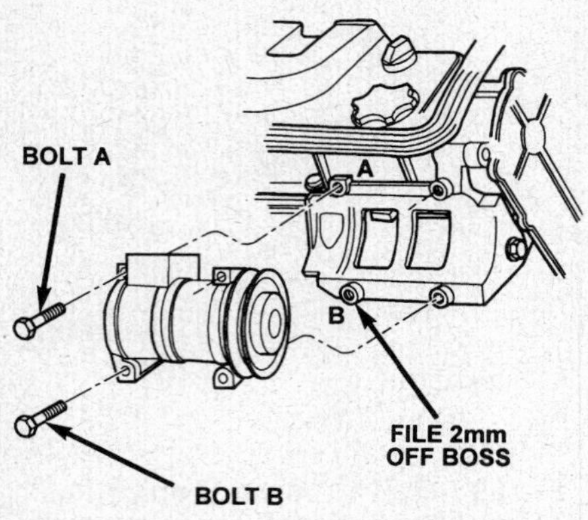

Fig. 13 A/C compressor mounting & bracket boss modification. 1998-99 Concorde, Intrepid, LHS & 300M

ambient conditions, the A/C expansion valve may produce a "Hum" sound.

To correct this condition, evacuate and recharge the A/C system to 1.69 lbs., then reprogram the PCM with the latest software revision.

UNWANTED AUTOMATIC TEMPERATURE CONTROL CHANGE TO MANUAL OPERATION

1998-99 Concorde, Intrepid, LHS & 300M

On these models, built before 7/20/98, this condition may occur if left in "Auto" mode when the ignition was turned Off and may appear when the ignition is turned back On.

This condition may be caused by servicing the A/C or radio without disconnecting and isolating the battery ground cable. This will set an erroneous DTC of "In-Car Temperature Sensor Failure" in the Body Control Module (BCM). This DTC's presence will result in the unrequested Auto to Manual change. This can be prevented by disconnecting and isolating the battery ground cable during electrical system service, then corrected by erasing the DTC.

This condition may also be caused by changing the blower speed while the ignition is turned Off. This is a normal ATC system operation and should be explained to the vehicle's owner.

COOLING FANS

NOTE: On Air Bag Equipped Models, Refer To "Air Bag System Precautions" Located In The Front Of This Manual For System Disarming & Arming Procedures.

NOTE: Refer To "Computer Relearn Procedures" Located In The Front Of This Manual When Battery Power To The Computer Has Been Interrupted.

NOTE: "Electrical Symbol And Wire Color Code Identification" Located In Front Of This Manual Can Be Used As An Aid When Using Wiring Circuits Found In This Section.

INDEX

PRECAUTIONS

AIR BAG SYSTEMS

Refer to "Air Bag System Precautions" in the front of this manual for system disarming and arming procedures.

BATTERY GROUND CABLE

Prior to service, disconnect battery ground cable and isolate as required.

DESCRIPTION

AVENGER, TALON & 1998-2000 SEBRING COUPE

Refer to **Figs. 1 through 3** for fan operation modes.

BREEZE, CIRRUS & STRATUS

Refer to **Figs. 4 through 7** for fan operating modes.

1998

Fan control is accomplished in two ways.

Switch conditions		Vehicle speed sensor km/h (mph)	Engine coolant temperature sensor °C (°F)	Fan revolving operation condition		
Air conditioning switch	Dual pressure switch			Radiator fan motor		Condenser fan motor
	Turn to ON at 1770 kPa (256 psi) or more			M/T	A/T	
OFF	OFF	45 (28) or less	95 (203) or less	OFF	OFF	OFF
			95 (203)–100 (210)	HIGH	Medium	OFF
			100 (210) or more	HIGH	HIGH	Medium
		45 (28)–80 (50)	90 (194) or less	OFF	OFF	OFF
			90 (194)–100 (210)	HIGH	Medium	OFF
			100 (210) or more	HIGH	HIGH	Medium
		80 (50) or more	100 (210) or less	OFF	OFF	OFF
			100 (210) or more	HIGH	HIGH	OFF
ON	OFF	19 (12) or less	100 (210) or less	HIGH	Medium	Medium
			100 (210)–115 (242)	HIGH	HIGH	HIGH
			115 (242) or more	HIGH	HIGH	HIGH
		19 (12)–80 (50)	100 (210) or less	HIGH	Medium	Medium
			100 (210)–115 (242)	HIGH	HIGH	HIGH
			115 (242) or more	HIGH	HIGH	HIGH
		80 (50) or more	100 (210) or less	OFF	OFF	OFF
			100 (210)–115 (242)	HIGH	HIGH	HIGH
			115 (242) or more	HIGH	HIGH	HIGH

CR1089500134000X

Fig. 1 Fan operating mode conditions. Avenger, Sebring Coupe & Talon w/2.0L engine less turbocharged engine

Switch conditions		Vehicle speed sensor km/h (mph)	Engine coolant temperature sensor °C (°F)	Fan revolving operation condition	
Air conditioning switch	Dual pressure switch			Radiator fan motor	Condenser fan motor
	Turn to ON at 1770 kPa (256 psi) or more				
OFF	OFF	45 (28) or less	95 (203) or less	OFF	OFF
			95 (203)–100 (210)	LOW	LOW
			100 (210) or more	HIGH	HIGH
		45 (28)–80(50)	90 (194) or less	OFF	OFF
			90 (194)–100 (210)	LOW	LOW
			100 (210) or more	HIGH	HIGH
		80 (50) or more	100 (210) or less	OFF	OFF
			100 (210) or more	HIGH	HIGH
ON	OFF	19 (12) or less	100 (210) or less	LOW	OFF
			100 (210)–115 (242)	HIGH	LOW
			115 (242) or more	HIGH	HIGH
		19 (12)–80(50)	100 (210) or less	LOW	OFF
			100 (210)–115 (242)	HIGH	LOW
			115 (242) or more	HIGH	HIGH
		80 (50) or more	100 (210) or less	OFF	OFF
			100 (210)–115 (242)	HIGH	HIGH
			115 (242) or more	HIGH	HIGH

CR1089500161000X

Fig. 2 Fan operating mode conditions. Avenger & Sebring Coupe w/2.5L engine

The fan always runs when the A/C pressure reaches 265 psi. The fan is also turned on by the temperature of the coolant which is sensed by the coolant temperature sensor. The sensor sends this temperature reading to the engine controller. The engine controller then turns on the fan through the fan relay.

1999–2002

Fan control is accomplished in three ways. The fans come on when the air conditioning pressure reaches a predetermined pressure, the fans are also activated by coolant temperature. Coolant temperature is sensed by a coolant sensor which sends a signal to the Powertrain Control Module (PCM). On models equipped with an automatic transaxle, the transmission fluid thermistor also can turn on the fan.

CONCORDE, INTREPID, LHS & 300M

Refer to **Figs. 8 through 10,** for specific fan operating modes.

Radiator fan control is accomplished in two ways. A pressure transducer on the compressor discharge line sends a signal to the Powertrain Control Module (PCM) which activates the fans. The fans are also activated when the coolant temperature sensor sends a signal to the PCM. The engine controller then sends a signal to the fan relay which turns the coolant fans on.

NEON

1998–99

Fan control is accomplished in two ways. The fan always runs when the compressor clutch is engaged. The fan is also activated by the temperature of the coolant which is sensed by the coolant temperature sensor. The coolant temperature sensor sends this signal to the engine controller which turns the fan on through the fan relay. Switching through the engine controller provides fan control for the following conditions:

1. Fan will not run when cranking engine no matter what coolant temperature is.
2. Fan will run when A/C clutch engaged and low pressure cutout switch is closed.
3. **At vehicle speeds over 40 mph,** fan will run only if coolant temperature reaches 230°F and fan will turn off when temperature drops to 220°F.
4. **At vehicle speeds under 40 mph,** fan will run when coolant temperature reaches 215°F and fan will turn off when temperature drops 200°F.
5. **At idle speed,** to prevent steaming, the fan will run only for three minutes, when ambient temperature is below 60°F and coolant temperature is between 100–195°F.

2000

Refer to **Fig. 11** for fan operating mode conditions.

2001–02

Refer to **Figs. 12** for fan operating mode conditions.

SEBRING CONVERTIBLE, SEBRING SEDAN & STRATUS SEDAN

The radiator has a single cooling fan, with a two speed motor. The fan is controlled by the Powertrain Control Module (PCM) which activates the cooling fan relays.

Refer to **Figs. 13 through 19** for fan operating mode conditions.

SYSTEM DIAGNOSIS & TESTING

Wiring Diagrams

AVENGER, SEBRING COUPE & 2001–02 STRATUS COUPE

Refer to **Figs. 20 through 27** for cooling fan wiring diagrams.

BREEZE, CIRRUS, 1998–2000 STRATUS & 2001–02 SEBRING SEDAN AND STRATUS SEDAN

Refer to **Fig. 28 through 30** for cooling fan wiring diagrams.

NEON

Refer to **Figs. 31 and 32** for cooling fan wiring diagrams.

SEBRING CONVERTIBLE

1998–2000

Refer to **Figs. 33 through 35** for cooling fan wiring diagrams.

2001–02

Refer to **Figs. 28 through 30** for cooling fan wiring diagrams.

TALON

Refer to **Figs. 36 through 39** for cooling fan wiring diagrams.

Switch conditions		Vehicle speed sensor km/h (mph)	Engine coolant temperature sensor °C (°F)	Fan revolving operation condition		
Air conditioning switch	Dual pressure switch			Radiator fan motor		Condenser fan motor
	Turn to ON at 1770 kPa (256 psi) or more			M/T	A/T	
OFF	OFF	45 (28) or less	95 (203) or less	OFF	OFF	OFF
			95 (203)–100 (210)	Medium	LOW	LOW
			100 (210) or more	HIGH	HIGH	HIGH
		45 (28)–80(50)	90 (194) or less	OFF	OFF	OFF
			90 (194)–100 (210)	Medium	LOW	LOW
			100 (210) or more	HIGH	HIGH	HIGH
		80 (50) or more	100 (210) or less	OFF	OFF	OFF
			100 (210) or more	HIGH	HIGH	HIGH
ON	OFF	19 (12) or less	100 (210) or less	Medium	LOW	OFF
			100 (210)–115 (242)	HIGH	HIGH	LOW
			115 (242) or more	HIGH	HIGH	HIGH
		19 (12)–80(50)	100 (210) or less	Medium	LOW	OFF
			100 (210)–115 (242)	HIGH	HIGH	LOW
			115 (242) or more	HIGH	HIGH	HIGH
		80 (50) or more	100 (210) or less	OFF	OFF	OFF
			100 (210)–115 (242)	HIGH	HIGH	HIGH
			115 (242) or more	HIGH	HIGH	HIGH

CR1089500135000X

Fig. 3 Fan operating mode conditions. Talon w/turbocharged engine

Radiator Fan Control			A/C Pressure	
A/C Off	**Low**	**High**		
Fan On:	104°C (220°F)	110°C (230°F)		
Fan Off:	99°C (210°F)	104°C (220°F)		
A/C On	Low	High	Low	High
Fan On:	99°C (210°F)	110°C (230°F)	1,466 Kpa (209 psi)	1,717 Kpa (249 psi)
Fan Off:	93°C (200°F)	104°C (220°F)	1,172 Kpa (170 psi)	1,579 Kpa (229 psi)
EATX Fluid Temperature			**Low Speed**	**High Speed**
Fan On:			116°C (240°F)	120°C (248°F)
Fan Off:			109°C (228°F)	116°C (240°F)

CR1089900256000X

Fig. 4 Fan operating mode conditions. Breeze & Stratus w/2.0L engine

Radiator Fan Control			A/C Pressure	
A/C Off	**Low**	**High**		
Fan On:	104°C (219°F)	110°C (230°F)		
Fan Off:	99°C (210°F)	105°C (221°F)		
A/C On	**Low**	**High**	**Low**	**High**
Fan On:	99°C (210°F)	110°C (230°F)	1,448 Kpa (210 psi)	1,718 Kpa (249 psi)
Fan Off:	93°C (199°F)	105°C (221°F)	1,207 Kpa (175 Psi)	1,585 Kpa (229 Psi)
EATX Fluid Temperature			**Low Speed**	**High Speed**
Fan On:			118°C (244°F)	122°C (252°F)
Fan Off:			116°C (240°F)	118°C (244°F)

CR1089900257000X

Fig. 5 Fan operating mode conditions. Breeze, Stratus & Sebring Sedan w/2.4L engine

CONCORDE, INTREPID, LHS & 300M

Refer to **Figs. 40 and 41** for cooling fan wiring diagrams.

COMPONENT DIAGNOSIS & TESTING

Coolant Temperature Sensor

AVENGER, TALON & 1998–2000 SEBRING COUPE

1. Disconnect engine coolant temperature sensor electrical connector and connect an ohmmeter between sensor terminals.
2. Measure resistance between terminals. When coolant temperature is at 77°F, resistance should be 9.0–11.0 kohms. When coolant temperature is at 212°F, resistance should be 600–800 ohms.
3. If resistance is not as specified, replace sensor.

BREEZE, CIRRUS & 1998–2000 STRATUS

1. Ensure ignition switch is in the OFF position, then disconnect wiring harness at coolant temperature sensor and connect an ohmmeter between sensor terminals.
2. Measure resistance between sensor terminals. Resistance should be 7.0–13.0 kohms.
3. Run engine until coolant temperature reaches approximately 200°F, then measure resistance. Resistance should be 700–1000 ohms.
4. Measure wiring harness resistance between Powertrain Control Module (PCM) terminal 26 and coolant sensor harness connector. Resistance should not exceed 1 ohm.
5. If resistance is not as specified, replace coolant sensor or repair wiring harness.

CONCORDE, INTREPID, LHS & 300M

1. With ignition in the OFF position, disconnect coolant temperature sensor connector.
2. Measure resistance between sensor terminals when engine is at 200°F.
3. If resistance is not 700–1000 ohms, replace sensor.

NEON

1. Ensure ignition is in the OFF position, then disconnect coolant temperature sensor electrical connector and connect a digital volt/ohmmeter between sensor terminals.
2. Measure resistance between sensor terminals. Resistance should be 7.0–13.0 kohms.
3. Run engine until coolant temperature reaches approximately 200°F, then measure resistance. Resistance should be 700–1000 ohms.
4. Measure wiring harness resistance between Powertrain Control Module (PCM) terminal 28 and coolant sensor harness connector. Resistance should not exceed 1 ohm.
5. Measure wiring harness resistance between PCM terminal 51 and coolant sensor harness connector. Resistance should not exceed 1 ohm.
6. If resistance is not as specified, replace coolant sensor or repair wiring harness.

SEBRING CONVERTIBLE

1. With key off, disconnect connector from coolant sensor.
2. Connect one lead of digital volt/ohm meter to each terminal of sensor.
3. With engine sensor at normal operating temperature of approximately 200°F, reading should be 700–1000 ohms.
4. With engine sensor at room temperature of approximately 70°F, reading should be 7–13 kohms.
5. If sensor measurements are not as indicated, replace sensor.

Radiator Fan Control			A/C Pressure	
A/C Off	**Low**	**High**		
Fan On:	104°C (220°F)	110°C (230°F)		
Fan Off:	98°C (208°F)	105°C (221°F)		
A/C On	Low	High	Low	High
Fan On:	99°C (210°F)	110°C (230°F)	1,448 Kpa (210 psi)	1,718 Kpa (249 psi)
Fan Off:	93°C (199°F)	105°C (221°F)	1,207 Kpa (175 psi)	1,585 kpa (229 psi)
EATX Fluid Temperature			**Low Speed**	**High Speed**
Fan On:			118°C (244°F)	122°C (252°F)
Fan Off:			116°C (240°F)	118°C (244°F)

CR1089900258000X

Fig. 6 Fan operating mode conditions. Cirrus & Stratus w/2.5L engine

Radiator Fan Control			A/C Pressure	
A/C Off	**Low**	**High**		
Fan On:	104°C (220°F)	110°C (230°F)		
Fan Off:	98°C (208°F)	105°C (221°F)		
A/C On	Low	High	Low	High
Fan On:	99°C (210°F)	110°C (230°F)	1,448 Kpa (210 psi)	1,718 Kpa (249 psi)
Fan Off:	93°C (199°F)	105°C (221°F)	1,207 Kpa (175 psi)	1,585 kpa (229 psi)
EATX Fluid Temperature			**Low Speed**	**High Speed**
Fan On:			118°C (244°F)	122°C (252°F)
Fan Off:			116°C (240°F)	118°C (244°F)

CR1080000290000X

Fig. 7 Fan operating mode conditions. 2001–02 Sebring & Stratus Sedan w/2.7L engine

Radiator Fan Control			A/C Pressure	
A/C Off	Low	High		
Fan On:	110°C (230°F)	113°C (235°F)		
Fan Off:	104°C (219°F *)	111°C (231°F)		
	***109°C (228°F) @ Vehicle speed greater than 12.8 Kmh (8 mph).**			
A/C On	Low	High	Low	High
Fan On:	105°C (221°F)	110°C (230°F)	1,448 Kpa (210 psi)	1,717 Kpa (249 psi)
Fan Off:	102°C (216°F)	106°C (223°F)	1207 Kpa (175 psi)	1,579 Kpa (229 psi)

CR1089800214000X

Fig. 8 Fan operating mode. 1998 Concorde & Intrepid

Engine Coolant Temperature Switch

TALON

1. Place sensor in oil up to mounting thread.
2. Connect a suitable ohmmeter across terminals of coolant temperature switch, then increase oil temperature.
3. Ensure switch is switched OFF when oil temperature at 234–244°F, replace sensor if necessary.

Thermo Sensor

TALON

1. Place sensor in hot water up to mounting thread.
2. Check for continuity between terminals on sensor.
3. Continuity should exist with water temperature at 180–190°F. Continuity should not exist with water temperature at 172°F or less.
4. If continuity is not as specified, replace sensor.

Fan Control Module

2001-02 SEBRING & STRATUS COUPE

1. Disconnect condenser fan motor electrical connector.
2. Start engine and allow it to idle.
3. Turn A/C switch on and maintain engine coolant temperature of 176°F or less.
4. Measure voltage between fan control module side connector terminal, **Fig. 42.**
5. Check that voltage changes repeatedly as follows:
   a. 0V.
   b. 5.6–10.8V.
   c. Battery positive voltage ± 2.6 V.
6. If voltage does not repeatedly change as indicated, replace radiator fan motor and fan control module.

Fan Control Relay

2001-02 SEBRING & STRATUS COUPE

Refer to **Figs. 43 and 44** for fan control relay location and **Fig. 44** for continuity check.

Fan Motor Relay

AVENGER, TALON & 1998-2000 SEBRING COUPE

Refer to **Fig. 45** when performing this test.

1. Remove radiator fan motor relay from relay box inside engine compartment.
2. Check for continuity between terminals 1 and 3. Continuity should exist.
3. Check for continuity between terminals 4 and 5. Continuity should not exist.
4. Connect 12 power supply between terminals 1 and 3.
5. Check for continuity between terminals 4 and 5. Continuity should exist.
6. If continuity is not as specified, replace relay.

NEON

1998-2002

Refer to **Fig. 46** for coolant fan control relay circuit test.

2001-02

Refer to 2001 Concorde, Intrepid, LHS & 300M "Low Speed Fan Control Relay" for fan motor relay testing.

Radiator Fan Motor

AVENGER & 1998-2000 SEBRING COUPE

1. Connect battery positive and negative terminals to fan motor connector terminals as shown in **Figs. 47 and 48.**
2. If fan motor does not operate normally, replace fan motor assembly.

BREEZE, CIRRUS & 1998-2000 STRATUS

1. Disconnect fan motor electrical connector.
2. Check low speed coolant fan motor as follows:
   a. Connect battery voltage to fan motor connector terminal No. 3.
   b. If low speed coolant fan operates, proceed to next step. If coolant fan does not operate, check circuit between connector terminal No. 1 and ground. If ground circuit is satisfactory, replace fan motor.
   c. Check circuit and relays for open or short.
3. Check high speed coolant fan motor as follows:
   a. Connect battery voltage to fan motor connector terminal No. 4.
   b. If high speed coolant fan operates, proceed to next step. If coolant fan does not operate, check circuit between connector terminal No. 2 and ground. If ground circuit is satisfactory, replace fan motor.
   c. Check circuit and relays for open or short.

CONCORDE, INTREPID, LHS & 300M

1998-2000

Refer to **Figs. 49 and 50,** for coolant fan motor connector view and diagnostic test.

NEON

1. Disconnect fan motor electrical connector.
2. Connect a 14 gauge jumper wire from battery positive terminal to fan motor terminal No. 1.
3. If fan motor does not operate normally, check circuit between fan motor electrical connector terminal No. 2 and ground.

ENGINE COOLANT TEMPERATURE							INTAKE (CHARGE) TEMPERATURE	
	A/C Off		A/C On		Engine @ Idle<2 Km/h (1 MPH) Vehicle Speed			
Fan Speed	Low	High	Low	High	Low	High	Low	High
Fan On:	106°C (223°F)	110°C (230°F)	105°C (221°F)	110°C (230°F)	99°C (210°F) - After 2nd Fan Cycle	110°C (230°F)	63°C (145°F) if coolant<93°C (199°F) 60°C (140°F) if coolant>99°C (210°F)	67°C (153°F)
Fan Off:	102°C (216°F)	107°C (225°F)	102°C (216°F)	106°C (223°F)	Fan on time = 4 minutes*	105°C (221°F)	Fan on time = 8 minutes*	Fan on time = 4 minutes*

*Minimum fan on time = 90 seconds

	A/C PRESSURE		TRANSMISSION OIL TEMPERATURE	
Fan Speed	Low	High	Low	High
Fan On:	1,448 Kpa (210 psi)	1,717 Kpa (249 psi)	109°C (228°F)	111°C (232°F)
Fan Off:	1,207 Kpa (175 psi)	1,503 Kpa (218 psi)	104°C (220°F)	109°C (228°F)

CR1089800262000X

Fig. 9 Fan operating mode conditions. 1999–2002 Concorde & Intrepid w/2.7L engine

ENGINE COOLANT TEMPERATURE					INTAKE (CHARGE) AIR TEMPERATURE	
	A/C Off/On		Engine @ Idle <2 Km/h (1 MPH) Vehicle Speed			
Fan Speed	Low	High	Low	High	Low	High
Fan On:	102°C (216°F)	110°C (230°F)	99°C (210°F) - After 2nd Fan Cycle	110°C (230°F)	63°C (145°F) if coolant<93°C (199°F) 60°C (140°F) if coolant>99°C (210°F)	67°C (153°F)
Fan Off:	99°C (210°F)	105°C (221°F)	Fan on time = 4 minutes*	105°C (221°F)	Fan on time = 8 minutes*	Fan on time = 4 minutes*

*Minimum fan on time = 90 seconds

	A/C PRESSURE		TRANSMISSION OIL TEMPERATURE	
Fan Speed	Low	High	Low	High
Fan On:	1,448 Kpa (210 psi)	1,717 Kpa (249 psi)	102°C (216°F)	109°C (228°F)
Fan Off:	1,207 Kpa (175 psi)	1,510 Kpa (219 psi)	98°C (208°F)	107°C (224°F)

CR1089800263000X

Fig. 10 Fan operating mode conditions. 1999–2002 Concorde, Intrepid, LHS & 300M w/3.2L & 3.5L engines

4. If ground circuit is satisfactory, replace fan motor.

SEBRING CONVERTIBLE

1. Disconnect fan motor electrical connector.
2. Check low speed fan operation as follows:
   a. Connect a jumper wire from battery positive terminal to fan motor terminal No. 2.
   b. If fan motor operates at low speed, proceed to next step. If fan motor does not operate normally, check circuit between fan motor electrical connector terminal No. 1 and ground. If ground circuit is satisfactory, replace fan motor.
   c. Check circuit and relay for open or short.
3. Check high speed fan operation as follows:
   a. Connect a jumper wire from battery positive terminal to fan motor terminal No. 3.
   b. If fan motor operates at high speed, proceed to next step. If fan motor does not operate normally, check circuit between fan motor electrical connector terminal No. 1 and ground. If ground circuit is satisfactory, replace fan motor.
   c. Check circuit and relay for open or short.
4. Check low speed fan operation as follows:
   a. Connect a jumper wire from battery positive terminal to fan motor terminal No. 2.
   b. If fan motor operates at low speed, proceed to next step. If fan motor does not operate normally, check circuit between fan motor electrical connector terminal No. 1 and ground. If ground circuit is satisfactory, replace fan motor.
   c. Check circuit and relay for open or short.

TALON

1. Disconnect fan motor connector and connect to battery positive and negative using jumper wires as shown, **Fig. 51.**

Accessory Drive Belts	Gauge
2.0/2.4/2.5L Engines	
Air Conditioning Compressor & Generator	NEW BELT: 150 LB.
Power Steering Pump	USED BELT: 90 LB.

CR1080100335000X

Fig. 11 Fan operating mode conditions. 2000 Neon

2. If fan does not run normally or makes abnormal noises, replace fan motor assembly.

2001 SEBRING & STRATUS COUPE

Refer to **Figs. 52 through 55** for radiator and condenser fan motor testing.

2002 SEBRING & STRATUS COUPE

Refer to **Figs. 56 and59** for radiator and condenser fan motor testing.

Low Speed Fan Control Relay

AVENGER, BREEZE, CIRRUS, TALON & 1998–2000 SEBRING CONVERTIBLE, SEBRING COUPE & STRATUS

Refer **Figs. 60 through 63,** for low coolant fan relay circuit connectors. Refer to **Fig. 64** for low coolant fan relay diagnostic procedures.

CONCORDE, INTREPID, LHS & 300M

1998–2000

Refer to **Figs. 65 and 66** for low speed coolant fan relay connector views. Refer to **Figs. 67 and 68** for relay diagnostic procedures.

2001–02

Refer to **Fig. 69** for low speed fan relay circuit test.

2001–02 SEBRING CONVERTIBLE, SEBRING SEDAN & STRATUS SEDAN

Refer to **Fig. 70** for low speed fan relay circuit testing.

High Speed Fan Control Relay

AVENGER, BREEZE, CIRRUS, TALON & 1998–2000 SEBRING & STRATUS

Refer to **Figs. 71 through 76,** for circuit connector views. Refer to **Fig. 77** for high speed coolant fan relay circuit diagnostic test.

CONCORDE, INTREPID, LHS & 300M

1998–2000

Refer to **Figs. 78 through 80,** for high speed coolant fan relay connector view and diagnostic test.

2001

Refer to **Fig. 81** for high speed fan control circuit test.

2001 SEBRING CONVERTIBLE & SEBRING & STRATUS SEDAN

Refer to **Fig. 82** for high speed fan relay circuit testing.

Radiator Fan Control			
A/C Off	**Vehicle Speed < 36 mph**	**Vehicle Speed ≥ 44 mph**	
Fan On:	97° C (210° F)	104° C (219° F)	
Fan Off:	94° C (201° F)	97° C (210° F)	WOT* < 113° C (235° F)
A/C On	Fan On—regardless of coolant temperature or vehicle speed.		
*WOT = Wide Open Throttle			

CR1080100336000X

Fig. 12 Fan operating mode conditions. 2001–02 Neon

Radiator Fan Control			A/C Pressure	
A/C Off	**Low**	**High**		
Fan On:	104°C (220°F)	110°C (230°F)		
Fan Off:	99°C (210°F)	104°C (220°F)		
A/C On	Low	High	Low	High
Fan On:	99°C (210°F)	110°C (230°F)	1,466 Kpa (209 psi)	1,717 Kpa (249 psi)
Fan Off:	93°C (200°F)	104°C (220°F)	1,172 Kpa (170 psi)	1,579 Kpa (229 psi)
EATX Fluid Temperature			**Low Speed**	**High Speed**
Fan On:			116°C (240°F)	120°C (248°F)
Fan Off:			109°C (228°F)	116°C (240°F)

CR1080100327000X

Fig. 13 Fan operating mode conditions. 2001 Sebring & Stratus Sedan w/2.0L engine

COMPONENT REPLACEMENT

Fan Motor

AVENGER & 1998–2000 SEBRING COUPE

1. Drain engine coolant into a suitable container.
2. Remove cooling fan motor, **Fig. 83.**
3. Reverse procedure to install.

BREEZE, CIRRUS & 1998–2000 STRATUS

1. Remove fan shroud and retaining clip at end of fan motor shaft, then slide fan from shaft. **Do not bend or strike fan blades during removal.**
2. Disconnect fan motor electrical connectors, then remove fan motor fasteners from motor support.
3. Separate motor from support.
4. Reverse procedure to install, noting the following:
   a. **Torque** short fasteners to 25 inch lbs.
   b. **Torque** long fasteners to 45 inch lbs.
   c. **Torque** fan shroud fasteners to 61 inch lbs.

CONCORDE, INTREPID, LHS & 300M

1. Disconnect electrical connector, **Fig. 84.**
2. Remove fan module to radiator clips and fasteners, **Fig. 84.**
3. Remove assembly from radiator, then remove fan blades as follows:
   a. Bench support motor and motor shaft.
   b. Remove fan retaining clip or nut. Surface or burr removal may be necessary before removing fans from shaft. **Do not let fan blades touch bench when removing.**
4. Remove motor fasteners from support, then motor from support.
5. Reverse procedure to install, noting the following:
   a. **Torque** right fan motor fasteners to 25 inch lbs. and left fan motor fasteners to 45 inch lbs.
   b. **Torque** shroud to radiator fasteners to 45 inch lbs.

NEON

1. Disconnect electrical connector from motor.
2. Drain cooling system below upper radiator hose level.
3. Remove upper radiator hose from radiator.
4. Remove radiator to battery strut.
5. **On models equipped with dual fan modules,** remove battery and battery tray.
6. **On all models,** remove fan module fasteners from radiator.
7. Lift fan shroud up and out of lower shroud attachment clips.
8. Reverse procedure to install.

SEBRING CONVERTIBLE

1. Remove upper radiator crossmember.
2. Disconnect fan motor electrical connector.
3. Remove fasteners attaching fan module to radiator.
4. Remove fan from motor shaft.
5. Remove motor fasteners from motor support, then the motor.
6. Reverse procedure to install, **torque** fasteners to 45 inch lbs.

TALON

Refer to **Figs. 85 and 86** for radiator fan motor replacement.

2001–02 SEBRING & STRATUS COUPE

Refer to **Fig. 87** for radiator fan motor replacement.

2001–02 SEBRING & STRATUS SEDAN

1. Remove upper radiator crossmember.
2. Disconnect radiator fan electrical connector.
3. Remove fasteners and upper clip attaching fan assembly to radiator.
4. Remove radiator fan assembly by carefully lifting upward.
5. Reverse procedure to install.

Radiator Fan Control			A/C Pressure	
A/C Off	Low	High		
Fan On:	104°C (220°F)	110°C (230°F)		
Fan Off:	99°C (210°F)	104°C (220°F)		
A/C On	Low	High	Low	High
Fan On:	99°C (210°F)	110°C (230°F)	1,466 Kpa (209 psi)	1,717 Kpa (249 psi)
Fan Off:	93°C (200°F)	104°C (220°F)	1,172 Kpa (170 psi)	1,579 Kpa (229 psi)
EATX Fluid Temperature			Low Speed	High Speed
Fan On:			109°C (228°F)	111°C (232°F)
Fan Off:			104°C (220°F)	109°C (228°F)

CR1080100330000X

Fig. 14 Fan operating mode conditions. 2002 Sebring Convertible, Sebring Sedan & Stratus Sedan w/2.0L engine

Radiator Fan Control			A/C Pressure	
A/C Off	Low	High		
Fan On:	104°C (219°F)	110°C (230°F)		
Fan Off:	99°C (210°F)	105°C (221°F)		
A/C On	Low	High	Low	High
Fan On:	99°C (210°F)	110°C (230°F)	1,448 Kpa (210 psi)	1,718 Kpa (249 psi)
Fan Off:	93°C (199°F)	105°C (221°F)	1,207 Kpa (175 Psi)	1,585 Kpa (229 Psi)
EATX Fluid Temperature			Low Speed	High Speed
Fan On:			109°C (228°F)	111°C (232°F)
Fan Off:			104°C (220°F)	109°C (228°F)

CR1080100325000X

Fig. 16 Fan operating mode conditions. 2002 Sebring Convertible, Sebring Sedan & Stratus Sedan w/2.4L engine

Radiator Fan Control			A/C Pressure	
A/C Off	Low	High		
Fan On:	102°C (215°F)	107°C (225°F)		
Fan Off:	96°C (205°F)	96°C (205°F)		
A/C On	Low	High	Low	High
Fan On:	102°C (215°F)	107°C (225°F)	1,448 Kpa (210 psi)	1,718 Kpa (249 psi)
Fan Off:	96°C (205°F)	96°C (205°F)	1,207 Kpa (175 Psi)	1,585 Kpa (229 Psi)
EATX Fluid Temperature			Low Speed	High Speed
Fan On:			118°C (244°F)	122°C (252°F)
Fan Off:			116°C (240°F)	118°C (244°F)

CR1089900260000X

Fig. 15 Fan operating mode conditions. 1998–2000 Sebring Convertible w/2.4L engine

Radiator Fan Control			A/C Pressure	
A/C Off	Low	High		
Fan On:	102°C (215°F)	107°C (224°F)		
Fan Off:	96°C (205°F)	101°C (213°F)		
A/C On	Low	High	Low	High
Fan On:	102°C (215°F)	107°C (224°F)	1,448 Kpa (210 psi)	1,718 Kpa (249 psi)
Fan Off:	96°C (205°F)	101°C (213°F)	1,207 Kpa (175 psi)	1,585 Kpa (229 psi)
EATX Fluid Temperature			Low Speed	High Speed
Fan On:			118°C (244°F)	122°C (252°F)
Fan Off:			116°C (240°F)	118°C (244°F)

CR1089500194000X

Fig. 17 Fan operating mode conditions. 1998 Sebring Convertible w/2.5L engine

Radiator Fan Control			A/C Pressure	
A/C Off	Low	High		
Fan On:	102°C (215°F)	107°C (224°F)		
Fan Off:	96°C (205°F)	103°C (217°F)		
A/C On	Low	High	Low	High
Fan On:	102°C (215°F)	107°C (224°F)	1,448 Kpa (210 psi)	1,718 Kpa (249 psi)
Fan Off:	96°C (205°F)	101°C (213°F)	1,207 Kpa (175 psi)	1,585 Kpa (229 psi)
EATX Fluid Temperature			Low Speed	High Speed
Fan On:			118°C (244°F)	122°C (252°F)
Fan Off:			116°C (240°F)	118°C (244°F)

CR1089900261000X

Fig. 18 Fan operating mode conditions. 1999–2000 Sebring Convertible w/2.5L engine

Radiator Fan Control			A/C Pressure	
A/C Off	Low	High		
Fan On:	104°C (220°F)	110°C (230°F)		
Fan Off:	98°C (208°F)	105°C (221°F)		
A/C On	Low	High	Low	High
Fan On:	99°C (210°F)	110°C (230°F)	1,448 Kpa (210 psi)	1,718 Kpa (249 psi)
Fan Off:	93°C (199°F)	105°C (221°F)	1,207 Kpa (175 psi)	1,585 kpa (229 psi)
EATX Fluid Temperature			Low Speed	High Speed
Fan On:			109°C (228°F)	111°C (232°F)
Fan Off:			104°C (220°F)	109°C (228°F)

CR1080100329000X

Fig. 19 Fan operating mode conditions. 2001–02 Sebring Convertible, Sebring Sedan & Stratus Sedan w/2.7L engine

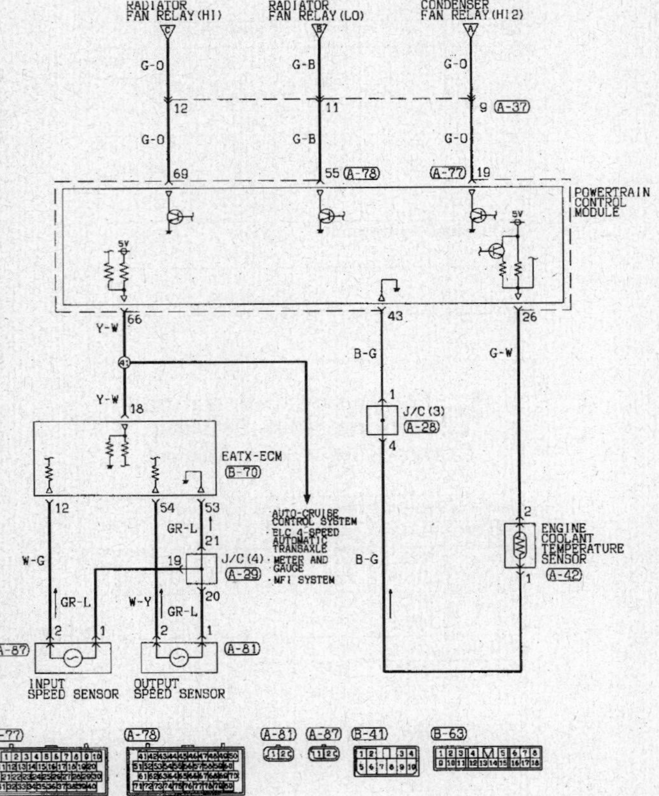

Fig. 20 Engine cooling fan wiring diagram (Part 2 of 2). 1998 Avenger & Sebring Coupe w/2.0L engine & automatic transaxle

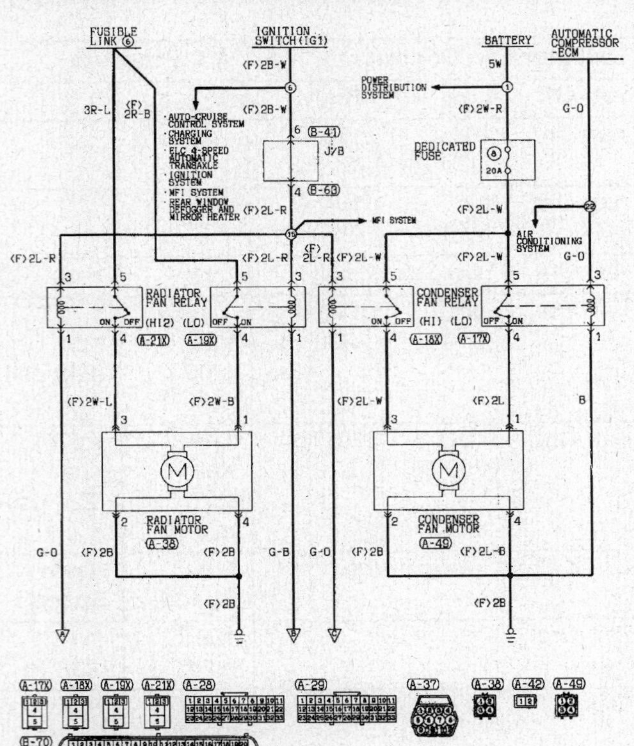

Fig. 20 Engine cooling fan wiring diagram (Part 1 of 2). 1998 Avenger & Sebring Coupe w/2.0L engine & automatic transaxle

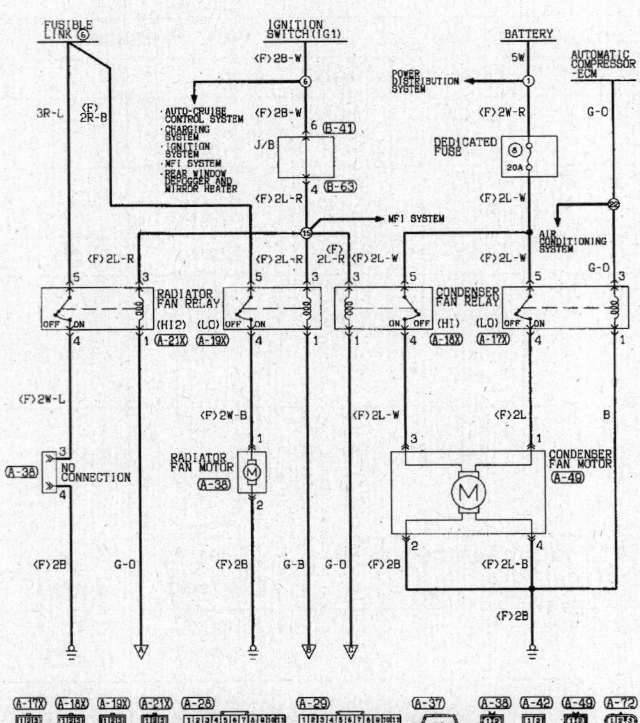

Fig. 21 Engine cooling fan wiring diagram (Part 1 of 2). 1998 Avenger & Sebring Coupe w/2.0L engine & manual transaxle

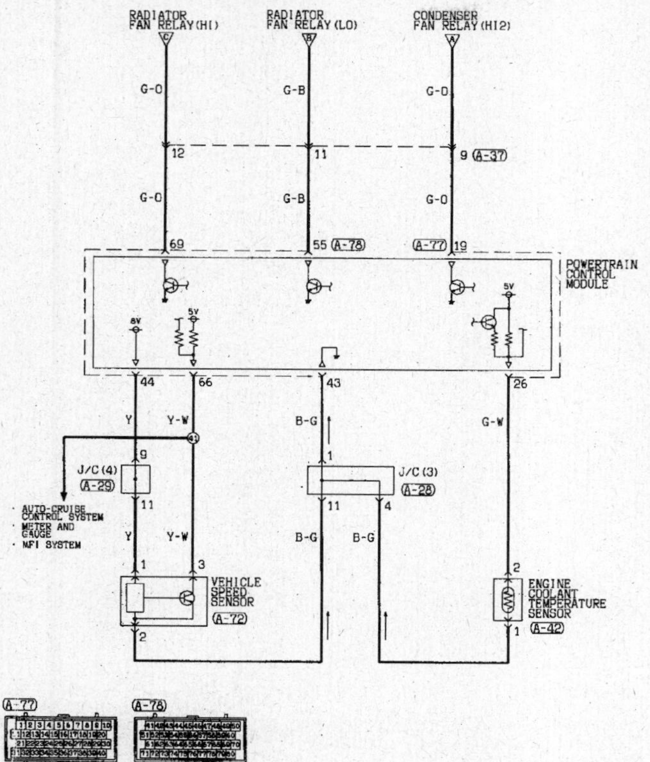

Fig. 21 Engine cooling fan wiring diagram (Part 2 of 2). 1998 Avenger & Sebring Coupe w/2.0L engine & manual transaxle

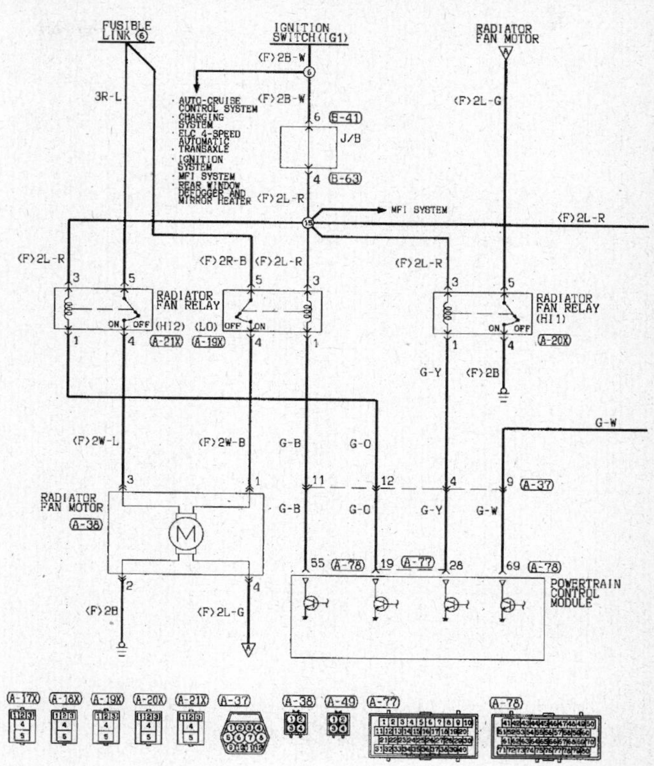

Fig. 22 Engine cooling fan wiring diagram (Part 1 of 3). 1998 Avenger & Sebring Coupe w/2.5L engine

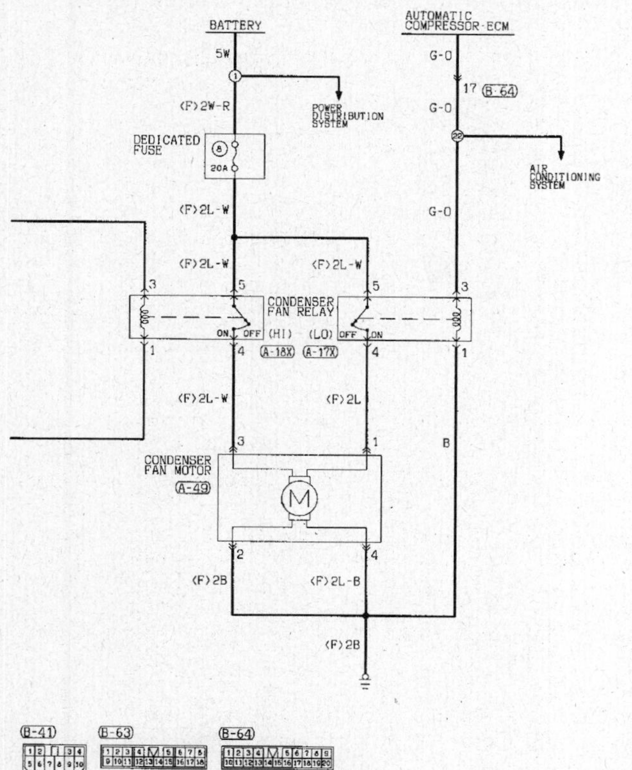

Fig. 22 Engine cooling fan wiring diagram (Part 2 of 3). 1998 Avenger & Sebring Coupe w/2.5L engine

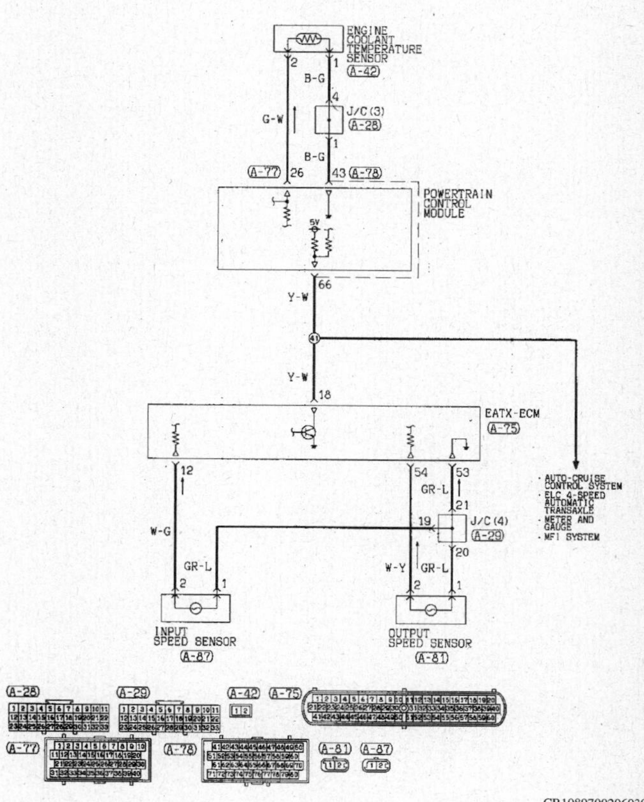

Fig. 22 Engine cooling fan wiring diagram (Part 3 of 3). 1998 Avenger & Sebring Coupe w/2.5L engine

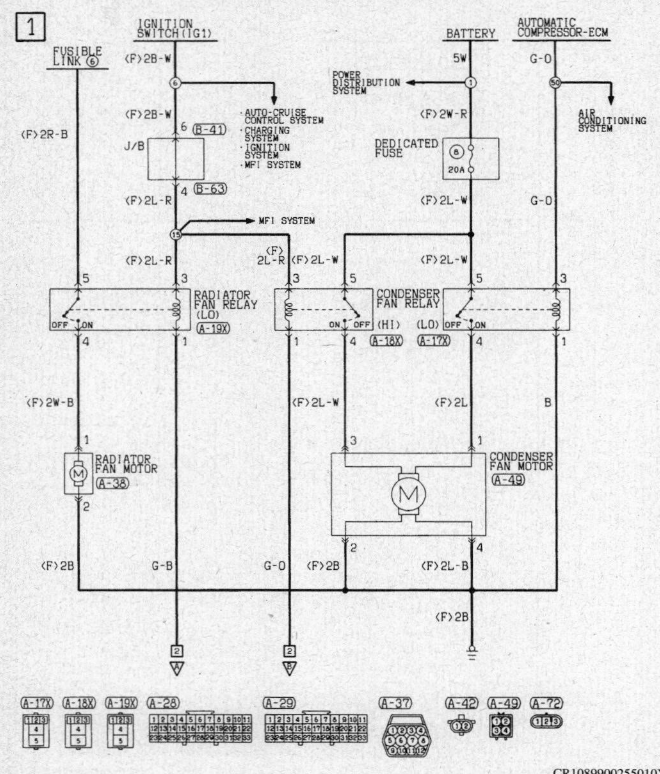

Fig. 23 Engine cooling fan wiring diagram (Part 1 of 2). 1999–2000 Avenger & Sebring Coupe w/DOHC engine

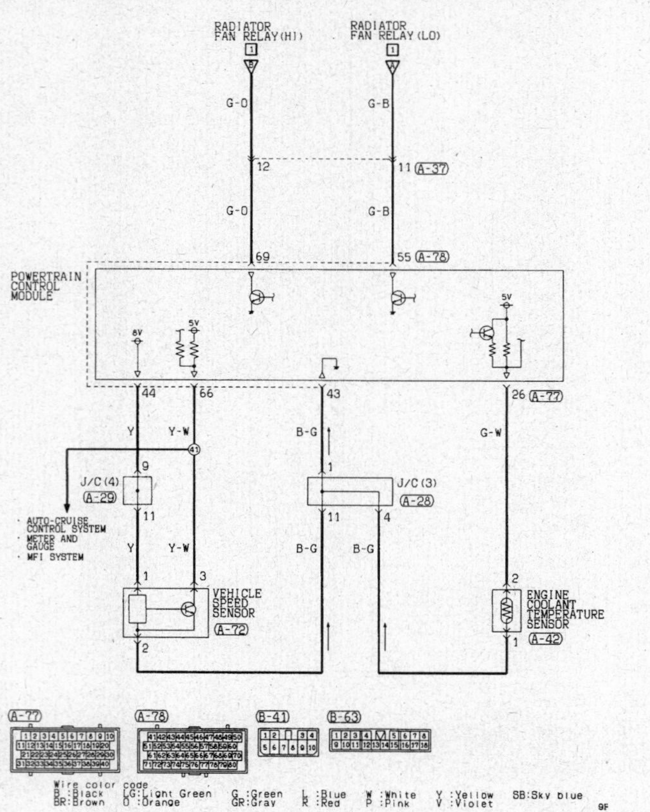

Fig. 23 Engine cooling fan wiring diagram (Part 2 of 2). 1999–2000 Avenger & Sebring Coupe w/DOHC engine & automatic transmission

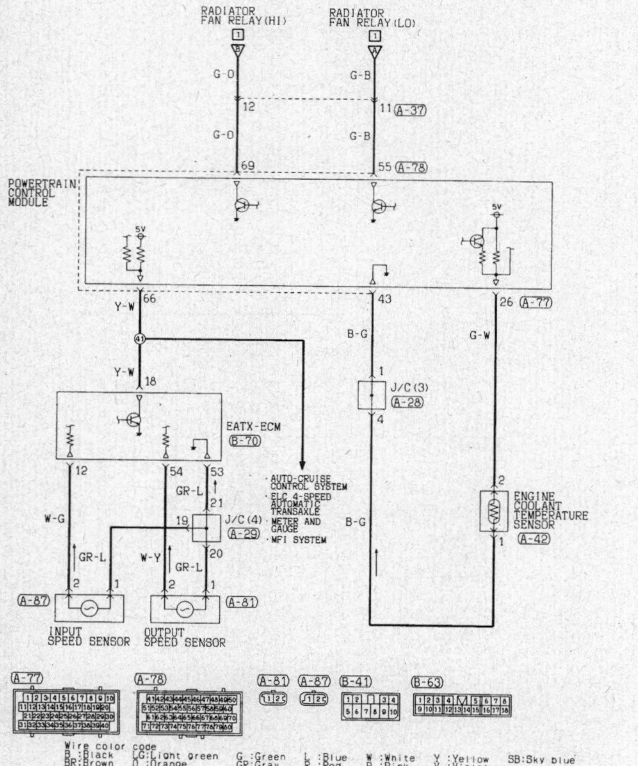

Fig. 23 Engine cooling fan wiring diagram (Part 2 of 2). 1999–2000 Avenger & Sebring Coupe w/DOHC engine & manual transmission

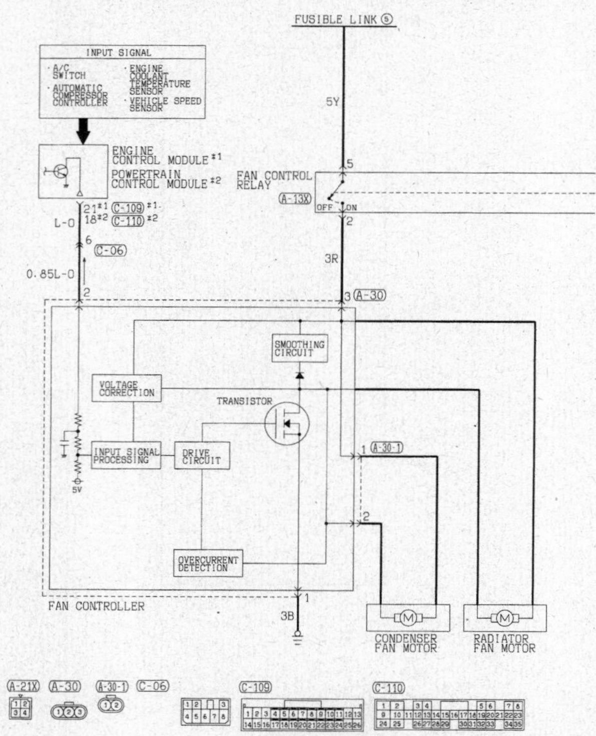

Fig. 24 Engine cooling fan wiring diagram (Part 1 of 2). 2001 Sebring & Stratus Coupe w/2.4L engine

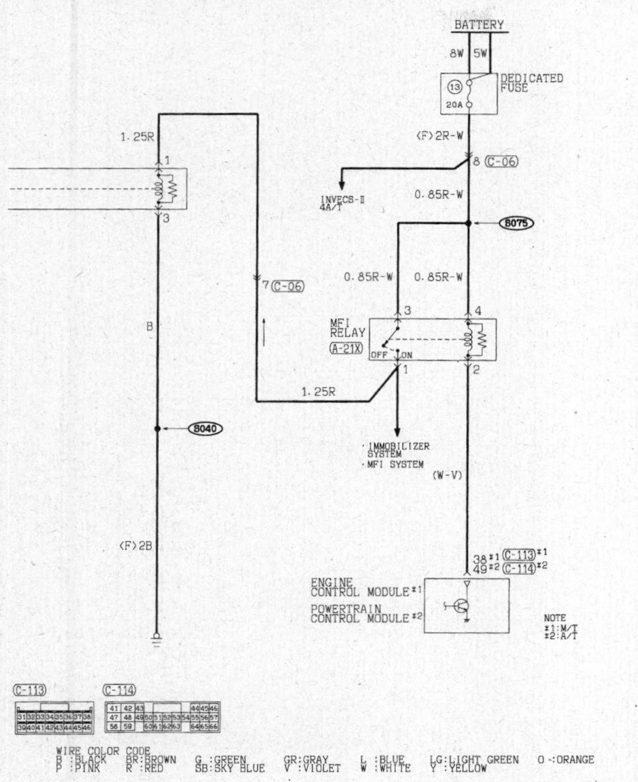

Fig. 24 Engine cooling fan wiring diagram (Part 2 of 2). 2001 Sebring & Stratus Coupe w/2.4L engine

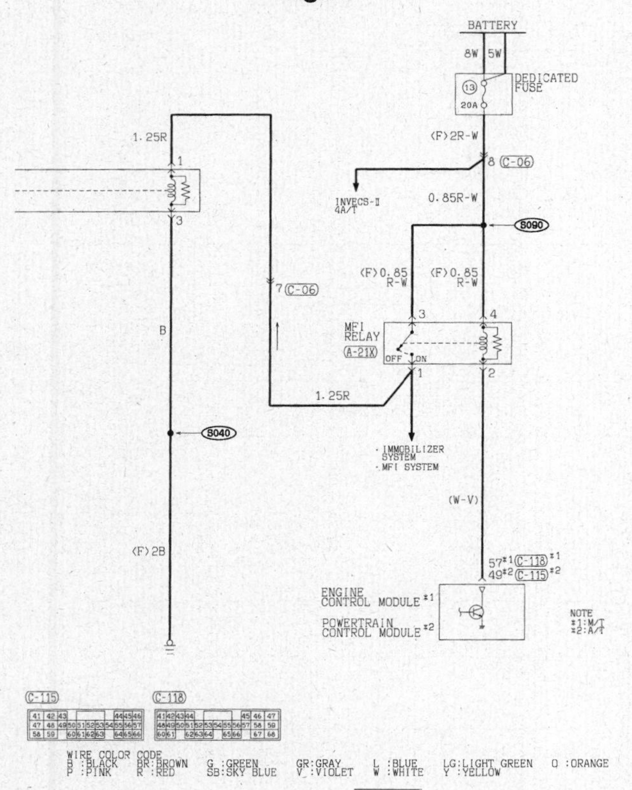

Fig. 25 Engine cooling fan wiring diagram (Part 2 of 2). 2001 Sebring & Stratus Coupe w/3.0L engine

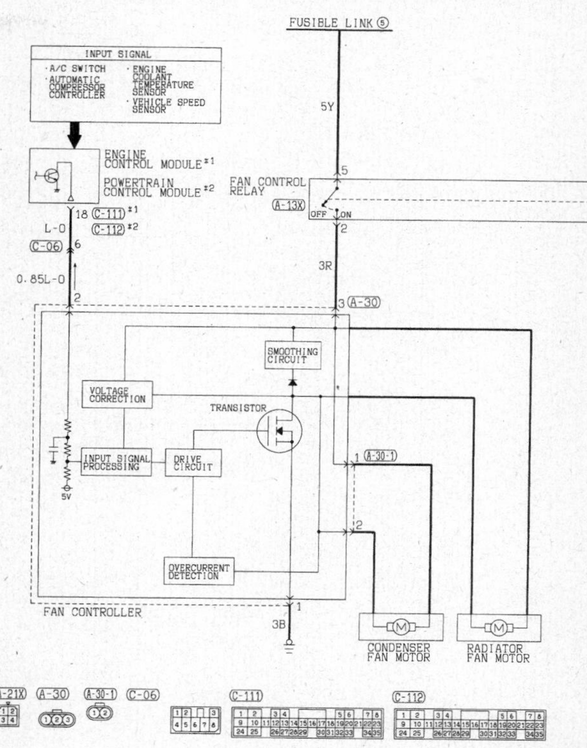

Fig. 25 Engine cooling fan wiring diagram (Part 1 of 2). 2001 Sebring & Stratus Coupe w/3.0L engine

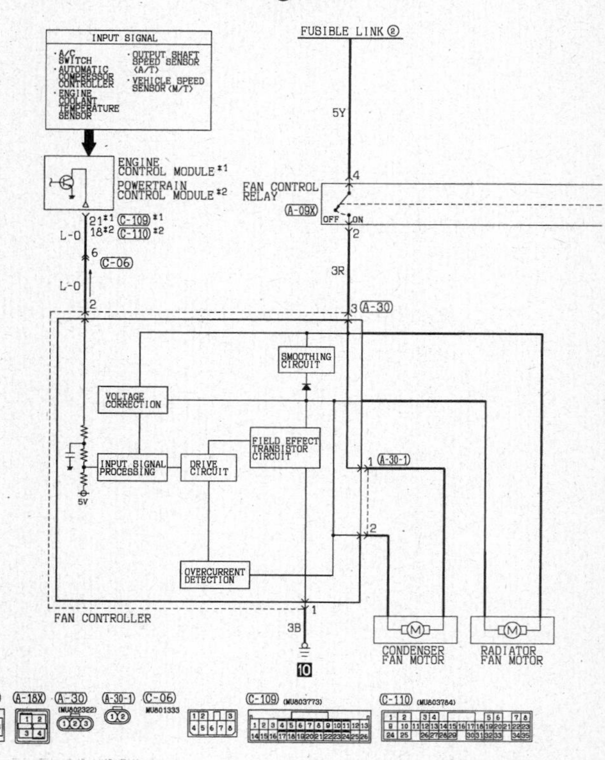

Fig. 26 Engine cooling fan wiring diagram (Part 1 of 2). 2002 Sebring/Stratus Coupe w/2.4L engine

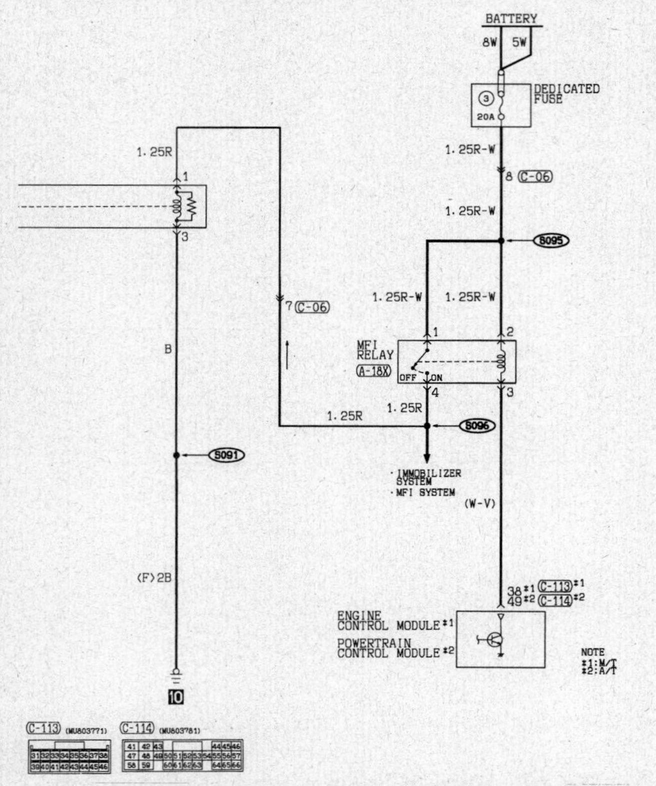
CR1080100331020X

Fig. 26 Engine cooling fan wiring diagram (Part 2 of 2). 2002 Sebring/Stratus Coupe w/2.4L engine

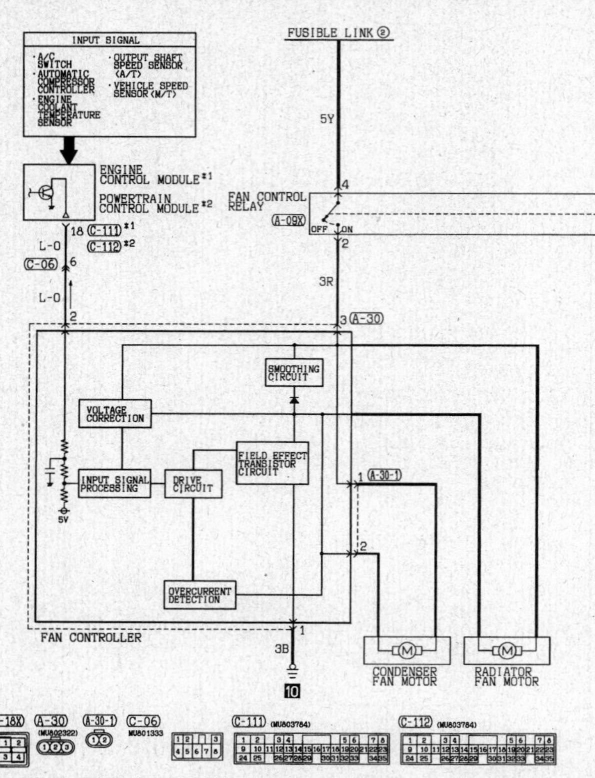
CR1080100332010X

Fig. 27 Engine cooling fan wiring diagram (Part 1 of 2). 2002 Sebring/Stratus Coupe w/3.0L engine

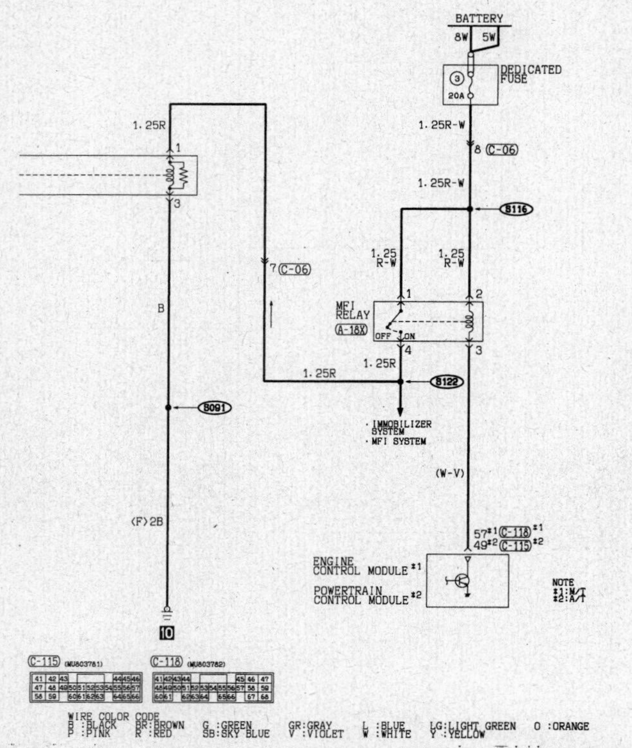
CR1080100332020X

Fig. 27 Engine cooling fan wiring diagram (Part 2 of 2). 2002 Sebring/Stratus Coupe w/3.0L engine

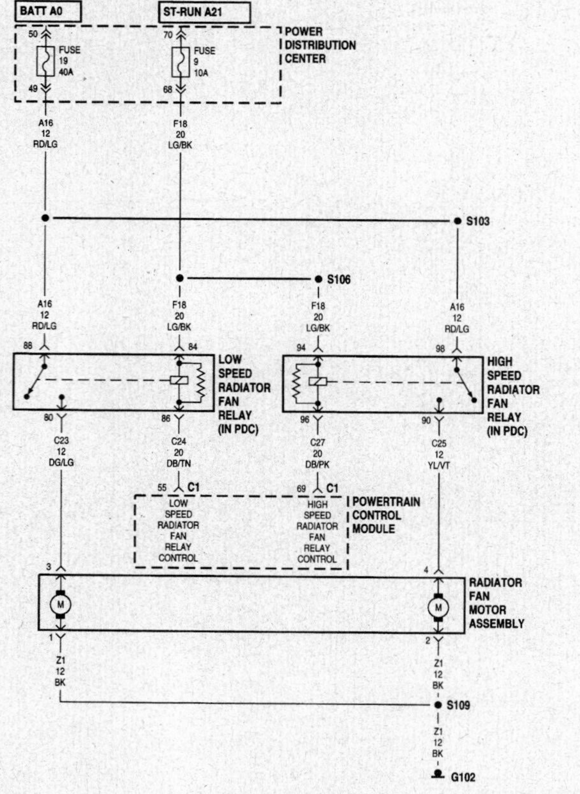
CR7029700399030X

Fig. 28 Engine cooling fan wiring diagram. Breeze, Cirrus & 1998–2000 Stratus

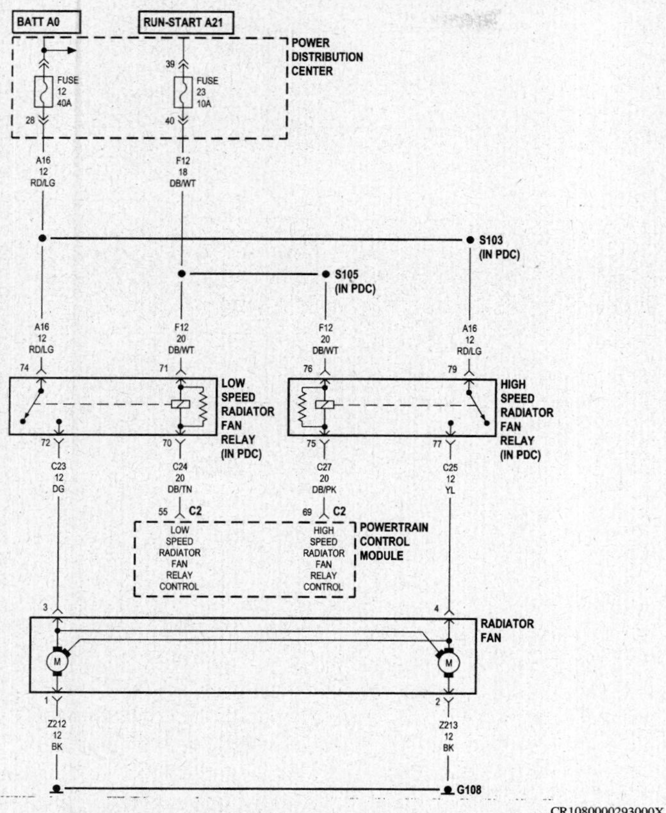

Fig. 29 Engine cooling fan wiring diagram. 2001 Sebring & Stratus Sedan

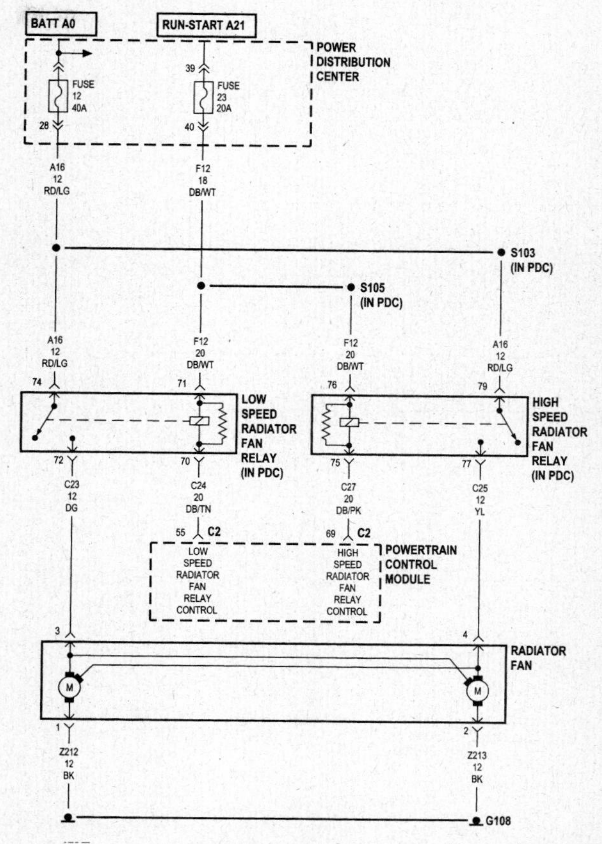

Fig. 30 Engine cooling fan wiring diagram. 2002 Sebring Sedan/Convertible and Stratus Sedan

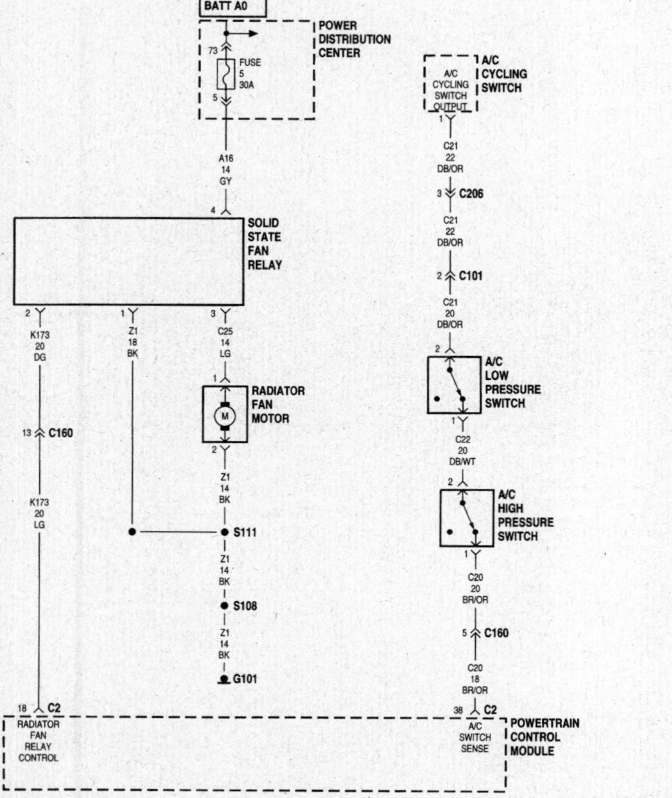

Fig. 31 Engine cooling fan wiring diagram. 1998–99 Neon

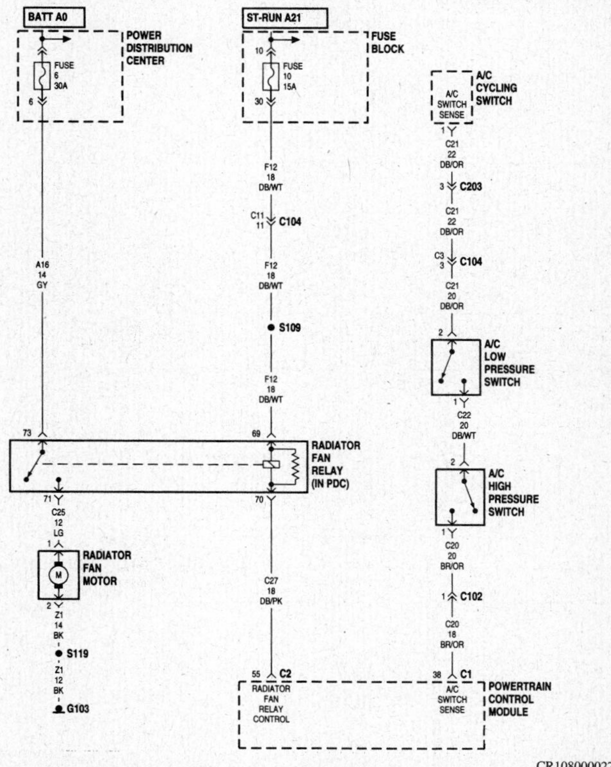

Fig. 32 Engine cooling fan wiring diagram. 2000–02 Neon

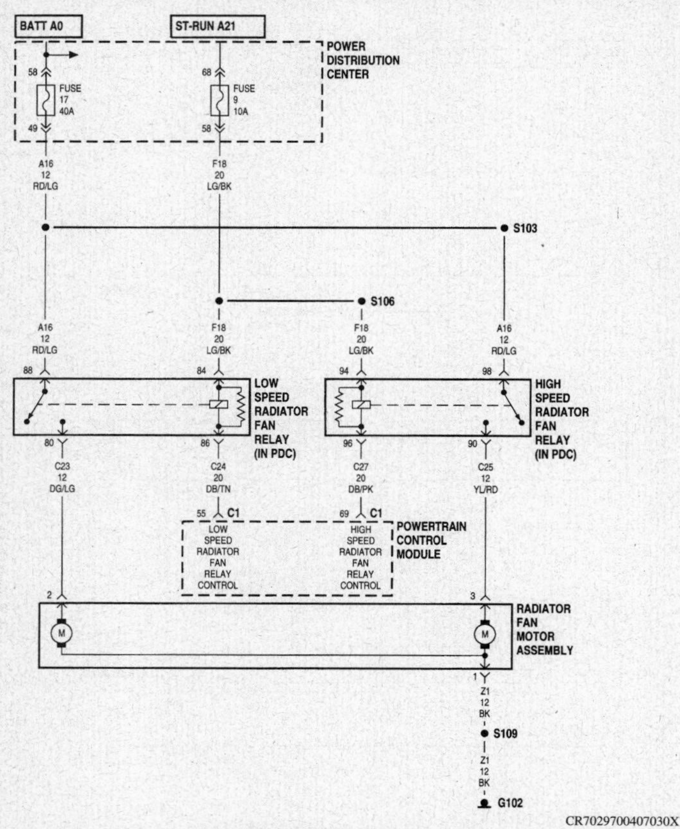

Fig. 33 Engine cooling fan wiring diagram. 1998 Sebring Convertible

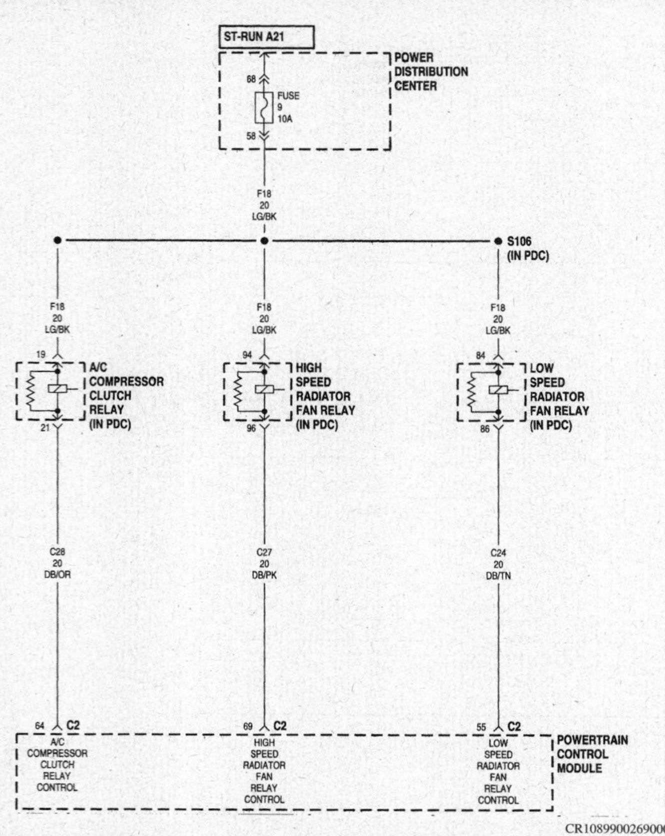

Fig. 34 Engine cooling fan wiring diagram. 1999 Sebring Convertible

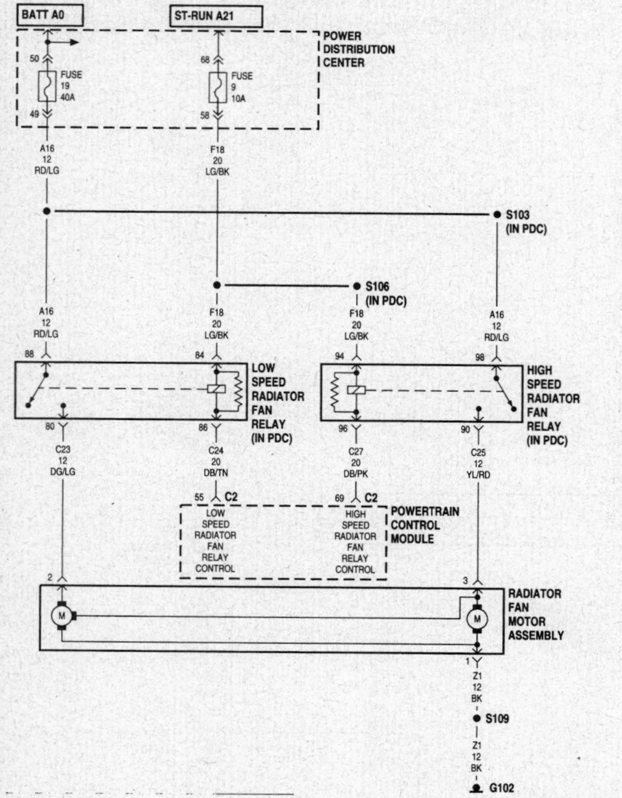

Fig. 35 Engine cooling fan wiring diagram. 2000 Sebring Convertible

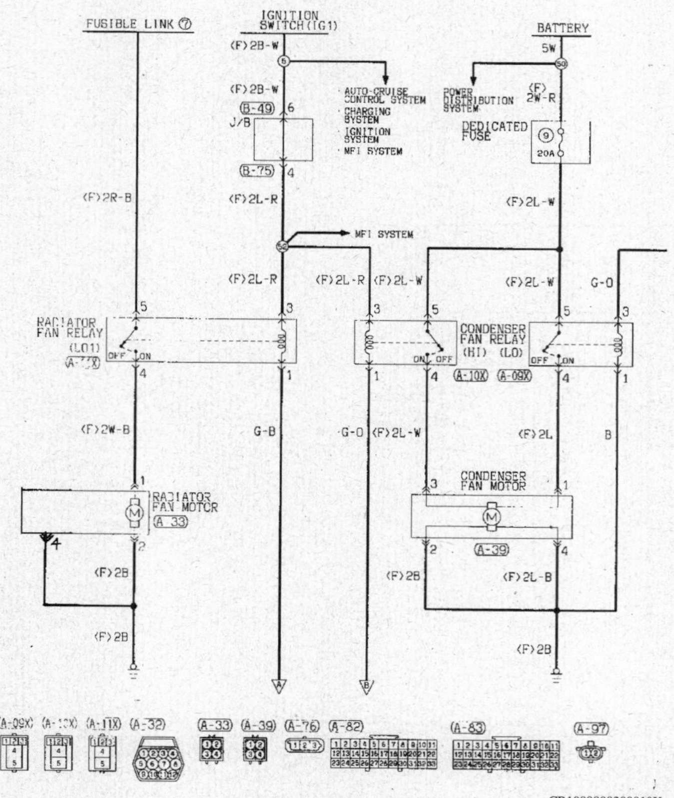

Fig. 36 Engine cooling fan wiring diagram (Part 1 of 2). Talon less turbo w/manual transaxle

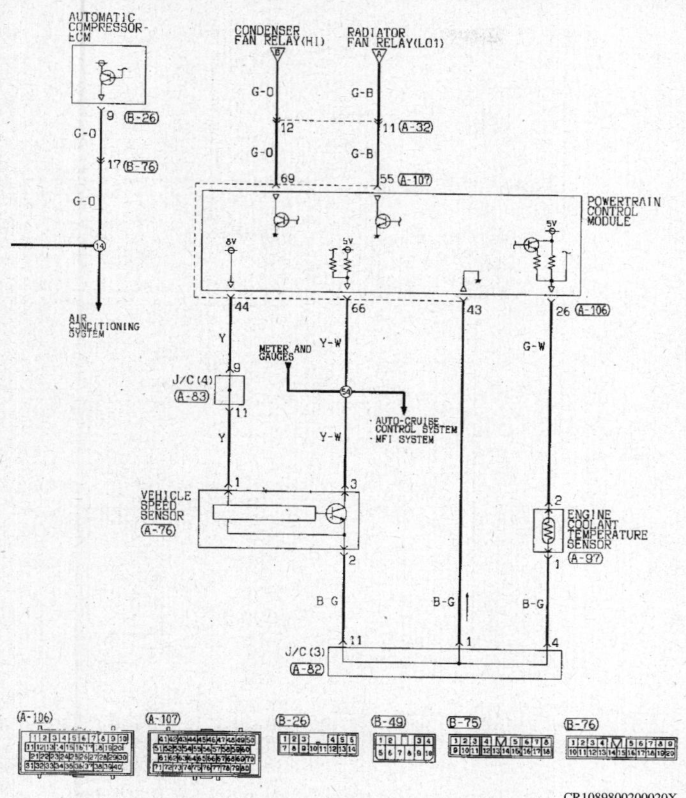

CR1089800200020X

Fig. 36 Engine cooling fan wiring diagram (Part 2 of 2). Talon less turbo w/manual transaxle

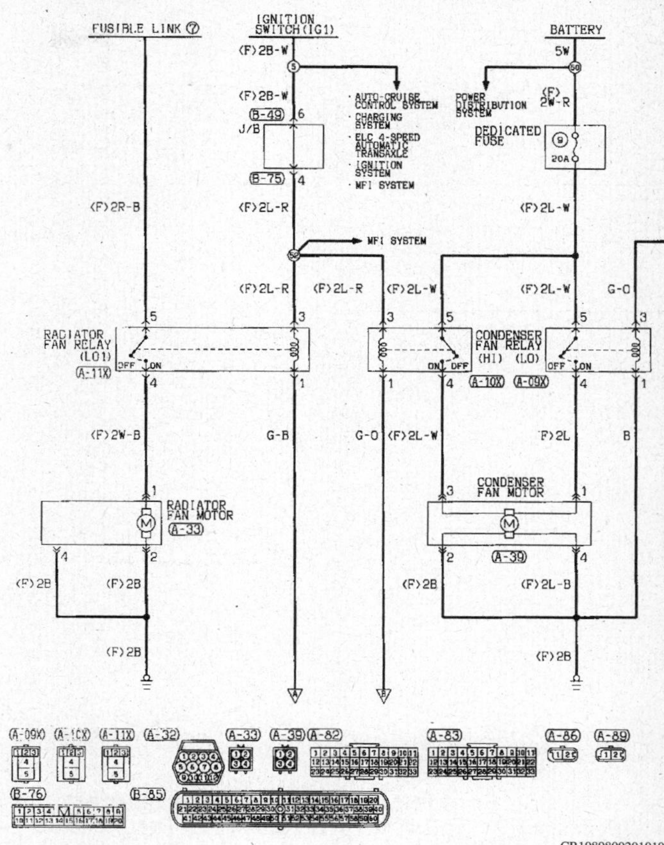

CR1089800201010X

Fig. 37 Engine cooling fan wiring diagram (Part 1 of 2). Talon less turbo w/automatic transaxle

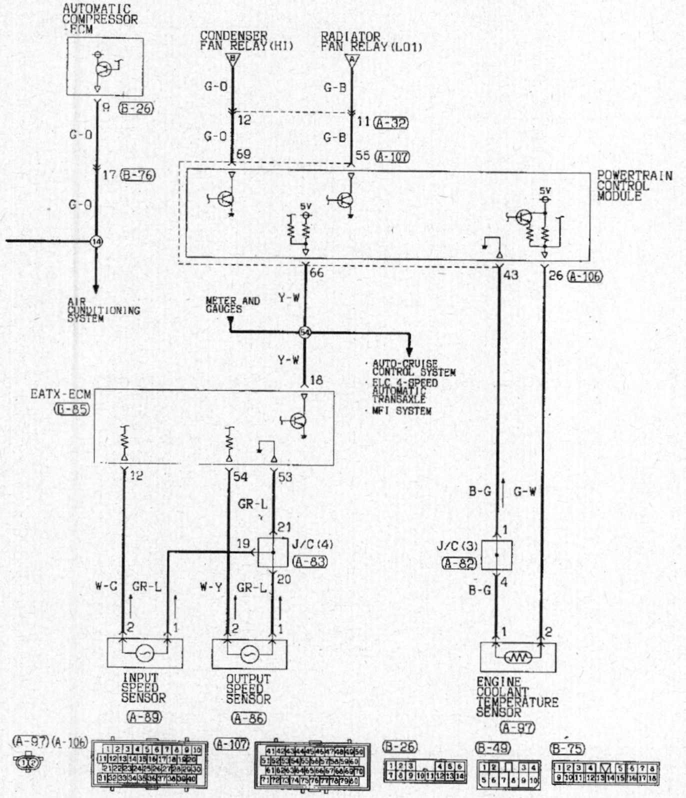

CR1089800201020X

Fig. 37 Engine cooling fan wiring diagram (Part 2 of 2). Talon less turbo w/automatic transaxle

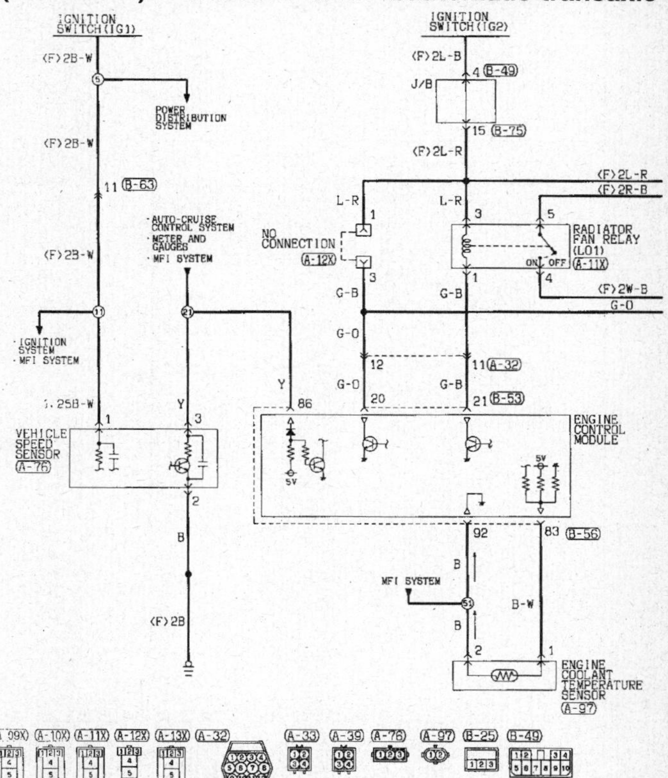

CR1089800202010X

Fig. 38 Engine cooling fan wiring diagram (Part 1 of 2). Talon w/turbo & manual transaxle

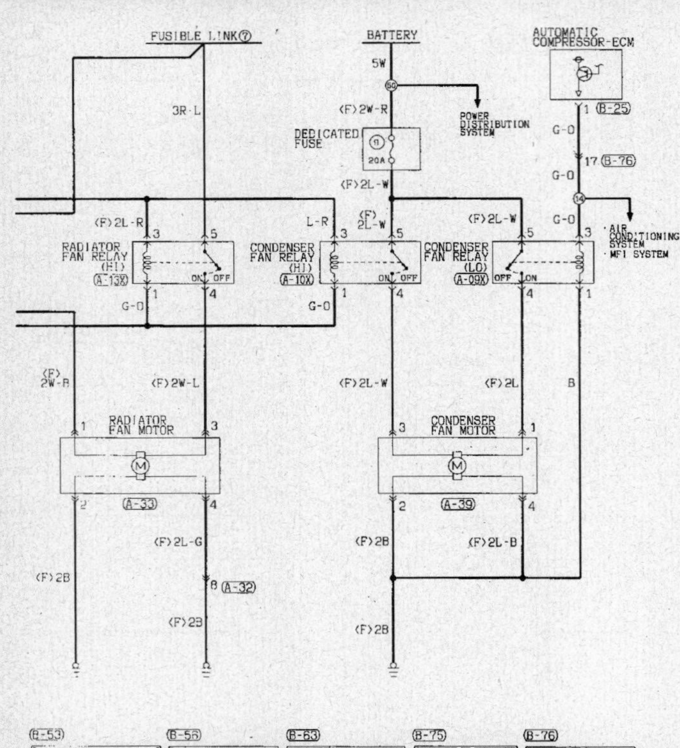

Fig. 38 Engine cooling fan wiring diagram (Part 2 of 2). Talon w/turbo & manual transaxle

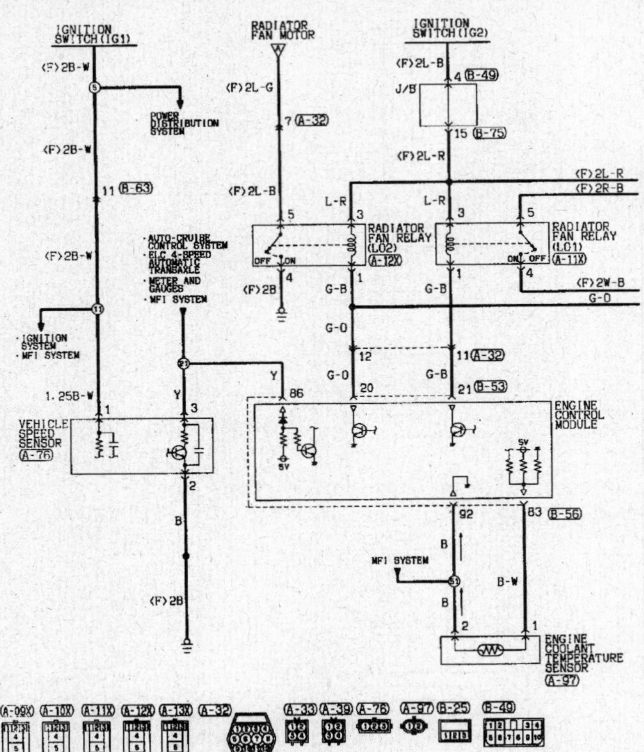

Fig. 39 Engine cooling fan wiring diagram (Part 1 of 2). Talon w/turbo & automatic transaxle

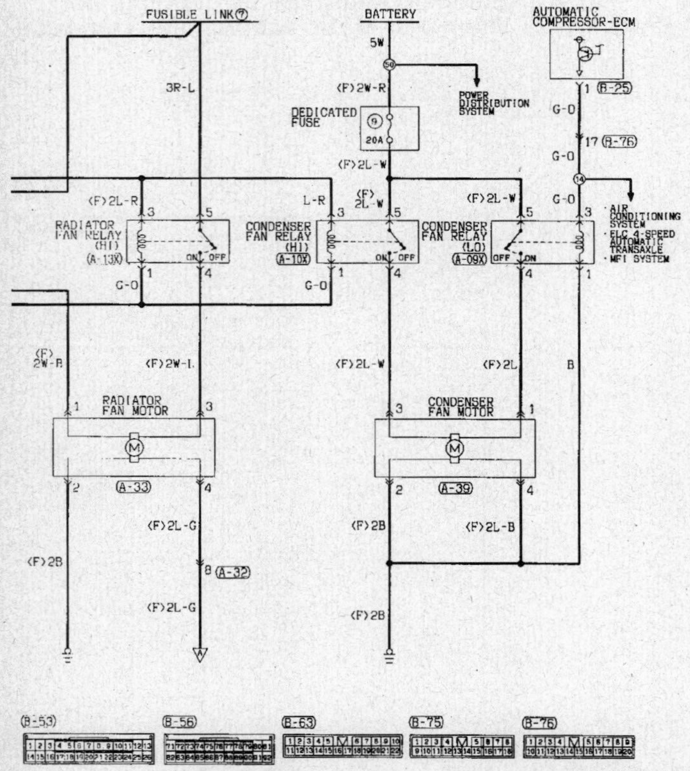

Fig. 39 Engine cooling fan wiring diagram (Part 2 of 2). Talon w/turbo & automatic transaxle

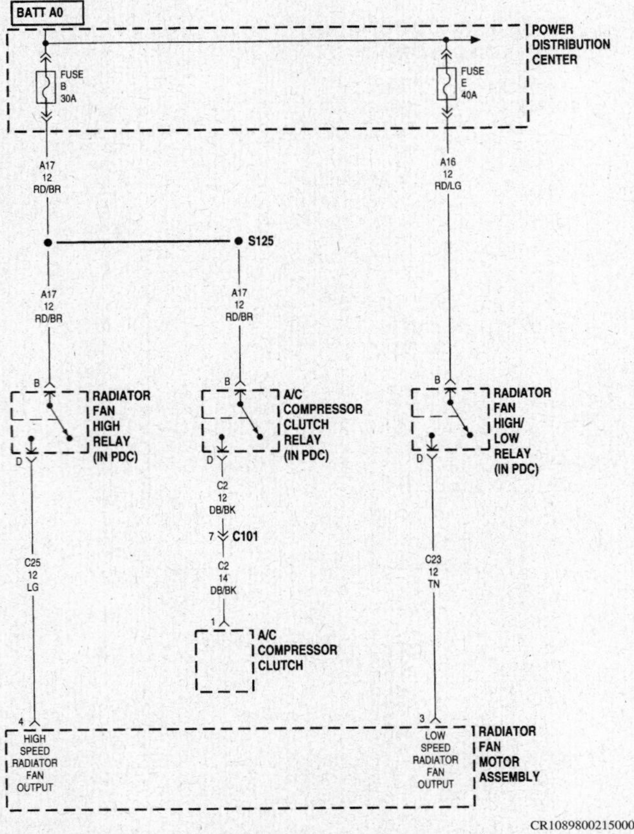

Fig. 40 Engine cooling fan wiring diagram. 1998–99 Concorde, Intrepid, LHS & 300M

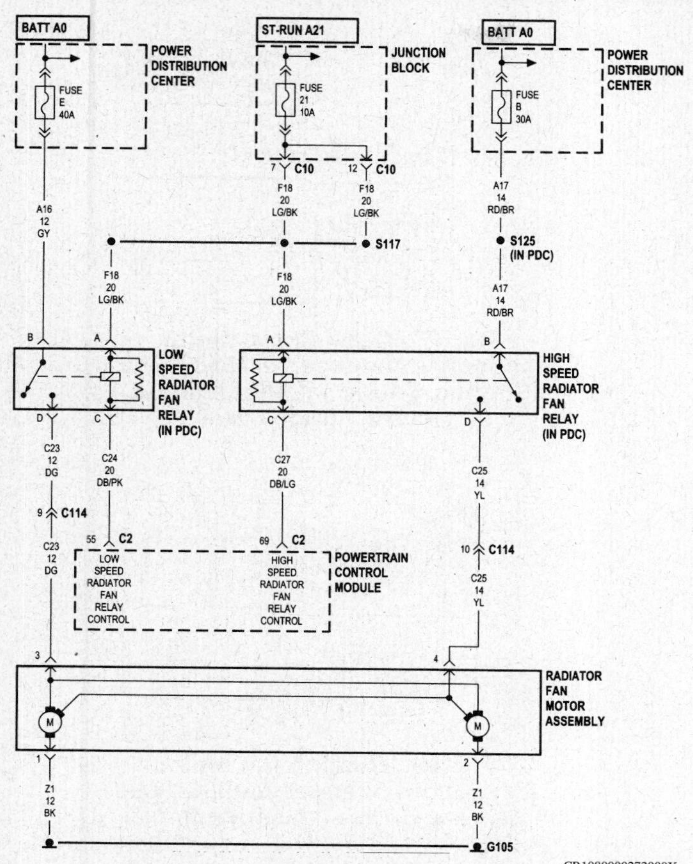

Fig. 41 Engine cooling fan wiring diagram. 2000–02 Concorde, Intrepid, LHS & 300M

TESTER CONNECTION	BATTERY VOLTAGE	SPECIFIED CONDITION
1 – 3	Not applied	Approximately 2Ω
2 – 5	Not applied	Open circuit
	Applied (Connect "+" to the terminal 3 and "–" to the terminal 1.)	Less than 2Ω

CR1080000295000X

Fig. 44 Fan control relay continuity check. 2001–02 Sebring & Stratus Coupe

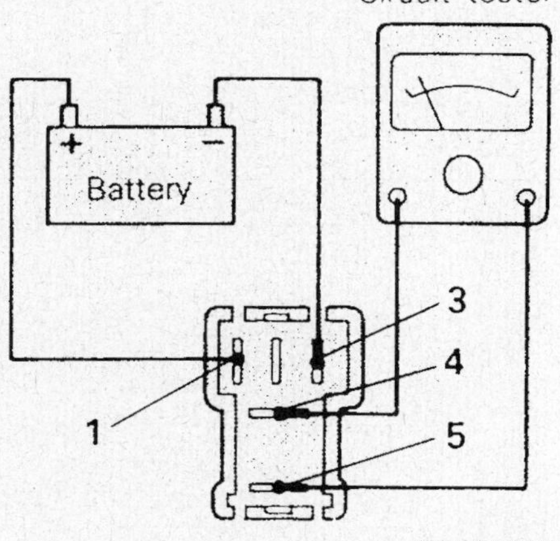

Fig. 45 Radiator fan motor relay test. Avenger, Talon & 1998–2000 Sebring Coupe

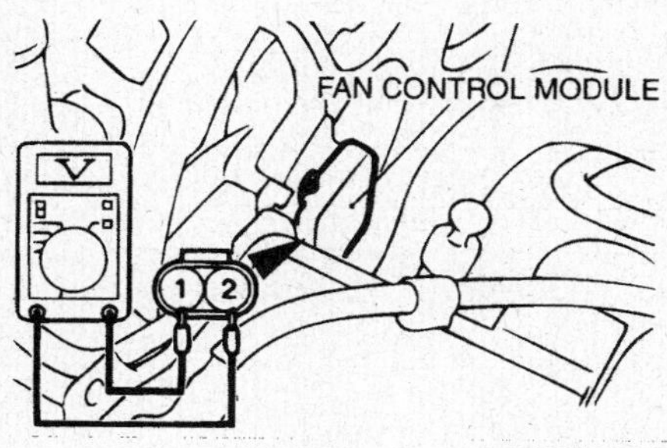

Fig. 42 Fan control module terminal identification. 2001–02 Sebring & Stratus Coupe

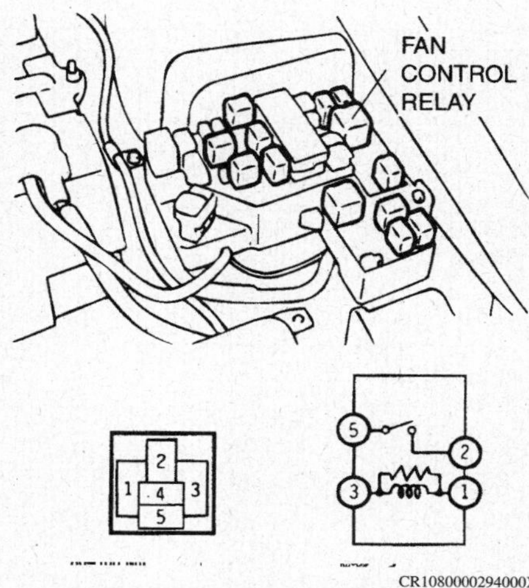

Fig. 43 Fan control relay location. 2001–02 Sebring & Stratus Coupe

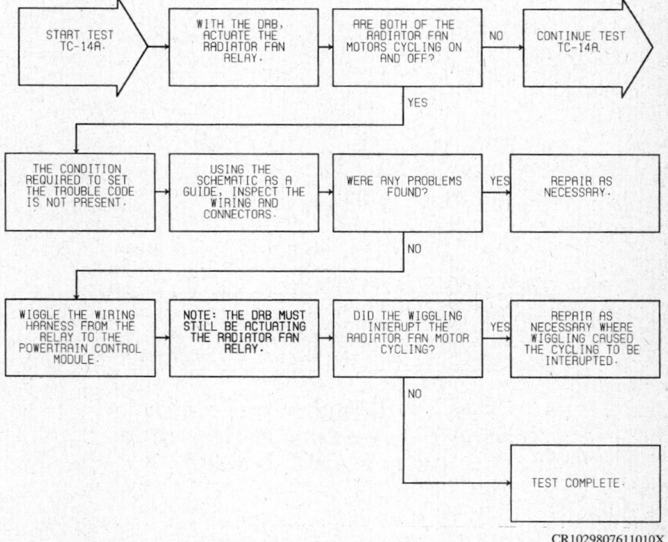

Fig. 46 Radiator Fan Control Relay Circuit (Part 1 of 2). Neon

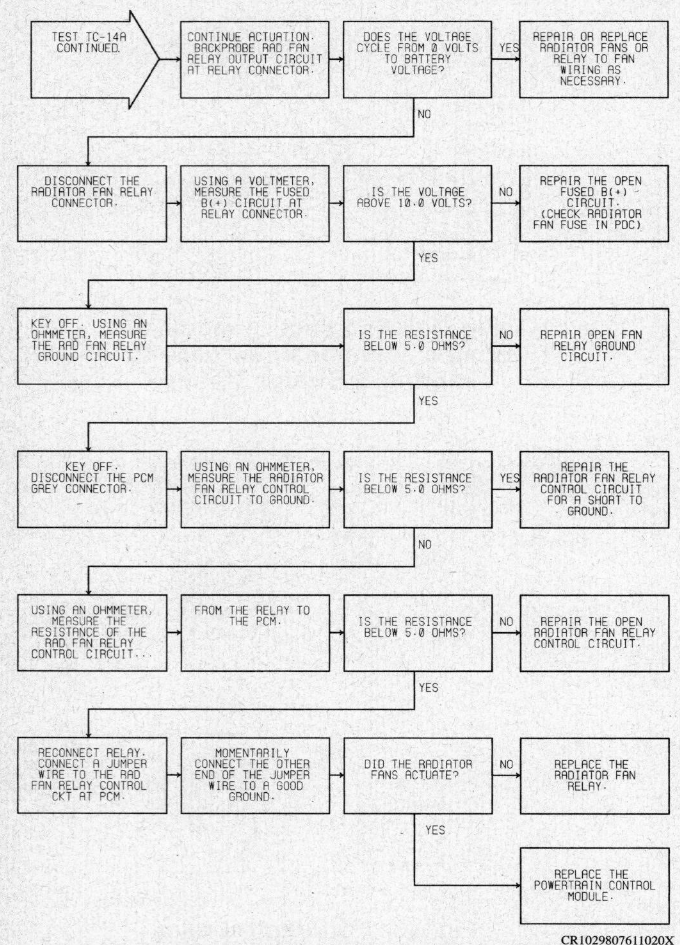

Fig. 46 Radiator Fan Control Relay Circuit (Part 2 of 2). Neon

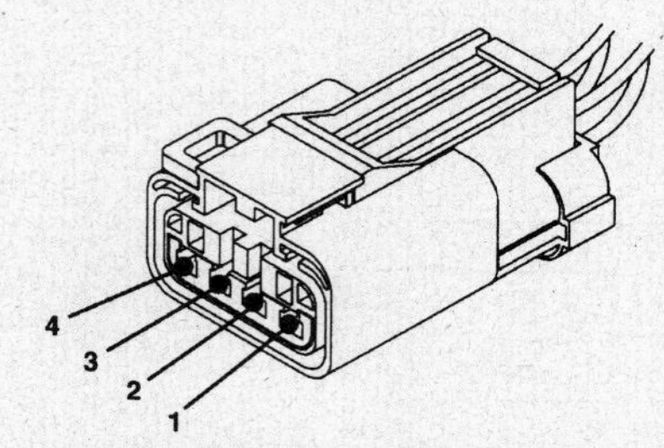

CAV	COLOR	FUNCTION
1	BK	GROUND
2	BK	GROUND
3	TN	LO SPEED RAD FAN RELAY OUTPUT
4	LG	HI SPEED RAD FAN RELAY OUTPUT

CR1089800249000X

Fig. 49 Radiator fan motor connector. 1998–2000 Concorde, Intrepid, LHS & 300M

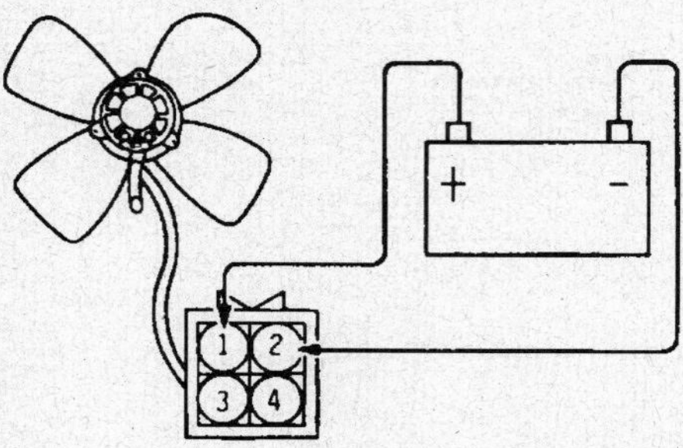

Fig. 47 Cooling fan motor inspection. Avenger & 1998–2000 Sebring Coupe w/2.0L engine & manual transaxle

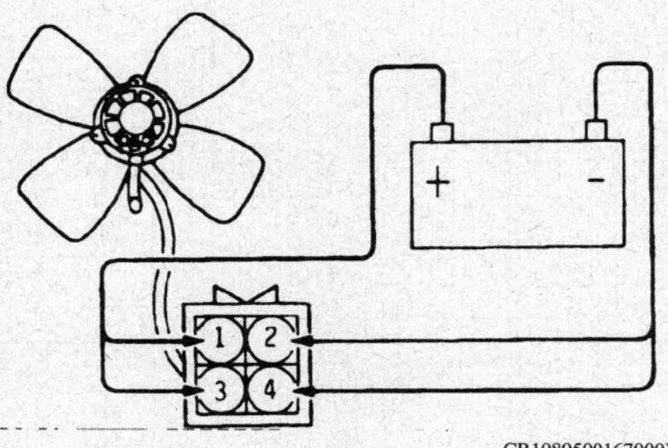

Fig. 48 Cooling fan motor inspection. Avenger & 1998–2000 Sebring Coupe w/2.0L engine & automatic transaxle & 2.5L engine

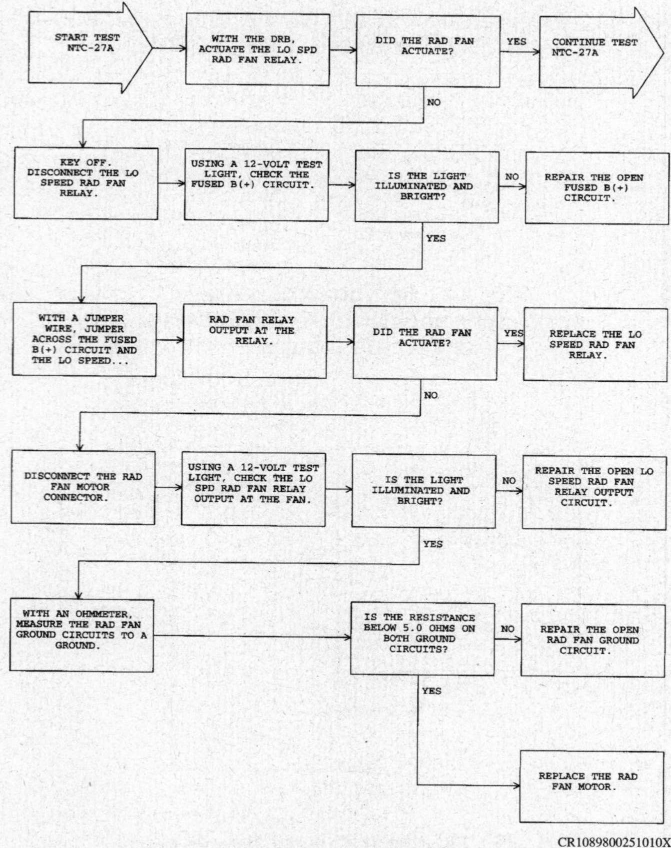

Fig. 50 Radiator fan motor test (Part 1 of 2). 1998–2000 Concorde, Intrepid, LHS & 300M

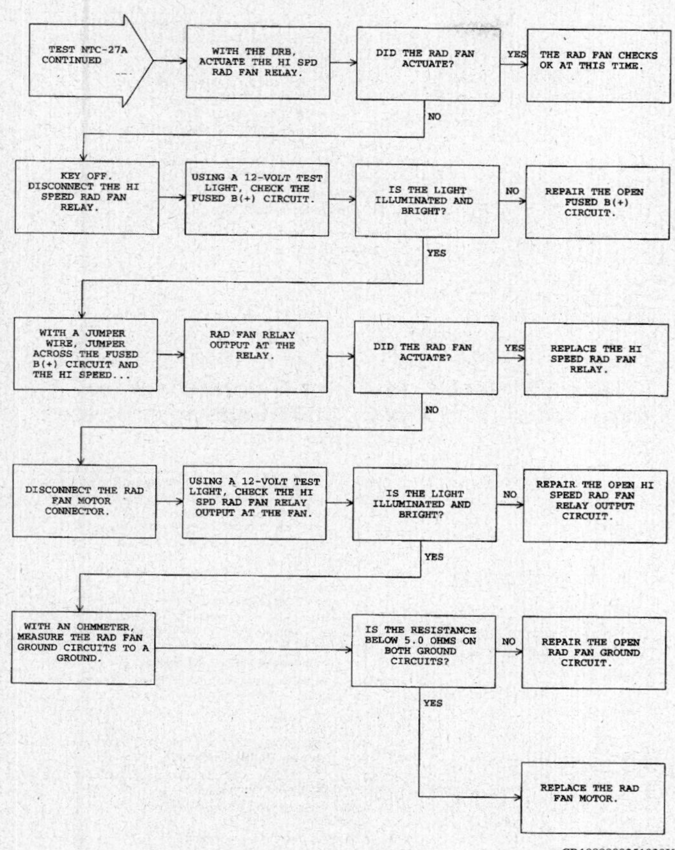

CR1089800251020X

Fig. 50 Radiator fan motor test (Part 2 of 2). 1998–2000 Concorde, Intrepid, LHS & 300M

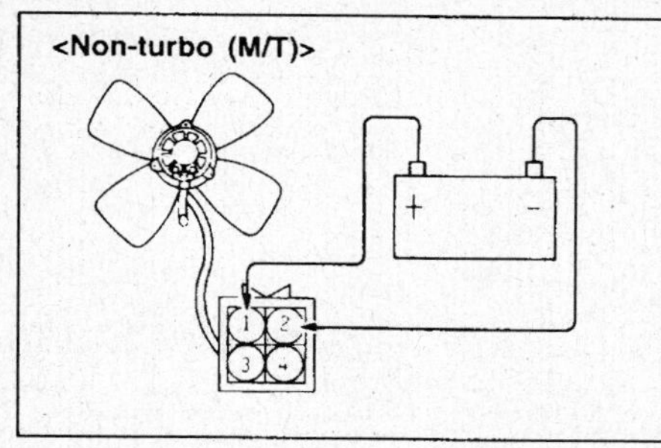

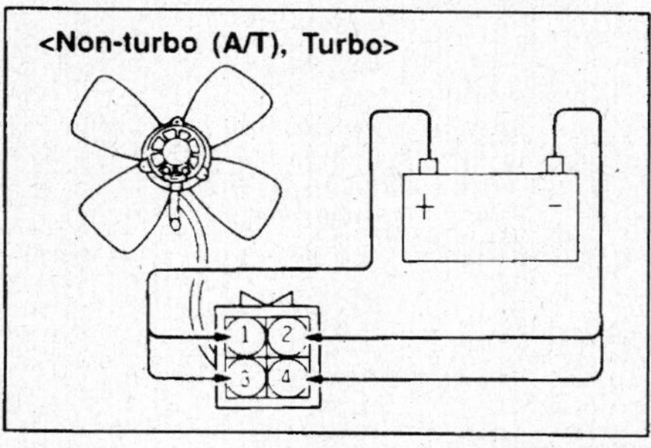

CR1089800207000X

Fig. 51 Fan motor terminal identification. Talon

CIRCUIT OPERATION

- The fan control module is powered from fusible link number 5.
- The ECM <M/T> or PCM <A/T> judges the required revolution speed of radiator fan motor and condenser fan motor using the input signals transmitted from A/C switch, automatic compressor controller, vehicle speed sensor and engine coolant temperature sensor, The ECM <M/T> or PCM <A/T> activates the fan control module to drive the radiator fan motor and condenser fan motor.

TECHNICAL DESCRIPTION

- The cause could be a malfunction of the fan control module power supply or ground circuit.
- The cause could also be a malfunction of the fan control module or the ECM <M/T> or PCM <A/T>.

TROUBLESHOOTING HINTS

- Malfunction of fusible link
- Malfunction of fan control relay
- Malfunction of fan control module
- Malfunction of ECM <M/T> or PCM <A/T>
- Damaged wiring harness or connector

DIAGNOSIS

Required Special Tool:
MB991223: Harness Set

STEP 1. Check the circuit at fan control module connector A-30.

(1) Disconnect fan control module connector A-30, and measure at the harness side connector.
(2) Measure the voltage between terminal number 3 and ground.
- When the ignition switch is turned to "ON" position, voltage should be battery positive voltage.

Q: Is the voltage battery positive voltage when the ignition switch is turned to "ON" position?
YES : Go to Step 7.
NO : Go to Step 2.

CONNECTOR A-30

STEP 2. Check the fan control relay.

Q: Is the fan control relay in good condition?
YES : Go to Step 3.
NO : Replace it, then go to Step 10.

CR1080000297010X

Fig. 52 Test 1: Radiator & condenser fan inoperative (Part 1 of 6). 2001 Sebring & Stratus Coupe

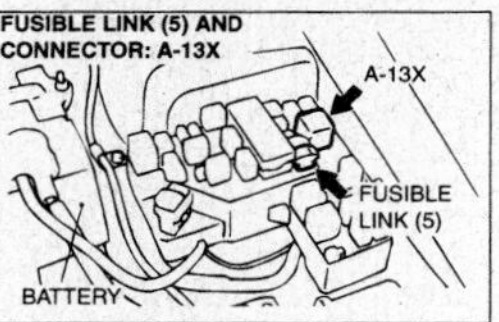

STEP 3. Check for continuity between fusible link number 5 and fan control relay connector A-13X.

Q: Are the harness wires between fusible link number 5 and fan control relay connector A-13X damaged?
YES : Repair or replace them, then go to Step 12.
NO : Go to Step 4.

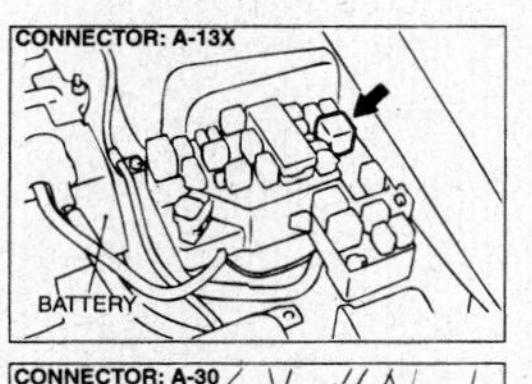

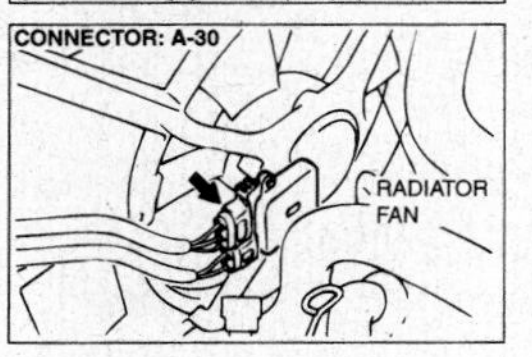
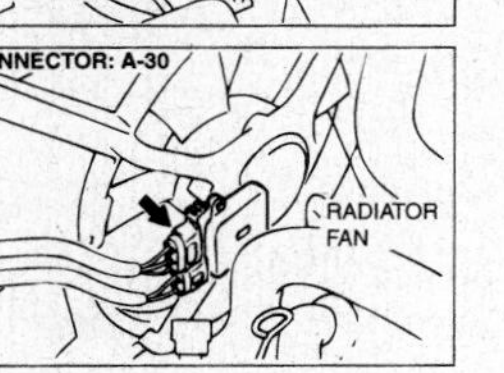

STEP 4. Check for continuity between fan control relay connector A-13X and fan control module connector A-30.

Q: Are the harness wires between fan control relay connector A-13X and fan control module connector A-30 damaged?
YES : Repair or replace them, then go to Step 12
NO : Go to Step 5.

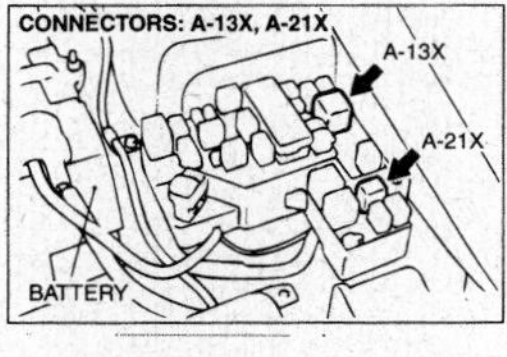

STEP 5. Check for continuity between MFI relay connector A-21X and fan control relay connector A-13X .

Q: Are the harness wires between MFI relay connector A-21X and fan control relay connector A-13X damaged?
YES : Repair or replace them, then go to Step 12.
NO : Go to Step 6.

CR1080000297020X

Fig. 52 Test 1: Radiator & condenser fan inoperative (Part 2 of 6). 2001 Sebring & Stratus Coupe

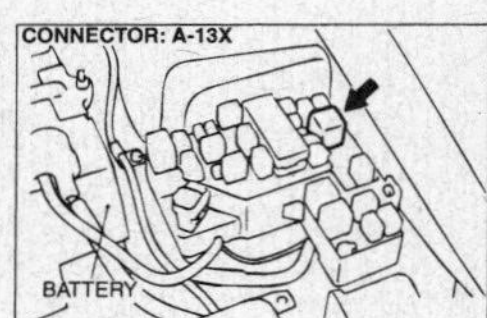

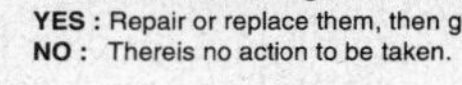

STEP 6. Check for continuity between fan control relay connector A-13X and ground.

Q: Are the harness wires between fan control relay connector A-13X and ground damaged?

YES : Repair or replace them, then go to Step 12.
NO : Thereis no action to be taken.

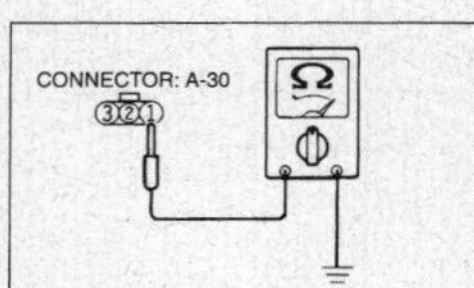

STEP 7. Check the circuit at fan control module connector A-30.

(1) Disconnect fan control module connector A-30, and measure at the harness side connector.
(2) Measure the resistance between terminal number 1 and ground.

Q: Is the resistance less than 2 ohm?

YES : Go to Step 9.
NO : Go to Step 8.

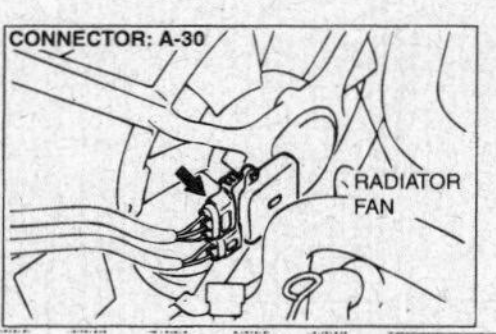

STEP 8. Check the harness wire between fan control module connector A-30 and ground.

Q: Are the harness wires between fan control module connector A-30 and ground damaged?

YES : Repair or replace them, then go to Step 12.
NO : There is no action to be taken.

CR1080000297030X

Fig. 52 Test 1: Radiator & condenser fan inoperative (Part 3 of 6). 2001 Sebring & Stratus Coupe

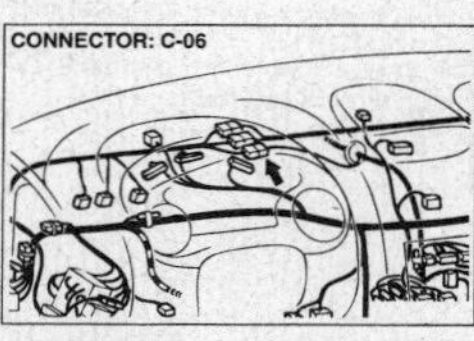

STEP 10. Check the harness wire between ECM connector C-109 <2.4L-M/T>, C-111 <3.0L-M/T>or PCM connector C-110 <2.4L-A/T> , C-112 <3.0L-A/T> and fan control module connector A-30.

NOTE: If intermediate connector C-06 is damaged, repair or replace it.

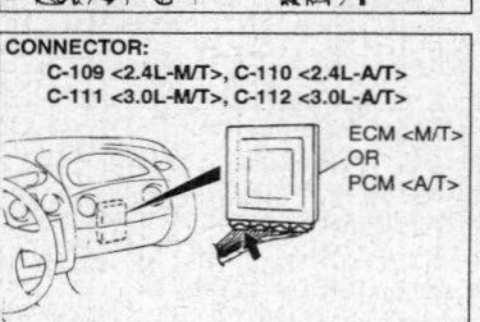

Q: Are the harness wires between ECM connector C-109 <2.4L-M/T>, C-111 <3.0L-M/T>or PCM connector C-110 <2.4L-A/T> , C-112 <3.0L-A/T> and fan control module connector A-30 damaged?

YES : Repair or replace them, then go to Step 12.
NO : Go to Step 11.

CR1080000297050X

Fig. 52 Test 1: Radiator & condenser fan inoperative (Part 5 of 6). 2001 Sebring & Stratus Coupe

Radiator Fan and Condenser Fan Drive Circuit

CIRCUIT OPERATION

- The fan control module is powered from fusible link number 5.
- The ECM <M/T> or PCM <A/T> judges the required revolution speed of radiator fan motor and condenser fan motor using the input signals transmitted from A/C switch, automatic compressor controller, vehicle speed sensor and engine coolant temperature sensor. The ECM <M/T> or PCM <A/T> activates the fan control module to drive the radiator fan motor and condenser fan motor.

TECHNICAL DESCRIPTION

The fan control module has variable control of the radiator fan motor and the condenser fan motor speeds using signals transmitted from the ECM <M/T> or PCM <A/T>.

TROUBLESHOOTING HINTS

- Malfunction of fan control relay
- Malfunction of fan control module
- Malfunction of ECM <M/T> or PCM <A/T>
- Malfunction of ECM <M/T> or PCM <A/T>

DIAGNOSIS

Required Special Tool:
MB991223: Harness Set

CR1080000298010X

Fig. 53 Test 2: Radiator & condenser fan do not change speed or stop (Part 1 of 3). 2001 Sebring & Stratus Coupe

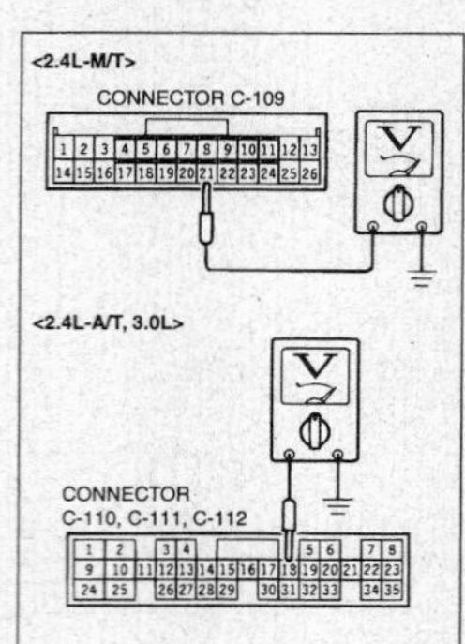

STEP 9. Check the circuit at ECM connector C-109 <2.4L-M/T>, C-111 <3.0L-M/T>or PCM connector C-110 <2.4L-A/T> , C-112 <3.0L-A/T>.

(1) Connect ECM connector C-109 <2.4L-M/T>, C-111 <3.0L-M/T> or PCM connector C-110 <2.4L-A/T>, C-112 <3.0L-A/T>.
(2) Start the engine and allow it to idle.
(3) Measure the voltage between terminal number 21 <2.4L-M/T> or 18 <2.4L-A/T, 3.0L> and ground.

Q: Is the voltage 0.7 volt or more when the radiator fan is operating?

YES : Go to Step 11.
NO : Go to Step 10.

CR1080000297040X

Fig. 52 Test 1: Radiator & condenser fan inoperative (Part 4 of 6). 2001 Sebring & Stratus Coupe

STEP 11. Check the fan control module at ECM connector C-109 <2.4L-M/T>, C-111 <3.0L-M/T>or PCM connector C-110 <2.4L-A/T> , C-112 <3.0L-A/T>.

(1) Disconnect ECM connector C-109 <2.4L-M/T>, C-111 <3.0L-M/T> or PCM connector C-110 <2.4L-A/T>, C-112 <3.0L-A/T>.
(2) Pull out pin 21 <2.4L-M/T> or 18 <2.4L-A/T, 3.0L> to disconnect it.
(3) Reconnect ECM connector C-109 <2.4L-M/T>, C-111 <3.0L-M/T> or PCM connector C-110 <2.4L-A/T>, C-112 <3.0L-A/T> with pin 21 <2.4L-M/T> or 18 <2.4L-A/T, 3.0L> still removed.
(4) Turn the ignition switch to "ON" position.

Q: Do the radiator fan motor and condenser fan motor operate?

YES : Replace the ECM <M/T> or PCM <A/T>. Then go to Step 12.
NO : Replace the radiator fan motor and fan control module assembly.Then go to Step 12 .

STEP 12. Check the symptoms.

Q: Do the radiator fan and condenser fan operate correctly?

YES : This diagnosis is complete.
NO : Return to Step 1.

CR1080000297060X

Fig. 52 Test 1: Radiator & condenser fan inoperative (Part 6 of 6). 2001 Sebring & Stratus Coupe

STEP 1. Check the fan control relay.
Refer to P.7-18.

Q: Is the fan control relay in good condition?

YES : Go to Step 2.
NO : Replace the part, then go to Step 6.

STEP 2. Check the harness wire between fan control relay connector A-13X and fan control module connector A-30.

Q: Are the harness wire between fan control relay connector A-13X and fan control module connector A-30 damaged?

YES : Repair or replace the part, then go to Step 6.
NO : Go to Step 3.

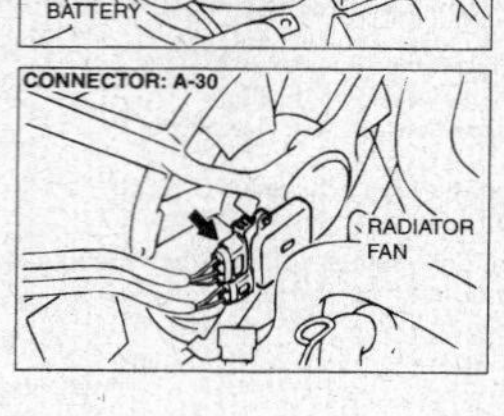

STEP 3. Check the circuit at ECM connector C-109 <2.4L-M/T>, C-111 <3.0L-M/T>or PCM connector C-110 <2.4L-A/T> , C-112 <3.0L-A/T>.

(1) Connect ECM connector C-109 <2.4L-M/T>, C-111 <3.0L-M/T> or PCM connector C-110 <2.4L-A/T>, C-112 <3.0L-A/T>.
(2) Start the engine and run it at idle. [Engine coolant temperature: 80°C (176°Φ) ορ λεσσ]
(3) Measure the voltage between terminal number 21 <2.4L-M/T> or 18 <2.4L-A/T, 3.0L> and ground.

Q: Is the voltage 0 - 0.3 volt when radiator fan is not operating?

YES : Go to Step 6.
NO : Go to Step 4.

CR1080000298020X

Fig. 53 Test 2: Radiator & condenser fan do not change speed or stop (Part 2 of 3). 2001 Sebring & Stratus Coupe

STEP 4. Check the harness wire between ECM connector C-109 <2.4L-M/T>, C-111 <3.0L-M/T>or PCM connector C-110 <2.4L-A/T> , C-112 <3.0L-A/T> and fan control module connector A-30.

NOTE: If intermediate connector C-06 is damaged, repair or replace it.

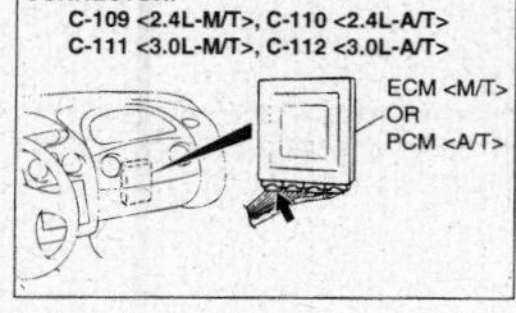

Q: Are the harness wires between ECM connector C-109 <2.4L-M/T>, C-111 <3.0L-M/T>or PCM connector C-110 <2.4L-A/T> , C-112 <3.0L-A/T> and fan control module connector A-30 damaged?

YES : Repair or replace them, then go to Step 6.
NO : Go to Step 5.

<2.4L-M/T>
CONNECTOR C-109
<2.4L-A/T, 3.0L>
CONNECTOR C-110, C-111, C-112

STEP 5. Check the fan control module at ECM connector C-109 <2.4L-M/T>, C-111 <3.0L-M/T>or PCM connector C-110 <2.4L-A/T> , C-112 <3.0L-A/T>.

(1) Connect ECM connector C-109 <2.4L-M/T>, C-111 <3.0L-M/T> or PCM connector C-110 <2.4L-A/T>, C-112 <3.0L-A/T>.
(2) Turn the ignition switch to " ON" position.
(3) Pull out the terminal number 21 <2.4L-M/T> or 18 <2.4L-A/T, 3.0L> and connect it to the body ground.

Q: Do the radiator fan motor and condenser fan motor stop?

YES : Replace the ECM <M/T> or PCM <A/T>. Then go to Step 6.
NO : Replace the radiator fan motor and fan control module assembly. Then go to Step 6 .

STEP 6. Check the symptoms.

Q: Do the radiator fan and condenser fan operate correctly?

YES : This diagnosis is complete.
NO : Return to Step 1.

CR1080000298030X

Fig. 53 Test 2: Radiator & condenser fan do not change speed or stop (Part 3 of 3). 2001 Sebring & Stratus Coupe

Radiator Fan and Condenser Fan Drive Circuit

CIRCUIT OPERATION

- The fan control module is powered from fusible link number 5.
- The ECM <M/T> or PCM <A/T> judges the required revolution speed of radiator fan motor and condenser fan motor using the input signals transmitted from A/C switch, automatic compressor controller, vehicle speed sensor and engine coolant temperature sensor. The ECM <M/T> or PCM <A/T> activates the fan control module to drive the radiator fan motor and condenser fan motor.

TECHNICAL DESCRIPTION

The cause could be a malfunction of the condenser fan motor or of the fan control module.

TROUBLESHOOTING HINTS

- Malfunction of condenser fan motor
- Malfunction of fan control module

DIAGNOSIS

STEP 1. Check the condenser fan motor.

Q: Is the condenser fan in good condition?

YES : Replace the radiator fan motor and fan control module assembly. Then go to Step 3.
NO : Go to Step 2.

STEP 2. Check the fan control module.
Refer to P.7-18.

Q: Is the fan control module in good condition?

YES : Go to Step 3.
NO : Replace the fan control module, then go to Step 3.

STEP 3. Check the symptoms.

Q: Does the condenser fan operate correctly?

YES : This diagnosis is complete.
NO : Return to Step1.

CR1080000300000X

Fig. 55 Test 4: Condenser fan inoperative. 2001 Sebring & Stratus Coupe

TECHNICAL DESCRIPTION

The cause could be a malfunction of the radiator fan motor or an open circuit between the fan control module and the radiator fan motor.

TROUBLESHOOTING HINTS

- Malfunction of radiator fan motor
- Malfunction of fan control module

CR1080000299010X

Fig. 54 Test 3: Radiator fan inoperative (Part 1 of 2). 2001 Sebring & Stratus Coupe

DIAGNOSIS

Replace the radiator fan motor and fan control module assembly.

Q: Does the radiator fan operate correctly?

YES : There is no action to be taken?
NO : Repair the wiring harness between the fan control module and the radiator fan motor.

CR1080000299020X

Fig. 54 Test 3: Radiator fan inoperative (Part 2 of 2). 2001 Sebring & Stratus Coupe

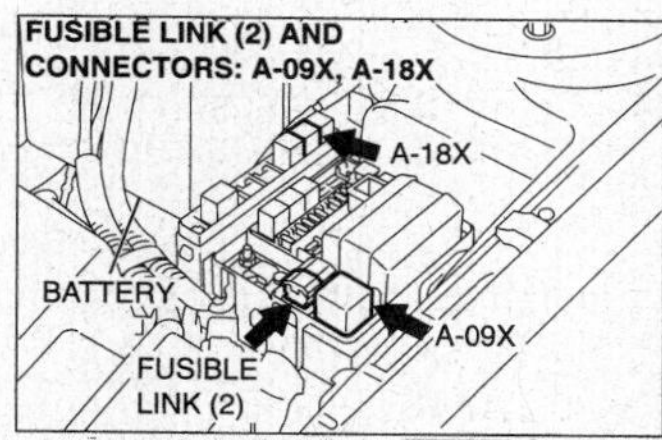

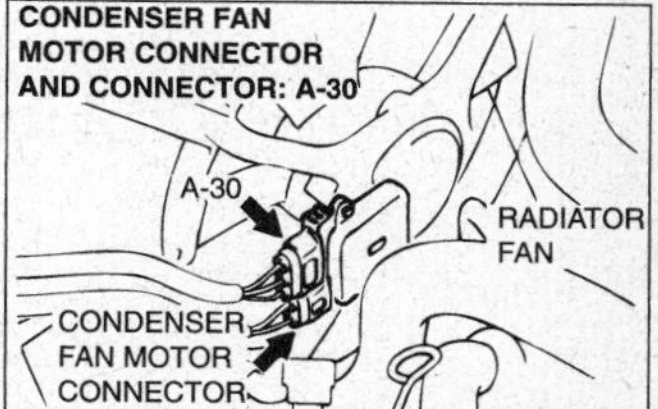

CR1080200331010X

Fig. 56 Radiator fan and condenser fan do not operate (Part 1 of 7). 2002 Sebring & Stratus Coupe

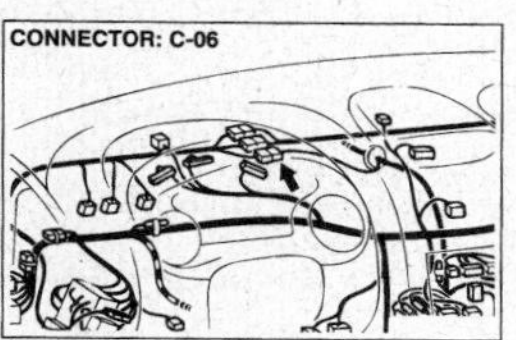

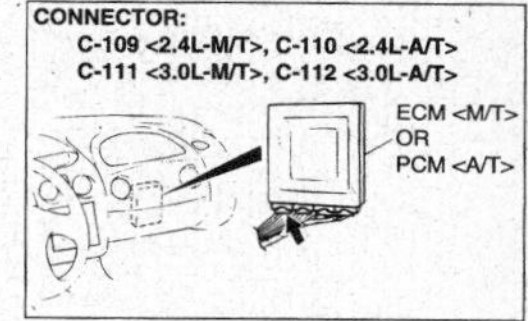

CIRCUIT OPERATION

- The fan control module is powered from fusible link number 2.
- The ECM <M/T> or PCM <A/T> judges the required revolution speed of radiator fan motor and condenser fan motor using the input signals transmitted from A/C switch, automatic compressor controller, vehicle speed sensor <M/T>, output shaft speed sensor <A/T> and engine coolant temperature sensor. The ECM <M/T> or PCM <A/T> activates the fan control module to drive the radiator fan motor and condenser fan motor.

TECHNICAL DESCRIPTION

- The cause could be a malfunction of the fan control module power supply or ground circuit.
- The cause could also be a malfunction of the fan control module or the ECM <M/T> or PCM <A/T>.

TROUBLESHOOTING HINTS

- Malfunction of fusible link
- Malfunction of fan control relay
- Malfunction of fan control module
- Malfunction of ECM <M/T> or PCM <A/T>
- Damaged wiring harness or connector

DIAGNOSIS

Required Special Tool:
MB991223: Harness Set

STEP 1. Check the fusible link number 2.

Q: Is the fusible link number 2 good condition?

YES : Go to Step 2.
NO : Replace it, then go to Step 13.

STEP 2. Check the circuit at fan control module connector A-30.

CONNECTOR A-30

(1) Disconnect fan control module connector A-30, and measure at the harness side connector.
(2) Measure the voltage between terminal number 3 and ground.
   - When the ignition switch is turned to "ON" position, voltage should be battery positive voltage.

Q: Is the voltage battery positive voltage when the ignition switch is turned to "ON" position?

YES : Go to Step 8.
NO : Go to Step 3.

CR1080200331020X

Fig. 56 Radiator fan and condenser fan do not operate (Part 2 of 7). 2002 Sebring & Stratus Coupe

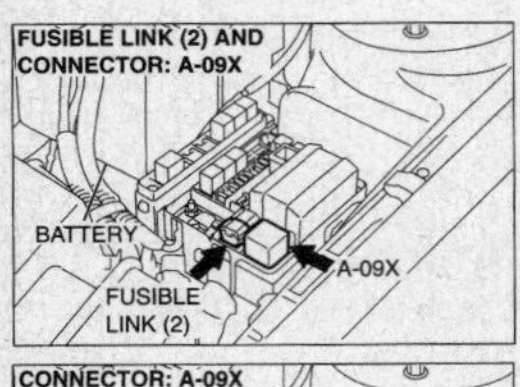

STEP 3. Check the fan control relay.
Refer to P.7-18.

Q: Is the fan control relay in good condition?

YES : Go to Step 4.
NO : Replace it, then go to Step 11.

CONNECTOR: A-09X
BATTERY
A-09X

STEP 4. Check for continuity between fusible link number 2 and fan control relay connector A-09X.

Q: Are the harness wires between fusible link number 2 and fan control relay connector A-09X damaged?

YES : Repair or replace them, then go to Step 13.
NO : Go to Step 5.

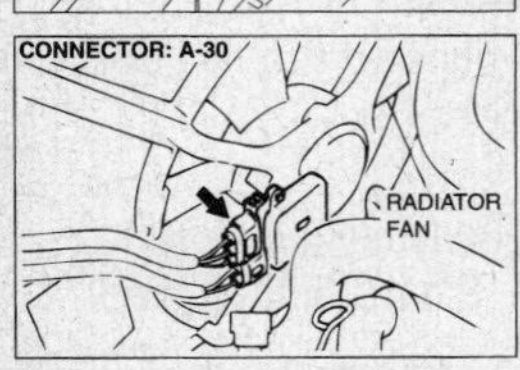

STEP 5. Check for continuity between fan control relay connector A-09X and fan control module connector A-30.

Q: Are the harness wires between fan control relay connector A-09X and fan control module connector A-30 damaged?

YES : Repair or replace them, then go to Step 13.
NO : Go to Step 6.

CR1080200331030X

Fig. 56 Radiator fan and condenser fan do not operate (Part 3 of 7). 2002 Sebring & Stratus Coupe

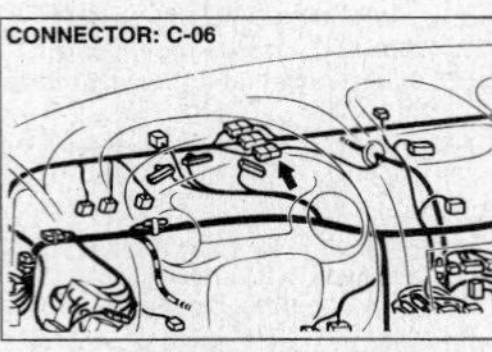

STEP 6. Check for continuity between MFI relay connector A-18X and fan control relay connector A-09X.
NOTE: If intermediate connector C-06 is damaged, repair or replace it.

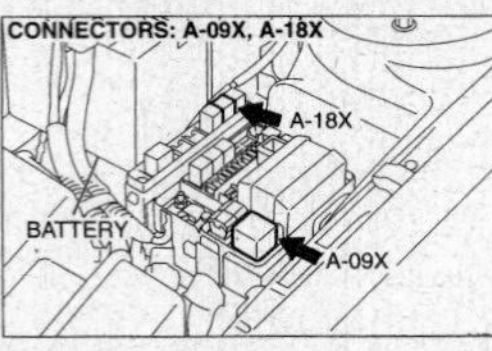

Q: Are the harness wires between MFI relay connector A-18X and fan control relay connector A-09X damaged?

YES : Repair or replace them, then go to Step 13.
NO : Go to Step 7.

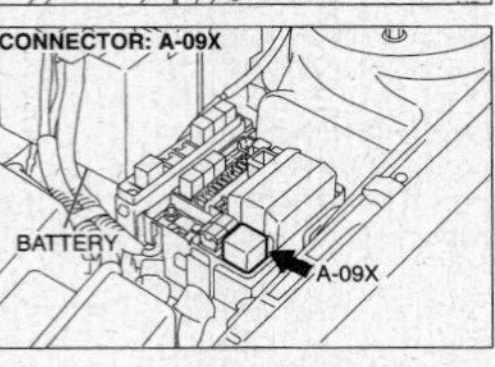

STEP 7. Check for continuity between fan control relay connector A-09X and ground.

Q: Are the harness wires between fan control relay connector A-09X and ground damaged?

YES : Repair or replace them, then go to Step 13.
NO : There is no action to be taken.

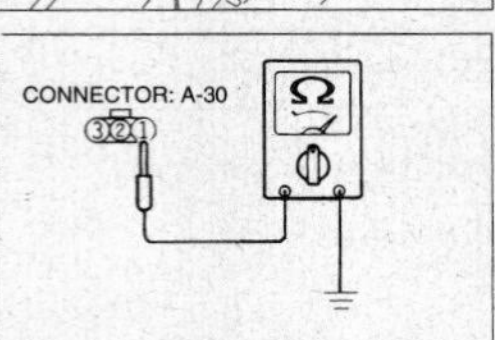

STEP 8. Check the circuit at fan control module connector A-30.

(1) Disconnect fan control module connector A-30, and measure at the harness side connector.
(2) Measure the resistance between terminal number 1 and ground.

Q: Is the resistance less than 2 ohm?

YES : Go to Step 10.
NO : Go to Step 9.

CR1080200331040X

Fig. 56 Radiator fan and condenser fan do not operate (Part 4 of 7). 2002 Sebring & Stratus Coupe

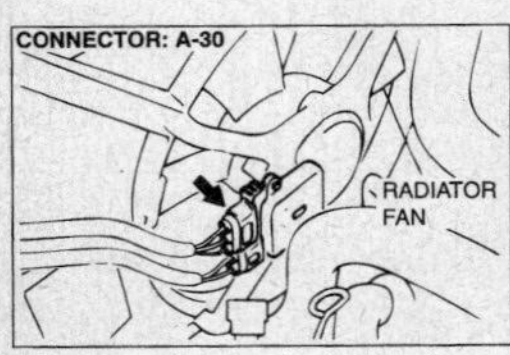

STEP 9. Check the harness wire between fan control module connector A-30 and ground.

Q: Are the harness wires between fan control module connector A-30 and ground damaged?

YES : Repair or replace them, then go to Step 13.
NO : There is no action to be taken.

<2.4L-M/T>
CONNECTOR C-109
<2.4L-A/T, 3.0L>
CONNECTOR
C-110, C-111, C-112

STEP 10. Check the circuit at ECM connector C-109 <2.4L-M/T>, C-111 <3.0L-M/T> or PCM connector C-110 <2.4L-A/T>, C-112 <3.0L-A/T>.

(1) Connect ECM connector C-109 <2.4L-M/T>, C-111 <3.0L-M/T> or PCM connector C-110 <2.4L-A/T>, C-112 <3.0L-A/T>.
(2) Start the engine and allow it to idle.
(3) Measure the voltage between terminal number 21 <2.4L-M/T> or 18 <2.4L-A/T, 3.0L> and ground.

Q: Is the voltage 0.7 volt or more when the radiator fan is operating?

YES : Go to Step 12.
NO : Go to Step 11.

CR1080200331050X

Fig. 56 Radiator fan and condenser fan do not operate (Part 5 of 7). 2002 Sebring & Stratus Coupe

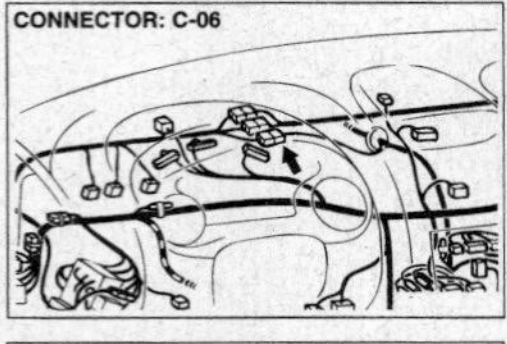

STEP 11. Check the harness wire between ECM connector C-109 <2.4L-M/T>, C-111 <3.0L-M/T> or PCM connector C-110 <2.4L-A/T>, C-112 <3.0L-A/T> and fan control module connector A-30.
NOTE: If intermediate connector C-06 is damaged, repair or replace it.

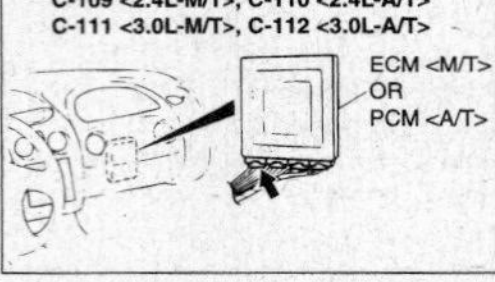

Q: Are the harness wires between ECM connector C-109 <2.4L-M/T>, C-111 <3.0L-M/T> or PCM connector C-110 <2.4L-A/T>, C-112 <3.0L-A/T> and fan control module connector A-30 damaged?

YES : Repair or replace them, then go to Step 13.
NO : Go to Step 12.

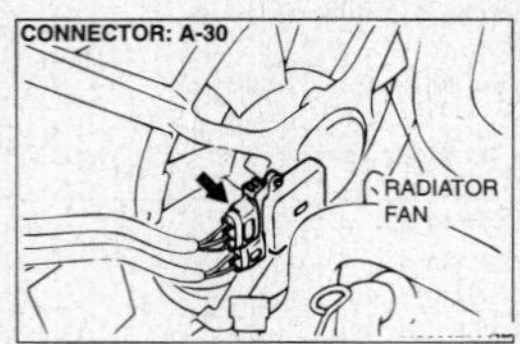

CR1080200331060X

Fig. 56 Radiator fan and condenser fan do not operate (Part 6 of 7). 2002 Sebring & Stratus Coupe

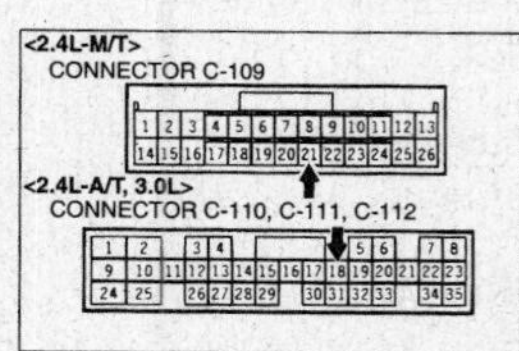

STEP 12. Check the fan control module at ECM connector C-109 <2.4L-M/T>, C-111 <3.0L-M/T> or PCM connector C-110 <2.4L-A/T>, C-112 <3.0L-A/T>.

(1) Disconnect ECM connector C-109 <2.4L-M/T>, C-111 <3.0L-M/T> or PCM connector C-110 <2.4L-A/T>, C-112 <3.0L-A/T>.
(2) Pull out pin 21 <2.4L-M/T> or 18 <2.4L-A/T, 3.0L> to disconnect it.
(3) Reconnect ECM connector C-109 <2.4L-M/T>, C-111 <3.0L-M/T> or PCM connector C-110 <2.4L-A/T>, C-112 <3.0L-A/T> with pin 21 <2.4L-M/T> or 18 <2.4L-A/T, 3.0L> still removed.
(4) Turn the ignition switch to "ON" position.

Q: Do the radiator fan motor and condenser fan motor operate?
YES : Replace the ECM <M/T> or PCM <A/T>. Then go to Step 13.
NO : Replace the radiator fan motor and fan control module assembly. Then go to Step 13.

STEP 13. Check the symptoms.

Q: Do the radiator fan and condenser fan operate correctly?
YES : This diagnosis is complete.
NO : Return to Step 1.

CR1080200331070X

Fig. 56 Radiator fan and condenser fan do not operate (Part 7 of 7). 2002 Sebring & Stratus Coupe

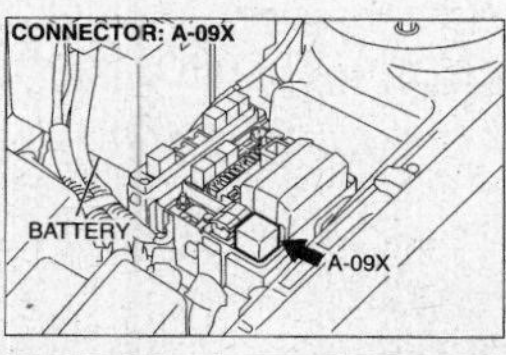

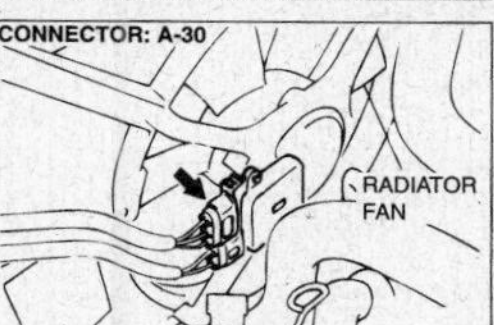

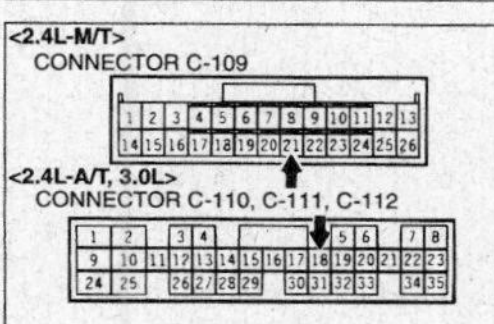

STEP 1. Check the fan control relay.

Q: Is the fan control relay in good condition?
YES : Go to Step 2.
NO : Replace the part, then go to Step 6.

STEP 2. Check the harness wire between fan control relay connector A-09X and fan control module connector A-30.
Q: Are the harness wire between fan control relay connector A-09X and fan control module connector A-30 damaged?
YES : Repair or replace the part, then go to Step 6.
NO : Go to Step 3.

STEP 3. Check the circuit at ECM connector C-109 <2.4L-M/T>, C-111 <3.0L-M/T> or PCM connector C-110 <2.4L-A/T>, C-112 <3.0L-A/T>.
(1) Connect ECM connector C-109 <2.4L-M/T>, C-111 <3.0L-M/T> or PCM connector C-110 <2.4L-A/T>, C-112 <3.0L-A/T>.
(2) Start the engine and run it at idle. [Engine coolant temperature: 80°C (176°F) or less]
(3) Measure the voltage between terminal number 21 <2.4L-M/T> or 18 <2.4L-A/T, 3.0L> and ground.

Q: Is the voltage 0 – 0.3 volt when radiator fan is not operating?
YES : Go to Step 6.
NO : Go to Step 4.

CR1080200332020X

Fig. 57 Radiator fan and condenser fan do not change speed or stop (Part 2 of 3). 2002 Sebring & Stratus Coupe

CIRCUIT OPERATION
- The fan control module is powered from fusible link number 2.
- The ECM <M/T> or PCM <A/T> judges the required revolution speed of radiator fan motor and condenser fan motor using the input signals transmitted from A/C switch, automatic compressor controller, vehicle speed sensor <M/T>, output shaft speed sensor <A/T> and engine coolant temperature sensor. The ECM <M/T> or PCM <A/T> activates the fan control module to drive the radiator fan motor and condenser fan motor.

TECHNICAL DESCRIPTION
The fan control module has variable control of the radiator fan motor and the condenser fan motor speeds using signals transmitted from the ECM <M/T> or PCM <A/T>.

TROUBLESHOOTING HINTS
- Malfunction of fan control relay
- Malfunction of fan control module
- Malfunction of ECM <M/T> or PCM <A/T>
- Damaged wiring harness or connector

CR1080200332010X

Fig. 57 Radiator fan and condenser fan do not change speed or stop (Part 1 of 3). 2002 Sebring & Stratus Coupe

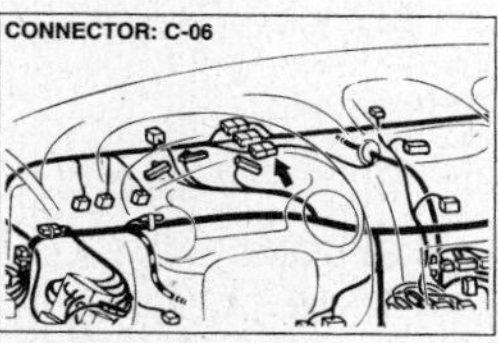

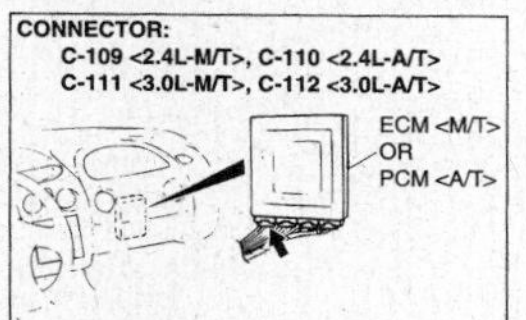

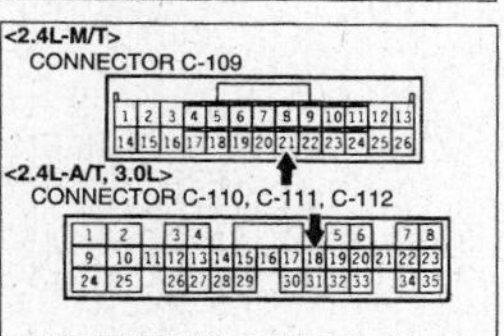

STEP 4. Check the harness wire between ECM connector C-109 <2.4L-M/T>, C-111 <3.0L-M/T> or PCM connector C-110 <2.4L-A/T>, C-112 <3.0L-A/T> and fan control module connector A-30.
NOTE: If intermediate connector C-06 is damaged, repair or replace it.

Q: Are the harness wires between ECM connector C-109 <2.4L-M/T>, C-111 <3.0L-M/T> or PCM connector C-110 <2.4L-A/T>, C-112 <3.0L-A/T> and fan control module connector A-30 damaged?
YES : Repair or replace them, then go to Step 6.
NO : Go to Step 5.

STEP 5. Check the fan control module at ECM connector C-109 <2.4L-M/T>, C-111 <3.0L-M/T> or PCM connector C-110 <2.4L-A/T>, C-112 <3.0L-A/T>.
(1) Connect ECM connector C-109 <2.4L-M/T>, C-111 <3.0L-M/T> or PCM connector C-110 <2.4L-A/T>, C-112 <3.0L-A/T>.
(2) Turn the ignition switch to "ON" position.
(3) Pull out the terminal number 21 <2.4L-M/T> or 18 <2.4L-A/T, 3.0L> and connect it to the body ground.

Q: Do the radiator fan motor and condenser fan motor stop?
YES : Replace the ECM <M/T> or PCM <A/T>. Then go to Step 6.
NO : Replace the radiator fan motor and fan control module assembly. Then go to Step 6.

STEP 6. Check the symptoms.

Q: Do the radiator fan and condenser fan operate correctly?
YES : This diagnosis is complete.
NO : Return to Step 1.

CR1080200332030X

Fig. 57 Radiator fan and condenser fan do not change speed or stop (Part 3 of 3). 2002 Sebring & Stratus Coupe

TECHNICAL DESCRIPTION
The cause could be a malfunction of the radiator fan motor or an open circuit between the fan control module and the radiator fan motor.

TROUBLESHOOTING HINTS
- Malfunction of radiator fan motor
- Malfunction of fan control module

DIAGNOSIS
Replace the radiator fan motor and fan control module assembly.

Q: Does the radiator fan operate correctly?
YES : There is no action to be taken?
NO : Repair the wiring harness between the fan control module and the radiator fan motor.

CR1080200333000X

Fig. 58 Radiator fan does not operate. 2002 Sebring & Stratus Coupe

STEP 3. Check the symptoms.

Q: Does the condenser fan operate correctly?
YES : This diagnosis is complete.
NO : Return to Step1.

CR1080200334020X

Fig. 59 Condenser fan does not operate (Part 2 of 2). 2002 Sebring & Stratus Coupe

Radiator Fan and Condenser Fan Drive Circuit

CIRCUIT OPERATION
- The fan control module is powered from fusible link number 2.
- The ECM <M/T> or PCM <A/T> judges the required revolution speed of radiator fan motor and condenser fan motor using the input signals transmitted from A/C switch, automatic compressor controller, vehicle speed sensor <M/T>, output shaft speed sensor <A/T> and engine coolant temperature sensor. The ECM <M/T> or PCM <A/T> activates the fan control module to drive the radiator fan motor and condenser fan motor.

TECHNICAL DESCRIPTION
The cause could be a malfunction of the condenser fan motor or of the fan control module.

TROUBLESHOOTING HINTS
- Malfunction of condenser fan motor
- Malfunction of fan control module

DIAGNOSIS

STEP 1. Check the condenser fan motor.

Q: Is the condenser fan in good condition?
YES : Go to Step 2.
NO : Replace the condenser fan motor. Then go to Step 3.

STEP 2. Check the fan control module.
Refer to P.7-18.

Q: Is the fan control module in good condition?
YES : Go to Step 3.
NO : Replace the fan control module, then go to Step 3.

CR1080200334010X

Fig. 59 Condenser fan does not operate (Part 1 of 2). 2002 Sebring & Stratus Coupe

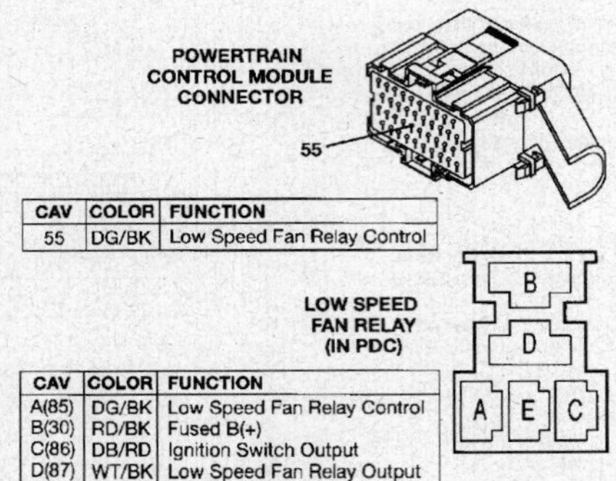

CAV	COLOR	FUNCTION
55	DG/BK	Low Speed Fan Relay Control

CAV	COLOR	FUNCTION
A(85)	DG/BK	Low Speed Fan Relay Control
B(30)	RD/BK	Fused B(+)
C(86)	DB/RD	Ignition Switch Output
D(87)	WT/BK	Low Speed Fan Relay Output

CR1089800224000X

Fig. 60 PCM connector. Avenger, Talon & 1998–2000 Sebring Coupe

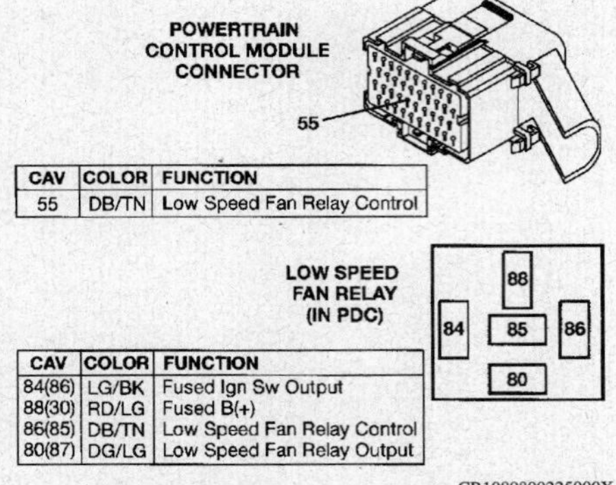

CAV	COLOR	FUNCTION
55	DB/TN	Low Speed Fan Relay Control

CAV	COLOR	FUNCTION
84(86)	LG/BK	Fused Ign Sw Output
88(30)	RD/LG	Fused B(+)
86(85)	DB/TN	Low Speed Fan Relay Control
80(87)	DG/LG	Low Speed Fan Relay Output

CR1089800225000X

Fig. 61 PCM connector. Breeze, Cirrus & 1998–2000 Sebring Convertible & Stratus

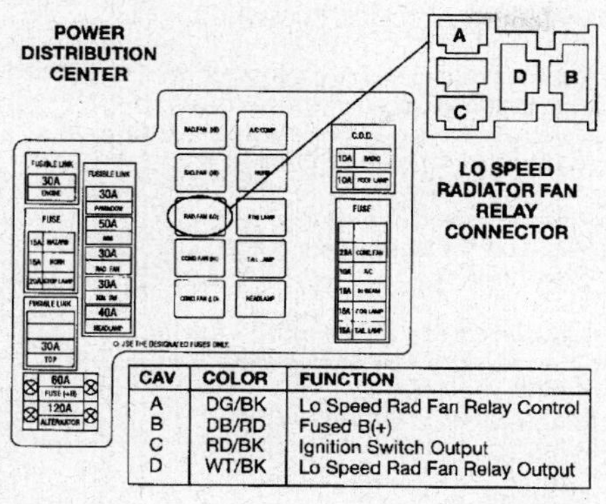

CAV	COLOR	FUNCTION
A	DG/BK	Lo Speed Rad Fan Relay Control
B	DB/RD	Fused B(+)
C	RD/BK	Ignition Switch Output
D	WT/BK	Lo Speed Rad Fan Relay Output

CR1089800220000X

Fig. 62 Low speed fan control relay connector. Avenger, Talon & 1998–2000 Sebring Coupe

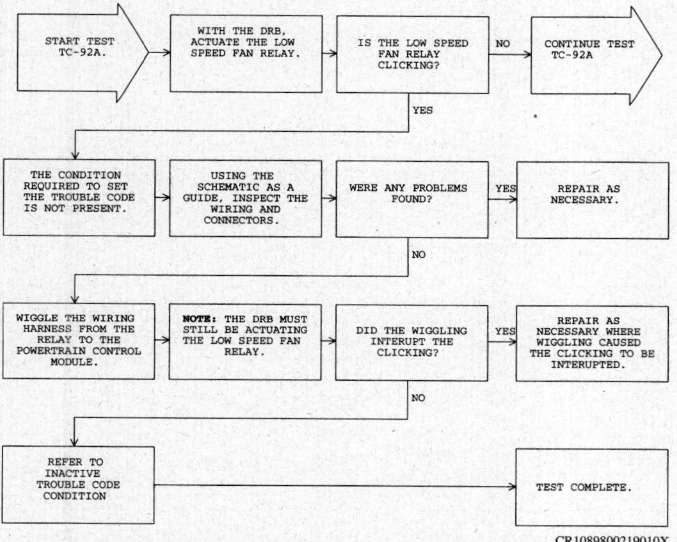

CR1089800219010X

Fig. 64 Low speed fan control relay circuit test (Part 1 of 3). Avenger, Breeze, Cirrus, Talon & 1998–2000 Sebring Convertible, Sebring Coupe & Stratus

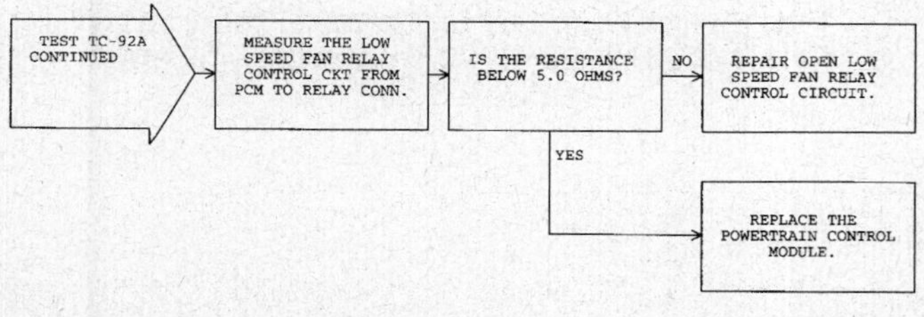

CR1089800219030X

Fig. 64 Low speed fan control relay circuit test (Part 3 of 3). Avenger, Breeze, Cirrus, Talon & 1998–2000 Sebring Convertible, Sebring Coupe & Stratus

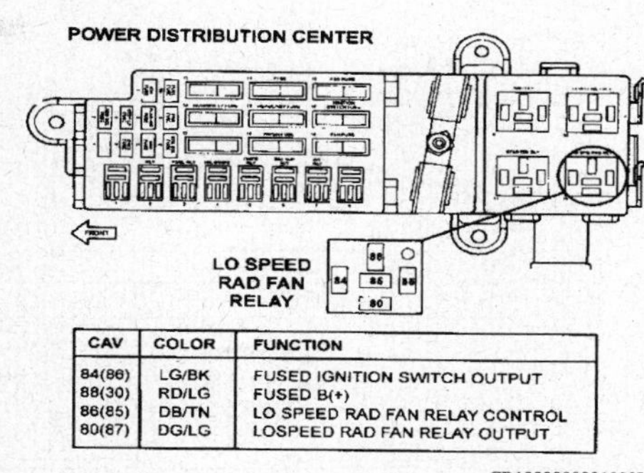

CAV	COLOR	FUNCTION
84(86)	LG/BK	FUSED IGNITION SWITCH OUTPUT
88(30)	RD/LG	FUSED B(+)
86(85)	DB/TN	LO SPEED RAD FAN RELAY CONTROL
80(87)	DG/LG	LOSPEED RAD FAN RELAY OUTPUT

CR1089800221000X

Fig. 63 Low speed fan control relay connector. Breeze, Cirrus & 1998–2000 Sebring Convertible & Stratus

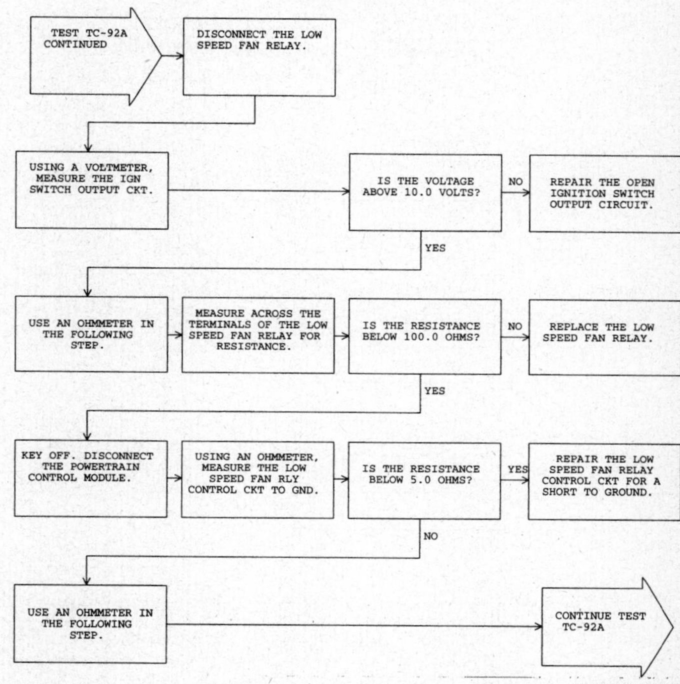

CR1089800219020X

Fig. 64 Low speed fan control relay circuit test (Part 2 of 3). Avenger, Breeze, Cirrus, Talon & 1998–2000 Sebring Convertible, Sebring Coupe & Stratus

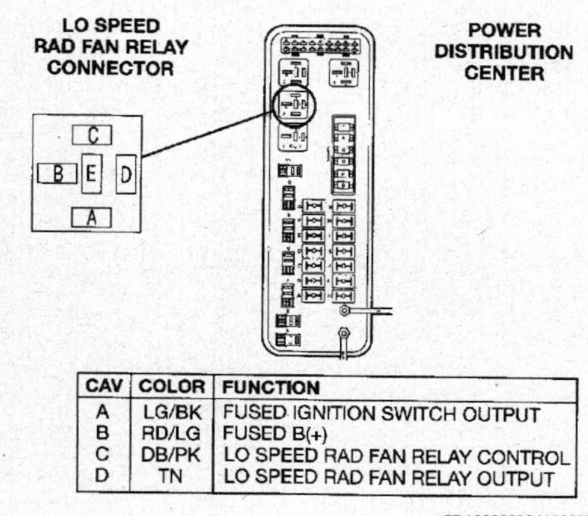

CAV	COLOR	FUNCTION
A	LG/BK	FUSED IGNITION SWITCH OUTPUT
B	RD/LG	FUSED B(+)
C	DB/PK	LO SPEED RAD FAN RELAY CONTROL
D	TN	LO SPEED RAD FAN RELAY OUTPUT

CR1089800241000X

Fig. 65 Low speed fan relay connector. 1998–2000 Concorde, Intrepid, LHS & 300M

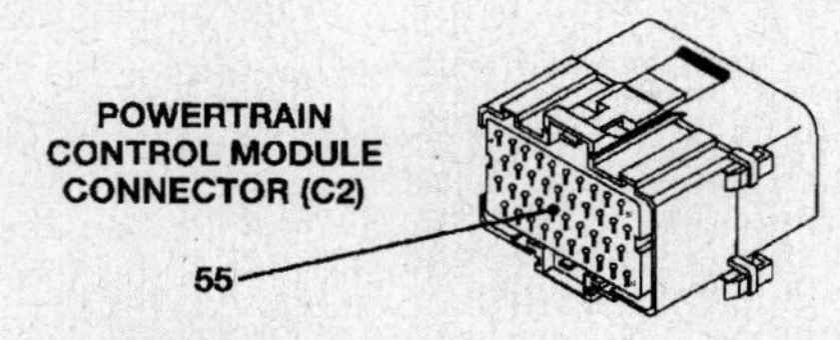

CAV	COLOR	FUNCTION
55	DB/PK	LOW SPEED FAN RELAY CONTROL

LOW SPEED FAN RELAY (IN PDC)

CAV	COLOR	FUNCTION
A	LG/BK	FUSED IGNITION SW OUTPUT
B	RD/LG	FUSED B(+)
C	DB/PK	LOW SPEED FAN RELAY CONTROL
D	TN	LOW SPEED FAN RELAY OUTPUT

CR1089800243000X

Fig. 66 PCM connector. 1998–2000 Concorde, Intrepid, LHS & 300M

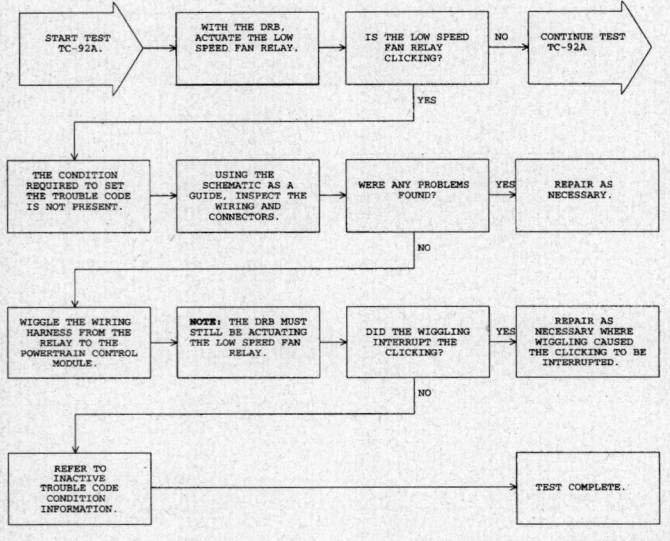

START TEST TC-92A.
WITH THE DRB, ACTUATE THE LOW SPEED FAN RELAY.
IS THE LOW SPEED FAN RELAY CLICKING?
NO
CONTINUE TEST TC-92A
YES
THE CONDITION REQUIRED TO SET THE TROUBLE CODE IS NOT PRESENT.
USING THE SCHEMATIC AS A GUIDE, INSPECT THE WIRING AND CONNECTORS.
WERE ANY PROBLEMS FOUND?
YES
REPAIR AS NECESSARY.
NO
WIGGLE THE WIRING HARNESS FROM THE RELAY TO THE POWERTRAIN CONTROL MODULE.
NOTE: THE DRB MUST STILL BE ACTUATING THE LOW SPEED FAN RELAY.
DID THE WIGGLING INTERRUPT THE CLICKING?
YES
REPAIR AS NECESSARY WHERE WIGGLING CAUSED THE CLICKING TO BE INTERRUPTED.
NO
REFER TO INACTIVE TROUBLE CODE CONDITION INFORMATION.
TEST COMPLETE.

CR1089800240010X

Fig. 68 Low speed fan control relay test (Part 1 of 3). 1998–2000 Concorde, Intrepid, LHS & 300M

INACTIVE TROUBLE CODE CONDITION

You have just attempted to simulate the condition that initially set the trouble code message. The following additional checks may assist you in identifying a possible intermittent problem:

— Visually inspect related wire harness connectors. Look for broken, bent, pushed out, or corroded terminals.

— Visually inspect the related harnesses. Look for chafed, pierced, or partially broken wire.

— Refer to any hotlines or technical service bulletins that may apply.

CR1089800239000X

Fig. 67 Inactive trouble code condition. 1998–2000 Concorde, Intrepid, LHS & 300M

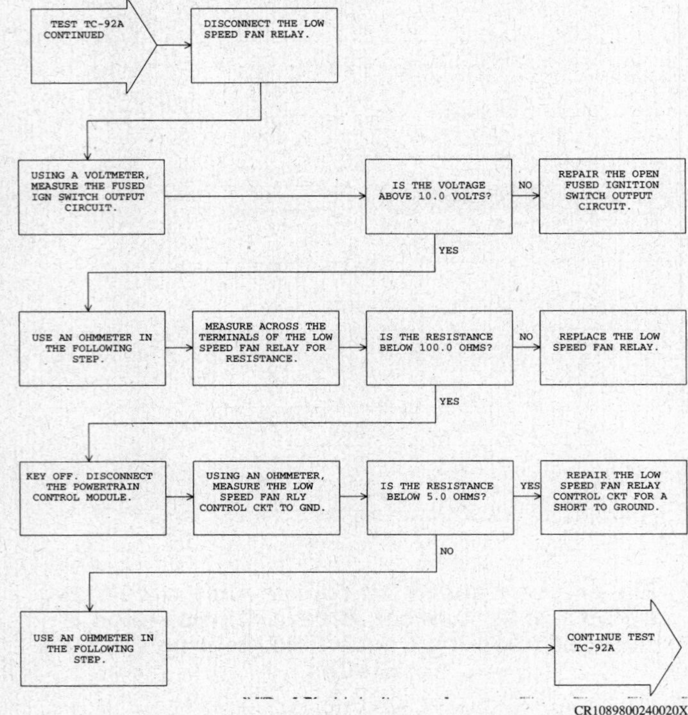

CR1089800240020X

Fig. 68 Low speed fan control relay test (Part 2 of 3). 1998–2000 Concorde, Intrepid, LHS & 300M

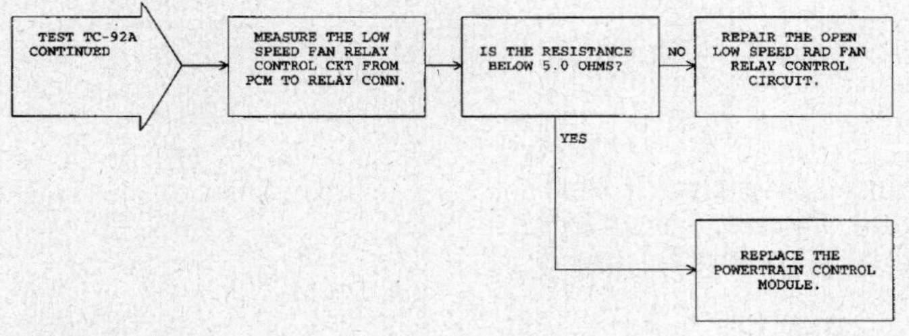

CR1089800240030X

Fig. 68 Low speed fan control relay test (Part 3 of 3). 1998–2000 Concorde, Intrepid, LHS & 300M

P1490-LOW SPEED FAN CONTROL RELAY CIRCUIT

When Monitored: With the ignition on. Battery voltage greater than 10 volts.

Set Condition: An open or shorted circuit is detected in the radiator fan relay control circuit.

POSSIBLE CAUSES
LOW SPEED RADIATOR FAN RELAY INTERMITTENT OPERATION
INTERMITTENT CONDITION
FUSED IGNITION SWITCH OUTPUT CIRCUIT
LOW SPEED RADIATOR FAN RELAY RESISTANCE
LOW SPEED RADIATOR FAN RELAY CONTROL CIRCUIT OPEN
LOW SPEED RADIATOR FAN RELAY CONTROL CIRCUIT SHORT TO GROUND
PCM

TEST	ACTION
1	Turn the ignition on. With the DRBIII®, actuate the Low Speed Radiator Fan Relay. Is the Low Speed Radiator Fan Relay operating? Yes → Go To 2 No → Go To 4
2	Turn the ignition on. With the DRBIII®, actuate the Low Speed Radiator Fan Relay. Wiggle the wiring harness from the Low Speed Radiator Fan Relay to the PCM while the relay is actuating. Did the Low Speed Radiator Fan Relay stop when wiggling the wiring harness? Yes → Repair as necessary. No → Go To 3

CR1080000304010X

Fig. 69 Low speed fan control relay circuit test (Part 1 of 3). 2001–02 Concorde, Intrepid, LHS & 300M

TEST	ACTION
3	**WARNING: WHEN THE ENGINE IS OPERATING, DO NOT STAND IN A DIRECT LINE WITH THE FAN. DO NOT PUT YOUR HANDS NEAR THE PULLEYS, BELTS OR FAN. DO NOT WEAR LOOSE CLOTHING.** **NOTE: The conditions that set the DTC are not present at this time. The following list may help in identifying the intermittent condition.** With the engine running at normal operating temperature, monitor the DRB parameters related to the DTC while wiggling the wiring harness. Look for parameter values to change and/or a DTC to set. Review the DRB Freeze Frame information. If possible, try to duplicate the conditions under which the DTC was set. Refer to any Technical Service Bulletins (TSB) that may apply. Visually inspect the related wiring harness. Look for any chafed, pierced, pinched, or partially broken wires. Visually inspect the related wiring harness connectors. Look for broken, bent, pushed out, or corroded terminals. Were any of the above conditions present? Yes → Repair as necessary No → Test Complete.
4	Turn the ignition off. Remove the Low Speed Radiator Fan Relay from the PDC. Turn the ignition on. Measure the voltage of the Fused Ignition Switch Output circuit in the PDC. Is the voltage above 11.0 volts? Yes → Go To 5 No → Repair the Fused Ignition Switch Output circuit. Check and replace any open fuses.
5	Turn the ignition off. Remove the Low Speed Radiator Fan Relay from the PDC. Measure the resistance of the Low Speed Radiator Fan Relay between the Fused Ignition Switch Output terminal and the Low Speed Radiator Fan Relay Control terminal. Using a jumper wire, momentarily jumper the Radiator Fan Relay Control circuit to ground. Is the resistance between 60 to 80 ohms? Yes → Go To 6 No → Replace the Low Speed Radiator Fan Relay.
6	Turn the ignition off. Remove the Low Speed Radiator Fan Relay from the PDC. Disconnect the PCM harness connector. Measure the resistance of the Low Speed Radiator Fan Relay Control circuit between the PDC and the PCM harness connector. Is the resistance below 5.0 ohms. Yes → Go To 7 No → Repair the Low Speed Radiator Fan Relay Control circuit for an open.

CR1080000304020X

Fig. 69 Low speed fan control relay circuit test (Part 2 of 3). 2001–02 Concorde, Intrepid, LHS & 300M

TEST	ACTION
7	Turn the ignition off. Remove the Low Speed Radiator Fan Relay from the PDC. Disconnect the PCM harness connector. Measure the resistance of the Low Speed Radiator Fan Relay Control circuit in the PDC to ground. Is the resistance below 5.0 ohms. Yes → Repair the Low Speed Radiator Fan Relay Control circuit for a short to ground. No → Go To 8
8	If there are no possible causes remaining, view repair. Repair Replace and program the Powertrain Control Module

CR1080000304030X

Fig. 69 Low speed fan control relay circuit test (Part 3 of 3). 2001–02 Concorde, Intrepid, LHS & 300M

P1490-LOW SPEED FAN CONTROL RELAY CIRCUIT

When Monitored: With the ignition on. Battery voltage greater than 10 volts.

Set Condition: An open or shorted circuit is detected in the radiator fan relay control circuit.

POSSIBLE CAUSES
LOW SPEED RADIATOR FAN RELAY INTERMITTENT OPERATION
INTERMITTENT CONDITION
FUSED IGNITION SWITCH OUTPUT CIRCUIT
LOW SPEED RADIATOR FAN RELAY RESISTANCE
LOW SPEED RADIATOR FAN RELAY CONTROL CIRCUIT OPEN
LOW SPEED RADIATOR FAN RELAY CONTROL CIRCUIT SHORT TO GROUND
PCM

TEST	ACTION
1	Turn the ignition on. With the DRBIII®, actuate the Low Speed Radiator Fan Relay. Is the Low Speed Radiator Fan Relay operating? Yes → Go To 2 No → Go To 4
2	Turn the ignition on. With the DRBIII®, actuate the Low Speed Radiator Fan Relay. Wiggle the wiring harness from the Low Speed Radiator Fan Relay to the PCM while the relay is actuating. Did the Low Speed Radiator Fan Relay stop when wiggling the wiring harness? Yes → Repair as necessary. No → Go To 3

CR1080000302010X

Fig. 70 Low speed fan control relay circuit test (Part 1 of 3). 2001–02 Sebring Convertible, Sebring Sedan & Stratus Sedan

TEST	ACTION
3	**WARNING: WHEN THE ENGINE IS OPERATING, DO NOT STAND IN A DIRECT LINE WITH THE FAN. DO NOT PUT YOUR HANDS NEAR THE PULLEYS, BELTS OR FAN. DO NOT WEAR LOOSE CLOTHING.** **NOTE: The conditions that set the DTC are not present at this time. The following list may help in identifying the intermittent condition.** With the engine running at normal operating temperature, monitor the DRB parameters related to the DTC while wiggling the wiring harness. Look for parameter values to change and/or a DTC to set. Review the DRB Freeze Frame information. If possible, try to duplicate the conditions under which the DTC was set. Refer to any Technical Service Bulletins (TSB) that may apply. Visually inspect the related wiring harness. Look for any chafed, pierced, pinched, or partially broken wires. Visually inspect the related wiring harness connectors. Look for broken, bent, pushed out, or corroded terminals. Were any of the above conditions present? Yes → Repair as necessary No → Test Complete.
4	Turn the ignition off. Remove the Low Speed Radiator Fan Relay from the PDC. Turn the ignition on. Measure the voltage of the Fused Ignition Switch Output circuit in the PDC. Is the voltage above 11.0 volts? Yes → Go To 5 No → Repair the Fused Ignition Switch Output circuit. Check and replace any open fuses.
5	Turn the ignition off. Remove the Low Speed Radiator Fan Relay from the PDC. Measure the resistance of the Low Speed Radiator Fan Relay between the Fused Ignition Switch Output terminal and the Low Speed Radiator Fan Relay Control terminal. Is the resistance between 60 to 80 ohms? Yes → Go To 6 No → Replace the Low Speed Radiator Fan Relay.
6	Turn the ignition off. Remove the Low Speed Radiator Fan Relay from the PDC. Disconnect the PCM harness connector. Measure the resistance of the Low Speed Radiator Fan Relay Control circuit between the PDC and the PCM harness connector. Is the resistance below 5.0 ohms. Yes → Go To 7 No → Repair the Low Speed Radiator Fan Relay Control circuit for an open.

CR1080000302020X

Fig. 70 Low speed fan control relay circuit test (Part 2 of 3). 2001–02 Sebring Convertible, Sebring Sedan & Stratus Sedan

TEST	ACTION
7	Turn the ignition off. Remove the Low Speed Radiator Fan Relay from the PDC. Disconnect the PCM harness connector. Measure the resistance of the Low Speed Radiator Fan Relay Control circuit in the PDC to ground. Is the resistance below 5.0 ohms. Yes → Repair the Low Speed Radiator Fan Relay Control circuit for a short to ground. No → Go To 8
8	If there are no possible causes remaining, view repair. Repair Replace and program the Powertrain Control Module

CR1080000302030X

Fig. 70 Low speed fan control relay circuit test (Part 3 of 3). 2001–02 Sebring Convertible, Sebring Sedan & Stratus Sedan

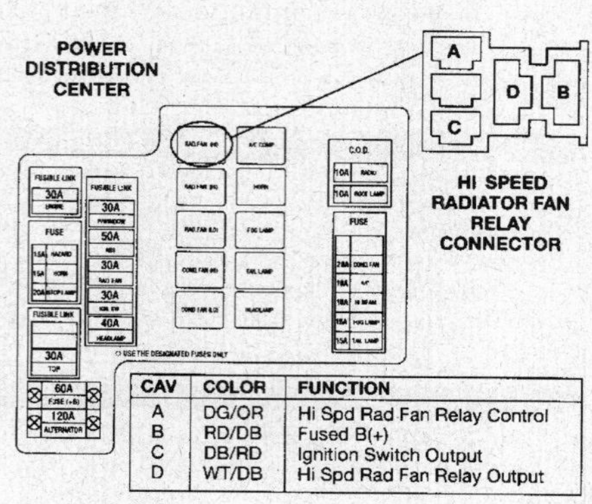

Fig. 71 High speed coolant fan relay connector. Avenger, Talon w/2.0L engine & 1998–2000 Sebring Coupe

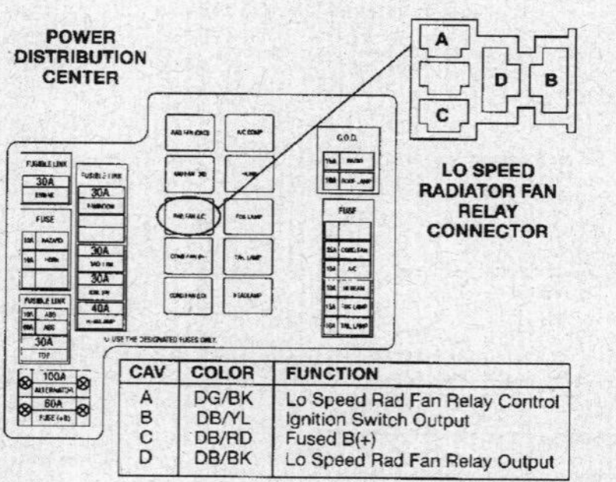

Fig. 72 High speed coolant fan relay connector. Avenger & Sebring Coupe w/2.5L engine

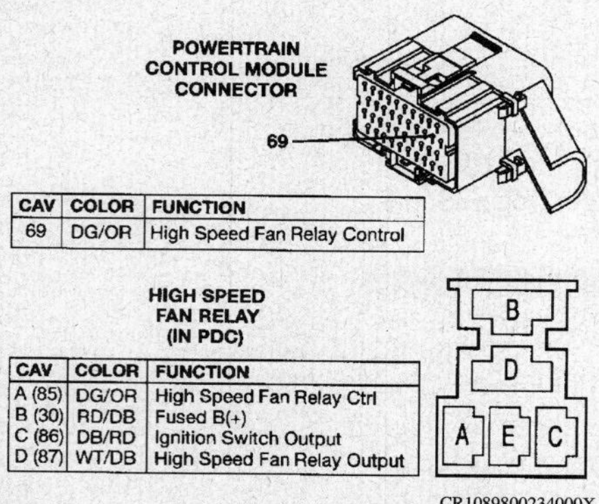

POWERTRAIN CONTROL MODULE CONNECTOR
69
CAV COLOR FUNCTION
69 DG/OR High Speed Fan Relay Control
HIGH SPEED FAN RELAY (IN PDC)
CAV COLOR FUNCTION
A (85) DG/OR High Speed Fan Relay Ctrl
B (30) RD/DB Fused B(+)
C (86) DB/RD Ignition Switch Output
D (87) WT/DB High Speed Fan Relay Output
B
D
A E C
CR1089800234000X

Fig. 73 PCM connector. Avenger, Talon w/2.0L engine & 1998–2000 Sebring Coupe

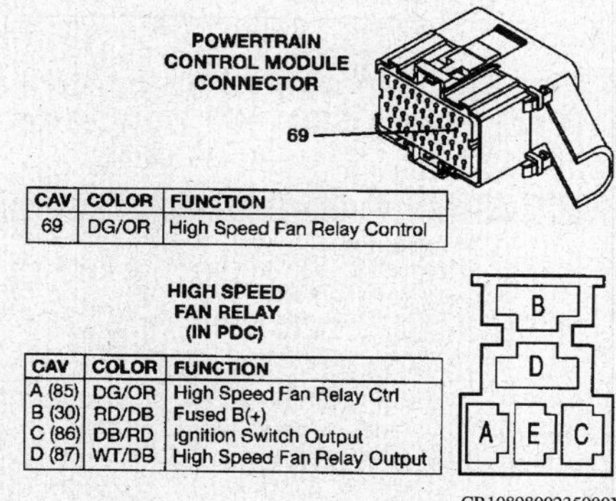

POWERTRAIN CONTROL MODULE CONNECTOR
69
CAV COLOR FUNCTION
69 DG/OR High Speed Fan Relay Control
HIGH SPEED FAN RELAY (IN PDC)
CAV COLOR FUNCTION
A (85) DG/OR High Speed Fan Relay Ctrl
B (30) RD/DB Fused B(+)
C (86) DB/RD Ignition Switch Output
D (87) WT/DB High Speed Fan Relay Output
B
D
A E C
CR1089800235000X

Fig. 74 PCM connector. Avenger & Sebring Coupe w/2.5L engine

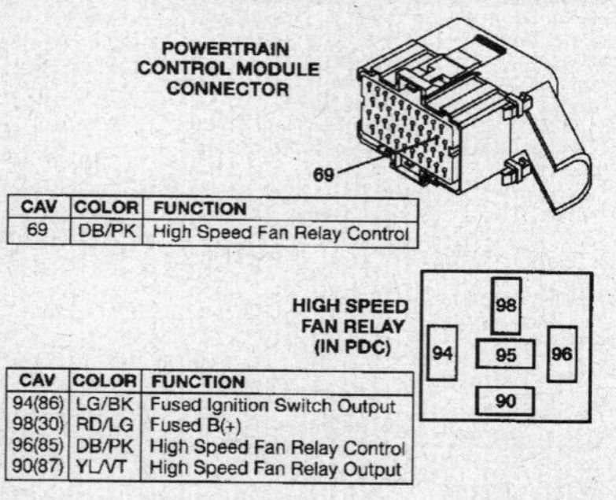

POWERTRAIN CONTROL MODULE CONNECTOR
69
CAV COLOR FUNCTION
69 DB/PK High Speed Fan Relay Control
HIGH SPEED FAN RELAY (IN PDC)
98
94 95 96
90
CAV COLOR FUNCTION
94(86) LG/BK Fused Ignition Switch Output
98(30) RD/LG Fused B(+)
96(85) DB/PK High Speed Fan Relay Control
90(87) YL/VT High Speed Fan Relay Output
CR1089800236000X

Fig. 75 PCM connector. Breeze, Cirrus & 1998–2000 Stratus

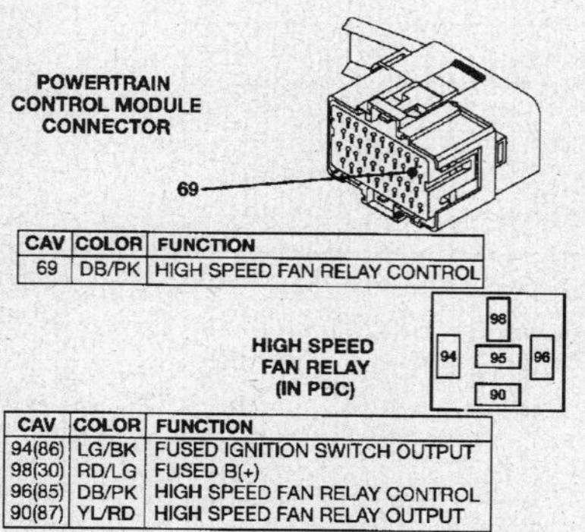

POWERTRAIN CONTROL MODULE CONNECTOR
69
CAV COLOR FUNCTION
69 DB/PK HIGH SPEED FAN RELAY CONTROL
HIGH SPEED FAN RELAY (IN PDC)
98
94 95 96
90
CAV COLOR FUNCTION
94(86) LG/BK FUSED IGNITION SWITCH OUTPUT
98(30) RD/LG FUSED B(+)
96(85) DB/PK HIGH SPEED FAN RELAY CONTROL
90(87) YL/RD HIGH SPEED FAN RELAY OUTPUT
CR1089800237000X

Fig. 76 PCM connector. 1998–2000 Sebring Convertible

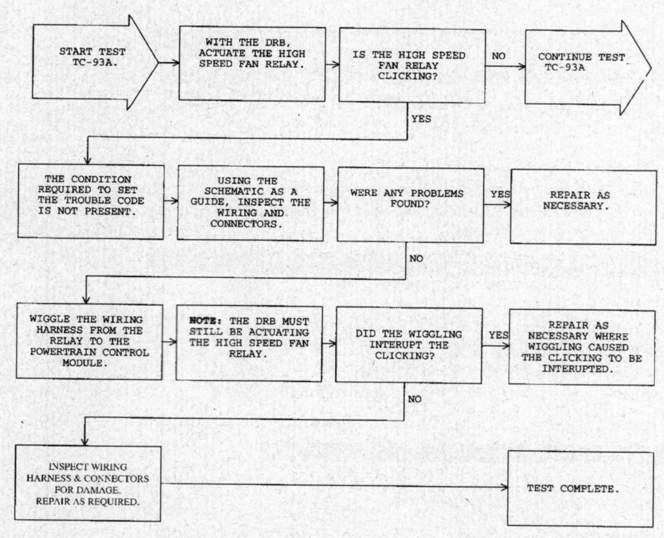

Fig. 77 High speed fan control relay circuit test (Part 1 of 3). Avenger, Breeze, Cirrus, Talon & 1998–2000 Sebring Convertible, Sebring Coupe & Stratus

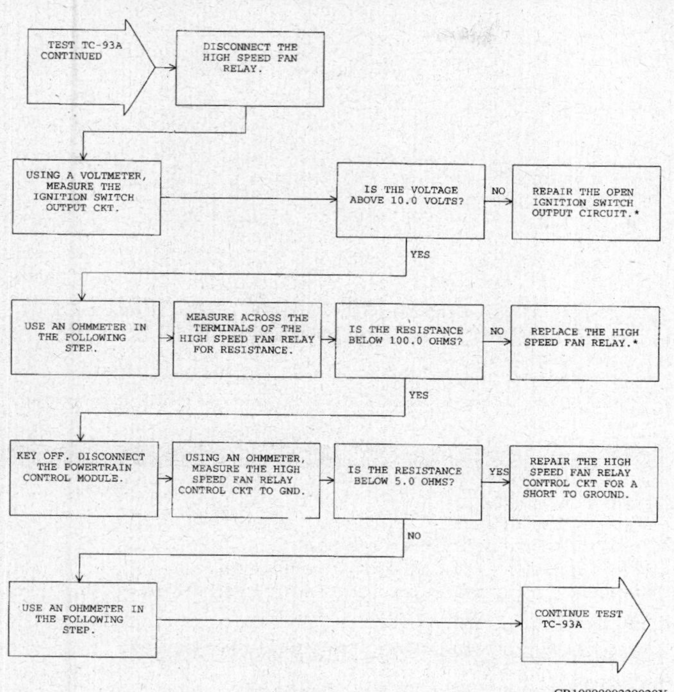

Fig. 77 High speed fan control relay circuit test (Part 2 of 3). Avenger, Breeze, Cirrus, Talon & 1998–2000 Sebring Convertible, Sebring Coupe & Stratus

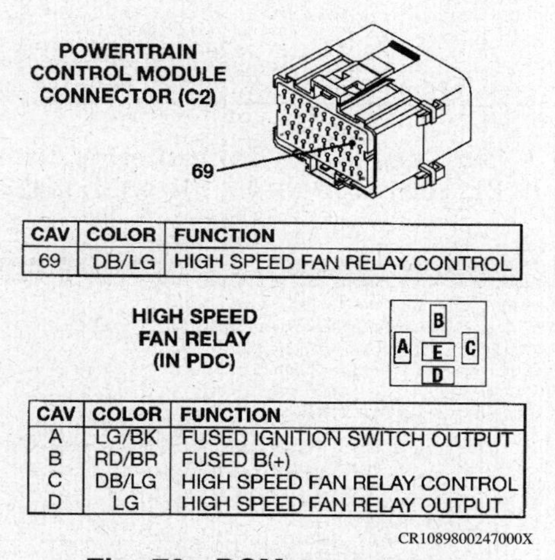

CAV	COLOR	FUNCTION
69	DB/LG	HIGH SPEED FAN RELAY CONTROL

CAV	COLOR	FUNCTION
A	LG/BK	FUSED IGNITION SWITCH OUTPUT
B	RD/BR	FUSED B(+)
C	DB/LG	HIGH SPEED FAN RELAY CONTROL
D	LG	HIGH SPEED FAN RELAY OUTPUT

Fig. 79 PCM connector. 1998–2000 Intrepid, Concorde, LHS & 300M

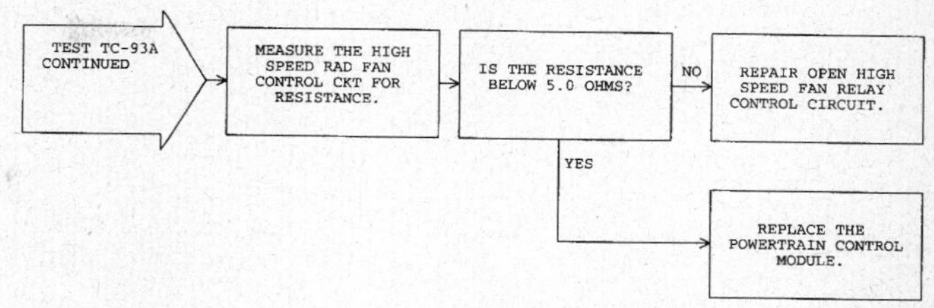

Fig. 77 High speed fan control relay circuit test (Part 3 of 3). Avenger, Breeze, Cirrus, Talon & 1998–2000 Sebring Convertible, Sebring Coupe & Stratus

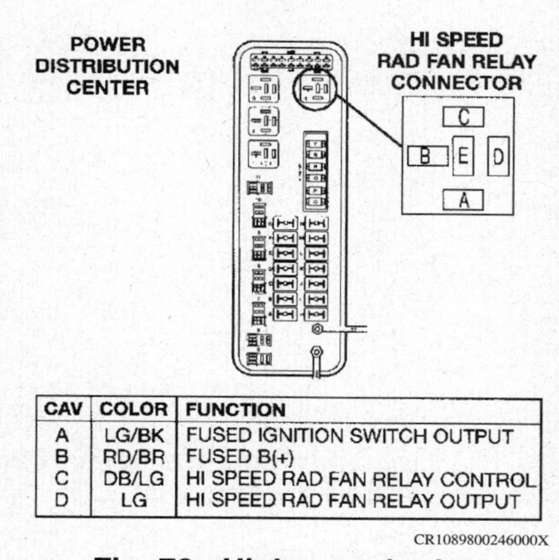

CAV	COLOR	FUNCTION
A	LG/BK	FUSED IGNITION SWITCH OUTPUT
B	RD/BR	FUSED B(+)
C	DB/LG	HI SPEED RAD FAN RELAY CONTROL
D	LG	HI SPEED RAD FAN RELAY OUTPUT

Fig. 78 High speed relay connector. 1998–2000 Intrepid, Concorde, LHS & 300M

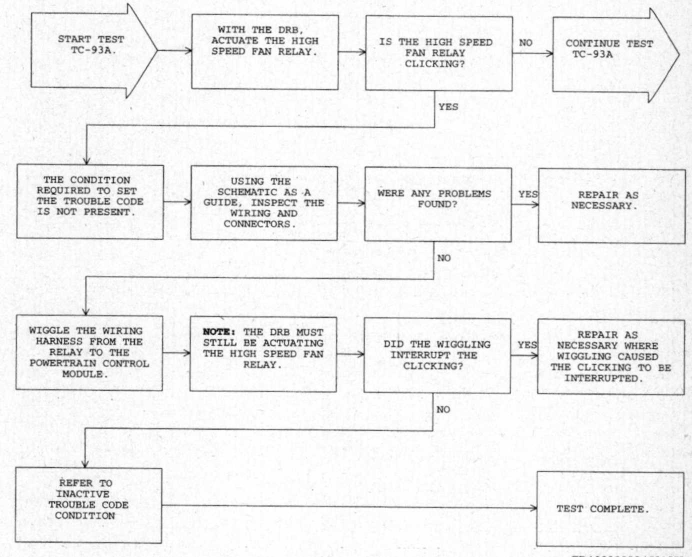

Fig. 80 High speed fan control relay (Part 1 of 3). 1998–2000 Intrepid, Concorde, LHS & 300M

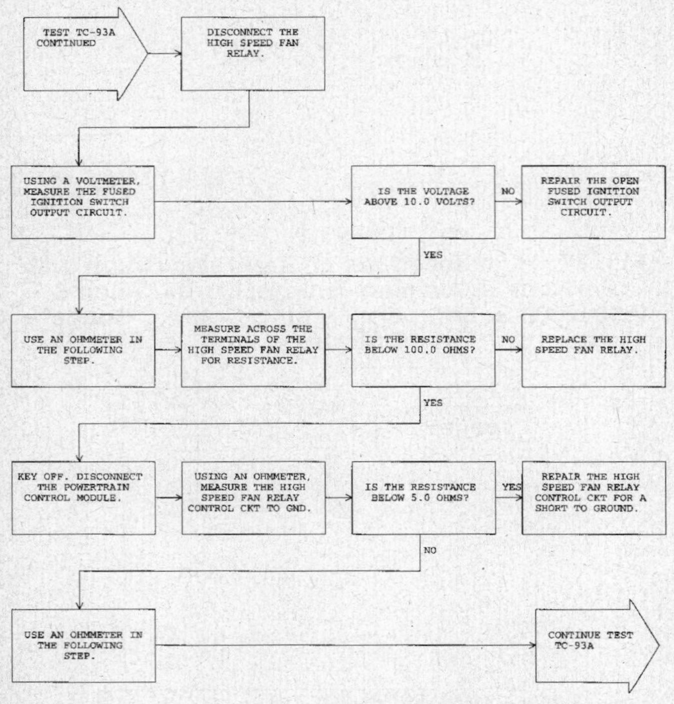

Fig. 80 High speed fan control relay (Part 2 of 3). 1998–2000 Intrepid, Concorde, LHS & 300M

TEST	ACTION
3	**WARNING: WHEN THE ENGINE IS OPERATING, DO NOT STAND IN A DIRECT LINE WITH THE FAN. DO NOT PUT YOUR HANDS NEAR THE PULLEYS, BELTS OR FAN. DO NOT WEAR LOOSE CLOTHING.** **NOTE: The conditions that set the DTC are not present at this time. The following list may help in identifying the intermittent condition.** With the engine running at normal operating temperature, monitor the DRB parameters related to the DTC while wiggling the wiring harness. Look for parameter values to change and/or a DTC to set. Review the DRB Freeze Frame information. If possible, try to duplicate the conditions under which the DTC was set. Refer to any Technical Service Bulletins (TSB) that may apply. Visually inspect the related wiring harness. Look for any chafed, pierced, pinched, or partially broken wires. Visually inspect the related wiring harness connectors. Look for broken, bent, pushed out, or corroded terminals. Were any of the above conditions present? Yes → Repair as necessary No → Test Complete.
4	Turn the ignition off. Remove the High Speed Radiator Fan Relay from the PDC. Turn the ignition on. Measure the voltage of the Fused Ignition Switch Output circuit in the PDC. Is the voltage above 11.0 volts? Yes → Go To 5 No → Repair the Fused Ignition Switch Output circuit. Check and replace any open fuses.
5	Turn the ignition off. Remove the High Speed Radiator Fan Relay from the PDC. Measure the resistance of the High Speed Radiator Fan Relay between the Fused Ignition Switch Output terminal and the High Speed Radiator Fan Relay Control terminal. Is the resistance between 60 to 80 ohms? Yes → Go To 6 No → Replace the High Speed Radiator Fan Relay.
6	Turn the ignition off. Remove the High Speed Radiator Fan Relay from the PDC. Disconnect the PCM harness connector. Measure the resistance of the High Speed Radiator Fan Relay Control circuit between the PDC and the PCM harness connector. Is the resistance below 5.0 ohms. Yes → Go To 7 No → Repair the High Speed Radiator Fan Relay Control circuit for an open.

CR1080000305020X

Fig. 81 High speed fan control relay circuit test (Part 2 of 3). 2001 Concorde, Intrepid, LHS & 300M

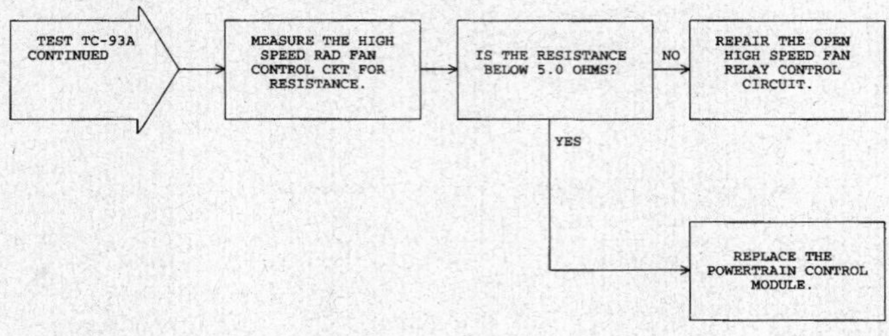

Fig. 80 High speed fan control relay (Part 3 of 3). 1998–2000 Intrepid, Concorde, LHS & 300M

When Monitored: With the ignition on. Battery voltage greater than 10.0 volts.

Set Condition: An open or shorted circuit is detected in the radiator fan relay control circuit.

POSSIBLE CAUSES
HIGH SPEED RADIATOR FAN RELAY INTERMITTENT OPERATION
INTERMITTENT CONDITION
FUSED IGNITION SWITCH OUTPUT CIRCUIT
HIGH SPEED RADIATOR FAN RELAY RESISTANCE
HIGH SPEED RADIATOR FAN RELAY CONTROL CIRCUIT OPEN
HIGH SPEED RADIATOR FAN RELAY CONTROL CIRCUIT SHORT TO GROUND
PCM

TEST	ACTION
1	Turn the ignition on. With the DRBIII®, actuate the High Speed Radiator Fan Relay. Is the High Speed Radiator Fan Relay operating? Yes → Go To 2 No → Go To 4
2	Turn the ignition on. With the DRBIII®, actuate the High Speed Radiator Fan Relay. Wiggle the wiring harness from the High Speed Radiator Fan Relay to the PCM while the relay is actuating. Did the High Speed Radiator Fan Relay stop when wiggling the wiring harness? Yes → Repair as necessary. No → Go To 3

CR1080000305010X

Fig. 81 High speed fan control relay circuit test (Part 1 of 3). 2001 Concorde, Intrepid, LHS & 300M

TEST	ACTION
7	Turn the ignition off. Remove the High Speed Radiator Fan Relay from the PDC. Disconnect the PCM harness connector. Measure the resistance of the High Speed Radiator Fan Relay Control circuit in the PDC to ground. Is the resistance below 5.0 ohms. Yes → Repair the High Speed Radiator Fan Relay Control circuit for a short to ground. No → Go To 8
8	If there are no possible causes remaining, view repair. Repair Replace and program the Powertrain Control Module

CR1080000305030X

Fig. 81 High speed fan control relay circuit test (Part 3 of 3). 2001 Concorde, Intrepid, LHS & 300M

P1489-HIGH SPEED FAN CONTROL RELAY CIRCUIT

When Monitored: With the ignition on. Battery voltage greater than 10.0 volts.

Set Condition: An open or shorted circuit is detected in the radiator fan relay control circuit.

POSSIBLE CAUSES
HIGH SPEED RADIATOR FAN RELAY INTERMITTENT OPERATION
INTERMITTENT CONDITION
FUSED IGNITION SWITCH OUTPUT CIRCUIT
HIGH SPEED RADIATOR FAN RELAY RESISTANCE
HIGH SPEED RADIATOR FAN RELAY CONTROL CIRCUIT OPEN
HIGH SPEED RADIATOR FAN RELAY CONTROL CIRCUIT SHORT TO GROUND
PCM

TEST	ACTION
1	Turn the ignition on. With the DRBIII®, actuate the High Speed Radiator Fan Relay. Is the High Speed Radiator Fan Relay operating? Yes → Go To 2 No → Go To 4
2	Turn the ignition on. With the DRBIII®, actuate the High Speed Radiator Fan Relay. Wiggle the wiring harness from the High Speed Radiator Fan Relay to the PCM while the relay is actuating. Did the High Speed Radiator Fan Relay stop when wiggling the wiring harness? Yes → Repair as necessary. No → Go To 3

CR1080000303010X

Fig. 82 High speed fan control relay circuit test (Part 1 of 3). 2001 Sebring Convertible & Sebring & Stratus Sedan

TEST	ACTION
3	**WARNING: WHEN THE ENGINE IS OPERATING, DO NOT STAND IN A DIRECT LINE WITH THE FAN. DO NOT PUT YOUR HANDS NEAR THE PULLEYS, BELTS OR FAN. DO NOT WEAR LOOSE CLOTHING.** **NOTE: The conditions that set the DTC are not present at this time. The following list may help in identifying the intermittent condition.** With the engine running at normal operating temperature, monitor the DRB parameters related to the DTC while wiggling the wiring harness. Look for parameter values to change and/or a DTC to set. Review the DRB Freeze Frame information. If possible, try to duplicate the conditions under which the DTC was set. Refer to any Technical Service Bulletins (TSB) that may apply. Visually inspect the related wiring harness. Look for any chafed, pierced, pinched, or partially broken wires. Visually inspect the related wiring harness connectors. Look for broken, bent, pushed out, or corroded terminals. Were any of the above conditions present? Yes → Repair as necessary No → Test Complete.
4	Turn the ignition off. Remove the High Speed Radiator Fan Relay from the PDC. Turn the ignition on. Measure the voltage of the Fused Ignition Switch Output circuit in the PDC. Is the voltage above 11.0 volts? Yes → Go To 5 No → Repair the Fused Ignition Switch Output circuit. Check and replace any open fuses.
5	Turn the ignition off. Remove the High Speed Radiator Fan Relay from the PDC. Measure the resistance of the High Speed Radiator Fan Relay between the Fused Ignition Switch Output terminal and the High Speed Radiator Fan Relay Control terminal. Is the resistance between 60 to 80 ohms? Yes → Go To 6 No → Replace the High Speed Radiator Fan Relay.
6	Turn the ignition off. Remove the High Speed Radiator Fan Relay from the PDC. Disconnect the PCM harness connector. Measure the resistance of the High Speed Radiator Fan Relay Control circuit between the PDC and the PCM harness connector. Is the resistance below 5.0 ohms. Yes → Go To 7 No → Repair the High Speed Radiator Fan Relay Control circuit for an open.

CR1080000303020X

Fig. 82 High speed fan control relay circuit test (Part 2 of 3). 2001 Sebring Convertible & Sebring & Stratus Sedan

TEST	ACTION
7	Turn the ignition off. Remove the High Speed Radiator Fan Relay from the PDC. Disconnect the PCM harness connector. Measure the resistance of the High Speed Radiator Fan Relay Control circuit in the PDC to ground. Is the resistance below 5.0 ohms. Yes → Repair the High Speed Radiator Fan Relay Control circuit for a short to ground. No → Go To 8
8	If there are no possible causes remaining, view repair. Repair Replace and program the Powertrain Control Module in accordance with the Service Information.

CR1080000303030X

Fig. 82 High speed fan control relay circuit test (Part 3 of 3). 2001 Sebring Convertible & Sebring & Stratus Sedan

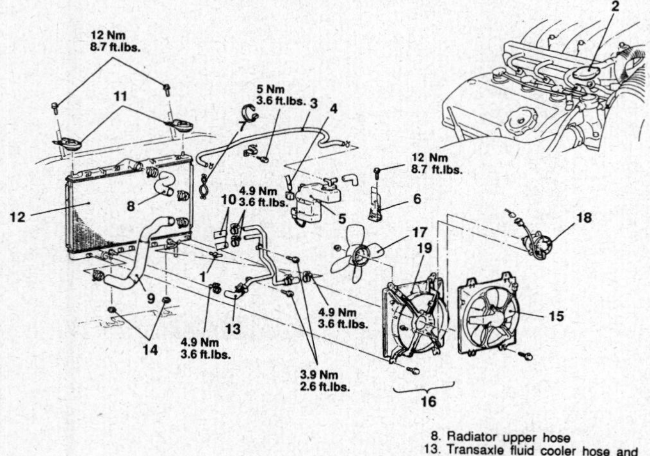

CR1089500168000X

Fig. 83 Cooling fan & fan motor removal. Avenger & Sebring Coupe

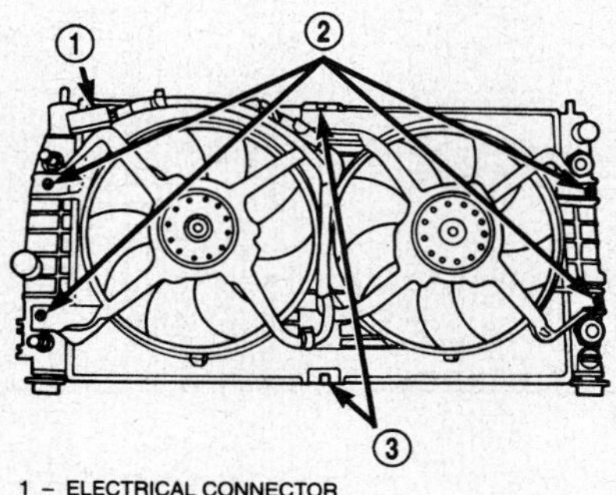

CR1080000273000X

Fig. 84 Fan module removal. Concorde, Intrepid, LHS & 300M

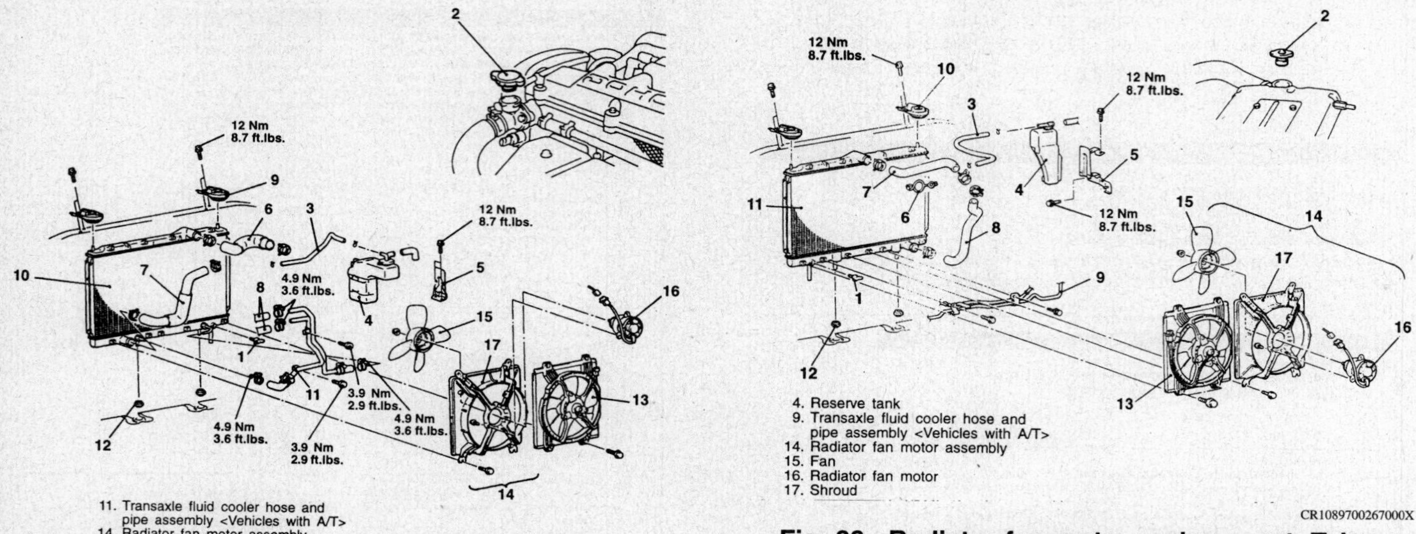

Fig. 85 Radiator fan motor replacement. Talon less turbocharged engine

Fig. 86 Radiator fan motor replacement. Talon w/turbocharged engine

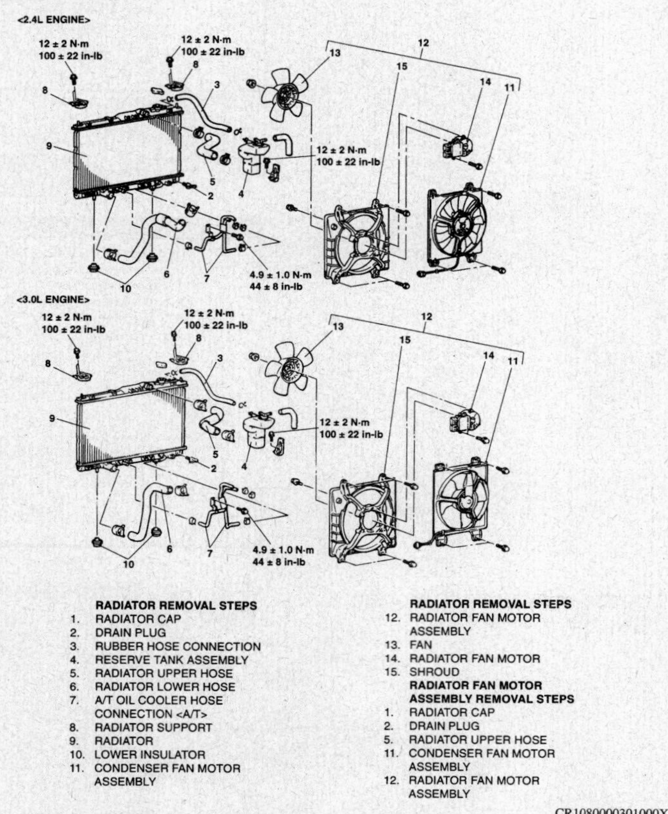

Fig. 87 Radiator fan replacement. 2001–02 Sebring & Stratus Coupe

STARTER MOTORS

TABLE OF CONTENTS

Application Chart

Model	Year	Engine	Starter	
			Manufacturer	Type
Avenger & Sebring Coupe	1998–2000	2.0L	Mitsubishi	Direct Drive
		2.5L	Mitsubishi	Gear Reduction
Breeze, Cirrus & Stratus	1998–99	2.0L	Bosch	Gear Reduction
		2.4L	Nippondenso	Gear Reduction
		2.5L	Melco	Gear Reduction
	2000	2.0L	Bosch	Direct Drive
		2.4L	Nippondenso	Gear Reduction
		2.5L	Melco	Direct Drive
Concorde, Intrepid, LHS & 300M	1998–99	2.7L	Nippondenso	Direct Drive
		3.2L	Nippondenso	Gear Reduction
		3.5L	Melco	Gear Reduction
	2000–02	2.7L	Melco	Direct Drive
		3.2L	Nippondenso	Gear Reduction
		3.5L	Nippondenso	Gear Reduction
Neon	1998–2002	2.0L	Bosch	Gear Reduction
Sebring Convertible	1998–2000	2.4L	Nippondenso	Gear Reduction
		2.5L	Melco	Gear Reduction
	2001–02	2.4L	Nippondenso	Gear Reduction
		2.7L	Melco	Direct Drive
Sebring & Stratus Coupe	2001–02	2.4L	Mitsubishi	Gear Reduction
		3.0L	Mitsubishi	Gear Reduction
Sebring & Stratus Sedan	2001–02	2.4L	Nippondenso	Gear Reduction
		2.7L	Melco	Direct Drive
Talon	1998	2.0L①	Mitsubishi	Direct Drive
		2.0L②	Mitsubishi	Gear Reduction

① — Non-turbocharged engine. ② — Turbocharged engine.

Bosch Starter Motors

NOTE: On Air Bag Equipped Models, Refer To "Air Bag System Precautions" Located In The Front Of This Manual For System Disarming & Arming Procedures.

NOTE: Refer To "Computer Relearn Procedures" Located In The Front Of This Manual When Battery Power To The Computer Has Been Interrupted.

INDEX

DESCRIPTION

Bosch starter motors incorporate an overrunning clutch type starter drive. A solenoid switch is mounted on the starter motor, **Fig. 1.**

The Bosch starter is a gear reduction type. It uses six permanent magnets in place of conventional wound field magnets to save weight, eliminate field winding to case shorts and improve cold start performance. The gear reduction system uses a planetary gear train to transmit armature rotation to the pinion shaft. A solenoid switch is mounted on the starter motor drive end shield.

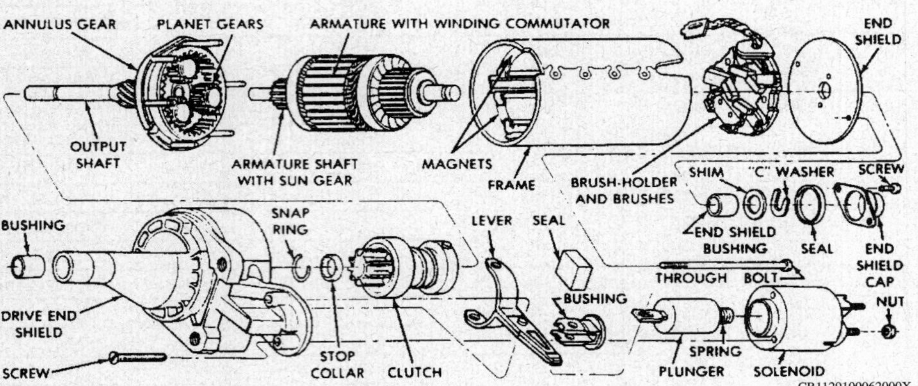

Fig. 1 Bosch starter motor

TROUBLESHOOTING

Refer to **Fig. 2** when troubleshooting the starting system.

SYMPTOM STARTER FAILS TO ENGAGE. NO SOUNDS	SYMPTOM STARTER FAILS TO ENGAGE. SOLENOID OR RELAY CLICKS	SYMPTOM STARTER ENGAGES, FAILS TO TURN ENGINE. DOME LIGHT DIMS	SYMPTOM STARTER ENGAGES, DRIVE CLUTCH SPINS OUT	SYMPTOM STARTER DOES NOT DISENGAGE AFTER ENGINE STARTS
POSSIBLE CAUSE	POSSIBLE CAUSE	POSSIBLE CAUSE	POSSIBLE CAUSE	POSSIBLE CAUSE
STARTER CONTROL CIRCUIT FAULTY	RESISTANCE TOO HIGH IN STARTER FEED CIRCUIT	RESISTANCE TOO HIGH IN STARTER FEED CIRCUIT	DRIVE CLUTCH FAULTY	IGNITION SWITCH FAULTY
IGNITION SWITCH FAULTY	STARTER CONTROL CIRCUIT FAULTY	ENGINE SEIZED	BROKEN TEETH ON RING GEAR	STARTER RELAY FAULTY
NEUTRAL SAFETY SWITCH (AUTO TRANS.) FAULTY OR MISADJUSTED	STARTER SOLENOID FAULTY	STARTER ASSEMBLY FAULTY	STARTER ASSEMBLY FAULTY	STARTER ASSEMBLY FAULTY
CLUTCH PEDAL SWITCH (MANUAL TRANS.) FAULTY OR MISADJUSTED	STARTER ASSEMBLY FAULTY			
STARTER RELAY FAULTY	REFER TO PROPER SERVICE AND TEST PROCEDURES FOR THE COMPONENTS INVOLVED			
STARTER ASSEMBLY FAULTY				

CR1129200128000X

Fig. 2 Starting system troubleshooting chart

DIAGNOSIS & TESTING

IN-VEHICLE TESTS

Before starting any tests, ensure the battery is fully charged and all connections are secure.

STARTER FEED CIRCUIT TEST

The following test will require a suitable volt-ohmmeter tester, accurate to .10 volt.

On models equipped with manual transaxle, apply parking brake and depress clutch pedal whenever a test step calls for turning the ignition to Start position.

1. Connect tester to battery remote terminals following manufacturer's instructions.
2. **On Breeze, Cirrus, Stratus and Neon,** disable ignition and fuel systems by disconnecting automatic shutdown (ASD) relay in power distribution center (PDC).
3. **On all models,** ensure all electrical accessories are off, transmission is in Park or Neutral position and parking brake is set.
4. Turn ignition to Start and observe tester.
5. **On 1998–99 models,** if voltage reads between 9.6–12.4 volts and amperage draw reads above 250 amps, perform test outlined under "Starter Feed Circuit Resistance Test."
6. **On 2000–02 models,** if voltage reads between 9.6–12.4 volts and amperage draw reads above 280 amps, perform test outlined under "Starter Feed Circuit Resistance Test."
7. **On all models,** if voltage reads 12.4 volts or more and amperage reads 0–10 amps, perform "Starter Control Circuit Test" in this section.
8. After starting system conditions have been corrected, ensure battery is fully charged.
9. **On 2000–02 models,** if voltage reads below 9.6 volts and amperage draw reads above 300 amps, replace starter motor as outlined under "Starter Motor, Replace."

10. **On all models,** disconnect all testing equipment and connect ignition system.
11. Start vehicle several times to ensure system is operating properly.

STARTER FEED CIRCUIT RESISTANCE (VOLTAGE DROP) TEST

Neon

Ensure when performing this test that wiring harnesses and components are connected properly. The following test will require a voltmeter accurate to .10 volt.

On models equipped with manual transaxle, apply parking brake and depress clutch pedal whenever a test step calls for turning the ignition to Start position.

1. Disable ignition and fuel system by disconnecting Automatic Shutdown (ASD) relay in power distribution center.
2. Connect negative lead of voltmeter to battery ground post, then the positive lead to negative battery cable clamp.
3. Turn ignition to Start and observe voltmeter.
4. If voltage is detected, correct poor contact between cable clamp and post.
5. Connect positive lead of voltmeter to positive battery terminal and negative lead to battery positive cable clamp.
6. Turn ignition to Start and observe voltmeter.
7. If voltage is detected, correct poor contact between cable clamp and post.
8. Connect negative lead of voltmeter to battery ground terminal, and positive lead to engine block near battery cable attaching point.
9. Turn ignition to Start.
10. If voltage reads above .2 volt, correct poor contact at ground cable attaching point.
11. If voltage reading is still above .2 volt after correcting poor contacts, replace ground cable.
12. Remove starter heat shield if required.
13. Connect positive voltmeter lead to starter motor housing and negative lead to battery ground terminal.
14. Turn ignition to Start.
15. If voltage reads above .2 volt, correct poor starter to engine ground.
16. Connect positive voltmeter lead to battery positive terminal, and negative lead to battery cable terminal on starter solenoid.
17. Turn ignition to Start.
18. If voltage reads above .2 volt correct poor contact at battery cable to solenoid connection.
19. If reading is still above .2 volt after correcting poor contacts, replace battery positive cable.
20. **On 1998–99 models,** if resistance tests do not detect feed circuit failures, remove starter motor and Perform Bench Test. Refer to "Bench Tests" in this section.
21. **On 2000–02 models,** if resistance tests do not detect feed circuit failures, replace starter motor as outlined under "Starter Motor, Replace."

Breeze, Cirrus, Sebring Convertible & Stratus

Ensure when performing this test that wiring harnesses and components are connected properly. The following test will require a voltmeter accurate to .10 volt.

On models equipped with manual transaxle, apply parking brake and depress clutch pedal whenever a test step calls for turning the ignition to Start position.

1. Disable ignition and fuel systems by disconnecting automatic shutdown relay in power distribution center.
2. Connect negative lead of voltmeter to remote battery ground terminal, and positive lead to engine block near battery cable attaching point.
3. Turn ignition to Start.
4. If voltage reads above .2 volt, clean or repair poor contact at ground cable attaching points.
5. If voltage reading is still above .2 volt after correcting poor contacts, replace ground cable.
6. Connect positive voltmeter lead to remote battery positive terminal, and negative lead to remote battery positive cable terminal on starter solenoid.
7. Turn ignition to Start.
8. If voltage reads above .2 volt, clean or repair poor contact at:
    a. Battery cable to solenoid connection.
    b. Battery cable to remote terminal.
    c. Battery cable to battery.
9. If reading is still above .2 volt after correcting poor contacts, replace battery positive cable.
10. If resistance tests do not detect feed circuit failure, replace starter as outlined under "Starter Motor, Replace."

STARTER CONTROL CIRCUIT TEST

The starter control circuit consists of the starter solenoid, starter relay, ignition switch, neutral safety switch and all related wiring and connections. Always perform the Starter Solenoid Test before the performing the Starter Relay Test.

On models equipped with manual transaxle, apply parking brake and depress clutch pedal whenever a test step calls for turning the ignition to Start position.

Starter Solenoid Test

1. Ensure battery is fully charged and in good condition.
2. Raise and support vehicle.
3. Inspect starter and starter solenoid for corrosion or loose wiring.
4. Lower vehicle and remove starter relay from connector.
5. Connect a remote starter switch or a jumper wire between battery remote positive post and terminal 87 on starter relay connector.
6. If engine cranks, starter and starter solenoid are operating properly. Perform starter relay test as described under "Starter Relay Test."
7. If engine does not crank or solenoid chatters, inspect wiring and connectors from relay to starter for loose or corroded connections.
8. Repeat test and, if engine still does not crank properly, repair or replace starter or starter solenoid as required.

Starter Relay Test

1. Remove starter relay from power distribution center.
2. With relay in de-energized position, continuity should exist between terminals 87A and 30, but not between terminals 87 and 30.
3. Measure resistance between terminals 85 and 86, which should be 70–80 ohms.
4. Connect battery positive lead to terminal 86 and ground lead to terminal 85. Relay should click.
5. With relay in energized position, continuity should exist between terminals 30 and 87, but not between terminals 87A and 30.
6. If any one inspection failed, replace relay.

Ignition Switch Test

After testing starter solenoid and relay, test ignition switch and wiring. Inspect all wiring for opens and shorts and all connectors for looseness or corrosion.

BENCH TESTS

STARTER SOLENOID

1. Disconnect field coil wire from field coil terminal.
2. Inspect for continuity between solenoid terminal and field coil terminal. Continuity should exist.
3. Inspect for continuity between solenoid terminal and solenoid housing. Continuity should exist.
4. If continuity does not exist in either test, replace solenoid assembly.

STARTER SPECIFICATIONS

Year	Free Speed Test			Minimum RPM	Cranking Amp Draw Test①
	Power Rating, KW	Max. Amps	Volts		
1998–99	.95	.95	12	—	150–280
2000–02	1.1	—	12	—	150–280

① — With engine @ operating temperature.

Mitsubishi Starter Motors

NOTE: On Air Bag Equipped Models, Refer To "Air Bag System Precautions" Located In The Front Of This Manual For System Disarming & Arming Procedures.

NOTE: Refer To "Computer Relearn Procedures" Located In The Front Of This Manual When Battery Power To The Computer Has Been Interrupted.

INDEX

DESCRIPTION

Mitsubishi starters are either direct drive or gear reduction type. The unit shown in **Fig. 1** is a direct drive starter motor with an overrunning clutch type starter drive. A solenoid switch is mounted on the starter motor. The unit shown in **Figs. 2 and 3** is a gear reduction type utilizing a planetary gear assembly to obtain higher rotational speeds with the same torque output.

TROUBLESHOOTING

STARTER MOTOR DOES NOT OPERATE AT ALL

1. Inspect starter coil.
2. Inspect for poor contact at battery terminals and starter.
3. Inspect park/neutral position switch.
4. Inspect clutch pedal position switch.
5. Inspect starter relay.
6. Inspect theft alarm starter relay.
7. Inspect key reminder switch.

DIAGNOSIS & TESTING

STARTER SOLENOID CONTINUITY INSPECTION

Direct Drive Starter

1. Disconnect wire from M (motor) terminal, **Fig. 4.**
2. Inspect for continuity between S (solenoid) terminal and M (motor) terminal. Continuity should exist.
3. Inspect for continuity between S terminal and solenoid housing. Continuity should exist.
4. If continuity is detected in both tests, solenoid is operating properly.
5. If continuity is not detected in either one of the tests, solenoid is faulty. Replace starter motor.

MAGNETIC SWITCH PULL-IN TEST

Gear Reduction Starter

1. Disconnect field coil wire from "M" terminal, **Figs. 5 through 8.**
2. Connect a 12 volt battery between terminals S and M. **This test must be performed quickly (in less than ten seconds) to prevent coil from burning.**
3. If pinion moves out, the pull-in coil is satisfactory.
4. If pinion does not move out, replace magnetic switch.

MAGNETIC SWITCH HOLD-IN TEST

Gear Reduction Starter

1. Disconnect field coil wire from terminal M of switch, **Figs. 9 through 12.**
2. Connect a 12 volt battery between terminal S and starter body. **This test must be performed quickly (in less than ten seconds) to prevent coil from burning.**
3. Pull out pinion by hand until it hits stopper.
4. If pinion remains out, switch is operating properly.
5. If pinion moves in, hold-in circuit is open. Replace magnetic switch.

FREE RUNNING TEST

1. Place starter motor assembly in a soft-jawed vise.
2. Connect a test voltmeter (100 ampere scale) and carbon pile rheostat in series with positive post of fully charged battery and starter motor terminal, **Figs. 13 through 16.**
3. Connect a voltmeter (15 volt scale) across starter motor.
4. Rotate carbon pile to full resistance position.
5. Connect battery ground cable to starter body.
6. Adjust rheostat until battery voltage shown by voltmeter matches voltage listed in "Starter Specifications" chart.
7. Confirm amperage is as indicated in "Starter Specifications" chart and starter motor turns smoothly and freely.

MAGNETIC SWITCH RETURN TEST

Gear Reduction Starter

1. Disconnect field coil wire from terminal M from magnetic switch, **Figs. 17 through 20.**
2. Connect a 12 volt battery between terminals M and starter body. **This test must be performed quickly (in less than ten seconds) to prevent coil from burning.**
3. Pull pinion out and release.
4. If pinion quickly returns to original position, switch is operating properly.
5. If pinion does not quickly return to original position, replace magnetic switch.

STARTER RELAY TEST

Refer to **Figs. 21 through 23** for starter relay location, **Figs. 24 through 27** for starter relay terminal identification and **Figs. 28 through 31** for starter relay continuity tests.

THEFT ALARM STARTER RELAY TEST

Refer to **Fig. 21** for theft alarm starter relay location, **Figs. 32 and 33** for starter relay terminal identification, then to **Figs. 34 and 35** for theft alarm starter relay continuity tests.

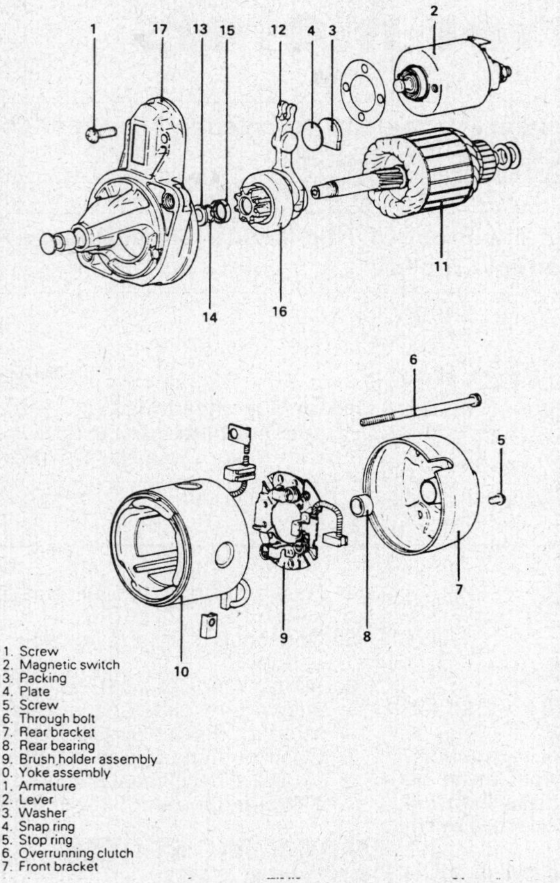

Fig. 1 Exploded view of Mitsubishi direct drive starter

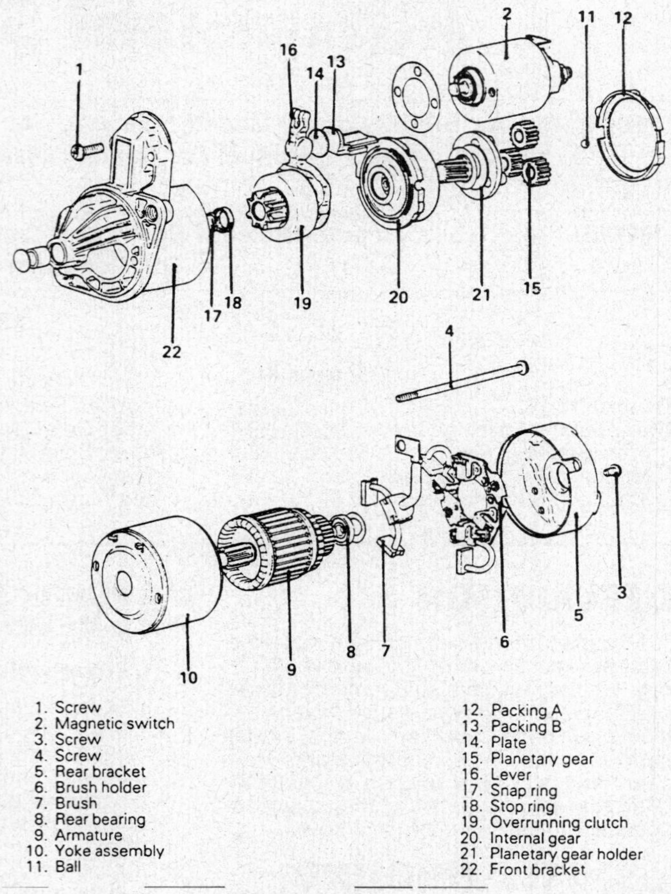

Fig. 2 Exploded view of Mitsubishi gear reduction starter. 1998–2000

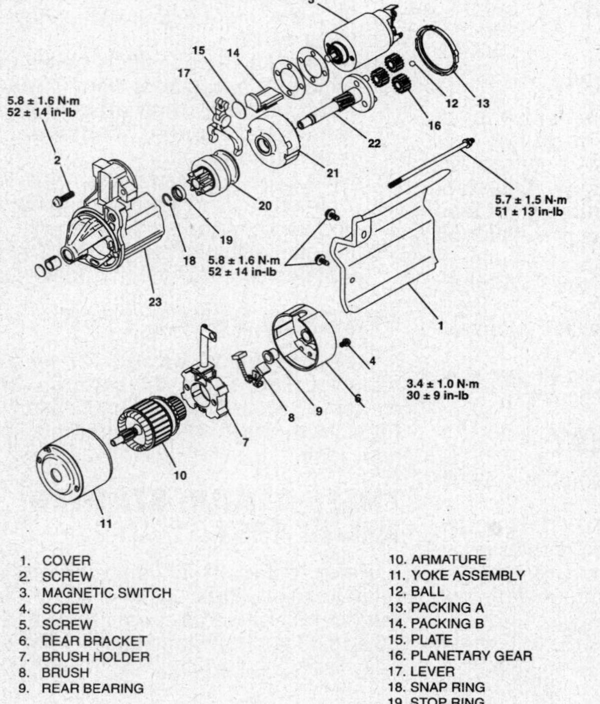

Fig. 3 Exploded view of Mitsubishi gear reduction starter. 2001–02

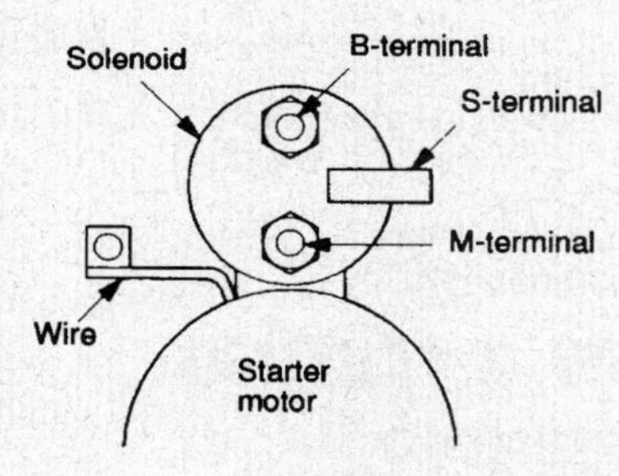

Fig. 4 Starter solenoid continuity inspection. Direct drive starter

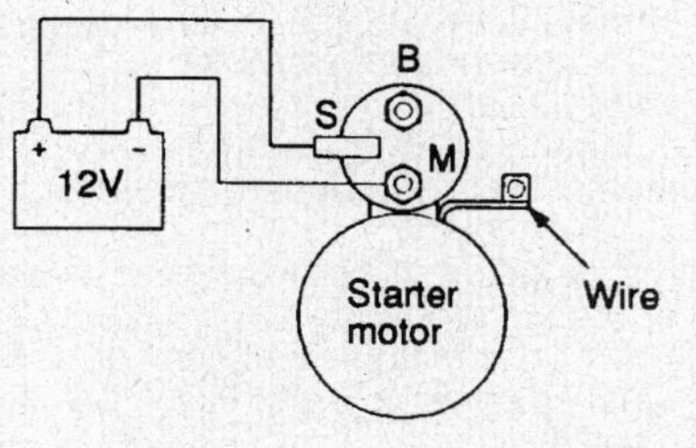

Fig. 5 Magnetic switch pull-in test. Avenger & 1998–2000 Sebring Coupe

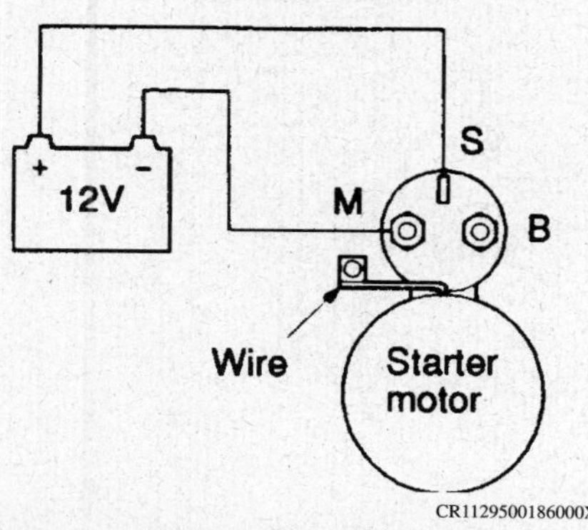

Fig. 6 Magnetic switch pull-in test. Talon

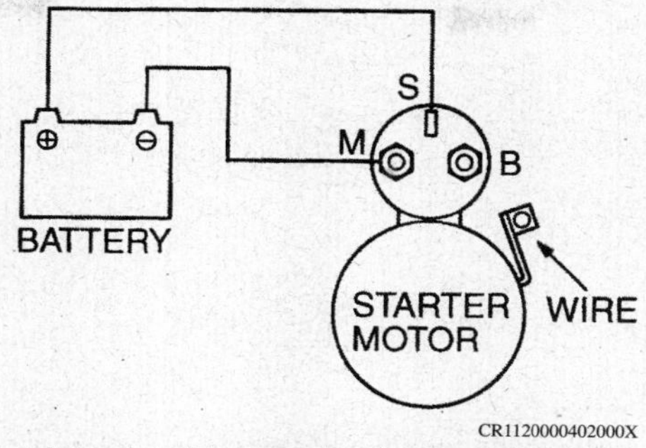

Fig. 7 Magnetic switch pull-in test. 2001–02 Sebring & Stratus Coupe w/2.4L engine

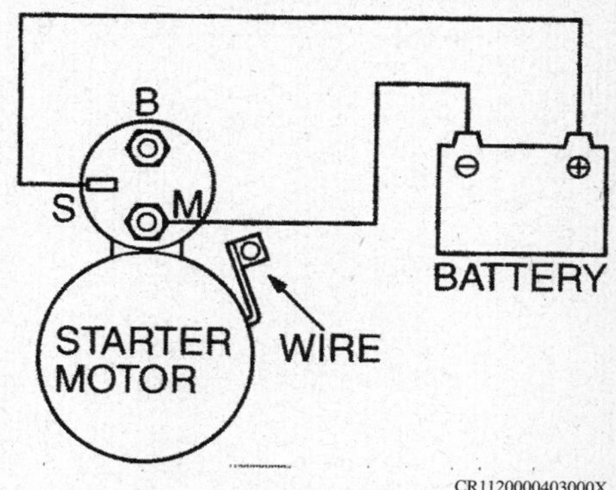

Fig. 8 Magnetic switch pull-in test. 2001–02 Sebring & Stratus Coupe w/3.0L engine

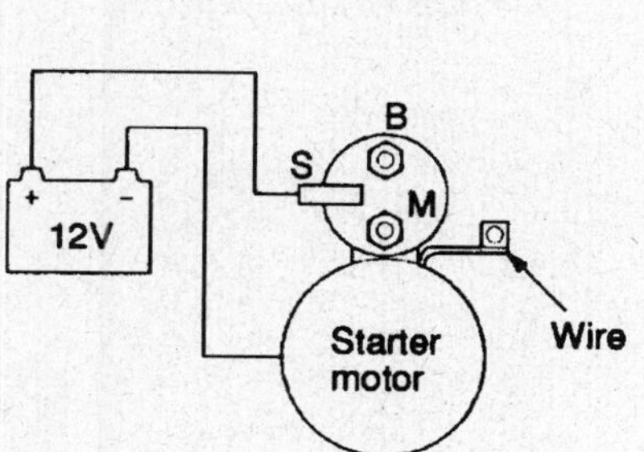

Fig. 9 Magnetic switch hold-in test. Avenger & 1998–2000 Sebring Coupe

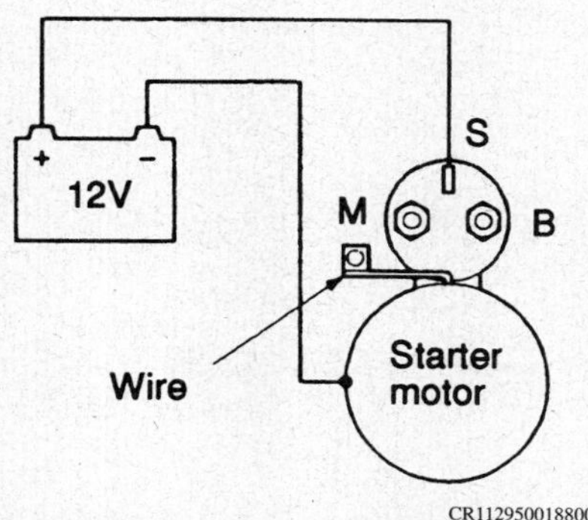

Fig. 10 Magnetic switch hold-in test. Talon

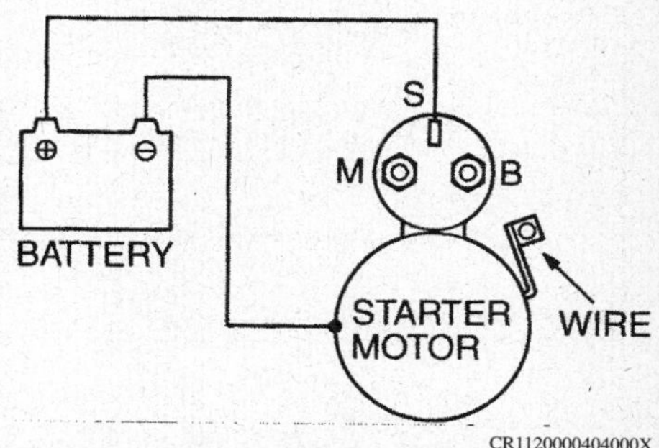

Fig. 11 Magnetic switch hold-in test. 2001–02 Sebring & Stratus Coupe w/2.4L engine

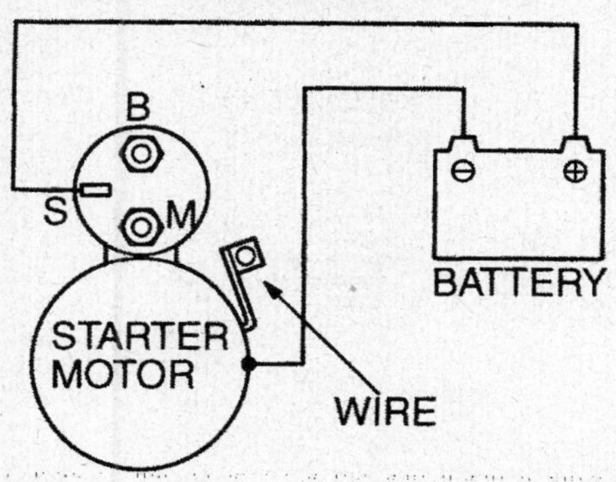

Fig. 12 Magnetic switch hold-in test. 2001–02 Sebring & Stratus Coupe w/3.0L engine

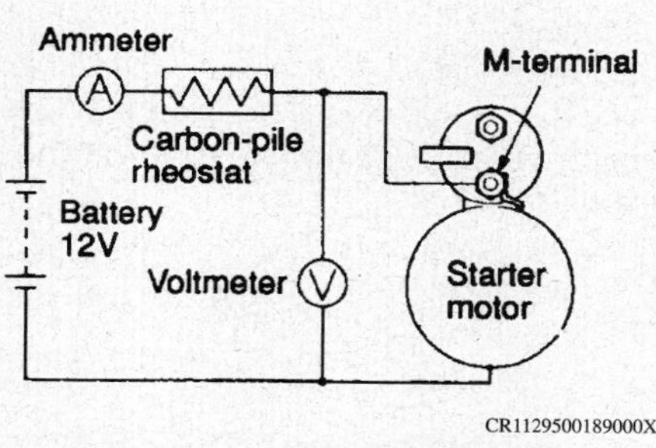

Fig. 13 Free running test. Avenger & 1998–2000 Sebring Coupe

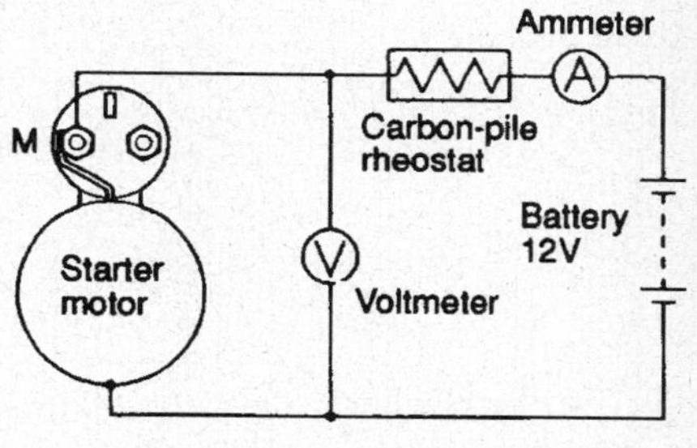

Fig. 14 Free running test. Talon

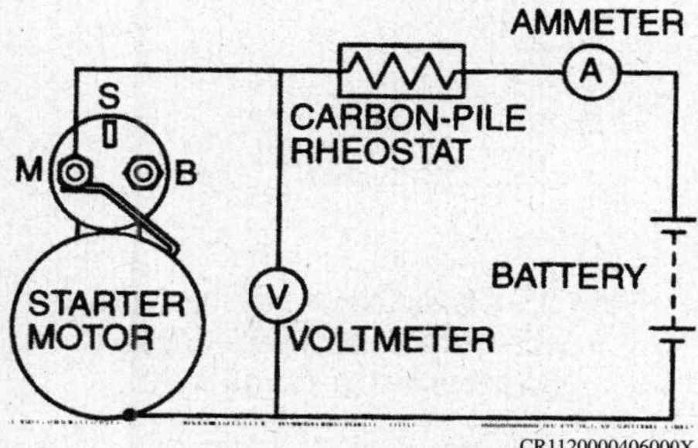

Fig. 15 Free running test. 2001–02 Sebring & Stratus Coupe w/2.4L engine

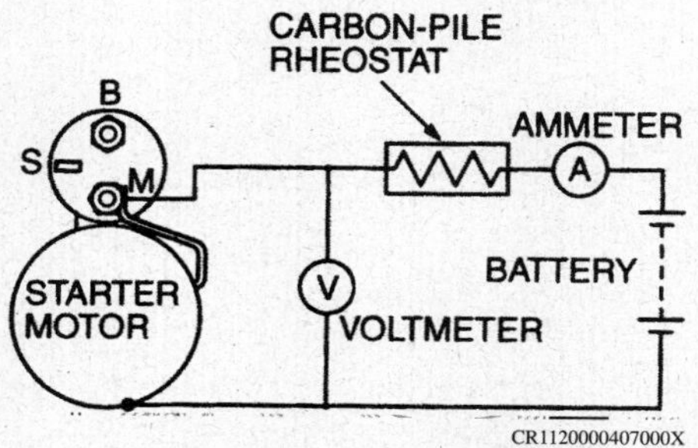

Fig. 16 Free running test. 2001–02 Sebring & Stratus Coupe w/3.0L engine

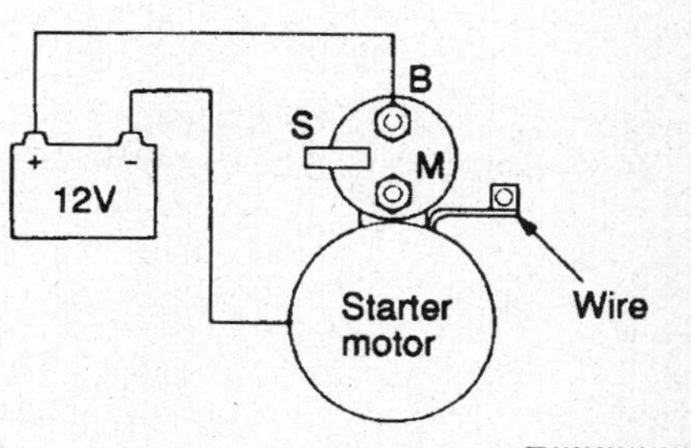

Fig. 17 Magnetic switch return test. Avenger & 1998–2000 Sebring Coupe

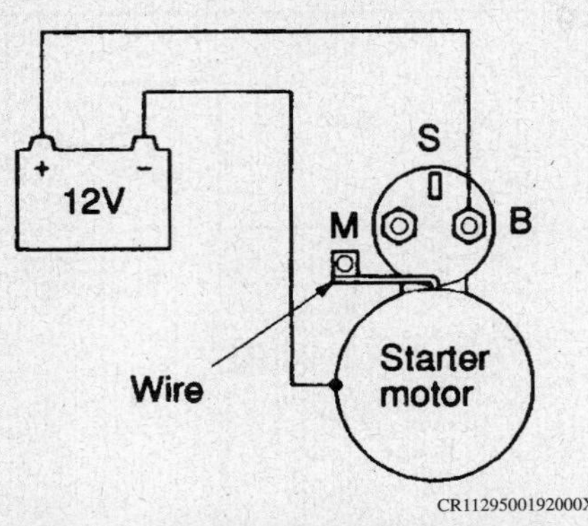

Fig. 18 Magnetic switch return test. Talon

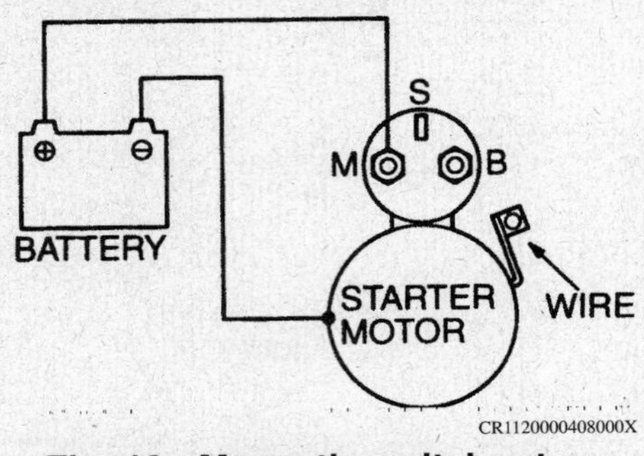

Fig. 19 Magnetic switch return test. 2001–02 Sebring & Stratus Coupe w/2.4L engine

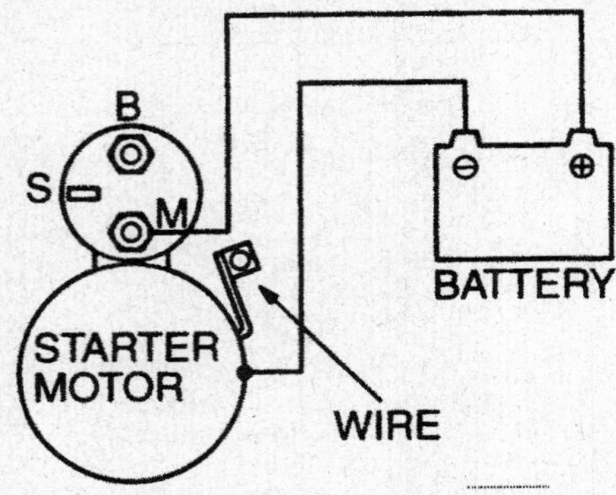

Fig. 20 Magnetic switch return test. 2001–02 Sebring & Stratus Coupe w/3.0L engine

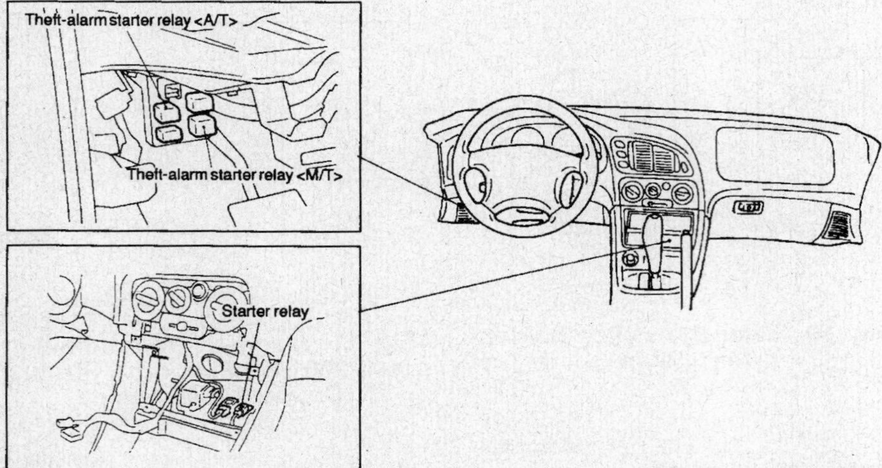

Fig. 21 Starter relay & theft alarm starter relay locations. 1998–2000 Sebring & Stratus Coupe

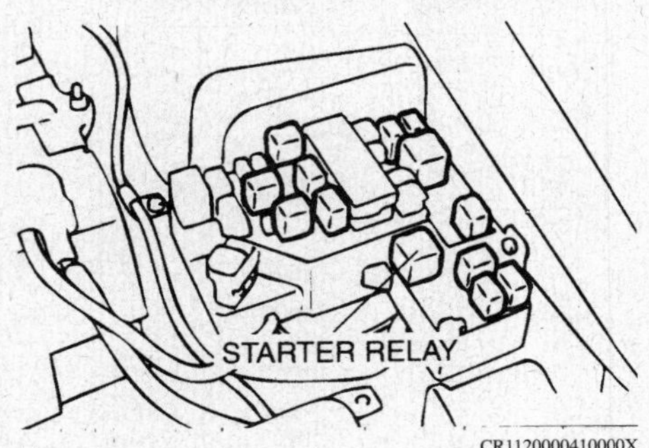

Fig. 22 Starter relay location. 2001 Sebring & Stratus Coupe

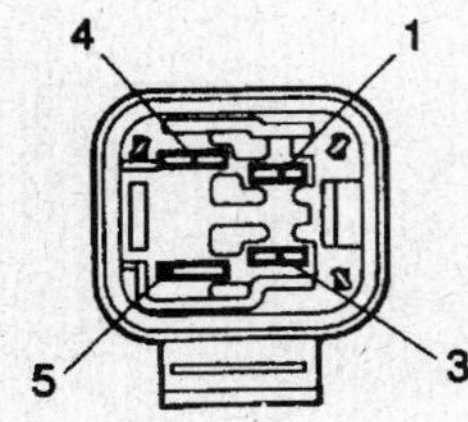

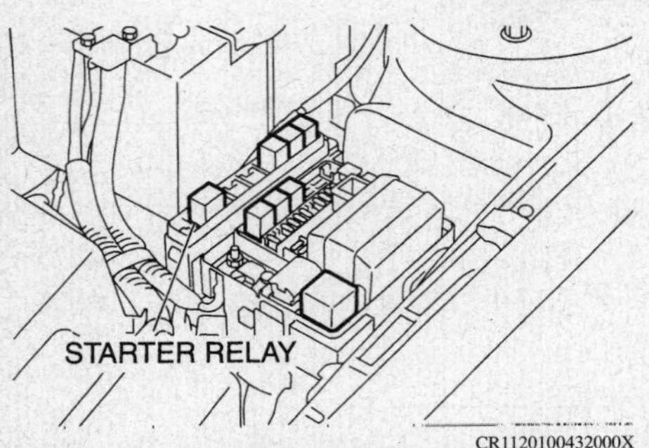

Fig. 23 Starter relay location. 2002 Sebring & Stratus Coupe

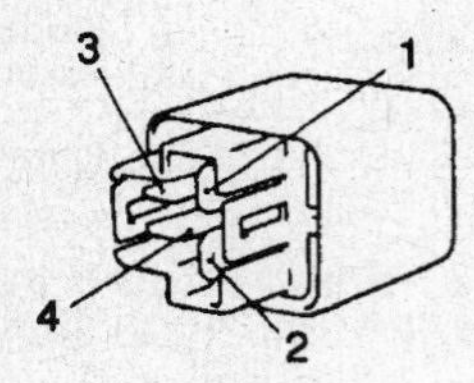

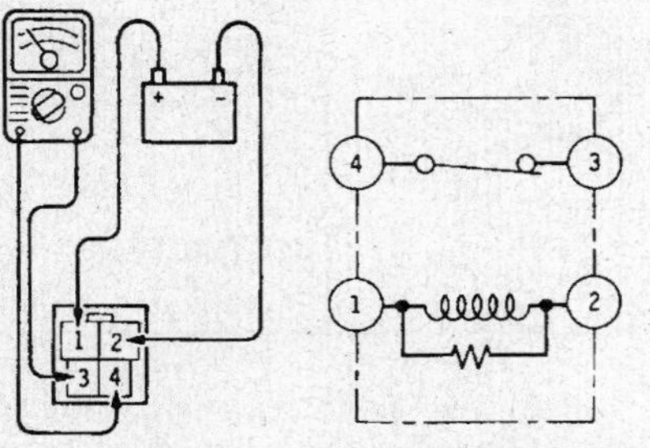

Fig. 24 Starter relay terminal identification. 1998–2000 w/ manual transaxle

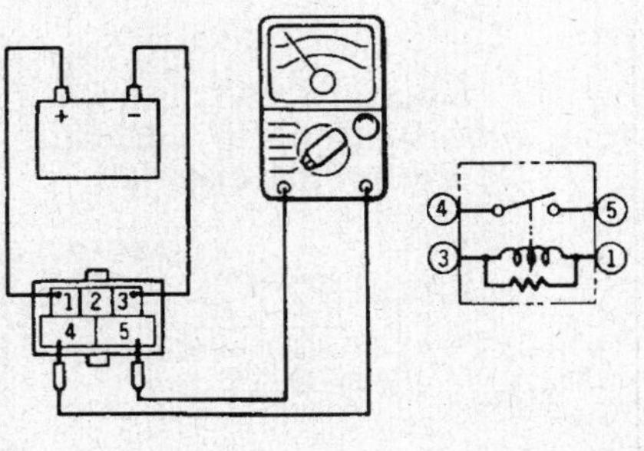

Fig. 25 Starter relay terminal identification. 1998–2000 w/automatic transaxle

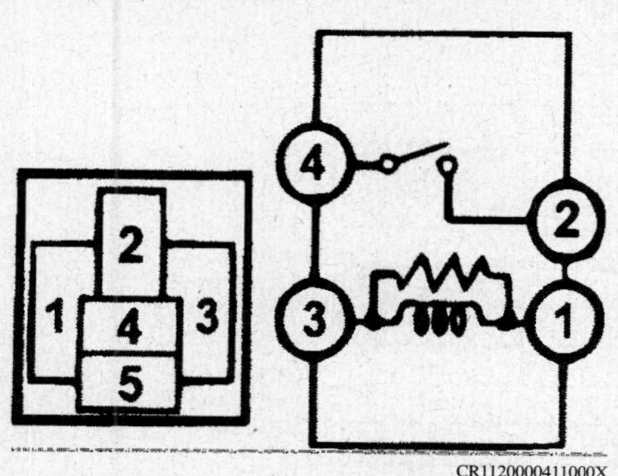

CR1120000411000X

Fig. 26 Starter relay terminal identification. 2001 Sebring & Stratus Coupe

Battery voltage	Terminal 1	2	3	4	5
Not applied	○	—	○		
Applied	⊕	- - -	⊖	○	○

NOTE
○—○ indicates that there is continuity between the terminals.
⊕- -⊖ indicates terminals to which battery voltage is applied.

CR1129500198000X

Fig. 29 Starter relay test. 1998–2000 w/Automatic transaxle

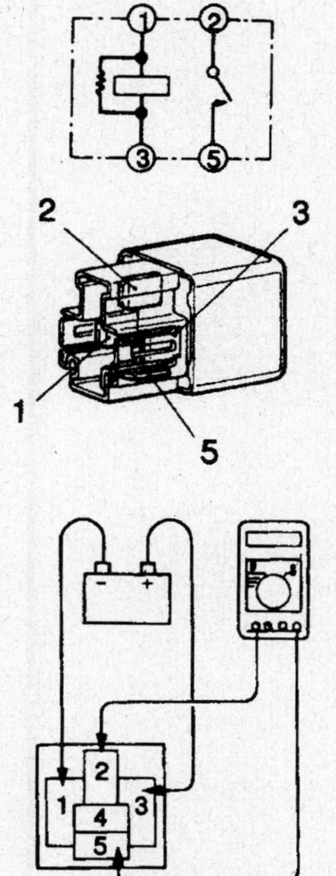

CR1129500199000X

Fig. 32 Theft alarm starter relay terminal identification. Manual transaxle

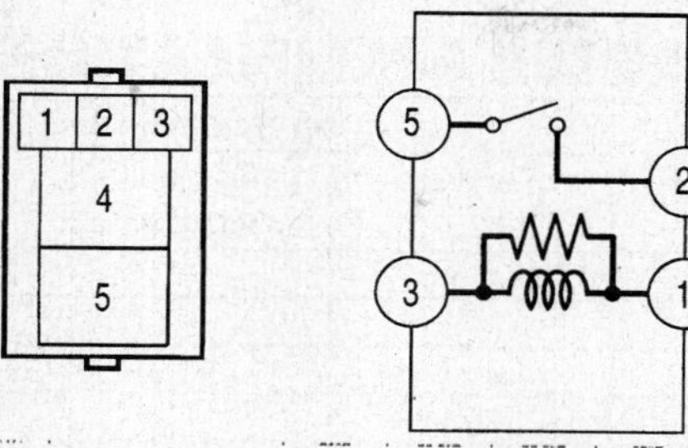

CR1120100431000X

Fig. 27 Starter relay terminal identification. 2002 Sebring & Stratus Coupe

TESTER CONNECTION	BATTERY VOLTAGE	SPECIFIED CONDITION
1 – 3	Not applied	Approximately 2Ω
2 – 4	Not applied	Open circuit
	Applied (Connect "+" to the terminal 3 and "–" to the terminal 1.)	Less than 2Ω

CR1120000412000X

Fig. 30 Starter relay test. 2001 Sebring & Stratus Coupe

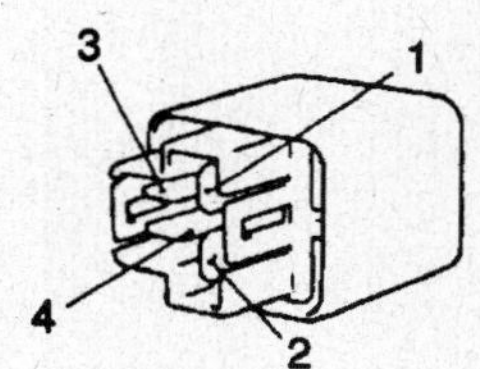

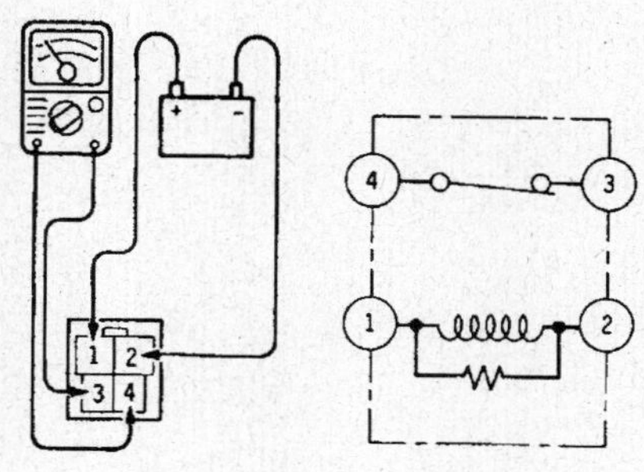

CR1129500200000X

Fig. 33 Theft alarm starter relay terminal identification. Automatic transaxle

Battery voltage	Terminal 1	2	3	4
Not applied	○—○		○—○	
Applied	⊕	⊖		

NOTE
○—○ indicates that there is continuity between the terminals.
⊕- -⊖ indicates terminals to which battery voltage is applied.

CR1129500197000X

Fig. 28 Starter relay test. 1998–2000 w/Manual transaxle

BATTERY VOLTAGE	TERMINAL NO. TO BE CONNECTED TO BATTERY	TERMINAL NO. TO PERFORM CONTINUITYTEST
Not applied	2 – 5	Open circuit
1 – Battery (–) terminal 3 – Battery (+) terminal	2 – 5	Less than 2 ohm

CR1120100433000X

Fig. 31 Starter relay test. 2002 Sebring & Stratus Coupe

Battery voltage	Terminal 1	2	3	5
Not applied	○	—	○	
Applied	⊖ - - -	- - -	⊕	
		○	—	○

NOTE
○—○ indicates that there is continuity between the terminals.
⊕- -⊖ indicates terminals to which battery voltage is applied.

CR1129500201000X

Fig. 34 Theft alarm starter relay test. Manual transaxle

Battery voltage	Terminal 1	2	3	4
Not applied	○—○		○—○	
Applied	⊕	⊖		

NOTE
○—○ indicates that there is continuity between the terminals.
⊕- -⊖ indicates terminals to which battery voltage is applied.

CR1129500202000X

Fig. 35 Theft alarm starter relay test. Automatic transaxle

STARTER SPECIFICATIONS

Model	Engine	Free Speed Test			Minimum RPM
		Power Rating	Max. Amps	Volts	
Avenger & Sebring & Stratus Coupe	2.0L	.95 kw	—	—	—
	2.4L	1.40 kw	—	—	—
	2.5L	1.20 kw	—	—	—
	3.0L	1.20 kw	—	—	—
Talon	2.0L①	.95 kw	—	—	—
	2.0L②	1.20 kw	—	—	—

① — Maximum, Turbocharged engine.
② — Minimum, Non-turbocharged engine.

Nippondenso Starter Motors

NOTE: On Air Bag Equipped Models, Refer To "Air Bag System Precautions" Located In The Front Of This Manual For System Disarming & Arming Procedures.

NOTE: Refer To "Computer Relearn Procedures" Located In The Front Of This Manual When Battery Power To The Computer Has Been Interrupted.

INDEX

DESCRIPTION

Nippondenso starters, **Figs. 1 and 2,** are either direct drive or gear reduction types. The direct drive starter has an overrunning clutch type starter drive and a solenoid switch is mounted on the starter motor. The structure of the gear reduction type starter differs from that of the direct drive type, but the electrical wiring is the same for both types.

DIAGNOSIS & TESTING

IN-VEHICLE TESTS

Before starting any tests, ensure the battery is fully charged and that all connections are good, then disable ignition system as follows:

On models equipped with manual transaxle, apply parking brake and depress clutch pedal whenever a test step calls for turning the ignition to Start position.

1. **On models equipped with distributor ignition system,** disconnect ignition coil cable from distributor cap, then connect a suitable jumper wire between coil cable end terminal and a good body ground.
2. **On models equipped with direct ignition system,** disconnect ignition coils electrical connector.
3. **On 2000–02 models,** disconnect Automatic Shutdown (ASD) relay in Power Distribution Center (PDC).

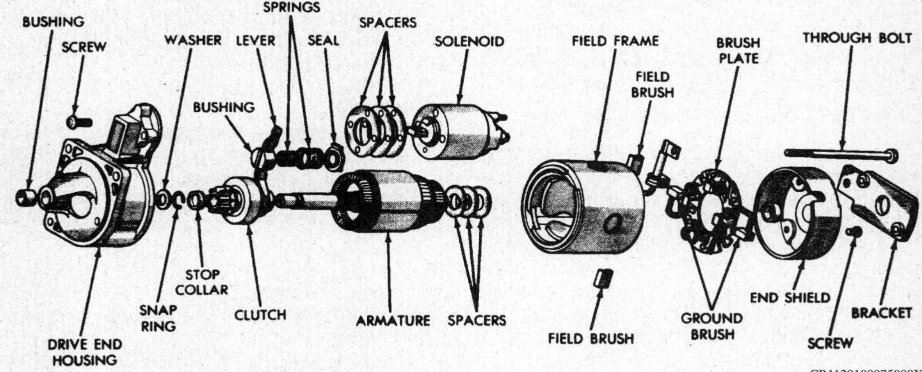

Fig. 1 Exploded view of Nippondenso direct drive starter

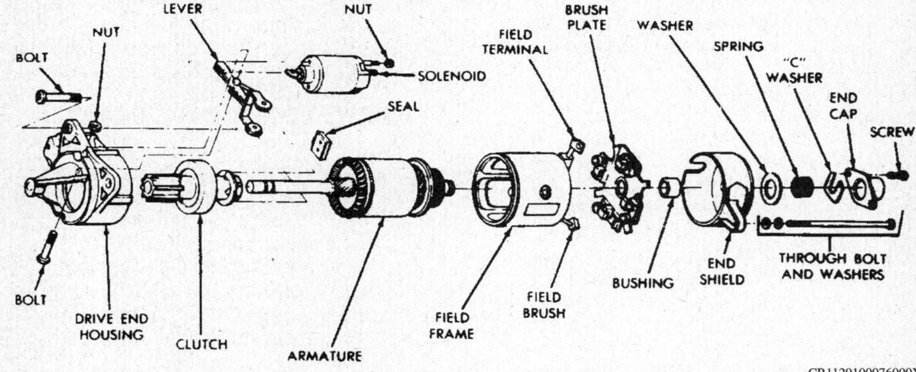

Fig. 2 Exploded view of Nippondenso gear reduction starter

STARTER FEED CIRCUIT TEST

Ensure when performing this test that wiring harnesses and components are connected properly. The following test will require a voltmeter accurate to .10 volt.

On models equipped with manual transaxle, apply parking brake and depress clutch pedal whenever a test step calls for turning the ignition to Start position.

1. Connect tester to battery terminals following manufacturer's instructions.
2. Ensure all electrical accessories are off, transmission is in Park or Neutral and parking brake is set.
3. Turn ignition to Start and observe tester.
4. **On 1998–99 models,** if voltage reads between 9.6–12.4 volts and amperage draw reads above 250 amps, perform test outlined under "Starter Feed Circuit Resistance (Voltage Drop) Test ."
5. **On 2000–02 models,** if voltage reads above 9.6 volts and amperage draw reads above 280 amps, inspect for engine seizure or a faulty starter.
6. **On 1998–99 models,** if voltage reads 12.4 volts or more and amperage reads 0–10 amps, perform test outlined under "Starter Control Circuit Test."
7. **On 2000–02 models,** if voltage reads 12.4 volts or more and amperage reads 0–10 amps, inspect and correct corroded cables and poor connections. If voltage reads below 9.6 volts and amperage reads above 300 amps, replace starter motor as outlined under "Starter Motor, Replace."
8. **On all models,** after starting system fault conditions have been corrected, ensure battery is fully charged.
9. Disconnect all testing equipment and connect ignition system.
10. Start vehicle several times to ensure system is operating properly.

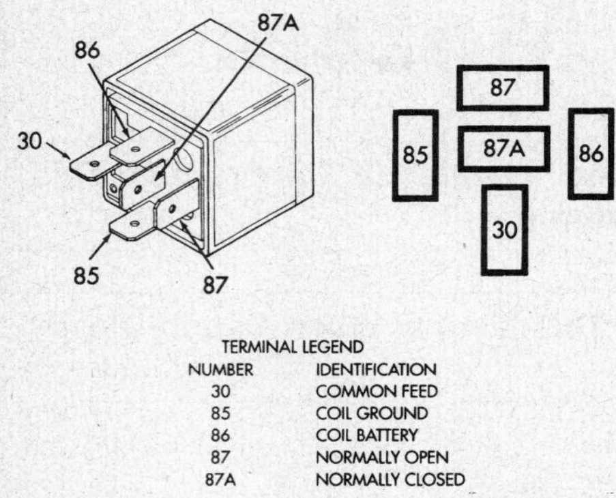

Fig. 3 Starter relay terminal identification. Breeze, Cirrus, Sebring Convertible & Stratus

STARTER FEED CIRCUIT RESISTANCE (VOLTAGE DROP) TEST

Concorde, Intrepid, LHS, 300M & 2001-02 Sebring Sedan & Convertible & Stratus Sedan

Ensure when performing this test that wiring harnesses and components are connected properly. The following test will require a voltmeter accurate to .10 volt.

On models equipped with manual transaxle, apply parking brake and depress clutch pedal whenever a test step calls for turning the ignition to Start position.

1. Disconnect Automatic Shutdown (ASD) relay in Power Distribution Center (PDC).
2. Connect negative lead of voltmeter to battery ground post, then the positive lead to negative battery cable clamp.
3. Turn ignition to Start and observe voltmeter.
4. If voltage is detected, correct poor contact between cable clamp and post.
5. Connect positive lead of voltmeter to positive battery terminal and negative lead to battery positive cable clamp.
6. Turn ignition to Start and observe voltmeter.
7. If voltage is detected, correct poor contact between cable clamp and post.
8. Connect negative lead of voltmeter to battery ground terminal, and positive lead to engine block near battery cable attaching point.
9. Turn ignition to Start.
10. If voltage reads above .2 volt, correct poor contact at ground cable attaching point.
11. If voltage reading is still above .2 volt after correcting poor contacts, replace ground cable.
12. Remove starter heat shield if required.
13. Connect positive voltmeter lead to starter motor housing and negative lead to battery ground terminal.
14. Turn ignition to Start.
15. If voltage reads above .2 volt, correct poor starter to engine ground.
16. Connect positive voltmeter lead to battery positive terminal, and negative lead to battery cable terminal on starter solenoid.
17. Turn ignition to Start.
18. If voltage reads above .2 volt correct poor contact at battery cable to solenoid connection.
19. If reading is still above .2 volt after correcting poor contacts, replace battery positive cable.
20. If resistance tests do not detect feed circuit failures, replace starter motor as outlined under "Starter Motor, Replace."

Breeze, Cirrus, Sebring Convertible & 1998-2000 Stratus

1. Connect negative lead of voltmeter to battery ground terminal, and positive lead to engine block near battery cable attaching point.
2. Turn and hold ignition switch in START position.
3. **On models equipped with manual transaxle,** apply parking brake and depress clutch pedal.
4. **On all models,** if voltage reads above .2 volt, clean or repair poor contact at ground cable attaching points.
5. If voltage still reads above .2 volt, clean or repair poor contact at:
   a. Battery cable to solenoid connection.
   b. Battery cable to remote terminal.
   c. Battery cable to battery.
6. If reading is still above .2 volt after correcting poor contacts, replace battery positive cable.
7. If resistance tests do not detect feed circuit failures, replace starter motor.

STARTER CONTROL CIRCUIT TEST

The starter control circuit consists of the starter solenoid, starter relay, ignition switch, neutral safety switch and all related wiring and connections.

On models equipped with manual transaxle, apply parking brake and depress clutch pedal whenever a test step calls for turning the ignition to Start position.

Starter Relay Test

1. Remove starter relay from power distribution center.
2. With relay in de-energized position, continuity should exist between terminals 87A and 30, but not between terminals 87 and 30.
3. Measure resistance between terminals 85 and 86, which should be 70–80 ohms.
4. Connect battery positive lead to terminal 86 and ground lead to terminal 85. Relay should click.
5. With relay in energized position, continuity should exist between terminals 30 and 87, but not between terminals 87A and 30.
6. If any one inspection failed, replace relay.

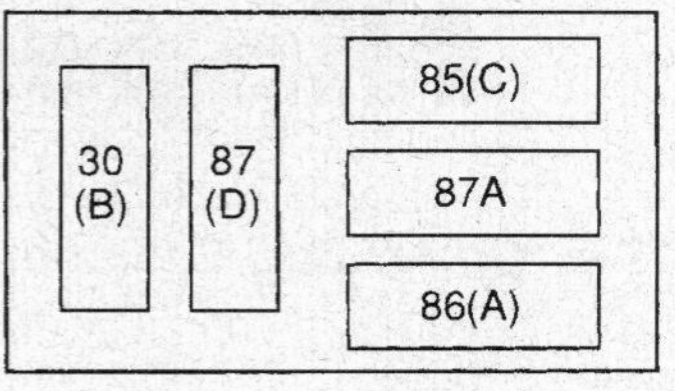

Starter Relay Pinout

CAV	COLOR	FUNCTION
30 (B)	RD	B (+)
85 (C)	TN	P/N POSITION SW.SENSE (AUTO)
86 (A)	YL	IGNITION SWITCH OUTPUT
87 (D)	LG	STARTER RELAY OUTPUT

CR1129100065000X

Fig. 4 Starter relay terminal identification. Concorde, Intrepid, LHS, 300M & 2001–02 Sebring Sedan & Convertible & Stratus Sedan

Starter Solenoid Test

1. Ensure battery is fully charged and in good condition.
2. Raise and support vehicle.
3. Inspect starter and starter solenoid for corrosion or loose wiring.
4. Lower vehicle.
5. Remove starter relay from connector.
6. Connect a remote starter switch or a jumper wire between battery positive post and terminal 87, **Figs. 3 and 4.**
7. If engine cranks, starter and starter solenoid are operating properly.
8. Perform starter relay test as described under "Starter Control Circuit Test."
9. If engine does not crank or solenoid chatters, inspect wiring and connectors from relay to starter for loose or corroded connections.
10. Repeat test and, if engine still does not crank properly, repair or replace starter or starter solenoid as required.

Ignition Switch Test

After testing starter solenoid and relay, test ignition switch and wiring. Inspect all wiring for opens or shorts and all connectors for looseness or corrosion.

BENCH TESTING

STARTER SOLENOID

Refer to "Bench Tests" in the "Bosch Starter Motors" section.

STARTER SPECIFICATIONS

Engine	Free Speed Test			Minimum RPM	Cranking Amp Draw Test①
	Power Rating, KW	Max. Amps	Volts		
2.4L	1.4	—	12	—	150–280
2.7L	1.4	—	12	—	150–280
3.2L	1.4	—	12	—	150–280
3.3L	1.2	—	12	—	150–280
3.5L	1.4	—	12	—	150–280

① — With engine @ operating temperature.

Melco Starters

NOTE: On Air Bag Equipped Models, Refer To "Air Bag System Precautions" Located In The Front Of This Manual For System Disarming & Arming Procedures.

NOTE: Refer To "Computer Relearn Procedures" Located In The Front Of This Manual When Battery Power To The Computer Has Been Interrupted.

INDEX

DESCRIPTION

Melco starters may be direct drive or gear reduction type starters. They have an overrunning clutch starter drive and a solenoid switch mounted on the starter motor.

DIAGNOSIS & TESTING

Refer to the "Nippondenso Starter Motors" section for Melco starter diagnosis and testing procedures.

STARTER SPECIFICATIONS

Engine	Free Speed Test		Cranking Amp Draw Test①
	Power Rating, KW	Volts	
2.5L	1.2	12	150–280
2.7L	1.4	12	150–280
3.5L	1.2	12	150–280

① — With engine @ operating temperature.

ALTERNATORS

NOTE: On Air Bag Equipped Models, Refer To "Air Bag System Precautions" Located In The Front of This Manual For System Disarming & Arming Procedures.

NOTE: Refer To "Computer Relearn Procedure" Located In The Front of This Manual When Battery Power To The Computer Has Been Interrupted.

NOTE: "Electrical Symbol & Wire Color Code Identification" Located In The Front of This Manual May Be Used As An Aid When Using Wiring Circuits Found In This Section.

TABLE OF CONTENTS

Melco & Nippondenso

INDEX

APPLICATION CHART

Model & Year	Engine	Type
1998		
Breeze, Cirrus & Stratus	2.0L & 2.4L	Nippondenso
Cirrus & Stratus	2.5L	Melco
Concorde & Intrepid	2.7L	Nippondenso
	3.2L & 3.5L	Melco
Neon	All	Melco
Sebring Convertible	All	Nippondenso
1999		
Breeze, Cirrus & Stratus	2.0L & 2.4L	Nippondenso
Cirrus & Stratus	2.5L	Melco
Concorde, Intrepid, LHS & 300M	2.7L	Nippondenso
	3.2L & 3.5L	Melco
Neon	All	Melco
Sebring Convertible	All	Nippondenso
2000		
Breeze, Cirrus & Stratus	2.0L & 2.4L	Nippondenso
Cirrus & Stratus	2.5L	Melco
Concorde, Intrepid, LHS & 300M	2.7L	Nippondenso
	3.2L & 3.5L	Melco
2001		
Concorde, Intrepid, LHS & 300M	2.7L	Nippondenso
	3.2L & 3.5L	Melco
Sebring Convertible & Sedan & Stratus Sedan	2.4L & 2.7L	Nippondenso
2002		
Concorde, Intrepid, LHS & 300M	2.7L & 3.5L	Nippondenso
Sebring Convertible & Sedan & Stratus Sedan	2.4L & 2.7L	Nippondenso

PRECAUTIONS

BATTERY GROUND CABLE

Prior to service, disconnect battery ground cable and isolate as required.

GENERAL INFORMATION

The power source of the charging system is the alternator. Current is transmitted from the field terminal of the regulator through a slip ring to the field coil and back to ground through another slip ring. The strength of the field regulates the output of the alternating current. This alternating current is then transmitted from the alternator to the rectifier where it is converted to direct current.

These alternators employ a three-phase stator winding in which the phase windings are electrically 120° apart. The rotor consists of a field coil encased between interleaved sections producing a magnetic field with alternate north and south poles. By rotating the rotor inside the stator, the alternating current is induced in the stator windings. This alternating current is rectified (changed to DC) by silicon diodes and brought out to the output terminal of the alternator.

DIODE RECTIFIERS

Six or more silicon diode rectifiers are used and act as electrical one-way valves. One half of the diodes have ground polarity and are pressed or screwed into a heat sink

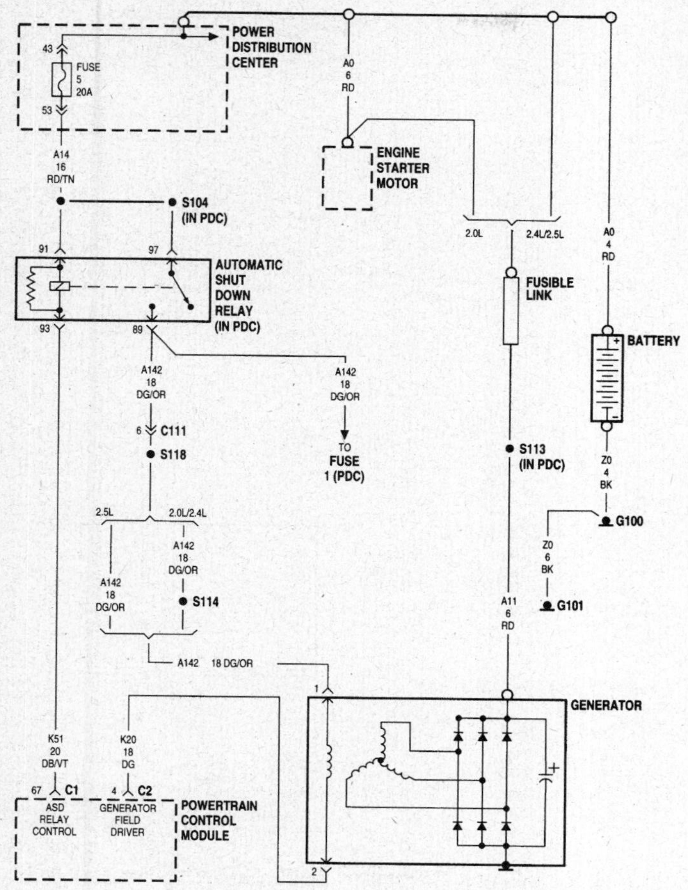

Fig. 1 Wiring diagram. 1998 Breeze, Cirrus, Sebring Convertible & Stratus

CR1129900312000X

Fig. 2 Wiring diagram. 1999 Breeze, Cirrus, Sebring Convertible & Stratus

which is grounded. The other diodes (ungrounded) are pressed or screwed into and insulated from the end head. These diodes are connected to the alternator output terminal.

Since the diodes have a high resistance to the flow of current in one direction and a low resistance in the opposite direction, they may be connected in a manner which allows current to flow from the alternator to the battery in the low resistance direction. The high resistance in the opposite direction prevents the flow of current from the battery to the alternator. Because of this feature no circuit breaker is required between the alternator and battery.

SERVICE PRECAUTIONS

1. Ensure battery polarity is proper when servicing units. Reversed battery polarity will damage rectifiers and regulators.
2. If booster battery is used for starting, use proper polarity in hookup.
3. When a fast charger is used to charge a vehicle battery, vehicle battery cables should be disconnected unless fast charger is equipped with a special alternator protector, in which case vehicle battery cables need not be disconnected. Also, fast chargers should never be used to start a vehicle, as damage to rectifiers will result.
4. Lead connections to grounded rectifiers (negative) should never be soldered, as excessive heat may damage rectifiers.
5. Unless system includes a load relay or field relay, grounding alternator output terminal will damage alternator and/or circuits. This is true even when system is not in operation, since no circuit breaker is used and battery voltage is applied to alternator output terminal at all times. Field or load relay acts as a circuit breaker in that it is controlled by ignition switch.
6. Before making any in-vehicle tests of alternator or regulator, battery should be inspected and circuit inspected for faulty wiring or insulation, loose or corroded connections and poor ground circuits.
7. Inspect alternator belt tension to ensure belt is tight enough to prevent slipping under load.
8. To prevent system damage, turn ignition off before making any test connections.
9. The vehicle battery must be fully charged or a fully charged battery may be installed for test purposes.

DESCRIPTION

The main components of the alternator are the rotor, stator, rectifier, end shields and drive pulley. Direct current is available at the output B terminal.

Alternator output is controlled by voltage regulator circuitry contained within the power and logic modules of the engine controller.

DIAGNOSIS & TESTING

WIRING DIAGRAMS

BREEZE, CIRRUS, SEBRING CONVERTIBLE & SEDAN & STRATUS SEDAN

Refer to **Figs. 1 through 5** for wiring diagrams.

CONCORDE, INTREPID, LHS, & 300M

Refer to **Figs. 6 and 7** for wiring diagrams.

NEON

Refer to **Fig. 8** for wiring diagram.

DIAGNOSTIC TESTS

1998

Refer to **Figs. 9 through 14** for diagnostic tests.

1999–2000

Refer to **Figs. 15 through 21** for diagnostic tests.

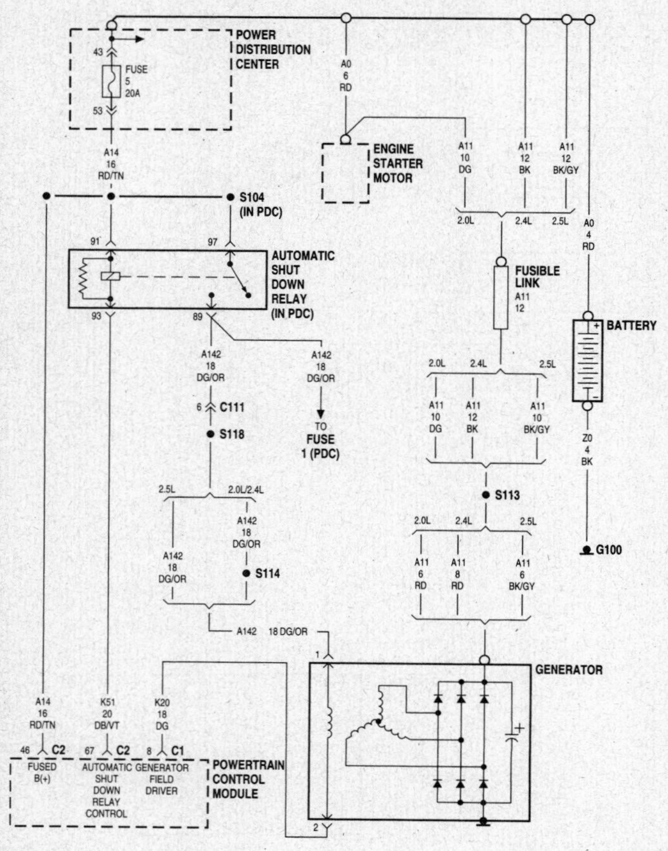

Fig. 3 Wiring diagram. 2000 Breeze, Cirrus, Sebring Convertible & Stratus

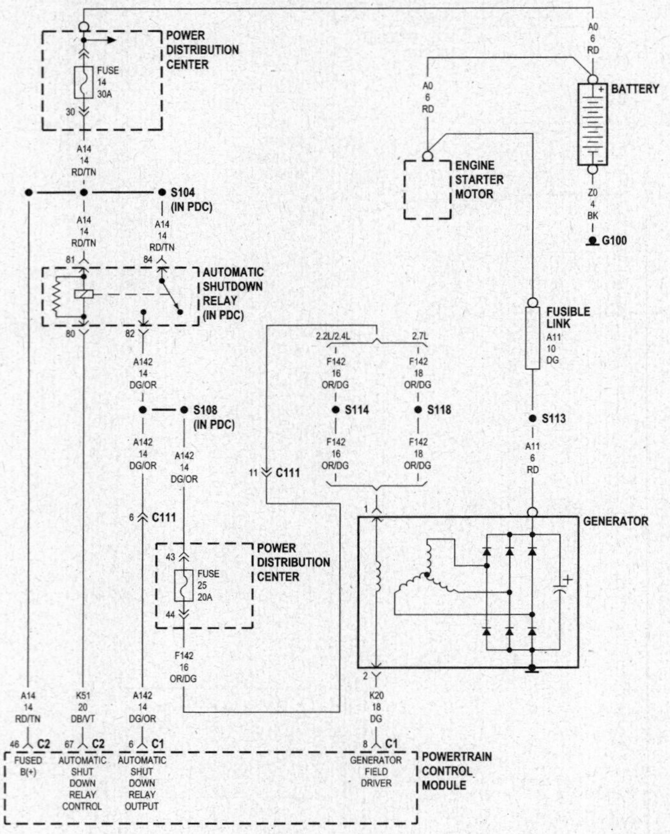

CR1120100393000X

Fig. 4 Wiring diagram. 2001 Sebring Sedan & Stratus Sedan

Breeze, Cirrus, Sebring Convertible & Stratus

Concorde, Intrepid, LHS & 300M

Refer to **Figs. 22 through 30** for diagnostic tests.

2001

Concorde, Intrepid, LHS & 300M

Refer to "Concorde, Intrepid, LHS & 300M" under "1999–2000" for diagnostic tests.

Sebring Convertible & Sedan & Stratus Sedan

Refer to **Figs. 31 through 37** for diagnostic tests.

2002

Concorde, Intrepid, LHS & 300M

Refer to **Figs. 38 through 42** for diagnostic tests.

Sebring Convertible & Sedan & Stratus Sedan

Refer to "Sebring Convertible & Sedan & Stratus Sedan" under "2001" for diagnostic tests.

OUTPUT WIRE VOLTAGE DROP TEST

1998

1. Prepare vehicle for test as follows:
   a. Ensure battery is in good condition and fully charged.
   b. Ensure battery cables are clean.
   c. Start engine and allow it to reach normal operating temperature.
   d. Turn engine off, then connect engine to a tachometer.
   e. Fully engage parking brake.
2. Start engine, then turn HVAC blower to High position.
3. Turn headlamps to high beam position.
4. Turn vehicle interior lamps on.
5. Bring engine speed up to 2400 RPM and hold.
6. Test positive circuitry as follows:
   a. Using a voltmeter, touch negative lead directly to battery positive terminal.
   b. Touch positive lead to battery positive terminal stud on alternator. There should be no higher than .6 volts.
   c. If voltage is higher than .6 volts, touch test lead to terminal mounting stud nut and then to wiring connector. If voltage is now below .6 volts, inspect for dirty, loose or poor connection and condition of alternator output wire to battery bullet connector.
7. Test ground circuitry as follows:
   a. Touch positive lead of voltmeter directly to battery ground post.
   b. Touch negative lead of voltmeter to alternator case. Voltage should be no higher than .3 volts.
   c. If voltage is higher than .3 volts, touch test lead to alternator case and then to engine block. If voltage is now below .3 volts, inspect for dirty, loose or poor connection.

CURRENT OUTPUT TEST

1998

A volt/amp tester equipped with both a battery load control (Carbon pile rheostat) and an inductive type pickup clamp are required for this test.

1. Prepare vehicle for test as follows:
   a. Ensure battery is in good condition and fully charged.
   b. Ensure battery cables are clean.

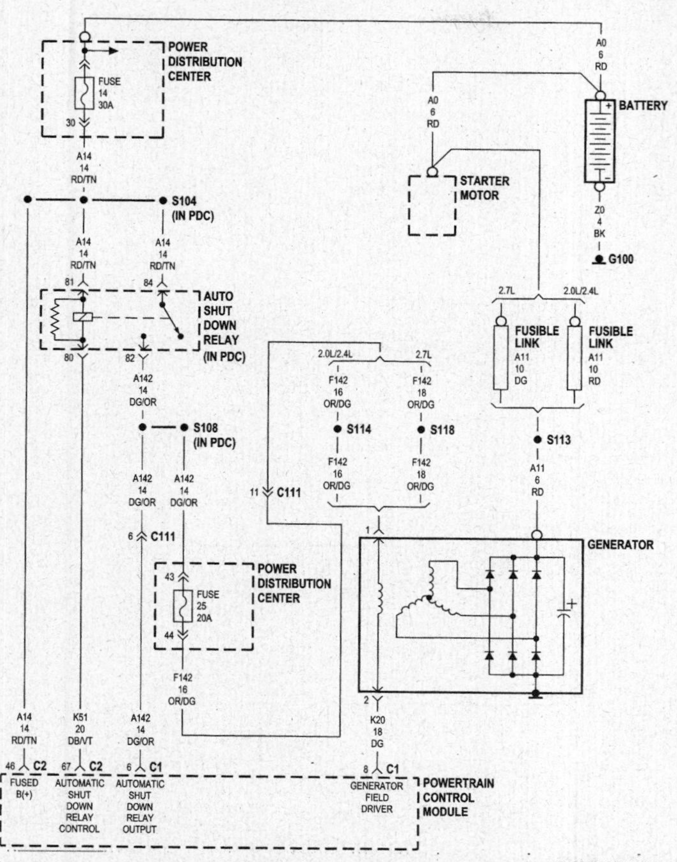

Fig. 5 Wiring diagram. 2002 Sebring Convertible & Sedan & Stratus Sedan

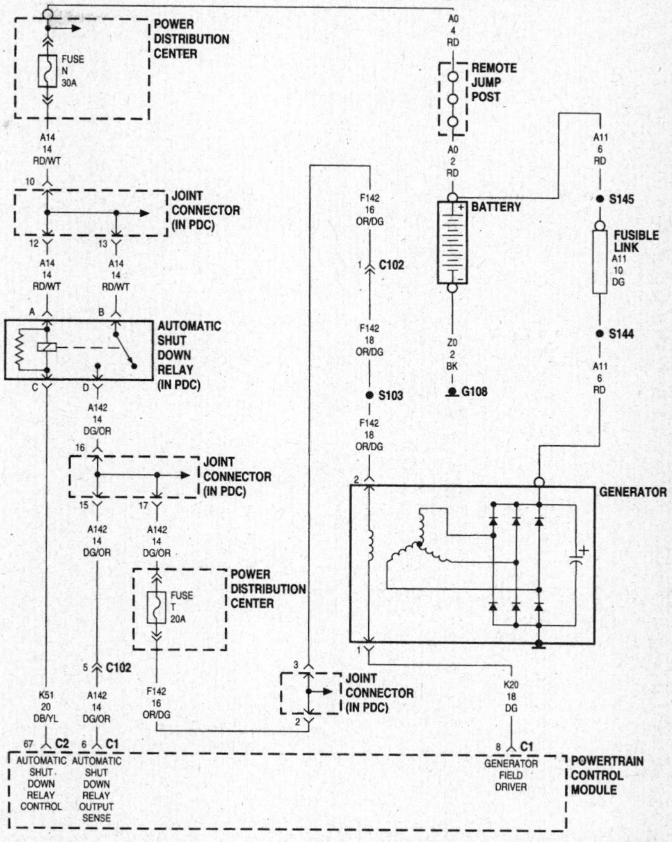

CR1129900258000X

Fig. 6 Wiring diagram. 1998–2001 Concorde, Intrepid, LHS & 300M

c. Ensure alternator drive belt is properly tensioned.
d. Start engine and allow it to reach normal operating temperature.
e. Stop engine, then turn off all electrical accessories and all vehicle lighting.
f. Fully engage parking brake.

2. Connect volt/amp tester leads to battery post or jump start posts. Ensure carbon pile rheostat control is in Open or off position before connecting leads.
3. Connect inductive clamp, then a tachometer to engine.
4. Fully apply parking brake.
5. Start engine and bring speed to 2500 RPM.
6. With engine speed held at 2500 RPM, slowly adjust rheostat control on tester to obtain highest amperage reading. **Do not allow voltage to drop below 12 volts. This load test must be performed within 15 seconds to prevent damage to test equipment.**
7. Record reading. If amperage does not meet specifications, refer to "Diagnostic Tests" in this section. Refer to "Alternator Specifications" in this section for specifications.
8. Rotate load control to off position.
9. Continue holding engine speed at 2500 RPM. If electronic voltage regulator circuitry is in good condition, amperage should drop below 15–20 amps.
10. Remove volt amp tester. If amperage does not meet specifications, refer to "Diagnostic Tests" in this section.

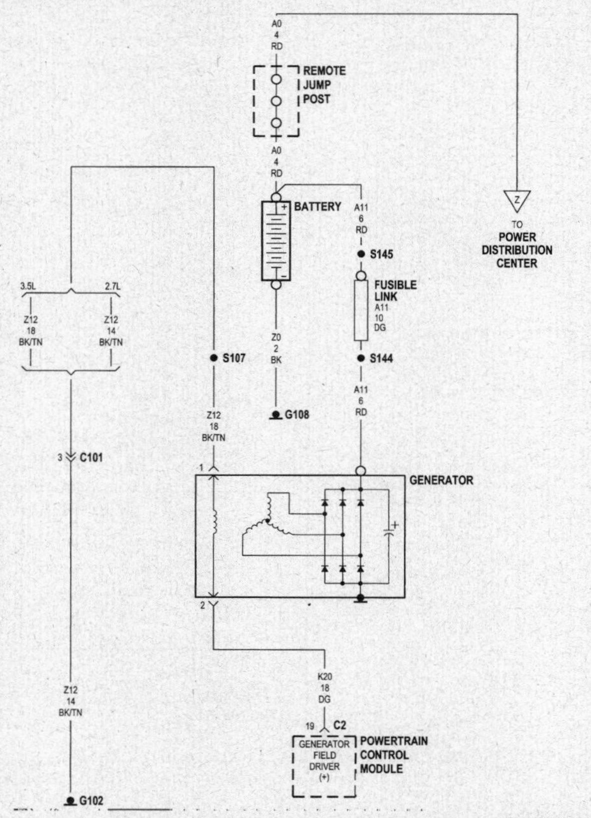

Fig. 7 Wiring diagram (Part 1 of 2). 2002 Concorde, Intrepid, LHS & 300M

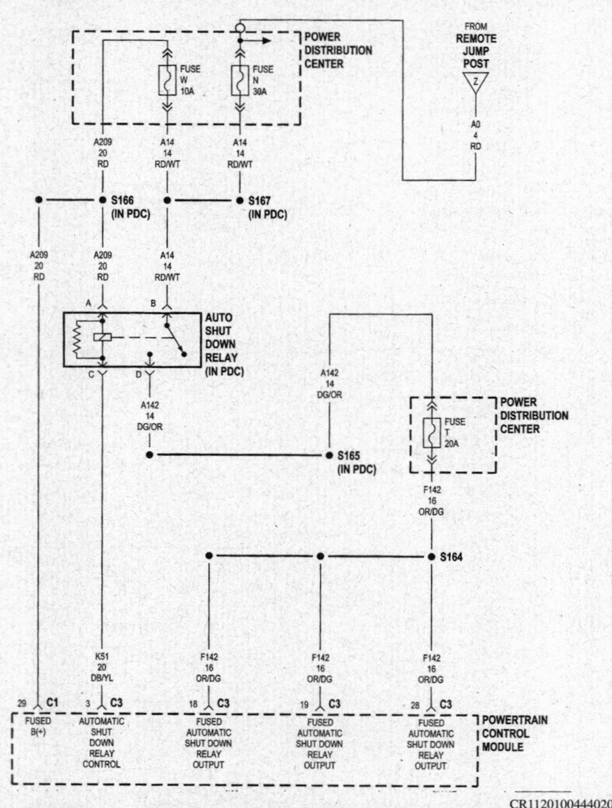

Fig. 7 Wiring diagram (Part 2 of 2). 2002 Concorde, Intrepid, LHS & 300M

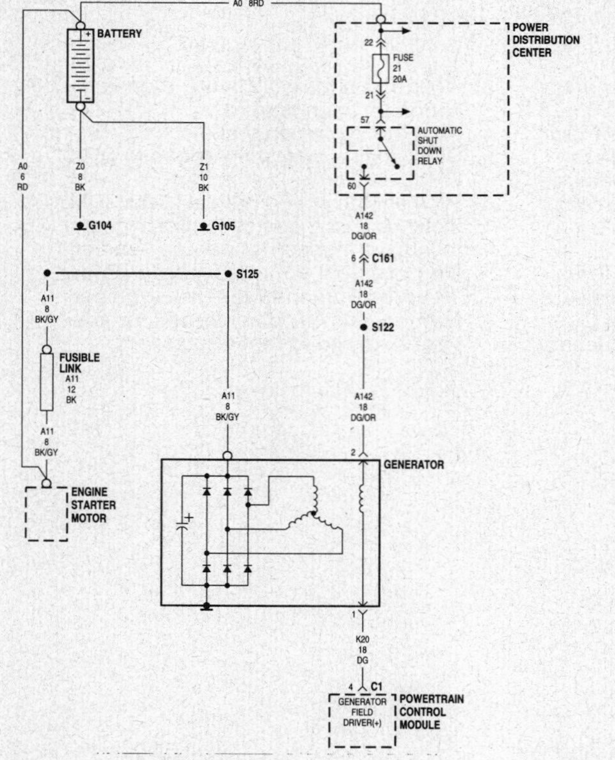

Fig. 8 Wiring diagram. Neon

DIAGNOSTIC CHART INDEX

Code/Test	Description	Page No.	Fig.No.
1998			
Test CH-1A	Charging System No Code Test	9-8	9
Test TC-5A	Charging System Voltage Too Low	9-8	10
Test TC-5B	Charging System Voltage Too Low	9-9	11
Test TC-6A	Charging System Voltage Too High	9-9	12
Test TC-6B	Charging System Voltage Too High	9-9	13
Test TC-11A	Alternator Field Not Switching Properly	9-10	14
1999–2000 BREEZE, CIRRUS, SEBRING CONVERTIBLE & STRATUS			
P0622	Alternator Field Not Switching Properly	9-11	15
P1492	Battery Temperature Sensor Voltage Out Of Range	9-11	16
P1493	Battery Temperature Sensor Voltage Out Of Range	9-11	16
P1594	Charging System Voltage Too High	9-12	17
P1682	Charging System Voltage Too Low	9-12	18
—	Charging System Diagnosis w/No Code	9-13	19
—	Verification Test VER-2A	9-14	20
—	Verification Test VER-3A	9-14	21
1999–2001 CONCORDE, INTREPID, LHS & 300M			
P0622	Alternator Field Not Switching Properly	9-14	22
P1478	Battery Temperature Sensor Voltage Out Of Limit	9-15	23
P1492	Ambient/Battery Temperature Sensor Voltage Out Of Range	9-15	24
P1493	Ambient/Battery Temperature Sensor Voltage Out Of Range	9-15	24
P1594	Charging System Voltage Too High	9-16	25
P1682	Charging System Voltage Too Low	9-16	26
—	Ambient/Battery Temperature Sensor Diagnosis	9-17	27
—	Charging System Diagnosis w/No Code	9-17	28
—	Verification Test VER-3	9-18	29
—	Verification Test VER-5	9-18	30
2002 CONCORDE, INTREPID, LHS & 300M			
P0562	Battery Voltage Low	9-21	38
P0563	Battery Voltage High	9-22	39
P0622	Alternator Field Control Circuit	9-23	40
P2503	Charging System Voltage Low	9-23	41
—	Verification Test VER-3	9-24	42
2001–02 SEBRING CONVERTIBLE & SEDAN & STRATUS SEDAN			
P0622	Alternator Field Not Switching Properly	9-18	31
P1492	Ambient/Battery Temperature Sensor Voltage Too High	9-19	32
P1493	Ambient/Battery Temperature Sensor Voltage Too Low	9-19	33
P1594	Charging System Voltage Too High	9-20	34
P1682	Charging System Voltage Too Low	9-20	35
—	Verification Test VER-3	9-21	36
—	Verification Test VER-5	9-21	37

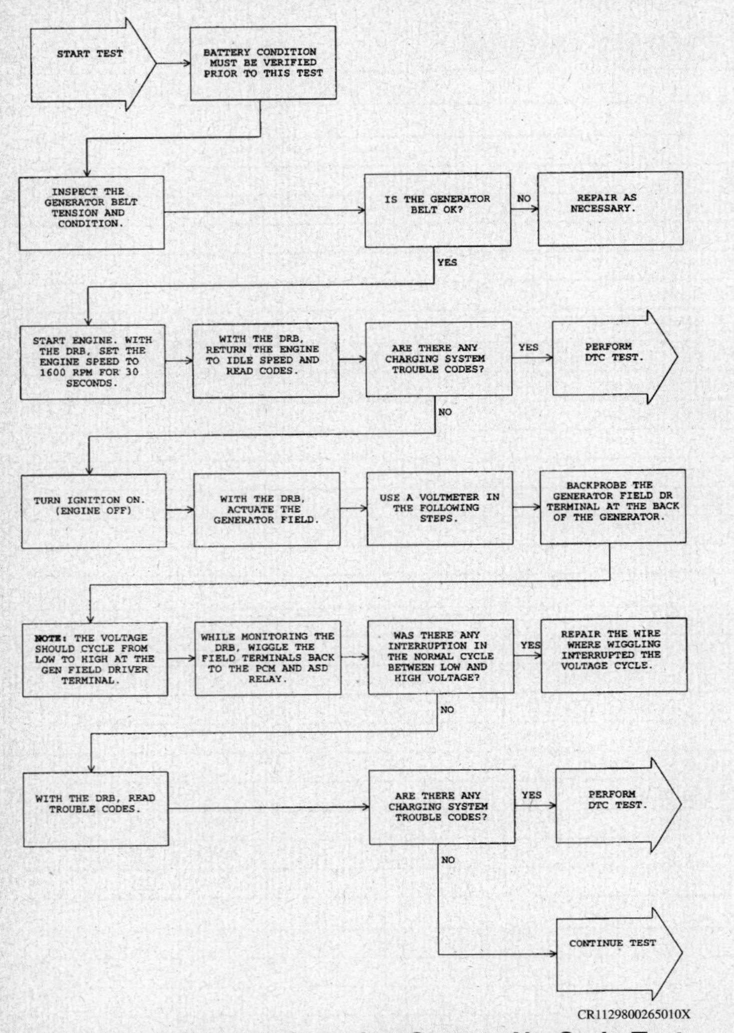

Fig. 9 Test CH-1A: Charging System No Code Test (Part 1 of 3). 1998

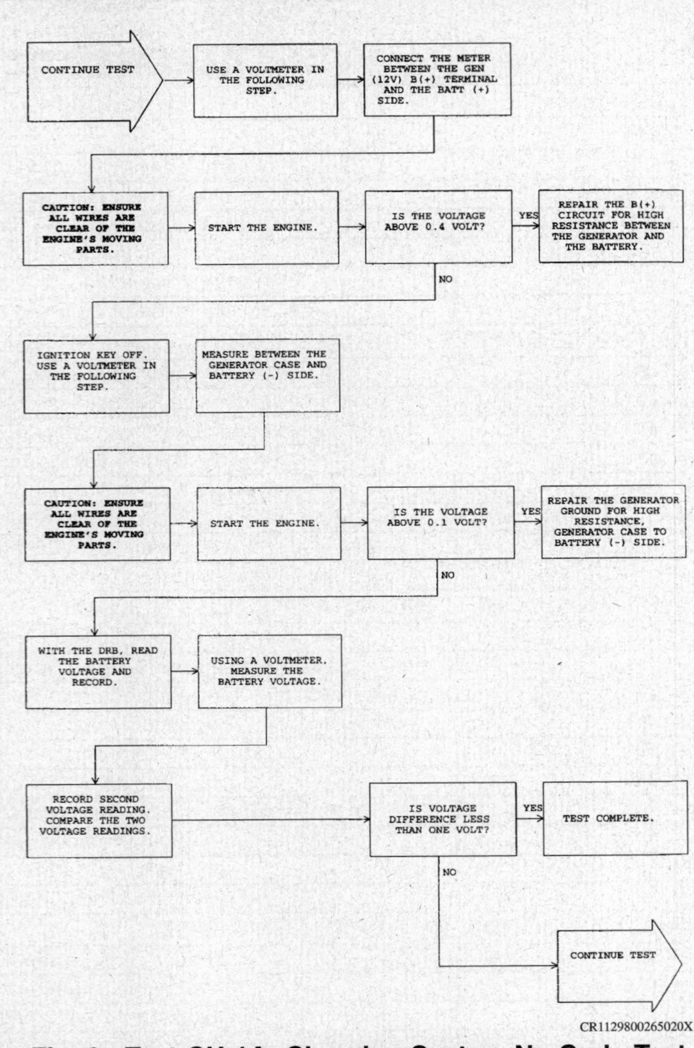

Fig. 9 Test CH-1A: Charging System No Code Test (Part 2 of 3). 1998

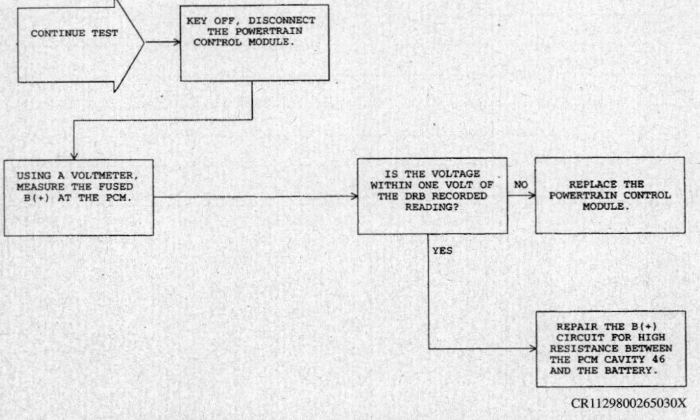

Fig. 9 Test CH-1A: Charging System No Code Test (Part 3 of 3). 1998

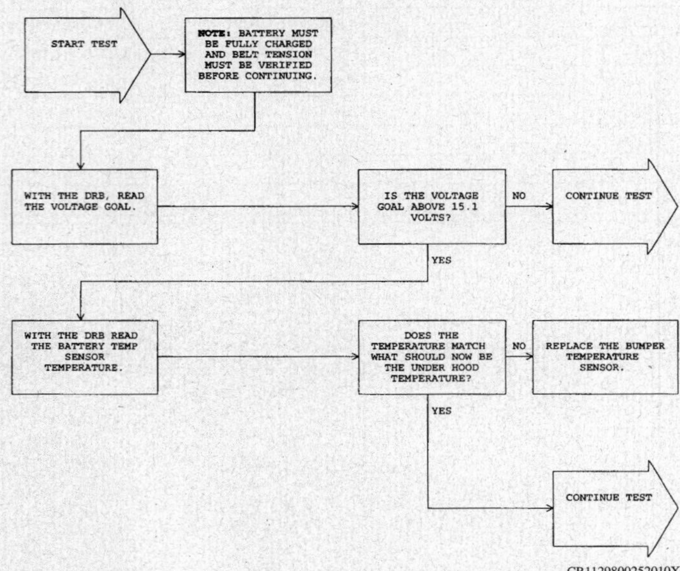

Fig. 10 Test TC-5A: Charging System Voltage Too Low (Part 1 of 2). 1998

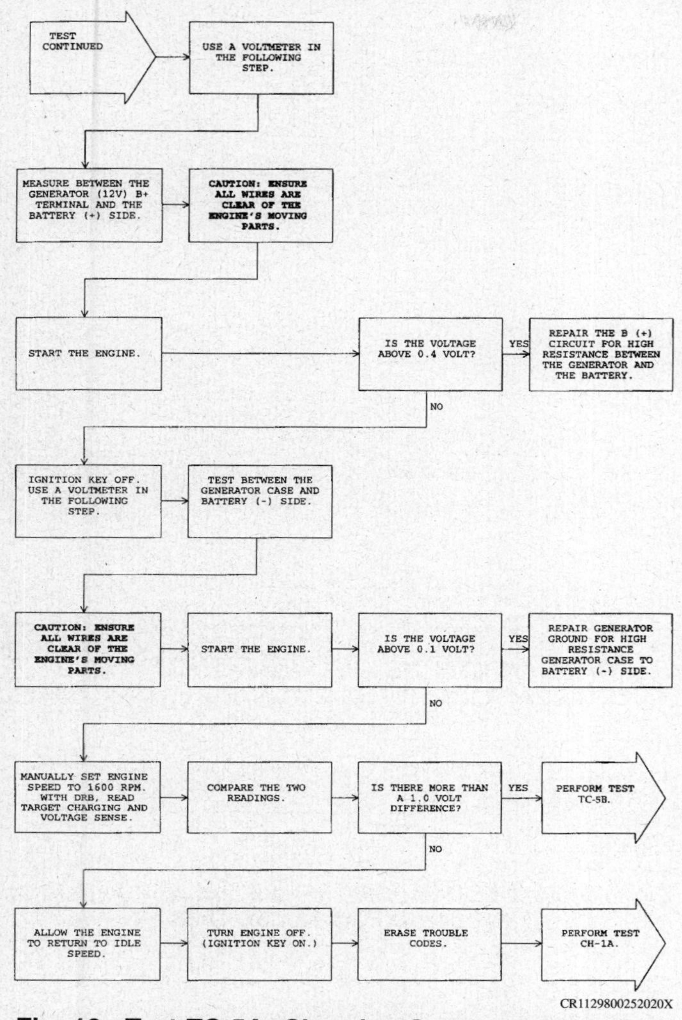

Fig. 10 Test TC-5A: Charging System Voltage Too Low (Part 2 of 2). 1998

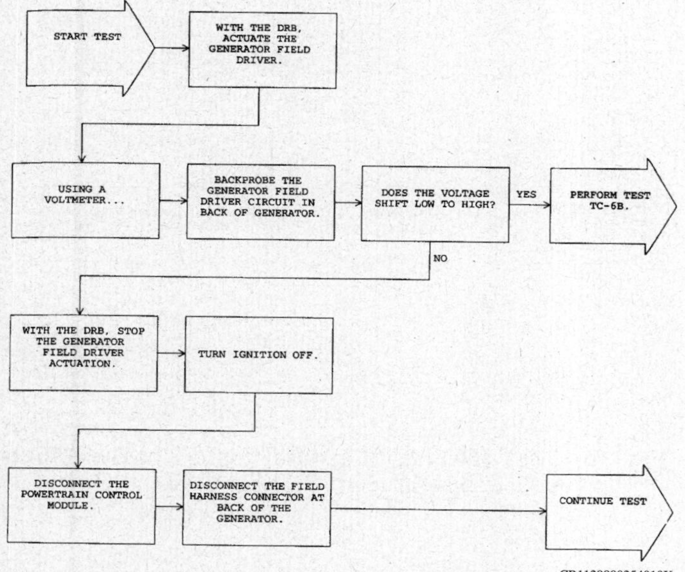

Fig. 12 Test TC-6A: Charging System Voltage Too High (Part 1 of 2). 1998

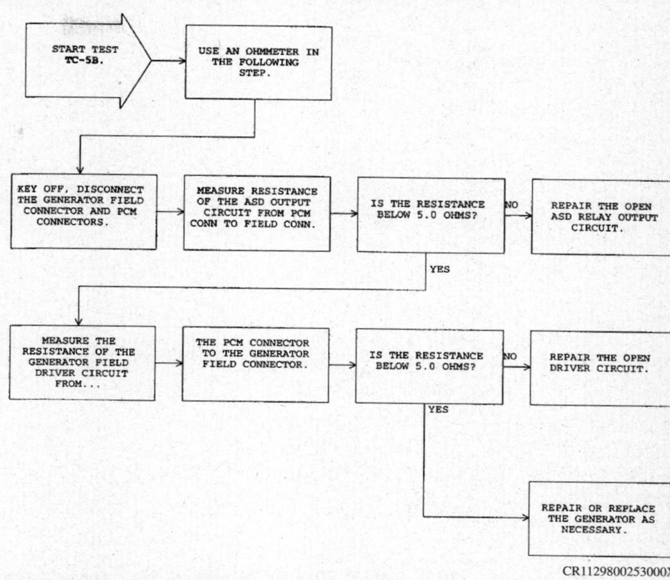

Fig. 11 Test TC-5B: Charging System Voltage Too Low. 1998

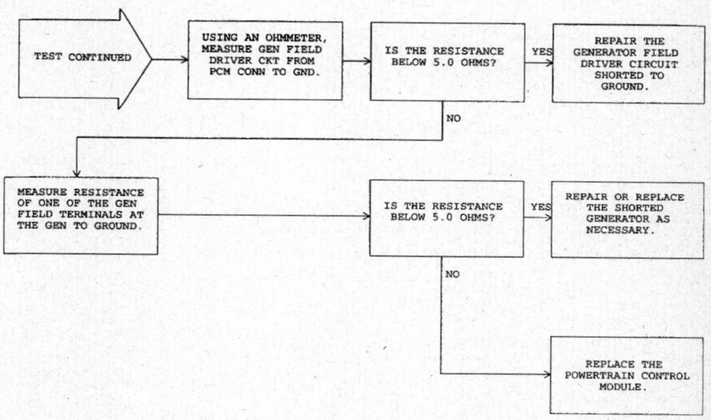

Fig. 12 Test TC-6A: Charging System Voltage Too High (Part 2 of 2). 1998

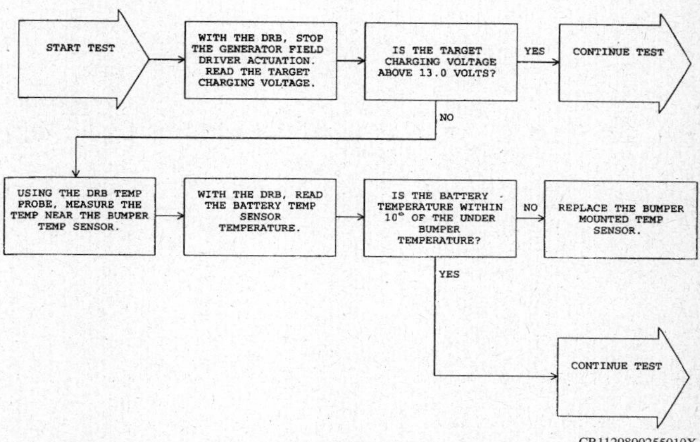

Fig. 13 Test TC-6B: Charging System Voltage Too High (Part 1 of 2). 1998

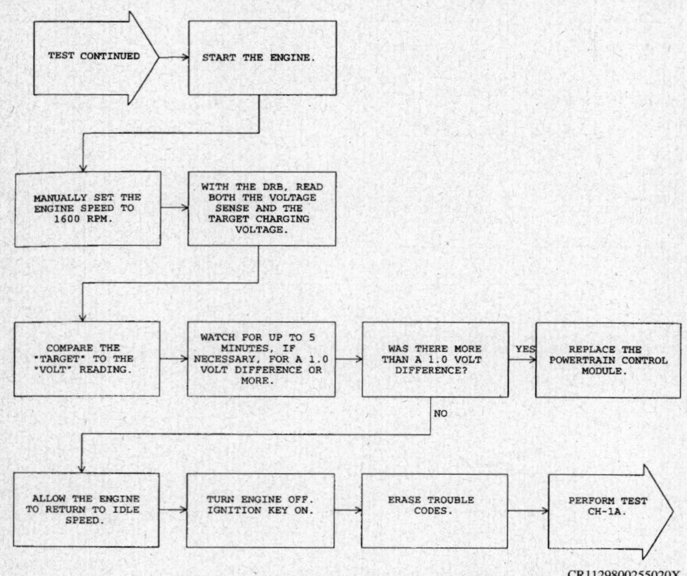

Fig. 13 Test TC-6B: Charging System Voltage Too High (Part 2 of 2). 1998

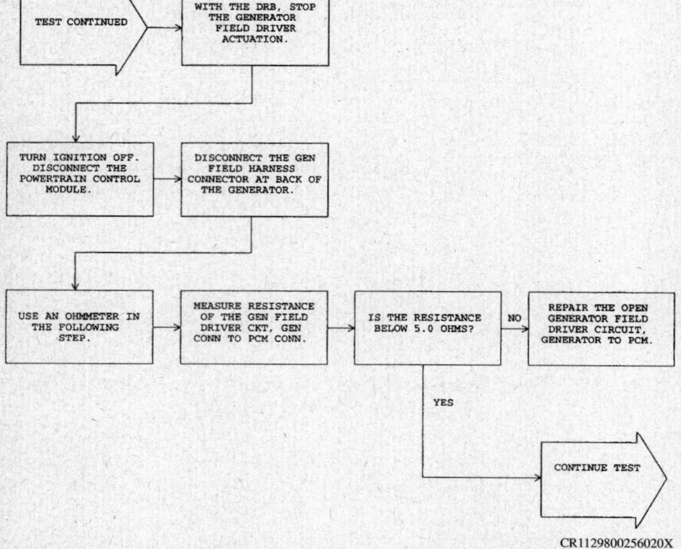

Fig. 14 Test TC-11A: Alternator Field Not Switching Properly (Part 2 of 3). 1998

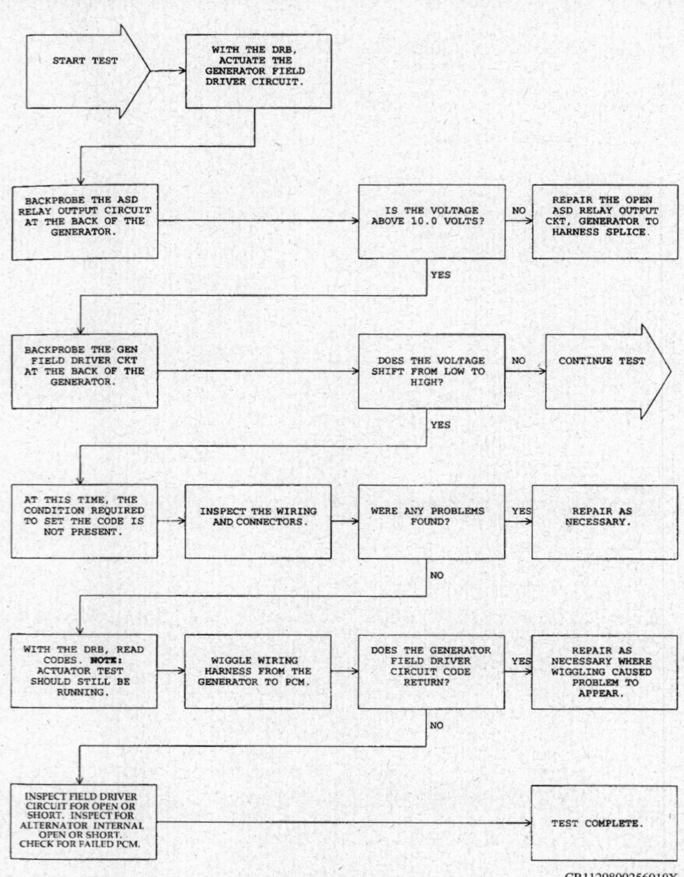

Fig. 14 Test TC-11A: Alternator Field Not Switching Properly (Part 1 of 3). 1998

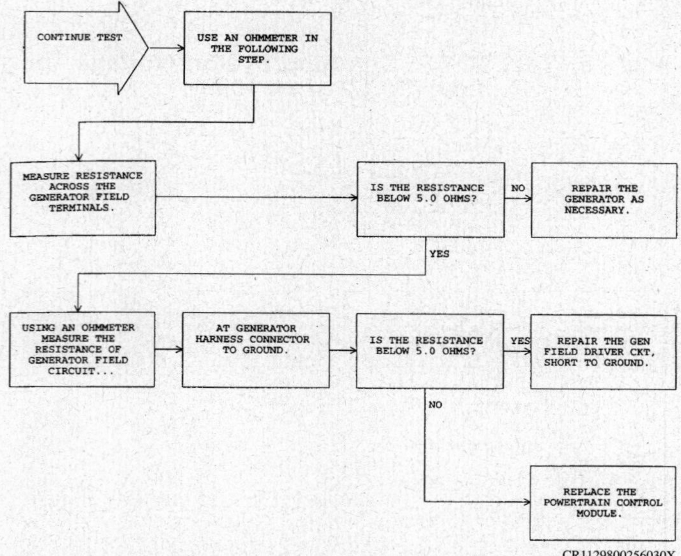

Fig. 14 Test TC-11A: Alternator Field Not Switching Properly (Part 3 of 3). 1998

TEST	ACTION	APPLICABILITY
1	Ignition On, Engine Not Running With the DRB, erase trouble codes. With the DRB, actuate the Generator Field Driver Circuit. Backprobe the ASD Relay Output Circuit at the back of the Generator. Record all DTC's and Freeze Frame Data. Is the voltage above 10.0 volts? Yes → Go To 2 No → Repair the open ASD Relay Output Circuit, Generator to Harness splice. Perform Powertrain Verification Test VER-3A.	All
2	Ignition On, Engine Not Running With the DRB, actuate the Generator Field Driver Circuit. Backprobe the Generator Field Driver Circuit at the back of the Generator. Does the voltage shift from low to high? Yes → Go To 3 No → Go To 5	All

CR1120000314010X

Fig. 15 Code P0622: Alternator Field Not Switching Properly (Part 1 of 3). 1999–2000 Breeze, Cirrus, Sebring Convertible & Stratus

TEST	ACTION	APPLICABILITY
8	If there are no potential causes remaining, replace the PCM. View repair options. Repair Replace the Powertrain Control Module. Perform Powertrain Verification Test VER-3A.	All

CR1120000314030X

Fig. 15 Code P0622: Alternator Field Not Switching Properly (Part 3 of 3). 1999–2000 Breeze, Cirrus, Sebring Convertible & Stratus

TEST	ACTION
1	Ignition On, Engine Not Running With the DRB, read the Battery Temperature Sensor (BTS) voltage. Is the BTS voltage below 0.4 volt? Yes → Go To 2 No → Go To 5

CR1120000315010X

Fig. 16 Codes P1492 & P1493: Battery Temperature Sensor Voltage Out of Range (Part 1 of 4). 1999–2000 Breeze, Cirrus, Sebring Convertible & Stratus

TEST	ACTION
3	Ignition On, Engine Not Running Actuate the Generator Field Driver Circuit. Wiggle Wiring Harness from the Generator to the PCM. Read codes. Does the Generator Field Driver circuit code return? Yes → Repair as necessary where wiggling caused problem to appear. Perform Powertrain Verification Test VER-3A. No → Go To 4
4	Ignition Off Using the schematic as a guide, inspect the Wiring and Connectors. Were any problems found? Yes → Repair as necessary. Perform Powertrain Verification Test VER-3A. No → Test Complete.
5	Ignition Off Disconnect the PCM. **Note: Check connectors - Clean/repair as necessary.** Disconnect the Generator Field Harness Connector at the back of the Generator. **Note: Check connectors - Clean/repair as necessary.** Using an Ohmmeter, measure the resistance across the Generator Field Terminals. Is the resistance below 5.0 ohms? Yes → Go To 6 No → Repair the Generator as necessary. Perform Powertrain Verification Test VER-3A.
6	Ignition Off Disconnect the Powertrain Control Module Harness Connector. Disconnect the Generator Field Harness Connector at the back of the Generator. **Note: Check connectors - Clean/repair as necessary.** Using an Ohmmeter, test the resistance of the Generator Field Driver Circuit from the Generator Connector to the PCM Connector. Is the resistance below 5.0 ohms? Yes → Go To 7 No → Repair open Generator Field Driver Circuit, Generator to PCM. Perform Powertrain Verification Test VER-3A.
7	Ignition Off Disconnect the Powertrain Control Module Harness Connector. Disconnect the Generator Field Harness Connector at the back of the Generator. **Note: Check connectors - Clean/repair as necessary.** Using an Ohmmeter, measure the resistance of the Generator Field Circuit at the Generator Harness Connector to ground. Is the resistance below 5.0 ohms? Yes → Repair the Generator Field Driver Circuit short to ground. Perform Powertrain Verification Test VER-3A. No → Go To 8

CR1120000314020X

Fig. 15 Code P0622: Alternator Field Not Switching Properly (Part 2 of 3). 1999–2000 Breeze, Cirrus, Sebring Convertible & Stratus

TEST	ACTION
2	Ignition On, Engine Not Running Disconnect the Battery Temperature Sensor (BTS). **Note: Check connectors - Clean/repair as necessary.** With the DRB, read the BTS voltage. Is the BTS voltage above 4.0 volts? Yes → Replace the BTS. Perform Powertrain Verification Test VER-2A. No → Go To 3
3	Ignition Off Disconnect the Battery Temperature Sensor (BTS). **Note: Check connectors - Clean/repair as necessary.** Disconnect the Powertrain Control Module. **Note: Check connectors - Clean/repair as necessary.** With an Ohmmeter, measure the BTS Sensor Signal Ckt at BTS Conn to ground. Is the resistance below 5.0 ohms? Yes → Repair the Sensor Signal Circuit for a short to ground. Perform Powertrain Verification Test VER-2A. No → Go To 4
4	If there are no potential causes remaining, replace the Powertrain Control Module. View repair options. Repair Replace the Powertrain Control Module. Perform Powertrain Verification Test VER-2A.
5	Ignition On, Engine Not Running With the DRB, read the Battery Temperature Sensor (BTS) voltage. Is the BTS voltage above 4.9 volts? Yes → Go To 6 No → Go To 11
6	Ignition Off Disconnect the BTS Electrical Connector. **Note: Check connectors - Clean/repair as necessary.** Disconnect the PCM Connector. **Note: Check connectors - Clean/repair as necessary.** Using an Ohmmeter, measure the resistance of the Sensor Ground Circuit between the BTS and the Powertrain Control Module. Is the resistance below 5.0 ohms? Yes → Go To 7 No → Repair the open BTS Sensor Ground Circuit. Perform Powertrain Verification Test VER-2A.

CR1120000315020X

Fig. 16 Codes P1492 & P1493: Battery Temperature Sensor Voltage Out of Range (Part 2 of 4). 1999–2000 Breeze, Cirrus, Sebring Convertible & Stratus

TEST	ACTION
7	Ignition On, Engine Not Running Disconnect the Battery Temperature Sensor (BTS). **Note: Check connectors - Clean/repair as necessary.** Connect a jumper wire between the BTS Signal and Sensor Ground at BTS Connectors. With the DRB, read the BTS voltage. Is the voltage below 1.0 volt? Yes → Replace the BTS. Perform Powertrain Verification Test VER-2A. No → Go To 8
8	Ignition Off Disconnect the Battery Temperature Sensor (BTS). **Note: Check connectors - Clean/repair as necessary.** Using a Voltmeter, measure the BTS Signal Circuit voltage. Is the voltage above 5.0 volts? Yes → Repair the BTS Signal Circuit for a short to voltage. Perform Powertrain Verification Test VER-2A. No → Go To 9
9	Ignition Off Disconnect the Battery Temperature Sensor (BTS). **Note: Check connectors - Clean/repair as necessary.** Disconnect the Powertrain Control Module. **Note: Check connectors - Clean/repair as necessary.** Using an Ohmmeter, measure the BTS Signal Circuit from the Sensor Connector to the PCM. Is the resistance below 5.0 ohms? Yes → Go To 10 No → Repair the open BTS Signal Circuit. Perform Powertrain Verification Test VER-2A.
10	If there are no remaining causes known, replace the PCM. View repair options. Repair Replace the PCM. Perform Powertrain Verification Test VER-2A.
11	Ignition On, Engine Not Running With the DRB, read the Battery Temperature Sensor (BTS) voltage. Using the schematic as a guide, wiggle the BTS Connector and Harness. Monitor the DRB display. Was there any BTS voltage change? Yes → Repair the Harness or Connector that caused the voltage change. Perform Powertrain Verification Test VER-2A. No → Go To 12

CR1120000315030X

Fig. 16 Codes P1492 & P1493: Battery Temperature Sensor Voltage Out of Range (Part 3 of 4). 1999–2000 Breeze, Cirrus, Sebring Convertible & Stratus

TEST	ACTION
1	Ignition On, Engine Not Running. **Note: Battery must be fully charged.** **Note: Generator Belt tension and condition must be checked before continuing.** With the DRB, actuate the Generator Field Driver. Using a voltmeter, backprobe the Generator Field Driver Circuit at the Generator. Does the voltage shift low to high? Yes → Go To 2 No → Go To 5
2	Ignition On, Engine Not Running. **Note: Battery must be fully charged.** **Note: Generator Belt tension and condition must be checked before continuing.** With the DRB, read the target charging voltage. Is the target charging voltage above 13.0 volts? Yes → Go To 4 No → Go To 3
3	Ignition On, Engine Not Running. Using the DRB temperature probe, measure the under hood temperature near PCM. With the DRB, read the Battery Temperature Sensor temperature. Is the battery temperature within 10F of the under hood temperature? Yes → Go To 4 No → Replace the Powertrain Control Module. Perform Powertrain Verification Test VER-3A.

CR1120000316010X

Fig. 17 Code P1594: Charging System Voltage Too High (Part 1 of 2). 1999–2000 Breeze, Cirrus, Sebring Convertible & Stratus

TEST	ACTION
12	Ignition Off Using the schematic as a guide, inspect the Wiring and Connectors. Were any problems found? Yes → Repair as necessary. Perform Powertrain Verification Test VER-2A. No → Test Complete.

CR1120000315040X

Fig. 16 Codes P1492 & P1493: Battery Temperature Sensor Voltage Out of Range (Part 4 of 4). 1999–2000 Breeze, Cirrus, Sebring Convertible & Stratus

TEST	ACTION
4	Start the engine. Manually set the engine speed to 1600 RPM. With the DRB, read both the voltage and the target charging voltage. Compare the "target" to the "volt" reading. Watch for up to 5 minutes, if necessary, for a 1.0 volt difference or more. Was there more than a 1.0 volt difference? Yes → Replace the PCM. Perform Powertrain Verification Test VER-3A. No → Refer to symptom CHARGING SYSTEM NO CODE
5	Ignition Off Disconnect the Powertrain Control Module. **Note: Check connectors - Clean/repair as necessary.** Disconnect the Field Harness Connector at back of Generator. **Note: Check connectors - Clean/repair as necessary.** Using an ohmmeter, measure the Generator Field Driver Circuit from PCM Connector to ground. Is the resistance below 5.0 ohms? Yes → Repair the Generator Field Driver Circuit shorted to ground. Perform Powertrain Verification Test VER-3A. No → Go To 6
6	Ignition Off Disconnect the Powertrain Control Module. **Note: Check connectors - Clean/repair as necessary.** Disconnect the Field Harness Connector at back of Generator. **Note: Check connectors - Clean/repair as necessary.** Using an ohmmeter, measure resistance of one of the Gen Field Terminals at the Gen to ground. Is the resistance below 5.0 ohms? Yes → Repair or replace the shorted Generator as necessary. Perform Powertrain Verification Test VER-3A. No → Go To 7
7	If there are no potential causes remaining, replace the PCM. View repair options. Repair Replace the Powertrain Control Module. Perform Powertrain Verification Test VER-3A.

CR1120000316020X

Fig. 17 Code P1594: Charging System Voltage Too High (Part 2 of 2). 1999–2000 Breeze, Cirrus, Sebring Convertible & Stratus

TEST	ACTION
1	Ignition On, Engine Not Running. **Note: Battery must be fully charged.** With the DRB, read the target charging voltage. Is the voltage goal above 15.1 volts? Yes → Go To 2 No → Go To 6
2	**Note: Battery must be fully charged.** Start the Engine. Manually set Engine Speed to 1600 rpm. With the DRB, read target charging voltage and charging voltage. Compare the two readings. Is there more than a 1.0 volt difference? Yes → Go To 3 No → Refer to CHARGING SYSTEM NO CODE

CR1120000317010X

Fig. 18 Code P1682: Charging System Voltage Too Low (Part 1 of 3). 1999–2000 Breeze, Cirrus, Sebring Convertible & Stratus

TEST	ACTION
3	Ignition Off **Note: Battery must be fully charged.** **Caution: Ensure all Wires are clear of the Engine's moving parts.** Using a Voltmeter, measure between the Generator (12V) B+ Terminal and the Battery (+) side. Start the Engine. Is the voltage above 0.4 volt? Yes → Repair the B (+) Circuit for high resistance between the Generator and Battery. Perform Powertrain Verification Test VER-3A. No → Go To 4
4	Ignition Key Off **Note: Battery must be fully charged.** **Caution: Ensure all Wires are clear of the Engine's moving parts.** With a Voltmeter, measure between the Generator Case and Battery (-) side. Start the Engine. Is the voltage above 0.1 volt? Yes → Repair Generator Ground for high resistance Generator Case to Battery (-) Side. Perform Powertrain Verification Test VER-3A. No → Go To 5
5	**Note: Battery must be fully charged.** Ignition On, Engine Not Running. With the DRB, read the Battery Temperature Sensor (BTS) temperature. Does the temperature match the under hood temperature? Yes → Go To 9 No → Replace the Battery Temperature Sensor. Perform Powertrain Verification Test VER-3A.
6	**Note: Battery must be fully charged.** Start the Engine. With the DRBIII, set Engine Speed to 1600 rpm. With the DRB, read target charging voltage and charging voltage. Compare the two readings. Is there more than a 1.0 volt difference? Yes → Go To 7 No → Refer to CHARGING SYSTEM NO CODE
7	Ignition Off **Note: Battery must be fully charged.** **Caution: Ensure all Wires are clear of the Engine's moving parts.** Using a Voltmeter, measure between the Generator (12V) B+ Terminal and the Battery (+) side. Start the Engine. Is the voltage above 0.4 volt? Yes → Repair the B (+) Circuit for high resistance between the Generator and Battery. Perform Powertrain Verification Test VER-3A. No → Go To 8

CR1120000317020X

Fig. 18 Code P1682: Charging System Voltage Too Low (Part 2 of 3). 1999–2000 Breeze, Cirrus, Sebring Convertible & Stratus

TEST	ACTION
1	Ignition Off **Note: Battery condition must be verified prior to this test.** Inspect the Generator Belt tension and condition. Is the Generator Belt OK? Yes → Go To 2 No → Repair as necessary.
2	Engine Running With the DRB, set the engine speed to 1600 RPM for 30 seconds. With the DRB, return the engine to idle speed and read codes. Are there any Charging System trouble codes? Yes → Refer to Symptom list for further diagnostic tests. Perform Powertrain Verification Test VER-3A. No → Go To 3
3	Ignition On, Engine Not Running With DRB, actuate the Generator Field. Using a Voltmeter, backprobe the Generator Field DR Terminal at the back of the Generator. **Note: The voltage should cycle from 0 to Battery voltage every 1.4 seconds at both terminals.** While monitoring the DRB, wiggle the field terminals back to the PCM and ASD relay. Was there any interruption in the normal cycle between 0 and Battery voltage? Yes → Repair the Wire where wiggling interrupted the voltage cycle. Perform Powertrain Verification Test VER-3A. No → Go To 4
4	Ignition On, Engine Running With DRB, read trouble codes. Are there any Charging System trouble codes? Yes → Refer to Symptom list for further diagnostic tests. No → Go To 5

CR1120000318010X

Fig. 19 Charging System Diagnosis w/No Code (Part 1 of 2). 1999–2000 Breeze, Cirrus, Sebring Convertible & Stratus

TEST	ACTION
8	Ignition Off **Note: Battery must be fully charged.** **Caution: Ensure all Wires are clear of the Engine's moving parts.** With a Voltmeter, measure between the Generator Case and Battery (-) side. Start the Engine. Is the voltage above 0.1 volt? Yes → Repair Generator Ground for high resistance Generator Case to Battery (-) Side. Perform Powertrain Verification Test VER-3A. No → Go To 9
9	Ignition Off Disconnect the Generator Field Connector. Disconnect the Powertrain Control Module Connectors. **Note: Check connectors - Clean/repair as necessary.** Using an Ohmmeter, measure resistance of the ASD Output Circuit from PCM Connector to Field Connector. Is the resistance below 5.0 ohms? Yes → Go To 10 No → Repair the ASD Relay Output Circuit open. Perform Powertrain Verification Test VER-3A.
10	Ignition Off Disconnect the Generator Field Connector. **Note: Check connectors - Clean/repair as necessary.** Disconnect the Powertrain Control Module Connectors. **Note: Check connectors - Clean/repair as necessary.** Using an Ohmmeter, measure resistance of the Generator Field Driver Circuit from PCM Connector to Generator Field Connector. Is the resistance below 5.0 ohms? Yes → Go To 11 No → Repair the open Driver Circuit. Perform Powertrain Verification Test VER-3A.
11	Turn Ignition off. If there are no potential causes remaining, replace the Generator. View repair options. Repair Replace the Generator. Perform Powertrain Verification Test VER-3A.

CR1120000317030X

Fig. 18 Code P1682: Charging System Voltage Too Low (Part 3 of 3). 1999–2000 Breeze, Cirrus, Sebring Convertible & Stratus

TEST	ACTION
5	Ignition Off **Caution: Ensure all wires are clear of the engine's moving parts.** Start the engine. Using a Voltmeter, measure the voltage between the Generator Case and Battery (-) side. Is the voltage above 0.1 volt? Yes → Repair Generator Ground High Resistance Generator Case to Battery (-) side. Perform Powertrain Verification Test VER-3A. No → Go To 6
6	Ignition Off Connect voltmeter between the Generator (12V) B+ Terminal and the Batt (+) side. **Caution: Ensure all Wires are clear of the Engine's moving parts.** Start the Engine. Is the voltage above 0.4 volt? Yes → Repair B+ Circuit for high resistance between the Generator and the Battery. Perform Powertrain Verification Test VER-3A. No → Go To 7
7	Ignition On, Engine Not Running With the DRB, read the Battery voltage and record. Using a Voltmeter, measure the Battery voltage B(+) to B(-) Terminal. Record second voltage reading. Compare the two voltage readings. Is the voltage difference less than one volt? Yes → Test Complete. No → Go To 8
8	Ignition On, Engine Not Running With the DRB, read the Battery voltage and record. Key off. Disconnect the Powertrain Control Module. **Note: Check connectors - Clean/repair as necessary.** Using a Voltmeter, measure the Fused B(+) at PCM. Is the voltage within one volt of the DRB recorded reading? Yes → Repair the B+ Circuit for high resistance between the PCM and the Battery. Perform Powertrain Verification Test VER-3A. No → Go To 9
9	Turn Ignition off. If there are no potential causes remaining, replace the PCM. View repair options. Repair Replace the PCM. Perform Powertrain Verification Test VER-3A.

CR1120000318020X

Fig. 19 Charging System Diagnosis w/No Code (Part 2 of 2). 1999–2000 Breeze, Cirrus, Sebring Convertible & Stratus

VERIFICATION TEST VER-2A
1. Road Test For Non-OBD II **2. Note: If the PCM has been changed and the correct VIN and mileage have not been programmed, a DTC will be set in the ABS and Air Bag modules. In addition, if the vehicle is equipped with a SKIM; Secret Key data must be updated to enable starting.** 3. For ABS and Air Bag Systems: ACTION: Enter correct VIN and mileage in PCM. Erase codes in ABS and Air Bag modules. 4. For SKIM Theft Alarm: ACTION: 5. Connect DRB to data link connector. 6. Go to Theft Alarm, SKIM, misc. and place SKIM in secured access mode, by using appropriate PIN code for vehicle. 7. 3. Select Update Secret Key data. Data will be transferred from SKIM to PCM. 8. Inspect the vehicle to ensure that all engine components are connected. 9. If there are any DTCs that have not been repaired, return to the symptom list and follow the path specified for that symptom. After all DTCs have been repaired, return to the appropriate Verification Test. **10. Note: If this verification procedure is being performed after a NO TROUBLE CODE test, do the following:** 11. Check to see if the initial symptom still exists. 12. If the initial or another symptom exists, the repair is not complete. Check for any Technical Service Bulletins or flash updates and return to the symptom list and restart diagnostic testing for this symptom if necessary. 13. Connect the DRB to the data link connector. 14. Using the DRB, erase any DTCs and reset all values. 15. Road test vehicle, use all accessories that may be related to this repair. 16. Using the DRB, read Global Good Trips. If Global Good Trips is zero, the repair is not complete. Check for any Technical Service Bulletins or flash updates and return to the symptom list and restart diagnostic testing for that symptom. 17. If another trouble code has set, return to the symptom list and restart diagnostic testing and follow the path specified for that symptom. 18. If there are no trouble codes or the Global Good Trip is not zero, the repair was successful and is now complete. Repair is not complete, refer to appropriate symptom.

CR1120000320000X

Fig. 20 Verification Test VER-2A. 1999–2000 Breeze, Cirrus, Sebring Convertible & Stratus

TEST	ACTION
1	Ignition On, Engine Not Running With the DRB actuate the Generator Field Driver Circuit. Using a 12-volt test light, backprobe the Generator Field Driver Circuit at the back of the Generator. Did the light blink? Yes → Go To 2 No → Go To 4
2	Ignition On, Engine Not Running With the DRB actuate the Generator Field Driver Circuit. **Note: Actuator Test should still be running.** Wiggle Wiring Harness from the Generator to PCM. With the DRB, read Codes. Does the Generator Field Driver (-) Circuit code return? Yes → Repair as necessary where wiggling caused problem to appear. Perform the Powertrain Verification Test - Ver 3 No → Go To 3
3	Turn ignition off. Using the schematic as a guide, inspect the Wiring and Connectors. Were any problems found? Yes → Repair as necessary. Perform the Powertrain Verification Test - Ver 3 No → Test Complete.

CR1129900321010X

Fig. 22 Code P0622: Alternator Field Not Switching Properly (Part 1 of 2). 1999–2001 Concorde, Intrepid, LHS & 300M

VERIFICATION TEST VER-3A
1. Charging Verification **2. Note: If the PCM has been changed and the correct VIN and mileage have not been programmed, a DTC will be set in the ABS and Air Bag modules. In addition, if the vehicle is equipped with a SKIM, Secret Key data must be updated to enable starting.** 3. For ABS and Air Bag Systems: ACTION: Enter correct VIN and mileage in PCM. Erase codes in ABS and Air Bag modules. 4. For SKIM Theft Alarm: ACTION: 5. Connect DRB to data link connector. 6. Go to Theft Alarm, SKIM, misc. and place SKIM in secured access mode, by using appropriate PIN code for vehicle. 7. Select Update Secret Key data. Data will be transferred from SKIM to PCM. 8. Inspect the vehicle to ensure that all engine components are connected. Reassemble and reconnect components as necessary. 9. Connect the DRB to the PCM data link connector and erase codes. **10. Note: Ensure no other Charging System problems remain by doing the following:** 11. Start the engine. 12. Perform generator output test 13. Raise the engine speed to 2000 RPM for at least 30 seconds. 14. Allow the engine to idle. 15. Turn the engine off. 16. Turn the ignition key on. 17. With the DRB, read trouble code messages. 18. If the repaired code has reset, or any other one has set, check all pertinent Technical Service Bulletins and return to the symptom list and restart diagnostic testing for this symptom if necessary. 19. If there are no codes, the repair is now complete. Repair is not complete, refer to appropriate symptom.

CR1120000319000X

Fig. 21 Verification Test VER-3A. 1999–2000 Breeze, Cirrus, Sebring Convertible & Stratus

TEST	ACTION
4	Ignition On, Engine Not Running Record all DTC's and freeze frame data, now erase Codes. Carefully inspect all Connectors for corrosion or spread Terminals before continuing. With the DRB actuate the Generator Field Driver Circuit. Backprobe the ASD Relay Output Circuit at back of Generator. Is the voltage above 10.0 volts? Yes → Go To 5 No → Repair the open ASD Relay Output Circuit. Perform the Powertrain Verification Test - Ver 3
5	Turn ignition off. Disconnect the PCM Connectors. Disconnect the Generator Field harness connector. Using an Ohmmeter, measure the Generator Field Driver Circuit from PCM Connector to ground. Is the resistance below 5.0 ohms? Yes → Repair the Generator Field Driver Circuit shorted to ground. Perform the Powertrain Verification Test - Ver 3 No → Go To 6
6	Turn ignition off. Disconnect the PCM harness connectors. Disconnect the Generator Field harness connector. **Note: Check Connectors - Clean/repair as necessary.** Using an Ohmmeter, measure the Generator Field Driver Circuit from PCM to Generator. Is the resistance below 5.0 ohms? Yes → Go To 7 No → Repair the open Generator Field Driver Circuit. Perform the Powertrain Verification Test - Ver 3
7	Turn ignition off. Disconnect the Generator Field harness connector at back of the Generator. **Note: Check connectors - Clean/repair as necessary.** Use an Ohmmeter in the following steps. Measure resistance across the Generator Field Terminals at the Generator. Is the resistance below 5.0 ohms? Yes → Repair the Generator as necessary. Perform the Powertrain Verification Test - Ver 3 No → Go To 8
8	If there are no possible causes remaining, replace the Powertrain Control Module. View repair options. Repair Replace the Powertrain Control Module. Perform the Powertrain Verification Test - Ver 3

CR1129900321020X

Fig. 22 Code P0622: Alternator Field Not Switching Properly (Part 2 of 2). 1999–2001 Concorde, Intrepid, LHS & 300M

TEST	ACTION
1	The Powertrain Control Module is reporting an internal trouble code and must be replaced. View repair options. Repair Replace the Powertrain Control Module.

CR1129900322000X

Fig. 23 Code P1478: Battery Temperature Sensor Voltage Out of Limit. 1999–2001 Concorde, Intrepid, LHS & 300M

TEST	ACTION
2	Disconnect the Ambient Temperature Sensor. Remove the Ambient Temperature Sensor. Using an ohmmeter, measure the resistance of the Ambient Temperature Sensor across the Sensor. Compare the readings with the Ambient Temp Sensor Specifications Do the readings compare with the values listed? Yes → Go To 3 No → Replace the Ambient Temperature Sensor. Perform the Powertrain Verification Test - Ver 5
3	Turn the ignition off. Disconnect the Ambient Temperature Sensor connector. Close all doors , insure all lights are off, then wait one minute. Measure the resistance of the sensor ground circuit to ground. Is the resistance below 30 ohms? No → Go To 4 Yes → Go To 6
4	Turn ignition off. Disconnect the Ambient Temperature Sensor connector. Disconnect the BCM connector. Measure the resistance of the Sensor Ground circuit between the Ambient Temperature Sensor connector and the BCM. Is the resistance below 5.0 ohms? No → Repair the open Sensor Ground circuit. Perform the Powertrain Verification Test - Ver 5 Yes → Go To 5
5	If there are no possible causes remaining, replace the BCM. View repair options. Repair Replace the BCM. Perform the Powertrain Verification Test - Ver 5
6	Turn ignition off. Disconnect the Ambient Temperature Sensor connectors. Disconnect the BCM connectors. Using an Ohmmeter, measure the resistance of the Ambient Temperature Sensor Signal circuit from the Sensor connector to the BCM connector. Is the resistance below 5.0 ohms? No → Repair the open circuit. Perform the Powertrain Verification Test - Ver 5 Yes → Go To 7

CR1129900323020X

Fig. 24 Codes P1492 & P1493: Ambient/Battery Temperature Sensor Voltage Out of Range (Part 2 of 3). 1999–2001 Concorde, Intrepid, LHS & 300M

TEST	ACTION
1	Turn ignition on. With the DRBIII®, read DTC's. Is the DTC Global Good Trip Counter displayed and equal to zero? Yes → Go To 2 No → Go To 11

CR1129900323010X

Fig. 24 Codes P1492 & P1493: Ambient/Battery Temperature Sensor Voltage Out of Range (Part 1 of 3). 1999–2001 Concorde, Intrepid, LHS & 300M

TEST	ACTION
7	Turn ignition off. Disconnect the Ambient Temperature Sensor connector. Disconnect the BCM connector. Using an Ohmmeter, measure the resistance between the Sensor Ground circuit and ground at the BCM. Is the resistance below 500K (500,000) ohms? No → Go To 8 Yes → Repair the Sensor Ground circuit for a partial short to ground. Perform the Powertrain Verification Test - Ver 5
8	Turn ignition off. Disconnect the Ambient Temperature Sensor connector. Disconnect the BCM connector. Using an Ohmmeter, measure the Ambient Temperature Sensor Signal circuit to ground. Is the resistance below 50K (50,000) ohms? Yes → Repair the Ambient Temperature Sensor signal circuit for a partial short to ground. Perform the Powertrain Verification Test - Ver 5 No → Go To 9
9	Turn ignition off. Disconnect the Ambient Temperature Sensor connector. Disconnect the BCM connector. Using an Ohmmeter, measure the resistance between the Ambient Temperature Sensor Signal circuit and the Sensor Ground circuit. Is the resistance below 50K (50,000) ohms? Yes → Repair the Ambient Temperature Sensor Signal Circuit for a short to the Sensor Ground Circuit. Perform the Powertrain Verification Test - Ver 5 No → Go To 10
10	If there are no possible causes remaining, replace the BCM. View repair options. Repair Replace the BCM. Perform the Powertrain Verification Test - Ver 5
11	Turn ignition off. **Note: Visually inspect the related wiring harness. Look for any chafed, pierced, pinched, or partially broken wires.** **Note: Visually inspect the related wire harness connectors. Look for broken, bent, pushed out, or corroded terminals.** **Note: Refer to any Technical Service Bulletins (TSB) that may apply.** Were any problems found? Yes → Repair wiring harness/connectors as necessary. Perform the Powertrain Verification Test - Ver 5 No → Test Complete.

CR1129900323030X

Fig. 24 Codes P1492 & P1493: Ambient/Battery Temperature Sensor Voltage Out of Range (Part 3 of 3). 1999–2001 Concorde, Intrepid, LHS & 300M

TEST	ACTION
1	Ignition On, Engine Not Running With DRB, actuate the Generator Field Driver. With a 12-volt test light, backprobe the Generator Field Driver Circuit in back of Generator. Did the light blink? Yes → Go To 2 No → Go To 5
2	Ignition On, Engine Not Running With the DRB, actuate the Generator Field Driver. With DRB, stop the Generator Field Driver actuation. With DRB, read the Target Charging voltage. Is the Target Charging voltage above 13 volts? Yes → Go To 3 No → Go To 4
3	Start the engine. Manually set the engine speed to 1600 RPM. With DRB, read both the Battery voltage and the Target Charging voltage. Compare the "Target Voltage" to the "Battery Voltage" reading. Monitor voltage for 5 minutes, if necessary. Look for a 1.0 volt difference or more. Was there more than a 1.0 volt difference? Yes → Replace the Powertrain Control Module. Perform the Powertrain Verification Test - Ver 3 No → Test Complete.

CR1129900324010X

Fig. 25 Code P1594: Charging System Voltage Too High (Part 1 of 2). 1999–2001 Concorde, Intrepid, LHS & 300M

TEST	ACTION
1	Turn Ignition Off. **Note: Battery must be fully charged.** **Note: Generator Belt tension and condition must be checked before continuing.** Start Engine. With the DRB, read the target charging voltage. Is the target charging voltage above 15.1 volts? Yes → Go To 2 No → Go To 3
2	Turn ignition off. **Note: Battery must be fully charged.** **Note: Generator Belt tension and condition must be checked before continuing.** Start engine and allow it to reach operating temperature. With the DRB, read the BTS temperature. Using a Thermometer, measure under hood temperature. Is the temperature within 10 F degrees of Battery temperature? Yes → Go To 3 No → Replace the PCM. Perform the Powertrain Verification Test - Ver 3

CR1129900325010X

Fig. 26 Code P1682: Charging System Voltage Too Low (Part 1 of 3). 1999–2001 Concorde, Intrepid, LHS & 300M

TEST	ACTION
4	Turn ignition off. **Note: Battery must be fully charged.** **Note: Generator Belt tension and condition must be checked before continuing.** Start engine and allow it to reach operating temperature. With the DRB, read the BTS temperature. Using a Thermometer, measure under hood temperature. Is the temperature within 10 F degrees of Battery temperature? Yes → Test Complete. No → Replace Powertrain Control Module. Perform the Powertrain Verification Test - Ver 3
5	Turn ignition off. Disconnect the PCM Connectors. Disconnect the Generator Field harness connector. Using an Ohmmeter, measure the Generator Field Driver Circuit from PCM Connector to ground. Is the resistance below 5.0 ohms? Yes → Repair the Generator Field Driver Circuit shorted to ground. Perform the Powertrain Verification Test - Ver 3 No → Go To 6
6	Turn ignition off. Disconnect the Field Harness Connector at back of the Generator. **Note: Check connectors - Clean/repair as necessary.** Measure resistance of the Generator Field Driver Circuit at the Generator to Ground. Is the resistance below 5.0 ohms? Yes → Repair or replace the shorted Generator as necessary. Perform the Powertrain Verification Test - Ver 3 No → Go To 7
7	If there are no possible causes remaining, replace the Powertrain Control Module. View repair options. Repair Replace the Powertrain Control Module. Perform the Powertrain Verification Test - Ver 3

CR1129900324020X

Fig. 25 Code P1594: Charging System Voltage Too High (Part 2 of 2). 1999–2001 Concorde, Intrepid, LHS & 300M

TEST	ACTION
3	Turn ignition on, engine not running. Using a Voltmeter, measure voltage between the Generator B(+) Terminal and the Battery (+) Post. **Caution: Ensure all wires are clear of the engine's moving parts.** Start engine. Is the voltage above 0.4 volt? Yes → Repair the B(+) Circuit for high resistance between the Generator and Battery. Perform the Powertrain Verification Test - Ver 3 No → Go To 4
4	Start engine. Warm the engine to operating temperature. **Caution: Ensure all wires are clear of the engine's moving parts.** Using a Voltmeter, measure voltage between the Generator case and Battery (-) Post. Is the voltage above 0.1 volt? Yes → Repair Generator Ground for high resistance, Generator Case to Battery (-) side. Perform the Powertrain Verification Test - Ver 3 No → Go To 5
5	Start engine. Turn on all accessories, manually set engine speed to 1600 RPM. With DRB, read Target Charging and Charging voltage. Compare the two readings. Is there more than a 1.0 volt difference? Yes → Go To 6 No → Test Complete.
6	Ignition On, Engine Not Running With the DRB, actuate the Generator Field. Using a Voltmeter, measure the voltage at both Generator Field Terminals. Is the voltage below 3.0 volts at either Terminal? Yes → Go To 7 No → Test Complete.
7	Ignition On, Engine Not Running Record all DTC's and freeze frame data, now erase Codes. Carefully inspect all Connectors for corrosion or spread Terminals before continuing. With the DRB actuate the Generator Field Driver Circuit. Backprobe the ASD Relay Output Circuit at back of Generator. Is the voltage above 10.0 volts? Yes → Go To 8 No → Repair the open ASD Relay Output Circuit. Perform the Powertrain Verification Test - Ver 3

CR1129900325020X

Fig. 26 Code P1682: Charging System Voltage Too Low (Part 2 of 3). 1999–2001 Concorde, Intrepid, LHS & 300M

TEST	ACTION
8	Turn ignition off. Disconnect the PCM Connectors. Disconnect the Generator Field harness connector. Using an Ohmmeter, measure the Generator Field Driver Circuit from PCM Connector to ground. Is the resistance below 5.0 ohms? Yes → Repair the Generator Field Driver Circuit shorted to ground. Perform the Powertrain Verification Test - Ver 3 No → Go To 9
9	Turn ignition off. Disconnect ASD Relay Connector. **Note: Check connectors - Clean/repair as necessary.** Disconnect the generator field connector. **Note: Check Connectors - Clean/repair as necessary.** Using an Ohmmeter, measure the ASD Relay Output Circuit from ASD Relay Connector to ground. Is the resistance below 5.0 ohms? Yes → Repair the ASD Relay Output Circuit shorted to ground. Perform the Powertrain Verification Test - Ver 3 No → Go To 10
10	Turn ignition off. Disconnect the PCM harness connectors. Disconnect the Generator Field harness connector. **Note: Check Connectors - Clean/repair as necessary.** Using an Ohmmeter, measure the Generator Field Driver Circuit from PCM to Generator. Is the resistance below 5.0 ohms? Yes → Go To 11 No → Repair the open Generator Field Driver Circuit. Perform the Powertrain Verification Test - Ver 3
11	If there are no possible causes remaining, replace the Powertrain Control Module. View repair options. Repair Replace the Powertrain Control Module. Perform the Powertrain Verification Test - Ver 3

CR1129900325030X

Fig. 26 Code P1682: Charging System Voltage Too Low (Part 3 of 3). 1999–2001 Concorde, Intrepid, LHS & 300M

TEST	ACTION
1	Turn ignition off. **Note: Battery condition must be verified prior to this test.** Inspect the Generator Belt tension and condition. Is the Generator Belt OK? Yes → Go To 2 No → Repair as necessary. Perform the Powertrain Verification Test - Ver 3
2	Start the Engine. Turn on all accessories. Raise engine speed to 2000 RPM for 30 seconds then return to idle. With the DRB III read DTC's. Are there any "Charging System" Trouble Codes? Yes → Refer to Symptom list for problems related to Charging. Perform the Powertrain Verification Test - Ver 3 No → Go To 3
3	Ignition On, Engine Not Running With the DRB, actuate the Generator Field. Using a 12-volt test light, backprobe the Generator Field Driver Terminal at the back of the Generator. **Note: The test light should blink On and Off every 1.4 seconds.** While monitoring the 12-volt test light, wiggle the Field Terminals back to the PCM and ASD Relay. Was there any interruption in the normal cycle of the test light? Yes → Repair the wire where wiggling interrupted the voltage cycle. Perform the Powertrain Verification Test - Ver 3 No → Go To 4

CR1129900326010X

Fig. 28 Charging System Diagnosis w/No Code (Part 1 of 3). 1999–2001 Concorde, Intrepid, LHS & 300M

TEST	ACTION
1	Turn ignition off. **Note: Visually inspect the related wiring harness. Look for any chafed, pierced, pinched, or partially broken wires.** **Note: Visually inspect the related wire harness connectors. Look for broken, bent, pushed out, or corroded terminals.** **Note: Refer to any Technical Service Bulletins (TSB) that may apply.** Were any problems found? Yes → Repair wiring harness/connectors as necessary. Perform the Powertrain Verification Test - Ver 5 No → Go To 2
2	Turn ignition on. With the DRB in sensors, read the "Ambient/Bat Tmp Deg" value and record the reading. Using a temp probe, measure the air temperature near the BTS. Is the recorded BTS temperature value within 10° of the temperature probe reading? Yes → Test Complete. No → Replace the BTS. Perform the Powertrain Verification Test - Ver 5

CR1129900327000X

Fig. 27 Ambient/Battery Temperature Sensor Diagnosis. 1999–2001 Concorde, Intrepid, LHS & 300M

TEST	ACTION
4	Ignition On, Engine Not Running With the DRB, read trouble codes. Are there any "Charging System" trouble codes? Yes → Refer to Symptom list for problems related to Charging. Perform the Powertrain Verification Test - Ver 3 No → Go To 5
5	Turn ignition on, engine not running. Using a Voltmeter, measure voltage between the Generator B(+) Terminal and the Battery (+) Post. **Caution: Ensure all wires are clear of the engine's moving parts.** Start engine. Is the voltage above 0.4 volt? Yes → Repair the B(+) Circuit for high resistance between the Generator and Battery. Perform the Powertrain Verification Test - Ver 3 No → Go To 6
6	Start engine. Warm the engine to operating temperature. **Caution: Ensure all wires are clear of the engine's moving parts.** Using a Voltmeter, measure voltage between the Generator case and Battery (-) Post. Is the voltage above 0.1 volt? Yes → Repair Generator Ground for high resistance, Generator Case to Battery (-) side. Perform the Powertrain Verification Test - Ver 3 No → Go To 7
7	Ignition On, Engine Not Running. With the DRB, read the Battery voltage and record the results. Using a Voltmeter, measure Battery voltage B(+) to B(-) Terminal and record the results. Compare the two voltage readings. Is the voltage difference less than one volt? Yes → Test Complete. No → Go To 8
8	Ignition On, Engine Not Running With the DRB, read the Battery voltage and record the results. Turn Ignition off. Disconnect the PCM. **Note: Check connectors - Clean/repair as necessary.** Turn Ignition on, with the engine off. Using a Voltmeter, measure the Fused B(+) at PCM Connector. Is the voltage within one volt of the DRB recorded reading? Yes → Go To 9 No → Repair the B(+) Circuit for high resistance between the PCM and the Battery. Perform the Powertrain Verification Test - Ver 3

CR1129900326020X

Fig. 28 Charging System Diagnosis w/No Code (Part 2 of 3). 1999–2001 Concorde, Intrepid, LHS & 300M

TEST	ACTION
9	If there are no possible causes remaining, replace the Powertrain Control Module. View repair options. Repair Replace the PCM. Perform the Powertrain Verification Test - Ver 3

CR1129900326030X

Fig. 28 Charging System Diagnosis w/No Code (Part 3 of 3). 1999–2001 Concorde, Intrepid, LHS & 300M

POWERTRAIN VERIFICATION TEST VER - 5
1. Inspect the vehicle to ensure that all engine components are properly installed and connected. Reassemble and reconnect components as necessary. 2. If any existing diagnostic trouble codes have not been repaired, go to Symptom List and follow path specified. 3. Connect the DRBIII® to the data link connector. 4. Ensure the fuel tank has at least a quarter tank of fuel. Turn off all accessories. 5. Perform steps 6 through 8 if the PCM has been replaced. Then proceed with the verification. If the PCM has not been replaced skip those steps and continue verification. 6. If PCM has been changed and correct VIN and mileage have not been programmed, a DTC will be set in ABS and Air bag modules. In addition, if vehicle is equipped with a Sentry Key Immobilizer Module (SKIM), Secret Key data must be updated to enable start. 7. For ABS and Air Bag systems: Enter correct VIN and Mileage in PCM. Erase codes in ABS and Air Bag modules. 8. For SKIM theft alarm: Connect DRB to data link conn. Go to Theft Alarm, SKIM, Misc. and place SKIM in secured access mode, by using the appropriate PIN code for this vehicle. Select Update the Secret Key data. Data will be transferred from SKIM to PCM. 9. If a Comprehensive Component DTC was repaired, perform steps 10-13. If a Major OBDII Monitor DTC was repaired skip those steps and continue verification. 10. After the ignition has been off for at least 10 seconds, restart the vehicle and run 2 minutes. 11. If the Good Trip counter changed to one or more and there are no new DTC's, the repair was successful and is now complete. Erase DTC's and disconnect the DRBIII®. 12. If the repaired DTC has reset, the repair is not complete. Check for any related TSB's or flash updates and return to the Symptom list. 13. If another DTC has set, return to the Symptom List and follow the path specified for that DTC. 14. With the DRBIII®, monitor the appropriate pre-test enabling conditions until all conditions have been met. Once the conditions have been met, switch screen to the appropriate OBDII monitor, (Audible beeps when the monitor is running). 15. If the monitor ran, and the Good Trip counter changed to one or more, the repair was successful and is now complete. Erase DTC's and disconnect the DRBIII®. 16. If the repaired OBDII trouble code has reset or was seen in the monitor while on the road test, the repair is not complete. Check for any related technical service bulletins or flash updates and return to Symptom List. 17. If another DTC has set, return to the Symptom List and follow the path specified for that DTC. Repair is not complete, refer to appropriate symptom.

CR1129900329000X

Fig. 30 Verification Test VER-5. 1999–2001 Concorde, Intrepid, LHS & 300M

TEST	ACTION	APPLICABILITY
1	Turn the ignition on. With the DRBIII®, actuate the Generator Field Driver circuit. Using a 12-volt test light connected to ground, backprobe the Generator Field Driver circuit in the back of the Generator. Does the test light illuminate brightly and flash? Yes → Go To 2 No → Go To 4	All
2	Turn the ignition on. With the DRBIII® actuate the Generator Field Driver circuit. Wiggle the wiring harness from the Generator to PCM. With the DRBIII®, read DTC's. Did the DTC reset? Yes → Repair as necessary . Perform POWERTRAIN VERIFICATION TEST VER - 3. No → Go To 3	All
3	Turn the ignition off. Using the schematic as a guide, inspect the Wiring and Connectors. Were any problems found? Yes → Repair as necessary. Perform POWERTRAIN VERIFICATION TEST VER - 3. No → Test Complete.	All

CR1120100394010X

Fig. 31 Code P0622: Alternator Field Not Switching Properly (Part 1 of 2). 2001–02 Sebring Convertible & Sedan & Stratus Sedan

POWERTRAIN VERIFICATION TEST VER - 3
1. Inspect the vehicle to ensure that all engine components are properly installed and connected. Reassemble and reconnect components as necessary. 2. Connect the DRB to the Data Link Connector and erase the codes. 3. If the PCM has been replaced perform steps 4 through 6 then continue the verification. 4. If PCM has been changed and correct VIN and mileage have not been programmed, a DTC will be set in ABS and Air bag modules. In addition, if vehicle is equipped with a Sentry Key Immobilizer Module (SKIM), Secret Key data must be updated to enable start. 5. For ABS and Air Bag systems: Enter correct VIN and Mileage in PCM. Erase codes in ABS and Air Bag modules. 6. For SKIM theft alarm: Connect DRB to data link conn. Go to Theft Alarm, SKIM, Misc. and place SKIM in secured access mode, by using the appropriate PIN code for this vehicle. Select Update the Secret Key data. Data will be transferred from SKIM to PCM. 7. Ensure no other charging system problems remain by doing the following: Start the engine. Perform generator output per service manual. 8. Raise the engine speed to 2000 rpm for at least 30 seconds. 9. Allow the engine to idle. 10. Turn the engine off. 11. Turn the ignition key on. 12. With the DRB, read trouble code messages. 13. If repaired code has reset, or any other one has set, check all pertinent Technical Service Bulletins and return to Symptom List if necessary. 14. If there are no codes, the repair is now complete. Repair is not complete, refer to appropriate symptom.

CR1129900328000X

Fig. 29 Verification Test VER-3. 1999–2001 Concorde, Intrepid, LHS & 300M

TEST	ACTION
4	**NOTE: Carefully inspect all Connectors for corrosion or spread Terminals before continuing.** Disconnect the Generator Field harness connector. Turn the ignition on. With the DRBIII® actuate the Generator Field Driver circuit. Using a 12-volt test light connected to ground, probe the ASD Relay Output circuit. Does the test light illuminate brightly? Yes → Go To 5 No → Repair the ASD Relay Output circuit. Perform POWERTRAIN VERIFICATION TEST VER - 3.
5	Turn the ignition off. Disconnect the PCM harness connector. Disconnect the Generator Field harness connector. Measure the resistance of the Generator Field Driver circuit from PCM harness connector to ground. Is the resistance below 5.0 ohms? Yes → Repair the Generator Field Driver circuit for a shorted to ground. Perform POWERTRAIN VERIFICATION TEST VER - 3. No → Go To 6
6	Turn the ignition off. Disconnect the PCM harness connector. Disconnect the Generator Field harness connector. Measure the resistance of the Generator Field Driver circuit from the PCM harness connector to the Generator Field harness connector. Is the resistance below 5.0 ohms? Yes → Go To 7 No → Repair the Generator Field Driver circuit for an open. Perform POWERTRAIN VERIFICATION TEST VER - 3.
7	Turn the ignition off. Disconnect the Generator Field harness connector. Measure the resistance across the Generator Field Terminals at the Generator. Is the resistance above 15.0 ohms? Yes → Replace the Generator. Perform POWERTRAIN VERIFICATION TEST VER - 3. No → Go To 8
8	Turn the ignition off. Disconnect the Generator Field harness connector. Measure the resistance across the Generator Field Terminals at the Generator. Is the resistance below 0.5 ohms? Yes → Replace the Generator. Perform POWERTRAIN VERIFICATION TEST VER - 3. No → Go To 9
9	If there is no more possible causes remaining, view repair. Repair Replace and program the Powertrain Control Module in accordance with the Service Information. Perform POWERTRAIN VERIFICATION TEST VER - 3.

CR1120100394020X

Fig. 31 Code P0622: Alternator Field Not Switching Properly (Part 2 of 2). 2001–02 Sebring Convertible & Sedan & Stratus Sedan

TEST	ACTION
1	Turn the ignition on. With the DRBIII®, read the Ambient Temperature Sensor voltage. Is the voltage above 4.8 volts? Yes → Go To 2 No → Go To 7
2	Turn the ignition off. Disconnect the Ambient Temperature Sensor harness connector. Turn the ignition on. Measure the voltage of the Ambient Temperature Sensor Signal circuit in the Ambient Temperature Sensor harness connector. Is the voltage above 5.2 volts? Yes → Repair the Ambient Temperature Sensor Signal circuit for a short to battery voltage. Perform POWERTRAIN VERIFICATION TEST VER - 5. No → Go To 3

CR1120100395010X

Fig. 32 Code P1492: Ambient/Battery Temperature Sensor Voltage Too High (Part 1 of 2). 2001–02 Sebring Convertible & Sedan & Stratus Sedan

TEST	ACTION
3	Turn the ignition off. Disconnect the Ambient Temperature Sensor harness connector. Connect a jumper wire between the Ambient Temperature Sensor Signal circuit and the Sensor ground circuit in the Ambient Temperature Sensor harness connector. Turn the ignition on. With the DRBIII®, read Ambient Temperature Sensor voltage. Is the voltage below 1.0 volt? Yes → Replace the Ambient Temperature Sensor. Perform POWERTRAIN VERIFICATION TEST VER - 5. No → Go To 4
4	Turn the ignition off. Disconnect the Ambient Temperature Sensor harness connector. Disconnect the PCM harness connector. Measure the resistance of the Ambient Temperature Sensor Signal circuit between the Ambient Temperature Sensor harness connector and the PCM harness connector. Is the resistance below 5.0 ohms? Yes → Go To 5 No → Repair the Ambient Temperature Sensor Signal circuit for an open. Perform POWERTRAIN VERIFICATION TEST VER - 5.
5	Turn the ignition off. Disconnect the Ambient Temperature Sensor harness connector. Disconnect the PCM harness connector. Measure the resistance of the Sensor ground circuit between the Ambient Temperature Sensor harness connector and the PCM harness connector. Is the resistance below 5.0 ohms? Yes → Go To 6 No → Repair the Sensor ground circuit for an open. Perform POWERTRAIN VERIFICATION TEST VER - 5.
6	If there are no possible causes remaining, view repair. Repair Replace and program the Powertrain Control Module Perform POWERTRAIN VERIFICATION TEST VER - 5.

CR1120100395020X

Fig. 32 Code P1492: Ambient/Battery Temperature Sensor Voltage Too High (Part 2 of 2). 2001–02 Sebring Convertible & Sedan & Stratus Sedan

TEST	ACTION
1	Turn the ignition on. With the DRBIII®, read the Ambient Temperature Sensor voltage. Is the voltage below 0.3 volt? Yes → Go To 2 No → Go To 6
2	Turn the ignition off. Disconnect the Ambient Temperature Sensor harness connector. Turn the ignition on. With the DRBIII®, read Ambient Temperature Sensor voltage. Is the voltage above 1.0 volt? Yes → Replace the Ambient Temperature Sensor. Perform POWERTRAIN VERIFICATION TEST VER - 5. No → Go To 3
3	Turn the ignition off. Disconnect the Ambient Temperature Sensor harness connector. Disconnect the PCM harness connector. Measure the resistance of the Ambient Temperature Sensor Signal circuit in the Ambient Temperature Sensor harness connector to chassis ground. Is the resistance below 100 ohms? Yes → Repair the Ambient Temperature Sensor Signal circuit for a short to ground. Perform POWERTRAIN VERIFICATION TEST VER - 5. No → Go To 4

CR1120100396010X

Fig. 33 Code P1493: Ambient/Battery Temperature Sensor Voltage Too Low (Part 1 of 2). 2001–02 Sebring Convertible & Sedan & Stratus Sedan

TEST	ACTION
4	Turn the ignition off. Disconnect the Ambient Temperature Sensor harness connector. Disconnect the PCM harness connector. Measure the resistance between the Ambient Temperature Sensor Signal circuit and the Sensor ground circuit in the Ambient Temperature Sensor harness connector. Is the resistance below 100 ohms? Yes → Repair the Ambient Temperature Sensor Signal circuit for a short to the Sensor ground circuit. Perform POWERTRAIN VERIFICATION TEST VER - 5. No → Go To 5
5	If there are no possible causes remaining, view repair. Repair Replace and program the Powertrain Control Module in accordance with the Service Information. Perform POWERTRAIN VERIFICATION TEST VER - 5.
6	**WARNING: WHEN THE ENGINE IS OPERATING, DO NOT STAND IN A DIRECT LINE WITH THE FAN. DO NOT PUT YOUR HANDS NEAR THE PULLEYS, BELTS OR FAN. DO NOT WEAR LOOSE CLOTHING.** **NOTE: The conditions that set the DTC are not present at this time. The following list may help in identifying the intermittent condition.** With the engine running at normal operating temperature, monitor the DRB parameters related to the DTC while wiggling the wiring harness. Look for parameter values to change and/or a DTC to set. Review the DRB Freeze Frame information. If possible, try to duplicate the conditions under which the DTC was set. Refer to any Technical Service Bulletins (TSB) that may apply. Visually inspect the related wiring harness. Look for any chafed, pierced, pinched, or partially broken wires. Visually inspect the related wiring harness connectors. Look for broken, bent, pushed out, or corroded terminals. Were any of the above conditions present? Yes → Repair as necessary Perform POWERTRAIN VERIFICATION TEST VER - 5. No → Test Complete.

CR1120100396020X

Fig. 33 Code P1493: Ambient/Battery Temperature Sensor Voltage Too Low (Part 2 of 2). 2001–02 Sebring Convertible & Sedan & Stratus Sedan

TEST	ACTION
1	**Note: Battery must be fully charged.** **Note: Generator Belt tension and condition must be checked before continuing.** Turn the ignition on. With DRBIII®, actuate the Generator Field Driver. With a 12-volt test light connected to ground, backprobe the Generator Field Driver circuit in the back of Generator Field harness connector. Does the test light illuminate brightly and flash? Yes → Go To 2 No → Go To 5
2	With DRBIII®, stop all actuation. Turn the ignition on. With DRBIII®, read the Target Charging voltage. Is the Target Charging voltage above 13 volts? Yes → Go To 3 No → Go To 4
3	Start the engine. With the DRBIII®, manually set the engine speed to 1600 RPM. With DRBIII®, read both the Battery voltage and the Target Charging voltage. Compare the Target Charging Voltage to the Battery Voltage reading. Monitor voltage for 5 minutes, if necessary. Look for a 1.0 volt difference or more. Was there more than a 1.0 volt difference? Yes → Replace the Powertrain Control Module in accordance with the Service Information. Perform POWERTRAIN VERIFICATION TEST VER - 3. No → Go To 4

CR1120100397010X

Fig. 34 Code P1594: Charging System Voltage Too High (Part 1 of 2). 2001–02 Sebring Convertible & Sedan & Stratus Sedan

TEST	ACTION
1	**NOTE: Inspect the vehicle for aftermarket accessories that may exceed the Generator System output.** Turn the ignition off. **NOTE: The battery must be fully charged.** **NOTE: The Generator belt tension and condition must be checked before continuing.** Start the engine. Allow the idle to stabilize. With the DRBIII®, read the Target Charging Voltage. Is the Target Charging Voltage above 15.1 volts? Yes → Go To 8 No → Go To 2
2	**WARNING: WHEN THE ENGINE IS OPERATING, DO NOT STAND IN A DIRECT LINE WITH THE FAN. DO NOT PUT YOUR HANDS NEAR THE PULLEYS, BELTS OR FAN. DO NOT WEAR LOOSE CLOTHING.** Turn the ignition on. **NOTE: Ensure all wires are clear of the engine's moving parts.** Measure the voltage between the Generator B+ Terminal and the Battery+ Post. Start the engine. Is the voltage above 0.4 volt? Yes → Repair the B+ circuit for high resistance between the Generator and Battery. Perform POWERTRAIN VERIFICATION TEST VER - 3. No → Go To 3

CR1120100398010X

Fig. 35 Code P1682: Charging System Voltage Too Low (Part 1 of 3). 2001–02 Sebring Convertible & Sedan & Stratus Sedan

TEST	ACTION
4	**WARNING: WHEN THE ENGINE IS OPERATING, DO NOT STAND IN A DIRECT LINE WITH THE FAN. DO NOT PUT YOUR HANDS NEAR THE PULLEYS, BELTS OR FAN. DO NOT WEAR LOOSE CLOTHING.** **NOTE: The conditions that set the DTC are not present at this time. The following list may help in identifying the intermittent condition.** With the engine running at normal operating temperature, monitor the DRB parameters related to the DTC while wiggling the wiring harness. Look for parameter values to change and/or a DTC to set. Review the DRB Freeze Frame information. If possible, try to duplicate the conditions under which the DTC was set. Refer to any Technical Service Bulletins (TSB) that may apply. Visually inspect the related wiring harness. Look for any chafed, pierced, pinched, or partially broken wires. Visually inspect the related wiring harness connectors. Look for broken, bent, pushed out, or corroded terminals. Were any of the above conditions present? Yes → Repair as necessary Perform POWERTRAIN VERIFICATION TEST VER - 3. No → Test Complete.
5	Turn the ignition off. Disconnect the PCM harness connector. Disconnect the Generator Field harness connector. Measure the resistance of the Generator Field Driver circuit from the PCM harness connector to ground. Is the resistance below 5.0 ohms? Yes → Repair the Generator Field Driver circuit shorted to ground. Perform POWERTRAIN VERIFICATION TEST VER - 3. No → Go To 6
6	Turn the ignition off. Disconnect the Generator Field harness connector. Measure resistance of the Generator Field Driver terminal on the Generator to ground. Is the resistance below 5.0 ohms? Yes → Repair or replace the shorted Generator as necessary. Perform POWERTRAIN VERIFICATION TEST VER - 3. No → Go To 7
7	If there are no possible causes remaining, view repair. Repair Replace and program the Powertrain Control Module Perform POWERTRAIN VERIFICATION TEST VER - 3.

CR1120100397020X

Fig. 34 Code P1594: Charging System Voltage Too High (Part 2 of 2). 2001–02 Sebring Convertible & Sedan & Stratus Sedan

TEST	ACTION
3	**WARNING: WHEN THE ENGINE IS OPERATING, DO NOT STAND IN A DIRECT LINE WITH THE FAN. DO NOT PUT YOUR HANDS NEAR THE PULLEYS, BELTS OR FAN. DO NOT WEAR LOOSE CLOTHING.** Start the engine. Warm the engine to operating temperature. **NOTE: Ensure all wires are clear of the engine's moving parts.** Measure the voltage between the Generator case and Battery ground post. Is the voltage above 0.1 volt? Yes → Repair Generator Ground for high resistance, Generator Case to Battery ground side. Perform POWERTRAIN VERIFICATION TEST VER - 3. No → Go To 4
4	Start the engine. **WARNING: WHEN THE ENGINE IS OPERATING, DO NOT STAND IN A DIRECT LINE WITH THE FAN. DO NOT PUT YOUR HANDS NEAR THE PULLEYS, BELTS OR FAN. DO NOT WEAR LOOSE CLOTHING.** Turn on all accessories, manually set engine speed to 1600 RPM. With DRBIII®, read Target Charging and Charging voltage. Compare the two readings. Is there more than a 1.0 volt difference? Yes → Go To 5 No → Go To 8
5	Turn the ignition off. Disconnect the PCM harness connector. Disconnect the Generator Field harness connector. Measure the resistance of the Generator Field Driver circuit from the PCM harness connector to Generator harness connector. Is the resistance below 5.0 ohms? Yes → Go To 6 No → Repair the Generator Field Driver circuit for an open. Perform POWERTRAIN VERIFICATION TEST VER - 3.
6	Disconnect the Generator Field harness connector. Turn the ignition on. With the DRBIII® actuate the Generator Field Driver. Using a 12-volt test light connected to ground, probe the ASD Relay Output circuit in the Generator harness connector. Does the test light illuminate brightly? Yes → Go To 7 No → Repair the ASD Relay Output circuit. Perform POWERTRAIN VERIFICATION TEST VER - 3.
7	If there is no possible causes remaining, view repair. Yes → Repair or replace the Generator as necessary.. Perform POWERTRAIN VERIFICATION TEST VER - 3.

CR1120100398020X

Fig. 35 Code P1682: Charging System Voltage Too Low (Part 2 of 3). 2001–02 Sebring Convertible & Sedan & Stratus Sedan

TEST	ACTION
8	**WARNING: WHEN THE ENGINE IS OPERATING, DO NOT STAND IN A DIRECT LINE WITH THE FAN. DO NOT PUT YOUR HANDS NEAR THE PULLEYS, BELTS OR FAN. DO NOT WEAR LOOSE CLOTHING.** **NOTE: The conditions that set the DTC are not present at this time. The following list may help in identifying the intermittent condition.** With the engine running at normal operating temperature, monitor the DRB parameters related to the DTC while wiggling the wiring harness. Look for parameter values to change and/or a DTC to set. Review the DRB Freeze Frame information. If possible, try to duplicate the conditions under which the DTC was set. Refer to any Technical Service Bulletins (TSB) that may apply. Visually inspect the related wiring harness. Look for any chafed, pierced, pinched, or partially broken wires. Visually inspect the related wiring harness connectors. Look for broken, bent, pushed out, or corroded terminals. Were any of the above conditions present? Yes → Repair as necessary Perform POWERTRAIN VERIFICATION TEST VER - 3. No → Test Complete.

CR1120100398030X

Fig. 35 Code P1682: Charging System Voltage Too Low (Part 3 of 3). 2001–02 Sebring Convertible & Sedan & Stratus Sedan

POWERTRAIN VERIFICATION TEST VER - 5
1. NOTE: If the PCM has been replaced and the correct VIN and mileage have not been programmed, a DTC will be set in the ABS Module, Airbag Module and the SKIM. **2. NOTE: If the vehicle is equipped with a Sentry Key Immobilizer System, Secret Key data must be updated. Refer to the Service Information for the PCM, SKIM and the Transponder (ignition key) for programming information.** 3. Inspect the vehicle to ensure that all engine components are properly installed and connected. Reassemble and reconnect components as necessary. 4. Connect the DRBIII® to the data link connector. 5. Ensure the fuel tank has at least a quarter tank of fuel. Turn off all accessories. 6. If a Comprehensive Component DTC was repaired, perform steps 5 - 8. If a Major OBDII Monitor DTC was repaired skip those steps and continue verification. 7. After the ignition has been off for at least 10 seconds, restart the vehicle and run 2 minutes. 8. If the Good Trip counter changed to one or more and there are no new DTC's, the repair was successful and is now complete. Erase DTC's and disconnect the DRBIII®. 9. If the repaired DTC has reset, the repair is not complete. Check for any related TSB's or flash updates and return to the Symptom list. 10. If another DTC has set, return to the Symptom List and follow the path specified for that DTC. 11. With the DRBIII®, monitor the appropriate pre-test enabling conditions until all conditions have been met. Once the conditions have been met, switch screen to the appropriate OBDII monitor, (Audible beeps when the monitor is running). 12. If the monitor ran, and the Good Trip counter changed to one or more, the repair was successful and is now complete. Erase DTC's and disconnect the DRBIII®. 13. If the repaired OBDII trouble code has reset or was seen in the monitor while on the road test, the repair is not complete. Check for any related technical service bulletins or flash updates and return to Symptom List. 14. If another DTC has set, return to the Symptom List and follow the path specified for that DTC. Are any DTCs present? Yes → Repair is not complete, refer to appropriate symptom. No → Repair is complete.

CR1120100400000X

Fig. 37 Verification Test VER-5. 2001–02 Sebring Convertible & Sedan & Stratus Sedan

POWERTRAIN VERIFICATION TEST VER - 3
1. NOTE: If the PCM has been replaced and the correct VIN and mileage have not been programmed, a DTC will be set in the ABS Module, Airbag Module and the SKIM. **2. NOTE: If the vehicle is equipped with a Sentry Key Immobilizer System, Secret Key data must be updated. Refer to the Service Information for the PCM, SKIM and the Transponder (ignition key) for programming information.** 3. Inspect the vehicle to ensure that all components related to the repair are connected properly. 4. With the DRBIII®, clear DTCs. 5. Perform generator output test. Refer to the appropriate service information as necessary. 6. Start the engine and set engine speed to 2000 RPM for at least thirty seconds. 7. Cycle the ignition key off and on. 8. With the DRBIII®, read the DTCs. If the DTC returns, or any other symptom or DTC is present, refer to the appropriate category and perform the corresponding symptom. 9. If there are no DTCs present and all components are functioning properly, the repair is complete. Are any DTCs present? Yes → Repair is not complete, refer to appropriate symptom. No → Repair is complete.

CR1120100399000X

Fig. 36 Verification Test VER-3. 2001–02 Sebring Convertible & Sedan & Stratus Sedan

Set Condition: The battery sensed voltage is 1 volt below the charging goal for 13.47 seconds. The PCM senses the battery voltage turns off the field driver and senses the battery voltage again. If the voltages are the same, the code is set. One trip Fault.

POSSIBLE CAUSES
INTERMITTENT CONDITION
B+ CIRCUIT HIGH RESISTANCE
GENERATOR GROUND HIGH RESISTANCE
GENERATOR OPERATION
GENERATOR FIELD GROUND CIRCUIT OPEN
GENERATOR FIELD CONTROL CIRCUIT SHORTED TO GROUND
GENERATOR FIELD CONTROL CIRCUIT OPEN
PCM

TEST	ACTION
1	**NOTE: Ensure the Battery is in good condition. Using the Midtronics Battery Tester, test the Battery before continuing.** **NOTE: Inspect the vehicle for aftermarket accessories that may exceed the Generator System output.** Turn the ignition off. **NOTE: Ensure the generator drive belt is in good operating condition.** **NOTE: Inspect the fuses in the PDC. If a fuse is found to be open use the wiring diagram/schematic as a guide, inspect the wiring and connectors for damage.** Ignition on, engine not running. With the DRBIII®, read DTCs and record the related Freeze Frame data. Is the Good Trip Counter displayed and equal to zero? Yes → Go To 2 No → Go To 9

CR1120100445010X

Fig. 38 Code P0562: Battery Voltage Low (Part 1 of 3). 2002 Concorde, Intrepid, LHS & 30M

TEST	ACTION
2	**WARNING: WHEN THE ENGINE IS OPERATING, DO NOT STAND IN A DIRECT LINE WITH THE FAN. DO NOT PUT YOUR HANDS NEAR THE PULLEYS, BELTS OR FAN. DO NOT WEAR LOOSE CLOTHING.** Ignition on, engine not running. **NOTE: Ensure all wires are clear of the engine's moving parts.** Measure the voltage between the Generator B+ Terminal and the Battery+ Post. Start the engine. Is the voltage above 0.4 of a volt? Yes → Repair the B+ circuit for high resistance between the Generator and Battery. Perform POWERTRAIN VERIFICATION TEST VER - 3. No → Go To 3
3	**WARNING: WHEN THE ENGINE IS OPERATING, DO NOT STAND IN A DIRECT LINE WITH THE FAN. DO NOT PUT YOUR HANDS NEAR THE PULLEYS, BELTS OR FAN. DO NOT WEAR LOOSE CLOTHING.** Start the engine. Allow the engine to reach normal operating temperature. **NOTE: Ensure all wires are clear of the engine's moving parts.** Measure the voltage between the Generator case and Battery ground post. Is the voltage above 0.1 of a volt? Yes → Repair Generator Ground for high resistance, Generator Case to Battery ground side. Perform POWERTRAIN VERIFICATION TEST VER - 3. No → Go To 4
4	Turn the ignition off. Disconnect the Generator Field harness connector. Using a 12-volt test light, jumper it across the Generator Field harness connector. Ignition on, engine not running. With the DRBIII®, actuate the Generator Field Driver circuit. Does the test light illuminate brightly and flash on and off? Yes → Replace the Generator. Perform POWERTRAIN VERIFICATION TEST VER - 3. No → Go To 5
5	Turn the ignition off. Disconnect the Generator Field harness connector. Using a 12-volt test connected to battery voltage, probe the Generator Ground circuit in the Generator Field harness connector. Does the test light illuminate brightly? Yes → Go To 6 No → Repair the open in the Generator Field Ground circuit. Perform POWERTRAIN VERIFICATION TEST VER - 3.

CR1120100445020X

Fig. 38 Code P0562: Battery Voltage Low (Part 2 of 3). 2002 Concorde, Intrepid, LHS & 300M

When Monitored: The engine running. The engine speed greater than 380 RPM.

Set Condition: Battery voltage is 1 volt greater than desired system voltage. One Trip Fault

POSSIBLE CAUSES
GENERATOR FIELD CONTROL CIRCUIT SHORTED TO GROUND
GENERATOR FIELD CONTROL CIRCUIT OPEN
GENERATOR FIELD GROUND CIRCUIT OPEN
INTERMITTENT CONDITION
GENERATOR OPERATION
GENERATOR FIELD CONTROL CIRCUIT SHORTED TO BATTERY VOLTAGE
PCM

TEST	ACTION
1	**NOTE: Ensure the Battery is in good condition. Using the Midtronics Battery Tester, test the Battery before continuing.** **NOTE: Inspect the vehicle for aftermarket accessories that may exceed the Generator System output.** Turn the ignition off. **NOTE: Ensure the generator drive belt is in good operating condition.** **NOTE: Inspect the fuses in the PDC. If a fuse is found to be open use the wiring diagram/schematic as a guide, inspect the wiring and connectors for damage.** Ignition on, engine not running. With the DRBIII®, read DTCs and record the related Freeze Frame data. Is the Good Trip Counter displayed and equal to zero? Yes → Go To 2 No → Go To 8
2	Turn the ignition off. Disconnect the Generator Field harness connector. Using a 12-volt test light, jumper it across the Generator Field harness connector. Ignition on, engine not running. With the DRBIII®, actuate the Generator Field Driver circuit. Does the test light illuminate brightly and flash on and off? Yes → Go To 4 No → Go To 3

CR1120100446010X

Fig. 39 Code P0563: Battery Voltage High (Part 1 of 3). 2002 Concord, Intrepid, LHS & 300M

TEST	ACTION
6	Ignition on, engine not running. Disconnect the Generator Field harness connector. Disconnect the PCM harness connector. Measure the resistance between ground and the Generator Field Control circuit in the Generator Field harness connector. Is the resistance below 100 ohms? Yes → Repair the Generator Field Control circuit for a short to ground. Perform POWERTRAIN VERIFICATION TEST VER - 3. No → Go To 7
7	Turn the ignition off. Disconnect the Generator Field harness connector. Disconnect the PCM harness connector. **CAUTION: DO NOT PROBE THE PCM HARNESS CONNECTORS. PROBING THE PCM HARNESS CONNECTORS WILL DAMAGE THE PCM TERMINALS RESULTING IN POOR TERMINAL TO PIN CONNECTION. INSTALL MILLER SPECIAL TOOL #8815 TO PERFORM DIAGNOSIS.** Measure the resistance of the Generator Field Control circuit from the Generator Field harness connector to the appropriate terminal of the special tool #8815. Is the resistance below 5.0 ohms? Yes → Go To 8 No → Repair the open in the Generator Field Control circuit. Perform POWERTRAIN VERIFICATION TEST VER - 3.
8	**NOTE: Before continuing, check the PCM harness connector terminals for corrosion, damage or terminal push out. Repair as necessary.** If there are no possible causes remaining, view repair. Repair Replace and program the Powertrain Control Module in accordance with the Service Information. Perform POWERTRAIN VERIFICATION TEST VER - 3.
9	**NOTE: Ensure the Battery is in good condition. Using the Midtronics Battery Tester, test the Battery before continuing.** **NOTE: The conditions that set the DTC are not present at this time. The following list may help in identifying the intermittent condition.** **WARNING: WHEN THE ENGINE IS OPERATING, DO NOT STAND IN A DIRECT LINE WITH THE FAN. DO NOT PUT YOUR HANDS NEAR THE PULLEYS, BELTS OR FAN. DO NOT WEAR LOOSE CLOTHING.** With the engine running at normal operating temperature, monitor the DRBIII® parameters related to the DTC while wiggling the wire harness. Look for parameter values to change and/or a DTC to set. Review the DRBIII® Freeze Frame information. If possible, try to duplicate the conditions under which the DTC was set. Refer to any Technical Service Bulletins (TSB) that may apply. Visually inspect the related wire harness. Look for any chafed, pierced, pinched, or partially broken wires. Visually inspect the related wire harness connectors. Look for broken, bent, pushed out, or corroded terminals. Were any of the above conditions present? Yes → Repair as necessary Perform POWERTRAIN VERIFICATION TEST VER - 3. No → Test Complete.

CR1120100445030X

Fig. 38 Code P0562: Battery Voltage Low (Part 3 of 3). 2002 Concorde, Intrepid, LHS & 300M

TEST	ACTION
3	Turn the ignition off. Disconnect the Generator Field harness connector. Disconnect the PCM harness connector. Measure the voltage on the Generator Field Control circuit at the Generator Field harness connector. Is the voltage above 1.0 volt? Yes → Repair the short to voltage in the Generator Field Control circuit. Perform POWERTRAIN VERIFICATION TEST VER - 3. No → Go To 4
4	Turn the ignition off. Disconnect the Generator Field harness connector. Using a 12-volt test connected to battery voltage, probe the Generator Ground circuit in the Generator Field harness connector. Does the test light illuminate brightly? Yes → Go To 5 No → Repair the open in the Generator Field Ground circuit. Perform POWERTRAIN VERIFICATION TEST VER - 3.
5	Ignition on, engine not running. Disconnect the Generator Field harness connector. Disconnect the PCM harness connector. Measure the resistance between ground and the Generator Field Control circuit in the Generator Field harness connector. Is the resistance below 100 ohms? Yes → Repair the Generator Field Control circuit for a short to ground. Perform POWERTRAIN VERIFICATION TEST VER - 3. No → Go To 6
6	Turn the ignition off. Disconnect the Generator Field harness connector. Disconnect the PCM harness connector. **CAUTION: DO NOT PROBE THE PCM HARNESS CONNECTORS. PROBING THE PCM HARNESS CONNECTORS WILL DAMAGE THE PCM TERMINALS RESULTING IN POOR TERMINAL TO PIN CONNECTION. INSTALL MILLER SPECIAL TOOL #8815 TO PERFORM DIAGNOSIS.** Measure the resistance of the Generator Field Control circuit from the Generator Field harness connector to the appropriate terminal of the special tool #8815. Is the resistance below 5.0 ohms? Yes → Go To 7 No → Repair the open in the Generator Field Control circuit. Perform POWERTRAIN VERIFICATION TEST VER - 3.
7	**NOTE: Before continuing, check the PCM harness connector terminals for corrosion, damage or terminal push out. Repair as necessary.** If there are no possible causes remaining, view repair. Repair Replace and program the Powertrain Control Module in accordance with the Service Information. Perform POWERTRAIN VERIFICATION TEST VER - 3.

CR1120100446020X

Fig. 39 Code P0563: Battery Voltage High (Part 2 of 3). 2002 Concord, Intrepid, LHS & 300M

TEST	ACTION
8	**NOTE: The conditions that set the DTC are not present at this time. The following list may help in identifying the intermittent condition.** **NOTE: Ensure the Battery is in good condition. Using the Midtronics Battery Tester, test the Battery before continuing.** **WARNING: WHEN THE ENGINE IS OPERATING, DO NOT STAND IN A DIRECT LINE WITH THE FAN. DO NOT PUT YOUR HANDS NEAR THE PULLEYS, BELTS OR FAN. DO NOT WEAR LOOSE CLOTHING.** With the engine running at normal operating temperature, monitor the DRBIII® parameters related to the DTC while wiggling the wire harness. Look for parameter values to change and/or a DTC to set. Review the DRBIII® Freeze Frame information. If possible, try to duplicate the conditions under which the DTC was set. Refer to any Technical Service Bulletins (TSB) that may apply. Visually inspect the related wire harness. Look for any chafed, pierced, pinched, or partially broken wires. Visually inspect the related wire harness connectors. Look for broken, bent, pushed out, or corroded terminals. Were any of the above conditions present? Yes → Repair as necessary Perform POWERTRAIN VERIFICATION TEST VER - 3. No → Test Complete.

CR1120100446030X

Fig. 39 Code P0563: Battery Voltage High (Part 3 of 3). 2002 Concord, Intrepid, LHS & 300M

TEST	ACTION
3	Turn the ignition off. Disconnect the Generator Field harness connector. Using a 12-volt test light, jumper it across the Generator Field harness connector. Ignition on, engine not running. With the DRBIII®, actuate the Generator Field Driver circuit. Does the test light illuminate brightly and flash on and off? Yes → Replace the Generator. Perform POWERTRAIN VERIFICATION TEST VER - 3. No → Go To 4
4	Turn the ignition off. Disconnect the Generator Field harness connector. Using a 12-volt test connected to battery voltage, probe the Generator Ground circuit in the Generator Field harness connector. Does the test light illuminate brightly? Yes → Go To 5 No → Repair the open in the Generator Field Ground circuit. Perform POWERTRAIN VERIFICATION TEST VER - 3.
5	Turn the ignition off. Disconnect the Generator Field harness connector. Disconnect the PCM harness connector. Measure the voltage on the Generator Field Control circuit in the Generator Field harness connector. Is the voltage above 1.0 volts? Yes → Repair the short to voltage in the Generator Field Control circuit. Perform POWERTRAIN VERIFICATION TEST VER - 3. No → Go To 6
6	Turn the ignition on. Disconnect the Generator Field harness connector. Disconnect the PCM harness connector. Measure the resistance between ground and the Generator Field Control circuit in the Generator Field harness connector. Is the resistance below 100 ohms? Yes → Repair the Generator Field Control circuit for a short to ground. Perform POWERTRAIN VERIFICATION TEST VER - 3. No → Go To 7
7	Turn the ignition off. Disconnect the Generator Field harness connector. Disconnect the PCM harness connector. **CAUTION: DO NOT PROBE THE PCM HARNESS CONNECTORS. PROBING THE PCM HARNESS CONNECTORS WILL DAMAGE THE PCM TERMINALS RESULTING IN POOR TERMINAL TO PIN CONNECTION. INSTALL MILLER SPECIAL TOOL #8815 TO PERFORM DIAGNOSIS.** Measure the resistance of the Generator Field Control circuit from the Generator Field harness connector to the appropriate terminal of the special tool #8815. Is the resistance below 5.0 ohms? Yes → Go To 8 No → Repair the open in the Generator Field Control circuit. Perform POWERTRAIN VERIFICATION TEST VER - 3.

CR1120100447020X

Fig. 40 Code P0622: Low (Part 2 of 3). 2002 Concorde, Intrepid, LHS & 300M

When Monitored: With the ignition on. Engine running.

Set Condition: When the PCM tries to regulate the generator field with no result during monitoring. One Trip Fault.

POSSIBLE CAUSES
WIRING HARNESS INTERMITTENT
GENERATOR OPERATION
GENERATOR FIELD GROUND CIRCUIT OPEN
GENERATOR FIELD CONTROL CIRCUIT SHORTED TO BATTERY VOLTAGE
GENERATOR FIELD CONTROL CIRCUIT SHORTED TO GROUND
GENERATOR FIELD CONTROL CIRCUIT OPEN
PCM

TEST	ACTION
1	Ignition on, engine not running. With the DRBIII®, read DTCs and record the related Freeze Frame data. Does the test light illuminate brightly and flash? Yes → Go To 2 No → Go To 3
2	With the DRBIII®, erase DTCs. **WARNING: WHEN THE ENGINE IS OPERATING, DO NOT STAND IN A DIRECT LINE WITH THE FAN. DO NOT PUT YOUR HANDS NEAR THE PULLEYS, BELTS OR FAN. DO NOT WEAR LOOSE CLOTHING.** Start the engine and allow it to idle. Wiggle the wire harness from the Generator to PCM. With the DRBIII®, read DTCs. Did the DTC reset? Yes → Repair as necessary . Perform POWERTRAIN VERIFICATION TEST VER - 3. No → Test Complete.

CR1120100447010X

Fig. 40 Code P0622: Alternator Field Control Circuit (Part 1 of 3). 2002 Concorde, Intrepid, LHS & 300M

TEST	ACTION
8	**NOTE: Before continuing, check the PCM connector terminals for corrosion, damage, or terminal push out. Repair as necessary.** If there are no possible causes remaining, view repair. Repair Replace and program the Powertrain Control Module in accordance with the Service Information. Perform POWERTRAIN VERIFICATION TEST VER - 3.

CR1120100447030X

Fig. 40 Code P0622: Battery Voltage Low (Part 3 of 3). 2002 Concorde, Intrepid, LHS & 300M

When Monitored: The engine running. The engine speed greater than 1157 RPM.

Set Condition: The battery sensed voltage is 1 volt below the charging goal for 13.47 seconds. The PCM senses the battery voltage turns off the field driver and senses the battery voltage again. If the voltages are the same, the code is set.

POSSIBLE CAUSES
B+ CIRCUIT HIGH RESISTANCE
GENERATOR GROUND HIGH RESISTANCE
GENERATOR OPERATION
INTERMITTENT CONDITION
GENERATOR FIELD GROUND CIRCUIT OPEN
GENERATOR FIELD CONTROL CIRCUIT SHORTED TO BATTERY VOLTAGE
GENERATOR FIELD CONTROL CIRCUIT SHORTED TO GROUND
GENERATOR FIELD CONTROL CIRCUIT OPEN
PCM

TEST	ACTION
1	**NOTE: Inspect the vehicle for aftermarket accessories that may exceed the Generator System output.** Turn the ignition off. **NOTE: The battery must be fully charged.** **NOTE: The Generator belt tension and condition must be checked before continuing.** Start the engine. Allow the idle to stabilize. With the DRBIII®, read the Target Charging Voltage. Is the Target Charging Voltage above 15.1 volts? Yes → Go To 2 No → Go To 3

CR1120100448010X

Fig. 41 Code P2503: Charging System Voltage Low (Part 1 of 4). 2002 Concorde, Intrepid, LHS & 300M

TEST	ACTION
2	**NOTE: The conditions that set the DTC are not present at this time. The following list may help in identifying the intermittent condition.** **WARNING: WHEN THE ENGINE IS OPERATING, DO NOT STAND IN A DIRECT LINE WITH THE FAN. DO NOT PUT YOUR HANDS NEAR THE PULLEYS, BELTS OR FAN. DO NOT WEAR LOOSE CLOTHING.** With the engine running at normal operating temperature, monitor the DRBIII® parameters related to the DTC while wiggling the wire harness. Look for parameter values to change and/or a DTC to set. Review the DRBIII® Freeze Frame information. If possible, try to duplicate the conditions under which the DTC was set. Refer to any Technical Service Bulletins (TSB) that may apply. Visually inspect the related wire harness. Look for any chafed, pierced, pinched, or partially broken wires. Visually inspect the related wire harness connectors. Look for broken, bent, pushed out, or corroded terminals. Were any of the above conditions present? Yes → Repair as necessary Perform POWERTRAIN VERIFICATION TEST VER - 3. No → Test Complete.
3	**WARNING: WHEN THE ENGINE IS OPERATING, DO NOT STAND IN A DIRECT LINE WITH THE FAN. DO NOT PUT YOUR HANDS NEAR THE PULLEYS, BELTS OR FAN. DO NOT WEAR LOOSE CLOTHING.** Ignition on, engine not running. **NOTE: Ensure all wires are clear of the engine's moving parts.** Measure the voltage between the Generator B+ Terminal and the Battery+ Post. Start the engine. Is the voltage above 0.4 of a volt? Yes → Repair the B+ circuit for high resistance between the Generator and Battery. Perform POWERTRAIN VERIFICATION TEST VER - 3. No → Go To 4
4	**WARNING: WHEN THE ENGINE IS OPERATING, DO NOT STAND IN A DIRECT LINE WITH THE FAN. DO NOT PUT YOUR HANDS NEAR THE PULLEYS, BELTS OR FAN. DO NOT WEAR LOOSE CLOTHING.** Start the engine. Warm the engine to operating temperature. **NOTE: Ensure all wires are clear of the engine's moving parts.** Measure the voltage between the Generator case and Battery ground post. Is the voltage above 0.1 of a volt? Yes → Repair Generator Ground for high resistance, Generator Case to Battery ground side. Perform POWERTRAIN VERIFICATION TEST VER - 3. No → Go To 5

CR1120100448020X

Fig. 41 Code P2503: Charging System Voltage Low (Part 2 of 4). 2002 Concorde, Intrepid, LHS & 300M

TEST	ACTION
10	If there are no possible causes remaining, view repair. Repair Replace and program the Powertrain Control Module in accordance with the Service Information. Perform POWERTRAIN VERIFICATION TEST VER - 3.

CR1120100448040X

Fig. 41 Code P2503: Charging System Voltage Low (Part 4 of 4). 2002 Concorde, Intrepid, LHS & 300M

TEST	ACTION
5	Turn the ignition off. Disconnect the Generator Field harness connector. Using a 12-volt test light, jumper it across the Generator Field harness connector. Ignition on, engine not running. With the DRBIII®, actuate the Generator Field Driver circuit. Does the test light illuminate brightly and flash on and off? Yes → Replace the Generator. Perform POWERTRAIN VERIFICATION TEST VER - 3. No → Go To 6
6	Turn the ignition off. Disconnect the Generator Field harness connector. Using a 12-volt test connected to battery voltage, probe the Generator Ground circuit in the Generator Field harness connector. Does the test light illuminate brightly? Yes → Go To 7 No → Repair the open in the Generator Field Ground circuit. Perform POWERTRAIN VERIFICATION TEST VER - 3.
7	Turn the ignition off. Disconnect the Generator Field harness connector. Disconnect the PCM harness connector. Measure the voltage on the Generator Field Control circuit at the Generator Field harness connector. Is the voltage above 1.0 volt? Yes → Repair the short to voltage in the Generator Field Control circuit. Perform POWERTRAIN VERIFICATION TEST VER - 3. No → Go To 8
8	Turn the ignition on. Disconnect the Generator Field harness connector. Disconnect the PCM harness connector. Measure the resistance between ground and the Generator Field Control circuit in the Generator Field harness connector. Is the resistance below 100 ohms? Yes → Repair the Generator Field Control circuit for a short to ground. Perform POWERTRAIN VERIFICATION TEST VER - 3. No → Go To 9
9	Turn the ignition off. Disconnect the Generator Field harness connector. Disconnect the PCM harness connector. **CAUTION: DO NOT PROBE THE PCM HARNESS CONNECTORS. PROBING THE PCM HARNESS CONNECTORS WILL DAMAGE THE PCM TERMINALS RESULTING IN POOR TERMINAL TO PIN CONNECTION. INSTALL MILLER SPECIAL TOOL #8815 TO PERFORM DIAGNOSIS.** Measure the resistance of the Generator Field Control circuit from the Generator Field harness connector to the appropriate terminal of the special tool #8815. Is the resistance below 5.0 ohms? Yes → Go To 10 No → Repair the open in the Generator Field Control circuit. Perform POWERTRAIN VERIFICATION TEST VER - 3.

CR1120100448030X

Fig. 41 Code P2503: Charging System Voltage Low (Part 3 of 4). 2002 Concorde, Intrepid, LHS & 300M

POWERTRAIN VERIFICATION TEST VER - 3
1. **NOTE: After completing the Powertrain Verification Test the Transmission Verification Test must be performed.** 2. **NOTE: If the PCM has been replaced and the correct VIN and mileage have not been programmed, a DTC will be set in the ABS Module, Airbag Module and the SKIM.** 3. **NOTE: If the vehicle is equipped with a Sentry Key Immobilizer System, Secret Key data must be updated. Refer to the Service Information for the PCM, SKIM and the Transponder (ignition key) for programming information.** 4. Inspect the vehicle to ensure that all components related to the repair are connected properly. 5. With the DRBIII®, clear DTCs. 6. Perform generator output test. Refer to the appropriate service information as necessary. 7. Start the engine and set engine speed to 2000 RPM for at least thirty seconds. 8. Cycle the ignition key off and on. 9. With the DRBIII®, read the DTCs. If the DTC returns, or any other symptom or DTC is present, refer to the appropriate category and perform the corresponding symptom. 10. If there are no DTCs present and all components are functioning properly, the repair is complete. Are any DTCs present? Yes → Repair is not complete, refer to appropriate symptom. No → Repair is complete.

CR1120100449000X

Fig. 42 Verification Test VER-3. 2002 Concorde, Intrepid, LHS & 300M

ALTERNATOR SPECIFICATIONS

Model & Year	Engine	Type	Rated Output Amps
1998			
Breeze, Cirrus & Stratus	2.0L & 2.4L	Nippondenso	74
Cirrus & Stratus	2.5L	Melco	74
Neon	All	Melco	75
Sebring Convertible	All	Nippondenso	74
1998–2001			
Concorde, Intrepid, LHS & 300M	2.7L	Nippondenso	105
	3.2L & 3.5L	Melco	110
1999			
Breeze, Cirrus & Stratus	2.0L & 2.4L	Nippondenso	74
Cirrus & Stratus	2.5L	Melco	74
Neon	All	Melco	75
Sebring Convertible	All	Nippondenso	74
2000			
Breeze, Cirrus & Stratus	2.0L & 2.4L	Nippondenso	74
Cirrus & Stratus	2.5L	Melco	74
Sebring Convertible	All	Nippondenso	74
2001			
Sebring Convertible & Sedan	All	Nippondenso	120
Stratus Sedan	All	Nippondenso	120
2002			
Concorde, Intrepid, LHS & 300M	2.7L	Nippondenso	105
	3.5L	Nippondenso	125
Sebring Convertible & Sedan & Stratus Sedan	2.4L & 2.7L	Nippondenso	120

Mitsubishi

INDEX

APPLICATION CHART

Model	Year	Engine	Part No.
Avenger & Sebring Coupe	1998–2000	2.0L	M04661998
		2.5L	M04609075
Neon	2000–01	2.0L	479422AA
	2002		479422AC
Sebring Coupe & Stratus Coupe	2002	2.4L	MD362870
		3.0L	MD373093
Talon	1998	Less Turbocharged Engine	M04661998
		With Turbocharged Engine	MD327513

PRECAUTIONS

BATTERY GROUND CABLE

Prior to service, disconnect battery ground cable and isolate as required.

GENERAL INFORMATION

The power source of the charging system is the alternator. Current is transmitted from the field terminal of the regulator through a slip ring to the field coil and back to ground through another slip ring. The strength of the field regulates the output of the alternating current. This alternating current is then transmitted from the alternator to the rectifier where it is converted to direct current.

These alternators employ a three-phase stator winding in which the phase windings are electrically 120° apart. The rotor consists of a field coil encased between interleaved sections producing a magnetic field with alternate north and south poles. By rotating the rotor inside the stator the alternating current is induced in the stator windings. This alternating current is rectified (changed to D.C.) by silicon diodes and brought out to the output terminal of the alternator.

DIODE RECTIFIERS

Six or more silicon diode rectifiers are used and act as electrical one-way valves. One half of the diodes have ground polarity and are pressed or screwed into a heat sink which is grounded. The other diodes (ungrounded) are pressed or screwed into and insulated from the end head. These diodes are connected to the alternator output terminal.

Since the diodes have a high resistance to the flow of current in one direction and a low resistance in the opposite direction, they may be connected in a manner which allows current to flow from the alternator to the battery in the low resistance direction. The high resistance in the opposite direction prevents the flow of current from the battery to the alternator. Because of this feature, no circuit breaker is required between the alternator and battery.

SERVICE PRECAUTIONS

1. Ensure battery polarity is proper when servicing units. Reversed battery polarity will damage rectifiers and regulators.
2. If booster battery is used for starting, use proper polarity in hookup.
3. When a fast charger is used to charge a vehicle battery, vehicle battery cables should be disconnected unless fast charger is equipped with a special alternator protector, in which case vehicle battery cables need not be disconnected. Also, fast chargers should never be used to start a vehicle, as damage to rectifiers will result.
4. Lead connections to grounded rectifiers (negative) should never be soldered, as excessive heat may damage rectifiers.
5. Unless system includes a load relay or field relay, grounding alternator output terminal will damage alternator and/or circuits. This is true even when system is not in operation, since no circuit breaker is used and battery is applied to alternator output terminal at all times. Field or load relay acts as a circuit breaker in that it is controlled by ignition switch.
6. Before making any in-vehicle tests of alternator or regulator, battery should be inspected and circuit inspected for faulty wiring or insulation, loose or corroded connections and poor ground circuits.
7. Inspect alternator belt tension to ensure belt is tight enough to prevent slipping under load.
8. To prevent system damage, turn ignition off before making any test connections.
9. The vehicle battery must be fully charged or a fully charged battery may be installed for test purposes.

DESCRIPTION

On these units, the regulator is incorporated into the alternator rear housing. The electronic voltage regulator has the ability to vary regulated system voltage upward or downward as temperature changes. No voltage regulator adjustments are required on these units.

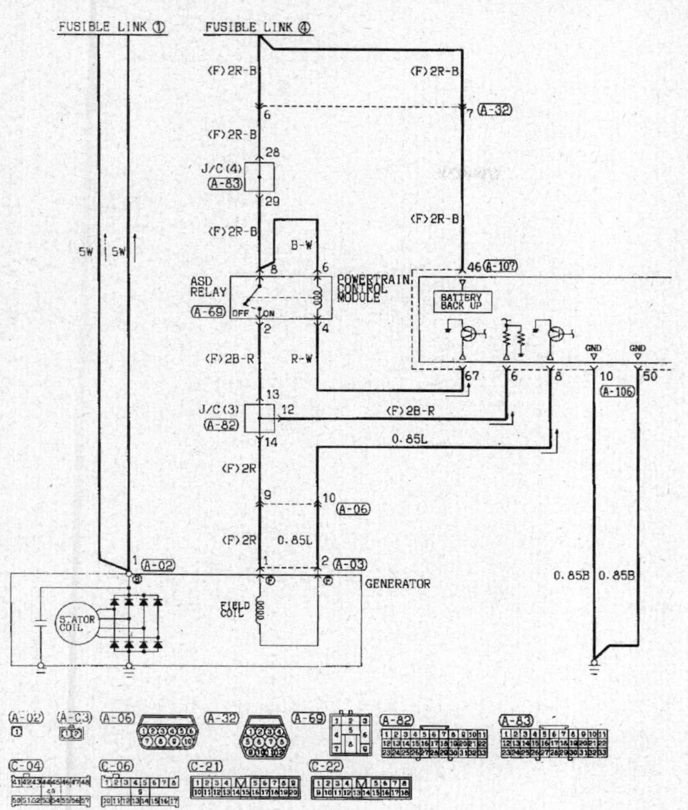

CR1129800226010X

Fig. 1 Wiring diagram (Part 1 of 2). Talon less turbocharged engine & Avenger & Sebring Coupe w/2.0L engine

CR1129800226020X

Fig. 1 Wiring diagram (Part 2 of 2). Talon less turbocharged engine & Avenger & Sebring Coupe w/2.0L engine

DIAGNOSIS & TESTING

WIRING DIAGRAMS

Refer to **Figs. 1 through 7** for wiring diagrams when diagnosing the charging system.

DIAGNOSTIC TESTS

2000–01 Neon

Refer to **Figs. 8 through 12** for diagnostic tests.

2002 Neon

Refer to **Figs. 13 through 20** for diagnostic tests.

ALTERNATOR OUTPUT WIRE VOLTAGE DROP TEST

1998–2000

1. Disconnect alternator output lead from alternator B terminal, **Figs. 21 and 22,** then connect a DC ammeter between terminal B and disconnected output lead, noting the following:
   a. Connect positive lead of ammeter to B terminal.
   b. Connect negative lead to disconnected output wire.
2. Connect a digital voltmeter between alternator B terminal and battery positive terminal, noting the following:
   a. Connect positive lead wire of voltmeter to B terminal.
   b. Connect negative lead wire to positive battery terminal.
3. Connect battery ground cable and leave hood open.
4. With engine running at approximately 2500 RPM, turn headlamps and other lamps on and off to adjust alternator load on ammeter to slightly above 30 amps.
5. Decrease engine speed gradually until value displayed on ammeter is 30 amps, then take a reading on voltmeter, noting the following:
   a. **On Talon less turbocharged engine, Avenger and 1998–2000 Sebring Coupe,** limit value should be .5 volts maximum.
   b. **On Talon with turbocharged engine,** limit value should be .3 volts maximum.
6. **On all models,** if alternator output is high and value does not decrease to 30 amps, set value at 40 amps and take a voltmeter reading, noting the following:
   a. Limit value should be .7 volts maximum.
   b. If value is still above limit value, a malfunction in alternator output wire may exist.
   c. Inspect wiring between alternator B terminal and battery positive terminal, including fusible link.
   d. If a terminal is not sufficiently tight or if harness has become discolored due to overheating, repair and test again.
7. Run engine at idle.
8. Turn all lamps and ignition off.
9. Disconnect battery ground cable, then the ammeter and voltmeter.
10. Connect alternator output wire to alternator B terminal.

2001–02

1. Disconnect and isolate battery ground cable.
2. Disconnect alternator output lead from alternator B terminal, **Fig. 22,** then connect a 0–100 amp DC ammeter in series between terminal B and disconnected output lead, noting the following:
   a. A clamp type ammeter which allows measurements to be taken without disconnecting the output wire is recommended.
   b. Connect positive lead of ammeter to B terminal.
   c. Connect negative lead to disconnected output wire.
3. Connect a digital voltmeter between alternator B terminal and battery positive terminal, noting the following:
   a. Connect positive lead wire of voltmeter to B terminal.

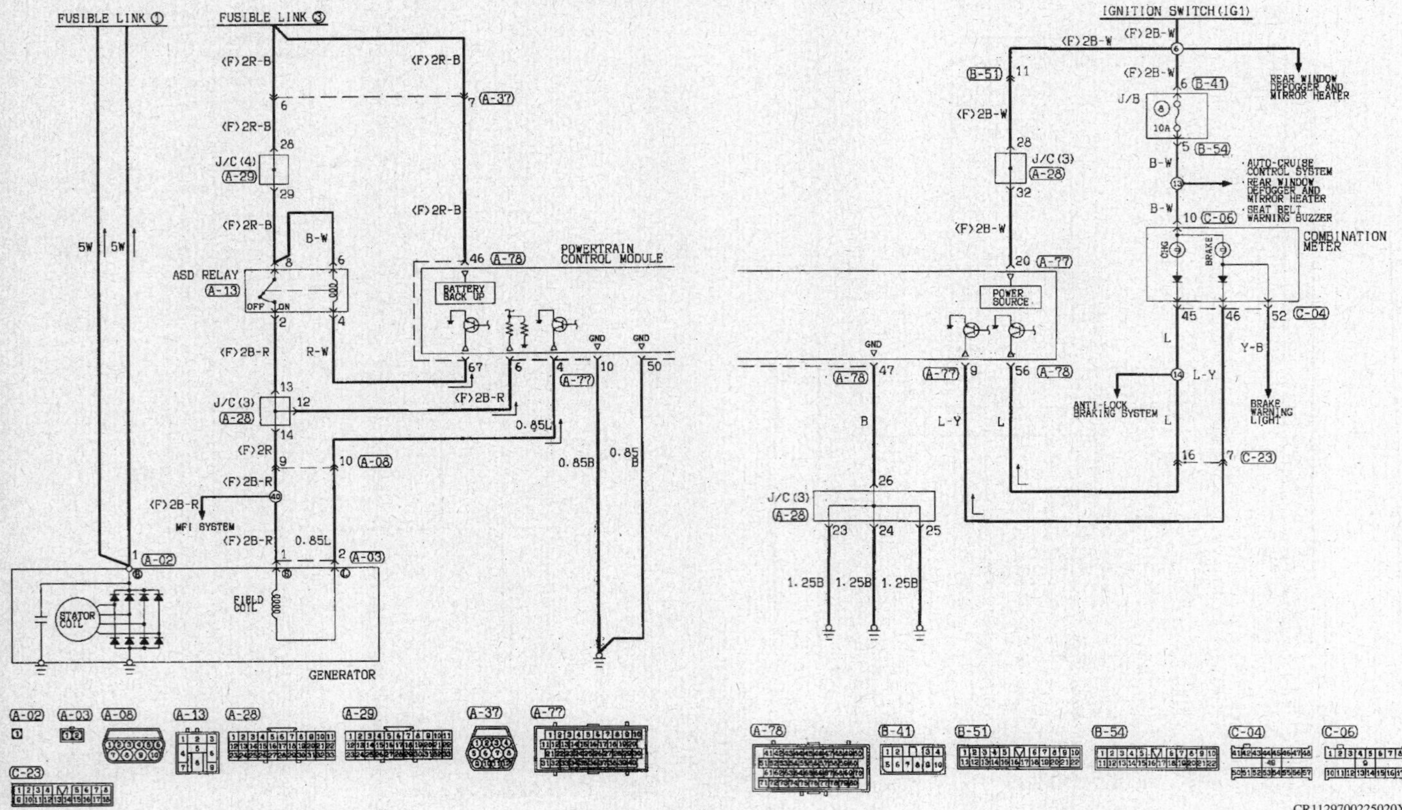

Fig. 2 Wiring diagram (Part 1 of 2). 1998–2000 Avenger & Sebring Coupe w/2.5L engine

Fig. 2 Wiring diagram (Part 2 of 2). 1998–2000 Avenger & Sebring Coupe w/2.5L engine

   b. Connect negative lead wire to positive battery terminal.
4. Connect battery ground cable and leave hood open.
5. With engine running at approximately 2500 RPM, turn headlamps and other lamps on and off to adjust alternator load on ammeter to slightly above 30 amps.
6. Decrease engine speed gradually until value displayed on ammeter is 30 amps, then take a reading on voltmeter. Limit value should be .3 volts maximum.
7. If alternator output is high and value does not decrease to 30 amps, set value to 40 amps and take a voltmeter reading. Limit value should be .4 volts maximum.
8. If value is still above limit value, a malfunction in alternator output wire may exist.
9. Inspect wiring between alternator B terminal and battery positive terminal, including fusible link.
10. If a terminal is not sufficiently tight or if harness has become discolored due to overheating, repair and test again.
11. After completing tests, run engine at idle.
12. Turn all lamps and ignition off.
13. Disconnect battery ground cable, then the ammeter and voltmeter.
14. Connect alternator output wire to alternator B terminal.

CURRENT OUTPUT TEST

1998–2000

1. Turn ignition off, then disconnect battery cables.
2. Disconnect wire from terminal B of alternator, **Figs. 23 and 24,** then connect an ammeter between B terminal and disconnected output wire, noting the following:
   a. Connect positive lead of ammeter to B terminal.
   b. Connect negative lead of ammeter to disconnected output wire.
3. Connect a voltmeter between alternator and ground, noting the following:
   a. Connect positive lead of voltmeter to B terminal.
   b. Connect negative lead of voltmeter to ground.
4. Connect battery ground cable. Leave hood open.
5. Ensure voltmeter reading is equal to battery voltage. If voltage is 0 volts, the cause is probably an open circuit in wire or fusible link between alternator B terminal and battery positive terminal.
6. Start engine and turn headlamps on.
7. Switch headlamps to high beam, turn HVAC blower switch to High, increase engine speed to approximately 2500 RPM and read maximum current output. Limit should be 70% of rated output.
8. Reading should be above limit value. If reading is below limit value and alternator output wire is in good condition, replace alternator.
9. Run engine at idle speed.
10. Turn ignition off.
11. Disconnect battery ground cable, then the ammeter and voltmeter.
12. Connect alternator output wire to generator B terminal.
13. Connect battery ground terminal.

2001–02

1. Disconnect wire from alternator terminal B, **Fig. 25,** then connect a 0–100 amp ammeter in series between B terminal and disconnected output wire, noting the following:
   a. A clamp type ammeter which allows measurements to be taken without disconnecting the output wire is recommended.
   b. Connect positive lead of ammeter to B terminal.
   c. Connect negative lead of ammeter to disconnected output wire.
2. Connect a 0–20 volt voltmeter between alternator and ground, noting the following:
   a. Connect positive lead of voltmeter to B terminal.
   b. Connect negative lead of voltmeter to ground.

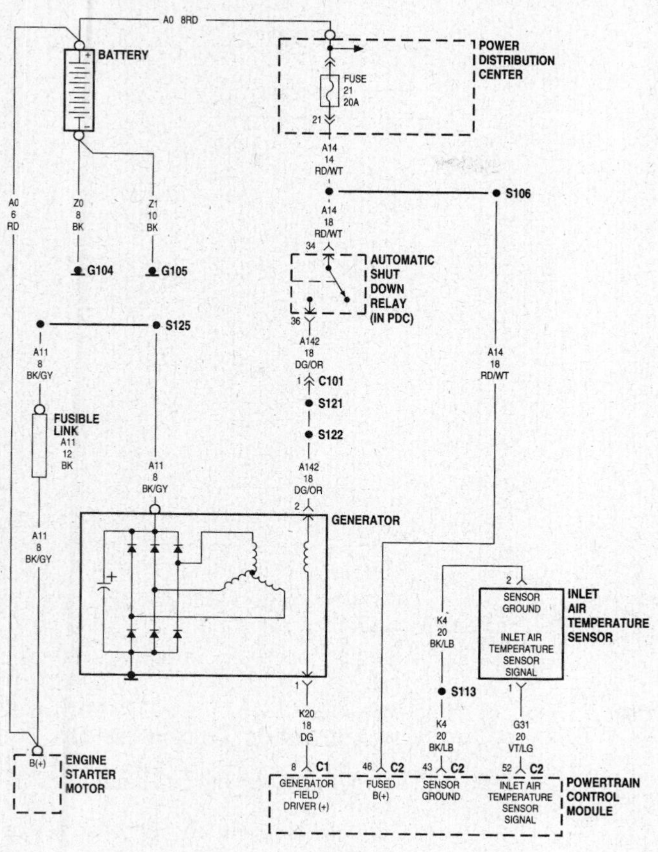

Fig. 3 Wiring diagram. Neon

CR1120100387010X

Fig. 4 Wiring diagram (Part 1 of 2). 2001 Sebring & Stratus Coupe w/Manual Transmission

3. Connect battery ground cable. Leave hood open.
4. Ensure voltmeter reading is equal to battery voltage. If voltage is 0 volts, the cause is probably an open circuit in wire or fusible link between alternator B terminal and battery positive terminal.
5. Turn headlamps on at low beam, then start engine.
6. Turn headlamps to high beam, HVAC blower switch to High, increase engine speed to approximately 2500 RPM and read maximum current output. Limit should be 70% of nominal current output.
7. Reading should be above limit value. If reading is below limit value and alternator output wire is in good condition, replace alternator.
8. Run engine at idle speed.
9. Turn ignition off.
10. Disconnect battery ground cable, then the ammeter and voltmeter.
11. Connect alternator output wire to generator B terminal.
12. Connect battery ground cable.

VOLTAGE REGULATOR TEST

Talon Less Turbocharged Engine, Avenger & 1998–2000 Sebring Coupe

1. Turn ignition off, then connect a digital voltmeter as illustrated in **Fig. 26,** noting the following:
   a. Connect positive lead of voltmeter to battery positive terminal.
   b. Connect negative lead of voltmeter to a secure ground or battery ground terminal.
2. Disconnect alternator output wire from alternator B terminal, then connect a DC ammeter in series between B terminal and output wire, noting the following:
   a. Connect positive lead of ammeter to B terminal.
   b. Connect negative lead to output wire.
3. Connect battery ground cable, then ensure all lamps and accessories are off.
4. Connect a tachometer and start engine.
5. Increase engine speed to approximately 2500 RPM.
6. Read voltmeter when current output by alternator becomes 10 amps or less, noting the following:
   a. If voltage reading is as specified in **Fig. 27,** voltage regulator is operating properly.
   b. If voltage is not within specifications, a voltage regulator or alternator malfunction exists.
7. Lower engine speed to idle speed.
8. Turn ignition off.
9. Disconnect battery ground cable, then the ammeter, voltmeter and tachometer.
10. Connect alternator output wire to B terminal.

Talon w/Turbocharged Engine

1. Turn ignition off.
2. Connect a digital voltmeter between alternator S terminal and ground, **Fig. 28,** noting the following:
   a. Connect positive lead of voltmeter to S terminal.
   b. Connect negative lead of voltmeter to a secure ground or to battery ground terminal.
3. Disconnect alternator output wire from alternator B terminal.
4. Connect a DC ammeter in series between B terminal and disconnected output wire, noting the following:
   a. Connect positive lead of ammeter to B terminal.
   b. Connect negative lead of ammeter to disconnect output wire.
5. Connect a tachometer to engine.
6. Connect battery ground terminal.
7. Turn ignition On.
8. Ensure reading on voltmeter is equal to battery voltage. If there is 0 volts, the cause is probably an open circuit in wire or fusible link between alternator S terminal and battery positive terminal.
9. Ensure all lamps and accessories are off.
10. Start engine and increase engine speed to approximately 2500 RPM.
11. Read voltmeter when current output by alternator becomes 10 amps or less, noting the following:
   a. If voltage is as specified in **Fig. 29,**

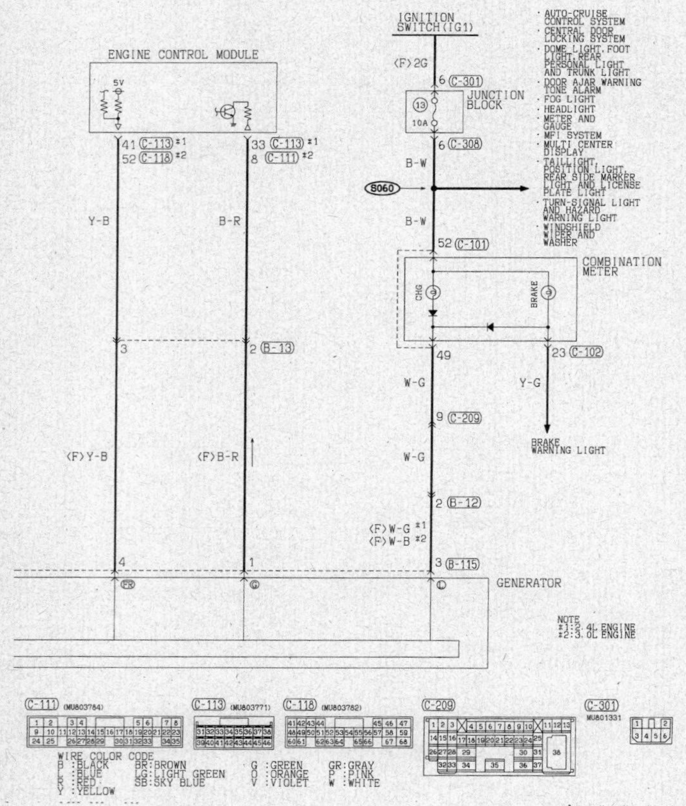

Fig. 4 Wiring diagram (Part 2 of 2). 2001 Sebring & Stratus Coupe w/Manual Transmission

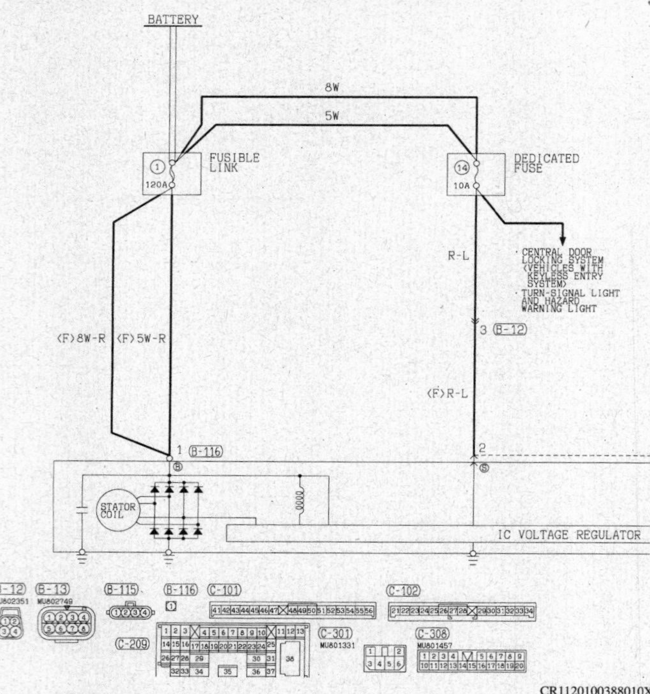

Fig. 5 Wiring diagram (Part 1 of 2). 2001 Sebring & Stratus Coupe w/Automatic Transmission

voltage regulator is operating properly.

b. If voltage is not as specified, a voltage regulator or alternator malfunction exists.

2001–02

1. Disconnect and isolate battery ground cable.
2. Using harness tool No. MB991519, or equivalent, connect a digital voltmeter between alternator S terminal and ground, **Fig. 30,** noting the following:
   a. Connect positive lead of voltmeter to S terminal.
   b. Connect negative lead of voltmeter to a secure ground or battery ground terminal.
3. Disconnect alternator output wire from alternator B terminal, then connect a 0–100 amp DC ammeter in series between B terminal and output wire, noting the following:
   a. Connect positive lead of ammeter to B terminal.
   b. Connect negative lead to disconnected output wire.
4. Connect battery ground cable, then ensure all lamps and accessories are off.
5. Connect a tachometer and turn ignition On.
6. Ensure voltmeter reading is equal to battery positive voltage. If voltage is 0 volts, the cause is probably an open circuit in wire or fusible link between alternator S terminal and battery positive terminal.
7. Ensure all lights and accessories are turned off.
8. Start engine and increase speed to approximately 2500 RPM.
9. Read voltmeter when current output by alternator becomes 10 amps or less, noting the following:
   a. If voltage reading is as specified in **Fig. 31,** voltage regulator is operating properly.
   b. If voltage is not within specification, a voltage regulator or alternator malfunction exists.
10. Lower engine speed to idle speed.
11. Turn ignition off.
12. Disconnect battery ground cable, then the ammeter, voltmeter and tachometer.
13. Connect alternator output wire to B terminal.

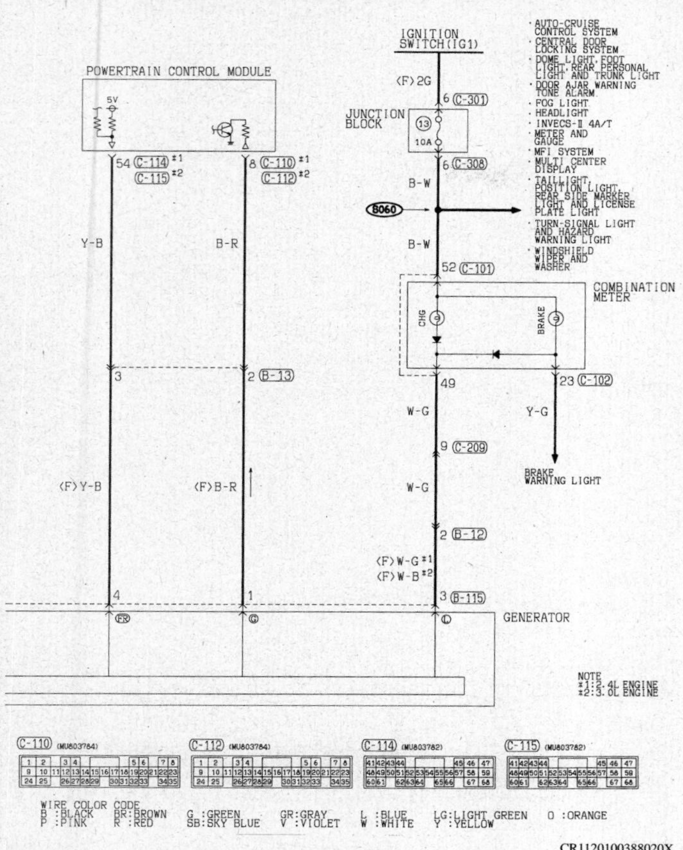

Fig. 5 Wiring diagram (Part 2 of 2). 2001 Sebring & Stratus Coupe w/Automatic Transmission

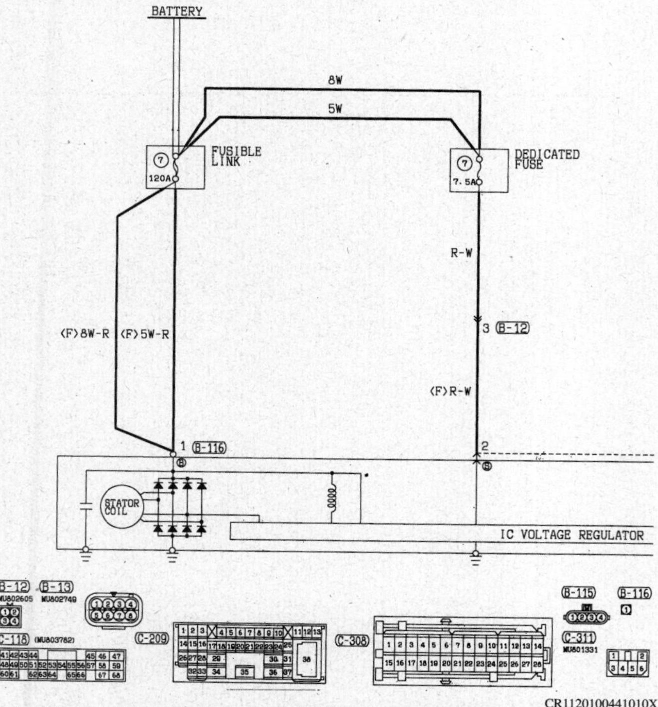

Fig. 7 Wiring diagram (Part 1 of 4). 2001-02 Sebring & Stratus Coupe w/Manual Transmission

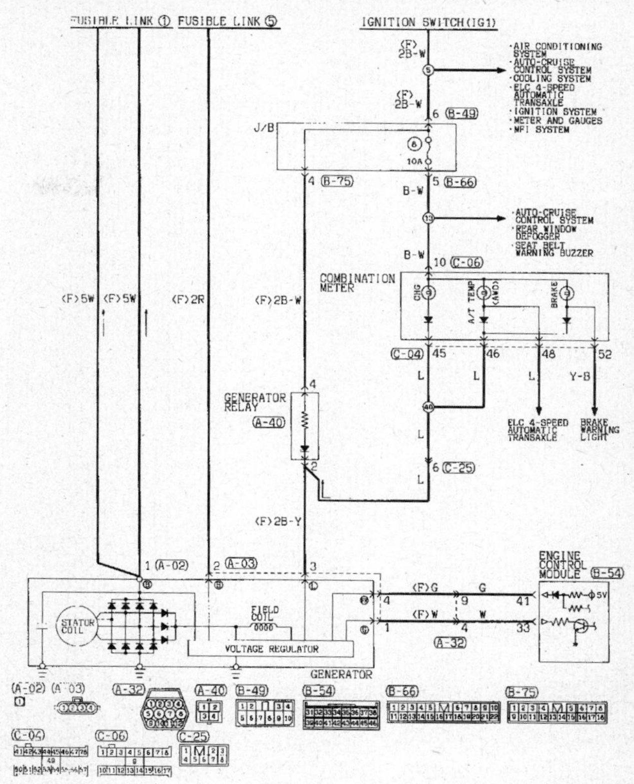

Fig. 6 Wiring diagram. Talon w/turbocharged engine

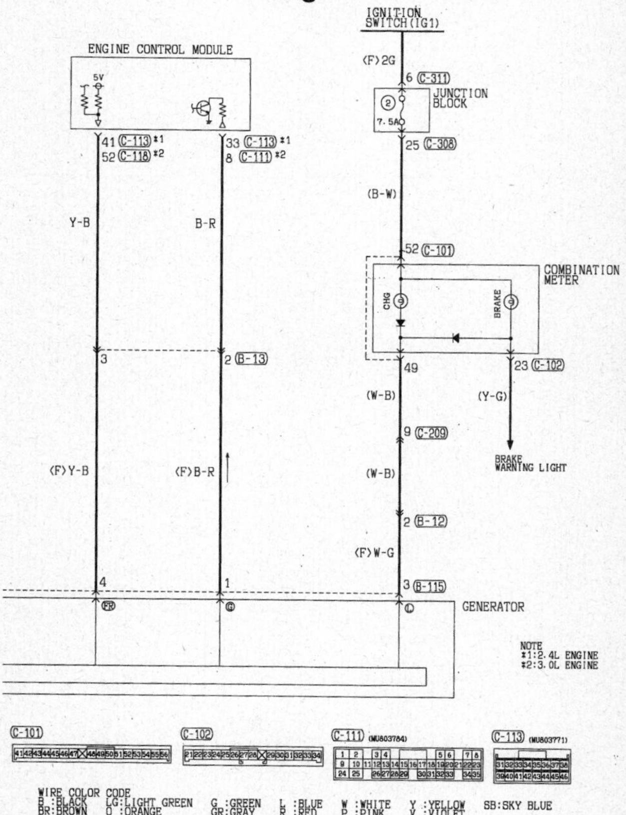

Fig. 7 Wiring diagram (Part 2 of 4). 2001-02 Sebring & Stratus Coupe w/Manual Transmission

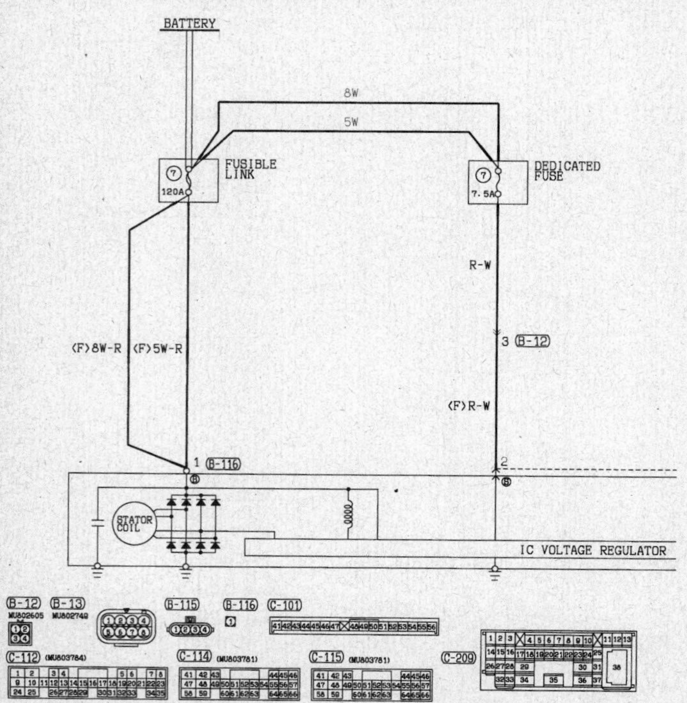

Fig. 7 Wiring diagram (Part 3 of 4). 2001-02 Sebring & Stratus Coupe w/Automatic Transmission

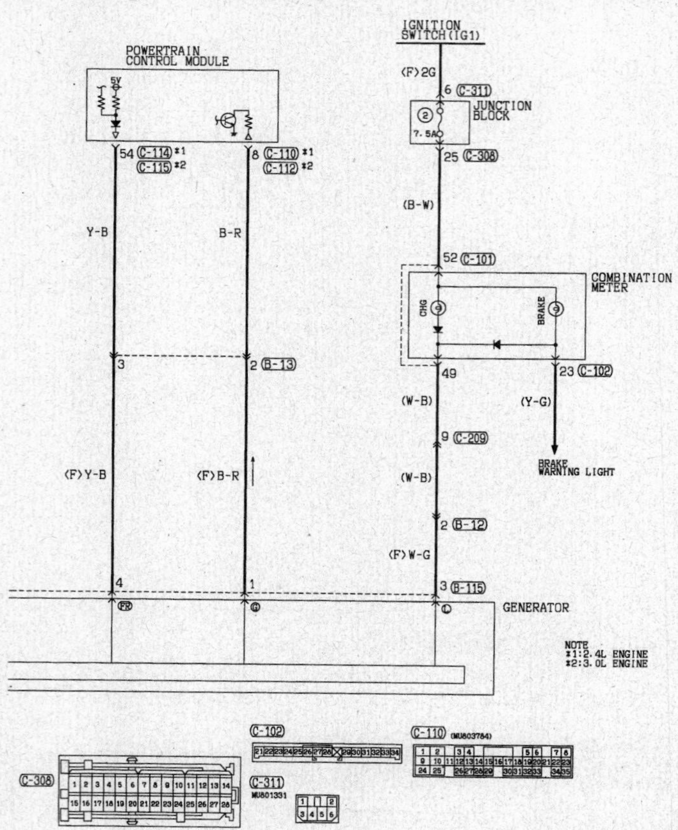

Fig. 7 Wiring diagram (Part 4 of 4). 2001-02 Sebring & Stratus Coupe w/Automatic Transmission

DIAGNOSTIC CHART INDEX

Code/Test	Description	Page No.	Fig No.
2000–01 NEON			
P0622	Alternator Field Not Switching Properly	9-33	8
P1594	Charging System Voltage Too High	9-34	9
P1682	Charging System Voltage Too Low	9-34	10
—	Charging System Diagnosis w/No Code	9-35	11
—	Verification Test VER-3A	9-35	12
2002 NEON			
P0562	Charging System Voltage Too Low	9-35	13
P0563	Charging System Voltage Too High	9-36	14
P0622	Generator Field Not Switching Properly	9-37	15
P0625	Generator Field Control Circuit Low	9-37	16
P0626	Generator Field Control High	9-38	17
P1594	Charging System Voltage Too High	9-38	18
P1682	Charging System Voltage Too Low	9-38	19
—	Verification Test VER-3	9-39	20

TEST	ACTION
1	Ignition On, Engine Not Running With the DRB actuate the Generator Field Driver Circuit. Using a 12-volt test light, backprobe the Gen Field Driver Circuit at the back of the Generator. Did the light blink? Yes → Go To 2 No → Go To 4
2	Ignition On, Engine Not Running With the DRB actuate the Generator Field Driver Circuit. **Note: Actuator Test should still be running.** Wiggle Wiring Harness from the Generator to PCM. With the DRB, read Codes. Does the Generator Field Driver (-) Circuit code return? Yes → Repair as necessary where wiggling caused problem to appear. Perform Powertrain Verification Test VER-3A. No → Go To 3
3	Turn ignition off. Using the schematic as a guide, inspect the Wiring and Connectors. Were any problems found? Yes → Repair as necessary. Perform Powertrain Verification Test VER-3A. No → Test Complete.
4	Ignition On, Engine Not Running Record all DTC's and freeze frame data, now erase Codes. Carefully inspect all Connectors for corrosion or spread Terminals before continuing. With the DRB actuate the Generator Field Driver Circuit. Backprobe the ASD Relay Output Circuit at back of Generator. Is the voltage above 10.0 volts? Yes → Go To 5 No → Repair the open ASD Relay Output Circuit. Perform Powertrain Verification Test VER-3A.
5	Turn ignition off. Disconnect the PCM Connectors. **Note: Check connectors - Clean/repair as necessary.** Disconnect the generator field connector. **Note: Check Connectors - Clean/repair as necessary.** Using an Ohmmeter, measure the Generator Field Driver Circuit from PCM Connector to ground. Is the resistance below 5.0 ohms? Yes → Repair the Generator Field Driver Circuit shorted to ground. Perform Powertrain Verification Test VER-3A. No → Go To 6

CR1120000331010X

Fig. 8 Code P0622: Alternator Field Not Switching Properly (Part 1 of 2). 2000–01 Neon

TEST	ACTION
6	Turn ignition off. Disconnect the PCM Connectors. Disconnect the generator field connector. **Note: Check Connectors - Clean/repair as necessary.** Using an Ohmmeter, measure the Generator Field Driver Circuit from PCM to Generator. Is the resistance below 5.0 ohms? Yes → Go To 7 No → Repair the open Generator Field Driver Circuit. Perform Powertrain Verification Test VER-3A.
7	Turn ignition off. Disconnect the Gen Field Harness Connector at back of the Generator. **Note: Check connectors - Clean/repair as necessary.** Use an Ohmmeter in the following steps. Measure resistance across the Generator Field Terminals at the Generator. Is the resistance below 5.0 ohms? Yes → Repair the Generator as necessary. Perform Powertrain Verification Test VER-3A. No → Go To 8
8	If there are no potential causes remaining, the PCM is assumed to be defective. View repair options. Repair Replace the Powertrain Control Module. Perform Powertrain Verification Test VER-3A.

CR1120000331020X

Fig. 8 Code P0622: Alternator Field Not Switching Properly (Part 2 of 2). 2000–01 Neon

TEST	ACTION
9	Ignition On, Engine Not Running With DRB, actuate the Generator Field Driver. With a 12-volt test light, backprobe the Generator Field Driver Circuit in back of Generator. Did the light blink? Yes → Go To 10 No → Go To 13
10	Ignition On, Engine Not Running With the DRB, actuate the Generator Field Driver. With DRB, stop the Generator Field Driver actuation. With DRB, read the Target Charging voltage. Is the Target Charging voltage above 13 volts? Yes → Go To 11 No → Go To 12
11	Start the engine. Manually set the engine speed to 1600 RPM. With DRB, read both the Battery voltage and the Target Charging voltage. Compare the "Target Voltage" to the "Battery Voltage" reading. Monitor voltage for 5 minutes, if necessary. Look for a 1.0 volt difference or more. Was there more than a 1.0 volt difference? Yes → Replace the Powertrain Control Module. Perform Powertrain Verification Test VER-3A. No → Test Complete.
12	Turn ignition off. **Note: Battery must be fully charged.** **Note: Generator Belt tension and condition must be checked before continuing.** Start engine and allow it to reach operating temperature. With the DRB, read the BTS temperature. Using a Thermometer, measure under hood temperature. Is the temperature within 10 F degrees of Battery temperature? Yes → Test Complete. No → Replace Powertrain Control Module. Perform Powertrain Verification Test VER-3A.
13	Turn ignition off. Disconnect the PCM Connectors. **Note: Check connectors - Clean/repair as necessary.** Disconnect the generator field connector. **Note: Check Connectors - Clean/repair as necessary.** Using an Ohmmeter, measure the Generator Field Driver Circuit from PCM Connector to ground. Is the resistance below 5.0 ohms? Yes → Repair the Generator Field Driver Circuit shorted to ground. Perform Powertrain Verification Test VER-3A. No → Go To 14

CR1120000332010X

Fig. 9 Code P1594: Charging System Voltage Too High (Part 1 of 2). 2000–01 Neon

TEST	ACTION
16	Turn Ignition Off. **Note: Battery must be fully charged.** **Note: Generator Belt tension and condition must be checked before continuing.** Start Engine. With the DRB, read the target charging voltage. Is the target charging voltage above 15.1 volts? Yes → Go To 17 No → Go To 18
17	Turn ignition off. **Note: Battery must be fully charged.** **Note: Generator Belt tension and condition must be checked before continuing.** Start engine and allow it to reach operating temperature. With the DRB, read the BTS temperature. Using a Thermometer, measure under hood temperature. Is the temperature within 10 F degrees of Battery temperature? Yes → Go To 18 No → Replace the PCM. Perform Powertrain Verification Test VER-3A.
18	Turn ignition on, engine not running. Using a Voltmeter, measure voltage between the Generator B(+) Terminal and the Battery (+) Post. **Caution: Ensure all wires are clear of the engine's moving parts.** Start engine. Is the voltage above 0.4 volt? Yes → Repair the B(+) Circuit for high resistance between the Generator and Battery. Perform Powertrain Verification Test VER-3A. No → Go To 19
19	Start engine. Warm the engine to operating temperature. **Caution: Ensure all wires are clear of the engine's moving parts.** Using a Voltmeter, measure voltage between the Generator case and Battery (-) Post. Is the voltage above 0.1 volt? Yes → Repair Generator Ground for high resistance, Generator Case to Battery (-) side. Perform Powertrain Verification Test VER-3A. No → Go To 20
20	Start engine. Turn on all accessories, manually set engine speed to 1600 RPM. With DRB, read Target Charging and Charging voltage. Compare the two readings. Is there more than a 1.0 volt difference? Yes → Go To 21 No → Test Complete.

CR1120000333010X

Fig. 10 Code P1682: Charging System Voltage Too Low (Part 1 of 3). 2000–01 Neon

TEST	ACTION
14	Turn ignition off. Disconnect the Field Harness Connector at back of the Generator. **Note: Check connectors - Clean/repair as necessary.** Measure resistance of the Generator Field Driver Circuit at the Generator to Ground. Is the resistance below 5.0 ohms? Yes → Repair or replace the shorted Generator as necessary. Perform Powertrain Verification Test VER-3A. No → Go To 15
15	If there are no potential causes remaining, the Powertrain Control Module is assumed to be defective. View repair options. Repair Replace the Powertrain Control Module. Perform Powertrain Verification Test VER-3A.

CR1120000332020X

Fig. 9 Code P1594: Charging System Voltage Too High (Part 2 of 2). 2000–01 Neon

TEST	ACTION
21	Ignition On, Engine Not Running With the DRB, actuate the Generator Field. Using a Voltmeter, measure the voltage at both Generator Field Terminals. Is the voltage below 3.0 volts at either Terminal? Yes → Go To 22 No → Test Complete.
22	Ignition On, Engine Not Running Record all DTC's and freeze frame data, now erase Codes. Carefully inspect all Connectors for corrosion or spread Terminals before continuing. With the DRB actuate the Generator Field Driver Circuit. Backprobe the ASD Relay Output Circuit at back of Generator. Is the voltage above 10.0 volts? Yes → Go To 23 No → Repair the open ASD Relay Output Circuit. Perform Powertrain Verification Test VER-3A.
23	Turn ignition off. Disconnect the PCM Connectors. **Note: Check connectors - Clean/repair as necessary.** Disconnect the generator field connector. **Note: Check Connectors - Clean/repair as necessary.** Using an Ohmmeter, measure the Generator Field Driver Circuit from PCM Connector to ground. Is the resistance below 5.0 ohms? Yes → Repair the Generator Field Driver Circuit shorted to ground. Perform Powertrain Verification Test VER-3A. No → Go To 24
24	Turn ignition off. Disconnect ASD Relay Connector. **Note: Check connectors - Clean/repair as necessary.** Disconnect the generator field connector. **Note: Check Connectors - Clean/repair as necessary.** Using an Ohmmeter, measure the ASD Relay Output Circuit from ASD Relay Connector to ground. Is the resistance below 5.0 ohms? Yes → Repair the ASD Relay Output Circuit shorted to ground. Perform Powertrain Verification Test VER-3A. No → Go To 25
25	Turn ignition off. Disconnect the PCM Connectors. Disconnect the generator field connector. **Note: Check Connectors - Clean/repair as necessary.** Using an Ohmmeter, measure the Generator Field Driver Circuit from PCM to Generator. Is the resistance below 5.0 ohms? Yes → Go To 26 No → Repair the open Generator Field Driver Circuit. Perform Powertrain Verification Test VER-3A.

CR1120000333020X

Fig. 10 Code P1682: Charging System Voltage Too Low (Part 2 of 3). 2000–01 Neon

TEST	ACTION
26	If there are no potential causes remaining, the PCM is assumed to be defective. View repair options. Repair Replace the Powertrain Control Module. Perform Powertrain Verification Test VER-3A.

CR1120000333030X

Fig. 10 Code P1682: Charging System Voltage Too Low (Part 3 of 3). 2000–01 Neon

TEST	ACTION
32	Start engine. Warm the engine to operating temperature. **Caution: Ensure all wires are clear of the engine's moving parts.** Using a Voltmeter, measure voltage between the Generator case and Battery (-) Post. Is the voltage above 0.1 volt? Yes → Repair Generator Ground for high resistance, Generator Case to Battery (-) side. Perform Powertrain Verification Test VER-3A. No → Go To 33
33	Ignition On, Engine Not Running. With the DRB, read the Battery voltage and record the results. Using a Voltmeter, measure Battery voltage B(+) to B(-) Terminal and record the results. Compare the two voltage readings. Is the voltage difference less than one volt? Yes → Test Complete. No → Go To 34
34	Ignition On, Engine Not Running With the DRB, read the Battery voltage and record the results. Turn Ignition off. Disconnect the PCM. **Note: Check connectors - Clean/repair as necessary.** Turn Ignition on, with the engine off. Using a Voltmeter, measure the Fused B(+) at PCM Connector. Is the voltage within one volt of the DRB recorded reading? Yes → Go To 35 No → Repair the B(+) Circuit for high resistance between the PCM and the Battery. Perform Powertrain Verification Test VER-3A.
35	If there are no potential causes remaining, the PCM is assumed to be defective. View repair options. Repair Replace the PCM. Perform Powertrain Verification Test VER-3A.

CR1120000334020X

Fig. 11 Charging System Diagnosis w/No Code (Part 2 of 2). 2000–01 Neon

VERIFICATION TEST VER-3A
1. Inspect the vehicle to ensure that all engine components are properly installed and connected. Reassemble and reconnect components as necessary. 2. Connect the DRB to the Data Link Connector and erase the codes. 3. If the PCM has been replaced perform steps 4 through 6 then continue the verification. 4. If PCM has been changed and correct VIN and mileage have not been programmed, a DTC will be set in ABS and Air bag modules. In addition, if vehicle is equipped with a Sentry Key Immobilizer Module (SKIM), Secret Key data must be updated to enable start. 5. For ABS and Air Bag systems: Enter correct VIN and Mileage in PCM. Erase codes in ABS and Air Bag modules. 6. For SKIM theft alarm: Connect DRB to data link conn. Go to Theft Alarm, SKIM, Misc. and place SKIM in secured access mode, by using the appropriate PIN code for this vehicle. Select Update the Secret Key data. Data will be transferred from SKIM to PCM. 7. Ensure no other charging system problems remain by doing the following: Start the engine. Perform generator output per service manual. 8. Raise the engine speed to 2000 rpm for at least 30 seconds. 9. Allow the engine to idle. 10. Turn the engine off. 11. Turn the ignition key on. 12. With the DRB, read trouble code messages. 13. If repaired code has reset, or any other one has set, check all pertinent Technical Service Bulletins and return to Symptom List if necessary. 14. If there are no codes, the repair is now complete.

CR1120000335000X

Fig. 12 Verification Test VER-3A. 2000–01 Neon

TEST	ACTION
27	Turn ignition off. **Note: Battery condition must be verified prior to this test.** Inspect the Generator Belt tension and condition. Is the Generator Belt OK? Yes → Go To 28 No → Repair as necessary. Perform Powertrain Verification Test VER-3A.
28	Start the Engine. Turn on all accessories. Raise engine speed to 2000 RPM for 30 seconds then return to idle. With the DRB III read DTC's. Are there any "Charging System" Trouble Codes? Yes → Refer to Symptom list for problems related to Charging. Perform Powertrain Verification Test VER-3A. No → Go To 29
29	Ignition On, Engine Not Running With the DRB, actuate the Generator Field. Using a 12-volt test light, backprobe the Generator Field Driver Terminal at the back of the Generator. **Note: The test light should blink On and Off every 1.4 seconds.** While monitoring the 12-volt test light, wiggle the Field Terminals back to the PCM and ASD Relay. Was there any interruption in the normal cycle of the test light? Yes → Repair the wire where wiggling interrupted the voltage cycle. Perform Powertrain Verification Test VER-3A. No → Go To 30
30	Ignition On, Engine Not Running With the DRB, read trouble codes. Are there any "Charging System" trouble codes? Yes → Refer to Symptom list for problems related to Charging. Perform Powertrain Verification Test VER-3A. No → Go To 31
31	Turn ignition on, engine not running. Using a Voltmeter, measure voltage between the Generator B(+) Terminal and the Battery (+) Post. **Caution: Ensure all wires are clear of the engine's moving parts.** Start engine. Is the voltage above 0.4 volt? Yes → Repair the B(+) Circuit for high resistance between the Generator and Battery. Perform Powertrain Verification Test VER-3A. No → Go To 32

CR1120000334010X

Fig. 11 Charging System Diagnosis w/No Code (Part 1 of 2). 2000–01 Neon

When Monitored: With the engine running for more than 30 seconds.

Set Condition: When battery voltage is less than 11.5 volts for more than 5 seconds.

POSSIBLE CAUSES
B+ CIRCUIT HIGH RESISTANCE
GENERATOR GROUND HIGH RESISTANCE
INTERMITTENT CONDITION
GENERATOR FIELD DRIVER CIRCUIT OPEN
ASD RELAY OUTPUT CIRCUIT OPEN
GENERATOR

TEST	ACTION
1	**NOTE: Inspect the vehicle for aftermarket accessories that may exceed the Generator System output.** Turn the ignition off. **NOTE: Verify that the battery is fully charged and capable of passing a load test before continuing.** **NOTE: The Generator belt tension and condition must be checked before continuing.** Start the engine. Allow the idle to stabilize. With the DRBIII®, read the Target Charging Voltage. Is the Target Charging Voltage above 15.1 volts? Yes → Go To 7 No → Go To 2
2	**WARNING: WHEN THE ENGINE IS OPERATING, DO NOT STAND IN A DIRECT LINE WITH THE FAN. DO NOT PUT YOUR HANDS NEAR THE PULLEYS, BELTS OR FAN. DO NOT WEAR LOOSE CLOTHING.** Turn the ignition on. **NOTE: Ensure all wires are clear of the engine's moving parts.** Measure the voltage between the Generator B+ Terminal and the Battery+ Post. Start the engine. Is the voltage above 0.4 volt? Yes → Repair the B+ circuit for high resistance between the Generator and Battery. Perform POWERTRAIN VERIFICATION TEST VER - 3. No → Go To 3

CR1120100434010X

Fig. 13 Code P0562: Charging System Voltage Too Low (Part 1 of 3). 2002 Neon

TEST	ACTION
3	**WARNING: WHEN THE ENGINE IS OPERATING, DO NOT STAND IN A DIRECT LINE WITH THE FAN. DO NOT PUT YOUR HANDS NEAR THE PULLEYS, BELTS OR FAN. DO NOT WEAR LOOSE CLOTHING.** Start the engine. Warm the engine to operating temperature. **NOTE: Ensure all wires are clear of the engine's moving parts.** Measure the voltage between the Generator case and Battery ground post. Is the voltage above 0.1 volt? Yes → Repair Generator Ground for high resistance, Generator Case to Battery ground side. Perform POWERTRAIN VERIFICATION TEST VER - 3. No → Go To 4
4	Start the engine. **WARNING: WHEN THE ENGINE IS OPERATING, DO NOT STAND IN A DIRECT LINE WITH THE FAN. DO NOT PUT YOUR HANDS NEAR THE PULLEYS, BELTS OR FAN. DO NOT WEAR LOOSE CLOTHING.** Turn on all accessories, manually set engine speed to 1600 RPM. With DRBIII®, read Target Charging and Charging voltage. Compare the two readings. Is there more than a 1.0 volt difference? Yes → Go To 5 No → Go To 7
5	Turn the ignition off. Disconnect the PCM harness connector. Disconnect the Generator Field harness connector. Measure the resistance of the Generator Field Driver circuit from the PCM harness connector to Generator harness connector. Is the resistance below 5.0 ohms? Yes → Go To 6 No → Repair the Generator Field Driver circuit for an open. Perform POWERTRAIN VERIFICATION TEST VER - 3.
6	Disconnect the Generator Field harness connector. Turn the ignition on. With the DRBIII® actuate the Generator Field Driver. Using a 12-volt test light connected to ground, probe the ASD Relay Output circuit in the Generator harness connector. Does the test light illuminate brightly? Yes → Repair or replace the Generator as necessary. Perform POWERTRAIN VERIFICATION TEST VER - 3. No → Repair the ASD Relay Output circuit. Perform POWERTRAIN VERIFICATION TEST VER - 3.

CR1120100434020X

Fig. 13 Code P0562: Charging System Voltage Too Low (Part 2 of 3). 2002 Neon

When Monitored: With the engine running for more than 30 seconds.

Set Condition: When battery voltage is greater than 1 volt over target voltage for more than 5 seconds.

POSSIBLE CAUSES
TARGET VOLTAGE DIFFERS FROM BATTERY VOLTAGE
INTERMITTENT CONDITION
GENERATOR FIELD DRIVER CIRCUIT SHORTED TO GROUND
GENERATOR FIELD
POWERTRAIN CONTROL MODULE

TEST	ACTION
1	**NOTE: Verify that the battery is fully charged and capable of pass a load test before continuing.** **Note: Generator Belt tension and condition must be checked before continuing.** Turn the ignition on. With DRBIII®, actuate the Generator Field Driver. With a 12-volt test light connected to ground, backprobe the Generator Field Driver circuit in the back of Generator Field harness connector. Does the test light illuminate brightly and flash? Yes → Go To 2 No → Go To 5
2	With DRBIII®, stop all actuation. Turn the ignition on. With DRBIII®, read the Target Charging voltage. Is the Target Charging voltage above 13.0 volts? Yes → Go To 3 No → Go To 4

CR1120100435010X

Fig. 14 Code P0563: Charging System Voltage Too High (Part 1 of 2). 2002 Neon

TEST	ACTION
7	**WARNING: WHEN THE ENGINE IS OPERATING, DO NOT STAND IN A DIRECT LINE WITH THE FAN. DO NOT PUT YOUR HANDS NEAR THE PULLEYS, BELTS OR FAN. DO NOT WEAR LOOSE CLOTHING.** **NOTE: The conditions that set the DTC are not present at this time. The following list may help in identifying the intermittent condition.** With the engine running at normal operating temperature, monitor the DRBIII® parameters related to the DTC while wiggling the wiring harness. Look for parameter values to change and/or a DTC to set. Review the DRBIII® Freeze Frame information. If possible, try to duplicate the conditions under which the DTC was set. Refer to any Technical Service Bulletins (TSB) that may apply. Visually inspect the related wiring harness. Look for any chafed, pierced, pinched, or partially broken wires. Visually inspect the related wiring harness connectors. Look for broken, bent, pushed out, or corroded terminals. Were any of the above conditions present? Yes → Repair as necessary Perform POWERTRAIN VERIFICATION TEST VER - 3. No → Test Complete.

CR1120100434030X

Fig. 13 Code P0562: Charging System Voltage Too Low (Part 3 of 3). 2002 Neon

TEST	ACTION
3	Start the engine. With the DRBIII®, manually set the engine speed to 1600 RPM. With DRBIII®, read both the Battery voltage and the Target Charging voltage. Compare the Target Charging Voltage to the Battery Voltage reading. Monitor voltage for 5 minutes, if necessary. Look for a 1.0 volt difference or more. Was there more than a 1.0 volt difference? Yes → Replace the Powertrain Control Module in accordance with the Service Information. Perform POWERTRAIN VERIFICATION TEST VER - 3. No → Go To 4
4	**WARNING: WHEN THE ENGINE IS OPERATING, DO NOT STAND IN A DIRECT LINE WITH THE FAN. DO NOT PUT YOUR HANDS NEAR THE PULLEYS, BELTS OR FAN. DO NOT WEAR LOOSE CLOTHING.** **NOTE: The conditions that set the DTC are not present at this time. The following list may help in identifying the intermittent condition.** With the engine running at normal operating temperature, monitor the DRBIII® parameters related to the DTC while wiggling the wiring harness. Look for parameter values to change and/or a DTC to set. Review the DRBIII® Freeze Frame information. If possible, try to duplicate the conditions under which the DTC was set. Refer to any Technical Service Bulletins (TSB) that may apply. Visually inspect the related wiring harness. Look for any chafed, pierced, pinched, or partially broken wires. Visually inspect the related wiring harness connectors. Look for broken, bent, pushed out, or corroded terminals. Were any of the above conditions present? Yes → Repair as necessary. Perform POWERTRAIN VERIFICATION TEST VER - 3. No → Test Complete.
5	Turn the ignition off. Disconnect the PCM harness connector. Disconnect the Generator Field harness connector. Measure the resistance of the Generator Field Driver circuit from the PCM harness connector to ground. Is the resistance below 5.0 ohms? Yes → Repair the Generator Field Driver circuit shorted to ground. Perform POWERTRAIN VERIFICATION TEST VER - 3. No → Go To 6
6	Turn the ignition off. Disconnect the Generator Field harness connector. Measure resistance of the Generator Field Driver terminal pin to ground. Is the resistance below 5.0 ohms? Yes → Repair or replace the shorted Generator as necessary. Perform POWERTRAIN VERIFICATION TEST VER - 3. No → Replace and program the Powertrain Control Module in accordance with the Service Information. Perform POWERTRAIN VERIFICATION TEST VER - 3.

CR1120100435020X

Fig. 14 Code P0563: Charging System Voltage Too High (Part 2 of 2). 2002 Neon

When Monitored: With the ignition on. Engine running.

Set Condition: When the PCM tries to regulate the generator field with no result during monitoring.

POSSIBLE CAUSES
WIRING HARNESS INTERMITTENT
INSPECT WIRING HARNESS
ASD RELAY OUTPUT CIRCUIT OPEN
GENERATOR FIELD DRIVER CIRCUIT SHORTED TO GROUND
GENERATOR FIELD DRIVER CIRCUIT OPEN
GENERATOR FIELD COIL OPEN
GENERATOR FIELD COIL SHORTED
POWERTRAIN CONTROL MODULE

TEST	ACTION
1	Turn the ignition on. With the DRBIII®, actuate the Generator Field Driver circuit. Using a 12-volt test light connected to ground, backprobe the Generator Field Driver circuit in the back of the Generator. Does the test light illuminate brightly and flash? Yes → Go To 2 No → Go To 4
2	Turn the ignition on. With the DRBIII® actuate the Generator Field Driver circuit. Wiggle the wiring harness from the Generator to PCM. With the DRBIII®, read DTC's. Did the DTC reset? Yes → Repair as necessary. Perform POWERTRAIN VERIFICATION TEST VER - 3. No → Go To 3
3	Turn the ignition off. Using the schematic as a guide, inspect the Wiring and Connectors. Were any problems found? Yes → Repair as necessary. Perform POWERTRAIN VERIFICATION TEST VER - 3. No → Test Complete.

CR1120100436010X

Fig. 15 Code P0622: Generator Field Not Switching Properly (Part 1 of 2). 2002 Neon

TEST	ACTION
4	**NOTE: Carefully inspect all Connectors for corrosion or spread Terminals before continuing.** Disconnect the Generator Field harness connector. Turn the ignition on. With the DRBIII® actuate the Generator Field Driver circuit. Using a 12-volt test light connected to ground, probe the ASD Relay Output circuit. Does the test light illuminate brightly? Yes → Go To 5 No → Repair the ASD Relay Output circuit. Perform POWERTRAIN VERIFICATION TEST VER - 3.
5	Turn the ignition off. Disconnect the PCM harness connector. Disconnect the Generator Field harness connector. Measure the resistance of the Generator Field Driver circuit from PCM harness connector to ground. Is the resistance below 100 ohms? Yes → Repair the Generator Field Driver circuit for a shorted to ground. Perform POWERTRAIN VERIFICATION TEST VER - 3. No → Go To 6
6	Turn the ignition off. Disconnect the PCM harness connector. Disconnect the Generator Field harness connector. Measure the resistance of the Generator Field Driver circuit from the PCM harness connector to the Generator Field harness connector. Is the resistance below 5.0 ohms? Yes → Go To 7 No → Repair the Generator Field Driver circuit for an open. Perform POWERTRAIN VERIFICATION TEST VER - 3.
7	Turn the ignition off. Disconnect the Generator Field harness connector. Measure the resistance across the Generator Field Terminals at the Generator. Is the resistance above 15.0 ohms? Yes → Replace the Generator. Perform POWERTRAIN VERIFICATION TEST VER - 3. No → Go To 8
8	Turn the ignition off. Disconnect the Generator Field harness connector. Measure the resistance across the Generator Field Terminals at the Generator. Is the resistance below 0.5 ohms? Yes → Replace the Generator. Perform POWERTRAIN VERIFICATION TEST VER - 3. No → Go To 9
9	If there is no more possible causes remaining, view repair. Repair Replace and program the Powertrain Control Module in accordance with the Service Information. Perform POWERTRAIN VERIFICATION TEST VER - 3.

CR1120100436020X

Fig. 15 Code P0622: Generator Field Not Switching properly (Part 2 of 2). 2002 Neon

When Monitored: With the engine running for more than 25 seconds.

Set Condition: When the Generator Field Circuit is open or shorted to ground.

POSSIBLE CAUSES
WIRING HARNESS INTERMITTENT
GENERATOR FIELD DRIVER CIRCUIT SHORTED TO GROUND
GENERATOR FIELD
GENERATOR FIELD DRIVER CIRCUIT OPEN
GENERATOR FIELD COIL OPEN
POWERTRAIN CONTROL MODULE

TEST	ACTION
1	**NOTE: Verify that the battery is capable of passing a load test and is fully charged before continuing.** Turn the ignition on. With the DRBIII®, actuate the Generator Field Driver circuit. Using a 12-volt test light connected to ground, backprobe the Generator Field Driver circuit in the back of the Generator. Does the test light illuminate brightly and flash? Yes → Go To 2 No → Go To 3
2	Turn the ignition off. Using a schematic as a guide, inspect the related Wiring and Connectors. Turn the ignition on, engine not running. With the DRBIII® actuate the Generator Field Driver circuit. Wiggle the wiring harness from the Generator to PCM. With the DRBIII®, read DTC's. Did the DTC reset? Yes → Repair as necessary. Perform POWERTRAIN VERIFICATION TEST VER - 3. No → Test Complete.

CR1120100437010X

Fig. 16 Code P0625: Generator Field Control Circuit Low (Part 1 of 2). 2002 Neon

TEST	ACTION
3	Turn the ignition off. Disconnect the PCM harness connector. Disconnect the Generator Field harness connector. Measure the resistance of the Generator Field Driver circuit from PCM harness connector to ground. Is the resistance below 5.0 ohms? Yes → Repair the Generator Field Driver circuit for a shorted to ground. Perform POWERTRAIN VERIFICATION TEST VER - 3. No → Go To 4
4	Turn the ignition off. Disconnect the Generator Field harness connector. Measure resistance of the Generator Field Driver terminal on the Generator to ground. Is the resistance below 5.0 ohms? Yes → Repair or replace the shorted Generator as necessary. Perform POWERTRAIN VERIFICATION TEST VER - 3. No → Go To 5
5	Turn the ignition off. Disconnect the PCM harness connector. Disconnect the Generator Field harness connector. Measure the resistance of the Generator Field Driver circuit from the PCM harness connector to the Generator Field harness connector. Is the resistance below 5.0 ohms? Yes → Go To 6 No → Repair the Generator Field Driver circuit for an open. Perform POWERTRAIN VERIFICATION TEST VER - 3.
6	Turn the ignition off. Disconnect the Generator Field harness connector. Measure the resistance across the Generator Field Terminals at the Generator. Is the resistance above 15.0 ohms? Yes → Replace the Generator. Perform POWERTRAIN VERIFICATION TEST VER - 3. No → Go To 7
7	If there is no more possible causes remaining, view repair. Repair Replace and program the Powertrain Control Module in accordance with the Service Information. Perform POWERTRAIN VERIFICATION TEST VER - 3.

CR1120100437020X

Fig. 16 Code P0625: Generator Field Control Circuit Low (Part 2 of 2). 2002 Neon

When Monitored: With the engine running for more than 25 seconds.

Set Condition: When the Generator Field circuit is shorted to B+.

POSSIBLE CAUSES
WIRING HARNESS INTERMITTENT
GENERATOR FIELD CKT SHORT TO VOLTAGE
POWERTRAIN CONTROL MODULE

TEST	ACTION
1	**NOTE: Verify that the battery is capable of passing a load test and is fully charged before continuing.** Turn the ignition on. With the DRBIII®, actuate the Generator Field Driver circuit. Using a 12-volt test light connected to ground, backprobe the Generator Field Driver circuit in the back of the Generator. Does the test light illuminate brightly and flash? Yes → Go To 2 No → Go To 3
2	Turn the ignition off. Using a schematic as a guide, inspect the related Wiring and Connectors. Turn the ignition on, engine not running. With the DRBIII® actuate the Generator Field Driver circuit. Wiggle the wiring harness from the Generator to PCM. With the DRBIII®, read DTC's. Did the DTC reset? Yes → Repair as necessary. Perform POWERTRAIN VERIFICATION TEST VER - 3. No → Test Complete.
3	Turn the ignition off. Disconnect PCM harness connector. Using a 12-volt test light connect to Ground (B-), backprobe the Generator Field circuit at the PCM harness connector. Does the test light illuminate brightly? Yes → Repair the Generator Field Driver circuit short to B+. Perform POWERTRAIN VERIFICATION TEST VER - 3. No → Replace and program the Powertrain Control Module in accordance with the Service Manual. Perform POWERTRAIN VERIFICATION TEST VER - 3.

CR1120100438000X

Fig. 17 Code P0626: Generator Field Control High. 2002 Neon

When Monitored: The engine running. The engine speed greater than 380 RPM.

Set Condition: Battery voltage is 1 volt greater than desired system voltage.

POSSIBLE CAUSES
TARGET VOLTAGE DIFFERS FROM BATTERY VOLTAGE
INTERMITTENT CONDITION
GENERATOR FIELD DRIVER CIRCUIT SHORTED TO GROUND
GENERATOR FIELD
POWERTRAIN CONTROL MODULE

TEST	ACTION
1	**Note: Battery must be fully charged.** **Note: Generator Belt tension and condition must be checked before continuing.** Turn the ignition on. With DRBIII®, actuate the Generator Field Driver. With a 12-volt test light connected to ground, backprobe the Generator Field Driver circuit in the back of Generator Field harness connector. Does the test light illuminate brightly and flash? Yes → Go To 2 No → Go To 5
2	With DRBIII®, stop all actuation. Turn the ignition on. With DRBIII®, read the Target Charging voltage. Is the Target Charging voltage above 13.0 volts? Yes → Go To 3 No → Go To 4
3	Start the engine. With the DRBIII®, manually set the engine speed to 1600 RPM. With DRBIII®, read both the Battery voltage and the Target Charging voltage. Compare the Target Charging Voltage to the Battery Voltage reading. Monitor voltage for 5 minutes, if necessary. Look for a 1.0 volt difference or more. Was there more than a 1.0 volt difference? Yes → Replace the Powertrain Control Module in accordance with the Service Information. Perform POWERTRAIN VERIFICATION TEST VER - 3. No → Go To 4

CR1120100439010X

Fig. 18 Code P1594: Charging System Voltage Too High. (Part 1 of 2). 2002 Neon

TEST	ACTION
4	**WARNING: WHEN THE ENGINE IS OPERATING, DO NOT STAND IN A DIRECT LINE WITH THE FAN. DO NOT PUT YOUR HANDS NEAR THE PULLEYS, BELTS OR FAN. DO NOT WEAR LOOSE CLOTHING.** **NOTE: The conditions that set the DTC are not present at this time. The following list may help in identifying the intermittent condition.** With the engine running at normal operating temperature, monitor the DRBIII® parameters related to the DTC while wiggling the wiring harness. Look for parameter values to change and/or a DTC to set. Review the DRBIII® Freeze Frame information. If possible, try to duplicate the conditions under which the DTC was set. Refer to any Technical Service Bulletins (TSB) that may apply. Visually inspect the related wiring harness. Look for any chafed, pierced, pinched, or partially broken wires. Visually inspect the related wiring harness connectors. Look for broken, bent, pushed out, or corroded terminals. Were any of the above conditions present? Yes → Repair as necessary. Perform POWERTRAIN VERIFICATION TEST VER - 3. No → Test Complete.
5	Turn the ignition off. Disconnect the PCM harness connector. Disconnect the Generator Field harness connector. Measure the resistance of the Generator Field Driver circuit from the PCM harness connector to ground. Is the resistance below 5.0 ohms? Yes → Repair the Generator Field Driver circuit shorted to ground. Perform POWERTRAIN VERIFICATION TEST VER - 3. No → Go To 6
6	Turn the ignition off. Disconnect the Generator Field harness connector. Measure resistance of the Generator Field Driver terminal pin to ground. Is the resistance below 5.0 ohms? Yes → Repair or replace the shorted Generator as necessary. Perform POWERTRAIN VERIFICATION TEST VER - 3. No → Replace and program the Powertrain Control Module in accordance with the Service Information. Perform POWERTRAIN VERIFICATION TEST VER - 3.

CR1120100439020X

Fig. 18 Code P1594: Charging System Voltage Too High. (Part 2 of 2). 2002

When Monitored: With the ignition on. Engine RPM greater than 1152 RPM. With no other charging system codes set.

Set Condition: The battery sensed voltage is 1 volt below the charging goal for 13.47 seconds. The PCM senses the battery voltage, then turns off the field driver, and then senses the battery voltage again. If the voltages are the same, the code is set.

POSSIBLE CAUSES
B+ CIRCUIT HIGH RESISTANCE
GENERATOR GROUND HIGH RESISTANCE
INTERMITTENT CONDITION
GENERATOR FIELD DRIVER CIRCUIT OPEN
ASD RELAY OUTPUT CIRCUIT OPEN
GENERATOR

TEST	ACTION
1	**NOTE: Inspect the vehicle for aftermarket accessories that may exceed the Generator System output.** Turn the ignition off. **NOTE: The battery must be fully charged.** **NOTE: The Generator belt tension and condition must be checked before continuing.** Start the engine. Allow the idle to stabilize. With the DRBIII®, read the Target Charging Voltage. Is the Target Charging Voltage above 15.1 volts? Yes → Go To 7 No → Go To 2
2	**WARNING: WHEN THE ENGINE IS OPERATING, DO NOT STAND IN A DIRECT LINE WITH THE FAN. DO NOT PUT YOUR HANDS NEAR THE PULLEYS, BELTS OR FAN. DO NOT WEAR LOOSE CLOTHING.** Turn the ignition on. **NOTE: Ensure all wires are clear of the engine's moving parts.** Measure the voltage between the Generator B+ Terminal and the Battery+ Post. Start the engine. Is the voltage above 0.4 volt? Yes → Repair the B+ circuit for high resistance between the Generator and Battery. Perform POWERTRAIN VERIFICATION TEST VER - 3. No → Go To 3

CR1120100440010X

Fig. 19 Code P1682: Charging System Voltage Too Low (Part 1 of 3). 2002 Neon

TEST	ACTION
3	**WARNING: WHEN THE ENGINE IS OPERATING, DO NOT STAND IN A DIRECT LINE WITH THE FAN. DO NOT PUT YOUR HANDS NEAR THE PULLEYS, BELTS OR FAN. DO NOT WEAR LOOSE CLOTHING.** Start the engine. Warm the engine to operating temperature. **NOTE: Ensure all wires are clear of the engine's moving parts.** Measure the voltage between the Generator case and Battery ground post. Is the voltage above 0.1 volt? Yes → Repair Generator Ground for high resistance, Generator Case to Battery ground side. Perform POWERTRAIN VERIFICATION TEST VER - 3. No → Go To 4
4	Start the engine. **WARNING: WHEN THE ENGINE IS OPERATING, DO NOT STAND IN A DIRECT LINE WITH THE FAN. DO NOT PUT YOUR HANDS NEAR THE PULLEYS, BELTS OR FAN. DO NOT WEAR LOOSE CLOTHING.** Turn on all accessories, manually set engine speed to 1600 RPM. With DRBIII®, read Target Charging and Charging voltage. Compare the two readings. Is there more than a 1.0 volt difference? Yes → Go To 5 No → Go To 7
5	Turn the ignition off. Disconnect the PCM harness connector. Disconnect the Generator Field harness connector. Measure the resistance of the Generator Field Driver circuit from the PCM harness connector to Generator harness connector. Is the resistance below 5.0 ohms? Yes → Go To 6 No → Repair the Generator Field Driver circuit for an open. Perform POWERTRAIN VERIFICATION TEST VER - 3.
6	Disconnect the Generator Field harness connector. Turn the ignition on. With the DRBIII® actuate the Generator Field Driver. Using a 12-volt test light connected to ground, probe the ASD Relay Output circuit in the Generator harness connector. Does the test light illuminate brightly? Yes → Repair or replace the Generator as necessary. Perform POWERTRAIN VERIFICATION TEST VER - 3. No → Repair the ASD Relay Output circuit. Perform POWERTRAIN VERIFICATION TEST VER - 3.

CR1120100440020X

Fig. 19 Code P1682: Charging System Voltage Too Low (Part 2 of 3). 2002 Neon

POWERTRAIN VERIFICATION TEST VER - 3
1. NOTE: If the PCM has been replaced and the correct VIN and mileage have not been programmed, a DTC will be set in the ABS Module, Airbag Module and the SKIM. **2. NOTE: If the vehicle is equipped with a Sentry Key Immobilizer System, Secret Key data must be updated. Refer to the Service Information for the PCM, SKIM and the Transponder (ignition key) for programming information.** 3. Inspect the vehicle to ensure that all components related to the repair are connected properly. 4. With the DRBIII®, clear DTCs. 5. Perform generator output test. Refer to the appropriate service information as necessary. 6. Start the engine and set engine speed to 2000 RPM for at least thirty seconds. 7. Cycle the ignition key off and on. 8. With the DRBIII®, read the DTCs. If the DTC returns, or any other symptom or DTC is present, refer to the appropriate category and perform the corresponding symptom. 9. If there are no DTCs present and all components are functioning properly, the repair is complete. Are any DTCs present? Yes → Repair is not complete, refer to appropriate symptom. No → Repair is complete.

CR1120100442000X

Fig. 20 Verification Test VER-3. 2002 Neon

TEST	ACTION
7	**WARNING: WHEN THE ENGINE IS OPERATING, DO NOT STAND IN A DIRECT LINE WITH THE FAN. DO NOT PUT YOUR HANDS NEAR THE PULLEYS, BELTS OR FAN. DO NOT WEAR LOOSE CLOTHING.** **NOTE: The conditions that set the DTC are not present at this time. The following list may help in identifying the intermittent condition.** With the engine running at normal operating temperature, monitor the DRBIII® parameters related to the DTC while wiggling the wiring harness. Look for parameter values to change and/or a DTC to set. Review the DRBIII® Freeze Frame information. If possible, try to duplicate the conditions under which the DTC was set. Refer to any Technical Service Bulletins (TSB) that may apply. Visually inspect the related wiring harness. Look for any chafed, pierced, pinched, or partially broken wires. Visually inspect the related wiring harness connectors. Look for broken, bent, pushed out, or corroded terminals. Were any of the above conditions present? Yes → Repair as necessary Perform POWERTRAIN VERIFICATION TEST VER - 3. No → Test Complete.

CR1120100440030X

Fig. 19 Code P1682: Charging System Voltage Too Low (Part 3 of 3). 2002 Neon

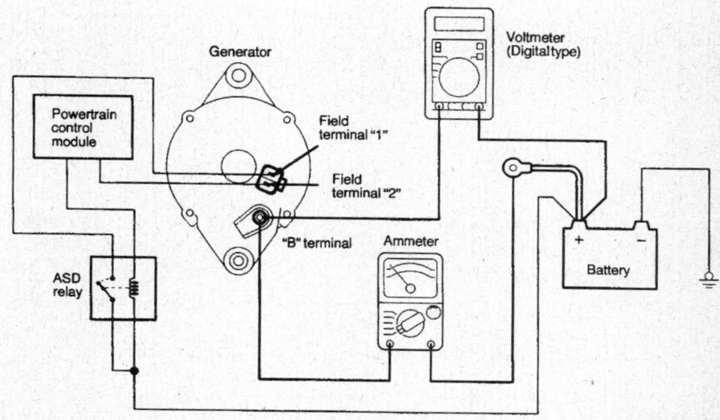

Fig. 21 Alternator output wire voltage drop test connection. Talon less turbocharged engine, Avenger & 1998–2000 Sebring Coupe

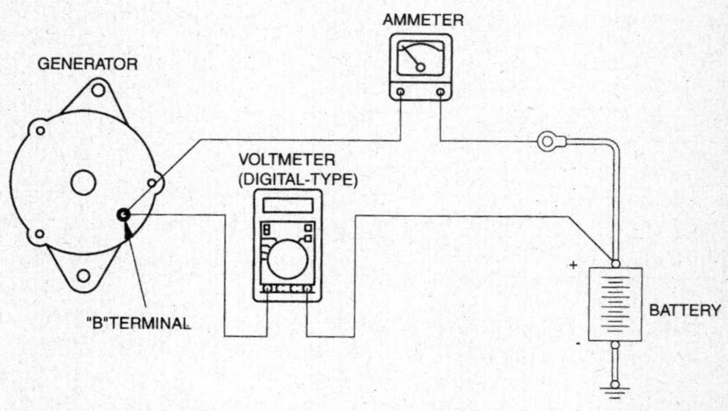

Fig. 22 Alternator output wire voltage drop test connection. Talon w/turbocharged engine & 2001–02 models

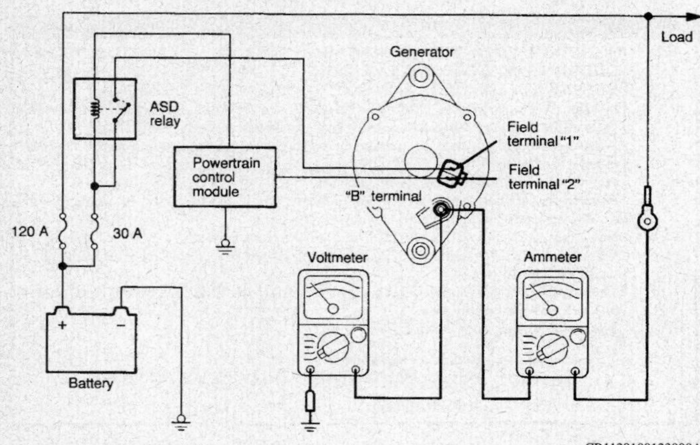

Fig. 23 Alternator output test connection. Talon less turbocharged engine, Avenger & 1998–2000 Sebring Coupe

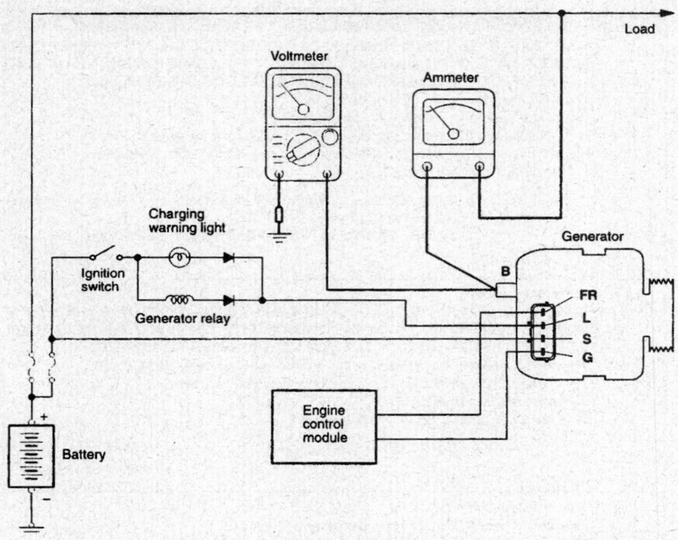

Fig. 24 Alternator output test connection. Talon w/turbocharged engine

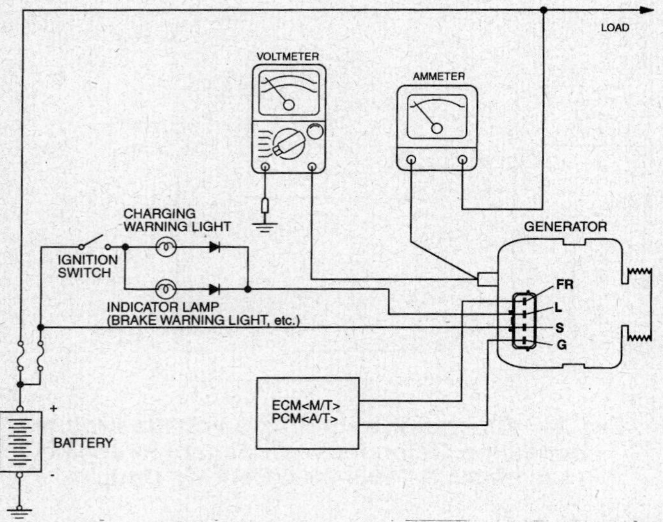

Fig. 25 Alternator output test connection. 2001–02

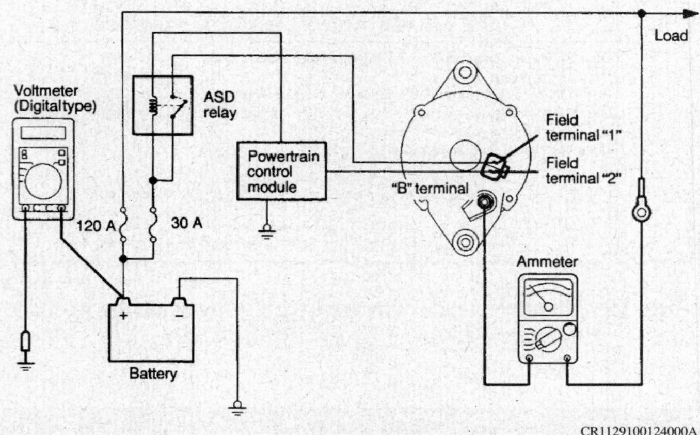

Fig. 26 Voltage regulator test connections. Talon less turbocharged engine, Avenger & 1998–2000 Sebring Coupe

Battery ambient temperature °C (°F)	Standard value V
–20 (–4)	14.07 – 15.07
0 (32)	13.89 – 14.89
20 (68)	13.58 – 14.58
40 (104)	13.15 – 14.15
62 (143.6)	12.84 – 13.84

CR1129900261000X

Fig. 27 Regulated voltage specifications. Talon less turbocharged engine, Avenger & 1998–2000 Sebring Coupe

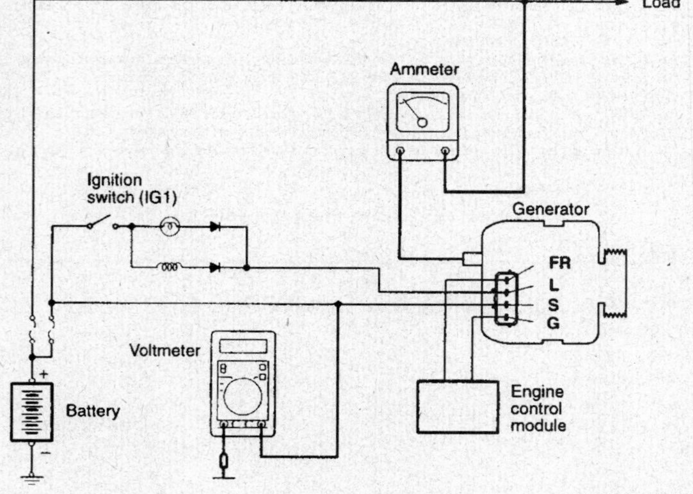

Fig. 28 Voltage regulator test connections. Talon w/turbocharged engine

Battery ambient temperature °C (°F)	Standard value V
–20 (–4)	14.2–15.4
20 (68)	13.9–14.9
60 (140)	13.4–14.6
80 (176)	13.1–14.5

CR1129800264000X

Fig. 29 Regulated voltage specifications. Talon less turbocharged engine, Avenger & 1998–2000 Sebring Coupe

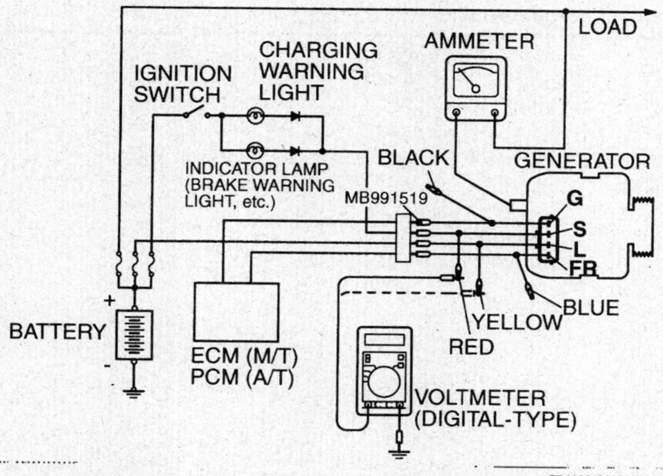

CR1120100391000X

Fig. 30 Voltage regulator test connections. 2001–02

INSPECTION TERMINAL	VOLTAGE REGULATOR AMBIENT TEMPERATURE [°C(°F)]	STANDARD VALUE (V)
Terminal "S"	-20 (-4)	14.2 - 15.4
	20 (68)	13.9 - 14.9
	60 (140)	13.4 - 14.5
	80 (176)	13.1 - 14.5

CR1120100392000X

Fig. 31 Regulated voltage specifications. 2001–02

ALTERNATOR SPECIFICATIONS

Model	Engine	Type	Rated Output Amps
Neon	2.0L	Mitsubishi	85
Sebring Coupe & Stratus Coupe	2.4L	Mitsubishi	95
	3.0L	Mitsubishi	85
Talon	2.0L①	Mitsubishi	75
	2.0L②	Mitsubishi	90

① — Turbocharged engine.
② — Less turbocharged engine.

STEERING COLUMNS

NOTE: On Air Bag Equipped Models, Refer To "Air Bag System Precautions" Located In The Front Of This Manual For System Disarming & Arming Procedures.

NOTE: Refer To "Computer Relearn Procedures" Located In The Front Of This Manual When Battery Power To The Computer Has Been Interrupted.

NOTE: Prior To Performing Any Service Operations Listed In This Section, Consult The "Technical Service Bulletins" Section For Related Information.

INDEX

PRECAUTIONS

AIR BAG SYSTEMS

Refer to "Air Bag System Precautions" in the front of this manual for system disarming and arming procedures.

BATTERY GROUND CABLE

Prior to service, disconnect battery ground cable and isolate as required.

COLUMN SERVICE

When servicing collapsible steering columns, care should be exercised since they are extremely susceptible to damage. Dropping of or leaning on column or striking sharp blows on end of steering shaft or shift levers could loosen or shear plastic fasteners which maintain column rigidity.

It is important only the specified screws, bolts and nuts be used during the assembly sequence and tightened to specifications to ensure proper breakaway action of column under impact. Avoid using excessively long bolts, as they may prevent a portion of the steering column from collapsing under impact.

If there is evidence of a sheared plastic shift tube injection, a new shift tube must be installed. If plastic injections are sheared but steering shaft is not bent, repairs may be possible using a service steering shaft repair kit containing instructions and dimensions for all steering columns. On some models, the mounting brackets will shear under impact and must also be replaced.

STEERING COLUMN

REPLACE

AVENGER & TALON & 1998–2000 SEBRING COUPE

Refer to **Fig. 1,** for steering column replacement. Remove steering wheel using puller tool No. MB-990803, or equivalent.

BREEZE & CIRRUS & 1998–2000 SEBRING CONVERTIBLE & STRATUS

1. Place front wheels in straight ahead position.
2. Remove lefthand end of instrument panel fuse panel cover and instrument panel cover mounting screw behind fuse panel.
3. Remove center bezel and instrument panel top cover.
4. Remove knee bolster.
5. Remove steering wheel speed control switches, then disconnect clockspring and horn ground wire.
6. Remove air bag module mounting bolts.
7. Disconnect clockspring electrical connection.
8. Remove steering wheel mounting nut and steering wheel using puller tool No. C-J2001-P, or equivalent.
9. Remove steering column upper shroud, tilt column to its highest position and remove lower shroud, **Fig. 2.**
10. Remove lockspring, halo light and ignition switch wiring harness connectors.
11. **On models equipped with automatic transmission,** place key cylinder in Off position and remove shifter/ignition interlock cable from key lock housing.
12. **On all models,** remove pinch bolt and separate steering coupler from steering gear.
13. Ensure steering column tilt lever is in locked position and insert 7/32 drill bit in each locking pin hole on upper steering column bracket.
14. Remove upper and lower steering column support bracket mounting nuts.
15. Remove steering column.
16. Reverse procedure to install, noting the following:
    a. Depress clockspring locking pins to disengage clockspring locking mechanism.
    b. Rotate clockspring fully clockwise until it does not turn. **Do not over tighten.**
    c. Rotate clockspring counterclockwise until yellow appears in clockspring centering window.
    d. Engage clockspring locking mechanism.

2001–02 SEBRING & STRATUS COUPE

Removal

1. **Wait at least 60 seconds after disconnecting battery ground cable before doing any work.**
2. Remove mounting screws and air bag module, **Fig. 3. Do not remove screws from holder.**
3. Disconnect air bag module clockspring connect by pressing lock toward outer

side using suitable flat-tipped screwdriver.

4. Remove mounting nut and steering wheel using puller tool No. MB-990803, or equivalent. **Do not hammer.**
5. Remove mounting screws and instrument panel under cover.
6. Remove mounting bolts, then the lower and upper column covers.
7. Remove mounting screws and clockspring
8. Remove mounting bolts and column switch.
9. **On models equipped with automatic transaxle,** remove cover and disconnect key interlock cable.
10. **On all models,** Remove mounting and pinch bolts, then the steering column.
11. Remove mounting bolt and steering cover.

Installation

1. Install steering cover securely in steering gear box groove. Ensure clearance is zero–.02 inch.
2. **Torque** steering cover mounting bolts to 36–52 inch lbs.
3. Install steering column. **Torque** pinch bolt to 12–14 ft. lbs. and mounting bolts to 78–122 inch lbs.
4. **On models equipped with automatic transaxle,** connect key interlock cable and install cover.
5. **On all models,** install column switch and **torque** mounting bolts to 14–22 ft. lbs.
6. Ensure front wheels are in straight ahead position.
7. Install clockspring.
8. Turn clockspring fully clockwise, then back approximately three counterclockwise turns to align mating marks.
9. Install upper and lower steering column covers.
10. Install instrument panel under cover.
11. Install steering wheel. **Ensure clockspring harness is not caught or tangled.**
12. **Torque** steering wheel mounting nut to 26–36 ft. lbs.
13. Turn steering all the way in both directions.
14. Connect clockspring air bag module connector.
15. Install air bag module. **Torque** mounting bolts to 61–95 inch lbs.

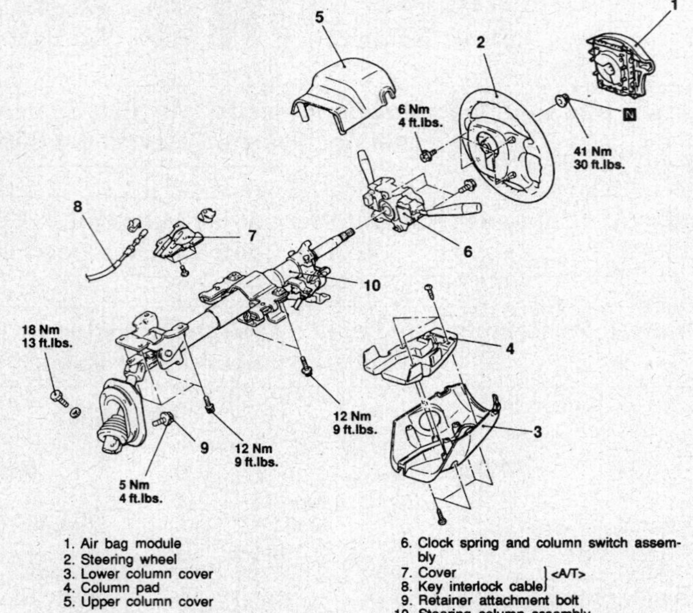

Fig. 1 Steering column replacement. Avenger & Talon & 1998–2000 Sebring Coupe

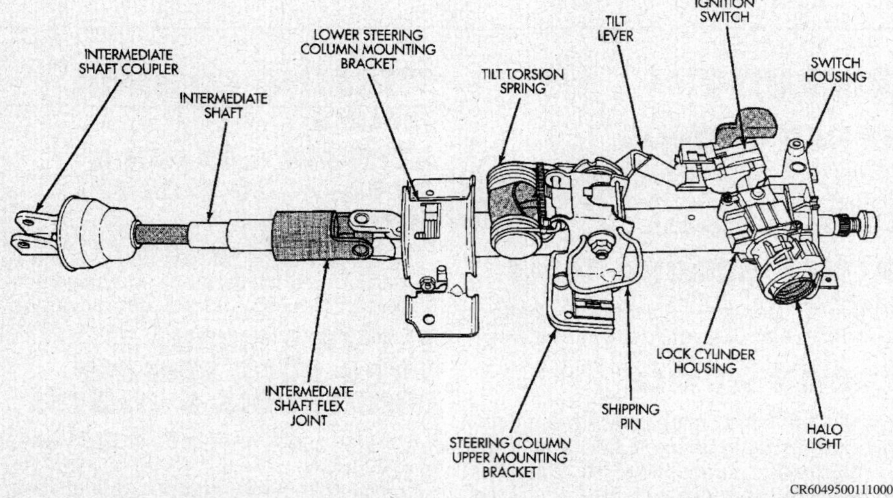

Fig. 2 Steering column replacement. Breeze & Cirrus & 1998–2000 Sebring Convertible & Stratus

2001–02 SEBRING CONVERTIBLE/SEDAN & STRATUS SEDAN

1. **Wait at least two minutes after disconnecting battery ground cable before doing any work.**
2. Place wheels in straight ahead position.
3. Remove fuse panel cover, then the instrument panel top cover attaching screws.
4. Remove radio bezel and climate control panel from top cover of instrument panel.
5. Remove instrument panel attaching screws from rear of climate control panel.
6. Remove knee bolster, then cruise control switches from steering wheel.
7. Remove air bag, then disconnect electrical connector from module, **Fig. 4.**
8. Remove steering wheel using a suitable steering wheel puller.
9. Remove upper shroud by pressing inward on upper shroud while pulling apart upper and lower shrouds.
10. Place column tilt in highest position, then remove lower shroud.
11. Remove electrical connectors from clockspring, ignition switch and multifunction switch.
12. **On models equipped with automatic transmissions,** proceed as follows:
    a. Place key cylinder in Off position.
    b. Depress locking tab on shifter/ignition interlock cable, **Fig. 5.** Remove cable from key lock housing.
13. **On all models,** remove wiring harness from steering column and place aside.
14. Remove pinch bolt from intermediate shaft **Fig. 6**, then slide shaft up and off steering gear.
15. Remove steering column attaching nuts and bolts, then column from vehicle.
16. Reverse procedure to install, noting the following:
    a. **Torque** steering column mounting brackets nuts and bolts to 150 inch lbs.
    b. **Torque** intermediate shaft coupler pinch bolt to 32 ft. lbs.

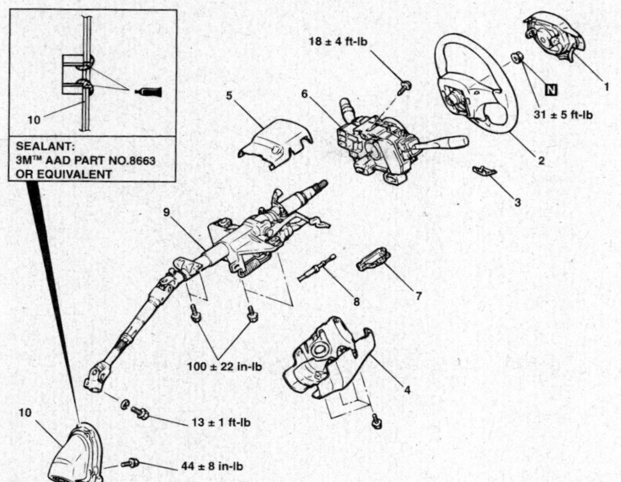

Fig. 3 Steering column replacement. 2001–02 Sebring & Stratus Coupe

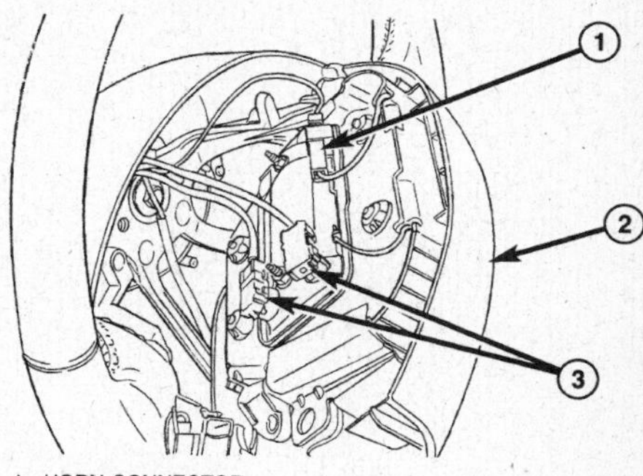

Fig. 4 Air bag electrical connector. 2001–02 Sebring Convertible/Sedan & Stratus Sedan

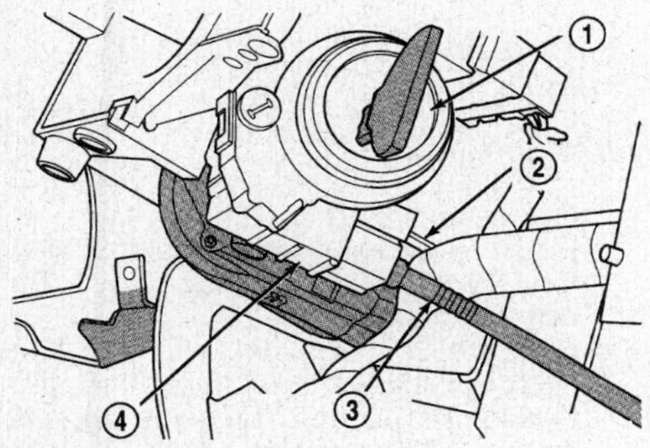

Fig. 5 Shifter/ignition interlock cable removal. 2001–02 Sebring Convertible/Sedan & Stratus Sedan

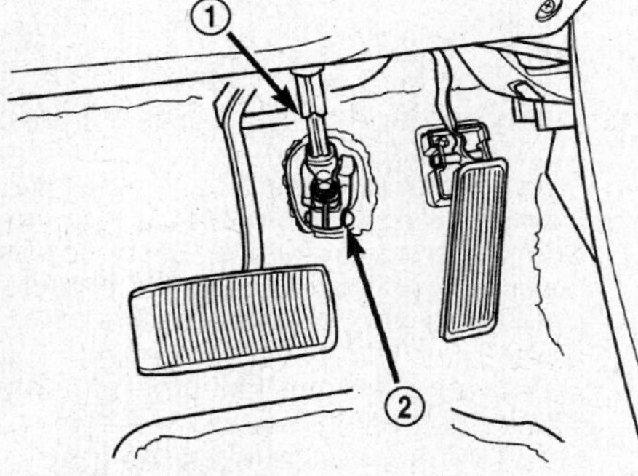

Fig. 6 Intermediate shaft pinch bolt removal. 2001–02 Sebring Convertible/Sedan & Stratus Sedan

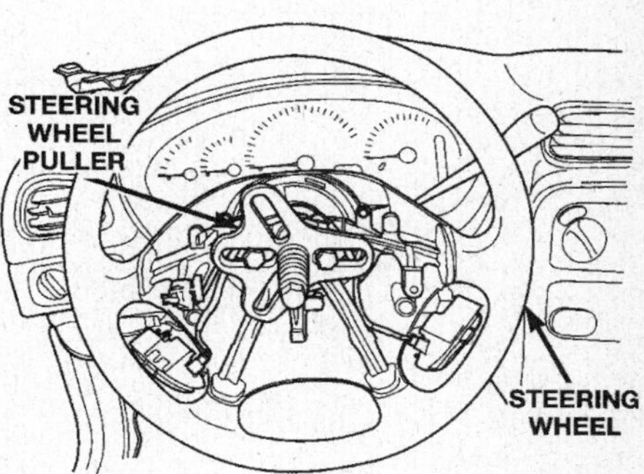

Fig. 7 Steering wheel removal. Concorde, Intrepid, LHS & 300M

c. Depress plastic locking pin to disengage clockspring mechanism. Rotate clockspring clockwise to end of travel.
d. Slowly rotate counterclockwise until yellow appears in centering window of clockspring and the drive pin on rotor will be in front of arrow on clockspring label. Engage clockspring.
e. **Torque** upper and lower shroud bolts to 17 inch lbs.
f. **Torque** steering wheel bolt to 40 ft. lbs.
g. **Torque** air bag module attaching screws to 17 inch lbs.
h. **Torque** cruise control switch attaching screws to 12 inch lbs.

CONCORDE, INTREPID, LHS & 300M

1. Remove instrument panel lefthand end fuse panel cover.
2. Remove lower instrument panel cover to instrument panel mounting bracket mounting screws from behind fuse panel cover.
3. Remove lower instrument panel cover.
4. Remove trunk release switch wiring harness connector.
5. Remove park release handle cable.
6. Remove mounting bolts and instrument panel reinforcement.
7. Remove diagnostic connector.
8. Ensure front wheels are in straight ahead position. If steering column is to be removed as one assembly, or without removing steering wheel, steering wheel must be turned to right 180° from straight ahead position and locked in place.
9. If removing steering wheel, proceed as follows:
   a. Remove steering wheel speed control switches.
   b. **Wait at least two minutes before starting to remove air bag.**
   c. Remove mounting bolts and air bag module.
   d. Disconnect lock and air bag electrical connector. **Do not twist connector lock when removing.**
   e. Disconnect clockspring horn switch wire.
   f. Remove steering wheel mounting nut.
   g. Remove steering wheel using suitable puller, **Fig. 7. Ensure puller bolts are fully seated in steering wheel threaded holes.**
10. Push in righthand seam between upper and lower shrouds.
11. When upper shroud unsnaps, pull upper shroud away from lower.
12. Remove steering column upper shroud by repeating previous steps on lefthand side..

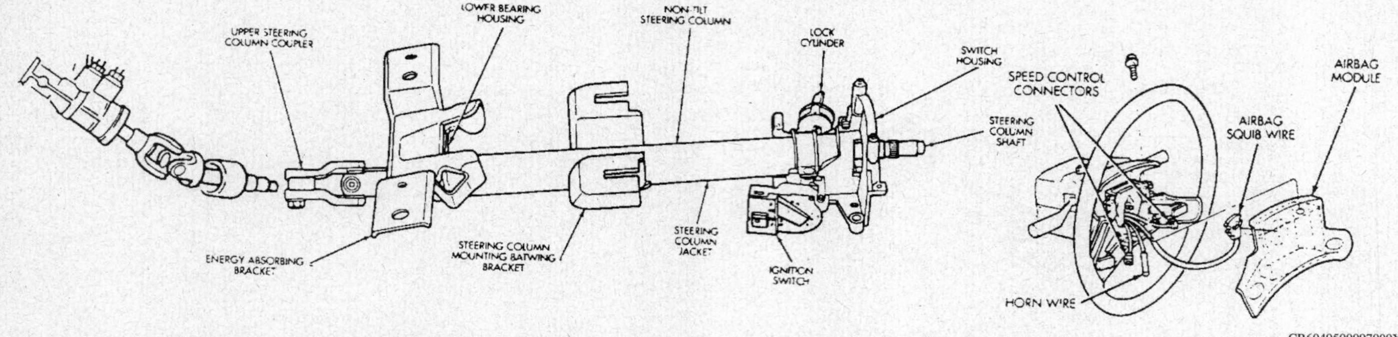

CR6049500097000X

Fig. 8 Steering column replacement. 1998–99 Neon w/standard column

CR6049500098000X

Fig. 9 Steering column replacement. 1998–99 Neon w/tilt column

13. Remove tilt lever.
14. Remove mounting screws and lower steering column shroud.
15. Remove clockspring wiring harness connectors.
16. Remove mounting screws and clockspring.
17. Disconnect module wire harness connector.
18. Remove retaining screw and unclip module from key cylinder halo bezel.
19. Disconnect multi-function switch wiring harness from routing clip.
20. Remove mounting screws and multi-function switch.
21. Remove mounting screws and ignition switch.
22. **On models equipped with floor mounted shifter,** depress lock tab and remove shifter/ignition interlock cable from key lock housing.
23. **On models equipped with steering column mounted shifter,** proceed as follows:
    a. Remove cable from shifter mechanism.
    b. Unlock cable lock, then remove shift cable by inserting suitable screwdriver between shift cable and shifter mechanism, and prying cable off pin.
24. **On all models,** remove mounting screws and cable mounting bracket.
25. Remove air ducts under steering column.
26. Remove retaining pin and steering column coupler pinch bolt.
27. Remove mounting bracket to support bracket mounting nuts and loosen steering column lower mounting bracket to support bracket mounting bolts.
28. Remove steering column support bracket by pulling rearward and out.
29. Reverse procedure to install, noting the following:
    a. **Torque** bracket to support bracket fasteners to 96 inch lbs.
    b. **Torque** coupler pinch bolt to 20 ft. lbs.
    c. **Torque** steering wheel mounting nut to 45 ft. lbs.
    d. **Torque** air bag module bolts to 96 inch lbs.

NEON

1998–99

1. Ensure front wheels are straight ahead.
2. Remove steering column cover trim panel and lower instrument panel cover liner, **Figs. 8 and 9.**
3. Remove steering wheel trim covers and speed control switches, as required.
4. Remove mounting bolts, lift air bag module and disconnect clockspring electrical connector, **Fig. 10.**
5. Disconnect horn switches clockspring electrical connectors, then remove steering wheel mounting nut and dampener weight.
6. Remove steering wheel using puller tool No. C-3428-B, or equivalent. **Do not use hammer.**
7. Place key lock cylinder in On position and depress lock cylinder retaining tab through tab access hole using suitable small screwdriver, **Fig. 11.**
8. Remove key lock cylinder and steering column lower shroud.
9. Tilt steering column to lowest position, remove upper shroud and slip retaining pin out of upper to lower column pinch bolt.
10. Remove pinch bolt nut, then separate upper and lower coupler shafts. **Pinch bolt cannot be removed from coupler assembly.**
11. Remove through bolt from lower steering column bearing housing and mounting bracket, then the upper steering column bracket bolts.
12. Lower steering column in instrument panel access opening, then disconnect wiring harness at wiper and multi-function switches, and disengage from clips.
13. Remove ignition switch and clockspring, wiring harness connectors.
14. Remove steering column.
15. Reverse procedure to install, noting the following:
    a. **Torque** upper steering column bracket to support bolts to 108 inch lbs.
    b. **Torque** pinch bolt nut to 21 ft. lbs.

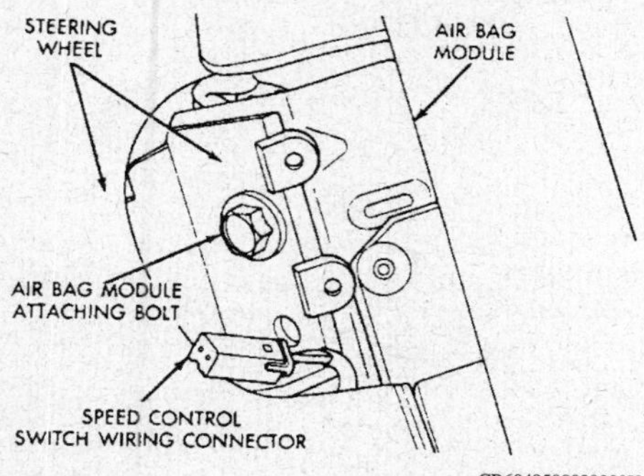

Fig. 10 Air bag module mounting bolt locations. 1998–99 Neon

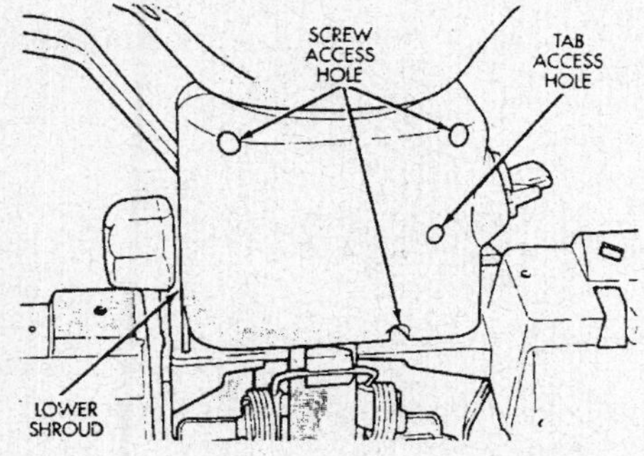

Fig. 11 Ignition key lock cylinder retaining tab access hole location. 1998–99 Neon

c. Ensure pinch bolt retaining pin is installed.
d. **Torque** steering wheel mounting nut to 45 ft. lbs.
e. **Torque** air bag mounting bolts to 84–96 inch lbs. **Use only original or correct replacement bolts when installing air bag module.**

2000–02

1. Ensure front wheels are in straight ahead position.
2. Remove screw to lefthand end of instrument panel above lefthand end cap.
3. Remove instrument panel top cover retaining clip from driver side and to access instrument panel.
4. Remove instrument cluster bezel.
5. Remove column covers screws and clips, then pull covers straight away from instrument panel.
6. Remove steering wheel speed control switches.
7. Remove steering wheel rear cover trim caps.
8. Remove air bag module mounting screws.
9. Disconnect clockspring and electrical connectors, then remove air bag module.
10. Remove mounting nut and steering wheel using suitable puller tool.
11. Remove ignition key from cylinder.
12. Remove upper and lower column shroud.

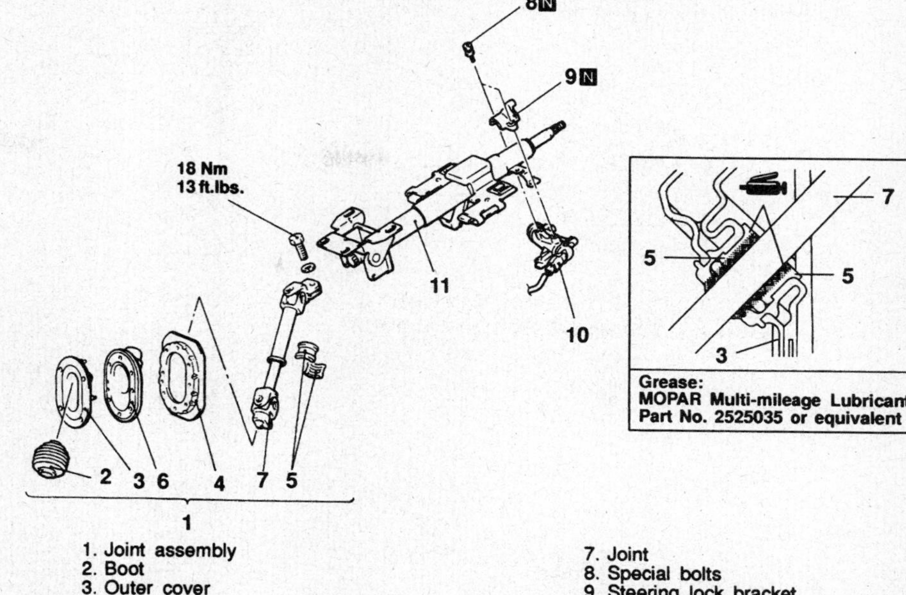

Fig. 12 Exploded view of steering column. Avenger & Talon & 1998–2000 Sebring Coupe

13. Remove steering column coupling retainer pin and coupling bolt, then separate upper and lower steering column couplings.
14. **On models equipped with automatic transaxle,** disconnect ignition interlock cable from steering column.
15. **On all models,** remove upper and lower steering column to instrument panel mounting nuts.
16. Lower steering column from instrument panel.
17. Disconnect clockspring, multi-function switch, windshield wiper switch and ignition switch wiring electrical connectors.
18. **On models equipped Sentry Key Immobilizer Module (SKIM),** disconnect electrical connector.
19. **On all models,** remove steering column.
20. When replacing steering column, remove the following:
    a. Ignition key cylinder.
    b. Clockspring.
    c. Multi-function switch.
    d. Ignition switch straight.
    e. **On models equipped with SKIM,** mounting screws and slide off non-halo ring.
21. **On all models,** reverse procedures to install noting the following:
    a. **Torque** mounting screws for SKIM to 24 inch lbs.
    b. **Torque** mounting nuts to instrument panel 13 ft. lbs.
    c. **Torque** coupler pinch bolt to 20 ft. lbs.
    d. **Torque** air bag module bolts to 90 inch lbs.

STEERING COLUMN SERVICE

AVENGER & TALON & 1998–2000 SEBRING COUPE

Refer to **Fig. 12** when servicing steering column.

Disassemble

Disassemble steering column in sequence, **Fig. 12,** noting the following:

1. Apply grease to inside lip of boot and remove boot while using suitable rod to widen lip of boot, **Fig. 13.**
2. Apply suitable grease to inside lip of inner cover and cover joint while using suitable rod to widen lip section, then widen inner cover from behind with suitable rod and pull cover to remove from joint, **Fig. 14.**
3. If steering lock cylinder is to be removed, cut special bolts at bracket side with hacksaw.

Inspection

1. Inspect steering shaft for play and round movement.
2. Inspect joints for play, damage, or rough movement.
3. Inspect joint bearing for wear and damage.
4. Inspect dust shield for damage.

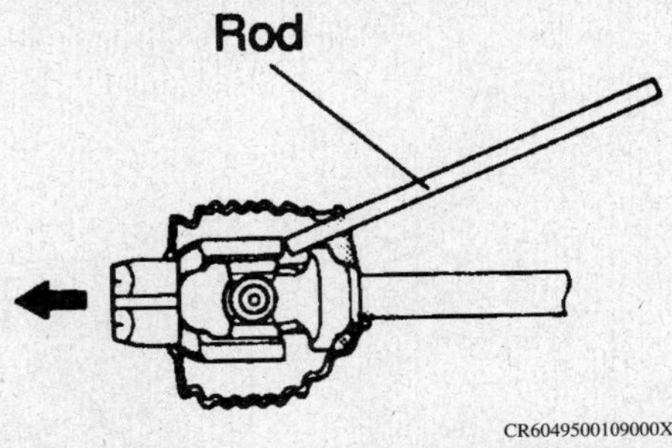

Fig. 13 Boot removal. Avenger & Talon & 1998–2000 Sebring Coupe

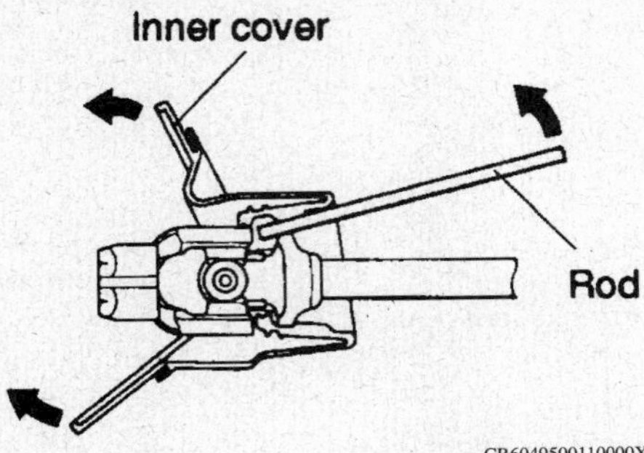

Fig. 14 Inner cover removal. Avenger & Talon & 1998–2000 Sebring Coupe

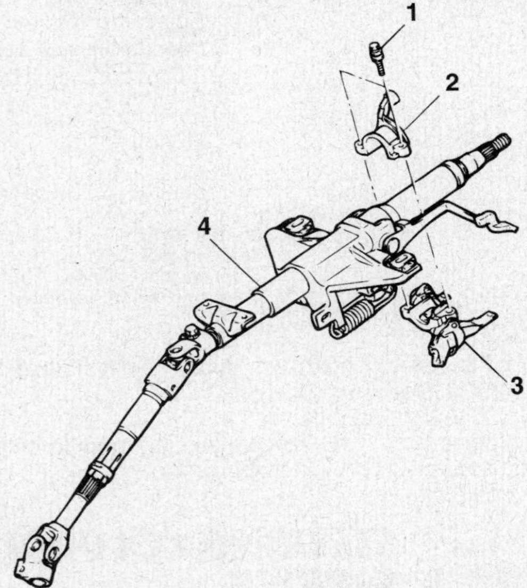

Fig. 15 Steering lock cylinder & bracket. 2001–02 Sebring & Stratus Coupe

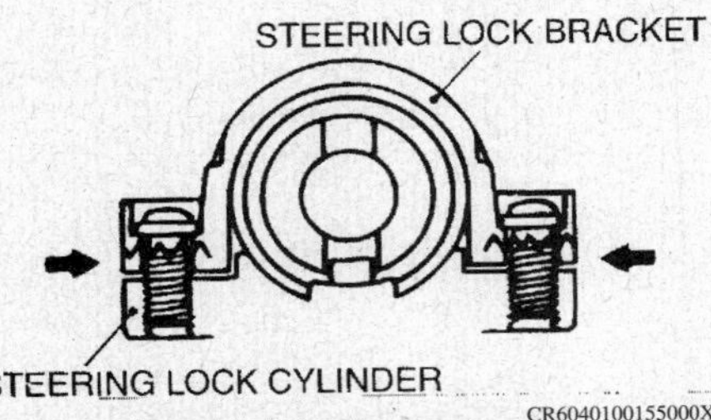

Fig. 16 Steering lock bracket bolt removal. 2001–02 Sebring & Stratus Coupe

Assemble

Disassemble steering column in reverse sequence, **Fig. 12,** noting the following:

1. When installing steering lock cylinder and steering lock bracket, temporarily install steering lock in alignment with column boss.
2. Ensuring steering lock operates correctly.
3. Tighten special bolts until heads twist off.
4. Cover inside lip of inner cover with suitable grease and pull outside of cover onto joint.
5. Fill inside of bearing with suitable multipurpose grease and install bearings to shaft on joint assembly.
6. Wrap vinyl tape 1½ times around concave circumferences of bearings, and press fit bearing into cover assembly.
7. Apply suitable grease to inside of lip section of boot and install boot to joint.

BREEZE & CIRRUS & 1998–2000 SEBRING CONVERTIBLE & STRATUS

The steering column used on this model, **Fig. 2,** has been designed to be serviced as an assembly except for wiring, switches, shrouds and the steering wheel. Most steering column components can be serviced without removing the column.

The only other serviceable component is the shaft coupler. If the coupler requires replacement because of a seized bearing, insufficient bearing staking or improper bearing seating, proceed as follows:

1. Remove steering column as previously described.
2. Install puller tool No. 6831-A, or equivalent, through center of roll pin in flex joint and install knurled nut.
3. Pry flex joint off of steering column shaft using suitable screw driver inserted between flex joint and steering column lower mounting bracket.
4. Reverse procedure to install.

2001–02 SEBRING & STRATUS COUPE

The steering column has been designed to be serviced as an assembly except for wiring, switches, shrouds and the steering wheel.

The only serviceable component is the steering lock cylinder, **Fig. 15.** To remove cylinder lock proceed as follows:

1. Using a hacksaw cut bolts at steering column lock bracket, **Fig. 16.** Discard old bolts.
2. Remove bracket and cylinder lock.
3. Install new steering lock cylinder in alignment with column boss. Do not completely tighten new twist off bolts.
4. Ensure lock is working properly. Tighten new bolts until head twists off.

2001–02 SEBRING CONVERTIBLE/SEDAN & STRATUS SEDAN

The steering column has been designed to be serviced as an assembly except for wiring, switches, key cylinder, shrouds and the steering wheel.

The only other serviceable component is the intermediate shaft. If the shaft requires replacement, proceed as follows:

1. Remove steering column as outlined under "Steering Column, Replace."
2. Remove roll pin from flex joint using

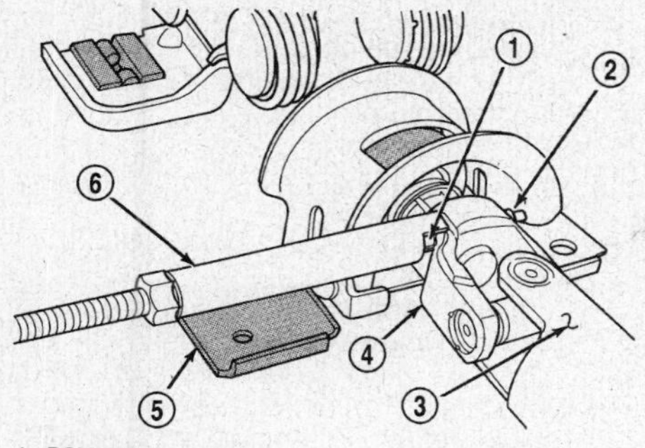

Fig. 17 Roll pin removal. 2001–02 Sebring Convertible/Sedan & Stratus Sedan

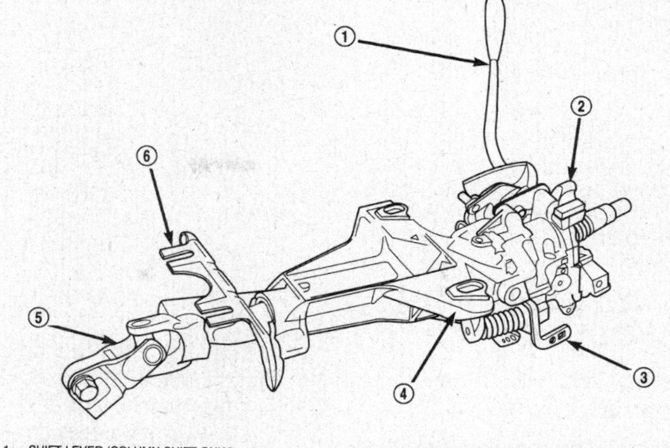

Fig. 18 Steering column components. Concorde, Intrepid, LHS & 300M

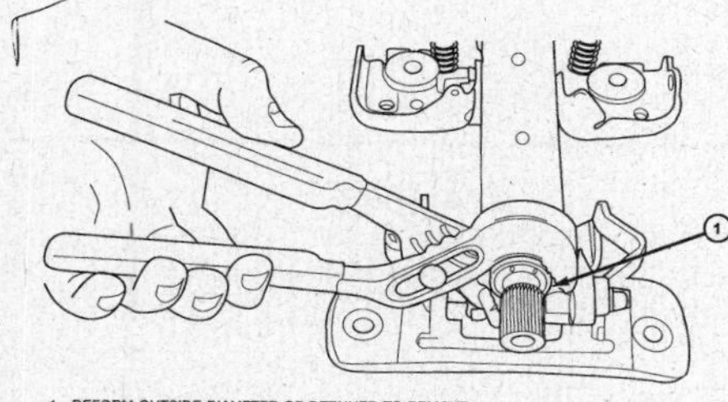

Fig. 19 Spring retainer removal. 2001 Sebring Convertible/Sedan & Stratus Sedan

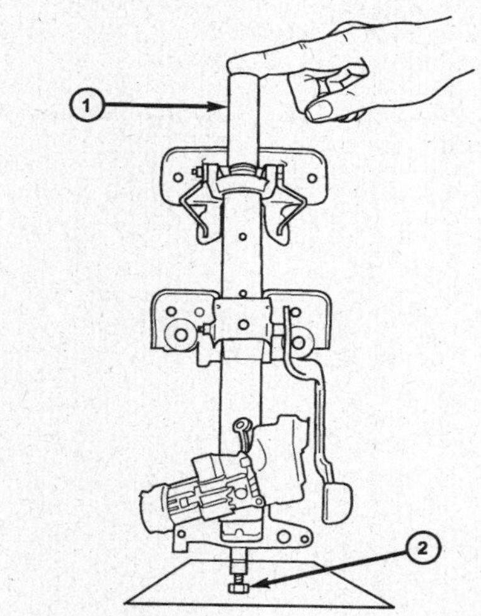

Fig. 20 Retainer installation. 2001 Sebring Convertible/Sedan & Stratus Sedan

remover/installer tool No. 6831-A, or equivalent, **Fig. 17.**

3. Using a suitable screwdriver pry intermediate shaft off steering column.
4. Reverse procedure to install.

CONCORDE, INTREPID, LHS & 300M

The steering column was been designed to be serviced as an assembly less wiring, switches, clockspring, gear shift lever, shift ignition interlock, brake lock solenoid, shrouds and steering wheel. **Fig. 18.**

The steering column intermediate shaft must be replaced as an entire assembly.

NEON

1998–99

The steering column used on this model, **Figs. 8 and 9,** has been designed to be serviced as an assembly except for wiring, switches, shrouds and the steering wheel. Most steering column components can be serviced without removing the column.

The only other serviceable component is the steering column shaft coupler. If the coupler requires replacement because of a seized bearing, insufficient bearing staking or improper bearing seating, proceed as follows:

1. Remove steering column as previously described.
2. Remove spring pin from coupler and slide coupler from end of steering shaft. **Ensure lower shaft coupler is supported during spring pin removal and installation to prevent bearing damage.**
3. Reverse procedure to install.

2000–02

The steering column on these models has been designed to be serviced as a complete assembly, only. The shaft, bearings and upper coupling are all serviced with the column.

The replaceable components on the steering column are the key cylinder, ignition switch, multi-function switch, trim shrouds, steering wheel, air bag module and the clockspring.

TECHNICAL SERVICE BULLETINS

STEERING CLUNKING OR RATTLE

1998–2000 Breeze, Cirrus, Neon, Sebring Convertible & Stratus

On some of these models there may be a steering clunking or rattle.

This condition may be caused by steering column preload.

To correct this condition, proceed as follows:

1. Adjust tilt steering column to full up position, if equipped.
2. Disconnect lower steering column intermediate shaft from steering gear shaft.
3. Attach intermediate shaft to steering gear using new pinch bolt (Neon part No. 05015627AA and Breeze, Cirrus, Sebring Convertible and Stratus part Nos. 06506112AA or 06036212AA).
4. **Torque** bolt to 20 ft. lbs. and install retaining clip/pin.

STEERING COLUMN CLICKING SOUND

2001 Sebring Convertible/ Sedan & Stratus Sedan

Some of these models may have a clicking noise from the upper steering column shaft.

To correct this condition proceed as follows:

1. Remove steering column as outlined under "Steering Column, Replace."
2. Remove multi-function switch from column, then the clockspring.

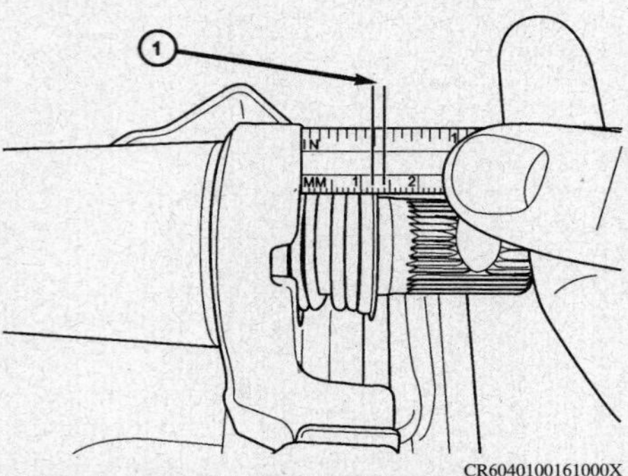

Fig. 21 Spring retainer measurement. 2001 Sebring Convertible/Sedan & Stratus Sedan

3. Remove spring retainer using suitable pliers by pinching outside of retainer and sliding it off the steering column shaft, **Fig. 19.**
4. Remove spring and plastic wedge, discard.
5. Remove shaft from upper end of steering column, discard.
6. Install new shaft part No. 0505087AA onto the column.
7. Install new steel wedge, part No. 04690570 and spring part No. 05057088AA.
8. Partially install steering wheel bolt onto column shaft.
9. Place column assembly on head of steering wheel bolt.
10. Install new retainer, part No. 04664130, **Fig. 20** onto shaft using a 7/8 inch deep well socket and hammer to tap retainer into place.
11. Distance between lower housing and outside face of retainer is 15/32–17/32 inch, **Fig. 21.**
12. If distance is less than 15/32–17/32 inch, remove retainer and install new one.
13. Remove steering wheel bolt, then install multi-function switch.
14. Install intermediate shaft, then steering column as outlined under "Steering Column, Replace."

POWER STEERING

TABLE OF CONTENTS

Power Steering Pressure Specifications

Model	Engine	Power Steering Pump Pressure, psi			Output Flow, Gallons Per Minute④
		Test Valve		Max Relief Pressure	
		Open	Closed		
1998					
Avenger	2.0L 2.5L	50–80①	1250–1350②	1250–1350	1.7
Breeze	2.0L 2.4L	50–80①	1195–1293②	1195–1293	1.5–2.0
Cirrus	2.5L	50–80①	1195–1293②	1195–1293	1.5–2.0
Concorde	2.7L 3.2L	50–80①	1250–1350②	1250–1350	2.1–2.5
Intrepid	2.7L 3.2L	50–80①	1250–1350②	1250–1350	2.1–2.5
Neon	2.0L	50–80①	1350–1450②	1350–1450	1.3–1.4
Sebring Convertible	2.4L 2.5L	50–80①	1195–1293②	1195–1293	1.5–2.0
Sebring Coupe	2.0L 2.5L	114–142	1209–1309③	1209–1309	—
Stratus	2.0L 2.4L 2.5L	50–80①	1195–1293②	1195–1293	1.5–2.0
Talon	2.0L	114–142	1209–1309③	1209–1309	—
1999					
Avenger	2.0L 2.5L	50–80①	1250–1350②	1250–1350	1.7
Breeze	2.0L 2.4L	50–80①	1195–1293②	1195–1293	1.5–2.0
Cirrus	2.5L	50–80①	1195–1293②	1195–1293	1.5–2.0
Concorde	2.7L 3.2L	50–125①	1250–1350②	1250–1350	2.1–2.5
Intrepid	2.7L 3.2L	50–125①	1250–1350②	1250–1350	2.1–2.5
LHS	3.5L	50–125①	1250–1350②	1250–1350	2.1–2.5
Neon	2.0L	50–80①	1350–1450②	1350–1450	1.3–1.4
Sebring Convertible	2.4L 2.5L	50–80①	1195–1293②	1195–1293	1.5–2.0
Sebring Coupe	2.0L 2.5L	114–142	1209–1309③	1209–1309	—

Continued

Model	Engine	Power Steering Pump Pressure, psi			Output Flow, Gallons Per Minute④
		Test Valve		Max Relief Pressure	
		Open	Closed		
1999					
Stratus	2.0L	50–80①	1195–1293②	1195–1293	1.5–2.0
	2.4L				
	2.5L				
300M	3.5L	50–125①	1250–1350②	1250–1350	2.1–2.5
2000					
Avenger	2.5L	50–80①	1250–1350②	1250–1350	1.7
Breeze	2.0L	50–80①	1195–1293②	1195–1293	1.3–1.6
	2.4L				
Cirrus	2.5L	50–80①	1195–1293②	1195–1293	1.3–1.6
Concorde	2.7L	50–125①	1250–1350②	1250–1350	2.1–2.5
	3.2L				
Intrepid	2.7L	50–125①	1250–1350②	1250–1350	2.1–2.5
	3.2L				
LHS	3.5L	50–125①	1250–1350②	1250–1350	2.1–2.5
Neon	2.0L	50–80①	1350–1450②	1350–1450	1.1–1.3
Sebring Convertible	2.5L	50–80①	1195–1293②	1195–1293	1.3–1.6
Sebring Coupe	2.5L	114–142	1209–1309③	1209–1309	—
Stratus	2.0L	50–80①	1195–1293②	1195–1293	1.3–1.6
	2.4L				
	2.5L				
300M	3.5L	50–125①	1250–1350②	1250–1350	2.1–2.5
2001–02					
Concorde	2.7L	50–125	1250–1350	1250–1350	2.1–2.5
	3.2L				
Intrepid	2.7L	50–125	1250–1350	1250–1350	2.1–2.5
	3.2L				
LHS	3.5L	50–125	1250–1350	1250–1350	2.1–2.5
Neon	2.0L	50–80①	1350–1450②	1350–1450	1.5–1.7
Sebring Coupe	2.4L	116–145	1209–1280⑤	1209–1280	—
	3.0L				
Stratus Coupe	2.4L	116–145	1209–1280⑤	1209–1280	—
	3.0L				
Sebring Sedan	2.4L	50–80①	1195–1293	1195–1293	—
	2.7L				
Stratus Sedan	2.4L	50–80①	1195–1293	1195–1293	—
	2.7L				
300M	3.5L	50–125	1250–1350	1250–1350	2.1–2.5

① — Initial pressure.
② — Do not leave valve closed for more than five seconds.
③ — Do not leave valve closed for more than 10 seconds.
④ — At 1500 RPM & minimum pressure.
⑤ — At 1000 RPM & minimum pressure.

Avenger, Sebring Coupe & Talon

NOTE: On Air Bag Equipped Models, Refer To "Air Bag System Precautions" Located In The Front Of This Manual For System Disarming & Arming Procedures.

NOTE: Refer To "Computer Relearn Procedures" Located In The Front Of This Manual When Battery Power To The Computer Has Been Interrupted.

NOTE: Prior To Performing Any Service Operations Listed In This Section, Consult The "Technical Service Bulletins" Section For Related Information.

INDEX

PRECAUTIONS

AIR BAG SYSTEMS

Refer to "Air Bag System Precautions" in the front of this manual for system disarming and arming procedures.

BATTERY GROUND CABLE

Prior to service, disconnect battery ground cable and isolate as required.

DESCRIPTION

POWER STEERING PUMP

A vane type oil pump with a fluid flow control system is used on these models. Two different type pumps are used as shown in **Figs. 1 through 3.**

STEERING GEAR

The steering gear and linkage are an integral rack and pinion type as shown in **Fig. 4.**

DIAGNOSIS & TESTING

ACCESSING DIAGNOSTIC TROUBLE CODES

A DRB, or equivalent scan tool, is required to access the speed proportional power steering diagnostic trouble codes. Connect the scan tool to the Data Link Connector (DLC) under the lefthand side of the instrument panel. The diagnostic cycle begins when the ignition is turned On.

CONNECTOR TERMINAL IDENTIFICATION

Refer to **Fig. 5,** for connector terminal identifications.

DIAGNOSTIC TESTS

Refer to "Breeze, Cirrus, Sebring Convertible & Stratus" for power steering system diagnostic tests.

CLEARING DIAGNOSTIC TROUBLE CODES

Record existing codes for future reference prior to clearing DTCs. To clear diagnostic trouble codes, select the "Erase DTCs" data screen on the DRB scan tool.

COMPONENT TESTING

Oil Pump Relief Pressure Test

1. Disconnect pressure hose from oil pump, then connect oil pump pressure test tools as shown in **Fig. 6.**
2. Bleed air, then turn steering wheel several times while vehicle is not moving.
3. Start engine and idle at 900–1100 RPM.
4. **On 1998–2000 models,** fully close shutoff valve on pressure gauge, then measure oil pump relief pressure to confirm that it is within 1209–1309 psi. **Pressure gauge shutoff valve must not remain closed for more than 10 seconds.**
5. **On 2001–02 models,** fully close shutoff valve on pressure gauge, then measure oil pump relief pressure to confirm that it is within 1209–1280 psi. **Pressure gauge shutoff valve must not remain closed for more than 10 seconds.**
6. **On all models,** if pressure is not as specified, replace oil pump.
7. Remove pressure test tools, then tighten pressure hose to specifications.
8. Bleed system.

No-Load Condition Pressure Test

1. Disconnect pressure hose from oil pump, then connect no-load condition pressure test tools as shown in **Fig. 7.**
2. Bleed air, then turn steering wheel several times while vehicle is not moving so fluid temperature rises.
3. Start engine and idle at 900–1100 RPM.
4. **On 1998–2000 models,** inspect and ensure hydraulic pressure is at standard value of 114–142 psi when no-load conditions are created by fully opening pressure gauge shutoff valve.
5. **On 2001–02 models,** inspect and ensure hydraulic pressure is at standard value of 116–145 psi when no-load conditions are created by fully opening pressure gauge shutoff valve.
6. **On all models,** if pressure is not as specified, condition's probable cause is oil line or steering gearbox. Inspect and repair as required.
7. Remove pressure test tools, then tighten pressure hose to specifications.
8. Bleed system.

Steering Gear Retention Hydraulic Pressure Test

1. Disconnect pressure hose from oil pump, then connect retention hydraulic pressure test tools as shown in **Fig. 8.**
2. Bleed air, then turn steering wheel several times while vehicle is not moving

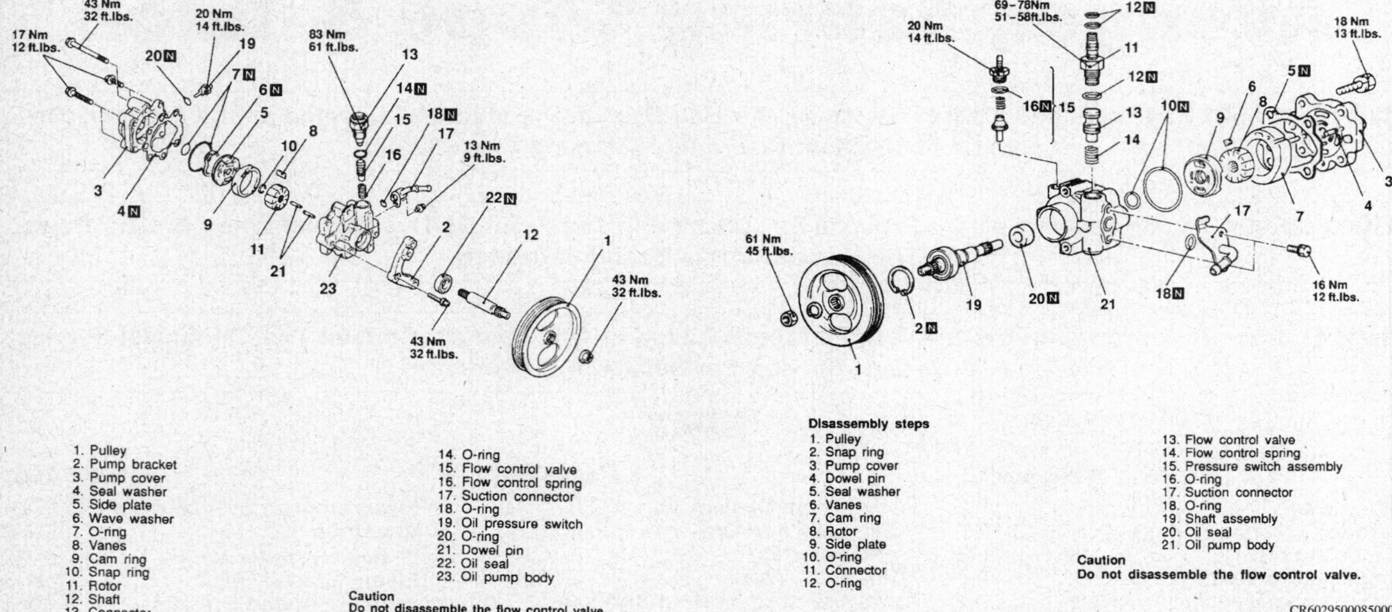

Fig. 1 Exploded view of power steering pump. 2.0L engine

Fig. 2 Exploded view of power steering pump. 2.5L engine

so fluid temperature rises.

3. Start engine, then idle at 900–1100 RPM.
4. Fully close, then fully open shutoff valve on pressure gauge.
5. **On 1998–2000 models,** turn steering wheel all way to left or right, then ensure retention hydraulic pressure is at standard value of 1209–1309 psi.
6. **On 2001–02 models,** turn steering wheel all way to left or right, then ensure retention hydraulic pressure is at standard value of 1209–1280 psi.
7. **On all models,** if pressure is not within standard value, overhaul steering gearbox.
8. Measure fluid pressure again.
9. Remove tools, then tighten pressure hose to specifications.
10. Bleed system.

Power Steering Pressure Switch Inspection

1. Disconnect pressure hose from oil pump, then connect power steering pressure switch test tools as shown in **Fig. 9.**
2. Bleed air, then turn steering wheel several times while vehicle is not moving so fluid temperature rises.
3. Idle engine.
4. Disconnect pressure switch connector, then place ohmmeter in position.
5. Gradually close shutoff valve at pressure gauge and increase hydraulic pressure.
6. **On 1998–2000 models,** turn steering wheel all way to left or right, then ensure retention hydraulic pressure is at standard value of 1209–1309 psi. Ensure hydraulic pressure activates switch at standard value of 213–284 psi.
7. **On 2001–02 models,** turn steering wheel all way to left or right, then ensure retention hydraulic pressure is at standard value of 1209–1280 psi. Ensure hydraulic pressure activates switch at standard value of 261–348 psi.
8. **On all models,** gradually open shutoff valve and reduce hydraulic pressure.
9. **On 1998–2000 models,** ensure hydraulic pressure deactivates switch at standard value of 114 psi or less.
10. **On 2001–02 models,** ensure hydraulic pressure deactivates switch at standard value of 116–348 psi.
11. **On all models,** emove tools, then tighten pressure hose to specifications.
12. Bleed system.

POWER STEERING SYSTEM SERVICE

Power Steering System Bleed

1. Raise and support front wheels.
2. Manually turn oil pump pulley several times.
3. Turn steering wheel all way left and right five or six times.
4. Disconnect high-tension cable, then crank starter motor intermittently, while turning steering wheel fully to left and right, five or six times for 15–20 seconds.
5. Refill fluid supply during air bleeding so level never falls below lower position of filter.
6. If air bleeding is done while engine is running, air will be broken up and absorbed into fluid. Ensure bleeding is done only while cranking.
7. Connect high-tension cable, then start engine.
8. Turn steering wheel to left and right until there are no air bubbles in reservoir.
9. Ensure fluid is not milky, then inspect fluid level.
10. Ensure level does not change when steering wheel is turned left or right.
11. Ensure level is within .2 inch when engine is stopped compared to when it is running.
12. If fluid level variation is more than .2 inch, air still exists in system, requiring additional bleeding.
13. If bleeding procedure is not complete, abnormal noises may be emitted from pump and flow control valve which may reduce pump life.

Component Service

OUTER TIE ROD & BOOT, REPLACE

Removal

Refer to **Fig. 10,** for tie rod and boot removal.

Installation

1. Using pliers, apply pressure to concave section of bellows band and tighten as shown in **Fig. 11.**
2. Using a plastic hammer, bend convex section of bellows band as shown in **Fig. 12.**
3. Pack tie rod dust cover with multi purpose grease, then apply specified sealant, 3M ATD Part No. 8663 or equivalent as shown in **Fig. 13.**
4. Using tool No. MB990776 or equivalent as shown in **Fig. 13,** install dust

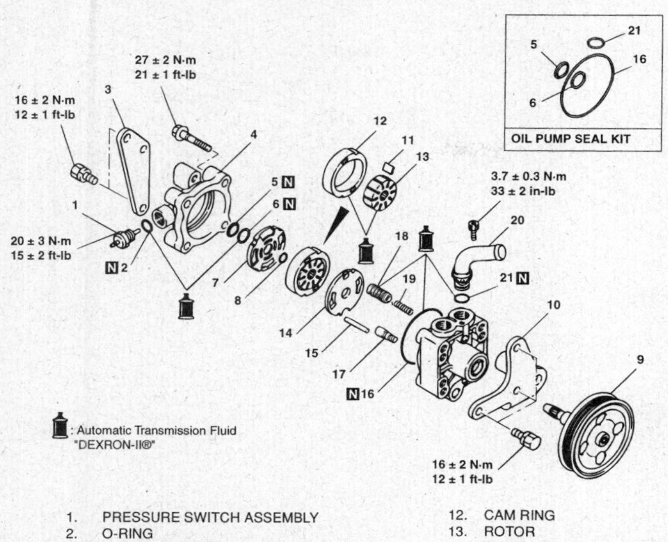

1. PRESSURE SWITCH ASSEMBLY
2. O-RING
3. REAR BRACKET <3.0L ENGINE>
4. REAR COVER
5. BACKUP RING
6. O-RING
7. SIDE PLATE (REAR)
8. SNAP RING
9. DRIVESHAFT ASSEMBLY
10. FRONT BRACKET <3.0L ENGINE>
11. VANE
12. CAM RING
13. ROTOR
14. SIDE PLATE (FRONT)
15. LOCK PIN
16. O-RING
17. VALVE SUBASSEMBLY
18. SPOOL ASSEMBLY
19. SPRING
20. SUCTION PIPE
21. O-RING

CR6020000221000X

Fig. 3 Exploded view of power steering pump. 2.4L & 3.0L engines

cover to tie rod end ball joint.

5. Install tie rod end to specified dimension as shown in **Fig. 14,** then tighten tie rod to specifications.

TECHNICAL SERVICE BULLETINS

BELT NOISE OR IRREGULAR WEAR

Talon & 1998-99 Avenger & Sebring Coupe

On these models, equipped with 2.0L non-turbocharged engines, the power steering belt may make noise or wear irregularly. These conditions may be caused by power steering pump pulley misalignment.

On models less A/C, visually inspect pump pulley alignment to the crankshaft pulley. If improper alignment is not clearly visible, use a suitable straightedge. The pump pulley should be close to parallel with the crankshaft pulley as shown in **Fig. 15.**

On models equipped with A/C, inspect pulley alignment by observing the way the belt rides on the idler pulley. If the belt rides over the idler's edge, the pump pulley will be misaligned as shown in **Fig. 16.**

If misalignment is discovered, perform repair procedures listed below.

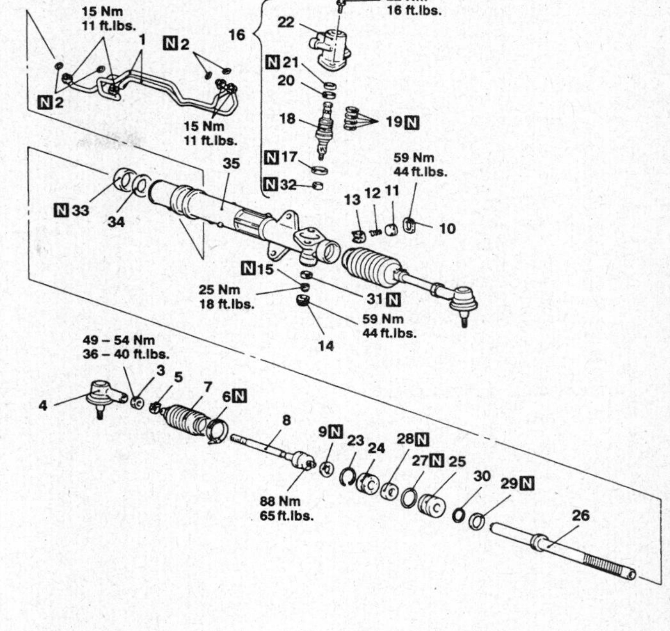

1. Feed tube
2. O-ring
3. Tie rod end locking nut
4. Tie rod end
5. Bellows clip
6. Bellows band
7. Bellows
8. Tie rod
9. Tab washer
- Total pinion torque adjustment
10. Locking nut
11. Rack support cover
12. Rack support spring
13. Rack support
14. End plug
15. Self-locking nut
16. Valve housing assembly
17. Oil seal
18. Pinion and valve assembly
19. Seal ring
20. Ball bearing
21. Oil seal
22. Valve housing
23. Circlip
24. Rack stopper
25. Rack bushing
26. Rack
27. O-ring
28. Oil seal
29. Seal ring
30. O-ring
31. Ball bearing
32. Needle roller bearing
33. Oil seal
34. Back-up washer
35. Rack housing

CR6029700191000X

Fig. 4 Exploded view of power steering gear

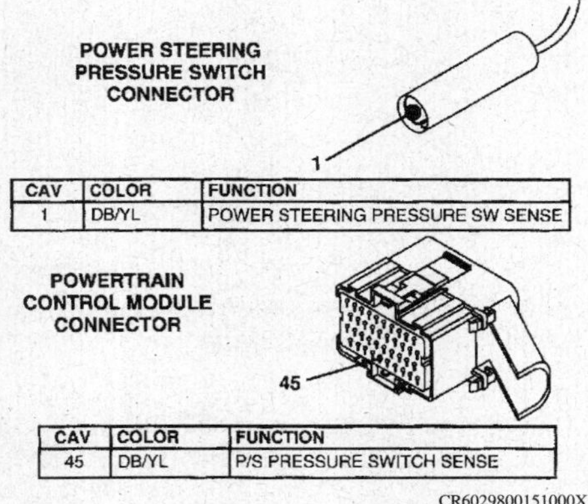
POWER STEERING PRESSURE SWITCH CONNECTOR

CAV	COLOR	FUNCTION
1	DB/YL	POWER STEERING PRESSURE SW SENSE

POWERTRAIN CONTROL MODULE CONNECTOR

CAV	COLOR	FUNCTION
45	DB/YL	P/S PRESSURE SWITCH SENSE

CR6029800151000X

Fig. 5 Connector terminal identification

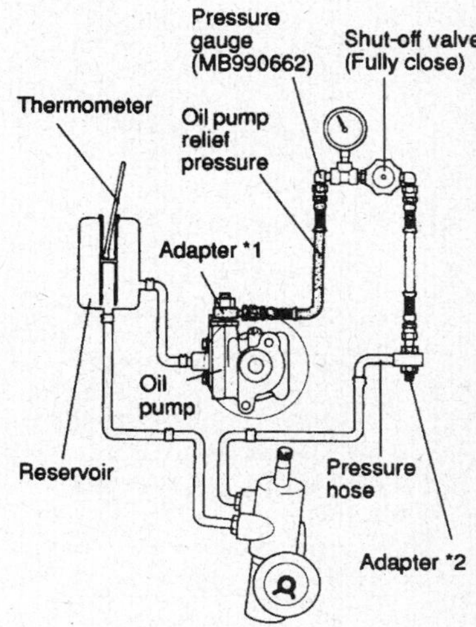

NOTE
*1: MB990993 or MB991217 <SOHC>
MB991548 <DOHC>
*2: MB990994 <SOHC>
MB991549 <DOHC>

CR6029500087000X

Fig. 6 Oil pump relief pressure test tool installation

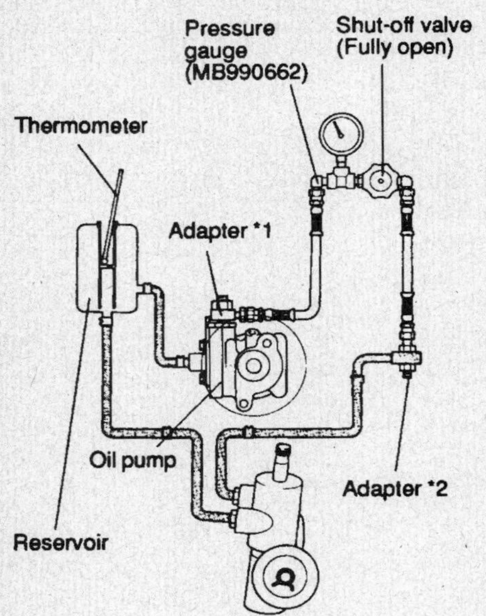

NOTE
*1: MB990993 or MB991217 <SOHC>
MB991548 <DOHC>

*2: MB990994 <SOHC>
MB991549 <DOHC>

CR6029500088000X

Fig. 7 No-load pressure test tool installation

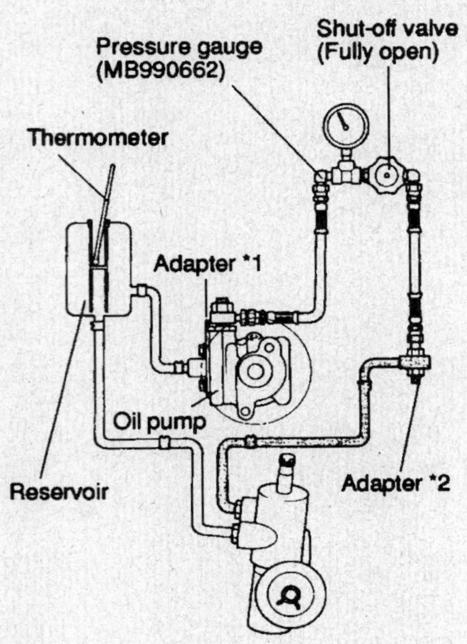

NOTE
*1: MB990993 or MB991217 <SOHC>
MB991548 <DOHC>

*2: MB990994 <SOHC>
MB991549 <DOHC>

CR6029500089000X

Fig. 8 Retention pressure test tool installation

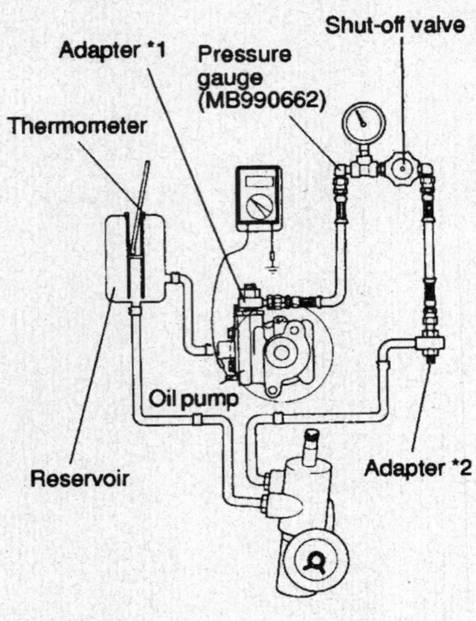

NOTE
*1: MB990993 or MB991217 <SOHC>
MB991548 <DOHC>

*2: MB990994 <SOHC>
MB991549 <DOHC>

CR6029500090000X

Fig. 9 Pressure switch test tool installation

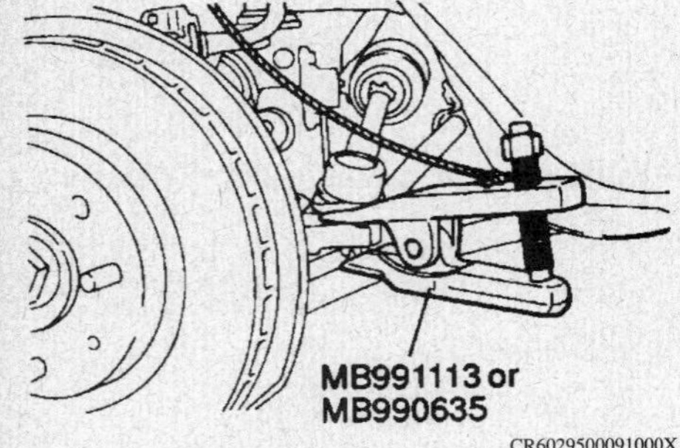

CR6029500091000X

Fig. 10 Tie rod removal

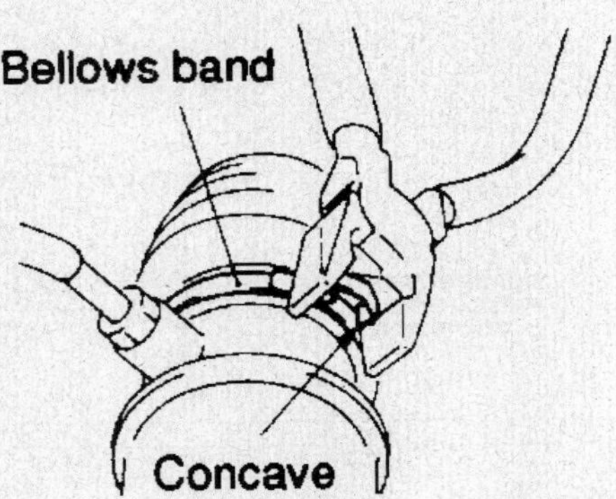

CR6029500092000X

Fig. 11 Concave section of band adjustment

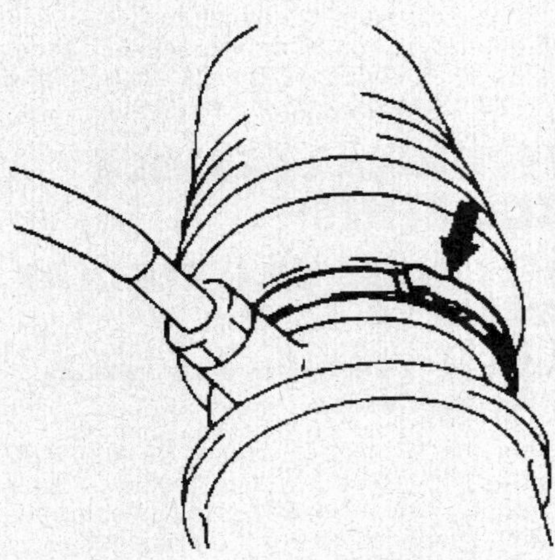

CR6029500093000X

Fig. 12 Convex section of band adjustment

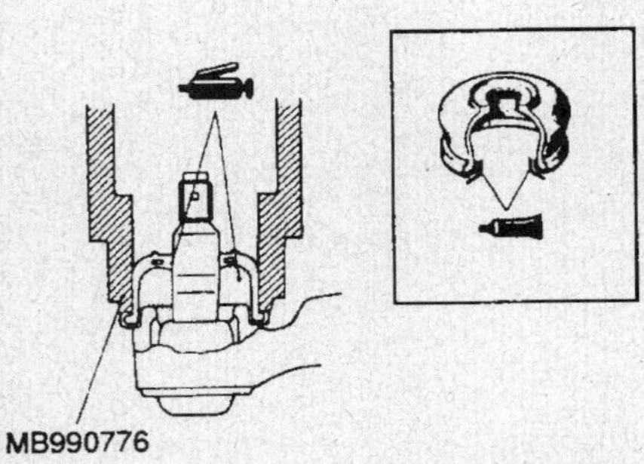

CR6029500094000X

Fig. 13 Dust cover sealant application

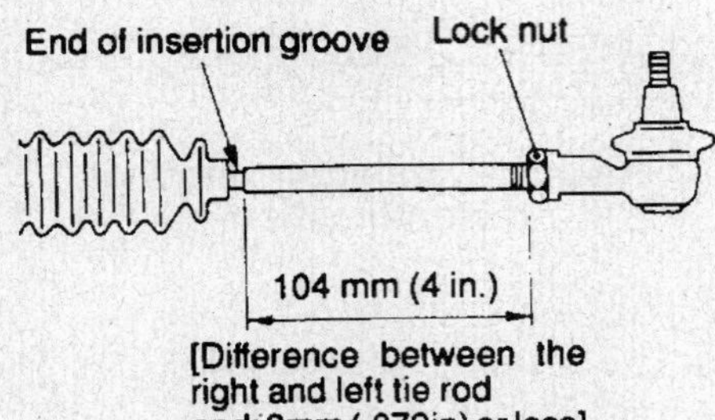

CR6029500095000X

Fig. 14 Tie rod replacement dimension

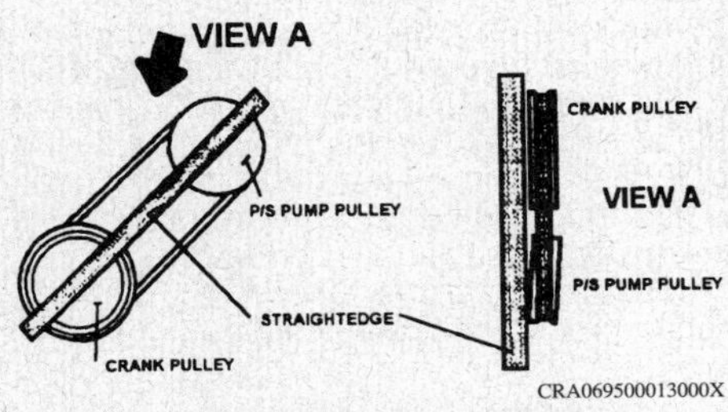

CRA069500013000X

Fig. 15 PS pump pulley & crankshaft pulley alignment inspection. Talon & 1998–99 Avenger & Sebring Coupe Less A/C

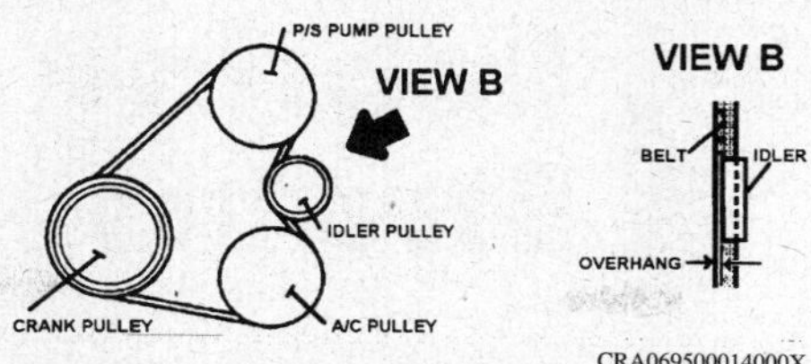

Fig. 16 PS pump pulley & idler pulley alignment inspection. Talon & 1998–99 Avenger & Sebring Coupe With A/C

TIGHTENING SPECIFICATIONS

Year	Component	Torque/Ft. Lbs.
1998–2002	Cooler Tube Assembly Bracket	100①
	Oil Pump	31
	Oil Pump Bracket	36
	Oil Reservoir	100①
	Outer Tie Rod End Locknut	36–40
	Outer Tie Rod To Steering Knuckle	18–25
	Pressure Hose To Pump②	42
	Pressure Hose To Pump③	13
	Pressure Tube To Rack	11
	Return Tube To Rack	11

① — Inch Lbs.
② — 2.0L, 2.4L & 3.0L Engines.
③ — 2.5L Engine.

Breeze, Cirrus, Sebring Convertible & Stratus

NOTE: On Air Bag Equipped Models, Refer To "Air Bag System Precautions" Located In The Front Of This Manual For System Disarming & Arming Procedures.

NOTE: Refer To "Computer Relearn Procedures" Located In The Front Of This Manual When Battery Power To The Computer Has Been Interrupted.

NOTE: Prior To Performing Any Service Operations Listed In This Section, Consult The "Technical Service Bulletins" Section For Related Information.

NOTE: For 2001–02 Stratus Coupe, Refer To The "Avenger, Sebring Coupe & Talon Section."

INDEX

PRECAUTIONS

AIR BAG SYSTEMS

Refer to "Air Bag System Precautions" in the front of this manual for system disarming and arming procedures.

BATTERY GROUND CABLE

Prior to service, disconnect battery ground cable and isolate as required.

DESCRIPTION

POWER STEERING PUMP

Constant Displacement

On models equipped with a TTA constant displacement, vane type pump as shown in **Fig. 1,** the pump utilizes a remote fluid reservoir, mounted at the rear of the cylinder head on the passenger side of the vehicle. In the event of a power steering failure, manual control can be maintained. However, under these conditions, steering effort will be significantly increased. No repairs are to be done on internal components of the TTA power steering pumps.

All vehicles equipped with this pump have a remote mounted power steering fluid reservoir. On models equipped with 2.0L and 2.4L engines the reservoir is

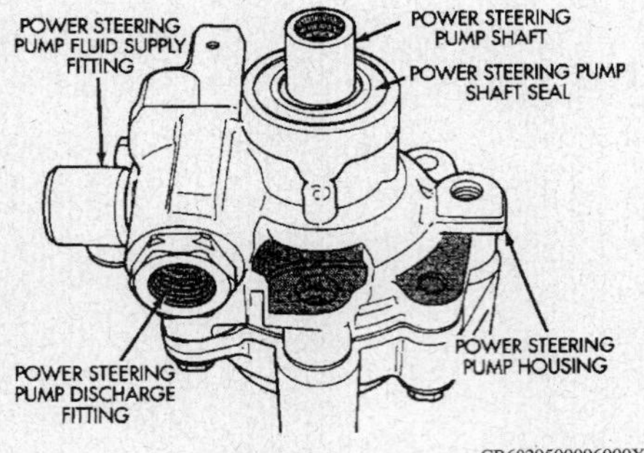

Fig. 1 Power steering pump

mounted to the rear of the cylinder head on the passenger side of the vehicle. On models equipped with 2.5L engines the reservoir is mounted to the front side of the engine between the cylinder heads.

Rectangular pumping vanes in the shaft driven rotor move power steering fluid from the intake to the cam ring pressure cavities of the pump. As the rotor begins to turn, centrifugal force throws the vanes against the inside surface of the cam ring to pickup residual oil. This oil is then forced into the cavities of the thrust plate through two crossover holes in the cam ring and pressure plate. The crossover holes empty into the high pressure area between the pressure plate and the housing end cover.

As the high pressure is filled, oil flows under the vanes in the rotor slots, forcing the vanes to follow the inside surface of the cam ring. As the vanes reach the restricted area of the cam ring, oil is forced out from between the vanes. When excess oil flow is generated during high speed operation, a regulated amount of oil returns to the pump intake side through a flow control valve. The flow control valve reduces the power required to drive the pump and holds down temperature buildup.

When steering conditions exceed maximum pressure requirements, such as when the wheels are turned against the stops, pressure built up in the steering gear exerts pressure on the spring end of the flow control valve. The high pressure lifts the relief valve ball from its seat and allows oil to flow through a trigger orifice located in the outlet fitting. This reduces pressure on the spring end of the flow control valve which then opens and allows the oil to return to the intake side of the pump. This action limits maximum pressure output of the pump to a safe level.

Under normal power steering pump operating conditions, pressure requirements of the pump are below maximum, causing the pressure relief valve to remain closed.

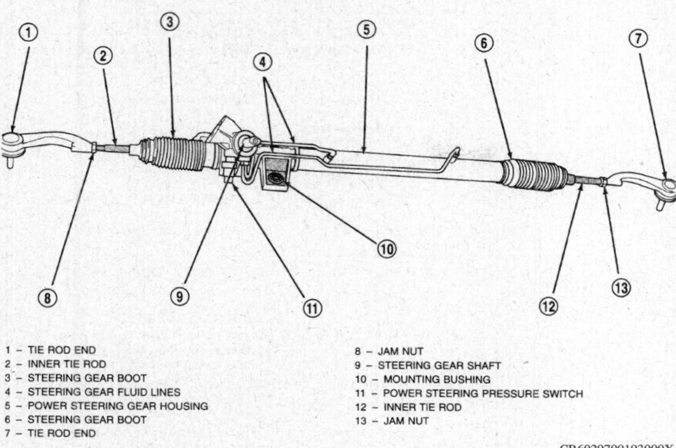

Fig. 2 Power steering gear assembly

CONDITION	POSSIBLE CAUSES	CORRECTION
OBJECTIONABLE HISS OR WHISTLE*	1. Damaged or mispositioned steering column shaft/coupling dash panel seal.	1. Reposition or replace steering column shaft/coupling dash panel seal.
	2. Noisy valve in power steering gear.	2. Replace power steering gear.
RATTLE OR CLUNK	1. Power steering gear loose on front suspension crossmember.	1. Inspect power steering gear mounting bolts. Replace as necessary. Tighten to the specified torque.
	2. Front suspension crossmember mounting fasteners loose at frame.	2. Tighten the front suspension crossmember mounting fasteners to the specified torque.
	3. Loose tie rod (outer or inner).	3. Check tie rod pivot points for wear. Replace worn/loose parts as required.
	4. Loose lower control arm mounting bolts at front suspension crossmember.	4. Tighten control arm mounting bolts to the specified torques.
	5. Loose shock assembly mounting fasteners at shock tower.	5. Tighten shock assembly fasteners to the specified torques.
	6. Power steering fluid pressure hose touching the body of the vehicle.	6. Adjust hose to proper position by loosening, repositioning, and tightening fitting to specified torque. Do not bend tubing.
	7. Internal power steering gear noise.	7. Replace power steering gear.
	8. Damaged front suspension crossmember.	8. Replace front suspension crossmember.

CR6029700192010X

Fig. 3 Power steering pump troubleshooting (Part 1 of 6)

CONDITION	POSSIBLE CAUSES	CORRECTION
POPPING NOISE	1. Worn outer tie rod.	1. Replace outer tie rod.
CHIRP OR SQUEAL (POWER STEERING PUMP)	1. Loose power steering pump drive belt.	1. Check and adjust power steering pump drive belt to specifications. Replace belt if worn or glazed.
WHINE OR GROWL (POWER STEERING PUMP)**	1. Low fluid level.	1. Fill power steering fluid reservoir to proper level and check for leaks (make sure all air is bled from the system fluid).
	2. Power steering hose touching vehicle body or frame.	2. Adjust hose to proper position by loosening, repositioning, and tightening fitting to specified torque. Do not bend tubing. Replace hose if damaged.
	3. Extreme wear of power steering pump internal components.	3. Replace power steering pump and flush system as necessary.
SUCKING AIR SOUND	1. Loose clamp on power steering fluid return hose.	1. Tighten or replace hose clamp.
	2. Missing O-Ring on power steering hose connection.	2. Inspect connection and replace O-Ring as required.
	3. Low power steering fluid level.	3. Fill power steering fluid reservoir to proper level and check for leaks.
	4. Air leak between power steering fluid reservoir and power steering pump.	4. Replace power steering pump (with reservoir).
SQUEAK OR RUBBING SOUND	1. Steering column shroud rubbing.	1. Realign shrouds as necessary.
	2. Steering column shaft rubbing.	2. Move or realign item rubbing shaft.
	3. Clockspring noisy.	3. Remove clockspring. Reinstall wheel. If noise is gone, replace clockspring.
	4. Steering gear internally noisy.	4. Replace steering gear.
SCRUBBING OR KNOCKING NOISE.	1. Incorrect tire or wheel size.	1. Replace incorrect size tire or wheel with size used as original equipment.
	2. Interference between steering gear and other vehicle components.	2. Check for bent or misaligned components and correct as necessary.
	3. Steering gear internal stops worn excessively allowing tires to be steered excessively far.	3. Replace steering gear.

CR6029700192020X

Fig. 3 Power steering pump troubleshooting (Part 2 of 6)

Variable Assist

The system provides additional steering assist while the vehicle is stationary and at low driving speeds. This additional power steering assist reduces the steering effort required by the driver for low speed driving and parking maneuvers. Variable assist speed proportional power steering then provides less power steering assist at highway speeds to maintain the firm responsive feel of the non-variable assist speed proportional power steering system.

The operational range of the variable assist speed proportional power steering system is from 0–60 mph. Maximum available power steering assist is provided at zero miles per hour. The power steering assist is then gradually reduced from vehicle speeds greater than zero to a maximum speed of 60 mph. The minimum power steering assist available is reached at a vehicle speed of approximately 60 mph.

Variable assist power steering is provided by controlling fluid pressure at the power steering gear. The pressure is controlled by regulating fluid flow from the steering gear back to the pump. A solenoid valve located on the steering gear is used to control power steering pressure by varying the size of an orifice which controls fluid flow from the steering gear back to the pump.

The variable assist speed proportional solenoid control valve is controlled by the steering gear mounted electronic solenoid control module (SCM). The SCM receives the vehicle speed signal sent from the transmission control module (TCM). Upon receiving the vehicle speed signal from the TCM, the SCM converts that speed signal into an electrical current usable by the solenoid control valve for controlling the variable assist of the power steering system.

STEERING GEAR

The power steering system consists of these six major components: the power steering gear, pump, fluid reservoir, supply and pressure hose, return hose and oil cooler. Turning of the wheel is converted into linear travel through the meshing of helical pinion teeth with rack teeth as shown in **Fig. 2.** Power assisted steering is provided by an open center, rotary type control valve which directs oil from the pump to either side of integral rack piston.

Road feel is controlled by the diameter of a torsion bar which initially steers the vehicle. This movement directs oil behind the integral rack piston which, in turn, builds up hydraulic pressure and assists in turning effort.

The drive tangs on the pinion of the power steering pump mate loosely with a stub shaft. This is to permit manual steering control to be maintained if the drive belt on the pump should break. However, under these conditions, steering effort will be increased.

TROUBLESHOOTING

Refer to **Fig. 3,** when troubleshooting the power steering system.

DIAGNOSIS & TESTING

ACCESSING DIAGNOSTIC TROUBLE CODES

A DRB or equivalent scan tool is required to access the speed proportional power steering diagnostic trouble codes. Connect the scan tool to the Data Link Connector (DLC) as shown in **Fig. 4.** The diagnostic cycle begins when the ignition is turned On.

CONNECTOR TERMINAL IDENTIFICATION

Refer to **Fig. 5,** for connector terminal identification.

DIAGNOSTIC TESTS

Refer to **Figs. 6 through 11,** for diagnostic and testing procedures.

CONDITION	POSSIBLE CAUSES	CORRECTION
STEERING WHEEL/ COLUMN CLICKING, CLUNKING OR RATTLING.	1. Steering column preload is not set properly.	1. Loosen steering column coupling pinch bolt to reset steering column preload. Replace pinch bolt and torque to specifications.
	2. Loose steering coupling pinch bolt.	2. Replace pinch bolt and torque to specifications.
	3. Steering column bearings.	3. Replace steering column.
STEERING WHEEL HAS FORE AND AFT LOOSENESS.	1. Steering wheel retaining nut not properly tightened and torqued.	1. Tighten the steering wheel retaining nut to its specified torque.
	2. Steering column preload is not set properly.	2. Loosen steering column coupling pinch bolt to reset steering column preload. Replace pinch bolt and torque to specifications.
	3. Steering column lower bearing spring retainer slipped on steering column shaft.	3. Replace steering column.
STEERING WHEEL OR DASH VIBRATES DURING LOW SPEED OR STANDSTILL STEERING MANEUVERS.	1. Air in the fluid of the power steering system.	1. Bleed air from system following the power steering pump initial operation service procedure.*
	2. Tires not properly inflated.	2. Inflate tires to the specified pressure.
	3. Excessive engine vibration.	3. Ensure that the engine is running properly.
	4. Loose tie rod end jam nut.	4. Tighten the inner to outer tie rod jam nut to the specified torque.
	5. Overcharged air conditioning system.	5. Check air conditioning pump head pressure and correct as necessary.
STEERING CATCHES, STICKS IN CERTAIN POSITIONS OR IS DIFFICULT TO TURN.	1. Low power steering fluid level.	1. Fill power steering fluid reservoir to specified level and check for leaks.
	2. Tires not inflated to specified pressure.	2. Inflate tires to the specified pressure.
	3. Lack of lubrication in front suspension control arm ball joints.	3. Lubricate ball joints if ball joints are not a lubricated-for-life type ball joint. If ball joint is a lubricated-for-life ball joint, replace ball joint or control arm.
	4. Worn upper or lower control arm ball joint.	4. Replace ball joint or control arm.
	5. Lack of lubrication in steering gear outer tie rod ends.	5. Lubricate tie rod ends if they are not a lubricated-for-life type. If tie rod end is a lubricated-for-life type, replace tie rod end.

CR6029700192030X

Fig. 3 Power steering pump troubleshooting (Part 3 of 6)

CONDITION	POSSIBLE CAUSES	CORRECTION
	6. Loose power steering pump drive belt.	6. Tighten the power steering pump drive belt to specifications. If drive belt is worn or glazed, replace belt.
	7. Faulty power steering pump flow control (Perform Power Steering System Flow and Pressure Test).	7. Replace power steering pump.
	8. Excessive friction in steering column or intermediate shaft.	8. Isolate and correct condition.
	9. Binding upper or lower control arm ball joint.	9. Replace the upper or lower ball joint.
	10. Excessive friction in power steering gear.	10. Replace power steering gear.
STIFF, HARD TO TURN, SURGE, MOMENTARY INCREASE IN EFFORT WHEN TURNING.	1. Tires not properly inflated.	1. Inflate tires to specified pressure.
	2. Low power steering fluid level.	2. Add power steering fluid as required to power steering fluid reservoir to obtain proper level. Check for leaks.
	3. Loose power steering pump drive belt.	3. Tighten the power steering pump drive belt to specifications. If drive belt is worn or glazed, replace belt.
	4. Lack of lubrication in control arm ball joints.	4. Lubricate ball joints if ball joints are not a lubricated-for-life type ball joint. If ball joint is a lubricated-for-life ball joint, replace ball joint or control arm.
	5. Low power steering pump pressure (Perform Power Steering System Flow and Pressure Test).	5. Replace the power steering pump as necessary.
	6. High internal leak in power steering gear (Perform Power Steering System Flow and Pressure Test).	6. Replace power steering gear.
STEERING WHEEL DOES NOT RETURN TO CENTER POSITION.	1. Tires not inflated properly.	1. Inflate tires to specified pressure.
	2. Improper front wheel alignment.	2. Check and adjust wheel alignment as necessary.
	3. Lack of lubrication in front suspension control arm ball joints.	3. Lubricate ball joints if ball joints are not a lubricated for life type of ball joint. If ball joint is a lubricated for life ball joint, replace ball joint or control arm.
	4. Steering column coupling joints misaligned.	4. Realign steering column coupling joints.
	5. Steering wheel rubbing.	5. Adjust steering column shrouds to eliminate rubbing condition.

CR6029700192040X

Fig. 3 Power steering pump troubleshooting (Part 4 of 6)

CLEARING DIAGNOSTIC TROUBLE CODES

Record existing codes for future reference prior to clearing DTCs. To clear diagnostic trouble codes, select the "Erase DTCs" data screen on the DRB scan tool.

POWER STEERING SYSTEM SERVICE

Power Steering System Bleed

To avoid personal injury, power steering fluid level should be inspected with engine Off. Use only approved fluid. Do not use automatic transmission fluid. Do not overfill fluid system.

1. Wipe filler cap clean, then inspect fluid level.
2. Dipstick should indicate "Full Cold" when fluid is at normal temperature approximately 70–80°F.
3. Fill power steering pump fluid reservoir to proper level with approved power steering fluid.
4. Start and run engine for a few seconds, then turn engine Off.
5. Add fluid as required.
6. Repeat previous procedure until fluid level remains constant after running engine.
7. Raise front wheels off ground, then start engine.
8. Slowly turn steering wheel right and then left, lightly contacting wheel stops.
9. Turn engine off and add fluid as required.
10. Lower vehicle and start engine.
11. Turn steering wheel slowly from lock to lock.
12. Stop engine, then inspect fluid and refill as required.
13. If fluid is extremely foamy, wait a few minutes, then repeat entire bleeding procedure.

Pump Pressure Inspection

NON-VARIABLE & ELECTRONICALLY CONTROLLED VARIABLE ASSIST

1. Inspect power steering pump drive belt tension and adjust as required.
2. Disconnect power steering fluid pressure hose at power steering pump.
3. Connect inlet hose on pressure gauge tool No. 6815, or equivalent, using required adapter to pressure fitting on power steering pump.
4. Connect pressure hose which was removed from power steering pump, using required adapter fitting, to outlet port of pressure gauge. **Pressure gauge is to be installed in series with power steering pressure hose, between pump and steering gear. It must also be installed so it is in proper direction of fluid flow.**
5. Completely open valve on gauge.
6. Start engine and let idle long enough to circulate fluid through flow/pressure test and get air out of fluid.
7. Turn off engine, then inspect fluid level and add as required.
8. Start engine and observe pressure gauge, which should read below 125 psi. If reading is above specification, inspect hoses for restrictions.
9. Initial pressure reading should be 50–80 psi and flow meter should read 1.3–1.6 GPM.
10. Close pressure gauge valve fully three times and record highest pressure each time. Readings must be above specification and within 50 psi of each other. **Do not leave valve closed for more than five seconds as pump could be damaged.**
11. Open test valve, then turn steering wheel to left and right positions until against stops, recording highest pressure at each position. **Do not force pump to operate against stops for more than 2–4 seconds as pump damage will result.**
12. Compare pressure gauge readings to pump specifications.
13. If highest output pressures are not same against either stop, steering

CONDITION	POSSIBLE CAUSES	CORRECTION
	6. Damaged, mis-positioned or un-lubricated steering column coupler to dash seal.**	6. Replace, reposition, or lubricate dash seal.
	7. Binding upper or lower control arm ball joint.	7. Replace the upper or lower control arm ball joint.
	8. Tight shaft bearing in steering column.	8. Replace the steering column.
	9. Excessive friction in steering column coupling.	9. Replace steering column coupling.
	10. Excessive friction in power steering gear.	10. Replace power steering gear.
EXCESSIVE STEERING WHEEL KICKBACK OR TOO MUCH STEERING WHEEL FREE PLAY.	1. Air in the fluid of the power steering system.	1. Bleed air from system following the the power steering pump initial operation service procedure. *
	2. Power steering gear loose on front suspension crossmember.	2. Inspect power steering gear mounting bolts. Replace as necessary. Tighten to the specified torque.
	3. Steering column coupling worn, broken or loose.	3. Replace steering column coupling.
	4. Free play in steering column.	4. Check all components of the steering system and repair or replace as required.
	5. Worn control arm ball joints.	5. Replace ball joint or control arm as required.
	6. Loose steering knuckle to ball joint stud pinch bolt.	6. Inspect pinch bolts, replace as necessary, and tighten to specified torque.
	7. Front wheel bearings loose or worn.	7. Replace wheel bearing or knuckle as necessary.
	8. Loose outer tie rod ends.	8. Replace outer tie rod ends that have excessive free play.
	9. Loose inner tie rod ends.	9. Replace power steering gear.
	10 Defective steering gear rotary valve.	10. Replace power steering gear.

NOTE: * Steering shudder can be expected in new vehicles and vehicles with recent steering system repairs. Shudder should dissipate after the vehicle has been driven several weeks.

CR6029700192050X

Fig. 3 Power steering pump troubleshooting (Part 5 of 6)

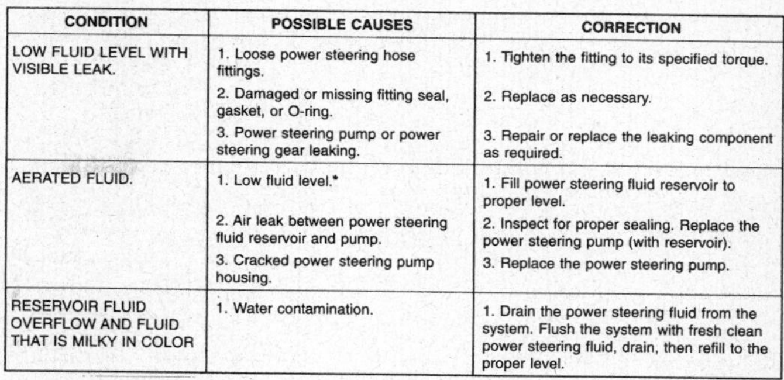

CONDITION	POSSIBLE CAUSES	CORRECTION
LOW FLUID LEVEL WITH VISIBLE LEAK.	1. Loose power steering hose fittings.	1. Tighten the fitting to its specified torque.
	2. Damaged or missing fitting seal, gasket, or O-ring.	2. Replace as necessary.
	3. Power steering pump or power steering gear leaking.	3. Repair or replace the leaking component as required.
AERATED FLUID.	1. Low fluid level.*	1. Fill power steering fluid reservoir to proper level.
	2. Air leak between power steering fluid reservoir and pump.	2. Inspect for proper sealing. Replace the power steering pump (with reservoir).
	3. Cracked power steering pump housing.	3. Replace the power steering pump.
RESERVOIR FLUID OVERFLOW AND FLUID THAT IS MILKY IN COLOR	1. Water contamination.	1. Drain the power steering fluid from the system. Flush the system with fresh clean power steering fluid, drain, then refill to the proper level.

CR6029700192060X

Fig. 3 Power steering pump troubleshooting (Part 6 of 6)

gear is leaking internally and must be replaced.

DROOP FLOW VARIABLE ASSIST

1. Set up power steering analyzer as follows:
   a. Connect together pressure hose tool No. 6713 and 6905 or equivalents as shown in **Fig. 12.**
   b. Install adapter tool No. 6866, or equivalent, on end of pressure hose, then the quick disconnect.
   c. Install pressure hose in inlet and outlet fitting of pressure/flow tester.
2. Inspect power steering pump drive belt tension and adjust as required.
3. Disconnect power steering fluid pressure hose at pump.
4. Install adapter tool No 6972-1, or equivalent, in pressure fitting on pump, then adapter tool No 6972-2, or equivalent, in banjo fitting on power steering fluid pressure hose and nut tool No. 6972-3, or equivalent, on adapter tool 6972-2 in banjo fitting as shown in **Fig. 13.**
5. Connect inlet hose of pressure/flow tester tool No. 6815, or equivalent, to pressure fitting on pump using adapter tool No. 6866 that was installed in pressure hose tool No. 6713, or equivalent as shown in **Fig. 14.**
6. Connect outlet hose on pressure/flow tester to adapter tool No. 6972-2, or equivalent, installed in pressure hose using quick disconnect.
7. Completely open valve on pressure/flow tester.
8. Start engine and idle long enough to circulate fluid through tester and extract air from fluid, then turn off engine.
9. Inspect and adjust fluid level as required, then start and idle engine.
10. Pressure gauge should read below 125 psi. If reading is above specification, inspect hoses for restrictions.
11. Initial pressure reading should be 50–80 psi and flow meter should read 1.3–1.6 GPM.
12. Close pressure gauge valve fully three times and record highest pressure each time. Readings must be above specification and within 50 psi of each other. **Do not leave valve closed for more than 2–4 seconds as pump will be damaged.**
13. Open test valve, then turn steering wheel to left and right positions until against stops, recording highest pressure at each position. **Do not force pump to operate against stops for more than 2–4 seconds as pump damage will result.**
14. Compare pressure gauge readings to pump specifications. If highest output pressures are not same against either stop, steering gear is leaking internally and must be replaced.

Component Service

POWER STEERING PUMP

On these models, the power steering pump is not serviceable except for the following items:

1. Power steering pump oil seals except for pump shaft seal.
2. Power steering pump reservoirs and related components.
3. Power steering pump reservoir filler cap/dipstick.
4. Power steering pump pulley.

Pulley, Replace

Refer to "Power Steering Pump, Replace" in the "Front Suspension & Steering" section of the "Breeze, Cirrus, Sebring Convertible & Stratus" chapter.

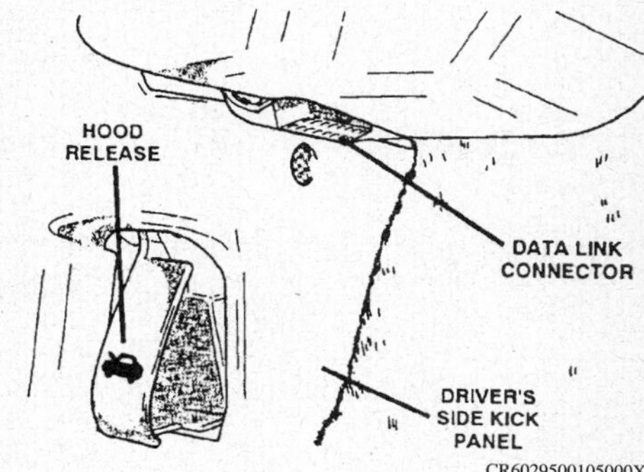

CR6029500105000X

Fig. 4 DLC location

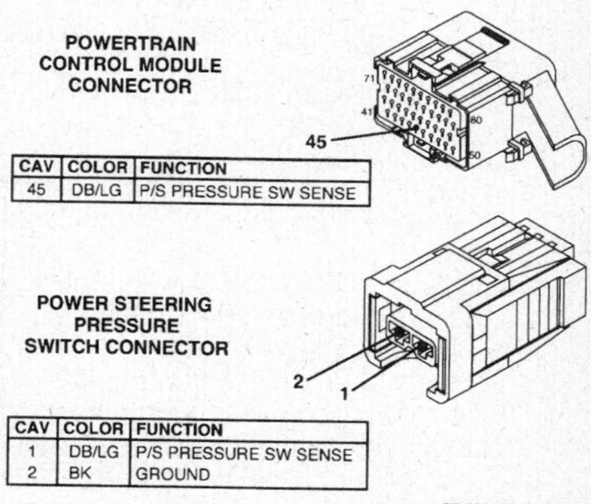

CAV	COLOR	FUNCTION
45	DB/LG	P/S PRESSURE SW SENSE

CAV	COLOR	FUNCTION
1	DB/LG	P/S PRESSURE SW SENSE
2	BK	GROUND

CR6029800152000X

Fig. 5 Connector terminal identification

1. Remove power steering pump from engine.
2. Place power steering pump in a vise while using puller tool No. C-4068, or C-4333, or equivalent as shown in **Fig. 15,** to remove pulley. **Ensure pump shaft does not turn. Do not hammer on pulley or shaft.**
3. Install pulley, noting the following:
   a. Place power steering pump in vise using power steering pump bracket.
   b. Place power steering pump pulley squarely on end of power steering pump shaft.

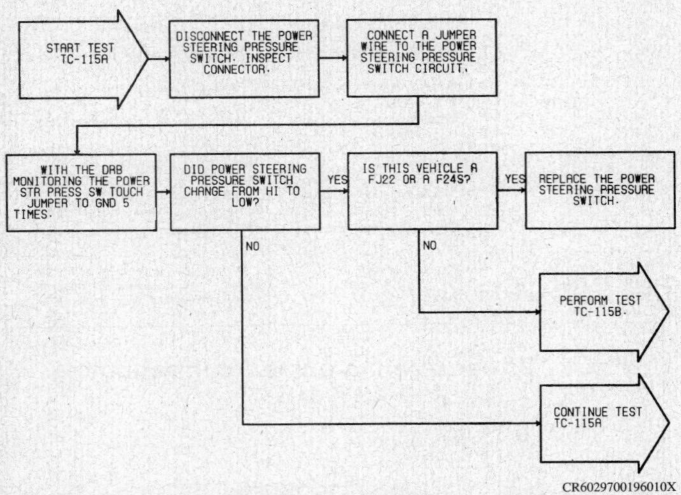

Fig. 6 Test TC-115A: PS Switch Failure (Part 1 of 2). 1998

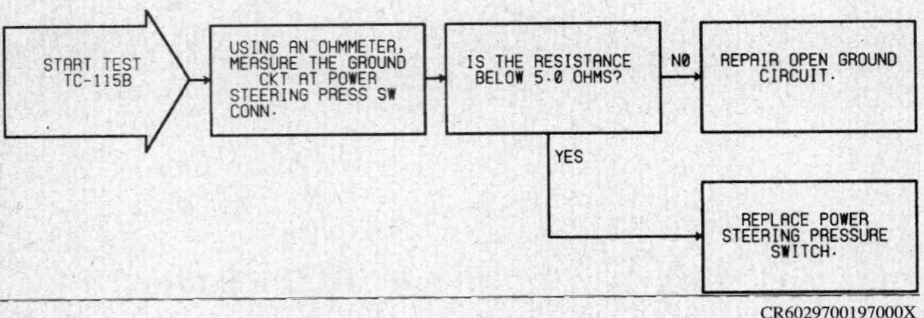

Fig. 7 Test TC-115B: PS Switch Failure. 1998

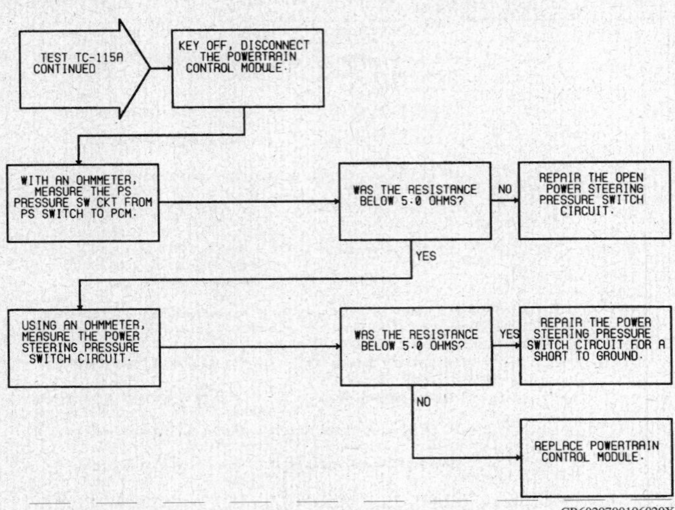

Fig. 6 Test TC-115A: PS Switch Failure (Part 2 of 2). 1998

TEST	ACTION
1	Ignition Off Disconnect the Power Steering Pressure Switch. **Note: Check connectors - Clean/repair as necessary.** Ignition on, engine not running. Connect a jumper wire to the Power Steering Pressure Switch Circuit. With the DRB monitoring the Power Steering Pressure Switch, touch jumper to ground 5 times. Did the Power Steering Pressure Switch change from high to low? Yes → Go To 2 No → Go To 4
2	Ignition Off Disconnect the Power Steering Pressure Switch. **Note: Check connectors - Clean/repair as necessary.** Using an Ohmmeter, measure the resistance of the Ground Circuit at the Power Steering Pressure Switch Connector. Is the resistance below 5.0 ohms? Yes → Go To 3 No → Repair the open Ground Circuit. Perform Powertrain Verification Test VER-5A.
3	If there are no potential causes remaining, replace the Power Steering Pressure Switch. View repair options. Repair Replace the Power Steering Pressure Switch. Perform Powertrain Verification Test VER-2A.

CR6029900194010X

Fig. 8 DTC P0551: PS Switch Failure (Part 1 of 2). 1999–2000

c. Install spacer tool No. 6936, or equivalent, on top of pulley as shown in **Fig. 16.**
d. Place installer tool No. C-4063B, or equivalent, in internal threads of power steering pump shaft and against spacer on power steering pump pulley as shown in **Fig. 17.**
e. Ensuring installer tool and pulley remain aligned with pump shaft, install pulley onto power steering pump shaft until spacer is against end of shaft. **When spacer is against shaft, power steering pump tool will no longer be able to turn.**
f. Remove installation tool, then install pump. Refer to "Power Steering Pump, Replace" for installation procedures.
g. Refill fluid and bleed system of air. Refer to "Power Steering System Bleed" for air bleeding procedure.

Flow Control Valve Fitting O-Ring, Replace

The power steering pump does not require removal from the engine for flow control valve O-ring replacement.

1. Remove power steering fluid pressure hose from power steering pump pressure fitting as shown in **Figs. 18 and 19.**
2. Remove pump discharge/flow control valve fitting from power steering pump housing as shown in **Figs. 20 and 21. Prevent flow control valve and spring from sliding out of housing bore.**
3. Remove and discard O-ring.
4. Reverse procedure to install, noting following:
   a. Clean and install flow control valve and spring in pump housing bore if required.
   b. Install new O-ring seal on fitting.
   c. Install pump discharge/flow control valve fitting in pump and tighten to specifications.
   d. Install power steering pressure hose on flow control valve fitting, then tighten tube nut to specifications.
   e. Refill fluid and bleed system of air. Refer to "Power Steering System Bleed" for air bleeding procedure.

Suction Port O-Ring Seal, Replace

The power steering pump must be removed from the vehicle for replacement of the suction port O-ring seal. Refer to "Power Steering Pump, Replace" section for removal procedure.

1. Remove power steering fluid supply hose from power steering pump suction port fitting.
2. Remove suction port fitting attaching bolt as shown in **Fig. 22.**
3. Remove and discard O-ring seal from suction port fitting.
4. Reverse procedure to install, noting following:
   a. Install new O-ring on suction fitting.
   b. Install suction port fitting to power steering pump. Install and securely

TEST	ACTION
4	Ignition Off Disconnect the Power Steering Pressure Switch. **Note: Check connectors - Clean/repair as necessary.** Disconnect the PCM. **Note: Check connectors - Clean/repair as necessary.** With an Ohmmeter, measure the Power Steering Pressure Switch Circuit from power steering switch to PCM. Was the resistance below 5.0 ohms? Yes → Go To 5 No → Repair the open Power Steering Pressure Switch Circuit. Perform Powertrain Verification Test VER-2A.
5	Ignition Off Disconnect the Power Steering Pressure Switch. **Note: Check connectors - Clean/repair as necessary.** Disconnect the PCM. **Note: Check connectors - Clean/repair as necessary.** Using an Ohmmeter, measure the Power Steering Pressure Switch Circuit resistance from power steering switch to ground. Was the resistance below 5.0 ohms? Yes → Repair the Power Steering Pressure Switch Circuit for a short to ground. Perform Powertrain Verification Test VER-2A. No → Go To 6
6	There are no other potential causes remaining. View repair options? Repair Replace the PCM. Perform Powertrain Verification Test VER-2A.

CR6029900194020X

Fig. 8 DTC P0551: PS Switch Failure (Part 2 of 2). 1999–2000

VERIFICATION TEST VER-2A	APPLICABILITY
1. Road Test For Non-OBD II **2. Note: If the PCM has been changed and the correct VIN and mileage have not been programmed, a DTC will be set in the ABS and Air Bag modules. In addition, if the vehicle is equipped with a SKIM; Secret Key data must be updated to enable starting.** 3. For ABS and Air Bag Systems: ACTION: Enter correct VIN and mileage in PCM. Erase codes in ABS and Air Bag modules. 4. For SKIM Theft Alarm: ACTION: 5. Connect DRB to data link connector. 6. Go to Theft Alarm, SKIM, misc. and place SKIM in secured access mode, by using appropriate PIN code for vehicle. 7. 3. Select Update Secret Key data. Data will be transferred from SKIM to PCM. 8. Inspect the vehicle to ensure that all engine components are connected. 9. If there are any DTCs that have not been repaired, return to the symptom list and follow the path specified for that symptom. After all DTCs have been repaired, return to the appropriate Verification Test. **10. Note: If this verification procedure is being performed after a NO TROUBLE CODE test, do the following:** 11. Check to see if the initial symptom still exists. 12. If the initial or another symptom exists, the repair is not complete. Check for any Technical Service Bulletins or flash updates and return to the symptom list and restart diagnostic testing for this symptom if necessary. 13. Connect the DRB to the data link connector. 14. Using the DRB, erase any DTCs and reset all values. 15. Road test vehicle, use all accessories that may be related to this repair. 16. Using the DRB, read Global Good Trips. If Global Good Trips is zero, the repair is not complete. Check for any Technical Service Bulletins or flash updates and return to the symptom list and restart diagnostic testing for that symptom. 17. If another trouble code has set, return to the symptom list and restart diagnostic testing and follow the path specified for that symptom. 18. If there are no trouble codes or the Global Good Trip is not zero, the repair was successful and is now complete. Repair is not complete, refer to appropriate symptom.	ENGINE - 2.5L V6, ENGINE - 2.0L I-4 SOHC and/or ENGINE - 2.4L I-4 DOHC

CR6029900195000X

Fig. 9 Verification Test VER-2A. 1999–2000

POSSIBLE CAUSES
POWER STEERING PRESSURE SWITCH OPERATION
GROUND CIRCUIT
POWER STEERING PRESSURE SWITCH SENSE CIRCUIT SHORTED TO GROUND
POWER STEERING PRESSURE SENSE CIRCUIT OPEN
PCM

TEST	ACTION
1	Turn the ignition off. Disconnect the Power Steering Pressure Switch harness connector. Turn the ignition on. With the DRBIII®, monitor the Power Steering Pressure Switch. Using a jumper wire, connect one end to the Power Steering Pressure Switch Sense circuit. With the other end of the jumper tap the ground circuit in the Power Steering Pressure Switch harness connector. Does the Power Steering Pressure Switch display change from HI to LOW? Yes → Replace the Power Steering Pressure Switch Perform POWERTRAIN VERIFICATION TEST VER - 5. No → Go To 2
2	Turn the ignition off. Disconnect Power Steering Pressure Switch harness connector. Using a 12-volt test light connected to 12-volts, probe the ground circuit in the Power Steering Pressure Switch harness connector. Does the test light illuminate? Yes → Go To 3 No → Repair the ground circuit for an open. Perform POWERTRAIN VERIFICATION TEST VER - 5.

CR6020100222010X

Fig. 10 DTC P0551: PS Switch Failure (Part 1 of 2). 2001–02

tighten suction port fitting attaching bolt.

c. Install power steering fluid supply hose on suction port fitting, ensure hose clamp is installed on hose past upset bead on suction port fitting.
d. Refill fluid and bleed system of air. Refer to "Power Steering System Bleed" for air bleeding procedure.

Fluid Reservoir, Replace

Use care when replacing power steering fluid hoses on power steering reservoir. Avoid excessive force when removing or installing hoses, as nipples on reservoir may break off.

1. Using a siphon pump, remove fluid from power steering fluid reservoir.
2. Raise and support vehicle.
3. Remove power steering fluid supply hose at power steering pump.
4. Drain remaining fluid from supply hose and power steering fluid reservoir until empty.
5. Lower vehicle.
6. Remove power steering fluid return and supply hose from power steering reservoir.
7. Remove reservoir attaching bolts on engine, then reservoir.
8. Reverse procedure to install, noting following:
   a. When installing return and supply hoses, ensure both hose clamps are installed on hose past upset bead on steering gear steel tube.
   b. Refill fluid and bleed system of air. Refer to "Power Steering System Bleed" for air bleeding procedure.

POWER STEERING PRESSURE SWITCH, REPLACE

The power steering power steering pressure switch as shown in **Fig. 23,** is to improve engine idle quality. The switch maintains idle speed when required due to increased power steering system pressure. Otherwise, this higher pressure would slow down the power steering pump, decreasing engine idle speed.

The pressure switch signals the Powertrain Control Module (PCM) that additional engine load is being applied by the power steering system. Engine idle is compensated for load by the signal from the pressure switch. As steering load increases or decreases, engine idle speed and quality are maintained.

The pressure switch is mounted directly on the power steering gear.

1. Raise and support vehicle.
2. Locate power steering switch on rear side of power steering gear, then disconnect its electrical connector.
3. Using a crowfoot and long extension, or equivalent, remove pressure switch from steering gear.
4. Reverse procedure to install, noting following:
   a. Install and hand tighten switch into gear until fully seated.
   b. Using a crowfoot and extension, or

TEST	ACTION
3	Turn the ignition off. Disconnect the Power Steering Pressure Switch harness connector. Disconnect the PCM harness connector. Measure the resistance of the Power Steering Pressure Switch Sense circuit in the PSP Switch harness connector to ground. Is the resistance below 100 ohms? Yes → Repair the Power Steering Pressure Sense circuit for a short to ground. Perform POWERTRAIN VERIFICATION TEST VER - 5. No → Go To 4
4	Turn the ignition off. Disconnect the Power Steering Pressure Switch harness connector. Disconnect the PCM harness connector. Measure the resistance of the Power Steering Pressure Switch Sense circuit between the PSP Switch harness connector and the PCM harness connector. Is the resistance below 5.0 ohms? Yes → Go To 5 No → Repair the Power Steering Pressure Sense circuit for an open. Perform POWERTRAIN VERIFICATION TEST VER - 5.
5	If there are no possible causes remaining, view repair. Repair Replace and program the Powertrain Control Module in accordance with the Service Information. Perform POWERTRAIN VERIFICATION TEST VER - 5.

CR6020100222020X

Fig. 10 DTC P0551: PS Switch Failure (Part 2 of 2). 2001–02

POWERTRAIN VERIFICATION TEST VER - 5
1. NOTE: If the PCM has been replaced and the correct VIN and mileage have not been programmed, a DTC will be set in the ABS Module, Airbag Module and the SKIM. **2. NOTE: If the vehicle is equipped with a Sentry Key Immobilizer System, Secret Key data must be updated. Refer to the Service Information for the PCM, SKIM and the Transponder (ignition key) for programming information.** 3. Inspect the vehicle to ensure that all engine components are properly installed and connected. Reassemble and reconnect components as necessary. 4. Connect the DRBIII® to the data link connector. 5. Ensure the fuel tank has at least a quarter tank of fuel. Turn off all accessories. 6. If a Comprehensive Component DTC was repaired, perform steps 5 - 8. If a Major OBDII Monitor DTC was repaired skip those steps and continue verification. 7. After the ignition has been off for at least 10 seconds, restart the vehicle and run 2 minutes. 8. If the Good Trip counter changed to one or more and there are no new DTC's, the repair was successful and is now complete. Erase DTC's and disconnect the DRBIII®. 9. If the repaired DTC has reset, the repair is not complete. Check for any related TSB's or flash updates and return to the Symptom list. 10. If another DTC has set, return to the Symptom List and follow the path specified for that DTC. 11. With the DRBIII®, monitor the appropriate pre-test enabling conditions until all conditions have been met. Once the conditions have been met, switch screen to the appropriate OBDII monitor, (Audible beeps when the monitor is running). 12. If the monitor ran, and the Good Trip counter changed to one or more, the repair was successful and is now complete. Erase DTC's and disconnect the DRBIII®. 13. If the repaired OBDII trouble code has reset or was seen in the monitor while on the road test, the repair is not complete. Check for any related technical service bulletins or flash updates and return to Symptom List. 14. If another DTC has set, return to the Symptom List and follow the path specified for that DTC. Are any DTCs present? Yes → Repair is not complete, refer to appropriate symptom. No → Repair is complete.

CR6020100223000X

Fig. 11 Verification Test VER-5. 2001–02

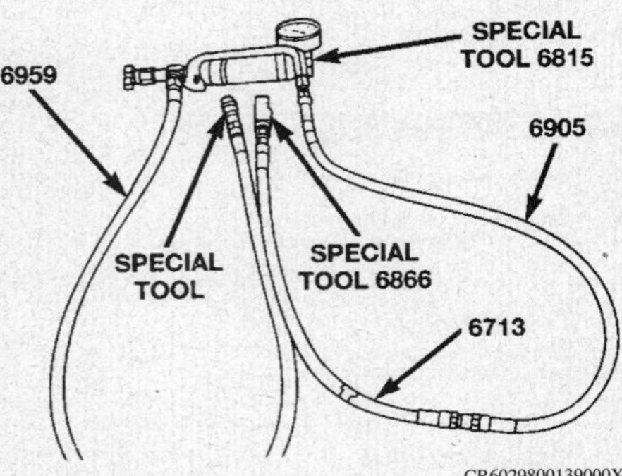

Fig. 12 Power steering flow/ pressure tester & fittings. Droop Flow Variable Assist

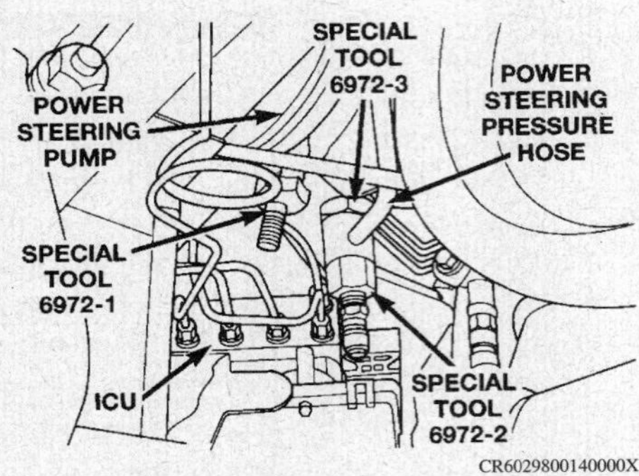

Fig. 13 Adapter fitting installation. Droop Flow Variable Assist

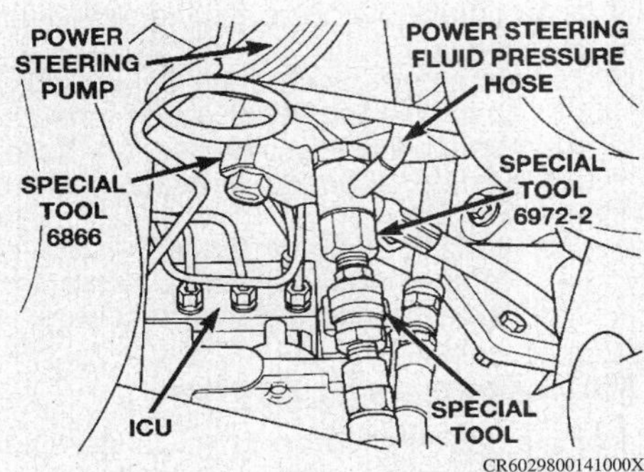

Fig. 14 Flow/pressure tester connections. Droop Flow Variable Assist

equivalent, tighten switch to specifications. **Do not overtighten. This may result in damage to switch port threads on steering gear.**

c. Connect pressure switch electrical connector, ensuring latch is securely engaged with locking tab.
d. Refill fluid and bleed system of air. Refer to "Power Steering System Bleed" for air bleeding procedure.
e. Inspect system for fluid leaks.

SOLENOID CONTROL MODULE, REPLACE

Replacement of the solenoid control module as shown in **Fig. 24,** can be done without removing steering gear from vehicle. The solenoid control module is mounted on the steering gear assembly fluid lines.

1. Disconnect solenoid control module electrical connectors as shown in **Fig. 25.**
2. Unclip locking tab, holding module to fluid lines, on bottom side of control module.
3. Rotate module upward, then remove two upper attaching clips from steering gear.
4. Reverse procedure to install, noting the following:
   a. Hook upper tabs on solenoid control module to upper steering gear fluid lines.
   b. Rotate module downward until locking tab on bottom of module is locked on lower power steering gear fluid line.
   c. Connect control module electrical connectors. Ensure connector seal is in good condition prior to installation.

SOLENOID CONTROL VALVE, REPLACE

Removal of the steering gear assembly from the vehicle is required when replacing the solenoid control valve as shown in **Fig. 26.** Refer to "Front Suspension & Steering" for power steering gear replacement procedures.

1. Disconnect solenoid control valve electrical connector at solenoid control module as shown in **Fig. 24.**
2. Using a suitable 1 5/16 inch crowfoot or equivalent, remove solenoid from steering gear.
3. Inspect O-ring seals on solenoid control valve for damage replace as required. Coat with fresh clean power steering fluid prior to installation.
4. Install solenoid control valve by hand until fully seated, then using crowfoot tool or equivalent, tighten to specifications.
5. Connect solenoid electrical connectors. Ensure connector seal is in good condition prior to installation.
6. Road test vehicle or test using DRB scan tool, or equivalent to confirm proper operation of variable assist speed proportional power steering gear.

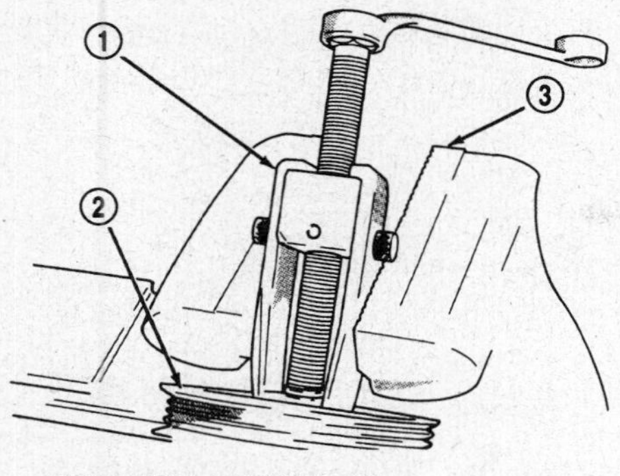

Fig. 15 Power steering pump pulley removal

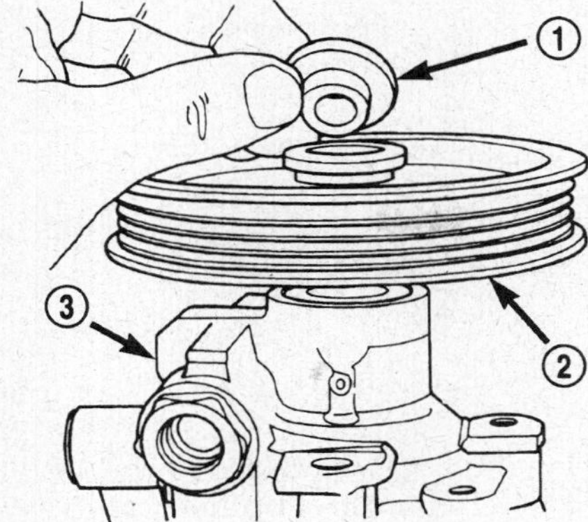

Fig. 16 Power steering pump pulley spacer

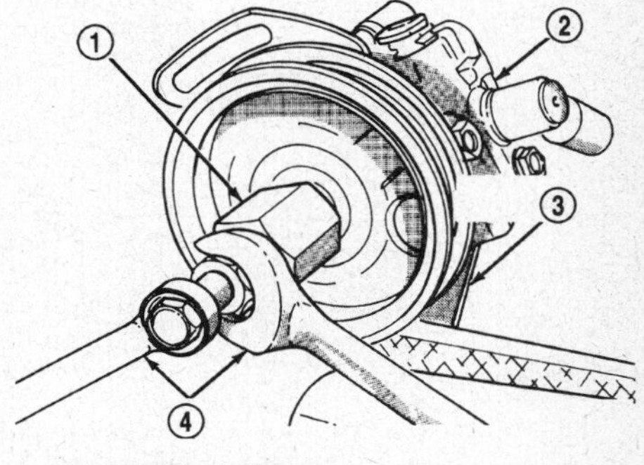

Fig. 17 Power steering pulley installer tool

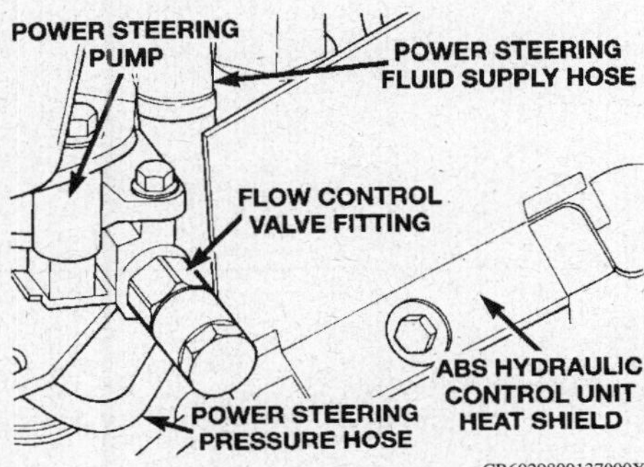

Fig. 18 Power steering pressure hose replacement. With droop flow variable assist power steering

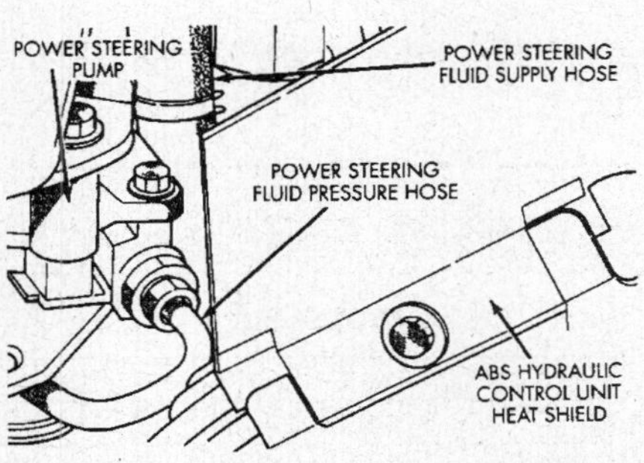

Fig. 19 Power steering pressure hose replacement. Less droop flow assisted power steering

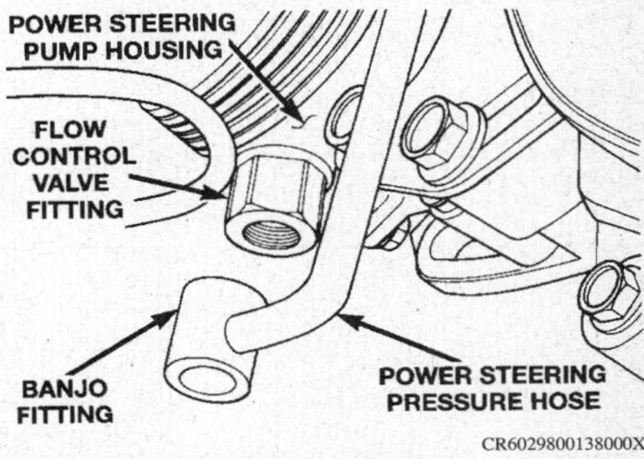

Fig. 20 Flow control valve replacement. With droop flow assisted power steering

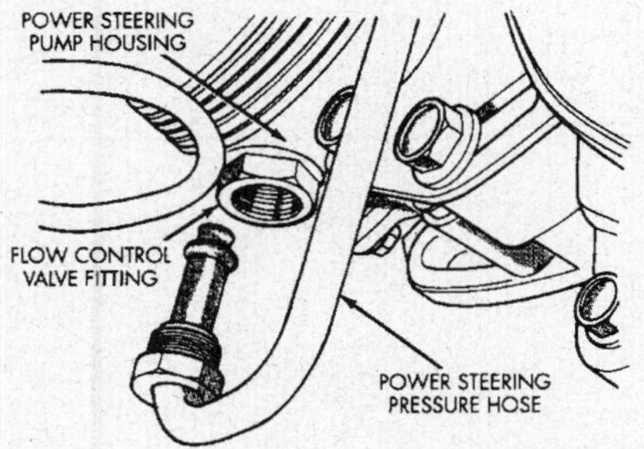

Fig. 21 Flow control valve replacement. Less droop flow assisted power steering

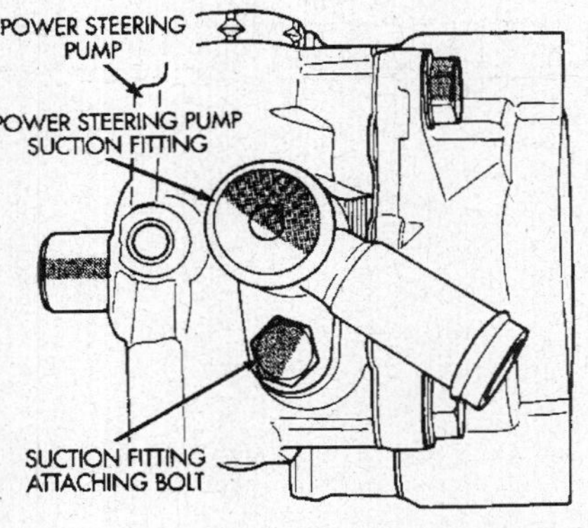

Fig. 22 Suction port fitting replacement

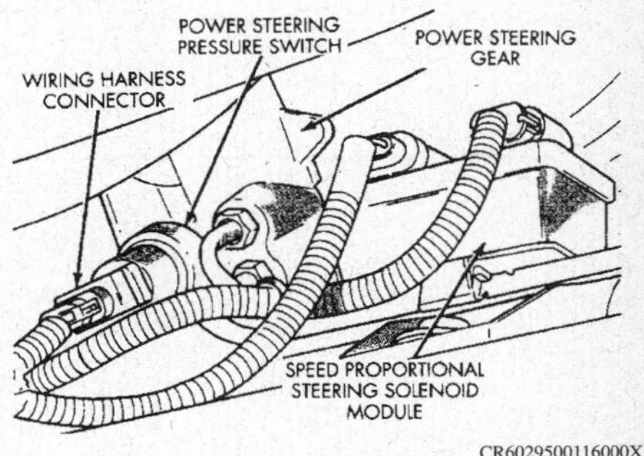

Fig. 23 Pressure switch replacement

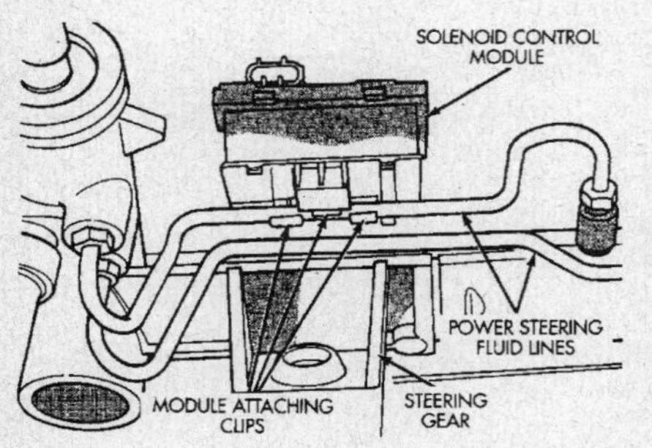

Fig. 24 Solenoid control module replacement

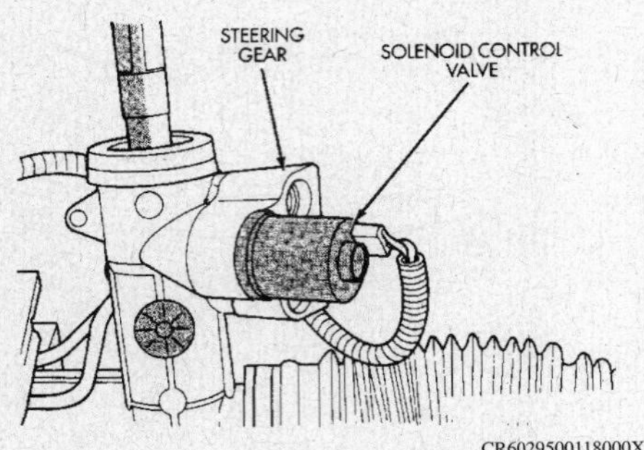

Fig. 25 Solenoid module electrical connectors

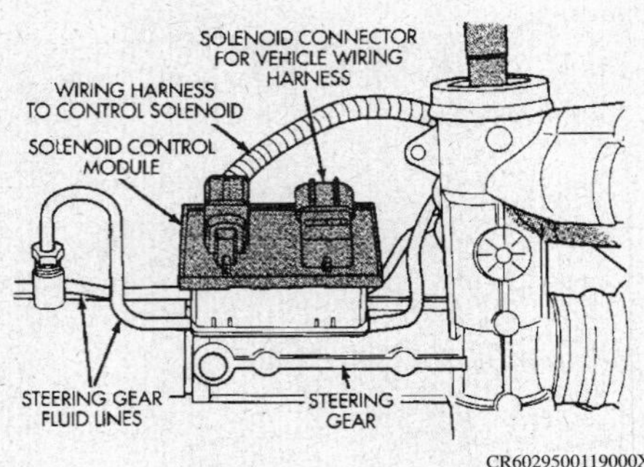

Fig. 26 Solenoid control valve replacement

TECHNICAL SERVICE BULLETINS

COLD ENGINE POWER STEERING NOISE

1998

On some of these models, the power steering pump may make noise following cold engine starts at temperatures below 10°F. Usually the noise will last less than one minute. The noise occurs with or without steering wheel input, increasing in duration and intensity as temperature decreases.

This condition may be caused by the power steering fluid. To correct this condition, replace power steering fluid part No. MS-5931 with improved cold temperature property power steering fluid part No. MS-9933 (5010304AA).

TIGHTENING SPECIFICATIONS

Year	Component	Torque/Ft. Lbs.
1998–2002	Discharge/Flow Control Valve Fitting	55
	Hose Tube Nuts	23
	Outer Tie Rod To Inner Tie Rod Lock Nut	55
	Pressure Switch	12
	Reservoir To Engine Bracket	21
	Solenoid Control Valve	10
	Steering Pump Bracket	40
	Tie Rod To Steering Knuckle	45

Concorde, Intrepid, LHS & 300M

NOTE: On Air Bag Equipped Models, Refer To "Air Bag System Precautions" Located In The Front Of This Manual For System Disarming & Arming Procedures.

NOTE: Refer To "Computer Relearn Procedures" Located In The Front Of This Manual When Battery Power To The Computer Has Been Interrupted.

NOTE: Prior To Performing Any Service Operations Listed In This Section, Consult The "Technical Service Bulletins" Section For Related Information.

INDEX

PRECAUTIONS

AIR BAG SYSTEMS

Refer to "Air Bag System Precautions" in the front of this manual for system disarming and arming procedures.

BATTERY GROUND CABLE

Prior to service, disconnect battery ground cable and isolate as required.

DESCRIPTION

Power assist is provided by an open center, rotary type control valve. It is used to direct oil from the power steering pump to either side of the integral steering rack piston. These vehicles may be equipped with three different types of power steering. They are base, firm-feel and speed-proportional power steering.

POWER STEERING PUMP

2.7L Engine

This belt driven constant flow rate power steering pump has an integral power steering fluid reservoir as shown in **Fig. 1.**

3.2L & 3.5L Engines

The belt driven power steering pump is a constant flow rate and displacement vane type. This power steering pump has a remotely mounted power steering fluid reservoir as shown in **Fig. 2.**

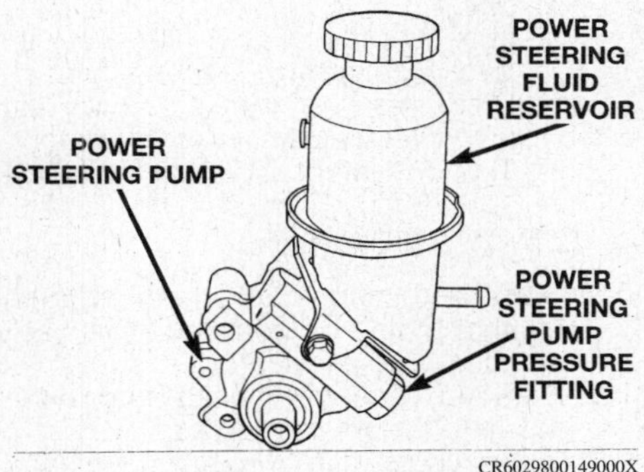

Fig. 1 Power steering pump. 2.7L engine

STEERING GEAR

The standard and firm-feel steering gears only differ internally, **Fig. 3** . The speed-sensitive variable-effort, speed-proportional steering is an electronically controlled, variable-effort type system, **Fig. 4.**

The rack and pinion power steering gear used on these models should not be serviced or adjusted. If a malfunction or internal fluid leak should occur, the complete steering gear must be replaced.

TROUBLESHOOTING

Refer to "Breeze, Cirrus, Sebring Convertible & Stratus" section for power steering system troubleshooting.

DIAGNOSIS & TESTING

ACCESSING DIAGNOSTIC TROUBLE CODES

A DRB III or equivalent scan tool is required to access the speed proportional power steering diagnostic trouble codes. Connect the scan tool to the Data Link Connector (DLC) as shown in **Fig. 5**. The diagnostic cycle begins when the ignition is turned On.

CONNECTOR TERMINAL IDENTIFICATION

Refer to **Figs. 6 and 7,** for connector terminal identification.

DIAGNOSTIC TESTS

1998

Refer to **Fig. 8,** for diagnostic test.

1999-2000

Refer to **Figs. 9 and 10** for diagnostic tests.

2001-02

Refer to **Figs. 11 through 14,** for diagnostic tests.

CLEARING DIAGNOSTIC TROUBLE CODES

Record existing codes for future reference prior to clearing DTCs. To clear diagnostic trouble codes, select the "Erase DTCs" data screen on the DRB scan tool.

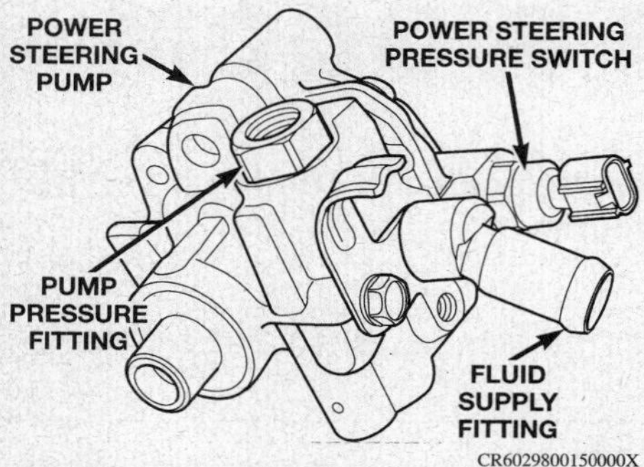

Fig. 2 Power steering pump. 3.2L & 3.5L engines

COMPONENT TESTING

POWER STEERING PUMP

Less Speed Proportional Steering

Refer to "Neon" section for power steering pump diagnosis and testing procedures.

POWER STEERING SYSTEM SERVICE

Power Steering System Bleed

1. Ensure power steering fluid remote reservoir is full, then start engine and turn steering wheel from stop to stop several times.
2. Stop engine and inspect fluid level again. If required, add fluid until proper fluid level is reached.
3. Repeat procedure until fluid level is consistent. Inspect system for leaks.

Component Service

FLUID COOLER, REPLACE

1. Using suitable siphon pump, remove as much power steering fluid as possible from reservoir.
2. Raise and support vehicle on a frame contact hoist or with suitable jack stands.
3. **On 300M models,** remove front fascia.
4. **On all models,** remove clamp and lower hose, then drain fluid into suitable container.
5. Remove clamp and upper hose.
6. Remove mounting clips and air dam from lower radiator support.
7. Remove mounting nuts and cooler.
8. Reverse procedure to install, noting following:
   a. Install air dam with new retaining clips.
   b. Ensure clamps are installed on hoses past cooler retention beads.
   c. Tighten mounting nuts to specifications.
   d. Fill and bleed power steering fluid.

1 – STEERING GEAR FLUID LINES
2 – STEERING GEAR BOOT
3 – RACK AND PINION STEERING GEAR
4 – CLAMP
5 – TIE ROD END
6 – ADJUSTMENT SLEEVE
7 – INNER TIE ROD
8 – ADJUSTMENT SLEEVE
9 – TIE ROD END
10 – CLAMP

CR6029800201000X

Fig. 3 Rack & pinion steering gear. Less speed proportional steering

RESERVOIR, REPLACE

2.7L Engine

1. Remove power steering pump as outlined in "Front Suspension & Steering" under "Concorde, Intrepid, LHS & 300M."
2. Remove mounting bolts and reservoir.
3. Reverse procedure to install, noting following:
   a. Lubricate reservoir O-ring seal with fresh clean power steering fluid.
   b. Press reservoir nipple straight into pump without rotating or twisting.
   c. Tighten fasteners to specifications.

3.2 & 3.5L Engines

1. Raise and support vehicle on a frame contact hoist or with suitable jack stands.
2. Remove reservoir hoses and drain fluid into suitable container.
3. Lower vehicle, then rotate reservoir's rear side toward engine, out of its bracket, then remove reservoir.
4. Reverse procedure to install, noting following:
   a. Ensure reservoir bottom tab is inserted into frame rail hole.
   b. Ensure clamps are installed on hoses past retention beads.
   c. Tighten mounting screw to specifications.

DRIVE PULLEY, REPLACE

Removal

1. Remove power steering pump as described in "Front Suspension & Steering Section." under "Concorde, Intrepid, LHS & 300M.".
2. Mount pump by mounting boss in suitable vise. Do not clamp pump body.
3. Using puller tool No. C-4333, or equivalent, remove pulley. **Do not use press or hammer on pump shaft.**

Installation

1. Place pulley squarely on shaft end and install spacer provided with pump or pulley into pulley hub.
2. Uninstall spacer tool No. 6936, or equivalent into pulley hub as shown in **Fig. 15.**
3. Thread installer tool No. C-4063, or equivalent, into pump shaft.
4. Holding installer tool with one wrench, turn installer hex down threaded rod pushing pulley onto shaft. Ensure tool and pulley remain aligned.
5. Ensure spacer is fully seated against shaft front, then remove tool and spacer.
6. Tighten all fasteners to specifications.

PRESSURE FITTING, REPLACE

1998–99

1. Remove power steering pump as outlined in "Front Suspension & Steering." under "Concorde, Intrepid, LHS & 300M."
2. Remove pressure fitting.
3. Reverse procedure to install with new O-ring seal. Tighten fitting to specifications.

2000–02

This is not a serviceable component.

PRESSURE SWITCH, REPLACE

1. **On models equipped with 3.2 and 3.5L engines,** raise and support vehicle.
2. **On all models,** disconnect wire harness electrical connector, then remove power steering pressure switch.
3. Reverse procedure to install. Tighten to specifications.

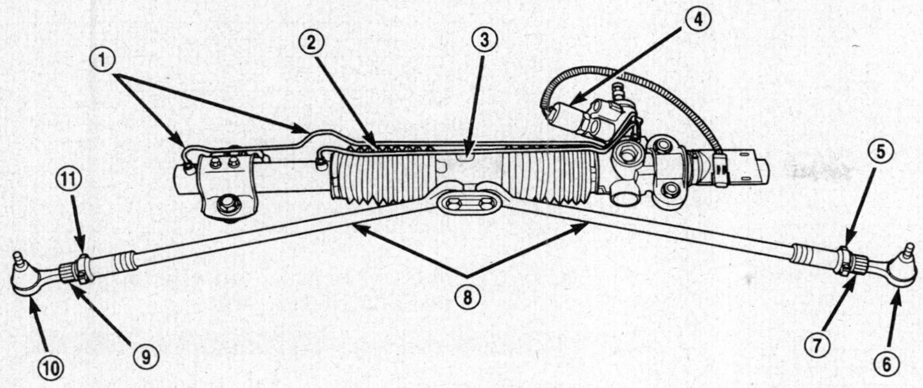

1 – STEERING GEAR FLUID LINES
2 – STEERING GEAR BOOT
3 – RACK AND PINION STEERING GEAR
4 – SOLENOID CONTROL VALVE
5 – CLAMP
6 – TIE ROD END
7 – ADJUSTMENT SLEEVE
8 – INNER TIE ROD
9 – ADJUSTMENT SLEEVE
10 – TIE ROD END
11 – CLAMP

CR6029800202000X

Fig. 4 Rack & pinion steering gear. With speed proportional steering

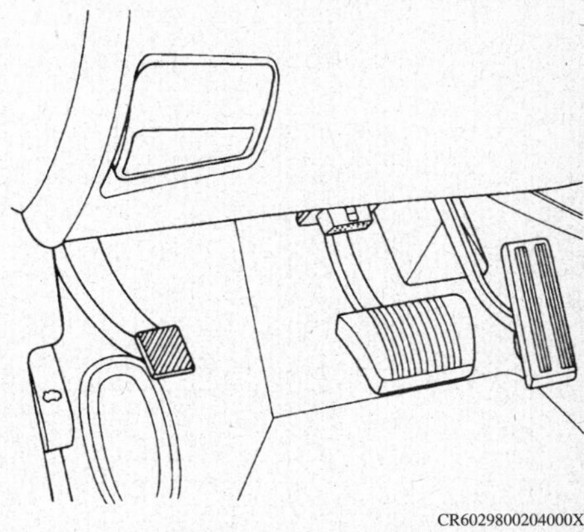

Fig. 5 Data link connector location

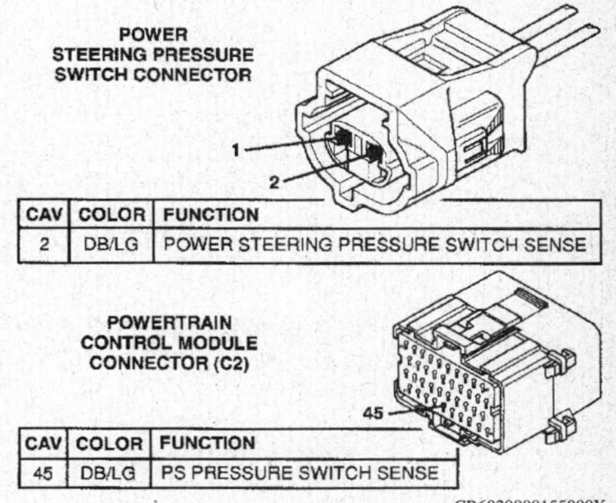

CAV	COLOR	FUNCTION
2	DB/LG	POWER STEERING PRESSURE SWITCH SENSE

CAV	COLOR	FUNCTION
45	DB/LG	PS PRESSURE SWITCH SENSE

Fig. 6 Connector terminal identification. 1998–2000

OUTER TIE ROD & BOOT, REPLACE

1. Raise and support vehicle, then remove tire and wheel assembly.
2. Loosen tie rod adjustment sleeve locknut.
3. Loosen, but do not remove, outer tie rod to steering arm nut.
4. Using tie rod replacement tool No. C-3894-A, or equivalent, remove tie rod end from steering arm.
5. Remove tie rod from adjustment sleeve.
6. Reverse procedure to install, noting following:
   a. Inspect toe setting prior to tightening adjustment sleeve locknut.
   b. Ensure maximum exposed thread requirements are not exceeded as shown in **Fig. 16.**

SOLENOID CONTROL VALVE CONTROL MODULE, REPLACE

1. Remove electrical connector from control module.
2. Depress two locking tabs on bottom of control module, then detach control module from steering gear end cap.
3. Rotate control module upward, until retaining tabs can be removed from steering gear end cap. Remove control module from steering gear.
4. Reverse procedure to install.

SOLENOID CONTROL VALVE, REPLACE

1. Remove solenoid control valve electrical connector from control module.
2. Remove power steering pressure and return hoses from steering gear, allowing fluid to drain into an approved container.
3. Using a suitable 1$\frac{5}{16}$ inch crowfoot wrench, loosen solenoid control valve from steering gear.
4. Remove control valve from steering gear.
5. Reverse procedure to install. Tighten valve to specifications.

TECHNICAL SERVICE BULLETINS

COLD ENGINE POWER STEERING NOISE

1998 Concorde & Intrepid & 1998–99 Concorde, Intrepid, LHS & 300M Built Through 7/31/98

On these models, the power steering pump may make noise following cold engine starts at temperatures below 10°F. The noise usually last less than one minute, occurring with and without steering wheel input and increasing in duration and intensity as temperatures decrease.

This condition may be caused by the power steering fluid. To correct this condition, replace power steering fluid with improved cold temperature property power steering fluid part No. MS-9933, (5010304AA) or equivalent.

STEERING GEAR/FRONT SUSPENSION RATTLE

1998–2000

Vehicles may exhibit rattle from front of vehicle which is more noticeable at slow speeds on rough road or over bumps. This rattle may sound like a front suspension component rattle.

If rattle can be isolated to the rack housing, inspect for pin holes in the convolutes of the bellows by expanding the convolutes left and right. The pinholes may be surrounded by rusty water stains. If pinholes exist and there is a rattle, replace power steering gear assembly. If pinholes cannot be seen, inspect steering gear assembly as follows:

1. Center steering gear.
2. Remove fluid level wire connector and master cylinder mounting nuts, then move master cylinder out of way.
3. Cut off clamp from rubber rack protector on left end of steering gear, then remove rack protector.
4. With vehicle off of ground, cycle rack all the way to the left. Approximately 3–4 inches of the rack should now be visible.
5. Inspect rack for any signs of corrosion. The rack will normally appear greasy and may look dark in color.
6. If rack is corroded, replace power steering rack assembly.
7. If there is no corrosion, install new rack protector and clamp and reassemble vehicle.

JUNCTION BLOCK BODY CONTROL MODULE - JB

CAV	CIRCUIT	FUNCTION
1	Z20	GROUND
2	M2	COURTESY LAMP DRIVER
3	S76	SPEED PROPORTIONAL STEERING SOLENOID (-)
4	S77	SPEED PROPORTIONAL STEERING SOLENOID (+)
5	G5	FUSED IGNITION SWITCH OUTPUT (RUN-START)
6	L7	PARK LAMP RELAY OUTPUT
7	M1	FUSED B(+)
8	P2	DECKLID RELEASE CONTROL
9	-	-
10	D25	PCI BUS (OTIS)
11	-	-
12	-	-
13	P109	DRIVER DOOR UNLOCK RELAY CONTROL
14	L307	LOW BEAM RELAY CONTROL
15	P38	DOOR LOCK RELAY CONTROL
16	L308	PARK LAMP RELAY CONTROL
17	L26	FOG LAMP RELAY CONTROL
18	X3	HORN RELAY CONTROL
19	P36	DOOR UNLOCK RELAY CONTROL
20	Z2	GROUND

CR6020000214000X

Fig. 7 Connector terminal identification (Part 1 of 3). 2001–02

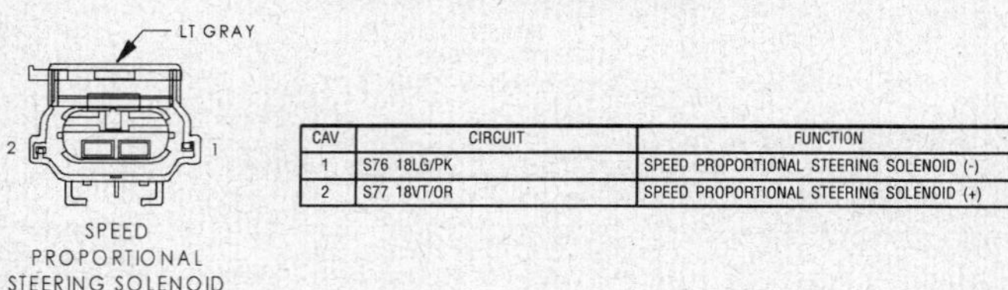

CAV	CIRCUIT	FUNCTION
1	S76 18LG/PK	SPEED PROPORTIONAL STEERING SOLENOID (-)
2	S77 18VT/OR	SPEED PROPORTIONAL STEERING SOLENOID (+)

CR6020000216000X

Fig. 7 Connector terminal identification (Part 3 of 3). 2001–02

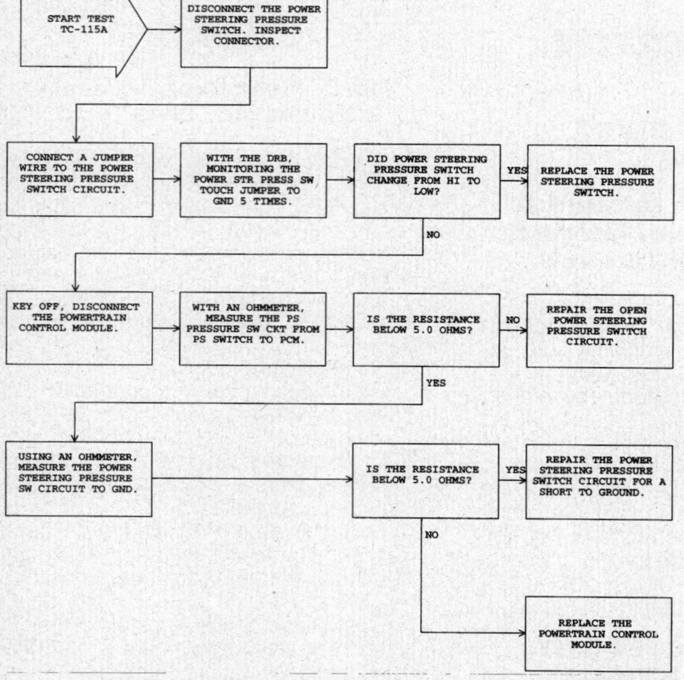

CR6029800205000X

Fig. 8 Test TC-115A: Power Steering Switch Failure. 1998

JUNCTION BLOCK - C10

GRAY

CAV	CIRCUIT	FUNCTION
1	L60 18TN	RIGHT TURN SIGNAL
2	L61 18LG	LEFT TURN SIGNAL
3	G9 20GY/BK	RED BRAKE WARNING INDICATOR DRIVER
4	L34 20GY/OR	FUSED RIGHT HIGH BEAM OUTPUT
5	-	-
6	L1 20VT/BK	BACK-UP LAMP FEED
7	F18 20LG/BK	FUSED IGNITION SWITCH OUTPUT (RUN-START)
8	S77 18VT/OR (EXCEPT BUILT-UP EXPORT)	SPEED PROPORTIONAL STEERING SOLENOID (+)
9	-	-
10	S76 18LG/PK (EXCEPT BUILT-UP EXPORT)	SPEED PROPORTIONAL STEERING SOLENOID (-)

CR6020000215000X

Fig. 7 Connector terminal identification (Part 2 of 3). 2001–02

TEST	ACTION
1	Turn Ignition On. With the DRB, read the DTC's. Is the Global Good Trip Counter displayed and equal to zero? Yes → Go To 2 No → Go To 7
2	Turn Ignition Off Disconnect the Power Steering Pressure Switch connector. Using an Ohmmeter, measure the resistance of the Ground Circuit at the Power Steering Pressure Switch connector to a good Ground. Is the resistance below 5.0 ohms? Yes → Go To 3 No → Repair the open Power Steering Pressure Switch Ground Circuit. Perform the Powertrain Verification Test - Ver 5.
3	Turn ignition off. Disconnect the Power Steering Pressure Switch Connector. Turn ignition on. Connect a Jumper Wire to the Power Steering Pressure Switch Sense Circuit. Using the DRB, while monitoring the Power Steering Pressure Switch, touch the Jumper Wire to the Ground Circuit at the Power Steering Pressure Switch harness connector several times. Did the Power Steering Pressure Switch status change from Hi to Low? Yes → Replace the Power Steering Pressure Switch. Perform the Powertrain Verification Test - Ver 5. No → Go To 4

CR6020000206010X

Fig. 9 DTC P0551: PS Switch Failure (Part 1 of 2). 1999–2000

TEST	ACTION
4	Turn Ignition Off. Disconnect the Power Steering Pressure Switch Connector. Disconnect the Powertrain Control Module connector. With an Ohmmeter, measure the Power Steering Pressure Switch Sense Circuit to ground at the PCM connector. Is the resistance below 5.0 ohms? Yes → Repair the Power Steering Pressure Switch Sense Circuit for a short to ground. Perform the Powertrain Verification Test - Ver 5. No → Go To 5
5	Turn Ignition Off. Disconnect the Power Steering Pressure Switch Connector. Disconnect the Powertrain Control Module connector. Using an Ohmmeter, measure resistance of Power Steering Pressure Switch Sense circuit from PCM connector to Sensor Connector. Is the resistance below 5.0 ohms? Yes → Go To 6 No → Repair the open Power Steering Switch Sense Circuit. Perform the Powertrain Verification Test - Ver 5.
6	If there are no possible causes remaining, replace the Powertrain Control Module. View repair options. Repair Replace the Powertrain Control Module. Perform the Powertrain Verification Test - Ver 5.
7	Turn ignition off. **Note: Visually inspect the related wiring harness. Look for any chafed, pierced, pinched, or partially broken wires.** **Note: Visually inspect the related wire harness connectors. Look for broken, bent, pushed out, or corroded terminals.** **Note: Refer to any Technical Service Bulletins (TSB) that may apply.** Were any problems found? Yes → Repair wiring harness/connectors as necessary. Perform the Powertrain Verification Test - Ver 5. No → Test Complete.

CR6020000206020X

Fig. 9 DTC P0551: PS Switch Failure (Part 2 of 2). 1999–2000

POWERTRAIN VERIFICATION TEST VER - 5
1. Inspect the vehicle to ensure that all engine components are properly installed and connected. Reassemble and reconnect components as necessary. 2. If any existing diagnostic trouble codes have not been repaired, go to Symptom List and follow path specified. 3. Connect the DRBIII® to the data link connector. 4. Ensure the fuel tank has at least a quarter tank of fuel. Turn off all accessories. 5. Perform steps 6 through 8 if the PCM has been replaced. Then proceed with the verification. If the PCM has not been replaced skip those steps and continue verification. 6. If PCM has been changed and correct VIN and mileage have not been programmed, a DTC will be set in ABS and Air bag modules. In addition, if vehicle is equipped with a Sentry Key Immobilizer Module (SKIM), Secret Key data must be updated to enable start. 7. For ABS and Air Bag systems: Enter correct VIN and Mileage in PCM. Erase codes in ABS and Air Bag modules. 8. For SKIM theft alarm: Connect DRB to data link conn. Go to Theft Alarm, SKIM, Misc. and place SKIM in secured access mode, by using the appropriate PIN code for this vehicle. Select Update the Secret Key data. Data will be transferred from SKIM to PCM. 9. If a Comprehensive Component DTC was repaired, perform steps 10-13. If a Major OBDII Monitor DTC was repaired skip those steps and continue verification. 10. After the ignition has been off for at least 10 seconds, restart the vehicle and run 2 minutes. 11. If the Good Trip counter changed to one or more and there are no new DTC's, the repair was successful and is now complete. Erase DTC's and disconnect the DRBIII®. 12. If the repaired DTC has reset, the repair is not complete. Check for any related TSB's or flash updates and return to the Symptom list. 13. If another DTC has set, return to the Symptom List and follow the path specified for that DTC. 14. With the DRBIII®, monitor the appropriate pre-test enabling conditions until all conditions have been met. Once the conditions have been met, switch screen to the appropriate OBDII monitor, (Audible beeps when the monitor is running). 15. If the monitor ran, and the Good Trip counter changed to one or more, the repair was successful and is now complete. Erase DTC's and disconnect the DRBIII®. 16. If the repaired OBDII trouble code has reset or was seen in the monitor while on the road test, the repair is not complete. Check for any related technical service bulletins or flash updates and return to Symptom List. 17. If another DTC has set, return to the Symptom List and follow the path specified for that DTC. Repair is not complete, refer to appropriate symptom.

CR6020000207000X

Fig. 10 Verification Test VER-5. 1999–2000

TEST	ACTION
3	Turn the ignition off. Disconnect the Speed Pro Steering Solenoid harness connector. Start the engine. Measure the voltage of the Speed Pro Steering Solenoid (+) circuit in the Speed Pro Steering Solenoid harness connector. Is there any voltage present? Yes → Repair the Seed Pro Steering Solenoid (+) circuit for a short to voltage. Perform SPEED PRO STEERING VERIFICATION TEST - VER 1. No → Go To 4
4	Turn the ignition off. Disconnect the Speed Pro Steering Solenoid harness connector. Start the engine. Measure the voltage of the Speed Pro Steering Solenoid (-) circuit in the Speed Pro Steering Solenoid harness connector. Is there any voltage present? Yes → Repair the Speed Pro Steering Solenoid (-) circuit for a short to voltage and replace the Body Control Module (BCM will be damaged). Perform BODY VERIFICATION TEST - VER 1. No → Go To 5
5	Turn the ignition off. Disconnect the Speed Pro Steering Solenoid harness connector. Remove the Body Control Module from the Junction Block. Measure the resistance of the Speed Pro Steering Solenoid (+) circuit to the Speed Pro Steering Solenoid (-) circuit in the Junction Block BCM Internal connector. Is the resistance below 100.0 ohms Yes → Repair the Speed Pro Steering Solenoid (+) circuit for a short to the Speed Pro Steering Solenoid (-) circuit. Perform SPEED PRO STEERING VERIFICATION TEST - VER 1. No → Go To 6
6	If there are no possible causes remaining, view repair. Repair Replace the Body Control Module. Perform BODY VERIFICATION TEST - VER 1.

CR6020000217020X

Fig. 11 Speed Pro Steering Circuit Short to Voltage (Part 2 of 2). 2001–02

TEST	ACTION
1	Start the engine. While turning the Steering Wheel, monitor the amount of force it takes to turn the Steering Wheel. With the DRBIII®, de-activate the Speed Pro Steering Solenoid for 15 seconds. Again turn the Steering Wheel and monitor the amount of force it takes to turn the Steering Wheel. Was the Steering Wheel harder to turn with the Speed Pro Steering Solenoid de-activated? Yes → System is operating properly at this time. Erase DTC, inspect the wiring and connectors and repair as necessary. Perform SPEED PRO STEERING VERIFICATION TEST - VER 1. No → Go To 2
2	Turn the ignition off. Disconnect the Speed Pro Steering Solenoid harness connector. Measure the resistance of the Speed Pro Steering Solenoid. Is the resistance between 5.7 and 6.3 ohms at 20 C (68° F)? Yes → Go To 3 No → Replace the Speed Pro Steering Solenoid. Perform SPEED PRO STEERING VERIFICATION TEST - VER 1.

CR6020000217010X

Fig. 11 Speed Pro Steering Circuit Short to Voltage (Part 1 of 2). 2001–02

TEST	ACTION
1	Start the engine. While turning the Steering Wheel, monitor the amount of force it takes to turn the Steering Wheel With the DRBIII®, de-activate the Speed Pro Steering Solenoid for 15 seconds. Again turn the steering wheel and monitor the amount of force it takes to turn the Steering Wheel. Was the Steering Wheel harder to turn while the Speed Pro Steering Solenoid was de-activated? Yes → System is operating properly at this time. Erase the DTC, inspect the wiring and connectors and repair as necessary. Perform SPEED PRO STEERING VERIFICATION TEST - VER 1. No → Go To 2
2	Turn the ignition off. Disconnect the Speed Pro Steering Solenoid harness connector. Measure the resistance of the Speed Pro Steering Solenoid. Is the resistance between 5.7 and 6.3 ohms at 20 C (68° F)? Yes → Go To 3 No → Replace the Speed Pro Steering Solenoid. Perform SPEED PRO STEERING VERIFICATION TEST - VER 1.

CR6020000218010X

Fig. 12 Speed Pro Steering Solenoid Circuit Open/Shorted to Ground (Part 1 of 2). 2001–02

TEST	ACTION
3	Turn the ignition off. Disconnect the Speed Pro Steering Solenoid harness connector. Measure the resistance between ground and the Speed Pro Steering Solenoid (+) circuit in the Speed Pro Steering Solenoid harness connector. Is the resistance below 100 ohms? Yes → Repair the Speed Pro Steering (+) circuit for a short to ground. Perform SPEED PRO STEERING VERIFICATION TEST - VER 1. No → Go To 4
4	Turn the ignition off. Disconnect the Speed Pro Steering Solenoid harness connector. Measure the resistance between ground and the Speed Pro Steering Solenoid (-) circuit in the Speed Pro Steering Solenoid harness connector. Is the resistance below 100 ohms? Yes → Repair the Speed Pro Steering (-) circuit for a short to ground. Perform SPEED PRO STEERING VERIFICATION TEST - VER 1. No → Go To 5
5	Turn the ignition off. Disconnect the Speed Pro Steering Solenoid harness connector. Remove the Body Control Module from the Junction Block. Measure the resistance of the Speed Pro Steering Solenoid (-) circuit between the Junction Block BCM connector and the Speed Pro Steering Solenoid harness connector. Is the resistance below 5.0 ohms? Yes → Go To 6 No → Repair the open Speed Pro Steering Solenoid (-) circuit. Perform SPEED PRO STEERING VERIFICATION TEST - VER 1.
6	Turn the ignition off. Disconnect the Speed Pro Steering Solenoid harness connector. Remove the Body Control Module from the Junction Block. Measure the resistance of the Speed Pro Steering Solenoid (+) circuit to the Speed Pro Steering Solenoid (-) circuit in the Junction Block BCM Internal connector. Is the resistance below 100.0 ohms Yes → Repair the Speed Pro Steering Solenoid (+) circuit for a short to the Speed Pro Steering Solenoid (-) circuit. Perform SPEED PRO STEERING VERIFICATION TEST - VER 1. No → Go To 7
7	Turn the ignition off. Disconnect the Speed Pro Steering Solenoid harness connector. Remove the Body Control Module from the Junction Block. Measure the resistance of the Speed Pro Steering Solenoid (+) circuit between the Junction Block BCM connector and the Speed Pro Steering Solenoid connector. Is the resistance below 5.0 ohms? Yes → Go To 8 No → Repair the open Speed Pro Steering Solenoid (+) circuit. Perform SPEED PRO STEERING VERIFICATION TEST - VER 1.
8	If there are no possible causes remaining, view repair. Repair Replace the Body Control Module. Perform BODY VERIFICATION TEST - VER 1.

CR6020000218020X

Fig. 12 Speed Pro Steering Solenoid Circuit Open/Shorted to Ground (Part 2 of 2). 2001–02

BODY VERIFICATION TEST - VER 1
1. Disconnect all jumper wires and reconnect all previously disconnected components and connectors. 2. If the Sentry Key Immobilizer Module (SKIM) or the Powertrain Control Module (PCM) was replaced, proceed to number 6. If the SKIM or PCM was not replaced, continue to the next number. 3. If the Body Control Module was replaced, turn the ignition on for 15 seconds (to allow the new BCM to learn VIN) or engine may not start (if VTSS equipped). If the vehicle is equipped with VTSS, use the DRBIII® and enable VTSS. 4. Program all other options as needed. 5. If any repairs were made to the HVAC System, disconnect the battery or, using the DRBIII®, recalibrate the HVAC doors. Proceed to number 13. 6. Obtain the Vehicle's unique PIN assigned to it's original SKIM from either the vehicle's invoice or from Chrysler's Customer Assistance Center (1-800-992-1997). 7. NOTE: Once Secured Access Mode is active, the SKIM will remain in that mode for 60 seconds. 8. With the DRBIII®, select THEFT ALARM, SKIM, MISCELLANEOUS and select SKIM REPLACED. Enter the 4 digit PIN to put the SKIM in Secured Access Mode. 9. The DRBIII® will prompt for the following steps. (1) Program the country code into the SKIM's memory. (2) Program the vehicle's VIN into the SKIM memory. (3) Transfer the vehicle's Secret Key data from the PCM. 10. Using the DRBIII®, program all customer keys into the SKIM memory. This requires that the SKIM be in Secured Access Mode, using the 4 digit PIN. 11. Note: If the PCM is replaced, the VIN and the unique Secret Key data must be transferred from the SKIM to the PCM. This procedure requires the SKIM to be placed in Secured Access Mode using the 4-digit PIN. 12. Note: If 3 attempts are made to enter Secured Access Mode using an incorrect PIN, Secured Access Mode will be locked out for 1 hour which causes the DRBIII® to display "Bus +\- Signals Open". To exit this mode, turn ignition to Run for 1 hour. 13. Ensure that all accessories are turned off and that the battery is fully charged. 14. Ensure that the Ignition is on. 15. With the DRBIII®, record and erase all DTCs from ALL modules. Start and run the engine for 2 minutes. Operate all functions of the system that caused the original concern. 16. Turn the ignition off and wait 5 seconds. Turn the ignition on and using the DRBIII®, read DTCs from ALL modules. Are any DTC's present or is the original condition still present? Yes → Repair is not complete, refer to appropriate symptom. No → Repair is complete.

CR6020000220000X

Fig. 14 Verification Test VER-1. 2001–02

TEST	ACTION
1	Start the engine. While turning the Steering Wheel, monitor the amount of force it takes to turn the Steering Wheel. With the DRBIII®, de-activate the Speed Pro Steering Solenoid for 15 seconds. Again turn the Steering Wheel and monitor the amount of force it takes to turn the Steering Wheel. Was the Steering Wheel harder to turn while the Speed Pro Steering Solenoid was de-activated? Yes → System is operating properly at this time. Erase the DTC, inspect the wiring and connectors and repair as necessary. Perform SPEED PRO STEERING VERIFICATION TEST - VER 1. No → Go To 2
2	Turn the ignition off. Disconnect the Speed Pro Steering Solenoid harness connector. Measure the resistance of the Speed Pro Steering Solenoid. Is the resistance between 5.7 and 6.3 ohms at 20 C (68° F)? Yes → Go To 3 No → Replace the Speed Pro Steering Solenoid. Perform SPEED PRO STEERING VERIFICATION TEST - VER 1.

CR6020000219010X

Fig. 13 Speed Pro Steering Solenoid Over Temperature (Part 1 of 2). 2001–02

TEST	ACTION
3	Using the wiring diagram/schematic as a guide, inspect the wiring and connectors from the BCM to the Speed Pro Steering Solenoid. Check for chafed, pinched, open or shorted wiring. Were there any problems found? Yes → Repair the Speed Pro Steering Solenoid wiring and/or connectors as necessary. Perform SPEED PRO STEERING VERIFICATION TEST - VER 1. No → Go To 4
4	If there are no possible causes remaining, view repair. Repair Replace the Body Control Module. Perform BODY VERIFICATION TEST - VER 1.

CR6020000219020X

Fig. 13 Speed Pro Steering Solenoid Over Temperature (Part 2 of 2). 2001–02

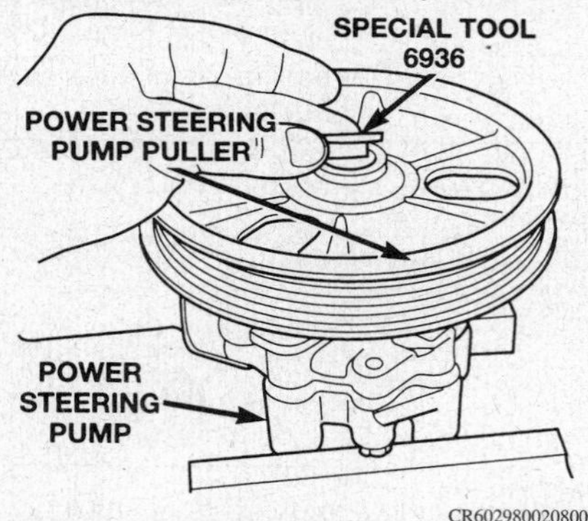

Fig. 15 Spacer tool installation into pulley

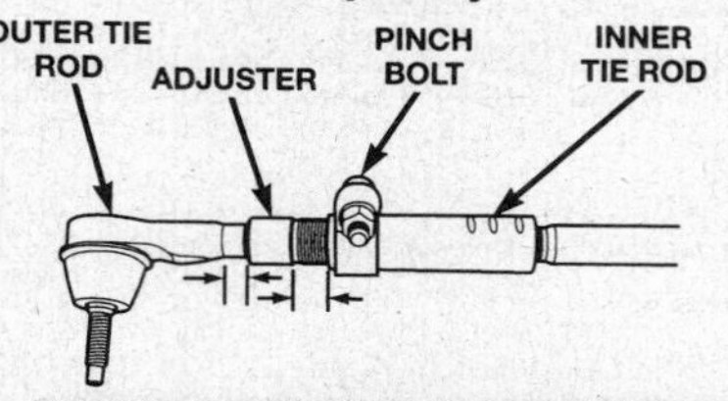

Fig. 16 Tie rod end thread requirements

TIGHTENING SPECIFICATIONS

Year	Component	Torque/Ft. Lbs.
1998–2002	Discharge Fitting	62
	Gear To Crossmember	43
	Hose Tube Nuts	35
	Pressure Switch	17
	Pump Mounting	21
	Reservoir Mounting (3.2 & 3.5L Engines)	108①
	Reservoir Mounting, Pulley Side (2.7L Engine)	10
	Reservoir Mounting, Rear (2.7L Engine)	18
	Solenoid Control Valve	12
	Tie Rod Adjuster Pinch (1998)	25
	Tie Rod Adjuster Pinch (1999–2002)	33
	Tie Rod Steering Arm	27
	Tie Rod Steering Gear	60

① — Inch Lbs.

Neon

NOTE: On Air Bag Equipped Models, Refer To "Air Bag System Precautions" Located In The Front Of This Manual For System Disarming & Arming Procedures.

NOTE: Refer To "Computer Relearn Procedures" Located In The Front Of This Manual When Battery Power To The Computer Has Been Interrupted.

NOTE: Prior To Performing Any Service Operations Listed In This Section, Consult The "Technical Service Bulletins" Section For Related Information.

INDEX

PRECAUTIONS

AIR BAG SYSTEMS

Refer to "Air Bag System Precautions" in the front of this manual for system disarming and arming procedures.

BATTERY GROUND CABLE

Prior to service, disconnect battery ground cable and isolate as required.

POWER STEERING PUMP APPLICATIONS

Due to the unique shaft bearings, flow control levels and pump displacements, the power steering pumps used on these models may not be interchanged with pumps from other vehicles.

On 2000 models, the only serviceable power steering pump components are the pulley and the pump itself. The reservoir is serviced with the pump.

DESCRIPTION

POWER STEERING PUMP

This model is equipped with a TTA constant displacement, vane type pump as shown in **Figs. 1 and 2,** a remote fluid reservoir mounts at the rear of the cylinder head on the passenger side of the vehicle. On 2000–02 models, the reservoir is serviced with the pump.

STEERING GEAR

The rack and pinion power steering gear used on these models should not be serviced or adjusted. If a malfunction or fluid leak should occur, the complete steering gear must be replaced.

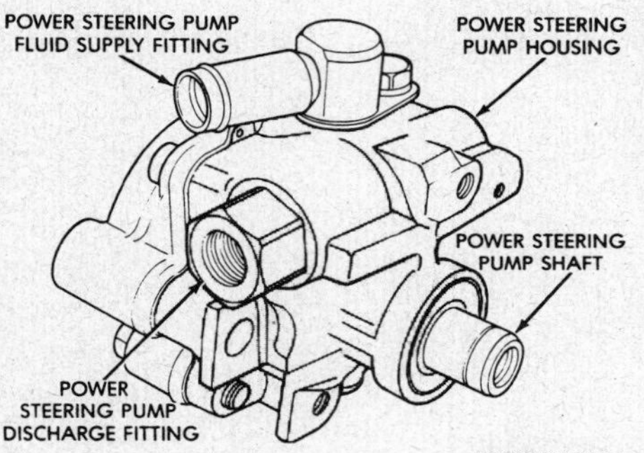

Fig. 1 TTA power steering pump. 1998–99

TROUBLESHOOTING

Refer to "Breeze, Cirrus, Sebring Convertible & Stratus" section for power steering system troubleshooting.

DIAGNOSIS & TESTING

ACCESSING DIAGNOSTIC TROUBLE CODES

A DRB or equivalent scan tool is required to access the speed proportional power steering diagnostic trouble codes. Connect the scan tool to the Data Link Connector (DLC) under lefthand side of instrument panel. The diagnostic cycle begins when the ignition is turned On.

CONNECTOR TERMINAL IDENTIFICATION

Refer to **Fig. 3,** for connector terminal identification.

DIAGNOSTIC TESTS

Refer to "Breeze, Cirrus, Sebring Convertible & Stratus" section for power steering system diagnostic tests.

CLEARING DIAGNOSTIC TROUBLE CODES

Record existing codes for future reference prior to clearing DTCs. To clear diagnostic trouble codes, select the "Erase DTCs" data screen on the DRB scan tool.

COMPONENT TESTING

Pump Pressure Inspection

1. Inspect power steering pump drive belt tension and adjust as required.
2. Disconnect power steering fluid pressure hose at steering gear or power steering pump.
3. Connect pressure/flow tester tool No C-6815, or equivalent, to both hoses using proper adapter fittings as shown in **Figs. 4 and 5.**
4. Connect spare pressure hose to gear or pump.
5. Open valve on pressure/flow tester to fully open position.
6. Start engine and let idle, then inspect

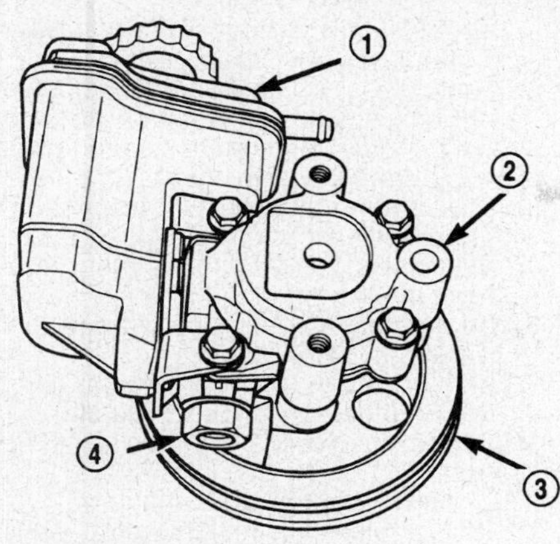

1 – POWER STEERING FLUID RESERVOIR
2 – POWER STEERING PUMP
3 – PULLEY
4 – PUMP PRESSURE FITTING

CR6020000210000X

Fig. 2 TTA power steering pump. 2000–02

steering fluid level and add as required.

7. Gauge should read below 125 psi. If pressure is not as specified, inspect hoses for restrictions. Initial pressure should be 50–80 psi.
8. Close valve fully three times and record highest pressure indicated each time. **Do not leave valve closed for more than five seconds as pump damage could occur.**
9. All three readings must be above specifications and within 50 psi of each other.
10. Open test valve and turn steering wheel left and right until against stops, then record highest indicated pressure at each position.
11. Compare pressure gauge readings to power steering pump specifications.
12. If highest output pressures are not same against either stop, steering gear is leaking internally and must be replaced.

POWER STEERING SYSTEM SERVICE

Power Steering System Bleed

1. Ensure power steering fluid reservoir is full, then start and run engine.
2. If fluid level drops after engine has been run, fill and run again until level remains constant.
3. Raise and support front of vehicle, then start engine and turn steering wheel slowly from stop to stop.
4. Stop engine and add fluid as required, then lower vehicle and start engine.
5. Turn steering wheel slowly from stop to stop, then stop engine again and add fluid as required.
6. Inspect fluid condition. If it appears extremely foamy, do not disturb vehicle for several minutes, then repeat bleed procedure. Inspect for leaks.

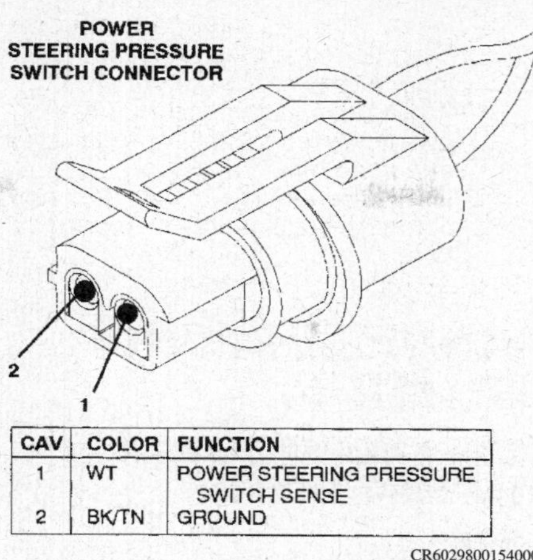

CAV	COLOR	FUNCTION
1	WT	POWER STEERING PRESSURE SWITCH SENSE
2	BK/TN	GROUND

CR6029800154000X

Fig. 3 Connector terminal identification

Component Service

POWER STEERING PRESSURE SWITCH, REPLACE

1. Raise and support vehicle.
2. Locate power steering switch on rear side of power steering gear, then disconnect its electrical connector.
3. Using a suitable 7⁄8 inch deepwell socket, remove pressure switch from steering gear.
4. Reverse procedure to install, noting following:
   a. Install and hand tighten switch into gear until fully seated.
   b. Using deepwell socket, tighten switch to specifications. **Do not overtighten. This may result in damage to switch port threads on steering gear.**
   c. Connect pressure switch electrical connector, ensuring latch is securely engaged with locking tab.
   d. Refill fluid and bleed system of air. Refer to "Power Steering System Bleed" for air bleeding procedure.
   e. Inspect system for fluid leaks.

POWER STEERING PUMP, REPLACE

On 1998–99 models, the power steering pump is not serviceable except for the pulley, reservoirs and related components, filler cap/dipstick and any oil seals other than the pump shaft seal.

On 2000–02 models, the only serviceable power steering pump components are the pulley and the pump itself. The reservoir is serviced with the pump.

POWER STEERING PUMP PULLEY, REPLACE

Refer to "Power Steering Pump, Replace" in the "Front Suspension & Steering" section of the "Neon" chapter.

1. Remove power steering pump from engine.
2. Place power steering pump in a vise while using puller tool No. C-4333, or equivalent to remove pulley, **Ensure pump shaft does not turn. Do not hammer on pulley or shaft.**
3. Place new pulley squarely on end of pump shaft.
4. Mount installer tool No. C-4063, or equivalent in pump shaft internal threads and against pulley.
5. Ensure installer and pulley remain aligned with shaft, then turn tool's outer nut and force pulley onto shaft until it is flush with end of shaft. When pulley is flush tool's outer nut will no longer turn.
6. Install pump onto engine. tighten fasteners to specifications.

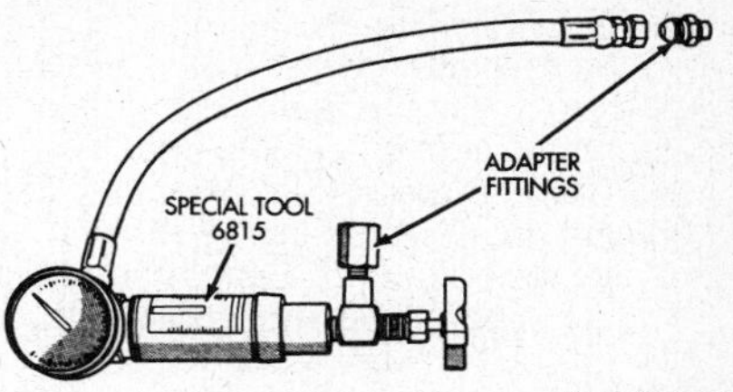

CR6029500078000A

Fig. 4 Pressure gauge tool connections. 1998–99

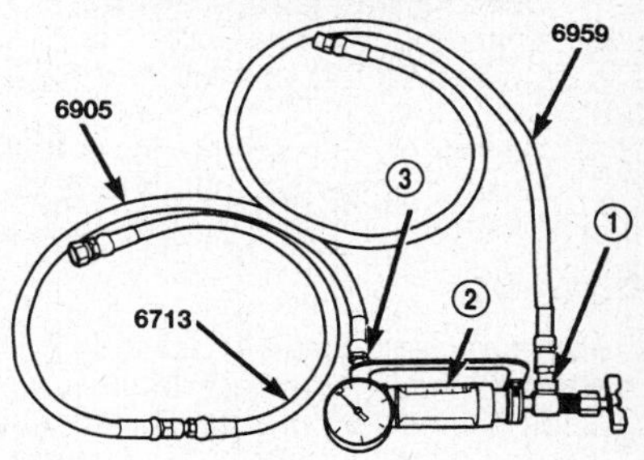

1 – OUTLET
2 – SPECIAL TOOL 6815
3 – INLET

CR6020000211000X

Fig. 5 Pressure gauge tool connections. 2000–02

STEERING GEAR, REPLACE

OUTER TIE ROD & BOOT

1998–99

1. Raise and support vehicle.
2. Remove required wheel and tire.
3. Loosen inner to outer tie rod jam nut.
4. Thread jam nut far enough up inner tie rod to pull collar away from outer tie rod end, then pull collar of end of outer tie rod.
5. Remove outer tie rod end to knuckle attaching nut by holding rod end stud stationary using a suitable 11⁄32 inch socket, then removing nut with a wrench.
6. Using tie rod end replacement tool No. MB990635, or equivalent, disconnect tie rod end from steering knuckle.
7. Unthread outer tie rod end from inner tie rod.
8. Reverse procedure to install, noting following:
   a. Install outer tie rod onto inner tie rod, ensuring lock nut is on inner tie rod. **Do not tighten nut at this time.**

b. Ensure collar is installed on inner tie rod with flat end against lock nut and open end facing outer tie rod.
c. Install tie rod end into knuckle.
d. Start tie rod end to knuckle attaching nut onto rod end stud.
e. While holding rod end stud stationary, tighten tie rod end to knuckle attaching nut.
f. Using a suitable crowfoot wrench and an 11⁄32 inch socket, tighten attaching nut to specifications. **Avoid twisting steering gear boot.**
g. Adjust front toe setting.
h. Tighten tie rod lock nut to specifications.
i. Adjust steering gear to inner tie rod boots at inner tie rods if they have twisted.

2000–02

1. Raise and support vehicle.
2. Remove required wheel and tire.
3. Loosen inner to outer tie rod jam nut.
4. Thread jam nut far enough up inner tie rod to pull collar away from outer tie rod end, then pull collar of end of outer tie rod.
5. Remove outer tie rod end to knuckle attaching nut by holding rod end stud stationary and loosening nut with a wrench.
6. Using tie rod end replacement tool No. MB991113, or equivalent, disconnect tie rod end from steering knuckle.
7. Remove tie rod heat shield.
8. Unthread outer tie rod end from inner tie rod.
9. Reverse procedure to install, noting following:
   a. Ensure jam nut is in place on inner tie rod.
   b. Thread outer tie rod end into inner tie rod.
   c. Position collar around end of outer tie rod.
   d. Thread jam nut down inner tie rod far enough to keep collar in place. Do not tighten nut at this time.
   e. Place heat shield on knuckle's steering arm. Ensure shield's hole is aligned with knuckle's hole and tangs on outside of shield with outside configuration of steering arm. Shield should now face outboard, away from steering gear and tie rod.
   f. Install outer tie rod end to knuckle.
   g. Start tie rod end to knuckle attaching nut onto rod end stud.
   h. While holding rod end stud stationary, tighten tie rod end to knuckle attaching nut.
   i. Using a suitable crowfoot wrench, tighten attaching nut to specifications.
   j. Adjust front toe setting.

TECHNICAL SERVICE BULLETINS

COLD ENGINE POWER STEERING NOISE

1998

On these models, power steering pump may make noise following cold engine starts at temperatures below 10°F. The noise usually lasts less than one minute, occurring with or without steering wheel input and increasing in duration and intensity as temperature decreases.

This condition may be caused by the power steering fluid. To correct this condition, replace power steering fluid with improved cold temperature property power steering fluid part No. MS-9933 (5010304AA), or equivalent.

POWER STEERING MOAN NOISE

2000

Power steering moan can be described as a low frequency noise emitted by the steering system with steering wheel inputs at low engine RPM. Although some noise is normally present during these conditions, moan is brought to an unacceptable level when power steering fluid is aerated. Inspect fluid level and top up if necessary. If moan is still apparent or fluid appears aerated, bleed power steering system using one of the following power steering system bleed procedures.

Bleeding with a vacuum pump:

1. Remove power steering fluid cap. Do not start vehicle until step 5.
2. Lift front wheels offo of ground just enough to allow for free turning of wheels. Turn steering wheel lock to lock three times.
3. Inspect fluid level in reservoir and fill to proper level if necessary.
4. Apply 15–20 in Hg of vacuum to power steering system at reservoir neck for five minutes, then release vacuum. Do not exceed 20 in Hg of vacuum.
5. Start engine and slowly turn steering wheel form lock to lock for 10 cycles while maitaining apporximately 2000 RPM engine speed.
6. Do not hold steering against lock, end of travel position.
7. After 10 cycles, allow engine to idle for three minutes before shutting off.
8. Inspect fluid level and top up as necessary.

Bleeding without a vacuum pump:

1. Do not start engine until step 4. Fill power steering system to recommended level at normal ambient temperature. Leave cap off.
2. Lift front wheels offo of ground just enough to allow for free turning of wheels. Turn steering wheel lock to lock three times.
3. Inspect fluid level in reservoir and top up if necessary.
4. Start engine and slowly turn steering wheel form lock to lock for 10 cycles while maitaining apporximately 2000 RPM engine speed.
5. Do not hold steering against lock, end of travel position.
6. After 10 cycles, allow engine to idle for three minutes before shutting off.
7. Inspect fluid level and top up as necessary.

LOW SPEED POWER STEERING MOAN

2000–01

A moan type sound may be heard during low speed steering wheel inputs at low engine RPM (low speed turns or parking lot maneuvers). Drive evhicle slowly through parking lot and make slow speed turns. If power steering moan is heard, replace power steering reservoir cap with revised part, number 05066063AA and inspect fluid level with included, new style dipstick. Correct fluid level as needed, do not overfill.

TIGHTENING SPECIFICATIONS

Year	Component	Torque/Ft. Lbs.
1998–2002	Outer Tie Rod End To Knuckle Nut	40
	Outer Tie Rod End Locknut (1998–99)	45
	Outer Tie Rod End Locknut (2000–02)	55
	Power Steering Hose Tube Nuts (2000–02)	25
	Power Steering Pressure Switch	70①
	Power Steering Pump Relief Valve Ball Seat	48①
	Pressure Hose Banjo Bolt	25

① — Inch lbs.

DISC BRAKES

TABLE OF CONTENTS

Application Chart

Model	Year	Type	Disc Brake Type
FRONT			
Avenger	1998–2000	⑥	6
Breeze & Cirrus	1998–2000	③	3
Concorde, Intrepid, LHS & 300M	1998–2002	④	4
Neon	1998–2002	④	4
Sebring Convertible	1998–2000	③	3
	2001–02	—	7
Sebring Coupe	1998–2002	⑥	6
Sebring Sedan	2001–02	—	7
Stratus	1998–2000	③	3
Stratus Coupe	2001–02	⑥	6
Stratus Sedan	2001–02	—	7
Talon AWD	1998	①	1
Talon FWD	1998	⑥	6
REAR			
Avenger	1998–2000	②	2
Concorde, Intrepid, LHS & 300M	1998–2002	⑤	5
Neon	1998–2002	⑤	5
Sebring Convertible	2001–02	—	8
Sebring Coupe	1998–2002	②	2
Sebring Sedan	2001–02	—	8
Stratus Coupe	2001–02	②	2
Stratus Sedan	2001–02	—	8
Talon	1998	②	2

① — MR56W & MR57W Dual Piston Floating Caliper Disc Brake, Front
② — MR45S, MR45V & MR58V Dual Pin Floating Caliper Disc Brake, Rear
③ — Allied Signal/Bosch Dual Pin Floating Caliper Disc Brake, Front
④ — Kelsey-Hayes Dual Pin Floating Caliper Disc Brake, Front
⑤ — Kelsey-Hayes Dual Pin Floating Caliper Disc Brake, Rear
⑥ — MR31S, MR34V, MR44V & MR46V Dual Pin Floating Caliper Disc Brake, Front

Type 1

NOTE: On Air Bag Equipped Models, Refer To "Air Bag System Precautions" Located In The Front Of This Manual For System Disarming & Arming Procedures.

NOTE: Refer To "Computer Relearn Procedures" Located In The Front Of This Manual When Battery Power To The Computer Has Been Interrupted.

NOTE: Prior To Performing Any Service Operations Listed In This Section, Consult The "Technical Service Bulletins" Section For Related Information.

INDEX

TROUBLESHOOTING

Refer to **Fig. 1,** for brake system troubleshooting.

LATERAL RUNOUT INSPECTION

1. Remove caliper support bolts, then caliper.
2. Inspect disc surface for grooves, cracks and rust.
3. Place a dial gauge approximately .2 inch from outer circumference of brake rotor.
4. Measure runout of rotor. Refer to "Disc Brake Specifications."
5. If runout of rotor is equal to or exceeds limit specified, change phase of rotor and hub then, measure runout again noting following:
   a. Before removing brake rotor, chalk both sides of wheel stud on side at which runout is greatest.
   b. Remove brake rotor and place dial gauge as shown in **Fig. 2.**
   c. Move hub in axial direction and measure play. If play exceeds .0020 inch disassemble hub knuckle and check each part.
   d. If play does not exceed limit specification, install brake rotor 180° away from chalk marks.
6. Check runout of brake rotor again.
7. If runout cannot be corrected by changing phase of rotor, replace or machine rotor.

PARALLELISM INSPECTION

1. Using a suitable micrometer, measure rotor thickness at eight positions, approximately 45° apart and .39 inch in from outer edge of disc.
2. If rotor is beyond limits for thickness, replace.
3. If thickness variation exceeds specification, replace or resurface brake rotor.

BRAKE SYSTEM BLEED

Bleeding the hydraulic brake system is necessary if air has entered the system. Symptoms can be noted by loss of brake operation, and/or a low or spongy brake pedal.

Pressure bleeding is recommended for all hydraulic brake systems. However, if pressure bleeding equipment is not available, the hydraulic system may be bled as described under "Manual Bleed."

PRESSURE BLEED

1. Use bleeder tank tool No. C-3496-B or equivalent, with required adapter for master cylinder reservoir.
2. Attach clear plastic hose to bleeder screw and feed hose into clear jar containing enough brake fluid to submerge end of hose.
3. Bleed system using sequence as follows:
   a. Left rear.
   b. Right front.
   c. Right rear.
   d. Left front.
4. Open bleeder screw one full turn or more to obtain steady stream.
5. Close bleeder screw after 4–8 ounces of air free fluid is bled into jar.
6. Repeat procedure to all remaining bleeder screws.

MANUAL BLEED

Refer to **Fig. 3,** for bleeding sequence of brake hydraulic system.

1. Attach clear plastic hose to bleeder screw and feed hose into clear jar containing enough brake fluid to submerge end of hose.
2. Pump brake pedal three to four times, hold pedal down.
3. Open bleeder screw at least one full turn.
4. Close bleeder screw and release brake pedal.
5. Repeat four to five times at each bleeder screw.
6. If pedal travel is excessive, repeat previous steps until all air is bled from system.
7. Test drive vehicle, ensure brakes are operating correctly.

BRAKE PAD SERVICE

The brake pads have wear indicators that contact brake rotor when brake pad thickness becomes .08 inch. The wear indicators emit a squealing sound to warn driver to have pads replaced and brake system checked.

1. Remove guide pin as shown in **Fig. 4.**
2. Lift caliper assembly, then slide assembly toward inside of wheel well until separated from lock pin.
3. Remove pad and wear indicator assemblies, inner and outer shims, then clip from caliper support.
4. Securely attach pad clip to caliper support.
5. Clean piston and insert into cylinder with tool No. MB990520 or equivalent.
6. Apply grease to attaching faces of pad and inner shim and to attaching faces of inner and outer shims.
7. Ensure piston boot does not catch and tear as caliper assembly and lockpin are installed.
8. Reverse procedure to install.

Symptom	Probable cause	Remedy
Vehicle pulls to one side when brakes are applied	Grease or oil on pad or lining surface	Replace
	Inadequate contact of pad or lining	Correct
	Auto adjuster malfunction	Adjust
	Drum out of round or uneven wear	Repair or replace as necessary
Insufficient braking power	Low or deteriorated brake fluid	Refill or change
	Air in brake system	Bleed air from system
	Overheated brake rotor due to dragging of pad or lining	Correct
	Inadequate contact of pad or lining	
	Brake booster malfunction	
	Clogged brake line	
	Grease or oil on pad or lining surface	Replace
	Proportioning valve malfunction	
	Auto adjuster malfunction	Adjust
Increased pedal stroke (Reduced pedal to floorboard clearance)	Air in brake system	Bleed air from system
	Worn lining or pad	Replace
	Broken vacuum hose	
	Faulty master cylinder	
	Brake fluid leaks	Correct
	Auto adjuster malfunction	Adjust
	Excessive push rod to master cylinder clearance	
Brake drag	Incomplete release of parking brake	Correct
	Clogged master cylinder return port	
	Incorrect parking brake adjustment	Adjust
	Incorrect push rod to master cylinder clearance	
	Faulty master cylinder piston return spring	Replace
	Worn brake pedal return spring	
	Broken rear drum brake shoe return spring	
	Lack of lubrication in sliding parts	Lubricate

CR4079100038010X

Fig. 1 Brake system troubleshooting (Part 1 of 3)

CALIPER SERVICE

REPLACEMENT

1. Remove brake pads as outlined under "Brake Pad Service."
2. Disconnect brake hose at caliper strut and brake caliper, then cap brake line.
3. Reverse procedure to install, noting following:
   a. Bleed brakes as outlined under "Brake System Bleed."

OVERHAUL

1. Remove caliper assembly as described previously.
2. Remove lockpin, bushing, caliper support, pin boot and boot ring as shown in **Fig. 4.**
3. Using compressed air, remove two piston boots and pistons. **To prevent damage to pistons, place a suitable block of wood in caliper when removing pistons.**
4. Using finger tip, remove piston seal.
5. Reverse procedure to assemble, noting following:
   a. Inspect cylinders and pistons for wear, damage and/or corrosion.
   b. Inspect caliper body and sleeve for wear.
   c. Apply suitable brake fluid to cylinders, then install piston seals into cylinder groove. **Do not wipe grease from piston seal.**
   d. Apply brake fluid to pistons and insert into cylinders by pushing downward into caliper. **Do not twist pistons into caliper.**
   e. Fill piston edges with grease supplied with seal and boot repair kit, then install piston boots.
   f. Lubricate sliding surface of guide, lockpins and boots with grease supplied with seal and boot repair kit.
   g. Install guide and lockpins. Ensure head marks match identification marks on caliper body.

ROTOR

REPLACE

1. Remove caliper from brake rotor as described in "Brake Pad Service."
2. Remove rotor. If necessary use a suitable soft face hammer to tap rotor free of hub.
3. Reverse procedure to install.

TECHNICAL SERVICE BULLETINS

ABS LIGHT ON, CANNOT COMMUNICATE w/DRB III

1998 Talon AWD

When performing ABS diagnostics, early model vehicles may not be able to communicate with DRB III due to a miswired data link connector.

1. Remove 16 way data link connector from mounting bracket.
2. Remove pin No. 8 (yellow/red) from connector. Cut female terminal from wire and strip ½ of insulation from end of wire.
3. Remove pin No. 7 (pink) from data link connector. Make a center splice approximately one inch behind female terminal. Remove ½ inch of insulation.
4. Wrap yellow/red wire around center splice of pink wire. Solder splice with rosin core solder.
5. Slide a piece of shrink tubing over splice and heat until it is shrunk and glue flows from both ends.
6. Reverse procedure to install.

ALTERNATE ABS DIAGNOSTIC CODE RETRIEVAL

1998 Avenger, Sebring & Talon

ABS diagnostic trouble codes can be accessed by actuating a procedure where ABS warning light will blink DTC. Follow procedure listed below to retrieve and erase ABS trouble codes.

1. Connect pin No. 1 of 16 way data link connector to ground.
2. Turn ignition switch ON. Diagnostic trouble codes will begin to flash on amber ABS warning light. First digit of code will be represented by slow flashes and second digit will be represented by quick flashes.
3. Diagnostic trouble code can be erased by turning ignition switch ON while brake pedal is depressed. Quickly operate brake pedal 10 times in succession. Each pedal depression must be within 1 second of last pedal depression. data link connector pin No. 1 must be connected to ground.
4. When code is erased, ABS warning lamp will flash quickly and continuously.

Symptom	Probable cause	Remedy
Insufficient parking brake function	Worn brake lining	Replace
	Grease or oil on lining surface	
	Parking brake cable sticking	
	Stuck wheel cylinder or caliper piston	
	Excessive parking brake lever stroke	Adjust the parking brake lever stroke or check the parking brake cable routing
	Auto adjuster malfunction	Adjust
Scraping or grinding noise when brakes are applied	Worn brake lining or pad	Replace
	Caliper to wheel interference	Correct or replace
	Dust cover to disc interference	
	Bent brake backing plate	
	Cracked drums or brake disc	
Squealing, groaning or chattering noise when brakes are applied	Missing or damaged brake pad anti-squeak shim	Replace
	Brake drums and linings, discs and pads worn or scored	Correct or replace
	Incorrect parts	
	Burred or rusted calipers	Clean or deburr
	Dirty, greased; contaminated or glazed linings	Clean or replace
	Drum brakes-weak, damaged or incorrect shoe hold-down springs, loose or damaged shoe hold-down pins and springs	Correct or replace
	Incorrect brake pedal or booster push rod setting	Adjust
Squealing noise when brakes are not applied	Bent or warped backing plate causing interference with drum	Replace
	Drum brakes-weak, damaged or incorrect shoe-to-shoe spring	
	Poor return of brake booster, master cylinder or wheel cylinder	
	Loose or extra brake parts	Retighten

CR4079100038020X

Fig. 1 Brake system troubleshooting (Part 2 of 3)

Symptom	Probable cause	Remedy
Squealing noise when brakes are not applied	Improper positioning of pads in caliper	Correct
	Improper installation of support mounting to caliper body	
	Improper machining of drum causing interference with backing plate or shoe	Replace drum
	Disc brakes-rusted, stuck	Lubricate or replace
	Worn, damaged or insufficiently lubricated wheel bearings	
	Incorrect brake pedal or booster push rod setting	Adjust
Groaning clicking or rattling noise when brakes are not applied	Stones or foreign material trapped inside wheel covers	Remove stones, etc.
	Loose wheel nuts	Retighten
	Disc brakes-loose installation bolt	
	Worn, damaged or dry wheel bearings	Lubricate or replace
	Disc brakes-failure of anti-rattle shim	Replace
	Disc brakes-wear on sleeve	
	Incorrect brake pedal or booster push rod setting	Adjust

CR4079100038030X

Fig. 1 Brake system troubleshooting (Part 3 of 3)

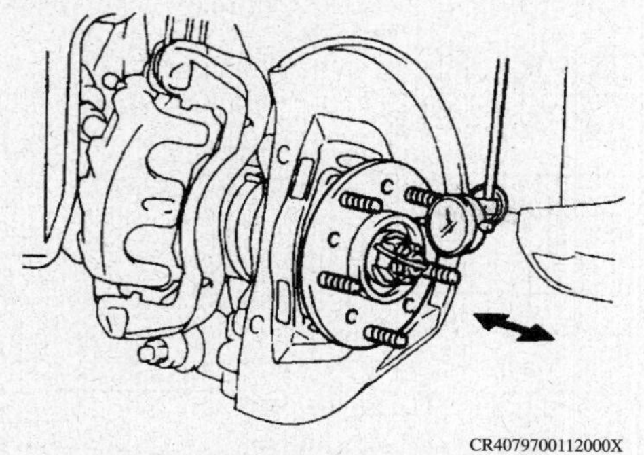

CR4079700112000X

Fig. 2 Dial gauge mounting

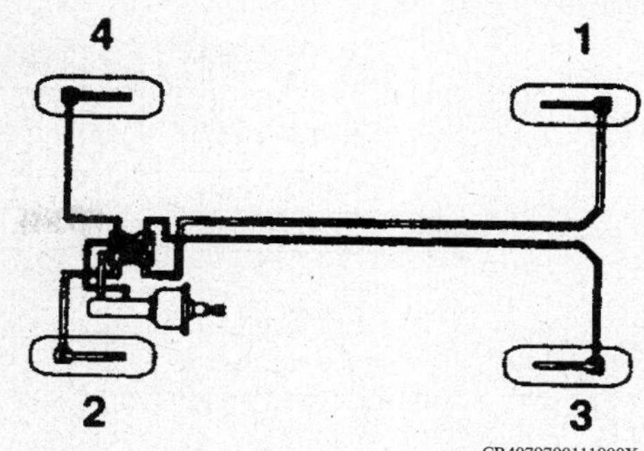

CR4079700111000X

Fig. 3 Bleed sequence

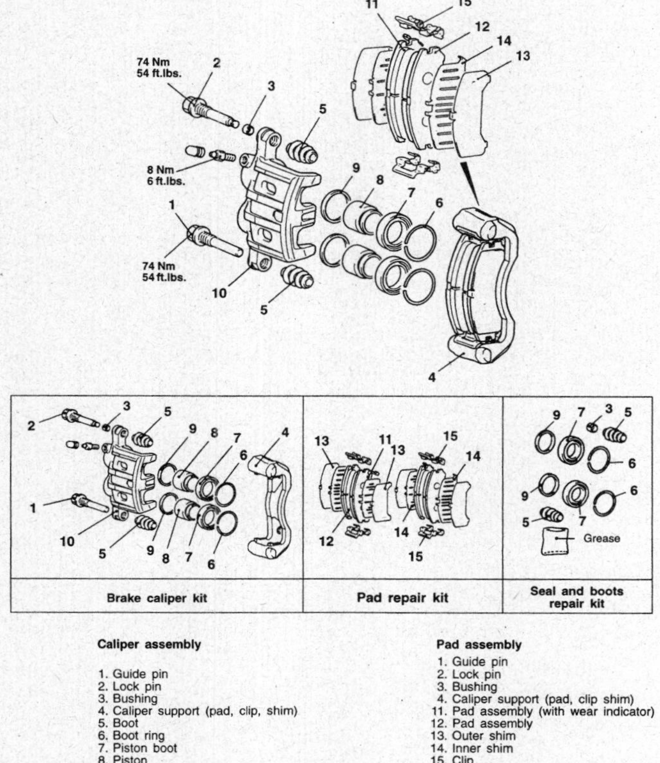

CR4079100043000X

Fig. 4 MR56W & MR57W dual piston floating caliper disc brake assembly

DISC BRAKE SPECIFICATIONS

ROTOR SPECIFICATIONS

Model	Year	Nominal Thickness, Inch	Minimum Allowable Thickness, Inch	Thickness Variation Parallelism, Inch	Lateral Runout (T.I.R.), Inch
Talon AWD	1998	.940	.880	.0006	.0031

CALIPER SPECIFICATIONS

Model	Year	Caliper Bore Dia. Inch
Talon AWD	1998	1.6875 x 2

TIGHTENING SPECIFICATIONS

Component	Torque/Ft. Lbs.
Bleed Screws	60–84①
Caliper Guide & Lockpins	54
Caliper Support To Front Axle	58–72
Wheel Lug Nuts	87–101

① — Inch lbs.

Type 2

NOTE: On Air Bag Equipped Models, Refer To "Air Bag System Precautions" Located In The Front Of This Manual For System Disarming & Arming Procedures.

NOTE: Refer To "Computer Relearn Procedures" Located In The Front Of This Manual When Battery Power To The Computer Has Been Interrupted.

INDEX

TROUBLESHOOTING

Refer to "Type 1" for system troubleshooting.

BRAKE SYSTEM BLEED

Bleeding the hydraulic brake system is necessary if air has entered the system. Symptoms can be noted by loss of brake operation, and/or a low or spongy brake pedal.

The hydraulic fluid is bled or flushed from system through bleeder valves located on calipers, wheel cylinders, and some master cylinders. Use only specified brake fluid when bleeding system. **Never reuse brake fluid that was removed from system.**

PRESSURE BLEED

Refer to "Type 1" for bleeding procedures.

MANUAL BLEED

Refer to "Type 1" for bleeding procedures.

BRAKE PAD SERVICE

Refer to **Fig. 1,** for MR45S and MR45V dual pin floating caliper disc brake assembly.

Refer to "Type 1" for brake pad service procedures.

CALIPER SERVICE

REPLACEMENT

1. Remove brake pads, as outlined under "Brake Pad Service."
2. Disconnect brake hose at brake caliper, then cap brake line.
3. Reverse procedure to install, noting following:
   a. Bleed brakes as outlined under "Brake System Bleed."

OVERHAUL

1. Remove caliper assembly as described previously.
2. Remove caliper support as shown in **Fig. 1.**
3. Remove pin boots and boot ring.
4. Position a suitable wood block in caliper body, then apply compressed air through brake hose fitting hole to remove piston and dust boot. **Apply air gently.**
5. Using finger tip, remove piston seal.
6. Reverse procedure to assemble, noting following:
   a. Inspect cylinder and piston for wear, damage and/or corrosion. Inspect caliper body and sleeve for wear.
   b. Apply brake fluid to inner cylinder, then install piston seal into cylinder groove. **Do not wipe grease from piston seal.**
   c. Apply brake fluid to pistons and insert into cylinders by pushing downward into caliper. **Do not twist pistons into caliper.**
   d. Fill piston edge with grease from seal and boot repair kit, then install piston boot.
   e. Lubricate bushing, pin boot and slide pins with grease from seal and boot repair kit.
   f. Install guide and lockpins. Ensure head marks match with identification marks on caliper body.

ADJUSTMENTS

PARKING BRAKE LEVER

Avenger, Sebring Coupe, Stratus Coupe & Talon

1. Pull parking brake lever with a force of approximately 45 ft. lbs. and count number of notches. Standard value is 5–7 notches for vehicles with drum brakes, and 3–5 notches on vehicles with drum in disc brakes.
2. If parking brake lever stroke is not as specified, adjust as follows:
   a. Remove inner compartment mat of floor console.
   b. Loosen adjusting nut to end of cable rod to free cable.
   c. Remove adjustment hole plug, then use a flat tipped screwdriver or equivalent, to turn adjuster.
   d. Turn adjuster in direction of arrow (Direction which expands shoes) so disc will not rotate.
   e. Return adjuster five notches in opposite direction.
   f. Turn adjusting nut to adjust parking brake lever stroke within standard value. **If number of brake lever notches engaged is less than standard value, cable has been excessively pulled.**
   g. Check to ensure there is no play between adjusting nut and pin.
   h. Raise and support rear of vehicle.
   i. Turn rear wheel with parking brake in released position to confirm rear brakes are not dragging.

PARKING BRAKE SHOE

1. Raise and support vehicle, then remove rear wheels.
2. **On models equipped with AWD,** disconnect drive axles from companion flange.
3. **On all models,** firmly apply, then release parking brake lever several times to seat and center parking brake shoes.
4. Remove adjusting hole plug from hub of brake disc.
5. Using a suitable tool, turn adjusting nut until brake disc cannot be turned by hand.
6. Back off adjusting nut five notches.
7. Repeat above steps on opposite side.
8. **On models equipped with AWD,** connect drive axles to companion flange.
9. **On all models,** firmly apply, then release parking brake lever several times to seat and center parking brake shoes.

10. Adjust parking brake lever as outlined under "Parking Brake Lever, Adjust"
11. Install rear wheels, then lower vehicle.

ROTOR

REPLACE

1. Remove caliper from brake rotor as described in "Brake Pad Service."
2. Remove parking brake adjustment hole plug from brake disc hub.
3. Remove rotor. If necessary use a suitable soft face hammer to tap rotor free of hub.
4. Reverse procedure to install, noting following:
   a. Adjust parking brake as outlined under "Adjustments."

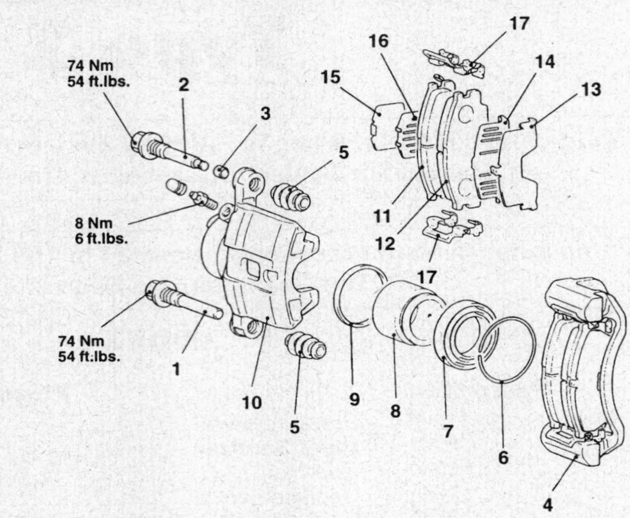

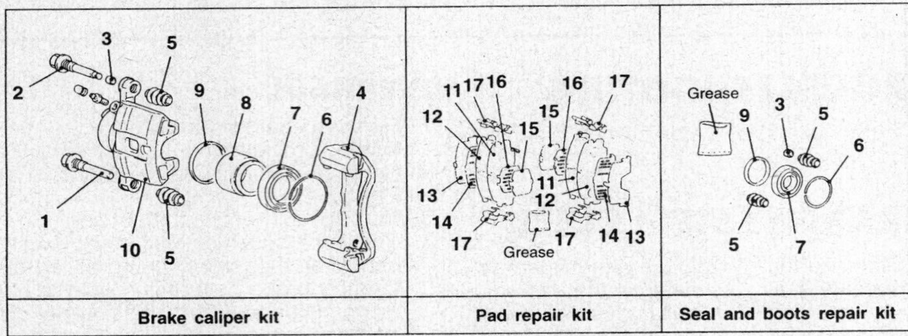

Caliper assembly

1. Guide pin
2. Lock pin
3. Bushing
4. Caliper support (pad, clip, shim)
5. Boot
6. Boot ring
7. Piston boot
8. Piston
9. Piston seal
10. Caliper body

Pad assembly

1. Guide pin
2. Lock pin
3. Bushing
4. Caliper support (pad, clip, shim)
11. Pad and wear indicator assembly
12. Pad assembly
13. Outer shim (stainless)
14. Outer shim (coated with rubber)
15. Inner shim (stainless)
16. Inner shim (coated with rubber)
17. Clip

CR4079100045000X

Fig. 1 MR45S, MR45V, MR58V dual pin floating caliper disc brake assembly

DISC BRAKE SPECIFICATIONS

ROTOR SPECIFICATIONS

<table>
<tr><th>Year</th><th>Model</th><th>Nominal Thickness, Inch</th><th>Minimum Allowable Thickness, Inch</th><th>Lateral Runout (T.I.R.), Inch</th></tr>
<tr><td>1998–2000</td><td>Avenger, Sebring Coupe & Talon</td><td rowspan="2">.390</td><td rowspan="2">.330</td><td rowspan="2">.0031</td></tr>
<tr><td>2001–02</td><td>Sebring Coupe & Stratus Coupe</td></tr>
</table>

CALIPER SPECIFICATIONS

Model	Caliper Bore Dia., Inch
All	1.375

TIGHTENING SPECIFICATIONS

Component	Torque/Ft. Lbs.
Backing Plate Bolts	36–43
Bleed Screws	60-84①
Brake Hose To Rear Caliper Banjo Bolt	18–25
Caliper Guide & Lockpins, Rear (MR45V & MR45S)	32
Caliper Guide & Lockpins, Rear (MR58V)	32
Caliper Support To Rear Axle	36–43
Wheel Lug Nuts	87–101

① — Inch lbs.

Type 3

NOTE: On Air Bag Equipped Models, Refer To "Air Bag System Precautions" Located In The Front Of This Manual For System Disarming & Arming Procedures.

NOTE: Refer To "Computer Relearn Procedures" Located In The Front Of This Manual When Battery Power To The Computer Has Been Interrupted.

INDEX

TROUBLESHOOTING

Refer to **Fig. 1,** for brake system troubleshooting procedures.

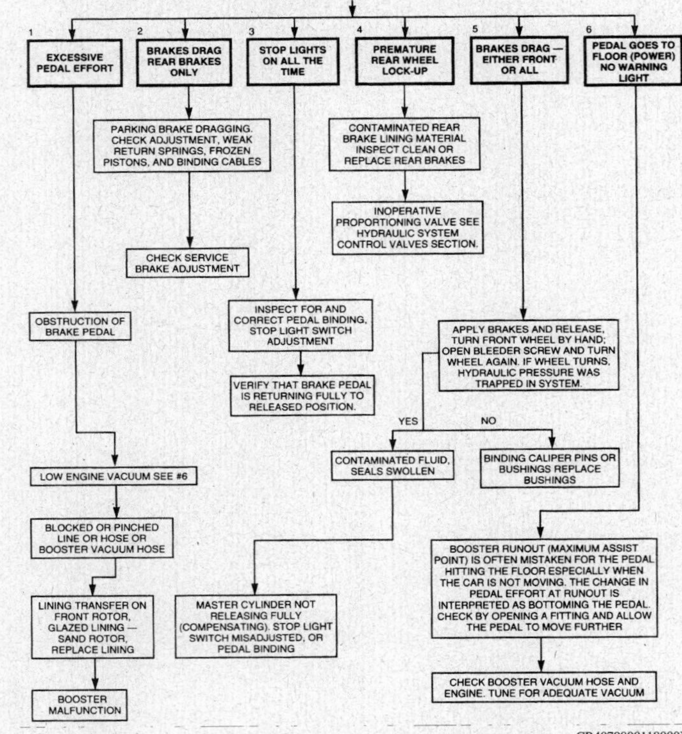

Fig. 1 Brake system troubleshooting

BRAKE SYSTEM BLEED

Bleeding hydraulic brake system is necessary if air has entered system. Symptoms can be noted by loss of brake operation, and/or a low or spongy brake pedal.

The hydraulic fluid is bled or flushed from system through bleeder valves located on calipers, wheel cylinders, and some master cylinders. Use only specified brake fluid when bleeding hydraulic brake system. **Never reuse old brake fluid removed from system.**

PRESSURE BLEED

Refer to "Type 1" for bleeding procedures.

MANUAL BLEED

Refer to "Type 1" for bleeding procedures.

BRAKE PAD SERVICE

1. Raise and support vehicle, then remove front wheel and tire assembly.
2. Remove caliper to steering knuckle attaching bolts.
3. Remove caliper from steering knuckle by rotating free end of caliper away from steering knuckle, then slide opposite end of caliper out from under machined abutment on steering knuckle. Support caliper on upper control arm. Do not allow it to hang on flex hose.
4. Remove outboard pad by prying pad retaining clip over raised area on caliper as shown in **Fig. 2.**
5. Pull inboard brake pad away from piston until retaining clip is free from cavity in piston.
6. Reverse procedure to install, noting following:
   a. Using a suitable tool, press caliper piston back into piston bore of caliper.
   b. Apply brake pedal several times, then inspect master cylinder brake fluid level and add fluid if necessary.

CALIPER SERVICE

REPLACEMENT

1. Remove caliper from brake rotor and brake pads from caliper as described in "Brake Pad Service."
2. Disconnect brake hose at brake caliper, then cap brake line.
3. Reverse procedure to install, noting following:
   a. Bleed brakes as outlined under "Brake System Bleed."

OVERHAUL

1. Remove caliper from brake rotor and brake pads from caliper as described in "Brake Pad Service."
2. Hang caliper on a wire away from rotor.

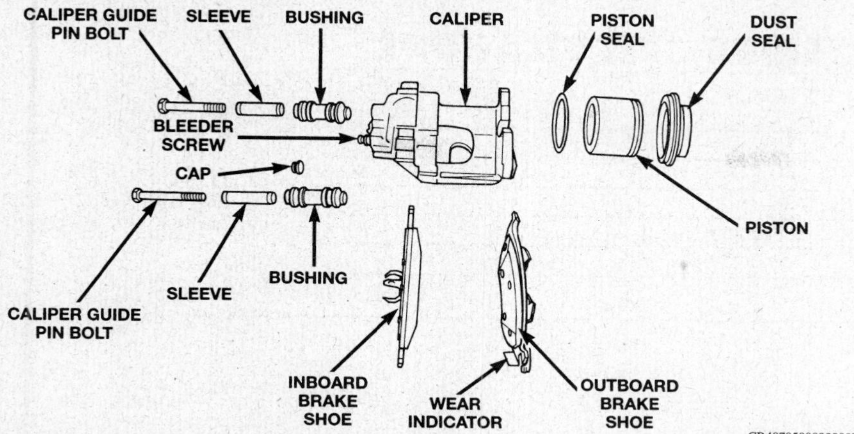

Fig. 2 Allied Signal/Bosch dual pin floating caliper disc brake assembly

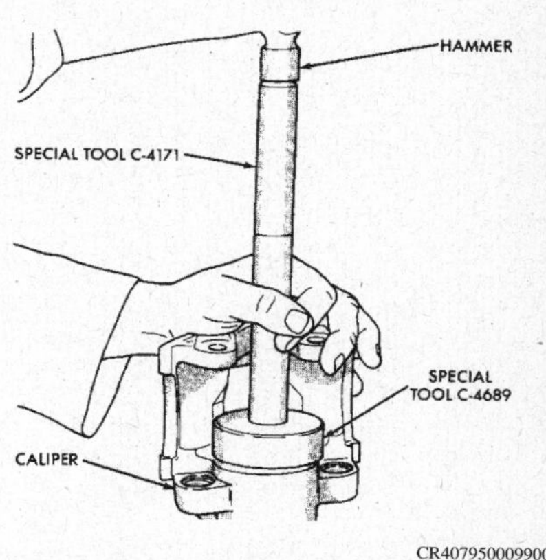

Fig. 3 Caliper piston boot installation

3. Place a small piece of wood between piston and caliper fingers.
4. Carefully depress brake pedal to hydraulically push piston out of bore, then apply and hold-down brake pedal to any position beyond first inch of brake travel. This will prevent master cylinder brake fluid loss.
5. Disconnect brake line from caliper. Plug brake line to avoid any additional brake fluid loss.
6. Mount brake caliper assembly in soft jawed vise. **Excessive vise pressure will cause bore distortion and binding of piston.**
7. Remove guide pin bushings from caliper.
8. Remove piston dust boot from caliper and discard.
9. Using a plastic trim stick, work piston seal out of its groove in caliper piston bore. **Do not use a screw driver or other metal tool for this procedure, because of possibility of scratching piston bore or burring edges of seal groove.**
10. Clean all parts using alcohol or a suitable solvent and wipe dry using a lint free cloth. **No lint residue can be left in caliper bore.**
11. Inspect piston bore for scoring or pitting. Light scratches or corrosion can usually be cleared from bores using crocus cloth. Bores that show deep scratches or scoring should be honed. **Bore diameter should not be honed more than .001 inch. If bore does not clean up within this specification, a new caliper housing should be installed.**
12. When honing brake caliper housing, coat stones and bore with brake fluid.
13. After honing bore, clean seal and boot grooves with a stiff non-metallic rotary brush. **Use extreme care in cleaning caliper after honing. Remove all dirt and grit by flushing caliper with brake fluid, wipe dry with a lint free cloth.**
14. Replace caliper piston if there is any pitting, scratches, or physical damage.
15. Dip new piston seal in clean brake fluid and install in caliper bore groove. Seal should be positioned at one area in groove and gently worked around groove, using only your fingers until properly seated. **Never reuse old piston seal.**
16. Coat new piston boot with clean brake fluid leaving a generous amount inside boot.
17. Coat dust boot with clean brake fluid, position over piston.
18. Install piston into caliper bore pushing it past piston seal until it bottoms in caliper bore.
19. Position dust boot in counterbore of caliper piston bore.
20. Using a hammer and piston caliper boot installer No. C-4689 and handle No. C-4171, or their equivalents, drive boot into counterbore of caliper as shown in **Fig. 3.**
21. Install guide pin bushings and dust boots.
22. Attach hydraulic brake line to caliper. **Always use new seal washers when installing brake line to caliper.**
23. Install brake pads and caliper assembly as described in "Caliper Service."
24. Bleed brake system as described in "Brake System Bleed."

ROTOR

REPLACE

1. Remove caliper from brake rotor as described in "Brake Pad Service."
2. Remove rotor. If necessary use a suitable soft face hammer to tap rotor free of hub.
3. Reverse procedure to install.

DISC BRAKE SPECIFICATIONS

ROTOR SPECIFICATIONS

Model	Year	Nominal Thickness, Inch	Minimum Allowable Thickness, Inch	Thickness Variation (Parallelism), Inch	Lateral Runout (T.I.R.), Inch	Finish, Micro-Inch
Breeze, Cirrus, Sebring Convertible & Stratus	1998–2000	.900–.911	.843	.0005	.005	15–80

CALIPER SPECIFICATIONS

Model	Caliper Piston O.D., Inch
Breeze, Cirrus, Sebring Convertible & Stratus	2.125

TIGHTENING SPECIFICATIONS

Component	Torque/Ft. Lbs.
Bleeder Screw	84①
Caliper Banjo Bolt	35
Caliper Guide Pin Bolts	16
Hydraulic Brake Line Fitting	26
Wheel Lug Nuts	100

① — Inch lbs.

Type 4

NOTE: On Air Bag Equipped Models, Refer To "Air Bag System Precautions" Located In The Front Of This Manual For System Disarming & Arming Procedures.

NOTE: Refer To "Computer Relearn Procedures" Located In The Front Of This Manual When Battery Power To The Computer Has Been Interrupted.

INDEX

DESCRIPTION

The single piston, floating caliper disc brake assembly as shown in **Fig. 1,** consists of rotor, caliper, pads and driving hub. The caliper is mounted to steering knuckle using bushings, sleeves and two thru bolts which thread directly into steering knuckle.

This assembly has an anti-rattle clip attached to outer pad and an inner pad-piston retainer clip.

All of braking force is taken directly by adapter. The caliper is a one piece casting with inboard side containing a single piston cylinder bore.

A square cut rubber piston seal is located in a machined groove in caliper bore and provides a seal between piston and caliper bore.

A molded rubber dust boot installed in a groove in cylinder bore and piston keeps contamination from caliper bore and piston. The boot mounts in caliper bore and in a groove in piston.

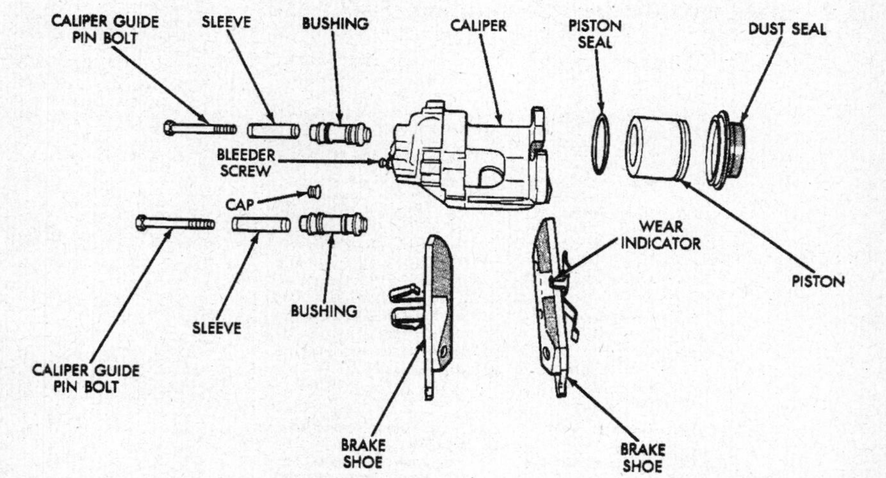

Fig. 1 Kelsey Hayes dual pin floating caliper disc brake assembly

TROUBLESHOOTING

Refer to **Fig. 2,** for system troubleshooting.

LATERAL RUNOUT INSPECTION

Refer to "Disc Brake Specifications" for runout specifications.

1. Raise and support vehicle, then remove wheels.
2. If applicable, ensure wheel bearings are properly adjusted.
3. Using suitable spacers install lug nuts or bolts, then tighten to specifications.
4. Mount a dial indicator to vehicle, then position dial indicator plunger so it contacts rotor at a point one inch from outer edge.
5. Rotate rotor and note dial indicator readings. Perform this inspection on both inboard and outboard rotor faces.
6. If runout exceeds specifications proceed as follows:
    a. Position rotor on hub, then inspect runout.
    b. If runout still exceeds specifications, replace or machine rotor.

PARALLELISM INSPECTION

Refer to "Disc Brake Specifications" for parallelism specifications.

1. Using a suitable micrometer, measure rotor at 12 equally spaced points at a radius approximately one inch from edge of disc.
2. **If measurements exceed specifications,** resurface or replace rotors as necessary.

BRAKE SYSTEM BLEED

Bleeding hydraulic brake system is necessary if air has entered system. Symptoms can be noted by loss of brake operation, and/or a low or spongy brake pedal.

The hydraulic fluid is bled or flushed from system through bleeder valves located on calipers, wheel cylinders, and some master cylinders. Use only specified brake fluid when bleeding system. **Never reuse old brake fluid removed from system.**

PRESSURE BLEED

Refer to "Type 1" for bleeding procedures.

MANUAL BLEED

Refer to "Type 1" for bleeding procedures.

BRAKE PAD SERVICE

REMOVAL

1. Raise and support vehicle.
2. Remove front wheel and tire assemblies.
3. Remove caliper assembly to steering knuckle guide pin bolts.
4. Remove caliper assembly from steering knuckle as follows:

RED BRAKE WARNING LAMP

CONDITION	POSSIBLE CAUSES	CORRECTION
RED BRAKE WARNING LAMP ON	1. Parking brake lever not fully released.	1. Release parking brake lever.
	2. Parking brake warning lamp switch on parking brake lever.	2. Inspect and replace switch as necessary.
	3. Brake fluid level low in reservoir.	3. Fill reservoir. Check entire system for leaks. Repair or replace as required.
	4. Brake fluid level switch.	4. Disconnect switch wiring connector. If lamp goes out, replace switch.
	5. Mechanical instrument cluster (MIC) problem.	5. Refer to Chassis Diagnostic Procedures manual.

BRAKE NOISE

CONDITION	POSSIBLE CAUSES	CORRECTION
DISC BRAKE CHIRP	1. Excessive brake rotor runout.	1. Follow brake rotor diagnosis and testing. Correct as necessary.
	2. Lack of lubricant on brake caliper slides.	2. Lubricate brake caliper slides.
DISC BRAKE RATTLE OR CLUNK	1. Broken or missing anti-rattle spring clips on shoes.	1. Replace brake shoes.
	2. Caliper guide pins loose.	2. Tighten guide pins.
DISC BRAKE SQUEAK AT LOW SPEED (WHILE APPLYING LIGHT BRAKE PEDAL EFFORT)	1. Brake shoe linings.	1. Replace brake shoes.
SCRAPING (METAL-TO-METAL).	1. Foreign object interference with brakes.	1. Inspect brakes and remove foreign object.
	2. Brake shoes worn out.	2. Replace brake shoes. Inspect rotors. Reface or replace as necessary.

CR4079900136010X

Fig. 2 Brake system troubleshooting (Part 1 of 3)

OTHER BRAKE CONDITIONS

CONDITION	POSSIBLE CAUSES	CORRECTION
BRAKES CHATTER	1. Disc brake rotor has excessive thickness variation.	1. Isolate condition as rear or front. Reface or replace brake rotors as necessary.
BRAKES DRAG (FRONT OR ALL)	1. Contaminated brake fluid.	1. Check for swollen seals. Replace all system components containing rubber.
	2. Binding caliper pins or bushings.	2. Replace pins and bushings
	3. Binding master cylinder.	3. Replace master cylinder.
	4. Binding brake pedal.	4. Replace brake pedal.
BRAKES DRAG (REAR ONLY)	1. Parking brake cables binding or froze up.	1. Check cable routing. Replace cables as necessary.
	2. Parking brake cable return spring not returning shoes.	2. Replace cables as necessary.
	3. Obstruction inside the center console preventing full return of the parking brake cables.	3. Remove console and remove obstruction.
BRAKES GRAB	1. Contaminated brake shoe linings.	1. Inspect and clean, or replace shoes. Repair source of contamination.
	2. Improper power brake booster assist.	2. Refer to Power Brake Booster in the diagnosis and testing section.
EXCESSIVE PEDAL EFFORT	1. Obstruction of brake pedal.	1. Inspect, remove or move obstruction.
	2. Low power brake booster assist.	2. Refer to power brake booster in the diagnosis and testing section.
	3. Glazed brake linings.	3. Reface or replace brake rotors as necessary. Replace brake shoes.
	4. Brake shoe lining transfer to brake rotor.	4. Reface or replace brake rotors as necessary. Replace brake shoes.
EXCESSIVE PEDAL TRAVEL (VEHICLE STOPS OK)	1. Air in brake lines.	1. Bleed brakes.
EXCESSIVE PEDAL TRAVEL (PEDAL GOES TO FLOOR - CAN'T SKID WHEELS)	1. Power brake booster runout (vacuum assist).	1. Check booster vacuum hose and engine tune for adequate vacuum supply. Refer to power brake booster in the diagnosis and testing section.
EXCESSIVE PEDAL TRAVEL (ONE FRONT WHEEL LOCKS UP DURING HARD BRAKING)	1. One of the two hydraulic circuits to the front brakes is malfunctioning.	1. Inspect system for leaks. Check master cylinder for internal malfunction.
PEDAL PULSATES/ SURGES DURING BRAKING	1. Disc brake rotor has excessive thickness variation.	1. Isolate condition as rear or front. Reface or replace brake rotors as necessary.

CR4079900136020X

Fig. 2 Brake system troubleshooting (Part 2 of 3)

CONDITION	POSSIBLE CAUSES	CORRECTION
PEDAL IS SPONGY	1. Air in brake lines.	1. Bleed brakes.
	2. Power brake booster runout (vacuum assist).	2. Check booster vacuum hose and engine tune for adequate vacuum supply. Refer to power brake booster in the diagnosis and testing section.
PREMATURE REAR WHEEL LOCKUP	1. Contaminated brake shoe linings.	1. Inspect and clean, or replace shoes. Repair source of contamination.
	2. Inoperative proportioning valve.	2. Test proportioning valves folowing procedure listed in diagnosis and testing section. Replace valves as necessary.
	3. Improper power brake booster assist.	3. Refer to power brake booster in the diagnosis and testing section.
STOP LAMPS STAY ON	1. Brake lamp switch out of adjustment.	1. Adjust brake lamp switch.
	2. Brake pedal binding.	2. Inspect and replace as necessary.
	3. Obstruction in pedal linkage.	3. Remove obstruction.
	4. Power Brake Booster not allowing pedal to return completely.	4. Replace power brake booster.
VEHICLE PULLS TO RIGHT OR LEFT ON BRAKING	1. Frozen brake caliper piston.	1. Replace frozen piston or caliper. Bleed brakes.
	2. Contaminated brake shoe lining.	2. Inspect and clean, or replace shoes. Repair source of contamination.
	3. Pinched brake lines.	3. Replace pinched line.
	4. Leaking piston seal.	4. Replace piston seal or brake caliper.
	5. Suspension problem.	5. Refer to the Suspension group.
PARKING BRAKE - EXCESSIVE LEVER TRAVEL	1. Rear parking brake shoes out of adjustment.	1. Adjust rear parking brake shoes.

CR4079900136030X

Fig. 2 Brake system troubleshooting (Part 3 of 3)

   a. Rotate top of caliper away from steering knuckle.
   b. Lift caliper off bottom machined abutment on steering knuckle.
5. Support caliper to prevent damage of flexible brake hose.
6. Remove outboard brake shoe by prying shoe retaining clip over raised area of caliper.
7. Pull inboard brake shoe away from piston until retaining clip is free from cavity in piston.
8. Reverse procedure to install, noting following:
   a. Using a suitable tool Press caliper piston back into piston bore of caliper.
   b. Apply brake pedal several times, then inspect master cylinder brake fluid level and add fluid if necessary.

CALIPER SERVICE

REPLACEMENT

1. Remove caliper from brake rotor and brake pads from caliper as described in "Brake Pad Service."
2. Disconnect brake hose at brake caliper, then cap brake line.
3. Reverse procedure to install, noting following:
   a. Bleed brakes as outlined under "Brake System Bleed."

OVERHAUL

Disassemble

1. Remove caliper assembly as described under "Brake Pad, Service."
2. Place a wood block between caliper piston and caliper fingers. With brake hose attached to caliper, carefully depress brake pedal to push piston out of caliper bore. Prop brake pedal to any position below first inch of brake pedal travel to prevent brake fluid loss.
3. If pistons are to be removed from both calipers, disconnect brake hose at frame bracket after removing piston, then cap brake line and repeat procedure to remove piston from other caliper.
4. Disconnect brake hose from caliper.
5. Mount caliper in a soft jawed vise.
6. Support caliper, then remove and discard dust boot.
7. Using a small wooden or plastic stick, remove seal from groove in piston bore and discard. **Do not use a screwdriver or other metal tool, as this may scratch caliper bore.**
8. Remove caliper bushings.

Assemble

1. Mount caliper in a soft jawed vise.
2. Lubricate piston seal with clean brake fluid and install seal in caliper bore groove. Ensure seal is properly seated.
3. Lubricate piston boot with clean brake fluid and position over piston.
4. Install piston and boot assembly, pushing it past piston seal until it bottoms in caliper bore.

5. Using a hammer and dust boot installer No. C-4689 with handle No. C-4171 or equivalents, drive dust boot into counterbore until properly seated.
6. On models where bushings require replacement, compress flanges of bushings and install on caliper housing. Ensure bushing flanges extend evenly over caliper housing on both sides. Remove Teflon sleeves from guide pin bushings prior to installing bushings into caliper. After bushings are installed into caliper, reinstall Teflon sleeves into bushings.
7. Connect brake hose to brake line at frame bracket.
8. Install caliper on vehicle as described under "Brake Pad Service."
9. Bleed brakes as outlined under "Brake System Bleed."

ROTOR

REPLACE

1. Remove caliper from brake rotor as described in "Brake Pad Service."
2. Remove parking brake adjustment hole plug from brake disc hub.
3. Remove rotor. If necessary use a suitable soft face hammer to tap rotor free of hub.
4. Reverse procedure to install, noting following:
   a. Adjust parking brake as outlined under "Adjustments."

Remove caliper as outlined under "Caliper Service," then remove rotor. Use a suitable soft face hammer if necessary to tap rotor free of hub.

DISC BRAKE SPECIFICATIONS

ROTOR SPECIFICATIONS

Model	Year	Nominal Thickness, Inch	Minimum Refinish Thickness, Inch	Thickness Variation (Parallelism), Inch	Lateral Runout (T.I.R.), Inch	Finish, Micro-Inch
Concorde, Intrepid, LHS & 300M	1998–2002	1.019–1.029	.960	.0005	.003	15–80
Neon	1998–99	.782–.792	.724	.0005	.005	15–80
	2000–02	.861–.871	.803	.0005	.005	15–80

CALIPER SPECIFICATIONS

Model	Caliper Piston O.D., Inch
Concorde, Intrepid, LHS & 300M	2.360
Neon	2.125

TIGHTENING SPECIFICATIONS

Component	Torque/Ft. Lbs.
Bearing Retainer Bolts	21
Bleed Screws	10
Brake Hose To Caliper Banjo Bolt	35
Brake Line Fitting	12
Caliper Mounting Bolts	16
Caliper Guide Pins	30
Front Brake Hose Intermediate Bracket	108①
Wheel Lug Nuts	85–110

① — Inch lbs.

Type 5

NOTE: On Air Bag Equipped Models, Refer To "Air Bag System Precautions" Located In The Front Of This Manual For System Disarming & Arming Procedures.

NOTE: Refer To "Computer Relearn Procedures" Located In The Front Of This Manual When Battery Power To The Computer Has Been Interrupted.

INDEX

DESCRIPTION

This single piston, floating caliper rear disc brake assembly as shown in **Fig. 1,** includes a hub assembly, adapter, rotor, caliper, shoes and pads. The parking brake system consists of a small duo-servo brake mounted to an adapter which expands out against the hat section on inside of rotor. The caliper has either a 1.338 or 1.42 inch piston located on inboard side.

The caliper floats on rubber bushings with metal sleeves on two bolts that are threaded into adapter. Two machined abutments on adapter position and align caliper and brake pads for movement fore and aft.

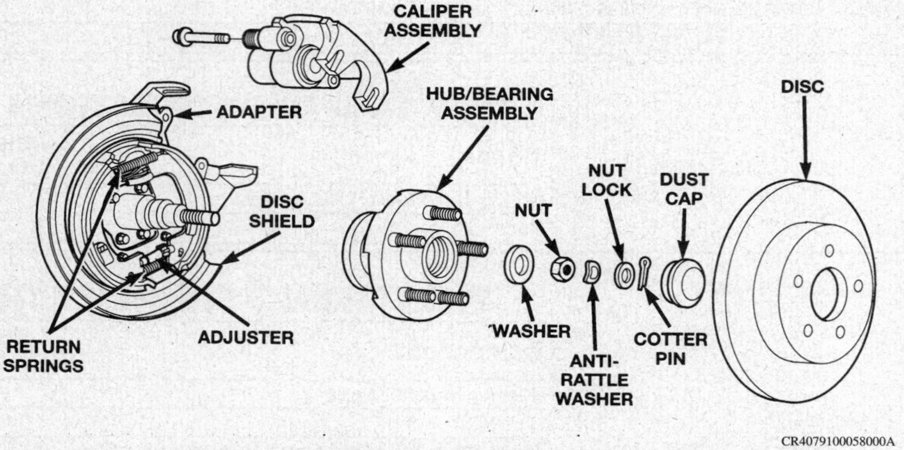

Fig. 1 Kelsey-Hayes dual pin floating caliper disc brake assembly

TROUBLESHOOTING

Refer to "Type 1" for system troubleshooting.

LATERAL RUNOUT INSPECTION

Refer to "Disc Brake Specifications" for runout specifications.

1. Raise and support vehicle, then remove wheels.
2. If applicable, ensure wheel bearings are properly adjusted.
3. Using suitable spacers install lug nuts or bolts, then tighten to specifications.
4. Mount a dial indicator to vehicle, then position dial indicator plunger so it contacts rotor at a point one inch from outer edge.
5. Rotate rotor and note dial indicator readings. Perform this inspection on both inboard and outboard rotor faces.
6. If runout exceeds specifications, proceed as follows:
   a. Position rotor on hub, then inspect runout.
   b. If runout still exceeds specifications, replace or machine rotor.

PARALLELISM INSPECTION

Refer to "Disc Brake Specifications" for parallelism specifications.

1. Using a suitable micrometer, measure rotor at 12 equally spaced points at a radius approximately one inch from edge of disc.
2. **If measurements exceed specifications,** resurface or replace rotor as necessary.

BRAKE SYSTEM BLEED

Bleeding hydraulic brake system is necessary if air has entered system. Symptoms can be noted by loss of brake operation, and/or a low or spongy brake pedal.

The hydraulic fluid is bled or flushed from the system through bleeder valves located on the calipers, wheel cylinders, and some master cylinders. Use only specified brake fluid when bleeding system. **Never reuse old brake fluid removed from system.**

PRESSURE BLEED

Refer to "Type 1" for bleeding procedures.

MANUAL BLEED

Refer to "Type 1" for bleeding procedures.

BRAKE PAD SERVICE

Refer to "Type 6" for service procedures.

CALIPER SERVICE

REPLACEMENT

1. Remove caliper from brake rotor and brake pads from caliper as described in "Brake Pad Service."
2. Disconnect brake hose at brake caliper, then cap brake line.
3. Reverse procedure to install, noting following:
   a. Bleed brakes as outlined under "Brake System Bleed."

OVERHAUL

1. Remove caliper from rotor as described under "Brake Pad Service."
2. Place a small piece of wood between piston and caliper fingers, then carefully depress brake pedal to hydraulically push piston out of bore. Prop brake pedal to any position below first inch of brake pedal travel to prevent brake fluid loss.
3. If pistons are to be removed from both calipers, disconnect brake hose at frame bracket after removing piston, then cap brake line and repeat procedure to remove piston from other caliper.
4. Disconnect brake hose from caliper.
5. Mount caliper in a soft jawed vise.
6. Support caliper, then remove and discard dust boot.
7. Using a small wooden or plastic stick, remove seal from groove in piston bore and discard. **Do not use a screwdriver or other metal tool, as this may scratch caliper bore.**
8. If necessary, remove bushing and sleeve assembly, as follows:
   a. Using fingers, push inner sleeve until it pops out of bushing, then pull inner sleeve completely out of bushing.
   b. Using fingers collapse one side of bushing. Pull opposite side of bushing to remove from caliper.
9. Using denatured alcohol or equivalent, thoroughly clean piston and caliper grooves, caliper housing and bushing mounting surfaces.
10. Dip new piston seal in clean brake fluid and install in groove in bore.
11. Coat new piston boot with clean brake fluid leaving a generous amount inside boot.
12. Coat piston with clean brake fluid, then position dust boot over piston.
13. Install piston into bore pushing it past piston seal until it bottoms in bore.
14. Position dust boot in counterbore, then using a hammer and installer No. C-4383-7 or equivalent, drive boot into counterbore of caliper.
15. If removed, install guide pin sleeve bushings as follows:
    a. Fold bushing in half lengthwise at solid middle section.
    b. Using fingers, insert folded bushing into caliper. Do not use sharp object to perform this step.
    c. Using wooden dowel, unfold bushing until it is fully seated in caliper. Flanges should be seated evenly on both sides of bushing hole.
16. If removed, install guide pin sleeve as follows:
    a. Hold end of bushing, then push sleeve through bushing until end of bushing is fully seated into seal groove of sleeve.
    b. Holding sleeve in place, install other end of bushing into seal groove.
    c. Ensure bushing is in seal groove on both sides.
17. Install brake fluid line, then install caliper as outlined under "Brake Pad Service."
18. Bleed brakes as outlined under "Brake System Bleed."

PARKING BRAKE SERVICE

PARKING BRAKE SHOES, REPLACE

1. Remove rear disc brake caliper assembly, as described under "Caliper Service," from adapter and rotor.
2. Remove rear rotor from hub, then dust cap.
3. Remove cotter pin, nut retainer, wave washer and rear hub/bearing assembly retaining nut and washer from rear spindle.
4. Remove rear hub and bearing assembly from rear spindle.
5. **On Neon and LH models,** remove rear brake shoe assembly hold-down clip.
6. **On all models,** turn brake shoe adjuster wheel until adjuster is at shortest length.
7. Remove adjuster assembly from parking brake assembly.
8. **On Neon and LH models,** remove lower shoe to shoe spring.
9. **On all models,** pull front parking brake shoe away from anchor pin, then remove front parking brake shoe and lower spring.
10. **On Neon and LH models,** pull rear brake shoe assembly away from anchor.
11. **On all models,** remove rear brake shoe and upper spring.
12. **On Neon and LH models,** remove front brake shoe hold-down clip, then brake shoe assembly.

ADJUSTMENTS

PARKING BRAKE

1. Release parking brake.
2. Raise and support vehicle.
3. Adjust parking brake cable until there is slack in cable.
4. Tighten adjusting nut until a slight drag is felt when rotating rear wheels.
5. Back off adjusting nut two full turns past point when both rear wheels rotate freely.
6. Inspect parking brake operation.

ROTOR

REPLACE

1. Remove caliper from brake rotor as described in "Brake Pad Service."
2. Remove parking brake adjustment hole plug from brake disc hub.
3. Remove rotor. If necessary use a suitable soft face hammer to tap rotor free of hub.
4. Reverse procedure to install, noting following:
   a. Adjust parking brake as outlined under "Adjustments."

DISC BRAKE SPECIFICATIONS

ROTOR SPECIFICATIONS

Model	Year	Nominal Thickness, Inch	Minimum Allowable Thickness, Inch	Thickness Variation (Parallelism), Inch	Lateral Runout (T.I.R.), Inch	Finish, Micro-Inch
Concorde, Intrepid, LHS & 300M	1998–2002	.458–.478	.409	.0005	.005	15–80
Neon	1998–99	.782–.792	.724	.0005	.005	15–80
	2000–02	.344–.364	.285	.0005	.005	15–80

CALIPER SPECIFICATIONS

Rotor Type	Caliper Piston O.D., Inch
Solid	1.34
Vented	1.42

TIGHTENING SPECIFICATIONS

Component	Torque/Ft. Lbs.
Bearing Retainer Bolts	21
Bleed Screws	10
Brake Hose To Caliper Banjo Bolt	35
Brake Line Fitting	12
Caliper Guide Pins	30
Caliper Mounting Bolts	16
Support Plate To Rear Axle	80
Wheel Lug Nuts	85–110

Type 6

NOTE: On Air Bag Equipped Models, Refer To "Air Bag System Precautions" Located In The Front Of This Manual For System Disarming & Arming Procedures.

NOTE: Refer To "Computer Relearn Procedures" Located In The Front Of This Manual When Battery Power To The Computer Has Been Interrupted.

INDEX

TROUBLESHOOTING

Refer to "Type 1" for system troubleshooting.

LATERAL RUNOUT INSPECTION

Refer to "Type 1" for system troubleshooting.

PARALLELISM INSPECTION

Refer to "Type 1" for system troubleshooting.

BRAKE SYSTEM BLEED

Bleeding hydraulic brake system is necessary if air has entered system. Symptoms can be noted by loss of brake operation, and/or a low or spongy brake pedal.

The hydraulic fluid is bled or flushed from system through bleeder valves located on calipers, wheel cylinders, and some master cylinders. Use only specified brake fluid when bleeding system. **Never reuse old brake fluid removed from system.**

PRESSURE BLEED

Refer to "Type 1" for bleeding procedures.

MANUAL BLEED

Refer to "Type 1" for bleeding procedures.

BRAKE PAD SERVICE

1. Raise and support vehicle, then remove tire and wheel assemblies.
2. Remove guide pin as shown in **Figs. 1 and 2,** then lift caliper body upward and secure with wire.
3. Remove inner shims, anti-squeak shims, brake pad assemblies and pad clips from support mounting.
4. Reverse procedure to install, noting following:
   a. Using a suitable tool Press caliper piston back into piston bore of caliper.
   b. Apply brake pedal several times, then inspect master cylinder brake fluid level and add fluid if necessary.

CALIPER SERVICE

REPLACEMENT

1. Remove caliper from brake rotor and brake pads from caliper as described in "Brake Pad Service."
2. Disconnect brake hose at brake caliper, then cap brake line.
3. Reverse procedure to install, noting following:
   a. Bleed brakes as outlined under "Brake System Bleed."

OVERHAUL

Avenger & Sebring Coupe

1. Remove caliper assembly as described previously.
2. Remove lockpin, bushing, caliper support, guide pin and lockpin boots as shown in **Figs. 1 and 2.**
3. Remove boot ring using a suitable flat blade screwdriver.
4. Position a shop towel in caliper body, then apply compressed air through brake hose fitting hole to remove piston and dust boot. **Apply air gently.**
5. Remove piston seal using finger tips. **Do not use screwdriver or other tool to prevent damage to inner cylinder.**
6. Reverse procedure to assemble, noting following:
   a. Inspect cylinder and piston for wear or damage and/or corrosion. Inspect caliper body and sleeve for wear.
   b. Apply suitable brake fluid to inner cylinder, then install piston seal into cylinder groove. **Do not wipe special grease from piston seal.**
   c. Apply suitable brake fluid to piston

and insert into cylinder without twisting.

d. Fill piston edge with grease from seal and boot repair kit or equivalent, then install piston boot.

e. Lubricate sliding surface of lockpin and guide pin boots, caliper support and bushing with grease from seal and boot repair kit.

f. Install guide and lockpins with their head marks matched with identification marks on caliper body.

ROTOR

REPLACE

1. Remove caliper from brake rotor as described in "Brake Pad Service."
2. Remove rotor. If necessary use a suitable soft face hammer to tap rotor free of hub.
3. Reverse procedure to install.

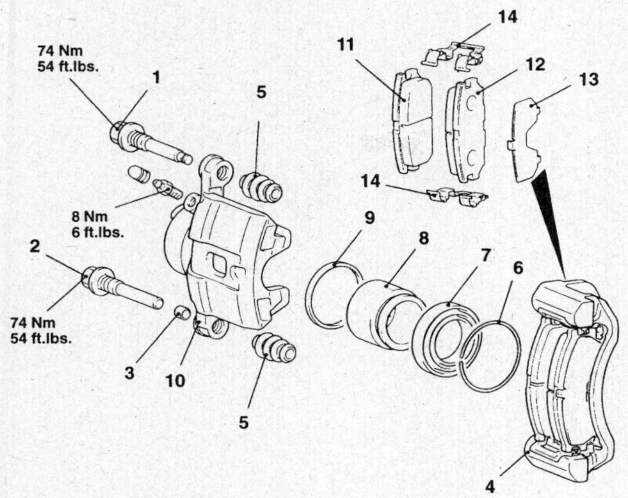

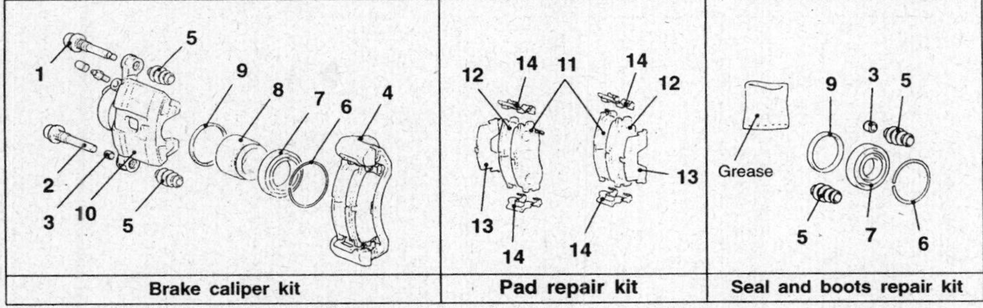

Caliper assembly

1. Guide pin
2. Lock pin
3. Bushing
4. Caliper support (pad, clip, shim)
5. Boot
6. Boot ring
7. Piston boot
8. Piston
9. Piston seal
10. Caliper body

Pad assembly

1. Guide pin
2. Lock pin
3. Bushing
4. Caliper support (pad, clip, shim)
11. Pad and wear indicator assembly
12. Pad assembly
13. Outer shim
14. Clip

CR4079100060000X

Fig. 1 Disc brake assembly. 1998–2000 Avenger & Sebring Coupe

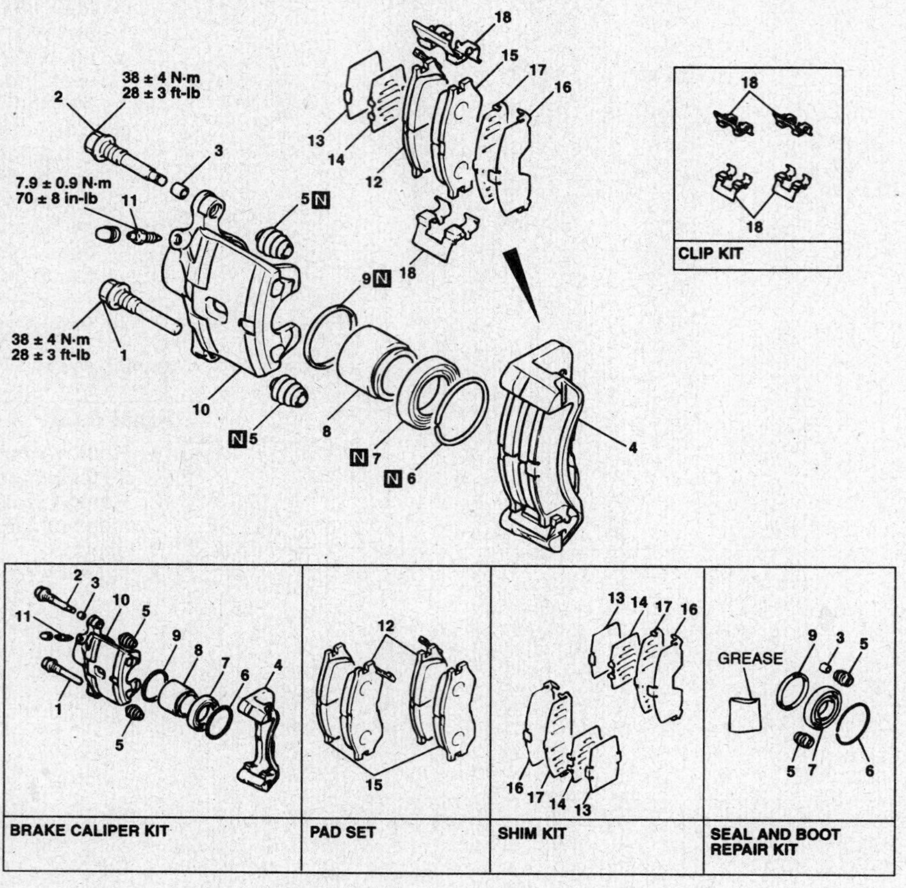

CALIPER ASSEMBLY DISASSEMBLY STEPS

1. GUIDE PIN
2. LOCK PIN
3. BUSHING
4. CALIPER SUPPORT, PAD, CLIP AND SHIM ASSEMBLY
5. PIN BOOT
6. BOOT RING
7. PISTON BOOT
8. PISTON
9. PISTON SEAL
10. CALIPER BODY
11. BLEEDER SCREW

PAD ASSEMBLY DISASSEMBLY STEPS

1. GUIDE PIN
2. LOCK PIN
3. BUSHING
4. CALIPER SUPPORT, PAD, CLIP AND SHIM ASSEMBLY
12. PAD AND WEAR INDICATOR ASSEMBLY
13. INNER SHIM B
14. INNER SHIM A
15. PAD ASSEMBLY
16. OUTER SHIM B
17. OUTER SHIM A
18. CLIP

CR40700001440000X

Fig. 2 Disc brake assembly. 2001–02 Sebring Coupe & Stratus Coupe

DISC BRAKE SPECIFICATIONS

ROTOR SPECIFICATIONS

Model	Year	Nominal Thickness, Inch	Minimum Allowable Thickness, Inch	Thickness Variation (Parallelism), Inch	Lateral Runout (T.I.R.), Inch
Avenger & Sebring Coupe	1998–2000	.940	.880	.0006	.0031
Talon	1998	.940	.880	.0006	.0031
Sebring Coupe & Stratus Coupe	2001–02	.900	.880	.0006	.0020

CALIPER SPECIFICATIONS

Model	Year	Caliper Bore Dia. Inch
Avenger & Sebring Coupe	1998–2000	2.375
Talon FWD	1998	2.375
Sebring Coupe & Stratus Coupe	2001–02	—

TIGHTENING SPECIFICATIONS

Component	Torque/Ft. Lbs.
Bleed Screws	50–84①
Caliper Guide & Lockpins	54
Caliper Support To Front Axle	65
Wheel Lug Nuts	87–101

① — Inch lbs.

Type 7

NOTE: On Air Bag Equipped Models, Refer To "Air Bag System Precautions" Located In The Front Of This Manual For System Disarming & Arming Procedures.

NOTE: Refer To "Computer Relearn Procedures" Located In The Front Of This Manual When Battery Power To The Computer Has Been Interrupted.

INDEX

TROUBLESHOOTING

LATERAL RUNOUT INSPECTION

1. Remove caliper as outlined in "Brake Pad Service" in this section.
2. Inspect disc surface for grooves, cracks and rust.
3. Tighten rotor to hub.
4. Place a dial indicator approximately 1 inch from outer circumference of brake rotor, **Fig. 1**.
5. Measure brake rotor runout and compare measurements to those listed in "Disc Brake Specifications" chart.
6. If runout of rotor is equal to or exceeds limit specified, change phase of rotor and hub then, measure runout again noting following:
   a. Before removing brake rotor, chalk both sides of wheel stud on side at which runout is greatest.
   b. Remove brake rotor and place dial gauge as shown in **Fig. 2.**
   c. Move hub in axial direction and measure play. If play exceeds .0020 inch, disassemble hub knuckle and inspect each part.
   d. If play does not exceed limit specification, install brake rotor 180° away from chalk marks.
7. Inspect runout of brake rotor again.
8. If runout cannot be corrected by changing phase of rotor, replace or machine rotor.

PARALLELISM INSPECTION

1. Measure rotor thickness at 12 positions with suitable micrometer, 1 inch in from outer edge of disc.
2. Compare measurements taken with those listed in "Disc Brake Specifications." chart.
3. If thickness variation exceeds specification, refer to replace or resurface brake rotor.

BRAKE SYSTEM BLEED

Bleeding hydraulic brake system is necessary if air has entered system. Symptoms can be noted by loss of brake operation, and/or a low or spongy brake pedal.

The hydraulic fluid is bled or flushed from system through bleeder valves located on calipers, wheel cylinders, and some master cylinders. Use only specified brake fluid when bleeding hydraulic brake system. **Never reuse old brake fluid removed from system.**

PRESSURE BLEED

Refer to "Type 1" for bleeding procedures.

MANUAL BLEED

Refer to "Type 1" for bleeding procedures.

BRAKE PAD SERVICE

1. Raise and support vehicle, then remove tire and wheel assemblies.
2. Remove anti-rattle spring from outboard side of caliper and adapter.

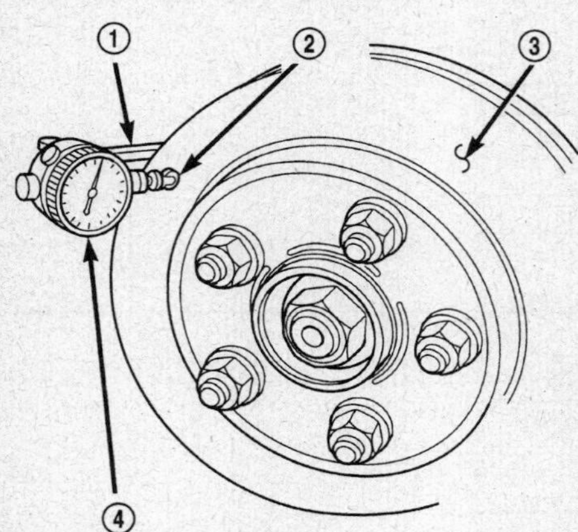

Fig. 1 Dial indicator mounting for rotor lateral runout

3. Remove caps over caliper guide pin bolts, then the guide pin bolts.
4. Remove caliper from caliper adapter and brake rotor.
5. Remove pads from caliper and from caliper adapter.
6. Reverse procedure to install, noting following:
   a. Using a suitable tool, press caliper piston back into piston bore of caliper.
   b. Apply brake pedal several times, then inspect master cylinder brake fluid level and add fluid if necessary.

CALIPER SERVICE

REPLACEMENT

1. Remove caliper from brake rotor and brake pads from caliper as described in "Brake Pad Service."
2. Disconnect brake hose at brake caliper, then cap brake line.
3. Reverse procedure to install, noting following:
   a. Bleed brakes as outlined under "Brake System Bleed."

OVERHAUL

Refer to "Caliper Overhaul" in "Type 3" section.

ROTOR

REPLACE

1. Remove caliper from brake rotor as described in "Brake Pad Service."

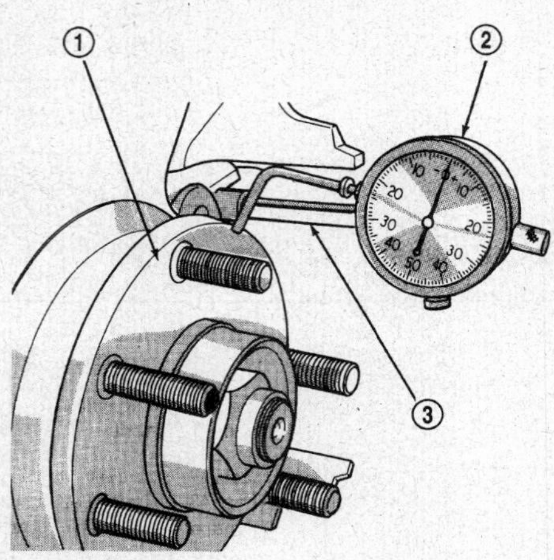

Fig. 2 Dial gauge mounting for hub lateral runout

2. Remove rotor retaining clips if equipped, and rotor, if necessary use a suitable soft face hammer to tap rotor free of hub.
3. Reverse procedure to install.

DISC BRAKE SPECIFICATIONS

ROTOR SPECIFICATIONS

Model	Year	Nominal Thickness, Inch	Minimum Allowable Thickness, Inch	Thickness Variation (Parallelism), Inch	Lateral Runout (T.I.R.), Inch	Rotor Micro Finish
Sebring Convertible, Sebring Sedan & Stratus Sedan	2001–02	.900–.911	.843	.0005	.004	15–80

TIGHTENING SPECIFICATIONS

Component	Torque/Ft. Lbs.
Bleed Screws	125①
Brake Hose Intermediate Bracket Bolt	105①
Brake Hose To Caliper (Banjo Bolt)	26
Brake Tube Nuts	145①
Caliper Adapter Mounting Bolt	60
Caliper Guide & Lockpins	26
Wheel Lug Nuts	100

① — Inch lbs.

Type 8

NOTE: On Air Bag Equipped Models, Refer To "Air Bag System Precautions" Located In The Front Of This Manual For System Disarming & Arming Procedures.

NOTE: Refer To "Computer Relearn Procedures" Located In The Front Of This Manual When Battery Power To The Computer Has Been Interrupted.

INDEX

TROUBLESHOOTING

LATERAL RUNOUT INSPECTION

Refer to "Type 7" for Inspection procedures.

PARALLELISM INSPECTION

Refer to "Type 7" for Inspection procedures.

BRAKE SYSTEM BLEED

Bleeding the hydraulic brake system is necessary if air has entered the system. Symptoms can be noted by loss of brake operation, and/or a low or spongy brake pedal.

The hydraulic fluid is bled or flushed from system through bleeder valves located on calipers, wheel cylinders, and some master cylinders. Use only specified brake fluid when bleeding hydraulic brake system. **Never reuse old brake fluid removed from system.**

PRESSURE BLEED

Refer to "Type 1" for bleeding procedures.

MANUAL BLEED

Refer to "Type 1" for bleeding procedures.

BRAKE PAD SERVICE

Refer to "Type 1" for brake pad service procedures.

CALIPER SERVICE

REPLACEMENT

1. Remove caliper from brake rotor and brake pads from caliper as described in "Brake Pad Service." in "Type 1" section.
2. Disconnect brake hose at brake caliper, then cap brake line.
3. Reverse procedure to install, noting following:
   a. Bleed brakes as outlined under "Brake System Bleed."

OVERHAUL

Refer to "Caliper Overhaul" in "Type 3" section.

ADJUSTMENTS

PARKING BRAKE LEVER

1. Remove center floor console, then lower parking brake handle.
2. Position lever to its fully released position.
3. Tighten adjusting nut on parking brake lever output cable until 26mm of thread is out past top edge of adjustment nut.
4. Actuate parking brake lever to its fully applied position (22 clicks) one time, then reposition lever to its fully released position.
5. Raise and support rear of vehicle.
6. Turn rear wheel with parking brake in released position to confirm rear brakes are not dragging.

PARKING BRAKE SHOE

1. Raise and support vehicle, then remove rear wheels.
2. Remove adjusting hole plug from hub of brake disc.
3. Using a suitable tool, turn adjusting nut until brake disc cannot be turned by hand.
4. Back off adjusting nut five notches.
5. Repeat above steps on opposite side.
6. Connect drive axles to companion flange.
7. Firmly apply, then release parking brake lever several times to seat and center parking brake shoes.
8. Adjust parking brake lever as outlined under "Parking Brake Lever, Adjust"
9. Install rear wheels, then lower vehicle.

DISC BRAKE SPECIFICATIONS

ROTOR SPECIFICATIONS

Model	Year	Nominal Thickness, Inch	Minimum Allowable Thickness, Inch	Thickness Variation (Parallelism), Inch	Lateral Runout (T.I.R.), Inch	Rotor Micro Finish
Sebring Convertible, Sebring Sedan & Stratus Sedan	2001	.350–.360	.285	.0005	.005	15–80
	2002	.350–.360	.285	.0005	.004	15–80

TIGHTENING SPECIFICATIONS

Component	Torque/Ft. Lbs.
Bleed Screws	125①
Brake Hose Intermediate Bracket Bolt	105①
Brake Hose To Caliper (Banjo Bolt)	26
Brake Tube Nuts	145①
Caliper Guide & Lockpins	26
Parking Brake Lever Mounting Bolts	21
Wheel Lug Nuts	100

① — Inch lbs.

DRUM BRAKES

TABLE OF CONTENTS

Application Chart

Model	Year	Type	Drum Brake Type
Avenger	1998–2000	—	2
Breeze, Cirrus & Stratus	1998–2000	Varga	1
Concorde, Intrepid & LHS	1998–99	Varga	1
Neon	1998–2002	Kelsey-Hayes	1
Sebring Convertible	1998–2000	Kelsey-Hayes	1
Sebring Coupe	1998–2000	—	2
	2001–02	—	2
Stratus Coupe	2001–02	—	2

Type 1

NOTE: On Air Bag Equipped Models, Refer To "Air Bag System Precautions" Located In The Front Of This Manual For System Disarming & Arming Procedures.

NOTE: Refer To "Computer Relearn Procedures" Located In The Front Of This Manual When Battery Power To The Computer Has Been Interrupted.

INDEX

PRECAUTIONS

When working on or around brake assemblies, care must be taken to prevent breathing asbestos dust. During routine service operations, the amount of asbestos dust from brake lining wear is at a low level due to a chemical breakdown during use. A few precautions will minimize exposure.

Do not sand or grind brake linings unless suitable exhaust ventilation equipment is used to prevent excessive asbestos exposure.

1. Wear a suitable respirator approved for asbestos dust use during all repair procedures.
2. When cleaning brake dust from brake parts, use a vacuum cleaner with a highly efficient filter system. If a suitable vacuum cleaner is not available, use a water soaked rag. **Do not use compressed air or dry brush to clean brake parts.**
3. Keep work area clean using same equipment as for cleaning brake parts.
4. Properly dispose of rags and vacuum cleaner bags by placing them in plastic bags.
5. Do not smoke or eat while working on brake systems.
6. Never use any fluid containing mineral oil to clean brake system components. This will damage the rubber caps and seals. If system contamination is suspected, inspect brake fluid in the reservoir for dirt, discoloration, or separation (breakdown) of the brake fluid into distinct layers. Drain and flush the hydraulic system with clean brake fluid if contamination is suspected.

INSPECTION

BRAKE DRUMS

Any time the brake drums are removed for brake service, the braking surface diameter should be inspected with a suitable brake drum micrometer at several points to determine if they are within the safe oversize limit stamped on the brake drum outer surface. If the braking surface diameter exceeds specifications, the drum must be replaced. If the braking surface diameter is

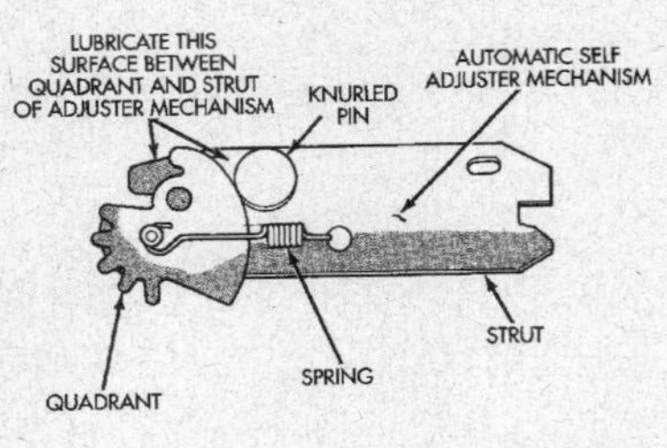

Fig. 1 Automatic self-adjuster mechanism. Breeze, Cirrus & Stratus

within specifications, drums should be cleaned and inspected for cracks, scores, deep grooves, taper, out of round and heat spotting. If drums are cracked or heat spotted, they must be replaced. Scoring and grooves in the braking surface can only be removed by machining with special equipment, as long as the braking surface is within specifications. Any brake drum showing taper or sufficient out of round to cause vehicle vibration or noise while braking should also be machined, removing only enough stock to true up the drum.

After a brake drum is machined, wipe the braking surface diameter with a denatured alcohol soaked cloth. If one brake drum is machined, the other should also be machined to the same diameter to maintain equal braking forces.

BRAKE LININGS & SPRINGS

Inspect brake linings for excessive wear, damage, oil, grease or brake fluid contamination. If any of the above conditions exist, brake linings should be replaced as an axle set to maintain equal braking forces. Examine brake shoe webbing, hold-down and return springs for signs of overheating indicated by a slight blue color. Any component which exhibits overheating signs should be replaced. Overheated springs lose their pull and could cause brake linings to wear out prematurely. Inspect all springs for sags, bends and external damage and replace as required.

Inspect hold-down retainers and pins for bends, rust and corrosion. Replace faulty components as required.

WHEEL CYLINDER

With brake drum removed, inspect the wheel cylinder for fluid leaks. Inspect wheel cylinder boots for cuts, tears, or heat cracks. Replace faulty components as required.

BACKING PLATE

Inspect backing plate shoe contact surface for grooves that may restrict shoe movement and cannot be removed by lightly sanding with emery cloth or other suitable abrasive. If backing plate exhibits above condition, it should be replaced. Also inspect for signs of cracks, warpage and excessive rust, indicating need for replacement.

ADJUSTER MECHANISM

Inspect the adjuster assembly as shown in **Figs. 1 and 2.** Use the following procedure to ensure adjuster mechanism operates properly:

1. Ensure quadrant rotates freely throughout its tooth contact range.
2. Ensure quadrant slides freely entire length of its mounting slot.
3. Inspect quadrant spring for any signs of damage.
4. Ensure knurled pin is securely attached to adjuster mechanism and teeth are not damaged.
5. Examine adjuster mechanism for excessive wear or damage. Replace as required.
6. If adjuster mechanism will be used again, apply a light coat of multipurpose lubricant, or equivalent, between quadrant and strut of adjuster mechanism.

PARKING BRAKE CABLE

Inspect parking brake cable end for kinks, fraying and elongation and replace as required. Use a small hose clamp to compress clamp where it enters backing plate during removal.

TROUBLESHOOTING

Refer to **Figs. 3 and 4,** for brake system troubleshooting.

BRAKE SERVICE

REMOVAL

BREEZE, CIRRUS & STRATUS

1. Raise and support vehicle on jack stands or centered on a hoist.
2. Remove rear wheel and tire assemblies.
3. Remove rubber plug from top of brake support plate.
4. Insert a suitable screwdriver into hole and turn adjuster towards front of car until it stops. This will fully release rear brake adjuster.
5. Remove brake drum.
6. Remove brake drum to hub/bearing retaining nuts, then the rear brake drum from hub and bearing assembly.
7. Remove actuator spring from automatic adjuster mechanism and trailing brake shoe as shown in **Fig. 5.**
8. Remove upper and lower return springs.
9. Remove brake shoe retainer and pin from leading brake shoe.
10. Remove leading brake shoe and adjuster mechanism as an assembly from brake support plate.
11. Remove brake shoe retainer and pin from trailing brake shoe.
12. Remove trailing brake shoe assembly from brake support plate.
13. Remove park brake cable from actuating lever. **Do not attempt to remove actuating lever from brake shoe assembly.**
14. Fully extend automatic adjuster mechanism in direction as shown in **Fig. 6,** then rotate and remove adjuster mechanism from leading brake shoe assembly.

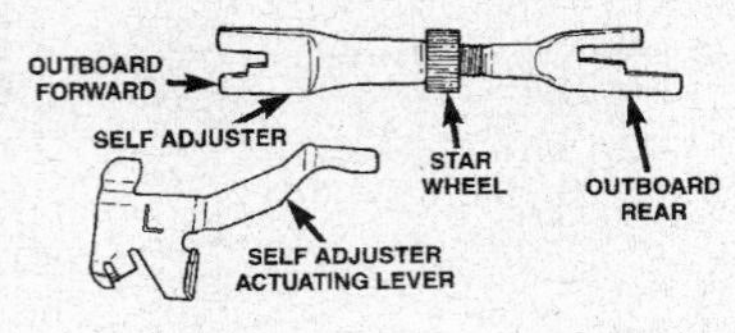

Fig. 2 Automatic self-adjuster mechanism. Except Breeze, Cirrus & Stratus

CONCORDE, INTREPID & LHS

1. Remove dust cap from hub and bearing assembly.
2. Remove cotter pin, nut retainer, wave washer, retaining nut and washer from rear spindle.
3. Remove hub and bearing assembly from spindle.
4. Remove automatic adjuster spring from adjuster lever.
5. Rotate automatic adjuster screw assembly until each shoe assembly is free from wheel cylinder boots.
6. Disconnect parking brake cable from lever.
7. Remove lower brake shoe assembly to anchor plate springs.
8. Remove brake shoe assembly to support plate hold-down springs.
9. Remove upper brake shoe return spring, then the automatic adjuster and adjuster lever from brake shoe support plate.
10. Separate brake shoes from automatic adjuster mechanism.
11. Remove automatic adjuster lever from leading brake shoe.

NEON

1998–99

Due to the automatic adjustment feature of the parking brake, only remove brake shoes from one side of the vehicle at a time. If the brake shoes are removed from both sides of vehicle at the same time the adjuster will remove all slack from park brake cables making shoe installation very difficult.

1. Raise and support vehicle.
2. Remove rear wheel and tire assemblies.
3. Remove rear brake drum to hub retaining clips (if equipped), then the drum from hub and bearing assembly.
4. Remove automatic adjuster lever actuating spring from leading shoe, then the automatic adjuster actuating lever.
5. Thread automatic adjuster star wheel all the way into adjuster.
6. Remove upper return spring from brake shoes.
7. Remove brake shoe lower return spring.
8. Remove hold-down spring and attaching pin from leading brake shoe.
9. Remove leading brake shoe from brake support plate.

SYMPTOM	CHART 1 MISC. COND.	CHART 2 WARNING LIGHT	CHART 3 POWER BRAKES	CHART 4 BRAKE NOISE	CHART 5 WHEEL BRAKES
Brake Warning Light On		X	NO	NO	
Excessive Pedal Travel	6	X	NO		O
Pedal Goes To The Floor	6	X			
Stop Light On Without Brakes	3				
All Brakes Drag	5				
Rear Brakes Drag	2	NO	NO		
Grabby Brakes			O		X
Spongy Brake Pedal		X	NO		
Premature Rear Brake Lockup	4	NO	NO		O
Excessive Pedal Effort	1		O		
Rough Engine Idle		NO	O		
Brake Chatter (Rough)		NO	NO		X
Surge During Braking		NO	NO		X
Noise During Braking		NO	NO	X	
Rattle Or Clunking Noise		NO	NO	X	
Pedal Pulsates During Braking		NO	NO		X
Pull To Right Or Left		NO	NO		X
No: Not A Possible Cause		X: Most Likely Cause		O: Possible Cause	

CR4089700045010X

Fig. 3 Brake system troubleshooting (Part 1 of 6). 1998

10. Remove automatic adjuster from trailing brake shoe and parking brake actuating lever.
11. Remove park brake actuating lever to trailing brake retaining clip.
12. Remove pin and hold-down spring from trailing brake shoe.
13. Remove trailing brake shoe from brake support plate and parking brake actuating lever.

2000–02

Due to the automatic adjustment feature of the parking brake, only remove brake shoes from one side of the vehicle at a time. If the brake shoes are removed from both sides of vehicle at the same time the adjuster will remove all slack from park brake cables making shoe installation very difficult.

1. Raise and support vehicle.
2. Remove rear wheel and tire assemblies.
3. Remove brake drum retaining clips, then the drum from hub/bearing assembly.
4. remove self-adjuster lever to brake shoe spring.
5. Remove self-adjustment lever from shoe.
6. Remove brake shoe to support plate hold-down clips and pins.
7. Remove lower brake shoe to anchor plate return spring.
8. Remove park brake lever pin to shoe retaining clip.
9. Remove leading and trailing brake shoes, upper return spring and self-adjuster screw from support plate as an assembly for disassembly on a workbench.

SEBRING CONVERTIBLE

1998–2000

Refer to "1998–99" under "Neon" for drum brake removal procedures.

INSTALLATION

BREEZE, CIRRUS & STRATUS

1. Using Mopar Multi-Purpose Lubricant, or equivalent, lubricate brake shoe contact areas on support plate as shown in **Fig. 7.**
2. Install park brake cable on park brake actuating lever of trailing brake shoe.
3. Install trailing brake shoe on support plate so it is squarely on shoe contact areas. **The leading and trailing shoes used on these models are unique for lefthand and righthand vehicle sides. When properly installed, the shoe web reinforcement plates will be facing toward brake support plates. The park brake actuating lever will be positioned behind brake shoe web as shown in Fig. 8.**
4. Install automatic self-adjuster on leading brake shoe assembly.
5. Install leading brake shoe and adjuster mechanism as an assembly on brake support plate.
6. Install brake retainer on retainer pin.
7. Install lower return spring onto leading and trailing brake shoes.
8. Install upper return spring (blue right-hand side, green lefthand side) on leading brake shoe, then on trailing shoe.
9. Install automatic adjuster actuator spring on trailing shoe, then hook it onto the adjuster mechanism.
10. Install rear brake drums on hubs, then the wheel and tire assembly.
11. Adjust rear brake shoes as outlined under "Adjustments."

CONCORDE, INTREPID & LHS

1. Lubricate shoe contact areas on support plate and anchor as shown in **Fig. 7.**
2. Assemble leading and trailing brake shoe assemblies, top shoe to shoe spring, automatic adjuster lever and adjuster, before mounting on vehicle. **Ensure automatic adjuster ends are above extruded pins in web of brake shoes.**
3. Install pre-assembled brake shoe assembly on support plate.
4. Install both lower brake shoe assembly to anchor plate return springs.
5. Install park brake cable on park brake lever of trailing brake shoe.
6. Rotate adjuster nut to remove free play from adjuster assembly.
7. Install automatic adjuster lever spring on leading brake shoe and automatic adjuster lever.
8. Install rear hub and bearing assembly on rear spindle.
9. Install wave washer, nut lock and cotter pin on spindle, then the dust cap.
10. Install brake drums, then the wheel and tire assemblies.

NEON

1998–99

1. Using Mopar Multi-Purpose Lubricant, or equivalent, lubricate all brake shoe contact areas on brake support plate and anchor as shown in **Fig. 9.**
2. Install wave washer on pin of parking brake actuating lever.
3. Install trailing brake shoe on parking brake actuating lever, then on the brake support plate.
4. Install parking brake actuating lever to trailing brake shoe retaining clip.
5. Install trailing brake shoe attaching pin and hold-down spring.
6. Install park brake actuating lever to trailing brake shoe retaining clip.
7. Install automatic adjuster on trailing

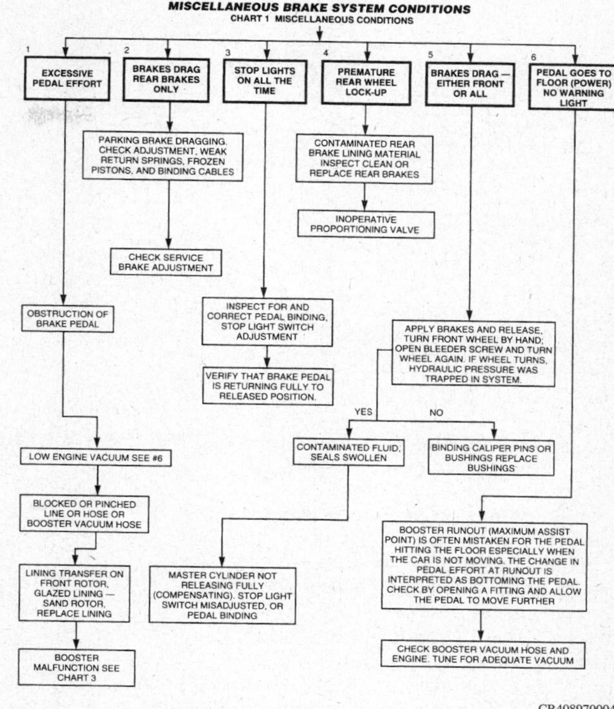

Fig. 3 Brake system troubleshooting (Part 2 of 6). 1998

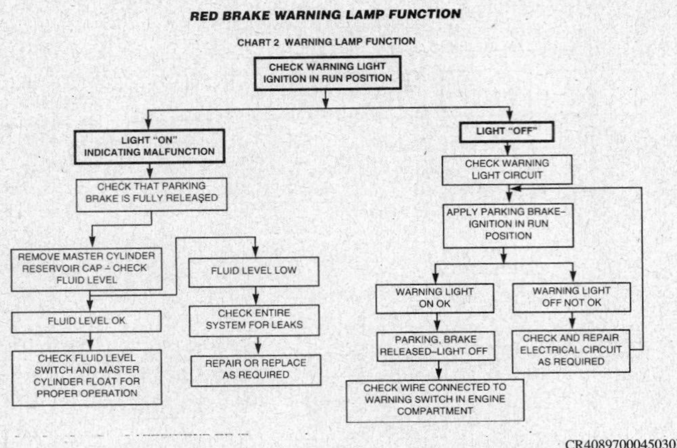

Fig. 3 Brake system troubleshooting (Part 3 of 6). 1998

brake shoe and parking brake actuating lever.

8. Install leading brake shoe on brake support with its attaching pin and hold-down spring.
9. Install brake shoe lower and upper return springs.
10. Install automatic adjuster actuating lever and spring on leading brake shoe.
11. Manually adjust brake shoes outward as far as possible, but not so far as to interfere with drum installation.
12. Install rear brake drums on hub, then adjust rear brake shoes as outlined under "Adjustments."
13. Install wheel and tire assembly. Tighten lugnuts in proper sequence to half specification, then repeat procedure and tighten in sequence to full specification.
14. Road test vehicle.

2000–02

1. Complete one side of vehicle before moving on to the other.
2. Using Mopar Multi-Purpose Lubricant, or equivalent, lubricate all brake shoe contact areas on brake support plate and anchor as shown in **Fig. 10.**
3. Assemble front and rear shoes, self-adjuster screw, and upper return spring as an assembly before installation on vehicle.
4. Install brake shoe components assembly onto vehicle.
5. Install wave washer on park brake lever pin.
6. Install both shoe to support plate hold-down pins and clips.
7. Install lower shoe to anchor plate return spring.
8. Install self-adjustment lever on leading brake shoe.
9. Install self-adjustment lever to shoe spring.
10. Adjust shoes out until drum drags lightly when installed. Do not over-adjust.
11. Install brake drum.
12. Repeat procedures on opposite side of vehicle.

POWER BRAKE SYSTEM DIAGNOSTICS

CHART 3 POWER BRAKES

BASIC TEST

ENGINE OFF. DEPRESS AND RELEASE BRAKE PEDAL SEVERAL TIMES TO REMOVE VACUUM FROM POWER UNIT.

DEPRESS PEDAL AND HOLD WITH LIGHT EFFORT OF 15 TO 25 LBS., AND START ENGINE.

IF POWER UNIT IS OPERATING, PEDAL WILL FALL SLIGHTLY AND THEN HOLD. LESS EFFORT WILL BE NEEDED TO APPLY PEDAL.

NO YES

IF PEDAL DOES NOT DROP, CONNECT VACUUM GAUGE TO SPEED CONTROL VACUUM PORT ON POWER UNIT. WITH ENGINE AT WARM IDLE CHECK FOR PROPER VACUUM.

NO YES

IF VACUUM SUPPLY IS BELOW 12 INCHES — REPLACE OR REPAIR VACUUM HOSE AND VACUUM FITTINGS. ALSO TUNE OR REPAIR ENGINE AS REQUIRED.

IF VACUUM SUPPLY IS 12 INCHES OR MORE — POWER UNIT IS DEFECTIVE AND SHOULD BE REPLACED.

WHEN ADEQUATE VACUUM SUPPLY IS OBTAINED, REPEAT BASIC TEST.

LOW VACUUM CAUSES EARLY BOOSTER RUNOUT WHICH CAN BE MISTAKEN FOR PEDAL GOES TO FLOOR CONDITION.

VACUUM LEAK TEST

REMOVE THE A/C VACUUM CONTROL LINE (IF SO EQUIPPED) FROM THE BOOSTER CHECK VALVE. CAP OFF THE NIPPLE.

REMOVE THE VACUUM HOSE OR RUBBER CAP FROM THE SPEED CONTROL OUTLET NIPPLE ON THE BOOSTER CHECK VALVE.

ATTACH A VACUUM GAUGE TO THE SPEED CONTROL NIPPLE ON THE BOOSTER CHECK VALVE. PLUG ANY REMAINING OPEN NIPPLES.

START THE ENGINE. ALLOW A WARM-UP PERIOD SO THAT THE ENGINE REACHES NORMAL IDLE SPEED.

LEAK TEST — BRAKES NOT APPLIED

WITH VACUUM LINE PLIERS (TOOL NUMBER C4390), CLOSE OFF THE VACUUM SUPPLY HOSE TO THE BOOSTER. IF VACUUM DROP EXCEEDS 1.0 INCH Hg IN ONE MINUTE, REPEAT PROCEDURE TO CONFIRM READINGS. LEAKAGE SHOULD BE LESS THAN 1.0 INCH Hg IN ONE MINUTE.

YES NO

LEAK TEST — BRAKES APPLIED

BOOSTER IS DEFECTIVE AND SHOULD BE REPLACED.

APPLY LIGHT EFFORT (APPROXIMATELY 15 POUNDS OF PEDAL FORCE) TO THE BRAKE PEDAL AND HOLD STEADY IN THIS POSITION. DO NOT MOVE THE PEDAL FROM THIS POSITION AS IT WILL AFFECT THE LEAKAGE READING.

USING VACUUM LINE PLIERS (TOOL NUMBER C4390), HAVE AN ASSISTANT CLOSE OFF THE VACUUM SUPPLY HOSE TO THE BRAKE BOOSTER. ALLOW FIVE SECONDS FOR STABILIZATION AND OBSERVE THE VACUUM GAUGE. IF VACUUM DROP EXCEEDS 3.0 INCHES Hg IN 15 SECONDS, REPEAT PROCEDURE TO CONFIRM READINGS. LEAKAGE SHOULD BE LESS THAN 3.0 INCHES Hg IN 15 SECONDS.

YES NO

BOOSTER IS NOT DEFECTIVE.

BOOSTER IS DEFECTIVE AND SHOULD BE REPLACED.

CR4089700045040X

Fig. 3 Brake system troubleshooting (Part 4 of 6). 1998

SEBRING CONVERTIBLE

1998–99

Refer to "1998–99" under "Neon" for drum brake installation procedures.

ADJUSTMENTS

SERVICE BRAKE

Breeze, Cirrus & Stratus

These vehicles are equipped with a fully automatic adjustment mechanism. In the event of brake shoe replacement the following initial adjustment procedure must be completed prior to driving the vehicle.

1. Ensure parking brake lever is fully released.
2. Depress brake pedal as far as possible 2–3 times. This will cause automatic adjuster to properly adjust rear brakes.
3. Apply and release park brake lever one time after service brakes have been adjusted.

Concorde, Intrepid, LHS, Neon & 1998–2000 Sebring Convertible

1. Ensure parking brake is in its fully released position.
2. Raise and support vehicle with a frame contact hoist or jack stands.
3. Remove brake adjusting hole plug from rear brake shoe support plate.
4. Insert a brake adjustment tool or a suitable thin screwdriver through adjusting hole in support plate and against star wheel of adjustment screw.
5. Rotate adjuster downward until a slight drag is felt when wheel is rotated.
6. Insert a thin screwdriver or welding rod into adjustment hole, then push adjustment lever out of engagement with star wheel. **Do not bend adjusting lever or distort lever spring.**
7. If brakes are now over-adjusted, insert a second screwdriver and engage it with star wheel while holding adjuster actuator lever away from star wheel.
8. Back off star wheel until there is no brake shoe drag. Repeat adjustment procedure.
9. Install brake adjusting hole plug.
10. Repeat procedure at other rear wheel.

PARKING BRAKE

Breeze, Cirrus & Stratus

These vehicles use a bent nail type park brake cable tensioner equalizer as shown in **Fig. 11.** The bent nail tension equalizer is to be used only one time to set cable tension. If park brake cables require adjustment during the life of vehicle a new tension equalizer must be installed.

1. Remove three screws attaching rear of center console.
2. **On models equipped with automatic transaxle,** remove shift knob from shifter using a suitable hex wrench.
3. **On models equipped with manual transaxle,** remove gearshift knob and shifter boot as follows:
   a. Push boot down to expose clips on shift knob and the handle's roll pin.

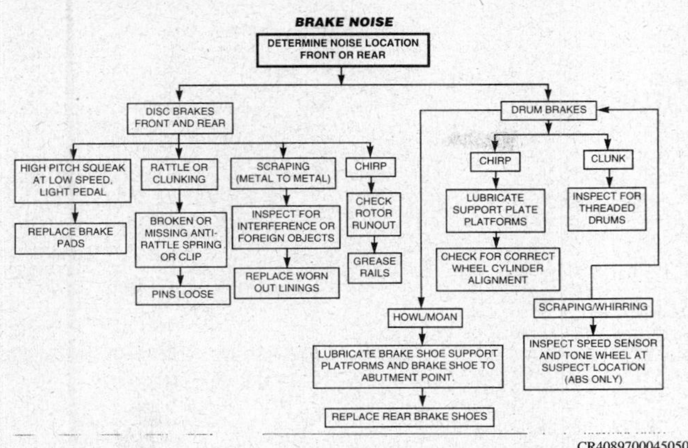

Fig. 3 Brake system troubleshooting (Part 5 of 6). 1998

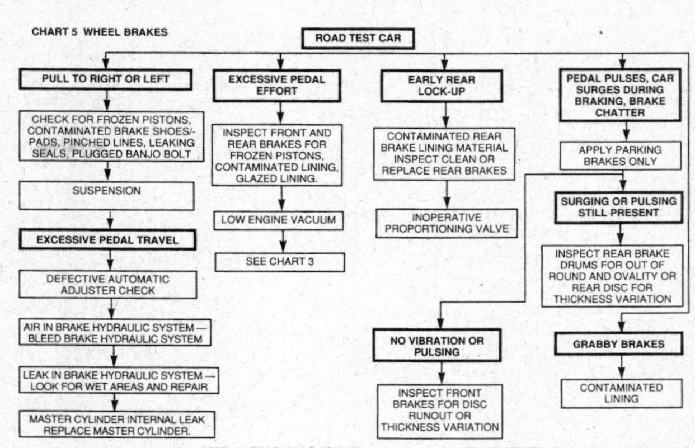

Fig. 3 Brake system troubleshooting (Part 6 of 6). 1998

RED BRAKE WARNING LAMP

CONDITION	POSSIBLE CAUSES	CORRECTION
RED BRAKE WARNING LAMP ON	1. Parking brake lever not fully released.	1. Release parking brake lever.
	2. Parking brake warning lamp switch on parking brake lever.	2. Inspect and replace switch as necessary.
	3. Brake fluid level low in reservoir.	3. Fill reservoir. Check entire system for leaks. Repair or replace as required.
	4. Brake fluid level switch.	4. Disconnect switch wiring connector. If lamp goes out, replace switch.
	5. Mechanical instrument cluster (MIC) problem.	5. Diagnose Instrument Cluster Fault Condition.
	6. ABS EBD malfunction.	6. Refer to ABS section

BRAKE NOISE

CONDITION	POSSIBLE CAUSES	CORRECTION
DISC BRAKE CHIRP	1. Excessive brake rotor runout.	1. Follow brake rotor diagnosis and testing. Correct as necessary.
	2. Lack of lubricant on brake caliper slides.	2. Lubricate brake caliper slides.
DISC BRAKE RATTLE OR CLUNK	1. Broken or missing anti-rattle spring clips on shoes.	1. Replace brake shoes.
	2. Caliper guide pins loose.	2. Tighten guide pins.
DISC BRAKE SQUEAK AT LOW SPEED (WHILE APPLYING LIGHT BRAKE PEDAL EFFORT)	1. Brake shoe linings.	1. Replace brake shoes.
DRUM BRAKE CHIRP	1. Lack of lubricant on brake shoe support plate where shoes ride.	1. Lubricate shoe contact areas on brake shoe support plates.
	2. Wheel cylinder out of alignment.	2. Loosen wheel cylinder mounting bolts, realign wheel cylinder with brake shoes and tighten mounting bolts.
DRUM BRAKE CLUNK	1. Drum(s) have threaded machined braking surface.	1. Reface or replace drake drums as necessary.
DRUM BRAKE HOWL OR MOAN	1. Lack of lubricant on brake shoe support plate where shoes ride and at the anchor.	1. Lubricate shoe contact areas on brake shoe support plates and at the anchor.
	2. Rear brake shoes.	2. Replace rear brake shoes.
DRUM BRAKE SCRAPING OR WHIRRING	1. ABS wheel speed sensor or tone wheel.	1. Inspect, correct or replace faulty component(s).
SCRAPING (METAL-TO-METAL)	1. Foreign object interference with brakes.	1. Inspect brakes and remove foreign object.
	2. Brake shoes worn out.	2. Replace brake shoes. Inspect rotors and drums. Reface or replace as necessary.

CR4089900044010X

Fig. 4 Brake system troubleshooting (Part 1 of 3). 1999–2002

CONDITION	POSSIBLE CAUSES	CORRECTION
BRAKES CHATTER	1. Rear brake drum out of round or disc brake rotor has excessive thickness variation.	1. Isolate condition as rear or front. Reface or replace brake drums or rotors as necessary.
BRAKES DRAG (FRONT OR ALL)	1. Contaminated brake fluid.	1. Check for swollen seals. Replace all system components containing rubber.
	2. Binding caliper pins or bushings.	2. Replace pins and bushings
	3. Binding master cylinder.	3. Replace master cylinder.
	4. Binding brake pedal.	4. Replace brake pedal.
BRAKES DRAG (REAR ONLY)	1. Parking brake cables binding or froze up.	1. Check cable routing. Replace cables as necessary.
	2. Parking brake cable return spring not returning shoes.	2. Replace cables as necessary.
	3. Service brakes not adjusted properly (rear drum brakes only).	3. Follow the procedure listed in the adjustment section.
	4. Obstruction inside the center console preventing full return of the parking brake cables.	4. Remove console and remove obstruction.
BRAKES GRAB	1. Contaminated brake shoe linings.	1. Inspect and clean, or replace shoes. Repair source of contamination.
	2. Improper power brake booster assist.	2. Refer to power brake booster in the diagnosis and testing section.
EXCESSIVE PEDAL EFFORT	1. Obstruction of brake pedal.	1. Inspect, remove or move obstruction.
	2. Low power brake booster assist.	2. Refer to power brake booster in the diagnosis and testing section.
	3. Glazed brake linings.	3. Reface or replace brake rotors as necessary. Replace brake shoes.
	4. Brake shoe lining transfer to brake rotor.	4. Reface or replace brake rotors as necessary. Replace brake shoes.
EXCESSIVE PEDAL TRAVEL (VEHICLE STOPS OK)	1. Air in brake lines.	1. Bleed brakes.
	2. Rear drum brake auto-adjuster malfunctioning.	2. Inspect and replace drum brake components as necessary. Adjust rear brakes.
EXCESSIVE PEDAL TRAVEL (PEDAL GOES TO FLOOR - CAN'T SKID WHEELS)	1. Power brake booster runout (vacuum assist).	1. Check booster vacuum hose and engine tune for adequate vacuum supply. Refer to power brake booster in the diagnosis and testing section.
EXCESSIVE PEDAL TRAVEL (ONE FRONT WHEEL LOCKS UP DURING HARD BRAKING)	1. One of the two hydraulic circuits to the front brakes is malfunctioning.	1. Inspect system for leaks. Check master cylinder for internal malfunction.

CR4089900044020X

Fig. 4 Brake system troubleshooting (Part 2 of 3). 1999–2002

   b. Using a suitable flat pry tool, pry knob clips away from roll pin.
   c. Pull straight up on shifter knob to remove it from handle.
   d. Squeeze shifter boot bezel base together, then pull upward on boot.
4. **On all models,** remove two screws attaching front of center console to gear selector or shifter.
5. Raise parking brake hand lever halfway up and remove center console from vehicle.
6. Lower the park brake lever handle.
7. Loosen adjusting nut on park brake cable output cable.
8. Using a screwdriver unlatch park brake output cable retainer, then the cable retainer from cable tension equalizer.
9. Remove cable tension equalizer from lever output cable and rear cables as shown in **Fig. 12.**
10. Install a new park brake cable tension equalizer on lever output cable and rear cables.
11. Install new park brake lever output cable to tension equalizer retaining clip.
12. Adjust cable tension as follows:
   a. Position park brake lever in its fully released position.
   b. Tighten adjusting nut on park brake lever output cable until ½ inch of thread is past top of adjusting nut.
   c. Pull park brake lever to its fully applied position one time, then release. **This will yield bent nail portion of tension equalizer approximately ¼ inch.** Maximum travel is 21 clicks.
13. Reverse procedures to install.

Concorde, Intrepid, LHS, Neon & Sebring Convertible

Due to the self-adjusting feature of the parking brake lever, adjustment of the parking brake system relies on proper brake shoe adjustment. Refer to "Adjustments."

CONDITION	POSSIBLE CAUSES	CORRECTION
PEDAL PULSATES/SURGES DURING BRAKING	1. Rear brake drum out of round or disc brake rotor has excessive thickness variation.	1. Isolate condition as rear or front. Reface or replace brake drums or rotors as necessary.
PEDAL IS SPONGY	1. Air in brake lines. 2. Power brake booster runout (vacuum assist).	1. Bleed brakes. 2. Check booster vacuum hose and engine tune for adequate vacuum supply. Refer to power brake booster in the diagnosis and testing section.
PREMATURE REAR WHEEL LOCKUP	1. Contaminated brake shoe linings. 2. Inoperative proportioning valve (non-ABS vehicles only). 3. ABS EBD not functioning. 4. Improper power brake booster assist.	1. Inspect and clean, or replace shoes. Repair source of contamination. 2. Test proportioning valves folowing procedure listed in diagnosis and testing section. Replace valves as necessary. 3. Refer to the ABS section 4. Refer to power brake booster in the diagnosis and testing section.
STOP LAMPS STAY ON	1. Brake lamp switch out of adjustment. 2. Brake pedal binding. 3. Obstruction in pedal linkage. 4. Power Brake Booster not allowing pedal to return completely.	1. Adjust brake lamp switch. 2. Inspect and replace as necessary. 3. Remove obstruction. 4. Replace power brake booster.
VEHICLE PULLS TO RIGHT OR LEFT ON BRAKING	1. Frozen brake caliper piston. 2. Contaminated brake shoe lining. 3. Pinched brake lines. 4. Leaking piston seal. 5. Suspension problem.	1. Replace frozen piston or caliper. Bleed brakes. 2. Inspect and clean, or replace shoes. Repair source of contamination. 3. Replace pinched line. 4. Replace piston seal or brake caliper. 5. Refer to the Suspension section.
PARKING BRAKE - EXCESSIVE HANDLE TRAVEL	1. Rear brakes out of adjustment.	1. Adjust rear drum brake shoes, or rear parking brake shoes on vehicles with rear disc brakes.

CR4089900044030X

Fig. 4 Brake system troubleshooting (Part 3 of 3). 1999–2002

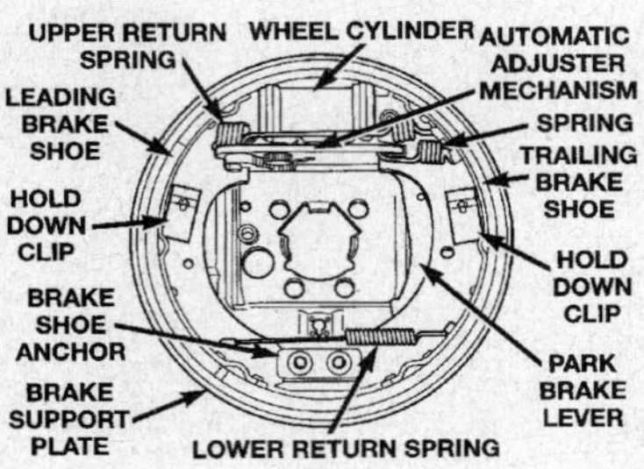

Fig. 5 Brake assembly. Breeze, Cirrus & Stratus

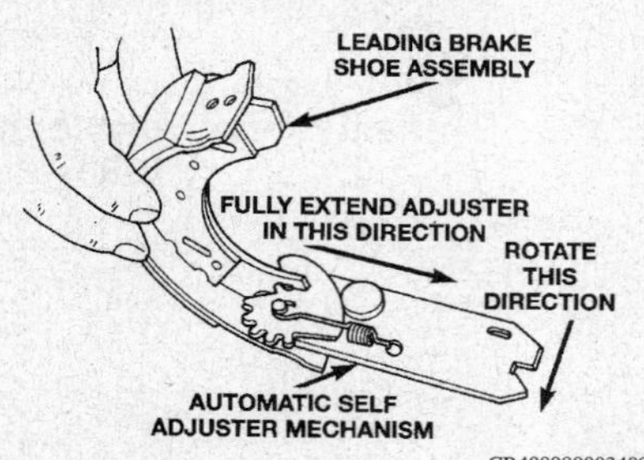

Fig. 6 Adjuster mechanism removal. Breeze, Cirrus & Stratus

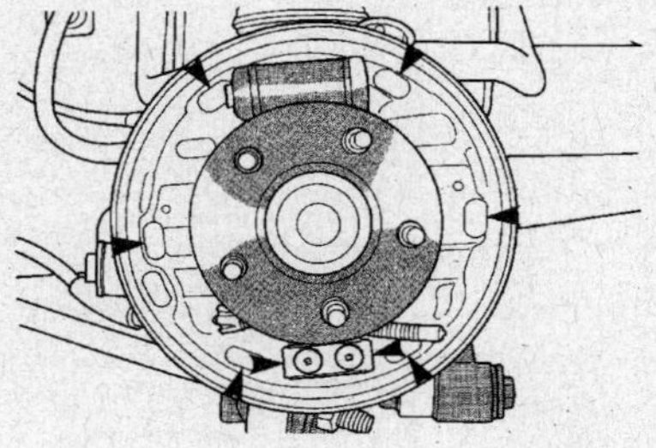

Fig. 7 Brake shoe contact areas. Breeze, Cirrus, Concorde, Intrepid, LHS & Stratus

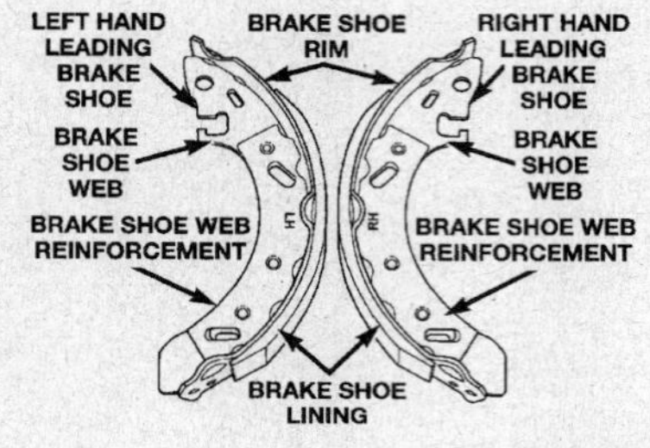

Fig. 8 Brake shoe installation. Breeze, Cirrus & Stratus

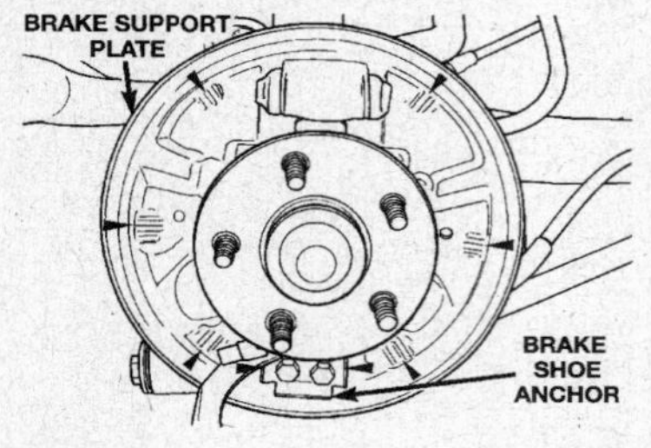

Fig. 9 Brake shoe contact areas. 1998–99 Neon & Sebring Convertible

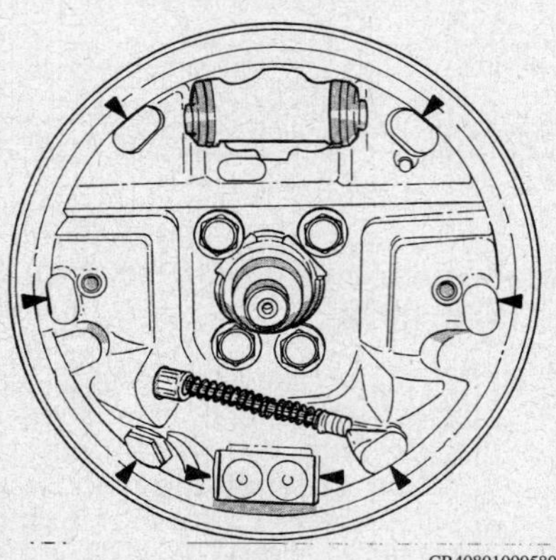

Fig. 10 Brake shoe contact areas. 2000-02 Neon

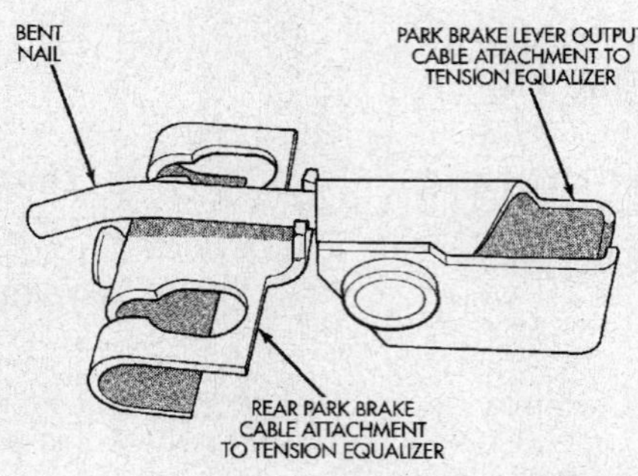

Fig. 11 Bent nail park brake cable tension equalizer. Breeze, Cirrus & Stratus

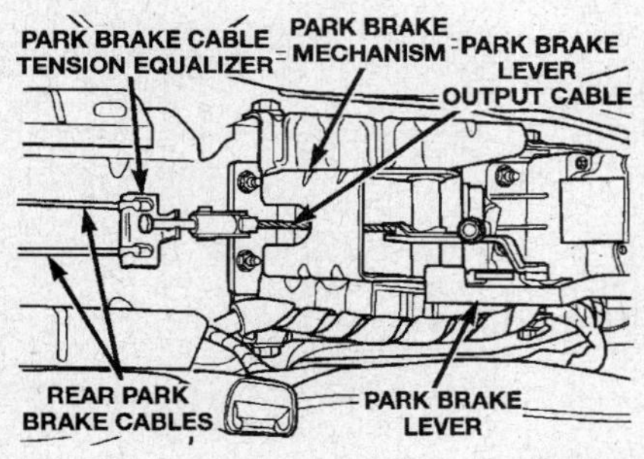

Fig. 12 Park brake assembly. Breeze, Cirrus & Stratus

DRUM BRAKE SPECIFICATIONS

Year	Model	Brake Drum Inside Dia. Inch	Rear Wheel Cylinder Bore Dia. Inch
1998	Concorde, Intrepid & LHS	①	—
1998–2000	Breeze, Cirrus, Neon, Sebring Convertible & Stratus	①	—
2001–02	Neon	①	—

① — Maximum refinishing diameter is stamped on outer face of drum.

TIGHTENING SPECIFICATIONS

Component	Torque/Ft. Lbs.
BREEZE, CIRRUS, SEBRING CONVERTIBLE & STRATUS	
Bearing Retainer Bolts	185
Brake Line Fittings	12
Support Plate To Rear Axle	46
Wheel Cylinder Bleed Screws	79②
Wheel Cylinder To Backing Plate	97②
Wheel Lugnuts	100①
CONCORDE, INTREPID & LHS	
Bearing Retainer Bolts	124
Brake Line Fittings	12
Support Plate To Rear Axle	80
Wheel Cylinder Bleed Screws	72②
Wheel Cylinder To Support Plate	72②
Wheel Lugnuts	85–115
NEON	
Bearing Retainer Bolts	160
Brake Line Fittings	12
Support Plate To Rear Axle (1998–99)	85
Support Plate To Rear Axle (2000)	55
Wheel Cylinder Bleed Screws	80②
Wheel Cylinder To Backing Plate (1998–99)	72②
Wheel Cylinder To Backing Plate (2000)	115②
Wheel Lugnuts	100①

① — Tighten in proper sequence to half specification, then repeat procedure and tighten to full specification.
② — Inch lbs.

Type 2

NOTE: On Air Bag Equipped Models, Refer To "Air Bag System Precautions" Located In The Front Of This Manual For System Disarming & Arming Procedures.

NOTE: Refer To "Computer Relearn Procedures" Located In The Front Of This Manual When Battery Power To The Computer Has Been Interrupted.

INDEX

PRECAUTIONS

When working on or around brake assemblies, care must be taken to prevent breathing asbestos dust. During routine service operations, the amount of asbestos dust from brake lining wear is at a low level due to a chemical breakdown during use. A few precautions will minimize exposure.

Do not sand or grind brake linings unless suitable local exhaust ventilation equipment is used to prevent excessive asbestos exposure.

1. Wear a suitable respirator approved for asbestos dust use during all repair procedures.
2. When cleaning brake dust from brake parts, use a vacuum cleaner with a highly efficient filter system. If a suitable vacuum cleaner is not available, use a water soaked rag. **Do not use compressed air or dry brush to clean brake parts.**
3. Keep work area clean using same equipment as for cleaning brake parts.
4. Properly dispose of rags and vacuum cleaner bags by placing them in plastic bags.
5. Do not smoke or eat while working on brake systems.
6. Never use any fluid containing mineral oil to clean brake system components. This will damage the rubber caps and seals. If system contamination is suspected, inspect brake fluid in the reservoir for dirt, discoloration, or separation (breakdown) of the brake fluid into distinct layers. Drain and flush the hydraulic system with clean brake fluid if contamination is suspected.

Symptom	Probable cause	Remedy
Vehicle pulls to one side when brakes are applied	Grease or oil on pad or lining surface	Replace
	Inadequate contact of pad or lining	Correct
	Auto adjuster malfunction	Adjust
	Drum out of round or uneven wear	Repair or replace as necessary
Insufficient braking power	Low or deteriorated brake fluid	Refill or change
	Air in brake system	Bleed air from system
	Overheated brake rotor due to dragging of pad or lining	Correct
	Inadequate contact of pad or lining	
	Brake booster malfunction	
	Clogged brake line	
	Grease or oil on pad or lining surface	Replace
	Proportioning valve malfunction	
	Auto adjuster malfunction	Adjust
Increased pedal stroke (Reduced pedal to floorboard clearance)	Air in brake system	Bleed air from system
	Worn lining or pad	Replace
	Broken vacuum hose	
	Faulty master cylinder	
	Brake fluid leaks	Correct
	Auto adjuster malfunction	Adjust
	Excessive push rod to master cylinder clearance	
Brake drag	Incomplete release of parking brake	Correct
	Clogged master cylinder return port	
	Incorrect parking brake adjustment	Adjust
	Incorrect push rod to master cylinder clearance	
	Faulty master cylinder piston return spring	Replace
	Worn brake pedal return spring	
	Broken rear drum brake shoe return spring	
	Lack of lubrication in sliding parts	Lubricate

CR4089200019010X

Fig. 1 Brake system troubleshooting (Part 1 of 3). 1998–2000

INSPECTION

BRAKE DRUMS

Any time the brake drums are removed for brake service, the braking surface diameter should be inspected with a suitable brake drum micrometer at several points to determine if they are within the safe oversize limit stamped on the brake drum outer surface. If the braking surface diameter exceeds specifications, the drum must be replaced. If the braking surface diameter is within specifications, drums should be cleaned and inspected for cracks, scores, deep grooves, taper, out of round and heat spotting. If drums are cracked or heat spotted, they must be replaced. Scoring and grooves in the braking surface can only be removed by machining with special equipment, as long as the braking surface is within specifications. Any brake drum showing taper or sufficiently out of round to cause vehicle vibration or noise while braking should also be machined, removing only enough stock to true up the drum.

After a brake drum is machined, wipe the braking surface diameter with a denatured alcohol soaked cloth. If one brake drum is machined, the other should also be machined to the same diameter to maintain equal braking forces.

BRAKE LININGS & SPRINGS

Inspect brake linings for excessive wear,

Symptom	Probable cause	Remedy
Insufficient parking brake function	Worn brake lining	Replace
	Grease or oil on lining surface	
	Parking brake cable sticking	
	Stuck wheel cylinder	
	Excessive parking brake lever stroke	Adjust the parking brake lever stroke or check the parking brake cable routing
	Auto adjuster malfunction	Adjust
Scraping or grinding noise when brakes are applied	Worn brake lining or pad	Replace
	Caliper to wheel interference	Correct or replace
	Dust cover to disc interference	
	Bent brake backing plate	
	Cracked drums or brake disc	
Squealing, groaning or chattering noise when brakes are applied	Missing or damaged brake pad anti-squeak shim	Replace
	Brake drums and linings, discs and pads worn or scored	Correct or replace
	Incorrect parts	
	Burred or rusted calipers	Clean or deburr
	Dirty, greased, contaminated or glazed linings	Clean or replace
	Drum brakes-weak, damaged or incorrect shoe hold-down springs, loose or damaged shoe hold-down pins and springs	Correct or replace
	Incorrect brake pedal or booster push rod setting	Adjust
Squealing noise when brakes are not applied	Bent or warped backing plate causing interference with drum	Replace
	Drum brakes-wear, damaged or incorrect shoe-to-shoe spring	
	Poor return of brake booster, master cylinder or wheel cylinder	
	Loose or extra brake parts	Retighten

CR4089200019020X

Fig. 1 Brake system troubleshooting (Part 2 of 3). 1998–2000

Symptom	Probable cause	Remedy
Squealing noise when brakes are not applied	Improper positioning of pads in caliper	Correct
	Improper installation of support mounting to caliper body	
	Improper machining of drum causing interference with backing plate or shoe	Replace drum
	Disc brakes-rusted, stuck	Lubricate or replace
	Worn, damaged or insufficiently lubricated wheel bearings	
	Incorrect brake pedal or booster push rod setting	Adjust
Groaning clicking or rattling noise when brakes are not applied	Stones or foreign material trapped inside wheel covers	Remove stones, etc.
	Loose wheel nuts	Retighten
	Disc brakes-loose installation bolt	
	Worn, damaged or dry wheel bearings	Lubricate or replace
	Disc brakes-failure of anti-rattle shim	Replace
	Disc brakes-wear on sleeve	
	Incorrect brake pedal or booster push rod setting	Adjust

CR4089200019030X

Fig. 1 Brake system troubleshooting (Part 3 of 3). 1998–2000

SYMPTOMS	INSPECTION PROCEDURE
Vehicle pulls to one side when brakes are applied	1
Insufficient braking power	2
Increased pedal stroke (Reduced pedal-to-floor board clearance)	3
Brake drag	4
Scraping or grinding noise when brake are applied	5
Squealing, groaning or chattering noise when brake are applied	6
Squealing noise when brakes are not applied	7
Groaning, clicking or rattling noise when brakes are not applied	8

CR4080100057000X

Fig. 2 Symptom chart. 2001–02

damage, oil, grease or brake fluid contamination. If any of the above conditions exist, brake linings should be replaced as an axle set to maintain equal braking forces. Examine brake shoe webbing, hold-down and return springs for signs of overheating indicated by a slight blue color. Any component which exhibits overheating signs should be replaced. Overheated springs lose their pull and could cause brake linings to wear out prematurely. Inspect all springs for sags, bends and external damage and replace as required.

Inspect hold-down retainers and pins for bends, rust and corrosion. If any of the above is found, replace as required.

BACKING PLATE

Inspect backing plate shoe contact surface for grooves that may restrict shoe movement and cannot be removed by lightly sanding with emery cloth or other suitable abrasive. If backing plate exhibits above condition, it should be replaced. Also inspect for signs of cracks, warpage and excessive rust, indicating need for replacement.

ADJUSTER MECHANISM

Inspect all components for rust, corrosion, bends and fatigue. Replace as required. On adjuster mechanism equipped with adjuster cable, inspect cable for kinks, fraying or elongation of eyelet and replace as required.

PARKING BRAKE CABLE

Inspect parking brake cable end for kinks, fraying and elongation and replace as required. Use a small hose clamp to compress clamp where it enters backing plate to remove.

TROUBLESHOOTING

Refer to **Fig. 1 through 10** for brake system troubleshooting.

BRAKE SERVICE

Refer to **Figs. 11 and 12,** for drum brake procedures.

ADJUSTMENTS

PARKING BRAKE

These brakes are equipped with self adjusting mechanisms. Periodic adjustments are not required. If stopping power is insufficient, or if brake pedal travel is excessive, brakes and self adjusting mechanism should be cleaned and inspected.

After performing brake service, adjust parking brake as follows:

1. Apply parking brake lever with a force of approximately 45 lbs. while counting number of clicks. Lever should click five to seven times.
2. If not within specifications, release parking brake lever and remove center console, if equipped.
3. Loosen adjusting nut on parking brake lever to free parking brake cables, then depress brake pedal several times to ensure shoe to drum clearance is properly maintained by self-adjusters.
4. Tighten adjusting nut until brake lever can be raised five to seven notches with a force of approximately 45 lbs. **If adjusting nut is tightened excessively, self-adjuster mechanism will be inoperative.**
5. After adjustment, raise rear of vehicle, ensuring brakes do not drag with parking brake lever released.

DIAGNOSIS

STEP 1. Check for oil, water, etc., on the pad or lining contact surface of all brakes.

Q: Is oil, water, etc., on the pad or lining contact surface?

YES : Replace the part and determine and repair source/cause of foreign material. Then go to Step 8.

NO : Go to Step 2.

STEP 2. Check the lining and brake drum contact (Vehicles equipped with rear drum brake).

(1) If equipped with rear disc brake, go to Step 5.

(2) Put chalk on the inner surface of the brake drum. Rub the lining against the drum inner surface.

NOTE: Clean off chalk after check.

Q: Does the lining wipe off or smudge the chalk across the full width of the lining?

YES : Go to Step 3.

NO : Replace the shoe and lining assemblies on both sides. Then go to Step 4.

CR4080100049010X

Fig. 3 Inspection 1: Vehicle pulls to one side when brakes are applied (Part 1 of 2). 2001–02

STEP 3. Check the auto adjuster function

Q: Is there fault?
YES : Repair it. Then go to step 8.
NO : Go to Step 4.

STEP 4. Check the brake drum inside diameter

Q: Is the brake drum inside diameter outside of specifications?
YES : Replace the part. Then go to Step 8.
NO : Go to Step 5.

STEP 5. Check disc brake pistons for smooth operation.
(1) With engine not running, depress the brake pedal rapidly several times to deplete booster vacuum reserves.
(2) Test each disc brake assembly one at a time.
a. 1) Remove the lower caliper bolt, then remove caliper from mount.
b. 2) Have an assistant slowly depress the brake pedal. Confirm piston(s) extend slowly and smoothly with no jumpiness. Repeat for each disc brake assembly.

Q: Do (does) the piston(s) move correctly?
YES : Go to Step 6.
NO : Disassemble and inspect brake assembly Then go to Step 8.

STEP 6. Check brake disc(s) for run out

Q: Is runout outside of specifications?
YES : Repair and replace as necessary. Then go to Step 8.
NO : Go to Step 7.

STEP 7. Check brake discs for correct thickness

Q: Is the thickness outside of specifications?
YES : Repair or replace as necessary. Then go to Step 8.
NO : Go to Step 8.

STEP 8. Check symptoms.
Q: Is the symptom eliminated?
YES : Repair complete.
NO : Start over at Step 1. If a new symptom appears, refer to the symptom chart.

CR4080100049020X

Fig. 3 Inspection 1: Vehicle pulls to one side when brakes are applied (Part 2 of 2). 2001–02

DIAGNOSIS

STEP 1. Check whether the brake fluid is low, is the correct fluid (A/T fluid, engine oil, etc.) or is contaminated (debris, sand, etc.).
Q: Is there fault?
YES : Refill or replace with the specified brake fluid DOT 3 or DOT 4. Bleed the brakes if necessary Then go to Step 9.
NO : Go to Step 2.

STEP 2. Check for spongy (not firm brakes).
(1) With engine not running, depress the brake pedal rapidly several times to deplete booster vacuum reserve.
(2) With the brake pedal fully released, depress the brake pedal slowly until it stops.
(3) With a measuring stick (ruler, etc.) next to the brake pedal, depress the pedal firmly and measure the distance the pedal traveled.

Q: Is the distance greater than 20 mm (0.8 inch)?
YES : Bleed the brakes to remove air in the fluid. Then go to Step 9.
NO : Go to Step 3.

STEP 3. Check the lining and brake drum contact (Vehicles equipped with rear drum brake).
(1) If equipped with rear disc brake, go to Step 4.
(2) Put chalk on the inner surface of the brake drum. Rub the lining against the drum inner surface.
NOTE: Clean off chalk after check.

Q: Does the lining wipe off or smudge the chalk across the full width of the lining?
YES : Go to Step 5.
NO : Replace the shoe and lining assemblies on both sides. Go to Step 9.

STEP 4. Check the auto adjuster function.
Q: Is there fault?
YES : Repair it. Then go to Step 9.
NO : Go to Step 6.

STEP 5. Check the brake booster function.
Q: Is there fault?
YES : Replace the part. Then go to Step 9.
NO : Go to Step 5.

CR4080100050010X

Fig. 4 Inspection 2: Insufficient braking power (Part 1 of 2). 2001–02

STEP 6. Check for pinched or restricted brake tube or hose.
Q: Is there pinched or restricted brake tube or hose?
YES : Replace that complete section of brake tube or brake hose. Then go to Step 9.
NO : Go to Step 7.

STEP 7. Check for oil, water, etc., on the pad or lining contact surfaces of all brakes.
Q: Is oil, water, etc., on the pad or lining contact surface?
YES : replace the part and determine and repair source/cause of foreign material. Recheck symptom. Then go to Step 9.
NO : Diagnosis is complete. If condition persists, go to Step 8.

STEP 8. Check the proportioning valve operation.

Q: Is there fault?
YES : Replace the part. Then go to Step 9.
NO : Go to Step 9.

STEP 9. Recheck symptom.
Q: Is the symptom eliminated?
YES : Diagnosis is complete.
NO : Start over at step 1. If a new symptom surfaces, refer to the symptom chart.

CR4080100050020X

Fig. 4 Inspection 2: Insufficient braking power (Part 2 of 2). 2001–02

DIAGNOSIS

STEP 1. Check for spongy (not firm brakes).
(1) With engine not running, depress the brake pedal rapidly several times to deplete booster vacuum reserve.
(2) With the brake pedal fully released, depress the brake pedal slowly until it stops.
(3) With a measuring stick (ruler, etc.) next to the brake pedal, depress the pedal firmly and measure the distance the pedal traveled.

Q: Is the distance greater than 20 mm (0.8 inch)?
YES : Bleed the brakes to remove air in the fluid. Then go to Step 8 .
NO : Go to Step 2.

STEP 2. Check the pad or lining for wear.
Q: Is the pad or lining thickness outside of specifications?
YES : Replace the part. Then go to Step 8.
NO : Go to Step 3.

STEP 3. Check the vacuum hose and check valve for damage.
Q: Is there damage?
YES : Replace the part. Then go to Step 8.
NO : Go to Step 4.

CR4080100051010X

Fig. 5 Inspection 3: Increased pedal stroke (Part 1 of 2). 2001–02

STEP 4. Check the master cylinder function.
Q: Is there fault?
YES : Repair it. Then go to Step 8.
NO : Go to Step 5.

STEP 5. Check for brake fluid leaks.
Q: Is there leaks?
YES : Check the connection for looseness, corrosion, etc. Clean and repair as necessary. If leaking in any tube or hose section, replace the complete tube or hose. Then go to Step 8.
NO : Go to Step 6.

STEP 6. Check the auto adjuster function.
Q: Is there fault?
YES : Repair the part. Then go to Step 8.
NO : Go to Step 7.

STEP 7. Check the clearance (too much) between the pushrod and primary piston.
Q: Is the clearance outside of specifications?
YES : Adjust the clearance. Then go to Step 8.
NO : Go to Step 8.

STEP 8. Recheck symptom.
Q: Is the symptom eliminated?
YES : Diagnosis is complete.
NO : Start over at step 1. If a new symptom surfaces, refer to the symptom chart.

CR4080100051020X

Fig. 5 Inspection 3: Increased pedal stroke (Part 2 of 2). 2001–02

DIAGNOSIS

STEP 1. Check the parking brake lever return.
Q: Is there fault?
YES : Repair it. Then go to Step 10.
NO : Go to Step 2.

CR4080100052010X

Fig. 6 Inspection 4: Brake drag (Part 1 of 3). 2001–02

STEP 2. Check the parking brake pull amount.
Q: Is there fault?
YES : Adjust it. Then go to Step 10.
NO : Go to Step 3.

STEP 3. Check the brake pedal return spring for deterioration.
Q: Is there deterioration?
YES : Replace the spring. Then go to Step 10.
NO : Go to Step 4.

STEP 4. Check the brake shoe springs for breakage.
Q: Are the brake shoe springs broken?
YES : Replace the spring. Then go to Step 10.
NO : Go to Step 5.

STEP 5. Check the amount of grease at each sliding section.
Q: Is the grease amount low?
YES : Apply grease. Then go to Step 10.
NO : Go to Step 6.

CR4080100052020X

Fig. 6 Inspection 4: Brake drag (Part 2 of 3). 2001–02

STEP 6. Check the clearance (too low) between the pushrod and primary piston.

Q: Is there fault?
YES : Adjust the clearance. Then go to Step 10.
NO : Go to Step 7.

STEP 7. Check the master cylinder piston return spring for damage and return port for clogging.
Q: Is there damage?
YES : Replace the part. Then go to Step 10.
NO : Go to Step 8.

STEP 8. Check port for clogging.
Q: Is the port clogged?
YES : Repair it. Then go to Step 10.
NO : Go to Step 9.

STEP 9. Check disc brake pistons for sticking.
Depress the brake pedal, then release. Confirm each wheel spins freely.
Q: Are all wheels stuck?
YES : Inspect that brake assembly. Then go to Step 10.
NO : Go to Step 10.

STEP 10. Recheck symptom.
Q: Is the symptom eliminated?
YES : Diagnosis is complete.
NO : Start over at step 1. If a new symptom surfaces, refer to the symptom chart.

CR4080100052030X

Fig. 6 Inspection 4: Brake drag (Part 3 of 3). 2001–02

DIAGNOSIS

STEP 1. Check the brake drums and lining or brake disc and pads for wear or cutting.
Q: Is there wear or cutting?
YES : Repair or replace the part. Then go to Step 7.
NO : Go to Step 2.

STEP 2. Check the calipers for rust.
Q: Is there rust?
YES : Remove the rust. Then go to Step 7.
NO : Go to Step 3.

STEP 3. Check the lining parts for damage.
If equipped with rear disc brakes, go to Step 6.
Q: Is there damage?
YES : Repair or replace the part. Then go to Step 7.
NO : Go to Step 4.

STEP 4. Check whether the lining is dirty or greasy.
Q: Is the lining dirty or greasy?
YES : Clean or replace the part. Then go to Step 7.
NO : Go to Step 5.

STEP 5. Check whether the shoe hold-down springs are weak or the shoe-hold-down pins and springs are loose or damaged.
Q: Is there fault?
YES : Repair or replace the part. Then go to Step 7.
NO : Go to Step 6.

STEP 6. Adjust the brake pedal or brake booster pushrod.
Q: Is the adjustment value come?
YES : Adjust. Then go to Step 7.
NO : Go to Step 7.

STEP 7. Recheck symptom.
Q: Is the symptom eliminated?
YES : Diagnosis is complete.
NO : Start over at step 1. If a new symptom surfaces, refer to the symptom chart.

CR4080100054000X

Fig. 8 Inspection 6: Squealing, groaning or chattering noise when brakes are applied. 2001–02

DIAGNOSIS

STEP 1. Check the front brakes, then rear brakes, for metal-to-metal condition.
Q: Is the metal-to-metal contact evicent?
YES : Repair or replace components. Then go to Step 6.
NO : Go to Step 2.

STEP 2. Check for interference between the caliper and wheel.
Q: Is there interference?
YES : Repair or replace the part. Then go to Step 6.
NO : Go to Step 3.

CR4080100053010X

Fig. 7 Inspection 5: Scraping or grinding noise when brakes are applied (Part 1 of 2). 2001–02

STEP 3. Check for interference between the dust cover and brake disc.
Q: Is there interference?
YES : Repair or replace the part. Then go to Step 6.
NO : Go to Step 4.

STEP 4. Check the brake drums or discs for cracks.
Q: Are there cracks?
YES : Repair or replace the part. Then go to Step 6.
NO : Go to Step 5.

STEP 5. Check for bent backing plate(s).
Q: Is(Are) the backing plate(s) bent?
YES : Repair or replace the part. Then go to Step 6.
NO : Go to Step 6.

STEP 6. Recheck symptom.
Q: Is the symptom eliminated?
YES : Diagnosis is complete.
NO : Start over at step 1. If a new symptom surfaces, refer to the symptom chart.

CR4080100053020X

Fig. 7 Inspection 5: Scraping or grinding noise when brakes are applied (Part 2 of 2). 2001–02

DIAGNOSIS

STEP 1. Check whether the backing plate is bent or loose and interfering with the drum

If equipped with rear disc brakes, go to Step 4.
Q: Is there fault?
YES : Replace the part. Then go to Step 10.
NO : Go to Step 2.

STEP 2. Check whether the drum is damaged due to interference with the backing plate or shoe.
Q: Is there damage?
YES : Replace the part. Then go to Step 10.
NO : Go to Step 3.

STEP 3. Check the brake drum for wear and the shoe-to-shoe spring for damage.
Q: Is there wear or damage?
YES : Replace the part. Then go to Step 10.
NO : Go to Step 4.

STEP 4. Check the brake discs for rust.
Q: Are the brake discs rusted?
YES : Remove the rust by using sand paper. If still rusted, turn the rotors with an on-the-car brake lathe. Then go to Step 10.
NO : Go to Step 5.

STEP 5. Check the brake pads for correct installation.
Q: Are the pads installed incorrectly?
YES : Repair it. Then go to Step 10.
NO : Go to Step 6.

STEP 6. Check the calipers for correct installation.
Q: Are the calipers installed incorrectly?
YES : Repair it. Then go to Step 10.
NO : Go to Step 7.

CR4080100055010X

Fig. 9 Inspection 7: Squealing noise when brakes are not applied (Part 1 of 2). 2001–02

STEP 7. Check the wheel bearings for deterioration or damage, and the quality and quantity.
Q: Are the wheel bearings damaged or out of grease?
YES : Apply grease or replace the part. Then go to Step 10.
NO : Go to Step 8.

STEP 8. Check whether the brake booster, master cylinder or wheel cylinder return is insufficient.
Q: Is the brake booster, master cylinder or wheel cylinder return insufficient?
YES : Replace the part. Then go to Step 10.
NO : Go to Step 9.

STEP 9. Adjust the brake pedal or brake booster pushrod.

Q: Is the adjustment value come?
YES : Adjust.Then go to Step 10.
NO : Go to Step 10.

STEP 10. Recheck symptom.
Q: Is the symptom eliminated?
YES : Diagnosis is complete.
NO : Start over at step 1. If a new symptom surfaces, refer to the symptom chart.

CR4080100055020X

Fig. 9 Inspection 7: Squealing noise when brakes are not applied (Part 2 of 2). 2001–02

DIAGNOSIS

STEP 1. Check whether foreign material has entered the wheel covers.
Q: Is there foreign material?
YES : Remove it. Then go to Step 5.
NO : Go to Step 2.

STEP 2. Check for looseness of the wheel nuts.
Q: Are the wheel nuts loose?
YES : Tighten to 98 ± 10 N·m (73 ± 7 ft-lb). Then go to Step 5.
NO : Go to Step 3.

STEP 3. Check for looseness of the caliper installation bolt.
Q: Is the caliper installation bolt loose?
YES : Tighten to 100 ± 10 N·m (74 ± 7 ft-lb) for the front caliper, or 60 ± 5 N·m (45 ± 3 ft-lb) for the rear caliper. Then go to Step 5.
NO : Go to Step 4.

CR4080100056010X

Fig. 10 Inspection 8: Groaning, clicking or rattling noise when brakes are not applied (Part 1 of 2). 2001–02

STEP 4. Check the wheel bearings for wear, damage or dryness.
Q: Is there fault?
YES : Apply grease or replace the part. Then go to Step 5.
NO : Go to Step 5.

STEP 5. Recheck symptom.
Q: Is the symptom eliminated?
YES : Diagnosis is complete.
NO : Start over at step 1. If a new symptom surfaces, refer to the symptom chart.

CR4080100056020X

Fig. 10 Inspection 8: Groaning, clicking or rattling noise when brakes are not applied (Part 2 of 2). 2001–02

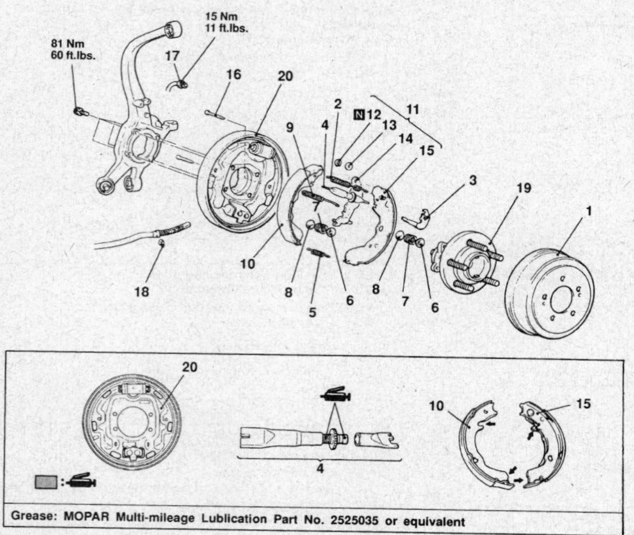

1. Brake drum
2. Shoe-to-lever spring
3. Adjuster lever
4. Auto adjuster assembly
5. Retainer spring
6. Shoe hold-down cup
7. Shoe hold-down spring
8. Shoe hold-down cup
9. Shoe-to-shoe spring
10. Shoe and lining assembly
11. Shoe and lever assembly
12. Retainer
13. Wave washer
14. Parking lever
15. Shoe and lining assembly
16. Shoe hold-down pin
17. Brake pipe connection
18. Snap ring
19. Rear hub assembly
20. Backing plate

CR4089500024000X

Fig. 11 Leading trailing drum brake assembly

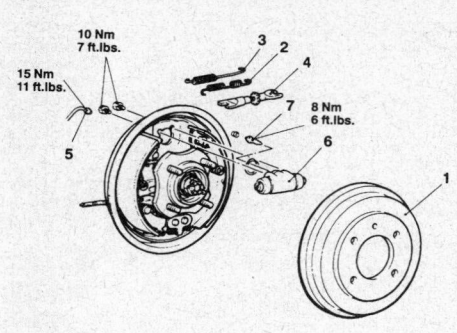

10 Nm
7 ft.lbs.
15 Nm
11 ft.lbs.
8 Nm
6 ft.lbs.

1. Brake drum
2. Retainer
3. Shoe-to-shoe spring
4. Auto adjuster assembly
5. Connection for the brake tube
6. Wheel cylinder
7. Bleeder screw

CR4089500023000X

Fig. 12 Rear drum brake wheel cylinder

DRUM BRAKE SPECIFICATIONS

Model	Brake Drum I.D. Inch		Rear Wheel Cylinder Bore I.D. Inch
	Standard	Maximum	
Avenger, Sebring Coupe & Stratus Coupe	9.0	9.08	.750

TIGHTENING SPECIFICATIONS

Component	Torque/Ft. Lbs.
AVENGER, SEBRING COUPE & STRATUS COUPE	
Backing Plate To Rear Axle	60
Brake Line Fittings	11
Wheel Cylinder Bleed Screw	96①
Wheel Cylinder To Backing Plate	84①
Wheel Lugnuts	65–80

① — Inch lbs.

HYDRAULIC BRAKE SYSTEMS

NOTE: On Air Bag Equipped Models, Refer To "Air Bag System Precautions" Located In The Front Of This Manual For System Disarming & Arming Procedures.

NOTE: Refer To "Computer Relearn Procedures" Located In The Front Of This Manual When Battery Power To The Computer Has Been Interrupted.

NOTE: Refer To "Anti-Lock Brakes" Chapter When Servicing ABS System.

INDEX

DESCRIPTION

MASTER CYLINDER

The master cylinder is a center valve master cylinder used for all applications. The brake fluid reservoir mounted on top and brake fluid level switch is mounted on the side of the reservoir.

The reservoir is indexed to prevent installation in the wrong direction. The cap diaphragm is slit to allow atmospheric pressure to equalize on both sides of diaphragm.

The primary and secondary outlet tubes of the master cylinder are connected to a junction block on non-ABS equipped vehicles. The master cylinder primary outlet port connects to the inboard port of the junction block, and the secondary outlet port connects to the outboard port of the junction block. The inboard port of the junction block supplies the right front and left rear brakes. The outboard port of the junction block supplies the left front and right rear brakes.

On vehicles equipped with ABS (with or without Traction Control) the master cylinder primary outlet port outlet tubes connect to the inboard port of the ICU, and the secondary outlet port outlet tubes connect to the outboard port of the ICU.

TROUBLESHOOTING

Refer to "Troubleshooting" in "Disc Brakes" for troubleshooting of the hydraulic brake system.

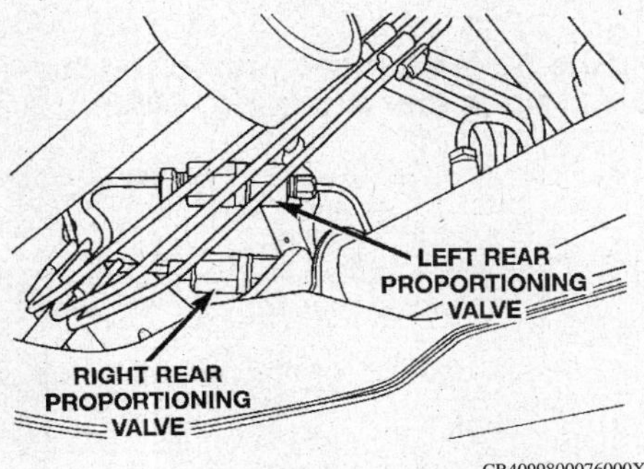

Fig. 1 Proportioning valve. 1998–2000 Breeze, Cirrus, Sebring Convertible & Stratus

DIAGNOSIS & TESTING

PROPORTIONING VALVE

AVENGER & TALON

1. Install suitable pressure gauges, one each on input side and output side of proportioning valve.
2. Bleed brake line and pressure gauge, then gradually depress brake pedal and observe gauge readings. Refer to "Hydraulic Brake Controls Specifications" chart.
3. Observe left and right output pressures.
4. Pressure difference between left and right should not be greater than 57 psi.
5. If gauge readings are not within specifications, replace proportioning valve.

BREEZE & CIRRUS

Less Anti-Lock Brake System

1. Road test vehicle to determine which rear wheel exhibits premature wheel skid.
2. Remove hydraulic brake line from proportioning valve that controls rear wheel which has premature skid as outlined in **Fig. 1.**
3. Remove proportioning valve from rear brake chassis tube.
4. Install pressure test fitting tool No. 8187 or equivalent, in inlet port of proportioning valve and **torque** tube nuts to 12 ft. lbs.
5. Install pressure fitting tool No. 8187-2 or equivalent, in outlet port of proportioning valve and **torque** tube nuts to 12 ft. lbs., as shown in **Fig. 2.**
6. Install proportioning valve with pressure test fittings installed, in chassis brake tube and **torque** tube nuts to 12 ft. lbs.
7. Install pressure gauge tool No. C-4007-A or equivalent, into each pressure test fitting.
8. Bleed air out of hose from pressure test fitting to pressure gauge to remove trapped air hose.
9. Apply pressure to brake pedal until reading on proportioning valve inlet gauge is within specifications.
10. Check pressure reading on proportioning valve outlet gauge. If outlet pressure is not within specifications when inlet pressure is obtained, replace proportioning valve.

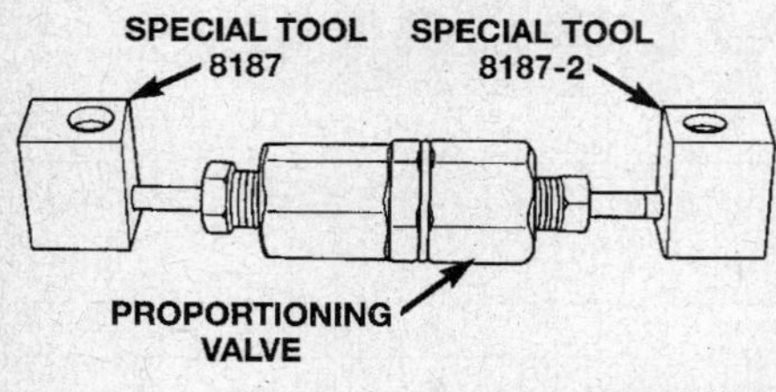

Fig. 2 Pressure test fittings

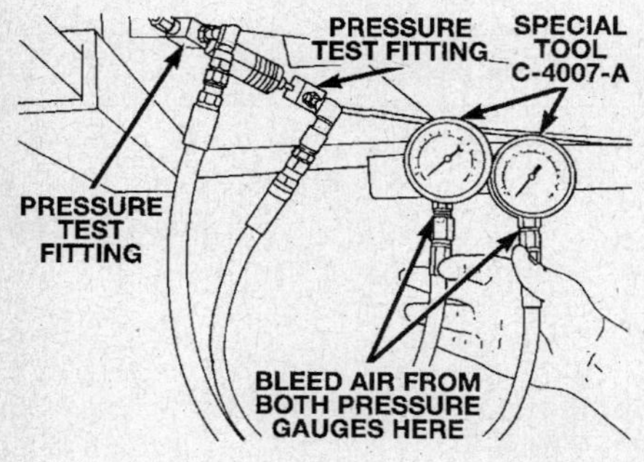

Fig. 5 Pressure gauge. 1998–2000 Breeze, Cirrus, Sebring Convertible & Stratus

11. Check rear wheel brake shoe linings for contamination, replace as required.
12. Install proportioning valve in rear brake line and hand tighten both tube nuts until fully seated.
13. **Torque** tube nuts at proportioning valve to 12 ft. lbs.
14. Bleed affected brake line as outlined under "Brake System Bleed."

Anti-Lock Brake System

1. Remove cover securing chassis brake tubes and fuel lines to vehicle floor pan.
2. Remove chassis brake tubes from proportioning valve controlling rear wheel which has premature wheel skid, **Fig. 3.**
3. Remove proportioning valve from rear brake chassis tube.
4. Remove routing clips for chassis brake tubes and fuel lines from floor pan.
5. Remove chassis brake tube that requires testing of its proportioning valve from routing clips.
6. Install pressure test fitting tool No. 6833-1, or equivalent, in inlet port of proportioning valve.
7. Install pressure test fitting tool No. 8187-2, or equivalent, in outlet port of valve and **torque** tube nuts to 12 ft. lbs, **Fig. 4.**
8. Install proportioning valve with pressure test fittings installed, in chassis brake tube. **Torque** tube nuts to 12 ft. lbs.
9. Install pressure gauge tool No. C-4007-A, or equivalent, into each pressure fitting, **Fig. 5.**
10. Apply pressure to brake pedal until reading on proportioning valve inlet gauge is within specifications.
11. Check pressure reading on proportioning valve outlet gauge.

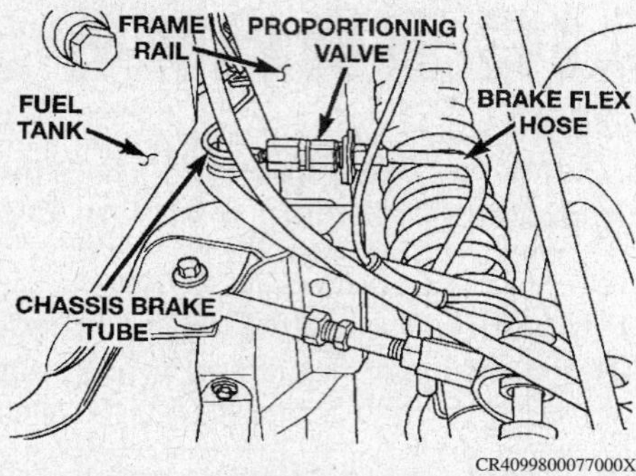

Fig. 3 Proportioning valve. 1998–2000 Breeze, Cirrus, Sebring Convertible & Stratus

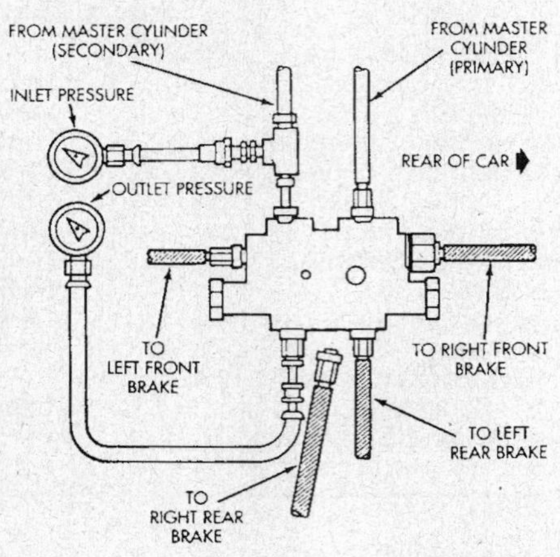

Fig. 6 Pressure connection for right rear skidding. 1998

12. If outlet pressure is not within specifications when inlet pressure is obtained, replace valve.
13. Check rear wheel brake shoe linings for contamination, replace as necessary.
14. Install chassis brake tube in routing clips.
15. Install routing clips for chassis brake tubes and fuel lines on floor pan.
16. Install cover securing chassis brake tubes and fuel lines to vehicle floor pan.
17. Install proportioning valve in chassis brake tube and **torque** valve to 12 ft. lbs.
18. Install brake tube on proportioning valve and **torque** to 12 ft. lbs.
19. Bleed affected brake line as described under "Brake System Bleed."

CONCORDE, INTREPID, LHS & 300M

1998–2001 Less ABS Brakes Less (TLEV) Teeves Low Emission Vehicle

To test the proportioning valve when the right rear or left rear wheel slides first, leave the front brakes connected to the valve and proceed as follows.

1. **On models where right rear slides first,** install two Pressure Gauge Set tool Nos. C-4007A or equivalent between brake line from master cylinder secondary port and brake valve assembly as shown in **Fig. 6.**
2. **On models where left rear slides first,** install two Pressure Gauge Set tool Nos. C-4007A or equivalent between brake line from master cylinder secondary port and brake valve assembly as shown in **Fig. 7.**
3. **On all rear wheel slides,** bleed hose and gauge set.
4. Observe pressure gauge readings as brake pedal is depressed, refer to "Hydraulic Brake Controls Specifications" chart.
5. If pressure readings are not within specifications for right or left wheel, replace combination valve. After installing a new combination valve, bleed hydraulic brake system as outlined under "Brake System Bleed."

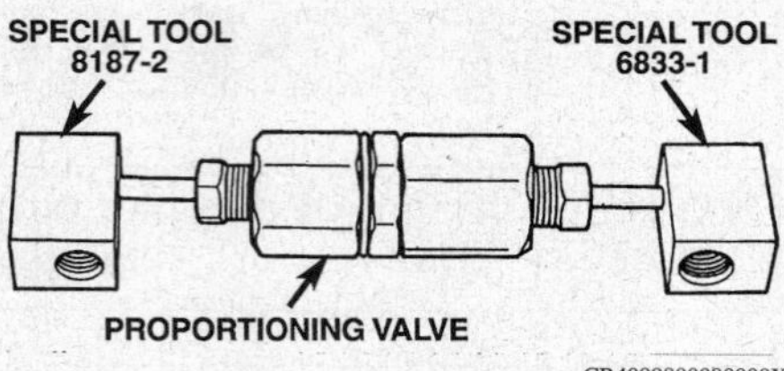

Fig. 4 Pressure test fittings. 1998–2000 Breeze, Cirrus, Sebring Convertible & Stratus

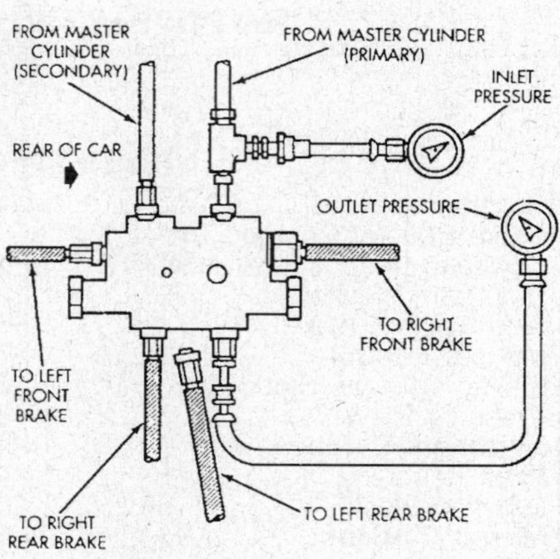

Fig. 7 Pressure connection for left rear skidding. 1998

1998–2001 ABS & Non-ABS (TLEV) Teeves Low Emission Vehicle

On vehicles with ABS system, refer to "Anti-Lock Brakes" section for testing procedures. All ABS components use an ISO type tubing flare. Ensure proper adapters with ISO type flare are used when installing test gauges.

1. Remove proportioning valve as shown in **Figs. 8 and 9,** from chassis brake tube.
2. **On 1998 models,** remove bracket attaching brake flex hose to side of frame rail as shown in **Fig. 8.**

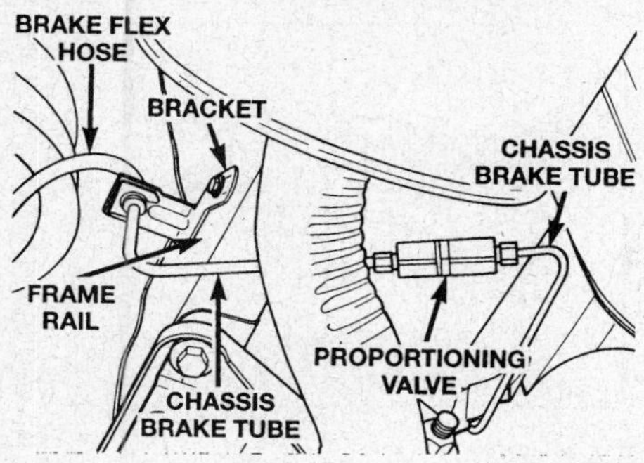

Fig. 8 Proportioning valve removal. 1998

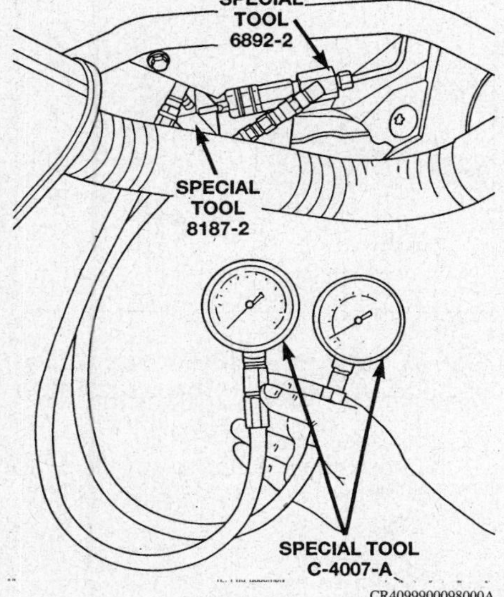

Fig. 11 Pressure test fittings. 1999–2001

3. **On 1998 models,** install Pressure Test Fitting tool No. 6892 or equivalent into inlet and outlet ports of proportioning valve.
4. **On 1999–2001 models,** remove retaining clip as shown in **Fig. 9.**
5. **On 1999–2001 models,** install Pressure Test Fitting tool No. 6892 or equivalent into inlet and outlet ports of proportioning valve.
6. **On all models,** remove routing bracket attaching brake tube to bottom of frame rail.
7. **On 1998 models,** install proportioning valve and Pressure Test Fitting tool No. 6892 or equivalent as an assembly into chassis brake tube as shown in **Fig. 10.**
8. **On 1999–2001 models,** install proportioning valve and Pressure Test Fittings tool No. 6892-2 and No. 8187-2 or equivalent as shown in **Fig. 11.**
9. **On all models,** install Pressure Gauge tool No. C-4007-A or equivalent into each pressure test fitting as shown in **Fig. 12.**
10. While recording inlet and outlet pressure gauges, have an assistant depress brake pedal. Note gauge readings, refer to "Hydraulic Brake

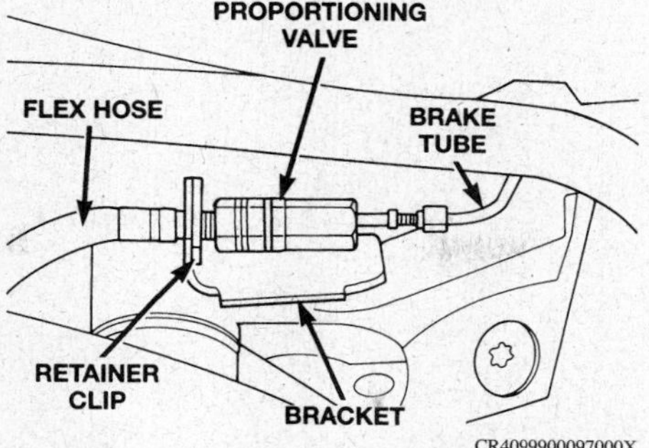

Fig. 9 Proportioning valve removal. 1999–2001 Concorde, Intrepid, LHS & 300M

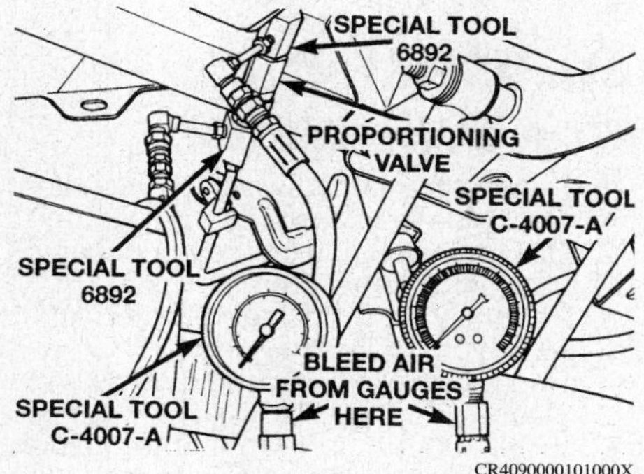

Fig. 12 Pressure gauge installation

Controls Specifications" chart.

11. If pressures are not within specifications replace proportioning valve.

NEON

Less ABS

1. Road test vehicle to determine which rear wheel exhibits premature wheel skid. Refer to **Fig. 13 ,** to determine which proportioning valve needs to be tested.
2. Remove hydraulic brake line from proportioning valve to be tested, then remove valve from master cylinder outlet port.
3. Install pressure test fitting tool No. 6805-1, 6805-2 or equivalent, into outlet port of master cylinder.
4. Install pressure test fitting tool No. 6805-1, 6805-2 or equivalent, into rear brake tube.
5. Install proportioning valve into pressure test fitting.
6. Install pressure test fitting tool No. 6805-3, 6805-4 or equivalent, into outlet port or proportioning valve.
7. Connect brake hydraulic line onto pressure test fitting on proportioning valve.
8. Install pressure gauge set tool No. C-4007-A or equivalent, into test fitting and bleed air from pressure gauge hose.
9. Apply pressure to brake pedal until reading on proportioning valve inlet test fitting is appropriate, then check pressure reading on outlet test fitting.
10. If proportioning valve is not within

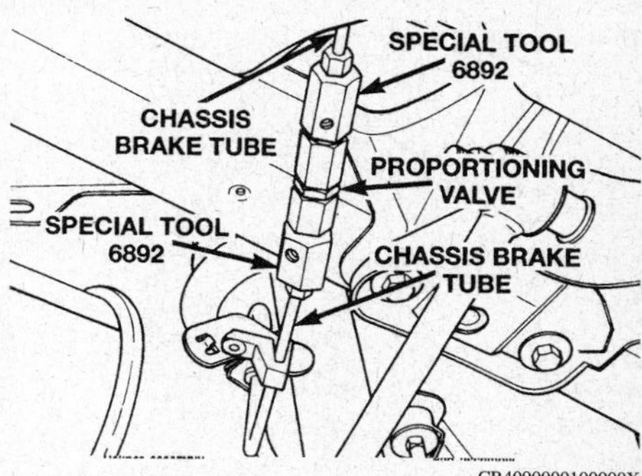

Fig. 10 Pressure test fittings. 1998

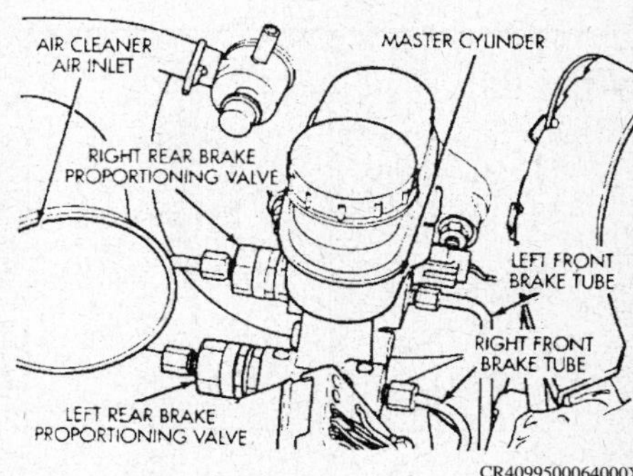

Fig. 13 Proportioning valve. Neon Less ABS

specifications when inlet pressure is obtained, replace valve.

11. Install proportioning valve into master cylinder body until O-ring is seated. **Torque** proportioning valve to 30 ft. lbs.
12. Install brake tube onto proportioning valve and **torque** nut to 12 ft. lbs.
13. Bleed brake line as outlined under "Brake System Bleed."

ABS

1. Road test vehicle to determine which rear wheel exhibits premature wheel skid. Refer to **Fig. 14,** to determine which proportioning valve needs to be tested.
2. Remove hydraulic brake line from proportioning valve to be tested, then remove valve from master cylinder outlet port.
3. Install pressure test fitting tool No. 6805–1 or 6805–2, or equivalent, into outlet port of master cylinder.
4. Install proportioning valve into pressure test fitting in master cylinder outlet port.
5. Install pressure test fitting tool No. 6805–3 or 6805–4, or equivalent, into outlet port of proportioning valve.
6. Connect brake hydraulic line onto pressure test fitting on proportioning valve.
7. Install pressure gauge set tool No. C-4007–A, or equivalent, into test fitting and bleed air from pressure gauge hose.
8. Apply pressure to brake pedal until reading on proportioning valve inlet test fitting is appropriate, then check

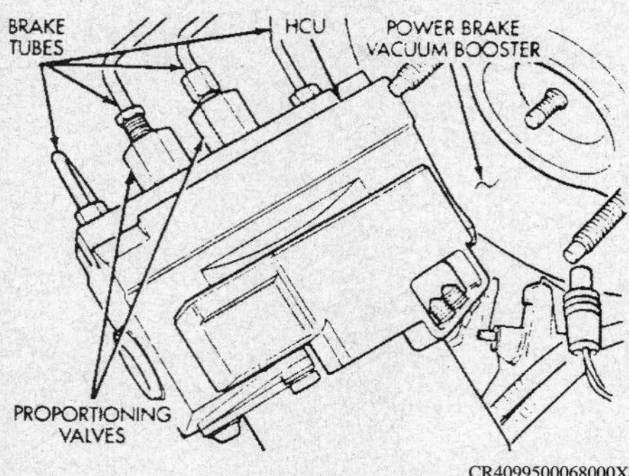

Fig. 14 Proportioning valve. Neon w/ABS

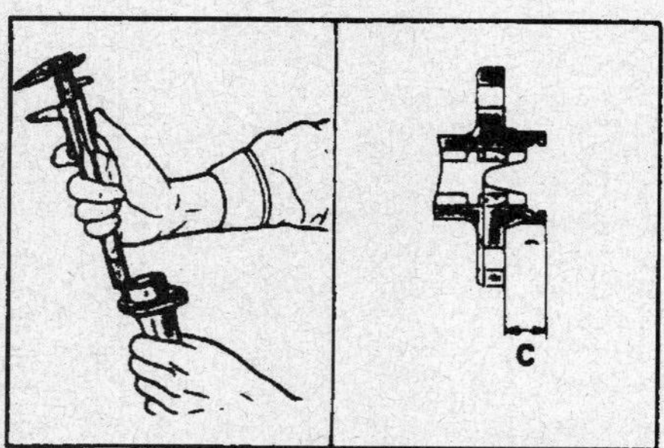

Fig. 17 Brake booster mounting surface. Avenger, Sebring & Talon

the pressure reading on the outlet test fitting.

9. If the pressure on the outlet test fitting is not within specifications, replace proportioning valve.
10. Install proportioning valve into master cylinder body until O-ring is seated, then **torque** proportioning valve to 30 ft. lbs.
11. Install brake tube onto proportioning valve and **torque** tube nut to 12 ft. lbs.
12. Bleed brake line as outlined under "Brake System Bleed."

SEBRING

Refer to "Avenger & Talon" for proportioning valve duagnostic procedures.

SEBRING CONVERTIBLE

1998–2000

Refer to "Breeze & Cirrus" for proportioning valve duagnostic procedures.

SEBRING COUPE

2001

Refer to "Avenger & Talon" for proportioning valve duagnostic procedures.

STRATUS

1998–2000

Refer to "Breeze & Cirrus" for proportioning valve duagnostic procedures.

STRATUS COUPE

2001

Refer to "Avenger & Talon" for proportioning valve duagnostic procedures.

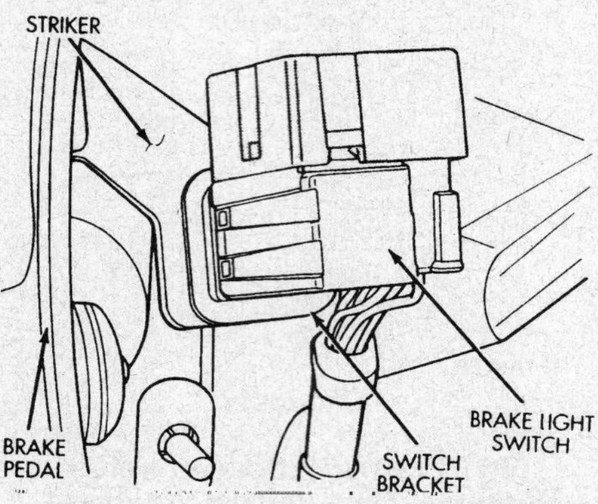

Fig. 15 Stop lamp switch installation

ADJUSTMENTS

STOP LAMP SWITCH

1. Rotate stop lamp switch 30° counterclockwise to release from bracket.
2. Disconnect wiring harness connector from stop lamp switch.
3. Pull outward on plunger of stop lamp switch until fully extended.
4. Depress brake pedal, holding down in place.
5. Install stop lamp switch onto bracket by aligning index key on switch with slot at top of square hole.
6. Rotate switch 30° clockwise to lock switch into bracket as shown in **Fig. 15.**
7. Connect wiring harness connector to stop lamp switch.
8. Pull back on brake pedal until pedal stops moving.
9. This will enable switch plunger to ratchet to correct position.

BRAKE BOOSTER PUSHROD TO PRIMARY PISTON CLEARANCE

AVENGER, SEBRING & TALON

1. With master cylinder removed from vehicle as outlined under "Component Replacement" proceed with following procedure.
2. Measure distance between master cylinder end face and piston as outlined in **Fig. 16.**
3. Position a square against edge of master cylinder, then measure and subtract thickness of square to determine dimension B.
4. Find dimension C by measuring distance between brake booster mounting surface and end face as outlined in **Fig. 17**
5. Measure distance between master cylinder mounting surface and pushrod end as outlined in **Fig. 18.**
6. Find dimension D by subtracting the squares thickness from the measurement taken.
7. Find brake booster to primary piston clearance dimension A as outlined in **Fig. 19,** using formula A=B–C–D. Refer to "Hydraulic Brake System Specifications" chart for proper clearance specifications.

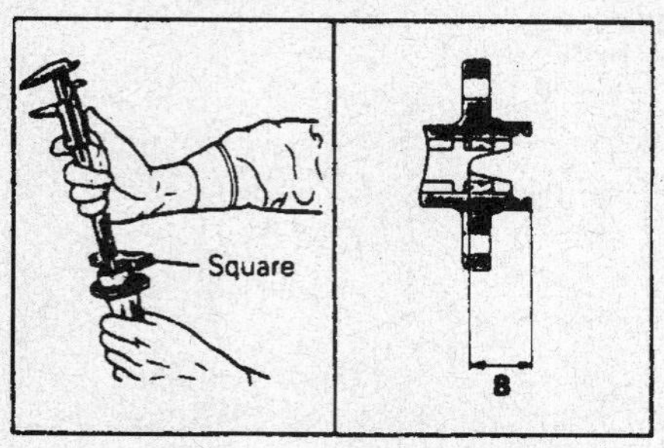

Fig. 16 Master cylinder end face piston measurement. Avenger, Sebring & Talon

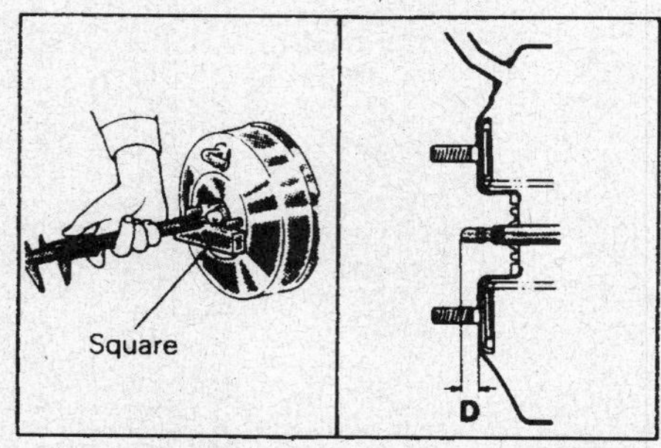

Fig. 18 Master cylinder mounting surface. Avenger, Sebring & Talon

8. If dimension A is not as specified, adjust brake booster pushrod as shown in **Fig. 20.**

COMPONENT REPLACEMENT

Fluid Reservoir

1. Remove reservoir caps.
2. Remove brake fluid from reservoir.
3. Remove master cylinder as outlined in "Master Cylinder, Replace" in this section.
4. Secure master cylinder in a suitable vise.
5. Remove two reservoir to master cylinder retaining pins as shown in **Fig. 21.**
6. Rock reservoir from side to side and remove from master cylinder. **Do not use any tools when removing reservoir from master cylinder, damage to reservoir may result.**
7. Remove sealing grommets
8. Reverse procedure to install, noting following:
   a. Lubricate new sealing grommets with brake fluid.
   b. Ensure reservoir is seated properly against sealing grommets.
   c. Refer to "Brake System Bleed" to bench bleed master cylinder. **These models use ISO style flares that are of metric dimension. Use ISO style tubing flares and metric tubing when performing any repairs.**

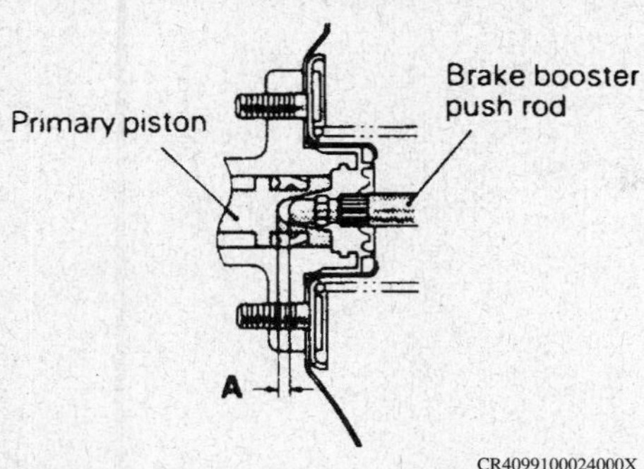

Fig. 19 Brake booster to primary piston clearance. Avenger, Sebring & Talon

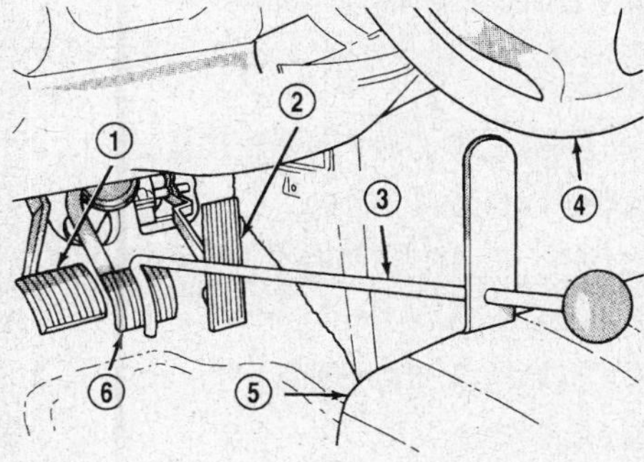

Fig. 22 Brake pedal holding tool

Junction Block

1. Depress and hold brake pedal one inch down using suitable tool as shown in **Fig. 22.**
2. **On 2001–02 Sebring Sedan & Stratus Sedan,** remove air cleaner housing assembly.
3. **On all models,** raise and support vehicle.
4. Remove left inner fender shield.
5. **On 2001–02 Concorde, Intrepid, LHS & 300M models,** proceed as follows:
   a. Remove screw from speed control servo to upper radiator closure panel as shown in **Fig. 23.**.
   b. Remove screw from washer filler tube to upper radiator closure panel.
   c. Remove nut and screw from transmission control module (TCM).
   d. Remove TCM with servo attached from mount with wiring harness attached, set aside.
   e. Remove two brake tubes coming from primary and secondary master cylinder ports at junction block.
6. **On all models,** remove 4 chassis brake tubes mounted across front top of junction block.
7. Remove two brake tubes from primary and secondary ports and top of junction block.

Fig. 20 Brake booster pushrod adjustment. Avenger, Sebring & Talon

8. Remove three bolts attaching junction block to mounting bracket.
9. Remove junction block.
10. Reverse procedure to install, noting following:
    a. **On 2001–02 Concorde, Intrepid, LHS & 300M models, torque** first mounting bolt to 19 ft. lbs.
    b. **On all models, torque** attaching bolts to junction block to 19 ft. lbs.
    c. **Torque** two tube fittings from primary and secondary ports to top rear corners of junction block to 12 ft. lbs.
    d. **Torque** four chassis brake tubes to junction block to 12 ft. lbs.
    e. **On 2001–02 Concorde, Intrepid, LHS & 300M models, torque** TCM mounting screw to 45 inch lbs.
    f. **On 2001–02 Concorde, Intrepid, LHS & 300M models, torque** TCM mounting nut to 107 inch lbs.
    g. **On all models,** bleed brake system as outlined under "Brake System Bleed."

Master Cylinder

AVENGER, SEBRING & TALON

1. Disconnect brake fluid level sensor.
2. Remove brake fluid reservoir.
3. Remove master cylinder.
4. Reverse Procedure to install, noting the following:
   a. Adjust clearance between brake booster pushrod and primary piston as outlined previously in this chapter.
   b. Bleed brakes as outlined in this chapter.

CONCORDE, INTREPID, LHS & 300M

1. Disconnect brake fluid level sensor

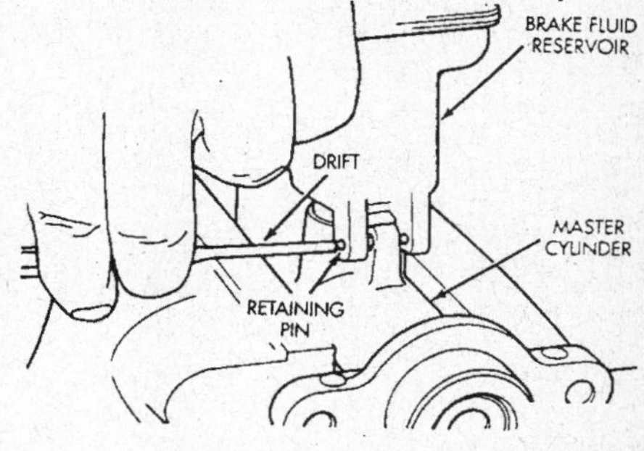

Fig. 21 Retaining pin removal

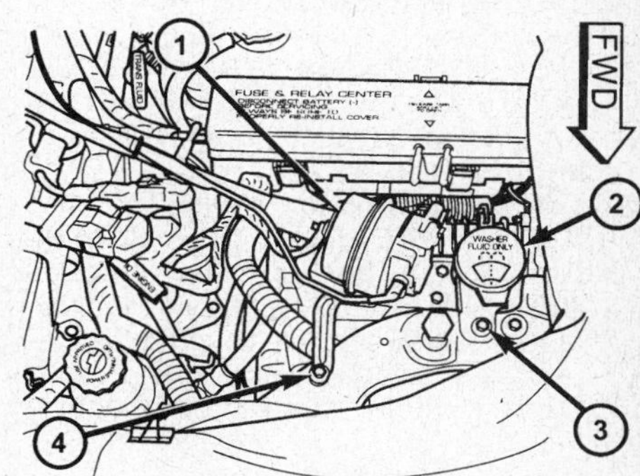

Fig. 23 Speed control servo & filler tube fastener removal. 2001–02 Concorde, Intrepid, LHS & 300M

wire connector from side of reservoir.

2. Disconnect primary and secondary brake lines from master cylinder, then install plugs at brake line outlets.
3. Remove master cylinder attaching nuts as shown in **Fig. 24,** then slide cylinder away from brake booster.
4. Reverse procedure to install noting following:
   a. **Torque** master cylinder to brake booster attaching nuts to 21 ft. lbs.
   b. **Torque** brake lines to master cylinder to 12 ft. lbs.

BREEZE & CIRRUS

When replacing master cylinder on Neon models equipped with ABS, vacuum in power booster must be pumped down before removing master cylinder to prevent booster from drawing in contaminants. This can be done by pumping the brake pedal until it is firm, with the ignition off.

1. **On Neon models equipped with ABS,** ensure engine is not running and brake pedal has been pumped until firm.
2. **On all models,** remove wiring harness connector from brake fluid level sensor mounted on fluid reservoir.
3. Disconnect the primary and secondary brake tubes from master cylinder housing.
4. Install suitable plugs at all open brake

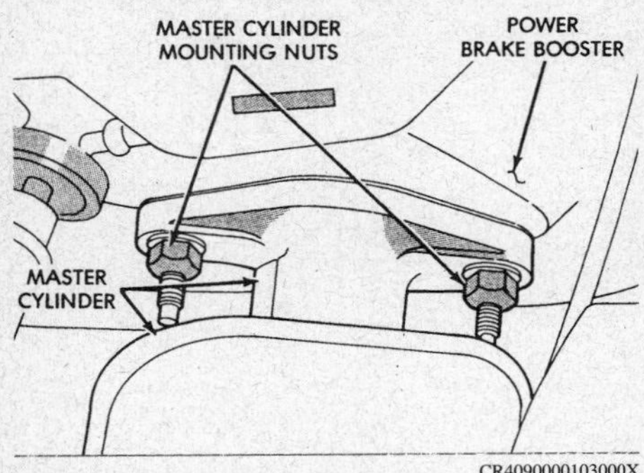

Fig. 24 Master cylinder removal. Concorde, Intrepid, LHS, 300M & 2001–02 Sebring Sedan & Stratus Sedan

tube outlets on master cylinder assembly.

5. **On Neon models equipped with ABS and all Breeze, Cirrus, Sebring Convertible and Stratus models,** clean area where master cylinder attaches to power brake vacuum booster using a suitable brake cleaner.
6. **On all models,** remove nuts attaching master cylinder to power brake vacuum booster.
7. Slide master cylinder forward out of power brake vacuum booster.
8. **On Neon models equipped with ABS, the vacuum seal in the front of the power brake vacuum booster must be replaced.** Remove vacuum seal in front of power brake vacuum booster by carefully inserting a suitable, small, screwdriver between master cylinder push rod and vacuum seal and prying seal out of booster, **Fig. 25. Do not attempt to pry seal out by inserting screwdriver between seal and booster.**
9. Reverse procedure to install noting the following:
   a. **On Neon models equipped with ABS,** Lubricate master cylinder push rod using suitable silicone lubricant, Slide vacuum seal onto master cylinder push rod with notches on seal pointing toward and seated against master cylinder housing.
   b. **On all models,** slide master cylinder assembly into power brake vacuum booster and position on mounting studs.
   c. Install mounting nuts and **torque** to 21 ft. lbs.

NEON

1998-2002

Refer to "Breeze & Cirrus" for master cylinder removal and installation procedures.

SEBRING COUPE

2001-02

Refer to **Fig. 26,** for removal and installation procedures.

SEBRING CONVERTIBLE

1998-2000

Refer to "Breeze & Cirrus" for master cylinder removal and installation procedures.

SEBRING SEDAN

2001-02

Refer to "Concorde, Intrepis, LHS & 300M" for master cylinder removal and installation procedures.

STRATUS

Refer to "Breeze & Cirrus" for master cylinder removal and installation procedures.

STRATUS SEDAN

2001-02

Refer to "Concorde, Intrepis, LHS & 300M" for master cylinder removal and installation procedures.

STRATUS COUPE

2001-02

Refer to **Fig. 26,** for removal and installation procedures.

Proportioning Valve

CONCORDE, INTREPID, LHS & 300M

1998-2000

Refer to "Diagnosis & Testing" for replacement procedure.

2001

This procedure applies to ABS and early production Non-ABS applications. Later production Non-ABS proportioning valves are located in the junction block and cannot be serviced separately.

1. Raise and support vehicle.
2. Clean debris away from proportioning valve and connections.
3. Remove chassis brake tube from proportioning valve.
4. Remove proportioning valve from from rear flex hose.
5. Reverse procedure to install, noting the folowing:
   a. Attach proportioning valve to rear flex hose, **torque** to 145 inch lbs.
   b. Attach chassis brake tube to proportioning valve, **torque** to 145 inch lbs.
   c. Bleed affected brake line.

2002

With ABS

These models use Electronic Variable Brake Proportioning, this is built into the Integral Control Unit (ICU).

Without ABS

These models use a proportioning valve that is integrated with the junction block. The proportioning valve cannot be serviced separately.

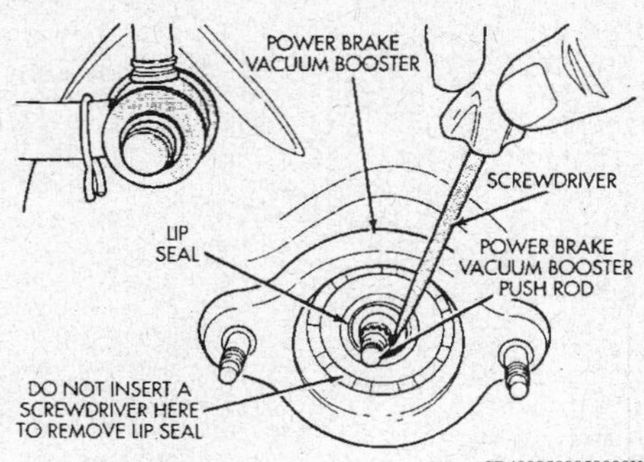

Fig. 25 Type 2 vacuum seal removal. Neon w/ABS

AVENGER & TALON

Refer to **Fig. 27** for proportioning valve replacement.

SEBRING CONVERTIBLE

2001-02

Refer to "2002" under "Concorde, Intrepid, LHS & 300M" for proportioning valve replacement procedure.

SEBRING COUPE

2001-02

Refer to "Avenger & Talon" for proportioning valve replacement procedure.

SEBRING SEDAN

2001-02

Refer to "2002" under "Concorde, Intrepid, LHS & 300M" for proportioning valbe replacement procedure.

STRATUS COUPE

2001-02

Refer to "Avenger & Talon" for proportioning valve replacement procedure.

STRATUS SEDAN

2001-02

Refer to "2002" under "Concorde, Intrepid, LHS & 300M" for proportioning valbe replacement procedure.

COMPONENT SERVICE

The only serviceable component on master cylinder(s) are the reservoir and sealing grommets. The master cylinder(s) are not to be serviced, they must be replaced as an assembly.

BRAKE SYSTEM BLEED

PRESSURE BLEED

Use bleeder tank tool No. C-3496-B or equivalent and adapter tool No. BB400-9A or equivalent to pressurize hydraulic system.

1. Attach a clear plastic hose to bleeder screw and submerge other end into clear container with clean brake fluid.

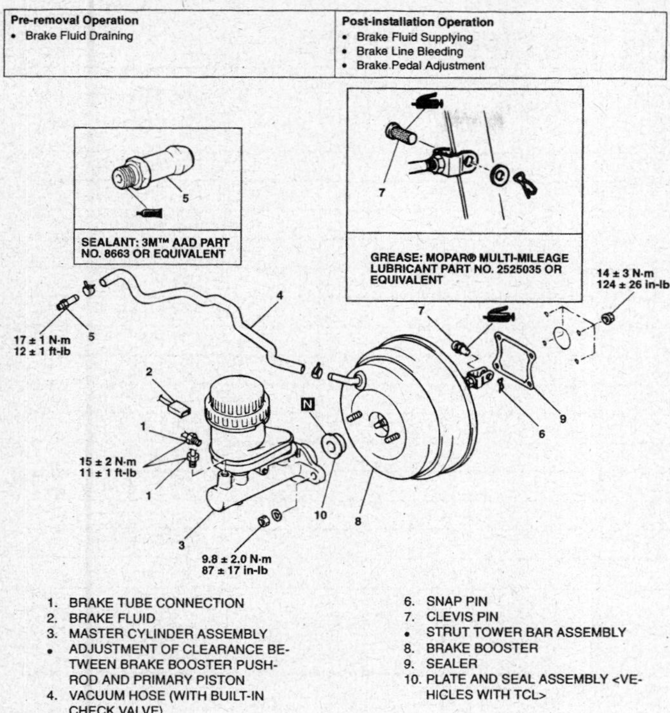

Fig. 26 Master cylinder. 2001–02 Sebring Coupe & Stratus Coupe

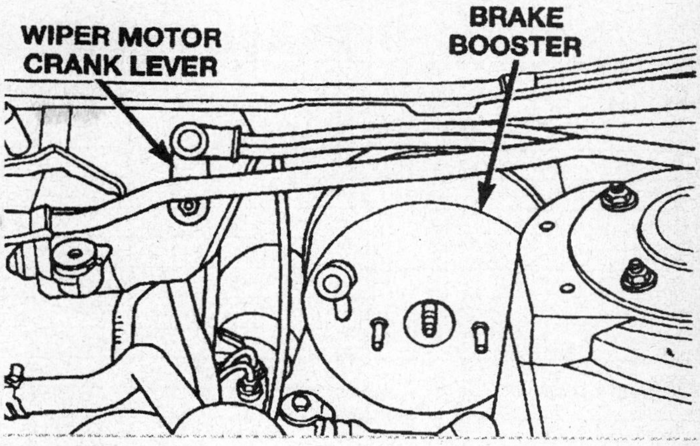

CR4090100121000X

Fig. 27 Proportioning valve replacement. Avenger & Talon & 2001–02 Sebring Coupe & Stratus Coupe

2. Open bleeder screw at least one full turn.
3. Bleed 4–8 ounces of fluid through system until air free flow is maintained.
4. Repeat procedure at all screws.
5. If pedal travel is excessive or has not improved, repeat procedure.

PRECAUTIONS

Normal pressure from the pressure bleeder should not be greater than 35 psi. On vehicles equipped with plastic reservoirs, do not exceed 25 psi. bleeding pressure.

MANUAL BLEED

On models with power brakes, if bleeding the hydraulic system without the engine running, first reduce vacuum in the power unit to zero by pumping the brake pedal several times with the engine off.

1. Remove rubber dust caps from all four bleeder screws.
2. Attach clear plastic tubing to bleeder screw and submerge other end of tube into a clear container of clean brake fluid.
3. Pump brake pedal three or four times and hold it down.
4. Open bleeder screw at least one full turn.
5. Release brake pedal only after bleeder screw is closed.
6. Repeat procedure four or five times at all bleeder screw locations. Ensure fluid level in master cylinder stays at proper level.
7. Test drive vehicle after a solid pedal is obtained.

MASTER CYLINDER BLEED

BENCH BLEEDING

When clamping master cylinder in vise for bleeding, carefully tighten vise just enough to hold master cylinder from moving. Excessive pressure can damage master cylinder.

1. Support master cylinder assembly and attach special bleeding tubes as shown in **Fig. 28.**
2. Fill reservoir with approved brake fluid.

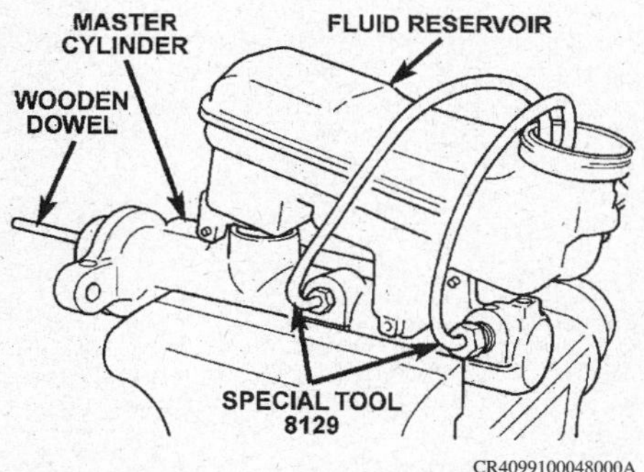

Fig. 28 Master cylinder bench bleeding

3. Using a wooden stick or dowel depress pushrod slowly and allow pistons to return under pressure of springs. Do this several times until all air bubbles are expelled.
4. Remove bleeding tubes from cylinder and install reservoir cover.
5. Install master cylinder onto vehicle as described under "Component Replacement."
6. Bleed hydraulic system as previously described.

ON-VEHICLE SERVICE

Master cylinders may be bled manually or by pressure bleeding. It is recommended that the master cylinder be bled before bleeding the wheel cylinders and calipers.

HYDRAULIC BRAKE SYSTEM SPECIFICATIONS

Model	Year	Master Cylinder Bore Dia. Inch	Booster to Primary Piston Clearance Inch	Wheel Bleed Sequence
Avenger & Sebring	1998–2000	1.001	.0255–.0334	LR, RF, RR, LF
Breeze & Cirrus	1998–2000	.874	—	LR, RF, RR, LF
Concorde, Intrepid, LHS & 300M	1998–2000	.937	—	RR, LF, LR, RF
	2001–02	.937	—	LR, RF, RR, LF
Neon	1998–99②	.875	—	LR, RF, RR, LF
	1998–99①	.827	—	LR, RF, RR, LF
	2000–02	③	—	LR, RF, RR, LF
Sebring Convertible	1998–2000	.874	—	LR, RF, RR, LF
	2001–02	—	—	LR, RF, RR, LF
Sebring Coupe	2001–02	1.06	.404–.415	RR, LF, LR, RF
Sebring Sedan	2001–02	—	—	LR, RF, RR, LF
Stratus	1998–2000	.874	—	LR, RF, RR, LF
Stratus Coupe	2001–02	1.06	.404–.415	RR, LF, LR, RF
Stratus Sedan	2001–02	—	—	LR, RF, RR, LF
Talon	1998	1.001	.0255–.0334	LR, RF, RR, LF

① — Front & rear disc brakes. ② — Front disc & rear drum brakes. ③ — With ABS .937; w/out ABS .875.

HYDRAULIC BRAKE CONTROLS SPECIFICATIONS

Model	Year	Valve Identification	Valve Tag Color①	Split Point psi/Slope	Inlet Pressure From Master Cylinder psi	Outlet Pressure To Rear Brakes psi
WITH ABS						
Avenger	1998–2000	③	—	391–462	996	569–640
Cirrus, Stratus & Breeze	1998–2000⑧	③	Bar Coded Label	500/.43	1000	600–700
	1999–2000⑨	③	Bar Coded Label	400/.34	1000	600–700
Concorde, Intrepid, LHS & 300M	1998⑥	③	Bar Coded Label	435/.43	1000	560–640
	1998⑦	③	Bar Coded Label	435/.43	1000	525–600
	1999⑨	③	Bar Coded Label	400	1000	600–700
	1999④	③	Bar Coded Label	500	1000	650–750
	2000⑪	③	Bar Coded Label	350/.34	1000	525–625
	2001–02	③	Bar Code Label	400/.34	1000	525–625
Neon	1998–99	③	Bar Coded Label	300/.34	1000	550–650
	2000–02	③	Black Band	300/.34	1000	550–650
Sebring Coupe	2001–02	⑬	—	—	—	—
Sebring Sedan	1998–2000	③	—	391–462	996	569–640
	2001–02	⑬	—	—	—	—
Sebring Convertible	1998–2000⑧	③	Bar Coded Label	600/.59	1000	800–900
	1999–2000②	③	Bar Coded Label	500/.43	1000	600–700
	2001–02	⑬	—	—	—	—
Stratus Coupe	2001–02	⑬	—	—	—	—
Stratus Sedan	2001–02	⑬	—	—	—	—
Talon⑤	1998	③	—	391–462	—	569–640

Continued

HYDRAULIC BRAKE CONTROLS SPECIFICATIONS—Continued

Model	Year	Valve Identification	Valve Tag Color①	Split Point psi/Slope	Inlet Pressure From Master Cylinder psi	Outlet Pressure To Rear Brakes psi
LESS ABS						
Avenger	1998–2000	③	—	320–391	925	462–533
Breeze & Cirrus	1998–2000	③	—	500/.43	1000	600–700
Concorde, Intrepid & LHS & 300M	1998	③	White Or Bar Coded Label	500/.43	1000	725–850
	1999	③	Bar Coded Label	400/.43	1000	600–700
	2000	③	Bar Coded Label	350/.34	1000	525–625
	2001–02	③	Bar Coded Label	400/.34	1000	525–625
Neon	1998–99⑧	③	Black	400/.43	1000	600–700
	1998–99②	③	Bar Code Label	300/.34	1000	550–650
	2000⑩	③	Bar Code Band	400/.43	1000	600–700
	2001–02	③	Purple	350/.34	1000	525–625
	2001–02	③	Red	300/.34	1000	480–580
Sebring Coupe	2001–02	⑫	—	—	—	—
Sebring Sedan	1998–2000	③	—	320–391	925	462–533
	2001–02	⑫	—	—	—	—
Sebring Convertible⑧	1998–2000	③	Black /Gold Stripe Or Bar Coded Label	600/.59	1000	800–900
	2001–02	⑫	—	—	—	—
Stratus	1998–2000	③	—	500/.43	1000	600–700
Stratus Coupe	2001–02	⑫	—	—	—	—
Stratus Sedan	2001–02	⑫	—	—	—	—
Talon⑤	1998	③	—	320–391	—	462–533

① — Color tag located under boot of valve stem.
② — 14 inch disc/disc.
③ — Proportioning Valve.
④ — 16 inch disc/disc system w/ABS & TCS. Sales code BR4.
⑤ — FWD.
⑥ — With ABS & Less TCS.
⑦ — With TCS & ABS
⑧ — 14 inch disc/drum.
⑨ — 15 & 16 inch disc/disc systems, w/ABS & w/ABS & TCS. Sales codes BRG, BR3 & BR3 + BNM.
⑩ — Disc/drum.
⑪ — All Sales Codes.
⑫ — Proportioning valves are included in Junction Block, they are not serviceable.
⑬ — Electronic variable brake proportioning.

POWER BRAKE UNITS

NOTE: On Air Bag Equipped Models, Refer To "Air Bag System Precautions" Located In The Front Of This Manual For System Disarming & Arming Procedures.

NOTE: Refer To "Computer Relearn Procedures" Located In The Front Of This Manual When Battery Power To The Computer Has Been Interrupted.

INDEX

DESCRIPTION

SYSTEM

These units are of the vacuum suspended type. Some units are of the single diaphragm type, while others are of the tandem diaphragm type, both single piston and double piston or split system type master cylinders are used.

The vacuum suspended diaphragm type units utilize engine manifold vacuum and atmospheric pressure for its power. It consists of three basic elements combined into a single power unit. The three basic elements of the single diaphragm type are:

1. A vacuum power section which includes a front and rear shell, a power diaphragm, a return spring and a pushrod.
2. A control valve, built integral with power diaphragm and connected through a valve rod to brake pedal, controls degree of brake application or release in accordance with pressure applied to brake pedal.
3. A hydraulic master cylinder, attached to vacuum power section which contains all elements of conventional brake master cylinder except for pushrod, supplies fluid under pressure to wheel brakes in proportion to pressure applied to brake pedal.

OPERATION

Upon application of the brakes, the valve rod and plunger move to the left in the power diaphragm to close the vacuum port and open the atmospheric port to admit air through the air cleaner and valve at the rear diaphragm chamber. With vacuum present in the rear chamber, a force is developed to move the power diaphragm, hydraulic pushrod and hydraulic piston or pistons to close the compensating port or ports and force fluid under pressure through the residual check valve or valves and lines into the front and rear wheel cylinders to actuate the brakes.

As pressure is developed within the master cylinder a counter force acting through the hydraulic pushrod and reaction disc against the vacuum power diaphragm and valve plunger sets up a reaction force opposing the force applied to the valve rod and plunger. This reaction force tends to close the atmospheric port and reopen the vacuum port. Since this force is in opposition to the force applied to the brake pedal by the driver it gives the driver a "feel" of the amount of brake applied. The proportion of reactive force applied to the valve plunger through reaction disc is designed into the Master-Vac to ensure maximum power consistent with maintaining pedal feel. The reaction force is in direct proportion to the hydraulic pressure developed within the brake system.

TROUBLESHOOTING

DECREASING BRAKE PEDAL TRAVEL

If a decreasing brake pedal is encountered, the power brake unit may be binding internally. To test the power brake unit for this condition proceed as follows:

1. Place transmission shift lever into Neutral and start engine.
2. Increase engine speed to approximately 1500 RPM, close throttle and completely depress brake pedal.
3. Slowly release brake pedal and stop engine.
4. Remove vacuum check valve and hose from power brake unit. Observe for backward movement of brake pedal.
5. If brake pedal moves backward, power brake unit has internal binding. Replace power brake unit.

HARD BRAKE PEDAL

An internal bind or a failed vacuum check valve would cause this condition. Refer to Previous to test power brake unit for an internal bind. To check for a failed vacuum check valve proceed as follows:

1. Start engine and increase engine speed to approximately 1500 RPM, then close throttle and stop engine.
2. Wait 90 seconds, then try brake action.
3. If brakes are not vacuum assisted for two or more applications, replace check valve.

DRAGGING BRAKES

If slow or incomplete release of brakes (dragging brakes) is encountered the power brake unit has an internal bind condition. Test for an internal bind condition as outlined under "Decreasing Brake Pedal Travel."

DIAGNOSIS & TESTING

Refer to **Fig. 1,** for diagnostic flowchart.

ADJUSTMENTS

PUSHROD ADJUSTMENT

Refer to "Adjustments" in the "Hydraulic Brake Systems" section for pushrod adjustment procedure.

GENERAL SERVICE

In order to properly service and repair available brake systems, a thorough understanding of the power assist systems is necessary. The vacuum assist diaphragm assembly multiplies the force exerted on the master cylinder piston in order to increase the hydraulic pressure delivered to the wheel cylinders or calipers while decreasing the effort necessary to obtain acceptable stopping performance.

Vacuum assist units get their energy by opposing engine vacuum to atmospheric pressure. A piston, cylinder and flexible diaphragm utilize this energy to provide brake assistance. The diaphragm is balanced with engine vacuum until the brake pedal is depressed, allowing atmospheric pressure to unbalance the unit and apply force to the brake system.

Brakes will operate even if the power unit fails. This means the conventional brake system and the power assist system are

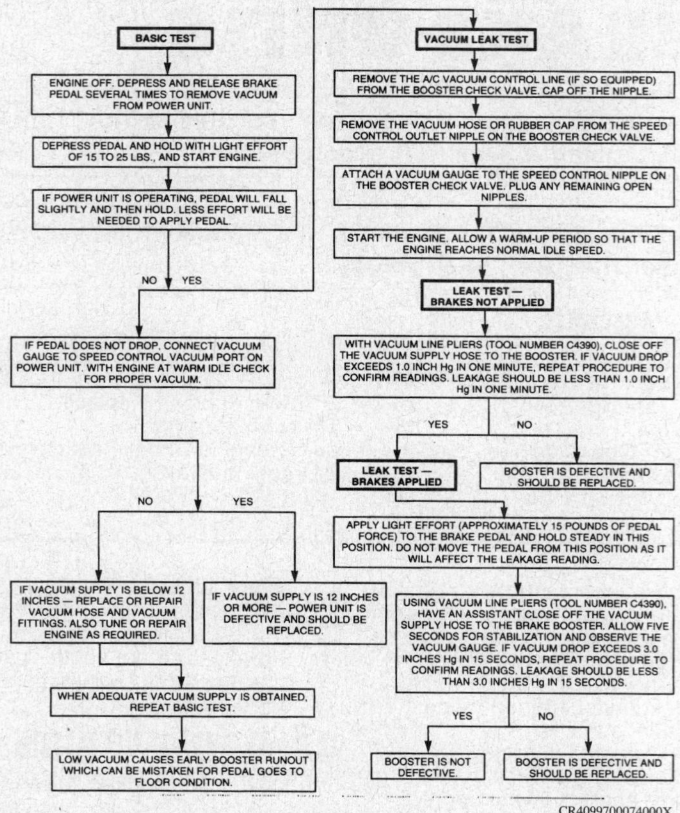

Fig. 1 Power brake system diagnosis

completely separate. Troubleshooting conventional and power assist systems are exactly the same until the power unit is reached. As with conventional hydraulic brakes, a spongy pedal still means air is trapped in the hydraulic system. Power brakes give higher line pressure, making leaks more critical.

BRAKE BOOSTER OPERATION TEST

1. Run engine for one or two minutes, then shut off.
   a. If brake pedal depresses fully first time but gradually becomes higher when depressed succeeding times, booster is operating properly.
   b. If pedal height remains unchanged, booster is defective.
2. With engine stopped, step on brake pedal several times, then step on brake pedal and start engine.
   a. If pedal moves downward slightly, booster is in good condition.
   b. If there is no change in pedal, booster is defective.
3. With engine running, step on brake pedal and stop engine, then hold pedal depressed for 30 seconds.
   a. If pedal height does not change, booster is in good condition.
   b. If pedal height rises, booster is defective.
4. Brake booster performance is satisfactory if it passes all three operating tests.
5. If brake booster does not pass all three tests, there may be a fault in check valve, vacuum hose or in booster itself.

CHECK VALVE OPERATION TEST

1. Remove vacuum hose. **Check valve is press fitted inside vacuum hose.**
2. Check operation of check valve by using a vacuum pump. Refer to **Fig. 2,** for vacuum pump connection locations.
3. Connect vacuum pump at brake booster side (A). A negative pressure (vacuum) should be created and held.
4. Connect vacuum pump at intake manifold side (B). A negative pressure (vacuum) is not created.
5. If check valve is defective, replace it as an assembly unit together with vacuum hose.

POWER BRAKE UNIT SERVICE

POWER BOOSTER, REPLACE

AVENGER & TALON

Refer to **Figs. 3 and 4** for power booster replacement procedures.

SEBRING

1998–2000

Refer to **Fig. 3** for power booster replacement procedures.

2001–02

Refer to **Fig. 5** for power booster removal procedures.

STRATUS

2001–02

Refer to **Fig. 5** for power booster removal procedures.

CONCORDE, INTREPID, LHS & 300M

Three different power brake vacuum boosters designs are used, although externally they appear the same. **On 1998–99 models** with standard brakes and ABS applications a Bendix booster is used. Traction control ABS applications use a Teves booster. **On 2000–02 models** a Bosch power brake booster is used in all brake applications, if power booster is to be replaced ensure the correct component is installed, refer to **Figs. 6 and 7** for brake booster assembly and identification.

Do not attempt to disassemble or service power brake unit. Brake unit is serviced only as a complete unit.

1. Remove caps from both wiper arms, then the wiper arm mounting nuts at pivots, **Fig. 8.**
2. Remove wiper arms from pivots by rocking them back and forth on pivots.
3. Remove wiper module and cowl cover from vehicle, **Fig. 9.**
4. Remove eight bolts mounting reinforcement to strut towers and one bolt mounting wiper module to reinforcement, then the reinforcement from vehicle **Fig. 10.**
5. Disconnect wire connector from brake fluid level sensor on right side of master cylinder reservoir.
6. Remove two master cylinder to brake booster attaching nuts, then slide master cylinder off mounting studs with brake lines attached.
7. Position master cylinder backwards on left engine valve cover.
8. Disconnect vacuum hose from booster check valve. **Do not remove check valve from booster.**
9. Rotate windshield wiper motor crank lever until lever is at the 12 o'clock position, **Fig. 11.**
10. From under instrument panel, position a small screwdriver between center tang of booster input rod to brake pedal pin retaining clip, then rotate screwdriver so retainer clip center tang passes over end of brake pedal pin and pull retainer clip off. Discard old retainer clip.
11. From under instrument panel remove four booster mounting nuts, slide booster up and to right on dash panel, then tilt outward and up to remove.
12. Reverse procedure to install noting following:
    a. **Torque** booster to dash panel and master cylinder to booster mounting nuts to 21 ft. lbs.
    b. When connecting booster input rod to brake pedal pin use a new retainer clip.
    c. Ensure brake lights work properly.

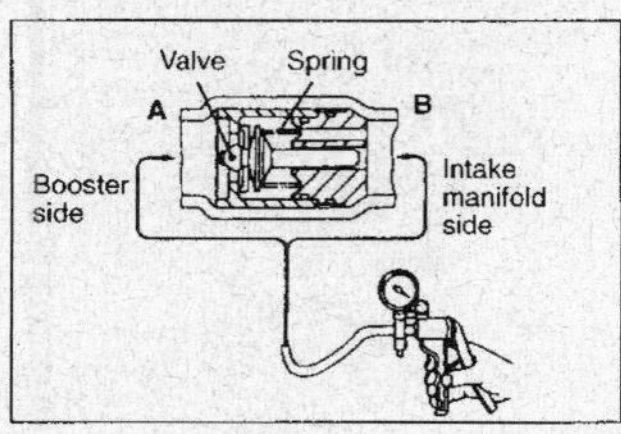

Vacuum pump connection	Accept/reject criteria
Connection at the brake booster side (A)	A negative pressure (vacuum) is created and held.
Connection at the intake manifold side (B)	A negative pressure (vacuum) is not created.

CR4099700073000X

Fig. 2 Vacuum pump connection locations

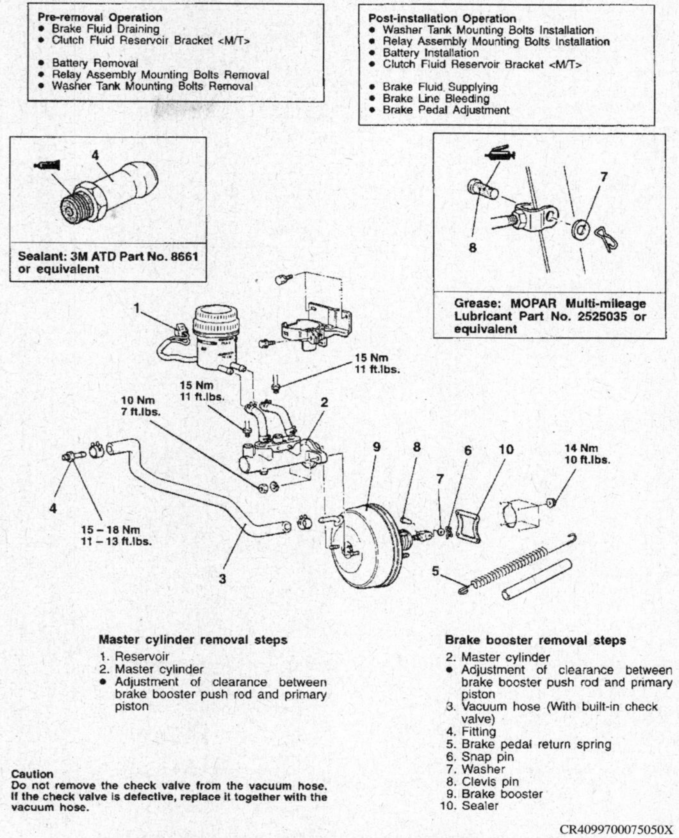

CR4099700075050X

Fig. 3 Brake booster & master cylinder replacement. Avenger & 1998–2000 Sebring

NEON

When repairing vehicles equipped with ABS systems, the vacuum in the power booster must be pumped down before removing the master cylinder to avoid drawing in any contamination. This can be done by pumping the brake with ignition off until a firm pedal is achieved.

1. **On models equipped with ABS systems,** ensure ignition switch is Off and brake pedal has been pumped until firm.
2. **On 2000–02 models,** proceed as follows:
   a. Remove battery from vehicle.
   b. Remove one bolt mounting air cleaner box, then disconnect electrical connector at air inlet sensor.
   c. Lift air cleaner box upward to clear alignment post, then move air cleaner box forward to access battery tray mounting bolts and remove battery tray from vehicle.
3. **On all models,** disconnect wiring harness from brake fluid level sensor mounted on fluid reservoir.
4. Disconnect primary and secondary brake tubes from master cylinder housing and plug outlets on master cylinder.
5. **On models equipped with ABS,** clean area where master cylinder attaches to power booster using a suitable cleaner.
6. **On all models,** remove mounting nuts and slide master cylinder forward out of booster.
7. **On models equipped with ABS,** vacuum seal in front of power brake vacuum booster must be replaced. Remove vacuum seal in front of power brake vacuum booster by carefully inserting a small screwdriver between master cylinder push rod and vacuum seal and prying seal out of booster. **Do not attempt to pry seal out by inserting screwdriver between seal and booster.**
8. **On all models,** disconnect vacuum hoses from power booster check valve. **Do not remove check valve from power booster.**
9. **On models equipped with ABS,** remove Integrated Hydraulic Control Unit (ICU) then remove the ICU mounting bracket from frame.
10. **On all models,** locate power booster input rod to brake pedal attachment under instrument panel.
11. Position a suitable small screwdriver between center tang on input rod to brake pedal pin retaining clip. **Discard old retaining clip.**
12. Rotate screwdriver to allow retaining clip center tang to pass over end of brake pedal pin. Discard retaining clip.
13. Remove power booster mounting nuts holding unit to dash panel.
14. Slide power booster forward until mounting studs clear dash, then tilt unit upward to remove.
15. Reverse procedure to install noting following:
    a. **On models equipped with ABS,** install new vacuum seal by lubricating master cylinder push rod using suitable silicone lubricant and slide vacuum seal onto master cylinder push rod with notches on seal pointing toward and seated against master cylinder housing.
    b. **On all models,** install power booster mounting nuts and **torque** to 21 ft. lbs.
    c. Install master cylinder mounting bolts and **torque** to 13 ft. lbs.
    d. Install a new brake booster input rod to brake pedal retaining clip.
    e. Connect brake tubes to master cylinder primary and secondary ports and **torque** tube nuts to 12 ft. lbs.

BREEZE, CIRRUS & 1998–2000 STRATUS

2.0L & 2.4L Engines

1. Remove remote ground cable from stud located on lefthand strut tower, then remove wiring harness connector from speed control servo.
2. Remove two speed control servo mounting bracket nuts, then move speed control servo out of way. **Do not remove speed control cable from servo.**
3. Remove vacuum harness connector and electrical connector from purge control solenoid.
4. Remove purge control solenoid bracket bolt, then remove purge control solenoid.
5. Remove vacuum hoses from check valve located on brake booster, then remove EGR transducer assembly and vacuum hoses.
6. Remove master cylinder assembly from brake booster. **Do not remove brake lines from master cylinder.**

Pre-removal Operation
- Brake Fluid Draining
- Clutch Fluid Reservoir Bracket <M/T>
- Battery Removal <Non-turbo>
- Relay Assembly Mounting Bolts Removal <Non-turbo>
- Washer Tank Mounting Bolts Removal <Non-turbo>
- Centermember Assembly Mounting Bolts Removal <Turbo>
- Engine Mount Bracket Removal <Turbo>
- Air Conditioning Compressor Mounting Bolts Removal <Turbo>
- Air Conditioning High Pressure Hose Clamp Mounting Bolts Removal<Turbo>
- Power Steering Pressure Hose, Pipe and Return Pipe Clamp Mounting Bolts Removal <Turbo>

Post-installation Operation
- Power Steering Pressure Hose, Pipe and Return Pipe Clamp Mounting Bolts Installation <Turbo>
- Air Conditioning High Pressure Hose Clamp Mounting Bolts Installation <Turbo>
- Air Conditioning Compressor Mounting Bolts Installation
- Engine Mount Bracket Installation <Turbo>
- Centermember Assembly Mounting Bolts Installation <Turbo>
- Washer Tank Mounting Bolts Installation <Non-turbo>
- Relay Assembly Mounting Bolts Installation <Non-turbo>
- Battery Installation<Non-turbo>
- Clutch Fluid Reservoir Bracket <M/T>
- Brake Fluid Supplying
- Brake Line Bleeding
- Brake Pedal Adjustment

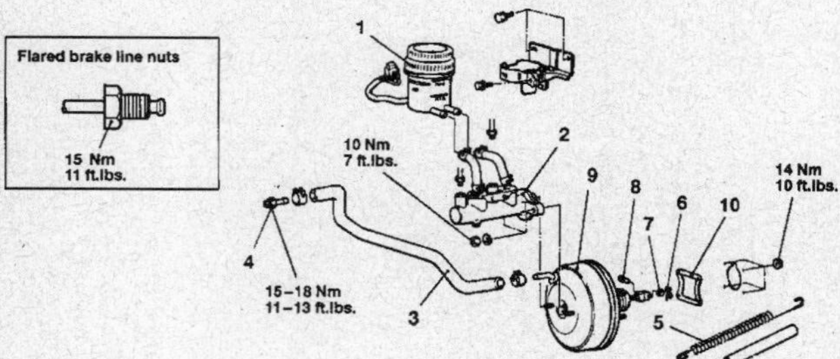

Master cylinder removal steps
1. Reservoir
2. Master cylinder
- Adjustment of clearance between brake booster push rod and primary piston

Caution
The check valve should not be removed from the vacuum hose. If the check valve is defective, replace it together with the vacuum hose.

Brake booster removal steps
2. Master cylinder
- Adjustment of clearance between brake booster push rod and primary piston
3. Vacuum hose (With built-in check valve)
4. Fitting
5. Brake pedal return spring
6. Snap pin
7. Washer
8. Clevis pin
9. Brake booster
10. Sealer

CR4099700075010X

Fig. 4 Brake booster & master cylinder replacement. Talon

Pre-removal Operation
- Brake Fluid Draining

Post-installation Operation
- Brake Fluid Supplying
- Brake Line Bleeding
- Brake Pedal Adjustment

SEALANT: 3M™ AAD PART NO. 8663 OR EQUIVALENT

GREASE: MOPAR® MULTI-MILEAGE LUBRICANT PART NO. 2525035 OR EQUIVALENT

14 ± 3 N·m
124 ± 26 in-lb

17 ± 1 N·m
12 ± 1 ft-lb

15 ± 2 N·m
11 ± 1 ft-lb

9.8 ± 2.0 N·m
87 ± 17 in-lb

1. BRAKE TUBE CONNECTION
2. BRAKE FLUID
3. MASTER CYLINDER ASSEMBLY
- ADJUSTMENT OF CLEARANCE BETWEEN BRAKE BOOSTER PUSHROD AND PRIMARY PISTON
4. VACUUM HOSE (WITH BUILT-IN CHECK VALVE)
5. FITTING
6. SNAP PIN
7. CLEVIS PIN
- STRUT TOWER BAR ASSEMBLY
8. BRAKE BOOSTER
9. SEALER
10. PLATE AND SEAL ASSEMBLY <VEHICLES WITH TCL>

CR4090000106000X

Fig. 5 Brake booster & master cylinder replacement. 2001–02 Sebring & Stratus

1. Disconnect brake booster input rod from brake pedal pin.
2. Remove brake booster mounting nuts and brake booster.
3. Reverse procedure to install. Install brake booster mounting nuts and **torque** to 21 ft. lbs.

2.5L Engine

1. Remove remote ground cable from stud located on lefthand strut tower, then remove wiring harness connector from speed control servo.
2. Remove PCV hose from intake manifold.
3. Remove bolt attaching air chamber to intake manifold and loosen clamp attaching air inlet hose to throttle body.
4. Remove air inlet hose, air cleaner lid and air chamber as an assembly.
5. Remove throttle cable and speed control cable from throttle body, then remove vacuum hose from throttle body.
6. Remove wiring harness connectors from Air Idle Speed (AIS) motor and throttle position sensor, then remove throttle body from intake manifold.
7. Remove throttle cable and speed control cable mounting bracket from intake manifold. **Do not remove cables from bracket.**
8. Remove EGR tube from intake manifold and EGR valve.
9. Remove two speed control servo mounting bracket nuts, then move speed control servo out of way. **Do not remove speed control cable from servo.**
10. Remove primary and secondary brake tubes from master cylinder assembly, then remove master cylinder from brake booster.
11. Remove vacuum harness connector and electrical connector from purge control solenoid.
12. Remove purge control solenoid bracket bolt, then remove purge control solenoid.
13. Remove dipstick and dipstick tube from transaxle as an assembly.
14. Remove vacuum hoses from check valve located on brake booster.
15. Disconnect brake booster input rod from brake pedal pin, then remove brake booster mounting nuts and brake booster.
16. Reverse procedure to install. Install brake booster mounting nuts and **torque** to 21 ft. lbs.

2001-02 SEBRING & STRATUS

1. Disconnect wiring harness connector and vacuum hose at speed control servo.
2. Remove speed control servo mounting nuts. Leave cable attached, leave servo out off to side.
3. Remove master cylinder from booster as outlined under "Hydraulic Brake Systems."
4. Remove vacuum hoses from check valve at power brake vacuum booster.
5. Remove electrical connector and mounting screw from purge solenoid mounted on frame rail, **Fig. 12.**
6. Locate power brake booster input rod to brake pedal attachment under instrument panel.
7. Insert small screwdriver between center tang on power brake booster input rod to brake pedal retaining clip, **Fig. 13.**
8. Rotate screwdriver to allow retaining clip center tang to pass over end of brake pedal pin, then pull retaining clip off brake pedal pin. **Discard retaining clip, replace with new clip during installation.**
9. Remove four nuts attaching power brake vacuum booster to dash panel. Nuts are accessible from under dash panel, **Fig. 14.**
10. Slide power brake vacuum booster straight forward until mounting studs clear dash panel, then remove.
11. Reverse procedure to install, noting following:
    a. **Torque** four power brake vacuum booster mounting nuts to 21 ft. lbs.
    b. **Torque** speed control servo mounting nuts to 55 inch lbs.

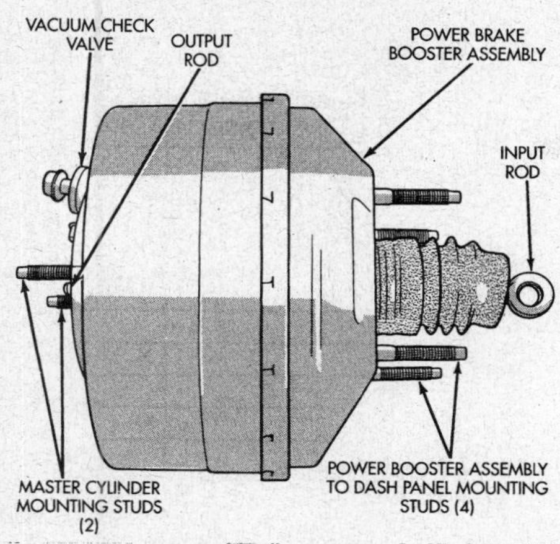

Fig. 6 Power brake booster assembly. Concorde, Intrepid, LHS & 300M

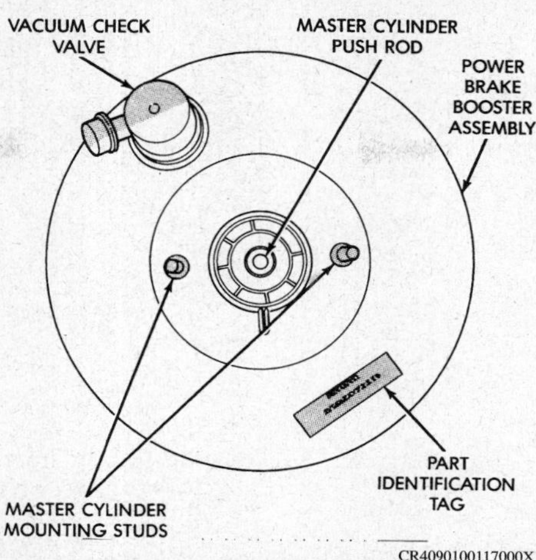

Fig. 7 Power brake booster identification. Concorde, Intrepid, LHS & 300M

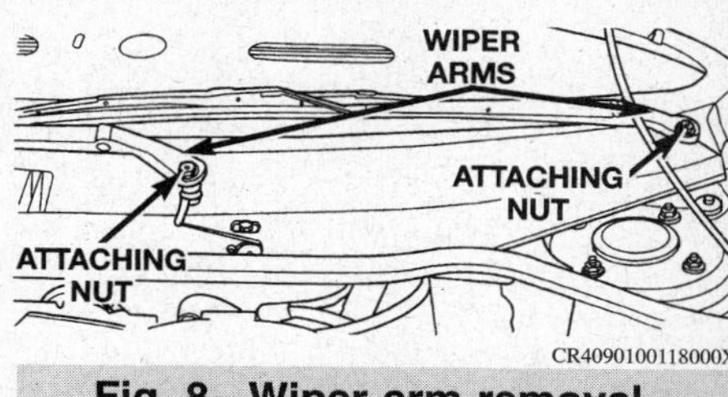

Fig. 8 Wiper arm removal. Concorde, Intrepid, LHS & 300M

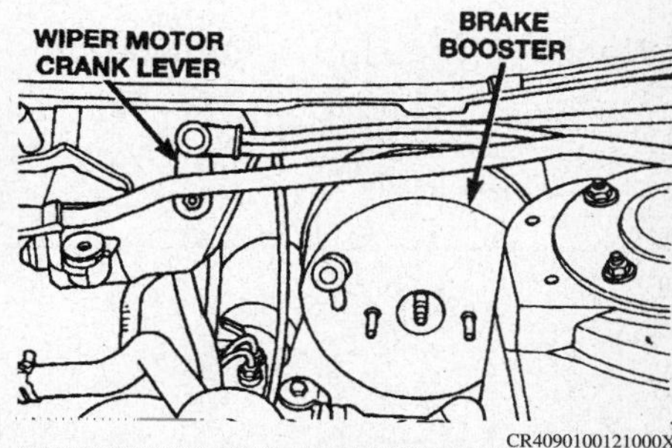

Fig. 11 Wiper crank lever position. Concorde, Intrepid, LHS & 300M

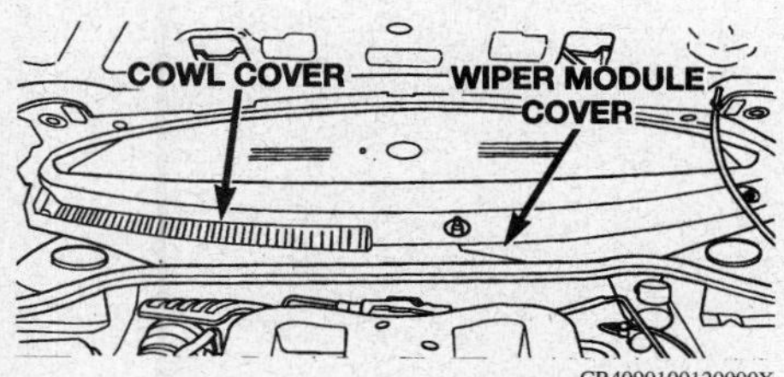

Fig. 9 Wiper module & cowl cover removal. Concorde, Intrepid, LHS & 300M

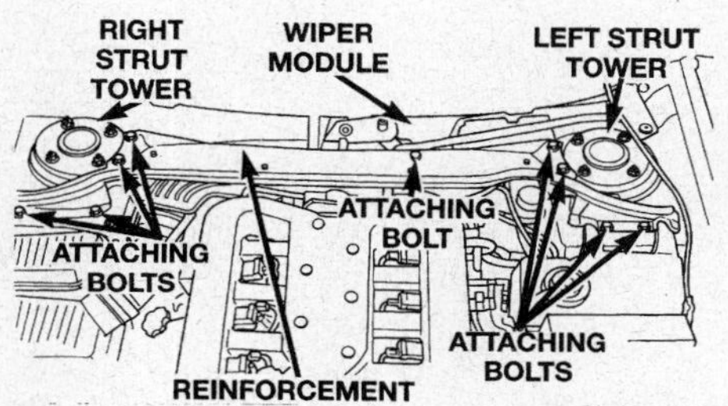

Fig. 10 Reinforcement & wiper module. Concorde, Intrepid, LHS & 300M

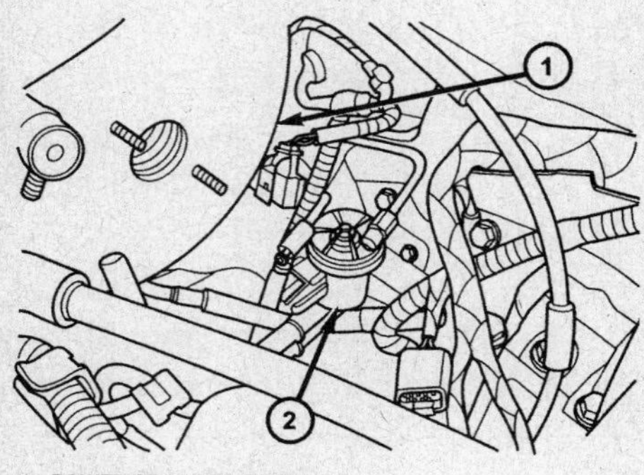

1 - POWER BRAKE BOOSTER
2 - PURGE SOLENOID

CR4090000108000X

Fig. 12 Purge solenoid location. Sebring & Stratus

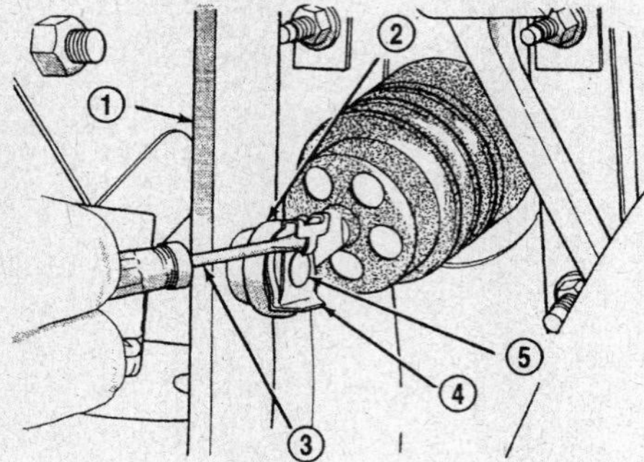

1 - BRAKE PEDAL
2 - INPUT ROD
3 - SCREWDRIVER
4 - RETAINING CLIP
5 - BRAKE PEDAL PIN

CR4090000109000X

Fig. 13 Input rod retaining pin. Sebring & Stratus

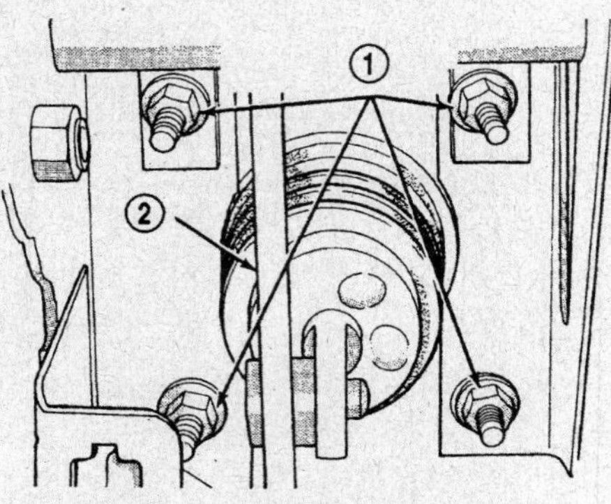

1 - POWER BRAKE BOOSTER MOUNTING NUTS
2 - BRAKE PEDAL

CR4090000110000X

Fig. 14 Power brake booster mounting nuts. Sebring & Stratus

AUTOMATIC TRANSAXLES

TABLE OF CONTENTS

Application Chart

Model	Year	Automatic Transmission/ Transaxle
Avenger	1998–2000	F4AC1
Breeze	1998–2000	41TE
Cirrus	1998–2000	41TE
Concorde	1998–2002	42LE
Intrepid	1998–2002	42LE
LHS	1998–2002	42LE
Neon	1998–2001	31TH
	2002	41TE
Sebring Convertible	1998–2002	41TE
Sebring Coupe	1998–2000	F4AC1
	2001–02	F4A42 (2.4L Engine)
		F4A51 (3.0L Engine)
Sebring Sedan	2001	41TE
Stratus	1998–2000	41TE
Stratus Coupe	2001–02	F4A42 (2.4L Engine)
		F4A51 (3.0L Engine)
Stratus Sedan	2001–02	41TE
Talon	1998	F4AC1, F4A33, W4A33
300M	1999–2002	42LE

F4A33 & W4A33 Automatic Transaxles

NOTE: On Air Bag Equipped Models, Refer To "Air Bag System Precautions" Located In The Front Of This Manual For System Disarming & Arming Procedures.

NOTE: Refer To "Computer Relearn Procedures" Located In The Front Of This Manual When Battery Power To The Computer Has Been Interrupted.

INDEX

PRECAUTIONS

AIR BAG SYSTEMS

Refer to "Air Bag System Precautions" in the front of this manual for system disarming and arming procedures.

BATTERY GROUND CABLE

Prior to service, disconnect battery ground cable and isolate as required.

IDENTIFICATION

The transaxle identification number is located at the top of the bellhousing, **Fig. 1.**

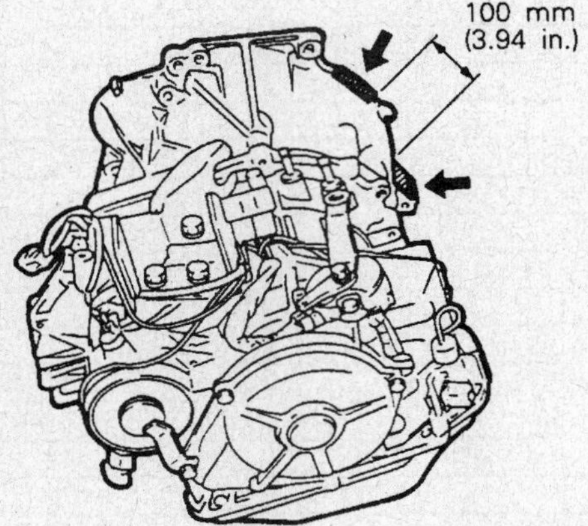

Fig. 1 Transaxle identification

DESCRIPTION

The Mitsubishi F4A33 is a fully automatic four-speed electronically controlled transaxle. This transaxle is used on the Talon equipped with FWD and turbocharged engines.

The Mitsubishi W4A33 is a fully automatic four-speed electronically controlled transaxle. This transaxle is used on the Talon equipped with AWD and turbocharged engines.

TROUBLESHOOTING

Refer to **Fig. 2** when troubleshooting the transaxle.

MAINTENANCE

Refer to "Lubricant Data" chart in the appropriate chassis chapter of this manual for transmission fluid specifications.

FLUID CHECK

1. With vehicle on level surface, start engine and operate at idle speed.
2. With parking brake applied, move shift lever through each gear, then place selector lever in N position.
3. Remove dipstick and check fluid level.
4. Transmission should be at operating temperature when checking fluid level (160–180°F).
5. Fluid level should be within Hot range on dipstick.
6. Adjust fluid level as required.

FLUID CHANGE

The automatic transaxle fluid should be changed every 30,000 miles on these units.

1. Remove plug and drain fluid into suitable container.
2. Loosen mounting bolts, tap pan at one corner to break loose and drain fluid into suitable container.
3. Remove oil pan and drain residual fluid.
4. Inspect oil filter for damage or obstructions. Replace as required.
5. Install drain plug with new gasket and tighten to specifications.
6. Clean transaxle case and oil pan mating surfaces.
7. Install oil pan with new gasket and tighten mounting bolts to specifications.
8. Add 4.2 quarts suitable automatic transmission fluid to transaxle through dipstick hole.
9. Run engine at idle for at least two minutes, then shift transaxle through all ranges and check fluid level.
10. Add sufficient fluid to bring level to lower mark on dipstick.
11. Run engine until normal operating temperature is reached.
12. Check dipstick and ensure fluid level is within Hot range.

ADJUSTMENTS

KICKDOWN SERVO

1. Thoroughly clean area around kickdown servo cover.
2. Remove snap ring and kickdown servo switch.
3. Install holding fixture tool No. MD998918 and adapter tool No. MD998915, or equivalents, **Fig. 3.** Ensure piston is not pushed in by tool. When installing adapter to brake pressure output port, tighten only by hand.
4. Loosen locknut past V channel in adjuster rod and tighten tool No. MD998916, or equivalent, (inner) until there is contact with locknut, **Fig. 4.**
5. Attach tool No. MD998916 (outer), or equivalent, to locknut. Turn outer tool to left and inner tool to right to lock locknut and inner tool.
6. Install torque wrench to inner tool. **Torque** locknut to 84 inch lbs.
7. Loosen locknut and **torque** to 43 inch lbs.
8. Back off inner tool 2–2¼ turns.
9. Attach outer tool to locknut. Turn outer tool to right and inner tool to left to unlock locknut and inner tool.

10. Tighten locknut by hand until it contacts piston, then tighten to specifications.
11. Remove holding fixture and install low reverse pressure port outlet plug.

TRANSAXLE

REPLACE

1. Drain transaxle fluid as described under "Maintenance."
2. Remove transaxle in numbered sequence, **Fig. 5,** noting the following:
   a. Raise transaxle to relieve weight off of mounts using suitable transmission jack and remove transaxle mount insulator bolt.
   b. Support engine using engine support fixture tool No. MZ203827, or equivalent.
   c. Loosen lateral lower arm and compression lower arm using ball joint puller tool No. MB991113-01, or equivalent. **Do not remove tie rod ends.**
   d. Remove driveshaft by applying pry bar to protrusion. **Remove driveshaft as an assembly with hub and knuckle**
   e. Remove inner shaft assembly from transaxle by tapping on center bearing bracket suitable plastic hammer.
   f. Support transaxle with suitable transaxle stand, rotate crankshaft and remove torque converter mounting bolts.
   g. Push torque converter toward transaxle.
   h. Remove coupling bolt at bottom and lower transaxle.
3. Reverse procedure to install.

Presumed cause \ Problem			Driving impossible or abnormal (before start-off): Starter motor won't function	Forward/backward movement impossible	Forward movement impossible	Backward movement impossible	Engine stalls when N → D or R	Clutch slips at D (stall rpm too high)	Clutch slips at R (stall rpm too high)	Stall rpm too low	Vehicle moves at P or N	Engine starts, or vehicle moves, between N R or N-D	Parking doesn't hold	Abnormal vibration-shock when shift to D-2-L-R
Engine	1	Abnormal idling rpm					⊗							×
	2	Performance malfunction					×			×				
Transaxle (power train)	3	Improper adjustment of manual linkage	×	⊗	⊗	⊗		⊗	⊗		⊗	⊗	⊗	⊗
	4	Malfunction of torque convertor		×	×	×				×				
	5	Operation malfunction of oil pump		×	×	×		×	×					
	6	Malfunction of one-way clutch			×			×						
	7	Damaged or worn gear or other rotating part, or improper adjustment of the preload												
	8	Malfunction of parking mechanism									×		×	
	9	Cracked drive plate, or loose bolt		×										
	10	Worn inside diameter of front clutch retainer				×			×					
Oil pressure system (including friction elements)	11	Low fluid level		⊗	⊗	⊗		×	×					
	12	Line pressure too low (seal damaged, leakage, looseness, etc.)		⊗	⊗	⊗		⊗	⊗					
	13	Malfunction of valve body (sticking valve, working cavity, adjustment, etc.)		⊗	⊗	⊗	×	×	×		×	×		×
	14	Malfunction of front clutch or piston				×			×					×
	15	Malfunction of rear clutch or piston			⊗			×						×
	16	Malfunction of kickdown band or piston												
	17	Improper adjustment of kickdown servo												
	18	Malfunction of low-reverse brake or piston		×		×			×					×
	19	O-ring of low-reverse brake circuit between valve body and case not installed				×			×					
	20	Malfunction of end clutch or piston (check ball hole, other)												
Electronic control system	21	Malfunction of inhibitors switch, damaged or disconnected wiring, or improper adjustment	×								×	×		×
	22	Malfunction of TPS, or improper adjustment												×
	23	Pulse generator (A) damaged or disconnected wiring, or short-circuit												
	24	Pulse generator (B) damaged or disconnected wiring, or short-circuit				×								
	25	Malfunction of kickdown servo switch												
	26	SCSV-A or B damaged or disconnected wiring, or short-circuit or sticking (valve open)												
	27	Malfunction of ignition signal system												
	28	Incorrectly grounded ground strap												
	29	PCSV damaged or disconnected wiring, or short-circuit												
	30	PCSV damaged or disconnected wiring (valve open)		⊗	⊗	⊗		×	×					
	31	DCCSV damaged or disconnecting wiring (valve closed)												
	32	DCCSV short-circuit or sticking (valve open)					⊗							
	33	Malfunction of overdrive control switch												
	34	Malfunction of accelerator switch, or improper adjustment												×
	35	Malfunction of oil-temperature sensor												
	36	Malfunction of lead switch												
	37	Poor contact of ignition switch												
	38	Malfunction of transaxle control unit												×

NOTE: ⊗ indicates items of high priority during inspection.
Abbreviations: TPS = Throttle position sensor SCSV = Shift control solenoid valve

CR5019000166010X

Fig. 2 Transaxle troubleshooting (Part 1 of 2)

SHIFT LOCK SYSTEM

ADJUSTMENTS

1. Move select lever to Reverse position and clamp shift lock cable.
2. Connect shift lock cable to select lever assembly and temporarily tighten nut.
3. Slide shift lock cable so distance between select lever assembly's detent pin and end of shift lock cable (distance A) is .04–.15 inch, **Fig. 6.**

	Transaxle malfunction of shift-shock (after start-off)																Abnormal noise, other			
	Won't shift from 2nd to 3rd	Won't shift to 4th	Overdrive control switch doesn't function	Doesn't shift according to shift pattern (shifting is possible)	Improper start-off (starts off from 2nd, etc.)	Excessive creeping or idling vibration	Excessive vibration-shock when shift 1-2 or 3-4	Excessive vibration-shock when shift 2-3 or 4-3	Excessive vibration-shock during upshift	Excessive vibration-shock during D-2 downshift	Sudden engine rpm increase during upshift	Sudden engine rpm increase during 3-2 shift, excessive vibration	Excessive vibration-shock only when cold	Excessive vibration-shock (other than already described)	Damper clutch won't function	Abnormal vibration in high-load region in low gear (approx. 1 Hz)	Abnormal noise from convertor housing together with engine rpm	Mechanical noise (clatter noise) from convertor housing	Abnormal noise inside transaxle case	3rd gear is held
1						×														
2					×		×	×	×	×			×	×		×				
3		×			×															×
4					×										×	×				
5												×					×			
6																				
7																			×	
8																				
9																		×		
10	×	×									×	×								×
11												×								×
12											⊗	⊗		×						×
13	×			×	×		×	×	×	×	×	×	×	×	×	×				×
14	×							×	×		×									×
15																				×
16							×				×	×								×
17							×				×	×		×						
18										×										×
19																				×
20		⊗					×				×									×
21		×			×															×
22				⊗			×	×	⊗	×	⊗	×		×	×	×				
23							×	×	×	×	×	×		×	×	×				×
24				×											×	×				×
25							×					×								×
26																				×
27							×	×	×	×	×	×		×	×					
28																				×
29																				×
30	×	×									×	×								×
31															×					
32																×				×
33		×	×																	
34					×	×									×					
35														×	×	×				
36																				×
37				×																×
38	×	×	×	×	×	×	×	×	×	×	×	×	×	×	×	×	×			×

PSCV = Pressure control solenoid valve
DCCSV = Damper clutch control solenoid valve

CR5019000166020X

Fig. 2 Transaxle troubleshooting (Part 2 of 2)

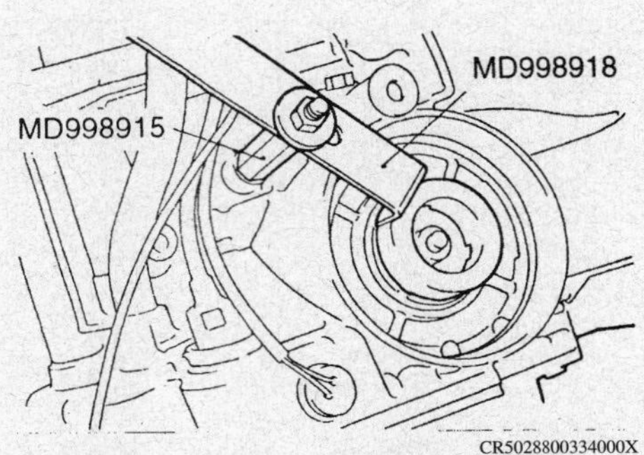

Fig. 3 Kickdown servo tools

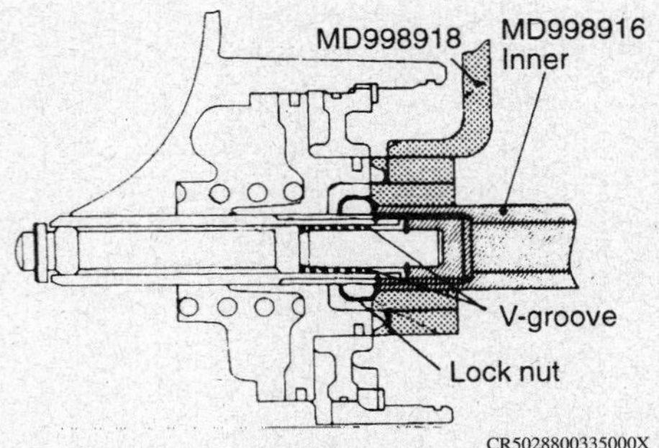

Fig. 4 Installing inner & outer adjustment tools

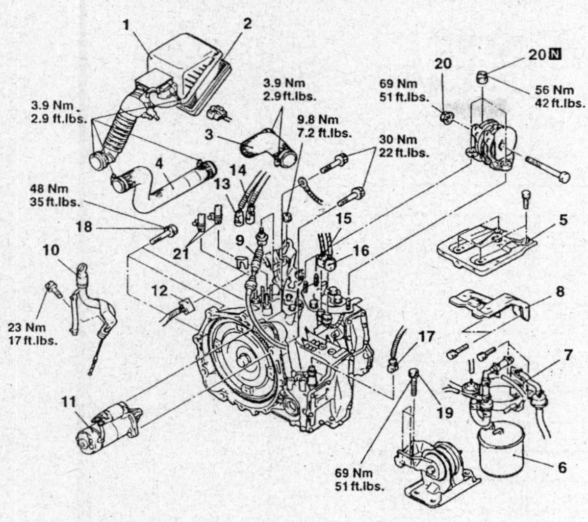

Removal steps

1. Air cleaner cover and air intake hose assembly
2. Air cleaner element
3. Air hose C
4. Air hose A
5. Battery tray
6. Evaporative emission canister
7. Evaporative emission canister holder
8. Battery tray stay
9. Transaxle control cable connection
10. Oil dipstick and guide assembly
11. Starter motor
12. Park/Neutral position switch connector
13. Oil temperature sensor connector
14. Kick down servo switch connector
15. Solenoid valve connector
16. Pulse generator connector
17. Speedometer connector
18. Transaxle assembly mounting bolts
19. Rear roll stopper bracket mounting bolts
20. Transaxle mounting bracket mounting nuts
21. Transaxle oil cooler hoses connection

- Supporting engine assembly

CR5029500776010X

Fig. 5 Transaxle replacement (Part 1 of 2)

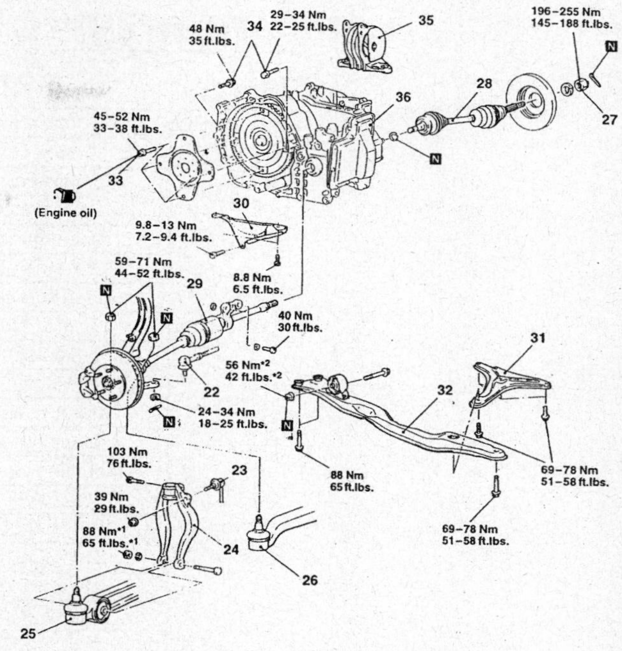

From under vehicles

22. Tie rod end ball joint and knuckle connection
23. Stabilizer link connection
24. Damper fork
25. Lateral lower arm ball joint and knuckle connection
26. Compression lower arm ball joint and knuckle connection
27. Drive shaft nut
28. Drive shaft
29. Drive shaft with inner shaft connection
30. Bell housing cover
31. Stay (R.H.)
32. Centermember assembly
33. Drive plate connecting bolts
34. Transaxle assembly mounting bolts
35. Transaxle mounting bracket
36. Transaxle assembly

Caution

*1: Indicates parts which should be temporarily tightened, and then fully tightened with the vehicle on the ground in the unladen condition.

*2: For tightening locations indicated by the symbol, first tighten temporarily, and then make the final tightening with the entire weight of the engine applied to the vehicle body.

CR5029500776020X

Fig. 5 Transaxle replacement (Part 2 of 2)

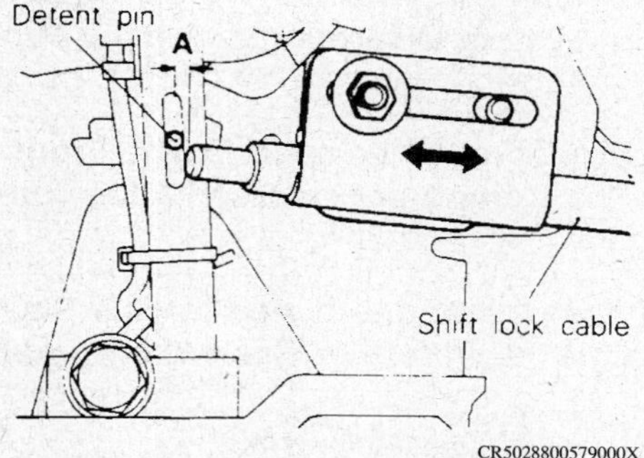

CR5028800579000X

Fig. 6 Shift lock cable adjustment

TIGHTENING SPECIFICATIONS

Year	Component	Torque/Ft. Lbs.
1998	Air Intake Hose Connections	36①
	Bell Housing Cover	84–108①
	Compression Arm Connection	44–52
	Crossmember To Body	51–58
	Crossmember To Righthand Stay	51–58
	Crossmember To Transaxle	42
	Damper Fork to Lateral Lower Arm	65
	Drain Plug	22–25
	Driveplate Connecting Bolt	33–38
	Kickdown Servo, Locknut	18–23
	Lateral Lower Arm Connection	44–52
	Mounting Bracket To Body	51
	Mounting Bracket To Transaxle	42
	Oil Level Gauge Bracket	17
	Oil Pan	96①
	Rear Roll Stopper Bracket	51
	Stabilizer Link To Damper Fork	29
	Starter Motor to Transaxle	22
	Tie Rod End Nut	18–25
	Torque Converter Connecting Bolt	33–38
	Transaxle Control Cable Connection	84①
	Transaxle Lower Coupling Bolts	35
	Transaxle Upper Coupling Bolts	22–25

① — Inch lbs.

F4AC1 Automatic Transaxle

NOTE: On Air Bag Equipped Models, Refer To "Air Bag System Precautions" Located In The Front Of This Manual For System Disarming & Arming Procedures.

NOTE: Refer To "Computer Relearn Procedures" Located In The Front Of This Manual When Battery Power To The Computer Has Been Interrupted.

NOTE: Prior To Performing Any Service Operations Listed In This Section, Consult The "Technical Service Bulletins" Section For Related Information.

INDEX

PRECAUTIONS

AIR BAG SYSTEMS

Refer to "Air Bag System Precautions" in the front of this manual for system disarming and arming procedures.

BATTERY GROUND CABLE

Prior to service, disconnect battery ground cable and isolate as required.

IDENTIFICATION

The vehicle information code plate is mounted onto the bulkhead of the engine compartment, **Fig. 1.** This plate shows model code (1), engine model (2 and 3), transaxle model (4) and vehicle color code (5).

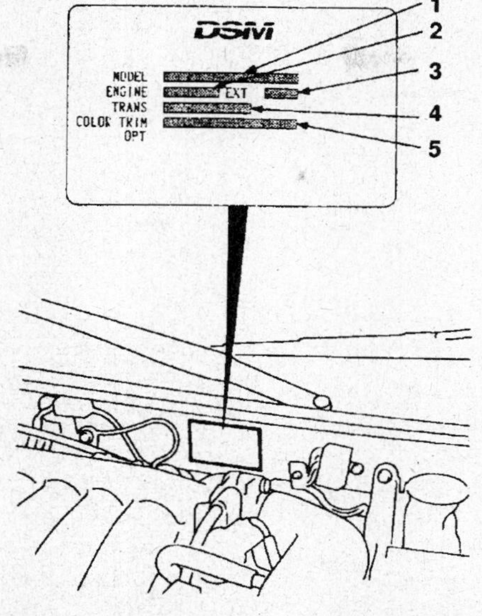

Fig. 1 Transaxle identification

DESCRIPTION

The F4AC1 automatic transaxle is a fully adaptive, electronically controlled four-speed full automatic transaxle. The F4AC1 transaxle uses a three element type torque converter with torque converter clutch.

The F4AC1 transaxle provides four forward speeds with ratios of 2.84:1, 1.57:1, 1.00:1 and .69:1. Reverse ratio is 2.21:1 and the final gear ratio is 4.08:1. The F4AC1 transaxle consists of damper, under drive, reverse, 2/4 and low/reverse clutches, **Fig. 2.** It is also equipped with output and input speed sensors.

TROUBLESHOOTING

Refer to **Fig. 3** when troubleshooting the transaxle.

MAINTENANCE

Refer to "Lubricant Data" chart in the appropriate chassis chapter of this manual for transmission fluid specifications.

FLUID CHECK

1. Place vehicle on level surface, start engine and operate at idle speed.
2. Shift transaxle through all gear ranges and return to Park position.
3. With parking brake applied, place selector lever in N position, then remove dipstick and check fluid level.
4. Transmission should be at operating temperature when checking fluid level (160–180°F).
5. Fluid level should be between Add and Full lines on dipstick.
6. Adjust automatic transmission fluid to bring fluid level within Add and Full lines on dipstick, as required.

FLUID CHANGE

This procedure as been revised by a Technical Service Bulletin.

The automatic transaxle fluid should be changed every 30,000 miles on these units.

1. Raise and support front of vehicle, then position suitable drain pan under transaxle.
2. Loosen transaxle oil pan bolts and tap pan at one corner to break it loose allowing fluid to drain.
3. Install new filter and O-ring on bottom of valve body and clean oil pan and magnet.
4. Install oil pan using Mopar Silicone Adhesive sealant, or equivalent. **Do not seal oil pan with RTV.**
5. Install oil pan and tighten mounting bolts to specifications.
6. Add four quarts transaxle fluid through filler tube.
7. Start engine and check fluid level as outlined under "Fluid Check."

ADJUSTMENTS

THROTTLE CONTROL CABLE

1. Ensure choke lever is away from cam follower.
2. Raise throttle cable (B) upward and loosen cable lower mounting bracket bolt, **Fig. 4.**
3. Move cable lower mounting bracket until clearance between nipple and top of cable cover (A) is .02–.06 inch.
4. Tighten cable lower mounting bracket bolt to specifications.
5. With throttle lever in wide open position, pull throttle cable upward to ensure cable has freedom of movement.

IN-VEHICLE REPAIRS

TRANSAXLE CONTROL CABLE

Refer to **Fig. 5** when replacing transaxle control cable.

TRANSAXLE

REPLACE

2.0L ENGINE

1. Remove transaxle assembly in numbered sequence, **Fig. 6,** noting the following:
   a. Support transaxle with suitable transaxle jack when removing mounting bracket nuts.
   b. Support engine using engine support fixture tool No. 7137, or equivalent.
   c. Loosen, but do not remove tie rod ends nut, lateral lower arm and compression lower arm joints using ball joint puller tool No. MB990635, or equivalent.
   d. Remove driveshaft by applying pry bar between transaxle case and driveshaft. **Remove driveshaft as an assembly with hub and knuckle.**
   e. Support transaxle with suitable transaxle stand, rotate crankshaft and remove torque converter mounting bolts.
   f. Push torque converter toward transaxle.
   g. Remove bottom coupling bolt and lower transaxle.
2. Reverse procedure to install.

2.5L ENGINE

1. Remove battery and washer fluid reservoir.
2. Remove radiator and under cover.
3. Remove transaxle in numbered sequence, **Fig. 7,** noting the following:
   a. Raise transaxle to relieve weight off of mounts using suitable transmission jack and remove transaxle mount insulator bolt.
   b. Support engine using engine support fixture tool No. 7137, or equivalent.
   c. Loosen, but do not remove tie rod ends nut, lateral lower arm and compression lower arm joints using ball joint puller tool No. MB990635, or equivalent.
   d. Remove driveshaft by applying pry bar between transaxle case and driveshaft. **Remove driveshaft as an assembly with hub and knuckle.**
   e. Support transaxle with suitable transaxle stand, rotate crankshaft and remove torque converter mounting bolts.
   f. Push torque converter toward transaxle.
   g. Remove bottom coupling bolt and lower transaxle.
4. Reverse procedure to install.

SHIFT LOCK SYSTEM

ADJUSTMENTS

SHIFT LOCK CABLE

1. Place selector lever in Park position.
2. Install cable so it is above red marking, **Fig. 8.**

INHIBITOR SWITCH & CONTROL CABLE

1. Place selector lever in Neutral position.

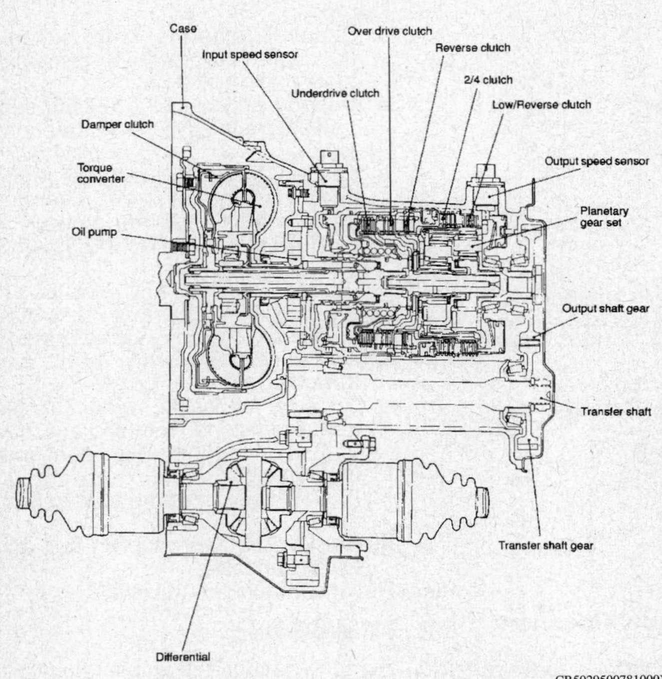

Fig. 2 Cross-sectional view of F4AC1 automatic transaxle

Probable cause \ Trouble symptom	Harsh engagement from Neutral(N) to Drive(D)	Harsh engagement from Neutral(N) to Reverse(R)	Delayed engagement from Neutral(N) to Drive(D)	Delayed engagement from Neutral(N) to Reverse(R)	Poor shift quality	Shifts erratically	Dives in Neutral(N)	Drags or locks	Grating, scraping, growling noise	Knocking noise	Buzzing noise during shifts only	Hard to fill oil blows out filler tube	Transaxle overheats	Harsh upshift	No upshift into overdrive	No torque converter control	Harsh downshifts	High shift efforts	Harsh torque converter control shift
Engine performance			×			×								×				×	×
Worn or faulty clutch(es) — Underdrive clutch			×									×	×	×			×		×
Worn or faulty clutch(es) — Overdrive clutch					×	×						×	×	×					
Worn or faulty clutch(es) — Reverse clutch												×	×			×		×	
Worn or faulty clutch(es) — 2-4 clutch			×			×						×		×					
Worn or faulty clutch(es) — Low/Reverse clutch			×									×		×				×	×
Clutch(es) dragging													×						
Insufficient clutch plate clearance							×						×						
Damaged clutch seal			×													×	×		
Worn or damaged accumulator sealing (s)			×													×	×	×	×
Faulty cooling system							×												
Engine coolant temperature too low				×	×														
Incorrect gear shift control linkage adjustment							×						×	×		×	×		
Shift linkage damaged		×																	
Chipped or damaged gear teeth											×	×							
Planetary gear sets broken or seized											×	×							
Bearings worn or damaged											×	×							
Driveshaft(s) bushing(s) worn or damaged											×								
Worn or broken reaction shaft support sealing			×											×	×	×	×		
Worn or damaged input shaft sealing				×												×	×		
Valve body malfunction or leakage		×	×	×						×			×	×	×	×	×	×	×
Hydraulic pressures too low				×		×	×							×	×	×	×		
Hydraulic pressures too high			×			×												×	×
Faulty oil pump				×			×							×		×	×		
Oil filter clogged								×						×	×	×	×		
Low fluid level			×	×			×			×				×	×	×	×		
High fluid level							×	×											
Aerated fluid			×	×			×	×		×				×	×	×	×		
Engine idle too low																×	×		
Engine idle too high			×				×											×	×
Normal solenoid operation									×										
Solenoid sound cover loose									×										
Sticking lockup piston	×																		
Torque converter failure				×			×												×

CR5029500782000X

Fig. 3 Troubleshooting symptoms chart

2. Loosen transaxle control cable to manual control cable lever coupling nut to free cable and lever.
3. Place manual control lever in Neutral position.
4. Turn inhibitor switch body to align end of manual control lever to flange of inhibitor switch body, **Fig. 9.**
5. Tighten inhibitor switch mounting bolts to specifications.
6. Loosen nut and lightly pull end of transaxle control cable in direction F, **Fig. 10.** Tighten nut to specifications.
7. Ensure selector lever is in Neutral position.
8. Ensure switch operates properly.

KEY INTERLOCK & SHIFT LOCK CABLE, REPLACE

Refer to **Fig. 11** when replacing key interlock or shift lock cables.

TECHNICAL SERVICE BULLETINS

TRANSAXLE SEEPAGE

1999

On some of these models, there may be transaxle case seepage.

This condition may be cause by cooler boss area case porosity.

To correct this condition, proceed as follows:

To correct this condition proceed as follows:

1. Remove throttle body to airbox air intake hose, air box cover, lefthand cooling fan module, Transaxle Control Module (TCM), TCM bracket and solenoid pack electrical connector.
2. Insert suitable air hammer with blunt punch attachment Snap-On tool No. PH59, or equivalent, into pocket formed by cooler boss web. (Refer to "41TE 4-Speed Electronic Automatic Transaxle" technical service bulletins for exact location.)
3. Operate air hammer in 15–20 second intervals moving in circular motion starting in center of pocket.
4. Repeat previous step.
5. Replace transaxle is leak continues.

INTERMITTENT LOSS OF SPEED CONTROL

1998–99

On some of these models built before Aug. 8, 1998, there may be intermittent loss of speed controls after input or output speed sensors have been replaced.

This condition may be caused by new sensor spreading connector terminals.

To correct this condition, replace connector (input part No. 05014469AA or output part No. 05014471AA).

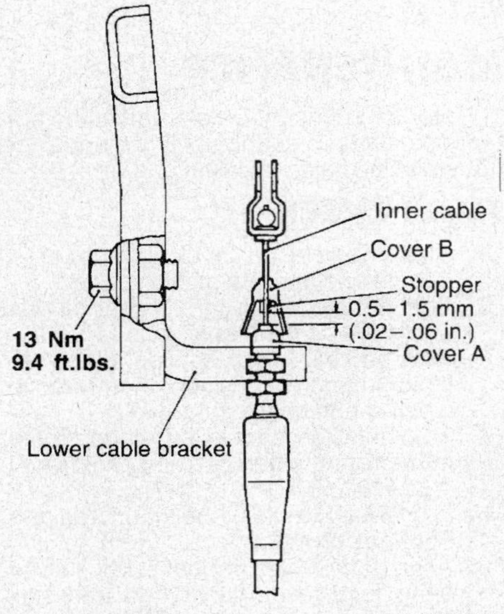

Fig. 4 Throttle control cable adjustment

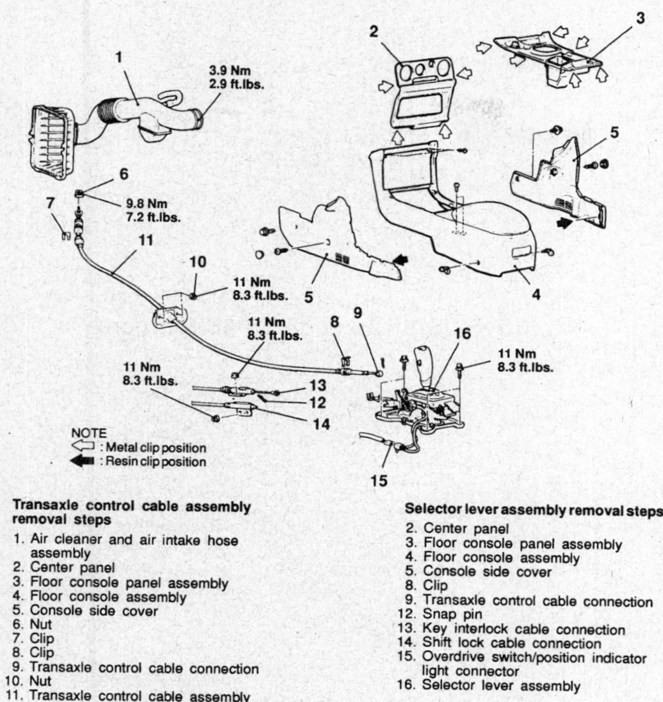
3.9 Nm
2.9 ft.lbs.
9.8 Nm
7.2 ft.lbs.
11 Nm
8.3 ft.lbs.
NOTE
: Metal clip position
: Resin clip position
Transaxle control cable assembly removal steps
1. Air cleaner and air intake hose assembly
2. Center panel
3. Floor console panel assembly
4. Floor console assembly
5. Console side cover
6. Nut
7. Clip
8. Clip
9. Transaxle control cable connection
10. Nut
11. Transaxle control cable assembly
Selector lever assembly removal steps
2. Center panel
3. Floor console panel assembly
4. Floor console assembly
5. Console side cover
8. Clip
9. Transaxle control cable connection
12. Snap pin
13. Key interlock cable connection
14. Shift lock cable connection
15. Overdrive switch/position indicator light connector
16. Selector lever assembly
CR5029500783000X

Fig. 5 Transaxle control cable replacement

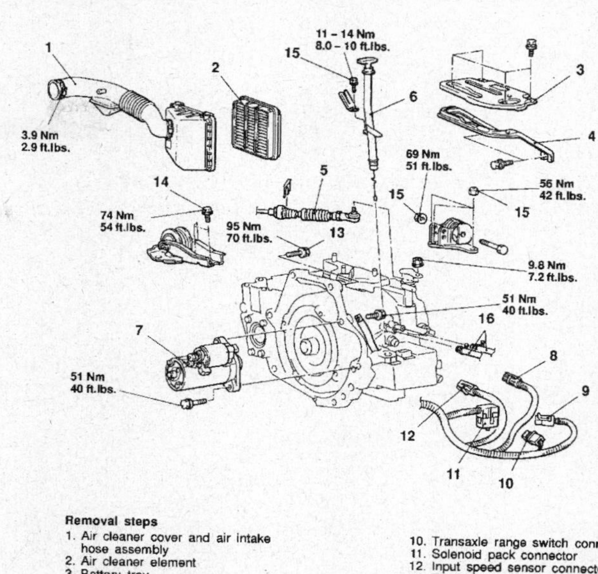
11 - 14 Nm
8.0 - 10 ft.lbs.
3.9 Nm
2.9 ft.lbs.
69 Nm
51 ft.lbs.
56 Nm
42 ft.lbs.
74 Nm
54 ft.lbs.
95 Nm
70 ft.lbs.
9.8 Nm
7.2 ft.lbs.
51 Nm
40 ft.lbs.
Removal steps
1. Air cleaner cover and air intake hose assembly
2. Air cleaner element
3. Battery tray
4. Battery tray stay
5. Transaxle control cable connection
6. Dipstick and guide assembly
7. Starter motor
8. Output speed sensor connector
9. Park/Neutral position switch connector
10. Transaxle range switch connector
11. Solenoid pack connector
12. Input speed sensor connector
13. Transaxle assembly mounting bolts
14. Rear roll stopper bracket mounting bolts
15. Transaxle mounting bracket mounting nuts
16. Transaxle oil cooler hoses connection
• Engine assembly supporting
CR5029500785010X

Fig. 6 Transaxle replacement (Part 1 of 2). Avenger, Sebring & Talon w/2.0L engine

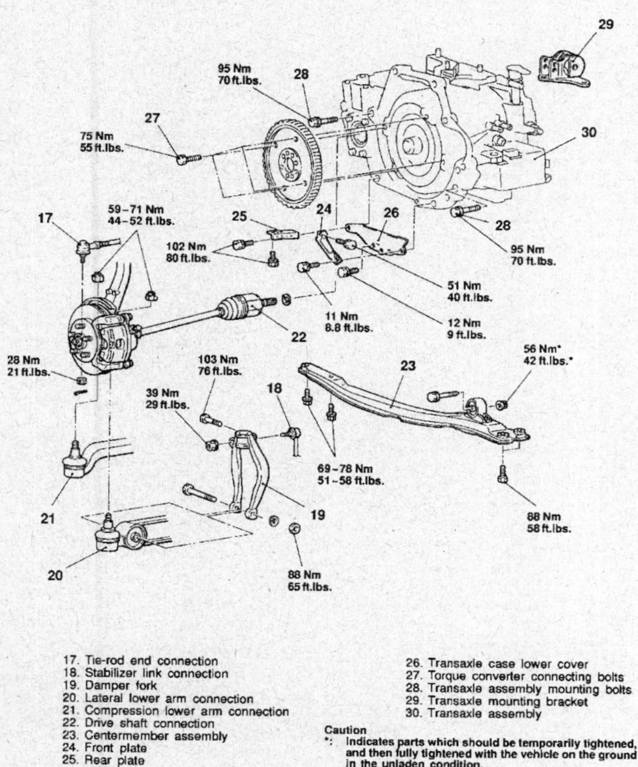
95 Nm
70 ft.lbs.
75 Nm
55 ft.lbs.
59-71 Nm
44-52 ft.lbs.
102 Nm
80 ft.lbs.
51 Nm
40 ft.lbs.
11 Nm
8.8 ft.lbs.
12 Nm
9 ft.lbs.
56 Nm*
42 ft.lbs.*
28 Nm
21 ft.lbs.
103 Nm
76 ft.lbs.
39 Nm
29 ft.lbs.
69-78 Nm
51-58 ft.lbs.
88 Nm
58 ft.lbs.
88 Nm
65 ft.lbs.
17. Tie-rod end connection
18. Stabilizer link connection
19. Damper fork
20. Lateral lower arm connection
21. Compression lower arm connection
22. Drive shaft connection
23. Centermember assembly
24. Front plate
25. Rear plate
26. Transaxle case lower cover
27. Torque converter connecting bolts
28. Transaxle assembly mounting bolts
29. Transaxle mounting bracket
30. Transaxle assembly
Caution
*: Indicates parts which should be temporarily tightened, and then fully tightened with the vehicle on the ground in the unladen condition.
CR5029500785020X

Fig. 6 Transaxle replacement (Part 2 of 2). Avenger & Sebring & Talon w/2.0L engine

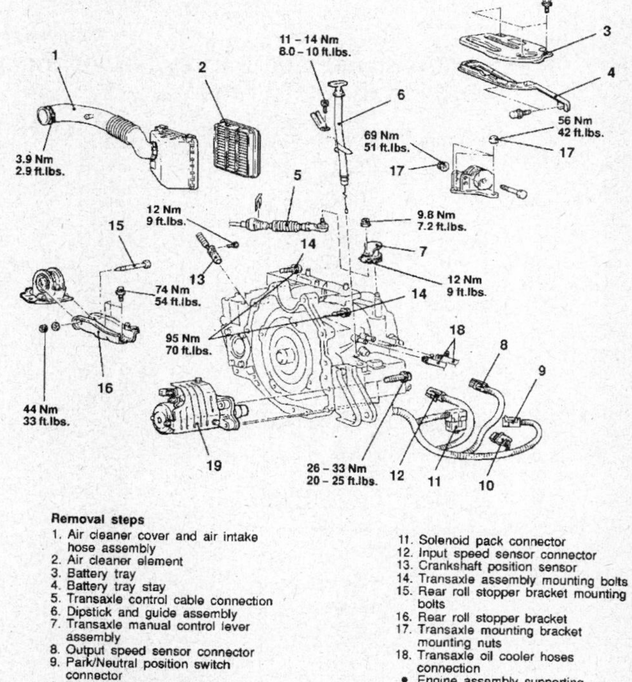
11 - 14 Nm
8.0 - 10 ft.lbs.
3.9 Nm
2.9 ft.lbs.
69 Nm
51 ft.lbs.
56 Nm
42 ft.lbs.
12 Nm
9 ft.lbs.
9.8 Nm
7.2 ft.lbs.
74 Nm
54 ft.lbs.
95 Nm
70 ft.lbs.
44 Nm
33 ft.lbs.
26 - 33 Nm
20 - 25 ft.lbs.
Removal steps
1. Air cleaner cover and air intake hose assembly
2. Air cleaner element
3. Battery tray
4. Battery tray stay
5. Transaxle control cable connection
6. Dipstick and guide assembly
7. Transaxle manual control lever assembly
8. Output speed sensor connector
9. Park/Neutral position switch connector
10. Transaxle range switch connector
11. Solenoid pack connector
12. Input speed sensor connector
13. Crankshaft position sensor
14. Transaxle assembly mounting bolts
15. Rear roll stopper bracket mounting bolts
16. Rear roll stopper bracket
17. Transaxle mounting bracket mounting nuts
18. Transaxle oil cooler hoses connection
• Engine assembly supporting
19. Starter motor
CR5029500786010X

Fig. 7 Transaxle replacement (Part 1 of 2). Avenger & Sebring w/2.5L engine

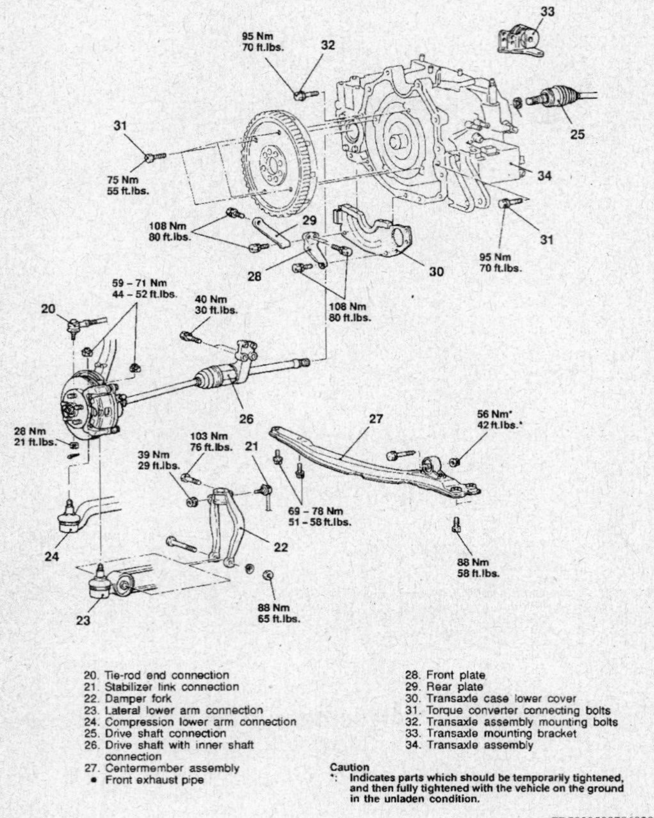

Fig. 7 Transaxle replacement (Part 2 of 2). Avenger & Sebring w/2.5L engine

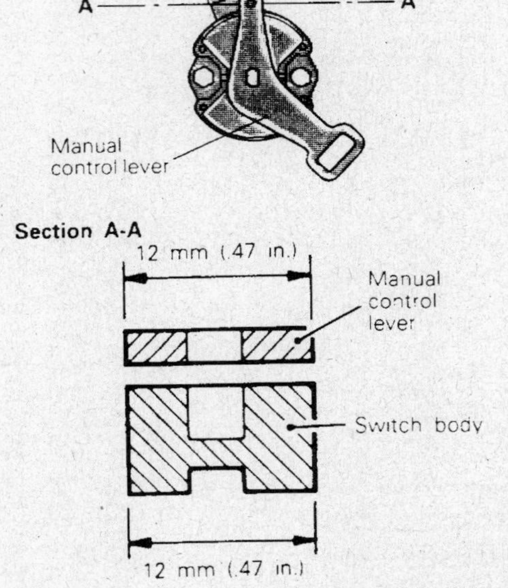

Fig. 9 Inhibitor switch adjustment

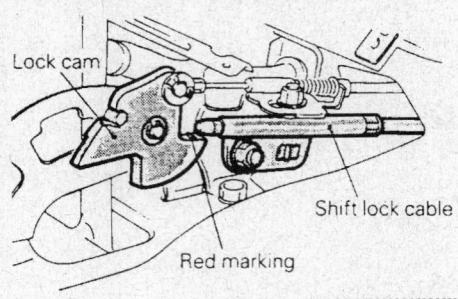

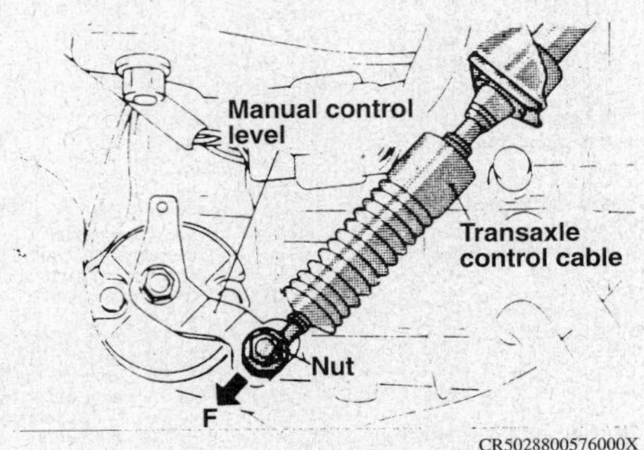

Fig. 8 Shift lock cable adjustment

Fig. 10 Control cable adjustment

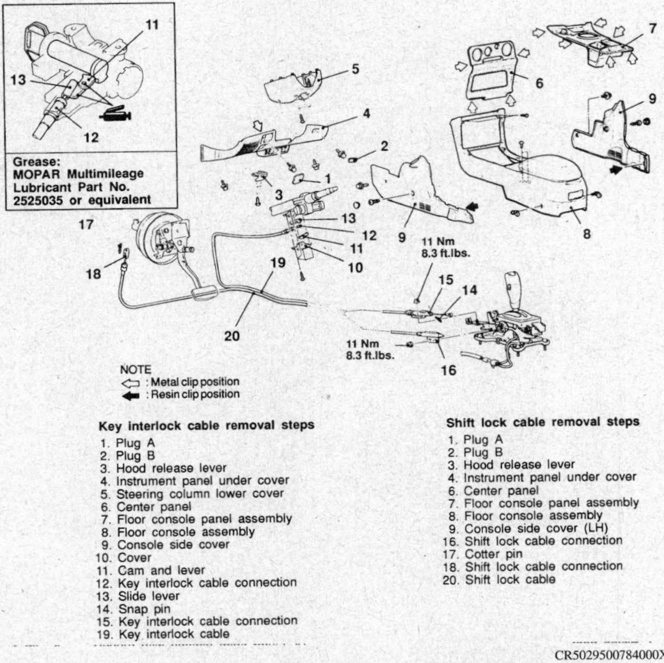

Fig. 11 Key interlock & shift lock cable replacement

TIGHTENING SPECIFICATIONS

Year	Component	Torque/Ft. Lbs.
1998–2000	Air Intake Hose Clamp	36③
	Centermember To Body	51–58
	Centermember To Transaxle	42
	Compression Lower Arm Nut	44–52
	Damper Fork To Lateral Lower Arm	65
	Damper Fork To Stabilizer	29
	Dipstick Guide Bracket	8–10
	Front Plate To Lower Cover	①
	Inhibitor Switch	84–96③
	Lateral Lower Arm Nut	44–52
	Lower Cover To Transaxle	108③
	Mounting Bracket To Body	51
	Mounting Bracket To Transaxle	42
	Oil Pan	14
	Rear Plate To Lower Cover	80
	Rear Roll Stopper To Transaxle	54
	Roll Stopper Bracket To Body	33
	Starter	②
	Throttle Cable Lower Mounting Bracket	10
	Tie Rod	21
	Torque Converter	55
	Transaxle	70
	Transaxle Control Cable	84③

① — DOHC engine 40 ft. lbs., SOHC engine 80 ft. lbs.
② — DOHC engine 40 ft. lbs., SOHC engine 20–25 ft. lbs.
③ — Inch lbs.

F4A42 & F4A51 4-Speed Automatic Transaxles

NOTE: On Air Bag Equipped Models, Refer To "Air Bag System Precautions" Located In The Front Of This Manual For System Disarming & Arming Procedures.

NOTE: Refer To "Computer Relearn Procedures" Located In The Front Of This Manual When Battery Power To The Computer Has Been Interrupted.

INDEX

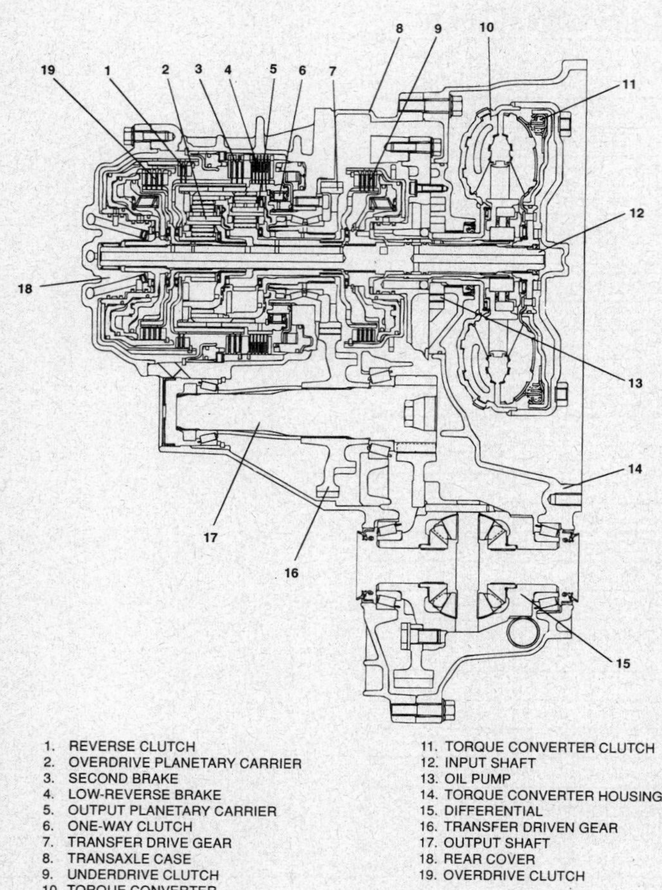

Fig. 1 Cross-sectional view of F4A42 automatic transaxle

1. REVERSE CLUTCH
2. OVERDRIVE PLANETARY CARRIER
3. SECOND BRAKE
4. LOW-REVERSE BRAKE
5. OUTPUT PLANETARY CARRIER
6. ONE-WAY CLUTCH
7. TRANSFER DRIVE GEAR
8. TRANSAXLE CASE
9. UNDERDRIVE CLUTCH
10. TORQUE CONVERTER
11. TORQUE CONVERTER CLUTCH
12. INPUT SHAFT
13. OIL PUMP
14. TORQUE CONVERTER HOUSING
15. DIFFERENTIAL
16. TRANSFER DRIVEN GEAR
17. OUTPUT SHAFT
18. REAR COVER
19. OVERDRIVE CLUTCH

CR5020001539000X

Fig. 2 Cross-sectional view of F4A51 automatic transaxle

PRECAUTIONS

AIR BAG SYSTEMS

Refer to "Air Bag System Precautions" in the front of this manual for system disarming and arming procedures.

BATTERY GROUND CABLE

Prior to service, disconnect battery ground cable and isolate as required.

DESCRIPTION

The F4A42 and F4A51 four-speed automatic transaxles have electronically controlled shift pattern, oil pressure (during shifting) and torque converter clutch. There is a three-element, one-step, two-phase torque converter with built-in torque converter clutch. The gear train has three sets of multi-plate clutches, two sets of multiphase brakes, one set of one-way clutch and two sets of planetary gears with sun gears, carriers, pinion gears and annulus gears.

The F4A42 transaxle provides four forward speeds with ratios of 2.842:1, 1.529:1, 1.00:1 and .712:1. Reverse ratio is 2.48:1 and the final gear ratio is 4.042:1. The torque converter stall torque ratio is 1.85.

The F4A51 transaxle provides four forward speeds with ratios of 2.842:1, 1.425:1, 1.00:1 and .731:1. Reverse ratio is 2.72:1 and the final gear ratio is 3.735:1. The torque converter stall torque ratio is 2.04.

These transaxles have four underdrive clutch discs, four overdrive clutch discs, two reverse clutch discs, six low-reverse brakes discs and two second brake discs, **Figs. 1 and 2.**

TROUBLESHOOTING

VEHICLE DOES NOT MOVE

1. Park/Neutral position switch malfunction.
2. Control cable malfunction.
3. Engine system malfunction.
4. Torque converter malfunction.
5. Oil pump malfunction.
6. PCM malfunction.

DOES NOT MOVE FORWARD

1. Line pressure abnormal.
2. Underdrive solenoid valve malfunction.
3. Underdrive clutch malfunction.
4. Valve body malfunction.
5. PCM malfunction.

DOES NOT MOVE BACKWARD

1. Reverse clutch pressure abnormal.
2. Low-reverse brake pressure abnormal.
3. Low-reverse solenoid valve malfunction.
4. Reverse clutch malfunction.
5. Low-reverse brake malfunction.
6. Valve body malfunction.
7. PCM malfunction.

DOES NOT MOVE FORWARD OR REVERSE

1. Line pressure abnormal.
2. Power train malfunction.
3. Oil pump malfunction.
4. Valve body malfunction.
5. Low fluid level.
6. PCM malfunction.

ENGINE STALLS MOVING SELECTOR LEVER N TO D OR N TO R

1. Engine system malfunction.
2. Torque converter clutch solenoid malfunction.
3. Valve body malfunction.
4. Torque converter clutch malfunction.
5. Torque converter malfunction.

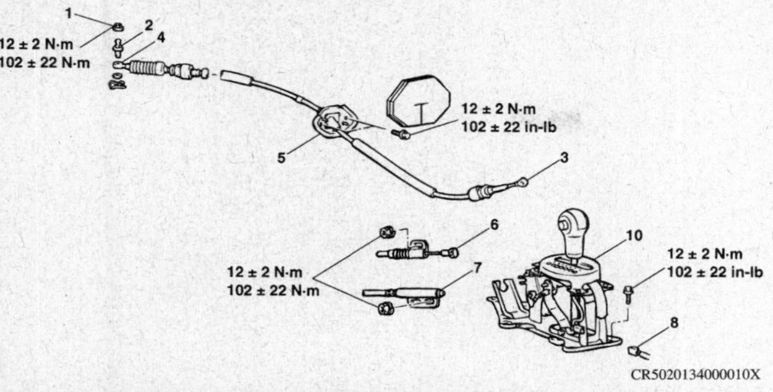

Fig. 3 Selector lever replacement (Part 1 of 2). Less sport mode

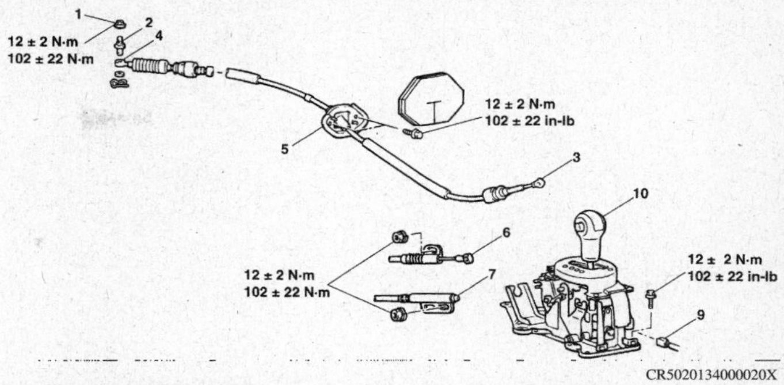

CR5020134000020X

Fig. 3 Selector lever replacement (Part 1 of 2). With sport mode

1. NUT
2. ADJUSTER
3. TRANSAXLE CONTROL CABLE ASSEMBLY CONNECTION (SELECTOR LEVER ASSEMBLY SIDE)
4. TRANSAXLE CONTROL CABLE ASSEMBLY (TRANSAXLE SIDE)
- HEATER/COOLER UNIT (REFER TO GROUP 24, HEATER/COOLER UNIT, HEATER CORE AND EVAPORATORP.24-28.)
5. TRANSAXLE CONTROL CABLE ASSEMBLY
3. TRANSAXLE CONTROL CABLE ASSEMBLY CONNECTION (SELECTOR LEVER ASSEMBLY SIDE)
6. KEY INTERLOCK CABLE CONNECTION (SELECTOR LEVER SIDE)
7. SHIFT LACK CABLE CONNECTION (SELECTOR LEVER SIDE)
8. A/T SELECTOR LEVER POSITION ILLUMINATION LIGHT CONNECTOR
9. HARNESS CONNECTOR
10. SELECTOR LEVER ASSEMBLY

CR5020134000030X

Fig. 3 Selector lever replacement (Part 2 of 2)

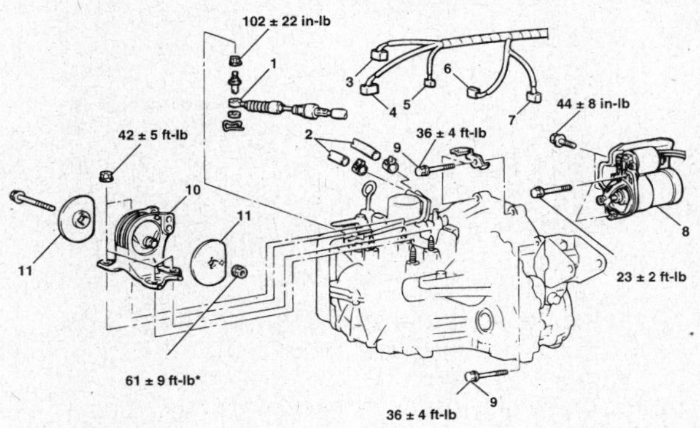

1. TRANSAXLE CONTROL CABLE CONNECTION
2. TRANSAXLE OIL COOLER HOSES CONNECTION
3. PATK/NEUTRAL SOLENOID VELVE ASSEMBLY CONNECTOR
4. A/T CONTROL SOLENOID VALVE ASSEMBLY CONNECTOR
5. INPUT SHAFT SPEED SENSOR CONNECTOR
6. OUTPUT SHAFT SPEED SENSOR CONNECTOR
7. VEHICLE SPEED SENSOR CONNECTOR
8. STARTER MOTOR
9. TRANSAXLE ASSEMBLY UPPER PART COUPLING BOLTS
10. TRANSAXLE MOUNT BRACKET
11. TRANSAXLE MOUNT STOPPER
- EMGINE ASSEMBLY SUPPORTING

CR5020001542010X

Fig. 4 Transaxle replacement (Part 1 of 2). 2.4L engine

6. PCM malfunction.

SHIFT SHOCKS SHIFTING N TO D & LONG DELAY

1. Abnormal underdrive clutch pressure.
2. Underdrive solenoid valve malfunction.
3. Underdrive clutch malfunction.
4. Valve body malfunction.
5. Throttle position sensor malfunction.
6. PCM malfunction.

SHIFT SHOCKS SHIFTING N TO R & LONG DELAY

1. Abnormal reverse clutch pressure.
2. Abnormal low-reverse brake pressure.
3. Low-reverse solenoid valve malfunction.
4. Reverse clutch malfunction.
5. Low-reverse brake malfunction.
6. Valve body malfunction.
7. Throttle position sensor malfunction.
8. PCM malfunction.

SHIFT SHOCKS SHIFTING N TO D, N TO R & LONG DELAY

1. Abnormal line pressure.
2. Valve body malfunction.
3. PCM malfunction.

SHIFT SHOCKS & SLIPPING

1. Abnormal line pressure.
2. Each solenoid valve malfunction.
3. Oil pump malfunction.
4. Valve body malfunction.
5. Each brake or clutch malfunction.
6. PCM malfunction.

ALL SHIFT POINTS EARLY OR LATE

1. Output shaft speed sensor malfunction.
2. Throttle position sensor malfunction.
3. Each solenoid valve malfunction.
4. Abnormal line pressure.
5. Valve body malfunction.
6. PCM malfunction.

SOME SHIFT POINTS EARLY OR LATE

1. Valve body malfunction.
2. PCM malfunction.

DOES NOT SHIFT

1. Park/neutral position switch malfunction.
2. Damaged harness and/or connector.
3. PCM malfunction.

POOR ACCELERATION

1. Engine system malfunction.
2. Clutch and brake systems malfunction.
3. PCM malfunction.

VIBRATION

1. Abnormal torque converter clutch pressure.
2. Engine system malfunction.
3. Torque converter clutch solenoid malfunction.
4. Valve body malfunction.
5. PCM malfunction.

SHIFTS DIFFERENTLY WITH A/C ENGAGED

1. Dual pressure switch malfunction.
2. Damaged harness and/or connector.
3. A/C system malfunction.
4. PCM malfunction.

WON'T DOWNSHIFT UNDER LOAD w/ AUTO-CRUISE ENGAGED

1. Damaged harness and/or connector.
2. PCM malfunction.
3. Auto-cruise control ECU malfunction.

SHIFT SWITCH

1. Park/neutral position switch malfunction.

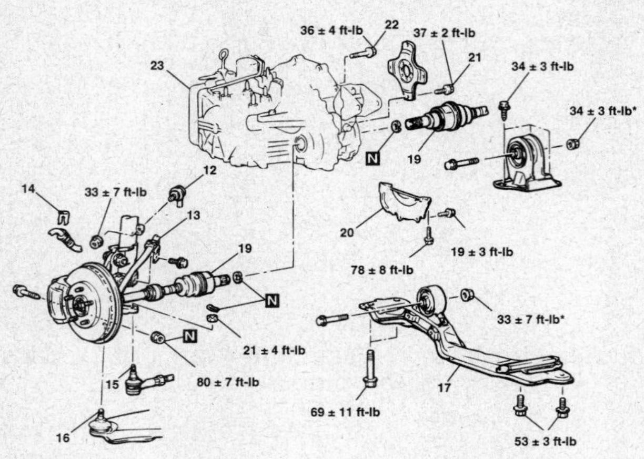

12. STABILIZER LINK CONNECTION <STRUT SIDE>
13. SPEED SNSOR CABLE CONNECTION <VEHICLES WITH ABS>
14. BRAKE HOSE CLAMP
15. TIE ROD END CONNECTION
16. LOWER ARM CONNECTION
17. CENTERMEMBER ASSEMBLY
18. REAR ROLL STOPPER
19. DRIVE SHAFT CONNECTION
20. BELL HOUSING COVER
21. DRIVE PLATE BOLTS
22. TRANASXLE ASSEMBLY LOWER PART COUPLING BOLTS
23. TRANSAXLE ASSEMBLY

CR5020001542020X

Fig. 4 Transaxle replacement (Part 2 of 2). 2.4L engine

2. Shift switch assembly select switch malfunction.
3. Damaged harness and/or connector.
4. PCM malfunction.

MAINTENANCE

Refer to "Lubricant Data" chart in the appropriate chassis chapter of this manual for transmission fluid specifications.

FLUID CHECK

1. Drive vehicle until automatic transaxle fluid temperature reaches normal (158–167°F).
2. Place vehicle on level surface.
3. Shift transaxle through all positions and return to N position.
4. Remove dipstick and check fluid level.
5. If fluid level is below HOT mark, add automatic transmission fluid to adjust level, as required.

FLUID CHANGE

1. Place suitable container under transaxle and oil cooler hose.
2. Disconnect transaxle and oil cooler hose
3. Start engine and run in N position. Let fluid drain. **Do not operate engine for more than one minute.**
4. Remove drain plug and drain case fluid into suitable container.
5. Add approximately 5.8 quarts of suitable ATF.
6. Start engine and run in N position. Let fluid drain into suitable container. **Do not operate engine for more than one minute.**
7. Adjust fluid level as required with approximately 3.7 quarts of suitable ATF.
8. Connect hose.
9. Start engine and idle for 1–2 minutes.
10. Check fluid level as outlined under "Fluid Check."

1. TRANSAXLE CONTROL CABLE CONNECTION
2. TRANSAXLE OIL COOLER HOSES CONNECTION
3. PARK/NEUTRAL POSITION SWITCH CONNECTIOR
4. A/T CONTROL SOLENOID VALVE ASSEMBLY CONNECTOR
5. INPUT SHAFT SPEED SENSOR CONNECTOR
6. OUTPUT SHAFT SPEED SENSOR CONNECTOR
7. VEHICLE SPEED SENSOR CONNECTOR
8. SARTER MOTOR
9. TRANSAXLE ASSEMBLY UPPER PART COUPLING BOLTS
10. TRANSAXLE MOUNT BRACKET
11. TRANSAXLE MOUNT STOPPER
- ENGINE ASSEMBLY SUPPORTING

CR5020001543010X

Fig. 5 Transaxle replacement (Part 1 of 2). 3.0L engine

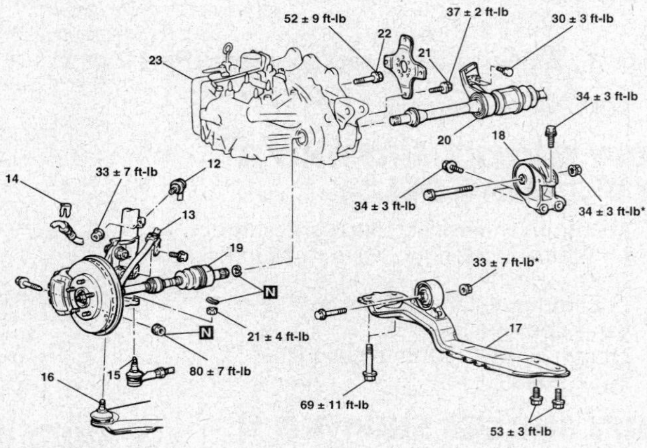

- LIFTING OP OF THE VEHICLE
12. STABILIZER LINK CONNECTION <STRUT SIDE>
13. SPEED SENSOR CABLE CONNECTION <VEHICLES WITH ABS>
14. BRAKE HOSE CLAMP
15. TIE ROD END CONNECTION
16. LOWER ARM CONNECTION
17. CENTERMEMBER ASSEMBLY
18. REAR ROLL STOPPER
19. DRIVE SHAFT CONNECTION
20. DRIVESHAFT AND INNER SHAFT CONNECTION
21. DTIVE PLATE BOLTS
22. TRANSAXLE ASSEMBLY LOWER PART COUPLING BOLTS
23. TRANSAXLE ASSEMBLY

CR5020001543020X

Fig. 5 Transaxle replacement (Part 2 of 2). 3.0L engine

ADJUSTMENTS

CONTROL CABLE & PARK/ NEUTRAL POSITION SWITCH

1. Set shift selector to N position.
2. Loosen control cable to manual control lever coupling nut.
3. Set manual control lever to neutral position.
4. Loosen park/neutral position switch body mounting bolts.
5. Turn park/neutral position switch so manual control lever and park/neutral position switch flange holes align. **Ensure switch does not move while tightening mounting bolts.**
6. Pull control cable toward manual control lever until taut.
7. Tighten adjusting nut to specifications.
8. Ensure selector and manual control

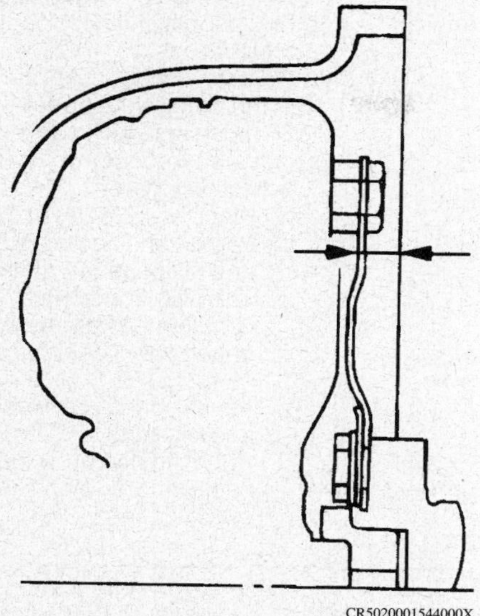

CR5020001544000X

Fig. 6 Torque converter clearance

lever positions match.

IN-VEHICLE REPAIRS

SHIFT SELECTOR, REPLACE

1. Remove air cleaner, then the battery and tray.
2. Remove mounting screws and instrument panel under cover.
3. Remove console box, then the mounting screws, lid and cover.
4. Remove door mirror control switch and disconnect harness.
5. Disconnect accessory socket harness.
6. Remove floor console indicator panel, then the mounting screws and floor console.
7. Remove mounting nut and transaxle control cable adjuster, **Fig. 3.**
8. Disconnect and remove control cable from selector lever and through firewall.
9. Remove key interlock and shift cables' connectors.
10. Disconnect selector lever electrical connectors.
11. Remove mounting bolts and shift selector.
12. Reverse procedure to install, noting the following:
    a. Place selector lever in N position.
    b. Fasten shift lock cable where cable end is above red mark.
    c. Install key interlock cable on lock cam.
    d. Install spring and washer on key interlock cable.
    e. Push lightly on lock cam toward cable and tighten mounting nut to specifications.
    f. Ensure selector lever is in N position when connecting control cable.
    g. Pull control cable toward manual control lever until taut, then tighten mounting bolt to specifications.
    h. Adjust cable as previously described.

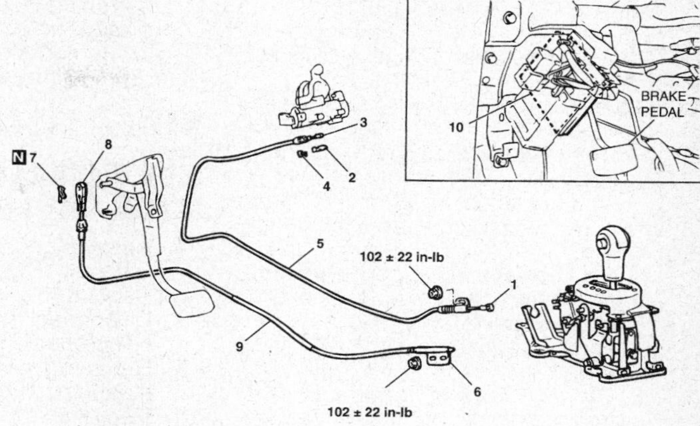

CR5020001541010X

Fig. 7 Key interlock & shift lock cables replacement (Part 1 of 2)

KEY INTERLOCK CABLE REMOVAL STEPS

1. KEY INTERLOCK CABLE CONNECTON (SELECTOR LEVER SIDE)
2. COVER
3. KEY INTERLOCK CABLE CONNECTON (STEERING LECK CYLINDER SIDE)
4. SLIDER
5. KEY INTERLOCK CABLE

SHIFT LOCK CABLE REMOVAL SEPS

6. SHIFT LOCK CABLE CONNECTION (SELECTOR LEVER SIDE)
7. COTTER PIN
8. SHIFT LOCK CABLE CONNECTION (BRAKE PEDAL SIDE)
9. SHIFT LOCK CABLE
10. ETACS-ECU

CR5020001541020X

Fig. 7 Key interlock & shift lock cables replacement (Part 2 of 2)

TRANSAXLE

REPLACE

1. Drain fluid into suitable container.
2. Remove under cover.
3. Remove battery and tray, then air cleaner.
4. Remove mounting nut and disconnect transaxle control cable, **Figs. 4 and 5.**
5. Disconnect transaxle oil cooler hoses.
6. Disconnect park/neutral solenoid valve, control solenoid valve, input haft speed sensor and output shaft speed sensor connectors.
7. Remove mounting bolts and starter motor. Secure started inside engine compartment with harness connected.
8. Support transaxle with suitable jack.
9. Remove transaxle upper part coupling bolts.
10. Remove mounting nut, through bolt, mount bracket and stopper.
11. Support engine with engine supporting tools Nos. MB991453 and MZ203827, or equivalent.
12. Raise and support vehicle.
13. Disconnect stabilizer link strut side.
14. Disconnect speed sensor and brake hose clamp.
15. Loose tie rod end mounting nut. **Do not remove.**
16. Disconnect tie rod end and lower arm using ball joint separate tool No. MB991113, or MB990635, or equivalent. Support separation tool with suitable clamp.
17. Remove mounting nut, bolts and through bolt, then the center member.
18. Remove mounting nut, bolts and through bolt, then the rear roll stopper.
19. **On models equipped with 2.4L engine,** remove driveshafts using suitable pry bar between transaxle case and shafts, noting the following:
    a. **Do not pull on driveshaft.**
    b. **Do not damage oil seal with pry bar or shaft spline.**
20. **On models equipped with 3.0L engine,** remove lefthand driveshaft using suitable pry bar between transaxle case and shaft, noting the following:
    a. **Do not pull on driveshaft.**
    b. **Do not damage oil seal with pry bar or shaft spline.**
21. **On models equipped with 3.0L engine,** remove righthand driveshaft and inner shaft using suitable pry bar between transaxle case and shaft, noting the following:
    a. **Do not pull on driveshaft.**
    b. **Do not damage oil seal with pry bar or shaft spline.**
    c. If inner shaft and transaxle are joined tightly, tape center bearing bracket lightly with suitable plastic hammer.
22. **On all models,** cover transaxle case with suitable shop towel.
23. Ensure transaxle is supported by suitable jack.
24. Remove drive plate mounting bolts while rotating crankshaft.

25. Ensure torque converter does not stay with engine by pressing it to transaxle side.
26. Remove lower part coupling bolts and transaxle.
27. Reverse procedure to install, noting the following:
    a. **On models equipped with 2.4L engine,** install torque converter into transaxle oil pump so clearance approximately .48 inch, **Fig. 6.**
    b. **On models equipped with 3.0L engine,** install torque converter into transaxle oil pump so clearance approximately .37 inch, **Fig. 6.**
    c. **On all models,** install transaxle mount stopper with arrow point toward engine.
    d. Temporarily tighten through bolts' nuts. Tighten to specification after vehicle has been lowered and engine weight is on body.
    e. Tighten mounting nuts and bolts to specifications.

SHIFT LOCK SYSTEM

KEY INTERLOCK & SHIFT LOCK CABLES, REPLACE

1. Remove console as described in "Shift Selector, Replace" under "In-Vehicle Repairs."
2. Disconnect key interlock cable from selector lever, **Fig. 7.**
3. Remove mounting screws and lower steering column cover.
4. Remove cover, then disconnect cable connector and slider from steering lock cylinder.
5. Remove key interlock cable.
6. Disconnect shift lock cable from selector lever.
7. Remove cotter pin and disconnect cable from brake pedal.
8. Remove shift lock cable.
9. Reverse procedure to install, noting the following:
    a. Place selector lever in N position.
    b. Fasten shift lock cable where cable end is above red mark.
    c. Turn ignition switch to Lock position, then install key interlock cable.
    d. Install key interlock cable on lock cam.
    e. Install spring and washer on key interlock cable.
    f. Push lightly on lock cam toward cable and tighten mounting nut to specifications.

TIGHTENING SPECIFICATIONS

Year	Component	Torque/Ft. Lbs.
2001–02	Bell Housing Cover To Engine (2.4L Engine)	70–86①
	Bell Housing Cover To Transaxle (2.4L Engine)	16–22
	Cable Arm	80–124①
	Center Member, Front	58–80
	Center Member, Front Roll Stopper	26–40
	Center Member, Rear	50–56
	Control	80–124①
	Control Cable	80–124①
	Detent Spring	10–18①
	Drain Plug	23–25
	Drive Plate	35–39
	Drive Shaft (3.0L Engine)	37–33
	Indicator Panel	10–18①
	Inner Shaft (3.0L Engine)	37–33
	Key Interlock Cable	80–124①
	Lever	80–124①
	Lower Arm	73–87
	Mount Bracket	37–47
	Mount Stopper	52–70
	Park/Neutral Position Switch	88–104①
	Rear Roll Stopper Bracket	31–37
	Selector	80–124①
	Shift Knob	14–18①
	Shift Lever	80–124①
	Shift Lock Cable	80–124①
	Shift Switch	35–53①
	Starter Cover (2.4L Engine)	36–52①
	Starter Motor	21–25
	Stabilizer Link	26–40
	Tie Rod End	17–25
	Transaxle Lower Part Coupling (2.4L Engine)	32–40
	Transaxle Lower Part Coupling (3.0L Engine)	43–61
	Transaxle Upper Part Coupling (2.4L Engine)	32–40

Continued

TIGHTENING SPECIFICATIONS—Continued

Year	Component	Torque/Ft. Lbs.
2001–02	Transaxle Upper Part Coupling, Bolt w/Flange (3.0L Engine)	43–61
	Transaxle Upper Part Coupling, Bolt w/Washer (3.0L Engine)	58–72

① — Inch lbs.

31TH 3-Speed Automatic Transaxle

NOTE: On Air Bag Equipped Models, Refer To "Air Bag System Precautions" Located In The Front Of This Manual For System Disarming & Arming Procedures.

NOTE: Refer To "Computer Relearn Procedures" Located In The Front Of This Manual When Battery Power To The Computer Has Been Interrupted.

INDEX

PRECAUTIONS

AIR BAG SYSTEMS

Refer to "Air Bag System Precautions" in the front of this manual for system disarming and arming procedures.

BATTERY GROUND CABLE

Prior to service, disconnect battery ground cable and isolate as required.

IDENTIFICATION

A seven-digit part number is stamped on a pad located at the rear of the transaxle on the transaxle oil pan flange. This number must be referred to when servicing the transaxle because of differences in some internal components.

DESCRIPTION

These transaxles combine a torque converter, three-speed automatic transaxle, final drive gearing and differential combined into one unit. The torque converter, transaxle and differential assemblies are housed in an integral aluminum diecast housing, **Fig. 1.** The differential oil sump is integral with the transaxle sump. Separate filling of the differential is not necessary.

The torque converter is connected to the crankshaft through a flexible driveplate. Converter cooling is accomplished by an oil-to-water type cooler, located in the radiator side tank. The torque converter cannot be disassembled.

The transaxle consists of two multiple disc clutches, an overrunning clutch, two servos, a hydraulic accumulator, two bands and two planetary gear assemblies to provide three forward and one reverse gear. The sun gear is connected to the front clutch retainer. The hydraulic system consists of an oil pump and a single valve body which contains all of the valves except the governor valves. Output torque from the main drive gears is transferred through helical gears to the transfer shaft. An integral ring gear on the transfer shaft drives the differential ring gear.

All vehicles except turbocharged models are equipped with a lock-up torque converter. The lock-up mode is activated only in direct drive (3rd gear) and is controlled by the engine control computer. A lock-up solenoid on the valve body transfer plate is powered by the computer to activate torque converter lock-up.

TROUBLESHOOTING

Refer to **Fig. 2** when troubleshooting transaxle.

MAINTENANCE

Refer to "Lubricant Data" chart in the appropriate chassis chapter of this manual for transmission fluid specifications.

FLUID CHECK

To check fluid level, apply the parking brake and operate engine at idle speed with transaxle in N or P position. Add fluid as required.

FLUID CHANGE

This procedure has been revised by Technical Service Bulletins.

On models built after April 24, 1999, transaxle is filled with fill for life ATF +4. Even if fluid discolor, fluid should not be change unless accompanied by burnt small and/or shift quality deterioration. Under severe conditions the fluid and filter should be changes every 48,000 miles.

On models other than previously mentioned, fluid and filter changes are not required for average passenger car use. Severe usage such as commercial type usage or prolonged operation in city traffic, requires that fluid be changed and bands adjusted every 15,000 miles. Whenever factory fill fluid is changed, only fluids labeled Mopar ATF +3 (Type 7176) should be used. Dexron II automatic transmission fluid should be used only if recommended fluid is not available.

Change the fluid and filter as follows:

1. Raise and support vehicle, then place suitable drain pan under transaxle oil pan.
2. Loosen transaxle oil pan mounting bolts and allow fluid to drain. Remove oil pan.
3. Replace oil filter and adjust bands as required.
4. Install oil pan and gasket using Mopar Silicone Rubber Adhesive Sealant, or equivalent. **Do not seal oil pan with RTV.**
5. Add four quarts of appropriate automatic transmission fluid through fill tube.
6. Start engine and allow to idle for at least two minutes.
7. With parking brake applied move selector lever momentarily to each position. Place selector lever in N or P position and check fluid level.
8. Adjust fluid to bring level to Add mark.
9. Check fluid level after transaxle has reached operating temperature. Level should be between Add and Full marks.

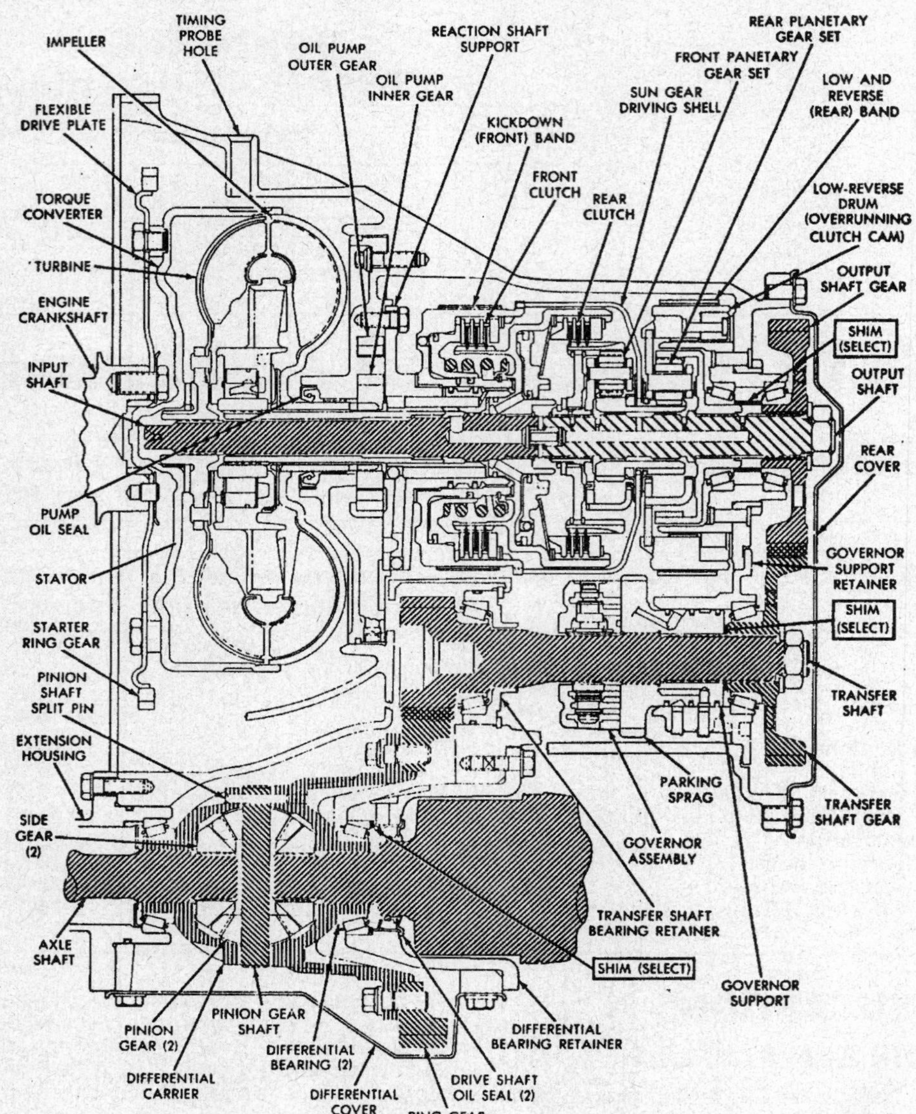

Fig. 1 Cross-sectional view of 31TH automatic transaxle

ADJUSTMENTS

BANDS

KICKDOWN BAND

1. Loosen locknut and back off nut approximately five turns, **Fig. 3.**
2. Ensure adjusting screw turns freely in transaxle case.
3. **Torque** band adjusting screw to 72 inch lbs.
4. Back off adjusting screw 2¼ turns. Tighten locknut to specifications while preventing adjusting screw from turning.

LOW-REVERSE BAND

1. Loosen locknut and back off nut approximately five turns.
2. **Torque** adjusting nut to 41 inch lbs.
3. Back off adjusting nut 3½ turns.
4. Tighten locknut to specifications.

GEARSHIFT LINKAGE

1. Set parking brake and remove floor console.
2. Place gear selector lever in P position and unsnap collar at shifter cable.
3. Move gear selector lever on transaxle to park position, then ensure both shifter lever and transaxle are in park position.
4. Rotate collar on shift cable adjuster until it seats against plastic housing, **Fig. 4. Collar must seat against plastic housing to achieve required detent lock position.**
5. Inspect adjustment as follows:
   a. Detent position for neutral and drive should be within limits of hand lever gate stops.
   b. Key start must occur only when shift lever is in neutral or park positions.

THROTTLE PRESSURE LINKAGE

1. Ensure engine is at operating temperature.
2. Release cross-lock on cable assembly by pulling upward.
3. Ensure cable is able to slide freely towards engine, against its stop.
4. Move transaxle throttle control lever fully clockwise, against its internal stop.
5. Press cross-lock downward into locked position.
6. Ensure proper operation of throttle cable.

IN-VEHICLE REPAIRS

VALVE BODY, REPLACE

1. Loosen transaxle oil pan mounting bolts and allow transaxle to drain into suitable container. Remove oil pan.
2. Remove mounting screws and oil filter.
3. Remove E-clip using suitable screwdriver and parking rod.
4. Remove mounting bolts, valve body and governor oil tubes.
5. Reverse procedure to install, noting the following:
   a. Tighten valve body mounting bolts to specifications.
   b. Install using Mopar Silicone Rubber Adhesive Sealant to oil pan. **Do not seal oil pan with RTV.**

GOVERNOR & TRANSFER SHAFT OIL SEAL, REPLACE

When cleaning or assembling the governor assembly, ensure governor valves move freely in governor body bores.

1. Remove mounting bolts and rear cover.
2. Remove transfer shaft gear mounting nut using transfer shaft gear tool No. L-4434, or equivalent, **Fig. 5.**
3. Remove transfer shaft gear and shim

CONDITION	POSSIBLE CAUSES	CORRECTION
HARSH ENGAGEMENT (FROM NEUTRAL TO DRIVE OR REVERSE)	1. Fluid Level Low	1. Add Fluid
	2. Throttle Linkage Misadjusted	2. Adjust linkage - setting may be too long.
	3. Excessive Pinion Backlash	3. Correct as needed.
	4. Hydraulic Pressure Incorrect	4. Check pressure. Remove, overhaul or adjust valve body as needed.
	5. Band Misadjusted.	5. Adjust rear band.
	6. Valve Body Check Balls Missing.	6. Inspect valve body for proper check ball installation.
	7. Clutch, band or planetary component Damaged.	7. Remove, disassemble and repair transmission as necessary.
	8. Converter Clutch (if equipped) Faulty.	8. Replace converter and flush cooler and line before installing new converter.
DELAYED ENGAGEMENT (FROM NEUTRAL TO DRIVE OR REVERSE)	1. Fluid Level Low.	1. Correct level and check for leaks.
	2. Filter Clogged.	2. Change filter.
	3. Gearshift Linkage Misadjusted.	3. Adjust linkage and repair linkage if worn or damaged.
	4. Rear Band Misadjusted.	4. Adjust band.
	5. Valve Body Filter Plugged.	5. Replace fluid and filter. If oil pan and old fluid were full of clutch disc material and/or metal particles, overhaul will be necessary.
	6. Oil Pump Gears Worn/Damaged.	6. Remove transmission and replace oil pump.
	7. Hydraulic Pressure Incorrect.	7. Perform pressure test, remove transmission and repair as needed.
	8. Reaction Shaft Seal Rings Worn/Broken.	8. Remove transmission, remove oil pump and replace seal rings.
	9. Rear Clutch/Input Shaft, Rear Clutch Seal Rings Damaged.	9. Remove and disassemble transmission and repair as necessary.
	10. Governor Valve Stuck.	10. Remove and inspect governor components. Replace worn or damaged parts.
	11. Regulator Valve Stuck.	11. Clean.

CR50299012140l0X

Fig. 2 Transaxle troubleshooting chart (Part 1 of 7)

CONDITION	POSSIBLE CAUSES	CORRECTION
NO DRIVE RANGE (REVERSE OK)	1. Fluid Level Low.	1. Add fluid and check for leaks if drive is restored.
	2. Gearshift Linkage/Cable Loose/Misadjusted.	2. Repair or replace linkage components.
	3. Rear Clutch Burnt.	3. Remove and disassemble transmission and rear clutch and seals. Repair/replace worn or damaged parts as needed.
	4. Valve Body Malfunction.	4. Remove and disassemble valve body. Replace assembly if any valves or bores are damaged.
	5. Transmission Overrunning Clutch Broken.	5. Remove and disassemble transmission. Replace overrunning clutch.
	6. Input Shaft Seal Rings Worn/ Damaged.	6. Remove and disassemble transmission. Replace seal rings and any other worn or damaged parts.
	7. Front Planetary Failed Broken.	7. Remove and repair.
NO DRIVE OR REVERSE (VEHICLE WILL NOT MOVE)	1. Fluid Level Low.	1. Add fluid and check for leaks if drive is restored.
	2. Gearshift Linkage/Cable Loose/Misadjusted.	2. Inspect, adjust and reassemble linkage as needed. Replace worn/damaged parts.
	3. Filter Plugged.	3. Remove and disassemble transmission. Repair or replace failed components as needed. Replace filter. If filter and fluid contained clutch material or metal particles, an overhaul may be necessary. Perform lube flow test. Flush oil. Replace cooler as necessary.
	4. Oil Pump Damaged.	4. Perform pressure test to confirm low pressure. Replace pump body assembly if necessary.
	5. Valve Body Malfunctioned.	5. Check press and inspect valve body. Replace valve body (as assembly) if any valve or bore is damaged. Clean and reassemble correctly if all parts are in good condition.
	6. Transmission Internal Component Damaged.	6. Remove and disassemble transmission. Repair or replace failed components as needed. Remove and disassemble transmission. Repair or replace failed components as needed.
	7. Park Sprag not Releasing - Check Stall Speed, Worn/Damaged/Stuck.	7. Remove, disassemble, repair.
	8. Torque Converter Damage.	8. Inspect and replace as required.

CR50299012140 20X

Fig. 2 Transaxle troubleshooting chart (Part 2 of 7)

using transfer shaft gear puller tool No. L-4407A, or equivalent, **Fig. 6.**

4. Remove governor support retainer and low-reverse band anchor pin.
5. Remove governor.
6. Remove transfer shaft retainer snap ring.
7. Remove transfer shaft and retainer using transfer shaft and bearing retainer removal tool No. L-4512, or equivalent, and suitable puller.
8. Remove transfer shaft retainer.
9. Remove transfer shaft retainer oil seal using suitable screwdriver.
10. Tap oil seal into shaft retainer using suitable tool.
11. Reverse procedure to install. Tighten transfer shaft gear mounting nut to specifications.

TRANSAXLE

REPLACE

The transaxle and converter must be removed as an assembly to prevent damage to the torque converter driveplate, pump bushing and oil seal. **The driveplate will not support a load. Do not allow the weight of the transaxle to rest on the driveplate.**

1. Pull Power Distribution Center (PDC) up and out of holding bracket. Position PDC aside.
2. Remove battery heat shield, battery and battery tray.
3. Disconnect cruise control, if equipped.
4. Disconnect vehicle speed sensor wiring, neutral safety switch and torque converter control wiring at transaxle.
5. Disconnect gear shift cable end from transaxle shift lever and remove bracket mounting bolt.
6. Remove throttle pressure control cable from lever and bracket mounting bolts.
7. Remove dipstick tube.
8. Remove transaxle cooler lines. Plug lines.
9. Remove throttle pressure control cable support bracket bolts, upper bellhousing bolts and upper starter bolt.
10. Install engine bridge fixture and support engine.
11. Raise and support vehicle, then remove front wheels.
12. Remove both front driveshafts. **When installing driveshafts, new driveshaft retaining clips must be used. Failure to use new clips may result in disengagement of inner constant-velocity joint.**
13. Remove exhaust flex joint to exhaust manifold mounting bolts and disconnect exhaust pipe from manifold.
14. Remove transaxle to rear lateral bending strut.
15. Remove lower starter bolt and lower dust shield screw.
16. Rotate engine clockwise and remove torque converter mounting bolts. Mark converter to flex plate for installation.
17. Support transaxle using suitable transaxle jack.
18. Remove through bolt, mounting bolt and lefthand transaxle mount.
19. Remove transaxle rear engine bolt.
20. Carefully work transaxle and torque converter rearward off engine block dowels and disengage converter hub from crankshaft end. **Attach small C-clamp to edge of bellhousing to hold torque converter in place during transaxle removal.**
21. Reverse procedure to install.

SHIFT LOCK SYSTEM

ADJUSTMENTS

1. Remove console.
2. Remove gearshift knob set screw and knob.
3. Remove gearshift indicator bezel and indicator lamp.
4. Install gearshift knob.
5. Place shifter in Park position.
6. **On 1998–99 models,** place ignition in Lock or Accessory position. **If cable is out of adjustment, grasp slug on interlock cable with suitable pair of pliers and pull back on cable. This will allow ignition to be placed in position.**
7. Ensure interlock cable is completely seated into shifter interlock lever and ignition is in Lock or Accessory position.
8. Pry up adjuster lock on interlock cable. **Spring on interlock cable should automatically adjust for slack in cable.**
9. Snap interlock cable adjuster lock onto cable.
10. Remove gearshift knob set screw and knob.
11. **On 2000–01 models,** adjust interlock cable/system by prying up on cable adjuster lock to release and allow cable to self adjust. Lock cable adjustment by pressing down on adjuster lock until bottomed at cable housing.
12. **On all models,** install indicator lamp, gearshift bezel and gearshift knob.

CONDITION	POSSIBLE CAUSES	CORRECTION
SHIFTS DELAYED OR ERRATIC (ALSO SHIFTS HARSH AT TIMES)	1. Fluid Level Low/High.	1. Correct fluid level and check for leaks if low.
	2. Fluid Filter Clogged.	2. Replace filter. If filter and fluid contained clutch material or metal particles, an overhaul may be necessary. Perform lube flow test.
	3. Throttle Linkage Misadjusted.	3. Adjust linkage as described in service section.
	4. Throttle Linkage Binding.	4. Check cable for binding. Check for return to closed throttle at transmission.
	5. Gearshift Linkage/Cable Misadjusted.	5. Adjust linkage/cable as described in service section.
	6. Governor Valve Sticking.	6. Inspect, clean or repair.
	7. Governor Seal Rings Worn/ Damaged.	7. Inspect/replace.
	8. Clutch or Servo Failure.	8. Remove valve body and air test clutch, and band servo operation. Disassemble and repair transmission as needed.
	9. Front Band Misadjusted.	9. Adjust band.
	10. Pump Suction Passage Leak.	10. Check for excessive foam on dipstick after normal driving. Check for loose pump bolts, defective gasket. Replace pump assembly if needed.
NO REVERSE (D RANGES OK)	1. Gearshift Linkage/Cable Misadjusted/Damaged.	1. Repair or replace linkage parts as needed.
	2. Rear Band Misadjusted/Worn.	2. Adjust band; replace.
	3. Valve Body Malfunction.	3. Remove and service valve body. Replace valve body if any valves or valve bores are worn or damaged.
	4. Rear Servo Malfunction.	4. Remove and disassemble transmission. Replace worn/damaged servo parts as necessary.
	5. Direct Clutch in Overdrive Worn	5. Disassemble overdrive. Replace worn or damaged parts.
	6. Front Clutch Burnt.	6. Remove and disassemble transmission. Replace worn, damaged clutch parts as required.
HAS FIRST/REVERSE ONLY (NO 1-2 OR 2-3 UPSHIFT)	1. Governor Valve, Shaft, Weights or Body Damaged/Stuck.	1. Remove governor assembly and clean or repair as necessary.
	2. Valve Body Malfunction.	2. Stuck 1-2 shift valve or governor plug.
	3. Front Servo/Kickdown Band Damaged/Burned.	3. Repair/replace.
MOVES IN 2ND OR 3RD GEAR, ABRUPTLY DOWNSHIFTS TO LOW	1. Valve Body Malfunction.	1. Remove, clean and inspect. Look for stuck 1-2 valve or governor plug.
	2. Governor Valve Sticking.	2. Remove, clean and inspect. Replace faulty parts.

CR5029901214030X

Fig. 2 Transaxle troubleshooting chart (Part 3 of 7)

CONDITION	POSSIBLE CAUSES	CORRECTION
NO LOW GEAR (MOVES IN 2ND OR 3RD GEAR ONLY)	1. Governor Valve Sticking.	1. Remove governor, clean, inspect and repair as required.
	2. Valve Body Malfunction.	2. Remove, clean and inspect. Look for sticking 1-2 shift valve, 2-3 shift valve, governor plug or broken springs.
	3. Front Servo Piston Cocked in Bore.	3. Inspect servo and repair as required.
	4. Front Band Linkage Malfunction	4. Inspect linkage and look for bind in linkage.
NO KICKDOWN OR NORMAL DOWNSHIFT	1. Throttle Linkage Misadjusted.	1. Adjust linkage.
	2. Accelerator Pedal Travel Restricted.	2. Floor mat under pedal, accelerator cable worn or brackets bent.
	3. Governor/Valve Body Hydraulic Pressures Too High or Too Low Due to Sticking Governor, Valve Body Malfunction or Incorrect Hydraulic Control Pressure Adjustments.	3. Perform hydraulic pressure tests to determine cause and repair as required. Correct valve body pressure adjustments as required.
	4. Valve Body Malfunction.	4. Perform hydraulic pressure tests to determine cause and repair as required. Correct valve body pressure adjustments as required.
	5. Valve Body Malfunction.	5. Sticking 1-2, 2-3 shift valves, governor plugs, 3-4 solenoid, 3-4 shift valve, 3-4 timing valve.
STUCK IN LOW GEAR (WILL NOT UPSHIFT)	1. Throttle Linkage Misadjusted/ Stuck.	1. Adjust linkage and repair linkage if worn or damaged. Check for binding cable.
	2. Gearshift Linkage Misadjusted.	2. Adjust linkage and repair linkage if worn or damaged.
	3. Governor/Valve Body, Governor Valve Stuck Closed; Loose Output Shaft Support or Governor Housing Bolts, Leaking Seal Rings or Valve Body Problem (i.e., Stuck 1- 2 Shift Valve/Gov. Plug).	3. Check line and governor pressures to determine cause. Correct as required.
	4. Front Band Out of Adjustment.	4. Adjust Band.
	5. Clutch or Servo Malfunction.	5. Air pressure check operation of clutches and bands. Repair faulty component.
CREEPS IN NEUTRAL	1. Gearshift Linkage Misadjusted.	1. Adjust linkage.
	2. Rear Clutch Dragging/Warped Welded.	2. Disassemble and repair.
	3. Valve Body Malfunction.	3. Perform hydraulic pressure test to determine cause and repair as required.

CR5029901214040X

Fig. 2 Transaxle troubleshooting chart (Part 4 of 7)

CONDITION	POSSIBLE CAUSES	CORRECTION
BUZZING NOISE	1. Fluid Level Low	1. Add fluid and check for leaks.
	2. Shift Cable Misassembled.	2. Route cable away from engine and bell housing.
	3. Valve Body Misassembled.	3. Remove, disassemble, inspect valve body. Reassemble correctly if necessary. Replace assembly if valves or springs are damaged. Check for loose bolts or screws.
	4. Pump Passages Leaking	4. Check pump for porous casting, scores on mating surfaces and excess rotor clearance. Repair as required. Loose pump bolts.
	5. Cooling System Cooler Plugged.	5. Flow check cooler circuit. Repair as needed.
	6. Overrunning Clutch Damaged.	6. Replace clutch.
SLIPS IN REVERSE ONLY	1. Fluid Level Low.	1. Add fluid and check for leaks.
	2. Gearshift Linkage Misadjusted.	2. Adjust linkage.
	3. Rear Band Misadjusted.	3. Adjust band.
	4. Rear Band Worn.	4. Replace as required.
	5. Hydraulic Pressure Too Low.	5. Perform hydraulic pressure tests to determine cause.
	6. Rear Servo Leaking.	6. Air pressure check clutch-servo operation and repair as required.
	7. Band Linkage Binding.	7. Inspect and repair as required.
SLIPS IN FORWARD DRIVE RANGES	1. Fluid Level Low.	1. Add fluid and check for leaks.
	2. Fluid Foaming.	2. Check for high oil level, bad pump gasket or seals, dirt between pump halves and loose pump bolts. Replace pump if necessary.
	3. Throttle Linkage Misadjusted.	3. Adjust linkage.
	4. Gearshift Linkage Misadjusted.	4. Adjust linkage.
	5. Rear Clutch Worn.	5. Inspect and replace as needed.
	6. Low Hydraulic Pressure Due to Worn Pump, Incorrect Control Pressure Adjustments, Valve Body Warpage or Malfunction, Sticking Governor, Leaking Seal Rings, Clutch Seals Leaking, Servo Leaks, Clogged Filter or Cooler Lines	6. Perform hydraulic and air pressure tests to determine cause.
	7. Rear Clutch Malfunction, Leaking Seals or Worn Plates.	7. Air pressure check clutch-servo operation and repair as required.
	8. Overrunning Clutch Worn, Not Holding (Slips in 1 Only).	8. Replace Clutch.
SLIPS IN LOW GEAR "D" ONLY, BUT NOT IN 1 POSITION	Overrunning Clutch Faulty.	Replace overrunning clutch.

CR5029901214050X

Fig. 2 Transaxle troubleshooting chart (Part 5 of 7)

SHIFT INTERLOCK CABLE, REPLACE

1. Remove console.
2. Remove gearshift knob set screw and knob.
3. Remove gearshift bezel and indicator lamp.
4. Pry up adjuster lock on interlock cable, remove cable core from plastic cam and release cable from shifter bracket.
5. Pull cable up and out of gearshift assembly.
6. Remove lower steering column cover and liner.
7. Lift top cover and cluster bezel until clips disengage to provide clearance.
8. Place ignition in On position.
9. Depress cylinder button while rotating cylinder to disengage it from column using suitable screwdriver in lower shroud access hole.
10. Remove upper and lower shrouds.
11. Disconnect and remove interlock cable.
12. Reverse procedure to install. Adjust interlock cable as described under "Adjustments."

SHIFT INTERLOCK, REPLACE

1. Remove lower steering column cover and liner.
2. Lift top cover and cluster bezel until clips disengage to provide clearance.
3. Place ignition in On position.
4. Depress cylinder button while rotating cylinder to disengage it from column using suitable screwdriver in lower shroud access hole.
5. Remove upper and lower shrouds.
6. Disconnect interlock cable from interlock assembly.
7. Remove mounting screws and interlock assembly.
8. Reverse procedure to install. **Torque** interlock assembly mounting screws to 21 inch lbs.

CONDITION	POSSIBLE CAUSES	CORRECTION
GROWLING, GRATING OR SCRAPING NOISES	1. Drive Plate Broken.	1. Replace.
	2. Torque Converter Bolts Hitting Dust Shield.	2. Dust shield bent. Replace or repair.
	3. Planetary Gear Set Broken/Seized.	3. Check for debris in oil pan and repair as required.
	4. Overrunning Clutch Worn/Broken.	4. Inspect and check for debris in oil pan. Repair as required.
	5. Oil Pump Components Scored/Binding.	5. Remove, inspect and repair as required.
	6. Output Shaft Bearing or Bushing Damaged.	6. Remove, inspect and repair as required.
	7. Clutch Operation Faulty.	7. Perform air pressure check and repair as required.
	8. Front and Rear Bands Misadjusted.	8. Adjust bands.
DRAGS OR LOCKS UP	1. Fluid Level Low.	1. Check and adjust level.
	2. Clutch Dragging/Failed	2. Air pressure check clutch operation and repair as required.
	3. Front or Rear Band Misadjusted.	3. Adjust bands.
	4. Case Leaks Internally.	4. Check for leakage between passages in case.
	5. Servo Band or Linkage Malfunction.	5. Air pressure check servo operation and repair as required.
	6. Overrunning Clutch Worn.	6. Remove and inspect clutch. Repair as required.
	7. Planetary Gears Broken.	7. Remove, inspect and repair as required (look for debris in oil pan).
WHINE/NOISE RELATED TO ENGINE SPEED	1. Fluid Level Low.	1. Add fluid and check for leaks.
	2. Shift Cable Incorrect Routing.	2. Check shift cable for correct routing. Should not touch engine or bell housing.
TORQUE CONVERTER LOCKS UP IN SECOND AND/OR THIRD GEAR	Lockup Solenoid, Relay or Wiring Shorted/Open.	Test solenoid, relay and wiring for continuity, shorts or grounds. Replace solenoid and relay if faulty. Repair wiring and connectors as necessary.
HARSH 1-2 OR 2-3 SHIFTS	Lockup Solenoid Malfunction.	Remove valve body and replace solenoid assembly.
NO START IN PARK OR NEUTRAL	1. Gearshift Linkage/Cable Misadjusted.	1. Adjust linkage/cable.
	2. Neutral Switch Wire Open/Cut.	2. Check continuity with test lamp. Repair as required.
	3. Neutral Switch Faulty.	3. Refer to service section for test and replacement procedure.
	4. Neutral Switch Connect Faulty.	4. Connectors spread open. Repair.
	5. Valve Body Manual Lever Assembly Bent/Worn/Broken.	5. Inspect lever assembly and replace if damaged.

CR5029901214060X

Fig. 2 Transaxle troubleshooting chart (Part 6 of 7)

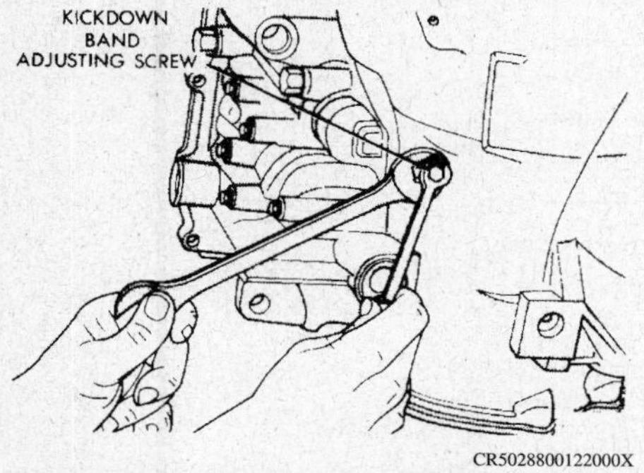

Fig. 3 Kickdown band adjustment

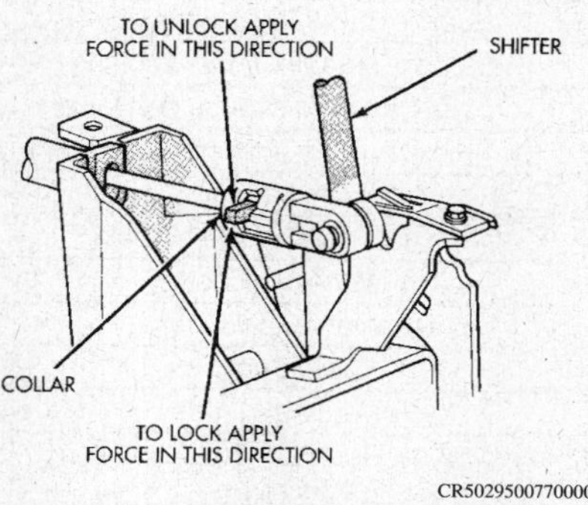

Fig. 4 Gearshift linkage adjustment

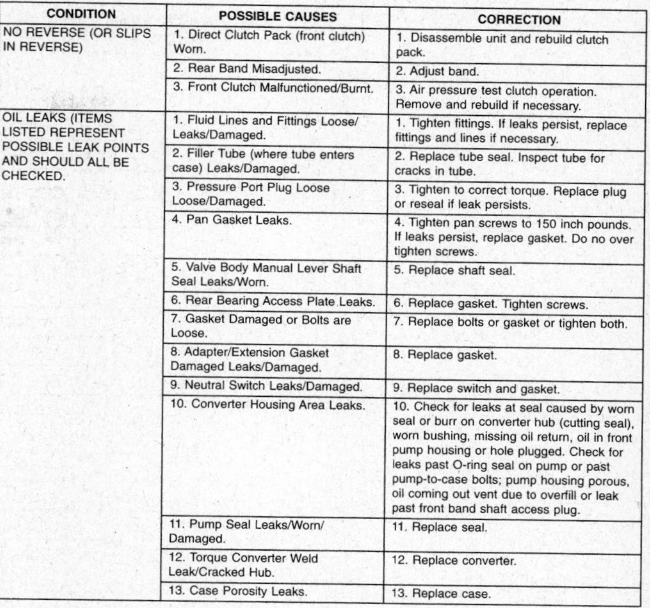

CONDITION	POSSIBLE CAUSES	CORRECTION
NO REVERSE (OR SLIPS IN REVERSE)	1. Direct Clutch Pack (front clutch) Worn.	1. Disassemble unit and rebuild clutch pack.
	2. Rear Band Misadjusted.	2. Adjust band.
	3. Front Clutch Malfunctioned/Burnt.	3. Air pressure test clutch operation. Remove and rebuild if necessary.
OIL LEAKS (ITEMS LISTED REPRESENT POSSIBLE LEAK POINTS AND SHOULD ALL BE CHECKED.	1. Fluid Lines and Fittings Loose/Leaks/Damaged.	1. Tighten fittings. If leaks persist, replace fittings and lines if necessary.
	2. Filler Tube (where tube enters case) Leaks/Damaged.	2. Replace tube seal. Inspect tube for cracks in tube.
	3. Pressure Port Plug Loose Loose/Damaged.	3. Tighten to correct torque. Replace plug or reseal if leak persists.
	4. Pan Gasket Leaks.	4. Tighten pan screws to 150 inch pounds. If leaks persist, replace gasket. Do no over tighten screws.
	5. Valve Body Manual Lever Shaft Seal Leaks/Worn.	5. Replace shaft seal.
	6. Rear Bearing Access Plate Leaks.	6. Replace gasket. Tighten screws.
	7. Gasket Damaged or Bolts are Loose.	7. Replace bolts or gasket or tighten both.
	8. Adapter/Extension Gasket Damaged Leaks/Damaged.	8. Replace gasket.
	9. Neutral Switch Leaks/Damaged.	9. Replace switch and gasket.
	10. Converter Housing Area Leaks.	10. Check for leaks at seal caused by worn seal or burr on converter hub (cutting seal), worn bushing, missing oil return, oil in front pump housing or hole plugged. Check for leaks past O-ring seal on pump or past pump-to-case bolts; pump housing porous, oil coming out vent due to overfill or leak past front band shaft access plug.
	11. Pump Seal Leaks/Worn/Damaged.	11. Replace seal.
	12. Torque Converter Weld Leak/Cracked Hub.	12. Replace converter.
	13. Case Porosity Leaks.	13. Replace case.

CR5029901214070X

Fig. 2 Transaxle troubleshooting chart (Part 7 of 7)

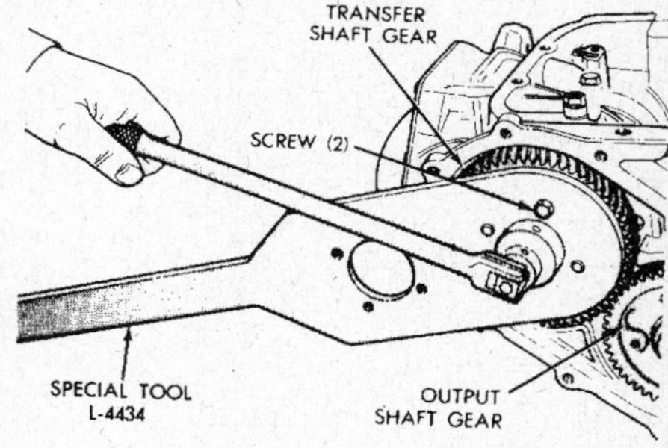

Fig. 5 Transfer shaft gear nut removal

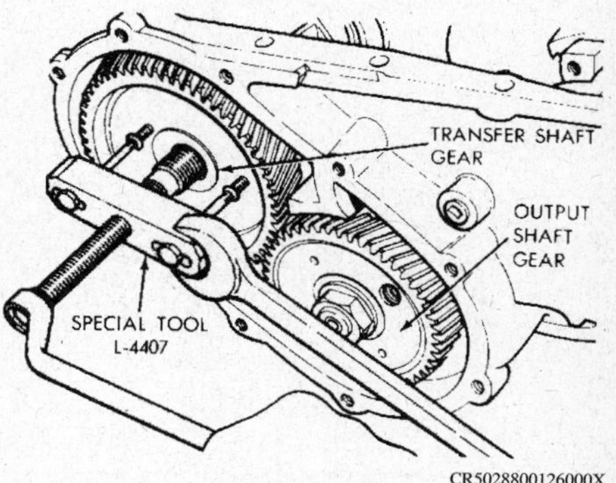

Fig. 6 Transfer shaft gear removal

TIGHTENING SPECIFICATIONS

Year	Component	Torque/Ft. Lbs.
1998–2001	Bellhousing Cover	108①
	Connector Assembly Cooler Line	21
	Cooler Hose Connector To Radiator	108①
	Differential Bearing Retainer To Case	21
	Differential Cover To Case	14
	Differential Extension Housing To Case	21
	Differential Ring Gear	70
	Flexplate To Crankshaft	70
	Flexplate To Torque Converter	50
	Front Motor Mount	40
	Governor Counterweight	21
	Governor To Support	60①
	Kickdown Band Adjustment Locknut	35
	Left Motor Mount	40
	Low Reverse Band Adjustment Locknut	10
	Lower Bellhousing Cover	30
	Manual Cable To Transaxle Case	21
	Manual Control Lever	108①
	Neutral Safety Switch	25
	Output Shaft Nut	200
	Pressure Check Plug	45①
	Pump To Case	23
	Reaction Shaft	21
	Rear Cover To Case	14
	Reverse Band Shaft Plug	60①
	Speedometer To Extension	60①
	Starter To Transaxle Bellhousing	40
	Throttle Cable To Transaxle Case	108①
	Throttle Lever To Transaxle Shaft	108①
	Transaxle Oil Pan To Case	14
	Transaxle To Cylinder Block	70
	Transaxle To Engine	70
	Transfer Shaft Gear	200
	Valve Body	108①
	Valve Body Filter	45①
	Valve Body Reverse Band Adjusting Locknut	10
	Valve Body	45①
	Valve Body Sprag Retainer To Transfer Case	21
	Valve Body Transfer Plate	45①
	Valve Body Transfer Plate To Case	108①

① — Inch lbs.

41TE 4-Speed Electronic Automatic Transaxle

NOTE: On Air Bag Equipped Models, Refer To "Air Bag System Precautions" Located In The Front Of This Manual For System Disarming & Arming Procedures.

NOTE: Refer To "Computer Relearn Procedures" Located In The Front Of This Manual When Battery Power To The Computer Has Been Interrupted.

NOTE: Prior To Performing Any Service Operations Listed In This Section, Consult The "Technical Service Bulletins" Section For Related Information.

INDEX

PRECAUTIONS

AIR BAG SYSTEMS

Refer to "Air Bag System Precautions" in the front of this manual for system disarming and arming procedures.

BATTERY GROUND CABLE

Prior to service, disconnect battery ground cable and isolate as required.

IDENTIFICATION

During production, the transaxle identification number (TIN) is stamped on a boss located on the transaxle housing. In addition to the TIN, each transaxle carries an assembly part number which is on a pad just above the oil pan at the rear of the transaxle. This assembly number must be referenced when ordering transaxle replacement parts.

DESCRIPTION

The 41TE electronic four-speed transaxle is a fully adaptive transaxle. The 41TE transaxle uses feedback sensors to adjust functions on a real time basis, similar to electronic anti-lock brake controls.

The 41TE transaxle provides four forward speeds with ratios of 2.84:1, 1.57:1, 1.00:1 and .069:1, and with torque converter lock-up available in second, direct, or overdrive gear. Reverse ratio is 2.21:1. The 41TE consists of three multiple disc input clutches, two multiple disc grounded clutches, four hydraulic accumulators and two planetary gear sets to provide four forward speeds and reverse ratio, **Fig. 1.** Electrical solenoids provide the transaxles shifting control. Sensors on the transaxle send control inputs to the electronic control unit located under the hood in a potted, diecast aluminum housing. The system can be diagnosed by accessing information from the electronic control unit memory. The transaxle and differential sump have a common oil sump with a communicating opening between the two.

TROUBLESHOOTING

Before attempting any repair on the 41TE transaxles, general engine performance, transmission fluid level and shift linkage must first be checked and adjusted, as required. Diagnosis of the Powertrain Control Module (PCM) must also be performed in the following steps: verification of complaint, verification of any related symptoms, symptom analysis, problem isolation, repair of isolated problem and verification of proper operation.

MAINTENANCE

Refer to "Lubricant Data" chart in the appropriate chassis chapter of this manual for transmission fluid specifications.

FLUID CHECK

Oil level should be checked every six months as follows:

1. Start engine and let idle with transaxle in Park or Neutral position for at least one minute.
2. Oil level, when properly filled, will read near Add mark when oil is cold, (70°F) and in Hot zone when oil is at normal operating temperature (180°F).
3. Adjust level as required.

FLUID CHANGE

This procedure has been revised by Technical Service Bulletins.

On Breeze, Cirrus and Stratus models built after Sept. 7, 1998, Sebring Convertible models built after May 21, 1999, and 2002 Neon transaxle is filled with fill for life ATF +4, Type 9602. Even if fluid discolor, fluid should not be change unless accompanied by burnt smell and/or shift quality deterioration. Under severe conditions the fluid and filter should be changes every 48,000 miles.

On models other than previously list, fluid and filter changes are not required for average passenger vehicle usage. If the vehicle is subjected to severe usage, the fluid and filter should be changed at 15,000 mile intervals. The magnet on the inside of the oil pan should also be cleaned with a clean, dry cloth at this time.

Change the fluid and filter as follows:

1. Raise and support vehicle, then place

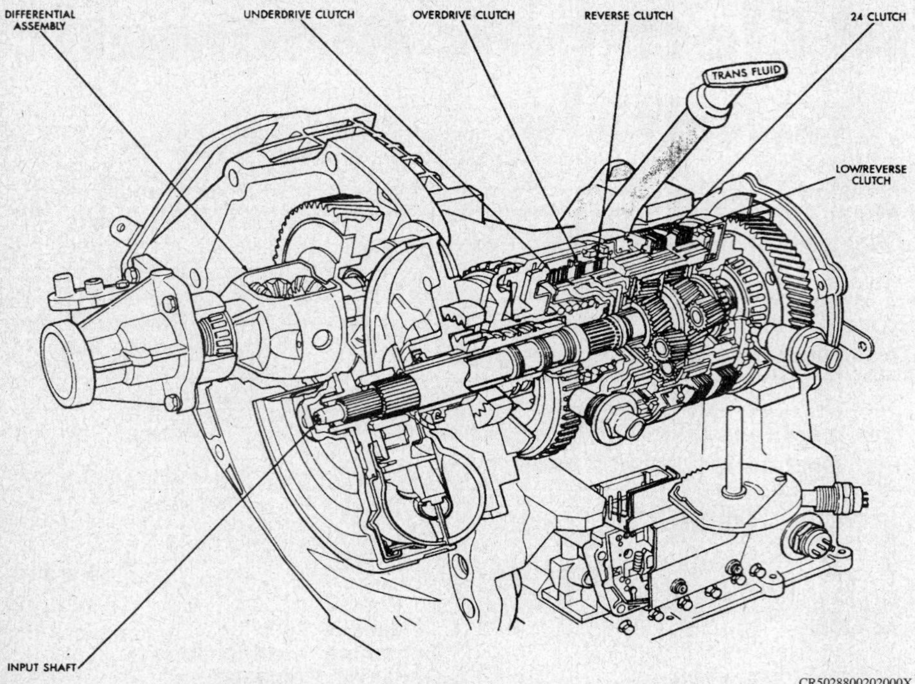

Fig. 1 Cross-sectional view of transaxle

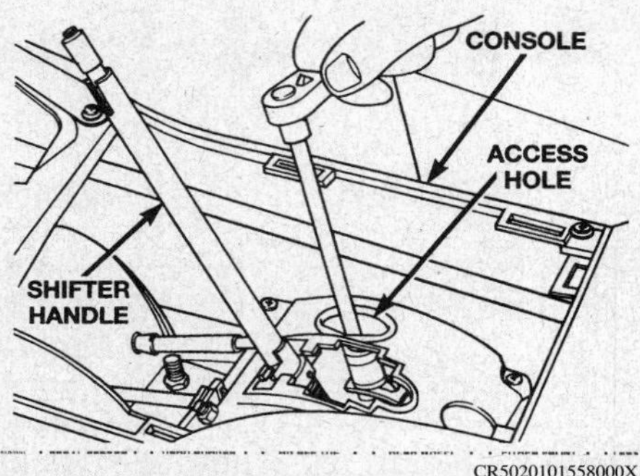

Fig. 2 Shift cable adjustment lever nut. Except Neon

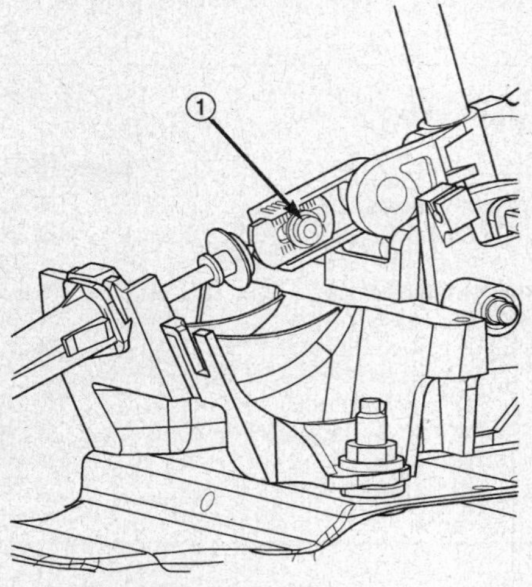

Fig. 3 Shift cable adjustment lever screw. Neon

suitable wide drain pan container under transaxle oil pan.

2. Loosen pan bolts and tap pan at one corner to break seal and allow fluid to drain. Remove pan.
3. Install new filter and O-ring on valve body.
4. Clean oil pan and magnet.
5. Install oil pan using Mopar Silicone Adhesive sealant, or equivalent. **Do not seal oil pan with RTV.**
6. Tighten pan mounting bolts to specifications.
7. Add four quarts of appropriate automatic transmission fluid through fill tube.
8. Start engine and allow to idle for at least one minute.
9. With parking and service brakes applied, move selector lever through range, pausing momentarily at each position. Return lever to P or N position.
10. Add fluid to bring level 1/8 inch below Add mark.
11. Check fluid level after transaxle is at normal operating temperature.

ADJUSTMENTS

GEARSHIFT LINKAGE

1. Set parking brake, then remove gearshift knob set screw and knob.
2. Remove gearshift selector bezel and lamp wiring.
3. Install gearshift knob and set screw.
4. **On all models except Neon,** place gearshift in P park position and loosen gearshift cable adjuster nut at shifter **Fig. 2.**
5. **On Neon models,** place gearshift in P park position and loosen gearshift cable adjustment screw at shifter, **Fig. 3.**
6. **On all models,** ensure shifter and transaxle are in P park position, then tighten nut at shifter
7. Detent position for neutral and drive should be with in limits of hand lever gate stops.
8. Key start must occur only when shift lever is in park or neutral positions.

IN-VEHICLE REPAIRS

SOLENOID, REPLACE

1. Remove air cleaner.
2. Remove Transmission Control Module (TCM) **Fig. 4.**
3. Disconnect and remove input speed sensor, **Fig. 5.**
4. Disconnect transmission cooler lines. Cap fitting.
5. Disconnect and remove solenoid pressure switch connector to transaxle case bolts, **Fig. 6.**
6. Remove solenoid pressure switch gasket.
7. Reverse procedures to install.

VALVE BODY, REPLACE

1. Raise and support vehicle.
2. Drain transaxle fluid as described under "Maintenance."
3. Remove air cleaner assembly.
4. **On Neon models,** remove throttle body assembly.
5. **On all models,** disconnect gearshift cable from manual valve lever.
6. Remove mounting bolts and oil pan.
7. Remove oil filter and valve body mounting bolts.
8. Push park rod rollers from guide bracket and remove valve body, **Fig. 7.**
9. Reverse procedure to install, noting the following:
   a. Guide park rollers into guide bracket.
   b. Tighten valve body mounting bolts to specifications.
   c. Install oil pan using Mopar Silicone Adhesive sealant, or equivalent. **Do not seal oil pan with RTV.**
   d. Tighten oil pan mounting bolts to specifications.

TRANSMISSION RANGE SENSOR (TRS), REPLACE

1. Disconnect TRS electrical connector.
2. Remove valve body as outlined under "Valve Body, Replace."
3. Remove manual shaft mounting screw and seal, then slide TRS off manual valve shaft.
4. Reverse procedure to install.

Fig. 4 Transmission control module

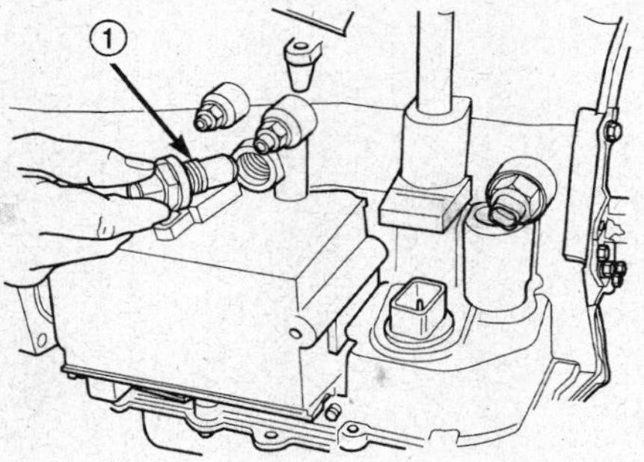

Fig. 5 Input speed sensor removal

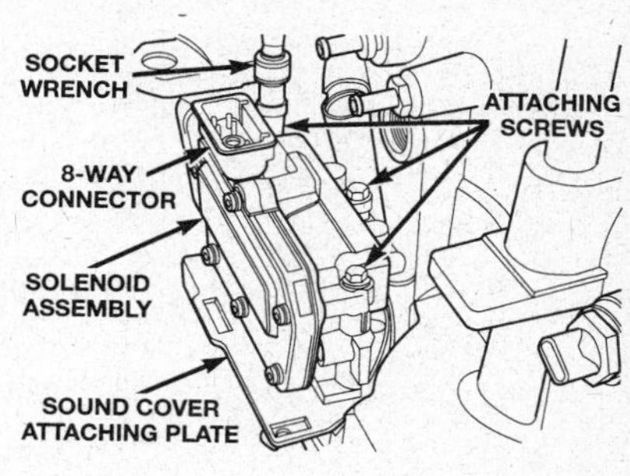

Fig. 6 Solenoid removal

TRANSAXLE

REPLACE

BREEZE, CIRRUS & 1998–2000 SEBRING CONVERTIBLE & STRATUS

1. Remove air cleaner duct.
2. Remove transaxle control module, wiring and solenoid pack connector.
3. Remove dipstick tube and oil cooler lines, then the shift cable at lever and transaxle clamp.
4. Install engine support fixture and remove lefthand upper transaxle mounting bolts.
5. Raise and support vehicle, then remove front wheels and both drive shafts.
6. Remove splash shields and remaining lefthand upper mount bolts.
7. Remove engine oil filter, starter and wiring.
8. Remove front motor mount bracket and rear mount bracket through-bolt.
9. Remove center member bolts, then the mounting bolts and rear mount bracket.
10. Remove radiator lower crossmember, then front and rear lateral bending strut brackets.
11. Remove flex plate cover.
12. Rotate lower engine pulley to line up converter bolts and remove converter bolts. **Mark converter for installation.**
13. Remove crank position sensor, if equipped.
14. Remove transaxle wiring, then loosen righthand side steering gear bolts and side K-frame bolts.
15. Remove sway bar mounts.
16. Support transaxle with suitable transmission jack and safety chain.
17. Remove upper and lower bell housing bolts.
18. Move K-frame rearward, lower and remove transaxle.
19. Reverse procedure to install.

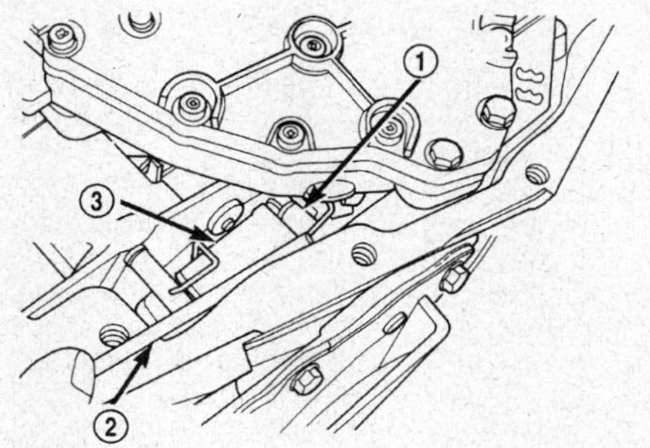

Fig. 7 Park rod rollers removal

2001–02 SEBRING CONVERTIBLE & STRATUS SEDANS

1. Remove air cleaner.
2. Remove dipstick tube. Plug dipstick tube hole.
3. Cut transaxle oil cooler lines off flush with fitting using suitable blade or hose cutter. Plug lines and fittings.
4. Disconnect solenoid/pressure switch assembly and transaxle range sensor connectors.
5. Disconnect input and output speed sensors connectors.
6. Disconnect manual valve lever shift cable and bracket.
7. Disconnect crankshaft position sensor.
8. Remove throttle body support bracket.
9. Disconnect oxygen sensor harness retainer.
10. Remove transaxle rear mount bracket.
11. Remove starter motor upper bracket.
12. Raise and support vehicle.
13. Remove halfshafts as described in "Front Wheel Drive Axles" chapter.
14. Remove mounting bolts, rear transaxle mount and bracket.
15. Remove mounting bolts, front transaxle mount and bracket.
16. Remove lower bracket and starter motor.
17. Remove dust shield and torque converter mounting bolts.
18. Support engine/transaxle with suitable jack. Ensure suitable wood block is placed between jack and engine oil pan.
19. Remove lefthand mount mounting bolts.
20. Carefully lower engine/transaxle to access and remove transaxle-to-engine mounting bolts.
21. Remove transaxle.
22. Reverse procedure to install. Tighten mounting bolts and nuts to specifications.

NEON

1. Remove battery hold-down, then battery.
2. Remove air cleaner/throttle body assembly.
3. Cut transaxle oil cooler hose off flush with end of fittings.
4. Disconnect input and output speed sensor electrical connectors.
5. Disconnect solenoid/pressure switch assembly, then gearshift cable from manual valve.
6. Disconnect gearshift cable from upper mount bracket, place aside.
7. Remove starter motor upper mounting bolts.
8. Raise vehicle on hoist.
9. Remove halfshafts, structural collar, then left lateral bending brace.
10. Remove starter, then power steering cooler to crossmember fasteners and place aside.
11. Remove right lateral bending brace to transaxle bolts, then converter dust shield.
12. Remove torque converter to drive plate bolts, then lower transaxle bellhousing to engine bolts.
13. Support engine with suitable screw jack and wood block.
14. Remove transaxle upper mount through bolt, then lower assembly with screw jack.
15. Place transmission jack under transaxle and secure.
16. Remove two transaxle bellhousing to block bolts, then remove transaxle.

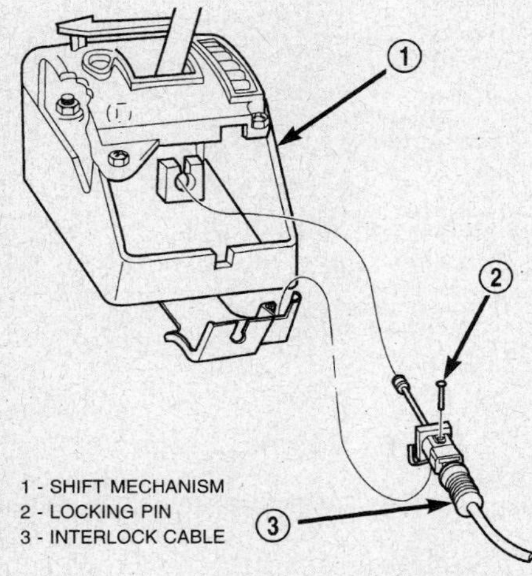

Fig. 8 Interlock cable locking pin. 2001–02

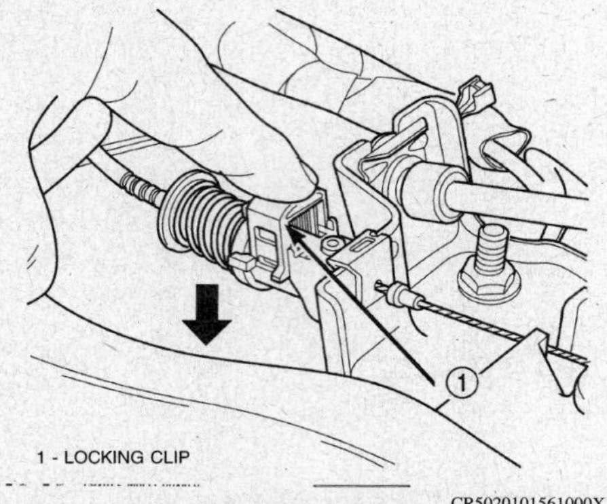

Fig. 9 Interlock cable locking clip. 2001–02

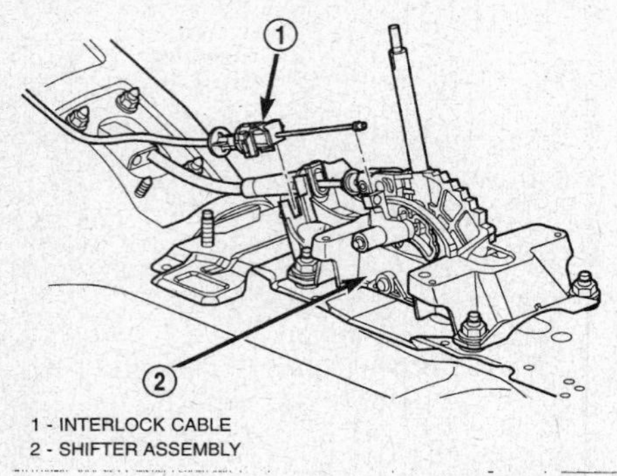

Fig. 10 Interlock cable at shifter assembly. Neon

17. Reverse procedure to install noting the following:
    a. Install cooler lines with service splice kit.
    b. Tighten nuts and bolts to specifications.

SHIFT LOCK SYSTEM

ADJUSTMENTS

1998–2000

1. Remove gearshift knob set screw and knob.
2. Remove floor console.
3. Loosen adjustment nut on interlock lever and place ignition in On position.
4. Remove interlock cable from shifter housing and slide cable out of interlock lever groove.
5. With ignition in Off position and key removed, interlock cable should not move.
6. With ignition in On position, cable should slide freely when pulled and return to bottomed out position when released.
7. If cable does not operate as specified, then cable is improperly installed or kinked.
8. Place shifter in P park position and slide interlock cable into adjustment lever groove.
9. Slip cable into housing until it snaps in place.
10. Ensure shift lever remains in P position and remove ignition key.
11. Loosen interlock cable adjustment nut. **When adjustment nut is loosened cable automatically indexes itself to correct position.**
12. Tighten adjustment nut, then install gearshift knob and set screw.

2001–02

1. Remove gearshift knob set screw and knob, then gearshift bezel to gain access to interlock cable adjuster lock.
2. Re-install gear shift knob and set screw.
3. Place shift lever in Park, then move ignition switch to Lock position and remove key.
4. If interlock cable is to be replaced remove lock pin, **Fig. 8.** This will allow cable to self adjust.
5. If interlock cable is not to be replaced, pull outward on cable locking clip to allow cable to self adjust, **Fig. 9.** Push clip down to lock into place.
6. Install gearshift bezel.
7. Verify proper operation.

SHIFT INTERLOCK CABLE, REPLACE

1998–2000

1. Remove gearshift knob set screw and knob.
2. Remove floor console.
3. Unsnap interlock cable from gearshift lever groove, then pull cable up and out of gearshift.
4. Remove lefthand instrument panel fuse panel cover and instrument panel top cover mounting screw.
5. Remove center bezel and instrument panel center top cover mounting screw.
6. Pull instrument panel top cover up enough to gain access to knee bolster screws.
7. Remove knee bolster screws and knee bolster.
8. Remove mounting screws and pull lower steering column shroud to clear ignition cylinder.
9. Hold tilt wheel lever down, then slide lower shroud forward and remove.
10. Tilt wheel to full down position and remove upper steering column shroud.
11. Place ignition in On position and remove interlock cable from housing.
12. Remove interlock cable from underside of instrument panel.
13. Reverse procedure to install. Adjust interlock cable as described in "Adjustments."

2001–02

Sebring Convertible & Sedan & Stratus Sedan

1. Remove gearshift knob set screw and knob, then gearshift bezel.
2. Release interlock cable adjuster end by inserting pointed object into shift bracket to disengage lock.
3. Unsnap interlock cable adjuster end from slot in gearshift mechanism bracket, then disconnect cable core from shifter.
4. Remove fuse panel cover from left end of instrument panel, then screws from instrument panel top cover.
5. Remove lower knee bolster, then lower steering column shroud.
6. Tilt wheel to down position, then remove upper shroud.
7. Disconnect interlock solenoid connector, then nylon cable retainer from lower column mounting stud.
8. Place ignition key in the On position, grasp interlock cable clip and connector. Remove cable from interlock housing.
9. Remove interlock cable from under instrument panel.
10. Reverse procedure to install.

Neon

1. Remove gearshift knob set screw and knob.
2. Remove center console assembly, then shifter bezel.
3. Disconnect shifter/ignition interlock cable from bracket, **Fig. 10.**
4. Remove cable core end from plastic cam of shifter mechanism and release cable from shifter bracket.
5. Remove steering column lower cover, then upper and lower column shrouds.
6. Disconnect brake Transmission Shift Interlock solenoid connector from interlock cable.
7. Rotate ignition key to Off or On position, squeeze interlock cable locking tab to remove cable from the interlock housing.
8. Release cable from retaining clips, then remove the cable from under steering column.

9. Reverse procedure to install.

SHIFT INTERLOCK, REPLACE

1998–2000

1. Remove lefthand instrument panel fuse panel cover and instrument panel top cover mounting screw.
2. Remove center bezel and remove instrument panel center mounting screw,
3. Pull instrument panel top cover up enough to gain access to knee bolster screws.
4. Remove knee bolster screws and knee bolster.
5. Remove mounting screws and pull lower shroud to clear ignition cylinder.
6. Hold tilt wheel lever down, then slide lower shroud forward and remove.
7. Tilt wheel to full down position and remove upper steering column shroud.
8. Place ignition in On position and remove interlock cable from housing.
9. Remove steering column mounting screws and interlock.
10. Reverse procedure to install. Tighten interlock mounting screws to specifications.

2001–02

1. **On Neon models,** remove steering column lower cover.
2. **On all models,** remove upper and lower shrouds.
3. Remove interlock cable.
4. Remove two attaching screws, then the interlock mechanism
5. Reverse procedure to install.

TECHNICAL SERVICE BULLETINS

TRANSAXLE SEEPAGE

1999

On some of these models, there may be transaxle case seepage.

This condition may be cause by cooler boss area case porosity.

To correct this condition, proceed as follows:

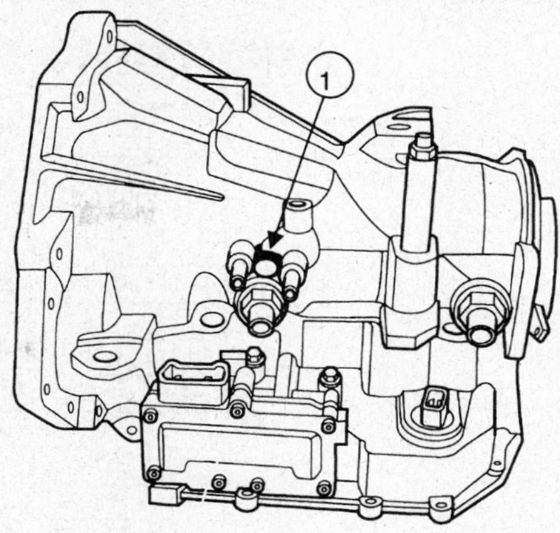

1 - POCKET FORMED BY METAL WEB

CR5020001241000X

Fig. 11 Cooler boss web. 1999

To correct this condition proceed as follows:

1. Remove transaxle control module (TCM), TCM bracket and solenoid pack electrical connector.
2. Insert suitable air hammer with blunt punch attachment Snap-On tool No. PH59, or equivalent, into pocket formed by cooler boss web, **Fig. 11.**
3. Operate air hammer in 15–20 second intervals moving in circular motion starting in center of pocket.
4. Repeat previous step.
5. Replace transaxle is leak continues.

INTERMITTENT LOSS OF SPEED CONTROL

1998–99

On some of these models built before Aug. 8, 1998, there may be intermittent loss of speed controls after input or output speed sensors have been replaced.

This condition may be caused by new sensor spreading connector terminals.

To correct this condition, replace connector (input part No. 05014469AA or output part No. 05014471AA).

DIFFERENTIAL FLUID LEAKAGE

1998–98

An auxiliary vent tube assembly has been released for service to provide improved differential case venting. In cold climate areas, under certain driving conditions, pressure can build up in the differential case forcing fluid out through the primary vent tube at the top of the differential. Fluid can collect on the top of the differential case and/or drip to the ground.

1. Clean all fluid from differential case.
2. Remove differential drain and fill plugs, then drain fluid into suitable container.
3. Install differential drain plug. **Torque** plug to 60 inch lbs.
4. Fill differential with 32 ounces of Mopar 75W-90 Gear Lubricant 04549624, or equivalent.
5. Install new differential fill plug (part No. 05011589AA). **Torque** plug to 35 ft. lbs.
6. Install new vent tube into fill plug and orient tube between ribs on differential cover.

TIGHTENING SPECIFICATIONS

Year	Component	Torque/Ft. Lbs.
1998–2002	Cooler Line Fittings	105①
	Differential Cover	14
	Differential Ring Gear	70
	Differential Bearing Retainer	21
	Driveplate	70
	Eight-Way Solenoid Connector	36①
	Extension Housing	21
	Input Speed Sensor	20
	Left Lateral Bending Brace (Neon)	80
	L/R Clutch Retainer	45①
	Neutral Safety Switch	25
	Oil Pan	14
	Oil Pump	20
	Output Gear	200
	Output Speed Sensor	20
	Output Gear Strap	17
	Pressure Tap	45①
	PRNDL Switch	25
	Reaction Shaft	20
	Right Lateral Brace To Transaxle Bolt (Neon)	60
	Shift Interlocks	21①
	Solenoid/Pressure Switch	35①
	Torque Converter (Except Neon)	55
	Torque Converter (Neon)	65
	Transaxle Range Sensor	45①
	Transaxle To Engine Block (Neon)	80
	Transaxle To Engine Block (2001–02)	70
	Transaxle Upper Mount To Rail Through Bolt (Neon)	87
	Transfer Gear Cover	15
	Transfer Gear	200
	Transfer Plate	96–108①
	Valve Body, Bolt	105①
	Valve Body, Screw	45①
	Vent Assembly	108①
	60-Way EATX Connector	36①

① — Inch lbs.

42LE 4-Speed Electronic Automatic Transaxle

NOTE: On Air Bag Equipped Models, Refer To "Air Bag System Precautions" Located In The Front Of This Manual For System Disarming & Arming Procedures.

NOTE: Refer To "Computer Relearn Procedures" Located In The Front Of This Manual When Battery Power To The Computer Has Been Interrupted.

NOTE: Prior To Performing Any Service Operations Listed In This Section, Consult The "Technical Service Bulletins" Section For Related Information.

INDEX

PRECAUTIONS

AIR BAG SYSTEMS

Refer to "Air Bag System Precautions" in the front of this manual for system disarming and arming procedures.

BATTERY GROUND CABLE

Prior to service, disconnect battery ground cable and isolate as required.

IDENTIFICATION

The 42LE four-speed transaxle identification code is printed on a bar code label. This label is located on the transaxle case, **Fig. 1.**

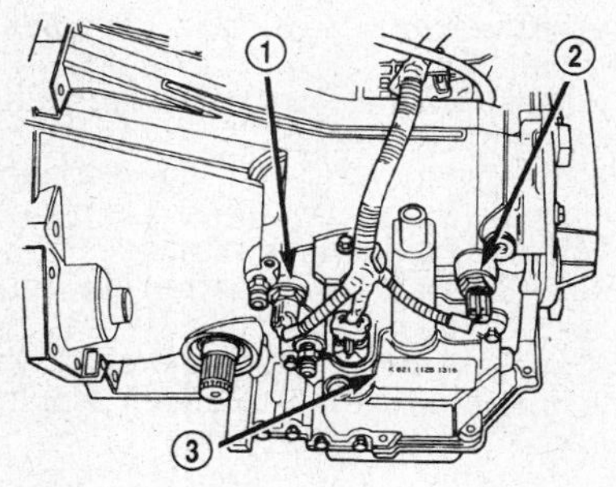

1 – INPUT SPEED SENSOR
2 – OUTPUT SPEED SENSOR
3 – IDENTIFICATION TAG

CR5029400667000X

Fig. 1 Transaxle identification tag location

DESCRIPTION

The 42LE transaxle provides forward ratios of 2.84, 1.57, 1.00 and .69 with torque converter clutch available in second, direct or overdrive gear. The reverse ratio is 2.21. The shift lever is conventional with six positions. When overdrive is selected the transaxle shifts normally through all four speeds with the torque converter clutch operational in third and overdrive; this position is recommended for most driving. The third position is tailored for use in hilly or mountainous driving. When third is selected, the transaxle uses only first, second and direct gear with second-direct shift delayed to 40 mph or greater. When operating in third or low positions, torque converter clutch application occurs in direct gear. If high engine coolant temperature occurs, the torque converter clutch will also engage in second gear.

TROUBLESHOOTING

Prior to attempting any repair on the 42LE transaxle, general engine performance, transaxle fluid level and shift linkage must first be checked and adjusted, as required. For specific symptom diagnosis, refer to **Figs. 2 through 5.**

MAINTENANCE

Refer to "Lubricant Data" chart in the appropriate chassis chapter of this manual for transmission fluid specifications.

FLUID CHECK

AUTOMATIC TRANSAXLE

To check automatic transaxle fluid level, proceed as follows:

1. With vehicle on level surface, start engine and operate at idle speed for at least of one minute.
2. Move selector through all transaxle ranges and place in Park position.
3. Remove dipstick and check fluid level.
4. Transaxle should be at operating temperature when checking fluid level (160–180°F). Fluid level should be within Hot range on dipstick.
5. Adjust level as required.

DIFFERENTIAL

The differential sump is checked separately from the transaxle, as follows:

1. Remove fill plug on transaxle, **Fig. 6.**
2. Fluid should be level with bottom of fill hole.
3. Add suitable petroleum based hypoid gear lubricant 75W-90, or equivalent, to bring level to bottom of fill hole. **Synthetic gear lubricants should not be used.**

FLUID CHANGE

AUTOMATIC TRANSAXLE

To change transaxle fluid and filter, proceed as follows:

1. Raise and support vehicle, then place suitable drain container under transaxle oil pan.
2. Loosen pan bolts and tap pan at one corner to break it loose allowing fluid to drain.
3. Remove oil pan and filter.
4. Install new filter and O-ring on bottom of valve body. Tighten filter mounting bolts to specifications.
5. Clean and install oil pan and magnet. Install transmission oil pan using 1/8 bead of Mopar Silicone Sealer, or equivalent. **Do not seal oil pan with RTV.** Tighten oil pan bolts to specifications.
6. Add four quarts of appropriate automatic transmission fluid through dipstick opening.
7. Start engine and allow to idle for at least one minute.
8. With parking and service brakes applied, move selector lever momentarily to each position, ending in Park or Neutral position.
9. **On 1998 models,** add fluid to bring level 1/4 inch above bottom hole of dipstick.
10. **On 1999–2002 models,** add fluid to bring level 1/8 inch below ADD mark on dipstick.
11. **On all models,** check fluid level after transaxle has reached normal operating temperature.

DIFFERENTIAL

To change differential fluid, proceed as follows:

1. Raise and support vehicle.
2. Drain fluid into suitable container by removing differential drain plug located on bottom of differential housing.
3. Install drain plug and tighten to specifications.
4. Remove differential fill plug located on differential side cover.
5. Fill differential with suitable petroleum based hypoid gear lubricant 75W-90, or equivalent, level with bottom of fill hole. Differential capacity is approximately 32 ounces.
6. Install fill plug and tighten to specifications.

ADJUSTMENTS

GEARSHIFT LINKAGE

COLUMN SHIFT

1. Remove upper steering column shroud and rotate cable adjuster into unlock position.
2. Ensure transaxle shift lever at transaxle is in Park position.
3. Tilt steering column to full down position and place shifter in Park position with key removed.
4. Adjust by rotating adjuster to lock position.
5. Install upper steering column shroud.

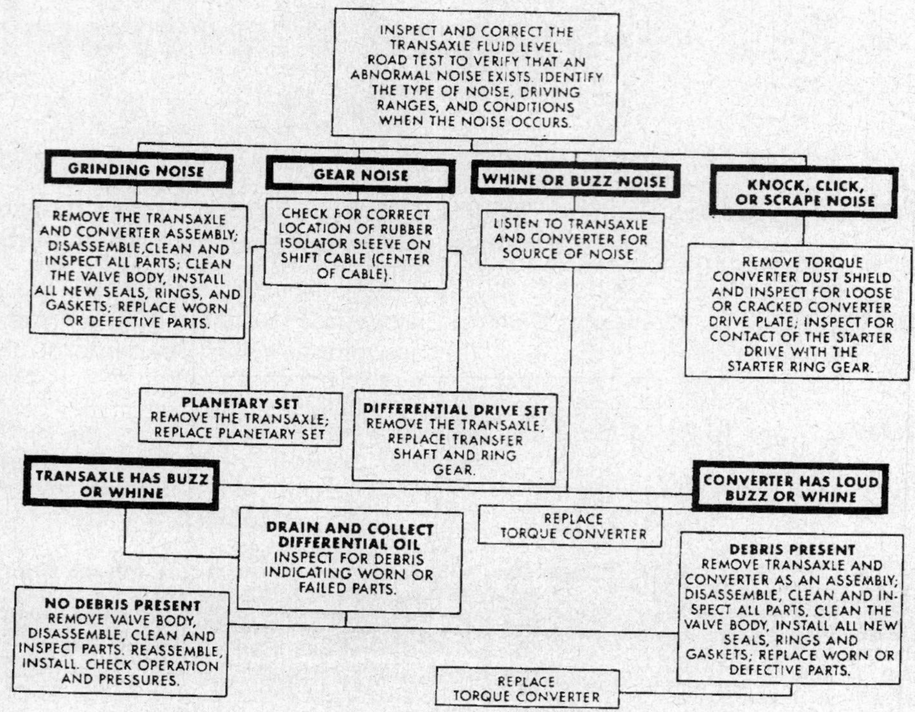

Fig. 2 Abnormal noise diagnosis

6. Inspect shifter for proper operation. Vehicle should start in Park or Neutral only.

FLOOR SHIFT

1. Remove shifter handle and console bezel, then loosen shifter cable adjuster nut.
2. Set shift lever in Park (most rearward) position at transaxle.
3. Place shifter in Park position and ignition in Lock position with key removed.
4. Tighten adjuster nut at shifter.
5. Install console bezel and shifter handle.
6. Check shifter for proper operation. Vehicle should start in Park or Neutral only.

IN-VEHICLE REPAIRS

VALVE BODY, REPLACE

The solenoid pack and manual valve lever position sensor are mounted on top side of valve body. They will remain attached to the valve body when the valve body is removed.

1. Disconnect MVLPS/TRS wiring connector and shift cable from shift lever at transaxle.
2. Move shift lever clockwise as far as possible and remove shift lever.
3. Remove mounting bolts and transaxle oil pan.
4. Remove oil filter from valve body.
5. Remove mounting bolts and valve body.
6. Reverse procedure to install. Install transmission oil pan using 1/8 bead of Mopar Silicone Sealer, or equivalent. **Do not seal oil pan with RTV.**

SOLENOID/PRESSURE SWITCH ASSEMBLY, REPLACE

1. Remove valve body as previously described.
2. Remove mounting screw, solenoid/pressure assembly and screen.
3. Reverse procedure to install. Tighten to specifications.

MANUAL VALVE LEVER POSITION SENSOR (MVLPS), REPLACE

1. Disconnect MVLPS electrical connector.
2. Remove valve body as previously described.
3. Remove manual shaft mounting screw and seal, then slide MVLPS off manual valve shaft.
4. Reverse procedure to install.

TRANSMISSION RANGE SENSOR (TRS), REPLACE

1. Disconnect TRS electrical connector.
2. Remove valve body as previously described.
3. Remove manual shaft mounting screw and seal, then slide TRS off manual valve shaft.
4. Reverse procedure to install.

INPUT & OUTPUT SPEED SENSOR, REPLACE

1. Disconnect speed sensor electrical connector. Ensure weather seal stays attached to connector.
2. Unscrew and remove sensor.

3. Inspect speed sensor O-ring. Replace as required.
4. Reverse procedure to install. Tighten sensor to specifications.

SHORT (RIGHT) STUB SHAFT SEAL, REPLACE

1. Place shift selector in N position, then raise and support vehicle.
2. Remove short driveshaft, then place alignment mark on outer adjuster and housing.
3. Remove outer adjuster lock.
4. Loosen outer adjuster using tool No. 6503, or equivalent.
5. Tighten to alignment mark using torque wrench. Record amount of torque required to return alignment marks to original location.
6. Remove adjuster.
7. Replace oil seal using press and seal remover tool No. 6558, or equivalent,
8. Inspect stub shaft for corrosion.
9. Lubricate O-ring, threads on adjuster, seal protector and seal lips with gear oil.
10. Install outer adjuster into transaxle case. **Torque** adjuster to within 10 ft. lbs. of torque reading previously recorded.
11. Rotate ring gear four revolutions in both directions to seat differential bearings.
12. Continue tightening outer adjuster until alignment marks line up in original location, then install adjuster lock.
13. Install new driveshaft retaining circlip, stub shaft O-ring and driveshaft.
14. Check differential fluid level. Adjust as required.

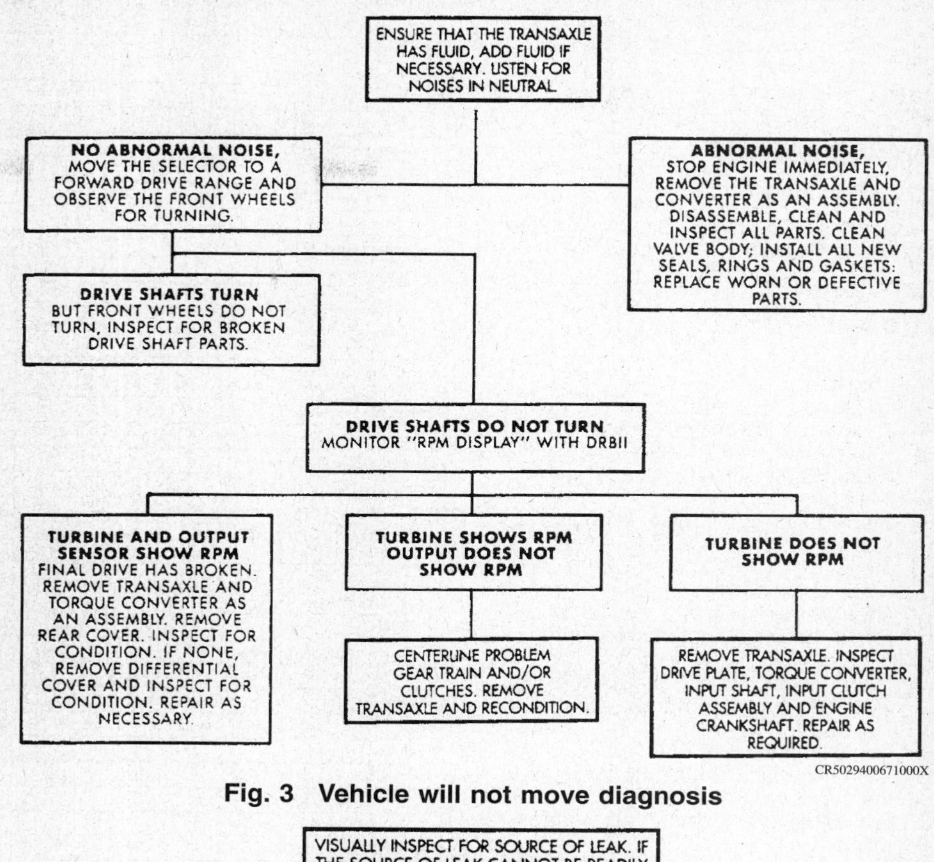

Fig. 3 Vehicle will not move diagnosis

VISUALLY INSPECT FOR SOURCE OF LEAK. IF THE SOURCE OF LEAK CANNOT BE READILY DETERMINED, CLEAN THE EXTERIOR OF THE TRANSAXLE. CHECK TRANSAXLE FLUID LEVEL. CORRECT IF NECESSARY.

THE FOLLOWING LEAKS MAY BE CORRECTED WITHOUT REMOVING THE TRANSAXLE:

MANUAL LEVER SHAFT OIL SEAL
PRESSURE GAUGE PLUGS
REAR COVER SEALANT
OIL PAN SEALANT
OIL COOLER FITTINGS
MANUAL VALVE LEVER POSITION SENSOR SEAL
SOLENOID VENT PLUG
SOLENOID WIRING CONNECTOR
DIFFERENTIAL SHORT STUB SHAFT SEAL

THE FOLLOWING LEAKS REQUIRE REMOVAL OF THE TRANSAXLE AND TORQUE CONVERTER FOR CORRECTION.

TRANSAXLE FLUID LEAKING FROM THE LOWER EDGE OF THE CONVERTER HOUSING; CAUSED BY FRONT PUMP SEAL, PUMP TO CASE SEAL, OR TORQUE CONVERTER WELD.

CRACKED OR POROUS TRANSAXLE CASE.
LONG STUB SHAFT SEAL.
TRANSFER SHAFT SEAL LEAKING FROM WEEP HOLE.

CR5029400672000X

Fig. 4 Fluid leak diagnosis

TRANSAXLE

REPLACE

1. Remove wiper blades, then the right and lefthand wiper module covers.
2. Remove steel cowl/strut support.
3. Remove engine air inlet tube.
4. Remove transaxle harness connectors at cowl area.
5. Remove upper bell housing stud nuts.
6. Disconnect heater hose tube and throttle body support bracket.
7. Remove upper bell housing studs.
8. Raise and support vehicle.
9. Loosen clamps, then separate rear exhaust from left and righthand catalytic converter pipes.
10. Remove rear exhaust system and exhaust pipes to transmission mount mounting nuts.
11. Loosen clamp and remove righthand extension.
12. Disconnect connector and remove crankshaft position sensor.
13. Remove dipstick tube.
14. Disconnect gear selector cable.
15. Disconnect transmission range, input and out sensors' connectors.
16. Disconnect and plug transaxle cooler lines at transaxle.
17. Remove lower control arm pinch bolts and pry lower control arms out of steering knuckles. **Do not allow drive shaft or CV joint to hang freely.**
18. Disconnect inner tripod joints from transaxle using suitable pry bar.
19. Pull bottom of knuckles and drive shafts outward to allow clearance during transaxle removal. Drive shafts do not have to be completely removed.
20. Disconnect oxygen sensor wiring and remove lefthand catalytic converter pipe.
21. Remove mounting bolts, then place starter between engine and frame.
22. Remove engine oil pan collar.
23. Remove torque converter bolts. Torque converter is indexed to flex plate. Mark torque converter location to ensure converter is installed correctly. **Driveplate to torque converter bolts and driveplate to crankshaft bolts must not be reused.**
24. Place suitable transmission jack under transaxle and secure it to jack.
25. Raise transaxle slightly to relieve weight on rear transaxle mount.
26. Remove rear crossmember bridge bolts and rear mount adapter plate mounting bolts.
27. Remove rear crossmember bridge, mount and adapter plate as an assembly.
28. Lower transaxle rear to gain access to bell housing bolts.
29. Remove side bell housing bolts and dipstick tube. **Be prepared to plug dipstick hole when removing dipstick to prevent fluid from spilling out of transaxle.**
30. Remove solenoid pack connector and transaxle.
31. Reverse procedure to install. Install transmission oil pan using ⅛ bead of

Mopar Silicone Sealer, or equivalent. **Do not seal oil pan with RTV.**

SHIFT LOCK SYSTEM

ADJUSTMENTS

COLUMN SHIFT

Adjust column shift as described under "In-Vehicle Repairs."

FLOOR SHIFT

1998–99

1. Remove gearshift knob and console bezel.
2. Loosen locking clip on interlock cable and place ignition in On position.
3. Remove interlock cable from shifter housing and slide cable out of interlock lever groove.
4. With ignition in Off position and key removed, interlock cable should not move.
5. With ignition in On position, cable should slide freely when pulled and return to bottomed out position when released.
6. If cable does not operate as specified, then cable is improperly installed or kinked.
7. Place shifter in P park position and slide interlock cable into adjustment lever groove.
8. Slip cable into housing until it snaps in place.
9. Ensure shift lever remains in P park position and remove ignition key .
10. Loosen locking clip on interlock cable. **When adjustment nut is loosened cable automatically indexes itself to correct position.**
11. Tighten adjustment nut, then install gearshift knob and set screw.

2000–02

1. Remove shifter handle and console bezel.
2. Move gear shifter to PARK and ignition key to LOCK position, **Fig. 7.**
3. If interlock cable is replaced, remove pin to allow cable to self adjust, **Fig. 8.**
4. If interlock cable is not being replaced, loosen locking clip on interlock cable to allow cable to self adjust. Press locking clip to secure adjustment.

COLUMN SHIFT, REPLACE

The interlock cassette slides into the housing behind the lock cylinder and the cable at the rear of the cassette attaches to a locking arm on the shifter assembly. **The column shift interlock system is adjusted only after installing a new cassette. It can not be adjusted more than once. If the system operates incorrectly, install and adjust a new interlock cassette.**

REMOVAL

1. Remove steering column upper and lower cover.
2. Depress tab on top of cassette.
3. Slide interlock cassette out of housing.
4. Remove cable from locking arm on shifter.

POSSIBLE CAUSE / CONDITION	HARSH ENGAGEMENT FROM NEUTRAL TO D	R	DELAYED ENGAGEMENT FROM NEUTRAL TO D	R	POOR SHIFT QUALITY	SHIFTS ERRATIC	DRIVES IN NEUTRAL	DRAGS OR LOCKS	GRATING, SCRAPING, GROWLING NOISE	ENGINE MISFIRE	BUZZING NOISE	BUZZING NOISE DURING SHIFTS ONLY	HARD TO FILL OIL BLOWS OUT FILLER TUBE	TRANSAXLE OVERHEATS	HARSH UPSHIFT	NO UPSHIFT INTO OVERDRIVE	NO TORQUE CONVERTER CLUTCH	HARSH DOWNSHIFTS	HIGH SHIFT EFFORTS	HARSH CONVERTER CLUTCH
Engine Performance	X	X				X									X			X		
Worn or faulty clutch(es)	X	X	X	X		X	X	X							X	X		X		
— Underdrive clutch	X		X			X	X	X										X		
— Overdrive clutch						X	X	X							X	X				
— Reverse clutch		X		X			X	X												
— 2/4 clutch						X		X							X			X		
— Low/reverse clutch	X	X				X		X										X		
Clutch(es) dragging							X													
Insufficient clutch plate clearance							X							X						
Damaged clutch seals			X	X														X		
Worn or damaged accumulator seal ring(s)	X	X	X	X														X		
Faulty cooling system														X						
Engine coolant temp. too low																X	X			
Incorrect gearshift control linkage adjustment			X	X		X	X							X						
Shift linkage damaged																			X	
Chipped or damaged gear teeth								X	X											
Planetary gear sets broken or seized								X	X											
Bearings worn or damaged								X	X											
Driveshaft(s) bushing(s) worn or damaged									X											
Worn or broken reaction shaft support seal rings			X	X	X	X												X		
Worn or damaged input shaft seal rings			X	X													X			
Valve body malfunction or leakage	X	X	X	X	X	X	X				X						X	X	X	
Hydraulic pressures too low			X	X	X	X								X	X		X			
Hydraulic pressures too high	X	X													X			X		
Faulty oil pump			X	X		X								X			X			
Oil filter clogged			X	X	X	X							X							
Low fluid level			X	X	X	X					X			X			X	X		
High fluid level													X	X						
Aerated fluid			X	X	X	X					X		X	X			X	X		
Engine idle speed too low			X	X																
Engine idle speed too high	X	X												X				X		
Normal solenoid operation												X								
Solenoid sound cover loose												X								
Sticking torque converter clutch position																				X
Torque Converter Failure	X													X			X			X
Drive Plate cracked or bent									X	X										

CR5029400673000X

Fig. 5 Symptom diagnosis chart

INSTALLATION

1. Ensure latch rotates freely on shifter gate.
2. Place shifter in P position and install cable over shifter locking arm hook.
3. Slide cassette into housing until it locks into place.
4. Push adjustment tab in until it stops. **Tab will click as it moves into position. Ensure tab is fully depressed.**
5. Install steering column upper and lower covers.

FLOOR SHIFT, REPLACE

1. Remove gearshift knob.
2. Remove bezel from shifter console and driver side under panel.
3. Remove mounting screw and tilt lever.
4. Remove upper and lower steering column covers, then loosen interlock cable locking clip.
5. Remove ignition key and remove shifter housing interlock cable by sliding cable out of interlock lever groove.
6. **On 2000–02 models,** remove Brake Transmission Shift Interlock (BTSI) solenoid connector.
7. **On all models,** remove interlock cable.
8. Reverse procedure to install. Adjust interlock cable as described under "Adjustments."

TECHNICAL SERVICE BULLETINS

DIFFERENTIAL FLUID LEAKAGE

1998–2000

On some of these models, differential fluid may leak in cold climates.

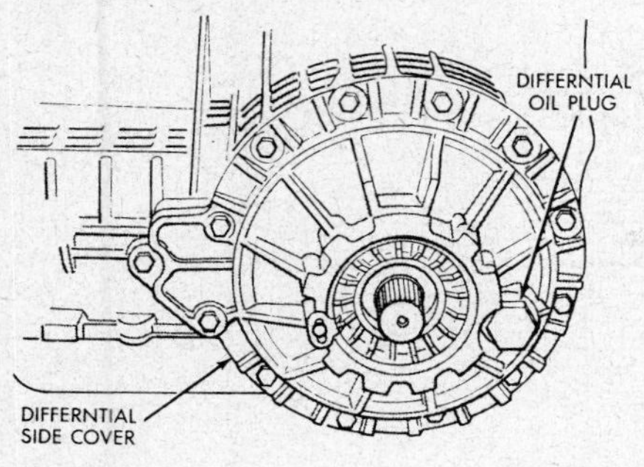

Fig. 6 Differential oil fill plug location

This condition may be caused by fluid being forced out primary vent tube at top of differential.

To correct this condition, proceed as follows:

1. Clean fluid from differential case.
2. Drain differential fluid into suitable container by removing differential drain and fill plugs.
3. Install differential drain plug. **Torque** plug to 60 inch lbs.
4. Fill differential with 32 ounces of Mopar 75W-90 Gear Lubricant 04549624, or equivalent.
5. Install new differential fill plug (part No. 05011589AA). **Torque** plug to 35 ft. lbs.
6. Install revised differential fill plug (part No. 05011589AA) orienting tube between differential cover ribs. **Torque** plug to 35 ft. lbs.

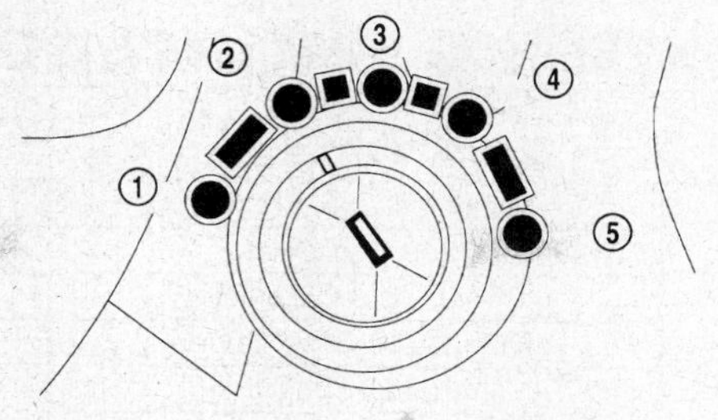

Fig. 7 Ignition key switch points. 2000–02

TRANSAXLE OUTPUT SPEED SENSOR WIRES FATIGUED

1999

On some of these models built between July 14, 1998, and Sept. 27, 1998, the transaxle wires either break or pull out of the output speed sensor connector.

This condition may be caused by the tie strap.

To correct this condition replace existing tie strap with revised unit (part No. 04856500).

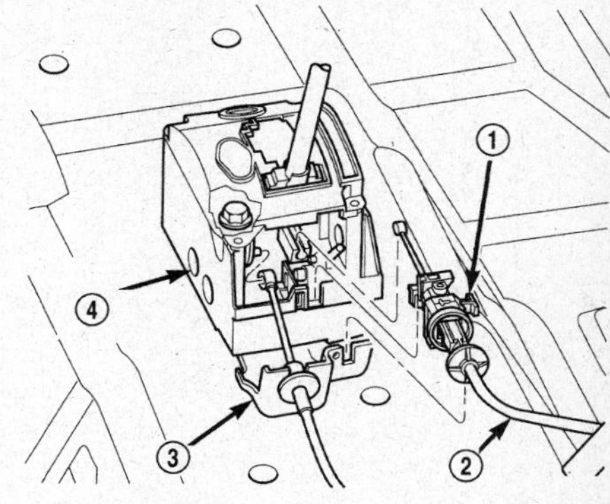

Fig. 8 Interlock cable. 2000–02

TIGHTENING SPECIFICATIONS

Year	Component	Torque/Ft. Lbs.
1998–2002	Adjuster Lock Bracket	45①
	Case End Cover	21
	Cooler Line Connector	155①
	Differential Case Cover	21
	Differential Drain Plug	62①
	Differential Fill Plug	35
	Differential Vent	100①
	Driveplate To Crankshaft	②
	Filter	45①
	Input Sensor	20
	Manual Lever To Valve Body	45①
	Mount	45
	Oil Pan	17
	Output Sensor	20
	Output Shaft Stake Nut	200
	Park Sprag Retainer	45①
	Pressure Check Plug	53①
	Pump	21
	Solenoid/Pressure Switch Assembly	35①
	Solenoid To Transfer Plate	53①
	Solenoid Wiring Connector Retainer	53①
	Torque Converter	③
	Transfer Plate To Case	108①
	Transfer Shaft Stake Nut	200
	Valve Body	105①
	Valve Body Screw	45①
	Wiring Harness Tie Down	53①

① — Inch lbs.
② — 1998–99, 75 ft. lbs.; 2000–02, 70 ft. lbs.
③ — 1998–99, 60 ft. lbs.; 2000–02, 65 ft. lbs.

FRONT WHEEL DRIVE AXLES

TABLE OF CONTENTS

Application Chart

Model	Year	Type No.
Avenger	1998–2000	1
Breeze	1998–2000	2
Cirrus	1998–2000	2
Concorde	1998–2002	2
Intrepid	1998–2002	2
LHS	1998–2002	2
Neon	1998–2002	2
Sebring Convertible	1998–2002	2
Sebring Coupe	1998–2002	1
Sebring Sedan	2001–02	2
Stratus	1998–2000	2
Stratus Coupe	2001–02	1
Stratus Sedan	2001–02	2
Talon	1998	1
300M	1999–2002	2

Type 1

NOTE: On Air Bag Equipped Models, Refer To "Air Bag System Precautions" Located In The Front Of This Manual For System Disarming & Arming Procedures.

NOTE: Refer To "Computer Relearn Procedures" Located In The Front Of This Manual When Battery Power To The Computer Has Been Interrupted.

INDEX

DRIVESHAFT

REPLACE

AVENGER

2.0L ENGINE

Do not apply vehicle load to the wheel bearing after removal of the driveshaft. If a load must be applied to the bearing in moving the vehicle, temporarily secure bearing with stub axle replacement tool No. MB-990998 or equivalent, as shown in Fig. 1.

1. Remove center cap and drive axle nut.
2. Raise and support vehicle, then remove front wheel.
3. Disconnect tie rod end connection, stabilizer link connection and compression lateral lower arm using steering linkage puller tool No. MB-991113 or equivalent.
4. Insert a suitable pry bar between transaxle case and outer case of double offset joint, then withdraw drive axle as shown in **Fig. 2.** Cover drive axle opening in transaxle. **Pry bar should not be inserted deeply between transaxle case and joint, as damage to oil seal may result.**
5. Reverse procedure to install. Position drive axle so raised inner diameter of washer is facing nut, then install and tighten drive axle nut to specifications.

2.5L ENGINE

Do not apply vehicle load to wheel bearing after removal of the driveshaft. If a load must be applied to the bearing in moving the vehicle, temporarily secure bearing with stub axle replacement tool No. MB-990998 or equivalent, as shown in Fig. 1.

1. Remove center cap and drive axle nut.
2. Raise and support vehicle, then remove front wheel.
3. Disconnect tie rod end connection, stabilizer link connection and compression lateral lower arm using steering linkage puller tool No. MB-991113 or equivalent.
4. When removing righthand driveshaft, lightly tap center bearing bracket with a plastic hammer and disconnect driveshaft and inner shaft from transaxle.
5. When removing lefthand driveshaft, insert a suitable pry bar to projecting part of driveshaft, then withdraw drive axle as shown in **Fig. 2.** Cover drive axle opening in transaxle.
6. Reverse procedure to install. Tighten drive axle nut to specifications.

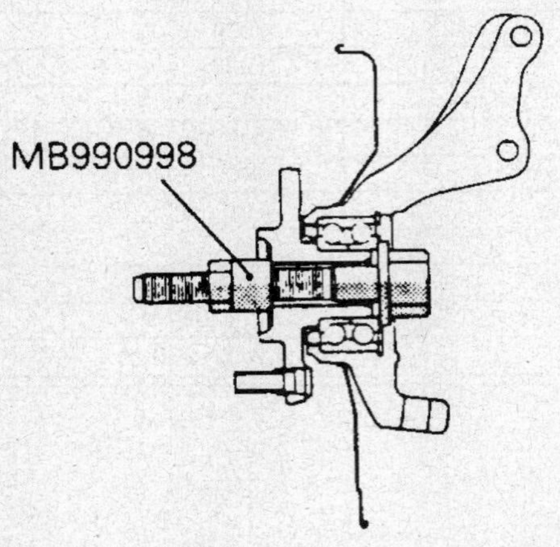

Fig. 1 Wheel bearing support tool installation. Avenger, Talon & 1998–2000 Sebring Coupe

SEBRING COUPE

1998–2000

Refer to "Avenger" for driveshaft replacement procedure.

2001–02

Do not apply pressure to wheel bearing by the vehicle weight to avoid possible damage when the driveshaft nut is loosened. Refer to **Fig. 3,** for removal and installation procedures, noting the following:

1. Do not remove nut from ball joint. Loosen it and use special tool No. MB99113 or MB990635 or equivalent, to avoid damage to ball joint threads as shown in **Fig. 4.**
2. Install special tool No. MB991354, MB990242 and MB990767 or equivalent, to push driveshaft out from hub as shown in **Fig. 5.**
3. **Do not pull on driveshaft, doing so will damage Tripod Joint. Do not insert pry bar as to damage oil seal.** Insert pry bar between transaxle case and driveshaft as shown in **Fig. 6.**
4. If inner shaft and transaxle are joined tightly, tap center bearing bracket slightly with plastic hammer to remove driveshaft.
5. Reverse procedure to install. Tighten drive axle to specifications.

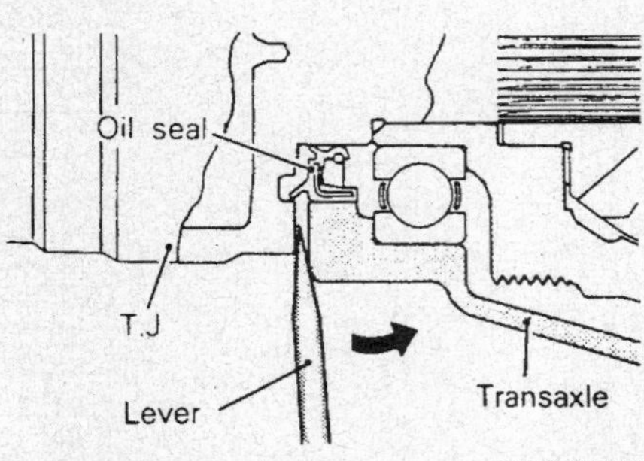

Fig. 2 Front drive axle removal. Avenger, Talon & 1998–2000 Sebring Coupe

STRATUS COUPE

Refer to "2001–02" under "Sebring Coupe" for driveshaft replacement procedure.

TALON

ALL WHEEL DRIVE (AWD)

Do not apply vehicle load to wheel bearing after removal of the driveshaft. If a load must be applied to bearing in moving the vehicle, temporarily secure bearing with stub axle replacement tool No. MB-990998 or equivalent, as shown in Fig. 1.

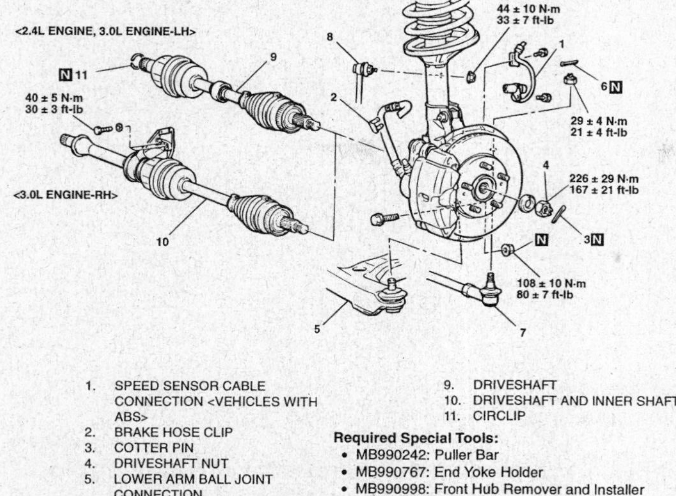

1. SPEED SENSOR CABLE CONNECTION <VEHICLES WITH ABS>
2. BRAKE HOSE CLIP
3. COTTER PIN
4. DRIVESHAFT NUT
5. LOWER ARM BALL JOINT CONNECTION
6. COTTER PIN
7. TIE ROD END CONNECTION
8. STABILIZER LINK CONNECTION
9. DRIVESHAFT
10. DRIVESHAFT AND INNER SHAFT
11. CIRCLIP

Required Special Tools:
- MB990242: Puller Bar
- MB990767: End Yoke Holder
- MB990998: Front Hub Remover and Installer
- MB991345: Puller Body

CR3030000478000X

Fig. 3 Driveshaft assembly removal. 2001–02 Sebring Coupe & Stratus Coupe

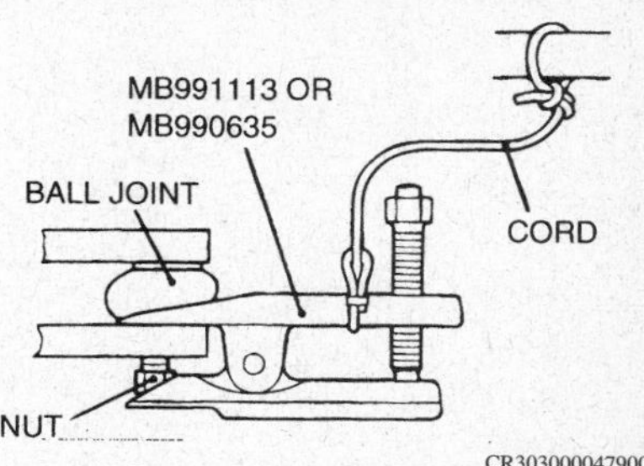

Fig. 4 Ball joint/tie rod end disconnection. 2001–02 Sebring Coupe & Stratus Coupe

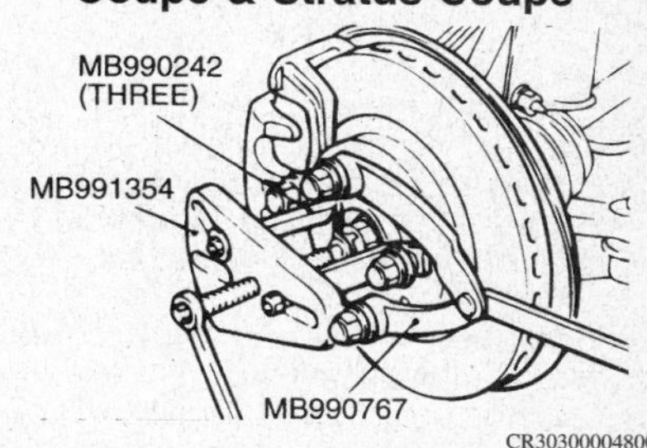

Fig. 5 Driveshaft/driveshaft inner shaft removal. 2001–02 Sebring Coupe & Stratus Coupe

1. Remove center cap and drive axle nut.
2. Raise and support vehicle, then remove front wheel.
3. Disconnect tie rod end connection, stabilizer link connection and compression lateral lower arm using steering linkage puller tool No. MB-991113 or equivalent.
4. When removing lefthand driveshaft, lightly tap center bearing bracket with a plastic hammer and disconnect driveshaft and inner shaft from transaxle.
5. When removing righthand driveshaft, insert a suitable pry bar to projecting part of driveshaft, then withdraw drive axle as shown in **Fig. 2.** Cover drive axle opening in transaxle.
6. Reverse procedure to install. Tighten drive axle nut to specifications.

FRONT WHEEL DRIVE (FWD)

Do not apply vehicle load to wheel bearing after removal of the driveshaft. If a load must be applied to the bearing in moving the vehicle, temporarily secure bearing with stub axle replacement tool No. MB-990998 or equivalent, as shown in Fig. 1.

1. Remove center cap and drive axle nut.
2. Raise and support vehicle, then remove front wheel.
3. Disconnect tie rod end connection, stabilizer link connection and compression lateral lower arm using steering linkage puller tool No. MB-991113 or equivalent.
4. Insert a suitable pry bar between transaxle case and outer case of double offset joint, then withdraw drive axle as shown in **Fig. 2.** Cover drive axle opening in transaxle. **Pry bar should not be inserted deeply between transaxle case and joint, as damage to oil seal may result.**
5. Reverse procedure to install. Position drive axle so raised inner diameter of washer is facing nut, then install and tighten drive axle nut to specifications.

DRIVESHAFT SERVICE

AVENGER & TALON w/FRONT WHEEL DRIVE (FWD)

DOUBLE OFFSET JOINT TYPE

When servicing the drive axle, do not disassemble the Birfield bell type or Rzeppa type constant velocity joint, as components on this type joint are precision fitted and are replaced only as a unit.

Disassemble

1. Remove Double Offset Joint (DOJ) boot bands, then remove circlip using a suitable screwdriver as shown in **Fig. 7.**
2. Remove DOJ outer race from DOJ joint assembly.
3. Remove snap ring, then remove DOJ inner race, cage and balls as an assembly. Clean bearing assembly without disassembling them.
4. Wind tape around drive axle splines, then remove DOJ and Birfield joint boot band and slide boots from drive axle. When inspecting Birfield joint, note amount of grease removed for reassembly.

Assemble

A special grease containing Molybdenum is used to lubricate the drive axle double offset joint and the Birfield joint. This special grease is included in the drive axle repair kit and must be used.

1. Wrap tape around drive axle splines to prevent damage to boots, then install Birfield joint and DOJ boots.
2. Apply special grease to DOJ joint assembly.
3. Install DOJ joint assembly on drive axle with chamfered side of cage facing splined end of shaft, then install snap ring.
4. Apply 1.4–2.1 ounces of special molybdenum grease to double offset joint outer race, then position outer race on drive axle.
5. Apply an additional .7–1.4 ounce of special molybdenum grease to DOJ boot, then install clip.
6. Add amount of special molybdenum grease to Birfield joint as removed during disassembly and inspection.
7. Install boots and boot bands for each joint. When installing boot bands for DOJ, position bands as shown in **Fig. 8,** so dimension "A" is 3.5 inches on two wheel drive models or 3.3 inches on four wheel drive models.

TRIPOD JOINT TYPE DRIVESHAFT

When servicing the drive axle, do not disassemble the Birfield bell type or Rzeppa type constant velocity joint, as components of this type joint are precision fitted and are replaced only as a unit.

Disassemble

1. Remove boot clamps, then remove boot from tripod joint housing and position on drive axle as shown in **Figs. 9 and 10.**
2. Pull drive axle from tripod joint housing, then remove snap ring and lift tripod joint spider from housing. Clean tripod joint spider and inspect for wear and damage. Also inspect joint needle roller bearings for smooth operation. **Do not disassemble tripod joint spider.**
3. Wind tape around drive axle splines, then remove bands for Rzeppa type joint and remove boots from drive axle.

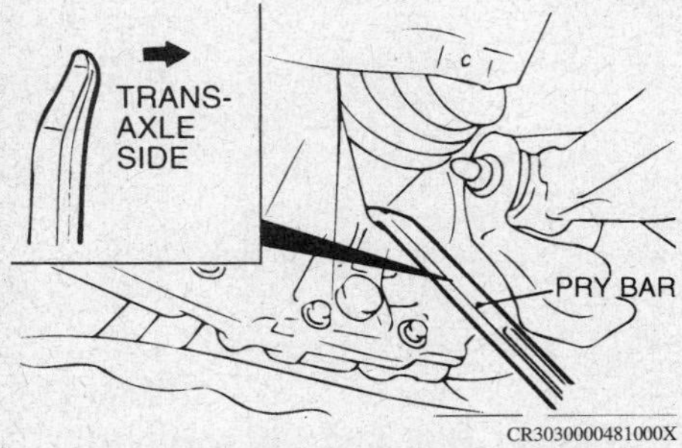

Fig. 6 Pry bar installation. 2001–02 Sebring Coupe & Stratus Coupe

If Rzeppa joint is to be reused, do not wipe away grease. Inspect grease for contamination and clean and replace grease only if required. Note amount of grease removed for use during reassembly.

4. **On models with inner shaft,** continue disassembly as follows:
   a. Using press and support fixture No. MB-991248 or equivalent, press inner shaft and seal plate out of tripod case.
   b. Using two inch steel pipe as support as shown in **Fig. 11,** press inner shaft from center bearing support.
   c. Using screwdriver, remove driveshaft side dust seal, then using same steel pipe press out center bearing and differential side dust seal.

Assemble

A special grease is used to lubricate the drive axle tripod joint and Rzeppa joint. This grease is included in the drive axle repair kit and must be used.

1. Press fit center bearing into center bearing support, then lubricate and press fit dust seals into center bearing.
2. Press fit inner shaft into center bearing, then the inner shaft assembly into Tripod case.
3. Apply grease to drive axle, then install boots.
4. Position tripod joint spider on drive axle, then install snap ring.
5. Apply 2.8–3.2 ounces of special grease to tripod joint housing, then insert drive axle and spider into housing.
6. Apply another 2.8–3.2 ounces of special grease to tripod joint boot.
7. Apply as much special grease as removed to Rzeppa joint, if required.
8. Install bands and boots for each joint. When installing boot bands for tripod joint, bands (dimension "A") must be positioned 3.1 inches apart as shown in **Fig. 8.**

SEBRING COUPE

1998–2000

Refer to "Avenger & Talon w/Front Wheel Drive (FWD)" for driveshaft service procedures.

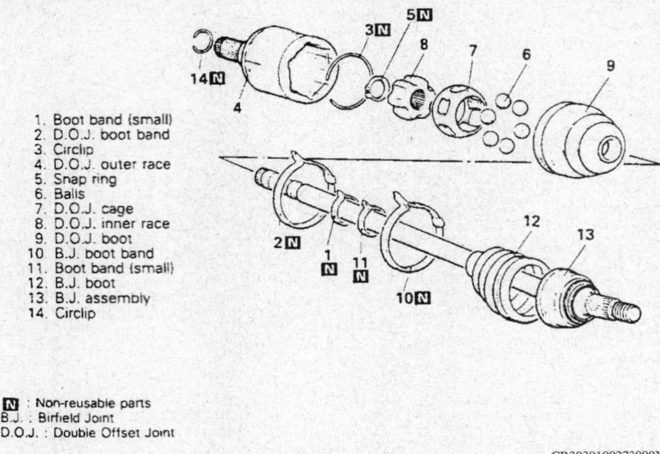

Fig. 7 Exploded view of double offset joint type front drive axle

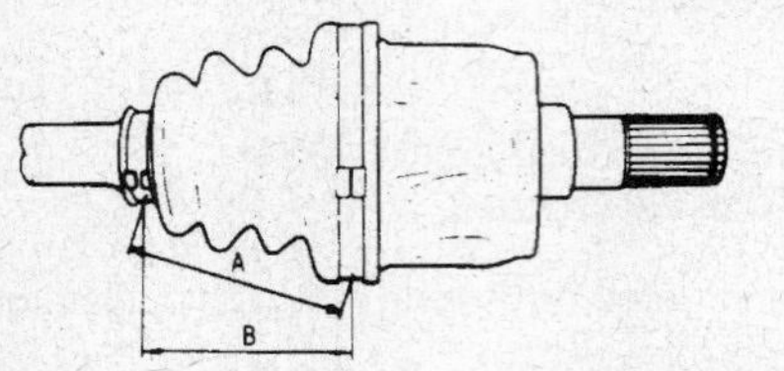

Fig. 8 Double offset joint or tripod joint boot length measurement

2001–02

When servicing the drive axle, never disassemble the Birfield Joint assembly except when replacing the Birfield Joint boot.

Disassembly

Refer to **Fig. 12,** when servicing driveshaft assembly, noting the following:

1. When removing inner shaft, install special tool No. MB991248 or MD998801 or equivalent, to remove inner shaft assembly and seal plate as shown in **Fig. 13.**
2. Remove inner shaft from center bearing bracket using special tool No. MB991248 or MD998801 or equivalent, as shown in **Fig. 14.**
3. Remove center bearing from center bearing bracket using special tool No. MB990930 and MB990938 or equivalent, as shown in **Fig. 15.**
4. Ensure plastic tape is around spline part on Birfield Joint assembly so that Tripod Joint boot is not damaged when they are removed.

Assemble

A special grease, lubricant part No. 2525035 or equivalent, is used to lubricate the drive axle. This grease is included in the drive axle repair kit. Refer to **Fig. 12,** when servicing driveshaft assembly, noting the following:

1. Install dynamic damper in position as shown in **Fig. 16.**
2. **There should be no grease adhered to rubber part of dynamic damper. Damper band and Tripod Joint boot band are different in shape, ensure proper band assembly is completed.** Secure damper bands.
3. Wrap plastic tape around shaft spline, then install Tripod Joint boot band and Tripod Joint boot.
4. Apply grease to spider axles and rollers of spider assembly.
5. Install chamfered portion of spider assembly's spline toward driveshaft, then install spider assembly to driveshaft as shown in **Fig. 17.**
6. Install center bearing into center bearing bracket using special tool No. MB990930 and MB990938 or equivalent, as shown in **Fig. 18.**
7. Install specified grease as shown in **Fig. 19,** use special tool No. MB990890 and MB990934 or equivalent, to press oil into seal. Apply grease to lip of dust seal. **Do not apply grease to outside of lip.**
8. Install special tool No. MB991172 or equivalent, to hold center bearing inner race, then press-in the inner shaft as shown in **Fig. 20.**
9. Install specified grease to inner shaft serration, then press inner shaft assembly into Tripod Joint case.
10. Install Tripod Joint case with specified grease and insert driveshaft, then refill Tripod Joint case with repair kit grease. **Grease from repair kit should be divided in half for use, at joint and inside boot.**
11. Position Tripod Joint outer race so that distance between boot bands is at standard value of 3.3 inch as shown in **Fig. 21.**
12. Remove part of Tripod Joint outer race to release air pressure inside boot.

STRATUS COUPE

Refer to "2001–02" under "Sebring Coupe" for driveshaft service procedures.

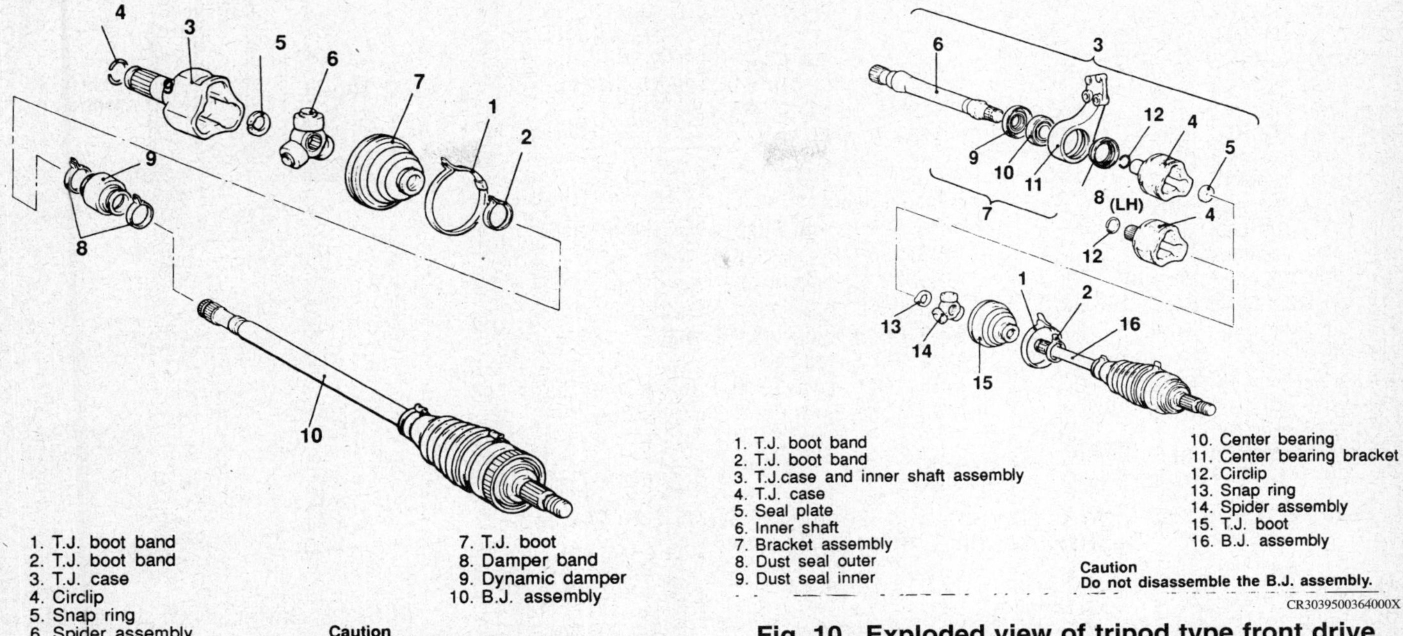

Fig. 9 Exploded view of tripod type front drive axle. Less inner shaft

Fig. 10 Exploded view of tripod type front drive axle. With inner shaft

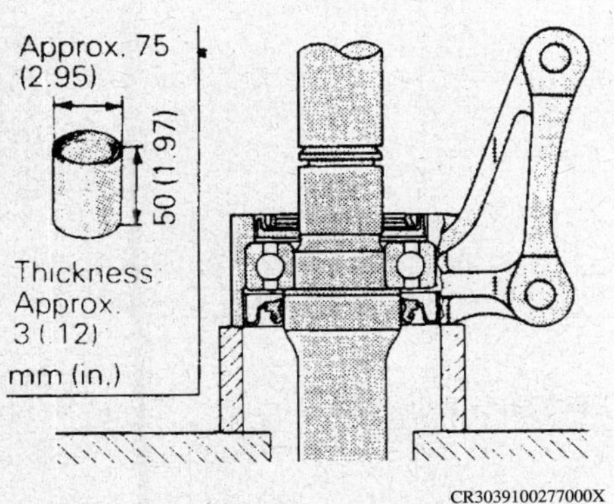

Fig. 11 Inner shaft removal

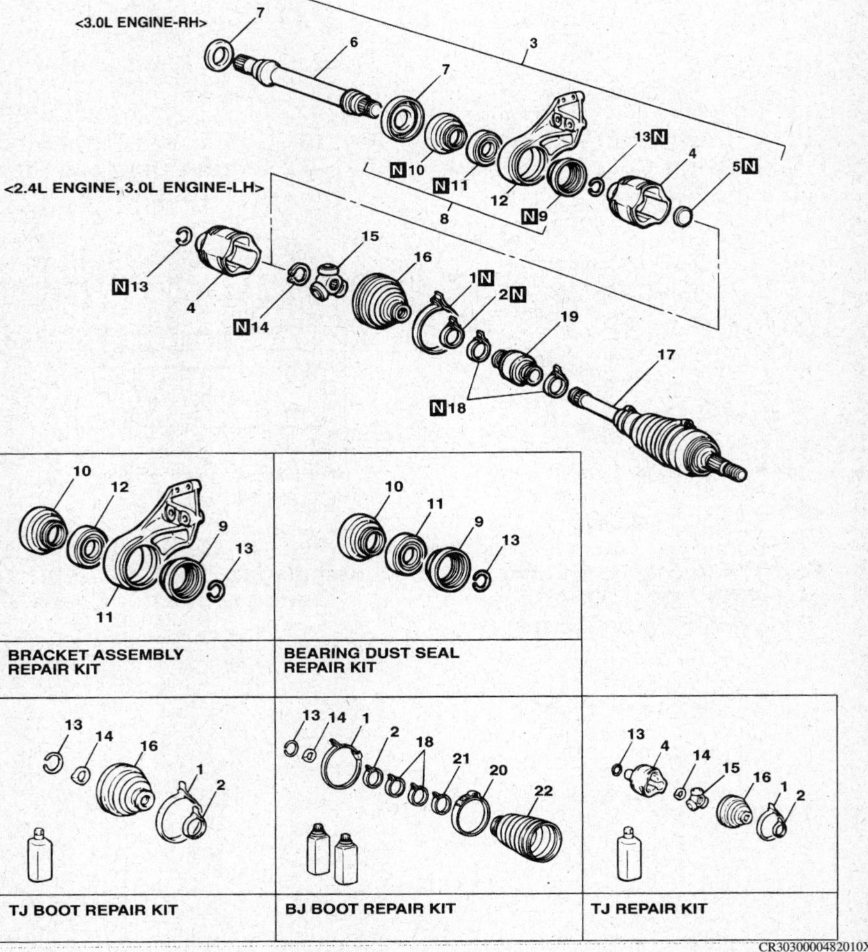

Fig. 12 Exploded view of driveshaft assembly (Part 1 of 2). 2001–02 Sebring Coupe & Stratus Coupe

1. TJ BOOT BAND (LARGE)
2. TJ BOOT BAND (SMALL)
3. TJ CASE INNER SHAFT ASSEMBLY
4. TJ CASE
5. SEAL PLATE
6. INNER SHAFT
7. DUST COVER
8. BRACKET ASSEMBLY
9. DUST SEAL OUTER
10. DUST SEAL INNER
11. CENTER BEARING
12. CENTER BEARING BRACKET
13. CIRCLIP
14. SNAP RING
15. SPIDER ASSEMBLY
16. TJ BOOT
17. BJ ASSEMBLY
18. DAMPER BAND <2.4L ENGINE, 3.0L ENGINE-LH>
19. DYNAMIC DAMPER <2.4L ENGINE, 3.0L ENGINE-LH>
20. BJ BOOT BAND (LARGE)
21. BJ BOOT BAND (SMALL)
22. BJ BOOT

NOTE: BJ: Birfield Joint
TJ: Tripod Joint

Required Special Tool:

- MB990890: Rear Suspension Bush Base
- MB990930: Installation Adapter
- MB990932: Installation Adapter
- MB990934: Installation Adapter
- MB990938: Installation Adapter
- MB991172: Adapter
- MB991248 or MD998801: Inner Shaft Remover
- MB991561: Boot Band Crimping Tool

CR3030000482020X

Fig. 12 Exploded view of driveshaft assembly (Part 2 of 2). 2001–02 Sebring Coupe & Stratus Coupe

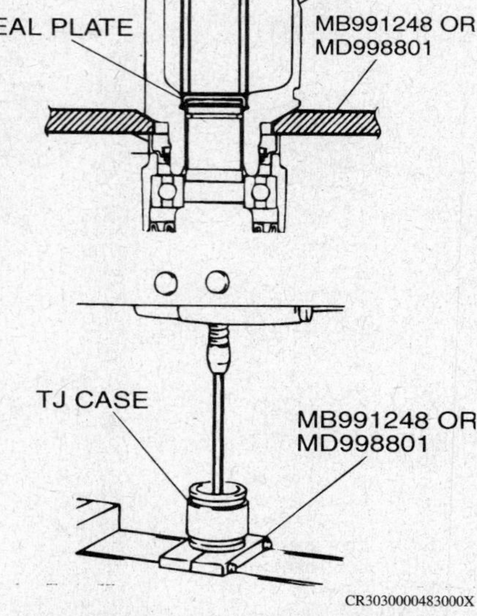

Fig. 13 Inner shaft assembly removal. 2001–02 Sebring Coupe & Stratus Coupe

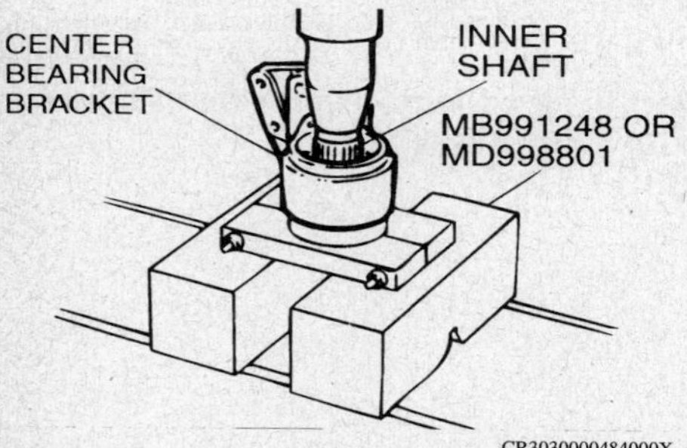

Fig. 14 Inner shaft removal. 2001–02 Sebring Coupe & Stratus Coupe

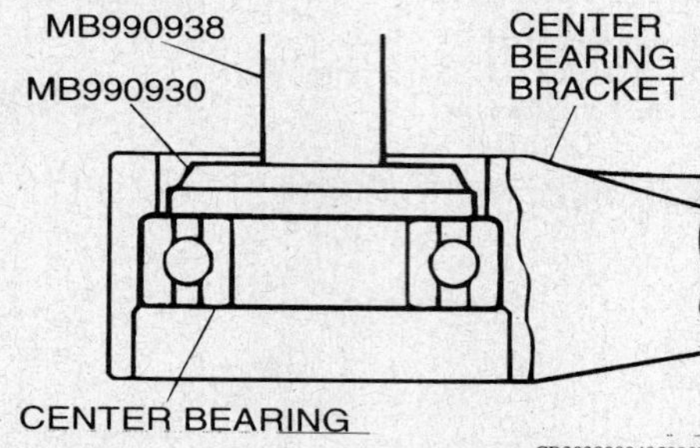

Fig. 15 Center bearing removal. 2001–02 Sebring Coupe & Stratus Coupe

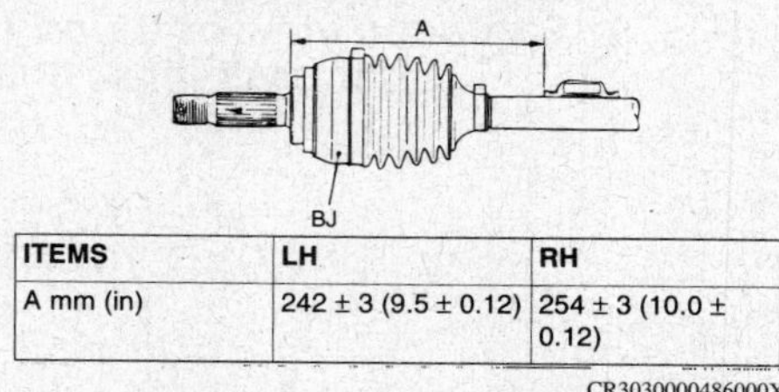

ITEMS	LH	RH
A mm (in)	242 ± 3 (9.5 ± 0.12)	254 ± 3 (10.0 ± 0.12)

CR3030000486000X

Fig. 16 Dynamic damper installation. 2001–02 Sebring Coupe & Stratus Coupe

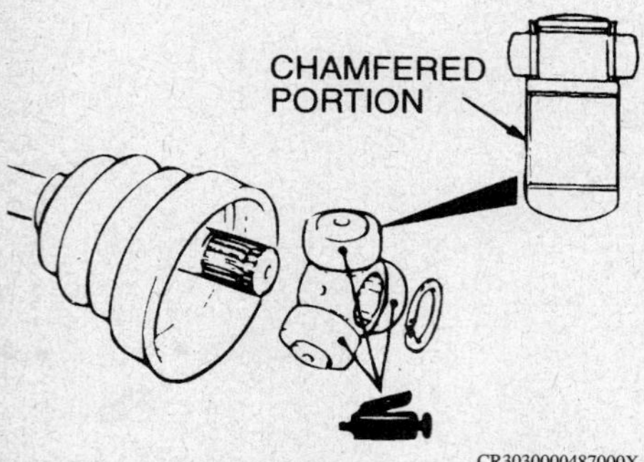

Fig. 17 Spider assembly installation. 2001–02 Sebring Coupe & Stratus Coupe

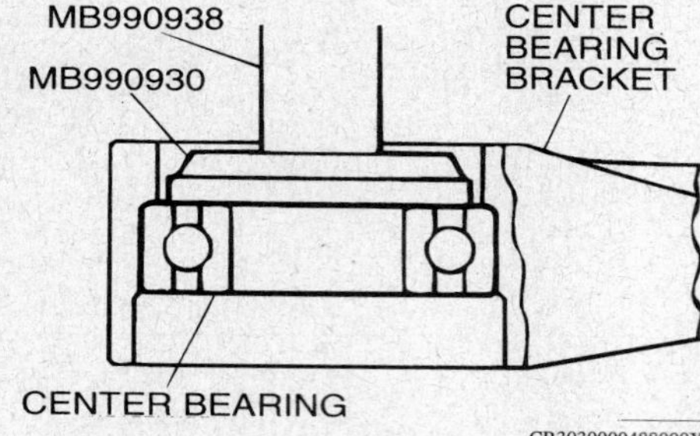

Fig. 18 Center bearing installation. 2001–02 Sebring Coupe & Stratus Coupe

DUST SEAL INNER

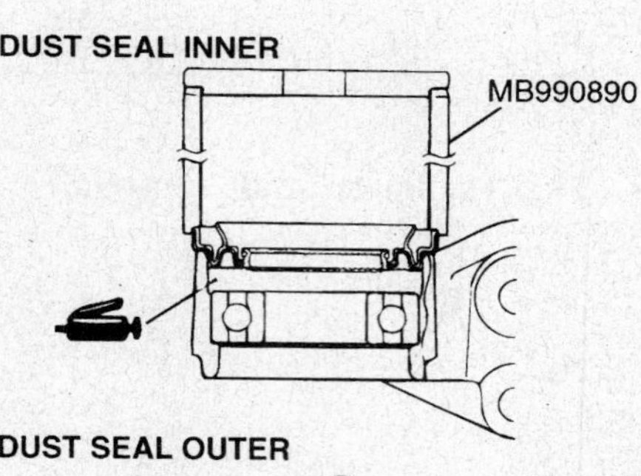

DUST SEAL OUTER

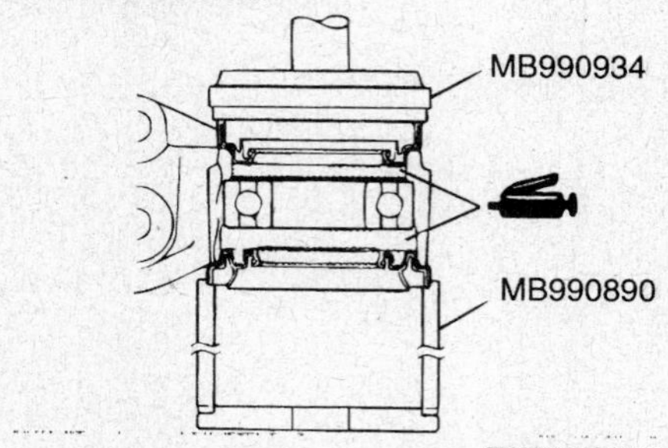

Fig. 19 Dust seal installation. 2001–02 Sebring Coupe & Stratus Coupe

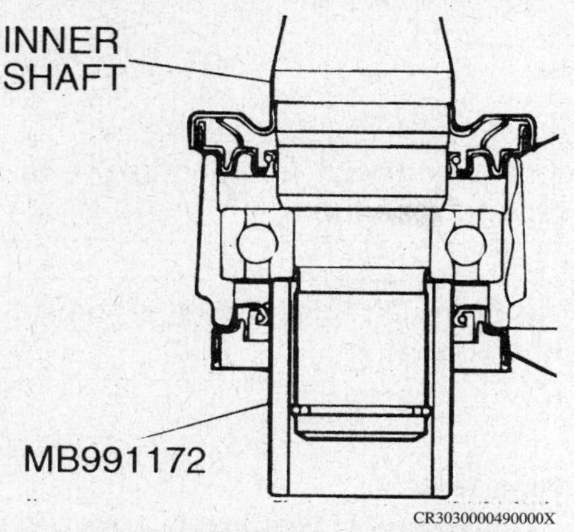

Fig. 20 Inner shaft installation. 2001–02 Sebring Coupe & Stratus Coupe

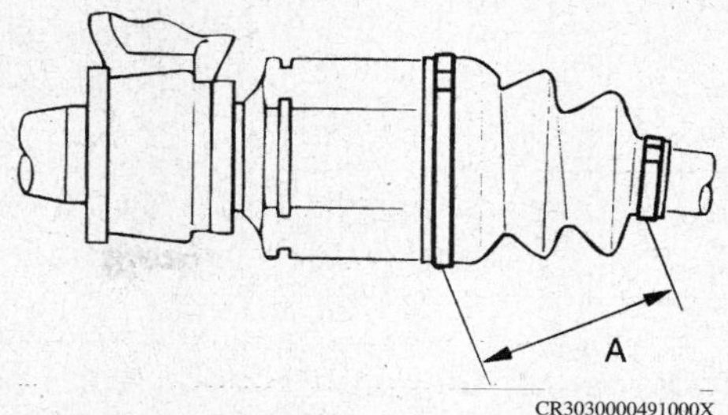

Fig. 21 Boot band installation. 2001–02 Sebring Coupe & Stratus Coupe

TIGHTENING SPECIFICATIONS

Component	Torque Ft. Lbs.
AVENGER, & TALON	
Damper Fork To Lateral Lower Arm	65
Driveshaft Nut	146–188
Lower Arm Ball Joint Nut	43–52
Stabilizer Link Nut	27–33
Tie Rod End & Ball Joint Nut	17–25
1998–2000 SEBRING COUPE	
Damper Fork To Lateral Lower Arm	65
Driveshaft Nut	146–188
Lower Arm Ball Joint Nut	43–52
Stabilizer Link Nut	27–33
Tie Rod End & Ball Joint Nut	17–25
2001–02 SEBRING COUPE & STRATUS COUPE	
Caliper Assembly Bolt	67–81
Center Bearing Bolt	27–33
Driveshaft Nut	146–188
Driveshaft & Inner Shaft Bracket	27–33
Dust Shield Bolt	61–95①
Front Strut Nut	203–239
Knuckle To Front Hub Bolt	58–72
Lower Arm Ball Joint Nut	73–87
Stabilizer Link Nut	26–40
Tie Rod End & Ball Joint Nut	17–25

① — Inch Lbs.

Type 2

NOTE: On Air Bag Equipped Models, Refer To "Air Bag System Precautions" Located In The Front Of This Manual For System Disarming & Arming Procedures.

NOTE: Refer To "Computer Relearn Procedures" Located In The Front Of This Manual When Battery Power To The Computer Has Been Interrupted.

INDEX

DRIVESHAFT IDENTIFICATION

These models use an "unequal length" system. The "unequal length" system has a short solid interconnecting shaft on one side with a longer tubular interconnecting shaft on the other as shown in **Figs. 1 through 3.**

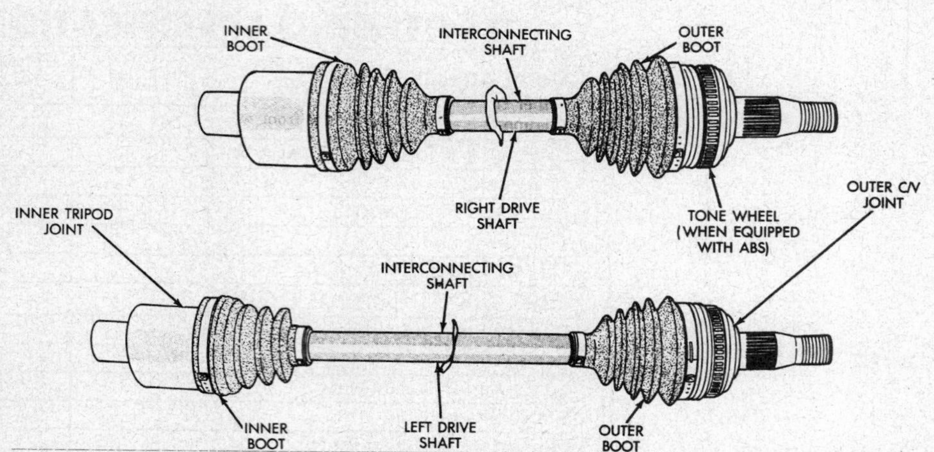

Fig. 1 Driveshaft identification. Concorde, Intrepid, LHS, & 300M

DRIVESHAFT

REPLACE

BREEZE, CIRRUS, SEBRING CONVERTIBLE & STRATUS

1. Remove cotter pin, locknut and spring washer from end of outer CV joint stub axle.
2. Apply service brakes, loosen hub bearing retaining nut, then raise and support vehicle.
3. Remove wheel and tire assemblies.
4. Remove brake caliper assembly as outlined in "Disc Brakes" section.
5. Remove brake rotor from front hub.
6. Remove tie rod end to steering knuckle attaching nut, then tie rod end from steering knuckle using removal tool No. MB-991113 or equivalent.
7. **On models equipped with ABS,** remove speed sensor cable routing bracket from strut assembly.
8. **On all models,** remove cotter pin and castle nut from stud of lower ball joint at steering knuckle.
9. Turn knuckle so front of knuckle is facing as far outboard as possible, then using a suitable hammer strike steering boss until steering knuckle separates from stud of lower ball joint. **Do not hit lower control arm or ball joint seal. No tool is to be inserted between steering knuckle and lower ball joint to separate them. Do not separate inner CV joint at this time. The driveshaft must be supported. Do not allow it to hang by inner CV joint.**
10. Pull steering knuckle aside and away from outer CV joint.
11. Insert suitable pry bar between transmission case and driveshaft, then pry driveshaft from transmission. **Do not pull on interconnecting shaft, nor insert pry bar deep enough to damage oil seal.** Pry against inner tripod joint until tripod snap ring is disengaged.
12. Hold inner tripod joint and interconnecting shaft of driveshaft assembly, then remove inner tripod joint from transaxle by pulling straight out. **Avoid letting spline or snap ring drag across transaxle to tripod joint oil seal lip.**
13. Reverse procedure to install, noting following:
    a. Ensure snap rings are securely seated in their grooves.
    b. Tighten steering knuckle to ball joint stud castle nut to specifications.
    c. Tighten tie rod end to steering knuckle attaching nut to specifications.
    d. Apply vehicle brakes when tightening hub nut to specifications.
    e. Ensure transaxle fluid is up to proper level.

CONCORDE, INTREPID, LHS, & 300M

1. Raise and support vehicle.
2. Remove wheel and tire assemblies.
3. Remove brake caliper assembly as outlined under the "Disc Brakes" section.
4. Remove brake rotor by pulling it straight off mounting studs.
5. Remove speed sensor cable routing bracket from strut assembly.
6. Remove stub axle and hub retaining nut.
7. Install puller tool No. 6790 or equivalent, on hub and bearing assembly using wheel lugnuts to secure it in place.
8. Install a lugnut on a wheel stud to protect its threads.
9. Insert a suitable flat-bladed pry tool to prevent hub from turning.
10. Using puller tool, force outer stub axle from hub and bearing assembly.
11. Dislodge inner tripod joint from stub shaft retaining ring on transaxle assembly.

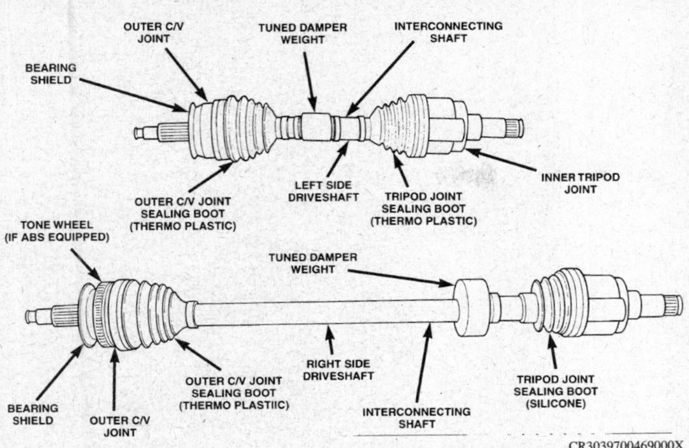

Fig. 2 Driveshaft identification. 1998–2000 Breeze & Cirrus

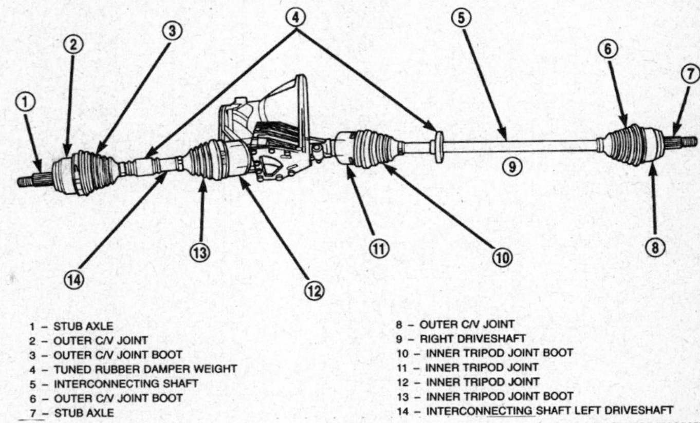

Fig. 3 Driveshaft identification. 1998–2002 Neon, Sebring Convertible, Stratus, Sebring & Stratus Sedan

12. Insert suitable pry bar between transmission case and driveshaft, then pry driveshaft from transmission as shown in **Fig. 4. Do not pull on driveshaft, nor insert pry bar deep enough to damage oil seal. Only pry inner joint from retaining snap ring. Do not attempt to remove inner tripod joint from transaxle stub shaft.**
13. Support steering knuckle, then disconnect and remove strut assembly from steering knuckle.
14. Hold outer CV joint assembly with one hand, grasp steering knuckle with the other hand and rotate it out and to the rear of the vehicle, until outer CV joint clears hub and bearing assembly.
15. Remove driveshaft inner tripod joint from transaxle stub shaft. **Do not pull on interconnecting shaft to remove inner tripod joint from stub shaft.**
16. Reverse procedure to install, noting following:
    a. Install new O-ring seal and tripod joint retaining circlip.
    b. Apply a thin, even bead of Mopar Multi-Purpose Lubricant or equivalent, grease around inner tripod joint splines where O-rings seats against joint.
    c. When installing outer CV joint into hub and bearing assembly, do not allow flinger disc as shown in **Fig. 5,** to become damaged.
    d. Tighten strut attaching bolts to specifications. **Strut bolts have a serrated shaft so do not turn bolts in steering knuckle. Turn nut on bolts, but do not turn bolts.**
    e. Install a new hub and bearing stub shaft retaining nut. Tighten, but do not torque nut at this time.
    f. Apply vehicle brakes and tighten new hub and bearing stub shaft nut to specifications. **Do not exceed the maximum specification as damage to driveshaft may occur.**

NEON

1998–99

If the vehicle will be moved on its wheels when a driveshaft has been removed, install a properly sized bolt and nut through the front hub. **Torque** to 150 ft. lbs. This ensures the hub bearing will not loosen.

1. Remove cotter pin, locknut and spring washer from end of outer CV joint stub axle.
2. Apply service brakes, then loosen hub bearing retaining nut.
3. Raise and support vehicle.
4. Remove wheel and tire assemblies.
5. Remove brake caliper assembly as outlined in the "Disc Brakes" section.
6. Remove brake rotor from front hub. Support caliper with suitable cord or wire. **Do not let it hang by brake hose.**
7. Remove tie rod end to steering knuckle attaching nut, then remove tie rod end from steering knuckle using removal tool No. MB-990635, MB-991113 or equivalent.
8. Remove nut and bolt clamping ball joint into steering knuckle, then separate ball joint stud from steering knuckle by prying down on lower control arm. **Do not damage ball joint seal. Do not separate inner CV joint at this time. Do not allow driveshaft to hang by inner CV joint. Driveshaft must be supported.**
9. Remove hub and bearing to stub axle retaining nut.
10. Install puller tool No. 6790 or equivalent, on hub and bearing assembly using lugnuts to secure it in place.
11. Install a lugnut on stud to protect threads.
12. Insert a suitable flat-bladed pry tool to prevent hub from turning.
13. Using puller tool, force outer stub axle from hub and bearing assembly, then Pull steering knuckle aside and away from outer CV joint.
14. Hold inner tripod joint and interconnecting shaft of driveshaft assembly, then remove inner tripod joint from transaxle by pulling straight out. **Do not let spline or snap ring damage oil seal.**
15. Reverse procedure to install, noting following:
    a. Tighten new steering knuckle to ball joint stud castle nut to specifications.
    b. Tighten tie rod end to steering knuckle attaching nut to specifications.
    c. Apply vehicle brakes and tighten hub nut to specifications.

2000–02

If the vehicle will be moved on its wheels when a driveshaft has been removed, install a properly sized bolt and nut through the front hub. Torque to 180 ft. lbs. This ensures the hub bearing will not loosen.

1. Disconnect and isolate battery ground cable.
2. Place transaxle in gated Park.
3. Raise and support vehicle.
4. Remove wheel and tire assembly.
5. **On models equipped with ABS,** disconnect front wheel speed sensor, then position harness aside.
6. **On all models,** remove ball joint to knuckle retaining nut and bolt.
7. Separate ball joint stud from knuckle by prying down on lower control arm. **Avoid damaging joint seal.**
8. Remove driveshaft from knuckle by pulling outward on knuckle while pressing in on driveshaft. Support outer end of driveshaft. If separation is difficult, proceed as follows:
    a. Install puller tool No. 6790 or equivalent, on hub and bearing using lugnuts to secure it in place.
    b. Install a axle nut to protect threads.
    c. Insert a suitable flat-bladed pry tool to prevent hub from turning.
    d. Using puller tool, force driveshaft outer stub axle from hub and bearing assembly.
    e. Remove axle nut, then pull knuckle assembly out and away from outer CV joint.
9. Support outer end of driveshaft assembly.
10. Remove inner tripod joints from transaxle side gears using a punch to dislodge inner joint retaining ring from side gear. For righthand side joint removal, position punch against inner

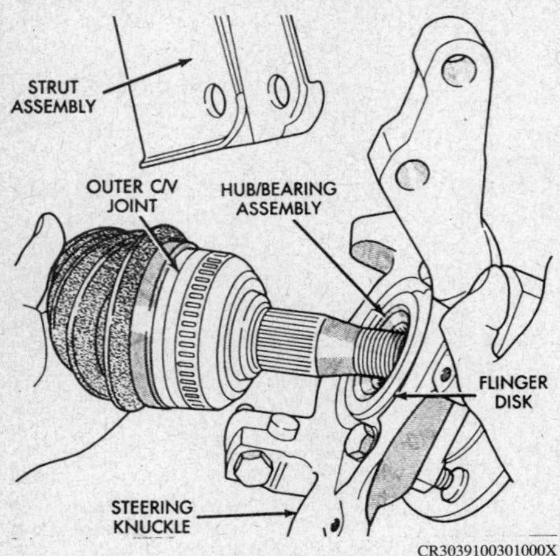

Fig. 4 Outer CV joint separation from hub. Concorde, Intrepid, LHS, & 300M

joint. For lefthand side joint removal, position punch in joint groove.

11. Position a suitable oil resistant container under driveshaft where it enters transaxle.
12. Hold inner tripod joint and driveshaft interconnecting shaft.
13. Remove inner joint from transaxle by pulling it straight out of side gear and oil seal. **Do not let spline or snap ring drag across oil sealing lip.**
14. Reverse procedure to install, noting following:
    a. Thoroughly clean spline and oil sealing surface on tripod joint, then lubricate oil seal sealing surface with transaxle fluid.
    b. Ensure snap ring is fully seated in its groove. The tripod joint will not be removable by hand when snap ring is properly installed.
    c. Install a new knuckle to ball joint stud bolt and nut. Tighten to specifications.
    d. Clean all dirt and debris from driveshaft outer stub shaft threads. Tighten hub nut to specifications.
    e. Inspect transaxle fluid level and correct as required.

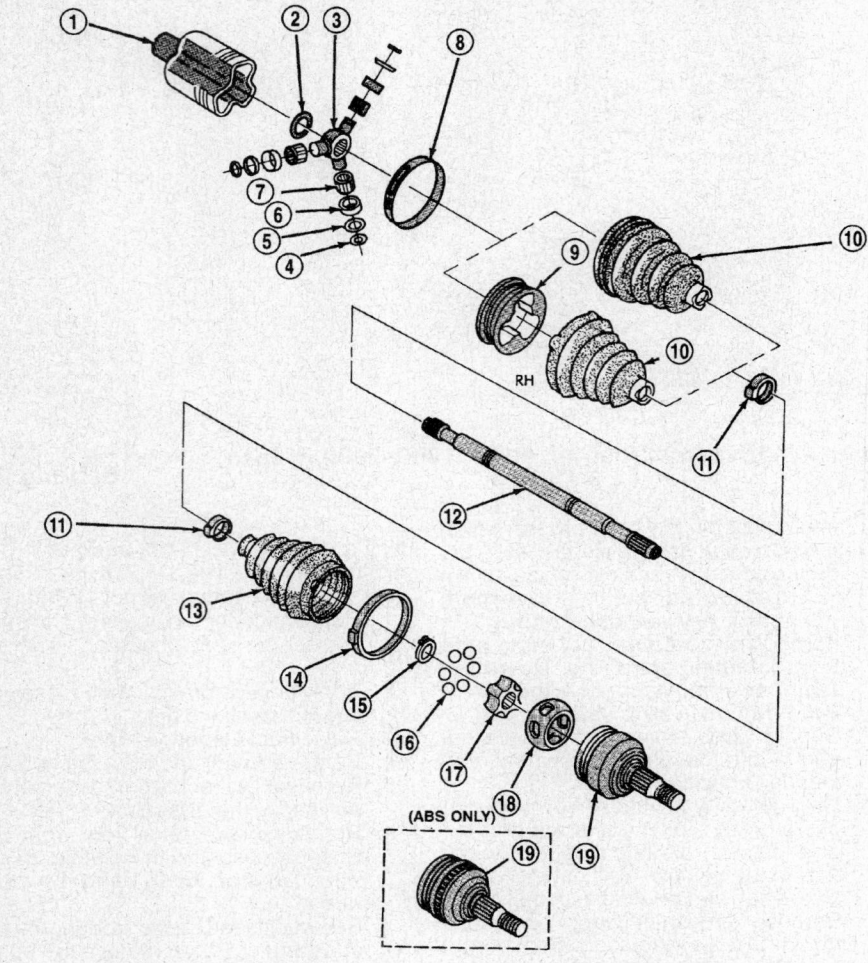

1 - HOUSING ASM, RETAINER
2 - RING, SPACER
3 - SPIDER, TRIPOD JOINT
4 - RING, RETAINING
5 - RETAINER, BALL & ROLLER
6 - BALL, TRIPOD JOINT
7 - ROLLER, NEEDLE
8 - CLAMP, SEAL RETAINING
9 - BUSHING, TRILOBAL TRIPOD
10 - SEAL, DRIVE AXLE INBOARD
11 - CLAMP, SEAL RETAINING
12 - SHAFT, AXLE (RH SHOWN, LH SIMILAR)
13 - SEAL, DRIVE AXLE OUTBOARD
14 - CLAMP, SEAL RETAINING
15 - RING, RACE RETAINING
16 - BALL, CHROME ALLOY
17 - RACE, C/V JOINT INNER
18 - CAGE, C/V JOINT
19 - RACE, C/V JOINT OUTER

CR3030000477000X

Fig. 5 Exploded view of driveshaft assembly

DRIVESHAFT SERVICE

The driveshaft assembly as shown in **Fig. 5,** is a non-serviceable item, except for the inner and outer driveshaft boots. If any failure of internal components is diagnosed during a road test or disassembly, the driveshaft will need to be replaced as an assembly.

INNER DRIVESHAFT BOOT, REPLACE

REMOVAL

1. Remove driveshaft as outlined under "Driveshaft, Replace."
2. Remove inner joint boot clamps, then slide boot down interconnecting shaft.
3. Remove interconnecting shaft and spider assembly out of joint housing. **Do not pull on interconnecting shaft.**
4. Remove snap ring, then spider assembly from interconnecting shaft using a brass drift if required. **Hold bearings in place on spider trunnions to prevent them from falling away. Do not hit outer tripod bearings when removing spider assembly.**
5. Remove joint boot from interconnecting shaft.
6. Clean and inspect spider assembly, tripod joint housing and interconnecting shaft for any signs of excessive wear. **If any excessive wear is present, replacement of entire driveshaft will be required.**

INSTALLATION

Two different types of boots are used on these models. One is a high temperature, soft and pliable type, the other is a normal temperature, soft and rigid type. The replacement boot must be of the same type which was removed.

1. **On Concorde, Intrepid, LHS, and 300M models,** install new boot clamps and boot onto interconnecting shaft. **Boot must be positioned on interconnecting shaft so only thinnest shaft groove is visible.**
2. **On Breeze, Cirrus, Neon, Sebring Convertible, Stratus and 2001–02 Sebring & Stratus Sedan models,** install new boot clamps and boot onto interconnecting shaft. **Boot must be positioned so raised bead on inside of boot is in groove on interconnecting shaft.**
3. **On all models,** install spider assembly onto interconnecting shaft, then the retaining snap ring. **Ensure retaining**

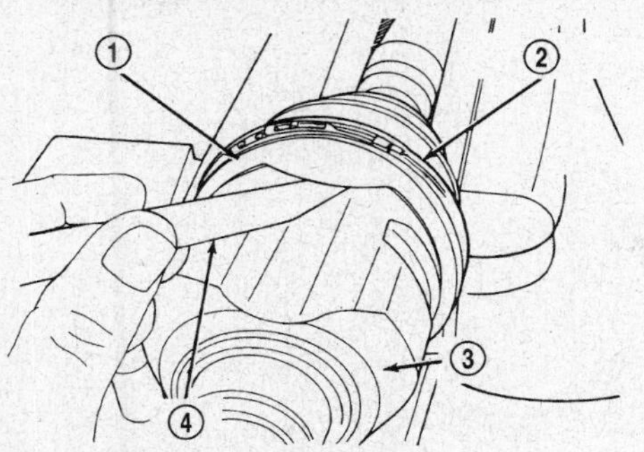

Fig. 6 Venting tripod joint assembly

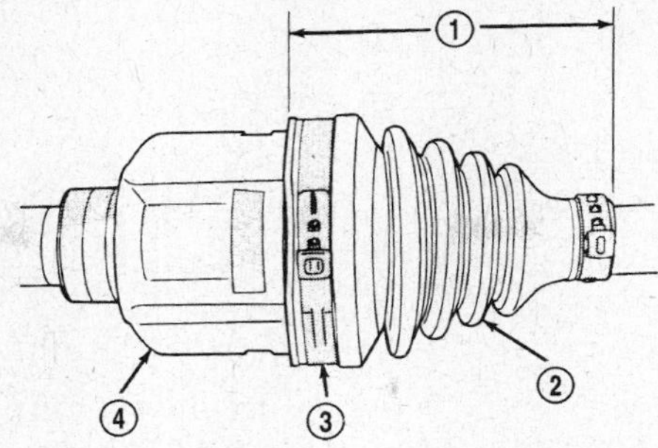

Fig. 7 Sealing boot edge to edge length

snap ring is fully installed and seated into its shaft groove.

4. Distribute ½ amount of grease provided in boot service package into tripod housing and remaining amount into boot. **Do not use any other type of grease.**
5. Install spider assembly into tripod housing.
6. Position boot over boot retaining groove on interconnecting shaft and install boot retaining clamp using crimper tool No. C-4975-A or equivalent.
7. Position boot into tripod housing retaining groove.
8. **On Breeze, Cirrus, Neon, Sebring Convertible, Stratus and 2001–02 Sebring & Stratus Sedan models,** proceed as follows:
   a. **This procedure determines correct air pressure inside inner tripod joint assembly prior to clamping boot to tripod joint housing. Failure to perform this procedure can adversely effect boot durability.**
   b. Insert a trim stick between joint and boot to vent inner joint assembly **Fig. 6.** If inner joint has a hard plastic boot, trim stick must be inserted between soft rubber insert and joint housing.
   c. With trim stick inserted between sealing boot and tripod joint housing, position interconnecting shaft so it sits in center of its travel in tripod joint housing.
   d. **On Models equipped with (Hytrel) hard plastic sealing boot,** insert trim stick between soft rubber and tripod housing not hard plastic sealing boot and soft rubber insert.
   e. **On all models** With trim stick inserted, position inner tripod joint on halfshaft until correct sealing boot edge to edge length is obtained, **Fig. 7. On models with hard plastic sealing boot** edge to edge length is 4.213 inches. **On models with soft sealing boot** edge to edge length is 4.134 inches.

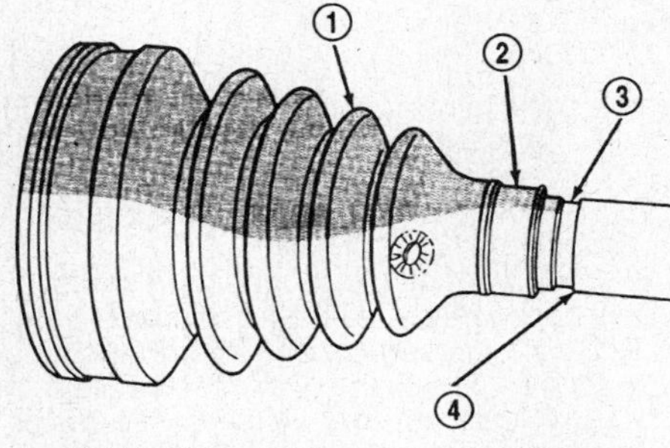

Fig. 9 Outer sealing boot installation. Neon, Sebring Convertible, 1998–2000 Breeze, Cirrus, Stratus & 2001–02 Sebring & Stratus Sedan

   f. Position boot to interface with tripod housing. Boot lobes must be properly aligned with tripod housing recesses.
9. **On models equipped with crimp type boot clamp,** proceed as follows:
   a. Clamp sealing boot onto tripod housing using crimper tool No. C-4975-A or equivalent.
   b. Place crimping tool over clamp bridge.
   c. Tighten nut on crimper tool until tool's jaws are completely closed together, face to face.
10. **On models equipped with latching type boot clamp,** proceed as follows:
   a. Clamp sealing boot onto tripod housing using clamp locking tool No. YA3050 or equivalent.
   b. Place tool's prongs in clamp hole.
   c. Squeeze tool together until clamp's top band is latched behind two tabs on lower clamp band.
11. **On all models,** install driveshaft as outlined under "Driveshaft, Replace."

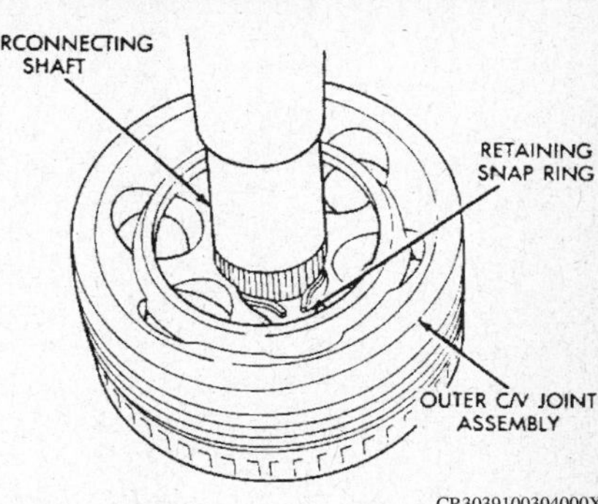

Fig. 8 Outer CV joint retaining snap ring location. Concorde, Intrepid, LHS, & 300M

OUTER DRIVESHAFT BOOT, REPLACE

CONCORDE, INTREPID, LHS, & 300M

Removal

1. Remove driveshaft as outlined under "Driveshaft, Replace."
2. Remove outer joint boot clamps, then slide boot down interconnecting shaft.
3. Remove grease to expose outer CV joint retaining ring as shown in **Fig. 8.**
4. Spread retaining ring and slide CV joint assembly off interconnecting shaft.
5. Remove and discard failed boot and clamps.
6. Clean and inspect spider assembly, CV joint and interconnecting shaft for any signs of excessive wear. **If any excessive wear is present, entire driveshaft replacement will be required.**

Installation

1. Install new boot clamps and boot onto interconnecting shaft.
2. Install CV joint onto interconnecting shaft by pushing shaft into CV joint until retaining snap ring is seated in groove on shaft as shown in **Fig. 8.**
3. Distribute ½ the amount of grease provided in boot service package into CV joint assembly and remaining amount into boot.
4. Position boot over boot retaining grove on interconnecting shaft. **Boot must be positioned on interconnecting shaft so only thinnest shaft groove is visible.**
5. Install boot retaining clamp using crimper tool No. C-4975-A or equivalent.
6. Position boot over boot retaining grove on CV joint housing and install boot retaining clamp using crimper tool. Ensure seal is not dimpled, stretched or distorted in any way.
7. Install driveshaft as outlined under "Driveshaft, Replace."

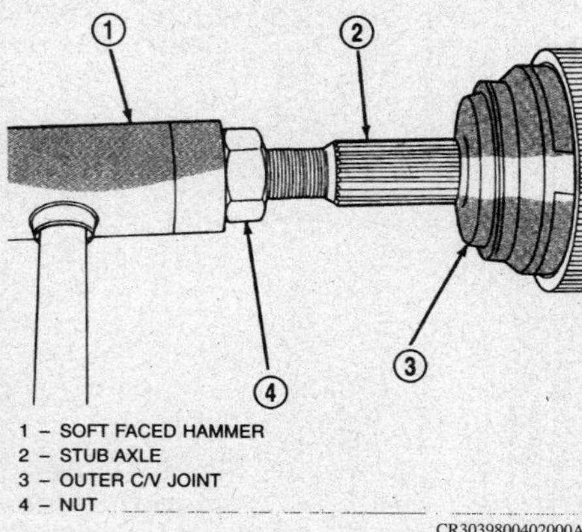

Fig. 10 Outer CV joint assembly installation. Neon, Sebring Convertible, 1998–2000 Breeze, Cirrus, Stratus & 2001–02 Sebring & Stratus Sedan

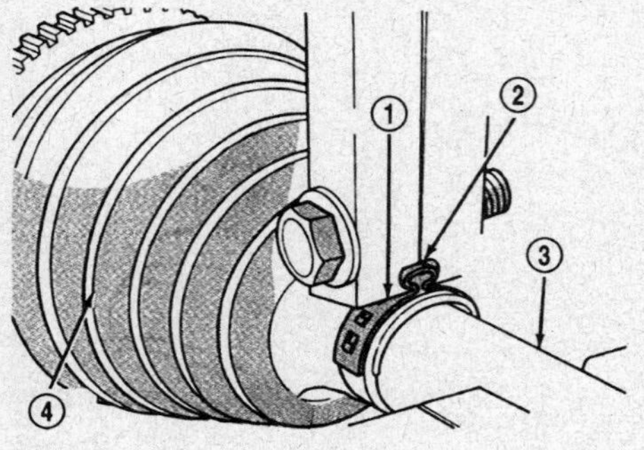

Fig. 11 CV boot clamp installation. Neon, Sebring Convertible, 1998–2000 Breeze, Cirrus, Stratus & 2001–02 Sebring & Stratus Sedan

NEON, SEBRING CONVERTIBLE, 1998–2000 BREEZE, CIRRUS, STRATUS & 2001–02 SEBRING & STRATUS SEDAN

Removal

1. Remove driveshaft as outlined under "Driveshaft, Replace."
2. Remove and discard large boot clamp retaining CV joint sealing boot to CV joint housing.
3. Remove and discard small clamp that retains outer CV joint sealing boot to interconnecting shaft.
4. Slide sealing boot from outer CV joint housing and slide it down interconnecting shaft.
5. Wipe away grease to expose outer CV joint and interconnecting shaft.
6. Remove outer CV joint from interconnecting shaft as follows:
   a. Support interconnecting shaft in a suitable soft jawed vice with protective jaw caps.
   b. Using a suitable soft faced hammer, strike end of CV joint housing to dislodge housing from internal circlip on interconnecting shaft.
   c. CV joint may have to be tapped off interconnecting shaft using a suitable soft faced hammer.
7. Remove large circlip from interconnecting shaft.
8. Slide boot off interconnecting shaft.
9. Thoroughly clean and inspect outer CV joint assembly and interconnecting joint for any signs of excessive wear. **If any components show signs of excessive wear, replace driveshaft assembly.**

Installation

1. Slide new sealing boot to interconnecting shaft retaining clamp and onto interconnecting shaft as shown in **Fig. 9. Ensure seal boot is positioned on interconnecting shaft so raised bead on inside of seal boot is in groove on interconnecting shaft.**
2. Align splines on interconnecting shaft with splines on cross of outer CV joint assembly and start outer CV joint onto interconnecting shaft.
3. Use a suitable soft faced hammer to install outer CV joint assembly onto interconnecting shaft as shown in **Fig. 10.**
4. Distribute ½ amount of grease provided in seal boot service package into outer CV joint assembly housing. **Do not use any other type of grease.**
5. Put remaining amount into sealing boot.
6. Install outer CV joint boot to interconnecting shaft clamp evenly on sealing boot.
7. Clamp sealing boot onto interconnecting shaft using clamp crimper tool No. C-4975-A or equivalent, as shown in **Fig. 11.**
8. Position outer CV joint sealing boot into its retaining groove on outer CV joint housing.
9. Install sealing boot to outer CV joint retaining clamp evenly on sealing boot.
10. Clamp sealing boot onto CV joint housing using clamp crimper tool No. C-4975-A or equivalent. **Ensure jaws of crimper tool are closed completely together.**
11. Install driveshaft as outlined under "Driveshaft, Replace."

TIGHTENING SPECIFICATIONS

Car/Year	Component	Torque Ft. Lbs.
BREEZE, CIRRUS, SEBRING CONVERTIBLE & STRATUS		
1998–99	Caliper To Knuckle Bolts	23
	Halfshaft To Hub Bearing Nut	180
	Knuckle To Ball Stud Nut	70
	Knuckle To Strut Bolt Nuts	125
	Tie Rod End To Knuckle	45
	Wheel Lugnuts	100
2000	Halfshaft To Hub Bearing Nut	105
	Knuckle To Ball Stud Nut	70
	Knuckle To Strut Bolt Nuts	125
	Tie Rod End To Knuckle	45
	Wheel Lugnuts	100
CONCORDE, INTREPID, LHS, & 300M		
1998–99	Caliper To Knuckle Bolts	14
	Halfshaft To Hub Bearing Nut	120
	Knuckle To Ball Stud Nut	70
	Knuckle To Strut Bolt Nuts	125
	Tie Rod End To Knuckle	45
	Wheel Lugnuts	100
2000–02	Halfshaft To Hub Bearing Nut	105
	Knuckle To Ball Stud Nut	70
	Knuckle To Strut Bolt Nuts	155
	Tie Rod End To Knuckle	27
	Wheel Lugnuts	100
NEON		
1998–99	Halfshaft To Hub Bearing Nut	135
	Knuckle To Ball Stud Nut	70
	Knuckle To Strut Bolt Nuts (1998-99 Less ACR Package)	40①
	Knuckle To Strut Bolt Nuts (1999 With ACR Package)	75①
	Tie Rod End To Knuckle	45
	Wheel Lugnuts	100
2000–02	Caliper To Knuckle Bolts	16
	Halfshaft To Hub Bearing Nut	180
	Knuckle To Ball Joint Stud Nut	70
	Knuckle To Strut Bolt Nuts	40①
	Tie Rod End To Knuckle	45
	Wheel Lugnuts	95

Continued

TIGHTENING SPECIFICATIONS—Continued

Car/Year	Component	Torque Ft. Lbs.
SEBRING & STRATUS SEDAN		
2001–02	Ball Joint To Knuckle Nut	70
	Halfshaft To Hub Bearing Nut	110
	Tie Rod To Knuckle Nut	41
	Wheel To Hub Nut	100

① — Rotate an additional 90.°

ALL-WHEEL DRIVE SYSTEMS

NOTE: Refer To "Front Drive Axles" For Procedures Not Found In This Section.

NOTE: On Air Bag Equipped Models, Refer To "Air Bag System Precautions" Located In The Front Of This Manual For System Disarming & Arming Procedures.

NOTE: Refer To "Computer Relearn Procedures" Located In The Front Of This Manual When Battery Power To The Computer Has Been Interrupted.

INDEX

DESCRIPTION

This system used on Talon is a full time All Wheel Drive (AWD) system. It has an optional limited slip differential for increased traction. The main components used in this system are the transfer case, rear drive axle, axle shafts and driveshaft.

TROUBLESHOOTING

Refer to **Fig. 1,** when troubleshooting system malfunctions.

AXLE SHAFT

REPLACE

Refer to "Rear Axle Hub & Carrier Service" for procedure.

DRIVESHAFT

REPLACE

Remove rear driveshaft in numbered sequence, **Fig. 2,** noting the following:

1. Remove drive shaft nut using removal tool No. MB990767, or equivalent.
2. Remove driveshaft by pushing the lower part of the knuckle to the outside of the vehicle, then separate the driveshaft from the differential carrier. At this time, use a suitable tire lever or similar tool to separate the driveshaft connection.
3. Reverse procedure to install noting the following:
   a. Ensure proper driveshaft placement. The right driveshaft has an orange boot band, while the left driveshaft has a green boot band.
   b. Ensure differential carrier oil seal is not damaged by driveshaft spline.
   c. Using special tool No. MB990767, or equivalent, tighten driveshaft nut to specifications, **Fig. 2.** Ensure there is no load on wheel bearings.

DRIVESHAFT SERVICE

DISASSEMBLE

1. Remove Tripod joint boot bands, **Fig. 3.**
2. Remove Tripod joint case.
3. Remove snap ring off Tripod joint end of driveshaft.
4. Remove spider assembly off driveshaft. **Do not service spider assembly.**
5. Wrap vinyl tape around splines of driveshaft then remove Tripod joint boot.
6. Remove Birfield joint bands.
7. Wrap vinyl tape around splines of driveshaft then remove Birfield joint boot.
8. Remove Birfield joint. **Do not service Birfield joint.**

INSPECTION

1. Check driveshaft for damage, bending or corrosion.
2. Check driveshaft spline for wear or damage.
3. Check Birfield joint for entry of water or foreign material.
4. Check spider assembly for roller rotation, wear or corrosion.
5. Check Birfield joint outer race for damage or corrosion.
6. Check boots for damage, cracking or wear.

ASSEMBLE

Reverse disassembly procedure to assemble, noting the following:

1. Wrap vinyl tape around spline on driveshaft then install Birfield joint and Tripod joint boots.
2. Fill inside of Birfield joint and Birfield joint boot with half of grease included in repair kit.
3. Secure boot bands with driveshaft at a 0° angle.
4. Apply grease to spider assembly then install spider assembly with chamfered spline end first.
5. Install Tripod joint on driveshaft.
6. Set Tripod joint boot bands 3.23–4.47 inches apart to adjust amount of air inside boot then tighten Tripod joint boot band securely.

DIFFERENTIAL CARRIER

REPLACE

1. Remove driveshafts as described in "Driveshaft, Replace."
2. Position a suitable jack under rear axle assembly, then drain differential gear oil.
3. Remove center exhaust system components as necessary.
4. Scribe mating marks on differential companion flange and flange yoke for assembly reference.
5. Remove differential to propeller shaft connection, then support propeller shaft with wire.
6. Remove dynamic damper to differential support member bolts.
7. Remove differential support member bolts, then the carrier, **Fig. 4.**

AXLE SHAFT

Symptom	Probable cause	Remedy
Noise while wheels are rotating	Brake drag	Replace
	Bent axle shaft	
	Worn or scarred axle shaft bearing	
Grease leakage	Worn or damaged oil seal	
	Malfunction of bearing seal	

DRIVE SHAFT

Symptom	Probable cause	Remedy
Noise	Wear, play or seizure of ball joint	Replace
	Excessive drive shaft spline looseness	

DIFFERENTIAL (LIMITED SLIP DIFFERENTIAL)

Symptom	Probable cause	Remedy
Abnormal noise during driving or gear changing*1	Excessive drive gear backlash	Adjust
	Insufficient drive pinion preload	
	Excessive differential gear backlash	Adjust or replace
	Worn spline of a side gear	Replace
	Loose companion flange self-locking nut	Retighten or replace
Abnormal noise when cornering	Damaged differential gears	Replace
	Damaged pinion shaft	
	Insufficient gear oil quantity	Replenish
Gear noise	Improper drive gear tooth contact adjustment	Adjust or replace
	Incorrect drive gear backlash	Adjust
	Improper drive pinion preload adjustment	

CR3039100178010X

Fig. 1 AWD troubleshooting chart (Part 1 of 2)

Symptom	Probable cause	Remedy
Gear noise	Damaged, broken, and/or seized tooth surfaces of the drive gear and drive pinion	Replace
	Damaged, broken, and/or seized drive pinion bearings	
	Damaged, broken, and/or seized side bearings	
	Damaged differential case	
	Inferior gear oil	
	Insufficient gear oil quantity	Replenish
Gear oil leakage	Worn or damaged front oil seal, or an improperly installed oil seal	Replace
	Damaged gasket	
	Loose companion flange self-locking nut	Retighten or replace
	Loose filler or drain plug	Retighten or apply adhesive
	Clogged or damaged vent plug	Clean or replace
Seizure	Insufficient drive gear backlash	Adjust
	Excessive drive pinion preload	
	Excessive side bearing preload	
	Insufficient differential gear backlash	
	Excessive clutch plate preload	
	Inferior gear oil	Replace
	Insufficient gear oil quantity	Replenish
Breakdown	Incorrect drive gear backlash	Adjust
	Insufficient drive pinion preload	
	Insufficient side bearing preload	
	Excessive differential gear backlash	
	Loose drive gear clamping bolts	Retighten
The limited slip differential does not function (on snow, mud, ice, etc.)	The limited slip device is damaged	Disassemble, check the functioning and replace the damaged parts

CR3039100178020X

Fig. 1 AWD troubleshooting chart (Part 2 of 2)

8. Reverse procedure to install, tighten bolts to specifications.

CARRIER INSPECTION & SERVICE

REAR AXLE TOTAL BACKLASH

If vehicle vibrates and has a booming sound due to system driveline imbalance. Total axle backlash should be checked. To check backlash, proceed as follows:

1. Place gearshift in neutral, apply parking brake, then raise and support vehicle.
2. Manually turn propeller shaft clockwise as far as it will go and scribe mating mark on companion flange dust cover and differential carrier, **Fig. 5.**
3. Manually turn shaft counterclockwise as far as it will go and measure movement of mating marks.
4. If axle total backlash is less than .2 inch (5 mm), backlash is satisfactory.
5. If backlash is more than .2 inch (5 mm), adjust as necessary.

GEAR OIL LEVEL CHECK

1. Remove filler plug and check oil level.
2. If oil level reaches bottom of filler plug hole, oil level is satisfactory.
3. If level does not reach bottom of filler plug hole, fill differential with Mopar Hypoid Gear Oil API classification GL-5, or equivalent.

REAR WHEEL BEARING ENDPLAY CHECK

1. Raise and support vehicle on axle stands.
2. Remove rear wheel and tire assembly, then disconnect parking brake cable from rear brake.
3. Remove caliper assembly and brake disc.
4. Position a dial indicator, **Fig. 6** and measure endplay when axle is moved in an axial direction.
5. If endplay is less than .002 inch, endplay is satisfactory.
6. If endplay exceeds .002 inch, replace rear wheel bearing.

REAR WHEEL BEARING ROTATION SLIDING RESISTANCE CHECK

1. Raise and support vehicle, then remove driveshaft as described under "Driveshaft, Replace."
2. Use bolt tool No. MB990998, or equivalent to mount rear hub onto lower arm, **Fig. 7.**
3. **Torque** nut of special bolt to 145–188 ft. lbs.
4. Rotate rear hub to seat bearing.
5. With bolt tool installed, measure wheel bearing starting torque using torque wrench, adapter and socket tool Nos. MB990998, MB990685 and MB990326, or equivalents.
6. Starting torque should be 9 inch lbs. or less and bearing must not feel rough when rotated.

LIMITED-SLIP DIFFERENTIAL CHECK

1. Block front wheels and move shift lever to neutral.
2. Release parking brake completely, then raise rear wheels and support with rigid jack stand.
3. Disconnect coupling of differential and propeller shaft.
4. Rotate one wheel slowly, ensure wheel on opposite side turns in the same direction.
5. If wheel turns in the opposite direction, replace viscous unit.

DIFFERENTIAL CARRIER SERVICE

EXCEPT LIMITED-SLIP

Pre-Disassemble Inspection

1. Support working base in a vise, and attach differential carrier to working base, **Fig. 8.**
2. Check final drive gear backlash as follows:
   a. Lock drive pinion in place, then mount dial indicator to differential carrier, **Fig. 9.**
   b. Measure backlash at four points or more on the circumference of the drive gear. Backlash should be within .004–.006 inch.
3. Mount dial indicator to differential carrier, **Fig. 10,** then measure drive gear runabout at the shoulder on the reverse side of drive gear. Runabout should not exceed .002 inch.
4. Lock side gear with a wedge, **Fig. 11,** then measure differential gear backlash with dial indicator on pinion gear.

Differential gear backlash should not exceed .008 inch.

5. Check final drive gear tooth contact as follows:
   a. Apply a thin, uniform coat of machine blue to both surfaces of drive gear teeth, **Fig. 12.**
   b. Insert a brass rod between differential carrier and differential case, then rotate companion flange by hand (once in normal direction, and once in reverse direction) while applying a load to drive gear, so revolution torque applied to the drive pinion is approximately 28–33 inch lbs., **Fig. 13.**
   c. Compare and adjust tooth contact pattern, **Fig. 14.**
   d. If correct tooth pattern cannot be obtained by adjustment, drive gear and drive pinion have exceeded their usage limit and both gears should be replaced as a set.

Disassemble

1. Support working base in a vise, and attach differential carrier to working base.
2. Remove differential cover and vent plug, **Fig. 15.**
3. Using two hammer shafts, or equivalent, slowly and carefully pry differential case assembly out of gear carrier. **Ensure side bearing outer race is not dropped when removing differential case assembly. Keep right and left side bearings separate, so they do not become mixed at time of reassembly.**
4. Using side bearing puller tool No. MB990810 and side bearing cup tool No. MB990811, or equivalents, pull out side bearing inner races, **Fig. 16.**
5. Scribe mating marks on differential case and drive gear, then loosen drive gear attaching bolts in diagonal sequence to remove drive gear.
6. Drive out lockpin with a punch and remove pinion gears, pinion washers, side gears, side gear spacers and differential case.
7. Scribe mating marks on drive pinion and companion flange. **Mating marks should not be made to contact surfaces of companion flange and propeller shaft.**
8. Using side bearing puller tool No. MB990810, or equivalent, drive out drive pinion together with drive pinion spacer and drive pinion front shims.
9. Mount companion flange attached to taper roller bearing puller tool No. C-293-PA and bearing remover tool No. C-293-45, or equivalents in a vise, **Fig. 17.** Pull drive pinion rear bearing inner race out of companion flange.
10. Remove drive pinion rear shim used for drive pinion height adjustment and drive pinion.
11. Remove oil seal, then drive out drive pinion front bearing from gear carrier.
12. Drive out drive pinion rear bearing outer race from gear carrier.

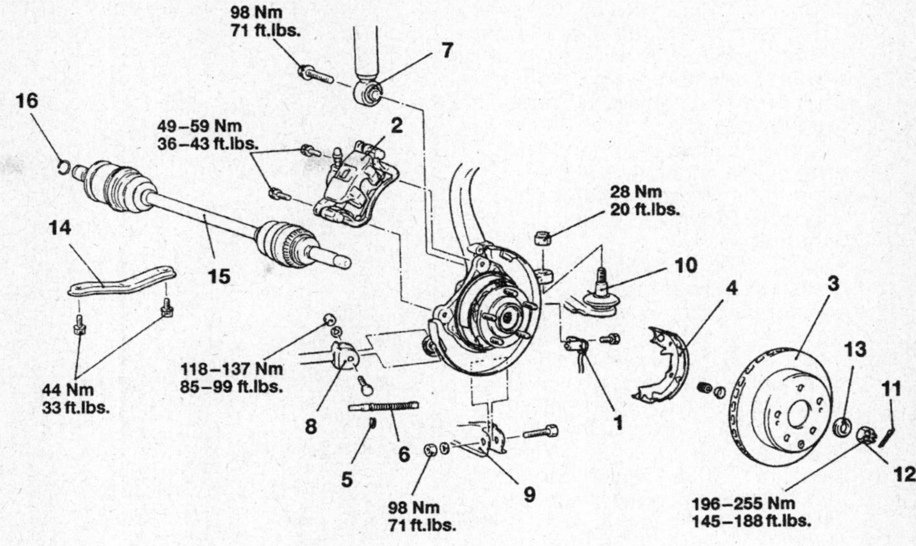

1. Rear wheel speed sensor <Vehicles with ABS>
2. Caliper assembly
3. Brake disc
4. Shoe and lining assembly
5. Clip
6. Parking brake cable
7. Shock absorber connection
8. Trailing arm connection
9. Lower arm connection
10. Toe control arm ball joint and knuckle connection
11. Cottor pin
12. Drive shaft nut
13. Washer
14. Differential mount support
15. Drive shaft
16. Circlip

CR3039500356000X

Fig. 2 Driveshaft replacement

Inspection

1. Check companion flange for wear or damage.
2. Check oil seal for wear or deterioration.
3. Check bearing for wear and discoloration.
4. Check gear carrier for cracks.
5. Check drive pinion and drive gear for wear or cracks.
6. Check side gears, pinion gears and pinion shaft for wear or damage.
7. Check side gear spline for wear or damage.

Assemble

1. Apply multipurpose grease to lip of oil seal, then using installer bar tool No. C-4171 and oil seal installer tool No. MB991115, or equivalents, press seal into gear carrier.
2. Using installer handle tool No. C-4171 and bearing installer tool Nos. MB990932 and MB990935, or equivalents, press drive pinion rear and front bearing outer races into gear carrier.
3. Adjust drive pinion height as follows:
   a. Install a pinion height gauge set tool Nos. MB990835 and MB990836, or equivalent, and drive pinion front and rear bearing inner races on gear carrier, **Fig. 18. Apply a thin coat of multipurpose grease to mating surface on washer of tool.**
   b. Tighten handle of special tool until standard value of drive pinion turning torque is obtained, **Fig. 19.**
   c. Measure drive pinion turning torque (without oil seal).
   d. Position special tool No. MB990835, or equivalent, in side bearing seat of gear carrier, **Fig. 20.** Select a drive pinion rear shim of a thickness which corresponds to the gap between special tools. **Clean side bearing seat thoroughly. When positioning special tool, ensure cutout sections of tool are in position shown, Fig. 20, and that special tool is in close contact with side bearing seat. When selecting drive pinion rear shims, keep number of drive shims to a minimum.**
   e. Fit selected drive pinion rear shims to drive pinion, then using bearing installer tool No. MB990728, or equivalent, press rear bearing inner race onto drive pinion, **Fig. 21.**
4. Adjust drive pinion preload as follows:
   a. Fit drive pinion front shims between drive pinion spacer and drive pinion front bearing inner race.
   b. **Torque** companion flange nut to 116–159 ft. lbs. using end yoke holder tool No. MB990767, or equivalent. **Do not install oil seal.**
   c. Using a torque wrench, measure drive pinion turning torque, **Fig. 22.**
   d. Compare measurement with **Fig. 19.** If turning torque is not within specification, adjust by replacing

drive pinion front shims or drive pinion spacer. **If a number of shims will be required to bring preload within specified value, reduce the number of shims by replacing the spacer.**

e. Remove companion flange and drive pinion, then drive oil seal into gear carrier front lip. Apply a thin coat of multipurpose grease to the oil seal lip.

f. Apply a thin coat of multipurpose grease to companion flange washer contacting surface prior to installing drive pinion.

g. Install drive pinion assembly and companion flange with mating marks aligned, and **torque** companion flange self-locking nut to 116–159 ft. lbs.

h. Measure drive pinion turning torque, and compare with specified value, **Fig. 23.** If turning torque is not within specified value, ensure companion flange self-locking nut is tightened within specification and oil seal is correctly installed.

5. Clean drive gear attaching bolts, then using a M10 X 1.25 tap, remove adhesive adhering to threaded holes of drive gear. Clean remaining material out of drive gear using compressed air.
6. Apply multipurpose adhesive Mopar Loctite No. 271, or equivalent to threaded holes of drive gear.
7. Install drive gear onto differential case with mating marks aligned. **Torque** drive gear attaching bolts in a diagonal sequence to 58–65 ft. lbs.
8. Using bearing installer tool No. MB990728, or equivalent, press side bearing inner races to differential case.
9. Adjust final drive gear backlash as follows:

a. Install side bearing spacers, which are thinner than those removed, to side bearing outer races and then mount differential case assembly into gear carrier. **Use side bearing spacers with the same thickness for both drive pinion and drive gear sides.**

b. Push differential case to one side of the gear carrier and measure clearance between gear carrier and side bearing, **Fig. 24.**

c. Measure thickness of side bearing spacers on one side, then select two pairs of spacers which correspond to that thickness plus one half of clearance plus .002 inch, **Fig. 25.** Install one pair each to drive pinion side and drive gear side.

d. Install side bearing spacers and differential case assembly to gear carrier, **Fig. 26.**

e. Tap side bearing spacers with a brass bar to fit them to side bearing outer race.

f. Align mating marks on gear carrier and bearing cap, then tighten bearing cap.

g. With drive pinion locked in place, measure final drive gear backlash with a dial indicator mounted on drive gear, **Fig. 9.**

h. Measure at four or more points around the circumference of the drive gear, backlash should be within .004–.006 inch (.11–.16 mm).

i. Change side bearing spacers, **Fig. 27,** and then adjust final drive gear backlash between drive gear and drive pinion. **When increasing number of side bearing spacers, use the same number of each, and as few as possible.**

j. Check drive gear and drive pinion for proper tooth contact, refer to "Pre-Disassemble Inspection" for adjustment procedure.

k. Measure drive gear runout at shoulder on reverse side of drive gear, **Fig. 10.** If drive gear runout exceeds .002 inch, reinstall by changing phase of drive gear and differential case, and measure.

10. Apply a semi-drying sealant to installation surface of differential cover and vent plug, **torque** cover bolts to 22–30 ft. lbs.

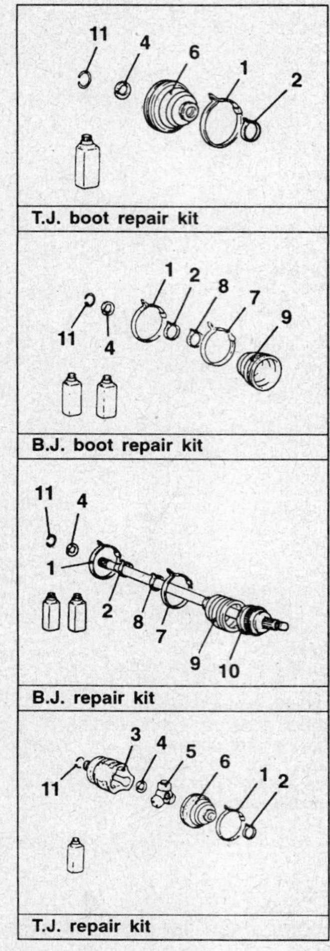

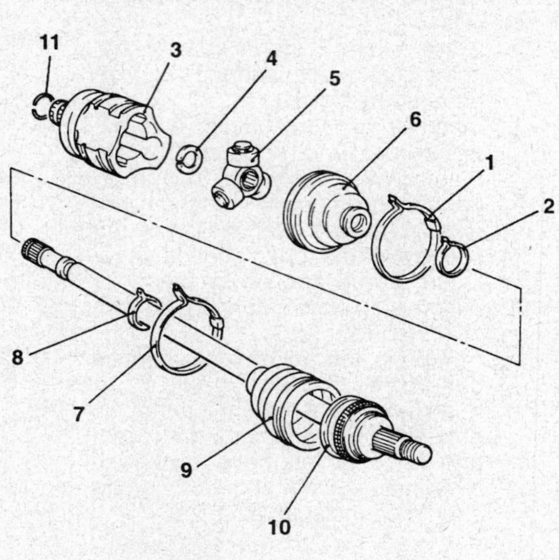

1. T.J. boot band (large)
2. T.J. boot band (small)
3. T.J. case
4. Snap ring
5. Spider assembly
6. T.J. boot
7. B.J. boot band (large)
8. B.J. boot band (small)
9. B.J. boot
10. B.J. assembly
11. Circlip

Caution
Do not disassemble the B.J. assembly.

CR3039500397000X

Fig. 3 Exploded view of driveshaft

LIMITED-SLIP

Pre-Disassemble Inspection

1. Secure differential case assembly in a vise so differential side gear (right) is facing upward, **Fig. 28.**
2. Insert a .0012 inch (.03 mm) feeler gauge at two places (diagonally) between differential case B and thrust washer, **Fig. 29. Do not insert feeler gauge in oil groove of differential case B.**
3. Insert side gear holding tool No. MB990990, or equivalent, at spline part of differential case B (right) and ensure side gear rotates, **Fig. 30.**
4. Insert a .0035 inch (.09 mm) feeler gauge to replace .0012 inch (.03 mm) feeler gauge.
5. Insert side gear holding tool No. MB990990, or equivalent, at spline part of differential case B (right) and

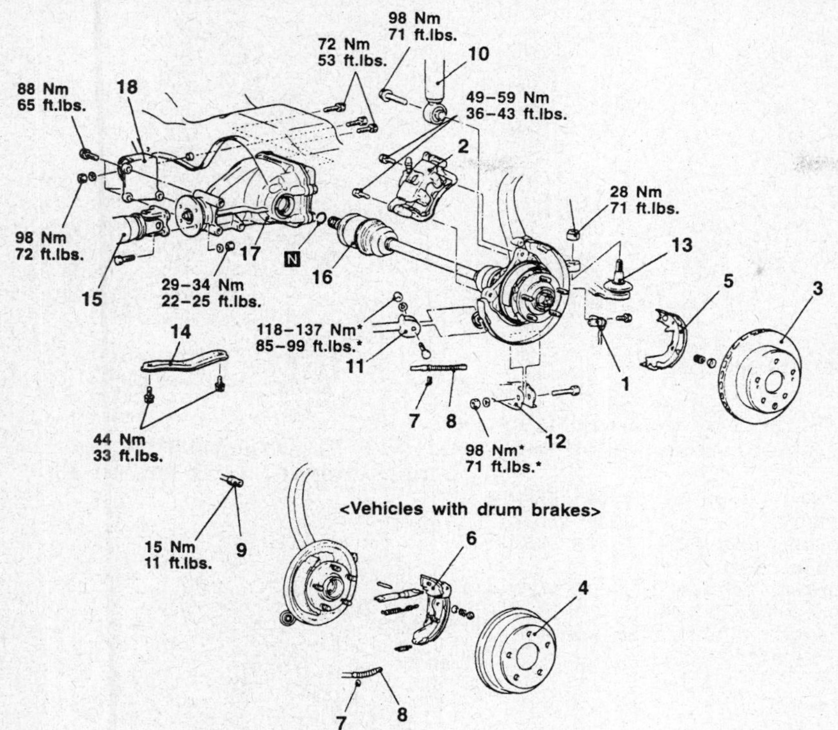

1. Rear wheel speed sensor <Vehicles with ABS>
2. Caliper assembly
3. Brake disc
4. Brake drum
5. Shoe and lever assembly
6. Shoe and lever assembly
7. Clip
8. Parking brake cable
9. Brake pipe connection
10. Shock absorber connection
11. Trailing arm connection
12. Lower arm connection
13. Toe control arm ball joint and knucle connection
14. Differential mount support
15. Propeller shaft connection
16. Drive shaft connection
17. Differential carrier
18. Differential mount bracket assembly

Caution
*: Indicates parts which should be temporarily tightened, and then fully tightened with the vehicle on the ground in the unladen condition.

CR3039500398000X

Fig. 4 Differential carrier replacement

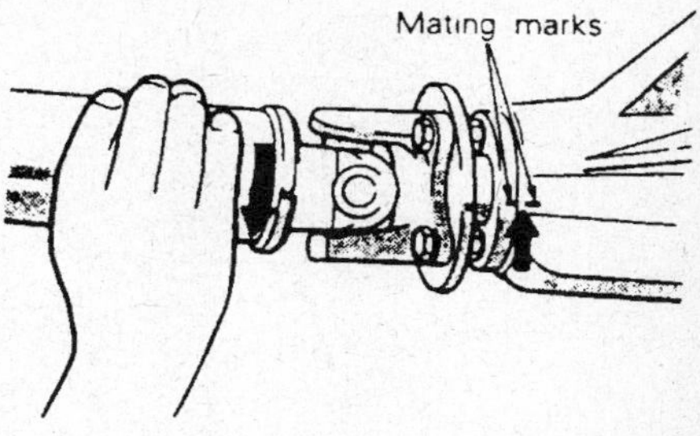

CR3039100179000X

Fig. 5 Rear axle total backlash check

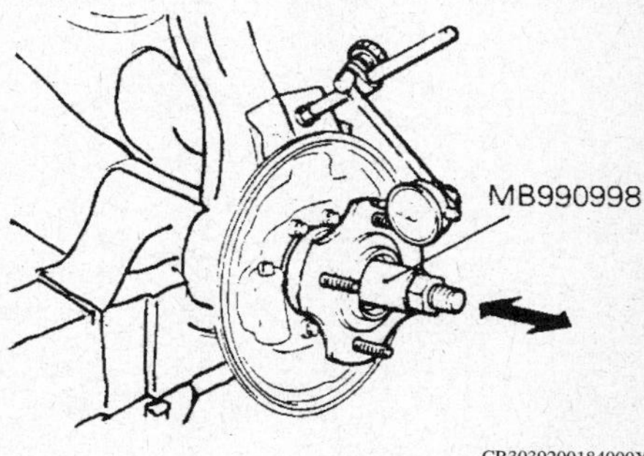

CR3039200184000X

Fig. 6 Rear wheel bearing endplay inspection

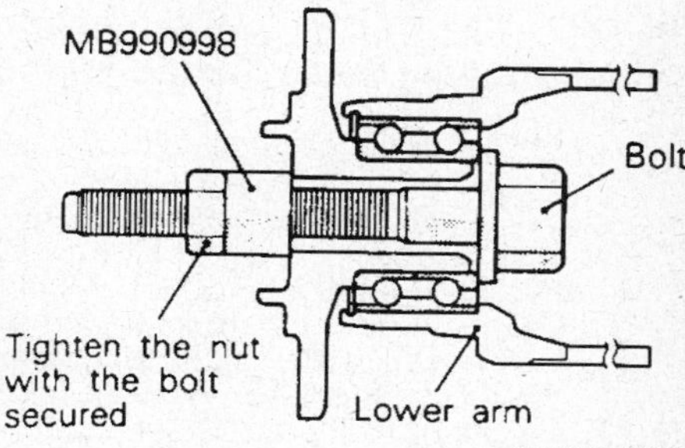

CR3039200183000X

Fig. 7 Bolt tool installation

ensure side gear does not rotate, **Fig. 30.**

6. Differential gear backlash (clearance in thrust direction of side gear) should be within .0012–.0035 inch (.03 mm–.09 mm). If clearance in the thrust direction of the side gear is within standard value range, backlash of differential gear is normal.
7. If clearance in thrust direction of side gear is not within specification, remove differential case A and make adjustment by adjusting thickness of the thrust washer (left).

Disassemble

1. Remove attaching screw from differential case A, **Fig. 31.**
2. Remove differential case B.
3. Remove left thrust washer. **Since thrust washer from left side is of a different thickness than the right side, it will be necessary to mark the washer in some manner for assembly reference.**
4. Remove viscous unit, pinion mate washer, differential pinion mate, pinion shaft and rightward differential side gear.
5. Remove right thrust washer. **Since thrust washer from right side is of a different thickness than the left side, it will be necessary to mark the washer for assembly reference.**

Inspection

1. Check gears and differential pinion shaft for unusual wear or damage.
2. Check spline part of right side differential gear for stepped wear or damage.
3. Check thrust washer and pinion mate washer for unusual wear of contact surfaces, heat damage or other damage.
4. Check contact surfaces of differential cases A and B for damage or wear, **Fig. 32.**
5. Check spline part of viscous unit for stepped wear or damage, and check contact surface with differential case B.
6. Check left side gear of viscous unit for unusual wear or damage.

Assemble

1. With pinion mate washer in position, **Fig. 33,** install to differential pinion mate to differential pinion shaft, and then install to differential case B.
2. If differential side gear and pinion mate gear have been replaced, select left side thrust washer as follows:
   a. Wash differential side gear and pinion mate gear in unleaded gasoline to remove all foreign material.
   b. Install previously used thrust washers (matching left and right sides), together with gears, viscous unit, pinion mate washer and pinion shaft to differential cases A and B. Using screws, secure temporarily.
   c. Secure differential case assembly in a vise so right side differential side gear is facing upward, **Fig. 28. Do not hold differential case too tightly.**
   d. Insert a .0012 inch feeler gauge at two places (diagonally) between differential case B and right side thrust washer. **Do not insert feeler gauge in oil groove of differential case B.**
   e. Insert side gear holding tool No. MB990990, or equivalent, at spline part of differential case B (right) and

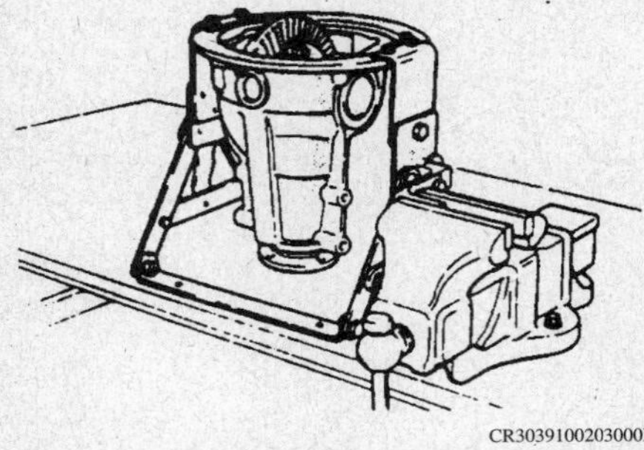

Fig. 8 Differential carrier positioned in working base. Less limited-slip

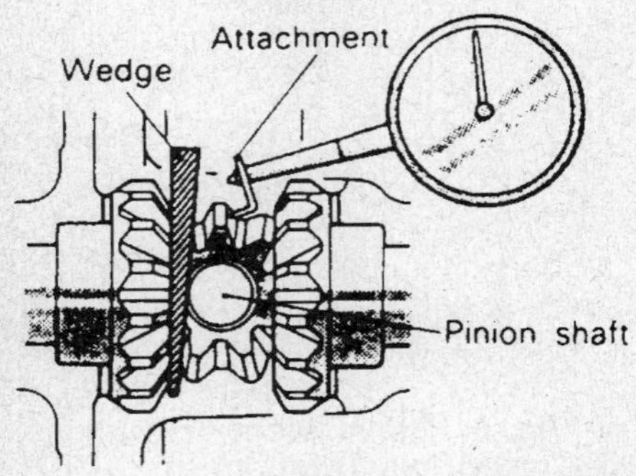

Fig. 11 Differential gear backlash measurement. Less limited-slip

ensure side gear does not rotate, **Fig. 30.**

f. Differential gear backlash (clearance in thrust direction of side gear) should be within .0012–.0035 inch (.03 mm–.09 mm). If clearance in the thrust direction of the side gear is within standard value range, backlash of differential gear is normal.

g. If clearance in thrust direction of side gear is not within specification, remove differential case A and make adjustment by selecting appropriate thrust washer from chart, **Fig. 34.**

3. After installing thrust washers, align mating marks of differential cases and reassemble.

PROPELLER SHAFT

REPLACE

1. Place suitable match marks on all propeller shaft components where disassembly will occur.
2. Place suitable supports under shaft sections to prevent over flexing of components during removal.
3. Remove bolts at flange yoke, **Fig. 35.**
4. Remove nuts and bolts from center bearing(s). **Note position and location of center bearing alignment spacers and shims as equipped.**
5. Remove shaft from vehicle, to prevent damage to joints and boot, do not allow over flexing of shaft.
6. Install output shaft blocker plug, tool No. MB991193, or equivalent into transfer assembly.

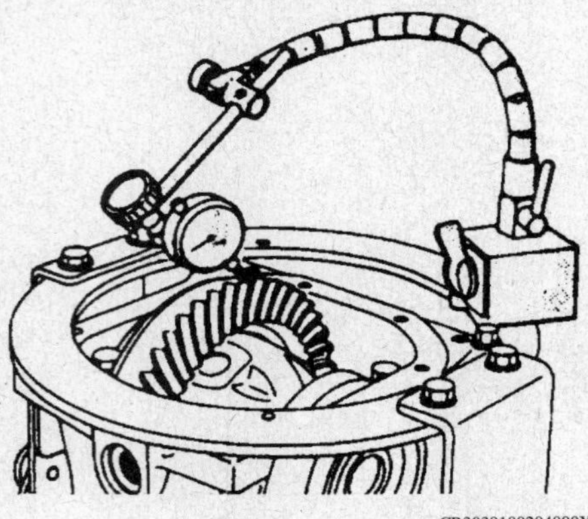

Fig. 9 Final drive gear backlash measurement. Less limited-slip

7. Reverse procedure to install, noting the following:
   a. Ensure alignment of all match marks.
   b. **Torque** differential flange yoke bolts to 22–25 ft. lbs.
   c. **Torque** center bearing mount nuts and bolts to 22 ft. lbs.

PROPELLER SHAFT SERVICE

LOBO JOINT, JOINT BOOT & COMPANION FLANGE

Removal

1. Place suitable match marks on all components to be disassembled **Fig. 35.**
2. Remove bolts retaining Lobo joint to companion flange, then separate joint from flange.
3. Using a suitable screwdriver, tap flange edge of boot off Lobo joint outer race.
4. **On models where outer race of joint can be removed,** proceed as follows:
   a. Place match marks on all components and note position of balls.
   b. Tilt edge of outer race until balls can removed from cage, then remove balls.
   c. Remove outer race and cage, then snap ring retaining inner race to shaft.
   d. Using a suitable fuller, remove inner race from shaft.
5. **On models where outer race of joint can not be removed,** remove snap ring retaining joint to shaft.
6. **On models where outer race of joint can not be removed,** using a suitable fuller carefully pull joint from shaft.
7. **On all models,** remove boot clamp then boot and if equipped, boot washer.

Cleaning & Inspection

Do not use solvents to clean boot, wipe clean only.

1. Using a suitable solvent, clean, then dry joint components.

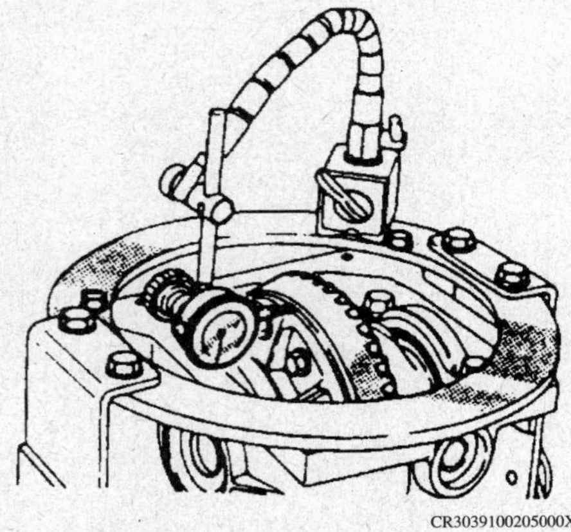

Fig. 10 Drive gear runout measurement. Less limited-slip

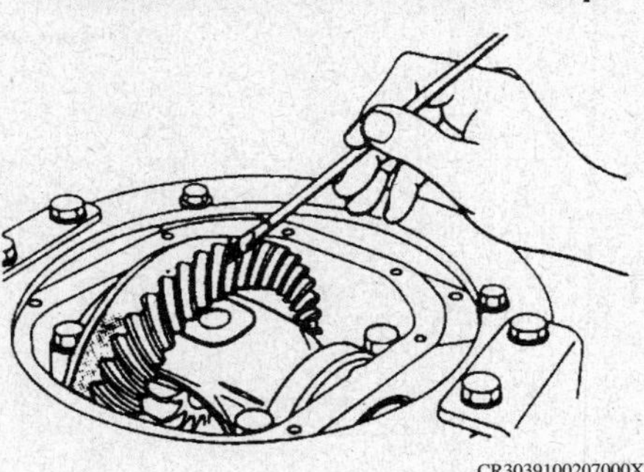

Fig. 12 Final drive gear tooth contact marking inspection. Less limited-slip

2. Check splines of shaft and joint for wear or damage.
3. Check ball grooves and balls for uneven wear, damage or rust.
4. Check cage for wear, rust or damage.
5. Inspect boot for tears, deterioration and chafing.

Installation

Note position of bosses in small end I.D. of boot for later assembly. These are used to ventilate boot and joint.

Ensure seat area on shaft for small end of joint is grease free when installing boot. Grease in this area will prevent proper ventilation of joint.

1. Place tape over shaft spline to protect boot during installation, then, as equipped, install boot washer, boot clamp and boot. Remove tape.
2. **On models where joint was disassembled,** reassemble joint, ensure match marks are aligned. Joint boot flange recess on outer race, spline recess of inner race and chamfer of cage should all be assembled on same side of joint.
3. **On all models,** pack joint and boot with 1.6–2.0 oz. of a suitable joint grease.
4. Using a suitable adhesive, position and secure joint gaskets.
5. Place joint on shaft splines so that bolt holes of boot flange and joint align, then using a suitable socket or tube and hammer drive joint onto shaft and

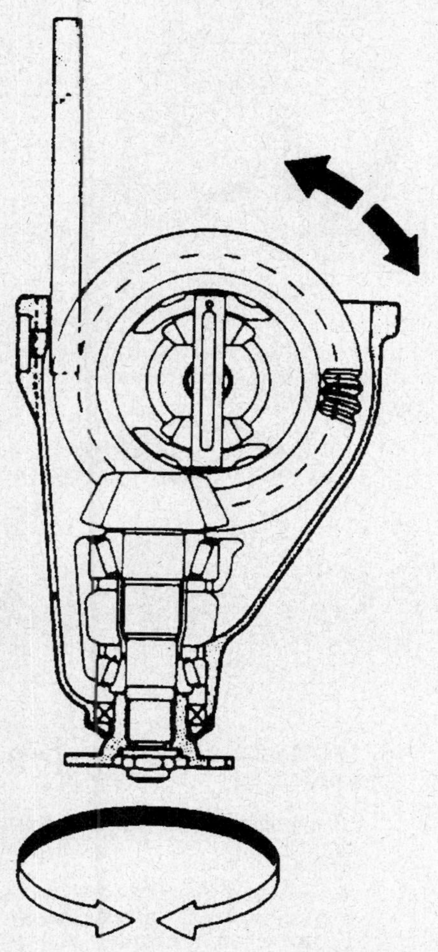

CR3039100208000X

Fig. 13 Final drive gear rotation. Less limited-slip

Standard tooth contact pattern

1 Narrow tooth side
2 Drive-side tooth surface (the side applying power during forward movement)
3 Wide tooth side
4 Coast-side tooth surface (the side applying power during reverse movement)

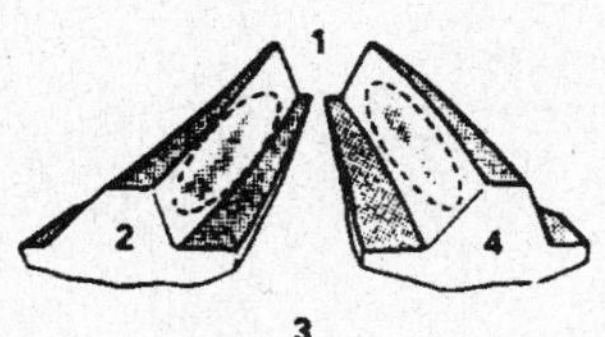

Problem	Solution
Tooth contact pattern resulting from excessive pinion height  The drive pinion is positioned too far from the center of the drive gear.	 Increase the thickness of the pinion height adjusting shim, and position the drive pinion closer to the center of the drive gear. Also, for backlash adjustment, position the drive gear farther from the drive pinion.
Tooth contact pattern resulting from insufficient pinion height  The drive pinion is positioned too close to the center of the drive gear.	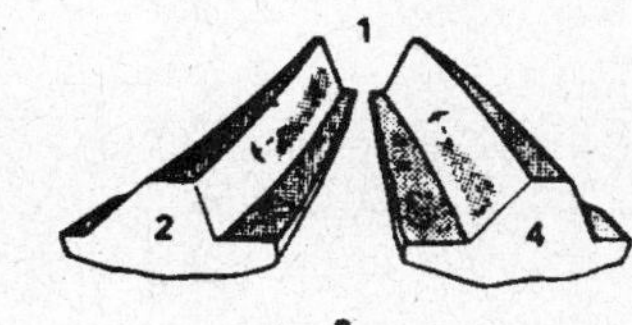 Decrease the thickness of the pinion height adjusting shim, and position the drive pinion farther from the center of the drive gear. Also, for backlash adjustment, position the drive gear closer to the drive pinion.

NOTE
(1) Tooth contact pattern is a method for judging the result of the adjustment of drive pinion height and final drive gear backlash. The adjustment of drive pinion hight and final drive gear backlash should be repeated until tooth contact patterns bear a similarity to the standard tooth contact pattern.

CR3039100209000X

Fig. 14 Final drive gear & drive pinion adjustment. Less limited-slip

install snap ring.

6. Tighten boot clamp, ensure clip of clamp is on opposite side of bosses on inside of boot small end used for ventilation of joint.
7. Align match marks on companion flange and joint, install bolts, then **torque** bolts as shown in **Fig. 35.**

UNJOINTED JOURNALS

Removal

1. Place match marks on all components to be disassembled, then remove snap rings retaining journal bearing, **Fig. 35.**
2. Remove journal bearings using suitable press tool, **Fig. 36** or equivalent.
3. Remove journal from yoke.

Installation

1. Position journal and journal bearings into yoke, then using press tool No. MB990840, or equivalent, press journal bearings into yoke and onto journal, **Fig. 36.**
2. Install and seat snap rings into yoke, then using a suitable brass punch and hammer, tap journal and bearings until seated against one snap ring.
3. Using a suitable feeler gauge, measure resulting clearance, standard value dimension (A), between journal bearing cap and snap ring, **Fig. 37.**
4. If standard value dimension is less than or exceeds .0008–.0024 inch, select a new PAIR of snap rings from table **Fig. 38,** to set clearance to standard value.
5. Center journal bearing in yoke and install snap rings.

CENTER BEARINGS

1. Remove Unjointed journal or Lobo joint as described under "Lobo Joint, Joint Boot & Companion Flange" or "Unjointed Journals" in this section.
2. Remove nut retaining companion flange or yoke, **Fig. 35.**
3. Using a suitable fuller, remove companion flange or yoke from shaft.
4. Using a suitable fuller, remove center bearing from shaft.
5. Reverse procedure to install, noting the following
   a. Using a suitable socket or tube and hammer, drive center bearing then companion flange or yoke onto shaft.
   b. Install washer and nut, then **torque** nut, **Fig. 35.**

REAR AXLE HUB & CARRIER SERVICE

Hub and carrier are serviceable as an assembly only.

1. Remove driveshaft as described under "Driveshaft, Replace" in this section.
2. Remove brake components as outlined under "Disc Brakes."
3. Remove bolts retaining hub & carrier to knuckle, then hub.

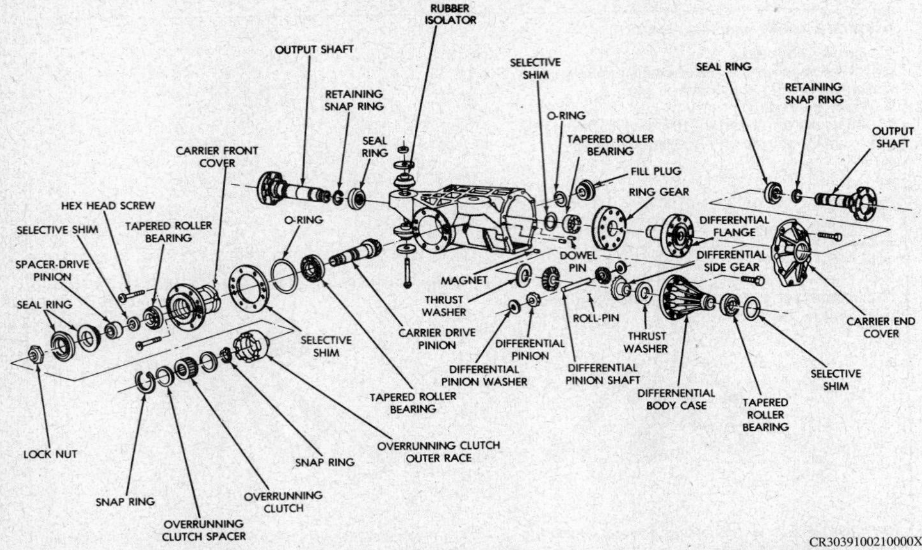

Fig. 15 Exploded view of differential carrier. Less limited-slip

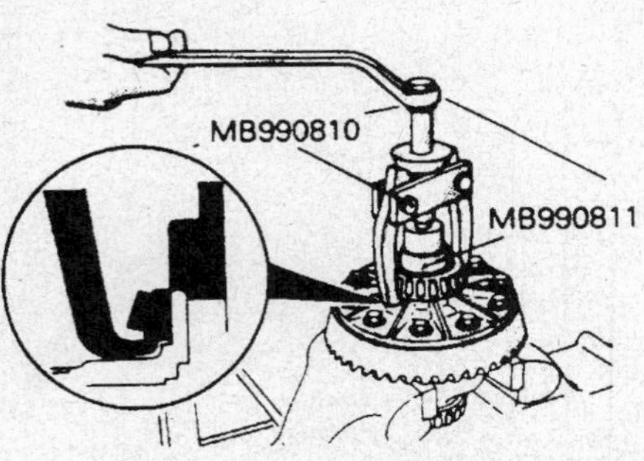

Fig. 16 Side bearing inner race removal. Less limited-slip

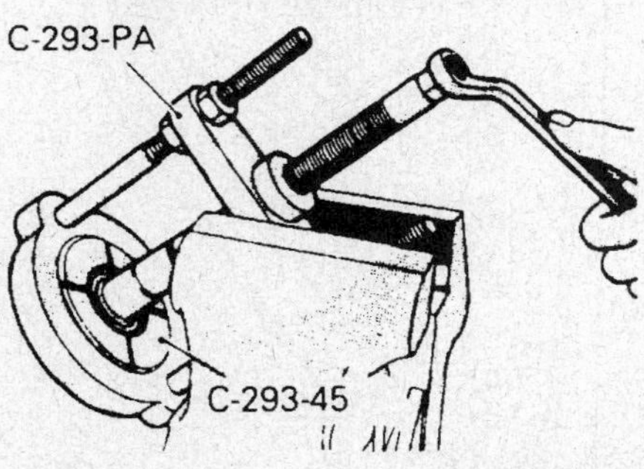

Fig. 17 Rear bearing inner race removal. Less limited-slip

4. Reverse procedure to install, **torque** hub and carrier bolts to 54–65 ft. lbs.

POWER TRANSFER UNIT

REPLACE

1. Remove two front exhaust pipe attaching nuts and lower exhaust pipe, **Fig. 39.**
2. Remove transfer assembly mounting bolts.
3. Remove driveshaft by moving transfer assembly to the left and lowering the front side. Suspend driveshaft with a piece of wire.
4. Reverse procedure to install, noting the following:
   a. **Torque** transfer assembly mounting bolts to 40–43 ft. lbs.
   b. **Torque** front exhaust pipe attaching nuts to 29–43 ft. lbs.

POWER TRANSFER UNIT SERVICE

DISASSEMBLE

1. Remove cover and cover gasket, **Fig. 40.**
2. Remove extension housing assembly and transfer case subassembly.
3. Remove spacer, O-ring and transfer case adapter subassembly.

SUBASSEMBLY SERVICE

Extension Housing Assembly

1. Remove air breather, **Fig. 41.**
2. Remove dust shield guard and oil seal from extension housing assembly.
3. Reverse procedure to assemble, noting the following:
   a. Use oil seal installer tool No. MD998304, or equivalent, when installing oil seal.
   b. Prior to installing air breather, apply 3M Super Weatherstripped No. 8001 or equivalent to air breather.

Transfer Case Subassembly

1. Remove transfer cover, **Fig. 42.**
2. Remove Oaring, spacer and outer race.
3. Remove drive bevel gear assembly, spacer and oil seal.
4. Reverse procedure to assemble, noting the following:
   a. Use oil seal installer tool No. MD998323, or equivalent, when installing oil seal.
   b. Using reload socket tool No. MB990326 and side gear holding tool No. MB990900, or equivalents, check turning torque of the drive bevel gear assembly as shown in **Fig. 43.** If turning torque is not within 1.23–1.81 ft. lbs., adjust by installing new spacers. Select spacers of nearly same thickness on both sides.

Transfer Case Adapter Subassembly

1. Onstage lockout and using special spanner tool No. MB991013, or equivalent, remove lockout, **Fig. 44.**
2. Using a press, remove driven gear bevel assembly.
3. Remove taper roller bearing, spacer, collar and outer races.
4. Reverse procedure to assemble, noting the following:
   a. When installing taper roller bearing, use installer cap tool No. MD998812, installer tube tool No. MD998814 and installer adapter tool No. MD998820, or equivalent, **Fig. 45.**
   b. **Torque** lockout to 102–115 ft. lbs., then stake lockout at two places.
   c. Using wrench adapter tool No. MD998806 and suitable torque wrench, or equivalents, check turning torque of the driven bevel gear assembly as shown in **Fig. 46.** If turning torque is not within .72–1.23 ft. lbs., adjust with adjusting spacer.

Drive Bevel Gear Assembly

1. Using bearing removal tool No. MD998801, or equivalent, remove taper roller bearings and drive bevel gear, **Fig. 47.**
2. Using installer cap tool No. MD998812 and installer adapter tool No. MD998827, or equivalent, install taper roller bearing above drive bevel gear, **Fig. 48.**
3. Using bearing installation tool No. MD998350, or equivalent, install taper roller bearing at opposite end drive bevel gear, **Fig. 48.**

Driven Bevel Gear Assembly

1. Using bearing removal tool No. MD998801, or equivalent, remove taper roller bearing from driven gear assembly, **Fig. 49.**
2. Use collar to install taper roller bearing onto driven bevel gear.

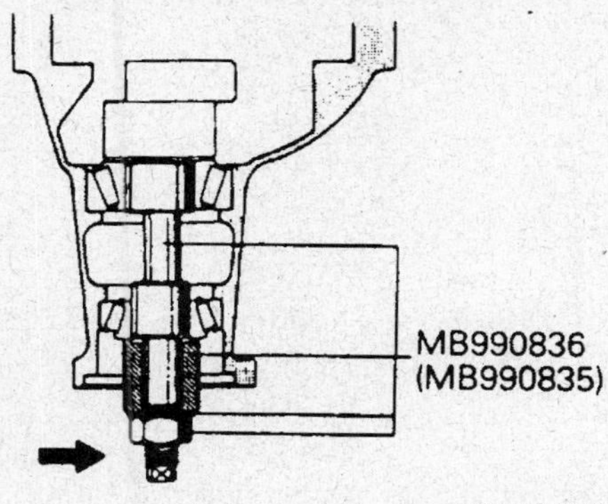

CR3039100214000X

Fig. 18 Drive pinion height adjustment. Less limited-slip

Bearing classification	Bearing lubrication	Rotation torque (starting friction torque) Nm (in.lbs.)
New	None (with rust-prevention oil)	0.9–1.2 (8–10)
New/reused	Oil application	0.4–0.5 (3–4)

NOTE
(1) Gradually tighten the nut of the special tool while checking the drive pinion turning torque.
(2) Because the special tool cannot be turned one turn, turn it several times within the range that it can be turned; then, after fitting to the bearing, measure the rotation torque.

CR3039100215000X

Fig. 19 Drive pinion turning torque specifications (less oil seal installed). Less limited-slip

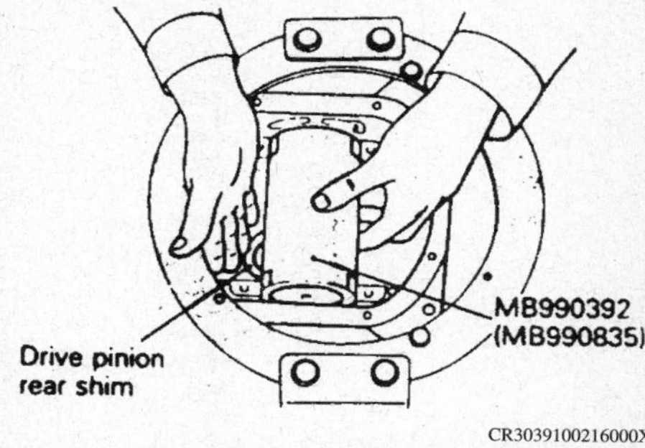

CR3039100216000X

Fig. 20 Selecting drive pinion adjustment shims. Less limited-slip

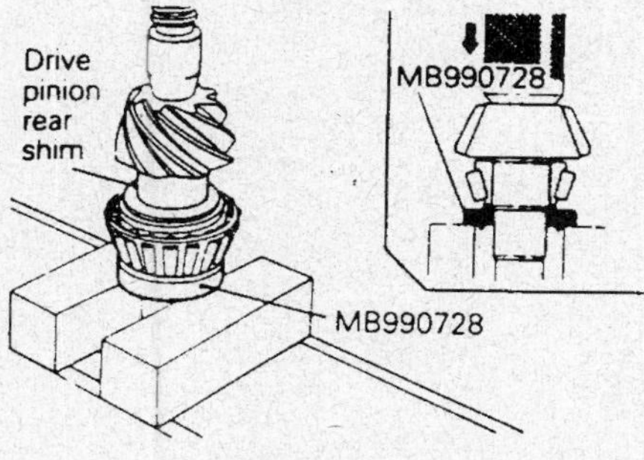

CR3039100217000X

Fig. 21 Drive pinion inner race installation. Less limited-slip

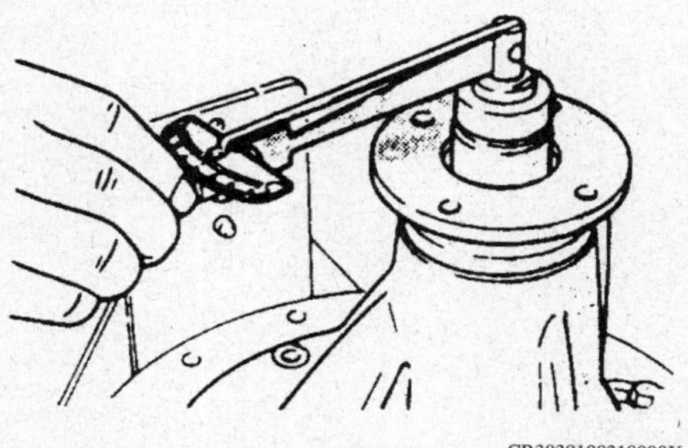

CR3039100218000X

Fig. 22 Drive pinion turning torque check. Less limited-slip

Bearing classification	Bearing lubrication	Rotation torque (starting friction torque) Nm (in.lbs.)
New	None (with rust-prevention oil)	1.0–1.3 (9–11)
New/reused	Oil application	0.5–0.6 (4–5)

CR3039100219000X

Fig. 23 Drive pinion turning torque specifications (w/oil seal installed). Less limited-slip

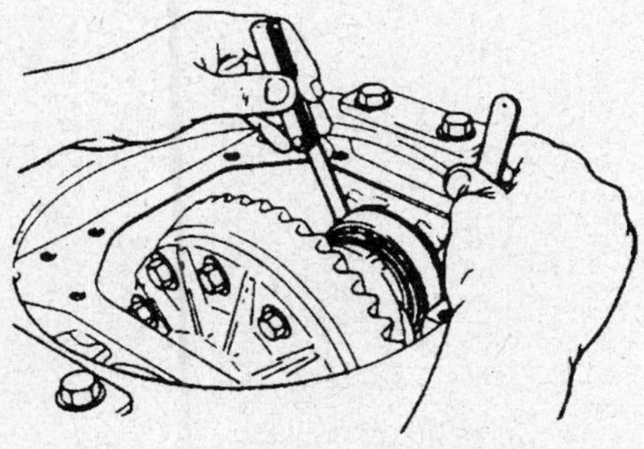

CR3039100222000X

Fig. 24 Gear carrier & side bearing clearance check. Less limited-slip

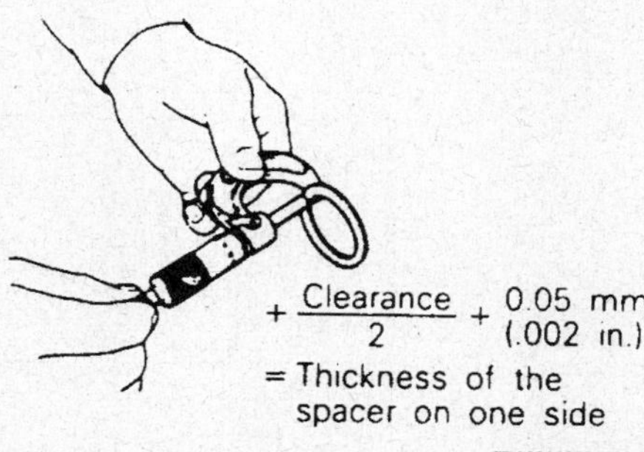

CR3039100223000X

Fig. 25 Side bearing spacers selection. Less limited-slip

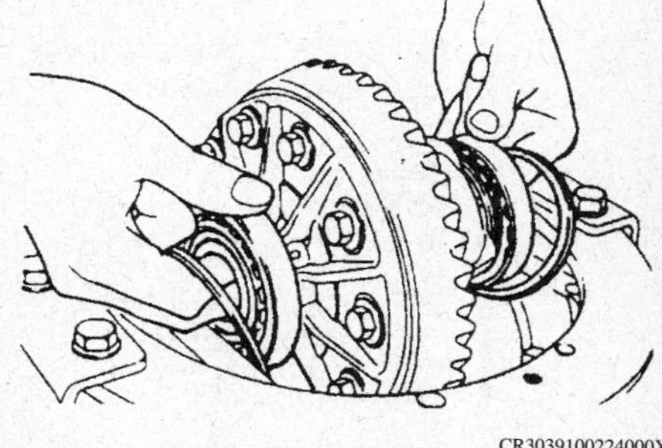

CR3039100224000X

Fig. 26 Side bearing spacers & differential case assembly installation. Less limited-slip

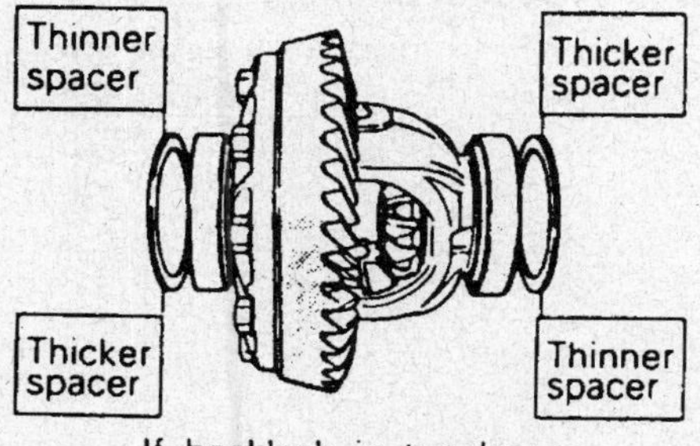

CR3039100225000X

Fig. 27 Side bearing spacers. Less limited-slip

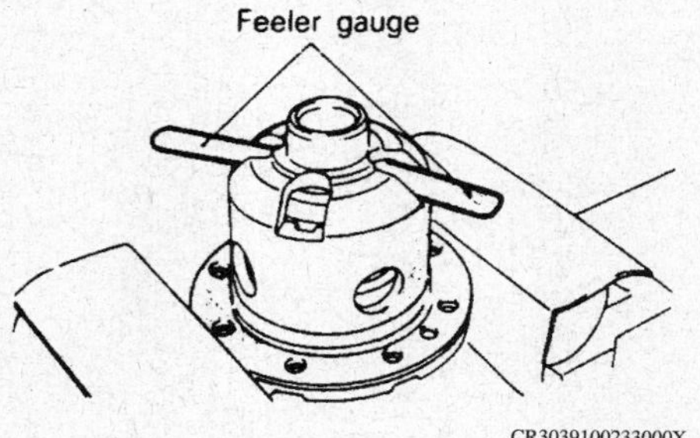

CR3039100233000X

Fig. 28 Differential case assembly mounting in vise. Limited-Slip

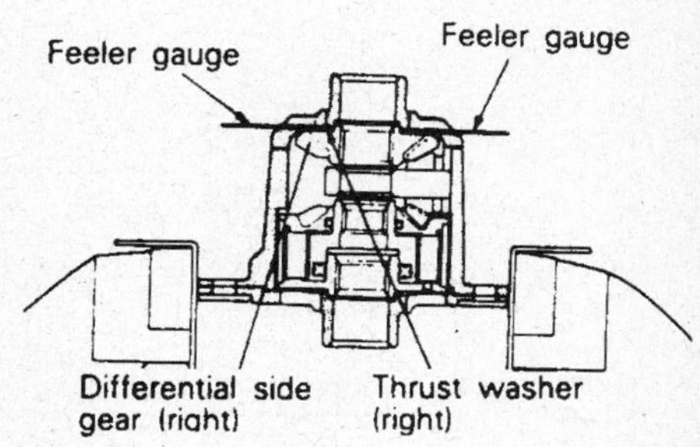

CR3039100234000X

Fig. 29 Feeler gauge insertion into differential case. Limited-Slip

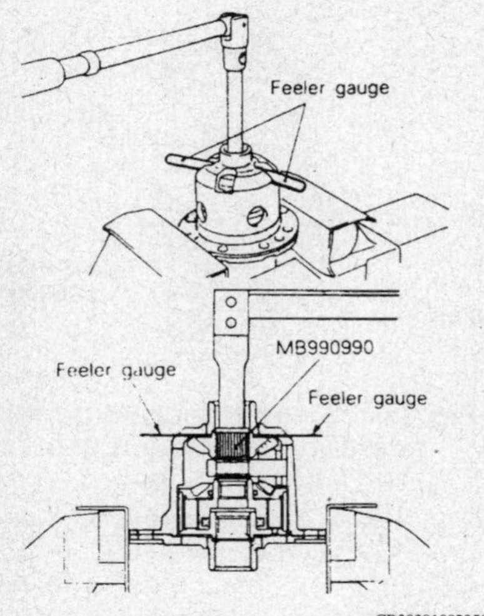

Fig. 30 Differential gear backlash inspection. Limited-Slip

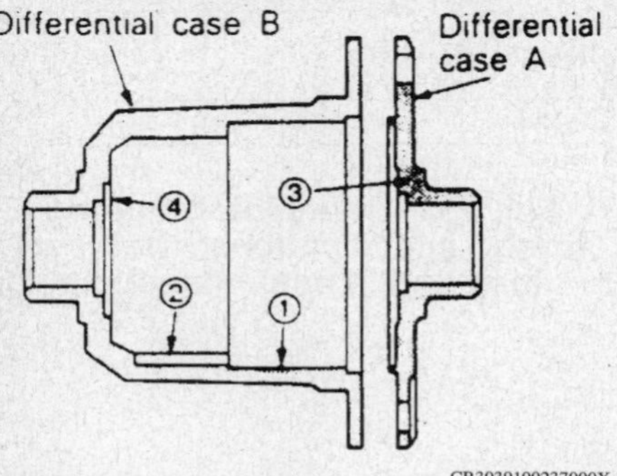

Fig. 32 Differential case contact surfaces. Limited-Slip

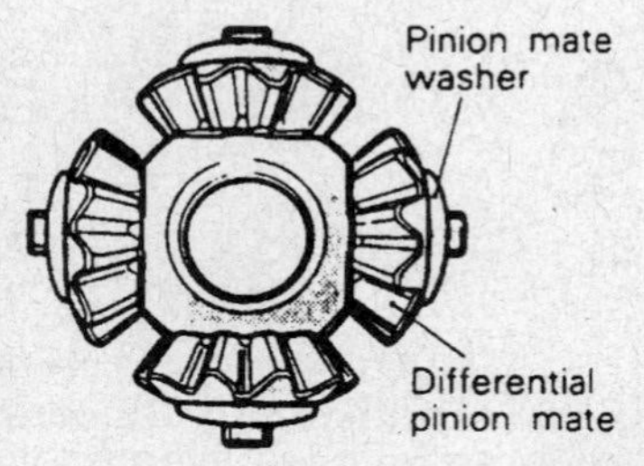

Fig. 33 Differential pinion mate installation. Limited-Slip

Thrust washer (left)	
Part No.	Thickness mm (in.)
MB569243	0.8 (.031)
	0.9 (.035)
	1.0 (.039)
	1.1 (.043)
	1.15 (.045)
	1.2 (.047)
	1.25 (.049)
	1.3 (.051)
	1.35 (.053)
	1.4 (.055)
	1.5 (.059)

CR3039100239000X

Fig. 34 Thrust washer thickness chart. Limited-Slip

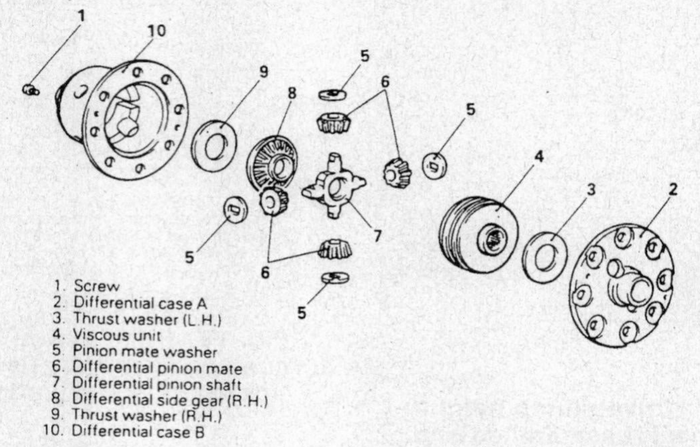

Fig. 31 Exploded view of differential carrier. Limited-Slip

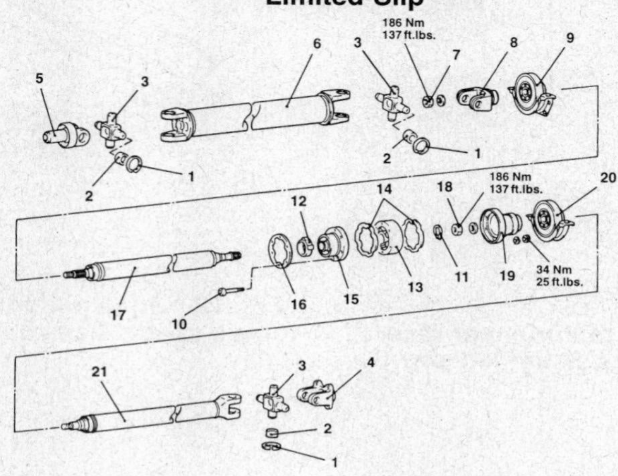

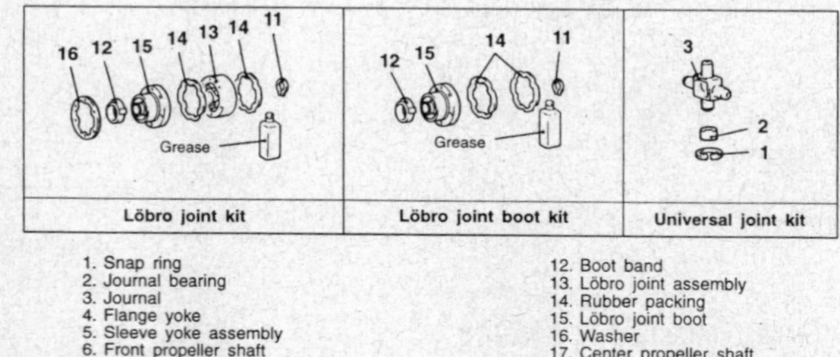

Fig. 35 Exploded view of propeller shaft

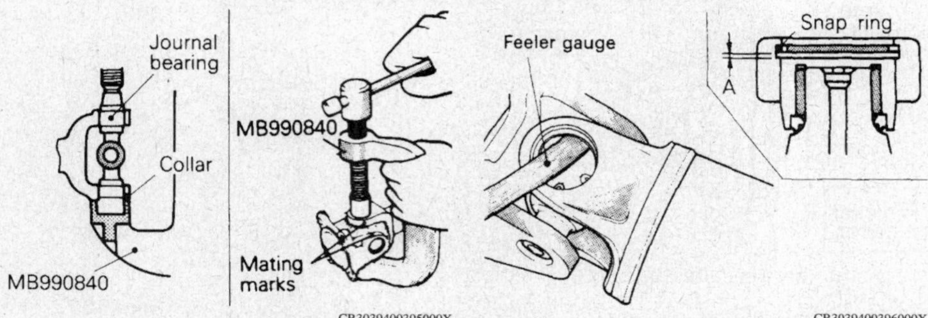

Fig. 36 Journal bearings replacement

Fig. 37 Journal bearing standard value clearance measurement

Snap Ring Thickness	Color
.0503	—
.0516	Yellow
.0528	Blue
.0539	Purple
.0551	Brown

Fig. 38 Journal bearing snap ring selection table

1. Front exhaust pipe connection
2. Transfer assembly

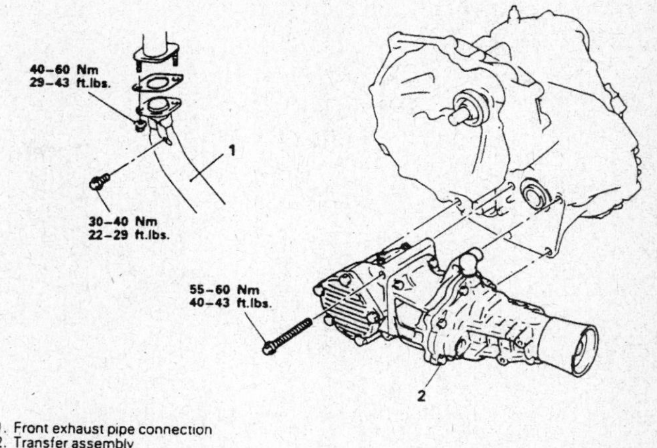

CR3039100191000X

Fig. 39 Transfer assembly replacement

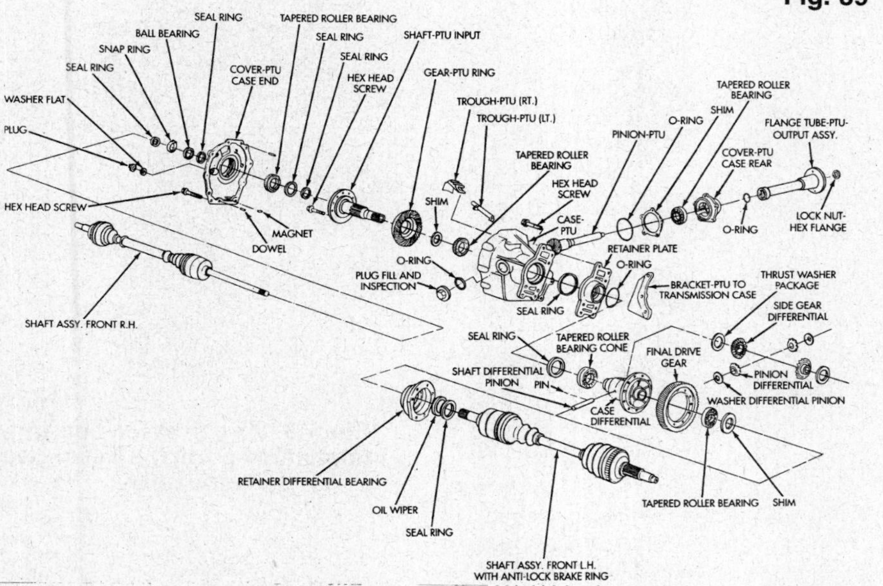

CR3039100243000X

Fig. 40 Exploded view of transfer assembly

1. Air breather
2. Dust seal guard
3. Oil seal
4. Extension housing

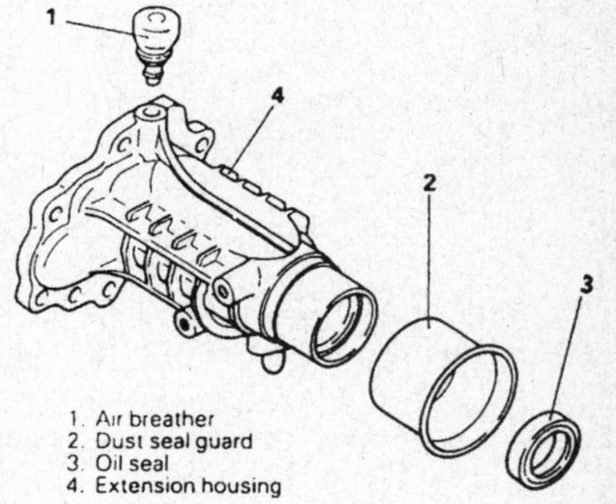

CR3039100244000X

Fig. 41 Extension housing assembly

1. Transfer cover
2. O-ring
3. Spacer
4. Outer race
5. Drive bevel gear assembly
6. Outer race
7. Spacer
8. Oil seal
9. Transfer case

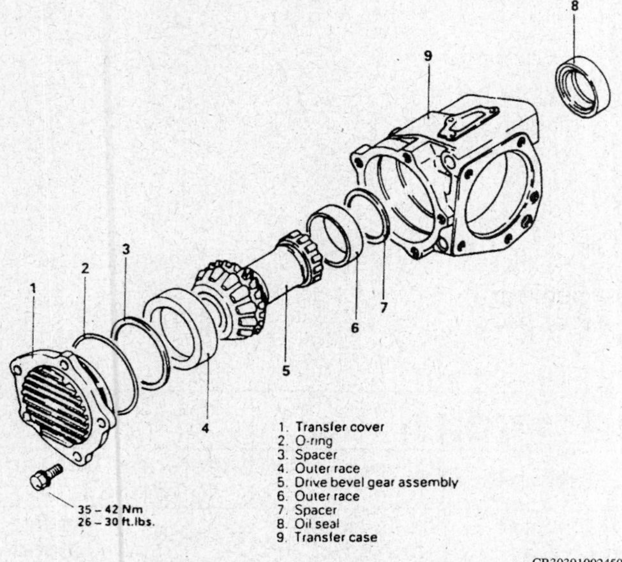

CR3039100245000X

Fig. 42 Exploded view of transfer case

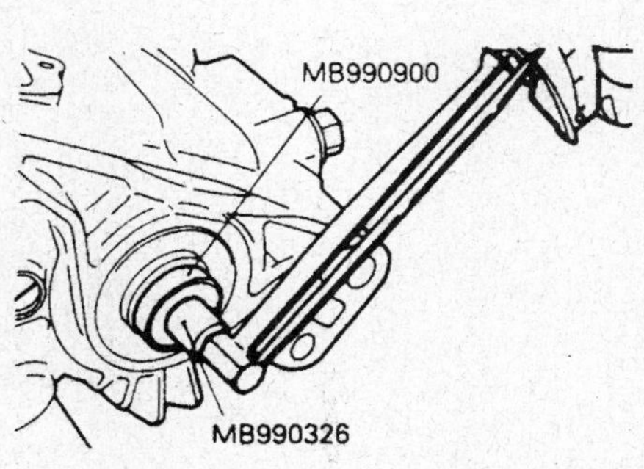

CR3039100246000X

Fig. 43 Turning drive torque of drive bevel gear assembly check

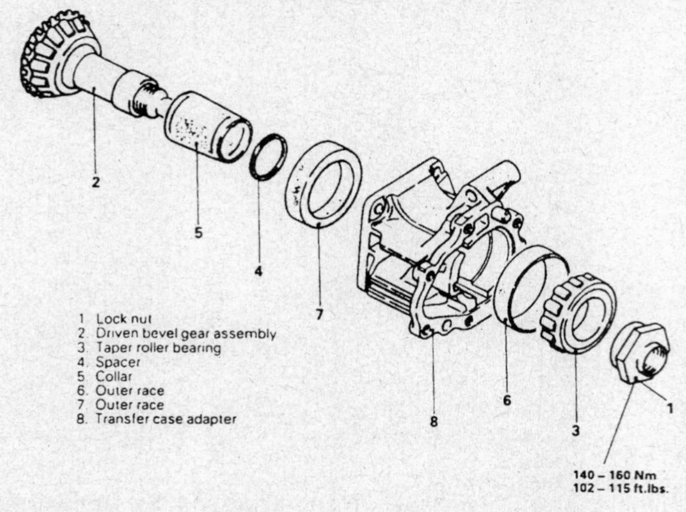

Fig. 44 Exploded view of transfer case adapter

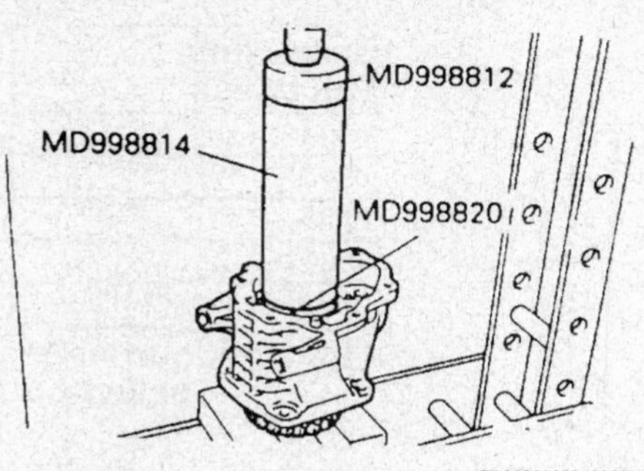

Fig. 45 Taper roller bearing installation

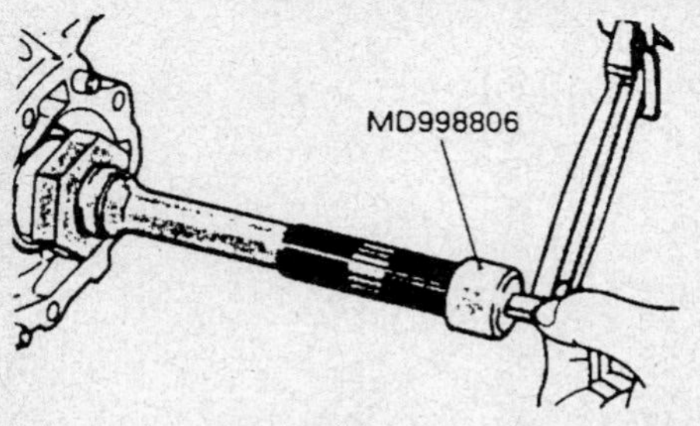

Fig. 46 Turning drive torque of driven bevel gear assembly check

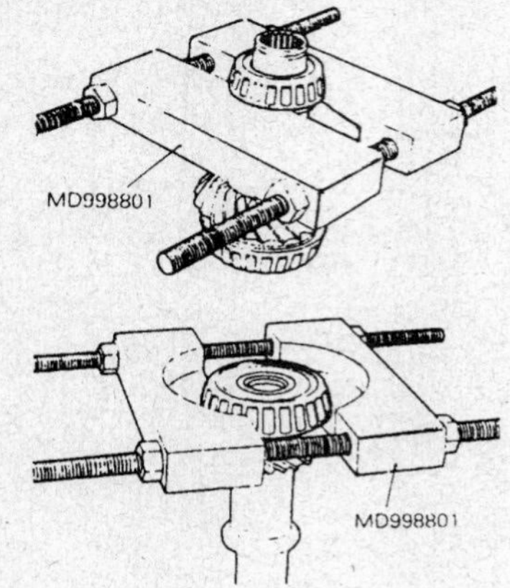

Fig. 47 Taper roller bearing removal from drive bevel gear assembly

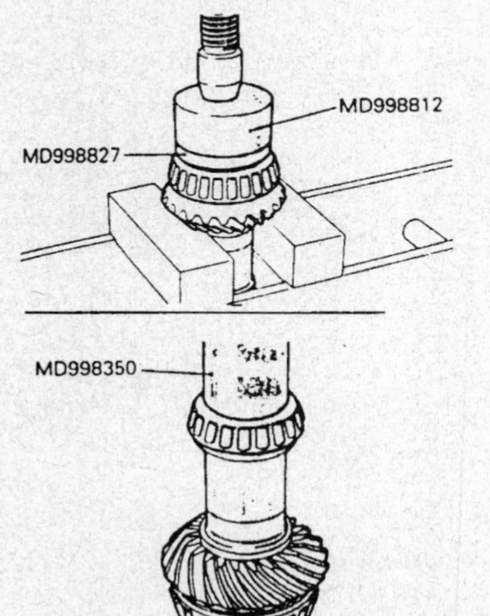

Fig. 48 Taper roller bearing installation on drive bevel gear assembly

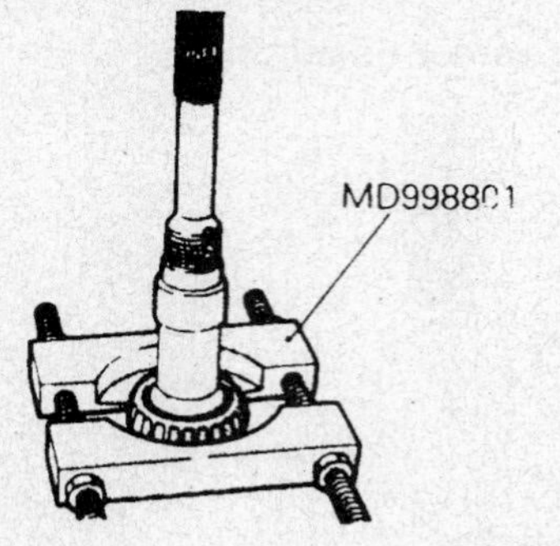

Fig. 49 Topper roller bearing removal from driven bevel gear assembly

REAR AXLE SPECIFICATIONS

Carrier Type	Ring Gear & Pinion Backlash		Pinion Bearing Reload			Differential Bearing Reload	
	Method	Adjustment	Method	With Seal Inch Lbs.	Less Seal Inch Lbs.	Method	Adjust-mend
Removal	Shim	.004–.006	Shim	—	8–10	Shim	.002

ENGINE REBUILDING SPECIFICATIONS

NOTE: For Engine Tightening Specifications, Refer To The Engine Section In The Appropriate Chassis Chapter Of This Manual.

INDEX

CYLINDER HEAD, VALVE GUIDE & VALVE SEATS

All measurements given in inches, unless otherwise specified.

Engine Liter	Year	Cylinder Head Warpage Limit①	Cylinder Head Overall Thickness②	Valve Guides (Standard)			Valve Seats			
				Inside Diameter	Stem To Guide Clearance		Angle, Degrees	Width		Runout
					Intake	Exhaust		Intake	Exhaust	
2.0L SOHC	1998–2002	.004	—	.2350–.2360	.0018–.0025	.0029–.0037	45.0	.035–.051	.035–.051	.002
2.0L DOHC	1998–99	.004	—	.2350–.2360	.0009–.0025	.0020–.0037	44.5–45.0	.035–.051	.035–.051	.002
2.0L Non-Turbo③	1998	.004	—	.2352–.2362	.0009–.0025	.0020–.0037	45.0–45.5	.035–.051	.035–.051	.002
2.0L Turbo③	1998	.008	5.193–5.201	.2600	.0008–.0020	.0020–.0035	—	.035–.051	.035–.051	—
2.4L DOHC	1998–2002	.004	—	.2350–.2360	.0018–.0025	.0029–.0037	45.0	.035–.051	.035–.051	.002
2.4L SOHC	2001–02	.007	—	.2400	.0008–.0019	.0012–.0027	45.0–44.0	.040–.050	.040–.050	—
2.5L	1998–2000	.008	4.720–4.730	.2360	.0008–.0020	.0016–.0028	45.0–45.5	.035–.051	.035–.051	—
2.7L	1998–2002	.003	—	.2353–.2363	.0009–.0026	.0020–.0037	45.0–45.5	.039–.059	.049–.069	.002
3.0L	2001–02	.007	4.720–4.730	.3200	.0008–.019	.0016–.0027	45.0-45.5	.040–.050	.049–.069	—
3.2L	1998–2000	.003	—	.2746–.2756	.0009–.0025	.0020–.0037	44.5–45.0	.030–.049	.049–.069	.002
	2001	.002	—	.2746–.2756	.0009–.0025	.0020–.0037	45.0–45.5	.030–.049	.049–.069	.002
3.5L	1999–2002	.008	—	.2746–.2756	.0009–.0026	.0020–.0037	45.00–45.50	.030–.049	.049–.069	.002

DOHC — Dual Overhead Cam
SOHC — Single Overhead Cam
① — Measurement is a combined total dimension of stock removal limit from cylinder head and block surface (deck) together.
② — Overall thickness, less warpage limit.
③ — Talon.

VALVE SPRINGS

All measurements given in inches, unless otherwise specified.

Engine	Year	Free Length		Installed Height	Spring Pressure, Lbs. @ Inches		Maximum Straightness Deviation
		Intake	Exhaust		Intake	Exhaust	
2.0L SOHC	1998–99	1.747	1.747	1.580	67 @ 1.57	67 @ 1.57	—
	2000–02	1.840	1.840	1.580	70 @ 1.57	70 @ 1.57	—
2.0L DOHC	1998–99	1.811	1.811	1.496	55–60 @ 1.50	55–60 @ 1.50	—
2.0L SOHC①	2001–02	2.130	2.130	1.580	72 @ 1.57	72 @ 1.57	—
2.0L Non-Turbo②	1998–2000	1.811	1.811	1.496	55–60 @ 1.50	55–60 @ 1.50	—
2.0L Turbo②	1998	1.850	1.850	1.570	54 @ 1.57	54 @ 1.57	4°
2.4L DOHC	1998–2002	1.905	1.905	1.496	76 @ 1.50	76 @ 1.50	—
2.4L SOHC	2001–02	2.000	2.000	1.740	60 @ 1.74	60 @ 1.74	2°
2.5	1998–2000	2.010	2.010	1.704	60 @ 1.74	60 @ 1.74	4°
2.7L	1998–2002	1.797	1.797	1.496	56–64 @ 1.50	56–64 @ 1.50	—
3.0L	2001–02	2.010	2.010	1.740	60 @ 1.74	60 @ 1.74	2°
3.2L	1998–2001	1.720	1.745	1.496	69.5–80.5 @ 1.50	70–81 @ 1.50	—
3.5L	1999	1.719	1.744	1.496	70–81 @ 1.496	56–64 @ 1.50	—
	2000–02	1.719	1.744	1.496	96.5–80.5 @ 1.50	71–79 @.1.50	—

DOHC — Dual Overhead Cam
SOHC — Single Overhead Cam

① — High Output R/T & ACR Neon.

② — Talon.

VALVES

All measurements given in inches, unless otherwise specified.

Engine	Year	Stem Diameter		Clearance		Stem Tip Height		Maximum Tip Refinish	Face Angle, Degrees	Margin (Minimum)	
		Intake	Exhaust	Intake	Exhaust	Intake	Exhaust			Intake	Exhaust
2.0L DOHC	1998–99	.2340	.2330	—	—	1.891	1.889	—	44.5–45.0	.050–.063	.038–.051
2.0L SOHC	1998–2000	.2340	.2330	—	—	1.77–1.81	1.71–1.75	—	45.0–45.5	.045–.058	.058–.071
2.0L SOHC	2001–02	.2337–.2344	.2326–.2333	—	—	1.760–1.800	1.710–.750	—	45.0–45.5	.045–.058	.058–.071
2.0L Non-Turbo①	1998	.2330	.2340	—	—	1.891	1.889	—	44.5–45.0	.050–.063	.038–.050
2.0L Turbo①	1998	.2600	.2590	—	—	—	—	—	45.0–45.5	.039	.059
2.4L DOHC	1998–2000	.2340	.2330	—	—	1.891	1.889	—	44.5–45.0	.050–.063	.038–.051
	2001–02	.2337–.2344	.2326–.2333	—	—	1.891	1.889	—	44.5–45.0	.050–.063	.038–.051
2.4L SOHC	2001–02	.2400	.2300	—	—	1.941	1.941	—	45.0–45.5	.020	.030
2.5L	1998–2000	.2360	.2360	—	—	1.940	1.940	—	45.0–45.5	.039	.047
2.7L	1998–2002	.2337–.2344	.2326–.2333	—	—	1.837–1.874	1.898–1.935	—	45.0–45.5	—	—
3.0L	2001–02	.2400	.2400	—	—	1.941–1.960	1.941–1.960	—	45.0–45.5	.040	.050
3.2L	1998–2001	.2730–.2737	.2719–.2726	—	—	1.668–1.719	1.760–1.811	—	44.5–45.0	—	—
3.5L	1999–2002	.2730–.2737	.2719–.2726	—	—	1.668–1.719	1.760–1.811	—	44.5–45.0	.040	.057

DOHC — Dual Overhead Cam.

SOHC — Single Overhead Cam.

① — Talon.

CAMSHAFT

All measurements given in inches, unless otherwise specified.

Engine	Year	Camshaft Journal Diameter	Camshaft Bearing Clearance	Camshaft Endplay	Lifter Bore Diameter	Lifter Diameter	Lifter To Bore Clearance
2.0L DOHC	1998–99	1.0210–1.0220	.0027–.0030	.0019–.0066	—	—	—
2.0L SOHC	1998	①	.0027–.0030	.0059	—	—	—
	1999	1.0210–1.0220	.0027–.0030	.002–.006	—	—	—
	2000	①	.0021–.0037	.002–.015	—	—	—
	2001–02	①	.0027–.0030④	.002–.015	—	—	—
2.0L Non-Turbo②	1998–2000	1.0217–1.0224	.0027–.0028	.0060	—	—	—
2.0L Non-Turbo③	1998	1.0217–1.0224	.0027–.0028	.0060	—	—	—
2.0L Turbo	1998	1.0220	—	—	—	—	—
2.4L DOHC	1998	1.0240–1.0250	.0027–.0030	.0019–.0066	—	—	—
	2000–02	1.0210–1.0220	.0027–.0030	.0019–.0066	—	—	—
2.4L SOHC	2001–02	1.8000	—	—	—	—	—
2.5L	1998–2000	1.7689	—	—	—	—	—
2.7L	1998–2002	.9449–.9441	.0020–.0035	.0051–.0110	.9469–.9476	—	—
3.0L	2002	1.8000	—	—	—	—	—
3.2L	1998–2001	1.6905–1.6913	.0030–.0047	.0040–.0140	—	—	—
3.5L	1998–2002	1.6905–1.6913	.0030–.0047	.0040–.0140	—	—	—

DOHC — Dual Overhead Cam
SOHC — Single Overhead Cam
① — Bearing journal No. 1, 1.6190–1.6199 inches; No. 2, 1.6340–1.6350 inches; No. 3, 1.6500–1.6510 inches; No. 4, 1.6660–1.6680 inches; No. 5, 1.6820–1.6829 inches.
② — Avenger & Sebring Coupe.
③ — Talon.
④ — 2002 Models, .0021–.0037 inches.

CRANKSHAFT, BEARINGS & RODS

All measurements given in inches, unless otherwise specified.

Engine	Year	Crankshaft				Bearing Clearance		Connecting Rods		Crankshaft Endplay
		Main Bearing Journal Diameter	Connecting Rod Journal Diameter	Max. Out Of Round (All)	Max. Taper (All)	Main Bearings	Connecting Rod Bearings	Pin Bore Diameter	Side Clearance	
2.0L②③	1998–2002	2.0469–2.0475	1.8894–1.8900	.0001	.0001	.0008–.0024	.0010–.0023	.8252–.8260	.0050–.0150	.0035–.0094
2.0L④	1998	2.0469–2.0475	1.8894–1.8900	.0001	.0001	.0008–.0024	.0010–.0023	.8252–.8260	.0050–.0150	.0035–.0094
2.0L①	1998–2000	2.0469–2.0475	1.8894–1.8900	.0001	.0001	.0009–.0024	.0010–.0023	.8252–.8260	.0050–.0150	.0035–.0094
2.0L Turbo④	1998	2.2400	—	.0004	.0004	.0008–.0016	—	—	.0039–.0098	.0020–.0071
2.4L DOHC	1998–2002	2.3610–2.3625	1.9670–1.9685	.0001	.0001	.0007–.0023	.0009–.0027	.8252–.8260	.0051–.0150	.0035–0094
2.4L SOHC	2001–02	2.2400	—	—	—	.0008–.0015	—	—	.0040–.0090	.0020–.0090
2.5L①	1998–2000	2.3600	—	—	—	.0008–.0016	—	—	.0039–.0098	.0020–.0098
2.5L②	1998–2000	2.3620	—	—	—	.0008–0016	—	—	.0039–.0098	.0020–.0100
2.7L	1998–2002	2.4997–2.5004	2.1067–2.1060	.0006	.0006	.0014–.0021	.0010–.0026	.8665–.8668	.0052–.0150	.0019–.0108
3.0L	2002–02	2.4000	—	.0003	—	.0008–.0015	—	.87	.0030–.0090	.002–.009
3.2L	1998–2001	2.5190–2.5200	2.2830–2.2840	.0006	.0006	.0007–.0030	.0007–.0034	.9452–.9455	—	.0040–.0120
3.5L	1999–2002	2.5190–2.5200	2.2830–2.2840	.0006	.0006	.0007–.0030	.0007–.0031	.9452–.9455	.0153	.0040–.0120

DOHC-Dual Overhead Cam.
SOHC- Single Overhead Cam.
① — Avenger & Sebring Coupe.
② — Breeze, Cirrus, Sebring Convertible & Stratus.
③ — Neon.
④ — Talon.

PISTONS, PINS & RINGS

All measurements given in inches, unless otherwise specified.

Engine	Year	Piston Diameter (Std.)	Piston Clearance	Piston Pin Diameter	Piston Pin To Piston Clearance	Piston Ring End Gap (Minimum)			Piston Ring Side Clearance		
						Compression		Oil	Compression		Oil
						Top	2nd		Top	2nd	
2.0L DOHC⑤	1998–99	3.4434–3.4441	.0007–.0020②	.8267–.8269	.0003–.0008	.0090–.0200	.0190–.0310	.0090–.0260	.0010–.0026	.0010–.0026	.0002–.0070
2.0L④	1998–99	3.4434–3.4441	.0004–.0017②	.8267–.8269	.0003–.0008	.0090–.0200	.0190–.0310	.0090–.0260	.0010–.0026	.0010–.0026	.0002–.0070
2.0L SOHC⑤	1998–2000	3.4434–3.4441	.0008–.0020②	.8267–.8269	.0003–.0008	.0090–.0200	.0190–.0310	.0090–.0260	.0010–.0026	.0010–.0026	.0002–.0070
2.0L SOHC⑤	2001–02	3.4432–3.4439	0008–.0020③	.8268–.8269	.0003–.0006	.0090–.0200	.0190–.0310	.0090–.0260	.0010–.0026	.0010–.0026	.0002–.0070
2.0L Non-Turbo⑥	1998	3.4434–3.4441	.0005–.0017②	.8267–.8269	.0003–.0008	.0090–.0200	.0190–.0310	.0090–.0260	.0010–.0026	.0010–.0026	.0002–.0070
2.0L Turbo⑥	1998	3.3340	.0012–.0020	.8700	—	.0098–.0138	.0157–.0217	.0039–.0157	.0016–.0031	.0008–.0028	—
2.4L DOHC	1998–2002	3.4434–3.4441	.0009–.0022①	.8660–.8662	.0001–.0007	.0098–.0200	.0090–.0180	.0098–.0250	.0011–.0031	.0011–.0031	.0004–.0070
2.4L SOHC	2001–02	3.40	.008–.0015	.87	.0008–.0019	.010–.013	.016–.021	.004–.015	..0012–.0027	.0012–.0027	—
2.5L	1998–2000	3.2900	.0008–.0016	—	—	.010–.016	.016–.022	.006–.019	.0012–.0028	.0007–.0024	—
2.7L	1998–2002	3.3845–3.3857	.0001–.0016	.8661–.8662	.0001–.0004	.0080–.0140	.0146–.0249	.0100–.0300	.0016–.0031	.0016–.0031	.0025–.0082
3.0L	2001–02	3.58	.0008–.015	.8700	—	.012–.017	.018–.023	.008–.023	.0012–.0027	.008–.0023	—
3.2L	1998–2001	3.6205–3.6221	-.0003–.0018	.9448–.9449	.0002–.0006	.0080–.0140	.0087–.0193	.0100–.0300	.0016–.0031	.0016–.0031	.0015–.0073
3.5L	1999–2002	3.7788–3.7796	-.0003–.0018	.9448–.9449	.0002–.0006	.0080–.0140	.0091–.0197	.0100–.0300	.0016–.0031	.0016–.0031	.0015–.0073

DOHC — Dual Overhead Cam
SOHC — Single Overhead Cam
① — Measured at 9/16 inch from bottom of skirt.
② — Measured at 11/16 inch from bottom of skirt.
③ — Measured at 0.420 inches from bottom of skirt.
④ — Breeze, Cirrus, & Stratus.
⑤ — Neon.
⑥ — Talon.

CYLINDER BLOCK

All measurements given in inches, unless otherwise specified.

Engine	Year	Cylinder Bore Diameter (Std.)	Cylinder Bore Taper (Max.)	Cylinder Bore Out Of Round (Max.)
2.0L (Except Turbo)	1998–2002	3.4446–3.4452	.002	.002
2.0L (Turbo)	1998	3.3500	—	—
2.4L DOHC	1998–2002	3.4446–3.4452	.002	.002
2.4L SOHC	2001–02	3.4100	0.02	.00[illegible]
2.5L	1998–2000	3.2900	.004	[illegible]
2.7L	1998–2002	3.3859	.002	[illegible]
3.0L	2001–02	3.5900	.002	[illegible]
3.2L	1998–2001	3.6220	.002	[illegible]
3.5L	1999–2002	3.7797–3.7803	.002	[illegible]

DOHC-Dual Overhead Cam.
SOHC- Single Overhead Cam.

OIL PUMP

All measurements given in inches, unless otherwise specified.

Engine	Year	Rotor Backlash	Rotor To Body Clearance	Rotor Endplay ①	Rotor Thickness (Minimum)		Outer Rotor Diameter (Minimum)	Maximum Cover Flatness Variation	Relief Spring Free Length	Relief Spring Pressure, Lbs. @ Inches
					Inner	Outer				
2.0L (Except Turbo)	1998–2002	.0080②	.0150	.0040	.301	.301	3.148	.003	2.390	18.0–19.0 @ 1.600
2.0L (Turbo)	1998	—	③	—	—	—	—	—	—	—
2.4L DOHC	1998–2002	.0080	.0150	.0040	.370	.370	3.148	.001	—	—
2.4L SOHC	2001–02	—	.004–.005	—	—	—	—	—	—	—
2.5L	1998–2000	.0024–.0071	.0039–.0071	.0015–.0035	—	—	—	—	—	—
2.7L	1998–2002	.0080	.0150	—	.373–.374	.373–.374	3.511	.001	—	—
3.0L	2001–02	.003–.007	.004–.007	.002–.003	—	—	—	—	—	—
3.2L	1998–2001	.0080	.0150	—	.563	.5630	3.149	.001	—	—
3.5L	1999–2002	.0080	.0150	.003	.563	.5630	3.149	.001	1.95	23–25

DOHC — Dual Overhead Cam.
SOHC — Single Overhead Cam.
① — Measured between pump cover mounting surface & end of gear using straightedge & feeler gauge.
② — Maximum inner & outer rotor tip clearance.
③ — Drive gear, .0031–.0055 inch; driven gear, .0024–.0047 inch

ENGINE REBUILDING SPECIFICATIONS

OIL PUMP

All measurements given in inches, unless otherwise specified.

Engine	Year	Rotor Backlash	Rotor To Body Clearance	Rotor Endplay ①	Rotor Thickness (Minimum)		Outer Rotor Diameter (Minimum)	Maximum Cover Flatness Variation	Relief Spring Free Length	Relief Spring Pressure, Lbs. @ Inches
					Inner	Outer				
2.0L (Except Turbo)	1998–2002	.0080②	.0150	.0040	.301	.301	3.148	.003	2.390	18.0–19.0 @ 1.600
2.0L (Turbo)	1998	—	③	—	—	—	—	—	—	—
2.4L DOHC	1998–2002	.0080	.0150	.0040	.370	.370	3.148	.001	—	—
2.4L SOHC	2001–02	—	.004–.005	—	—	—	—	—	—	—
2.5L	1998–2000	.0024–.0071	.0039–.0071	.0015–.0035	—	—	—	—	—	—
2.7L	1998–2002	.0080	.0150	—	.373–.374	.373–.374	3.511	.001	—	—
3.0L	2001–02	.003–.007	.004–.007	.002–.003	—	—	—	—	—	—
3.2L	1998–2001	.0080	.0150	—	.563	.5630	3.149	.001	—	—
3.5L	1999–2002	.0080	.0150	.003	.563	.5630	3.149	.001	1.95	23–25

DOHC — Dual Overhead Cam.
SOHC — Single Overhead Cam.
① — Measured between pump cover mounting surface & end of gear using straightedge & feeler gauge.

② — Maximum inner & outer rotor tip clearance.

③ — Drive gear, .0031–.0055 inch; driven gear, .0024–.0047 inch

ENGINE REBUILDING SPECIFICATIONS

PISTONS, PINS & RINGS

All measurements given in inches, unless otherwise specified.

Engine	Year	Piston Diameter (Std.)	Piston Clearance	Piston Pin Diameter	Piston Pin To Piston Clearance	Piston Ring End Gap (Minimum)			Piston Ring Side Clearance		
						Compression		Oil	Compression		Oil
						Top	2nd		Top	2nd	
2.0L DOHC⑤	1998–99	3.4434–3.4441	.0007–.0020②	.8267–.8269	.0003–.0008	.0090–.0200	.0190–.0310	.0090–.0260	.0010–.0026	.0010–.0026	.0002–.0070
2.0L④	1998–99	3.4434–3.4441	.0004–.0017②	.8267–.8269	.0003–.0008	.0090–.0200	.0190–.0310	.0090–.0260	.0010–.0026	.0010–. 0026	.0002–.0070
2.0L SOHC⑤	1998–2000	3.4434–3.4441	.0008–.0020②	.8267–.8269	.0003–.0008	.0090–.0200	.0190–.0310	.0090–.0260	.0010–.0026	.0010–.0026	.0002–.0070
2.0L SOHC⑤	2001–02	3.4432–3.4439	0008–.0020③	.8268–.8269	.0003–.0006	.0090–.0200	.0190–.0310	.0090–.0260	.0010–.0026	.0010–.0026	.0002–.0070
2.0L Non-Turbo⑥	1998	3.4434–3.4441	.0005–.0017②	.8267–.8269	.0003–.0008	.0090–.0200	.0190–.0310	.0090–.0260	.0010–.0026	.0010–.0026	.0002–.0070
2.0L Turbo⑥	1998	3.3340	.0012–.0020	.8700	—	.0098–.0138	.0157–.0217	.0039–.0157	.0016–.0031	.0008–.0028	—
2.4L DOHC	1998–2002	3.4434–3.4441	.0009–.0022①	.8660–.8662	.0001–.0007	.0098–.0200	.0090–.0180	.0098–.0250	.0011–. 0031	.0011–.0031	.0004–.0070
2.4L SOHC	2001–02	3.40	.008–.0015	.87	.0008–.0019	.010–.013	.016–.021	.004–.015	..0012–.0027	.0012–.0027	—
2.5L	1998–2000	3.2900	.0008–.0016	—	—	.010–.016	.016–.022	.006–.019	.0012–.0028	.0007–.0024	—
2.7L	1998–2002	3.3845–3.3857	.0001–.0016	.8661–.8662	.0001–.0004	.0080–.0140	.0146–.0249	.0100–.0300	.0016–.0031	.0016–.0031	.0025–.0082
3.0L	2001–02	3.58	.0008–.015	.8700	—	.012–.017	.018–.023	.008–.023	.0012–.0027	.008–.0023	—
3.2L	1998–2001	3.6205–3.6221	-.0003–.0018	.9448–.9449	.0002–.0006	.0080–.0140	.0087–.0193	.0100–.0300	.0016–.0031	.0016–.0031	.0015–.0073
3.5L	1999–2002	3.7788–3.7796	-.0003–.0018	.9448–.9449	.0002–.0006	.0080–.0140	.0091–.0197	.0100–.0300	.0016–.0031	.0016–.0031	.0015–.0073

DOHC — Dual Overhead Cam
SOHC — Single Overhead Cam
① — Measured at 9/16 inch from bottom of skirt.
② — Measured at 11/16 inch from bottom of skirt.
③ — Measured at 0.420 inches from bottom of skirt.
④ — Breeze, Cirrus, & Stratus.
⑤ — Neon.
⑥ — Talon.

CYLINDER BLOCK

All measurements given in inches, unless otherwise specified.

Engine	Year	Cylinder Bore Diameter (Std.)	Cylinder Bore Taper (Max.)	Cylinder Bore Out Of Round (Max.)
2.0L (Except Turbo)	1998–2002	3.4446–3.4452	.002	.002
2.0L (Turbo)	1998	3.3500	—	—
2.4L DOHC	1998–2002	3.4446–3.4452	.002	.002
2.4L SOHC	2001–02	3.4100	0.02	.002
2.5L	1998–2000	3.2900	.004	.004
2.7L	1998–2002	3.3859	.002	.003
3.0L	2001–02	3.5900	.002	.003
3.2L	1998–2001	3.6220	.002	.003
3.5L	1999–2002	3.7797–3.7803	.002	.003

DOHC-Dual Overhead Cam.
SOHC- Single Overhead Cam.

FORD MOTOR COMPANY

Page No.

FORD

LINCOLN

MERCURY

GENERAL SERVICE

Power Brake Units . . . 18-1
Power Steering . . . 14-1
Rear Drive Axles . . . 21-1
Speed Controls (Volume 2) . . . 2-1
Starter Motors . . . 11-1
Steering Columns . . . 13-1
Supplemental Restraint Systems (Volume 2) . . . 4-1
Wiper Systems (Volume 2) . . . 3-1

FORD MOTOR COMPANY

Page No.

FORD

LINCOLN

MERCURY

GENERAL SERVICE

Page No.

Power Brake Units 18-1
Power Steering 14-1
Rear Drive Axles 21-1
Speed Controls (Volume 2) 2-1
Starter Motors 11-1
Steering Columns 13-1
Supplemental Restraint Systems (Volume 2) 4-1
Wiper Systems (Volume 2) 3-1

CONTOUR, COUGAR & MYSTIQUE

NOTE: Refer To The Rear Of This Manual For Manufacturer's Special Service Tool Suppliers.

INDEX OF SERVICE OPERATIONS

Specifications

GENERAL ENGINE SPECIFICATIONS

Year	Engine Liter①	Fuel System	Bore & Stroke, Inches	Compression Ratio	Net HP @ RPM②	Maximum Torque, Ft. Lbs. @ RPM	Normal Oil Pressure, psi
1998–2000	2.5L⑤	SEFI	3.25 X 3.13	10.0	195 @ 6625	165 @ 5625	—
1998–2002	2.0L	SEFI	3.34 X 3.46	9.6	125 @ 5500	130 @ 4000	③
	2.5L④	SEFI	3.25 X 3.13	9.7	170 @ 6250	165 @ 4250	③

SEFI — Sequential Electronic Fuel Injection

① — Eighth digit of Vehicle Identifications Number (VIN) denotes engine code.

② — Net rating, as installed on vehicle.

③ — 2.5L engine & 1998 2.0L engine; 20–45 psi w/engine hot @ 1500 RPM. 1999–2002 w/2.0L engine; 35–65 psi w/engine hot @ 2000 RPM.

④ — Except Contour SVT.

⑤ — Contour SVT.

TUNE UP SPECIFICATIONS

Engine (Code)③	Spark Plug Gap, Inch	Ignition Timing; °BTDC				Curb Idle Speed⑦		Fast Idle Speed⑦		Fuel Pump Pressure, psi ②	Valve Clearance, Inch
		Firing Order Fig.①	Man. Trans.	Auto Trans.	Mark Fig.	Man. Trans.	Auto Trans.	Man. Trans.	Auto Trans.		
1998–2002											
2.0L (3)	.052	A	⑧	⑧	④	⑤	⑤	⑤	⑤	30-45	⑨
2.5L (L)	.052	B	⑧	⑧	④	⑤	⑤	⑤	⑤	45-60	⑥

BTDC — Before Top Dead Center

① — Before disconnecting wires from distributor coil unit, determine location of ignition wires, as position may have been altered from that shown at end of this chart.

② — Wrap shop towel around diagnostic valve to prevent fuel spillage. Connect suitable fuel pressure gauge to fuel diagnostic valve. Place ignition switch in On position to energize fuel pump & check pressure gauge reading.

③ — Eighth digit of Vehicle Identification Number (VIN) denotes engine code.

④ — Equipped w/crankshaft position sensor.

⑤ — Controlled by Idle air control valve.

⑥ — Valve clearance is hydraulically controlled, no adjustment is necessary.

⑦ — When adjusting idle speed, set parking brake & chock drive wheels.

⑧ — Non-adjustable.

⑨ — Intake, .0043–.0071 inch; exhaust, .0106–.0134 inch.

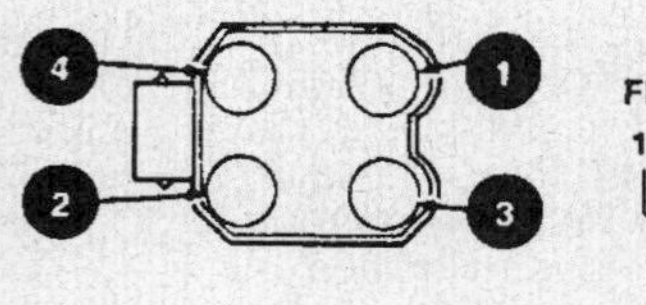

FIRING ORDER:
1- 3- 4- 2

FM1139500409000X

Fig. A

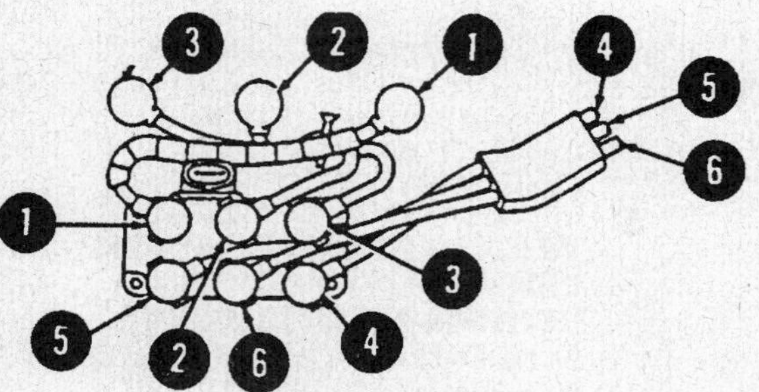

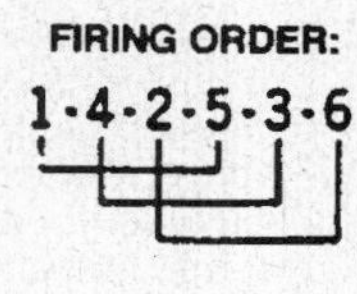

FM1139500410000X

Fig. B

FRONT WHEEL ALIGNMENT SPECIFICATIONS

Model	Caster Angle, Degrees		Camber Angle, Degrees		Total Toe, Inch①		Toe-Out On Turns, Degrees		Ball Joint Wear, Inch
	Limits	Desired	Limits	Desired	Limits	Desired	Outer Wheel	Inner Wheel	
1998									
Contour & Mystique	+1.23 to +3.31	+2.27	-1.83 to +.77	-.53	-.170 to +.170	0	—	—	.015②
1999									
Contour & Mystique	+1.23 to +3.31	+2.27	-1.83 to +.77	-.53	-.170 to +.170	0	—	—	.015②
Cougar	+1.23 to +3.31	+2.27	-1.83 to +.77	-.53	-.170 to +.170	0	—	—	.015②
2000									
Contour & Mystique	+1.23 to +3.31	+2.27	-1.83 to +.77	-.53	-.170 to +.170	0	—	—	.015②
Cougar	+1.23 to +3.31	+2.27	-1.83 to +.77	-.53	-.170 to +.170	0	—	—	.015②
2001–02									
Cougar	+1.23 to +3.31	+2.27	-1.83 to +.77	-.53	-.170 to +.170	0	—	—	.015②

① — Toe-in (+), toe-out (-).

② — Refer to "Ball Joint Inspection," in "Front Suspension & Steering" section, for inspection procedure.

REAR WHEEL ALIGNMENT SPECIFICATIONS

Model	Camber Angle, Degrees		Total Toe, Degrees①	
	Limits	Desired	Limits	Desired
1998–2000				
All	-1.82 to +.76	-.53	+.12 to +.52	+.32
2001–02				
All	-1.98 to +.58	-.70	+.12 to +.52	+.32

① — Toe-in (+), toe-out (-).

VEHICLE RIDE HEIGHT

Model	Year	Body Style	Manufacturer's Original Tire Size	Measurement Points & Specifications②					
				Front			Rear		
				Dim.	Specification		Dim.	Specification	
					Inches	mm		Inches	mm
Contour	1998–2000	All	①	A	7.21	183	B	7.18	182
Mystique	1998–2000	All	①	A	7.21	183	B	7.18	156

A Dim. — Distance from Front Rocker Panel to Ground
B Dim. — Distance from Rear Rocker Panel to Ground
Dim. — Dimension
① — See door sticker or inside of glove box for manufacturer's original tire size specifications. If tires on vehicle do not match manufacturer's original tire size & measurement is not within limits, it will be necessary to refer to the "Non-Standard Tire & Wheel Size Adjustment To Ride Height Specification & Tire Size Adjustment Charts" in the front of this manual for approximate changes in ride height specifications.
② — Measurement is w/fuel, radiator coolant & engine oil full, spare tire, jack, hand tools & mats in designated positions & tires properly inflated.

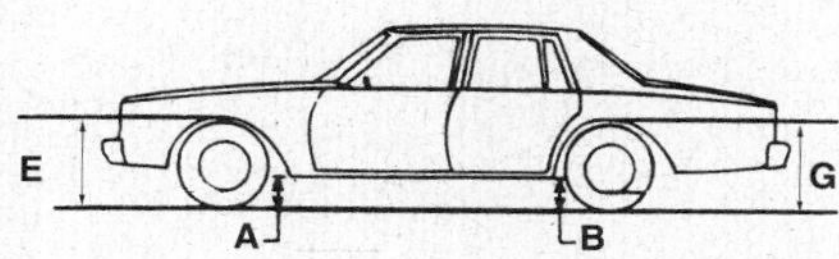

Dimensions A, B, E & G

FLUID CAPACITIES & COOLING SYSTEM DATA

Year	Engine (Code)③	Coolant Capacity, Qts.		Coolant Type	Radiator Cap Relief Pressure, Lbs.	Thermo Opening Temp., Deg. F	Fuel Tank, Gals.	Engine Oil Refill, Qts.②	Transaxle Oil	
		Auto-matic Trans.	Manual Trans.						Manual Trans., Pts.	Auto-matic Trans., Qts.①
1998	2.0L	7.5	7	⑤	13-18	191	15	4.5	4.2	9
	2.5L	9.1	8.9	⑤	13-18	187	15	5.5	4.2	10
1999–2002	2.0L	7.5	7	⑤	13-18	191	④	4	2.9	9
	2.5L	9.1	8.9	⑤	13-18	187	④	5.8	2.9	10

① — Approximate. Make final check w/dipstick.
② — Includes filter.
③ — Eighth digit of Vehicle Identification Number (VIN) denotes engine code.
④ — Cougar; 15.5 gallons. Contour & Mystique; 15 gallons.
⑤ — 1998–99 Ford Premium Cooling System Fluid – E2FZ-19549-AA or B; 2000–01 Ford Premium Cooling System Fluid – F6AZ-19544-AA; 2002 Motorcraft Specialty Orange Engine Coolant VC-2 – WSS-M97B44-P, or equivalents.

LUBRICANT DATA

Year	Model	Lubricant Type				
		Transaxle		Hydraulic Clutch Fluid	Power Steering	Brake System
		Manual	Automatic			
1998–2002	All	Mercon	Mercon	DOT 3	Premium Power Steering Fluid①	DOT 3

① — Premium power steering fluid meeting Ford specification number ESW-M2C-33–F.

Electrical

NOTE: On Air Bag Equipped Models, Refer To "Air Bag System Precautions" Located In The Front Of This Manual For System Disarming & Arming Procedures.

NOTE: Refer To "Computer Relearn Procedures" Located In The Front Of This Manual When Battery Power To The Computer Has Been Interrupted.

INDEX

PRECAUTIONS

BATTERY GROUND CABLE

Prior to service, disconnect battery ground cable and isolate as required.

AIR BAG SYSTEMS

Refer to "Air Bag System Precautions" in front of this manual for system disarming and arming procedures.

FUEL PRESSURE RELIEF

1. Remove air cleaner outlet tube.
2. Remove Schrader valve cap.
3. Connect fuel pressure gauge tool No. T80L-9974-B, or equivalent, to Schrader valve.
4. When relieving fuel pressure, catch any displaced fuel in a suitable container. Turn tap on fuel pressure gauge fully counterclockwise to relieve fuel pressure.

FUSE PANEL & FLASHER LOCATION

Fuse junction panel is located to left of steering column and is attached to instrument panel

Indicator flasher is located at turn and emergency warning indicator switch at steering column tube.

FUEL PUMP RELAY LOCATION

Fuel pump relay is located in front lefthand corner of engine compartment, in engine compartment fuse box.

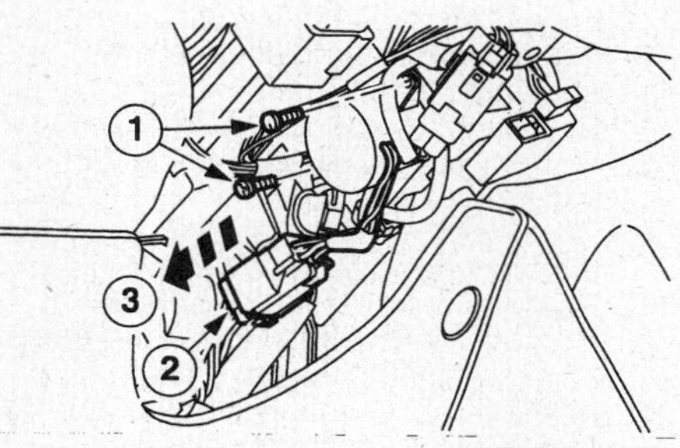

Fig. 1 Ignition switch replacement

RELAY CENTER LOCATION

Relays are contained in power distribution box, located in engine compartment on lefthand fender apron.

STARTER

REPLACE

CONTOUR & MYSTIQUE

2.0L ENGINE

1. Remove air cleaner.
2. The engine ground cable is secured by one of the starter motor bolts. Remove starter motor upper bolts.
3. Cut cable ties, then raise and support vehicle.
4. Disconnect starter motor electrical connectors.
5. Remove starter motor.
6. Reverse procedure to install. **Torque** starter motor bolts to 15–20 ft. lbs.

2.5L ENGINE

1. Remove engine air cleaner.
2. Remove fuel supply and return tubes from fuel tube support bracket located on accelerator cable bracket and fuel tube support bracket.
3. **On models equipped with automatic transaxle,** remove gear selector cable and gear shift cable bracket from transaxle.
4. **On all models,** remove engine air cleaner mounting bracket from engine and transaxle support.
5. Remove connector retaining nut from starter solenoid.
6. Remove starter motor to transaxle case retaining bolt at rear of start motor.
7. Remove two starter motor retaining bolts from top of starter.
8. Lift starter motor to disengage alignment pins from transaxle case. Carefully remove starter motor from vehicle.
9. Reverse procedure to install, noting the following:
   a. **Torque** starter motor bolts to 15-21 ft. lbs.
   b. **Torque** engine air cleaner mounting bracket to engine and transaxle support insulator bolts to 15-21 ft. lbs.
   c. **Torque** B terminal nut to 6-10 ft. lbs.
   d. **Torque** S terminal nut to 40-55 inch lbs.

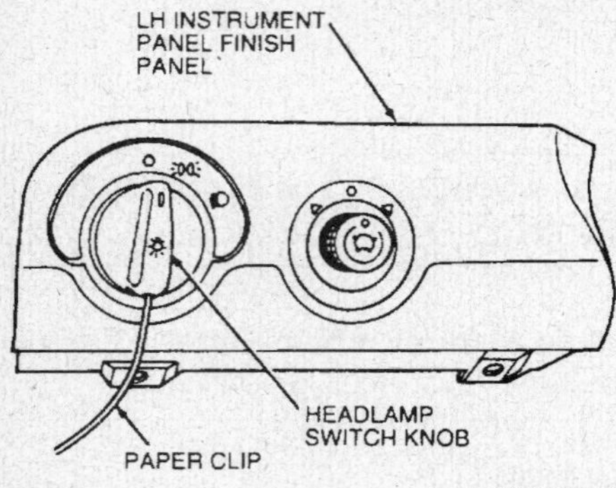

Fig. 2 Headland switch knob removal

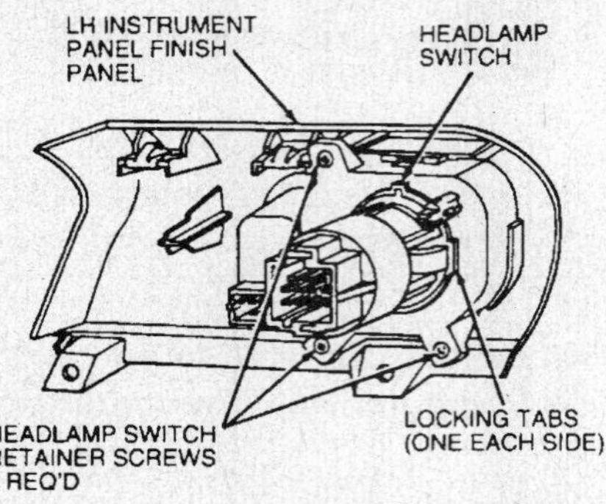

Fig. 3 Headland switch removal

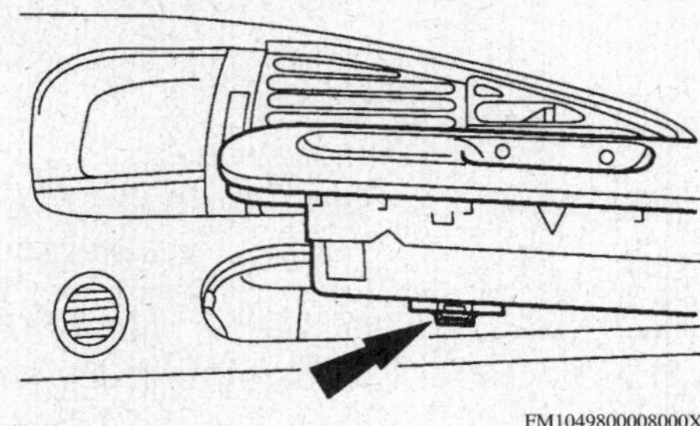

Fig. 4 Clock removal. Contour

COUGAR

2.0L ENGINE

Refer to "Contour & Mystique" for replacement procedure.

2.5L ENGINE

1999–2000

1. Remove air cleaner, then the air cleaner bracket.
2. Disconnect starter motor electrical connectors.
3. Remove shift cable bracket bolts, then disconnect shift cable.
4. Remove starter motor support bracket.
5. Relieve fuel pressure as outlined in "Precautions."
6. Using fuel line tool No. 310-D005 or 310-D004, or equivalents, disconnect fuel return and supply lines.
7. Remove starter motor bolts and starter motor.
8. Reverse procedure to install, noting the following:
   a. **Torque** starter bolts and starter bracket bolts to 18 ft. lbs.
   b. **Torque** B terminal nut to 108 inch lbs.
   c. **Torque** S terminal nut to 40-55 inch lbs.

2001–02

1. Drain cooling system into a suitable container.
2. Remove lower intake manifold as outlined under "Intake Manifold Replace."
3. Remove air cleaner, then the air cleaner bracket.
4. Disconnect starter motor electrical connectors.
5. Remove shift cable bracket bolts, then disconnect shift cable.
6. Remove starter motor support bracket, then the Schrader valve cap.
7. Relieve fuel pressure as outlined in "Precautions."
8. Using fuel line tool No. 310-D005 or 310-D004, or equivalents, disconnect fuel return and supply lines.
9. Disconnect cooling system hoses from crossover pipe, then the coolant temperature sensor electrical connector.
10. Remove accelerator cable guide, then the PCV pipe nut and hose.
11. Remove water crossover pipe, then the starter retaining bolts and starter motor
12. Reverse procedure to install. Tighten bolts to specifications.

ALTERNATOR

REPLACE

2.0L ENGINE

1. Remove the intake air resonator as follows:
   a. Disconnect air cleaner outlet pipe.
   b. Remove bolts and nuts, then the resonator.
2. **On Cougar models,** detach coolant hose from the retaining clip.
3. **On all models,** disconnect vacuum pipe underneath.
4. Remove radiator splash shield.
5. Disconnect cable and wiring from alternator.
6. Disconnect ground cable on eye hook, then raise and support vehicle.
7. Remove radiator splash shield.
8. Remove right front wheel, then splash shield bolts and splash shield.
9. Remove accessory drive belt, then alternator lower retaining bolts.
10. Lower vehicle and remove alternator upper retaining bolt.
11. There is a very limited amount of space in which to remove the alternator. Do not overdress or damage any hoses or cables. Lift alternator clear of engine.
12. Reverse procedure to install. **Torque** alternator bolt to 33 ft. lbs.

2.5L ENGINE

CONTOUR & MYSTIQUE

1. Remove alternator drive belt form alternator pulley.
2. Raise and support vehicle, then remove righthand wheel and tire.
3. Remove righthand outer tie rod end from righthand spindle.
4. Remove exhaust system Y pipe as follows:
   a. Remove front and rear Y pipe flange fasteners from exhaust manifolds.
   b. Remove stud bolt and nut retainer from oil pan, then remove two remaining nuts and bolts from U pipe outlet connection.
   c. Discard exhaust converter inlet gasket, then remove Y pipe.
5. Disconnect wire harness attachments to integral alternator/voltage regulator, then remove alternator brace bolts and brace from alternator.
6. Remove righthand halfhearted as described in "Front Wheel Drive Axles" section.
7. Remove alternator bolts from bracket, then rotate alternator and remove through righthand side of vehicle.
8. Remove bracket bolts and bracket from cylinder block.
9. Reverse procedure to install, noting following:
   a. **Torque** alternator bracket bolts to 15–22 ft. lbs.
   b. **Torque** alternator bolts to 29–40 ft. lbs.
   c. **Torque** alternator brace bolts to 15–22 ft. lbs.
   d. **Torque** output terminal nut to 84–96 inch lbs.

COUGAR

1. Remove alternator drive belt form alternator pulley.
2. Using tie rod separator tool No. 211–001 or equivalent, separate tie rod from wheel knuckle.
3. Disconnect alternator electrical connector.
4. Remove alternator rear support bracket bolt, then alternator upper and lower bolts.
5. Remove alternator through wheel opening.
6. Reverse procedure to install, noting the following:
   a. **Torque** alternator bracket bolts to 18 ft. lbs.
   b. **Torque** alternator bolts to 33 ft. lbs.
   c. **Torque** tie rod end nut to 35 ft. lbs.

COIL PACK

REPLACE

1. Disconnect ignition coil electrical connector and spark plug wires from coil.
2. Remove ignition coil mounting screws.
3. Reverse procedure to install. **Torque** coil mounting screws to 48 inch lbs.

IGNITION LOCK

REPLACE

NON-FUNCTIONAL LOCK CYLINDER

REMOVAL

Following procedure is for vehicles in

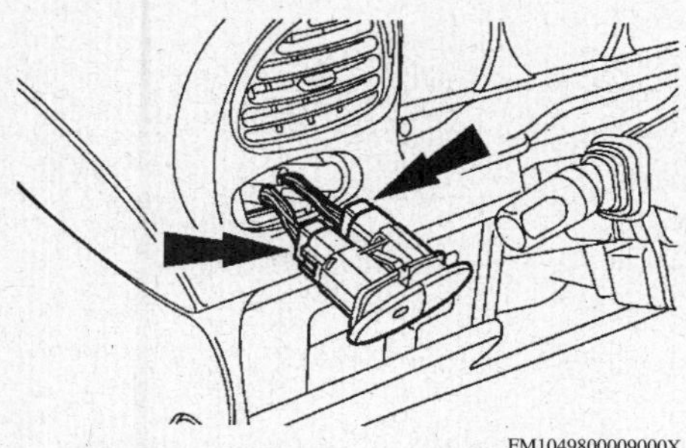

Fig. 5 Rear window defroster switch panel. Contour

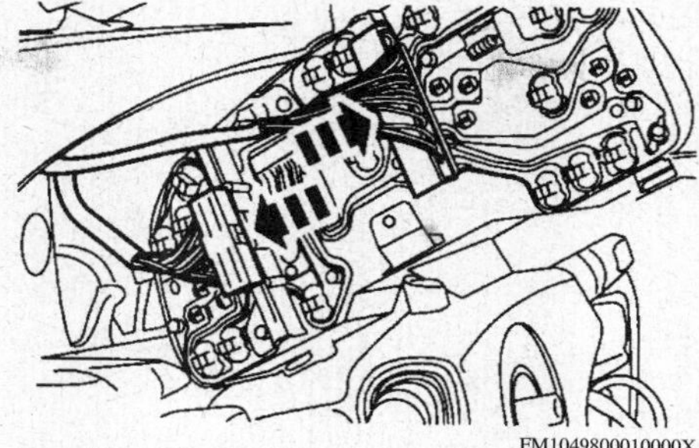

Fig. 6 Instrument cluster removal. Contour

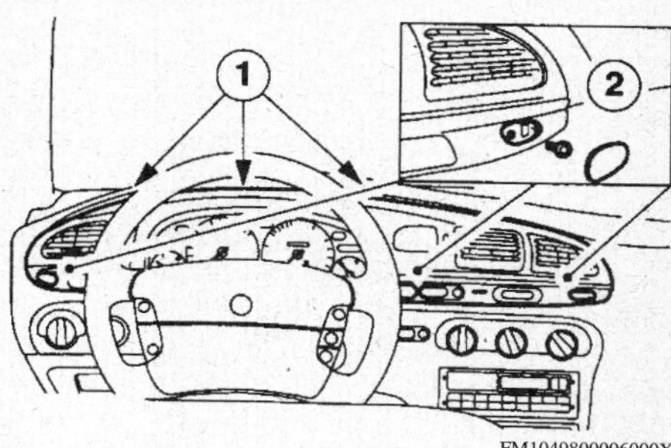

Fig. 7 Instrument cluster bezel removal. Mystique

which ignition switch lock cylinder is inoperative and ignition switch lock cylinder cannot be rotated due to a lost or broken lock cylinder key, unknown key number or with an ignition switch lock cylinder cap damaged and/or broken to extent key cannot be rotated.

1. Remove upper and lower steering column shroud screws, then shrouds.
2. Using ⅛ inch drill, drill out ignition switch lock cylinder pin.
3. Pull lock cylinder from steering column housing, then inspect housing for damage. If damaged, replace steering column as described in "Steering Columns" section.

INSTALLATION

1. Thoroughly clean all drill shavings and other foreign materials from steering column housing.
2. Install new lock cylinder by turning it to accessory position and pressing in pin.
3. Insert ignition switch lock cylinder into lock cylinder housing, then turn lock cylinder to OFF position. This permits pin to extend into lock cylinder housing hole.
4. Rotate lock cylinder, using key, to check for proper operation.
5. Install steering column shrouds, then shroud screws.
6. Connect battery ground cable.

FUNCTIONAL LOCK CYLINDER

1. Remove steering column lower shroud.
2. Remove anti-theft system transceiver screw and transceiver.
3. Insert and turn the key to accessory, then depress the retainer and remove ignition switch lock cylinder.
4. Reverse procedure to install.

IGNITION SWITCH

REPLACE

1. Remove steering column shroud screws, then shrouds.
2. Disconnect ignition switch electrical connector
3. Remove two ignition switch attaching screws, then the ignition switch, **Fig. 1.**
4. Reverse procedure to install.

CLUTCH START SWITCH

REPLACE

1. Disconnect harness connector from clutch pedal position switch.
2. Rotate switch approximately 45° and pull switch from bracket.
3. Reverse procedure to install.

TRANSAXLE RANGE SENSOR

REPLACE

1. Place manual control lever in NEUTRAL position.
2. Remove battery tray, then disconnect electrical harness from sensor, remove two retaining bolts and sensor.
3. Reverse procedure to install, noting following:
   a. Ensure manual control lever is in NEUTRAL position.
   b. Align TR sensor slots using TR sensor tool No. T94P-70010-AH, or equivalent.
   c. **Torque** TR sensor bolts to 84–108 inch lbs.
   d. **Torque** MAF sensor bolts to 25 inch lbs.
   e. **Torque** engine air cleaner tube clamps to 24–48 inch lbs.

HEADLAMP SWITCH

REPLACE

CONTOUR & MYSTIQUE

1. Remove two lefthand finish panel to instrument panel screws.
2. Pull straight outward on lefthand finish panel to release finish panel clips.
3. Grasp headland switch knob and slide small pin into hole in bottom of headland switch knob to release locking tab, **Fig. 2.**
4. Pull knob straight away from headland switch, then remove three headland switch retainer to lefthand instrument panel finish panel screws.
5. Press locking tabs on headland switch retainer and separate retainer, **Fig. 3.**
6. Press locking tabs on headland switch and remove headland switch from headland switch retainer.
7. Reverse procedure to install.

COUGAR

1. Remove instrument panel lower panel.
2. Remove lamp switch panel screws and detach instrument panel from clips.
3. Disconnect electrical connectors and remove switch.
4. Reverse procedure to install.

STOP LIGHT SWITCH

REPLACE

1. Disconnect stop lamp switch electrical connector.
2. Remove switch by rotating 90° counterclockwise and pulling toward rear of vehicle.
3. Reverse procedure to install.

MULTI-FUNCTION SWITCH

REPLACE

1. Remove steering column upper shroud screws, then upper shroud.
2. Press multi-function switch locking tab, then slide switch up and off of steering column.
3. Press locking tabs on multi-function switch electrical connector and remove connector from switch.
4. Reverse procedure to install.

STEERING WHEEL

REPLACE

1. Remove air bag module screws and air bag module.
2. Disconnect air bag wire harness from driver side air bag module, then remove module from steering wheel.
3. Center front wheels to straight ahead position, then disconnect speed control wire harness from steering wheel.
4. Remove steering wheel bolt.
5. Route air bag sliding contact assembly wire harness through steering wheel opening while lifting steering wheel off shaft.
6. Reverse procedure to install, noting following:
   a. Ensure front wheels are in straight-ahead position.
   b. Ensure steering wheel and steering shaft alignment marks are aligned and air bag contact wire is not pinched.
   c. **Torque** new steering wheel bolt to 37 ft. lbs.
   d. **Torque** air bag module screws to 8–10 ft. lbs.
   e. Verify air bag warning indicator.

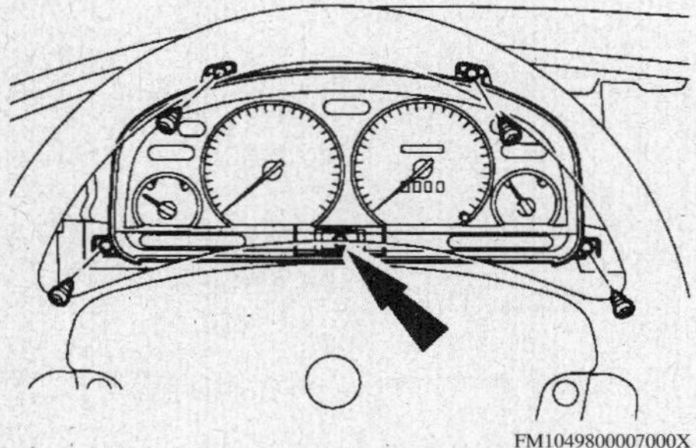

Fig. 8 Instrument cluster removal. Mystique

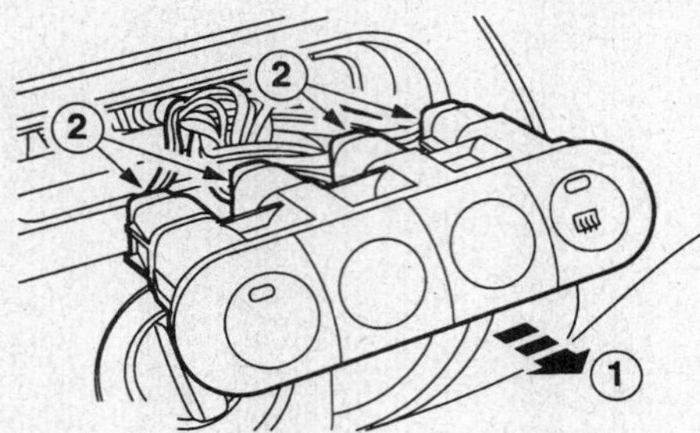

Fig. 9 Center switch removal. Cougar

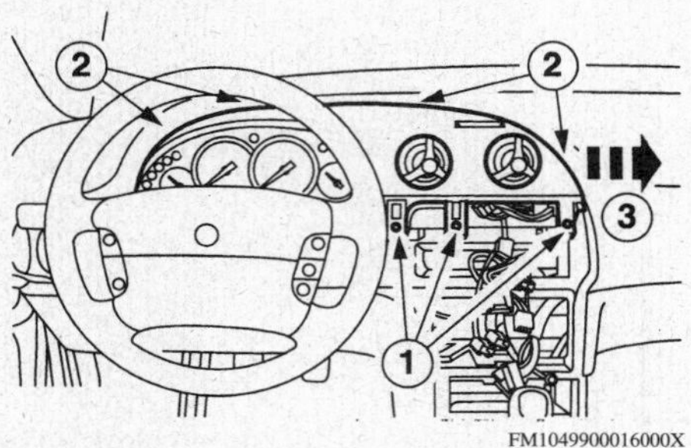

Fig. 10 Instrument cluster bezel removal. Cougar

INSTRUMENT CLUSTER

REPLACE

CONTOUR

1. Disconnect and remove clock, **Fig. 4.**
2. Remove lefthand lower instrument panel trim panel.
3. Remove headland switch panel.
4. Push rear window defroster switch panel outward and disconnect electrical connectors, **Fig. 5.**
5. Remove five instrument cluster bezel retaining screws, then the bezel.
6. Remove instrument cluster and disconnect electrical connectors, **Fig. 6.**
7. Reverse procedures to install.

MYSTIQUE

1. Remove instrument cluster bezel attaching screws, then the cluster bezel, **Fig. 7.**
2. Disconnect electrical connectors.
3. Remove instrument cluster, then disconnect electrical connectors, **Fig. 8.**
4. Reverse procedure to install.

COUGAR

1. Remove ashtray and cigar lighter bezel, then the radio.
2. Remove center switch assembly and disconnect electrical connectors, **Fig. 9.**
3. Remove heater control panel and radio unit bezel.
4. Remove heater control radio unit bezel, then disconnect electrical connectors and vacuum line.
5. Remove instrument panel lower trim panel.
6. Remove lamp switch panel and disconnect electrical connectors.
7. Remove instrument cluster bezel screws, release the clips and bezel, **Fig. 10.**
8. Pull instrument cluster forward, then release locking tangs and disconnect electrical connectors.
9. Remove cluster from vehicle.
10. Reverse procedure to install.

RADIO

REPLACE

1. Record preset stations.
2. Install radio removing tool No. T87P-19061-A, or equivalent, into radio chassis, then push tools in approximately 1 inch to release retaining clips, **Fig. 11. Do not use excessive force when installing radio removing tool to avoid damaging retaining clips. Damaging clips will make removing radio chassis difficult and may cause damage.**
3. Apply light spreading force on tools and pull radio chassis out of instrument panel.
4. Disconnect wiring connectors and antenna cable.
5. Reverse procedure to install. Check radio chassis operation, then reset preset radio stations.

WIPER MOTOR

REPLACE

FRONT

1. Ensure wiper motor is in the park position, then remove wiper arms.
2. Remove cowl grille, then the wiper motor and linkage.
3. Mark position of wiper pivot arm in relation to wiper motor mounting bracket, **Fig. 12,** then remove windshield wiper linkage to upper cowl panel bolts, **Fig. 13.**
4. Remove wiper motor nut and bolt from mounting plate and linkage.
5. Disconnect harness from wiper motor.
6. Reverse procedure to install, noting the following:
   a. **Torque** wiper motor mounting plate bolts to 106 inch lbs.
   b. **Torque** wiper motor output arm bolt to 19 ft. lbs.
   c. **Torque** wiper linkage bolts to 72 inch lbs.
   d. **Torque** wiper pivot arm nuts to 18 ft. lbs.
   e. **Torque** wiper motor bolts to 106 inch lbs.

REAR

1. Open wiper cover and loosen the nut.
2. Open liftgate and remove liftgate trim panel.
3. Loosen ground connection and bolts, then disconnect rear wiper motor electrical connector.
4. Remove rear window wiper motor.
5. Reverse procedure to install.

WIPER SWITCH

REPLACE

Refer to "Multi-Function Switch, Replace" for replacement.

CENTRAL TIMER MODULE

REPLACE

CONTOUR & MYSTIQUE

1. Pull central timer module straight away from fuse junction panel, then remove from vehicle.
2. Reverse procedure to install.

BLOWER MOTOR

REPLACE

1. Working from inside vehicle, remove push pins and upper foothill trim panel from passenger side.
2. Disconnect blower motor wire harness electrical connector.
3. Carefully lift retaining lug on A/C blower motor flange, **Fig. 14,** and rotate blower motor counterclockwise approximately 30° to disengage it from A/C evaporator housing.
4. Pull blower motor out of A/C evaporator housing.
5. Reverse procedure to install. After inserting blower motor into A/C evaporator housing, turn clockwise until retaining lug engages.

HEATER CORE

REPLACE

1. Drain coolant into a suitable container.
2. Raise and support vehicle, then disconnect heater hoses from heater core.
3. Disconnect vacuum line from engine.
4. Lower vehicle.
5. Remove floor console as follows:
   a. **On models with manual transaxle,** remove gearshift knob, spring, damping sleeve and gearshift lever boot.
   b. **On models with armrest,** raise armrest to gain access.
   c. **On models less armrest,** remove rear cup holder to gain access.
   d. **On all models,** remove ashtray and cigar lighter bezel.
   e. Remove stowage tray by pushing

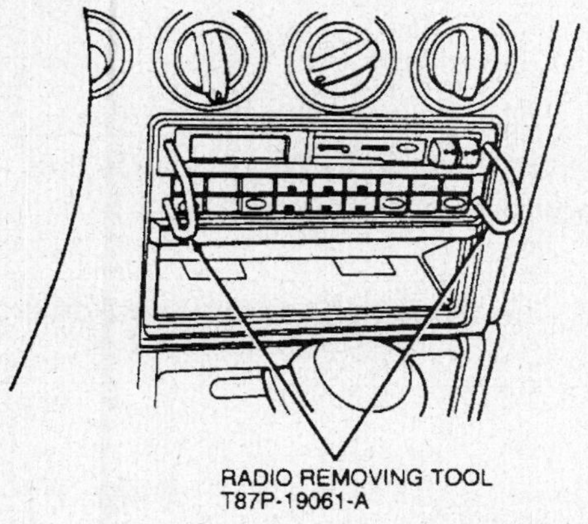

Fig. 11 Radio chassis removal

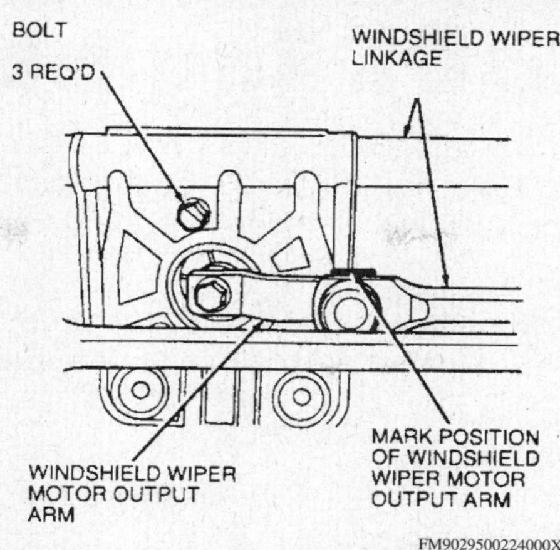

Fig. 12 Wiper pivot arm position marking

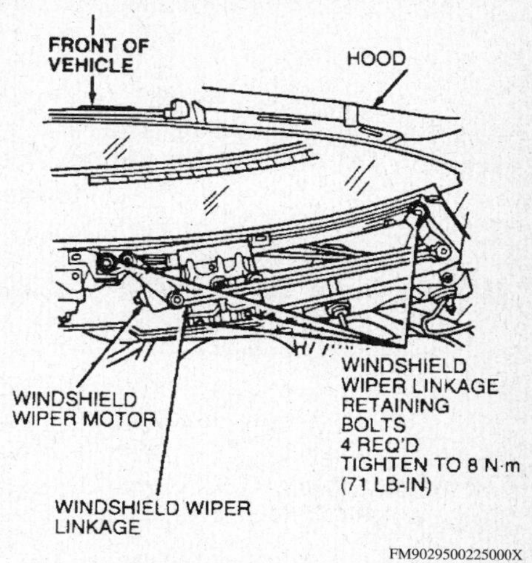

Fig. 13 Wiper linkage removal

down on the power socket aperture and pulling out stowage tray.

f. Remove floor console front screws.
g. Fully raise parking brake control lever, then remove console and disconnect cigar lighter/power socket electrical connector.

6. Remove air bag diagnostic monitor and position to one side.
7. Disconnect vacuum supply line from vacuum reservoir tank.
8. Remove screws from heater outlet floor duct.
9. Remove heater outlet floor duct screw from heater/evaporator core housing, then slide air duct upwards and release retaining tabs on each side and remove the heater outlet floor duct.
10. Remove four heater core cover retaining clips, then the cover and core.
11. Reverse procedure to install.

EVAPORATOR CORE

REPLACE

1. Recover refrigerant from A/C system as outlined in "Air Conditioning" section.
2. Drain coolant into a suitable container.
3. Remove instrument panel as outlined in "Dash Panel Service."
4. Raise and support vehicle, then disconnect heater hoses from heater core and vacuum line from engine.

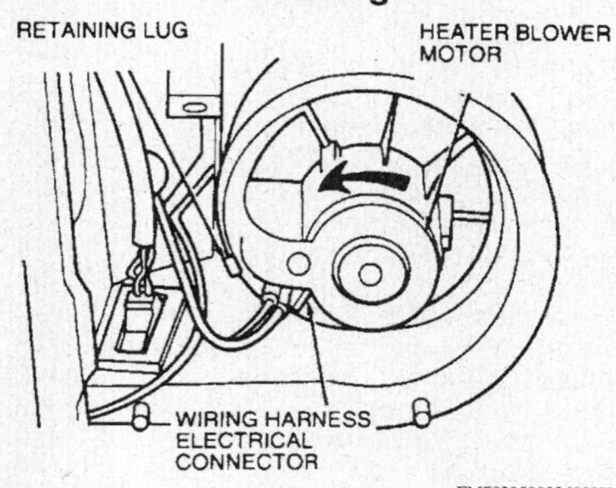

Fig. 14 Blower motor replacement

5. Lower vehicle and disconnect blower motor and resistor electrical connector.
6. **On models equipped with 2.5L engine,** remove ignition.
7. **On all models,** pull clips off air conditioning lines.
8. Disconnect line to accumulator/drier at the evaporator using tool No. T84L-19623-B, or equivalent. Seal line and evaporator with plugs.
9. Disconnect line from condenser at the evaporator using tool No. T84L-19623-B, or equivalent.
10. Remove nut on heater/evaporator core housing.
11. Remove lower defroster air duct screw from heater/evaporator core housing and release retaining tabs.
12. Disconnect right and lefthand air hose from heater/evaporator core housing.
13. Disconnect air distributor from heater/air conditioning assembly.
14. Remove heater/evaporator core housing.
15. Separate heater/air conditioning housing.
16. Remove screws at front of heater/air conditioning housing and rubber seal.
17. Remove evaporator nut, unclip vacuum hose and disconnect housing parts.
18. Remove evaporator.
19. Reverse procedure to install, noting the following:
    a. Install new Rings and coat them with refrigerant oil.
    b. When installing a new evaporator, install gaskets as they were on the old evaporator.

2.0L Engine

NOTE: On Air Bag Equipped Models, Refer To "Air Bag System Precautions" Located In The Front Of This Manual For System Disarming & Arming Procedures.

NOTE: Refer To "Computer Relearn Procedures" Located In The Front Of This Manual When Battery Power To The Computer Has Been Interrupted.

INDEX

PRECAUTIONS

BATTERY GROUND CABLE

Prior to service, disconnect battery ground cable and isolate as required.

AIR BAG SYSTEMS

Refer to "Air Bag System Precautions" in front of this manual for system disarming and arming procedures.

COOLING SYSTEM

This engine has an aluminum cylinder head and requires a special corrosion inhibiting coolant to avoid cooling system damage. Use only specified coolant in this engine.

FUEL SYSTEM PRESSURE RELIEF

1. Remove engine air intake resonators from air cleaner assembly.
2. Connect multipolar Fuel Injection (MFI) fuel pressure gauge tool No. T80L-9974-B, or equivalent, to fuel pressure relief valve cap on fuel injection supply manifold.
3. Open manual valve on gauge tool to relieve fuel system pressure.

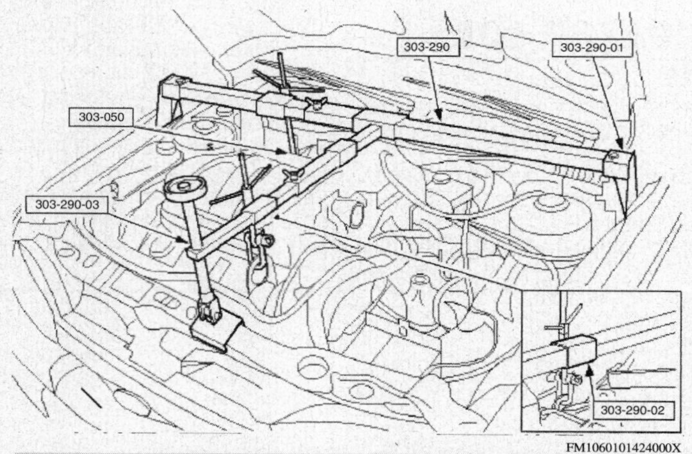

Fig. 1 Engine mount replacement

COMPRESSION PRESSURE

Compression pressure should be checked with engine at normal operating temperature, spark plugs removed and throttle plate wide open. Cylinder compression pressure is considered within specification if lowest reading cylinder is within 75 percent of highest reading and no reading is lower than 101 psi.

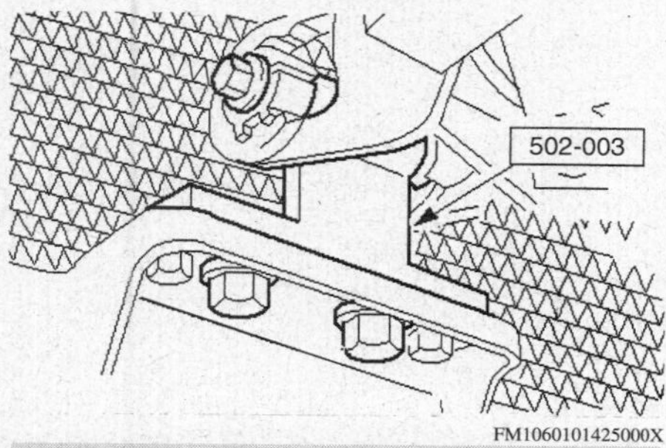

Fig. 2 Powertrain alignment gauge

ENGINE MOUNT

REPLACE

REMOVAL

1. Remove coolant expansion tank hose from clip, bolts, then water pump pulley shield.
2. Install engine support bar tool No. 303-290, adapters, tool Nos. 303-290-01, 303-290-02 and 303-290-03 and engine lifting bracket tool no. 303-050, or equivalents, **Fig. 1.**
3. Remove ignition wires, then retainer from upper front engine support bracket, place aside.
4. Remove power steering pressure line bracket bolt, then ground strap.
5. Disconnect power steering pressure line and position it aside.
6. Remove upper front engine support bracket nuts, then support bracket. **Mark on engine support bracket the position of nuts.**
7. Remove bolts and position radiator coolant expansion tank to one side.
8. Remove three bolts, then upper front engine support insulator.

INSTALLATION

1. Raise and support vehicle.
2. Remove through bolt, then lefthand front engine support insulator.
3. Replace lefthand engine support insulator with powertrain alignment gauge tool No. 502-003, or equivalent, **Fig. 2.** Tighten through bolt finger tight.
4. Remove righthand engine support insulator through bolt, then loosen mounting bolts.
5. Lower vehicle.
6. Install front engine support insulator, then radiator coolant expansion tank.
7. Install upper front engine support bracket. **Use new nuts and ensure nuts align with marks on engine support bracket.**
8. Remove the three bar engine support and universal lifting eye.
9. Raise and support vehicle.
10. Install righthand engine support insulator bolt. **Ensure righthand engine support insulator is center in transaxle bracket and in front to rear alignment before tightening through bolt.**
11. Remove powertrain alignment gauge, then install lefthand support insulator and through bolt. **Ensure lefthand engine support insulator is centered in transaxle bracket and in front to rear alignment before tightening through bolt.**
12. Lower vehicle, install power steering pressure line to power steering pump.
13. Install ignition wires and retainer to upper front engine support bracket stud.
14. Install water pump pulley shield.

ENGINE

REPLACE

AUTOMATIC TRANSAXLE

1. Move selector lever to "D."
2. Raise and support vehicle and remove front wheels.
3. Remove radiator splash shield and brace on both sides.
4. Drain engine coolant into a suitable container.
5. Lower vehicle and remove battery.
6. Remove air intake tube, then disconnect mass air flow and intake air temperature sensor connectors.
7. Remove air cleaner and crankcase ventilation hose.
8. Secure condenser core on hood lock panel.
9. Using an allen key to stop the piston rod from turning, loosen suspension strut locknuts five turns on both sides. Hold the suspension strut steady.
10. Disconnect engine wiring harness and automatic transaxle ground cable, then remove cable tie.
11. Unclip the wiring harness and disconnect transaxle range switch electrical connector.
12. Disconnect crankshaft position sensor and engine coolant temperature sensor electrical connectors.
13. Remove selector cable abutment bracket, then unclip selector cable from the selector lever and disconnect selector cable.
14. Disconnect throttle cable by pulling out the clip and unhooking the cable.
15. Remove upper accessory drive belt cover, then raise and support vehicle.
16. Remove righthand splash shield, then loosen and remove accessory drive belt.
17. Disconnect lower suspension arm ball joints and the stabilizer link rods, then ABS wiring harness bracket from the suspension strut. **Do not damage boot and ABS sensor ring.**
18. Disconnect radiator at the bottom and both heated oxygen sensor electrical connectors. Cut cable ties.
19. Remove power steering hoses from subframe.
20. Remove vehicle speed sensor retaining clip bolt, then vehicle speed sensor.
21. Disconnect brake booster vacuum line from of intake manifold.
22. Remove righthand engine support insulator bolts and engine support insulator.
23. Remove steering gear heat shield, then power steering line bracket and coolant line bracket.

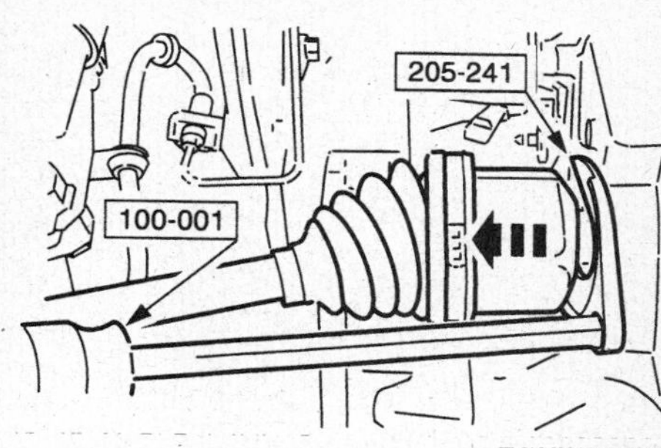

Fig. 3 Halfshaft removal

24. Remove front exhaust tube and discard the gasket.
25. Using tool No. T97P-3504-A, or equivalent, remove steering gear two bolts and secure it with wire out of the way.
26. If necessary raise automatic transaxle slightly with a transmission jack to remove lefthand engine support insulator nuts, center bolt and insulator.
27. Remove suction accumulator bolts.
28. Remove subframe. Take out rubber guides from the lower radiator supports. Support subframe using a suitable powertrain lift.
29. Drain automatic transmission fluid into a suitable container and install drain plug.
30. Using a slide hammer tool No. T50T-100-A and halfshaft remover tool No. T86P-3514-A, or equivalents, remove lefthand halfshaft, **Fig. 3. To avoid damage to the halfshaft joints and boots, do not bend the inner halfshaft joint more than 18 degrees and the outer one no more than 45 degrees.**
31. Disconnect fluid tube and close off openings with suitable plugs.
32. Disconnect turbine shaft speed sensor electrical connector.
33. Remove fluid cooler tube from transaxle.
34. Remove righthand drive halfshaft and intermediate shaft. Secure righthand drive halfshaft out of the way with mechanics wire.
35. Disconnect coolant hose from heater coolant tube and remove the bracket.
36. Disconnect lower coolant hose and lower vehicle.
37. Disconnect the two ground cables and hoses from oil cooler.
38. Disconnect fan motor and power steering pressure switch electrical connectors, then remove upper coolant hose.
39. Remove tube/hose (A/C) bracket and the power steering line.
40. Remove upper bolts from the power steering pump, wiring clamp from the fender apron panel and coolant hoses.
41. Raise and support vehicle and disconnect A/C compressor electrical connector.
42. Separate radiator from condenser core.
43. Remove A/C compressor bolts, then

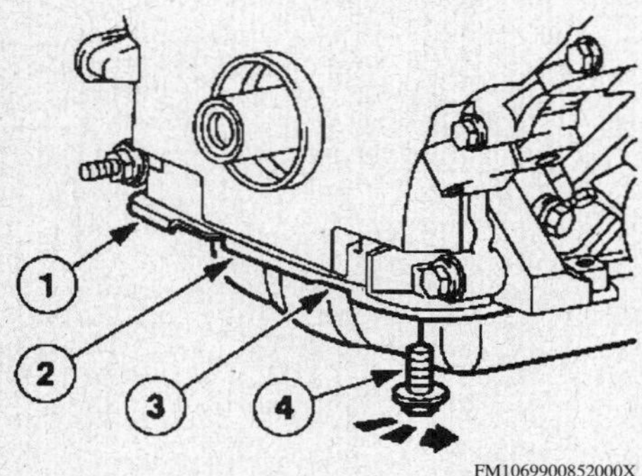

Fig. 4 Manual gear lever alignment tool installation. Cougar, Contour & Mystique

secure the compressor with mechanics wire and position it to one side.

44. Remove power steering pump and position it to one side.
45. Disconnect heater coolant hose, then lower the vehicle.
46. Remove power steering reservoir (push fit) and lay it to one side, then disconnect main wiring harness from the powertrain control module.
47. Disconnect vacuum hoses from intake manifold.
48. Relieve fuel pressure as outlined in "Precautions," then disconnect fuel lines using quick disconnect connect tool Nos. D87L-9280-A or D87L-9280-B, or equivalents.
49. Raise and support vehicle.
50. Carefully lower vehicle and place engine/transaxle assembly on powertrain lift and secure it with retaining straps.
51. Remove coolant expansion tank and position it to one side. Disconnect speed control cable (if equipped) from the coolant expansion tank.
52. Remove front engine mounting bracket nuts and loosen bolts two turns.
53. Remove rear engine mounting bracket.
54. Raise vehicle and pull out powertrain lift with the engine/automatic transaxle assembly from underneath the vehicle.
55. Reverse procedure to install.

MANUAL TRANSAXLE

CONTOUR & MYSTIQUE

1. Put gearshift lever into neutral, then using gear lever alignment tool No. T97P-7025-A, or equivalent, lock shifter into neutral, **Fig. 4.**
2. Raise and support vehicle, then remove both front tires.
3. Remove radiator splash shield and brace on both sides.
4. Drain engine coolant into a suitable container, then lower vehicle.
5. Remove battery, then disconnect mass air flow and intake air temperature sensor connectors.
6. Remove air cleaner body, crankcase ventilation hose and air hose.
7. Tie up air conditioning condenser on hood lock panel.
8. Loosen suspension strut locknuts five turns on both sides.
9. Disconnect engine wiring harness connector and automatic transaxle ground cable. Remove cable tie.
10. Brake fluid may leak out. Pull out clip and pull off the pipe and remove slave cylinder pipe from the transaxle and tie it up.
11. Pull out the clip and disconnect accelerator cable.
12. Remove upper drive belt cover and raise and support vehicle.
13. Remove lower wheel arch trim panels.
14. Loosen and remove drive belt.
15. Disconnect lower suspension arm ball joints and the stabilizer link rods, then ABS wiring harness bracket from suspension strut. **Do not damage boot and ABS sensor ring.**
16. Disconnect radiator at the bottom and disconnect both heated oxygen sensor connectors. Cut cable ties.
17. Remove power steering hoses from subframe.
18. Disconnect brake booster vacuum line from the intake manifold.
19. Remove steering gear bolt using steering gear wrench tool No. T97P-3504-A, or equivalent and righthand engine roll restrictor.
20. Remove bracket for righthand engine roll restrictor from transaxle.
21. Remove steering gear heat shield using steering gear heat shield wrench tool No. 21-066, or equivalent. Secure steering gear with mechanic's wire out of the way.
22. Disconnect front exhaust tube and remove the gasket.
23. If necessary raise transaxle slightly with a transmission jack and remove the lefthand engine roll restrictor nuts, center through bolt and roll restrictor.
24. Disconnect air conditioning dehydrator.
25. Support subframe using a suitable powertrain lift. Remove subframe and take out rubber guides from the lower radiator supports.
26. **To avoid to damage the halfshaft joints and boots, do not bend the inner halfshaft joint more than 18 degrees and the outer one no more than 45 degrees.**
27. Using slide hammer tool No. T50T-100-A and halfshaft remover tool No. T86-P3514-A, or equivalents, remove left and righthand halfshafts, **Fig. 3.** Secure halfshafts with wire.
28. Disconnect coolant hose from heater coolant tube and remove bracket.
29. Disconnect lower coolant hose and lower vehicle.
30. Disconnect two ground cables, then the fan motor and power steering pressure switch connectors.
31. Remove A/C line bracket and the power steering hose.
32. Remove upper bolts from power steering pump, then the wiring clamp from fender apron panel and coolant hoses.
33. Raise and support vehicle.
34. Disconnect A/C compressor electrical connector.
35. Separate radiator from condenser by disconnecting electrical connector

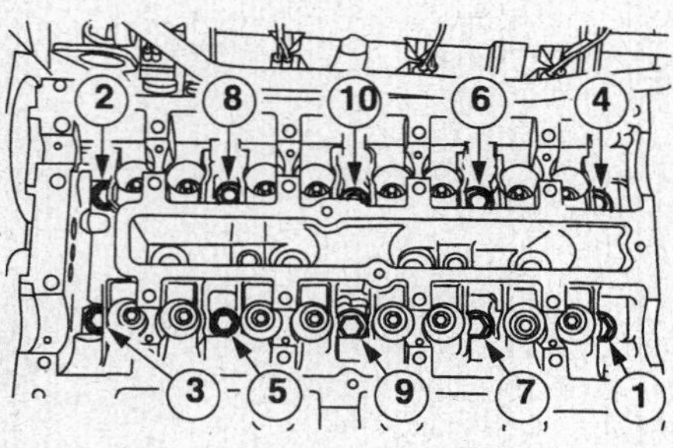

Fig. 5 Cylinder head removal sequence

from fan motor ballast resistor and removing one bolt on each side. Lower radiator to remove.

36. Remove A/C compressor and secure it out of the way with mechanics wire.
37. Remove power steering pump and secure it out of the way with mechanics wire.
38. Disconnect shift cable from the transaxle, release abutment bracket by twisting it counterclockwise and remove the cable from the bracket.
39. Disconnect shift cable from gear selector lever, release abutment bracket by twisting it counterclockwise remove the cable from the bracket.
40. Lower vehicle.
41. Remove power steering reservoir (push fit) and lay it to one side, then disconnect main wiring harness from PCM.
42. Disconnect vacuum hoses from intake manifold.
43. Disconnect battery leads and connectors, and cut cable ties.
44. Relieve fuel pressure as outlined in "Precautions."
45. Using fuel line quick disconnect tool No. D87L-9280-A/B, equivalent, disconnect fuel lines.
46. Raise and support vehicle.
47. Carefully lower vehicle and place the engine/transaxle assembly on Montagetisch GV2166, or equivalent and secure it with straps.
48. Disconnect coolant recovery tank and lay it to one side, then the speed control cable (if equipped) from the coolant recovery tank.
49. Remove front engine mounting bracket nuts and loosen bolts two turns.
50. Remove rear engine mounting bracket.
51. Raise vehicle and pull out powertrain lift with the engine/transaxle assembly from underneath the vehicle.
52. Separate transaxle from the engine.
53. Reverse procedure to install.

COUGAR

1. Put gearshift lever into neutral, then using gear lever alignment tool No. T97P-7025-A, or equivalent, lock shifter into neutral, **Fig. 4.**
2. Disconnect hose and remove hood bolts and hood.
3. Use an allen key to stop piston rod from turning and loosen suspension strut locknut five turns on both sides.

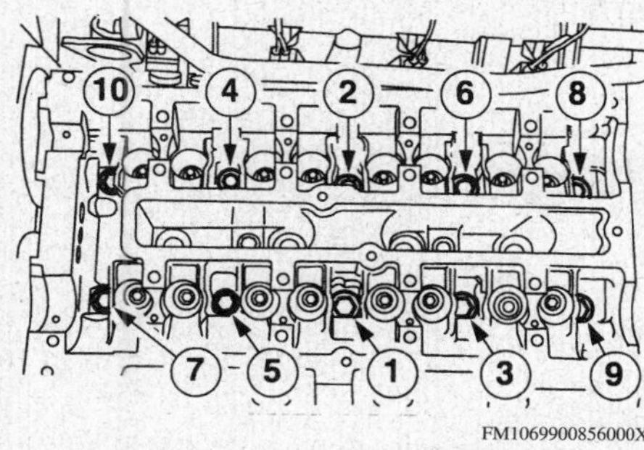

Fig. 6 Cylinder head bolt tightening sequence

4. Raise and support vehicle, then remove front wheels.
5. Remove radiator splash shield and brackets on both sides.
6. Drain engine coolant into a suitable container.
7. Disconnect mass air flow and intake air temperature sensor electrical connectors, then remove air intake tube.
8. Remove crankcase ventilation hose and air hose.
9. Unhook rubber ring and remove the air cleaner.
10. Remove battery, then loosen central junction box and position it to one side.
11. Remove four battery bracket bolts and two ground cables.
12. Remove power steering reservoir (push fit) and position it to one side, then disconnect main wiring harness from PCM.
13. Remove ground cable from engine lifting eye and disconnect power steering pressure switch.
14. Disconnect speed control cable from throttle valve, then gently move cable up and down and pull it out off the retaining bush. Press retaining bush out of bracket.
15. Disconnect throttle cable by unhooking cable and pulling off plastic clip, then lay throttle cable to one side.
16. Disconnect vacuum hoses from intake manifold.
17. Remove heat shield, coolant hose brackets, then pull out the engine oil level indicator tube.
18. Remove coolant hose from coolant pipe and the coolant hose from the water pump.
19. Remove three-way catalytic converter from exhaust manifold.
20. Disconnect A/C compressor electrical connector.
21. Disconnect engine coolant temperature sensor electrical connector.
22. Disconnect fan motor electrical connector and remove upper coolant hoses.
23. Remove clamp from fender apron panel and coolant hoses.
24. Remove upper accessory drive belt cover.
25. Pull out clip, then disconnect from slave cylinder, then remove slave cylinder from transaxle and tie it up.
26. Disconnect ground cable from transaxle.
27. Raise and support vehicle.
28. Remove righthand fender splash shields.
29. Loosen and remove accessory drive belt, then disconnect brake booster vacuum line from the intake manifold.
30. Remove radiator brackets and disconnect both heated oxygen sensor (HO2S) electrical connectors. Cut cable ties.
31. Disconnect front exhaust tube and discard the gasket.
32. Disconnect lower suspension arm ball joints from the wheel knuckles and ABS wiring harness bracket from suspension strut. **Do not damage boot and ABS sensor ring.**
33. **To avoid to damage the halfshaft joints and boots, do not bend the inner halfshaft joint more than 18 degrees or outer halfshaft no more than 45 degrees.**
34. Using slide hammer tool No. T50T-100-A and halfshaft remover tool No. T86-P3514-A, or equivalents, remove left and right halfshafts, **Fig. 3.** Secure halfshafts with wire.
35. Remove righthand engine support insulator center bolt and engine support insulator.
36. Remove bracket for righthand engine support insulator from transaxle.
37. If necessary raise transaxle slightly with a transmission jack, then remove lefthand engine support insulator and three way catalytic converter (TWC).
38. Remove suction accumulator bracket bolts, then the lower coolant hose.
39. Disconnect heater coolant hoses, then remove compressor bolts and position compressor with mechanics wire to one side.
40. Disconnect shift cable from gear shift lever, then release abutment bracket by turning it counterclockwise and removing cable from bracket.
41. Disconnect shift cable from gear selector lever, then release abutment bracket by turning it counterclockwise and removing cable from bracket. Release adjustment mechanism by pressing it in.
42. Lower vehicle, then relieve fuel pressure as outlined under "Precautions."
43. Using fuel line quick disconnect tool No. D87L-9280-A/B, or equivalent, disconnect fuel lines.
44. Disconnect coolant expansion tank and position it to one side, then the speed control cable (if equipped) from the coolant expansion tank.
45. Remove TWC bracket.
46. Install lifting bracket tool No. T70P-6000 and spreader bar tool No. D93P–6001-A3, or equivalents, and a suitable floor crane, raise engine/transaxle assembly slightly to remove pressure from the support insulator.
47. Remove front engine support insulator nuts and loosen bolts two turns.
48. Mark up position, then remove rear transaxle support insulator nuts and bolts.
49. Raise engine/transaxle assembly, until power steering pump is accessible, then remove power steering pump bolts and position pump aside with mechanics.
50. Remove engine/transaxle assembly.
51. Separate transaxle from engine.
52. Reverse procedure to install.

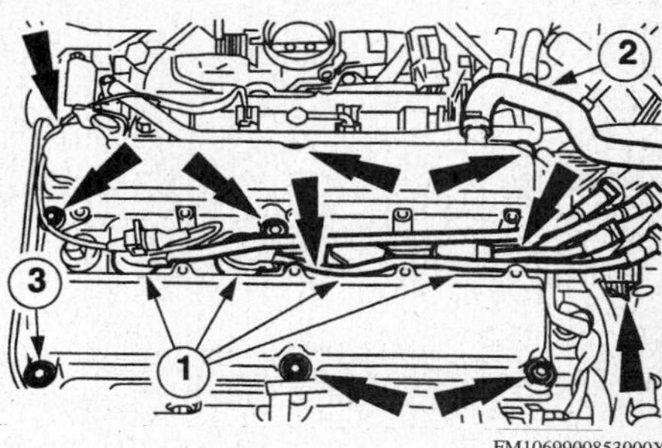

Fig. 7 Valve cover loosening sequence. 1999–2002

INTAKE MANIFOLD

REPLACE

1. Remove air cleaner outlet tube.
2. Disconnect throttle position sensor, idle air control and engine control sensor wiring.
3. Relieve fuel system pressure as outlined under "Precautions."
4. Remove fuel supply manifold.
5. Remove engine wiring harness screws and position aside.
6. Disconnect vacuum supply hoses from the intake manifold by squeezing tabs, twisting hoses and pulling away from intake manifold.
7. Disconnect brake booster vacuum line from intake manifold.
8. Remove fuel charging wiring, then accessory drive belt.
9. Remove alternator bolts and position out of the way.
10. Remove seven intake manifold bolts and two nuts, then the intake manifold.
11. Remove manifold gasket and discard.
12. Reverse procedure to install.

EXHAUST MANIFOLD

REPLACE

1. Remove heat shield, coolant hose bracket and engine lifting eye and pull out engine oil dipstick tube.
2. **When repairing exhaust system or removing exhaust components, disconnect heated oxygen sensor (HO2S) at the wiring harness to prevent damage to sensors and the harness.** Disconnect HO2S wiring connector.
3. Remove catalytic converter from exhaust manifold.
4. Raise and support vehicle.
5. Loosen catalytic converter bracket bolt and drop converter down so the studs clear the exhaust manifold.
6. Lower vehicle.
7. Remove exhaust manifold bolts, manifold and gasket.
8. Reverse procedure to install.

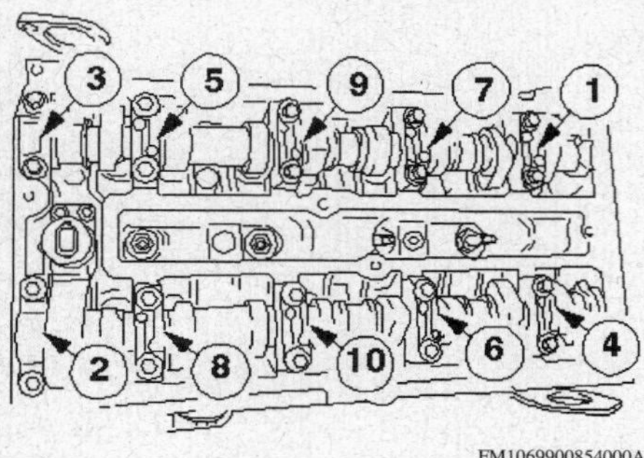

Fig. 8 Camshaft bearing caps loosening sequence. 1999–2002

CYLINDER HEAD

REPLACE

1998

1. Drain engine coolant from radiator and cylinder block drain plugs.
2. Remove intake manifold as outlined under "Intake Manifold, Replace."
3. Remove exhaust manifold as outlined under "Exhaust Manifold, Replace."
4. Remove camshafts as outlined under "Camshaft, Replace."
5. Remove valve tappets from cylinder head, then support front of engine with wood block between crankshaft pulley and front subframe.
6. Remove righthand engine lifting eye bolt, then the righthand eye.
7. Remove power steering pump mounting and cylinder head support brackets.
8. Remove camshaft timing belt tensioner pulley, then the front cover from front of cylinder head.
9. Remove thermostat housing as outlined under "Thermostat, Replace."
10. Disconnect ignition coil electrical connectors by squeezing locking tabs and twisting while pulling upward.
11. Remove ignition coil attaching bolts, then the coil and bracket.
12. Remove spark plugs from cylinder head.
13. Remove cylinder head bolts in sequence, **Fig. 5.**
14. Remove cylinder head and head gasket from cylinder block.
15. If necessary, remove lefthand engine lifting eye from cylinder head.
16. Inspect cylinder head and cylinder block, then replace components as required.
17. Reverse procedure to install, noting following:
    a. Clean intake manifold, valve cover and cylinder head gasket surfaces.
    b. Using sequence in **Fig. 6, torque** cylinder head bolts in three steps. First step 18 ft. lbs., second step 33 ft. lbs, then an additional 105.°

1999–2002

The maximum amount by which the engine management system will adjust the camshaft timing (VCT control unit) is limited to 2 degrees. As a result of this an extremely high degree of accuracy is required for any work which affects the valve timing.

1. Raise and support vehicle.
2. Remove engine undershield and front righthand wheel.
3. Remove radiator splash shield and drain coolant into a suitable container.
4. Remove righthand lower wheel arch cover.
5. Loosen water pump belt pulley bolts, then working clockwise, loosen and remove drive belt.
6. Remove water pump belt pulley and drive belt idler pulley.
7. Remove crankshaft vibration damper, then the lower timing belt cover.
8. It should be possible to insert locating pins free of strain in subframe and body locating bores. Check position of subframe and realign later if necessary.
9. **On models equipped with manual transaxle,** loosen bolts of righthand engine roll restrictor two turns.
10. **On models equipped with automatic transaxle,** loosen bolt of righthand engine roll restrictor two turns.
11. **On all models,** align subframe, if necessary as follows:
    a. Remove locating pins.
    b. Loosen subframe bolts two turns.
    c. Subframe must not move during tightening operation.
    d. With locating pins fitted, tighten four bolts, diagonally.
12. Remove lower power steering pump bolts, then disconnect brake booster line and crankcase ventilation hose from intake manifold.
13. Disconnect oil pressure switch connector and knock sensor.
14. Lower vehicle.
15. Remove intake pipe, pull out plug of mass air flow sensor and intake air temperature sensor.
16. Remove air cleaner, disconnect crankcase ventilation hose and intake hose.
17. Disconnect speed control cable from throttle valve. Move cable up and down slightly and pull it out of the retaining bush.
18. Disconnect accelerator cable, unhook cable and remove plastic clip, then position cable to one side.
19. Disconnect cylinder head wiring harness connector and vacuum hoses, then remove upper wiring rail bolts from intake manifold.
20. Remove undershield, then disconnect starter motor positive lead. **Do not bend fusible element when removing the nut as there is a risk of it breaking.**
21. Disconnect radio interference suppressor, ignition coil, engine coolant temperature sensor and power steering pressure switch. Position wiring to one side.
22. Disconnect coolant hoses and lay them to one side.
23. Remove thermostat housing and disconnect connector from camshaft position sensor.
24. Remove bracket for PCV line.
25. Remove upper bolts, coolant hose bracket and engine lifting eye, pull out engine oil dipstick tube, bracket for the tube/hose (A/C), lower bolts and heat shield.

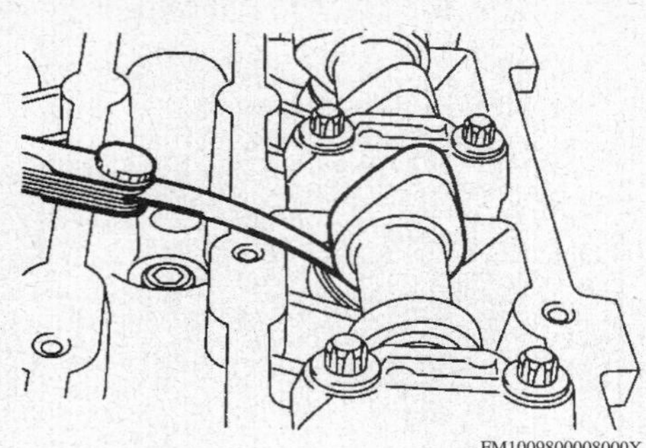

Fig. 9 Valve clearance measurement

26. Disconnect catalytic converter from exhaust manifold, then remove heated oxygen sensor.
27. Remove belt pulley cover.
28. Remove power steering pump, coolant expansion tank, power steering pump bracket from cylinder head.
29. Remove alternator bolts, alternator and alternator bracket.
30. Raise and support vehicle.
31. **On models equipped with a manual transaxle,** remove lefthand engine roll restrictor and bracket.
32. **On models equipped with automatic transaxle,** slightly lifting engine with a transmission jack, remove left hand engine roll restrictor.
33. **On all models,** install gauge tool No. T94P-6000-AH, or equivalent, in place of lefthand engine roll restrictor.
34. Lower vehicle and support engine with a jack.
35. Remove front engine mounting, then the upper timing belt cover.
36. Disconnect solenoid valve connector and remove the cylinder head cover plate.
37. Using sequence, **Fig. 7,** remove cylinder head cover.
38. Remove center timing belt cover/front engine mounting bracket.
39. Loosen bolt and release timing belt tensioner by turning it clockwise. Loosen bolt four turns and unhook the timing belt tensioner.
40. Remove timing belt, unscrew blanking plug from exhaust camshaft timing belt pulley. **Hold the camshaft by the hexagon with an open ended wrench to stop it from turning.**
41. Using timing belt pulley holding tool, tool No. T74P-6256-B, or equivalent to stop timing belt pulley from turning, remove exhaust camshaft timing belt pulley. .
42. Remove intake camshaft timing belt pulley.
43. Remove bolts from the VCT oil feed flange and upper timing case.
44. Loosen camshaft bearing caps in sequence, **Fig. 8.** Working evenly in several stages, loosen each bolt two turns at a time.
45. Remove intake camshaft and exhaust camshaft with VCT control unit.
46. Remove valve tappets.

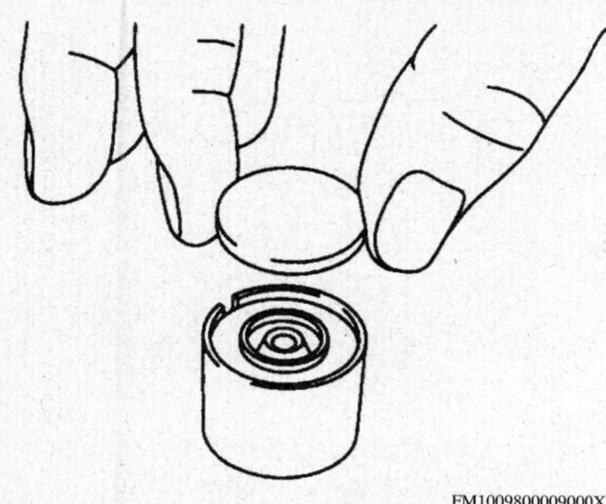

Fig. 10 Shim installation. 1998–June 1999

47. Remove cylinder head bolts in sequence, **Fig. 5.**
48. Remove cylinder head from block.
49. Reverse procedure to install, noting the following:
    a. **Cylinder head bolts must be replaced with new bolts.**
    b. **On 1999 Cougar and 1999–2000 Contour and Mystique models,** using sequence in **Fig. 6, torque** cylinder head bolts in three steps. First step 18 ft. lbs., second step 33 ft. lbs, then an additional 105.°
    c. **On 2000–02 Cougar models,** using sequence in **Fig. 6, torque** cylinder head bolts in three steps. First step 15 ft. lbs., second step 30 ft. lbs, then an additional 90.°

VALVE COVER

REPLACE

1. Disconnect oil feed sensor connector, then remove crankcase ventilation tube.
2. Position throttle cable out of the way and speed control cable if equipped, then remove eight bolts and appearance cover.
3. Remove spark plug wires.
4. Remove four bolts and position front cover out of the way.
5. Position throttle cable and the speed control cable if equipped out of the way, remove the bolts and valve cover. Refer to loosening sequence in "Cylinder Head, Replace."
6. Reverse procedure to install, noting the following:
    a. Inspect valve cover gasket and O-rings for damage or signs of leakage, replace as necessary.
    b. Tighten all bolts to specification.

CAMSHAFT LOBE LIFT SPECIFICATIONS

Camshaft lobe lift for intake and exhaust is .245 inch.

VALVE CLEARANCE SPECIFICATIONS

Intake valve clearance is .004–.007 inch, exhaust valve clearance is .010–.013.

VALVE ADJUSTMENT

1. Remove valve covers as described under "Valve Cover, Replace."
2. Rotate crankshaft until camshaft reaches base circle and measure valve clearance with a feeler gauge, **Fig. 9.**
3. Repeat for all valves and note measurement.
4. If valve clearance is not within specifications, remove camshafts as outlined under "Camshaft, Replace."
5. **On models built before June 1999,** measure and insert shim, **Fig. 10,** of required thickness as follows:
    a. Intake valve: required shim = current shim + measured clearance –.006 inch.
    b. Exhaust valve: required shim = current shim + measured clearance – .012 inch.
6. **On model built after June 1999,** proceed as follows:
    a. Measure required tappet thickness.
    b. Remove adjusting tappet and read size from back face of tappet. Number on the tappet corresponds to tappet thickness.
    c. Determine tappet thickness required and insert correct tappet.
    d. Intake valve: tappet thickness required = thickness of current tappet + measured valve clearance –.006 inch.
    e. Exhaust valve: tappet thickness required = thickness of current tappet + measured valve clearance –.012 inch.
7. **On all models,** install camshaft as outlined under "Camshaft, Replace."
8. Install valve cover as outlined under "Valve Cover, Replace." and tighten bolts to specification.

HYDRAULIC VALVE TAPPETS

REPLACE

1. Remove camshafts as described under "Camshaft, Replace."
2. If camshafts and valve tappets are to be reused, mark tappet locations for assembly.
3. Remove valve tappets.
4. If valve tappet is pitted, scored, excessively worn or if plunger is not free in body, replace tappet.
5. Reverse procedure to install.

FRONT COVER

REPLACE

1. Remove bolts and position power steering line out of the way.
2. Remove front engine support insulator.
3. Remove upper engine front cover studs, bolts and cover.
4. Remove splash shields bolts and splash shields.
5. Loosen but do not remove water pump pulley bolts.
6. Turn belt tensioner clockwise and remove accessory drive belt.

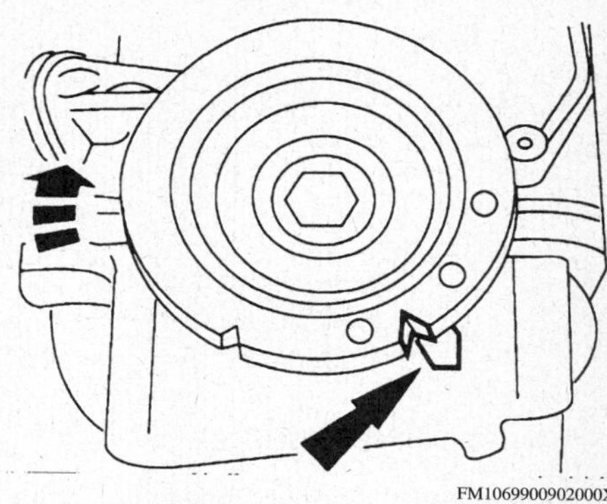

Fig. 11 Crankshaft timing marks

7. Remove idler pulley and water pump pulley.
8. Remove center engine front cover bolts and center engine front cover.
9. Remove bolt and crankshaft pulley.
10. Remove bolts and lower engine front cover.
11. Reverse procedure to install.

TIMING BELT

REPLACE

1998

REMOVAL

With timing belt removed, avoid turning camshaft or crankshaft. If movement is required, exercise extreme caution to avoid valve damage caused by piston contact.

1. Rotate crankshaft until No. 1 cylinder reaches TDC, **Fig. 11.**
2. Remove power steering line retaining bolts, then position line out of way.
3. Remove engine front support insulator.
4. Remove engine front upper cover retaining bolts and studs, then the cover.
5. Loosen righthand front wheel lugnuts.
6. Raise and support vehicle with jackstands.
7. Remove righthand front wheel and tire.
8. Remove righthand front splash shield.
9. Loosen, but do not remove water pump pulley bolts.
10. Rotate serpentine belt tensioner clockwise, then remove belt.
11. Remove idler pulley.
12. Remove water pump pulley bolts and pulley.
13. Remove engine front center cover retaining bolts, then the cover.
14. Remove crankshaft pulley retaining bolt, then the pulley by using a suitable puller tool.
15. Remove engine front lower cover retaining bolts, then the cover.
16. Disconnect oil feed sensor connector.
17. Remove crankcase ventilation tube.
18. Position throttle and speed control cables aside.
19. Remove engine appearance cover retaining bolts, then the cover.
20. Tag spark plug wires, then disconnect them at spark plugs.

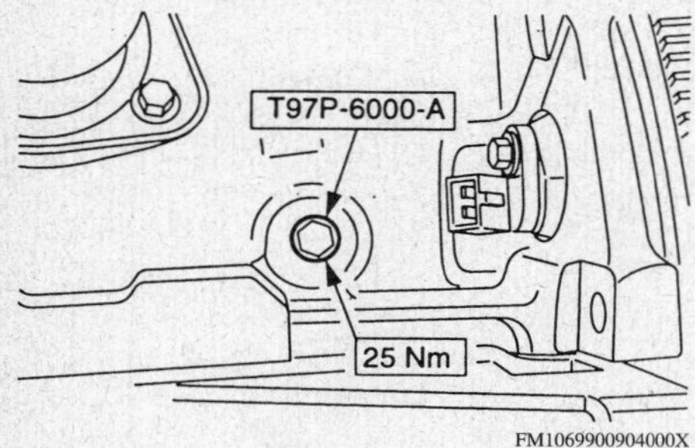

Fig. 12 Blanking plug removed

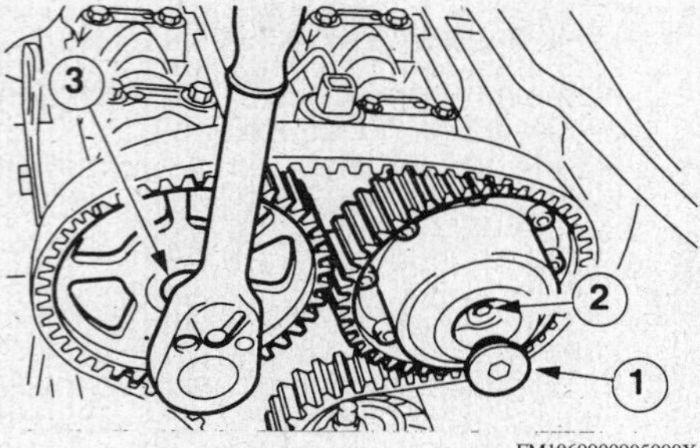

Fig. 13 Loosening camshaft sprockets. 1999–2002

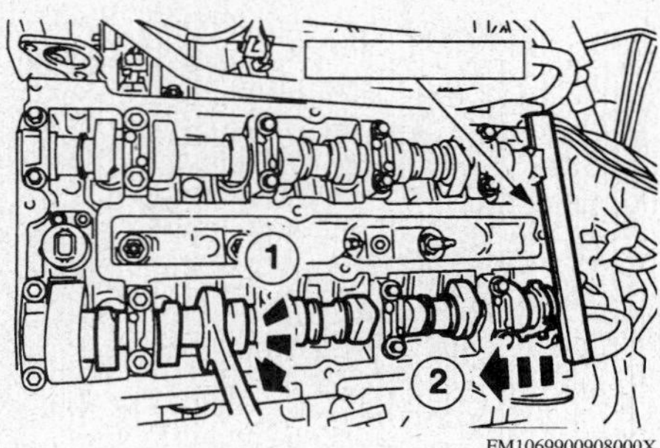

Fig. 14 Camshaft locking tool installation. 1999–2002

21. Remove four upper front cover bolts, then position cover aside.
22. Remove nine valve cover retaining bolts, then the cover.
23. Note timing belt tensioner's alignment marks, then loosen tensioner pulley bolt.
24. Rotate tensioner pulley clockwise, then remove timing belt.

INSTALLATION

1. Install camshaft alignment tool No. T94P-6256-CH, or equivalent.
2. Remove blanking plug at side of engine block, install timing peg tool No. T97P-6000-A, or equivalent, **Fig. 12. Torque** peg to 18 ft. lbs.
3. Ensure camshafts are properly positioned with alignment tool in place.
4. Install new timing belt, starting at crankshaft.
5. Rotate timing belt tensioner and ensure marks are properly aligned, then **torque** tensioner bolt to 18 ft. lbs.
6. Remove timing peg tool and install blanking plug into block. **Torque** plug to 18 ft. lbs.
7. Remove camshaft alignment tool.
8. Install valve cover. **Torque** retaining bolts to 60 inch lbs.
9. Install upper front cover.
10. Connect spark plug wires at spark plugs.
11. Install engine appearance cover.
12. Connect throttle and speed control cables.
13. Install crankcase ventilation tube.
14. Connect oil feed sensor connector.
15. Install crankshaft pulley. **Torque** retaining bolt to 83 ft. lbs.
16. Install water pump pulley. **Torque** bolts to 17 ft. lbs.
17. Install idler pulley. **Torque** retaining bolt to 34 ft. lbs.
18. Rotate serpentine belt tensioner clockwise, then install belt.
19. Install righthand front splash shield.
20. Install righthand front wheel and tire.
21. Lower vehicle to ground, then tighten wheel lugnuts.
22. Install engine front upper cover.
23. Install engine front support insulator.
24. Move power steering line back to its original position, then tighten retaining bolts.
25. Connect battery ground cable.
26. Start engine and inspect for proper operation. **Some abnormal drive symptoms may appear for approximately 10 miles while vehicle relearns its adaptive strategy.**

1999–2002

REMOVAL

With timing belt removed, avoid turning camshaft or crankshaft. If movement is required, exercise extreme caution to avoid valve damage caused by piston contact.

1. Loosen righthand front wheel lugnuts.
2. Raise and safely support vehicle.
3. Remove righthand front wheel and tire.
4. Remove righthand front splash shield.
5. **On Cougar models,** remove engine undercover.
6. **On all models,** remove serpentine belt.
7. Loosen water pump pulley bolts.
8. Loosen belt tensioner in a clockwise direction, then remove tensioner.
9. Remove water pump and belt idler pulleys.
10. Insert a suitable tool into access hole in bottom of transaxle case to prevent engine rotation.
11. Using a suitable puller tool, remove crankshaft pulley.
12. Remove lower portion of engine front cover.
13. Loosen righthand engine support insulator center bolt two turns.
14. Loosen lefthand engine support insulator center bolt two turns.
15. Lower vehicle.
16. Remove coolant expansion tank fasteners, then position tank aside.
17. Disconnect speed control cable from coolant expansion tank.
18. Position a suitable floor jack and a block of wood under engine oil pan.
19. Mark engine front support insulator mounting position.
20. Raise up slightly on floor jack to take pressure off engine front support insulator, then remove insulator.
21. Disconnect power steering pipe bracket from engine lifting eye.
22. Remove upper and center portions of engine front cover.
23. Unhook throttle and speed control cables from engine appearance cover.
24. Disconnect solenoid valve electrical connector.
25. Remove engine appearance cover.
26. Tag spark plug wires, then disconnect at spark plugs.
27. Disconnect crankcase ventilation hose.
28. Working diagonally from outside to inside, remove valve cover attaching bolts, then the valve cover.
29. Remove spark plugs.
30. Rotate crankshaft until No. 1 cylinder is approximately at TDC position.
31. Note timing belt tensioner alignment marks, then loosen tensioner bolt.
32. Rotate belt tensioner clockwise to release tension.
33. Loosen belt tensioner bolt four turns, then unhook tensioner.
34. Using a suitable wrench, hold camshafts by hexagons.
35. Remove blanking plug (1), **Fig. 13,** from exhaust camshaft sprocket.
36. Loosen exhaust camshaft sprocket (2), then the intake camshaft sprocket (3).
37. Remove timing belt.

INSTALLATION

1. Remove tool from access hole in bottom of transaxle case.
2. Rotate crankshaft until No. 1 cylinder reaches TDC, **Fig. 11.**
3. Using a suitable wrench (1), **Fig. 14,** hold camshafts by hexagons and turn in direction of engine rotation.
4. Install camshaft alignment tool No. T94P-6256-CH, or equivalent, **Fig. 15.**
5. Ensure crankshaft is still resting against timing peg. **Do not rotate crankshaft.**
6. Ensure timing belt tensioner lug is not hooked in sheet metal cover during belt installation.
7. Install new timing belt. Start at crankshaft sprocket, work in a counterclockwise direction and keep belt under tension, **Fig. 16.**
8. Hook belt tensioner into sheet metal cover and loosely turn bolt in.
9. Rotate belt tensioner counterclockwise until pointer and mark are properly aligned. **Torque** tensioner bolt to 18 ft. lbs.
10. Use holding tool No. T74P-6256-B, **Fig. 17,** or equivalent to prevent intake camshaft sprocket from turning.
11. **Torque** intake camshaft sprocket to 50 ft. lbs.
12. Using a suitable wrench, hold exhaust camshaft by its hexagon. **Torque** exhaust camshaft sprocket to 44 ft. lbs.
13. Remove timing peg and install blanking plug. **Torque** to 18 ft. lbs.
14. Remove camshaft locking tool.
15. Hold exhaust camshaft by its hexagon.

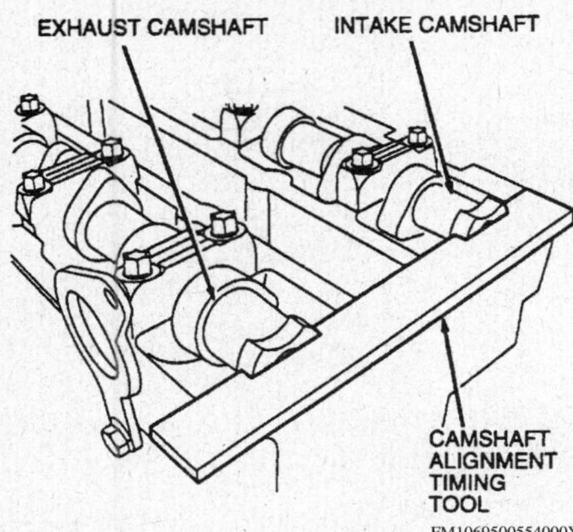

Fig. 15 Camshaft alignment. 1999–2002

Torque exhaust camshaft sprocket again to 89 ft. lbs.

16. Ensure camshaft timing is properly set by installing aligning tool No. T94P-6256-CH, or equivalent, onto camshafts. If aligning tool refuses to fit into both slots, loosen tensioner and both camshaft sprocket bolts, then tension timing belt again.
17. Install a new blanking plug onto exhaust camshaft sprocket. **Torque** to 27 ft. lbs.
18. Install valve cover. **Torque** mounting bolts to 62 inch lbs.
19. Install spark plugs. **Torque** to 11 ft. lbs.
20. Connect crankcase ventilation hose.
21. Connect spark plug wires.
22. Install engine appearance cover.
23. Connect solenoid valve electrical connector.
24. Hook throttle and speed control cables at engine appearance cover.
25. Install center and upper portions of engine front cover.
26. Connect power steering pipe bracket at engine lifting eye.
27. Raise up slightly on floor jack, then install engine support insulator. **Torque** fasteners to 60 ft. lbs.
28. Install coolant expansion tank.
29. Connect speed control cable at coolant expansion tank.
30. Raise and safely support vehicle.
31. **On models equipped with automatic transaxle,** ensure center bolt is properly centered in righthand engine support insulator. **Torque** bolt to 86 ft. lbs.
32. **On models equipped with manual transaxle,** ensure center bolt is properly centered in righthand engine support insulator. **Torque** bolt to 34 ft. lbs.
33. **On all models,** ensure center bolt is properly centered in lefthand engine support insulator. **Torque** bolt to 86 ft. lbs.
34. Install lower portion of engine front cover.
35. Insert a suitable tool into access hole in bottom of transaxle case to prevent engine rotation.
36. Install crankshaft pulley. **Torque** retaining bolt to 85 ft. lbs.
37. Install serpentine belt idler and water pump pulleys.

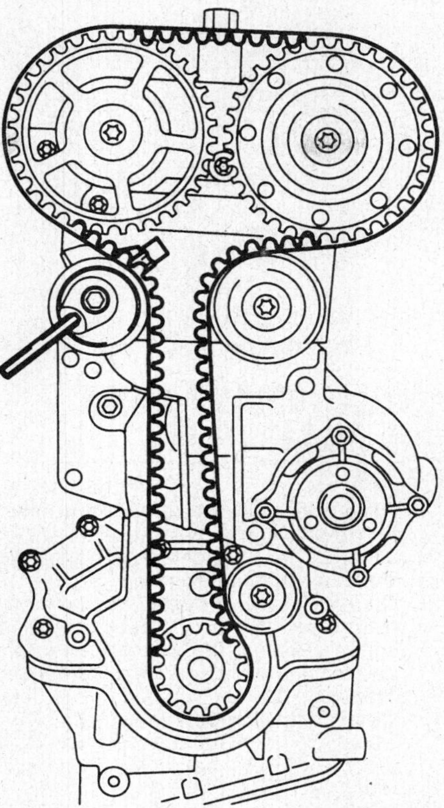

Fig. 16 Timing belt installation. 1999–2002

38. Rotate serpentine belt tensioner clockwise and install belt.
39. **Torque** water pump pulley bolts to 13 ft. lbs.
40. **On Cougar models,** install engine undercover.
41. **On all models,** install righthand splash shield.
42. Install righthand front wheel and tire.
43. Lower vehicle to ground.
44. Tighten righthand front wheel lugnuts.
45. Connect battery ground cable.
46. Start engine and inspect for proper operation. **Some abnormal drive symptoms may appear for approximately 10 miles while vehicle relearns its adaptive strategy.**

CAMSHAFT

REPLACE

REMOVAL

1. Before removal of camshaft, measure valve clearance as outlined in "Valve Adjustment."
2. Remove timing belt as described under "Timing Belt, Replace."
3. Remove camshaft sprockets.
4. Remove valve cover as described under "Valve Cover, Replace."
5. Mark cylinder head camshaft journal cap number on outside edge of camshaft journal caps and cylinder head. **Cylinder head camshaft journal caps and cylinder head should be numbered to ensure they are assembled in original positions. Keep camshaft journal caps from cylinder head together. Do not mix with camshaft journal caps from another cylinder head. Failure to do so may result in engine damage.**

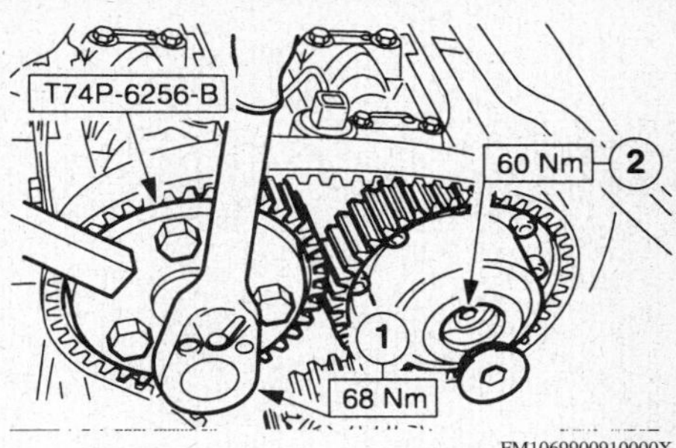

Fig. 17 Tightening camshaft sprockets. 1999–2002

6. Remove cylinder head camshaft journal cap bolts in pairs, loosening one turn at a time, beginning at rear of cylinder head, **Fig. 18.** Remove cylinder head camshaft journal thrust caps last to ensure proper camshaft position in cylinder head.
7. Remove intake and exhaust camshaft and camshafts.
8. Inspect camshafts and cylinder head for wear or damage. Replace components as required.

INSTALLATION

1. Ensure crankshaft is at Top Dead Center (TDC) of No. 1 cylinder.
2. Lubricate camshafts with engine assembly lubricant part No. D9AZ-19579-D, or equivalent.
3. Install camshafts into cylinder head. Camshafts are marked for identification. Intake camshaft also has additional cam lobe for camshaft position sensor.
4. Apply a ⅛ inch bead of silicone gasket and sealant part No. F1AZ-19562-A, or equivalent, to sealing surfaces of camshaft journal thrust caps and cylinder head.
5. Loosely install cylinder head camshaft journal caps and bolts. **Install camshaft journal thrust caps last.**
6. **Torque** camshaft journal cap bolts in sequence, **Fig. 19,** in several steps, with final step to 11 ft. lbs.
7. Install valve cover as described under "Valve Cover, Replace."
8. Install camshaft front seals as described under "Camshaft Front Seals, Replace."
9. Install camshaft sprockets.
10. Install timing belt as described under "Timing Belt, Replace."

CAMSHAFT FRONT SEALS

REPLACE

1998

1. Remove timing belt as described under "Timing Belt, Replace."

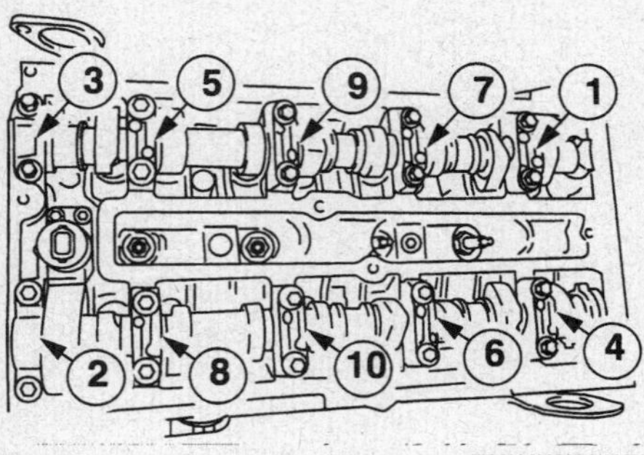

Fig. 18 Camshaft journal cap removal sequence

2. Remove camshaft sprockets, then using seal remover tool No. T92C-6700-CH, or equivalent, remove camshaft front oil seal from camshaft journal thrust caps.
3. Lubricate camshaft front oil seals with clean engine oil.
4. Using camshaft seal replacer tool No. T81P-6700-A, or equivalent, and rubber mallet, install camshaft front oil seals into camshaft journal thrust caps, **Fig. 20.**
5. Install camshaft sprockets.
6. Install timing belt as described under "Timing Belt, Replace."

1999–2002

1. Remove timing belt as described under "Timing Belt, Replace."
2. Remove camshaft sprockets, camshaft bearing cap No. 5, then the camshaft oil seals,
3. Reverse procedure to install, noting the following:
   a. Thinly coat camshaft bearing cap Nos. 0 and 5 with sealer.
   b. Bring oil feed ring hole right to the top.
   c. If lug is not centered between oil bores and mark, install a new exhaust camshaft timing belt pulley.

CRANKSHAFT SEAL

REPLACE

1. Remove timing belt as described under "Timing Belt, Replace," then the crankshaft sprocket and washer.
2. Using seal remover tool No. T92C-6700-CH, or equivalent, remove crankshaft front seal from oil pump.
3. Clean and inspect crankshaft front seal bore.
4. Lubricate crankshaft front oil seal bore and crankshaft front seal with engine assembly lubricant D9AZ-19579-D, or equivalent.
5. Using seal replacer tool No. T81P-6700-A, or equivalent, install crankshaft front seal.
6. Install crankshaft timing sprocket, then timing belt as described under "Timing Belt, Replace."

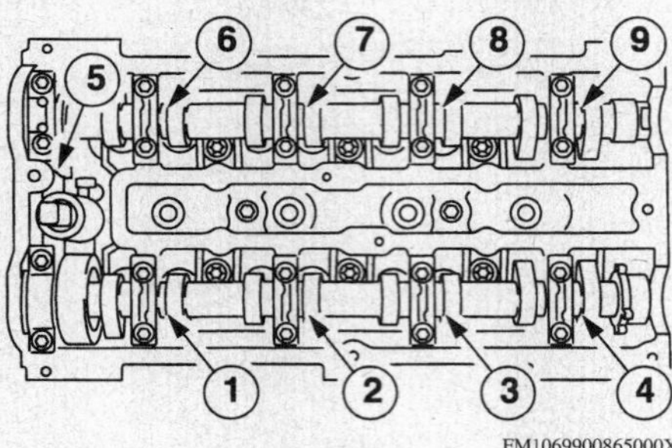

Fig. 19 Camshaft journal cap tightening sequence

CRANKSHAFT REAR OIL SEAL

REPLACE

1. **On models equipped with automatic transaxle,** remove transaxle as described in "Automatic Transaxle/Transmission" section.
2. **On models equipped with manual transaxle,** remove transaxle, then clutch pressure plate and clutch disc as described under "Clutch & Manual Transaxle."
3. **On all models,** observe position of flywheel on crankshaft flange, then remove flywheel bolts, flywheel and reinforcement plate.
4. Using seal remover tool No. T92C-6700-CH, or equivalent, remove rear oil seal.
5. Reverse procedure to install. Install oil seal using crankshaft rear seal replacer tool No. T88P-6701-B1, or equivalent, and three flywheel bolts.

OIL PAN

REPLACE

1. Remove heat shield and coolant hose bracket.
2. Remove engine lifting eye and pull out the engine oil dipstick tube.
3. Remove catalytic converter from exhaust manifold.
4. Raise vehicle.
5. Remove bolt and retaining clip for catalytic converter, then the catalytic converter from exhaust system.
6. Disconnect heated oxygen sensor connector, then remove catalytic converter from bracket.
7. Drain engine oil into a suitable container.
8. Remove oil pan bolts, then oil pan.
9. Reverse procedure to install, noting the following:
   a. **Do not damage mating faces.** Using a spatula or scraper remove any traces of sealer or gasket residue from mating faces.
   b. The mating faces must be free of oil and gasket residue. Clean oil pan to remove any oil residue or sludge.
   c. Apply a 3 mm bead of sealer to mating face of the oil pan, then install oil pan within 10 minutes of applying the sealer.
   d. Using sequence, **Fig. 21** and **torque** oil pan bolts in two steps, first 53 inch lbs, then to 88 inch lbs.

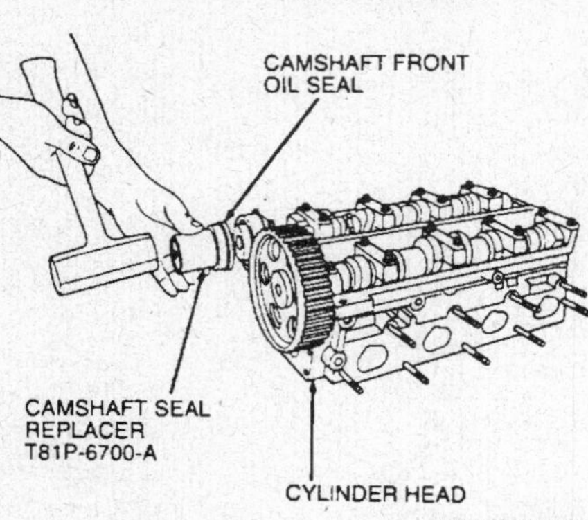

Fig. 20 Camshaft front seal installation. 1998

OIL PUMP

REPLACE

1. Remove timing belt as described under "Timing Belt, Replace," then the crankshaft sprocket.
2. Remove oil pan as described under "Oil Pan, Replace."
3. Remove oil pump screen cover and tube as described under "Oil Pump Service."
4. Remove lower A/C bracket bolts, then lower crankcase to transmission bolts.
5. Remove lower crankcase to upper crankcase bolts and lower crankcase.
6. Remove oil pump bolts, then the pump from cylinder block.
7. Reverse procedure to install, noting following:
   a. Clean oil pump to cylinder block gasket sealing surfaces with wire brush. Use care to prevent damaging sealing surfaces.
   b. Rotate oil pump inner rotor to align with flats on crankshaft, then install pump with new gasket flush to cylinder block at oil pan sealing surface, using straight edge. Clearance between oil pan and oil pump sealing surfaces should not exceed .012–.031 inch.
   c. Fill crankcase to proper level with specified engine oil, then run engine and check for leaks.

BELT TENSION DATA

Drive belts have an automatic drive belt tensioner and do not require adjustment.

Automatic belt tensioner has a drive belt wear indicator mark, **Fig. 22.** If indicator mark is not between tabs on front cover, belt is worn or an incorrect belt is installed.

SERPENTINE DRIVE BELT

ROUTING

Refer to **Fig. 23** for belt routing.

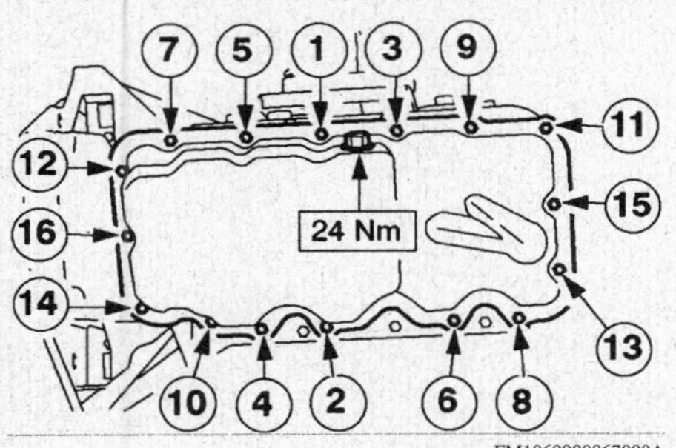

FM1069900867000A

Fig. 21 Oil pan tightening sequence

BELT REPLACEMENT

Minor cracks in V-grooved portion of drive belt are considered normal and acceptable. Drive belt should be replaced if it has chunks missing from ribs, severe glazing or frayed cords.

1. Raise and support vehicle.
2. Using a 13 mm wrench, loosen drive belt tensioner pulley mounting bolt, then rotate drive belt tensioner away from accessory drive belt.
3. Lift belt over pulley flanges and remove.
4. Reverse procedure to install. Ensure drive belt is properly installed on each pulley, with all V-grooves making proper contact with each pulley, **Fig. 24.**

TENSIONER REPLACEMENT

1. Remove drive belt as described under "Belt Replace."
2. Loosen belt tensioner bolts completely, then remove tensioner from front of engine.
3. Install tensioner and bolts to front of engine, then tighten bolts to specifications.
4. Install drive belt as described under "Belt Replace."

COOLING SYSTEM BLEED

These engines do not require a specific bleed procedure. To ensure coolant level is satisfactory, start the engine, turn heater control to its maximum heat and vent positions. After engine reaches normal operating temperature, hot air should be blowing from the A/C vents. If cool air is blowing from the vents, coolant level is low, turn engine off and add coolant as necessary.

THERMOSTAT

REPLACE

1. Remove engine air intake resonators from air cleaner assembly.
2. Drain engine cooling system so engine coolant level is below thermostat, then disconnect upper radiator hose and overflow hose from water hose connection.
3. Remove water outlet connection bolts, then the connection from thermostat housing, **Fig. 25.**

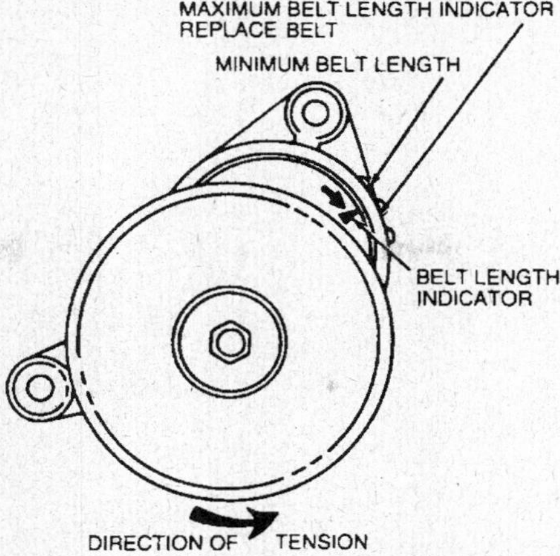

FM1069500412000X

Fig. 22 Drive belt wear indicator mark

4. Remove thermostat and seal from housing.
5. Reverse procedure to install.

WATER PUMP

REPLACE

1. Drain engine coolant into a suitable container.
2. Remove righthand front wheel and lower splash shield.
3. Lower vehicle.
4. Disconnect hoses and remove coolant expansion tank.
5. Loosen water pump pulley bolts, then remove accessory drive belt.
6. Remove water pump pulley bolts and pulley.
7. Remove water pump bolts, then the water pump.
8. Reverse procedure to install.

RADIATOR

REPLACE

CONTOUR & MYSTIQUE

1. Drain engine coolant into a suitable container.
2. Disconnect fan resistor, cooling fan, A/C and A/C low pressure electrical connectors.
3. Disconnect ground cable from frame.
4. **On models equipped with automatic transaxle,** disconnect transaxle upper and lower cooling lines.
5. **On all models,** disconnect radiator upper and lower hoses.
6. Secure A/C condenser and remove bolts
7. Remove radiator four bolts and radiator.
8. Reverse procedure to install.

COUGAR

1. Drain engine coolant into a suitable container.
2. Remove motor, fan and shroud.
3. Remove upper shield and secure condenser.
4. Disconnect radiator upper cooling hose.

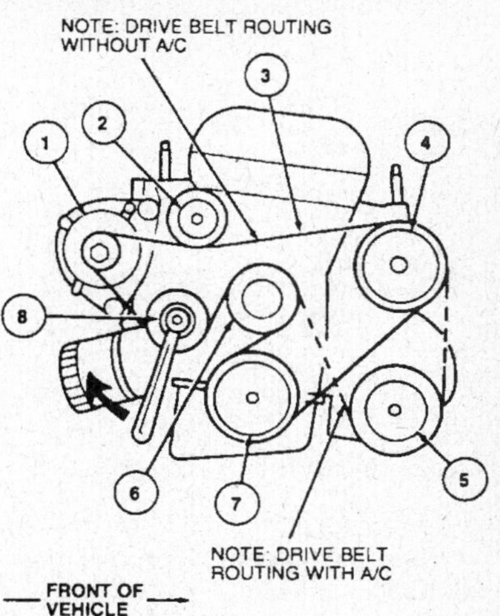

Item	Description
1	Generator
2	Drivebelt Idler Pulley
3	Accessory Drive Belt
4	Power Steering Pump Pulley
5	A/C Compressor
6	Water Pump Pulley
7	Crankshaft Pulley
8	Drive Belt Tensioner

FM1069500410000X

Fig. 23 Drive belt routing

5. **On models equipped with automatic transaxle,** disconnect radiator upper cooling hose.
6. **On all models,** disconnect radiator lower cooling hose and detach air conditioning condenser.
7. Remove radiator.
8. Reverse procedure to install.

FUEL PUMP

REPLACE

CONTOUR & MYSTIQUE

1. Relieve fuel system pressure as described under "Precautions."
2. Remove rear seat cushion.
3. Remove plastic grommet from floor pan, then disconnect fuel pump module electrical connector.
4. Disconnect fuel and vapor return tubes from fuel pump module.
5. Disconnect fuel lines by compressing tabs on both sides of each nylon push connect fitting and ease fuel line out of module.
6. Turn pump locking retainer ring counterclockwise using fuel tank sender wrench tool No. D84P-9275-A, or equivalent.
7. Remove fuel pump module, then immediately cover opening in fuel tank in order to prevent fuel system contamination.
8. Remove fuel pump module O-ring seal and discard.
9. Reverse procedure to install, noting the following:
   a. Apply light coat of premium long-life grease part No. XG-1-C,-K, or

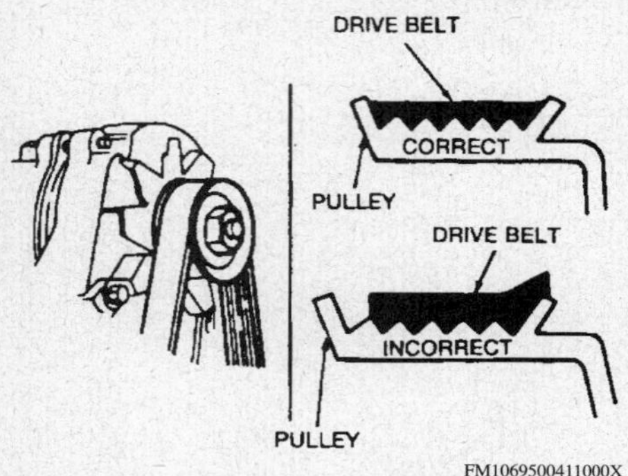

Fig. 24 Drive belt installation

equivalent, on new O-ring seal, then install seal to groove on fuel tank.

b. Ensure locating keys are in keyways and O-ring seal remains in place.
c. Ensure all locking tabs are under fuel tank lock ring tabs.
d. Install multi-port fuel pressure gauge tool No. T80L-9974-B, or equivalent, to fuel pressure relief valve cap on fuel supply injection manifold.
e. Turn ignition switch to Run position for three seconds, five to 10 times until pressure gauge reads at least 30 psi, then check for leaks at fittings.

COUGAR

1. Remove fuel tank.
2. Fuel supply line connectors are white or are identified by a white band. Fuel return line connectors are red or are identified by a red band. Disconnect fuel feed pipe.

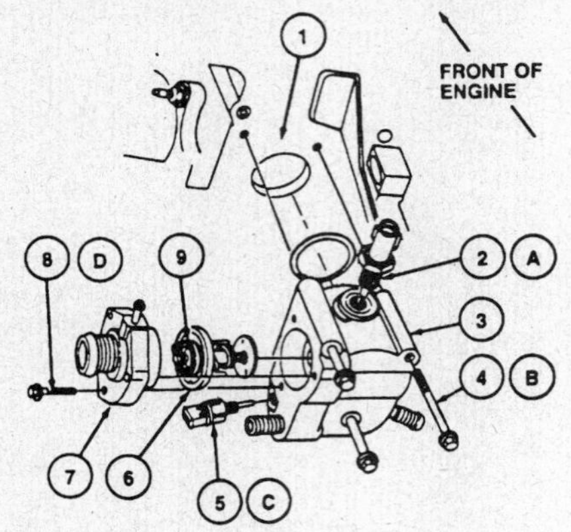

Item	Description
1	Cylinder Block
2	Engine Coolant Temperature Sensor
3	Water Thermostat Housing
4	Bolt (3 Req'd)
5	Water Temperature Indicator Sender Unit
6	O-Ring
7	Water Hose Connection
8	Bolt (3 Req'd)
9	Water Thermostat
A	Tighten to 10-14 N-m (89-124 Lb-In)
B	Tighten to 18-22 N-m (13-16 Lb-Ft)
C	Tighten to 7-10 N-m (62-89 Lb-In)
D	Tighten to 8-11 N-m (71-97 Lb-In)

FM1089500091000X

Fig. 25 Thermostat replacement

3. Remove fuel pump locking ring using fuel sender ring wrench tool No. D84P-9275-A, or equivalent.
4. Remove fuel pump.
5. Reverse procedure to install. Install new O-ring.

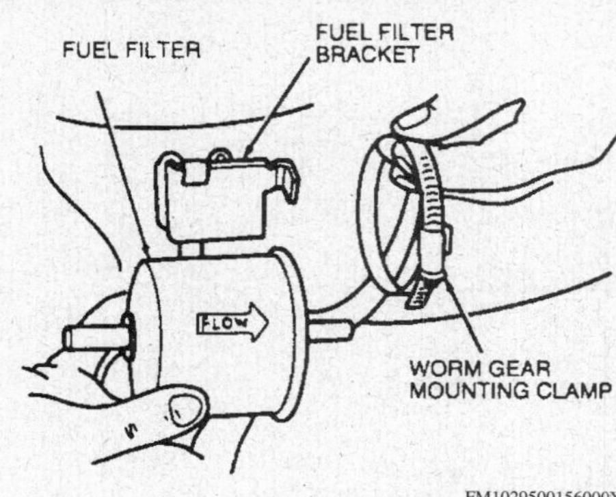

Fig. 26 Inline fuel filter replacement

FUEL FILTER

REPLACE

IN-TANK

1. Remove fuel pump as described under "Fuel Pump, Replace."
2. Remove filter mounted on fuel pump inlet.
3. Reverse procedure to install.

INLINE

1. Relieve fuel system pressure as described under "Precautions."
2. Remove push connect fittings at both ends of fuel filter, then install retainer clips in each connect fitting.
3. Remove fuel filter from bracket by loosening worm gear mounting clamp enough to allow filter to pass through, **Fig. 26.**
4. Reverse procedure to install, noting the following:
   a. Locate fuel filter against tab at lower end of bracket. Ensure proper direction of fuel flow, **Fig. 26.**
   b. Tighten worm gear mounting clamp to specifications.

TIGHTENING SPECIFICATIONS

Year	Component	Torque/Ft. Lbs.
1998–2002	Accelerator Cable Bracket	72–108①
	Air Cleaner Bracket	15–22
	Battery Ground Cable To Engine At Transaxle Stud Bolt Nut	15–22
	Camshaft Journal Cap	④
	Camshaft Sprocket Bolt	47–53
	Catalytic Converter Bracket Bolts	72–108①
	Catalytic Converter Clamp Bolt	15–22
	Catalytic Converter To Exhaust Manifold Nuts	26–33
	Center & Lower Timing Belt Cover Bolts	60-72①
	Crankshaft Pulley Bolt	81–89
	Cylinder Head Bolts	②
	Drive Belt Idler Pulley Bolt	30
	Drive Belt Tensioner Bolts	15–22
	EGR Valve To Exhaust Manifold Tube Nut	44

Continued

TIGHTENING SPECIFICATIONS—Continued

Year	Component	Torque/Ft. Lbs.
1998–2002	Engine Air Cleaner Tube Clamps	24–48①
	Engine & Transaxle Support Insulator Nuts	62
	Engine & Transaxle Support Insulator To Front Fender Apron Bolts	52–70
	Engine Lifting Eye	⑥
	Engine Rear Plate Bolts	79–86③
	Exhaust Manifold Heat Shield Nuts	72–108①
	Exhaust Manifold Nuts	13–16
	Exhaust Manifold Shield Retainers	72–108①
	Flywheel Bolts	81
	Flywheel Nuts	54–64③
	Front Engine Support Bracket To Front Sub-Frame Bolts	20
	Front Engine Support Bracket To Transaxle Bolts	⑤
	Front Engine Support Insulator Bolt	20
	Front Engine Support Insulator Through Bolt	20
	Front Stabilizer Bar Link To Stabilizer Bar Nuts	35
	Heated Oxygen Sensor	44
	Heater Water Tube Bolt	72–108①
	Intake Manifold Bolts	13
	Lefthand Engine Support Insulator Through Bolt	62
	Lower Engine Rear Plate Bolts	72–108①
	Main Bearing Cap Bolts	63
	Oil Level Indicator Tube Bolt	72–108①
	Oil Pan Drain Plug	20
	Oil Pan	⑨
	Oil Pump Screen Cover & Tube Bolts	72–96①
	Power Steering Pump Mounting Bracket Support Bracket Bolts	29–41
	Radiator Coolant Recovery Reservoir Bolts	72–108①
	Radiator Supports To Front Sub-Frame Bolts	72–96①
	Righthand Front Engine Support Insulator Through Bolt	62
	Self-Locking Oil Pump Screen Cover & Tube Support Nut	13–15
	Shift Cable Bracket Bolts	15–19
	Shift Rod Bolt	17
	Stabilizer Nut	41
	Steering Shaft To Joint Bolt	18
	Thermostat Housing	15
	Throttle Body Bolts & Nuts	72–108①
	Tie Rod End Stud Nuts	⑧
	Timing Belt Pulley	26–30
	Timing Belt Tensioner Pulley	72–96①
	Transaxle Oil Cooler Lines	17
	Transaxle To Engine Bolts	25–34
	Upper Front Engine Support Bolts	52–70
	Upper Front Engine Support Bracket Self-Locking Nuts	52-70

Continued

TIGHTENING SPECIFICATIONS—Continued

Year	Component	Torque/Ft. Lbs.
1998–2002	Upper Timing Belt Cover Bolts	27–44①
	Valve Cover Bolts	⑦
	VCT Oil Feed Flange To Cylinder Head	84①
	Water Hose Connection Bolts	71–97
	Water Pump Pulley Bolts	89–124
	Wheel Knuckle To Lower Arm Bolts	37–43
	Wheel Lug Nuts	94
	Worm Gear Mounting Clamp	15–25①

①— Inch lbs.
②— Refer to "Cylinder Head, Replace."
③— Tighten in alternating sequence.
④— Refer to "Camshaft, Replace" for procedure.
⑤— Lefthand side, 30–40 ft. lbs.; righthand side, 40–55 ft. lbs.
⑥— Lefthand side, 10–13 ft. lbs.; righthand side, 30–40 ft. lbs.
⑦— Refer to "Valve Cover, Replace" for procedure.
⑧— Refer to "Engine, Replace" for procedure.
⑨— Refer to "Oil Pan, Relace" for procedure.

2.5L Engine

NOTE: On Air Bag Equipped Models, Refer To "Air Bag System Precautions" Located In The Front Of This Manual For System Disarming & Arming Procedures.

NOTE: Refer To "Computer Relearn Procedures" Located In The Front Of This Manual When Battery Power To The Computer Has Been Interrupted.

INDEX

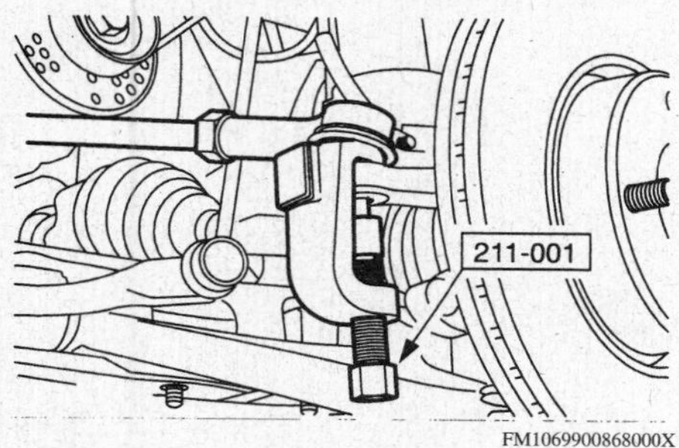

Fig. 1 Tie rod end removal. Cougar

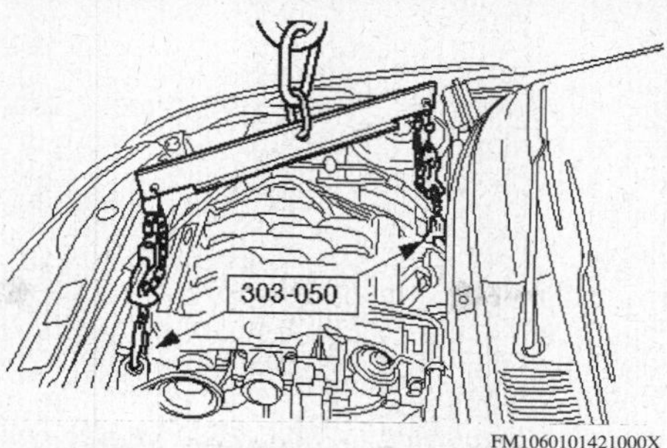

Fig. 2 Engine lifting tool. Cougar w/manual transaxle

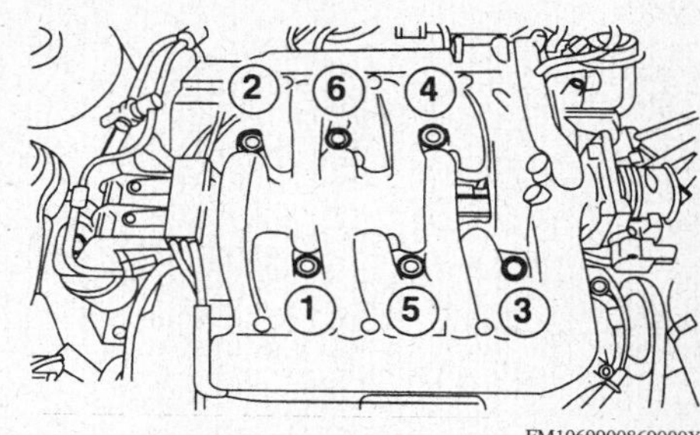

Fig. 3 Upper intake removal sequence

PRECAUTIONS

BATTERY GROUND CABLE

Prior to service, disconnect battery ground cable and isolate as required.

AIR BAG SYSTEMS

Refer to "Air Bag System Precautions" in front of this manual for system disarming and arming procedures.

COOLING SYSTEM

This engine has an aluminum cylinder head and requires a special corrosion inhibiting coolant to avoid cooling system damage. Use only specified coolant in this engine.

FUEL SYSTEM PRESSURE RELIEF

Fuel supply lines will remain pressurized for long periods of time after engine shutdown. Pressure must be relieved before servicing fuel system.

1. Remove engine air cleaner as follows:
   a. Remove engine air intake resonators.
   b. Disconnect engine control sensor wiring connectors from Mass Air Flow (MAF) sensor and Intake Air Temperature (IAT) sensor.
   c. Remove engine air cleaner to body O-ring retainer.
   d. Remove engine air cleaner body and intake tube from bracket and intake tube and duct.
2. Connect Multi-Port Fuel Injection (MFI) fuel pressure gauge tool No. T80L-9974-B, or equivalent, to fuel pressure relief valve cap on fuel injection supply manifold.
3. Open manual valve on gauge tool to relieve fuel system pressure.

COMPRESSION PRESSURE

Compression pressure should be checked at normal operating temperature with spark plugs removed and throttle plate wide open. Cylinder compression pressure is considered within specification if lowest reading cylinder is within 75 percent of highest reading.

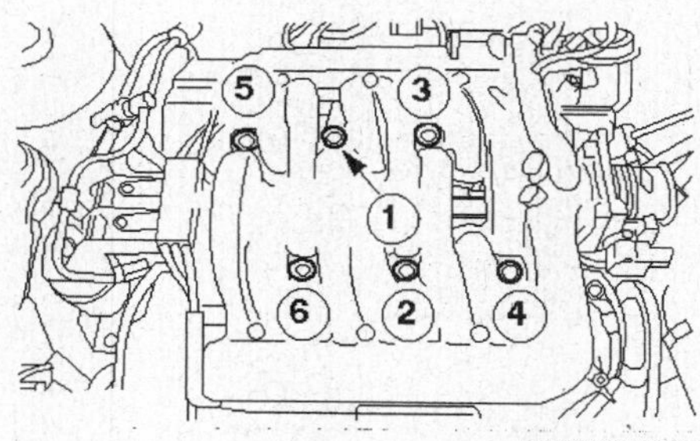

Fig. 4 Upper intake manifold bolt tightening sequence

ENGINE MOUNT

REPLACE

Refer to "Engine Mount, Replace" in the "2.0L Engine" section for procedure.

ENGINE

REPLACE

CONTOUR & MYSTIQUE

1. Remove air intake box assembly, then the battery cables from retaining clips.
2. Use wire or tie strap to secure radiator.
3. Recover A/C system as outlined in "Air Conditioning" section.
4. Remove coolant and power steering reservoir caps.
5. Raise and support vehicle, then remove both front wheels.
6. Remove lower radiator splash shield and drain engine coolant into a suitable container.
7. **On models equipped with automatic transaxle,** remove drain plug and drain transaxle fluid, then disconnect lower transaxle cooler line.
8. **On all models,** disconnect power steering cooler lines and drain fluid.
9. Disconnect lower radiator hose and A/C compressor electrical connector.
10. Remove lower radiator support brackets.
11. **On models equipped with manual transaxle,** disconnect exhaust after converter pipe and remove the hanger.
12. **On models equipped with automatic transaxle,** disconnect exhaust after flex pipe and remove hanger.
13. **On all models,** remove exhaust crossover pipe.
14. Disconnect A/C condenser tube/hose and remove front heat shield.
15. Disconnect heater core hoses and drain remaining coolant.
16. Remove bolts and right side, front and rear inner splash shield.
17. Remove bolt and position bumper bracket aside.
18. **On models equipped with manual transaxle,** remove flywheel access cover.
19. **On models equipped with automatic transaxle,** remove four torque converter nuts.
20. **On all models,** remove A/C accumulator drier bolts, then the intermediate shaft pinch bolt.
21. Disconnect left and right stabilizer bar link rod and position stabilizer bar link rod out of the way.
22. Remove left and right wheel speed sensors and brake calipers.
23. Lower vehicle and remove water pump pulley cover.
24. Relieve fuel pressure as outlined in "Precautions."
25. Remove safety clips and disconnect fuel lines using fuel line disconnect tool Nos. D87L-9280-A (3/8 inch) or D87L-9280-B (1/2 inch), or equivalent.
26. **On SVT models,** disconnect accelerator and speed control cables.
27. **On all models,** disconnect bulkhead connector.
28. Drain power steering fluid reservoir, then pull it out (push fit) and lay to one side.
29. Disconnect PCM electrical connector module.
30. Disconnect coolant expansion tank hoses.
31. Disconnect power steering line and position it out of the way.
32. **On models equipped with automatic transaxle,** remove shifter cable and position out of the way.
33. **On all models,** disconnect upper intake vacuum supply lines.
34. Disconnect upper radiator hose and heater control vacuum hoses.
35. Remove A/C accumulator tub/hose from bracket, then safety clip away from the A/C accumulator tube/hose.
36. **On models equipped with manual transaxle,** disconnect clutch slave cylinder hydraulic pipe.
37. **On all models,** raise and support vehicle.
38. Position powertrain fixture tool No.

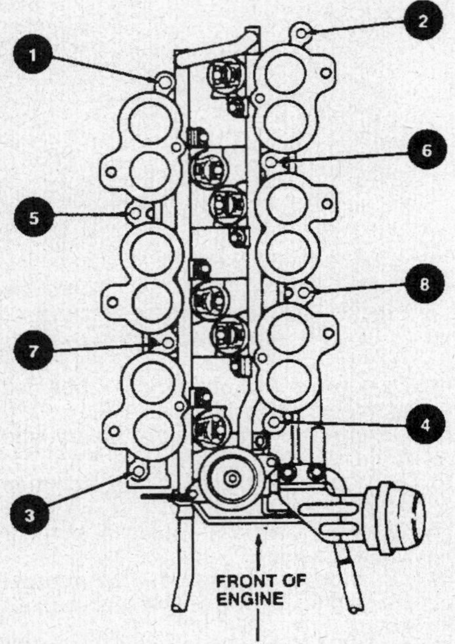

Fig. 5 Lower intake manifold bolt removal sequence

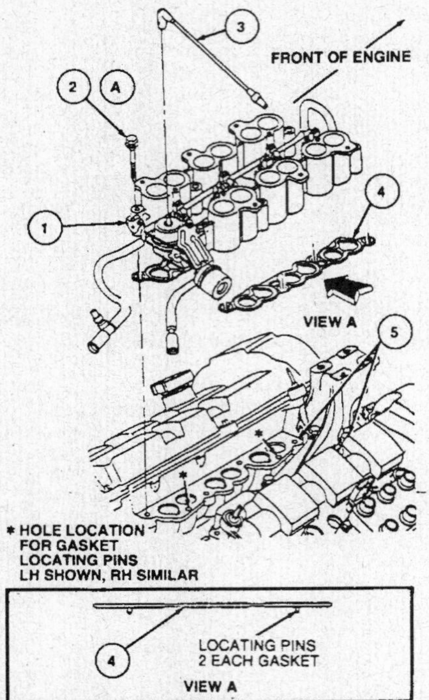

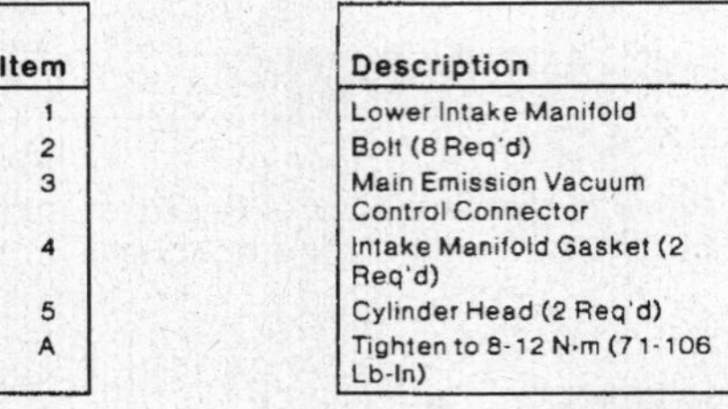

Item	Description
1	Lower Intake Manifold
2	Bolt (8 Req'd)
3	Main Emission Vacuum Control Connector
4	Intake Manifold Gasket (2 Req'd)
5	Cylinder Head (2 Req'd)
A	Tighten to 8-12 N·m (71-106 Lb-In)

FM1059500073000X

Fig. 6 Lower intake manifold replacement

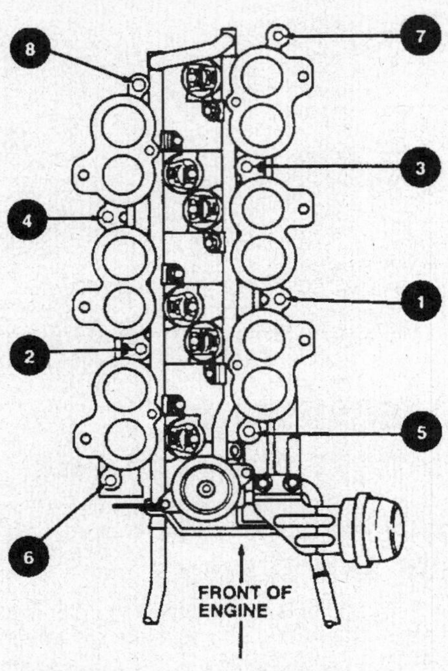

Fig. 7 Intake manifold bolt tightening sequence

134-00250, or equivalent under supporting plate and raise the jack.

39. Remove left and right subframe bolts.
40. Remove spark plug wiring rail from front engine mounting bracket.
41. Remove upper front engine support bracket nuts, then the rear transaxle mount nuts.
42. **On models equipped with manual transaxle,** disconnect shifter cables and position shifter bracket aside.
43. **On all models,** remove left and right strut pinch bolts,
44. Lower engine/transaxle assembly from vehicle, or raise vehicle off of the assembly.
45. Remove left and right halfshaft.
46. Remove front rear roll restrictor through bolts.
47. Lift engine/transaxle assembly off of subframe with a suitable floor crane.
48. Do not let torque converter drop out of transaxle. Separate transaxle from engine.
49. Reverse procedure to install.

COUGAR

AUTOMATIC TRANSAXLE

1. Remove front wheels, battery and hood.
2. Remove coolant hose from clip, then the water pump pulley cover bolts and cover.
3. Remove air cleaner, then drain engine coolant into a suitable container.
4. Disconnect accelerator and speed control cables from bracket.
5. Remove transaxle selector cable bolts and cable.
6. Remove bolt from bulkhead connector and disconnect electrical connector.
7. Loosen central junction box and position it to one side.
8. Disconnect ground cable and fan motor connector.
9. Remove four battery bracket bolts, battery bracket and two ground cables.
10. Relieve fuel pressure as outlined in "Precautions."
11. Disconnect fuel lines using fuel line disconnect tool Nos. D87L-9280-A (3/8 inch) or D87L-9280-B (1/2 inch), or equivalent.
12. Disconnect all heater hoses.
13. Disconnect suction accumulator electrical connector and evaporative emission hose.
14. Loosen both suspension strut nuts five turns.
15. Disconnect upper intake vacuum supply line and heater control vacuum hoses.
16. Drain power steering fluid reservoir into a suitable container, then pull reservoir out (push fit) and position it to one side.
17. Disconnect power steering lines and position to one side.
18. Disconnect PCM and ground cable.
19. Disconnect coolant expansion tank hoses, then remove the tank.
20. Remove upper transaxle cooling tube. Close off openings with plugs for transaxle opening
21. Remove fan, then raise and support vehicle.
22. Drain engine oil into a suitable container.
23. Disconnect heated oxygen sensor electrical connector.
24. Remove dual converter Y-pipe, then righthand fender splash shields.
25. Remove righthand control arm, then intermediate shaft bearing with the righthand front drive halfshaft from the transaxle and tie it up using cable ties.
26. Disconnect stabilizer link rod, then using the stabilizer link rod tool No. 211-001, or equivalent, **Fig. 1,** remove tie rod end.
27. Disconnect ABS wiring harness bracket from suspension strut. **Do not damage boot and ABS sensor ring.**
28. Remove lefthand front drive halfshaft from transaxle and hang it up.
29. Disconnect and remove HO2S electrical connector.
30. Remove transaxle cooling lines.
31. Remove coolant hose from the radiator.
32. Disconnect A/C compressor electrical connector.
33. Remove condenser core and tie it up.
34. Remove radiator and disconnect HO2S sensor.
35. Remove coolant pipe.
36. Remove accessory drive belt, then the compressor heat shield.
37. Remove compressor bracket bolts and secure compressor to one side with

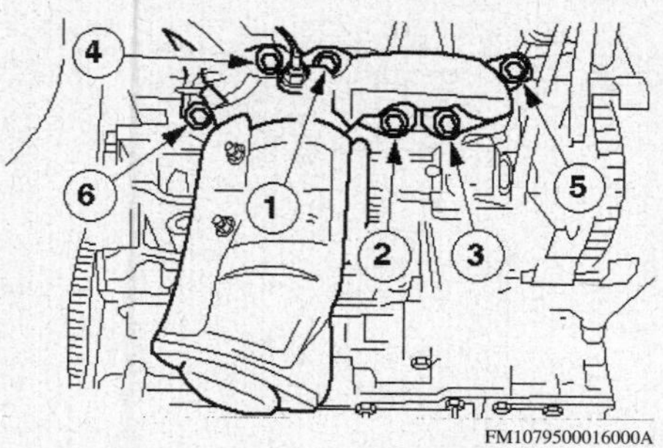

Fig. 8 Exhaust manifold tightening sequence

mechanics wire.

38. Remove lefthand support insulator nuts, center bolt and insulator.
39. Remove center bolt from righthand support insulator.
40. Lower vehicle.
41. Using lifting bracket tool No. T70P-6000, or equivalent, and a suitable floor crane raise engine slightly to remove pressure from support insulator.
42. Remove upper front support insulator from side member, then rear support insulator from side member.
43. Remove engine and transaxle as an assembly.
44. Separate transaxle from engine.
45. Reverse procedure to install.

MANUAL TRANSAXLE

1. Remove battery, then the hood.
2. Remove water pump pulley cover.
3. Remove air cleaner, then drain brake fluid into suitable container.
4. **On models equipped with speed control,** disconnect accelerator and speed control cables.
5. **On models less speed control,** disconnect accelerator.
6. **On all models,** disconnect bulkhead connector, then loosen central junction box and place aside.
7. Remove fan motor electrical connectors from battery tray.
8. Remove three battery ground straps, then battery tray.
9. Disconnect fuel lines, then coolant hoses. Place aside.
10. Remove ground strap from transaxle bolt.
11. Disconnect suction accumulator and two fan motor electrical connectors.
12. Disconnect engine coolant temperature sensor, then reverse lamp connector.
13. Disconnect evaporative emission hose, then upper intake vacuum supply lines and heater control vacuum hoses.
14. Loosen suspension strut lock nuts five turns on both sides.
15. Drain power steering reservoir, then pull it out and place it aside.
16. Disconnect power steering lines.
17. Remove powertrain control module (PCM) cover plate.
18. Disconnect PCM electrical connector, then the coolant expansion tank hoses.
19. Remove coolant level sensor electrical connector, then the expansion tank.
20. Remove oil level indicator, then the oxygen sensor electrical connector bracket.
21. Loosen fan from radiator, then raise and support vehicle.
22. Remove radiator splash shield, then drain cooling system into suitable container.
23. Drain transmission fluid into suitable container.
24. Remove coolant hose from radiator, then drain engine oil.
25. Disconnect A/C compressor electrical connector, then remove condenser core from radiator.
26. Remove radiator and fans.
27. Disconnect oxygen sensor connector, then remove coolant pipe.
28. Remove Y-pipe and three-way catalytic converter.
29. Remove righthand front fender splash shield, then accessory drive belt.
30. Remove compressor heat shield, then compressor bracket bolts. Place compressor aside.
31. Disconnect shifter cables and brackets.
32. Remove both control arms, then the righthand front driveshaft from intermediate shaft bearing using a suitable copper drift. Secure aside.
33. Using a suitable tire lever remove the lefthand front drive halfshaft from transaxle and secure it to one side.
34. Remove lefthand support insulator through bolt, then the bracket.
35. Remove righthand support insulator through bolt, support insulator, then the bracket.
36. Lower vehicle. Install engine lifting bracket tool No. 303-050 or equivalent, **Fig. 2.**
37. Remove starter motor bracket and ground cable from transaxle flange.
38. Remove the ACL bracket, then the rear upper support insulator.
39. Raise engine slightly, then remove front upper support through bolt and insulator.
40. Remove engine/transaxle assembly from vehicle.
41. Reverse procedure to install. Tighten all nuts and bolts to specifications.

INTAKE MANIFOLD

REPLACE

UPPER

1. Remove air cleaner and water pump pulley shield.
2. Disconnect exhaust gas recirculation valve, accelerator and speed control cables, then remove accelerator cable bracket.
3. Disconnect black retainer, two vacuum supply lines from the upper intake and vacuum regulator solenoid vacuum hose.
4. Disconnect positive crankcase ventilation hose, throttle position sensor and Idle air control valve electrical connector.

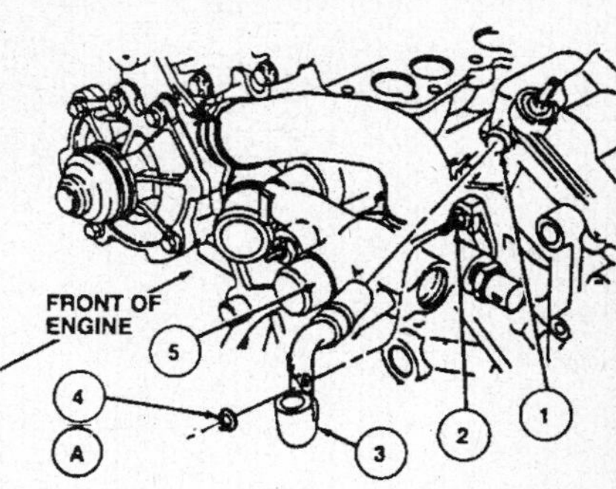

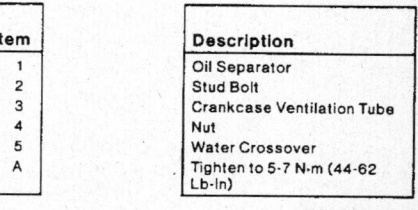

Item	Description
1	Oil Separator
2	Stud Bolt
3	Crankcase Ventilation Tube
4	Nut
5	Water Crossover
A	Tighten to 5-7 N·m (44-62 Lb-In)

FM1069500416000X

Fig. 9 Cylinder head replacement

5. Disconnect EGR vacuum regulator solenoid electrical connector.
6. Remove intake bolts in sequence, **Fig. 3.**
7. Reverse procedure, noting the following:
   a. New gaskets must be used, position gasket on the lower intake manifold.
   b. **Torque** bolts in sequence to 84 inch lbs., **Fig. 4.**

LOWER

1. Relieve fuel system pressure as described under "Precautions."
2. Remove upper intake manifold as outlined previously.
3. Disconnect fuel supply and return lines from fuel injection supply manifold.
4. Disconnect engine control sensor wiring from fuel injectors and valve cover studs. Position wiring aside.
5. Disconnect vacuum supply line from fuel pressure regulator and Intake Manifold Runner Control (IMRC) vacuum solenoid. Position line aside.
6. Remove fuel injection supply manifold and fuel injectors from lower intake manifold.
7. Remove IMRC vacuum solenoid from lower intake manifold.
8. Remove lower intake manifold to cylinder head bolts in sequence, **Fig. 5.**
9. Remove lower intake manifold from cylinder heads, then the intake manifold gaskets from cylinder heads, **Fig. 6.** Discard gaskets.
10. Reverse procedure to install, noting following:
    a. Verify IMRC vacuum solenoid and plate operation using hand vacuum pump. Install new intake manifold gaskets.
    b. **Torque** lower intake manifold bolts in sequence, **Fig. 7,** to 72–108 inch lbs.

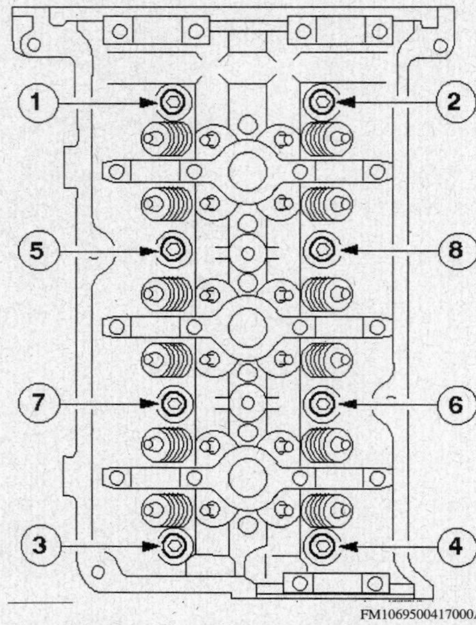

Fig. 10 Cylinder head bolt removal sequence

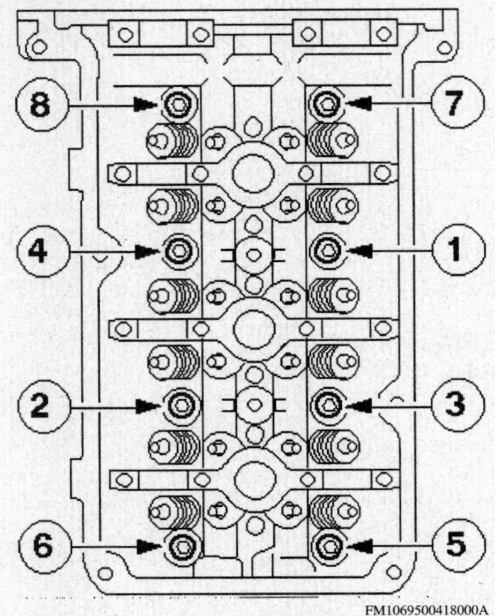

Fig. 11 Cylinder head bolt tightening sequence

EXHAUST MANIFOLD

REPLACE

RIGHTHAND

1. Disconnect engine control sensor extension wire from righthand heated oxygen sensor.
2. Raise and support vehicle, then remove alternator and bracket as described under "Electrical."
3. Remove converter outlet flange nuts, then the muffler and converter outlet gasket from converter.
4. Remove converter nuts and exhaust pipe flange hold down springs.
5. Remove converter and inlet gasket from Y pipe, then discard gasket.
6. Remove front and rear Y pipe flange fasteners from exhaust manifolds.
7. Remove stud bolt and nut retainer from oil pan, then the Y pipe.
8. Remove righthand halfshaft support bearing bracket from support bearing and cylinder block as described in "Front Wheel Drive Axles" section.
9. Remove heated oxygen sensor from righthand exhaust manifold using oxygen sensor wrench tool No. T94P-9472-A, or equivalent. If excessive force is necessary to remove sensor, lubricate sensor with penetrating oil before removal.
10. Loosen EGR valve to exhaust manifold tube from exhaust manifold.
11. Remove exhaust manifold nuts from cylinder head studs, then the manifold and manifold gasket from engine.
12. Reverse procedure to install, noting following:
    a. **Torque** exhaust manifold nuts in sequence, **Fig. 8,** to 15 ft. lbs.
    b. Tighten EGR valve to exhaust manifold tube nuts and heated oxygen sensor to specifications.

LEFTHAND

1. Disconnect lefthand heated oxygen sensor from engine control sensor wiring.
2. Raise and support vehicle.
3. Remove front and rear flange pipe fasteners from exhaust manifolds, then the stud bolt and nut retainer from oil pan.
4. Remove two remaining nuts and bolts from Y-pipe outlet connection.
5. Discard exhaust converter inlet gasket, then remove Y-pipe.
6. Remove lower radiator hose tube bracket nuts from stud bolts, then the exhaust manifold nuts from lefthand cylinder head studs.
7. Position lower radiator hose tube aside, then remove lefthand exhaust manifold and gasket from engine.
8. Remove heated oxygen sensor from lefthand exhaust manifold using oxygen sensor wrench tool No. T94P-9472-A, or equivalent. If excessive force is necessary to remove sensor, lubricate sensor with penetrating oil before removal.
9. Reverse procedure to install. **Torque** lefthand exhaust manifold nuts in sequence, **Fig. 8,** to 15 ft. lbs.

CYLINDER HEAD

REPLACE

1. Drain engine coolant from radiator and cylinder block drain plugs.
2. Remove upper and lower intake manifolds as described under "Intake Manifold, Replace."
3. Remove alternator and alternator bracket as outlined in "Electrical" section.
4. Remove heated oxygen sensor from righthand exhaust manifold using oxygen sensor wrench tool No. T94P-9472-A, or equivalent. If excessive force is necessary to remove sensor, lubricate sensor with penetrating oil before removal.
5. **On lefthand cylinder head,** remove lefthand exhaust manifold as outlined under "Exhaust Manifold, Replace," then the water pump as described under "Water Pump, Replace."
6. **On both cylinder heads,** remove front cover as described under "Front Cover, Replace."
7. Remove camshafts as described under "Camshaft, Replace," then the

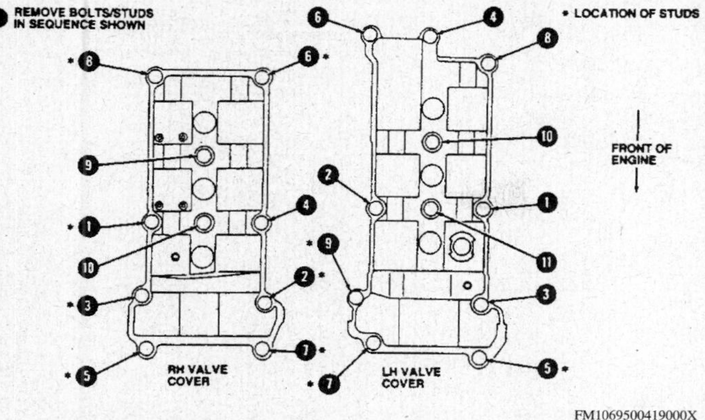

Fig. 12 Valve cover bolt removal sequence

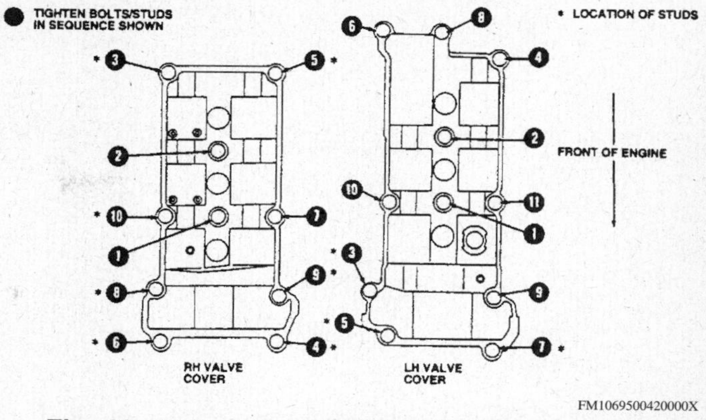

FM1069500420000X

Fig. 13 Valve cover bolt tightening sequence

valve tappets as described under "Hydraulic Valve Tappets, Replace."

8. Install upper front engine support insulator and front engine support bracket to front of engine and righthand front fender apron.
9. Remove three bar engine support tool No. D88L-6000-A, or equivalent.
10. **On righthand cylinder head,** proceed as follows:
    a. Disconnect hoses from EGR pressure sensor to exhaust manifold tube, then the pressure sensor electrical connector.
    b. Disconnect interior vacuum source hose from main emission vacuum harness, then the fuel vapor hose from PCV valve.
    c. Disconnect EGR transducer electrical connector.
    d. Remove EGR exhaust manifold tube from vehicle, then the fuel charging wiring bracket from EGR transducer bracket.
11. **On both cylinder heads,** loosen engine air cleaner tube clamps on outlet tube, then disconnect crankcase ventilation hoses and IAC valve tube from air cleaner outlet tube fitting.
12. Remove air cleaner outlet tube from MAF sensor and throttle body.
13. Disconnect engine control sensor wiring connector form MAF and IAT sensor.
14. Remove engine air cleaner to body O-ring retainer, then the air cleaner body and intake tube from bracket.
15. Remove engine air cleaner intake tube and duct.
16. Remove crankcase ventilation tube from water crossover and oil separator, **Fig. 9.**
17. Remove water crossover bolt and stud bolt from righthand cylinder head, then the crossover, position aside.
18. **On lefthand cylinder head,** remove oil level dipstick.
19. **On both cylinder heads,** remove cylinder head bolts in sequence, **Fig. 10.**
20. Remove cylinder heads. Remove righthand cylinder head with exhaust manifold and EGR transducer bracket attached.
21. Remove exhaust manifold and EGR transducer bracket from righthand cylinder head.
22. Reverse procedure to install, noting following:
    a. Clean cylinder heads, lower intake manifold valve cover and cylinder gasket surfaces. If cylinder heads were removed to replace cylinder gasket, check flatness of cylinder heads and cylinder block gasket surfaces.
    b. Install new head gaskets on cylinder block.
    c. **Cylinder head bolts are torque-to-yield designed and must be replaced with new bolts. If reused, damage to engine may occur.**
    d. Using sequence shown in **Fig. 11,** tighten cylinder head bolts in six steps: first step, **torque** bolts 29 ft. lbs.; second step, tighten bolts an additional 90°; third step, loosen bolts one full turn; fourth step, **torque** bolts to 29 ft. lbs.; fifth step, tighten bolts an additional 90°; sixth step, tighten bolts an additional 90.°
    e. Inspect water crossover O-rings for wear or damage.
    f. Lubricate water crossover O-rings with specified engine coolant.

VALVE COVER

REPLACE

RIGHTHAND

1. Remove upper intake manifold as described under "Intake Manifold, Replace."
2. Remove ignition wires from ignition coils and spark plugs.
3. Disconnect engine control sensor wiring from ignition coil and radio ignition interference capacitor.
4. Remove EGR vacuum regulator control from upper intake manifold.
5. Disconnect ignition wires by squeezing locking tabs and twisting while pulling upward.
6. Remove ignition coil attaching bolts, then the ignition coil.
7. Remove radio ignition interference capacitor, then disconnect coil ground wire.
8. Remove crankcase ventilation tube from righthand valve cover.
9. Remove fuel charging wiring retainer and inline connector wiring bracket nuts and bracket from righthand valve cover stud bolts. Position bracket and fuel charging wiring aside.
10. Remove engine control sensor wiring nuts, then the wiring from righthand valve cover stud bolts. Position engine control sensor wiring aside.
11. Loosen valve cover bolts and stud bolts in sequence, **Fig. 12.**
12. Carefully remove valve cover from cylinder head, then the gaskets from cover.
13. Reverse procedure to install, noting following:
    a. Clean valve cover sealing surfaces using shop towel and suitable metal cleaner.
    b. Apply .31 inch diameter bead of black silicone rubber sealant, part No. F4AZ-19562-B, or equivalent, at two places on valve cover sealing surfaces where front cover and cylinder heads contact.
    c. Install new valve cover gaskets onto valve cover.
    d. Within six minutes of applying sealer, **torque** valve cover bolts and studs to 89 inch lbs. using sequence shown in **Fig. 13.**

LEFTHAND

1. Remove upper intake manifold as described under "Intake Manifold, Replace."
2. Remove crankcase ventilation tube from lefthand valve cover, then fuel charging wiring brackets from lefthand valve cover stud bolts. Position fuel charging wiring aside.
3. Remove ignition wires from spark plugs and valve cover, then loosen valve cover bolts and stud bolts in sequence, **Fig. 12.**
4. Carefully remove valve cover from lefthand cylinder head, then gaskets from cover.
5. Reverse procedure to install, noting following:
    a. Clean valve cover sealing surfaces using shop towel and suitable metal cleaner.
    b. Apply .31 inch diameter bead of black silicone rubber sealant, part No. F4AZ-19562-B, or equivalent,

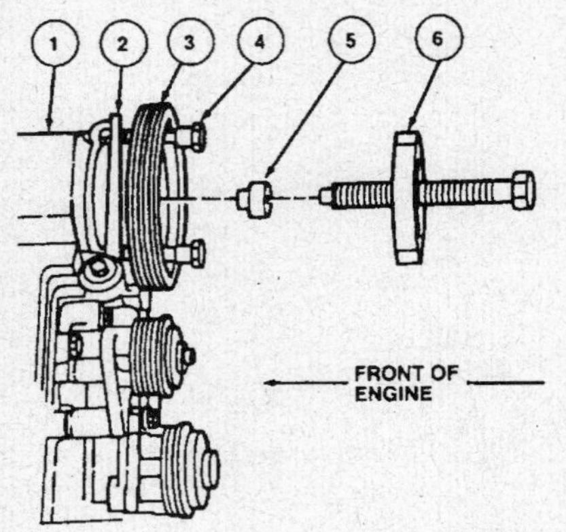

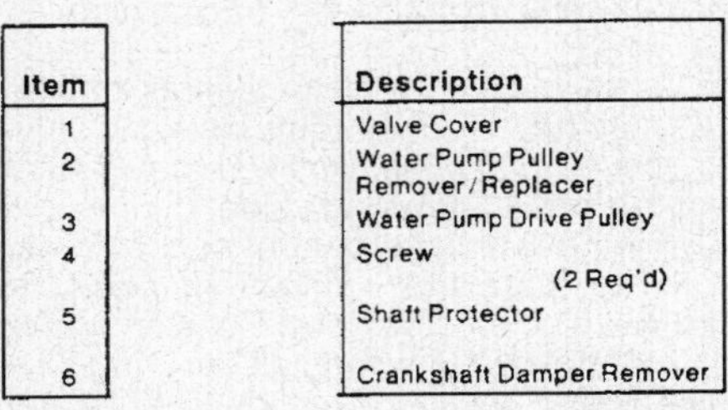

Item	Description
1	Valve Cover
2	Water Pump Pulley Remover/Replacer
3	Water Pump Drive Pulley
4	Screw (2 Req'd)
5	Shaft Protector
6	Crankshaft Damper Remover

FM1069500421000X

Fig. 14 Water pump drive pulley removal. 1998–99

at two places on valve cover sealing surfaces where front cover and cylinder heads contact and two places on rear of cylinder head where camshaft seal retainer contacts cylinder head.

c. Install new valve cover gaskets onto valve cover.

d. Within six minutes of applying sealer, **torque** valve cover bolts and studs to 89 inch lbs. using sequence shown in **Fig. 13.**

VALVE ARRANGEMENT

FRONT TO REAR

Lefthand Intake: ....Secondary-Primary-Secondary-Primary-Secondary-Primary.

Righthand Intake: ....Primary-Secondary-Primary-Secondary-Primary-Secondary.

CAMSHAFT LOBE LIFT SPECIFICATIONS

Camshaft lobe lift for primary and secondary intake and exhaust is .188 inch with zero allowable lobe lift loss.

VALVE CLEARANCE SPECIFICATIONS

Valve clearance is hydraulically controlled and not adjustable.

VALVE ADJUSTMENT

Valve clearance is hydraulically controlled and not adjustable.

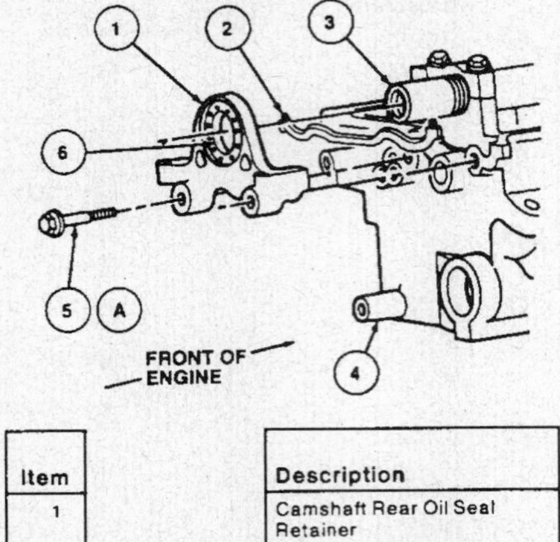

Item	Description
1	Camshaft Rear Oil Seal Retainer
2	Oil Seal Retainer Gasket
3	LH Intake Camshaft
4	LH Cylinder Head
5	Bolt (2 Req'd)
6	Camshaft Rear Oil Seal
A	Tighten to 8-12 N·m (71-106 Lb-In)

FM1069500422000X

Fig. 15 Rear camshaft rear oil seal retainer removal. 1998–99

CAMSHAFT FOLLOWERS

REPLACE

1998-99

1. Remove valve covers and gaskets as described under "Valve Cover, Replace."
2. Remove crankshaft pulley bolt from front of crankshaft, then rotate crankshaft to position crankshaft keyway to 11 o'clock position and No. 1 cylinder at Top Dead Center (TDC).
3. Verify alignment arrows on camshafts are aligned. If arrows are not aligned, rotate crankshaft one complete revolution.
4. Rotate crankshaft to position crankshaft keyway to three o'clock location. This will position righthand cylinder head camshafts to neutral position (base circle).
5. Rotate water pump drive belt tensioner clockwise to release water pump drive belt tension, remove water pump drive belt, then carefully release drive belt tensioner.
6. Remove battery, then using crankshaft damper remover tool No. T58P-6316-D and water pump pulley remover/replacer tool No. T94P-6312-AH, or equivalents, with shaft protector and screw, remove water pump drive pulley from lefthand intake camshaft, **Fig. 14.**
7. Remove camshaft rear oil seal bolts, then the retainer and gasket from lefthand cylinder head, **Fig. 15.**
8. Remove cylinder head camshaft journal thrust cap bolts and thrust caps from righthand cylinder head. **Remove cylinder head camshaft journal thrust caps first to prevent damage to cylinder head camshaft journal thrust caps. Cylinder head camshaft journal caps are numbered to ensure they are assembled in their original position. Do not mix camshaft journal caps.**

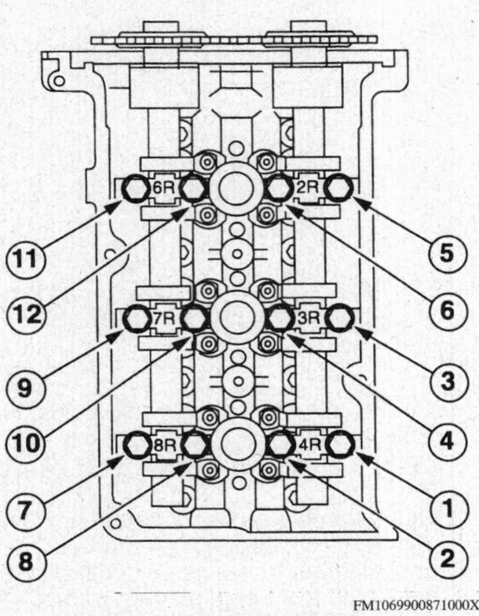

FM1069900871000X

Fig. 16 Right camshaft journal cap bolt removal sequence. 1998–99

9. Loosen remaining righthand cylinder head camshaft journal cap bolts seven to eight turns in sequence, **Fig. 16,** in several passes (approximately one to two turns each pass) to allow camshafts to be raised from righthand cylinder head. Do not completely remove bolts.
10. With righthand cylinder head camshaft journal caps and camshafts loose on righthand cylinder head, remove rocker arms. **If camshaft followers are to be reused, mark position or rocker arms to ensure they are assembled in original positions.**
11. Rotate crankshaft two revolutions and position crankshaft keyway to 11 o'clock location. This will position lefthand cylinder head camshafts to neutral position (base circle).
12. Verify alignment arrows on camshafts are aligned.
13. Remove cylinder head camshaft journal thrust cap bolts and thrust caps from lefthand cylinder head. **Remove cylinder head camshaft journal thrust caps first to prevent damage to cylinder head camshaft journal thrust caps. Cylinder head camshaft journal caps are numbered to ensure they are assembled in their original position. Do not mix camshaft journal caps.**
14. Loosen remaining lefthand cylinder head camshaft journal cap bolts seven to eight turns in sequence, **Fig. 17,** in several passes (approximately one to two turns each pass) to allow camshafts to be raised from lefthand cylinder head. Do not remove bolts completely.
15. With lefthand cylinder head camshaft journal caps and camshafts loose on

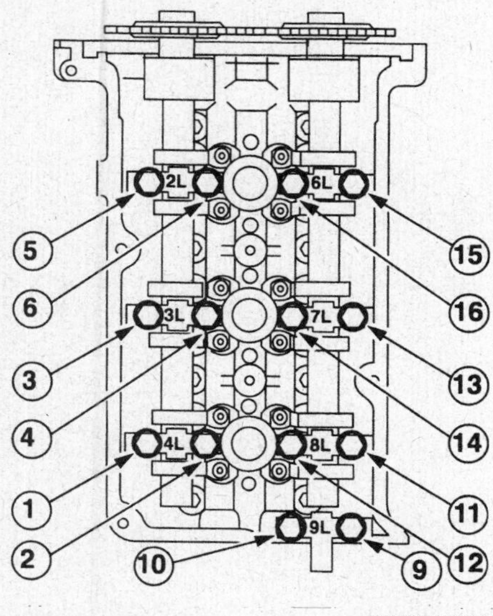

Fig. 17 Left camshaft journal cap bolt removal sequence. 1998–99

lefthand cylinder head, remove rocker arms. **If camshaft followers are to be reused, mark positions of rocker arms to ensure they are assembled in original positions.**

16. Reverse procedure to install, noting the following:
    a. **Ensure camshaft followers are installed in original locations. Crankshaft keyway must be at 11 o'clock position before installing followers. Failure to do so may lead to engine damage.**
    b. Lubricate rocker arms with suitable engine assembly lubricant, then install rocker arms onto lefthand cylinder head under camshafts.
    c. With lefthand cylinder head rocker arms installed under camshafts, **torque** lefthand cylinder head camshaft journal cap bolts in sequence, **Fig. 18,** in several passes, to 6–9 ft. lbs.
    d. With righthand cylinder head rocker arms installed under camshafts, **torque** righthand cylinder head camshaft journal cap bolts in sequence, **Fig. 19,** in several passes, to 6–9 ft. lbs. Install cylinder head camshaft journal thrust cap last to ensure damage to No. 1 journal cap does not occur.
    e. Using power steering pump pulley replacer tool No. T91P-3A733-A, screw tool No. T94P-6312-AH and replacer cup tool No. T94P-6312-AH, or equivalents, install water pump drive pulley on lefthand intake camshaft, **Fig. 20.**
    f. Tighten crankshaft pulley bolt in four steps: first step, **torque** bolt to 89 ft. lbs.; second step, loosen bolt one full turn; third step, **torque** bolt to 35–39 ft. lbs.; fourth step, tighten an additional 85–95.°

2000–02

1. Remove valve covers and gaskets as

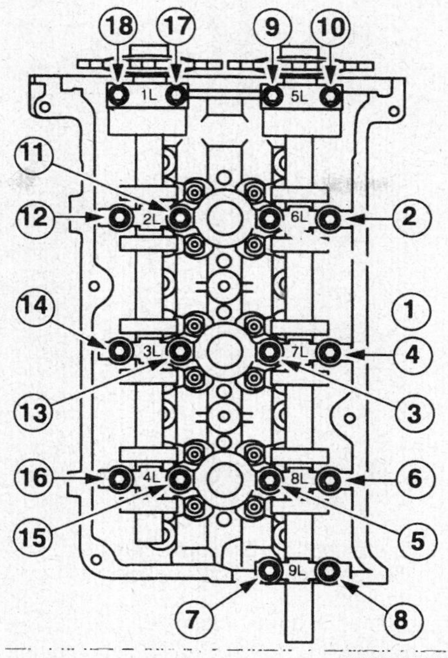

Fig. 18 Lefthand camshaft journal cap bolt tightening sequence. 1998–99

described under "Valve Cover, Replace."

2. **Piston must be at bottom of its stroke with both valves closed. Any loss of air pressure will allow to fall into cylinder.** Remove spark plug.
3. Install adapter into spark plug bore, then connect compressed air supply at 102–144 psi.
4. Using valve spring compressor tool No. T94P-6565-BH or equivalent, compress valve spring and remove roller follower.
5. Reverse procedure to install.

HYDRAULIC LASH ADJUSTER

REPLACE

Mark the position of camshaft follower and hydraulic lash adjuster to ensure they are assembled in their original position if they are to be reused.

1. Remove camshaft followers as described under "Camshaft Followers, Replace."
2. Remove hydraulic lash adjusters.
3. Lubricate adjusters with engine assembly lubricant, then install. Ensure lash adjusters are installed in original positions.

FRONT COVER

REPLACE

1. Remove lefthand and righthand valve covers as described under "Valve Cover, Replace."
2. Remove oil pan as described under "Oil Pan, Replace."
3. Remove alternator and power steering pump.

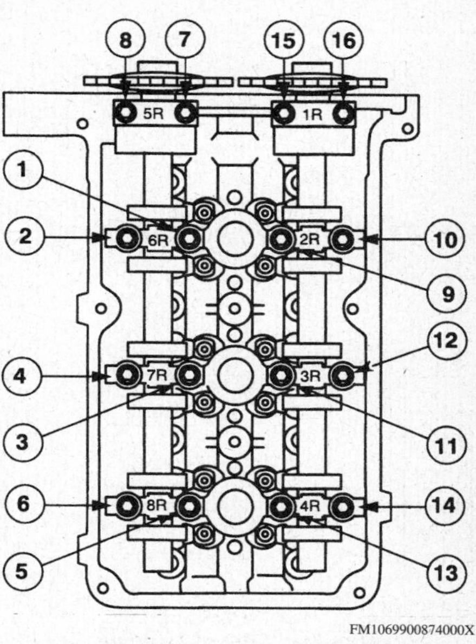

Fig. 19 Righthand camshaft journal cap bolt tightening sequence. 1998–99

4. Disconnect camshaft and crankshaft position sensor electrical connectors and remove.
5. Remove front cover bolts and studs in sequence, **Fig. 21,** then the cover.
6. Reverse procedure to install, noting the following:
    a. Prior to applying sealer clean front cover to cylinder block and cylinder head sealing surfaces with metal surface cleaner F4AZ-19A536-RA.
    b. Engine front cover must be installed in a two step sequence.
    c. Install bolts and studs in the indicated sequence, **Fig. 22,** tighten in two steps. First tighten seven bolts and studs one quarter turn (90°) after engine front cover contacts cylinder block and cylinder heads.
    d. Second, install remaining engine front cover bolts and studs and **torque** in sequence, **Fig. 23** to 18 ft. lbs.
    e. Lubricate new O-rings with engine oil before installation.
    f. Install position sensors and bolts.

TIMING CHAIN

REPLACE

REMOVAL

1. Remove front cover as described under "Front Cover, Replace."
2. Remove camshaft oil seal retainer, **Fig. 24.**
3. Remove crankshaft position sensor pulse wheel.
4. Install crankshaft pulley bolt and washer and rotate crankshaft keyway clockwise to the 11 o'clock position and engine at TDC of cylinder of No. 1. Roller finger follower marks on back of camshaft sprockets must line up with one another, **Figs. 25 and 26.**

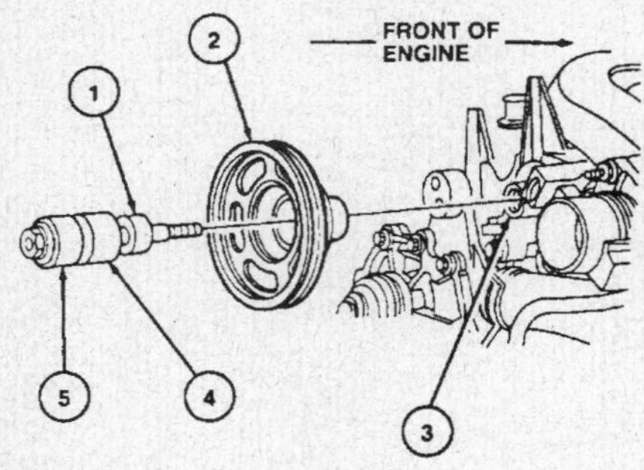

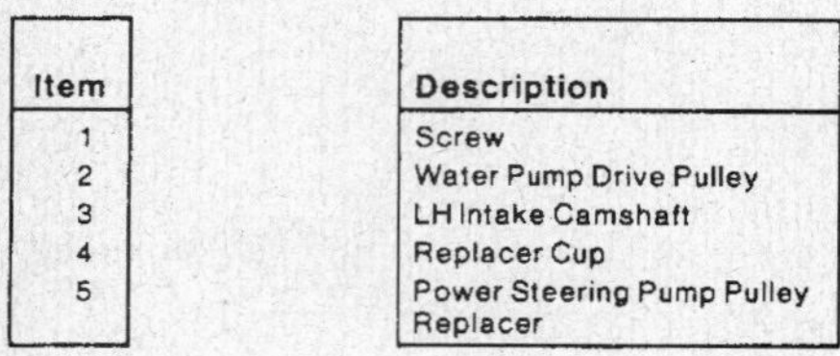

Item	Description
1	Screw
2	Water Pump Drive Pulley
3	LH Intake Camshaft
4	Replacer Cup
5	Power Steering Pump Pulley Replacer

FM1069500425000X

Fig. 20 Water pump drive pulley installation. 1998–99

5. Rotate crankshaft clockwise to position crankshaft keyway in 3 o'clock position.
6. Mark position of all chain drive components to ensure they are assembled in their original positions.
7. Remove righthand chain tensioner and tensioner arm bolts, chain tensioner and tensioner adapter plate.
8. Remove righthand timing chain guide and timing chain.
9. Remove right camshaft as follows:
   a. Remove camshaft thrust caps Nos. 1R and 5R. **Fig. 27.**
   b. Loosen camshaft bearing caps in sequence, **Fig. 27,** in several passes.
   c. Remove bearing caps.
10. Remove righthand camshaft followers as outlined in "Camshaft Follower, Replace."
11. Rotate crankshaft clockwise two revolutions until keyway is in the 11 o'clock position.
12. Remove crankshaft pulley bolt and washer.
13. Remove lefthand chain tensioner and tensioner arm.
14. Remove lefthand timing chain fixed chain guide and timing chain.
15. Remove lefthand camshaft as follows:
   a. Remove camshaft thrust caps Nos. 1L and 5L. **Fig. 28.**
   b. Loosen camshaft bearing caps in sequence, **Fig. 28,** in several passes.
   c. Remove bearing caps.
16. Remove lefthand camshaft followers as outlined in "Camshaft Follower, Replace."
17. Remove righthand and lefthand timing chain sprockets.

INSTALLATION

1. Install crankshaft pulley washer and bolt.
2. Install righthand and lefthand timing chain sprocket, washer and bolt.
3. Turn crankshaft clockwise to position key to the 11 o'clock position.

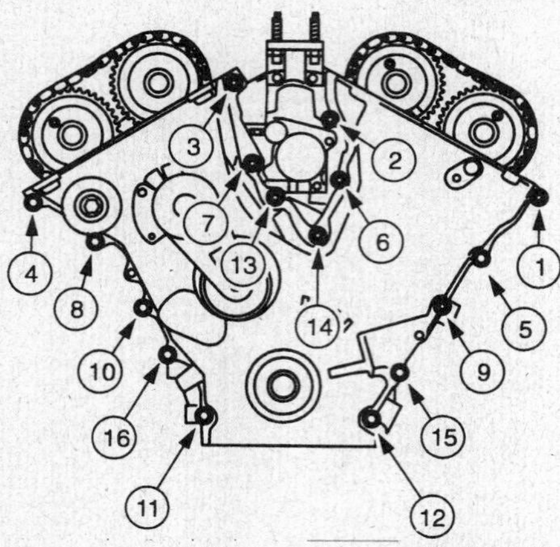

FM1069900875000X

Fig. 21 Front engine cover bolt removal sequence

4. Remove crankshaft pulley bolt and washer.
5. Lubricate camshafts with engine assembly lubricator.
6. **On 1998–99 models,** align timing flags on the rear of lefthand camshaft sprockets, **Fig. 29.**
7. **On all models,** install lefthand chain guide and bolts (black material), then timing chain. **The colored links of timing chain and the marks on the timing sprockets must line up.**
8. Set tensioner as follows:
   a. Position timing chain tensioner in a vise with jaw protectors.
   b. During tensioner compression, do not release ratchet stem until tensioner piston is fully bottomed in its bore or damage to the ratchet stem will result.
   c. Hold timing chain tensioner ratchet lock mechanism away from the ratchet stem with a small pick.
   d. Slowly compress timing chain tensioner. **Piston should retract with minimal force. If binding occurs, reposition tensioner to eliminate side loading.**
   e. Retain piston with a paper clip. **Wire must remain in timing chain tensioner until tensioner is installed onto engine with the piston bottomed in the bore.**
9. Install lefthand tensioner arm (black material), tensioner adapter plate and timing chain tensioner.
10. Install righthand chain guide and bolts (tan material), then timing chain. **The colored links of timing chain and the marks on the timing sprockets must line up.**
11. Set tensioner as outlined in step 7.
12. Install righthand tensioner arm (tan material), tensioner adapter plate and timing chain tensioner.
13. Install lefthand roller finger followers.
14. Install lefthand camshaft bearing caps and tighten to sequence, **Fig. 30.** Do not install thrust caps until camshaft journal caps are installed.
15. Install crankshaft pulley bolt and washer.

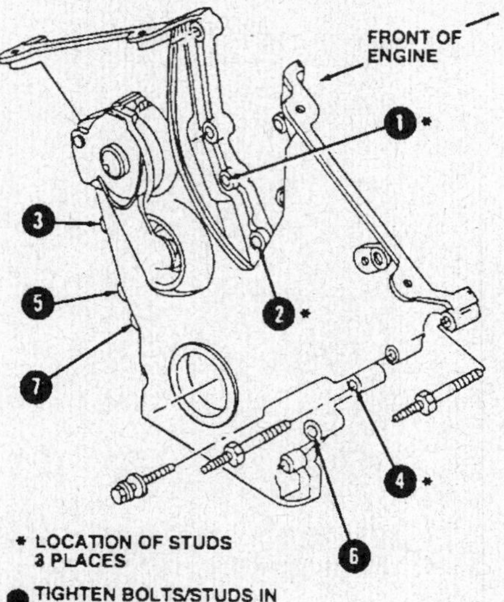

FM1069500428000X

Fig. 22 Front cover bolt & stud bolt installation sequence

16. Rotating crankshaft counterclockwise may cause the timing chains to bind and may cause engine damage. Rotate engine clockwise to locate crankshaft keyway to 3 o'clock position.
17. Install righthand roller finger followers.
18. Install righthand camshaft bearing caps and tighten to sequence, **Fig. 30.** Do not install thrust caps until camshaft journal caps are installed.
19. Remove righthand and lefthand chain tensioner retaining wires.
20. Remove crankshaft pulley bolt and washer.
21. Install camshaft oil seal retainer.
22. Install pulse wheel with keyway in the slot stamped 25, color code blue.
23. Install new camshaft oil seal.
24. Install engine front cover as outlined.

TIMING CHAIN TENSIONER

REPLACE

Refer to "Timing Chain, Replace."

CAMSHAFT

REPLACE

Refer to "Timing Chain, Replace" for camshaft replacement procedures.

CRANKSHAFT SEAL

REPLACE

1. Raise and support vehicle, then remove righthand front wheel and tire assembly.
2. Remove righthand splash shield from fender apron for access to crankshaft pulley.
3. Remove accessory drive belt as described under "Serpentine Drive Belt."
4. Remove crankshaft pulley bolt and washer from crankshaft, then, using

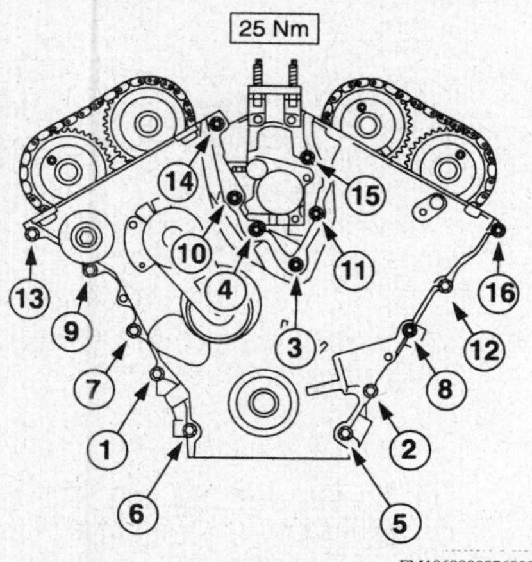

Fig. 23 Front engine cover tightening sequence

crankshaft damper remover tool No. T58P-6316-D, or equivalent, remove crankshaft pulley from crankshaft.

5. Using seal remover tool No. T92C-6700-CH, or equivalent, remove crankshaft front seal from front cover.
6. Reverse procedure to install, noting following:
   a. Lubricate seal sealing surfaces with suitable engine assembly lubricant, then, using crankshaft seal replacer tool No. T88T-6701-A and crankshaft damper replacer tool No. T74P-7316-B, or equivalents, install crankshaft front seal into front cover.
   b. Clean crankshaft pulley sealing surfaces with suitable metal cleaner to remove all residues which could interfere with sealer's ability to adhere.
   c. Apply black silicone rubber part No. F4AZ-19562-B, or equivalent, to front of crankshaft on inside diameter surface of pulley at keyway.
   d. Install crankshaft pulley using crankshaft damper replacer tool No. T74P-6316-B, or equivalent, and washer from bolt.
   e. **Torque** crankshaft pulley bolt to 89 ft. lbs., loosen bolt one full turn, **torque** bolt to 35–39 ft. lbs., then rotate bolt an additional 85–95.°

CRANKSHAFT REAR OIL SEAL

REPLACE

1. **On models equipped with manual transaxle,** remove transaxle and clutch assembly as outlined under "Clutch & Manual Transaxle" section.
2. **On models equipped with automatic transaxle,** remove transaxle as outlined in "Automatic Transaxle/ Transmission" section.
3. **On all models,** observe position of flywheel on crankshaft flange, then remove flywheel bolts.
4. Install rear crankshaft seal remover tool No. T95P-6701-EH, or equivalent, **Fig. 31.** Install slide hammer and remove rear crankshaft seal. **Avoid scratching or damaging the oil seal sealing surfaces on the crankshaft and cylinder block.**
5. Reverse procedure to install, noting the following:
   a. Clean and inspect crankshaft rear oil seal sealing surfaces.
   b. Lubricate crankshaft flange, crankshaft rear oil seal bore and oil seal lip with Engine Assembly Lubricant D9AZ-19579-D, or equivalent.
   c. Alternately tighten bolt until crankshaft rear oil seal is flush with the cylinder block, using rear main seal replacer tool No. T82L-6701-A, or equivalent, **Fig. 32.**

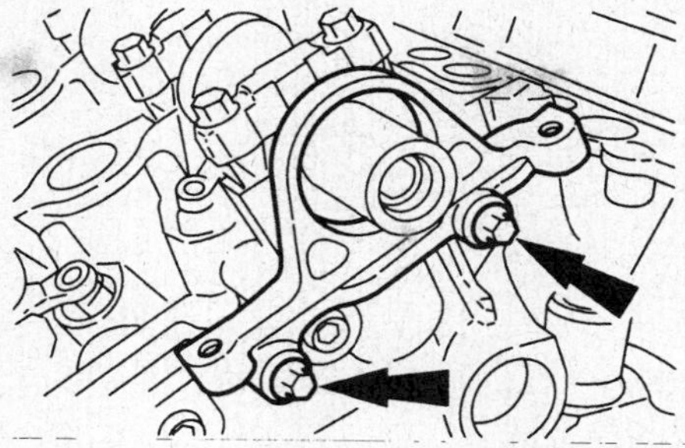

Fig. 24 Camshaft oil seal removal

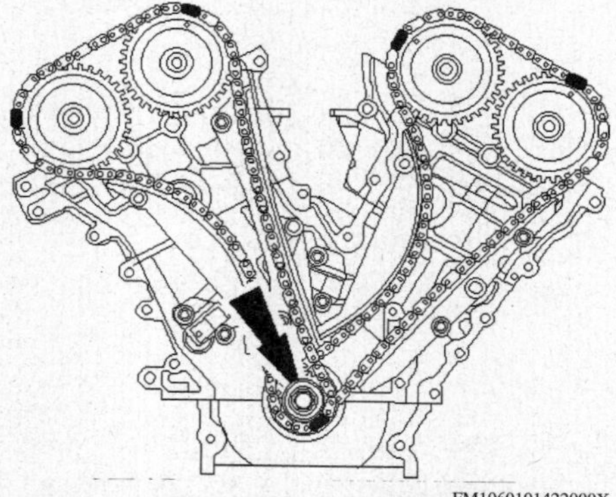

Fig. 26 Crankshaft & camshaft alignment. 2000–02

OIL PAN

REPLACE

1. Remove exhaust Y-pipe, then the exhaust support bracket nuts and support bracket.
2. Remove A/C compressor heat shield nuts and heat shield.
3. Drain engine oil into a suitable container.
4. Remove flywheel access cover and oil pan bolts from transaxle housing.
5. Remove oil pan bolts and studs in sequence, **Fig. 33.** Discard gasket
6. Reverse procedure to install, noting the following:
   a. Position oil pan and loosely install bolts and studs.
   b. Install oil pan to transaxle housing bolts.

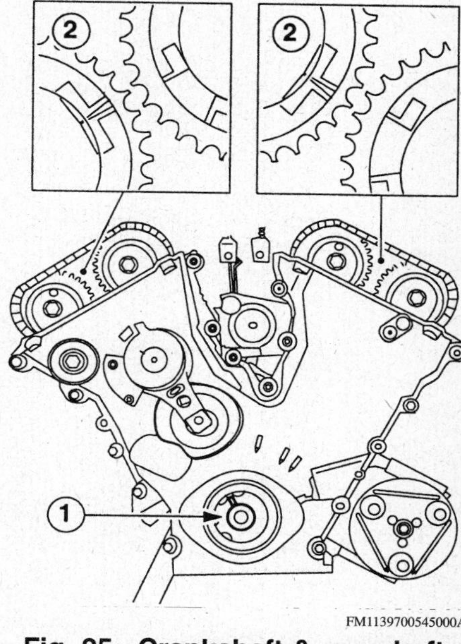

Fig. 25 Crankshaft & camshaft alignment. 1998–99

   c. Using sequence shown in **Fig. 34** tighten bolts to specification.

OIL PUMP

REPLACE

1. Remove oil pan and oil pump screen cover and tube as described under "Oil Pan, Replace."
2. Remove front cover as described under "Front Cover, Replace."
3. Remove timing chains as described under "Timing Chain, Replace."
4. Remove crankshaft sprocket, then the oil pump bolts in sequence, **Fig. 35.**
5. Remove pump from cylinder block.
6. Reverse procedure to install, noting the following:
   a. **Torque** oil pump bolts in sequence, **Figs. 36,** to 72–108 inch lbs.
   b. Fill crankcase to proper level with specified engine oil, then run engine and check for leaks.

BELT TENSION DATA

Drive belts have an automatic drive belt tensioner and do not require adjustment.

The automatic belt tensioner is a spring loaded device which sets and maintains drive belt tension. Drive belts should not require tension adjustment for the life of the drive belt.

SERPENTINE DRIVE BELT

ROUTING

Refer to **Figs. 37 through 39** for belt routing.

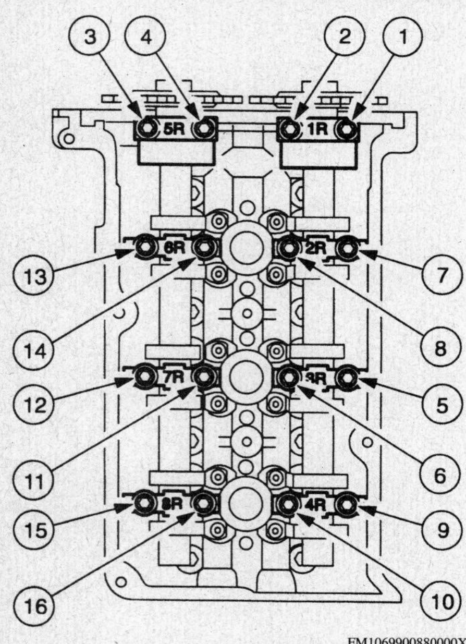

Fig. 27 Righthand camshaft cap bolts loosening sequence

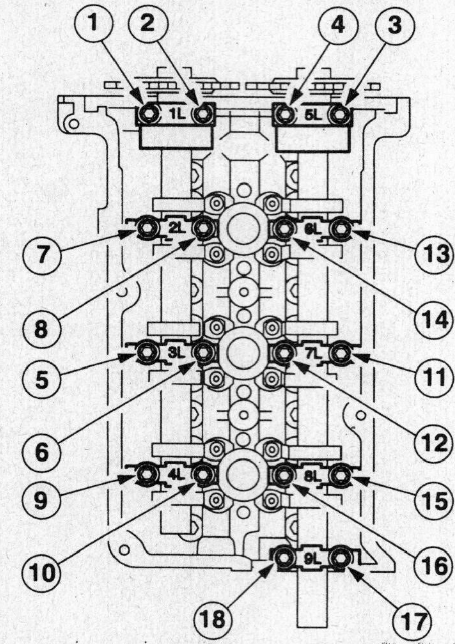

Fig. 28 Lefthand camshaft cap bolt loosening sequence

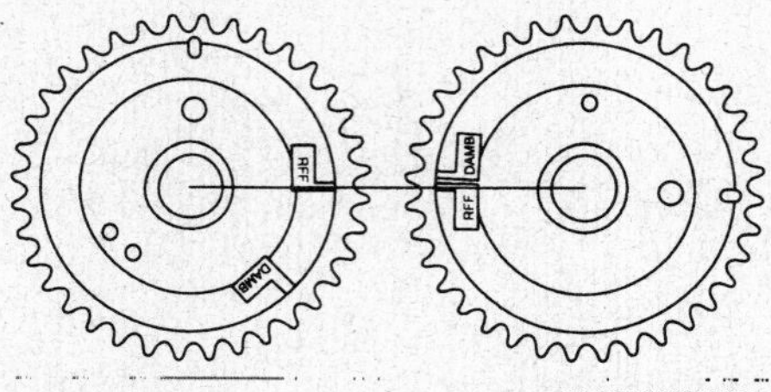

Fig. 29 Lefthand camshaft flag alignment. 1998–1999

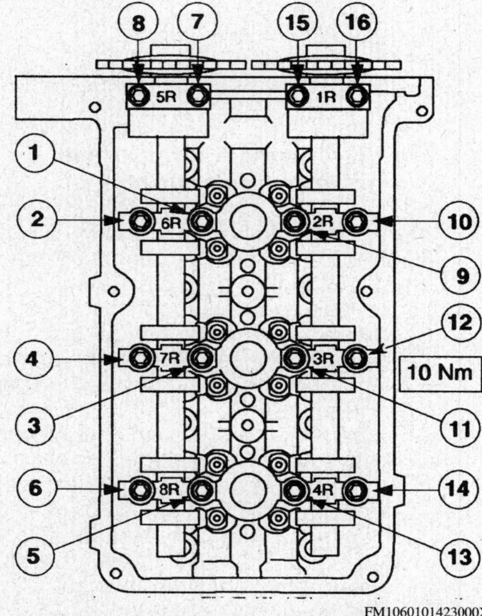

Fig. 30 Camshaft cap bolt tightening sequence

BELT REPLACEMENT

WATER PUMP

1. Remove engine cover, then rotate drive belt tensioner clockwise by hand.
2. Lift drive belt over pulley flanges and remove.
3. Reverse procedure to install.

ACCESSORY DRIVE

1. Raise and support vehicle.
2. Use a breaker bar installed in the ⅜ inch square hole in drive belt tensioner to rotate the drive belt.
3. Lift drive belt over the pulley flanges and remove.
4. Reverse procedure to install.

TENSIONER REPLACEMENT

ACCESSORY DRIVE

1. Remove drive belt as described under "Belt Replace."
2. Loosen belt tensioner bolts completely, then remove tensioner from front of engine.
3. Align drive belt tensioner spring to slot in front cover, then install tensioner onto front cover. Tighten tensioner bolt to specifications.
4. Install drive belt as described under "Belt Replace."

WATER PUMP

1. Remove tensioner bolt and tensioner from water pump.
2. Align tab on tensioner with hole in mounting area on water pump, then install tensioner onto pump. Tighten bolts to specifications.

COOLING SYSTEM BLEED

These engines do not require a specific bleed procedure. To ensure coolant level is satisfactory, start the engine, turn heater control to its maximum heat and vent positions. After engine reaches normal operating temperature, hot air should be blowing from the A/C vents. If cool air is blowing from the vents, coolant level is low, turn engine off and add coolant as necessary.

THERMOSTAT

REPLACE

1. Drain engine cooling system so engine coolant level is below water thermostat.
2. Remove engine cover, if equipped
3. Disconnect radiator hoses from thermostat housing, then remove housing.
4. Remove housing bolts, then separate thermostat housings.
5. Remove O-ring seal and thermostat from housing.
6. Reverse procedure to install.

WATER PUMP

REPLACE

CONTOUR & MYSTIQUE

1. Drain cooling system into a suitable container.
2. Remove water pump drive belt tensioner.
3. Raise and support vehicle.
4. Remove water pump bolts, pump and gasket.
5. Reverse procedure to install.

COUGAR

1. Remove battery, then air cleaner.
2. Remove thermostat housing, then engine cover.
3. Rotate belt tensioner clockwise by hand, then remove belt.
4. **On models equipped with automatic transmission,** disconnect transmission range selector electrical connector.
5. **On all models,** remove water pump bolts, coolant hoses, then the water pump.
6. Remove water pump from housing.
7. Reverse procedure to install. Replace gasket and O-ring.

RADIATOR

REPLACE

Refer to "2.0L Engine" for radiator replacement.

FUEL PUMP

REPLACE

Refer to "2.0L Engine" for fuel pump replacement.

FUEL FILTER

REPLACE

Refer to "2.0L Engine" for fuel filter replacement.

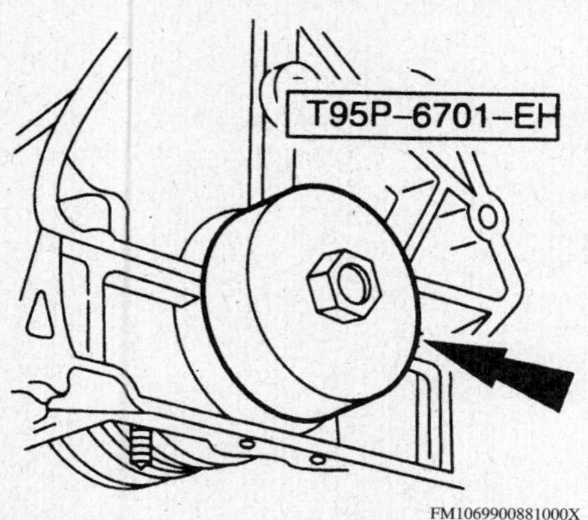

FM1069900881000X

Fig. 31 Rear crankshaft seal remover tool installation

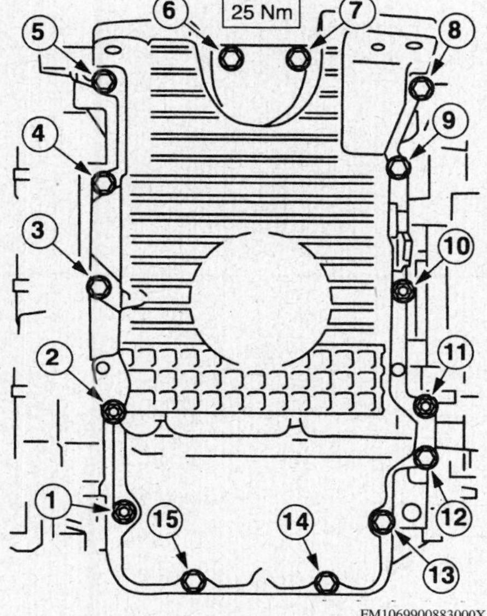

FM1069900883000X

Fig. 34 Oil pan tightening sequence

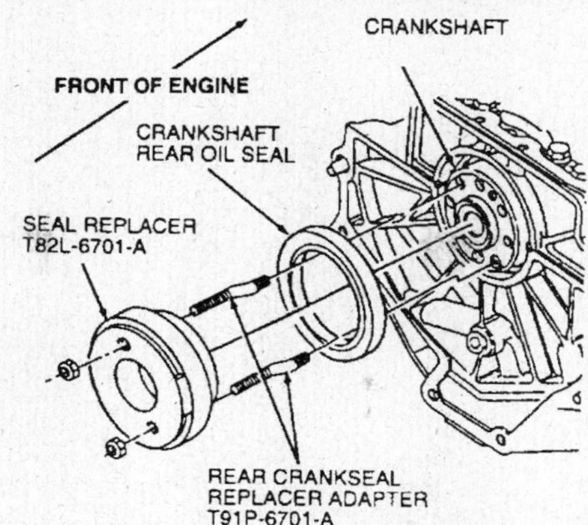

NOTE: LUBRICATE CRANKSHAFT FLANGE AND REAR OIL SEAL BORE WITH ENGINE ASSY LUBRICANT D9AZ-19579-D OR EQUIVALENT MEETING FORD SPECIFICATION ESR-M99C80-A PRIOR TO INSTALLATION OF SEAL

FM1069500436000X

Fig. 32 Crankshaft rear oil seal installation

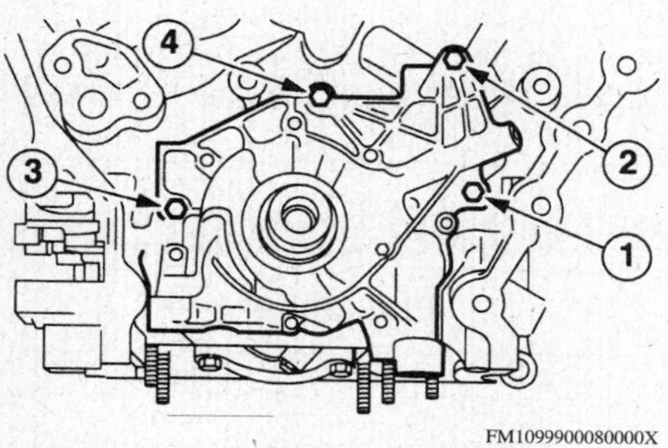

FM1099900080000X

Fig. 35 Oil pump bolt removal sequence

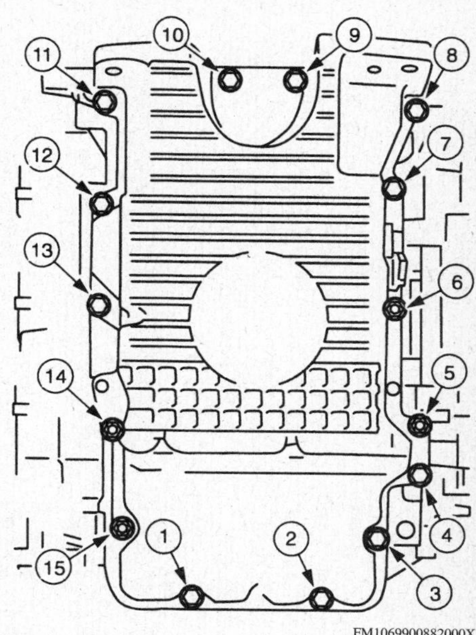

FM1069900882000X

Fig. 33 Oil pan removal sequence

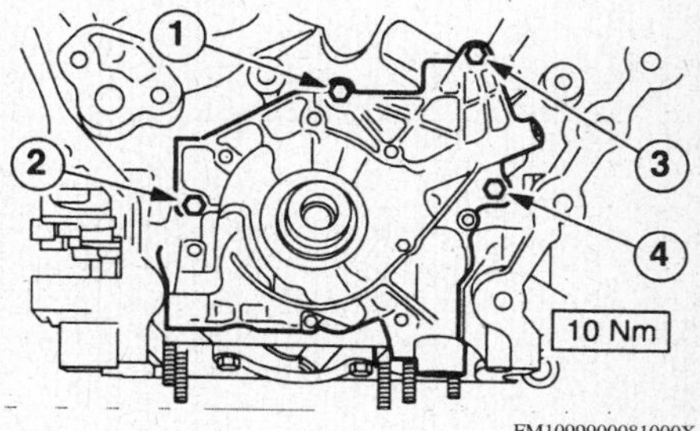

FM1099900081000X

Fig. 36 Oil pump bolt tightening sequence

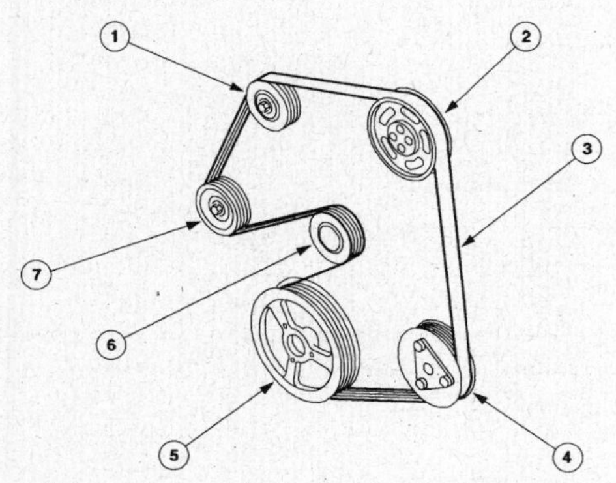

Item	Description
1	Belt idler pulley
2	Power steering pump pulley
3	Accesory drive belt
4	Air conditioning pump pulley

Item	Description
5	Crankshaft pulley
6	Belt tensioner
7	Generator pulley

FM1069500438000A

Fig. 37 Accessory drive belt routing. With A/C built before January 1999

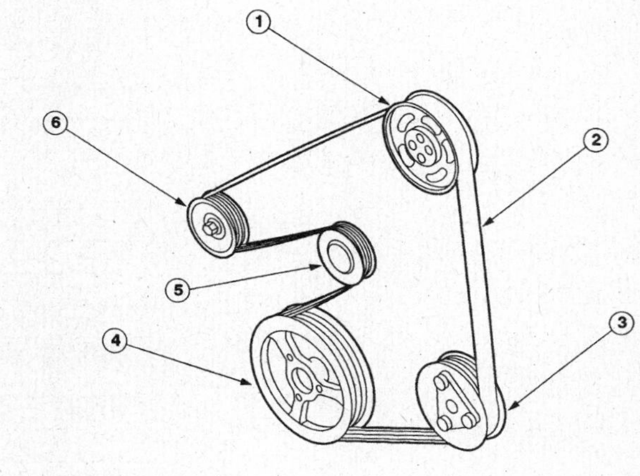

Item	Description
1	Power steering pump pulley
2	Accesory drive belt
3	Air conditioning pump pulley

Item	Description
4	Crankshaft pulley
5	Belt tensioner
6	Generator pulley

FM1069500439000A

Fig. 38 Accessory drive belt routing. With A/C built after January 1999

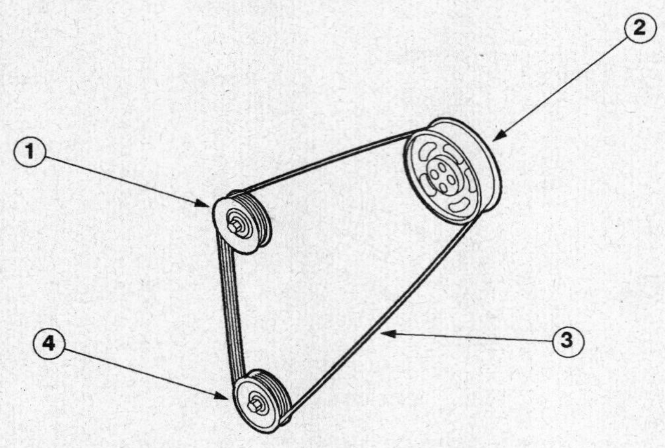

Item	Description
1	Belt tensioner
2	Water pump pulley
3	Water pump belt
4	Water pump drive pulley

FM1069500440000A

Fig. 39 Water pump drive belt routing

TIGHTENING SPECIFICATIONS

Year	Component	Torque/Ft. Lbs.
1998–2002	A/C Compressor Bolts	15–22
	A/C Condenser Core To Radiator Bolts	60①
	A/C Hose Bracket To Front Cover Nut	72–108①
	Accelerator Cable Bracket To Throttle Body Bolts	72–108①
	Accessory Drive Belt Tensioner Bolt	15–22
	Battery Ground Cable To Engine/ Transaxle Stud Nut	15–22
	Camshaft Journal Cap Bolts	72–108①
	Camshaft Journal Thrust Cap Bolts	72–108①
	Camshaft Rear Oil Seal Retainer Bolts	72–108①
	Crankcase Ventilation Tube	44–62①
	Crankshaft Pulley Bolt	⑦
	Cylinder Head Bolts	②
	Drive Belt Idler Pulley Bolt	15–22
	EGR Valve To Exhaust Manifold Tube Nut	26–33
	Engine Air Cleaner Tube Clamps	24–48①
	Engine Rear Plate Bolts	54–64③
	Engine & Transaxle Support Insulator Nuts	④
	Exhaust Manifold Nuts	15
	Fan Shroud Nuts	24–48①
	Flywheel Bolts	59③
	Front Engine Support Bracket Nuts	61
	Front Engine Support Bracket To Sub-Frame Bolts	20

Continued

TIGHTENING SPECIFICATIONS—Continued

Year	Component	Torque/Ft. Lbs.
1998–2002	Front Stabilizer Link To Front Stabilizer Bar Nuts	35
	Front Tie Rod End Nuts	⑥
	Front Wheel Knuckle To Front Suspension Lower Arm Bolts	40
	Heated Oxygen Sensor	30
	Inline Fuel Filter Worm Gear Mounting Clamp	15–25①
	Intake Manifold Bolts	⑤
	Lower Radiator Hose Tube Nuts	72–108①
	Lower Radiator Support Bolts	72–96①
	Muffler Inlet Flange Nuts	26–33
	Oil Pan Drain Plug	19
	Oil Pan Retaining Bolts & Studs (1998–99)	18
	Oil Pan To Transaxle Bolts	25–34
	Oil Pan To Transaxle Housing Bolts	25–34
	Oil Pump Bolts	72–108①
	Oil Pump Screen Cover & Tube Bolts	72–108①
	Oil Pump Screen Cover & Tube Support Nut	15–22
	Power Steering Pressure Hose Bracket Bolt	72–108①
	Power Steering Pump Bolts	18
	Power Steering Pump Pulley Bolts	18
	Power Steering Pump Support Nuts	72–108①
	Radiator To Front Sub-Frame Bolts	72–96①
	Shift Cable Bracket Bolts	17
	Shift Rod Bolt	17
	Stabilizer Bar Nut	41
	Steering Shaft Pinch Bolt	18
	Thermostat Housing Bolts	18
	Three-Way Catalytic Converter Nuts	27
	Transaxle Oil Cooler Line Bracket Nuts	20
	Transaxle Oil Cooler Tube To Fitting	21
	Transaxle Stabilizer Bar Nut	41
	Transaxle To Engine Bolts	30
	Torque Converter To Flywheel Nuts	59
	Upper Intake Manifold Bolts	84①
	Valve Cover Bolts	72–108①
	Water Crossover Pipe (Bypass Tube) To Cylinder Head Bolts	72–108①
	Water Pump Bolts	13
	Water Pump Drive Belt Tensioner Bolt	72–108①
	Wheel Lug Nuts	94

①— Inch lbs.
②— Refer to "Cylinder Head, Replace."
③— Tighten in an alternating sequence.
④— Automatic transaxle, 30–41 ft. lbs.; manual transaxle, 52–70 ft. lbs.
⑤— Refer to "Intake Manifold, Replace."
⑥— Refer to "Engine, Replace."
⑦— Refer to "Crankshaft Seal, Replace."

Clutch & Manual Transaxle

NOTE: Refer To "Air Bag System Precautions" Located In The Front Of This Manual For System Disarming & Arming Procedures.

NOTE: Refer To "Computer Relearn Procedures" Located In The Front Of This Manual When Battery Power To The Computer Has Been Interrupted.

INDEX

PRECAUTIONS

BATTERY GROUND CABLE

Prior to service, disconnect battery ground cable and isolate as required.

AIR BAG SYSTEMS

Refer to "Air Bag System Precautions" in front of this manual for system disarming and arming procedures.

FUEL SYSTEM PRESSURE RELIEF

Fuel supply lines will remain pressurized for long periods of time after engine shutdown. Pressure must be relieved before servicing fuel system.

1. Remove engine air cleaner as follows:
    a. Remove engine air intake resonators as described under "Engine Air Intake Resonators, Replace."
    b. Disconnect engine control sensor wiring connectors from Mass Air Flow (MAF) sensor and Intake Air Temperature (IAT) sensor.
    c. Remove engine air cleaner to body O-ring retainer.
    d. Remove engine air cleaner body and intake tube from bracket and intake tube and duct.
2. Connect Multi-Port Fuel Injection (MFI) fuel pressure gauge tool No. T80L-9974-B, or equivalent, to fuel pressure relief valve cap on fuel injection supply manifold.
3. Open manual valve on gauge tool to relieve fuel system pressure.

ADJUSTMENTS

CLUTCH PEDAL

1998

Clutch pedal mechanism is self-adjusting, no adjustment is required.

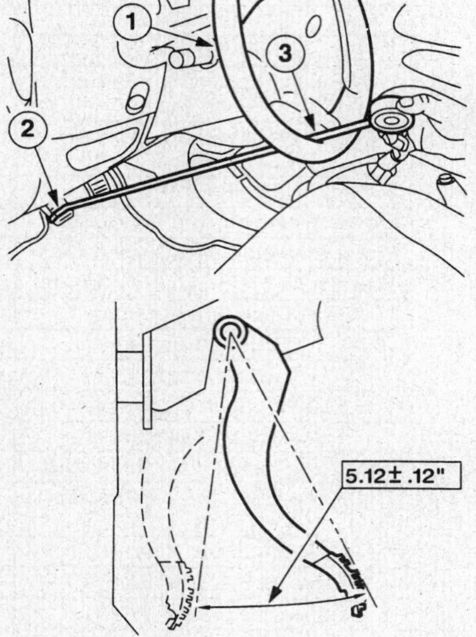

Fig. 1 Clutch pedal adjustment. 1999–2002

1999-2002

1. Turn steering wheel from straight ahead position approximately 30° to left.
2. Attach cable ties to clutch pedal (second groove from the bottom) and tighten.
3. Install a steel rule with cable ties and pass through the steering wheel.
4. Read measurement, depress clutch pedal as far as stop and read measurement again, **Fig. 1.**
5. Pedal travel should not be restricted by mats or clutch master cylinder.
6. Adjust clutch pedal travel to 5–5¼ inches at pedal stop screw.

HYDRAULIC SYSTEM SERVICE

HYDRAULIC SYSTEM BLEED

Pump clutch pedal at least 30 times to ensure no air is in system.

1. Clean top and side of fluid reservoir to avoid fluid contamination.
2. Attach suitable hose to bleeder valve at clutch slave cylinder, then submerge other end in suitable container of clean brake fluid. **Ensure clutch reservoir is full at all times.**
3. While depressing clutch, slightly open bleeder valve, then observe air bubbles in fluid at end of hose.
4. Close bleeder valve before releasing clutch pedal.
5. Top off fluid in brake master cylinder reservoir, then install diaphragm and reservoir cap.
6. Replace air cleaner outlet tube and MAF sensor assembly.
7. Depress clutch ten times and check clutch is functioning properly.

CLUTCH SLAVE CYLINDER, REPLACE

1. Remove transaxle as outlined under "Transaxle, Replace."
2. Disconnect slave cylinder to clutch master cylinder tube.
3. Remove clutch slave cylinder attaching bolts, then the cylinder.
4. Remove clutch slave cylinder bleed tube.
5. Reverse procedure to install. Bleed hydraulic system

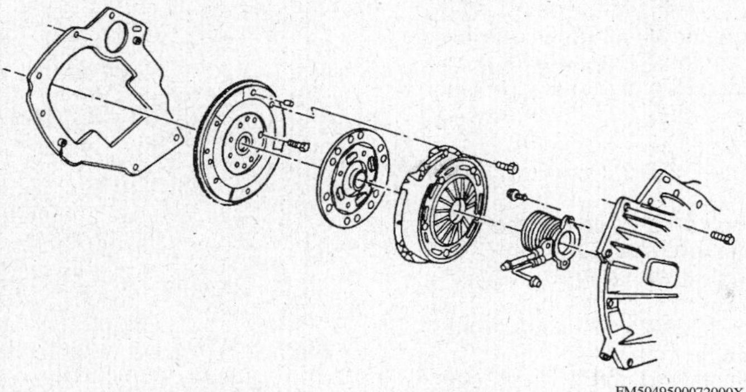

Fig. 2 Exploded view of clutch assembly

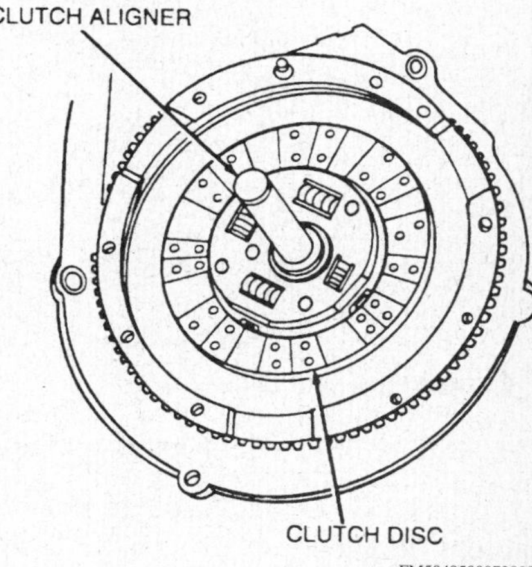

Fig. 3 Clutch aligning tool

CLUTCH

REPLACE

REMOVAL

1. Remove transaxle as described under "Transaxle, Replace."
2. Mark assembled position of clutch pressure plate to flywheel.
3. Loosen clutch pressure plate retaining bolts evenly until clutch pressure plate spring pressure is released, then remove clutch pressure plate and clutch disc, **Fig. 2.**

INSTALLATION

1. Clean clutch pressure plate and flywheel surfaces. **Do not use cleaners with a petroleum base.**
2. Install the clutch disc using clutch aligner tool No. 309-204, or equivalent, **Fig. 3.**
3. Install the clutch pressure plate, then holding flywheel in place using flywheel holding tool No. T74P-6375–A, or equivalent, tighten pressure plate attaching bolts to specification, **Fig. 4.**
4. Connect slave cylinder tube coupling.
5. Install transaxle as outlined under "Transaxle, Replace."
6. Bleed clutch hydraulic system.

TRANSAXLE

REPLACE

1998

1. Disconnect battery positive cable and remove battery.
2. Secure radiator and engine cooling fan motor, fan blade and shroud to radiator support with suitable wire.
3. Loosen but do not remove upper shock absorber mounting nuts.
4. Remove mass air flow sensor and air cleaner outlet tube with resonator.
5. Remove engine air cleaner and lower bracket.
6. Install engine support tool No. D88L-6000-A, or equivalent.
7. Disconnect back-up lamp electrical connector.
8. Remove bolt holding ground strap to transaxle, then the engine and transaxle support insulator
9. Disconnect hydraulic line and grommet from bracket.
10. Remove rubber inspection cover from transaxle clutch housing.
11. Disconnect hydraulic line fitting and position aside.
12. Remove upper transaxle to engine bolt, then the upper starter bolts and ground strap.
13. **On models equipped with 2.0L engine,** remove exhaust manifold heat shield and disconnect catalytic converter at exhaust manifold.
14. **On all models,** remove front tire and wheel assemblies.
15. Raise and support vehicle.
16. **On models equipped with 2.0L engine,** remove catalytic converter.
17. **On models equipped with 2.5L engine,** remove catalytic converter Y-pipe.
18. **On all models,** remove vehicle speed sensor electrical connector and remove speedometer cable.
19. Remove lower radiator air deflector.
20. Push shift rod completely forward and remove shift rod pinch bolt, then pull shift rod back and remove from transaxle.
21. Remove shift control stabilizer bar and bracket from righthand engine support insulator bracket.
22. Remove underbody heat shield from under shift control.
23. Position and secure shift rod and stabilizer bar to allow transaxle removal.
24. Remove suction accumulator/drier from front subframe.
25. Remove left and right side halfshafts and intermediate shafts.
26. Remove righthand engine support insulator bracket.
27. Remove lefthand engine support insulator through-bolt.
28. Lower vehicle.
29. Adjust engine support tool No. D88L-6000-A, or equivalent, to remove tension at righthand front engine support bracket.
30. Remove righthand engine support bracket through-bolt.
31. Raise and properly support vehicle, then remove front subframe.
32. Lower vehicle and loosen front mount nuts five turns.
33. Using suitable floor jack and wood block under transaxle, release tension from engine support tool. Lower transaxle to limits of front engine mount movement.
34. Adjust engine support tool No. D88L-6000-A, or equivalent, to hold engine.
35. Remove floor jack and wood block
36. Secure transmission jack No. 014–002, or equivalent, to transaxle.
37. Remove remaining starter bolts and position aside, support starter motor with suitable wire.
38. Remove engine oil pan to transaxle bolts.
39. Remove remaining bolts and separate transaxle from engine and remove from vehicle.
40. Reverse procedure to install.

1999–2002

2.0L ENGINE

1. Remove battery and engine air cleaner.
2. Loosen suspension strut nut five turns on both sides.
3. Disconnect intake air temperature sensor electrical connector.
4. Remove air cleaner outlet tube clamp and air cleaner outlet tube.
5. Use wire or tie strap to secure radiator.
6. Disconnect ground cable from transaxle and position it aside.
7. Disconnect reverse lamp switch connector.
8. Remove clip and disconnect clutch slave cylinder hydraulic line. **Be careful not to spill brake fluid onto painted surfaces.**
9. Disconnect clutch slave cylinder hydraulic line from bracket, then remove push pin and position aside.
10. Remove upper bellhousing and upper starter motor bolts.
11. Install support bar as shown, **Fig. 5.**
12. Remove lefthand transaxle support insulator nuts, bolts and insulator.
13. Remove lefthand transaxle support insulator studs.
14. Raise and support vehicle and remove both front wheels.
15. Remove lower wheel arch covers.
16. Disconnect lower suspension arm ball joints and stabilizer link rods, then ABS wiring harness bracket from suspension strut. **Do not damage boot and ABS sensor ring.**

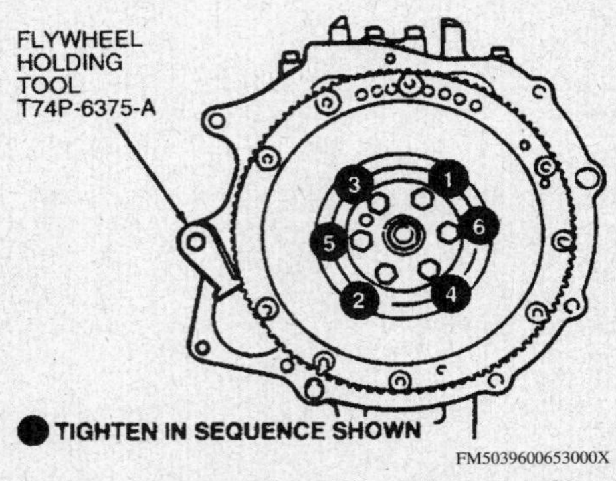

Fig. 4 Flywheel holding tool

17. Remove righthand halfshaft and intermediate shaft. Secure righthand halfshaft out of the way with mechanic's wire.
18. **To avoid damage to joints and boots, do not bend inner halfshaft joint more than 18° or outer halfshaft more than 45.°**
19. Remove lefthand halfshaft using halfshaft remover tool Nos. T86P-3514-A1, T86P-3514-A2 and slide hammer T50T-100-A, or equivalents.
20. Secure halfshaft out of the way with mechanic's wire, then plug transmission openings with auxiliary plugs.
21. Remove rear and front roll restrictor bolts and the rear roll restrictors.
22. Remove suction accumulator bracket bolts.
23. Remove radiator splash shield and radiator support brackets.
24. Disconnect starter motor connectors and remove starter motor.
25. Remove three-way catalytic converter.
26. Disconnect shifter cables and bracket.
27. Disconnect VSS connector.
28. Remove power steering hose bracket bolt and nut.
29. Remove power steering line bracket bolt, then steering gear to subframe bolt.
30. Secure steering gear using mechanics wire, then remove subframe bolts and subframe.
31. Position a suitable hi-lift transmission jack and secure holding strap to transaxle.
32. Remove lower front bellhousing bolts, then the remaining bellhousing bolts.
33. Separate transaxle from engine.
34. Reverse procedure to install.

2.5L ENGINE

1. Remove battery, then loosen both front nuts five turns.
2. Lock steering wheel, then using wire or tie strap to secure radiator.
3. Remove engine air cleaner, then the water pump cover.
4. Disconnect accelerator and speed control cables.
5. Disconnect ground cable from transaxle and position it aside.
6. Disconnect power steering reservoir hose and drain power steering reservoir.
7. Disconnect vehicle speed sensor and reverse lamp switch connectors.
8. Relieve fuel pressure as outlined in "Precautions."
9. Remove safety clips and disconnect fuel lines, using fuel line disconnect tool Nos. D87L-9280-A (3/8 inch) or D87L-9280-B (1/2 inch), or equivalent.
10. Disconnect starter motor connectors, then remove air cleaner bracket and starter motor bracket.
11. Remove clutch slave cylinder hydraulic pipe. **Do not spill brake fluid onto painted surfaces.**
12. Install engine support bar, **Fig. 5.**
13. Remove lefthand transaxle support insulator nuts, bolts and support insulator.
14. Remove lefthand transaxle support insulator studs.
15. Remove four upper bellhousing bolts.
16. Raise and support vehicle and remove both front wheels.
17. Disconnect lower suspension arm ball joints and stabilizer link rods, then ABS wiring harness bracket from suspension strut. **Do not damage boot and ABS sensor ring.**
18. **To avoid damage to joints and boots, do not bend inner halfshaft joint more than 18° and the outer halfshaft more than 45.°**
19. Remove righthand halfshaft and intermediate shaft. Secure halfshaft out of the way with mechanic's wire.

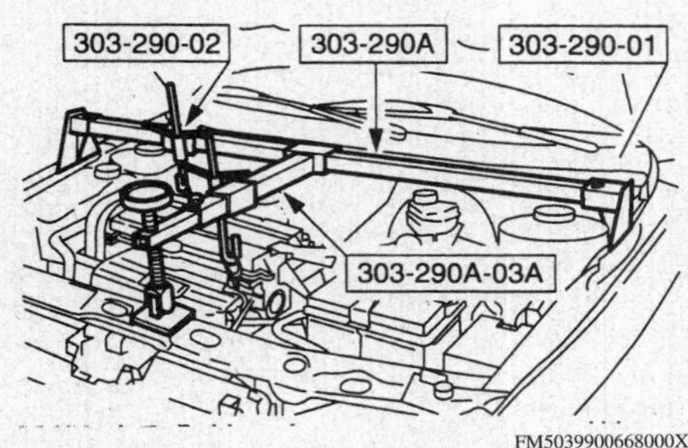

Fig. 5 Engine support bar tool installation. 1999–2002

20. Remove lefthand halfshaft using halfshaft remover tool Nos. T86P-3514-A1, T86P-3514-A2 and slide hammer T50T-100-A, or equivalents. Secure halfshaft out of the way with mechanic's wire, then plug transmission openings with auxiliary plugs.
21. Remove radiator splash shield.
22. Remove secondary three way catalytic converter, then the radiator support brackets.
23. Remove bolt and position bumper bracket aside.
24. Remove suction accumulator bracket bolts, then the heated oxygen sensor connector from subframe.
25. Remove intermediate shaft pinch bolt.
26. Remove front and rear roll restrictors.
27. Remove rear roll restrictor bracket.
28. Loosen subframe bolts and lower subframe.
29. Disconnect shifter cables and bracket.
30. Remove power steering line bracket bolt and disconnect power steering line from steering gear.
31. Remove subframe bolts and subframe.
32. Position hi lift transmission jack and secure holding strap to transaxle.
33. Remove lower rear and front bellhousing bolts.
34. Lower engine and transaxle assembly.
35. Separate transaxle from engine.
36. Reverse procedure to install.

TIGHTENING SPECIFICATIONS

Year	Component	Torque/Ft. Lbs.
1998–2002	Back-Up Lamp Switch	84①
	Clutch Bleed Screw	84–108①
	Clutch Bleed Tube Fitting	10
	Clutch Master Cylinder Nuts	84①
	Clutch Pressure Plate To Flywheel	22
	Clutch Slave Cylinder Mounting	10
	Flywheel Attaching Bolts	②
	Front Engine Support Bracket	61
	Front Shock Absorber Upper Mounting	34
	Righthand Engine Support Bracket	62
	Selector Housing	89①
	Shift Stabilizer Bar	28–38
	Shift Rod	14–18
	Starter Motor Bolts	20–30
	Transaxle Case To Clutch Housing	28–38
	Transaxle To Engine	28–38
	Wheel Lug Nuts	62

① — Inch lbs.
② — 2.5L engine, 59 ft. lbs.; 2.0L engine, 83 ft. lbs.

Rear Suspension

NOTE: On Air Bag Equipped Models, Refer To "Air Bag System Precautions" Located In The Front Of This Manual For System Disarming & Arming Procedures.

NOTE: Refer To "Computer Relearn Procedures" Located In The Front Of This Manual When Battery Power To The Computer Has Been Interrupted.

INDEX

DESCRIPTION

Rear suspension has a quadralink design, **Fig. 1,** This is basically two horizontal, pressed steel, lateral arms each side of the vehicle, attached to a pressed steel crossmember at the inner pivots and cast iron spindle assemblies at the outer pivots. The lateral arms control the toe change of the rear wheels. The third link of the quadralink system is a tie bar which connects the wheel spindle to a forward body mounted bracket. The fourth link is a MacPherson strut mounted on top of the wheel spindle. The strut controls the camber and reacts to braking torque. The tie bar and lateral arms connect through rubber bushes, the strut is mounted to the spindle assembly. The rear lateral arm joint to the crossmember allows toe adjustment by rotation of a cam bolt. The system has additional roll control by use of a stabilizer bar, connected between the crossmember and the front lateral arms. A hub and bearing assembly runs on the wheel spindle and locates on the brake drum or disc, and the wheel.

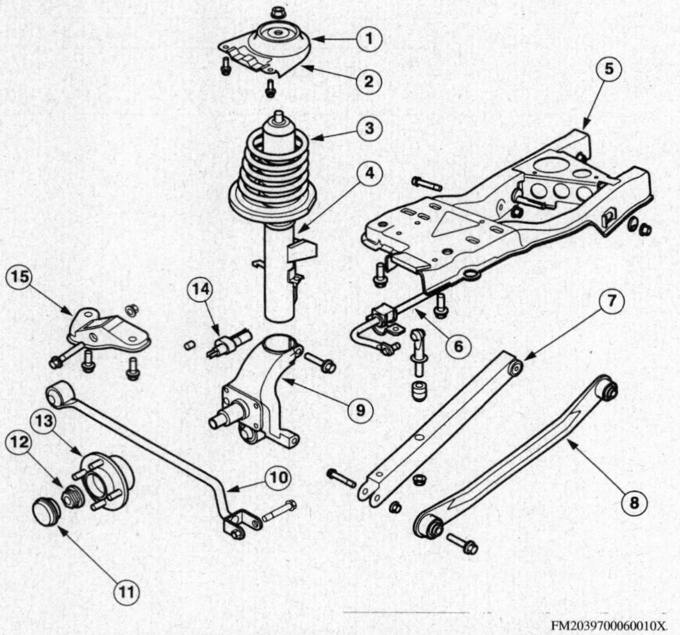

FM2039700060010X

Fig. 1 Exploded view of rear suspension (Part 1 of 2)

HUB & BEARING

REPLACE

1. Raise and support vehicle, then remove wheel.
2. **On models equipped with rear disc brakes,** remove caliper and brake rotor. **It is not necessary to disconnect hydraulic line from caliper; support caliper aside to prevent hydraulic line damage.**
3. **On models equipped with rear drum brakes,** remove brake drum retainer, then drum.
4. **On all models,** remove and discard rear axle wheel hub retainer, then remove wheel hub. **Do not use an impact wrench to loosen retainer; spindle damage may result.**
5. Reverse procedure to install. Tighten new retainer and wheel lug nuts to specifications.

WHEEL BEARING

ADJUST

Wheel bearings are pre-greased and sealed; as a result, they require no periodic maintenance. Their cartridge design prohibits adjustment.

REAR WHEEL SPINDLE

REPLACE

1. Raise and support vehicle, then remove wheel and rear anti-lock brake sensor.
2. Remove rear wheel hub and bearing assembly as described under "Hub & Bearing, Replace."
3. **On models equipped with rear disc brakes,** remove disc brake shield.
4. **On models equipped with rear drum brakes,** proceed as follows:
   a. Remove brake backing plate and position aside.
   b. Disconnect stabilizer bar link from lateral arm.
5. **On all models,** disconnect rear suspension tie rod and bushing at spindle, **Fig. 2.**
6. Disconnect rearward and forward suspension arms with bushings from spindle, then remove strut to spindle pinch bolt.
7. Remove spindle from strut assembly.
8. Reverse procedure to install, noting the following:
   a. When installing rear suspension arms, tie rods and their respective bushings on the spindle, tighten bolts snugly, but do not tighten to

Item	Description
1	Body mounting cup
2	Spring seat
3	Spring
4	Strut
5	Crossmember
6	Stabilizer bar
7	Front lower arm
8	Rear lower arm
9	Wheel spindle
10	Tie-bar
11	Dust cap
12	Hub retaining nut
13	Hub and bearing assembly
14	Wheel speed sensor
15	Tie-bar mounting bracket

FM2039700060020X

Fig. 1 Exploded view of rear suspension (Part 2 of 2)

specifications until all other components have been installed and vehicle weight is on the wheels.

b. **Do not use an impact wrench to tighten new wheel hub retainer, as spindle damage may result.**
c. Tighten all bolts and nuts to specifications.

STRUT

REPLACE

1. Raise and support vehicle, then remove wheel.
2. Detach anti-lock brake sensor wiring from strut assembly, then remove sensor.
3. **On models equipped with drum brakes,** clamp and disconnect rear brake hose from brake tube, then remove hose and retainer from strut assembly.
4. **On models equipped with disc brakes,** remove brake hose.
5. **On all models,** remove wheel spindle to suspension unit pinch bolt.
6. Remove wheel spindle from suspension unit.
7. Raise suspension unit of a jack and remove suspension unit from crossmember.
8. Remove suspension unit.

STRUT SERVICE

1. Position strut assembly in Rotunda strut spring compressor tool No. 014–00781, or equivalent, then compress spring.
2. Remove top nut, bracket, bushing and spring seat, **Fig. 3,** then slowly release

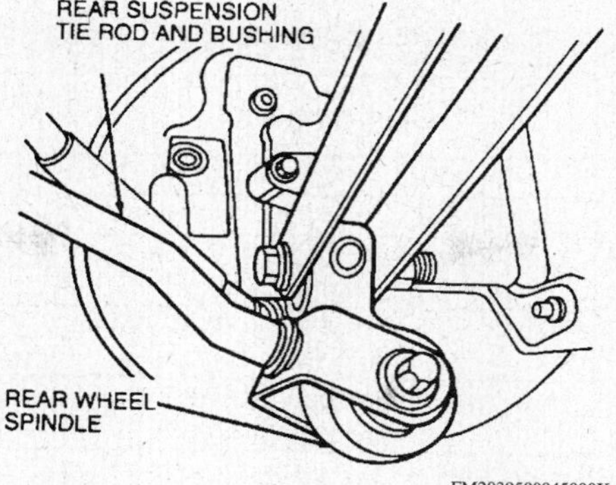

FM2039500045000X

Fig. 2 Rear spindle assembly

spring compressor tool.

3. Remove spring, dust shield and jounce bumper.
4. Reverse procedure to assemble. Tighten top nut to specifications.

CONTROL ARM

REPLACE

LOWER

FRONT ARM

1. Raise and support vehicle, then remove wheel.
2. Remove stabilizer bar link and bushing from front lateral arm, then front lateral arm from spindle.
3. Remove tie bar from spindle carrier, then release three exhaust mounting and support exhaust system.
4. Support crossmember and remove crossmember bolts and lower.
5. Reverse procedure to install, noting following:
   a. When installing forward arm and bushing to crossmember bolt and nut, ensure bolt head faces fuel tank. Tighten bolt and nut snugly, but do not final tighten until vehicle weight is resting upon rear wheels.
   b. Tighten all bolts and nuts to specifications.

REAR ARM

1. Raise and support vehicle, then remove wheel and disconnect rear arm from spindle.
2. Remove rear lateral arm from crossmember.
3. Reverse procedure to install, noting following:
   a. When installing rearward arm, connect to spindle and tighten bolts and nuts snugly, but do not final tighten until vehicle weight is resting upon rear wheels. **Tighten wheel lug nuts to specifications before lowering vehicle.**
   b. After vehicle weight is resting on rear wheels, tighten rearward arm bolts and nuts to specifications.

TIE ROD

REPLACE

1. Raise and support vehicle, then re-

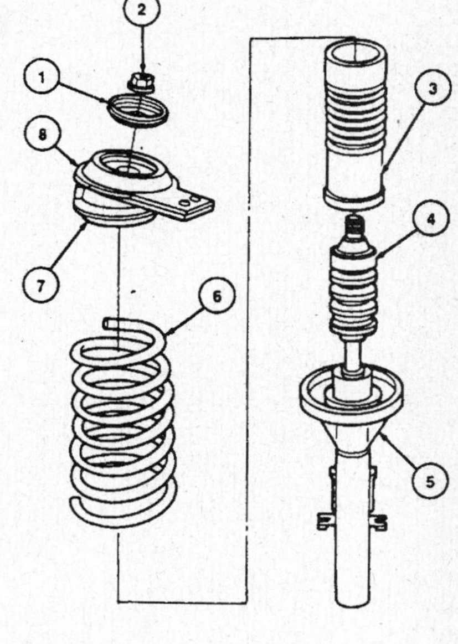

Item	Description
1	Rear Shock Absorber Bracket
2	Shock Absorber Mounting Nut
3	Rear Shock Absorber Dust Boot
4	Rear Suspension Jounce Bumper
5	Shock Absorber
6	Rear Spring
7	Spring Seat
8	Shock Absorber Bushing

FM2039500047000X

Fig. 3 Exploded view of strut assembly

move wheel and disconnect parking brake cable and conduit from forward tie rod bracket.

2. Remove exhaust rubber from tie bar bracket.
3. Remove tie strap securing parking brake rear cable and conduit to rear suspension tie rod and bushing.
4. Disconnect tie rod and bushing assembly at spindle.
5. Remove bolts, tie rod and bushing assembly, then the front bracket from vehicle.
6. Remove bolt and tie rod and bushing assembly from front bracket.
7. Reverse procedure to install.

STABILIZER BAR

REPLACE

1. Raise and support vehicle.
2. Remove stabilizer bar links and bushings from front lateral arms.
3. Remove stabilizer bar bushings.
4. Remove righthand tie bar from wheel spindle, then the stabilizer bar.
5. Reverse procedure to install.

TIGHTENING SPECIFICATIONS

Year	Component	Torque/Ft. Lbs.
1998–2002	Anti-Lock Sensor Bolt	90①
	Drum Brake Backing Plate Bolts	33–40
	Rearward Rear Suspension Arm To Crossmember Bolt	52–79
	Spindle To Forward Rear Suspension Arm Bolt	52–79
	Spindle To Rearward Rear Suspension Arm Bolt	75–102
	Stabilizer Bar Bracket Bolts	14–19
	Stabilizer Bar Link To Rear Suspension Arm	22–30
	Strut Mounting Bolts	17–22
	Strut Top Nut	30–43
	Strut To Spindle Pinch Bolt	52–72
	Tie Rod Forward Bracket To Body Bolts	75–102
	Tie Rod To Spindle Bolt	75–102
	Wheel Hub Retainer	214
	Wheel Lug Nuts	94

① — Inch lbs.

Front Suspension & Steering

NOTE: On Air Bag Equipped Models, Refer To "Air Bag System Precautions" Located In The Front Of This Manual For System Disarming & Arming Procedures.

NOTE: Refer To "Computer Relearn Procedures" Located In The Front Of This Manual When Battery Power To The Computer Has Been Interrupted.

INDEX

PRECAUTIONS

BATTERY GROUND CABLE

Prior to service, disconnect battery ground cable and isolate as required.

AIR BAG SYSTEMS

Refer to "Air Bag System Precautions" in front of this manual for system disarming and arming procedures.

DESCRIPTION

Front suspension utilizes McPherson struts, a stabilizer bar, lower control arms and a tubular perimeter frame. Steering control is maintained by an integral power rack and pinion steering gear coupled with a belt driven, vane type power steering pump. Power steering fluid is contained in a remote reservoir.

WHEEL BEARING

ADJUST

Wheel bearings are pre-greased and sealed; as a result, they require no periodic maintenance. Their cartridge design prohibits adjustment.

HUB & BEARING

REPLACE

1. Raise and support vehicle, then remove wheel, caliper and rotor. **It is not necessary to disconnect brake hydraulic line to caliper, but it is necessary to prevent caliper from hanging on brake hose by supporting it from vehicle chassis.**
2. Remove front brake anti-lock sensor and tie rod end cotter pin, then loosen tie rod end to knuckle nut.
3. Separate tie rod end from knuckle using rod end remover tool No. 3290-D, or equivalent, then insert steel rod into front disc brake rotor to prevent turning and remove front axle wheel hub retaining nut.
4. Separate halfshaft from wheel hub using special tools as shown in **Fig. 1. Support halfshaft during separation from wheel hub.**
5. Reverse procedure to install. Tighten bolts and nuts to specifications.

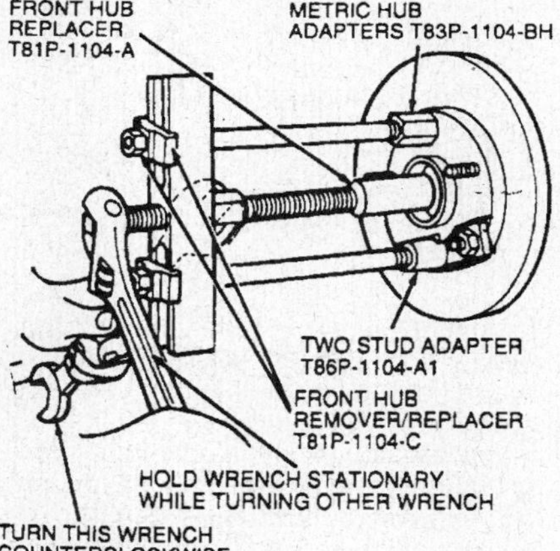

Fig. 1 Hub assembly removal

BALL JOINT INSPECTION

1. Raise and support vehicle.
2. Attach dial indicator with bracketry tool No. 4201-C, or equivalent, at ball joint to be checked.
3. To measure lateral movement between front wheel knuckle and front suspension arm lower ball joint, grasp tire at top and bottom and slowly move tire in and out.
4. Record radial play from dial indicator. If reading exceeds .015 inch, replace ball joint.

BALL JOINT

REPLACE

REMOVAL

1. Raise and support vehicle, then remove wheel and lower arm as described under "Control Arm, Replace."
2. Drill a .118 inch pilot hole through each rivet, **Fig. 2,** then drill a .354 inch hole in rivets to a depth of .472 inch.
3. Using a .275–.314 inch diameter punch, drive rivets out, then remove ball joint from vehicle.

INSTALLATION

1. Allow protective cover to remain on ball joint to protect seal, then position ball joint in lower arm.
2. Install three bolts and nuts in lower arm as shown, **Fig. 3,** to replace rivets.
3. Install lower arm as described under "Control Arm, Replace," then install wheel and lower vehicle.

STRUT

REPLACE

1. Raise and support vehicle, then remove wheel and, while holding piston rod with a hex wrench as shown in **Fig. 4,** remove strut top nut.
2. Disconnect stabilizer bar link from strut assembly, then disengage brake hose and anti-lock brake sensor wiring from strut brackets.

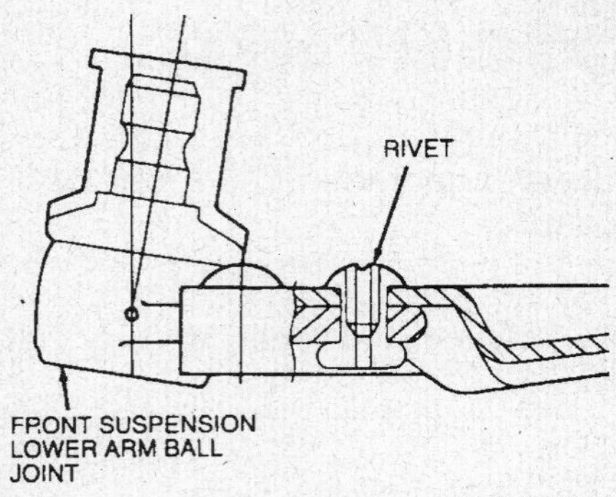

Fig. 2 Ball joint rivets

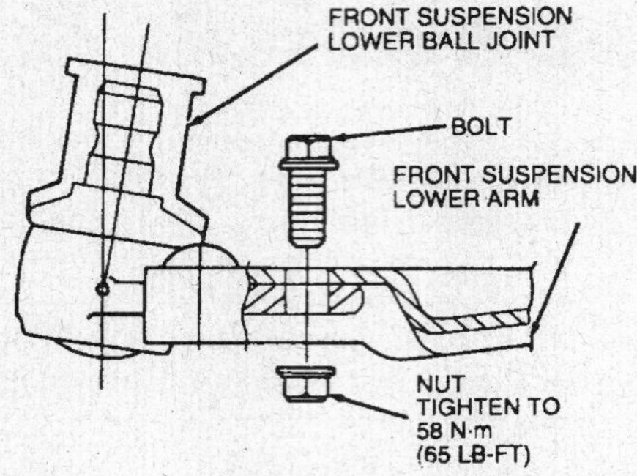

Fig. 3 Ball joint bolt installation

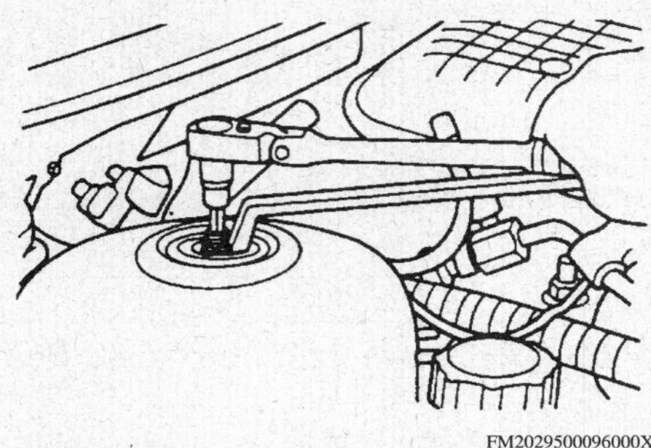

Fig. 4 Strut top nut replacement

3. Remove strut to knuckle pinch bolt, then strut assembly.
4. Reverse procedure to install, noting following:
   a. Install strut top nut as shown in **Fig. 4** before tightening strut to knuckle pinch bolt.
   b. During stabilizer bar link installation, avoid damaging ball joint seal.
   c. Tighten bolts and nuts to specifications.

COIL SPRING & STRUT SERVICE

1. Remove strut assembly as described under "Strut, Replace," then position assembly in Rotunda spring compressor tool No. 086–00029, or equivalent.
2. Compress coil spring and remove thrust bearing retainer nut, thrust bearing, spring seat and dust shield, **Fig. 5.**
3. Release spring compressor tension and remove coil spring from strut assembly, then remove jounce bumper, **Fig. 5.**
4. Reverse procedure to assemble, noting following:
   a. Compress coil spring for installation using Rotunda spring compressor tool No. 086-0029B, or equivalent.
   b. Ensure coil spring seats properly in spring seat notch.
   c. Tighten thrust bearing nut to specifications.

CONTROL ARM

REPLACE

LOWER

LEFT SIDE

1. Support radiator assembly.
2. **On models equipped with 2.0L engine,** remove heat shield and catalytic converter retaining nuts from exhaust manifold.
3. **On all models,** raise and support vehicle, then remove 3–way catalytic converter, then disconnect steering column lower yoke.
4. **On models equipped with manual transaxle,** disconnect gearshift rod and clevis.
5. **On all models,** remove lower front radiator cover, radiator supports and ball joint to knuckle pinch bolts.
6. Remove lower arm ball joints from knuckle, then disconnect power steering cooler lines at righthand front subframe and stabilizer bar link at front stabilizer bar.
7. Remove front and rear engine mount through bolts, then position Rotunda powertrain lift tool No. 014–00765, or equivalent, under front subframe.
8. Remove lower arm bushing to subframe nuts, then lower subframe to gain access to lower suspension mounting bolts.
9. Remove four lower arm to subframe bolts and nuts, **Fig. 6,** then separate lower arm from subframe.
10. Reverse procedure to install, noting following:
    a. Install lower arm bolts as shown, **Fig. 6.**
    b. Tighten all bolts and nuts to specifications.

RIGHT SIDE

1. Raise and support vehicle, then remove wheel and ball joint to knuckle pinch bolt.
2. Separate lower arm ball joint from knuckle, then remove four lower arm bushing to subframe bolts, **Fig. 6.**
3. Reverse procedure to install, noting following:
   a. Install lower arm bolts as shown, **Fig. 6.**
   b. Tighten all bolts and nuts to specifications.

STEERING KNUCKLE

REPLACE

1. Remove hub as described under "Hub & Bearing, Replace," then remove pinch bolt securing knuckle to lower arm ball joint.
2. Remove strut to knuckle pinch bolt, then knuckle, **Fig. 7.**
3. Reverse procedure to install, noting following:
   a. Install new pinch bolts and nuts on knuckle mounts.
   b. Tighten all bolts and nuts to specifications.

STABILIZER BAR

REPLACE

1. Raise and support vehicle, then remove both front wheels.
2. Remove stabilizer bar link from strut assembly, **Fig. 8,** then use ball joint remover tool No. D88L-3006-A, or equivalent, to remove link from stabilizer bar. **Avoid damaging stabilizer bar link ball joint seal during removal. Link assembly must be replaced if seal is damaged.**
3. Remove four stabilizer bar insulator bracket to subframe bolts, then stabilizer bar.
4. Reverse procedure to install, noting following:
   a. **Avoid damaging stabilizer bar link ball joint seal during installation. Link assembly must be replaced if seal is damaged.**
   b. Tighten bolts and nuts to specifications.

TIE ROD END

REPLACE

1. Remove and discard cotter pin and nut from tie rod end, then use tie rod end remover tool No. 3290-D, or equivalent, to separate tie rod end from steering knuckle.
2. While holding tie rod end with a suitable wrench, loosen jam nut slightly. **Allow jam nut to remain as close to its original position as possible for tie rod end installation depth reference.**
3. Using suitable pliers, remove tie rod end from tie rod.
4. Reverse procedure to install, noting following:
   a. Thread new tie rod end onto tie rod only until it reaches jam nut, then secure with jam nut until wheel alignment can be inspected and set.
   b. Install a new tie rod end stud nut and cotter pin.
   c. Tighten tie rod end to knuckle nut and tie rod end jam nut to specifications.
   d. Set front wheel toe to specifications as described in "Wheel Alignment" section.

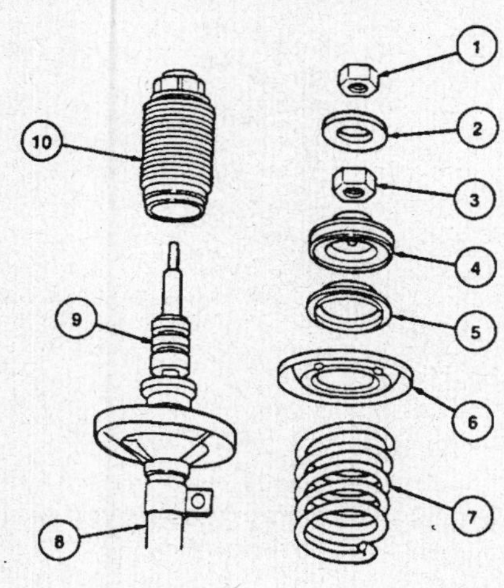

Item	Description
1	Nut
2	Retainer
3	Upper Mount Retainer Nut
4	Upper Mount
5	Bearing
6	Spring Seat
7	Front Coil Spring
8	Front Shock Absorber
9	Jounce Bumper
10	Dust Shield

FM2029500097000X

Fig. 5 Exploded view of strut assembly

POWER STEERING GEAR

REPLACE

1. Center the steering wheel and lock in position.
2. Working from inside passenger compartment, remove clamp plate bolt securing steering column shaft to flexible coupling.
3. Rotate clamp plate to disengage from steering gear pinion shaft, then carefully remove floor seal.
4. Remove pinch bolt from flexible coupling, then slide coupling from steering gear pinion shaft.
5. Using a suction gun, or equivalent fluid suction tool, remove as much power steering fluid from pump auxiliary reservoir as possible.
6. Disconnect power steering return hose from pump auxiliary reservoir, then raise and support vehicle.
7. Remove front subframe assembly, then remove steering gear cover plate from subframe as shown, **Fig. 9.**
8. Disconnect pressure and return hose unions from power steering gear, then remove two bolts securing gear to subframe.
9. Separate steering gear from subframe. **Do not attempt to disassemble any part of steering gear. If any steering gear service is necessary, entire unit must be replaced.**
10. Remove spindle connecting rods and boots from steering gear assembly.
11. Reverse procedure to install, noting following:
    a. Install new plastic seals on hydraulic lines.
    b. Tighten all bolts and nuts to specifications.
    c. Refill power steering fluid reservoir and bleed system as described under "Power Steering System Bleed."
    d. If tie rod ends were loosened during procedure, inspect and adjust wheel alignment as described in "Wheel Alignment" section.

POWER STEERING PUMP

REPLACE

2.0L ENGINE

1. Raise and support vehicle, then remove lower splash shield.
2. Rotate drive belt tensioner clockwise and remove drive belt.
3. Disconnect power steering pump high pressure line union and drain fluid into suitable container.
4. Disconnect power steering low pressure hose.
5. Remove four power steering pump bolts, then the pump.
6. Reverse procedures to install.

2.5L ENGINE

1. Rotate drive belt tensioner clockwise, then remove drive belt.
2. Disconnect power steering line and hose from pump.
3. Support engine using engine support tool No. D88L-6000-A, or equivalent, then remove engine mount bracket, **Fig. 10.**
4. Drain cooling system , then remove coolant expansion tank.
5. Remove engine mount attaching bolts, then the engine mount.
6. Holding center of power steering pump pulley with a suitable hex head wrench, remove four power steering pump attaching bolts.
7. Remove pump bracket attaching bolt, then the retaining plate nuts and bolts, **Fig. 11.**
8. Remove power steering pump attaching bolts, then the pump.
9. Reverse procedures to install.

POWER STEERING SYSTEM BLEED

LESS AIR EVACUATOR TOOL

1. Raise and support front of vehicle, then fill power steering pump reservoir until fluid level is between MIN and MAX marks.

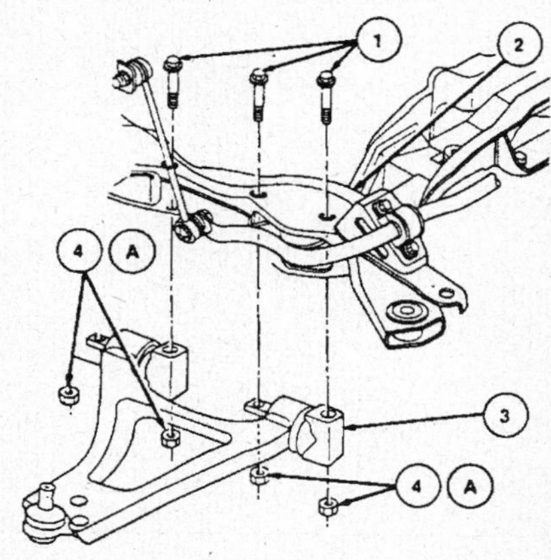

Item	Description
1	Bolts (4 Req'd)
2	Sub-frame
3	Front Suspension Lower Arm
4	Nuts (4 Req'd)
A	Tighten to 130 N·m (96 Lb-Ft)

FM2029500098000X

Fig. 6 Lower arm replacement

2. Disconnect Ignition Control Module (ICM) lead to prevent engine from starting, then crank engine for 30 seconds.
3. Check fluid level and add as necessary; then, while cranking engine again for 30 seconds, rotate steering wheel from lock to lock repeatedly. **Do not hold wheel at either lock more than five seconds, power steering pump damage may result.**
4. Check and add fluid as necessary, then reconnect ICM and lower vehicle.

WITH AIR EVACUATOR TOOL

1. Fill pump reservoir to MAX mark.
2. Start engine and slowly turn steering wheel from lock to lock
3. Switch engine off and check fluid level, add fluid as necessary.
4. Connect a suitable stopper to hand vacuum pump tube and insert into reservoir filler neck.
5. Start engine and slowly turn steering wheel to right, just off stop.
6. Turn engine off and apply 5 inches Hg of vacuum pressure until air is purged from system, minimum of five minutes. If pressure drops by more than 2 inches Hg in five minutes, system should be checked for leaks.
7. Depressurize system at vacuum pump, then repeat bleed operation turning steering wheel to left, just off stop.
8. If noise level is still unacceptable, leave vehicle standing overnight then repeat bleed procedure.

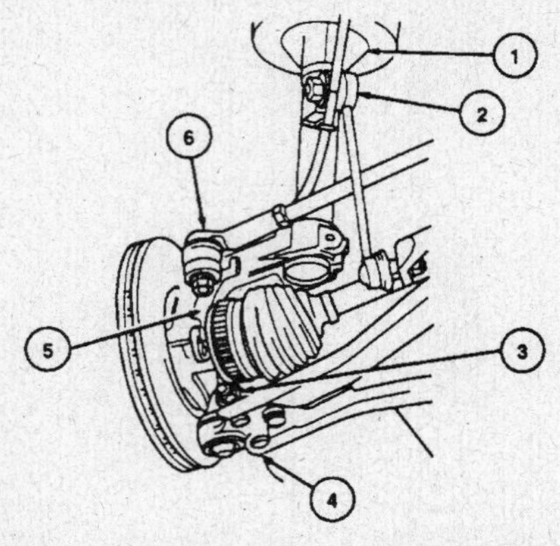

Item	Description
1	Front Shock Absorber
2	Stabilizer Bar Link
3	Lower Ball Joint-To-Knuckle Pinch Bolt
4	Front Suspension Lower Arm
5	Front Wheel Knuckle
6	Front Wheel Spindle Connecting Rod

FM2029500099000X

Fig. 7 Knuckle assembly

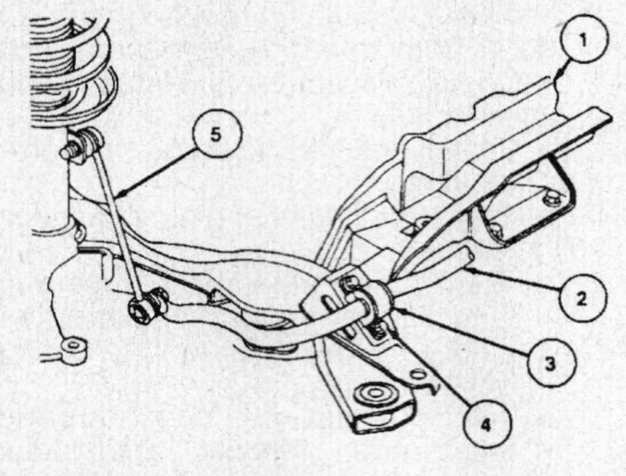

Item	Description
1	Front Sub-Frame
2	Stabilizer Bar
3	Stabilizer Bar Bracket
4	Stabilizer Bar Bracket Bolt (4 Req'd)
5	Stabilizer Bar Link

FM2029500100000X

Fig. 8 Stabilizer bar assembly

STEERING GEAR COVER PLATE

STEERING GEAR

FRONT SUB-FRAME

FM6029500193000X

Fig. 9 Steering gear cover plate removal

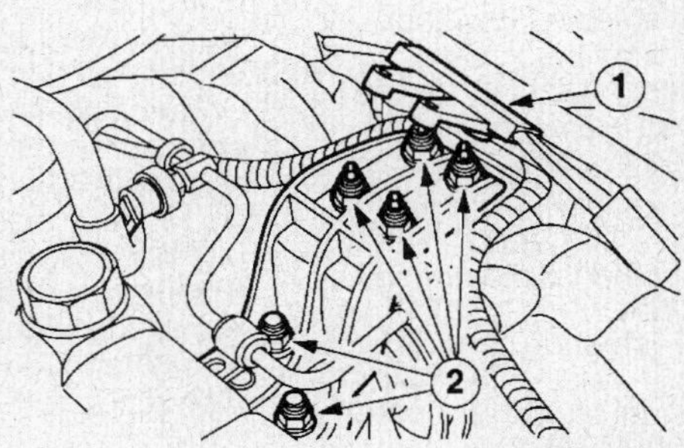

Fig. 10 Engine mount bracket. 2.5L engine

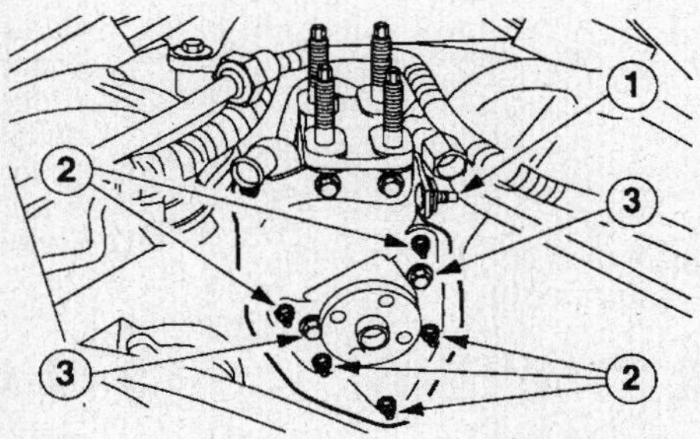

Fig. 11 Retaining plate & bracket. 2.5L engine

TIGHTENING SPECIFICATIONS

Year	Component	Torque/Ft. Lbs.
1998–2002	Engine Mount Through Bolts	40–55
	Exhaust Manifold Heat Shield Bolts & Nuts	53①
	Lower Arm To Subframe Bolts	96
	Lower Ball Joint Pinch Bolt	65
	Power Steering Hose To Bracket Bolts & Nut	53①
	Power Steering Hose To Power Steering Pump Fittings	48
	Power Steering Hose Union To Steering Gear	23
	Power Steering Pump Mounting Bolts	18
	Power Steering Pump Pulley Bolts (2.5L)	96①
	Stabilizer Bar Insulator Mounting Bracket To Subframe Bolts	37
	Stabilizer Bar Link Nut	37
	Steering Gear Cover Plate To Subframe	37
	Steering Gear To Subframe Bolts	101
	Steering Shaft Clamp Plate Bolt	18
	Steering Shaft Flex Coupling Pinch Bolt	21
	Strut Thrust Bearing Nut	44
	Strut To Front Wheel Knuckle Pinch Bolt	62
	Strut Top Mounting Nut	37
	Tie Rod End Jam Nut	35–50
	Tie Rod End To Knuckle Nut	18–22
	Traction Assist Module Bolts	53①
	Wheel Hub Retainer	210
	Wheel Lug Nuts	94

① — Inch lbs.

Wheel Alignment

INDEX

PRELIMINARY INSPECTION

1. Ensure all tires are inflated to proper pressure.
2. Inspect tire for wear patterns that may indicate improper wheel alignment, tire imbalance or damage due to bulges or separation.
3. Inspect suspension for modifications such as trailer towing equipment or heavy duty handling components.
4. Inspect vehicle for signs of overloading or sagging; ensure luggage compartment does not contain heavy objects.
5. Road test vehicle to isolate area of concern.

FRONT WHEEL ALIGNMENT

All wheel alignment inspections must be performed on an alignment rack leveled to within 1⁄16 inch side to side and front to rear. Alignment equipment must be capable of compensating for wheel runout and of measuring left and right front wheel toe independently.

CASTER & CAMBER

Front wheel caster and camber are preset by manufacturer and are not adjustable. If caster and camber are not as indicated under "Front Wheel Alignment Specifications," inspect suspension components for damage, modification or excessive wear.

TOE

1. Start engine and rotate steering wheel back and forth several times, then place it in its centered position (wheels straight ahead).
2. Stop engine and lock steering wheel in position, then loosen steering ball stud dust seal outer clamp and slide off end of seal to prevent seal from twisting during adjustment.
3. Loosen tie rod end jam nuts, then adjust left and right tie rod ends until each wheel's toe measurement is ½ of total toe as specified under "Front Wheel Alignment Specifications."
4. **Torque** tie rod end jam nuts to 35–46 ft. lbs., then position steering ball stud dust seal outer clamp over seal and tighten securely. **Ensure seal is not twisted.**

REAR WHEEL ALIGNMENT

1. Loosen bolt attaching rear suspension arm and bushing to subframe.
2. Rotate alignment cam to obtain specified toe.
3. **Torque** rear suspension arm and bushing retaining nut to 62 ft. lbs.

CROWN VICTORIA & GRAND MARQUIS

NOTE: Refer To Rear Of This Manual For Vehicle Manufacturer's Special Service Tool Suppliers.

INDEX OF SERVICE OPERATIONS

Specifications

GENERAL ENGINE SPECIFICATIONS

Engine Liter (VIN)①	Fuel System	Bore & Stroke	Compression Ratio	Net H.P. @ RPM②	Maximum Torque Ft. Lbs. @ RPM	Normal Oil Pressure, psi
1998–99						
4.6L (W)	SEFI	3.55 x 3.54	9.0	⑥	④	—
4.6L (9)⑤	SEFI	3.55 x 3.54	10.0	175 @ 4500	235 @ 3500	—
2000						
4.6L (W)	SEFI	3.55 x 3.54	9.0	200 @ 4250	275 @ 3000	40–70③
4.6L (9)⑤	SEFI	3.55 x 3.54	10.0	175 @ 4500	235 @ 3500	40–70③
2001–02						
4.6L (W)	SEFI	3.55 x 3.54	9.4	⑦	⑧	40–70③
4.6L (9)⑤	SEFI	3.55 x 3.54	10.0	175 @ 4500	235 @ 3500	40–70③

SEFI — Sequential Multi-Port Electronic Fuel Injection
① — The eighth digit of VIN denotes engine code.
② — Ratings are net-as installed in vehicle.
③ — At 200°F.
④ — 275 @ 3000 RPM w/single exhaust; 285 @ 3000 RPM w/dual exhaust.
⑤ — Natural Gas Vehicle (NGV).
⑥ — 200 @ 4250 RPM w/single exhaust; 215 @ 4500 RPM w/dual exhaust.
⑦ — 220 @ 4750 RPM w/single exhaust; 235 @ 4750 RPM w/dual exhaust.
⑧ — 265 @ 4000 RPM w/single exhaust; 275 @ 4000 RPM w/dual exhaust.

TUNE UP SPECIFICATIONS

Engine Liter (VIN)①	Spark Plug Gap	Ignition Timing, BTDC				Curb Idle Speed, RPM③		Fast Idle Speed, RPM③		Fuel Pump Pressure, psi	Valve Clearance, Inch
		Firing Order Fig.	Man. Trans.	Auto. Trans.	Mark Fig.	Man. Trans.	Auto. Trans.	Man. Trans.	Auto. Trans.		
4.6L (W)	0.054	A⑩	—	10⑤	②	—	⑥	—	⑥	30–45⑦	⑧
4.6L (9)⑨	0.044	A⑩	—	10⑤	②	—	⑥	—	⑥	80–120④	⑧

BTDC — Before Top Dead Center
① — The eighth digit of Vehicle Identification Number (VIN) denotes engine code.
② — Equipped w/crankshaft sensor.
③ — When checking idle speed, set parking brake & block drive wheels.
④ — Locate vehicle in a well ventilated area away from heat, spark & flame producing equipment. Using extreme caution, connect a suitable natural gas approved fuel pressure gauge to the fuel pressure Schrader valve. Release fuel pressure in fuel injection supply manifold back to fuel tanks. Place ignition switch in On position, then start engine if possible. Place ignition switch in Off position. After two minutes, check fuel pressure reading on gauge.
⑤ — Non-adjustable.
⑥ — Idle speed is controlled by an automatic idle speed control. No adjustment is required.
⑦ — Wrap shop towel around fuel diagnostic valve to prevent fuel spillage. Connect suitable fuel pressure gauge to fuel diagnostic valve. Place ignition switch in On position to energize fuel pump & check pressure gauge reading.
⑧ — Equipped w/hydraulic lifters.
⑨ — Natural Gas Vehicle.
⑩ — Equipped w/coil on spark plug ignition. Cylinder numbering front to rear, righthand bank, 1-2-3-4; lefthand bank 5-6-7-8. Firing order, 1-3-7-2-6-5-4-8.

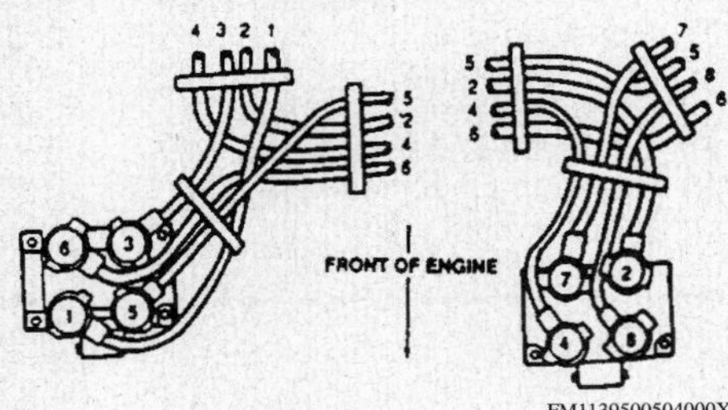

Fig. A

FRONT WHEEL ALIGNMENT SPECIFICATIONS

Year	Caster Angle, Degrees		Camber Angle, Degrees				Total Toe-In, Inch	Toe Out On Turns, Deg.		Ball Joint Wear
	Limits	Desired	Limits		Desired			Outer Wheel	Inner Wheel	
			Left	Right	Left	Right				
1998–2002	+4.75 to +6.25	+5.5	−1.25 to +0.25	−1.25 to +0.25	−0.5	−0.5	1⁄16	18.51	20	①②

① — Refer to “Ball Joint Inspection” in “Front Suspension & Steering” section.

② — Lower ball joint backlash, 0.03937 inch maximum; Upper ball joint backlash, 0.015 inch maximum; Ball joint endplay, 0.02 inch maximum.

VEHICLE RIDE HEIGHT SPECIFICATIONS

Model	Year	Body Style	Manufacturer's Original Tire Size	Measurement Points & Specifications②					
				Front③			Rear③		
				Dim.	Specification⑤		Dim.	Specification④	
					Inches	mm		Inches	mm
Crown Victoria	1998–2002	Base	①	1	1.2	29.6	2	5.4	138.0
		Air Suspension	①	1	1.1	27.4	2	5.2	132.4
		Handling Package	①	1	1.0	26.0	2	5.2	132.4
		Police/NGV	①	1	1.0	26.4	2	5.2	132.3
Grand Marquis	1998–2002	Base	①	1	1.2	29.6	2	5.4	138.0
		Air Suspension	①	1	1.1	27.4	2	5.2	132.4
		Handling Package	①	1	1.0	26.0	2	5.2	132.4

1 Dim. — Distance from lower control arm bolt head center to ground minus distance from ball stud center to ground.

2 Dim. — Distance between top of rear axle and inner frame reinforcement.

Dim. — Dimension

① — See door sticker or inside of glove box for manufacturer's original tire size specifications. If tires on vehicle do not match manufacturer's original tire size & measurement is not within limits, it will be necessary to refer to the “Non-Standard Tire & Wheel Size Adjustment To Ride Height Specification & Tire Size Adjustment Charts” in the front of this manual for approximate changes in ride height specifications.

② — Measurement is with fuel, radiator coolant and engine oil full, spare tire, jack, hand tools and mats in designated positions and tires properly inflated.

③ — Ride height lean (side to side) should be within 0.50 inch (12.7 mm).

④ — ± 0.3 inch (7.6 mm).

⑤ — ± 0.5 inch (12.7 mm).

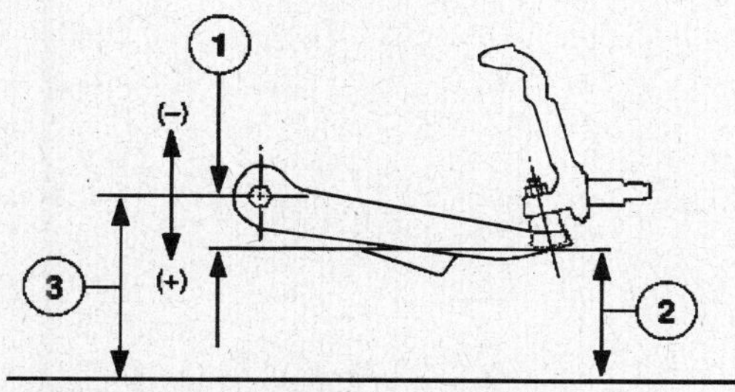

Item	Description
1	Ride height
2	Measurement (center of ball stud to ground)
3	Measurement (center of bolt head to ground)

FM2020100206000X

Front ride height measurement

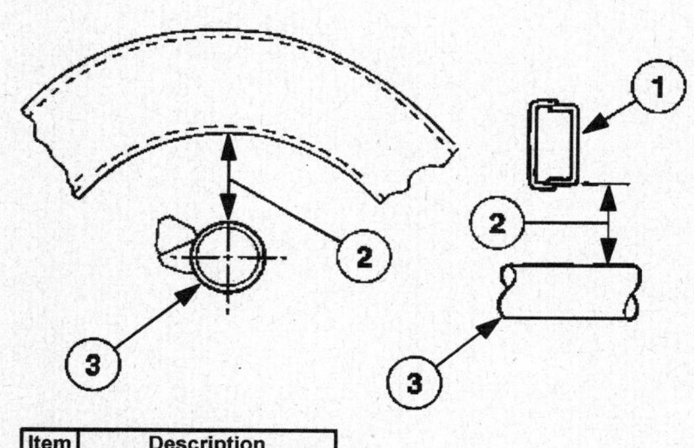

Item	Description
1	Inner frame reinforcement
2	Ride height
3	Rear axle

FM2030100153000X

Rear ride height measurement

FLUID CAPACITIES & COOLING SYSTEM DATA

Year	Coolant Capacity, Qts.	Coolant Type	Radiator Cap Relief Pressure, psi	Thermo. Opening Temp.	Fuel Tank Gals.	Engine Refill Qts.	Transmission Oil		
							Man. Trans. Pts.	Auto. Trans. Qts.①	Rear Axle Oil Pts.
1998–2002	17.9	⑤	16	192	19	5②	—	13.9③	3.75④

① — Approximate, make final check w/dipstick.
② — Includes filter. Final check is made w/dipstick.
③ — 2000–02 police model, 12.8 qts.
④ — Traction-Lok axles, add 4 oz. of Ford Motor Co. Friction Modifier No. C8AZ-19B546-A, or equivalent.
⑤ — Always fill cooling system with same coolant that is present in the system. Do not mix coolant types. For models w/green coolant use ethylene glycol, Motorcraft Premium Engine Coolant VC-4 (in Oregon VC-5), or equivalent meeting Ford specification ESE-M97B44-A. For models w/orange coolant use coolant Motorcraft Premium Gold Engine Coolant VC-7-A meeting Ford specifications WSS-M97B51-A1.

LUBRICANT DATA

Year	Model	Lubricant Type				
		Transmission		Rear Axle	Power Steering	Brake System
		Manual	Automatic			
1998	All	—	Mercon V	80-90W①③	②	DOT 3 or 4
1999–2002	All	—	Mercon V	80-90W①③	Mercon ATF	DOT 3 or 4

① — Premium thermally stable rear axle lubricant part No. XY-80W90-QL, or equivalent, meeting Ford specification WSP-M2C197-A.
② — Premium power steering fluid meeting Ford Specification ESW-M2C33-F
③ — Traction-Lok axles, add 4 oz. of Ford Motor Co. Friction Modifier No. C8AZ-19B546-A, or equivalent.

Electrical

NOTE: On Air Bag Equipped Models, Refer To "Air Bag System Precautions" Located In The Front Of This Manual For System Disarming & Arming Procedures.

NOTE: Refer To "Computer Relearn Procedures" Located In The Front Of This Manual When Battery Power To The Computer Has Been Interrupted.

NOTE: Prior To Performing Any Service Operations Listed In This Section, Consult The "Technical Service Bulletins" Section For Related Information.

INDEX

PRECAUTIONS

AIR BAG SYSTEMS

Refer to "Air Bag System Precautions" in the front of this manual for system disarming and arming procedures.

BATTERY GROUND CABLE

Prior to service, disconnect battery ground cable and isolate as required.

FUSE PANEL & FLASHER LOCATION

The fuse panel is located behind the lefthand side of the instrument panel.

The emergency flashers are located on the lefthand rear of the trunk, front flasher is located in righthand rear of engine compartment and the rear flasher is located center rear of trunk.

FUEL PUMP RELAY LOCATION

The fuel pump relay is located on the lefthand side of engine compartment, in the relay center.

RELAY CENTER LOCATION

The relay center is located on the lefthand side of the engine compartment.

STARTER

REPLACE

1. Raise and support front of vehicle.
2. Remove starter motor solenoid terminal cover and disconnect cables.
3. Remove bolt, then position transmission cooler lines and bracket aside.
4. Remove two upper mounting bolts, lower bolt and starter motor.
5. Reverse procedure to install, noting the following:
   a. **Torque** starter bolts to 15–20 ft. lbs.
   b. **Torque** S-terminal cable eyelet with washer nut to 40–57 inch lbs.
   c. **Torque** starter cable B-terminal nut to 72–120 inch lbs.
   d. **Torque** transmission cooler line bracket bolt to 84 inch lbs.

COIL PACK

REPLACE

1. Disconnect engine control sensor wiring from ignition coil and radio ignition interference capacitor.
2. Disconnect ignition wires by squeezing locking tabs and twisting while pulling upward.
3. Remove ignition coil mounting screws and ignition coil with radio ignition interference capacitor.
4. Reverse procedure to install, noting the following:
   a. **Torque** coil pack mounting bolts to 40–61 inch lbs.
   b. Apply dielectric compound No. D7AZ-19A331-A, or equivalent, to ignition wire boots.

COIL UNITS

REPLACE

1. **On 1999–2002 models,** remove air cleaner outlet tube.
2. **On all models,** remove fuel rail and disconnect engine control sensor wiring connector from coil per plug units.
3. Remove mounting bolts and coil per plug units.
4. Reverse procedure to install. **Torque** mounting bolts to 72–108 inch lbs.

IGNITION LOCK

REPLACE

FUNCTIONING

The following procedures are for vehicles that have a functioning ignition switch lock cylinder, ignition key is available, or the lock cylinder key numbers are known and key can be made.

1. Turn lock cylinder to Run position.
2. Insert 1/8 inch diameter wire pin or small drift punch in hole in trim shroud under lock cylinder.
3. Depress retaining pin while pulling out on lock cylinder to remove from column housing.
4. Install lock cylinder by turning to Run position and depressing retaining pin.
5. Insert lock cylinder into housing.
6. Ensure cylinder is fully seated and aligned in interlocking washer before turning key to OFF position. This will permit cylinder retaining pin to extend into cylinder housing hole.
7. Lock cylinder using key.
8. Ensure correct mechanical operation in all positions.

NON-FUNCTIONING

The following procedure is for vehicles that have a inoperative ignition lock cylinder and the ignition switch cannot be rotated because of a lost or broken lock cylinder key, unknown key number, or an ignition switch cap that has been damaged to the extent that the key cannot be rotated.

1. Remove steering wheel as described under "Steering Wheel, Replace."
2. Twist ignition cap or bezel using suitable channel lock or vise-grip type pliers until it separates from ignition switch.
3. Drill down middle of key slot approximately 1¾ inches using suitable 3/8 inch diameter drill until ignition switch lock cylinder breaks loose from breakaway base of ignition switch lock cylinder.
4. Remove lock cylinder and drill shavings from steering column tube flange.
5. Remove steering column upper bearing retainer, steering column lock housing bearing, ignition switch lock cylinder and steering column lock gear. Thoroughly clean all drill shavings and other foreign material from casting.
6. Install new ignition lock cylinder as described under "Lock Cylinder, Functioning."

IGNITION SWITCH

REPLACE

1998

1. Remove self-tapping screws, steering column shroud and tilt lever, as required.
2. Remove instrument panel lower steering column cover.
3. Disconnect ignition switch electrical connector.
4. Rotate ignition key lock cylinder to Run position and remove two ignition switch mounting screws.
5. Disconnect ignition switch from actuator.
6. Reverse procedure to install, noting the following:
   a. Move switch slightly back and forth to align mounting holes with column mounting holes.
   b. Ensure proper operation of ignition switch in all positions.

1999–2002

1. Remove pin-type retainers and position lefthand instrument panel insulator aside.
2. Disconnect courtesy lamp and remove lefthand instrument panel insulator.
3. Remove lower instrument panel steering column opening cover.
4. Remove five bolts and instrument panel steering column opening cover reinforcement.
5. Disconnect ignition switch electrical connector.
6. Ensure ignition key is in Off position.
7. Remove ignition switch bolts and switch.
8. Reverse procedure to install, noting the following:
   a. **Torque** ignition switch bolts to 7–11 inch lbs.
   b. **Torque** reinforcement bolts to 31–45 inch lbs.
   c. **Torque** instrument panel insulator bolts to 19–26 inch lbs.

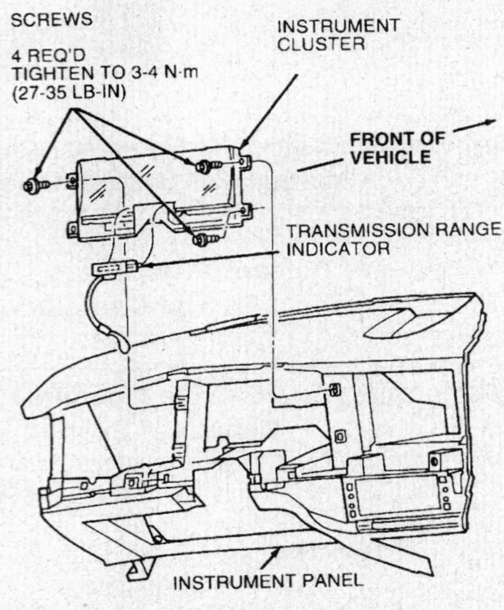

Fig. 1 Instrument cluster replacement

HEADLAMP SWITCH

REPLACE

1998

1. Remove knob from headlamp switch by grasping knob and pulling out.
2. Remove instrument panel finish panel from instrument panel.
3. Disconnect main wiring connectors from headlamp switch.
4. Remove mounting nut and headlamp switch.
5. Reverse procedure to install.

1999–2002

1. Remove instrument panel cluster finish panel.
2. Unclip switch and remove headlamp switch.
3. Reverse procedure to install.

STOP LIGHT SWITCH

REPLACE

REMOVAL

The switch side plate nearest brake pedal is slotted, it is not necessary to remove brake master cylinder push rod and one spacer washer from brake pedal pin.

1. Lift locking tab and disconnect connector.
2. Remove hairpin retainer and slide switch, pushrod, nylon washers and bushings away from brake pedal.

INSTALLATION

1. Position switch so U-shaped side is nearest brake pedal and directly over or under pin.
2. Slide switch down or up trapping master cylinder pushrod and black bushing between switch and side plates.
3. Push switch and pushrod firmly toward brake pedal arm.
4. Assemble outside white plastic washer to pin and install hairpin retainer to trap whole assembly.
5. Ensure switch wire harness has sufficient length to travel with switch during full stroke of brake pedal.
6. Inspect switch for proper operation.

MULTI-FUNCTION SWITCH

REPLACE

1. Tilt column to lowest position and remove tilt lever, as required.
2. Remove ignition lock cylinder.
3. Remove mounting screws, then the upper and lower shrouds.

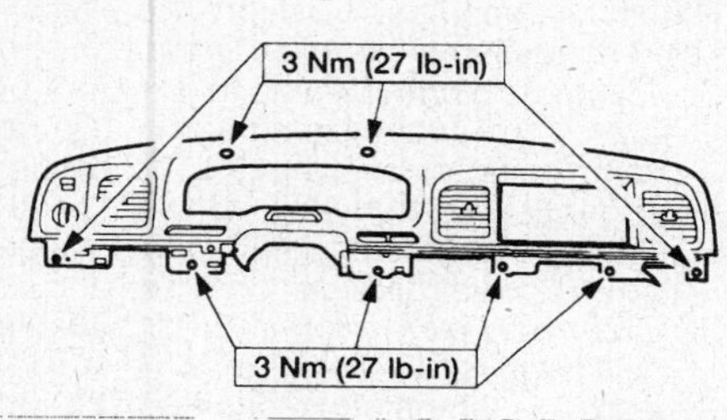

Fig. 2 Instrument panel cluster finish trim panel replacement. 1999–2002

4. Remove two multi-function switch to steering column casting mounting screws.
5. Disconnect switch.
6. Disconnect two electrical connectors.
7. Reverse procedure to install. **Torque** mounting screws to 18–26 inch lbs.

TURN SIGNAL SWITCH

REPLACE

Refer to "Multi-Function Switch, Replace."

STEERING WHEEL

REPLACE

1. Center front wheels to straight ahead position.
2. Remove driver's air bag module as outlined in "Passive Restraint Systems" chapter.
3. Disconnect speed control wire harness from steering wheel.
4. Remove and discard steering wheel mounting bolt.
5. **On 1998 models,** remove steering wheel using steering wheel puller tool No. T67L-3600-A, or equivalent.
6. **On 1999–2002 models,** remove steering wheel using steering wheel puller tool No. T77F-4220-B1, or equivalent.
7. **On all models,** route contact wire harness through steering wheel as wheel is lifted off of shaft.
8. Reverse procedure to install, noting the following:
   a. Align steering wheel and shaft marks.
   b. Route contact wire harness through steering wheel opening at three o'clock position.
   c. Ensure air bag contact wire is not pinched and speed control wiring does not get trapped between steering wheel and contact.
   d. **Torque** steering wheel mounting bolt to 25–34 ft. lbs.
   e. **Torque** air bag module mounting nuts to 108 inch lbs.

INSTRUMENT CLUSTER

REPLACE

1998

STANDARD CLUSTER

1. Remove lefthand instrument panel molding and righthand instrument panel molding.
2. **On Crown Victoria models,** remove six mounting screws and lower instrument panel steering column cover.
3. **On Grand Marquis models,** remove five mounting screws and instrument panel steering column cover.
4. **On all models,** remove screws and lower steering column shroud.
5. Remove screw fastening transmission range indicator column bracket to steering column.
6. Disconnect cable loop from pin on shift lever.
7. Remove column bracket from steering column.
8. Disconnect instrument cluster connectors.
9. Reverse procedure to install. Adjust transmission range indicator as follows:
   a. Place transmission selector lever arm and support on steering column in 1 position.
   b. Place loop on indicator cable over retainer pin on shift lever and secure cable bracket with screw.
   c. Shift selector lever arm and support into overdrive position.
   d. Adjust thumb wheel on steering column so entire width of pointer falls within letter D (overdrive).
   e. When properly adjusted, entire width of pointer must fall within width of letter D (overdrive) and must touch remaining letters or numerals when viewed parallel to center line of steering column from driver's position.

ELECTRONIC CLUSTER

1. Set parking brake.
2. Unsnap center molding on left and righthand sides of instrument panel.
3. Remove steering column cover and column shroud.
4. Remove auto dim and auto lamp switches' knobs, as required.
5. Remove 13 mounting screws and pull instrument panel out.
6. Move shift lever to 1 position.
7. Disconnect warning lamp module, switch module and center panel switches' connectors, as required.
8. Remove instrument panel. **Do not damage cluster lens.**
9. Disconnect electrical connector from front of cluster.
10. Disconnect PRNDL assembly from cluster by carefully bending bottom tab down and pulling assembly forward.
11. Pull cluster out and disconnect electrical connectors on rear of cluster.
12. Remove instrument cluster, **Fig. 1.**
13. Reverse procedure to install.

1999–2002

1. Remove audio unit.
2. Remove left and righthand instrument panel finish panels, then disconnect electrical connectors.
3. Place gearshift lever in 1 position.
4. Place steering column in full tilt position.
5. Remove screws and disconnect electrical connectors, **Fig. 2.**
6. Remove instrument panel cluster finish panel.
7. Remove lower steering column cover.
8. Remove instrument panel steering column opening cover reinforcement.
9. Disconnect transmission range indicator cable and position aside.
10. Remove four mounting screws and instrument cluster.
11. Reverse procedure to install.

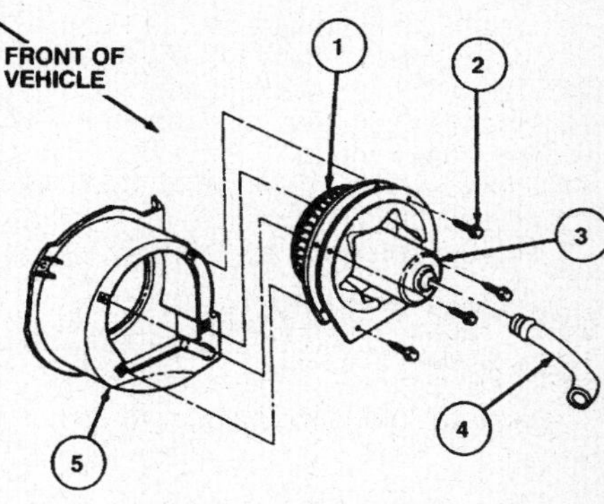

Item	Description
1	A/C Blower Wheel
2	Screw (4 Req'd)
3	A/C Blower Motor
4	Blower Motor Housing Tube
5	A/C Evaporator Core Housing

FM7029800509000X

Fig. 3 Blower motor replacement. 1998

RADIO

REPLACE

1. Release retaining clips by pushing radio removal tools No. T87P-19061-A, or equivalents, into face plate.
2. Slightly spread tools and pull radio from dash.
3. Disconnect power, antenna and speaker leads.
4. Reverse procedure to install. Ensure rear bracket is engaged on lower support rail.

WIPER MOTOR

REPLACE

1998

1. Remove wiper arm and blade.
2. Unsnap and remove windshield wiper motor and linkage cover.
3. Remove windshield wiper motor output arm clip by lifting locking tab and pulling clip away from pin.
4. Remove mounting screws and wiper motor.
5. Reverse procedure to install.

1999–2002

1. Remove cowl top vent panel.
2. Remove evaporative emission canister purge valve and set aside.

3. Remove mounting bolts, then position mounting arm and pivot shaft aside.
4. Remove wiper motor cover.
5. Remove clip and disconnect linkage from wiper motor.
6. Remove mounting bolts and wiper motor.
7. Reverse procedure to install.

WIPER SWITCH

REPLACE

Refer to "Multi-Function Switch, Replace."

BLOWER MOTOR

REPLACE

1998

1. Working in righthand wheel opening, remove three radiator coolant recovery reservoir to fender splash panel nuts and move reservoir away from blower motor.
2. Disconnect blower motor from main wiring harness at snap lock connector.
3. Depress locking tab and slide two harness connectors from face of blower motor.
4. Remove blower motor housing tube from blower motor, **Fig. 3.**
5. Remove four blower motor mounting plate mounting screws and wiring support bracket.
6. Turn blower motor and wheel slightly to right so bottom edge of mounting plate follows contour of front fender splash panel.
7. While still in evaporator core housing, lift blower motor up and maneuver if out of housing.
8. Reverse procedure to install.

1999–2002

1. Disconnect wire harness connectors.
2. Remove hose, mounting screws and blower motor.
3. If wheel is to be reused, clean corrosion from blower motor shaft.
4. Remove push clip and blower motor wheel.
5. Reverse procedure to install.

HEATER CORE

REPLACE

1. Remove heater outlet floor duct.
2. Remove instrument panel as outlined in "Dash Panel Service" chapter.
3. Disconnect heater water hoses from heater core tubes.
4. Plug heater water hoses' ends and core tubes.
5. Remove evaporator core housing upper lefthand corner mounting nut.
6. Disconnect two vacuum supply hoses from vacuum source. Push grommet and vacuum supply hose into passenger compartment.
7. Disconnect wiring harness from air conditioning electronic blend door actuator.

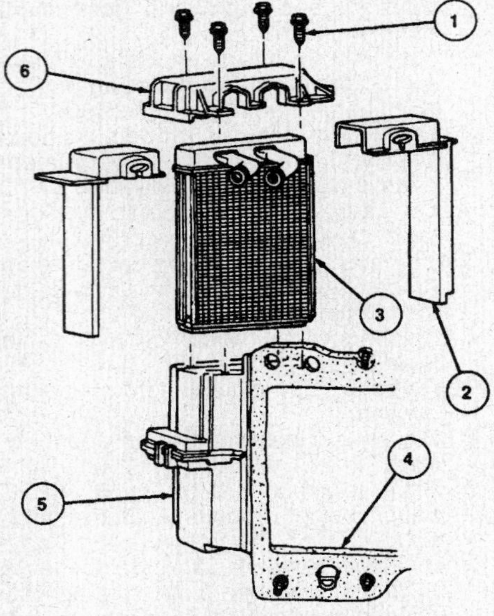

Item	Description
1	Screw (4 Req'd)
2	Heater Core Case Seal
3	Heater Core
4	Heater Dash Gasket
5	Heater Air Plenum Chamber
6	Heater Core Cover

FM7029800510000X

Fig. 4 Heater core replacement

8. Disconnect white vacuum hose from heater and air conditioning air inlet duct door vacuum control motor.
9. Remove nuts from studs along lower flange of heater air plenum chamber.
10. Disconnect connectors to air conditioning electronic blend door actuator and module on side of heater air plenum chamber.
11. Remove heater air plenum chamber by pulling rearward.
12. Remove four mounting screws and heater core cover, **Fig. 4.**
13. Pull heater core from heater air plenum chamber.
14. Reverse procedure to install. Ensure heater core case seal is properly positioned.

EVAPORATOR CORE

REPLACE

Whenever an evaporator core is replaced, replace the suction accumulator/drier.

1. Recover air conditioning refrigerant system as outlined in "Air Conditioning" chapter
2. Remove heater blower motor switch resistor.
3. Disconnect evaporator to compressor suction line from suction accumulator/drier using suitable spring lock coupling disconnect tools.
4. Plug openings. Position hose away from suction accumulator/drier.
5. Disconnect condenser to evaporator tube from evaporator core inlet tube using suitable spring lock coupling disconnect tools.
6. Position condenser to evaporator tube away from evaporator core housing.
7. Drain radiator coolant into suitable container.
8. Loosen clamps and disconnect heater water hoses from heater core tubes.
9. Remove two purge valve mounting bracket to cowl top extension mounting nuts. Position purge valve and bracket away from evaporator core housing.
10. Remove radiator coolant recovery reservoir. Position forward, away from evaporator core housing.
11. Disconnect air conditioning blower motor lead from main wiring harness, then remove hard shell connector from air conditioning blower motor speed control and air conditioning cycling switch.
12. Disconnect main wire harness (which crosses evaporator core housing) at hard shell connecting point and position it away from evaporator core housing.
13. Remove instrument panel lower insulator from bottom of instrument panel on passenger side by disengaging four push pins and disconnecting power point electrical connector.
14. Fold carpeting back on righthand side of floor. Remove air conditioning recirculating air duct bottom lefthand screw.
15. Raise and support vehicle, then remove righthand front tire and wheel assembly.
16. Remove mounting bolts from rear of righthand fender apron. Position apron down in rear to improve access to evaporator core housing.
17. From engine side of instrument panel, remove three nuts from evaporator mounting studs and two screws from top of evaporator core housing, **Fig. 5.**
18. Pull bottom of evaporator core housing away from instrument panel to disconnect two bottom studs.
19. Move top of evaporator core housing away from instrument panel, disconnect it from top stud, then maneuver case up and over fender apron.
20. Remove six evaporator core housing halves mounting screws, **Fig. 6.**
21. Separate evaporator core housing halves and carefully cutting evaporator case instrument panel seal at seams using suitable razor blade.
22. Disconnect suction accumulator/drier inlet from evaporator core outlet tube.
23. Remove suction accumulator/drier and evaporator core mounting bracket screw, then the suction accumulator/drier from evaporator core.
24. Remove mounting screw from inlet tube bracket and evaporator core.
25. Reverse procedure to install.

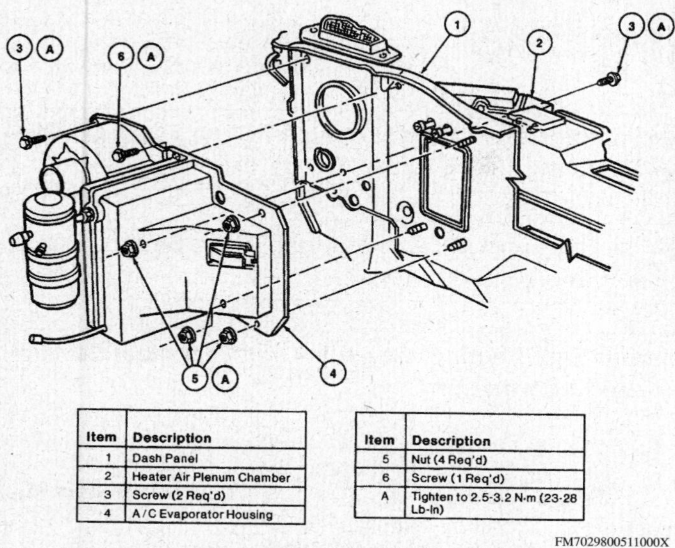

Item	Description
1	Dash Panel
2	Heater Air Plenum Chamber
3	Screw (2 Req'd)
4	A/C Evaporator Housing

Item	Description
5	Nut (4 Req'd)
6	Screw (1 Req'd)
A	Tighten to 2.5-3.2 N·m (23-28 Lb-In)

FM7029800511000X

Fig. 5 Evaporator core housing removal

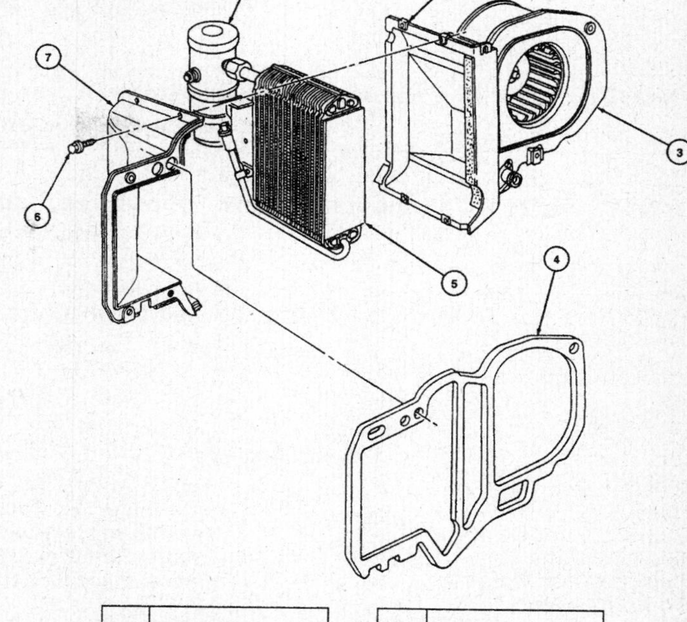

Item	Description
1	Suction Accumulator/Drier
2	Spring Nut (4 Req'd)
3	A/C Evaporator Core Housing
4	A/C Evaporator Case Dash Panel Seal

Item	Description
5	A/C Evaporator Core
6	Screw (6 Req'd)
7	A/C Evaporator Core Housing (LH)

FM7029800512000X

Fig. 6 Evaporator core replacement

TECHNICAL SERVICE BULLETINS

REPEATED HEATER CORE FAILURE

On some of these models there may be repeated heater core leaks.

This condition may be caused by a chemical reaction (electrolysis).

To correct this condition, proceed as follows:

1. Place positive probe of suitable digital volt/ohm meter in engine coolant and negative probe on battery negative terminal.
2. Adjust engine to 2000 RPM.
3. If more than 0.4 volt is recorded, flush coolant and check voltage, again.
4. If voltage is still excessive, inspect body/battery grounds.
5. If condition still exists, add extra grounds to heater core and engine, as follows:
   a. Secure 16 gauge stranded copper wire to heater core inlet tube using suitable hose clamp.
   b. Secure other end of wire to existing body sheet metal fastener.
   c. Secure another extra ground between existing engine and body sheet metal fasteners.
   d. Ensure there is continuity between added grounds and battery negative terminal.
6. If condition still exists, install restrictor as follows:
   a. Cut line as close to engine block as possible.
   b. Install restrictor (part No. F1UZ-18D406-A) on inlet hose with arrow facing coolant flow direction (toward heater core).
   c. Secure with two suitable hose clamps.
7. Bleed cooling system trapped air as follows:
   a. Disconnect heater hose at right-hand front or rear of engine.
   b. Remove thermostat and housing.
   c. Fill engine with suitable coolant until mixture is seen at engine side heater hose connection.
   d. Connect heater hose, then install thermostat and housing.
   e. Fill degas bottle to coolant fill level mark.
   f. Fun engine to normal operating temperature.
   g. Select max heat and blower speeds

4.6L Engine

NOTE: On Air Bag Equipped Models, Refer To "Air Bag System Precautions" Located In The Front Of This Manual For System Disarming & Arming Procedures.

NOTE: Refer To "Computer Relearn Procedures" Located In The Front Of This Manual When Battery Power To The Computer Has Been Interrupted.

NOTE: Prior To Performing Any Service Operations Listed In This Section, Consult The "Technical Service Bulletins" Section For Related Information.

INDEX

PRECAUTIONS

Air Bag Systems

Refer to "Air Bag System Precautions" in the front of this manual for system disarming and arming procedures.

Battery Ground Cable

Prior to service, disconnect battery ground cable and isolate as required.

Fuel System Pressure Relief

GASOLINE ENGINE

The fuel system remains under high pressure even when the engine is not running. To avoid injury or fire, release pressure from the fuel system before disconnecting any fuel line. Proceed as follows:

1. Ensure ignition switch is in Off position.
2. Remove fuel tank cap to release residual fuel pressure.
3. Connect fuel pressure gauge tool No. T80L-9974-B, or equivalent, to fuel rail valve located on fuel rail.
4. Gradually open testing kit valve to relieve fuel pressure in system.
5. Drain fuel into suitable container or return to fuel tank.
6. When repair is completed, turn ignition On and Off several times to pressurize fuel system. **Do not start engine.**
7. Inspect for fuel leaks at pressure regulator, fuel injectors and fuel fittings. Repair as required.

NATURAL GAS ENGINE

SYSTEM

When servicing any component of the fuel charging system, fuel pressure should be released using the following procedures.

When venting fuel system, venting into a vent stack is recommended, **Fig. 1.** If using a vent stack, ensure local regulations are followed. Before venting occurs, battery should be disconnected and isolated, as required.

Natural gas O-rings are identified with a yellow stripe. Do not use unapproved O-rings.

Before performing pressure relief procedures, refer to "Fuel Tank Solenoid Valve Test" to determine status of fuel tank solenoid valves.

If a manual override tool has been used to open fuel tank solenoid valve, solenoid valve must be replaced, Fig. 2.

Do not vent fuel tank unless tank or fuel tank solenoid valve is being replaced. Unnecessary venting of good tanks will damage fuel tank solenoid valve.

FUEL TANK SOLENOID VALVE TEST

Prior to relieving fuel pressure on NGV vehicles, the following diagnosis should be

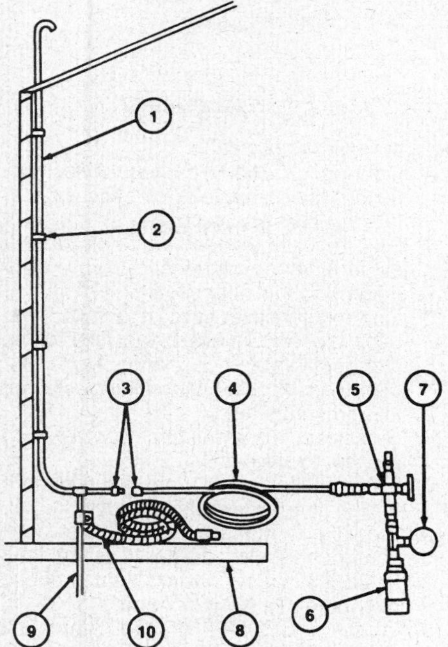

Item	Description
1	1/2 Inch Pipe
2	Vent Stack Support
3	Vent Stack Connectors
4	Rotunda Venting Hose
5	Rotunda Fuel Filter Neck Venting Kit
6	Fill Valve Connector
7	Gauge
8	Building Floor
9	Support / Grounding Rod
10	Grounding Cable

FM1029900308000X

Fig. 1 Typical vent stack installation

performed to determine whether or not the fuel tank solenoid valve is stuck open or closed.

1. Inspect fuel system and determine if any of the following apply:
    a. Damaged fuel tanks.
    b. Damaged fuel tank solenoid valve.
    c. Damaged lines or hoses.
    d. Damaged fuse or relay.
    e. Damaged power distribution box.
    f. Damaged, loose or corroded electrical connections.
2. If any of preceding conditions were found during visual inspection, repair as require.
3. If none of preceding conditions were found during visual inspection, refer to symptom chart, **Fig. 3.**
4. **On 1998 models,** refer to **Fig. 4** for pinpoint test A.
5. **On 1999 models,** refer to **Fig. 5** for pinpoint test A.
6. **On 2000–02 models,** refer to **Fig. 6** for pinpoint tests A.
7. If fuel tank solenoid valve requires replacement, refer to **MOTOR's "Domestic Engine Performance & Driveability Manual"** for procedure.

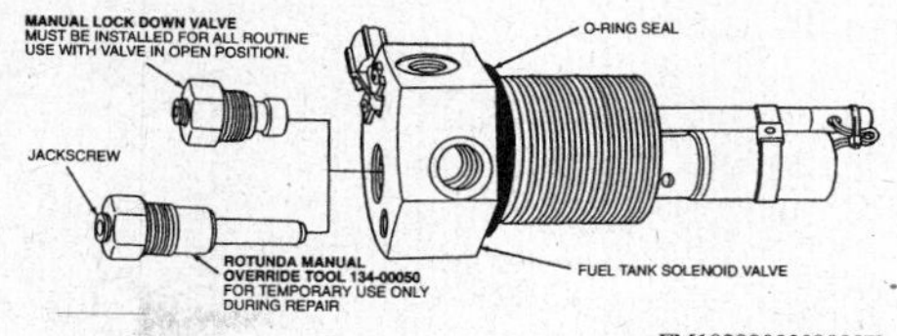

FM1029900309000X

Fig. 2 Fuel tank solenoid valve replacement

LINE PRESSURE

1998

1. Remove fuel pump relay from power distribution box.
2. When using fuel tester kit, ensure tester kit valve is closed.
3. Connect fuel rail pressure test and venting kit tool No. 134-00116 and Rotunda venting hose tool No. 134-00118, or equivalents, to Schrader valve on fuel supply manifold.
4. Connect Rotunda grounding cable tool No. 134-00121, or equivalent, to fuel supply manifold and ground.
5. Slowly open testing kit valve to relieve fuel pressure. **Five psi of fuel pressure will remain in fuel supply manifold. High pressure still exists in fuel tanks and upstream of quarter turn manual fuel line shut of valve if closed.**
6. **If fuel tubes continue to vent or pressure remains after one minute, fuel tank solenoids are stuck open. Do not disconnect fuel tubes while still under pressure.** Close bleed valve on fuel rail pressure tester and remove.
7. Inspect all connections at fuel injection supply manifold, fuel injectors and fuel line push connect fittings.
8. Connect wire sockets Nos. 87 and 30 in fuel pump relay socket of power distribution box using suitable jumper wire constructed of six inches of 18 gauge wire and two spade terminals.
9. Inspect fuel system for leaks using Rotunda combustible gas detector tool No. 055-00107, or equivalent. Service all leaks, as required.
10. Start engine and inspect for presence of any leaks.
11. Perform PCM self test as outlined in **MOTOR's "Domestic Engine Performance & Driveability Manual."**
12. Inspect coolant for presence of natural gas. If present, replace fuel pressure regulator.
13. Install fuel pump relay to power distribution box.

1999–2002

1. Connect grounding cable tool No. 134-00121, or equivalent, to fuel supply manifold and ground.
2. Ensure bleed valve on fuel rail pressure test kit is closed before installing.
3. Install fuel rail pressure test kit tool No. 134-00116, or equivalent, to fuel supply manifold Schrader valve.
4. Connect vent hose to pressure test kit and vent stack.
5. Slowly open bleed valve of fuel rail pressure tester and allow fuel lines to vent to atmosphere for one minute. If pressure gauge still registers 95–125 psi, refer to **MOTOR's "Domestic Engine Performance & Driveability Manual."**

TANK PRESSURE

1998 w/Solenoid Stuck Open Or Normally Functioning

When venting fuel tanks, tanks must be vented according to solenoid operation in the following sequence; stuck open, functioning normally, stuck closed or inoperative.

1. Ensure all solenoid valves are in locked position.
2. Connect Rotunda fuel filter neck venting kit tool No. 134-00117 and vent hose tool No. 134-00118, or equivalents, to vent stack and vehicle fuel fill valve.
3. Connect Rotunda grounding cable tool No. 134-00121, or equivalent, to rear of fuel filler valve and ground.
4. Remove fuel pump relay from power distribution box.
5. Connect wire sockets Nos. 87 and 30 in fuel pump relay socket of power distribution box using suitable jumper wire constructed of six inches of 18 gauge wire and two spade terminals.
6. Slowly open manual lockout valve on affected tank.
7. Slowly open manual backflow valve on fuel filler valve.
8. Pressure on fuel filter neck venting kit gauge should read tank pressure is solenoid valve was identified as stuck open.
9. Slowly open bleed valve on fuel filter neck venting kit and allow tank to vent to atmosphere. Venting process may take one hour or more.
10. Close bleed valve on filter neck venting kit. Ensure fuel line pressure is zero psi.
11. Remove manual lockdown valve.
12. **Ensure jackscrew in manual override tool is retracted fully (counterclockwise) prior to installation into fuel tank solenoid valve. If tool is installed in vent position, fuel will be immediately released.**
13. Install Rotunda manual override tool No. 134-00050, or equivalent, to tank solenoid and **torque** to 28–31 ft. lbs.
14. Turn override tool jackscrew clockwise until fuel flows.
15. Vent system until fuel flow stops.
16. Remove override tool.
17. Install manual lockdown valve into fuel

tank solenoid valve and **torque** to 28–31 ft. lbs.

18. **Torque** manual valve lockdown valve jackscrew to 62–79 inch lbs.
19. Repeat procedure on remaining tanks, as required.
20. Close manual backflow valve on fuel filter valve when tank contents have vented and **torque** to 62–79 inch lbs.

1998 w/Solenoid Stuck Closed Or Inoperative

When venting fuel tanks, tanks must be vented according to solenoid operation in the following sequence; stuck open, functioning normally, stuck closed or inoperative.

1. Ensure all solenoid valves should be in locked position.
2. Connect Rotunda fuel filter neck venting kit tool No. 134-00117 and vent hose tool No. 134-00118, or equivalents, to vent stack and vehicle fuel fill valve.
3. Connect Rotunda grounding cable tool No. 134-00121, or equivalent to rear of fuel filler valve and ground.
4. Remove solenoid valve manual lockout.
5. **Ensure jackscrew in manual override tool is retracted fully (counterclockwise) prior to installation into fuel tank solenoid valve. If tool is installed in vent position, fuel will be immediately released.**
6. Install Rotunda manual override tool No. 134-00050, or equivalent and **torque** to 28–31 ft. lbs.
7. Turn override tool jackscrew clockwise until fuel flows.
8. Ensure pressure reading of fuel filler neck vent kit gauge reads tank pressure.
9. Slowly open bleed valve on neck vent kit and bleed tank to atmosphere. Vent process may take one hour or more.
10. Remove manual override tool from solenoid valve.
11. Retract manual lock down jackscrew, then install lockdown. **Torque** to 62–79 inch lbs.
12. Close bleed valve on neck vent kit. Ensure tank pressure is zero psi.
13. Close manual backflow valve on fuel filler valve and **torque** to 62–79 inch lbs.
14. Remove neck vent kit and vent stack.
15. Repeat vent procedure on remaining tanks, as required.

1999–2002 w/Solenoid Normally Operating

1. Remove vapor vent box from fuel tank, as required.
2. Disconnect fuel tank electrical connectors and **torque** manual lockdown jackscrews to 80 inch lbs. on fuel tanks not to be vented. If neither of rear or upper tanks need to be vented, rear upper fuel tank rack harness connector may be disconnected without removing rear or upper fuel tank rack vent box.
3. Connect grounding cable 134-00121, or equivalent, to back side of fuel fill valve at fuel line connection and ground.
4. Ensure manual bleed valve on fuel vent kit is closed before connecting to fuel filler valve.
5. Connect fuel filler neck venting kit tool No. 134-00117, or equivalent, to fuel filler valve.
6. Connect vent hose tool No. 134-00118, or equivalent, to filler neck vent kit and vent stack.
7. Remove fuel valve relay from power distribution box.
8. Connect wire sockets Nos. 87 and 30 in fuel pump relay socket of power distribution box using suitable jumper wire constructed of six inches of 18 gauge wire and two spade terminals.
9. Slowly open manual backflow valve on fuel filler valve using suitable 3/16 inch Allen wrench.
10. Ensure gauge on fuel filler neck vent kit indicates tank pressure.
11. Slowly open bleed valve on fuel filler neck vent kit and allow fuel tank to vent to atmosphere. Venting process may take one hour or more.
12. Close bleed valve on fuel filler neck vent kit. Ensure gauge pressure is zero psi.
13. Remove fuel tank solenoid manual lockdown valve.
14. **Ensure jackscrew in manual override tool is retracted fully (counterclockwise) prior to installation into fuel tank solenoid valve. If tool is installed in vent position, fuel will be immediately released.**
15. Install Rotunda manual override tool No. 134-00050, or equivalent, to tank solenoid and **torque** to 30 ft. lbs.
16. Turn override tool jackscrew clockwise until fuel flows.
17. Vent system until fuel flow stops.
18. Close manual backflow valve on fuel filler valve after tank has been vented.
19. Vent fuel lines as outlined under.
20. Remove manual override tool from fuel tank solenoid valve.
21. Install fuel tank solenoid manual lockdown valve and **torque** to 30 ft. lbs.
22. **Torque** manual lockdown valve jackscrew on fuel tank solenoid valve to 80 inch lbs.
23. Repeat procedure until affected tanks are vented.

Condition	Possible Source	Action
• Unable to Vent Fuel Tanks or Fuel Lines	• Damaged fuel tank solenoids. • Damaged lines or hoses. • Circuitry.	• GO to Pinpoint Test A.

FM1029900301000X

Fig. 3 NGV fuel tank solenoid valve symptom chart

1999–2002 w/Solenoid Stuck Open

1. Disconnect fuel tank electrical connectors and **torque** manual lockdown jackscrews to 80 inch lbs. on fuel tanks not to be vented. If neither of rear or upper tanks need to be vented, rear upper fuel tank rack harness connector may be disconnected without removing rear or upper fuel tank rack vent box.
2. Remove vent box from upper fuel tank rack, as required.
3. Connect grounding cable tool No. 134-00121, or equivalent, to back side of fuel fill valve and ground.
4. Ensure manual bleed valve on fuel filler neck vent kit is closed before connecting to fuel filler valve.
5. Connect fuel filler vent kit tool No. 134-00117, or equivalent, to fuel filler valve.
6. Connect vent hose tool No. 134-00118, or equivalent, to filler neck vent kit and vent stack.
7. Slowly open manual backflow valve on fuel filler valve.
8. Ensure filler neck vent kit pressure gauge indicates tank pressure.
9. Slowly open bleed valve on filler neck vent kit and allow contents of fuel tank to vent to atmosphere. Vent process may take one hour or more.
10. Close bleed valve on fuel filler neck vent kit. Ensure pressure is zero psi.
11. Remove fuel tank solenoid manual lockdown valve.
12. **Ensure jackscrew in manual override tool is retracted fully (counterclockwise) prior to installation into fuel tank solenoid valve. If tool is installed in vent position, fuel will be immediately released.**
13. Install Rotunda manual override tool No. 134-00050, or equivalent, to tank solenoid and **torque** to 30 ft. lbs.
14. Turn override tool jackscrew clockwise until fuel flows.
15. Open manual bleed valve on fuel filler neck vent kit and vent system until fuel flow stops.
16. Close manual backflow valve on fuel filler valve after tank has been vented.
17. Vent fuel lines.
18. Remove manual override tool from fuel tank solenoid valve.
19. Install fuel tank solenoid manual lockdown valve and **torque** to 30 ft. lbs.
20. **Torque** manual lockdown valve jackscrew on fuel tank solenoid valve to 80 inch lbs.
21. Repeat procedure until affected tanks are vented.

1999–2002 w/Solenoid Stuck Closed

1. Disconnect fuel tank electrical connectors and **torque** manual lockdown jackscrews to 80 inch lbs. on fuel tanks not to be vented. If neither of rear or upper tanks need to be vented, rear upper fuel tank rack harness connector may be disconnected without removing rear or upper fuel tank rack vent box.
2. Remove vent box from upper fuel tank rack, as required.
3. Connect grounding cable tool No. 134-00121, or equivalent, to back side of fuel fill valve and ground.

	Test Step	Result	Action to Take
A1	CHECK FOR OPEN SOLENOID		
	NOTE: Battery must be fully charged to perform solenoid diagnostics. • **Close bleed valve on vent tool.** • **Connect Rotunda Fuel Filter Neck Venting Kit 134-00117 or equivalent and attach Rotunda Ground Cable 134-00121 or equivalent.** • **Disconnect tank No. 3 and No. 4 solenoid valve connectors.** 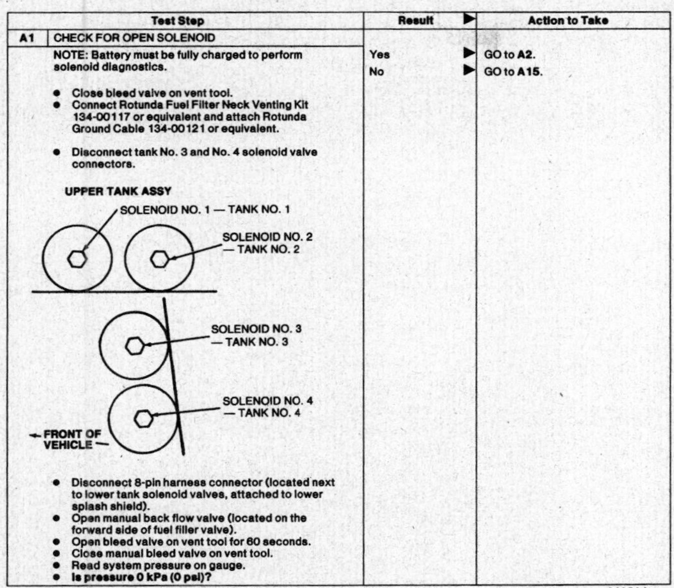 • **Disconnect 8-pin harness connector (located next to lower tank solenoid valves, attached to lower splash shield).** • **Open manual back flow valve (located on the forward side of fuel filler valve).** • **Open bleed valve on vent tool for 60 seconds.** • **Close manual bleed valve on vent tool.** • **Read system pressure on gauge.** • **Is pressure 0 kPa (0 psi)?**	**Yes** **No**	GO to **A2**. GO to **A15**.

FM1029900302010X

Fig. 4 Pinpoint Test A: Fuel tank solenoid valve diagnosis (Part 1 of 9). 1998

	Test Step	Result	Action to Take
A3	CHECK POWER SUPPLY TO FUEL TANK NO. 4 SOLENOID VALVE		
	• Connect NGS or equivalent to data link connector. • Select PCM. • Select ACTIVE COMMAND MODES. • Select OUTPUT TEST MODE. • Using a voltmeter connected to ground, connect second lead to fuel tank No. 4 solenoid connector Circuit 787 (PK/BK). 787 (PK/BK) V 57 (BK) • NOTE: This procedure will supply power to the fuel tank solenoid valve for approximately 30-60 seconds. If time expires, cycle START/STOP button on NGS Tester to restore power. • Push START button. • Read voltage. • Push STOP button. • **Is voltage B+?**	Yes No	GO to **A4**. SERVICE Circuit 787 (PK/BK) for open. REPEAT Step A2.
A4	CHECK CIRCUIT 57 (BK) AT FUEL TANK NO. 4 SOLENOID		
	• Using an ohmmeter connected to ground, measure resistance at fuel tank No. 4 solenoid connector Circuit 57 (BK). • **Is resistance 5 ohms or less?**	Yes	MARK fuel tank No. 4 solenoid valve "Stuck Closed." Solenoid will be replaced after completing diagnostics. GO to **A5**.
		No	SERVICE Circuit 57 (BK) for open. REPEAT Step A2.
A5	CHECK FUEL TANK NO. 3 SOLENOID		
	• Open manual bleed valve on Rotunda Fuel Filter Neck Venting Kit 134-00117 or equivalent and vent system pressure to 0 kPa (0 psi). • Close manual bleed valve on Rotunda Fuel Filter Neck Venting Kit 134-00117 or equivalent. • Connect fuel tank No. 3 solenoid connector. • Connect NGS to data link connector. • Select PCM. • Select ACTIVE COMMAND MODES. • Select OUTPUT TEST MODE. • Make sure manual lock down on fuel tank No. 3 solenoid valve is open. • NOTE: This procedure will supply power to the fuel tank solenoid valve for approximately 30-60 seconds. If time expires, cycle START/STOP button on NGS to restore power. • Push START button. • Read system pressure on Rotunda Fuel Filter Neck Venting Kit 134-00117 or equivalent gauge. • Push STOP button. • Disconnect fuel tank No. 3 solenoid connector. • **Did pressure read 0 kPa (0 psi) when triggered ON?**	Yes No	GO to **A6**. MARK fuel tank No. 3 solenoid as "Good" and GO to **A8**.

FM1029900302030X

Fig. 4 Pinpoint Test A: Fuel tank solenoid valve diagnosis (Part 3 of 9). 1998

	Test Step	Result	Action to Take
A2	CHECK FUEL TANK NO. 4 SOLENOID VALVE		
	• Connect fuel tank No. 4 solenoid valve connector. • Connect Rotunda New Generation Star (NGS) Tester 007-00500 or equivalent to data link connector. • Select PCM. • Select ACTIVE COMMAND MODES. • Select OUTPUT TEST MODE. • Make sure manual lock down valve on fuel tank No. 4 solenoid valve is open. MANUAL LOCK DOWN VALVE FUEL TANK SOLENOID VALVE JACKSCREW • NOTE: This procedure will supply power to the fuel tank solenoid valve for approximately 30-60 seconds. If time expires, cycle START/STOP button on NGS to restore power. • Push START button. • Read system pressure on Rotunda Fuel Filter Neck Venting Kit 134-00117 or equivalent. • Push STOP button. • Disconnect fuel tank No. 4 solenoid valve connector. • **Did system pressure read 0 kPa (0 psi) when triggered ON?**	Yes No	GO to **A3**. MARK fuel tank No. 4 solenoid valve as "Good" and GO to **A5**.

FM1029900302020X

Fig. 4 Pinpoint Test A: Fuel tank solenoid valve diagnosis (Part 2 of 9). 1998

	Test Step	Result	Action to Take
A6	CHECK POWER SUPPLY TO FUEL TANK NO. 3 SOLENOID VALVE		
	• Connect NGS to data link connector. • Select PCM. • Select ACTIVE COMMAND MODES. • Select OUTPUT TEST MODE. • Using a voltmeter connected to ground, connect second lead to Circuit 787 (PK/BK) at fuel tank solenoid connector. • NOTE: This procedure will supply power to the fuel tank solenoid valve for approximately 30-60 seconds. If time expires, cycle START/STOP button on NGS to restore power. • Push START button. • Read voltage. • Push STOP button. • **Is voltage B+?**	Yes No	GO to **A7**. SERVICE Circuit 787 (PK/BK) for open. REPEAT Step A5.
A7	CHECK CIRCUIT 57 (BK) AT FUEL TANK NO. 3 SOLENOID VALVE		
	• Using an ohmmeter connected to ground, measure resistance at fuel tank No. 3 solenoid connector Circuit 57 (BK). • **Is resistance 5 ohms or less?**	Yes	MARK fuel tank No. 3 solenoid valve "Stuck Closed." Solenoid will be replaced after completing diagnostics. GO to**A8**.
		No	SERVICE Circuit 57 (BK) for open. REPEAT Step A5.
A8	CHECK FUEL TANK NO. 2 SOLENOID VENT		
	NOTE: Battery must be fully charged to perform solenoid diagnostics. • Open manual bleed valve on Rotunda Fuel Filter Neck Venting Kit 134-00117 or equivalent and vent system pressure to 0 kPa (0 psi) • Close manual bleed valve on vent tool. • Install Rotunda Electrical Harness for Venting Tanks 134-00120 or equivalent between upper tank assembly 8-pin and harness connectors. • Connect NGS to data link connector. • Select PCM. • Select ACTIVE COMMAND MODES. • Select OUTPUT TEST MODE. • Hold Rotunda Electrical Harness for Venting Tanks 134-00120 or equivalent to tank No. 2 position. • NOTE: This procedure will supply power to the fuel tank solenoid valve for approximately 30-60 seconds. If time expires, cycle START/STOP button on NGS to restore power. • Push START button. • Read system pressure on Rotunda Fuel Filter Neck Venting Kit 134-00117 or equivalent gauge. • Release Rotunda Electrical Harness for Venting Tanks 134-00120 or equivalent switch. • Push STOP button. • **Did pressure read 0 kPa (0 psi) when triggered ON?**	Yes No	NOTE: Fuel tank No. 2 solenoid valve may be "Stuck Closed". GO to **A9**. MARK fuel tank No. 2 solenoid valve as "Good". GO to **A9**.

FM1029900302040X

Fig. 4 Pinpoint Test A: Fuel tank solenoid valve diagnosis (Part 4 of 9). 1998

	Test Step	Result	Action to Take
A9	CHECK POWER SUPPLY TO FUEL TANK NO. 1 SOLENOID VALVE		
	• Open manual bleed valve on Rotunda Fuel Filter Neck Venting Kit 134-00117 or equivalent and vent system pressure 0 kPa (0 psi). • Close manual bleed valve on Rotunda Fuel Filter Neck Venting Kit 134-00117 or equivalent. • Connect NGS to data link connector. • Select PCM. • Select ACTIVE COMMAND MODES. • Select OUTPUT TEST MODE. • Switch Rotunda Electrical Harness for Venting Tanks 134-00120 or equivalent to tank No. 1 position. • NOTE: This procedure will supply power to the fuel tank solenoid valve for approximately 30-60 seconds. If time expires, cycle START/STOP button on NGS to restore power. • Push START button. • Read system pressure on Rotunda Fuel Filter Neck Venting Kit 134-00117 or equivalent gauge. • Release Rotunda Electrical Harness for Venting Tanks 134-00120 switch. • Push STOP button. • **Did pressure read 0 kPa (0 psi) when triggered ON?**	Yes ▶ No ▶	NOTE: Fuel tank No. 1 solenoid valve may be "Stuck Closed." GO to **A10**. MARK fuel tank No. 1 solenoid valve "Good." REPLACE all solenoids marked stuck closed. If fuel tank No. 2 solenoid valve was marked may be "Stuck Closed," GO to **A10**. If all solenoids were marked "Good," solenoids operating properly at this time. RETURN to venting procedure.
A10	CHECK CIRCUIT 57 (BK) TO UPPER TANK ASSEMBLY		
	• Open manual bleed valve on Rotunda Fuel Filter Neck Venting Kit 134-00117 or equivalent and vent system pressure to 0 kPa (0 psi). • Close manual bleed valve on Rotunda Fuel Filter Neck Venting Kit 134-00117 or equivalent. • Remove upper fuel tank rack assembly vapor vent box as described. • Using an ohmmeter, measure resistance of Circuit 57 (BK) between fuel tank No. 1 and No. 2 solenoid valve connectors and upper tank assembly 8-pin harness connector Pin 1. • **Is resistance 5 ohms or less on both circuits?**	Yes ▶ No ▶	GO to **A11**. SERVICE Circuit 57 (BK) for open. Install upper tank assembly as described. GO to **A8**.
A11	CHECK CIRCUIT 787 (PK/BK)		
	• Using an ohmmeter, measure resistance between upper tank assembly 8-pin harness connector Pin 6 and fuel tank No. 2 solenoid valve connector Circuit 787 (PK/BK) and upper tank assembly 8-pin harness connector Pin 5 and fuel tank No. 1 solenoid valve connector Circuit 787 (PK/BK). • **Is resistance 5 ohms or less for each circuit?**	Yes ▶ No ▶	GO to **A12**. SERVICE suspect circuit for open. Install upper tank assembly as described. GO to **A8**.
A12	CHECK FUEL TANK SOLENOID VALVE FOR MANUAL LOCK DOWNS		
	• Install upper tank assembly without vent box installed, make all fuel line and electrical connections as described in the installation procedure. • Check fuel tank No. 1 and No. 2 solenoid valves manual lock downs. • **Are manual lock downs open?**	Yes ▶ No ▶	REPLACE all solenoids marked "Stuck Closed." If fuel tank No. 1 or No. 2 solenoid valve was marked may be "Stuck Closed," REPLACE at this time. RESTORE vehicle. RETEST system. GO to **A13**.

FM1029900302050X

Fig. 4 Pinpoint Test A: Fuel tank solenoid valve diagnosis (Part 5 of 9). 1998

	Test Step	Result	Action to Take
A16	CHECK FOR OPEN FUEL TANK SOLENOID IN UPPER TANK ASSEMBLY		
	• Using a 3/16 allen wrench, tighten manual lock down jackscrew on fuel tank No. 3 and No. 4 solenoid valves to within 7-9 N·m (62-79 lb-in). • Open bleed valve on Rotunda Fuel Filter Neck Venting Kit 134-00117 or equivalent for 60 seconds. • Close bleed valve on Rotunda Fuel Filter Neck Venting Kit 134-00117 or equivalent. • Read pressure on Rotunda Fuel Filter Neck Venting Kit 134-00117 or equivalent gauge. MANUAL LOCK DOWN VALVE FUEL TANK SOLENOID VALVE JACKSCREW • **Is pressure 0 kPa (0 psi)?**	Yes ▶ No ▶	GO to **A21**. GO to **A17**.
A17	CHECK CIRCUIT 787 (PK/BK)		
	• Open manual bleed valve on Rotunda Fuel Filter Neck Venting Kit 134-00117 or equivalent and vent system pressure to 0 kPa (0 psi). • Close bleed valve on Rotunda Fuel Filter Neck Venting Kit 134-00117 or equivalent. • Remove upper fuel tank rack assembly vapor vent box as described. • Using an ohmmeter, measure resistance of Circuit 787 (PK/BK) between upper tank assembly 8-pin harness connector Pin 6 and fuel tank No. 2 solenoid valve connector, and between upper tank assembly 8-pin harness connector Pin 5 and fuel tank No. 1 solenoid valve connector. • **Is resistance 5 ohms or less for each circuit?**	Yes ▶ No ▶	GO to **A18**. SERVICE suspect circuit for open. RESTORE vehicle. RETEST system.
A18	CHECK CIRCUIT 57 (BK)		
	• Using an ohmmeter, measure resistance of Circuit 57 (BK) between fuel tank No. 1 and No. 2 solenoid valve connectors and upper tank assembly 8-pin harness connector. • **Is resistance 5 ohms or less?**	Yes ▶ No ▶	GO to **A19**. SERVICE Circuit 57 (BK) for open. GO to **A19**.

FM1029900302070X

Fig. 4 Pinpoint Test A: Fuel tank solenoid valve diagnosis (Part 7 of 9). 1998

	Test Step	Result	Action to Take
A13	CHECK FUEL TANK NO. 2 SOLENOID VALVE MANUAL LOCK DOWN		
	• Make sure bleed valve on Rotunda Fuel Filter Neck Venting Kit 134-00117 or equivalent is closed. • Open fuel tank No. 2 solenoid valve manual lock down. • Open bleed valve on Rotunda Fuel Filter Neck Venting Kit 134-00117 or equivalent for 60 seconds. • Close bleed valve on Rotunda Fuel Filter Neck Venting Kit 134-00117 or equivalent. • Read system pressure. • **Is system pressure 0 kPa (0 psi)?**	Yes ▶ No ▶	If fuel tank No. 1 solenoid valve manual lock down is open, GO to **A8**. If closed GO to **A14**. Mark fuel tank No. 2 solenoid valve "Stuck Open." GO to **A15**.
A14	CHECK FUEL TANK NO. 1 SOLENOID LOCK DOWN		
	• Using a 3/16 allen wrench, tighten manual lock down jackscrew on fuel tank No. 2 solenoid valve to within 7-9 N·m (62-79 lb-in). • Open fuel tank No. 1 solenoid valve manual lock down. • Open bleed valve on Rotunda Fuel Filter Neck Venting Kit 134-00117 or equivalent for 60 seconds. • Close bleed valve on Rotunda Fuel Filter Neck Venting Kit 134-00117 or equivalent. • Read system pressure. • **Is system pressure 0 kPa (0 psi)?**	Yes ▶ No ▶	GO to **A8**. MARK fuel tank No. 1 solenoid valve "Stuck Open." GO to **A15**.
A15	CHECK FOR SHORT TO B+		
	• Ignition switch OFF. • Using a voltmeter, measure for voltage at tank side of 8-pin harness connector Pin 1, Circuit 57 (BK), Pin 5, Circuit 787 (PK/BK) and Pin 6, Circuit 787 (PK/BK). • Measure for voltage at fuel tank No. 3 and No. 4 solenoid connectors Circuit 787 (PK/BK). 787 (PK/BK) V 57 (BK) • **Is voltage B+ on any circuit?**	Yes ▶ No ▶	SERVICE suspect circuit for short to B+. GO to **A1**. GO to **A16**.

FM1029900302060X

Fig. 4 Pinpoint Test A: Fuel tank solenoid valve diagnosis (Part 6 of 9). 1998

	Test Step	Result	Action to Take
A19	CHECK FUEL TANK NO. 2 SOLENOID VALVE OPERATION		
	NOTE: Battery must be fully charged to perform solenoid diagnostics • Make sure manual bleed valve is closed on Rotunda Fuel Filter Neck Venting Kit 134-00117 or equivalent. • Install upper fuel tank assembly without vent box installed, make all fuel line and electrical connections as described. • Tighten fuel tank No. 1 solenoid valve manual lock down jackscrew to 7-9 N·m (62-79 lb-in). • Open fuel tank No. 2 solenoid valve manual lock down. • Connect Rotunda Electrical Harness for Venting Tanks 134-00120 or equivalent to harness 8-pin connector. • Connect fuel tank No. 2 solenoid valve connector. • Make sure fuel tank No. 1 solenoid valve connector is disconnected. • Connect NGS or equivalent to data link connector. • Select PCM. • Select ACTIVE COMMAND MODES. • Select OUTPUT TEST MODE. • Hold Rotunda Electrical Harness for Venting Tanks 134-00120 or equivalent to tank No. 2 position. • NOTE: This procedure will supply power to the fuel tank solenoid valve for approximately 30-60 seconds. If time expires, cycle START/STOP button on NGS to restore power. Push START button. • Read system pressure on Rotunda Fuel Filter Neck Venting Kit 134-00117 or equivalent gauge. • Release Rotunda Electrical Harness for Venting Tanks 134-00120 or equivalent switch. • Press STOP button. • **Is pressure 0 kPa (0 psi) when triggered ON?**	Yes ▶ No ▶	MARK fuel tank No. 2 solenoid valve "Does Not Operate." Solenoid will be replaced after completing diagnostics. GO to **A20**. MARK fuel tank No. 2 solenoid valve "Good" and GO to **A20**.
A20	CHECK FUEL TANK NO. 1 SOLENOID VALVE OPERATION		
	• Open manual bleed valve on Rotunda Fuel Filter Neck Venting Kit 134-00117 or equivalent and vent system pressure to 0 kPa (0 psi). • Close manual bleed valve on Rotunda Fuel Filter Neck Venting Kit 134-00117 or equivalent. • Disconnect fuel tank No. 2 solenoid valve connector. • Connect fuel tank No. 1 solenoid valve connector. • Tighten fuel tank No. 1 solenoid valve manual lock down jackscrew to 7-9 N·m (62-79 lb-in). • Connect NGS or equivalent to data link connector. • Select PCM. • Select ACTIVE COMMAND MODES. • Select OUTPUT TEST MODE. • Hold Rotunda Electrical Harness for Venting Tanks 134-00120 or equivalent to tank No. 1 position. • NOTE: This procedure will supply power to the fuel tank solenoid valve for approximately 30-60 seconds. If time expires, cycle START/STOP button on NGS to restore power. • Push START button. • Read system pressure on Rotunda Fuel Filter Neck Venting Kit 134-00117 or equivalent gauge. • Release Rotunda Electrical Harness for Venting Tanks 134-00120 or equivalent switch. • Press STOP button. • **Is pressure 0 kPa (0 psi) when triggered ON?**	Yes ▶ No ▶	MARK fuel tank No. 1 solenoid valve "Does Not Operate." Solenoid will be replaced after completing diagnostics. GO to **A21**. MARK fuel tank No. 1 solenoid "Good" and GO to **A21**.

FM1029900302080X

Fig. 4 Pinpoint Test A: Fuel tank solenoid valve diagnosis (Part 8 of 9). 1998

	Test Step	Result	▶	Action to Take
A21	CHECK FUEL TANK NO. 3 SOLENOID VALVE FOR STUCK OPEN CONDITION			
	• Disconnect Rotunda Electrical Harness for Venting Tanks 134-00120 or equivalent. • Tighten fuel tank No. 1 solenoid valve manual lock down jackscrew to 7-9 N-m (62-79 lb-in). • Open manual bleed valve on Rotunda Fuel Filter Neck Venting Kit 134-00117 or equivalent and vent system pressure to 0 kPa (0 psi). • Close manual bleed valve on Rotunda Fuel Filter Neck Venting Kit 134-00117 or equivalent. • Open fuel tank No. 3 solenoid valve manual lock down jackscrew. • Read system pressure. • **Is pressure 0 kPa (0 psi)?**	Yes No	▶ ▶	GO to **A22**. MARK fuel tank No. 3 solenoid valve as "Stuck Open." Solenoid will be replaced after completing diagnostics. GO to **A23**.
A22	CHECK FUEL TANK NO. 3 SOLENOID VALVE OPERATION			
	• Connect fuel tank No. 3 solenoid connector. • Connect Rotunda New Generation Star (NGS) Tester 007-00500 or equivalent to data link connector. • Select PCM. • Select ACTIVE COMMAND MODES. • Select OUTPUT TEST MODE. • NOTE: This procedure will supply power to the fuel tank solenoid valve for approximately 30-60 seconds. If time expires, cycle START/ STOP button on New Generation Star (NGS) Tester to restore power. • Push START button. • Read system pressure on Rotunda Fuel Filter Neck Venting Kit 134-00117 or equivalent gauge. • Push STOP button. • **Did pressure read 0 kPa (0 psi) when triggered ON?**	Yes No	▶ ▶	MARK fuel tank No. 3 solenoid valve "Stuck Closed." Solenoid will be replaced after completing diagnostics. GO to **A23**. GO to **A23**.
A23	CHECK FUEL TANK NO. 4 SOLENOID VALVE STUCK OPEN CONDITION			
	• Open manual bleed valve on Rotunda Fuel Filter Neck Venting Kit 134-00117 or equivalent and vent system pressure to 0 kPa (0 psi). • Close manual bleed valve on Rotunda Fuel Filter Neck Venting Kit 134-00117 or equivalent. • Tighten fuel tank No. 1 solenoid valve manual lock down jackscrew to 7-9 N-m (62-79 lb-in). • Open fuel tank No. 4 solenoid valve manual lock down jackscrew. • Read system pressure. • **Is pressure 0 kPa (0 psi)?**	Yes No	▶ ▶	GO to **A24**. MARK fuel tank No. 4 solenoid valve as "Stuck Open." REPLACE all solenoids marked "Stuck Closed." "Stuck Open" or "Does Not Operate." RESTORE vehicle. RETEST system.
A24	CHECK FUEL TANK NO. 4 SOLENOID VALVE OPERATION			
	• Disconnect fuel tank No. 3 solenoid valve connector. • Connect fuel tank No. 4 solenoid valve connector. • Connect NGS or equivalent to data link connector. • Select PCM. • Select ACTIVE COMMAND MODES. • Select OUTPUT TEST MODE. • NOTE: This procedure will supply power to the fuel tank solenoid valve for approximately 30-60 seconds. If time expires, cycle START/ STOP button on NGS to restore power. • Push START button. • Read system pressure on Rotunda Fuel Filter Neck Venting Kit 134-00117 or equivalent gauge. • Push STOP button. • **Did pressure read 0 kPa (0 psi) when triggered ON?**	Yes No	▶ ▶	MARK fuel tank No. 4 solenoid valve "Stuck Closed." REPLACE all solenoids marked "Stuck Open," "Stuck Closed" or "Does Not Operate." RESTORE vehicle. RETEST system. MARK fuel tank No. 4 solenoid valve as "Good." REPLACE all solenoids marked "Stuck Closed," "Stuck Open," or "Does Not Operate." RESTORE vehicle. RETEST system.

FM1029900302090X

Fig. 4 Pinpoint Test A: Fuel tank solenoid valve diagnosis (Part 9 of 9). 1998

TEST CONDITIONS	TEST DETAILS/RESULTS/ACTIONS
A2 CHECK FUEL TANK NO. 4 SOLENOID VALVE	
NOTE: Make sure the manual lock-down jackscrew on fuel tank No. 4 solenoid valve is open. **NOTE:** This procedure will supply power to the fuel tank solenoid valve for approximately 30-60 seconds. If time expires, cycle the start/stop button on the NGS Tester to restore power.	
1 Tank No. 4 Solenoid Connector C417 2 NGS Tester 3	4 Select the proper output test mode on the NGS Tester and press the start button. 5 Observe the system pressure on the Fuel Filler Neck Venting Kit Gauge. 6 Press the stop button on the NGS Tester. • Was the pressure on the gauge 0 kPa (0 psi) when triggered on? → **Yes** GO to **A3**. → **No** Mark No. 4 solenoid valve "good." GO to **A5**.

FM1029900303020X

Fig. 5 Pinpoint Test A: Fuel tank solenoid valve diagnosis (Part 2 of 20). 1999

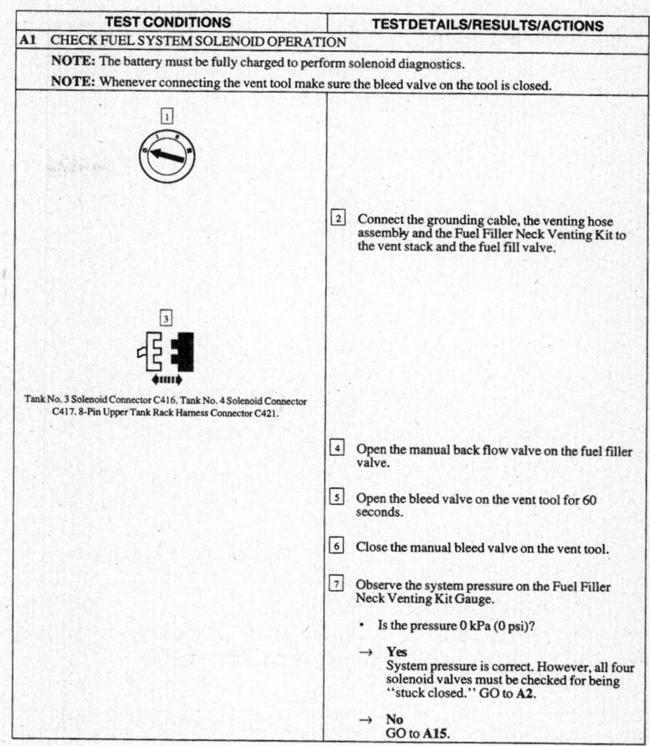

TEST CONDITIONS	TEST DETAILS/RESULTS/ACTIONS
A1 CHECK FUEL SYSTEM SOLENOID OPERATION	
NOTE: The battery must be fully charged to perform solenoid diagnostics. **NOTE:** Whenever connecting the vent tool make sure the bleed valve on the tool is closed.	
1 3 Tank No. 3 Solenoid Connector C416. Tank No. 4 Solenoid Connector C417. 8-Pin Upper Tank Rack Harness Connector C421.	2 Connect the grounding cable, the venting hose assembly and the Fuel Filler Neck Venting Kit to the vent stack and the fuel fill valve. 4 Open the manual back flow valve on the fuel filler valve. 5 Open the bleed valve on the vent tool for 60 seconds. 6 Close the manual bleed valve on the vent tool. 7 Observe the system pressure on the Fuel Filler Neck Venting Kit Gauge. • Is the pressure 0 kPa (0 psi)? → **Yes** System pressure is correct. However, all four solenoid valves must be checked for being "stuck closed." GO to **A2**. → **No** GO to **A15**.

FM1029900303010X

Fig. 5 Pinpoint Test A: Fuel tank solenoid valve diagnosis (Part 1 of 20). 1999

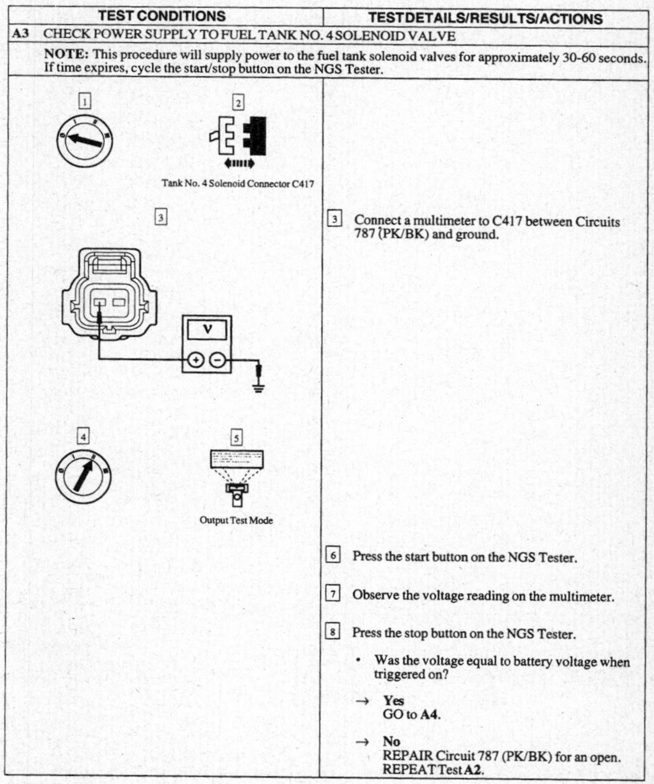

TEST CONDITIONS	TEST DETAILS/RESULTS/ACTIONS
A3 CHECK POWER SUPPLY TO FUEL TANK NO. 4 SOLENOID VALVE	
NOTE: This procedure will supply power to the fuel tank solenoid valves for approximately 30-60 seconds. If time expires, cycle the start/stop button on the NGS Tester.	
1 2 Tank No. 4 Solenoid Connector C417 3 V 4 5 Output Test Mode	3 Connect a multimeter to C417 between Circuits 787 (PK/BK) and ground. 6 Press the start button on the NGS Tester. 7 Observe the voltage reading on the multimeter. 8 Press the stop button on the NGS Tester. • Was the voltage equal to battery voltage when triggered on? → **Yes** GO to **A4**. → **No** REPAIR Circuit 787 (PK/BK) for an open. REPEAT Test **A2**.

FM1029900303030X

Fig. 5 Pinpoint Test A: Fuel tank solenoid valve diagnosis (Part 3 of 20). 1999

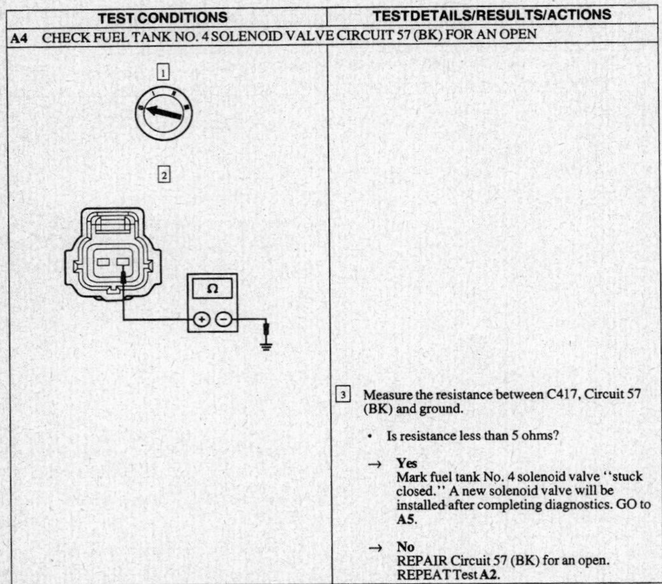

TEST CONDITIONS	TEST DETAILS/RESULTS/ACTIONS
A4 CHECK FUEL TANK NO. 4 SOLENOID VALVE CIRCUIT 57 (BK) FOR AN OPEN	
1 2	3 Measure the resistance between C417, Circuit 57 (BK) and ground. • Is resistance less than 5 ohms? → **Yes** Mark fuel tank No. 4 solenoid valve "stuck closed." A new solenoid valve will be installed after completing diagnostics. GO to **A5**. → **No** REPAIR Circuit 57 (BK) for an open. REPEAT Test **A2**.

FM1029900303040X

Fig. 5 Pinpoint Test A: Fuel tank solenoid valve diagnosis (Part 4 of 20). 1999

TEST CONDITIONS	TEST DETAILS/RESULTS/ACTIONS
A6 CHECK POWER SUPPLY TO FUEL TANK NO. 3 SOLENOID VALVE	
NOTE: This procedure will supply power to the fuel tank solenoid valves for approximately 30-60 seconds. If time expires, cycle the start/stop button on the NGS Tester.	
1 2 Tank No. 3 Solenoid Connector C416 3 4 5 Output Test Mode	3 Connect a multimeter to C416 between Circuits 787 (PK/BK) and ground. 6 Press the start button on the NGS Tester. 7 Observe the voltage reading on the multimeter. 8 Press the stop button on the NGS Tester. • Was the voltage equal to battery voltage when triggered on? → **Yes** GO to **A7**. → **No** REPAIR Circuit 787 (PK/BK) for an open. REPEAT Test **A5**.

FM1029900303060X

Fig. 5 Pinpoint Test A: Fuel tank solenoid valve diagnosis (Part 6 of 20). 1999

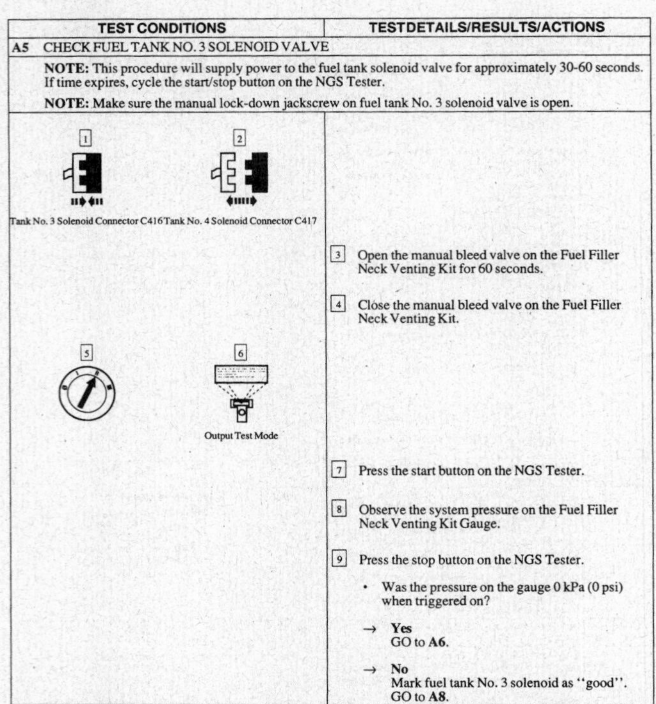

TEST CONDITIONS	TEST DETAILS/RESULTS/ACTIONS
A5 CHECK FUEL TANK NO. 3 SOLENOID VALVE	
NOTE: This procedure will supply power to the fuel tank solenoid valve for approximately 30-60 seconds. If time expires, cycle the start/stop button on the NGS Tester. **NOTE:** Make sure the manual lock-down jackscrew on fuel tank No. 3 solenoid valve is open.	
1 2 Tank No. 3 Solenoid Connector C416 Tank No. 4 Solenoid Connector C417 5 6 Output Test Mode	3 Open the manual bleed valve on the Fuel Filler Neck Venting Kit for 60 seconds. 4 Close the manual bleed valve on the Fuel Filler Neck Venting Kit. 7 Press the start button on the NGS Tester. 8 Observe the system pressure on the Fuel Filler Neck Venting Kit Gauge. 9 Press the stop button on the NGS Tester. • Was the pressure on the gauge 0 kPa (0 psi) when triggered on? → **Yes** GO to **A6**. → **No** Mark fuel tank No. 3 solenoid as "good". GO to **A8**.

FM1029900303050X

Fig. 5 Pinpoint Test A: Fuel tank solenoid valve diagnosis (Part 5 of 20). 1999

TEST CONDITIONS	TEST DETAILS/RESULTS/ACTIONS
A7 CHECK FUEL TANK NO. 3 SOLENOID VALVE CIRCUIT 57 (BK) FOR AN OPEN	
1 2	2 Measure the resistance between C416 Circuit 57 (BK) and ground. • Is the resistance less than 5 ohms? → **Yes** Mark fuel tank No. 3 solenoid valve "stuck closed." A new solenoid valve will be installed after completing diagnostics. GO to **A8**. → **No** REPAIR Circuit 57 (BK) for an open. REPEAT Test **A5**.
A8 CHECK FUEL TANK NO. 2 SOLENOID VALVE	
NOTE: The battery must be fully charged to perform solenoid valve diagnostics. **NOTE:** This procedure will supply power to the fuel tank solenoid valves for approximately 30-60 seconds. If time expires, cycle the start/stop button on the NGS Tester.	
1 2 Tank No. 3 Solenoid Valve Connector C416	3 Open the manual bleed valve on the Fuel Filler Neck Venting Kit for 60 seconds. 4 Close the manual bleed valve on the Fuel Filler Neck Venting Kit.

FM1029900303070X

Fig. 5 Pinpoint Test A: Fuel tank solenoid valve diagnosis (Part 7 of 20). 1999

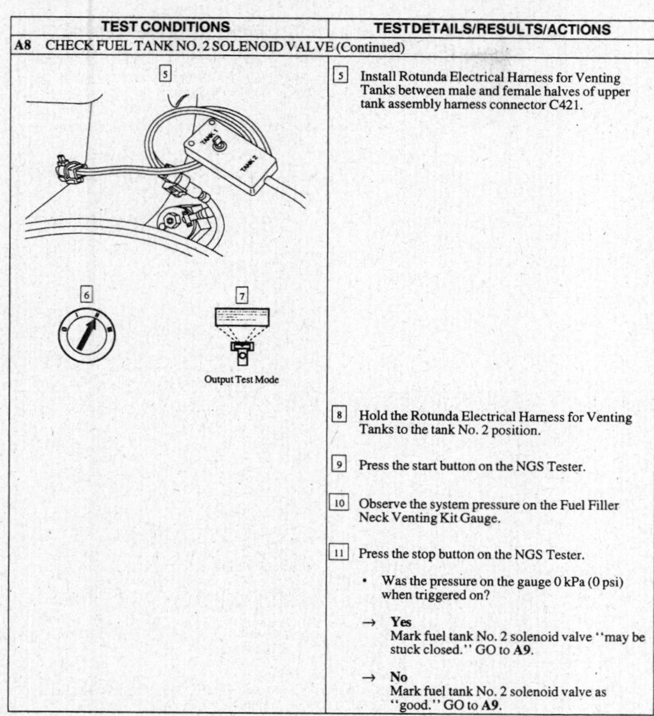

TEST CONDITIONS	TESTDETAILS/RESULTS/ACTIONS
A8 CHECK FUEL TANK NO. 2 SOLENOID VALVE (Continued)	
5	5 Install Rotunda Electrical Harness for Venting Tanks between male and female halves of upper tank assembly harness connector C421.
6 7 Output Test Mode	8 Hold the Rotunda Electrical Harness for Venting Tanks to the tank No. 2 position.
	9 Press the start button on the NGS Tester.
	10 Observe the system pressure on the Fuel Filler Neck Venting Kit Gauge.
	11 Press the stop button on the NGS Tester. • Was the pressure on the gauge 0 kPa (0 psi) when triggered on? → **Yes** Mark fuel tank No. 2 solenoid valve "may be stuck closed." GO to **A9**. → **No** Mark fuel tank No. 2 solenoid valve as "good." GO to **A9**.

FM1029900303080X

Fig. 5 Pinpoint Test A: Fuel tank solenoid valve diagnosis (Part 8 of 20). 1999

TEST CONDITIONS	TESTDETAILS/RESULTS/ACTIONS
A9 CHECK FUEL TANK NO. 1 SOLENOID VALVE (Continued)	
	9 Press the stop button on the NGS Tester. • Was the pressure on the gauge 0 kPa (0 psi) when triggered on? → **Yes** Fuel tank No. 1 solenoid valve "may be stuck closed." GO to **A10**. → **No** Mark fuel tank No. 1 solenoid valve "good." To complete diagnostics, install a new solenoid valve if the solenoid valve is marked "stuck closed." If fuel tank No. 2 solenoid valve was marked "may be stuck closed," GO to **A10**. If all solenoid valves were marked "good," diagnostics are complete. RESTORE the vehicle and test the system for normal operation.
A10 CHECK UPPER TANK RACK CIRCUIT 57 (BK)	
NOTE: At this point in the diagnostics it is necessary to access the upper fuel tank rack harness connections. Due to packaging considerations, it will be necessary to remove the upper tank rack assembly to remove the upper tank rack vent box.	
1	2 Disconnect and remove the Rotunda Electrical Harness for Venting Tanks from upper tank rack assembly harness connector C421.
	3 Open the manual bleed valve on the Fuel Filter Neck Venting Kit and vent system pressure to 0 kPa (0 psi).
	4 Close the manual bleed valve on the Fuel Filter Neck Venting Kit.
	5 Remove the upper fuel tank rack assembly.
	6 Remove the upper fuel tank rack assembly vent box.

FM1029900303100X

Fig. 5 Pinpoint Test A: Fuel tank solenoid valve diagnosis (Part 10 of 20). 1999

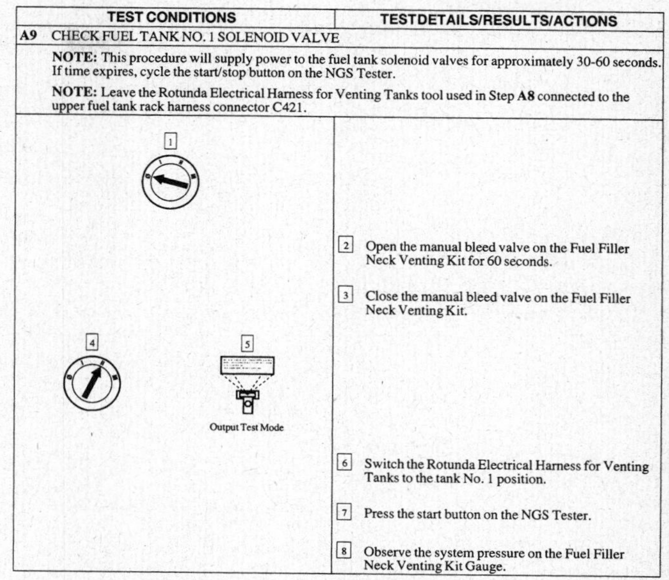

TEST CONDITIONS	TESTDETAILS/RESULTS/ACTIONS
A9 CHECK FUEL TANK NO. 1 SOLENOID VALVE	
NOTE: This procedure will supply power to the fuel tank solenoid valves for approximately 30-60 seconds. If time expires, cycle the start/stop button on the NGS Tester. **NOTE:** Leave the Rotunda Electrical Harness for Venting Tanks tool used in Step **A8** connected to the upper fuel tank rack harness connector C421.	
1	2 Open the manual bleed valve on the Fuel Filler Neck Venting Kit for 60 seconds.
	3 Close the manual bleed valve on the Fuel Filler Neck Venting Kit.
4 5 Output Test Mode	6 Switch the Rotunda Electrical Harness for Venting Tanks to the tank No. 1 position.
	7 Press the start button on the NGS Tester.
	8 Observe the system pressure on the Fuel Filler Neck Venting Kit Gauge.

FM1029900303090X

Fig. 5 Pinpoint Test A: Fuel tank solenoid valve diagnosis (Part 9 of 20). 1999

TEST CONDITIONS	TESTDETAILS/RESULTS/ACTIONS
A10 CHECK UPPER TANK RACK CIRCUIT 57 (BK) (Continued)	
7 Tank No. 1 Solenoid Valve Connector C414 8 Tank No. 2 Solenoid Valve Connector C415	9 With the upper fuel tank rack assembly removed, measure the resistance from both fuel tank No. 1 solenoid valve connector C414, Circuit 57 (BK) and fuel tank No. 2 solenoid connector C415, Circuit 57 (BK) to the upper tank rack assembly harness 8-pin connector C421 pin 1. • Is the resistance less than 5 ohms on both circuits? → **Yes** GO to **A11**. → **No** REPAIR Circuit 57 (BK) for an open. GO to **A11**.
A11 CHECK UPPER TANK RACK CIRCUIT 787 (PK/BK)	
	1 Measure the resistance between the upper tank rack assembly 8-pin harness connector C421 pin 6 and fuel tank No. 2 solenoid valve connector C415 Circuit 787 (PK/BK).
	2 Measure the resistance between the upper tank rack assembly 8-pin harness connector C421 pin 5 and fuel tank No. 1 solenoid valve connector C414, Circuit 787 (PK/BK). • Is the resistance less than 5 ohms on both circuits? → **Yes** GO to **A12**. → **No** REPAIR Circuit 787 (PK/BK) for an open. INSTALL the complete upper tank rack assembly (including the vent box) in the vehicle. REPEAT Test **A8**.

FM1029900303110X

Fig. 5 Pinpoint Test A: Fuel tank solenoid valve diagnosis (Part 11 of 20). 1999

TEST CONDITIONS	TEST DETAILS/RESULTS/ACTIONS
A12 CHECK UPPER FUEL TANK RACK ASSEMBLY MANUAL LOCK-DOWNS	
	1 With the upper fuel tank rack assembly still removed, check the fuel tank No. 1 and No. 2 solenoid valves manual lock-downs. • Are the manual lock-downs open? → **Yes** INSTALL new upper fuel tank rack assembly solenoids if marked "may be stuck closed." INSTALL the complete upper tank rack assembly (including vent box) in the vehicle. REPEAT Test **A8**. → **No** INSTALL the upper tank rack assembly without the vent box. Make all fuel line connections. GO to **A13**.
A13 CHECK FUEL TANK NO. 2 SOLENOID VALVE MANUAL LOCK-DOWN	
NOTE: Make sure the bleed valve on the Fuel Filler Neck Venting Kit is closed before proceeding with this test.	
	1 Open fuel tank No. 2 solenoid valve manual lock-down jackscrew. 2 Open the bleed valve on the Fuel Filler Neck Venting Kit for 60 seconds. 3 Close the bleed valve on the Fuel Filler Neck Venting Kit. 4 Observe the system pressure on the Fuel Filler Neck Venting Kit Gauge. • Is the pressure on the gauge 0 kPa (0 psi)? → **Yes** Mark fuel tank No. 2 solenoid valve "good." GO to **A14**. → **No** Mark fuel tank No. 2 solenoid valve "stuck open." GO to **A14**.
A14 CHECK FUEL TANK NO. 1 SOLENOID VALVE MANUAL LOCK-DOWN	
	1 Tighten the manual lock-down jackscrew on fuel tank No. 2 solenoid valve to 9 Nm (79 lb/in). 2 Open fuel tank No. 1 solenoid valve manual lock-down jackscrew.

FM1029900303120X

Fig. 5 Pinpoint Test A: Fuel tank solenoid valve diagnosis (Part 12 of 20). 1999

TEST CONDITIONS	TEST DETAILS/RESULTS/ACTIONS
A16 ISOLATE UPPER AND LOWER TANK RACK ASSEMBLIES	
	1 Tighten the manual lock-down jackscrew on fuel tank No. 3 and No. 4 solenoid valves to 9 Nm (79 lb/in). 2 Open the manual bleed valve on the Fuel Filler Neck Venting Kit for 60 seconds. 3 Close the manual bleed valve on the Fuel Filler Neck Venting Kit. 4 Observe the system pressure on the Fuel Filler Neck Venting Kit Gauge. • Is the pressure on the gauge 0 kPa (0 psi)? → **Yes** GO to **A21**. → **No** GO to **A17**.
A17 CHECK FUEL TANK NO. 1 CIRCUIT 787 (PK/BK)	
NOTE: At this point in the diagnostics it is necessary to access the upper fuel tank rack harness connectors. Due to packaging considerations, it will be necessary to remove the upper tank rack assembly to remove the upper tank rack vent box.	
1	
	2 Make sure the manual lock-downs on fuel tank No. 3 and No. 4 are still closed from Step **A16**. 3 Open the manual bleed valve on the Fuel Filler Neck Venting Kit and vent the system pressure to 0 kPa (0 psi). 4 Close the manual bleed valve on the Fuel Filler Neck Venting Kit. 5 Remove the upper tank rack assembly.

FM1029900303140X

Fig. 5 Pinpoint Test A: Fuel tank solenoid valve diagnosis (Part 14 of 20). 1999

TEST CONDITIONS	TEST DETAILS/RESULTS/ACTIONS
A14 CHECK FUEL TANK NO. 1 SOLENOID VALVE MANUAL LOCK-DOWN (Continued)	
	3 Open the bleed valve on the Fuel Filler Neck Venting Kit for 60 seconds. 4 Close the bleed valve on the Fuel Filler Neck Venting Kit. 5 Observe the system pressure on the Fuel Filler Neck Venting Kit Gauge. • Is the system pressure on the Fuel Filler Neck Venting Kit Gauge 0 kPa (0 psi)? → **Yes** Mark fuel tank No. 1 solenoid valve "good." GO to **A8** to retest the upper tank rack. → **No** MARK fuel tank No. 1 solenoid valve "stuck open." INSTALL new upper fuel tank rack assembly solenoid valves if marked "stuck open." RESTORE the vehicle. TEST the system for normal operation.
A15 CHECK ALL SOLENOID CIRCUITS 787 (PK/BK) FOR A SHORT TO B+	
1	
2	2 Measure the voltage at fuel tank No. 3 (C416) and No. 4 (C417) solenoid connectors Circuit 787 (PK/BK) and ground. Also measure the voltage at the upper fuel tank rack assembly harness connector C421 (male side of connector, pins 5 and 6) Circuits 787 (PK/BK) and ground. • Is battery voltage present on any connector 787 (PK/BK) circuit? → **Yes** REPAIR Circuit 787 (PK/BK) for a short to B+. REPEAT Test **A1**. → **No** GO to **A16**.

FM1029900303130X

Fig. 5 Pinpoint Test A: Fuel tank solenoid valve diagnosis (Part 13 of 20). 1999

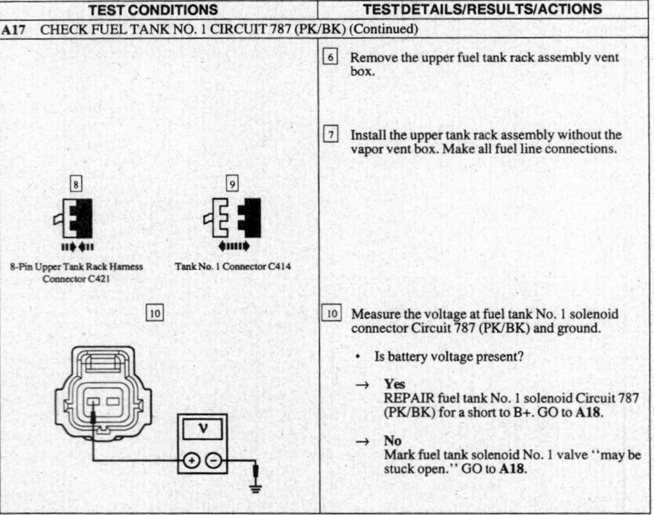

TEST CONDITIONS	TEST DETAILS/RESULTS/ACTIONS
A17 CHECK FUEL TANK NO. 1 CIRCUIT 787 (PK/BK) (Continued)	
	6 Remove the upper fuel tank rack assembly vent box. 7 Install the upper tank rack assembly without the vapor vent box. Make all fuel line connections.
8 8-Pin Upper Tank Rack Harness Connector C421 9 Tank No. 1 Connector C414	
10	10 Measure the voltage at fuel tank No. 1 solenoid connector Circuit 787 (PK/BK) and ground. • Is battery voltage present? → **Yes** REPAIR fuel tank No. 1 solenoid Circuit 787 (PK/BK) for a short to B+. GO to **A18**. → **No** Mark fuel tank solenoid No. 1 valve "may be stuck open." GO to **A18**.

FM1029900303150X

Fig. 5 Pinpoint Test A: Fuel tank solenoid valve diagnosis (Part 15 of 20). 1999

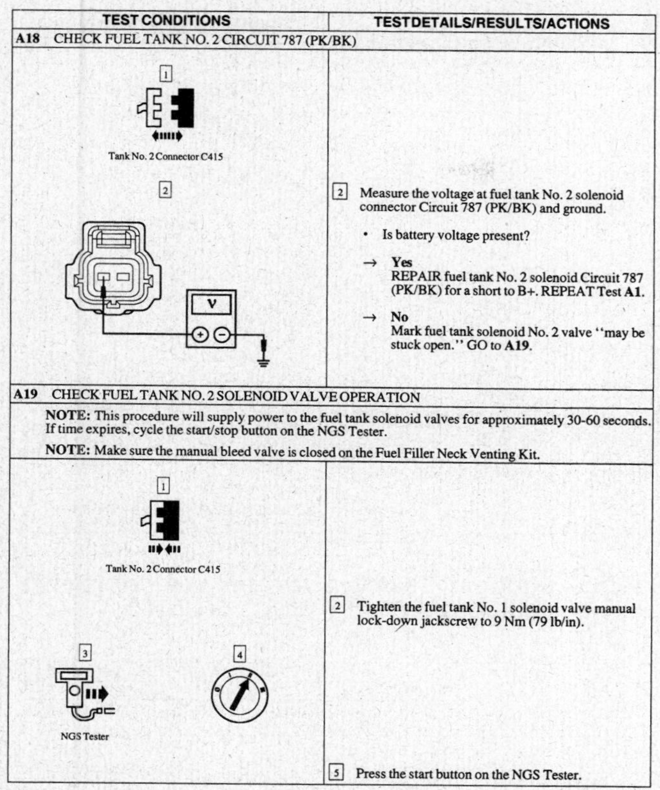

TEST CONDITIONS	TEST DETAILS/RESULTS/ACTIONS
A18 CHECK FUEL TANK NO. 2 CIRCUIT 787 (PK/BK)	
1 Tank No. 2 Connector C415	
2	2 Measure the voltage at fuel tank No. 2 solenoid connector Circuit 787 (PK/BK) and ground. • Is battery voltage present? → **Yes** REPAIR fuel tank No. 2 solenoid Circuit 787 (PK/BK) for a short to B+. REPEAT Test **A1**. → **No** Mark fuel tank solenoid No. 2 valve "may be stuck open." GO to **A19**.
A19 CHECK FUEL TANK NO. 2 SOLENOID VALVE OPERATION	
NOTE: This procedure will supply power to the fuel tank solenoid valves for approximately 30-60 seconds. If time expires, cycle the start/stop button on the NGS Tester. **NOTE:** Make sure the manual bleed valve is closed on the Fuel Filler Neck Venting Kit.	
1 Tank No. 2 Connector C415	2 Tighten the fuel tank No. 1 solenoid valve manual lock-down jackscrew to 9 Nm (79 lb/in).
3 NGS Tester; 4	5 Press the start button on the NGS Tester.

FM1029900303160X

Fig. 5 Pinpoint Test A: Fuel tank solenoid valve diagnosis (Part 16 of 20). 1999

TEST CONDITIONS	TEST DETAILS/RESULTS/ACTIONS
A19 CHECK FUEL TANK NO. 2 SOLENOID VALVE OPERATION (Continued)	
6 Output Test Mode	7 Observe the system pressure on the Fuel Filler Neck Venting Kit Gauge. 8 Press the stop button on the NGS Tester. • Was the pressure on the gauge 0 kPa (0 psi) when triggered on? → **Yes** Mark fuel tank No. 2 solenoid valve "stuck open." A new solenoid will be installed after completing diagnostics. GO to **A20**. → **No** Mark fuel tank No. 2 solenoid valve "good." GO to **A20**.
A20 CHECK FUEL TANK NO. 1 SOLENOID VALVE OPERATION	
NOTE: This procedure will supply power to the fuel tank solenoid valve for approximately 30-60 seconds. If time expires, cycle the start/stop button on the NGS Tester.	
1	2 Open the manual bleed valve on the Fuel Filler Neck Venting Kit and vent the system pressure to 0 kPa (0 psi). 3 Close the manual bleed valve on the Fuel Filler Neck Venting Kit. 4 Open the fuel tank No. 1 solenoid valve manual lock-down jackscrew. 5 Tighten the fuel tank No. 2 solenoid valve manual lock-down jackscrew to 9 Nm (79 lb/in).

FM1029900303170X

Fig. 5 Pinpoint Test A: Fuel tank solenoid valve diagnosis (Part 17 of 20). 1999

TEST CONDITIONS	TEST DETAILS/RESULTS/ACTIONS
A20 CHECK FUEL TANK NO. 1 SOLENOID VALVE OPERATION (Continued)	
6 Tank No. 2 Connector C415; 7 Tank No. 1 Connector C414; 8; 9 Output Test Mode	10 Press the start button on the NGS Tester. 11 Observe the system pressure on the Fuel Filler Neck Venting Kit Gauge. 12 Press the stop button on the NGS Tester. • Was the pressure on the gauge 0 kPa (0 psi) when triggered on? → **Yes** Mark fuel tank No. 1 solenoid valve "stuck open." INSTALL new upper tank rack assembly valves if marked "stuck open." RESTORE the vehicle and repeat Test **A1**. → **No** Mark fuel tank No. 1 solenoid valve "good." RESTORE the vehicle. TEST the system for normal operation.
A21 CHECK FUEL TANK NO. 3 SOLENOID VALVE FOR STUCK OPEN CONDITION	
1	2 Open the manual lock-down jackscrew on fuel tank No. 3 solenoid valve. 3 Make sure the manual lock-down jackscrew on fuel tank No. 4 solenoid valve is still closed from Step **A16**. 4 Open the manual bleed valve on the Fuel Filler Neck Venting Kit for 60 seconds. 5 Close the manual bleed valve on the Fuel Filler Neck Venting Kit.

FM1029900303180X

Fig. 5 Pinpoint Test A: Fuel tank solenoid valve diagnosis (Part 18 of 20). 1999

TEST CONDITIONS	TEST DETAILS/RESULTS/ACTIONS
A21 CHECK FUEL TANK NO. 3 SOLENOID VALVE FOR STUCK OPEN CONDITION (Continued)	
	6 Observe the system pressure on the Fuel Filler Neck Venting Kit Gauge. • Is the pressure on the gauge 0 kPa (0 psi)? → **Yes** Mark fuel tank No. 3 solenoid valve "good." GO to **A22**. → **No** Mark fuel tank No. 3 solenoid valve "stuck open." A new solenoid valve will be installed when diagnostics are complete. GO to **A22**.
A22 CHECK FUEL TANK NO. 4 SOLENOID FOR STUCK OPEN CONDITION	
1	2 Close the manual lock-down jackscrew fuel tank No. 3 solenoid valve to 9 Nm (79 lb/in). 3 Open the manual bleed valve on the Fuel Filler Neck Venting Kit and vent the system pressure to 0 kPa (0 psi). 4 Close the manual bleed valve on the Fuel Filler Neck Venting Kit. 5 Open the manual lock-down jackscrew on fuel tank No. 4 solenoid valve. 6 Open the manual bleed valve on the Fuel Filler Neck Venting Kit for 60 seconds. 7 Close the manual bleed valve on the Fuel Filler Neck Venting Kit.

FM1029900303190X

Fig. 5 Pinpoint Test A: Fuel tank solenoid valve diagnosis (Part 19 of 20). 1999

TEST CONDITIONS	TEST DETAILS/RESULTS/ACTIONS
A22 CHECK FUEL TANK NO. 4 SOLENOID FOR STUCK OPEN CONDITION (Continued)	
	8 Observe the system pressure on the Fuel Filler Neck Venting Kit Gauge. • Is the pressure on the gauge 0 kPa (0 psi)? → **Yes** Mark fuel tank No. 4 solenoid valve "good." If No. 3 solenoid valve was marked "stuck open," INSTALL a new solenoid valve at this time. RESTORE the vehicle. Test the system for normal operation. → **No** Fuel tank No. 4 solenoid valve is stuck open. INSTALL a new fuel tank No. 4 solenoid valve. INSTALL new solenoid valves for all other solenoid valves marked "stuck open." RESTORE the vehicle. TEST the system for normal operation.

FM1029900303200X

Fig. 5 Pinpoint Test A: Fuel tank solenoid valve diagnosis (Part 20 of 20). 1999

TEST CONDITIONS	TEST DETAILS/RESULTS/ACTIONS
A1 CHECK FUEL SYSTEM SOLENOID OPERATION (Continued)	
	6 Close the manual bleed valve on the vent tool. 7 Observe the system pressure on the Fuel Filler Neck Venting Kit Gauge. • Is the pressure 0 kPa (0 psi)? → **Yes** System pressure is correct. However, all six solenoid valves must be checked for being "stuck closed." GO to **A2**. → **No** GO to **A15**.
A2 CHECK FUEL TANK NO. 4 SOLENOID VALVE **Note:** Make sure the manual lock-down jackscrew on fuel tank No. 4 solenoid valve is open. **Note:** This procedure will supply power to the fuel tank solenoid valve for approximately 30-60 seconds. If time expires, cycle the start/stop button on the scan tool to restore power.	
1 Tank No. 4 Solenoid Connector C417 2 scan tool 3	4 Select the correct output test mode on the scan tool and press the start button. 5 Observe the system pressure on the Fuel Filler Neck Venting Kit Gauge. 6 Press the stop button on the scan tool. • Was the pressure on the gauge 0 kPa (0 psi) when triggered on? → **Yes** GO to **A3**. → **No** Mark No. 4 solenoid valve "good." GO to **A5**.

FM1029900362020X

Fig. 6 Pinpoint Test A: Fuel tank solenoid valve diagnosis (Part 2 of 26). 2000–02

TEST CONDITIONS	TEST DETAILS/RESULTS/ACTIONS
A1 CHECK FUEL SYSTEM SOLENOID OPERATION **Note:** The battery must be fully charged to carry out solenoid diagnostics. **Note:** Whenever connecting the vent tool make sure the bleed valve on the tool is closed.	
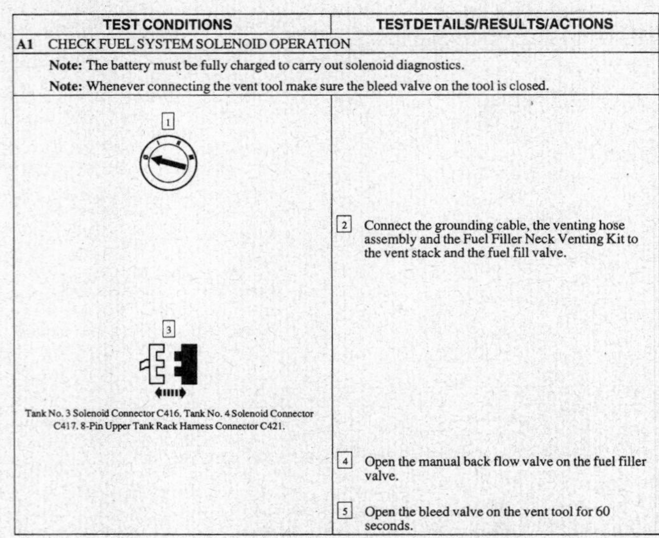	2 Connect the grounding cable, the venting hose assembly and the Fuel Filler Neck Venting Kit to the vent stack and the fuel fill valve. 4 Open the manual back flow valve on the fuel filler valve. 5 Open the bleed valve on the vent tool for 60 seconds.

FM1029900362010X

Fig. 6 Pinpoint Test A: Fuel tank solenoid valve diagnosis (Part 1 of 26). 2000–02

TEST CONDITIONS	TEST DETAILS/RESULTS/ACTIONS
A3 CHECK POWER SUPPLY TO FUEL TANK NO. 4 SOLENOID VALVE **Note:** This procedure will supply power to the fuel tank solenoid valves for approximately 30-60 seconds. If time expires, cycle the start/stop button on the scan tool.	
1 2 Tank No. 4 Solenoid Connector C417 3 V 4 5 Output Test Mode	3 Connect a multimeter to C417 between circuits 787 (PK/BK) and ground. 6 Press the start button on the scan tool. 7 Observe the voltage reading on the multimeter. 8 Press the stop button on the scan tool. • Was the voltage equal to battery voltage when triggered on? → **Yes** GO to **A4**. → **No** REPAIR circuit 787 (PK/BK) for an open. REPEAT Test **A2**.

FM1029900362030X

Fig. 6 Pinpoint Test A: Fuel tank solenoid valve diagnosis (Part 3 of 26). 2000–02

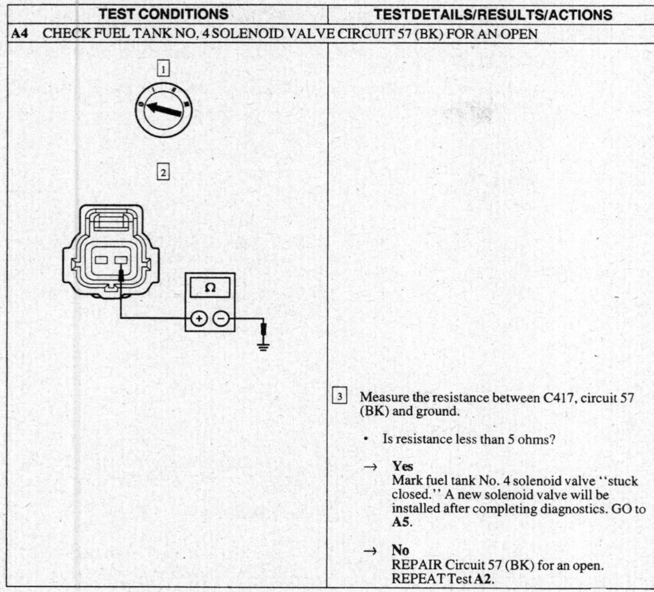

TEST CONDITIONS	TEST DETAILS/RESULTS/ACTIONS
A4 CHECK FUEL TANK NO. 4 SOLENOID VALVE CIRCUIT 57 (BK) FOR AN OPEN	
1 2	3 Measure the resistance between C417, circuit 57 (BK) and ground. • Is resistance less than 5 ohms? → **Yes** Mark fuel tank No. 4 solenoid valve "stuck closed." A new solenoid valve will be installed after completing diagnostics. GO to **A5**. → **No** REPAIR Circuit 57 (BK) for an open. REPEAT Test **A2**.

FM1029900362040X

Fig. 6 Pinpoint Test A: Fuel tank solenoid valve diagnosis (Part 4 of 26). 2000–02

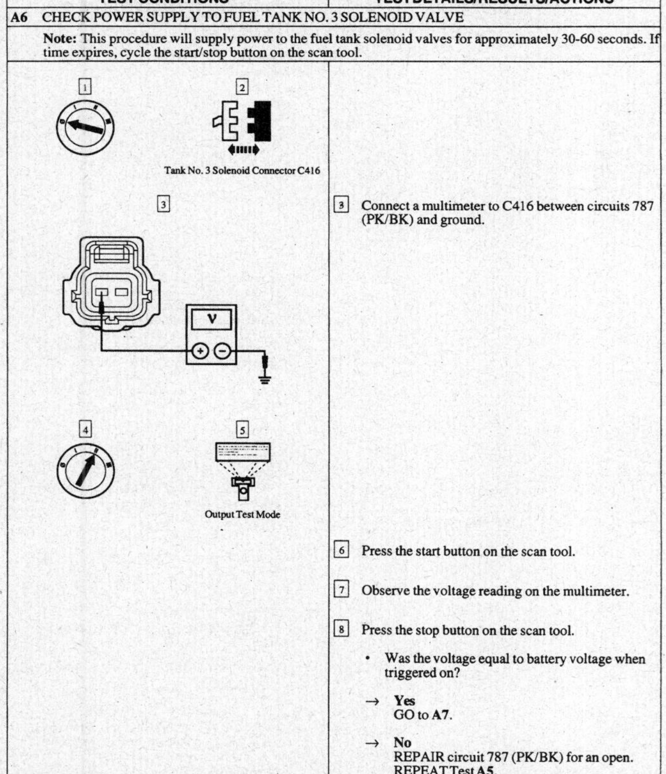

TEST CONDITIONS	TEST DETAILS/RESULTS/ACTIONS
A6 CHECK POWER SUPPLY TO FUEL TANK NO. 3 SOLENOID VALVE	
Note: This procedure will supply power to the fuel tank solenoid valves for approximately 30-60 seconds. If time expires, cycle the start/stop button on the scan tool.	
1 2 Tank No. 3 Solenoid Connector C416 3 4 5 Output Test Mode	3 Connect a multimeter to C416 between circuits 787 (PK/BK) and ground. 6 Press the start button on the scan tool. 7 Observe the voltage reading on the multimeter. 8 Press the stop button on the scan tool. • Was the voltage equal to battery voltage when triggered on? → **Yes** GO to **A7**. → **No** REPAIR circuit 787 (PK/BK) for an open. REPEAT Test **A5**.

FM1029900362060X

Fig. 6 Pinpoint Test A: Fuel tank solenoid valve diagnosis (Part 6 of 26). 2000–02

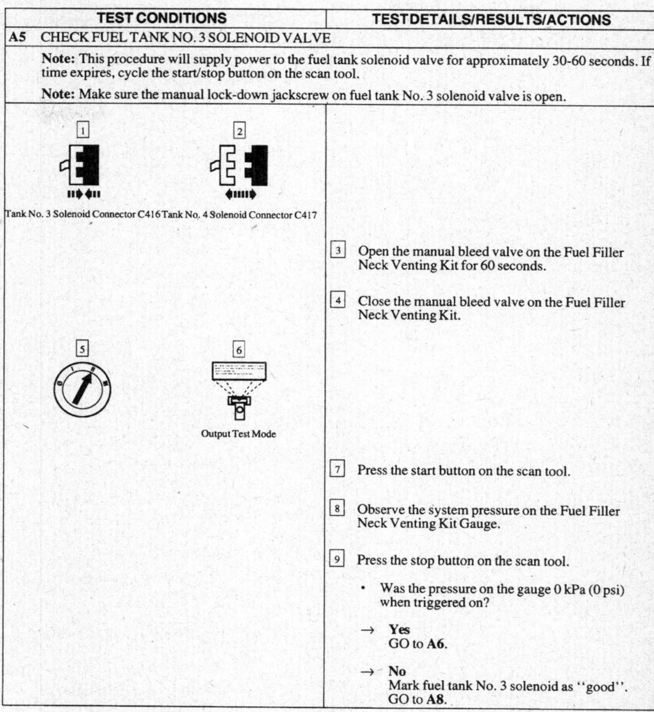

TEST CONDITIONS	TEST DETAILS/RESULTS/ACTIONS
A5 CHECK FUEL TANK NO. 3 SOLENOID VALVE	
Note: This procedure will supply power to the fuel tank solenoid valve for approximately 30-60 seconds. If time expires, cycle the start/stop button on the scan tool. **Note:** Make sure the manual lock-down jackscrew on fuel tank No. 3 solenoid valve is open.	
1 Tank No. 3 Solenoid Connector C416 2 Tank No. 4 Solenoid Connector C417 5 6 Output Test Mode	3 Open the manual bleed valve on the Fuel Filler Neck Venting Kit for 60 seconds. 4 Close the manual bleed valve on the Fuel Filler Neck Venting Kit. 7 Press the start button on the scan tool. 8 Observe the system pressure on the Fuel Filler Neck Venting Kit Gauge. 9 Press the stop button on the scan tool. • Was the pressure on the gauge 0 kPa (0 psi) when triggered on? → **Yes** GO to **A6**. → **No** Mark fuel tank No. 3 solenoid as "good". GO to **A8**.

FM1029900362050X

Fig. 6 Pinpoint Test A: Fuel tank solenoid valve diagnosis (Part 5 of 26). 2000–02

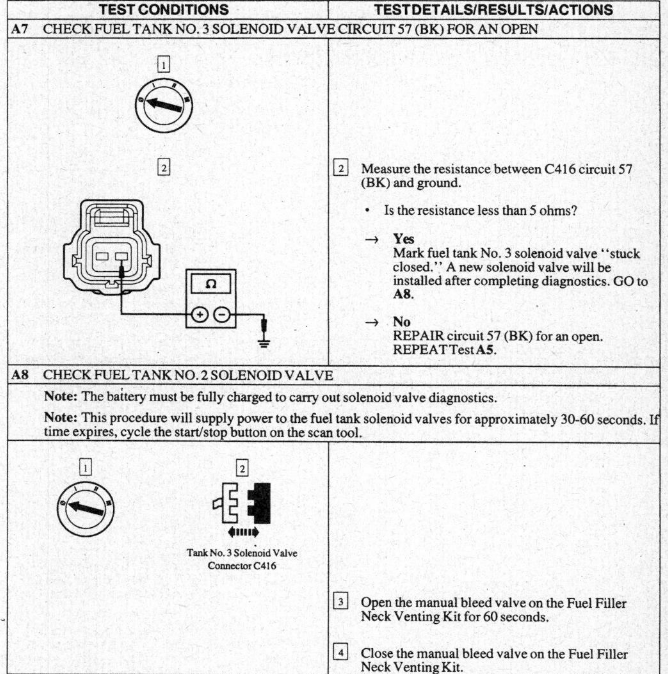

TEST CONDITIONS	TEST DETAILS/RESULTS/ACTIONS
A7 CHECK FUEL TANK NO. 3 SOLENOID VALVE CIRCUIT 57 (BK) FOR AN OPEN	
1 2	2 Measure the resistance between C416 circuit 57 (BK) and ground. • Is the resistance less than 5 ohms? → **Yes** Mark fuel tank No. 3 solenoid valve "stuck closed." A new solenoid valve will be installed after completing diagnostics. GO to **A8**. → **No** REPAIR circuit 57 (BK) for an open. REPEAT Test **A5**.
A8 CHECK FUEL TANK NO. 2 SOLENOID VALVE	
Note: The battery must be fully charged to carry out solenoid valve diagnostics. **Note:** This procedure will supply power to the fuel tank solenoid valves for approximately 30-60 seconds. If time expires, cycle the start/stop button on the scan tool.	
1 2 Tank No. 3 Solenoid Valve Connector C416	3 Open the manual bleed valve on the Fuel Filler Neck Venting Kit for 60 seconds. 4 Close the manual bleed valve on the Fuel Filler Neck Venting Kit.

FM1029900362070X

Fig. 6 Pinpoint Test A: Fuel tank solenoid valve diagnosis (Part 7 of 26). 2000–02

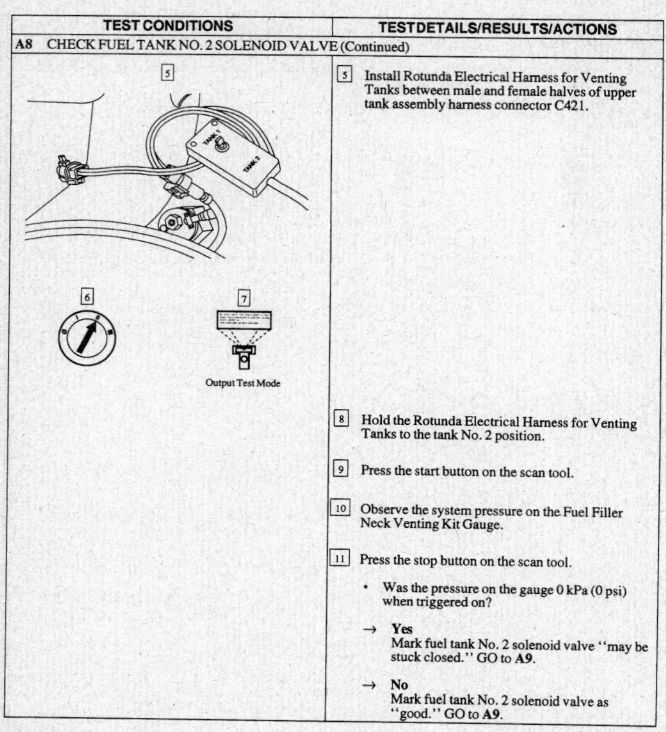

TEST CONDITIONS	TEST DETAILS/RESULTS/ACTIONS
A8 CHECK FUEL TANK NO. 2 SOLENOID VALVE (Continued)	
5 / 6 / 7 Output Test Mode	5 Install Rotunda Electrical Harness for Venting Tanks between male and female halves of upper tank assembly harness connector C421.
	8 Hold the Rotunda Electrical Harness for Venting Tanks to the tank No. 2 position.
	9 Press the start button on the scan tool.
	10 Observe the system pressure on the Fuel Filler Neck Venting Kit Gauge.
	11 Press the stop button on the scan tool. • Was the pressure on the gauge 0 kPa (0 psi) when triggered on? → **Yes** Mark fuel tank No. 2 solenoid valve "may be stuck closed." GO to **A9**. → **No** Mark fuel tank No. 2 solenoid valve as "good." GO to **A9**.

FM1029900362080X

Fig. 6 Pinpoint Test A: Fuel tank solenoid valve diagnosis (Part 8 of 26). 2000–02

TEST CONDITIONS	TEST DETAILS/RESULTS/ACTIONS
A9 CHECK FUEL TANK NO. 1 SOLENOID VALVE (Continued)	
	9 Press the stop button on the scan tool. • Was the pressure on the gauge 0 kPa (0 psi) when triggered on? → **Yes** Fuel tank No. 1 solenoid valve "may be stuck closed." GO to **A10**. → No Mark fuel tank No. 1 solenoid valve "good." To complete diagnostics, install a new solenoid valve if the solenoid valve is marked "stuck closed." If fuel tank No. 2 solenoid valve was marked "may be stuck closed," GO to **A10**. If all solenoid valves were marked "good," diagnostics are complete. RESTORE the vehicle and test the system for normal operation.
A10 CHECK UPPER AND REAR TANK RACK CIRCUIT 57 (BK)	
Note: At this point in the diagnostics it is necessary to access the upper and rear fuel tank rack harness connections. Due to packaging considerations, it will be necessary to remove the upper and rear tank rack assemblies to remove the upper and rear tank rack vent boxes.	
1	
	2 Disconnect and remove the Rotunda Electrical Harness for Venting Tanks from the upper and rear tank rack assembly harness connectors C420F.
	3 Open the manual bleed valve on the Fuel Filter Neck Venting Kit and vent system pressure to 0 kPa (0 psi).
	4 Close the manual bleed valve on the Fuel Filter Neck Venting Kit.
	5 Remove the upper and rear fuel tank rack assemblies.

FM1029900362100X

Fig. 6 Pinpoint Test A: Fuel tank solenoid valve diagnosis (Part 10 of 26). 2000–02

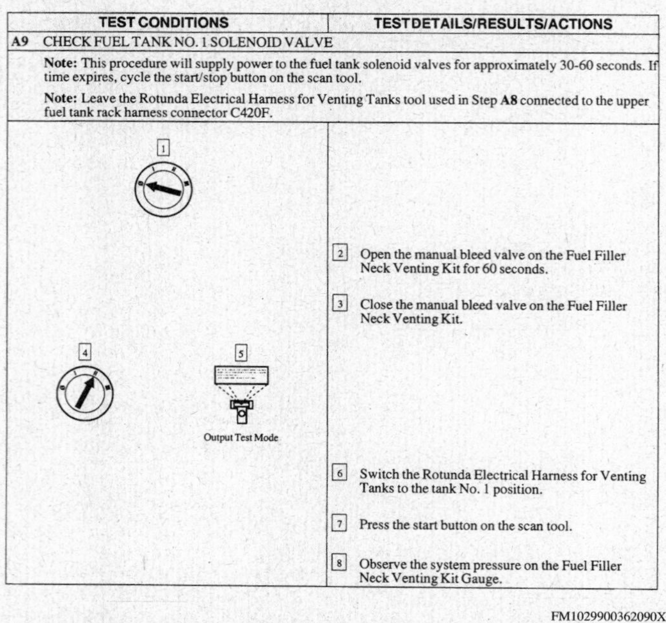

TEST CONDITIONS	TEST DETAILS/RESULTS/ACTIONS
A9 CHECK FUEL TANK NO. 1 SOLENOID VALVE	
Note: This procedure will supply power to the fuel tank solenoid valves for approximately 30-60 seconds. If time expires, cycle the start/stop button on the scan tool. **Note:** Leave the Rotunda Electrical Harness for Venting Tanks tool used in Step **A8** connected to the upper fuel tank rack harness connector C420F.	
1	
	2 Open the manual bleed valve on the Fuel Filler Neck Venting Kit for 60 seconds.
	3 Close the manual bleed valve on the Fuel Filler Neck Venting Kit.
4 / 5 Output Test Mode	
	6 Switch the Rotunda Electrical Harness for Venting Tanks to the tank No. 1 position.
	7 Press the start button on the scan tool.
	8 Observe the system pressure on the Fuel Filler Neck Venting Kit Gauge.

FM1029900362090X

Fig. 6 Pinpoint Test A: Fuel tank solenoid valve diagnosis (Part 9 of 26). 2000–02

TEST CONDITIONS	TEST DETAILS/RESULTS/ACTIONS
A10 CHECK UPPER AND REAR TANK RACK CIRCUIT 57 (BK) (Continued)	
	6 Remove the upper and rear fuel tank rack assembly vent boxes.
7 Tank No. 1 Solenoid Valve Connector C416 8 Tank No. 2 Solenoid Valve Connector C417 9 Tank No. 5 Solenoid Valve Connector C418 10 Tank No. 6 Solenoid Valve Connector C419	
	11 With the upper and rear fuel tank rack assemblies removed, measure the resistance between fuel tank No. 1 solenoid valve connector C416 circuit 57 (BK), fuel tank No. 2 solenoid connector C417 circuit 57 (BK), fuel tank No. 5 solenoid connector C418 circuit 57 (BK), fuel tank No. 6 solenoid connector C419 circuit 57 (BK), and ground. • Is the resistance less than 5 ohms on both circuits? → **Yes** GO to **A11**. → **No** REPAIR circuit 57 (BK) for an open. GO to **A11**.
A11 CHECK UPPER AND REAR TANK RACK CIRCUIT 787 (PK/BK)	
	1 Measure the resistance between connector C466 at the inertial fuel shut-of switch, and solenoid valve connectors C418, C419, C416 and C417, (PK/BK) circuit 787. • Is the resistance less than 5 ohms on both circuits? → **Yes** GO to **A12**. → **No** REPAIR circuit 787 (PK/BK) for an open. INSTALL complete upper and rear tank rack assemblies (including the vent boxes) in the vehicle. REPEAT Test **A8**.

FM1029900362110X

Fig. 6 Pinpoint Test A: Fuel tank solenoid valve diagnosis (Part 11 of 26). 2000–02

TEST CONDITIONS	TEST DETAILS/RESULTS/ACTIONS
A12 CHECK UPPER FUEL TANK RACK ASSEMBLY MANUAL LOCK-DOWNS	
	1 With the upper and rear fuel tank rack assemblies still removed, check the fuel tank No. 1 and No. 2 solenoid valves manual lock-downs. • Are the manual lock-downs open? → **Yes** INSTALL new upper fuel tank rack assembly solenoids if marked "may be stuck closed." INSTALL the complete upper tank rack assembly (including vent box) in the vehicle. REPEAT Test **A8**. → **No** INSTALL the upper and rear tank rack assemblies without the vent boxes. Make all fuel line connections. GO to **A13**.
A13 CHECK FUEL TANK NO. 2 SOLENOID VALVE MANUAL LOCK-DOWN	
Note: Make sure the bleed valve on the Fuel Filler Neck Venting Kit is closed before proceeding with this test.	
	1 Open fuel tank No. 2 solenoid valve manual lock-down jackscrew. 2 Open the bleed valve on the Fuel Filler Neck Venting Kit for 60 seconds. 3 Close the bleed valve on the Fuel Filler Neck Venting Kit. 4 Observe the system pressure on the Fuel Filler Neck Venting Kit Gauge. • Is the pressure on the gauge 0 kPa (0 psi)? → **Yes** Mark fuel tank No. 2 solenoid valve "good." GO to **A14**. → **No** Mark fuel tank No. 2 solenoid valve "stuck open." GO to **A14**.
A14 CHECK FUEL TANK NO. 1 SOLENOID VALVE MANUAL LOCK-DOWN	
	1 Tighten the manual lock-down jackscrew on fuel tank No. 2 solenoid valve to 9 Nm (79 lb/in). 2 Open fuel tank No. 1 solenoid valve manual lock-down jackscrew.

FM1029900362120X

Fig. 6 Pinpoint Test A: Fuel tank solenoid valve diagnosis (Part 12 of 26). 2000–02

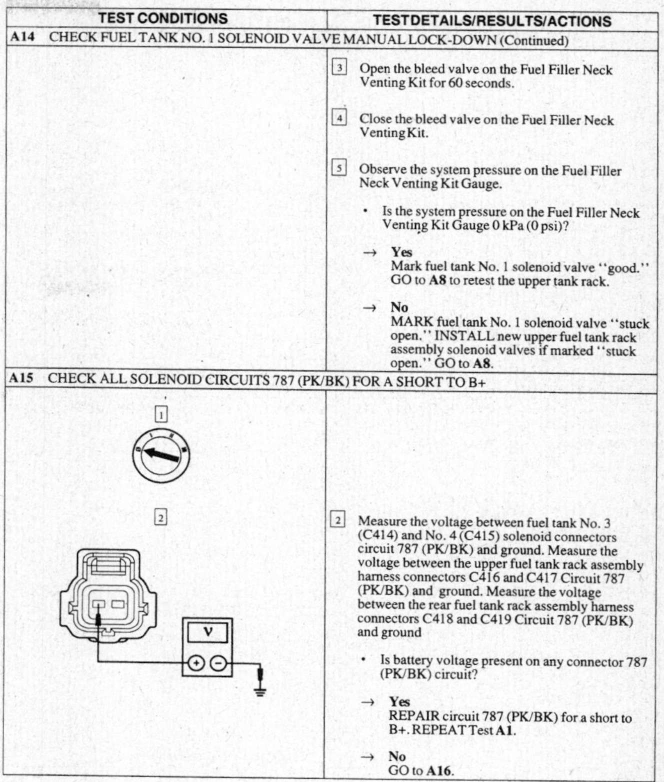

TEST CONDITIONS	TEST DETAILS/RESULTS/ACTIONS
A14 CHECK FUEL TANK NO. 1 SOLENOID VALVE MANUAL LOCK-DOWN (Continued)	
	3 Open the bleed valve on the Fuel Filler Neck Venting Kit for 60 seconds. 4 Close the bleed valve on the Fuel Filler Neck Venting Kit. 5 Observe the system pressure on the Fuel Filler Neck Venting Kit Gauge. • Is the system pressure on the Fuel Filler Neck Venting Kit Gauge 0 kPa (0 psi)? → **Yes** Mark fuel tank No. 1 solenoid valve "good." GO to **A8** to retest the upper tank rack. → **No** MARK fuel tank No. 1 solenoid valve "stuck open." INSTALL new upper fuel tank rack assembly solenoid valves if marked "stuck open." GO to **A8**.
A15 CHECK ALL SOLENOID CIRCUITS 787 (PK/BK) FOR A SHORT TO B+	
1 2	2 Measure the voltage between fuel tank No. 3 (C414) and No. 4 (C415) solenoid connectors circuit 787 (PK/BK) and ground. Measure the voltage between the upper fuel tank rack assembly harness connectors C416 and C417 Circuit 787 (PK/BK) and ground. Measure the voltage between the rear fuel tank rack assembly harness connectors C418 and C419 Circuit 787 (PK/BK) and ground • Is battery voltage present on any connector 787 (PK/BK) circuit? → **Yes** REPAIR circuit 787 (PK/BK) for a short to B+. REPEAT Test **A1**. → **No** GO to **A16**.

FM1029900362130X

Fig. 6 Pinpoint Test A: Fuel tank solenoid valve diagnosis (Part 13 of 26). 2000–02

TEST CONDITIONS	TEST DETAILS/RESULTS/ACTIONS
A16 ISOLATE UPPER AND LOWER TANK RACK ASSEMBLIES	
Note: At this point in the diagnostics it is necessary to remove the rear rack assembly.	
	1 Tighten the manual lock-down jackscrew on fuel tank No. 3 and No. 4 solenoid valves to 9 Nm (79 lb/in). 2 Open the manual bleed valve on the Fuel Filler Neck Venting Kit for 60 seconds. 3 Close the manual bleed valve on the Fuel Filler Neck Venting Kit. 4 Observe the system pressure on the Fuel Filler Neck Venting Kit Gauge. • Is the pressure on the gauge 0 kPa (0 psi)? → **Yes** GO to **A21**. → **No** GO to **A17**.
A17 CHECK FUEL TANK NO. 1 CIRCUIT 787 (PK/BK)	
Note: At this point in the diagnostics it is necessary to access the upper fuel tank rack harness connectors. Due to packaging considerations, it will be necessary to remove the upper tank rack assembly to remove the upper tank rack vent box.	
1	2 Make sure the manual lock-downs on fuel tank No. 3 and No. 4 are still closed from Step **A16**. 3 Open the manual bleed valve on the Fuel Filler Neck Venting Kit and vent the system pressure to 0 kPa (0 psi). 4 Close the manual bleed valve on the Fuel Filler Neck Venting Kit. 5 Remove the upper tank rack assembly.

FM1029900362140X

Fig. 6 Pinpoint Test A: Fuel tank solenoid valve diagnosis (Part 14 of 26). 2000–02

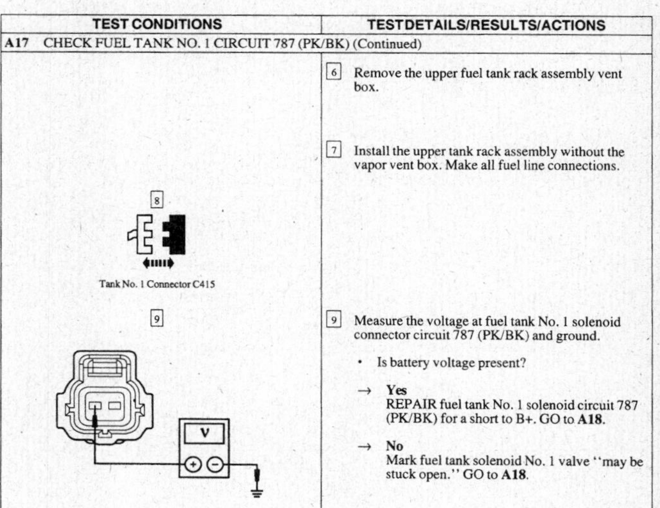

TEST CONDITIONS	TEST DETAILS/RESULTS/ACTIONS
A17 CHECK FUEL TANK NO. 1 CIRCUIT 787 (PK/BK) (Continued)	
	6 Remove the upper fuel tank rack assembly vent box. 7 Install the upper tank rack assembly without the vapor vent box. Make all fuel line connections.
8 Tank No. 1 Connector C415 9	9 Measure the voltage at fuel tank No. 1 solenoid connector circuit 787 (PK/BK) and ground. • Is battery voltage present? → **Yes** REPAIR fuel tank No. 1 solenoid circuit 787 (PK/BK) for a short to B+. GO to **A18**. → **No** Mark fuel tank solenoid No. 1 valve "may be stuck open." GO to **A18**.

FM1029900362150X

Fig. 6 Pinpoint Test A: Fuel tank solenoid valve diagnosis (Part 15 of 26). 2000–02

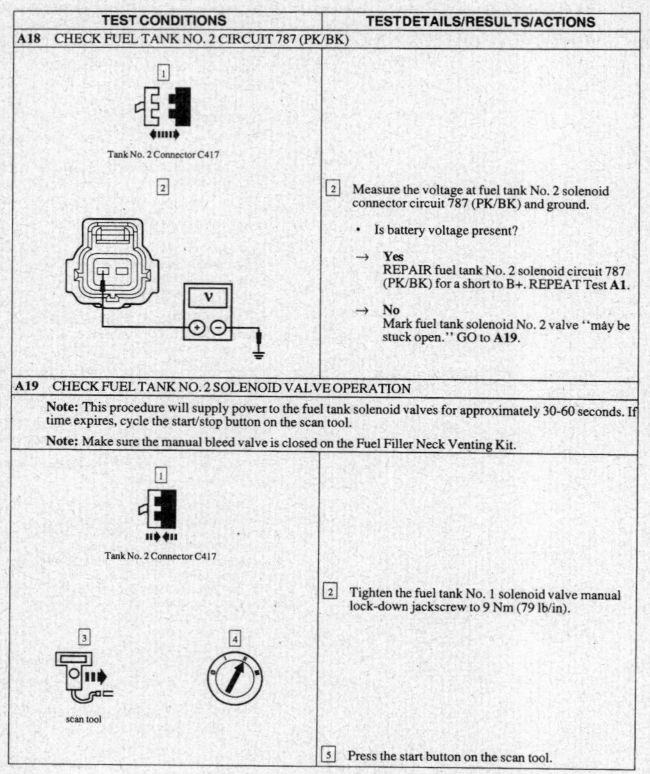

TEST CONDITIONS	TEST DETAILS/RESULTS/ACTIONS
A18 CHECK FUEL TANK NO. 2 CIRCUIT 787 (PK/BK)	
1 Tank No. 2 Connector C417	
2	2 Measure the voltage at fuel tank No. 2 solenoid connector circuit 787 (PK/BK) and ground. • Is battery voltage present? → **Yes** REPAIR fuel tank No. 2 solenoid circuit 787 (PK/BK) for a short to B+. REPEAT Test **A1**. → **No** Mark fuel tank solenoid No. 2 valve "may be stuck open." GO to **A19**.
A19 CHECK FUEL TANK NO. 2 SOLENOID VALVE OPERATION	
Note: This procedure will supply power to the fuel tank solenoid valves for approximately 30-60 seconds. If time expires, cycle the start/stop button on the scan tool. **Note:** Make sure the manual bleed valve is closed on the Fuel Filler Neck Venting Kit.	
1 Tank No. 2 Connector C417	2 Tighten the fuel tank No. 1 solenoid valve manual lock-down jackscrew to 9 Nm (79 lb/in).
3 scan tool 4	5 Press the start button on the scan tool.

FM1029900362160X

Fig. 6 Pinpoint Test A: Fuel tank solenoid valve diagnosis (Part 16 of 26). 2000–02

TEST CONDITIONS	TEST DETAILS/RESULTS/ACTIONS
A20 CHECK FUEL TANK NO. 1 SOLENOID VALVE OPERATION (Continued)	
6 Tank No. 2 Connector C417 7 Tank No. 1 Connector C416 8 9 Output Test Mode	10 Press the start button on the scan tool. 11 Observe the system pressure on the Fuel Filler Neck Venting Kit Gauge. 12 Press the stop button on the scan tool. • Was the pressure on the gauge 0 kPa (0 psi) when triggered on? → **Yes** Mark fuel tank No. 1 solenoid valve "stuck open." INSTALL new upper tank rack assembly valves if marked "stuck open." GO to **A21**. → **No** Mark fuel tank No. 1 solenoid valve "good." GO to **A21**.
A21 CHECK FUEL TANK NO. 3 SOLENOID VALVE FOR STUCK OPEN CONDITION	
1	2 Open the manual lock-down jackscrew on fuel tank No. 3 solenoid valve. 3 Make sure the manual lock-down jackscrew on fuel tank No. 4 solenoid valve is still closed from Step **A16**. 4 Open the manual bleed valve on the Fuel Filler Neck Venting Kit for 60 seconds. 5 Close the manual bleed valve on the Fuel Filler Neck Venting Kit.

FM1029900362180X

Fig. 6 Pinpoint Test A: Fuel tank solenoid valve diagnosis (Part 18 of 26). 2000–02

TEST CONDITIONS	TEST DETAILS/RESULTS/ACTIONS
A19 CHECK FUEL TANK NO. 2 SOLENOID VALVE OPERATION (Continued)	
6 Output Test Mode	7 Observe the system pressure on the Fuel Filler Neck Venting Kit Gauge. 8 Press the stop button on the scan tool. • Was the pressure on the gauge 0 kPa (0 psi) when triggered on? → **Yes** Mark fuel tank No. 2 solenoid valve "stuck open." A new solenoid will be installed after completing diagnostics. GO to **A20**. → **No** Mark fuel tank No. 2 solenoid valve "good." GO to **A20**.
A20 CHECK FUEL TANK NO. 1 SOLENOID VALVE OPERATION	
Note: This procedure will supply power to the fuel tank solenoid valve for approximately 30-60 seconds. If time expires, cycle the start/stop button on the scan tool.	
1	2 Open the manual bleed valve on the Fuel Filler Neck Venting Kit and vent the system pressure to 0 kPa (0 psi). 3 Close the manual bleed valve on the Fuel Filler Neck Venting Kit. 4 Open the fuel tank No. 1 solenoid valve manual lock-down jackscrew. 5 Tighten the fuel tank No. 2 solenoid valve manual lock-down jackscrew to 9 Nm (79 lb/in).

FM1029900362170X

Fig. 6 Pinpoint Test A: Fuel tank solenoid valve diagnosis (Part 17 of 26). 2000–02

TEST CONDITIONS	TEST DETAILS/RESULTS/ACTIONS
A21 CHECK FUEL TANK NO. 3 SOLENOID VALVE FOR STUCK OPEN CONDITION (Continued)	
	6 Observe the system pressure on the Fuel Filler Neck Venting Kit Gauge. • Is the pressure on the gauge 0 kPa (0 psi)? → **Yes** Mark fuel tank No. 3 solenoid valve "good." GO to **A22**. → **No** Mark fuel tank No. 3 solenoid valve "stuck open." A new solenoid valve will be installed when diagnostics are complete. GO to **A22**.
A22 CHECK FUEL TANK NO. 4 SOLENOID FOR STUCK OPEN CONDITION	
1	2 Close the manual lock-down jackscrew fuel tank No. 3 solenoid valve to 9 Nm (79 lb/in). 3 Open the manual bleed valve on the Fuel Filler Neck Venting Kit and vent the system pressure to 0 kPa (0 psi). 4 Close the manual bleed valve on the Fuel Filler Neck Venting Kit. 5 Open the manual lock-down jackscrew on fuel tank No. 4 solenoid valve. 6 Open the manual bleed valve on the Fuel Filler Neck Venting Kit for 60 seconds. 7 Close the manual bleed valve on the Fuel Filler Neck Venting Kit.

FM1029900362190X

Fig. 6 Pinpoint Test A: Fuel tank solenoid valve diagnosis (Part 19 of 26). 2000–02

TEST CONDITIONS	TEST DETAILS/RESULTS/ACTIONS
A22 CHECK FUEL TANK NO. 4 SOLENOID FOR STUCK OPEN CONDITION (Continued)	
	8 Observe the system pressure on the Fuel Filler Neck Venting Kit Gauge. • Is the pressure on the gauge 0 kPa (0 psi)? → **Yes** Mark fuel tank No. 4 solenoid valve "good." If No. 3 solenoid valve was marked "stuck open," INSTALL a new solenoid valve at this time. GO to **A23**. → **No** Fuel tank No. 4 solenoid valve is stuck open. INSTALL a new fuel tank No. 4 solenoid valve. GO to **A23**.
A23 CHECK FUEL TANK NO. 6 SOLENOID VALVE	
Note: Install the rear rack assembly fuel without the vent boxes. Make sure the manual lock-down jackscrew on fuel tank No. 6 solenoid valve is open. **Note:** This procedure will supply power to the fuel tank solenoid valve for approximately 30-60 seconds. If time expires, cycle the start/stop button on the scan tool to restore power.	
1 Tank No. 6 Solenoid Connector C419 2 scan tool 3	4 Select the correct output test mode on the scan tool and press the start button. 5 Observe the system pressure on the Fuel Filler Neck Venting Kit Gauge. 6 Press the stop button on the scan tool. • Was the pressure on the gauge 0 kPa (0 psi) when triggered on? → **Yes** Fuel tank no. 6 solenoid may be "stuck closed." GO to **A24**. → **No** Mark No. 6 solenoid valve "good." GO to **A24**.

FM1029900362200X

Fig. 6 Pinpoint Test A: Fuel tank solenoid valve diagnosis (Part 20 of 26). 2000–02

TEST CONDITIONS	TEST DETAILS/RESULTS/ACTIONS
A24 CHECK FUEL TANK NO. 5 SOLENOID VALVE	
Note: This procedure will supply power to the fuel tank solenoid valves for approximately 30-60 seconds. If time expires, cycle the start/stop button on the scan tool. **Note:** Install the Rotunda Electrical Harness for Venting Tanks 134-00120 or equivalent to the rear fuel tank rack harness connector C420F.	
1	2 Open the manual bleed valve on the Fuel Filler Neck Venting Kit for 60 seconds. 3 Close the manual bleed valve on the Fuel Filler Neck Venting Kit.
4 5 Output Test Mode	6 Switch the Rotunda Electrical Harness for Venting Tanks to the tank No. 1 position. 7 Press the start button on the scan tool. 8 Observe the system pressure on the Fuel Filler Neck Venting Kit Gauge. 9 Press the stop button on the scan tool. • Was the pressure on the gauge 0 kPa (0 psi) when triggered on? → **Yes** Fuel tank No. 5 solenoid valve "may be stuck closed." GO to **A25**. → **No** Mark fuel tank No. 5 solenoid valve "good." GO to **A25**.

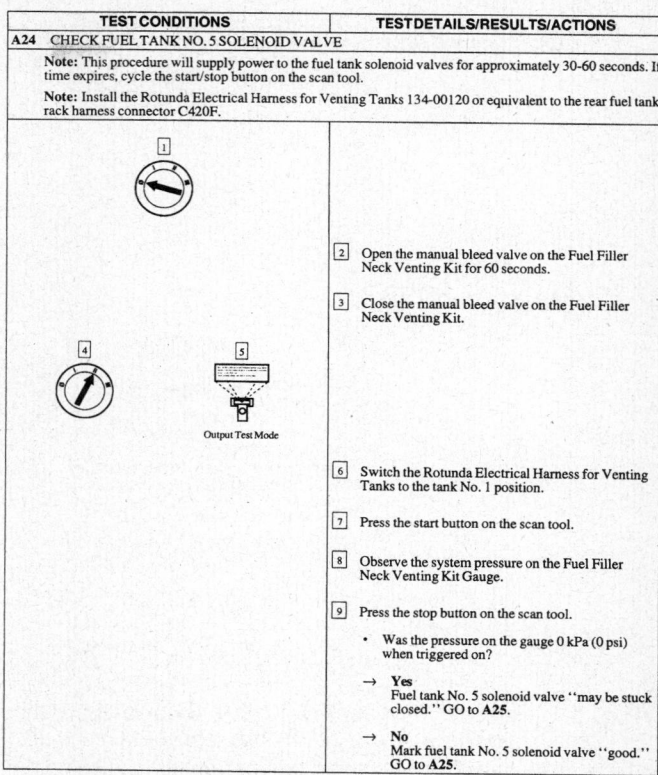

FM1029900362210X

Fig. 6 Pinpoint Test A: Fuel tank solenoid valve diagnosis (Part 21 of 26). 2000–02

TEST CONDITIONS	TEST DETAILS/RESULTS/ACTIONS
A25 CHECK REAR FUEL TANK RACK ASSEMBLY MANUAL LOCK-DOWNS	
	1 With the rear fuel tank rack assembly installed without the vent box, check the fuel tank No. 5 and No. 6 solenoid valves manual lock-downs. • Are the manual lock-downs open? → **Yes** INSTALL new solenoids for those marked "stuck closed." If no. 5 or 6 solenoid valve was marked may be "stuck closed," INSTALL a new solenoid at this time. RESTORE the vehicle. RETEST the system for normal operation. → **No** GO to **A26**.
A26 CHECK FUEL TANK NO. 6 SOLENOID VALVE MANUAL LOCK-DOWN	
Note: Make sure the bleed valve on the Fuel Filler Neck Venting Kit is closed before proceeding with this test.	
	1 Open fuel tank No. 6 solenoid valve manual lock-down jackscrew. 2 Open the bleed valve on the Fuel Filler Neck Venting Kit for 60 seconds. 3 Close the bleed valve on the Fuel Filler Neck Venting Kit. 4 Observe the system pressure on the Fuel Filler Neck Venting Kit Gauge. • Is the pressure on the gauge 0 kPa (0 psi)? → **Yes** If fuel tank no. 5 solenoid valve manual lock down is open GO to **A23**. If closed GO to **A27**. → **No** Mark fuel tank No. 6 solenoid valve "stuck open." GO to **A15**.
A27 CHECK FUEL TANK NO. 5 SOLENOID VALVE MANUAL LOCK-DOWN	
	1 Tighten the manual lock-down jackscrew on fuel tank No.6 solenoid valve to 9 Nm (79 lb/in). 2 Open fuel tank No. 5 solenoid valve manual lock-down jackscrew.

FM1029900362220X

Fig. 6 Pinpoint Test A: Fuel tank solenoid valve diagnosis (Part 22 of 26). 2000–02

TEST CONDITIONS	TEST DETAILS/RESULTS/ACTIONS
A27 CHECK FUEL TANK NO. 5 SOLENOID VALVE MANUAL LOCK-DOWN (Continued)	
	3 Open the bleed valve on the Fuel Filler Neck Venting Kit for 60 seconds. 4 Close the bleed valve on the Fuel Filler Neck Venting Kit. 5 Observe the system pressure on the Fuel Filler Neck Venting Kit Gauge. • Is the system pressure on the Fuel Filler Neck Venting Kit Gauge 0 kPa (0 psi)? → **Yes** GO to **A23**. → **No** MARK fuel tank No. 5 solenoid valve "stuck open." GO to **A15**.
A28 CHECK FUEL TANK NO. 6 SOLENOID VALVE OPERATION	
Note: The battery must be fully charged to carry out solenoid valve diagnostics. **Note:** This procedure will supply power to the fuel tank solenoid valves for approximately 30-60 seconds. If time expires, cycle the start/stop button on the scan tool.	
1 2 Upper and Lower Rack Solenoid Valve Connectors C420F, C421M	3 Open the manual bleed valve on the Fuel Filler Neck Venting Kit for 60 seconds. 4 Close the manual bleed valve on the Fuel Filler Neck Venting Kit.

FM1029900362230X

Fig. 6 Pinpoint Test A: Fuel tank solenoid valve diagnosis (Part 23 of 26). 2000–02

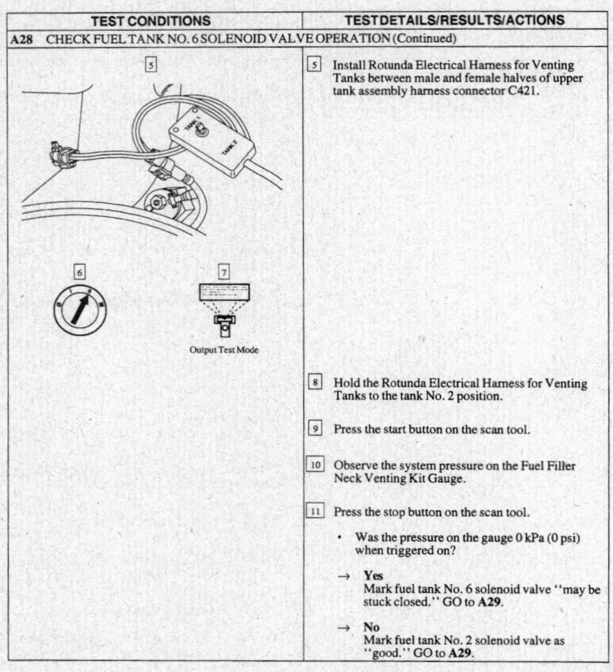

TEST CONDITIONS	TEST DETAILS/RESULTS/ACTIONS
A28 CHECK FUEL TANK NO. 6 SOLENOID VALVE OPERATION (Continued)	
5	5 Install Rotunda Electrical Harness for Venting Tanks between male and female halves of upper tank assembly harness connector C421.
6 7 Output Test Mode	8 Hold the Rotunda Electrical Harness for Venting Tanks to the tank No. 2 position.
	9 Press the start button on the scan tool.
	10 Observe the system pressure on the Fuel Filler Neck Venting Kit Gauge.
	11 Press the stop button on the scan tool.
	• Was the pressure on the gauge 0 kPa (0 psi) when triggered on?
	→ **Yes** Mark fuel tank No. 6 solenoid valve "may be stuck closed." GO to **A29**.
	→ **No** Mark fuel tank No. 2 solenoid valve as "good." GO to **A29**.

FM1029900362240X

Fig. 6 Pinpoint Test A: Fuel tank solenoid valve diagnosis (Part 24 of 26). 2000–02

TEST CONDITIONS	TEST DETAILS/RESULTS/ACTIONS
A29 CHECK FUEL TANK NO. 5 SOLENOID VALVE OPERATION (Continued)	
	9 Press the stop button on the scan tool.
	• Was the pressure on the gauge 0 kPa (0 psi) when triggered on?
	→ **Yes** MARK fuel tank no. 5 solenoid valve "Does not Operate." INSTALL new solenoids for those marked "Stuck Closed" at this time. RESTORE the vehicle. TEST the system for normal operation.
	→ **No** Mark fuel tank No. 5 solenoid valve "good." To complete diagnostics, install a new solenoid valve if the solenoid valve is marked "stuck closed." If fuel tank No. 6 solenoid valve was marked "may be stuck closed," INSTALL A new solenoid at this time. If all solenoid valves were marked "good," diagnostics are complete. RESTORE the vehicle. TEST the system for normal operation.

FM1029900362260X

Fig. 6 Pinpoint Test A: Fuel tank solenoid valve diagnosis (Part 26 of 26). 2000–02

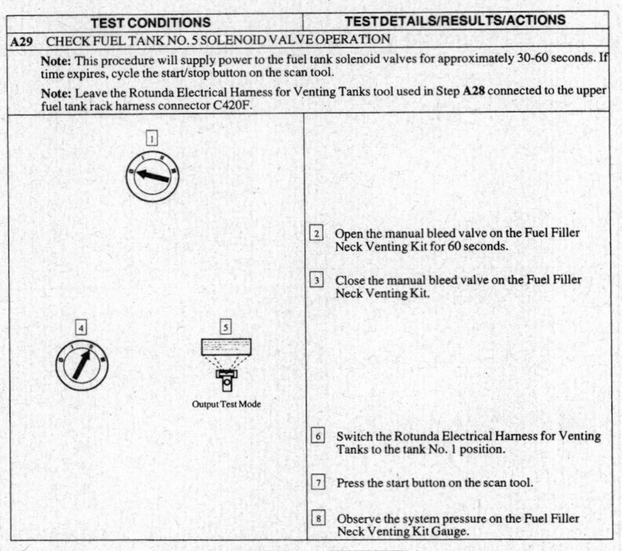

TEST CONDITIONS	TEST DETAILS/RESULTS/ACTIONS
A29 CHECK FUEL TANK NO. 5 SOLENOID VALVE OPERATION	
Note: This procedure will supply power to the fuel tank solenoid valves for approximately 30-60 seconds. If time expires, cycle the start/stop button on the scan tool.	
Note: Leave the Rotunda Electrical Harness for Venting Tanks tool used in Step **A28** connected to the upper fuel tank rack harness connector C420F.	
1	2 Open the manual bleed valve on the Fuel Filler Neck Venting Kit for 60 seconds.
	3 Close the manual bleed valve on the Fuel Filler Neck Venting Kit.
4 5 Output Test Mode	6 Switch the Rotunda Electrical Harness for Venting Tanks to the tank No. 1 position.
	7 Press the start button on the scan tool.
	8 Observe the system pressure on the Fuel Filler Neck Venting Kit Gauge.

FM1029900362250X

Fig. 6 Pinpoint Test A: Fuel tank solenoid valve diagnosis (Part 25 of 26). 2000–02

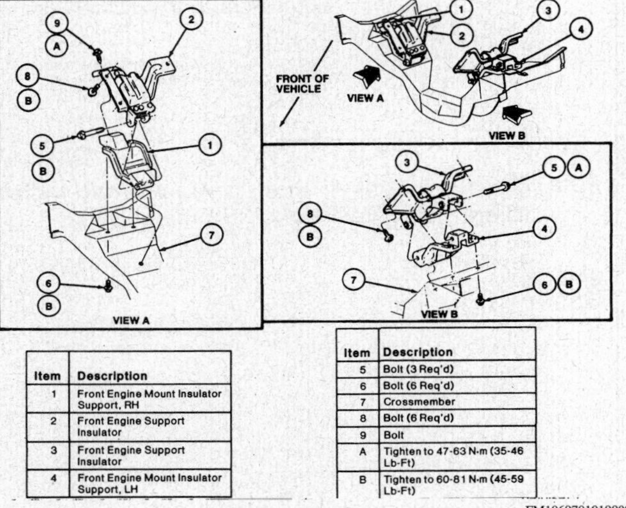

Item	Description
1	Front Engine Mount Insulator Support, RH
2	Front Engine Support Insulator
3	Front Engine Support Insulator
4	Front Engine Mount Insulator Support, LH

Item	Description
5	Bolt (3 Req'd)
6	Bolt (6 Req'd)
7	Crossmember
8	Bolt (6 Req'd)
9	Bolt
A	Tighten to 47-63 N·m (35-46 Lb-Ft)
B	Tighten to 60-81 N·m (45-59 Lb-Ft)

FM1069701019000X

Fig. 7 Engine mount replacement. 1998

1. Ensure manual bleed valve on fuel filler neck vent kit is closed before connecting to fuel filler valve.
2. Connect fuel filler vent kit tool No. 134-00117, or equivalent, to fuel filler valve.
3. Connect vent hose tool No. 134-00118, or equivalent, to filler neck vent kit and vent stack.
4. Open manual bleed valve on fuel filler neck vent kit for one minute to bleed residual fuel system pressure. Close manual bleed valve.
5. Remove manual lockdown valve from fuel tank solenoid valve of fuel tank to be vented.
6. **Ensure jackscrew in manual override tool is retracted fully (counterclockwise) prior to installation into fuel tank solenoid valve. If tool is installed in vent position, fuel will be immediately released.**
7. Install Rotunda manual override tool No. 134-00050, or equivalent, to tank solenoid and **torque** to 30 ft. lbs.
8. Turn override tool jackscrew clockwise until fuel flows.
9. Slowly open manual backflow valve on fuel filler valve and ensure pressure gauge on vent kit reads tank pressure.
10. Slowly open bleed valve on fuel filler neck vent kit and allow tank to vent to atmosphere. Vent process may take one hour or more.
11. Vent tank until fuel flow stops.
12. Close manual backflow valve on fuel filler valve when tank venting is complete.
13. Vent fuel lines.
14. Remove manual override tool from fuel tank solenoid valve.
15. Install fuel tank solenoid manual lockdown valve and **torque** to 30 ft. lbs.
16. **Torque** manual lockdown valve jackscrew on fuel tank solenoid valve to 80 inch lbs.
17. Repeat procedure until affected tanks are vented.

COMPRESSION PRESSURE

Cylinder compression pressure should be 134–250 psi at an engine cranking speed of 180 RPM minimum. The compression in each cylinder should fall within the specified compression pressure range with no more than a 75% variance in compression.

ENGINE MOUNT

REPLACE

1998

1. Remove air cleaner outlet tube.
2. Drain engine coolant into suitable container.

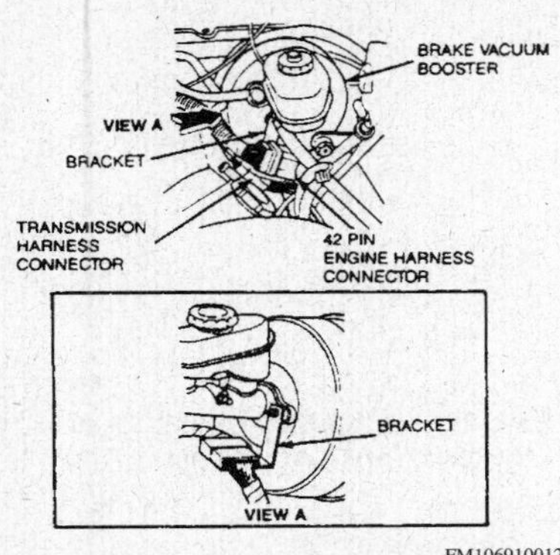

Fig. 8 Engine & transmission harness connectors replacement. 1998

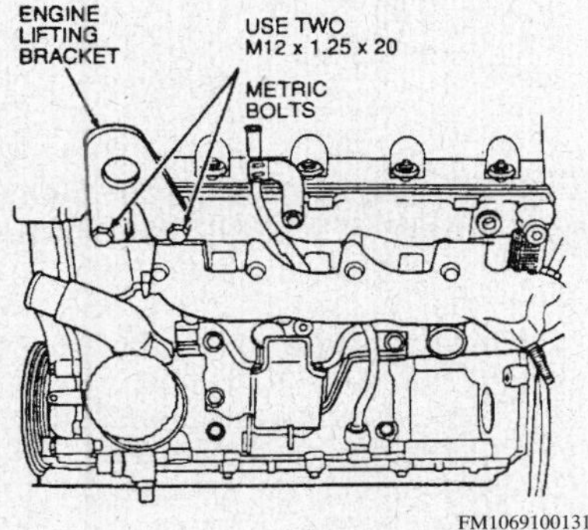

Fig. 11 Engine lift bracket installation. 1998

3. Remove cooling fan blade and fan shroud.
4. Relieve system fuel pressure as outlined under "Precautions."
5. Remove upper radiator hose.
6. Remove windshield wiper motor and mounting bracket.
7. Evacuate air conditioning system as outlined in "Air Conditioning" chapter.
8. Disconnect air conditioning manifold and tube at air conditioning compressor.
9. Remove air conditioning manifold mounting bolt and tube to righthand coil bracket.
10. Remove engine harness connector from wiring bracket on power brake booster.
11. Disconnect transmission harness connector.
12. Disconnect heater hose, then remove upper stud bolt and lower water hose to righthand side cylinder head bolt.
13. Remove heater blower motor switch resistor.
14. Remove upper righthand front engine mount insulator to front engine mount insulator support bolt.
15. Disconnect vacuum hoses from EGR control valve and EGR valve to exhaust manifold tube.
16. Remove EGR control valve.
17. Disconnect both heated oxygen sensors.
18. Raise and support vehicle.
19. Remove two through bolts from lefthand front engine support insulator and one through bolt from righthand

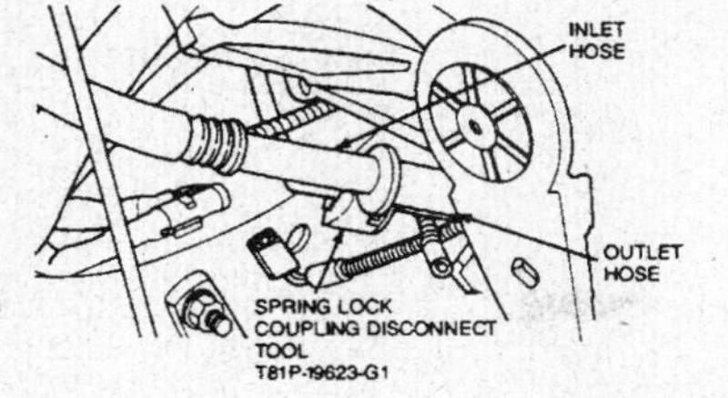

Fig. 9 Compressor lines removal. 1998

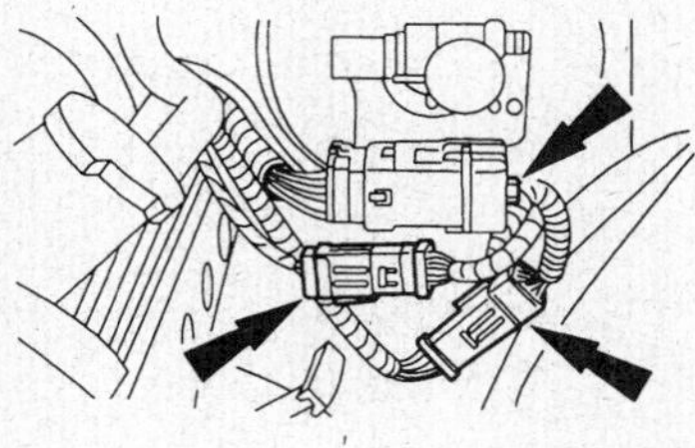

Fig. 12 Engine bulkhead connectors replacement. 1999–2002

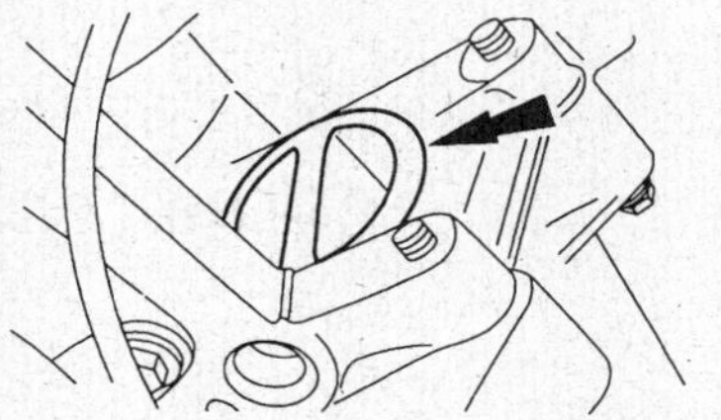

Fig. 14 Torque converter nut access plug replacement. 1999–2002

front engine support insulator, **Fig. 7.**

20. Remove EGR valve to exhaust manifold tube line nut from righthand exhaust manifold and remove EGR valve to exhaust manifold tube.
21. Disconnect exhaust system from exhaust manifolds.
22. Lower exhaust system and wire to crossmember to hold in position.
23. Position suitable jack and wood block under oil pan rearward of oil pan drain plug.
24. Raise engine approximately four inches.
25. Install suitable wood block under oil pan and lower engine onto wood block.
26. Remove three mounting bolts from both front engine support and remove insulators.
27. Reverse procedure to install.

1999-2002

1. For righthand engine mount, remove starter.
2. For lefthand engine mount, remove oil dipstick tube.
3. Support vehicle engine with suitable engine support device
4. Remove mounting bolts and mount(s).
5. Reverse procedure to install.

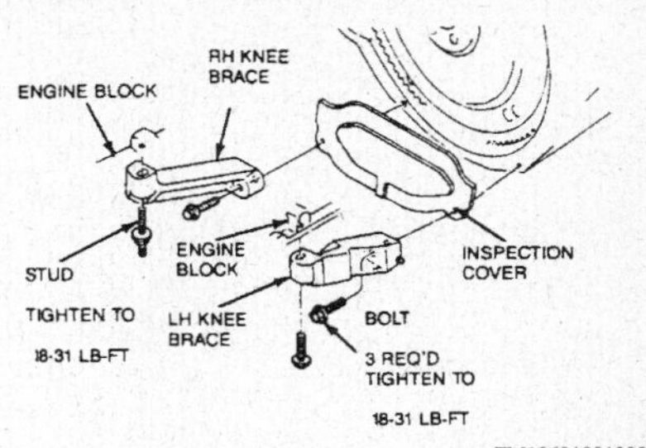

Fig. 10 Transmission line bracket removal. 1998

Fig. 13 Ground wire mounting bolt replacement. 1999–2002

ENGINE

REPLACE

1998

1. Mark hinges position for installation alignment and remove hood.
2. Drain coolant into suitable container.
3. Recover refrigerant as outlined in "Air Conditioning" chapter.
4. Relieve fuel system pressure as described under "Precautions."
5. Disconnect fuel lines.
6. Remove engine cooling fan, shroud and radiator.
7. Remove wiper module and bracket.
8. Remove air inlet tube and 42-pin electrical harness connector from bracket at brake vacuum booster, **Fig. 8.**
9. Disconnect 42-pin connector and transmission harness electrical connector. Position connectors aside.
10. Disconnect accelerator, speed control cables and throttle valve cable.
11. Disconnect purge solenoid electrical connector and vacuum hose.
12. Disconnect power distribution and starter relay power supply.
13. Disconnect vacuum hose from throttle body port.
14. Disconnect heater hoses.
15. Disconnect alternator electrical harness at fender apron and junction box.
16. Remove air conditioning compressor inlet and outlet hoses using suitable hose too, **Fig. 9.**
17. Disconnect power steering pump EVO sensor electrical connector.
18. Disconnect dash panel body ground strap, then raise and support vehicle.
19. Drain engine oil into suitable container.
20. Disconnect exhaust pipes at manifolds, lower exhaust system and suspend with suitable wire from crossmember.

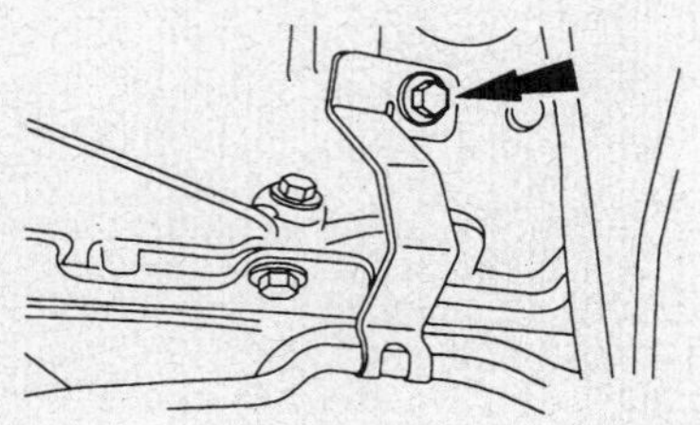

Fig. 15 Transmission cooler line bracket. 1999–2002

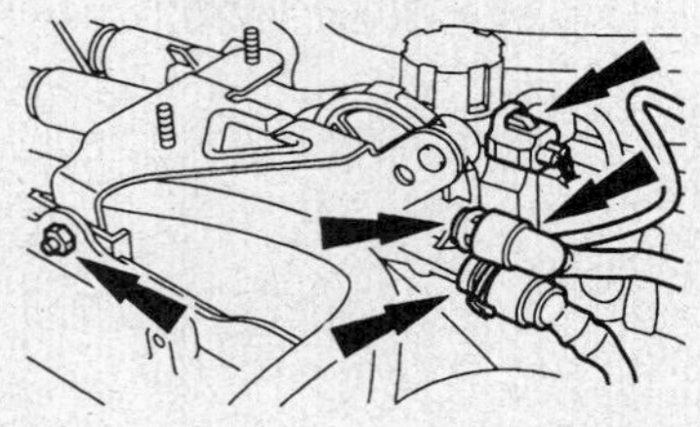

Fig. 18 Evaporative emission canister purge valve replacement. 1999–2002

21. Remove transmission line bracket mounting nut.
22. Remove engine to transmission knee braces mounting bolts and stud, **Fig. 10.**
23. Remove starter motor.
24. Disconnect power steering pump and position aside.
25. Remove plug to access torque converter mounting nuts.
26. Rotate crankshaft and remove four mounting nuts.
27. Remove six engine to transmission mounting bolts.
28. Remove engine mount through bolts.
29. Lower vehicle and support transmission with suitable jack.
30. Install engine lift brackets and connect suitable lift, **Fig. 11.**
31. Raise engine and separate from transmission.
32. Remove engine.
33. Reverse procedure to install.

1999-2002

1. Remove hood.
2. Evacuate air conditioning system as outlined in "Air Conditioning" chapter.
3. Remove air cleaner outlet tube.
4. Relieve fuel pressure as outlined under "Precautions."
5. Disconnect fuel lines.
6. Remove wiper arm and pivot shaft.
7. Raise and support vehicle.
8. Drain engine coolant and oil into suitable containers.
9. Disconnect lower radiator hose from oil filter adapter.
10. **On models equipped with oil cooler,** disconnect two coolant hoses, remove oil cooler and secure to front of engine.
11. **On all models,** remove battery.
12. Disconnect hoses from transmission fluid cooler and power steering cooler.
13. Remove radiator upper sight shield
14. Position clamp and disconnect upper radiator hose from water hose connec-

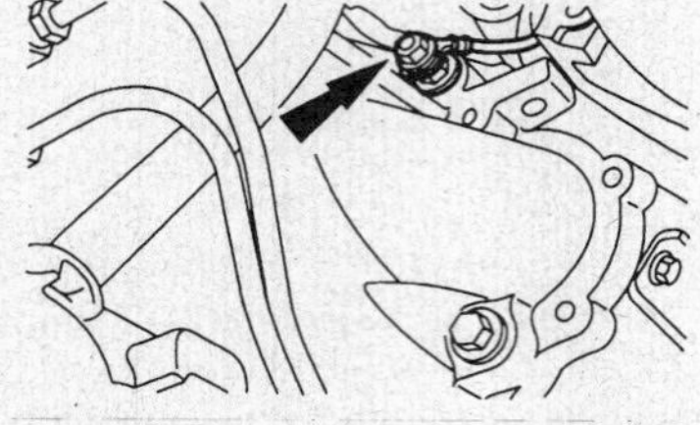

Fig. 16 Starter nut & ground wire replacement. 1999–2002

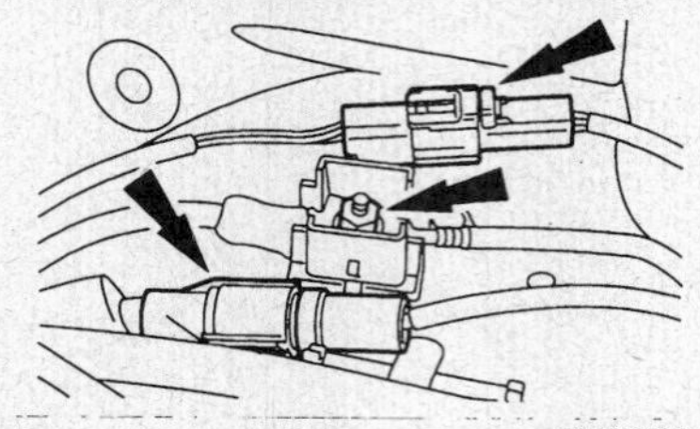

Fig. 19 Electrical connectors replacement. 1999–2002 righthand inner fender

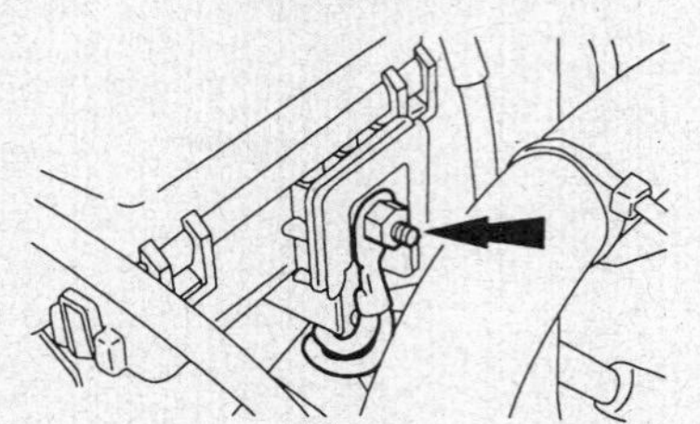

Fig. 21 Cover, nut & wiring replacement. 1999–2002 w/natural gas engine

tion. Secure hose to radiator.

15. Disconnect fan motor electrical connector and position aside.
16. Remove nuts and separate lines from air conditioning condenser core.
17. Remove mounting bolts, support brackets and radiator.
18. Disconnect engine bulkhead connectors, **Fig. 12.**
19. Disconnect accelerator and speed control actuator cables.
20. **On models equipped with gasoline engine,** remove accelerator and speed control actuator cables from clips and position aside.
21. **On all models,** disconnect main vacuum supply hose.
22. Remove ground wire bolt, **Fig. 13.**
23. Raise and support vehicle, then remove starter motor.
24. Support exhaust system and remove mounting nuts.
25. Remove torque converter inspection cover.
26. Remove torque converter nut access plug, **Fig. 14.**
27. Remove transmission cooler line bracket bolt, **Fig. 15.**
28. Remove nut and ground wire, **Fig. 16.**
29. Remove five starter bolts and one stud, **Fig. 17.**

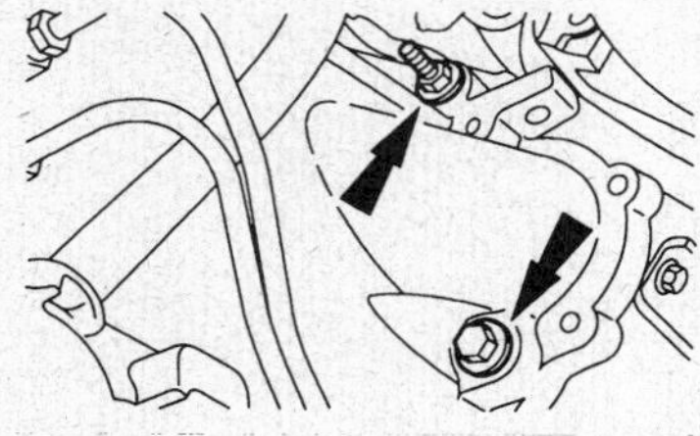

Fig. 17 Starter bolts & stud replacement. 1999–2002

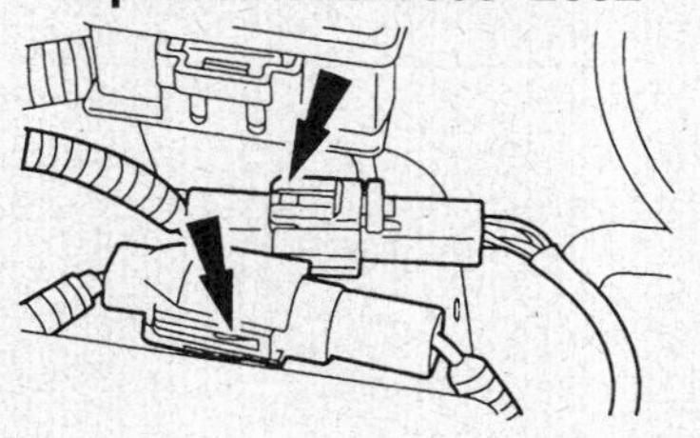

Fig. 20 Electrical connectors replacement. 1999–2002 w/natural gas engine

30. **On models equipped with gasoline engine,**
    a. Remove evaporative emission canister purge valve, **Fig. 18.**
    b. Position clamps aside and remove heater hoses.
    c. Remove nut and disconnect electrical connectors on righthand inner fender, **Fig. 19.**
31. **On models equipped with natural gas engine,** proceed as follows:
    a. Disconnect electrical connectors, **Fig. 20.**
    b. Remove cover, nut and wiring, **Fig. 21.**
32. **On all models,** remove bolt and body ground, **Fig. 22.**
33. Disconnect air conditioning cycling switch electrical connector and remove nut, **Fig. 23.**
34. Disconnect air conditioning lines.
35. Disconnect and unplug righthand heated oxygen sensor connector.
36. Disconnect lefthand heated oxygen sensor and separate transmission harness from rear of lefthand cylinder head.
37. Disconnect power steering pressure hose.
38. Remove bolt from bracket, **Fig. 24.**
39. Raise and support vehicle.
40. Remove lefthand engine mount through bolts, **Fig. 25.**
41. Remove righthand engine mount through bolt, **Fig. 26.**
42. Lower vehicle.
43. Install suitable engine lifting equipment.
44. Support transmission.
45. Remove engine.
46. Reverse procedure to install.

INTAKE MANIFOLD

REPLACE

1998

1. Drain coolant into suitable container.

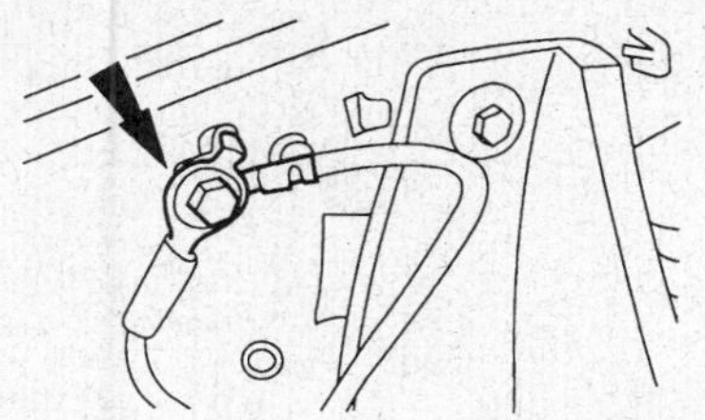

Fig. 22 Body ground wires replacement. 1999–2002

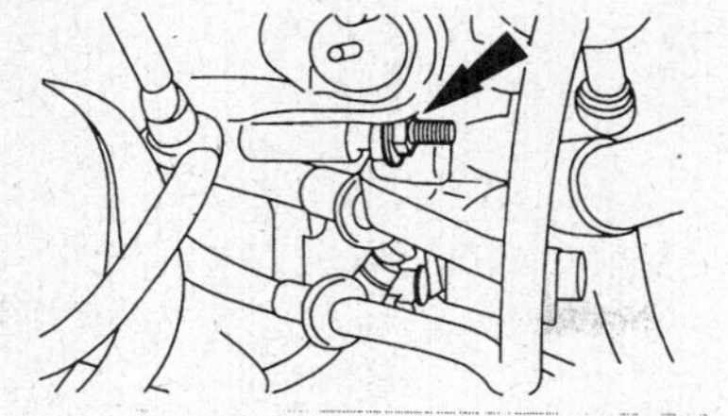

Fig. 23 Air conditioning line bracket replacement. 1999–2002

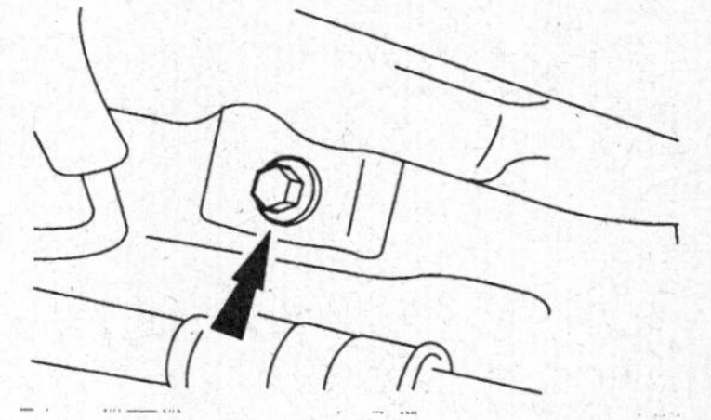

Fig. 24 Bracket bolt replacement 1999–2002

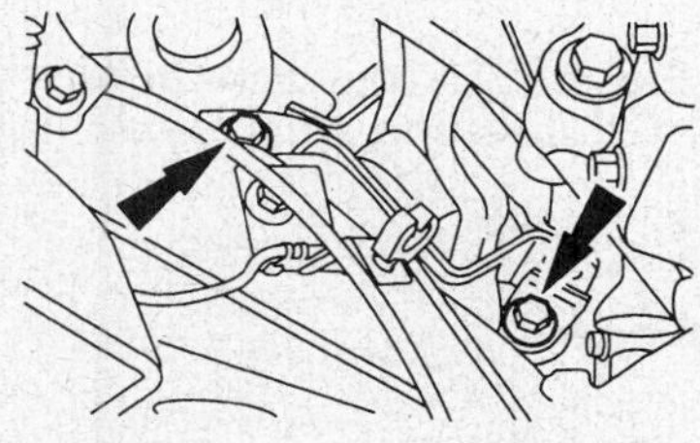

Fig. 25 Lefthand engine mount through bolts replacement. 1999–2002

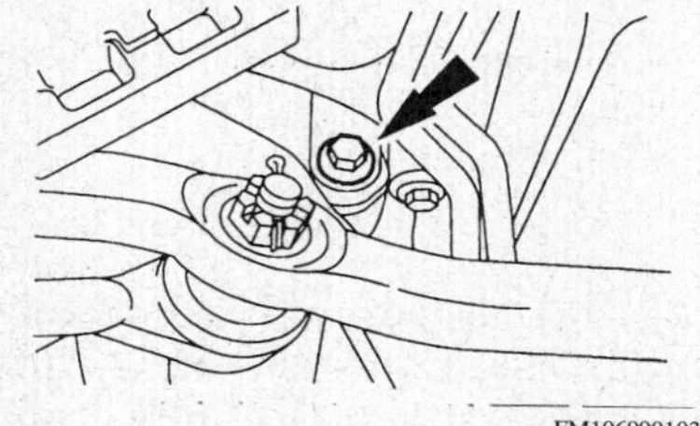

Fig. 26 Righthand engine mount through bolt replacement. 1999–2002

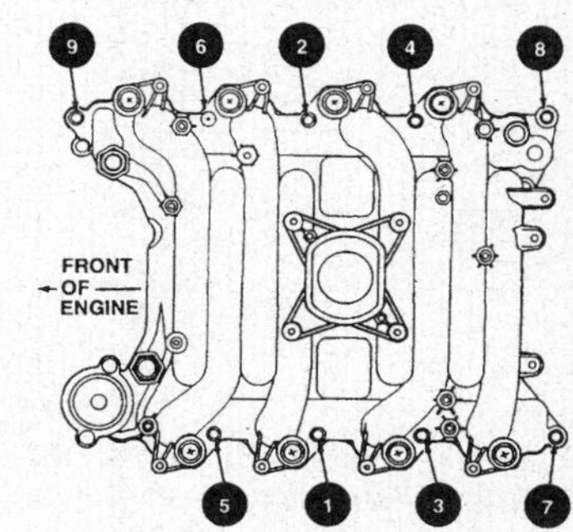

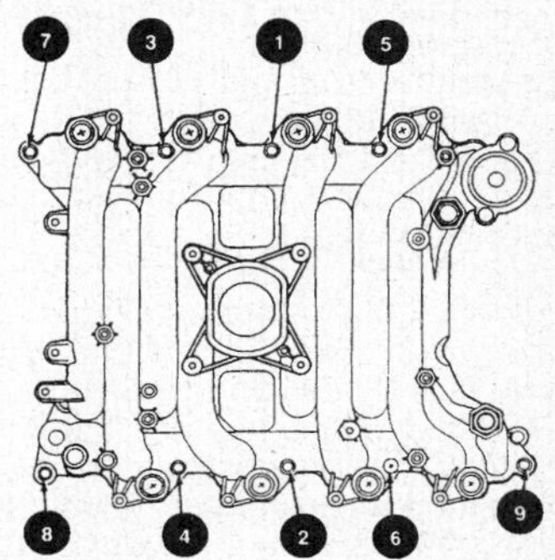

Fig. 27 Intake manifold tightening sequence

2. Remove air cleaner outlet tube.
3. Relieve fuel system fuel pressure as described under "Precautions."
4. Remove wiper governor and air inlet tube.
5. Release belt tensioner and remove accessory drive belt.
6. Raise and support vehicle.
7. Disconnect fuel charging wiring from crankshaft position sensor and air conditioning clutch.
8. Remove oil bypass filter.
9. Disconnect fuel charging wiring from oil pressure sensor, oil filter adapter bracket and power steering pump and move wiring aside.
10. Disconnect EGR valve to exhaust manifold tube from righthand exhaust manifold.
11. Disconnect EGR back pressure transducer hoses from EGR valve to exhaust manifold tube.
12. Disconnect fuel charging wring from heated oxygen sensors.
13. Lower vehicle.
14. Disconnect fuel charging wiring from eight ignition coils.
15. Disconnect alternator wiring from power distribution box at front fender apron and alternator.
16. Remove alternator and bracket.
17. Remove positive crankcase ventilation valve from valve cover.
18. Disconnect vacuum hose from throttle body adapter vacuum port.
19. **On models equipped with natural gas engine,** disconnect fuel pressure regulator coolant hoses from heater water hoses.
20. **On all models,** remove heater water hoses.
21. Disconnect engine control sensor extension wire from 42-pin connector and eight-pin transmission connector located at power brake booster.
22. **On models equipped with gasoline engine,** disconnect engine control sensor extension wire from EVR sensor, idle air control valve, EGR transducer, throttle position sensor, ignition coils and fuel injectors.
23. **On all models,** remove fuel charging wiring retainers from valve cover stud bolts.
24. Remove fuel charging wiring and transmission wiring from bracket on rear of lefthand cylinder head.
25. Disconnect accelerator cable and speed control actuator cable using suitable screwdriver.
26. **On models equipped with gasoline engine,** proceed as follows:
    a. Remove two bolts and intake manifold shield.
    b. Disconnect main emission vacuum control connector from fuel injection supply manifold and evaporative emission valve.
    c. Disconnect EGR valve to exhaust manifold tube from EGR valve and remove EGR valve to exhaust manifold tube.
    d. Remove accelerator cable bracket stud bolt.
    e. Remove five mounting bolts from throttle body adapter to intake manifold.
27. **On all models,** remove to water hose connection to intake manifold bolts. Position water hose connection and upper radiator hose aside.
28. **On models equipped with natural gas engine,** throttle body adapter, accelerator cable bracket, EGR valve, idle air control valve and EGR valve to exhaust manifold tube remain attached to intake manifold.
29. **On all models,** fuel charging wiring, fuel injection supply manifold and fuel injector nozzle tip remain attached to intake manifold.
30. Remove nine mounting, intake manifold and gaskets.
31. Reverse procedure to install, noting the following:
    a. Clean cylinder head and intake manifold surfaces.
    b. Install new intake manifold gaskets.
    c. Tighten manifold bolts in sequence, **Fig. 27.**

1999–2002

GASOLINE ENGINE

1. Drain engine coolant into suitable container.
2. Remove air cleaner outlet tube.
3. Relieve fuel pressure as outlined under "Precautions."
4. Remove wiper arm and pivot shaft.
5. Remove drive belt.
6. Raise and support vehicle.
7. Disconnect electrical connectors at crankshaft position sensor and air conditioning compressor.
8. Remove oil filter.
9. Disconnect oil pressure sensor electrical connector and power steering switch electrical connector.
10. Disconnect EGR valve from manifold.

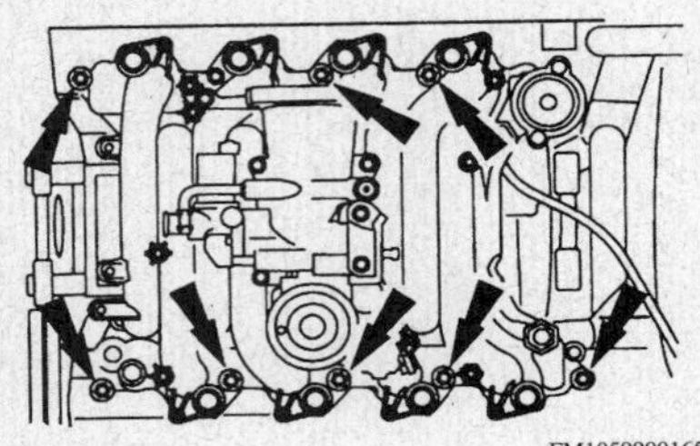

Fig. 28 Intake manifold initial tightening sequence. 1999–2002 w/gasoline engine

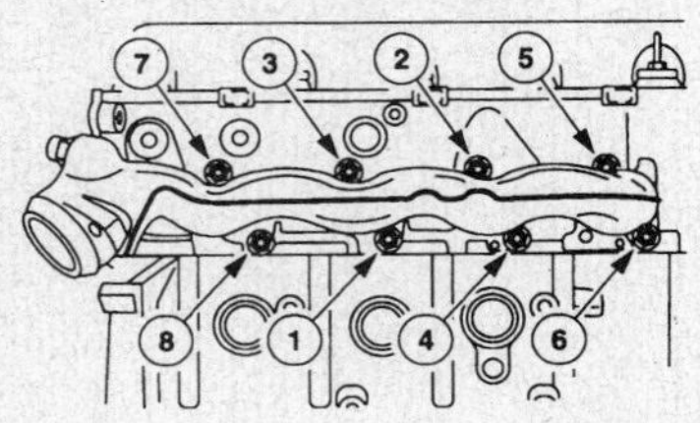

Fig. 31 Exhaust manifold tightening sequence, righthand side. 1999–2002

11. Disconnect two differential pressure feedback hoses.
12. Disconnect righthand heated oxygen sensor electrical connector.
13. Disconnect fuel charging wiring electrical connectors from ignition coils and fuel injectors.
14. Disconnect accelerator cable and speed control actuator cable.
15. Remove cables from EGR tube heat shield and position aside.
16. Remove EGR tube heat shield.
17. Disconnect evaporative emissions return tube, main chassis vacuum supply line and EGR valve vacuum supply.
18. Disconnect PCV tube at two locations and remove.
19. Disconnect electrical connector from EGR vacuum regulator.
20. Disconnect vacuum line from evaporative emission canister purge valve.
21. Disconnect alternator cable and position aside.
22. Remove upper mounting bracket and electrical connector from alternator.
23. Remove upper radiator and heater hose.
24. Disconnect electrical connector from idle air control valve and throttle position sensor.
25. Disconnect EGR tube from EGR valve.
26. Remove lefthand oxygen sensor and transmission electrical connectors from wiring bracket, then the bracket.
27. Remove throttle body.
28. Separate fuel charging wiring pushpin connector from crash bracket, then remove bolt, stud and crash bracket.
29. Disconnect vacuum lines and remove vacuum harness.
30. Remove fuel injection supply manifold and fuel injectors as an assembly.
31. Remove all eight ignition coils.
32. Remove water outlet adapter, thermostat and gasket.
33. Remove intake manifold and gaskets,

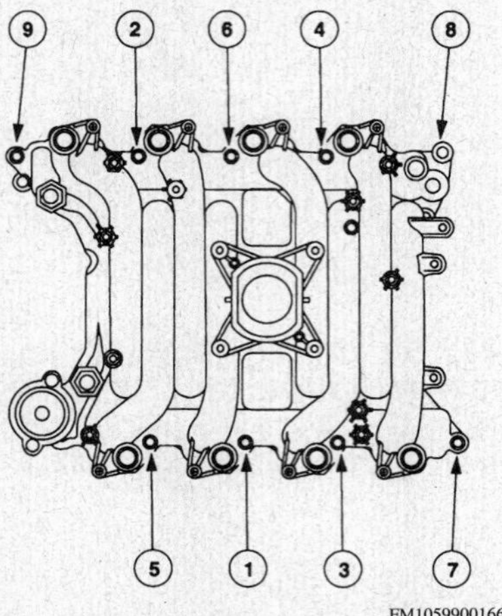

Fig. 29 Intake manifold bolt tightening sequence. 1999–2002 w/gasoline engine

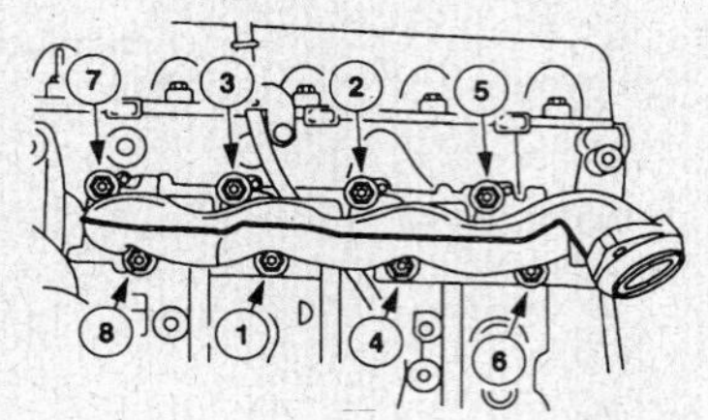

Fig. 32 Exhaust manifold tightening sequence, lefthand side. 1999–2002

clean gasket sealing surfaces.

34. Reverse procedure to install, noting the following:
    a. Install new gaskets.
    b. Install intake manifold and hand tighten bolts, **Fig. 28.**
    c. Install ignition coils and tighten bolts.
    d. Install fuel injection supply manifold and tighten studs.
    e. Install crash bracket loosely.
    f. Install thermostat and water outlet adapter loosely with bolts.
    g. Tighten intake manifold bolts in sequence, **Fig. 29.**

NATURAL GAS ENGINE

1. Remove wiper arm & pivot shaft.
2. Remove air cleaner outlet tube.
3. Relieve fuel pressure as outlined under "Precautions"
4. Disconnect fuel charging wiring electrical connectors from ignition coils and fuel injectors.
5. Disconnect fuel charging electrical connectors from fuel pressure, fuel pump temperature and engine coolant temperature sensors.
6. Remove isolation valve wiring lead from upper alternator support bracket and disconnect connector.
7. Disconnect alternator battery cable.
8. Remove power distribution box access cover, nut and wiring.
9. Disconnect fuel charging wiring electrical connectors from the following components:

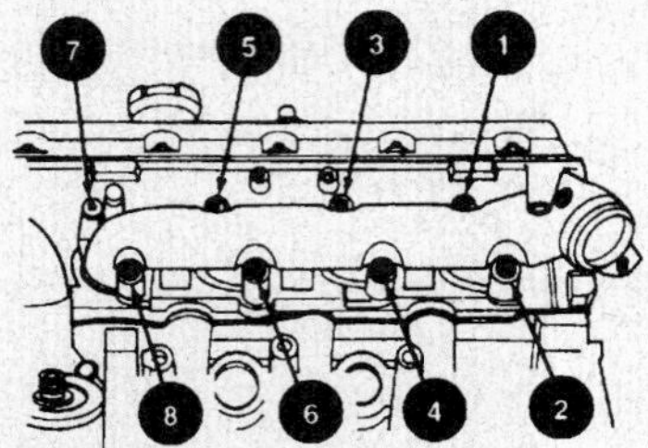

Fig. 30 Exhaust manifold tightening sequence

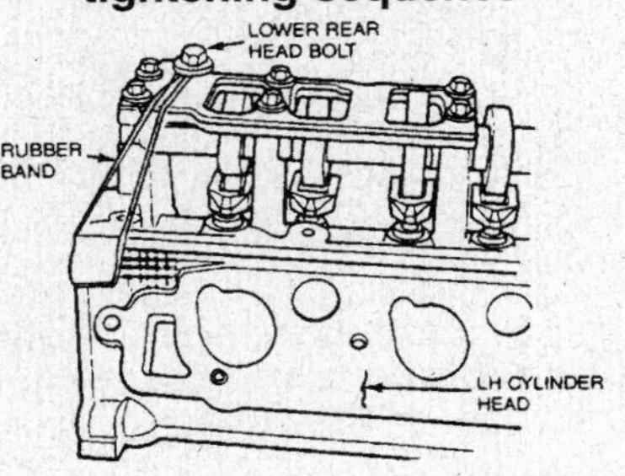

Fig. 33 Lefthand lower rear head bolt removal

   a. Inner fender splash shield connectors.
   b. Air conditioning pressure transducer.
   c. Cylinder head temperature sensor jumper.
   d. Camshaft position sensor.
   e. Alternator.
   f. Throttle position sensor.
   g. Radio ignition interference capacitor.
   h. EGR vacuum regulator solenoid.
   i. Differential pressure feedback EGR.
   j. Idle air control valve.

10. Disconnect throttle cable and speed control actuator cable from throttle body.
11. Remove mounting bolt, then position cables and bracket aside.
12. Remove fuel charging wiring mounting bolts and position harness aside.
13. Disconnect fuel lines and hoses from differential pressure feedback EGR and vacuum line from EGR valve.
14. Disconnect main chassis vacuum line.
15. Disconnect crankcase vent tube at two locations and remove.
16. Disconnect vacuum lines from throttle body adapter and EGR vacuum regulator solenoid.
17. Disconnect EGR tube from EGR valve.
18. Remove isolation valve bolts.
19. Remove fuel injection supply manifold and fuel injectors as an assembly.
20. Disconnect heater hose from intake manifold.
21. Disconnect upper radiator hose from water outlet adapter.
22. Remove all eight ignition coils.
23. Remove upper alternator support bracket.

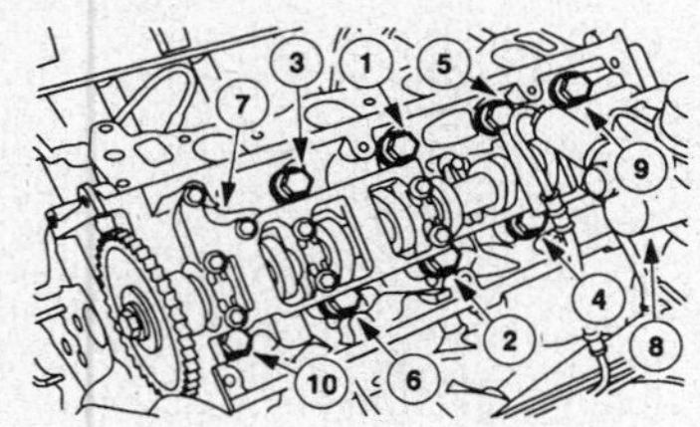

Fig. 34 Cylinder head bolt tightening sequence. Lefthand side

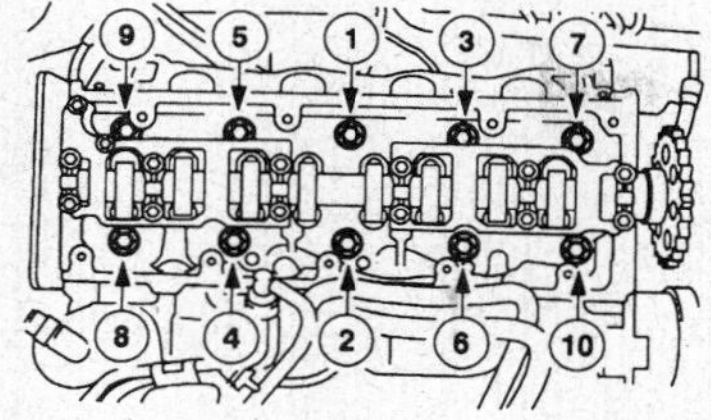

Fig. 35 Cylinder head bolt tightening sequence. Righthand side

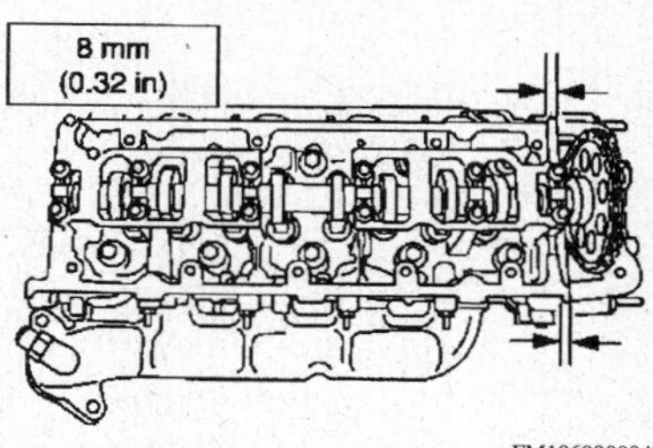

Fig. 36 Sealant application locations. 1999–2002

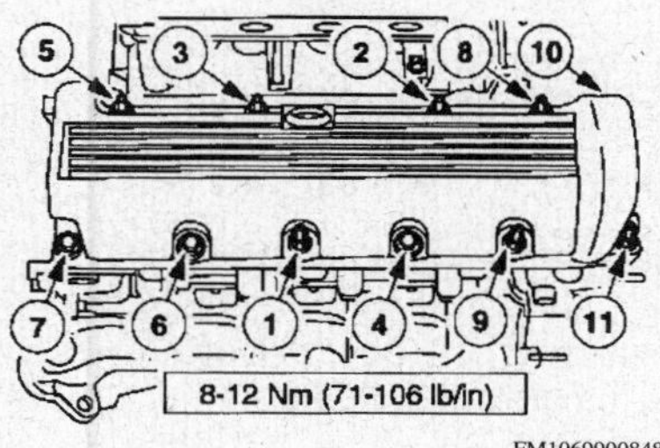

Fig. 37 Righthand cam cover tightening sequence. 1999–2002

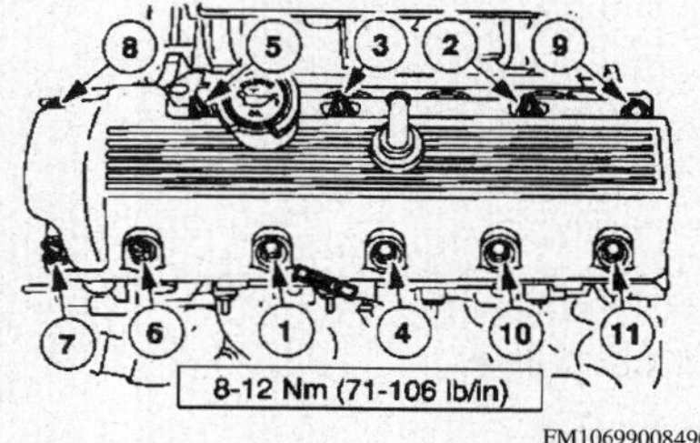

Fig. 38 Lefthand cam cover bolt tightening sequence. 1999–2002

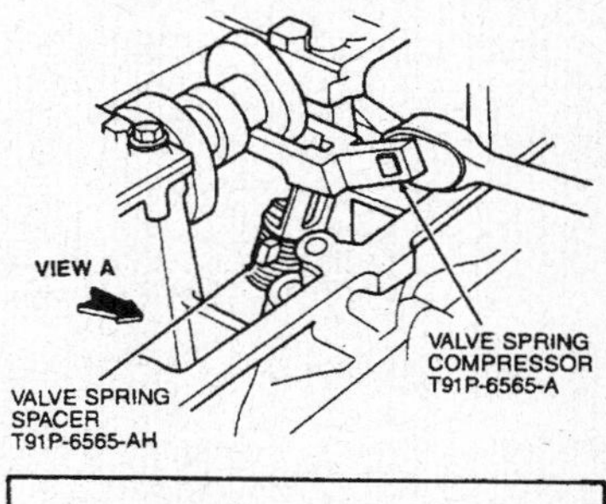

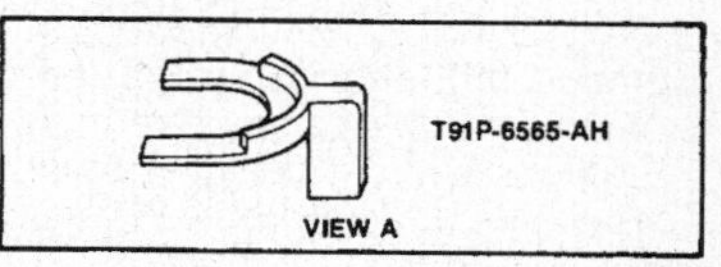

Fig. 39 Valve spring compression

24. Remove water outlet adapter, thermostat and O-ring.
25. Remove mounting bolts and intake manifold.
26. Remove intake manifold gaskets and clean all surfaces.
27. Reverse procedure to install, noting the following:
    a. Install new intake manifold gaskets.
    b. Tighten bolts in sequence, **Fig. 27.**

EXHAUST MANIFOLD

REPLACE

1998

1. Remove air cleaner outlet tube and drain coolant into suitable container.
2. Remove cooling fan and shroud.
3. Relieve fuel system pressure as described under "Precautions."
4. Disconnect fuel lines and remove upper radiator hose.
5. Remove wiper governor and support bracket.
6. Recover air conditioning refrigerant as outlined in "Air Conditioning" chapter.
7. Disconnect air conditioning compressor outlet hose at compressor, then remove hose to front cover stud bolt.
8. Disconnect 42-pin electrical and transmission harness connectors.
9. Disconnect heater water hose and remove righthand cylinder head ground strap nut.
10. **On models equipped with natural gas engine,** remove heater water hose to righthand cylinder head upper stud and lower bolts, then move it aside.
11. **On all models,** remove heater blower motor switch resistor.
12. Remove righthand front engine support insulator to front sub frame bolt.
13. Disconnect both heated oxygen sensors.
14. Raise and support vehicle.
15. Remove oil bypass filter.
16. Two through bolts are required for lefthand front engine support insulator and one through bolt is required for righthand front engine support insulator.
17. Remove EGR valve to exhaust manifold tube nut from righthand exhaust manifold.
18. Disconnect three-way catalytic converter from left and righthand exhaust manifold.
19. Lower exhaust and secure to crossmember.
20. For lefthand exhaust manifold, remove front engine support insulator from cylinder block and eight exhaust manifold nuts.
21. Remove lefthand exhaust manifold and two gaskets.
22. Position suitable screw type jackstand and block of wood under oil pan, rearward of oil drain hold.
23. Raise engine approximately four inches.
24. For righthand exhaust manifold, remove eight exhaust manifold to cylinder head and studs nuts.
25. Remove righthand exhaust manifold and gasket.
26. Reverse procedure to install. Position manifold to cylinder head and tighten bolts in sequence, **Fig. 30.**

1999–2002

1. Raise and support vehicle.
2. Disconnect oxygen sensor connectors.
3. Remove exhaust manifold to catalytic converter nuts and disconnect converters at exhaust inlet pipes.
4. Remove catalytic converters.
5. Disconnect EGR tube at exhaust manifold connector.
6. Remove nuts, exhaust manifolds and gaskets.
7. Reverse procedure to install, tighten manifold nuts in sequence, **Figs. 31 and 32.**

CYLINDER HEAD

REPLACE

1998

1. Remove intake manifold.
2. Raise and support vehicle.
3. Remove power steering pump mounting bolts. **Bolts do not come all the way out.**
4. Position power steering pump aside.
5. Remove crankshaft pulley and four oil pan to engine front cover mounting bolts.
6. Disconnect three-way catalytic converters from left and righthand exhaust manifolds.
7. Lower exhaust system and secure to crossmember with suitable wire.
8. Remove starter motor wiring harness retainer from rear of cylinder head.
9. Lower vehicle.
10. Remove power steering reservoir and bracket.
11. Remove water pump pulley, then disconnect positive battery cable at power distribution box and harness.
12. Remove pushpin from positive battery cable on back of cylinder head. Position aside.
13. Remove righthand valve cover mounting bolts, stud bolts and cover.
14. Remove air conditioning high pressure line mounting nut from front cover stud bolt.
15. Remove eight stud bolts, seven bolts and front cover.

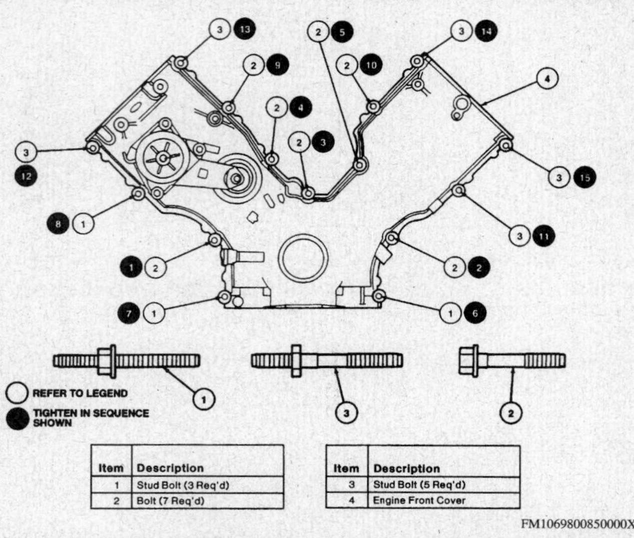

Item	Description
1	Stud Bolt (3 Req'd)
2	Bolt (7 Req'd)

Item	Description
3	Stud Bolt (5 Req'd)
4	Engine Front Cover

Fig. 40 Front cover tightening sequence. 1998

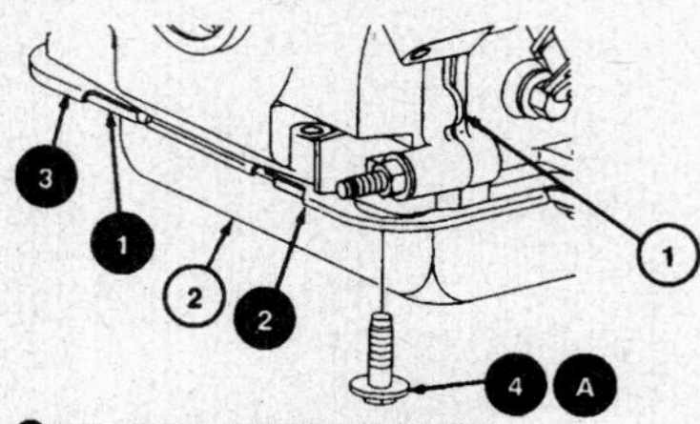

● TIGHTEN IN SEQUENCE SHOWN

○ REFER TO LEGEND

Item	Description
1	Engine Front Cover
2	Oil Pan
3	Bolt (4 Req'd)
4	Tighten in sequence in two steps: 1 Tighten to 20 N-m (14 Lb-Ft). 2 Tighten an additional 60 degrees.

FM1069800851000X

Fig. 41 Oil pan to front cover bolt tightening sequence. 1998

16. Remove timing chain as described under "Timing Chain, Replace."
17. Remove lefthand cylinder head bolts.
18. Lower rear bolt cannot be removed because of interference with brake vacuum booster. Use suitable rubber band or similar item to hold bolt away from engine, **Fig. 33.**
19. Remove lefthand cylinder head.
20. Remove heater return line to righthand cylinder head ground strap.
21. **On models equipped with gasoline engines,** remove two retainers and EVR sensor.
22. **On all models,** remove two heater tube to righthand cylinder head bolts.
23. Remove righthand cylinder head bolts. **Lower rear bolt cannot be removed because of evaporator housing interference.** Hold bolt away from engine using suitable rubber band, **Fig. 33.**
24. Remove righthand cylinder head.
25. Reverse procedure to install, noting the following:
    a. Rotate crankshaft counterclockwise 45° to ensure pistons are below top of engine block deck face.
    b. **Torque** head bolts to 28–31 ft. lbs. in sequence, **Figs. 34 and 35.**
    c. Tighten bolts an additional 85–95° in sequence.
    d. Loosen head bolts at least one full turn.
    e. **Torque** head bolts to 28–31 ft. lbs. in sequence again.
    f. Tighten bolts an additional 85–95° in sequence.
    g. Final tighten head bolts an additional 85–95° in sequence.
    h. Rotate crankshaft clockwise 45°. This will position crankshaft at TDC No. 1. **Crankshaft must only be rotated in clockwise direction and only as far as TDC.**

1999–2002

RIGHTHAND SIDE

1. Remove intake manifold as outlined under "Intake Manifold, Replace"
2. Remove valve covers as outlined under "Valve Cover, Replace."
3. Remove engine front cover as outlined under "Front Cover, Replace."
4. Remove spark plugs.
5. Remove evaporator housing.
6. Position clamp aside and remove coolant hose.
7. Remove nut and cylinder head ground strap.
8. Disconnect EGR transducer.
9. Remove ground strap stud.
10. Remove water bypass tube. Replace O-rings, as required.
11. Remove timing chains as outlined under "Timing Chain, Replace"
12. Remove left and righthand timing chain guides.
13. Remove any remaining hardware or wiring from cylinder head.
14. Raise and support vehicle.
15. Disconnect left and righthand exhaust manifolds.
16. Lower vehicle.
17. Loosen righthand side cylinder head bolts in three one turn passes in sequence, **Fig. 35.**
18. Remove cylinder head and gasket.
19. Clean gasket sealing surfaces and bolt holes.
20. Reverse procedure to install, noting the following:
    a. Install new gasket.
    b. **Torque** bolts to 28–31 ft. lbs. in sequence, **Fig. 35.**
    c. Tighten bolts an additional 85–95°.
    d. Loosen bolts at least one full turn (360°).
    e. **Torque** bolts to 28–31 ft. lbs. in sequence.
    f. Tighten bolts an additional 85–95°.
    g. Tighten bolts additional 85–95°.

LEFTHAND SIDE

1. Remove intake manifold as outlined under "Intake Manifold, Replace"
2. Remove timing chains as outlined under "Timing Chain, Replace"
3. Remove lefthand side exhaust manifold.
4. Disconnect radio ignition interference capacitor and remove engine control sensor wiring.
5. Remove oil dipstick tube. Replace O-rings, as required.
6. Remove lefthand and righthand timing chain guide.
7. Cylinder No. 8 head bolt cannot be completely removed, it will be necessary to support cylinder No. 8 head bolt with rubber band or tape to keep bolt from interfering with removal, **Fig. 33.**
8. Loosen cylinder head bolts in three one turn passes in sequence, **Fig. 34.**
9. Remove cylinder head and gasket.
10. Reverse procedure to install, noting the following:
    a. Install new gasket.
    b. **Torque** bolts to 28–31 ft. lbs. in sequence, **Fig. 34.**
    c. Tighten bolts an additional 85–95°.
    d. Loosen bolts at least one full turn (360°).
    e. **Torque** bolts to 28–31 ft. lbs. in sequence.
    f. Tighten bolts an additional 85–95°.
    g. Tighten bolts an additional 85–95°.

VALVE COVER

REPLACE

1998

RIGHTHAND SIDE

1. Disconnect positive battery cable at power distribution box.
2. Remove mounting bolt from positive battery cable bracket located on rear of righthand cylinder head. Position bracket aside.
3. Disconnect fuel charging wiring from crankshaft position sensor, air conditioning clutch, ignition coils and radio ignition interference capacitor. Position harness aside.
4. Disconnect vent hose from evaporative emission canister purge valve.

5. Remove PCV valve and position aside.
6. Remove mounting bolts and camshaft cover.
7. Reverse procedure to install.

LEFTHAND SIDE

1. Remove air outlet tube.
2. Relieve fuel pressure as outlined under "Precautions."
3. Disconnect fuel lines.
4. Raise and support vehicle.
5. Remove oil bypass filter.
6. Disconnect fuel charging wiring from power steering pump, oil pressure sensor and oil filter adapter bracket.
7. Lower vehicle.
8. Disconnect fuel charging wiring from camshaft position sensor and valve cover studs.
9. Remove windshield wiper governor.
10. **On 1998 models,** disconnect ignition coils.
11. **On all models,** disconnect 42-pin connector and transmission harness connector from fuel charging wiring at power brake booster.
12. Remove mounting bolts and camshaft cover.
13. Reverse procedure to install.

1999–2002

RIGHTHAND SIDE

1. Raise and support vehicle.
2. Disconnect Crankshaft Position (CKP) sensor and air conditioning compressor electrical connectors.
3. Lower vehicle and disconnect air conditioning cycling switch connector.
4. Relieve fuel pressure as outlined under "Precautions."
5. Disconnect fuel lines.
6. Disconnect ignition coils and fuel injector connectors.
7. Disconnect fuel injector electrical connectors.
8. Remove Positive Crankcase Ventilation (PCV) tube and position aside.
9. Remove Evaporative Emission (EVAP) canister purge valve.
10. Position hold-down clamp and remove hose from bypass tube.
11. Disconnect harness retainers from valve cover and position harness aside.
12. Remove studs, bolts and cam cover.
13. Reverse procedure to install, noting the following:
    a. Apply silicone gasket and sealant No. F7AZ-19554-EA, or equivalent, **Fig. 36.**
    b. Tighten bolts in sequence, **Fig. 37.**

LEFTHAND SIDE

1. Raise and support vehicle.
2. Remove oil bypass filter.
3. Disconnect Power Steering Pressure (PSP) switch and oil pressure sensor connectors.
4. Lower vehicle.
5. Disconnect cylinder head temperature sensor jumper wire connector.
6. Remove bolt and two studs and position bracket aside.
7. Disconnect Camshaft Position (CMP) sensor connector.
8. Disconnect alternator connector and fuel charging wiring connectors from coils and fuel injectors.
9. Disconnect Idle Air Control (IAC) valve and Throttle Position (TP) sensor connector.
10. Disconnect 42-pin connector, 16-pin connector and transmission connector.
11. Remove six bolts, five studs and cam cover.
12. Reverse procedure to install, noting the following:
    a. Apply silicone gasket and sealant No. F7AZ-19554-EA, or equivalent, **Fig. 36.**
    b. Adjust engine oil level.
13. Tighten bolts in sequence, **Fig. 38.**

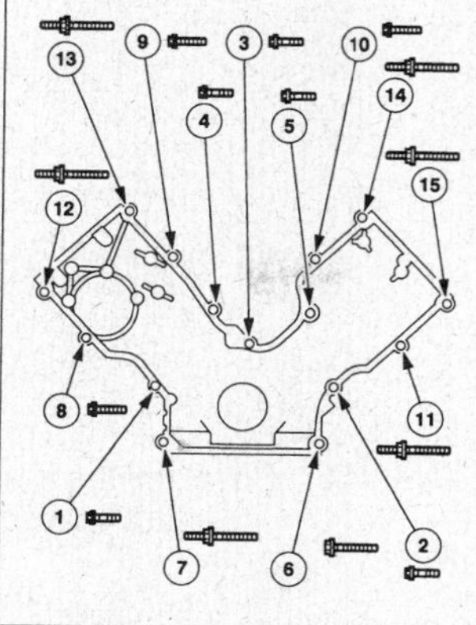

Item	Description
1	Bolt, Hex Flange Head Pilot, M8 x 1.25 x 53
2	Bolt, Hex Flange Head Pilot, M8 x 1.25 x 53
3	Bolt, Hex Flange Head Pilot, M8 x 1.25 x 53

Item	Description
4	Bolt, Hex Flange Head Pilot, M8 x 1.25 x 53
5	Bolts, Hex Flange Head Pilot, M8 x 1.25 x 53
6	Bolt, Hex-Head Pilot, M10 x 1.5 x 1.5 x 103.1
7	Stud, Hex-Head Pilot, M10 x 1.5 x 1.5 x 103.1
8	Screw and Washer, Hex Pilot, M10 x 1.5 x 57.5
9	Screw and Washer, Hex Pilot, M10 x 1.5 x 57.5
10	Screw and Washer, Hex Pilot, M10 x 1.5 x 57.5
11	Stud and Washer, Hex Head Pilot, M10 x 1.5 x M8 x 1.25 x 109.6
12	Stud and Washer, Hex Head Pilot, M10 x 1.5 x M8 x 1.25 x 109.6
13	Stud and Washer, Hex Head Pilot, M10 x 1.5 x M8 x 1.25 x 109.6
14	Stud and Washer, Hex Head Pilot, M10 x 1.5 x M8 x 1.25 x 109.6
15	Stud and Washer, Hex Head Pilot, M10 x 1.5 x M8 x 1.25 x 109.6

FM1069901038000X

Fig. 42 Front cover tightening sequence. 1999–2002

VALVE ARRANGEMENT

FRONT TO REAR

Right Bank ....I-E-I-E-I-E-I-E
Left Bank ....E-I-E-I-E-I-E-I

CAMSHAFT LOBE LIFT SPECIFICATIONS

Year	Intake, Inch	R. Exhaust, Inch	L. Exhaust, Inch
1998–2002	0.2591	0.2593	0.2597

VALVE ADJUSTMENT

These engines are equipped with hydraulic valve lash adjusters. The intake and exhaust valves cannot be adjusted.

ROCKER ARMS

REPLACE

1. Remove camshaft covers as outlined under "Valve Cover, Replace."
2. Position piston of cylinder at bottom of stroke and camshaft lobe at base circle.
3. Install valve spring spacer tool No. T91P-6565-AH, or equivalent, between spring coils.
4. Compress valve spring using valve spring compressor tool No. T91P-6565-AH, or equivalent, and remove rocker arm, **Fig. 39.**
5. Remove valve spring compressor and spacer.
6. Repeat previous steps for remaining cylinders, as required.
7. Reverse procedure to install. Apply clean engine oil to valve stem and tip, rocker arm roller contact surfaces and valve tappet.

HYDRAULIC LIFTERS

REPLACE

1. Remove rocker arms as outlined under "Rocker Arms, Replace."
2. Remove valve tappets from cylinder heads.
3. Clean and inspect valve tappets.
4. Reverse procedure to install, noting the following:
    a. Apply clean engine oil to valve stem and tip, rocker arm roller contact surfaces and valve tappets and cylinder head valve tappet bore.
    b. Valve tappets must have no more than 0.039 inches of plunger travel prior to installation.

VALVE SPRING & VALVE STEM OIL SEAL

REPLACE

REMOVAL

If, during this procedure, air pressure has forced the piston to the bottom of the cylinder, any loss of air pressure will

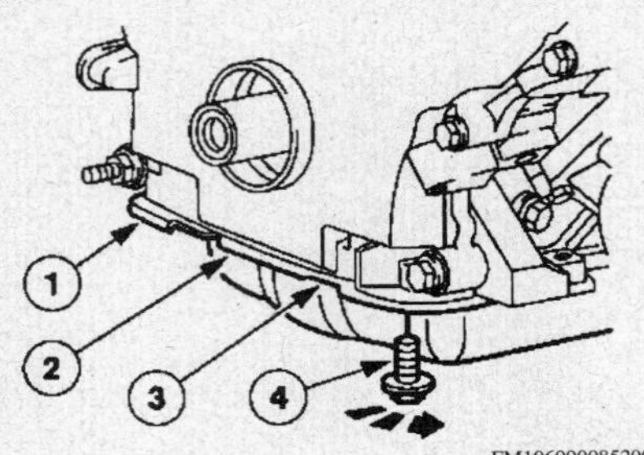
1
2
3
4

FM1069900852000X

Fig. 43 Oil pan to front cover bolt tightening sequence. 1999–2002

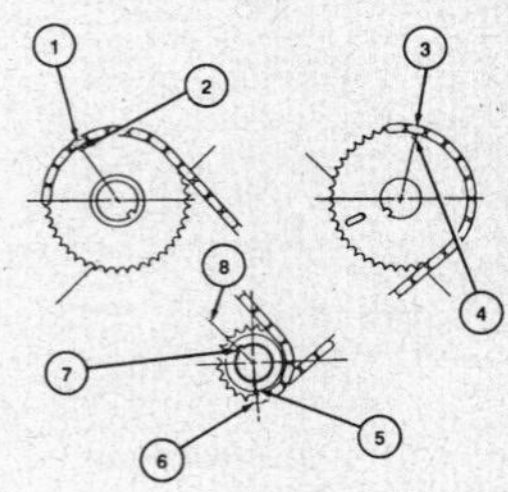

Item	Part Number	Description
1	—	RH Camshaft Timing Chain Mark
2	—	RH Camshaft Sprocket Mark
3	—	LH Camshaft Timing Chain Mark
4	—	RH Camshaft Sprocket Mark
5	—	Crankshaft Sprocket Mark
6	—	Crankshaft Timing Chain Mark
7	6306	Crankshaft Sprocket
8	—	Crankshaft Keyway Center Line

FM1069100143000X

Fig. 46 Lefthand timing chain installation

allow the valve to fall into the cylinder. A rubber band, tape or string wrapped around the end of the valve stem will prevent this and still allow enough travel to check the valve for binding and excess guide to valve stem clearance.

1. Remove camshaft covers as described under "Valve Cover, Replace."
2. Remove rocker arms/roller followers as described under "Rocker Arms, Replace."
3. Remove spark plug and position piston at top of stroke with both valves closed.
4. Install suitable air line with adapter in spark plug opening and apply air pressure.
5. Install valve spring spacer tool No. T91P-6565-AH, or equivalent, between valve spring coils.
6. Compress valve spring using valve spring compressor tool No. T91P-6565-A, or equivalent.
7. Remove keys, retainer and valve spring.
8. Remove valve stem seal using suitable locking pliers.
9. Repeat previously steps as required until all seals are removed.

INSTALLATION

Piston must be at Top Dead Center (TDC) of cylinder being serviced.

1. Remove air pressure and inspect valve stem for damage. Rotate valve and check valve stem tip eccentric

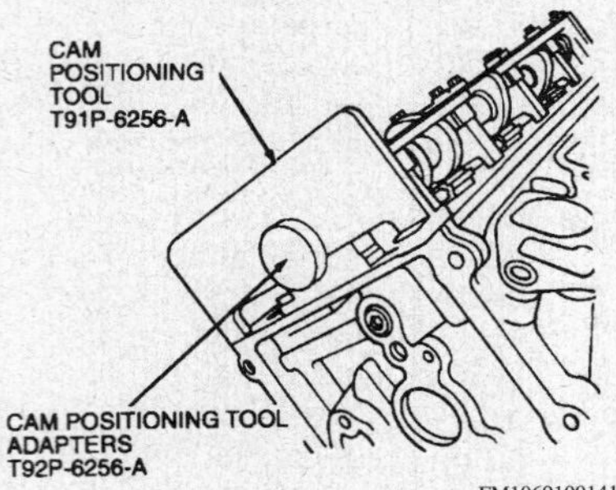
CAM POSITIONING TOOL T91P-6256-A
CAM POSITIONING TOOL ADAPTERS T92P-6256-A

FM1069100141000A

Fig. 44 Camshaft positioning tool installation

movement during rotation.
2. Position valve up and down through normal travel and check stem for binding. **If valve has been damaged. It will be necessary to remove cylinder head for service.**
3. If valve condition is good, apply engine oil to valve stem and hold valve closed.
4. Apply air pressure in cylinder.
5. Install valve stem seal using valve stem seal replacer tool No. T91P-6571-A, or equivalent.
6. Position valve spring and retainer over valve stem.
7. Compress valve spring using valve spring spacer tool No. T91P-6565-AH, or equivalent, between coils.
8. Install valve spring retainer key using valve spring compressor tool No. T91P-6565-A, or equivalent.
9. Turn off air supply and remove adapter from spark plug opening.
10. Install spark plug, roller follower and camshaft cover.
11. Start engine and inspect for leaks.

FRONT COVER

REPLACE

1998

The cam covers must be removed before engine front cover.

1. Remove drive belt and water pump pulley.
2. Raise and support vehicle.
3. Remove power steering mounting bolts. **Front lower belt will not come all the way out.**
4. Wire power steering pump aside.
5. Remove four oil pan to engine front cover bolts.
6. Remove crankshaft pulley bolt and washer.
7. Remove crankshaft pulley using crankshaft damper remover tool No. T58P-6316-D, or equivalent.
8. Lower vehicle.
9. Remove air conditioner high pressure line to righthand cover stud nuts.
10. Remove both valve covers.
11. Disconnect fuel charging wiring from camshaft position sensor.
12. Position power steering hoses aside.
13. Remove two power steering reservoir bracket nuts and one bolt.
14. Remove mounting bolt and belt idler pulley.

NOTE: WITH EITHER CHAIN POSITIONED AS SHOWN, MARK EACH END AND USE MARKS AS TIMING MARKS

FM1069100142000X

Fig. 45 Timing chain marks

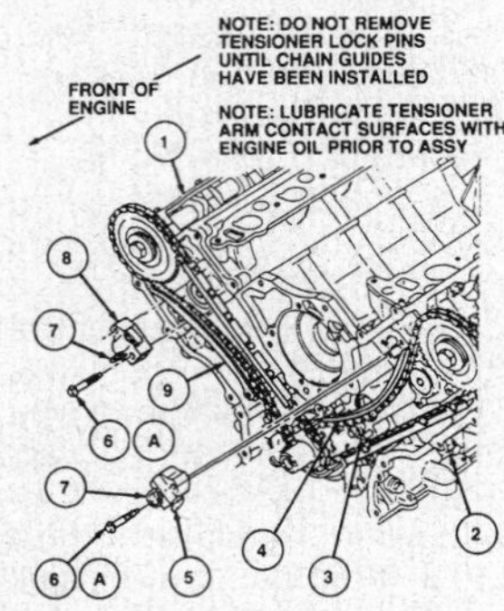
NOTE: DO NOT REMOVE TENSIONER LOCK PINS UNTIL CHAIN GUIDES HAVE BEEN INSTALLED
FRONT OF ENGINE
NOTE: LUBRICATE TENSIONER ARM CONTACT SURFACES WITH ENGINE OIL PRIOR TO ASSY

Item	Part Number	Description
1	6049	Cylinder Head (RH)
2	6049	Cylinder Head (LH)
3	N806007	Dowel
4	6L253	Timing Chain Tensioner Arm (LH)
5	6L266	Timing Chain Tensioner (LH)
6	N606543-S2	Bolt (2 Req'd)
7	—	Lock Pin (Part of 6L266)
8	6L266	Timing Chain Tensioner (RH)
9	6L253	Timing Chain Tensioner Arm (RH)
A	—	Tighten to 20-30 N·m (15-22 Lb-Ft)

FM1069100144000X

Fig. 47 Tensioner arm installation

15. Disconnect fuel charging wiring and remove crankshaft position sensor.
16. Remove eight stud bolts, seven bolts and front cover.
17. Reverse procedure to install, noting the following:
    a. Apply silicone gasket and sealant No. E3AZ-19562-A, or equivalent, in damper keyway.
    b. Ensure crankshaft key and keyway are aligned, using crankshaft damper replacer tool No. T47P-6316-B, or equivalent.
    c. Install crankshaft damper.
    d. Tighten bolts in sequence, **Fig. 40.**
    e. **Torque** four oil pan to engine front cover bolts to 15 ft. lbs. in sequence, **Fig. 41.**
    f. Final tighten bolts an additional 60°.

1999–2002

1. Remove both cam covers and water pump.
2. Raise and support vehicle.
3. Remove power steering bolts and position pump aside.
4. Drain engine oil into suitable container.
5. Remove oil pan to front cover bolts.
6. Remove crankshaft front seal.
7. Remove belt idler pulley.
8. Remove front cover bolts and stud bolts.
9. Remove engine front cover from front cover to cylinder block dowel.
10. Reverse procedure to install, noting the following:
    a. If engine front cover is not secured within four minutes, sealant must be removed and sealing area cleaned with metal surface cleaner

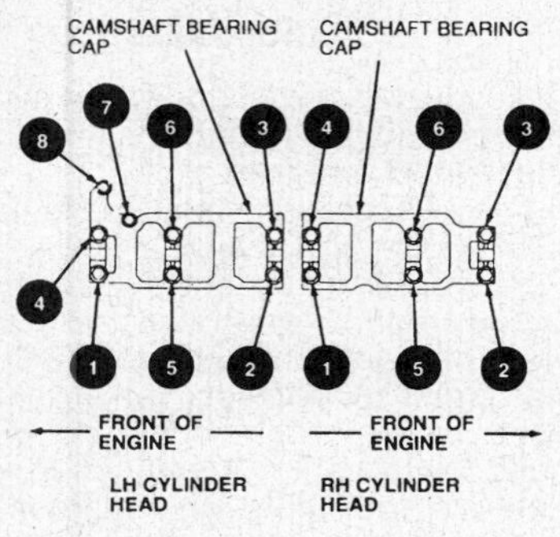

Fig. 48 Camshaft cap cluster tightening sequence

No. F4AZ-19A536-RA, or equivalent. Allow to dry until there is no sign of wetness, or for four minutes, whichever is longer.

b. Apply silicone along cylinder head-to-block surface and oil pan-to-cylinder block surface.
c. Use silicone gasket and sealant No. F7AZ-19554-EA, or equivalent.
d. Ensure crankshaft key and keyway are aligned, using crankshaft damper replacer tool No. T74P-6316-B, or equivalent.
e. Install crankshaft pulley.
f. **Torque** bolts 1–7 to 15–22 ft. lbs. in sequence, **Fig. 42.**
g. **Torque** bolts 6–15 to 29–40 ft. lbs. in sequence.
h. **Torque** four oil pan to engine front cover bolts to 15 ft. lbs. in sequence, **Fig. 43.**
i. Final tighten bolts an additional 60° in sequence.

FRONT COVER SEAL

REPLACE

1. Release belt tensioner and remove serpentine drive belt.
2. Raise and support vehicle, then remove crankshaft damper mounting bolt and washer.
3. Remove crankshaft damper using crankshaft damper removal tool No. T58P-6316-D, or equivalent.
4. Remove front cover seal using front cover seal removal tool No. T74P-6700-A, or equivalent.
5. Reverse procedure to install, noting the following:
   a. Install front cover seal using replacement tool No. T88T-6701-A, or equivalent.
   b. Apply silicone gasket and sealant part No. F6AZ-19562-AA, or equivalent, in damper keyway.
   c. Ensure crankshaft key and keyway are aligned.
   d. Install crankshaft damper using crankshaft damper replacer tool No. T74P-6316-B, or equivalent.
   e. **Torque** bolt to 66 ft. lbs.
   f. Loosen one complete turn.
   g. **Torque** bolts to 35–39 ft. lbs.
   h. Final tighten bolts an additional 85–95°.

TIMING CHAIN

REPLACE

REMOVAL

Do not rotate the crankshaft and/or camshaft with the timing chains removed and the cylinder heads installed. Rotation of camshaft or crankshaft may result in valve and/or piston damage.

If engine has jumped time, cylinder heads must be removed to repair damage to valves and/or pistons.

1. Remove components to access timing chains, as required.
2. Remove crankshaft position sensor tooth wheel and rotate engine to cylinder No. 1 TDC.
3. Prevent accidental rotation of camshafts by installing cam positioning tools No. T92P-6256-A, or equivalents, to flats on camshafts, **Fig. 44.**
4. Remove two bolts and righthand tensioner.
5. Remove righthand tensioner arm, two mounting bolts and righthand chain guide.
6. Remove righthand camshaft sprocket mounting bolt, washer, gear and spacer, as required.
7. Remove two mounting bolts and lefthand tensioner.
8. Remove tensioner arm, mounting bolts and lefthand chain guide.
9. Remove lefthand chain and camshaft gears.
10. Remove lefthand camshaft sprocket mounting bolt, washer, gear and spacer, as required.

INSTALLATION

If engine has jumped time, ensure all repairs to engine components and/or valve train are completed. Then rotate engine counterclockwise 45° to position pistons below top of deck face. Install cylinder heads.

1. Prevent camshafts from rotating using cam positioning tools No. T92P-6256-A, or equivalent.
2. Install timing chain guides (both sides) and tighten bolts.
3. Position left and righthand camshaft spacers and gears on camshaft, if removed.
4. Install washer and camshaft gear mounting bolt. **Do not tighten now.**
5. Install lefthand crankshaft gear. Ensure tapered portion of gear faces away from engine block.
6. If copper links of timing chain are not visible, split chain in half and mark two opposing links, **Fig. 45.**
7. Install lefthand timing chain on camshaft gear. Ensure copper link is aligned with timing mark of camshaft gear, **Fig. 46.**
8. Install lefthand timing chain on crankshaft gear. Ensure copper link is aligned with timing mark on crankshaft gear.
9. Install righthand crankshaft gear. Ensure tapered portion of gear faces toward engine block.
10. Install righthand timing chain on camshaft gear. Ensure copper link is

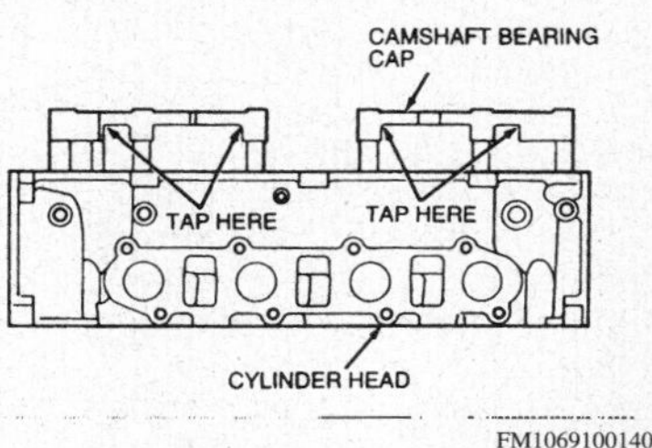

Fig. 49 Camshaft replacement

aligned with timing mark of camshaft gear.

11. Install righthand timing chain on crankshaft gear. Ensure copper link is aligned with crankshaft gear.
12. Lubricate tensioner arm contact surfaces with engine oil, then install left and righthand tensioner arms on dowels. **Fig. 47.**
13. Install left and righthand timing chain tensioners and tighten. **Do not remove lockpins until timing chain guides are installed.**
14. Install chain guides and tighten.
15. Remove lockpins from timing chain tensioners and ensure all timing marks are aligned.
16. Remove cam positioning tools and install all components removed during removal procedure.

CAMSHAFT

REPLACE

1. Remove cooling fan and shroud.
2. Relieve fuel system pressure as described under "Precautions."
3. Remove camshaft covers as described under "Valve Cover, Replace."
4. Remove front cover as described under "Front Cover, Replace."
5. Remove timing chains as described under "Timing Chain, Replace."
6. Rotate crankshaft counterclockwise 45°. Ensure pistons are below top of engine deck face. **Crankshaft must be in position prior to rotating camshafts or piston and/or valve damage may result.**
7. Install valve spring compressor tool No. T91P-6565-A, or equivalent, under camshaft and on valve spring retainer.
8. Install valve spring spacer tool No. T91P-6565-AH, or equivalent, between spring coils and camshaft to prevent damage.
9. With camshaft at base circle, compressing valve spring and remove followers by rotating camshaft, as required.
10. Repeat previous steps until all roller followers are removed.
11. Remove camshaft cap cluster mounting bolt, **Fig. 48.**
12. Tap upward, then remove cap and camshaft, **Fig. 49.**
13. Reverse procedure to install. Tighten camshaft cap cluster, **Fig. 48.**

PISTON & ROD ASSEMBLY

If old pistons are serviceable, ensure

they are installed on original rods. Check side clearance between connecting rods and crankshaft journal. Correct clearance is 0.00059–0.01772 inch.

1. Assemble pistons, pins, bearings, caps, nuts and bolts in original positions.
2. Install pistons with notch to front of engine.
3. Alternatively tighten connecting rod caps.
4. Rotate crankshaft to ensure smooth operation.

CRANKSHAFT REAR OIL SEAL

REPLACE

1. Lower transmission and support using suitable jack.
2. Remove flywheel.
3. Remove crankshaft oil slinger using rear crankshaft slinger remover tool No. T95P-6701-AH and slide hammer tool No. T50T-100-A, or equivalents.
4. Remove crankshaft rear oil seal using rear crankshaft seal remover tool No. T95P-6701-EH and slide hammer tool No. T50T-100-A, or equivalents.
5. Remove crankshaft rear oil seal retainer, as required.
6. Reverse procedure to install, noting the following:
   a. Use suitable plastic scraping tool to remove all traces of old sealant. **Do not use metal scrapers, wire brushes, power abrasive discs or other abrasive means to clean sealing surfaces.**
   b. Clean sealing surfaces with metal surface cleaner No. F4AZ-19A536-RA, or equivalent. Allow to dry until there is no sign of wetness, or four minutes, whichever is longer.
   c. Use silicone gasket and sealant No. F7AZ-19554-EA, or equivalent.

OIL PAN

REPLACE

1998

1. Remove air inlet tube.
2. Drain engine coolant into suitable container.
3. Remove cooling fan and shroud.
4. Relieve fuel system pressure as described under "Precautions."
5. Disconnect fuel lines.
6. Remove upper radiator hose, wiper module and support bracket.
7. Evacuate air conditioning system as outlined in "Air Conditioning" chapter.
8. Disconnect air conditioning compressor outlet hose.
9. Remove hose to righthand coil bracket bolt.
10. Disconnect engine electrical harness 42-pin connector from bracket on brake vacuum booster.
11. Remove righthand cylinder head ground strap mounting nut.
12. Remove heater hose to cylinder head upper stud and lower bolt.
13. Remove blower motor resistor.

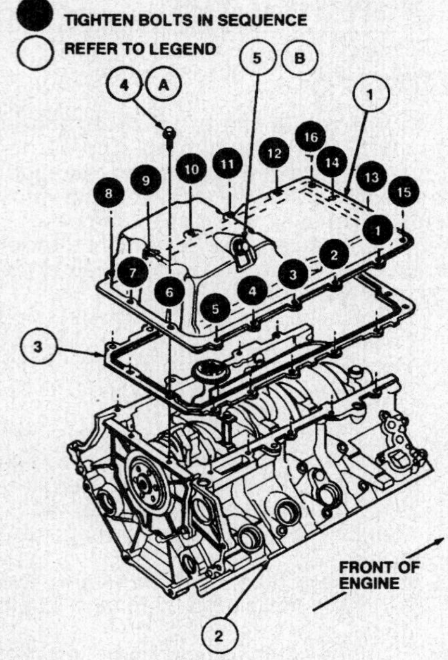

Item	Description
1	Oil Pan
2	Cylinder Blocks
3	Oil Pan Gasket
4	Bolt (16 Req'd)
5	Oil Pan Drain Plug
A	Tighten to 20 N·m (15 Lb-Ft Then an Additional 60 Degrees)
B	Tighten to 11-16 N·m (9-11 Lb-Ft)

FM1069800853000X

Fig. 50 Oil pan tighten sequence. 1998

14. Raise and support vehicle.
15. Drain engine oil into suitable container.
16. Install oil pan drain plug with new gasket.
17. Remove righthand engine mount to lower engine bracket mounting bolt.
18. Disconnect exhaust system from manifolds.
19. Lower exhaust and secure to crossmember with wire.
20. Position suitable jack and block of wood below oil pan, rearward of drain plug.
21. Raise engine approximately four inches, then insert two 2.5–2.75 inches thick wood blocks under each engine mount.
22. Lower engine onto wood blocks and remove jack from below oil pan.
23. Loosen 16 mounting bolts and remove oil pan. **It may be necessary to loosen, without removing, two nuts on rear transmission mount and raise extension housing of transmission slightly to remove oil pan.**
24. Reverse procedure to install. Tighten bolts in sequence, **Fig. 50.**

1999–2002

1. Remove air cleaner outlet tube.
2. Remove wiper arm and pivot shaft.
3. Remove drive belt, fan motor and shroud.
4. Relieve fuel system pressure as described under "Precautions."
5. Disconnect fuel lines.
6. Remove Exhaust Gas Recirculation (EGR) tube.
7. Remove alternator and blower motor speed control.
8. Remove righthand engine mount bolt.
9. Raise and support vehicle.
10. Remove two lefthand engine mount bolts.
11. Remove four nuts and support exhaust.
12. Remove bolt for transmission line support bracket.
13. Loosen nuts for transmission mount.
14. Lower vehicle.
15. Remove second righthand motor mount bolt from top.
16. Raise engine with suitable floor crane and support engine.
17. Raise and support vehicle.
18. Remove mounting bolts and position oil pan aside. Remove oil pickup tube bolts.
19. Remove oil pickup tube bracket bolt.
20. Remove O-ring and inspect.
21. Remove oil pan and gasket through front.
22. Reverse procedure to install. Tighten oil pan bolts in sequence, **Fig. 51.**

OIL PUMP

REPLACE

1. Remove camshaft covers as described under "Valve Cover, Replace."
2. Remove front cover as described under "Front Cover, Replace."
3. Remove oil pan as described under "Oil Pan, Replace."
4. Remove timing chains as described under "Timing Chain, Replace."
5. Remove mounting bolts and oil pump, **Fig. 52.**
6. Reverse procedure to install. Align oil pump inner rotor with flat of crankshaft.

BELT TENSION DATA

Automatic belt tensioners are spring loaded devices which set and maintain drive belt tension. The drive belt should not require tension adjustment . Automatic tensioners have belt wear indicator marks. If indicator mark is not between indicator lines, belt is worn or an incorrect belt is installed.

SERPENTINE DRIVE BELT

BELT ROUTING

Refer to **Figs. 53 and 54** for drive belt routing.

REPLACEMENT

1. Rotate tensioner away from belt using suitable breaker bar installed in ½ inch square hole in tensioner arm.
2. Lift old belt over alternator pulley flange and remove.

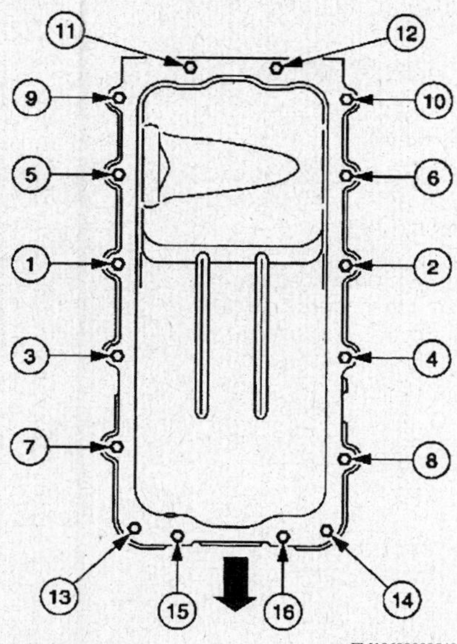

Fig. 51 Oil pan tighten sequence. 1999–2002

3. When installing, position new belt over pulleys. Ensure all V-grooves make proper contact with pulley.
4. Ensure belt is properly installed on each pulley.

COOLING SYSTEM BLEED

1. Place heater temperature switch in maximum heat position.
2. Start engine and allow to idle. While engine is idling, feel for hot air at air conditioning vents.
3. If air discharge remains cool and engine coolant temperature gauge does not move, engine coolant level is low in engine and must be filled.
4. Stop engine, allow to cool and fill cooling system.
5. Start engine and allow to idle until normal operating temperature is reached, noting the following:
   a. Hot air should discharge from air conditioning vents.
   b. Engine coolant temperature gauge should maintain stabilized reading in middle of NORMAL range.
   c. Upper radiator hose should feel hot to touch.
6. Shut engine off and allow to cool.
7. Inspect engine for coolant leaks.
8. Adjust engine coolant level in overflow bottle, as required.

THERMOSTAT

REPLACE

1. Drain coolant into suitable container until level is below upper radiator hose and thermostat housing.
2. **On 1999–2002 models,** remove engine appearance cover.
3. **On all models,** disconnect upper radiator hose at thermostat housing.
4. Remove two thermostat housing mounting bolts.

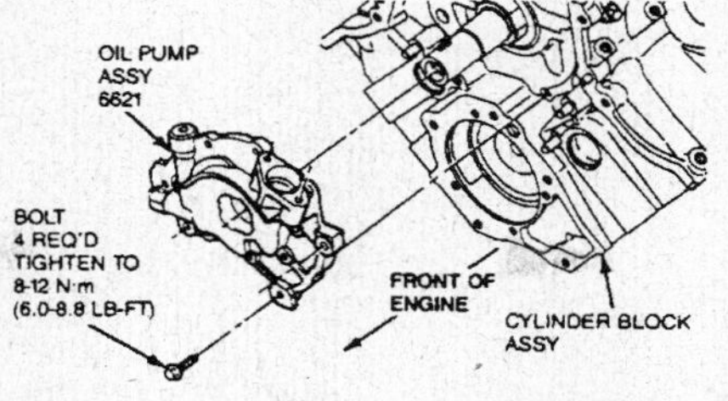

Fig. 52 Oil pump assembly

5. Remove O-ring seal and thermostat from intake manifold. Replace O-ring, as required.
6. Reverse procedure to install.

WATER PUMP

REPLACE

1. Drain coolant into suitable container.
2. Loosen water pump mounting bolts, release belt tensioner and remove accessory drive belt.
3. Remove mounting bolts and water pump pulley.
4. Loosen mounting bolts and remove water pump.
5. Reverse procedure to install. Replace O-ring.

RADIATOR

REPLACE

1998

1. Drain engine coolant into suitable container.
2. Remove fan shroud.
3. Disconnect upper, lower and overflow hoses from radiator.
4. Remove radiator upper support mounting bolts and supports.
5. Remove two mounting bolts on each side of radiator, connecting radiator, oil cooler and air conditioning condenser core.
6. Tilt radiator toward engine, then lift oil cooler and air conditioning condenser core disconnecting from radiator end tanks retaining tabs.
7. Remove radiator by pulling up.
8. Reverse procedure to install.

1999–2002

1. Raise and support vehicle.
2. Drain engine coolant into suitable container.
3. Remove fan blade, motor and shroud.
4. Release three hold downs and remove radiator sight shield.
5. Remove upper and lower radiator hoses from radiator.
6. Remove radiator support bolts and supports.
7. Remove bolts and position air conditioning condenser core and transmission oil cooler away from radiator.
8. Remove radio.
9. Reverse procedure to install.

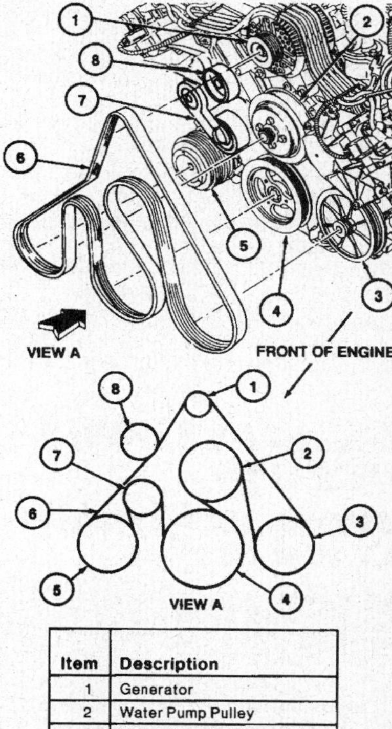

Item	Description
1	Generator
2	Water Pump Pulley
3	Power Steering Pump Pulley
4	Crankshaft Pulley
5	A / C Compressor
6	Drive Belt
7	Drive Belt Tensioner
8	Belt Idler Pulley

FM1069100145000A

Fig. 53 Serpentine drive belt routing. 1998–99

FUEL PUMP

REPLACE

1. Relieve fuel system pressure as described under "Precautions."
2. Drain fuel tank into suitable container, then raise and support vehicle.
3. Remove fuel tank and disconnect pressure transducer connector on top rear corner of fuel tank.
4. Remove six mounting bolts and fuel pump module.
5. Reverse procedure to install, noting the following:
   a. Turn ignition from Off to On position for three seconds using fuel pressure gauge tool No. T80L-9974-B, or equivalent, on fuel charging Schraeder valve.
   b. Repeat off to on switching 5–10 times until pressure gauge shows at least 35 psi.

FUEL FILTER

REPLACE

1. Turn engine off and relieve fuel system pressure as described under "Precautions."
2. Raise and support vehicle.
3. Remove push connect fittings at both ends of filter. Install new retainer clips in each push connect fitting.

4. Remove two mounting bolts and fuel filter from metal bracket.
5. Remove filter from retainer. Record direction of flow. Arrow points to open end of retainer.
6. Remove rubber insulator rings from filter.
7. Reverse procedure to install, noting the following:
   a. Replace insulator if filter moves freely.
   b. **On 1998 models, torque** fuel filter clamp to 72–108 inch lbs.
   c. **On 1999–2002 models, torque** fuel filter clamp to 18–26 inch lbs.
   d. **On all models,** start engine and inspect for fuel leaks.

TECHNICAL SERVICE BULLETINS

BUZZING OR RATTLING EXHAUST SYSTEM

1998-99

On some of these models there may be a buzzing or rattling from the exhaust system.

This condition may be caused by loose catalytic converter, catalytic pipes, muffler pipes and/or muffler heat shields.

To correct this condition secure heat shields with suitable worm clamps. **Torque** clamps to 60 inch lbs.

FUEL PUMP WHINING/ BUZZING THROUGH RADIO SPEAKER

1998-2001

On some of these models there may be a whining or buzzing in speakers.

This condition may be caused by fuel pump electrical noise.

To correct this condition install an electronic noise Radio Frequency Interference

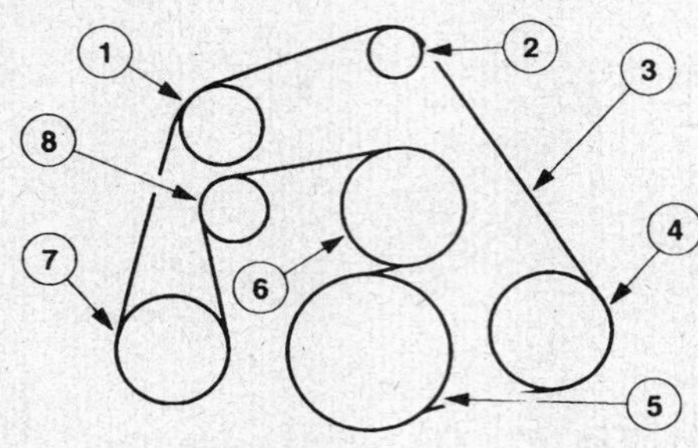

Item	Description
1	Belt idler pulley
2	Generator pulley
3	Drive belt
4	Power steering pump pulley
5	Crankshaft pulley
6	Water pump pulley
7	A/C clutch pulley
8	Drive belt tensioner pulley

FM1069901042000X

Fig. 54 Serpentine drive belt routing. 2000–02

(RFI) filter (part No. F1PZ-18B925-A) on fuel pump inside the fuel tank, as follows:

1. Remove fuel pump sender from fuel tank as described under "Fuel Pump, Replace."
2. Cut fuel pump wires three inches from flange. Discard wires.
3. Connect RFI filter connectors to fuel pump spade terminal.
4. Cut and solder both RFI filter red and black wires to flange red and black wires.
5. Install suitable heat shrink tubing over solder connectors.
6. Secure RFI filter to fuel pump using suitable bundling strap.
7. Install fuel pump sender.

ROUGH IDLE

1998-99

On some of these models equipped with single exhaust there may be engine roughness at idle.

This condition may be caused by exhaust system resonance.

To correct this condition install exhaust system mass damper on righthand Y pipe as follows:

1. Raise and support vehicle.
2. Remove righthand catalytic converter to Y pipe bolts and flag nuts. Discard bolts and nuts.
3. Remove gasket between converter and Y pipe. Discard gasket and clean flanges, as required.
4. Install new gasket (part No. E9AZ-5E241-A) between flanges.
5. Install mass damper (part No. F2VY-5F240-A) with mass toward righthand side and damper bracket on Y pipe flange.
6. **Torque** new bolts (part No. 56143-S100) and nuts (part No. 391188-S100) to 26–33 ft. lbs.

ENGINE MOUNTS LACK DURABILITY

1998-2001

On some of these models the engine mounts may lack satisfactory durability under severe operating conditions encountered by police, taxi or limo/livery service where there is extended idling at high ambient temperature.

This condition may be caused by extreme heat generated by engine.

To correct this condition install revised engine mounts with built-in heat shields (lefthand part No. F8VZ-6028-AA and righthand part No. F8VZ-6028-BA).

TIGHTENING SPECIFICATIONS

Year	Component	Torque/Ft. Lbs.
1998–2002	Air Conditioning Compressor	15–22
	Alternator	15–22
	Camshaft Bearing Caps	71–107①
	Camshaft Gear	82–95
	Connecting Rod	③
	Front Cover	15–22
	Cylinder Head	⑤
	Damper	④
	ECT Sensor	12–17
	EGR Tube Connector	33–48
	EGR Valve	15–22
	EGR Valve Line	26–33
	Engine Mount	45–59
	Engine Mount Through Bolt	15–22
	Engine To Transmission	30–44
	Engine To Transmission Brace	18–31
	Exhaust Manifold	14–16
	Exhaust Pipe To Exhaust Manifold	20–30
	Flywheel	54–64
	Front Cover	⑥
	Fuel Rail	71–106
	Fuel Tank Strap	22–30
	HEGO Sensors	27–33
	Intake Manifold	15–22
	Main Bearing Cap	22–25
	Oil Filter Adapter	15–22
	Oil Inlet Tube To Main Bearing Cap	15–22
	Oil Inlet Tube To Oil Pump	72–106①
	Oil Pan Drain Plug	98–143①
	Oil Pan To Cylinder Block	15–22
	Oil Pump To Cylinder Block	72–107①
	Power Steering Pump To Engine	15–22
	Rear Engine Mount	35–47
	Rear Engine Mount To Crossmember	51–67
	Rear Oil Seal Retainer	71–106①
	Spark Plug	②
	Thermostat	15–22
	Throttle Body & Adapter	71–106①
	Timing Chain Guides	71–106①
	Timing Chain Tensioner	15–22
	Torque Converter	22–25
	Water Pump	15–22
	Water Pump Pulley	15–22

① — Inch lbs.

② — On 1998 models, torque to 7–15 ft. lbs.; 1999–2002 models, torque to 15 ft. lbs.

③ — On 1998 models, torque to 15–18 ft. lbs.; then to 30–33 ft. lbs.; and final tighten an additional 90–120°. On 1999–2002 models, torque to 30–33 ft. lbs. and final tighten an additional 90–120°.

④ — Refer to "Front Cover Seal, Replace" for tightening specifications and sequence

⑤ — Refer to "Cylinder Head, Replace" for tightening specifications and sequence.

⑥ — On 1998 models, torque bolts to 15–22 ft. lbs.; 1999–2002 models, torque bolts 1–7 to 15–22 ft. lbs, torque bolts 6– 15 to 29–40 ft. lbs.

Rear Axle & Suspension

NOTE: On Air Bag Equipped Models, Refer To "Air Bag System Precautions" Located In The Front Of This Manual For System Disarming & Arming Procedures.

NOTE: Refer To "Computer Relearn Procedure" Located In The Front Of This Manual When Battery Power To The Computer Has Been Interrupted.

INDEX

PRECAUTIONS

AIR BAG SYSTEMS

Refer to "Air Bag System Precautions" in the front of this manual for system disarming and arming procedures.

AIR SUSPENSION PRESSURE RELIEF

Before servicing any air suspension components, disconnect power to system by turning air suspension switch OFF or by disconnecting battery ground cable.

Do not remove an air spring under any circumstances when there is pressure in the air spring. Do not remove any component supporting an air spring without either exhausting the air or providing support for air spring. Refer to "Functional Test" in the "Active Suspension Systems" chapter to vent air from spring.

BATTERY GROUND CABLE

Prior to service, disconnect battery ground cable and isolate as required.

DESCRIPTION

The rear suspension is composed of the upper and lower suspension arms, lateral arm, Watts link pivot, rear stabilizer bar and air or coil springs, **Fig. 1.**

REAR AXLE

REPLACE

1. **On models with air suspension,** turn air suspension switch to Off position, then vent air from system as outlined in "Active Suspension Systems" chapter.
2. **On all models,** raise and support vehicle and position safety stands below rear frame crossmember.
3. Mark driveshaft flange and pinion flange for correct alignment during installation.
4. Remove four mounting bolts and disconnect driveshaft.
5. Remove rear wheels, calipers and brake discs. Support caliper with suitable wire.
6. Remove rear disc rotor, parking brake rear cable and conduit from parking brake cable equalizer. Reroute parking brake rear cable and conduit aside.
7. Remove anti-lock brake sensors. Reroute anti-lock brake sensor wiring.
8. Remove rear stabilizer bar from rear stabilizer bar link and bushing.
9. Remove rear stabilizer bar bracket bolts, rear stabilizer bar brackets and rear stabilizer bar.
10. Remove rear air springs height sensor, as required.
11. Separate Watts linkage from rear axle housing.
12. Remove bellcrank stud nut. **Do not damage bellcrank stud threads.**
13. Secure rear axle to jack using additional support straps.
14. Support rear axle housing with suitable jack.
15. Remove lower mounting nuts and shock absorbers from brackets.
16. Remove lower control arm retainer, then the upper control arm mounting nuts and bolts.
17. Unseat air springs and lower rear axle.
18. Reverse procedure to install.

REAR AXLE SHAFT

REPLACE

REMOVAL

1. **On models with air suspension,** turn air suspension switch to Off position, then vent air from system as outlined in "Active Suspension Systems" chapter.
2. **On all models,** raise and support vehicle, then remove rear wheel and tire assembly.
3. Remove disc brake calipers and rotors, then the rear anti-lock brake sensor.
4. Drain rear axle fluid into suitable container, by removing cover.
5. Remove differential pinion shaft lock bolt and differential pinion shaft, **Fig. 2.**
6. Push flanged end of axle shafts toward center of vehicle and remove C-lock from button end of axle shaft, **Fig. 3.**
7. Remove axle shaft from housing. **Do not damage oil seal and ABS sensor ring.**

INSTALLATION

1. Ensure O-ring is present on spline end of axle shaft.
2. Slide axle shaft into axle housing. **Do not damage bearing seal or ABS sensor ring.**
3. Start splines into side gear and push firmly until button end of axle shaft can be seen in differential case.
4. Install C-lock on button end of axle shaft splines. Push shaft outboard until splines engage and C-lock seats in counterbore of differential side gear.
5. Position differential pinion shaft through case and pinion gears, aligning hole in shaft with lock bolt hose.
6. Apply rear axle lubricant No. E0AZ-19554-BA, or equivalent, to pinion shaft lock bolt and tighten.
7. Install cover and tighten.
8. Install ABS speed sensor, rotors and calipers.

SHOCK ABSORBER

REPLACE

1. **On models with air suspension,** turn air suspension switch to Off position, then vent air from system as outlined in "Active Suspension Systems" chapter.

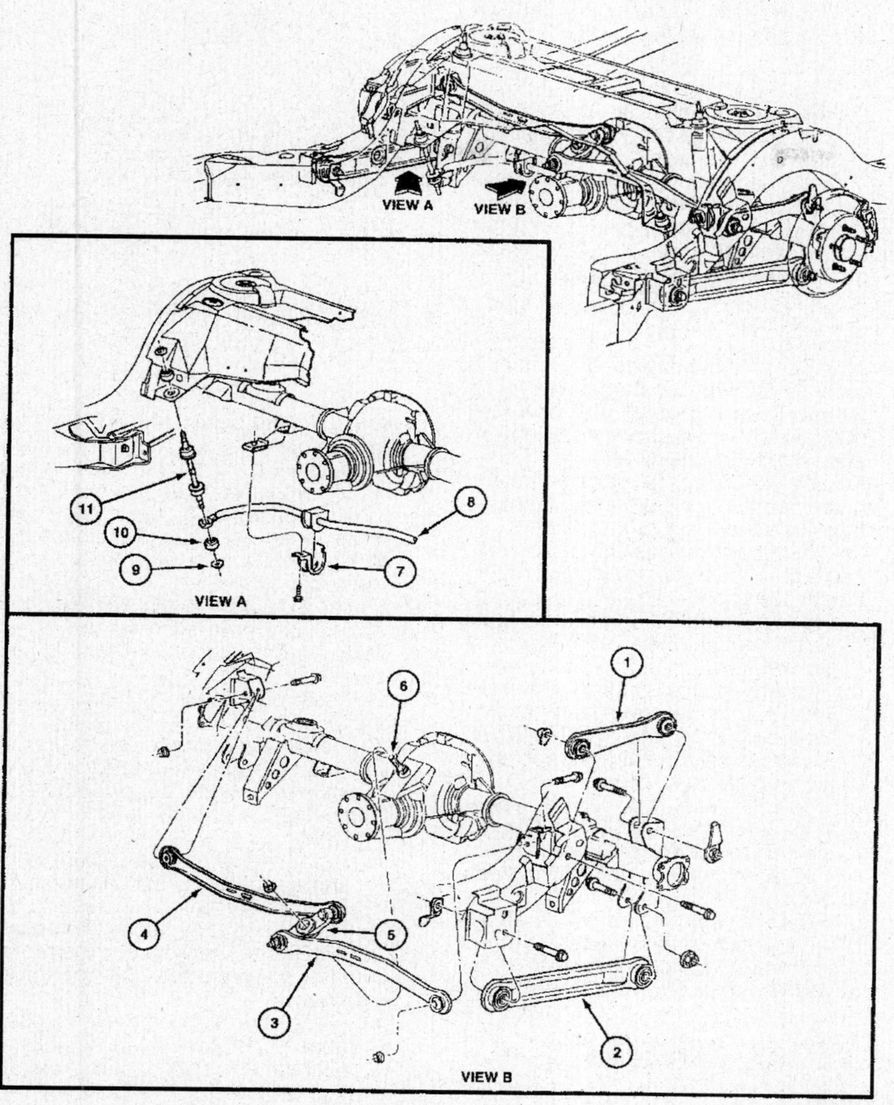

Fig. 1 Exploded view of rear suspension (Part 1 of 2)

2. **On all models,** raise and support vehicle.
3. **On models equipped with plastic dust tube,** place suitable open end wrench on hex stamped into dust tube's metal cap.
4. **On models equipped with steel dust tube** grasp tube to prevent stud rotation when loosening mounting nut.
5. **On all models,** remove shock absorber mounting nut, washer and insulator from stud on upper side of frame.
6. Compress shock absorber to clear hole in frame, then remove inner insulator and washer from upper stud.
7. Remove self-locking nut and disconnect shock absorber lower stud from mounting bracket on rear axle tube.
8. Reverse procedure to install.

COIL SPRING

REPLACE

1998

1. Raise rear of vehicle and support at frame. Support rear axle with suitable jack.
2. Remove rear stabilizer bar.
3. Disconnect lower studs of two shock absorbers from mounting brackets on rear axle.
4. Unsnap parking brake rear cable and conduit from upper arm retainer before lowering rear axle housing.
5. Lower hoist and axle housing until rear springs are released.
6. Remove rear spring and rear spring center mounting insulators.

Item	Description
1	Rear Suspension Upper Arm
2	Rear Suspension Lower Arm
3	Lateral Arm, LH (Part of 4264)
4	Lateral Arm, RH (Part of 4264)
5	Watts Link Pivot (Part of 4264)

Item	Description
6	Watts Link Pivot Stud
7	Stabilizer Bar Bracket
8	Stabilizer Bar and Isolator Assy
9	Stabilizer Bar Link Retaining Nut
10	Stabilizer Bar Bushing
11	Stabilizer Bar Link

FM2039800059020X

Fig. 1 Exploded view of rear suspension (Part 2 of 2)

7. Reverse procedure to install. Install insulator between upper seat and spring, as required.

1999-2002

1. Mark rear shock absorber relative to protective sleeve with vehicle in static, level ground position (curb height).
2. Raise and support vehicle on suitable hoist.
3. Remove both wheel and tire assemblies.
4. Remove nuts and bushings, then rotate stabilizer bar off links.
5. Support rear axle.
6. All vehicles are equipped with gas pressurized shock absorbers which will extend unassisted. **Do not apply heat or flame to shock absorbers during removal or component servicing.**
7. Remove nuts and disconnect shock absorbers. Discard nuts.
8. Lower axle, then remove springs and spring insulators.
9. Reverse procedure to install.

AIR SPRING

REPLACE

1998

1. Turn air suspension switch to Off position, then vent air from system as outlined in "Active Suspension Systems" chapter.
2. Remove heat shield and rear air spring retainer.
3. Remove air spring solenoid valve.
4. Insert air spring remover T90P-5310-A, or equivalent, between axle tube and spring seat on forward side of axle with its flat end resting on air spring piston knob.
5. Remove spring piston to axle spring seat by pushing downward, forcing piston and clip off axle spring seat.
6. Remove spring.
7. Reverse procedure to install.

1999-2002

1. Turn air suspension switch to Off position, then vent air from system as outlined in "Active Suspension Systems" chapter.
2. Remove rear air spring retainer.
3. Lift bottom of air spring off rear axle.
4. Disconnect electrical connector.

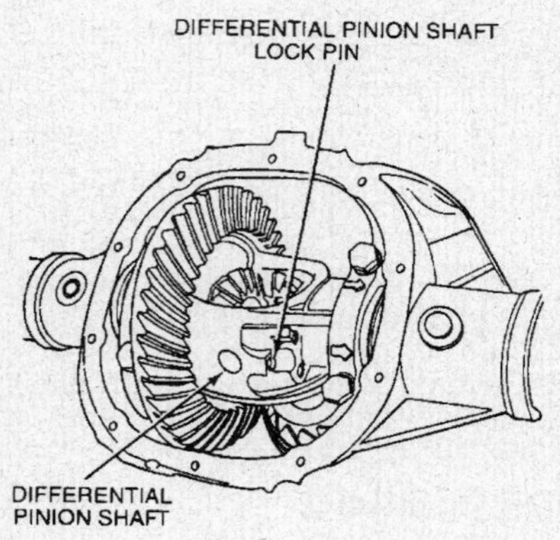

Fig. 2 Differential pinion shaft replacement

5. Push on red retaining ring and disconnect air line.
6. Remove air spring.
7. Reverse procedure to install.

CONTROL ARM

REPLACE

LOWER

1. **On models with air suspension,** turn air suspension switch to Off position, then vent air from system as outlined in "Active Suspension Systems" chapter.
2. **On all models,** mark rear suspension shock tube relative to protective sleeve with vehicle on level ground.
3. Raise and support vehicle, then remove wheel and tire assembly.
4. Support rear axle.
5. Remove and discard rear suspension lower arm pivot bolt and nut from axle bracket.
6. Remove and discard rear suspension lower arm pivot bolt and nut from frame bracket.
7. Remove rear suspension lower arm.
8. Reverse procedure to install, noting the following:
   a. Rear suspension lower arm bolts must be tightened with vehicle at curb height.
   b. Rear suspension lower arms are interchangeable from side to side with "OUTBOARD" stamped on side of arm for positioning during installation.
   c. Position rear suspension lower arm to frame bracket and install new pivot bolt and nut. Insert bolt so nut faces inboard. **Do not tighten now.**
   d. Raise axle to compresses shock absorber to previously established alignment mark (curb height).
   e. Tighten rear suspension lower arm to frame bracket pivot bolt.

UPPER

1. **On models with air suspension,** turn air suspension switch to Off position, then vent air from system as outlined in "Active Suspension Systems" chapter.
2. **On all models,** mark rear suspension shock absorber relative to protective sleeve with vehicle in static, level ground position (curb height).
3. Raise and support vehicle.
4. Support rear axle.
5. Remove and discard rear suspension upper arm pivot bolt and nut from axle bracket. **Do not use excessive force when removing pivot bolt and flag nut on righthand upper suspension arm to axle bracket.**
6. Remove and discard rear suspension upper arm pivot bolt and nut from frame bracket.
7. Remove rear suspension upper arm.
8. Reverse procedure to install, noting the following:
   a. Rear suspension upper arm bolts must be tightened with vehicle at curb height.
   b. Rear suspension upper arms are interchangeable from side to side with "FRONT" and "OUTBOARD" stamped on side of arms for positioning during installation.
   c. Position rear suspension upper arm to frame bracket and install new pivot bolt and nut. Insert bolt so nut faces inboard. **Do not tighten now.**
   d. Raise axle to compresses shock absorber to previously established alignment mark (curb height).
   e. Tighten bolts.

LATERAL CONTROL ARM

REPLACE

1. **On models with air suspension,** turn air suspension switch to Off position, then vent air from system as outlined in "Active Suspension Systems" chapter.
2. **On all models,** mark rear suspension shock absorber relative to protective sleeve with vehicle in static, level ground position (curb height).
3. Raise and support vehicle.
4. Support rear axle.
5. Disconnect height sensor from mounting bracket.
6. Remove and discard both lateral arm pivot bolts and nuts.
7. Watts link pivot stud is coated with dry adhesive and must be replaced whenever pivot nut or stud is loosened or removed using new Watts link pivot nut and stud service kit.

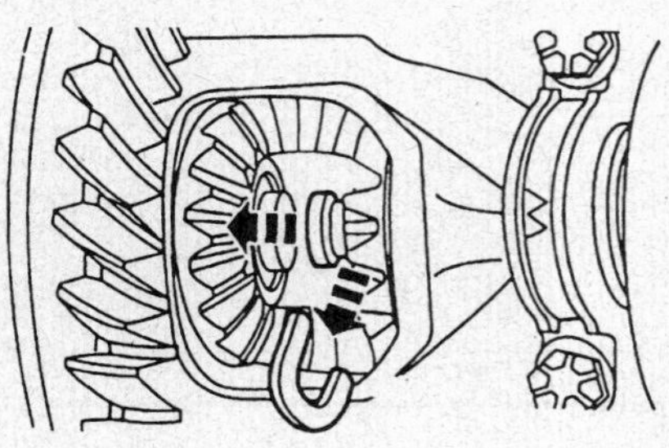

Fig. 3 Axle shaft C-lock replacement

8. If Watts link pivot stud on axle loosens while removing pivot nut, continue to loosen pivot stud until open end wrench can inserted to hold pivot stud. While holding pivot stud, remove and discard pivot nut.
9. Lower axle until Watts link is free of pivot stud. Remove lateral arm.
10. Remove and discard Watts link pivot stud.
11. Reverse procedure to install, noting the following:
    a. Install new Watts link pivot stud.
    b. Rear suspension lateral arm pivot bolts and Watts link pivot nut must be tightened with vehicle at curb height.
    c. Install lateral arm on pivot stud ensuring righthand arm flange faces front of vehicle.
    d. Raise axle until lateral arm aligns with frame brackets and install new pivot bolts and nuts. **Do not tighten now.**
    e. Raise axle to compresses shock absorber to previously established alignment mark (curb height). Tighten bolts.

STABILIZER BAR

REPLACE

1. **On models with air suspension,** turn air suspension switch to Off position, then vent air from system as outlined in "Active Suspension Systems" chapter.
2. **On all models,** raise and support vehicle.
3. Support rear axle using hi-lift jack tool No. 014-00942, or equivalent.
4. Remove both stabilizer bar link lower mounting nuts and bushings.
5. Remove upper mounting nuts, bushings and both stabilizer bar links.
6. Remove mounting bolts, both stabilizer bars and brackets.
7. Reverse procedure to install.

TIGHTENING SPECIFICATIONS

Year	Component	Torque/Ft. Lbs.
1998–2002	Caliper Locating Pin	21–26
	Driveshaft Flange Bolt	70–95
	Height Sensor Mounting Bracket To Lateral Arm	9–12
	Lateral Arm To Frame Bracket	65–88
	Lateral Arm To Watts Link Pivot	60–77
	Lower Arm To Axle & Frame	95–127
	Lower Arm To Frame	120–150
	Pinion Shaft Lock Bolt	15–29
	Rear Cover	25–34
	Shock Absorber To Axle Bracket	57–75
	Shock Absorber Upper	26–34
	Stabilizer Bar Bracket Bolt To Axle	16–21
	Stabilizer Link Nut To Stabilizer Bar	13–16
	Upper Arm To Axle	65–88
	Upper Arm To Frame	95–127
	Watts Link Pivot, Nut	158–212
	Watts Link Pivot, Stud	189–211
	Wheel Lug Nut	80–106

Front Suspension & Steering

NOTE: On Air Bag Equipped Models, Refer To "Air Bag System Precautions" Located In The Front Of This Manual For System Disarming & Arming Procedures.

NOTE: Refer To "Computer Relearn Procedure" Located In The Front Of This Manual When Battery Power To The Computer Has Been Interrupted.

NOTE: Prior To Performing Any Service Operations Listed In This Section, Consult The "Technical Service Bulletins" Section For Related Information.

INDEX

PRECAUTIONS

AIR BAG SYSTEMS

Refer to "Air Bag System Precautions" in the front of this manual for system disarming and arming procedures.

BATTERY GROUND CABLE

Prior to service, disconnect battery ground cable and isolate as required.

WHEEL BEARING

ADJUST

These models are equipped with sealed bearing units which do not require adjustment or maintenance. If the bearing is found to be defective, then the hub and bearing must be replaced as an assembly.

WHEEL BEARING

REPLACE

1. Raise and support front of vehicle, then remove wheel and tire assembly.
2. Remove grease cap from hub.
3. Remove disc brake caliper with brake hose attached. Suspend caliper from suspension with suitable wire. **Do not allow caliper to hang from brake hose.**
4. Remove brake rotor.
5. Remove nut, then the hub and bearing, **Fig. 1.** If hub is difficult to remove, use hub removal tool No. T81P-1104-C, or equivalent.
6. Reverse procedure to install. Install new hub nut.

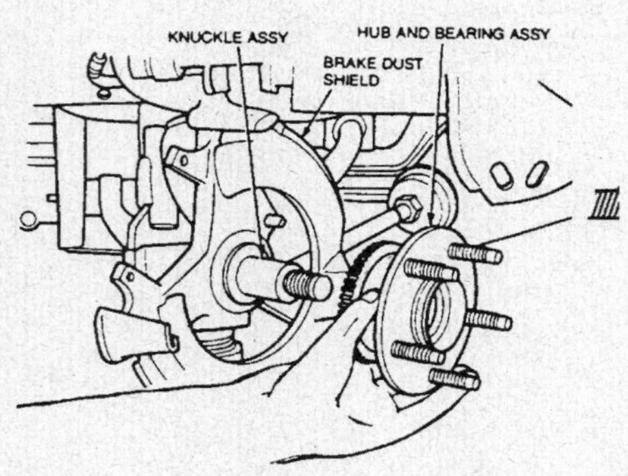

Fig. 1 Hub & wheel bearing assembly

BALL JOINT INSPECTION

On models equipped with air suspension, turn switch to Off position prior to raising and supporting vehicle.

Refer to "Specifications" section maximum backlash and endplay measurements.

1. Raise and support vehicle.
2. Inspect ball joint boos for tears. Replace ball joint as required.
3. Inspect wheel bearings.
4. Support lower control arm with suitable safety stand.
5. While assistant pushes and pulls equally on top and bottom of tire, observe any relative lateral backlash between upper control arm and front wheel spindle. Replace ball joint if lateral backlash is at or exceeds specifications.
6. While assistant moves tire up and down, observe any relative endplay between upper arm and front wheel spindle. Replace ball joint if endplay is at or exceeds specifications.
7. Remove tire and wheel assembly.
8. Separate lower arm from front wheel spindle. Disconnect mounting bolts and nuts.
9. Measure lateral backlash using suitable dial indicator while moving ball joint side to side. Replace ball joint if lateral backlash is at or exceeds specifications.
10. Measure endplay using suitable dial indicator while moving ball joint up and down. Replace ball joint if endplay is at or exceeds specifications.

BALL JOINT

REPLACE

LOWER

1. Raise and support vehicle.
2. Remove front wheel spindle.
3. Remove and discard joint boot seal.
4. Press out arm bushing joint using U-joint tool No. T74P-4635-C, ball joint remover tool No. D89P-3010-A, and receiving cup tool No. D84P-3395-A4, or equivalents, **Fig. 2.**
5. Reverse procedure to install, noting the following:
   a. When installing new front suspension arm bushing joint, protective cover must be left in place. It may be necessary to cut off end of cover to allow it to pass through receiving cup.
   b. Install ball joint with ball joint replacer tool No. D89P-3010-B, receiving cup tool No. D84P-3395-A4 and

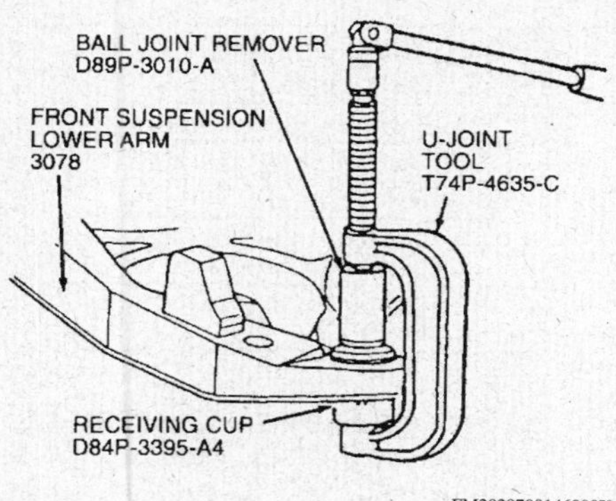

Fig. 2 Lower ball joint removal

U-joint tool No. T74P-4635-C, or equivalents, **Fig. 3.**

c. Inspect wheel alignment.

UPPER

1. Raise and support vehicle, then remove wheel and tire assembly.
2. Position suitable jack under lower control arm at ball joint.
3. Remove mounting nut and punch bolt from upper ball joint stud.
4. Mark position of alignment cams.
5. Remove ball joint mounting nuts.
6. Remove ball joint and separate ball joint stud from spindle by spreading slot with suitable pry bar.
7. Reverse procedure to install.

COIL SPRING

REPLACE

1. Raise and support vehicle, then remove wheel and tire assembly.
2. Remove two front shock absorber to suspension lower arm mounting bolts.
3. Remove upper nut, retainer, grommet and front shock absorber.
4. **On 1998 models,** proceed as follows:
   a. Remove steering center link from pitman arm.
   b. Support vehicle with safety stands under jacking pads.
   c. Lower hoist.
5. **On all models,** install one plate with pivot ball seat facing downward into coils of front coil spring, using coil spring compressor tool D78P-5310-A, or equivalent.
6. Rotate plate so it is flush with upper surface of front suspension lower arm.
7. Install other plate with pivot ball seat facing upward into coils of front coil spring.
8. Insert upper ball joint nut through coils of front coil spring so nut rests in upper plate. This pin can only be inserted one way into upper ball nut because of stepped-hole design.
9. Insert compression rod into opening in front suspension lower arm, through upper and lower plate and upper ball nut.
10. Insert securing pin through upper ball nut and compression rod, **Fig. 4.**
11. With upper ball nut secured, turn upper plate so it walks up coil until it contacts

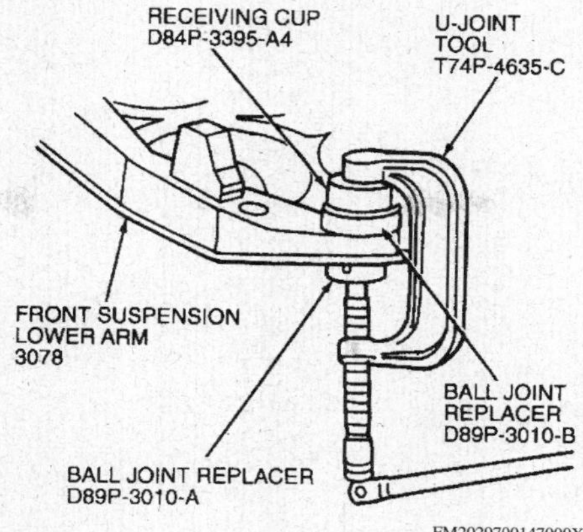

Fig. 3 Lower ball joint installation

upper front spring insulator. Back nut off one-half turn.

12. Install lower ball nut and thrust washer on compression rod and screw on forcing nut, **Fig. 5.**
13. Tighten forcing nut until front coil spring is compressed enough so it is free in its front spring insulator.
14. Remove two front lower arm pivot bolts, disconnect lower arm from crossmember and remove coil spring.
15. If new front coil spring is to be installed proceed as follows:
    a. Mark position of upper and lower plates on front coil spring.
    b. Compress new front coil spring for installation with an assistant.
    c. Measure compressed length and amount of curvature of old front coil spring.
16. Loosen forcing nut to relieve spring tension and remove tools from front coil spring.
17. Reverse procedure to install.

SHOCK ABSORBER

REPLACE

1. Remove upper shock absorber nut.
2. Raise and support vehicle.
3. Remove two lower screws and shock absorber.
4. Reverse procedure to install.

CONTROL ARM

REPLACE

1998

LOWER

1. Raise and support front of vehicle, then remove front wheel and tire assemblies.
2. Remove brake caliper, rotor, dust shield and ABS sensor, as required.
3. Remove jounce bumper, as required.
4. Remove shock absorber.
5. Disconnect steering sector shaft arm drag link from steering gear sector shaft arm.
6. Loosen lower ball joint stud nut one or two turns.
7. Tap front wheel spindle sharply, near

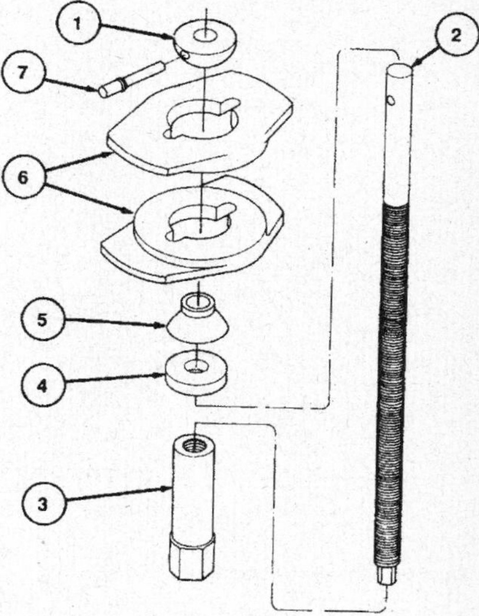

Item	Description
1	Upper Ball (Part of 204-D001 (D78P-5310-A))
2	Compression Rod (Part of 204-D001 (D78P-5310-A))
3	Forcing Nut (Part of 204-D001 (D78P-5310-A))
4	Thrust Washer (Part of 204-D001 (D78P-5310-A))
5	Lower Ball Nut (Part of 204-D001 (D78P-5310-A))
6	Plate (Part of 204-D001 (D78P-5310-A))
7	Pin (Part of 204-D001 (D78P-5310-A))

FM2029700148000X

Fig. 4 Compression rod assembly

lower stud, with suitable hammer to loosen stud in front wheel spindle.

8. Place suitable floor jack under front suspension lower arm.
9. Compress ball joint with tool and loosen spindle stud by tapping spindle near upper stud.
10. Remove ball joint press tool and position suitable jack under lower control arm.
11. Remove coil spring using suitable coil spring compression tool.
12. Remove ball joint nut and lower control arm, **Fig. 6.**
13. Reverse procedure to install, noting the following:
    a. Ensure coil spring is properly aligned.
    b. Check wheel alignment.

UPPER

1. Raise and support front of vehicle, then remove front wheel and tire assemblies.
2. Remove upper ball joint mounting nut cotter pin and loosen upper ball joint nut 1–2 turns. **Do not remove nut from stud.**
3. Compress ball joint with ball joint press tool T57P-3006-B, or equivalent, between upper and lower ball joint studs.
4. Loosen spindle stud by tapping spindle

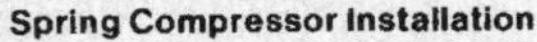
Spring Compressor Installation

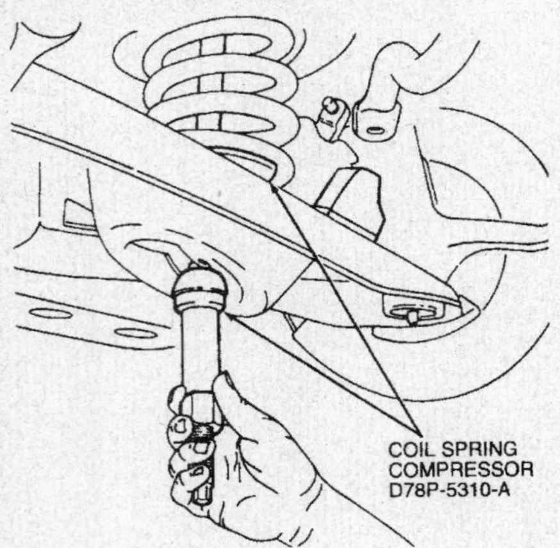

Spring Compressor Location

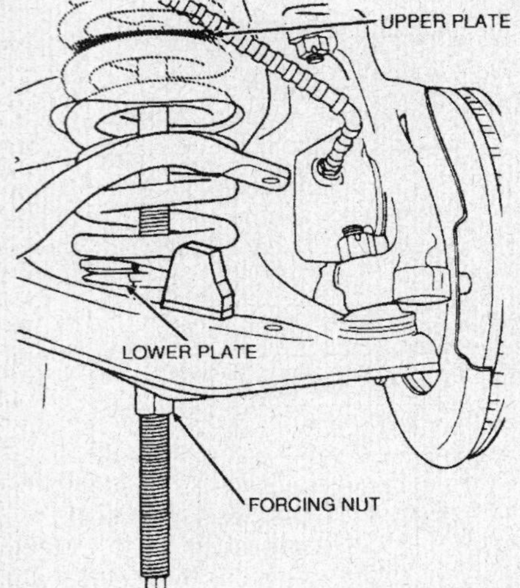

FM2029700149000X

Fig. 5 Spring compressor installation

near upper stud.

5. Remove ball joint press tool and position suitable jack under lower control arm.
6. Remove upper mounting bolts and upper control arm.
7. Reverse procedure to install. Check wheel alignment.

1999–2002

LOWER

1. Raise and support vehicle, then remove wheel and tire assembly.
2. Remove cotter pin and nut from tie rod end.
3. Remove tie rod end from front wheel spindle using tie rod end removal tool No. 211-001, or equivalent.
4. Remove coil spring as outlined under "Coil Spring, Replace"
5. Remove and discard lower ball joint nut.
6. Remove ball joint from steering knuckle using pitman arm puller tool No. 211-003, or equivalent.

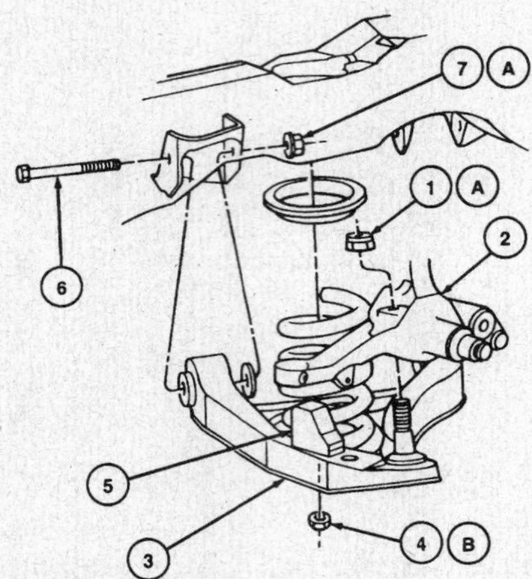

Item	Description
1	Nut (2 Req'd)
2	Front Wheel Spindle
3	Front Suspension Lower Arm
4	Nut (2 Req'd)

FM2029700150010X

Fig. 6 Lower arm replacement (Part 1 of 2). 1998

7. Remove lower control arm.
8. Reverse procedure to install.

UPPER

1. Raise and support vehicle, then remove wheel and tire assembly.
2. Place suitable jack under front suspension lower arm and lower vehicle until lower arm begins to move.
3. Secure front wheel spindle to frame using suitable piece of safety wire.
4. Remove upper steering knuckle bolt and nut to release upper ball joint from knuckle.
5. Remove mounting bolts, nuts and control arm.
6. Reverse procedure to install. Check wheel alignment.

STABILIZER BAR

REPLACE

1. Raise and support vehicle.
2. Remove stabilizer bar link nuts.
3. Remove four stabilizer bar brackets mounting nuts and lower arm stabilizer bar insulator from stabilizer bar.
4. **On 1998 models,** pry locking tab away from frame and slide stud out. Tap stud with suitable hammer, as required.
5. **On all models,** remove stabilizer bar.
6. Reverse procedure to install.

POWER STEERING GEAR

REPLACE

1. Remove stone shield, as required.
2. Disconnect steering gear pressure and return lines . Plug lines and ports.

Item	Description
5	Front Suspension Bumper
6	Bolt (4 Req'd)
7	Nut (4 Req'd)
A	Tighten to 148-201 N·m (109-148 Lb-Ft)
B	Tighten to 34-47 N·m (26-34 Lb-Ft)

FM2029700150020X

Fig. 6 Lower arm replacement (Part 2 of 2). 1998

3. Remove flex coupling to steering gear and column clamp bolt.
4. Raise and support vehicle.
5. Remove sector shaft nut.
6. Remove pitman arm using pitman arm puller tool No. T64P-3590-F, or equivalent.
7. Support steering gear and remove mounting bolts.
8. Remove steering gear by working if free of flex coupling.
9. Reverse procedure to install.

POWER STEERING PUMP

REPLACE

1. Disconnect power steering pump return line and allow power steering pump fluid to drain into suitable container.
2. Disconnect power steering pump pressure hose from pump fitting.
3. Disconnect drive belt, then remove pulley and power steering pump.
4. Reverse procedure to install, noting the following:
   a. **Do not overtighten pressure hose fitting.**
   b. Swivel and/or endplay of fitting is normal and does not indicate loose fitting.

TECHNICAL SERVICE BULLETINS

BUZZING FELT IN STEERING WHEEL ON RIGHTHAND TURNS AT LOW RPMS

1998

On some of these models equipped less police or taxi packages there may be a vibration or buzzing felt in the steering wheel on righthand turns at 590–1100 RPM.

This condition may be caused by valve resonance and power steering pump pulsations.

To correct this condition replace the power steering pressure hose (kit part No. F8AZ-3A719-AA). Attach hose bracket to the engine stud between the crankshaft and power steering pump pulleys. **Torque** nut to 53–72 inch lbs.

TIGHTENING SPECIFICATIONS

Year	Component	Torque/Ft. Lbs
1998–2002	Axle Nut	189–254
	Ball Joint To Lower Spindle	107–129
	Ball Joint To Upper Spindle	56–76
	Brake Caliper	24
	Flex Coupling to Gear Input Shaft	20–30
	Lower Arm To Crossmember	110–148
	Lower Arm To Frame	110–148
	Pinch Bolt & Nut	56–76
	Pitman Arm	35–46
	Pressure Hose To Gear	16–25
	Quick Connect Tube	35–45
	Return Hose To Gear	26–34
	Shock Absorber, Top Stud	25–33
	Shock Absorber, Lower Bolt	10–12
	Stabilizer Bar Link To Spindle	20–25
	Stabilizer Link To Bar	34–46
	Steering Gear To Side Rail	50–65
	Steering Pump To Engine	15–22
	Tie Rod End To Spindle	35–46
	Upper Ball Joint To Upper Arm	107–129
	Wheel Lug Nut	85–104

Wheel Alignment

INDEX

PRELIMINARY INSPECTION

1. Ensure all tires are inflated to proper pressure.
2. Inspect tire for wear patterns for improper wheel alignment, tire imbalance or damage because of bulges or separation.
3. Inspect suspension for modifications such as trailer towing equipment or heavy duty handling components.
4. Inspect vehicle for signs of overloading or sagging.
5. Ensure luggage compartment does not contain heavy objects.
6. Road test vehicle to isolate area of concern.

FRONT WHEEL ALIGNMENT

CASTER & CAMBER

Adjusting cams are provided for caster and camber adjustment, **Fig. 1.**

1. Check caster and camber and record readings.
2. Vehicle within minimum to maximum tolerances may require alignment adjustment to nominal setting because side to side setting is out of specification.
3. If adjustment is required, loosen two nuts on top of adjusting cams.
4. Turn hex cams as required to obtain desired valve.
5. Hold each cam and **torque** nuts to 109–148 ft. lbs.
6. Check toe-in and steering wheel spoke position. Adjust both at same time, as required.

TOE-IN & STEERING WHEEL SPOKE POSITION

After adjusting caster and camber, check steering wheel spoke position with front wheels in straight ahead position. If spokes are not in normal position, adjusted while toe is being adjusted.

1. Loosen two clamp bolts on each front wheel spindle tie rod adjusting sleeve, **Fig. 2.**
2. Adjust toe-in. If steering wheel spokes are in normal position, lengthen or shorten both rods equally to obtain correct toe.
3. If steering wheel spokes are not correct, make required rod adjustments to obtain correct toe-in and steering wheel alignment.
4. When toe-in and steering wheel position are both correct, lubricate clamp, bolts and nuts.
5. **Torque** clamp bolts on both connecting rod sleeves to 20–22 ft. lbs.
6. Sleeve position should not be changed when clamp bolts are tightened for proper clamp bolt orientation.

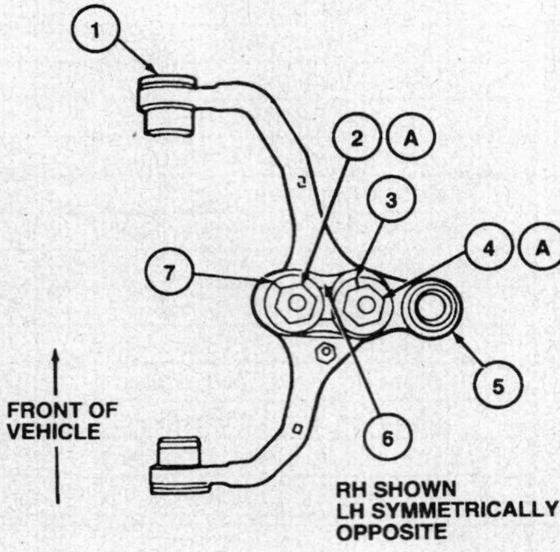

Item	Description
1	Front Suspension Lower Arm
2	Camber Adjust
3	Reference Mark
4	Caster Adjust
5	Front Suspension Upper Ball Joint
6	RH Identification on Forging

FM2049700059010X

Fig. 1 Caster & camber adjustment (Part 1 of 2)

Item	Description
7	Reference Mark
A	Turn Adjusting Cams Clockwise to Increase and Counterclockwise to Decrease

FM2049700059020X

Fig. 1 Caster & camber adjustment (Part 2 of 2)

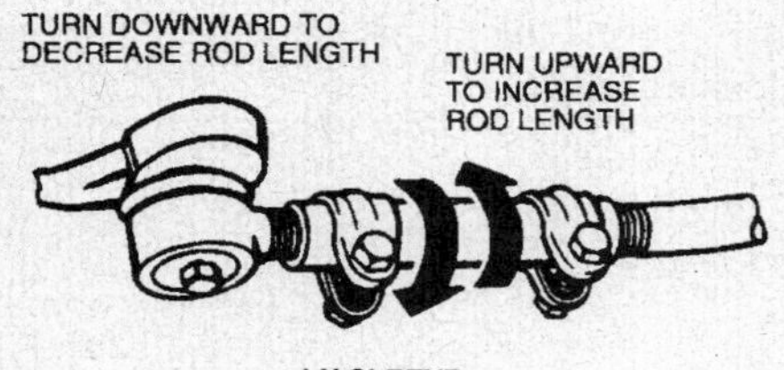

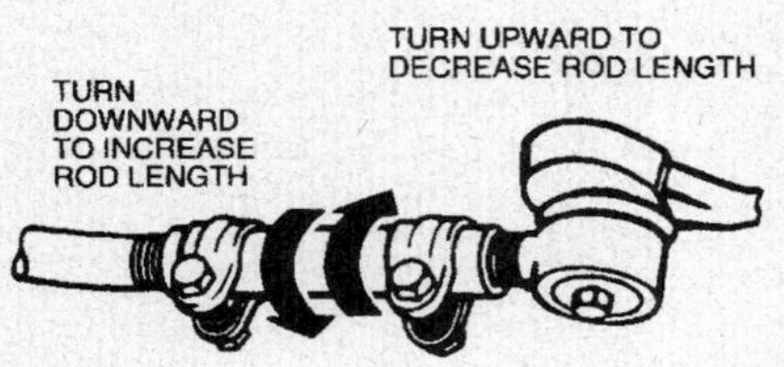

FM2049700060000X

Fig. 2 Toe adjustment

ESCORT, TRACER & ZX2

NOTE: Refer To Rear Of This Manual For Vehicle Manufacturer's Special Service Tool Suppliers.

INDEX OF SERVICE OPERATIONS

Specifications

GENERAL ENGINE SPECIFICATIONS

Year & Engine	Fuel System	Bore & Stroke, Inches	Compression Ratio	Net H.P. @ RPM	Maximum Torque Ft. Lbs. @ RPM	Normal Oil Pressure, psi
1998–2002						
2.0L SOHC	SEFI	3.34 x 3.46	①	110 @ 5000	125 @ 3750	35–65
2.0L DOHC	SEFI	3.34 x 3.46	9.6	130 @ 5750	127 @ 4250	54–80

SEFI — Sequential Electronic Fuel Injection

① — 1998–2000, 9.2:1; 2001–02, 9.35:1.

TUNE UP SPECIFICATIONS

Engine	Spark Plug Gap, Inch	Ignition Timing, °BTDC				Curb Idle Speed③		Fast Idle Speed		Fuel Pump Pressure, psi	Valve Clearance, Inch
		Firing Order Fig.④	Man. Trans.	Auto. Trans.	Timing Mark Fig.	Man. Trans.	Auto. Trans.	Man. Trans.	Auto. Trans.		
1998–2002											
2.0L SOHC	.052–.056①	③	10	10	⑦	⑥	⑥	⑥	⑥	35–55	⑧
2.0L DOHC	.052–.056	③	②	②	⑦	⑥	⑥	⑥	⑥	35–55	⑤

BTDC — Before Top Dead Center.

N — Neutral

① — 2002 models spark plug gap @ .044 inches.

② — Computer controlled, non-adjustable.

③ — Firing order, 1-3-4-2. Refer to Fig. 3-2, for spark plug wire connections @ ignition coil pack.

④ — Before disconnecting wires from distributor cap, determine location of No. 1 wire in cap, as distributor position may have been altered from that outlined @ the end of this chart.

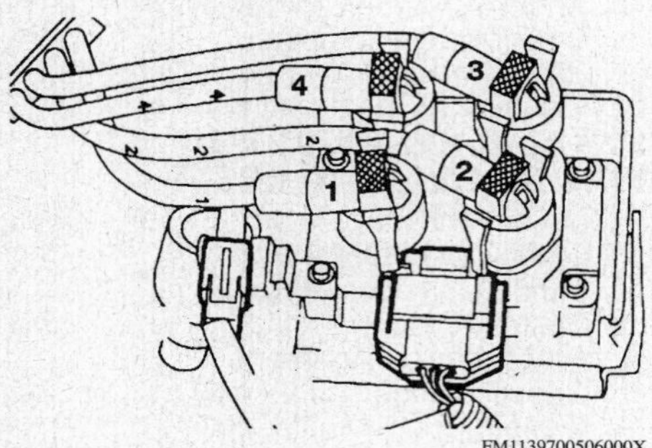

Fig. A

⑤ — Intake, .0043–.0071 inch; exhaust, .016–.0134 inch.

⑥ — Idle speed controlled by an automatic idle speed control.

⑦ — Equipped with a crankshaft position sensor. Timing is not adjustable.

⑧ — Equipped with hydraulic lash adjusters.

FRONT WHEEL ALIGNMENT SPECIFICATIONS

Year	Model	Caster Angle, Degrees		Camber Angle, Degrees		Total Toe, Inch	Steering Axis Inclination, Deg.	Maximum Steering Angle, Deg.		Ball Joint Wear
		Limits	Desired	Limits	Desired			Inner	Outer	
1998–2002	Escort & Tracer	+1.2 to +3.2	+2.2	–.4 to +1.4	+.4	–.5 to +.45	13.25	—	—	①
	ZX2	+1.55 to +3.15	+2.3	–.35 to +1.15	+.4	0 to +.16	0 to +.4	—	—	①

① — Refer to "Ball Joint Inspection" under "Front Suspension & Steering."

REAR WHEEL ALIGNMENT SPECIFICATIONS

Year	Model	Camber Angle, Degrees Limits	Camber Angle, Degrees Desired	Total Toe, Inch	Thrust Angle, Deg.
1998–2002	Escort & Tracer	–2.18 to –.12	–1.2	–.1 to +.5	—
	ZX2	–2.22 to –.11	–1.11	–.1 to +.5	—

VEHICLE RIDE HEIGHT SPECIFICATIONS

Model	Year	Body Style	Manu-facturer's Original Tire Size	Front Dim.	Front Specification Inches	Front Specification mm	Rear Dim.	Rear Specification Inches	Rear Specification mm
Escort	1998–2000	All	①	A	5.9	151	B	5.9	151
Tracer		Except Wagon	①	A	6.06	155	B	6.06	154
		Wagon	①	A	5.87	151	B	5.87	149

Measurement Points & Specifications②

A Dim. — Distance from Front Rocker Panel to Ground.
B Dim. — Distance from Rear Rocker Panel to Ground.
Dim. — Dimension.
N/A — Not Available.
① — See door sticker or inside of glove box for manufacturers original tire size specifications. If tires on vehicle do not match manufacturers original tire size & measurement is not within limits, it will be necessary to refer to the "Non-Standard Tire & Wheel Size Adjustment To Ride Height Specification & Tire Size Adjustment Charts" in the front of this manual for approximate changes in ride height specifications.
② — Measurement is with fuel, radiator coolant and engine oil full, spare tire, jack, hand tools and mats in designated positions and tires properly inflated.

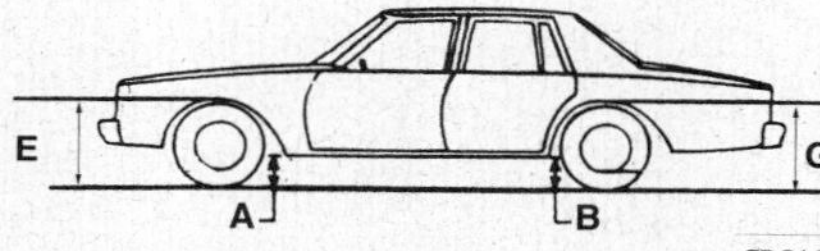

Dimensions A & B

FLUID CAPACITIES & COOLING SYSTEM DATA

Year/ Engine/ VIN	Coolant Capacity, Qts. Manual Transaxle	Coolant Capacity, Qts. Automatic Transaxle	Coolant Type	Radiator Cap Relief Pressure, Lbs.	Thermo. Opening Temp.	Fuel Tank Gals.	Engine Oil Refill Qts.①	Transaxle Oil Manual Transaxle Pints	Transaxle Oil Auto. Transaxle Qts.②
1998–2002									
2.0L/P	5.8	7.9	⑤	16	188–195	12.8	4.0	—	5.7③
2.0L/3	7.0	7.5	⑤	16	212	12.8	4.5	④	5.7③

① — Includes filter.
② — Approximate. Make final inspection w/dipstick.
③ — Without converter drained.
④ — Remove vehicle speed sensor from Transaxle. Add specified fluid and use speed sensor to inspect level. Full mark is at point between top & bottom of vehicle speed sensor gear.
⑤ — Some vehicle cooling systems are filled with "Motorcraft Premium Engine Coolant VC-4" (in Oregon VC-5) or equivalent meeting Ford specification ESE-M97B44-A **green color.** Others are filled with "Motorcraft Premium Gold Engine Coolant VC-7-A" meeting Ford specification WSS-M97B51–A1 **yellow color.** Always fill cooling system with same coolant that is present in the system. Do not mix coolant types.

LUBRICANT DATA

Year	Lubricant Type			
	Transaxle		Power Steering	Brake System
	Manual	Automatic		
1998–2002	75W-90 GL-4	Mercon	Mercon	DOT 3

Electrical

NOTE: On Air Bag Equipped Models, Refer To "Air Bag System Precautions" Located In The Front Of This Manual For System Disarming & Arming Procedures.

NOTE: Refer To "Computer Relearn Procedures" Located In The Front Of This Manual When Battery Power To The Computer Has Been Interrupted.

INDEX

PRECAUTIONS

BATTERY GROUND CABLE

Prior to service, disconnect battery ground cable and isolate as required.

AIR BAG SYSTEMS

Refer to "Air Bag System Precautions" in the front of this manual for system disarming and arming procedures.

FUSE PANEL & FLASHER LOCATION

These vehicles use two fuse panels. The passenger compartment fuse panel is located below the instrument panel, to the left of the steering wheel. The engine compartment fuse panel is located on the left side of the engine compartment.

The flasher unit is located at the relay panel behind the lefthand side of the instrument panel.

FUEL PUMP RELAY LOCATION

Fuel pump output is controlled by the Constant Control Relay Module (CCRM), located in the front lefthand corner of the engine compartment.

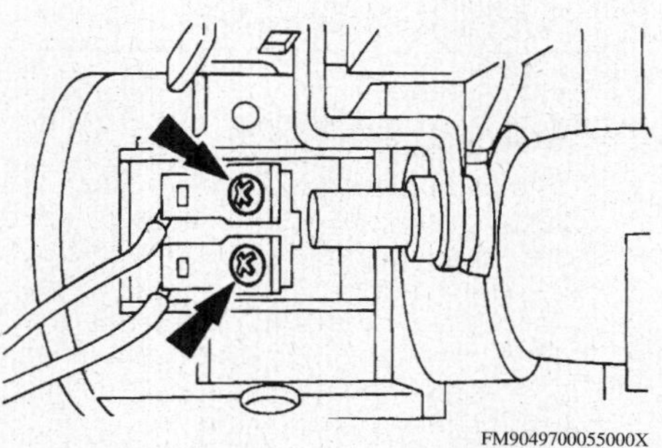

Fig. 1 Ignition key reminder switch screws

RELAY CENTER LOCATION

The relay panel is located behind the lefthand side of the instrument panel, above the I/P fuse panel.

STARTER

REPLACE

SOHC ENGINE

1. Remove air duct from throttle body to resonance chamber.
2. Remove starter motor upper mount bolts, then raise and support vehicle.
3. Disconnect "S" terminal connector from starter solenoid. When disconnecting connector from "S" terminal, grasp connector and depress plastic tab to remove.
4. Remove "B" terminal attaching nut and disconnect cable from terminal.
5. Remove starter motor lower mounting bolt, then the starter motor.
6. Reverse procedure to install. **Torque** upper and lower mounting bolts to 18–20 ft. lbs., and "B" terminal attaching nut to 84–144 inch lbs.

DOHC ENGINE

1. Remove air cleaner outlet tube, then raise and support vehicle.
2. Remove lower starter bolt, then lower vehicle.
3. Remove remaining two bolts, then raise and support vehicle.
4. Remove starter motor from block mounting surface, then the connector retaining nut.
5. Remove starter from vehicle.
6. Reverse procedure to install. **Torque** connector nut to 60 inch lbs., and mounting bolts to 15–20 ft. lbs.

COIL PACK

REPLACE

1. Disconnect ignition coil electrical connector.
2. Disconnect spark plug wires from ignition coil by squeezing locking tabs to release coil boot retainers.
3. Remove four ignition coil retaining bolts and noise filter condenser.

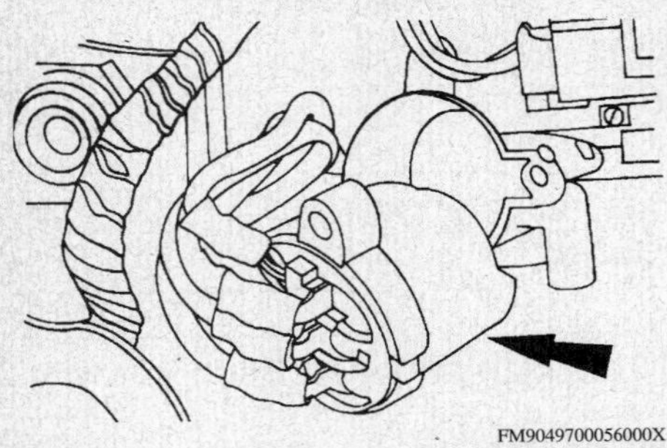

Fig. 2 Ignition switch removal

4. Save noise filter condenser for installation with new ignition coil.
5. Reverse procedure to install. **Torque** bolts to 40–60 inch lbs.

IGNITION LOCK

REPLACE

1. Remove combination switch as outlined under "Multi-Function Switch, Replace."
2. Disconnect ignition switch electrical connectors.
3. Remove ignition/shifter interlock cable mounting bracket bolt and position bracket and cable aside.
4. Groove head of ignition switch lock cylinder bracket bolts with hammer and chisel.
5. Remove ignition switch lock cylinder bracket bolts, ignition switch lock cylinder and bracket. Discard bolts.
6. Reverse procedure to install. Tighten lock cylinder bracket bolts until bolt heads break off.

IGNITION SWITCH

REPLACE

1. Remove upper and lower steering column shrouds.
2. Disconnect ignition switch electrical connector.
3. Remove ignition switch electrical connector cover screws.
4. Remove ignition key reminder switch screws, **Fig. 1.**
5. Remove ignition switch, **Fig. 2.**
6. Reverse procedure to install.

HEADLAMP SWITCH

REPLACE

The headlamp, fog lights and turn signal switches are serviced with the multi-function switch as a unit. Refer to "Multi-Function Switch, Replace" for procedure.

FOG LAMP SWITCH

REPLACE

The headlamp, fog lamp and turn signal switches are serviced with the multi-function switch. Refer to "Multi-Function Switch, Replace" for procedure.

STOP LIGHT SWITCH

REPLACE

1. Disconnect stop lamp switch electrical connector.
2. Remove stop lamp locknut, then the stop lamp switch.
3. Reverse procedure to install, adjust stop lamp switch by turning the switch until it contacts the brake pedal, then turn an additional half turn.

MULTI-FUNCTION SWITCH

REPLACE

1. Remove driver's air bag sliding contact as outlined under "Passive Restraint Systems."
2. Remove upper and lower steering column shrouds.
3. Remove turn signal switch, windshield wiper switch and hazard/flasher switch from multi-function switch.
4. Disconnect electrical connectors.
5. Remove mounting screws, then the multi-function switch housing.
6. Reverse procedure to install.

TURN SIGNAL SWITCH

REPLACE

The headlamp, fog lights and turn signal switches are serviced with the multi-function switch as a unit. Refer to "Multi-Function Switch, Replace" for procedure.

DIMMER SWITCH

REPLACE

ESCORT & TRACER

1. Detach hood release cable from left lower dash trim panel, then remove four retaining screws and left lower dash trim panel.
2. Disconnect electrical connector from dimmer switch, then squeeze two lock tabs and remove dimmer switch through front of trim panel.
3. Reverse procedure to install.

ZX2

1. Remove instrument panel upper finish panel insert, then the hood latch release handle retaining nut.
2. Remove instrument panel steering column cover attaching screw, then the cover.
3. Disconnect light switch rheostat resistor electrical connector.
4. Depress locking tabs and remove light switch from instrument panel steering column cover.
5. Reverse procedure to install.

STEERING WHEEL

REPLACE

1. Ensure front wheels are in straight-ahead position.
2. Remove driver side air bag module as outlined under "Passive Restraint Systems."

Fig. 3 I/P finish panel removal. Escort & Tracer

3. Remove steering wheel bolt.
4. Using steering wheel puller tool, remove steering wheel.
5. Reverse procedure to install. **Torque** steering wheel mounting bolt to 34–46 ft. lbs.

INSTRUMENT CLUSTER

REPLACE

ESCORT & TRACER

1. If equipped with tilt steering wheel, tilt steering wheel downward.
2. Remove hood latch release handle bolt.
3. Remove five retaining screws and the instrument panel finish panel, **Fig. 3.**
4. Remove four instrument cluster mounting screws, then pull cluster from instrument panel and disconnect electrical connectors at back of instrument cluster.
5. Reverse procedure to install.

ZX2

1. Remove instrument panel upper finish panel insert, then hood latch release handle attaching nut.
2. Remove instrument panel steering column cover attaching screw, then the cover.
3. Disconnect light switch rheostat resistor electrical connector.
4. Remove instrument panel upper finish panel attaching screws, then the panel.
5. Disconnect power mirrors switch electrical connector.
6. Remove four instrument cluster retaining screws, then disconnect three electrical connectors.
7. Remove instrument cluster from vehicle.
8. Reverse procedure to install.

RADIO

REPLACE

1. Set temperature control switch to Cold position.
2. Disconnect heater temperature cable.
3. Using radio removal tool No. T87P-19061-A, or equivalent, pull out Integrated Control Panel (ICP), **Fig. 4.**
4. Disconnect radio antenna lead, then the radio electrical connectors.
5. Remove radio from instrument panel.
6. Reverse procedure to install.

WIPER MOTOR

REPLACE

FRONT

1. Ensure windshield wiper motor is in the Off position and wiper pivot arms are parked in the highest position on the windshield.
2. Remove windshield wiper pivot arms.
3. Raise and support hood, then remove five center cowl top vent grille retainers and screws.
4. Remove two outer cowl top vent grille retainers and screws.
5. Lift clip up and off windshield wiper mounting arm and pivot shaft.
6. Slide windshield wiper mounting arm and pivot shaft off windshield wiper motor.
7. Disconnect windshield wiper motor electrical connector, then remove wiper motor bolts and wiper motor.
8. Reverse procedure to install. **Torque** wiper motor mounting bolts to 60–84 inch lbs.

REAR

1. Lift wiper arm attaching nut cover and remove nut, then pull wiper arm from pivot shaft.
2. Remove shaft seal from outer bushing attaching nut, then remove outer bushing attaching nut and outer bushing.
3. Remove liftgate trim panel as follows:
   a. Remove three push-in retainers and hi-mount stop lamp cover.
   b. Remove liftgate seaming welt from along trim panel, then disengage 10 retaining clips and remove trim panel.
   c. Remove cargo area lamp.
4. Disconnect wiper motor electrical connector, then remove three wiper motor mounting bolts and wiper motor.
5. Reverse procedure to install noting the following:
   a. **Torque** wiper motor mounting bolts to 60–84 inch lbs., and outer bushing attaching nut to 35–52 inch lbs.
   b. Turn wiper switch to the ON position and allow pivot shaft to move through three or four cycles, then turn wiper switch off.
   c. Position wiper arm on pivot shaft so tip of blade is .79–.98 inch from rear window molding.
   d. **Torque** wiper arm attaching nut to 60–84 inch lbs.

WIPER SWITCH

REPLACE

The windshield wiper switch is serviced with the multi-function switch as a unit. Refer to "Multi-Function Switch, Replace" for procedure.

WIPER TRANSMISSION

REPLACE

ESCORT & TRACER

1. With hood closed, remove seven screw covers from cowl grille screws.

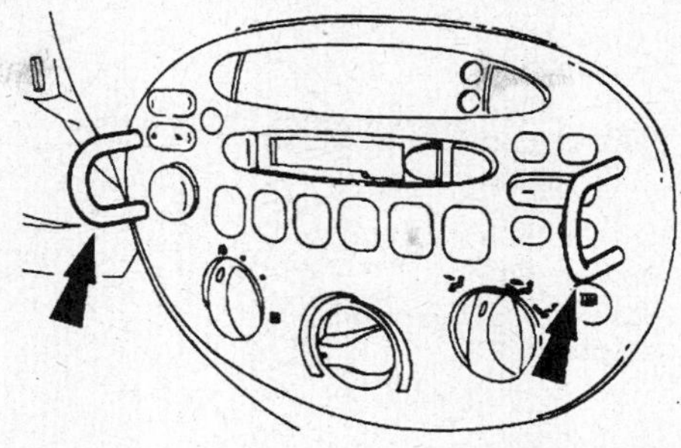

Fig. 4 Radio removal

2. Remove seven cowl grille screws, the cowl grille.
3. Pry up four baffle retaining clips, then remove baffle trim piece.
4. Remove two retaining screws from each pivot shaft, then the pivot shaft and wiper linkage assembly.
5. Reverse procedure to install. **Torque** pivot shaft retaining screws to 60–84 inch lbs.

ZX2

1. Remove windshield wiper pivot arms, then raise and support hood.
2. Remove five center cowl top vent grille retainers and screws, then the two outer cowl top vent grille retainers, screws and washers.
3. Remove pushpins from left and right air distribution flange baffles.
4. Remove windshield wiper mounting arm and pivot shaft retaining clip, then slide arm and shaft off windshield wiper motor.
5. Remove windshield wiper mounting arm and pivot shaft attaching screws, then pull arm and pivot shaft out through right air distribution flange baffle opening.
6. Reverse procedure to install. **Torque** pivot shaft retaining screws to 60–84 inch lbs.

BLOWER MOTOR

REPLACE

ESCORT & TRACER

1. Remove trim panel below glove compartment.
2. Remove wiring bracket and bolt, then disconnect blower motor electrical connector.
3. Remove three blower motor attaching bolts, then blower motor.
4. Remove blower wheel retaining clip, then blower wheel from blower motor.
5. Reverse procedure to install.

ZX2

1. Remove three blower motor retaining screws, then the blower motor.
2. Disconnect blower motor electrical connector.
3. Remove blower motor wheel retainer and blower wheel.
4. Reverse procedure to install. **Torque** blower motor retaining screws to 21–23 inch lbs.

HEATER CORE

REPLACE

ESCORT & TRACER

1. Disconnect heater hoses at bulkhead.
2. Disconnect mode selector and temperature control cables from cams and retaining clips.
3. Loosen heater to blower clamp, then remove three heater unit mounting nuts, **Fig. 5.**
4. Remove instrument panel as outlined under "Dash Panel Service."
5. Disconnect antenna lead from retaining clip, then remove heater unit.
6. Remove insulator, then four brace capscrews and brace.
7. Disconnect vacuum control motor vacuum connector.
8. Remove windshield defroster nozzle connectors.
9. Loosen A/C evaporator outlet duct clamp screw.
10. Remove lower heater core housing retaining nut.
11. Remove upper heater core housing retaining nuts and the heater core housing.
12. Remove heater dash panel seal.
13. Remove screws and the heater core cover.
14. Remove heater core from heater unit.
15. Reverse procedure to install.

ZX2

1. Drain coolant into a suitable container.
2. Remove air cleaner outlet tube, then disconnect heater hoses from heater core.
3. Remove instrument panel as outlined under "Dash Panel Service" section.
4. Disconnect antenna lead from heater core housing, then the vacuum control motor vacuum connector.
5. Disconnect vacuum lines from A/C evaporator housing retainer.
6. Remove windshield defroster nozzle pushpins and attaching screws.
7. Loosen A/C evaporator outlet duct clamp screw, then remove lower heater core housing retaining nut.
8. Remove upper heater core housing retaining nuts and heater core housing.
9. Remove heater dash panel seal, then the screws and heater core cover.
10. Remove heater core.
11. Reverse procedure to install.

EVAPORATOR CORE

REPLACE

ESCORT & TRACER

Do not disassemble A/C evaporator housing. If the evaporator core must be replaced, replace the entire A/C evaporator as a unit.

1. Recover refrigerant as outlined under "Air Conditioning."
2. Disconnect A/C vacuum line from evaporator housing.
3. Disconnect rear condenser to evaporator tube spring lock coupling.

4. Disconnect accumulator/drier spring lock coupling.
5. Remove instrument panel as outlined under "Dash Panel Service."
6. Loosen A/C evaporator outlet duct clamp bolt.
7. Disconnect A/C blower motor electrical connector.
8. Disconnect vacuum control motor vacuum connector.
9. Disconnect vacuum lines from A/C evaporator housing retainer.
10. Remove four A/C evaporator housing retaining nuts and the evaporator housing.
11. Reverse procedure to install.

ZX2

1. Recover refrigerant as outlined under "Air Conditioning."
2. Disconnect A/C vacuum line, then remove spring lock coupling from rear condenser to evaporator line.
3. Remove suction line support clip retaining nuts.
4. Disconnect suction line spring lock coupling.

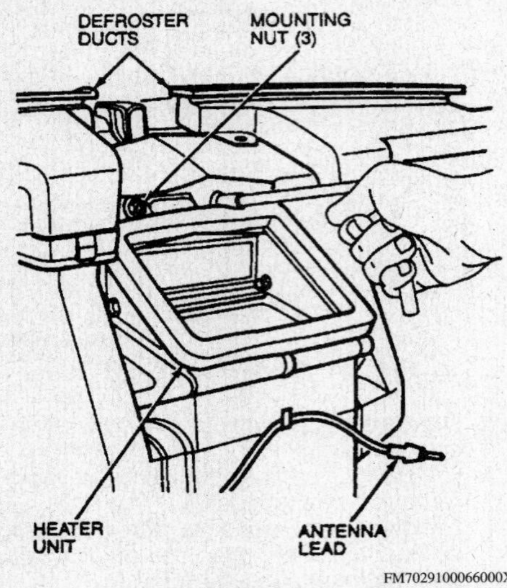

Fig. 5 Heater unit removal. Escort & Tracer

5. Remove instrument panel as outlined under "Dash Panel Service."
6. Remove righthand windshield defroster nozzle pushpins and screws, then the defroster nozzle.
7. Loosen A/C evaporator outlet duct clamp bolt, then disconnect A/C blower motor electrical connector.
8. Disconnect vacuum control motor vacuum connector, then the vacuum lines from A/C evaporator housing retainer.
9. Remove nuts and A/C evaporator housing, then disconnect vacuum line.
10. Remove screws and A/C vacuum reservoir tank and bracket.
11. Remove two inlet duct door vacuum control motor retaining nuts.
12. Remove push nut and vacuum control motor, then the air inlet duct attaching screws.
13. Remove blower motor and heater blower motor switch resistor.
14. Remove evaporator tube and drain tube dash panel seals.
15. Remove evaporator core.
16. Reverse procedure to install.

2.0L SOHC Engine

NOTE: On Air Bag Equipped Models, Refer To "Air Bag System Precautions" Located In The Front Of This Manual For System Disarming & Arming Procedures.

NOTE: Refer To "Computer Relearn Procedures" Located In The Front Of This Manual When Battery Power To The Computer Has Been Interrupted.

INDEX

PRECAUTIONS

AIR BAG SYSTEMS

Refer to "Air Bag System Precautions" in the front of this manual for system disarming and arming procedures.

BATTERY GROUND CABLE

Prior to service, disconnect battery ground cable and isolate as required.

FUEL SYSTEM PRESSURE RELIEF

1998-2001

Remove the schrader valve cap, **Fig. 1**, at the end of the fuel injection supply manifold and attach fuel pressure gauge No. T80L-9974-B. Open the pressure gauge manual valve to relieve fuel system pressure.

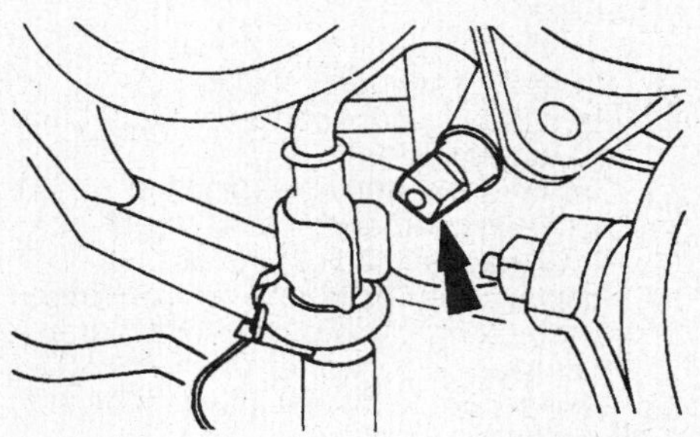

Fig. 1 Schrader valve cap location. 1998–2001

2002

1. Remove fuel pump fuse.
2. Start engine and let it run until it stalls.
3. Crank engine over two more times to remove all fuel pressure.
4. Turn ignition Off, then install fuel pump fuse.

COMPRESSION PRESSURE

1998-99

1. Run engine to warm to normal operating temperature.
2. Turn ignition switch to Off position, then remove spark plugs.
3. Place Transaxle in Park position (A/T) or Neutral position (M/T) and apply parking brake.
4. Block throttle plate in wide open position.
5. Install compression gauge into spark plug hole.
6. Install auxiliary starter switch in starting circuit.
7. Crank engine, using auxiliary starter switch, a minimum of five compression strokes and record highest reading. Note the number of compression strokes required to obtain highest reading.
8. Repeat test on each cylinder, cranking engine approximately the same number of compression strokes.
9. Compression pressure are within specification if the lowest reading cylinder is within 75% of the highest reading.

2000-02

1. Relieve fuel system pressure as outlined under "Precautions."
2. Remove spark plugs.
3. Install compression tester.
4. Install an auxiliary starter switch in the starting circuit.
5. With ignition switch Off, crank engine using auxiliary starter at least five times and record highest reading.
6. Repeat test on each cylinder, cranking engine same number of strokes per cylinder.
7. Install components as required, installing spark plugs into indicated cylinder.
8. Reset PCM fault memory as outlined under "Computer Relearn Procedures."

ENGINE

REPLACE

1. Remove hood.
2. Recover refrigerant as outlined under "Air Conditioning."
3. Remove battery and battery tray.
4. Remove air cleaner outlet tube.
5. Disconnect vacuum hoses from Exhaust Gas Recirculation (EGR) valve (A), brake booster (B), throttle body (C), fuel pressure regulator (D) and intake manifold (E), **Fig. 2.**
6. Disconnect two vacuum lines (A), remove two bolts (B) and position vacuum tree (C) aside, **Fig. 3.**
7. Disconnect speed control cable (if equipped), accelerator cable and throttle valve control actuating cable from throttle control lever.
8. Disconnect shift cable from bracket and set aside.
9. Disconnect two main engine/fuel charging wiring connectors.
10. Disconnect Constant Control Relay Module (CCRM) electrical connector and remove the CCRM and bracket.
11. Disconnect EGR backpressure transducer electrical connector, two vacuum hoses and remove the transducer.
12. Disconnect transmission range sensor electrical connector, transaxle solenoid connector, then remove two bolts, CCRM and bracket.

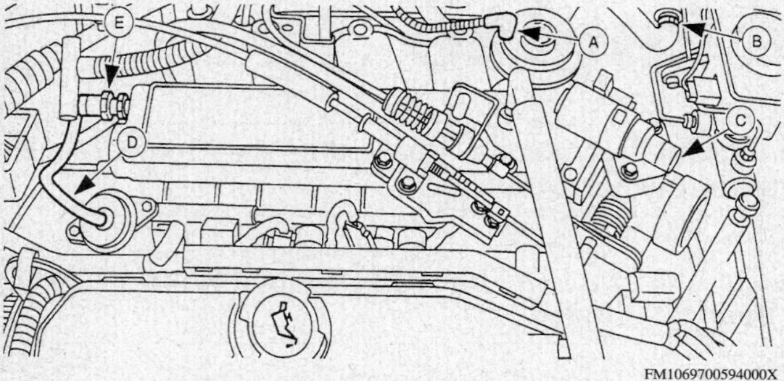

Fig. 2 Vacuum hose locations

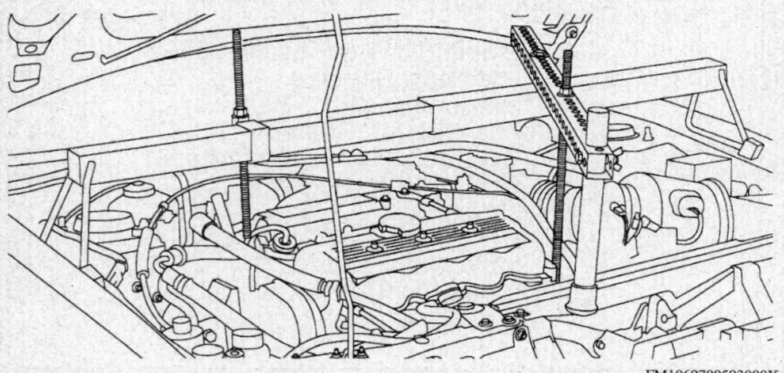

Fig. 4 Engine support tool installation

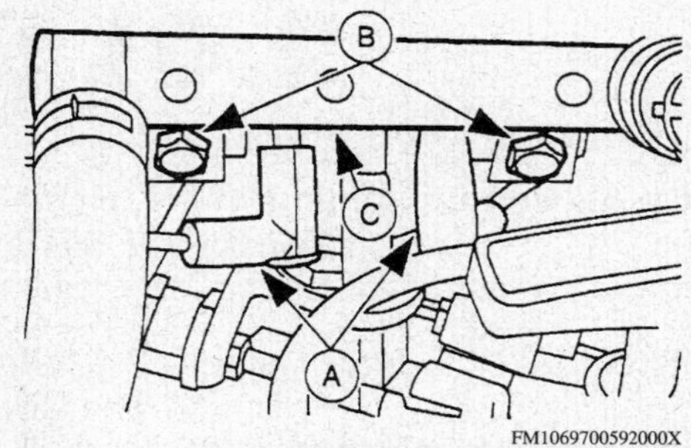

Fig. 3 Vacuum tree

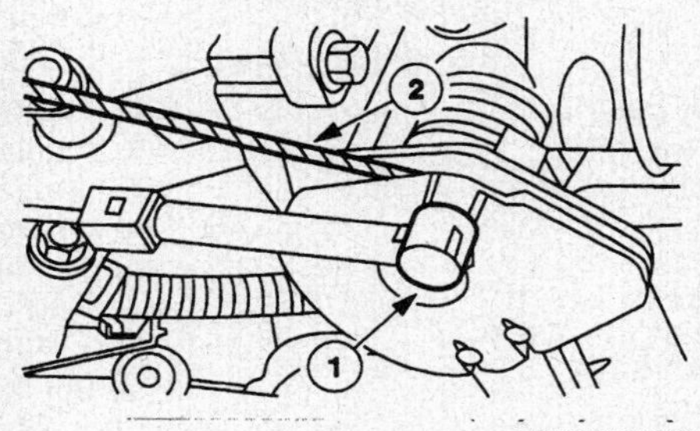

Fig. 5 Accelerator cable & throttle control cable removal

13. Disconnect transmission range sensor electrical connector, transaxle solenoid electrical connector and turbine speed connector.
14. Disconnect vehicle speed sensor electrical connector.
15. Disconnect upstream Heated Oxygen Sensor (HO2S) electrical connector mounted on cooling fan shroud.
16. Disconnect downstream HO2S electrical connector.
17. Remove screw and position ground strap aside.
18. Disconnect engine cooling fan electrical connector.
19. Remove three bolts and position power steering pressure hose aside.
20. Use disconnect tool No. D87L-9280-B (½ inch), or equivalent, to disconnect fuel return line from fuel injection supply manifold.
21. Remove exhaust manifold heat shield.
22. Remove four exhaust manifold to catalytic converter nuts.
23. Remove upper starter bolt and position bracket aside.
24. Disconnect transaxle fluid cooler lines from transaxle.
25. Remove A/C line bracket bolt.
26. Disconnect A/C manifold and tube spring lock coupling at accumulator/drier.
27. Disconnect A/C manifold and tube spring lock coupling at condenser.
28. Remove accessory drive belt, automatic tensioner and accessory drive belt tensioner (models equipped with A/C).
29. Drain fluid from power steering reservoir.
30. Position drain pan under power steering reservoir and disconnect power steering lines.
31. Raise and support vehicle.
32. Remove lug nuts and front wheel and tire assemblies.
33. Remove lefthand splash shield.
34. Remove righthand splash shield.
35. Drain coolant and engine oil.
36. Remove four bolts and crossmember.
37. Remove catalytic converter bolts and the catalytic converter.
38. Remove front wheel driveshafts and joints.
39. Disconnect S-terminal wire and the B-terminal nut and cable from starter solenoid.
40. Disconnect oil pressure switch electrical connector.
41. Disconnect A/C compressor electrical connector.
42. Remove four bolts and the A/C compressor and manifold lines.
43. Remove hose clamp and disconnect lower radiator hose from radiator.
44. Remove camshaft pulley bolt and the pulley.
45. Lower vehicle.
46. Loosen heater hose clamp at water outlet connection and disconnect heater hose.
47. Loosen heater hose clamp at bulkhead and remove heater hose.
48. Disconnect upper radiator hose and remove radiator.
49. Disconnect alternator electrical connectors.
50. Disconnect battery positive cable from alternator.
51. Attach engine lifting bracket tool No. T70P-6000, or equivalent, on left rear side of cylinder head.
52. Install three-bar engine support tool No. D88L-6000-A, or equivalent, **Fig. 4.**
53. Raise and support vehicle.
54. Remove transaxle support crossmember.
55. Lower vehicle.
56. Remove four nuts and transaxle mount.
57. Remove righthand engine support insulator through bolt.
58. Attach suitable lifting eye on transaxle and use for balance, if required.
59. Attach suitable lifting device and remove engine and transaxle assembly.
60. Separate transaxle from engine.
61. Mount engine on stand and remove lifting device.
62. Reverse procedure to install, tighten to specifications.

INTAKE MANIFOLD

REPLACE

1. Drain coolant system into suitable container.
2. Remove air cleaner outlet tube.
3. Disconnect vacuum hoses, **Fig. 2.**
4. Disconnect speed control cable, if required, then the accelerator cable and throttle control lever, **Fig. 5.**
5. Remove speed control cable bracket bolt, **Fig. 6.**
6. Disconnect idle air control valve (A) and throttle position sensor (B) connectors, **Fig. 7.**
7. Remove oil dipstick tube bracket bolt from manifold.
8. Disconnect EGR manifold tube, **Fig. 8.**
9. Raise and support vehicle.
10. Remove oil dipstick tube.
11. Remove four manifold nuts, **Fig. 9.**
12. Lower vehicle.
13. Remove nuts, then the intake manifold, discarding used gasket, **Fig. 10.**
14. Reverse procedure to install, tighten to specifications.

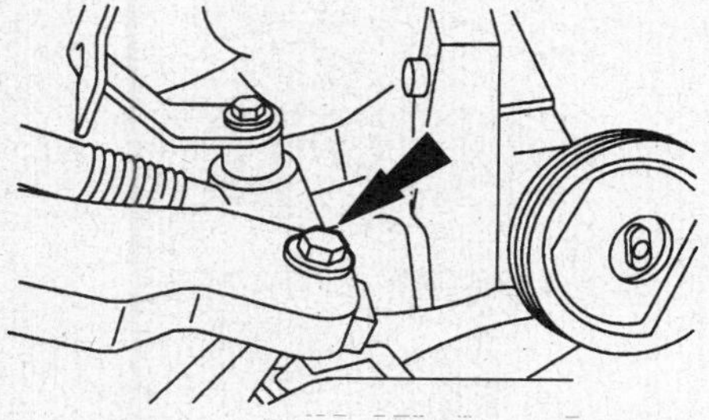

Fig. 6 Speed control bracket bolt removal

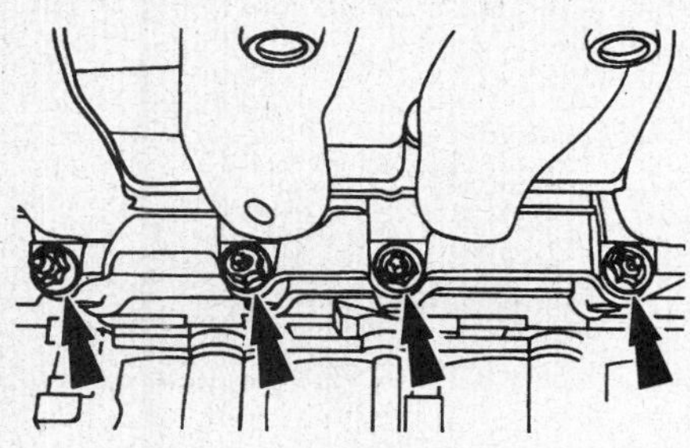

Fig. 9 Intake manifold nut removal

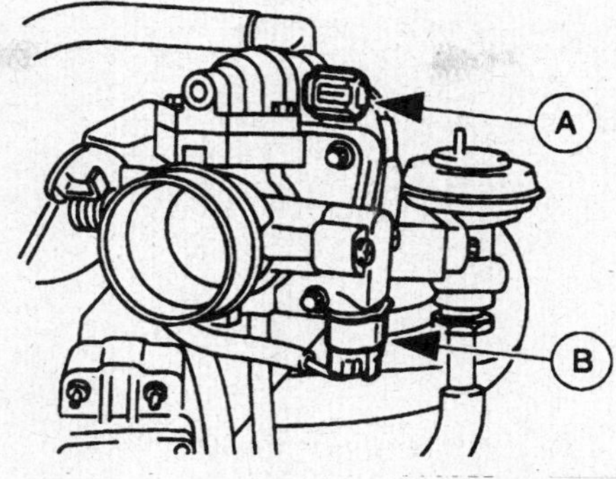

Fig. 7 Idle air control valve & throttle position sensor connectors removal

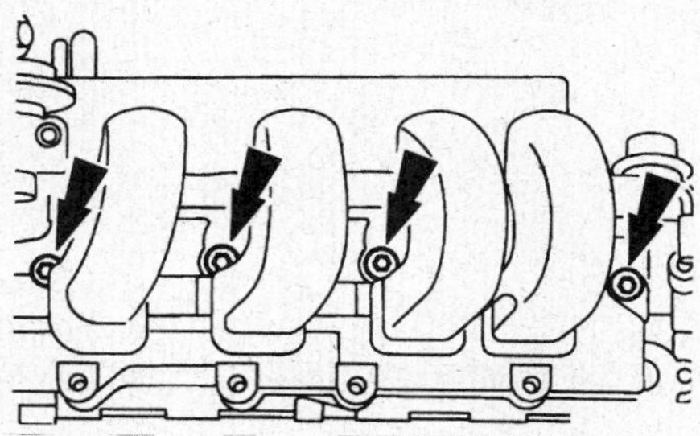

Fig. 10 Intake manifold & nut removal

Fig. 8 EGR manifold bolt removal

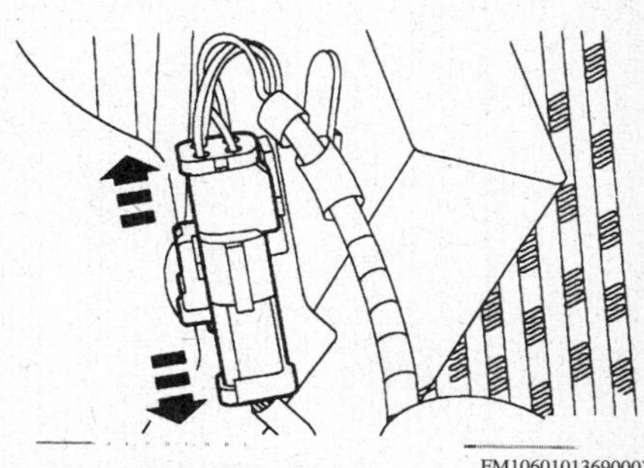

Fig. 11 HO2S connector removal

EXHAUST MANIFOLD

REPLACE

1. Remove engine drive belt as outlined under "Serpentine Drive Belt."
2. Disconnect forward HO2S electrical connector mounted to cooling fan shroud, **Fig. 11.**
3. Remove five exhaust shield nuts, then the shield.
4. Remove two EGR tubes to exhaust manifold nuts and studs, **Fig. 12.**
5. Remove bolts (A) an position power steering hose (B) aside, **Fig. 13.**
6. Loosen lower alternator bolt, remove upper bolt then pivot alternator forward, **Fig. 14.**
7. Remove exhaust manifold to TWC nuts, **Fig. 15.**
8. Remove exhaust nuts, then the exhaust manifold and gasket, **Fig. 16.**
9. Reverse procedure to install, tighten to specifications.

FUEL INJECTION SUPPLY MANIFOLD

REPLACE

1. Disconnect crankshaft position sensor electrical connector, **Fig. 17.**
2. Disconnect two main engine harness electrical connectors above righthand front wheel well, **Fig. 18.**
3. Disconnect four fuel injector electrical connectors, **Fig. 19.**
4. Disconnect fuel pressure sensor electrical connector, **Fig. 20.**
5. Disconnect camshaft position sensor electrical connector, **Fig. 21.**
6. Remove wiring harness routing rail pulling upward from fuel injection supply manifold.
7. Disconnect fuel inlet line from fuel injection supply manifold using suitable disconnect tool.
8. Disconnect fuel supply line from fuel injection supply manifold using suitable disconnect tool.
9. Remove two fuel injection supply manifold bolts, **Fig. 22.**
10. Disengage fuel injection supply manifold from fuel injectors, then remove manifold.
11. Reverse procedure to install, tighten to specifications.

CYLINDER HEAD

REPLACE

1. Remove timing belt as outlined under "Timing Belt, Replace."
2. Remove air cleaner intake tube and outlet half of engine air cleaner.
3. Disconnect vacuum hoses from Exhaust Gas Recirculation (EGR) valve (A), brake booster (B), throttle body (C), fuel pressure regulator (D) and intake manifold (E), **Fig. 2.**
4. Disconnect speed control cable, accelerator cable and throttle valve control actuating cable from throttle control lever.
5. Remove two speed control cable bracket bolts and position bracket and cables aside.
6. Disconnect two fuel charging wiring electrical connectors.
7. Disconnect crankshaft position sensor electrical connector.
8. Disconnect upstream heated oxygen sensor electrical connector mounted on cooling fan shroud.
9. Disconnect fuel supply line and fuel return line from fuel injection supply manifold using tool No. D87L-9280-A, or equivalent.
10. Remove power steering pressure hose bracket and position hose aside.
11. Loosen alternator lower bolt, remove alternator upper bolt and tilt alternator forward.
12. Remove oil dipstick tube bracket bolt from intake manifold.
13. Disconnect EGR tube from EGR valve.
14. Disconnect EGR tube from exhaust manifold.
15. Remove exhaust manifold shield.
16. Remove exhaust manifold to catalytic converter nuts.
17. Raise and support vehicle.
18. Drain coolant into a suitable container.
19. Remove righthand splash shield.
20. Remove oil dipstick tube from cylinder block.
21. Disconnect A/C compressor electrical connector.
22. Remove A/C compressor mounting bolts and suspend compressor with wire.
23. Loosen lower four bolts and one nut securing front engine accessory drive bracket about 4 turns. Do not remove.
24. Lower vehicle.
25. Remove uppermost front engine accessory drive bracket to cylinder head bolt.
26. Remove A/C line bracket to front engine accessory drive bracket bolt.

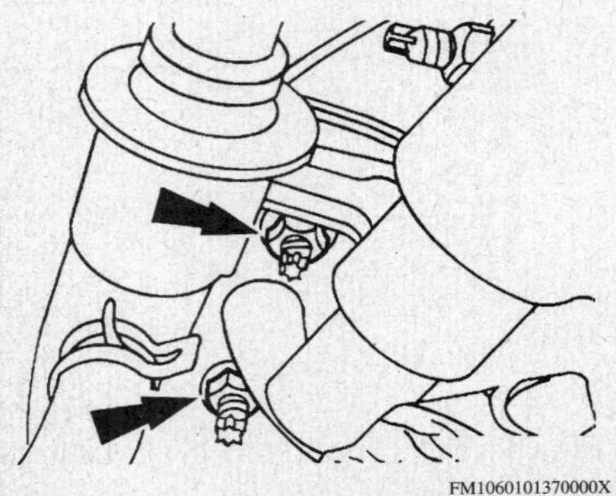

Fig. 12 EGR nut & stud removal

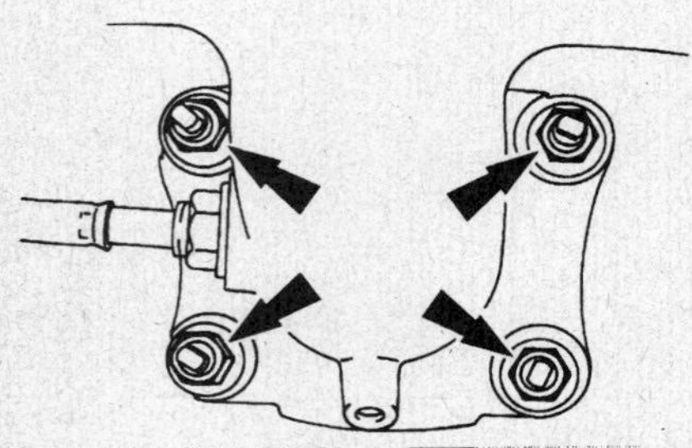

Fig. 15 Exhaust manifold to TWC nut removal

27. Remove valve cover.
28. Disconnect upper radiator hose from thermostat housing water hose connection.
29. Disconnect heater hose from thermostat housing.
30. Remove cylinder head bolts, cylinder head and gasket.
31. Reverse procedure to install, noting the following:
    a. **Torque** bolts to 30–44 ft. lbs., in sequence, **Fig. 23.**
    b. Back off bolts ½ turn.
    c. **Torque** bolts in same sequence to 30–44 ft. lbs.
    d. Turn bolts, in same tightening sequence, an additional 180° in two steps of 90° each.

VALVE ADJUSTMENT

This engine uses hydraulic valve lash adjusters. Valve clearance is adjusted automatically.

TIMING BELT

REPLACE

REMOVAL

1. Remove drive belt and drive belt tensioner as outlined under "Serpentine Drive Belt."
2. Remove front cover, **Fig. 24.**
3. Raise and support vehicle, then remove righthand wheel and tire assembly.
4. Remove righthand splash shield.
5. Remove crankshaft pulley attaching bolt, then the pulley.

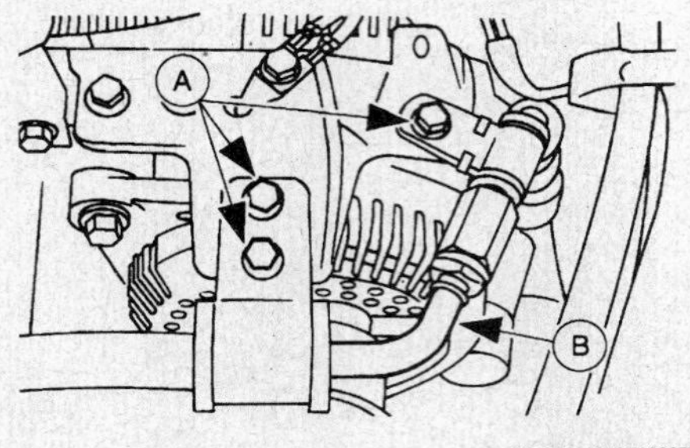

Fig. 13 Power steering hose removal

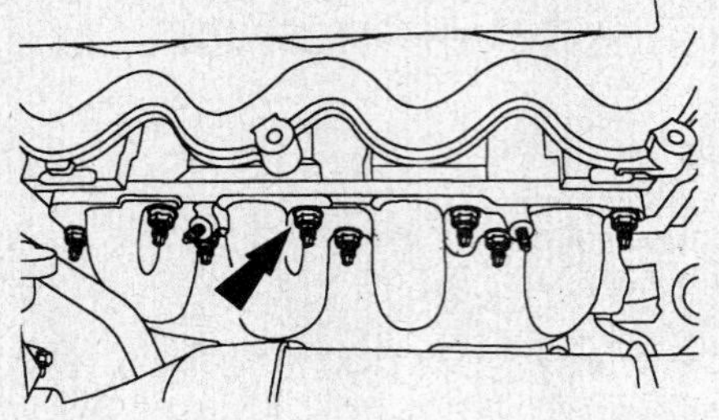

Fig. 16 Exhaust manifold removal

6. Align timing marks, **Fig. 25.**
7. Loosen timing belt tensioner bolt.
8. Using an 8 mm Allen wrench, turn timing belt counterclockwise ¼ turn.
9. Insert ⅛ inch drill bit to lock timing belt tensioner in place.
10. Remove timing belt.

INSTALLATION

1. Install timing belt in a counterclockwise direction, over the crankshaft pulley, over the camshaft pulley, under the timing belt tensioner, then over the water pump sprocket. **During installation, maintain the belt span between the crankshaft and camshaft sprockets.**
2. Remove ⅛ inch drill bit holding timing belt tensioner in position.
3. Allow tensioner to tension timing belt, then tighten tensioner bolt to specification.
4. Rotate crankshaft two turns in normal direction of rotation.
5. Ensure crankshaft and camshaft timing marks are aligned, **Fig. 25.** If timing mark are not aligned, timing belt must be removed and reinstalled.
6. Install engine front cover, then the crankshaft pulley.
7. Install splash shield, then the wheel and tire assembly.
8. Lower vehicle, then install accessory drive belt tensioner and drive belt.

CAMSHAFT

REPLACE

1. Remove engine air cleaner.
2. Remove three bolts, valve cover and gasket.

Fig. 14 Alternator forward pivot

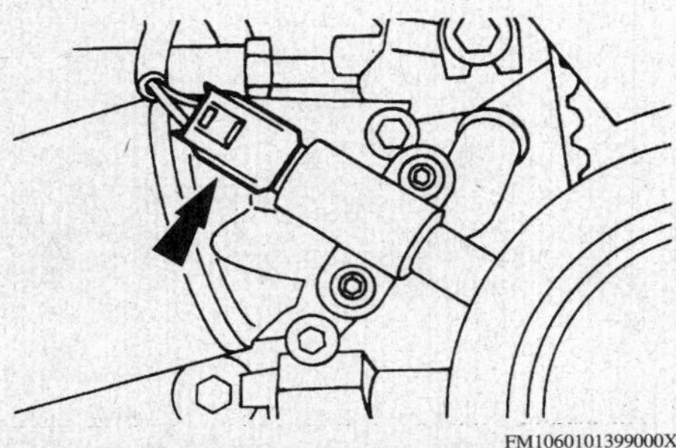

Fig. 17 Crankshaft sensor electrical connector removal

3. Remove camshaft front seal.
4. Remove ignition coil as outlined under "Ignition Coil, Replace" in "Electrical" section.
5. Remove ignition coil bracket, **Fig. 26.**
6. Remove valve tappet guide plate retainer, plate then the eight valve tappets.
7. Remove two bolts and camshaft thrust plate, **Fig. 27.**
8. Remove and discard cup plug from rear of cylinder head.
9. Remove camshaft from rear of cylinder head, **Fig. 28.**
10. Reverse procedure to install, tighten to specifications.

OIL PAN

REPLACE

1. Remove TWC converter assembly.
2. Drain engine oil into suitable container.
3. Remove bolts (A) and TWC to oil pan bracket (B), **Fig. 29.**
4. Remove oil pan bolts in numbered sequence, **Fig. 30.**
5. Reverse procedure to install, tighten to specifications.

OIL PUMP

REPLACE

1. Remove timing belt as outlined under "Timing Belt, Replace."
2. Raise and support vehicle.
3. Remove oil pan as outlined under "Oil Pan, Replace."

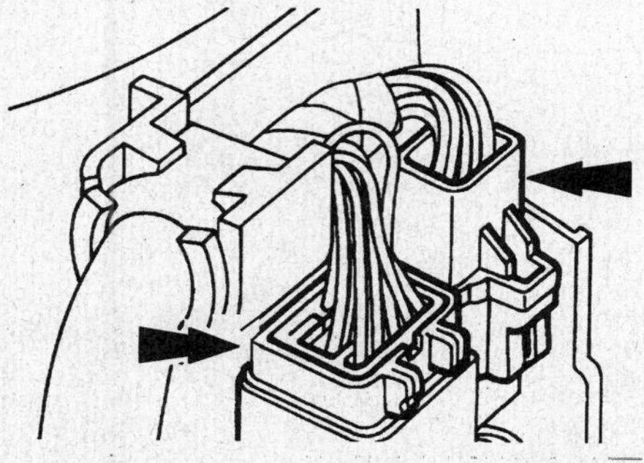

Fig. 18 Main engine harness removal

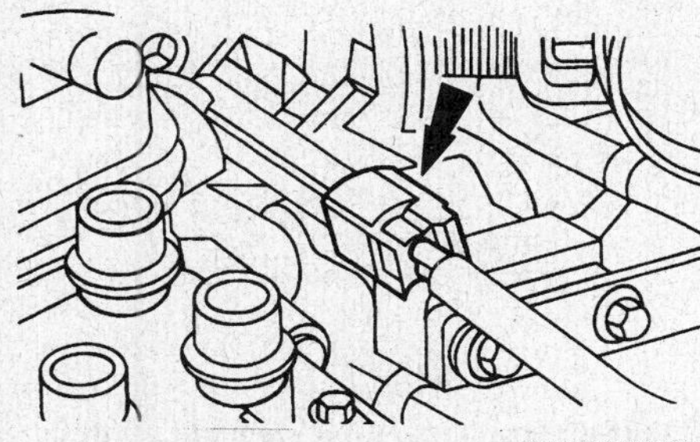

Fig. 21 Camshaft sensor connector removal

4. Disconnect crankshaft position sensor electrical connector.
5. Remove two bolts and the oil pump screen cover and tube, **Fig. 31.**
6. Remove oil pump and gasket, **Fig. 32.**
7. Reverse procedure to install. Tighten to specifications.

BELT TENSION DATA

No manual drive belt tension adjustments are required. The drive belt tensioner automatically adjusts belt tension.

SERPENTINE DRIVE BELT

Refer to **Figs. 33 and 34,** for serpentine drive belt routing.

COOLING SYSTEM BLEED

After filling cooling system, run engine for approximately 12 minutes with radiator pressure cap off, then top off radiator. Secure cap, then and with engine running, fill coolant reservoir to FULL HOT mark with coolant.

THERMOSTAT

REPLACE

1. Remove air cleaner outlet tube.
2. Drain coolant into suitable container.
3. Disconnect water temperature indicator sender unit and engine coolant temperature sensor electrical connectors, **Fig. 35.**

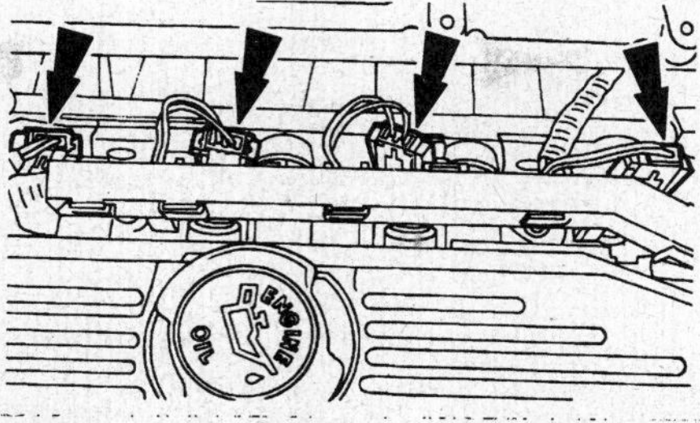

Fig. 19 Fuel injector connector removal

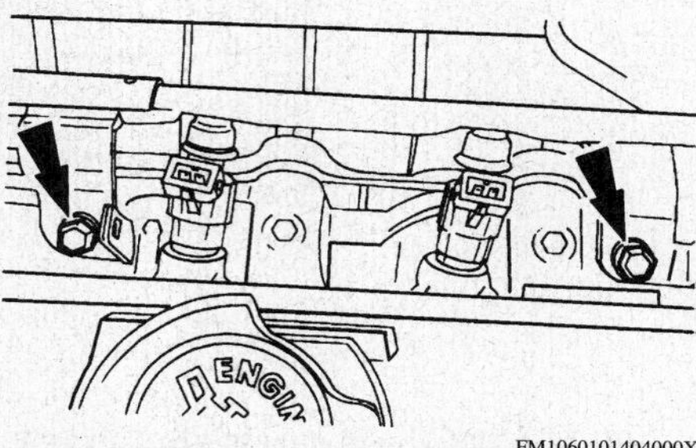

Fig. 22 Fuel injection supply manifold bolt removal

4. Disconnect upper radiator hose, then the heater coolant hose at thermostat housing, **Fig. 36.**
5. Remove thermostat housing bolts, thermostat housing then the thermostat, **Fig. 37.**
6. Reverse procedure to install, noting the following:
   a. Fill coolant system as outlined under "Specifications."
   b. Tighten to specifications.
   c. Inspect cooling system for leaks.

RADIATOR

REPLACE

1. Raise and support vehicle.
2. Drain coolant from radiator into suitable container.
3. Remove righthand splash shield bolts, then the splash shield, **Fig. 38.**
4. Disconnect lower radiator hose and lower oil cooler outlet tube, **Fig. 39.**
5. Remove two oil cooler tube bracket bolts.
6. Lower vehicle.
7. Disconnect connector at fan motor, **Fig. 40.**
8. Remove radiator cap and disconnect overflow hose.
9. Remove four radiator support bracket bolts and the radiator, **Fig. 41.**
10. Remove radiator and shroud assembly.
11. Remove fan motor, blade and shroud assembly, **Fig. 42.**
12. Reverse procedure to install, tighten to specifications. Fill cooling system and bleed as outlined under "Cooling System, Bleed."

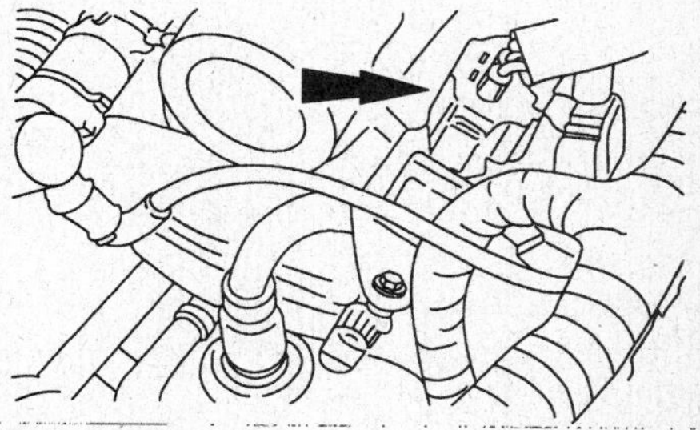

Fig. 20 Fuel pressure connector removal

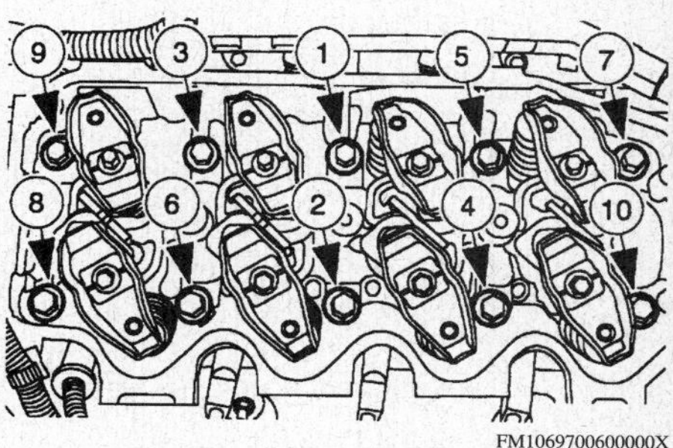

Fig. 23 Cylinder head bolt tightening sequence

WATER PUMP

REPLACE

1. Drain coolant into a suitable container.
2. Remove timing belt as outlined under "Timing Belt, Replace."
3. Remove timing belt tensioner bolt and timing belt tensioner.
4. Remove lower radiator hose from water pump.
5. Lower vehicle.
6. Disconnect heater hose from water pump.
7. Remove three bolts (A), one stud (B) and the water pump (C), **Fig. 43.**
8. Reverse procedure to install. Tighten to specifications.

FUEL PUMP

REPLACE

1. Remove rear seat cushion, then locate fuel pump access cover and disconnect fuel pump electrical connector.
2. Remove four fuel pump access cover screws then the access cover plate.
3. Remove fuel line clips and disconnect fuel lines from top of fuel pump.
4. Remove fuel pump locking retainer ring then the fuel pump.
5. Reverse procedure to install.

FUEL FILTER

REPLACE

1. Place suitable container under fuel filter.
2. Loosen fuel filter bracket clamp.
3. Remove fuel line clips.
4. Disconnect fuel tubes, then remove fuel filter, **Fig. 44.**
5. Reverse procedure to install.

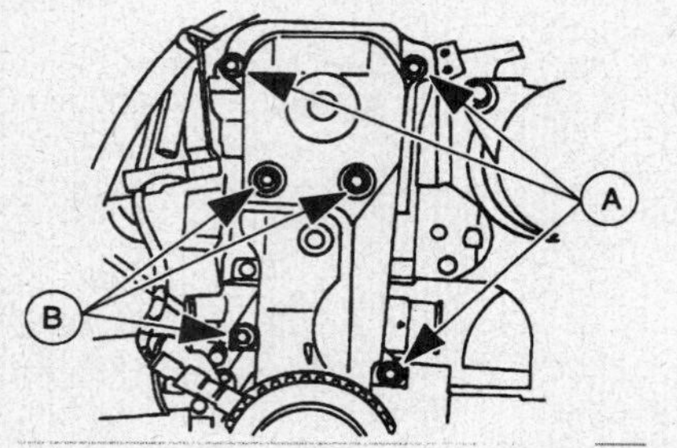

Fig. 24 Engine front cover removal

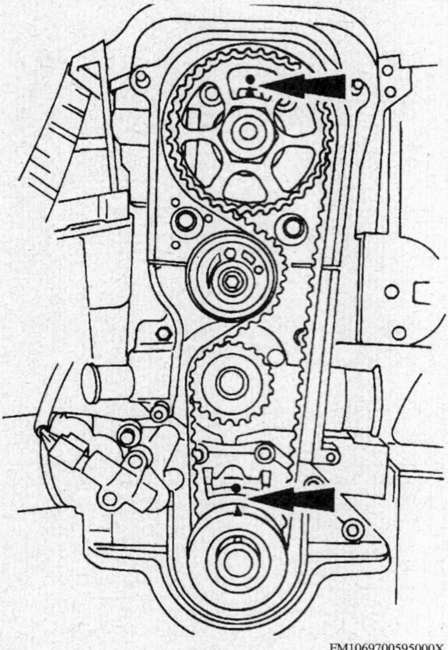

Fig. 25 Timing mark alignment

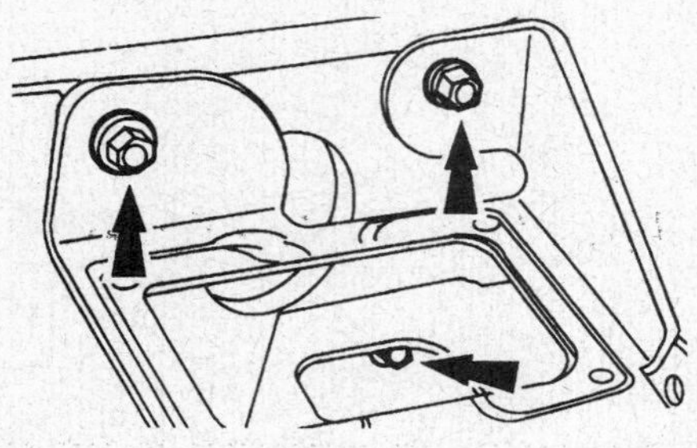

Fig. 26 Ignition coil bracket removal

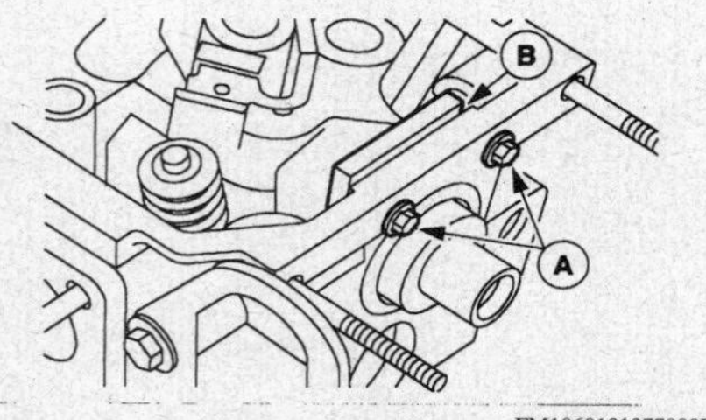

Fig. 27 Camshaft thrust plate removal

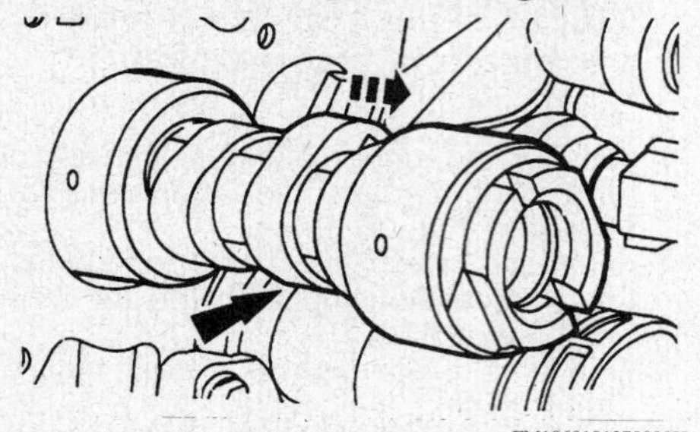

Fig. 28 Camshaft removal

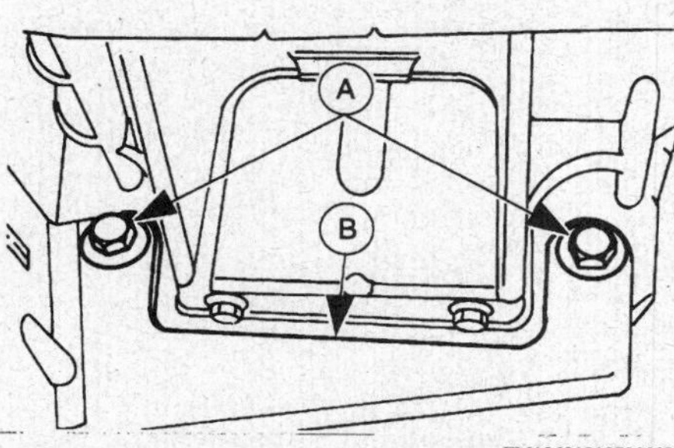

Fig. 29 Oil pan bracket bolt removal

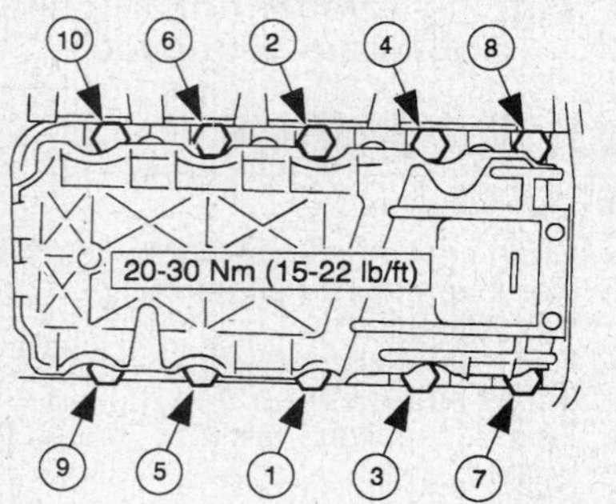

Fig. 30 Oil pan bolt removal

Fig. 31 Oil pump screen cover removal

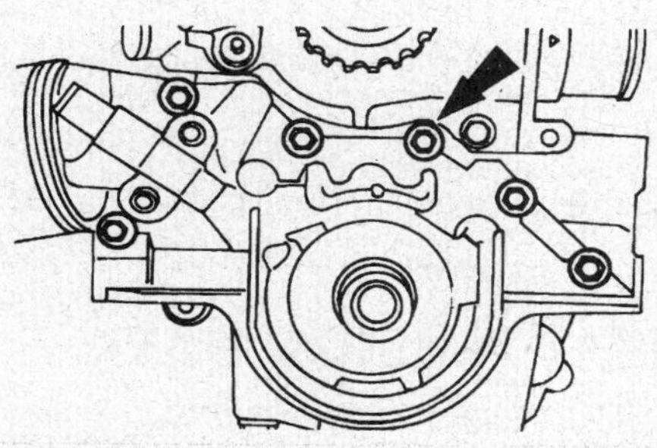

Fig. 32 Oil pump removal

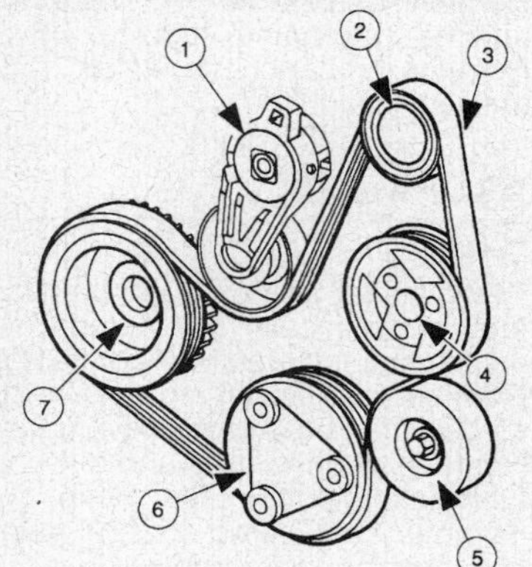

Item	Part Number	Description
1	6B209	Drive Belt Tensioner
2	10346	Generator
3	8620	Drive Belt
4	3A733	Power Steering Pump Pulley
5	6C348	Accessory Drive Belt Routing Pulley
6	19703	A/C Compressor
7	6A312	Crankshaft Pulley

FM1069700596000X

Fig. 33 Drive belt routing. Models with A/C

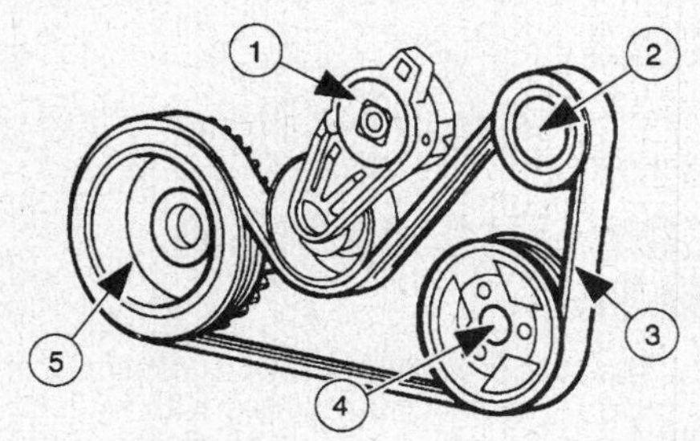

Item	Part Number	Description
1	6B209	Drive Belt Tensioner
2	10346	Generator
3	8620	Drive Belt
4	3A733	Power Steering Pump Pulley
5	6A312	Crankshaft Pulley

FM1069700597000X

Fig. 34 Drive belt routing. Models less A/C

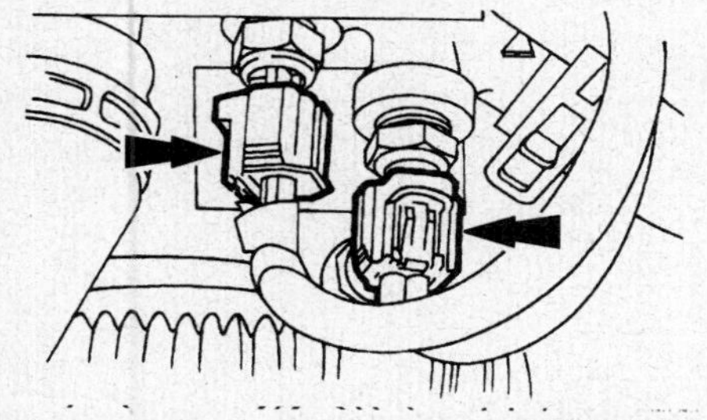

Fig. 35 Sender unit & sensor removal

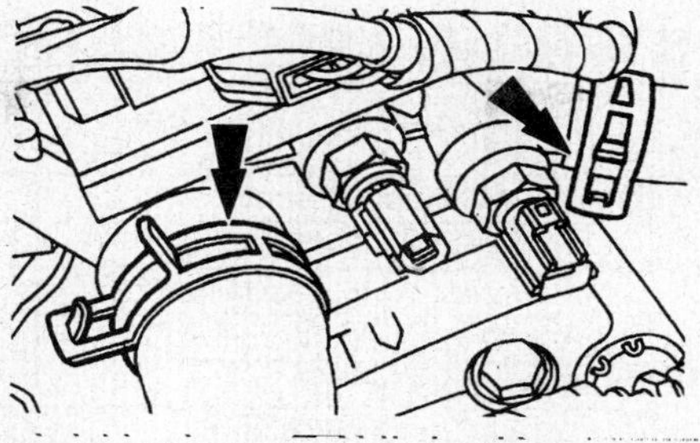

Fig. 36 Upper radiator hose & heater coolant hose removal

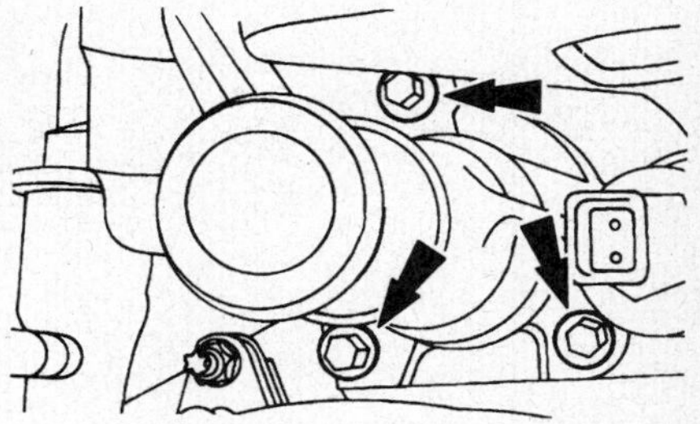

Fig. 37 Thermostat bolts & thermostat removal

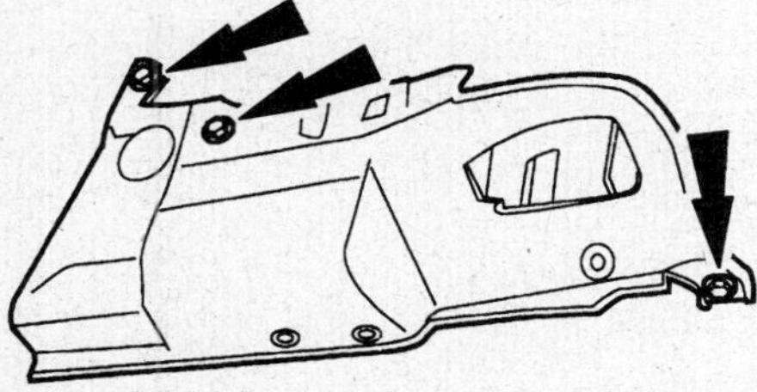

Fig. 38 Splash shield removal

Fig. 39 Lower radiator hose removal

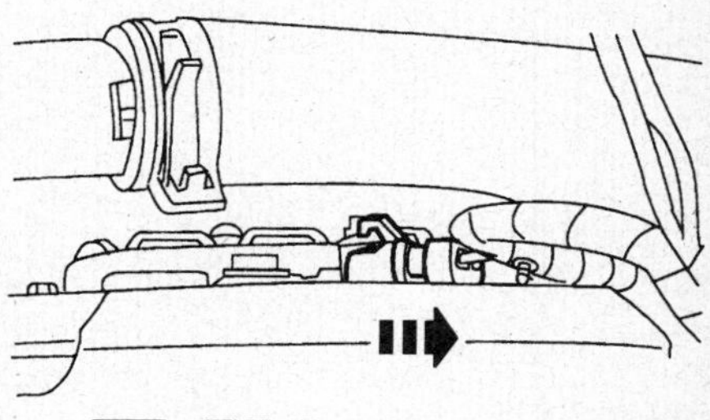

Fig. 40 Fan motor connector removal

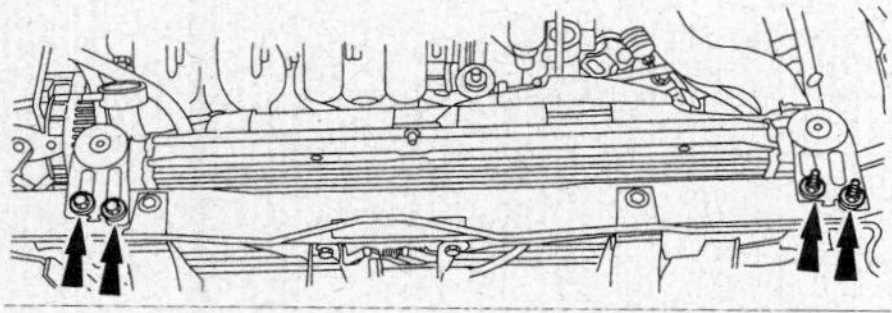

Fig. 41 Radiator support bracket bolt removal

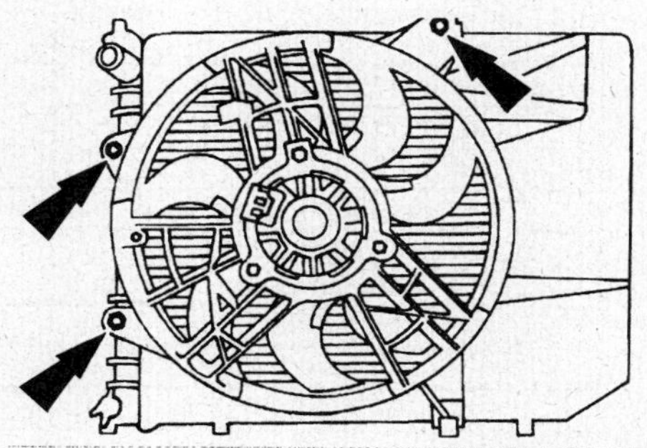

Fig. 42 Fan motor, blade & shroud assembly removal

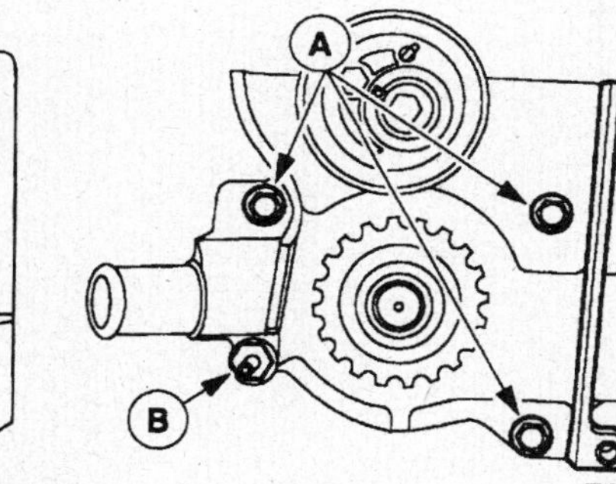

Fig. 43 Water pump replacement

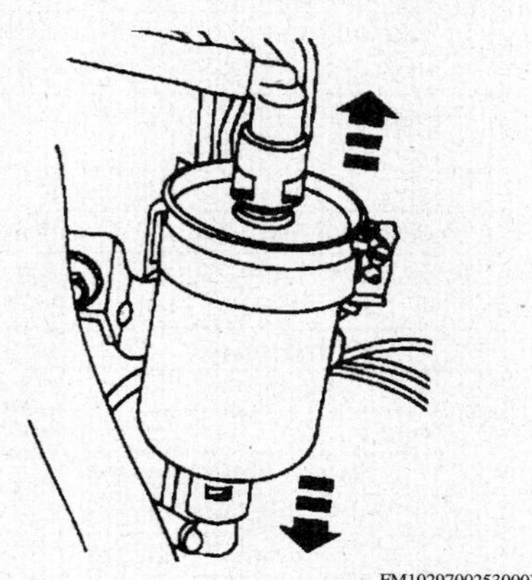

Fig. 44 Fuel filter replacement

TIGHTENING SPECIFICATIONS

Year	Component	Torque/Ft. Lbs.
1998–2002	A/C Compressor Bolts	15–22
	A/C Line Bracket Bolt	15–18
	Alternator Lower Mounting Bolt	15–22
	Alternator Upper Mounting Bolt	30–40
	Camshaft Position Sensor Bolt	15–22
	Camshaft Sprocket Bolt	70–85
	Camshaft Thrust Plate Bolts	6–10
	Catalytic Converter Bracket Bolts	15–20
	Catalytic Converter To Exhaust Mounting Nuts	26–34
	Catalytic Converter To Oil Pan Bracket Bolts	30–40
	Connecting Rod Cap Nuts	26–30
	Constant Control Relay Module	72–96①
	Crankshaft Main Bearing Cap Bolts	66–79
	Crankshaft Pulley Bolt	81–96
	Cylinder Head Bolts	②
	EGR Manifold Tube	15–20
	Engine Front Cover Bolts & Nuts	72–96①
	Engine Mounting Bracket Bolts	31–42
	Exhaust Manifold Heat Shield	45–61①
	Exhaust Manifold Nuts	15–18
	Flywheel Bolts	54–67
	Front Engine Accessory Drive Bracket Bolts/Nut	30–40
	Fuel Injection Supply Manifold Bolts	15–22
	Ignition Coil Bracket Bolts	72–96①
	Ignition Coil Mounting Bolts	40–61①
	Intake Manifold Nuts	15–22
	Intake Manifold Runner Control Actuator Bolts	72–96①
	LH Splash Shield Bolts	69–98①
	Engine Mount Nuts	50–69
	Oil Dipstick Tube Bolt	72–96①
	Oil Pan Baffle Bolts	15–22
	Oil Pan Bolts	15–22
	Oil Pan Drain Plug	15–22
	Oil Pump Bolts	8–12
	Oil Pump Screen Cover & Tube Bolts	72–96①
	Oil Pressure Sensor Switch	8–12
	Power Steering Pressure Hose Bracket	64–87①
	Power Steering Pump Bolts	30–41
	Power Steering Pump Pulley Bolts	15–22
	Righthand Engine Support Insulator Through Bolt	50–69
	Righthand Splash Shield	72–96①
	Rocker Arm Bolts	17–22
	Speed Control Cable Bracket Bolts	64–87①
	Starter Mounting Bolt	18–20
	Timing Belt Tensioner Bolt	15–22
	Thermostat Housing	8–12
	Valve Cover Bolts	72–96①
	Water Outlet Connection Bolts	8–11
	Water Pump Bolts	15–22

① — Inch Lbs.
② — Refer to "Cylinder Head, Replace" for tightening sequence.

2.0L DOHC Engine

NOTE: For Procedures Not Outlined In This Section, Refer To "Contour, Cougar & Mystique."

NOTE: On Air Bag Equipped Models, Refer To "Air Bag System Precautions" Located In The Front Of This Manual For System Disarming & Arming Procedures.

NOTE: Refer To "Computer Relearn Procedures" Located In The Front Of This Manual When Battery Power To The Computer Has Been Interrupted.

INDEX

PRECAUTIONS

AIR BAG SYSTEMS

Refer to "Air Bag System Precautions" in the front of this manual for system disarming and arming procedures.

BATTERY GROUND CABLE

Prior to service, disconnect battery ground cable and isolate as required.

FUEL SYSTEM PRESSURE RELIEF

1998–2001

Remove the schrader valve cap from the end of the fuel injection supply manifold, **Fig. 1.** Attach fuel pressure gauge No. T80L-9974-B, or equivalent, to the schrader valve cap opening. Open the pressure gauge manual valve to relieve fuel system pressure.

2002

1. Remove fuel pump fuse.
2. Start engine and let it run until it stalls.
3. Crank engine over two more times to remove all fuel pressure.
4. Turn ignition Off, then install fuel pump fuse.

COMPRESSION PRESSURE

1998–99

Compression pressure should be inspected at normal operating temperature with spark plugs removed and throttle plate wide open. Cylinder compression pressure is considered within specification if lowest reading cylinder is within 75 percent of highest reading.

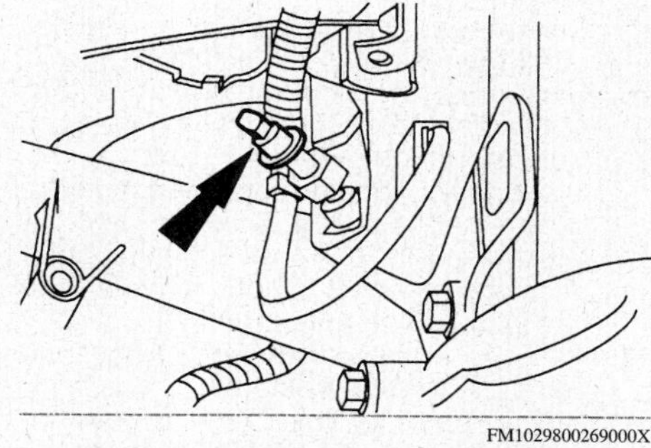

Fig. 1 Schrader valve cap location. 1998–2001

2000–02

1. Perform "Fuel System Pressure Relief" as outlined under "Precautions."
2. Remove spark plugs.
3. Install compression tester.
4. Install an auxiliary starter switch in the starting circuit.
5. With ignition switch Off, crank engine using auxiliary starter at least five times and record highest reading.
6. Repeat test on each cylinder, cranking engine same number of strokes per cylinder.
7. Install components as required, installing spark plugs into indicated cylinder.
8. Reset PCM fault memory as outlined under "Computer Relearn Procedures."

ENGINE

REPLACE

1. Remove hood.
2. Remove battery and battery tray.
3. Remove air cleaner assembly.
4. Remove throttle return spring and constant control relay module bracket as an assembly.
5. Disconnect heated oxygen sensor.
6. Drain coolant into suitable container.
7. Recover refrigerant as outlined under "Air Conditioning."
8. Remove catalytic converter, then the splash shield.
9. Disconnect starter motor wiring, then remove accessory drive belt.
10. Remove A/C compressor, then disconnect lower radiator hose and heater hose.
11. Disconnect power steering pressure line.
12. **On models equipped with automatic transaxle,** remove torque converter inspection cover and converter nuts.
13. **On all models,** remove front roll restrictor nuts and restrictor.
14. Remove axle shafts as outlined under "Front Wheel Drive Axles," then disconnect transaxle cooler lines.
15. **On models equipped with automatic transaxle,** remove transaxle cooler line bolts and transaxle cooler lines, then disconnect transaxle shift cable.
16. **On models equipped with manual transaxle,** disconnect transaxle control rod and support.

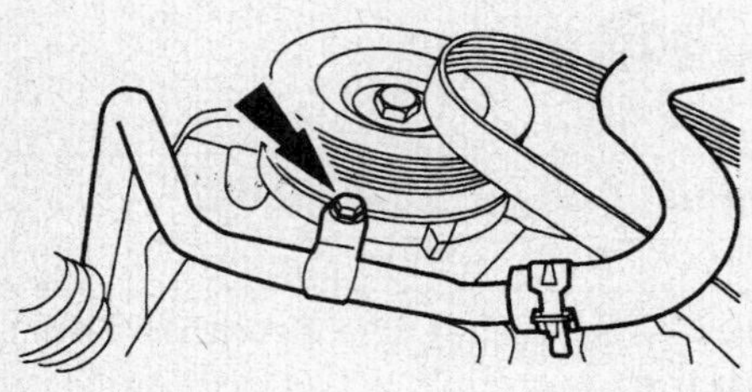

Fig. 2 Heater line bolt removal

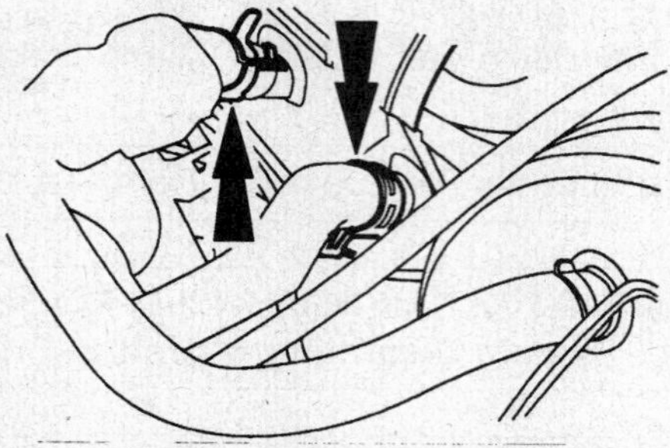

Fig. 3 Heater hose removal

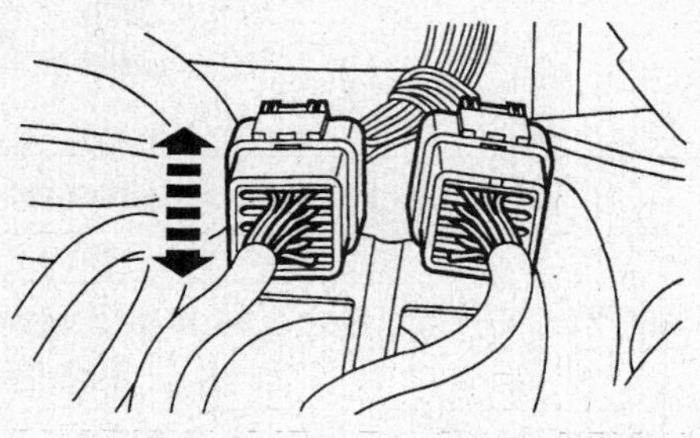

Fig. 4 Main engine control connector removal

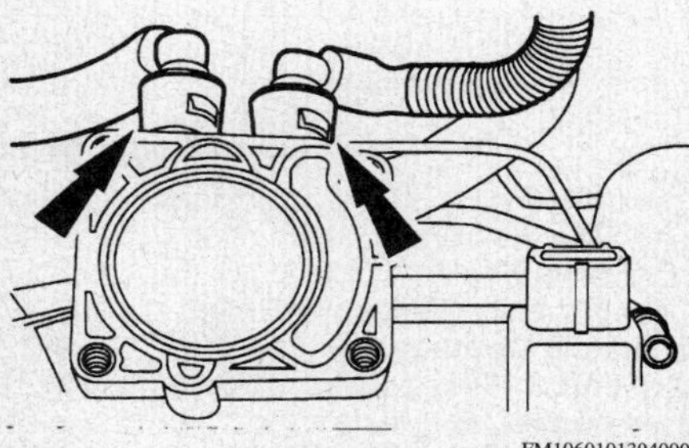

Fig. 5 Vacuum hose removal

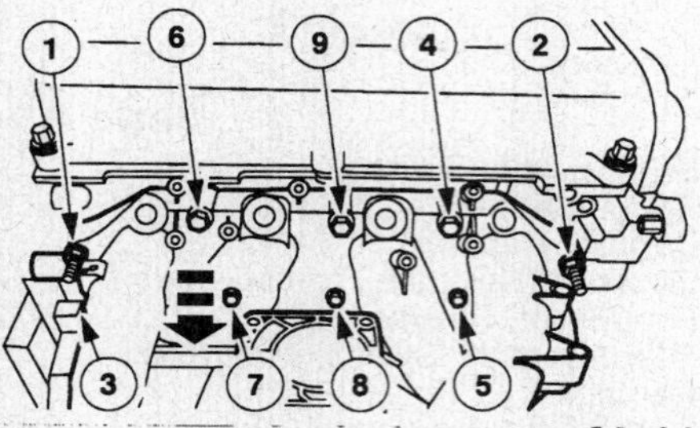

Fig. 6 Intake manifold removal

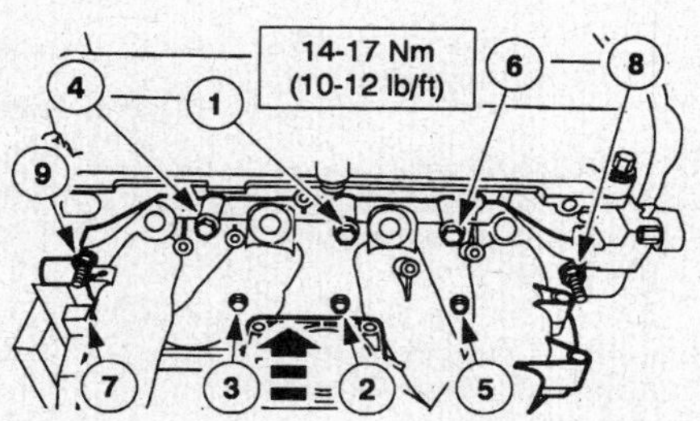

Fig. 7 Intake manifold nut & bolt installation

17. **On all models,** disconnect fuel charging wiring from transaxle internal wiring harness connector, turbine shaft speed sensor, transaxle range sensor and heated oxygen sensor connectors.
18. Remove radiator, fan shroud and fan motor as an assembly.
19. Disconnect accelerator cable and speed control actuator cable.
20. Disconnect power steering return hose, then remove radiator coolant recovery reservoir.
21. Disconnect alternator wiring and vacuum lines.
22. Disconnect fuel charging wiring harness connectors, then the heater water hoses, vehicle speed sensor and the ground strap.
23. Disconnect fuel line, then support engine with suitable lifting device.
24. Remove remaining engine mount nuts and bolts.
25. Remove engine and transaxle as an assembly with engine lifting brackets T70P-6000 or equivalent, and engine lift.
26. Reverse procedure to install, noting the following:
    a. Install axle shafts as outlined under "Front Wheel Drive Axles."
    b. Fill engine oil to specification and fill and bleed cooling system as outlined under "Cooling System Bleed."
    c. Charge A/C system as outlined under "Air Conditioning."
    d. Tighten to specifications.

INTAKE MANIFOLD

REPLACE

1. Remove air cleaner outlet tube, then disconnect throttle position sensor wiring.
2. Remove throttle body from intake manifold.
3. Raise and support vehicle.
4. Drain coolant into a suitable container.
5. Remove heater line bolt, **Fig. 2.**
6. Lower vehicle.
7. Disconnect heater hoses from heater core, **Fig. 3.**
8. Disconnect main engine control sensor wiring and remove connectors from mounting bracket, **Fig. 4.**
9. Disconnect vacuum supply hoses from intake manifold, **Fig. 5.**
10. Disconnect crankcase ventilation hose from valve cover, then remove fuel charging wiring and drive belt.
11. Remove alternator mounting bolt and position alternator aside.
12. Disconnect fuel line, then remove intake manifold attaching bolts and nuts in numbered sequence, **Fig. 6.**
13. Reverse procedure to install, noting the following:
    a. Tighten intake manifold bolts and nuts in numbered sequence, **Fig. 7.**
    b. Tighten to specifications.

EXHAUST MANIFOLD

REPLACE

1. Disconnect fan motor wiring, then remove fan shroud.
2. Raise and support vehicle.
3. Disconnect HO2S wiring connector.
4. Remove catalytic converter from exhaust manifold, then lower vehicle.
5. Remove oil dipstick tube bracket bolt.
6. Remove exhaust manifold heat shield.
7. Remove exhaust manifold attaching bolts and studs in numbered sequence, **Fig. 8.**
8. Reverse procedure to install, noting the following:
    a. Tighten exhaust manifold in numbered sequence, **Fig. 9.**
    b. Tighten to specifications.

FUEL INJECTION SUPPLY MANIFOLD

REPLACE

1. Disconnect spring lock coupling with tool Nos. D87L-9280-A or D87L-9280-B, or equivalent.
2. Remove air cleaner outlet tube, then the throttle body.
3. Disconnect fuel injector electrical connectors.
4. Disconnect fuel pressure sensor vacuum line and electrical connector.
5. Disconnect fuel temperature sensor wiring connector, then remove fuel charging wiring and position aside, **Fig. 10.**
6. Disconnect vacuum line and wiring from fuel pressure sensor.
7. Disconnect fuel temperature sensor wiring connector.
8. Remove fuel charging wiring, **Fig. 10.**
9. Remove fuel injection supply manifold bolts, then the manifold.
10. Reverse procedure to install.

CYLINDER HEAD

REPLACE

1998–2000

1. Remove air cleaner outlet tube.
2. Remove timing belt as outlined under "Timing Belt, Replace."
3. Disconnect vacuum hoses from PCV valve, throttle body, intake manifold and fuel pressure sensor.

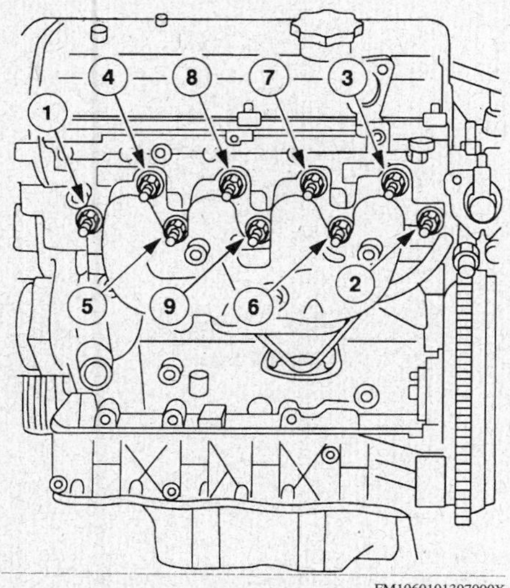

Fig. 8 Exhaust manifold removal

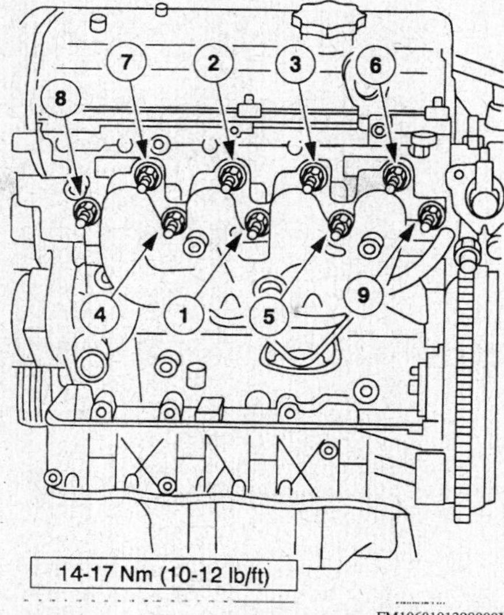

Fig. 9 Exhaust manifold installation

4. Disconnect speed control cable and accelerator cable from control lever.
5. Disconnect fuel charging wiring electrical connectors at main engine connector.
6. Disconnect crankshaft position sensor and heated oxygen sensor connectors.
7. Disconnect fuel line, then remove power steering pump and bracket as an assembly.
8. Remove alternator, then the oil dipstick tube.
9. Raise and support vehicle, then drain coolant into a suitable container.
10. Remove splash shield bolts and shield, then disconnect A/C compressor electrical connector.
11. Remove A/C compressor and position aside.
12. Lower vehicle, then disconnect spark plug wires and remove plugs.
13. Remove valve cover, then disconnect upper radiator hose from thermostat housing.
14. Disconnect heater water hose from thermostat housing, then remove camshafts, ignition coil and bracket.
15. Remove water thermostat housing, then the cylinder head.
16. Remove cylinder head gasket and discard.
17. Reverse procedure to install, noting the following:
    a. Install new head gasket on cylinder block.
    b. **Torque** cylinder head bolts in three steps in sequence, **Fig. 11,** first step to 12–18 ft. lbs.; second step to 26–33 ft. lbs.; third step an additional 90.°

2001-02

1. Remove air cleaner outlet tube.
2. Remove camshafts as outlined under “Camshaft, Replace.”
3. Remove thermostat housing.
4. Remove coolant recovery reservoir.
5. Relieve fuel system pressure as outlined under “Precautions.”
6. Disconnect fuel line.
7. Remove power steering pump and bracket assembly.
8. Remove alternator.
9. Remove oil dipstick and tube.
10. Disconnect speed control cables, accelerator cables, main engine electrical connectors and crankshaft position sensor electrical connector.
11. Raise and support vehicle.
12. Remove splash shield bolts, then the splash shield.
13. Lower vehicle.
14. Remove cylinder head bolts, then the cylinder head and gasket.
15. Reverse procedure to install, noting the following:
    a. Do not use abrasive grinding discs to remove gasket material, use only plastic scrapers. Do not gouge or scratch aluminum sealing surface.
    b. Install new head gasket and new head bolts. Head bolts are torque to yield design and cannot be re-used.
    c. **Torque** cylinder heads bolts in three stages in numbered sequence, **Fig. 11.**
    d. Stage 1: **Torque** bolts to 15 ft. lbs.
    e. Stage 2: **Torque** bolts to 30 ft. lbs.
    f. Stage 3: Tighten bolts an additional 105°.

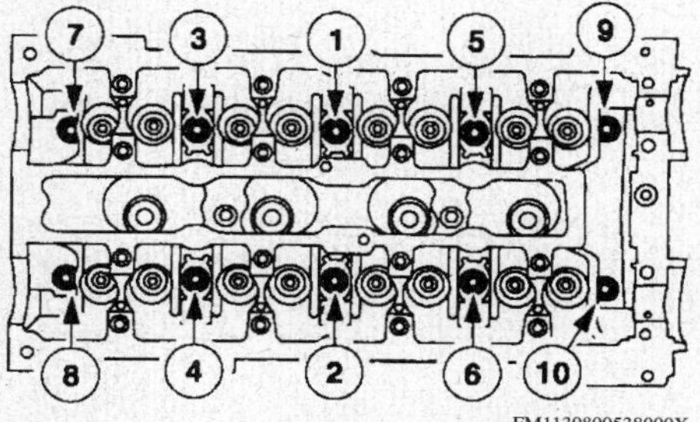

Fig. 11 Cylinder head tightening sequence

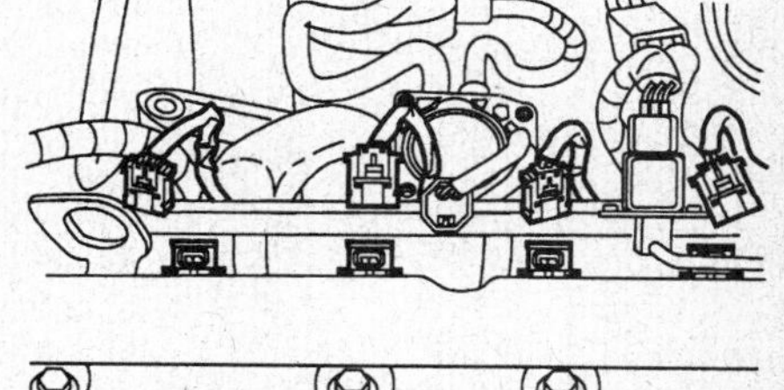

Fig. 10 Fuel charging wiring removal

VALVE COVER

REPLACE

1. Disconnect crankcase ventilation hose from fitting on valve cover.
2. Disconnect oil control solenoid electrical connector, then remove appearance cover.
3. Position accelerator cable and speed control cable aside.
4. Remove spark plug wires, then the upper timing belt cover, **Fig. 12.**
5. Remove valve cover bolts, then the cover, **Fig. 13.**
6. Reverse procedure to install.

TIMING BELT COVER

REPLACE

1. Remove upper timing belt cover bolts, then the cover, **Fig. 12.**
2. Loosen water pump pulley bolts.
3. Remove drive belt as outlined under “Serpentine Drive Belt.”
4. Remove idler pulley.
5. Remove water pump pulley bolts, then the pump, **Fig. 14.**
6. Raise and support vehicle.
7. Remove middle timing belt cover bolts, then the cover, **Fig. 15.**
8. Remove crankshaft pulley assembly.
9. Remove lower timing cover bolts, then the cover, **Fig. 16.**
10. Reverse procedure to install, tighten to specifications.

TIMING BELT

REPLACE

1. Remove the catalytic converter, if required.
2. Remove the spark plugs.
3. Rotate the crankshaft clockwise until the No. 1 cylinder reaches TDC, **Fig. 17.**
4. Remove the bolt, then install the Ford crankshaft TDC timing peg No. T97P-6000-A, or equivalent, **Fig. 18.**
5. Remove the timing belt upper cover attaching bolts, then the cover.
6. Raise and support the front of the vehicle with jack stands.
7. Remove the splash shield.
8. Loosen the water pump pulley bolts.
9. Remove the accessory drive belt.
10. Remove the accessory drive belt idler pulley.

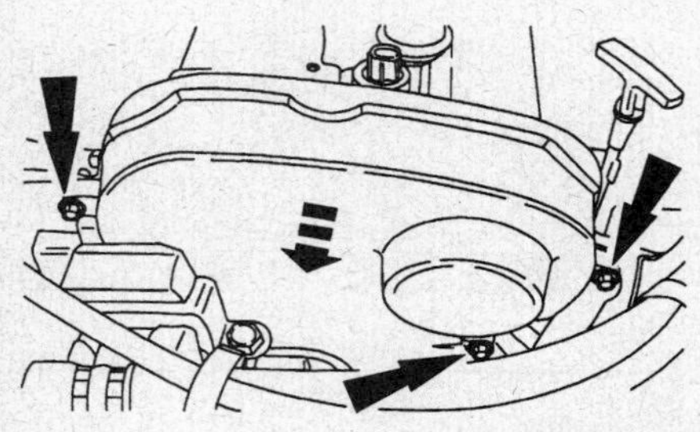

Fig. 12 Upper timing belt cover removal

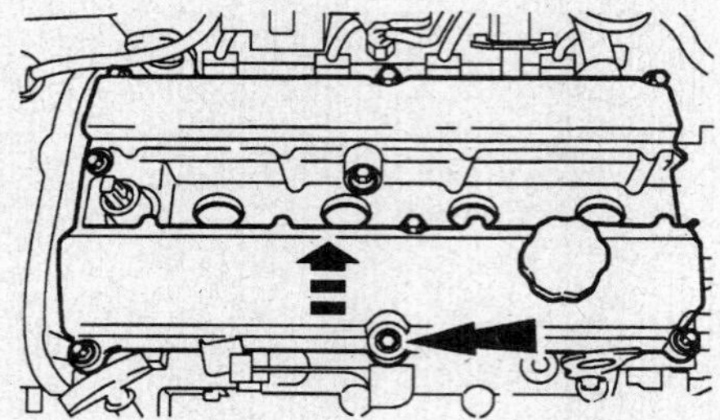

Fig. 13 Valve cover removal

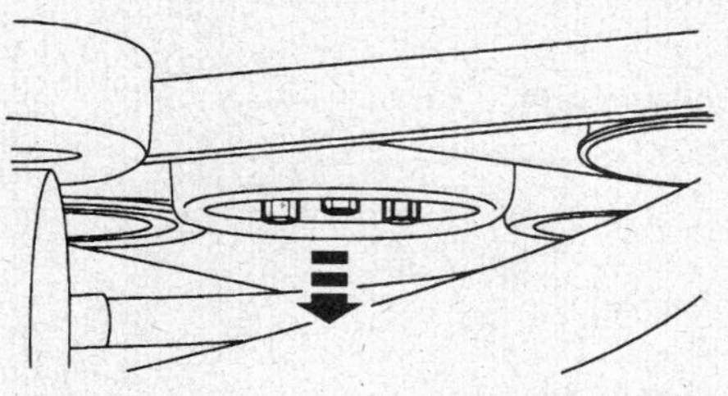

Fig. 14 Water pump pulley bolt removal

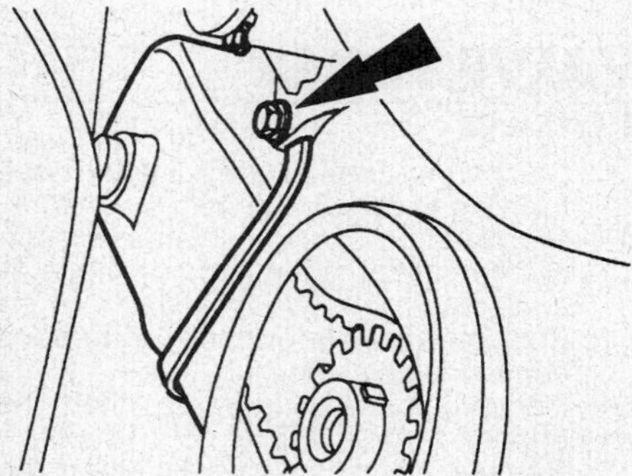

Fig. 15 Middle timing belt cover removal

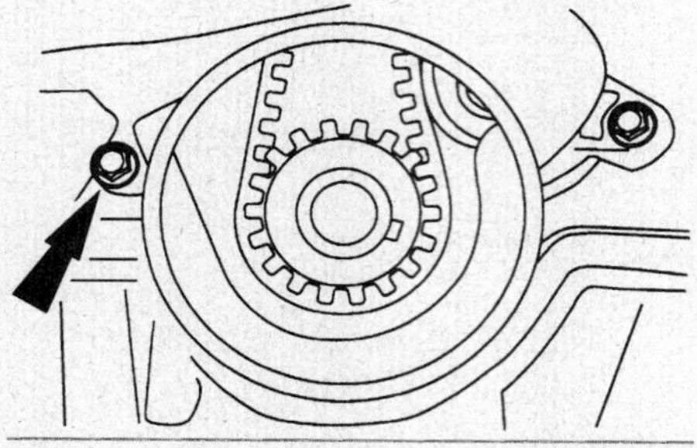

Fig. 16 Lower timing chain cover removal

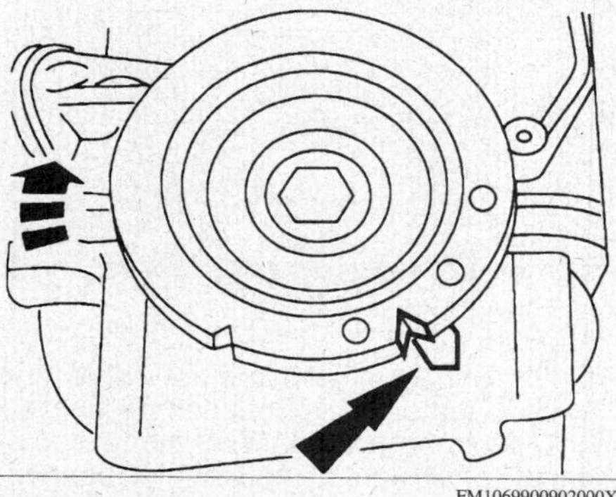

Fig. 17 Crankshaft timing marks

11. Remove the water pump pulley.
12. Remove the center timing belt cover.
13. Remove the crankshaft pulley.
14. Remove the timing belt lower cover.
15. Lower the vehicle.
16. Disconnect the PCV hose from the valve cover fitting.
17. Disconnect the oil control solenoid electrical connector.
18. Remove the appearance cover.
19. Position the accelerator control and speed control cables aside.
20. Remove the ignition wires and brackets.
21. Remove the valve cover, then discard the gasket.
22. Align the camshafts using Ford camshaft alignment tool No. T94P-6256-CH, or equivalent. It may be necessary to rotate the exhaust camshaft clockwise to install the alignment tool, **Fig. 19.**
23. Loosen the timing belt tensioner pulley bolt.
24. Release belt tension by disconnecting the tensioner tab from the timing cover backplate.
25. Carefully slide the timing belt off the camshaft and crankshaft sprockets.
26. Ensure the camshafts are properly aligned using the camshaft alignment tool.
27. Rotate the crankshaft clockwise against the TDC timing peg.
28. Engage the timing belt tensioner tab into the upper timing cover backplate.
29. With timing belt tensioner bolt backed out four full turns, position the tensioner so the location tab is at approximately the four o'clock position, **Fig. 20.** Line up the hex key slot in the tensioner adjusting washer with the pointer which is located behind the pulley.
30. Starting at the crankshaft and working counterclockwise, install the new timing belt.
31. Rotate the timing belt tensioner locating tab counterclockwise and insert the locating tab into the slot in the rear timing cover, **Fig. 21.**
32. Position the hex key slot in the tensioner adjusting washer to the 4 o'clock position, **Fig. 21.**
33. Tighten the tensioner bolt enough to seat the tensioner firmly against the rear timing belt cover, but still loose enough to allow the tensioner adjusting washer to be rotated with a 6 mm hex wrench.
34. Install a 6 mm hex wrench, rotate the adjusting washer counterclockwise until the notch in the pointer is centered over the index line on the locating tab, **Fig. 22.** During the adjustment the pointer will move in a clockwise direction.
35. While holding the adjusting washer in position, **torque** tensioner attaching bolt to 16–20 ft. lbs, **Fig. 23.** After tightening the tensioner bolt, ensure the tensioner pointer is still aligned with the index line. If not, repeat steps 33 through 36.
36. Remove the TDC peg, then install the bolt.
37. Remove the camshaft alignment tool.
38. Reverse steps 1 through 3 and 6 through 22 to complete the timing belt installation, noting the following:
    a. Install accessory drive belts.
    b. Install a new valve cover gasket and apply a 0.1 inch bead of silicone rubber sealer meeting Ford specification WSE-M4G323-A4, or equivalent, in two places where the front camshaft bearing cap meets the cylinder head.
    c. Tighten to specifications.

CAMSHAFT

REPLACE

1. Remove timing belt as outlined under "Timing Belt, Replace," then the valve cover and camshaft sprockets.
2. Remove oil control solenoid flange bolts and flange, **Fig. 24.**
3. Remove camshaft journal caps in sequence, **Fig. 25.**
4. Remove camshafts, then the oil control sensor and bushing.
5. Inspect camshafts for wear.
6. Reverse procedure to install, noting the following:
    a. Verify valve clearance as outlined under "Valve Clearance Specifications."
    b. Install oil control solenoid bushing and flange on exhaust camshaft, **Fig. 26.**
    c. Install camshaft journal caps, **Fig. 27,** tighten cap bolts to specifications.
    d. Tighten to specifications.

CRANKSHAFT SEAL

REPLACE

1. Remove timing belt as outlined under "Timing Belt, Replace."
2. Remove crankshaft sprocket and timing belt guide washer.

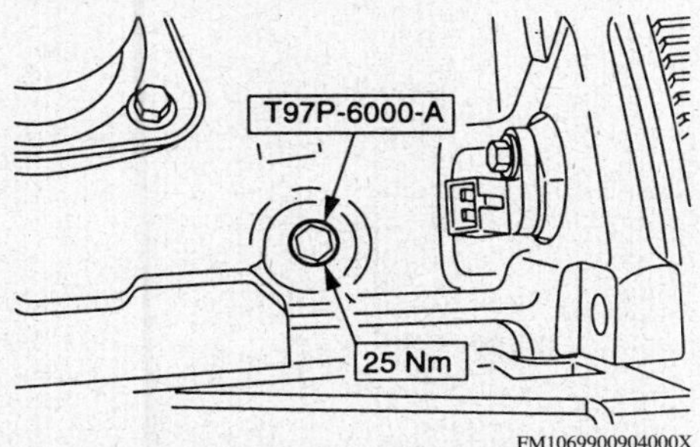

Fig. 18 Timing peg installation

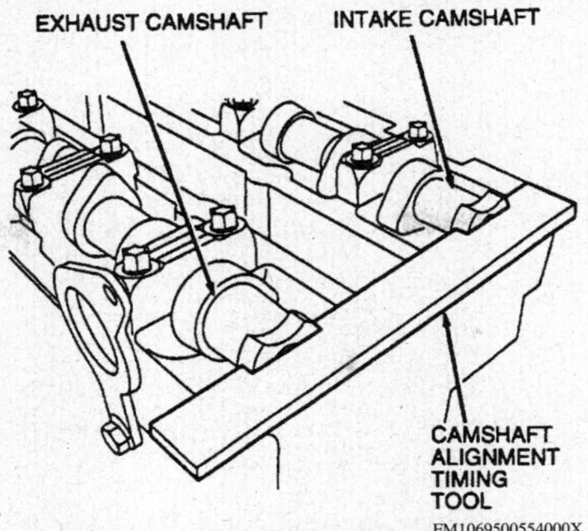

Fig. 19 Camshaft alignment

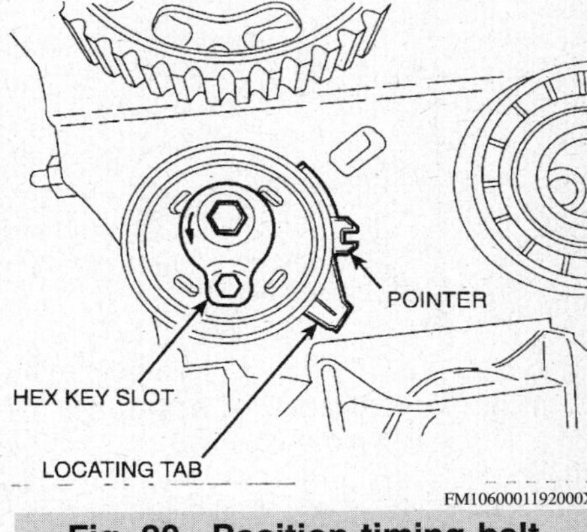

Fig. 20 Position timing belt tensioner

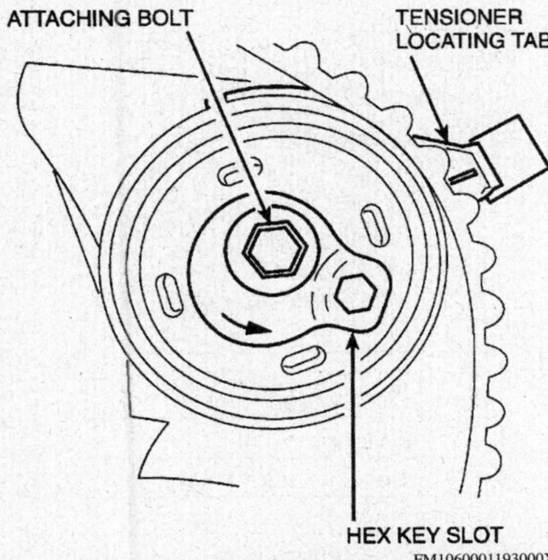

Fig. 21 Position timing belt tensioner adjusting washer

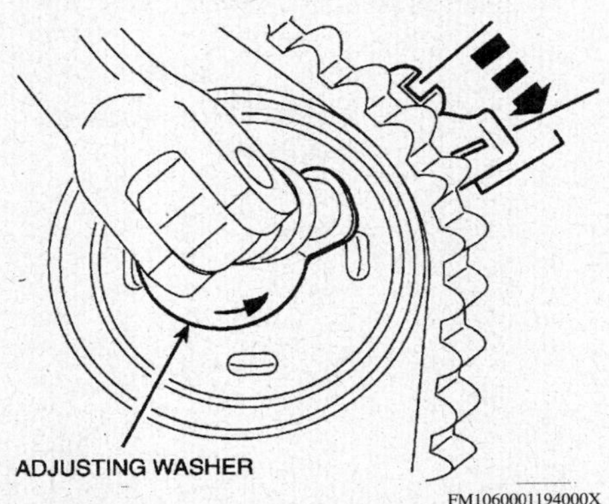

Fig. 22 Aligning timing belt tensioner

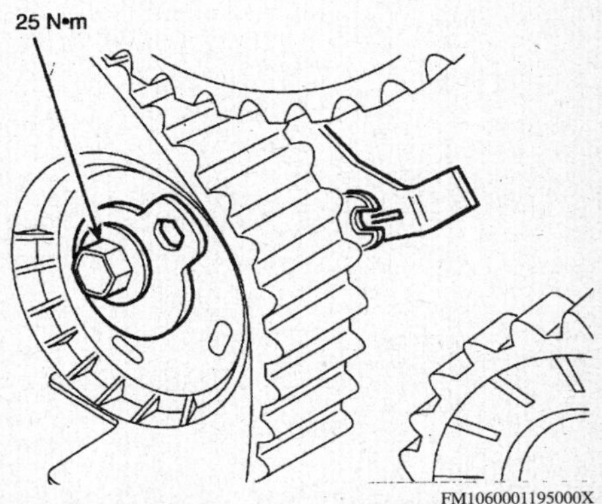

Fig. 23 Tightening timing belt tensioner bolt

3. Use care to avoid damaging crankshaft surface, then using seal remover T92C-6700-CH, or equivalent, remove front seal from oil pump.
4. Reverse procedure to install. Use oil pump replacer T81P-6700-A, or equivalent to install seal.

CRANKSHAFT REAR OIL SEAL

REPLACE

1. **On models equipped with automatic transaxle,** remove transaxle as outlined under "Automatic Transmissions/ Transaxles" section.
2. **On models equipped with manual transaxle,** remove transaxle, then clutch pressure plate and clutch disc as outlined under "Clutch & Manual Transaxle."
3. **On all models,** use care to avoid damaging cranking sealing surface, then using Seal Remover T92C-6700-CH, or equivalent, remove seal.
4. Inspect crankshaft rear oil seal area, then coat seal and seal area with engine oil.
5. Ensure edges of crankshaft rear oil seal are not rolled over, then using crankshaft rear seal pilot tool No. T88P-6701-B2 and crankshaft rear seal replacer tool No. T88P-6701-B1, or equivalents, install rear oil seal.

OIL PAN

REPLACE

1. Raise and support vehicle, then drain engine oil into a suitable container.
2. Remove catalytic convertor.
3. Remove seventeen oil pan bolts evenly, then the oil pan.
4. Reverse procedure to install, noting the following:
   a. Clean and inspect mounting faces of oil pan and cylinder block.
   b. Apply .1 inch continuous bead of silicone gasket and sealant F6AZ-19562-AA, or equivalent, to oil pan. **Install oil pan within four minutes after sealer has been applied.**
   c. **Torque** oil pan bolts in numbered sequence to 15–22 ft. lbs., **Fig. 28.**

OIL PUMP SERVICE

OIL PUMP SCREEN COVER & TUBE

1. Remove oil pan as outlined under "Oil Pan, Replace."
2. Remove oil pump screen bolts and discard oil pump inlet tube.
3. Reverse procedure to install.

BELT TENSION DATA

Automatic drive belt tensioners are spring loaded devices which set and maintain drive belt tension. The drive belt should not require tension adjustment for the life to the belt. Automatic drive belt tensioners have drive belt wear indicator marks. If the indicator mark is not approximately in the middle between MIN and MAX tabs on the engine front cover, the drive belt is worn or an incorrect drive belt is installed.

SERPENTINE DRIVE BELT

Refer to **Fig. 29,** for serpentine drive belt routing.

COOLING SYSTEM BLEED

1. Select maximum heater temperature and blower motor speed settings. Position control to discharge air through the vents.
2. Start engine and allow to idle. While engine is idling, feel for hot air at the vents.
3. If air discharge remains cool and engine coolant temperature gauge does not move, coolant level is low and must be filled. Stop engine, allow to cool and fill coolant.
4. Start engine and allow to idle until normal operating temperature is reached.

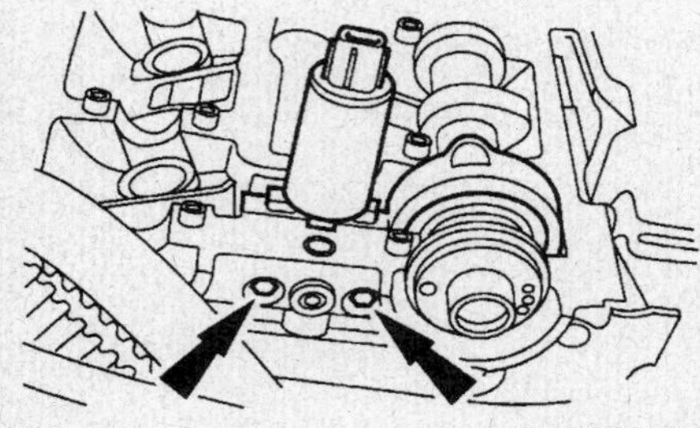

Fig. 24 Oil control solenoid flange removal

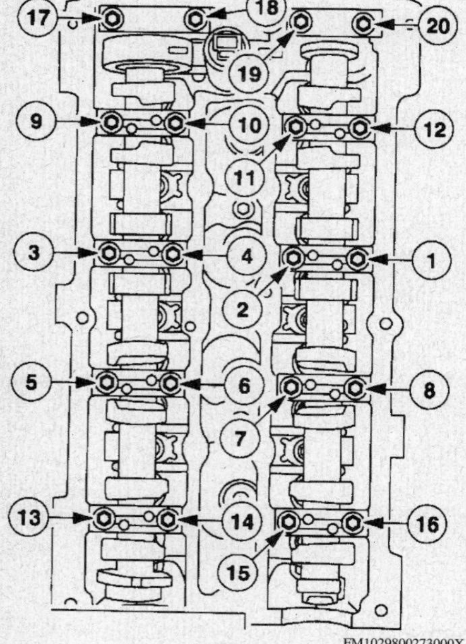

Fig. 27 Camshaft tightening sequence

Hot air should blow from vents and the engine temperature gauge should maintain a stabilized reading in the NORMAL range and the upper radiator hose should feel hot to the touch.

THERMOSTAT

REPLACE

1. Drain coolant into suitable container.
2. Disconnect camshaft position sensor electrical connector, **Fig. 30.**
3. Remove water hose connection bolts, then the connection to one side, **Fig. 31.**
4. Remove water thermostat and seal from housing, **Fig. 32.**
5. Reverse procedure to install, tighten to specifications.

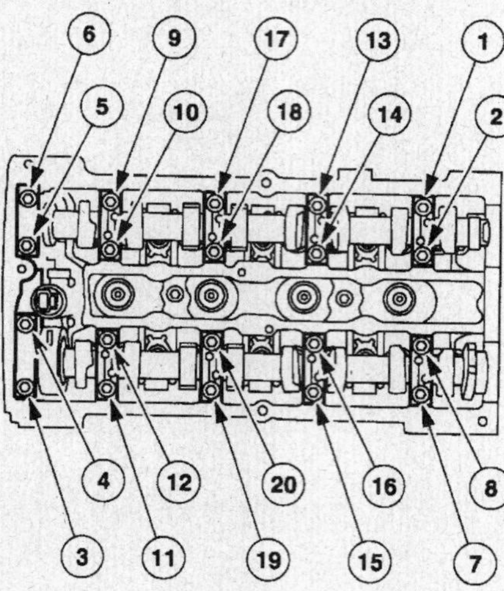

Fig. 25 Camshaft loosening sequence

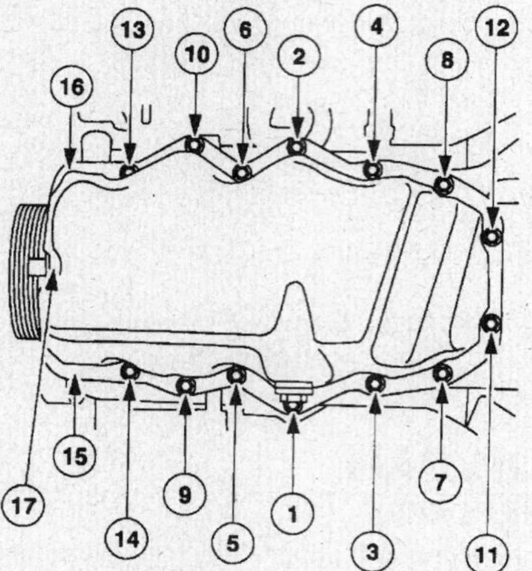

Fig. 28 Oil pan tightening sequence

RADIATOR

REPLACE

Refer to "2.0L SOHC Engine" for "Radiator, Replace" procedure.

WATER PUMP

REPLACE

1. Raise and support vehicle.
2. Drain radiator into a suitable container.
3. Remove splash shield bolts, then the splash shield.
4. Loosen water pump pulley attaching

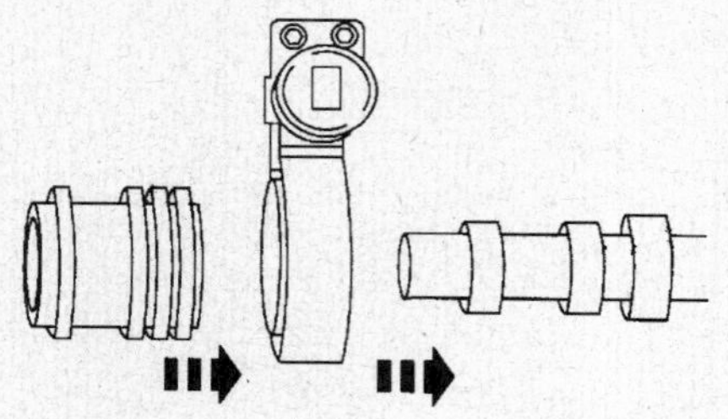

Fig. 26 Oil control solenoid bushing & flange installation

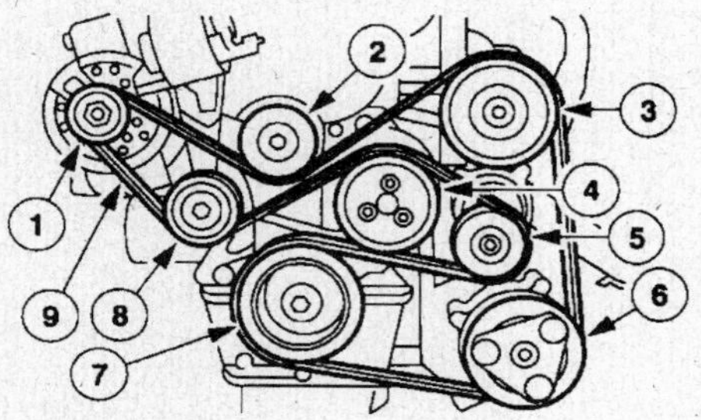

Item	Description
1	Generator
2	Drive Belt Idler Pulley
3	Power Steering Pump Pulley
4	Water Pump Pulley
5	Drive Belt Tensioner
6	A/C Compressor
7	Crankshaft
8	Drive Belt Idler Pulley
9	Accessory Drive Belt

Fig. 29 Serpentine drive belt routing

bolts, then remove drive belt.

5. Remove A/C compressor bolts and position compressor aside, **Fig. 33.**
6. Remove water pump from middle timing belt cover, **Fig. 34.**
7. Reverse procedure to install, tighten to specifications.

FUEL PUMP

REPLACE

Refer to "2.0L SOHC Engine" for "Fuel Pump, Replace" procedure.

FUEL FILTER

REPLACE

Refer to "2.0L SOHC Engine" for "Fuel Filter, Replace" procedure.

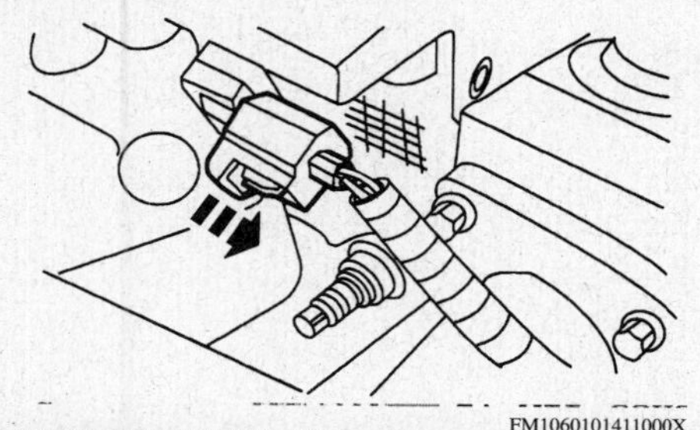

Fig. 30 Camshaft position sensor connector removal

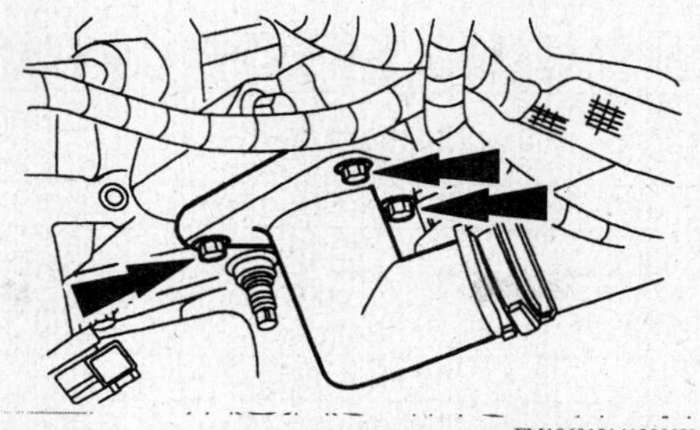

Fig. 31 Water hose removal

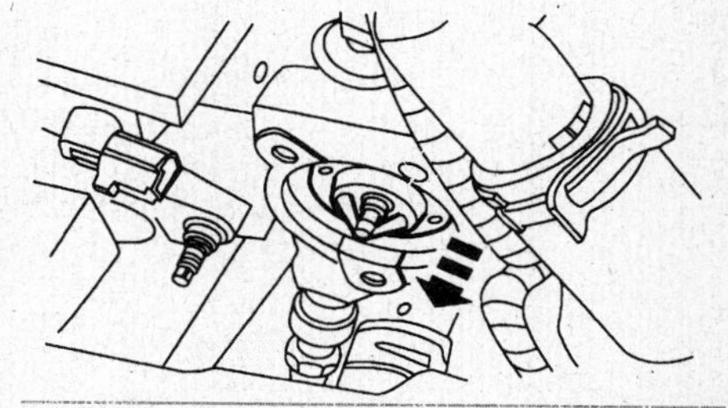

Fig. 32 Water thermostat removal

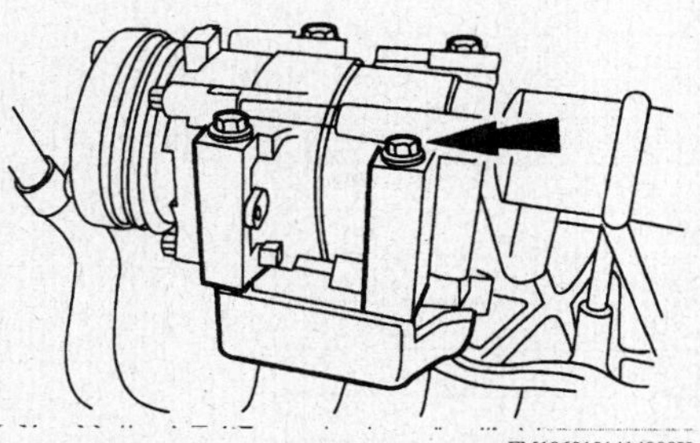

Fig. 33 A/C compressor removal

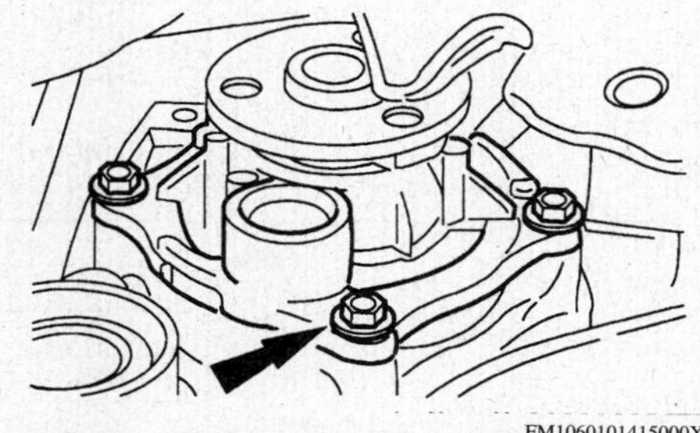

Fig. 34 Water pump removal

TIGHTENING SPECIFICATIONS

Year	Component	Torque/Ft. Lbs.
1998– 2002	A/C Compressor Bolts	15–22
	A/C Line Bracket Bolt	15–18
	Accelerator & Speed Control Bracket Bolts	72–84①
	Alternator Bolt	34
	Appearance Cover	48–84①
	Camshaft Position Sensor Bolt	48–84①
	Catalytic Converter Bracket Bolts	15–20
	Catalytic Converter To Exhaust Mounting Nuts	30–40
	Catalytic Converter To Oil Pan Bracket Bolts	30–40
	Constant Control Relay Module	72–96①
	Crankshaft Pulley Bolt	81–89
	Cylinder Head Bolts	②
	Exhaust Camshaft Sprocket Bolt	88
	Exhaust Camshaft Sprocket Plug	26–30
	Exhaust Manifold Heat Shield	72–96①
	Exhaust Manifold Nuts	11–12
	Flywheel Bolts	54–67
	Front Roll Restrictor Nuts	48–65
	Front Roll Restrictor Bolts	50–69
	Front Engine Support Isolator Bolt	50–69
	Ignition Coil Bracket Bolts	14–16
	Ignition Coil Mounting Bolts	40–61①
	Intake Camshaft Sprocket Bolt	48–53
	Intake Manifold Nuts	12–15
	Engine Mount Nuts	50–69
	Oil Control Solenoid Flange Bolt	72–96①
	Oil Dipstick Tube Bolt	72–96①
	Oil Pan Bolts	③
	Oil Pan Drain Plug	29–41
	Oil Pump Bolts	84–108①
	Oil Pump Screen Cover & Tube Bolts	72–96①
	Oil Pressure Sensor Switch	19
	Power Steering Pump Bolts	30–41
	Rear Engine Support Isolator Nuts & Bolts	50–69
	Rear Roll Restrictor Nuts	28–38
	Splash Shield Bolts	72–96①
	Timing Belt Tensioner Bolt	18
	Valve Cover Bolts	60–72①
	Water Pump Bolts	16

① — Inch Lbs.

② — Refer to "Cylinder Head, Replace" for tightening procedure.

③ — Refer to "Oil Pan, Replace" for tightening procedure.

Clutch & Manual Transaxle

NOTE: On Air Bag Equipped Models, Refer To "Air Bag System Precautions" Located In The Front Of This Manual For System Disarming & Arming Procedures.

NOTE: Refer To "Computer Relearn Procedures" Located In The Front Of This Manual When Battery Power To The Computer Has Been Interrupted.

INDEX

ADJUSTMENTS

CLUTCH

The Escort and Tracer use a hydraulic clutch control system. This system consists of a fluid reservoir, master cylinder, pressure line and slave cylinder. The clutch master cylinder is mounted on the bulkhead near the brake master cylinder. This hydraulic system utilizes brake fluid from the brake master cylinder reservoir. This system has no provisions for adjustment.

CLUTCH PEDAL

To determine if the pedal height requires adjustment, measure the distance from the bulkhead to the upper center of pedal pad. The distance should be 8.35–8.54 inches. Use the following procedure if adjustment is required.

1. Disconnect clutch switch electrical connector.
2. Loosen clutch switch locknut.
3. Turn clutch switch until correct height is achieved.
4. **Torque** locknut to 10–13 ft. lbs.
5. Connect electrical connector.

CLUTCH PEDAL FREEPLAY

To determine if the pedal freeplay requires adjustment, depress clutch pedal by hand until clutch resistance is felt. Measure the distance between upper pedal height and where the resistance is felt. Freeplay should be .22–.59. Use the following procedure if adjustment is required.

1. Loosen clutch pedal pushrod locknut.
2. Turn pushrod until pedal freeplay is within specification.
3. Ensure that disengagement height is correct when the pedal is fully depressed. Minimum disengagement height is 1.6 inches.
4. **Torque** pushrod locknut to 108–144 inch lbs.

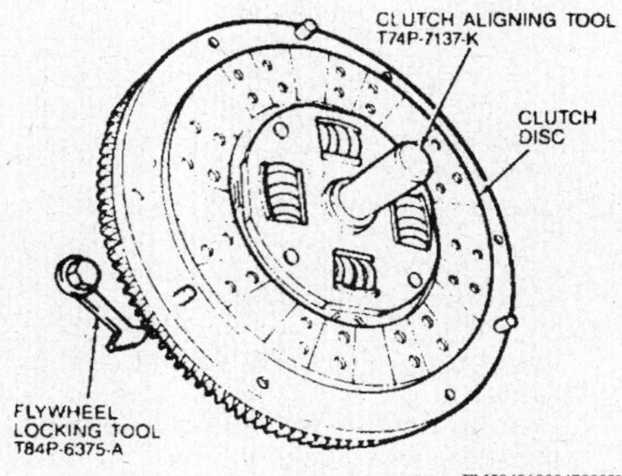

Fig. 1 Clutch disc installation. Escort & Tracer

HYDRAULIC SYSTEM SERVICE

CLUTCH SLAVE CYLINDER, REPLACE

1. Disconnect pressure line from slave cylinder, then plug line to prevent leakage.
2. Remove slave cylinder retaining bolts, then cylinder.
3. Reverse procedure to install, tighten to specifications.

HYDRAULIC CLUTCH BLEED

The clutch hydraulic system must be bled whenever the pressure line is disconnected.

The fluid in the reservoir must be maintained at the ¾ level or higher during air bleeding.

1. Remove bleeder cap from slave cylinder and attach vinyl hose to bleeder screw, place other end of hose in container.
2. Slowly pump clutch pedal several times.
3. With clutch pedal depressed, loosen bleeder screw to release trapped air.
4. Tighten bleeder screw.
5. Repeat steps 2 through 4 until no air bubbles appear in fluid.

CLUTCH MASTER CYLINDER, REPLACE

Escort & Tracer

1. Remove battery and battery tray assembly.
2. Disconnect clutch pressure line from master cylinder.
3. Using needle nose vise grips, or equivalent. clamp off brake fluid feed line to clutch master cylinder.
4. Disengage clamp, then remove brake fluid feed hose from clutch master cylinder.
5. From inside vehicle, remove master cylinder retaining nut.
6. From inside engine compartment, remove master cylinder retaining nut, then master cylinder.
7. Align clutch pedal pushrod, then install master cylinder. **Torque** retaining nuts to 14–19 ft. lbs.
8. Connect master cylinder pressure line, then **torque** pressure line retaining nut to 10–16 ft. lbs.
9. Install hose and clamp assembly, then battery and tray.
10. Bleed air from system.

ZX2

1. Disconnect clutch master cylinder hose from clutch master cylinder and plug it to prevent excess fluid loss.
2. Disconnect lower clutch slave cylinder tube from clutch master cylinder.
3. Remove clutch master cylinder nut from inside passenger compartment.
4. Remove clutch master cylinder nut and clutch master cylinder from engine compartment.
5. Reverse procedure to install.

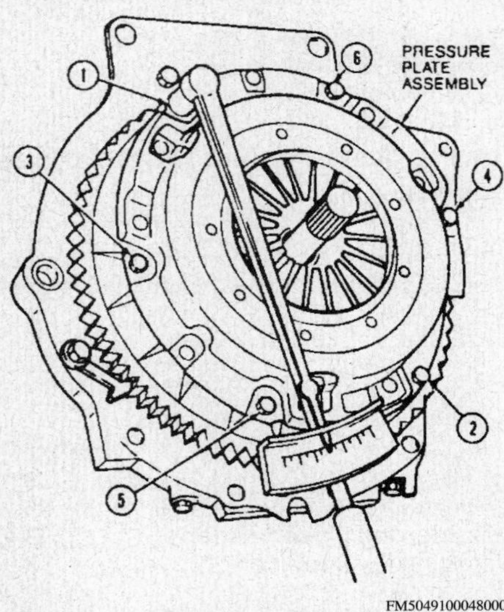

Fig. 2 Pressure plate tightening sequence

CLUTCH

REPLACE

ESCORT & TRACER

1. Remove manual transaxle as outlined under "Transaxle, Replace."
2. Install flywheel locking tool Nos. T84P-6375-A and T74P-7137-K, or equivalents, into a transaxle mounting hole on engine block, then engage tooth of locking tool into flywheel ring gear.
3. Loosen pressure plate cover attaching bolts evenly to avoid distorting cover. If same pressure plate and cover are to be installed, mark cover and flywheel so pressure plate can be installed in its original position.
4. Remove pressure plate and clutch disc from flywheel.
5. Reverse procedure to install, noting the following:
   a. Clean splines on clutch disc and transaxle input shaft, then apply a small amount of Clutch Grease P/N C1AZ-19590-B, or equivalent, to clutch disc and input shaft splines. **Avoid getting grease on clutch face.**
   b. Position clutch disc plate onto flywheel, **Fig. 1.**
   c. Ensure three dowel pins on flywheel are aligned with dowel pins on pressure plate.
   d. Finger tighten cover attaching bolts, then align clutch disc using tool No. T74P-7137-K, or equivalent.
   e. Evenly **torque** bolts to 13–20 ft. lbs., in sequence, **Fig. 2.**
   f. Remove alignment tool, then install transaxle then bleed clutch as outlined under "Hydraulic System Service."

ZX2

1. Remove manual transaxle as outlined under "Transaxle, Replace."
2. Use dial indicator and dial indicator bracket to inspect clutch pressure plate diaphragm fingers, **Fig. 3.** Rotate pressure plate to inspect diaphragm fingers runout.

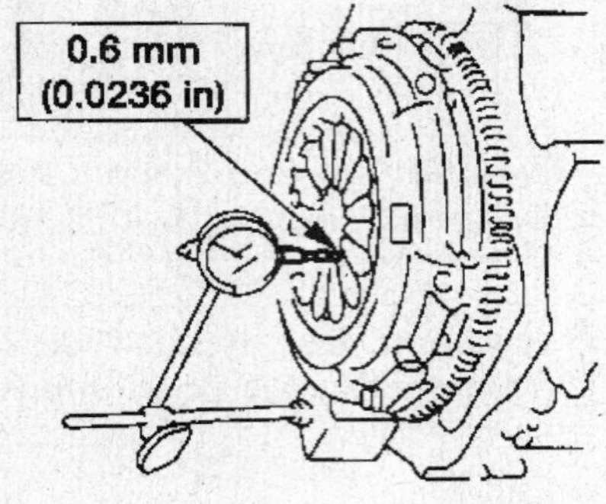

Fig. 3 Clutch pressure plate diaphragm fingers inspection. ZX2

3. Install flywheel holding tool T74P-6375-A and clutch aligner tool T74P-7137-K, or equivalents.
4. Remove clutch pressure plate bolts evenly to prevent pressure plate damage, if components are to be reused, mark position of clutch pressure plate and flywheel.
5. Use a slide caliper and measure the depth to rivet heads. Replace clutch disc if any rivet head measurement is not within specification, **Fig. 4.**
6. If clutch disc is saturated with oil, inspect rear engine crankshaft seal for leakage.
7. Use an emery cloth to remove minor imperfections in the clutch disc lining surface. Inspect clutch disc for oil or grease saturation, worn or loose facings, warpage or loose rivets at hub, loose or broken torsion dampening springs and wear or rust on splines. Replace clutch disc if any of these conditions are present.
8. Inspect clutch disc run out. Replace clutch disc if runout is not within .0276 inch.
9. Inspect clutch release fork for cracks, distortion, excessive wear on release bearing contact surface and damaged tines.
10. Use clutch aligner and position clutch disc on flywheel.
11. Position clutch pressure plate on flywheel, then install pressure plate bolts, then using sequence, **Fig. 2, torque** bolts to 17–32 ft. lbs., in several steps.
12. Remove alignment tool, then install transaxle and bleed clutch hydraulic system as outlined under "Hydraulic System Service."

TRANSAXLE

REPLACE

1. Remove battery and battery tray.
2. Remove air cleaner outlet tube.
3. Remove engine air cleaner
4. Disconnect Constant Control Relay Module (CCRM) electrical connector.
5. Remove CCRM bracket bolt and nut.

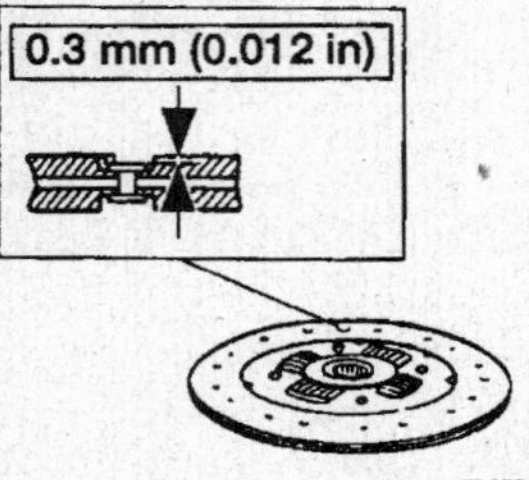

Fig. 4 Clutch disc inspection. ZX2

6. Remove CCRM bracket as an assembly.
7. Disconnect clutch slave cylinder tube from hydraulic clutch hose, then plug hose.
8. Disconnect back-up lamp electrical connector.
9. Remove electrical connector support bracket.
10. Disconnect vehicle speed sensor electrical connector.
11. Install three-bar engine support tool No. D88L-6000-A, or equivalent.
12. Remove three lefthand engine support insulator mounting bracket nuts.
13. Remove two upper transaxle to engine bolts.
14. Raise and support vehicle.
15. Remove wheel and tire assembly.
16. Remove lefthand splash shield.
17. Remove drain plug and drain transaxle.
18. Remove front engine crossmember bolts and front engine crossmember.
19. Disconnect A/C line from retainer located on front of engine support crossmember.
20. Remove engine support crossmember and lefthand engine mount nuts.
21. Remove transaxle mount nuts.
22. Remove front wheel driveshaft and joints.
23. Install two transaxle plugs (P/N T88C-7025-AH, or equivalent) into transaxle and hold differential side gears.
24. Remove gearshift stabilizer bar and support nut.
25. Remove stabilizer bar and support from transaxle.
26. Remove transaxle gearshift rod nut.
27. Remove transaxle gearshift bolt, then the gearshift rod and the clevis from input shift shaft.
28. Remove starter as outlined under "Starter, Replace" in "Electrical" section.
29. Disconnect lower clutch slave cylinder tube and plug to prevent excess fluid loss.
30. Remove two clutch slave cylinder nuts then the clutch slave cylinder.
31. Remove two lower transaxle to engine bolts.
32. Position transaxle jack, tool No. 014-00210, or equivalent, under transaxle and secure transaxle to jack.
33. Remove middle transaxle to engine bolts, then carefully lower transaxle out of vehicle.
34. Reverse procedure to install.

TIGHTENING SPECIFICATIONS

Year	Component	Torque/Ft. Lbs.
ESCORT & TRACER		
1998–2002	Back-Up Lamp Switch	15–21
	Front Transaxle Support Insulator Bolts	12–17
	Lower Transaxle To Engine Bolt	27–38
	Middle Transaxle To Engine Bolts	27–38
	Shift Rail Guide Bolt	7–12
	Transaxle Case To Flywheel Housing Bolts	14–19
	Transaxle Drain Plug	29–40
	Transaxle Gearshift Rod Nut	12–17
	Transaxle Mount Nuts	28–38
	Upper Transaxle To Engine Bolt	47–66
	Vehicle Speed Sensor Bolt	72–108①
	Wheel Lug Nuts	66–87
ZX2		
1998–2002	Back-Up Lamp Switch	14–18
	Clutch Slave Cylinder Nuts	12–17
	Engine Isolator Through Bolts	50–68
	Engine Isolator Nuts	28–37
	Engine Support Crossmember Bolts	47–65
	Front Engine Crossmember	48–65
	Left Engine Support Insulator Nuts	50–68
	Left Support Insulator Nuts & Bolts	32–44
	Left Support Insulator To Transaxle Nuts	50–68
	Lower Rear Support Insulator bolts	50–68
	Lower Transaxle To Engine Bolts	28–38
	Middle Transaxle To Engine Bolts	28–38
	Shift Rail Guide Bolt	7–12
	Transaxle Case To Flywheel Housing Bolts	14–19
	Transaxle Drain Plug	29–40
	Transaxle Gearshift Rod Nut	12–17
	Upper Transaxle To Engine Bolts	28–38
	Vehicle Speed Sensor (VSS) Bolt	72–96①

① — Inch lbs.

Rear Suspension

NOTE: On Air Bag Equipped Models, Refer To "Air Bag System Precautions" Located In The Front Of This Manual For System Disarming & Arming Procedures.

NOTE: Refer To "Computer Relearn Procedures" Located In The Front Of This Manual When Battery Power To The Computer Has Been Interrupted.

INDEX

DESCRIPTION

The rear strut and spring assemblies can be disassembled to replace any of the individual components, **Figs. 1 and 2.** The rear strut and spring assemblies can be replaced independently. The rear wheel hubs cannot be disassembled. The rear wheel hubs contain the rear wheel bearings and must be replaced as an assembly. The lefthand and righthand rear wheel spindles can be replaced individually. The rear suspension arm bushings can be replaced individually, only the toe can be adjusted on the rear suspension.

HUB & BEARING

REPLACE

1. Raise and support vehicle.
2. **On models equipped with disc brakes,** remove brake caliper and rotor as outlined under "Disc Brakes."
3. **On models equipped with drum brakes,** remove drum brake as outlined under "Drum Brakes."
4. **On all models,** unstake rear axle wheel hub retainer (1), **Fig. 3.**
5. Remove rear axle wheel hub retainer (2), then discard, **Fig. 3.**
6. Remove wheel hub (3), **Fig. 3.**
7. Reverse procedure to install, noting the following:
   a. Install suitable press with steel plate to install new anti-lock brake sensor indicator to wheel hub, **Fig. 4,** as required.
   b. Tighten to specifications.

REAR WHEEL SPINDLE

REPLACE

1. Raise and support vehicle.
2. Remove rear wheel hub as outlined under "Hub & Bearing, Replace."
3. **On models equipped with disc brakes,** remove rear disc plate shield as outlined under "Disc Brakes."
4. **On models equipped with drum brakes,** remove brake backing plate as outlined under "Drum Brakes."
5. **On models equipped with anti-lock brakes,** remove anti-lock brake system sensor bracket bolt, **Fig. 5.**
6. Remove anti-lock brake system sensor bolt, then the sensor, **Fig. 6.**
7. **On all models,** remove lower strut and spring assembly nuts, **Fig. 7.**
8. Remove rear suspension trailing link bolt, **Fig. 8.**
9. Remove rear suspension arm and bushing nut, then the rear wheel spindle, **Fig. 9.**
10. Reverse procedure to install, tighten to specifications.

STRUT

REPLACE

1. Remove high mount stop lamp cover and lamp.
2. Remove package tray trim panel pushpins, then the panel.
3. Remove upper strut and spring assembly nuts, **Fig. 10.**
4. Raise and support vehicle.
5. Slide brake hose clip off, position aside, **Fig. 11.**
6. **On models equipped with anti-lock brakes,** remove anti-lock brake system sensor bracket bolt.
7. **On all models,** remove lower strut and spring assembly bolts, then the strut and spring assembly, **Fig. 12.**
8. Reverse procedure to install, tighten to specifications.

SHOCK ABSORBER

REPLACE

1. Remove strut and spring assembly as outlined under "Strut, Replace."
2. Compress rear spring using tool No. 014-00781, or equivalent, to compress rear spring, **Fig. 13.**
3. Remove shock absorber top mounting cover, **Fig. 14.**
4. Remove piston rod nut, **Fig. 14.**
5. Remove retainer, then the shock absorber insulator, **Fig. 14.**
6. Remove spring compressor.
7. Remove rear shock components, **Fig. 15.**
8. Reverse procedure to install, tighten to specifications.

COIL SPRING

REPLACE

Refer to "Shock Absorber, Replace" for replacement procedure.

CONTROL ARM

REPLACE

1. Remove wheel and tire assemblies.
2. Install floor jack to support vehicle under rear floor crossmember.
3. Remove rear stabilizer bar end bolt and nut, **Fig. 16.**
4. Remove retainer, upper rear stabilizer bar end bushings, retainer spacer, lower rear stabilizer bar end bushings, then the retainer, **Fig. 16.**
5. Remove rear crossmember bolts, **Fig. 17.**
6. Remove rear suspension arm and bushing nut, **Fig. 18.**
7. Remove rear suspension arm and bushing bolt, then the rear suspension arm and bushing, **Fig. 19.**
8. Reverse procedure to install, tighten to specifications.

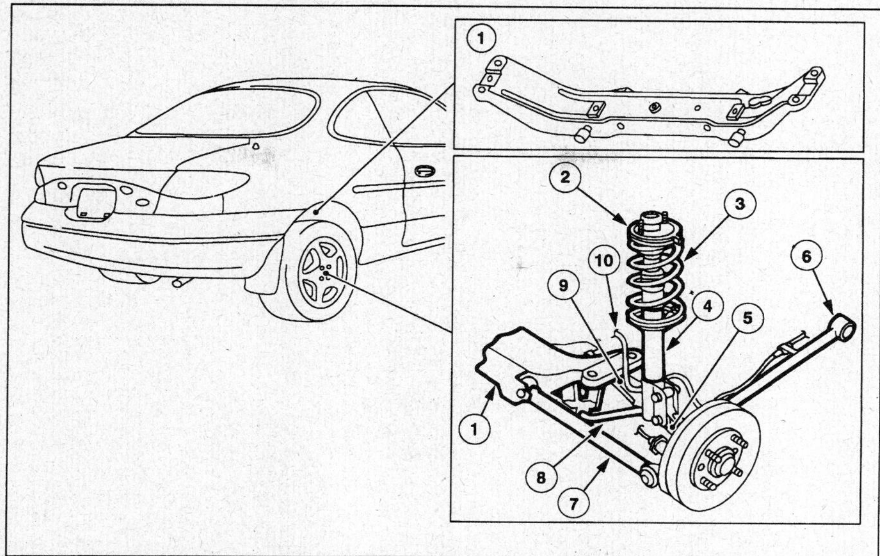

Item	Description
1	Rear Floor Cross Member
2	Rear Shock Absorber Insulator
3	Rear Spring
4	Rear Shock Absorber
5	Rear Wheel Spindle
6	Rear Suspension Tie Rod and Bushing

Item	Description
7	Rear Suspension Arm and Bushing (Rear)
8	Rear Stabilizer Bar
9	Rear Suspension Arm and Bushing (Front)
10	Rear Wheel Brake Hose

FM1060101416000X

Fig. 1 Rear suspension components

REAR CROSSMEMBER

REPLACE

1. Remove rear stabilizer bar as outlined under "Stabilizer Bar, Replace."
2. Remove two brake hose support brackets and disconnect hose.
3. Remove three-way connector bolt, **Fig. 20.**
4. **Locate alignment of both alignment shims prior to removal.** Remove rear suspension alignment shims and bolts, **Fig. 21.**
5. Install suitable jack under rear floor crossmember.
6. Remove rear floor crossmember bolts, **Fig. 17.**
7. Remove rear suspension arm and bushing nut.
8. Remove rear suspension arm and bushing bolt, then the rear suspension arm and bushing, **Fig. 19.**
9. Lower rear floor crossmember, then remove from vehicle.
10. Reverse procedure to install, tighten to specifications.

STABILIZER BAR

REPLACE

1. Raise and support vehicle.
2. Remove rear stabilizer links as outlined under "Control Arm, Replace."
3. Remove two stabilizer bar bracket bolts, then the stabilizer bar, **Fig. 22.**
4. Reverse procedure to install, tighten to specifications.

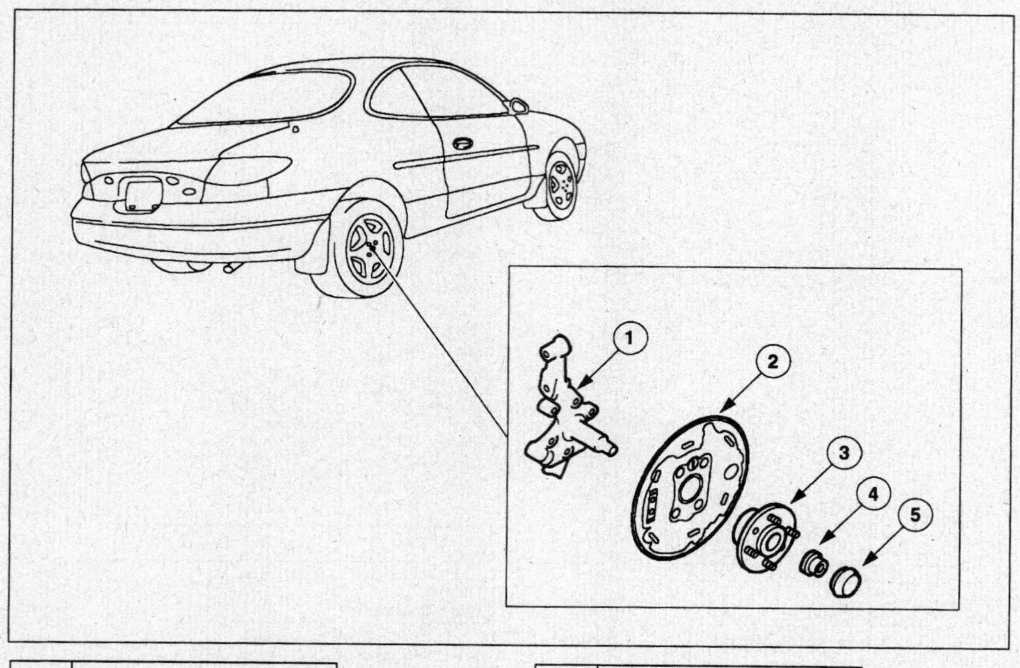

Item	Description
1	Rear Wheel Spindle
2	Brake Backing Plate
3	Wheel Hub

Item	Description
4	Rear Axle Wheel Hub Retainer
5	Hub Grease Cap

FM1060101417000X

Fig. 2 Rear wheel bearing & hub system components

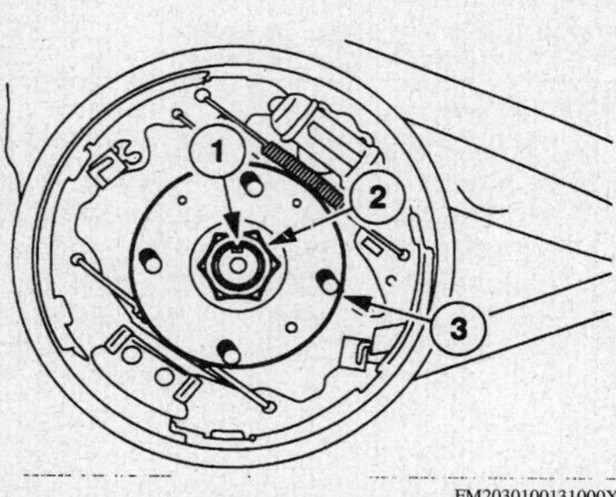

Fig. 3 Rear wheel hub removal

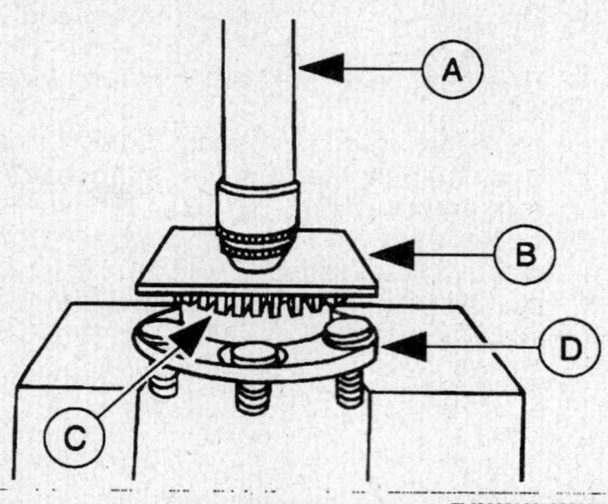

Fig. 4 Anti-lock brake sensor installation

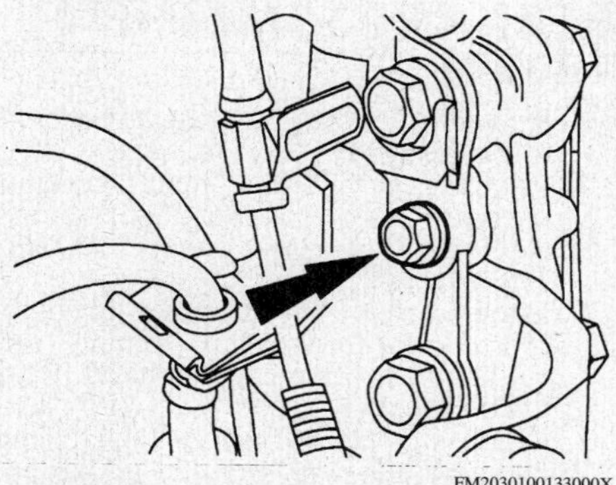

Fig. 5 Anti-lock brake bracket bolt removal

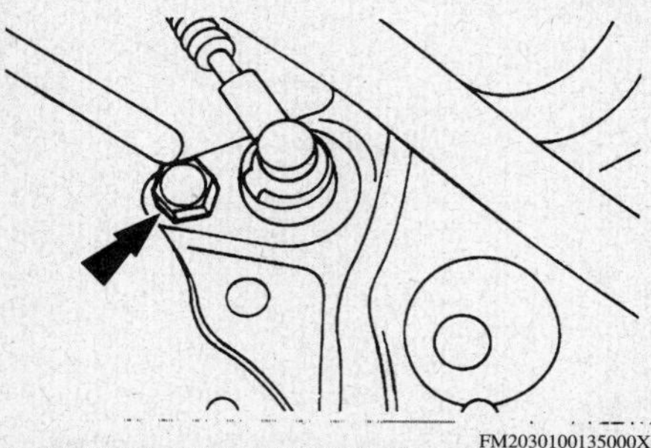

Fig. 6 Anti-lock brake sensor bolt removal

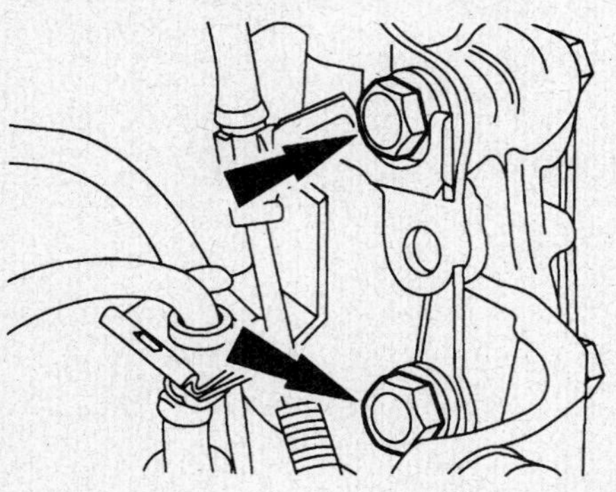

Fig. 7 Lower strut & spring removal

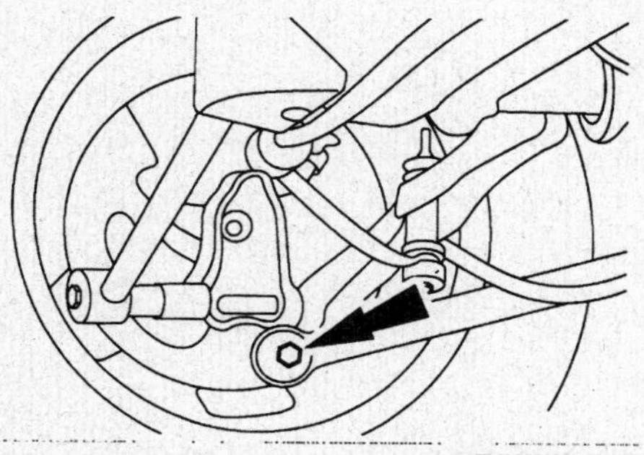

Fig. 8 Trailing link bolt removal

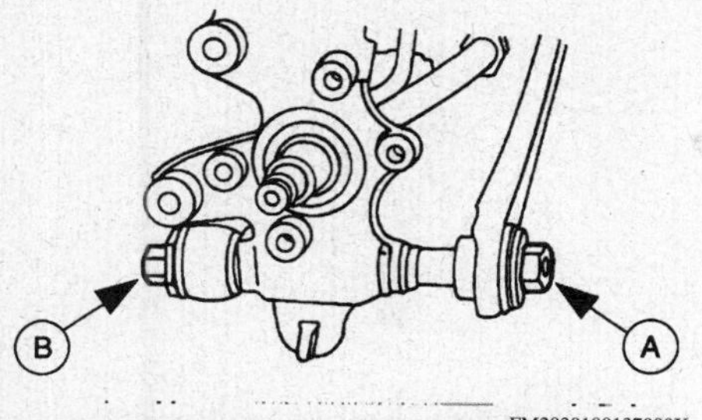

Fig. 9 Rear wheel spindle removal

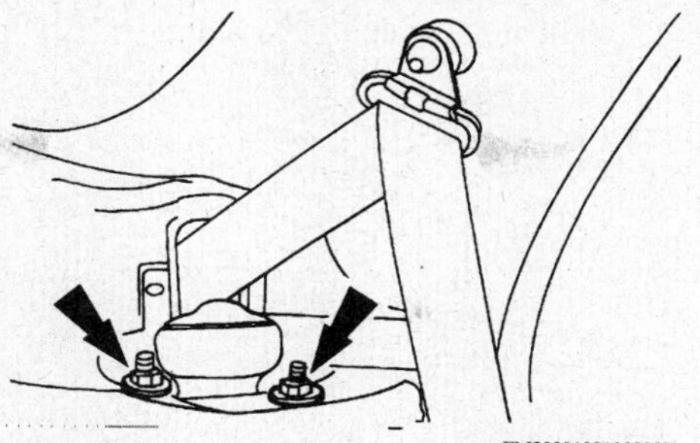

Fig. 10 Upper strut & spring nut removal

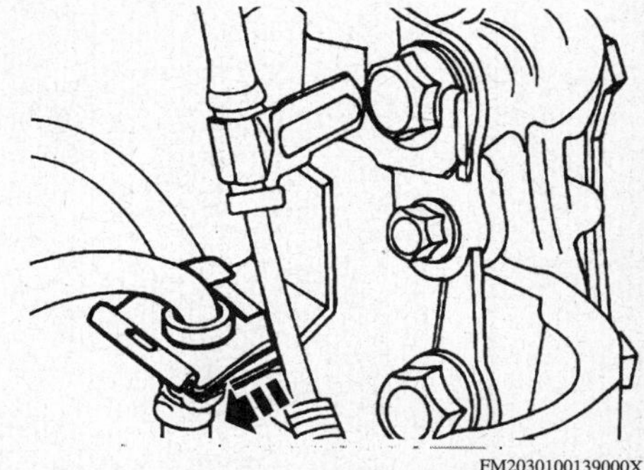

Fig. 11 Brake hose clip removal

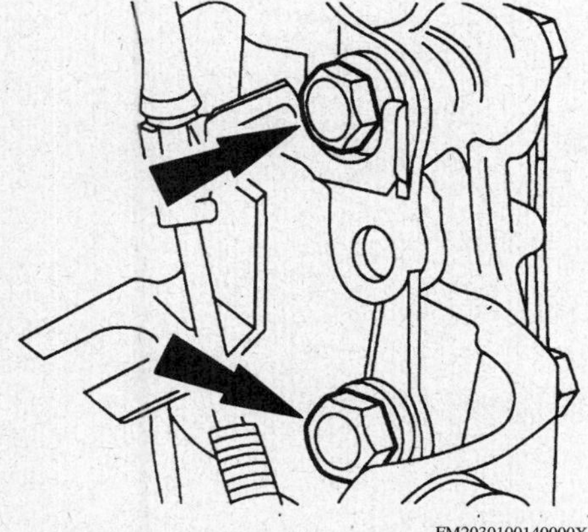

Fig. 12 Lower strut & spring bolt removal

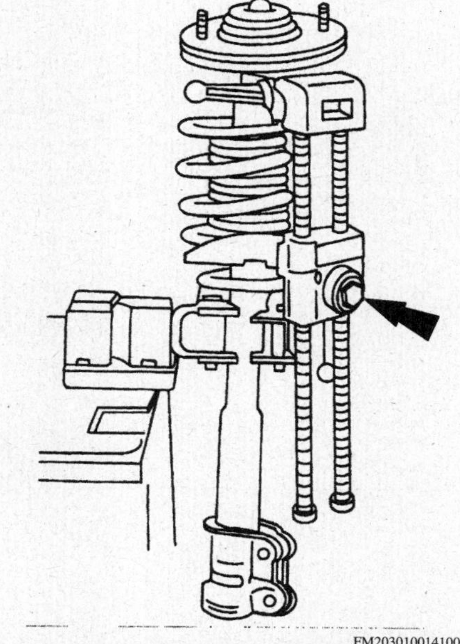
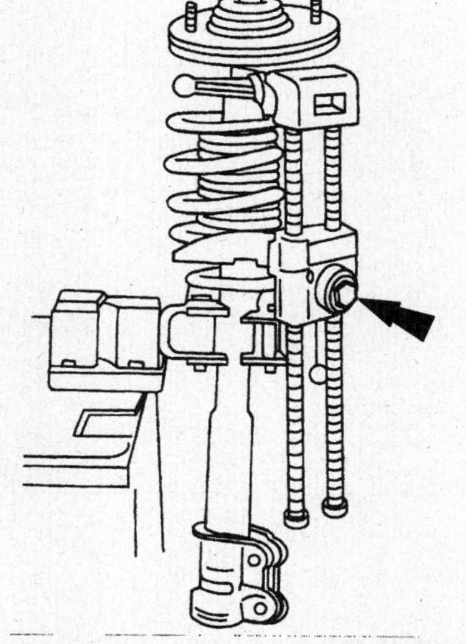

Fig. 13 Rear spring compression

FM2030100142000X

Fig. 14 Top mounting cover & component removal

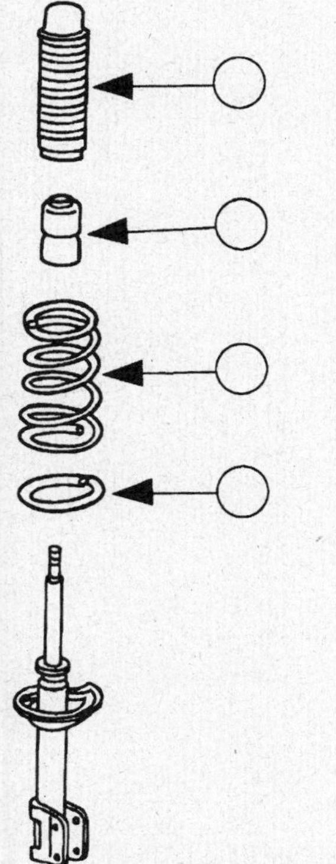

Fig. 15 Rear shock removal

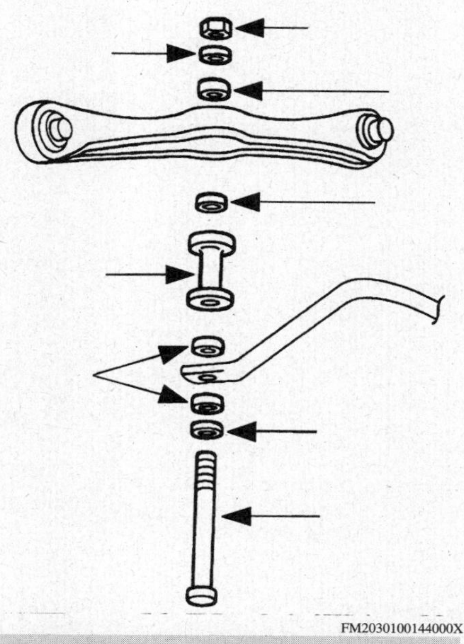

Fig. 16 Rear stabilizer bar link removal

Fig. 17 Rear crossmember bolt removal

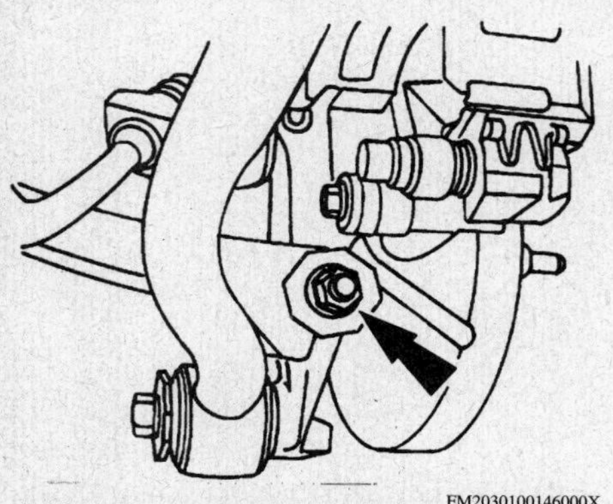

Fig. 18 Rear suspension arm & bushing nut removal

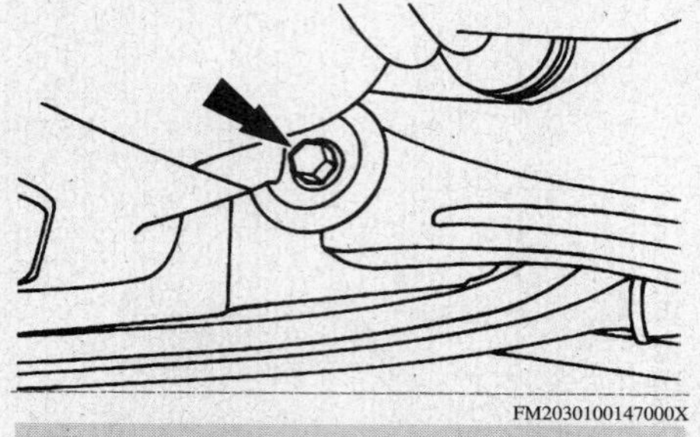

Fig. 19 Rear suspension arm & bushing bolt removal

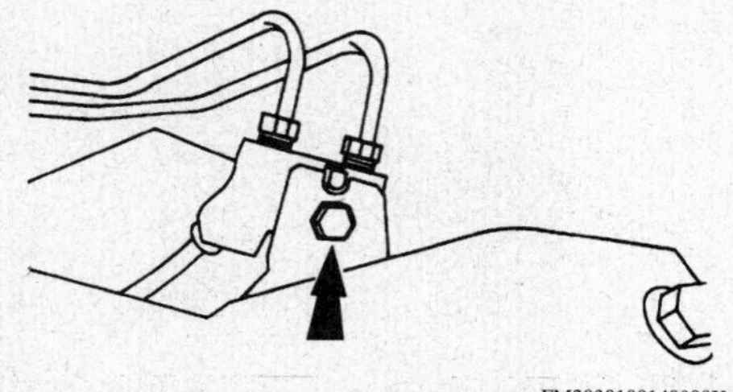

Fig. 20 Three-way bolt removal

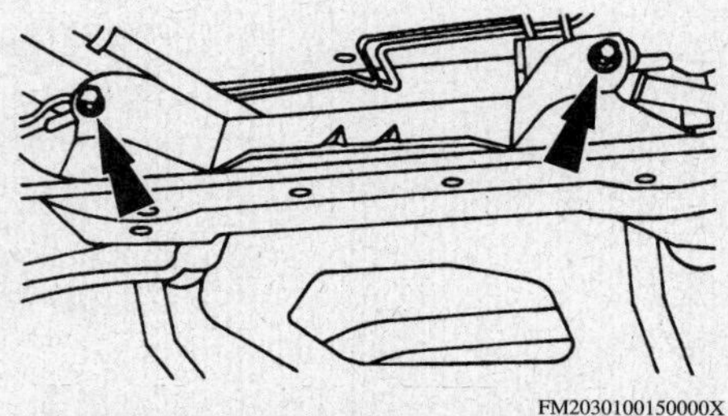

Fig. 21 Rear suspension alignment shims & bolt removal

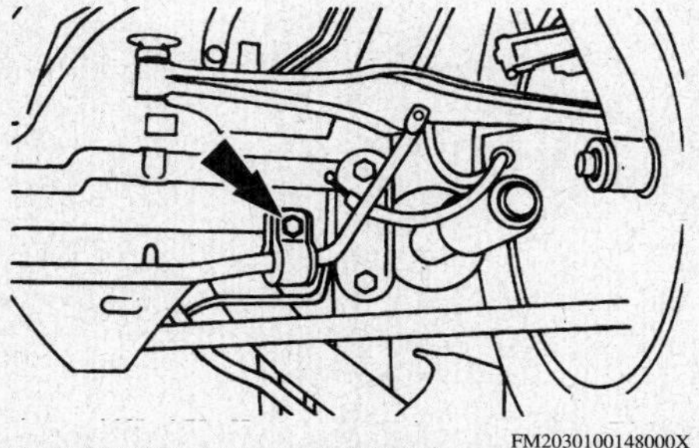

Fig. 22 Stabilizer bar removal

TIGHTENING SPECIFICATIONS

Year	Component	Torque/Ft. Lbs.
1998–2002	Anti-Lock Brake System Sensor Bolt	14–18
	Lower Strut & Spring Assembly Nuts	76–100
	Piston Rod Nut	41–49
	Rear Axle Wheel Hub Retainer	130–174
	Rear Anti-Lock Brake System Sensor Bracket Bolt	14–18
	Rear Floor Crossmember Nuts	34–46
	Rear Suspension Arm & Bushing Front Bolt	63–86
	Rear Suspension Arm & Bushing Front Nut	64–86
	Rear Suspension Arm & Bushing Rear Nut	64–86
	Rear Suspension Trailing Link Bolt	69–94
	Rear Wheel Disc Brake Shield Bolts	34–44
	Stabilizer Bar Bracket Bolts	32–43
	Upper Strut & Spring Assembly Nuts	34–46
	Wheel Lug Nuts	74–100

Front Suspension & Steering

NOTE: On Air Bag Equipped Models, Refer To "Air Bag System Precautions" Located In The Front Of This Manual For System Disarming & Arming Procedures.

NOTE: Refer To "Computer Relearn Procedures" Located In The Front Of This Manual When Battery Power To The Computer Has Been Interrupted.

INDEX

DESCRIPTION

The front suspension is a McPherson strut design with cast steering knuckles. The shock absorber strut assembly includes a mounting block, a thrust bearing, an upper spring seat, a rubber spring seat, a bound stopper and coil spring mounted to the shock strut, **Fig. 1.**

The front wheels and brake rotors are supported by a sealed roller bearing mounted in the steering knuckle. A snap ring holds the bearing in the knuckle. The halfshaft is secured to the front hub assembly with a staked nut. The staked nut cannot be reused, **Fig. 2.**

WHEEL BEARING

REPLACE

1. Remove front wheel knuckle as outlined under "Steering Knuckle, Replace."
2. Remove and discard inner wheel bearing oil seal.
3. Press wheel hub from the front wheel knuckle using bearing puller attachment tool No. 205-D064 (D84L-1123-A) or equivalent, **Fig. 3.**
4. Remove retainer ring from the front wheel knuckle, **Fig. 4.**
5. Press front wheel bearing from front wheel knuckle using bearing pulling attachment tool, **Fig. 5.**
6. Reverse procedure to install.

STEERING KNUCKLE

REPLACE

1. Raise and support vehicle.
2. Remove wheel and tire assembly.
3. Remove brake caliper bolts and rotor, then secure caliper with wire as outlined under "Disc Brakes."
4. Carefully raise staked portion of front axle wheel hub retainer, then remove retainer, **Fig. 6.**
5. Remove cotter pin and tie rod end nut from tie rod end, **Fig. 7.**
6. Separate tie rod end nut from front wheel knuckle using tie rod end separator tool No. T85M-3395-A, or equivalent, **Fig. 8.**
7. **On models equipped with anti-lock brakes,** remove anti-lock brake sensor, **Fig. 9.**
8. **On all models,** remove ball joint nut and through bolt.
9. Separate front suspension lower arm ball joint from front wheel knuckle, **Fig. 10.**
10. Remove two strut mounting bolts from front wheel knuckle.
11. Separate strut assembly from front wheel knuckle and remove knuckle.
12. Reverse procedure to install, tighten to specifications.

BALL JOINT INSPECTION

1. Raise and support vehicle.
2. Grasp lower edge of tire (A) and move wheel in and out from pivot center line (B), **Fig. 11.**
3. Ball joint should be replaced if excessive movement is felt (more than 1/32 inch).

BALL JOINT

REPLACE

1. Raise and support vehicle.
2. Remove wheel and tire assembly.
3. Remove ball joint nut and through bolt.
4. Separate front suspension lower arm ball joint from front wheel knuckle.
5. Remove two ball joint nuts and front suspension lower arm ball joint.
6. Reverse procedure to install, tighten to specifications.

COIL SPRING

REPLACE

1. Remove front shock/strut assembly as outlined under "Strut, Replace."
2. Remove cap from top of shock/strut assembly.
3. Secure shock/strut assembly mounting block in a vise, then turn piston rod nut one full revolution to loosen.
4. Install an appropriate spring compressor onto shock/strut spring, then compress spring.
5. Remove nut, mounting block, thrust bearing, upper spring seat, rubber spring seat, coil spring and bound stopper **Fig. 12.**
6. Reverse procedure to install, tighten to specifications.

STRUT

REPLACE

1. Raise and support vehicle, then remove front wheel.
2. Remove clip securing flexible brake hose to shock/strut assembly.
3. Remove two nuts and bolts securing shock/strut assembly to steering knuckle.
4. Remove upper mounting block nuts on strut tower, then remove shock/strut assembly, **Fig. 12.**
5. Reverse procedure to install noting the following:
   a. Position shock/strut assembly into wheel housing, ensure direction indicator on mounting block faces inboard.
   b. Tighten upper mounting block to strut tower nuts to and shock/strut assembly bolts to specification.

CONTROL ARM

REPLACE

1. Raise and support vehicle.
2. Remove stabilizer bar nuts, washers, bushings, sleeves and bolts, **Fig. 13.**
3. Remove lower control arm front bushing bolt and washer, then the bolts securing lower control arm rear bushing retaining strap.
4. Remove nut and bolt securing lower

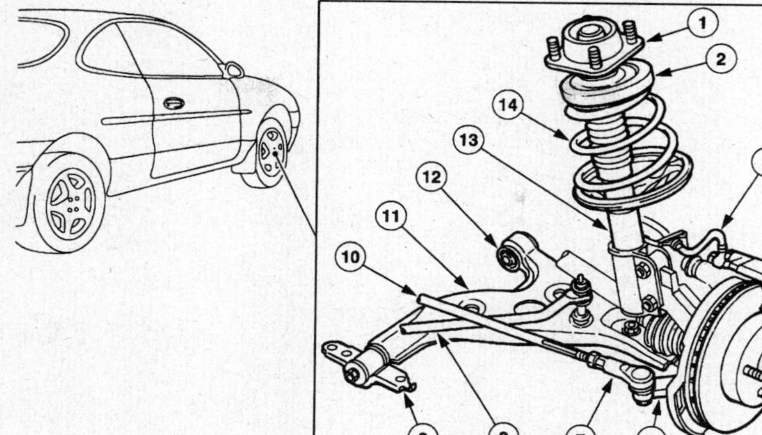

Item	Description
1	Front Shock Absorber Mounting Bracket
2	Upper Spring Seat (Part of 18198)
3	Front Brake Hose
4	Disc Brake Caliper
5	Front Disc Brake Rotor
6	Front Wheel Knuckle
7	Tie Rod End

Item	Description
8	Front Stabilizer Bar
9	Front Suspension Lower Arm Mounting Bolt Bushing (Rear)
10	Front Wheel Spindle Tie Rod
11	Front Suspension Lower Arm
12	Front Suspension Lower Arm Mounting Bolt Bushing (Front)
13	Front Shock Absorber
14	Front Coil Spring

FM2020100184000X

Fig. 1 Front suspension components

ball joint to steering knuckle, then separate steering knuckle from lower ball joint.

5. Remove lower control arm bolts, then the control arm, **Fig. 14.**
6. Reverse procedure to install noting the following:
   a. Tighten lower control arm pivot bolt nut, ball joint retaining bolt and nut, lower control arm rear bushing retaining strap bolts and lower control arm front pivot bolt to specification.
   b. Install stabilizer bar bolts, sleeves, bushings, washers and nuts and tighten so that .67–.75 inch of thread is showing.

STABILIZER BAR

REPLACE

1. Support engine with three bar engine support tool No. D88L-6000-A, or equivalent.
2. Raise and support vehicle.
3. Remove front wheel and tire assembly.
4. Remove crossmember bolts, then the crossmember, **Fig. 15.**
5. Remove steering gear mounting bracket nuts, **Fig. 16.**
6. Position steering gear slightly forward, then remove stabilizer bar nuts, washers, bushings, sleeves and bolts from lower control arm.
7. Remove front stabilizer bar link, **Fig. 13.**
8. Remove transaxle insulator nuts and rear engine support to vehicle frame nuts, **Fig. 17.**
9. Lower end of transaxle support crossmember, **Fig. 18.**
10. Install position high lift trans jack to support subframe, **Fig. 19.**
11. Remove two subframe to frame nuts.
12. Remove front subframe to vehicle attaching nuts, **Fig. 20.**
13. Lower subframe.
14. Remove four stabilizer bar bolts from subframe, then the front stabilizer bar, **Fig. 21.**
15. Reverse procedure to install, noting the following:
    a. Tighten front stabilizer bar link nuts to indicate 0.67–0.75 inch thread is exposed.
    b. Tighten to specifications.

POWER STEERING GEAR

REPLACE

1. Turn ignition switch to ACC position.
2. Remove five nuts, then the steering column tube boot.
3. Remove steering column input shaft coupling to steering gear input shaft and control bolt.
4. Raise and support vehicle.
5. Remove front wheel assemblies.
6. Remove and discard cotter pin from tie rod end nut.
7. Remove tie rod end nut, then use tie rod end separator tool No. T85M-3395-A, or equivalent, to separate tie rod from wheel knuckle, **Fig. 22.**
8. Remove righthand splash shield.
9. Remove crossmember.
10. Disconnect power steering return hose and plug the line.
11. Remove strap attaching hoses to steering gear housing.
12. **On models equipped with manual transaxle, proceed as follows:**
    a. Disconnect transmission gearshift rod and clevis from transaxle.
    b. remove extension bar nut and disconnect gearshift lever stabilizer bar and support from transaxle.
13. **On all models,** remove steering gear mounting brackets.
14. Remove two nuts from each bracket.
15. Remove two steering gear mounting brackets.
16. Remove pushpin and position righthand boot shield aside.
17. Remove steering gear assembly from righthand side of vehicle.
18. Reverse procedure to install.

POWER STEERING PUMP

REPLACE

SOHC ENGINE

1. Remove power steering pump reservoir.
2. Remove power steering pump pulley.
3. Raise and support vehicle.
4. Remove six bolts and righthand splash shield.
5. Disconnect power steering pressure hose.

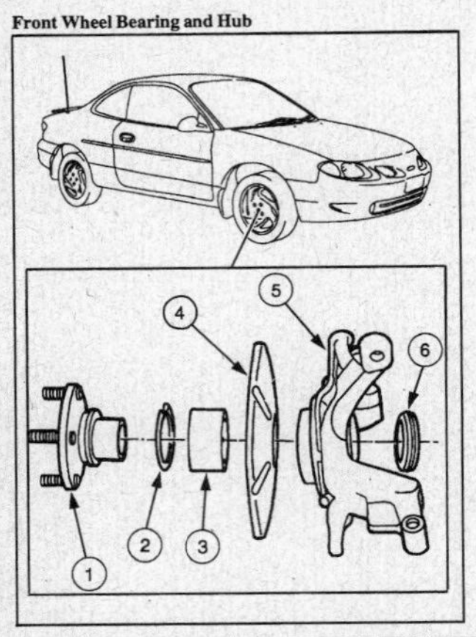

Item	Description
1	Wheel Hub
2	Retainer Ring
3	Front Wheel Bearing
4	Front Disc Brake Rotor Shield
5	Front Wheel Knuckle
6	Inner Wheel Bearing Oil Seal

FM2020100185000X

Fig. 2 Front wheel bearing & hub

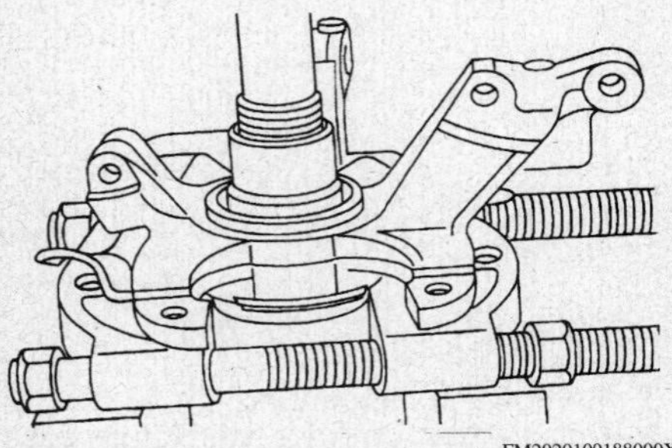

Fig. 5 Bearing removal

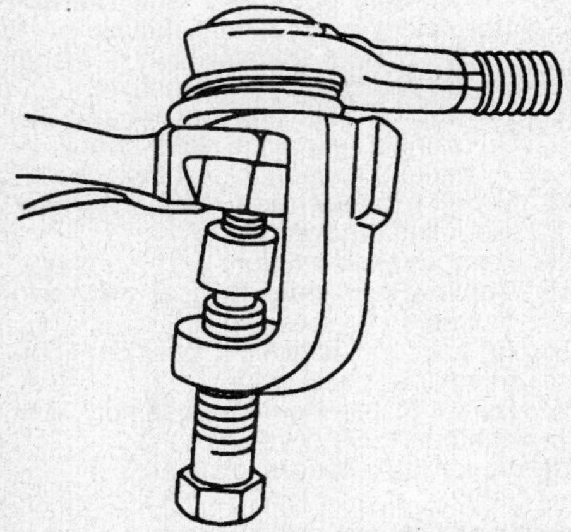

Fig. 8 Tie rod separator tool installation

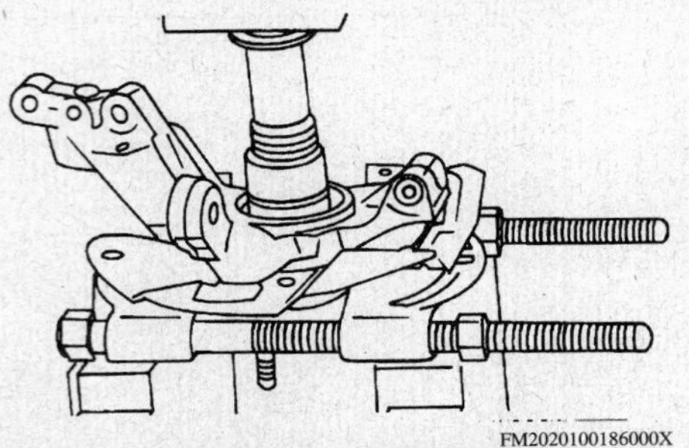
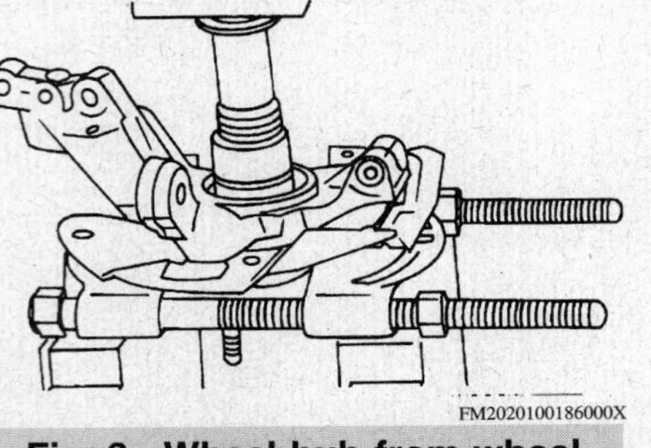

Fig. 3 Wheel hub from wheel knuckle removal

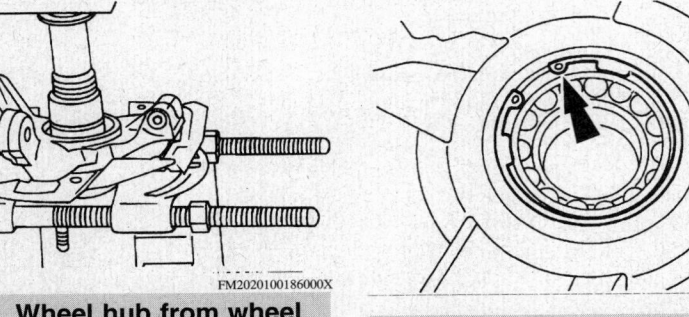

Fig. 4 Retaining ring removal

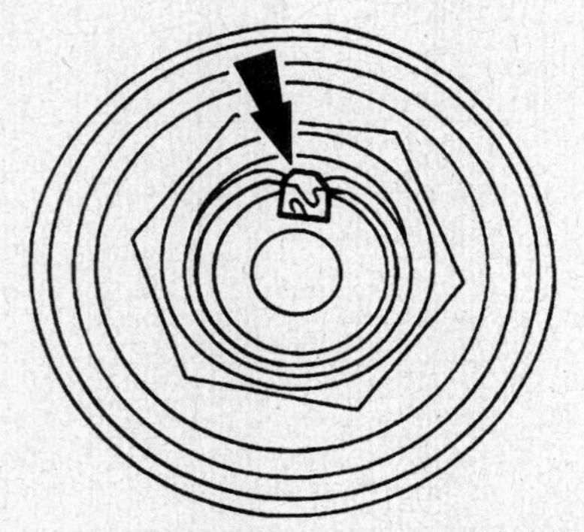

Fig. 6 Wheel hub retainer removal

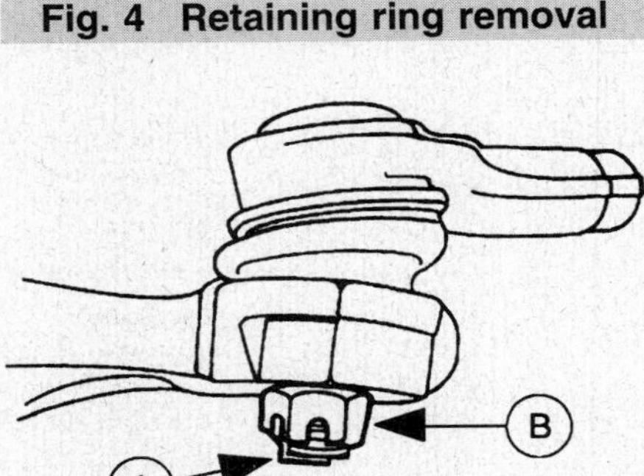

Fig. 7 Cotter pin & nut removal

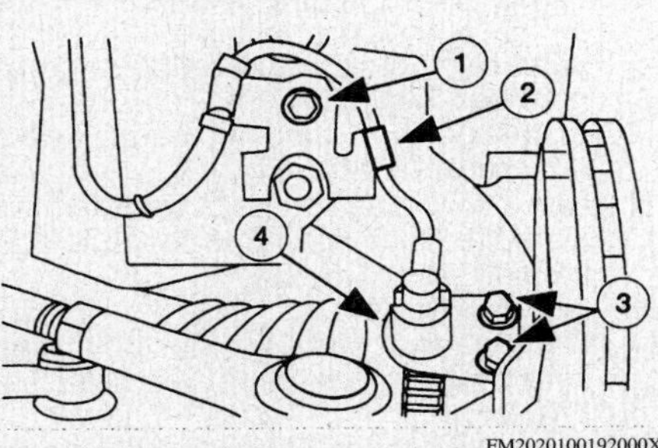

Fig. 9 Anti-lock brake sensor removal

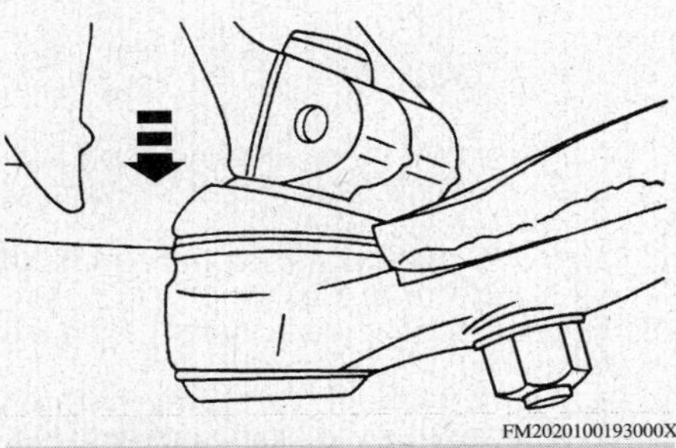

Fig. 10 Front suspension lower arm ball joint removal

6. Lower vehicle.
7. Loosen clamp and disconnect power steering reservoir to pump hose.
8. Remove power steering pump mounting bolts (A) and the pump (B), **Fig. 23.**
9. Reverse procedure to install.

DOHC ENGINE

1. Disconnect radiator overflow tube and position aside.
2. Remove A/C hose clamp bolt, then unclip speed control cable from A/C hose bracket.
3. Remove A/C hose bracket, then raise and support vehicle.
4. Remove lower right splash shield bolts and shield.
5. Turn belt tensioner bolt clockwise and remove accessory drive belt.
6. Disconnect power steering pressure hose from power steering pump, then lower vehicle.
7. Remove power steering hose brackets, then disconnect heated oxygen sensor connector.
8. Remove engine block ground bracket, then disconnect power steering return hose from power steering pump.
9. Raise and support vehicle, then remove power steering pressure hose from vehicle.
10. Lower vehicle, then remove four pump bolts and pump.
11. Discard power steering pump heat shield.
12. Reverse procedure to install. Install new power steering pump heat shield.

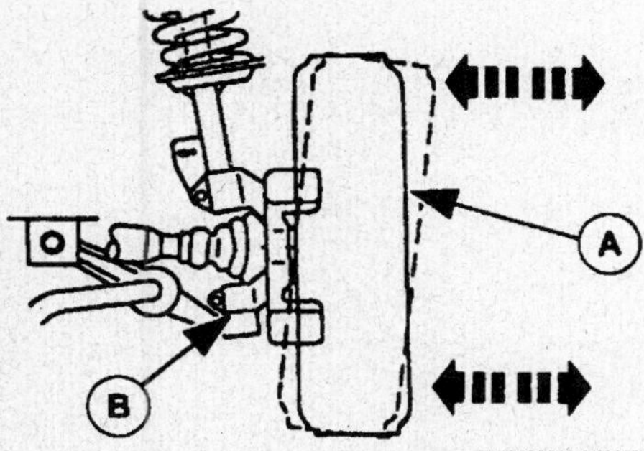

Fig. 11 Ball joint inspection

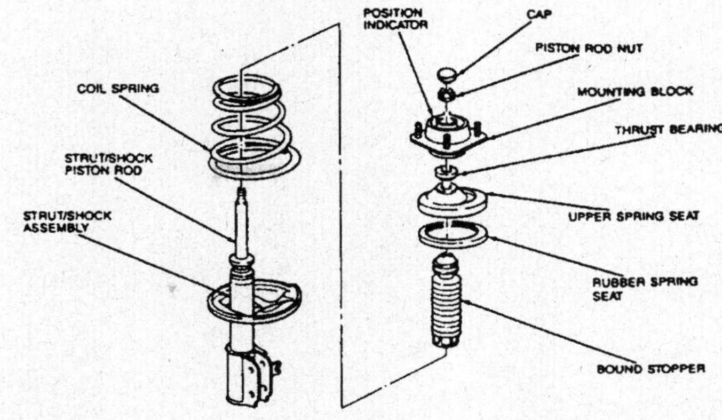

Fig. 12 Exploded view of front strut assembly

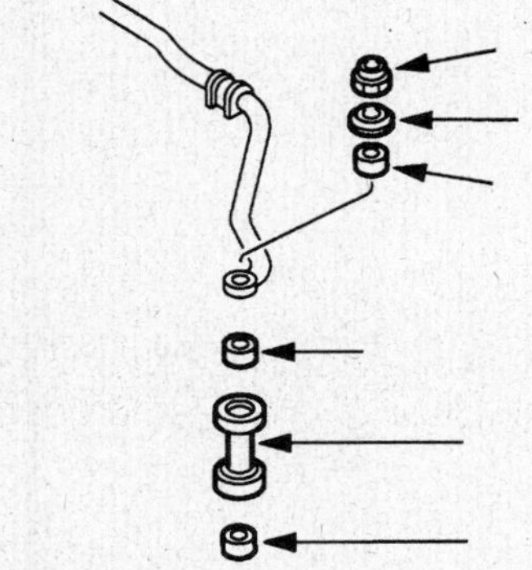

Fig. 13 Stabilizer bar link removal

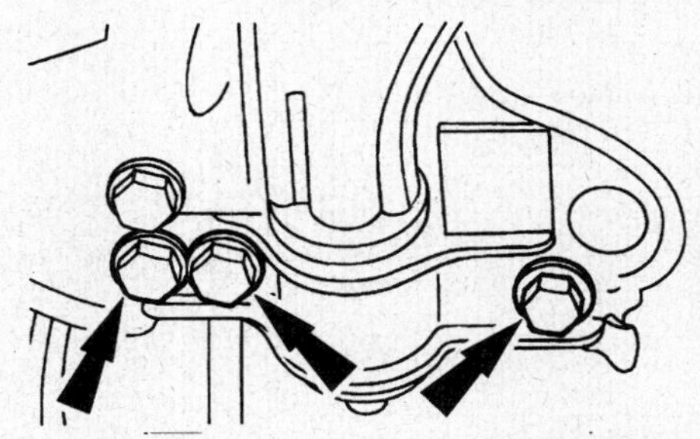

Fig. 14 Lower control arm removal

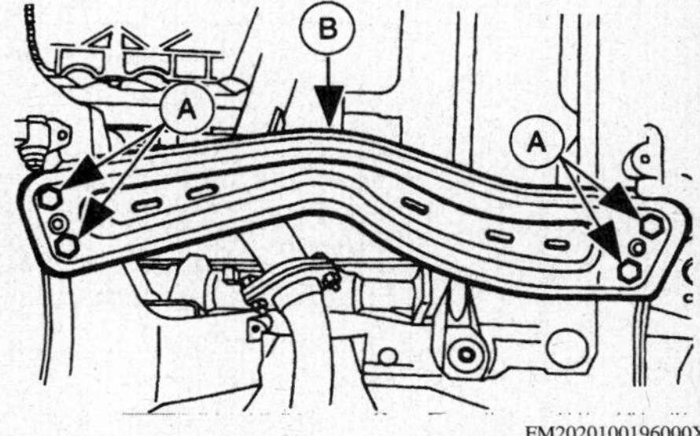

Fig. 15 Crossmember removal

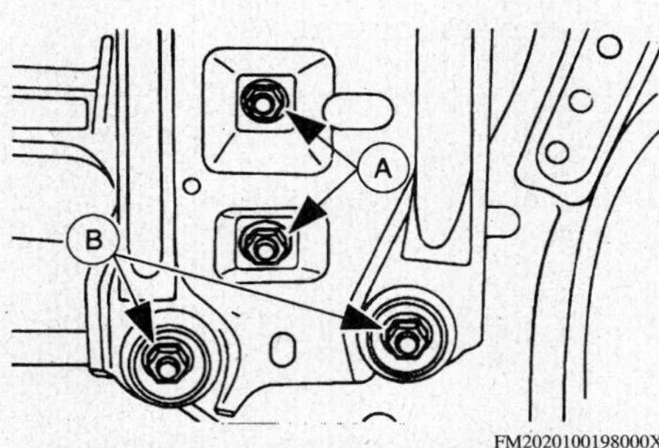

Fig. 17 Transaxle insulator nut removal

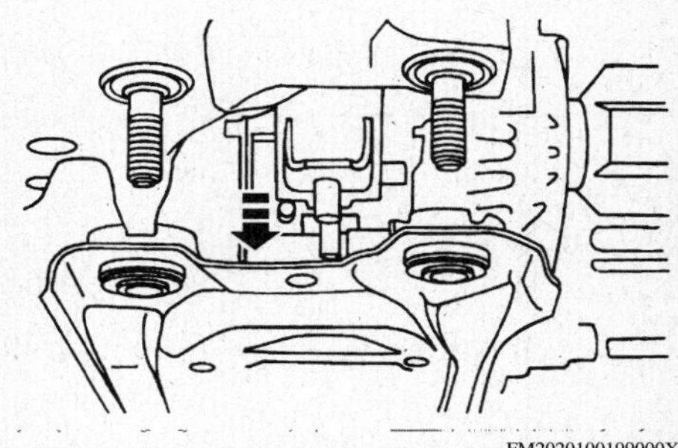

Fig. 18 Transaxle support crossmember removal

Fig. 16 Steering gear mounting bracket nut removal

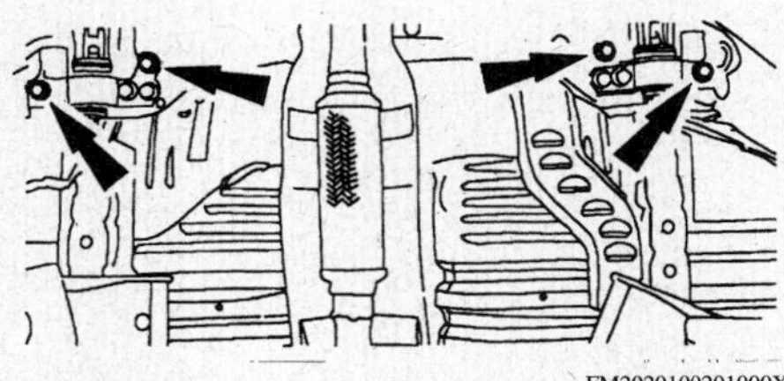

Fig. 20 Front subframe nut removal

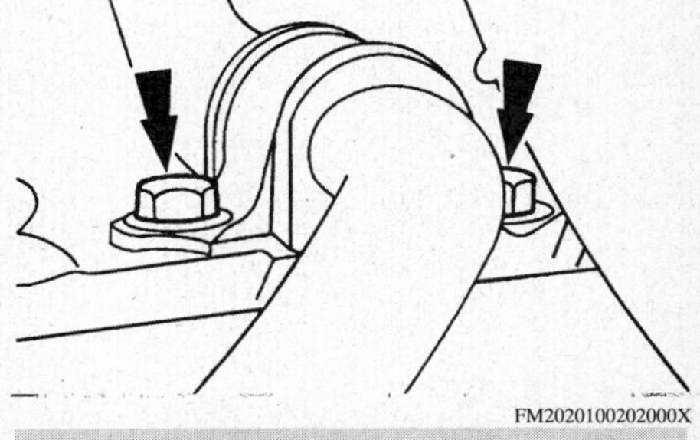

Fig. 21 Stabilizer bar removal

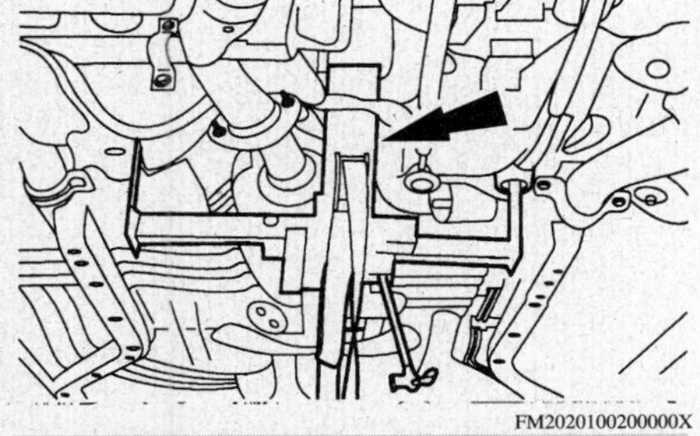

Fig. 19 Subframe removal

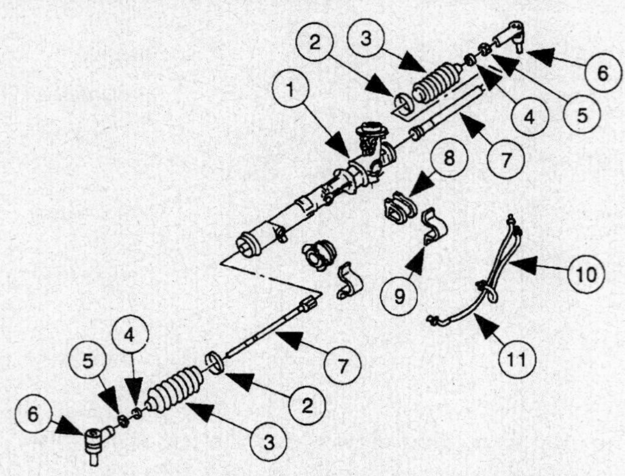

Item	Description
1	Steering Gear
2	Inner Front Suspension Steering Ball Stud Dust Seal (Part of 3332)
3	Front Suspension Steering Ball Stud Dust Seal
4	Outer Front Suspension Steering Ball Stud Dust Seal (Part of 3332)
5	Tie Rod End Jam Nut (Part of 3A130)
6	Tie Rod End
7	Front Wheel Spindle Tie Rod
8	Steering Gear Insulator
9	Steering Gear Mounting Bracket
10	Power Steering Left Turn Pressure Hose
11	Power Steering Right Turn Pressure Hose

FM6029700218000X

Fig. 22 Power steering gear components

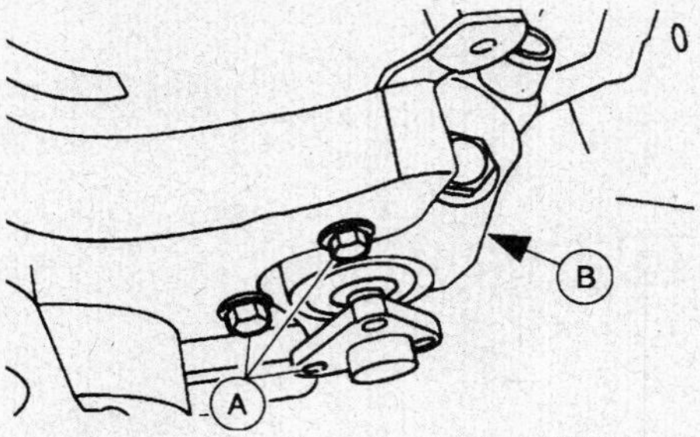

FM6029700217000X

Fig. 23 Power steering pump replacement. SOHC engine

TIGHTENING SPECIFICATIONS

Year	Component	Torque/Ft. Lbs.
1998–2002	Crossmember Bolts	69–97
	Engine Block Ground Bracket	71–89①
	Front Wheel Spindle Tie Rod	40–50
	Lower Alternator Bolt	15–22
	Lower Power Steering Hose Retaining Bracket Bolt	70–96①
	Power Steering Fluid Cooler Bracket Bolts	70–96①②
	Power Steering Pressure Hose Bracket Bolts	71–89①②
	Power Steering Pressure Hose Fitting	20–25②
	Power Steering Pressure Hose To Pump Fitting	40–54
	Power Steering Pressure Hose To Steering Gear Fitting	21–25
	Power Steering Pressure Hose Bracket Bolts	70–96①③
	Power Steering Pump Bolts	30–41③
	Power Steering Pump Bolts	15–22②
	Power Steering Pulley Bolts	15–22
	Power Steering Pump Reservoir Bolts	70–96①
	Power Steering Return Hose Retainer Bracket Bolts	70–96①③
	Power Steering Return Hose To Steering Gear Fitting	20–25
	Righthand Splash Shield Bolts	69–98①
	Steering Column Input Shaft Coupling To Steering Gear Input Shaft Pinch Bolt	30–36
	Steering Column Tube Boot Bolts	18–52①
	Steering Gear Mounting Bracket Bolts	28–38
	Tie Rod End Jam Nut	25–37
	Tie Rod End Nut	25–33
	Upper Alternator Bolt	30–40
	Upper Power Steering Hose Bracket Bolts	30–40②
	Wheel Lug Nuts	74–100

① — Inch lbs.

② — DOHC.

③ — SOHC.

Wheel Alignment

INDEX

PRELIMINARY INSPECTION

1. Inspect tires for proper inflation and similar tread wear.
2. Inspect hub and bearing for excessive wear, repair as required.
3. Inspect ball joints.
4. Inspect tie rod ends for excessive looseness.
5. Inspect wheel and tire runout.
6. Inspect vehicle ride height.
7. Inspect rack and pinion for looseness at frame.
8. Ensure proper strut operation.
9. Inspect suspension and steering components for damage, replace as required.

FRONT WHEEL ALIGNMENT

CAMBER

1. Raise and support vehicle.
2. Remove front shock absorber upper mounting bracket nuts.
3. Push front shock absorber upper mounting bracket downward and turn to desired position to set camber/caster, **Fig. 1.**
4. **Torque** front shock absorber upper mounting bracket nuts to 35–47 ft. lbs.

TOE

The lefthand and righthand front wheel spindle rods are both righthand threaded.

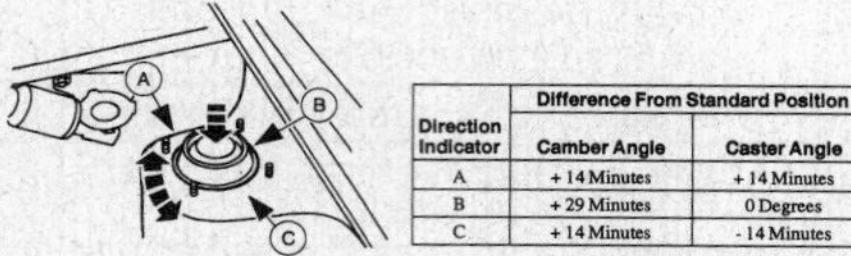

Direction Indicator	Difference From Standard Position	
	Camber Angle	Caster Angle
A	+ 14 Minutes	+ 14 Minutes
B	+ 29 Minutes	0 Degrees
C	+ 14 Minutes	- 14 Minutes

Fig. 1 Camber adjustment specifications

To increase the toe-in, turn the righthand front wheel spindle tie rod toward the front of the vehicle and turn the lefthand front wheel spindle tie rod the same amount toward the rear of the vehicle. One turn of the front wheel spindle tie rod (both sides) makes a toe-in change of 0.24 inch.

1. Loosen lefthand and righthand tie rod end jam nuts, **Fig. 2.**
2. Turn front wheel spindle tie rods equally until toe-in setting is within specifications.
3. **Torque** tie rod end jam nuts to 25–29 ft. lbs.

REAR WHEEL ALIGNMENT

TOE

1. Loosen lefthand and righthand rear suspension arm and bushing bolt.
2. Turn lefthand and righthand adjusting cams together until toe is with specifications, **Fig. 3.**
3. **Torque** lefthand and righthand rear suspension arm and bushing bolt to 63–86 ft. lbs.

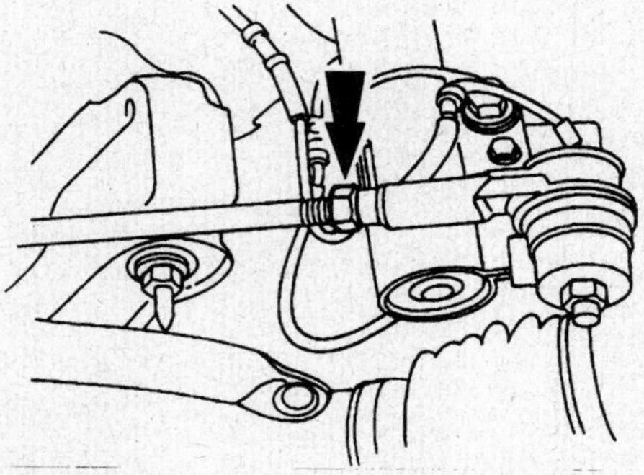

Fig. 2 Tie rod end jam nut

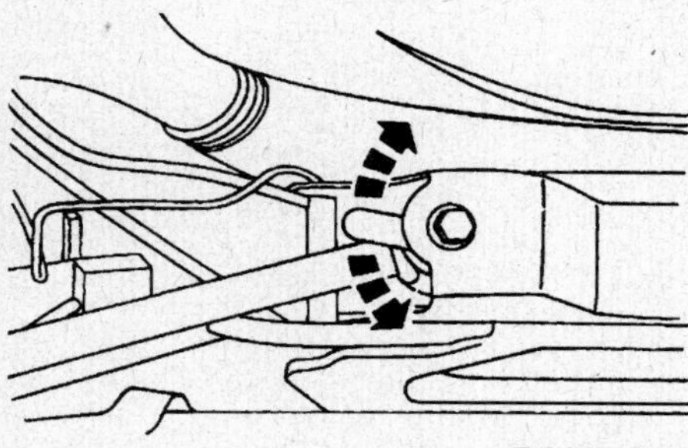

Fig. 3 Rear toe adjustment

CONTINENTAL, MARK VIII & TOWN CAR

NOTE: Refer To Rear Of This Manual For Vehicle Manufacturer's Special Service Tool Suppliers.

INDEX OF SERVICE OPERATIONS

Specifications

GENERAL ENGINE SPECIFICATIONS

Year	Engine Liter	Fuel System	Bore & Stroke	Compression Ratio	Net HP @ RPM③	Maximum Torque, Ft. Lbs. @ RPM	Normal Oil Pressure, psi
1998	4.6L SOHC	SFI	3.55 × 3.54	9.00	④	⑤	20–45
	4.6L DOHC	SFI	3.55 × 3.54	9.85	①	⑥	20–45
1999–2000	4.6L SOHC	SFI	3.55 × 3.54	9.00	⑦	⑧	20–45
	4.6L DOHC	SFI	3.55 × 3.54	9.85	275 @ 5750	275 @ 4750	20–45
2001–02	4.6L SOHC	SFI	3.55 × 3.54	9.40	⑨	②	20–45
	4.6L DOHC	SFI	3.55 × 3.54	9.85	275 @ 5750	275 @ 4750	20–45

SFI — Sequential Fuel Injection
SOHC — Single Overhead Cam
DOHC — Dual Overhead Cam
① — Continental, 260 @ 5750; Mark VIII standard equipment, 280 @ 5500; Mark VIII LSC, 290 @ 5750.
② — Single exhaust, 265 @ 4000; dual exhaust, 275 @ 4000.
③ — Ratings are net.
④ — Single exhaust, 200 @ 4500; dual exhaust, 220 @ 4500.
⑤ — Single exhaust, 265 @ 3500; dual exhaust, 275 @ 3500.
⑥ — Continental, 265 @ 4750; Mark VIII standard equipment, 285 @ 4500; Mark VIII LSC, 295 @ 4500.
⑦ — Single exhaust, 205 @ 4250; dual exhaust, 220 @ 4500.
⑧ — Single exhaust, 280 @ 3000; dual exhaust, 290 @ 3500.
⑨ — Single exhaust, 220 @ 4750; dual exhaust, 235 @ 4750.

TUNE UP SPECIFICATIONS

Year & Engine/ Liter	Spark Plug Gap, Inch	Ignition Timing, °BTDC: Firing Order, Fig.④	Ignition Timing, °BTDC: Degrees	Ignition Timing, °BTDC: Timing Mark, Fig.	Curb Idle Speed, RPM	Fast Idle Speed, RPM	Fuel Pump Pressure, psi	Valve Clearance③
1998								
4.6L SOHC	.054	⑦	10②	⑤	⑥	⑥	35–40①	.0177–.0335
4.6L DOHC	.054	⑦	10②	⑤	⑥	⑥	35–40①	.0315–.0472
1999–2002								
4.6L SOHC	.054	⑦	10②	⑤	⑥	⑥	35–40①	.0177–.0335
4.6L DOHC	.054	⑦	10②	⑤	⑥	⑥	35–40①	.0018–.0033

BTDC — Before Top Dead Center
DOHC — Dual Overhead Cam
SOHC — Single Overhead Cam
① — Wrap shop towel around fuel diagnostic valve to prevent fuel spillage. Connect a suitable fuel pressure gauge to fuel diagnostic valve. Energize fuel pump & note fuel pressure gauge reading.
② — Not adjustable.
③ — With cylinder at top dead center, hold steady pressure on lifter until fully collapsed to measure clearance.
④ — Before disconnecting wires from distributor cap, determine location of No. 1 wire in cap, as distributor position may have been altered from that illustrated at the end of this chart.
⑤ — Equipped w/crankshaft sensor.
⑥ — Idle speeds are controlled by the automatic idle control.
⑦ — 1-3-7-2-6-5-4-8; PCM controls eight separate ignition coils, each coil is mounted directly above its respective spark plug.

FRONT WHEEL ALIGNMENT SPECIFICATIONS

Year	Model	Caster Angle, Degrees: Limits	Caster Angle, Degrees: Desired	Camber Angle, Degrees: Limits	Camber Angle, Degrees: Desired	Total Toe, Degrees: Limits	Total Toe, Degrees: Desired
1998	Continental	+3.40 to +5.40	+4.4	–.40 to +.40	0	–.450 to +.050	–.200
	Mark VIII	+4.75 to +6.25	+5.5	–1.25 to +.25	–.50	0 to +.500	+.250
	Town Car	+5.25 to +6.75	+6.0	–1.25 to +.25	–.50	–.375 to +.125	–.125
1999	Continental	+3.40 to +5.40	+4.4	–.40 to +.40	0	–.450 to +.050	–.200
	Town Car	+5.25 to +6.75	+6.0	–1.25 to +.25	–.50	–.375 to +.125	–.125
2000–02	Continental	+3.40 to +5.40	+4.4	–1.30 to –.10	–.70	–.450 to +.050	–.200
	Town Car	+5.25 to +6.75	+6.0	–1.25 to +.25	–.50	–.375 to +.125	–.125

REAR WHEEL ALIGNMENT SPECIFICATIONS

Year	Model	Camber Angle, Degrees		Total Toe, Inch	
		Limits	Desired	Limits	Desired
1998	Mark VIII	–1 to 0	–.5	–.13 to .37	+.12
1998–2002	Continental	–1.2 to +.2	-.7	-.05 to +.45	+.20

VEHICLE RIDE HEIGHT SPECIFICATIONS

Model	Year	Body Style	Manu-facturer's Original Tire Size	Measurement Points & Specifications②					
				Front			Rear		
				Dim.	Specification		Dim.	Specification	
					Inches	mm		Inches	mm
Continental	1998	All	①	A	8.75	222	B	8.37	213
	1999–2002	All	P225/ 60HR16	E	④	④	G	④	④
Mark VIII	1998	All	①	I	24.5	620	J	24.25	614
Town Car	1998–2002	All	①	E	③	③	G	③	③

A Dim. — Distance from Front Rocker Panel to Ground.
B Dim. — Distance from Rear Rocker Panel to Ground.
E Dim. — Ground to Front Wheel Opening Through Centerline of Wheel.
G Dim. — Ground to Rear Wheel Opening Through Centerline of Wheel.
I Dim. — Bottom of Front Rim to Wheel Opening.
J Dim. — Bottom of Rear Rim to Wheel Opening.

Dim. — Dimension.

N/A — Not Available.

① — See door sticker or inside of glove box for manufacturers original tire size specifications. If tires on vehicle do not match manufacturers original tire size & measurement is not within limits, it will be required to refer to the "Non-Standard Tire & Wheel Size Adjustment To Ride Height Specification & Tire Size Adjustment Charts."

② — Measurement is with fuel, radiator coolant and engine oil full, spare tire, jack, hand tools and mats in designated positions and tires properly inflated.

③ — Ride height side to side should be within 0.50″ (13 mm).

④ — Ride height side to side should be within 0.50″ (13 mm). Ride height front to rear should be with in 0.60″ (14.5 mm).

Dimensions A, B, E & G

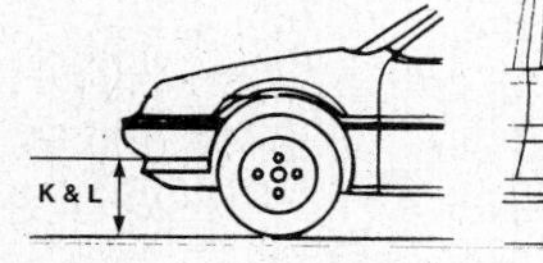

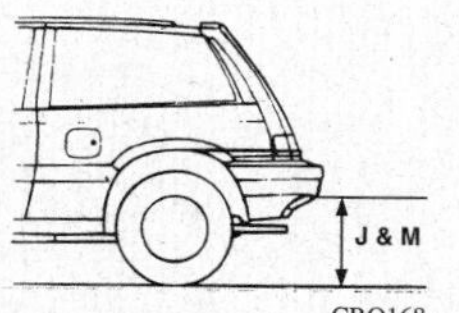

Dimension J

FLUID CAPACITIES & COOLING SYSTEM DATA

Year	Engine	Coolant Capacity, Qts.	Coolant Type	Radiator Cap Relief Pressure, psi	Thermo. Opening Temp., Deg. F	Fuel Tank, Gal.	Engine Oil Refill, Qts.②	Automatic Trans., Qts.②	Rear Axle Oil, Pints④
1998–2000	4.6L SOHC	14	⑥	16	196	③	5①	13.6	3.75
	4.6L DOHC	16	⑥	16	210	18	6①	14.0	3.0
2001–02	4.6L SOHC	15.8	⑥	16	196	20	5①	⑤	3.75
	4.6L DOHC	16	⑥	16	210	20	6①	13.7	—

① — With filter change.
② — Approximate. Make final inspection w/dipstick.
③ — 18–20 gal. depending on vehicle options.
④ — Differential w/tractional, add 4 oz. friction modifier.
⑤ — Except Signature Touring Sedan, 13.9 qts.; Signature Touring Sedan, 12.8 qts.
⑥ — Some vehicle cooling systems are filled with "Motorcraft Premium Engine Coolant VC-4" (in Oregon VC-5) or equivalent meeting Ford specification ESE-M97B44-A **green color.** Others are filled with "Motorcraft Premium Gold Engine Coolant VC-7-A" meeting Ford specification WSS-M97B51–A1 **yellow color.** Always fill cooling system with same coolant that is present in the system. Do not mix coolant types.

LUBRICANT DATA

Year	Lubricant Type			
	Automatic Transmission/ Transaxle	Rear Axle	Power Steering	Brake System
1998–2002	Mercon V	①	Mercon	DOT 3

① — Use premium axle lubricant P/N XY-80W90-QL, or an equivalent meeting Ford specification WSP-M2C197-A. On models equipped with traction lock axles, add four ounces of friction modifier P/N C8AZ-19B546-A, or equivalent meeting Ford specification EST-M2C118-A.

Electrical

NOTE: On Air Bag Equipped Models, Refer To "Air Bag System Precautions" Located In The Front Of This Manual For System Disarming & Arming Procedures.

NOTE: Refer To "Computer Relearn Procedures" Located In The Front Of This Manual When Battery Power To The Computer Has Been Interrupted.

NOTE: Prior To Performing Any Service Operations Listed In This Section, Consult The "Technical Service Bulletins" Section For Related Information.

INDEX

PRECAUTIONS

AIR BAG SYSTEM

Refer to "Air Bag System Precautions" in the front of this manual for system disarming and arming procedures.

BATTERY GROUND CABLE

Prior to service, disconnect battery ground cable and isolate as required.

FUSE PANEL & FLASHER LOCATION

CONTINENTAL

The fuse panel is located under the instrument panel to the lefthand side of the steering column.

The turn signal and hazard flashers are located in and are a component of the Lighting Control Module (LCM) found under the righthand side of the instrument panel.

MARK VIII

The fuse panel is located under the instrument panel to the lefthand side of the steering column.

The turn signal and hazard flashers are located in and are a component of the Lighting Control Module (LCM) found under the lefthand side of the instrument panel.

TOWN CAR

The instrument panel fuse panel is located behind the lefthand side of the instrument panel to the left of the steering column.

The engine compartment power distribution box is located on the rear lefthand side of the engine compartment.

The turn signal and hazard flashers are a component of the Lighting Control Module (LCM), located behind the instrument panel.

RELAY CENTER LOCATION

CONTINENTAL

The relay center, known as the Constant Control Relay Module (CCRM), is located on the radiator support in the lower front center of the engine compartment. The relay center contains the following relays: fuel pump, A/C fan, PCM power and A/C control.

MARK VIII

The relay center, known as the Variable Control Relay Module (VCRM), is located in the lower front center of engine compartment, on the radiator support. The relay center contains the following relays, low speed fuel pump, A/C fan, PCM power and the A/C control relay.

TOWN CAR

The relay center is located on top of the lefthand wheelwell in the engine compartment.

FUEL PUMP RELAY LOCATION

CONTINENTAL

The fuel pump relay is a component of the CCRM. The fuel pump control module is located at the front righthand side of the luggage compartment.

MARK VIII

The low speed fuel pump relay is a component of the VCRM. The high speed fuel pump relay is located in the engine compartment fuse box.

TOWN CAR

The fuel pump relay is located in the power distribution box.

STARTER

REPLACE

When servicing starter or performing any maintenance in the area of starter, note the heavy gauge input lead connected to the starter solenoid is hot at all times. Ensure protective cap is installed over terminal and is replaced after service. When battery has been disconnected and reconnected, some abnormal drive symptoms may occur while the EEC processor relearns its adaptive strategy. The vehicle may need to be driven 10 miles or more to relearn strategy.

1. Raise and support vehicle.
2. **On Continental models,** remove lower air deflector.
3. **On all models,** disconnect starter cable and push-on connector at starter solenoid. **When disconnecting hard shell connector at "S" terminal, pull plastic shell straight out. Do not pull on wire.**
4. Remove starter mounting bolts and the starter. It may be required to turn wheels to left or right to gain clearance for removal.
5. Reverse procedure to install, noting the following:
   a. **Torque** starter mounting bolts to 20–27 ft. lbs.
   b. **On Town Car models,** replace red solenoid cap.

COIL PACK

REPLACE

The PCM controls the eight separate ignition coils. Each coil is mounted directly above its respective spark plug.

1. Remove air cleaner outlet tube.
2. Remove righthand and lefthand spark plug/ignition coil covers.
3. Pull ignition coil wire from spark plug.
4. Disconnect connector from ignition coil.
5. Remove ignition coil from spark plug.
6. Inspect coil for cracks, dirt and carbon fouling.
7. Reverse procedure to install. **Torque** spark plug/ignition coil covers to 89 inch lbs.

IGNITION LOCK

REPLACE

FUNCTIONAL LOCK

MARK VIII

1. Turn lock cylinder key to Run position.
2. Using a 1/8 inch drift, depress lock cylinder retaining pin through access hole and remove lock cylinder, **Note position of bearing retainer prior to removal.**
3. Remove blue plastic bearing retainer by inserting suitable screwdriver with a 90° bend on its tip between bearing retainer and bearing, then prying upward.
4. Insert tip of screwdriver into "double-D" slot of bearing, then rotate 90°, removing bearing.
5. Remove lock drive gear. Note position of lock drive gear relative to rack teeth.
6. Reverse procedure to install. Noting the following:
   a. Position of steering column lock gear is proper if last tooth on drive gear steering column lock gear is meshed with the last tooth on rack.
   b. Position steering column upper bearing retainer in lock cylinder housing and rotate "double-D" slot 90°.
   c. Press blue plastic steering column upper bearing retainer into lock cylinder housing, ensure original position.
   d. Line up flats of steering column lock gear with flats of washer by pulling down on the steering column lock cam.
   e. Install ignition switch assembly.
   f. Inspect for proper starting in Park and Neutral, no start in drive and reverse and locked in lock position.

CONTINENTAL & TOWN CAR

1. Turn ignition lock cylinder to Run position.
2. Press ignition switch lock cylinder release pin while pulling on lock cylinder.
3. Reverse procedure to install.

NON-FUNCTIONAL LOCK

CONTINENTAL & MARK VIII

Removal

1. Using puller tool No. T77F-4220-B1, or equivalent, remove steering wheel.
2. Disconnect key warning switch electrical connector.
3. **On models equipped with ignition switch cap,** use channel–lock or vise–grip type pliers to twist cap from lock cylinder.
4. **On all models,** using a 1/8 inch drill bit, drill out retaining pin. **Do not drill deeper than 1/2 inch.**
5. Place a chisel at base of ignition lock cylinder cap, then strike chisel with sharp blows to break cap away from cylinder.
6. Using a 3/8 inch drill bit, drill down middle of ignition lock key slot 1 3/4 inches until lock cylinder breaks loose from breakaway base of lock cylinder.
7. Remove lock cylinder and drill shavings from lock cylinder housing.
8. Remove retainer, washer, ignition switch and actuator, then clean all drill shavings from casting.
9. Inspect lock cylinder housing and replace if any damage is present.

Installation

1. Install actuator and ignition switch.
2. Install trim and electrical components.
3. Install new ignition lock cylinder.
4. Install steering wheel.
5. Ensure lock operates properly.

TOWN CAR

1. Using puller tool No. T77F-4220-B1, or equivalent, remove steering wheel, then twist cap from ignition switch lock cylinder.
2. Drill out lock cylinder retaining pin with a 1/8 inch drill bit.
3. Drill down middle of ignition key slot with a 3/8 inch drill bit until ignition switch lock cylinder breaks loose.
4. Remove ignition switch lock cylinder, then the bearing retainer from steering column.
5. Remove steering column lock housing bearing and steering column lock gear from steering column.
6. Clean all drill shavings from steering column.
7. Reverse procedure to install.

IGNITION SWITCH

REPLACE

CONTINENTAL

1. Remove lefthand instrument panel steering column opening cover.
2. Remove hood latch release handle mounting bolts, then position handle aside.
3. Remove parking brake handle mounting bolts, then position handle aside.
4. Remove instrument panel steering column opening cover reinforcement.
5. Loosen ignition switch electrical connector bolt, then disconnect the connector.
6. Remove ignition switch mounting screws, then the switch.
7. Reverse procedure to install, noting the following:
   a. **Torque** ignition switch mounting screws to 47–64 inch lbs.
   b. **Torque** ignition switch electrical connector mounting bolt to 7–10 inch lbs.
   c. **Torque** parking brake handle and hood release handle mounting bolts to 24–33 inch lbs.

MARK VIII

1. Remove ignition switch lock cylinder. Refer to "Ignition Lock, Replace."

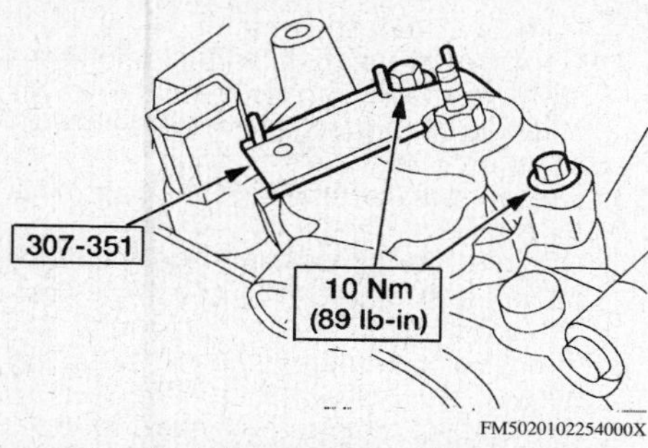

Fig. 1 TR sensor alignment. Continental

2. Remove bolts and instrument panel steering column cover.
3. Position ignition switch cylinder bracket aside by disconnecting electrical connectors and removing bolts.
4. Disconnect ignition/shifter interlock cable.
5. Remove ignition switch cylinder bracket.
6. Remove ignition switch.
7. Reverse procedure to install.

TOWN CAR

1. Remove lefthand instrument panel sound insulator pushpins, then disconnect insulator panel courtesy lamp electrical connector.
2. Remove sound insulator from instrument panel.
3. Remove lower steering column opening cover mounting screws, then the steering column opening cover.
4. Remove instrument panel steering column opening cover reinforcement.
5. Loosen ignition switch electrical connector mounting bolt, then disconnect connector.
6. Ensure ignition switch is in Off position.
7. Remove ignition switch mounting bolts, then the switch.
8. Reverse procedure to install, noting the following:
   a. **Torque** ignition switch mounting bolts to 47–64 inch lbs.
   b. **Torque** electrical connector mounting bolt to 7–10 inch lbs.
   c. **Torque** steering column reinforcement mounting bolts to 31–45 inch lbs.

NEUTRAL SAFETY SWITCH

REPLACE

CONTINENTAL

The Transmission Range (TR) sensor is located on the outside of the transmission. It completes the start circuit in Park or Neutral and the backup lamp circuit in Reverse. The sensor also opens and closes a set of four switches that are monitored by the Powertrain Control Module (PCM) to determine the position of the manual lever (PRND21).

1. Apply parking brake.
2. Place gearshift lever in Neutral, then remove engine air cleaner.
3. Disconnect TR sensor electrical connector.
4. Remove manual control lever to manual shaft mounting nut, then the manual control lever from transaxle.
5. Remove TR sensor mounting bolts, then the sensor.
6. Reverse procedure to install, adjusting sensor as follows:
   a. Loosely install TR sensor mounting bolts.
   b. Ensure manual shift lever is in Neutral position.
   c. Align TR sensor using TR sensor alignment tool No. T97L-70010-A (307-351) or equivalent, **Fig. 1**, then **torque** mounting bolts to 89 inch lbs.

MARK VIII & TOWN CAR

The Transmission Range (TR) sensor is located on the outside of the transmission. It completes the start circuit in Park or Neutral and the backup lamp circuit in reverse. The sensor also opens and closes a set of four switches that are monitored by the Powertrain Control Module (PCM) to determine the position of the manual lever (PRND21).

1. Turn air suspension switch off, then raise and support vehicle.
2. Disconnect TR sensor electrical connector.
3. Disconnect transmission shift linkage.
4. Remove TR sensor mounting bolts, then the sensor.
5. Reverse procedure to install, adjusting sensor as follows:
   a. Install TR sensor mounting bolts loosely.
   b. Ensure manual shift lever is in the Neutral position.
   c. Align TR sensor slots with TR sensor alignment tool No. T97L-70010-A, or equivalent, **Fig. 2.**
   d. **Torque** mounting bolts to 62–88 inch lbs.

HEADLAMP SWITCH

REPLACE

CONTINENTAL

Uploading module configuration information to the scan tool is required prior to removing the Lighting Control Module (LCM). This information needs to be downloaded into the new module after installation.

1. Remove instrument panel steering column opening cover.
2. Remove LCM to instrument panel mounting screws.
3. Pull LCM from instrument panel, then disconnect electrical connectors.
4. Reverse procedure to install. Use Worldwide Diagnostic System (WDS) 418-F224 New Generation STAR (NGS) tester tool No. 418-F052, or an equivalent scan tool to download module configuration information to the new LCM.

MARK VIII

1. Remove headlamp switch knob by pulling it off.

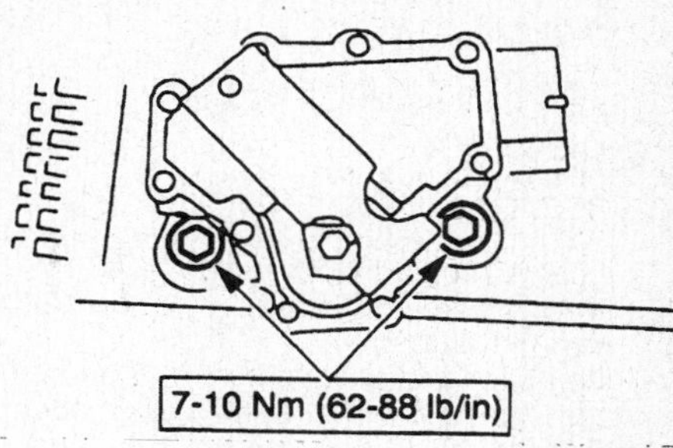

Fig. 2 TR sensor alignment. Mark VIII & Town Car

2. Remove lamp switch knob applique by pulling at lefthand end to unsnap it from the finish panel and twist out bulb socket.
3. Remove two screws mounting lefthand end of finish panel to the instrument panel.
4. Remove two screws at top of cluster opening mounting finish panel to the instrument panel.
5. Remove upper steering column cover by pulling up on forward edge to unsnap four snap-in tabs.
6. Pull lefthand end of finish panel rearward far enough to disconnect two wiring connectors.
7. Remove two screws mounting switch to center finish panel.
8. Reverse procedure to install.

TOWN CAR

1. Pull radio out from instrument cluster finish panel with radio removal tool No. T87P-19061-A, or equivalent.
2. Disconnect radio electrical connectors and antenna cable, then remove radio.
3. Remove instrument cluster finish panel mounting screws and pull cluster finish panel rearward.
4. Disconnect clock, headlamp switch and dimmer switch electrical connectors.
5. Remove instrument cluster finish panel and position aside.
6. Remove headlamp switch mounting screws, then the headlamp switch.
7. Reverse procedure to install.

STOP LIGHT SWITCH

REPLACE

CONTINENTAL & MARK VIII

1. Disconnect wires at switch connector.
2. Remove hair pin retainer, then slide switch, pushrod and nylon washers and bushing away from brake pedal and remove switch, **Fig. 3.**
3. Reverse procedure to install.

TOWN CAR

1. Remove lower insulator panel from lefthand side of instrument panel.
2. Disconnect courtesy lamp from lower insulator panel.
3. Disconnect Brake Pedal Position (BPP) switch electrical connector.
4. Remove cotter pin, sleeve and BPP switch.

5. Reverse procedure to install.

MULTI-FUNCTION SWITCH

REPLACE

1. Remove ignition lock cylinder.
2. Place tilt column in lowest position and remove tilt lever.
3. Remove column shroud mounting screws, then the upper and lower shrouds.
4. Remove wiring harness retainer, then disconnect electrical connectors.
5. Remove multi-function switch to steering column mounting screws, then the multi-function switch.
6. Reverse procedure to install.

STEERING WHEEL

REPLACE

1. Ensure front wheels are in straight-ahead position.
2. Disconnect back-up power supply and remove air bag module as outlined in "Passive Restraint Systems."
3. Disconnect speed control wiring harness from steering wheel.
4. Remove and discard steering wheel mounting bolt.
5. Using steering wheel puller tool No. T67L-3600-A, or equivalent, remove steering wheel.
6. Reverse procedure to install, noting the following:
   a. Ensure all electrical connectors and wiring are properly routed to avoid pinching.
   b. Install new steering wheel bolt.
   c. **On 1998–2000 models, torque** steering wheel bolt to 33 ft. lbs.
   d. **On 2001–02 models, torque** steering wheel bolt to 30 ft. lbs.

INSTRUMENT CLUSTER

REPLACE

CONTINENTAL

1. Remove lefthand instrument panel insulator.
2. Remove courtesy lamp.
3. Remove instrument panel lower cover.
4. Remove hood release handle mounting screws, then position the handle aside.
5. Remove parking brake handle mounting screws, then position the handle aside.
6. Remove steering column opening cover reinforcement.
7. Remove steering column shroud attaching screws, then the shrouds.
8. Disconnect electrical connectors and wiring as required in preparation for lowering the steering column.
9. Remove steering column mounting nuts, then lower the column to floor.
10. Remove instrument panel finish panel.
11. Remove instrument cluster finish panel.
12. Disconnect electrical connectors at clock and message center.
13. Carefully pull instrument cluster out of instrument panel, then disconnect transaxle range indicator, if equipped.
14. Reverse procedure to install, noting the following:
    a. Ensure all electrical connectors and wiring are properly routed to avoid pinching.
    b. **Torque** steering column mounting nuts to 10–12 ft. lbs.
    c. **Torque** steering column impact absorber nuts to 10–14 ft. lbs.
    d. When replacing instrument cluster, it will be required to cycle ignition to Run using two encoded ignition keys. Clear all DTCs. Test system for normal operation.
    e. Passive Anti-Theft System (PATS) must be configured after instrument cluster has been replaced. For additional reprogramming information, refer to HELP Screen on NGS Tester configuration card.

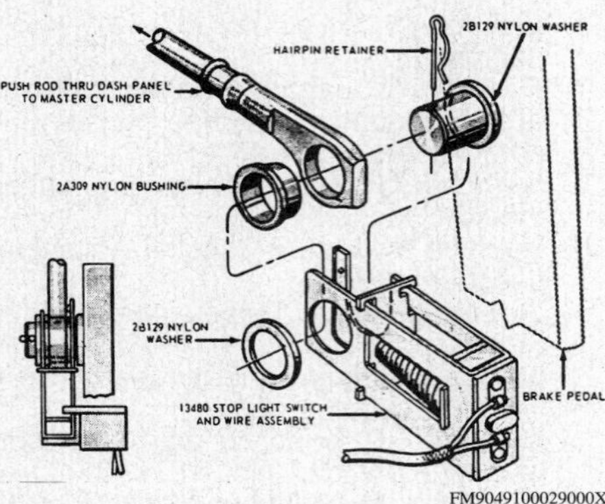

Fig. 3 Stop lamp switch. Continental, Mark VIII

MARK VIII

1. Remove instrument panel finish panel.
2. Remove four cluster to finish panel mounting screws. Do not remove screws securing lens and mask to backplate.
3. Rotate cluster face down and disconnect instrument cluster connector.
4. Slide cluster to right of instrument panel opening and unhook instrument panel harness from hook on back of instrument cluster.
5. Remove cluster assembly from panel.
6. Reverse procedure to install.

TOWN CAR

1. Pull radio out from instrument cluster finish panel with radio removal tool No. T87P-19061-A, or equivalent.
2. Disconnect radio electrical connectors and antenna cable, then remove radio.
3. Remove instrument cluster finish panel mounting screws and pull cluster finish panel rearward.
4. Disconnect clock, headlamp switch and dimmer switch electrical connectors.
5. Remove instrument cluster finish panel and position aside.
6. Remove lower steering column cover mounting bolts.
7. Position parking brake release aside.
8. Remove lower steering column cover from instrument panel.
9. Remove steering column reinforcement mounting bolts, then the lower steering column reinforcement from instrument panel.
10. Disconnect transmission range indicator cable.
11. Remove transmission range indicator cable bracket mounting bolt, then position cable aside.
12. Remove instrument cluster mounting screws and pull cluster rearward.
13. Disconnect cluster electrical connectors, then remove cluster from instrument panel.
14. Reverse procedure to install, noting the following:
    a. When replacing instrument cluster, it will be required to cycle ignition to Run using two encoded ignition keys. Clear all DTCs. Test system for normal operation.
    b. Passive Anti-Theft System (PATS) must be configured after instrument cluster has been replaced. For additional reprogramming information, refer to HELP Screen on NGS Tester configuration card.

RADIO

REPLACE

1. Remove instrument panel trim and insulation panels as required to access radio mounting fasteners and electrical connectors.
2. **On Town Car models,** proceed as follows:
   a. Install radio removal tool No. T87P-19061-A, or equivalent, into radio face plate.
   b. Push tool in approximately one inch to release retaining clips.
   c. Apply a light spreading force on tools and slowly pull radio from instrument panel.
3. **On all models,** disconnect wiring connectors and antenna cable.
4. Reverse procedure to install.

WIPER MOTOR

REPLACE

CONTINENTAL

1. Remove the wiper pivot arm cap and nut, then the arm.
2. Remove cowl top vent panels.
3. Disconnect wiper motor electrical connector.
4. Remove mounting arm and pivot shaft assembly bolts, then the arm and shaft assembly.
5. Remove wiper motor crank bolt, then disconnect the crank.
6. Remove wiper motor mounting bolts, then the motor.
7. Reverse procedure to install, noting the following:
   a. **Torque** motor mounting bolts to 10–13 ft. lbs.
   b. **Torque** motor crank bolt to 12–16 ft. lbs.
   c. **Torque** mounting arm and pivot shaft assembly bolts to 79–106 inch lbs.

MARK VIII

1. Turn ignition On.
2. Turn on windshield wipers and cycle to mid-wipe position, then turn ignition Off.
3. Remove lefthand and righthand wiper arms.
4. Remove cowl top to hood seal.
5. Remove lefthand and righthand cowl vent screens.
6. Remove four mounting screws and washers, then the cowl top extension.
7. Disconnect two wiring connectors from motor.
8. Remove mounting bolts and washer assemblies from wiper module.
9. Lift module slightly to disengage support bracket from dash panel mounting stud. Move module sideways approximately two inches toward passenger side and remove module from vehicle.
10. Disconnect linkage drive arm from motor crankpin after removing clip.
11. Remove wiper motor's three mounting screws and remove motor from module.
12. Reverse procedure to install. **Cycle motor and turn off wiper switch to ensure wiper linkage is in park position before installing blade and arm assemblies to pivot shafts.**

TOWN CAR

1. Remove windshield wiper pivot arm mounting nuts.
2. Remove wiper pivot arms from pivot shafts.
3. Remove cowl top vent panels.
4. Remove wiper mounting arm and pivot shaft assembly mounting nuts and bolt.
5. Position wiper mounting arm and pivot shaft assembly aside and disconnect electrical connector.
6. Remove wiper motor output shaft bolt.
7. Remove wiper motor mounting bolts, then the wiper motor.
8. Reverse procedure to install, noting the following:
   a. **Torque** wiper motor mounting bolts to 72–89 inch lbs.
   b. **Torque** wiper motor output shaft bolt to 10–12 ft. lbs.

WIPER SWITCH

REPLACE

Refer to "Multi-Function Switch, Replace" for replacement procedure.

BLOWER MOTOR

REPLACE

CONTINENTAL

1. Remove instrument panel insulator fasteners.
2. Disconnect courtesy lamp and remove insulator.
3. Remove righthand scuff plate.
4. Remove instrument panel upper finish panel and disconnect A/C sunload sensor wire harness connector.
5. Remove screws retaining righthand and center instrument panel to dash panel.
6. Remove righthand instrument panel to cowl retaining nut.
7. Disconnect blower motor electrical connector.
8. Remove blower motor mounting screws, then the motor.
9. Reverse procedure to install. **Torque** righthand instrument panel to cowl retaining nut to 89–123 inch lbs., and blower motor to 18–26 ft. lbs.

MARK VIII

1. Lower glove compartment door to gain access to rear of evaporator case.
2. Disconnect blower motor electrical connector.
3. Remove A/C evaporator air control venturi and in-vehicle temperature sensor aspirator hose.
4. Remove pulse width modulator (blower motor speed controller).
5. Remove screw and pull blower motor assembly out of blower motor housing.
6. Pull push nut off blower motor shaft and remove blower wheel from shaft.
7. Reverse procedure to install.

TOWN CAR

1. Remove windshield washer fluid reservoir mounting nut, then position reservoir aside.
2. Remove righthand fender apron mounting screws and position apron aside.
3. Disengage wire harness connector from retainer, then disconnect blower motor electrical connector.
4. Disconnect rubber hose from blower motor.
5. Remove blower motor mounting screws, then the motor.
6. Reverse procedure to install.

HEATER CORE

REPLACE

CONTINENTAL

1. Remove instrument panel as outlined under "Dash Panel Service."
2. Drain coolant into an approved container until level is below that of heater core.
3. Disconnect powertrain control module (PCM) electrical connector.
4. Disconnect hoses at heater core.
5. Remove metal cover retaining screws, then the cover.
6. Remove A/C electronic blend door actuator.
7. Remove A/C air intake flue damper assist spring.
8. Depress locking ramp, then remove A/C damper door shaft from air temperature control door shaft. **Do not attempt to bend A/C damper door shaft . This is brittle and will break.**
9. Remove A/C evaporator case outlet door shaft. **Do not attempt to bend lever. This is brittle and will break.**
10. Remove heater core cover screws, then the cover.
11. Remove heater core cover seal.
12. Remove heater core.
13. Reverse procedure to install, **torque** mounting screws to 18–26 inch lbs.

MARK VIII

1. Drain radiator coolant into an approved container.
2. Remove instrument panel as outlined under "Dash Panel Service."
3. Remove seal from heater core tubes.
4. Remove A/C electronic door actuator motor, three screws, from A/C evaporator housing.
5. Remove heater core cover and seal from A/C evaporator housing.
6. Disconnect heater hoses from heater tubes.
7. Carefully pull evaporator assembly away from dash panel and remove evaporator case from vehicle.
8. Reverse procedure to install.

TOWN CAR

1998–2000

1. Position driver seat as far back as possible, then remove seat track covers.
2. Remove mounting bolts from front of seat.
3. Move seat forward as far as possible and remove seat track covers.
4. Remove mounting nuts from rear of seat.
5. Disconnect seat electrical connectors, then remove driver seat from vehicle.
6. Position passenger front seat as far back as possible, then remove seat track covers.
7. Remove mounting bolts from front of seat.
8. Move seat as far forward as possible and remove seat track covers.
9. Remove mounting nuts from rear of seat.
10. Disconnect seat electrical connectors, then remove passenger front seat from vehicle.
11. Remove front center seat.
12. Remove carpet from front floor.
13. Remove rear seat airflow duct push-pin, then the rear seat airflow duct.
14. Remove instrument panel as outlined in "Dash Panel Service."
15. Drain coolant from radiator until level is below heater core.
16. Remove windshield wiper mounting arm and pivot shaft as outlined previously.
17. Remove cowl top extension mounting nut.
18. Disconnect wiper motor electrical connector, then remove cowl top extension.
19. Disconnect vacuum hoses and electrical connector from evaporative emissions canister purge valve.
20. Remove evaporative emissions canister purge valve mounting nuts, then the valve.
21. Disconnect heater water hoses from heater core.
22. Remove plenum chamber mounting nut from cowl.

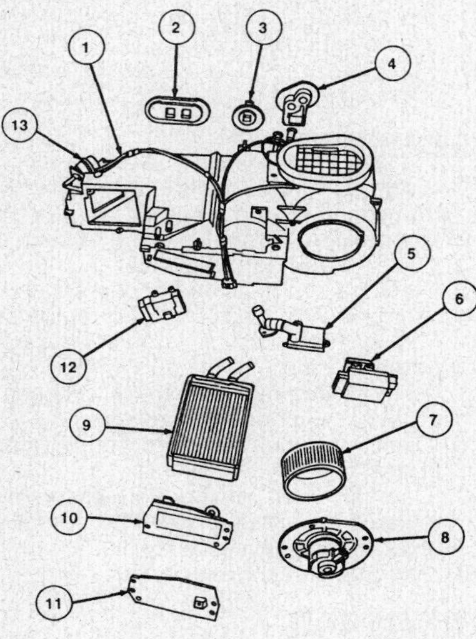

Item	Description
1	Evaporator Case Assy
2	Heater Core Tube Seal to Dash
3	Seal
4	A/C Evaporator Tube Seal
5	Muffler Assy
6	Pulse Width Modulator Assy (Blower Motor Speed Controller)
7	Wheel
8	Blower Motor Assy
9	Heater Core Assy
10	Heater Core Cover Seal
11	Heater Core Access Cover
12	Blend Door Actuator Motor Assy
13	Vacuum Motor Assy

FM7029100053000A

Fig. 4 Exploded view of evaporator case. Mark VIII

23. Remove windshield washer fluid reservoir mounting nut, then position reservoir aside.
24. Remove righthand fender apron mounting screws, then position apron aside.
25. Remove A/C evaporative core housing mounting nut and bolt.
26. Disconnect vacuum hoses and electrical connectors from plenum chamber.
27. Remove mounting nuts from plenum chamber lower flange.
28. Remove mounting nut from plenum chamber upper flange, then the plenum chamber from instrument panel carrier.
29. Remove heater core cover mounting screws.
30. Remove heater core cover and seal from plenum chamber.
31. Remove heater core from plenum chamber.
32. Reverse procedure to install.

2001–02

1. Remove instrument panel as outlined under "Dash Panel Service."
2. Drain coolant into an approved container until level is below that of heater core.
3. Remove windshield wiper arms.
4. Remove cowl top cover.
5. Remove fresh air inlet duct.
6. Remove windshield wiper mounting arm and pivot shaft with cowl extension as an assembly.
7. Disconnect heater hoses at heater core.
8. Remove nut at cowl side stud.
9. Remove screw and nut from evaporator core housing.
10. Disconnect all required vacuum hoses and electrical connectors.
11. Position carpet back from plenum chamber.
12. Cut each side of rear footwell duct and bend duct back. **Do not cut too much of duct. Ensure to cut only to the point of allowing heater floor duct to be removed with plenum chamber as an assembly.**
13. Remove nuts from plenum chamber lower flange.
14. Remove nut from plenum chamber upper flange, then remove chamber.
15. Remove heater core cover screws, then the cover.
16. Remove heater core cover seal, then the core.
17. Reverse procedure to install, noting the following:
    a. Ensure to sufficiently seal rear footwell duct to heater outlet floor duct.
    b. Close rear footwell duct around heater outlet floor duct, install a suitable tie strap, then position back the carpet.

EVAPORATOR CORE

REPLACE

CONTINENTAL

On 1999–2002 models, the evaporator core is serviced as a core and housing assembly. The core, internal doors, seals and door linkage arrive with the housing. The blower motor and wheel assembly, heater core and cover, dash panel seals and vacuum actuators will all require transferal to the new housing.

1. Remove seats from vehicle.
2. Remove rear seat airflow duct.
3. Remove instrument panel as outlined in "Dash Panel Service."
4. Drain coolant into an approved container until level is below that of heater core.
5. Recover refrigerant as outlined in "Air Conditioning" section.
6. Disconnect PCM electrical connector.
7. Disconnect heater hoses at heater core.
8. Disconnect vacuum supply hose.
9. Disconnect condenser to evaporator tube and evaporator to accumulator tube spring lock couplings from evaporator core.
10. Disconnect evaporator housing electrical connectors.
11. Remove nuts and washers at cowl panel.
12. Remove evaporator housing mounting screws.

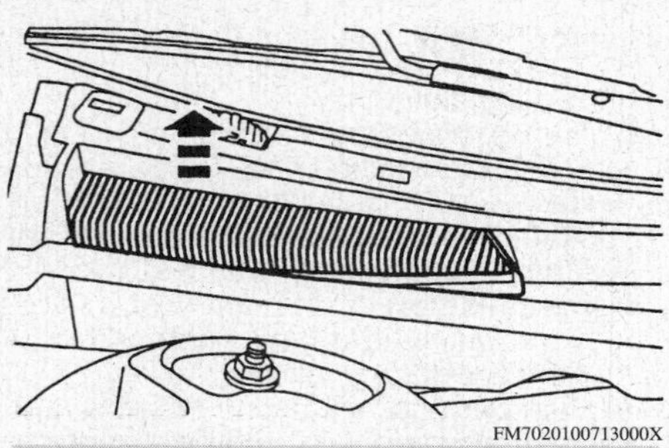

Fig. 5 Cabin air filter removal

13. Remove metal cover mounting screws, then the cover.
14. Remove screws and A/C electronic blend door actuator.
15. Remove A/C air intake flue damper assist spring.
16. Depress locking ramp and remove A/C damper door shaft from air temperature control door shaft. **Do not attempt to bend A/C damper door shaft. This is brittle and will break.**
17. Remove the A/C evaporator case outlet door shaft. **Do not attempt to bend lever. This is brittle and will break.**
18. Remove A/C tube dash panel seal and evaporator drain tube seal.
19. Remove 15 screws and evaporator housing cover.
20. Remove evaporator core.
21. Reverse procedure to install, noting the following:
    a. Lubricate replacement evaporator core with proper amount of PAG refrigerant oil.
    b. Fill cooling system with proper coolant.
    c. Charge A/C refrigerant system.

MARK VIII

1. Remove instrument panel.
2. Remove seal from heater core tubes, **Fig. 4.**
3. Remove blend door actuator to evaporator case mounting screws.
4. Remove actuator from case.
5. Remove access cover and seal from evaporator case.
6. Drain coolant from radiator and disconnect heater hoses from heater core, as required.
7. Pull heater core and seals from evaporator case.
8. Reverse procedure to install. Fill radiator with specified coolant and inspect system operation.

TOWN CAR

On 2001–02 models, the evaporator core is not available separately. It is serviced only with the evaporator core housing assembly. Transferring the components from the old evaporator core housing to the new one will be required.

1. Recover refrigerant as outlined in "Air Conditioning" section.
2. Drain coolant into an approved container.
3. Remove screws and righthand cowl vent screen.

4. Disconnect vacuum hoses and electrical connector from EVAP canister purge valve.
5. Remove EVAP canister purge valve.
6. Remove heater hoses from heater core.
7. Remove windshield washer fluid reservoir mounting screw, then position reservoir aside.
8. Disengage four wire harness retainers from top of righthand fender apron.
9. Remove righthand front wheel and tire.
10. Remove righthand front fender apron.
11. Disconnect electrical connectors from A/C cycling switch and blower motor.
12. Disconnect evaporator to compressor suction line from suction accumulator/dryer.
13. Disconnect suction accumulator/dryer from evaporator core.
14. Remove accumulator mounting bracket to evaporator core housing screw, then the suction accumulator/dryer.
15. Disconnect condenser to evaporator tube from evaporator core.
16. Remove righthand instrument panel insulator.
17. Remove in-vehicle temperature sensor hose and elbow from evaporator housing.
18. Remove nuts at top and bottom of evaporator housing.
19. Remove screws and nut near blower motor.
20. Separate housing portions, then remove blower motor and evaporator core.
21. Disconnect electrical connector.
22. Remove evaporator core cover.
23. Reverse procedure to install, noting the following:
    a. Lubricate A/C O-ring seals with PAG refrigerant compressor oil P/N F7AZ-19589-DA (Motorcraft YN-12-C), or an equivalent meeting Ford specification WSH-M1C231-B.
    b. Evacuate and recharge refrigerant system.
    c. Fill cooling system with proper coolant.

CABIN AIR FILTER

REPLACE

Under normal operating conditions, cabin air filter should be replaced every 15,000 miles. Under severe operating conditions replace, cabin air filter should be replaced every 12,000 miles. In dusty areas, change cabin air filter as required.

1. Open hood.
2. Pull the hood pad away from righthand cowl vent screen.
3. Remove righthand cowl vent screen.
4. Remove water shield.
5. Remove cabin air filter element from filter housing, **Fig. 5.**
6. Reverse procedure to install.

TECHNICAL SERVICE BULLETINS

INSTRUMENT CLUSTER WARNING LIGHTS LIT DIMLY

Continental

On some of these models the instrument cluster warning light(s) may be dimly lit.

This condition may be caused by the ignition switch. To correct this condition, replace ignition switch.

4.6L Engine

NOTE: On Air Bag Equipped Models, Refer To "Air Bag System Precautions" Located In The Front Of This Manual For System Disarming & Arming Procedures.

NOTE: Refer To "Computer Relearn Procedures" Located In The Front Of This Manual When Battery Power To The Computer Has Been Interrupted.

INDEX

PRECAUTIONS

AIR BAG SYSTEMS

Refer to "Air Bag System Precautions" in the front of this manual for system disarming and arming procedures.

BATTERY GROUND CABLE

Prior to service, disconnect battery ground cable and isolate as required.

FUEL SYSTEM PRESSURE RELIEF

Fuel supply lines will remain pressurized after the engine is shutoff. Pressure must be relieved prior to any fuel system servicing. Relieve fuel system pressure as follows:

1. Remove fuel tank cap.
2. Attach fuel pressure gauge tool No. T80L-9974-B, or equivalent to fuel rail pressure relief Schrader valve.
3. Place tool outlet hose in an approved container.
4. Slowly open valve of tool to relieve pressure.

COMPRESSION PRESSURE

The compression in the cylinder with the lowest reading should fall within 75% of that of the highest reading cylinder.

ENGINE MOUNT

REPLACE

CONTINENTAL

1998

Engine Mount

1. Turn off air suspension. Switch is located in trunk under flap of compartment trim.
2. Raise and safely support vehicle.
3. Position a suitable jack and wood block under engine.
4. Remove nut mounting mounts to subframe.
5. Raise engine only sufficiently to allow mount removal. **Do not raise engine excessively or separation of inner CV joints may occur. If required, remove driveshafts as outlined under "Front Wheel Drive Axles."**
6. Remove mount to engine support bracket bolts, then the mount.
7. Reverse procedures to install. Tighten to specifications.

Transaxle Mount

1. Turn off air suspension. Switch is located in trunk under flap of compartment trim.
2. Raise and support vehicle, then remove lefthand front wheel assembly.
3. Place a suitable transmission jack under transaxle.
4. Raise jack sufficiently to take load off transaxle mount.
5. Remove nut and bolts mounting mount to subframe and transaxle.
6. Raise transaxle only sufficiently to allow mount removal. **Do not raise transaxle excessively or separation of inner CV joints may occur. If required, remove driveshafts as outlined under "Front Wheel Drive Axles."**
7. Remove bolts mounting support bracket to transaxle.
8. Remove mount by rotating counterclockwise.

9. Reverse procedures to install. Tighten to specifications.

1999–2002

Engine Mount

1. Turn off air suspension system.
2. Raise and safely support vehicle.
3. Drain coolant into an approved container.
4. Disconnect lower radiator hose at coolant inlet.
5. Lower the vehicle.
6. Disconnect upper radiator hose at coolant outlet.
7. Remove PCV valve from valve cover.
8. Disconnect main vacuum supply tube.
9. Remove radiator upper sight shield.
10. Remove windshield wiper mounting arm and pivot shaft.
11. Remove nut and position engine control sensor wiring aside.
12. Disconnect heater hose at tube.
13. Disconnect PCM electrical connector.
14. Disconnect ground wires as required.
15. Install lefthand engine lifting bracket from 3-bar engine support set tool No. 303-290-A, or equivalent on righthand (rear) side of engine.
16. Install righthand engine lifting bracket on lefthand (front) side of engine.
17. Raise and safely support vehicle.
18. **If replacing righthand engine mount,** remove righthand front wheel and tire.
19. Remove radiator air deflector.
20. **If replacing lefthand engine mount,** remove oil filter.
21. Remove engine support insulator bolts and nut, then the insulator.
22. Remove engine support insulator bracket bolts, then the bracket.
23. Reverse procedure to install, noting the following:
    a. Apply threadlock P/N 262 E2FZ-19554-B, or an equivalent meeting Ford specification WSK-M2G351-A6, to fasteners for engine mount, support and insulator.
    b. Tighten all fasteners to specifications.

Transaxle Mount

1. Turn off air suspension system.
2. Remove lefthand front wheel and tire.
3. Remove lefthand front fender splash shield and position aside.
4. Position a suitable transaxle jack under the transaxle.
5. Remove transaxle upper support insulator nut.
6. Remove transaxle upper support bracket bolts and bracket.
7. Remove transaxle upper support insulator bolts and insulator.
8. Reverse procedure to install. Tighten all fasteners to specifications.

MARK VIII

ENGINE MOUNTS

All self locking or Loctite coated type fasteners must be replaced with new self locking fasteners. All residual locking compound must be removed from tapped holes before new bolts are installed.

Removal

1. Remove engine appearance cover, then air cleaner outlet tube.
2. Install suitable lifting eyes to engine, then install suitable engine support frame and lift engine sufficiently to relieve tension on mounts. **Do not lift engine too high as lines and wiring may be damaged.**
3. Raise and support vehicle, then remove front wheel assemblies.
4. Remove motor mount though bolts.
5. Prepare subframe for lowering by disconnecting all engine wiring and equipment clipped or attached to it.
6. Mark steering shaft coupling for later alignment, then disconnect at pinch bolt.
7. Support front suspension lower control arms with suitable jacks.
8. Disconnect lower control arms from shock strut, then lower jacks to allow control arms to hang freely.
9. Place suitable jacks under subframe, positioned to allow subframe to be lowered and motor mounts to be accessed.
10. Remove subframe mounting bolts, then lower subframe.
11. Remove mounting bolts of mount(s) to be replaced, then the mount.

Installation

1. Place new motor mount(s) into position and loosely install engine to motor mount mounting bolts.
2. Position sub frame to body with jacks, loosely install bolts, then align subframe as follows:
    a. With subframe in loose contact with body, place two alignment pins made from suitable ¾ inch OD diameter tubing or pipe through holes in subframe and into holes in body.
    b. Tighten one bolt in each corner of subframe, remove alignment pins.
    c. Tighten subframe mounting bolts to specification, then tighten motor mount bolts to specifications.
3. Using suitable jacks, position lower control arms into shock struts, then install lower shock strut bolts and tighten to specifications.
4. Align and install steering coupling, then tighten pinch bolt to specifications.
5. Attach all wiring lines and hoses to subframe using suitable clips and fasteners.
6. Install motor mount to subframe through bolts, then tighten to specifications.
7. Install wheel assemblies, lower vehicle, then tighten lug bolts to specifications.
8. Remove engine support frame and lifting eyes.
9. Install air cleaner outlet tube, engine appearance cover and battery ground cable.
10. Inspect and adjust front wheel alignment.

TRANSMISSION MOUNT

1. Raise and support vehicle.
2. Support transmission using a suitable jack.
3. Remove and/or lower exhaust components as required to allow removal of transmission crossmember.
4. Remove bolts mounting mount to transmission and crossmember.
5. Remove bolts mounting crossmember to body, then remove crossmember and mount
6. Reverse procedure to install. Tighten to specifications.

TOWN CAR

Righthand Mount

1. Remove starter motor as outlined under "Electrical" section.
2. Using a suitable lifting device, support engine.
3. Remove three righthand engine mount mounting bolts.
4. Remove righthand engine mount.
5. Reverse procedure to install. Tighten all fasteners to specifications.

Lefthand Mount

1. Remove oil dipstick tube.
2. Using a suitable lifting device, support engine.
3. Remove three lefthand engine mount mounting bolts.
4. Remove lefthand engine mount.
5. Reverse procedure to install. Tighten all fasteners to specifications.

ENGINE

REPLACE

CONTINENTAL

On these models, the engine will be separated from the transaxle during removal.

1. Drain coolant into an approved container.
2. Turn air suspension system off.
3. Remove lefthand dash closeout panel, then disconnect courtesy lamp.
4. Remove steering column boot.
5. Place matchmarks to ensure proper assembly, then remove steering column coupler pinch bolt and disconnect steering column from steering gear.
6. Remove air cleaner outlet tube.
7. Remove bolt and position roll restrictor aside.
8. Raise and safely support vehicle.
9. Lower the vehicle, then recover A/C system as outlined under "Air Conditioning."
10. Relieve fuel system pressure as outlined in "Precautions," then disconnect fuel line.
11. Disconnect main chassis vacuum supply hose.
12. Disconnect PCM ground straps.
13. Disconnect engine control sensor wiring from PCM.
14. Remove nut retaining engine control sensor wiring to righthand valve cover.

15. Disconnect engine control sensor wiring from main engine wiring harness, MAF sensor and TP sensor.
16. Remove accelerator cable snow shield.
17. Disconnect accelerator and speed control actuator cables from throttle body.
18. Remove bolts and accelerator cable bracket and position it aside.
19. Disconnect manual control cable from transaxle shift selector.
20. Disconnect engine control sensor wiring from three main engine compartment wiring harness connectors.
21. Remove bolt from retaining bracket and position main engine compartment harness aside.
22. Disconnect EVAP return line.
23. Disconnect transaxle cooler inlet and outlet tubes.
24. Remove engine oil dipstick.
25. Disconnect heater hoses from water bypass tube and engine connections as required.
26. Disconnect power steering return hose and allow fluid to drain into an approved container.
27. Remove nut and bolt and position alternator battery lead aside.
28. Raise vehicle on a suitable hoist, as required.
29. Remove front wheels and tires, then fully raise vehicle.
30. Disconnect and remove righthand and lefthand height sensor links.
31. Separate righthand and lefthand tie rod ends from front wheel knuckles.
32. Separate righthand and lefthand halfshafts from front wheel knuckles.
33. Remove radiator lower air deflector.
34. Remove dual converter Y-pipe.
35. Disconnect power steering cooler line and allow fluid to drain into an approved container.
36. Disconnect refrigerant lines from A/C compressor.
37. Disconnect lower radiator hose and bypass hose.
38. Disconnect starter motor wiring and electrical connectors.
39. Remove inspection cover.
40. Mark torque converter and flexplate for proper alignment at installation, then remove four nuts.
41. Support front subframe with a suitable powertrain jack and universal powertrain removal bracket.
42. Remove four subframe mounting bolts, then lower the subframe.
43. Install spreader bar set tool No. D93P-6001-A3 (303-D089), or equivalent.
44. Support engine and transaxle with spreader bar and suitable floor crane.
45. Disconnect electrical connector from EVO sensor.
46. Disconnect power steering return hose from the steering gear and allow fluid to drain into an approved container.
47. Disconnect turbine shaft speed sensor, transaxle range (TR) sensor and internal transmission wiring harness electrical connectors.
48. Disconnect engine righthand support insulator.
49. Remove all bellhousing to engine block bolts.
50. Remove engine righthand support insulator bracket.
51. Separate engine from transaxle.
52. Carefully remove engine from vehicle.
53. Reverse procedure to install, noting the following:
    a. Ensure torque converter to flexplate marks are properly aligned.
    b. Apply threadlock P/N 262 E2FZ-19554-B, or an equivalent meeting Ford specification WSK-M2G351-A6, to fasteners for engine mount, support and insulator.
    c. Install new castle nuts at tie rod ends.
    d. Ensure matchmarks at steering column to steering gear are properly aligned.
    e. Tighten all fasteners to specifications.

MARK VIII

1. Remove battery and air cleaner outlet tube.
2. Drain engine cooling system into a suitable container.
3. Remove windshield wiper.
4. Recover A/C system refrigerant as outlined under "Air Conditioning."
5. Disconnect secondary air injection valve inlet tube from secondary air injection pump outlet hose.
6. Remove fan motor.
7. Relieve fuel system pressure as outlined under "Precautions."
8. Disconnect 42-pin connector at rear of lefthand valve cover.
9. Position power distribution box out of way.
10. Disconnect alternator wires from power distribution box.
11. Disconnect headlamp dash panel junction wire and alternator wire connectors.
12. Remove accelerator and cruise control cables.
13. Disconnect evaporative emission hose at upper intake manifold.
14. Disconnect chassis vacuum supply hose.
15. Disconnect heater water hose and heater water hose behind righthand cylinder head.
16. Remove alternator mounting bracket.
17. Remove upper radiator hose and water bypass hose from water outlet tube.
18. Disconnect radiator overflow hose.
19. Remove power steering pressure line from bracket, then the pressure and return hoses.
20. Disconnect transmission cooling tubes and lower radiator hose from radiator.
21. Remove A/C compressor lines.
22. Raise and support vehicle, then remove front tires.
23. Disconnect righthand and lefthand air suspension height sensor connectors.
24. Remove stabilizer bar link from front stabilizer bar.
25. Disconnect righthand and lefthand tie rod ends.
26. Disconnect righthand and lefthand lower front wheel spindles.
27. Disconnect righthand and lefthand front spring and shock from front suspension lower arm strut.
28. Remove dual converter Y-pipe, then the starter motor.
29. Remove steering coupling at pinch bolt joint.
30. Remove ground strap from righthand fender apron.
31. Mark rear driveshaft yoke and axle flange so they may be installed in original positions.
32. Remove four bolts from rear axle universal joint flange to driveshaft centering socket yoke.
33. Disconnect nuts and position rear driveshaft aside.
34. Remove lefthand front shock absorber strut cover cup.
35. Disconnect neutral switch wiring connectors near lefthand fender wall.
36. Remove power brake booster hose from lower intake manifold.
37. Disconnect vacuum hoses near lefthand fender wall.
38. Disconnect fuel lines from fuel rail.
39. Remove shift cable and bracket.
40. Position a suitable powertrain lift and transmission support bracket under engine.
41. Remove crossmember.
42. Lower engine.
43. Disconnect transmission lines.
44. Remove transmission dipstick tube bolt from cylinder head.
45. Remove torque converter bolts.
46. Remove transmission housing bolts.
47. Remove flywheel bolts.
48. Remove engine rear plate.
49. Reverse procedure to install, tighten all fasteners to specification.

TOWN CAR

1. Drain engine coolant into an approved container.
2. Mark hinge positions for installation alignment, then remove hood.
3. Recover A/C refrigerant as outlined in "Air Conditioning" section.
4. Relieve fuel pressure as outlined under "Precautions."
5. Remove lefthand and righthand cowl extensions as required.
6. Remove wiper mounting arm and pivot shaft.
7. Raise and support vehicle, then disconnect lower radiator hose.
8. Lower vehicle and disconnect degas bottle supply hose.
9. Remove battery.
10. Disconnect hoses from transmission fluid cooler and power steering fluid cooler.
11. Remove radiator upper sight shield, then the engine appearance cover.
12. Remove upper radiator hose.
13. Disconnect cooling fan motor electrical connector.
14. Disconnect A/C condenser lines.
15. Remove radiator support brackets, then the radiator.
16. Loosen two air inlet duct clamp screws, then disconnect air inlet duct.
17. Remove air cleaner outlet tube mounting nut, then the air cleaner outlet tube.

18. Disconnect engine bulkhead connectors.
19. Disconnect accelerator and speed control actuator cables.
20. Remove accelerator and speed control actuator cables from retaining clips and position aside.
21. Disconnect main vacuum supply hose.
22. Remove engine ground mounting bolt from cowl.
23. Remove starter motor as outlined in "Electrical" section.
24. Remove exhaust pipe to manifold mounting nuts, then support the exhaust system.
25. Remove fuel line support bracket mounting bolt.
26. Remove engine ground wire mounting nut from transmission housing.
27. Remove inspection cover.
28. Mark torque converter and flexplate for proper alignment at installation, then remove four nuts from studs.
29. Remove transmission housing to engine mounting bolts and stud.
30. Disconnect vacuum hoses and electrical connector from EVAP canister purge valve.
31. Remove EVAP canister purge valve mounting nuts, then the valve.
32. Disconnect heater hoses from heater core.
33. Remove connector bracket mounting nut, then disconnect electrical connectors on top of righthand fender apron.
34. Disconnect A/C cycling switch electrical connector, then remove the switch.
35. Remove nut, then disconnect A/C lines from compressor.
36. Disconnect fuel lines from fuel rail.
37. Disconnect righthand and lefthand heated oxygen sensor electrical connectors.
38. Disconnect power steering pressure hose.
39. Disconnect lower radiator hose from oil filter adapter.
40. Raise and support vehicle, then remove lefthand and righthand engine mount mounting bolts.
41. Disconnect two coolant hoses and remove oil cooler.
42. Lower the vehicle and install suitable engine lifting device.
43. Support transmission and remove engine from vehicle.
44. Reverse procedure to install. Tighten all fasteners to specifications.

INTAKE MANIFOLD

REPLACE

TOWN CAR

1. Drain cooling system into a suitable container.
2. Remove wiper module and air inlet tube.
3. Release belt tensioner and remove accessory drive belt.
4. Disconnect ignition plug wires from spark plugs. **Do not pull on wires.**
5. Disconnect ignition wire brackets from valve cover studs.
6. Disconnect ignition coils, CID sensor and ignition wires from coils.

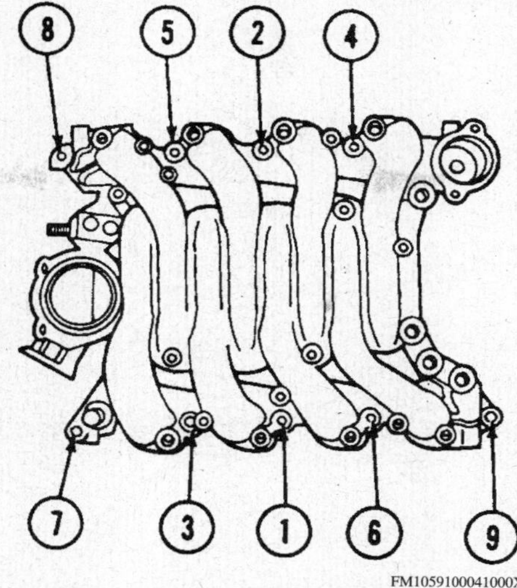

Fig. 1 Intake manifold tightening sequence. Town Car

7. Remove ignition wire tray and ignition wire assembly.
8. Disconnect alternator wiring harness from junction block, fender apron and alternator.
9. Disconnect electrical connectors at ECT and engine temperature sending unit at bottom of coolant bypass tube.
10. Remove coolant bypass tube
11. Remove alternator and mounting bracket.
12. Disconnect the following vacuum lines:
    a. Chassis vacuum supply hose.
    b. Fuel pressure regulator vacuum harness.
    c. Righthand and lefthand intake manifold runner controls (IMRC).
    d. Intake manifold connection.
    e. Crankcase vent.
    f. Throttle body.
    g. PCV.
13. Disconnect and remove upper engine wiring harness from intake manifold.
14. Disconnect eight fuel injector connectors.
15. Remove EGR valve.
16. Disconnect IAC and TPS electrical connectors.
17. Remove intake manifold.
18. Raise and support vehicle.
19. Disconnect oil sending unit and EVO sensor, then position aside.
20. Disconnect EGR tube from righthand exhaust manifold, then lower the vehicle.
21. Disconnect 42-pin connector, A/C compressor, HDR sensor and canister purge solenoid.
22. Remove PCV valve from valve cover, then disconnect canister purge vent hose from PCV valve.
23. Disconnect accelerator and speed control cables from throttle body, then remove accelerator cable bracket from intake manifold and position aside.
24. Disconnect throttle valve cable from throttle body.
25. Disconnect vacuum hose from throttle body adapter port.
26. Disconnect both HEGO sensors and heater supply hose.
27. Remove thermostat housing, then disconnect upper hose and position aside.
28. Remove bolts mounting intake manifold, then the intake manifold and gaskets.
29. Reverse procedure to install, noting the following:
    a. Clean cylinder head and intake manifold surfaces.
    b. Install new intake manifold gaskets.
    c. **Torque** manifold mounting bolts to 72–108 inch lbs. in sequence, **Fig. 1.**

MARK VIII

UPPER, LOWER & INTAKE MANIFOLD RUNNER CONTROL (IMRC)

1. Drain cooling system into a suitable container.
2. Remove water bypass tube.
3. Remove alternator.
4. Disconnect accelerator and cruise control cables.
5. Disconnect evaporative emission hose from upper intake manifold.
6. Disconnect throttle position sensor connector.
7. Disconnect crankcase ventilation hose from intake manifold.
8. Disconnect idler air control valve connector.
9. Loosen EGR tube nut from EGR valve.
10. Disconnect EGR valve vacuum hose.
11. Remove bolts and remove upper intake manifold.
12. Remove fuel injection supply manifold.
13. Remove bolts and remove lower intake manifold.
14. Disconnect righthand and lefthand intake manifold runner control cable.
15. Remove intake manifold runner control and upper and lower gaskets. **Ensure new lower IMRC gaskets are used during installation.**
16. Reverse procedure to install noting the following:
    a. **Torque** lower intake manifold outer bolts to 72–84 inch lbs., then an additional 85–95°, **Fig. 2.**
    b. **Torque** remaining lower intake manifold bolts to 15–22 ft. lbs., in sequence, **Fig. 3.**

CONTINENTAL

1998

1. Drain engine cooling system into a suitable container.
2. Remove air cleaner outlet tube.
3. Relive fuel system pressure as outlined under "Precautions."
4. Disconnect fuel line.
5. Disconnect alternator wiring harness, then remove mounting bracket.
6. Remove water bypass tube.
7. Disconnect accelerator cable and speed control actuator cable from throttle body.
8. Remove accelerator cable bracket and position out of way.
9. Disconnect chassis vacuum supply tube.

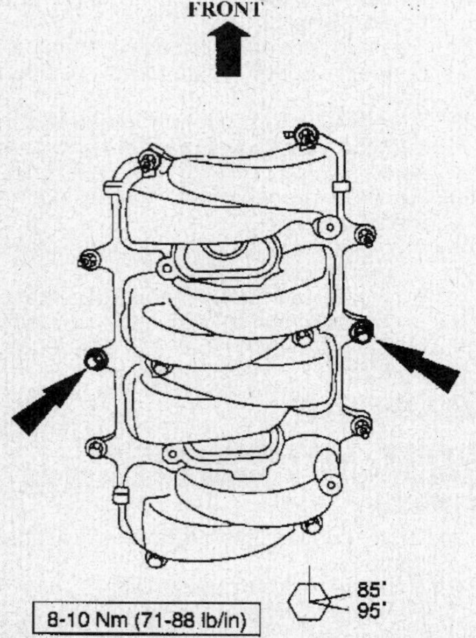

Fig. 2 Lower intake outer bolt location. Mark VIII

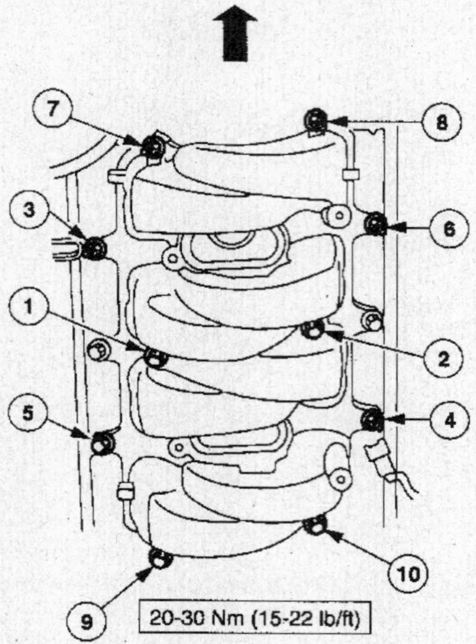

Fig. 3 Lower intake tightening sequence. Mark VIII

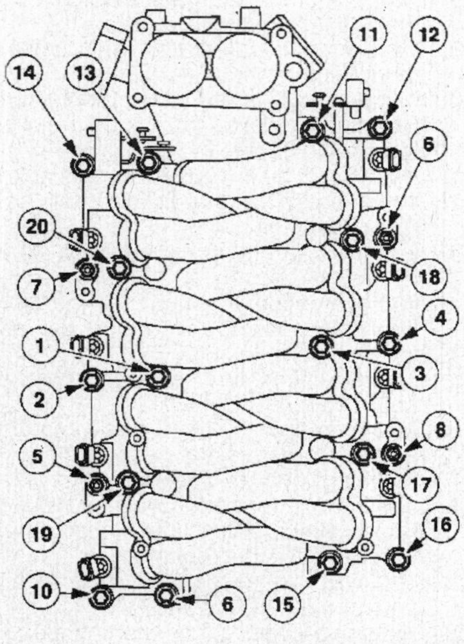

Fig. 4 Intake manifold loosening & tightening sequence. 1998 Continental

10. Disconnect crankcase ventilation tube.
11. Disconnect vacuum lines at fuel injection supply manifold.
12. Disconnect intake manifold runner control actuator cables.
13. Disconnect main emissions hose.
14. Disconnect heater hose.
15. Disconnect engine control wiring from:
    a. Idle air control valve.
    b. Throttle position sensor.
    c. Fuel temperature sensor.
    d. Fuel injectors.
16. Disconnect EGR to exhaust manifold tube and EGR vacuum line.
17. Disconnect fuel injection supply manifold.
18. Loosen bolts and studs in three even steps in sequence, **Fig. 4,** and remove.
19. Remove intake manifold.
20. Remove intake manifold runner controls.
21. Remove and discard runner gaskets and intake manifold gaskets.
22. Remove EGR valve, idle air control valve and throttle body.
23. Clean all sealing surfaces.
24. Reverse procedure to install noting the following:
    a. Tighten idle air control valve and EGR valve to specifications.
    b. **Torque** intake manifold bolts 5, 7, 9 and 11, **Fig. 4,** to 9–11 ft. lbs.
    c. **Torque** remaining bolts to 13–16 ft. lbs.
    d. Rotate all bolts an additional 85–95° in sequence.
    e. **Torque** bolts in **Fig. 5** to 71–89 inch lbs., then rotate an additional 85–95°.

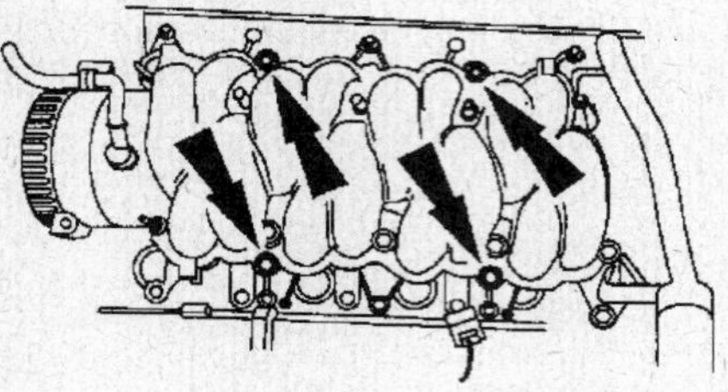

Fig. 5 Manifold bolt location. 1998 Continental

1999–2002

1. Drain coolant into an approved container.
2. Remove air cleaner outlet tube.
3. Relive fuel system pressure as outlined in "Precautions."
4. Disconnect fuel line.
5. Remove two nuts retaining engine sensor control wiring to valve covers.
6. Remove nut and bolt, then position alternator battery lead aside.
7. Disconnect alternator electrical connector.
8. Remove alternator mounting bracket.
9. Disconnect coolant hoses from water bypass tube.
10. Disconnect ECT sensor electrical connector.
11. Remove studs bypass tube. Discard O-rings.
12. Separate MAF sensor connector from accelerator snow shield.
13. Remove bolt and pushpin, then the snow shield.
14. Disconnect accelerator and speed control actuator cables from throttle body.
15. Remove bolts and accelerator cable bracket, then position it aside.
16. Disconnect chassis vacuum supply tube, PCV tube and engine vacuum supply line.
17. Disconnect the fuel pressure sensor vacuum line and the electrical connector.
18. Disconnect EVAP return line.
19. Disconnect heater hose.
20. Disconnect vacuum lines from EGR vacuum regulator solenoid and EGR valve.
21. Remove engine wiring harness covers.
22. Disconnect electrical connectors at fuel injectors.
23. Disconnect engine control sensor wiring electrical connectors from IAC valve, TP sensor and MAF sensor.
24. Disconnect EGR tube at EGR valve.
25. Disconnect ignition coils as required.
26. Disconnect starter motor electrical connectors.
27. Remove engine wiring harness holders from intake manifold studs, then position the harness aside.
28. Loosen and remove the bolts and the studs in three stages in sequence illustrated, **Fig. 6,** then remove the intake manifold assembly.
29. Remove and discard intake manifold gaskets.
30. Reverse procedure to install, noting the following:
    a. Clean all gasket sealing surfaces.
    b. **Torque** intake manifold fasteners to 89 inch lbs., in numbered sequence, **Fig. 6.**

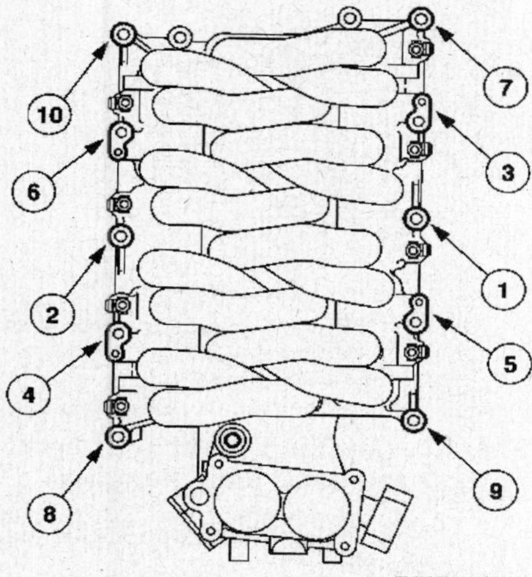

Fig. 6 Intake manifold fastener loosening & tightening sequence. 1999–2002 Continental

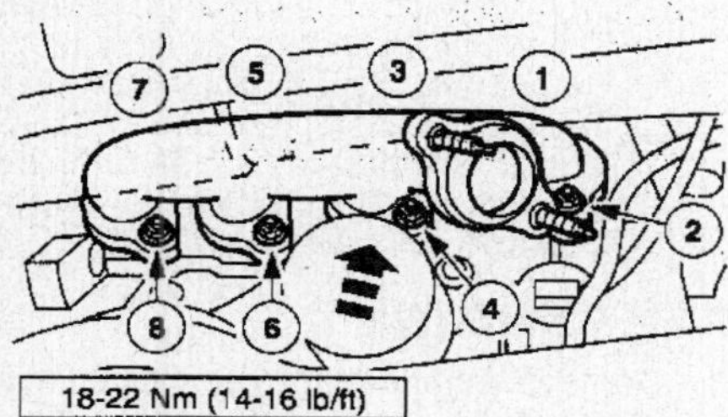

Fig. 9 Lefthand exhaust manifold tightening sequence. Continental

INTAKE MANIFOLD RUNNER CONTROL (IMRC)

REPLACE

Remove intake manifold runner control as outlined under "Intake Manifold, Replace."

EXHAUST MANIFOLD

REPLACE

CONTINENTAL

Righthand

1. Raise and support vehicle.
2. Remove righthand front wheel and tire assembly.
3. Remove radiator air deflector.
4. Remove dual converter Y-pipe.
5. Remove four bolts to exhaust manifold connector, then the gasket.
6. Disconnect EGR valve tube from exhaust manifold.
7. Remove engine support insulator strut.
8. Remove exhaust manifold.
9. Reverse procedure to install, noting the following:
   a. Tighten exhaust manifold nuts to specifications in sequence, **Fig. 7.**

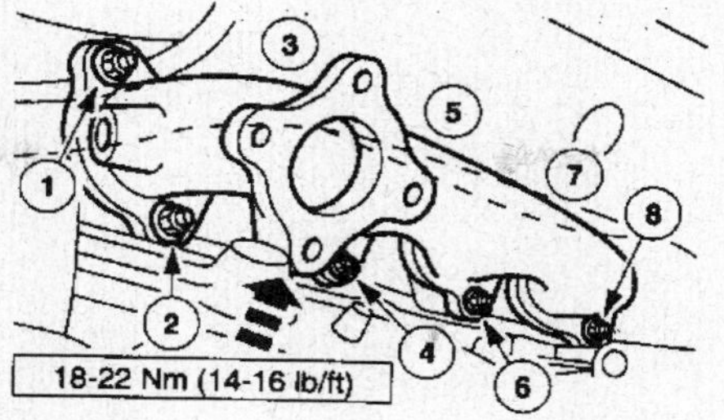

Fig. 7 Righthand exhaust manifold tightening sequence. Continental

   b. **Torque** exhaust manifold connector bolts to 13–17 ft. lbs., in numbered sequence, **Fig. 8,** then **torque** to 31–39 ft. lbs., in numbered sequence.

Lefthand

1. Recover A/C system refrigerant as outlined under "Air Conditioning."
2. Raise and support vehicle.
3. Remove radiator air deflector.
4. Remove dual converter Y-pipe.
5. Disconnect A/C suction discharge manifold from A/C compressor.
6. Remove manifold.
7. Reverse procedure to install. Tighten exhaust manifold nuts to specifications in sequence, **Fig. 9.**

MARK VIII

Righthand

1. Disconnect righthand heated oxygen sensors.
2. Remove dual converter Y-pipe.
3. Disconnect exhaust air tube from exhaust manifold.
4. Remove nuts, then the exhaust manifold.
5. Reverse procedure to install, tighten exhaust manifold nuts to specifications in sequence, **Fig. 10.**

Lefthand

1. Raise and support vehicle.
2. Disconnect lefthand heated oxygen sensors.
3. Remove dual converter Y-pipe.
4. Disconnect exhaust air tube from exhaust manifold.
5. Disconnect EGR valve to exhaust manifold tube from lefthand converter.
6. Remove nuts, then the manifold.
7. Reverse procedure to install, tighten manifold nuts to specifications in sequence, **Fig. 10.**

TOWN CAR

Righthand

1. Raise and safely support vehicle.
2. Remove righthand front wheel and tire.
3. Disconnect exhaust pipe at manifold.
4. Disconnect EGR tube at the exhaust manifold connector.
5. Remove exhaust manifold mounting nuts, then the manifold.
6. Reverse procedure to install. Tighten

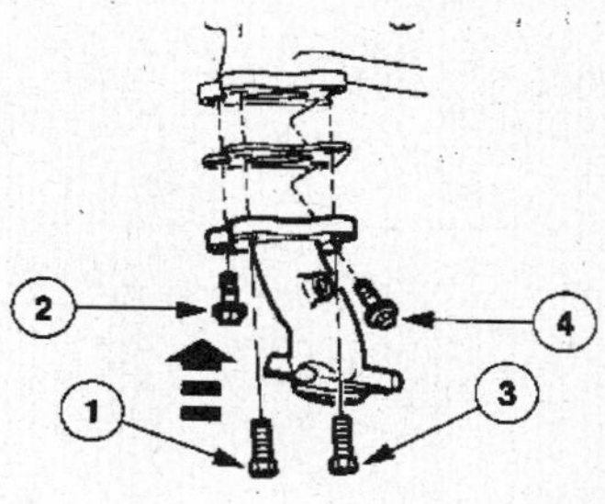

Fig. 8 Righthand exhaust manifold connector tightening sequence. Continental

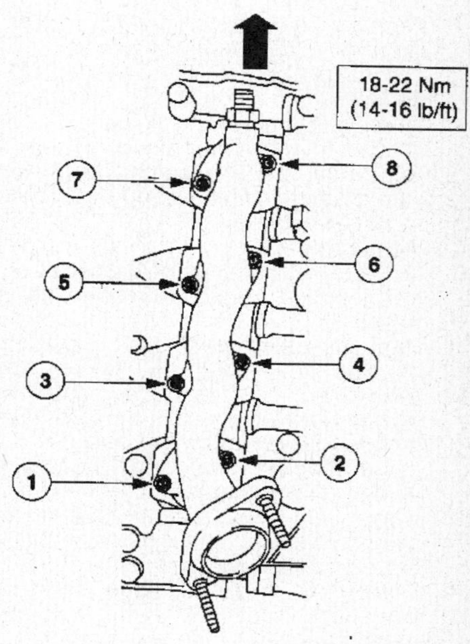

Fig. 10 Exhaust manifold tightening sequence. Mark VIII

manifold nuts to specifications as illustrated in **Fig. 11.**

Lefthand

1. Raise and safely support vehicle.
2. Remove lefthand front wheel and tire.
3. Disconnect exhaust pipe at manifold.
4. Remove exhaust manifold mounting nuts, then the manifold.
5. Reverse procedure to install. Tighten manifold nuts to specifications as illustrated in **Fig. 11.**

CYLINDER HEAD

REPLACE

SOHC ENGINE

1. Drain cooling system, then remove cooling fan and shroud.
2. Remove air inlet tube and wiper module.
3. Release belt tensioner, then remove accessory drive belt.
4. Disconnect ignition wires from spark plugs. **Do not pull on ignition wire(s).**

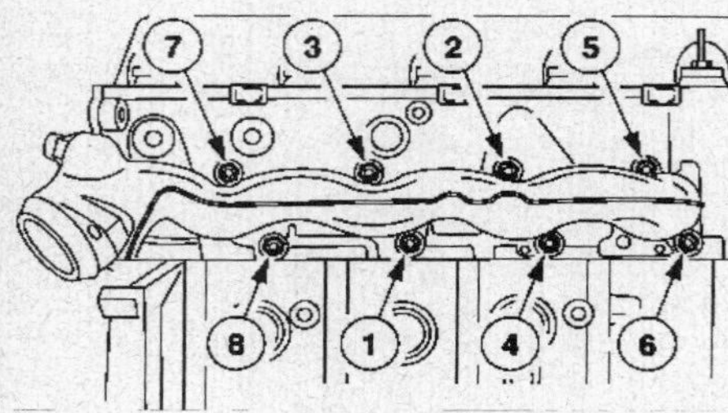

Fig. 11 Righthand exhaust manifold nut tightening sequence. Town Car

5. Disconnect ignition wire brackets from valve cover studs.
6. Remove bolt mounting A/C high pressure line to righthand coil bracket.
7. Disconnect both ignition coils and CID sensor.
8. Remove righthand and lefthand coil bracket to front cover mounting nuts.
9. Slide ignition coil brackets and ignition wire assembly off mounting studs, then remove from vehicle.
10. Remove water pump pulley, then disconnect alternator wiring harness from junction block, fender apron and alternator.
11. Remove alternator and mounting bracket.
12. Disconnect positive battery cable at power distribution box, then remove mounting bolt from positive battery cable bracket located on righthand side of cylinder head.
13. Disconnect vent hose from canister purge solenoid, then place positive battery cable aside.
14. Disconnect canister purge solenoid vent hose from PCV valve, then remove PCV valve from valve cover.
15. Remove 42-pin engine harness connector from mounting bracket on brake vacuum booster, then disconnect and position aside.
16. Disconnect HDR sensor, A/C compressor clutch and canister purge solenoid electrical connectors.
17. Raise and support vehicle.
18. Remove bolts mounting power steering pump to engine block and cylinder front cover. **Front lower bolt on power steering will not come all the way out.**
19. Remove bolts mounting oil pan to front cover.
20. Remove crankshaft damper mounting bolt and washer from crankshaft.
21. Install crankshaft damper remover tool No. T58P-6316-D, or equivalent on damper, then pull damper from crankshaft.
22. Disconnect EVO sensor and oil sending unit and position aside.
23. Disconnect EGR tube from righthand exhaust manifold.
24. Disconnect exhaust for righthand and lefthand manifolds, then suspend with wire.
25. Remove bolt mounting starter wiring harness to rear of righthand cylinder head, then lower the vehicle.
26. Remove righthand and lefthand valve

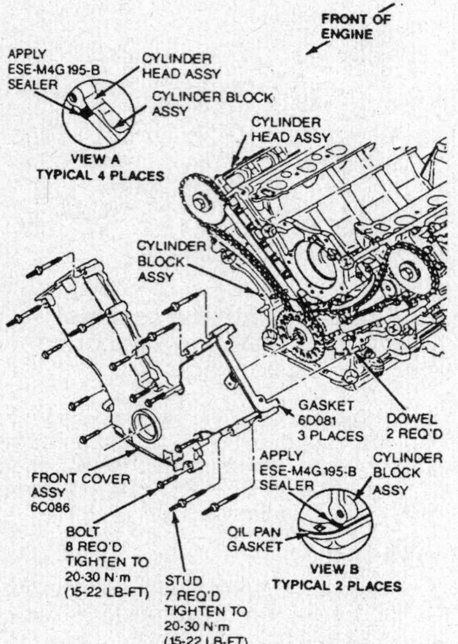

Fig. 12 Front cover removal. SOHC engine

cover to cylinder head.

27. Disconnect accelerator and speed control cables.
28. Remove accelerator bracket from intake manifold and position aside.
29. Disconnect throttle valve cable from throttle body, then the vacuum hose from throttle body elbow port.
30. Disconnect both HEGO sensor and heater supply hose.
31. Remove thermostat housing, then disconnect upper hose and position aside.
32. Remove bolts mounting intake manifold, then the intake manifold and gaskets, **Fig. 12.**
33. Remove timing chain as outlined under "Timing Chain, Replace."
34. Remove lefthand cylinder head mounting bolts. **The lower rear bolt cannot be removed due to interference with the brake vacuum booster. Use a rubber band or similar item to hold bolt away from engine, Fig. 13.**
35. Remove lefthand cylinder head.
36. Remove ground strap mounting heater return line to righthand cylinder head.
37. Remove bolts mounting EVR sensor, then the sensor.
38. Remove bolts mounting righthand cylinder head. **The lower rear bolt cannot be removed due to interference with the evaporator housing. Use a rubber band or similar item to hold bolt away from engine, Fig. 14.**
39. Remove righthand cylinder head.
40. Reverse procedure to install, noting the following:
    a. Rotate crankshaft counterclockwise 45° to ensure all pistons are below top of engine block deck face.
    b. **Torque** cylinder head bolts to 28–

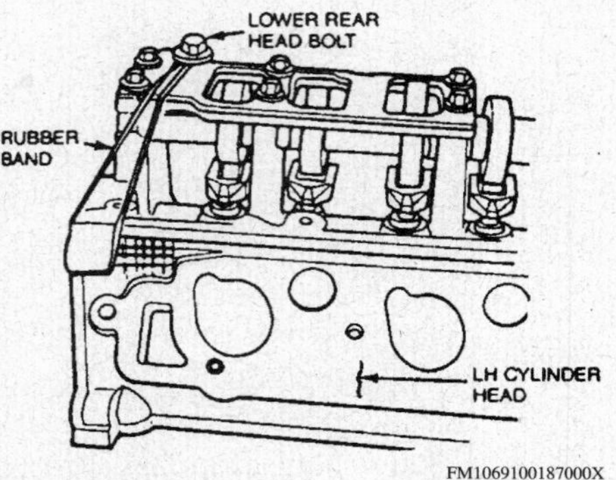

Fig. 13 Lefthand lower rear head bolt removal. SOHC engine

31 ft. lbs., in numbered sequence, **Fig. 15.**
    c. Tighten bolts an additional 85–95° in numbered sequence.
    d. Loosen all bolts a minimum of 360°.
    e. **Torque** bolts to 28–31 ft. lbs., in numbered sequence.
    f. Tighten bolts an additional 85–95°.
    g. Tighten bolts another 85–95°.
    h. Rotate crankshaft clockwise 45°. This will position crankshaft at TDC No. 1. **Crankshaft must only be rotated in the clockwise direction and only as far as TDC.**

DOHC ENGINE

1. Remove engine from vehicle as outlined under "Engine, Replace."
2. Remove valve covers as outlined under "Valve Cover, Replace."
3. Remove engine front cover as outlined under "Front Cover, Replace."
4. Remove intake manifold as outlined under "Intake Manifold, Replace."
5. Remove crankshaft position sensor pulse wheel.
6. Remove rocker arms as outlined under "Hydraulic Lifters, Replace."
7. Remove exhaust manifolds as outlined under "Exhaust Manifold, Replace."
8. Rotate engine to No. 1 cylinder TDC, **Fig. 16.**
9. Install camshaft positioning tool No. T93P-6256-A, or equivalent to camshafts, **Fig. 17.**
10. Remove primary timing chain as outlined under "Timing Chain, Replace." **Do not remove camshaft sprocket and secondary timing chain at this time.**
11. Remove heater hose tube from righthand cylinder head.
12. Loosen cylinder head bolts in sequence, **Fig. 18.**
13. Remove and discard cylinder head bolts.
14. Remove cylinder head and gaskets, discard gaskets.
15. If head casting is to be replaced, remove secondary timing chain and sprockets as outlined under outlined under "Timing Chain, Replace," then remove camshafts as outlined under "Camshaft, Replace."
16. Reverse procedure to install, noting the following:

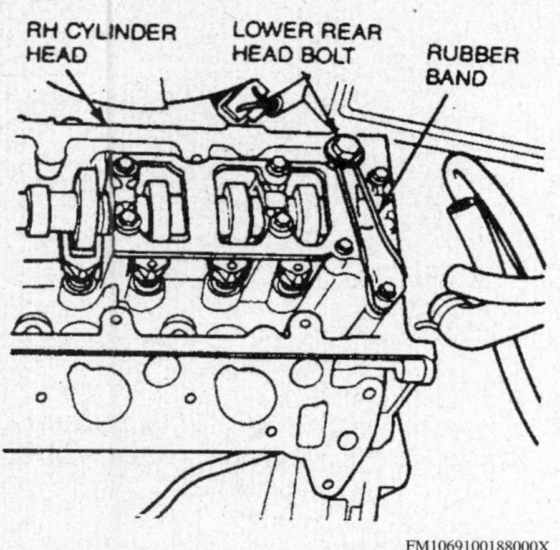

Fig. 14 Righthand lower rear head bolt removal. SOHC engine

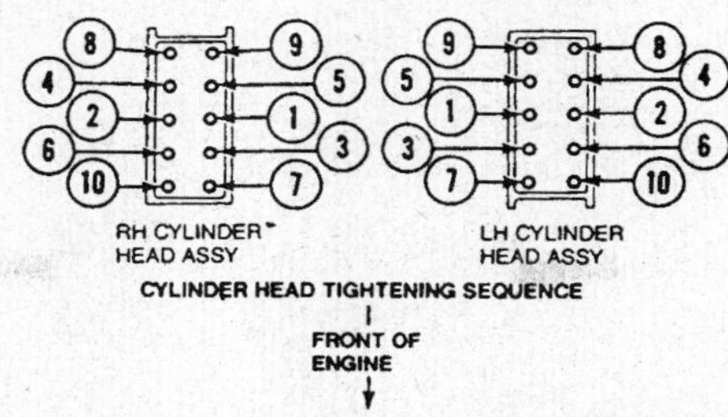

Fig. 15 Cylinder head tightening sequence. SOHC engine

FM1069300462000X

Fig. 16 Setting engine to No. 1 cylinder TDC. DOHC engine

a. **Use new cylinder head bolts and gaskets.**
b. Lightly oil new cylinder head bolts with clean motor oil.
c. **Torque** cylinder head bolts to 27–32 ft. lbs., in numbered sequence, **Fig. 15.**
d. Tighten bolts an additional 85–95° in sequence.
e. Tighten bolts an additional 85–95° in sequence.

VALVE COVER

REPLACE

CONTINENTAL

1998–2000

Righthand Side

1. Drain cooling system into a suitable container.
2. Remove water bypass tube.
3. Relieve fuel system pressure as outlined under "Precautions."
4. Disconnect fuel tube.
5. Disconnect heater hose.
6. Remove PCV valve from righthand valve cover.
7. Remove main chassis vacuum supply tube.
8. Disconnect powertrain control module grounds.
9. Disconnect engine control sensor wiring from powertrain control module.
10. Remove bolts and ignition coil cover.
11. Disconnect engine control sensor wiring from ignition coils.
12. Remove nuts and position engine control sensor wiring out of way.
13. Remove four ignition coils.
14. Remove cross vehicle support arm.
15. Remove eight bolts and two studs from valve cover, then the valve cover.
16. Reverse procedure to install noting the following:
    a. Ensure sealing surfaces are clean and dry before assembly of valve cover.
    b. Install new spark plug bore O-ring seals.
    c. Apply Silicone Gasket and Sealant F6AZ-19562-AA, or equivalent in two places where engine front cover meets cylinder head. **Valve cover bolts and studs must be installed and tightened to specifications within four minutes of sealant application.**
    d. Tighten valve cover bolts to specifications in sequence, **Fig. 19.**

Lefthand Side

1. Drain cooling system into a suitable container.
2. Remove water bypass hose, then the crankcase ventilation tube from lefthand valve cover.
3. Remove ignition coil cover from lefthand valve cover, then the ignition coils.
4. Remove two nuts and position fuel charging wiring out of way.
5. Disconnect air suspension relay.
6. Remove bolts and position air suspension relay out of way.
7. Remove valve cover bolts and studs, then the valve cover.
8. Reverse procedure to install noting the following:
    a. Ensure sealing surfaces are clean and dry before assembly of valve cover.
    b. Install new spark plug bore O-ring seals.
    c. Apply Silicone Gasket and Sealant F6AZ-19562-AA, or equivalent in two places where engine front cover meets cylinder head. **Valve cover bolts and studs must be installed and tightened to specifications within four minutes of sealant application.**
    d. Tighten valve cover bolts to specifications in sequence, **Fig. 20.**

2001–02

Righthand Side

1. Remove cross vehicle support.
2. Remove water bypass tube.
3. Relieve fuel system pressure as outlined under "Precautions," then disconnect fuel line.
4. Disconnect main vacuum supply tube and PCV valve and tube
5. Remove wiring harness retaining nut from valve cover.
6. Disconnect heater hose from heater water outlet tube.
7. Disconnect powertrain control module grounds.
8. Disconnect engine control sensor wiring from PCM.
9. Remove ignition coil cover, ignition coil electrical connectors and ignition coils.
10. Remove nut retaining engine control sensor wiring from front of valve cover.
11. Disconnect fuel injection pressure sensor.
12. Remove engine control sensor wiring cover.
13. Disconnect four fuel injectors and position wiring harness out of way.
14. Remove bolts and studs from valve cover, then the valve cover.
15. Reverse procedure to install, noting the following:
    a. Install new spark plug bore O-rings and valve cover gaskets.
    b. Apply silicone gasket and sealant meeting Ford specification to two places where engine front cover meets valve cover.
    c. Position valve cover and tighten

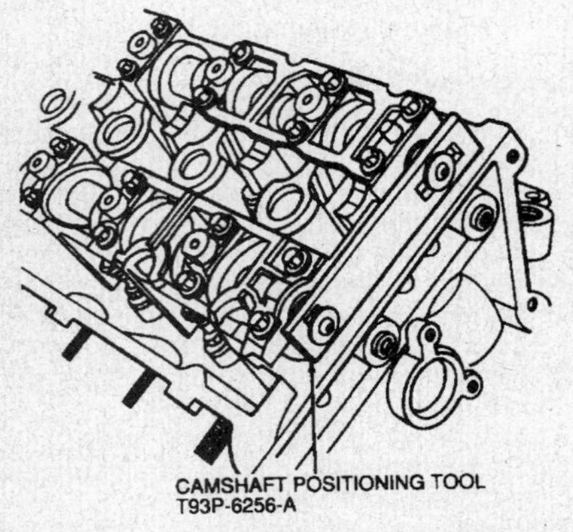

Fig. 17 Camshaft positioning tool installation. DOHC engine

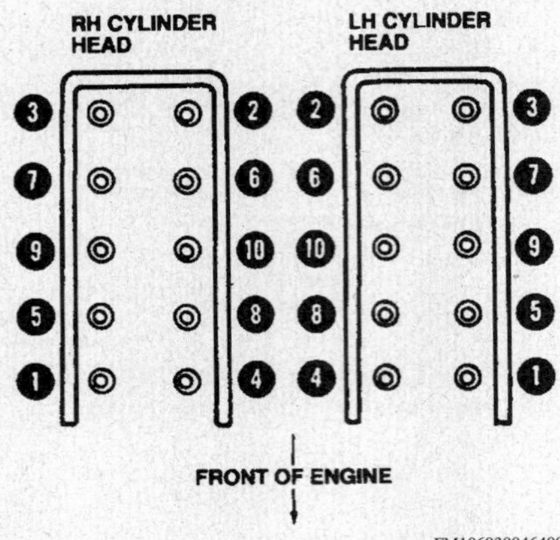

Fig. 18 Cylinder head bolt loosening sequence. DOHC engine

bolts in sequence, **Fig. 19,** to specified value.

Lefthand Side

1. Remove water bypass tube.
2. Remove crankcase ventilation tube from valve cover.
3. Remove two nuts securing engine control sensor wiring harness to valve cover.
4. Disconnect camshaft position sensor.
5. Remove ignition coil cover, disconnect coil wiring harness connectors, then remove ignition coils.
6. Disconnect air suspension relay electrical connector, then remove bolt and position air suspension relay and bracket out of way.
7. Remove bolts and studs, then the valve cover.
8. Reverse procedure to install, noting the following:
   a. Install new spark plug bore O-rings and valve cover gaskets.
   b. Apply silicone gasket and sealant meeting Ford specification to two places where engine front cover meets valve cover.
   c. Position valve cover and tighten bolts in sequence, **Fig. 20,** to specified value.

MARK VIII

Righthand Side

1. Remove ignition coils from righthand cylinder head.
2. Remove upper intake manifold assembly as outlined under "Intake Manifold, Replace."
3. Remove crankcase ventilation tube from valve cover.
4. Remove valve cover bolts, then the valve cover.
5. Reverse procedure to install noting the following:
   a. Ensure sealing surfaces are clean and dry before assembly of valve cover.
   b. Install new spark plug bore O-ring seals.
   c. Apply Silicone Gasket and Sealant F6AZ-19562-AA, or equivalent in two places where engine front cover meets cylinder head. **Valve cover bolts and studs must be installed and tightened to specifications within four minutes of sealant application.**
   d. Tighten valve cover bolts to specifications in sequence, **Fig. 19.**

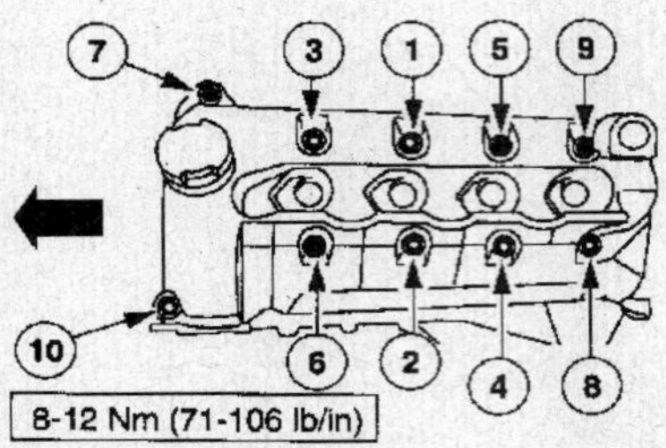

Fig. 20 Lefthand valve cover tightening sequence. Mark VIII & Continental

Lefthand Side

1. Remove windshield wiper module assembly.
2. Remove nuts and position EGR vacuum regulator control out of way.
3. Remove positive crankcase ventilation valve from valve cover and position aside.
4. Remove ignition coils from lefthand cylinder head.
5. Remove bolts and position master cylinder aside.
6. Remove front shock absorber strut cover cup.
7. Disconnect vacuum harness from EAS solenoid near lefthand fender wall.
8. Position power distribution box and bracket aside.
9. Disconnect fuel injector wiring and position aside.
10. Disconnect 42-pin electrical connector at rear of lefthand valve cover.
11. Disconnect engine wiring from fender apron.
12. Remove bolts, then the valve cover.
13. Reverse procedure to install, noting the following:

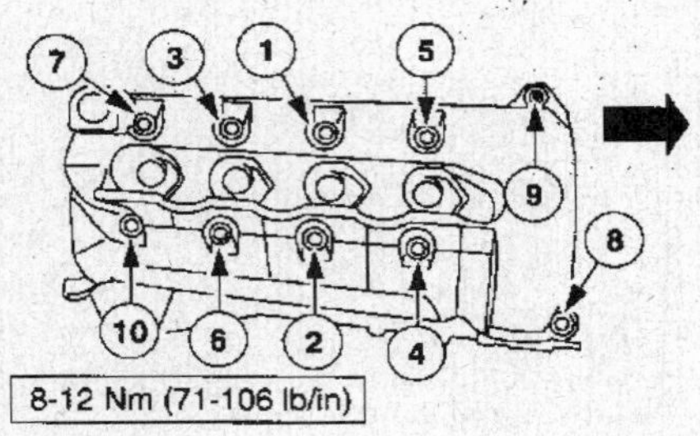

Fig. 19 Righthand valve cover tightening sequence. Mark VIII & Continental

   a. Ensure sealing surfaces are clean and dry before assembly of valve cover.
   b. Install new spark plug bore O-ring seals.
   c. Apply Silicone Gasket and Sealant F6AZ-19562-AA, or equivalent in two places where engine front cover meets cylinder head. **Valve cover bolts and studs must be installed and tightened to specifications within four minutes of sealant application.**
   d. Tighten valve cover bolts to specifications in sequence, **Fig. 20.**

TOWN CAR

Righthand Side

1. Raise and support vehicle.
2. Disconnect Crankshaft Position (CKP) sensor and A/C compressor electrical connectors.
3. Lower vehicle and disconnect A/C cycling switch.
4. Disconnect fuel lines.
5. Disconnect ignition coils from each spark plug.
6. Disconnect fuel injector connectors.
7. Remove crankcase ventilation tube and the evaporative emission canister purge valve.
8. Remove wiring harness hold-down clamp, then separate harness from valve cover.
9. Remove valve cover mounting bolts and studs.
10. Reverse procedure to install.

Lefthand Side

1. Raise and support vehicle.
2. Remove oil bypass filter.
3. Disconnect power steering and oil pressure switch connectors.
4. Lower vehicle and disconnect purge canister connector.
5. Remove power steering bracket bolts and stud, then position bracket aside.
6. Disconnect electrical connectors at Camshaft Position (CMP) sensor and alternator.
7. Disconnect coils from spark plugs.
8. Disconnect fuel injector electrical connectors.
9. Disconnect Idle Air Control (IAC) valve and Throttle Position (TP) sensor electrical connectors.

10. Remove valve cover mounting bolts and studs.
11. Reverse procedure to install.

VALVE ARRANGEMENT

FRONT TO REAR

Town Car
Righthand Side.........I-E-I-E-I-E-I-E
Lefthand Side............E-I-E-I-E-I-E-I

Continental & Mark VIII
Righthand Side..S-P-E-E-S-P-E-E-S-P-E-E-S-P-E-E①
Lefthand Side.E-E-P-S-E-E-P-S-E-E-P-S-E-E-P-S

①—S-Secondary Intake; P-Primary Intake; E-Exhaust.

CAMSHAFT LOBE LIFT SPECIFICATIONS

Engine	Intake, Inch	Exhaust, Inch
SOHC	.2591	.2597
DOHC	.2200	.2186

VALVE ADJUSTMENT

This engine has automatic hydraulic lifters. No valve adjustment is required.

VALVE SPRING & VALVE STEM OIL SEAL

REPLACE

REMOVAL

If, during this procedure, air pressure has forced the piston to the bottom of the cylinder, any loss of air pressure will allow the valve to fall into the cylinder. A rubber band, tape or string wrapped around the end of the valve stem will prevent this and still allow enough travel to inspect the valve for binding and excess guide to valve stem clearance.

1. Remove valve covers as outlined under "Valve Cover, Replace."
2. Remove roller followers as outlined under "Hydraulic Lifters, Replace."
3. Remove spark plug, then position piston at top of stroke with both valves closed.
4. Install suitable air line with adapter in spark plug opening, then apply air pressure. Failure of air pressure to hold the valves closed is an indication of valve or valve seat damage that may require cylinder head removal.
5. Install .40 inch shim between spring coils.
6. Using valve spring compressor tool No. T91P-6565-A, or equivalent, compress valve spring.
7. Remove keepers, retainer and valve spring.
8. Use suitable locking pliers, remove valve stem seal.
9. Repeat previous steps as required.

INSTALLATION

1. **Piston must be at Top Dead Center (TDC) of cylinder being serviced.**
2. Remove air pressure, then inspect valve stem for damage. Rotate valve and inspect valve stem tip eccentric movement during rotation.
3. Position valve up and down through normal travel and inspect the stem for binding. **If the valve has been damaged, it will be required to remove cylinder head for service.**
4. If valve condition is good, apply engine oil to valve stem and hold valve closed, then apply air pressure in cylinder.
5. Using valve stem seal replacer tool No. T88T-6571-A, or equivalent, install valve stem seal.
6. Position valve spring and retainer over valve stem.
7. Install .40 inch shim between spring coils.
8. Compress valve spring, then install keepers.
9. Turn off air supply, then remove adapter from spark plug opening.
10. Install spark plug, then roller follower and valve cover.
11. Start engine and inspect for leaks.

FRONT COVER

REPLACE

REMOVAL

1. Drain cooling system into a suitable container.
2. Remove water outlet tube and water bypass tube hoses.
3. Remove air cleaner outlet tube.
4. Remove fan assembly, then the drive belt.
5. Remove water pump pulley, then the hoses from secondary air injection diverter valve.
6. Remove bolt from secondary air injection manifold tube.
7. Disconnect secondary air injection manifold tube from diverter valve.
8. Remove nuts, then the secondary air injection diverter valve.
9. Disconnect power steering pump connector.
10. Remove bolts from battery to starter relay cable and bracket.
11. Drain engine oil into a suitable container.
12. Remove bolts from oil pan to engine front cover.
13. Disconnect camshaft sensor connector.
14. Remove power steering pump and power steering pump reservoir.
15. Remove crankshaft pulley bolt.
16. Remove crankshaft pulley using crankshaft damper remover tool No. TP58P-6316-D, or equivalent.
17. Remove lefthand and righthand valve covers as outlined under "Valve Cover, Replace."
18. Remove serpentine belt idler pulley and tensioner.
19. Disconnect crankshaft position sensor connector.
20. Remove bolts, then the engine front cover.

INSTALLATION

1. Apply Silicone Gasket Sealant F6AZ-19562-AA, or equivalent along head to block surface and block to oil pan (six places), **Fig. 21.**
2. Install engine front cover on dowel pins on front of cylinder block.
3. Loosely install bolts and studs to front cover.
4. Tighten front cover bolts to specifications in sequence, **Fig. 22.**
5. Tighten oil pan bolts to specifications in sequence, **Fig. 23,** then an additional 60°.
6. Install belt idler pulley, install bolt and tighten to specifications.
7. Install drive belt tensioner and tighten to specifications.
8. Install crankshaft pulley as follows:
   a. Apply silicone gasket and sealant F6AZ-19562-AA, or equivalent to woodruff key slot on crankshaft pulley.
   b. Install crankshaft pulley using crankshaft damper replacer tool No. T74P-6316-D, or equivalent.
   c. Install and **torque** crankshaft bolt to 66 ft. lbs.
   d. Loosen crankshaft bolt at least 360°.
   e. **Torque** crankshaft bolt to 35–39 ft. lbs.
   f. Rotate crankshaft bolt an additional 85–90°.
9. Install water pump pulley.
10. Install righthand and lefthand valve covers as outlined under "Valve Cover, Replace."
11. Connect crankshaft position sensor connector.
12. Install power steering pump and power steering pump reservoir.
13. Connect camshaft sensor connector.
14. Install oil pan drain plug.
15. Install bolts from battery to starter relay cable and bracket.
16. Connect power steering pump connector.
17. Install secondary air injection diverter valve.
18. Connect secondary air injection manifold tube to diverter valve.
19. Install bolt to secondary injection manifold tube.
20. Connect hoses and vacuum line to secondary air injection diverter valve.
21. Install drive belt, fan assembly, air cleaner outlet tube, water outlet tube and water bypass tube hoses.
22. Connect battery ground cable.
23. Fill engine with oil to specification.
24. Fill engine cooling system to specification.

FRONT COVER SEAL

REPLACE

CONTINENTAL

1. Remove drive belt.
2. Disconnect upper motor mount.
3. Raise and support vehicle.

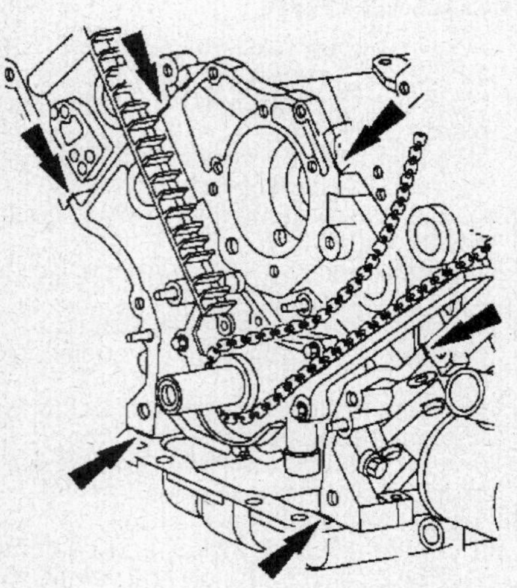
FM1069800792000X

Fig. 21 Silicone installation

4. Remove righthand front wheel and tire assembly.
5. Remove righthand inner fender.
6. Support engine, transaxle and front sub frame with a suitable powertrain lift and universal powertrain removal bracket.
7. Remove front subframe brackets.
8. Lower engine transaxle and front subframe as an assembly, as required.
9. Remove crankshaft pulley using crankshaft damper remover tool No. TP58P-6316-D, or equivalent.
10. Using front cover seal remover tool No. T74P-6700-A, or equivalent, remove front cover seal.
11. Reverse procedure to install, noting the following:
    a. Lubricate engine front cover seal and front cover with clean engine oil.
    b. Use crankshaft seal replacer tool No. T88T-6701-A, or equivalent to install oil seal.
    c. Apply silicone gasket and sealant F6AZ-19562-AA, or equivalent to woodruff key slot on crankshaft pulley.
    d. Install crankshaft pulley using crankshaft damper replacer tool No. T74P-6316-D, or equivalent.
    e. Install and **torque** crankshaft bolt to 66 ft. lbs.
    f. Loosen crankshaft bolt at least 360°.
    g. **Torque** crankshaft bolt to 35–39 ft. lbs.
    h. Tighten crankshaft bolt an additional 85–90°.

MARK VIII & TOWN CAR

1. Disconnect diverter valve hoses.
2. Disconnect tube from both exhaust manifolds and diverter valve.
3. Remove nuts from bracket and remove secondary air injection diverter valve.
4. Remove serpentine drive belt.

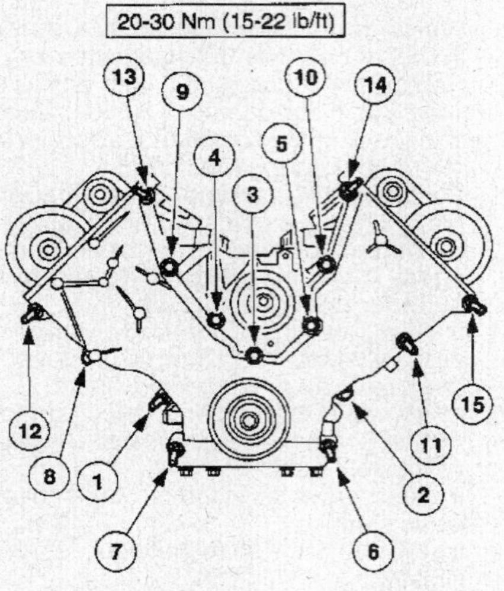

FM1069800793000X

Fig. 22 Front cover tightening sequence

5. Remove crankshaft pulley bolt.
6. Remove crankshaft pulley using crankshaft damper remover tool No. TP58P-6316-D, or equivalent.
7. Using front cover seal remover tool No. T74P-6700-A, or equivalent, remove front cover seal.
8. Reverse procedure to install noting the following:
    a. Lubricate engine front cover seal and front cover with clean engine oil.
    b. Use crankshaft seal replacer tool No. T88T-6701-A, or equivalent to install oil seal.
    c. Apply silicone gasket and sealant F6AZ-19562-AA, or equivalent to woodruff key slot on crankshaft pulley.
    d. Install crankshaft pulley using crankshaft damper replacer tool No. T74P-6316-D, or equivalent.
    e. Install and **torque** crankshaft bolt to 66 ft. lbs.
    f. Loosen crankshaft bolt at least 360°.
    g. **Torque** crankshaft bolt to 35–39 ft. lbs.
    h. Rotate crankshaft bolt an additional 85–90°.

TIMING CHAIN

REPLACE

These engines have an interference fit design. If engine has jumped time, damage will result to cylinder, valve and piston assemblies.

At no time, when the timing chains are removed and the cylinder heads are installed, may the crankshaft and/or camshaft be rotated unless all rocker arms have been removed. Rotation may result in valve and/or piston damage.

SOHC and DOHC engines have a primary timing chain. DOHC engines also use a secondary timing chain between intake and exhaust camshafts.

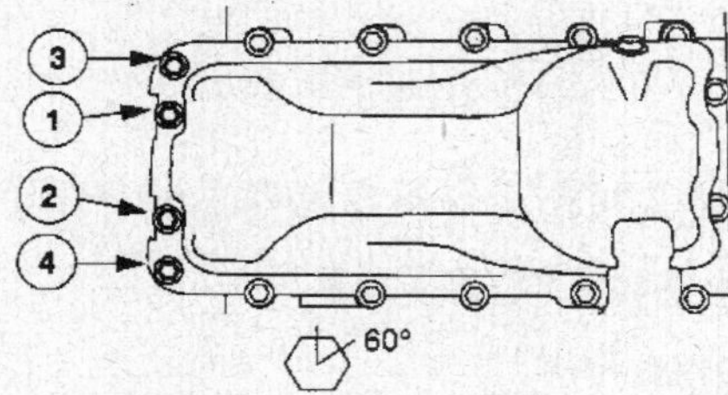

FM1069800794000X

Fig. 23 Oil pan to front cover tightening sequence

Before loosening or tightening camshaft sprocket nuts and bolts, ensure camshaft positioning and locking devices are in place.

PRIMARY

Removal

1. **On Continental models,** remove engine as outlined under "Engine, Replace."
2. **On all models,** remove valve covers as outlined under "Valve Cover, Replace."
3. Remove rocker arms as outlined under "Hydraulic Lifters, Replace."
4. Remove front engine cover as outlined under "Front Engine Cover, Replace."
5. **On models equipped with SOHC engine,** remove oil pan.
6. **On all models,** remove crankshaft position pulse wheel, then rotate engine to No. 1 TDC, **Figs. 16 and 24.**
7. **On models equipped with SOHC engine,** install cam positioning tool No. T91P-6256-A, or equivalent on camshaft flats, **Fig. 25.**
8. **On models equipped with DOHC engine,** install camshaft positioning tool No. T93P-6256-A, **Fig. 17,** and camshaft holding tool No. T93P-6256-AH, **Fig. 26,** or equivalents to camshafts.
9. **On all models,** remove righthand tensioner mounting bolts, then remove tensioner and arm.
10. Remove righthand chain guide mounting bolts, then remove chain guide. **Note length of bolts for installation.**
11. Remove righthand timing chain, then remove righthand crankshaft sprocket. **Note position of sprocket for installation.**
12. Remove righthand camshaft gear mounting bolt, washer, gear and spacer (spacer used only on SOHC engines), if required.
13. Remove lefthand tensioner mounting bolts, then remove tensioner and arm.
14. Remove lefthand chain guide mounting bolts, then remove chain guide. **Note length of bolts for later installation.**
15. Remove lefthand timing chain, then remove lefthand crankshaft sprocket. **Note position of gear for later installation.**
16. Remove lefthand camshaft gear mounting bolt, washer, sprocket and spacer (spacer used only on SOHC engines), if required.

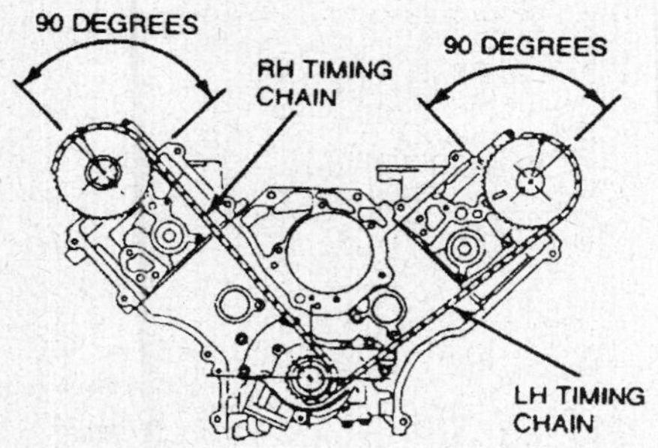

Fig. 24 Engine rotation to TDC

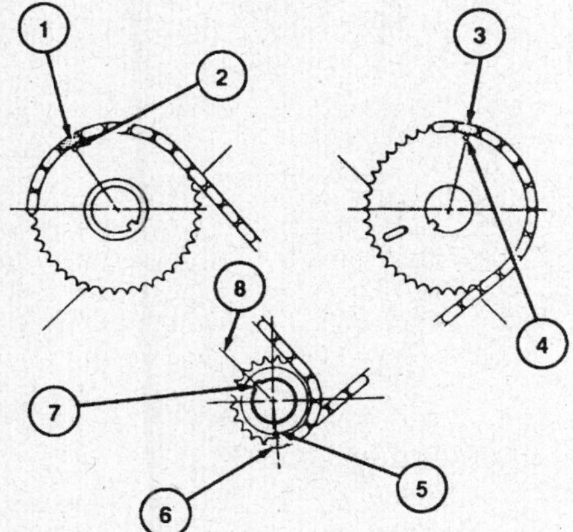

Item	Description
1	RH Camshaft Timing Chain Mark
2	RH Camshaft Sprocket Mark
3	LH Camshaft Timing Chain Mark
4	RH Camshaft Sprocket Mark
5	Crankshaft Sprocket Mark
6	Crankshaft Timing Chain Mark
7	Crankshaft Sprocket
8	Crankshaft Keyway Center Line

FM1069300467000X

Fig. 27 Crankshaft to camshaft timing

Installation

If engine has jumped time, ensure all repairs to engine components and/or valve train are completed. During timing chain installation ensure all rocker arm have been remove, if cam or crank should turn with rockers installed engine damage will result.

1. Rotate engine until keyway is 45° counterclockwise from vertical.
2. **On models equipped with DOHC engines,** ensure secondary timing chain and tensioner are properly installed.
3. **On models equipped with SOHC engines,** install cam positioning tool No. T91P-6256-A, or equivalent, on camshaft flats, **Fig. 25.**
4. **On models equipped with DOHC engines,** install camshaft positioning tool No. T93P-6256-A, **Fig. 17,** and camshaft holding tool No. T93P-6256-AH, or equivalents, **Fig. 26,** to camshafts.

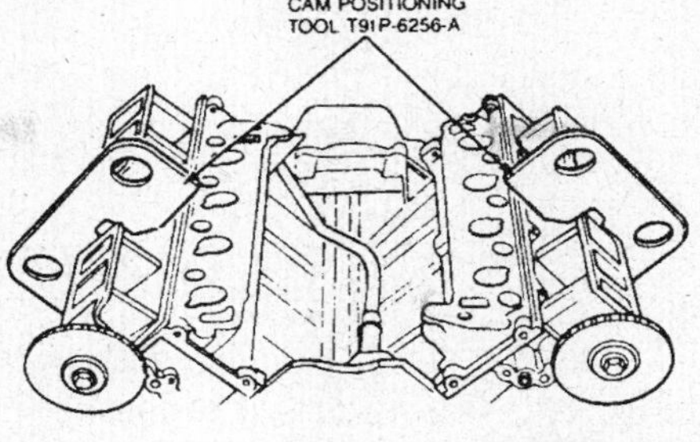

Fig. 25 Camshaft positioning tool. SOHC engine

5. **On all models,** if removed, install primary timing chain cam sprockets onto camshaft, tighten nuts finger tight at this time
6. Install lefthand timing chain onto camshaft sprocket, ensure one of the colored links of timing chain is aligned with timing marks of camshaft sprocket, **Fig. 27.**
7. Install lefthand timing chain onto crankshaft sprocket. Ensure one of the colored links of timing chain is aligned with timing marks of crankshaft sprocket. Ensure tapered boss of crankshaft sprocket is facing away from engine block, **Fig. 28.**
8. Bleed timing chain tensioner as outlined under "Timing Chain Tensioner, Bleed."
9. Install lefthand chain rail, tensioner and arm. Tighten to specifications.
10. Using a suitable C-clamp across both timing chain rails, remove all slack from timing chain, then release timing chain tensioner.
11. Repeat above procedures for righthand timing chain. Note that crankshaft sprocket tapered boss faces toward engine block, **Fig. 28.**
12. Tighten camshaft sprocket nuts to specifications.
13. Install crankshaft position pulse wheel.
14. **On models equipped with SOHC engines,** install oil pan.
15. **On all models,** install front engine cover as outlined under "Front Engine Cover, Replace."
16. Install rocker arms as outlined under "Hydraulic Lifters, Replace."
17. Install valve covers as outlined under "Valve Cover, Replace."
18. **On Continental models,** install engine as outlined under "Engine, Replace."

SECONDARY

Ensure camshaft locking tools are in place before loosening or tightening cam sprocket bolts. Engine damage will result if tools are not properly installed.

1. Remove primary timing chain as outlined above.
2. Compress and lock spring loaded secondary timing chain tensioner.
3. Remove mounting bolt from intake camshafts. **Note position of all spacers sprockets and washers for later assembly.**
4. Remove secondary timing chain and sprockets.
5. Remove bolts mounting secondary timing chain tensioner to head, then remove tensioner.
6. Reverse procedure to install. Tighten to specifications.

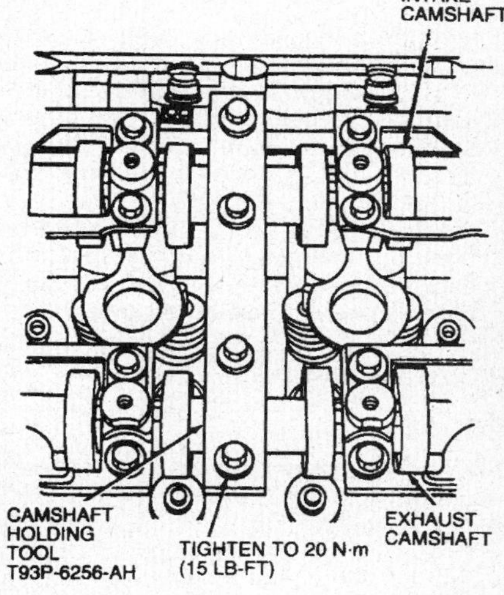

Fig. 26 Camshaft holding tool. DOHC engine

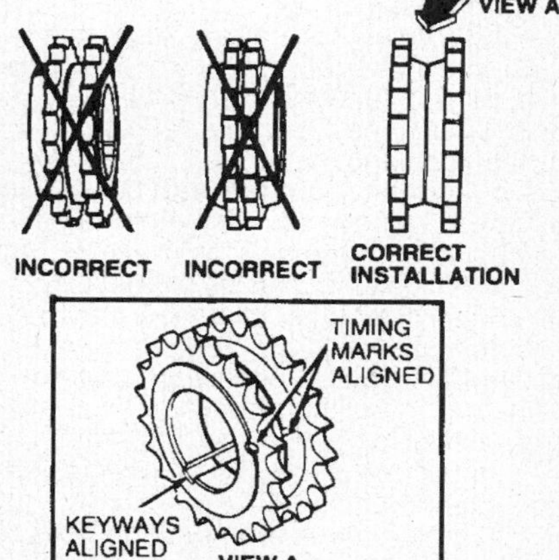

Fig. 28 Crankshaft sprocket position

TIMING CHAIN TENSIONER BLEED

1. Position timing chain tensioner in suitable soft-jawed vise.
2. Using suitable tool, position ratchet lock mechanism from ratchet stem, then slowly compress tensioner plunger by rotating vise handle. **Tensioner must be compressed slowly or internal seal damage may result.**
3. When tensioner plunger bottoms in

tensioner bore, continue holding ratchet lock mechanism, then push ratchet mechanism down until flush with tensioner face.

4. While holding ratchet stem flush to tensioner face, release ratchet lock mechanism, then install paper clip or suitable tool to lock tensioner in collapsed position, **Fig. 29.**
5. **Do not remove paper clip or suitable tool until timing chain, tensioner arm, tensioner and timing chain guide are installed on engine.**

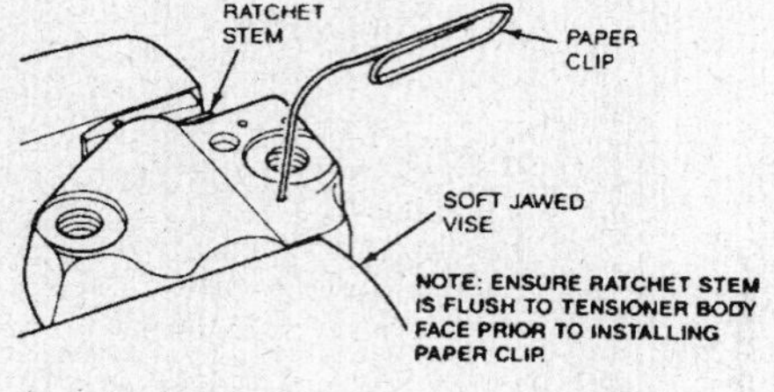

Fig. 29 Timing chain tensioner bleed

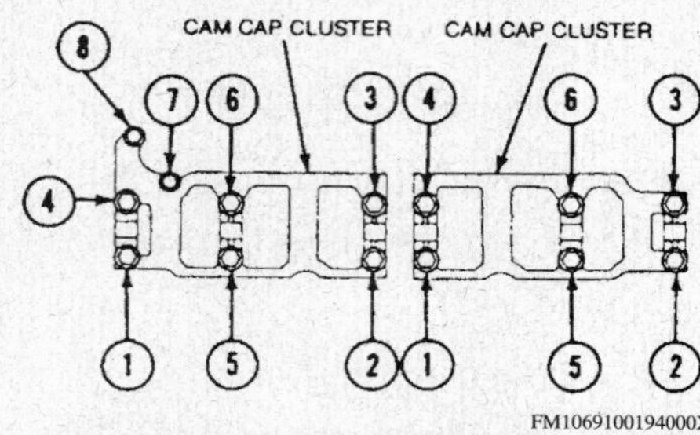

Fig. 30 Camshaft cap cluster assembly. SOHC engine

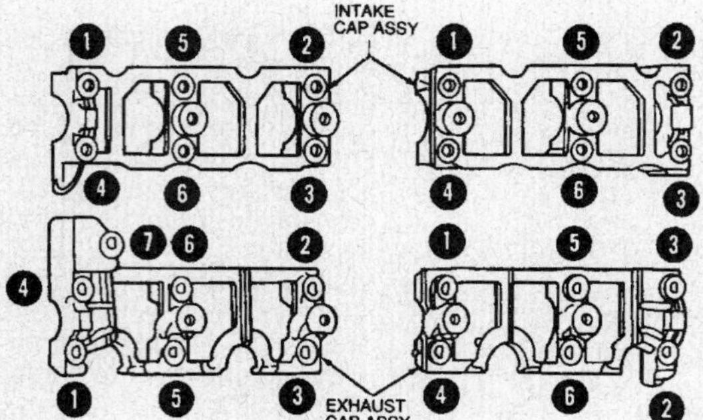

Fig. 31 Camshaft cap cluster assembly. DOHC engine

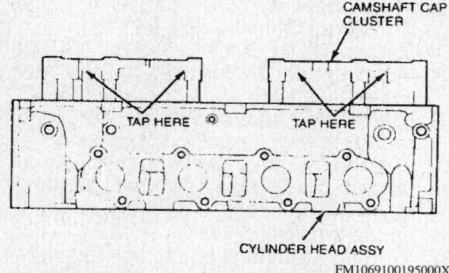

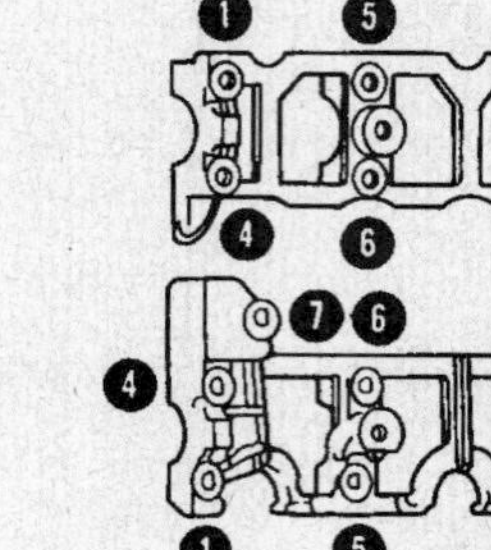

CAMSHAFT CAP CLUSTER
TAP HERE
TAP HERE
CYLINDER HEAD ASSY
FM1069100195000X

Fig. 32 Camshaft cap cluster removal. SOHC engine

CAMSHAFT

REPLACE

1. Remove timing chains as outlined under "Timing Chain, Replace."
2. Rotate crankshaft key counterclockwise 45° from vertical. Ensure pistons are below top of engine deck face. **Crankshaft must be in position prior to rotating camshafts or piston and/ or valve damage may result if all rocker arms have not been removed.**
3. Remove camshaft cap cluster assembly mounting bolts, **Figs. 30 and 31.**
4. **On models equipped with SOHC engine,** tap upward on camshaft cap, **Fig. 32,** then carefully remove camshaft cap and camshaft.
5. **On models equipped with DOHC engines,** remove first the exhaust then the intake camshaft cap cluster, tap upward on camshaft cap, **Fig. 32,** then carefully remove camshaft cap and camshaft.
6. **On all models,** reverse procedure to install, noting the following:
   a. Refer to **Figs. 30 and 31,** for camshaft cap cluster bolt tightening sequence.
   b. Tighten mounting nuts and bolts to specifications.

PISTON & ROD ASSEMBLY

If the old pistons are serviceable, make certain that they are installed on the rods from which they were removed. Measure side clearance between connecting rods and crankshaft journal, which should be .015–.040 inch.

MAIN & ROD BEARINGS

Main bearing vertical bolts and rod bolts used in these engines are of the "Torque To Yield" type and can not be reused. Ensure replacement bolts are available before servicing main or rod bearings.

DOHC ENGINE

Refer to **Figs. 33 and 34,** for main bearing cap removal and tightening sequences, noting the following:

1. Seat bearing caps using a brass hammer.
2. **Torque** vertical main bearing bolts 1–20 to 72–108 inch lbs.
3. **Torque** vertical main bearing bolts 1–10 to 16–21 ft. lbs., and main bearing bolts 11–20 to 28–32 ft. lbs.
4. Rotate vertical main bearing bolts 1–20 an additional 85–90°.
5. **Torque** main bearing cap adjusting screws 21–30 in sequence to 80–97 inch lbs., then in sequence to 14–17 ft. lbs.
6. **Torque** main bearing cap side bolts 31–40 to 84 inch lbs., then in sequence to 14–17 ft. lbs.

SOHC ENGINE

Refer to **Fig. 35,** for main bearing cap removal and tightening sequence. **Torque** bolts to 22–25 ft. lbs., then tighten each bolt an additional 85–90°.

CRANKSHAFT REAR OIL SEAL

REPLACE

1. Remove transmission as outlined in "Automatic Transmission/Transaxles" section.
2. Remove flywheel.
3. Using rear crankshaft slinger remover tool No. T-95P-6701-AH, or equivalent and a suitable slide hammer, remove crankshaft oil slinger.
4. Remove crankshaft rear oil seal using rear crankshaft seal remover tool No. T95P-6701-BH, or equivalent and a suitable slide hammer.
5. Reverse procedure to install, noting the following:
   a. Use crankshaft seal replacer tool No. T-95P-6701-AH and rear crankshaft seal adapter tool No. T-95P-6701-DH, or equivalents to install rear oil seal.
   b. With rear crankshaft seal adapter still installed, use rear crankshaft slinger replacer and rear crankshaft seal replacer to install crankshaft oil slinger.

OIL PAN

REPLACE

CONTINENTAL

1. Drain engine oil into a suitable container.

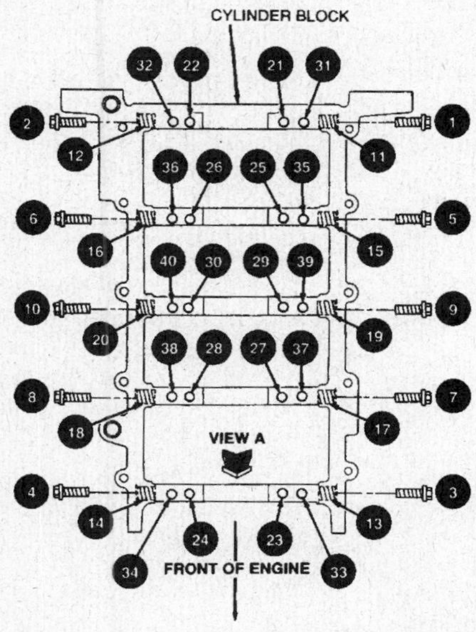
CYLINDER BLOCK
VIEW A
FRONT OF ENGINE
FM1069300472000X

Fig. 33 Main bearing cap removal sequence. DOHC engine

2. Remove dual converter Y-pipe.
3. Disconnect sensor wiring from low oil level sensor and oil pan rail.
4. Remove 16 bolts, then the oil pan.
5. Reverse procedure to install, noting the following:
   a. Tighten oil pan bolts to specifications in sequence, **Fig. 36,** then in sequence an additional 60°.
   b. Fill engine with clean oil to specification.

MARK VIII

1. Drain engine oil into a suitable container.
2. Install engine lifting set tool No. 014-00340, or equivalent on engine.
3. Install three-bar engine support tool No. D88L-6000-A, or equivalent to engine lifting set.
4. Raise and safely support vehicle.
5. Remove bolts from front engine support insulators.
6. Raise and support engine with three bar engine support. **Ensure no damage occurs to lines and hoses at rear of engine.**
7. Remove front tires, then the tie rod ends from front wheel spindles.
8. Remove front suspension lower arm from front wheel spindles.
9. Remove stabilizer bar link from front stabilizer bar.
10. Disconnect front air spring and shock from front suspension lower arm strut.
11. Remove front fender splash shield.
12. Disconnect anti-lock brake sensor.
13. Drain power steering fluid into an approved container.
14. Disconnect steering coupling at pinch bolt joint, then the power steering pressure and return hoses.
15. Remove wiring harnesses from front sub frame.
16. Support front subframe with suitable adjustable jacks at four points.
17. Remove eight front subframe to body

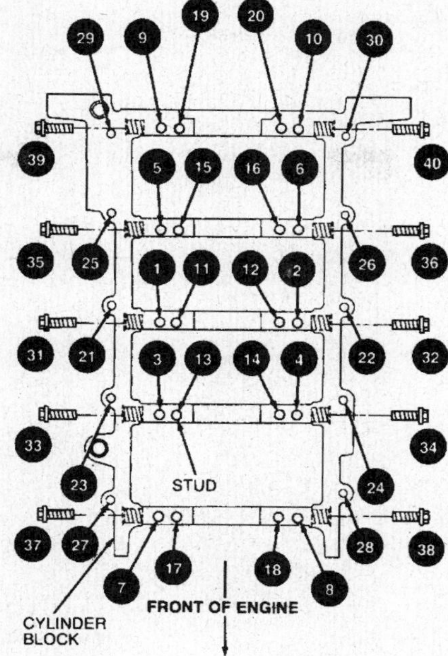
STUD
FRONT OF ENGINE
CYLINDER BLOCK
FM1069300473000X

Fig. 34 Main bearing cap tightening sequence. DOHC engine

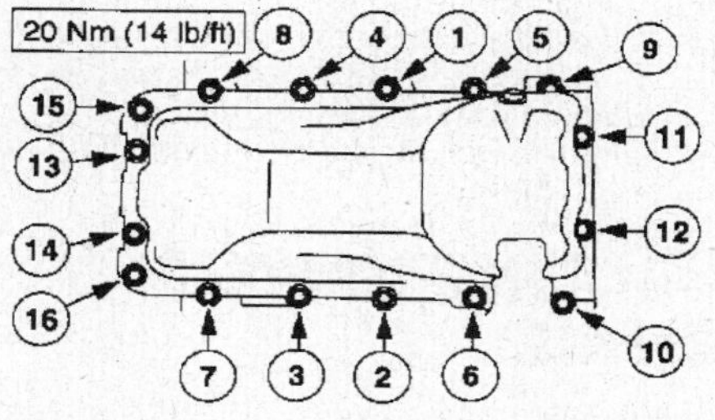
20 Nm (14 lb/ft)
FM1069800796000X

Fig. 36 Oil pan tightening sequence. Mark VIII & Continental

mounting bolts, then lower the subframe.

18. Disconnect sensor wiring from low oil level sensor and oil pan rail.
19. Remove oil pan bolts, then the oil pan.
20. Remove bolts from oil pump screen and cover, then the oil pump screen cover and tube.
21. Remove oil pan gasket.
22. Reverse procedure to install noting the following:
    a. Tighten oil pump screen and cover bolts to specifications illustrated in **Fig. 37.**
    b. **Torque** oil pan bolts to specifications in sequence, **Fig. 36,** then tighten in sequence an additional 60°.
    c. Fill engine with clean oil to specification.

TOWN CAR

1. Disconnect ground and positive battery cables.
2. Remove air inlet tube.

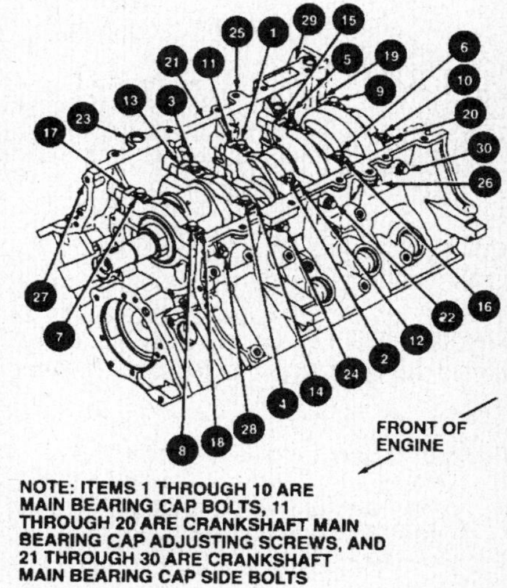
FRONT OF ENGINE
NOTE: ITEMS 1 THROUGH 10 ARE MAIN BEARING CAP BOLTS, 11 THROUGH 20 ARE CRANKSHAFT MAIN BEARING CAP ADJUSTING SCREWS, AND 21 THROUGH 30 ARE CRANKSHAFT MAIN BEARING CAP SIDE BOLTS
FM1069300474000X

Fig. 35 Main bearing cap tightening sequence. SOHC engine

3. Drain cooling system, then remove cooling fan and shroud.
4. Relieve fuel system pressure as outlined under "Precautions," then disconnect fuel lines.
5. Remove upper radiator hose.
6. Remove wiper module and support bracket.
7. Discharge A/C system.
8. Disconnect A/C compressor outlet hose, then remove hose assembly to righthand coil bracket mounting bolt.
9. Remove engine electrical harness 42-pin connector from bracket on brake vacuum booster.
10. Disconnect engine electrical connector, then disconnect transmission harness electrical connector.
11. Disconnect throttle valve cable at throttle body.
12. Disconnect heater outlet hose.
13. Remove righthand cylinder head grounds strap mounting nut.
14. Remove heater outlet hose assembly to righthand cylinder head upper mounting stud, then loosen lower bolt and position aside.
15. Remove blower motor resistor.
16. Remove righthand engine mount to lower engine bracket mounting bolt.
17. Disconnect EGR valve vacuum hoses and tube.
18. Remove EGR valve to intake manifold mounting bolts.
19. Raise and support vehicle, then drain engine oil.
20. Remove righthand front engine mount two through bolts, then remove lefthand front engine mount through bolt.
21. Remove EGR tube line mounting nut at righthand exhaust manifold, then remove EGR valve assembly.
22. Disconnect exhaust pipes at exhaust manifolds, then lower and support exhaust at crossmember.
23. Position suitable jack and wood block under oil pan, rearward of drain plug,

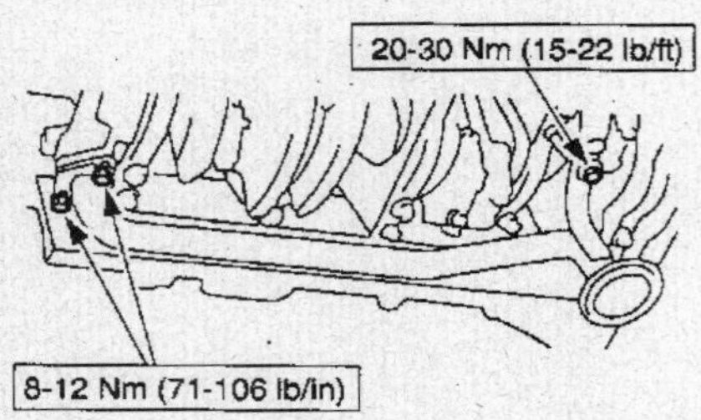

Fig. 37 Oil pump screen & cover bolts torque specifications. Mark VIII

then raise engine approximately 4 inches.

24. Install two wood blocks approximately 2.50–2.75 inches thick under each engine mount.
25. Lower engine to wood blocks, then remove jack.
26. Remove oil pan mounting bolts. It may be required to loosen rear transmission mount mounting nuts and with suitable jack, then raise extension housing slightly to remove oil pan.
27. Remove oil pan, discard pan gasket.
28. Reverse procedure to install. Refer to **Fig. 38,** for oil pan bolt tightening sequence and specifications.

OIL PUMP

REPLACE

1. Remove valve covers as outlined under "Valve Cover, Replace."
2. Remove front cover as outlined under "Front Engine Cover, Replace."
3. Remove oil pan as outlined under "Oil Pan, Replace."
4. Remove timing chains as outlined under "Timing Chain, Replace."
5. Remove oil pump mounting bolts, then remove oil pump, **Fig. 39.**
6. Reverse procedure to install, noting the following:
   a. Align oil pump inner rotor with flat of crankshaft.
   b. Tighten oil pump mounting bolts to specifications.

BELT TENSION DATA

Automatic belt tensioners are spring loaded devices which set and maintain the drive belt tension. The belt should not require tension adjustments during its lifetime. Automatic tensioners have belt wear indicator marks. If the indicator mark is not between the indicator lines, the belt is worn or an improper belt is installed.

SERPENTINE DRIVE BELT

BELT ROUTING

Refer to **Figs. 40 through 42,** for drive belt routing.

BELT REPLACEMENT

1. Rotate tensioner away from belt using a breaker bar installed in ½ inch square hole in tensioner arm.
2. Lift old belt over alternator pulley flange and remove.
3. When installing new belt over pulleys. Ensure all "V" grooves make proper contact with pulley.
4. Ensure belt is properly installed on each pulley.

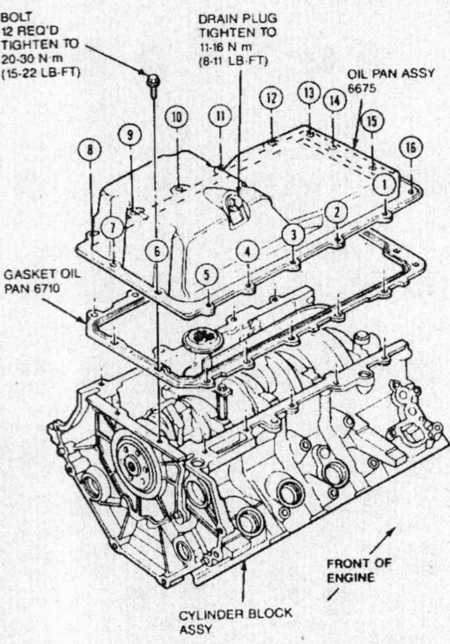

Fig. 38 Oil pan tightening sequence. Town Car

COOLING SYSTEM BLEED

A pressurized reservoir system is used which constantly separates the air from the cooling system. When the thermostat is open, coolant flows through a small hose from the top of the radiator outlet tank to the reservoir. The reservoir separates any entrapped air from the coolant and replenishes the system through the lower hose. The reservoir serves as the location for service fill, coolant expansion during warm up, system pressurization from the pressure cap and air separation during operation. The reservoir is designed to have approximately ½–1 quart of air when cold to allow for coolant expansion.

Add coolant to the minimum level on the reservoir.

THERMOSTAT

REPLACE

DOHC ENGINE

1. Drain coolant level below upper radiator hose and thermostat housing.
2. Disconnect lower radiator, coolant recovery and engine return hoses at thermostat housing, **Fig. 43,** then remove two thermostat housing mounting bolts.
3. Remove O-ring seal and thermostat from thermostat housing. Inspect O-ring for damage and replace if required.
4. Reverse procedure to install. Tighten to specifications.

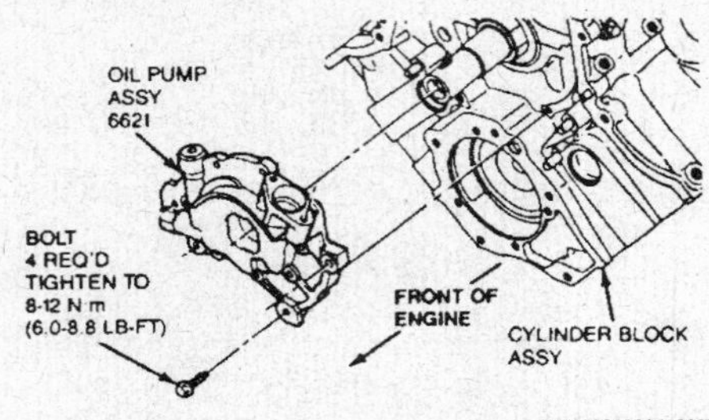

Fig. 39 Oil pump assembly

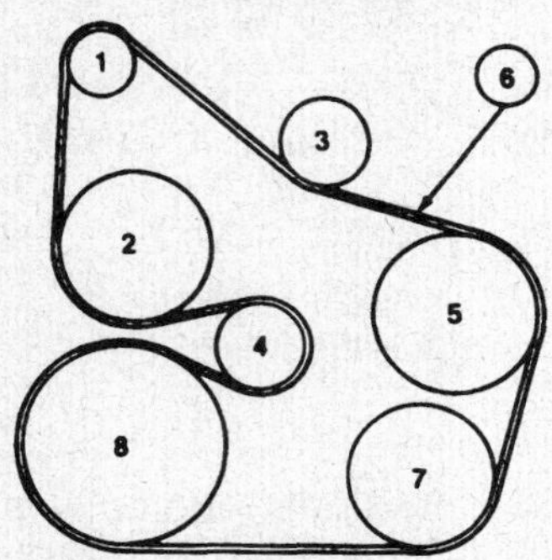

Item	Description
1	Generator
2	Water Pump Pulley
3	Belt Idler Pulley
4	Drive Belt Tensioner
5	Power Steering Pump
6	Drive Belt
7	A / C Compressor
8	Crankshaft Pulley

FM1069300469000X

Fig. 40 Drive belt routing. Continental

SOHC ENGINE

1. Drain coolant level below upper radiator hose and thermostat housing.
2. Disconnect upper radiator hose at thermostat housing, then remove two thermostat housing mounting bolts.
3. Remove O-ring seal and thermostat from intake manifold. Inspect O-ring for damage and replace if required.
4. Reverse procedure to install. Tighten to specifications.

WATER PUMP

REPLACE

1. Drain cooling system into suitable container, then remove engine cooling fan and shroud.
2. Release belt tensioner, then remove accessory drive belt, **Fig. 44.**
3. Remove water pump pulley mounting bolts, then remove water pump pulley.
4. Remove water pump mounting bolts, then remove water pump.

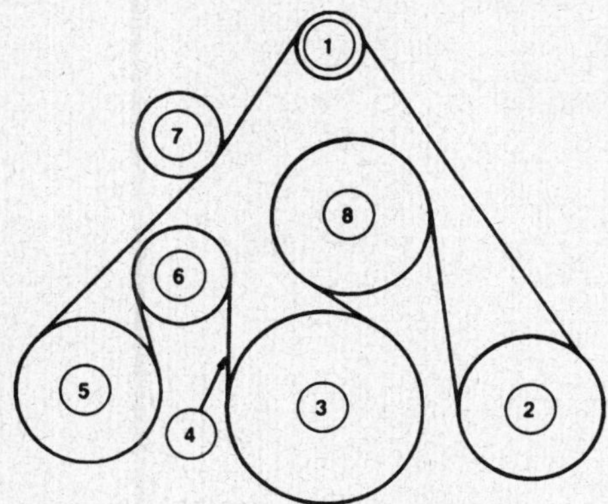

Item	Description
1	Generator
2	Power Steering Pump
3	Crankshaft Pulley
4	Drive Belt
5	A / C Compressor
6	Drive Belt Tensioner
7	Belt Idler Pulley
8	Water Pump

FM1069300470000X

Fig. 41 Drive belt routing. Mark VIII & 1998–99 Town Car

5. Reverse procedure to install. Tighten mounting bolts to specifications.

RADIATOR

REPLACE

1. Drain engine coolant, then disconnect de-aeration hose and both radiator hoses.
2. Disconnect automatic transmission fluid inlet and outlet lines. Use a back-up wrench to hold fitting when removing transmission cooler lines.
3. **On models equipped with fan shroud,** proceed as follows:
   a. Remove upper shroud mounting bolts at radiator support.
   b. Remove A/C condenser core to radiator upper mounting bolts.
   c. Lift fan shroud enough to disengage lower retaining clips and lay shroud over fan.
4. **On all models,** remove radiator upper support mounting bolts, then the supports.
5. Reverse procedure to install, noting the following:
   a. Operate engine, inspect automatic transmission, radiator and coolant recovery tank for proper fluid level.

FUEL PUMP

REPLACE

1. Relieve fuel system pressure as outlined under "Precautions."

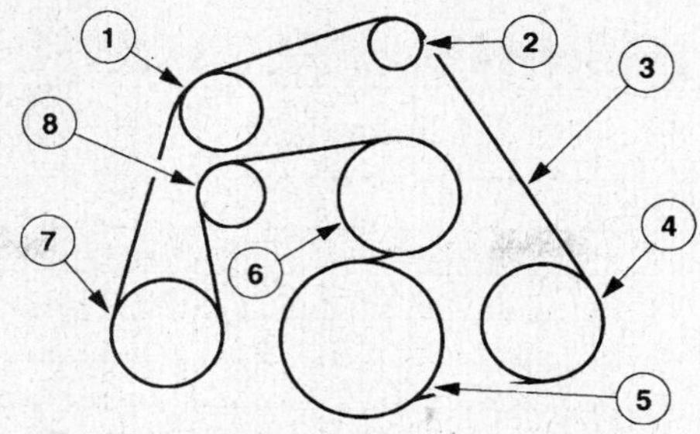

Item	Description
1	Belt idler pulley
2	Generator pulley
3	Drive belt
4	Power steering pump pulley
5	Crankshaft pulley
6	Water pump pulley
7	A/C clutch pulley
8	Drive belt tensioner pulley

FM1060101420000X

Fig. 42 Drive belt routing. 2000–02 Town Car

2. Using suitable tool, drain fuel tank at fuel filler neck.
3. Raise and support vehicle.
4. Disconnect fuel supply and return line fittings and vent line.
5. Disconnect fuel pump and sender electrical connectors.
6. Remove fuel tank mounting support straps, then carefully lower fuel tank assembly. Ensure dirt does not enter tank or fuel system.
7. Using fuel tank sender wrench No. D74P-9275-A, or equivalent, turn fuel pump locking ring counterclockwise, then remove locking ring.
8. Remove fuel pump assembly, then remove and discard seal ring.
9. Reverse procedure to install, noting the following:
   a. Once fuel pump is installed, using fuel pressure gauge tool No. T80L-9974-B, or equivalent on the fuel charging assembly Schrader valve.
   b. Turn ignition from Off to On position for three seconds.
   c. Repeat Off to On switching 5–10 times until pressure gauge shows at least 35 psi.

FUEL FILTER

REPLACE

1. Turn engine off and relieve fuel system pressure as outlined under "Precautions."
2. Raise and support vehicle.
3. Remove push connect fittings at both ends of fuel filter. Install new retainer clips in each push connect fitting.
4. Remove fuel filter and retainer from metal bracket by removing two retainer bolts.
5. Remove filter from retainer. Note direction of flow arrow.
6. Remove rubber insulator rings from filter.
7. Reverse procedure to install, noting the following:
   a. Replace insulator(s) if filter moves freely after retainer installation.
   b. **Torque** mounting bolts to 27–44 inch lbs.
   c. Start engine and inspect for leaks.

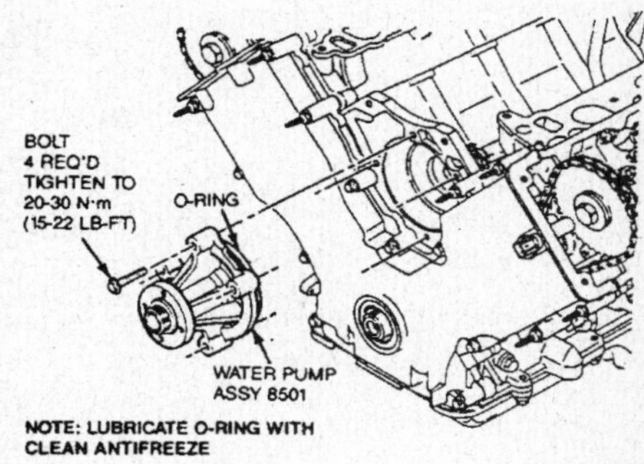

FM1089100059000X

Fig. 44 Water pump replacement

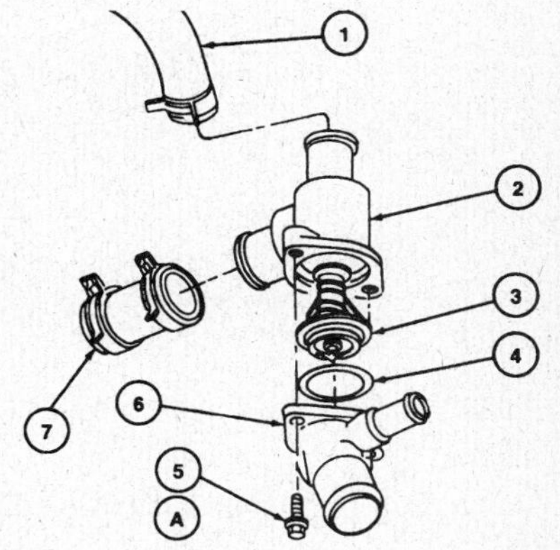

Item	Description
1	Water Bypass Hose
2	Lower Water Thermostat Housing
3	Water Thermostat
4	O-Ring Seal
5	Bolt (2 Req'd)
6	Upper Water Thermostat Housing
7	Engine Return Hose
A	Tighten to 20-30 N·m (15-22 Lb-Ft)

FM1069300471000X

Fig. 43 Thermostat housing. DOHC engine

TIGHTENING SPECIFICATIONS

Year	Component	Torque/Ft. Lbs.
DOHC ENGINE		
1998–2002	Alternator Brackets To Cylinder Block	15–22
	Belt Idler Pulley	15–22
	Belt Tensioner	15–22
	Camshaft	81–95
	Camshaft Cover	72–108⑥
	Camshaft Sprocket	81–95
	Crankshaft Damper	114–121
	Crankshaft Pulley	⑧
	Connecting Rod	18–24④
	Cylinder Front Cover	15–22
	Cylinder Head	③
	Drive Belt Tensioner	15–22
	EGR Tube Connector	30–33
	EGR Valve To Intake Manifold	15–22
	EGR Valve To Exhaust Manifold Tube	26–33
	Engine Insulators	15–22
	Engine To Transmission	30–44
	Exhaust Manifold Studs	96–108⑥
	Exhaust Manifold To Cylinder Head	15–22
	Exhaust Pipe To Exhaust Manifold	20–30
	Flywheel	54–64
	Front Engine Cover	15–22
	Front Engine Mount	45–59
	Front Engine Mount Through Bolts	15–22
	Fuel Filer	27–44⑥
	Heater Outlet Hose	15–22
	Idle Air Control	14
	IMRC Bolts To Intake	⑦
	Intake Manifold To Cylinder Head	53–64
	Low Oil Level Sensor	15–22
	Lower Control Arm To Strut	118–162
	Main Bearing	⑤
	Oil Filter Adapter	15–22
	Oil Inlet Tube To Main Bearing Cap	15–22
	Oil Inlet Tube To Oil Pump	72–108⑥
	Oil Pan Drain Plug	8–12
	Oil Pan To Cylinder Block	14
	Oil Pump To Cylinder Block	72–108⑥
	Oxygen Sensor	27–33
	Power Steering Pump Reservoir	72–96⑥
	Power Steering Pump To Engine	15–22
	Powertrain Frame	73–100
	Pulley To Crankshaft	②
	Rear Axle Assembly To Rear Subframe	72–89
	Rear Engine Mount, Bolt	50–70
	Rear Engine Mount, Nut	35–50
	Rear Engine Support	15–22
	Spark Plug	84–96⑥
	Thermostat Housing	15–22
	Throttle Body	72–108⑥
	Torque Converter	22–25

Continued

TIGHTENING SPECIFICATIONS—Continued

Year	Component	Torque/Ft. Lbs.
DOHC ENGINE		
1998–2002	Upper Control Arm To Steering Knuckle	50–68
	Upper Manifold	15–22
	Valve Cover	72–108⑥
	Water Bypass Tube	72–96⑥
	Water Pump To Cylinder Block	15–22
	Water Pump To Pulley	15–22
SOHC ENGINE		
1998–2002	Accelerator Cable Bracket	72–96⑥
	Alternator To Cylinder Block	15–22
	Camshaft	81–95
	Camshaft Cover	72–108⑥
	Connecting Rod	29–34①
	Crankshaft Damper	114–121
	Crankshaft Pulley	⑧
	Cylinder Front Cover	15–22
	Cylinder Head	③
	Damper To Crankshaft	114–121
	Engine To Transmission	30–44
	EGR Valve To Intake Manifold	15–22
	Exhaust Manifold To Cylinder Head	15–22
	Exhaust Pipe To Exhaust Manifold	20–30
	Front Engine Mount	45–59
	Front Engine Mount Through Bolts	15–22
	Fuel Filter	27–44⑥
	Intake Manifold To Cylinder Head	53–64
	Main Bearing Cap Adjusting	⑤
	Main Bearing Cap Side	⑤
	Main Bearing Cap Vertical	⑤
	Oil Inlet Tube To Main Bearing Cap	15–22
	Oil Inlet Tube To Oil Pump	72–106⑥
	Oil Pan Drain Plug	8–12
	Oil Pan To Cylinder Block	14
	Oil Pump To Cylinder Block	72–108⑥
	Rear Engine Mount, Bolt	50–70
	Rear Engine Mount, Nut	35–50
	Spark Plug	84–96⑥
	Thermostat Housing	15–22
	Torque Converter	15–22
	Valve Cover	72–108⑥
	Water Pump To Cylinder Block	15–22
	Water Pump To Pulley	15–22

①— Tighten an additional 90–120°.
②— Refer to "Front Cover Seal, Replace." for tightening specifications and sequence.
③— Refer to "Cylinder Head, Replace" for tightening specifications and sequence.
④— Tighten an additional 85–90°.
⑤— Refer to "Main & Rod Bearings" for tightening specifications and sequence.
⑥— Inch lbs.
⑦— Refer to "Intake Manifold, Replace" for tightening specifications and sequence.
⑧— Refer to "Front Cover, Replace" for tightening specifications and sequence.

Rear Axle & Suspension

NOTE: On Air Bag Equipped Models, Refer To "Air Bag System Precautions" Located In The Front Of This Manual For System Disarming & Arming Procedures.

NOTE: Refer To "Computer Relearn Procedures" Located In The Front Of This Manual When Battery Power To The Computer Has Been Interrupted.

NOTE: Prior To Performing Any Service Operations Listed In This Section, Consult The "Technical Service Bulletins" Section For Related Information.

INDEX

DESCRIPTION

CONTINENTAL

The rear suspension utilizes a fully independent rear suspension which includes lower suspension arms, suspension upper arm and bushings, spring, tension strut and bushing, wheel spindle, shock absorbers, stabilizer bar & fasteners, **Figs. 1 through 3.**

The air suspension system incorporates a rear load leveling system that maintains the vehicle at the proper ride height under varying conditions of vehicle load, and an optional road calibrated suspension ride control system that varies the damping of the shock absorbers between soft and firm, **Fig. 4.**

MARK VIII

This system employs constant velocity (CV) joints at both its inboard and outboard wheel ends for vehicle operating smoothness, **Figs. 5 and 6.** The CV joints are connected by an interconnecting shaft which is splined at both ends and retained in the inboard and outboard CV joints by circlips.

The inboard CV joint stub shaft is splined and held in the differential side gear by a circlip. The outboard CV joint stub shaft is pressed into the hub and secured with a free spinning locknut. The CV joints are lube-for-life with a special CV joint grease and require no periodic lubrication. The CV boots should be periodically inspected and replaced immediately when damage or grease leakage is evident.

Halfshaft removal from the differential is accomplished by applying a load to the back face of the inboard CV joint assembly to overcome the circlip. The outboard joint end must be pressed from the hub. The inboard tripod CV joints can be disassembled and serviced. Other then the CV boot, the outboard CV joint is serviced only as an assembly with the shaft.

TOWN CAR

The gear set, **Fig. 7,** consists of a ring gear and an overhung drive pinion which is supported by two opposed tapered roller bearings. Pinion bearing preload is maintained by a collapsible spacer on the pinion shaft and adjusted by the pinion nut. The differential case is a one piece design with two openings to allow assembly of internal components and lubricant flow. The pinion shaft is retained with a threaded bolt assembled to the case. The differential case is mounted in the carrier between two opposed tapered roller bearings. The bearings are retained in the carrier by removable bearing caps. Differential bearing preload and ring gear backlash are adjusted by the use of shims located between the differential bearing cups and the carrier housing. Axle shafts are held in the housing by C-locks positioned in a slot on the axle shaft splined end, **Fig. 8.**

REAR AXLE

REPLACE

MARK VIII

1. Remove righthand wheel cover, then loosen lug nuts.
2. Raise vehicle on a frame contact type hoist.
3. Remove wheel and tire assembly.
4. Remove righthand and lefthand hand brake sensors.
5. Remove rear suspension arm and bushing bolt. Wire upper suspension arm to top of rear shock absorber so it does not interfere with or damage CV joint boot when halfshaft is removed.
6. Using a paint marker, mark position of rear suspension arm and bushing in relation to rear wheel knuckle with bushings in relaxed position.
7. Install front hub remover and replacer tool Nos. T81P-1104-C with metric hub remover adapters T83P-1104-BH on hub adapter T86P-1104-A1, or equivalents to righthand wheel studs. Turn wrench counterclockwise until halfshaft is free in rear hub.
8. Remove rear suspension arm and bushing to rear suspension arm and bushing mounting bolts.
9. Remove rear wheel knuckle assembly from driveshaft and joint assembly.
10. Carefully rest halfshaft on rear suspension arm and bushing, then secure rear wheel knuckle to top of rear shock absorber using suitable wire or rope.
11. Inboard CV joint stud shaft pilot bearing housing seal must be replaced whenever halfshaft is removed. Remove righthand halfshaft from rear axle housing using CV Joint Remover tool No. T89P-3514-A, or equivalent.
12. Remove halfshaft from vehicle. Install differential plug T89P-4850-B, or equivalent into rear axle housing to prevent lubricant loss.
13. Mark driveshaft centering socket yoke in relation to rear axle universal joint flange. Remove driveshaft mounting bolts.

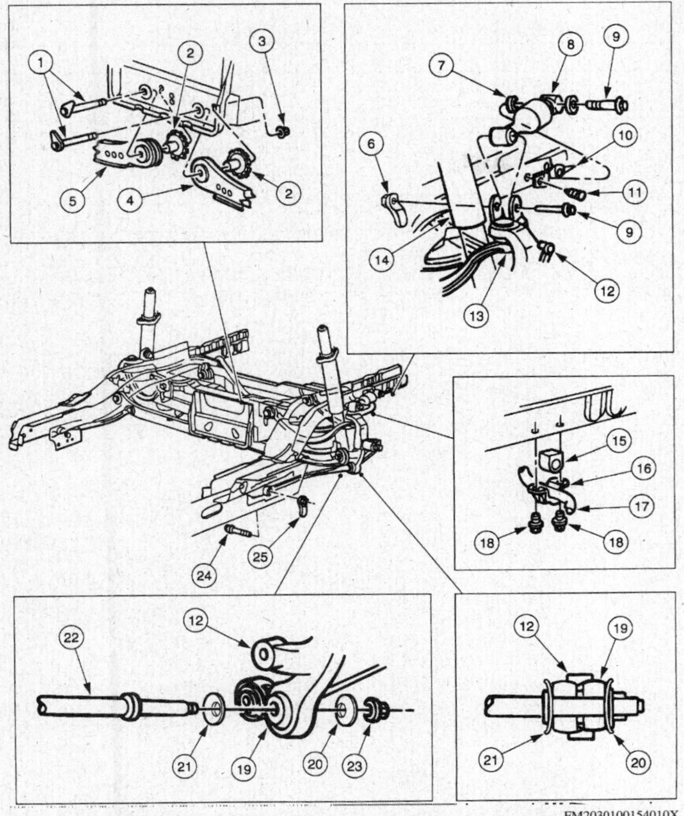

FM2030100154010X

Fig. 1 Rear suspension components (Part 1 of 2). Continental

Item	Description
1	Bolt (4 Req'd)
2	Rear Suspension Arm Adjusting Cam (4 Req'd)
3	Nut (4 Req'd)
4	Rear Lower Suspension Arm (Front LH and Rear RH)
5	Front Lower Suspension Arm (Front RH and Rear LH)
6	Nut (2 Req'd)
7	Washer (4 Req'd)
8	Rear Suspension Damper
9	Bolt (4 Req'd)
10	Damper Bracket
11	Bolt (4 Req'd)
12	Rear Wheel Spindle
13	Rear Suspension Arm and Bushing
14	Shock Absorber
15	Lower Suspension Arm Stabilizer Bar Insulator (2 Req'd)
16	Stabilizer Bar Bracket
17	Rear Stabilizer Bar
18	Bolt (4 Req'd)
19	Rear Suspension Tie Rod Bushing (4 Req'd)
20	Washer (2 Req'd)
21	Washer (2 Req'd)
22	Rear Suspension Tension Strut and Bushing
23	Nut (2 Req'd)
24	Bolt (2 Req'd)
25	Nut Assy (2 Req'd)

FM2030100154020X

Fig. 1 Rear suspension components (Part 2 of 2). Continental

12. Remove shock absorber lower retainer nuts and shock absorbers from retainer brackets.
13. Remove lower control arm retainer and upper control arm retainer nuts and bolts.
14. Unseat air springs, then lower the rear axle from vehicle.
15. Reverse procedure to install. Tighten all fasteners to specifications.

14. Slide driveshaft forward and rest on driveshaft center bridge support reinforcement.
15. With transmission jack supporting rear axle housing, remove axle differential rear insulator to crossmember mounting nuts.
16. Remove rear axle differential rear insulator from axle housing cover.
17. Remove axle front mounting bolts, nuts, bushings and washers.
18. **Do no damage CV joint boot.** Inboard CV joint stub shaft pilot bearing housing seal must be replaced whenever a halfshaft (CV joint) has been removed from rear axle housing.
19. Remove lefthand halfshaft (inboard CV joint) from rear axle housing using CV Joint Remover tool No. T89P-3514-A, or equivalent. Push tool inward (toward rear axle housing).
20. Lower rear axle housing. While lowering rear axle housing, move to righthand and disengage rear axle housing from lefthand inboard CV joint stub shaft.
21. Install Differential Plug tool No. T89P-4850-B, or equivalent, in lefthand side of rear axle housing and lower rear axle housing from vehicle.
22. Reverse procedure to install, noting the following:
    a. **New hub retainer nut, CV joint stub shaft circlips and differential seals must be installed.**
    b. Tighten to specifications.

TOWN CAR

1. Turn air suspension Off.
2. Raise vehicle and position safety stands below rear frame crossmember.
3. Mark driveshaft flange and pinion flange for proper alignment during installation. Remove four driveshaft retainer bolts and disconnect driveshaft.
4. Remove rear wheels, rear disc brake calipers and brake discs, then position caliper aside with suitable wire or rope.
5. Remove rear disc rotor and parking brake rear cable and conduit from the parking brake cable equalizer. Route parking brake rear cable and conduit out of the way.
6. Remove anti-lock brake sensors Reroute anti-lock brake sensor wiring.
7. Remove rear stabilizer bar from rear stabilizer bar link and bushing.
8. Remove rear stabilizer bar bracket bolts, rear stabilizer bar brackets and the rear stabilizer bar.
9. If equipped with rear air springs, remove height sensor.
10. Do not to damage threads on bellcrank stud, separate the Watts linkage from rear axle housing. Remove retainer nut from bellcrank stud.
11. Support straps to secure rear axle to jack and support rear axle housing with a suitable jack.

REAR AXLE SHAFT

REPLACE

TOWN CAR

Removal

1. Turn air suspension switch OFF.
2. Raise and support vehicle. Remove rear wheel and tire assembly.
3. Remove disc brake calipers and rotors and anti-lock brake sensors.
4. Drain rear axle fluid by removing cover.
5. Remove differential pinion shaft lock bolt and differential pinion shaft, **Fig. 9.**
6. Push flanged end of axle shafts toward center of vehicle and remove "C" lock from button end of axle shaft, **Fig. 8.**
7. Remove axle shaft from housing. **Use extreme caution not to damage oil seal and ABS sensor ring.**

Installation

1. Ensure O-ring is present on spline end of axle shaft.
2. Carefully slide axle shaft into axle housing. **Use extreme caution to not damage bearing seal or ABS sensor ring.**
3. Start splines into side gear and push firmly until button end of axle shaft can be seen in differential case.
4. Install C-lock on button end of axle shaft splines. Push shaft outboard until

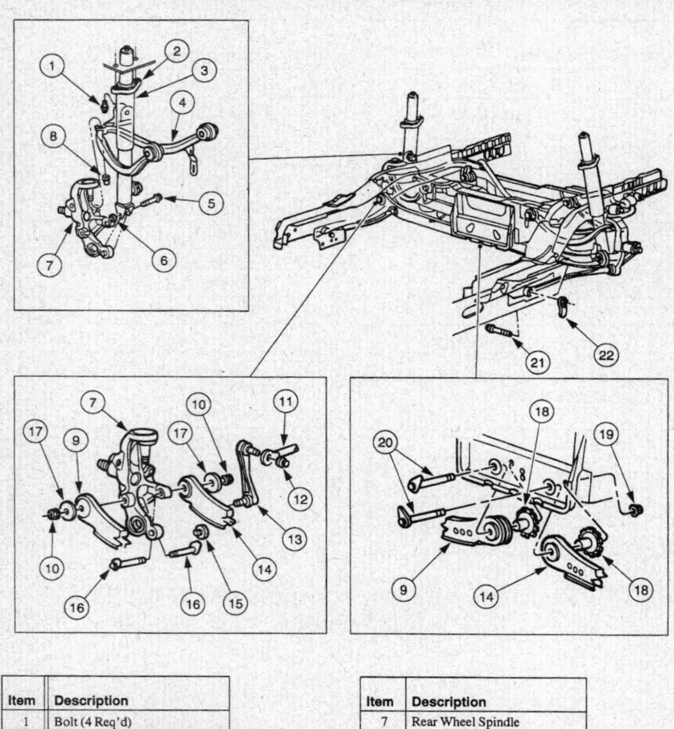

Item	Description
1	Bolt (4 Req'd)
2	Rear Shock Absorber Bracket
3	Shock Absorber
4	Rear Suspension Arm and Bushing
5	Bolt (2 Req'd)
6	Nut

Item	Description
7	Rear Wheel Spindle
8	Nut (2 Req'd)
9	Front Lower Suspension Arm (RH)
10	Nut (4 Req'd)
11	Rear Stabilizer Bar

FM2030100155010X

Fig. 2 Rear shock absorber & components (Part 1 of 2). Continental

Item	Description
12	Nut (2 Req'd)
13	Rear Stabilizer Bar Link
14	Rear Lower Suspension Arm (Rear RH and Front LH)
15	Nut (2 Req'd)
16	Bolt (4 Req'd)

Item	Description
17	Bolt (4 Req'd)
18	Rear Suspension Arm Adjusting Cam (4 Req'd)
19	Nut (4 Req'd)
20	Washer (4 Req'd)
21	Bolt (2 Req'd)
22	Nut Assy (2 Req'd)

FM2030100155020X

Fig. 2 Rear shock absorber & components (Part 2 of 2). Continental

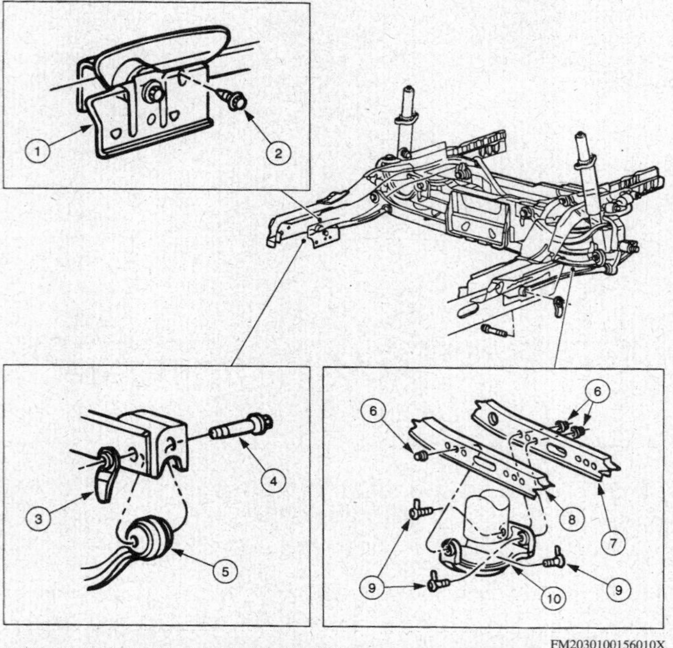

FM2030100156010X

Fig. 3 Rear subframe & components (Part 1 of 2). Continental

splines engage and the C-lock seats in counterbore of differential side gear.

5. Position differential pinion shaft through case and pinion gears, aligning hole in shaft with lock bolt hose. Apply rear axle lubricant E0AZ-19554-BA, or equivalent to pinion shaft lock bolt. Tighten to specifications.
6. Install cover and tighten to specifications.
7. Install ABS speed sensor, rotors and calipers. Tighten to specifications.

REAR HALFSHAFT

REPLACE

MARK VIII

Do not begin this removal procedure unless following components are available: new hub retainer nut, new inboard CV joint stub shaft circlip and new differential oil seal. Once removed, these components must not be used again during assembly. Their torque holding ability is diminished during removal.

1. Remove wheel cover/hub cover and remove hub retainer nut, then loosen wheel nuts.
2. Raise and support vehicle on a frame contact hoist.
3. Remove rear wheel and tire assembly.
4. Remove anti-lock brake sensors.
5. Pull back on parking brake release lever and at same time pull on cable. This will slacken cable so cable end can be removed from brake caliper attachment.
6. Remove upper and lower brake caliper mounting bolts.
7. Remove caliper assembly from rotor, then carefully wire caliper to brake junction bracket.
8. Remove brake rotor push nuts and remove rotor.
9. Remove upper control arm bolts and nuts, then wire upper control arm to upper shock absorber so that it does not damage CV joint boots when halfshaft is removed.
10. Using a paint marker, mark position of lower control arm in relation to knuckle with lower bushings in their relaxed position. When upper control arm bolt is removed from knuckle, lower bushings will return to their relaxed positions. **Failure to mark this position will result in bushing wind-up on assembly and improper ride height, causing misalignment and premature tire wear.**
11. Install hub remover T81P-1104-C, or equivalent to hub studs, **Fig. 10.**
12. Turn wrench counterclockwise until halfshaft is free in hub.
13. Remove lower control arm mounting bolts.
14. Remove knuckle assembly while supporting outboard CV joint and boot. Carefully rest halfshaft on lower control arm.
15. Insert CV joint removal tool No. T89P-3514-A, or equivalent, between differential housing and CV joint. Push tool outward until CV joint becomes free from differential side gear. **Extreme care must be taken to prevent damage to the differential oil seal, differential housing, sensor ring and/or CV joint and boot.**
16. Remove halfshaft from vehicle, then plug differential housing to prevent loss of lubricant.
17. Reverse procedure to install, noting the following:
    a. Install new differential oil seal and circlip on inboard CV joint.
    b. Ensure to align reference marks on

Item	Description
1	Bracket (2 Req'd)
2	Bolt (2 Req'd)
3	Nut (4 Req'd)
4	Bolt (4 Req'd)
5	Rear Suspension Arm and Bushing
6	Nut (6 Req'd)
7	Rear Lower Suspension Arm (Rear RH and Front LH)
8	Front Lower Suspension Arm (Front RH and Rear LH)
9	Bolt (6 Req'd)
10	Spring Seat (2 Req'd)

FM2030100156020X

Fig. 3 Rear subframe & components (Part 2 of 2). Continental

lower control arm to marks on knuckle/bushing assembly.

c. **On models equipped with rear disc brakes,** tighten caliper mounting bolts to specifications.

d. **On models equipped with anti-lock brakes,** tighten brake sensor mounting bolts to specifications.

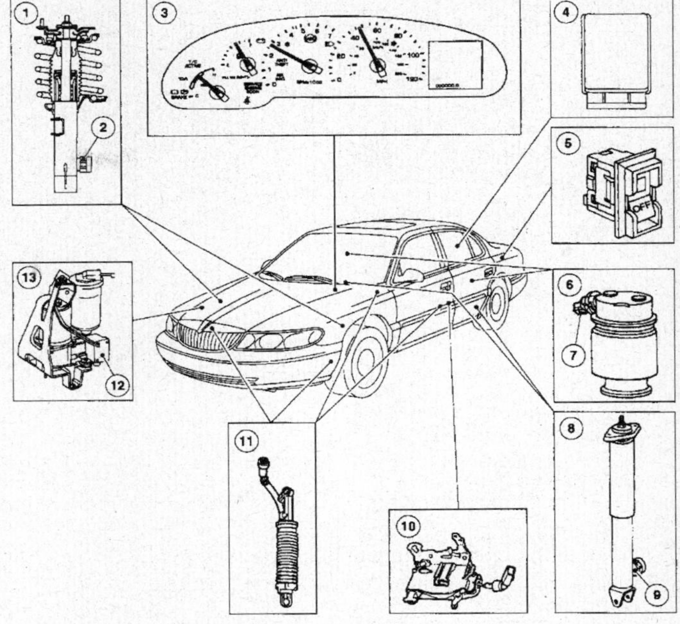

Item	Description
1	Front Spring and Shock Absorber Assembly
2	Shock Actuator (Part of 3C098)
3	Message Center Indicator
4	Vehicle Dynamic Module (VDM)
5	Rear Suspension Leveler Compressor Switch
6	Rear Air Spring

FM2019800374010X

Fig. 4 Air suspension components (Part 1 of 2). Continental

Item	Description
7	Air Spring Solenoid
8	Shock Absorber
9	Shock Actuator
10	Lamp Switch
11	Air Suspension Height Sensor
12	Vent Solenoid
13	Air Compressor

FM2019800374020X

Fig. 4 Air suspension components (Part 2 of 2). Continental

PROPELLER SHAFT

REPLACE

MARK VIII

1. Lower the fuel tank. Refer to "Fuel Pump, Replace" in the "4.6L Engine" section.
2. Remove mounting bolts and subframe center support member.
3. Remove subframe crossmember.
4. Place an index mark on rear axle universal joint flange and driveshaft centering socket yoke.
5. Separate driveshaft centering socket yoke from rear axle universal joint flange.
6. Remove driveshaft.
7. Reverse procedure to install.

TOWN CAR

To maintain proper drive line balance, mark the driveshaft, universal joints, slip yoke and companion flange before removing the shaft assembly so it can be reinstalled in its original position.

1. Remove companion flange to drive pinion flange mounting bolts.
2. Pull driveshaft rearward until slip yoke clears transmission extension housing.
3. Reverse procedure to install.

SHOCK ABSORBER

REPLACE

MARK VIII

Turn air suspension switch off before replacing shock absorber.

1. Open luggage compartment to gain access to upper shock absorber attachment.
2. Remove rubber cap from shock absorber stud, then remove nut, washer and insulator.
3. Raise vehicle and support rear axle.
4. Remove lower shock absorber protective cover, then remove cross bolt and nut from lower shock absorber mounting bracket.
5. From underneath vehicle, compress shock absorber to clear hole in upper shock tower, then remove shock absorber. **These models are equipped with gas pressurized shock absorbers which extend unassisted during removal. Do not apply heat or flame to the shock absorber tube during removal.**
6. Reverse procedure to install. Tighten mounting bolts to specifications.

CONTINENTAL & TOWN CAR

Turn air suspension switch off before raising vehicle.

1. Raise and support vehicle.
2. Support rear axle with suitable jack.
3. Release air pressure from air springs.
4. Remove shock absorber upper mounting nut, washer and insulator, **Fig. 11.**
5. Remove self-locking mounting nut from lower shock absorber stud, discard nut.
6. Remove shock absorber.
7. Reverse procedure to install.

COIL SPRING

REPLACE

TOWN CAR

These models are equipped with an air spring. Refer to "Active Suspension Systems" for air spring replacement.

CONTROL ARM

REPLACE

CONTINENTAL

Upper

1. Turn air suspension switch Off.

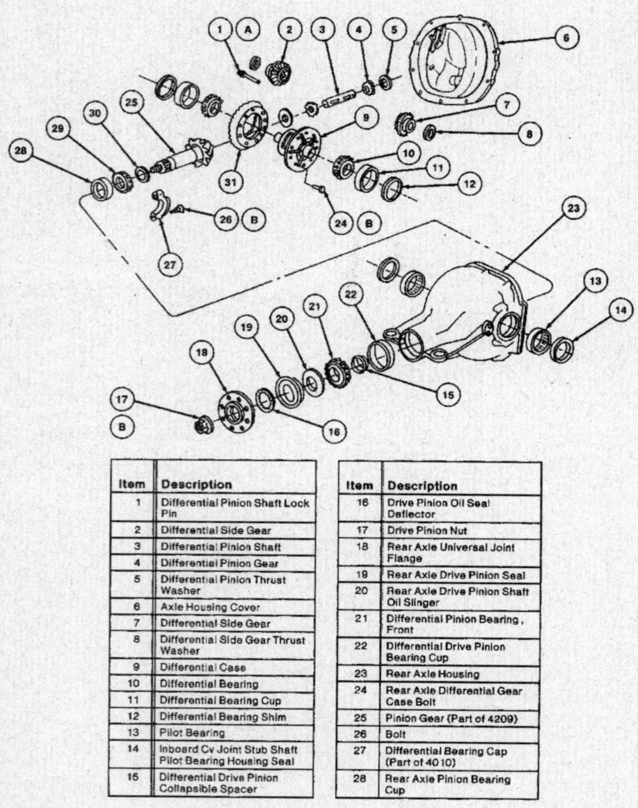

Item	Description
1	Differential Pinion Shaft Lock Pin
2	Differential Side Gear
3	Differential Pinion Shaft
4	Differential Pinion Gear
5	Differential Pinion Thrust Washer
6	Axle Housing Cover
7	Differential Side Gear
8	Differential Side Gear Thrust Washer
9	Differential Case
10	Differential Bearing
11	Differential Bearing Cup
12	Differential Bearing Shim
13	Pilot Bearing
14	Inboard Cv Joint Stub Shaft Pilot Bearing Housing Seal
15	Differential Drive Pinion Collapsible Spacer

Item	Description
16	Drive Pinion Oil Seal Deflector
17	Drive Pinion Nut
18	Rear Axle Universal Joint Flange
19	Rear Axle Drive Pinion Seal
20	Rear Axle Drive Pinion Shaft Oil Slinger
21	Differential Pinion Bearing, Front
22	Differential Drive Pinion Bearing Cup
23	Rear Axle Housing
24	Rear Axle Differential Gear Case Bolt
25	Pinion Gear (Part of 4209)
26	Bolt
27	Differential Bearing Cap (Part of 40 10)
28	Rear Axle Pinion Bearing Cup

FM3039700317010X

Fig. 5 Exploded view of rear axle assembly (Part 1 of 2). Mark VIII

2. Raise and support vehicle.
3. Remove wheel and tire assembly.
4. Deflate air spring.
5. Disconnect air suspension height sensor from ball stud pin on rear suspension arm and bushing.
6. Remove lower shock absorber mounting nut and bolt.
7. Loosen but do not remove upper ball joint to upper rear suspension arm nut.
8. Using a suitable joint removal tool, separate ball joint from rear suspension arm and bushing and remove nut.
9. Remove rear upper suspension arm to body nuts and bolts.
10. Remove rear suspension arm and bushing.
11. Reverse procedure to install.

Lower

1. Turn air suspension to Off position.
2. Raise and support vehicle.
3. Remove tire and wheel assembly.
4. Deflate air spring.
5. Remove air spring seat and air spring.
6. Remove brake anti-lock sensor wiring, rear parking brake cable conduit and routing clips from front lower suspension arm.
7. Remove front lower suspension arm to rear wheel spindle nut, washer and bolt.
8. Remove front lower suspension arm to body nut and bolt and front lower suspension arm.
9. Remove rear suspension arm adjusting cam from front lower suspension arm, if damaged.
10. Reverse procedure to install.

TOWN CAR

Upper

If both rear suspension arms and bushings are to be replaced, remove and replace one rear suspension arm and bushing at a time to prevent axle from slipping or rolling sideways.

1. Turn air suspension switch Off.
2. Raise and support vehicle.
3. Support frame side rails with suitable jackstands, then support rear axle assembly.
4. Lower rear axle assembly and support under differential pinion nose as well as under rear axle assembly.

Item	Description
29	Differential Pinion Bearing, Rear
30	Drive Pinion Bearing Adjustment Shim

Item	Description
31	Ring Gear (Part of 4209)
A	Tighten to 20-41 N·m (15-30 Lb-Ft)
B	Tighten to 95-115 N·m (70-84 Lb-Ft)

FM3039700317020X

Fig. 5 Exploded view of rear axle assembly (Part 2 of 2). Mark VIII

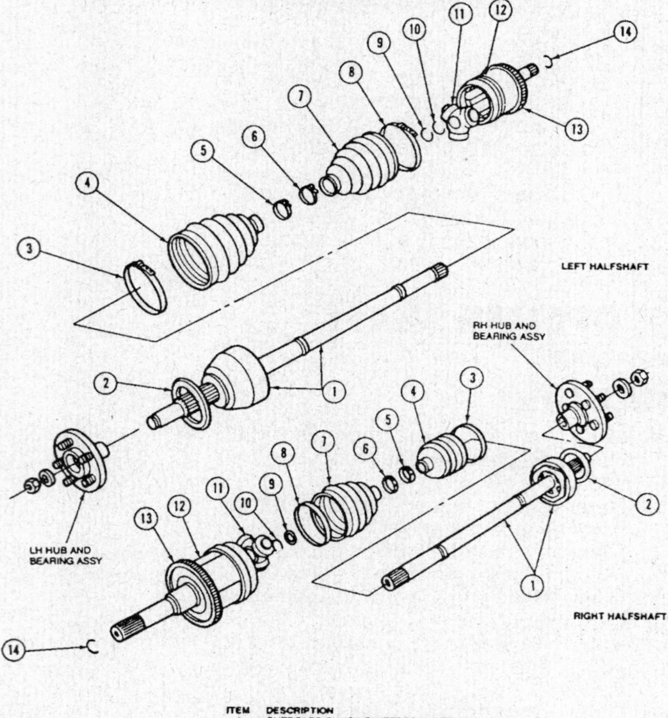

ITEM	DESCRIPTION
1.	OUTBOARD CV JOINT/INTERCONNECTING SHAFT ASSY
2.	DUST SEAL
3.	BOOT CLAMP (LARGE OUTBOARD)
4.	BOOT (OUTBOARD)
5.	BOOT CLAMP (SMALL OUTBOARD)
6.	BOOT CLAMP (SMALL INBOARD)
7.	BOOT (INBOARD)
8.	BOOT CLAMP (LARGE INBOARD)
9.	STOP RING
10.	CIRCLIP
11.	TRIPOD ASSY
12.	INBOARD JOINT OUTER RACE
13.	SENSOR RING (ANTI-SKID)
14.	CIRCLIP

FM3039100210000X

Fig. 6 Rear wheel drive halfshaft system. Mark VIII

5. Unsnap parking brake rear cable and conduit from upper arm retainer.
6. Remove and discard nut and bolt retaining rear suspension arm and bushing to rear axle housing.
7. Disconnect rear suspension arm and bushing from housing.
8. Remove and discard nut and bolt that secures rear suspension arm and bushing to frame bracket, then remove rear suspension arm and bushing.
9. Reverse procedure to install.

Lower

1. Turn air suspension to Off position.
2. Mark rear suspension shock absorber relative to protective sleeve with vehicle in a static level, ground condition.
3. Remove rear stabilizer as outlined under "Stabilizer Bar, Replace."
4. Raise and support vehicle and place

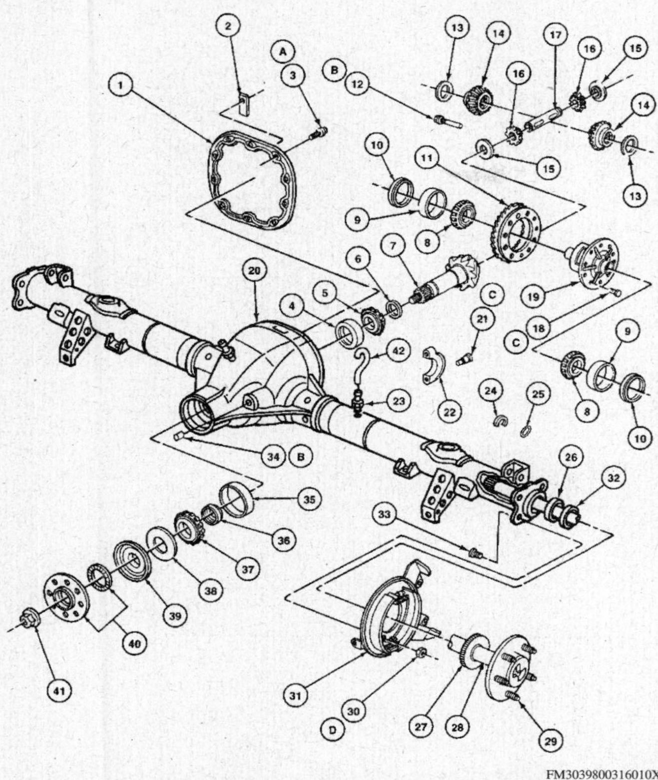

Fig. 7 Exploded view of rear axle (Part 1 of 2). Town Car

Item	Description
1	Axle Housing Cover
2	Identification Tag
3	Axle Housing Cover Bolt
4	Rear Axle Pinion Bearing Cup
5	Differential Pinion Bearing (Rear)
6	Drive Pinion Bearing Adjustment Shim
7	Drive Pinion (Part of 4209)
8	Differential Bearing (RH)
9	Differential Bearing Cup
10	Differential Bearing Shim
11	Ring Gear (Part of 4209)
12	Differential Pinion Shaft Lock Pin
13	Differential Side Gear Thrust Washer
14	Differential Side Gear
15	Differential Pinion Thrust Washer
16	Differential Pinion Gear
17	Differential Pinion Shaft
18	Rear Axle Differential Gear Case Bolt
19	Differential Case
20	Rear Axle Housing
21	Bolt
22	Differential Bearing Cap (Part of 4010)
23	Rear Axle Housing Vent
24	U-Washer

Item	Description
25	Rear Axle Shaft O-Ring
26	Rear Wheel Bearing
27	Rear Brake Anti-Lock Sensor Indicator
28	Axle Shaft
29	Lug Bolt
30	Nut
31	Rear Wheel Disc Brake Adapter
32	Inner Wheel Bearing Oil Seal
33	Bolt
34	Fill Plug
35	Differential Drive Pinion Bearing Cup
36	Differential Drive Pinion Collapsible Spacer
37	Differential Pinion Bearing (Front)
38	Rear Axle Drive Pinion Shaft Oil Slinger
39	Rear Axle Drive Pinion Seal
40	Rear Axle Universal Joint Flange
41	Drive Pinion Nut
42	Formed Vent Hose
A	Tighten to 38-52 N·m (28-38 Lb-Ft)
B	Tighten to 20-40 N·m (15-30 Lb-Ft)
C	Tighten to 95-115 N·m (70-84 Lb-Ft)
D	Tighten to 27-40 N·m (20-30 Lb-Ft)

FM3039800316020X

Fig. 7 Exploded view of rear axle (Part 2 of 2). Town Car

suitable jackstands under rear axle assembly.

5. Lower hoist until shock absorbers are fully extended to relieve rear spring pressure.
6. Support rear axle assembly under differential pinion nose as well as under rear axle assembly.
7. Remove and discard lower arm pivot bolt and nut from axle bracket.
8. Disengage rear suspension lower arm from bracket.
9. Remove and discard pivot bolt and nut from frame bracket and remove rear suspension arm.
10. Reverse procedure to install.

MARK VIII

Lower

1. Turn air suspension switch to off position, then raise and support vehicle and remove wheel assembly.
2. Vent air springs to atmosphere by removing air spring solenoid.
3. Remove two air spring to lower control arm mounting bolts, then the air spring from lower arm.
4. Remove control arm to frame and control arm to axle bracket pivot bolts and nuts.
5. Remove lower control arm.
6. Reverse procedure to install.

Upper

Always replace control arm in pairs. If

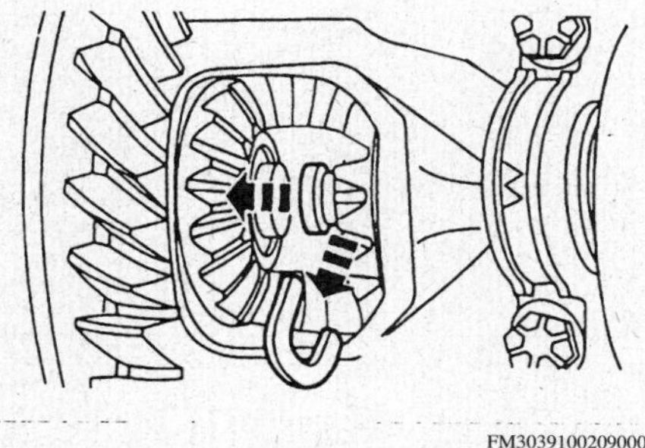

Fig. 8 Axle shaft "C" lock. Town Car

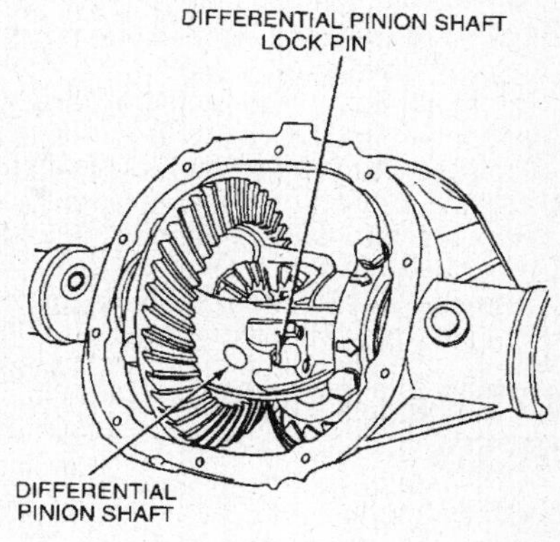

Fig. 9 Differential pinion shaft removal. Town Car

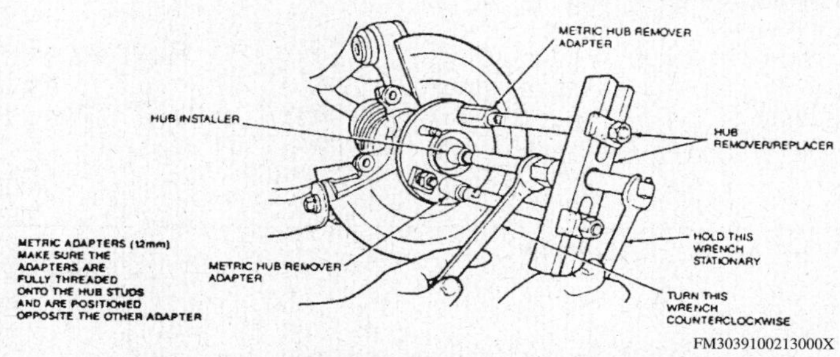

Fig. 10 Mounting hub removal tool. Mark VIII

one arm requires replacement, replace the same arm on the opposite side of the vehicle.

1. Turn air suspension switch off.
2. Raise and support vehicle, then disconnect rear height sensor from side arm. Note position of sensor adjustment bracket to aid in reassembly.
3. Remove upper arm to axle and upper arm to frame bracket pivot bolts and nuts.
4. Remove upper control arm.
5. Reverse procedure to install.

STABILIZER BAR

REPLACE

CONTINENTAL

1. If required, disconnect air suspension electrical wiring and all related components that will interfere with stabilizer bar removal.
2. Raise and support vehicle.
3. Remove stabilizer bar to link mounting nuts, washers and insulators.
4. Remove U-bracket mounting bolts, then the stabilizer bar.
5. Reverse procedure to install, using new mounting fasteners.

MARK VIII & TOWN CAR

1. Turn air suspension switch Off, then raise and support vehicle.
2. Remove both rear wheel and tire assemblies.
3. Disconnect emergency brake cables from stabilizer bar.
4. Remove both stabilizer bar link upper mounting nuts and insulators.
5. Remove links from stabilizer bar eyelets by pushing bar ends up and rotating out of the way.
6. Remove both stabilizer bar bracket bolts.
7. Remove brackets from T-slots in subframe.
8. Remove rear muffler hanger mounting nuts.
9. Remove stabilizer bar from vehicle.
10. Reverse procedure to install.

LATERAL LINK

REPLACE

TOWN CAR

1. Turn air suspension switch off.
2. Raise and support vehicle.
3. Support rear axle with a suitable jack.
4. Release air pressure from air spring, then disconnect height sensor from mounting bracket.
5. Remove and discard both lateral arm assembly pivot bolts and nuts to frame brackets, **Fig. 11.**
6. Remove and discard Watts link pivot nut.

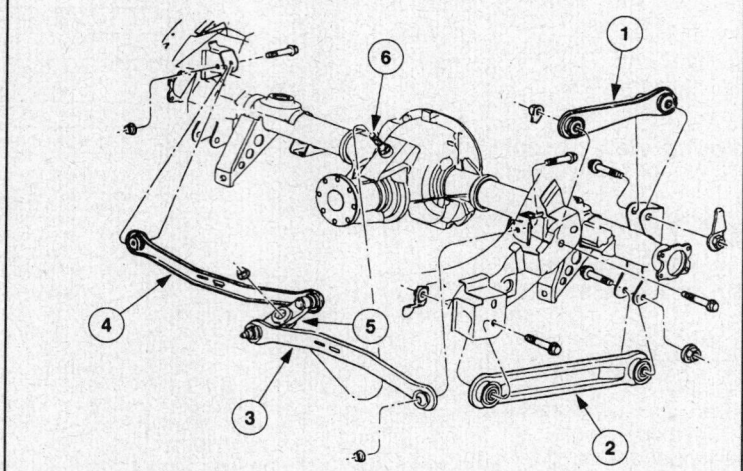

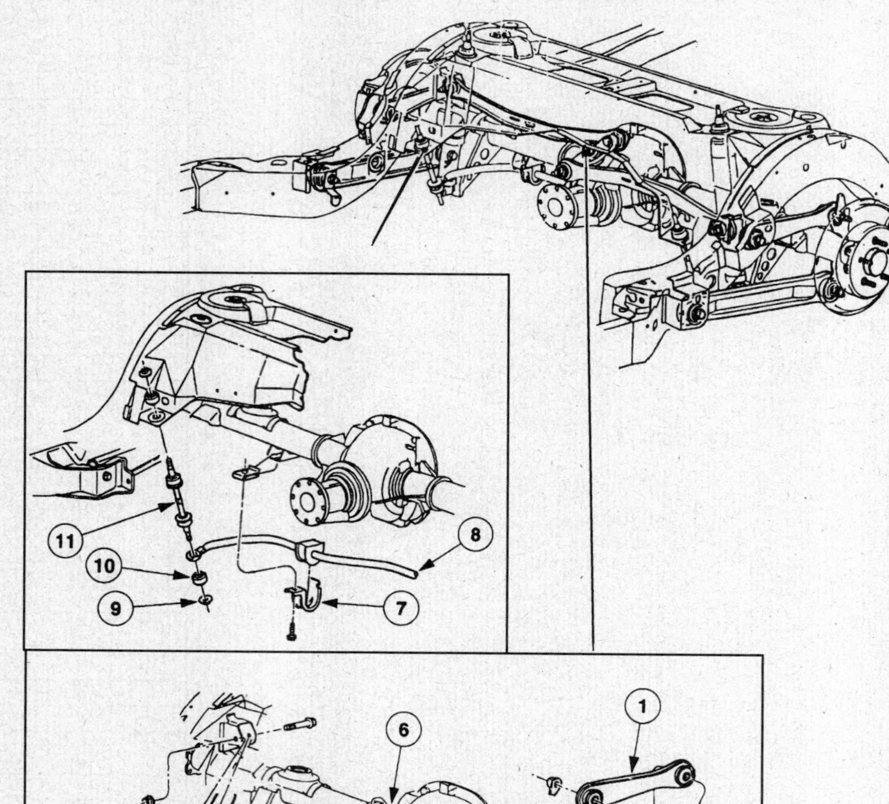

Item	Description
1	Rear Suspension Upper Arm
2	Rear Suspension Lower Arm
3	Lateral Arm, LH
4	Lateral Arm, RH
5	Watts Link Pivot

Item	Description
6	Watts Link Pivot Stud
7	Stabilizer Bar Bracket
8	Stabilizer Bar and Isolator Assy
9	Stabilizer Bar Link Retaining Nut
10	Stabilizer Bar Bushing
11	Stabilizer Bar Link

FM2039800062000X

Fig. 11 Rear suspension components. Continental & Town Car

7. Lower axle until Watts link is free of pivot stud.
8. Remove lateral arm assembly.
9. Remove and discard Watts link pivot stud.
10. Reverse procedure to install.

TIGHTENING SPECIFICATIONS

Year	Component	Torque/Ft. Lbs.
CONTINENTAL		
1998–2002	Anti-Lock Brake Sensor Bolt	53②
	Disc Brake Adapter To Caliper Bolt	64–88
	Disk Brake Shield Bolts	89②
	Lower Suspension Arm To Body Nut	59
	Lower Suspension Arm To Rear Wheel Spindle Nuts	59
	Rear Spring Seat To Lower Suspension Arm Nut	50–68
	Rear Stabilizer Bar Link To Rear Lower Suspension Arm Nut	30
	Rear Stabilizer Bar Link To Rear Stabilizer Bar Nut	30
	Shock Absorber Lower Mounting Nut	59
	Shock Absorber Mass Damper	21
	Shock Absorber Upper Mounting Bolts	30
	Stabilizer Bar Bracket To Body Bolt	22
	Tension Strut To Body Bolt	77
	Tension Strut To Rear Wheel Spindle	41
	Upper Ball Joint Nut	59
	Upper Suspension Arm To Body Nut	85
	Wheel Hub Retainer	188–254
	Wheel Lug Nuts	85–104
MARK VIII		
1998	ABS Sensor	14–20
	Air Spring To Lower Arm	25–35
	Brake Backing Plate	20–40
	Caliper Mount	80–100
	Clevis Bracket To Axle	55–70
	Differential Bearing Cap	70–85
	Differential Pinion Shaft Lock	15–30
	Lower Arm To Axle	90–100
	Lower Arm To Frame	80–105
	Oil Filler Plug	15–30
	Pivot Bolts	100
	Rear Cover	①
	Rear Muffler Hanger	17–24
	Ring Gear	70–85
	Sensor Lower Bracket To Frame	84–120②
	Sensor Upper Bracket To Frame	10–12
	Shock Absorber Cross Bolt	59
	Shock Absorber To Clevis Bracket	45–60
	Shock Absorber To Frame	17–27
	Shock Absorber Upper Mount	24–26
	Stabilizer Bar Bracket To Subframe	25–34
	Stabilizer Bar To Axle	13–20
	Stabilizer Bar To Body	13–18
	Upper Arm To Axle	70–100
	Upper Arm To Frame	80–105
	Wheel Lug	85–104

Continued

TIGHTENING SPECIFICATIONS—Continued

Year	Component	Torque/Ft. Lbs.
TOWN CAR		
1998–2002	Height Sensor Mounting Bracket To Lateral Arm	9–12
	Lateral Arm To Frame Bracket	65–88
	Lateral Arm To Watts Link Pivot	60–77
	Lower Suspension Arm To Axle Bracket	95–127
	Lower Suspension Arm To Frame Bracket	95–127
	Shock Absorber To Axle Bracket	57–75
	Shock Absorber To Upper Mount Nut	26–34
	Stabilizer Bar Bracket To Axle	16–21
	Stabilizer Link Nut To Stabilizer Bar	13–16
	Stabilizer Link Upper Nut To Frame	13–16
	Upper Suspension Arm To Axle Bracket	65–88
	Upper Suspension Arm To Frame Bracket	95–127
	Watts Link Pivot	158–212
	Watts Link Pivot Stud	189–211
	Wheel Lug	85–105

① — Torque plastic cover to 15–20 ft. lbs., or metal cover to 25–35 ft. lbs.

② — Inch lbs.

Front Suspension & Steering

NOTE: On Air Bag Equipped Models, Refer To "Air Bag System Precautions" Located In The Front Of This Manual For System Disarming & Arming Procedures.

NOTE: Refer To "Computer Relearn Procedures" Located In The Front Of This Manual When Battery Power To The Computer Has Been Interrupted.

INDEX

PRECAUTIONS

AIR BAG SYSTEMS

Refer to "Air Bag System Precautions" in the front of this manual for system disarming and arming procedures.

AIR SUSPENSION SYSTEM

Always place the air suspension switch in the Off position before performing any work, or whenever raising the front suspension.

WHEEL BEARING

ADJUST

MARK VIII & TOWN CAR

On these models the wheel bearings are preset and cannot be adjusted.

WHEEL BEARING

REPLACE

MARK VIII & TOWN CAR

1. Raise and support front of vehicle, then remove wheel and tire assembly.
2. Remove grease cap from hub.
3. Remove brake caliper and suspend from chassis with wire. Do not allow caliper to hang from brake hose.
4. Remove push clips, if equipped, then the brake rotor, **Fig. 1.**
5. Remove hub nut, then remove hub and bearing assembly. If difficulty is encountered, use front hub remover tool No. T81P-1104-C, or equivalent to remove hub and bearing assembly.
6. Reverse procedure to install, noting the following:

ROTOR ASSY
DUST CAP
HUB AND BEARING ASSY
WITHOUT ABS
HUB NUT TIGHTEN TO 255-345 N·m (188-254 LB-FT)
ROTOR ASSY
DUST CAP
HUB AND BEARING ASSY
HUB NUT TIGHTEN TO 255-345 N·m (188-254 LB-FT)
WITH ABS
FM3039100221000X

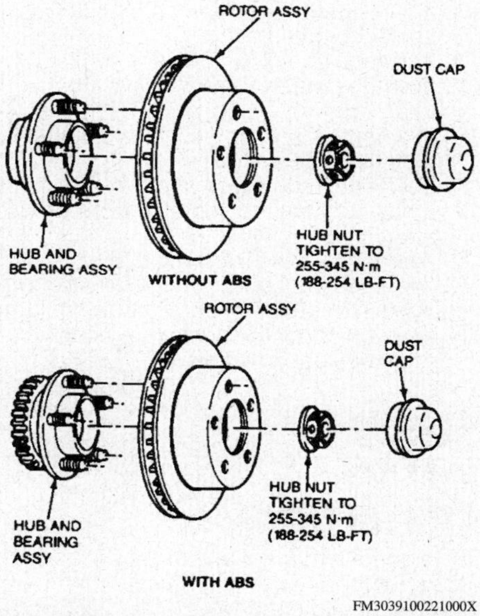

Fig. 1 Hub & bearing assembly. Mark VIII & Town Car

   a. A new hub and bearing mounting nut should be installed.
   b. Tighten hub bearing nut to specifications.

CONTINENTAL

Wheel hub is not pressed into front wheel knuckle. Do not use a slide hammer or strike back of inner bearing race to remove a stuck wheel hub. Damage to bearing or wheel hub will occur. Apply rust penetrant and inhibitor to the inboard and outboard wheel hub/knuckle mating surface and remove wheel hub from front wheel knuckle.

1. Turn air suspension switch to Off position.
2. Raise and support vehicle.
3. Remove wheel and tire assembly.
4. Remove brake disc.
5. Remove and discard front axle wheel hub retainer.
6. Ensure steering column is in the unlocked position.
7. Remove and discard front suspension lower ball joint nut, then using a suitable joint removal tool, separate ball joint from lower suspension arm.
8. Using Hub remover/replacer tool No. T81P-1104–C, or equivalent, press front driveshaft joint out of wheel hub.
9. Remove and discard three wheel hub mounting bolts.
10. Remove wheel hub and bearing assembly.

BALL JOINT INSPECTION

UPPER

Town Car

1. Support vehicle on floor jacks placed beneath lower control arms.
2. Grasp lower edge of tire and move wheel in and out.
3. As wheel is being moved in and out, observe upper end of spindle and upper arm.
4. Any movement between upper end of spindle and upper arm indicates ball joint wear and loss of preload. If such

movement is observed, replace upper ball joint. **During the foregoing inspection, the lower ball joint will be unloaded and may move. Disregard all such movement of the lower joint. Also, do not mistake loose wheel bearings for a worn ball joint.**

LOWER

Mark VIII

1. Raise and support vehicle under subframe.
2. Attach dial indicator at ball joint to be inspected so as to measure lateral movement between the spindle and the arm. Either upper or lower ball joint may be inspected in this manner.
3. Hold tire at top and bottom and slowly move tire in and out. Note reading on dial indicator. If reading exceeds .015 inch, replace ball joint.

Town Car

These models are equipped with lower ball joint wear indicators. To inspect ball joint for wear, support vehicle in normal driving position with both ball joints loaded. Observe the checking surface of the ball joint, and if it is inside the cover, replace the ball joint.

BALL JOINT

REPLACE

CONTINENTAL

The ball joint is not serviceable. If the ball joint requires replacement, the front wheel knuckle must be replaced.

MARK VIII

These ball joints are not serviceable. If they require replacement, the control arm and ball joint must be replaced as an assembly. Tighten ball joint stud to specifications.

TOWN CAR

1. Raise and support vehicle, then remove wheel and tire assembly. Position jack stands under both sides of frame just to the rear of lower control arm.
2. Position a suitable jack under lower control arm.
3. Remove nut from upper ball joint to steering knuckle pinch bolt, then tap out pinch bolt.
4. Mark positions of caster and camber adjusting cams for use during installation, **Fig. 2.**
5. Remove two bolts mounting ball joint to upper control arm.
6. Using a suitable pry bar, spread slot to release ball joint from steering knuckle and remove.
7. Reverse procedure to install. Align caster and camber marks made during removal. After completing installation, inspect front wheel alignment.

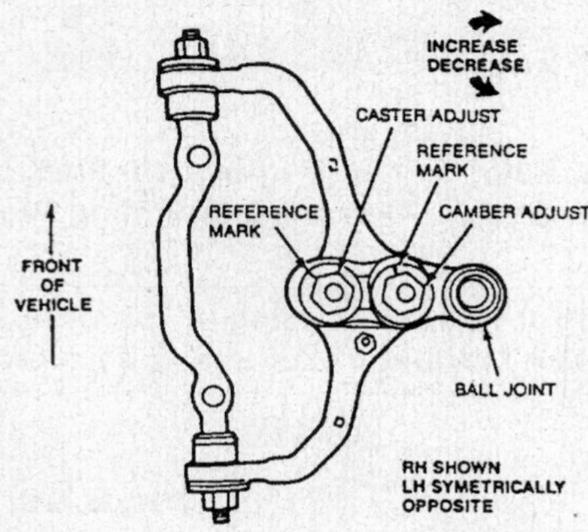

Fig. 2 Upper control assembly. Town Car

COIL SPRING

REPLACE

CONTINENTAL

Refer to "Strut, Replace" for coil spring replacement procedure.

TOWN CAR

1. Raise and support vehicle.
2. Remove wheel and tire assembly.
3. Disconnect stabilizer bar link from lower control arm.
4. Remove shock absorber.
5. Remove steering center link from Pitman arm.
6. Compress coil spring with a suitable spring compressor.
7. Remove two lower control arm pivot bolts and disengage arm from crossmember.
8. Remove spring from vehicle.
9. Reverse procedure to install. Tighten stabilizer bar to lower control arm nuts and lower control arm to crossmember bolts to specifications.

STRUT

REPLACE

CONTINENTAL

1. Remove hub nut and loosen the upper strut mounting nuts, **Fig. 3.**
2. Raise and support vehicle. **Do not lift vehicle from lower control arm.**
3. Disconnect air suspension electrical wiring and all related components that will interfere with strut removal.
4. Remove wheel and tire assembly.
5. Remove brake caliper and suspend with wire, then disconnect tie rod end.
6. Remove stabilizer bar link nut, then remove link from strut.
7. Remove lower control arm to steering knuckle pinch nut and bolt, then spread joint as required and disengage control arm from knuckle.
8. Using a suitable hub installation/removal tool, press axle from hub/rotor assembly. Wire axle shaft as required to maintain level position. **Do not permit axle shaft to move outward during disengagement from hub, since damage to CV joints could result.**
9. Remove strut to steering knuckle pinch bolt, then spread joint and remove steering knuckle and hub assembly.
10. Remove strut upper mounting nuts, then remove strut from vehicle.
11. Reverse procedure to install. Tighten to specifications.

SHOCK ABSORBER

REPLACE

MARK VIII

These models are equipped with gas pressurized shock absorbers which extend unassisted during removal. Do not apply heat or flame during removal.

1. Raise and support vehicle.
2. Remove shock actuator.
3. Remove upper shock mount to body nuts from inside luggage compartment.
4. Remove bolt and nut at lower arm, then remove shock absorber.
5. Reverse procedure to install.

TOWN CAR

1. Remove nut, washer and bushing from upper end of shock absorber.
2. Raise and support vehicle.
3. Remove screws mounting shock absorber to lower control arm and remove shock absorber.
4. **These models are equipped with gas pressurized shock absorbers which extend unassisted during removal. Do not apply heat or flame during removal.**
5. Reverse procedure to install.

CONTROL ARM

REPLACE

LOWER

Continental

1. Raise and support vehicle.
2. Disconnect air suspension electrical wiring and all related components that will interfere with control arm removal.
3. Remove wheel and tire assembly, then the tension strut nut and washer.
4. Separate ball joint from lower arm using suitable joint removal tool.
5. Remove lower control arm inner pivot bolt and nut, then the lower control arm.
6. Reverse procedure to install. Tighten to specifications.

Mark VIII

Do not begin procedure unless a new hub retainer nut is available. Once removed, this component cannot be used again during assembly.

1. Raise and support front of vehicle, then remove rear knuckle/hub assembly.
2. Deflate rear air springs and disengage height sensor from lower arm ball stud attachment (lefthand only). Ensure the

integral lower air spring clip is disengaged from lower arm.

3. Disconnect rear stabilizer bar straps from emergency brake cables (both sides).
4. Remove rear stabilizer bar link nuts at their lower arm attachment ends.
5. Remove link bushings and push link ends up and out of lower arm, then rotate bar and link assembly out of the way.
6. Mark toe adjustment cam-to-subframe position. Loosen both pivot attachment nuts at lower arm to subframe positions but do not remove bolts.
7. Remove shock absorber to lower control arm bolt.
8. Remove inner pivot bolts and nuts.
9. Remove lower control arm from vehicle.
10. Reverse procedure to install, noting the following:
    a. Tighten lower control arm to toe compensating link nut to specifications.
    b. Ensure air spring assembly is fully seated and the spring is not kinked.

Town Car

1. Raise and support front of vehicle, then remove front wheels.
2. Remove brake caliper, rotor, dust shield and ABS sensor, if equipped.
3. Remove jounce bumper, if equipped.
4. Remove shock absorber.
5. Disconnect steering center link from Pitman arm.
6. Remove lower ball joint mounting nut cotter pin, then loosen lower ball joint nut one or two times, **Fig. 4. Do not remove nut from stud at this time.**
7. Tap spindle boss sharply to relieve stud pressure, then tap near lower stud to loosen stud in spindle.
8. Position a suitable jack under lower control arm.
9. Install suitable coil spring compression tool, then remove coil spring.
10. Remove ball joint nut, then the lower control arm assembly.
11. Reverse procedure to install, noting the following:
    a. Tighten ball joint mounting nut to specifications.
    b. Ensure coil spring is properly aligned, **Fig. 4.**
    c. Tighten control arm to crossmember mounting bolts and nuts to specifications.
    d. Inspect wheel alignment.

UPPER

Mark VIII

1. Raise and support vehicle.
2. Remove wheel and tire assembly, **Fig. 5.**
3. Support knuckle and hub assembly.
4. Support knuckle and hub assembly so it cannot swing outward.
5. Remove inner and outer pivot bolts and nuts at upper control arm.
6. Reverse procedure to install. Tighten inner pivot nut to specifications.

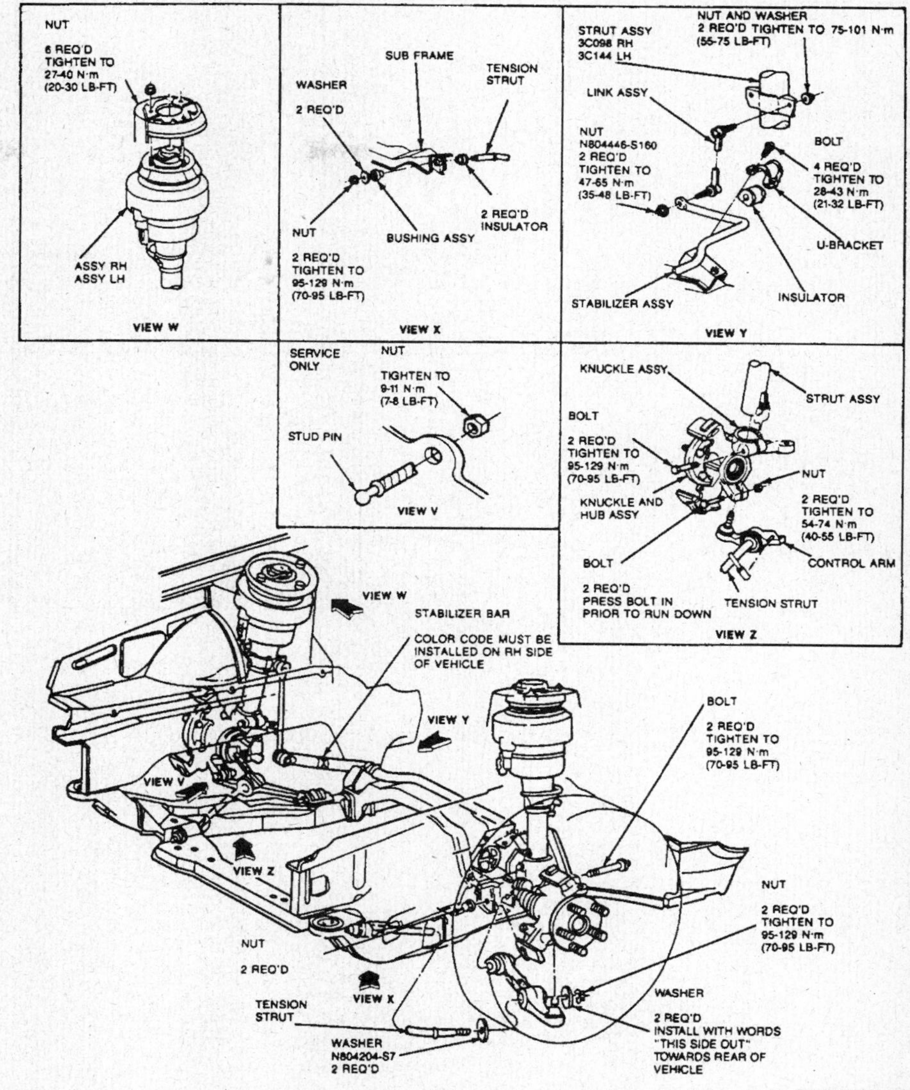

Fig. 3 Front suspension components. Continental

Town Car

1. Raise and support vehicle, then remove wheel and tire assembly. Position jack stands under both side of frame just to the rear of lower control arm.
2. Position a suitable jack under lower control arm.
3. Remove nut from upper ball joint to steering knuckle pinch bolt, then tap out pinch bolt.
4. Mark positions of caster and camber adjusting cams for use during installation, **Fig. 2.**
5. Using a suitable pry bar, spread slot to release ball joint from steering knuckle.
6. Remove upper control arm mounting bolts, then remove upper arm assembly, **Fig. 4.**
7. Reverse procedure to install. Align caster and camber marks made during removal. After completing installation, inspect front end alignment.

STABILIZER BAR

REPLACE

CONTINENTAL

1. Turn air suspension switch to off position.
2. Raise and support vehicle.
3. Position safety stands behind front subframe.
4. Remove and discard stabilizer bar link retaining nut.
5. Position another set of safety stands under front subframe.
6. Remove bolts and brackets as required to lower rear of subframe enough to gain access to stabilizer bar brackets.
7. Remove stabilizer bar brackets, then the stabilizer bar.
8. Reverse procedure to install.

MARK VIII

1. Turn air suspension switch off, then raise and support vehicle.

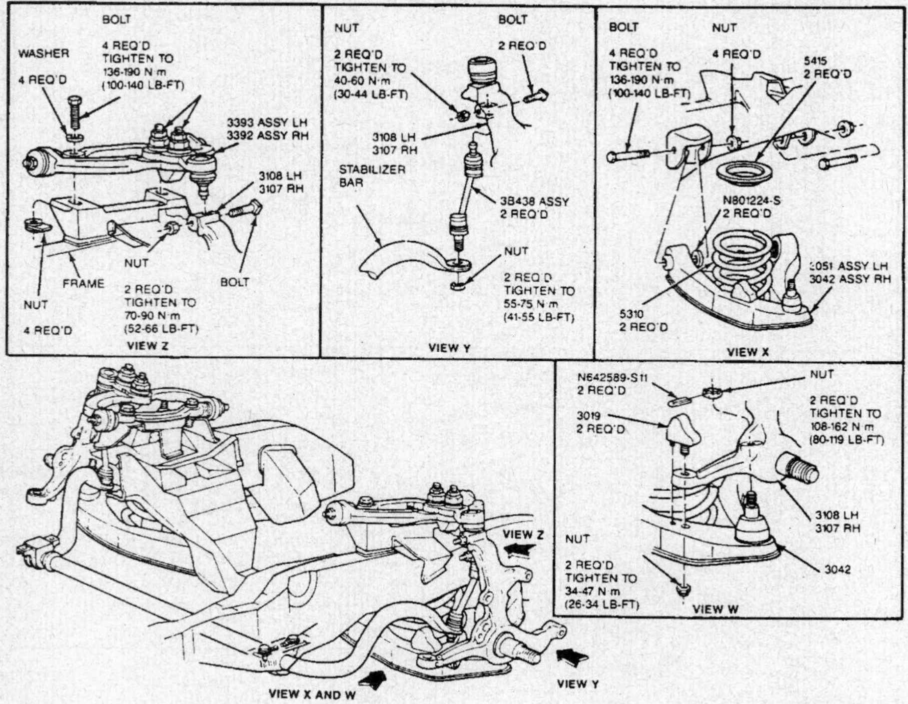

Fig. 4 Front suspension. Town Car

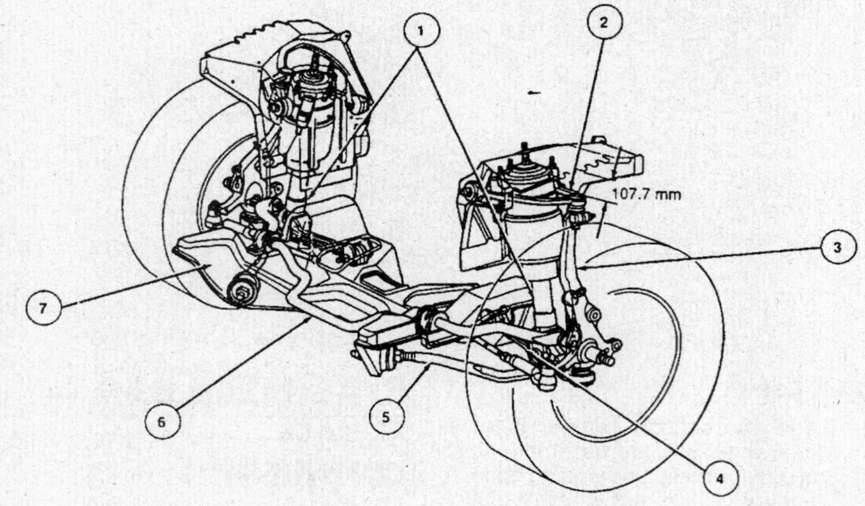

Item	Description	Item	Description
1	Spring / Shock Assy	4	Lower Control Arm
2	Upper Control Arm	5	Tension Strut (2 Req'd)
		6	Stabilizer Bar
3	Spindle	7	Front Subframe Assy

FM2029100054000X

Fig. 5 Front Suspension. Mark VIII

2. Remove both rear wheel and tire assemblies.
3. Disconnect emergency brake cables from stabilizer bar.
4. Remove both stabilizer bar link upper mounting nuts and insulators.
5. Remove links from stabilizer bar eyelets by pushing bar ends up and rotating out of the way.
6. Remove both stabilizer bar bracket bolts.
7. Remove brackets from T-slots in subframe.
8. Remove rear muffler hanger mounting nuts.
9. Remove stabilizer bar from vehicle.
10. Reverse procedure to install.

TOWN CAR

1. Raise and support vehicle.
2. Remove stabilizer bar mounting clamps, then the stabilizer bar mounting bolts from each stabilizer link.
3. Remove stabilizer bar assembly, **Fig. 4.**
4. Reverse procedure to install.

POWER STEERING GEAR

REPLACE

CONTINENTAL

1. Remove instrument panel lower trim panel.
2. Remove steering column lower trim panel and reinforcement panel.
3. Remove universal joint pinch bolt, then the bolt at intermediate shaft to steering gear coupling.
4. Slide shaft upward to remove from steering gear, then downward to remove from steering column.
5. Loosen retaining screw, then disconnect engine compartment wiring harness.
6. Remove bolt and position upper motor mount out of way.
7. Remove ground strap mounting bolt.
8. Raise and support vehicle.
9. Separate tie rod ends from steering knuckle.
10. Disconnect height sensors.
11. Disconnect heated oxygen sensors.
12. Remove catalytic converter and brackets.
13. Remove subframe insulator braces.
14. Remove steering gear nuts.
15. Support subframe with suitable lifting device, then remove rear subframe bolts and loosen front subframe bolts.
16. Lower lifting device.
17. Remove pushpins and heat shield, then the heat shield bracket.
18. Disconnect wiring at steering gear.
19. Rotate steering gear to clear bolt from subframe then pull to left to access power steering lines.
20. Disconnect pressure and return lines at steering gear.
21. Remove steering gear through left wheelwell.
22. Reverse procedure to install.

TOWN CAR

1. Remove stone shield, if equipped.
2. Disconnect pressure and return lines from steering gear. Plug lines and ports in gear to prevent entry of dirt.
3. Remove two bolts that secure flex coupling to steering gear and to column.
4. Raise vehicle and remove sector shaft nut.
5. Use a puller to remove Pitman arm.
6. Support steering gear, then remove mounting bolts.
7. Work steering gear free of flex coupling and remove it from car.
8. Reverse procedure to install.

MARK VIII

1. Raise and support vehicle, then remove front wheel and tire assemblies.
2. Remove cotter pins at outer tie rod ends and castellated nuts at each end. Discard cotter pins.
3. Separate tie rod end studs from spindles using tie rod end remover tool No. 3290-D, or equivalent.
4. Place suitable container under vehicle, then disconnect and plug power steering return line hose.
5. Disconnect power steering pressure line at intermediate fitting.
6. Remove steering shaft mounting bolt.
7. Remove rack to subframe bolts and nuts.
8. Lower rack as required to remove pressure line inlet tube. Remove and discard plastic seal on inlet tube.
9. Cut tie strap securing pressure line to each tube.
10. Remove steering rack from vehicle.
11. Reverse procedure to install. Tighten steering rack mounting bolts and steering shaft mounting bolt to specifications.

POWER STEERING PUMP

REPLACE

CONTINENTAL

1. Remove radiator upper sight shield.
2. Disconnect power steering reservoir pump hose.
3. Evacuate air conditioning system as outlined under "Air Conditioning."
4. Remove A/C compressor.
5. Remove routing bracket, disconnect power steering pressure hose, then remove power steering pump.
6. Reverse procedure to install.

MARK VIII

1. Disconnect fluid return hose from reservoir and drain power steering fluid into a container.
2. Remove pressure hose from pump fitting. Do not remove fitting from pump.
3. Disconnect belt from pulley. If required, remove pulley from pump installing pulley removal tool No. T75L-3733-A, or equivalent so small diameter threads engage in pump shaft. While holding small hex head, rotate tool nut to remove pulley. Do not apply in and out pressure on pump shaft as this will damage internal thrust areas.
4. Remove pump.
5. If pulley was removed, install tool and while holding small hex head, turn tool nut clockwise to install pulley. Pulley must be flush within .010 inch of end of pump. Do not apply in and out pressure on shaft. Remove tool.

TOWN CAR

1. Disconnect power steering pump return line and allow power steering pump fluid to drain into an approved container.
2. Disconnect power steering pump pressure hose from pump fitting.
3. Disconnect drive belt from power steering pump pulley, remove pulley, then remove pump.
4. Reverse procedure to install. **Torque** pump to mounting bracket bolts to 30–45 ft. lbs. **On Ford model CII power steering pump, torque** pressure hose to pump fitting to 10–15 ft. lbs. Endplay on this fitting is normal and does not indicate a loose fitting.

TIGHTENING SPECIFICATIONS

Year	Component	Torque/Ft. Lbs.
CONTINENTAL		
1998–2000	Control Arm To Knuckle	40–55
	Control Arm To Subframe	70–95
	Front Bolts To Support Bracket	30–41
	Intermediate Shaft To Steering Column	15–25
	Outlet Fitting To Valve Cover	25–34
	Pivot Bolt	45–57
	Pressure Hose Tube Nut To Pump Pressure Fitting	20–25
	Pump To Bracket	30–45
	Return Hose To Pump Hose Clamp	8–24
	Stabilizer Bar Bracket To Subframe	21–32
	Stabilizer Bar Link Assembly To Bar	35–48
	Stabilizer Bar Link Assembly To Strut	55–75
	Strut To Knuckle	70–95
	Strut To Top Mount	35–50
	Strut Top Mount To Body	22–32
	Support Bracket To Cylinder Head	15–22
	Tension Strut To Control Arm	70–95
	Tension Strut To Subframe	70–95
	Tie Rod Ball Socket Assembly To Rack	55–65
	Tie Rod End To Spindle Nut	35–47
	Tie Rod End To Steering Knuckle	23–25
	Wheel Lug	85–104

Continued

TIGHTENING SPECIFICATIONS—Continued

Year	Component	Torque/Ft. Lbs.
CONTINENTAL		
2001–02	Combination Power Steering And Transmission Fluid Cooler Mounting	62–88①
	Front Wheel Spindle Tie Rod To Rack	67–81
	Intermediate Hose Connection	42–53
	Intermediate Shaft To Steering Column	16–24
	Intermediate Shaft To Steering Gear	31–37
	Power Steering Oil Pressure Switch	62–123①
	Power Steering Pump To Engine bolts	15–22
	Power Steering Return Hose Bracket To Subframe	80–106①
	Power Steering Secondary VAPS Actuator To Steering Gear Bolt	25–30
	Pressure Line Fitting	
	Pressure Line Fitting At Pump	31–39
	Pressure Line Fitting Into Banjo Bolt	25–30
	Reservoir Bolts	54–61①
	Return Line Fitting	25–30
	Steering Gear to Subframe Mounting Bolt & Nut	84–112
	Subframe To Body Bolts	100–144
	Tie Rod End To Spindle Arm Nut	35–46
	Tie Rod End To Tie Rod jam Nut	35–46
	Vehicle Dynamics Module Connector Screw	45–61①
	Wheel Lug Nuts	85–104
MARK VIII		
1998	Air Compressor To Bracket	30–40①
	Ball Joint To Spindle	100–120
	Compressor Bracket To Frame	30–40①
	Front Bolts To Support Bracket	30–45
	Hub Bearing	189–254
	Inner Pivot Nut	50–68
	Lower Arm To No. 2 Crossmember	110–150
	Lower Control Arm To Toe Compensating Link	83–113
	Pinion Bearing Plug	40–60
	Pinion Bearing Locknut	30–40
	Pivot Bolt	30–45
	Pressure Hose Fitting To Pump	10–15
	Pump Bracket To Rear Support	18–24
	Pump To Bracket	30–45
	Rear Support To Engine Head	30–45
	Return Hose To Pump	12–24①
	Sensor Lower Attachment To Arm	8–12
	Sensor Upper Attachment To Frame	26–34
	Shock Strut Upper Mount	55–92
	Shock Upper Mount To Body	62–75
	Spindle To Shock Strut	140–200
	Stabilizer Bar Mounting Clamp	40–55
	Stabilizer Bar To Lower Arm	9–12
	Steering Gear To No. 2 Crossmember	90–100
	Steering Rack	100–144
	Steering Shaft	20–30

Continued

TIGHTENING SPECIFICATIONS—Continued

Year	Component	Torque/Ft. Lbs.
MARK VIII		
1998	Support Bracket To Engine	30–45
	Support Bracket To Water Pump	30–45
	Tie Rod Ball Socket Assembly To Rack	55–65
	Tie Rod End To Jam Nut	35–50
	Tie Rod End To Spindle	35–47
	Wheel Lug	85–104
TOWN CAR		
1998–2002	Air Compressor To Bracket	30–40①
	Ball Joint To Spindle	100–120
	Compressor Bracket To Frame	30–40①
	Front Bolts To Support Bracket	30–45
	Hub Bearing	189–254
	Inner Pivot Nut	50–68
	Lower Arm To No. 2 Crossmember	110–150
	Lower Control Arm To Toe Compensating Link	83–113
	Pinion Bearing Locknut	30–40
	Pinion Bearing Plug	40–60
	Pivot Bolt	30–45
	Pressure Hose Fitting To Pump	10–15
	Pump Bracket To Rear Support	18–24
	Pump To Bracket	30–45②
	Rear Support To Engine Head	30–45
	Return Hose To Pump	12–24①
	Sensor Lower Attachment To Arm	8–12
	Sensor Upper Attachment To Frame	26–34
	Shock Strut Upper Mount	55–92
	Shock Upper Mount To Body	62–75
	Spindle To Shock Strut	140–200
	Stabilizer Bar Mounting Clamp	40–55
	Stabilizer Bar To Lower Arm	9–12
	Steering Gear To No. 2 Crossmember	90–100
	Steering Rack	100–144
	Steering Shaft	20–30
	Support Bracket To Engine	30–45
	Support Bracket To Water Pump	30–45
	Tie Rod Ball Socket Assembly To Rack	55–65
	Tie Rod End To Jam	35–50
	Tie Rod End To Spindle	35–47
	Wheel Lug	85–104

① — Inch lbs.
② — On Ford model CII power steering pump, 10–15 ft. lbs.

Wheel Alignment

INDEX

PRELIMINARY INSPECTION

Prior to performing the front wheel alignment, a preliminary inspection should be made to determine the condition of the vehicle's suspension components. The following inspections and procedures should be made prior to performing front wheel alignment:

1. Vehicle must be leveled by performing the air suspension system test.
2. Inflate tires to specified pressure (cold).
3. Measure vehicle ride height.
4. Inspect all suspension and steering components for looseness.
5. Inspect existing caster, camber, and toe settings prior to alignment.
6. Inspect all suspension fasteners for proper tightness.
7. Alignment equipment must be capable of four wheel alignment.
8. Alignment rack must be leveled to 1/16 of an inch, side to side and front to rear and be equipped with wheel runout compensation.

Do not attempt to adjust alignment by heating or bending.

FRONT WHEEL ALIGNMENT

MARK VIII & TOWN CAR

Caster and camber can be adjusted by loosening the bolts that attach the upper suspension arm to the shaft at the frame side rail, and moving the arm assembly in or out in the elongated bolt holes. Since any movement of the arm affects both caster and camber, both factors should be balanced against one another when making the adjustment.

Caster

1. To adjust caster, install adjusting tool, **Fig. 1.**

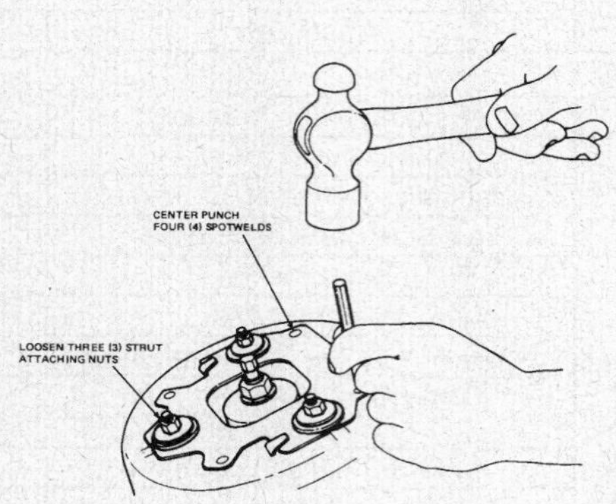

Fig. 1 Caster & camber adjustment tools. Mark VIII & Town Car

2. Loosen both upper arm inner shaft mounting bolts and move either front or rear of the shaft in or out as required to increase or decrease caster angle, then tighten bolt to retain adjustment.

Camber

1. Loosen both upper arm inner mounting bolts and move both front and rear ends of shaft inward or outward as required to increase or decrease camber angle.
2. Tighten bolts, inspect caster again and adjust if required.

Toe-In

Position the front wheels in the straight-ahead position, then turn both tie rod adjusting sleeves an equal amount until the desired toe-in setting is obtained.

CONTINENTAL

Toe-In

To adjust toe-in, lock steering wheel in straight ahead position using suitable steering wheel holder. Loosen, then slide off small outer clamps from steering boot to prevent boot from twisting during adjustment procedure. Loosen tie rod adjusting and jam nuts, then adjust length of lefthand and righthand tie rods until each wheel has 1/2 the desired total toe specification. After adjustment is completed, tighten jam nuts, install outer clamps and remove steering wheel holder.

REAR WHEEL ALIGNMENT

CONTINENTAL

Camber

Camber is factory set and cannot be adjusted.

Toe-In

Toe-in is adjusted by rotating the cams located inside the rear inner lower control arm bushings.

MARK VIII

Caster & Camber

The recommended adjustment sequence for rear alignment is to set the camber and then the toe. Toe should be inspected prior to final tightening.

1. Loosen rear upper suspension arm nut.
2. Rotate pivot bolt and cam to desired camber setting.
3. Tighten nut while holding pivot bolt and cam stationary.

Toe

1. Loosen nut on rear suspension lower arm pivot bolt.
2. Rotate pivot bolt and cam to desired toe setting.
3. Tighten nut to while holding pivot bolt and cam stationary.
4. Inspect toe settings after tightening.

LS & THUNDERBIRD

NOTE: Refer To The Rear Of This Manual For Manufacturer's Special Service Tool Suppliers.

INDEX OF SERVICE OPERATIONS

Specifications

GENERAL ENGINE SPECIFICATIONS

Year	Engine Liter	Engine VIN Code①	Fuel System	Bore x Stroke, Inches	Comp. Ratio	Net HP @ RPM	Maximum Torque, Ft. Lbs. @ RPM	Normal Oil Pressure, psi
2000–02	3.0L	S	SFI	3.50 x 3.13	10.5	210 @ 6500	205 @ 4750	20–45②
	3.9L	A	SFI	3.38 x 3.35	10.5	252 @ 6100	267 @ 4300	—

① — The eighth digit of the VIN denotes engine code.

② — At operating temperature & 1500 RPM.

TUNE UP SPECIFICATIONS

Year	Engine	Spark Plug Gap	Firing Order	Curb Idle Speed	Fuel Pump Pressure, psi	Valve Clearance, Inch Intake	Valve Clearance, Inch Exhaust
2000–02	3.0L	.051–.057	1-4-2-5-3-6	①	39–55	.007–.009	.013–.015
	3.9L	.039–.043	1-5-4-2-6-3-7-8	①	39–65	.007–.009	.009–.011

① — Idle speed is electronically controlled and is non-adjustable.

FRONT WHEEL ALIGNMENT SPECIFICATIONS

Year	Caster Angle, Degrees		Caster Split		Camber Angle, Degrees		Camber Split		Toe-In, Degrees	Ball Joint Wear, Inch①
	Limits	Desired	Limits	Desired	Limits	Desired	Limits	Desired		
2000–02	+7.6 to +8.6	+8.1	-.7 to +.7	0	-.65 to +.35	-.15	-.7 to +.7	0	-.09 to +.41	1/32

① — Radial play.

REAR WHEEL ALIGNMENT SPECIFICATIONS

Year	Camber, Degrees		Toe-In, Degrees		Toe-In Split		Ball Joint Wear, Inch①
	Limits	Desired	Limits	Desired	Limits	Desired	
2000–02	-1.75 to -.25	-1	-.13 to +.37	+.12	-.01 to +.49	+.24	1/32

① — Radial play.

VEHICLE RIDE HEIGHT SPECIFICATIONS

Year	Front, Inches①	Rear, Inches①	Ride Height Difference, Inches	
			Side To Side	Front To Rear
2000–02	. 2.1–2.7②	.7–1.3 ③	0.5	0.6

① — See door sticker or inside of glove box for manufacturers original tire size specifications. If tires on vehicle do not match manufacturers original tire size & measurement is not within limits, it will be necessary to refer to the "Non-Standard Tire & Wheel Size Adjustment To Ride Height Specification & Tire Size Adjustment Charts" in the front of this manual for approximate changes in ride height specifications.

② — Measure front vehicle ride height as shown **Fig. A.**

③ — Measure rear vehicle ride height as shown **Fig. B.**

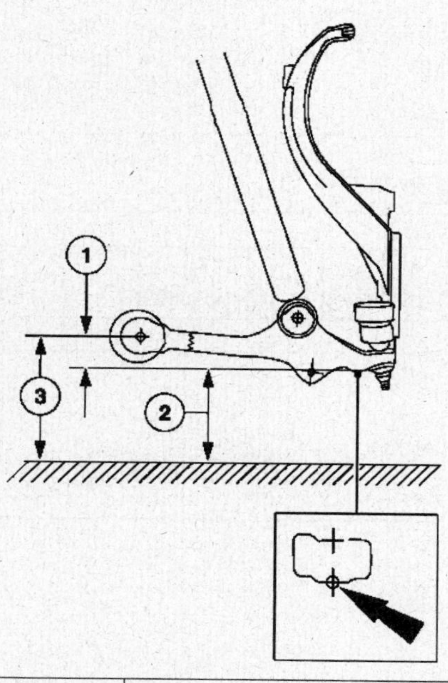

Item	Description
1	Ride height = B-A
2	Measurement A
3	Measurement B

FM2049900063000X

Fig. A Front ride height measurement

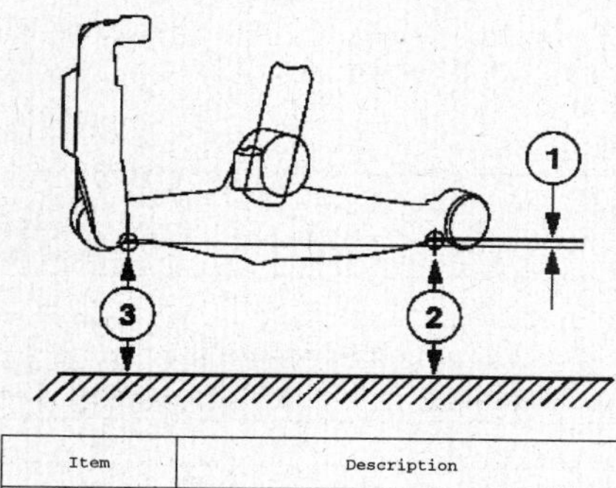

Item	Description
1	Ride height = A-B
2	Measurement A
3	Measurement B

FM2049900064000X

Fig. B Rear ride height measurement

FLUID CAPACITIES & COOLING SYSTEM DATA

Year	Engine	Coolant Capacity, Qts.		Coolant Type	Radiator Cap Relief Pressure, Lbs.	Thermo. Opening Temp.	Fuel Tank, Gals.	Engine Oil Refill, Qts.④	Rear Axle, Pts.③	Transmission Oil	
		Less A/C	With A/C							Man. Trans., Pts.	Auto. Trans., Qts.
2000–02	3.0L	10.6	10.6	Ethylene Glycol	16	①	18	6.9	3	②	11.9
	3.9L	11.3	11.3	Ethylene Glycol	16	①	18	6.0	3	—	11.9

① — Thermostat begins to open at 192–199°F and is fully open at 219°F.

② — Fill transmission to .02 inch below lower edge of fill plug bore.

③ — Fill 1⁄8–3⁄16 inch from bottom of filler hole.

④ — Includes engine oil filter.

LUBRICANT DATA

Year	Lubricant Type					
	Transmission		Rear Axle	Power Steering	Brake System	Hydraulic Clutch Fluid
	Manual	Automatic				
2000–02	Mercon ATF	Mercon V XT-5-Q-M	①	②	DOT 3	DOT 3

① — Use 75W-140 synthetic rear axle lubricant F1TZ–19580–B, or equivalent, meeting Ford specification WSL–M2C192–A.

② — Use Motorcraft Mercon multi-purpose ATF transmission fluid XT-2-QDX, or equivalent, meeting Ford specification Mercon.

Electrical

NOTE: On Air Bag Equipped Models, Refer To "Air Bag System Precautions" Located In The Front Of This Manual For System Disarming & Arming Procedures.

NOTE: Refer To "Computer Relearn Procedures" Located In The Front Of This Manual When Battery Power To The Computer Has Been Interrupted.

INDEX

PRECAUTIONS

AIR BAG SYSTEMS

Refer to "Air Bag System Precautions" in the front of this manual for system disarming and arming procedures.

BATTERY GROUND CABLE

Prior to service, disconnect battery ground cable and isolate as required.

ELECTROSTATIC DISCHARGE

Electronic modules are sensitive to electrical charges. Ensure modules are not exposed to these charges or damage may result.

MODULE CONFIGURATION

Newly released modules will require configuration after being installed on the vehicle. All configurable modules will be packaged in a kit which contains a warning label and multi-language sheet which lists requirements to configure the modules.

There are two types of configuration data. The first type is used by the module so that it can interact with the vehicle correctly. The second type is customer preference driven. These are items that the customer may or may not want to have enabled. To program customer driven preferences, a Ford service function card (FSF) and the New Generation Star Tester (NGS), tool No. 007-00500, or equivalents must be used to toggle preferences on or off.

The New Generation Star Tester (NGS), tool No. 007-00500, or equivalent, must be used to retrieve configuration data from the old module before it is removed from the vehicle. This information will be transferred into the new module so that the new module will contain the same settings as the old module.

The following modules require configuration when being replaced; Anti-Lock Brake System (ABS) module, ABS module with traction control, Interactive Vehicle Dynamic (IVD) module, Instrument Cluster Module (ICM), ICM with message center, Message Center Module (MCM), Rear Electronic Module (REM), Front Electronic Module (FEM), Driver Door Module (DDM), Dual Automatic Temperature Control (DATC) module, Remote Emergency Satellite Cellular Unit (RESCU) module, Audio Control Module (ACM), Steering Column Lock Module (SCLM) and the Powertrain Control Module (PCM) when it is replaced on models equipped with a manual transmission. If configuring the PCM, a NGS tester flash cable tool No. 007-00531, or equivalent, must be used.

To perform the configuration process, proceed as follows:

1. Connect New Generation Star Tester tool No. 007-00500 with Ford service function (FSF) card to vehicle DLC.
2. Follow scan tool instructions to upload configuration data.
3. Install new module. **NGS will not retain configuration data for more than 24 hours.**
4. Download stored configuration information to new module using FSF card and NGS tester.
5. If unable to carry out configuration process, proceed as follows:
   a. Inspect for signs of electrical damage.
   b. If NGS does not communicate with vehicle, ensure program card is correctly installed, vehicle connections are secure and that ignition switch is in run position.
   c. If NGS still does not communicate with vehicle, diagnose module

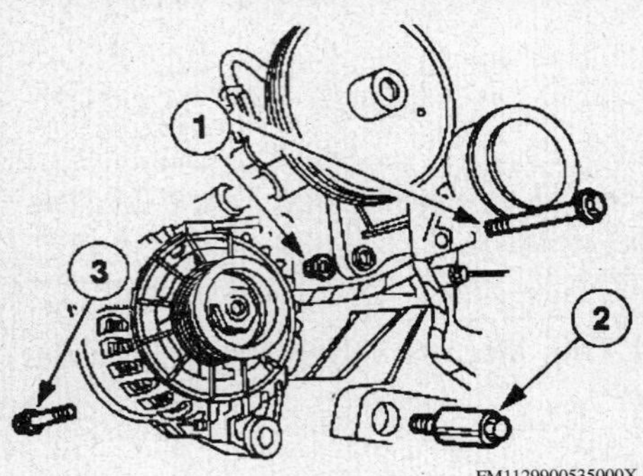

Fig. 1 Alternator bolt tightening sequence. 3.9L engine

communications network concern.

FUSE PANEL & FLASHER LOCATION

BATTERY JUNCTION BOX

The battery junction box is located under the rear righthand side of the luggage compartment floor lining.

CENTRAL JUNCTION BOX

The central junction box is located under the righthand side of the instrument panel.

INTERIOR AUXILIARY JUNCTION BOX

The interior auxiliary junction box is located under the lefthand side of the instrument panel. This junction box contains a power junction stud and the DLC.

UNDERHOOD AUXILIARY JUNCTION BOX

The underhood auxiliary junction box is located on the rear righthand side of the engine compartment.

TRAILER TOW AUXILIARY JUNCTION BOX

The trailer tow auxiliary junction box is located in the rear center of the luggage compartment.

FLASHER

The flashing function is controlled by the front electronic module. The module is located at the lefthand "A" pillar.

FUEL PUMP RELAY LOCATION

The fuel pump relay is located under the luggage compartment floor lining in the battery junction box.

STARTER

REPLACE

1. Raise and support vehicle.
2. Remove ground strap from starter mounting stud.
3. Remove starter cable cover from starter, then the starter cables.
4. Remove starter attaching bolts, then the starter.
5. Reverse procedure to install. **Torque** starter attaching bolts to 18 ft. lbs.

ALTERNATOR

REPLACE

3.0L ENGINE

1. Remove accessory drive belt.
2. Raise and support vehicle.
3. Remove lower splash shield.
4. Support alternator, then remove attaching bolts.
5. Disconnect alternator electrical connections and remove alternator.
6. Reverse procedure to install, noting the following:
   a. **Torque** alternator electrical connectors to 71 inch lbs.
   b. **Torque** alternator mounting bolts to 33 ft. lbs.

3.9L ENGINE

1. Remove engine appearance cover.
2. Disconnect IAT sensor, breather hose and idle air control valve inlet tube.
3. Remove air intake tube support nut and washer.
4. Loosen tube clamps and remove tube.
5. Remove accessory drive belt.
6. Raise and support vehicle, then remove front lower splash shield.
7. Support alternator, then remove attaching bolts.
8. Turn alternator as necessary, then remove positive cable from alternator.
9. Lower alternator and disconnect electrical connector.
10. Rotate alternator as necessary, then remove.
11. Reverse procedure to install, noting the following:
    a. **Torque** alternator electrical connector to 71 inch lbs.
    b. Using sequence, **Fig. 1, torque** alternator attaching bolts to 15 ft. lbs., then tighten an additional 90.°

IGNITION COIL

REPLACE

These engines use a coil on plug ignition system with an individual coil mounted on top of each spark plug.

3.0L ENGINE

1. Remove engine appearance cover.
2. If replacing righthand ignition coils, remove upper intake manifold as outlined under "Intake Manifold, Replace."
3. Disconnect coil electrical connector.
4. Remove coil attaching bolts, then the ignition coil.
5. Reverse procedure to install, noting the following:
   a. Ensure coils are seated and boot is not damaged. If boot is damaged, coil must be replaced.
   b. **Torque** coil attaching bolts to 53 inch lbs.

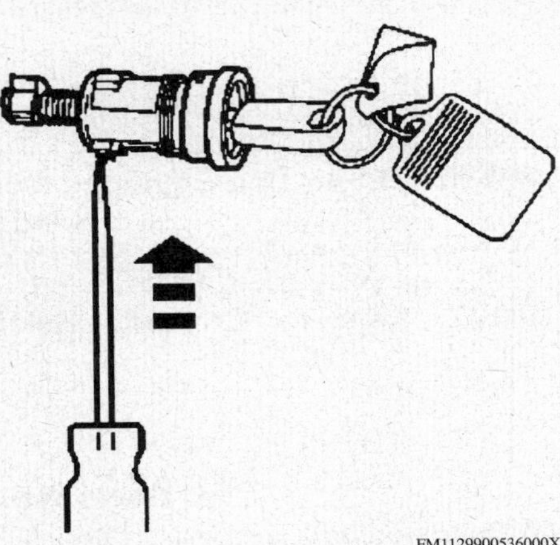

Fig. 2 Ignition lock cylinder removal

3.9L ENGINE

1. Remove engine appearance cover.
2. Disconnect IAT sensor, breather hose and idle air control valve inlet tube.
3. Remove air intake tube support nut and washer.
4. Loosen tube clamps and remove tube.
5. Remove ignition coil cover.
6. Disconnect coil electrical connectors.
7. Remove coil attaching bolts, then the ignition coils.
8. Reverse procedure to install. **Torque** attaching bolts to 44 inch lbs.

IGNITION LOCK

REPLACE

1. Remove steering column lower cover.
2. Remove hood release handle attaching bolts, then the release handle assembly.
3. Remove lower dash heater duct from below steering column.
4. Remove steering column opening cover reinforcement.
5. Place ignition switch in run position.
6. Depress ignition switch lock cylinder tab using a suitable screwdriver, **Fig. 2.**
7. Remove ignition switch lock cylinder.
8. Reverse procedure to install.

IGNITION SWITCH

REPLACE

1. Adjust steering column to full tilt down and full extended position.
2. Remove hood release handle attaching bolts, then the release handle assembly.
3. Disconnect electrical connectors, then remove lower steering column cover.
4. Disconnect electrical connectors and remove outer instrument panel finish panel, **Fig. 3.**
5. Remove inner instrument panel finish panel, then the instrument cluster finish panel attaching screws.
6. Disconnect in-car air temperature sensor electrical connector and remove instrument cluster finish panel.

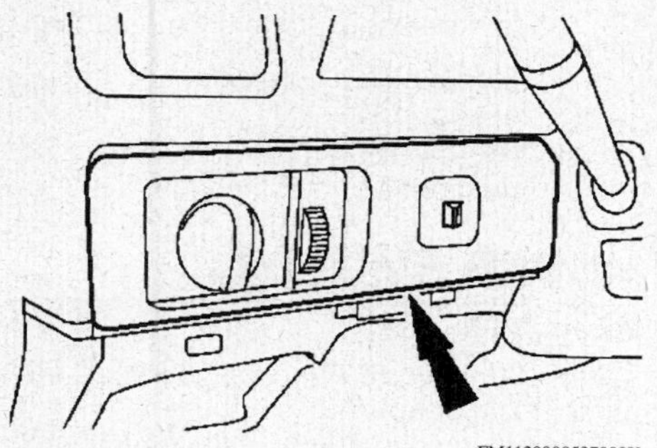
Fig. 3 Outer instrument panel finish panel removal

7. Remove steering column reinforcement attaching bolts, then the reinforcement.
8. Disconnect ignition switch electrical connector and remove ignition switch lock cylinder assembly attaching screws.
9. Remove ignition switch lock cylinder assembly, **Fig. 4.**
10. With ignition switch in the OFF position, remove set screw, then the ignition switch, **Fig. 5.**
11. Reverse procedure to install.

CLUTCH START SWITCH

REPLACE

1. Disconnect clutch pedal position switch electrical connector.
2. Lift switch retaining tag, then remove switch, **Fig. 6.**
3. Reverse procedure to install.

NEUTRAL SAFETY SWITCH

REPLACE

Refer to "Digital Transmission Range (TR) Sensor, Replace" for replacement procedure.

DIGITAL TRANSMISSION RANGE (TR) SENSOR

REPLACE

REMOVAL

1. Raise and support vehicle.
2. Disconnect oxygen sensor and catalyst monitor electrical connectors.
3. Remove three-way catalytic converter attaching nuts, then the catalytic converter from the exhaust system.
4. Remove heat shield retaining nuts, then the heat shield.
5. Make index marks on bolts, washers and nuts, to indicate installation position of driveshaft flex coupling to transmission flange and pinion flanges.
6. Make index marks on front driveshaft companion flange and transmission flange, then remove companion flange to transmission flange attaching bolts. **Do not remove driveshaft flex coupling retaining bolts.**

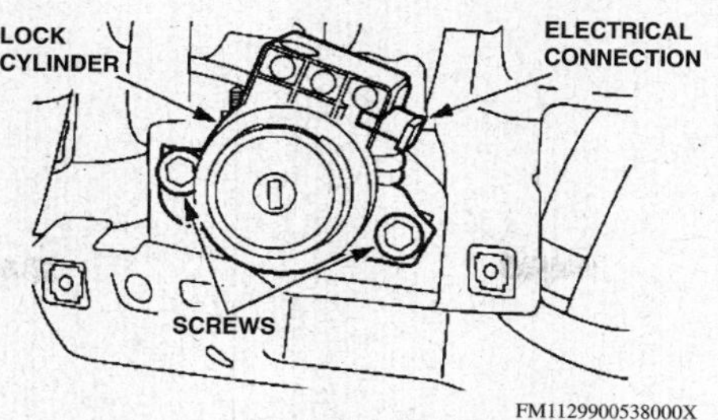

Fig. 4 Ignition switch lock cylinder assembly removal

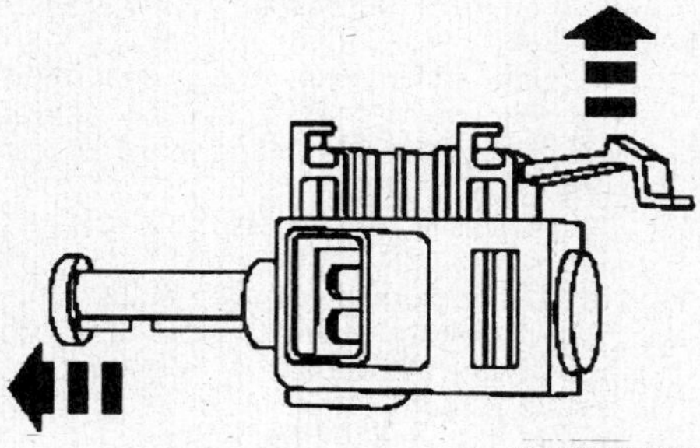
Fig. 6 Clutch pedal position switch

7. Slide front driveshaft assembly rearward and support transmission with a suitable transmission jack. Ensure transmission is properly secured to jack using a safety chain.
8. Remove transmission mount, then lower transmission to gain access to digital TR sensor.
9. Disconnect shift cable.
10. Disconnect TR sensor electrical connector, then remove sensor.

INSTALLATION

1. Place TR sensor flush against boss on transmission case, then loosely install sensor attaching bolts.
2. Place manual lever in neutral position.
3. Align TR sensor using sensor alignment tool No. T97L-70010-A, or equivalent.
4. **Torque** sensor screws evenly to 89 inch lbs., then connect TR sensor electrical connector.
5. Connect shift cable and install rear transmission support.
6. Adjust shift cable as outlined under "Automatic Transmissions/ Transaxles."
7. Align index marks made during "Removal" procedure, then **torque** companion flange to transmission flange bolts to 60 ft. lbs.
8. Install heat shield and catalytic converter, lower vehicle.

HEADLAMP SWITCH

REPLACE

1. Remove lower instrument panel steering column cover.
2. Remove outer instrument panel finish panel located on lefthand side of steering column.
3. Release four retaining clips, then remove headlamp switch from outer instrument panel finish panel.
4. Reverse procedure to install.

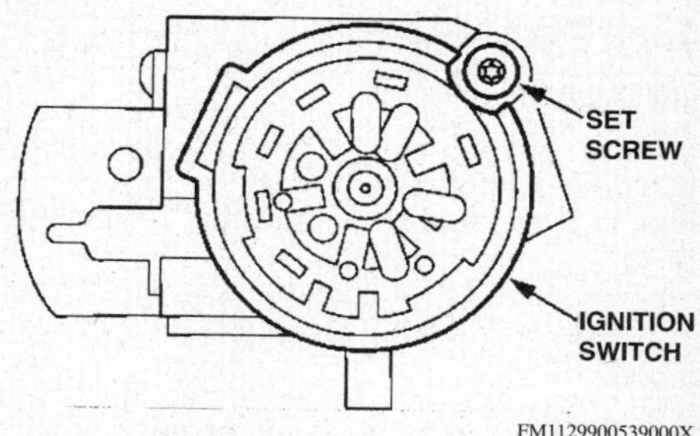

Fig. 5 Ignition switch removal

STOP LIGHT SWITCH

REPLACE

1. Remove instrument panel insulator.
2. Disconnect and remove brake pedal position switch.
3. Reverse procedure to install.

MULTI-FUNCTION SWITCH

REPLACE

1. Remove steering wheel as outlined under "Steering Wheel, Replace."
2. Remove hood release handle attaching bolts, then the release handle assembly.
3. Disconnect electrical connectors, then remove lower steering column cover.
4. Disconnect electrical connectors and remove outer instrument panel finish panel, **Fig. 3.**
5. Remove inner instrument panel finish panel, then the instrument cluster finish panel attaching screws.
6. Disconnect in-car air temperature sensor electrical connector and remove instrument cluster finish panel.
7. Apply two strips of masking tape across air bag sliding contact to prevent rotation.
8. Depress three clips and position air bag sliding contact aside.
9. Disconnect multi-function switch electrical connector, then remove switch.
10. Reverse procedure to install.

STEERING WHEEL

REPLACE

1. Ensure front wheels are in straight ahead position.
2. Remove driver's air bag module as outlined under "Air Bag Systems."
3. Remove horn switch.
4. Loosen steering wheel attaching bolt.
5. Loosen steering wheel using differential bearing cone removal tool No. T77F-4220-B1, or equivalent, **Fig. 7.**
6. Remove steering wheel puller, then the steering wheel attaching bolt and steering wheel. Discard steering wheel attaching bolt.
7. Reverse procedure to install. **Torque** new steering wheel attaching bolt to 30 ft. lbs.

INSTRUMENT CLUSTER

REPLACE

Prior to removal of instrument cluster, module configuration must be retrieved. Refer to "Module Configuration" for procedure.

1. Remove hood release handle attaching bolts, then the release handle assembly.
2. Disconnect electrical connectors, then remove lower steering column cover.
3. Disconnect electrical connectors and remove outer instrument panel finish panel, **Fig. 3.**
4. Remove inner instrument panel finish panel, then the instrument cluster finish panel attaching screws.
5. Disconnect in-car air temperature sensor electrical connector and remove instrument cluster finish panel.
6. Remove floor heat duct.
7. Remove steering column reinforcement.
8. Loosen steering column attaching bolts and lower steering column.
9. Place a suitable cloth over upper steering column cover to prevent damage to instrument cluster lens.
10. Remove instrument cluster attaching bolts, then the instrument cluster.
11. Reverse procedure to install. Download module configuration from NGS tester into new module.

RADIO

REPLACE

Prior to radio removal, module configuration must be retrieved. Refer to "Module Configuration" for procedure.

1. Remove A/C register finish panel.
2. Remove ash tray finish panel.
3. Remove audio/climate control assembly attaching bolts.
4. Disconnect electrical connectors and antenna cable.
5. Remove audio/climate control unit.
6. Separate audio unit from audio/climate control assembly.
7. Reverse procedure to install. Download module configuration from NGS tester into new module.

WIPER MOTOR

REPLACE

LS

1. Remove wiper pivot arm retaining nuts, then the pivot arms.
2. Remove two part pin retainers and separate velcro attachment of rubber hinge cover to rear outboard corner of cowl vent screen.
3. Lift cowl vent screen to release clips.
4. Remove cowl vent screen.
5. Remove strut tower support brace.
6. Remove coolant overflow bottle and position aside.
7. Remove wiper mounting arm and pivot shaft bolts.
8. Disconnect drain boot from windshield wiper mounting arm and pivot shaft assembly.

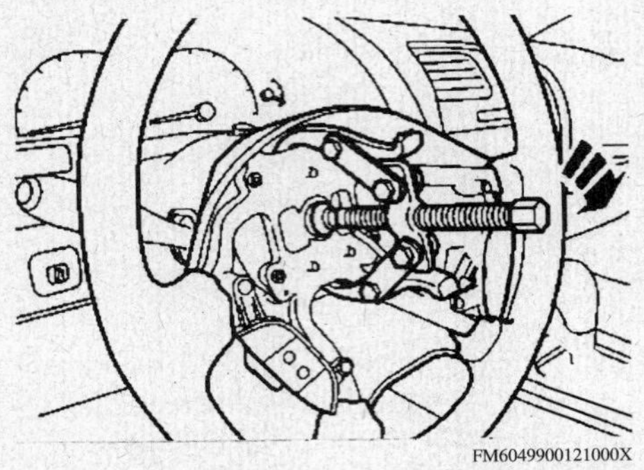

Fig. 7 Steering wheel removal

9. Position windshield wiper mounting arm and pivot shaft assembly aside, then loosen upper windshield wiper motor bolt.
10. Rotate wiper output arm to 6 o'clock position.
11. Remove lower wiper motor bolts.
12. Rotate bottom of wiper mounting arm and pivot shaft assembly upward.
13. Remove windshield wiper mounting arm and pivot shaft assembly.
14. Remove remaining wiper motor attaching bolts, then the wiper motor.
15. Reverse procedure to install, noting the following:
    a. **Torque** wiper pivot arm nuts to 18 ft. lbs.
    b. **Torque** strut support brace bolts to 15 ft. lbs.
    c. **Torque** mounting arm and pivot shaft bolts to 108 inch lbs.
    d. **Torque** wiper motor crank bolt and attaching bolts to 108 inch lbs.

THUNDERBIRD

1. Remove wiper arm pivot arm retaining nuts, then the pivot arms.
2. Remove lefthand and righthand cowl vent screen extension panels.
3. Disconnect windshield washer nozzle hoses from engine main wiring harness at lower righthand side of engine compartment.
4. Remove cowl vent screen pin-type retainers, then the cowl vent screen.
5. Remove strut tower support brace.
6. Remove degas bottle and position aside. Route degas bottle lower hose in front of brake booster.
7. Remove wiper mounting arm and pivot shaft retaining bolts.
8. Disconnect drain boot from wiper mounting arm and pivot shaft assembly.
9. Position wiper arm and pivot shaft assembly aside, then loosen wiper motor attaching bolt.
10. Rotate wiper output arm to the 6 o'clock position, then remove lower wiper motor bolts.
11. Remove wiper mounting arm and pivot shaft assembly by rotating upward.
12. Remove wiper motor upper attaching bolt and crank bolt, then the wiper motor.
13. Reverse procedure to install, noting the following:
    a. **Torque** wiper motor attaching bolts to 11 ft. lbs.
    b. **Torque** wiper motor crank bolt and to 13 ft. lbs.
    c. **Torque** strut support brace bolts to 15 ft. lbs.
    d. **Torque** mounting arm and pivot shaft bolts to 108 inch lbs.

WIPER SWITCH

REPLACE

Refer to "Multi-Function Switch, Replace" for procedure.

WIPER TRANSMISSION

REPLACE

Refer to "Wiper Motor, Replace" for procedure.

BLOWER MOTOR

REPLACE

1. Remove passenger side floor duct.
2. Remove blower motor cover.
3. Disconnect blower motor electrical connector.
4. Remove blower motor.
5. Reverse procedure to install.

CABIN AIR FILTER

REPLACE

LS

1. Remove wiper pivot arm retaining nuts, then the pivot arms.
2. Remove two part pin retainers and separate velcro attachment of rubber hinge cover to rear outboard corner of cowl vent screen.
3. Lift cowl vent screen to release clips.
4. Remove righthand cowl cover.
5. Push on righthand corner of filter to release clip.
6. Release lefthand clip and remove cabin air filter.
7. Reverse procedure to install.

THUNDERBIRD

1. Remove left and right cowl side trim pieces.
2. Remove wiper arms retaining nuts, then the wiper arms.
3. Remove cowl vent screen pin-type retainers, then the vent screen.
4. Push on righthand corner of cabin air filter and release righthand clip.
5. Release lefthand clip, then the cabin air filter.
6. Reverse procedure to install.

HEATER CORE

REPLACE

LS

1. Recover A/C refrigerant as outlined in "Air Conditioning" chapter.
2. Disconnect heater hose assembly from heater core.
3. Remove cabin air filter as outlined under "Cabin Air Filter, Replace."
4. Remove strut tower support brace.

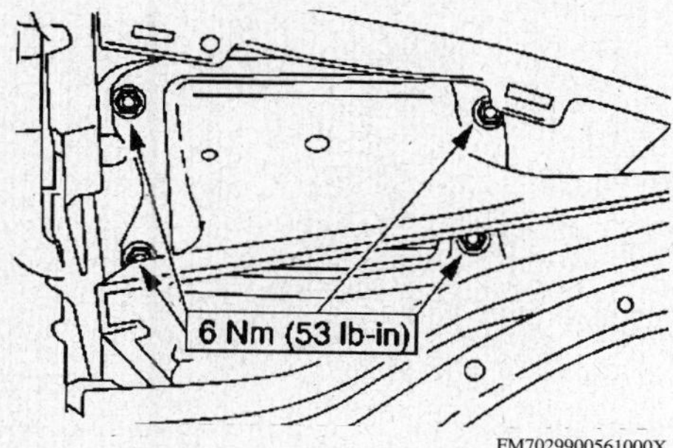

Fig. 8 Cabin air filter housing bolt locations

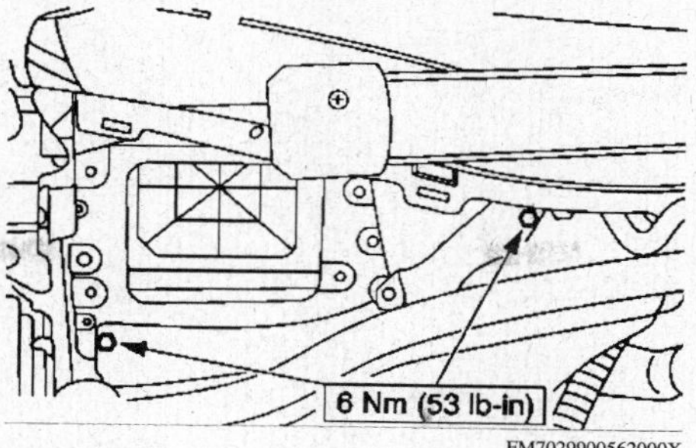

Fig. 9 Plenum panel removal

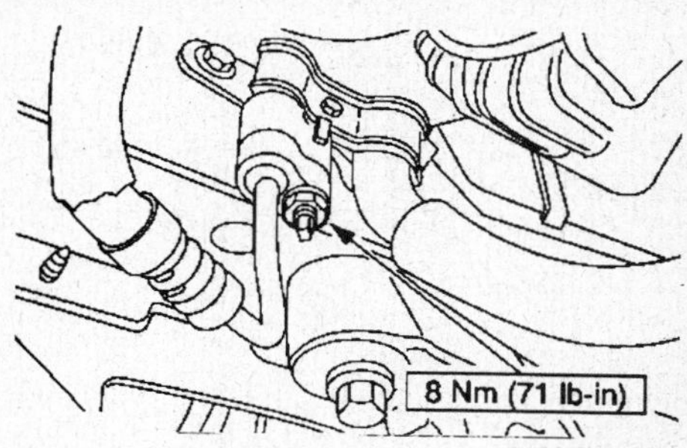

Fig. 10 Peanut fitting location

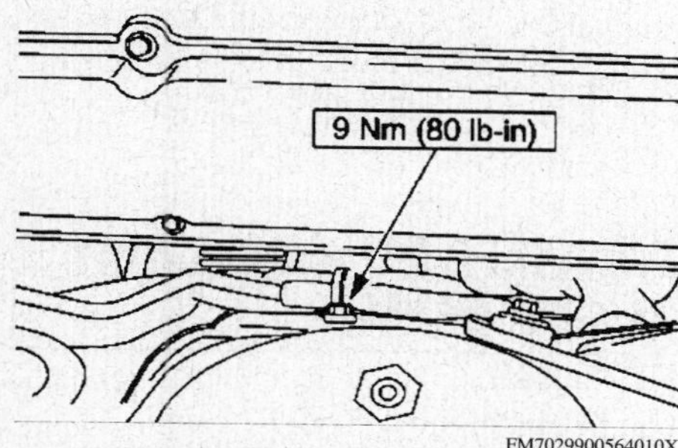

Fig. 11 A/C line bracket location (Part 1 of 2)

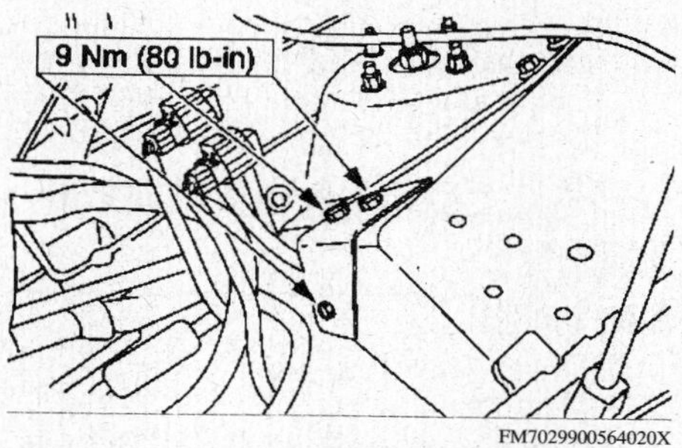

Fig. 11 A/C line bracket location (Part 2 of 2)

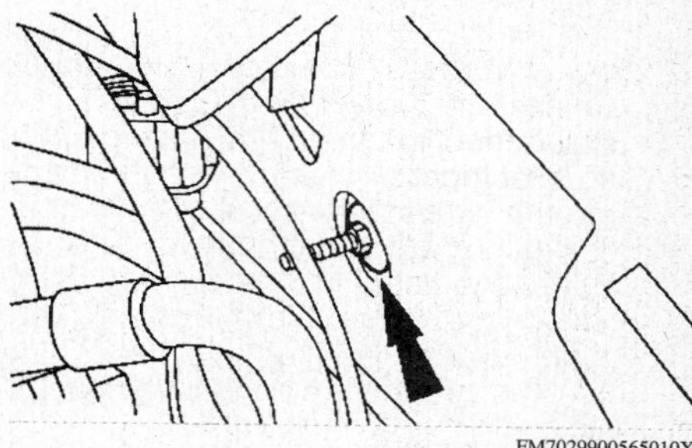

Fig. 12 Engine compartment evaporator housing bolt location (Part 1 of 3)

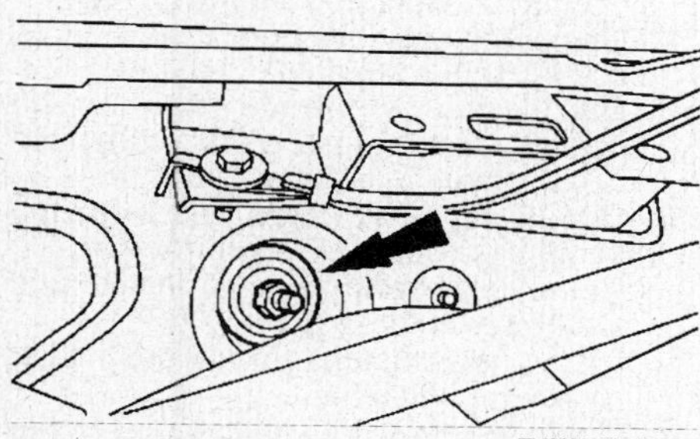

Fig. 12 Engine compartment evaporator housing bolt location (Part 2 of 3)

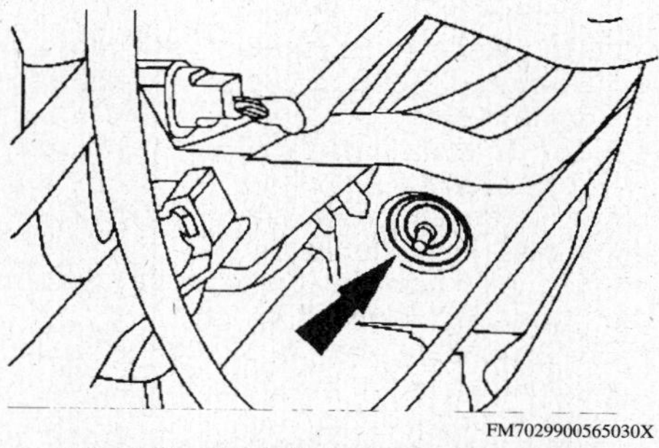

Fig. 12 Engine compartment evaporator housing bolt location (Part 3 of 3)

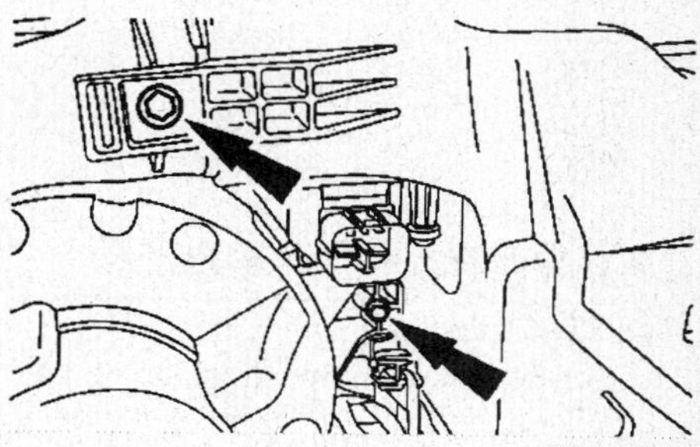

Fig. 13 Evaporator housing to air inlet housing screw location

5. Remove cabin air filter housing attaching bolts, **Fig. 8.**
6. Remove plenum panel attaching bolts, then the plenum panel, **Fig. 9.**
7. Disconnect coolant recovery line.
8. Remove forward heater hose mounting bolt at righthand shock tower.
9. Raise and support vehicle.
10. Remove rear heater hose mounting bolt from body side and position heater hose assembly aside.
11. Disconnect spring lock coupling using spring lock coupling tool T84L-19623-B, or equivalent.
12. Remove nut and disconnect peanut fitting, **Fig. 10.**
13. Remove peanut fitting bracket bolt.
14. Remove A/C line bracket bolts, **Fig. 11.**
15. Remove thermostatic expansion valve manifold and tube assembly.
16. Remove instrument panel as outlined under "Dash Panel Service."
17. Disconnect electrical connector at top of evaporator core housing.
18. Remove cowl top attaching bolt.
19. Remove evaporator housing attachment bolt.
20. Remove the following nuts located in engine compartment, **Fig. 12.**
21. Remove evaporator core housing.
22. Remove evaporator core housing to air inlet housing screws, **Fig. 13.**
23. Disengage clip and separate evaporator core housing from air inlet housing.
24. Remove housing gasket.
25. Remove nine screws, then disengage clip and separate evaporator core housing halves.
26. Disconnect bypass door connector and position harness aside.
27. Remove screws as shown in **Fig. 14.**
28. Remove heater core.
29. Reverse procedure to install noting the following:
    a. Lubricate A/C O-ring seal using PAG refrigerant oil YN–12–C, F7AZ–19589–DA, or equivalent, meeting Ford specification WSH–M1C231–B.
    b. **Torque** A/C peanut fitting to 71 inch lbs.
    c. **Torque** expansion valve fitting to 15 ft. lbs.
    d. **Torque** evaporator housing to engine compartment nuts and cowl top attachment bolt to 62 inch lbs.
    e. **Torque** evaporator housing bolt to 44 inch lbs.
    f. Ensure heater hoses are correctly connected to heater core.

THUNDERBIRD

1. Recover refrigerant as outlined in "Air Conditioning" chapter.
2. Partially drain cooling system into suitable container, then disconnect heater hose from heater core.
3. Remove manifold and tube assembly to expansion valve retaining bolt, then disconnect assembly from expansion valve. Discard O-rings.
4. Remove instrument panel as outlined in "Dash Panel Service" chapter.
5. Disconnect electrical connector located on top of evaporator core housing.

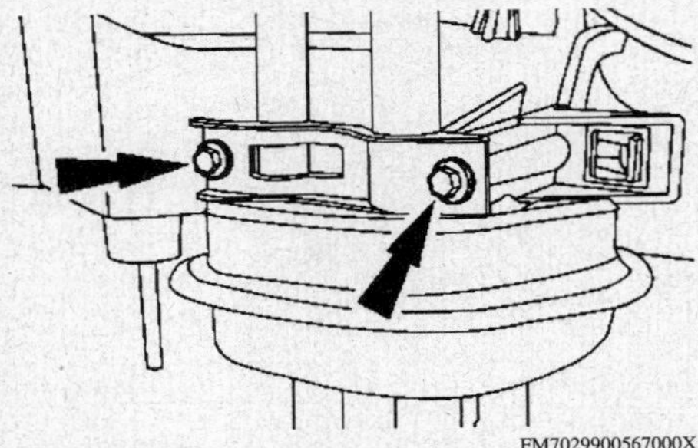

Fig. 14 Heater core cover screw location

6. Remove cowl top and evaporator housing attaching bolts.
7. Remove evaporator housing to bulkhead retaining nuts and washers from engine compartment side of bulkhead.
8. Remove evaporator housing to bulkhead retaining nut and washer from passenger compartment side of bulkhead.
9. Remove evaporator core housing from vehicle.
10. Remove evaporator core housing to air inlet housing attaching screws.
11. Release clip and separate evaporator core housing from air inlet housing.
12. Remove evaporator core housing screws, then separate housing halves.
13. Remove heater core retaining screws, then the heater core.
14. Remove heater core tube gasket.
15. Reverse procedure to install.

EVAPORATOR CORE

REPLACE

1. Remove evaporator housing and separate housing halves as outlined in "Heater Core, Replace."
2. Remove evaporator core from housing.

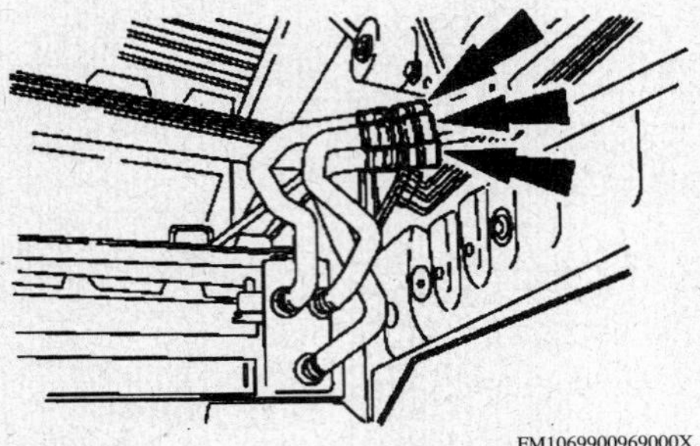

Fig. 15 Dual coolant flow valve

3. Remove evaporator core to thermostatic expansion valve fittings, then the expansion valve from evaporator core.
4. Reverse procedure to install.

DUAL COOLANT FLOW VALVE

REPLACE

1. Ensure engine is cold.
2. Wrap a suitable shop towel around pressure relief cap, then remove cap. **Ensure coolant does not come into contact with accessory drive belt.**
3. Open radiator draincock and drain coolant into a suitable container.
4. **On models equipped with an oil cooler,** disconnect coolant return hose at oil cooler.
5. **On models equipped with 3.9L engine,** remove auxiliary coolant pump as outlined under "Auxiliary Coolant Flow Pump, Replace."
6. **On all models,** disconnect coolant valve electrical connector.
7. Place identification marks on dual coolant flow valve for installation reference, **Fig. 15.**
8. Raise and support vehicle.
9. Remove coolant valve mounting nut and bolt.

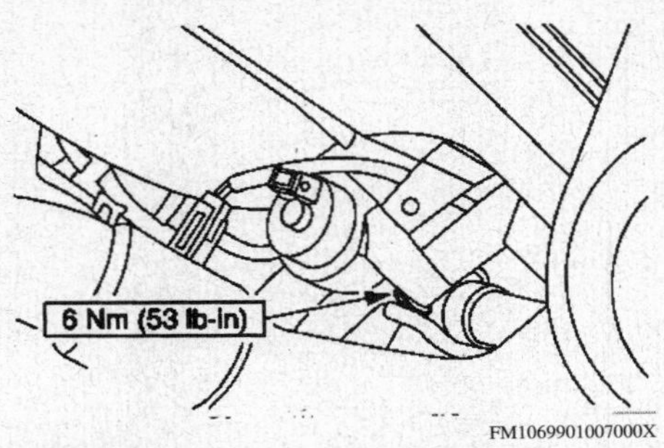

Fig. 16 Auxiliary coolant pump removal

10. Raise valve and disconnect coolant supply and return lines.
11. Remove coolant flow valve.
12. Reverse procedure to install.

AUXILIARY COOLANT FLOW PUMP

REPLACE

1. Ensure engine is cold.
2. Wrap a suitable shop towel around pressure relief cap, then remove cap.
3. **Ensure coolant does not come into contact with accessory drive belt.**
4. Open radiator draincock and drain coolant into a suitable container.
5. **On models equipped with an oil cooler,** disconnect coolant return hose at oil cooler.
6. **On all models,** disconnect auxiliary coolant pump electrical connector.
7. Remove coolant pump to fan shroud attaching bolts, **Fig. 16.**
8. Disconnect coolant pump hoses, then remove pump.
9. Reverse procedure to install. **Torque** auxiliary coolant pump attaching bolts to 53 inch lbs.

3.0L Engine

NOTE: On Air Bag Equipped Models, Refer To "Air Bag System Precautions" Located In The Front Of This Manual For System Disarming & Arming Procedures.

NOTE: Refer To "Computer Relearn Procedures" Located In The Front Of This Manual When Battery Power To The Computer Has Been Interrupted.

INDEX

PRECAUTIONS

AIR BAG SYSTEMS

Refer to "Air Bag System Precautions" in the front of this manual for system disarming and arming procedures.

BATTERY GROUND CABLE

Prior to service, disconnect battery ground cable and isolate as required.

FUEL SYSTEM PRESSURE RELIEF

1. Remove schrader valve cap and install fuel pressure gauge tool No. T80L-9974-B, or equivalent, to schrader valve.
2. Slowly open manual valve on pressure gauge and drain fuel into a suitable container.

QUICK DISCONNECT HOSES

R-CLIP

When working with R-clip type connections, **Fig. 1**, do not use tools to disconnect. Use of tools may deform clip components and could cause leaks.

To disconnect, bend shipping tab downward, **Fig. 1.** Spread R-clip and push clip into fitting. Separate fitting from tube.

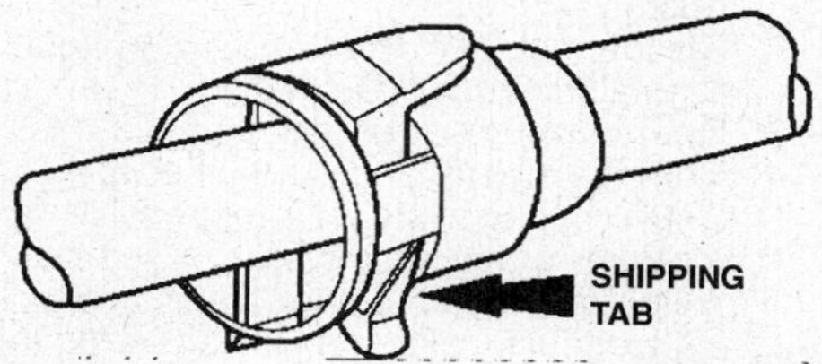

Fig. 1 R-clip connection

To install, first inspect fitting and tube for damage and ensure connections are clean. Apply a light coat of clean 5W-30 motor oil to male end of tube. Insert R-clip into fitting. Align tube and fitting, then insert tube into fitting and push together until a click is heard. Pull on connection to ensure it is fully engaged.

SPRING LOCK

When working with spring lock type connections, **Fig. 2,** spring lock tool set No. T84L-19623-B, or equivalent, must be used to disconnect fittings. When connecting spring lock type fittings, inspect and clean both coupling ends. Lubricate fuel line O-ring seals with clean 5W-30 motor oil. When connection is made, pull on line to ensure it is fully engaged.

VAPOR TUBE

To disconnect vapor tube connections, squeeze fitting (1) and disconnect vapor tube from fitting (2), **Fig. 3.** To connect, ensure fittings are clean and free from damage. Push tube onto fitting until it snaps into place. Pull on connection to verify fitting is secure.

COMPRESSION PRESSURE

Before performing compression test, ensure the following conditions are met: crankcase oil is of correct viscosity and at correct level, ensure battery is fully charged and engine is at normal operating temperature.

1. Turn ignition switch to off position.
2. Remove all spark plugs.
3. Set throttle plates to wide open position.
4. Install a suitable compression gauge in No. 1 cylinder.
5. Install an auxiliary starter switch in starting circuit.
6. With ignition switch off, use auxiliary starter switch to crank engine a minimum of five compression strokes.
7. Note number of compression strokes necessary to reach highest reading and record highest reading.
8. Repeat test on each cylinder, cranking engine same number of compression strokes.
9. Indicated compression pressures are

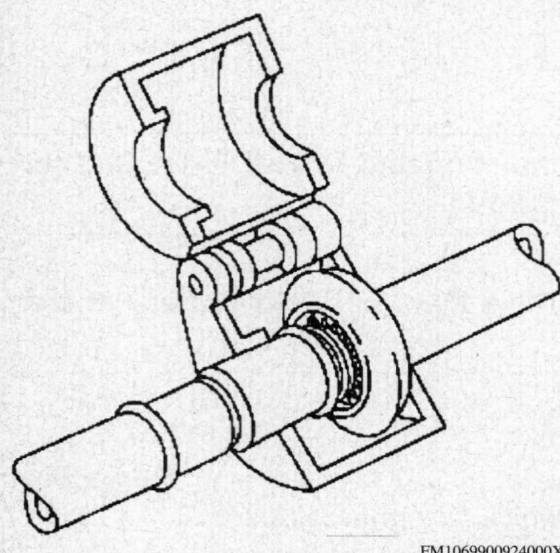

Fig. 2 Spring lock connection

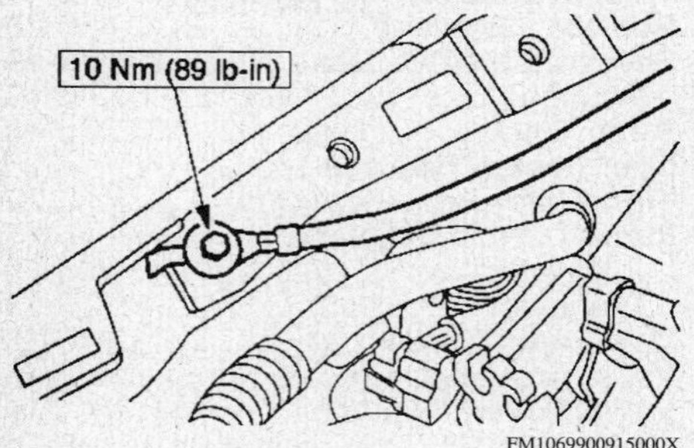

Fig. 5 Ground strap location

considered within specifications if lowest reading cylinder is within 75 percent of highest reading.

ENGINE MOUNT

REPLACE

1. Remove cowl vent screen as outlined under "Wiper Motor, Replace."
2. Remove strut brace.
3. Remove wire harness bracket, **Fig. 4.**
4. Disconnect intake manifold tuning valve electrical connector.
5. Remove intake manifold tuning valve attaching bolts, then the valve.
6. Remove cabin air filter plenum as outlined under "Heater Core, Replace."
7. Remove engine mount upper nut.
8. Raise and support vehicle.
9. Remove engine mount lower nut.
10. Raise engine and remove mount.
11. Reverse procedure to install noting the following:
    a. **Ensure intake manifold tuning valve is fully seated into intake before installing bolts.**
    b. **Torque** intake manifold tuning valve to 89 inch lbs.
    c. **Torque** upper mount nut to 30 ft. lbs.
    d. **Torque** lower mount nut to 46 ft. lbs.

ENGINE

REPLACE

When carrying out operations which involve the removal and installation of the driveshaft, always check the joint angles and make the necessary adjustments as outlined under "Driveline Angle Measurement" in "Rear Axle & Suspension" section.

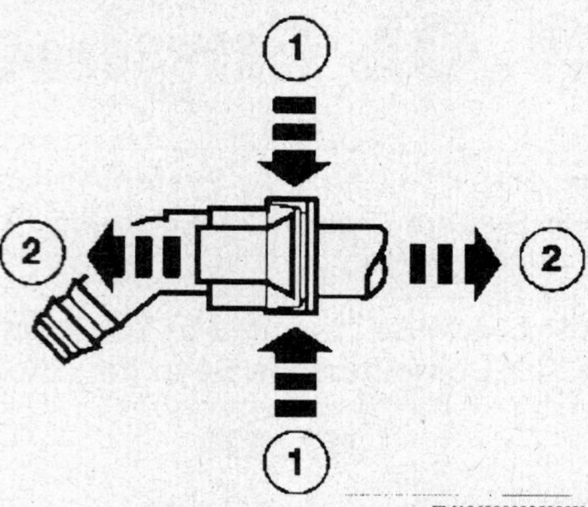

Fig. 3 Vapor tube connection

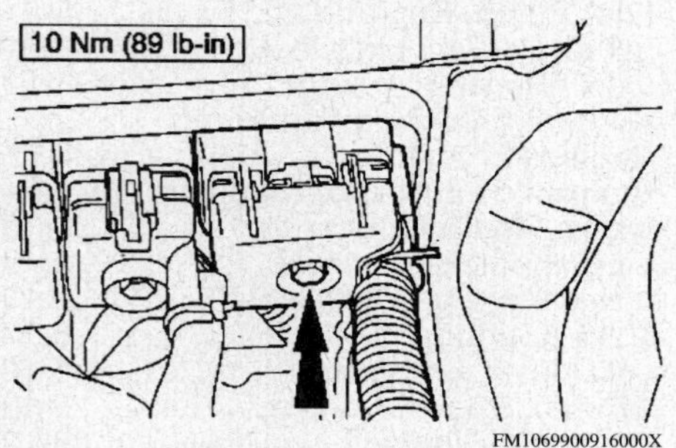

Fig. 6 Main engine harness connector

1. Disconnect IAT sensor electrical connector.
2. Disconnect aspirator and PCV hose from air cleaner outlet tube.
3. Remove air cleaner outlet tube.
4. Remove engine appearance cover.
5. Drain cooling system as follows:
    a. Ensure engine is cold.
    b. Wrap a suitable shop towel around pressure relief cap, then remove cap.
    c. **Ensure coolant does not come into contact with accessory drive belt.**
    d. Open radiator draincock and drain coolant into a suitable container.
    e. **On models equipped with oil cooler,** disconnect coolant return hose at oil cooler.
6. **On all models,** recover A/C refrigerant as outlined under "Air Conditioning."
7. Remove upper radiator sight shield, then the upper radiator support brackets.
8. Disconnect A/C pressure switch connector.
9. Remove power steering reservoir bolts and position reservoir aside.
10. Disconnect fuel lines.
11. Disconnect brake aspirator vacuum hose, then remove right and left cowl trim panels.
12. Unclip chassis vacuum lines from support bracket, then disconnect lines.
13. Remove strut brace support.
14. Remove cabin air filter plenum as outlined under "Heater Core, Replace."

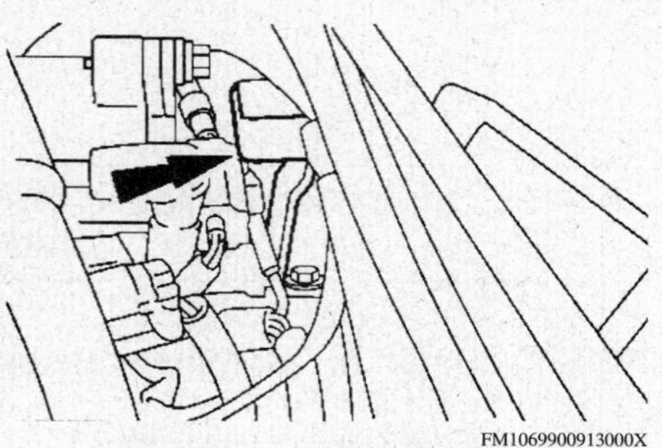

Fig. 4 Wire harness bracket removal

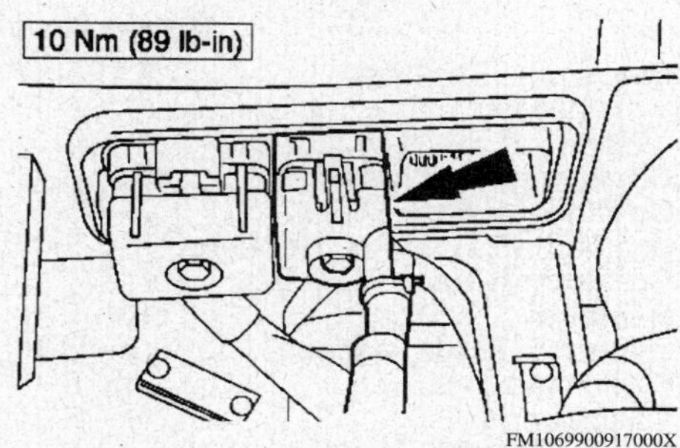

Fig. 7 Main transmission harness connector

15. Disconnect main vacuum hose from rear of intake manifold.
16. Disconnect throttle and speed control cables and unclip from bracket.
17. Remove ground strap bolt, **Fig. 5.**
18. Disconnect main engine wiring harness and transmission harness connectors, **Figs. 6 and 7.**
19. Disconnect fuel charging wiring, **Fig. 8.**
20. Disconnect wiring harness retainer from bracket.
21. Remove A/C line mounting bracket.
22. Remove hydraulic cooling fan reservoir and position aside.
23. Unclip line from frame as shown in **Fig. 9.**
24. Raise and support vehicle.
25. Drain engine oil.
26. Remove right and left splash shields.
27. Remove A/C manifold bolt, then position manifold aside.
28. Place reference marks on dual coolant flow valve coolant lines for installation reference.
29. Disconnect coolant hoses from dual coolant flow valve using quick disconnect tool No. T85T-18539-AH, or equivalent, **Fig. 10.**
30. Remove exhaust system and heat shields.
31. Remove driveshaft as outlined under "Rear Axle & Suspension."
32. Disconnect shift cable at transmission.
33. Remove shift cable bracket bolt.
34. Remove front tires.
35. Disconnect right and left front ABS sensors.
36. Remove front calipers as outlined under "Disc Brakes" and position aside.
37. Disconnect stabilizer link lower mounts and upper ball joints.
38. Remove lower strut mount bolts.

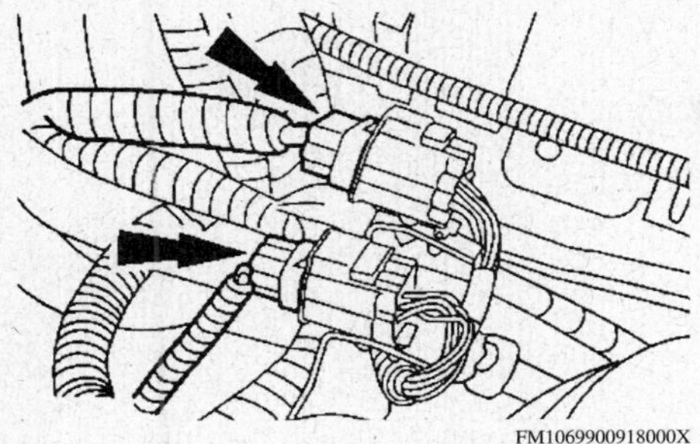

Fig. 8 Fuel charging wiring connectors

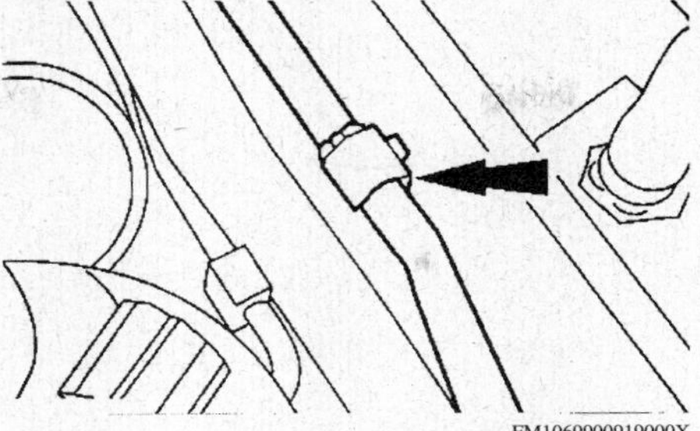

Fig. 9 Frame line location

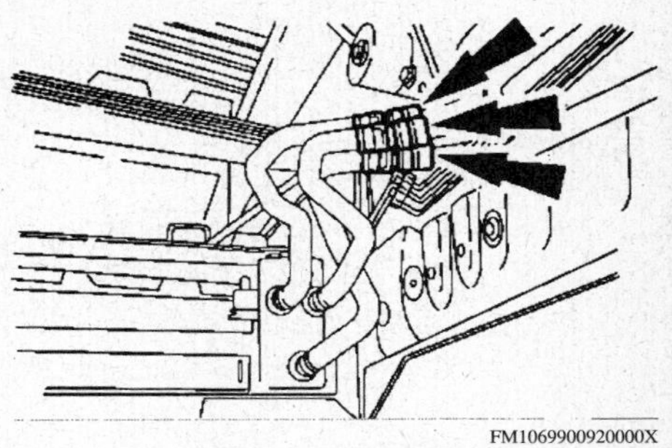

Fig. 10 Dual coolant flow valve

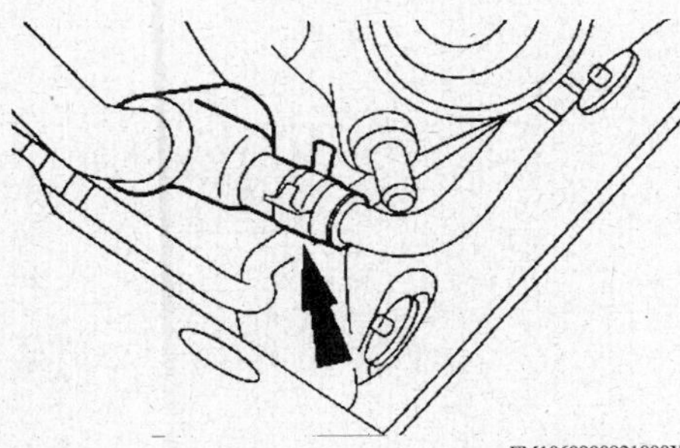

Fig. 11 Hose disconnect location

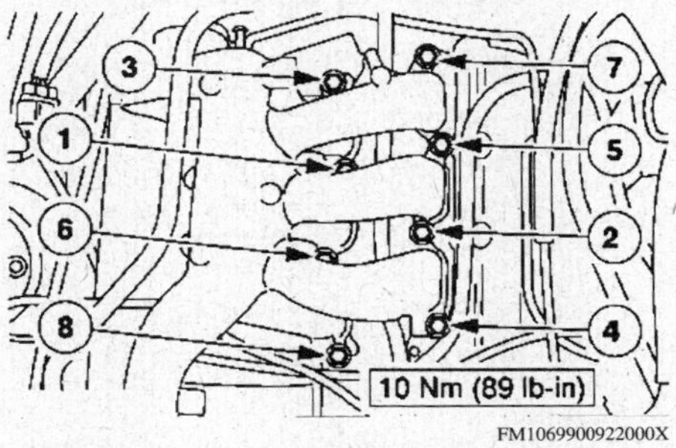

Fig. 12 Upper intake manifold bolt tightening sequence

39. Disconnect starter wiring harness at starter.
40. Disconnect power steering pressure electrical connectors.
41. Remove steering shaft clamp bolt.
42. Remove torque converter nuts.
43. Disconnect hose as shown in **Fig. 11.**
44. Support rear of vehicle using suitable safety stands.
45. Support engine, transmission, front and center crossmembers and cooling system with a suitable powertrain lift and transmission support bracket.
46. Remove four transmission crossmember bolts.
47. Remove four front and four center crossmember bolts.
48. Lower engine and transmission assembly from vehicle.
49. Install two engine lifting brackets tool No. 303-050, or equivalent, to engine.
50. Using a suitable engine lift and spreader bar, support engine and transmission in front subframe.
51. Disconnect two wire harness retainers and position harness aside.
52. Remove starter, then the oxygen sensor bracket.
53. Remove upper then lower transmission to engine attaching bolts.
54. Remove right and left engine mount upper attaching nuts.
55. Remove accessory drive belt.
56. Disconnect power steering pump electrical connector.
57. Remove power steering pump and position aside.
58. Disconnect hydraulic cooling fan pump electrical connector.
59. Remove hydraulic cooling fan pump and position aside.
60. Disconnect upper radiator hose.
61. **On models equipped with automatic transmission,** disconnect cooler line bracket from oil pan, then remove transmission cooler lines from transmission and plug fittings.
62. **On models equipped with oil cooler,** disconnect oil cooler hoses.
63. **On all models,** remove remaining transmission to engine attaching bolts and separate transmission from engine.
64. **On models equipped with manual transmission,** remove clutch assembly.
65. **On all models,** remove flywheel.
66. Unclip right and left wire harness retainers.
67. Remove rear separator plate assembly.
68. Mount engine to a suitable workstand, then remove lifting equipment.
69. Reverse procedure to install.

INTAKE MANIFOLD

REPLACE

UPPER INTAKE MANIFOLD

1. Drain cooling system as follows:
   a. Ensure engine is cold.
   b. Wrap a suitable shop towel around pressure relief cap, then remove cap.
   c. **Ensure coolant does not come into contact with accessory drive belt.**
   d. Open radiator draincock and drain coolant into a suitable container.
   e. **On models equipped with oil cooler,** disconnect coolant return hose at oil cooler.
2. **On all models,** remove air cleaner outlet tube.
3. Disconnect TP sensor and IAC electrical connectors.
4. Disconnect speed control and accelerator cables and position aside.
5. Disconnect coolant hoses, PCV hose and vapor purge hose from throttle body.
6. Disconnect EGR vacuum hose, then the EGR tube.
7. Remove cowl vent screen.
8. Remove vacuum hoses and cruise control cables from mounting brackets.
9. Disconnect differential pressure feedback EGR electrical connector.
10. Remove differential pressure feedback EGR transducer and position aside.
11. Remove fuel pressure sensor shield.
12. Disconnect vacuum hose from rear of intake manifold.
13. Disconnect intake manifold tuning valve electrical connector.
14. Disconnect exhaust vacuum regulator electrical connector and vacuum line.
15. Remove upper intake support bolt.
16. Remove upper intake attaching bolts, then the upper intake manifold. Inspect gaskets and discard as necessary.
17. Reverse procedure to install. Using sequence, **Fig. 12,** tighten manifold bolts to specifications.

LOWER INTAKE MANIFOLD

1. Remove upper intake manifold as outlined under "Upper Intake Manifold."
2. Disconnect fuel lines.
3. Remove fuel line bracket bolt.
4. Disconnect fuel pressure sensor vacuum line, then the fuel charging wiring harness connector.
5. Disconnect crankcase ventilation tube and position aside.
6. Remove lower intake manifold attaching bolts, then the manifold. **Fuel injection supply manifold and lower intake manifold must be removed as an assembly.**
7. Reverse procedure to install, noting the following:
   a. Inspect fuel injector O-rings and replace as necessary.
   b. Inspect lower intake manifold gaskets and replace as necessary.
   c. Using sequence **Fig. 13,** tighten manifold bolts to specifications.

EXHAUST MANIFOLD

REPLACE

LEFTHAND

1. Remove heat shield.
2. Remove three upper nuts on manifold.

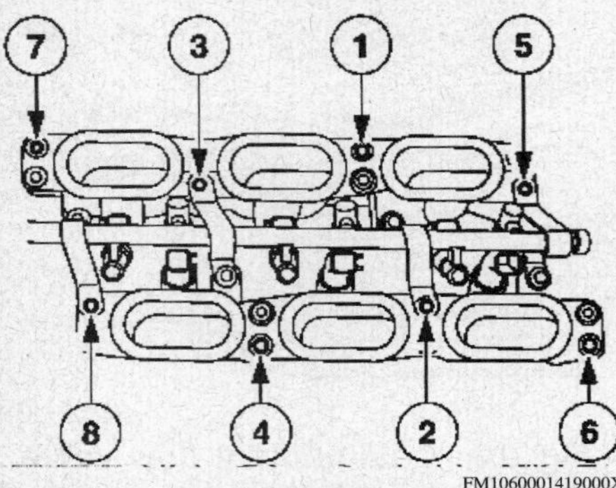

Fig. 13 Lower intake manifold tightening sequence

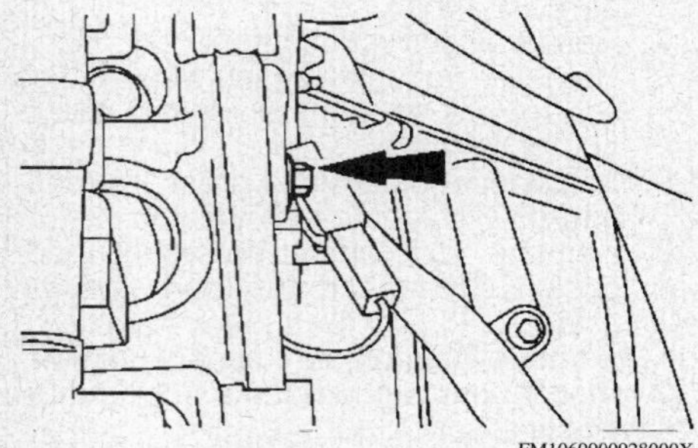

Fig. 16 Lefthand noise suppressor bolt location

3. Remove secondary air tube from exhaust manifold.
4. Remove dual converter Y-pipe.
5. Remove three lower nuts and exhaust manifold.
6. Reverse procedure to install. Install new gasket, then using sequence, **Fig. 14,** tighten nuts to specifications.

RIGHTHAND

1. Remove heat shield.
2. Remove secondary air tube from exhaust manifold.
3. Remove dual Y-pipe.
4. Disconnect EGR valve to exhaust manifold tube.
5. Remove manifold attaching nuts, then the manifold.
6. Reverse procedure to install. Install new gasket, then using sequence, **Fig. 14,** tighten nuts to specifications.

CYLINDER HEAD

REPLACE

When cleaning cylinder head surfaces, do not use metal scrapers, wires brushes, power abrasive discs or other abrasive methods to clean sealing surfaces. Use only a plastic scraping tool to remove all traces of gasket material.

Cylinder head bolts are of torque-to-yield style and must be replaced when removed.

Lefthand and righthand cylinder head gaskets are not interchangeable.

LEFTHAND

1. Remove camshafts as outlined under "Camshaft, Replace."
2. Remove exhaust manifold as outlined under "Exhaust Manifold, Replace."
3. Remove lower intake manifold as outlined under "Intake Manifold, Replace."
4. Remove cylinder head ground strap, stud and bolt, **Fig. 15.**
5. Remove noise suppressor bolt, **Fig. 16.**
6. Disconnect coolant outlet hose from thermostat housing.
7. Remove thermostat housing.
8. Remove oil level indicator tube stud bolt.
9. Remove cylinder head bolts in sequence, **Fig. 17.**
10. Reverse procedure to install. Using sequence, **Fig. 18,** tighten cylinder head bolts as follows:
    a. First step, **torque** to 22 ft. lbs.
    b. Second step, tighten an additional 90.°
    c. Third step, loosen all bolts 360.°
    d. Fourth step, **torque** to 22 ft. lbs.
    e. Fifth step, tighten an additional 90.°
    f. Sixth step, tighten an additional 90.°

RIGHTHAND

1. Remove camshafts as outlined under "Camshaft, Replace."
2. Remove exhaust manifold as outlined under "Exhaust Manifold, Replace."
3. Remove lower intake manifold as outlined under "Intake Manifold, Replace."
4. Remove noise suppressor bolt, **Fig. 19.**
5. Disconnect outlet hose from thermostat housing.
6. Remove thermostat housing.
7. Remove cylinder head bolts in sequence, **Fig. 17.**

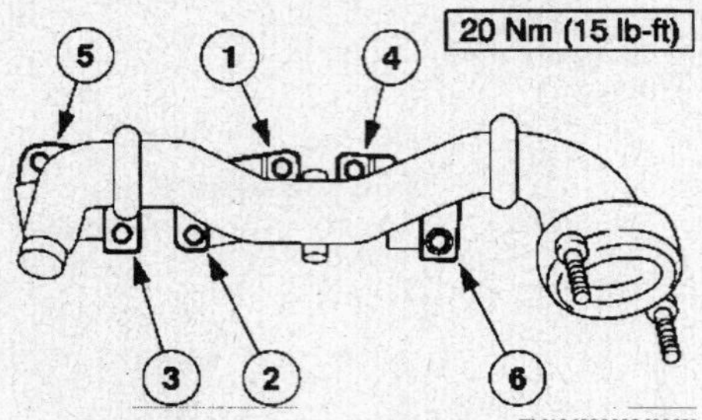

Fig. 14 Exhaust manifold tightening sequence

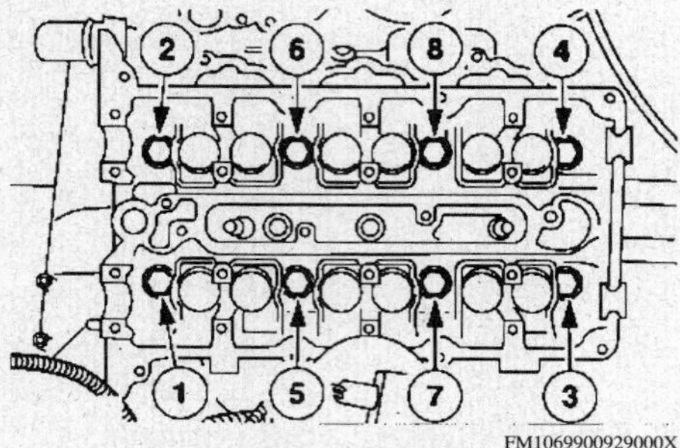

Fig. 17 Cylinder head bolt removal sequence

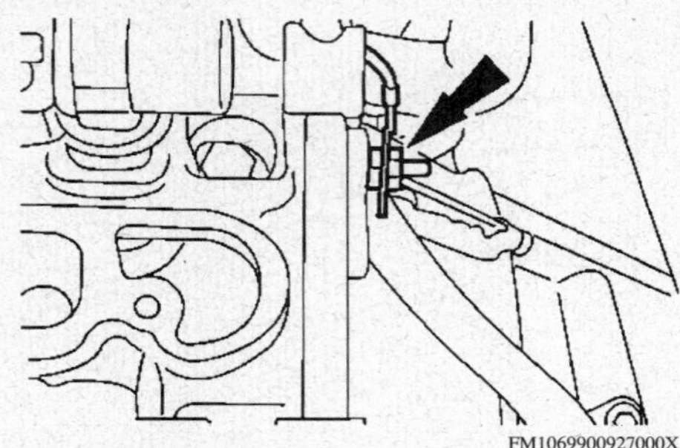

Fig. 15 Lefthand cylinder head ground strap location

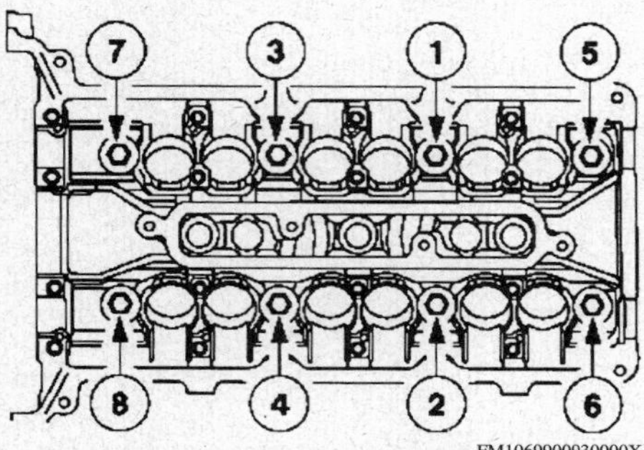

Fig. 18 Cylinder head bolt tightening sequence

8. Reverse procedure to install. Using sequence, **Fig. 18,** tighten cylinder head bolts as follows:
    a. First step, **torque** to 22 ft. lbs.
    b. Second step, tighten an additional 90.°
    c. Third step, loosen all bolts 360.°
    d. Fourth step, **torque** to 22 ft. lbs.
    e. Fifth step, tighten an additional 90.°
    f. Sixth step, tighten an additional 90.°

VALVE COVER

REPLACE

LEFTHAND

1. Remove lefthand ignition coils as outlined under "Ignition Coil, Replace" in the "Electrical" section.
2. Remove cylinder head temperature sensor.
3. Remove vacuum hoses from appearance cover support bracket.
4. Remove appearance cover support bracket.
5. Disconnect PCV tube and position aside.
6. Remove ignition coil harness from retainers.
7. Remove studs, bolts and valve cover.
8. Reverse procedure to install. Apply a .2 inch bead of silicone gasket sealant part No. F7AZ-19554-EA, or equivalent, to front cover joints, then using sequence **Fig. 20,** tighten to specifications.

RIGHTHAND

1. Remove upper intake manifold as outlined under "Intake Manifold, Replace."

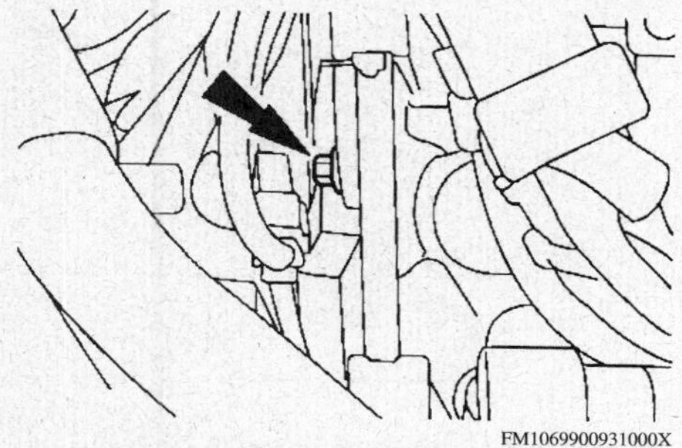

Fig. 19 Righthand noise suppressor bolt location

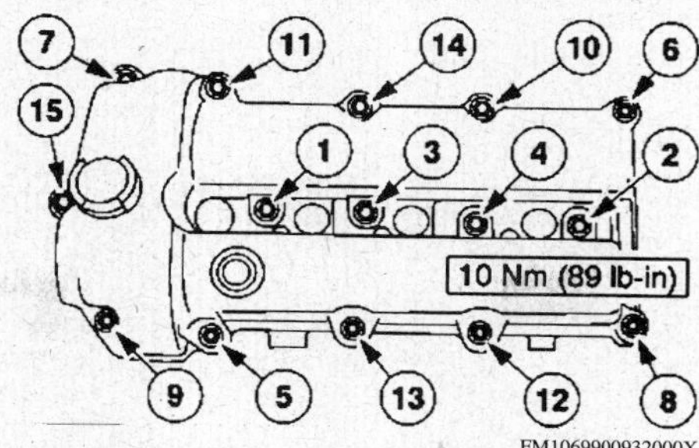

Fig. 20 Valve cover tightening sequence

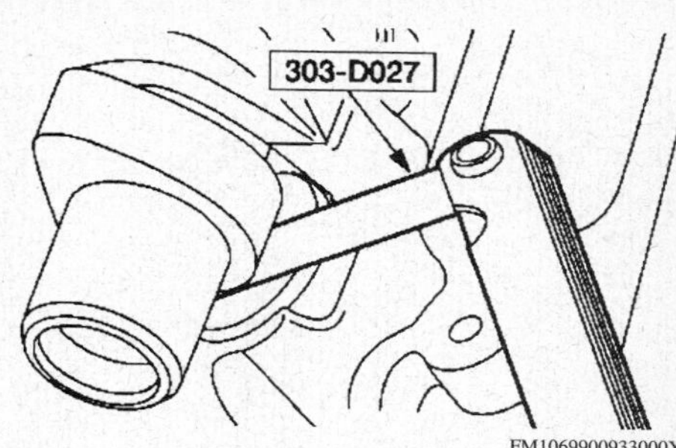

Fig. 21 Valve lash measurement

2. Disconnect PCV tube and position aside.
3. Remove righthand ignition coils as outlined under "Ignition Coil, Replace" in "Electrical" section.
4. Remove wiring harness retainer from stud.
5. Remove upper intake manifold support bracket and position aside.
6. Remove wiring harness bracket nuts and position aside.
7. Remove valve cover attaching bolts and studs, then the valve cover.
8. Reverse procedure to install. Apply a .2 inch bead of silicone gasket sealant part No. F7AZ-19554-EA, or equivalent, to front cover joints, then using sequence **Fig. 20,** tighten to specifications.

VALVE ARRANGEMENT

Inner .... I-I-I-I-I-I
Outer .... E-E-E-E-E-E

VALVE ADJUSTMENT

Rotating the engine in a counterclockwise direction will cause engine damage.

When marking shims, the only approved method is using a permanent marker. Scratches or paint on shim will cause incorrect lash adjustment and severe engine damage.

When measuring valve lash, ensure camshaft lobes are 180° away from each valve tappet.

1. Remove right and left valve covers as outlined under "Valve Cover, Replace."
2. Rotate engine clockwise to position camshaft lobe away from shim surface.
3. Using feeler gauge set tool No. D81L-4201-A, or equivalent, measure clearance between camshaft and shim surface, **Fig. 21.** Refer to "Tune Up Specifications" chart in "Specifications" section for correct valve clearance.
4. Use a suitable marker to mark position of timing chain in relation to camshaft sprockets to ensure timing remains correct.
5. Place alignment marks on camshaft caps for installation reference. Caps should be marked for location and orientation.
6. Remove camshaft thrust cap and rear camshaft cap from camshaft that requires adjustment.
7. Install camshaft lift tools, tool No. 303-659, or equivalents and hand tighten. Taller tool should be installed in place of rear camshaft cap to allow camshaft to be lifted for shim removal.
8. Remove center camshaft caps.
9. Mark location of each shim.
10. Use a rubber tipped air gun and compressed air to remove shims that require adjustment.
11. Measure and record thickness of each shim to correspond with valve clearance.
12. To calculate required shim thickness, use the following formula: original shim thickness + measured clearance – desired clearance = required shim thickness.
13. After correct shim thickness has been calculated, reverse procedure to install, noting the following:
    a. Apply a coat of clean 5W-30 motor oil to replacement shims and install shims.
    b. Apply a coat of clean 5W-30 motor oil to camshaft journals and bearing caps.
    c. Rotate crankshaft in clockwise direction to rotate camshafts two full revolutions. Recheck valve clearance and timing.

CRANKSHAFT DAMPER

REPLACE

1. Remove accessory drive belt.
2. Remove secondary air valve, bracket and tube.
3. Raise and support vehicle.
4. Remove front center splash panel.
5. Remove crankshaft pulley bolt and washer.
6. Remove crankshaft damper using damper removal tool No. 303-D121, or equivalent. **Ensure removal tool grabs inside of damper or damage will occur.**
7. Reverse procedure to install, noting the following:
    a. Ensure all damper and crankshaft surfaces are clean.
    b. Apply silicone gasket and sealant part No. F7AZ-19554-EA, or equivalent, to end of keyway slot.
    c. Lubricate outside sealing surface of crankshaft pulley with clean 5W-30 motor oil.
    d. Install damper using damper installer tool No. T74P-6316-B, or equivalent.
    e. Tighten crankshaft pulley bolt in four steps: First step, **torque** to 89 ft. lbs.; second step, loosen 360°; third step, **torque** to 37 ft. lbs.; fourth step, tighten an additional 90.°

FRONT COVER

REPLACE

1. Remove right and left valve covers as outlined under "Valve Cover, Replace."
2. Support engine with three bar engine support kit tool No. 303-F072, or equivalent.
3. Raise and support vehicle.
4. Remove splash shields.
5. Ensure engine is cold, then wrap a suitable shop towel around pressure relief cap and remove cap. **Ensure coolant does not come into contact with accessory drive belt.**
6. Open radiator draincock and drain coolant into a suitable container.
7. **On models equipped with oil cooler,** disconnect coolant return hose at oil cooler.
8. **On all models,** disconnect upper water pump hose, then the upper and lower radiator hoses.
9. Disconnect and remove radiator hose assembly.
10. Disconnect lower water pump hose.
11. Remove accessory drive belt.
12. Remove water pump as outlined under "Water Pump, Replace."
13. Remove oil pan as outlined under "Oil Pan, Replace."
14. Remove power steering pump as outlined under "Power Steering Pump, Replace" in "Front Suspension & Steering" section.
15. Remove hydraulic cooling fan pump as outlined under "Hydraulic Cooling Fan Pump, Replace"
16. Remove idler pulley, then the belt tensioner.
17. Remove crankshaft damper as outlined under "Crankshaft Damper, Replace."
18. Remove crankshaft front oil seal using seal removal tool No. T92C-6700-CH, or equivalent.
19. Remove front cover attaching bolts, then the front cover.
20. Reverse procedure to install, noting the following:

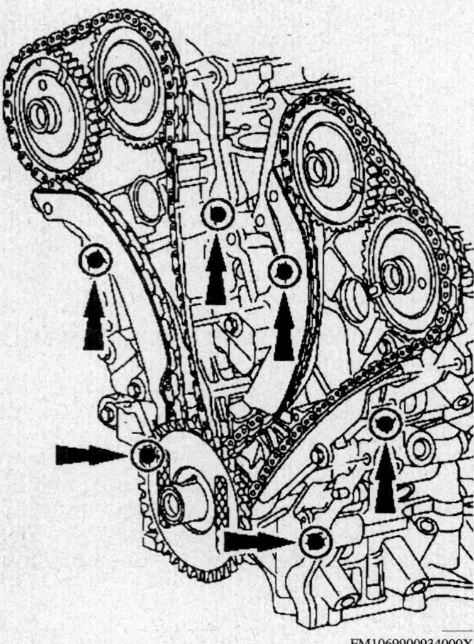

Fig. 22 Front cover sealant application points

a. Apply a .24 inch diameter dot of silicone gasket and sealant part No. F7AZ-19554-EA, or equivalent, **Fig. 22.** Ensure front cover is installed within 6 minutes of sealer application.
b. Install front cover, then using sequence **Fig. 23,** tighten cover bolts to specifications.
c. Install front crankshaft seal using seal installer tool No. T88T-6701-1, or equivalent.

FRONT COVER SEAL

REPLACE

1. Remove crankshaft damper as outlined under "Crankshaft Damper, Replace."
2. Remove front cover seal using seal remover tool No. T92C-6700-CH, or equivalent.
3. Reverse procedure to install, noting the following:
   a. Lubricate inside diameter of seal using clean 5W-30 motor oil.
   b. Install front cover seal using seal installer tool No. T88T-6701-A, or equivalent.

TIMING CHAIN

REPLACE

Rotating the engine in a counterclockwise direction will cause engine damage.

REMOVAL

1. Remove front cover as outlined under "Front Cover, Replace."
2. Remove ignition pulse ring.
3. Reinstall crankshaft damper bolt and washer.

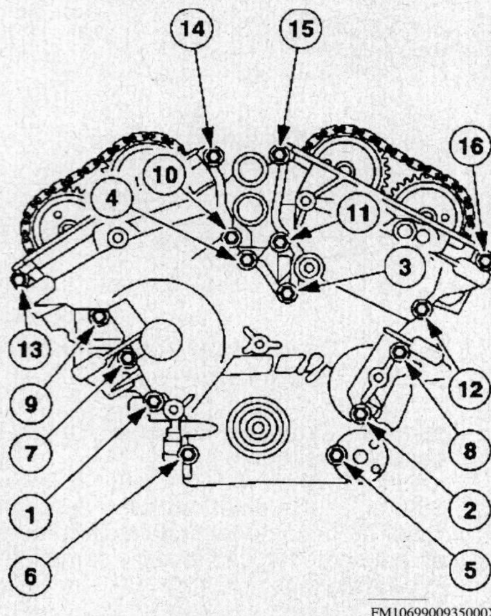

Fig. 23 Front cover tightening sequence

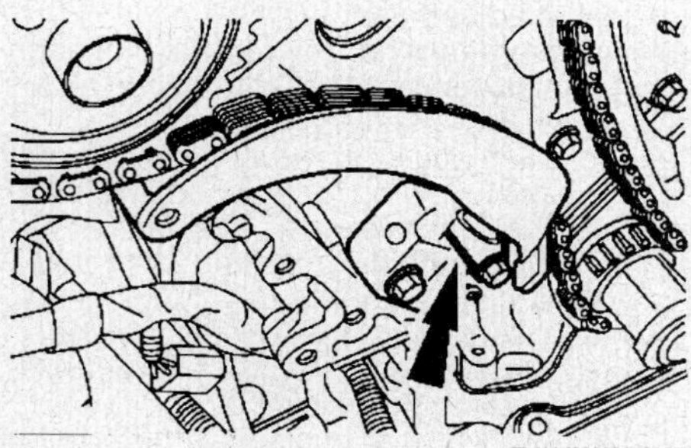

Fig. 25 Timing chain tensioner retention

4. Rotate crankshaft clockwise until keyway is positioned in 9 o'clock position, **Fig. 24.**
5. If timing chain tensioner and chain are to be reused, place identification marks on them for installation reference. **Do not interchange right and left timing components.**
6. Place a suitable paper clip into righthand timing chain tensioner before removing bolts, **Fig. 25.**
7. Remove righthand timing chain tensioner and arm.
8. Remove righthand timing chain, then the chain guide.
9. Install a suitable paper clip into lefthand timing chain tensioner.
10. Remove lefthand timing chain tensioner and arm, then the timing chain and guide.

INSTALLATION

Ensure crankshaft keyway remains in 9 o'clock position until cams are properly positioned or valve damage will occur.

1. Verify crankshaft keyway is in 9 o'clock position, **Fig. 24.**
2. Rotate right and left camshafts to locate them to neutral positions, **Fig. 26.**
3. Place lefthand chain tensioner into a suitable soft-jawed vise.

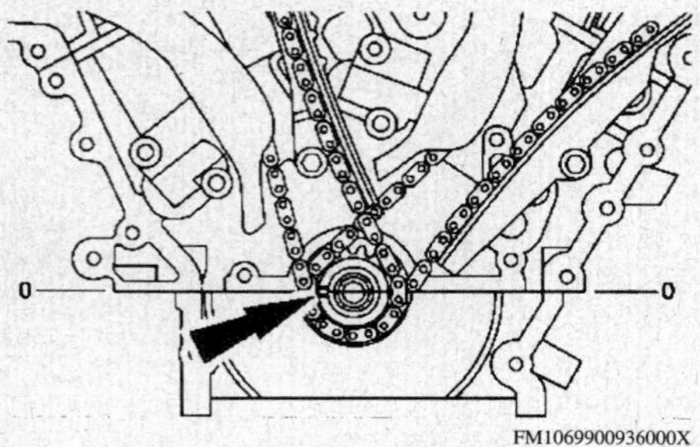

Fig. 24 Crankshaft keyway alignment

4. Hold tensioner ratchet lock mechanism away from ratchet stem using a suitable pick, **Fig. 27.**
5. **During tensioner compression, do not release ratchet stem until tensioner piston is fully bottomed in bore or stem will become damaged.** Slowly compress chain tensioner.
6. Retain lefthand tensioner piston using a suitable paper clip, **Fig. 28.**
7. Rotate crankshaft clockwise to 11 o'clock position.
8. Remove crankshaft damper bolt and washer.
9. Install lefthand timing chain guide and tighten to specifications. Ensure short bolt is installed into upper hole and long bolt into lower hole.
10. Install lefthand timing chain. Align gold timing chain index link with marks on camshaft and crankshaft sprockets, **Fig. 29.**
11. Install left timing chain tensioner and tighten to specifications. Ensure tensioner piston is fully engaged in tensioner arm.
12. Remove paper clip from left tensioner and install crankshaft damper bolt and washer.
13. Rotate crankshaft clockwise until keyway is positioned between 2 o'clock and 3 o'clock position.
14. Ensure gold timing chain index links on lefthand timing chain are still aligned with timing index marks on crankshaft and camshaft sprockets, **Fig. 30.**
15. Place righthand chain tensioner into a suitable soft-jawed vise.
16. Hold tensioner ratchet lock mechanism away from ratchet stem using a suitable pick, **Fig. 27.**
17. **During tensioner compression, do not release ratchet stem until tensioner piston is fully bottomed in bore or stem will become damaged.** Slowly compress chain tensioner.
18. Retain righthand tensioner piston using a suitable paper clip, **Fig. 28.**
19. Install righthand timing chain guide and tighten to specifications.
20. Install righthand timing chain. Align gold chain index marks with camshaft and crankshaft alignment marks, **Fig. 31.**
21. Install right timing chain tensioner and tighten to specifications.
22. Remove paper clip from righthand tensioner.
23. Ensure gold timing index links on righthand timing chain are still aligned with

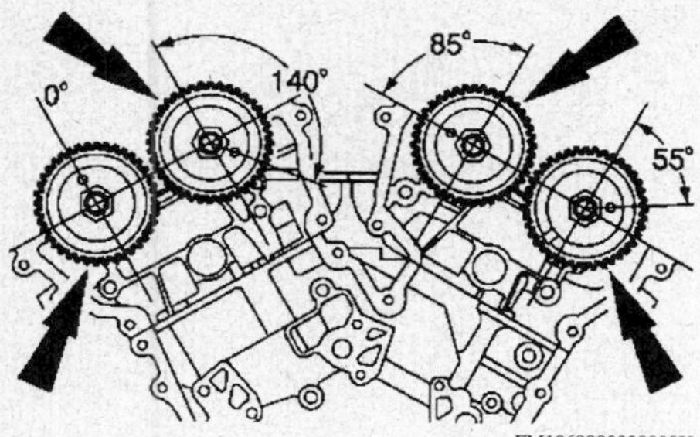

Fig. 26 Camshaft neutral positions

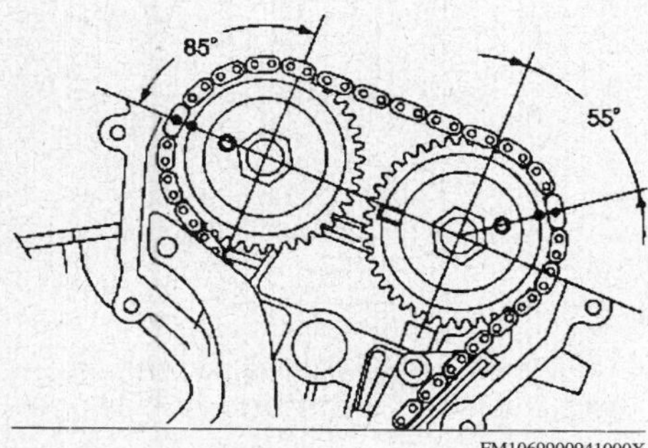

Fig. 29 Primary lefthand timing chain alignment mark inspection

timing index marks on camshaft and crankshaft sprockets, **Fig. 32.**

24. Remove crankshaft damper bolt and washer.
25. Install ignition pulse ring.
26. Install front cover as outlined under "Front Cover, Replace."

CAMSHAFT

REPLACE

When removing camshafts, camshaft journal thrust caps must be removed prior to loosening other camshaft journal cap bolts.

When installing camshafts, camshaft bearing caps must be installed prior to installing thrust caps.

Camshaft journal caps and cylinder heads are numbered to ensure they are assembled in their original positions.

REMOVAL

1. Remove upper intake manifold as outlined under "Intake Manifold, Replace."
2. Remove front cover as outlined under "Front Cover, Replace."
3. Remove timing chains as outlined under "Timing Chain, Replace."
4. Remove camshaft journal thrust caps, **Fig. 33.**
5. Remove remaining camshaft journal caps, then the camshafts.

INSTALLATION

1. Ensure all bearing caps are installed to original positions.
2. Lubricate camshafts and all bearing surfaces with clean 5W-30 motor oil.
3. Install camshaft bearing caps. **Do not tighten bolts at this time.**

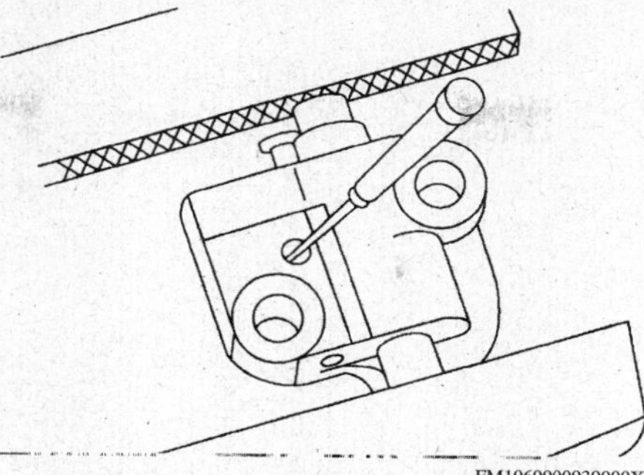

Fig. 27 Timing chain tensioner ratchet lock access hole

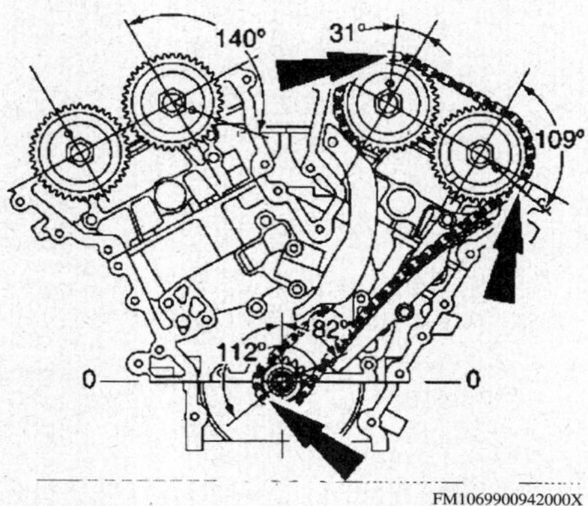

Fig. 30 Secondary lefthand timing chain alignment mark inspection

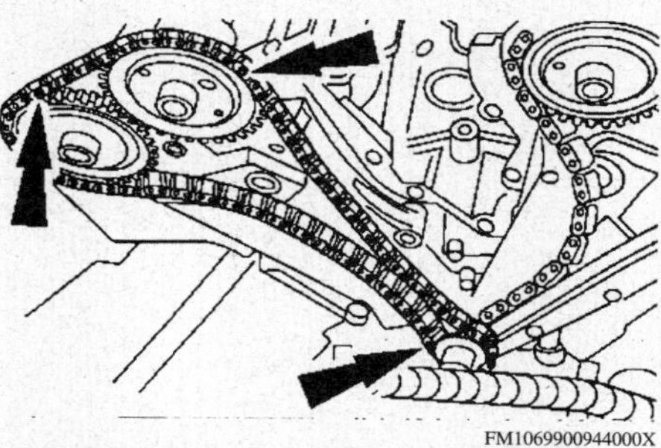

Fig. 32 Secondary righthand timing chain alignment mark inspection

4. Install camshaft thrust caps. **Do not tighten bolts at this time.**
5. Using sequences **Figs. 34 and 35,** tighten camshaft bearing caps to specifications.
6. If new camshafts were installed, adjust valve lash as outlined under "Valve Adjustment."
7. **Verify crankshaft keyway is in the 9 o'clock position before rotating camshafts or engine damage will result.**
8. Rotate camshafts to ensure they are not binding. If binding occurs, ensure bearing caps are in original positions. Loosen all bearing caps in reverse order and retighten.
9. Install timing chains as outlined under "Timing Chain, Replace."
10. Install front cover as outlined under "Front Cover, Replace."
11. Install upper intake manifold as outlined under "Intake Manifold, Replace."

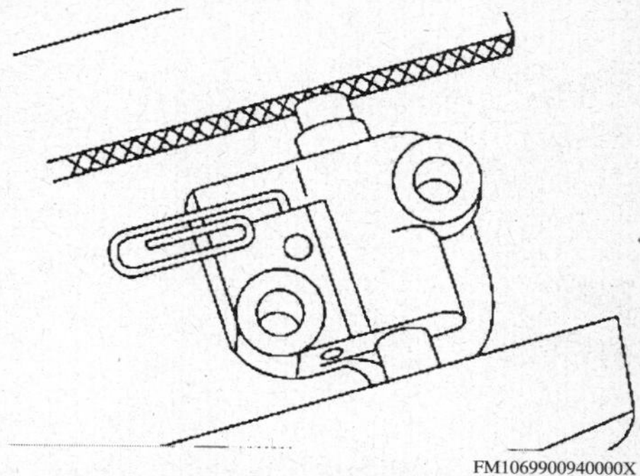

Fig. 28 Timing chain tensioner piston retention

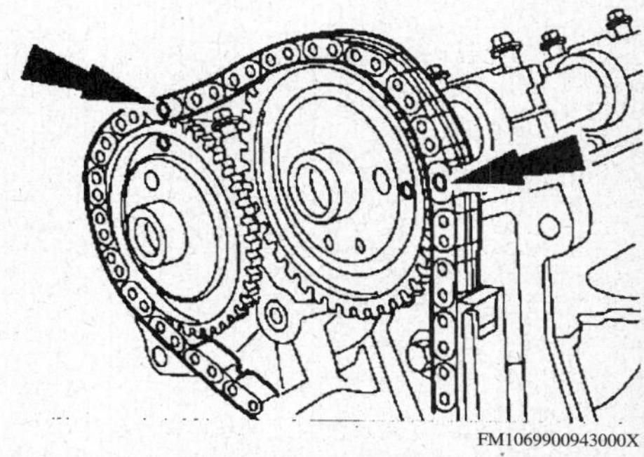

Fig. 31 Primary righthand timing chain alignment mark inspection

PISTON & ROD ASSEMBLY

When removing pistons and connecting rods, place reference marks on all parts involved for installation reference.

Connecting rod bearing caps are cracked and split from connecting rods during the manufacturing process. When assembling parts, ensure all mating surfaces are clean and ensure identification marks on cap and rod are aligned.

Connecting rod bolts are of torque-to-yield design and must be replaced when removed.

Connecting rod bolts are of torque-to-yield design and must be replaced once taken apart. When installing pistons, ensure arrow on piston is facing toward front of engine. For connecting rod bolt tightening specifications refer to "Tightening Specifications."

MAIN BEARINGS

When cleaning gasket surfaces, do not use metal scrapers, wires brushes, power abrasive discs or other abrasive methods to clean sealing surfaces. Use only a plastic scraping tool to remove all traces of gasket material.

Lower cylinder block bolts and studs are of torque-to-yield design and must be replaced when removed.

To select and install main bearings, proceed as follows:

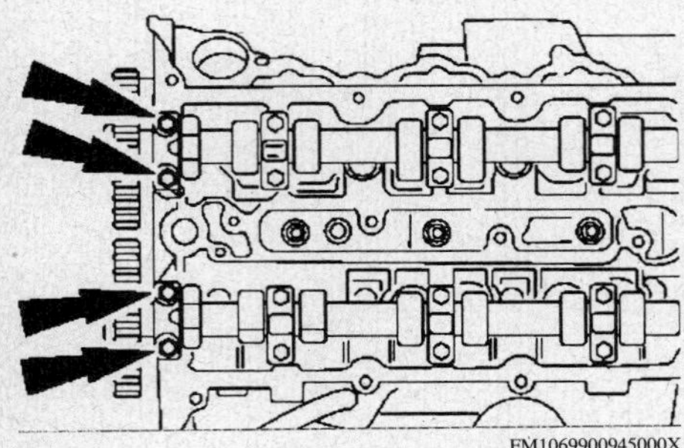

Fig. 33 Camshaft journal thrust cap location

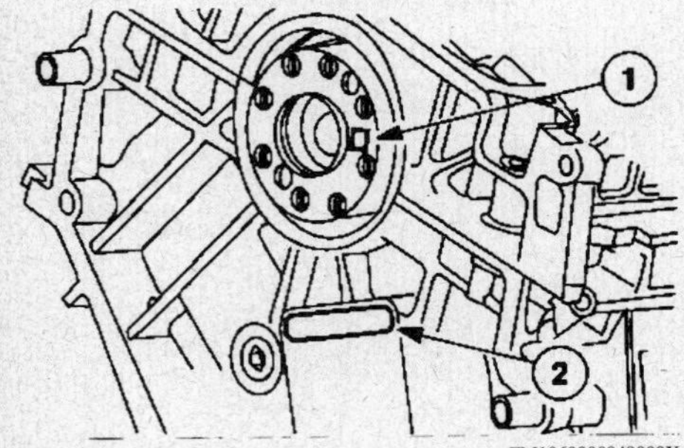

Fig. 36 Cylinder block and crankshaft bearing reference marks

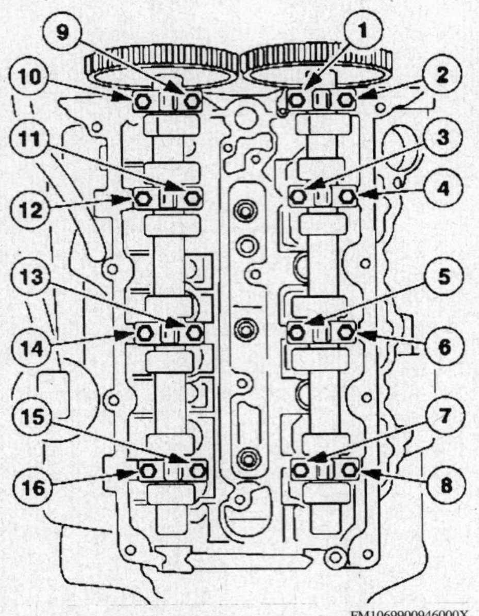

Fig. 34 Lefthand camshaft bearing cap tightening sequence

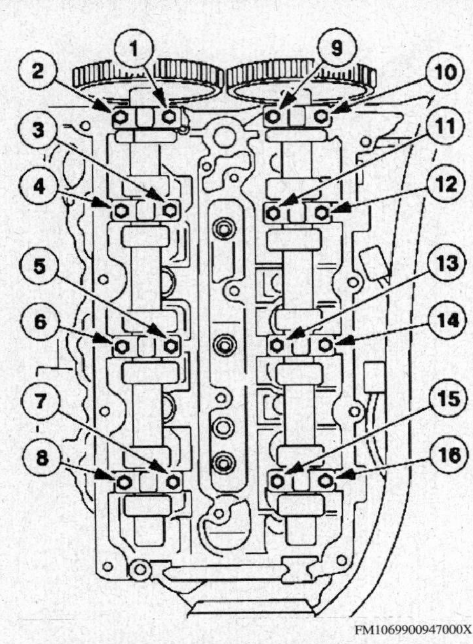

Fig. 35 Righthand camshaft bearing cap tightening sequence

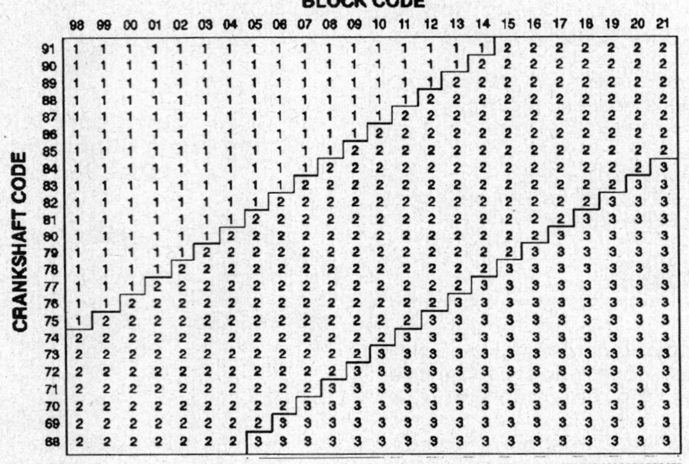

BLOCK CODE

CRANKSHAFT CODE	98	99	00	01	02	03	04	05	06	07	08	09	10	11	12	13	14	15	16	17	18	19	20	21
91	1	1	1	1	1	1	1	1	1	1	1	1	1	1	1	1	1	2	2	2	2	2	2	2
90	1	1	1	1	1	1	1	1	1	1	1	1	1	1	1	1	2	2	2	2	2	2	2	2
89	1	1	1	1	1	1	1	1	1	1	1	1	1	1	1	2	2	2	2	2	2	2	2	2
88	1	1	1	1	1	1	1	1	1	1	1	1	1	1	2	2	2	2	2	2	2	2	2	2
87	1	1	1	1	1	1	1	1	1	1	1	1	1	2	2	2	2	2	2	2	2	2	2	2
86	1	1	1	1	1	1	1	1	1	1	1	1	2	2	2	2	2	2	2	2	2	2	2	2
85	1	1	1	1	1	1	1	1	1	1	1	2	2	2	2	2	2	2	2	2	2	2	2	2
84	1	1	1	1	1	1	1	1	1	1	2	2	2	2	2	2	2	2	2	2	2	2	2	3
83	1	1	1	1	1	1	1	1	1	2	2	2	2	2	2	2	2	2	2	2	2	2	3	3
82	1	1	1	1	1	1	1	1	2	2	2	2	2	2	2	2	2	2	2	2	2	3	3	3
81	1	1	1	1	1	1	1	2	2	2	2	2	2	2	2	2	2	2	2	2	3	3	3	3
80	1	1	1	1	1	1	2	2	2	2	2	2	2	2	2	2	2	2	2	3	3	3	3	3
79	1	1	1	1	1	2	2	2	2	2	2	2	2	2	2	2	2	2	3	3	3	3	3	3
78	1	1	1	1	2	2	2	2	2	2	2	2	2	2	2	2	2	3	3	3	3	3	3	3
77	1	1	1	2	2	2	2	2	2	2	2	2	2	2	2	2	3	3	3	3	3	3	3	3
76	1	1	2	2	2	2	2	2	2	2	2	2	2	2	2	3	3	3	3	3	3	3	3	3
75	1	2	2	2	2	2	2	2	2	2	2	2	2	2	3	3	3	3	3	3	3	3	3	3
74	2	2	2	2	2	2	2	2	2	2	2	2	2	3	3	3	3	3	3	3	3	3	3	3
73	2	2	2	2	2	2	2	2	2	2	2	2	3	3	3	3	3	3	3	3	3	3	3	3
72	2	2	2	2	2	2	2	2	2	2	2	3	3	3	3	3	3	3	3	3	3	3	3	3
71	2	2	2	2	2	2	2	2	2	2	3	3	3	3	3	3	3	3	3	3	3	3	3	3
70	2	2	2	2	2	2	2	2	2	3	3	3	3	3	3	3	3	3	3	3	3	3	3	3
69	2	2	2	2	2	2	2	2	3	3	3	3	3	3	3	3	3	3	3	3	3	3	3	3
68	2	2	2	2	2	2	2	3	3	3	3	3	3	3	3	3	3	3	3	3	3	3	3	3

FM1069900948000X

Fig. 37 Bearing grade selection chart

1. Read code on crankshaft flange (1), and code on engine block rear face (2), **Fig. 36.**
2. First 2 numbers after asterisk make up code for main No. 1 and next two numbers for main No. 2. The first 2 numbers after second asterisk make up code for main No. 3 and last two numbers for main No. 4. Refer to **Fig. 37** for bearing grade selection chart.
3. As an example, if block code is *0609*0711* and crankshaft code is *8480*8082*, main No. 1 will use grade 1 bearings as determined by intersection of 06 block column and 84 crankshaft row, **Fig. 37.** Using these codes as an example, main Nos. 2, 3 and 4 will use grade 2.
4. Install upper main bearing and upper thrust bearing to cylinder block in proper locations.
5. Lubricate bearings using clean 5W-30 motor oil, then install crankshaft to cylinder block.
6. Install lower main bearings and lower thrust bearing into lower cylinder block in proper locations.
7. Ensure all gasket surfaces are clean using Ford Metal Surface Cleaner part No. F4AZ-19A536-RA, or equivalent. Allow to dry until there is no sign of wetness present.
8. Apply a .12 inch bead of silicone gasket sealant part No. F7AZ-19554-EA, or equivalent, to lower cylinder block. End bead of gasket material .24 inch from rear crankshaft seal bore on both sides, **Fig. 38.** Bolts and studs must be tightened within four minutes of applying sealant.
9. Install lower cylinder block studs (1) and bolts (2), **Fig. 39.**
10. Install new bolts and studs, then using sequence, **Fig. 40,** tighten bolts as follows:
    a. Bolts 1–8, **torque** to 18 ft. lbs.
    b. Bolts 9–16, **torque** to 30 ft. lbs.
    c. Bolts 1–16, tighten an additional 90.°
    d. Bolts 17–22, **torque** to 18 ft. lbs.
11. Remove excess sealer from front cover and rear seal bore inner diameter areas.
12. Rotate crankshaft in clockwise direction to verify free rotation.

CRANKSHAFT REAR OIL SEAL

REPLACE

1. **On models equipped with automatic transmissions,** remove transmission as outlined in "Automatic Transmission/Transaxle" chapter.
2. **On models equipped with manual transmissions,** remove transmission as outlined in "Clutch & Manual Transmission" section.
3. **On all models,** remove flywheel.
4. Remove rear crankshaft seal using seal removal tool No. T95P-6701-EH and slide hammer tool No. 307-005, or equivalents.
5. Lubricate outer lips and inner seal of new crankshaft rear seal with clean 5W-30 motor oil.
6. Install rear oil seal using seal installer tool No. T82L-6701-A and rear adapter bolts tool No. T91P-6701-A, or equivalents.
7. Install flywheel with elongated hole over crankshaft dowel.
8. Install flywheel bolts, then using sequence, **Fig. 41,** tighten to specifications.

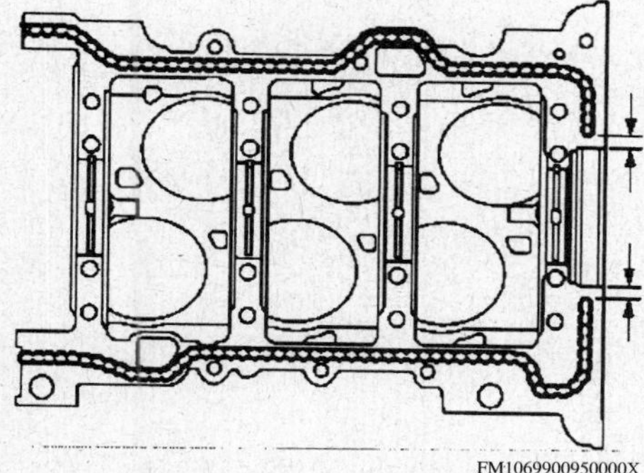

Fig. 38 Lower cylinder block sealant application

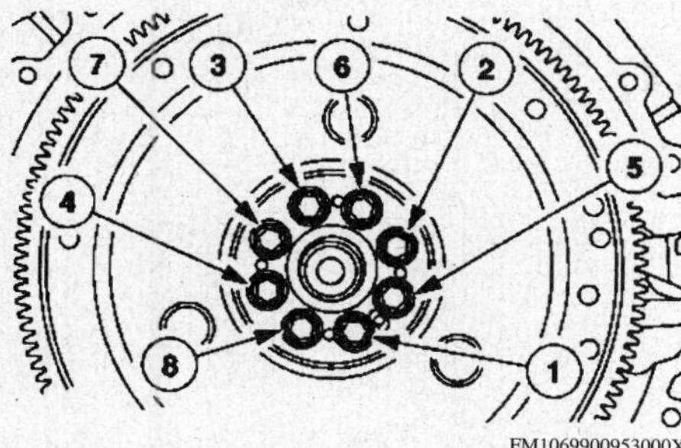

Fig. 41 Flywheel tightening sequence

9. **On models equipped with automatic transmissions,** install transmission as outlined in "Automatic Transmission/Transaxle" chapter.
10. **On models equipped with manual transmissions,** install transmission as outlined in "Clutch & Manual Transmission" section.

OIL PAN

REPLACE

1. Support engine using three bar engine support tool No. 303-F072, or equivalent.
2. Raise and support vehicle.
3. Drain engine oil.
4. Remove alternator as outlined under "Alternator, Replace" in "Electrical" section.
5. Remove A/C compressor mounting bolts, then support compressor aside using suitable mechanics wire.
6. Remove electronic thermactor air bracket bolts.
7. Remove power steering line from oil pan stud.
8. Remove steering gear attaching nuts and support steering gear.
9. Remove right and left control arm through bolts, then the right and left motor mount nuts.
10. Remove left and right subframe bolts, **Figs. 42 and 43.**
11. Remove transmission cooler line bracket nut.
12. Remove transmission to oil pan bolts.
13. Remove oil pan attaching bolts.
14. Pry subframe downward and remove oil pan.

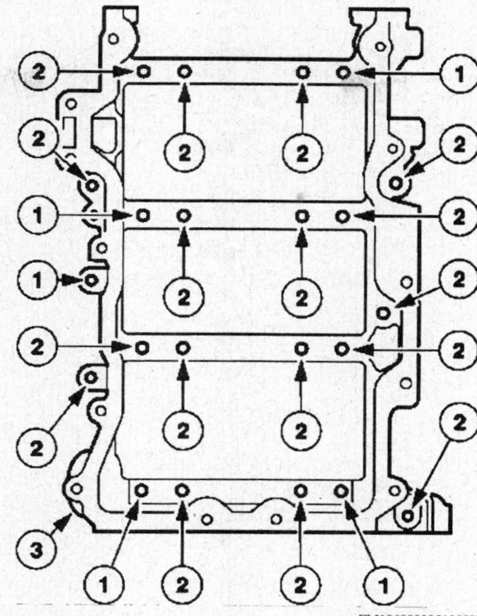

Fig. 39 Lower cylinder block bolt identification

15. Reverse procedure to install, noting the following:
    a. Install new gasket to oil pan.
    b. Apply a .4 inch dot of silicone gasket sealant part No. F7AZ-19554-EA or equivalent, to oil pan as shown in **Fig. 44.** Oil pan must be installed and bolts tightened within six minutes of sealant application.
    c. Install oil pan, then using sequence, **Fig. 45,** tighten bolts to specification.
    d. Ensure vehicle suspension alignment is within specifications, refer to "Front Wheel Alignment Specifications" in "Specifications" section.

OIL PUMP

REPLACE

1. Remove timing chains as outlined under "Timing Chain, Replace."
2. Remove oil pan as outlined under "Oil Pan, Replace."
3. Remove oil pump screen tube.
4. Remove oil pump attaching bolts, then the oil pump, **Fig. 46.**
5. Reverse procedure to install.

OIL COOLER

REPLACE

1. Ensure engine is cold.
2. Wrap a suitable shop towel around pressure relief cap, then remove cap. **Ensure coolant does not come into contact with accessory drive belt.**
3. Open radiator draincock and drain coolant into a suitable container.
4. Disconnect coolant hoses at oil cooler.
5. Remove oil cooler attaching bolt, then the oil cooler.
6. Reverse procedure to install, noting the following:
    a. Position oil cooler and gasket.
    b. Install attaching bolt, then rotate

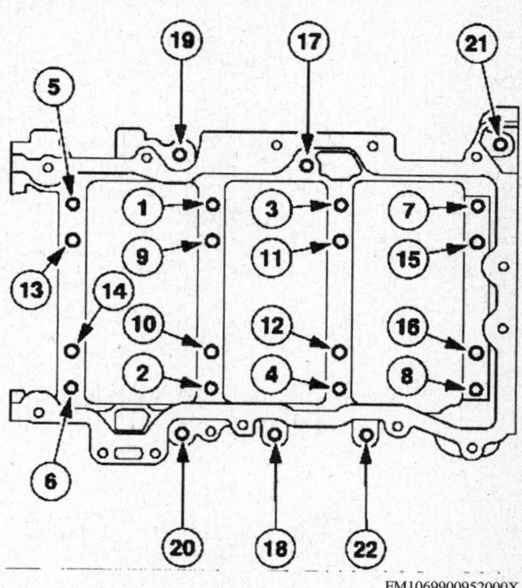

Fig. 40 Lower cylinder block tightening sequence

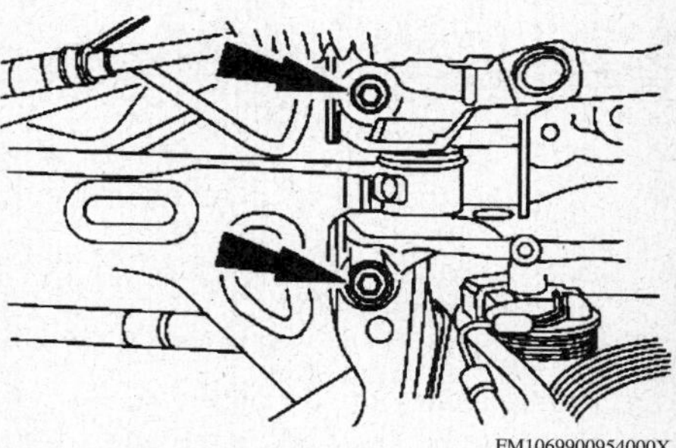

Fig. 42 Lefthand subframe bolt location

cooler clockwise until locating pin hits the stop.

SERPENTINE DRIVE BELT

TENSION

Vehicle is equipped with an automatic belt tensioner and tension is not adjustable. Refer to **Fig. 47** to inspect tensioner.

ROUTING

Refer to **Fig. 48** for serpentine drive belt routing.

COOLING SYSTEM BLEED

1. Open engine air bleed fitting, **Fig. 49.**
2. Open heater air bleed fitting, **Fig. 50.**
3. Add coolant to overflow bottle. Allow system to equalize until no more coolant can be added.
4. Close engine air bleed when coolant begins to escape.
5. Install cap to overflow bottle.
6. Start and run engine at idle speed with heater air bleed open. Turn heater to MAX position.
7. Close heater air bleed when a steady stream of coolant starts to flow.
8. Allow engine to idle for 5 minutes, then

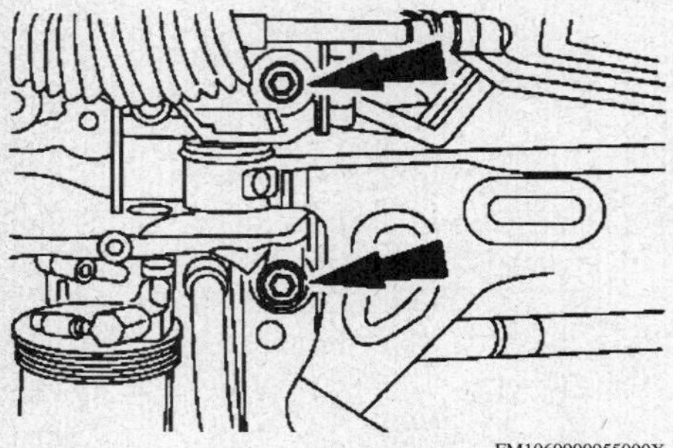

Fig. 43 Righthand subframe bolt location

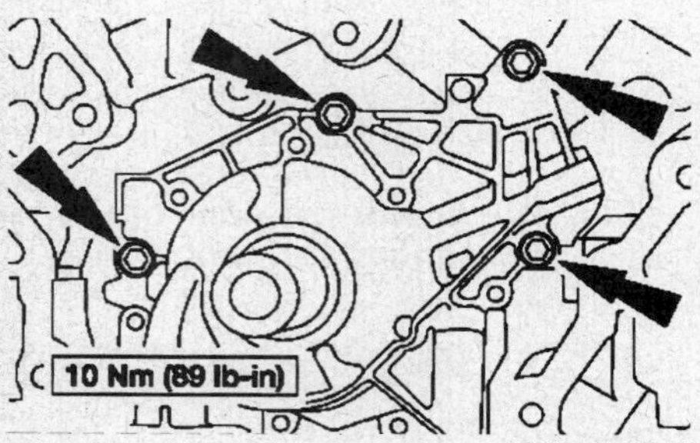

Fig. 46 Oil pump removal

add coolant to overflow bottle until it reaches MAX mark.
9. Reopen heater air bleed to release any trapped air, then close.
10. Operate engine at 1500 RPM for 3–5 minutes or until hot air comes from heater.
11. Return to idle and verify hot air is still coming from heater.
12. Turn engine off and allow to cool. After engine has cooled, add coolant to overflow bottle to bring level to MAX cold fill mark.

THERMOSTAT

REPLACE

1. Ensure engine is cold.
2. Wrap a suitable shop towel around pressure relief cap, then remove cap. **Ensure coolant does not come into contact with accessory drive belt.**
3. Open radiator draincock and drain coolant into a suitable container.
4. Disconnect coolant hoses at oil cooler.
5. Remove air cleaner outlet tube.
6. Disconnect hoses from thermostat housing, **Fig. 51.**
7. Remove thermostat housing, then the thermostat and seal.
8. Reverse procedure to install.

WATER PUMP

REPLACE

1. Ensure engine is cold.
2. Wrap a suitable shop towel around pressure relief cap, then remove cap. **Ensure coolant does not come into contact with accessory drive belt.**
3. Open radiator draincock and drain coolant into a suitable container.
4. Disconnect coolant hoses at oil cooler.

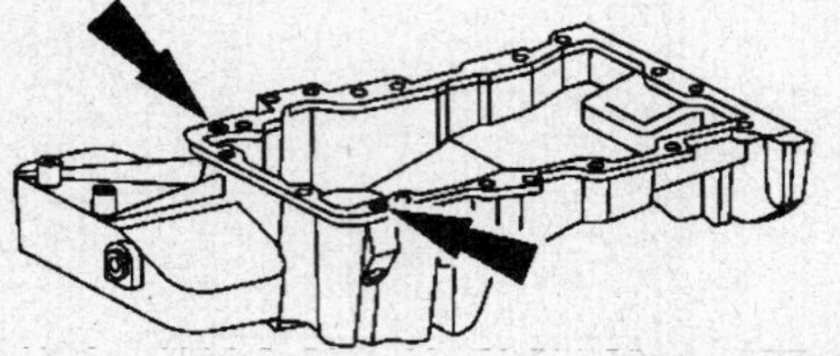

Fig. 44 Oil pan sealant application points

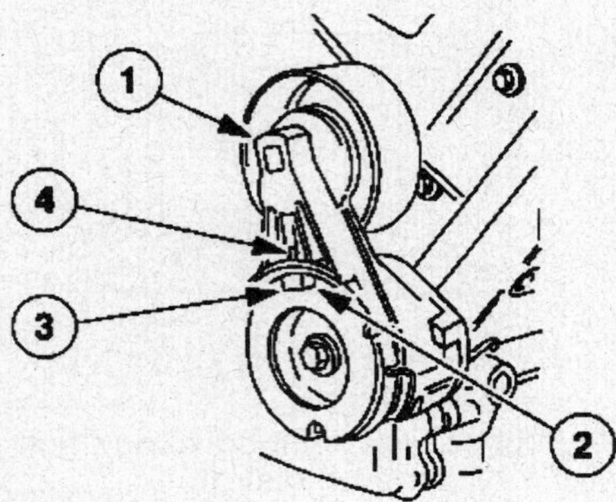

Item	Description
1	Belt tension relief point
2	Unacceptable belt wear range
3	Acceptable belt installation and wear range
4	Belt length indicator

FM1069900959000X

Fig. 47 Belt tensioner inspection

5. Remove air cleaner outlet tube.
6. Disconnect engine vent hose, **Fig. 49.**
7. Disconnect upper and lower radiator hoses, then the heater supply and water pump hoses.
8. Remove water crossover assembly.
9. Disconnect water inlet hose from coolant outlet tube.
10. Disconnect and remove water inlet hose from pump.
11. Remove serpentine drive belt.
12. Remove water pump attaching bolts and studs, then the water pump. Record location of water pump studs for installation reference.
13. Reverse procedure to install.

RADIATOR

REPLACE

1. Ensure engine is cold.
2. Wrap a suitable shop towel around pressure relief cap, then remove cap. **Ensure coolant does not come into contact with accessory drive belt.**
3. Open radiator draincock and drain coolant into a suitable container.
4. Disconnect coolant hoses at oil cooler.
5. Remove upper radiator sight shield.
6. Remove air cleaner outlet tube.

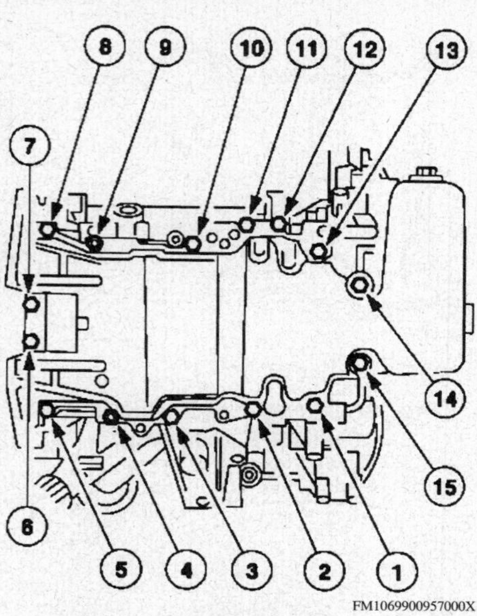

Fig. 45 Oil pan tightening sequence

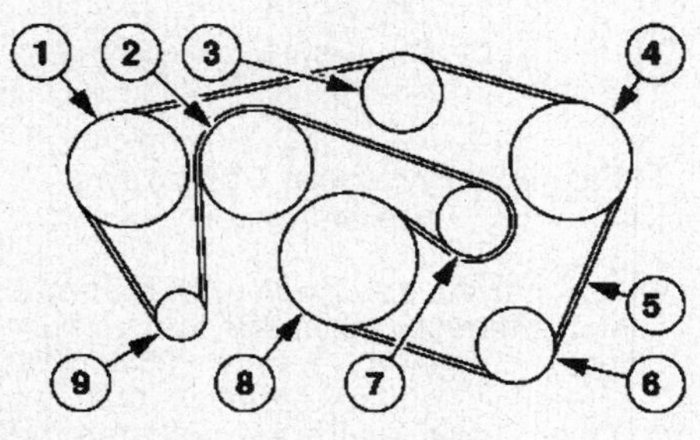

Item	Description
1	Hydraulic fan pump pulley
2	Water pump pulley
3	Belt idler pulley
4	Power steering pump pulley
5	Drive belt
6	A/C clutch pulley
7	Drive belt tensioner
8	Crankshaft vibration damper
9	Generator pulley

FM1069900960000X

Fig. 48 Serpentine drive belt routing

7. Remove radiator support brackets, then the upper radiator hose.
8. Remove receiver drier attaching bolt and position receiver drier aside.
9. Disconnect high pressure cooling fan line, then the return hose.
10. Separate return hose from fan shroud and position aside.
11. Remove fan shroud.
12. Support A/C condenser using suitable mechanics wire.
13. Raise and support vehicle.
14. Remove right and left splash shields, then the radiator air deflector.
15. Disconnect lower radiator hose.

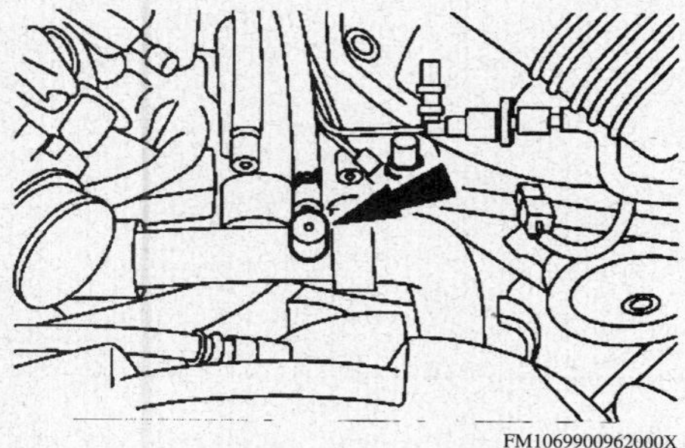

Fig. 49 Engine air bleed location

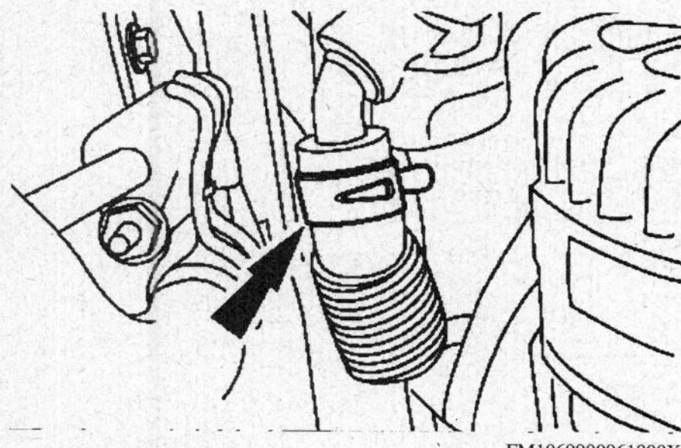

Fig. 52 Hose location

16. Remove condenser to radiator attaching bolts.
17. Remove condenser support brackets, then the radiator through bottom of vehicle.
18. Reverse procedure to install.

HYDRAULIC FAN MOTOR

REPLACE

Refer to "Radiator, Replace" for procedure.

HYDRAULIC COOLING FAN PUMP

REPLACE

1. Remove accessory drive belt.
2. Remove lower cooling fan pump bolt.
3. Disconnect hose and allow to drain, **Fig. 52.**
4. Disconnect cooling fan pump electrical connector.
5. Remove high pressure line bracket.
6. Disconnect high pressure line.
7. Remove two upper pump bolts, then the cooling fan pump.
8. Reverse procedure to install.

FUEL PUMP

REPLACE

The fuel system contains two pumps. One is the "fuel delivery module" which provides fuel pressure to the engine. The second pump is a "jet pump" or "transfer" pump which maintains fuel levels in both sides of the fuel tank.

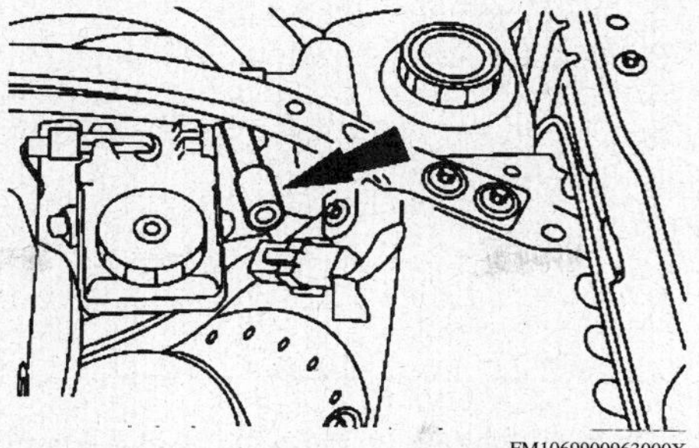

Fig. 50 Heater air bleed location

Fig. 53 Transfer pump fuel line connections

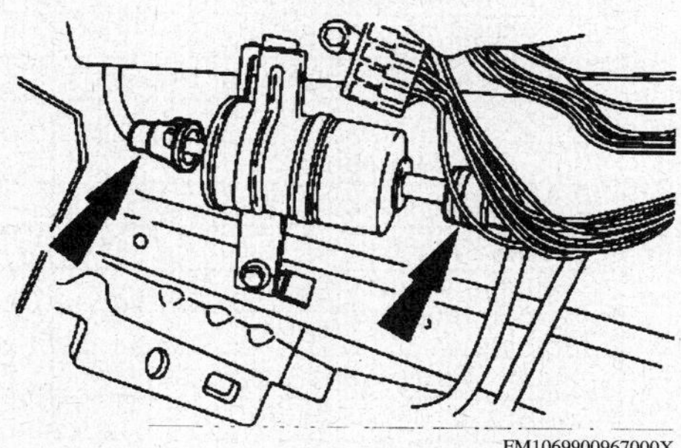

Fig. 55 Fuel filter

The jet pump is located on the lefthand side of the fuel tank and contains a fuel level sensor and a check valve which maintains system pressure after the pump is shut off.

The fuel delivery module is located on the righthand side of the fuel tank and contains a fuel level sensor and an inlet screen on the bottom of the pump.

To disconnect fuel lines from pumps, press down on fuel line connector while pressing release tabs. Pull straight up to remove.

Whenever fuel pumps are removed, new fuel pump gaskets must be installed.

FUEL DELIVERY MODULE

1. Relieve fuel pressure as outlined under "Precautions."
2. Drain fuel tank as follows:
   a. Release rear seat mini-buckle.
   b. Depress two seat cushion latches, then remove rear seat cushion and insulation.
   c. Remove fuel pump access covers. Ensure all fuel pump connectors are fully seated.
   d. Remove black connector elbow on transfer pump, **Fig. 53.**
   e. Attach a fuel line draining connector to a suitable fuel storage tanker hose and outlet fitting on transfer pump.
   f. Siphon fuel until tank side is empty.
   g. Attach fuel draining connector to fuel delivery module, **Fig. 54,** and repeat steps d, e and f.
3. Disconnect remaining fuel line from fuel delivery module.
4. Disconnect fuel delivery module electrical connector.
5. Loosen fuel pump lockring using fuel sender wrench tool No. 310-069, or equivalent.
6. Remove fuel delivery module lockring.
7. Position pump flange clear of pump opening, then press lock tabs and release pump from tank mounting flange.
8. Lift pump straight up and out of retainer cup, then tilt while in tank to drain fuel from reservoir.
9. Straighten and lift straight up and out of tank. Drain excess fuel into a suitable container.
10. Reverse procedure to install.

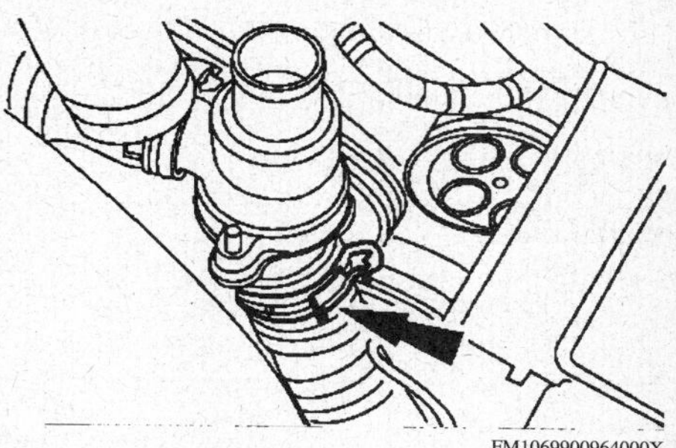

Fig. 51 Thermostat housing location

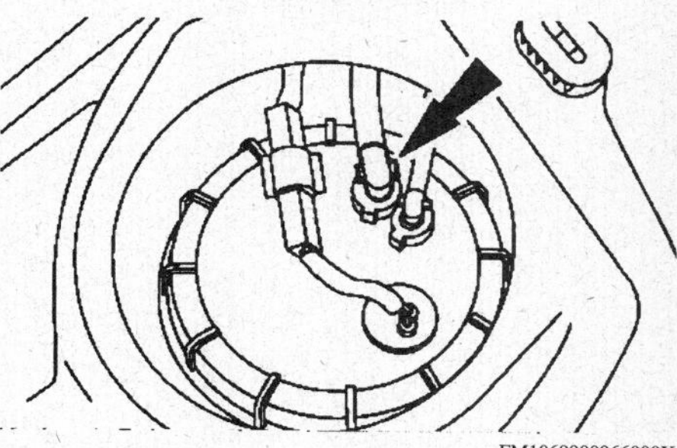

Fig. 54 Fuel delivery module fuel line connections

JET (TRANSFER) PUMP

1. Relieve fuel pressure as outlined under "Precautions."
2. Drain fuel tank as outlined under "Fuel Delivery Module."
3. Ensure fuel line connectors are fully seated prior to pressing release tabs.
4. Disconnect fuel lines from transfer pump.
5. Disconnect electrical connector from transfer pump.
6. Loosen transfer pump lockring using fuel sender wrench tool No. 310-069, or equivalent.

7. Remove lockring, then the transfer pump.
8. Reverse procedure to install.

FUEL FILTER

REPLACE

1. Relieve fuel pressure as outlined under "Precautions."
2. Raise and support vehicle.
3. Remove left front wheel.
4. Remove splash shield fasteners.
5. Disconnect fuel line R-clip fittings, **Fig. 55.**
6. Remove fuel filter attaching bolt, then the filter.
7. Reverse procedure to install.

TIGHTENING SPECIFICATIONS

Year	Component	Torque, Ft. Lbs.
2000–02	A/C Compressor	18
	Alternator	35
	Belt Tensioner	35
	Camshaft Bearing Caps	89①
	CKP Sensor	89①
	CMP Sensor	89①
	Connecting Rod	②
	Coolant Inlet Tube	18
	Coolant Outlet Tube	18
	Crankshaft Damper	③
	Cylinder Head	④
	Dipstick Tube	89①
	EGR Tube To EGR Valve	30
	Engine Appearance Cover Bracket	53
	Engine Mount Lower Nut	46
	Engine Mount Upper Nut	46
	Exhaust Manifold Heat Shield	89①
	Exhaust Manifold To Cylinder Head	15
	Exhaust Pipe To Exhaust Manifold	30
	Flywheel	59
	Front Brake Caliper	76
	Front Cover	18
	Front & Center Crossmember Bolts	76
	Front Intake Manifold Support Nut	89①
	Hydraulic Cooling Fan Pump	18
	Hydraulic Cooling Fan Reservoir	108①
	Idler Pulley	18
	Lower Control Arm Through Bolt	129
	Lower Cylinder Block	⑤
	Lower Intake Manifold To Cylinder Head	89①
	Lower Stabilizer Link Nut	41
	Lower Strut Mount Bolts	129
	Main Bearing Cap	⑤
	Oil Cooler	42
	Oil Pan	18
	Oil Pan To Transmission Bolts	35
	Oil Pump	89①
	Oil Pump Screen	89①
	Power Steering Pump	18
	Power Steering Reservoir	108①
	Radiator Support Brackets	89①
	Starter Motor	18
	Steering Gear Nuts	76
	Steering Shaft Clamp Bolt	18
	Subframe	77

Continued

TIGHTENING SPECIFICATIONS—Continued

Year	Component	Torque, Ft. Lbs.
2000–02	Thermostat Housing	96①
	Timing Chain Guide	18
	Timing Chain Tensioner	18
	Torque Converter Nuts	23–28
	Transmission Crossmember	41
	Transmission Cooler Lines	15
	Transmission To Engine Bolts	35
	Transmission To Oil Pan Bolts	35
	Upper Ball Joint	66
	Upper Intake Manifold Support Bracket Bolt	89①
	Upper Intake Manifold Support Bracket Nut	53①
	Upper Intake Manifold To Lower Intake Manifold	89①
	Valve Cover	89①
	Water Pump	18
	Wheel Lug Nuts	100

①— Inch lbs.
②— Tighten using new bolts in 3 steps as follows: 1st step, 17 ft. lbs.; second step, 32 ft. lbs.; 3rd step, additional 90.°
③— Refer to "Crankshaft Damper, Replace."
④— Refer to "Cylinder Head, Replace."
⑤— Refer to "Main Bearings."

3.9L Engine

NOTE: On Air Bag Equipped Models, Refer To "Air Bag System Precautions" Located In The Front Of This Manual For System Disarming & Arming Procedures.

NOTE: Refer To "Computer Relearn Procedures" Located In The Front Of This Manual When Battery Power To The Computer Has Been Interrupted.

INDEX

PRECAUTIONS

AIR BAG SYSTEMS

Refer to "Air Bag System Precautions" in the front of this manual for system disarming and arming procedures.

BATTERY GROUND CABLE

Prior to service, disconnect battery ground cable and isolate as required.

FUEL SYSTEM PRESSURE RELIEF

1. Remove schrader valve cap and install fuel pressure gauge tool No. T80L-9974-B, or equivalent, to schrader valve.
2. Slowly open manual valve on pressure gauge and drain fuel into a suitable container.

QUICK DISCONNECT HOSES

R-CLIP

When working with R-clip type connections, **Fig. 1,** do not use tools to disconnect. Use of tools may deform clip components and could cause leaks.

To disconnect, bend shipping tab downward, **Fig. 1.** Spread R-clip and push clip into fitting. Separate fitting from tube.

To install, first inspect fitting and tube for damage and ensure connections are clean.

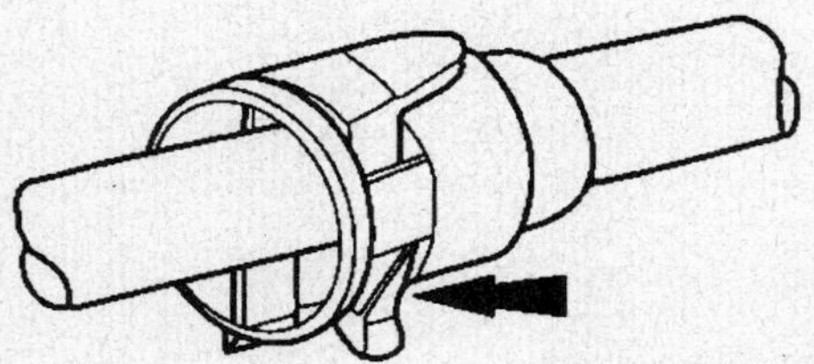

Fig. 1 R-clip connection

Apply a light coat of clean 5W-30 motor oil to male end of tube. Insert R-clip into fitting. Align tube and fitting, then insert tube into fitting and push together until a click is heard. Pull on connection to ensure it is fully engaged.

SPRING LOCK

When working with spring lock type connections, **Fig. 2**, spring lock tool set No. T84L-19623-B or equivalent, must be used to disconnect fittings. When connecting spring lock type fittings, inspect and clean both coupling ends. Lubricate fuel line O-ring seals with clean 5W-30 motor oil. When connection is made, pull on line to ensure it is fully engaged.

VAPOR TUBE

To disconnect vapor tube connections, squeeze fitting (1) and disconnect vapor tube from fitting (2), **Fig. 3.** To connect, ensure fittings are clean and free from damage. Push tube onto fitting until it snaps into place. Pull on connection to verify fitting is secure.

COMPRESSION PRESSURE

Before performing compression test, ensure the following conditions are met: crankcase oil is of correct viscosity and at correct level, ensure battery is fully charged and engine is at normal operating temperature.

1. Turn ignition switch to off position.
2. Remove all spark plugs.
3. Set throttle plates to wide open position.
4. Install a suitable compression gauge in No. 1 cylinder.
5. Install an auxiliary starter switch in starting circuit.
6. With ignition switch off, use auxiliary starter switch to crank engine a minimum of five compression strokes.
7. Note number of compression strokes necessary to reach highest reading and record highest reading.
8. Repeat test on each cylinder, cranking engine same number of compression strokes.
9. Indicated compression pressures are considered within specifications if lowest reading cylinder is within 75 percent of highest reading.

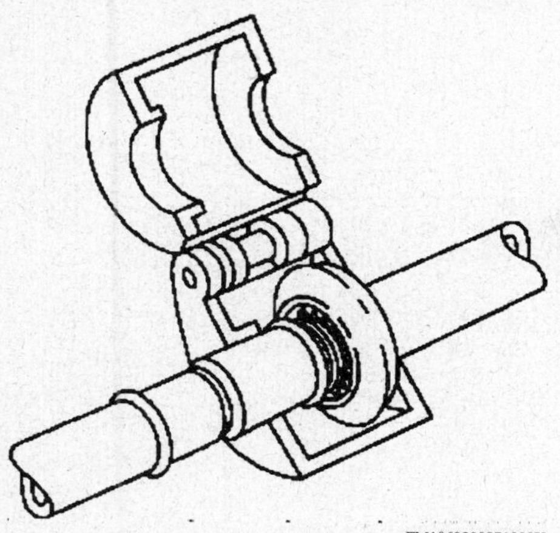
FM1069900971000X

Fig. 2 Spring lock connection

ENGINE MOUNT

REPLACE

1. Using engine lifting eye kit tool No. D81L-6001-D and three bar engine support kit tool No. D88L-6000-A, or equivalents, support engine.
2. Raise and support vehicle.
3. Remove upper and lower engine mount nuts.
4. Remove engine mount and bracket.
5. Reverse procedure to install.

ENGINE

REPLACE

When carrying out operations which involve the removal and installation of the driveshaft, always check the joint angles and make the necessary adjustments as outlined under "Driveline Angle Measurement" in "Rear Axle & Suspension" section.

1. Remove air cleaner and outlet tube.
2. Remove engine appearance cover.
3. Drain cooling system as follows:
   a. Ensure engine is cold.
   b. Wrap a suitable shop towel around pressure relief cap, then remove cap.
   c. **Ensure coolant does not come into contact with accessory drive belt.**
   d. Open radiator draincock and drain coolant into a suitable container.
   e. **On models equipped with oil cooler,** disconnect coolant return hose at oil cooler.
4. **On all models,** remove upper radiator sight shield.
5. Remove upper radiator support brackets.
6. Recover refrigerant as outlined under "Air Conditioning."
7. Disconnect A/C pressure switch.
8. Release power steering line from frame rail.
9. Remove power steering reservoir and position aside.
10. Disconnect fuel lines.
11. Disconnect evaporative canister purge hose, then the main vacuum supply hose.

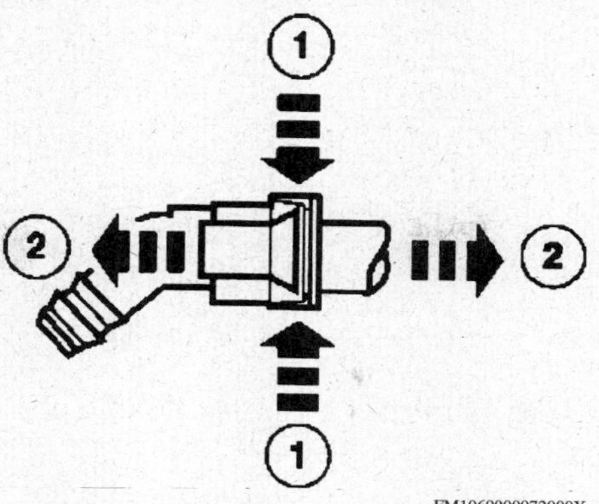

FM1069900972000X

Fig. 3 Vapor tube connection

12. Remove cowl panels.
13. Remove cowl panel support bracket.
14. Disconnect throttle and speed control cables, then the engine ground strap.
15. Remove cabin air filter and plenum as outlined under "Heater Core, Replace."
16. Disconnect powertrain bulkhead connectors located on rear side of right-hand strut tower and position aside.
17. Remove cowl to engine insulation panel.
18. Disconnect remaining bulkhead connectors.
19. Place reference marks on heater hoses for installation reference.
20. Disconnect four heater hoses at water control valve.
21. Remove hydraulic cooling fan reservoir and position aside.
22. Disconnect water valve electrical connector from radiator support and position harness aside.
23. Raise and support vehicle.
24. Remove front wheels.
25. Remove front anti-lock brake sensors.
26. Remove front calipers as outlined in "Disc Brakes" chapter and position aside.
27. Remove two sway bar link lower bolts.
28. Hold ball joint external hex, then remove upper ball joint nuts.
29. Separate upper ball joints from spindles.
30. Remove lower strut mount bolts.
31. Remove left, right and center splash shields.
32. Remove retaining nut, then disconnect A/C high pressure line.
33. Disconnect low pressure A/C quick disconnect coupler.
34. Remove exhaust system.
35. Remove driveshaft as outlined under "Propeller Shaft, Replace" in "Rear Axle & Suspension" section.
36. Disconnect shift cable and shift cable bracket bolt.
37. Disconnect hydraulic cooling fan lines from righthand frame rail.
38. Disconnect power steering lines from lefthand frame rail.
39. Disconnect steering gear electrical connectors.
40. Disconnect steering coupling.
41. Disconnect starter motor electrical connectors, then the alternator electrical connector.

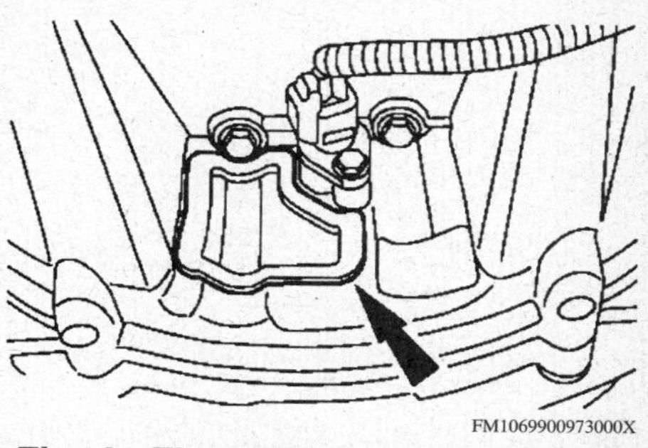
FM1069900973000X

Fig. 4 Flywheel inspection cover

FM1069900974000X

Fig. 5 Front & center support bolt location

42. Remove flywheel inspection cover, **Fig. 4.**
43. Place reference marks on torque converter stud, nut and adapter plate for installation reference.
44. Remove eight torque converter nuts from flywheel spacer.
45. **On models equipped with engine block heater,** disconnect engine block heater plug at grille opening.
46. **On all models,** support rear of vehicle using suitable safety stands.
47. Support engine transmission, front suspension, front and center crossmemebers and cooling system using a suitable powertrain lift and transmission support bracket. Disconnect transmission support system as necessary.
48. Remove four front and four center support bolts, **Fig. 5.**
49. Lower entire powertrain assembly from vehicle.
50. Disconnect engine block heater.
51. Disconnect A/C manifold hose from compressor.
52. Disconnect power steering pump and hydraulic cooling fan return hoses. Drain fluid into a suitable container.
53. Remove lower radiator hose bolts.
54. Disconnect radiator hoses, then the heater hoses.
55. Remove transmission cooler line bracket nut.
56. Disconnect transmission cooler lines, then the power steering pressure line.
57. Remove power steering line bracket.
58. Install engine lifting eye kit tool No. D81L-6001-D, or equivalent, to engine.
59. Remove six lower transmission bolts.

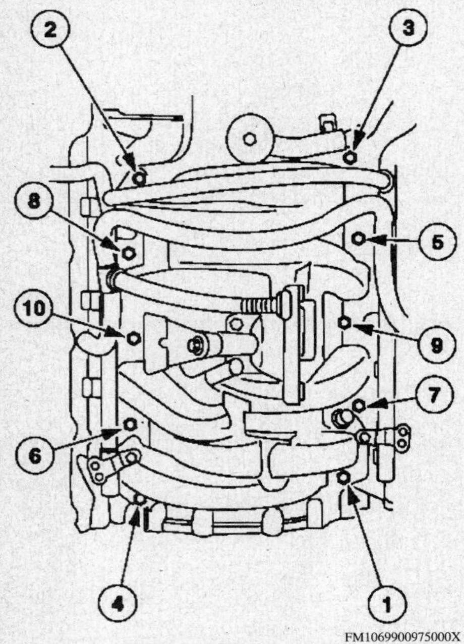

Fig. 6 Intake manifold loosening & tightening sequence

60. Install spreader bar tool No. D93P-6001-A3, or equivalent, to engine lifting eyes.
61. Attach a suitable engine crane to spreader bar and support engine and transmission.
62. Remove engine mount upper nuts.
63. Remove engine and transmission from subframe and place on floor.
64. Remove wiring harness attaching nuts, then the remaining transmission to engine attaching bolts.
65. Separate engine from transmission, then mount engine to a suitable stand.
66. Reverse procedure to install.

INTAKE MANIFOLD

REPLACE

When cleaning cylinder head surfaces, do not use metal scrapers, wires brushes, power abrasive discs or other abrasive methods to clean sealing surfaces. Use only a plastic scraping tool to remove all traces of gasket material.

1. Remove air cleaner outlet tube.
2. Ensure engine is cold.
3. Wrap a suitable shop towel around pressure relief cap, then remove cap. **Ensure coolant does not come into contact with accessory drive belt.**
4. Open radiator draincock and drain coolant into a suitable container.
5. Disconnect coolant return hose at oil cooler.
6. Remove wiper motor and arm assembly as outlined under "Wiper Motor, Replace" in "Electrical" section.
7. Remove engine compartment brace.
8. Disconnect accelerator and speed control cables.
9. Disconnect main vacuum hose and vacuum harness.

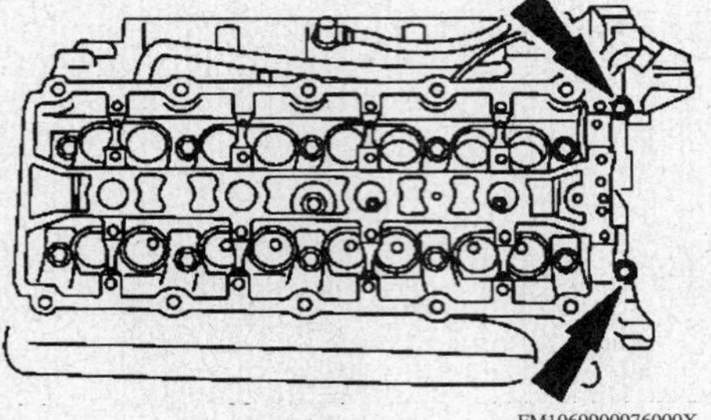

Fig. 7 Front cylinder head bolt location

10. Disconnect EGR vacuum line, then the EGR valve to exhaust manifold tube.
11. Disconnect camshaft position sensor, then the evaporative emission canister purge valve line.
12. Remove fuel pressure sensor connector.
13. Disconnect inline vacuum connector to fuel pressure sensor.
14. Relieve fuel pressure as outlined under "Precautions."
15. Disconnect fuel line, then the knock sensor and cylinder head temperature sensor connectors from bracket.
16. Raise wiring harness, then disconnect lefthand fuel injector connectors.
17. Disconnect idle air control, TP sensor and crankcase ventilation tube.
18. Disconnect coolant hoses from throttle body.
19. Raise wiring harness and disconnect righthand fuel injectors.
20. Remove manifold attaching bolts in sequence, **Fig. 6.**
21. Reverse procedure to install. Using sequence, **Fig. 6,** tighten bolts to specification.

EXHAUST MANIFOLD

REPLACE

LEFTHAND

1. Remove dipstick tube.
2. Raise and support vehicle.
3. Remove exhaust catalyst pipe.
4. Remove eight exhaust manifold attaching bolts, then the manifold.
5. Reverse procedure to install.

RIGHTHAND

1. Raise and support vehicle.
2. Disconnect exhaust catalyst from manifold.
3. Disconnect starter motor electrical connectors.
4. Disconnect EGR tube from exhaust manifold.
5. Remove eight exhaust manifold attaching bolts, then the manifold.
6. Reverse procedure to install.

CYLINDER HEAD

REPLACE

When cleaning cylinder head surfaces, do not use metal scrapers, wires brushes, power abrasive discs or other abrasive methods to clean sealing surfaces. Use only a plastic scraping tool to remove all traces of gasket material.

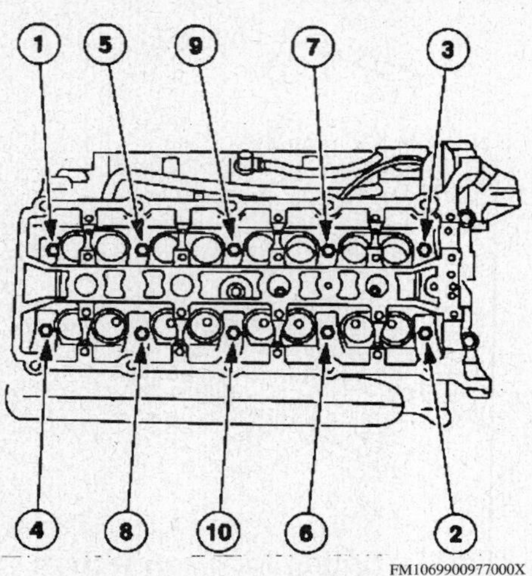

Fig. 8 Righthand cylinder head removal sequence

Cylinder head bolts should be replaced when removed.

When marking shims, the only approved method is using a permanent marker. Scratches or paint on shim will cause incorrect lash adjustment and severe engine damage.

1. Remove intake manifold as outlined under "Intake Manifold, Replace."
2. Remove engine sound insulator.
3. Remove camshafts as outlined under "Camshaft, Replace."
4. Place reference marks on bucket and shim tappets for installation reference, then remove as necessary.
5. Remove water crossover tube.
6. Disconnect cylinder head temperature sensor, then the camshaft position sensor.
7. Raise and support vehicle.
8. Disconnect exhaust system from exhaust manifolds.
9. Disconnect EGR tube from exhaust manifold, then lower vehicle.
10. Remove right and left front cylinder head bolts, **Fig. 7.**
11. Remove righthand cylinder head bolts in sequence, **Fig. 8.**
12. Remove righthand cylinder head and gasket.
13. Remove lefthand cylinder head bolts in sequence, **Fig. 9. Bolt (2), Fig. 9, cannot be fully removed. Retain bolt (2) above decking surface using a rubber band when removing cylinder head.**
14. Remove lefthand cylinder head and gasket.
15. Reverse procedure to install. Using sequences, **Figs. 10 and 11,** tighten cylinder head bolts as follows:
    a. First step, finger tighten.
    b. Second step, **torque** to 15 ft. lbs.
    c. Third step, **torque** to 26 ft. lbs.
    d. Fourth step, **torque** to 33 ft. lbs.
    e. Fifth step, tighten an additional 90.°
    f. Sixth step, tighten an additional 90.°
    g. **Torque** front cylinder head bolts to

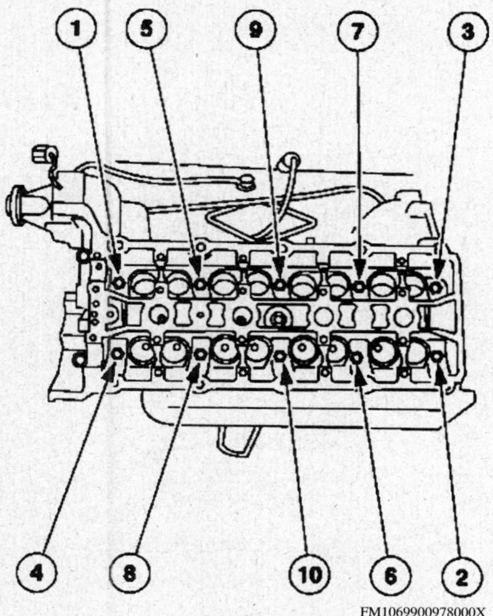

Fig. 9 Lefthand cylinder head removal sequence

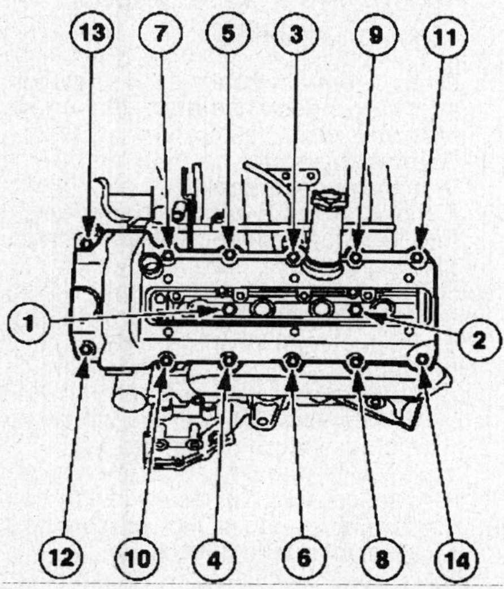

Fig. 12 Lefthand valve cover loosening & tightening sequence

15 ft. lbs., then an additional 90.°

VALVE COVER

REPLACE

LEFTHAND

1. Remove engine appearance cover.
2. Remove air cleaner housing.
3. Disconnect crankcase ventilation tube.
4. Relieve fuel system pressure as outlined under "Precautions."
5. Disconnect fuel line.
6. Disconnect evaporative emission canister purge valve hose, then the air assist tube.
7. Remove vapor management valve appearance cover and disconnect hose.
8. Position evaporative emission canister purge valve, engine vacuum regulator and bracket aside.
9. Position engine wiring harness upward, then remove ignition coil cover and ignition coils.
10. Disconnect three front and one rear wiring harness retainers.
11. Remove fuel line bracket bolt.
12. Remove reservoir attaching bolts and position aside.
13. Remove oil level indicator tube.
14. Remove brake line bracket, then the lefthand valve cover attaching bolts in sequence, **Fig. 12.**
15. Reverse procedure to install, noting the following:
    a. Apply a .12 inch bead of silicone gasket and sealant part No. F7AZ-19554-EA or equivalent, to cover joints, **Fig. 13.**
    b. Using sequence **Fig. 12,** tighten bolts to specification.

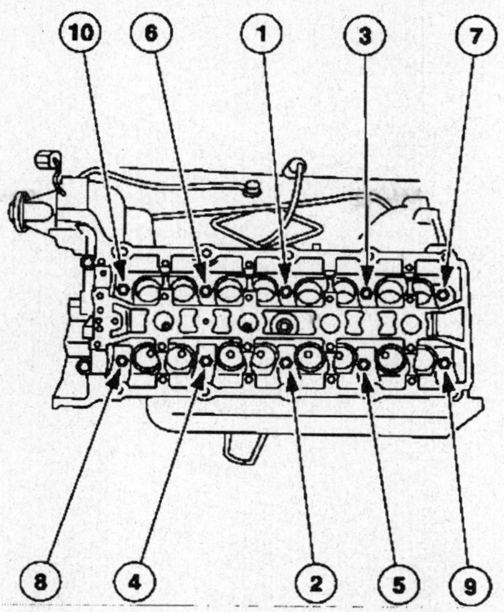

Fig. 10 Lefthand cylinder head tightening sequence

RIGHTHAND

1. Remove air cleaner outlet tube.
2. Remove hydraulic cooling fan reservoir and position aside.
3. Disconnect crankcase ventilation hose.
4. Disconnect wiring harness brackets and position aside.
5. Remove ignition coil cover, then disconnect ignition coils.
6. Raise engine wiring harness and disconnect fuel injectors.
7. Disconnect three front and one rear wiring harness retainer, then remove ignition coils.
8. Remove right valve cover attaching bolts in sequence, **Fig. 14,** then the valve cover.
9. Reverse procedure to install, noting the following:
    a. Apply silicone gasket and sealant part No. F7AZ-19554-EA, or equivalent, to cover joints, **Fig. 13.**
    b. Using sequence, **Fig. 14,** tighten valve cover bolts to specification.

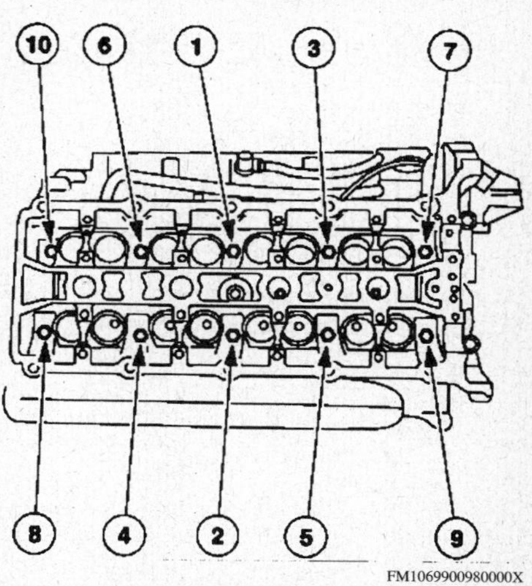

Fig. 11 Righthand cylinder head tightening sequence

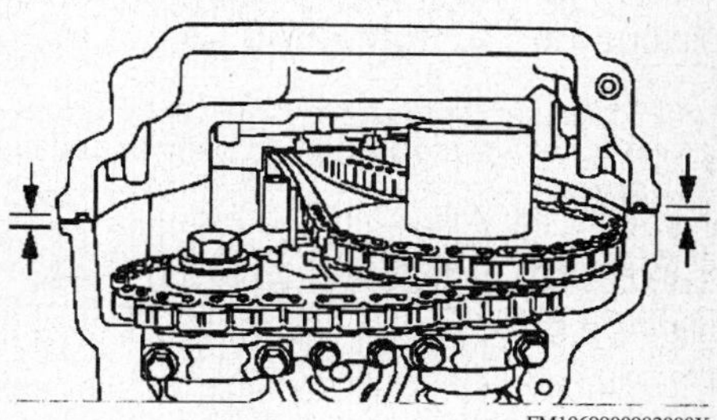

Fig. 13 Valve cover sealant application points

VALVE ARRANGEMENT

Inner .... I-I-I-I-I-I-I-I
Outer .... E-E-E-E-E-E-E-E

VALVE ADJUSTMENT

1. Remove valve covers as outlined under "Valve Cover, Replace."
2. Remove spark plugs.
3. When measuring valve clearance, ensure camshaft is on base circle, **Fig. 15.**
4. Using a suitable feeler gauge, measure and record all valve clearances. Refer to "Tune Up Specifications" chart in "Specifications" section for valve clearance specifications.
5. If adjustment is necessary, remove camshafts as outlined under "Camshaft, Replace."
6. Remove shims from bucket tappet. Shims are marked for thickness (example, 2.22 mm will read 222 on shim.)
7. Select shims using the following formula: required shim thickness = measured clearance plus base shim thickness minus most desirable clearance. Desirable clearance is .006 inch for intake and .012 inch for exhaust.

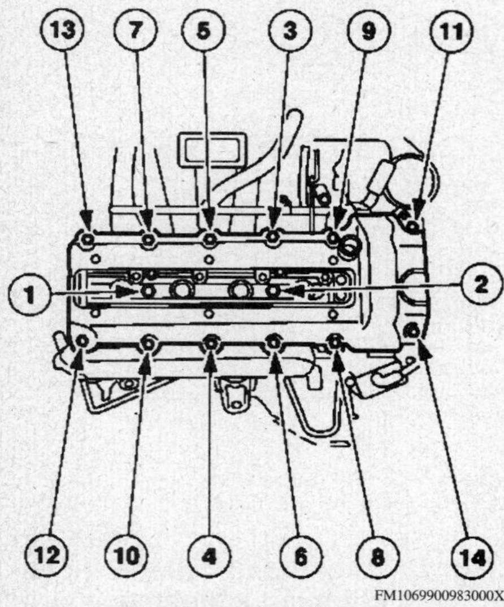

Fig. 14 Righthand valve cover loosening & tightening sequence

8. Reverse procedure to install. Ensure new valve clearance is within specifications.

CRANKSHAFT DAMPER

REPLACE

1. Remove hydraulic cooling fan as outlined under "Radiator, Replace."
2. Remove accessory drive belt.
3. Remove crankshaft pulley attaching bolt.
4. Remove crankshaft damper using damper remover tool No. T58P-6316-D, or equivalent.
5. Reverse procedure to install, noting the following:
   a. Apply silicone gasket and sealant part No. F7AZ-19554-EA, or equivalent, to damper keyway.
   b. Install damper using damper installation tool No. T74P-6316-B, or equivalent.
   c. Tighten damper bolt as follows: First step, **Torque** bolt to 59 ft. lbs.; second step, loosen bolt 2 full turns; third step, **torque** bolt to 37 ft. lbs.; fourth step, tighten an additional 90.°

FRONT COVER

REPLACE

1. Ensure engine is cold.
2. Wrap a suitable shop towel around pressure relief cap, then remove cap. **Ensure coolant does not come into contact with accessory drive belt.**
3. Open radiator draincock and drain coolant into a suitable container.
4. **On models equipped with oil cooler,** disconnect coolant return hose at oil cooler.
5. **On all models,** remove valve covers as outlined under "Valve Cover, Replace."
6. Remove cooling fan as outlined under "Radiator, Replace."
7. Loosen water pump bolts.

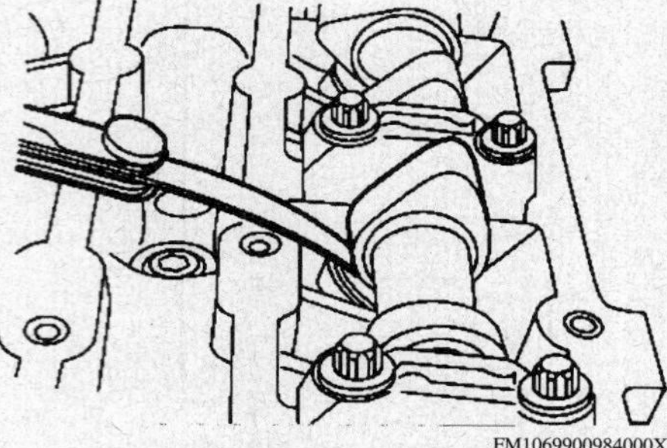

Fig. 15 Valve clearance measurement

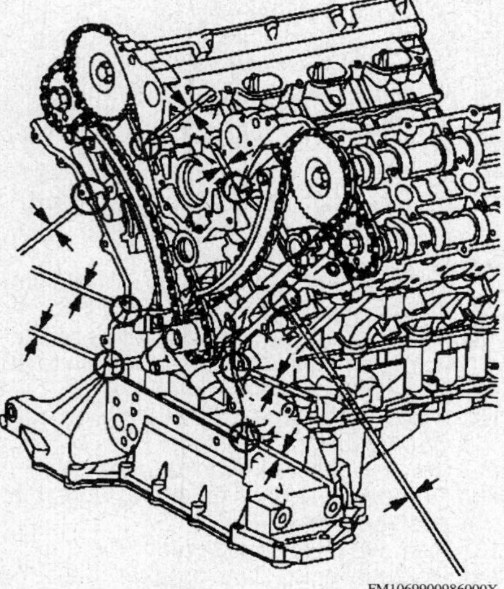

Fig. 17 Front cover sealant application points

8. Remove accessory drive belts.
9. Remove water pump pulley, then cover alternator.
10. Remove lower radiator hose bolts.
11. Disconnect upper radiator hose from water crossover.
12. Disconnect heater hose.
13. Remove idler pulleys.
14. Remove crankshaft damper as outlined under "Crankshaft Damper, Replace."
15. Recover refrigerant as outlined in "Air Conditioning." chapter.
16. Raise and support vehicle.
17. Remove splash shields.
18. Remove power steering hose bracket and position aside.
19. Remove A/C compressor manifold from compressor.
20. Disconnect compressor electrical connector.
21. Remove A/C compressor attaching bolts, then the compressor.
22. Drain power steering reservoir, then disconnect reservoir hose.
23. Remove power steering pump and position aside.
24. Remove power steering pump bracket.
25. Remove alternator as outlined under "Alternator, Replace" in "Electrical" section.

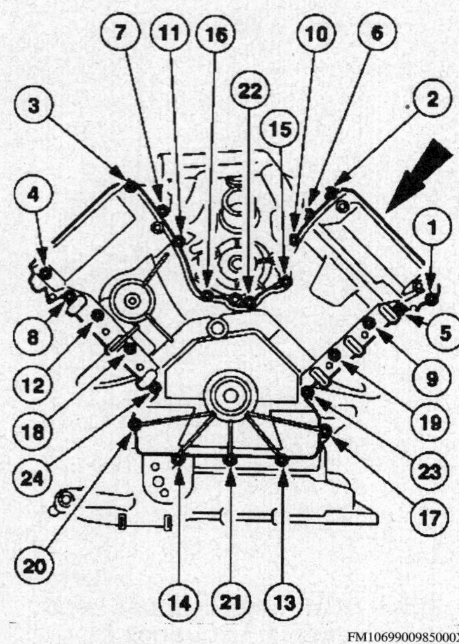

Fig. 16 Front cover removal sequence

26. Drain hydraulic cooling fan reservoir and disconnect hydraulic fan pump reservoir hose.
27. Remove hydraulic cooling fan pump, then the pump bracket.
28. Remove front cover bolts in sequence, **Fig. 16.** Clean gasket surfaces using a plastic scraper.
29. Reverse procedure to install, noting the following:
    a. Inspect front cover gaskets.
    b. Apply a .12 inch wide bead of silicone gasket and sealant part No. F7AZ-19554-EA, or equivalent, to eight points shown in **Fig. 17.**
    c. Install front cover and tighten in sequence **Fig. 18** as follows: first step, **torque** to 44 inch lbs.; second step, **torque** to 89 inch lbs.

FRONT COVER SEAL

REPLACE

1. Remove crankshaft damper as outlined under "Crankshaft Damper, Replace."
2. Remove front seal using seal removal tool No. 303-409, or equivalent.
3. Reverse procedure to install. Install new seal using seal installer tool No. 303-646, or equivalent.

TIMING CHAIN

REPLACE

PRIMARY

REMOVAL

There are no timing alignment marks for this engine. The proper alignment is achieved using a crankshaft locking tool and camshaft positioning/locking tools.

1. Remove front cover as outlined under "Front Cover, Replace."
2. Raise and support vehicle.

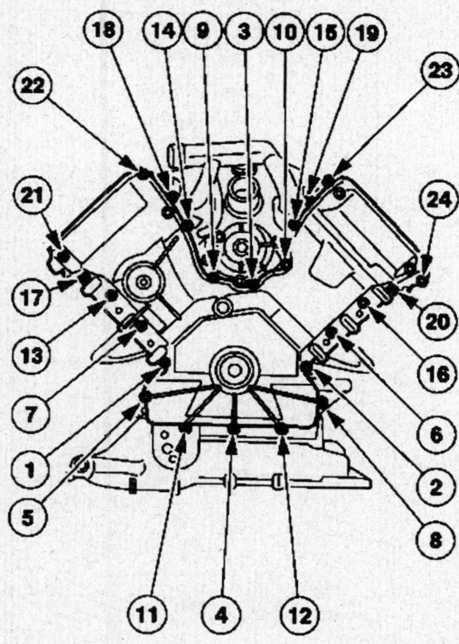

Fig. 18 Front cover tightening sequence

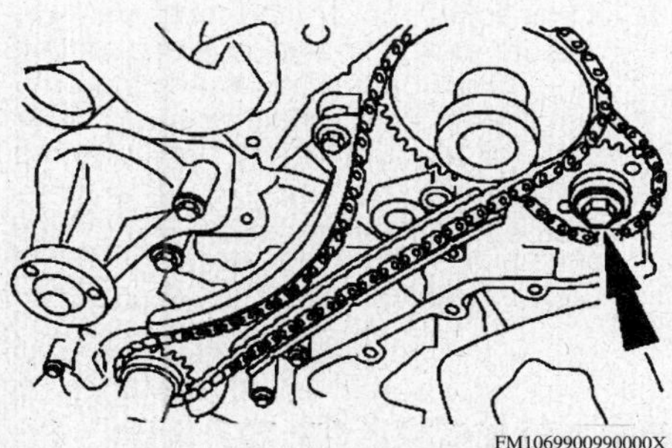

Fig. 21 Lefthand outer camshaft bolt

3. Remove crankshaft position sensor, then the torque converter access cover.
4. Turn crankshaft to 45° ATDC and ensure crankshaft keyway is at 6 o'clock position.
5. Install crankshaft positioning tool No. 303-645, or equivalent, to ignition pulse wheel.
6. Lower vehicle, then install camshaft locking tool No. 303-530, or equivalent, to righthand cylinder head.
7. Loosen outer camshaft bolt, **Fig. 19.**
8. Loosen camshaft damper bolt and slide camshaft sprockets forward on bolts, **Fig. 20.**
9. Remove righthand timing chain tensioner and blanking plate.
10. Remove tensioner arm, then the timing chain guide.
11. Remove righthand primary timing chain and crankshaft sprocket as an assembly.
12. Remove camshaft locking tool from righthand cylinder head.
13. Install camshaft locking tool to lefthand cylinder head.
14. Loosen outer camshaft bolt, **Fig. 21.**

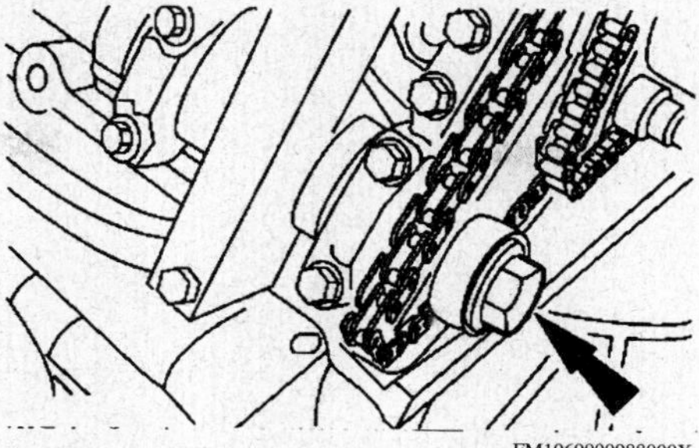

Fig. 19 Righthand outer camshaft bolt

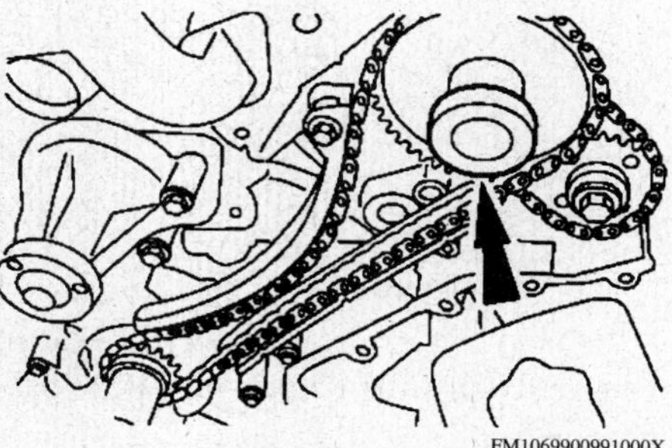

Fig. 22 Lefthand camshaft damper bolt

15. Loosen lefthand camshaft damper bolt and slide camshaft sprockets forward on bolts, **Fig. 22.**
16. Remove lefthand timing chain tensioner and blanking plate, then the tensioner arm.
17. Remove lefthand timing chain guide.
18. Remove left timing chain and crankshaft gear as an assembly.

INSTALLATION

There are no timing alignment marks for this engine. The proper alignment is achieved using a crankshaft locking tool and camshaft positioning/locking tools.

1. Insert a suitable wire into timing chain tensioner and dislodge check ball, **Fig. 23.**
2. Compress tensioner using finger pressure, then remove wire.
3. If timing mark on left timing chain crankshaft gear is facing toward rear of engine, install right timing chain crankshaft gear with mark facing forward. If timing mark on left timing chain crankshaft gear is facing toward front of engine, install right timing chain crankshaft gear with mark facing toward rear of engine.
4. Ensure camshaft holding tool is installed on left cylinder head.
5. Position timing chain over left intake camshaft sprocket.
6. Position crankshaft gear into timing chain.
7. Position timing chain and crankshaft gear over crankshaft as an assembly.
8. Install left timing chain guide and tensioner arm.
9. Position left blanking plate as shown in **Fig. 24. If blanking plate is not positioned as shown, oil galley will not seal resulting in low oil pressure and engine damage.**

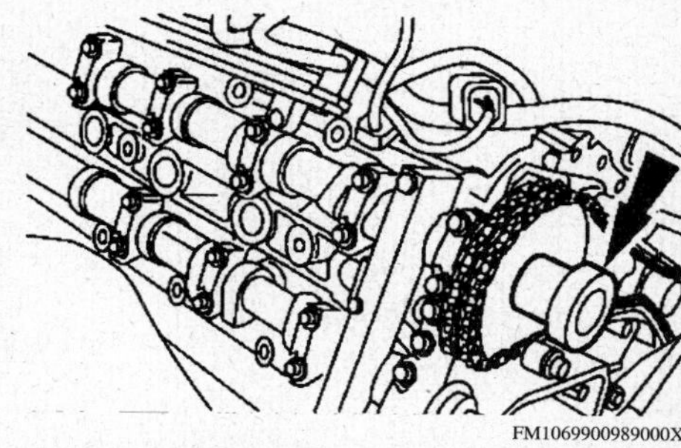

Fig. 20 Righthand camshaft damper bolt

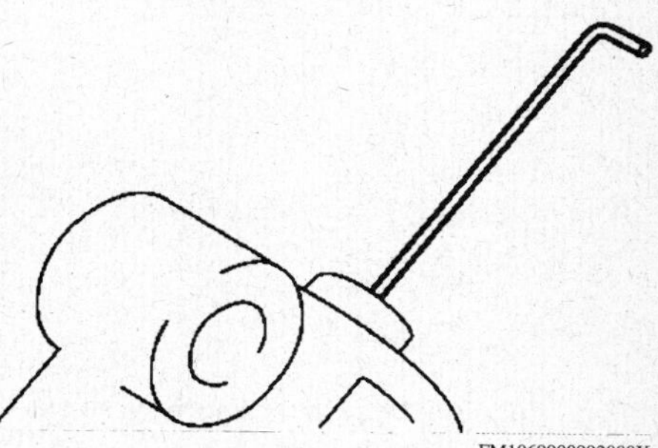

Fig. 23 Timing chain tensioner reset

10. Install left timing chain tensioner and blanking plate.
11. Install a suitable tie strap to take up timing chain slack, **Fig. 25.**
12. Apply tension to left exhaust camshaft sprocket using timing chain tensioning tool No. 303-532, or equivalent. Tighten camshaft sprocket bolts as follows: First step, **torque** to 15 ft. lbs.; second step, tighten an additional 90.°
13. Install camshaft holding tool to right cylinder head. It may be necessary to adjust camshafts to install holding tool.
14. If timing mark on left timing chain crankshaft gear is facing toward rear of engine, install right timing chain crankshaft gear with mark facing forward. If timing mark on left timing chain crankshaft gear is facing toward front of engine, install right timing chain crankshaft gear with mark facing toward rear of engine.
15. Position timing chain over right intake camshaft sprocket.
16. Place crankshaft gear into timing chain.
17. Install timing chain and crankshaft gear over crankshaft as an assembly.
18. Install right chain guide and tensioner arm.
19. Position right blanking plate as shown in **Fig. 26. If blanking plate is not positioned as shown, oil galley will not seal resulting in low oil pressure and engine damage.**
20. Install right timing chain tensioner and blanking plate.
21. Install a suitable tie strap to take up timing chain slack, **Fig. 25.**
22. Exhaust camshaft sprocket bolt must be fully tightened before tightening intake camshaft sprocket bolt.

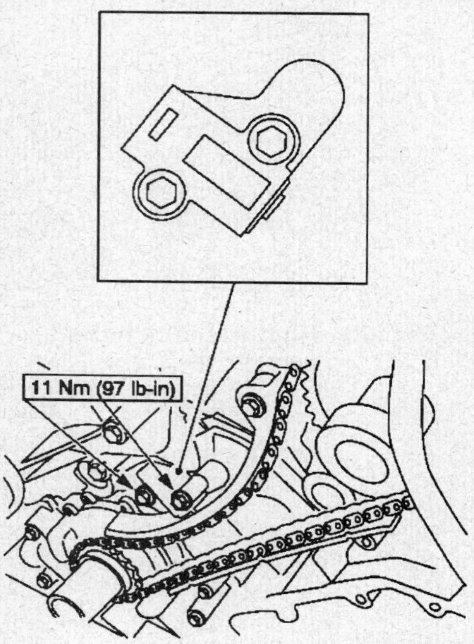

Fig. 24 Lefthand blanking plate installation

23. Apply tension to right exhaust camshaft sprocket using timing chain tensioning tool No. 303-532, or equivalent. Tighten sprocket bolts as follows: First step, **torque** to 15 ft. lbs.; second step, tighten an additional 90.°
24. Remove camshaft locking tool and tie straps.
25. Raise and support vehicle.
26. Remove crankshaft locking tool.
27. Install crankshaft position sensor and torque converter cover.
28. Lower vehicle.
29. Install front cover as outlined under "Front Cover, Replace."

SECONDARY

There are no timing alignment marks for this engine. The proper alignment is achieved using a crankshaft locking tool and camshaft positioning/locking tools.

1. Remove primary timing chains as outlined under "Primary."
2. Remove exhaust camshaft sprocket bolt, then the intake camshaft sprocket bolt.
3. Remove sprockets, damper and chain as an assembly.
4. Remove secondary timing chain tensioner.
5. Reverse procedure to install, noting the following:
   a. Insert a wire into tensioner check valve.
   b. Apply hand pressure until tensioner is fully collapsed, then remove wire.
   c. When installing secondary timing chains, ensure camshaft holding tool No. 303-530, or equivalent, is in place.

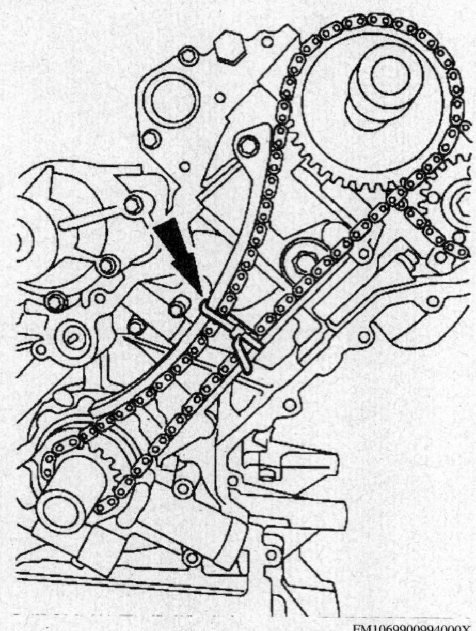

Fig. 25 Timing chain installation

TIMING CHAIN TENSIONER

REPLACE

Refer to "Timing Chain, Replace" for procedure.

CAMSHAFT

REPLACE

REMOVAL

1. Remove primary and secondary timing chains as outlined under "Timing Chain, Replace."
2. Remove camshaft locking tool.
3. Place reference marks on all camshaft bearing caps and record locations for installation reference.
4. Remove right and left camshaft bearing caps, then the camshafts. Place reference marks on shims and bucket tappets and record all locations for installation reference. **A permanent marker is the only approved method of marking shims and bucket tappets. Scratches or paint on shims will result in incorrect lash adjustments and engine damage.**

INSTALLATION

1. Apply clean 5W-30 motor oil to all camshaft journals, camshaft caps and camshaft lobes.
2. Install left and right cylinder head camshafts, then using sequence, **Figs. 27 and 28,** tighten bolts as follows:
   a. First step, hand tighten.
   b. Second step, **torque** bolts to 53 inch lbs.
   c. Third step, tighten an additional 90.°

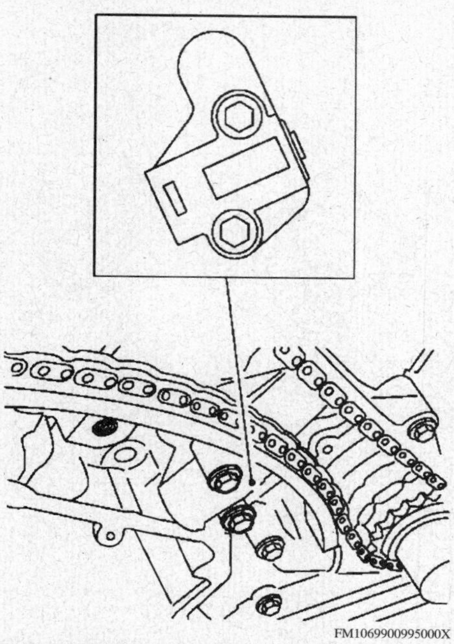

Fig. 26 Righthand blanking plate installation

3. If any valve train components were replaced, perform valve lash adjustment as outlined under "Valve Adjustment."
4. Install camshaft locking tool No. 303-530, or equivalent, to left cylinder head.
5. Install primary and secondary timing chains as outlined under "Timing Chain, Replace."

CRANKSHAFT REAR OIL SEAL

REPLACE

1. Raise and support vehicle.
2. **On models equipped with automatic transmission,** remove transmission as outlined in "Automatic Transmissions/Transaxles" chapter.
3. **On models equipped with manual transmission,** remove transmission as outlined in "Clutch & Manual Transmission" section.
4. **On all models,** remove flywheel.
5. Remove rear crankshaft oil seal using screw tool No. T95T-5310-AR2 and seal remover/installer tool No. 303-647, or equivalents.
6. Reverse procedure to install, noting the following:
   a. Lubricate outer lips and inner seal of new oil seal before installation.
   b. Install new seal using seal remover/installer tool No. 303-647, or equivalent.
   c. Using sequence, **Fig. 29,** tighten flywheel bolts in two steps: First step, **torque** to 11 ft. lbs.; second step, **torque** to 81 ft. lbs.

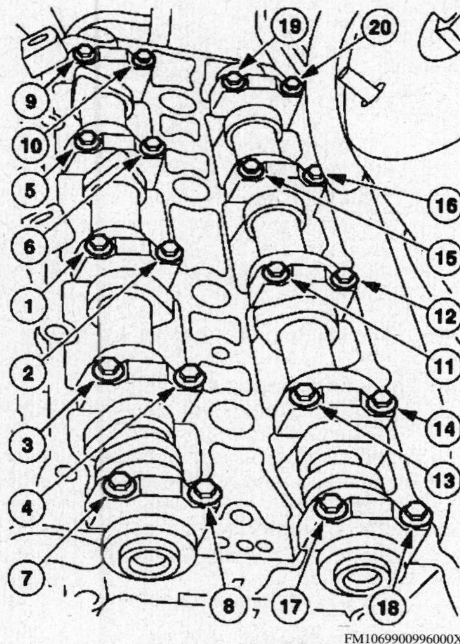

Fig. 27 Left cylinder head camshaft tightening sequence

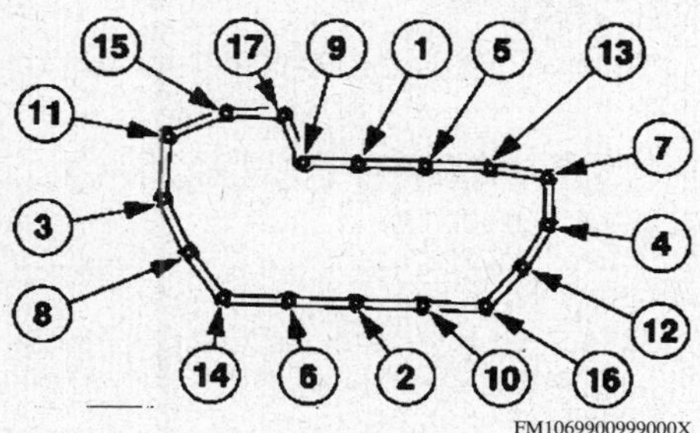

Fig. 30 Oil pan tightening sequence

OIL PAN

REPLACE

1. Raise and support vehicle.
2. Drain engine oil.
3. Remove oil pan attaching bolts, then the oil pan.
4. Reverse procedure to install, noting the following:
   a. Inspect oil pan gasket and replace as necessary.
   b. Using sequence, **Fig. 30,** tighten bolts in two steps: First step, **torque** to 44 inch lbs.; second step, **torque** to 108 inch lbs.

OIL PUMP

REPLACE

1. Remove primary timing chains as outlined under "Timing Chain, Replace."
2. Remove oil pump attaching bolts, then the oil pump.
3. Reverse procedure to install.

OIL COOLER

REPLACE

1. Ensure engine is cold.
2. Wrap a suitable shop towel around pressure relief cap, then remove cap. **Ensure coolant does not come into contact with accessory drive belt.**
3. Open radiator draincock and drain coolant into a suitable container.
4. Disconnect coolant return hose at oil cooler.
5. Remove center air deflector, then the oil filter.
6. Disconnect oil cooler coolant hoses.
7. Remove oil cooler attaching bolts, then the oil cooler.
8. Reverse procedure to install.

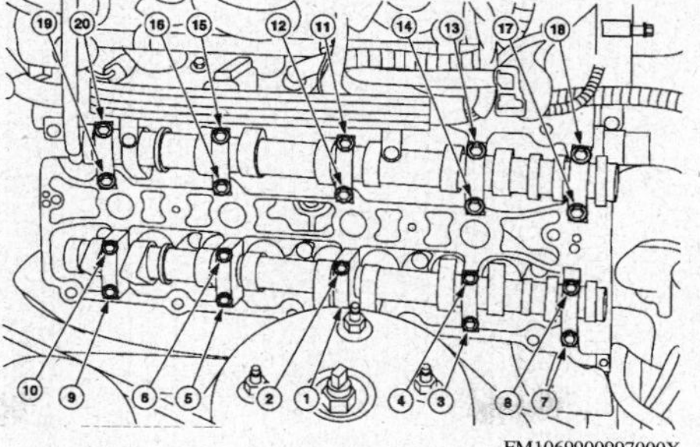

Fig. 28 Right cylinder head camshaft tightening sequence

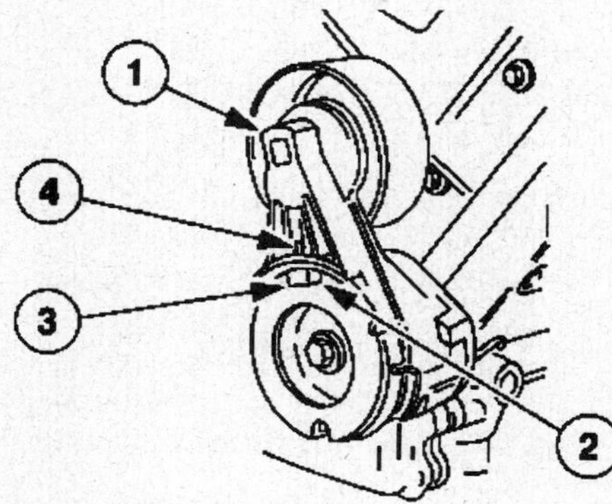

Item	Description
1	Belt tension relief point
2	Unacceptable belt wear range
3	Acceptable belt installation and wear range
4	Belt length indicator

FM1069901000000X

Fig. 31 Belt tensioner inspection

SERPENTINE DRIVE BELT

TENSION DATA

Vehicle is equipped with an automatic belt tensioner. Belt tension is not adjustable. Refer to **Fig. 31** to inspect tensioner.

ROUTING

Refer to **Fig. 32** for serpentine drive belt routing.

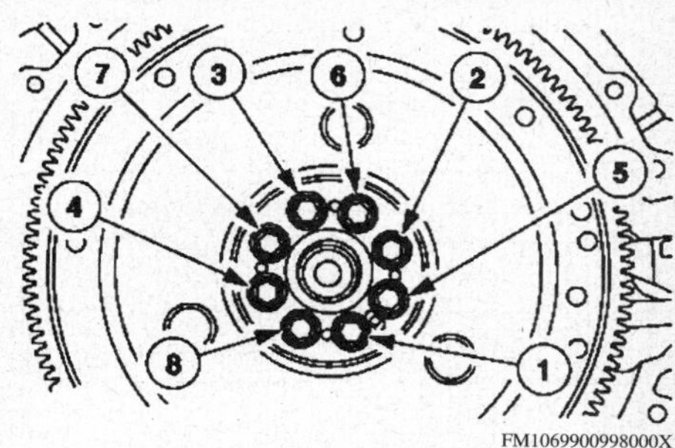

Fig. 29 Flywheel tightening sequence

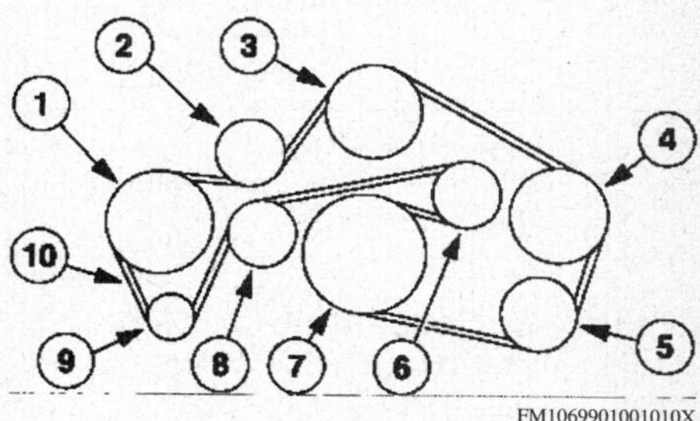

Fig. 32 Serpentine drive belt routing (Part 1 of 2)

COOLING SYSTEM BLEED

1. Remove engine fill cap, **Fig. 33.**
2. Open heater air bleed, **Fig. 34.**
3. Add coolant to overflow bottle allowing system to equalize until no more coolant can be added.
4. Install overflow bottle cap.
5. Add as much coolant as possible to engine fill cap opening. Ensure coolant does not come in contact with accessory drive belt.
6. Install engine fill cap.
7. Start engine and turn heater to Max position.
8. Close heater bleed when a steady stream of coolant is present.
9. Allow engine to idle for five minutes adding coolant to overflow bottle as needed to maintain cold fill Max mark.
10. Re-open heater air bleed to release any trapped air and close again.
11. Operate engine at 2000 RPM for 3–5 minutes or until hot air comes from heater.
12. Return engine to idle and verify hot air is still coming from heater.
13. Turn engine off and allow to cool.
14. Add coolant to overflow bottle to bring level to cold fill Max level.

THERMOSTAT

REPLACE

1. Ensure engine is cold.
2. Wrap a suitable shop towel around pressure relief cap, then remove cap. **Ensure coolant does not come into contact with accessory drive belt.**
3. Open radiator draincock and drain coolant into a suitable container.

Item	Description
1	Hydraulic fan pump pulley
2	Belt idler pulley—unflanged
3	Water pump pulley
4	Power steering pump pulley
5	A/C clutch pulley
6	Drive belt tensioner
7	Crankshaft vibration damper
8	Belt idler pulley—flanged
9	Generator pulley
10	Drive belt

FM1069901001020X

Fig. 32 Serpentine drive belt routing (Part 2 of 2)

4. **On models equipped with oil cooler,** disconnect coolant return hose at oil cooler.
5. **On all models,** remove air cleaner outlet tube.
6. Remove coolant tube from front of engine, **Fig. 35.**
7. Remove coolant tube bracket studs.
8. Disconnect lower radiator hose from thermostat housing.
9. Remove thermostat housing cover, then the thermostat, **Fig. 36.**
10. Reverse procedure to install.

WATER PUMP

REPLACE

1. Ensure engine is cold.
2. Wrap a suitable shop towel around pressure relief cap, then remove cap. **Ensure coolant does not come into contact with accessory drive belt.**
3. Open radiator draincock and drain coolant into a suitable container.
4. **On models equipped with oil cooler,** disconnect coolant return hose at oil cooler.
5. **On all models,** loosen water pump pulley bolts.
6. Remove accessory drive belt.
7. Remove water pump pulley bolts, then the pulley.
8. Remove water pump attaching bolts, then the water pump. Inspect water pump O-ring seal and replace as necessary.
9. Reverse procedure to install, noting the following:

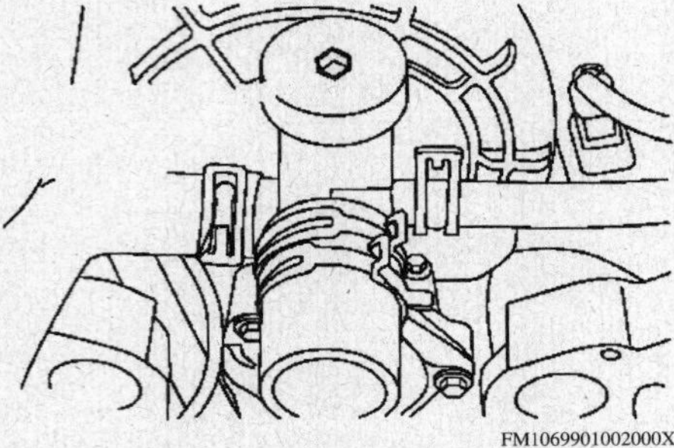

FM1069901002000X

Fig. 33 Engine fill cap location

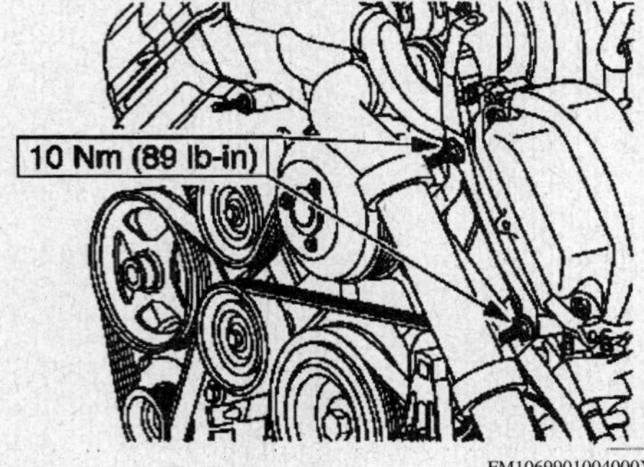

FM1069901004000X

Fig. 35 Coolant tube removal

a. Lubricate water pump O-ring using premium engine coolant part No. E2FZ-19549-AA, or equivalent.
b. Bleed cooling system as outlined under "Cooling System Bleed."

RADIATOR

REPLACE

1. Ensure engine is cold.
2. Wrap a suitable shop towel around pressure relief cap, then remove cap. **Ensure coolant does not come into contact with accessory drive belt.**
3. Open radiator draincock and drain coolant into a suitable container.
4. **On models equipped with oil cooler,** disconnect coolant hoses at oil cooler.
5. **On all models,** remove upper radiator sight shield.
6. Remove air cleaner outlet tube.
7. Remove radiator support brackets, then the upper radiator hose.
8. Remove receiver drier attaching bolt and position receiver drier aside.
9. Remove electric water pump bolt and position aside, **Fig. 37.**
10. Disconnect high pressure cooling fan line, then the return hose.
11. Separate return hose from fan shroud and position aside.
12. Remove fan shroud.
13. Support A/C condenser using suitable mechanics wire.

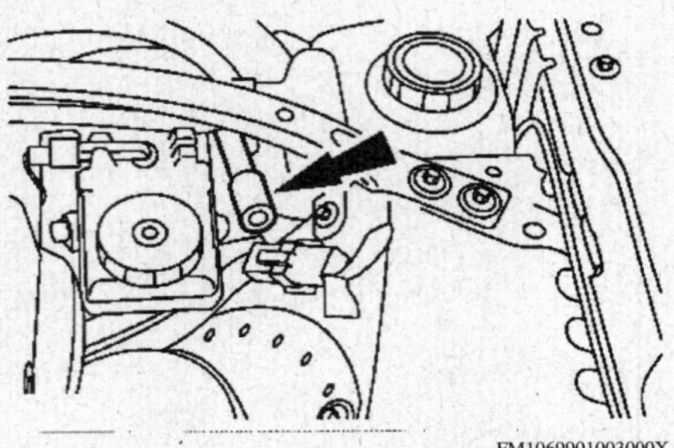

FM1069901003000X

Fig. 34 Heater air bleed location

14. Raise and support vehicle.
15. Remove right and left splash shields, then the radiator air deflector.
16. Disconnect lower radiator hose.
17. Remove condenser to radiator attaching bolts.
18. Remove condenser support brackets, then the radiator through bottom of vehicle.
19. Reverse procedure to install.

HYDRAULIC FAN MOTOR

REPLACE

Refer to "Radiator, Replace" for procedure.

HYDRAULIC COOLING FAN PUMP

REPLACE

1. Remove alternator as outlined under "Alternator, Replace" in the "Electrical" section.
2. Disconnect hose and drain fluid into suitable container, **Fig. 38.**
3. Disconnect fan pump electrical connector.
4. Remove high pressure line bracket and disconnect high pressure line.
5. Remove cooling fan pump attaching bolts, then the cooling fan.
6. Reverse procedure to install.

FUEL PUMP

REPLACE

Refer to "Fuel Pump, Replace" in the "3.0L Engine" section for fuel pump replacement procedures.

FUEL FILTER

REPLACE

Refer to "Fuel Filter, Replace" in the "3.0L Engine" section for fuel filter replacement procedures.

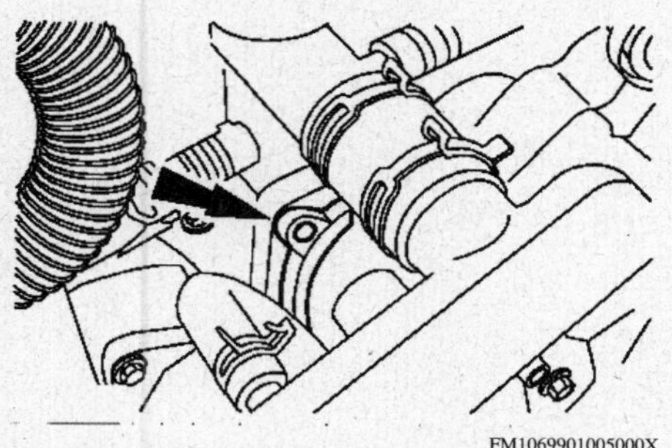
FM1069901005000X

Fig. 36 Thermostat housing cover removal

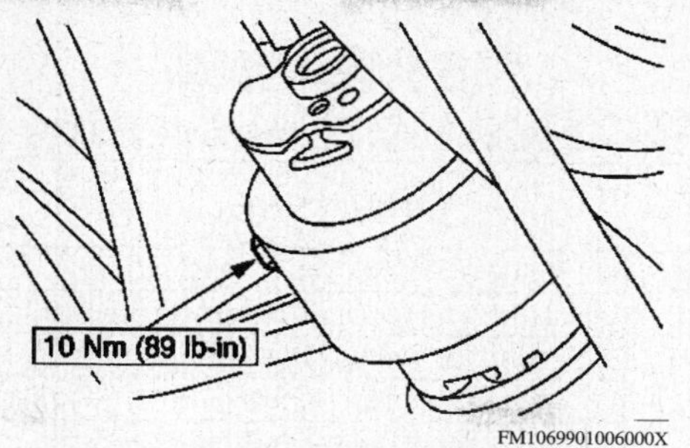

FM1069901006000X

Fig. 37 Electric water pump location

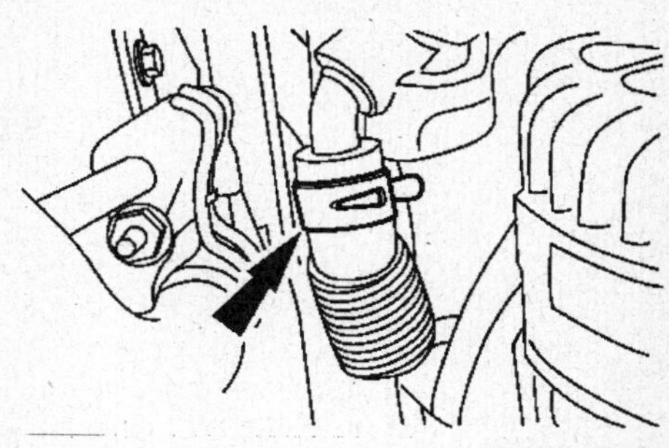
FM1069901008000X

Fig. 38 Fan pump hose location

TIGHTENING SPECIFICATIONS

Year	Component	Torque, Ft. Lbs.
2000–02	A/C Compressor	18
	A/C Manifold To Compressor	15
	Alternator	⑤
	Belt Tensioner	37
	Camshaft Bearing Caps	⑩
	Camshaft Sprockets	15⑦
	Condenser To Radiator Bolts	89①
	Cowl Panel Support Bracket	80①
	Crankshaft Damper	③
	Crankshaft Position Sensor	89①
	Cylinder Head	②
	EGR Tube To EGR Valve	30
	EGR Tube To Exhaust Manifold	30
	Electric Water Pump Attaching Bolt	89①
	Engine Mount Bracket To Cylinder Block	34
	Engine Mount Upper & Lower Nuts	30
	Exhaust Catalyst To Exhaust Manifold	30
	Exhaust Manifold To Cylinder Head	18
	Flywheel	⑧
	Front Cover	④
	Front & Center Support Bolts	76
	Hydraulic Cooling Fan Pump	18
	Hydraulic Cooling Fan Pump Bracket	18
	Hydraulic Cooling Fan Reservoir Lower Bolt	106①
	Hydraulic Cooling Fan Reservoir Upper Bolt	53①
	Idler Pulley	18
	Intake Manifold	15
	Lower Strut Mount Bolts	129
	Lower Sway Bar Link	41
	Oil Cooler	43
	Oil Pan	⑨
	Oil Pump	53①⑦
	Power Steering Pressure Line	89①
	Power Steering Pump Bracket	18
	Power Steering Pump To Bracket	18
	Power Steering Reservoir Lower Bolt	106①
	Power Steering Reservoir Upper Bolt	53①
	Primary Timing Chain Guide	97①

Continued

TIGHTENING SPECIFICATIONS—Continued

Year	Component	Torque, Ft. Lbs.
2000–02	Primary Timing Chain Tensioner	97①
	Receiver/Drier Bracket	8
	Secondary Timing Chain Tensioner	97①
	Steering Coupling	26
	Thermostat Housing	80①
	Torque Converter To Flywheel	28
	Transmission Cooler Lines	89①
	Transmission To Engine Bolts	35
	Upper Ball Joint Nuts	66
	Upper Radiator Support Brackets	89①
	Valve Cover	89①
	Water Pump	71①⑦
	Water Pump Pulley	89①⑥
	Wheel Lug Nuts	100

①— Inch lbs.
②— Refer to "Cylinder Head, Replace."
③— Refer to "Crankshaft Damper, Replace."
④— Refer to "Front Cover, Replace."
⑤— Refer to "Alternator, Replace" in "Electrical" section.
⑥— Tighten an additional 45.°
⑦— Tighten an additional 90.°
⑧— Refer to "Crankshaft Rear Oil Seal, Replace" for tightening procedure.
⑨— Refer to "Oil Pan, Replace" for tightening procedure.
⑩— Refer to "Camshaft, Replace."

Clutch & Manual Transmission

NOTE: On Air Bag Equipped Models, Refer To "Air Bag System Precautions" Located In The Front Of This Manual For System Disarming & Arming Procedures.

NOTE: Refer To "Computer Relearn Procedures" Located In The Front Of This Manual When Battery Power To The Computer Has Been Interrupted.

INDEX

PRECAUTIONS

AIR BAG SYSTEMS

Refer to "Air Bag System Precautions" in the front of this manual for system disarming and arming procedures.

BATTERY GROUND CABLE

Prior to service, disconnect battery ground cable and isolate as required.

DESCRIPTION

The clutch system consists of a flywheel, clutch disc, pressure plate, master cylinder, clutch release hub and bearing.

The clutch master cylinder transmits fluid pressure to the slave cylinder which moves the clutch release hub and bearing.

The clutch master cylinder uses brake fluid and shares a common reservoir with brake master cylinder.

MAINTENANCE

FLUID CHECK

Fluid level should be within .02 inch below lower edge of fill plug bore, **Fig. 1.**

FLUID CHANGE

1. Raise and support vehicle.
2. Remove fill plug, **Fig. 1.**
3. Remove drain plug and drain fluid into a suitable container, **Fig. 2.**
4. Install drain plug and fill transmission as outlined under "Fluid Check."

ADJUSTMENTS

The hydraulic clutch system adjusts automatically to compensate for clutch disc wear. The clutch linkage is not adjustable.

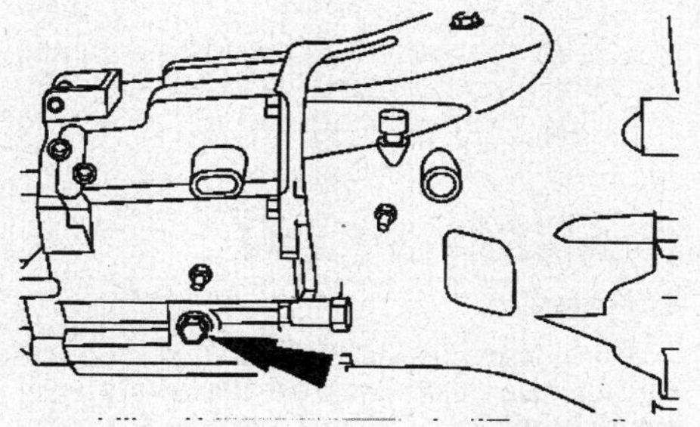

Fig. 1 Transmission fill plug

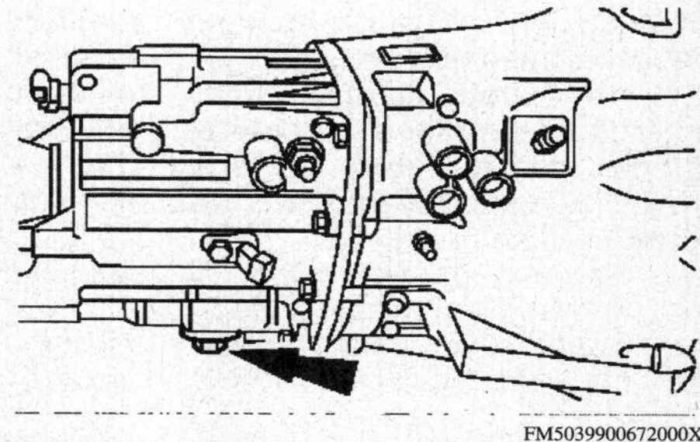

Fig. 2 Transmission drain plug

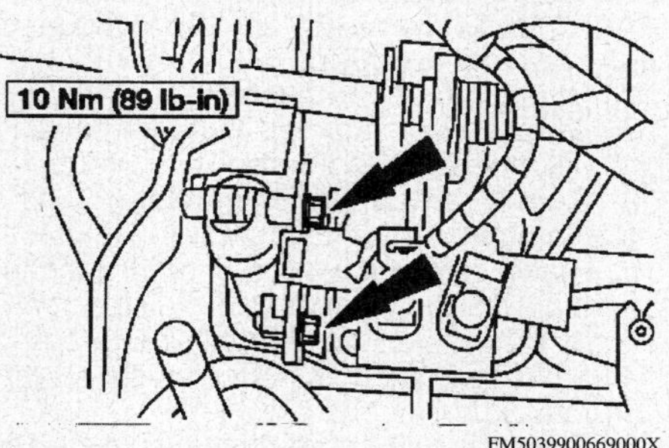

Fig. 3 Clutch master cylinder removal

HYDRAULIC SYSTEM SERVICE

CLUTCH SYSTEM BLEED

1. Raise and support vehicle.
2. Remove dust cover, then the bleeder screw cover.
3. Attach a bleed jar to bleed nipple and open bleeder screw one turn.
4. Depress clutch pedal repeatedly until emerging fluid is free of bubbles. Ensure fluid reservoir is kept full during bleed procedure.
5. After bleed procedure is complete, tighten bleeder screw and verify proper clutch operation by depressing clutch pedal 10 times.
6. Ensure fluid level is between Min and Max marks.

CLUTCH MASTER CYLINDER, REPLACE

1. Disconnect footwell lamp electrical connector.
2. Remove clutch pedal position switch bracket bolts and position bracket aside.
3. Remove snap ring and disconnect clutch master cylinder pushrod.
4. Remove snap ring from hydraulic line, then disconnect line from elbow.
5. Remove clutch master cylinder attaching nuts, then the master cylinder, **Fig. 3.**
6. Reverse procedure to install. Bleed clutch hydraulic system.

SLAVE CYLINDER, REPLACE

1. Remove transmission as outlined under "Transmission, Replace."
2. Remove hydraulic tube connector, **Fig. 4.**
3. Remove slave cylinder attaching bolts, then the slave cylinder.
4. Reverse procedure to install. Bleed clutch hydraulic system.

HYDRAULIC TUBES, REPLACE

1. Remove snap ring and tube from clutch master cylinder connector.

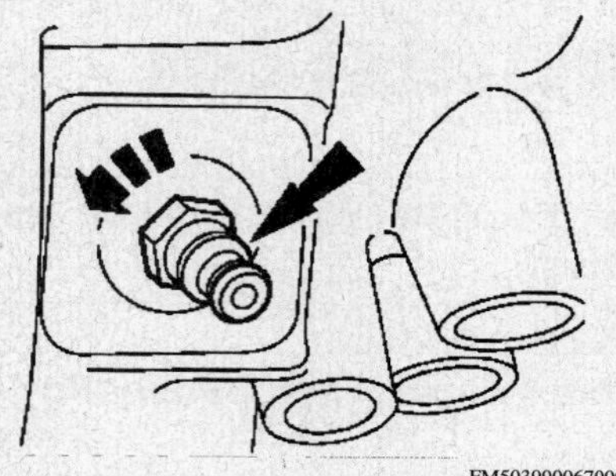

Fig. 4 Hydraulic tube connector

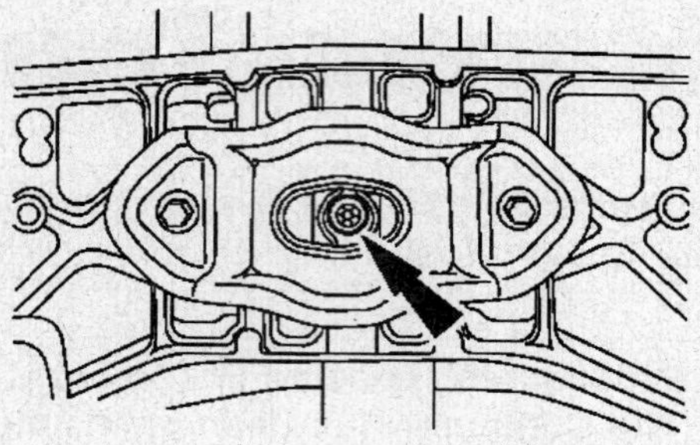

Fig. 5 Support insulator removal

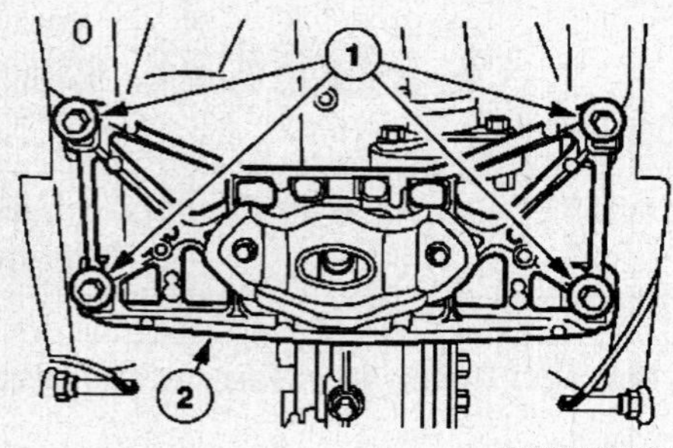

Fig. 6 Transmission support removal

2. Disconnect clutch slave cylinder hydraulic line.
3. Remove hydraulic tube bracket nut.
4. Remove hydraulic tube and bracket.
5. Reverse procedure to install. Install new O-ring to slave cylinder port and bleed clutch hydraulic system.

CLUTCH

REPLACE

When carrying out operations which involve the removal and installation of the driveshaft, always check the joint angles and make the necessary adjustments as outlined under "Driveline Angle Measurement" in "Rear Axle & Suspension" section.

1. Remove transmission as outlined under "Transmission, Replace."
2. Support clutch plate using clutch alignment tool No. T74P-7137-K, or equivalent.
3. Remove pressure plate attaching bolts in a uniform sequence.
4. Remove clutch disc and pressure plate.
5. Reverse procedure to install noting the following:
   a. Align clutch disc using clutch alignment tool No. T74P-7137-K, or equivalent.
   b. Tighten pressure plate to specifications using a diagonal sequence.

PILOT BEARING

REPLACE

When carrying out operations which involve the removal and installation of the driveshaft, always check the joint angles and make the necessary adjustments as outlined under "Driveline Angle Measurement" in "Rear Axle & Suspension" section.

1. Remove transmission as outlined under "Transmission, Replace."
2. Remove clutch as outlined under "Clutch, Replace."
3. Remove pilot bearing from crankshaft using slide hammer tool No. T58L-101-B, or equivalent.
4. Reverse procedure to install. Install pilot bearing using installer tool No. T85T-7137-A, or equivalent.

TRANSMISSION

REPLACE

When carrying out operations which involve the removal and installation of the driveshaft, always check the joint angles and make the necessary adjustments as outlined under "Driveline Angle Measurement" in "Rear Axle & Suspension" section.

1. Raise and support vehicle.
2. Remove selector rod locating pin and disconnect selector rod.
3. Remove intermediate muffler.
4. Remove center heat shield.
5. Place reference marks on transmission flange, driveshaft flexible coupling, flange bolts, nuts, washers and balance add on nuts for installation reference.
6. Support front section of driveshaft. **Do not loosen or remove flexible coupling from driveshaft.**
7. Loosen driveshaft yoke locknut and move driveshaft front section toward center bearing.
8. Disconnect right and left catalyst monitor sensor electrical connectors.
9. Remove wiring harness from top of transmission.
10. Disconnect VSS and reverse light switch connectors.
11. Remove wiring harness from transmission.
12. Place a suitable transmission jack under transmission and secure transmission to jack.
13. Remove support insulator, **Fig. 5.**
14. Remove transmission support, **Fig. 6.**
15. Remove slave cylinder supply tube retaining clip, then the tube.
16. Plug slave cylinder tube to prevent fluid loss.
17. Remove transmission to engine attaching bolts.
18. Disconnect starter motor ground cable and remove starter wiring harness.
19. Remove starter motor, then the transmission.
20. Reverse procedure to install, noting the following:
    a. Install new O-ring to slave cylinder tube.
    b. Bleed clutch hydraulic system.

TIGHTENING SPECIFICATIONS

Year	Component	Torque, Ft. Lbs.
2000–02	Clutch Hydraulic Tube Bracket	89①
	Clutch Master Cylinder	89①
	Driveshaft Yoke Locknuts	66
	Pressure Plate To Flywheel	17
	Slave Cylinder	16
	Starter Motor	18
	Support Insulator	30
	Transmission Drain Plug	37
	Transmission Fill Plug	37
	Transmission Flex Coupling Balance Nuts	18
	Transmission Flex Coupling Nuts	63
	Transmission To Engine Bolts	35

① — Inch lbs.

Rear Axle & Suspension

NOTE: On Air Bag Equipped Models, Refer To "Air Bag System Precautions" Located In The Front Of This Manual For System Disarming & Arming Procedures.

NOTE: Refer To "Computer Relearn Procedures" Located In The Front Of This Manual When Battery Power To The Computer Has Been Interrupted.

NOTE: Prior To Performing Any Service Operations Listed In This Section, Consult The "Technical Service Bulletins" Section For Related Information.

INDEX

PRECAUTIONS

AIR BAG SYSTEMS

Refer to "Air Bag System Precautions" in the front of this manual for system disarming and arming procedures.

BATTERY GROUND CABLE

Prior to service, disconnect battery ground cable and isolate as required.

DESCRIPTION

The rear axle is an integral-type housing hypoid gear design, **Fig. 1.** The ring and pinion consists of an eight inch ring gear and an overhung drive pinion which is supported by two opposed tapered roller bearings. Pinion preload is maintained by a drive pinion collapsible spacer on the pinion shaft and is adjusted by the pinion nut. Differential bearing preload and ring gear backlash are adjusted by differential bearing shims located between differential bearing cup and rear axle housing.

Halfshafts are held in the differential case by a driveshaft bearing retainer circlip which engages a step in the differential side gear.

The suspension is an independent design featuring upper and lower control arms, shock absorber and spring assembly, adjustable toe links, stabilizer bar and wheel knuckles. Refer to **Fig. 2** for rear suspension components.

When servicing suspension components, always use new appropriate nuts and bolts when removed.

When carrying out operations which involve the removal and installation of the driveshaft, always check the joint angles and make the necessary adjustments as outlined under "Driveline Angle Measurement."

REAR AXLE

REPLACE

1. Remove halfshafts as outlined under "Rear Halfshaft, Replace."
2. Remove exhaust system and heat shield as necessary.
3. Place reference marks on pinion flange, flex coupling and driveshaft to pinion flange bolts, nuts, washers and weighted washers for installation reference.
4. Support driveshaft, then remove driveshaft to pinion flange bolts and nuts. **Do not remove flex coupling on driveshaft flange.**
5. Loosen driveshaft yoke adjuster nut using driveshaft coupler wrenches, tool No. 205-474, or equivalents.
6. Remove center bearing mounting bolts and shims. Mark position of shims for installation reference.
7. Slide rear driveshaft to full forward position and tighten adjuster nut.
8. Position a suitable jack under axle housing and secure axle to jack.
9. Remove three axle mounting nuts, **Fig. 3.**
10. Lower axle housing from vehicle.
11. Reverse procedure to install.

STUB SHAFT BEARING & SEAL

REPLACE

1. Remove halfshaft as outlined under "Rear Halfshaft, Replace."
2. Remove stub shaft bearing housing seal and bearing using bearing cup remover tool No. T77F-1102-A and slide hammer tool No. T50T–100–A, or equivalents.
3. Lubricate new bearing with SAE 75W-140 synthetic rear axle lubricant F1TZ-19580–B, or equivalent.
4. Install bearing into rear axle housing bore using bearing replacer tool No. T89P-1244-A and handle tool No. T80T-4000-W, or equivalents.
5. Lubricate lip of seal with premium long life grease XG-1-C, or equivalent.
6. Install seal using seal replacer tool No. T89P-4850-A and handle tool No. T80T-4000-W, or equivalents.
7. Install halfshaft as outlined under "Rear Halfshaft, Replace."

PINION FLANGE & SEAL

REPLACE

REMOVAL

1. Raise and support vehicle, then remove rear wheels.

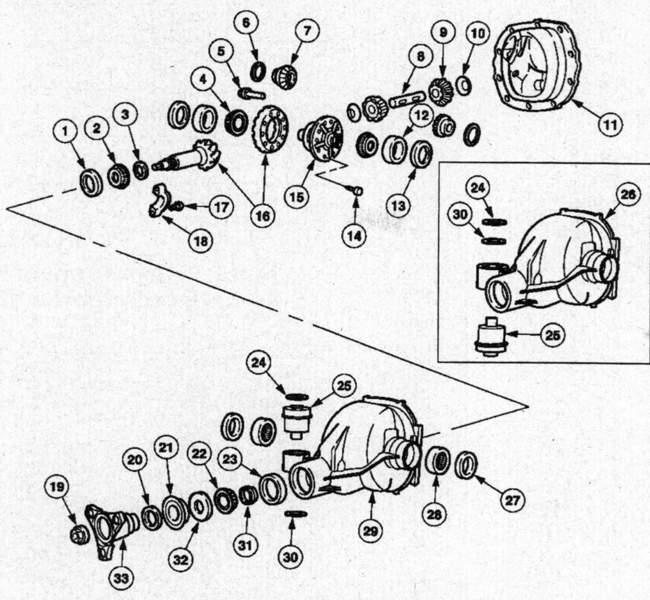

Item	Description
1	Rear axle pinion bearing cup
2	Pinion bearing
3	Drive pinion bearing adjustment shim
4	Differential bearing
5	Differential pinion shaft lock bolt
6	Differential side gear thrust washer
7	Differential side gear
8	Differential pinion shaft
9	Differential pinion gear
10	Differential pinion thrust washer
11	Differential housing cover
12	Differential bearing cup
13	Differential bearing shim
14	Rear axle ring gear case bolt
15	Differential case

FM2039900064010X

Fig. 1 Exploded view of rear axle (Part 1 of 2)

16	Ring gear and pinion
17	Bolt
18	Differential bearing cap (part of 4010)
19	Pinion nut
20	Drive pinion oil seal deflector
21	Rear axle drive pinion seal
22	Pinion bearing
23	Differential drive pinion bearing cup
24	Front mount shim
25	Rear axle differential front lower insulator
26	Rear axle housing (aluminum)
27	Inboard CV joint stub shaft pilot bearing housing seal
28	Inboard CV joint stub shaft pilot bearing housing
29	Rear axle housing (nodular iron)
30	Rear axle differential front lower insulator cap
31	Differential drive pinion collapsible spacer
32	Rear axle drive pinion shaft oil slinger
33	Rear axle pinion flange

FM2039900064020X

Fig. 1 Exploded view of rear axle (Part 2 of 2)

2. Remove rear brake calipers and position aside as outlined under "Disc Brakes."
3. Disconnect propeller shaft as outlined under "Propeller Shaft, Replace."
4. Record torque necessary to maintain rotation of pinion gear using a suitable inch lb. torque wrench.
5. Install flange holding tool No. 205-478, or equivalent, then the cotter pin, **Fig. 4.**
6. Remove and discard pinion nut using a suitable breaker bar.
7. Place a reference mark on pinion flange in relation to drive pinion stem for installation reference, **Fig. 5.**
8. Remove flange from axle using flange removal tool No. 307-408, or equivalent.
9. Remove pinion seal.

INSTALLATION

1. Lubricate new seal using premium long life grease XG-1-C, or equivalent.
2. Install seal using seal installer tool No. T79P-4676-A, or equivalent.
3. Lubricate pinion flange spines using SAE 75W-140 synthetic rear axle lubricant F1TZ–19580–B, or equivalent.
4. Polish pinion flange seal journal using suitable crocus cloth.
5. Align pinion flange with drive pinion shaft.
6. Install flange using holding tool No. 205-478 and pinion flange installer tool No. 205-479, or equivalents.
7. Install cotter pin, **Fig. 4.**
8. Install a new pinion nut.
9. Hold pinion flange using a suitable flange holding tool, tighten new pinion nut until proper preload is reached. Refer to "Tightening Specifications" for proper pinion preload. **If necessary to reduce preload, a new collapsible spacer and pinion nut must be installed.**

REAR HALFSHAFT

REPLACE

Halfshaft assemblies are not serviceable. If wear or damage is present, replace entire halfshaft assembly. When servicing halfshafts, ensure excessive angle is not applied to CV joints and that joints are not pulled apart or separated.

The halfshafts on models equipped with 3.9L engine are larger in diameter and are not interchangeable with halfshafts on models equipped with a 3.0L engine.

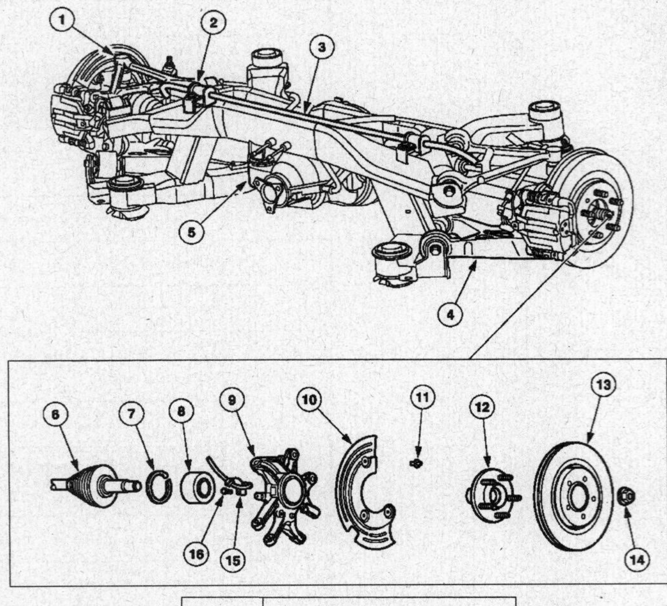

Item	Description
1	Upper arm
2	Stabilizer bar link
3	Stabilizer bar retaining bracket
4	Stabilizer bar
5	Lower arm
6	Axle shaft
7	Snap ring
8	Wheel hub bearing
9	Knuckle
10	Rear brake disc shield
11	Rivet

FM2039900065010X

Fig. 2 Rear suspension components (Part 1 of 2)

12	Hub'
13	Rear brake disc
14	Hub retainer
15	ABS sensor
16	Screw

FM2039900065020X

Fig. 2 Rear suspension components (Part 2 of 2)

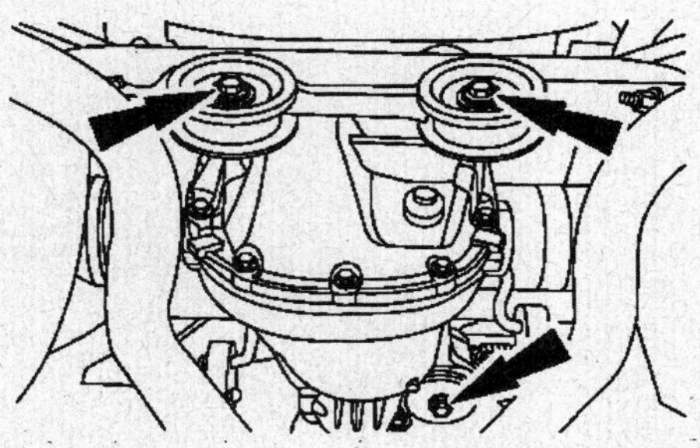

FM2039900066000X

Fig. 3 Axle mounting nuts

1. Raise and support vehicle.
2. Remove rear tires.
3. Remove and discard axle wheel hub nut.
4. Remove rear brake rotors as outlined in "Disc Brakes" chapter.
5. Remove ABS sensors as outlined in "Anti-Lock Brakes" chapter.
6. Remove lower knuckle attaching bolt.
7. Press CV joint from hub using hub remover/replacer tool No. T81P-1104-C, hub remover adapter tool No. T86P-1104-A1 and hub remover adapter tool No. T83P-1104-BH, or equivalents.
8. Raise and support knuckle, then remove CV joint from hub.
9. Separate CV joint from differential side gear using halfshaft removal tool No. 205-472, or equivalent. Ensure crown of tool forks face away from axle housing.
10. Remove halfshaft from axle housing.
11. Install differential plug tool No. T89P-4850-B, or equivalent, to differential.
12. Reverse procedure to install, noting the following:
    a. Install new axleshaft circlip.
    b. Before installing halfshaft into differential housing, install seal protector tool No. 205-461.
    c. Slide CV joint into housing until splines are past seal, then remove seal protector tool.
    d. Ensure halfshaft is fully seated into differential.
    e. Install new wheel hub nut.

DRIVELINE ANGLE MEASUREMENT

1. Park vehicle on a level surface.
2. Remove exhaust heat shield attaching bolts and slide shield as far forward as possible to expose driveshaft to axle coupling.
3. Rotate driveshaft several times by hand to neutralize center support bearing and flex couplings.
4. Place pinion angle level gauge tool No. T86P-4602-A, or equivalent, on left frame rail with tool facing passenger side, **Fig. 6.**
5. Zero angle gauge tool using thumbscrew.
6. Mark location where tool was zeroed. **When measuring driveline angle, bolts should not be removed from flange.**
7. Measure transmission angle "A," **Fig. 7,** as follows:
    a. Remove one nut from flex coupling to transmission flange.
    b. Install driveline adapter tool No. 205-449, or equivalent, to front of flex coupling and tighten nut. Ensure adapter contacts flex coupling bolt sleeve to obtain accurate reading.
    c. Place pinion angle gauge in angle adapter with angle gauge facing passenger side and record reading.
8. Measure front driveshaft angle "B," **Fig. 7,** as follows:
    a. Remove one nut from flex coupling to front driveshaft connection.
    b. Install driveline adapter tool No. 205-449, or equivalent, to front of flex coupling and tighten nut. Ensure adapter contacts flex coupling bolt sleeve to obtain accurate reading.
    c. Place pinion angle gauge in angle adapter with angle gauge facing passenger side and record reading.
9. Measure rear driveshaft angle "C," **Fig. 7,** as follows:
    a. Remove one nut from flex coupling to rear driveshaft connection.
    b. Install driveline adapter tool No. 205-449, or equivalent, to front of flex coupling and tighten nut. Ensure adapter contacts flex coupling bolt sleeve to obtain accurate reading.
    c. Place pinion angle gauge in angle adapter with angle gauge facing passenger side and record reading.
10. Measure differential pinion angle "D," **Fig. 7,** as follows:

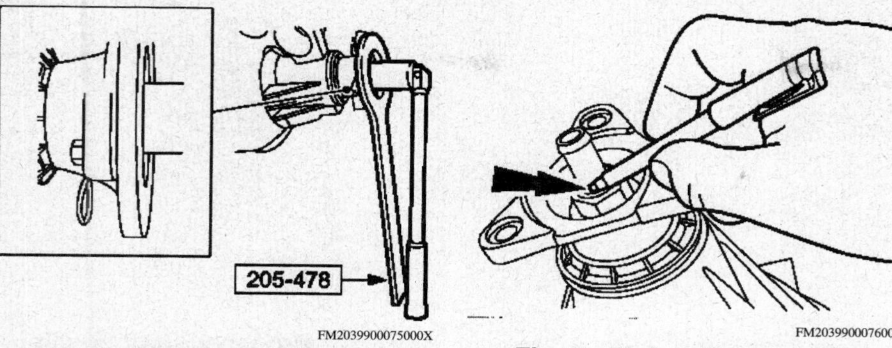

Fig. 4 Flange holding tool installation

Fig. 5 Pinion flange marks

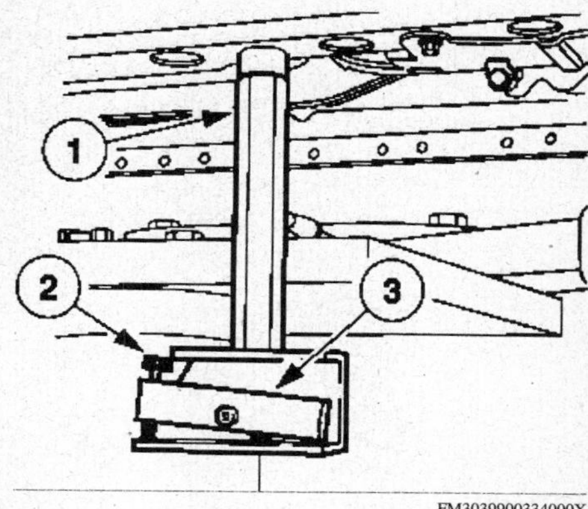

Fig. 6 Pinion angle gauge setup

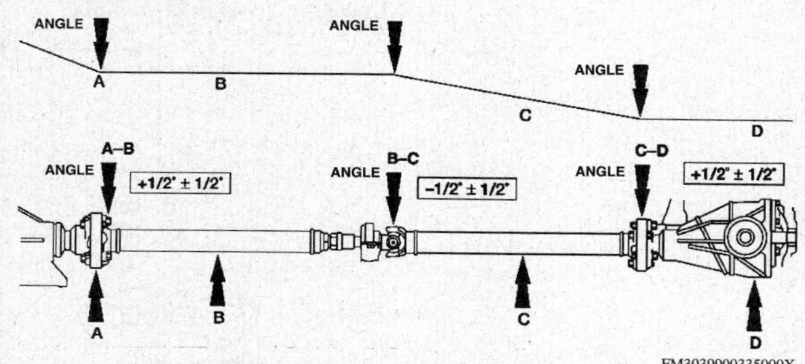

Fig. 7 Driveline angle inspection points

Part Number	Thickness, Inch
W704775	.079
W704776	.118
W704777	.157
W704778	.020
W704779	.240
W704780	.280

Fig. 8 Driveshaft washer selection

a. Remove one nut from flex coupling to pinion flange connection.
b. Install driveline adapter tool No. 205-449, or equivalent, to front of flex coupling and tighten nut. Ensure adapter contacts flex coupling bolt sleeve to obtain accurate reading.
c. Place pinion angle gauge in angle adapter with angle gauge facing passenger side and record reading.

11. Calculate angles of joints 1, 2 and 3 as follows, referring to **Fig. 7,** for driveline angle specifications:
    a. A-B=Joint 1.
    b. B-C=Joint 2.
    c. C-D=Joint 3.
12. If adjustment is necessary, install appropriate center support bearing adjusting washers. Ensure left and right washers are of equal thickness.
13. Refer to **Fig. 8** for washer selection chart.

PROPELLER SHAFT

REPLACE

1. Raise and support vehicle.
2. Remove muffler and extension pipe, then the body brace.
3. Remove heat shield.
4. Inspect and record driveline angles as outlined under "Driveline Angle Measurement."
5. Place reference marks on bolts, washers, nuts and flex coupling to transmission flange and pinion flange for installation reference.
6. Remove driveshaft to axle flange attaching nuts. **Do not remove flex coupling to driveshaft attaching bolts, Fig. 9.**
7. Loosen driveshaft length adjustment nut using driveshaft coupler wrenches, tool No. 205-474, or equivalents.
8. Remove transmission flange to driveshaft attaching nuts. **Do not remove flex coupling to driveshaft attaching bolts.**
9. Slide front shaft assembly rearward, then hand tighten adjustment nut to prevent separation of front and rear shafts.
10. Remove center bearing support brace nuts, then the driveshaft assembly.
11. Reverse procedure to install, noting the following:
    a. Add one gram of premium long life grease XG-1-C, or equivalent, to both alignment bushing cavities.
    b. Apply Threadlock 262 E2FZ–19554–B, or equivalent, to driveshaft to flange nuts and bolts.

U-JOINT

REPLACE

The single center U-joint is of a lubed for life design that requires no periodic lubrication. This U-joint is staked to the yoke and is not removable.

PROPELLER SHAFT CENTER BEARING

REPLACE

1. Remove propeller shaft as outlined under "Propeller Shaft, Replace."
2. Place alignment marks on driveshaft assemblies for installation reference.
3. Loosen adjustment nut and separate front and rear shaft assemblies.
4. Place propeller shaft in a suitable vise and clamp at driveshaft weld yoke.
5. Remove retaining ring and center bearing and bracket assembly using 2 jaw puller tool No. D80L-1002-L and bearing puller tool No. D84L-1123-A, or equivalents.
6. Reverse procedure to install. Install center bearing and retaining ring to driveshaft using driveshaft alignment bushing remover tube tool No. 205-D073, or equivalent, and a suitable hammer.

PROPELLER SHAFT ALIGNMENT BUSHING

REMOVAL

1. Remove propeller shaft as outlined under "Propeller Shaft, Replace."
2. Place alignment marks on front and rear driveshaft assemblies for installation reference.
3. Loosen length adjustment nut and separate front and rear shaft assemblies.
4. Remove flex coupling nuts, then the bolts and flex coupling.
5. Place driveshaft end yoke into a suitable vise.
6. Remove alignment bushing inner core using blind hole puller set tool No. D80L-100A, driveshaft alignment bushing remover tube tool No. 205-D073 and handle tool No. T80T-4000-W, or equivalents, **Fig. 10.**
7. Remove bushing shell using removal tools, **Fig. 11.**

INSTALLATION

There are six bushings in each flex coupling. Three bushings protrude from each side of coupling. Arrows on the

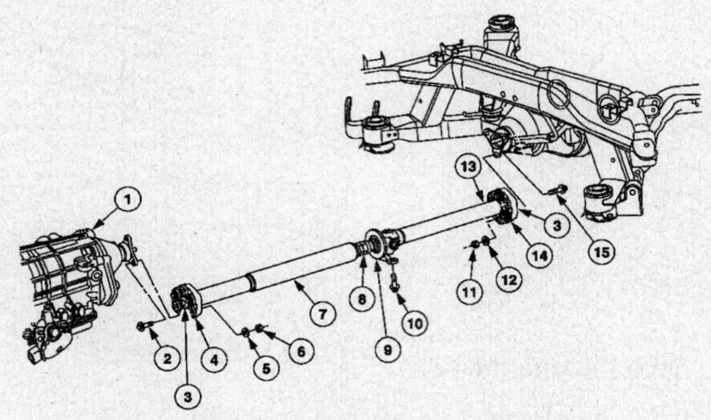

Item	Description
1	Transmission
2	Bolt
3	Alignment bushing
4	Flex coupling
5	Washer
6	Nut
7	Shaft assembly, front
8	Nut, length adjustment
9	Center bearing and bracket assembly
10	Bolt
11	Nut
12	Washer
13	Shaft assembly, rear
14	Flex coupling
15	Bolt

FM2039900077000X

Fig. 9 Driveshaft components

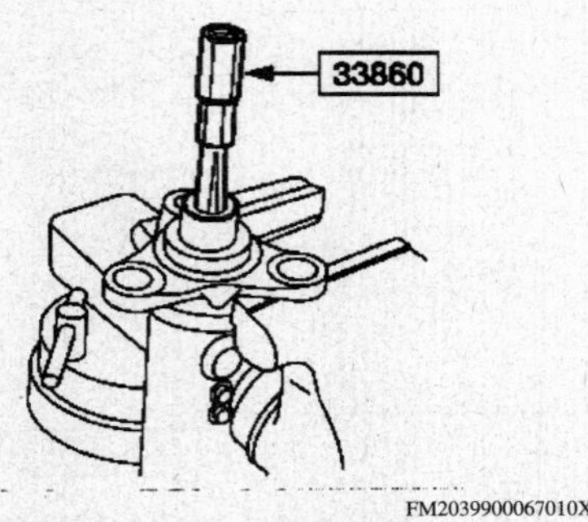

FM2039900067010X

Fig. 10 Propeller shaft bushing inner core removal (Part 1 of 4)

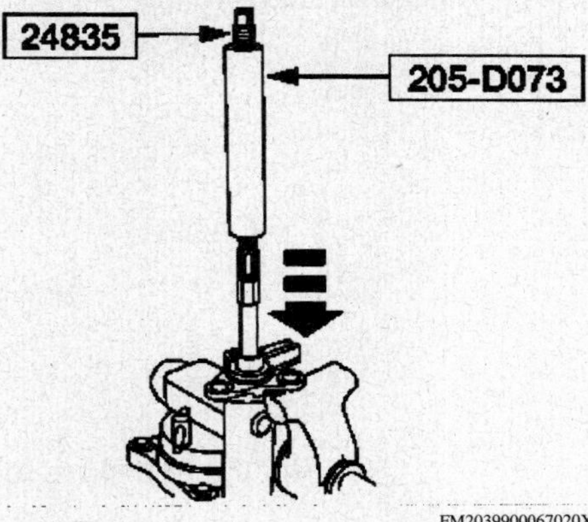

FM2039900067020X

Fig. 10 Propeller shaft bushing inner core removal (Part 2 of 4)

side of coupling point toward protruding end of bushing. When installing flex coupling, protruding end of bushing must seat in driveshaft flange counterbore or damage will occur to coupling during operation.

1. Align bushing with propeller shaft, then install using handle tool No. T80T-4000-W and alignment bearing installer tool No. 205-D074, or equivalents.
2. Install flex coupling as follows:
   a. Position protruding end of bushing against driveshaft flange, **Fig. 12.**
   b. Apply Threadlock 262 E2FZ–19554–B, or equivalent, to flex coupling bolts and nuts, then install. Ensure bolt heads seat against driveshaft flange and nuts against flex coupling. Bolt heads are serrated and must be held in place while nut is tightened.
3. Align front and rear propeller shaft reference marks, then assemble both shafts. Finger tighten nut to prevent separation of shaft assembly.
4. Add one gram of premium long life grease XG–1–C, or equivalent, to both alignment bushing cavities before installing propeller shaft.
5. Install propeller shaft as outlined under "Propeller shaft, Replace."

HUB & BEARING

REPLACE

1. Remove knuckle as outlined under "Knuckle, Replace."
2. Drill out dust shield rivets using a .22 inch drill bit. If larger bit is needed, it should not exceed .24 inch.
3. Remove dust shield.
4. Place knuckle in a suitable press. Ensure knuckle is level and is supported as close to bearing bore as possible. Knuckle extremities should not be used for support.
5. Remove hub from knuckle using step plate adapter set tool No. D80L-630-A and bearing puller tool No. T71P-4621-B, or equivalents. When hub is pressed from bearing, bearing inner race will also be removed. **Do not install race back into bearing.**
6. Remove bearing retaining snap ring.
7. Support knuckle in press as close to bearing bore as possible.
8. Remove bearing from knuckle using appropriate step plate adapter.
9. If hub is reused, remove inner bearing race from hub using a suitable press and bearing puller tool No. T71P-4621-B, or equivalent.
10. Reverse procedure to install, noting the following:
    a. Attach dust shield using aluminum rivets.
    b. When installing hub to bearing, ensure bearing inner race is properly supported.

BALL JOINT INSPECTION

1. Raise and support vehicle.
2. Inspect wheel bearings as outlined under "Wheel Bearing Inspection."
3. Position a suitable safety stand under lower suspension arm.
4. Grasp tire at top and bottom and attempt to move inward and outward.
5. If movement is more than 1⁄32 inch replace control arm.

WHEEL BEARING INSPECTION

1. Raise and support vehicle.
2. Ensure brake pads are retracted enough to allow free movement of tire.
3. Grasp tire at top and bottom and move wheel inward and outward while lifting weight of tire off bearing.
4. If tire is loose on spindle or does not rotate freely, install new hub and bearing as necessary.

STRUT

REPLACE

When working with strut, do not apply heat during removal or service.

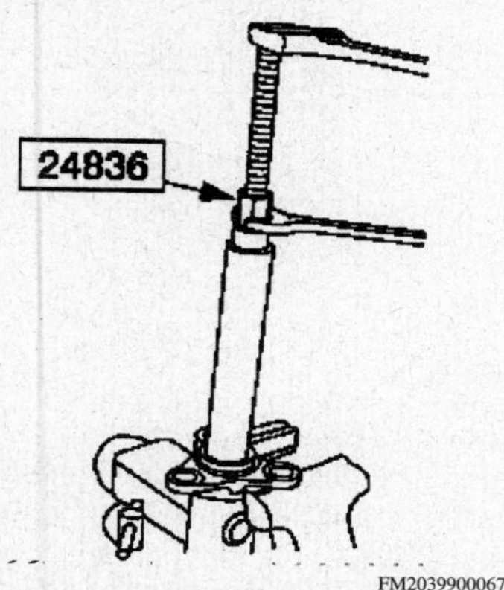

Fig. 10 Propeller shaft bushing inner core removal (Part 3 of 4)

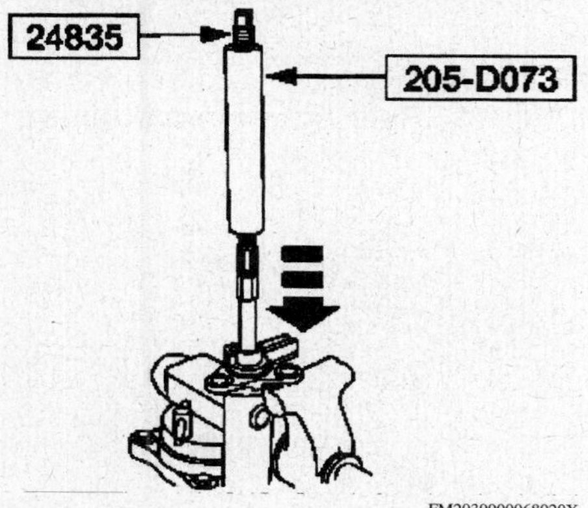

Fig. 11 Propeller shaft bushing shell removal (Part 2 of 4)

1. Open luggage compartment.
2. Remove carpet, then the spare tire.
3. Remove trim covers to access strut upper attaching bolts.
4. Remove four strut upper attaching nuts and discard, **Fig. 13.**
5. Raise and support vehicle.
6. Remove strut lower attaching bolt and nut and discard.
7. Remove strut assembly from vehicle.
8. Reverse procedure to install.

STRUT SERVICE

DISASSEMBLE

When working with strut, do not apply heat during removal or service.

If reusing components, place alignment marks on all parts for installation reference.

1. Remove strut as outlined under "Strut, Replace."
2. Place strut into a suitable vise, **Fig. 14.**
3. Compress spring using a suitable spring compressor.
4. Remove center nut while holding shock absorber rod, **Fig. 15.**
5. Remove upper mount and dust boot.
6. Release spring and remove from strut.

ASSEMBLE

1. Inspect all strut components for damage or wear. If spring paint is damaged, a new spring should be installed.

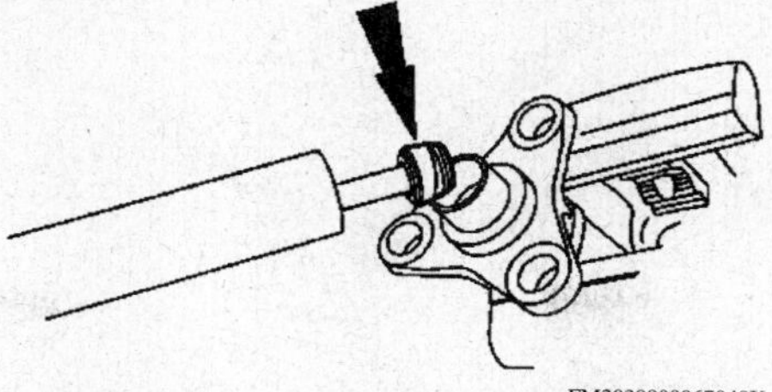

Fig. 10 Propeller shaft bushing inner core removal (Part 4 of 4)

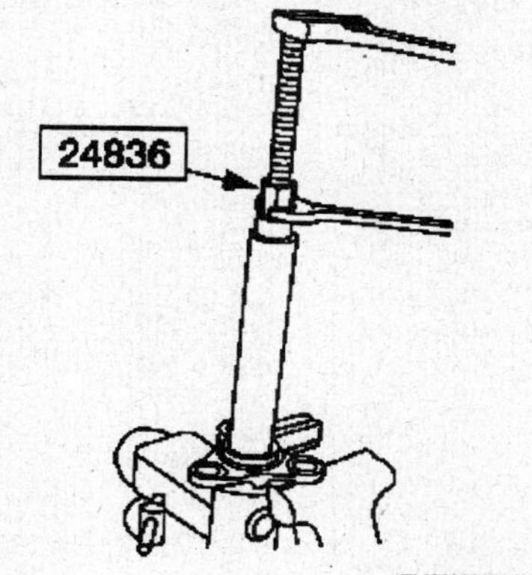

Fig. 11 Propeller shaft bushing shell removal (Part 3 of 4)

2. Compress spring using a suitable spring compressor.
3. Position upper mount and dust boot on spring. Ensure all parts are properly aligned.
4. Install new upper strut mount nut.
5. Remove strut from spring compressor and vise.
6. Install strut as outlined under "Strut, Replace."

BALL JOINT

REPLACE

Refer to "Control Arm, Replace" for ball joint replacement.

CONTROL ARM

REPLACE

LOWER

REMOVAL

If lower arm bushings require service, entire lower control arm must be replaced.

1. With vehicle at a static level position, remove hub cap and measure distance from center of hub to lip of fender, **Fig. 16.**
2. Raise and support vehicle, then remove rear wheels.
3. Remove rear brake rotor as outlined in "Disc Brakes" chapter.
4. Remove lower strut to control arm attaching bolt and nut, discard nut and bolt.
5. Remove lower stabilizer link to control arm attaching nut, discard nut.

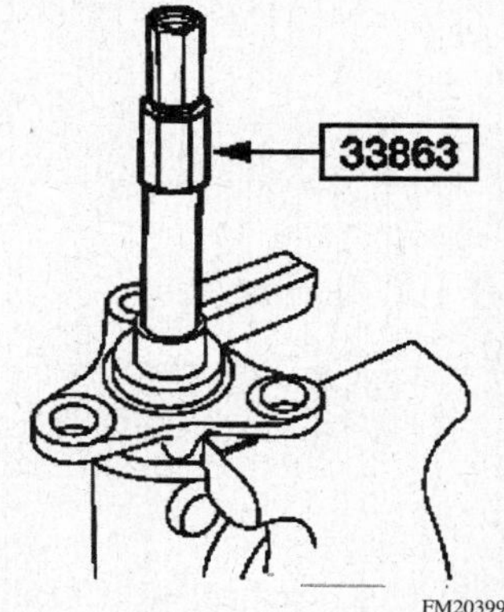

Fig. 11 Propeller shaft bushing shell removal (Part 1 of 4)

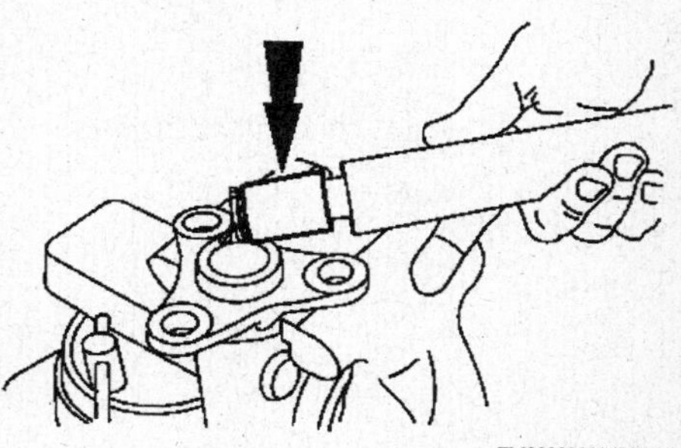

Fig. 11 Propeller shaft bushing shell removal (Part 4 of 4)

6. Remove lower knuckle to control arm attaching nut and bolt, discard nut and bolt.
7. Remove lower arm to subframe attaching bolts and nuts, discard nuts and bolts.
8. Remove lower control arm.

INSTALLATION

Do not tighten lower arm to subframe or knuckle bolts and nuts until curb height is at correct level.

1. Connect lower arm to subframe.
2. Install knuckle to lower arm.
3. Connect stabilizer bar link to lower suspension arm.
4. Install strut to lower control arm.
5. Position a suitable jackstand under lower arm and raise suspension until distance between center of hub and lip of fender is as recorded during removal procedure.
6. Tighten lower arm attaching nuts and remove jackstand.
7. Install rear rotors as outlined in "Disc Brakes" chapter.
8. Install wheels, then lower vehicle.

UPPER

Removal

If upper arm bushings and ball joints require service, entire upper control arm must be replaced.

1. With vehicle at a static level position, remove hub cap and measure distance from center of hub to lip of fender, **Fig. 16.**
2. Raise and support vehicle.

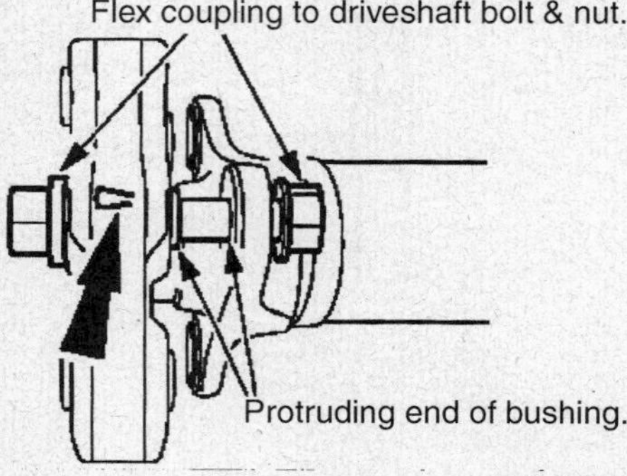

Fig. 12 Flex coupling installation

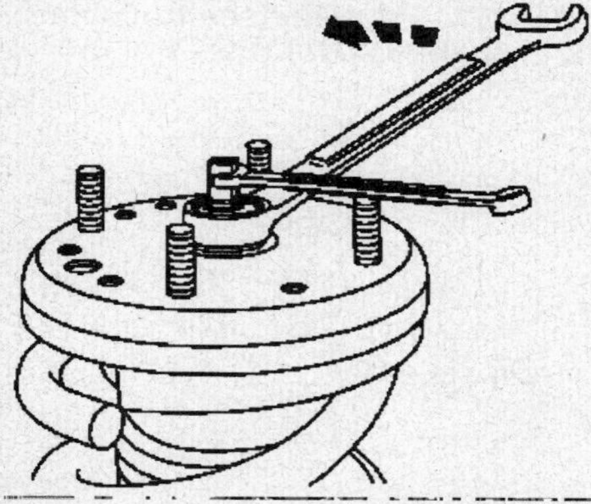

Fig. 15 Rear strut center nut removal

3. Remove rear wheels.
4. Unclip ABS sensor wire retainer from suspension arm.
5. Disconnect and remove ABS sensor and position aside.
6. Remove and discard upper ball joint to knuckle nut, then separate knuckle from ball joint.
7. Remove upper arm to subframe nuts and bolts, discard nuts and bolts.
8. Remove upper suspension arm.

Installation

Do not tighten upper arm to subframe or knuckle nuts and bolts until suspension is at proper curb height.

1. Install upper arm to subframe and knuckle.
2. Clip ABS sensor wire to upper suspension arm.
3. Position a suitable jack under suspension lower arm.
4. Raise suspension until distance between center of hub and lip of fender is as recorded during removal procedure.
5. Tighten upper arm to subframe and knuckle attaching nuts.
6. Lower suspension and remove jack.
7. Install wheels and lower vehicle.

TOE LINK

REPLACE

1. Raise and support vehicle.
2. Remove rear wheels.

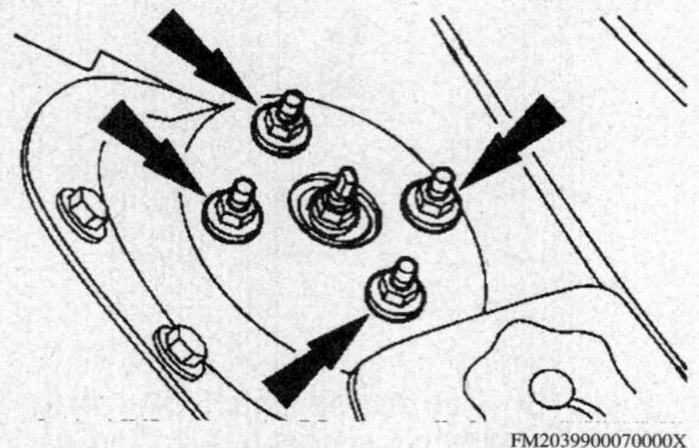

Fig. 13 Strut upper attaching nuts

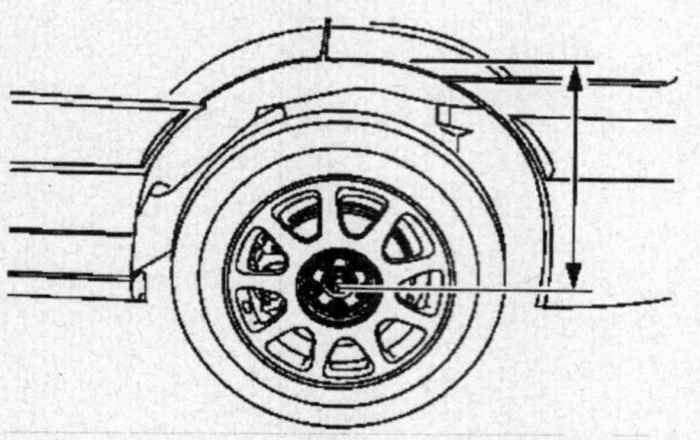

Fig. 16 Curb height measurement

3. Disconnect toe link from knuckle, **Fig. 17.**
4. Remove toe link from subframe, then the toe link.
5. Reverse procedure to install. Use new toe link attaching nuts and ensure wheel alignment is within specifications. Refer to "Specifications" section.

KNUCKLE

REPLACE

1. With vehicle at a static level position, remove hub cap and measure distance from center of hub to lip of fender, **Fig. 16.**
2. Raise and support vehicle, then remove rear wheels.
3. Remove and discard hub nut.
4. Remove rear rotors as outlined in "Disc Brakes" section.
5. Disconnect toe link from knuckle.
6. Remove ABS sensor and position aside.
7. Disconnect lower suspension arm from knuckle.
8. Support axleshaft.
9. Remove axleshaft from hub using hub remover/replacer tool No. T81P-1104-C, hub remover adapter tool No. T86P-1104-A and hub remover adapters tool No. T83P-1104-BH, or equivalents.
10. Remove upper ball joint from knuckle, then the knuckle.
11. Reverse procedure to install, noting the following:
    a. Before tightening knuckle attaching bolts, raise suspension and ensure distance between center of hub and lip of fender is as recorded in step No. 1.
    b. When servicing suspension components, always use new nuts and bolts.

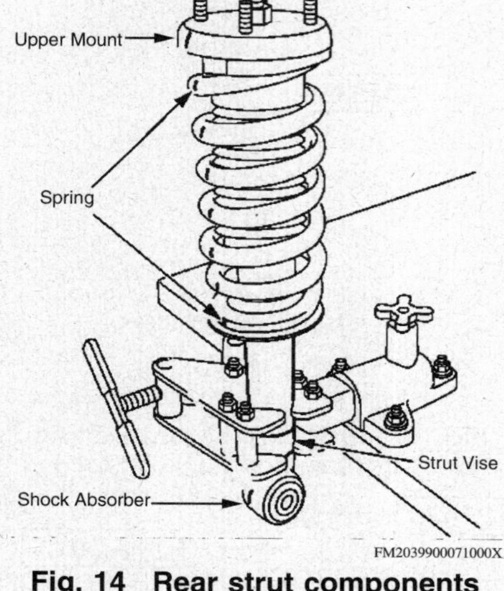

Fig. 14 Rear strut components

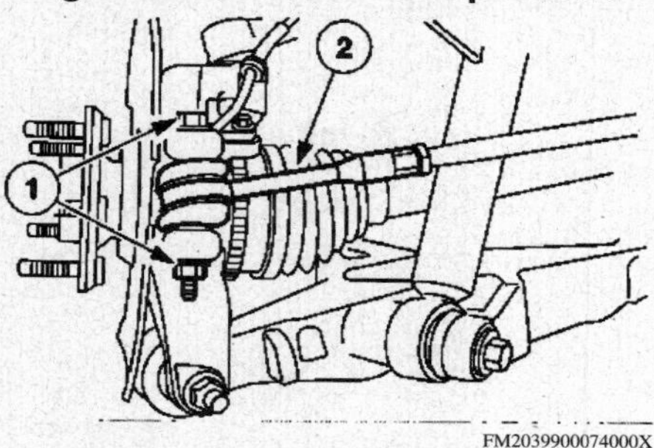

Fig. 17 Toe link removal

STABILIZER BAR

REPLACE

1. With vehicle at a static level position, remove hub cap and measure distance from center of hub to lip of fender, **Fig. 16.**
2. Raise and support vehicle, then remove wheels.
3. Disconnect propeller shaft from axle as outlined under "Propeller Shaft, Replace."
4. Place Rotunda powertrain lift tool No. 014-00765, or equivalent, under rear subframe.
5. Place reference marks on all subframe attaching bolts for installation reference.
6. Remove subframe attaching bolts and lower subframe eight inches.
7. Remove stabilizer link caps from right and left stabilizer links.
8. Disconnect right and left stabilizer links from stabilizer bar.
9. Remove stabilizer bar brackets and bushings.
10. Secure right and left knuckles to subframe using suitable mechanics wire.
11. Disconnect right and left upper control arms from subframe.
12. Remove stabilizer bar.
13. Reverse procedure to install, noting the following:
    a. Before tightening knuckle attaching bolts, raise suspension and ensure distance between center of hub and

lip of fender is as recorded in step No. 1.
b. When servicing suspension components, always use new nuts and bolts.

STABILIZER BAR LINK

REPLACE

1. Raise and support vehicle, then remove rear wheels.
2. Disconnect stabilizer bar link from suspension lower arm.
3. Remove protective cap from stabilizer bar link.
4. Remove stabilizer link from stabilizer bar.
5. Reverse procedure to install. When servicing suspension components, always use new nuts and bolts.

TECHNICAL SERVICE BULLETINS

DROANING NOISE ON ACCELERATION AT HIGHWAY SPEEDS

Some vehicles may exhibit a moaning or droning noise during light acceleration while transmission is in 5th gear at highway speeds. Noise will disappear if the transmission is shifted to 4th gear or when lifting the throttle. The noise may be due to the body reacting to a resonant frequency generated by the powertrain. To correct this condition, install revised larger diameter rear halfshafts. Larger diameter halfshafts will reduce the resonant frequencies generated by the powertrain.

TIGHTENING SPECIFICATIONS

Year	Component	Torque, Ft. Lbs.
2000–02	Anti-Lock Brake Sensor Bolt	89①
	Axle Fill Plug	25
	Center Bearing Bolts	32
	Driveshaft Length Adjustment Nut	58
	Flex Coupling To Driveshaft Nuts	60
	Front Differential Mounting Bolts	52
	Hub Nut	221
	Lower Arm & Bushing To Knuckle Pivot Bolt Nut	111
	Lower Arm & Bushing To Subframe Pivot Bolt & Nut	111
	Pinion Nut	②
	Rear Differential Mounting Bolts	76
	Shock & Spring Assembly To Lower Arm	98
	Stabilizer Bar Bracket Bolts	41
	Stabilizer Bar Link Nuts	35
	Subframe To Body Bolts	76
	Toe Link Nuts	41
	Upper Arm & Bushing To Subframe Pivot Bolt Nut	66
	Upper Ball Joint Nut	66
	Upper Shock Absorber Rod To Upper Shock Mount Nut	37
	Upper Shock Absorber Mount To Body Nuts	21
	Yoke Adjuster Nut	66
	Wheel Lug Nuts	100

① — Inch lbs.
② — Tighten until proper preload specification is achieved as follows: used bearings, 8–10 inch lbs.; new bearings, 16–28 inch lbs.

Front Suspension & Steering

NOTE: On Air Bag Equipped Models, Refer To "Air Bag System Precautions" Located In The Front Of This Manual For System Disarming & Arming Procedures.

NOTE: Refer To "Computer Relearn Procedures" Located In The Front Of This Manual When Battery Power To The Computer Has Been Interrupted.

INDEX

PRECAUTIONS

AIR BAG SYSTEMS

Refer to "Air Bag System Precautions" in the front of this manual for system disarming and arming procedures.

BATTERY GROUND CABLE

Prior to service, disconnect battery ground cable and isolate as required.

DESCRIPTION

The front suspension is an aluminum short-arm-long-arm that features struts, stabilizer bar and stabilizer bar links, **Fig. 1.**

When servicing suspension components, always use new nuts and bolts.

HUB & BEARING

REPLACE

1. Raise and support vehicle.
2. Remove front wheels.
3. Remove brake rotor as outlined in "Disc Brakes" chapter.
4. Remove inner fender splash shield and position aside.
5. Disconnect ABS wheel speed sensor and separate from wire retainers. **Do not remove ABS sensor from hub unless new sensor and wire are being installed.**
6. Remove wheel hub and bearing attaching bolts and discard, **Fig. 2.**
7. Remove wheel hub and bearing from knuckle. **Do not use a slide hammer or strike back of wheel hub and bearing to remove. Hub and bearing should slide out from knuckle.**
8. Reverse procedure to install, noting the following:
   a. Ensure knuckle bore is clean enough to allow hub and bearing to be seated by hand.
   b. Apply Motorcraft high temperature nickel anti-seize lubricant F6AZ–9L494–AA, or equivalent, to bearing carrier and wheel knuckle
   c. Install new suspension attaching bolts and nuts.

BALL JOINT INSPECTION

1. Raise and support vehicle.
2. Inspect wheel bearings as outlined under "Wheel Bearing Inspection."
3. Position a suitable safety stand under lower suspension arm.
4. Grasp tire at top and bottom and attempt to move inward and outward.
5. If movement is more than $1/32$ inch on upper or lower ball joint, replace control arm.

WHEEL BEARING INSPECTION

1. Raise and support vehicle.
2. Ensure brake pads are retracted enough to allow free movement of tire.
3. Grasp tire at top and bottom and move wheel inward and outward while lifting weight of tire off bearing.
4. If tire is loose on spindle or does not rotate freely, install new hub and bearing.

STRUT

REPLACE

Do not use heat to remove strut attaching bolts.

1. Raise and support vehicle, then remove front wheels.
2. Disconnect stabilizer bar link from control arm and discard nut.
3. Remove and discard strut to lower control arm attaching bolt.
4. Remove strut to body attaching bolts, **Fig. 3. Do not remove strut center nut.**
5. Reverse procedure to install. Install new suspension attaching bolts and nuts.

COIL SPRING & STRUT SERVICE

Do not use heat to remove strut attaching bolts.

1. Remove strut as outlined under "Strut, Replace."
2. Mount strut in a suitable vise, **Fig. 4.**
3. Place reference marks on all strut components for assembly reference.
4. Compress spring using a suitable spring compressor.
5. Hold shock absorber center rod and remove center nut from strut.
6. Remove upper mount and dust boot.
7. Release pressure from spring and remove from spring compressor.
8. Reverse procedure to install, noting the following:
   a. Inspect spring, upper and lower spring seats, mount and insulator for damage. If spring coating is damaged, replace spring.
   b. Install new strut attaching nuts and bolts.

CONTROL ARM

REPLACE

LOWER

REMOVAL

1. Ensure ignition switch is off in unlocked position.

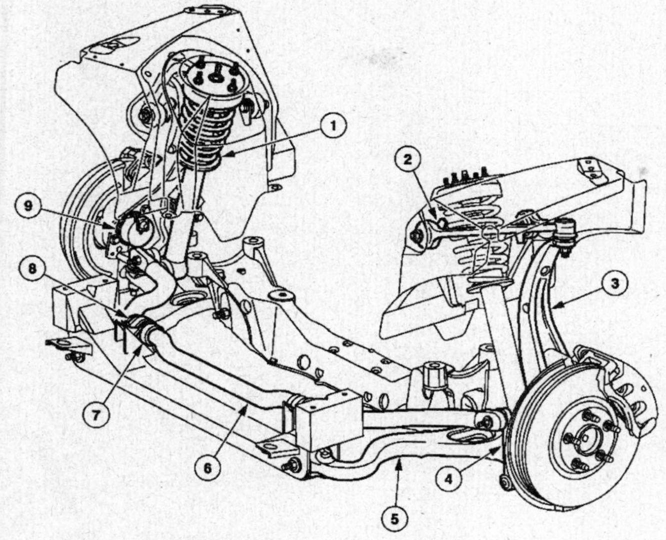

Item	Description
1	Shock absorber and spring assy
2	Upper arm and bushing
3	Wheel knuckle
4	Stabilizer bar link
5	Lower arm and bushing
6	Stabilizer bar
7	Stabilizer bar bushing
8	Stabilizer bar bracket
9	Wheel hub and bearing

FM2029900148000X

Fig. 1 Front suspension components

2. Raise and support vehicle, then remove wheels.
3. Remove splash shields as necessary.
4. Disconnect stabilizer bar link from lower control arm and discard nut.
5. Disconnect strut from lower control arm, then discard nut and bolt.
6. Disconnect lower control arm from steering knuckle and discard nut.
7. Remove front lower control arm bolt and nut, then discard nut and bolt.
8. Remove two nuts and bolts (1), then loosen nut and bolt (2) and rotate steering gear rack (3) to access lower control arm rear bolt, **Fig. 5.**
9. Remove and discard rear lower control arm nut and bolt.

INSTALLATION

1. Position lower control arm and install new caster adjustment cam bolt with cam lobe pointed downward, ensure cam is seated between cam guides on No. 1 crossmember, **Fig. 6.**
2. Install nut. **Do not fully tighten nut until wheel alignment is performed.** Refer to "Wheel Alignment" section.
3. Install new camber adjustment cam bolt with cam lobe pointed downward, ensure cam is seated in groove of No. 2 crossmember and nut, **Fig. 7.**
4. Install nut. **Do not fully tighten nut until wheel alignment is performed.** Refer to "Wheel Alignment" section.
5. Connect lower ball joint to control arm. Ensure tapered washer is installed on ball joint.
6. Connect stabilizer link and strut to lower arm.
7. Install splash shields.
8. Tighten bolts and nuts loosened when repositioning steering gear.
9. Install wheels, then lower vehicle and ensure wheel alignment is within specifications.

LEFT UPPER

1. Remove hub cap.
2. Measure and record distance from lip of fender to center of wheel hub, **Fig. 8.**
3. Remove air cleaner.
4. Remove upper control arm nut and discard, **Fig. 9.**
5. Raise and support vehicle, then remove front wheel.
6. Remove strut as outlined under "Strut, Replace."
7. Secure knuckle to body using suitable mechanics wire.
8. Disconnect upper control arm from

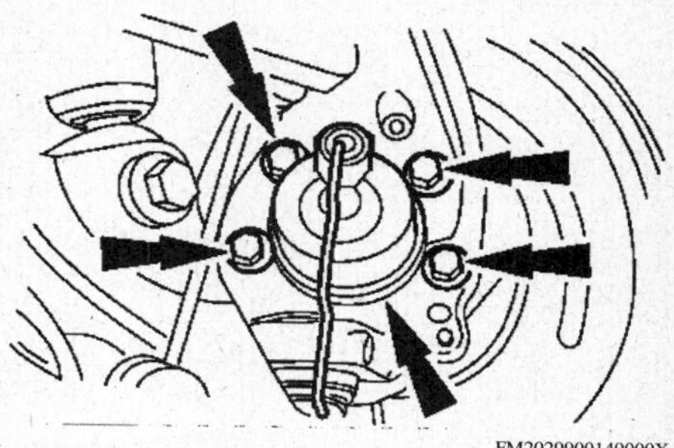

FM2029900149000X

Fig. 2 Wheel hub & bearing removal

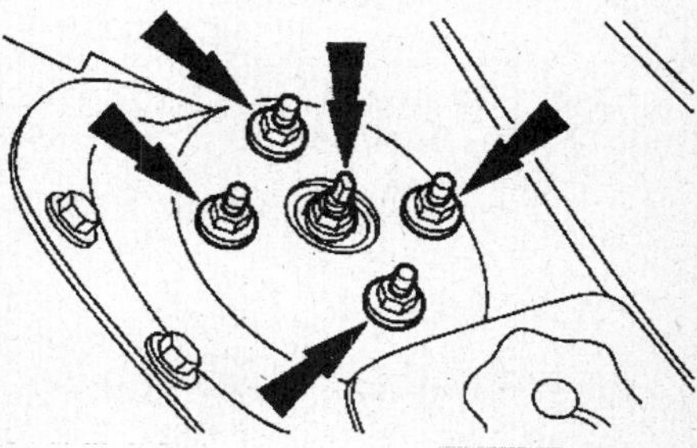

FM2029900150000X

Fig. 3 Strut attaching bolts

steering knuckle and discard nut.

9. Remove control arm from body and discard nuts and bolts.
10. Reverse procedure to install, noting the following:
    a. Ensure suspension is at distance measured in step No. 2, before tightening control arm attaching bolts.
    b. When servicing suspension components, always use new nuts and bolts.

RIGHT UPPER

1. Remove hub cap.
2. Measure and record distance from lip of fender to center of wheel hub, **Fig. 8.**
3. Remove and discard nut from engine compartment, **Fig. 10.**
4. Disconnect wiring harness and brackets as necessary to access control arm attaching bolts and nuts.
5. Remove upper control arm attaching nut and discard.
6. Remove strut as outlined under "Strut, Replace."
7. Secure knuckle to body using suitable mechanics wire.
8. Disconnect upper ball joint from steering knuckle and discard nut.
9. Remove upper arm attaching bolts and nuts, then the upper arm. Discard attaching bolts and nuts.
10. Reverse procedure to install, noting the following:
    a. Ensure suspension is at distance measured in step No. 2, before tightening control arm attaching bolts.
    b. When servicing suspension components, always use new nuts and bolts.

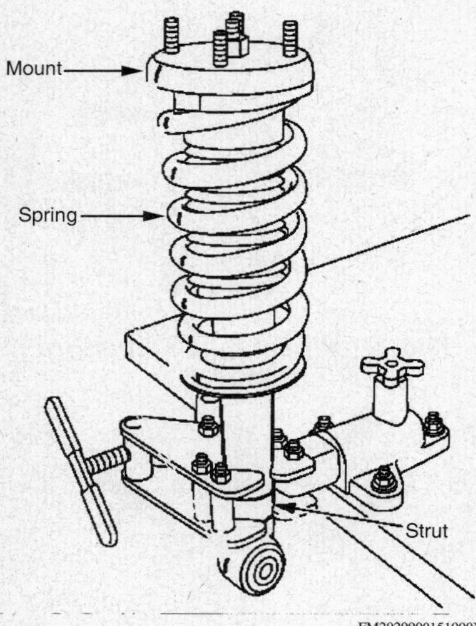

Fig. 4 Front strut components

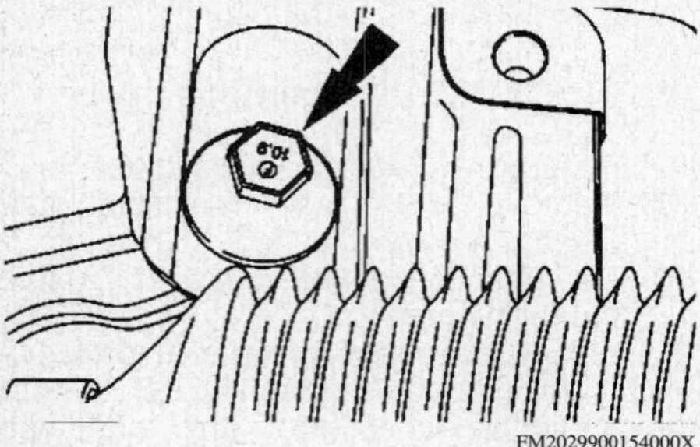

Fig. 7 Camber adjustment bolt installation

STEERING KNUCKLE

REPLACE

1. Remove wheel hub and bearing as outlined under "Hub & Bearing, Replace."
2. Disconnect tie rod, upper control arm and lower control arm from steering knuckle and discard nuts.
3. Remove steering knuckle from vehicle.
4. Reverse procedure to install, noting the following:
   a. Support steering knuckle using a suitable jackstand during installation.
   b. When servicing suspension components always use new nuts and bolts.

STABILIZER BAR

REPLACE

1. Remove air cleaner.
2. Remove stabilizer bracket bolt, **Fig. 11.**
3. Raise and support vehicle, then remove front wheels.
4. Remove right, left and center splash shields.
5. Disconnect stabilizer bar link from control arm and stabilizer bar, discard nuts.

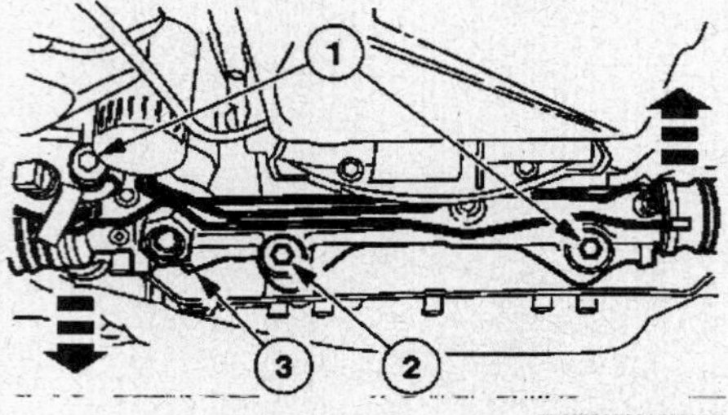

Fig. 5 Steering gear bolts

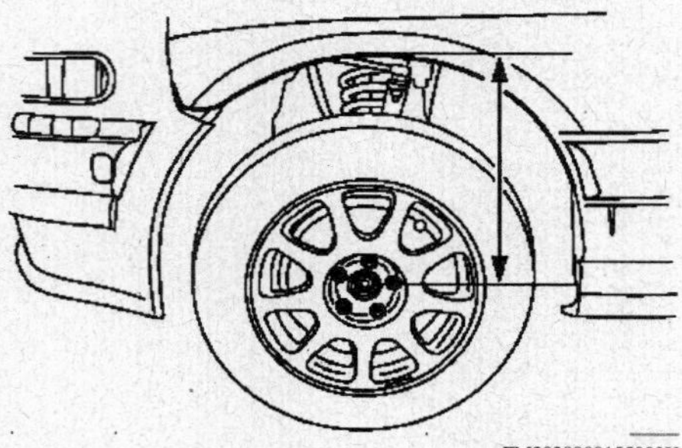

Fig. 8 Curb height measurement

6. Disconnect strut from left lower control arm, discard bolt and nut.
7. Disconnect lower control arm from left steering knuckle, discard nut.
8. Remove heater water valve bracket and position valve aside.
9. Remove stabilizer bar brackets and bushings. Remove right front bolt first.
10. Remove stabilizer bar through left wheel well.
11. Reverse procedure to install. When servicing suspension components, always use new nuts and bolts.

TIE ROD

REPLACE

Refer to "Power Steering" chapter for inner and outer tie rod replacement procedures.

POWER STEERING GEAR

REPLACE

1. Raise and support vehicle, then remove front wheels.
2. Disconnect tie rod ends from steering knuckles and discard nuts.
3. Disconnect power steering gear electrical connector.
4. Loosen steering shaft bolt.
5. Remove pinch bolt and disconnect intermediate shaft.
6. Remove power steering hose bracket.
7. Disconnect power steering hoses from steering gear. Plug hose ends at gear.
8. Remove steering gear attaching nuts, bolts and gear. Discard attaching nuts and bolts.
9. Reverse procedure to install, noting the following:
   a. Install new seal to power steering

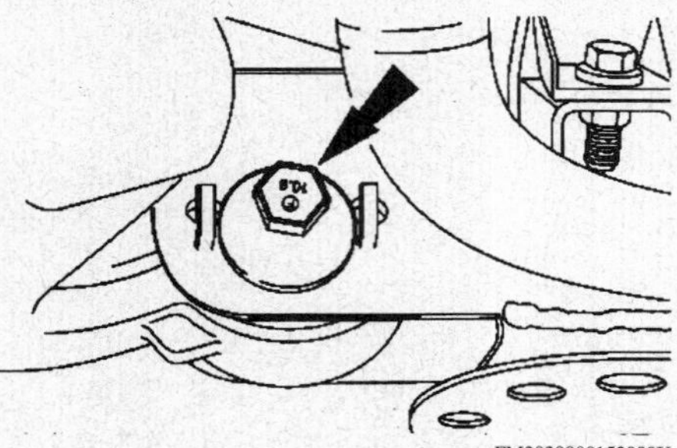

Fig. 6 Caster adjustment bolt installation

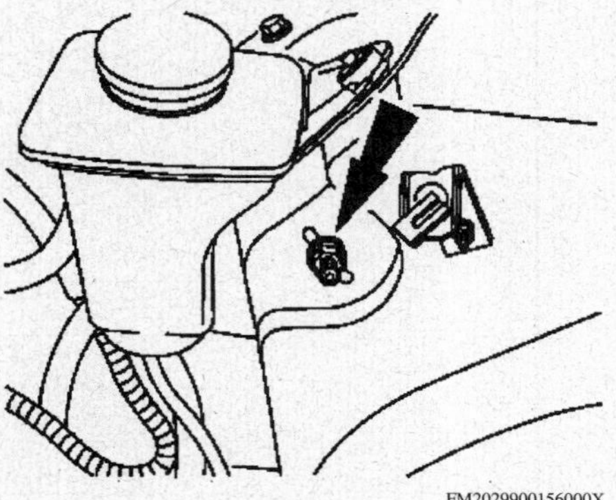

Fig. 9 Upper control arm attaching nut location

lines using teflon seal replacer set tool No. D90P-3517-A, or equivalent.
   b. When servicing suspension components, always use new nuts and bolts.
   c. Fill system and inspect for leaks. Ensure wheel alignment is within specifications.

POWER STEERING PUMP

REPLACE

3.0L ENGINE

1. Remove engine appearance cover.
2. Remove air cleaner and outlet tube.
3. Remove accessory drive belt.
4. Disconnect power steering reservoir to pump hose and drain fluid into a suitable container.
5. Raise and support vehicle, then remove front wheels.
6. Remove lower power steering pump shield, **Fig. 12.**
7. Remove power steering hose bracket bolt, then disconnect hose from pump.
8. Remove pump attaching bolts, then the pump.
9. Reverse procedure to install, noting the following:
   a. Install new O-rings to power steering hoses using telfon seal replacer set tool No. D90P-3517-A, or equivalent.
   b. Tighten upper pump attaching bolts after lower bolts are installed.
   c. Fill power steering system and inspect for leaks.

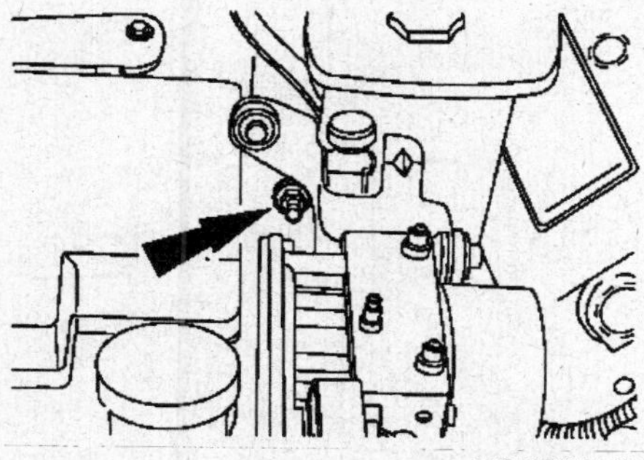

Fig. 10 Engine compartment nut location

Fig. 12 Power steering pump shield (Part 2 of 2)

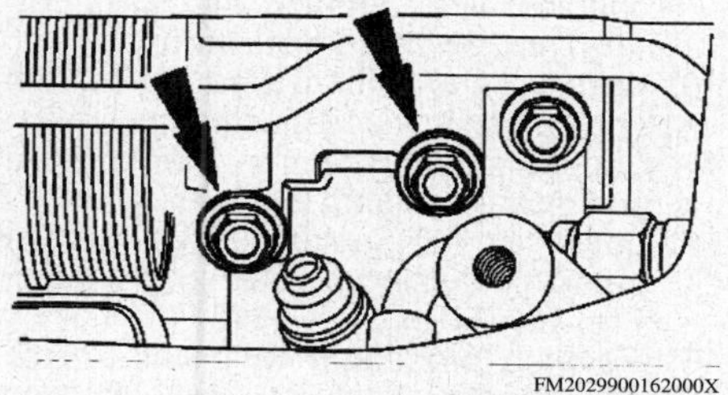

Fig. 15 Power steering pump bolts

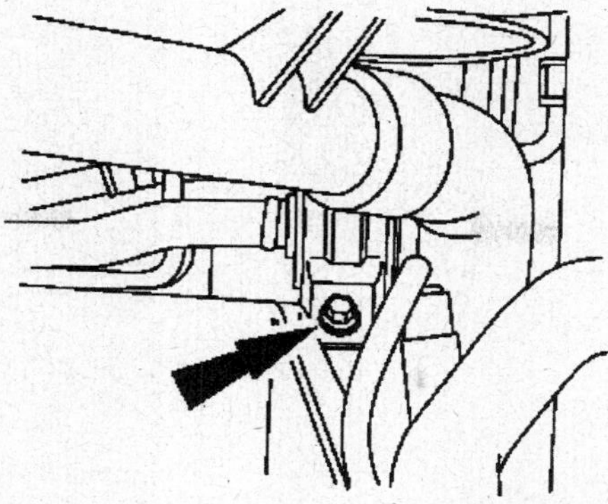

Fig. 11 Stabilizer bracket bolt removal

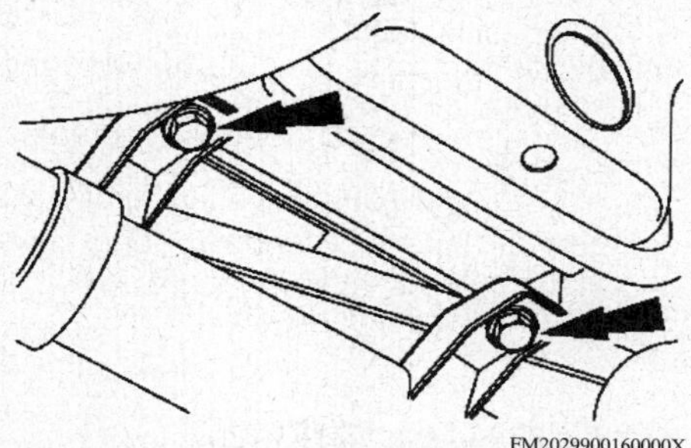

Fig. 13 Coolant tube bolt location

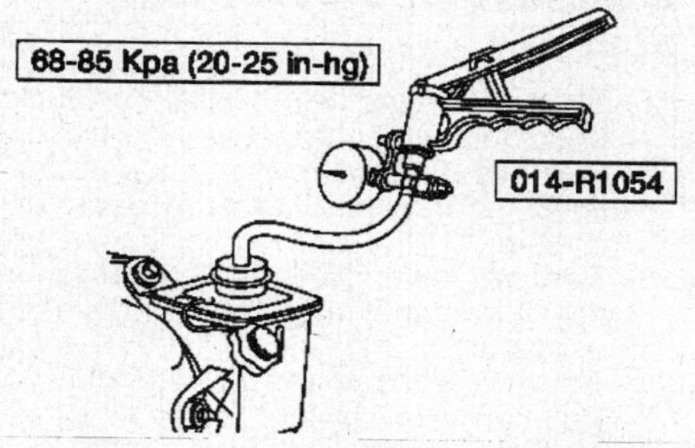

Fig. 16 Power steering vacuum bleed

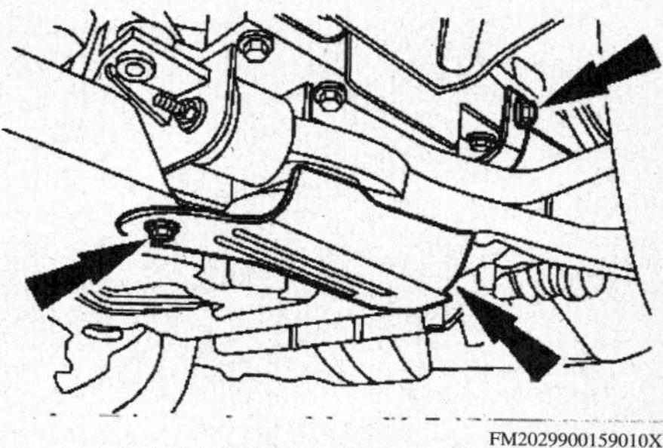

Fig. 12 Power steering pump shield (Part 1 of 2)

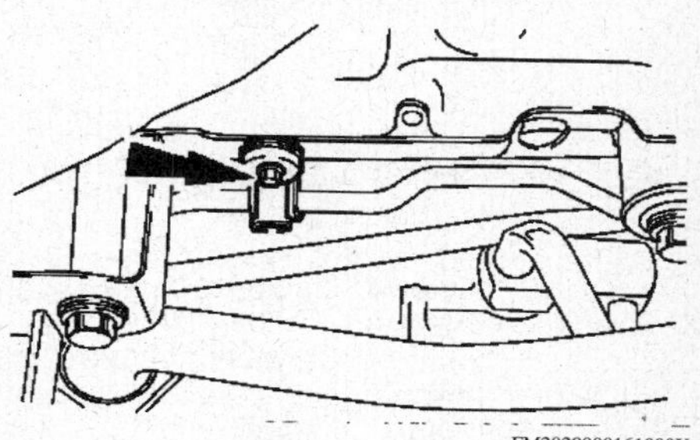

Fig. 14 Power steering line bracket

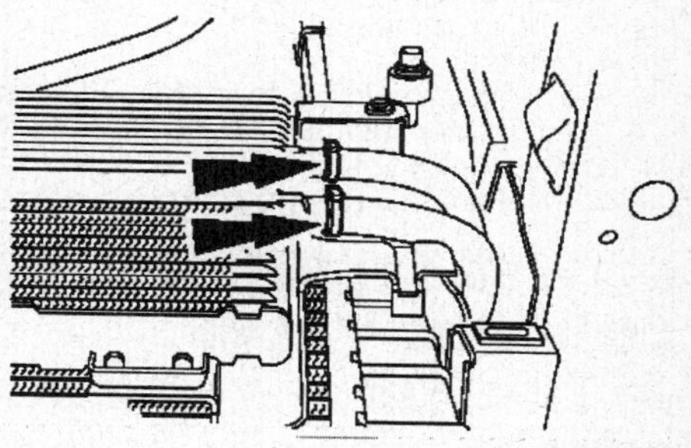

Fig. 17 Power steering fluid cooler

3.9L ENGINE

1. Remove engine appearance cover.
2. Remove air cleaner and outlet tube.
3. Remove coolant tube attaching bolts, **Fig. 13.**
4. Remove accessory drive belt.
5. Disconnect power steering reservoir to pump hose and drain fluid into suitable container.
6. Remove power steering reservoir attaching bolts and position reservoir aside.
7. Raise and support vehicle, then remove front wheels.
8. Remove power steering pump shields, **Fig. 12.**
9. Remove pump line bracket bolt, **Fig. 14.**
10. Disconnect power steering pump electrical connector and wire retainer.
11. Remove A/C compressor attaching bolts and position compressor aside.
12. Disconnect power steering pressure hose from pump.
13. Remove pump attaching bolts, **Fig. 15.**
14. Lower vehicle, then remove remaining pump attaching bolts and pump.
15. Reverse procedure to install, noting the following:
    a. Install new O-ring seals to power steering lines using teflon seal replacer set tool No. D90P-3517-A, or equivalent.
    b. Upper bolts should only be tightened after lower bolts are installed.

POWER STEERING SYSTEM BLEED

1. Ensure power steering reservoir is filled to proper level.
2. Install vacuum tester tool No. 014-R1054, or equivalent, to reservoir, **Fig. 16.**
3. Start and run engine at idle speed.
4. Apply maximum vacuum for at least three minutes. Maintain vacuum with vacuum pump.
5. Remove vacuum tester.
6. Add Motorcraft Mercon multi-purpose ATF transmission fluid XT–2–QDX, or equivalent, fluid to bring reservoir to proper level.
7. Attach vacuum tester to reservoir and apply maximum vacuum. Cycle steering wheel from stop to stop every 30 seconds for 5 minutes. **Do not hold steering wheel against stops for more than 5 seconds.**
8. Remove vacuum tester and install reservoir cap.
9. Ensure fluid is at proper level and inspect system for leaks.
10. Repeat procedure as necessary.

POWER STEERING FLUID COOLER

REPLACE

1. Recover refrigerant as outlined under "Air Conditioning."
2. Remove right, left and center splash shields.
3. **On models equipped with 3.9L engine,** disconnect air intake tube and position aside.

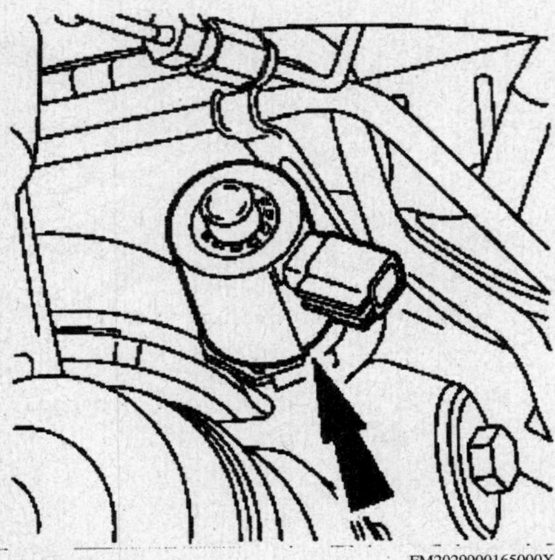

Fig. 18 Power steering control valve actuator

4. **On all models,** disconnect A/C lines from condenser.
5. Support condenser, then remove condenser attaching bolts and condenser.
6. Remove and discard fluid cooler clamps, **Fig. 17.**
7. Disconnect fluid cooler hoses and drain into a suitable container.
8. Remove cooler attaching bolts, then the cooler.
9. Reverse procedure to install. Tighten fluid cooler clamps using CV boot clamp tool No. T95P-3514-A, or equivalent. Refill and purge air from system.

POWER STEERING CONTROL VALVE ACTUATOR

REPLACE

1. Raise and support vehicle.
2. Disconnect steering control valve electrical connector.

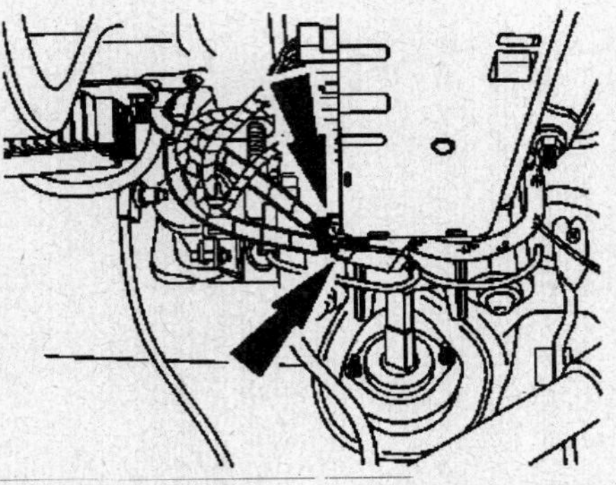

Fig. 19 Steering wheel rotation sensor removal (Part 1 of 2)

3. Remove power steering hose bracket and position aside.
4. Disconnect and plug power steering hoses.
5. Remove control valve actuator, **Fig. 18.**
6. Reverse procedure to install. Install new O-rings to power steering lines using teflon seal replacer set tool No. D90P-3517-A, or equivalent.

STEERING WHEEL ROTATION SENSOR

REPLACE

1. Ensure wheels are in straight ahead position, then center steering wheel.
2. Remove driver air bag module as outlined in "Passive Restraint Systems" chapter.
3. Remove lower steering column opening finish panel, then the hood release assembly.
4. Remove lefthand lower heater duct.
5. Pull carpet away from console tunnel and remove bracket bolts.

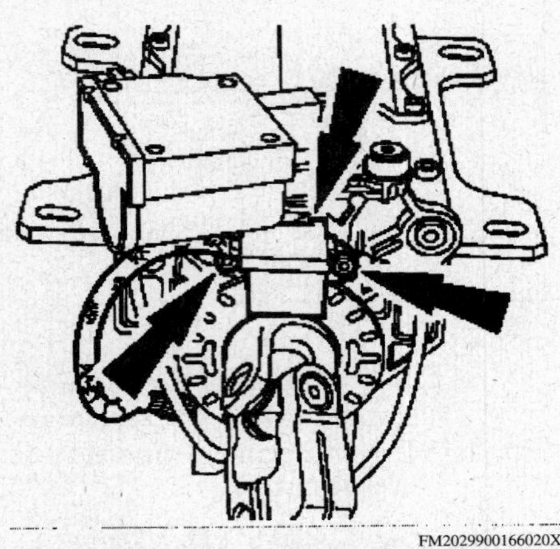

Fig. 19 Steering wheel rotation sensor removal (Part 2 of 2)

6. Remove steering column opening reinforcement.
7. Disconnect steering wheel rotation sensor, then the electric tilt/telescoping motor electrical connectors.
8. Disconnect lower steering column electrical connectors.
9. Secure steering column shaft and steering column using suitable mechanics wire. **Ensure steering column and shaft do not rotate.**
10. Remove and discard steering column shaft pinch bolt and disconnect shaft.
11. Support steering column, then remove and discard column locknuts.
12. Lower steering column, then remove sensor attaching screws and sensor, **Fig. 19.**
13. Reverse procedure to install. Install new steering column locknuts and pinch bolt.

TIGHTENING SPECIFICATIONS

Year	Component	Torque, Ft. Lbs.
2000–02	A/C Compressor	18
	Control Valve Actuator	22
	Engine Control Wiring Bracket	44①
	Heater Water Valve Bracket	44①
	Hub & Bearing To Knuckle	66
	Intermediate Shaft Bolt	18
	Intermediate Shaft To Gear Pinch Bolt	26
	Lower Arm To Frame	129
	Lower Arm To Knuckle	111
	Power Steering Cooler To Radiator	89①
	Power Steering Hose Brackets	89①
	Power Steering Pressure Hose	23
	Power Steering Return Hose To Gear	23
	Power Steering Pump	18
	Power Steering Reservoir Lower Bolt	9
	Power Steering Reservoir Upper Bolt	53①
	Radiator Tube To Engine	89①
	Stabilizer Bar Bracket	41
	Stabilizer Bar Link	41
	Steering Column Lock Nuts	30
	Steering Column Opening Reinforcement Bolts	15
	Steering Column Shaft To Intermediate Shaft Pinch Bolt	26
	Steering Gear Lock Nuts	76
	Steering Sensor Mounting Bolts	27①
	Strut To Body	21
	Strut To Lower Arm	129
	Tie Rod End To Knuckle	74
	Upper Control Arm To Body	35
	Upper Control Arm To Knuckle	66
	Upper Strut Rod To Upper Mount	37
	Wheel Lug Nuts	100

① — Inch lbs.

Wheel Alignment

INDEX

PRELIMINARY INSPECTION

1. Inspect all suspension and steering components for looseness and wear and correct as necessary.
2. Inspect tires for similar tread and proper air pressure.
3. Ensure vehicle ride height is within specifications.

FRONT WHEEL ALIGNMENT

CASTER & CAMBER

If vehicle is equipped with hex head bolts in lower control arm, new cam bolts and lock nuts must be installed before adjusting suspension. If new bolts are to be installed, refer to "Control Arm, Replace" under "Front Suspension & Steering."

1. In order to turn camber and caster cams, loosen lower control arm attaching nuts, **Figs. 1 and 2.**
2. Rotate caster adjustment bolt until caster is within specifications.
3. Rotate camber adjustment bolt while supporting lower control arm by hand until camber is within specifications. Adjustments to camber may affect toe setting. Toe and camber may need to be adjusted at the same time. Refer to "Toe" to adjust toe settings.
4. Tighten lower control arms to specifications and recheck alignment. Readjust as necessary.

TOE

1. Start engine and center steering wheel.

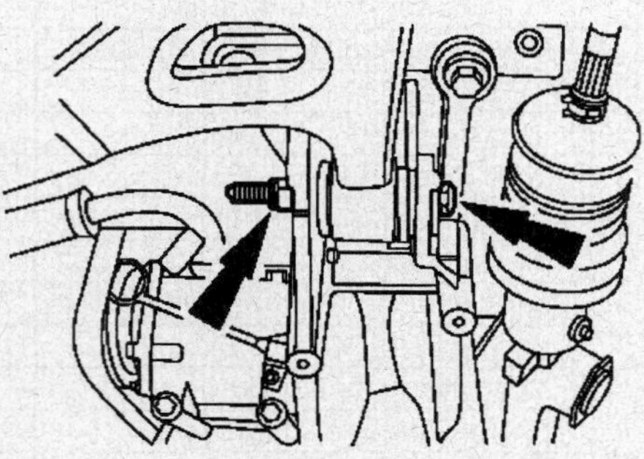

Fig. 1 Camber adjustment bolt

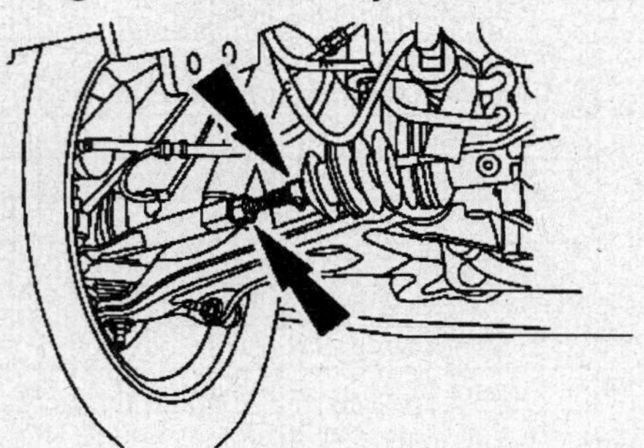

Fig. 3 Tie rod adjustment

2. Turn engine off and hold steering wheel in straight ahead position by attaching a rigid link from steering wheel to brake pedal.
3. Remove tie rod boot clamps, then loosen jam nuts, **Fig. 3.**
4. Clean and lubricate nuts and tie rod threads.
5. Rotate inner tie rod link to adjust to. Do not allow bellows to twist when tie rod is rotated.
6. Ensure toe is within specifications and tighten jam nuts.
7. Recheck alignment settings and adjust as necessary.

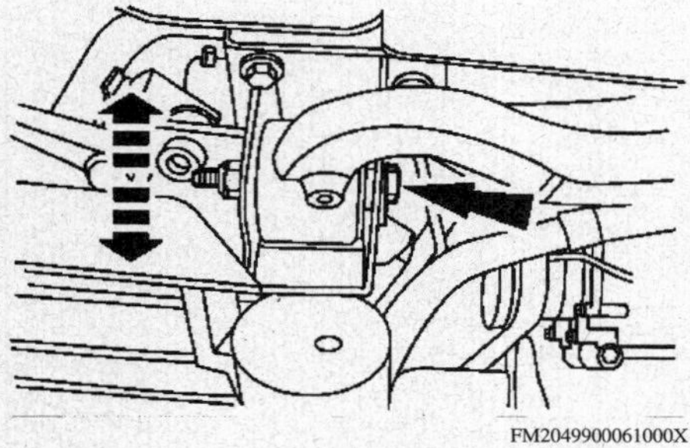

Fig. 2 Caster adjustment bolt

REAR WHEEL ALIGNMENT

CASTER & CAMBER

Caster and camber are not adjustable on the rear suspension.

TOE

1. Clean toe link threads and nut.
2. Loosen toe link jam nut and turn toe link until alignment is within specifications.
3. Tighten jam nut.
4. Ensure alignment is within specifications.

MUSTANG

NOTE: Refer To The Rear Of This Manual For Vehicle Manufacturer's Special Service Tool Suppliers.

INDEX OF SERVICE OPERATIONS

MUSTANG

Specifications

GENERAL ENGINE SPECIFICATIONS

Year	Engine Liter (VIN)①	Fuel System	Bore & Stroke	Compression Ratio	Net H.P. @ RPM②	Maximum Torque Ft. Lbs. @ RPM	Normal Oil Pressure, psi
1998	3.8L (4)	SEFI	3.81 × 3.39	9.0	150 @ 4000	215 @ 2750	40–60③
	4.6L DOHC (V)	SEFI	3.55 × 3.54	9.5	305 @ 5800	300 @ 4800	20–45④
	4.6L OHV (X)	SEFI	3.55 × 3.54	9.0	225 @ 4750	290 @ 3500	20–45④
1999	3.8L (4)	SEFI	3.81 × 3.39	9.4	190 @ 5250	220 @ 2750	40–125③
	4.6L (V) DOHC	SEFI	3.81 × 3.39	9.0	260 @ 5250	300 @ 4000	20–45④
	4.6L (X) SOHC	SEFI	3.55 × 3.54	9.1	250 @ 4750	290 @ 3500	20–45④
2000–01	3.8L (4)	SEFI	3.81 × 3.39	9.4	190 @ 5250	220 @ 2750	40–125③
	4.6L (V) DOHC	SEFI	3.55 × 3.54	9.0	260 @ 5250	302 @ 4000	20–45④
	4.6L (X) SOHC	SEFI	3.55 × 3.54	9.9	320 @ 6000	317 @ 4750	20–45④
2002	3.8L (4)	SEFI	3.81 × 3.39	9.4	193 @ 5500	225 @ 2800	40–125③
	4.6L (V) DOHC	SEFI	3.55 × 3.54	9.0	260 @ 5250	302 @ 4000	20–45④
	4.6L (X) SOHC	SEFI	3.55 × 3.54	9.9	320 @ 6000	317 @ 4750	20–45④

DOHC — Double overhead cams, four valves per cylinder.
SEFI — Sequential Multi-Port Electronic Fuel Injection.
SOHC — Single overhead cam, two valves per cylinder.
OHV — Overhead valve, two valves per cylinder.
① — Eighth digit denotes engine code.
② — Net rating as installed in-vehicle.
③ — Engine hot @ 2500 RPM.
④ — Engine hot @ 1500 RPM.

TUNE UP SPECIFICATIONS

Year & Engine	Spark Plug Gap	Ignition Timing BTDC				Curb Idle Speed		Fast Idle Speed		Fuel Pump Pressure, psi	Valve Lash, Inch
		Firing Order Fig.	Man. Trans.	Auto. Trans.	Mark Fig.	Man. Trans.	Auto Trans.	Man. Trans.	Auto. Trans.		
1998											
3.8L	.054	A②	10⑥	10⑥	⑦	⑤	⑤	⑤	⑤	30–45①	④
4.6L	.054	③	10⑥	10⑥	⑦	⑤	⑤	⑤	⑤	30–45①	④
1999–2002											
3.8L	.054	A②	10⑥	10⑥	⑦	⑤	⑤	⑤	⑤	30–50①	④
4.6L	.054	③	10⑥	10⑥	⑦	⑤	⑤	⑤	⑤	30–50①	④

BTDC — Before Top Dead Center

① — Wrap shop towel around fitting to prevent fuel spillage, then connect suitable fuel pressure gauge to fuel diagnostic valve on fuel rail assembly. Gradually open fuel pressure gauge test valve to relieve fuel system pressure & drain fuel into suitable container. Close fuel pressure gauge test valve. Turn ignition On. Access output test mode on scan tool & operate fuel pump to obtain maximum fuel pressure. Fuel pump will operate for approximately 8 seconds. Inspect fuel pressure gauge reading.

② — Cylinder numbering front to rear, righthand bank, 1, 2, 3 ; lefthand bank, 4, 5, 6. Firing order 1-4-2-5-3-6.

③ — Cylinder numbering front to rear: righthand bank 1, 2, 3, 4; lefthand bank 5, 6, 7, 8. Firing order 1-3-7-2-6-5-4-8. Refer to **Fig. B** for ignition coil tower terminal numbering.

④ — Equipped w/hydraulic valve tappets.

⑤ — Idle speed controlled by an automatic idle speed control.

⑥ — Non-adjustable. Do not attempt to inspect base timing. False readings will be received.

⑦ — Equipped w/crankshaft position sensor.

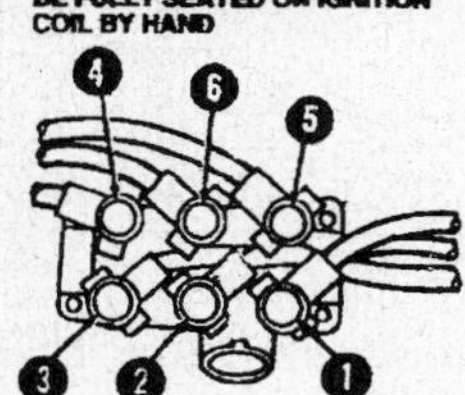

Fig. A

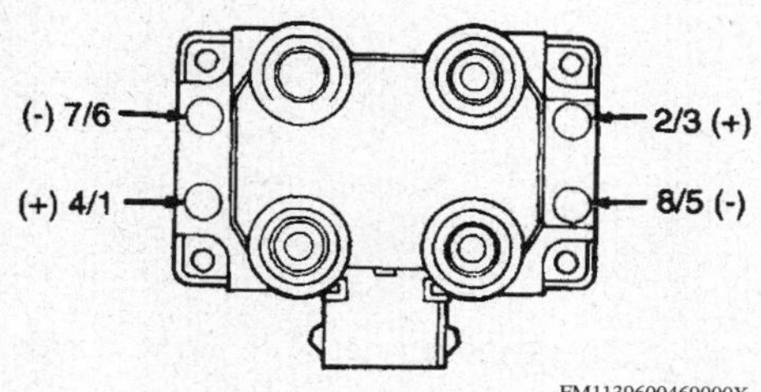

Fig. B

FRONT WHEEL ALIGNMENT SPECIFICATIONS

Caster Angle, Degrees①		Camber Angle, Degrees		Total Toe, Degrees②		Toe Out On Turns, Degrees	
Limits	Desired	Limits	Desired	Limits	Desired	Outer Wheel	Inner Wheel
1998							
+2.45 to +3.95	+3.2	–1.35 to +0.15	–.6	0 to +0.50	+0.25	19.84	20
1999–2001							
+2.45 to +3.95	+3.2	–1.25 to +0.25	–.5	0 to +0.50	+0.25	—	—
2002							
+2.45 to +3.95	+3.2	–1.00 to -0.20	–.6	+0.10 to +0.40	+0.25	—	—

① — Difference side to side, lefthand minus righthand should not exceed 0.75°.

② — Toe-In (+). Toe-Out (–).

REAR WHEEL ALIGNMENT SPECIFICATIONS

Model	Caster Angle, Degrees	Camber Angle, Degrees		Toe-In, Degrees	
		Limits	Desired	Limits	Desired
1999–2001 Cobra	—	-0.9 to -0.5	-0.7	+0.1 to +0.40	+0.25

VEHICLE RIDE HEIGHT SPECIFICATIONS

Model	Year	Body Style	Manu-facturer's Original Tire Size	Measurement Points & Specifications②					
				Front③			Rear③		
				Dim.	Specification Inches	Specification mm	Dim.	Specification Inches	Specification mm
Mustang	1998	Coupe Base	①	L	10.18	258	M	14.09	357
		Coupe GT	①	L	10.18	258	M	14.18	360
		Convertible	①	L	10.18	258	M	14.09	357
		Convertible GT	①	L	10.09	256	M	14.09	357
	1999–2001	Base & GT	①	1	0.2	4	2	5.00	128
		Cobra	①	1	0.2	4	1	1.40	36
	2002	Base & GT	①	1	0.2	4	2	5.00	128

E Dim. — Ground to Front Wheel Opening Through Centerline of Wheel

G Dim. — Ground to Rear Wheel Opening Through Centerline of Wheel

L Dim. — Ground to Bottom of Front Bumper

M Dim. — Ground to Bottom of Rear Bumper

1 Dim. — Front suspension: Height from ground to center of lower control arm mounting bolt minus height from ground to bottom of steering knuckle.

1 Dim. —Rear suspension: Height from ground to center of lower control arm mounting bolt minus height from ground to center of steering knuckle lower mounting bolt.

2 Dim. —Rear axle arch center to body reinforcement at closest point.

Dim. — Dimension

N/A — Not Available

① — See door sticker or inside of glove compartment for manufacturer's original tire size specifications. If tires on vehicle do not match manufacturer's original tire size & measurement is not within limits, it will be necessary to refer to the "Non-Standard Tire & Wheel Size Adjustment To Ride Height Specification & Tire Size Adjustment Charts" in the front of this manual for approximate changes in ride height specifications.

② — Measurement is with fuel, radiator coolant and engine oil full, spare tire, jack, hand tools and mats in designated positions and tires properly inflated.

③ — Ride height side to side should be within 0.50″ (13 mm). Ride height front to rear should be with in 0.75″ (19 mm).

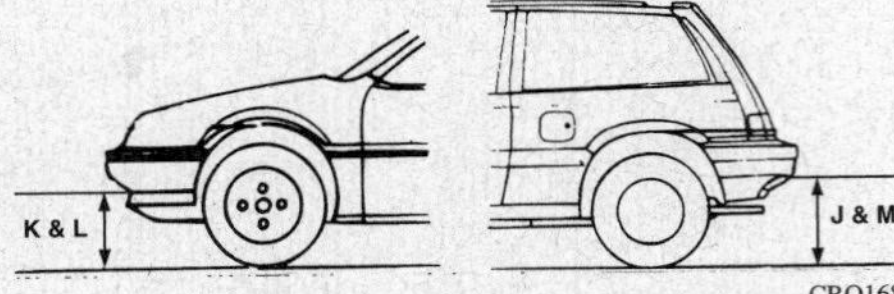

Dimensions J, K, L & M. 1998

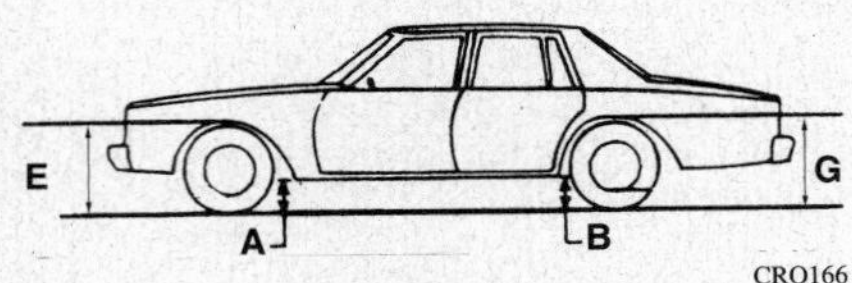

Dimensions A, B, E & G. 1998

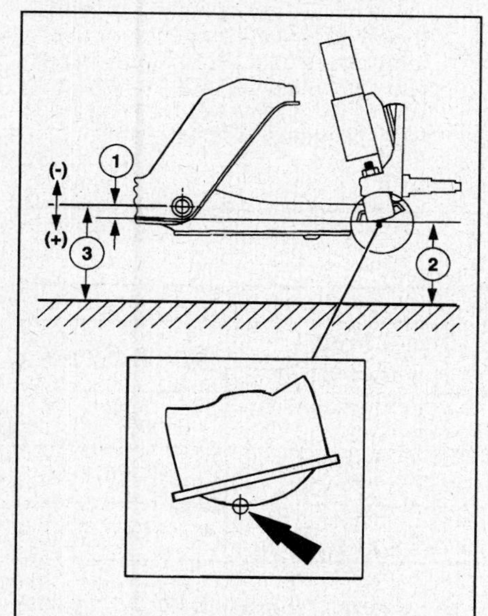

Item	Description
1	Ride height = B - A
2	Measurement A
3	Measurement B

FM2020100207000X

Front ride height. 1999–2002

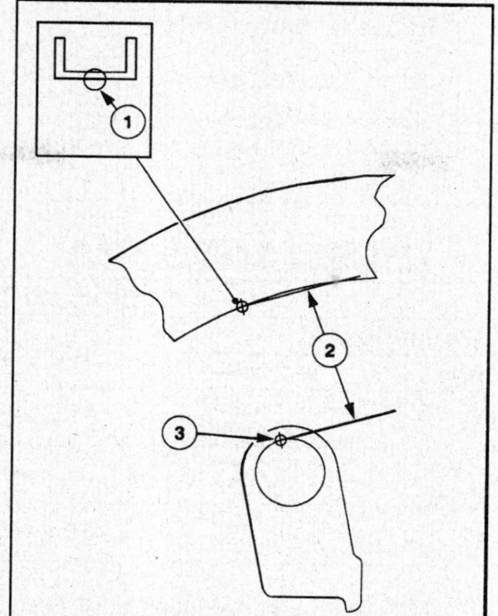

Item	Description
1	Body reinforcement
2	Ride height (shortest distance)
3	Rear axle

FM2030100158000X

Rear ride height. 1999–2002 base & GT

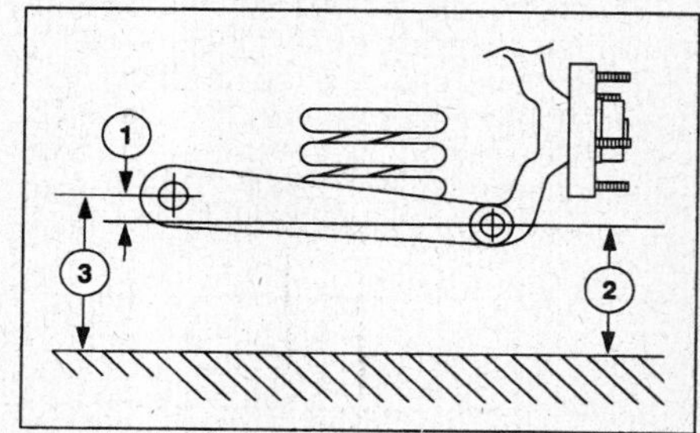

Item	Description
1	Ride height = B - A
2	Measurement A
3	Measurement B

FM2030100159000X

Rear ride height. 1999–2001 Cobra

FLUID CAPACITIES & COOLING SYSTEM DATA

Year	Engine (VIN①)	Cooling Capacity, Qts.		Coolant Type	Radiator Cap Relief Pressure, Lbs.	Thermo. Opening Temp. Deg. F	Fuel Tank Gals.	Engine Oil Refill Qts.⑦	Transmission Oil		Rear Axle Oil Pints
		Less A/C	With A/C						Man. Trans. Pints	Auto. Trans. Qts.③	
1998	3.8L (4)	11.8	11.8	⑨	16	192–199④	15.7	5	5.6	13.9	3.50
	4.6L (V)	14.1	14.1	⑨	16	188–196④	15.7	6②	6.4–6.7	12.8	3.75⑧
	4.6L (X)	14.1	14.1	⑨	16	188–196④	15.7	⑤	6.4–6.7	12.8	3.75⑧
1999	3.8L (4)	19.2	19.2	⑩	16	192–199④	15.7	5	5.6	13.9	⑥
	4.6L (V)	19.2	19.2	⑩	16	189–196④	15.7	6②	6.6	12.8	3.00⑧
	4.6L (X)	19.2	19.2	⑩	16	189–196④	15.7	5②	6.6	12.8	3.75⑧
2000	3.8L (4)	19.2	19.2	⑩	16	192–199④	15.7	5	5.6	13.9	⑥
	4.6L (V)	19.2	19.2	⑩	16	189–196④	15.7	6②	6.6	12.8	2.60–2.90⑧
	4.6L (X)	19.2	19.2	⑩	16	189–196④	15.7	5②	6.6	12.8	3.75⑧
2001	3.8L (4)	19.2	19.2	⑩	16	192–199④	15.7	5	5.6	13.9	3.25–3.50
	4.6L (V)	19.2	19.2	⑩	16	189–196④	15.7	6②	6.6	12.8	2.60–2.90⑧
	4.6L (X)	19.2	19.2	⑩	16	189–196④	15.7	5②	7.5	12.8	3.50–3.75⑧
2002	3.8L (4)	11.8	11.8	⑩	16	192–199④	15.7	5	5.6	13.9	3.25–3.50
	4.6L (V)	—	—	—	—	—	—	—	—	—	—
	4.6L (X)	14.1	14.1	⑩	16	189–196④	15.7	5②	7.5	12.8	3.50–3.75⑧

① — Eighth digit of Vehicle Identification Number (VIN) denotes engine code.

② — ±0.25 qts.

③ — Approximate. Make final inspection w/dipstick.

④ — Fully open at 219°F.

⑤ — With oil cooler 6.675 qts. ± 0.125 qts.; less oil cooler 6.425 ± 0.125 qts.

⑥ — With 3.25:1 ratio, 6.9 pts; w/3.50:1 ratio, 7.4 pts.

⑦ — Includes filter.

⑧ — Models equipped with Traction-Lok axle, add 4 ounces of additive friction modifier.

⑨ — Always fill cooling system with same coolant that is present in the system. Do not mix coolant types. For models w/green coolant use ethylene glycol, Premium Engine Coolant Fluid VC-4-A (in Oregon VC-5), or equivalent meeting Ford specifications ESE-M97B44-A. For models w/orange coolant use Dex-Cool or Extended Life Engine Coolant F6AZ-19544-AA, or equivalent meeting Ford specifications WSS-M97B44-D.

⑩ — Always fill cooling system with same coolant that is present in the system. Do not mix coolant types. For models w/green coolant use ethylene glycol, Premium Engine Coolant Fluid VC-4-A (in Oregon VC-5), or equivalent meeting Ford specifications ESE-M97B44-A.

LUBRICANT DATA

Year	Model	Lubricant Type				
		Transmission		Rear Axle	Power Steering	Brake System
		Automatic	Manual			
1998–2000	All	Mercon V	Mercon ATF XT-2-QDX	80W-90①②	Mercon ATF XT-2-QDX	DOT 3
2001–02	3.8L Engine	Mercon V	Mercon ATF XT-2-QDX	80W-90①	Mercon ATF XT-2-QDX	DOT 3
	4.6L Engines	Mercon V	Mercon ATF XT-2-QDX	75W-140②	Mercon ATF XT-2-QDX	DOT 3

① — Thermally Stable Rear Axle Lubricant XY-80W90-QL.

② — On models equipped w/Traction-Lok axle, add 4 ounces of friction modifier C8AZ-19B546-A, or equivalent meeting Ford specification EST-M2C118-A.

Electrical

NOTE: On Air Bag Equipped Models, Refer To "Air Bag System Precautions" Located In The Front Of This Manual For System Disarming & Arming Procedures.

NOTE: Refer To "Computer Relearn Procedures" Located In The Front Of This Manual When Battery Power To The Computer Has Been Interrupted.

NOTE: Prior To Performing Any Service Operations Listed In This Section, Consult The "Technical Service Bulletins" Section For Related Information.

INDEX

PRECAUTIONS

AIR BAG SYSTEMS

Refer to "Air Bag System Precautions" in front of this manual for system disarming and arming procedures.

BATTERY GROUND CABLE

Prior to service, disconnect battery ground cable and isolate as required.

FUSE PANEL & FLASHER LOCATION

1998

The fuse panel is located on lefthand side of steering column, under instrument panel.

A power distribution center containing engine fuses and relays for horn, starter and fog lamps is located on lefthand side of engine compartment, behind radiator.

The combination turn signal and emergency warning indicator flasher is attached by a bracket to lower lefthand instrument panel reinforcement, above fuse holder.

1999–2002

The fuse panel is located below and to the left of the steering column near the brake pedal. To access these fuses, remove the panel cover.

There is also a power distribution and relay box located in the engine compartment, adjacent to the battery.

RELAY CENTER LOCATION

1998

The relay panel is located in the righthand front corner of the engine compartment, mounted to the upper radiator support.

1999–2002

A relay and power distribution box is located under the hood. Ensure its cover is intact when filling fluid reservoirs or servicing the battery.

FUEL PUMP RELAY LOCATION

1998

The fuel pump relay is part of the Constant Control Relay Module (CCRM), located on a bracket behind the engine coolant reservoir.

1999–2002

The fuel pump relay is located in the underhood relay and power distribution box.

STARTER

REPLACE

1998

1. Raise and support front of vehicle.
2. Disconnect S-terminal connector. **Pull on connector only.**
3. Disconnect starter cable from starter.
4. Remove mounting bolts and starter motor.
5. Reverse procedure to install, noting the following:
   a. **Torque** starter bolts to 15–19 ft. lbs.
   b. **Torque** starter cable nut to 84–108 inch lbs.

1999–2002

1. Raise and safely support vehicle.
2. **On models equipped with 3.8L engine,** remove ground cable nut.
3. **On all models,** remove solenoid protective cap and wiring nuts. Position wiring aside.
4. Remove mounting bolts and starter motor.
5. Reverse procedure to install, noting the following:
   a. **Torque** starter mounting bolts to 17 ft. lbs.
   b. **Torque** solenoid B-terminal nut to 108 inch lbs.
   c. **Torque** solenoid terminal nut to 53 inch lbs.
   d. **On models equipped with 3.8L engine, torque** ground cable nut to 17 ft. lbs.
   e. **On models equipped with 4.6L engine, torque** HO2S bracket nut to 18 ft. lbs.

ALTERNATOR

REPLACE

1998

1. Disconnect alternator and voltage regulator wire harness attachments.
2. Disconnect alternator drive belt from pulley.
3. **On models equipped with 4.6L engine,** remove mounting bolts and alternator mounting bracket.
4. **On all models,** remove mounting bolts and alternator.
5. Reverse procedures to install noting the following:
   a. **On models equipped with 4.6L engine, torque** mounting bolts 15–22 ft. lbs.

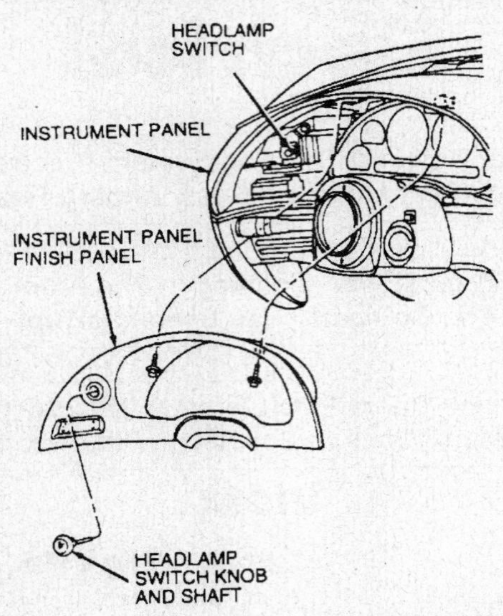

Fig. 1 Headlamp switch replacement. 1998

   b. **On models equipped with 3.8L engine, torque** upper bolt 16–21 ft. lbs. and lower bolt 30–40 ft. lbs.
   c. **On all models, torque** output terminal nut 60–84 inch. lbs.

1999–2002

1. Remove serpentine drive belt from alternator pulley. Leave belt in place to ease installation.
2. **On models equipped with 4.6L SOHC engine,** remove mounting bolts and alternator upper bracket, then disconnect alternator electrical connector by pressing tab. **Do not pull on tab.**
3. **On all models,** disconnect alternator electrical connections.
4. Remove mounting bolts and alternator.
5. Reverse procedure to install, noting the following:
   a. **On models equipped with 3.8L engine, torque** alternator lower mounting bolt to 35 ft. lbs. and upper bolt to 18 ft. lbs.
   b. **On models equipped with 4.6L engines, torque** alternator lower mounting bolts to 18 ft. lbs. and upper bolts to 89 inch lbs.
   c. **On all models, torque** battery positive cable nut to solenoid to 72 inch lbs.

IGNITION COIL PACK

REPLACE

1998

1. Disconnect fuel charging wiring connectors and radio ignition interference capacitor.
2. Release boot retainers by squeezing locking tabs.
3. Remove ignition wires by twisting while pulling.
4. Remove mounting screws and coil.
5. Reverse procedure to install. **Torque** mounting screws to 44–61 inch lbs.

1999–2002

3.8L ENGINE

1. Disconnect electrical connectors, as required.
2. Tag spark plug wires, squeeze locking tabs and disconnect. Position wires aside.
3. Record radio ignition interference capacitor location.
4. Remove mounting bolts and coil.
5. Reverse procedure to install, noting the following:
   a. Ensure radio ignition interference capacitor is located under proper coil mounting bolt.
   b. **Torque** coil mounting bolts to 53 inch lbs.
   c. Apply silicone brake caliper grease and dielectric compound No. D7AZ-19A331-A, or equivalent, to inside of each wire coil boot.

4.6L ENGINE

On these engines, the ignition coil is located on the spark plug.

1. Remove the air cleaner outlet tube.
2. Disconnect the ignition coil.
3. Remove mounting bolt and ignition coil.
4. Remove remaining ignition coils, as required.
5. Reverse procedure to install, noting the following:
   a. Ensure ignition coil spring is correctly located inside boot and tip is not damaged.
   b. **Torque** mounting bolts to 89 inch lbs.

IGNITION LOCK

REPLACE

FUNCTIONING

1. Turn ignition to switch to Run position.
2. Remove ignition switch by depressing retaining pin with suitable drift punch in hole in upper steering column shroud under switch.
3. Reverse procedure to install. Ensure lock cylinder operates properly.

NON-FUNCTIONING

1. Remove steering wheel as outlined under "Steering Wheel, Replace."
2. Twist ignition switch lock cylinder cap with suitable locking-type pliers until it separates from ignition switch lock cylinder.
3. Center punch retaining pin with suitable small pilot punch through access hole in lower steering column shroud, then drill it out with 1/8 inch diameter drill.
4. Drill down middle of key slot using 3/8 inch diameter bit approximately 1 3/4 inches until lock cylinder breaks loose.
5. Remove ignition switch lock cylinder.
6. Record positions of column lock gear, bearing and retainer.
7. Remove bearing retainer, steering column lock housing bearing, ignition switch lock cylinder and steering column lock gear.

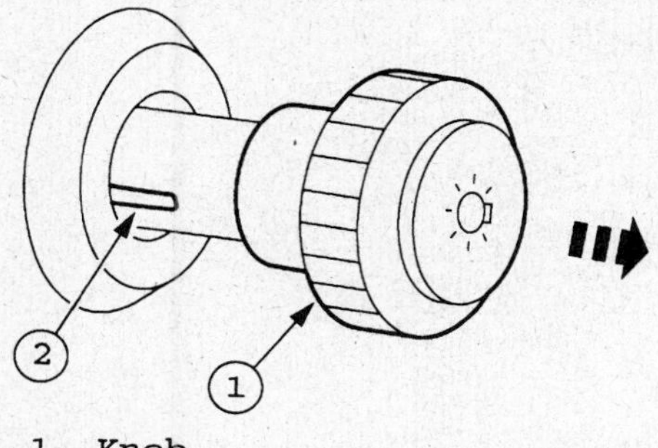

Fig. 2 Headlamp switch knob replacement. 1999–2002

8. Reverse procedures to install, noting the following:
   a. Repair steering column lock cylinder housing, as required.
   b. Ensure components are properly aligned and oriented.
   c. Coat lock gear and housing with ignition lock grease No. F0AZ-19584-A, or equivalent.

BRAKE PEDAL ARM (BRAKES NOT APPLIED)

PEDAL MOVEMENT AS BRAKES ARE APPLIED

Item	Description
1	Master Cylinder Push Rod
2	Brake Pedal Arm Pin
3	Stoplight Switch
4	Stoplight Switch Actuating Pin
5	Stoplight Switch Contacts
6	Stoplight Switch Spring
7	Stoplight Switch Pressure Plate
8	Plastic Bushing
9	Push Rod Eye

FM9049400043000X

Fig. 3 Stop lamp switch replacement. 1998

IGNITION SWITCH

REPLACE

1998

1. Disconnect ignition switch electrical connector.
2. Ensure ignition switch lock cylinder is in Run position.
3. Remove two ignition switch mounting screws and disconnect it from actuator pin.
4. Reverse procedure to install, noting the following:
   a. Adjust ignition switch by sliding carrier to switch Run position. **Replacement ignition switch should already be set in Run position.**
   b. **Torque** mounting screws to 60–84 inch lbs.

1999–2002

1. Remove mounting screws and steering column lower cover.
2. Remove mounting screws and instrument panel reinforcement.
3. Loosen mounting bolt and disconnect ignition switch electrical connector.
4. Ensure ignition switch is in Off position.
5. Remove mounting screws and ignition switch.
6. Reverse procedure to install, noting the following:
   a. **Torque** ignition switch mounting screws to 53 inch lbs.
   b. **Torque** instrument panel reinforcement mounting screws to 80 inch lbs.
   c. **Torque** steering column lower cover mounting screws to 80 inch lbs.

CLUTCH START SWITCH

REPLACE

1998

1. Disconnect clutch pedal position switch harness connector.
2. Disconnect locating tab lock and rotate switch approximately 90° clockwise.
3. Remove switch lock plate and pry switch off clutch pushrod by hand.
4. Reverse procedure to install. An audible click will be heard when clutch pedal position switch is mounted properly.

1999–2002

1. Disconnect clutch pedal position switch electrical connector.
2. Record switch's positioning.
3. Remove mounting bolt and switch.
4. Reverse procedure to install. Tighten mounting bolt securely and inspect for proper operation.

NEUTRAL SAFETY SWITCH

REPLACE

1998

1. Place manual control lever in Neutral position.
2. Raise and support vehicle.
3. Disconnect Transmission Range (TR) sensor electrical harness.
4. Remove two mounting bolts and TR sensor.
5. Reverse procedure to install, noting the following:
   a. Ensure manual control lever is in Neutral position.
   b. Align TR sensor slots using transmission range sensor alignment (MLPS alignment) tool No. T92P-70010-AH, or equivalent.
   c. **Torque** sensor bolts to 84–108 inch lbs.
   d. Ensure engine starts in Park or Neutral, only.

1999–2002

On these models the neutral safety switch is incorporated into the digital Transmission Range (TR) sensor.

1. Apply parking brake and place transmission in Neutral position.
2. Raise and safely support vehicle.
3. Disconnect TR sensor electrical connector.
4. Disconnect range selector cable.
5. Remove mounting bolts and TR sensor.
6. Reverse procedure to install, noting the following:
   a. Ensure shift lever shaft is in Neutral position.
   b. Align sensor slots using TR sensor alignment tool No. T97L-70010-A, or equivalent.
   c. **Torque** sensor mounting bolts to 62–89 inch lbs.
   d. Ensure starter cranks in Park or Neutral position, only.

HEADLAMP SWITCH

REPLACE

1998

1. Pull headlamp switch to full On position.

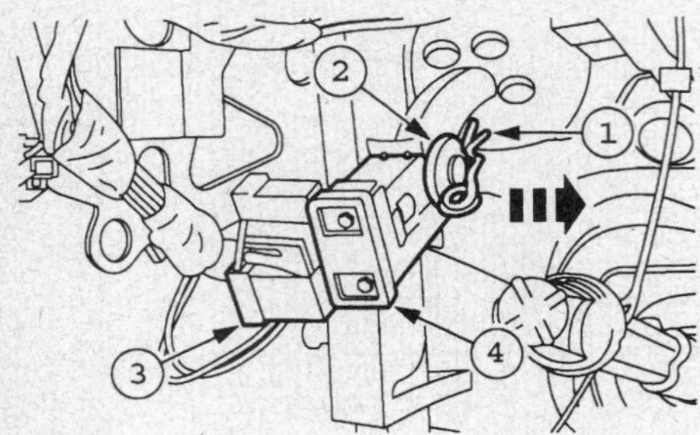

1. Linkage Clip
2. Retainer
3. Connector
4. Switch

FM9019900385000X

Fig. 4 Stop lamp switch replacement. 1999–2002

2. Depress shaft release button on headlamp switch by reaching through instrument panel opening , then remove headlamp switch knob and shaft, **Fig. 1.**
3. Remove two screws above instrument cluster, then pull instrument panel finish panel to unsnap clip above lefthand register.
4. Pull cluster to unsnap three clips on righthand side vertical/horizontal edge and remove panel.
5. Remove nut and pull headlamp switch through instrument cluster opening.
6. Disconnect wiring and remove headlamp switch.
7. Reverse procedure to install.

1999–2002

1. Pull headlamp switch to full On position.
2. Pull and remove knob by inserting suitable thin tool into slot, **Fig. 2.**
3. Remove mounting screws and instrument cluster finish retaining panel.
4. Remove mounting screws and headlamp switch.
5. Disconnect headlamp switch electrical connector.
6. Reverse procedure to install.

STOP LIGHT SWITCH

REPLACE

1998

REMOVAL

1. Disconnect wires at connector.
2. Remove hairpin retainer, then slide switch, pushrod and nylon washers and bushing away from pedal, **Fig. 3.**
3. Remove switch

INSTALLATION

1. Position stop lamp switch so U-shaped side is nearest brake pedal and directly over/under pin.
2. Slide stop lamp switch up/down, trapping master cylinder pushrod and blade bushing between stop lamp switch side plates.
3. Push stop lamp switch and pushrod assembly firmly toward brake pedal arm.

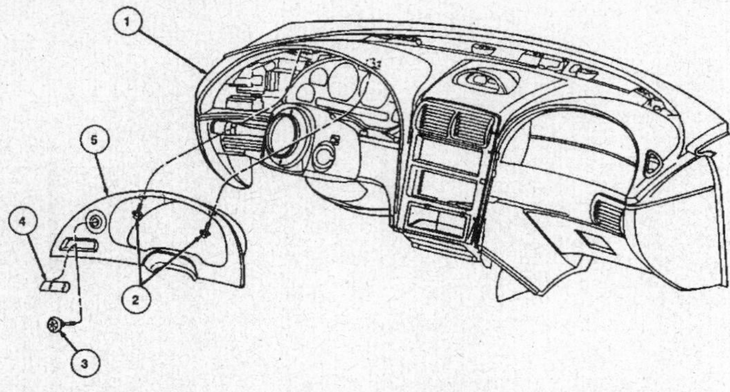

Item	Description
1	Instrument Panel
2	Screw and Washer Assy (2 Req'd)
3	Light Switch Knob

Item	Description
4	Instrument Panel Control Opening Cover
5	Instrument Panel Finish Panel

FM1049700013000X

Fig. 5 Instrument cluster bezel replacement. 1998

4. Assemble outside white plastic washer to pin and install hairpin retainer to trap whole assembly.
5. Assemble wire harness connector to stop lamp switch and install wires in retaining clip. **Stop lamp switch wire harness must have sufficient length to travel with switch during full stroke of brake pedal. If wire length is insufficient, reroute harness or service, as required.**

1999–2002

1. Remove stop lamp switch linkage clip and retainer, **Fig. 4.**
2. Disconnect switch electrical connector and remove switch.
3. Reverse procedure to install.

MULTI-FUNCTION SWITCH

REPLACE

1998

1. Place ⅛ diameter wire pin in steering column shroud hole under ignition switch lock cylinder, then depress retaining pin while pulling out on ignition switch lock cylinder.
2. Remove four mounting screws and steering column shroud.
3. Disconnect multi-function switch electrical connectors.
4. Remove two mounting screws and multi-function switch.
5. Reverse procedures to install, noting the following:
   a. **Torque** multi-function switch screws to 19–25 inch lbs.
   b. **Torque** steering column shroud mounting screws to 6–8 inch lbs.

1999–2002

1. Remove ignition lock cylinder as outlined under "Ignition Lock, Replace."
2. Remove tilt wheel handle.
3. Remove mounting screws, then the steering column upper and lower shrouds.
4. Remove multi-function switch mounting screws.
5. Disconnect electrical connectors and remove multi-function switch.
6. Reverse procedure to install. **Torque** multi-function switch mounting screws to 18–26 inch lbs.

STEERING WHEEL

REPLACE

1998

1. Remove driver's air bag models as outlined in "Passive Restraint Systems" chapter.
2. Disconnect horn and speed control wire harness from steering wheel.
3. Remove and discard steering wheel bolt.
4. Remove steering wheel using steering wheel remover tool No. T67L-3600-A, or equivalent, noting the following:
   a. Route air bag sliding contact assembly wire harness through steering wheel as steering wheel is lifted off steering column.
   b. **Ensure control assembly wire harness does not get caught on steering wheel when lifting wheel off steering column.**
5. Reverse procedure to install, noting the following:
   a. **Ensure air bag sliding contact wire is not pinched or air bag monitor will detect a fault condition.**
   b. Route air bag sliding contact assembly wire harness through steering wheel opening at three o'clock position.
   c. Position steering wheel on steering column. Steering wheel and column gear input shaft coupling alignment marks should be aligned.
   d. **Torque** steering wheel bolt to 22–33 ft. lbs.

1999–2002

1. Remove driver's air bag models as outlined in "Passive Restraint Systems" chapter.

2. Remove and discard steering wheel mounting bolt.
3. Remove steering wheel using suitable puller tool.
4. Reverse procedure to install, noting the following:
   a. Install new steering wheel mounting bolt.
   b. **Torque** mounting bolt to 23–32 ft. lbs.

INSTRUMENT CLUSTER

REPLACE

1998

1. Remove headlamp switch knob as outlined under "Headlamp Switch, Replace."
2. Remove two upper screws and instrument cluster bezel, **Fig. 5.**
3. Remove four screws and pull instrument cluster away from instrument panel.
4. Disconnect two cluster printed circuit connectors from back plate and remove cluster. **Do not remove gauge pointer if gauges are being removed from cluster assembly. Magnetic gauges cannot be calibrated.**
5. Reverse procedure to install.

1999–2002

1. Remove headlamp switch knob as outlined under "Headlamp Switch, Replace."
2. Remove mounting screws and instrument cluster finish retaining panel.
3. Remove mounting screws and cluster out.
4. Disconnect electrical connector.
5. Remove instrument cluster.
6. Reverse procedure to install.

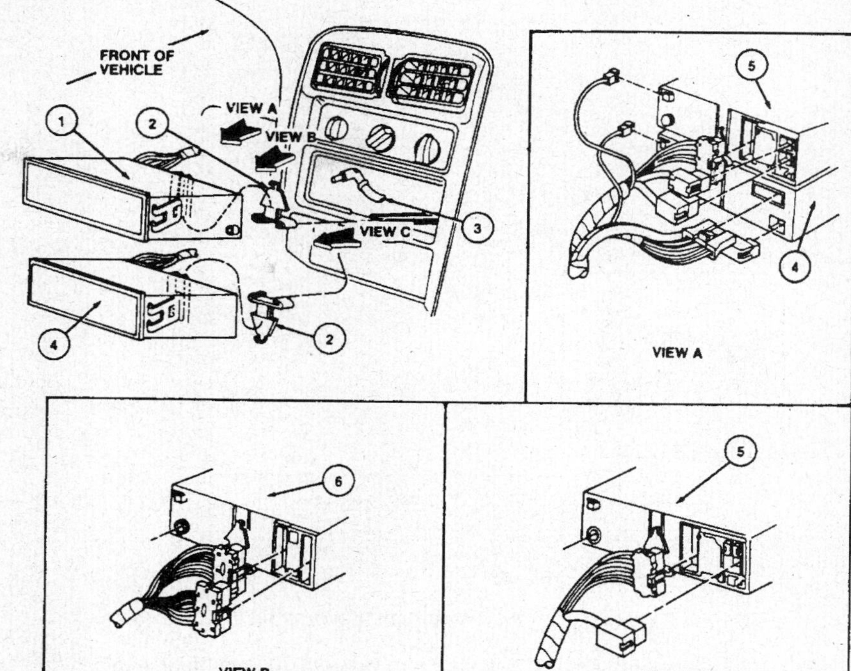

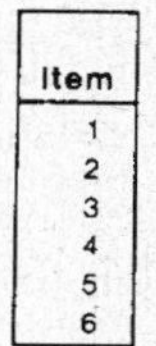

Item	Description
1	ESR Radio Chassis, ESC Radio Chassis and PAC Radio Chassis
2	Radio Chassis Support
3	Radio Antenna Lead In Cable
4	Digital Audio Compact Disc Player
5	ESC Radio Chassis, PAC Radio Chassis
6	ESR Radio Chassis

FM9039400008000X

Fig. 6 Radio replacement. 1998

RADIO

REPLACE

1998

1. Insert radio removing tools No. T87P-19061, or equivalent, into face plate approximately one inch.
2. Release clips by spreading radio face plate removal tools using light pressure, **Fig. 6.**
3. Remove radio, then disconnect antenna and electrical connectors.
4. Remove stereo tape cartridge container or digital audio compact disc player, as required.
5. Reverse procedure to install.

1999–2000

1. Insert radio removal tool No. T87P-19061-A, or equivalent into face plate. **Do not use excessive force.**
2. Pull radio out of instrument panel.
3. Disconnect radio electrical connectors and antenna lead-in cable.
4. Reverse procedure to install.

2001–02

1. Remove instrument panel center finishing panel.
2. Remove mounting screws and radio.
3. Disconnect electrical connector and antenna lead-in cable.
4. Reverse procedure to install.

WIPER MOTOR

REPLACE

The internal permanent magnets used in the windshield wiper motor are of a ceramic material. Care must be exercised in handling the motor to avoid damaging the magnets. The motor must not be struck or tapped with a hammer or other object.

1. Turn windshield wipers on. When blades reach full upright travel on glass, turn ignition switch Off.
2. Remove windshield wiper pivot arms and blades.
3. Remove cowl top vent grille.
4. Disconnect wiper motor adapter and connecting linkage clip from motor arm.
5. Remove linkage drive arm from windshield wiper motor.
6. Disconnect wiper motor electrical connector and remove motor to cowl mounting fasteners.
7. Remove wiper motor.
8. Reverse procedures to install. **Torque** wiper motor mounting screws to 10–12 ft. lbs.

WIPER SWITCH

REPLACE

Refer to "Multi-Function Switch, Replace." for replacement procedure.

WIPER TRANSMISSION

REPLACE

1998

1. Turn windshield wipers on. When blades reach full upright travel on glass, turn ignition switch to Off position.
2. Remove windshield wiper pivot arm and wiper blade from wiper mounting arm and pivot shaft, **Fig. 7.**
3. Remove cowl top vent grille and wiper adapter.
4. Remove windshield wiper mounting arm and pivot shaft arm clip.
5. Remove mounting screws, then guide wiper mounting arm and pivot shafts from righthand side of cowl chamber.
6. Reverse procedure to install noting the following:

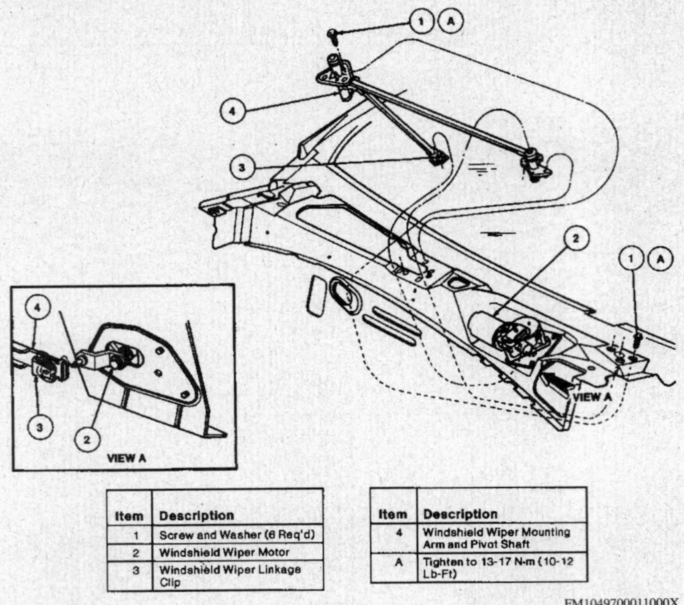

Item	Description
1	Screw and Washer (6 Req'd)
2	Windshield Wiper Motor
3	Windshield Wiper Linkage Clip

Item	Description
4	Windshield Wiper Mounting Arm and Pivot Shaft
A	Tighten to 13-17 N·m (10-12 Lb-Ft)

Fig. 7 Exploded view of wiper transmission. 1998

a. Ensure wiper motor is in park position before installing pivot arm and wiper blade.
b. Set windshield wiper blade to specified dimensions, **Fig. 8.**
c. **Torque** windshield wiper mounting arm and pivot shaft screws 10–12 ft. lbs.

1999–2002

1. Turn windshield wipers on. When blades reach full upright travel on glass, turn ignition Off.
2. Remove windshield wiper pivot arms and blades.
3. Remove cowl top vent grille.
4. Remove linkage drive arm from windshield wiper motor.
5. Lower hood, then remove mounting bolts and wiper transmission through righthand cowl chamber opening.
6. Reverse procedure to install, noting the following:
   a. Install retaining clip onto end of wiper transmission linkage.
   b. **Torque** transmission mounting bolts to 11 ft. lbs.
   c. Cycle wipers back to park position, then install arms and blades.

BLOWER MOTOR

REPLACE

1998

1. Disconnect jumper wire harness from main harness electrical connector and blower motor switch resistor.
2. Remove three mounting screws and pull blower motor out of evaporator housing.
3. Remove heater blower motor cover and stiffener plate.
4. Disconnect blower motor jumper wire harness.
5. Reverse procedure to install. Install gasket material to new air conditioning blower motor.

1999–2002

1. Disconnect jumper wire harness from main harness electrical connector.
2. Disconnect main harness at blower motor resistor.
3. Remove blower motor mounting screws.
4. Separate cover and motor.
5. Disconnect blower motor jumper harness.
6. Remove blower motor.
7. Reverse procedure to install.

HEATER CORE

REPLACE

1998

1. Remove evaporator case as outlined under "Evaporator Case, Replace."
2. Disconnect vacuum harness from evaporator and position aside.
3. Remove four mounting screws and heater core access cover.
4. Remove heater dash panel seal from heater inlet and outlet tubes, then pull heater core out of case.
5. Reverse procedure to install.

1999–2002

1. Remove evaporator core housing as outlined under "Evaporator Core, Replace."
2. Remove foam sealing strip.
3. Remove mounting screws and heater core cover.
4. Remove heater core.
5. Reverse procedure to install.

EVAPORATOR CASE

REPLACE

1998

1. Remove instrument panel as outlined in "Dash Panel Service" chapter.

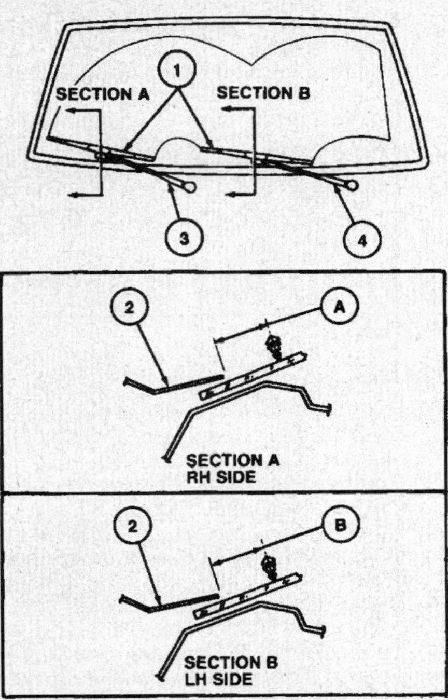

Item	Description
1	Windshield Wiper Blade
2	Cowl Vent Screen
3	Windshield Wiper Pivot Arm (RH)
4	Windshield Wiper Pivot Arm (LH)
A	55-81 mm (2.16-3.18 inches)
B	56-80 mm (2.20-3.14 inches)

FM1049700012000X

Fig. 8 Windshield wiper blade dimensions. 1998

2. Place suitable container under heater water hose connections.
3. Disconnect heater water hoses from heater core tubes.
4. Disconnect back vacuum supply hose from engine compartment vacuum source.
5. Recover air conditioning system as outlined in "Air Conditioning" chapter.
6. Remove evaporator housing to cowl panel mounting nut.
7. Remove one screw attaching evaporator housing bottom of to cowl panel from inside passengers' compartment.
8. Remove evaporator case support bracket to cowl top panel and mounting bracket to cowl top panel mounting screws, **Fig. 9.**
9. Disconnect blower motor wire harness connector.
10. Pull evaporator housing away from cowl panel and remove.
11. Reverse procedures to install noting the following:
    a. **Torque** evaporator housing to cowl top bracket nut and screw to 84–120 inch lbs.
    b. **Torque** bottom housing to cowl panel screw to 15–19 inch lbs.
    c. **Torque** evaporator housing to cowl

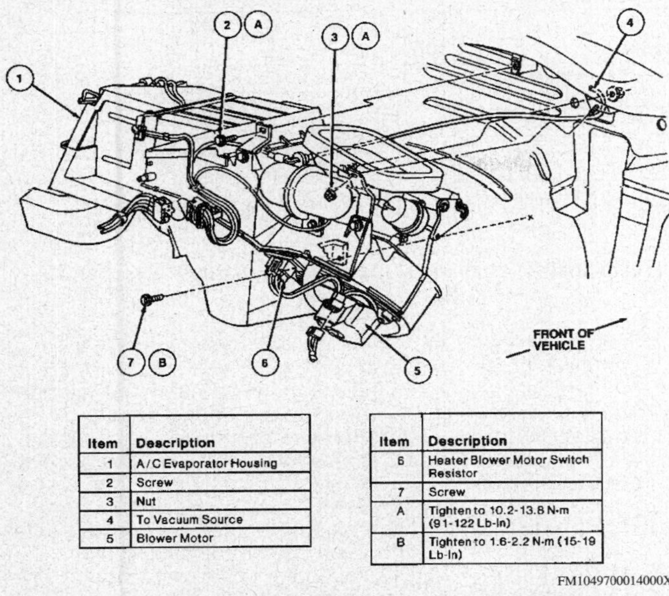

Item	Description
1	A/C Evaporator Housing
2	Screw
3	Nut
4	To Vacuum Source
5	Blower Motor

Item	Description
6	Heater Blower Motor Switch Resistor
7	Screw
A	Tighten to 10.2-13.8 N-m (91-122 Lb-In)
B	Tighten to 1.6-2.2 N-m (15-19 Lb-In)

Fig. 9 Evaporator housing & components. 1998

panel mounting nut to 59–83 inch lbs.

EVAPORATOR CORE

REPLACE

1998

Whenever an evaporator core is replaced, it is necessary to replace suction accumulator/drier.

Before an evaporator core is replaced, it must be leak tested in-vehicle as outlined in "Air Conditioning" chapter.

If it is necessary to replace an evaporator core, new core is serviced with a service replacement evaporator housing which has new core. All vacuum control motors, heater core, vacuum reservoir tank and bracket, blower motor, vacuum lines and air ducts from old evaporator housing must be transferred to new evaporator housing, **Fig. 10.**

1. Remove evaporator core case as outlined under "Evaporator Case, Replace."
2. Remove heater core as outline under "Heater Core, Replace."
3. Remove three mounting screws and vacuum line from vacuum control motor.
4. Remove recirculating air duct.
5. Remove air conditioning vacuum reservoir tank and bracket.
6. Remove vacuum hose harness from attachment points.
7. Remove vacuum control motor arm from air conditioning damper door cam.
8. Disconnect vacuum hose harness from control motor.
9. Remove two mounting screws and vacuum motor.
10. Disconnect jumper wire harness from heater blower motor switch resistor.
11. Remove two mounting screws and heater blower motor switch resistor.
12. Remove blower motor as outlined under "Blower Motor, Replace."
13. Remove mounting screws and heater outlet floor duct.
14. Remove mounting screw and evaporator case support bracket
15. Remove mounting screw and evaporator case mounting bracket.
16. Remove evaporator drain tube seal from evaporator housing.
17. Reverse procedures to install.

1999–2002

1. Recover refrigerant as outlined in "Air Conditioning" chapter.
2. Drain coolant into suitable container.
3. Remove instrument panel as outlined in "Dash Panel Service" chapter.
4. Place suitable container under heater water hose connections.
5. Disconnect heater hoses at underhood core fittings.
6. Disconnect vacuum connector near firewall.
7. Remove air conditioning accumulator.
8. Disconnect air conditioning liquid line.
9. Remove evaporator core housing nuts and screws at firewall.
10. Remove evaporator core housing bolts from inside passenger compartment.
11. Remove evaporator core housing.
12. Reverse procedure to install. **Torque** evaporator core housing bolts to 71 inch lbs.

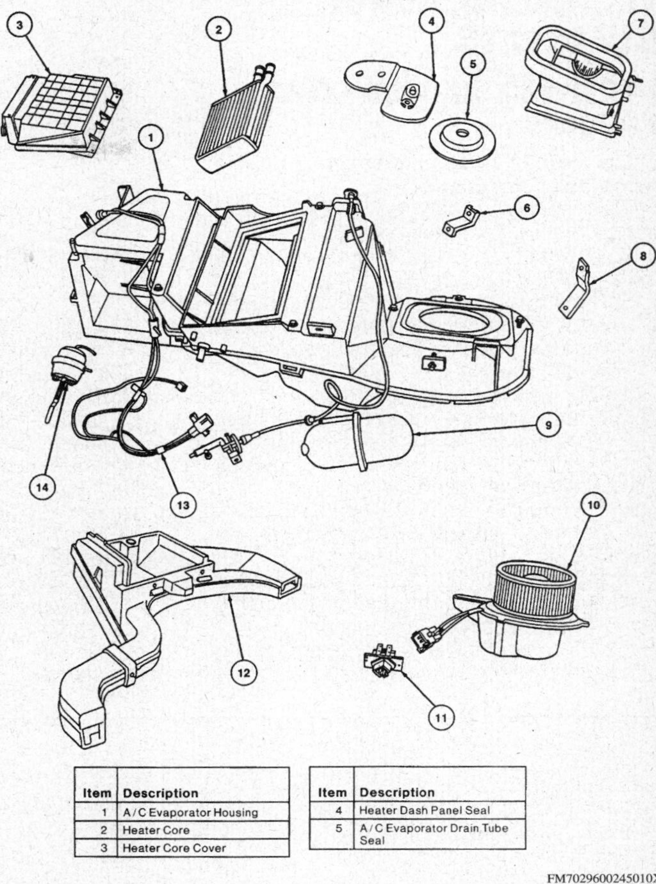

Item	Description
1	A/C Evaporator Housing
2	Heater Core
3	Heater Core Cover

Item	Description
4	Heater Dash Panel Seal
5	A/C Evaporator Drain Tube Seal

Fig. 10 Evaporator core replacement (Part 1 of 2). 1998

TECHNICAL SERVICE BULLETINS

REPEATED HEATER CORE FAILURE

On some of these models there may be repeated heater core leaks.

This condition may be caused by a chemical reaction (electrolysis).

To correct this condition, proceed as follows:

1. Place positive probe of suitable digital volt/ohm meter in engine coolant and negative probe on battery negative terminal.
2. Adjust engine to 2000 RPM.
3. If more than 0.4 volt is recorded, flush coolant and check voltage, again.
4. If voltage is still excessive, inspect body/battery grounds.
5. If condition still exists, add extra grounds to heater core and engine, as follows:
   a. Secure 16 gauge stranded copper wire to heater core inlet tube using suitable hose clamp.
   b. Secure other end of wire to existing body sheet metal fastener.
   c. Secure another extra ground between existing engine and body sheet metal fasteners.
   d. Ensure there is continuity between added grounds and battery negative terminal.
6. If condition still exists, install restrictor as follows:
   a. Cut line as close to engine block as possible.
   b. Install restrictor (part No. F1UZ-18D406-A) on inlet hose with arrow facing coolant flow direction (toward heater core).
   c. Secure with two suitable hose clamps.
7. Bleed cooling system trapped air as follows:
   a. Disconnect heater hose at right-hand front or rear of engine.
   b. Remove thermostat and housing.
   c. Fill engine with suitable coolant until mixture is seen at engine side heater hose connection.
   d. Connect heater hose, then install thermostat and housing.
   e. Fill degas bottle to coolant fill level mark.
   f. Fun engine to normal operating temperature.
   g. Select max heat and blower speeds

Item	Description
6	A/C Evaporator Case Mounting Bracket
7	A/C Recirculating Air Duct
8	A/C Evaporator Case Support Bracket
9	A/C Vacuum Reservoir Tank and Bracket

Item	Description
10	Blower Motor
11	Heater Blower Motor Switch Resistor
12	Heater Outlet Floor Duct
13	Vacuum Hose Harness
14	Vacuum Control Motor

FM7029600245020X

Fig. 10 Evaporator core replacement (Part 2 of 2). 1998

3.8L Engine

NOTE: On Air Bag Equipped Models, Refer To "Air Bag System Precautions" Located In The Front Of This Manual For System Disarming & Arming Procedures.

NOTE: Refer To "Computer Relearn Procedures" Located In The Front Of This Manual When Battery Power To The Computer Has Been Interrupted.

NOTE: Prior To Performing Any Service Operations Listed In This Section, Consult The "Technical Service Bulletins" Section For Related Information.

INDEX

PRECAUTIONS

AIR BAG SYSTEMS

Refer to "Air Bag System Precautions" in the front of this manual for system disarming and arming procedures.

BATTERY GROUND CABLE

Prior to service, disconnect battery ground cable and isolate as required.

FUEL SYSTEM PRESSURE RELIEF

Fuel supply tubes will remain pressurized for long periods of time after engine shutdown. This pressure must be relieved before beginning fuel system service or personal injury and vehicle damage may occur. A valve is provided on the fuel injection supply manifold for this purpose.

1. Remove engine air cleaner.
2. Connect EFI/CFI fuel pressure gauge tool No. T80L-9974-B, or equivalent, to fuel pressure relief valve on fuel injection supply manifold.
3. Open manual valve on fuel pressure gauge tool to relieve fuel system pressure.

COMPRESSION PRESSURE

When inspecting cylinder compression, lowest cylinder must be within 75% of highest cylinder. Perform compression test with engine at normal operating temperature, spark plugs and air cleaner removed and the throttle propped wide open.

ENGINE MOUNT

REPLACE

Whenever self-locking mounting bolts and nuts are removed, they must be replaced with new self-locking bolts and nuts.

1. Remove fan shroud mounting screws and air tube from remote air cleaner.
2. Raise and support vehicle, then support engine using suitable jack and wood block placed below engine.
3. Remove insulator to front subframe through bolts, **Fig. 1.**
4. Disconnect shift linkage and raise engine enough to clear front subframe brackets.
5. Remove accessories and oil cooler line attaching clips from engine support brackets.
6. Remove mounting bolts, insulator and bracket.
7. Reverse procedure to install.

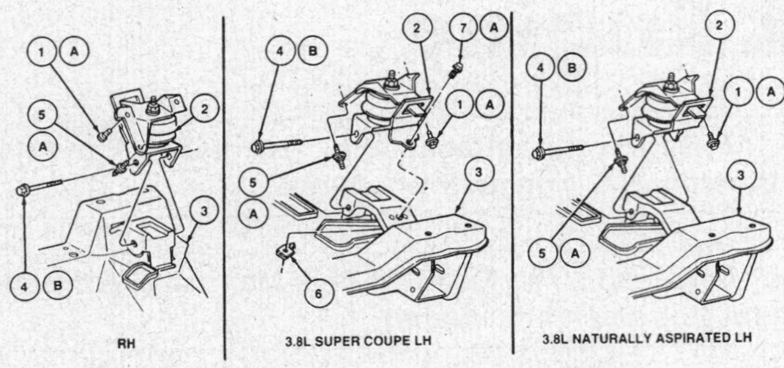

Item	Part Number	Description
1	N803098-S100	Bolt (2 Req'd)
2	6038	Front Engine Support Insulator
3	5C145	Front Sub-Frame
4	N805748-S36	Bolt
5	N805803-S36	Stud

Item	Part Number	Description
6	N805968-S36	U-Nut
7	N605918-S56	Bolt
A	—	Tighten to 34-47 N·m (25-35 Lb-Ft)
B	—	Tighten to 47-68 N·m (35-50 Lb-Ft)

FM1069100113000X

Fig. 1 Engine mount replacement

ENGINE

REPLACE

1998

REMOVAL

1. Drain engine cooling system into suitable container.
2. Disconnect underhood lamp wiring connector.
3. Mark hinge position and remove hood.
4. Disconnect alternator to voltage regulator wiring assembly and remove radiator upper sight shield.
5. Release tensioner and remove drive belt.
6. Disconnect Intake Air Temperature (IAT) sensor wire harness and crankcase ventilation tube from air cleaner outlet tube.
7. Loosen clamps and disconnect outlet tube air cleaner from throttle body.
8. Disconnect from Mass Air Flow (MAF) sensor and remove outlet tube .
9. Disconnect electric fan motor.
10. Disconnect constant control relay module wiring connector and remove radiator coolant recovery reservoir.
11. Remove radiator electric motor, fan blade and fan shroud as an assembly.
12. Remove upper radiator hose.
13. **On models equipped with automatic transmission,** disconnect transmission oil cooler inlet and outlet tubes.
14. **On all models,** disconnect heater inlet and heater return tube hoses.
15. Disconnect lower radiator hose at water pump, then remove mounting bolts and radiator.
16. Disconnect power steering pressure hose.
17. Remove power steering pump and bracket and position aside.
18. Remove Mass Air Flow (MAF) sensor, then disconnect power steering pressure switch at wiring connector.
19. **On models equipped with air conditioning,** proceed as follows:
    a. Disconnect air conditioning clutch from fuel charging wiring.
    b. Recover air conditioning system refrigerant as outlined in "Air Conditioning" chapter.
    c. Disconnect air conditioning compressor lines. Cap or plug open lines.
    d. Remove mounting bolts and air conditioning compressor.
20. **On all models,** remove wiring shield, then disconnect accelerator cable and speed control actuator from throttle body.
21. Remove accelerator cable bracket and position aside with cables.
22. Relieve fuel system pressure as outlined under "Precautions."
23. Disconnect fuel supply and return hoses.
24. Disconnect fuel charging wiring from engine control sensor wiring at 40-pin connector.
25. Disconnect main vacuum source hose and direct ignition control module at wiring connector.
26. Disconnect fuel vapor hose.
27. **On models equipped with air conditioning,** remove air conditioning compressor mounting bracket with drive belt tensioner attached.
28. **On all models,** raise and support vehicle, then drain engine oil into suitable container.
29. Remove oil bypass filter.
30. Disconnect heated oxygen sensors.
31. Remove dual converter and pipe.
32. Remove engine rear plate inspection plug.
33. **On models equipped with automatic transmission,** remove torque converter bolts.
34. **On all models,** remove engine to transmission bolts.
35. **On models equipped with automatic transmission,** remove transmission oil cooler line retainers from righthand front engine support insulator.
36. **On all models,** remove front engine support insulator to crossmember nuts.
37. Remove starter motor as outlined in "Electrical" section.
38. Remove ground cable, then starter motor wire harness retainers on both left and righthand sides.
39. Partially lower vehicle and position suitable floor jack under transmission.
40. Remove engine using suitable lifting equipment.

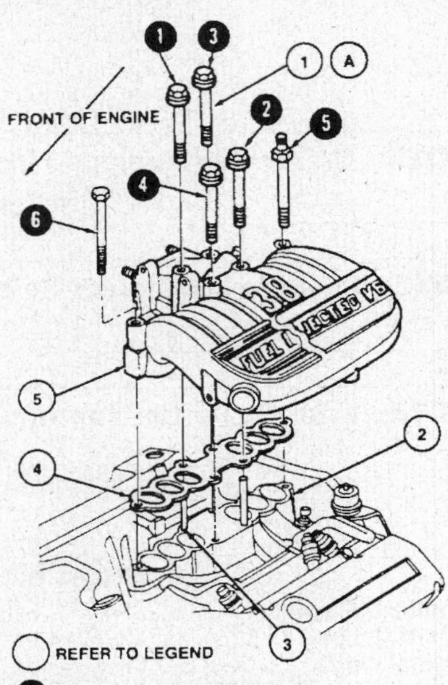

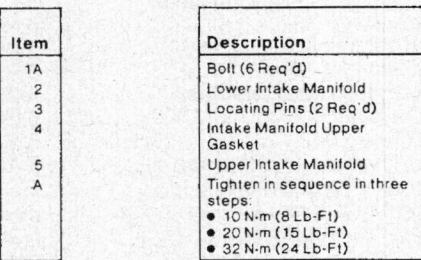

Item	Description
1A	Bolt (6 Req'd)
2	Lower Intake Manifold
3	Locating Pins (2 Req'd)
4	Intake Manifold Upper Gasket
5	Upper Intake Manifold
A	Tighten in sequence in three steps: • 10 N·m (8 Lb-Ft) • 20 N·m (15 Lb-Ft) • 32 N·m (24 Lb-Ft)

FM1059400060000X

Fig. 2 Upper intake manifold bolt tightening sequence. 1998

INSTALLATION

Lightly oil all bolt and stud threads before installation, except those specifying special sealant.

1. Position engine in engine compartment using suitable engine lifting equipment.
2. Install two engine to transmission bolts.
3. Lower engine onto front engine support insulators and remove lifting equipment. **Seat lefthand side front engine support insulator locating pin before righthand side front engine support insulator.**
4. Remove floor jack from under transmission and tighten two engine to transmission bolts.
5. Raise and support vehicle, then tighten all engine to transmission bolts.
6. **On models equipped with automatic transmission,** install and tighten torque converter bolts.
7. **On all models,** install engine rear plate inspection plug and front engine support insulator nuts.

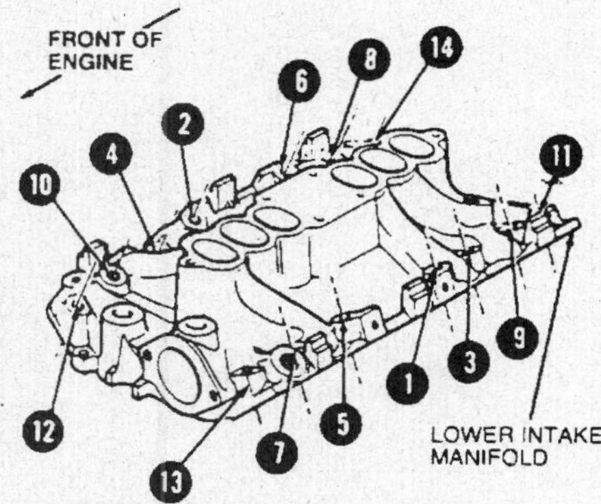

Fig. 3 Lower intake manifold bolt tightening sequence. 1998

8. Install starter motor as outlined under "Electrical."
9. **On models equipped with automatic transmission,** install transmission oil cooler line bracket.
10. **On all models,** install dual converter and pipe.
11. Connect heated oxygen sensor.
12. Install oil bypass filter and lower vehicle.
13. **On models equipped with air conditioning,** install air conditioning compressor mounting bracket with drive belt tensioner attached.
14. **On all models,** connect fuel vapor hose.
15. Install radiator coolant recovery reservoir and connect constant control relay module at wiring connector.
16. Connect main vacuum source hose, then fuel charging wiring to engine control sensor wiring at 40-pin connector.
17. Connect ignition control module at wiring connector.
18. Remove fuel and return lines' plugs, then connect lines.
19. Install accelerator cable bracket, then connect accelerator cable and speed control actuator to throttle body.
20. Install wiring shield.
21. **On models equipped with air conditioning,** proceed as follows:
    a. Install air conditioning compressor and tighten mounting bolts.
    b. Remove air conditioning compressor lines' caps or plugs and connect lines to compressor.
    c. Connect air conditioning clutch to fuel charging wiring.
22. **On all models,** connect power steering pressure switch at wiring connector and install MAF sensor.
23. Install power steering pump and bracket, then connect power steering hoses.
24. Install radiator and connect lower radiator hose to water pump.
25. Install heater inlet and heater return tube hoses.
26. **On models equipped with automatic transmission,** install transmission cooler lines.

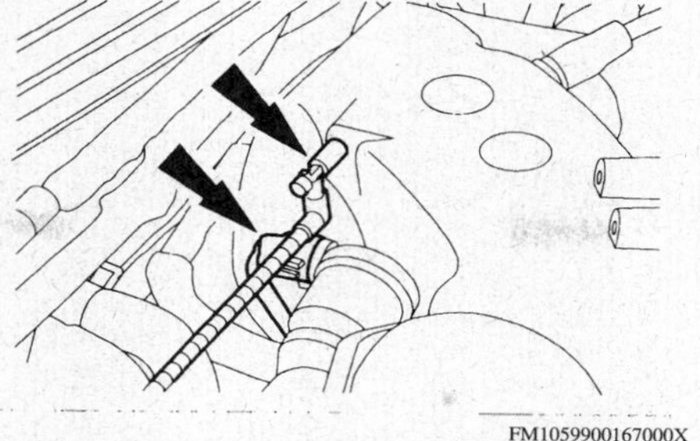

Fig. 4 Vacuum tube at upper intake manifold replacement. 1999–2002

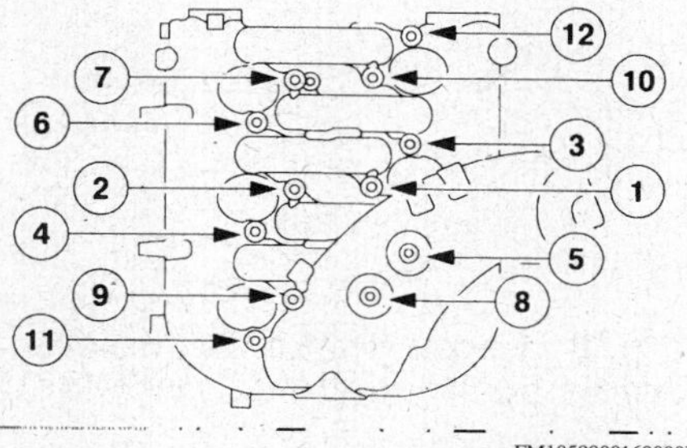

Fig. 6 Upper intake manifold bolt tightening sequence. 1999–2002

27. **On all models,** install upper radiator hose.
28. Install radiator electric motor, fan blade and fan shroud as an assembly.
29. Connect electric fan motor to engine control sensor wiring.
30. Install radiator coolant recovery reservoir, then the constant control relay module at wiring connector.
31. Position drive belt and install radiator upper sight shield.
32. Position air cleaner outlet tube and connect it to MAF sensor.
33. Connect air cleaner outlet tube to throttle body and install tube clamps to tube.
34. Connect crankcase ventilation tube to air cleaner outlet tube.
35. Connect wire harness to IAT sensor.
36. Install hood.
37. Connect underhood lamp wiring and battery ground cable.
38. Fill crankcase and cooling systems to proper level with specified fluids.
39. **On models equipped with air conditioning,** drain, evacuate, pressure test and charge air conditioning system as outlined in "Air Conditioning" chapter.

1999–2002

1. Recover air conditioning refrigerant as outlined in "Air Conditioning" chapter.
2. Drain coolant into suitable container.
3. Relieve fuel system pressure as outlined under "Precautions."
4. Disconnect hood ground strap and underhood lamp electrical connector.
5. Mark hinge positions, then remove bolts and hood.
6. Disconnect vacuum hose near firewall.
7. Disconnect battery positive cable at alternator and alternator electrical connectors.

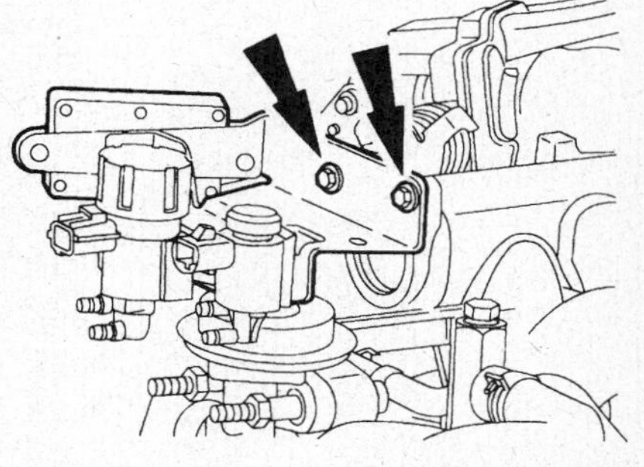

Fig. 5 Solenoid bracket replacement. 1999–2002

8. Disconnect power steering pump fluid lines and drain into suitable container.
9. Disconnect lower radiator hose at water pump.
10. Disconnect upper radiator hose at coolant outlet.
11. Remove coolant reservoir.
12. Disconnect accelerator cable.
13. Remove mounting bolt and position accelerator cable bracket aside.
14. Remove air cleaner assembly and outlet tube.
15. Disconnect air conditioning manifold and tube.
16. Disconnect air conditioning compressor electrical connector.
17. Disconnect fuel supply line using fuel line disconnection set tool No. T90T-9550-S, or equivalent.
18. Disconnect vacuum hose at righthand rear corner of engine compartment.
19. Disconnect heater hoses at underhood core fittings and drain into suitable containers.
20. Disconnect 42-pin electrical connector at righthand rear corner of engine compartment and position wiring harness aside.
21. Disconnect vacuum tube and connector at rear of TBI.
22. Disconnect EVAP return tube.
23. Raise and support vehicle.
24. Remove starter motor as outlined in "Electrical" section.
25. Disconnect electrical connectors at left and righthand O2 sensors.
26. Remove dual converter mounting nuts.
27. Remove left and righthand exhaust manifold flange nuts.
28. Remove Y-pipe.
29. Disconnect engine ground strap.
30. Drain engine oil into suitable container.
31. **On models equipped with automatic transmission,** remove inspection cover and four torque converter to flexplate nuts. Discard nuts.
32. **On all models,** remove bellhousing upper and lower bolts.
33. **On models equipped with automatic transmission,** remove transmission fluid filler tube.
34. **On all models,** remove left and righthand engine mount nuts.
35. Lower vehicle.
36. Support transmission using suitable

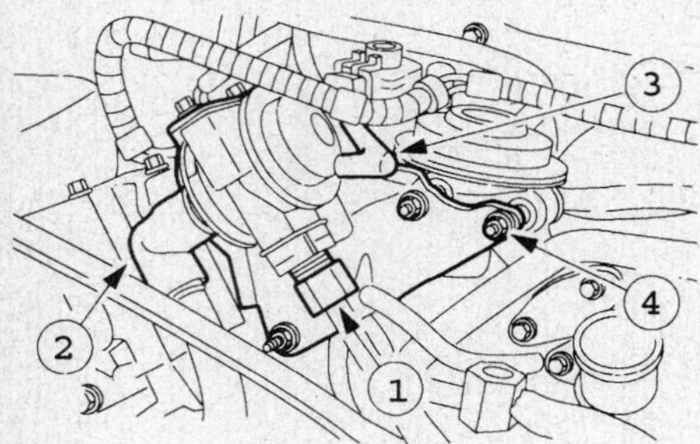

1. Tube Nut
2. Air Tube
3. Vacuum Tube
4. Nut

FM1059900170000X

Fig. 7 Exhaust air supply valve replacement. 1999–2002

floor jack and block of wood.

37. Install engine lifting brackets tool No. D94L-6001-A, or equivalent.
38. Connect spreader bar tool No. D93L-6001-A3, or equivalent, to brackets.
39. Lift engine up and out of engine compartment, then mount on suitable stand using suitable crane or skyhook.
40. Reverse procedure to install, noting the following:
    a. **On models equipped with automatic transmission,** install four new torque converter to flexplate nuts.
    b. **On all models,** install oil pan drain plug and close radiator petcock.

INTAKE MANIFOLD

REPLACE

1998

UPPER

1. Disconnect Intake Air Temperature (IAT) sensor wire harness and crankcase ventilation tube from air cleaner outlet tube.
2. Loosen air cleaner tube clamps and disconnect outlet tube from throttle body.
3. Disconnect from Mass Air Flow (MAF) sensor and remove outlet tube.
4. Disconnect accelerator cable at throttle body and speed control actuator.
5. Remove bracket bolts and position accelerator cable aside.
6. Disconnect vacuum lines at intake manifold and electrical connectors, as required.
7. Disconnect one crankcase ventilation tube at upper intake manifold and PCV valve.
8. Remove throttle body, as required, then EGR valve from upper intake manifold.
9. Remove engine support and wiring retainer bracket nut and bolt at lefthand front of intake manifold. Set bracket aside with ignition wires.
10. Record upper intake manifold bolts/studs locations.
11. Remove bolts, studs, upper intake manifold and gasket.

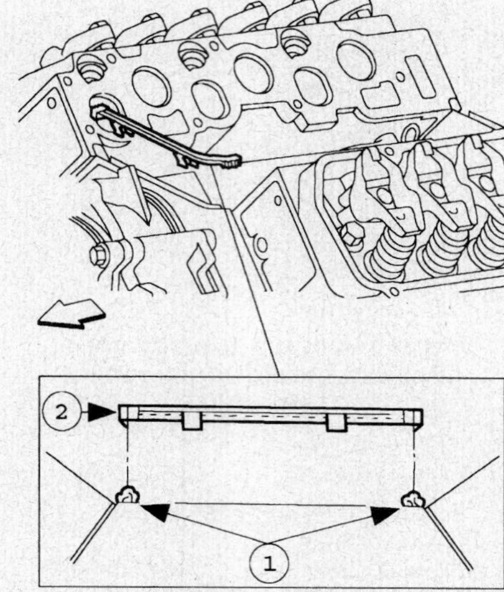

1. Sealant Beads
2. End Seals

FM1059900171000X

Fig. 8 Lower intake manifold end seals bead locations. 1999–2002

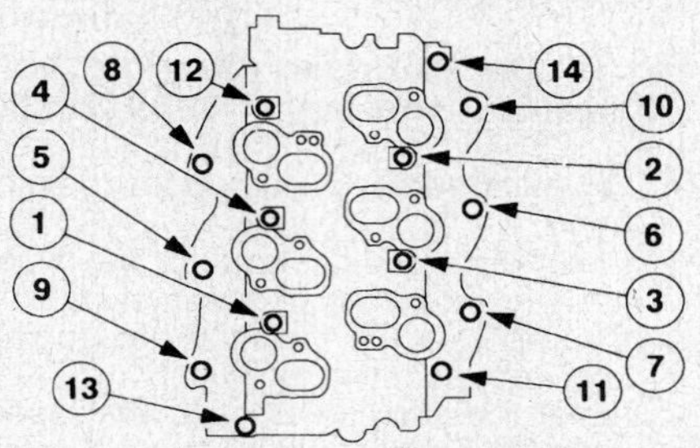

FM1059900173000X

Fig. 10 Lower intake manifold bolt tightening sequence. 1999–2002

12. Reverse procedure to install, noting the following:
    a. **Torque** upper intake manifold mounting bolts to 96 inch lbs. in sequence, **Fig. 2.**
    b. **Torque** mounting bolts to 15 ft. lbs. in sequence.
    c. Finally **torque** bolts to 24 ft. lbs. in sequence.

LOWER

1. Drain engine cooling system into suitable container.
2. Remove upper intake manifold as described under "Upper."
3. Remove fuel injector and fuel injection supply manifold.
4. Remove heater water outlet hose.
5. Remove mounting bolts, studs and lower intake manifold, noting the following:
    a. Intake manifold is sealed at each end with RTV type sealer.
    b. To break seal, it may be necessary to pry on front of manifold with suitable screwdriver blade. **Do not damage machined surfaces.**
6. Remove and discard intake manifold

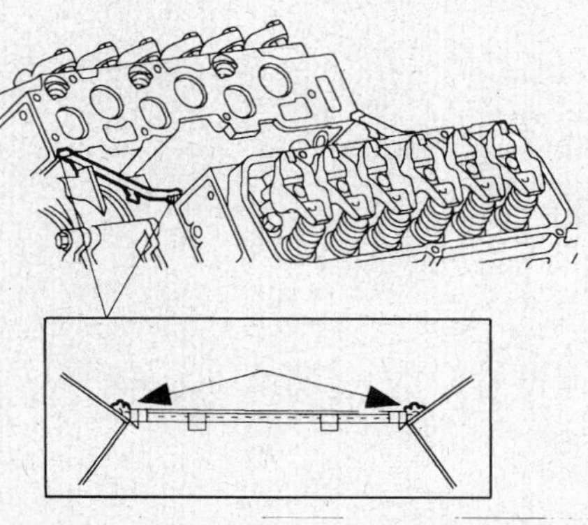

FM1059900172000X

Fig. 9 Lower intake manifold sealant bead locations. 1999–2002

gasket and end seals.

7. If lower intake manifold is to be disassembled, proceed as follows:
    a. Remove water outlet connection and water thermostat.
    b. Remove engine coolant temperature sensor.
    c. Water bypass tube is pressed in and is not serviceable.
    d. Remove heater elbow.
    e. Remove all vacuum and electrical fittings.
8. Reverse procedure to install, noting the following:
    a. Lightly oil all bolt and stud threads before installation.
    b. When using silicone rubber sealer, assembly must occur within 15 minutes after sealer application. After this time, sealer may start to set and its effectiveness may be reduced.
    c. Ensure lower intake manifold, cylinder head and cylinder block mating surfaces are clean and free of old gasket and sealing material. Clean with suitable solvent.
    d. If intake manifold was disassembled, apply coat of pipe sealant with Teflon part No. D8AZ-19554-A, or equivalent, to all vacuum fittings, heater elbows and electrical fittings.
    e. Install lower intake manifold bolts and stud bolt in original locations.
    f. **Torque** lower intake manifold bolts and stud to 96 inch lbs. in sequence, **Fig. 3.**
    g. **Torque** bolts to 15 ft. lbs. in sequence.

1999–2002

UPPER

1. Remove air cleaner outlet tube.
2. Disconnect vacuum tube and the Idle Air Control (IAC) solenoid, **Fig. 4.**
3. Disconnect Throttle Position (TP) sensor and EVAP return tube.
4. Disconnect accelerator cable from TBI and position aside.
5. Remove solenoid bracket bolts, **Fig. 5.**
6. Disconnect PCV tube and vacuum tubes, as required.
7. Remove mounting bolts and position ignition coil aside.
8. Record remove upper intake manifold

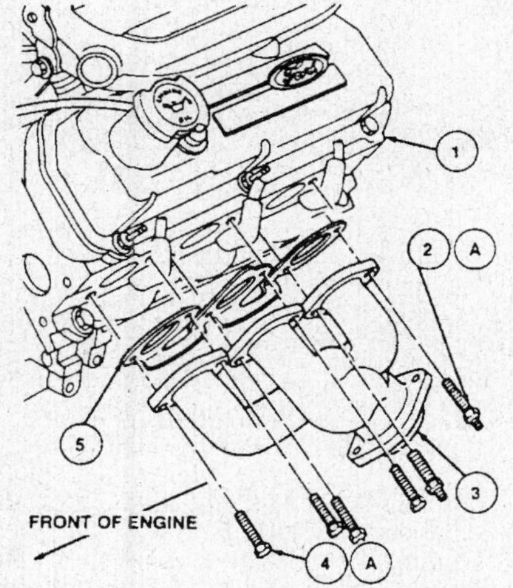

Item	Description
1	Cylinder Head
2A	Stud (3 Req'd)
3	LH Exhaust Manifold
4A	Bolt (3 Req'd)
5	Exhaust Manifold Gasket
A	Tighten to 20-33 N-m (15-22 Lb-Ft)

FM1059400062000X

Fig. 11 Lefthand exhaust manifold replacement. 1998

mounting bolts' locations.

9. Remove upper intake manifold. Discard gasket.
10. Reverse procedure to install, noting the following:
    a. Install new upper to lower intake manifold gasket.
    b. Ensure mounting bolts are in original proper locations.
    c. **Torque** manifold mounting bolts to 53 inch lbs. in sequence, **Fig. 6.**
    d. **Torque** mounting bolts to 71 inch lbs. in sequence.
    e. Finally, tighten bolts an additional 90°.

LOWER

1. Drain coolant into suitable container.
2. Remove upper intake manifold as outlined under "Upper."
3. Relieve fuel system pressure as outlined under "Precautions."
4. Disconnect fuel pressure sensor electrical connector.
5. Disconnect fuel injection supply manifold.
6. Disconnect engine wiring harness and position it aside.
7. Disconnect heater hose at rear of engine.
8. Position spark plug wire loom aside and remove stud bolt.
9. Disconnect EGR valve vacuum tube.
10. **On models equipped with exhaust air supply valve assembly,** proceed as follows:
    a. Loosen tube nut, **Fig. 7.**
    b. Disconnect air tube.
    c. Disconnect vacuum tube.
    d. Remove nuts.
11. **On all models,** loosen EGR hex tube nut and disconnect tube.
12. Disconnect radiator upper hose and bypass hose.
13. Disconnect electrical connectors, as required.
14. Remove bypass tube bolt.
15. Remove mounting bolts, then the fuel injection supply manifold and injectors as an assembly.
16. Record lower intake manifold mounting bolts' locations.
17. Remove mounting bolts and lower intake manifold. Discard gaskets and end seals.
18. Reverse procedure to install, noting the following:
    a. Apply beads of silicone gasket sealant No. F7AZ-19554-EA, or equivalent, to end seal mounting points, **Fig. 8.**
    b. Apply beads of sealant to lower intake manifold mounting locations, **Fig. 9.**
    c. Install lower intake manifold within four minutes of sealant application.
    d. Ensure manifold mounting bolts are installed in original locations.
    e. **Torque** manifold mounting bolts to 44 inch lbs. in sequence, **Fig. 10.**
    f. **Torque** mounting bolts to 89 inch lbs. in sequence.

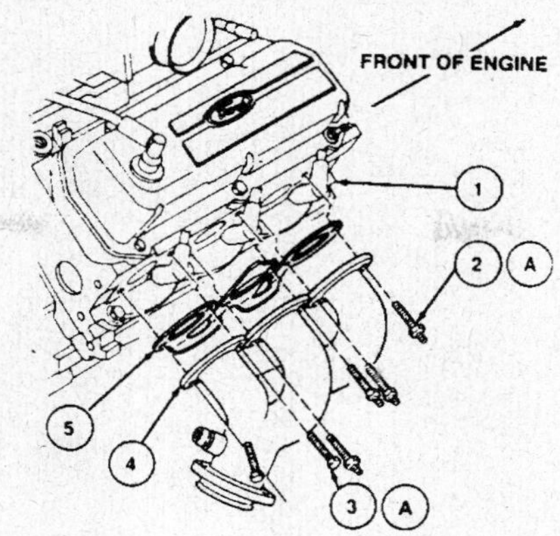

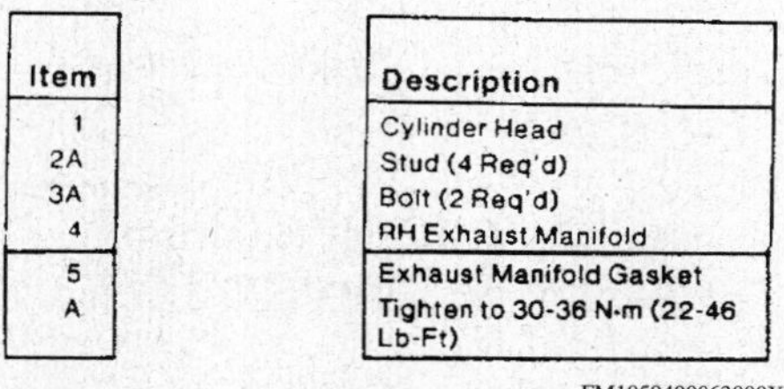

Item	Description
1	Cylinder Head
2A	Stud (4 Req'd)
3A	Bolt (2 Req'd)
4	RH Exhaust Manifold
5	Exhaust Manifold Gasket
A	Tighten to 30-36 N-m (22-46 Lb-Ft)

FM1059400063000X

Fig. 12 Righthand exhaust manifold replacement. 1998

EXHAUST MANIFOLD

REPLACE

1998

LEFTHAND

1. Remove oil level indicator tube support bracket.
2. Disconnect heated oxygen sensor from fuel charging wiring and ignition wires from spark plugs.
3. Raise and support vehicle.
4. Remove exhaust manifold to converter and pipe nuts, then lower vehicle.
5. Remove exhaust manifold bolts, then the lefthand exhaust manifold and gasket, **Fig. 11.**
6. If installing new manifold, remove oxygen sensor.
7. Reverse procedure to install, noting the following:
    a. Lightly oil all bolt and stud threads before installation, except those specifying special sealant.
    b. Coat heated oxygen sensor threads with high temperature anti-seize compound. **Do not allow anti-seize compound to enter sensor flutes.**
    c. Position exhaust manifold and exhaust manifold gasket on cylinder head, then install pilot bolt (lower front bolt hole on No. 5 cylinder).
    d. Slight warpage in exhaust manifold may cause misalignment between bolt holes in cylinder head and exhaust manifold.
    e. Elongate holes in exhaust manifold to correct misalignment, as required.
    f. **Do not elongate pilot hole.**

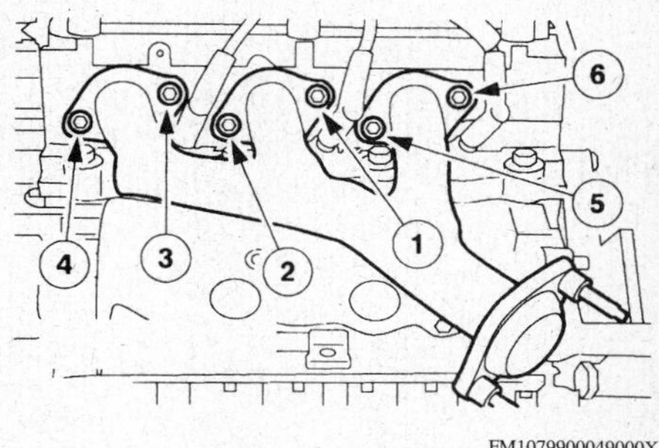

FM1079900049000X

Fig. 13 Lefthand exhaust manifold bolt tightening sequence. 1999–2002

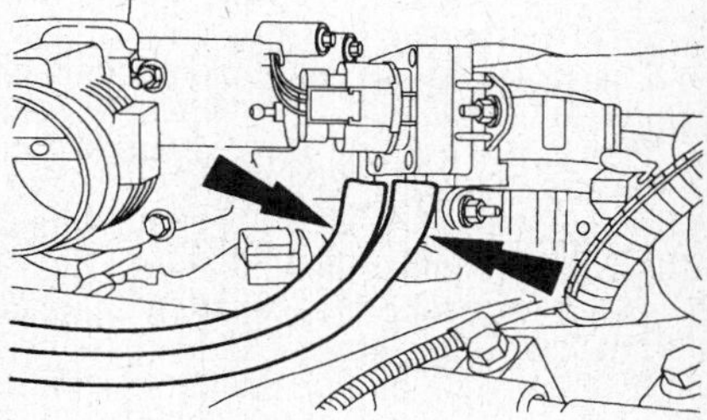

FM1059900174000X

Fig. 14 TBI hose replacement. 1999–2002

RIGHTHAND

1. Disconnect coil ignition wire from ignition coil and ignition wires from spark plugs.
2. Remove spark plugs, then raise and support vehicle.
3. Disconnect EGR valve to exhaust manifold tube from exhaust manifold.
4. **On models equipped with automatic transmission,** remove transmission fluid level indicator tube.

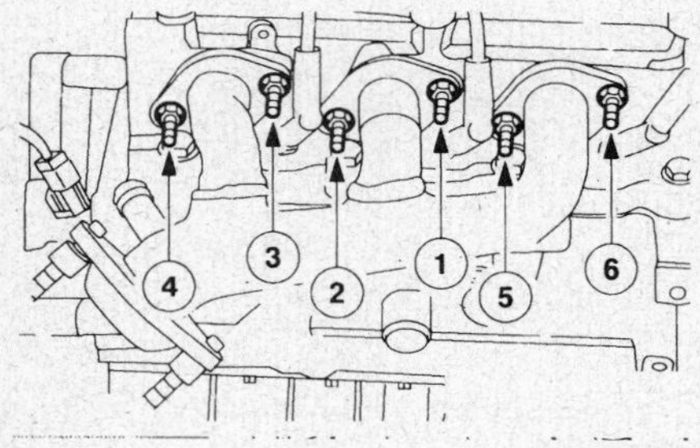

Fig. 15 Righthand exhaust manifold bolt tightening sequence. 1999–2002

5. **On all models,** remove heater inlet tube and hose.
6. Remove exhaust manifold to dual converter Y-pipe nuts, then lower vehicle.
7. Remove mounting bolts, exhaust manifold and gasket, **Fig. 12.**
8. If installing new manifold, remove heated oxygen sensor.
9. Reverse procedure to install, noting the following:
   a. Lightly oil all bolt and stud threads before installation, except those specifying special sealant.
   b. Coat heated oxygen sensor threads with high temperature anti-seize compound. **Do not allow anti-seize compound to enter sensor flutes.**
   c. Position exhaust manifold and exhaust manifold gasket on cylinder head and start two bolts.
   d. Slight warpage in exhaust manifold may cause misalignment between bolt holes in cylinder head and exhaust manifold.
   e. Elongate holes in exhaust manifold to correct misalignment, as required.
   f. **Do not elongate pilot hole.**

1999–2002

LEFTHAND

1. Raise and support vehicle.
2. Remove lefthand manifold flange nuts, then lower vehicle.
3. Remove engine oil dipstick tube.
4. **On models equipped with exhaust air supply valve,** loosen tube nut at front of exhaust manifold.
5. **On all models,** remove mounting nuts and exhaust manifold. Discard gasket.
6. Reverse procedure to install, noting the following:
   a. Install new exhaust manifold gasket.
   b. Tighten manifold mounting bolts in sequence, **Fig. 13.**

RIGHTHAND

1. Remove air cleaner outlet tube.
2. Disconnect two TBI hoses, **Fig. 14.**
3. **On models equipped with exhaust air supply valve assembly,** proceed as follows:
   a. Loosen tube nut, **Fig. 7.**
   b. Disconnect air tube.
   c. Disconnect vacuum tube.
   d. Remove nuts and valve assembly.

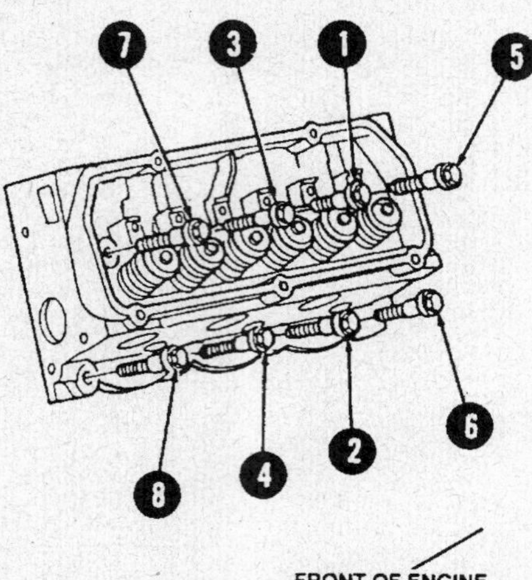

Fig. 16 Cylinder head bolt tightening sequence. 1998

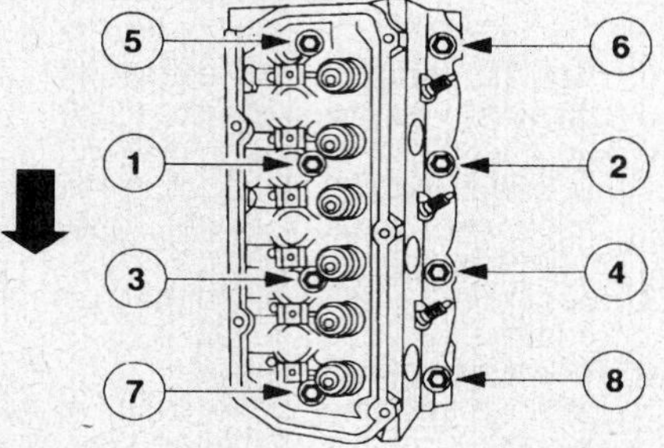

Fig. 18 Cylinder head bolt tightening sequence. 1999–2002

4. **On all models,** loosen EGR hex tube nut, disconnect vacuum lines and remove tube.
5. Raise and support vehicle.
6. Remove righthand manifold flange nuts, then lower vehicle.
7. **On models equipped with exhaust air supply valve assembly,** loosen tube nut at front of righthand exhaust manifold.
8. **On all models,** remove mounting nuts and manifold. Discard gasket.
9. Reverse procedure to install, noting the following:
   a. Install new exhaust manifold gasket.
   b. Tighten manifold mounting bolts in sequence, **Fig. 15.**

CYLINDER HEAD

REPLACE

1998

LEFTHAND

Removal

1. Drain engine cooling system.
2. Disconnect wire harness from Intake Air Temperature (IAT) sensor and crankcase ventilation tube from air cleaner outlet tube.

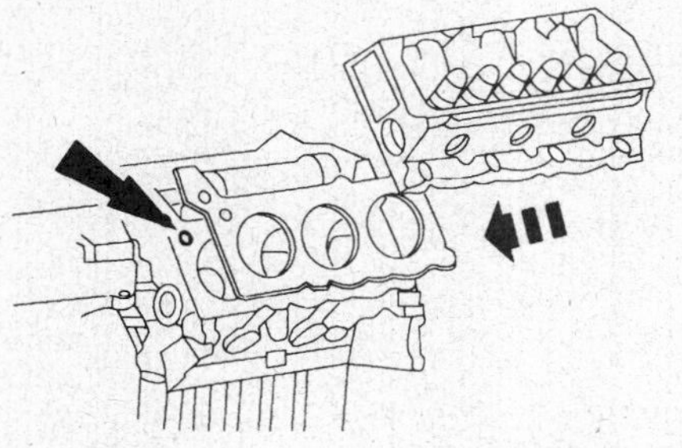

Fig. 17 Cylinder head gasket orientation. 1999–2002

3. Loosen air cleaner tube clamps and disconnect outlet tube from throttle body.
4. Disconnect from Mass Air Flow (MAF) sensor and remove tube.
5. Loosen tensioner and remove drive belts.
6. Remove oil filler cap.
7. Remove power steering pump front mounting bracket bolts.
8. Remove alternator and belt idler pulley.
9. Remove power steering pump/alternator bracket bolts.
10. Place pump/bracket assembly aside with hoses connected and in position to prevent fluid leakage.
11. Remove upper intake manifold as outlined under "Intake Manifold, Replace."
12. Remove valve cover as outlined under "Valve Cover, Replace."
13. Remove fuel injection supply manifold.
14. Remove lower intake manifold as outlined under "Intake Manifold, Replace."
15. Remove exhaust manifolds as outlined under "Exhaust Manifold, Replace."
16. Loosen rocker arm fulcrum bolts enough to allow rocker arm to be lifted off pushrod, then rotate to one side.
17. Remove pushrods and identify for installation in original positions.
18. Remove bolts and cylinder head. Discard bolts and gaskets.

Installation

Install new cylinder head bolts.

1. Lightly oil all bolts and stud bolt threads before installation, except those specifying special sealant.
2. Clean cylinder head, intake manifold, rocker arm cover and head gasket surfaces. If cylinder head was removed for head gasket replacement, inspect flatness of cylinder head and cylinder block gasket surfaces.
3. Position new head gasket onto cylinder block using dowels for alignment, then position cylinder heads onto cylinder block.
4. **Torque** new cylinder head bolts to 15 ft. lbs. in sequence, **Fig. 16.**
5. **Torque** head bolts to 29 ft. lbs.
6. **Torque** bolts to 36 ft. lbs.
7. Back off cylinder head bolts, one at a

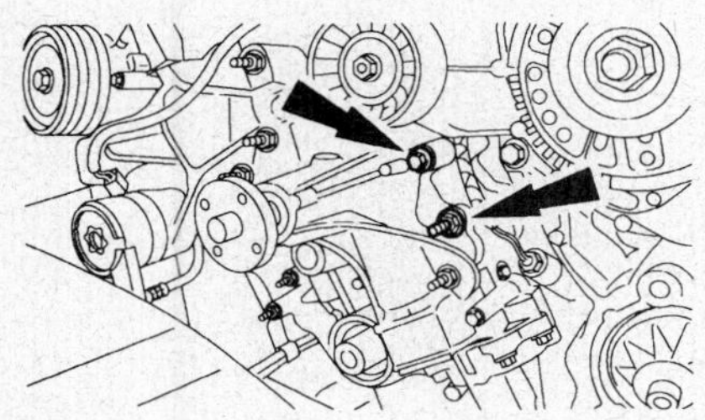

FM1069901045000X

Fig. 19 Front cover capscrew location. 1999–2002

time, 2–3 turn. **Do not loosen all bolts at same time. Only work on one bolt at a time.**

8. **Torque** long bolts to 29–37 ft. lbs. in sequence
9. Tighten long bolts an additional 180° in sequence.
10. **Torque** short bolts to 15–22 ft. lbs. in sequence
11. Tighten short bolts an additional 180° in sequence.
12. Dip each pushrod end in engine assembly lubricant D9AZ-19579-D, or equivalent.
13. Install pushrods in original positions and lubricate rocker arms with engine assembly lubricant.
14. Install rocker arms.
15. Install exhaust manifolds as outlined under "Exhaust Manifold, Replace."
16. Install lower intake manifold as outlined under "Intake Manifold, Replace."
17. Install fuel injection supply manifold.
18. Position rocker arm and new valve cover on cylinder head.
19. Ensure ignition wire routing clip stud bolts are properly position.
20. Install and tighten rocker arm bolts.
21. Install upper intake manifold as outlined under "Intake Manifold, Replace."
22. Install and tighten spark plugs, then connect ignition wires to spark plugs.
23. Install oil filler cap.
24. Install alternator/power steering pump mounting bracket and alternator.
25. Install accessory drive belt tensioner.
26. Install power steering pump and support bracket.
27. Install drive belt.
28. Connect battery ground cable.
29. Install outlet tube and connect tube to MAF sensor.
30. Connect outlet tube to throttle body, then tighten air cleaner tube clamps on outlet tube.
31. Connect crankcase ventilation tube to air cleaner outlet tube and wire harness to IAT sensor.
32. Connect battery ground cable.
33. Install outlet tube and connect tube to MAF sensor.
34. Connect outlet tube to throttle body, then tighten air cleaner tube clamps on outlet tube.
35. Connect crankcase ventilation tube to air cleaner outlet tube and wire harness to IAT sensor.

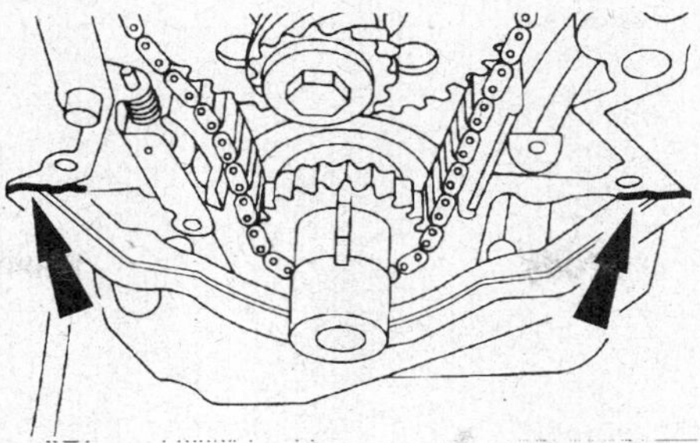

FM1069901046000X

Fig. 20 Sealant application before gasket installation. 1999–2002

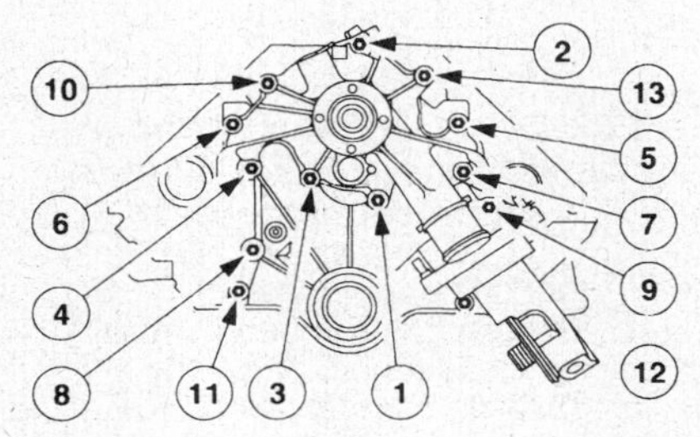

FM1069901048000X

Fig. 22 Front cover bolt tightening sequence. 1999–2002

RIGHTHAND

Removal

1. Drain engine cooling system.
2. Disconnect wire harness from Intake Air Temperature (IAT) sensor and crankcase ventilation tube from air cleaner outlet tube.
3. Loosen air cleaner tube clamps and disconnect outlet tube from throttle body.
4. Disconnect from Mass Air Flow (MAF) sensor and remove tube.
5. Loosen tensioner and remove drive belts.
6. Remove drive belt.
7. **On models equipped with air conditioning,** remove mounting bracket bolts and place air conditioning compressor aside with hoses connected.
8. **On models less air conditioning,** remove idler pulley.
9. **On all models,** remove positive crankcase ventilation valve.
10. Remove upper intake manifold as outlined under "Intake Manifold, Replace."
11. Remove valve cover as outlined under "Valve Cover, Replace."
12. Remove fuel injection supply manifold.
13. Remove lower intake manifold as outlined under "Intake Manifold, Replace."
14. Remove exhaust manifolds as outlined under "Exhaust Manifold, Replace."
15. Loosen rocker arm fulcrum bolts enough to allow rocker arm to be lifted off pushrod, then rotate to one side.
16. Remove pushrods and identify for installation in original positions.
17. Remove bolts and cylinder head. Discard bolts and gasket.

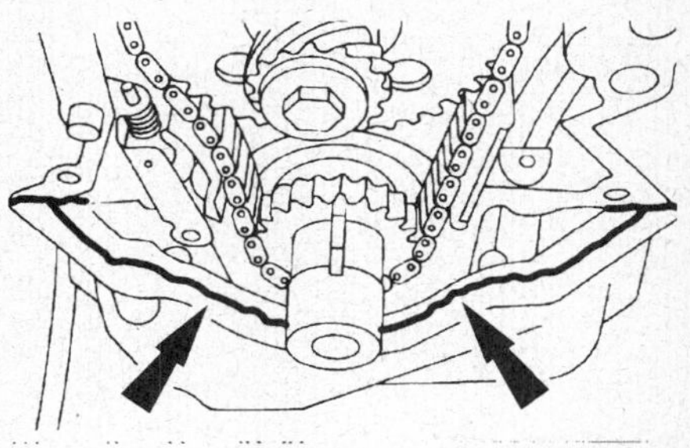

FM1069901047000X

Fig. 21 Sealant application after gasket installation. 1999–2002

Installation

Install new cylinder head bolts.

1. Lightly oil all bolts and stud bolt threads before installation, except those specifying special sealant.
2. Clean cylinder head, intake manifold, rocker arm cover and head gasket surfaces. If cylinder head was removed for head gasket replacement, inspect flatness of cylinder head and cylinder block gasket surfaces.
3. Position new head gasket onto cylinder block using dowels for alignment, then position cylinder heads onto cylinder block.
4. **Torque** new cylinder head bolts to 15 ft. lbs. in sequence, **Fig. 16.**
5. **Torque** head bolts to 29 ft. lbs.
6. **Torque** bolts to 36 ft. lbs.
7. Back off cylinder head bolts, one at a time, 2–3 turn. **Do not loosen all bolts at same time. Only work on one bolt at a time.**
8. **Torque** long bolts to 29–37 ft. lbs. in sequence
9. Tighten long bolts an additional 180° in sequence.
10. **Torque** short bolts to 15–22 ft. lbs. in sequence
11. Tighten short bolts an additional 180° in sequence.
12. Dip each pushrod end in engine assembly lubricant D9AZ-19579-D, or equivalent.
13. Install pushrods in original positions and lubricate rocker arms with engine assembly lubricant.
14. Install rocker arms.
15. Install exhaust manifolds as outlined under "Exhaust Manifold, Replace."
16. Install lower intake manifold as outlined under "Intake Manifold, Replace."
17. Install fuel injection supply manifold.
18. Position rocker arm and new valve cover on cylinder head.
19. Ensure ignition wire routing clip stud bolts are properly position.
20. Install and tighten rocker arm bolts.
21. Install upper intake manifold as outlined under "Intake Manifold, Replace."
22. Install and tighten spark plugs, then connect ignition wires to spark plugs.
23. Install PCV valve.

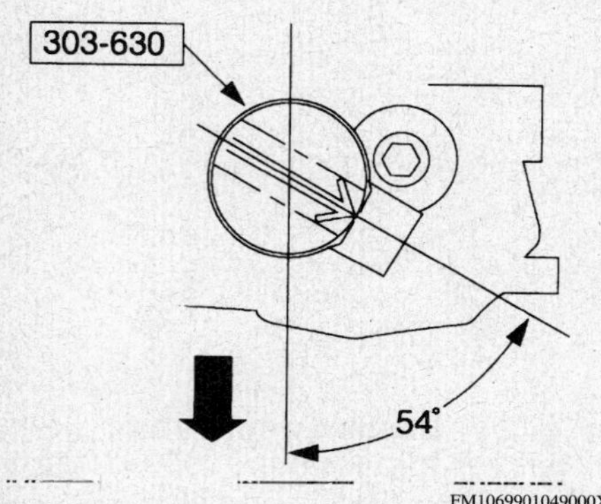

Fig. 23 Camshaft synchronizer assembly installation. 1999–2002

24. **On models equipped with air conditioning,** install mounting and supporting brackets, then the air conditioning compressor.
25. **On all models,** install drive belt.
26. Connect battery ground cable.
27. Install outlet tube and connect tube to MAF sensor.
28. Connect outlet tube to throttle body, then tighten air cleaner tube clamps on outlet tube.
29. Connect crankcase ventilation tube to air cleaner outlet tube and wire harness to IAT sensor.

1999–2002

LEFTHAND

1. Drain coolant into suitable container.
2. Remove exhaust manifold as outlined under "Exhaust Manifold, Replace."
3. Remove lower intake manifold as outlined under "Intake Manifold, Replace."
4. Mark locations and position spark plug wires aside.
5. Disconnect PCV valve.
6. Remove mounting bolts and position ignition coil aside.
7. Remove lefthand valve cover. Discard gasket.
8. Keeping in order for installation in original position, remove mounting bolts, rocker arms and pushrods.
9. Remove serpentine belt.
10. Remove power steering pump pulley using pulley remover tool No. T69L-10300-B, or equivalent.
11. Remove power steering pump and alternator mounting brackets.
12. Remove exhaust manifold mounting studs.
13. Record long and short cylinder head bolts' locations.
14. Remove and discard cylinder head bolts.
15. Remove cylinder head.
16. Reverse procedure to install, noting the following:
    a. Ensure all gasket surfaces are clean and flat.
    b. Install new head gaskets with small hole to front of engine, **Fig. 17.**
    c. Lubricate new cylinder head bolts with clean 5W-30 engine oil.
    d. Place cylinder head in position.
    e. Install new cylinder head long bolts,

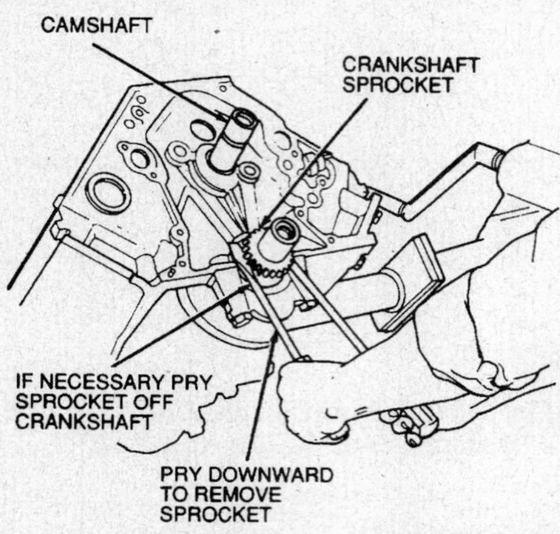

Fig. 24 Camshaft sprocket, crankshaft sprocket & timing chain replacement

then the short ones.
    f. **Torque** cylinder head bolts to 15 ft. lbs. in sequence, **Fig. 18.**
    g. **Torque** bolts to 30 ft. lbs. in sequence.
    h. **Torque** bolts to 37 ft. lbs. in sequence.
    i. Back off cylinder head bolts one at a time. **Do not loosen all bolts at once. Work on one bolt at a time.**
    j. **Torque** long bolts to 33 ft. lbs. in sequence.
    k. Tighten long bolts an additional 180° in sequence.
    l. **Torque** short bolts to 18 ft. lbs. in sequence.
    m. Tighten short bolts an additional 180° in sequence.
    n. **Torque** rocker arm bolts to 44 inch lbs.
    o. **Torque** bolts to 26 ft. lbs.
    p. Install TBI with new mounting gasket.
    q. **Torque** TBI mounting nuts and bolts to 80 inch lbs.
    r. Tighten nuts and bolts an additional 85–90°.

RIGHTHAND

1. Drain coolant into suitable container.
2. Remove exhaust manifold as outlined under "Exhaust Manifold, Replace."
3. Remove lower intake manifold as outlined under "Intake Manifold, Replace."
4. Disconnect crankcase ventilation hose.
5. Disconnect transducer vacuum hoses.
6. **On models equipped with exhaust air supply valve assembly, Fig. 7,** proceed as follows:
    a. Loosen tube nut.
    b. Disconnect air and vacuum tubes.
    c. Remove nuts valve assembly.
7. **On all models,** disconnect and remove EGR tube.
8. Mark locations and position spark plug wires aside.
9. Remove air cleaner outlet tube.
10. Disconnect throttle and speed control cables.
11. Remove mounting nuts, bolts and TBI.

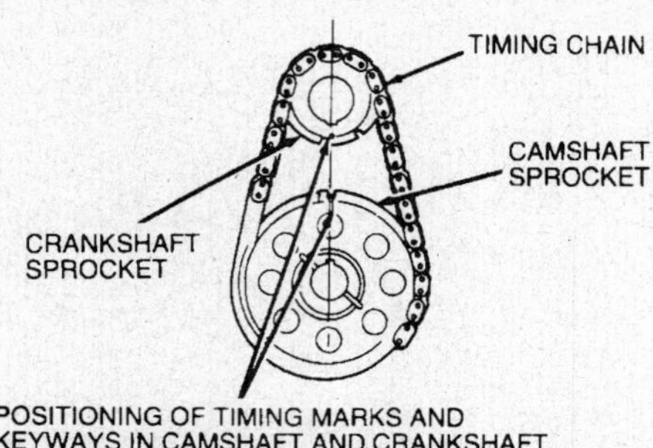

Fig. 25 Timing chain alignment marks

Discard gasket.
12. Remove righthand valve cover. Discard gasket.
13. Remove serpentine belt.
14. Recover air conditioning refrigerant as outlined in "Air Conditioning" chapter.
15. Disconnect air conditioning manifold and tube assembly.
16. Disconnect air conditioning compressor clutch electrical connector.
17. Remove air conditioning compressor mounting bracket.
18. Remove exhaust manifold mounting studs.
19. Record long and short cylinder head bolts' locations.
20. Remove and discard cylinder head bolts.
21. Remove cylinder head.
22. Reverse procedure to install, noting the following:
    a. Ensure all gasket surfaces are clean and flat.
    b. Install new head gaskets with small hole to front of engine, **Fig. 17.**
    c. Lubricate new cylinder head bolts with clean 5W-30 engine oil.
    d. Place cylinder head in position.
    e. Install new cylinder head long bolts, then the short ones.
    f. **Torque** cylinder head bolts to 15 ft. lbs. in sequence, **Fig. 18.**
    g. **Torque** bolts to 30 ft. lbs. in sequence.
    h. **Torque** bolts to 37 ft. lbs. in sequence.
    i. Back off cylinder head bolts one at a time. **Do not loosen all bolts at once. Work on one bolt at a time.**
    j. **Torque** long bolts to 33 ft. lbs. in sequence.
    k. Tighten long bolts an additional 180° in sequence.
    l. **Torque** short bolts to 18 ft. lbs. in sequence.
    m. Tighten short bolts an additional 180° in sequence.
    n. **Torque** rocker arm bolts to 44 inch lbs.
    o. **Torque** bolts to 26 ft. lbs.
    p. Install TBI with new mounting gasket.
    q. **Torque** TBI mounting nuts and bolts to 80 inch lbs.
    r. Tighten nuts and bolts an additional 85–90°.

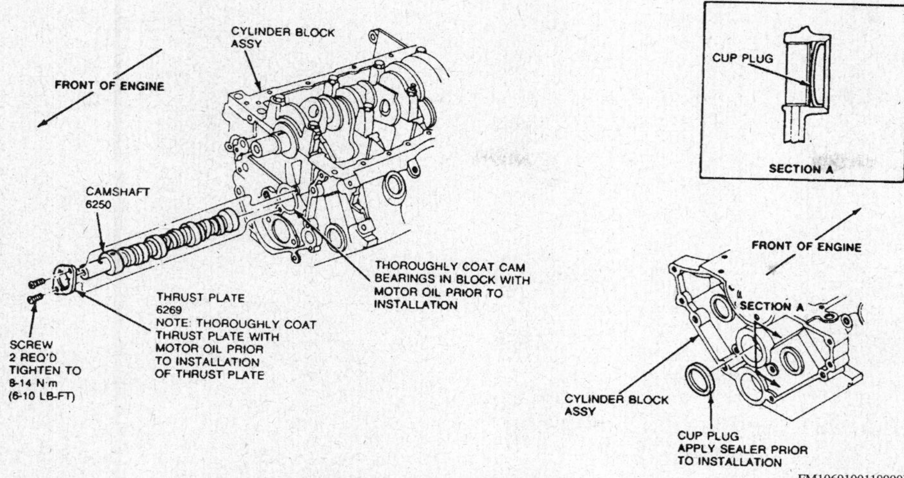

Fig. 26 Camshaft replacement

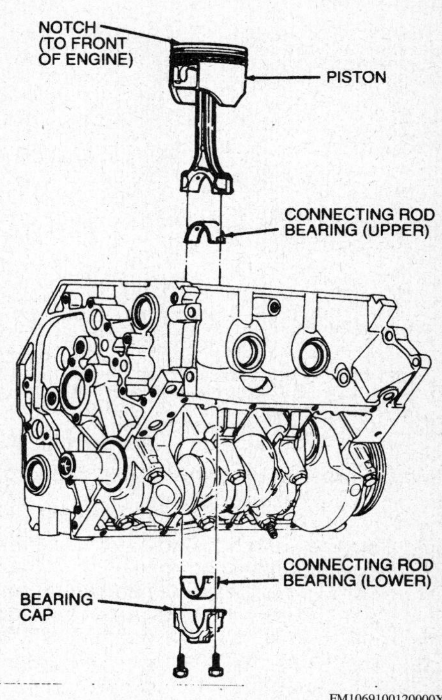

Fig. 27 Piston & rod assembly

VALVE COVER

REPLACE

1998

1. Disconnect spark plugs' ignition wires and routing clips from valve cover bolt studs.
2. **On lefthand valve cover,** remove oil filler cap and crankcase ventilation hose.
3. **On righthand valve cover,** remove positive crankcase ventilation valve.
4. **On both valve covers,** remove mounting screws, valve cover screws and gasket.
5. Reverse procedure to install. Lightly oil bolt and stud threads before installation.

1999–2002

LEFTHAND

1. Mark and position spark plug wires aside.
2. Disconnect PCV valve.
3. Remove mounting bolts and position ignition coil aside.
4. Remove cover and discard gasket.
5. Reverse procedure to install.

RIGHTHAND

1. Mark and position spark plug wires aside.
2. Disconnect crankcase ventilation hose.
3. Disconnect transducer vacuum hoses.
4. **On models equipped with exhaust air supply valve assembly, Fig. 7,** proceed as follows:
   a. Loosen tube nut.
   b. Disconnect air and vacuum tubes.
   c. Remove nuts and valve assembly.
5. **On all models,** disconnect and remove EGR tube.
6. Mark and position spark plug wires aside.
7. Remove air cleaner outlet tube.
8. Disconnect throttle and speed control cables.
9. Remove mounting nuts, bolts and TBI. Discard gasket.
10. Remove cover and discard gasket.
11. Reverse procedure to install.

VALVE ARRANGEMENT

FRONT TO REAR

Right Side .... I-E-I-E-I-E
Left Side .... E-I-E-I-E-I

CAMSHAFT LOBE LIFT SPECIFICATIONS

Engine	Intake, Inch	Exhaust, Inch
3.8L	0.245	0.259

VALVE CLEARANCE SPECIFICATIONS

Correct valve clearance is 0.09–0.19 inch.

VALVE ADJUSTMENT

This engine is equipped with hydraulic valve lash adjusters. No adjustment is required.

ROCKER ARMS

REMOVAL

1. Remove valve covers.
2. Remove seat mounting bolts and rocker arms.

INSTALLATION

1. Lubricate all rocker arms with engine assembly lubricant D9AZ-19579-D, , or equivalent.
2. **Rocker arm seats must be fully seated in cylinder head and pushrods must be seated in rocker arm sockets prior to final tightening.**
3. Rotate crankshaft until valve tappet rests onto heel (base circle) of camshaft lobe.
4. Position rocker arms over pushrods.
5. Install rocker arm seats.
6. Tighten rocker arm seat mounting bolts.
7. Repeat procedure for each rocket arm.
8. Final tightening with camshaft may be in any position.
9. Install valve cover.

VALVE GUIDES

Valve guides consist of holes bored in the cylinder head. For service the guide holes can be reamed oversize to accommodate valves with oversize stems of 0.015 and 0.030 inch.

HYDRAULIC LIFTERS

REPLACE

Before replacing a lifter for noisy operation, ensure the noise is not caused by improper valve to rocker arm clearance or by worn rocker arms or pushrods.

REMOVAL

1. Disconnect ignition wires at spark plugs using spark plug wire remover tool No. T74P-666-A, or equivalent.
2. Remove ignition wire routing clips from studs on valve cover mounting bolts. Lay ignition wires with routing clips toward front of engine.
3. Remove upper intake manifold as outlined under "Intake Manifold, Replace."
4. Remove valve covers and lower intake manifold as outlined under "Intake Manifold, Replace."
5. Loosen rocker arms seat mounting bolt sufficiently to allow rocker arm to be lifted off pushrod and rotated to one side.

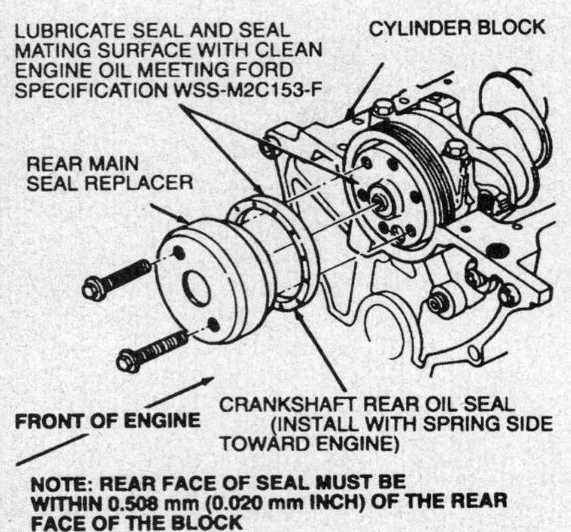

Fig. 28 Crankshaft rear seal installation

6. Remove pushrods and mark for installation in original positions.
7. Remove four bolts holding two tappet guide plates and retainers in place (bolts are held captive in retainers).
8. Remove six valve tappet guide plates from adjacent valve tappets.
9. Remove lifters using suitable magnet and mark for installation in original positions.
10. If lift is stuck in bores because excessive varnish or gum deposits, rotate it back and forth using suitable claw-type tool.

INSTALLATION

1. Lean cylinder head and valve sealing surfaces using suitable solvent.
2. Lightly oil bolts and stud threads before installation, except those specifying special sealant.
3. Lubricate each lift and bore with engine assembly lubricant No. D9AZ-19579-D, or equivalent.
4. Install each lifer in bore from which it was removed.
5. If new lifters are being installed, inspect for free fit in bore.
6. Align flats on side of lifter and install six valve tappet guide plates between adjacent valve lifters (ensure word "up" is showing).
7. Install two tappet guide plates and retainers and tighten four captive bolts.
8. Dip each push rod end in engine assembly lubricant No. D9AZ-19579-D, or equivalent.
9. Install pushrods in original positions.
10. Lubricate all rocker arms with engine assembly lubricant No. D9AZ-19579-D, or equivalent.
11. **Rocker arm seats must be fully seated in cylinder heads and pushrods must be seated in rocker arm sockets prior to final tightening.**
12. Rotate crankshaft until valve tappet rests onto heel (base circle) of camshaft lobe.
13. Position rocker arms over push rods.
14. Tighten rocker arm seat mounting bolts.
15. Repeat procedure for each rocket arm.
16. Final tightening with camshaft may be in any position.
17. Tighten rocker arm seat mounting bolts.
18. Repeat procedure for each rocket arm.
19. Final tightening with camshaft may be in any position.
20. Install lower intake manifold.
21. Install upper intake manifold.
22. Install routing clips and connect ignition wires to spark plugs.

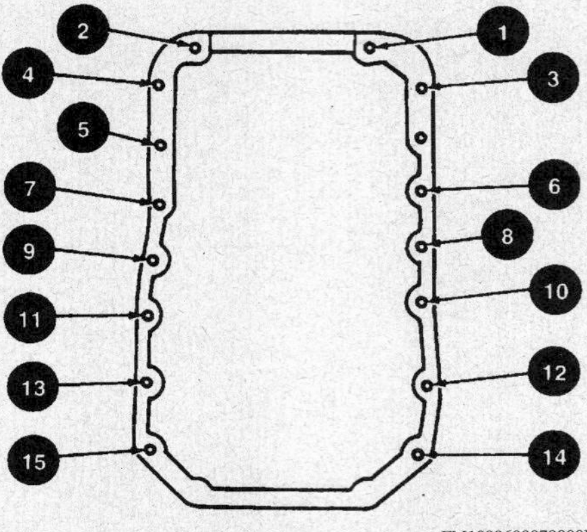

Fig. 29 Oil pan bolt tightening sequence. 1998

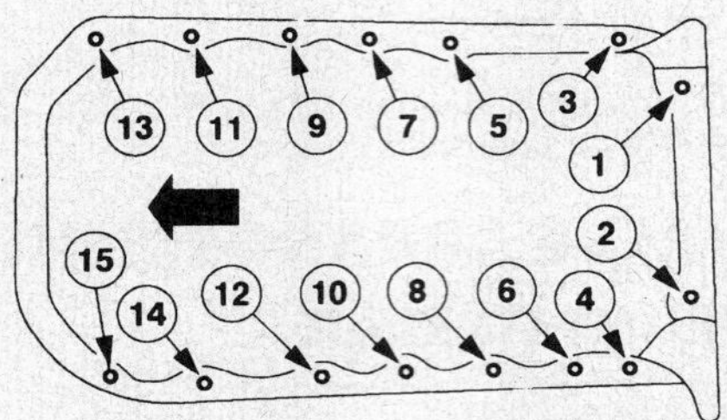

Fig. 31 Oil pan bolt tightening sequence. 1999–2002

FRONT COVER

REPLACE

1998

1. Drain engine cooling system into suitable container.
2. Remove air cleaner and outlet tube.
3. Remove cooling fan motor, fan blade and fan shroud assembly.
4. Remove drive belt and water pump pulley.
5. Remove power steering pump bracket mounting bolts and lay pump aside.
6. **On models with air conditioning,** remove compressor front support bracket leaving air conditioning compressor in place.
7. **On all models,** remove heater water outlet tube mounting bolts, then the tube and O-ring from water pump.
8. Disconnect upper radiator hose at water hose connection, then the fuel charging wiring from Camshaft Position (CMP) sensor.
9. Remove hold-down clamp, then lift CMP sensor and housing out of front cover.
10. Raise and support vehicle.
11. Remove crankshaft pulley and vibration damper using crankshaft damper remover tool No. T58P-6316-D and vibration damper remover adapter tool No. T82L-6316-B, or equivalents. **Crankshaft vibration damper and pulley are initially balanced as a unit so if vibration damper and pulley have to be separated, mark so they maybe assembled in same position.**
12. Remove oil bypass filter and disconnect lower radiator hose at water pump.
13. Remove oil pan as outlined under "Oil Pan, Replace."
14. Lower vehicle and remove front cover mounting bolts.
15. Remove front cover and water pump as an assembly.
16. Remove front cover gasket, as required, Crankshaft Position (CKP) sensor shield, CKP sensor and oil pump.
17. Reverse procedures to install.

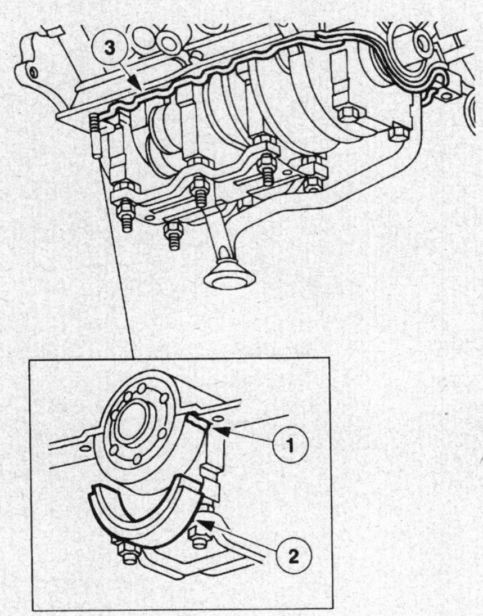

Fig. 30 Oil pan sealant locations. 1999–2002

1999-2002

1. Drain coolant into suitable container.
2. Remove serpentine belt.
3. Raise and support vehicle.
4. Rotate crankshaft pulley in engine's normal running direction until piston No. 1 reaches TDC mark.
5. Remove bolt and pulley using crankshaft pulley remover tool Nos. T58P-6316-D and T82L-6316-B, or equivalents.
6. Remove bolts and water pump pulley.
7. Remove power steering pump and bracket with hoses intact. Position pump aside.
8. Loosen nut and disconnect EGR valve tube.
9. Disconnect upper radiator and bypass hoses above front cover.
10. Disconnect connector, then remove mounting bolts and CMP sensor.
11. Remove heater water outlet tube.

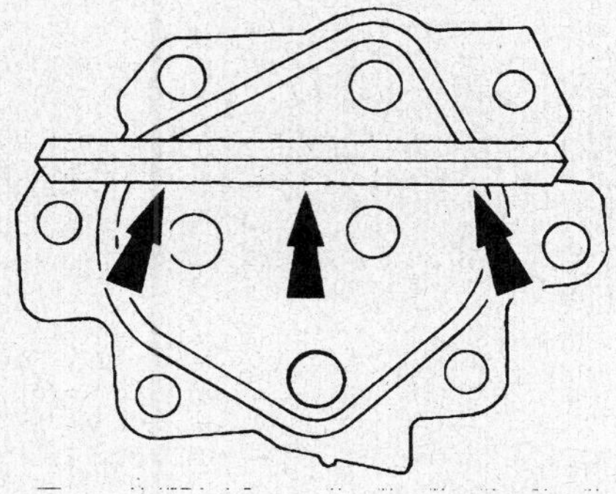

Fig. 32 Oil pump cover & front cover surface inspections. 1999–2002

12. Ensure piston No. 1 is still at TDC.
13. Remove camshaft synchronizer mounting bolt, washer and sensor. **Oil pump intermediate shaft should be removed with synchronizer.**
14. Disconnect radiator lower hose at water pump.
15. Disconnect CKP sensor.
16. Remove engine front wiring harness pin-style retainer.
17. Record locations, types and sizes of front cover mounting bolts, nuts and screws. Pay attention to the hidden cap screw, **Fig. 19.**
18. Slide front cover off alignment dowels. Discard gasket.
19. Reverse procedure to install, noting the following:
    a. Ensure gasket surfaces are clean and flat.
    b. Before installing front cover gasket, apply small portion of silicone gasket sealant No. F7AZ-19554-EA, or equivalent, **Fig. 20.**
    c. Install new front cover gasket.
    d. After installing front cover gasket, apply silicone gasket sealant to top of oil pan surface, **Fig. 21.**
    e. Install cover mounting bolts are in original positions.
    f. **Torque** bolts to 18 ft. lbs. in sequence, **Fig. 22.**
    g. Tighten mounting bolts an additional 90°. **Bolt No. 12 is not included in staged tightening.**
    h. Coat camshaft synchronizer gear with clean 10W-30 engine oil.
    i. Install synchro positioning tool No. 303-630, or equivalent by rotating tool until it engages synchronizer housing notch and armature.
    j. Install synchronizer housing assembly so tool's arrow is 54° from engine centerline, **Fig. 23.**

TIMING CHAIN

REPLACE

The front cover contains the oil pump gears and the water pump. If a new front cover is to be installed, remove water pump and oil pump gears from old front cover.

REPLACE

1. Remove front cover as outlined under "Front Cover, Replace."

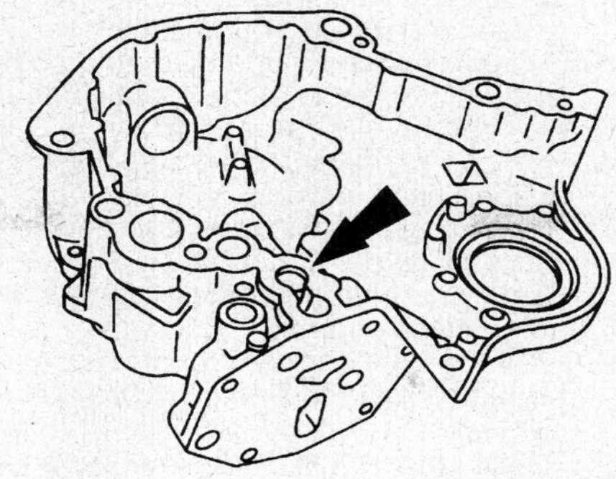

Fig. 33 Oil pump pressure relief valve removal. 1999–2002

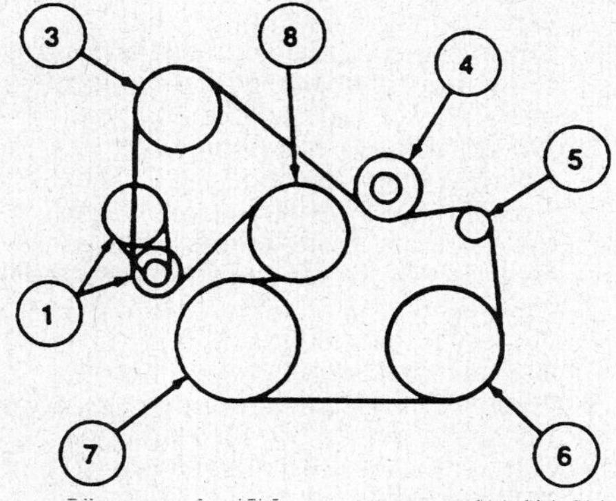

Fig. 35 Serpentine drive belt routing. 1998

2. Remove camshaft sprocket retainer bolt and washer from end of camshaft.
3. Remove distributor drive gear.
4. If crankshaft sprocket is difficult to remove, loosen crankshaft sprocket by prying, using suitable pair of large pry bars positioned on both sides of crankshaft sprocket.
5. Remove camshaft sprocket, crankshaft sprocket and timing chain at the same time, **Fig. 24.**
6. Remove timing chain vibration damper from front of cylinder blocks by pulling back on ratchet mechanism and installing pin through hole in bracket to relieve tension.

INSTALLATION

1. With timing chain vibration damper in compressed position, install timing chain vibration damper and mounting bolts to front of cylinder blocks.
2. Rotate crankshaft to position piston No. 1 at TDC and keyway at 12 o'clock.
3. Lubricate timing chain with clean engine oil.
4. Install camshaft sprocket, crankshaft sprocket and timing chain at same time. Ensure timing marks properly positioned , **Fig. 25.**
5. Install distributor drive gear.
6. Install mounting bolt and washer at end of camshaft.
7. Remove timing chain vibration damper retaining pin.
8. Install front cover.

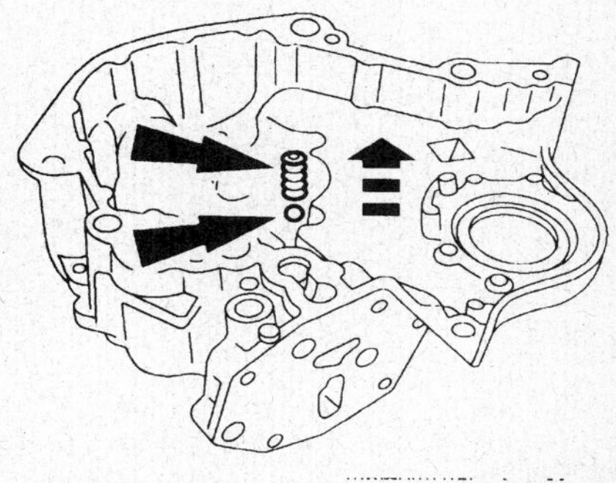

Fig. 34 Oil pressure relief valve ball & spring. 1999–2002

CAMSHAFT

REPLACE

1. Drain cooling system into suitable container.
2. Remove radiator as outlined under "Radiator, Replace."
3. Recover refrigerant as outlined in "Air Conditioning" chapter.
4. Remove condenser as outlined in "Air Conditioning" chapter.
5. Remove camshaft position sensor and housing.
6. Remove upper and lower intake manifolds as outlined under "Intake Manifold, Replace."
7. Remove hydraulic lifters as outlined under "Hydraulic Lifter, Replace."
8. Remove front cover as outlined under "Front Cover, Replace."
9. Remove timing chain as outlined under "Timing Chain, Replace."
10. Remove camshaft sprocket spacer.
11. Remove oil pan as outlined under "Oil Pan, Replace."
12. Remove camshaft thrust plate.
13. Remove camshaft by pulling toward front of engine, **Fig. 26. Do not damage camshaft bearings.**
14. Reverse procedure to install. Lubricate cam lobes and bearing surfaces with oil conditioner No. D9AZ-19579-D, or equivalent.

PISTON & ROD ASSEMBLY

When installed, piston and rod assembly should have the notch or arrow in piston head toward front of engine, **Fig. 27.** Side clearance between connecting rods at each crankshaft journal should be 0.0047–0.0114 Inch.

PISTONS, PINS & RINGS

Pistons are available in standard sizes and oversizes of 0.003, 0.020, 0.030 and 0.040 inch. Piston rings are available in standard sizes and oversizes of 0.020, 0.030 and 0.040 inch. Piston pins are available in standard size and oversizes of 0.001 and 0.002 inch.

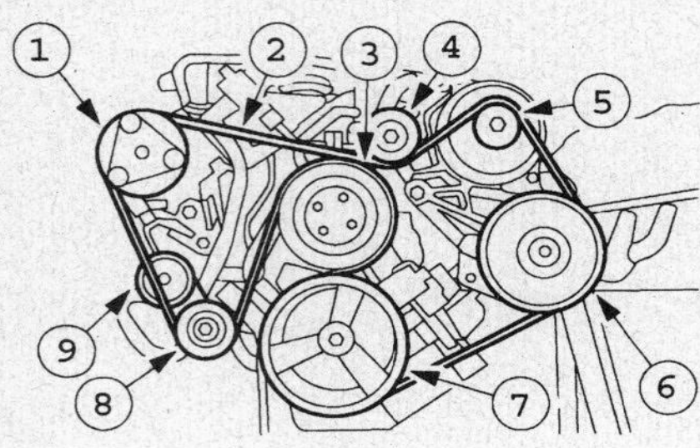

1. Air Conditioning Compressor
2. Belt
3. Water Pump
4. Idler
5. Alternator
6. Power Steering Pump
7. Crankshaft
8. Tensioner Pulley
9. Tensioner

FM1069901050000X

Fig. 36 Serpentine drive belt routing. 1999–2002

MAIN & ROD BEARINGS

Main and rod bearings are available in standard sizes and undersizes of 0.001, 0.002, 0.010, 0.020 and 0.030 inch.

CRANKSHAFT REAR OIL SEAL

REPLACE

A one piece crankshaft rear oil seal is used for replacement on all engines. The complete crankshaft rear oil seal can be replaced without removing crankshaft.

REMOVAL

1. Remove transmission as outlined in "Clutch & Manual Transmission" section or "Automatic Transmissions/ Transaxles" chapter.
2. Punch one hole into crankshaft rear oil seal metal surface between lip and cylinder blocks using suitable sharp tool
3. Remove oil seal using jet plug remover tool No. T77L-9533-B, or equivalent.

INSTALLATION

1. Lubricate new seal with clean engine oil.
2. Install seal using seal installation tool No. T82L-6701-A, or equivalent.
3. Tighten bolts alternately to seat seal properly, **Fig. 28.**

OIL PAN

REPLACE

1998

1. Disconnect wire harness from Intake Air Temperature (IAT) sensor and crankcase ventilation tube from air cleaner outlet tube.
2. Loosen air cleaner tube clamps and disconnect outlet tube from throttle body.
3. Disconnect from Mass Air Flow (MAF) sensor and remove outlet tube.
4. Remove two mounting bolts and position radiator upper sight shield aside.
5. Remove hood weather seal.
6. Remove windshield wipers as outlined in "Electrical" section.
7. Remove lefthand cowl vent screen and wiper module.
8. Raise and support vehicle using suitable engine support.
9. Remove front engine support insulator through bolts and partially lower vehicle.
10. Raise engine with engine support, then raise and support vehicle.
11. Remove starter motor as outlined in "Electrical" section.
12. Drain engine oil into suitable container.
13. Remove oil bypass filter, starter motor wire and ground strap.
14. **On models equipped with automatic transmission,** remove automatic transmission oil cooler lines.
15. **On all models,** remove oil pan to bellhousing bolts. and bolts at Crankshaft Position (CKP) sensor lower shield.
16. Remove remaining oil pan bolts.
17. Remove pinch bolt and separate steering shaft.
18. Support front subframe with suitable transmission jack.
19. Remove six front subframe rearward bolts and loosen two forward bolts.
20. Remove lower shock absorber to front suspension lower arm bolts and nuts.
21. Lower front subframe.
22. Remove oil pan. Empty residual oil from pan into suitable container.
23. Remove oil pump screen cover and tube mounting bolts, then the support bracket nut.
24. Remove oil pump screen cover and tube, then discard oil pump inlet tube gasket.
25. Reverse procedure to install, noting the following:
    a. Apply silicone gasket and sealant F1AZ019652-A, or equivalent, to oil pan.
    b. When using silicone rubber (RTV) sealer, assembly must occur within 15 minutes after sealer application.
    c. Seat lefthand before righthand side locating pin.
    d. Tighten bolts in sequence, **Fig. 29.**

1999–2002

1. Remove air cleaner outlet tube.
2. Remove radiator upper sight shield and coolant reservoir.
3. Raise and support vehicle using engine lift bracket tool set No. D94L-6001-A and engine support tool No. 303-F072, or equivalents, and suitable hoist
4. Remove left and righthand engine mount nuts, then lower vehicle.
5. Raise engine with engine support, then raise and support vehicle.
6. Drain engine oil into suitable oil pan.
7. Remove starter motor as outlined in "Electrical" section.
8. Position wiring harness bracket aside.
9. Remove bellhousing lower bolts.
10. Remove oil pan bolts.

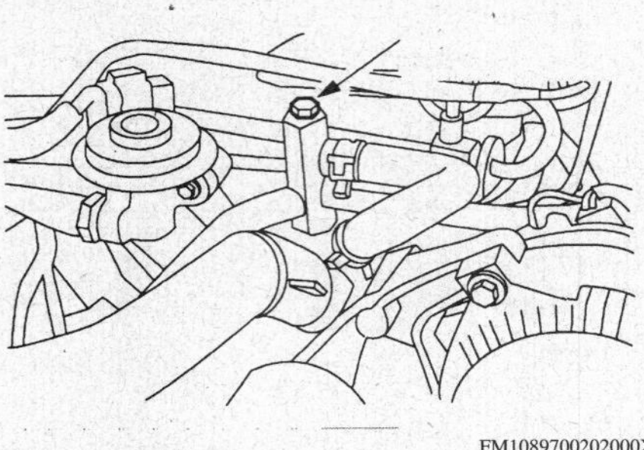

FM1089700202000X

Fig. 37 Cooling system vent plug

11. Support front subframe with suitable jack.
12. Remove four lower and two upper front subframe bolts.
13. Loosen two forward front subframe bolts.
14. Lower front subframe.
15. Remove oil pan. Empty residual oil into suitable container.
16. Reverse procedure to install, noting the following:
    a. Apply silicone gasket sealant No. F7AZ-19554-EA, or equivalent, to oil pan and block sealing surfaces , **Fig. 30.**
    b. **When using silicone rubber (RTV) sealer, assembly must occur within 15 minutes after sealer application. After this time, sealer may start to set and its sealing effectiveness may be reduced.**
    c. Install oil and loosely install bolts.
    d. **Torque** oil pan mounting bolts to 44 inch lbs. in sequence, **Fig. 31.**
    e. **Torque** mounting bolts to 89 inch lbs. in sequence.

OIL PUMP

REPLACE

1998

1. Remove oil bypass filter, as required.
2. Remove oil pump and filter body to front cover bolts.
3. Remove oil pump and filter body from front cover.
4. Inspect O-ring for distortion and wear. Replace as required.
5. Reverse procedure to install.

1999–2002

This procedure has been revised by a Technical Service Bulletin.

Some 2000–01 models built between Nov. 27, 2000, and May 30, 2001, may be equipped with a new Liquid Injection Sealing (LIS) oil pump. This oil pump cannot be repaired and must be replaced with suitable oil pump and O-ring.

1. Raise and support vehicle.
2. Drain engine oil into suitable container.
3. Remove engine oil filter.
4. Remove oil pump cover, mounting bolts and filter pad housing.
5. Separate oil pump drive and driven gears from cover. Discard O-ring.
6. Measure warpage across oil pump

cover and front cover mounting surfaces, **Fig. 32.** If surface is warped more than 0.0016 inch, replace oil pump cover or front cover.
7. Remove front cover as outlined under "Front Cover, Replace."
8. Flip cover over and remove plug over oil pump pressure relief valve, **Fig. 33.**
9. Remove pressure relief valve ball and spring, **Fig. 34.**
10. Reverse procedure to install, noting the following:
    a. Clean components in suitable solvent.
    b. Lubricate oil pump components with clean 5W-30 engine oil.
    c. Assemble pressure relief valve ball and spring with new plug.

OIL PUMP SERVICE

1998

DISASSEMBLY

1. Remove oil pump as outlined under "Oil Pump, Replace."
2. Lift pump gears out of pocket and filter body.
3. Remove oil pump body seal and discard.

INSPECTION

1. Clean front cover and oil pump and filter body sealing surfaces.
2. Measure across front cover mounting surface for wear or warpage using suitable straightedge and feeler gauge.
3. If surface is wrapped more than 0.0016 inch, replace front cover as outlined under "Front Cover, Replace."

ASSEMBLY

1. Lightly pack gear pockets with petroleum jelly or coat all gear surfaces with engine assembly lubricant No. D9AZ-19579-D, or equivalent. **Do not use chassis lubricants.**
2. Install gears in oil pump and filter body pocket. Ensure petroleum jelly fills all voids between gears and pockets.
3. Position oil pump body seal, then install oil pump and filter body to front cover using alignment dowels on front cover.

OIL PRESSURE RELIEF VALVE

Disassembly

1. Drill hole through valve plug.
2. Remove plug with slide hammer or by prying.
3. Remove spring and pressure relief valve from bore.

Inspection

1. Thoroughly clean pressure relief valve bore and pressure relief valve to remove any metal chips which may have entered bore during drilling.
2. Inspect pressure relief valve and valve bore for wear, scoring or galling. If inspection determines part(s) to be unserviceable, replace pressure relief valve and/or oil pump and filter body.
3. Measure clearance between pressure

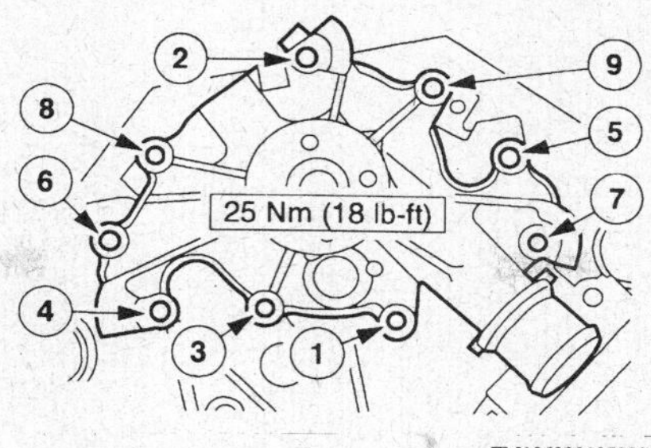

Fig. 38 Water pump fastener tightening sequence. 1999–2002

relief valve and bore. Valve should slip into bore without side play or binding.
4. Inspect spring for signs of fatigue or collapse.

Assemble

1. Lubricate pressure relief valve with engine oil and install in bore. End with smaller diameter goes in first.
2. Position spring in bore and install new plug.
3. Plug can be tapped into bore using suitable plastic tipped hammer.
4. Ensure plug is 0.01 inch below machined surface.

1999–2002

This procedure has been revised by a Technical Service Bulletin.

Some 2000–01 models built between Nov. 27, 2000, and May 30, 2001, may be equipped with a new Liquid Injection Sealing (LIS) oil pump. The LIS oil pump has a blue paint stripe along righthand edge when viewed from above. This oil pump cannot be repaired and must be replaced with suitable oil pump and O-ring.

Refer to "Oil Pump, Replace" for procedure.

SERPENTINE DRIVE BELT

Conditions requiring belt replacement are excessive wear, rib chunk-out, severe glazing and frayed cords. Replace any belt exhibiting any one of these conditions. Cracks on rib side of a belt are considered acceptable.

If the belt has chunks missing from its ribs, it should be replaced. If two or more adjacent ribs have lost sections ½ inch or longer, or if missing chunks are creating a noise or vibration condition, replace the belt.

BELT ROUTING

Refer to **Figs. 35 and 36** for serpentine drive belt routing.

BELT REPLACEMENT

1. Lift or rotate automatic tensioner.
2. Remove belt.
3. Install new belt over pulleys. Ensure all V-grooves make proper contact with pulley.
4. Rotate tensioner over belt.

COOLING SYSTEM BLEED

1. Remove vent plug, **Fig. 37.**
2. Fill radiator completely and install radiator cap.
3. Fill coolant reservoir and degas bottle to full cold mark.
4. Set heater control to full hot, high fan and set controls so air vents from dash vents.
5. Start and operate engine until fully warmed up while observing water temperature gauge as follows:
    a. If system is functioning properly, temperature will indicate normal and hot air will be felt at dash outlets.
    b. If system is not functioning properly, temperature gauge will not read and/or no hot air will be felt at dash vents.
6. If system is not functioning properly, allow engine to cool then repeat procedure.
7. If system is functioning properly, allow engine to cool, then fill coolant reservoir to full cold mark as required.
8. Install vent plug.

THERMOSTAT

REPLACE

1. Partially drain cooling system into suitable container.
2. Disconnect upper radiator hose at thermostat housing.
3. Remove two mounting bolts, housing and gaskets.
4. Reverse procedure to install.

WATER PUMP

REPLACE

1998

1. Drain cooling system into suitable container.
2. Remove radiator electric motor, fan blade and fan shroud as an assembly.
3. Rotate drive belt tensioner and remove drive belt.
4. Remove bolts and water pump pulley.
5. Remove power steering pump pulley and water pump to power steering pump brace.
6. Remove heater water outlet tube bolts and heater water outlet tube from water pump.
7. Disconnect lower radiator hose from water pump.
8. Remove water pump bolts, stud, nuts and water pump. Discard housing gasket. **Do not damage mating surfaces.**
9. Reverse procedure to install, noting the following:
    a. Lightly oil all bolt and stud threads before installation, except those specifying special sealant.
    b. Apply gasket and trim adhesive No. D7AZ-19B508-B, or equivalent, to water pump housing gasket.
    c. Coat water pump bolt No. 1 threads of with pipe sealant with Teflon

D8AZ-19554-A, or equivalent, before installing.

1999-2002

1. Drain coolant into suitable container.
2. Loosen water pump pulley bolts.
3. Remove serpentine belt.
4. Remove power steering pump pulley using pulley remover tool No. T69L-10300-B, or equivalent.
5. Remove bolts and water pump pulley.
6. Remove mounting bolts and position power steering pump aside with hoses attached.
7. Remove mounting bolts and power steering pump mounting bracket.
8. Disconnect radiator lower hose at water pump.
9. Remove mounting bolts and position power steering fluid reservoir aside with hoses attached.
10. Disconnect Camshaft Position (CMP) sensor electrical connector.
11. Remove mounting bolt and CMP sensor.
12. Remove stud, bolts and nuts and water pump.
13. Reverse procedure to install, noting the following:
    a. Install new water pump gasket.
    b. Tighten stud, bolts and nuts in sequence, **Fig. 38.**

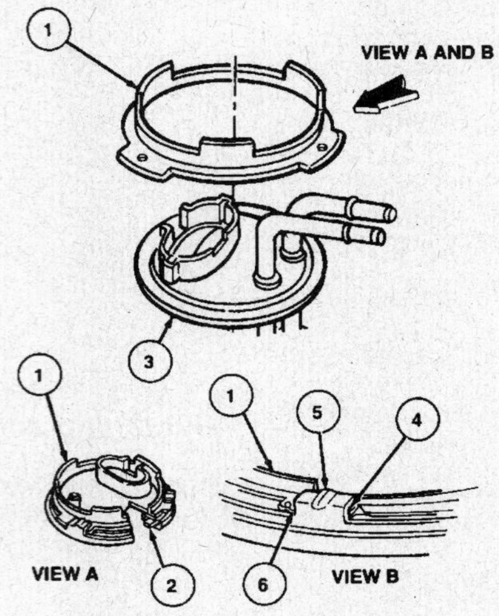

Item	Description
1	Fuel Pump Locking Retainer Ring
2	Fuel Pump Mounting Gasket
3	Fuel Pump Module
4	Stop
5	Tab
6	Detent

FM1029100137000A

Fig. 39 Fuel pump ring removal

RADIATOR

REPLACE

1998

REMOVAL

1. **On models equipped with automatic transmission,** disconnect automatic transmission fluid cooler inlet and outlet lines from radiator using disconnect tool No. T82L-9500-AH, or equivalent.
2. **On all models,** drain cooling system into suitable container.
3. Disconnect upper and lower radiator hoses, then the overflow hose.
4. Remove two upper shroud bolts at radiator support, then lift fan shroud enough to disconnect lower clips and lay shroud back over fan.
5. Remove bolts and radiator upper support.
6. Remove radiator.

INSTALLATION

1. **On models equipped with automatic transmission,** if installing new radiator, transfer oil cooler line connectors to new radiator using pipe sealant with suitable oil resistant sealer.
2. **On all models,** position radiator into vehicle.
3. Install upper supports and bolts.
4. **On models equipped with automatic transmission,** connect oil cooler lines.
5. **On all models,** install radiator electric motor, fan blade and fan shroud as an assembly by inserting two lower legs to radiator support with two bolts.
6. Install radiator support upper brackets and bolts.
7. Close petcock, then position hose clamps at least 2 inches from each hose end.
8. Slide upper, lower and overflow hoses on connections.
9. Tighten clamps. **Ensure clamps are beyond bead and place in center of clamping surface of connections. New hose clamps must be installed inside hose alignment marks.**

1999-2002

1. Drain radiator and degas bottle coolant into suitable container.
2. Disconnect cooling fan motor electrical connector and separate fan harness from shroud.
3. Remove fan shroud left and righthand mounting bolts.
4. Remove cooling fan, motor and shroud as an assembly.
5. Remove radiator sight shield.
6. Disconnect radiator upper hose at radiator.
7. **On models equipped with automatic transmission,** remove lower and upper cooler tube fittings.
8. **On all models,** raise and support vehicle.
9. Disconnect radiator lower hose at radiator and lower vehicle.
10. Remove supports and radiator.
11. Reverse procedure to install.

FUEL PUMP

REPLACE

1. Relieve fuel pressure as described under "Precautions."
2. Drain fuel tank into suitable container.
3. Raise and support vehicle.
4. Mark lines to be installed in original positions.
5. Disconnect and cap fuel tank fuel and vent lines.
6. Remove exhaust pipe and shield as required to gain access to fuel tank.
7. Mark electrical connections to be installed in original positions.
8. Disconnect electrical connectors from fuel sender and pump.
9. Disconnect fuel filler tube.
10. Remove support straps and fuel tank.
11. Remove fuel pump by rotating lock ring counterclockwise using fuel tank sender wrench No. T74P-9275-A, or equivalent, **Fig. 39.**
12. Reverse procedure to install.

FUEL FILTER

REPLACE

1. Relieve fuel system pressure as described under "Precautions."
2. Raise and support vehicle.
3. Remove push connect fittings at both ends of filter.
4. Remove fuel filter from bracket by loosening worm gear clamp. Record direction of flow arrow as installed in bracket to ensure proper direction of fuel flow through replacement filter.
5. Reverse procedure to install.

TECHNICAL SERVICE BULLETINS

BUZZING OR RATTLING EXHAUST SYSTEM

1998-99

On some of these models there may be a buzzing or rattling from the exhaust system.

This condition may be caused by loose catalytic converter, catalytic pipes, muffler pipes and/or muffler heat shields.

To correct this condition secure heat shields with suitable worm clamps. **Torque** clamps to 60 inch lbs.

FUEL PUMP WHINING/ BUZZING THROUGH RADIO SPEAKER

1998-2001

On some of these models there may be a whining or buzzing in speakers.

This condition may be caused by fuel pump electrical noise.

To correct this condition install an electronic noise Radio Frequency Interference (RFI) filter (part No. F1PZ-18B925-A) on fuel pump inside the fuel tank, as follows:

1. Remove fuel pump sender from fuel tank as described under "Fuel Pump, Replace."
2. Cut fuel pump wires three inches from flange. Discard wires.
3. Connect RFI filter connectors to fuel pump spade terminal.
4. Cut and solder both RFI filter red and black wires to flange red and black wires.
5. Install suitable heat shrink tubing over solder connectors.
6. Secure RFI filter to fuel pump using suitable bundling strap.
7. Install fuel pump sender.

ENGINE OIL CONTAMINATED w/COOLANT, UNDETERMINED COOLANT LOSS

1998

On these models, coolant may leak into the engine oiling system at the intake manifold gaskets or front cover gasket.

To correct this condition, install revised front cover and intake gaskets.

On engines built through April 24, 1998, install intake gasket kit part No. F6ZZ-9433-AA. **Ensure side gasket bead material is blue. Do not install gaskets with any other bead color.**

When installing the lower intake manifold, hand-tighten the center bolts to ease installation of the remaining bolts. The new gaskets have a slightly thicker side gasket bead material.

TIGHTENING SPECIFICATIONS

Year	Component	Torque/Ft. Lbs.
1998	Air Conditioning Compressor	30–45
	Alternator	45–57
	Camshaft Sprocket	30–37
	Camshaft Thrust Plate	72–120①
	Connecting Rod	15–18⑦
	Coolant Temperature Switch	96–144①
	Crankshaft Dampener	104–132
	Crankshaft Position Sensor	72–108 ①
	Crankshaft Position Sensor Shield	18–35①
	Crankshaft Pulley To Dampener	20–28
	Crankshaft Stud	72–102①
	Crankcase Ventilation Tube Bracket	15–22
	Cylinder Head	⑥
	Dual Converter & Pipe To Exhaust Manifold	16–23
	ECT Sensor	11–14
	EGR Valve To Exhaust Manifold	25–35
	EGR Valve To Intake Manifold	15–22
	EGR Valve To Manifold Tube Connector	34–47
	Engine Support & Wiring Bracket	15–22
	Engine Support Insulator	72–98
	Engine Support Insulator Through Bolt	35–50
	Engine To Transmission	⑤
	Exhaust Manifold	23–26
	Fan Clutch Assembly	12–18
	Fan Shroud	24–48①
	Flywheel	54–64
	Front Cover	15–22
	Fuel Injection Supply Manifold	72–84①
	Fuel Rail	72–96①
	Fulcrum Bolt	①
	Heated Oxygen Sensor	28–33
	Heater Tube Support Bracket	15–22
	Heater Water Outlet Tube To Water Pump	71–105①
	Ignition Wire Routing Clip	71–102①
	Intake Manifold, Lower	③
	Intake Manifold, Upper	③
	Lower Shock Absorber To Front Suspension Lower Arm	103–144
	Low Oil Level Sensor	20–30
	Main Bearing Cap	81–89
	Oil Drain Plug	15–25
	Oil Filter Adapter To Front Cover	18–22
	Oil Inlet Tube To Cylinder Block	15–22
	Oil Inlet Tube To Main Bearing Cap	30–40
	Oil Level Indicator Tube Support Bracket	15–22
	Oil Pan	79–105①
	Oil Pickup Tube	15–22
	Oil Pump & Filter Body	④
	Oil Pump Intermediate Shaft	15–22
	Oil Pump Screen Cover & Tube	15–22
	Oil Pump Screen Cover & Tube Bracket	30–40

Continued

TIGHTENING SPECIFICATIONS—Continued

Year	Component	Torque/Ft. Lbs.
1998	Power Steering Brace, Lower	18–24
	Power Steering Brace, Upper	30–45
	Radiator	71–92.5①
	Radiator Hose Clamps	20–30①
	Rocker Arm	84–108①⑪
	Rocker Arm Cover	84–108①
	Spark Plugs	7–15
	Steering Shaft Pinch Bolt	30–42
	Thermostat Housing	15–22
	Throttle Body	15–22
	Torque Converter	20–34
	Valve Lifter Guide Plate	84–120①
	Water Outlet Connection	15–22
	Water Pump, Bolt & Stud	15–22
	Water Pump, Nut	53–71①
	Water Pump Pulley	12–18
1999–2002	Accelerator Cable Bracket	89①
	Air Conditioning Compressor Bracket, Bolt & Nut	35
	Air Conditioning Compressor Bracket, Stud	18
	Alternator Bracket	18
	Alternator Bracket To Head	30
	Alternator Positive Cable	89①
	Automatic Transmission Oil Cooler Tube Bracket	20
	Bulkhead 42-Pin Electrical Connector	89①
	Camshaft Position Sensor	27①
	Camshaft Synchronizer Drive Gear To Camshaft	33
	Camshaft Synchronizer To Front Cover	18
	Camshaft Thrust Plate	108①
	Connecting Rod Cap	18⑧
	Coolant Reservoir To Head	89①
	Coolant Reservoir To Bracket	80①
	Cooling System Vent Plug	108①
	Crankshaft Main Bearing	37⑨
	Crankshaft Pulley	118
	Cylinder Head	⑥
	EGR Transducer Bracket	89①
	EGR Tube	30
	Engine Mount Ground Strap	20
	Engine Mount	52
	Engine Mount Bracket	52
	Engine Mount To Subframe Nut	85
	Engine To Transmission	30
	Exhaust Air Supply Tube	22
	Exhaust Air Supply Valve	89①
	Exhaust Manifold, Nut	24
	Exhaust Manifold, Stud	71①
	Fan Shroud	80①
	Flywheel	59
	Front Cover To Block	18
	Front Subframe To Body	66
	Front Subframe To Shock Tower	85

Continued

TIGHTENING SPECIFICATIONS—Continued

Year	Component	Torque/Ft. Lbs.
1999–2002	Fuel Supply Manifold	89①
	Hood Ground Strap	108①
	Hood Hinge	108①
	Ignition Coil To Intake Manifold	53①
	Intake Manifold, Lower	③
	Intake Manifold, Upper	③
	Main Bearing Bridge	24
	Motor Mount Bracket	52
	Motor Mount To Motor Mount	52
	Motor Mount To Subframe	85
	Oil Dipstick Tube	89①
	Oil Pan Baffle	35
	Oil Pan Drain Plug	19
	Oil Pan To Block	②
	Oil Pan To Bellhousing	33
	Oil Pickup Tube To Baffle	35
	Oil Pickup Tube To Block	18
	Oil Pump Cover To Front Cover	18
	Power Steering Pressure Tube	30
	Power Steering Pump	18
	Power Steering Pump Bracket	71①
	Power Steering Pump Bracket To Block	15
	Radiator Support	22
	Rocker Arm Pivot	⑥
	Steering Column Pinch	35
	Throttle Cable Bracket	89①
	Timing Chain Tensioner	108①
	Torque Converter	27
	Valve Cover	89①
	Valve Lifter Guide Plate	108①
	Water Outlet Tube	89①
	Water Pump Pulley	18
	Wire Harness	20
	42-Pin Connector	89①

①— Inch lbs.

②— Refer to "Oil Pan, Replace" for tightening specifications and sequence.

③— Refer to "Intake Manifold, Replace" for tightening specifications and sequence.

④— M8 bolts, 18–22 ft. lbs.; M6 bolts, 72–96 inch lbs.

⑤— Automatic transmission, 40–50 ft. lbs.; manual transmission, 28–38 ft. lbs.

⑥— Refer to "Cylinder Head, Replace" for tightening specifications and sequence.

⑦— Torque to 30–33 ft. lbs., finally tighten an additional 90–120°.

⑧— Torque to 33 ft. lbs.; finally tighten additional 105°.

⑨— On 1999 models, tighten an additional 115–125°; on 2000 models, tighten an additional 120°; on 2001–02 models, tighten an additional 90°.

4.6L Engine

NOTE: For Procedures Not Found In This Section, Refer To "4.6L Engine" Section In "Continental, Mark VIII & Town Car" Chapter.

NOTE: On Air Bag Equipped Models, Refer To "Air Bag System Precautions" Located In The Front Of This Manual For System Disarming & Arming Procedures.

NOTE: Refer To "Computer Relearn Procedures" Located In The Front Of This Manual When Battery Power To The Computer Has Been Interrupted.

NOTE: Prior To Performing Any Service Operations Listed In This Section, Consult The "Technical Service Bulletins" Section For Related Information.

INDEX

PRECAUTIONS

AIR BAG SYSTEMS

Refer to "Air Bag System Precautions" in front of this manual for system disarming and arming procedures.

BATTERY GROUND CABLE

Prior to service, disconnect battery ground cable and isolate as required.

FUEL SYSTEM PRESSURE RELIEF

Fuel supply tubes will remain pressurized for long periods of time after engine shutdown. This pressure must be relieved before beginning fuel system service or personal injury or damage to vehicle may occur. A valve is provided on fuel injection supply manifold for this purpose.

1. Connect EFI/CFI fuel pressure gauge tool No. T80L-9974-B, or equivalent, to fuel pressure relief valve on fuel injection supply manifold.
2. Place outlet hose of tool into suitable fuel container.
3. Open manual valve on fuel pressure gauge tool to relieve fuel system pressure.

COMPRESSION PRESSURE

When inspecting cylinder compression, lowest cylinder must be within 75% of highest cylinder. Perform compression test with engine at normal operating temperature, spark plugs and air cleaner removed and the throttle propped wide open.

ENGINE MOUNT

REPLACE

1998

1. Raise and support vehicle.
2. Support engine using suitable jack with wood block placed under engine.
3. Remove engine support to crossmember mounting nuts.
4. Raise engine until support is free of crossmember.
5. Remove support to block stud bolts and bolts, then the engine.
6. Reverse procedure to install. Install new self-locking bolts and nuts.

1999–2002

1. Install lift bracket tool No. D93P-6001-A3, or equivalent.

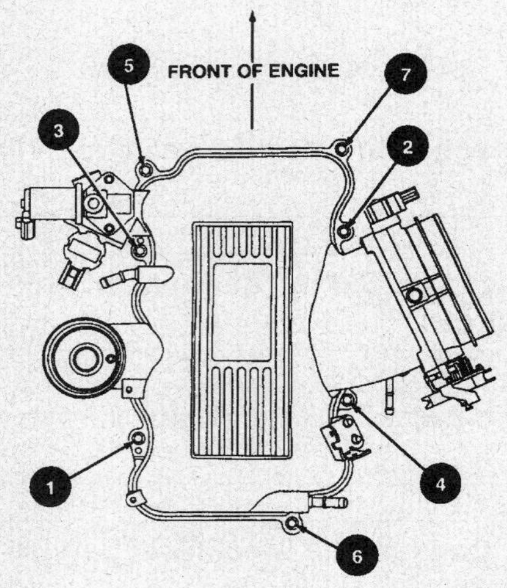

Fig. 1 Upper intake manifold tightening sequence. 1998 DOHC engine

2. Install engine support tool No. 303-290-A, or equivalent.
3. Remove starter motor as outlined in "Electrical" section.
4. Remove engine mount nuts and lower vehicle.
5. Raise engine using support tool.
6. Raise vehicle and remove engine mount.
7. Reverse procedure to install.

ENGINE

REPLACE

DOHC

1998

1. Mark bolt for installation alignment and remove hood.
2. Remove engine compartment braces.
3. Remove air cleaner outlet.
4. Recover air conditioning refrigerant as outlined in "Air Conditioning" chapter. Cap air conditioning fittings.
5. Drain cooling system into suitable container and remove coolant recovery reservoir.
6. Remove cooling fan motor and shroud, then disconnect upper radiator hose at water bypass tube.
7. Disconnect secondary air injection diverter valve vacuum regulator control connector and secondary air injection pump hose from diverter valve.
8. Relieve fuel system pressure as outlined under "Precautions."
9. Disconnect fuel lines from fuel supply manifold.
10. Disconnect 42-pin connector and other engine wiring from firewall.
11. Disconnect accelerator and speed control cables from engine.
12. Disconnect canister purge and chassis vacuum hoses from engine.
13. Disconnect alternator wiring from alternator and engine wiring connectors at power distribution box.
14. **On models equipped with automatic transmission,** disconnect transmission cooler lines.
15. **On all models,** remove power steering return and pressure hoses from pump.
16. Drain power steering pump into suitable container.
17. Disconnect return line hose and remove power steering reservoir.
18. Connect suitable lifting eye to rear of righthand cylinder head.
19. Raise and support vehicle.
20. Disconnect air conditioning lines from compressor. Cap air conditioning lines and fittings.
21. Drain engine oil into suitable container.
22. Remove dual converter Y-pipe and lower radiator hose.
23. Remove starter as outlined in "Electrical" section.
24. Remove transmission as outlined in "Clutch & Manual Transmission" section or "Automatic Transmission/ Transaxle" chapter.
25. Disconnect heater hoses from tubes at rear of righthand cylinder head.
26. Remove left and righthand engine support through bolts' nuts.
27. Lower vehicle.
28. Connect suitable lifting eye to front of lefthand cylinder head.
29. Connect suitable lifting equipment to lifting eyes.
30. Remove engine.
31. **On models equipped with manual transmission,** place on stable surface to remove clutch and pressure plate, as required.
32. **On all models,** mount engine to suitable work stand.
33. Reverse procedure to install.

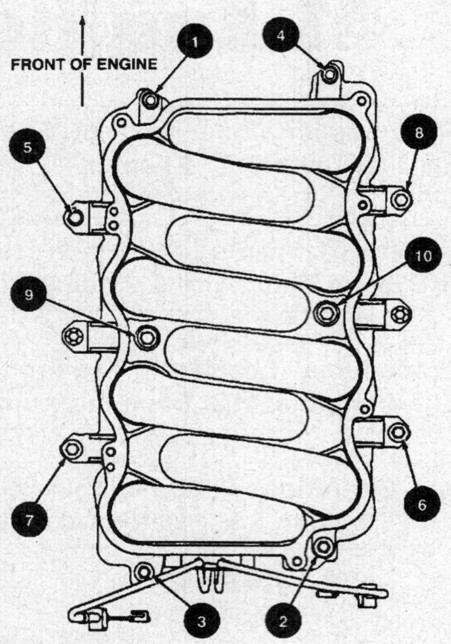

Fig. 2 Lower intake manifold loosening sequence. 1998 DOHC engine

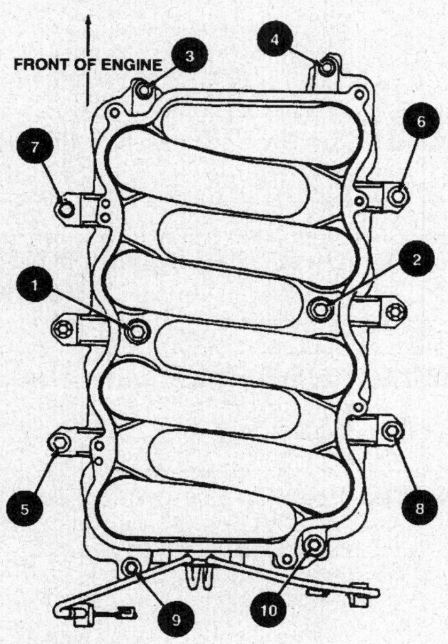

Fig. 3 Lower intake manifold tightening sequence. 1998 DOHC engine

1999–2001

1. Drain coolant into suitable container.
2. Recover air conditioning refrigerant as outlined in "Air Conditioning" chapter.
3. Remove air cleaner and outlet tube.
4. Relieve fuel system pressure as outlined under "Precautions."
5. Disconnect fuel lines, as required.
6. Remove radiator upper hose.
7. Disconnect throttle and speed control cables, then the return spring.
8. Remove bracket mounting bolts, then throttle and speed control cables aside.
9. Disconnect EVAP emissions return line.
10. Disconnect 16- and 42-pin electrical connectors.
11. Separate wiring harness at three firewall locations.
12. Disconnect TBI electrical connectors.
13. Disconnect HVAC vacuum supply hoses.
14. Place suitable container firewall fittings and disconnect heater hoses.
15. Remove nuts and wiring support bracket.
16. Disconnect electrical connectors near underhood power distribution box.
17. Slide underhood power distribution box access cover up, then remove nut and battery cables.
18. Disconnect low coolant sensor electrical connector.
19. Disconnect coolant hose at bypass tube.
20. Remove transmission shift lever knob.
21. Remove console panel shifter plate. Lift boot over lever.
22. Remove mounting bolts and shift lever.
23. Remove mounting screws inner boot.
24. Remove four mounting bolts and shifter assembly.

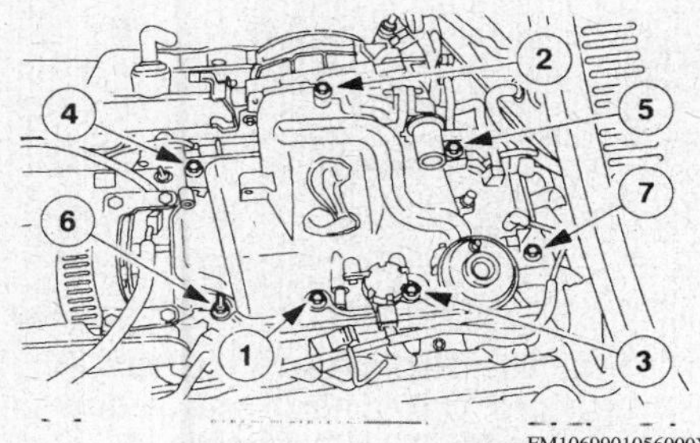

Fig. 4 Upper intake manifold bolt tightening sequence. 1999–2001 DOHC engine

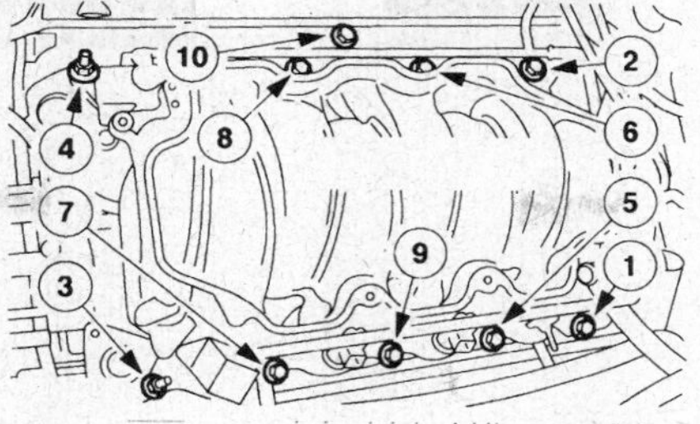

Fig. 5 Lower intake manifold fastener tightening sequence. 1999–2001 DOHC engine

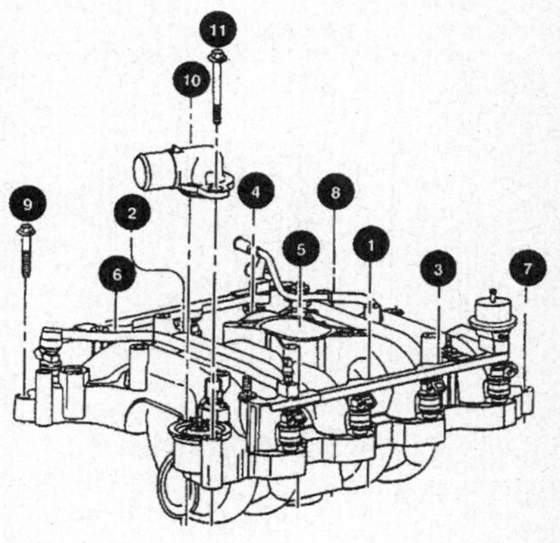

Fig. 6 Intake manifold tightening sequence. 1998 SOHC engine

25. Raise and support vehicle.
26. Remove front wheels and tires assemblies.
27. Disconnect front wheel speed sensor electrical connectors.
28. Remove mounting bolts and position front brake caliper aside with suitable wire or rope.
29. Remove mounting fasteners and three-way catalytic converter,
30. Disconnect air conditioning compressor inlet and outlet lines.
31. Position air conditioning muffler aside.
32. Remove starter motor as outlined in "Electrical" section.
33. Position wiring harness at front of engine aside.
34. Disconnect engine oil pressure sensor electrical connector.
35. Remove mounting nut and engine power ground cable.
36. Disconnect hose from engine oil filter adapter.
37. Remove radiator lower hose.
38. Disconnect clutch cable at transmission.
39. Disconnect power steering high pressure line.
40. Disconnect lower power steering line from fluid cooler.
41. Disconnect hose at power steering fluid reservoir.
42. Remove mounting bolt and power steering pump anti-rotation clip.
43. Disconnect power steering pump high pressure line fitting.
44. Separate steering shaft from steering gear. Discard bolt.
45. Remove pin-style retainers, then position left and righthand splash shields aside.
46. Remove stabilizer bar clamp nuts.
47. Remove mounting bolts and inspection cover.
48. Remove exhaust air supply valve tube nuts at exhaust manifolds.
49. Position universal powertrain lift and extension.
50. Mark crossmember for installation alignment.
51. Remove crossmember to body and frame bolts.
52. Remove engine and transmission.
53. Install engine righthand lifting bracket tool No. D93P-6001-A1, and lefthand lifting bracket tool No. D93P-6002-A2, or equivalents.

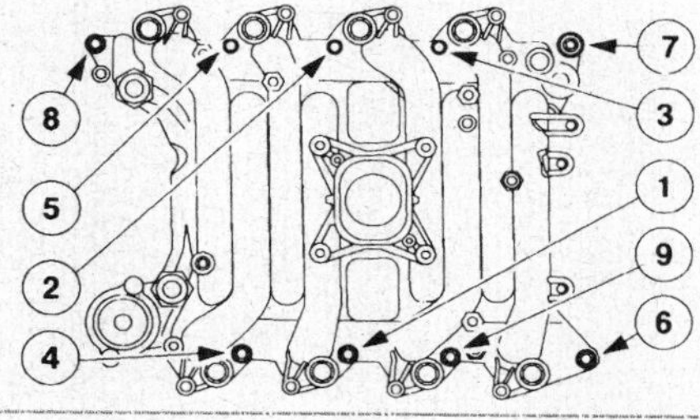

Fig. 7 Intake manifold bolt tightening sequence. 1999–2001 SOHC engine

54. Install suitable engine lifting crank or skyhook.
55. Remove motor mount nuts.
56. Disconnect transmission wiring.
57. Remove transmission to engine bolts.
58. Raise and separate engine from front A-frame.
59. Reverse procedure to install.

SOHC

1998

1. Mark bolt for installation alignment and remove hood.
2. Remove engine compartment braces.
3. Remove air cleaner outlet.
4. Recover air conditioning refrigerant as outlined in "Air Conditioning" chapter. Cap air conditioning fittings.
5. Drain cooling system into suitable container and remove coolant recovery reservoir.
6. Remove cooling fan motor and shroud, then disconnect upper radiator hose at water bypass tube.
7. Relieve fuel system pressure as outlined under "Precautions."
8. Disconnect fuel lines from fuel supply manifold.
9. Disconnect 42-pin connector and other engine wiring from firewall.
10. Disconnect accelerator and speed control cables from engine.
11. Disconnect canister purge and chassis vacuum hoses from engine.
12. Disconnect alternator wiring from alternator and engine wiring connectors at power distribution box.
13. **On models equipped with automatic transmission,** disconnect transmission cooler lines.
14. **On all models,** remove power steering return and pressure hoses from pump.
15. Drain power steering pump into suitable container.
16. Disconnect return line hose and remove power steering reservoir.
17. Connect suitable lifting eye to rear of righthand cylinder head.
18. Raise and support vehicle.
19. Disconnect air conditioning lines from compressor. Cap air conditioning lines and fittings.
20. Drain engine oil into suitable container.
21. Remove dual converter Y-pipe and lower radiator hose.
22. Remove starter as outlined in "Electrical" section.
23. Remove transmission as outlined in "Clutch & Manual Transmission" section or "Automatic Transmission/ Transaxle" chapter.
24. Disconnect heater hoses from tubes at rear of righthand cylinder head.
25. Remove left and righthand engine support through bolts' nuts.
26. Lower vehicle.
27. Connect suitable lifting eye to front of lefthand cylinder head.
28. Connect suitable lifting equipment to lifting eyes.
29. Remove engine.
30. **On models equipped with manual transmission,** place on stable surface to remove clutch and pressure plate, as required.
31. **On all models,** mount engine to suitable work stand.
32. Reverse procedure to install.

1999–2002

1. Drain coolant into suitable container.
2. Recover air conditioning refrigerant as outlined in "Air Conditioning" chapter.
3. Mark hinge locations, then disconnect ground strap and underhood lamp electrical connector.
4. Remove hood and battery.
5. Remove air cleaner and outlet tube.
6. Remove degas bottle.
7. Relieve fuel system pressure as outlined under "Precautions."
8. Disconnect fuel lines, as required.
9. Disconnect radiator upper hose at water outlet.

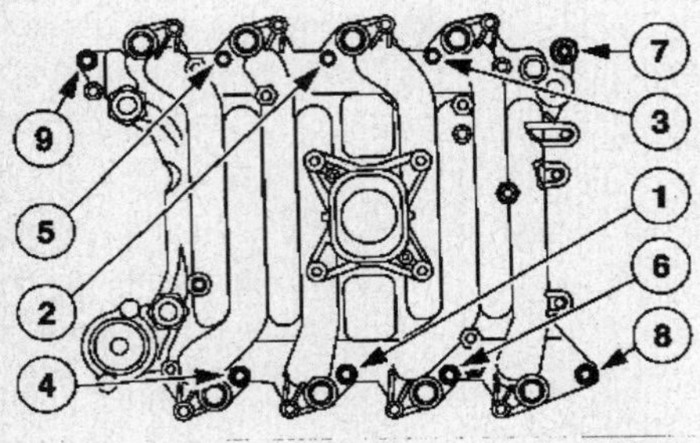

Fig. 8 Intake manifold bolt tightening sequence. 2002 SOHC engine

10. Disconnect throttle and speed control cables, then the return spring.
11. Remove bracket mounting bolts, then position throttle and speed control cables aside.
12. Disconnect HVAC vacuum supply hoses.
13. Place suitable drain pan under firewall fittings and disconnect heater hoses.
14. Remove mounting bolt and disconnect bulkhead multi-pin electrical connector.
15. Separate wiring harness at three firewall locations.
16. Disconnect TBI electrical connectors.
17. Remove safety clip and disconnect manifold suction tube.
18. Disconnect air conditioning pressure cycling switch electrical connector.
19. Separate liquid tube from air conditioning condenser.
20. Disconnect power steering hose from fluid reservoir.
21. Disconnect engine to body or frame ground wires.
22. Disconnect fusible link and electrical connector near battery tray.
23. Disconnect ground connector near washer fluid reservoir.
24. Slide underhood power distribution box access cover up, then remove nut and battery cables.
25. Separate degas sensor electrical connector from battery tray.
26. Raise and support vehicle.
27. Disconnect HO2S electrical connectors.
28. Remove exhaust pipe to manifold flange nuts.
29. Remove starter as outlined in "Electrical" section.
30. Remove nine bellhousing to engine bolts.
31. Disconnect engine to body lower ground strap.
32. Remove serpentine belt.
33. Position suitable drain pan under power steering pump.
34. Disconnect power steering fluid lines at pump.
35. Remove power steering pump pulley using power steering pump pulley remover tool No. T69L-10300-B, or equivalent.
36. Remove mounting bolts and power steering pump.
37. Lower vehicle.

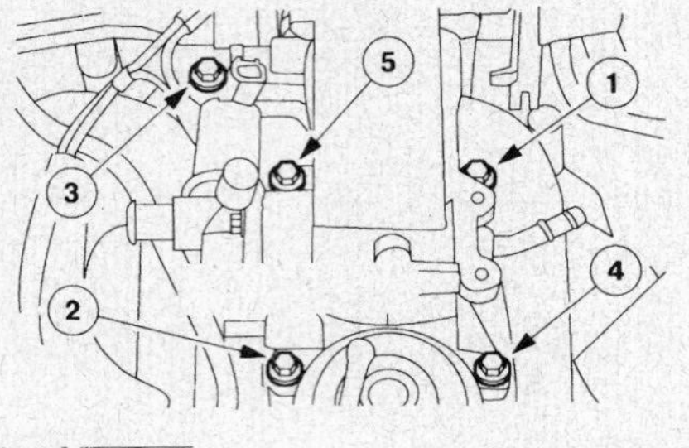

Fig. 9 TBI bolt tightening sequence. 1999–2002 SOHC engine

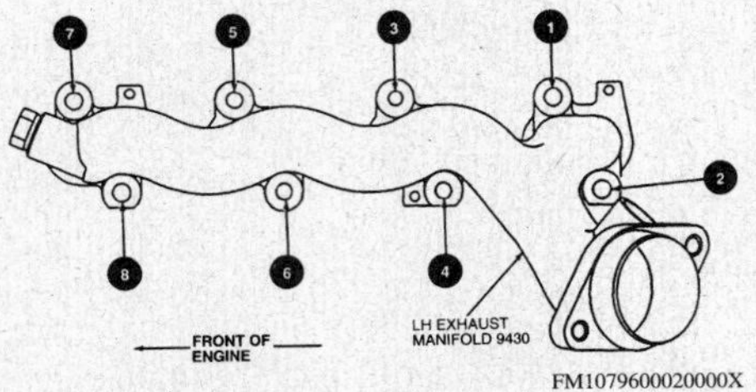

Fig. 11 Lefthand exhaust manifold tightening sequence. 1998 DOHC engine

38. Remove safety clip and disconnect receiver-dryer suction tube.
39. Remove safety clip and disconnect evaporator core line.
40. Disconnect air conditioning line at rear of condenser.
41. Remove two nuts at righthand exhaust manifold.
42. Raise and support vehicle.
43. Remove six remaining righthand exhaust manifold nuts. **Do not remove exhaust manifold now.**
44. Lower vehicle.
45. Remove alternator as outlined in "Electrical" section.
46. Install engine lifting bracket tool No. 303-639, or equivalent.
47. Raise engine using suitable crane or skyhook.
48. Remove righthand exhaust manifold from bottom of engine compartment.
49. Install engine lifting brackets tool No. 303-D074, or equivalent.
50. Support transmission with suitable floor jack and wooden block.
51. Connect spreader bar tool No. D93P-6001-A3, or equivalent to crane or skyhook.
52. Connect spreader bar to lifting brackets.
53. Raise engine slightly and disconnect transmission wiring pin at support bracket.
54. Remove engine.
55. If engine will be mounted on stand, remove rear seal as outlined under "Crankshaft Rear Oil Seal, Replace."
56. Reverse procedure to install.

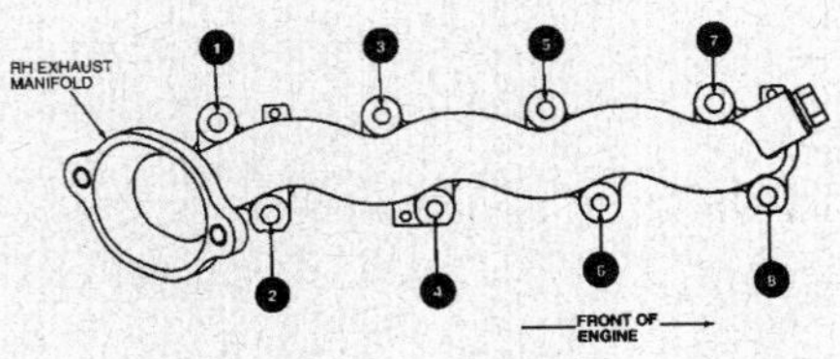

Fig. 10 Righthand exhaust manifold tightening sequence. 1998 DOHC engine

INTAKE MANIFOLD

REPLACE

DOHC Engine

1998

UPPER

1. Turn ignition and wipers on, then turn ignition Off when wipers reach mid cycle (straight up).
2. Remove wiper module.
3. Drain engine cooling system into suitable container, then relieve fuel system pressure as outlined under "Precautions."
4. Remove air cleaner outlet tube.
5. Remove engine drive belt as outlined under "Serpentine Drive Belt."
6. Remove ignition wire covers from valve covers.
7. Disconnect ignition wires at spark plugs and coils. **Do not pull on wires. Pull on caps only.**
8. Remove ignition wires and guides from engine.
9. Disconnect wiring connectors from alternator and mounting bracket.
10. Remove alternator to intake manifold mounting brackets.
11. Disconnect and remove water bypass tube.
12. Mark and disconnect all wiring connectors to upper intake manifold components.
13. Remove alternator from engine.
14. Disconnect accelerator and speed control cables and brackets.
15. Mark and disconnect all vacuum hose connections to intake manifold components.
16. Disconnect PCV hose, then remove idle air control valve inlet tube.
17. Disconnect and remove as required for bolt access:
    a. EGR valve.
    b. Idle Air Control (IAC) valve.
    c. Throttle body.
18. Remove upper intake manifold mounting bolts, then upper intake manifold.
19. Reverse procedure to install, noting the following:
    a. Tighten bolts to specifications.
    b. Ensure mating surfaces of manifolds are clean and free of burrs and

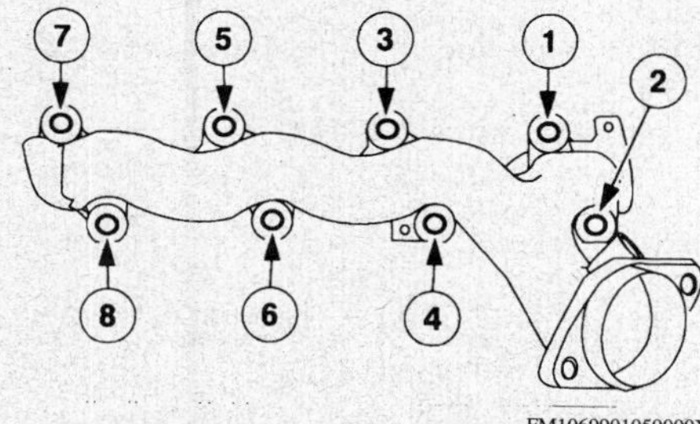

Fig. 12 Lefthand exhaust manifold nut tightening sequence. 1999–2001

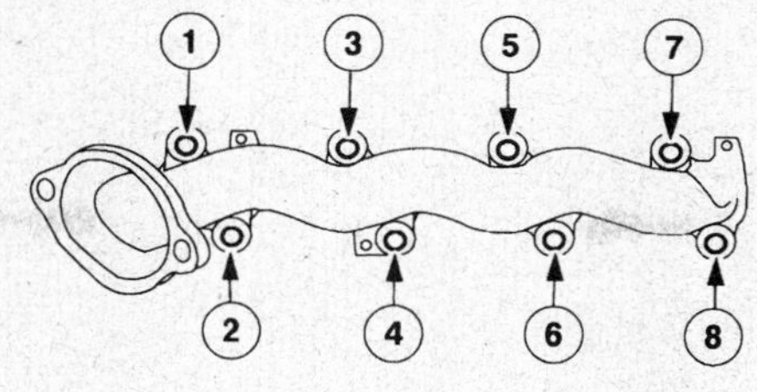

Fig. 13 Righthand exhaust manifold nut tightening sequence. 1999–2001

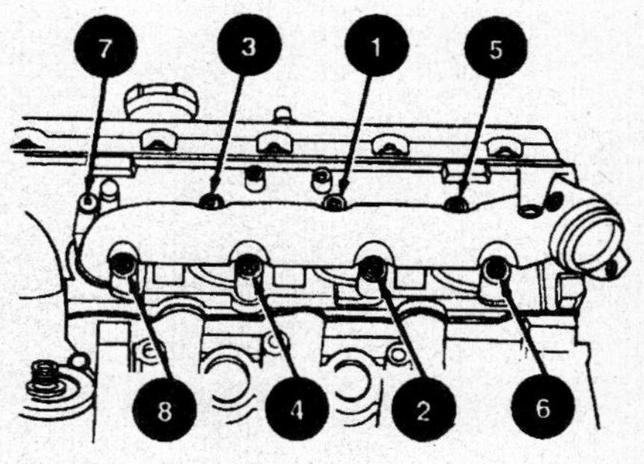

Fig. 14 Exhaust manifold tightening sequence. 1998 SOHC engine

gouges and seal is properly positioned.

c. Install upper intake manifold and lightly tighten bolts in sequence, **Fig. 1.**
d. Tighten bolts in sequence.
e. Lubricate coolant bypass tube O-rings with suitable rubber lubricant. **Use extreme care not to cut O-rings during installation.**
f. Use suitable ohmmeter to ensure a good ground for temperature sender mounted on coolant bypass tube.
g. Fill and bleed cooling system as outlined under "Cooling System Bleed."
h. **Do not allow engine coolant to come into contact with serpentine belt and pulleys. If required, remove belt and flush with clean water.**

LOWER

Removal

1. Remove upper intake manifold as outlined under "Intake Manifold, Replace."
2. Disconnect connectors from fuel manifold and fuel injectors, then disconnect wiring harness and mounting clips.
3. Loosen then remove intake manifold bolts and stud bolts in sequence, **Fig. 2.**
4. Disconnect wiring from IMRC controller while lifting intake manifold assembly from engine.
5. Remove fuel manifolds with injectors from intake manifold.
6. Remove left and righthand lower intake manifolds with IMRC from intake manifold. Discard all gaskets and load limit spacers.

Installation

1. Ensure all mating surfaces are clean and free of old adhesive, burrs and gouges.
2. Remove protective backing from adhesive surface of gaskets for lower intake manifolds with IMRC, then position gaskets onto both lower manifolds with IMRC. Ensure tapered pins of lower manifolds properly align with IMRC.
3. Install both lower manifolds with IMRC to intake manifold. **Tighten bolts only finger tight at this time.**

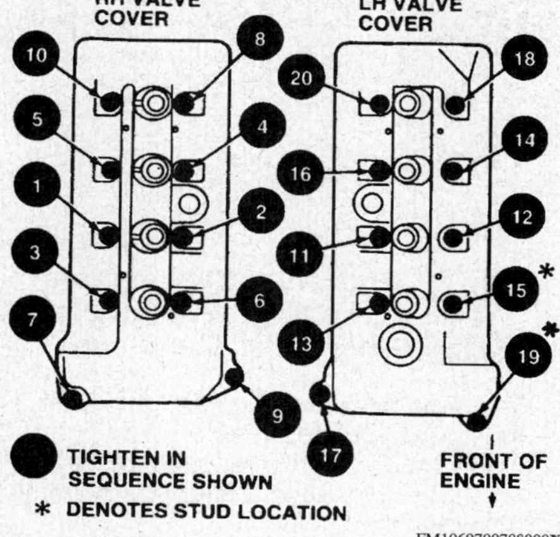

Fig. 15 Valve cover tightening sequence. 1998

4. Install fuel injectors and fuel supply manifold to intake manifold.
5. Place new intake manifold gaskets into position on cylinder head, ensuring proper location of gasket alignment pins.
6. Guide manifold assembly into position while connecting IMRC wiring.
7. Install bolts 7–10, **Fig. 3. Do not tighten bolts at this time.**
8. Install and tighten remaining bolts and stud bolts.
9. Tighten bolts and stud bolts to specifications in sequence, **Fig. 3.**
10. **Torque** lower intake manifold with IMRC to intake manifold bolts to 71–105 inch lbs.
11. Connect IMRC cables and levers.
12. Connect fuel manifold and fuel injector wiring connectors, then install retaining clips.
13. Install upper intake manifold as outlined under "Upper."

1999-2001

UPPER

1. Remove air cleaner outlet tube.
2. Disconnect accelerator and speed control cables, then the return spring.
3. Remove accelerator and speed control cable bracket bolts, then position cables aside.
4. Disconnect TPS electrical connector.
5. Disconnect EVAP emissions return hose.
6. Disconnect IAC control valve electrical connector.
7. Disconnect differential pressure feedback EGR.
8. Disconnect main vacuum supply and EGR vacuum lines.
9. Disconnect differential pressure feedback EGR hoses.
10. Disconnect EGR valve to exhaust tube from EGR valve.
11. Disconnect EGR vacuum regulator solenoid vacuum lines and electrical connector.
12. Remove PCV valve and tube as a unit.
13. Remove upper intake manifold mounting bolts in sequence, **Fig. 4.**
14. Remove upper intake manifold. Discard gasket.
15. Reverse procedure to install, noting the following:
    a. Clean and inspect all gasket sealing surfaces.
    b. Install new upper to lower intake gasket.
    c. Position upper intake manifold, then tighten bolts in sequence, **Fig. 4.**

LOWER

1. Remove upper intake manifold as outlined under "Upper.".
2. Relieve fuel system pressure as outlined under "Precautions."
3. Remove coolant bypass tube.
4. Remove alternator as outlined in "Electrical" section.
5. Disconnect fuel pressure sensor electrical connector and vacuum line.
6. Disconnect all fuel injector electrical connectors.
7. Separate fuel charging wiring from three injection supply manifold studs.
8. Remove lower intake manifold mounting bolts and studs in sequence, **Fig. 5.**
9. Remove lower intake manifold.
10. Reverse procedure to install, noting the following:
    a. Clean and inspect all gasket surfaces.
    b. Install new manifold mounting gaskets.
    c. Position lower intake manifold and tighten in sequence, **Fig. 5.**

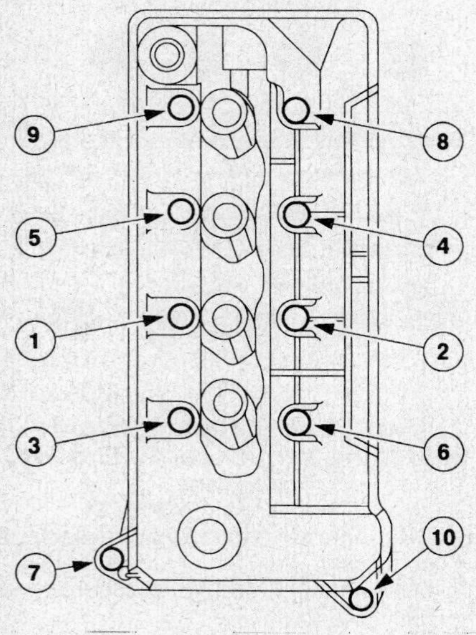

Fig. 16 Lefthand valve cover bolt tightening sequence. 1999–2001 DOHC engine

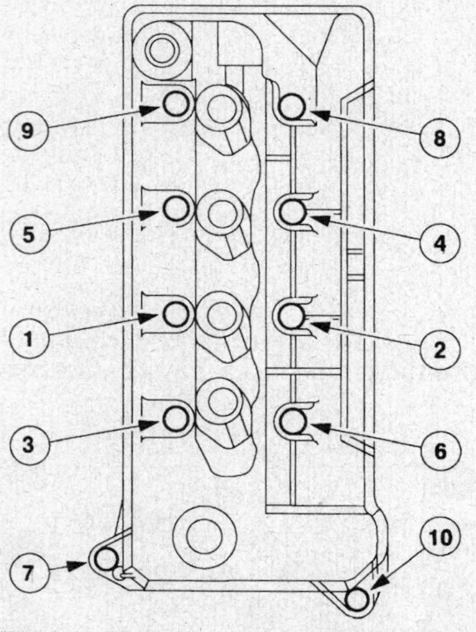

Fig. 17 Righthand valve cover bolt tightening sequence. 1999–2001 DOHC engine

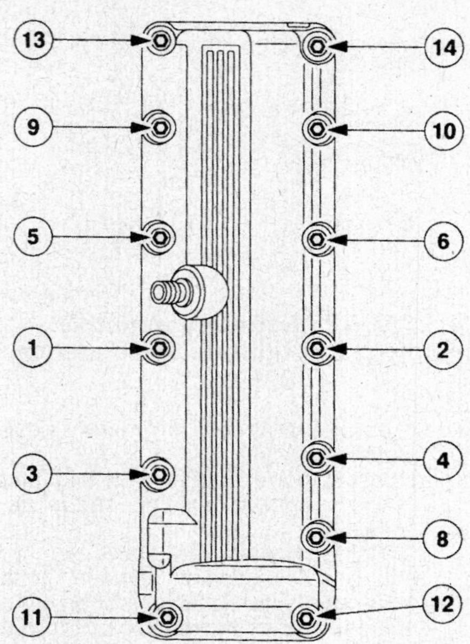

Fig. 18 Lefthand valve cover bolt tightening sequence. 1999–2000 SOHC engine

SOHC Engine

1998

1. Drain engine cooling system into suitable container, then relieve fuel system pressure as outlined under "Precautions."
2. Remove air cleaner outlet tube.
3. Remove serpentine belt as outlined under "Serpentine Drive Belt."
4. Disconnect ignition wires at spark plugs, then remove ignition wires and guides from valve cover studs.
5. Disconnect ignition coils and camshaft position sensor electrical connectors.
6. Remove ignition coils and disconnect alternator wiring connectors.
7. Remove alternator to intake manifold mounting brackets and engine.
8. Raise and support vehicle.
9. Disconnect engine oil pressure sensor and power steering variable orifice pressure sensor wiring connectors. Position wiring aside.
10. Disconnect EGR tube and remove righthand exhaust manifold.
11. Disconnect accelerator and speed control cables and brackets. Position and secure cables aside.
12. Disconnect vacuum hose from throttle body.
13. Disconnect heater water hose from intake manifold.
14. Remove mounting bolts, then position and secure hose and thermostat housing aside.
15. Remove nine remaining mounting bolts and intake manifold.
16. Reverse procedure to install, noting the following:
    a. Ensure mating surfaces of manifold and heads are clean, and free of burrs and gouges.
    b. Ensure alignment tabs of new intake gaskets are aligned with cylinder head holes.
    c. Install and lightly tighten manifold bolts 1–9 in sequence, **Fig. 6.**
    d. Tighten bolts in sequence.
    e. Position new O-ring seal for thermostat housing, then install housing and tighten bolts.

1999-2002

1. Drain coolant into suitable container.
2. Remove air cleaner outlet tube.
3. Relieve fuel system pressure as outlined under "Precautions."
4. Disconnect fuel lines, as required.
5. Remove radiator upper hose.
6. Disconnect accelerator and speed control cables, then the return spring.
7. Remove accelerator and speed control cable bracket bolts, then position cables aside.
8. Remove breather tube at valve cover.
9. Disconnect EVAP emissions return line.
10. Disconnect differential pressure feedback EGR electrical connector.
11. Disconnect differential pressure feedback EGR transducer hoses.
12. Disconnect EGR vacuum regulator solenoid electrical connector and vacuum supply.
13. Remove EGR vacuum regulator solenoid bracket from intake manifold.
14. Disconnect EGR tube from EGR valve.
15. Remove PCV valve and hose as a unit.
16. Disconnect EGR valve vacuum lines.
17. Disconnect IAC valve electrical connector.
18. Disconnect main vacuum supply from TBI base adapter.
19. Disconnect TPS electrical connector.
20. Remove mounting bolts, then the TBI and adapter as an assembly. Replace gasket as required.
21. Disconnect fuel pressure sensor electrical connector and fuel charging ground wire.
22. Disconnect ignition coil and fuel injector electrical connectors.
23. Disconnect HVAC vacuum supply lines and remove harness.
24. Remove four fuel supply manifold mounting studs.
25. Remove injectors and supply manifold as a unit.
26. Remove mounting bolts and ignition coils.
27. Remove alternator as outlined in "Electrical" section.
28. Disconnect heater hose at rear of intake manifold.
29. Unclip harness at manifold and position engine wiring harness aside.
30. Disconnect coolant temperature sender electrical connector.
31. Remove thermostat housing, thermostat and O-ring. Replace O-ring, as required.
32. Remove intake manifold mounting bolts in sequence, **Figs. 7 and 8. Gaskets can be used again if not damaged.**
33. Reverse procedure to install, noting the following:
    a. Clean and inspect all gasket sealing surfaces.
    b. Replace any gaskets and O-rings, as required.
    c. Tighten intake manifold mounting

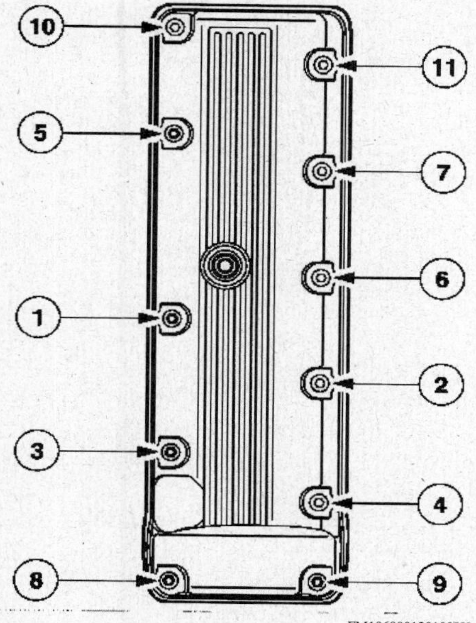

Fig. 19 Lefthand valve cover bolt tightening sequence. 2001–02 SOHC engine

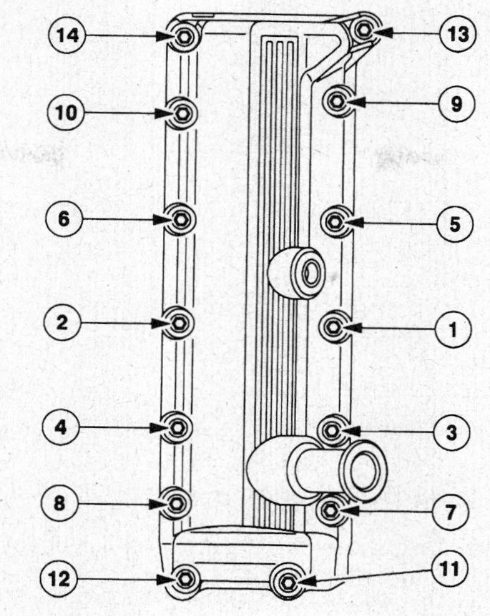

Fig. 20 Righthand valve cover bolt tightening sequence. 1999–2000 SOHC engine

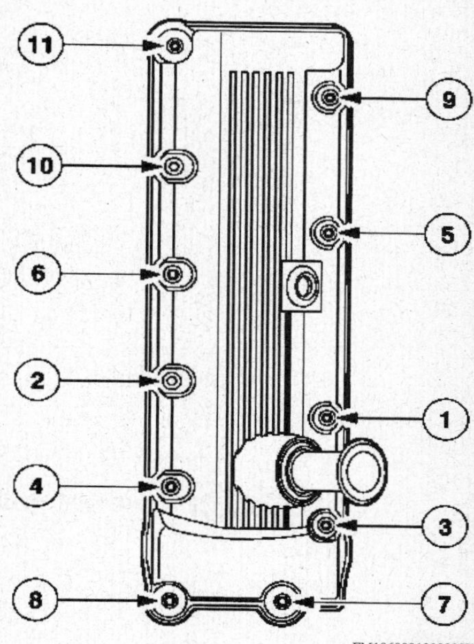

Fig. 21 Righthand valve cover bolt tightening sequence. 2001–02 SOHC engine

bolts in sequence, **Fig. 7.**

d. **Torque** TBI mounting bolts n sequence, **Fig. 9.**

EXHAUST MANIFOLD

REPLACE

DOHC

1998

Righthand

1. Remove air cleaner outlet tube.
2. Disconnect secondary air injection tube.
3. Remove upper mounting nuts from exhaust manifold.
4. Raise and support vehicle.
5. Remove dual converter Y-pipe.
6. Remove lower mounting nuts and exhaust manifold . Discard gaskets.
7. Reverse procedure to install, noting the following:
   a. Ensure mating surfaces are clean and free of burrs and gouges.
   b. Tighten exhaust manifold bolts in sequence, **Fig. 10.**

Lefthand

1. Install suitable lifting hooks and engine support frame.
2. Raise engine to relieve pressure on motor mounts.
3. Raise and support vehicle, then remove front tire and wheel assemblies.
4. Remove EGR and secondary air injection tubes from lefthand exhaust manifold.
5. Remove dual converter Y-pipe.
6. Disconnect left and righthand ball joints and tie rod ends from hub and spindle.
7. Disconnect steering coupling at pinch bolt.
8. Support subframe with suitable adjustable jacks.
9. Remove motor mount and subframe bolts.
10. Lower subframe to allow manifold removal clearance.
11. Remove mounting bolts and exhaust manifold. Discard gaskets.
12. Reverse procedure to install, noting the following:
    a. Ensure mating surfaces of manifold and head are clean, and free of burrs and gouges.
    b. Ensure new intake gaskets align with cylinder head holes.
    c. Install and lightly tighten manifold bolts in sequence, **Fig. 11.**
    d. Tighten mounting bolts in sequence.

1999–2001

1. Raise and support vehicle.
2. Disconnect exhaust pipe HO2S electrical connectors.
3. **If removing lefthand manifold on models equipped with DOHC engine,** disconnect EGR tube at manifold.
4. **On all models,** remove exhaust pipe flange to manifold bolts.
5. Remove mounting nuts, manifold and gasket. Discard gasket.
6. Reverse procedure to install, noting the following:
   a. Install new manifold gaskets.
   b. Tighten manifold mounting nuts in sequence, **Figs. 12 and 13.**

SOHC

1998

Lefthand

1. Remove bolt for oil dipstick tube.
2. Raise and support vehicle.
3. Disconnect heated oxygen sensors' wire connectors.
4. Remove EGR tube from manifold.
5. Disconnect dual converter Y-pipe from exhaust manifolds and support from subframe with suitable wire.
6. Disconnect steering shaft and position aside.
7. Remove lefthand motor mount bracket from engine, as required for clearance.
8. Remove mounting nuts and manifold. Discard gaskets.
9. Reverse procedure to install, noting the following:
   a. Ensure mating surfaces of manifold and head are clean, and free of burrs and gouges.
   b. Ensure new intake gaskets align with cylinder head holes.
   c. Install and lightly tighten manifold bolts in sequence, **Fig. 14.**
   d. Tighten mounting bolts in sequence.

Righthand

1. Raise and support vehicle.
2. Disconnect heated oxygen sensors' wire connectors.
3. Disconnect dual converter Y-pipe from exhaust manifolds and support from subframe with suitable wire.
4. Remove mounting nuts and manifold. Discard gaskets.
5. Reverse procedure to install, noting the following:
   a. Ensure mating surfaces of manifold and head are clean, and free of burrs and gouges.
   b. Ensure new intake gaskets aligns with cylinder head holes.
   c. Install and lightly tighten manifold bolts in sequence, **Fig. 14.**
   d. Tighten mounting bolts in sequence.

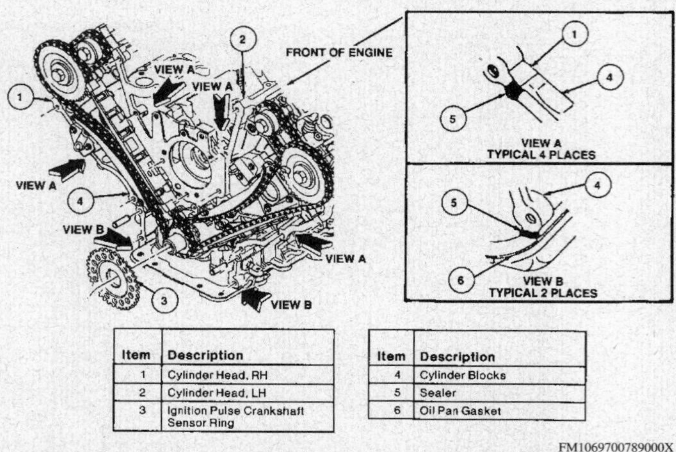

Item	Description
1	Cylinder Head, RH
2	Cylinder Head, LH
3	Ignition Pulse Crankshaft Sensor Ring

Item	Description
4	Cylinder Blocks
5	Sealer
6	Oil Pan Gasket

Fig. 22 Sealant points. 1998 DOHC engine

1999–2002

Refer to "DOHC."

CYLINDER HEAD

REPLACE

Refer to "4.6L Engine" section in "Continental, Mark VIII & Town Car" chapter.

VALVE COVER

REPLACE

DOHC

1998

1. Remove engine compartment brace and air cleaner outlet tube.
2. Remove four mounting screws and ignition wire cover.
3. Disconnect ignition wires from spark plugs. **Do not pull on ignition wires.**
4. Remove mounting bolts and valve cover.
5. Reverse procedures to install, noting the following:
   a. Use silicone gasket and sealant F6AZ-19562-AA, or equivalent.
   b. Tighten valve cover bolts in sequence, **Fig. 15.**

1999–2001

Lefthand

1. Turn engine off and depress brake pedal several times.
2. Disconnect brake fluid level sensor electrical connector.
3. Position suitable drain pan and disconnect brake fluid lines on lower side of master cylinder.
4. Position suitable drain pan and disconnect power steering fluid return line hose.
5. Disconnect power steering pressure lines at hydro-booster. Discard Teflon seals.
6. Remove self-locking pin in hydro-booster linkage.
7. Remove stop lamp switch and hydro-booster pushrod from brake pedal pin.
8. Remove hydro-booster mounting nuts at firewall.
9. Remove brake hydro-booster unit.
10. Disconnect clutch cable at clutch pedal and position aside.
11. Remove lefthand bank ignition coils.
12. Remove mounting bolts and valve cover.
13. Reverse procedure to install, noting the following:
   a. Apply a 0.32 inch bead of silicone gasket sealant No. F7AZ-19554-EA, or equivalent, to valve cover sealing surfaces. **Do not allow more than four minutes to elapse.**
   b. Tighten valve cover bolts and studs in sequence, **Fig. 16.**
   c. Install new power steering pressure line Teflon seals.
   d. Tighten all fasteners to specifications.
   e. Bleed brake and power steering fluid systems.

Righthand

1. Remove righthand bank ignition coils.
2. Relieve fuel system pressure as outlined under "Precautions."
3. Disconnect fuel lines, as required.
4. Disconnect EVAP emissions return tube.
5. Remove mounting bolts and valve cover.
6. Reverse procedure to install, noting the following:
   a. Apply 0.32 inch bead of silicone gasket sealant No. F7AZ-19554-EA, or equivalent, to valve cover sealing surfaces. **Do not allow more than four minutes to elapse.**
   b. Tighten valve cover bolts and studs in sequence, **Fig. 17.**
   c. Tighten all fasteners to specifications.

SOHC

1998

Righthand

1. Remove air cleaner outlet tube, then disconnect 42- and eight-pin connectors leading to Mass Air Flow (MAF) and Intake Air Temperature (IAT) sensors.

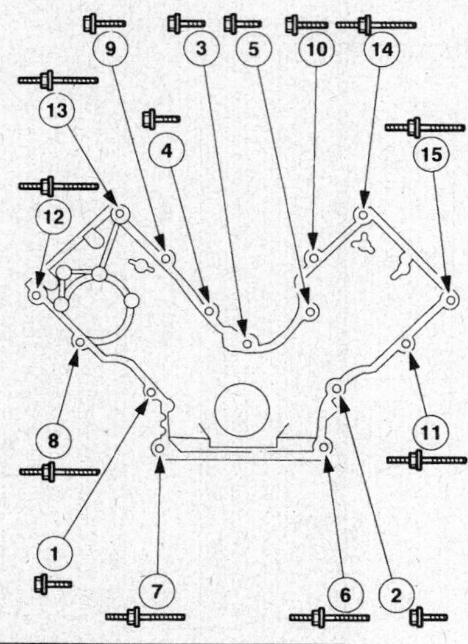

Item	Description
1	Bolt, Hex Flange Head Pilot, M8 x 1.25 x 53
2	Bolt, Hex Flange Head Pilot, M8 x 1.25 x 53
3	Bolt, Hex Flange Head Pilot, M8 x 1.25 x 53
4	Bolt, Hex Flange Head Pilot, M8 x 1.25 x 53
5	Bolt, Hex Flange Head Pilot, M8 x 1.25 x 53
6	Stud, Hex-Head Pilot, M8 x 1.5 x 1.5 x 103.1
7	Stud, Hex-Head Pilot, M8 x 1.5 x 1.5 x 103.1
8	Stud, Hex Pilot, M8 x 1.5 x 57.5
9	Screw and Washer, Hex Pilot, M8 x 1.5 x 57.5
10	Screw and Washer, Hex Pilot, M8 x 1.5 x 57.5
11	Stud and Washer, Hex-Head Pilot, M8 x 1.5 x M8 x 1.25 x 91.0
12	Stud and Washer, Hex-Head Pilot, M8 x 1.5 x M8 x 1.25 x 91.0
13	Stud and Washer, Hex-Head Pilot, M8 x 1.5 x M8 x 1.25 x 91.0
14	Stud and Washer, Hex-Head Pilot, M8 x 1.5 x M8 x 1.25 x 91.0
15	Stud and Washer, Hex-Head Pilot, M8 x 1.5 x M8 x 1.25 x 91.0

FM1069901065000X

Fig. 23 Front cover fastener locations. 1999–2001 DOHC engine

2. Remove air conditioning line to righthand front fender apron mounting nut.
3. Lift air conditioning line and feed 42-pin connector under air conditioning line. Position line aside.
4. Relieve fuel system pressure as outlined under "Precautions."
5. Disconnect fuel lines.
6. Disconnect ignition wires from spark plugs. **Do not pull on ignition wires.**
7. Remove ignition wires and ignition wire separators from valve cover studs. Position wires aside.

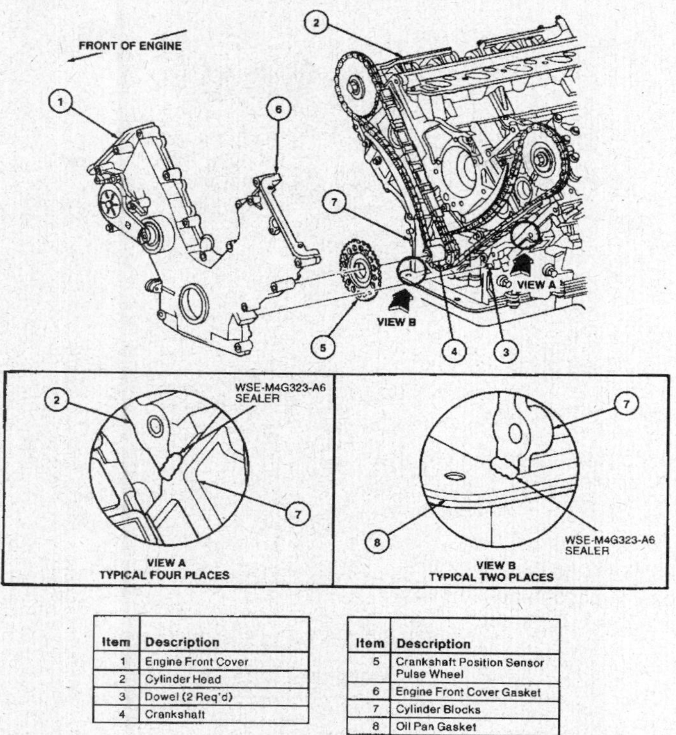

Item	Description
1	Engine Front Cover
2	Cylinder Head
3	Dowel (2 Req'd)
4	Crankshaft

Item	Description
5	Crankshaft Position Sensor Pulse Wheel
6	Engine Front Cover Gasket
7	Cylinder Blocks
8	Oil Pan Gasket

FM1069700790000X

Fig. 24 Sealant points. 1998 SOHC engine

8. Remove Positive Crankcase Ventilation (PCV) valve from crankcase ventilation grommet.
9. Remove bolts, stud bolts and valve cover.
10. Reverse procedures to install noting the following:
    a. Use silicone gasket and sealant F6AZ-19562-AA, or equivalent.
    b. Tighten valve cover bolts in sequence, **Fig. 15.**

Lefthand

1. Remove air cleaner outlet tube.
2. Disconnect speed control actuator cable from throttle body. Position cable aside.
3. Disconnect engine control sensor extension wire from electronic variable orifice and oil pressure sensors. Position wire aside.
4. Disconnect ignition wires from spark plugs. **Do not pull on ignition wires.**
5. Remove ignition wires and separators from studs.
6. Remove bolts, stud bolts and valve cover.
7. Reverse procedure to install noting the following:
    a. Use silicone gasket and sealant F6AZ-19562-AA, or equivalent.
    b. Tighten valve cover bolts in sequence, **Fig. 15.**

1999–2002

Lefthand

1. Remove bracket bolt and position oil dipstick tube aside.
2. Disconnect breather tube at valve cover grommet.
3. Disconnect engine wiring harness at valve cover retaining clips.
4. Remove bolts, studs and valve cover.
5. Reverse procedure to install, noting the following:
    a. Apply 0.32 inch bead of silicone gasket sealant No. F7AZ-19554-EA, or equivalent, to valve cover sealing surfaces. **Do not allow more than four minutes to elapse.**
    b. Tighten valve cover bolts and studs in sequence, **Figs. 18 and 19.**

Righthand

1. Remove air cleaner outlet tube.
2. Relieve fuel system pressure as outlined under "Precautions."
3. Disconnect fuel lines, as required.
4. Disconnect engine wiring harness at valve cover retaining clips.
5. Disconnect PCV valve and hose at valve cover grommet. Position them aside.
6. Remove bolts, studs and valve cover.
7. Reverse procedure to install, noting the following:
    a. Apply 0.32 inch bead of silicone gasket sealant No. F7AZ-19554-EA, or equivalent, to valve cover sealing surfaces. **Do not allow more than four minutes to elapse.**
    b. Tighten valve cover bolts and studs in sequence, **Figs. 20 and 21.**

VALVE ARRANGEMENT

Refer to "4.6L Engine" section in "Continental, Mark VIII & Town Car" chapter.

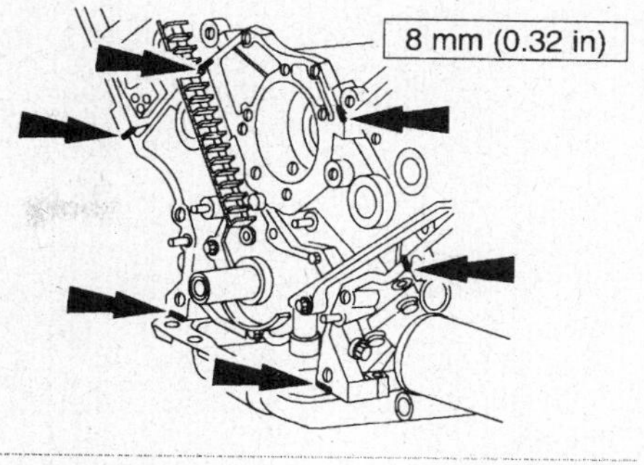

FM1069901063000X

Fig. 25 Front cover sealant application locations. 1999–2002

CAMSHAFT LOBE LIFT SPECIFICATIONS

Refer to "4.6L Engine" section in "Continental, Mark VIII & Town Car" chapter.

VALVE ADJUSTMENT

Refer to "4.6L Engine" section in "Continental, Mark VIII & Town Car" chapter.

FRONT COVER

REPLACE

DOHC

1998

1. Remove strut tower support brace and air cleaner outlet tube.
2. Drain engine cooling system into suitable container.
3. Remove water bypass tube to water thermostat housing hose and upper radiator hose at water bypass tube.
4. Remove cooling fan motor, fan shroud and fan blade.
5. Remove engine control sensor wiring support bracket mounting bolt from lefthand center of front cover.
6. Remove strap retaining fuel charging wiring to front cover.
7. Remove drive belt and loosen water pump pulley bolts.
8. Remove water pump pulley and lower water pump to cylinder block mounting bolt.
9. Remove power steering pump reservoir to lefthand ignition coil bracket bolts and stud bolt
10. Raise and support vehicle.
11. Remove power steering pressure hose to pump bracket mounting bolt.
12. Remove power steering pump to cylinder blocks and front cover mounting bolts. **Front lower bolt on power steering pump will not come all the way out.**
13. Position power steering pump and reservoir aside.
14. Remove four oil pan to front cover mounting bolts, then the crankshaft pulley mounting bolt and washer.
15. Remove crankshaft pulley using remover tool No. T58P-6316-D, or equivalent.

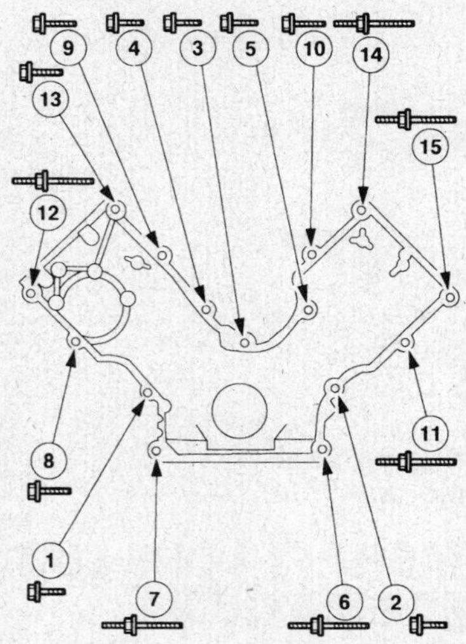

Item	Description
1	Bolt, Hex Flange Head Pilot, M8 x 1.25 x 53
2	Bolt, Hex Flange Head Pilot, M8 x 1.25 x 53
3	Bolt, Hex Flange Head Pilot, M8 x 1.25 x 53
4	Bolt, Hex Flange Head Pilot, M8 x 1.25 x 53
5	Bolt, Hex Flange Head Pilot, M8 x 1.25 x 53
6	Stud, Hex-Head Pilot, M10 x 1.5 x 1.5 x 103.1
7	Stud, Hex-Head Pilot, M10 x 1.5 x 1.5 x 103.1
8	Screw and Washer, Hex Pilot, M10 x 1.5 x 57.5
9	Screw and Washer, Hex Pilot, M10 x 1.5 x 57.5
10	Screw and Washer, Hex Pilot, M10 x 1.5 x 57.5
11	Stud and Washer, Hex-Head Pilot, M10 x 1.5 x M8 x 1.25 x 109.6
12	Stud and Washer, Hex-Head Pilot, M10 x 1.5 x M8 x 1.25 x 109.6
13	Stud and Washer, Hex-Head Pilot, M10 x 1.5 x M8 x 1.25 x 109.6
14	Stud and Washer, Hex-Head Pilot, M10 x 1.5 x M8 x 1.25 x 109.6
15	Stud and Washer, Hex-Head Pilot, M10 x 1.5 x M8 x 1.25 x 109.6

FM1069901064000X

Fig. 26 Front cover fastener locations. 1999–2002 SOHC engine

16. Lower vehicle and remove valve covers as outlined under "Valve Cover, Replace."
17. Disconnect fuel charging wiring from both ignition coils and CMP sensor.
18. Remove three righthand ignition coil bracket to front cover mounting bolts.
19. Remove three nuts and one bolt retaining lefthand ignition coil bracket to front cover.
20. Slide both ignition coil brackets and wires off mounting studs.

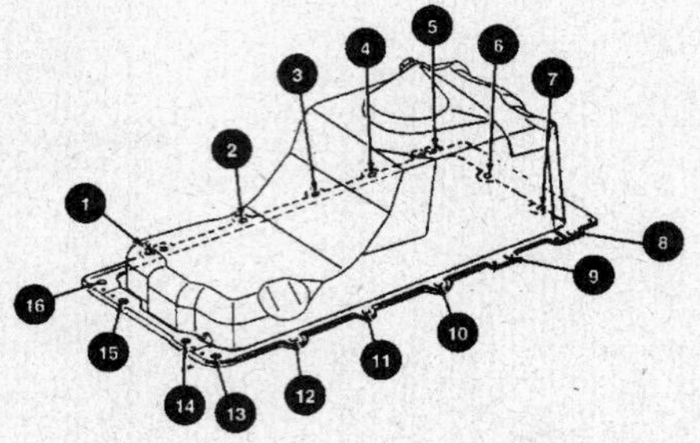

FM1069600461000X

Fig. 27 Oil pan bolt tightening sequence. 1998 DOHC engine

21. Remove mounting bolt and belt idler pulley.
22. Remove nine stud bolts and six bolts retaining front cover to engine.
23. Remove four oil pan to front cover bolts.
24. Remove front cover.
25. Reverse procedures to install. Apply 0.315–0.472 inch bead of silicone gasket sealant F6AZ-19562-AA, or equivalent, **Fig. 22.**

1999–2001

1. Remove valve covers as outlined under "Valve Cover, Replace."
2. Drain coolant from radiator and degas bottle into suitable container.
3. Disconnect cooling fan motor electrical connector, then separate fan harness from shroud.
4. Remove fan shroud left and righthand mounting bolts.
5. Remove cooling fan, motor and shroud as an assembly.
6. Remove mounting bolts and water pump pulley.
7. Raise and support vehicle.
8. Drain engine oil into suitable container.
9. Remove mounting bolt and crankshaft pulley using puller tool No. T58P-6316-D, or equivalent.
10. Remove mounting nut and position air conditioning muffler aside.
11. Remove mounting bolts and position power steering pump aside.
12. Disconnect CKP sensor electrical connector.
13. Remove front oil pan to front cover bolts.
14. Remove crankshaft front oil seal using seal remover tool No. T74P-6700-A, or equivalent.
15. Lower vehicle.
16. Disconnect CMP sensor electrical connector.
17. Remove serpentine belt idler pulley.
18. Mark locations, then remove front cover mounting bolts and studs.
19. Remove front cover. Discard gaskets.
20. Reverse procedure to install, noting the following:
    a. Apply silicone gasket sealer part No. F7AZ-19554-EA, or equivalent, **Fig. 25.**
    b. Install bolts and studs in original locations, **Fig. 23.**
    c. **Torque** oil pan to front cover bolts to 18 inch lbs.

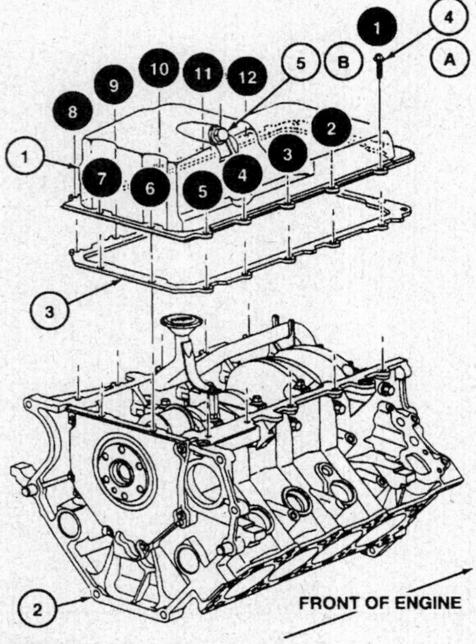

TIGHTEN BOLTS IN SEQUENCE

REFER TO LEGEND

Item	Description
1	Oil Pan
2	Cylinder Blocks
3	Oil Pan Gasket
4	Bolt
5	Drain Plug (Part of 6675)
A	Tighten to 20 N·m (15 Lb-Ft) Then Rotate 60 Degrees
B	Tighten to 11-16 N·m (9-11 Lb-Ft)

FM1099600079000X

Fig. 28 Oil pan bolt tightening sequence. 1998 SOHC engine

    d. **Torque** bolts to 15 ft. lbs.
    e. Finally, tighten bolts an additional 60°.
    f. Install new crankshaft pulley oil seal using installer and aligner tool No. T88T-6701-A, or equivalent.
    g. Apply silicone gasket sealer to crankshaft pulley keyway slot. **Do not allow more than four minutes to elapse.**
    h. Install crankshaft pulley using installer tool No. T74P-6316-B, or equivalent.
    i. **Torque** crankshaft pulley bolt to 66 ft. lbs., then loosen one full turn. **Torque** bolt to 37 ft. lbs.
    j. Finally tighten bolt an additional 85–95°.

SOHC

1998

1. Remove valve covers as outlined under "Valve Cover, Replace."
2. Remove oil pan as outlined under "Oil Pan, Replace."
3. Remove cooling fan motor, blade and shroud.
4. Loosen water pump pulley bolts and

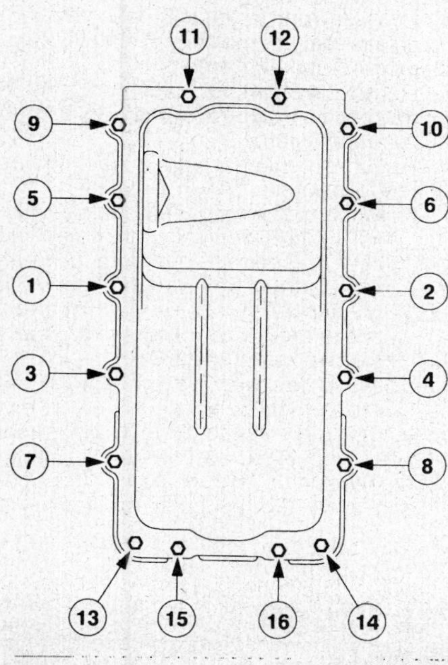

Fig. 29 Oil pan bolt tightening sequence. 1999–2002

remove drive belt.
5. Remove water pump pulley.
6. Raise and support vehicle.
7. Remove power steering pump to cylinder blocks and engine front cover mounting bolts. **Front lower bolt on power steering pump will not come all the way out.**
8. Remove crankshaft pulley bolt and retaining washer from crankshaft.
9. Remove crankshaft pulley using puller tool No. T58P-6316-D, or equivalent.
10. Lower vehicle.
11. Remove lefthand coil bracket mounting bolts and position power steering oil reservoir aside.
12. Disconnect fuel charging wiring from both ignition coils and CMP sensor.
13. Remove three righthand ignition coil bracket to front cover mounting bolts and lefthand ignition coil from bracket. Position aside.
14. Remove three lefthand ignition coil bracket to front cover mounting bolts.
15. Slide righthand ignition coil bracket and wires off mounting studs. Lay assembly on top of engine.
16. Remove mounting bolts and belt idler pulley.
17. Disconnect fuel charging wiring from CKP sensor.
18. Remove nine stud bolts, six bolts and front cover.
19. Reverse procedure to install. Apply 0.31–0.47 inch bead of silicone gasket sealant F6AZ-19562-AA, or equivalent, **Fig. 24.**

1999–2002

1. Remove mounting nuts and position RFI capacitor aside.
2. Remove valve covers as outlined under "Valve Cover, Replace."
3. Drain coolant from radiator and degas bottle into suitable container.
4. Disconnect cooling fan motor electrical connector and separate fan harness from shroud.
5. Remove fan shroud left and righthand mounting bolts.
6. Remove cooling fan, motor and shroud as an assembly.
7. Remove serpentine belt.
8. Remove mounting bolts and water pump pulley.
9. Remove mounting nut and position air conditioning muffler aside.
10. Raise and support vehicle.
11. Drain engine oil into suitable container.
12. Position power steering pump aside.
13. Disconnect CKP sensor electrical connector.
14. Remove battery cable support nuts at front of engine.
15. Remove bolt and crankshaft pulley using puller tool No. T58P-6316-D, or equivalent.
16. Remove crankshaft front seal using seal remover tool No. T74P-6700-A, or equivalent.
17. Remove oil pan to front cover bolts.
18. Lower vehicle.
19. Position suitable drain pan under and remove power steering fluid reservoir.
20. Disconnect CMP electrical connector.
21. Remove serpentine belt idler pulley.
22. Mark locations, then remove front cover mounting bolts and studs.
23. Remove front cover. Discard gaskets.
24. Reverse procedure to install, noting the following:
    a. Apply silicone gasket sealer part No. F7AZ-19554-EA, or equivalent , **Fig. 25.**
    b. Ensure bolts and studs are in original locations, **Fig. 26.**
    c. **Torque** oil pan to front cover bolts to 18 inch lbs.
    d. **Torque** bolts to 15 ft. lbs.
    e. Finally, tighten bolts an additional 60°.
    f. Install new crankshaft pulley oil seal using installer and aligner tool No. T88T-6701-A, or equivalent.
    g. Apply silicone gasket sealer to crankshaft pulley keyway slot. **Do not allow more than four minutes to elapse.**
    h. Install crankshaft pulley using installer tool No. T74P-6316-B, or equivalent.
    i. **Torque** crankshaft pulley bolt to 66 ft. lbs., then loosen one full turn. **Torque** bolt to 37 ft. lbs.
    j. Finally tighten bolt an additional 90°.

FRONT COVER SEAL

REPLACE

Refer to "4.6L Engine" section in "Continental, Mark VIII & Town Car" chapter.

TIMING CHAIN

REPLACE

Refer to "4.6L Engine" section in "Continental, Mark VIII & Town Car" chapter.

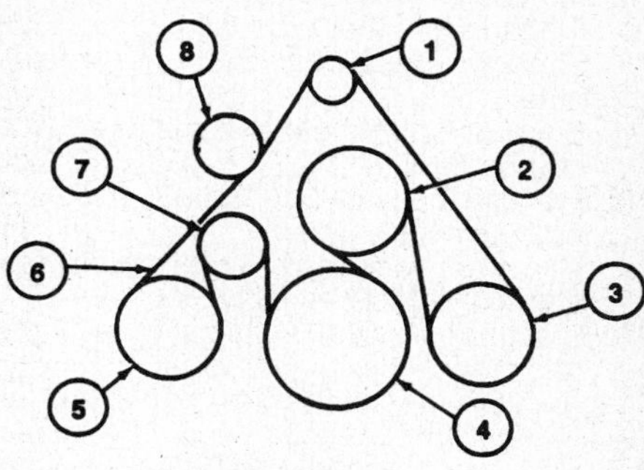

Fig. 30 Serpentine belt routing. 1998

TIMING CHAIN TENSIONER BLEED

Refer to "4.6L Engine" section in "Continental, Mark VIII & Town Car" chapter.

CAMSHAFT

REPLACE

Refer to "4.6L Engine" section in "Continental, Mark VIII & Town Car" chapter.

PISTON & ROD ASSEMBLY

Refer to "4.6L Engine" section in "Continental, Mark VIII & Town Car" chapter.

MAIN & ROD BEARINGS

Refer to "4.6L Engine" section in "Continental, Mark VIII & Town Car" chapter.

CRANKSHAFT SEAL

REPLACE

Refer to "4.6L Engine" section in "Continental, Mark VIII & Town Car" chapter.

OIL PAN

REPLACE

DOHC

1998

1. Remove engine dipstick.
2. Install suitable lifting eyes and engine lifting frame.
3. Raise engine to release pressure on motor mounts.
4. Raise and support vehicle, then remove front wheel and tire assemblies.
5. Disconnect left and righthand tie rod ends, then the ball joints from hub and spindles.

6. Disconnect steering coupling at pinch bolt joint and remove engine mount nuts.
7. Support subframe with suitable adjustable jacks.
8. Remove bolts, then separate strut and front spindle.
9. Remove bolts and lower subframe enough to allow oil pan removal.
10. Disconnect oil pan sensors' wiring connectors.
11. Remove mounting bolts, pan and gasket. Discard gasket.
12. Reverse procedure to install, noting the following:
    a. Apply suitable silicone sealer to areas where block meets front and rear engine covers.
    b. Tighten oil pan bolts to specifications in sequence, **Fig. 27.**

1999–2001

1. Remove air cleaner outlet tube.
2. Remove radiator sight shield.
3. Support engine using engine lifting bracket tool No. D93P-6001-A2, and engine support kit tool No. 303-F072, or equivalents.
4. Raise and support vehicle.
5. Remove left and righthand engine mount nuts.
6. Lower vehicle and raise engine.
7. Raise and support vehicle.
8. Drain engine oil into suitable container.
9. Compress front coil springs using compressor tool No. D78P-5310-A, or equivalent.
10. Position suitable jack stand under subframe.
11. Remove four subframe side bolts.
12. Loosen front subframe bolts. **Do not completely remove bolts.**
13. Lower front subframe.
14. Remove mounting bolts and pan. **If gasket is in good condition it may be used again.**
15. Reverse procedure to install, noting the following:
    a. Apply silicone gasket sealant No. F7AZ-19554-EA, or equivalent, to rear oil seal retainer to block sealing surface and at front cover to block mating surface. **Do not allow more than four minutes to elapse before installing oil pan.**
    b. Move oil pan into position and loosely install bolts.
    c. **Torque** bolts to 18 inch lbs. in sequence, **Fig. 29.**
    d. **Torque** bolts to 15 ft. lbs. in sequence.
    e. Finally, tighten bolts an additional 60°.

SOHC

1998

1. Remove engine compartment brace from front fender aprons and dash panel.
2. Raise and support vehicle, then drain engine oil into suitable container.
3. Remove mounting bolts and front subframe crossmember reinforcement.
4. Remove motor mount to front subframe crossover nuts.

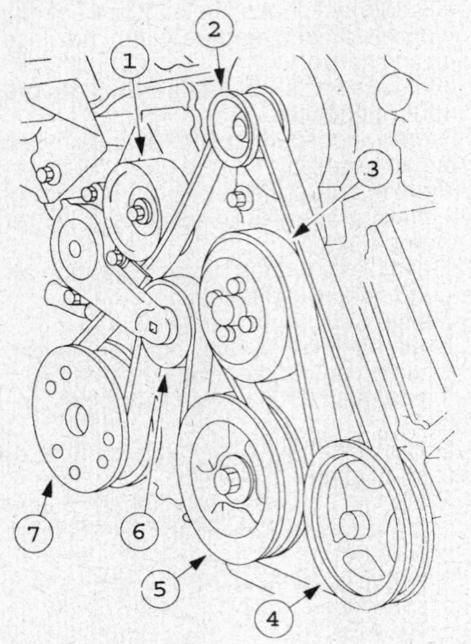

Fig. 31 Serpentine belt routing. 1999 & 2000 early production

5. Remove transmission housing cover.
6. Raise engine approximately four inches using suitable safety stand. Position suitable wooded block under crankshaft pulley.
7. Install 2½–2¾-inch wood blocks under each front engine support insulator.
8. Remove mounting bolts and oil pan. **It may be necessary to adjust engine height several times for sufficient removal clearance.**
9. Reverse procedure to install, noting the following:
    a. **Torque** oil pan bolts to 14 ft. lbs. in sequence, **Fig. 28.**
    b. Tighten bolts an additional 60°.

1999–2002

1. Remove air cleaner outlet tube.
2. Remove radiator sight shield.
3. Install engine lifting bracket tool No. D93P-6001-A2, or equivalent to lefthand front corner of engine.
4. Install engine support tool No. 303-290-A, or equivalent.
5. Raise and support vehicle.
6. Drain engine oil into suitable container.
7. Remove left and righthand engine mount nuts.
8. Lower vehicle.
9. Raise engine using support tool.
10. Raise and support vehicle.
11. Compress front coil springs using compressor tool No. D78P-5310-A, or equivalent.
12. Position suitable jack stand under subframe.
13. Remove four engine mount bolts.
14. Loosen front subframe bolts. **Do not completely remove bolt.**
15. Lower front subframe.
16. Remove mounting bolts and pan. **If gasket is in good condition it may be used again.**
17. Reverse procedure to install, noting the following:
    a. Apply silicone gasket sealant No. F7AZ-19554-EA, or equivalent, to rear oil seal retainer to block sealing surface and at front cover to block mating surface. **Do not allow more than four minutes to elapse before installing oil pan.**
    b. Move oil pan into position and loosely install bolts.
    c. **Torque** bolts to 18 inch lbs. in sequence, **Fig. 29.**
    d. **Torque** bolts 15 ft. lbs.
    e. Finally tighten bolts an additional 60°.

OIL PUMP

REPLACE

Refer to "4.6L Engine" section in "Continental, Mark VIII & Town Car" chapter.

BELT TENSION DATA

These models are equipped with an automatic drive belt tensioner. No adjustment or maintenance is required.

SERPENTINE DRIVE BELT

Always use square drive tool in hole in tensioner to move tensioner. Never pry on tensioner pulley. When releasing drive belt tensioner, never allow tensioner to snap back. Damage to tensioner or personal injury could result.

Do not allow engine coolant to remain on serpentine belt or pulleys. If required, remove belt and flush with clean water.

REMOVAL

1. Insert suitable square drive tool into square hole in tensioner arm and rotate tensioner away from belt.
2. Lift belt from pulley, then slowly release tensioner.
3. Remove belt from vehicle.

ROUTING

Refer to for **Figs. 30 through 32** belt routing.

INSTALLATION

1. Route belt.
2. Ensure belt is properly seated in pulley grooves.
3. Insert suitable square drive tool into square hole in tensioner arm and rotate tensioner away from belt.
4. Position belt under tensioner and slowly release tensioner onto belt.

COOLING SYSTEM BLEED

1. Fill radiator completely full and install radiator cap.
2. Fill coolant reservoir and degas bottle to full cold mark.
3. Set heater control to full hot, high fan and set controls so air vents from dash vents.
4. Start and operate engine until fully warmed up while observing water temperature gauge.
5. If system is functioning properly, temperature will indicate normal and hot air will be felt at dash outlets.
6. If system is not functioning properly, temperature gauge will not read and/or no hot air will be felt at dash vents.
7. If system is not functioning properly, allow engine to cool and repeat procedure.
8. If system is functioning properly, allow engine to cool and fill coolant reservoir to full cold mark, as required.

THERMOSTAT

REPLACE

Refer to "4.6L Engine" section in "Continental, Mark VIII & Town Car" chapter.

WATER PUMP

REPLACE

1. Drain engine coolant into suitable container.
2. Loosen water pump pulley mounting bolts.
3. Remove serpentine belt as outlined under "Serpentine Drive Belt."
4. Remove mounting bolts, water pump and gasket. Discard gasket.
5. Reverse procedure to install.

RADIATOR

REPLACE

1998

1. Disconnect transmission cooler lines using quick disconnect tool No. T82L-9500-AH, or equivalent.
2. Drain cooling system into suitable container.
3. Disconnect radiator hoses.
4. Remove cooling fan and shroud as an assembly.
5. Remove coolant reservoir and bracket.
6. Remove upper support bracket and radiator.
7. Reverse procedure to install. Ensure coolant hoses and clamps are properly positioned and tightened.

1999–2002

1. Drain coolant from radiator and degas bottle into suitable container.
2. Disconnect cooling fan motor electrical connector and separate fan harness from shroud.
3. Remove fan shroud left and righthand mounting bolts.

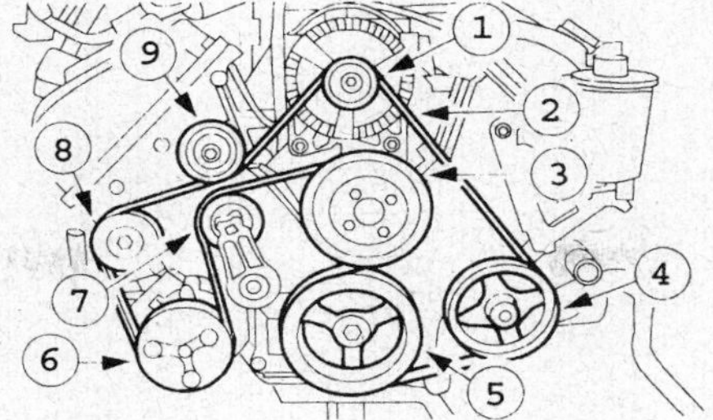

1. Alternator
2. Belt
3. Water Pump
4. Power Steering Pump
5. Crankshaft
6. Air Conditioning Compressor
7. Tensioner
8 & 9. Idler Pulleys

FM1069901052000X

Fig. 32 Serpentine belt routing. 2000 late production & 2001–02

4. Remove cooling fan, motor and shroud as an assembly.
5. Remove radiator sight shield.
6. Disconnect radiator upper hose at radiator.
7. **On models equipped with automatic transmission,** remove lower and upper cooler tube fittings.
8. **On all models,** raise and support vehicle.
9. Disconnect radiator lower hose at radiator. Lower vehicle.
10. Remove supports and radiator.
11. Reverse procedure to install.

FUEL PUMP

REPLACE

1998

1. Relieve fuel system pressure as outlined under "Precautions."
2. Remove fuel from fuel tank by pumping into suitable fuel storage tanker.
3. Raise and support vehicle, then remove fuel tank filler line.
4. Support fuel tank with suitable jack and remove support straps.
5. Partially lower fuel tank, then disconnect fuel lines and electrical connectors.
6. Lower fuel tank and place on suitable work surface.
7. Remove fuel pump/level sensor retaining ring using wrench tool No. D84P-9275-A, or equivalent.
8. Mark notches' location and position for installation alignment.
9. Remove fuel pump/level sensor
10. Reverse procedure to install. Lubricate new sealing O-ring to hold it in position during installation.

1999–2002

1. Relieve fuel system pressure as outlined under "Precautions."
2. Drain fuel from fuel tank into suitable container using draining tool No. 310-F013 and storage tanker tool No. 164-R3202, or equivalents.
3. Raise and support vehicle.
4. Remove filler pipe mounting bolt and disconnect pipe hose connections to tank.
5. Disconnect fuel tank electrical connector.
6. Disconnect vapor tube fitting at lefthand front side of tank.
7. Place suitable jack stand under tank.
8. Remove front two bolts from fuel tank support straps and position lefthand strap aside.
9. Remove righthand rear bolt and support strap.
10. Partially lower tank and disconnect fuel lines using suitable spring lock coupler tools.
11. Cut pipe-to-tank grommet's outer edge to ease filler pipe removal and remove grommet.
12. Lower and remove tank. Move tank to suitable bench.
13. Remove sender unit orientation for installation alignment and remove mounting bolts.
14. Pull sender unit up until locking tabs are accessible. **Avoid damaging filter, float arm, tubing and wiring.**
15. Remove sender by reaching through opening and squeeze locking tabs together.
16. Reverse procedure to install, noting the following:
    a. Install mounting bolts finger tight, then tighten in sequence, **Fig. 33.**
    b. Lubricate filler pipe check valve area and new tank-to-filler pipe grommet with Serfactant (Merpol), or equivalent.

FUEL FILTER

REPLACE

1. Relieve fuel system pressure as outlined under "Precautions."
2. Raise and support vehicle.
3. Remove push connector fittings from fuel filter ends using suitable spring lock coupler tools
4. Loosen worm gear clamp, and remove filter from bracket. Record flow arrow to ensure proper direction of fuel flow through filter.
5. Reverse procedure to install using new retainer clips in each fitting.

TECHNICAL SERVICE BULLETINS

COOLANT LEAK

1999–2000 w/SOHC ENGINE

On some of these models built between July 1, 1998, and June 30, 2000, there may be a leak or weep of coolant from righthand side intake manifold gasket at righthand rear corner of head-to-manifold joint.

This condition may be caused by the righthand side intake manifold gasket.

To correct this condition install revised righthand side intake manifold gasket (part No. YL3Z-9439-AA).

BUZZING OR RATTLING EXHAUST SYSTEM

1998–99

On some of these models there may be a buzzing or rattling from the exhaust system.

This condition may be caused by loose catalytic converter, catalytic pipes, muffler pipes and/or muffler heat shields.

To correct this condition secure heat shields with suitable worm clamps. **Torque** clamps to 60 inch lbs.

FUEL PUMP WHINING/ BUZZING THROUGH RADIO SPEAKER

1998–2001

On some of these models there may be a whining or buzzing in speakers.

This condition may be caused by fuel pump electrical noise.

To correct this condition install an electronic noise Radio Frequency Interference (RFI) filter (part No. F1PZ-18B925-A) on fuel pump inside the fuel tank, as follows:

1. Remove fuel pump sender from fuel tank as described under "Fuel Pump, Replace."
2. Cut fuel pump wires three inches from flange. Discard wires.
3. Connect RFI filter connectors to fuel pump spade terminal.
4. Cut and solder both RFI filter red and black wires to flange red and black wires.
5. Install suitable heat shrink tubing over solder connectors.
6. Secure RFI filter to fuel pump using suitable bundling strap.

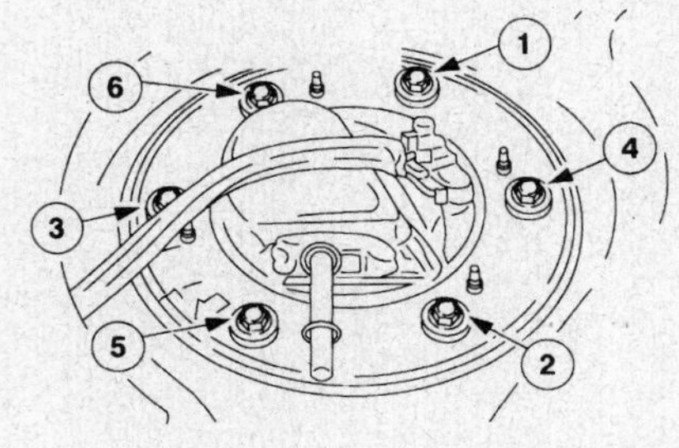

Fig. 33 Fuel tank sender unit bolt tightening sequence. 1999–2002

7. Install fuel pump sender.

DRIVE BELT BROKEN, FRAYED OR COMES OFF

1998

On some of these models built before Aug. 15, 1997, the accessory drive belt may be broken, frayed and/or come off engine.

This condition may be caused by engine deceleration.

To correct this condition, proceed as follows:

1. Remove and discard belt.
2. Inspect water pump pulley. If new flanged pulley is installed, proceed to next step. If raised flange pulley is not installed, proceed as follows:
   a. Remove and discard pulley.
   b. Install revised water pump pulley (part No. F6ZZ-8509-AA).
   c. **Torque** mounting bolts to 15–22 ft. lbs.
3. Inspect power steering pump pulley. If new flanged pulley is installed, proceed to next step. If raised flange pulley is not installed, proceed as follows:
   a. Remove and discard pulley.
   b. Install revised power steering pump pulley (part No. F7ZZ-3A733-AA).
   c. Pulley must be pressed on to 0.026 inch past shaft end.
   d. **Torque** mounting bolts to 15–22 ft. lbs.
4. Remove single fastener orientation clip from bottom of power steering pump.
5. Install revised power steering orientation clip (part No. F7ZZ-3E523-AA).
6. Inspect automatic belt tensioner, noting the following:
   a. If tensioner positive stop is installed over tensioner and part number stamped on bottom of positive stop is F7ZE-19A439-AB, remove and discard positive stop and belt tensioner.
   b. If tensioner positive stop is not installed, remove mounting bolts and nut.
   c. Discard tensioner, belt guide and mounting bolts. Retain mounting nut.
7. Install revised tensioner (part No. F7AZ-6B209-CB) using one existing stud and two new studs (part No. N807336-S2).
8. **Torque** studs and nuts to 15–22 ft. lbs.
9. Install new drive belt (part No. F7AZ-8620-AA).
10. Install revise tensioner positive stop (part No. F7ZZ-19A439-AC) onto two studs.
11. **Torque** stop bracket mounting nuts to 15–22 ft. lbs.

TIGHTENING SPECIFICATIONS

Year	Component	Torque/Ft. Lbs.
1998	Accelerator Cable Bracket	70–105①
	Alternator	15–22
	Ball Joint To Spindle	109–149
	Camshaft	81–95
	Camshaft Cover	72–108⑥
	Camshaft Sprocket (DOHC)	81–95
	Clutch Pressure To Flywheel	19–24
	Cylinder Head	③
	Drive Belt Tensioner & Idler Pulley	15–22
	EGR Tube Connector	33–48
	EGR Vacuum Regulator	45–60①
	EGR Valve To Exhaust Tube	30–33
	EGR Valve To Manifold	15–22
	Engine Lifting Eyes	30–37
	Engine Support To Crossmember	94–126
	Engine Support To Engine, Large Bolt	44–60
	Engine Support To Engine, Small Bolt	25–33
	Exhaust Manifold	13–16
	Front Strut To Spindle	141–191
	Fuel Injection Supply Manifold	70–105①
	Idle Air Control Valve	70–105①
	Ignition Coil To Engine	15–22
	Ignition Wire Cover	45–60①
	Intake Manifold To Cylinder Head	15–22
	Intake Manifold, Upper To Lower	71–105①
	Low Oil Sensor	20–30
	Oil Cooler To Oil Filter Adapter	59–74
	Oil Pan (DOHC)	15–22
	Oil Pan (SOHC)	②
	Oil Pan Drain Plug	96–144①
	Stabilizer Bar Link	11–16
	Sub Frame To Body	70–96
	Throttle Body To Intake	71–105.6①
	Tie Rod To Spindle	35–47
	Valve Cover	72–108①
	Water Pump Pulley	15–22
	Water Pump To Block	15–22
	Wheel Lug Nut	85–105
1999–2002	Accelerator Cable Bracket	72–96①
	Air Conditioning Compressor	18
	Air Conditioning Muffler	15
	Alternator	18
	Alternator Brace	89①
	Battery Cable To Alternator	89①
	Battery Cable Support Bracket	15
	Belt Idler Pulley	18
	Belt Tensioner	18
	Camshaft	81–95
	Camshaft Cover	89①
	Camshaft Position Sensor	89①
	Camshaft Sprocket (DOHC)	81–95
	Clutch Pressure Plate	26
	Connecting Rod (DOHC)	18–24⑦
	Connecting Rod (SOHC)	18⑨
	Crankshaft Damper	114–121

Continued

TIGHTENING SPECIFICATIONS—Continued

Year	Component	Torque/Ft. Lbs.
1999–2002	Crankshaft Position Sensor	89①
	Crankshaft Pulley	④
	Crankshaft Rear Seal Retainer	89①
	Cylinder Head	③
	Drive Belt Tensioner	18
	EGR Sensor Bracket	89①
	EGR Tube Connector	30–33
	EGR Vacuum Regulator Solenoid Bracket	89①
	EGR Valve	18
	EGR Tube To EGR Valve	26
	EGR Tube To Exhaust Manifold	30
	Engine Coolant Temperature Sensor	11
	Engine Mount, Nut	111
	Engine Mount To Block	52
	Exhaust Manifold, Nut	18
	Exhaust Manifold, Stud	84–120①
	Exhaust Manifold Stud (DOHC)	96–108⑥
	Exhaust Manifold Stud (SOHC)	84–120①
	Exhaust Pipe To Exhaust Manifold	20–30
	Flywheel	59
	Front Brake Caliper	23
	Front Cover	④
	Front Engine Mount	45–59
	Front Engine Mount Through Bolts	15–22
	Fuel Filer	27–44①
	Fuel Rail	89①
	Fuel Tank Sender	89①
	Heater Hose Fitting Studs To Manifold	18
	Idle Air Control Valve	89①
	Ignition Coil	53①
	Ignition Coil Cover	89①
	Intake Manifold	18
	Intake Manifold To Cylinder Head	53–64
	Main Bearing	⑧
	Oil Dipstick Tube	89①
	Oil Filter (SOHC)	11
	Oil Filter (DOHC)	37
	Oil Filter Adapter	15–22
	Oil Filter Adapter Insert	43
	Oil Inlet Tube To Main Bearing Cap	15–22
	Oil Inlet Tube To Oil Pump	72–108①
	Oil Pan	②
	Oil Pan Drain Plug	120①
	Oil Pump	89①
	Oil Pump Screen Cover & Tube To Main Cap Stud Spacer	18
	Oil Pump Screen Cover & Tube To Pump	89①
	Oxygen Sensor	27–33
	Power Steering Pump	18
	Power Steering Reservoir	89①
	Powertrain Frame	73–100
	Pressure Plate	47①
	Rear Engine Mount, Bolt	50–70

Continued

TIGHTENING SPECIFICATIONS—Continued

Year	Component	Torque/Ft. Lbs.
1999–2002	Rear Engine Mount, Nut	35–50
	Rear Engine Support	15–22
	Rear Seal Retainer	89①
	RFI Capacitor	89①
	Serpentine Belt Idler Pulley	18
	Serpentine Belt Tensioner	18
	Spark Plug	13
	Subframe	85
	Thermostat Housing	15–22
	Throttle Body	⑤
	Throttle Cable Bracket	89①
	Timing Chain Tensioner	18
	Torque Converter (DOHC)	22–25
	Torque Converter (SOHC)	18
	Transmission Filler Tube	35
	Transmission Shift Lever	27
	Transmission Shift Lever Inner Boot	89①
	Transmission Shift Lever Plate To Transmission	13
	Valve Cover	89①
	Water Bypass Tube	72–96①
	Water Drain Plug	15
	Water Outlet	18
	Water Pump	18
	Water Pump Pulley	18
	Wheel Lug Nuts	95
	Wiring Harness	89①

①— Inch pounds.

②— Refer to "Oil Pan, Replace" for tightening specifications and sequence.

③— Refer to "Cylinder Head, Replace" for tightening specifications and sequence.

④— Refer to "Front Cover, Replace" for tightening specifications and sequence.

⑤— Refer to "Intake Manifold, Replace" for tightening specifications and sequence.

⑥— Tighten an additional 90–120°.

⑦— Tighten an additional 85–90°.

⑧— Refer to "Main & Rod Bearings" for tightening specifications and sequence.

⑨— Torque to 30 ft. lbs.; then tighten an additional 90°.

Clutch & Manual Transmission

NOTE: On Air Bag Equipped Models, Refer To "Air Bag System Precautions" Located In The Front Of This Manual For System Disarming & Arming Procedures.

NOTE: Refer To "Computer Relearn Procedures" Located In The Front Of This Manual When Battery Power To The Computer Has Been Interrupted.

NOTE: Prior To Performing Any Service Operations Listed In This Section, Consult The "Technical Service Bulletins" Section For Related Information.

INDEX

PRECAUTIONS

AIR BAG SYSTEMS

Refer to "Air Bag System Precautions" in front of this manual for system disarming and arming procedures.

BATTERY GROUND CABLE

Prior to service, disconnect battery ground cable and isolate as required.

ADJUSTMENTS

CLUTCH PEDAL

1998

A self-adjusting type clutch mechanism is used. Adjust mechanism consists of a spring-loaded ratchet quadrant attached to clutch cable. Adjust the clutch every 5000 miles as follows:

1. Grasp clutch pedal and pull upward.
2. Slowly depress clutch pedal.
3. If click is heard during procedure, adjustment was required and has been accomplished.

1999–2002

On these models a self-adjusting type clutch mechanism is used. It automatically adjusts itself to compensate for clutch plate wear. No periodic attention is required. If the brake or clutch pedal are being replaced their bushings should be lubricated with a light film of clean engine oil.

CLUTCH PEDAL POSITION (CPP) SWITCH

The clutch pedal position switch is self-adjusting. Press the clutch pedal to the floor to reset.

CLUTCH

REPLACE

1998

The clutch pedal must be lifted to disconnect adjusting mechanism during clutch release lever cable installation.

Under no circumstances should a prying instrument such as a screwdriver or a pry bar be used to install or remove the clutch release lever cable from the clutch and brake pedal pivot shaft.

REMOVAL

1. Lift clutch pedal to upper most position to disconnect clutch and brake pedal pivot shaft, **Fig. 1.**
2. Push clutch and brake pedal pivot shaft forward, then disconnect clutch release lever cable from clutch and brake pedal pivot shaft. Allow it to slowly swing rearward.
3. Raise and support vehicle.
4. Remove clutch release lever dust shield.
5. Disconnect clutch release lever cable from clutch release shaft.
6. Remove retaining clip and clutch release lever cable from flywheel housing.
7. Remove starter motor as outlined in "Electrical" section.
8. Remove engine rear plate to front lower flywheel housing bolts.
9. Remove transmission as outlined under "Transmission, Replace."
10. Move flywheel housing back far enough to clear clutch pressure plate, then remove housing.
11. Remove clutch release shaft from flywheel housing by pulling it through window in flywheel housing until retainer spring disconnects from pivot.
12. Remove clutch release hub and bearing from clutch release shaft.
13. Loosen six clutch pressure plate bolts evenly.
14. If same clutch pressure plate is to be installed, mark plate and flywheel so pressure plate can be installed in its original position.
15. Remove clutch pressure plate and clutch disc from flywheel.

INSTALLATION

Avoid touching clutch disc face, dropping components or contaminating them with oil or grease.

1. Position clutch disc and pressure plate assembly on flywheel.
2. Align three flywheel housing to block dowels with clutch pressure plate. Replace bent, damaged or missing dowels.
3. Start threading clutch pressure plate bolts into place. **Do not tighten now.**
4. Align clutch disc using suitable alignment tool inserted in pilot bearing.
5. Alternately tighten bolts a few turns at a time until all bolts are tight.
6. Install transmission to flywheel housing.
7. Install engine rear plate to flywheel front lower housing bolts, then connect clutch release cable to flywheel housing and retaining clip.
8. Connect clutch release lever cable to clutch release shaft and install clutch release lever dust shield.
9. Install starter motor as outlined in "Electrical" section.
10. Lower vehicle.
11. Lift clutch pedal to disconnect clutch and brake pedal pivot shaft.
12. Push clutch and brake pedal pivot shaft forward, then hook end of clutch release lever cable over rear of clutch and brake pedal pivot shaft.

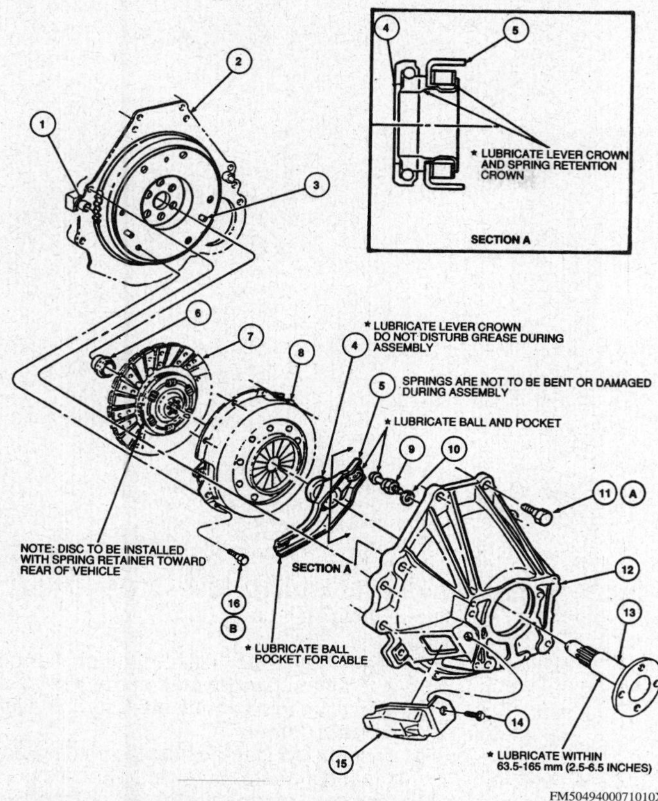

Fig. 1 Clutch disc & pressure plate replacement (Part 1 of 2).1998

Item	Description
1	Flywheel Housing to Block Dowel (2 Req'd)
2	Rear Face of Block and Flywheel (Part of 6010)
3	Flywheel-To-Clutch Pressure Plate Dowel (3 Req'd)
4	Clutch Release Hub and Bearing
5	Clutch Release Lever
6	Pilot Bearing (Install with Seal Toward Rear of Vehicle)
7	Clutch Disc
8	Clutch Pressure Plate
9	Clutch Release Lever Stud
10	Washer
11	Bolt (6 Req'd) (3.8L) Bolt (6 Req'd) (4.6L)

Item	Description
12	Flywheel Housing
13	Main Drive Gear Bearing Retainer
14	Bolt
15	Clutch Release Lever Dust Shield (Installed After Cable Assy)
16	Screw and Washer Assy (6 Req'd) (3.8L) Screw and Washer Assy (6 Req'd) (4.6L)

FM5049400071020X

Fig. 1 Clutch disc & pressure plate replacement (Part 2 of 2). 1998

13. Cycle clutch pedal several times to adjust clutch release lever cable.

1999–2002

REMOVAL

1. Remove transmission as outlined under "Transmission, Replace."
2. Mark pressure plate and flywheel to ease installation, **Figs. 2 and 3.**
3. Loosen pressure plate to flywheel bolts evenly, then remove them.
4. Remove pressure plate and disc.

INSTALLATION

1. Clean flywheel with an alcohol based solvent to remove all traces of oil film. **Do not use petroleum based solvent.**
2. Align clutch disc to flywheel using clutch alignment tool No. T74P-7137-K, or equivalent.
3. Install pressure plate using alignment tool and alignment marks.
4. **On models equipped with 3.8L engine, torque** pressure plate to flywheel bolts to 24 ft. lbs. in sequence, **Fig. 4.**
5. **On models equipped with 4.6L SOHC engine, torque** pressure plate to flywheel bolts to 26 ft. lbs. in sequence, **Fig. 4.**
6. **On models equipped with 4.6L DOHC engine,** proceed as follows:
   a. **Torque** pressure plate to flywheel bolts to 33 ft. lbs. in sequence, **Fig. 4.**
   b. Finally, tighten bolts an additional 60°.
7. **On all models,** remove alignment tool.
8. Install transmission.

TRANSMISSION

REPLACE

1998

T45 TRANSMISSION

1. Working inside vehicle, remove gearshift lever boot and console panel gear shift plate.
2. Remove two mounting bolts and gearshift lever. Isolator lever from transmission stub shaft.
3. Raise and support vehicle.
4. Mark driveshaft for installation alignment in original position.
5. Remove driveshaft from rear axle and slide out of transmission output shaft.
6. Install extension housing seal replacer tool No. T96P-7127-A, or equivalent into extension housing to prevent fluid loss.
7. Remove eight mounting bolts and dual converter H-pipe.
8. Remove mounting bolt and clutch release lever dust shield, then disconnect clutch cable.
9. Remove two rear transmission support to transmission support crossmember mounting nuts.
10. Support engine and transmission with suitable jack.
11. Remove two rear engine support bolts' nuts.
12. Raise jack slightly and remove transmission support crossmember.
13. Disconnect backup lamp switch wiring harness and speedometer sensor electrical connector from extension housing.
14. Disconnect battery cable and ignition wire from starter motor.
15. Remove three mounting bolts and starter motor.
16. Support cylinder blocks and balancer.
17. Remove seven clutch housing to cylinder block mounting bolts.
18. Move transmission rearward until input shaft clears clutch pressure plate. Lower engine to obtain clearance removal clearance, as required.
19. Reverse procedures to install.

T50D TRANSMISSION

1. Working inside vehicle, remove gearshift lever boot and console panel gear shift plate.
2. Remove two mounting bolts and gearshift lever. Isolator lever from transmission stub shaft.
3. Raise and support vehicle.
4. Mark driveshaft for installation alignment in original position.
5. Disconnect driveshaft from rear axle universal joint flange, then slide it off transmission output and fifth gear drive shaft.
6. Install extension housing seal replacer tool No. T61L-7657-A, or equivalent, into extension housing to prevent lubricant leakage.
7. Remove four mounting bolts and dual converter Y-pipe.
8. Remove two rear transmission support to rear engine support nuts, then bolts.
9. Support engine and transmission with suitable transmission jack.
10. Remove nuts and two rear engine support bolts.
11. Remove rear engine support bolts.
12. Raise jack slightly and remove rear engine support.

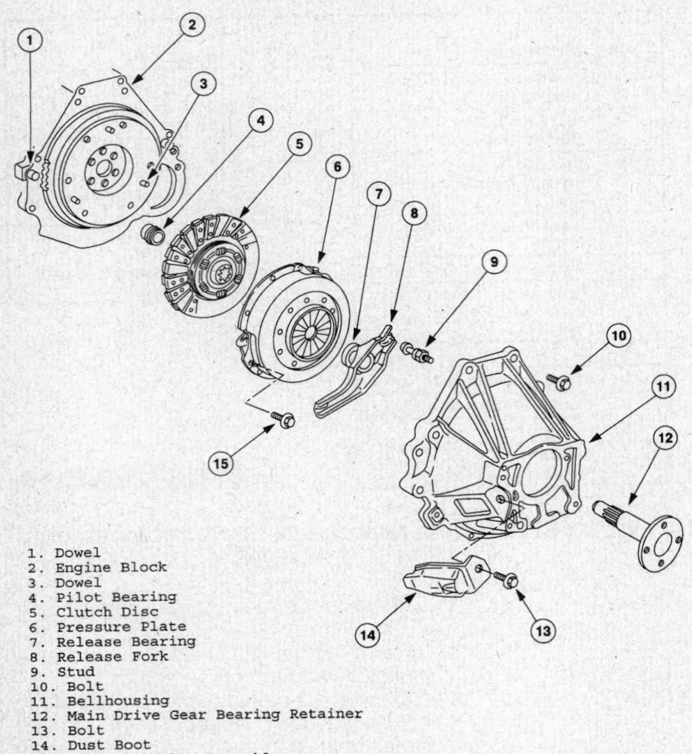

Fig. 2 Exploded view of clutch. 1999–2002 w/3.8L engine

1. Flywheel
2. Dowel
3. Pilot Bearing
4. Clutch Disc
5. Pressure Plate
6. Release Fork
7. Stud
8. Bolt
9. Bellhousing
10. Bolt
11. Dust Boot
12. Release Bearing
13 & 14. Bolts
15. Engine Block
16. Bolt
17. Dowel

FM5049900104000X

Fig. 3 Exploded view of clutch. 1999–2002 w/4.6L engine

13. Disconnect wiring back-up lamp switch harness.
14. Remove speedometer cable bolt and speedometer drive gear from transmission.
15. Remove four transmission to flywheel housing bolts.
16. Move transmission and jack rearward until transmission input shaft clears flywheel housing. Lower engine to obtain clearance removal clearance, as required.
17. Reverse procedure to install. Apply pipe sealant with Teflon D8AZ-19554-A, or equivalent, to transmission case plug in clockwise direction prior to installation.

1999–2002

T45 & TR3650 TRANSMISSIONS

1. Remove shift lever knob.
2. Remove console panel gearshift plate, then lift boot up and over lever.
3. Remove mounting bolts and lever.
4. Raise and support vehicle.
5. Disconnect HO2S electrical connectors.
6. Remove left and righthand exhaust pipe to manifold and muffler nuts.
7. Remove dual converter H-pipe.
8. Mark driveshaft at companion flange and pinion flange, then at the slip yoke and transmission tail shaft for installation alignment.
9. Disconnect back-up lamp switch electrical connector and wiring harness.
10. Remove starter motor as outlined in "Electrical" section.
11. Disconnect Output Shaft Speed (OSS) sensor electrical connector and wiring harness.
12. Remove clutch release lever cover.
13. Disconnect clutch release cable from clutch release fork. **Do not depress clutch pedal while transmission is removed.**
14. Remove retainer and disconnect clutch cable at transmission.
15. If transmission will be disassembled, drain lubricant into suitable container.
16. Support transmission with suitable jack.
17. Remove mounting bolts and crossmember.
18. Remove inspection cover.
19. Lower transmission and remove upper bellhousing bolts.
20. Lower and remove transmission.
21. Reverse procedure to install. Apply Teflon pipe sealant No. D8AZ-19554-A, or equivalent, to filler plug threads.

T50D TRANSMISSION

1. Lift clutch pedal up and secure it in place.
2. Remove shift lever knob.
3. Remove console panel gearshift plate, then lift boot up and over lever.
4. Remove mounting bolts and shift lever.
5. Raise and support vehicle.
6. Disconnect HO2S electrical connectors.
7. Remove left and righthand exhaust pipe to manifold and muffler nuts.
8. Remove dual converter Y-pipe.
9. Mark driveshaft at companion flange and pinion flange, then at the slip yoke and transmission tail shaft for installation alignment
10. Disconnect back-up lamp switch electrical connector and wiring harness.
11. Remove starter motor as outlined in "Electrical" section.
12. Disconnect OSS sensor electrical connector and wiring harness.
13. Remove clutch release lever cover.
14. Disconnect clutch release cable from clutch release fork. **Do not depress clutch pedal while transmission is removed.**
15. Remove retainer and disconnect clutch cable at transmission.
16. If transmission will be disassembled, drain lubricant into suitable container.
17. Support transmission with suitable jack.
18. Remove mounting bolts and crossmember.
19. Remove inspection cover.
20. Lower transmission and remove upper bellhousing bolts.
21. Lower and remove transmission.
22. Reverse procedure to install.

TECHNICAL SERVICE BULLETINS

CLUTCH VIBRATION

On some of these models there may be a vibration that is heard or felt in pedal between idle and 2300 RPM. This vibration goes away when pedal is depressed approximately one inch.

This condition may be caused by lack of reserve, quadrant binding, improper clutch cable routing, lack of release lever preload, improper or failed release bearing, improper pressure plate-to-flywheel bolt tightening or out-of-parallel pressure plate finger height.

To correct this condition, proceed as follows:

1. Set parking brake with clutch depressed, engine idling and shift control in 3rd gear.
2. Move shift lever to position halfway between 3rd gear and neutral.
3. Slowly release clutch pedal. Gear clash should be heard if attempt is made to shift into 3rd gear with pedal up.
4. Maintain light pressure on shift lever and slowly press clutch pedal to floor.
5. Measure distance between where gear clash stops (and shift selector slides easily into 3rd gear) and clutch pedal reaches floor. If clutch reserve is not at least 0.75 inch, replace disc and pressure plate.
6. Pull clutch pedal to upstop and allow quadrant to freely rotate against spring load.
7. Cycle clutch pedal and inspect for vibration.
8. Ensure clutch cable is routed properly and cable isolator grommet is seated in cowl.
9. Raise and support vehicle.
10. Remove transmission dust cover and prop clutch pedal to upstop.
11. Pull clutch release lever toward vehicle rear.
12. Ensure there is enough spring and cable tension to seat release bearing against clutch plate fingers by releasing clutch release lever.
13. Measure release force using spring scale tool No. T74P-3504-Y, or equivalent.
14. If release force is less than 3.5 lbs., quadrant is not functioning properly. Remove clutch pedal prop.
15. If condition has not been corrected, remove transmission.
16. Ensure picot stud fits in release lever pocket center. Replace lever if spring tabs are bent.
17. Ensure proper release bearing (part No. F7ZR-7548-AA is stamped on bearing rear flange) is installed.
18. Ensure pressure plate-to-flywheel bolts are properly tightened.
19. Measure pressure plate finger height variation using suitable dial indicator. Replace pressure plate if lowest to highest finger height variation is more than 0.04 inch.
20. Measure flywheel run-out at clutch disc contract surface with suitable dial indicator.
21. Install new flywheel if run-out is more than 0.008 inch.
22. Ensure pilot bearing is not damaged, worn or improperly installed. Replace as required.

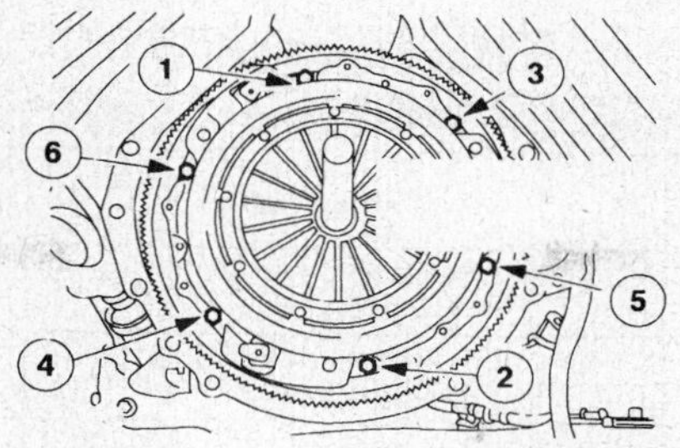

Fig. 4 Pressure plate to flywheel bolt tightening sequence. 1999–2002

CLUTCH VIBRATION/NOISE

1998

On some of these models there may be a vibration/noise felt when the clutch is engaged and foot is lightly touching the pedal. The vibration disappears once pressure is applied to the pedal.

This condition may be caused by reduction of throw-out bearing grease.

To correct this condition install revised throw-out bearing (part No. F7ZZ-7548-AA). **Do not replace clutch disc unless there are obvious signs of damage.** Do not replace pressure plate unless there is more than 0.039 inch height variation between highest and lowest finger.

TIGHTENING SPECIFICATIONS

Year	Component	Torque/Ft. Lbs.
1998	Driveshaft Nuts	70–95
	Dual Converter H- Or Y-Pipe	20–30
	Flywheel Housing To Case (T45)	15–25
	Flywheel Housing To Cylinder Block	28–38
	Gearshift Lever To Transmission	20–25
	Pressure Plate To Flywheel	②
	Transmission Extension Housing (T45)	15–25
	Transmission Extension Housing (T50D)	45–64
	Transmission To Flywheel Housing (T50D)	45–64
	Transmission Extension Housing Support	25–35
	Transmission Support	35–50
1999–2002	Back-Up Lamp Switch	27
	Bellhousing To Block	55
	Bellhousing To Case (T45)	20
	Brake Booster	18
	Brake Pedal Support Bracket	18
	Case Cover (T50D)	108①
	Companion To Pinion Flanges	83
	Clutch Housing	23
	Clutch Pedal	30
	Clutch Release Lever Cable Bracket	89①
	Clutch Release Lever Cable To Bulkhead	35①

Continued

TIGHTENING SPECIFICATIONS—Continued

Year	Component	Torque/Ft. Lbs.
1999–2002	Clutch Release Lever Cable To Crossmember	71①
	Clutch Release Lever Cable To Master Cylinder	71①
	Countershaft Rear Bearing Retainer	15
	Crossmember To Frame	30
	Crossmember To Transmission Support	43
	Drain Plug	17
	Driveshaft Centering Yoke	83
	Dual Converter Y-Pipe To Manifold	30
	Dual Converter Y Pipe To Muffler	26
	Engine Plate To Transmission	20
	Extension Housing (TR3650)	23
	Extension Housing (T50D)	40
	Fifth/Reverse Lockout	15
	Filler Plug	13
	Gear Shift Lever To Extension Housing	13
	Gear Shift Lever To Stub Shaft	27
	HO2S Bracket (4.6L Engine)	18
	Inner Shift Boot	89①
	Input Shaft Bearing Retainer	15
	Inspection Cover	20
	Instrument Panel Reinforcement	80①
	OSS	89①
	Pressure Plate To Flywheel	②
	Shift Lever Reverse Pin	30
	Shift Lever To Extension Housing	13
	Shift Lever To Stub Shaft	27
	Starter Motor	17
	Starter Solenoid B-Terminal	108①
	Starter Solenoid Terminal	53①
	Steering Column Cover	80①
	Tailshaft Housing To Case	40
	Transmission To Engine	55

①— Inch lbs.

②— Refer to "Clutch, Replace" for tightening specifications and sequence.

Rear Axle & Suspension

NOTE: On Air Bag Equipped Models, Refer To "Air Bag System Precautions" Located In The Front Of This Manual For System Disarming & Arming Procedures.

NOTE: Refer To "Computer Relearn Procedures" Located In The Front Of This Manual When Battery Power To The Computer Has Been Interrupted.

NOTE: Prior To Performing Any Service Operations Listed In This Section, Consult The "Technical Service Bulletins" Section For Related Information.

INDEX

DESCRIPTION

EXCEPT 1999-2001 COBRA

This rear axle is an integral design hypoid with center line of pinion set below center line of ring gear, **Fig. 1.** Semi-floating axle shafts are retained in housing by ball bearings and bearing retainers at axle ends.

The differential is mounted on two opposed tapered roller bearings which are retained in housing by removable caps. The differential bearing preload and drive gear backlash is adjusted by nuts located behind each differential bearing cup.

The drive pinion assembly is mounted on two opposed tapered roller bearings. The pinion bearing preload is adjusted by a collapsible spacer on pinion shaft. The pinion and ring gear tooth contact is adjusted by shims between rear bearing cone and pinion gear.

1999-2001 COBRA

On these models the hypoid type axle has an 8.8-inch ring gear and a one-piece differential case, **Fig. 2.** Two opposed pinion bearings support the drive pinion gear in the differential housing. Two pinion gears engage the differential side gears with their halfshaft splines.

REAR AXLE

REPLACE

EXCEPT 1999-2001 COBRA

1. Raise and support vehicle, then position safety stands under rear frame crossmember.
2. Drain axle lubricant into suitable container by removing axle housing cover.
3. Remove wheels, rear disc brake calipers and rear disc brake rotors as outlined in "Disc Brakes" chapter.
4. Remove lockpin and differential pinion shaft.
5. Remove rear brake anti-lock sensor.
6. Remove rear axle shaft U-washers by pushing axle shafts inward.
7. Remove axle shafts.
8. Remove brake junction block to axle housing cover bolt and brake hose support bracket from clips. Position hose aside.
9. Mark driveshaft centering socket yoke and rear axle universal joint flange for installation alignment.
10. Disconnect driveshaft at rear axle universal joint flange and wire it to underbody.
11. Support rear axle housing with suitable jackstands or hoist.
12. Disconnect rear brake hose from rear brake hose to rear axle housing clips.
13. Disconnect rear axle housing vent from rear axle housing.
14. Disconnect lower shock absorber studs from rear shock absorber lower mounting bracket.
15. Remove rear suspension arm and bushing nuts and bolts from axle housing rear bracket mountings.
16. Lower rear axle housing until rear springs are released, then lift out rear springs.
17. Remove rear suspension lower arm to rear axle housing nuts and bolts, then disconnect both rear suspension lower arms from rear axle housing.
18. Lower rear axle housing and remove it.
19. Reverse procedure to install, noting the following:
    a. Tighten differential pinion shaft lockpin using stud and bearing mount tool No. E0AZ-19554-BA, or equivalent.
    b. Tighten axle housing cover bolt in crosswise pattern.
    c. Apply threadlock and sealer E0AZ-19554-AA, or equivalent, to rear axle housing vents threads.

1999-2001 COBRA

1. Park vehicle at curb height and on level ground.
2. Mark rear shock absorber positions relative to their upper sleeves for installation alignment.
3. Raise and safely support vehicle, then

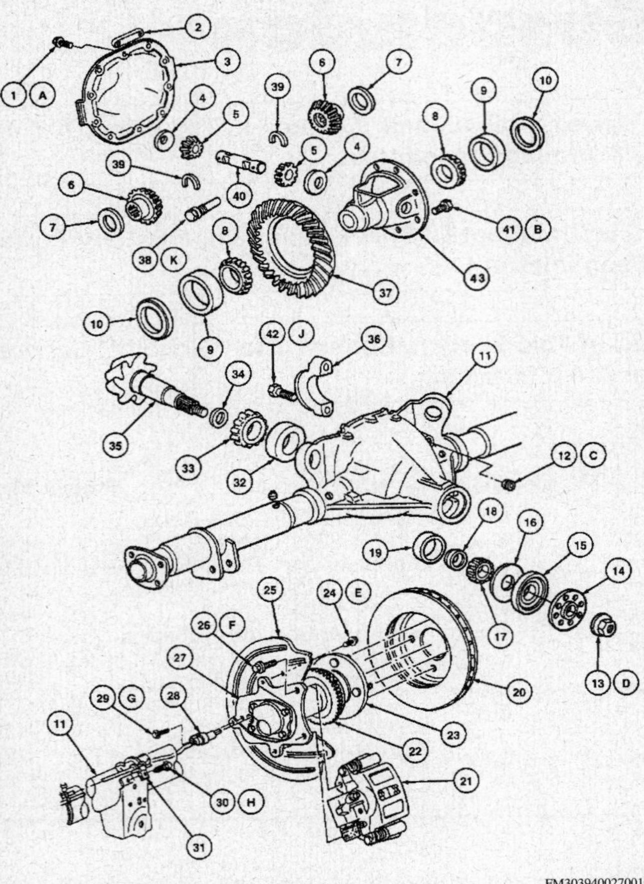

Fig. 1 Exploded view of integral rear axle (Part 1 of 2). Less Traction-Lok or 1999–2001 Cobra

Item	Description
1	Bolt
2	Rear Axle Brake Line Clip
3	Axle Housing Cover
4	Differential Pinion Thrust Washer
5	Differential Pinion Gear
6	Differential Side Gear
7	Differential Side Gear Thrust Washer
8	Differential Bearing
9	Differential Bearing Cup
10	Differential Bearing Shim
11	Rear Axle Housing
12	Filler Plug
13	Pinion Nut
14	Rear Axle Universal Joint Flange
15	Rear Axle Drive Pinion Seal
16	Rear Axle Drive Pinion Shaft Oil Slinger
17	Differential Pinion Bearing
18	Differential Drive Pinion Collapsible Spacer
19	Differential Drive Pinion Bearing Cup
20	Rear Disc Brake Rotor
21	Rear Disc Brake Caliper
22	Rear Brake Anti-Lock Sensor Indicator
23	Axle Shaft Flange (Part of 4234)
24	Bolt (3 Req'd)
25	Rear Wheel Disc Brake Shield
26	Caliper Anchor Bolt
27	Left Hand Rear Disc Brake Adapter
	Right Hand Rear Disc Brake Adapter

Item	Description
28	Rear Brake Anti-Lock Sensor
29	Bolt
30	Bolt
31	Clip
32	Rear Axle Pinion Bearing Cup
33	Differential Pinion Bearing
34	Drive Pinion Bearing Adjustment Shim
35	Drive Pinion (Part of 4209)
36	Bearing Cap (Part of 4010)
37	Ring Gear (Part of 4209)
38	Differential Pinion Shaft Lock Pin
39	U-Washer
40	Differential Pinion Shaft
41	Rear Axle Differential Gear Case Bolt
42	Bolt (Part of 4010)
43	Differential Case
A	Tighten to 24-38 N·m (18-28 Lb-Ft)
B	Tighten to 95-115 N·m (70-85 Lb-Ft)
C	Tighten to 20-41 N·m (15-30 Lb-Ft)
D	Tighten to 190 N·m (140 Lb-Ft)
E	Tighten to 8-12 N·m (6-9 Lb-Ft)
F	Tighten to 87-119 N·m (64-87.7 Lb-Ft)
G	Tighten to 5-7 N·m (40-60 Lb-In)
H	Tighten to 10-14 N·m (7-10 Lb-Ft)
J	Tighten to 102-122 N·m (75-90 Lb-Ft)
K	Tighten to 20-41 N·m (15-30 Lb-Ft)

FM3039400270020X

Fig. 1 Exploded view of integral rear axle (Part 2 of 2). Less Traction-Lok or 1999–2001 Cobra

remove rear wheel and tire assemblies.

4. Remove exhaust system.
5. Record transverse bar fastener for installation alignment.
6. Remove mounting nuts and pinion nose crossmember.
7. Mark driveshaft companion flange to pinion flange for installation alignment.
8. Remove and discard companion flange to pinion flange bolts.
9. Position driveshaft aside with suitable wire or rope.
10. Disconnect parking brake cables and conduits from parking brake lever and calipers.
11. Separate parking brake cables and conduits from knuckles.
12. Remove rear brake rotors.
13. Remove rear brake calipers and support brackets from knuckles as an assembly. Position calipers aside with suitable wire or rope.
14. Remove rear brake anti-lock sensors and position aside.
15. Support lower suspension arm and bushing with suitable jack stand.
16. Remove and discard lower suspension arm nuts and bolts.
17. Remove and discard toe link cotter pins and nuts.
18. Disconnect toe links from knuckles using separator tool No. T64P-3590-F, or equivalent.
19. Mark cam bolt to upper control arms and bushings for installation alignment.
20. Remove and discard lower control arm bushing nuts and bolts.
21. Disconnect knuckles from lower control arms.
22. Mark upper control arm cam bolts for installation alignment.
23. Remove and discard upper control arm bushing nuts and bolts.
24. Disconnect knuckles from upper control arms.
25. Separate CV joint from side gear using halfshaft removal tool No. 205-475, or equivalent, to overcome circlip. **Ensure tool fork crowns face away from differential housing. Position tool between CV joint and housing.**
26. Install seal protector tool No. 205-461, or equivalent.
27. Remove halfshaft and knuckle assemblies.
28. Install differential plug tool No. T89P-4850-B, or equivalent, into housing bores.
29. Support differential housing with suitable transmission jack.
30. Remove differential to frame mounting bolts.
31. Lower and remove axle.
32. Reverse procedure to install, noting the following:
    a. Replace differential mounting bushings, as required.
    b. Install seal protector tool No. 205-461, or equivalent, before install halfshafts.
    c. Ensure inboard CV joints circlips are properly seated.
    d. Ensure transverse bar is in place and bolt passes through it. **Do not tighten until vehicle is on ground and shock absorber marks are aligned.**
    e. Install new cam bolts and nuts at control arms and bushings. **Do not tighten until vehicle is on ground and shock absorber marks are aligned.**
    f. Apply high temperature nickel anti-seize lubricant part No. F6AZ-9L494-AA, or equivalent, to rear brake anti-lock sensors at axle housing contact points.

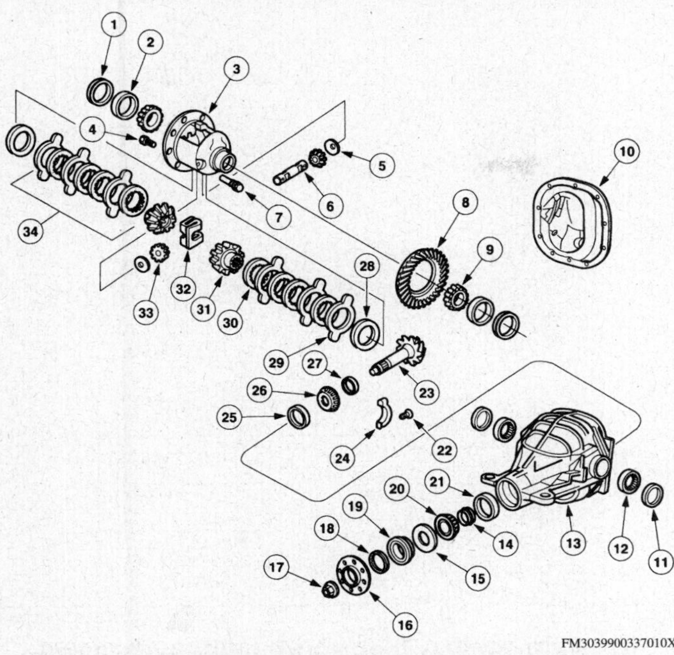

Fig. 2 Exploded view of rear axle (Part 1 of 2). 1999–2001 Cobra

Item	Description
1	Differential bearing shim
2	Differential bearing cup
3	Differential case
4	Differential ring gear case bolt
5	Differential pinion thrust washer
6	Differential pinion shaft
7	Differential pinion shaft lock bolt
8	Differential ring gear
9	Differential bearing
10	Differential housing cover
11	Inboard CV joint stub shaft pilot bearing housing seal
12	Inboard CV joint stub shaft pilot bearing
13	Differential housing
14	Differential drive pinion collapsible spacer
15	Rear axle drive pinion shaft oil slinger
16	Rear axle pinion flange
17	Pinion nut
18	Drive pinion oil seal deflector
19	Rear axle drive pinion seal
20	Pinion bearing
21	Differential drive pinion bearing cup
22	Bolt
23	Drive pinion gear
24	Differential bearing cap
25	Rear axle pinion bearing cup
26	Pinion bearing
27	Drive pinion bearing adjustment shim
28	Rear axle differential clutch shim
29	Clutch plate
30	Clutch disc
31	Differential side gear
32	Differential clutch spring
33	Differential pinion gear
34	Differential clutch pack

FM3039900337020X

Fig. 2 Exploded view of rear axle (Part 2 of 2). 1999–2001 Cobra

g. Adjust wheel alignment, as required.

REAR AXLE SHAFT

REPLACE

EXCEPT 1999-2001 COBRA

1. Raise and support vehicle, then remove rear wheel and tire assembly.
2. Remove brake drum as outlined in "Drum Brakes" chapter or rear disc brake calipers and rear disc brake rotors as outlined in "Disc Brakes" chapter.
3. Remove axle housing cover and drain axle lubricant into suitable container.
4. Remove lockpin and differential pinion shaft.
5. Remove rear brake anti-lock sensor.
6. Push axle shaft flanged end toward vehicle center, then remove C-lock from axle shaft button end.
7. Remove axle shaft from housing. **Do not damage oil seal.**
8. Reverse procedure to install.

1999-2001 COBRA

Refer to "Rear Axle, Replace" for this procedure.

AXLE DAMPER

REPLACE

1. Raise vehicle and support rear axle, then the rear wheel and tire assembly.
2. Remove axle damper front retaining pivot bolt and rear mounting nut, **Fig. 3.**
3. Remove damper and washers.
4. Reverse procedure to install.

PROPELLER SHAFT

REPLACE

EXCEPT 1999-2001 COBRA

REMOVAL

1. Mark rear driveshaft yoke and drive pinion flange relationship for installation alignment.
2. Disconnect rear U-joint from companion flange, **Fig. 4.**
3. Wrap tape around loose bearing caps to prevent them from falling off spider.
4. Pull driveshaft toward rear of vehicle until slip yoke clears transmission extension housing and seal.
5. Install suitable plug into extension housing to prevent lubricant leakage.

INSTALLATION

1. Lubricate slip yoke splines with suitable grease, then remove plug from transmission extension.
2. Inspect housing seal for damage. Replace as required.
3. Align slip yoke index mark with transmission output shaft mark and install driveshaft assembly. **Do not allow slip yoke to bottom on output shaft with excessive force.**
4. Install driveshaft so index mark on rear flange is aligned with index mark on axle companion flange to ensure original driveline balance.
5. When installing new driveshaft assembly, align factory made yellow paint mark at rear of driveshaft tube with factory made yellow paint mark on axle companion flange.

1999-2001 COBRA

1. Raise and support vehicle.
2. Remove exhaust hangers from rubber mounts.
3. Remove two mounting nuts on left-hand side exhaust flange.
4. Lower the muffler pipe to clear flange, then move muffler forward to disconnect third exhaust hanger.
5. Mark driveshaft companion flange to pinion flange for installation alignment.
6. Mark driveshaft yoke to transmission tailshaft for installation alignment.
7. Remove and discard companion flange to pinion flange bolts.
8. Lower driveshaft rear it clears axle housing.
9. Pull driveshaft rearward out of transmission.
10. Reverse procedure to install.

SHOCK ABSORBER

REPLACE

These vehicles are equipped with gas pressurized shock absorbers which will extend unassisted. Do not apply heat or flame to shock absorber tube during removal.

EXCEPT 1999-2001 COBRA

1. Open luggage compartment and remove rubber cap, as required.
2. Remove shock absorber upper stud nut, washer and insulator.
3. Raise and support vehicle, then support rear axle.
4. Remove shock absorber lower stud nut, washer and insulator.
5. Compress shock absorber to clear upper shock tower.
6. Remove shock absorber.
7. Reverse procedure to install.

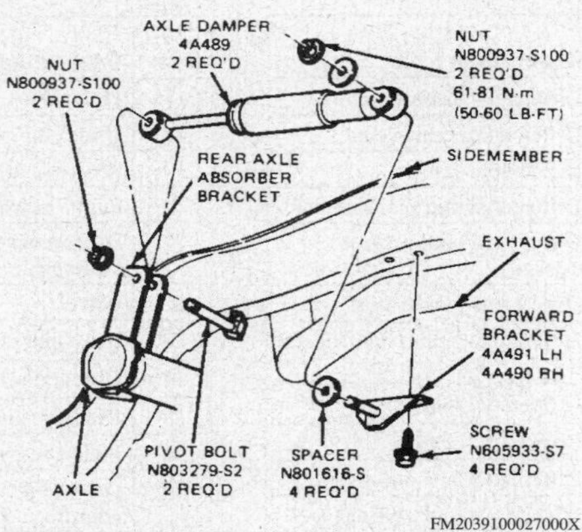

Fig. 3 Axle damper replacement

Item	Description	Item	Description
1	Needle Rollers (Part of 4635)	9	Driveshaft
2	Grease Seal (Part of 4635)	10	Driveshaft Centering Socket Yoke
3	Bearing Cup (Part of 4635)	11	Rear Axle Universal Joint Flange
4	Thrust Washer (Part of 4635)	12	Bolt (4 Req'd)
5	Spider (Part of 4635)	13	Universal Joint
6	Universal Joint	14	End Yoke (Part of 4635)
7	Driveshaft Slip Yoke		
8	Snap Ring (8 Req'd) (Part of 4635)		

FM3039400241000X

Fig. 4 Driveshaft & universal joint replacement. Single Cardan type U-joint

1999-2001 COBRA

1. Open luggage compartment and position carpet aside.
2. Remove and discard shock absorber mounting nut, washer and insulator.
3. Raise and support vehicle.
4. Remove and discard shock absorber lower mounting bolt and nut.
5. Remove shock absorber, then the insulator and washer.
6. Reverse procedure to install, noting the following:
   a. Install new lower insulator and washer onto shock absorber.
   b. **Ensure hardened washer sits between lower control arm and bushing and the absorber.**
   c. Install new upper insulator, washer and nut.

COIL SPRING

REPLACE

EXCEPT 1999-2001 COBRA

1. Raise rear of vehicle and support at rear body crossmember.
2. Remove stabilizer bar, as required, **Fig. 5.**
3. Lower axle housing until shock absorbers are fully extended. Support axle housing with suitable jack.
4. Support control arm with suitable jack under lower control arm rear pivot bolt. Remove pivot bolt.
5. Lower control arm until spring tension is relieved, then remove coil spring and insulator.
6. Reverse procedure to install. Tighten lower control arm pivot bolt with suspension at curb height.

1999-2001 COBRA

1. Raise and support vehicle.
2. Support No. 1 crossmember with suitable jack stand.
3. Remove rear tire and wheel assemblies.
4. Remove both mufflers.
5. Remove driveshaft as outlined under "Propeller Shaft, Replace."
6. Disconnect parking brake cables and conduits at parking brake levers, rear brake calipers and rear knuckles.
7. Remove parking brake cable brackets at coil spring seats.
8. Remove rear brake line to axle mounting bolts, then position lines aside.
9. Remove mounting bolts and rear wheel speed sensors.
10. Disconnect ABS sensor wiring harness at subframe.
11. Support lower control arms and bushings with suitable jack stands.
12. Discard shock absorber lower mounting nuts and bolts.
13. Lower control arms and bushings, then remove jack stands.
14. Support rear subframe using powertrain lift tool No. 014-00765, or equivalent.
15. Remove and discard subframe front mounting nuts.
16. Remove and discard subframe rear mounting nuts and bolts.
17. Lower subframe and allow it to pivot on its front bolts.
18. Remove springs and insulators.
19. Reverse procedure to install, noting the following:
    a. Install new lower insulator and washer onto shock absorber.
    b. **Ensure hardened washer sits between lower control arm and bushing and the absorber.**
    c. Adjust wheel alignment, as required.

CONTROL ARM

REPLACE

EXCEPT 1999-2001 COBRA

UPPER

Removal

1. Raise rear of vehicle and support at rear body crossmember.
2. Remove rear and front pivot bolts, then the upper control arm.

Installation

1. Position upper control arm into side rail bracket, then install front pivot bolt. **Do not tighten bolt now.**
2. Raise rear axle until upper control arm rear pivot bolt hole is aligned with hole in axle housing, then install rear pivot bolt. **Do not tighten bolt now.**
3. Position suspension at curb height, then tighten front pivot bolt.

LOWER

1. Raise and support vehicle, then support body at rear crossmember.
2. Lower hoist until rear shock absorbers are fully extended, then place suitable transmission jack under lower arm to axle pivot bolt.
3. Remove and discard lower control arm front pivot bolt and nut, **Fig. 5.**
4. Remove control arm.
5. Reverse procedure to install.

1999-2001 COBRA

UPPER

1. Park vehicle at curb height and on level ground.
2. Mark rear shock absorber positions relative to their upper sleeves.
3. Raise and support vehicle, then remove rear wheel and tire assemblies.
4. Remove rear brake rotor.
5. Remove coil springs as outlined under "Coil Spring, Replace."
6. Raise subframe into position, then remove and discard front bolts.
7. Mark upper control arm and bushing cam bolt position for installation alignment.
8. Remove and discard upper control arm bushing nut and bolt.

9. Disconnect knuckle from upper control arm.
10. Remove and discard upper control arm nut and bolt.
11. Remove upper control arm.
12. Reverse procedure to install, noting the following:
    a. Install new cam bolts and nuts at control arms and bushings. **Do not tighten until vehicle is on ground and shock absorber marks are aligned.**
    b. Adjust wheel alignment, as required.

LOWER

1. Park vehicle at curb height and on level ground.
2. Mark rear shock absorber positions relative to their upper sleeves.
3. Mark transverse bar fastener for installation alignment.
4. Remove coil springs as outlined under "Coil Spring, Replace."
5. Disconnect lower control arm from knuckle. Discard nut and bolt.
6. Disconnect lower control arm from subframe. Discard nuts and bolts.
7. Reverse procedure to install, noting the following:
    a. Install lower control arm with new fasteners. **Do not tighten until vehicle is on ground and shock absorber marks are aligned.**
    b. Ensure transverse bar is in place and bolt passes through it. **Do not tighten until vehicle is on ground and shock absorber marks are aligned.**
    c. Adjust wheel alignment, as required.

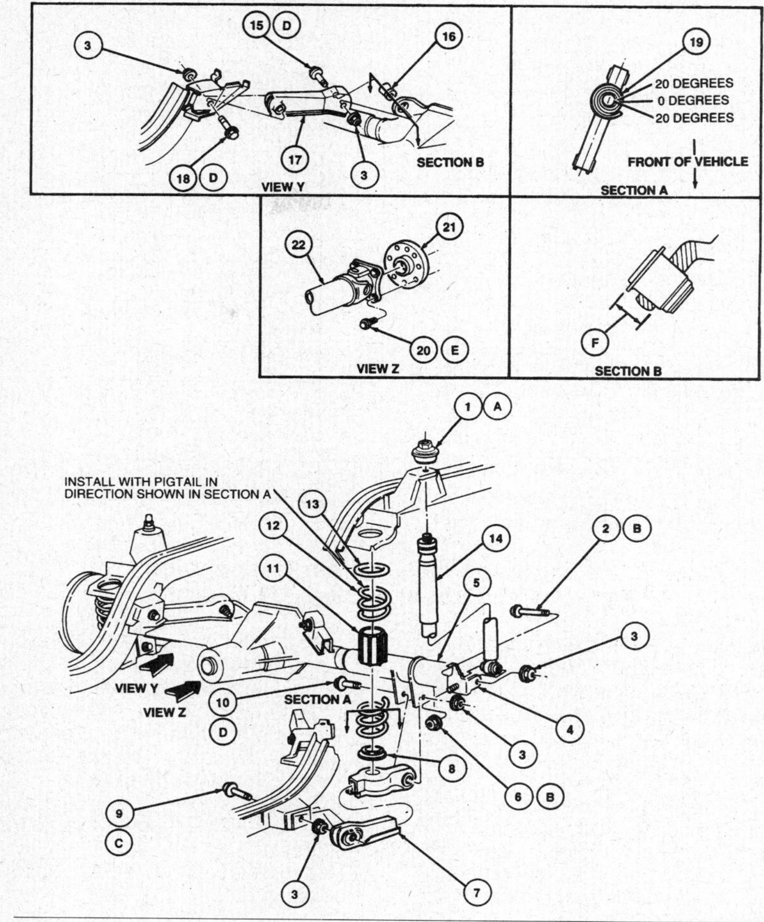

Fig. 5 Exploded view of rear suspension (Part 1 of 2). Except 1999–2001 Cobra

CONTROL ARM BUSHING

REPLACE

EXCEPT 1999–2001 COBRA

1. Remove control arm as outlined under "Control Arm, Replace."
2. Remove bushing using bushing remover and installer set tool No. T78P-5638-A, or equivalent, **Fig. 6.**
3. Reverse procedure to install using suitable installer tool, **Fig. 7.**

1999–2001 COBRA

1. Remove upper control arm as outlined under "Control Arm, Replace."
2. Remove bushing using bushing remover and installer set tool No. T79P-5638-A, or equivalent.
3. Reverse procedure to install. Ensure bushing is properly installed, **Fig. 8.**

STABILIZER BAR

REPLACE

EXCEPT 1999–2001 COBRA

1. Raise and support rear of vehicle.
2. Remove four bolts attaching stabilizer bar to brackets on lower control arms.
3. Remove stabilizer bar from vehicle.
4. Reverse procedure to install.

1999–2001 COBRA

1. Remove rear coil springs as outlined under "Coil Spring, Replace" in this section.
2. Raise subframe into position, then remove and discard its front bolts.
3. Lower the subframe out of vehicle.
4. Remove stabilizer link and nuts. Discard nuts.
5. Remove stabilizer bar brackets and bolts. Discard bolts.
6. Remove stabilizer bar and bushings.
7. Reverse procedure to install.

TECHNICAL SERVICE BULLETINS

VIBRATION/SHAKE AT 62 MPH

1998 CONVERTIBLE w/4.6L ENGINE

On some of these models there may be a vibration/shake at a steady 62 mph on smooth roads.

This condition may be caused by interaction between the body and suspension modes.

To correct this condition, proceed as follows:

1. Ensure tires are properly inflated and balanced.
2. Ensure wire lateral and radial runout is less than 0.045 inch.
3. Eliminate stressed or bound conditions, by normalizing engine and transmission mounts.
4. Inspect for loose suspension bolts and nuts, control arms, steering rack, engine mounts, crossmembers, etc.
5. Replace worn suspension and steering components, as required.
6. Install revised engines mounts with higher stiffness (lefthand part No. XR3Z-6038-DB and righthand part No. XR3Z-6038-DA).
7. Install underbody rails (lefthand part No. XR3Z-76101W09-AA and righthand part No. XR3Z-76101W08-AA), using Mig welder and standard body gas metal arc welding repair procedures, **Fig. 9.**
8. Welds should be a minimum 0.2 inch and at least 2.95 inches long on both sides of rail an at both front and rear ends.

Item	Description
1	Nut, Insulator Assy (Part of 18198)
2	Bolt (2 Req'd)
3	Nut (2 Req'd)
4	Rear Shock Absorber Lower Mounting Bracket (2 Req'd)
5	Axle
6	Nut (2 Req'd)
7	Rear Suspension Lower Arm (2 Req'd)
8	Rear Spring Insulator (2 Req'd)
9	Bolt (2 Req'd)
10	Bolt
11	Rear Spring Damper (2 Req'd)
12	Rear Spring (2 Req'd)
13	Rear Spring Insulator (2 Req'd)
14	Rear Shock Absorber (2 Req'd)
15	Bolt (2 Req'd)

Item	Description
16	Rear Suspension Arm Bushing (2 Req'd)
17	Rear Suspension Arm and Bushing (2 Req'd)
18	Bolt (2 Req'd)
19	Pigtail
20	Bolt (4 Req'd)
21	Rear Axle Universal Joint Flange
22	Driveshaft
A	Tighten to 34-46 N·m (25-34 Lb-Ft)
B	Tighten to 76-103 N·m (57-75 Lb-Ft)
C	Tighten to 98-132 N·m (71-79 Lb-Ft)
D	Tighten to 98-132 N·m (71-79 Lb-Ft)
E	Tighten to 56-77 N·m (41-56 Lb-Ft)
F	Install to 35.5-36.5 mm (1.39-1.43 In)

FM2039100026020X

Fig. 5 Exploded view of rear suspension (Part 2 of 2). Except 1999–2001 Cobra

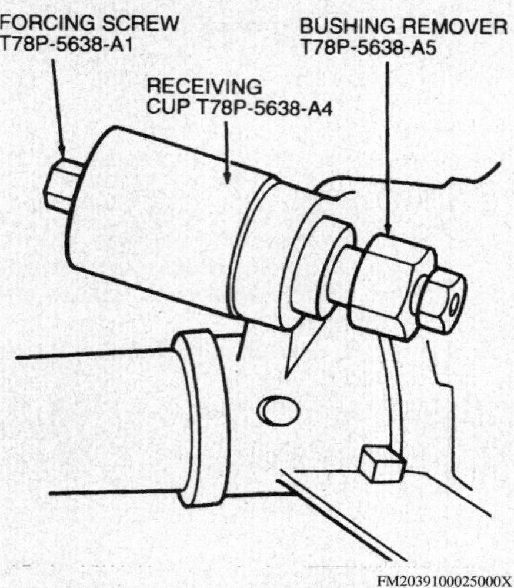

Fig. 6 Upper control arm axle bracket bushing removal. Except 1999–2001 Cobra

9. Welded area should be treated for corrosion using super sealant No. F3AZ-19515-SA, or equivalent.
10. **On models equipped with automatic transmission,** transfer shift cable retainer from body to underbody rails' bracket.
11. **On all models,** replace rear shock absorbers using new upper mount hardware (stiffer rubber isolator with white mark and 0.079 inch shorter steel spacer) included in kit (part No, F8ZZ-18125-BB).
12. Replace front struts using new upper mounting hardware (stiffer rubber isolator with white mark and 0.079 inch shorter steel spacer) included in kit (part No. F8ZZ-18124-BB). Use existing jounce bumper and dust shield.

REAR SUSPENSION SQUEAK

1999 COBRA

On some of these models there may be a rear suspension squeak when driving slowly over speed bumps.

This condition may be caused by lower control arm bushing outer sleeve rubbing on outboard subframe ear.

To correct this condition, proceed as follows:

1. Raise and support vehicle.
2. If there are signs of contact between lower control arm bushings and subframe ear, remove both rear wheel and tire assemblies.
3. Remove both rear exhaust pipe support brackets' bolts.
4. Press out four exhaust pipe rubber hangers and allow exhaust system rear to hang.
5. Remove both lower control arm bracket bolts's nuts, then move bolts back approximately one inch. **Do not remove bolts.**
6. Install spacer washers (part No. XR3Z-5561-AA) in front of bushing.
7. Push bolts back in and install nuts. **Do not tighten now.**
8. Tack weld washer to subframe ears.
9. Place suitable tall screw-type jack at vehicle front under front crossmember just below steering gear. **Do not raise vehicle with jack stand.**
10. Compress lower control arm without raising vehicle using suitable transmission jack.
11. **Torque** lower control arm bolt to 184 ft. lbs.

COASTDOWN REAR AXLE WHINE

1999–2001 MODELS w/3.8L ENGINE

On some of these models there may be a whining during coastdown from 60–35 mph. This noise disappears at less than 35 mph.

This condition may be caused by a variation in tooth contact between the differential ring gear and pinion, and by the original upper control arm bushings inability to isolate the noise.

To correct this condition, proceed as follows:

1. Raise and support vehicle.
2. Replace driveshaft, noting the following:
   a. **On models equipped with automatic transmission,** ensure driveshaft front yellow dot aligns with dot on transmission output shaft end.
   b. **On all models,** ensure driveshaft rear yellow dot aligns with corresponding pinion flange dot.
3. Remove two rear upper control arms.
4. Install two revised upper control arms (part No. 1R3Z-5500-AA). **Do not tighten mounting bolts now.**
5. Place suitable screw-type jack at vehicle front under front crossmember just below steering gear. **Do not raise vehicle with jack stand.**
6. Raise axle assembly as far as possible without raising vehicle using suitable transmission jack.
7. **Torque** two upper arm-to-frame bolts to 66 ft. lbs.
8. **Torque** two upper arm-to-axle bolts to 76 ft. lbs.

HIGHWAY SPEED VIBRATION

2000 COBRA

On some of these models there may be a vibration felt in seat or steering wheel at 65–78 mph in 4th or 5th gear without the brakes applied. Vibration disappears when speeds slows below 65 mph.

This condition may be caused by the driveshaft and/or differential being out of balance.

To correct this condition if vibration occurs in both 4th and 5th gears, install revised driveshaft differential (kit part No. YR3Z-4B490-AA).

To correct this condition if vibration occurs in 5th gear only, change index position of front driveshaft to transmission output shaft in 90° increments.

1999 COBRA

On some of these models there may be a vibration felt in seat or steering wheel at 65 mph in 4th or 5th gear

This condition may be caused by an unisolated driveline vibration.

To correct this condition proceed as follows:

1. Raise and support vehicle.
2. Support rear differential with suitable screw-type jack stand.
3. Remove two differential mount insulator bolts from front.
4. Install revised damper (part No. 1R3Z-4B424-A) and revised differential mount insulators (two upper part Nos. F3SZ-4B424-A and two lower part Nos. F3SZ-4B432-B).
5. **Torque** mounting bolts to 52 ft. lbs.
6. Connect suitable Electronic Vibration

TIGHTENING SPECIFICATIONS—Continued

Year	Component	Torque/Ft. Lbs.
COBRA		
1999–2001	ABS Sensor	17
	Axle Shaft To Hub	240
	Brake Fluid Line To Caliper	30
	Brake Rotor Dust Shield	89①
	Differential Insulator, Front	52
	Differential Insulator, Rear	76
	Driveshaft To Companion Flange	83
	Lower Control Arm & Bushing To Knuckle	85
	Lower Control Arm & Bushing To Subframe	184
	Lubricant Filler Plug	25
	Pinion Nose Crossmember	184
	Parking Brake Cable Bracket	11
	Shock Absorber, Lower	98
	Shock Absorber, Upper	30
	Stabilizer Bar Bracket	41
	Stabilizer Bar Link	35
	Subframe Rear Bracket	59
	Subframe To Body	76
	Subframe To Rear Bracket	76
	Toe Link	35
	Upper Control Arm	66
	Wheel Hub Retainer	251
	Wheel Lug Nuts	95

① — Inch lbs.

Front Suspension & Steering

NOTE: On Air Bag Equipped Models, Refer To "Air Bag System Precautions" Located In The Front Of This Manual For System Disarming & Arming Procedures.

NOTE: Refer To "Computer Relearn Procedures" Located In The Front Of This Manual When Battery Power To The Computer Has Been Interrupted.

INDEX

DESCRIPTION

The front suspension is of a modified McPherson strut design using shock struts and coil springs, **Fig. 1.** The springs are mounted between the lower control arm and a crossmember spring pocket.

WHEEL BEARING

ADJUST

Wheel bearings are not adjustable.

HUB & BEARING

REPLACE

1. Raise and support vehicle, then remove wheel and tire assembly.
2. Remove and discard front hub cap grease seal.
3. Remove two mounting bolts and front disc brake caliper. **Do not let front disc brake caliper assembly hang by front brake hose. Suspend it with suitable wire or rope.**
4. Remove front disc brake rotor. Discard factory push-on nuts.
5. Remove and discard front axle wheel hub retainer.
6. Remove wheel hub and bearing. If assembly cannot be removed by hand, use front hub remover/replacer tool No. T81P-1104-C, or equivalent.
7. Reverse procedure to install. Install new wheel hub retainer and hub cap grease seal.

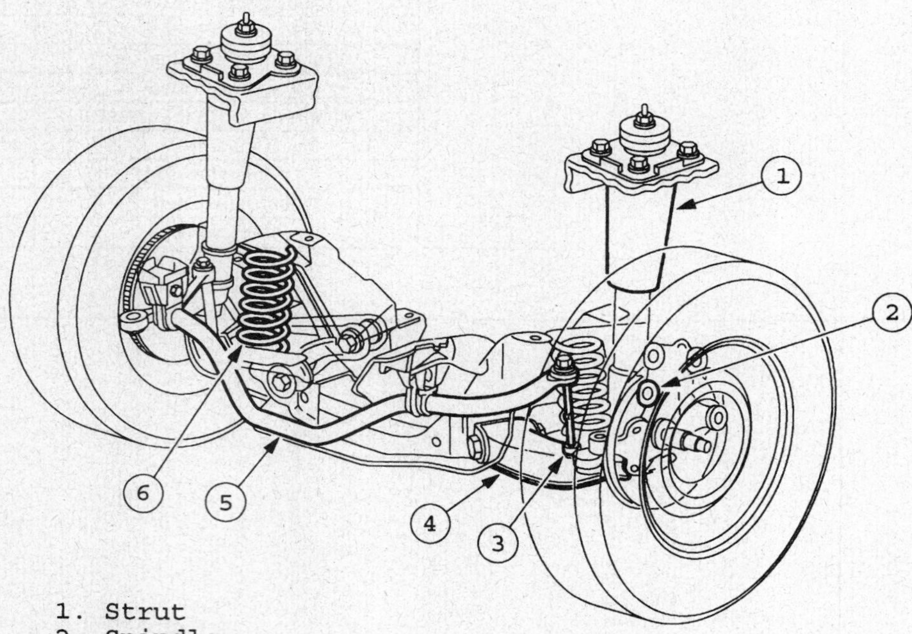

Fig. 1 Exploded view of front suspension

FRONT WHEEL SPINDLE

REPLACE

1. Raise and support vehicle, then remove front wheel and tire assembly.
2. Remove front brake anti-lock sensor from spindle.
3. Remove disc brake caliper, rotor and dust shield.
4. Remove wheel hub and front stabilizer bar from lower arm.
5. Remove tie rod end from wheel spindle using tie rod end remover tool No. 3290-D, or equivalent. **Do not remove nut from ball joint stud now.**
6. Loosen ball joint nut one or two turns, then tap spindle boss sharply to relieve stud pressure.
7. Compress front coil spring using suitable floor jack under front suspension lower arm as outlined under "Coil Spring, Replace."
8. Remove stud nut and front anti-lock sensor bracket.
9. Remove two mounting bolts and front wheel spindle.
10. Reverse procedures to install.

BALL JOINT INSPECTION

1. Raise and support front of vehicle.

2. Ensure front wheel hub and bearing assemblies are in good condition.
3. Place suitable jack stands under lower control arms.
4. Position suitable dial indicator between spindle and ball joint.
5. Grasp tire at top and bottom, then slowly move inward and outward.
6. **On 1998 models,** replace ball joint if movement is more than 0.015 inch.
7. **On 1999–2002 models,** replace lower control arm if movement more than 0.031 inch.

BALL JOINT

REPLACE

1998

1. Remove front wheel spindle as outlined under "Front Wheel Spindle, Replace."
2. Remove and discard joint boot seal.
3. Press out front suspension arm bushing joint using U-joint tool No. T74P-4635-C, or equivalent , and ball joint remover tool No. D84P-3395-A4, or equivalent, **Fig. 2.**
4. Reverse procedure to install, noting the following:
   a. When installing new front ball joint, protective cover must be left in place during installation to protect ball joint seal. It may be necessary to cut off end of cover to allow it to pass through receiving cup.
   b. Install ball joint using ball joint replacer tool No. D89P-3010-B, cup tool No. D84P-3395-A4 and C-frame tool No. T74P-4635C, or equivalents, **Fig. 3.**

1999–2002

On these models the ball joint and lower control arm must be replaced as a unit.

COIL SPRING

REPLACE

1. Park vehicle at curb height and on level ground.
2. Mark front strut positions to upper sleeves for installation alignment.
3. Raise and support vehicle.
4. Allowing front suspension lower arms to hang free, then remove wheel and tire assembly.
5. Remove brake caliper and support aside using suitable wire or rope.
6. Disconnect front wheel spindle connecting rod or end assembly from front wheel spindle using tie rod end remover tool No. 3290-D, or equivalent.
7. Disconnect stabilizer bar link from lower control arm.
8. Remove mounting bolts and position steering gear so suspension arm bolt may be removed.
9. Compress coil spring using coil spring compressor tool No. D78P-5310-A, or equivalent.
10. Remove suspension arm-to-crossmember nuts and bolts.
11. Remove compression rod and coil spring.

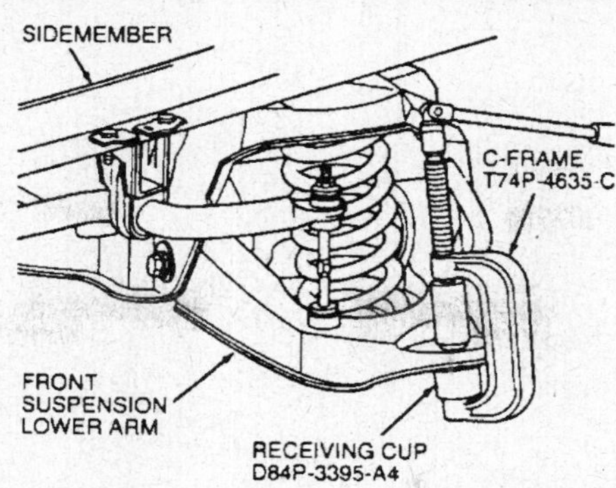

Fig. 2 Control arm ball joint removal. 1998

12. Reverse procedure to install. Ensure lower spring end is positioned between two holes in lower control arm spring pocket.

STRUT

REPLACE

1. Place ignition in unlocked position.
2. Raise and support vehicle.
3. Remove front wheel and tire assembly.
4. Remove disc brake caliper and position aside with suitable wire or rope.
5. Remove mounting bolt and ABS wheel speed sensor.
6. Disconnect ABS sensor wiring harness at bracket.
7. Support lower control arm with suitable jack stand.
8. Remove two strut to front wheel spindle mounting nuts.
9. Lower lower control arm and remove jack stand.
10. Lower vehicle.
11. Remove strut upper mounting nuts and bolts. Discard nuts.
12. Remove strut.
13. Reverse procedures to install.

CONTROL ARM

REPLACE

1. Park vehicle at curb height and on level ground.
2. Mark front strut positions to upper sleeves for installation alignment.
3. Raise and support vehicle. Allowing front suspension lower arms to hang free.
4. Remove wheel and tire assembly.
5. Remove front disc brake caliper, then position it aside with suitable wire or rope, as required to obtain working room.
6. Remove front disc brake rotor and front disc brake rotor shield as outlined in "Disc Brakes" chapter.
7. Disconnect front wheel spindle connecting rod or end from front wheel spindle using tie rod end remover tool No. 3290-D, or equivalent.
8. Remove mounting bolts and steering gear so front suspension lower arm bolt is accessible.
9. Disconnect front stabilizer link from front suspension lower arm.
10. Loosen ball joint nut one or two turns, then tap spindle boss sharply to relieve stud pressure. **Do not remove ball joint nut now.**
11. Compress spring using spring compressor tool No. D78P-5310-A, or equivalent.
12. Remove and discard ball joint stud nut, then the front shock absorber and spindle assembly. Wire aside to obtain working room.
13. Remove and discard front suspension lower arm to crossmember nuts and bolts.
14. Remove front suspension lower arm and coil spring.
15. Reverse procedure to install, noting the following:
    a. Ensure spring end is positioned between two holes in front suspension lower arm pocket.
    b. Adjust wheel alignment, as required.

STABILIZER BAR

REPLACE

1. Raise and support vehicle.
2. Disconnect stabilizer bar from each link.
3. Remove insulator clamps, insulators and stabilizer bar.
4. Reverse procedure to install. Tighten clamp to side rail bolts and stabilizer bar to link nuts.

STABILIZER BAR BUSHING

REPLACE

Refer to "Stabilizer Bar, Replace," for stabilizer bar bushing replacement procedure.

POWER STEERING GEAR

REPLACE

1998

1. Turn ignition switch to On position.
2. Place front wheels in straight-ahead position.
3. Raise and support vehicle, then position drain pan to catch power steering lines' fluid.
4. Remove front wheels and tire assemblies, as required.
5. Remove flexible coupling to power steering gear input shaft and control bolt.
6. Remove two front wheel spindle connecting end cotter pins and nuts.
7. Separate studs from spindle arms using tie rod end remover tool No. 3290-D, or equivalent.
8. Remove two steering gear to No. 2 front crossmember nuts, insulator washers and bolts.
9. Remove front rubber insulators, then position steering gear to allow access to hydraulic lines.
10. Disconnect hydraulic lines and remove steering gear.

11. Reverse procedure to install, noting the following:
    a. **Hydraulic lines are designed to swivel when properly tightened. Do not attempt to eliminate looseness by overtightening fittings, or plastic seals may be damaged.**
    b. Ensure all rubber insulators are pushed completely inside steering gear housing before installing bolts.
    c. If front wheel spindle connecting rod or ends were loosened, adjust front end alignment, as required.

1999-2002

1. Place front wheels in straight-ahead position. **Do not lock steering column.**
2. Raise and support vehicle, then remove front wheel and tire assemblies.
3. Remove tie rod end to spindle nut. Discard cotter pin.
4. Separate tie rod end from spindle using tie rod end separator tool No. 3290-D, or equivalent.
5. Remove and discard steering column intermediate shaft pinch bolt.
6. Lower vehicle.
7. Place front wheels in straight-ahead position and lock steering column. **Do not rotate steering wheel when lower column shaft is disconnected.**
8. Disconnect intermediate shaft coupling.
9. Remove steering gear mounting nuts, washers and bolts. Position gear forward.
10. Position drain pan to catch power steering lines' fluid.
11. Disconnect power steering hoses, then remove and discard O-rings. Plug all open ports,
12. Remove steering gear.
13. Reverse procedure to install, noting the following:
    a. Install new O-rings using seal replacement tool set No. D90P-3517-A, or equivalent.

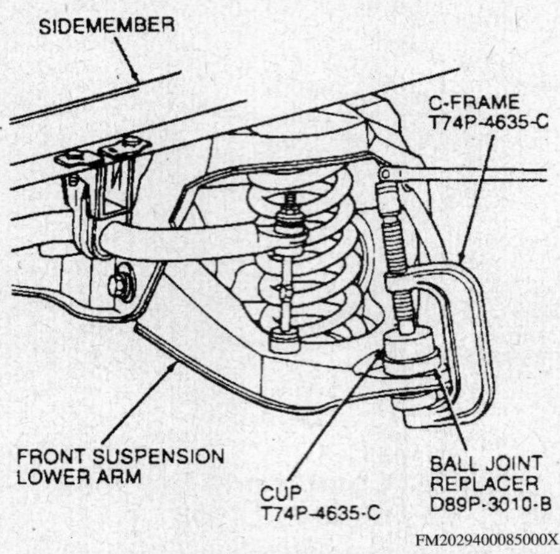

Fig. 3 Control arm ball joint installation. 1998

    b. Install new shaft coupling pinch bolt.

POWER STEERING PUMP

REPLACE

1998

1. Disconnect power steering pump reservoir return hose and allow fluid to drain into suitable container.
2. Disconnect power steering pump fitting pressure hose.
3. Remove pump mounting bracket.
4. Remove drive belt and pulley.
5. Remove power steering pump.
6. Reverse procedure to install. Endplay of pressure hose to pump fitting is normal and does not indicate a loose fitting. **Do not overtighten.**

1999-2002

TYPE CII

1. Remove serpentine drive belt.
2. Position drain pan to catch power steering lines' fluid.
3. Disconnect power steering hose, remove and discard O-ring. Plug open ports.
4. Remove pump pulley using removal tool No. T69L-10300-B, or equivalent.
5. Remove mounting bolts and power steering pump.
6. Reverse procedure to install, noting the following:
    a. Install pump pulley using installer tool No. T65P-3A733-C, or equivalent.
    b. Install new O-ring using seal replacement tool set No. D90P-3517-A, or equivalent.

TYPE CIII

1. Remove serpentine drive belt.
2. Raise and support vehicle.
3. Remove pump pulley using removal tool No. T69L-10300-B, or equivalent.
4. Remove mounting bolt and bracket.
5. Position drain pan to catch power steering lines' fluid.
6. Disconnect power steering hoses, then remove and discard O-rings. Plug open ports.
7. Remove mounting bolts and power steering pump.
8. Reverse procedure to install, noting the following:
    a. Inspect pump pulley for paint marks in hub web area. **If two paint marks are visible, discard pulley and install new one.**
    b. If there is only one or no mark, mark web area and that pulley is ready to install.
    c. Install pump pulley using installer tool No. T91P-3A733-A, or equivalent.
    d. Install new O-ring using seal replacement tool set No. D90P-3517-A, or equivalent.

TIGHTENING SPECIFICATIONS

Year	Component	Torque/Ft. Lbs.
1998	Ball Joint To Spindle	109–149
	Front Axle Wheel Hub Retainer	221–295
	Front Suspension Lower Arm To No. 2 Crossmember	141–191
	Shock Absorber To Wheel Spindle	141–191
	Stabilizer Bar Link	11–16
	Stabilizer Bar Mounting Clamp To Bracket	44–59
	Steering Gear To Crossmember	90–99
	Strut Lower Mounting To Spindle	141–199
	Strut To Upper Mounting Bracket	55–92
	Strut Upper Mount To Body	25–34
	Tie Rod End To Spindle	35–47
	Wheel Lug Nuts	85–105
1999–2002	ABS Sensor	53①
	ABS Sensor Wire Bracket	21
	Ball Joint To Spindle	129
	Lower Control Arm	148
	Stabilizer Bar Bracket	52
	Stabilizer Bar Link	14
	Steering Gear To Crossmember	52
	Strut To Spindle	148
	Strut Upper Mount	30
	Strut, Upper	74
	Tie Rod To Spindle	41
	Wheel Hub & Bearing Retainer	258
	Wheel Lug Nuts	95

① — Inch lbs.

Wheel Alignment

INDEX

PRELIMINARY INSPECTION

1. Inspect tires for proper inflation and similar tread wear.
2. Inspect hub and bearing for excessive wear. Replace as required.
3. Inspect ball joints.
4. Inspect tie rod ends for excessive looseness.
5. Measure wheel and tire runout.
6. Inspect rack and pinion for looseness at frame.
7. Ensure proper strut operation.
8. Inspect suspension and steering components for damage. Replace as required.
9. Inspect vehicle ride height.

FRONT WHEEL ALIGNMENT

BASIC INSPECTION

Inspect front wheel alignment under following curb load conditions:

1. Spare tire, wheel, jack and jack handle in proper positions.
2. Front seats in rearmost positions.
3. All other loading and aftermarket equipment removed.
4. All tires inflated to specified cold pressure.
5. All excessive mud, dirt and road deposit accumulation removed from chassis and underbody.

CASTER

Caster angle is preset during production and not adjustable. **However, if caster is still not within specifications by 0.6° after all other sources have been inspected and corrected as required, perpendicular slot cutting is allowed at the tops of the strut towers. Each millimeter of adjustment will yield approximately 0.12° in caster change. Do not cut any slots longer than 0.2 inch in any direction.**

CAMBER

1. Remove camber plate pop rivet.
2. Loosen two strut mount to body apron nuts and one strut mount to body apron bolt.
3. Move top of shock strut as required to bring camber angle within specifications.
4. Tighten nuts. **It is not necessary to replace pop rivet.**

TOE-IN

1. Determine if steering shaft and steering wheel marks are in alignment and in top position.
2. Loosen clamp screw on tie rod bellows and free seal on rod to prevent bellows from twisting.
3. Loosen tie rod jam nut.
4. Turn tie rod inner end to correct adjustment to specifications using suitable pliers, **Do not use pliers on tie rod threads.** Turning to reduce number of threads showing will increase toe-in. Turning in opposite direction will reduce toe-in.
5. Tighten nut.

REAR WHEEL ALIGNMENT

1999–2001 COBRA

On these models the independent rear suspension alignment is adjustable for camber and toe. After performing preliminary inspections, proceed as follows:

1. Loosen upper control arm pivot nuts.
2. Rotate bolts and cams until camber is within range.
3. Tighten nuts.
4. Loosen toe control jam nuts, then rotate toe link until toe is within range.
5. Tighten nuts.

SABLE & TAURUS

NOTE: Refer To The Rear Of This Manual For Vehicle Manufacturer's Special Service Tools.

INDEX OF SERVICE OPERATIONS

Specifications

GENERAL ENGINE SPECIFICATIONS

Liter/VIN Code②	Fuel System	Bore & Stroke	Comp. Ratio	Net H.P. @ RPM	Maximum Torque/Ft. Lbs. @ RPM	Normal Oil Pressure, psi
1998–99						
3.0L/S	SFI	3.50 x 3.13	—	200 @ 5750	200 @ 4500	45④
3.0L/U	SFI	3.50 x 3.14	—	145 @ 5250	170 @ 3250	40–60①
3.0L/1	SFI	3.50 x 3.14	—	145 @ 5250	170 @ 3250	40–60①
3.0L/2	SFI	3.50 x 3.14	—	145 @ 5250	170 @ 3250	40–60①
3.4L/N	SFI	3.25 x 3.13	—	235 @ 6100	230 @ 4800	20–45③
2000–02						
3.0L 2V	SFI	3.50 x 3.14	9.28:1	155@4900	185@3950	40–60①
3.0L 4V	SFI	3.50 x 3.13	10:1	200@5650	200@4400	45⑤

SFI — Sequential Fuel Injection
① — At 2500 RPM w/engine at operating temperature.
② — The eighth digit of the VIN denotes engine code.
③ — At 1500 RPM w/engine at operating temperature.
④ — With engine at operating temperature.
⑤ — At 445 RPM with engine hot.

TUNE UP SPECIFICATIONS

Liter/VIN Code①	Spark Plug Gap	Ignition Timing, °BTDC				Curb Idle Speed, RPM		Fast Idle Speed, RPM		Fuel Pump Pressure, psi	Valve Clearance
		Firing Order Fig. ②	Man. Trans.	Auto. Trans.	Mark Fig.	Man. Trans.	Auto. Trans.	Man. Trans.	Auto. Trans.		
1998–99											
3.0L/S	.054	B	—	10⑦	⑧	—	④	—	④	35–45⑨	⑥
3.0L/U	.044	A	—	10⑦	⑧	—	④	—	④	35–45⑨	⑥
3.0L/1	.044	A	—	10⑦	⑧	—	④	—	④	35–45⑨	⑥
3.0L/2	.044	A	—	10⑦	⑧	—	④	—	④	35–45⑨	⑥
3.4L/N	.044	③	—	10⑦	⑧	—	④	—	④	35–45⑨	⑤
2000–02											
3.0L 2V	.044	⑩	—	A	⑦	—	④	—	④	35–55⑪	⑥
3.0L 4V	.054	A	—	⑦	⑧	—	④	—	④	35–55⑪	⑥

BTDC — Before Top Dead Center
D — Drive
① — The eighth digit of the VIN denotes engine code.
② — Before disconnecting wires from distributor cap or coil, determine location of wire, as position may have been altered from that mounting at end of this chart.
③ — Cylinder numbering front to rear: righthand bank, 1, 2, 3, 4; lefthand bank, 5, 6, 7, 8. Firing order: 1-5-4-2-6-3-7-8.
④ — Idle speed is controlled by an automatic idle control system.
⑤ — Intake, .006–.010 inch @ room temperature; exhaust, .010–.014 inch @ room temperature.
⑥ — Equipped w/hydraulic valve lifters; no provision for adjustment.
⑦ — Non-adjustable.
⑧ — Equipped w/crankshaft position sensor.
⑨ — Engine running.
⑩ — Cylinder numbering front to rear, right bank, 1, 2, 3; left bank, 4, 5, 6. Firing order 1–4–2–5–3–6, Fig. A.
⑪ — Connect suitable fuel pressure gauge. Place ignition switch in on position. Access output mode on scan tool and operate fuel pump to obtain maximum fuel pressure. Pump will operate for approximately 8 seconds.

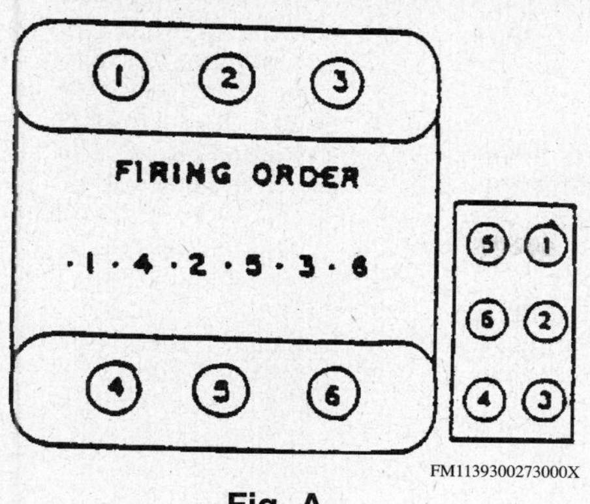

Fig. A

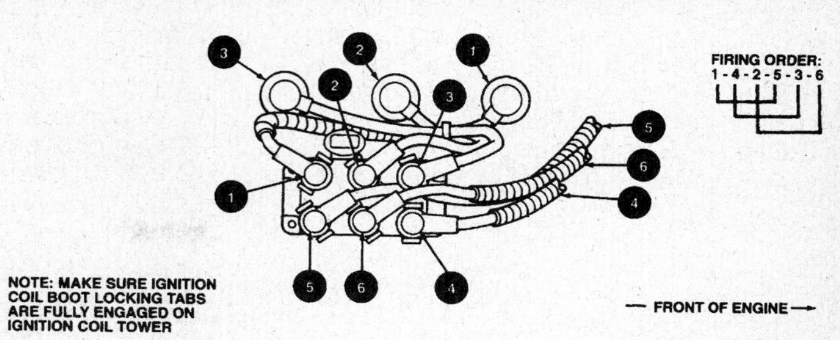

Fig. B

FRONT WHEEL ALIGNMENT SPECIFICATIONS

Model	Caster Angle, Degrees		Camber Angle, Degrees				Total Toe, Degrees①		Ball Joint Wear
	Limits	Desired	Limits		Desired		Limits	Desired	
			Left	Right	Left	Right			
All	+2.8 to +4.8	+3.8	-1.1 to +.1	-1.1 to +.1	-.5	-.5	-.45 to +.05	-.20	②

① — Turning angle at outside wheel on turns w/inner wheel @ 20° is 18.25.°

② — Refer to "Ball Joint Inspection" in "Front Suspension & Steering" section.

REAR WHEEL ALIGNMENT SPECIFICATIONS

Model	Camber Angle, Degrees①		Total Toe-In, Degrees	
	Limits	Desired	Limits	Desired
All	-1.3 to -.1	-.6	-.13 to +.37	+.12

① — Not adjustable.

VEHICLE RIDE HEIGHT SPECIFICATIONS

Model	Year	Body Style	Manufacturer's Original Tire Size	Measurement Points & Specifications					
				Front			Rear		
				Dim.	Specification		Dim.	Specification	
					Inches	mm		Inches	mm
Sable	1998–2000	Except Wagon	①	A	8.20	208	B	6.50	165
		Wagon	①	A	8.31	211	B	6.68	169
	2001–02	Wagon	①	E	27.80–28.15	700–720	G	27.47–27.85	692–712
		4 Door	①	E	27.89–28.27	703–723	G	27.22–27.60	686–706
Taurus	1998–2000	Except Wagon	①	A	8.20	208	B	6.50	165
		Wagon	①	A	8.31	211	B	6.81	172
		SHO	①	A	8.81	223	B	7.40	188
		4 Door	①	E	27.63-29.38	702-746	G	26.75-28.50	679-724
	2001–02	Wagon	①	E	27.80–28.15	700–720	G	27.47–27.85	692–712
		4 Door	①	E	27.89–28.27	703–723	G	27.22–27.60	686–706

A Dim. — Distance from Front Rocker Panel to Ground
B Dim. — Distance from Rear Rocker Panel to Ground
E Dim. — Ground to Front Wheel Opening Through Centerline of Wheel
G Dim. — Ground to Rear Wheel Opening Through Centerline of Wheel
Dim. — Dimension
① — See door sticker or inside of glove box for manufacturer's original tire size specifications. If tires on vehicle do not match manufacturer's original tire size & measurement is not within limits, it will be necessary to refer to the Non-Standard Tire & Wheel Size Adjustment To Ride Height Specification & Tire Size Adjustment Charts.

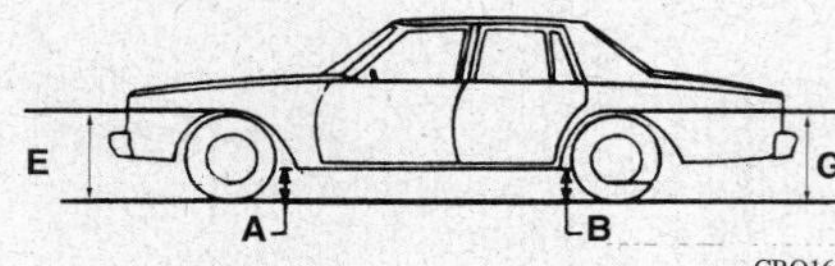

Dimensions A, B, E & G

FLUID CAPACITIES & COOLING SYSTEM DATA

Model	Engine Liter/VIN④	Coolant Capacity, Qts.	Coolant Type	Radiator Cap Relief Pressure, Lbs.	Thermo. Opening Temp. °F	Fuel Tank Gals.	Engine Oil Refill, Qts.②	Transaxle Capacity	
								Manual Trans., Pts.	Auto. Trans., Qts.①
1998–99									
All	3.0L/U, 1 & 2	11.6	⑥	16	197	⑤	4.5	—	③
	3.0L/S	10.5	⑥	16	197	16.0	5.8	—	③
SHO	3.4L/N	10.8	⑥	16	197	16.0	6.7	—	③
2000–02									
All	3.0L 2V	12.6	⑥	16	179	16	4.5	—	③
	3.0L 4V	10.6	⑥	16	179	16	5.8	—	③

① — Approximate; make final inspection w/dipstick.
② — Includes filter.
③ — Models w/AX4S transaxle, 12.25 qts.; models w/AX4N transaxle, 13.50 qts.
④ — The eighth digit of the VIN denotes engine code.
⑤ — Standard tank, 16.0 gals.; Flex Fuel tank, 18 gals.
⑥ — For models w/green coolant use ethylene glycol. For models w/orange coolant use coolant meeting Ford specifications.

LUBRICANT DATA

Year	Transaxle		Power Steering	Brake System
	Manual	Automatic		
1998–2002	—	Mercon V	①	DOT 3

① — Motorcraft MERCON Multi-Purpose ATF part No. XT-2-QDX, or equivalent.

Electrical

NOTE: On Air Bag Equipped Models, Refer To "Air Bag System Precautions" Located In The Front Of This Manual For System Disarming & Arming Procedures.

NOTE: Refer To "Computer Relearn Procedures" Located In The Front Of This Manual When Battery Power To The Computer Has Been Interrupted.

NOTE: Prior To Performing Any Service Operations Listed In This Section, Consult The "Technical Service Bulletins" Section For Related Information.

INDEX

PRECAUTIONS

AIR BAG SYSTEMS

Refer to "Air Bag System Precautions" in the front of this manual for system disarming and arming procedures.

BATTERY GROUND CABLE

Prior to service, disconnect battery ground cable and isolate as required.

FUSE PANEL & FLASHER LOCATION

The fuse panel is located under the instrument cluster or instrument panel, left of the steering column. The combination turn signal/hazard flasher is located behind on the lefthand side instrument panel reinforcement above the fuse panel.

RELAY CENTER LOCATION

The relay panel/power distribution center is located at the front center of the engine compartment, attached to the radiator support. This panel contains the PCM relay, low fan control relay, high fan control relay and A/C WAC relay.

FUEL PUMP RELAY LOCATION

The fuel pump relay is located at the front center of the engine compartment, in the power distribution center.

STARTER

REPLACE

When servicing the starter motor, note that the heavy gauge input lead connected to the starter solenoid is hot at all times. Ensure the protective cap is installed over the terminal and is replaced after service.

1998–99

1. Raise and support vehicle.
2. Disconnect engine control sensor wiring and starter battery cable from starter solenoid. **When disconnecting hard-shell connector of engine control sensor wiring at S-terminal, grasp plastic shell and pull straight off. Do not pull on wire. Replace any part of connector that is damaged during removal.**
3. Remove upper and lower starter mounting bolts, then the starter motor.
4. Reverse procedure to install. **Torque** upper and lower mounting bolts to 16–21 ft. lbs. and starter battery cable to solenoid nut to 84–120 inch lbs.

2000–02

1. Raise and support vehicle.
2. Remove lower air deflector.
3. Remove solenoid safety cap from starter solenoid.
4. Remove cables to starter solenoid and ground stud.
5. Remove bolts and stud, then the starter.
6. Reverse procedure to install.

ALTERNATOR

REPLACE

3.0L ENGINE

VIN S Engine

1. Remove accessory drive belt from alternator.

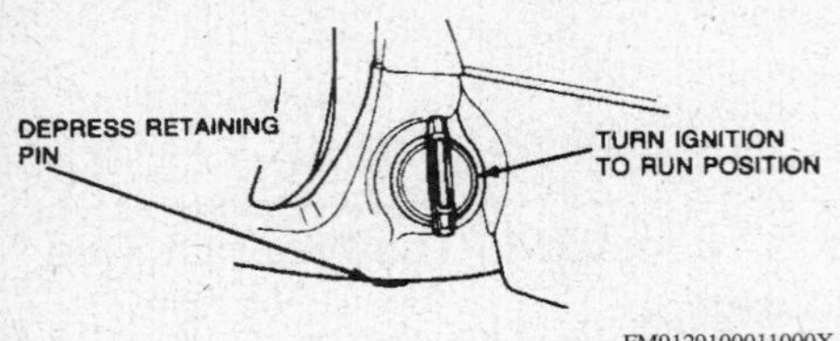

Fig. 1 Ignition lock cylinder removal

2. Remove nut, then position engine control sensor wiring and hose bracket out of the way.
3. Loosen alternator pulley nut, then Remove inboard upper alternator bolt.
4. Loosen outboard upper alternator bolt.
5. Disconnect electrical harness connector and output terminal wiring.
6. Raise and support vehicle, then remove wheel and tire assembly.
7. Remove alternator splash shield, then outboard upper alternator bolt.
8. Remove lower alternator bolt.
9. Remove alternator pulley nut, then the alternator.
10. Reverse procedure to install, noting the following:
    a. **Torque** alternator mounting bolts to 15–22 ft. lbs.
    b. **Torque** alternator output nut to 80–106 inch lbs.
    c. **Torque** alternator pulley nut to 60–100 ft. lbs.

VIN U, 1 & 2 Engines

The alternator is not internally serviceable.

1. Disconnect the electrical connectors from the integral alternator/voltage regulator.
2. Loosen the alternator pivot bolt, then remove the mounting brace bolt from the alternator.
3. Disengage the accessory drive belt from the alternator pulley.
4. Remove alternator brace.
5. Remove the alternator pivot bolt, then the alternator/voltage regulator.
6. Reverse procedure to install, noting the following:
    a. **Torque** mounting nut and mounting brace bolt to 15–22 ft. lbs. and alternator brace bolts to 72–96 inch lbs.
    b. **Torque** pivot bolt to 30–40 ft. lbs.
    c. **Torque** alternator output nut (B+) to 60–84 inch lbs.

3.4L ENGINE

1. Remove right side cowl vent screen.
2. Raise and support vehicle, then remove right front wheel assembly.
3. Remove right tie-rod, then accessory drive belt from alternator.
4. Disconnect electrical harness connector and output terminal wiring.
5. Remove nut and position engine control sensor wiring out of the way.
6. Remove one bolt and two stud bolts, then the alternator from vehicle.
7. Reverse procedure to install, noting the following:
    a. **Torque** alternator mounting bolt and stud bolts to 15–22 ft. lbs.
    b. **Torque** engine control sensor wiring mounting nut to 11–14 ft. lbs.
    c. **Torque** alternator output nut to 80–106 inch lbs.

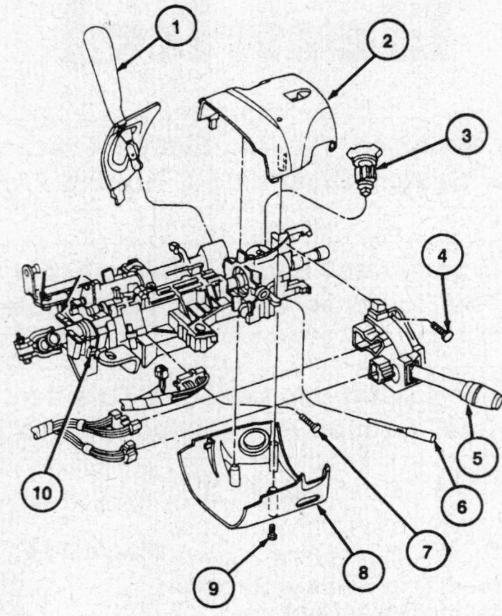

Item	Description
1	Gearshift Lever
2	Upper Steering Column Shroud
3	Ignition Lock Assy
4	Screw (2 Req'd)
5	Multi-Function Switch
6	Tilt Steering Column Lock Lever
7	Screw
8	Steering Column Shroud
9	Screw (3 Req'd)
10	Ignition Switch

FM9129600018000X

Fig. 2 Ignition switch removal

IGNITION LOCK

REPLACE

1. Place ignition switch in Run position and, working through steering column lower shroud, **Fig. 1,** depress lock cylinder retaining pin with suitable ⅛ inch drill or drift punch.
2. Pull ignition lock cylinder from housing.
3. Rotate replacement lock cylinder to Run position and, while depressing retaining pin, insert lock cylinder into housing. To ensure proper installation, rotate ignition switch through travel.

IGNITION SWITCH

REPLACE

1. Remove lower instrument panel steering column cover, **Fig. 2.**
2. Turn ignition lock to Run position.
3. Disconnect ignition switch electrical connector.
4. Remove mounting screws and ignition switch.
5. Reverse procedure to install, noting the following:

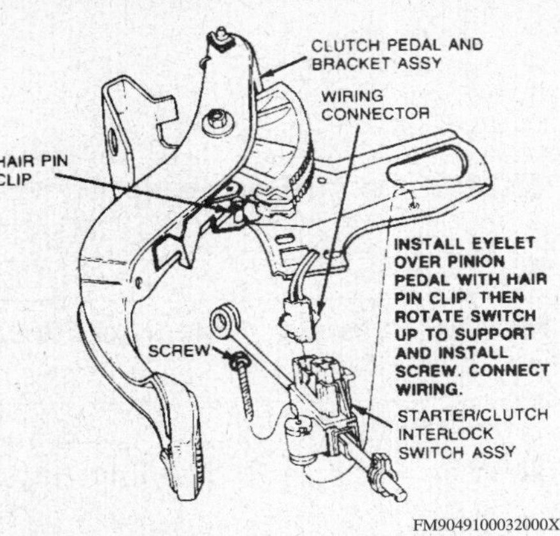

Fig. 3 Starter/clutch interlock switch replacement

    a. Ensure ignition lock is in Run position when installing ignition switch.
    b. **Torque** ignition switch mounting screws to 50–69 inch lbs.
    c. Inspect ignition switch for proper function, including Start and Accessory positions.

CLUTCH START SWITCH

REPLACE

REMOVAL

1. Remove panel above clutch pedal and disconnect starter/clutch interlock switch wiring.
2. Remove mounting screw, hairpin clip and starter/clutch interlock switch.
3. Depress barb at end of rod and pull rod from clutch pedal.

INSTALLATION

1. Install switch with self-adjusting clip about one inch from end of rod. **During installation of switch, clutch pedal must be fully up, otherwise switch may become misadjusted.**
2. Insert eyelet end of rod over clutch pedal pin and install hairpin clip, **Fig. 3.**
3. Align switch mounting hole with mounting bracket hole, install and tighten mounting screw.
4. Adjust starter/clutch interlock switch by pressing clutch pedal to floor.
5. Connect wiring connector and install panel above clutch pedal.

NEUTRAL SAFETY SWITCH

REPLACE

Neutral safety switch functions are incorporated into the transaxle range sensor. The following procedure covers range sensor replacement.

1. Place manual control lever in Neutral position.
2. Remove engine air cleaner and air cleaner outlet tube.
3. Disconnect transmission range sensor electrical connector.
4. Remove manual control lever from transaxle.

5. Remove mounting bolts and transmission range sensor.
6. Reverse procedure to install, noting the following:
   a. Ensure manual control lever is in Neutral position.
   b. Install transmission range sensor and mounting bolts loosely.
   c. Align position sensor using manual lever position sensor alignment tool No. T92P-70010-AH, or equivalent.
   d. **Torque** sensor mounting bolts to 84–108 inch lbs.
   e. **Torque** manual lever mounting bolts to 8–11 ft. lbs.

HEADLAMP SWITCH

REPLACE

1. Pry headlamp switch housing from instrument panel.
2. Depress release button on headlamp switch and pull away from instrument panel.
3. Disconnect headlamp switch electrical connectors and remove switch.
4. Reverse procedure to install.

STOP LIGHT SWITCH

REPLACE

1. Lift stop lamp switch harness wiring connector locking tab and remove connector.
2. Remove hairpin retainer and white nylon washer, and slide switch and pushrod assembly away from brake pedal. Remove switch by sliding up and/or down. **Since switch side plate nearest switch is slotted, it is not necessary to remove master cylinder pushrod, black bushing or one white bushing nearest brake pedal from brake pedal pin, Fig. 4.**
3. Position switch so U-shaped side is nearest brake pedal and directly over brake pedal pin. **The black bushing must be in position in pushrod eyelet with washer face on side away from pedal arm.**
4. Slide switch up and down as necessary to trap black plastic bushing and pushrod between two switch side plates, and push switch and pushrod assembly towards brake pedal arm.
5. Install white nylon washer on pedal pin and hairpin retainer. **Do not substitute other types of pin retainers. Replace only with production type hairpin retainer.**
6. Connect wire harness connector to switch and inspect brake lamps for proper operation. Brake lamps should illuminate with less than six pounds of force applied at brake pedal pad.

MULTI-FUNCTION SWITCH

REPLACE

1. **On models equipped with tilt steering column,** move column to lowest position, and remove tilt lever and key release lever.

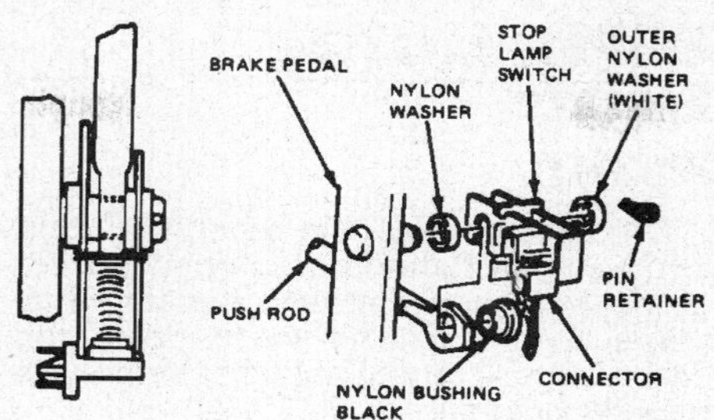

Fig. 4 Stop lamp switch installation

2. **On all models,** remove ignition lock as outlined under "Ignition Lock, Replace."
3. Remove upper and lower steering column shrouds.
4. Remove multi-function switch mounting screws and disengage switch from casting.
5. Disconnect electrical connectors, then remove switch.
6. Reverse procedure to install. **Torque** multi-function switch mounting screws to 18–27 inch lbs. and tilt lever mounting screw to 6–8 inch lbs.

STEERING WHEEL

REPLACE

1. Center front wheels to straight-ahead position.
2. Disconnect speed control wire harness from steering wheel.
3. Remove driver's air bag module as outlined under "Air Bag Systems."
4. Remove and discard steering wheel mounting bolt.
5. Using steering wheel puller tool No. T67L-3600-A, or equivalent, remove steering wheel. Route contact assembly wire harness through steering wheel as wheel is lifted off shaft.
6. Reverse procedure to install, noting the following:
   a. Ensure front wheels are in straight-ahead position.
   b. Route contact assembly wire harness through steering column opening at three o'clock position.
   c. Align steering shaft alignment marks.
   d. **Torque** new steering wheel mounting bolt to 26–34 ft. lbs.

INSTRUMENT CLUSTER

REPLACE

ANALOG

Column Shift

1. Remove ignition switch lock cylinder as outlined under "Ignition Lock, Replace."
2. Remove upper and lower steering column shrouds.
3. Remove instrument panel steering column cover from instrument panel.
4. Remove integrated control panel from instrument panel.
5. Tilt steering wheel to its lowest possible position.
6. Remove finish panel from instrument panel.
7. Detach PRNDL cable loop from column shift selector tube.
8. Remove adjustment nut from PRNDL cable, then cable from bracket.
9. Remove mounting screws and pull cluster toward steering wheel.
10. Reach behind instrument cluster and disconnect three electrical connectors.
11. Remove cluster assembly from instrument panel.
12. Reverse procedure to install.

Floor Shift

1. Remove ignition switch lock cylinder as outlined under "Ignition Lock, Replace."
2. Remove upper and lower steering column shrouds.
3. Remove mounting screws and finish panel from instrument panel.
4. Tilt steering wheel to its lowest possible position.
5. Remove instrument cluster mounting screws and pull top of cluster toward steering wheel.
6. Reach behind instrument cluster and disconnect three electrical connectors.
7. Remove cluster.
8. Reverse procedure to install.

ELECTRONIC

1. Remove lower trim panels.
2. Remove steering column cover and PRNDL cable to cluster mounting screws.
3. Pull cluster trim panel rearward, disconnect switch module and remove trim panel.
4. Remove mounting screws and pull cluster bottom rearward.
5. Reach behind and underneath cluster, and disconnect electrical connectors.
6. Pull cluster bottom rearward to remove.
7. Reverse procedure to install.

RADIO

REPLACE

1998-99

1. Install radio removal tool No. T87P-19061-A, or equivalent, to radio face plate and push tool inward about 1–1½ inches to release radio clips. **Do not push tool with excessive force or radio damage may result.**
2. Apply light even force on tool and pull radio from instrument panel.
3. **On models equipped with automatic temperature control,** disconnect sensor hose and elbow.
4. **On all models,** disconnect radio electrical connectors and antenna lead.
5. Reverse procedure to install.

2000-02

Each audio control is part of the Integrated Control Panel (ICP) and cannot be repaired separately. On the sedan model, the CD changer is located in the LH side of the

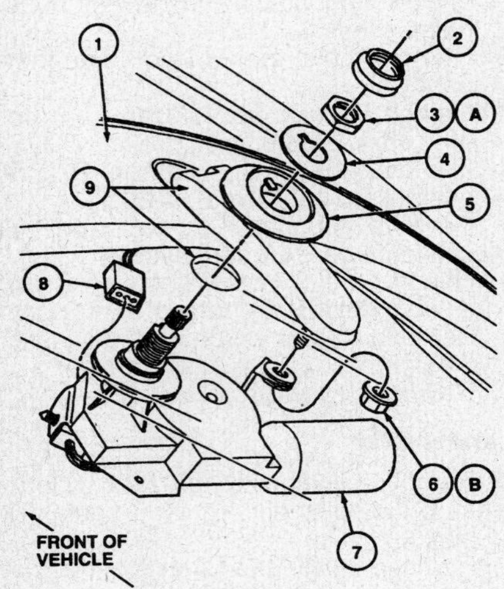

Item	Description
1	Liftgate
2	Windshield Wiper Output Arm Cover
3	Nut
4	Washer
5	Bezel
6	Nut and Washer
7	Windshield Wiper Motor
8	Rear Window Wiper/Washer Wire
9	Liftgate Window
A	Tighten to 15-20 N·m (11-15 Lb-Ft)
B	Tighten to 5-7 N·m (44-62 Lb-In)

FM9029600401000X

Fig. 5 Rear wiper motor removal

luggage compartment. On the wagon, it is located in the RH side of the rear quarter panel. On the six-passenger model it is located in the center console.

INTEGRATED CONTROL PANEL (ICP)

Refer to "Radio, Replace" as outlined previously

AUDIO UNIT

Four Door

1. Remove left side luggage compartment trim panel.
2. Disconnect wiring and antenna lead in cable from audio unit.
3. Remove retaining nuts, then the audio unit.
4. Reverse procedure to install.

Wagon

1. Remove left hand spare tire trim panel, then the spare tire.
2. Disconnect wiring connectors and antenna lead in cable.
3. Remove retaining screws and retaining nut, then the audio unit.
4. Reverse procedure to install.

WIPER MOTOR

REPLACE

FRONT

On these models, the wiper mounting arm and pivot shafts are connected together with non-removable plastic ball joints. Except for the wiper motor, the entire wiper transmission assembly is non-serviceable.

1. Remove wiper arm mounting nuts from pivot shafts. **Note normal park positions of wiper arms and blades.**
2. Turn ignition On and wiper switch to LO. When arms and blades to move to a straight up-and-down position, turn ignition Off.
3. Remove wiper arms from pivot shafts.
4. Turn eight plastic cowl vent screen nuts 1/4 turn counterclockwise.
5. Remove clips mounting vent screen to inner panels.
6. Remove screws mounting wiper assembly to cowl and assembly.
7. Reverse procedure to install, noting the following:
   a. Turn ignition switch to On position and wiper control switch to Low or High.
   b. Turn wiper control switch to Off position after wipers have cycled once or twice. This will allow them to park properly and will prevent damage.
   c. **Torque** wiper assembly screws to 84–120 inch lbs.
   d. Install wiper arms and blades in their previously noted park positions.
   e. **Torque** pivot arm nuts to 22–29 ft. lbs.

REAR

1. Open liftgate and remove window wiper motor cover, **Fig. 5.**
2. Disconnect rear window wiper/washer electrical connector.
3. Unscrew and remove windshield wiper output arm cover.
4. Remove outside mounting nut, washer and bezel.
5. Remove wiper motor to liftgate window hinge mounting nut.
6. Remove wiper motor from liftgate.
7. Reverse procedure to install.

WIPER SWITCH

REPLACE

FRONT

The windshield wiper switch is an integral part of the multi-function switch. Refer to "Multi-Function Switch, Replace" for replacement procedures.

REAR

1. Pull rear wiper/washer switch straight out of instrument panel.
2. Disconnect electrical connector and remove switch.
3. Reverse procedure to install.

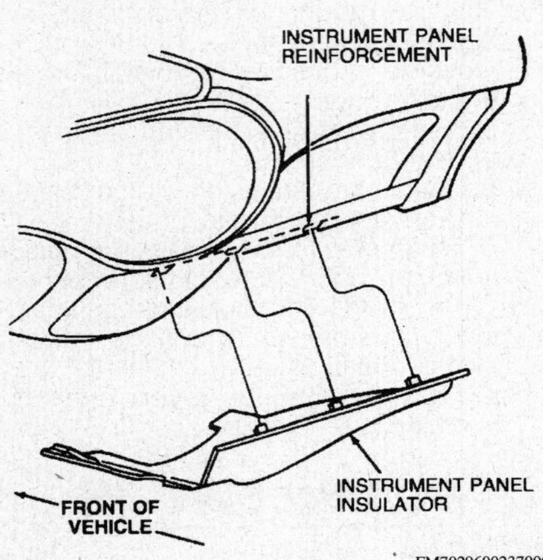

FM7029600237000X

Fig. 6 Instrument panel insulator panel removal

WIPER TRANSMISSION

REPLACE

The wiper mounting arm and pivot shafts are connected by non-removable plastic ball joints. Except for the wiper motor, the wiper transmission is non-serviceable. Refer to "Wiper Motor, Replace" for procedures.

BLOWER MOTOR

REPLACE

1. Pull instrument panel insulator from lower righthand side instrument panel reinforcement, **Fig. 6.**
2. Disconnect blower motor electrical connector.
3. Remove mounting screws and blower motor from A/C evaporator housing.
4. Reverse procedure to install.

CABIN AIR FILTER

REPLACE

1. Remove right side cowel vent screen.
2. Remove water shield.
3. Remove cabin air filter.
4. Reverse procedure to install.

HEATER CORE

REPLACE

1. Drain coolant into a suitable container.
2. Remove instrument panel as outlined in "Dash Panels."
3. Disconnect heater hoses from heater core and plug heater core tubes.
4. Remove four A/C electronic door actuator motor to A/C evaporator housing mounting screws, **Fig. 7.**
5. Disengage spring from heater core cover and remove spring from lever, **Fig. 8.**
6. Gently depress locking ramp and remove lever from secondary A/C air temperature control door end. **Do not bend any part of lever. It is brittle and will break.**
7. Rotate primary A/C air temperature

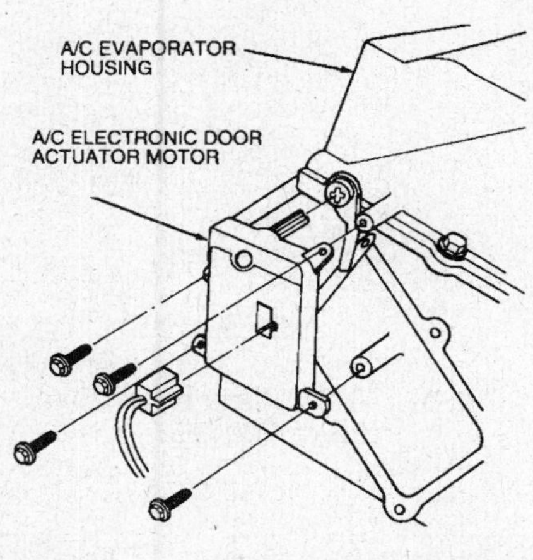

Fig. 7 A/C electronic door actuator motor removal

door shaft downward, swing metal link and remove from pin.

8. Remove three heater core cover mounting screws.
9. Remove heater core cover and heater core cover seal from A/C evaporator housing.
10. Remove heater core and seal from A/C evaporator housing by pushing on heater core tubes.
11. Reverse procedure to install.

EVAPORATOR CORE

REPLACE

1998–99

Whenever an evaporator core is replaced, the suction accumulator/dryer must also be replaced.

1. Drain coolant into a suitable container.
2. Recover A/C system as outlined under "Air Conditioning."
3. Disconnect heater hoses from heater core and plug heater core tubes.
4. Disconnect vacuum supply hose from in-line vacuum check valve in engine compartment.
5. Disconnect liquid line and accumulator from evaporator core at dash panel. Cap refrigerant lines and evaporator core to prevent entrance of dirt and excess moisture.
6. Remove instrument panel as outlined in "Dash Panels."
7. Remove mounting screw and evaporator case to instrument panel shake brace.
8. Remove screws holding floor register and floor ducts to bottom of evaporator case.
9. Remove evaporator housing to dash panel mounting nuts, located in engine compartment.
10. Remove support bracket to cowl top panel mounting screws.
11. Remove evaporator housing to Powertrain Control Module (PCM) mounting bracket mounting nut.
12. Carefully pull evaporator housing assembly away from dash panel and remove. **Whenever evaporator case is removed it will be necessary to replace suction accumulator/dryer.**
13. Remove foam seals from evaporator core tubes.
14. Remove A/C electronic door actuator motor to evaporator housing mounting screws, **Fig. 7.**
15. Disengage spring from heater core cover and remove spring from lever, **Fig. 8.**
16. Gently depress locking ramp and remove lever from secondary A/C air temperature control door end. **Do not bend any part of lever. It is brittle and will break.**
17. Rotate primary A/C air temperature control door shaft downward, swing metal link and remove from pin.
18. Remove screws from around evaporator housing flange joint.
19. Using suitable side cutters, or equivalent, cut all snap loops around evaporator housing flange joint.
20. Separate upper evaporator housing from lower evaporator housing, **Fig. 9.**
21. Remove evaporator from lower evaporator housing.
22. Reverse procedure to install.

2000–02

The evaporator core is serviced as a core and housing assembly. The evaporator core, internal doors, seals and door linkage are included with the housing. Transfer the blower motor and wheel assembly, heater core and cover, dash panel seals and vacuum actuators to the new housing.

1. Recover refrigerant as outlined under "Air Conditioning."
2. Drain coolant into suitable container.
3. Remove instrument panel as outlined under"Dash Panel Service"
4. Remove right side cowl vent screen, then the water shield.
5. Disconnect vacuum supply hose, **Fig. 10.**
6. Using suitable pinching pliers, clamp heater hoses, then disconnect hoses and cap all fittings.
7. Disconnect evaporator outlet spring lock coupling and cap evaporator outlet tube and suction accumulator tube.
8. Remove hold down bolts from A/C pipe clamps, **Fig. 11.**
9. Disconnect evaporator inlet spring lock coupling and cap evaporator inlet tube and condenser to evaporator line tube.
10. Remove three nuts at dash panel, **Fig. 12.**
11. Remove heater outlet floor duct.
12. Remove evaporator housing support bracket mounting nuts, **Fig. 13.**
13. Remove heater/evaporator core housing assembly.
14. Reverse procedure to install.

TECHNICAL SERVICE BULLETINS

NO CRANK

1998

On these models, the starter may not crank.

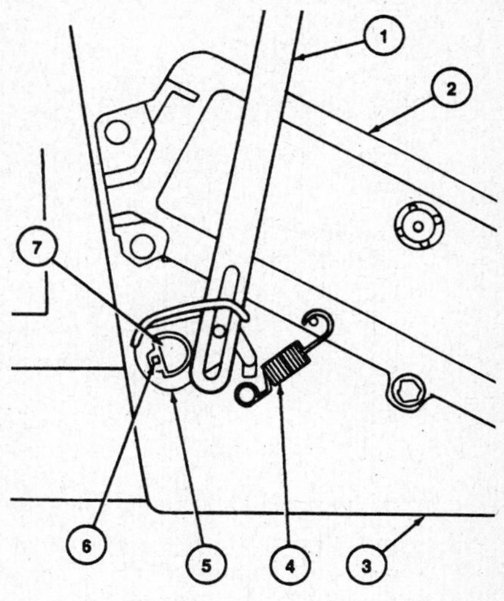

Item	Description
1	Metal Link
2	Heater Core Cover
3	A/C Evaporator Housing
4	Spring
5	Lever
6	Locking Ramp (Part of Secondary A/C Air Temperature Control Door Shaft)
7	Secondary A/C Air Temperature Control Door Shaft

FM7029600239000X

Fig. 8 Spring & metal link removal

This condition may be caused by an excessive current drain discharging the battery. To correct this condition, proceed as follows:

1. Isolate excessive drain by removing fuses.
2. If drain cannot be isolate, measure current drain. Current drain for VIN U, 1 and 2 engines should be 16 mAmps, and for VIN N and S engines, 20.5 mAmps.
3. If current drain is with specifications, inspect Anti-Lock Brake System (ABS) module connector C1507 for water entry or corrosion signs and repair as necessary.

FRONT WIPERS OPERATE WHILE SWITCH IS IN OFF POSITION

1999

The front windshield wipers may operate while the multifunction switch is in the Off position on some vehicles. This may be caused by a resistance drift in the multifunction switch or a partially plugged in connector. Perform diagnostics on wiper system. If uncommanded wiper operation is still present and no other symptoms apply to vehicle being serviced, replace multifunction switch with revised part. Do not attempt to repair vehicle by replacing GEM or wiper control module.

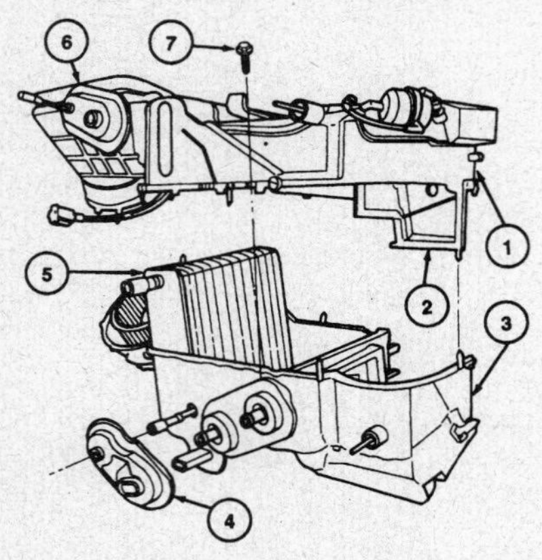

Item	Description
1	A/C Evaporator Housing Upper Half
2	Heater Air Damper Door
3	A/C Evaporator Housing Lower Half
4	Foam Seal (Evaporator Core Inlet)
5	A/C Evaporator Core
6	Foam Seal (Evaporator Core Outlet)
7	Screw (17 Req'd)

Fig. 9 Evaporator removal. 1998–99

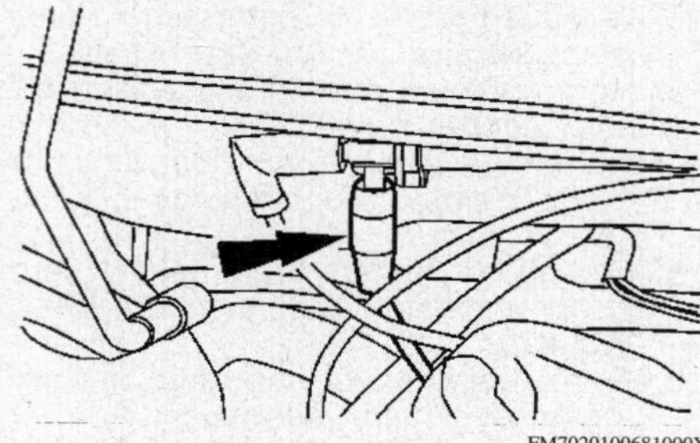

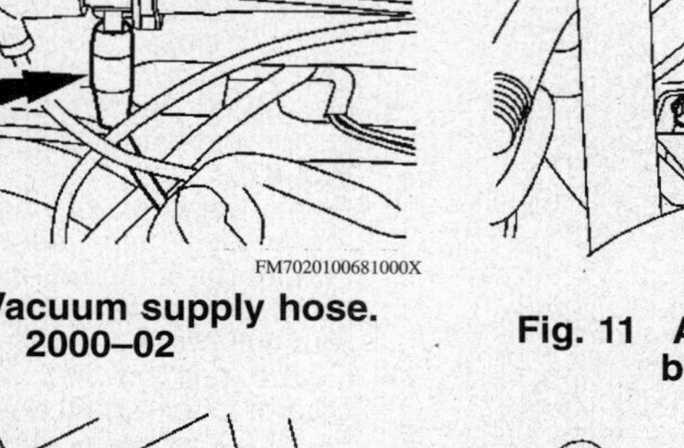

Fig. 10 Vacuum supply hose. 2000–02

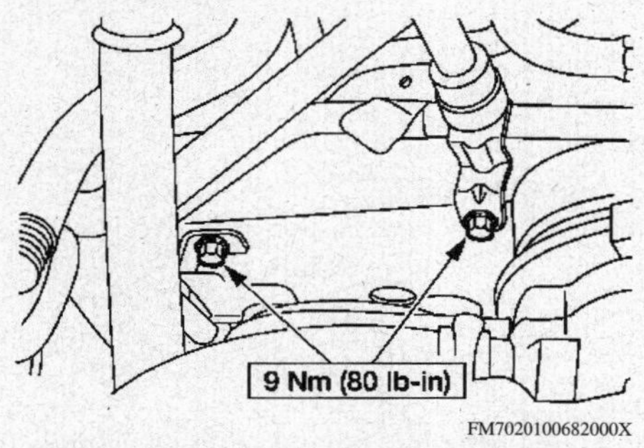

Fig. 11 A/C clamp hold down bolts. 2000–02

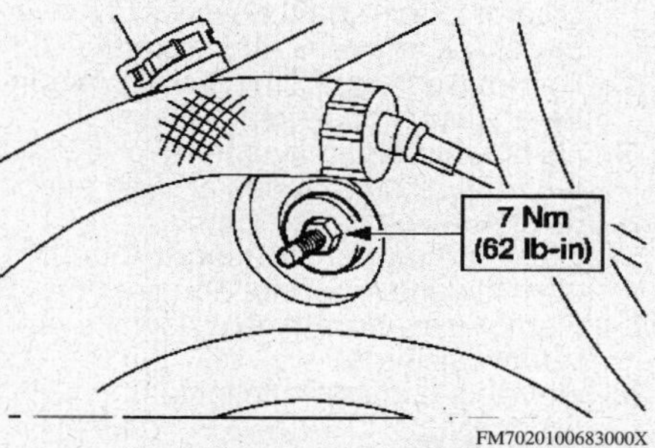

Fig. 12 Evaporator housing mounting nuts. 2000–02

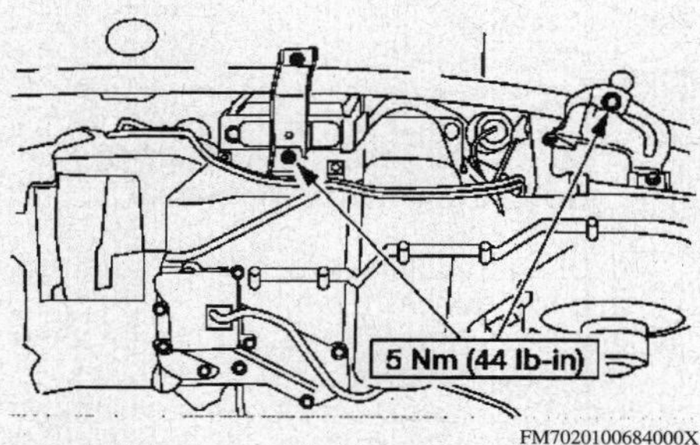

Fig. 13 Evaporator housing mounting support nuts. 2000–02

3.0L Engine

NOTE: On Air Bag Equipped Models, Refer To "Air Bag System Precautions" Located In The Front Of This Manual For System Disarming & Arming Procedures.

NOTE: Refer To "Computer Relearn Procedures" Located In The Front Of This Manual When Battery Power To The Computer Has Been Interrupted.

NOTE: Prior To Performing Any Service Operations Listed In This Section, Consult The "Technical Service Bulletins" Section For Related Information.

INDEX

PRECAUTIONS

AIR BAG SYSTEMS

Refer to "Air Bag System Precautions" in the front of this manual for system disarming and arming procedures.

FLEXIBLE FUEL MODELS

Flexible Fuel (FF) vehicles use unique methanol-compatible components. Certain gasoline-only components may appear identical to these FF vehicle components. Under no circumstances should these components be interchanged.

FUEL SYSTEM PRESSURE RELIEF

When releasing fuel pressure on flexible fuel vehicles, use methanol resistant gloves and eye protection. Avoid prolonged skin contact with liquid or breathing of vapors.

If methanol fuel should be spilled on paint, flush immediately with cold water. **Do not wipe, or paint damage may occur.**

Fuel supply lines will remain pressurized for long periods of time after engine shutdown. This pressure must be relieved before any service is attempted. A valve is provided on the fuel rail assembly for this purpose.

1. Remove air cleaner assembly.
2. Connect pressure gauge tool No. T80L-9974-A or T80L-9974-B, or equivalent, onto fuel rail assembly fuel valve.
3. Open manual valve on pressure gauge tool.
4. To pressurize fuel system, proceed as follows:
   a. Install pressure gauge tool onto fuel rail pressure fitting.
   b. Turn ignition On for three seconds, 5–10 times until pressure gauge indicates 13 psi.

BATTERY GROUND CABLE

Prior to service, disconnect battery ground cable and isolate as required.

COMPRESSION PRESSURE

When inspecting cylinder compression, the lowest cylinder must be within 75 percent of the highest cylinder. Perform compression inspection with engine at normal operating temperature, spark plugs removed and throttle wide open.

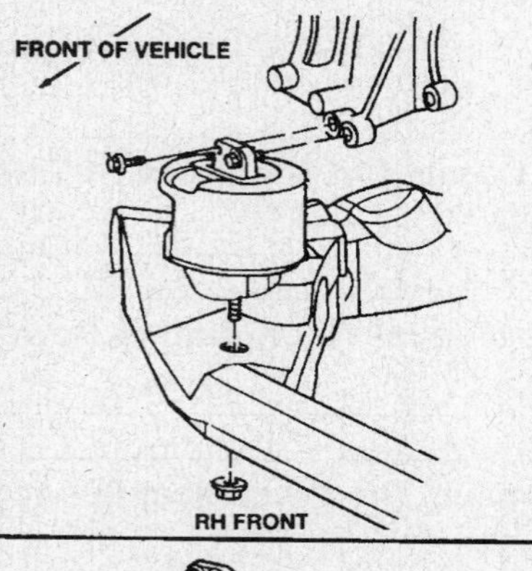

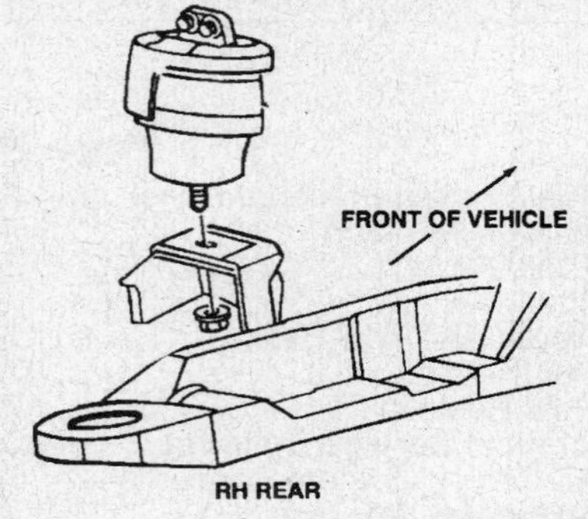

Fig. 1 Engine mounts. VIN U, 1 & 2 engines

ENGINE MOUNT

REPLACE

LEFTHAND & RIGHTHAND FRONT ENGINE SUPPORT INSULATORS

1. Raise and support vehicle.
2. Place jack and wood block in suitable place under engine block.
3. Remove lefthand and righthand front engine support insulator to subframe mounting nuts, **Figs. 1 and 2.**
4. Raise jack assembly enough to remove load from lefthand and righthand engine support insulators.
5. Remove bolts from lefthand and righthand engine support insulators, then the insulators from subframe.
6. Reverse procedure to install.

ENGINE & TRANSAXLE SUPPORT INSULATOR

1. Raise and support vehicle. Remove lefthand front tire and wheel assembly.
2. Support transaxle assembly with suitable transmission jack.
3. Remove engine and transaxle support insulator to rear engine and transaxle bracket mounting nut, **Fig. 3.**
4. Remove two engine and transaxle support insulator to subframe through bolts.
5. Raise transaxle assembly enough to remove load from engine and transaxle support insulator and remove support insulator from subframe.
6. Reverse procedure to install.

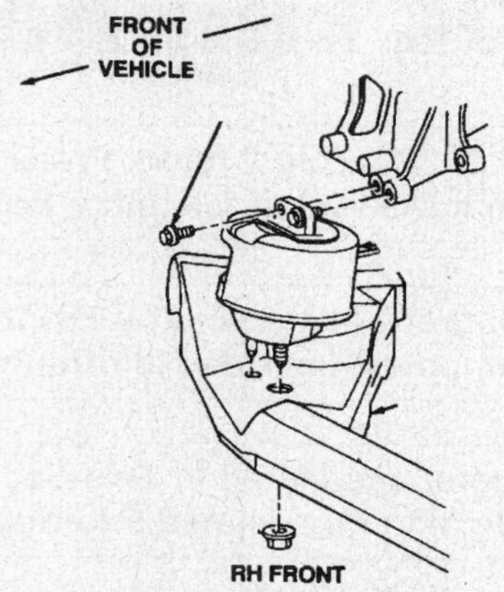

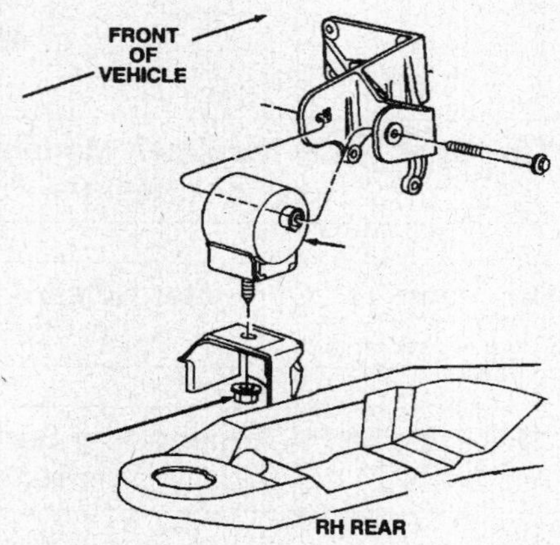

Fig. 2 Engine mounts. VIN S engine

ENGINE

REPLACE

1998-99

1. Disconnect steering coupling at pinch bolt joint inside passenger compartment.
2. **On VIN S engine,** remove cowl extension and wiper arm.
3. **On all models,** disconnect engine control sensor wiring from intake air temperature sensor.
4. Disconnect crankcase ventilation tube and aspirator hose from air cleaner outlet tube.
5. Remove air cleaner outlet tube.
6. Drain engine coolant and recover A/C system.
7. Relieve fuel system pressure as outlined under "Precautions."
8. Disconnect fuel tubes from fuel injection supply manifold.
9. Disconnect chassis vacuum supply hose and evaporative emission hose from upper intake manifold, and position hoses out of way.
10. Remove electrical ground straps from dash panel.
11. Disconnect engine control sensor wiring from Powertrain Control Module (PCM) and position wiring out of way.
12. Remove connectors for engine control sensor wiring from mounting bracket on power brake booster and disconnect sensor wiring at two connectors.
13. Disconnect engine control sensor wiring from MAF sensor and evaporative emission canister purge valve.
14. Remove shield, and disconnect accelerator cable and speed control actuator cable from throttle body. Position cable aside.
15. Remove accelerator bracket from throttle body.
16. Remove transmission range sensor and manual control lever to transaxle manual lever shaft mounting nut.
17. Remove connectors for engine control sensor from mounting bracket on top of transaxle and disconnect wiring at two connectors.
18. Disconnect wiring connectors from secondary air injection pump relay located on mounting bracket on top of transaxle.
19. Disconnect fluid cooler inlet tube from transaxle.
20. Disconnect heater hoses from water pump and water hose connection.
21. Disconnect upper radiator hose and de-gas tube from water hose connection.
22. Remove power steering return hose from power steering oil reservoir and drain.
23. Disconnect alternator wiring harness from alternator and remove wiring harness mounting clip from alternator mounting bracket.
24. Disconnect A/C compressor lines from A/C compressor.
25. Slightly raise and support vehicle. Remove tire and wheel assemblies.
26. Remove righthand and lefthand stabilizer bar links from stabilizer bar.
27. Separate righthand and lefthand front suspension lower control arm ball joints from wheel knuckles.
28. Separate lefthand and righthand tie rod ends from front wheel knuckle.
29. Remove lefthand and righthand halfshafts from front wheel knuckles as outlined in "Front Drive Axles."
30. Raise and support vehicle.
31. Remove splash shield from radiator support and drain engine oil into a suitable container.
32. **On VIN S engine,** remove heated oxygen sensors from converter Y-pipe.
33. **On all models,** remove dual converter Y-pipe.
34. Disconnect power steering pressure hose from power steering/transaxle fluid cooler connection and position hose out of way.
35. Disconnect lower radiator hose from radiator and radiator overflow hose.
36. Disconnect starter motor electrical connectors and remove starter motor.
37. Disconnect lower fluid cooler tube from transaxle.
38. Support front subframe, engine and transaxle assembly using Rotunda powertrain lift tool No. 014-00765 and universal powertrain removal bracket tool No. 014-00766, or equivalents.
39. Remove four front subframe mounting

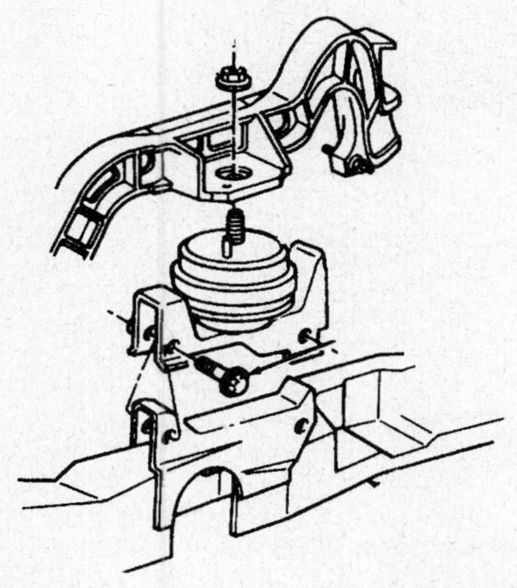

Fig. 3 Engine & transaxle mount

bolts, and lower engine, transaxle and front subframe.
40. Disconnect power steering hose from power steering pump.
41. Install engine lifting brackets tool No. T70P-6000, or equivalent.
42. Connect Rotunda separator bar tool No. 014-00793, or equivalent, to lifting brackets.
43. Remove engine and transaxle mounts as outlined under "Engine Mount, Replace."
44. Lift engine and transaxle from front subframe.
45. **On VIN S engine,** remove flywheel to torque converter mounting nuts.
46. **On all models,** lower engine and transaxle and support transaxle on a level surface.
47. Remove transaxle to cylinder block bolts and separate engine from transaxle.
48. Reverse procedure to install.

2000–02

1. Drain cooling system into suitable container.
2. Remove cowl vent screen and cowl vent extension.
3. Remove engine air cleaner and air cleaner outlet tube.
4. Recover refrigerant from A/C system as outlined under "Air Conditioning."
5. Relieve fuel system pressure as outlined under "Precautions."
6. Position steering column input shaft coupling aside.
7. Remove snow shield, **Fig. 4.**
8. Disconnect accelerator cable, speed control actuator cable and throttle return spring from throttle body, then position accelerator cable bracket aside.
9. Disconnect chassis vacuum hose, **Fig. 5.**
10. Disconnect manual control lever cable from lever, then disconnect cable from bracket and set aside.
11. Disconnect 42 pin and transmission range sensor electrical connectors.
12. Disconnect upper radiator hoses and heater hoses from thermostat housing.

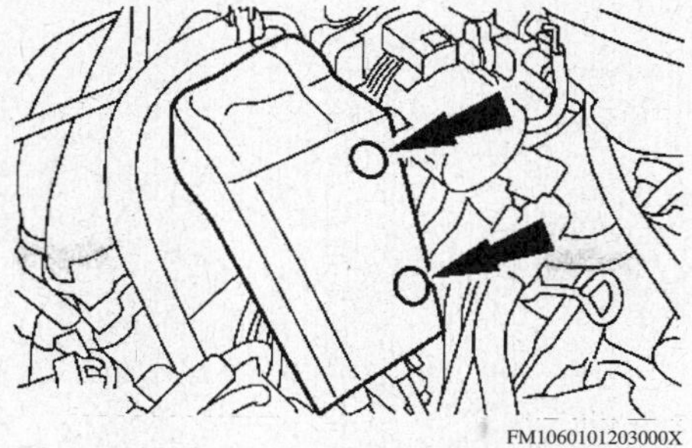

Fig. 4 Snow shield. 2000–02

13. Remove battery.
14. Remove nut, **Fig. 6,** then the ground strap electrical connector.
15. Disconnect left side exhaust manifold flange.
16. Disconnect power steering return hose.
17. Disconnect alternator electrical connectors and position wire harness aside.
18. Disconnect A/C suction tube from accumulator drier.
19. Disconnect fuel supply hose.
20. Remove engine roll restrictor brace, then the restrictor.
21. Disconnect degas hose from degas bottle.
22. Disconnect heater water hose.
23. Disconnect electrical ground connectors, **Fig. 7.**
24. Disconnect evaporative emissions canister purge valve electrical connector.
25. Disconnect powertrain control module electrical connector.
26. Raise and support vehicle.
27. Remove valance panel.
28. Disconnect catalyst monitor sensor electrical connector.
29. Remove catalytic converters and Y-pipe assemblies.
30. Remove front wheels.
31. Disconnect A/C discharge tube.
32. Disconnect lower radiator hose from water pump, then the radiator support bracket.
33. Disconnect lower radiator hose from radiator and degas bottle supply hose.
34. Disconnect transmission oil cooler hose.
35. Disconnect wire harness electrical connector.
36. Disconnect auxiliary oil cooler assembly.
37. Drain engine oil into suitable container.
38. Remove starter motor, engine rear plate, then the torque converter nuts.
39. Disconnect stabilizer links from stabilizer bar, then separate lower control arms from steering knuckles.
40. Separate tie rod ends from steering knuckles.
41. Remove both halfshafts from steering knuckles.
42. Position engine removal cradle tool No. 014–00765, or equivalent, beneath engine assembly.
43. Remove four subframe to body bolts, **Fig. 8.**
44. Lower engine, transmission and subframe assembly out of vehicle.

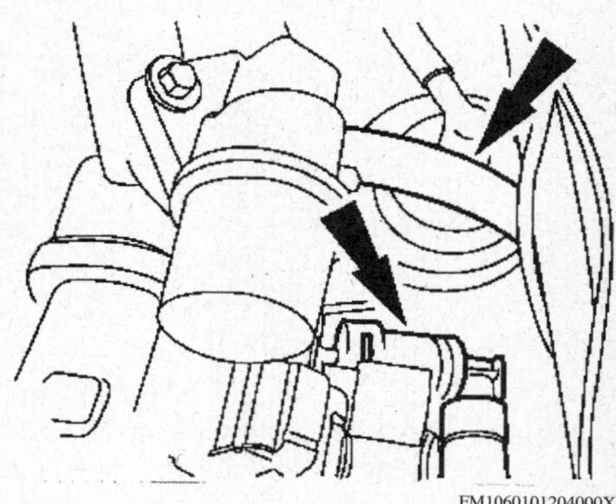

Fig. 5 Chassis vacuum hose. 2000–02

45. Reverse procedure to install.

INTAKE MANIFOLD

REPLACE

UPPER INTAKE MANIFOLD

VIN U, 1 & 2 ENGINES

1998–99

1. Remove air cleaner outlet tube.
2. Remove accelerator cable shield from accelerator cable bracket.
3. Remove accelerator retracting spring and disconnect accelerator cable and speed control actuator cable from throttle lever.
4. Remove accelerator bracket mounting bolts from side of throttle body and position bracket out of way.
5. Remove fuel pressure regulator vacuum hose.
6. Completely loosen EGR valve to exhaust manifold tube nut at EGR valve.
7. Disconnect EGR backpressure transducer hoses from EGR valve to exhaust manifold tube.
8. Remove crankcase ventilation hose, aspirator vacuum supply hose and evaporative emission return tube from fittings underneath upper intake manifold.
9. Disconnect engine control sensor wiring connections to idle air control valve, throttle position sensor, EGR backpressure transducer and EGR vacuum regulator solenoid.
10. Drain engine coolant and disconnect de-gas tube from radiator coolant recovery reservoir and lower intake manifold fitting.
11. Remove upper alternator brace mounting nuts and bolts, then brace.
12. Remove engine control sensor wiring bracket from throttle body mounting stud bolt and position wiring out of way.
13. Remove intake manifold support from throttle body and righthand cylinder head.
14. Loosen and remove upper intake manifold mounting bolts and stud bolts. **Note their locations for proper installation.**
15. Lift and remove upper intake manifold from lower intake manifold.

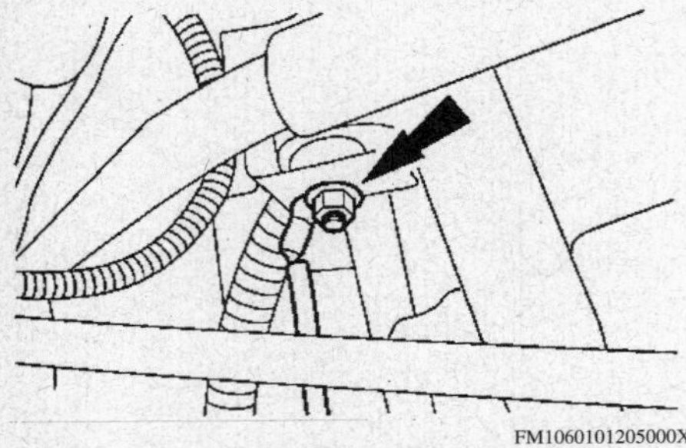

Fig. 6 Ground strap electrical connector. 2000–02

16. Reverse procedure to install, noting the following:
    a. Lightly oil all bolt and stud bolt threads prior to installation.
    b. Clean and inspect all sealing surfaces of intake manifold and throttle body.

2000–02

1. Remove air cleaner assembly and air cleaner outlet tube.
2. Remove snow shield, then the accelerator cable, speed control actuator cable and throttle return spring from throttle body.
3. Remove accelerator cable bracket and set aside.
4. Disconnect vacuum hoses and evaporative emissions return tube.
5. Disconnect idle air control valve and throttle position sensor.
6. Disconnect engine wiring harness from intake manifold support bracket.
7. Remove upper intake manifold support bracket.
8. Disconnect positive crankcase ventilation (PCV) tube from upper intake manifold.
9. Disconnect EGR tube from EGR valve.
10. Disconnect vacuum tube from EGR valve.
11. Disconnect vacuum tube from upper intake manifold and electronic vacuum regulator (ER) and disconnect electrical connector from EVR.
12. Disconnect wiring harness retaining clip and spark plug wire holder.
13. Remove bolts, then the upper intake manifold.
14. Reverse procedure to install, noting the following:
    a. Clean all sealing surfaces.
    b. Inspect upper intake manifold gaskets and replace as necessary.
    c. Install bolts in sequence, **Fig. 9.**
    d. **Torque** bolts in two stages, first finger tighten, then to 89 inch lbs.

VIN S ENGINE

1998–99

1. Remove air cleaner outlet tube.
2. Remove accelerator cable shield from accelerator cable bracket.
3. Remove accelerator retracting spring and disconnect accelerator cable and speed control actuator cable from throttle lever.
4. Remove accelerator spring, cable bracket and throttle body.

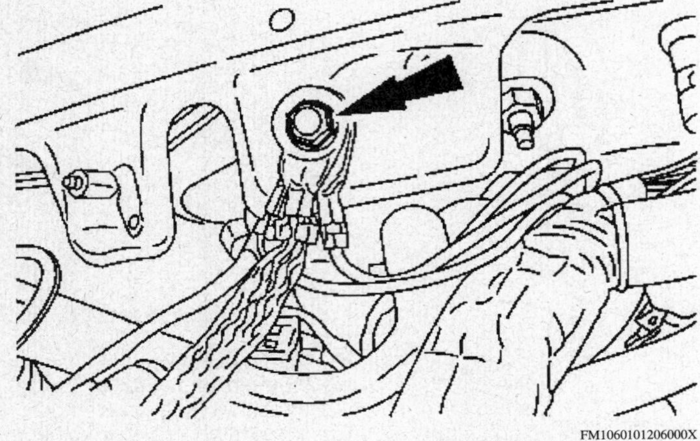

Fig. 7 Ground electrical connectors. 2000–02

5. Disconnect engine control sensor wiring from throttle position sensor and idle air control valve.
6. Remove evaporative emission hose from upper intake manifold.
7. Remove crankcase vent connector and hose from upper intake manifold to PCV valve.
8. Disconnect main emission vacuum control connector from upper intake manifold and secondary air injection diverter valve.
9. Remove EGR valve, secondary air diverter valve bracket and position bracket out of way.
10. Remove upper intake manifold mounting bolts in sequence, **Fig. 10.**
11. Remove manifold gaskets and discard.
12. Reverse procedure to install, noting the following:
    a. Always use new manifold gaskets.
    b. **Torque** upper intake manifold bolts to 96–108 inch lbs. in sequence. **Fig. 11.**

2000–01

1. Remove air cleaner outlet tube.
2. Remove accelerator cable splash shield.
3. Disconnect throttle cable, and cruise control cable.
4. Disconnect throttle position sensor and idle air control valve electrical connectors, then the harness from throttle body.
5. Disconnect exhaust gas recirculation (EGR) vacuum regulator and vacuum supply hoses.
6. Disconnect PCV and EVAP vacuum hoses.
7. Remove EGR valve and EGR valve vacuum regulator valve.
8. Remove eight bolts, then the upper intake manifold.
9. Reverse procedure to install, noting the following:
    a. Install new gaskets when installing.
    b. Position upper intake manifold and **torque** bolts in sequence, **Fig. 12** to 89 inch lbs.

LOWER INTAKE MANIFOLD

VIN U, 1 & 2 ENGINES

1998–99

1. Remove upper intake manifold as outlined under "Upper Intake Manifold."
2. Relieve fuel system pressure as outlined under "Precautions."
3. Disconnect fuel lines as follows:
    a. Remove clip from spring lock coupling.
    b. Position fuel line disconnect tool No. D87L-9280-A or No. D87L-9280-B, or equivalent, onto coupling, **Fig. 13.**
    c. Push disconnect tool into cage opening to release female fitting from garter spring.
    d. Pull male and female fittings apart, and remove disconnect tool from coupling.
    e. Inspect coupling for missing or damaged O-rings. If either O-ring is damaged, both O-rings have to be replaced.
4. Remove vacuum lines. **Mark vacuum lines for installation.**
5. Disconnect engine control sensor wiring from camshaft position sensor, ignition coil and water temperature sending unit.
6. Disconnect engine control sensor wiring retainers from valve cover stud bolts.
7. Carefully disconnect all fuel injector connectors and position sensor wiring out of way.
8. Remove ignition wires from spark plugs, then the harness retainers from valve cover stud bolts.
9. Remove camshaft position sensor.
10. Remove ignition coil from rear of left-hand cylinder head.
11. Remove valve covers as outlined under "Valve Cover, Replace."
12. Loosen cylinder No. 3 intake valve rocker arm seat mounting bolt and rotate rocker arm off of push rod and away from top of valve stem, and remove push rod.
13. Remove lower intake manifold Torx bolts, and using a pry bar, break seal

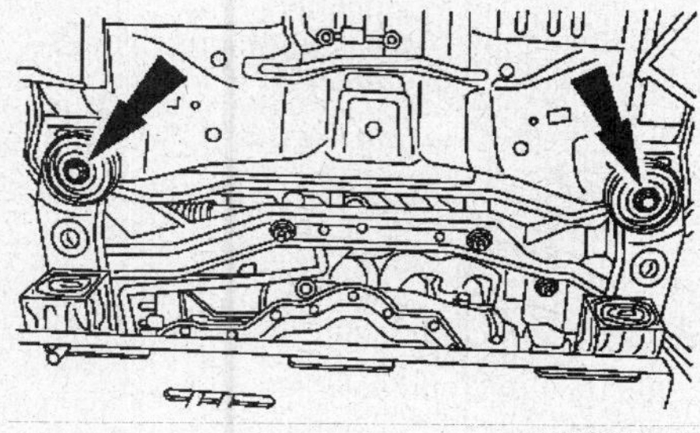

Fig. 8 Subframe to body bolts. 2000–02

between lower intake manifold and cylinder block.

14. Remove lower intake manifold, fuel injection supply manifold and fuel injectors as an assembly.
15. Reverse procedure to install, noting the following:
    a. Lightly oil bolts and studs prior to installation.
    b. Clean all mating surfaces. When scraping old gasket material lay a clean cloth in valve lifter valley to catch gasket material.
    c. Apply a drop of silicone rubber part No. D6AZ-19562-AA, or equivalent, to intersection of cylinder block and cylinder head, **Fig. 14.**
    d. Install front and rear intake manifold seals, **Fig. 14.**
    e. **Torque** bolts to 15–22 ft. lbs., then to 20–24 ft. lbs.
    f. Prior to installing camshaft position sensor coat entire surface of sensor with engine assembly lubricant part No. D9AZ-19579-D, or equivalent.
    g. Apply clean engine oil to No. 3 intake valve, push rod and rocker arm.
    h. Prior to tightening rocker arm, rotate crankshaft to position camshaft lobe straight down and away from valve lifter.

2000–02

1. Disconnect fuel supply line.
2. Remove upper intake manifold as outlined previously.
3. Remove both valve covers.
4. Disconnect engine control sensor wiring harness from fuel injectors.
5. Remove fuel injection supply manifold and fuel injectors as an assembly.
6. Disconnect heater hose and coolant temperature sender.
7. Disconnect engine coolant temperature sensor and degas bottle hose.
8. Disconnect upper radiator hose from thermostat housing.
9. Remove camshaft position sensor.
10. Remove lower intake manifold.
11. Reverse procedure to install, noting the following:
    a. Clean all surfaces. Apply a drop of silicone gasket and sealant at four cylinder block to cylinder head seams, **Fig. 15.**
    b. Position gaskets and end seals.
    c. Install manifold and tighten bolts in

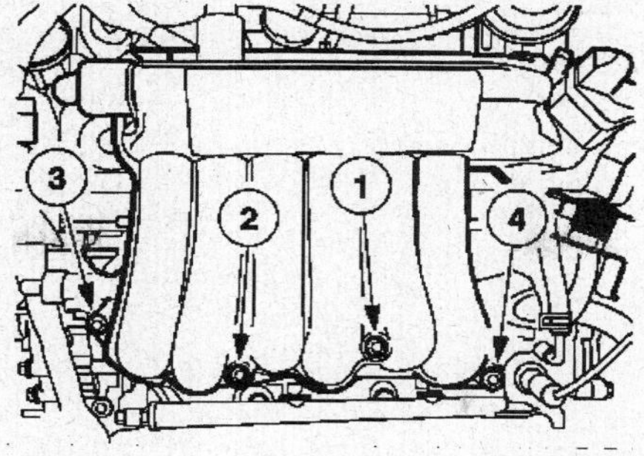

Fig. 9 Upper intake manifold bolt tightening sequence. 2000–02 VIN U engines

sequence, **Fig. 16** in two stages.
    d. First stage: **Torque** bolts to 11 ft. lbs.
    e. Second stage: **Torque** bolts to 24 ft. lbs.

VIN S ENGINE

1998–99

1. Remove upper intake manifold as outlined under "Upper Intake Manifold."
2. Relieve fuel system pressure as outlined under "Precautions."
3. Disconnect fuel lines as follows:
    a. Remove clip from spring lock coupling.
    b. Position fuel line disconnect tool No. D87L-9280-A or No. D87L-9280-B, or equivalent, onto coupling, **Fig. 13.**
    c. Push disconnect tool into cage opening to release female fitting from garter spring.
    d. Pull male and female fittings apart, and remove disconnect tool from coupling.
    e. Inspect coupling for missing or damaged O-rings. If either O-ring is damaged, both O-rings have to be replaced.
4. Remove vacuum lines. **Mark vacuum lines for installation.**
5. Disconnect intake manifold runner actuator control cable from lower intake manifold lever and bracket. **Do not loosen or bend intake manifold runner control actuator cable retainer bracket. Bracket alignment is important and potential actuator damage may occur.**
6. Disconnect ignition wires from lefthand cylinder head (cylinder Nos. 4, 5 and 6) and position wires out of way.
7. Remove fuel injection supply manifold and fuel injectors from lower intake manifold.
8. Remove lower intake manifold mounting bolts in sequence, **Fig. 17.**
9. Remove intake manifold and gaskets from cylinder head, discard gaskets.
10. Reverse procedure to install, noting the following:
    a. Always use new gaskets.
    b. **Torque** lower intake manifold bolts to 96–108 inch lbs. in sequence-,**Fig. 18.**
    c. Inspect intake manifold runner con-

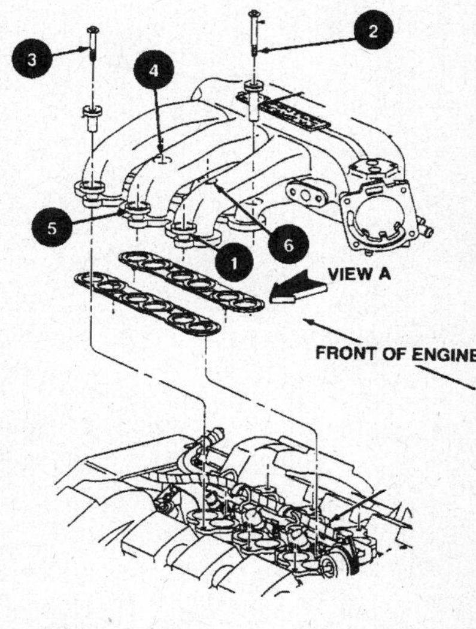

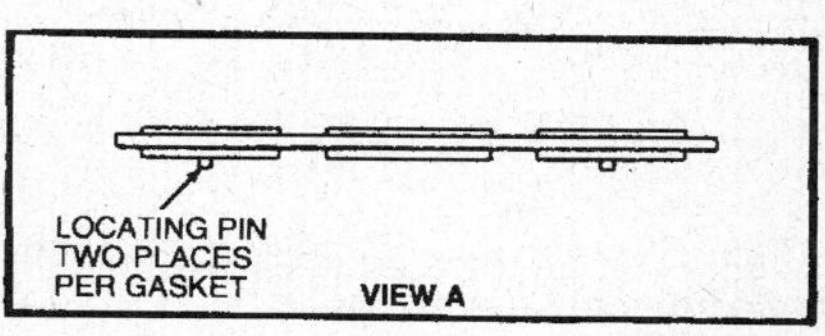

Fig. 10 Upper intake manifold bolt removal sequence. 1998–99 VIN S engine

trol plate operation.

2000–02

1. Relieve fuel system pressure as outlined under "Precautions."
2. Remove upper intake manifold as outlined previously.
3. Disconnect fuel line spring lock coupling.
4. Disconnect fuel injector electrical connectors.
5. Remove bolts in sequence, **Fig. 17,** then remove lower intake manifold.
6. Remove fuel rail and injectors from manifold.
7. Reverse procedure to install, noting the following:
    a. Install new gaskets.
    b. Inspect fuel injector O-ring seals and replace as necessary.
    c. Lubricate new O-ring seals lightly with SAE 5W-20 motor oil meeting Ford specification. Do not use silicone grease or injector clogging may occur.
    d. **Torque** bolts in sequence, **Fig. 18,** to 89 inch lbs.

EXHAUST MANIFOLD

REPLACE

VIN U, 1 & 2 ENGINES

1998–99

Lefthand

1. Relieve fuel system pressure as outlined under "Precautions."

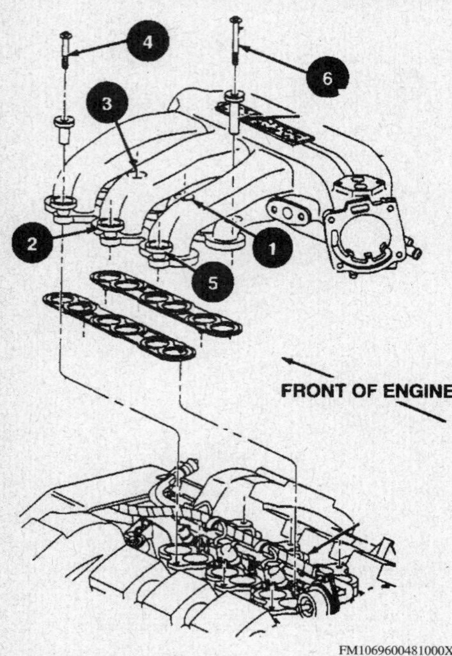

Fig. 11 Upper intake manifold bolt tightening sequence. 1998–99 VIN S engine

2. Remove dipstick tube support bracket and exhaust pipe to manifold mounting nuts.
3. Remove engine control sensor wiring from oil level indicator tube bracket.
4. Remove oil level dipstick and dipstick tube.
5. Remove Y-pipe mounting nuts.
6. Remove exhaust manifold to cylinder head mounting bolts and manifold.
7. Reverse procedure to install. Lightly lubricate nuts and bolts with engine oil, and tighten to specifications.

Righthand

1. Relieve fuel system pressure as outlined under "Precautions."
2. Remove EGR backpressure transducer hoses from EGR valve to exhaust manifold tube.
3. Using suitable back-up wrench on EGR tube lower adapter, remove EGR tube from exhaust manifold.
4. Remove mounting nuts and heat shield.
5. Remove coolant bypass tube.
6. Remove exhaust pipe to manifold mounting nuts.
7. Remove exhaust manifold to cylinder head mounting bolts and manifold.
8. Reverse procedure to install, noting the following:
   a. Lightly lubricate nuts and bolts with engine oil.
   b. Tighten manifold mounting bolts to specifications.
   c. Tighten exhaust pipe to manifold mounting nuts to specifications.
   d. Tighten EGR tube to specifications.

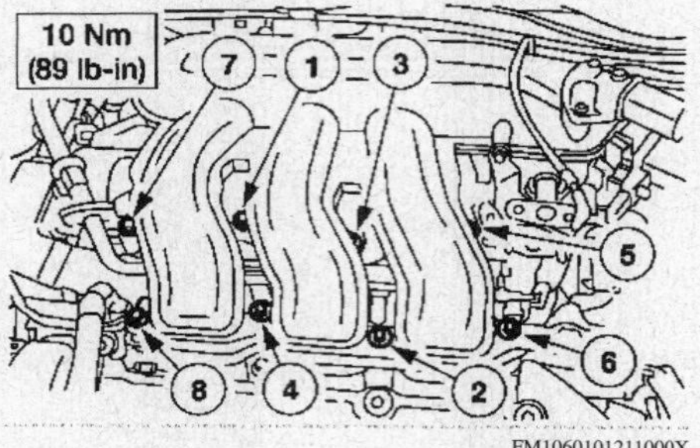

Fig. 12 Upper intake manifold bolt tightening sequence. 2000–02 VIN S engine

2000-02

Lefthand

1. Disconnect heated oxygen sensor electrical connector.
2. Remove oil level indicator tube.
3. Disconnect power steering pressure line from power steering pump
4. Remove nut from power steering line hold down bracket and position hose to one side.
5. Disconnect secondary air injection tube from exhaust manifold.
6. Separate dual converter Y-pipe from exhaust manifold.
7. Remove four exhaust manifold bolts and two stud bolts.
8. Remove exhaust manifold and gasket.
9. reverse procedure to install, noting the following:
   a. Install new gasket with exhaust manifold.
   b. Tighten bolts in sequence, **Fig. 19,** in two stages.
   c. Stage one: **Torque** bolts to 8 ft. lbs.
   d. Stage two: **Torque** bolts to 16 ft. lbs.

Righthand

1. Remove cowl vent screen and cowl extension.
2. Disconnect oxygen sensor electrical connector.
3. Remove exhaust manifold to exhaust gas recirculation tube.
4. Remove exhaust manifold heat shield.
5. Disconnect catalytic converter from exhaust manifold.
6. Remove six bolts from exhaust manifold, then the exhaust manifold.
7. Reverse procedure to install, noting the following:
   a. Install new exhaust manifold gasket.
   b. Tighten bolts in sequence, **Fig. 20,** in two stages.
   c. Stage one: **Torque** bolts to 89 inch lbs.
   d. Stage two: **Torque** bolts to 16 ft. lbs.

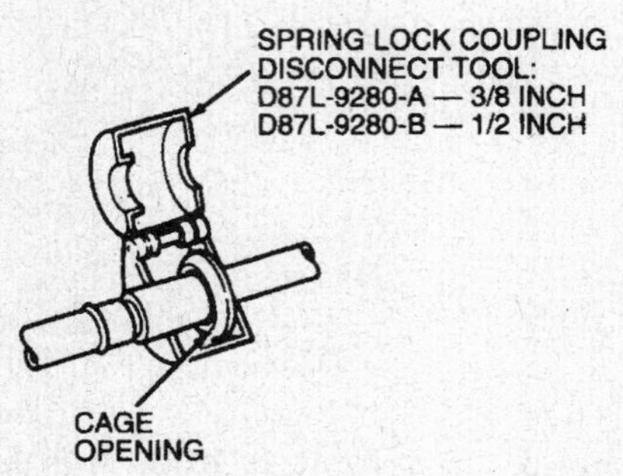

Fig. 13 Fuel line tool installation

VIN S ENGINE

1998-99

Lefthand

1. Raise and support vehicle.
2. Remove dual converter Y-pipe.
3. Remove secondary air injection manifold tube from exhaust manifold.
4. Remove lower exhaust manifold mounting nuts.
5. Remove lefthand exhaust manifold and gasket from cylinder head, discard gasket.
6. Reverse procedure to install.

Righthand

1. Remove upper intake manifold as outlined under "Intake Manifold, Replace."
2. Remove ignition coil from righthand valve cover.
3. Remove EGR valve to exhaust manifold tube.
4. Remove secondary air injection manifold tube.
5. Raise and support vehicle, and remove dual converter Y-pipe.
6. Remove lower exhaust manifold mounting nuts and lower vehicle.
7. Remove upper exhaust manifold mounting nuts.
8. Remove righthand exhaust manifold and gasket from cylinder head, discard gasket.
9. Reverse procedure to install.

2000-02

Lefthand

1. Remove left side exhaust manifold to pipe nuts.
2. Remove coolant tube bracket bolt.
3. Disconnect and unclip the left side heated oxygen sensor electrical connector from coolant tube.
4. Raise and support vehicle.
5. Remove pin type retainers and bolts, then the front splash shield.
6. Remove lower exhaust manifold nuts.
7. Remove coolant tube lower bracket.
8. Lower vehicle.
9. Remove upper nuts, then the exhaust manifold.

10. Reverse procedure to install, noting the following:
    a. Install new exhaust manifold gasket.
    b. **Torque** nuts in sequence, **Fig. 21,** to 15 ft. lbs.
    c. **Torque** manifold to pipe nuts to 30 ft. lbs.

Righthand

1. Remove cowl panel grille.
2. Remove right side valve cover.
3. Disconnect exhaust gas recirculation tube from exhaust manifold.
4. Raise and support vehicle.
5. Remove manifold to Y-pipe nuts.
6. Remove engine support insulator nut.
7. Lower vehicle.
8. Using suitable engine lifting device, raise engine until exhaust manifold can be removed.
9. Remove nuts in sequence, **Fig. 22.**
10. Reverse procedure to install, noting the following:
    a. Install new exhaust manifold gasket.
    b. **Torque** exhaust manifold nuts in sequence, **Fig. 23,** to 15 ft. lbs.

Intake Manifold Gasket

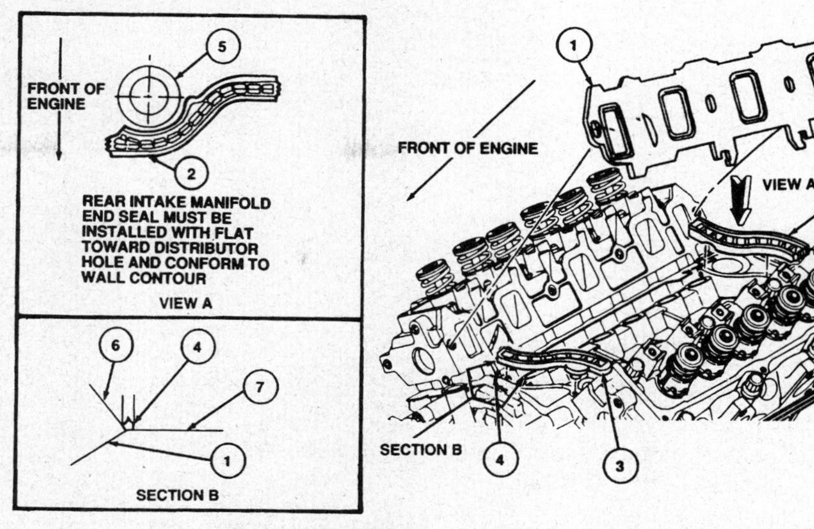
FRONT OF ENGINE
REAR INTAKE MANIFOLD END SEAL MUST BE INSTALLED WITH FLAT TOWARD DISTRIBUTOR HOLE AND CONFORM TO WALL CONTOUR
VIEW A
SECTION B
FRONT OF ENGINE
VIEW A
SECTION B

Item	Description
1	Intake Manifold Gasket (2 Req'd)
2	End Seal
3	End Seal
4	Silicone Rubber (4 Places)

Item	Description
5	Distributor Hole
6	Cylinder Head (2 Req'd)
7	Cylinder Block

FM1069600483000X

Fig. 14 Lower intake manifold. 1998–99 VIN U, 1 & 2 engines

CYLINDER HEAD

REPLACE

VIN U, 1 & 2 ENGINES

1998–99

1. Relieve fuel system pressure as outlined under "Precautions."
2. Rotate crankshaft to 0° TDC of compression stroke.
3. Drain cooling system.
4. Remove air cleaner outlet tube.
5. Remove upper and lower intake manifolds as outlined under "Intake Manifold, Replace."
6. Using a ½ inch drive breaker bar inserted into the automatic belt tensioner, rotate and relax tension on serpentine belt, and remove belt. Remove alternator if lefthand side cylinder head is being removed.
7. Remove mounting bolts, power steering pump and bracket as an assembly with hoses attached. Position pump and bracket assembly aside in an upright position to prevent leakage of fluid.
8. If lefthand side cylinder head is being removed, remove coil bracket and dipstick tube. If righthand side cylinder head is being removed, remove ground strap and throttle cable support bracket.
9. Remove exhaust manifolds, then the PCV valve and valve covers.
10. Loosen remaining rocker arm fulcrum bolts enough to allow rocker arms to be swung aside and pushrods removed. Keep pushrods in order so they can be installed in original positions.
11. Remove cylinder head mounting bolts, then the cylinder head and gasket. Discard gaskets and bolts.
12. Reverse procedure to install, noting the following:
    a. Lightly oil new cylinder head bolts threads prior to installation.
    b. Replace any damaged gasket alignment dowels.
    c. **On 1998 models, torque** cylinder head bolts to 52–66 ft. lbs., in sequence, **Fig. 24,** then loosen bolts in sequence one full turn.
    d. **Torque** cylinder head bolts, to 34–40 ft. lbs., then to 63–73 ft. lbs. in sequence.
    e. **On 1999 models, torque** cylinder head bolts to 35–39 ft. lbs. in sequence, **Fig. 24,** then loosen bolts in sequence one full turn.
    f. **Torque** cylinder head bolts to 20–24 ft. lbs. in sequence.
    g. **Torque** cylinder head bolts 85–95° in sequence shown, then final tighten an additional 85–95.°
    h. **On all models,** prior to installation, lubricate rocker arm assemblies and dip each pushrod end in oil conditioner part No. D9AZ-19579-C, or other suitable heavy engine oil.
    i. Starting with engine at TDC compression No. 1 cylinder, rotate crankshaft one full turn clockwise, and install No. 2 and No. 5 exhaust, and No. 1 and No. 4 intake push rod and rocker arm assembly.
    j. **Torque** rocker arm bolts to 6–11 ft. lbs., then to 20–28 ft. lbs.
    k. Rotate crankshaft ⅓ turn clockwise, and install remaining push rod and rocker arm assemblies.
    l. **Torque** rocker arm bolts to 6–11 ft. lbs., then to 20–28 ft. lbs.
    m. Ensure all rocker arm bolts are fully seated to their shoulder after tightening.
    n. If any valve train components were replaced or intermixed, inspect valve clearance as outlined under "Valve Clearance Specifications."

2000–02

Righthand

1. Remove lower intake manifold as outlined previously.
2. Disconnect crankshaft position sensor electrical connector.
3. Disconnect oxygen sensor electrical connector.
4. Disconnect wire harness ground connections.
5. Disconnect powertrain control module electrical connectors.
6. Disconnect evaporative emissions canister purge valve electrical connector.
7. Position spark plug wires aside.
8. Disconnect exhaust gas recirculation (EGR) tube.
9. Remove exhaust manifold heat shield.
10. Loosen exhaust manifold to catalytic converter bolts.
11. Remove six exhaust manifold to cylinder head bolts.
12. Disconnect engine wire harness locator.
13. Separate catalytic converter heat shield from cylinder head.
14. Remove eight cylinder head bolts, then the cylinder head.
15. Reverse procedure to install, noting the following:

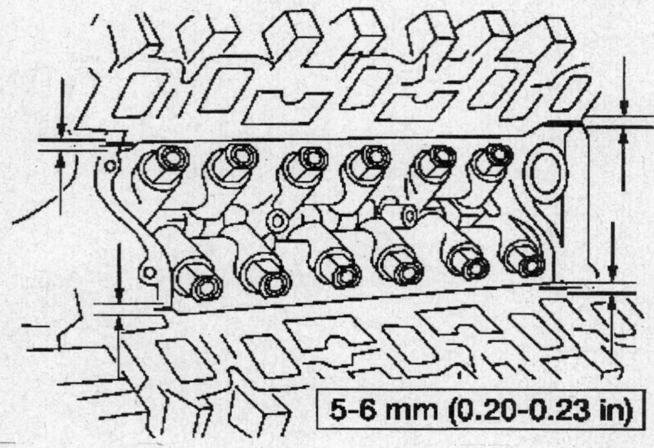

Fig. 15 Silicone gasket sealant placement. 2000–02 VIN U engine

FM1060101213000X

Fig. 16 Lower intake manifold bolt tightening sequence. 2000–02 VIN U engine

a. Clean all gasket surfaces and inspect cylinder head and block for flatness.
b. When installing new head gaskets, "V" notch in gasket faces front of engine.
c. Install cylinder head, new gasket and bolts and tighten in sequence, **Fig. 25,** in five stages.
d. Stage 1: **Torque** bolts to 37 ft. lbs.
e. Stage 2: Loosen bolts one full turn.
f. Stage 3: **Torque** bolts to 22 ft. lbs.
g. Stage 4: Tighten each bolt 90°.
h. Stage 5: Tighten each bolt an additional 90°.

Lefthand

1. Remove lower intake manifold as outlined previously.
2. Remove accessory drive belt.
3. Remove engine anti-roll strut brace.
4. Disconnect alternator electrical connector.
5. Remove alternator.
6. Remove accessory drive belt idler pulley and tensioner pulley.
7. Remove spark plug wires.
8. Remove left side exhaust manifold.
9. Remove power steering pump and bracket assembly.
10. Remove eight cylinder head bolts, then the cylinder head.
11. Reverse procedure to install, noting the following:
    a. Clean all gasket surfaces, inspect cylinder head and block surfaces for flatness.
    b. When installing new head gaskets, "V" notch faces front of engine.
    c. Install cylinder head, new gasket, and cylinder head bolts and tighten in sequence, **Fig. 25,** in five stages.
    d. Stage 1: **Torque** bolts to 37 ft. lbs.
    e. Stage 2: Loosen bolts one full turn
    f. Stage 3: **Torque** bolts to 22 ft. lbs.
    g. Stage 4: Tighten bolts an additional 90°.
    h. Stage 5: Tighten bolts an additional 90° again.

VIN S ENGINE

1998–99

1. Remove engine as outlined under "Engine, Replace."
2. Remove upper and lower intake manifolds as outlined under "Intake Manifold, Replace."
3. Remove engine control sensor wiring mounting nuts and bolts.
4. Remove mounting nut, crankcase ventilation tube from oil separator and water bypass tube stud bolt.
5. Remove radiator and heater hoses from water bypass tube.
6. Remove water bypass tube from cylinder head.
7. Remove power steering pump from engine front cover.
8. Remove A/C compressor mounting bracket from water pump brace.
9. Remove mounting brackets and A/C compressor
10. Remove alternator.
11. Remove water pump to engine front cover mounting bolts.
12. Install flywheel holding tool No. T74P-6375-A, or equivalent, to cylinder block and engage flywheel.
13. Remove crankshaft accessory drive pulley and bracket assembly from engine front cover. **Crankshaft drive pulley shaft has lefthand thread.**
14. Remove crankshaft pulley retainer bolt and washer from crankshaft.
15. Using front damper puller tool No. T58P-6316-D, or equivalent, remove crankshaft pulley from crankshaft.
16. Remove flywheel holding tool from cylinder block.
17. Remove ignition coil from righthand valve cover.
18. Remove valve cover retainer bolts and studs for both lefthand and righthand valve covers.
19. Remove valve covers from cylinder heads.
20. Remove spark plugs.
21. Remove oil level dipstick, dipstick tube and O-ring from lefthand cylinder head and cylinder block.
22. Remove lefthand and righthand exhaust manifolds and gaskets from cylinder heads.
23. Drain engine oil, and remove oil pan and gasket from cylinder block.
24. Remove drive belt tensioner from righthand side of engine front cover.
25. Remove camshaft and crankshaft position sensors from front cover.
26. Remove front cover mounting bolts in sequence, **Fig. 26.**
27. Remove engine front cover and gasket, discard gasket.
28. Remove crankshaft position sensor pulse ring from crankshaft.
29. Rotate crankshaft clockwise to position crankshaft keyway to 11 o'clock location. **Rotating crankshaft in a counterclockwise direction may make timing chain bind and cause engine damage.**
30. Ensure alignment arrows on camshafts are aligned. If arrows are not aligned, rotate crankshaft clockwise one complete revolution.
31. Rotate crankshaft so keyway is in three o'clock position. This will position righthand cylinder head camshafts to neutral position (base circle).
32. Remove mounting bolts and righthand timing chain tensioner.
33. Remove cylinder head camshaft journal thrust cap bolts and thrust caps from righthand cylinder head. **Cylinder head camshaft journal caps and cylinder heads are numbered to ensure they are assembled in their original positions. Do not mix with camshaft journals from another head.**
34. Loosen remaining righthand cylinder head camshaft journal cap bolts in sequence, **Fig. 27.**
35. Remove righthand timing chain tensioner arm and righthand timing chain. **Mark position of tensioner arm and timing chain guide for installation.**
36. Remove righthand timing chain guide and crankshaft sprocket.
37. Remove righthand cylinder head camshaft journal caps and bolts, camshafts, rocker arms and valve lifters. **Mark position of rocker arms and**

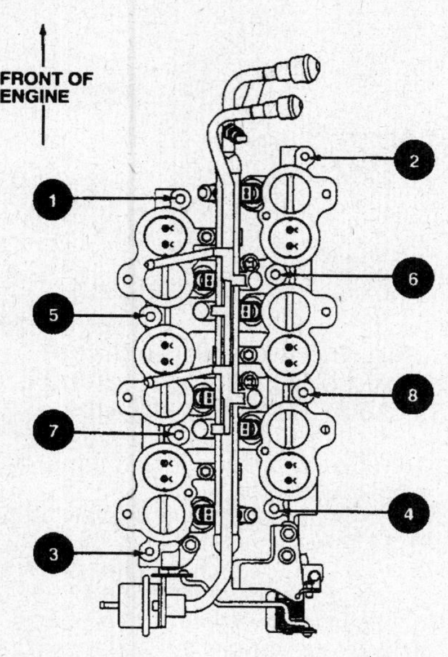

Fig. 17 Lower intake manifold bolt removal sequence. VIN S engine

valve lifters for installation.

38. Rotate crankshaft clockwise two revolutions and position crankshaft keyway to 11 o'clock location. This will position crankshaft to neutral position (base circle).
39. Ensure alignment arrows on camshafts are aligned. If arrows are not aligned, rotate crankshaft clockwise one complete revolution.
40. Remove mounting bolts and lefthand timing chain tensioner.
41. Remove cylinder head camshaft journal thrust cap bolts and thrust caps from lefthand cylinder head. **Cylinder head camshaft journal caps and cylinder heads are numbered to ensure they are assembled in their original positions. Do not mix with camshaft journals from another head.**
42. Loosen remaining lefthand cylinder head camshaft journal cap bolts in sequence, **Fig. 27.**
43. Remove lefthand timing chain tensioner arm and lefthand timing chain. **Mark position of tensioner arm and timing chain guide for installation.**
44. Remove lefthand timing chain guide and crankshaft sprocket.
45. Remove lefthand cylinder head camshaft journal caps and bolts, camshafts, rocker arms and valve lifters. **Mark position of rocker arms and valve lifters for installation.**
46. Remove EGR backpressure transducer mounting bracket and EGR backpressure transducer from righthand cylinder head.
47. Remove cylinder head mounting bolts and washers in sequence, **Fig. 28.**
48. Remove cylinder head and gasket from cylinder block.
49. Reverse procedure to install, noting the following:
    a. Place timing chain tensioners in a soft jawed vise, and slowly compress tensioner piston and bleed oil from tensioner, **Fig. 29.**
    b. Use new gasket and cylinder head bolts. **Cylinder head bolts must not be used again. These bolts are torque-to-yield designed and engine damage could result.**
    c. **Torque** cylinder head bolts to 28–31 ft. lbs. in sequence, **Fig. 30,** then tighten 85–95.°
    d. Loosen cylinder head bolts one full turn.
    e. **Torque** to 28–31 ft. lbs. and tighten 85–95.°
    f. Finally, tighten cylinder head bolts and additional 85–95.°
    g. Ensure timing chains are installed properly as outlined under "Timing Chain, Replace."
    h. Apply 7⁄16 inch bead of black silicone rubber part No. F4AZ-19562-B, or equivalent, in six locations on cylinder block, **Fig. 31.** Install front cover within six minutes of applying sealant.
    i. When installing crankshaft damper, apply black silicone rubber part No. F4AZ-19562-B to inside diameter of crankshaft damper keyway.

2000–02

Righthand

1. Remove coolant bypass tube.
2. Remove camshafts as outlined under "Camshafts."
3. Raise and support vehicle.
4. Remove right side exhaust manifold to pipe bolts.
5. Lower vehicle.
6. Disconnect exhaust gas recirculation (EGR) tube from exhaust manifold.
7. Remove camshaft followers and hydraulic lash adjusters.
8. Remove exhaust manifold as outlined under "Exhaust Manifold, Replace"
9. Remove cylinder head bolts in sequence, **Fig. 28.**
10. Remove cylinder head, discard gasket and bolts. Bolts are torque to yield design and cannot be re-used.
11. Reverse procedure to install, noting the following:
    a. Cylinder head bolts must be replaced with new bolts.
    b. Install new head gasket, and bolts, then tighten in sequence, **Fig. 30,** in six stages.
    c. Stage 1: **Torque** bolts to 30 ft. lbs.
    d. Stage 2: Tighten bolts 90°.
    e. Stage 3: Loosen bolts one full turn.
    f. Stage 4: **Torque** bolts to 30 ft. lbs.
    g. Stage 5: Tighten bolts 90°.
    h. Stage 6: Tighten bolts an additional 90°.

Lefthand

1. Remove coolant bypass tube.
2. Remove exhaust manifold.
3. Remove water pump as outlined under "Water Pump, Replace."
4. Remove camshafts as outlined under "Camshaft, Replace."
5. Remove camshaft followers and hydraulic lash adjusters.
6. Remove exhaust manifold.
7. Remove cylinder head bolts in sequence, **Fig. 28,** then the cylinder head.
8. Discard gasket and bolts.
9. Reverse procedure to install, noting the following:
    a. Install cylinder head with new bolts and head gasket.
    b. Install bolts and tighten in sequence, **Fig. 30,** in six stages.
    c. Stage 1: **Torque** bolts to 30 ft. lbs.
    d. Stage 2: Tighten bolts 90°.
    e. Stage 3: Loosen bolts one full turn.
    f. Stage 4: **Torque** bolts to 30 ft. lbs.
    g. Stage 5: Tighten bolts 90°.
    h. Stage 6: Tighten bolts an additional 90°.

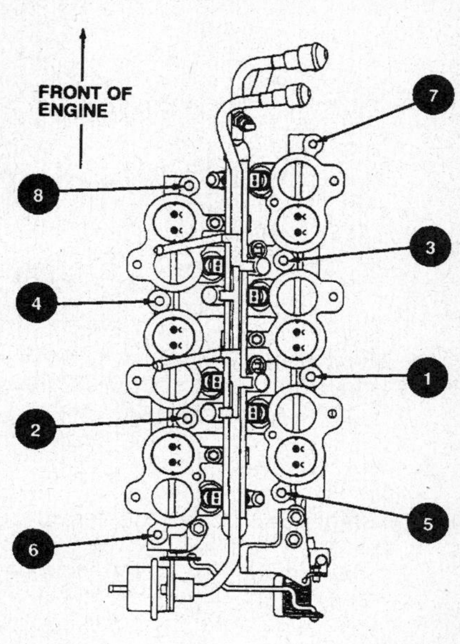

Fig. 18 Lower intake manifold bolt tightening sequence. VIN S engine

VALVE COVER

REPLACE

VIN U, 1 & 2 ENGINES

1998–99

1. Relieve fuel system pressure as outlined under "Precautions."
2. Disconnect spark plug wires from spark plugs.
3. Remove spark plug wire separators from valve cover mounting bolt studs.
4. If lefthand side valve cover is being removed, performing the following:
    a. Disconnect crankcase breather hose and remove oil filler cap.
    b. Remove fuel injector harness standoffs from inboard rocker arm cover studs and position harness out of way.
5. If righthand side rocker arm cover is removed, proceed as follows:
    a. Remove upper intake manifold as outlined under "Intake Manifold, Replace."

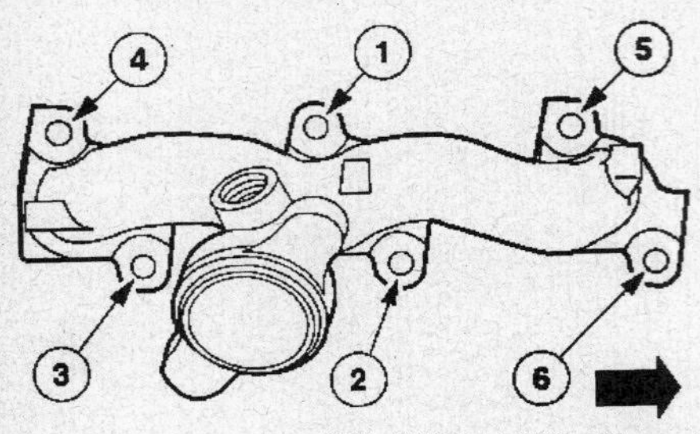

Fig. 19 Exhaust manifold bolt tightening sequence. 2000–02 VIN U, 1 & 2 engines

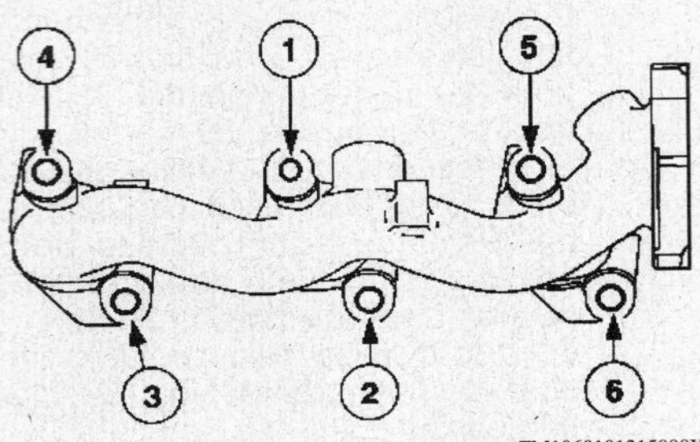

Fig. 20 Right side exhaust manifold tightening sequence. 2000–02 VIN U, 1 & 2 engines

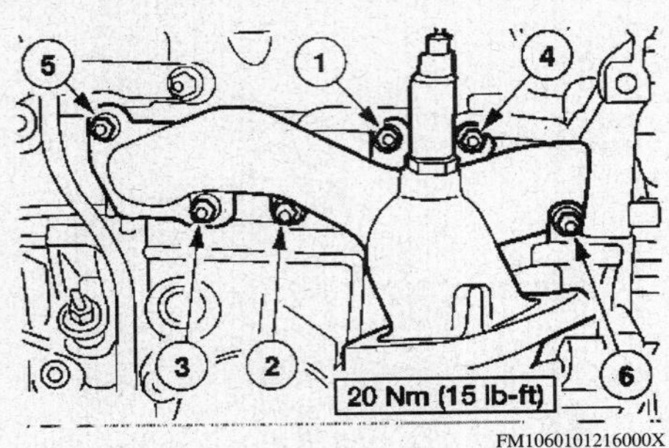

Fig. 21 Left side exhaust manifold tightening sequence. 2000–02 VIN S engines

   b. Disconnect EGR tube and heater hoses.
   c. Remove PCV valve and move fuel injector harness out of way.
6. Remove rocker arm cover mounting bolts and cover.
7. Reverse procedure to install, noting the following:
   a. Lightly oil bolt and stud threads prior to installation.
   b. Apply bead of RTV sealant at cylinder head to intake manifold rail step.
   c. Tighten rocker arm cover mounting bolts and EGR tube to specifications.

2000–02

Righthand

1. Remove upper intake manifold as outlined under “Intake Manifold, Replace.”
2. Position degas bottle aside.
3. Position fuel charge harness aside.
4. Position spark plug wires aside.
5. Remove valve cover.
6. Reverse procedure to install, noting the following:
   a. Do not clean valve cover with solvent or damage to cover may occur.
   b. Apply a bead of silicone gasket and sealant in two places where cylinder head and intake manifold meet.
   c. Install bolts and tighten to specification.

Lefthand

1. Remove ignition coil.
2. Disconnect crankcase ventilation hose.
3. Position engine wiring harness from front and back of valve cover aside.
4. Remove radio suppressor.
5. Remove spark plug wire retainers, then position spark plug wires aside.
6. Remove valve cover.
7. Reverse procedure to install, noting the following:
   a. Do not clean valve cover with solvent or damage to cover may occur.
   b. Apply a bead of silicone gasket and sealant in two places where cylinder head and intake manifold meet.
   c. Install bolts and tighten to specification.

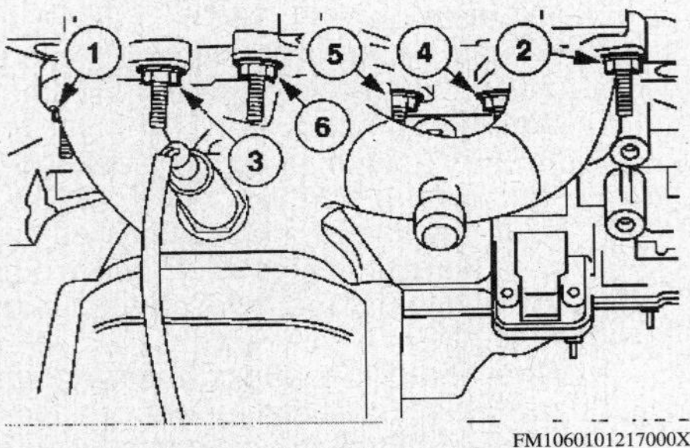

Fig. 22 Righthand side exhaust manifold bolt loosening sequence. 2000–02 VIN S engine

VIN S ENGINE

1998–99

Righthand

1. Remove upper intake manifold as outlined under “Intake Manifold, Replace.”
2. Remove ignition wires from ignition coil and spark plugs.
3. Remove ignition coil.
4. Remove crankcase ventilation tube from righthand valve cover.
5. Remove engine control sensor wiring and evaporative emission hose mounting nuts and stud bolts from righthand valve cover. Position emission hose out of way.
6. Remove mounting bolts, valve cover and gaskets.
7. Reverse procedure to install, noting the following:
   a. Apply a 5⁄16 inch bead of black silicone rubber part No. F4AZ-19562-B, or equivalent, at two places on valve cover sealing surfaces where engine front cover and cylinder head contact.
   b. Install new gasket.
   c. Install valve cover within six minutes of applying sealer.

Lefthand

1. Remove crankcase ventilation tube from lefthand valve cover.
2. Remove engine control sensor wiring mounting nuts and stud bolts from valve cover. Position sensor wiring out of way.
3. Remove ignition wires from spark plugs and valve cover.
4. Remove mounting bolts, stud bolts and valve cover.
5. Reverse procedure to install, noting the following:
   a. Apply a 5⁄16 inch bead of black silicone rubber part No. F4AZ-19562-B, or equivalent, at two places on valve cover sealing surfaces where engine front cover and cylinder head contact, **Fig. 32.**
   b. Install new gasket.
   c. Install valve cover within six minutes of applying sealer.

2000–02

Righthand

1. Remove upper intake manifold as outlined under “Intake Manifold, Replace.”
2. Remove ignition coil and bracket.
3. Remove spark plug wires.
4. Disconnect differential pressure feedback exhaust gas recirculation electrical connector.
5. Remove wiring harness nut and position harness aside.
6. Disconnect crankcase ventilation tube from valve cover.
7. Remove bolts and studs, then the valve cover.
8. Reverse procedure to install, noting the following:
   a. Install new valve cover gasket.
   b. Apply a 5mm dot of silicone gasket and sealant to front cover cylinder head joints.
   c. Position valve cover, install bolts and tighten to specification, in sequence, **Fig. 33,** to 89 inch lbs.

Lefthand

1. Disconnect crankcase ventilation tube from valve cover.
2. Remove water pump drive belt cover.
3. Remove spark plug wire using a slight twisting motion to break seal.
4. Disconnect spark plug wire holder and position out of way.
5. Disconnect wiring harness from valve cover and position out of way.
6. Remove bolts and studs, then the valve cover.
7. Reverse procedure to install, noting the following:
   a. Install new valve cover gasket.
   b. Apply a 5mm dot of silicone gasket

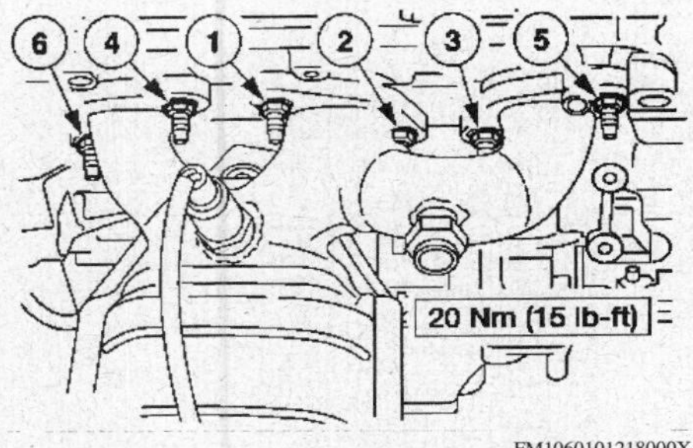

Fig. 23 Righthand side exhaust manifold bolt tightening sequence. 2000–02 VIN S engine

sealant to front cover to cylinder head joints.

c. Install valve cover bolts in sequence, **Fig. 34,** and tighten to specification.

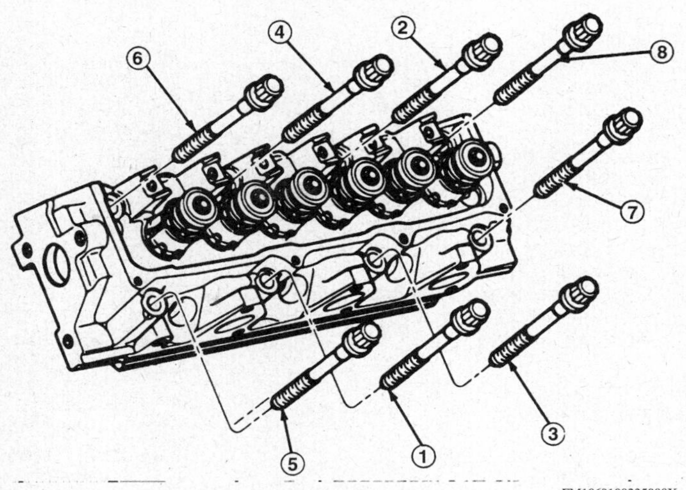

Fig. 24 Cylinder head bolt tightening sequence. 1998–99 VIN U, 1 & 2 engines

VALVE ARRANGEMENT

VIN U, 1 & 2 ENGINES

Front To Rear

Righthand Side...............I-E-I-E-I-E
Lefthand Side ....E-I-E-I-E-I

CAMSHAFT LOBE LIFT SPECIFICATIONS

VIN U, 1 & 2 ENGINES

1998–99

Exhaust.......................... .260 inch
Intake .... .260 inch

2000–02

Exhaust..................................264
Intake.....................................251

VIN S ENGINE

Exhaust.......................... .188 inch
Intake .... .188 inch

VALVE CLEARANCE SPECIFICATIONS

VIN U, 1 & 2 ENGINES

If any valve train component is replaced or if valve train components become intermixed, valve clearance will have to be inspected on those valves.

1. Using a suitable pry bar, apply pressure to push rod side of rocker arm until hydraulic lifter has bled down and bottomed out.
2. Ensure clearance between valve stem and rocker arm is .085 and .185 inch.

VALVE ADJUSTMENT

Hydraulic valve lifters are used in this engine. No adjustment is required.

HYDRAULIC LIFTERS

REPLACE

VIN U, 1 & 2 ENGINES

Before replacing a hydraulic valve lifter for noisy operation, ensure the noise is not caused by improper rocker arm to stem clearance, worn rocker arms, pushrods or valve tips.

1. Set engine to TDC compression No. 1 cylinder.
2. Remove intake manifold as outlined under "Intake Manifold, Replace."
3. Loosen remaining rocker arm fulcrum mounting bolts enough to swing rocker arm aside to allow pushrods to be removed and remove pushrods. Keep pushrods in order so they can be returned to original positions.
4. Remove bolts from roller lifter guide retainer plate, **Fig. 35,** and lift retainer plate from engine.
5. Remove roller lifter guide from lifter pair by lifting straight up.
6. **If lifters are stuck in their bores by excessive varnish or gum buildup, use a suitable claw type puller to remove roller lifters with a rocking and twisting motion.**
7. Place roller lifter lifters in a rack so they can be installed in original positions.
8. Reverse procedure to install, noting the following:
   a. Ensure word UP and/or button is facing upward when installing roller lifter guide plates.
   b. Lubricate lifters, lifter bores, rocker arms and pushrods with oil conditioner part No. D9AZ-19579-A, or suitable heavy engine oil.
   c. Starting with engine at TDC compression No. 1 cylinder, rotate crankshaft one full turn clockwise, and install No. 2 and No. 5 exhaust, and No. 1 and No. 4 intake push rod, and rocker arm assembly.
   d. **Torque** rocker arm bolts to 6–11 ft. lbs., then to 20–28 ft. lbs.
   e. Rotate crankshaft ⅓ turn clockwise, and install remaining push rod and rocker arm assemblies.
   f. **Torque** rocker arm bolts to 6–11 ft. lbs., then to 20–28 ft. lbs.
   g. Ensure all rocker arm bolts are fully seated to their shoulder after tightening.
   h. If any valve train components were replaced or intermixed, inspect valve clearance as outlined under "Valve Clearance Specifications."

FRONT COVER

REPLACE

VIN U, 1 & 2 ENGINES

1998–99

Removal

1. Relieve fuel system pressure as outlined under "Precautions."
2. Loosen four water pump pulley bolts with drive belt in place.
3. Using a ½ inch drive breaker bar inserted into serpentine belt auto tensioner, rotate tensioner to relieve tension until belt may be removed, and remove belt.
4. Drain cooling system, and remove lower radiator hose and heater hose from water pump.
5. Remove crankshaft pulley and damper as outlined under "Front Cover Seal, Replace."
6. Drain and remove oil pan as outlined under "Oil Pan, Replace."
7. Remove timing cover to block mounting bolts. Timing cover and water pump may be removed as an assembly by not removing bolts Nos. 11–15, **Fig. 36.**
8. After cover is pulled away from block, remove water pump pulley and bolts.
9. Inspect timing chain deflection for excessive wear.

Installation

1. Lightly oil all bolts and stud threads before installation except those specifying sealant.

2. Clean all gasket material from gasket selaing areas.
3. Inspect crankshaft front seal for wear or damage, replace as necessary.
4. Align engine front cover over cylinder block dowel.
5. Install crankshaft front oil seal protector onto crankshaft.
6. Install engine front cover and water pump as an assembly onto cylinder block with water pump pulley loosely attached to water pump hub.
7. Hand start front cover retaining bolts. Apply suitable sealant meeting Ford specifications, to bolts No. 1, 2 and 3, **Fig. 36.**
8. **Torque** bolts No. 1 through No. 10 to 18 ft. lbs., and No. 11 through No. 15 to 88 inch lbs.
9. Clean inside of oil pan and install.
10. Hand tighten water pump pulley retaining bolts.
11. Install crankshaft damper and crankshaft pulley. Tighten damper retaining bolt and four pulley retaining bolts to specification.
12. If crankshaft position sensor was removed from front cover, install and tighten bolts to specification.
13. Install drive belt tensioner and drive belt.
14. Tighten water pump pulley retaining bolts to specification.
15. Install lower radiator and heater hoses.
16. Fill and bleed cooling system.
17. Fill crankcase with proper amount and type engine oil.
18. Start engine and inspect for leaks.

2000–02

1. Drain coolant into suitable container.
2. Remove engine anti-roll strut brace.
3. Remove engine roll restrictor.
4. Remove coolant expansion tank.
5. Loosen water pump pulley bolts.
6. Raise and support vehicle
7. Remove crankshaft damper.
8. Disconnect lower radiator hose.
9. Remove crankshaft position sensor.
10. Remove oil pan as outlined under "Oil Pan, Replace."
11. Lower vehicle.
12. Remove alternator and support brace.
13. Remove accessory drive belt, drive belt idler pulley and drive belt tensioner.
14. Remove A/C compressor bracket.
15. Disconnect heater hose.
16. Remove water pump pulley.
17. Remove engine front cover and water pump as an assembly.
18. Reverse procedure to install, noting the following:
    a. Apply pipe sealant with Teflon to bolts No. 1, 2, 3, 6 and 7, **Fig. 36.**
    b. **Torque** bolts in sequence to 18 ft. lbs.

VIN S ENGINE

1998–99

1. Remove engine as outlined under "Engine, Replace."
2. Remove crankcase ventilation tube mounting nut, tube from oil separator and water bypass tube stud bolt.

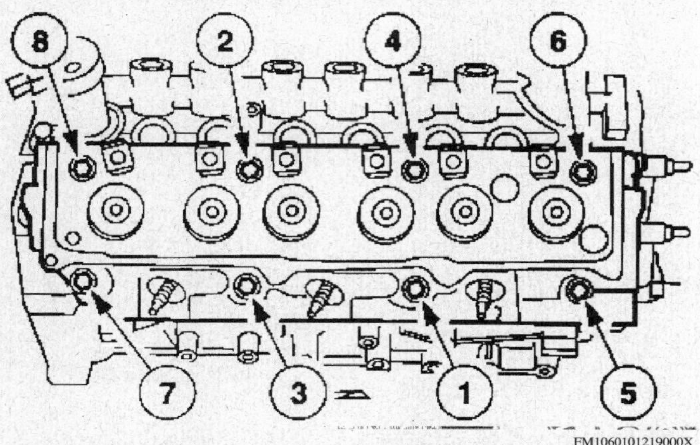

Fig. 25 Cylinder head bolt torque sequence. 2000–02 VIN U, 1 & 2 engines

3. Remove power steering pump from engine front cover.
4. Remove A/C compressor mounting bracket from water pump brace.
5. Remove mounting brackets and A/C compressor
6. Remove alternator.
7. Remove water pump to engine front cover mounting bolts.
8. Install flywheel holding tool No. T74P-6375-A, or equivalent, to cylinder block and engage flywheel.
9. Remove crankshaft accessory drive pulley and bracket assembly from engine front cover. **Crankshaft drive pulley shaft has a lefthand thread.**
10. Remove crankshaft pulley retainer bolt and washer from crankshaft.
11. Using front damper puller tool No. T58P-6316-D, or equivalent, remove crankshaft pulley from crankshaft.
12. Remove flywheel holding tool from cylinder block.
13. Drain engine oil, and remove oil pan and gasket from cylinder block.
14. Remove drive belt tensioner from righthand side of engine front cover.
15. Remove camshaft and crankshaft position sensors from front cover.
16. Remove front cover mounting bolts and studs in sequence, **Fig. 26.**
17. Remove engine front cover and gasket, discard gasket.
18. Reverse procedure to install, noting the following:
    a. Apply 7/16 inch bead of black silicone rubber part No. F4AZ-19562-B, or equivalent, in six locations on cylinder block, **Fig. 31.** Install front cover within six minutes of applying sealant.
    b. **Torque** front cover bolts to 15–22 ft. lbs. in sequence, **Fig. 37.**
    c. When installing crankshaft damper, apply black silicone rubber part No. F4AZ-19562-B, or equivalent, to inside diameter of crankshaft damper keyway.

2000–02

1. Remove left and right valve covers.
2. Remove power steering pump
3. Raise and support vehicle.
4. Remove oil pan as outlined under "Oil Pan, Replace."
5. Remove retaining nut and position power steering pressure line and muffler out of way.
6. Remove alternator, crankshaft pulley and crankshaft position sensor.
7. Remove A/C compressor to front cover bracket.
8. Disconnect camshaft position sensor.
9. Remove belt tensioner.
10. Remove engine cooling fan.
11. Install suitable engine support tool.
12. Remove two upper A/C compressor bolts.
13. Remove two upper A/C compressor bolts and position A/C compressor aside.
14. Lower vehicle.
15. Remove A/C bracket.
16. Remove bolts and studs, then the front cover.
17. Reverse procedure to install, noting the following:
    a. Install new gaskets in front cover.
    b. Apply a .24 inch bead of gasket and sealer to cylinder block to lower block and cylinder head mating surfaces. Front cover must be installed and bolts tightened within six minutes of applying sealant.
    c. Position cover, install bolts and **torque** in sequence, **Fig. 37,** to 18 ft. lbs.

FRONT COVER SEAL

REPLACE

VIN U, 1 & 2 ENGINES

1. Loosen accessory drive belts and remove righthand front wheel.
2. Remove four crankshaft pulley to damper mounting bolts, and remove accessory drive belt and pulley.
3. Remove vibration damper mounting bolt, and using suitable puller, vibration damper.
4. Using flat bladed screwdriver or other suitable tool, pry seal from front timing cover. **Use caution not to damage front cover or crankshaft.**
5. Lubricate replacement seal lip with clean engine oil and install seal with suitable seal installer.

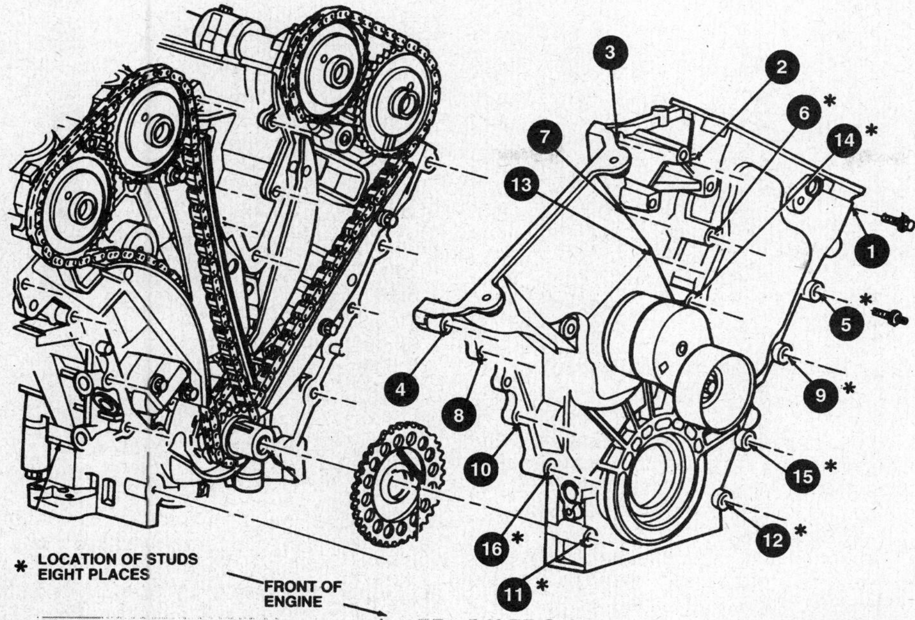

Fig. 26 Front cover bolt removal sequence. VIN S engine

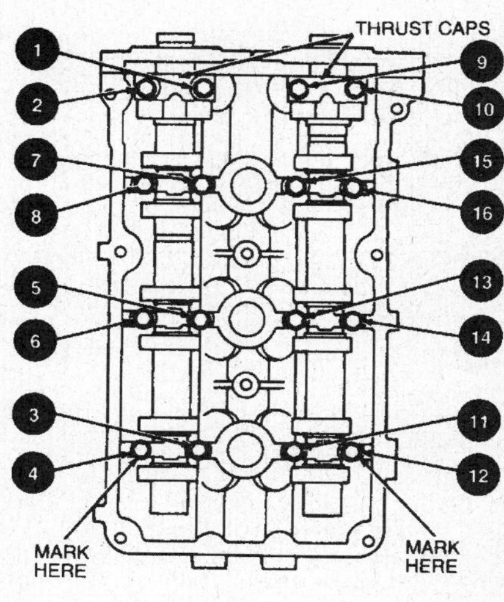

Fig. 27 Camshaft journal cap bolt removal sequence. VIN S engine

6. Lubricate inner hub surface of vibration damper with clean engine oil and apply RTV sealant to keyway of inner hub surface of vibration damper.
7. Install vibration damper and tighten mounting bolt to specifications.
8. Install crankshaft pulley and tighten bolts to specifications.
9. Install accessory drive belts and righthand front wheel.
10. Start engine and inspect for oil leaks.

TIMING CHAIN

REPLACE

VIN U, 1 & 2 ENGINES

1. Remove front engine cover as outlined under "Front Cover, Replace"
2. Rotate crankshaft until No. 1 piston is at TDC and timing marks are aligned, **Fig. 38.**
3. Remove camshaft sprocket mounting bolt and washer.
4. Inspect timing chain deflection for excessive wear.
5. Slide sprockets and timing chain forward and remove as an assembly.
6. Reverse procedure to install, noting the following:
   a. Slide timing chain and sprockets on with timing marks aligned, **Fig. 39.**
   b. The camshaft bolt is a special oil transferring part. **Do not replace with a standard bolt.**
   c. Tighten to specifications.

VIN S ENGINE

1998–99

1. Remove engine as outlined under "Engine, Replace."
2. Remove front cover as outlined under "Front Cover, Replace."
3. Remove crankshaft position sensor pulse ring from crankshaft.
4. Rotate crankshaft clockwise to position crankshaft keyway to 11 o'clock location. **Rotating crankshaft in a counterclockwise direction may cause timing chain to bind and cause engine damage.**
5. Ensure alignment arrows on righthand camshafts are aligned. If arrows are not aligned, rotate crankshaft clockwise one complete revolution.
6. Rotate crankshaft so keyway is in three o'clock position. This will position righthand cylinder head camshafts to neutral position (base circle).
7. Remove mounting bolts and righthand timing chain tensioner.
8. Remove righthand timing chain tensioner arm and righthand timing chain. **Mark position of tensioner arm and timing chain guide for installation reference.**
9. Remove righthand timing chain guide and crankshaft sprocket.
10. Rotate crankshaft clockwise two revolutions and position crankshaft keyway to 11 o'clock location. This will position crankshaft to neutral position (base circle).
11. Ensure alignment arrows on lefthand camshafts are aligned. If arrows are not aligned, rotate crankshaft clockwise one complete revolution.
12. Remove lefthand timing chain tensioner mounting bolts and lefthand timing chain tensioner.
13. Remove lefthand timing chain tensioner arm and lefthand timing chain. **Mark position of tensioner arm and timing chain guide for installation reference.**
14. Remove lefthand timing chain guide and crankshaft sprocket.
15. Reverse procedure to install, noting the following:
   a. Place timing chain tensioners in a soft jawed vise.
   b. Slowly compress tensioner piston and bleed oil from tensioner, **Fig. 29.**
   c. Ensure timing marks on sprockets and timing chain links are aligned, **Fig. 40.**
   d. Install front cover as outlined under "Front Cover, Replace."

2000–02

1. Remove engine front cover as outlined under "Front Cover, Replace."
2. Remove ignition pulse wheel.
3. Install damper bolt, remove spark plugs, then rotate crankshaft clockwise to position crankshaft keyway in the 11 o'clock position.
4. Verify that camshaft are correctly located in the TDC position for No. 1 cylinder. If not, rotate crankshaft one additional turn and re-check.
5. Rotate crankshaft clockwise 120° to the 3 o'clock position to place righthand camshafts in the neutral position and verify that camshafts are correctly positioned.
6. Remove righthand timing chain tensioner arm and timing chain guide, then the timing chain.
7. Rotate crankshaft clockwise two times to position crankshaft keyway in the 11 o'clock position to position camshafts in a neutral position.
8. Remove lefthand timing chain tensioner and tensioner arm, then the timing chain.
9. Remove damper bolt from crankshaft.
10. Reverse procedure to install, noting the following:
   a. Position chain tensioner in a soft jawed vise, hold chain tensioner ratchet lock mechanism away from ratchet stem with a small pick, then slowly compress timing chain tensioner.
   b. Retain tensioner piston with a .06 inch wire or paper clip, **Fig. 29.**

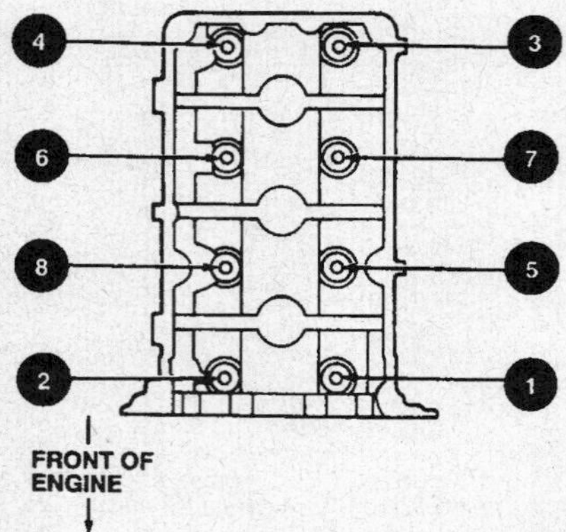

Fig. 28 Cylinder head bolt removal sequence. VIN S engine

a. Ensure timing marks on sprockets and timing chain are aligned, **Fig. 40.**

CAMSHAFT

REPLACE

VIN U, 1 & 2 ENGINES

1. Remove engine and mount in suitable work stand.
2. Remove front cover and timing chain as outlined under "Timing Chain, Replace."
3. Remove intake manifolds and hydraulic valve lifters as outlined under "Hydraulic Valve Lifters, Replace."
4. Remove camshaft thrust plate and carefully pull camshaft from cylinder block. Use caution to avoid damaging bearings, journals and lobes.
5. Reverse procedure to install, noting the following:
   a. Tighten camshaft thrust plate mounting screws to specifications.
   b. Lubricate lifters, lifter bores, rocker arms and pushrods with oil conditioner part No. D9AZ-19579-A, or suitable heavy engine oil.

VIN S ENGINE

1. Remove timing chain and gears as outlined under "Timing Chain, Replace."
2. Remove upper intake manifold as outlined under "Intake Manifold, Replace."
3. Remove both valve covers as outlined under "Valve Cover, Replace."
4. Remove camshaft journal cap bolts in sequence, **Fig. 27.**
5. Remove camshafts and rocker arms, mark rocker arms for installation reference.
6. Reverse procedure to install, tighten camshaft mo8unting bolts to specification.

PISTON & ROD ASSEMBLY

Assemble the rod to the piston with the

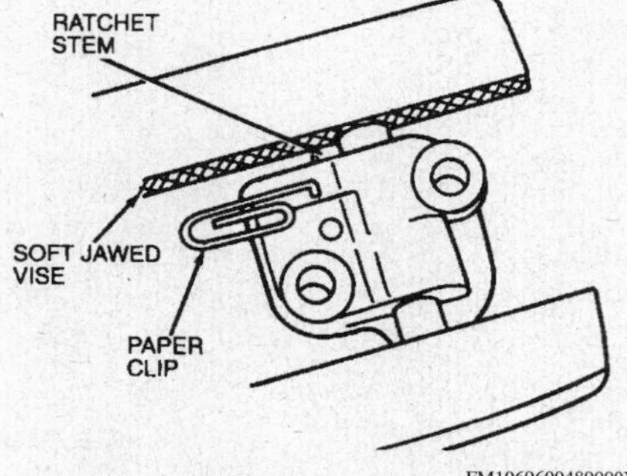

Fig. 29 Timing chain tensioner. VIN S engine

notch on the piston dome on the same side as the button on the connecting rod identification marks. Assemble piston and rod assembly in engine with notch in dome facing front of engine, **Fig. 41.**

After installation, inspect connecting rod big end side clearance. Clearance should be .006–.014 inch.

MAIN & ROD BEARINGS

Main bearings are available in standard sizes and undersizes of .001 and .002 inch.

CRANKSHAFT REAR OIL SEAL

REPLACE

1. Remove transaxle and flywheel.
2. Remove rear cover plate.
3. Using a suitable tool, punch a hole into seal metal surface between lip and block. Using slide hammer tool No. T77L-9533-B, or equivalent, remove seal.
4. Coat crankshaft seal area and seal lip with engine oil, and using tool No. T82L-6701-A, or equivalent, install seal.
5. Install rear cover plate and two dowels.
6. Install flywheel and tighten bolts to specifications.

OIL PAN

REPLACE

VIN U, 1 & 2 ENGINES

1998–99

This procedure has been revised by a Technical Service Bulletin.

1. Relieve fuel system pressure as outlined under "Precautions."
2. Remove oil dipstick.
3. Raise and support vehicle.
4. **On models with low oil level sensor,** remove retainer clip at sensor and disconnect sensor electrical connector.
5. **On all models,** drain crankcase.
6. Remove starter motor and disconnect Exhaust Gas Oxygen (EGO) sensor electrical connector.
7. Remove Y-pipe and catalytic converter assembly.

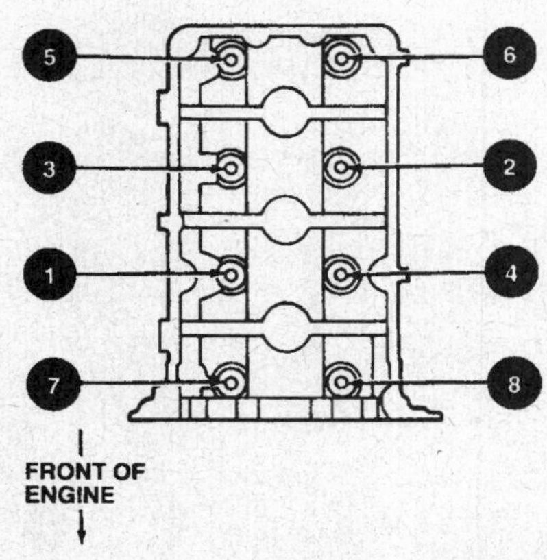

Fig. 30 Cylinder head bolt tightening sequence. VIN S engine

8. Remove lower engine/flywheel dust cover from converter/flywheel housing.
9. Remove oil pan to cylinder block and front cover mounting screws, **Fig. 42,** and oil pan and gasket.
10. Reverse procedure to install, noting the following:
    a. Carefully remove all traces of old RTV sealant from oil pan and engine block.
    b. Install oil pan gasket applying Weatherstrip & Rubber Adhesive No. E8Z-19552-A, or equivalent, to gasket surface that mates with engine block.
    c. Apply Weatherstrip & Rubber Adhesive No. E8Z-19552-A, or equivalent, to entire engine block sealing surface including front cover and rear main bearing cap. Do not apply sealant to front cover-to-block and rear bearing cap-to-block parting lines.
    d. Seal parting lines with bead of Silicone Gasket Sealant No. F7AZ-195540-EA, or equivalent.
    e. Install oil pan by carefully aligning bolt holes.
    f. Tighten four corner bolts to specifications, then tighten remaining bolts to specifications, back to front.
    g. Ensure all bolts are tighten to specifications.
    h. Finish installing oil pan.
    i. Start engine and allow to reach operating temperature (cooling fan should cycle at least once.)
    j. Stop engine and tighten oil pan bolts to specifications.
    k. Inspect oil pan gasket for extreme shifting out of place.

2000–02

1. Raise and support vehicle.
2. Remove dual converter Y-pipe
3. Remove starter motor.
4. Remove engine rear plate.
5. Drain engine oil into suitable container.
6. Remove oil pan.
7. Reverse procedure to install, noting the following:
   a. Apply weatherstrip adhesive to

gasket mating surface of cylinder block assembly and to cylinder block assembly mating surface of oil pan gasket.

b. Apply a bead of silicone gasket and sealant in two places where cylinder block meets front cover and in two places where rear main bearing cap meets cylinder block.

c. Position oil pan gasket, then the oil pan.

d. Install bolts and tighten in three stages.

e. Stage 1: **Torque** four corner bolts to 9 ft. lbs.

f. Stage 2: **Torque** remaining bolts from back to front to 9 ft. lbs.

g. Stage 3: Check all bolts for correct tightness.

VIN S ENGINE

1998–99

This procedure has been revised by a Technical Service Bulletin.

1. Raise and support vehicle.
2. Remove dual converter Y-pipe and drain engine oil.
3. Remove oil pan mounting bolts from transaxle housing.
4. Remove access plug from engine rear plate.
5. Remove transaxle support bracket from oil pan and transaxle.
6. Remove oil pan mounting bolts and stud bolts in sequence, **Fig. 43.**
7. Remove oil pan and oil pan gasket.
8. Reverse procedure to install, noting the following:
   a. Carefully remove all traces of old RTV sealant from oil pan and engine block.
   b. Install oil pan gasket applying Weatherstrip & Rubber Adhesive No. E8Z-19552-A, or equivalent, to gasket surface that mates with engine block.
   c. Apply Weatherstrip & Rubber Adhesive No. E8Z-19552-A, or equivalent, to entire engine block sealing surface including front cover and rear main bearing cap. Do not apply sealant to front cover-to-block and rear bearing cap-to-block parting lines.
   d. Seal parting lines with bead of Silicone Gasket Sealant No. F7AZ-195540-EA, or equivalent.
   e. Install oil pan by carefully aligning bolt holes.
   f. Tighten four corner bolts to specifications, then tighten remaining bolts to specifications, back to front.
   g. Ensure all bolts are tighten to specifications.
   h. Finish installing oil pan.
   i. Start engine and allow to reach operating temperature (cooling fan should cycle at least once.)
   j. Stop engine and tighten oil pan bolts to specifications.
   k. Inspect oil pan gasket for extreme shifting out of place.

2000–02

1. Raise and support vehicle.

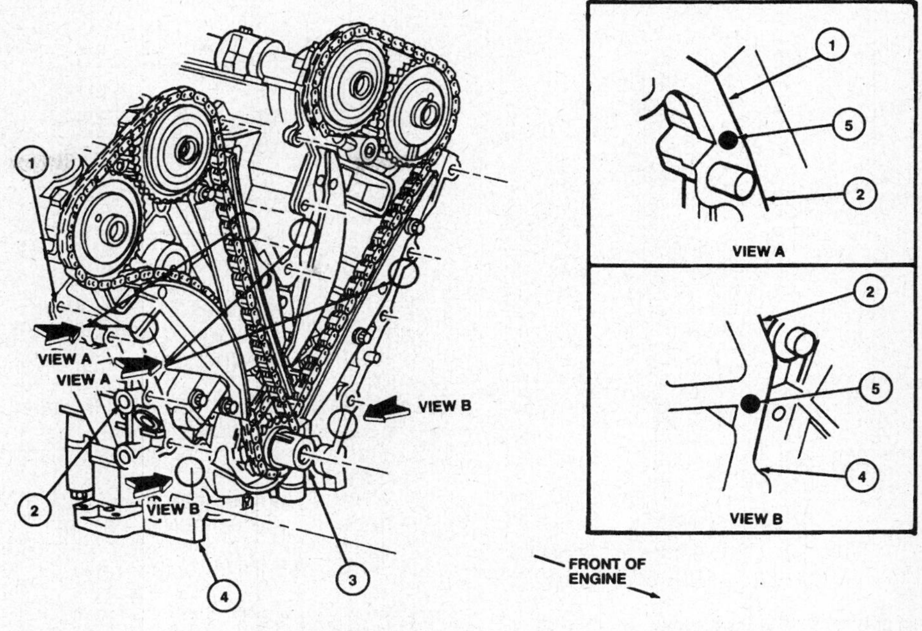

Item	Description
1	RH Cylinder Head
2	Upper Cylinder Block
3	Crankshaft
4	Lower Cylinder Block
5	Black Silicone Rubber

Item	Description
6	Engine Front Cover
7	Stud Bolt (8 Req'd)
8	Crankshaft Position Sensor Pulse Ring
A	Tighten to 20-30 N·m (15-22 Lb-Ft)

FM1069600491000X

Fig. 31 Front cover sealer locations. VIN S engine

2. Remove right front wheel and inner splash shield.
3. Remove dual converter Y-pipe.
4. Drain engine oil into suitable container.
5. Remove engine to transaxle bracket.
6. Remove torque converter inspection cover.
7. Remove oil pan.
8. Reverse procedure to install, noting the following:
   a. Clean all sealing surfaces on engine and oil pan with metal surface cleaner meeting Ford specification.
   b. Position new gasket on oil pan.
   c. Apply a .40 inch diameter dot of silicone gasket and sealer meeting Ford specification to areas indicated, **Fig. 44.**
   d. Position oil pan and tighten bolts in sequence, **Fig. 45.**

OIL PUMP

REPLACE

VIN U, 1 & 2 ENGINES

1. Remove oil pan as outlined under "Oil Pan, Replace."
2. Remove oil pump mounting bolts, **Fig. 46.**
3. Remove oil pump and intermediate shaft.
4. If necessary, pull intermediate shaft from oil pump.
5. Reverse procedure to install. When installing intermediate shaft into replacement pump, ensure shaft retainer clicks into position.

VIN S ENGINE

1. Remove timing chains as outlined under "Timing Chain, Replace."
2. Remove mounting bolts and oil pump from crankshaft.
3. Reverse procedure to install.

OIL PUMP SERVICE

VIN U, 1 & 2 ENGINES

1. Wash all parts in suitable solvent and dry with compressed air.
2. Ensure all dirt and particles are removed.
3. Inspect inner pump housing for wear or damage.
4. Inspect pump cover mating surface for wear. Scuff marks are normal. If surface is worn or grooved, replace pump assembly.
5. Inspect rotor for nicks, burrs or score marks, and remove imperfections with suitable oil stone.
6. Using suitable feeler gauge, measure inner tip to outer rotor tip clearance, **Fig. 47.** Clearance should be .0024–.0071 inch.
7. Install suitable straightedge and measure rotor endplay, **Fig. 48.** Clearance should be .0012–.0035 inch.
8. If any clearance does not meet specifications, replace oil pump assembly.

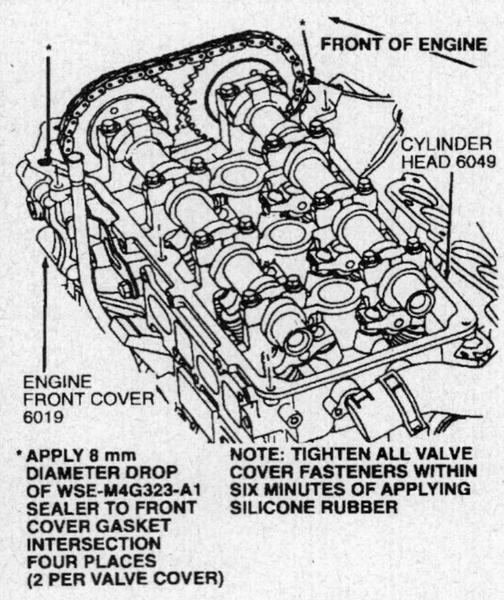

Fig. 32 Valve cover sealer locations. VIN S engine

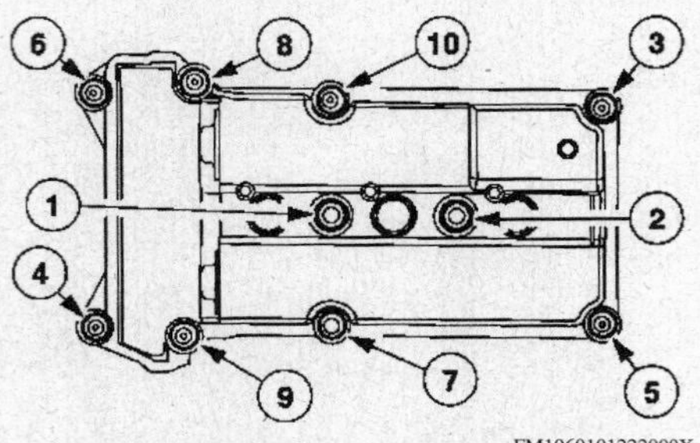

Fig. 33 Righthand valve cover tightening sequence. 2000–02 VIN S engine

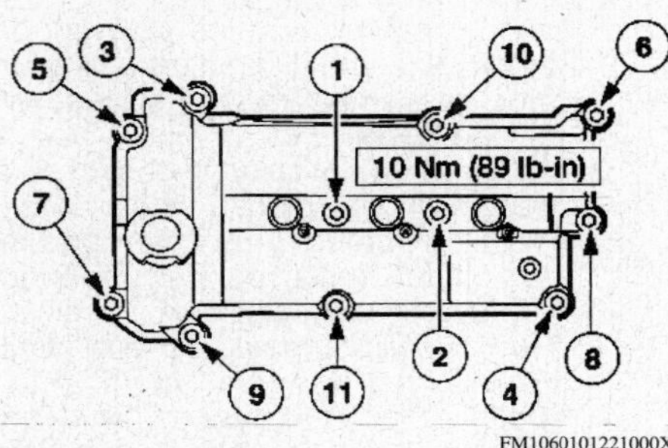

Fig. 34 Lefthand valve cover tightening sequence. 2000–02 VIN S engine

BELT TENSION DATA

Belt	New, Lbs.	Used, Lbs.
5-Rib	140–160	110–130
6-Rib	①	①

① — Automatic tensioner.

SERPENTINE DRIVE BELT

BELT ROUTING

Refer to **Figs. 49 and 50** for serpentine drive belt routing.

BELT, REPLACE

1. **On VIN U, 1 and 2 engines,** rotate drive belt tensioner in a clockwise direction.
2. **On VIN S engine,** rotate drive belt tensioner in a counterclockwise direction.
3. **On all models,** remove serpentine drive belt.
4. Reverse procedure to install. Ensure spring keeper releases.

COOLING SYSTEM BLEED

1. Select maximum blower motor and heater temperature settings. Set controls to discharge air through instrument panel A/C vents.
2. Start engine, and allow it to idle. Feel for hot air at A/C vents.
3. **If air discharge remains cool and engine coolant temperature gauge does not move, coolant level is low and must be filled. Stop engine, allow to cool. Add coolant to bring level to top of Cold Fill mark on degas bottle.**
4. Start engine and allow to idle until operating temperature is reached. Hot air should now blow through A/C vents, temperature gauge should rest in NORMAL range, and upper radiator hose should feel hot to touch.
5. Stop engine, allow to cool and inspect for leaks.
6. **When engine coolant level indicator flashes,** approximately one to 1 ½ quarts of coolant may now be added to de-gas bottle after proper refill.

THERMOSTAT

REPLACE

REMOVAL

1. Drain cooling system below level of upper radiator hose.
2. Remove upper radiator hose and thermostat housing mounting bolts.
3. Remove housing and thermostat as an assembly, discarding old gasket. Clean sealing surfaces with gasket scraper. Ensure not to gouge aluminum surfaces as these gouges may form leaks.

INSTALLATION

1. Install thermostat into housing, ensuring jiggle valve is up in relation to housing.
2. Position gasket onto housing using bolts as holding device, and install housing assembly and mounting bolts.
3. Install upper radiator hose.
4. Fill and bleed cooling system with recommended amount and mixture as outlined under "Cooling System Bleed."
5. Start engine and inspect for leaks.

WATER PUMP

REPLACE

VIN U, 1 & 2 ENGINES

1998–99

1. Drain cooling system into a suitable container.
2. Disconnect heater hose from water pump.
3. With drive belt still tight, loosen water pump pulley to pump hub mounting bolts.
4. Remove drive belt as outlined under "Serpentine Drive Belt." **The pump pulley cannot be removed at this time because of insufficient clearance between body and pump.**
5. Remove drive belt tensioner.
6. Remove water pump mounting bolts, **Fig. 36,** and lift water pump and pulley assembly up and out of vehicle. Remove pulley.
7. Lightly lubricate all bolts and stud threads with oil.
8. Position pulley on replacement pump and install pump/pulley assembly. Tighten mounting bolts to specifications as outlined under "Front Cover, Replace," in sequence, **Fig. 36.**
9. Install water pump pulley to pump hub mounting bolts and tighten to specifications.
10. Reverse procedure to install.

2000–02

1. Drain cooling system into suitable container.
2. Remove accessory drive belt.
3. Remove engine anti roll strut brace and strut.
4. Remove accessory drive belt tensioner.
5. Remove roll restrictor bracket.
6. Remove bolts and water pump pulley.
7. Disconnect water pump inlet hose and crankshaft position sensor.
8. Remove support bracket.
9. Remove water pump.
10. Reverse procedure to install, noting the following:
    a. Tighten bolts in sequence, **Fig. 51.**
    b. **Torque** numbers 1 through 7 to 18 ft. lbs.
    c. **Torque** numbers 8 through 12 to 89 inch lbs.

VIN S ENGINE

1998–99

1. Drain engine cooling system.
2. Remove drive belt as outlined under "Serpentine Drive Belt."
3. Remove radiator and heater hoses from water pump.
4. Remove mounting bolts and water pump.
5. Reverse procedure to install.

2000–02

1. Raise and support vehicle.
2. Drain cooling system into suitable container.
3. Remove splash shield.
4. Disconnect water hose from bottom of water pump.

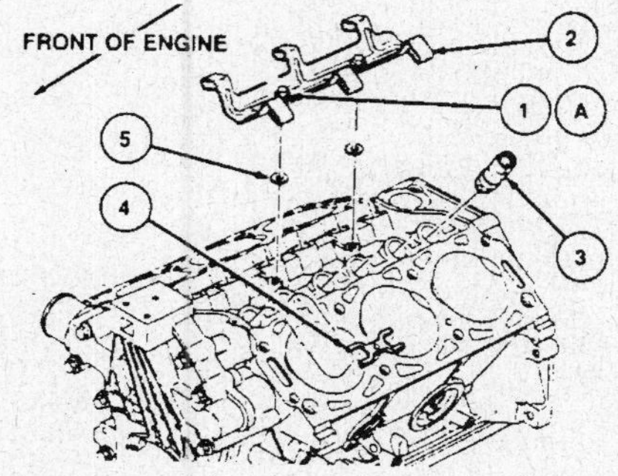

Item		Description
1A		Bolt (2 Req'd) (Part of 6K654)
2		Tappet Guide Plate and Retainer
3		Valve Tappet (12 Req'd)
4		Valve Tappet Guide Plate (6 Req'd)
5		Washer (2 Req'd) (Part of 6K564)
A		Tighten to 10-14 N·m (8-10 Lb-Ft)

FM1069500392000X

Fig. 35 Roller lifter removal. VIN U, 1 & 2 engines

5. Remove radiator lower tube bolt.
6. Lower vehicle.
7. Remove air cleaner assembly, battery and battery tray.
8. Remove water pump belt.
9. Remove radiator upper front tube bolt.
10. Disconnect upper radiator hose and engine vent hose.
11. Disconnect transmission 10 pin connector.
12. Remove radiator bypass hose assembly.
13. Disconnect thermostat housing and position aside.
14. Disconnect hose from water pump.
15. Remove water pump.
16. Reverse procedure to install, noting the following:
    a. Tighten water pump bolts in two stages.
    b. Stage 1: **Torque** bolts to 89 inch lbs.
    c. Stage 2: Tighten bolts an additional 90°.

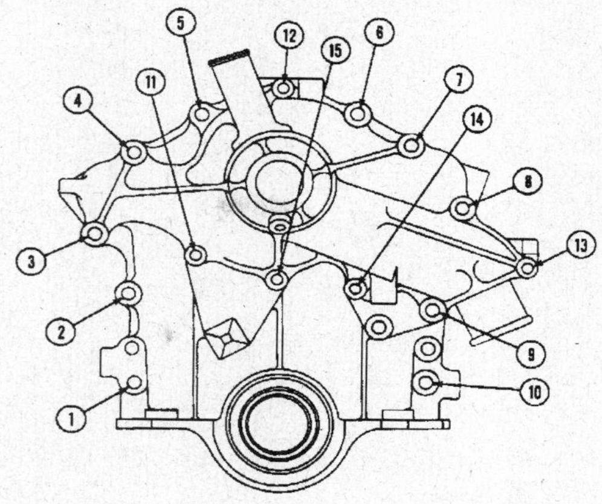

FASTENER AND HOLE NO.	FASTENERS		
	PART NO.	SIZE	FASTENER APPLICATION
1	N804113-S8	M8 x 1.25 x 43.5	F/C TO BLOCK
2	N804113-S100	M8 x 1.25 x 43.5	F/C TO BLOCK
3	N804811-S100	M8 x 1.25 x 70	W/P & F/C TO BLOCK
4	N804811-S8	M8 x 1.25 x 70	W/P & F/C TO BLOCK
5	N605909-S8	M8 x 1.25 x 42	F/C TO BLOCK
6	N804811-S8	M8 x 1.25 x 70	W/P & F/C TO BLOCK
7	N804811-S8	M8 x 1.25 x 70	W/P & F/C TO BLOCK
8	N804811-S8	M8 x 1.25 x 70	W/P & F/C TO BLOCK
9	N804811-S8	M8 x 1.25 x 70	W/P & F/C TO BLOCK
10	N605909-S8	M8 x 1.25 x 42	F/C TO BLOCK
11	N804168-S8	M6 x 1 x 25	W/P TO F/C
12	N804168-S8	M6 x 1 x 25	W/P TO F/C
13	N804168-S8	M6 x 1 x 25	W/P TO F/C
14	N804168-S8	M6 x 1 x 25	W/P TO F/C
15	N804168-S8	M6 x 1 x 25	W/P TO F/C

W/P — Water Pump Assy
F/C — Front Cover Assy
T/P — Timing Pointer

FM1069100236000X

Fig. 36 Timing cover & water pump removal. VIN U, 1 & 2 engines

RADIATOR

REPLACE

1998–99

1. Remove air cleaner, battery and battery tray.
2. Raise and support vehicle.
3. Drain cooling system into suitable container.
4. Remove four bolts retaining lower radiator hose shield and remove shield.
5. Disconnect lower radiator hose.
6. Disconnect lower transmission oil cooler tube from radiator using suitable fuel line disconnect tool.
7. Remove two lower radiator mounts.
8. Remove front bumper cover.
9. Lower vehicle.
10. Remove four bolts retaining hood latch support and position hood latch support aside.
11. Disconnect upper radiator hose and radiator overflow hose from radiator.
12. Remove power distribution box, harness and bracket and position power distribution box aside.
13. Remove upper radiator support.
14. Remove engine control sensor wiring harness and position aside.
15. Disconnect cooling fans from engine control sensor wiring.
16. Remove one nut from power steering/transmission cooler bracket.
17. Remove three bolts and one stud from A/C condenser core.
18. Position A/C condenser core forward and support with mechanics wire.
19. Disconnect upper transmission oil cooler tube from radiator using suitable fuel line disconnect tool.
20. Remove both lower radiator brackets.
21. Lower radiator two inches, then tilt forward and lift radiator clear of vehicle.
22. Reverse procedure to install

2000–02

1. Remove battery and battery tray.
2. Drain cooling system into suitable container.
3. Disconnect upper radiator hose.
4. Disconnect degas return hose.
5. Using suitable disconnect tool, disconnect upper transmission cooler line.
6. Remove A/C condenser retaining bolts.
7. Raise and support vehicle.
8. Disconnect lower radiator hose and transmission cooler line.
9. Remove bolts retaining condenser to radiator.
10. Remove bolt retaining power steering cooler to radiator.
11. Remove nuts and radiator support bracket.
12. Remove radiator.
13. Reverse procedure to install.

FUEL PUMP

REPLACE

1. Relieve fuel system pressure as outlined under "Precautions."
2. **On flexible fuel models,** remove fuel from tank as follows:
    a. Remove foam and rubber protective cover from special quick disconnect fitting on fuel drain tube found on righthand side of fuel tank.
    b. Attach adapter hose tool No. 034-00020, or equivalent, to suitable fuel storage tank.
    c. Pump out fuel from tank.
3. **On non-flexible fuel models,** remove fuel from fuel tank by pumping fuel out of fuel filler neck using a suitable fuel storage tanker.
4. **On all models,** raise and support vehicle.
5. Disconnect and remove fuel filler neck.
6. Support fuel tank and remove tank support straps.
7. Lower fuel tank partially and remove

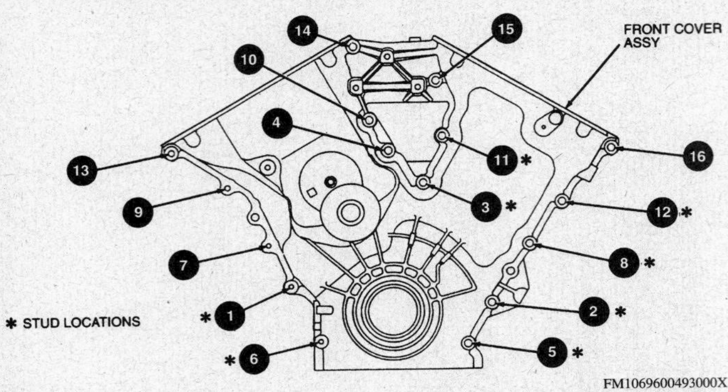

Fig. 37 Front cover bolt tightening sequence. VIN S engine

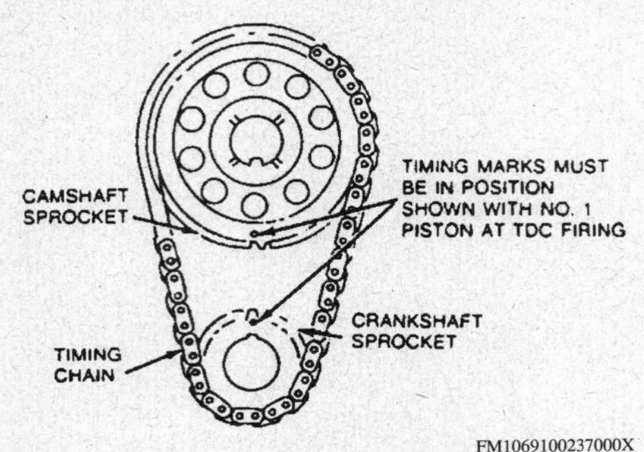

Fig. 38 Timing chain alignment. VIN U, 1 & 2 engines

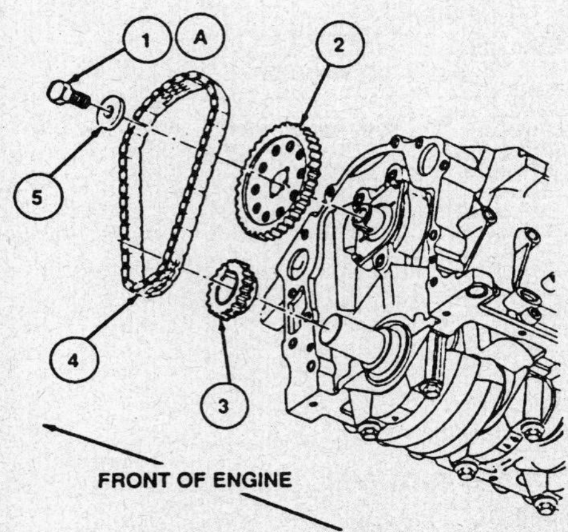

Item	Description
1A	Bolt
2	Camshaft Sprocket
3	Crankshaft Sprocket
4	Timing Chain Lubricate With Oil
5	Washer-Cam Sprocket
A	Tighten to 50-70 N·m (37-51 Lb-Ft)

FM1069100238000X

Fig. 39 Timing chain installation. VIN U, 1 & 2 engines

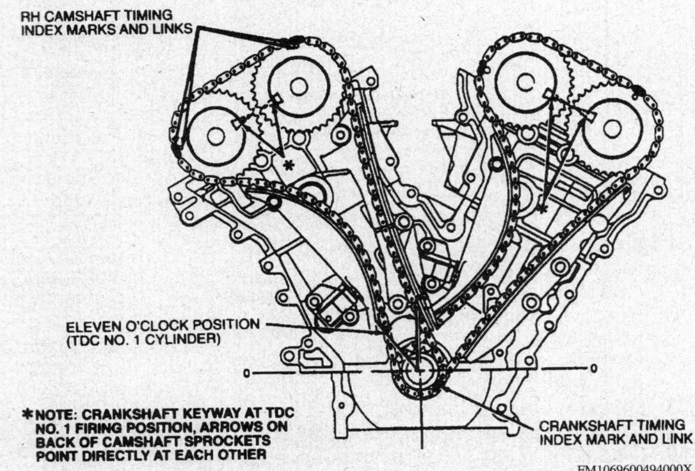

Fig. 40 Timing mark alignment. VIN S engine

fuel lines, electrical connectors and vent lines from tank.

8. Remove tank and place on suitable workbench.
9. Turn fuel pump locking ring counterclockwise and remove locking ring.
10. Remove fuel pump, bracket and gasket assembly.
11. Reverse procedure to install.

FUEL FILTER

REPLACE

1. Relieve fuel system pressure as outlined under "Precautions."
2. Twist push connect fittings at each end of filter until they move freely on tube.
3. Bend and break shipping tab from hairpin clip, and spread two clip legs approximately ⅛ inch, **Fig. 52.**
4. Remove clip from tube and fitting by pulling gently on triangular end.
5. Separate fitting and hose assembly from fuel filter.
6. Install retainer clips in each connect fitting.
7. Loosen worm gear mounting clip and remove filter from bracket, **Fig. 53.**
8. Reverse procedure to install.

TECHNICAL SERVICE BULLETINS

ALL COOLING SYSTEM CONCERNS

1998

This bulletin applies to vehicle built from 9/1/1997 through 1/23/1998 equipped with 3.0L gasoline Vulcan engine or 3.0L E85 ethanol Vulcan engine.

Cooling system concerns such as stuck thermostat, vibration or thumping from engine, leaking heater core, coolant overflow, high temperature gauge readings, fluctuating temperature gauge, contaminated/ corroded coolant, heater hose leaks, leaking head gasket and lack of heat, may be caused by bank to bank coolant flow imbalance. A revised water pump and coolant bypass kit is available to correct this concern.

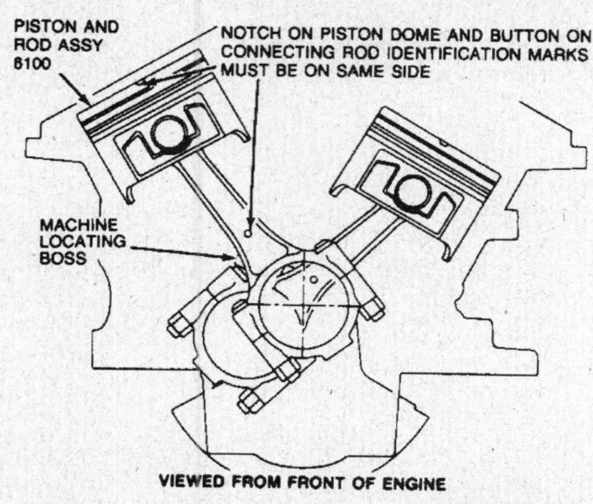

Fig. 41 Piston & rod assembly

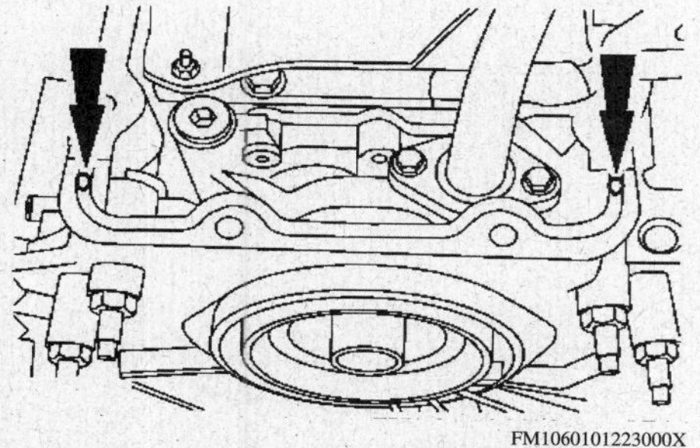

Fig. 44 Silicone gasket and sealer placement. 2000–02 VIN S engine

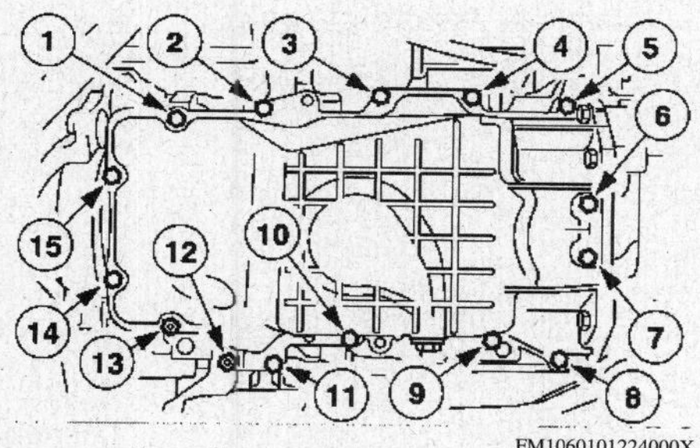

Fig. 45 Oil pan bolt tightening sequence. 2000–02 VIN S engine

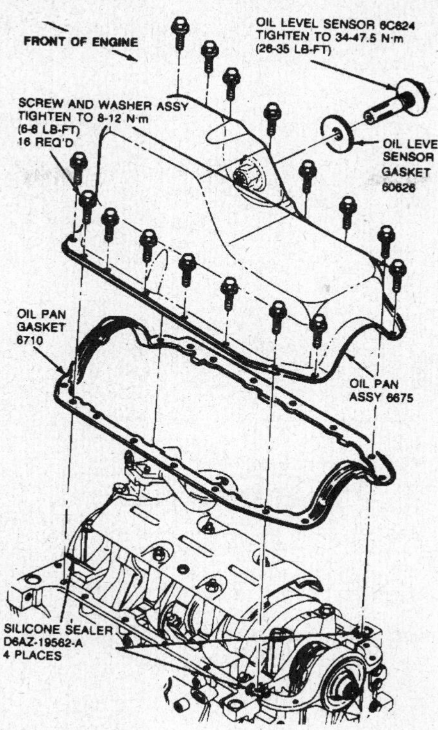

Fig. 42 Oil pan. 1998–99 VIN U, 1 & 2 engines

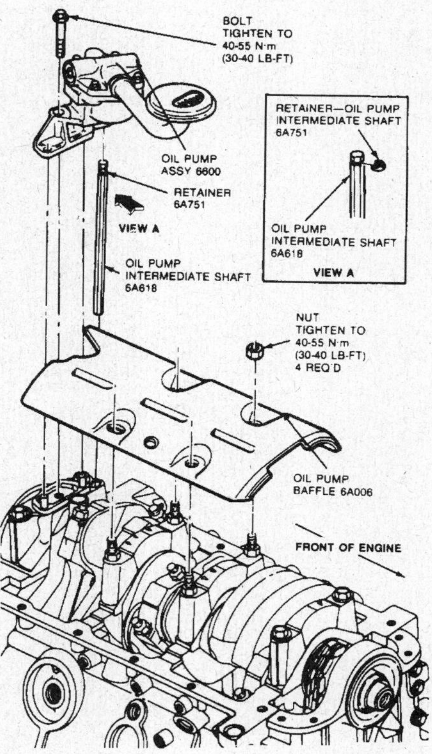

Fig. 46 Oil pump removal. VIN U, 1 & 2 engines

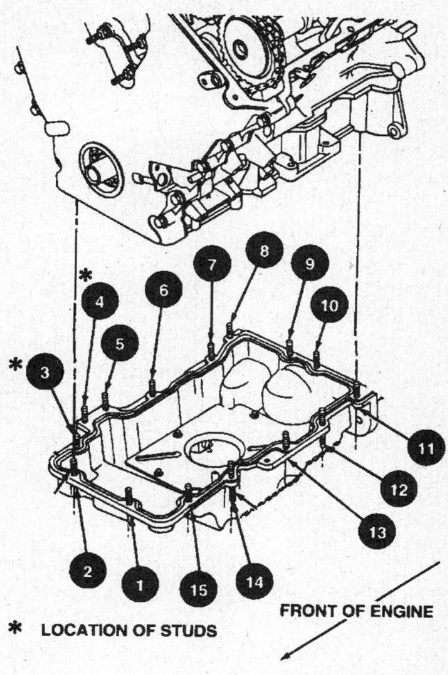

Fig. 43 Oil pan bolt removal sequence. 1998–99 VIN S engine

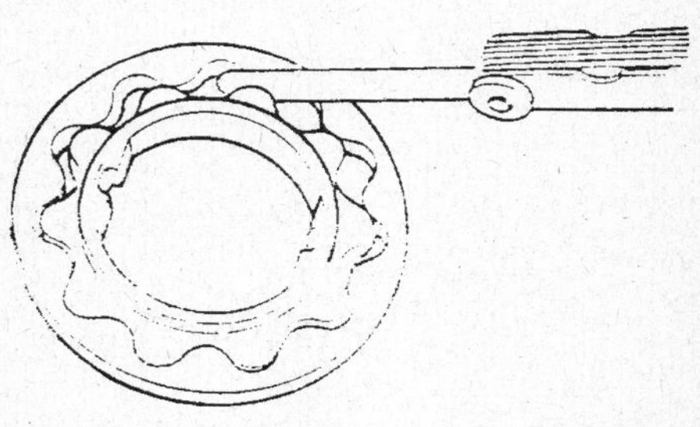

Fig. 47 Oil pump tip clearance. VIN U, 1 & 2 Engines

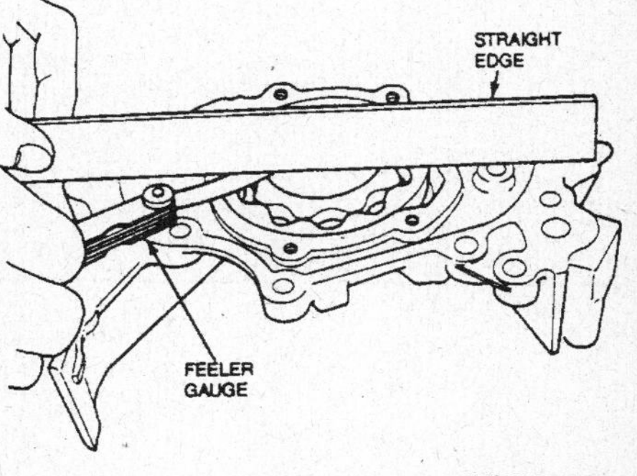

Fig. 48 Oil pump rotor endplay. VIN U, 1 & 2 Engines

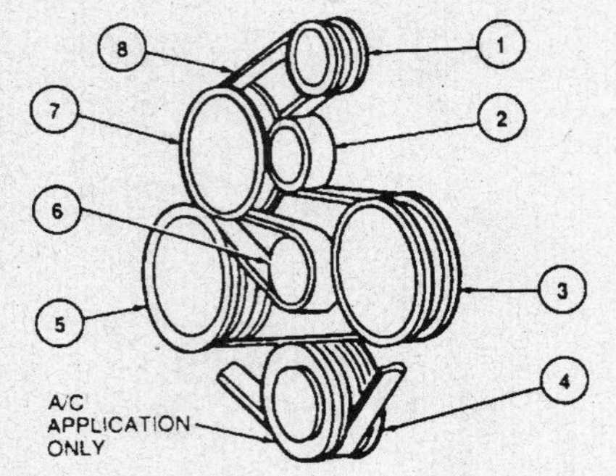

Item	Description
1	Generator
2	Drive Belt Tensioner
3	Power Steering Pump
4	A/C Compressor
5	Crankshaft Pulley
6	Idler Pulley
7	Water Pump
8	Drive Belt

FM1069500393000X

Fig. 49 Serpentine belt routing. VIN U, 1 & 2 engines

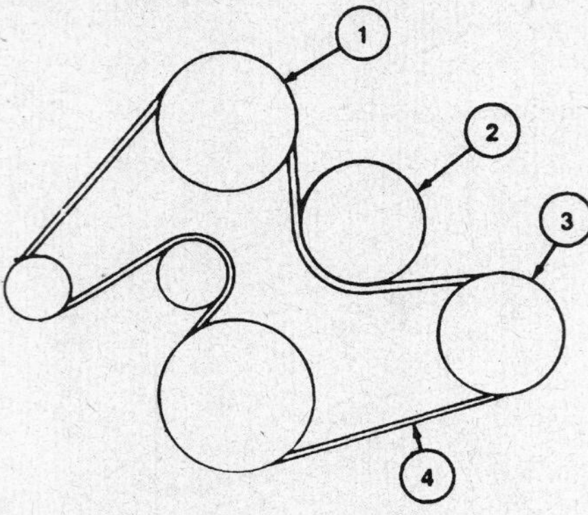

Item	Description
1	Power Steering Pump
2	Water Pump
3	A/C Compressor
4	Drive Belt

FM1069600497000X

Fig. 50 Serpentine belt routing. VIN S engine

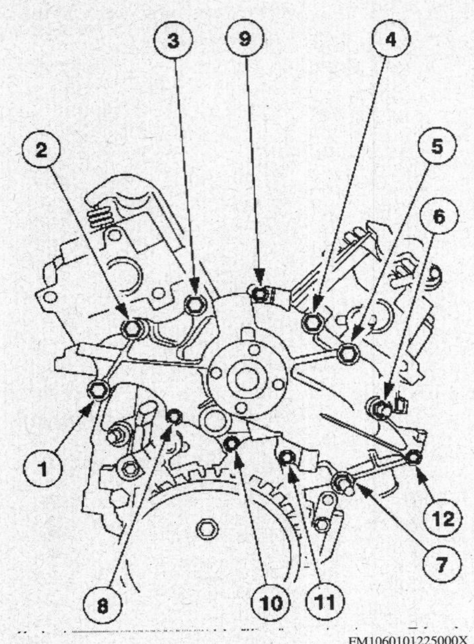

FM1060101225000X

Fig. 51 Water pump bolt tightening sequence. 2000–02 VIN U, 1 & 2 engines

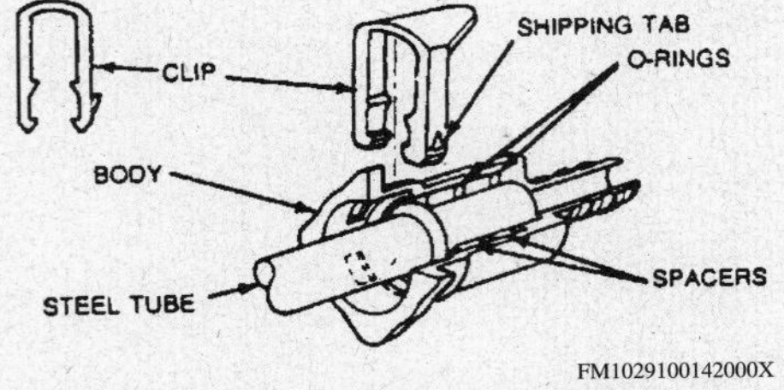

FM1029100142000X

Fig. 52 Push connect fitting removal

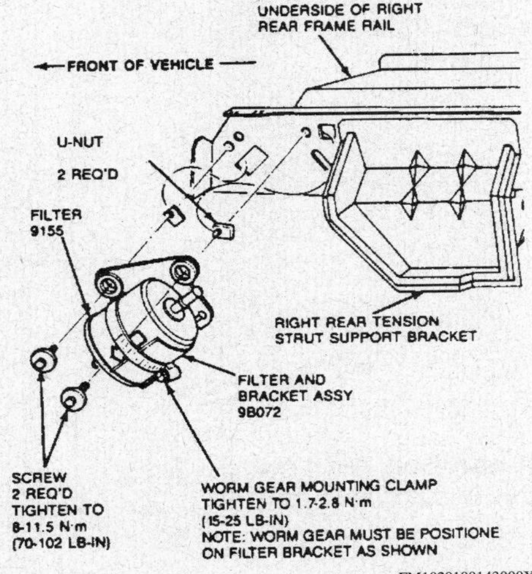

FM1029100143000X

Fig. 53 Fuel filter replacement

TIGHTENING SPECIFICATIONS

Year	Component	Torque/Ft. Lbs.
VIN U, 1 & 2 ENGINES		
1998–99	A/C Compressor Mounting	35
	Alternator Brace To Upper Intake Manifold	9–14
	Alternator To Bracket	27
	Alternator To Cylinder Head	35
	Camshaft Position Sensor Housing Mounting	18
	Camshaft Sprocket To Camshaft	37–51
	Camshaft Thrust Plate	84⑥
	Coil & Bracket To Cylinder Head	30–40
	Connecting Rod	23–28
	Crankshaft Damper To Crankshaft	93–121
	Crankshaft Position Sensor	45–61⑥
	Crankshaft Pulley To Damper	30–44
	Cylinder Head	①
	De-gas Tube To Upper Intake Manifold	72–108⑥
	EGR Tube To EGR Valve & Exhaust Manifold	26–47
	EGR Tube Retainer To Exhaust Manifold	30–34
	EGR Valve To Upper Intake Manifold	15–22
	Engine Front Cover, Bolts 1–10	15–22
	Engine Front Cover, Bolts 11–15	72–108⑥
	Engine To Transaxle/Torque Converter Assembly	30–44
	Exhaust Manifold	15–18
	Flywheel To Crankshaft	54–64
	Front Subframe To Body	57–76
	Fuel Injection Supply Manifold To Intake Manifold	72–108⑥
	Ignition Coil Bracket	30–40
	Intake Manifold Support To RH Cylinder Head	30–40
	Intake Manifold Support To Throttle Body	72–108⑥
	Intake Manifold To Cylinder Head	15–22⑤
	Main Bearing Cap	56–62
	Oil Filter Insert To Cylinder Block	20–29
	Oil Galley & Cooling Jacket Plugs	14
	Oil Level Indicator Tube To Exhaust Manifold	12–14
	Oil Pan Drain Plug	9–11
	Oil Pan To Cylinder Block	84–120⑥
	Oil Pressure Sensor	12–16
	Oil Pump To Cylinder Block	30–40
	Power Steering Pump To Cylinder Block	30–40
	RH Exhaust Manifold Heat Shield	72–108⑥
	Spark Plug	7–15
	Throttle Cable Bracket	13
	Torque Converter	20–33
	Transmission Range Sensor	12–16
	Upper Intake Manifold To Lower Intake Manifold	15–22
	Valve Tappet Guide Plate To Cylinder Block	84–120⑥
	Water Bypass Tube	15–22

Continued

TIGHTENING SPECIFICATIONS—Continued

Year	Component	Torque/Ft. Lbs.
VIN U, 1 & 2 ENGINES		
1998–99	Water Outlet Connection To Intake Manifold	84–120⑥
	Water Pump Pulley To Hub	15–22
	Water Pump To Front Cover (No. 4–9)	15–22
	Water Pump To Front Cover (No. 11–15)	72–108⑥
	Wiring Retainer Bracket	15–22
	Y-Pipe To Exhaust Manifold	25–34
2000–02	A/C Compressor To Bracket	18
	A/C Compressor Bracket To Engine	35
	A/C Compressor Bracket Stabilizer	18
	A/C Manifold & Tube Nut	89⑥
	Accelerator Cable Bracket To Throttle Body	13
	Accessory Drive Belt Idler Pulley To Engine	35
	Accessory Drive Belt Tensioner Pulley	35
	Camshaft Position Sensor	18⑥
	Camshaft Sprocket	46
	Camshaft Synchronizer Clamp	18
	Camshaft Thrust Plate	89⑥
	Crankshaft Damper	107
	Crankshaft Pulley To Damper	35
	Cylinder Head	①
	EGR Tube, Right Exhaust	30
	EGR Tube, EGR Valve	30
	EGR Valve	18
	Engine Rear Insulator To Front Subframe	40
	Engine Rear Insulator To Transaxle Bracket	72
	Engine Rear Plate To Transaxle	9
	Engine Roll Restrictor	35
	Engine Roll Restrictor To Front Cover & Alternator	18
	Exhaust Manifold Heat Shield	89⑥
	Flywheel To Crankshaft	59
	Fuel Injection Supply Manifold To Intake Manifold	89⑥
	Halfshaft To Steering Knuckle	190
	Lower Control Arm To Steering Knuckle	59
	Oil Filter Mounting Boss	25
	Oil Pan To Cylinder Block	⑦
	Oil Pan Drain Plug	10
	Oil Pump To Crankshaft	35
	Power Steering Pressure Line To Power Steering Pump	35
	Power Steering Pump Bracket To Cylinder Head	35
	Right Engine Insulator To Front Subframe	66
	Right Engine Insulator Bracket To Transaxle	44
	Right Engine Insulator Through Bolt	89
	Secondary Air Injection Tube	30

Continued

TIGHTENING SPECIFICATIONS—Continued

Year	Component	Torque/Ft. Lbs.
VIN U, 1 & 2 ENGINES		
2000–02	Spark Plugs	11
	Starter Motor	18
	Transaxle to Engine	37
	Valve Cover To Cylinder Head	9
	Valve Tappet Guide Plate Retainer Bolts	
VIN S ENGINE		
1998–99	A/C Compressor	15–22
	Accelerator Bracket To Throttle Body	8–12
	Accessory Drive Crankshaft Pulley Bracket	15–22
	Accessory Drive Crankshaft Pulley To Damper	70–77
	Alternator	15–22
	Battery Ground Cable To Engine	15–22
	Camshaft Position Sensor	72–108⑥
	Connecting Rod	29–33③
	Crankcase Ventilation Tube	44–62⑥
	Crankshaft Damper To Crankshaft	②
	Crankshaft Position Sensor	72–108⑥
	Cylinder Head	①
	Cylinder Head Camshaft Journal Cap	72–108⑥
	Drive Belt Idler Pulley	15–22
	EGR Vacuum Regulator Solenoid	44–61⑥
	EGR Valve	15–22
	Engine To Transaxle	25–33
	Exhaust Manifold	13–16
	Flywheel To Crankshaft	54–64
	Front Axle Wheel Hub Retainer	170–202
	Front Subframe To Body	57–75
	Front Wheel Knuckles To Suspension Lower Arms	67–80
	Idle Air Control Valve	72–108⑥
	Ignition Coil	72⑥
	Lower Intake Manifold	71–106⑥
	Oil Filter Mounting Insert To Cylinder Block	20–29
	Oil Pan Baffle	15–22
	Oil Pan Drain Plug	16–22
	Oil Pan To Cylinder Block	15–22
	Oil Pan To Transaxle	25–33
	Oil Pressure Sensor	9–12
	Oil Pump Screen Cover & Tube	15–22
	Oil Pump To Cylinder Block	72–108⑥
	Oil Separator	72–108⑥
	Oxygen Sensor	26–34
	Power Steering Pump	72–108⑥
	Powertrain Control Module	32
	RH Engine Support Insulator	75–102
	Secondary Air Injection Diverter Valve Bracket	72–108⑥
	Shift Cable Bracket	15–19
	Shift Rod To Transaxle	17
	Spark Plugs	7–15

Continued

TIGHTENING SPECIFICATIONS—Continued

Year	Component	Torque/Ft. Lbs.
VIN S ENGINE		
1998–99	Stabilizer Bar To Transaxle	30–40
	Starter Motor	15–22
	Steering Shaft & Joint Bolt	18
	Thermostat Housing	72–108⑥
	Throttle Body	72–108⑥
	Tie Rod End Stud	35–46
	Timing Chain Guide	15–22
	Timing Chain Tensioner	15–22
	Torque Converter To Flywheel	20–34
	Transaxle Support Bracket	15–22
	Transmission Oil Cooler Line	18–22
	Transmission Range Sensor	12–16
	Upper Front Engine Support Insulator	50–70
	Upper Intake Manifold	72–108⑥
	Valve Cover	72–108⑥
	Water Bypass Tube	72–108⑥
	Water Pump	15–22④
	Water Pump To Housing	16–18
	Wheel Lug	95
2000–02	A/C Compressor	18
	Accessory Drive Belt Tensioner	18
	Alternator Mounting	18
	Ball Joint Nuts	59
	Camshaft Cap Bolts	89⑥
	Camshaft Position Sensor	89⑥
	Camshaft Oil Seal Retainer	89⑥
	Crankshaft Position Sensor	89⑥
	Cylinder Head Bolts	①
	EGR Tube	30
	EGR Valve Bolts	18
	Engine Mount Bolts	52
	Exhaust Manifold	15
	Flexplate Bolts	59
	Fuel Rail Bolts	89⑥
	Halfshaft Nuts	191
	Knock Sensor	13
	Left Engine Support Insulator Bolts	52
	Left Engine Support Insulator Nut	66
	Lower Intake Manifold Bolts	89⑥
	Oil Pan Bolts & Studs	18
	Oil Pan To Transaxle	30
	Oil Pump Bolts	89⑥
	Oil Separator Bolts	89⑥
	Power Steering Pressure Line Nut	27
	Power Steering Pump Bolts	18
	Right Engine Support Insulator Nut	66
	Right Engine Support Insulator Through Bolt	89
	Shifter Cable Nut	13
	Spark Plugs	11
	Steering Shaft Pinch Bolt	18
	Subframe Bolts	76
	Timing Chain Guide	18
	Timing Chain Tensioner	18

Continued

TIGHTENING SPECIFICATIONS—Continued

Year	Component	Torque/Ft. Lbs.
VIN S ENGINE		
2000–02	Torque Converter To Flex Plate	27
	Upper Intake Manifold Bolts	89⑥
	Y-Pipe Nuts	30
	Y-Pipe To Exhaust Manifold	30

① — Refer to "Cylinder Head, Replace."
② — Torque to 89 ft. lbs., then loosen one full turn. Torque 27–32 ft. lbs., then tighten an additional 85–95.°
③ — Final tighten an additional 90–120.°
④ — Final tighten an additional 85–95.°
⑤ — Final torque to 20–24 ft. lbs.
⑥ — Inch lbs.
⑦ — Refer to "Oil Pan, Replace."

3.4L Engine

NOTE: On Air Bag Equipped Models, Refer To "Air Bag System Precautions" Located In The Front Of This Manual For System Disarming & Arming Procedures.

NOTE: Refer To "Computer Relearn Procedures" Located In The Front Of This Manual When Battery Power To The Computer Has Been Interrupted.

INDEX

PRECAUTIONS

AIR BAG SYSTEMS

Refer to "Air Bag System Precautions" in the front of this manual for system disarming and arming procedures.

FUEL SYSTEM PRESSURE RELIEF

Fuel supply lines will remain pressurized for long periods of time after engine shutdown. This pressure must be relieved before any service is attempted. A valve is provided on the fuel injection supply manifold for this purpose. To relieve system pressure, proceed as follows:

1. Remove fuel tank filler cap.
2. Remove air cleaner assembly.
3. Connect pressure gauge tool No. T80L-9974-B, or equivalent, to fuel pressure relief valve.
4. Open manual valve on gauge to relieve pressure.

BATTERY GROUND CABLE

Prior to service, disconnect battery ground cable and isolate as required.

COMPRESSION PRESSURE

When inspecting cylinder compression, the lowest cylinder must be within 75 percent of the highest cylinder. Perform compression inspection with engine at normal operating temperature, spark plugs removed and throttle wide open.

ENGINE MOUNT

REPLACE

FRONT

Removal

1. Raise and support vehicle.
2. Place jack and wooden block in suitable location under engine block.
3. Remove nuts mounting lefthand and righthand front engine support insulators to subframe, **Fig. 1.**
4. Raise engine enough to unload insulators.
5. Remove remaining bolts from lefthand insulator and front support insulator.
6. Remove through bolt from righthand front support insulator and insulator from front engine support mounting bracket.

Installation

1. Attach lefthand front support insulator with two bolts. Tighten to specifications.
2. Attach righthand front support insulator to case rear bracket with one through bolt. Tighten to specifications.
3. Lower engine down onto subframe. **Prevent front engine support bracket from rotating when tightening to avoid noise, vibration and harshness conditions.**
4. Install lefthand and righthand insulator to subframe mounting nuts. Tighten to specifications.

REAR

Refer to the "3.0L (VIN S, U, 1 & 2) Engines" section for procedures.

ENGINE

REPLACE

1. Remove battery and tray.
2. Remove oil filler cap and engine appearance cover.
3. Disconnect engine control sensor wiring from engine air/fuel ratio control bracket and mass air flow sensor.
4. Disconnect air cleaner outlet tube from throttle body.
5. Release air cleaner cover.
6. Disconnect crankcase ventilation hose from air cleaner outlet tube.
7. Remove air cleaner and outlet tube as an assembly.
8. Remove windshield wiper module.
9. Remove main vacuum connector mounting nuts and supply hose from connector.
10. Remove wiper motor connector and grommet from cowl top extension and remove extension.
11. Remove accelerator cable splash shield.
12. Disconnect speed control and accelerator cables from throttle body.

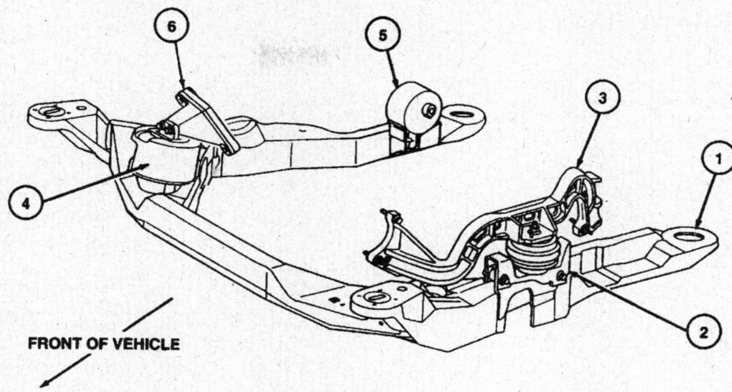

Item	Description
1	Front Sub-Frame
2	Engine and Transmission Support Insulator
3	Rear Engine Support Bracket

Item	Description
4	Front Engine Support Insulator, LH
5	Front Engine Support Insulator, RH
6	Front Engine Support Bracket

FM1069600599000X

Fig. 1 Engine & transaxle mounts

13. Remove speed control and accelerator cable mounting bolts, and position cables aside.
14. Disconnect main engine control harness connector and transaxle range sensor connector.
15. Position transaxle shift cable and bracket aside.
16. Remove power steering reservoir cap.
17. Drain engine coolant and oil into suitable containers.
18. Raise and support vehicle.
19. Disconnect power steering return hose from lefthand end of steering fluid cooler, allowing fluid to drain into a suitable container.
20. Disconnect upper fluid cooler tube from lefthand end of transaxle fluid cooler, allow fluid to drain into a suitable container.
21. Disconnect upper fluid cooler tube from lefthand rubber line.
22. Lower vehicle to ground.
23. Disconnect heater water hose at heater water tubes.
24. Disconnect canister purge valve vacuum hose.
25. Disconnect main vacuum hose at intake manifold.
26. Disconnect engine control sensor wiring from powertrain control module bracket.
27. Remove engine ground strap bolt and position strap aside.
28. Disconnect engine control sensor wiring from canister purge valve solenoid.
29. Relieve fuel pressure as outlined under "Precautions."
30. Disconnect fuel supply and return tubes from fuel injection supply manifold.
31. Disconnect power steering pump to reservoir hose at pump.
32. Disconnect de-gas tubes from radiator recovery reservoir.
33. Recover A/C as outlined under "Air Conditioning."
34. Disconnect engine control sensor wiring connector from A/C pressure cutoff switch.
35. Loosen A/C manifold to compressor mounting bolt.
36. Disconnect A/C pressure cutoff switch from compressor and position aside.
37. Disconnect upper radiator hose at water pump.
38. Disconnect lower radiator hose at water pump and position aside.
39. Disconnect battery to starter relay cable, remove mounting nut and move cable aside.
40. Remove front wheels.
41. Disconnect catalyst monitor sensors and heated oxygen sensor.
42. Remove dual three-way converter and pipe.
43. Disconnect battery cable at alternator.
44. Disconnect ride level sensors at front suspension lower arm.
45. Remove stabilizer bar link to front suspension mounting nuts.
46. Disconnect tie rod end from knuckle.
47. Remove wheel hub mounting nuts.
48. Disconnect ball joints from suspension lower arm.
49. Position knuckle and shock absorber assemblies aside.
50. Secure drive axle shafts to subframe.
51. Remove four flexplate to torque converter nuts.
52. Remove lower four transaxle to engine block bolts.
53. Remove steering column pinch bolt from intermediate shaft coupling and separate coupling from steering gear.
54. Support front subframe, engine, and transaxle assembly with Rotunda powertrain lift tool No. 014-00765 and universal powertrain removal bracket tool No. 014-00766, or equivalents.
55. Remove subframe mounting bolts.
56. Lower engine, transaxle and subframe.
57. Disconnect engine control sensor wiring connector from secondary air injection pump.
58. Disconnect engine control sensor wiring connector from transaxle and transaxle speed sensor.
59. Disconnect engine control sensor wiring connector from power steering pressure switch.
60. Remove power steering lefthand turn pressure hose mounting nut at power steering pump and move hose aside.
61. Remove upper engine block to transaxle bolts.
62. Remove righthand front drive axle assembly.
63. Remove righthand front engine support insulator bracket mounting bolts.
64. Remove lefthand front upper engine support insulator to bracket bolts.
65. Lift engine from transaxle.
66. Reverse procedure to install.

INTAKE MANIFOLD

REPLACE

UPPER

1. Relieve fuel system pressure as outlined under "Precautions."
2. Remove engine appearance cover.
3. Remove righthand half of cowl vent screen.
4. Remove throttle body.
5. Disconnect main emission vacuum supply hose from surge tank fitting and EGR valve, and position hose aside.
6. Disconnect vacuum tube from manifold vacuum union.
7. Remove transducer mounting bracket from surge tank and position bracket aside.
8. Remove manifold supports from surge tank and cylinder head.
9. Remove EGR valve.
10. Remove mounting bolts and tank stays from front and rear of surge tank.
11. Remove radio ignition capacitor bracket and position capacitor aside.
12. **Remove intake manifold mounting bolts in an alternating sequence.**
13. Reverse procedure to install. Tighten manifold mounting bolts in an alternating sequence to specifications.

LOWER

1. Remove upper intake manifold as outlined under "Upper Intake Manifold."
2. Disconnect fuel injection supply and return lines from supply manifold.
3. Disconnect intake manifold runner control deactivation cable.
4. Remove deactivation cable from bracket and position aside.
5. Disconnect engine control sensor wiring from injectors and wiring retainers, and move wiring out of way.
6. Remove supply manifold and injectors from lower intake manifold.
7. Remove manifold to cylinder head bolts in an alternating sequence and manifold.
8. Reverse procedure to install, noting the following:
   a. Ensure intake manifold runner control plate operates properly.
   b. Tighten manifold mounting bolts in an alternating sequence to specifications.

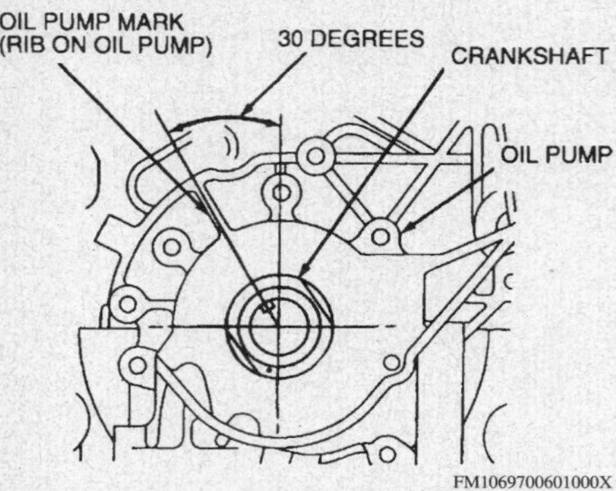

Fig. 2 Crankshaft & oil pump timing mark alignment

EXHAUST MANIFOLD

REPLACE

LEFTHAND SIDE

1. Raise and support vehicle.
2. Remove dual converter Y-pipe and lower exhaust manifold mounting nuts.
3. Lower vehicle, and remove secondary air injection manifold tube and heat shield from manifold.
4. Remove oil dipstick tube mounting bolt.
5. Remove upper manifold mounting nuts.
6. Remove manifold and gasket.
7. Reverse procedure to install. Tighten fasteners to specifications.

RIGHTHAND SIDE

1. Remove secondary air injection manifold tube from manifold.
2. Remove heat shield.
3. Raise and support vehicle.
4. Remove EGR valve to manifold tube from manifold.
5. Disconnect EGR valve to manifold tube from EGR transducer.
6. Remove dual converter Y-pipe and lower manifold mounting nuts.
7. Lower vehicle and remove manifold heat shield.
8. Remove upper manifold mounting nuts.
9. Remove manifold and gasket.
10. Reverse procedure to install. Tighten all fasteners to specifications.

CYLINDER HEAD

REPLACE

1. Remove engine as outlined under "Engine, Replace," and mount on suitable stand.
2. Remove accessory drive belt.
3. Remove A/C compressor, alternator and alternator bracket.
4. Remove water pump drive belt.
5. Remove water pump drive pulley from lefthand intake camshaft.
6. Disconnect main emission vacuum supply hose from surge tank fitting, air injection diverter valve and EGR valve.
7. Disconnect engine control sensor wiring from EGR backpressure transducer, EGR vacuum regulator solenoid and secondary vacuum valve.
8. Remove transducer mounting bolts from surge tank.
9. Disconnect EGR pressure sensor valve hoses from EGR valve to exhaust manifold tube and remove transducer mounting bracket.
10. Remove EGR valve to exhaust manifold tube from EGR valve and exhaust manifold.
11. Remove intake manifold supports from surge tank and cylinder head, and surge tank.
12. Disconnect engine control sensor wiring connections from idle air control valve and throttle position sensor.
13. Remove water bypass hose from throttle body.
14. Remove idle air control valve and gasket, and throttle body from engine air inlet connector.
15. Remove upper intake manifold.
16. Disconnect engine control sensor wiring from the following components:
    a. Water temperature sending units.
    b. Ignition coils.
    c. Radio ignition capacitor.
    d. Fuel injectors.
    e. Camshaft and crankshaft position sensors.
    f. Oil pressure sending unit.
    g. Engine control sensor extension wiring.
    h. Intake manifold runner control deactivation motor.
17. Remove engine control sensor wiring from engine assembly.
18. Remove exhaust air supply tube from exhaust manifolds and secondary air injection diverter valve.
19. Remove secondary air injection diverter valve from exhaust air supply valve mounting bracket.
20. Remove exhaust manifolds.
21. Remove lower intake manifolds.
22. Remove upper radiator hose from water crossover.
23. Remove water crossover from righthand cylinder head.
24. Remove oil cooler to water pump hoses at water pump.
25. Remove water pump.
26. Remove valve covers.
27. Remove spark plugs.
28. Remove power steering pump pulley, pump, and pump support.
29. Remove crankshaft pulley using steering wheel puller tool No. T67L-3600-A, or equivalent.
30. Remove camshaft and crankshaft position sensors.
31. Remove crankshaft front seal from engine front cover using locknut pin remover tool No. T78P-3504-N, or equivalent.
32. Remove engine front cover.
33. Remove crankshaft position sensor pulse ring from crankshaft.
34. Rotate crankshaft to place number one piston at top dead center by aligning crankshaft keyway groove with oil pump mark, **Fig. 2.**
35. Ensure camshaft sprocket timing marks are on top, and if not, rotate crankshaft one complete revolution.

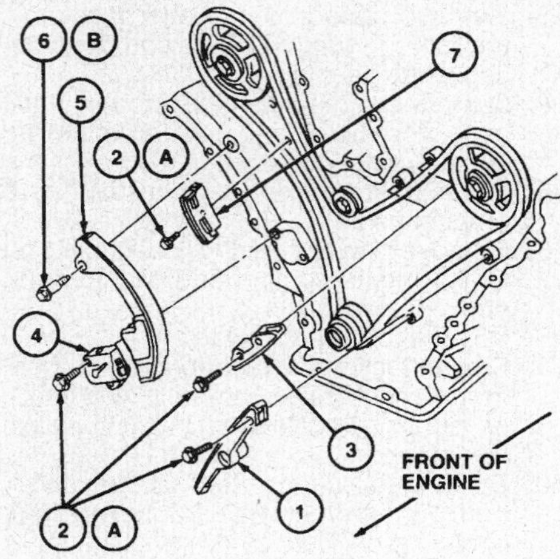

Item	Description
1	Timing Chain Guide
2	Timing Chain/Belt Tensioner Bolt (6 Req'd)
3	Timing Chain Guide, LH
4	Timing Chain Tensioner
5	Timing Chain Tensioner Arm
6	Timing Chain Tensioner Pivot Bolt
7	Timing Chain Guide
A	Tighten to 18-27 N·m (14-19 Lb-Ft)
B	Tighten to 34-53 N·m (25-39 Lb-Ft)

FM1069700602000X

Fig. 3 Timing chain guide & tensioner

36. Remove timing chain guides, tensioner arm and tensioner, **Fig. 3.**
37. Using a small screwdriver, release tensioner ratchet/pawl mechanism through tensioner access hole.
38. Compress tensioner rack and piston into tensioner housing by inserting a small wire into top of piston, and gently unseat oil check ball. **Compress tensioner by hand and leave in a compressed state for installation purposes.**
39. While tensioner is compressed, insert a .060 inch drill bit or wire into small hole above ratchet. This engages lock groove in rack of tensioner, **Fig. 4.**
40. Remove balance shaft driven gear and sprocket key from dynamic balance shaft.
41. Remove balance shaft thrust plate from engine block.
42. Thread balance shaft replacer tool No. T96P-6A333-AH, or equivalent, into balance shaft.
43. Thread impact slide hammer tool No. T50T-100-A, or equivalent, into replacer, and pull shaft and front bearing out.
44. Thread impact slide hammer into replacer and insert remover through inside diameter of rear bearing, and pull rear bearing out.
45. Remove timing chain sprocket tensioners from cylinder heads.
46. **Note camshaft journal caps and cylinder head numbering. This will ensure caps are returned to their**

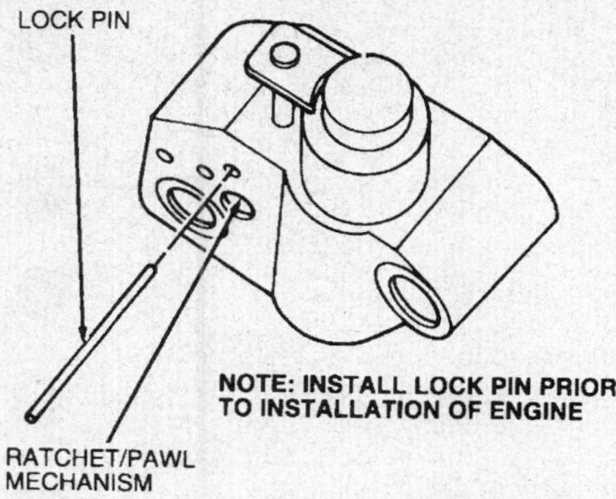

Fig. 4 Tensioner lock pin installation

original locations.

47. **Remove camshaft journal thrust caps first.**
48. Loosen remaining journal cap bolts in sequence, **Fig. 5.**
49. Remove camshafts.
50. Remove timing chain crankshaft sprocket.
51. Remove cylinder head mounting bolts and washers in sequence, **Fig. 6.**
52. Reverse procedure to install, noting the following:
    a. Install new torque-to-yield cylinder head bolts.
    b. **Torque** cylinder head bolts to 20–23 ft. lbs. in sequence, **Fig. 7,** then tighten an additional 85–95.°
    c. **Ensure No. 1 piston is at top dead center, Fig. 2.**
    d. Apply a .08–.11 inch bead of silicone gasket and sealant part No. F6AZ-19562-AA, or equivalent, to lefthand cylinder head intake camshaft journal cap.
    e. Install camshaft journal caps in their original locations and loosely install mounting bolts.
    f. **Torque** journal cap bolts to 60–108 inch lbs. in sequence, **Fig. 8,** then to 12–15 ft. lbs.

VALVE COVER

REPLACE

1. Remove engine appearance cover.
2. Remove righthand half of cowl vent screen.
3. Disconnect main emission vacuum supply hose from surge tank fitting, air injection diverter valve and EGR valve.
4. Disconnect vacuum tube from intake manifold vacuum union.
5. Disconnect EGR valve to exhaust manifold tube from bottom of EGR valve.
6. Position power steering lefthand turn pressure hose aside.
7. Position transducer mounting bracket aside.
8. Remove surge tank.
9. Remove ignition coils.
10. Remove radio ignition capacitor mounting nut.
11. Disconnect crankcase ventilation tube from valve cover.

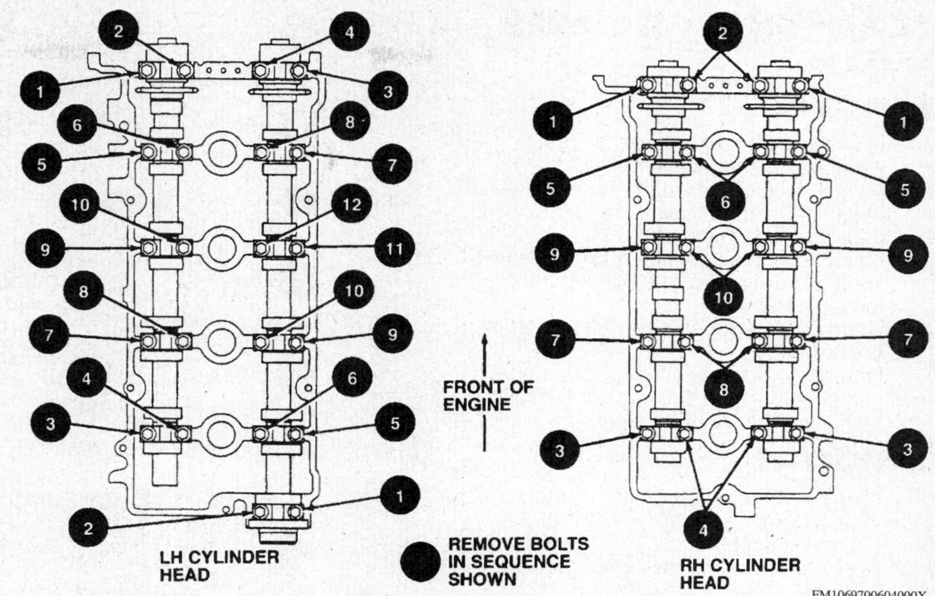

Fig. 5 Camshaft journal cap bolt loosening sequence

12. Position engine control sensor wiring aside.
13. Remove valve cover bolts and cover.
14. Reverse procedure to install, noting the following:
    a. Clean cover sealing surfaces with a shop towel and metal surface cleaner part No. F4AZ-19A536-RA, or equivalent.
    b. Apply a .31 inch diameter bead of silicone rubber sealer part No. F4AZ-19562-B, or equivalent, on cover sealing surfaces where engine front cover and cylinder heads contact.
    c. The old gasket may be used again if it is not damaged.
    d. Position cover on cylinder head within six minutes of sealer application.

CAMSHAFT LOBE LIFT SPECIFICATIONS

Exhaust .... .335 inch
Intake .... .323 inch

VALVE CLEARANCE SPECIFICATIONS

To inspect valve clearances, proceed as follows:

1. **Camshaft lobes must be directed 90° or more away from valve lifters.**
2. Insert feeler gauge at 90° angle to camshaft.
3. Ensure intake valve clearance at room temperature is .006–.010 inch.
4. Ensure exhaust valve clearance at room temperature is .010–.014 inch.

VALVE ADJUSTMENT

Because hydraulic valve lifters are used in this engine, no periodic valve adjustment is required. However, should any valve train components be replaced or intermixed, clearances on those valves must be inspected and corrected. To adjust valve clearances, proceed as follows:

1. Insert lifter compressor tool No. T89P-6500-A, or equivalent, under camshaft next to lobe and rotate down to depress bucket valve lifter, **Fig. 9.**
2. Insert lifter holder tool No. T96P-6500-AH, or equivalent, and remove compressor tool, **Fig. 10.**
3. Direct a jet of compressed air toward hole in face of valve adjusting spacer to lift spacer off lifter. **Wear eye protection during this procedure.**
4. Determine size of adjusting spacer by numbers on bottom face of spacer or by measuring with micrometer. Install spacer that will provide needed clearance.
5. Install new spacer with numbers facing down.
6. Repeat procedure for each valve by rotating crankshaft as needed.
7. After all valves have been inspected, ensure spacers are fully seated in their lifters.

HYDRAULIC LIFTERS

REPLACE

1. Remove camshafts as outlined under "Cylinder Head, Replace."
2. Remove lifters and valve adjusting spacers.
3. Reverse procedure to install, noting the following:
    a. Lubricate lifters and valve adjusting spacers with engine assembly lubricant part No. D9AZ-19579-D, or equivalent, prior to installation.
    b. Install lifters in their original locations, with valve adjusting spacer numbered sides facing down.

CRANKSHAFT DAMPER

REPLACE

REMOVAL

1. Raise and support vehicle on hoist.
2. Remove righthand front wheel.
3. Remove forward righthand splash shield from front fender apron to access crankshaft damper.
4. Remove accessory drive belt as outlined under "Separated Accessory Drive System."
5. Remove damper bolt and washer from crankshaft.
6. Remove damper from crankshaft using steering wheel puller tool No. T67L-3600-A, or equivalent.

INSTALLATION

1. Clean sealing surfaces with metal surface cleaner part No. F4AZ-19A536-RA, or equivalent.
2. Apply black silicone rubber part No. F4AZ-19562-B, or equivalent, to front of crankshaft on inside diameter surface of damper at keyway.
3. Install damper using vibration damper and seal replacer tool No. T82L-6316-A, or equivalent, and crankshaft damper bolt washer.
4. Install mounting bolt and tighten as follows:
   a. **Torque** bolt to 78–99 ft. lbs.
   b. Loosen bolt at least one full turn.
   c. **Torque** bolt to 35–39 ft. lbs.
   d. Rotate bolt an additional 85–95.°
5. Install drive belt and splash shield.

FRONT COVER

REPLACE

1. Remove front cover assembly, **Fig. 11.**
2. Clean cover to engine block and cylinder head sealing surfaces with metal surface cleaner part No. F4AZ-19A536-RA, or equivalent.
3. Apply a .118 inch bead of black silicone rubber part No. F4AZ-19562-B, or equivalent, in eight gasket surface joints and five mounting bosses on engine block, **Fig. 12.**
4. Install front cover with bolts and stud bolts in proper locations, **Fig. 13.**
5. Tighten bolts in sequence, **Fig. 14.**

FRONT COVER SEAL

REPLACE

1. Remove engine front cover as outlined under "Front Cover, Replace."
2. Remove crankshaft front seal using locknut pin remover tool No. T78P-3504-N, or equivalent.
3. Reverse procedure to install, noting the following:
   a. Install new seal using vibration damper and seal replacer tool No. T82L-6316-A, or equivalent.

TIMING CHAIN

REPLACE

1. Remove engine front cover as outlined under"Front Cover, Replace."

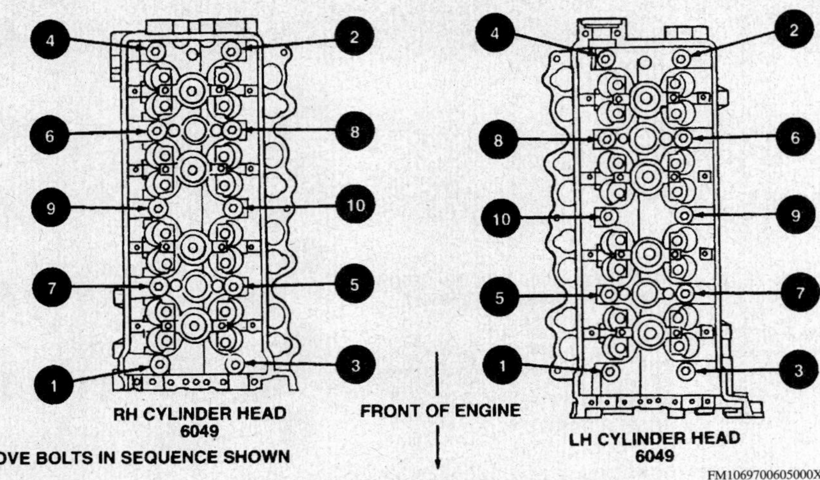

Fig. 6 Cylinder head bolt loosening sequence

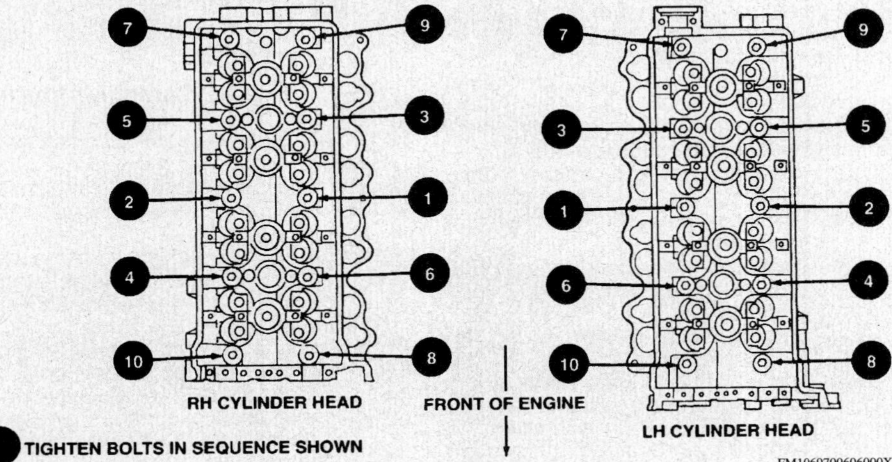

Fig. 7 Cylinder head bolt tightening sequence

2. Rotate crankshaft to place number one piston at top dead center by aligning crankshaft keyway groove with oil pump mark, **Fig. 2.**
3. Ensure camshaft sprocket timing marks are on top, and if not, rotate crankshaft one complete revolution.
4. Using a small screwdriver, release tensioner ratchet/pawl mechanism through tensioner access hole.
5. Compress tensioner rack and piston into tensioner housing by inserting a small wire into top of piston, and gently unseat oil check ball. **Compress tensioner by hand, and leave in a compressed state for future installation.**
6. While tensioner is compressed, insert a .060 inch drill bit or wire into small hole above ratchet. This engages lock groove in rack of tensioner, **Fig. 4.**
7. Remove timing chain.
8. Reverse procedure to install, noting following:
   a. Ensure number one cylinder piston is in top dead center position.
   b. Timing chain and sprocket marks must be properly aligned, **Fig. 15.**

CAMSHAFT

REPLACE

Refer to "Cylinder Head, Replace" for camshaft removal and installation procedure.

PISTON & ROD ASSEMBLY

Assemble piston with its front mark, **Fig. 16**, aligned with the connecting rod's front mark. These markings must also face the front of the engine on installation.

Torque new torque-to-yield connecting rod cap bolts in several alternating passes to 30–33 ft. lbs., then rotate an additional 90–120.° After installation, ensure big end side clearance is .006–.012 inch. Maximum service limit is .0137 inch.

MAIN & ROD BEARINGS

Main bearings are available in standard sizes and undersizes of .001 and .002 inch.

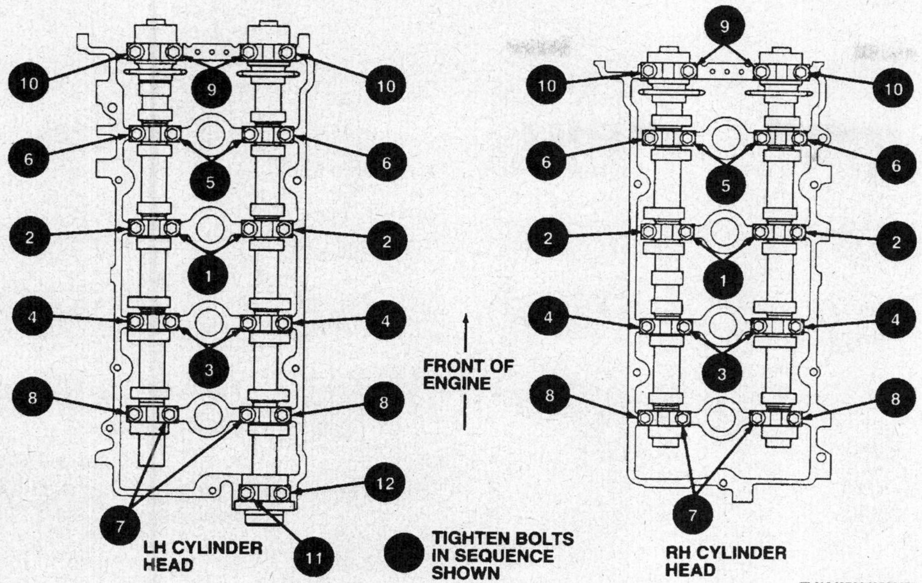

Fig. 8 Camshaft journal cap bolt tightening sequence

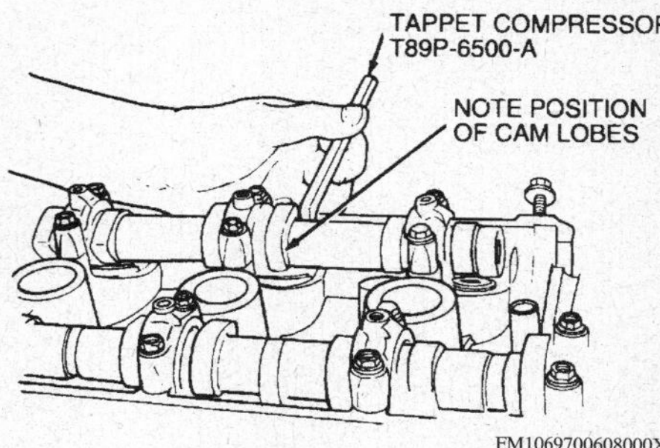

Fig. 9 Valve lifter depression

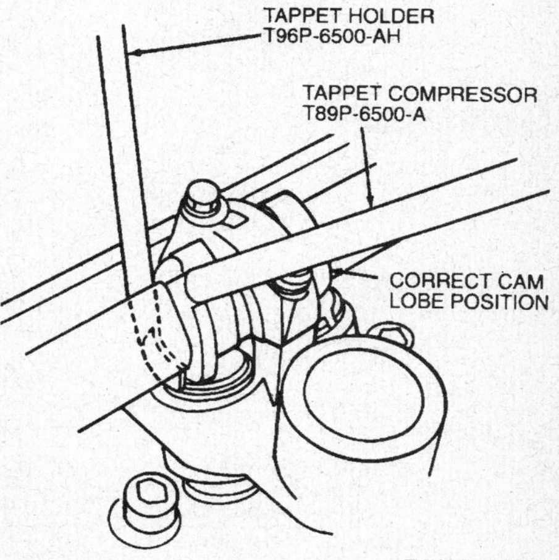

Fig. 10 Lifter holder tool insertion

CRANKSHAFT REAR OIL SEAL

REPLACE

REMOVAL

This engine uses a one-piece crankshaft rear seal, which must be replaced with the same type. The complete seal is replaceable without removing the crankshaft.

1. Remove transaxle assembly as outlined in "Automatic Transmissions/ Transaxles" chapter.
2. Remove flexplate.
3. Position seal remover tool No. T95P-6701-EH, or equivalent, on end of crankshaft, and rotate tool clockwise to thread remover into seal lip until tight.
4. Install impact slide hammer tool No. T50T-100-A, or equivalent, into remover and pull seal from engine block.

INSTALLATION

1. Clean and inspect all sealing surfaces.
2. Lubricate crankshaft flange and oil seal bore with engine assembly lubricant part No. D9AZ-19579-D, or equivalent.
3. Install new seal using seal replacer tool No. T82L-6701-A, and adapter tool No. T91P-6701-A, or equivalents.
4. Tighten bolts in an alternating sequence to evenly seat seal. Ensure seal is flush to rear of block or does not protrude more than .020 inch.

OIL PAN

REPLACE

1. Raise and support vehicle.
2. Drain engine oil into a suitable container.
3. Remove dual converter Y-pipe.
4. Remove oil pan mounting bolts from transaxle housing and engine block, then pan.
5. Reverse procedure to install, noting the following:
   a. After cleaning all sealing surfaces with metal surface cleaner part No. F4AZ-19A536-RA, or equivalent, apply a .16 inch thickness bead of black silicone rubber part No. F4AZ-19562-B, or equivalent, to surfaces where pan, front cover and block meet.
   b. Tighten oil pan bolts to specifications in sequence, **Fig. 17.**
   c. Tighten oil drain plug to specifications.

OIL PUMP

REPLACE

1. Remove timing chain as outlined under "Timing Chain, Replace."
2. Remove oil pump screen cover and tube from pump.
3. Remove mounting nuts and oil pan baffle from lower engine block mounting studs.
4. Remove oil pump mounting bolts in sequence, **Fig. 18.**
5. Carefully remove pump from block.
6. Reverse procedure to install, noting following:
   a. Rotate oil pump inner rotor to align with flat on crankshaft.
   b. Carefully install pump onto crankshaft until seated against engine block.
   c. Tighten pump mounting bolts to specifications in sequence, **Fig. 19.**

OIL PUMP SERVICE

This type of oil pump has no serviceable internal components. If any component does not meet specifications, the entire pump must be replaced.

1. Wash all parts in suitable solvent and dry with compressed air.
2. Ensure all dirt and particles are removed.
3. Inspect inner pump housing for wear or damage.
4. Inspect pump cover mating surface for wear. Scuff marks are normal. If surface is worn or grooved, replace pump assembly.
5. Inspect rotor for nicks, burrs or score marks, and remove imperfections with suitable oil stone.
6. Using a suitable feeler gauge, measure inner tip to outer rotor tip clearance. Clearance should be .0024–.0071 inch.
7. Using a suitable straightedge and feeler gauge, measure rotor endplay. Endplay should be .0012–.0035 inch.
8. If any clearance does not meet specifications, replace oil pump assembly.

BELT TENSION DATA

On these models, belt tension is automatically maintained by the tensioner assembly and no adjustment is required.

SEPARATED ACCESSORY DRIVE SYSTEM

BELT ROUTING

Refer to **Figs. 20 and 21** for drive belt routing.

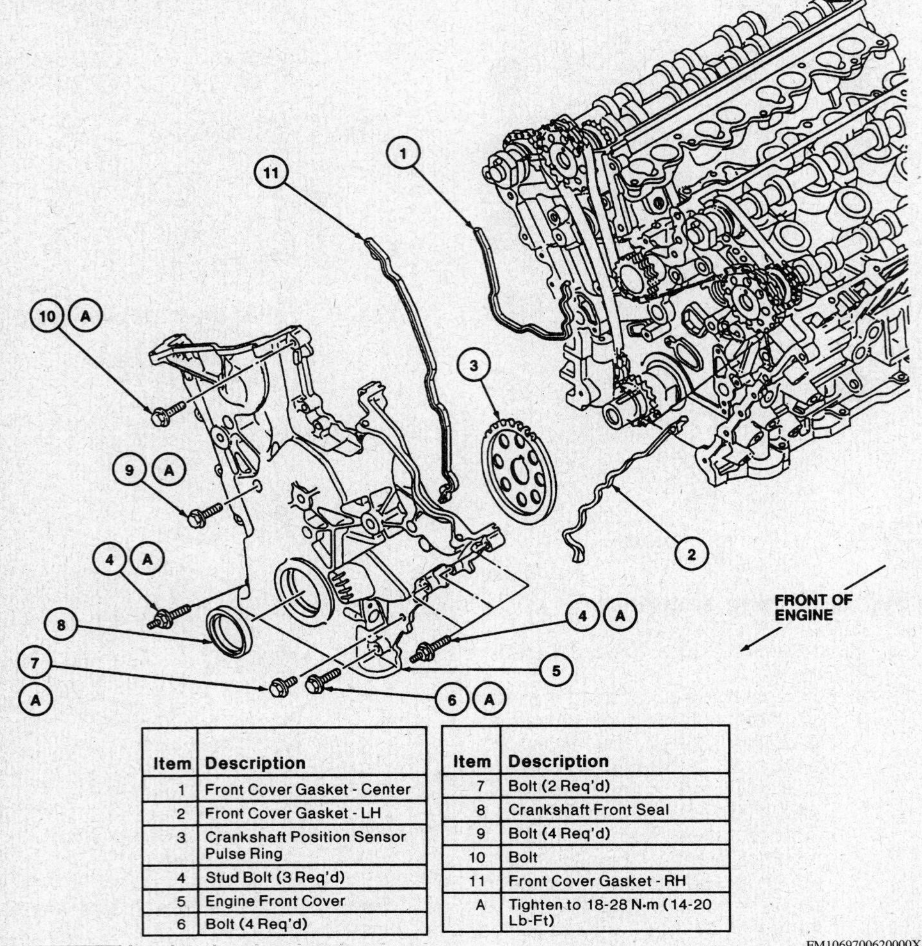

Item	Description
1	Front Cover Gasket - Center
2	Front Cover Gasket - LH
3	Crankshaft Position Sensor Pulse Ring
4	Stud Bolt (3 Req'd)
5	Engine Front Cover
6	Bolt (4 Req'd)

Item	Description
7	Bolt (2 Req'd)
8	Crankshaft Front Seal
9	Bolt (4 Req'd)
10	Bolt
11	Front Cover Gasket - RH
A	Tighten to 18-28 N-m (14-20 Lb-Ft)

FM1069700620000X

Fig. 11 Engine front cover removal

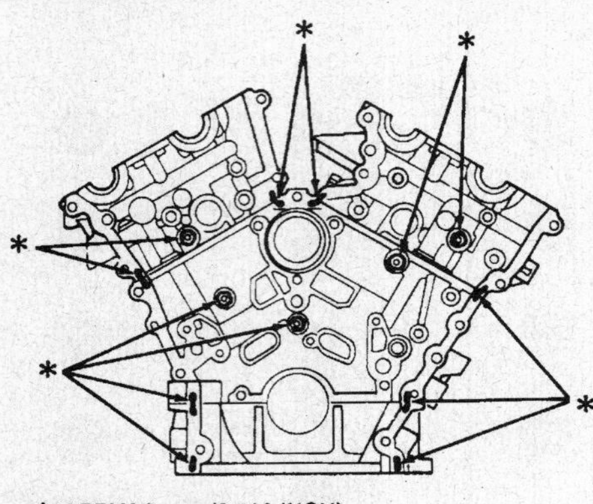

* APPLY 3 mm (0.118 INCH) BEAD OF SEALANT MEETING FORD SPECIFICATIONS (WSE-M4G321-A1) PRIOR TO INSTALLATION

FM1069700611000X

Fig. 12 Engine front cover sealer locations

BELT REPLACEMENT

Accessory Drive Belt

1. Raise and support vehicle.
2. Use a 3/8 inch ratchet on lifting lug to rotate tensioner counterclockwise and engage spring keeper.
3. Remove belt from tensioner.
4. Lower vehicle and remove belt.
5. Reverse procedure to install, noting the following:
   a. Install belt over all pulleys except tensioner.
   b. Raise and support vehicle.
   c. Rotate tensioner and install belt. Ensure V-grooves make proper contact with pulleys and spring keeper has released.

Water Pump Drive Belt

1. Rotate belt tensioner clockwise by hand and remove belt from tensioner.
2. Remove belt from water pump pulley.
3. Reverse procedure to install. Ensure V-grooves make proper contact with pulleys.

COOLING SYSTEM BLEED

1. Select maximum blower motor and heater temperature settings. Set controls to discharge air through instrument panel A/C vents.
2. Start engine and allow it to idle. Feel for hot air at A/C vents.
3. **If air discharge remains cool and engine coolant temperature gauge does not move, coolant level is low and must be corrected. Stop engine and allow it to cool. Add coolant to bring level to top of Cold Fill mark on de-gas bottle.**
4. Start engine and allow it to idle until operating temperature is reached. Hot air should now blow through A/C vents, temperature gauge should rest in Normal range and upper radiator hose should feel hot to touch.
5. Stop engine, allow it to cool and inspect for leaks.
6. When engine coolant level indicator flashes, approximately 1–1½ quarts of coolant may now be added to de-gas bottle after proper refill.

THERMOSTAT

REPLACE

1. Raise and support vehicle.
2. Drain coolant into a suitable container until level is below that of thermostat.
3. Disconnect lower radiator hose from thermostat housing.
4. Remove battery, power distribution box and battery tray.
5. Disconnect upper radiator hose and position aside.
6. Disconnect lower radiator hose at thermostat housing.
7. Remove mounting bolts and thermostat housing.
8. Remove O-ring seal and thermostat.
9. Reverse procedure to install, noting the following:
   a. Tighten thermostat housing bolts in an alternating sequence to specifications.
   b. Fill de-gas bottle until coolant reaches minimum cold fill level.

WATER PUMP

REPLACE

1. Raise and support vehicle.
2. Drain coolant into a suitable container.
3. Remove engine appearance cover.
4. Remove battery and battery tray.
5. Remove drive belt from water pump and pump pulley.
6. Disconnect throttle body supply and return hoses, heater core return hose and oil cooler hose from water pump.
7. Remove thermostat from water pump housing.
8. Remove bolts and collar mounting water pump housing from lefthand cylinder head.
9. Disconnect water inlet and outlet hoses from water pump, and remove water pump.
10. Remove mounting bolt and belt idler pulley from pump housing.
11. Reverse procedure to install, noting the following:
    a. Tighten all fasteners to specifications.
    b. Fill de-gas bottle until coolant reaches minimum cold fill level.

RADIATOR

REPLACE

1. Remove battery and tray.

2. Remove engine appearance cover.
3. Raise and support vehicle.
4. Drain coolant into a suitable container.
5. Remove lower radiator hose shield.
6. Disconnect lower radiator hose at radiator.
7. Disconnect lower transaxle cooler tube from radiator using fuel line disconnect tool No. T90T-9550-S, or equivalent.
8. Remove lower radiator mounts.
9. Remove front bumper cover.
10. Lower vehicle, remove hood latch support bolts and position support aside.
11. Disconnect upper radiator hose and overflow hose at radiator.
12. Remove power distribution box, harness and bracket, and position box and harness aside.
13. Remove upper radiator support.
14. Remove engine control sensor wiring mounting screws and position wiring aside.
15. Disconnect engine cooling fans from sensor wiring.
16. Remove nut from power steering/transaxle cooler bracket.
17. Remove three bolts and one stud nut from A/C condenser core.
18. Position condenser core forward and secure it with mechanic's wire.
19. Disconnect upper transaxle oil cooler tube from radiator using fuel line disconnect tool No. T90T-9550-S, or equivalent.
20. Remove lower radiator brackets.
21. Lower radiator two inches.
22. Tilt radiator forward and lift it clear of vehicle.
23. Reverse procedure to install, noting the following:
    a. Tighten both lower radiator brackets and hood latch support assembly bolts to specifications.
    b. Fill de-gas bottle until coolant reaches minimum cold fill level.

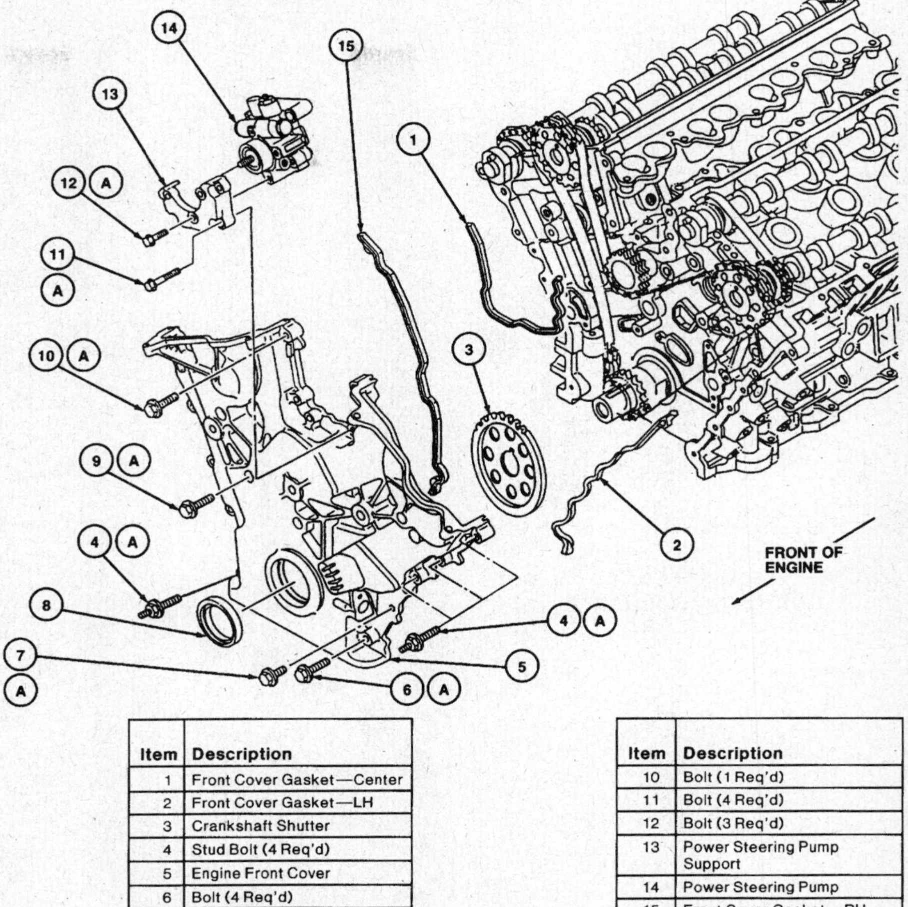

Item	Description
1	Front Cover Gasket—Center
2	Front Cover Gasket—LH
3	Crankshaft Shutter
4	Stud Bolt (4 Req'd)
5	Engine Front Cover
6	Bolt (4 Req'd)
7	Bolt (2 Req'd)
8	Crankshaft Front Seal
9	Bolt (4 Req'd)

Item	Description
10	Bolt (1 Req'd)
11	Bolt (4 Req'd)
12	Bolt (3 Req'd)
13	Power Steering Pump Support
14	Power Steering Pump
15	Front Cover Gasket—RH
A	Tighten to 18-28 N.m (14-20 Lb-Ft)

FM1069700621000X

Fig. 13 Engine front cover installation

FUEL PUMP

REPLACE

REMOVAL

On these models, the fuel pump is incorporated into the fuel tank sending unit and must be replaced as a complete assembly.

1. Relieve fuel system pressure as outlined under "Precautions."
2. Raise and support vehicle.
3. Drain fuel tank through filler pipe.
4. Remove vent hose clamps at metal lines and hoses.
5. Using fuel line disconnect tool No. T90T-9550-S, or equivalent, disconnect rear fuel supply and vapor tubes at push-connect fittings for fuel filter and base, and fuel tube retainer behind fuel filter and base.
6. Disconnect tank electrical connector at lefthand side of filter and base.
7. Disconnect push-connect fitting at upper righthand rear corner of tank.
8. Place a safety stand under tank and remove bolts at rear of safety straps, allowing straps to swing out of way.
9. **On flexible fuel vehicles,** remove plastic shield and fuel tank as an assembly.
10. **On all models,** lower tank safely to ground.
11. Place tank on workbench and clean any accumulated dirt around fuel pump module mounting flange.
12. Turn retainer ring counterclockwise using fuel tank sender wrench tool No. T74P-9275-A, or equivalent, and remove ring.
13. Pull module sender plate up out of tank until locking tabs are accessible.
14. Squeeze locking tabs together and remove module from tank.

INSTALLATION

1. Apply a light coating of premium long-life grease part No. XG-1-C, or an equivalent, meeting Ford specification ESA-M1C75-BA, on a new O-ring seal to hold in place during assembly.
2. Install O-ring into groove.
3. Install fuel module carefully into tank so that filter, hoses and float rod do not bind. When module is engaged, a distinct click will sound, and two outside locking tabs will engage into retainer.
4. Install tank into vehicle, add at least 10 gallons of fuel and inspect for leaks.
5. Install MFI fuel pressure gauge tool No. T80L-9974-B, or equivalent, as outlined in "Fuel System Pressure Relief" procedure under "Precautions."
6. Turn ignition to Run position for three seconds at least five to ten times until gauge reads at least 30 psi.

FUEL FILTER

REPLACE

1. Relieve fuel system pressure as outlined under "Precautions."
2. Twist push connect fittings at each end of filter until they move freely on tube.
3. Bend and break shipping tab from hairpin clip, and spread two clip legs approximately ⅛ inch.
4. Remove clip from tube and fitting by pulling gently on triangular end.
5. Separate fitting and hose assembly from fuel filter.
6. Install retainer clips in each connect fitting.
7. Loosen worm gear mounting clip and remove filter from bracket.
8. Reverse procedure to install.

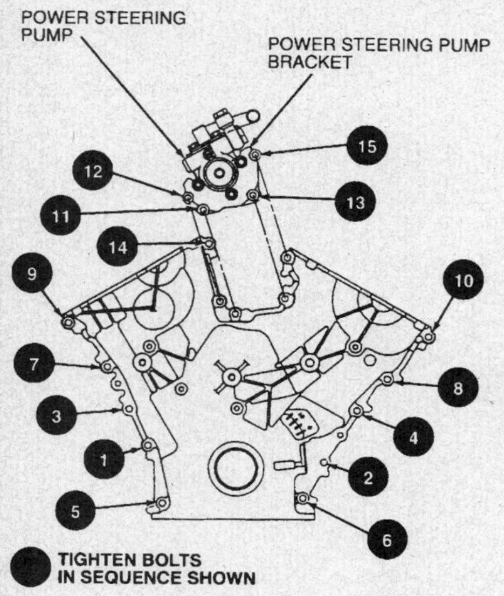

Fig. 14 Engine front cover bolt tightening sequence

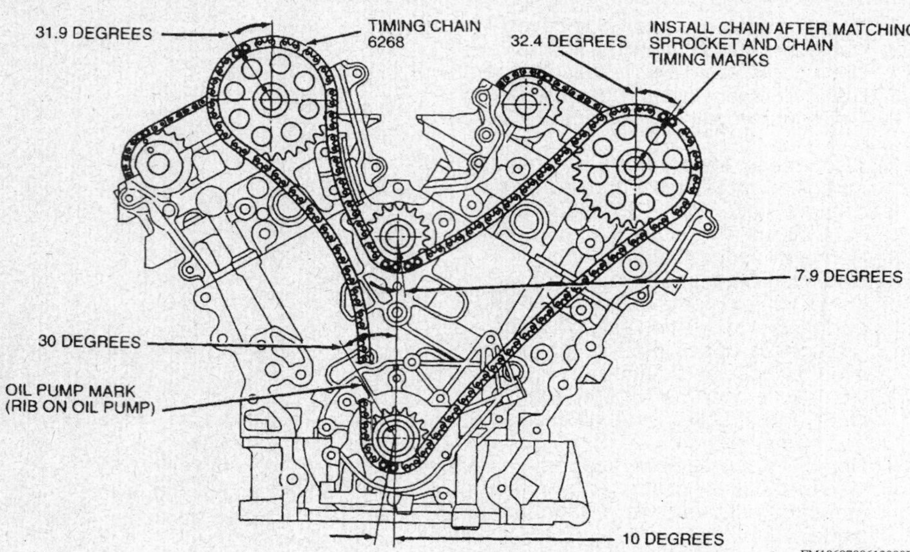

Fig. 15 Timing mark alignment

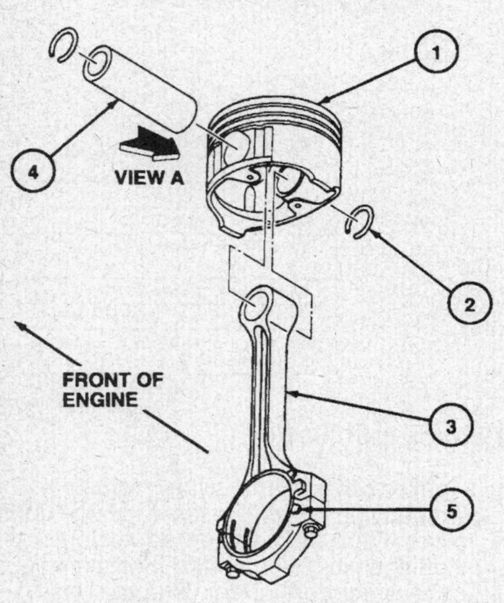

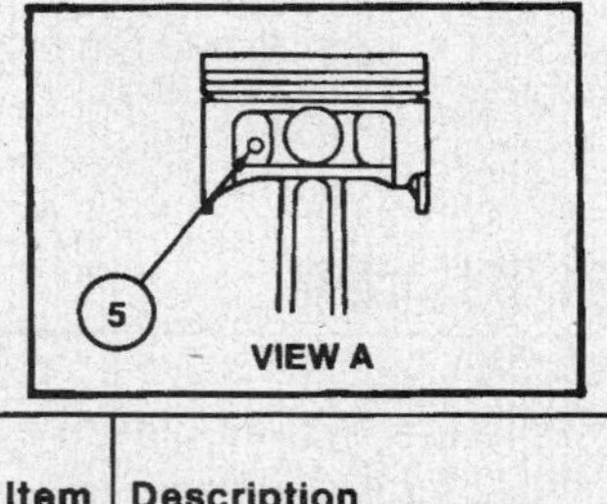

Item	Description
1	Piston, Pin and Ring
2	Piston Pin Retainer (2 Req'd)
3	Connecting Rod
4	Piston Pin
5	Front Mark

FM1069700614000X

Fig. 16 Piston & rod assembly

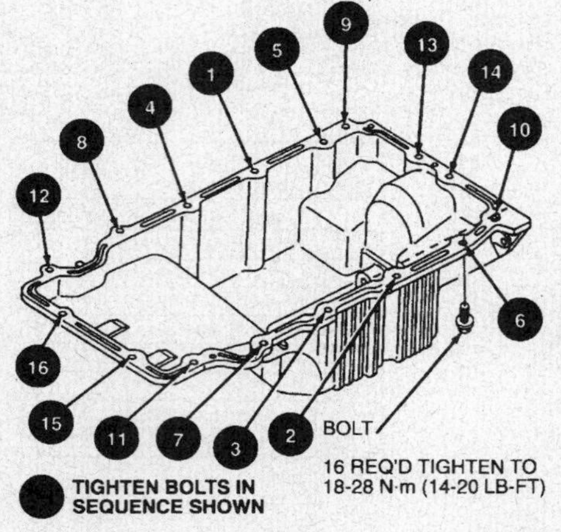

Fig. 17 Oil pan bolt tightening sequence

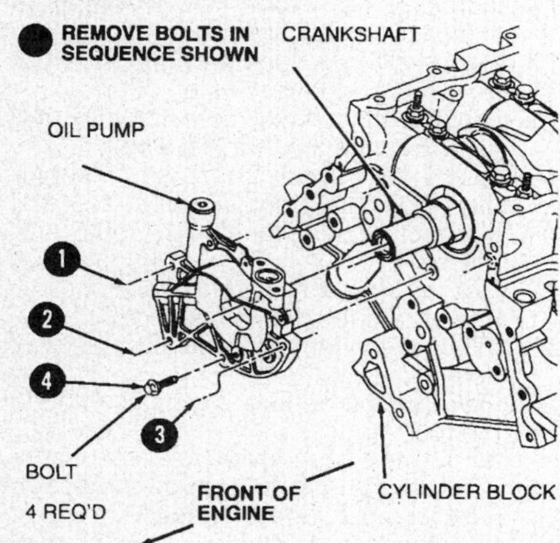

Fig. 18 Oil pump bolt removal sequence

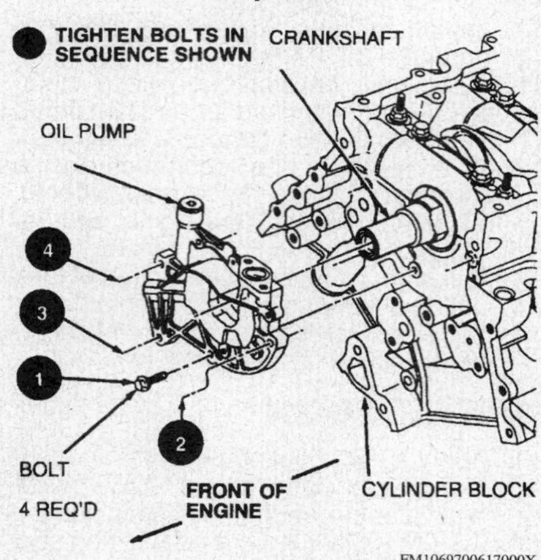

Fig. 19 Oil pump bolt tightening sequence

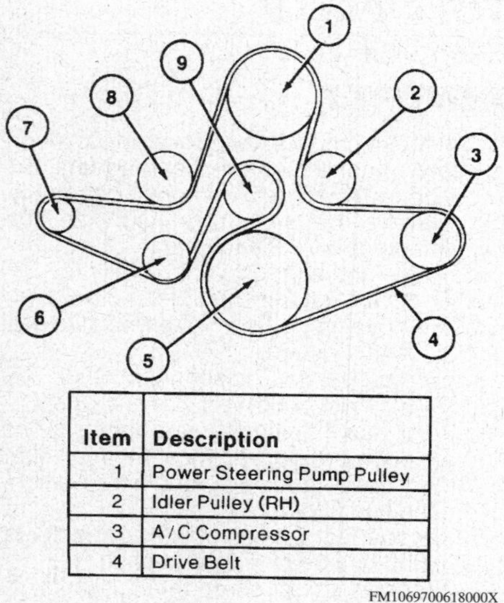

Item	Description
1	Power Steering Pump Pulley
2	Idler Pulley (RH)
3	A/C Compressor
4	Drive Belt

FM1069700618000X

Fig. 20 Accessory drive belt routing

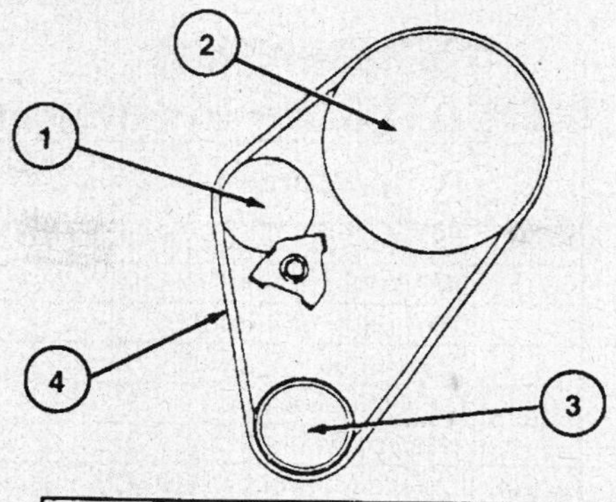

Item	Description
1	Drive Belt Tensioner
2	Crankshaft Pulley
3	Water Pump
4	Drive Belt

FM1069700619000X

Fig. 21 Water pump drive belt routing

TIGHTENING SPECIFICATIONS

Year	Component	Torque/Ft. Lbs.
1998–99	Access Drive Tensioner Assembly To Alternator Bracket	23–28
	A/C Compressor Mounting	17–27
	Alternator Bracket To Cylinder Block	28–41
	Alternator Bracket To Cylinder Head	17–27
	Alternator To Bracket	28–41
	Balance Shaft Sprocket Balancer	34–42
	Camshaft Bearing Caps To Cylinder Head	①
	Camshaft Position Sensor To Cylinder Head	72–108④
	Camshaft Timing Sprocket To Camshaft	48–70
	Connecting Rod Cap	②
	Crankshaft Damper	③
	Crankshaft Position Sensor	72–108④
	Cylinder Block Bearing Holder	16–22
	Cylinder Head	①
	Cylinder Head Water Jacket Plug	53–63
	Engine Front Cover	14–20
	Engine Front Cover To Idler Pulley	27–38
	Engine Mount Insulator To Subframe	57–75
	Engine Mount Lefthand Front Support Insulator	44–59
	Engine Mount Righthand Front Support Insulator	39–53
	Engine To Transaxle	25–33
	EGR Tube To EGR Valve	19–25
	EGR Tube To Exhaust Manifold	19–25
	EGR Valve mounting	12–16
	Exhaust Manifold Shield	12–16
	Exhaust Manifold Stud	11–19

Continued

TIGHTENING SPECIFICATIONS—Continued

Year	Component	Torque/Ft. Lbs.
1998–99	Flexplate To Crankshaft	55–61
	Front Axle Wheel Hub Retainer	170–202
	Front Subframe To Body	57–76
	Hood Latch Support	18–25
	Intake Manifold	14–20
	Knuckle To Lower Control Arm	50–67
	Lower Intake Manifold To Cylinder Head	14–20
	Oil Cooler To Cooler Adapter	30–36
	Oil Drain Plug	15–25
	Oil Pan	14–20
	Oil Pump	7–10
	Radiator Lower Bracket	72–108④
	Secondary Air Injection Tube To Manifold	30–33
	Stabilizer Link To Bar	30–40
	Thermostat Housing	72–108④
	Tie Rod End	35–46
	Timing Chain Tensioner Arm To Righthand Cylinder Head	25–39
	Torque Converter	20–33
	Valve Cover Bolts & Stud	72–108④
	Water Outlet To Cylinder Block	72–108④
	Water Pump	14–20
	Water Pump Belt Idler Pulley	7–12
	Water Pump Drive Pulley To Intake Camshaft	7–12
	Y-Pipe To Exhaust Manifold	25–33

①— Refer to "Cylinder Head, Replace."
②— Refer to "Piston & Rod Assembly."
③— Refer to "Crankshaft Damper, Replace."
④— Inch lbs.

Rear Suspension

NOTE: On Air Bag Equipped Models, Refer To "Air Bag System Precautions" Located In The Front Of This Manual For System Disarming & Arming Procedures.

NOTE: Refer To "Computer Relearn Procedures" Located In The Front Of This Manual When Battery Power To The Computer Has Been Interrupted.

INDEX

DESCRIPTION

SEDAN

These models utilize an independent rear suspension. Each side consists of a McPherson strut, an upper mount and washers, two parallel lower control arms, a tension strut, a spindle and a stabilizer bar mounted on the strut.

The top of the McPherson strut is attached to the inner body side panel, while the lower end of the strut is attached to the spindle with a pinch clamp and bolt. The parallel lower control arms attach to the underbody with nuts and bolts. The tension strut attaches to the lower part of the spindle and to the underbody, **Fig. 1.**

WAGON

These models also utilize an independent rear suspension. Each side consists of an upper and lower control arm, a shock absorber, a two-piece spindle tension control strut and a coil spring.

The top of the shock absorber is attached to the body side panel by a rubber insulated top mount assembly and to the lower control arms by two nuts. The upper control arm attaches to the crossmember and the upper part of the spindle. The lower control arm attaches to the underbody and lower part of the spindle. The coil spring operates against the lower control arm and is located inboard of the shock absorber, **Fig. 2.**

WHEEL BEARING

ADJUST

The rear wheel bearings are of a sealed cartridge design and are not adjustable.

REAR WHEEL SPINDLE

REPLACE

SEDAN

1998–99

Removal

1. Raise and support vehicle. Remove tire and wheel assembly. **Do not raise vehicle by tension strut or strut may be damaged.**
2. **On models equipped with rear disc brakes,** proceed as follows:
   a. Remove brake caliper and adapter, and hang them out of way.
   b. Brake rotor and wheel hub.
   c. Remove brake shield and anti-lock sensor.
3. **On models equipped with rear drum brakes,** proceed as follows:
   a. Remove brake drum and brake hose to strut mounting clip.
   b. Remove mounting bolts and brake backing plate. Wire plate out of way.
4. **On all models,** remove control arm to spindle mounting bolts, washers and nuts, tension strut nut, washer and bushing.
5. Remove spindle to strut pinch bolt and spindle.

Installation

1. Position replacement spindle onto tension strut and onto shock strut.
2. Install new strut to spindle pinch bolt. Do not tighten at this time.
3. Install tension strut bushing, washer and new nut. Do not tighten at this time.
4. Install new control arm to spindle mounting bolts.
5. Using suitable jack, raise lower control arm to normal curb height.
6. Tighten spindle to strut bolt, tension strut nut and control arm to spindle mounting nuts to specifications.
7. **On models equipped with rear disc brakes,** install brake caliper, adapter, brake rotor, wheel hub, brake shield and anti-lock sensor.
8. **On models equipped with rear drum brakes,** install brake backing plate, brake hose to strut mounting clip, and brake drum.

2000–02

1. Remove hub cap or wheel cover.
2. Measure distance from center of hub to lip of fender with vehicle in level static ground position (curb height).
3. Remove wheel hub and bearing.
4. Remove brake hose from shock absorber.
5. Remove rear anti-lock brake sensor.
6. Do not allow brake components to hang from brake hose.
7. Remove brake backing plate and support with suitable mechanics wire.
8. Remove lower control arm nuts, washers and flag bolts.
9. Remove and discard spindle pinch bolt, then remove rear spindle.
10. If necessary, use a suitable large screwdriver to spread pinch joint to aid in removal.
11. Reverse procedure to install, noting the following:
    a. Cupped side of lower arm mounting washers must face away from bushing.
    b. Install all nuts and bolts loosely then position suitable floor jack under rear suspension and raise to previously measured curb height.
    c. Tighten all suspension nuts and bolts to specification.

WAGON

1998–99

Removal

1. Raise and support vehicle. Remove tire and wheel assembly. **If vehicle is raised on frame contact hoist, position suitable jack under lower control arm to raise arm to normal curb height.**
2. **On models equipped with rear disc brakes,** proceed as follows:
   a. Remove brake caliper and adapter, and hang out of way.
   b. Remove brake rotor and wheel hub.
   c. Remove brake shield and anti-lock sensor.
3. **On models equipped with rear drum brakes,** remove brake drum, wheel bearings and brake backing plate.
4. **On all models,** remove upper control arms to crossmember mounting nuts and bolts.
5. Remove bolt, one washer, adjusting cam and nut mounting spindle to lower control arm.
6. Remove spindle and upper control arm as an assembly, then upper control arm to spindle mounting nut and spindle.

Installation

1. Install upper control arms to spindle using a new nut. Do not tighten at this time.
2. Position spindle and upper control arm assembly on lower control arm. Install new nut and washer, existing adjusting cam and new nut. Do not tighten at this time.
3. Position front and rear upper control arms to body bracket, and install new nuts and bolts. Do not tighten at this time.
4. Ensure lower control arm is at normal curb height.
5. Tighten upper control arms to body bracket mounting bolts, upper control arms to spindle mounting nut and spindle to lower control arm mounting nut to specifications.

2000–02

1. Remove hub cap or wheel cover.
2. Measure distance from center of hub to lip of fender with vehicle in a level static ground position (curb height).
3. Remove wheel hub and bearing.
4. Remove disc brake shield and anti-lock wheel sensor.
5. Place suitable jackstand under lower control arm and slightly raise suspension.
6. Remove and discard bolt and nut, **Fig. 3.**
7. Disconnect shock absorber, remove washer and bushing.
8. Using suitable joint removal tool, disconnect upper arm.
9. Remove wheel spindle, discard nuts and flag bolts.
10. Reverse procedure to install, noting the following:
    a. Install new flag bolts, nuts and washers.
    b. Before tightening suspension nuts and bolts, raise suspension with suitable floor jack to previously measured curb height.

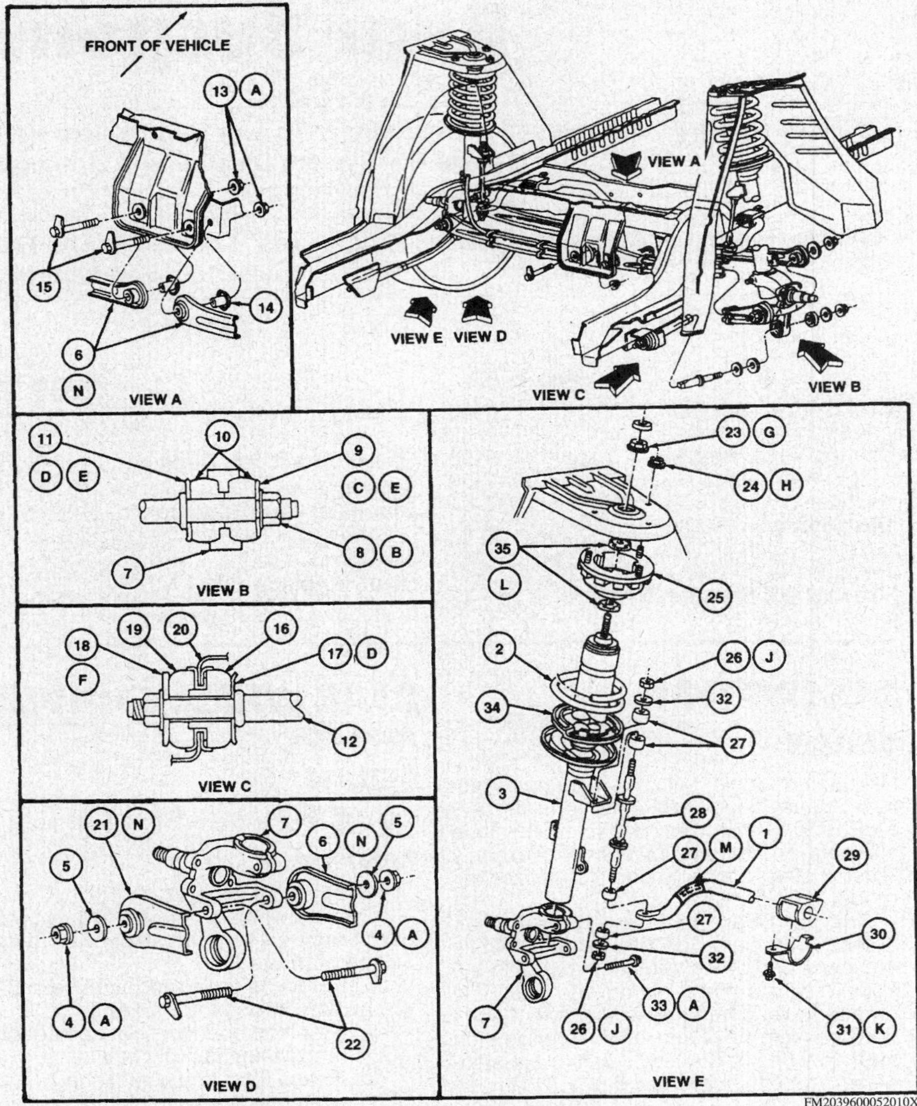

Fig. 1 Rear suspension (Part 1 of 2). Sedan

STRUT

REPLACE

SEDAN

1. Position suitable jack or hoist under vehicle, and raise just enough to contact body. **Do not raise vehicle by tension strut, or strut may be damaged.**
2. **On 1998–99 models,** working in trunk, loosen, but do not remove, three strut to inner body mounting nuts.
3. **On 2000–02 models,** remove rear parcel shelf.
4. **On all models,** raise and support vehicle. Remove tire and wheel assembly.
5. Remove brake differential valve to control arm mounting bolt.
6. Using suitable wire, suspend control arm to body to ensure proper support after strut removal.
7. Remove brake hose to shock strut bracket mounting clip and position hose aside.
8. If equipped with stabilizer bar, remove U-bracket from body, stabilizer bar mounting nut, washer and insulator. Separate stabilizer bar from link.
9. Remove tension strut to spindle mounting nut, washer and insulator, and move spindle rearward enough to separate it from tension strut.
10. Remove strut to spindle pinch bolt, and using a pry bar or other suitable tool, separate pinch joint as necessary to allow for strut removal.
11. Remove strut from pinch joint and lower vehicle as necessary to allow removal of three strut to inner body mounting bolts loosened previously. Remove strut. **During strut removal,**

use care not to stretch rear brake hose or kink steel brake line.

12. Reverse procedure to install, using new mounting parts. Tighten to specifications, in following order: stabilizer link to strut, strut pinch bolt, tension strut to spindle, stabilizer link to stabilizer bar, stabilizer bar U-bracket and strut top mount.

STRUT SERVICE

SEDAN

1. Remove strut assembly as outlined under "Strut, Replace."
2. Remove mounting nut, washer, insulator and link from strut.
3. Mark location of insulator to top mount. Place strut, spring and upper mount assembly in suitable spring compressor, and compress spring.
4. While preventing strut shaft from turning with a 10 mm six-point deep well socket on top of shaft, remove mounting nut with oxygen sensor wrench tool No. T94P-9472-A, or equivalent. **If strut is to be used again, do not use vise grips or pliers to hold strut shaft as damage will result.**
5. Carefully loosen spring compressor tool, and remove top mount bracket assembly, spring insulator and spring, **Fig. 4.**
6. Reverse procedure to install, noting following:
   a. When installing spring on strut, ensure spring is properly located in upper and lower spring seats, **Fig. 5.**
   b. When tightening strut nut, prevent strut shaft from turning.

Item	Description
1	Rear Stabilizer Bar
2	Rear Spring
3	Shock Absorber
4	Nut (4 Req'd)
5	Washer (4 Req'd)
6	Rear Lower Suspension Arm (2 Req'd)
7	Rear Wheel Spindle
8	Nut (4 Req'd)
9	Washer (2 Req'd)
10	Rear Suspension Tie Rod Bushing (4 Req'd)
11	Washer (2 Req'd)
12	Rear Suspension Tension Strut (2 Req'd)
13	Nut (4 Req'd)
14	Rear Suspension Arm Adjusting Cam Kit (4 Req'd)
15	Bolt (4 Req'd)
16	Rear Strut Body End Bushing Inner (2 Req'd)
17	Washer (2 Req'd)
18	Washer (2 Req'd)
19	Bushing - Outer (2 Req'd)
20	Body
21	Forward Lower Suspension Arm (2 Req'd)
22	Bolt (4 Req'd)
23	Nut (2 Req'd)
24	Nut (6 Req'd)
25	Rear Shock Absorber Bracket (2 Req'd)
26	Nut (4 Req'd)
27	Lower Suspension Arm Stabilizer Bar Insulator (8 Req'd)
28	Rear Stabilizer Bar Link (2 Req'd)

Item	Description
29	Lower Suspension Arm Stabilizer Bar Insulator (2 Req'd)
30	Stabilizer Bar Bracket (2 Req'd)
31	Bolt (2 Req'd)
32	Washer (4 Req'd)
33	Bolt (2 Req'd)
34	Rear Spring Center Mounting Insulator (Part of 18080)
35	Washer (2 Req'd)
A	Tighten to 68-92 N·m (50-68 Lb-Ft)
B	Tighten to 47-63 N·m (35-46 Lb-Ft)
C	Stamped Rear
D	Stamped This Side Out
E	Assemble N802855-S36 and N801335-S36 As Shown
F	Assemble 5B536 and 5B537 As Shown
G	Tighten to 53-71 N·m (39-53 Lb-Ft)
H	Tighten to 25-34 N·m (19-26 Lb-Ft)
J	Tighten to 7-9 N·m (62-79 Lb-In)
K	Tighten to 34-46 N·m (25-33 Lb-Ft)
L	Dished-Side Down
M	Color Code Must Be Installed on RH Side Of Vehicle
N	Arm Assemblies Must Be Installed As Shown. Trim Flange To Be Rearward On Front Arms And Left Rear Arm. Trim Flange To Be Forward On Right Rear Arm All Arms Are Stamped Bottom On Lower Surface

FM2039600052020X

Fig. 1 Rear suspension (Part 2 of 2). Sedan

TENSION STRUT

REPLACE

SEDAN

1. Raise vehicle on frame contact hoist using lift pads located rearward of front wheels and forward of rear wheels. Raise hoist only enough to contact body.
2. Working inside trunk, loosen, but do not remove, three strut to inner body mounting nuts.
3. Raise vehicle, and remove tire and wheel assembly.
4. Remove and discard tension strut to spindle mounting nut.
5. Remove and discard tension strut to body mounting nut.
6. While moving spindle rearward, remove tension strut.
7. Install new inner washers and bushings on both ends of tension strut, **Fig. 6.**
8. Install tension strut end into body bracket, outer bushing, washers and nut. Do not tighten nut at this time.
9. While moving spindle rearward, install tension strut in spindle, outer bushing, washer and nut.
10. Ensure bushings are properly seated in mountings, **Fig. 6.**
11. Support spindle with suitable jack stand, and working inside trunk, remove three strut to inner body mounting nuts. Install new nuts and tighten to specifications.
12. Remove jack stand, and install tire and wheel assembly.
13. Lower vehicle.

WAGON

Removal

1. Raise vehicle on frame contact hoist.
2. Remove wheel and tension strut to lower control arm mounting nut and bolt.
3. Remove tension strut to body bracket mounting nut and bolt, and tension strut.

Installation

1. Insert front end of replacement torsion strut in body bracket, and install new mounting nut and bolt. Do not tighten at this time.
2. Position rear end of torsion strut in lower control arm and install new mounting nut and bolt.
3. Tighten torsion strut to body bracket mounting nut and bolt to specifications.
4. Install wheel and tire assembly.

SHOCK ABSORBER

REPLACE

WAGON

1. Raise and support rear of vehicle. Remove tire and wheel assembly. **If a frame contact hoist is used, support lower control arm with floor jack. If a twin post lift is used, support body with floor jacks on lifting pads forward of tension strut body bracket.**
2. Loosen shock absorber to lower control arm mounting nuts. Do not remove nuts at this time.
3. Lower vehicle and remove rear compartment access panels.
4. Remove shock absorber top mounting nut, washer and insulator.
5. Raise and support vehicle.
6. Remove absorber to lower control arm mounting nuts and absorber. **The shock absorbers are gas filled and will require an effort to collapse for removal.**

7. If absorbers are to be used again, do not grip their shafts with pliers or vise grips, as this will damage shafts' surface finish and result in fluid leaks.
8. Reverse procedure to install. **Use a new bushing repair kit on top of absorber.** Tighten all fasteners to specifications.

COIL SPRING

REPLACE

WAGON

Removal

1. Raise vehicle on frame contact hoist, and using suitable floor jack, raise lower control arm to normal curb height.
2. Remove tire and wheel assembly.
3. Remove brake hose bracket from body.
4. Remove shock absorber.
5. Install spring cage tool No. 164-R3555, or equivalent, on spring.
6. Remove and discard upper ball joint nut, and separate joint from spindle.
7. Slowly lower rear suspension arm and bushing, and remove spring and its insulators.

Installation

1. Install lower spring insulator on control arm. Ensure insulator is seated properly.
2. Position upper insulator on spring and install spring on lower control arm. Ensure spring is properly seated.
3. Slowly raise suspension arm and bushing, and guide upper insulator onto upper spring seat on underbody.
4. Position upper ball joint into suspension arm and bushing.
5. Install shock absorber, stabilizer bar and bracket.
6. Remove spring cage tool.
7. Install brake hose bracket to body.
8. Install tire and wheel assembly.
9. Lower vehicle and inspect rear wheel alignment.

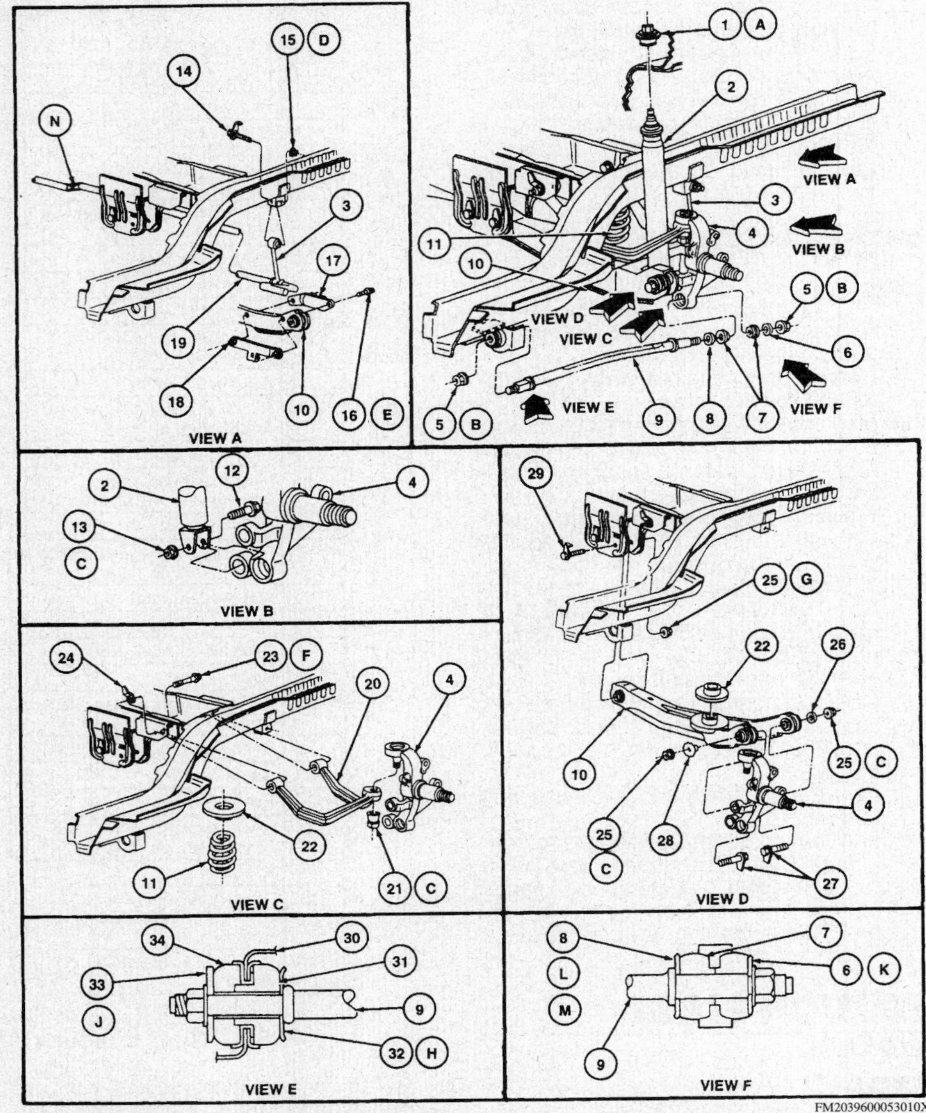

Fig. 2 Rear suspension (Part 1 of 2). Wagon

CONTROL ARM

REPLACE

LOWER

SEDAN

Removal

1. Raise and support vehicle, **but not by tension strut and bushing.**
2. Disconnect brake proportioning valve from lefthand side front control arm, parking brake cable and conduit from control arms.
3. Remove control arm to spindle mounting bolt, nut and washer.
4. Remove control arm to body bracket mounting bolt and nut, then control arm.

Installation

1. Position control arm (and cam, where required, **Fig. 7,**) at body bracket, and install new nut and bolt. Do not tighten at this time. **When installing control arms, offset must face up (the arms are stamped "bottom" on lower edge). flange edge of righthand side rear arm stamping must face front of vehicle. Other three must face rear of vehicle. During installation, note that control arms have two adjustment cams that fit inside bushings at control arm to body attachment. Cam is installed from rear on lefthand arm and from front on righthand arm, Fig. 7.**
2. Position outer end of arm at spindle, and install new bolt, washer and nut. Tighten nut to specifications.
3. Tighten control arm to body bracket mounting nut to specifications.
4. Attach parking brake cables and brake proportioning valve to control arms.
5. Lower vehicle, inspect rear toe and adjust as necessary.

WAGON

Removal

1. Raise and support rear of vehicle.
2. Remove tire and wheel assembly.
3. Remove rear spring as outlined under "Coil Spring, Replace."
4. Remove lower control arm to body bracket mounting bolt and control arm.

Installation

1. Position lower control arm in body bracket, and install new nut and bolt with bolt head toward front of vehicle. Do not tighten at this time.
2. Install rear spring as outlined under "Coil Spring, Replace."
3. Using suitable jack, support lower control arm at normal curb height and tighten control arm to body bracket mounting bolt to specifications.
4. Tighten lower control arm to spindle mounting bolt to specifications.

Item	Description
1	Upper Shock Absorber Nut (2 Req'd)
2	Shock Absorber (2 Req'd)
3	Rear Stabilizer Bar Link and Bushing
4	Rear Wheel Spindle
5	Nut (4 Req'd)
6	Washer (2 Req'd)
7	Rear Suspension Tie Rod Bushing (4 Req'd)
8	Washer (2 Req'd)
9	Rear Suspension Tension Strut and Bushing (2 Req'd)
10	Rear Suspension Arm and Bushing
11	Rear Spring (2 Req'd)
12	Bolt (2 Req'd)
13	Nut (2 Req'd)
14	Bolt (2 Req'd)
15	Nut (2 Req'd)
16	Bolt (4 Req'd)
17	Stabilizer Bar Bracket
18	Nut and Retainer Assembly (2 Req'd)
19	Rear Stabilizer Bar
20	Rear Suspension Arm and Bushing
21	Nut (2 Req'd)
22	Rear Spring Insulators (4 Req'd)
23	Bolt (4 Req'd)
24	Nut (4 Req'd)
25	Nut (2 Req'd)
26	Washer (2 Req'd)
27	Bolt (4 Req'd)
28	Rear Suspension Arm Adjusting Cam Kit (2 Req'd)
29	Bolt (2 Req'd)
30	Body
31	Rear Strut Body End Bushing Inner (2 Req'd)
32	Washer (2 Req'd)
33	Sleeve (2 Req'd)
34	Bushing Outer(2 Req'd)
A	Tighten to 25-34 N·m (19-25 Lb-Ft)
B	Tighten to 47-63 N·m (35-46 Lb-Ft)
C	Tighten to 68-92 N·m (50-67 Lb-Ft)
D	Tighten to 60-80 N·m (45-59 Lb-Ft)
E	Tighten to 19-26 N·m (14-19 Lb-Ft)
F	Tighten to 98-132 N·m (73-97 Lb-Ft)
G	Tighten to 54-71 N·m (40-52 Lb-Ft)
H	Stamped "This Side Out"
J	Assemble 5B536 and 5B537 As Shown
K	Stamped "Rear"
L	Stamped "This Side Out"
M	Assemble N802855-S36 and N801335-S36 As Shown
N	Color Code Must Be Installed On

FM2039600053020X

Fig. 2 Rear suspension (Part 2 of 2). Wagon

5. Install tire and wheel assembly, and lower vehicle.

UPPER

WAGON

Removal

1. Raise vehicle on frame contact hoist, and using suitable floor jack, raise lower control arm to normal curb height.
2. Remove wheel and tire assembly, then brake hose bracket from body.
3. Loosen spindle to upper control arms mounting nut.
4. Loosen spindle to lower control arm mounting nut.
5. Remove and discard upper ball joint nut, and separate joint from spindle.
6. Remove upper control arms to body brackets mounting nuts and bolts. Ensure spindle does not fall outward.
7. Carefully tilt upper part of spindle outward until upper control arms are clear of body brackets. Wire spindle in this position.
8. Remove spindle to upper control arms mounting nut and upper control arms.

Installation

1. Install upper control arms on spindle and install new nut. Do not tighten at this time.
2. Position upper control arms in body brackets, and install new nuts and bolts. Tighten to specifications. Remove wire from spindle.
3. Tighten control arms to spindle mounting nuts to specifications.
4. Install brake hose bracket on body, and tire and wheel assembly.
5. Remove floor jack and lower vehicle.
6. Inspect rear wheel alignment and adjust as necessary.

STABILIZER BAR

REPLACE

SEDAN

1. Raise and support vehicle, **but not by tension strut and bushing.**
2. Remove stabilizer bar to link mounting nuts, washers and insulators from both sides.
3. Remove U-bracket mounting bolts and stabilizer bar.
4. Remove link to strut mounting nuts, washers and insulators.
5. Inspect mounting parts for damage and replace as necessary.
6. Reverse procedure to install. Use new mounting parts, and tighten all fasteners to specifications.

WAGON

1. Raise and support vehicle.
2. Place jackstands under rear suspension arm and bushings so bar links and bushings are neutralized.
3. Remove U-bracket mounting nuts and bolts from either side, and slide U-brackets and insulators from stabilizer bar.
4. Remove link to body bracket mounting nuts and bolts, and stabilizer and link assemblies.
5. Slide link assemblies from stabilizer bar.
6. Inspect all components for damage and replace as necessary.
7. Reverse procedure to install. Use new mounting parts, and tighten all fasteners to specifications.

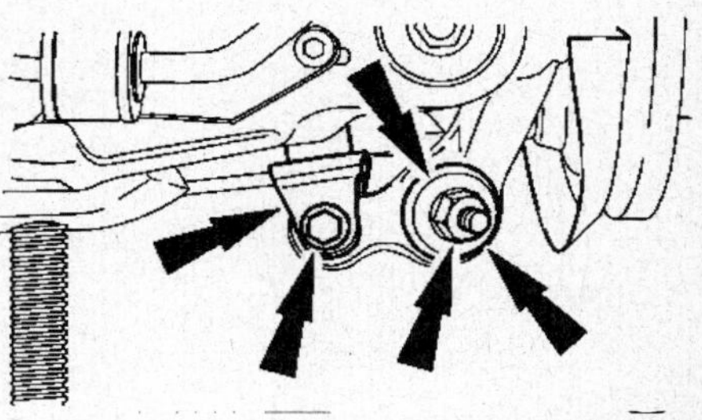

FM1060101226000X

Fig. 3 Rear spindle replacement. 2000–02 Wagon

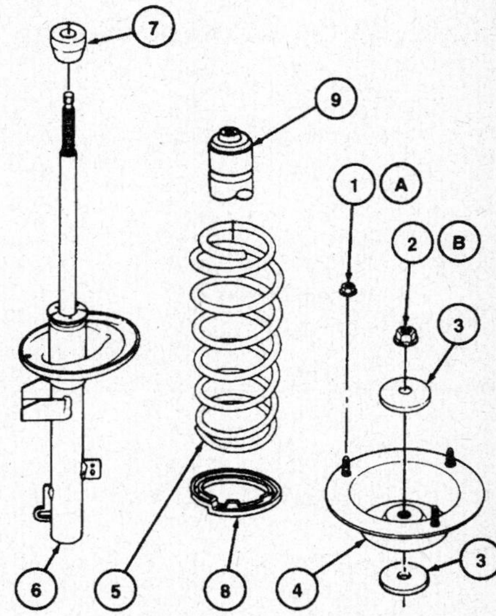

Item	Description
1	Nut (3 Req'd)
2	Nut
3	Washer (2 Req'd)
4	Rear Shock Absorber Bracket
5	Rear Spring
6	Shock Absorber
7	Rear Shock Absorber Jounce Bumper (Part of 18080)
8	Rear Spring Center Mounting insulator (Part of 18080)
9	Dust Boot (Part of 18080)
A	Tighten to 25-34 N·m (19-25 Lb-Ft)
B	Tighten to 53-71 N·m (39-53 Lb-Ft)

FM2039600054000X

Fig. 4 Rear strut & spring components

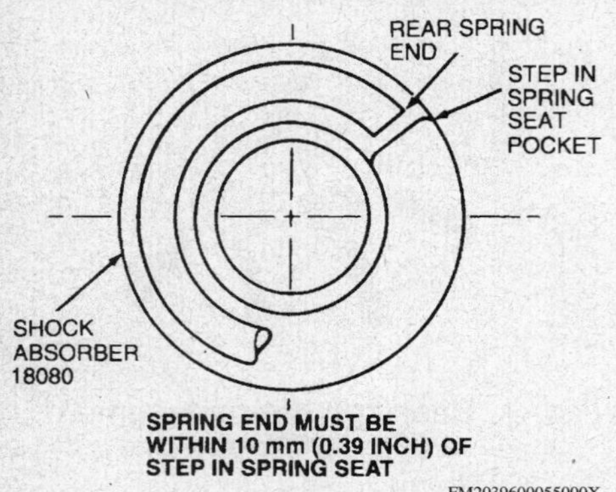

Fig. 5 Spring & seat positioning

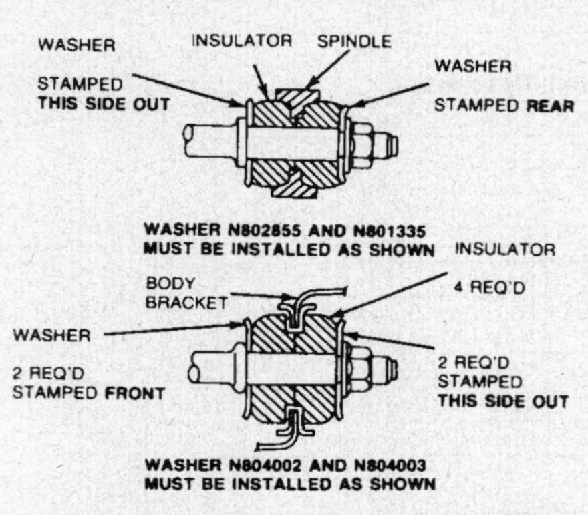

Fig. 6 Tension strut bushing installation. Sedan

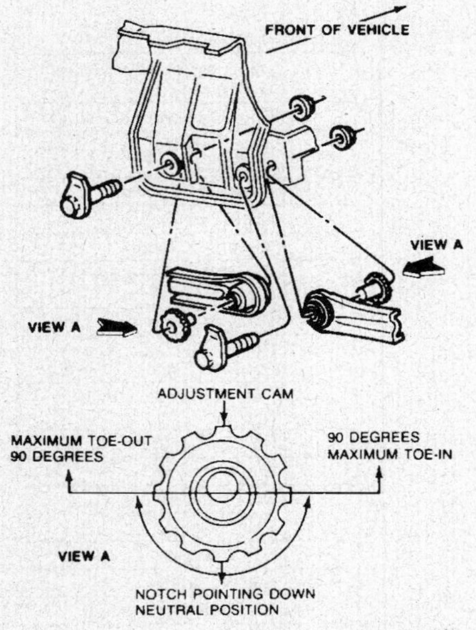

Fig. 7 Lower control arm bushing & cam installation. Sedan

TIGHTENING SPECIFICATIONS

Year	Component	Torque/Ft. Lbs.
SEDAN		
1998–2002	Brake Hose Bracket	9–12
	Control Arm To Body	73–97
	Control Arm To Spindle	50–67
	Stabilizer Bar Link To Stabilizer Bar	60–84①
	Stabilizer Bar Link To Strut	60–84①
	Stabilizer U-Bracket To Body	25–34
	Strut Rod Nut	39–53
	Strut Top Mount To Body	19–26
	Strut To Spindle	50–67
	Strut To Top Mount	35–50
	Tension Strut To Body	35–50
	Tension Strut To Spindle	35–50
	Wheel Bearing	188–254
	Wheel Lug	85–105
WAGON		
1998–2002	Brake Hose Bracket	9–12
	Lower Control Arm To Body	40–52
	Shock Absorber To Body	19–27
	Shock Absorber To Lower Suspension Arm	12–20
	Shock Absorber To Lower Suspension Spindle	50–67
	Spindle To Lower Control Arm	50–67
	Stabilizer Bar U-Bracket To Lower Suspension Arm	20–30
	Stabilizer Link Assembly To Body	44–59
	Tension Strut To Body	35–46
	Tension Strut To Spindle	35–46
	Upper Ball Joint	50–68
	Upper Control Arms To Body	70–95
	Upper Control Arms To Spindle	150–190
	Upper Suspension Arm To Spindle	40–55
	Wheel Bearing	188–254
	Wheel Lug	85–105

① — Inch lbs.

Front Suspension & Steering

NOTE: On Air Bag Equipped Models, Refer To "Air Bag System Precautions" Located In The Front Of This Manual For System Disarming & Arming Procedures.

NOTE: Refer To "Computer Relearn Procedures" Located In The Front Of This Manual When Battery Power To The Computer Has Been Interrupted.

NOTE: Prior To Performing Any Service Operations Listed In This Section, Consult The "Technical Service Bulletins" Section For Related Information.

INDEX

DESCRIPTION

This suspension is of the gas filled McPherson strut type, **Fig. 1.** The strut top mount consists of a rubber insulated bearing and seat and coil spring insulator. The top mount is attached to the body side apron by three bolts. The lower part of the strut is mounted in the steering knuckle and is retained by a pinch bolt. A forged lower control arm is attached to the subframe and to the steering knuckle. A tension strut is connected to the lower control arm and to the forward part of the subframe.

WHEEL BEARING

REPLACE

1. Turn ignition switch to OFF position and place steering column in unlocked position.
2. Remove wheel hub retainer nut, raise and support vehicle.
3. Remove cotter pin and nut from tie rod end stud. Discard cotter pin and nut.
4. Using tie rod end remover tool No. 3290-D, and tie rod adapter tool No. T81P-3504-W, or equivalents, remove tie rod end from front wheel knuckle. **Do not use power tools to remove nut. Avoid damaging rod boot seal.**
5. Remove stabilizer bar link from front wheel knuckle.
6. Remove disc brake caliper and wire aside.
7. Remove anti-lock brake sensor.
8. Remove and discard lower ball joint nut.
9. Using Rotunda spring compressor tool No. 164-R-3571, or equivalent, compress front coil spring until lower ball joint clears front suspension lower arm.
10. Using suitable special service tools, push front axle from hub.
11. Remove and discard three hub and bearing retainer bolts from front wheel knuckle.
12. **Wheel hub is not pressed into front wheel knuckle. Do not use a slide hammer to remove a stuck wheel hub. Do not strike back of inner bearing race.**
13. If bearing carrier is corroded to front wheel knuckle, apply a rust penetrant part No. D7AZ-19A501-AA, or equivalent, to inboard and outboard wheel hub/knuckle mating surface and allow to soak. Using a suitable pry bar, pry wheel hub from knuckle assembly.
14. Reverse procedure to install, noting the following:
    a. If wheel hub is damaged or if any endplay is detectable, replace wheel hub.
    b. Remove any foreign material from knuckle bearing bore.
    c. Lightly lubricate mating surfaces of bearing and front wheel knuckle.

BALL JOINT INSPECTION

1. Raise vehicle until wheels fall to a full down position.
2. Grasp lower edge of tire and move wheel assembly in and out.
3. As wheel is being moved, observe lower end of knuckle and lower control arm. Any movement would indicate abnormal ball joint wear.
4. If movement is observed, replace lower control arm assembly.

BALL JOINT

REPLACE

The ball joint must be replaced with the control arm as an assembly.

STRUT

REPLACE

1. Place ignition switch in Off position and ensure steering wheel is not locked.
2. Remove hub nut and loosen three strut mounting nuts.
3. Raise and support vehicle. **Do not raise vehicle with lower control arm.**
4. **On SHO models,** disconnect height sensor wiring connector.
5. **On all models,** remove wheel and tire assembly.
6. Remove brake caliper and wire it aside.
7. Remove brake rotor and tie rod end. **Do not use power tools to remove tie rod nut. Avoid damaging boot seal.**
8. Remove nut and stabilizer bar link from strut.
9. Remove lower control arm to steering knuckle pinch nut and bolt, and slightly spread joint and remove lower control arm.
10. Using suitable hub remover/installer, press axle from hub. Wire axle shaft to body to maintain level position. **Do not allow axle shaft to move outward. Overextension of constant velocity (CV) joint could result in separation of internal parts, which could cause CV joint failure.**
11. Remove strut to steering knuckle pinch bolt, spread joint slightly, and remove steering knuckle and hub assembly.

12. Remove mounting nuts and strut assembly.
13. Reverse procedure to install. Tighten all fasteners to specifications in following order: strut to steering knuckle pinch bolt, lower control arm to steering knuckle pinch bolt, stabilizer bar assembly to strut, tie rod end mounting nut, and strut mounting nuts. With vehicle on ground, tighten hub nut to specifications.

COIL SPRING & STRUT SERVICE

1. Compress strut spring with Rotunda coil spring compressor tool No. 164-R3571, or equivalent.
2. Using a 10 mm box wrench, restrain strut shaft, and remove strut mounting nut with suitable 21 mm crowfoot socket. **Do not allow strut shaft to rotate.**
3. Loosen compressor tool, remove strut top mount bracket assembly, bearing and seat assembly, and spring, **Fig. 2.**
4. Reverse procedure to install.

CONTROL ARM

REPLACE

1. Turn ignition switch to OFF position and place steering column in unlocked position.
2. Raise and support vehicle.
3. **On SHO models,** disconnect height sensor wiring connector.
4. **On all models,** remove and discard lower ball joint nut.
5. Using ball joint remover tool No. T96P-3010-A and tie rod end remover tool No. T81P-3504-W, or equivalents, separate ball joint from knuckle.
6. Using Rotunda spring compressor tool No. 164-R-3571, or equivalent, compress front coil spring until lower ball joint clears front suspension lower arm.
7. Remove forward lower suspension arm mounting nut and bolt.
8. Remove rear lower suspension arm mounting nut and bolt, and suspension arm from the vehicle.
9. Reverse procedure to install.

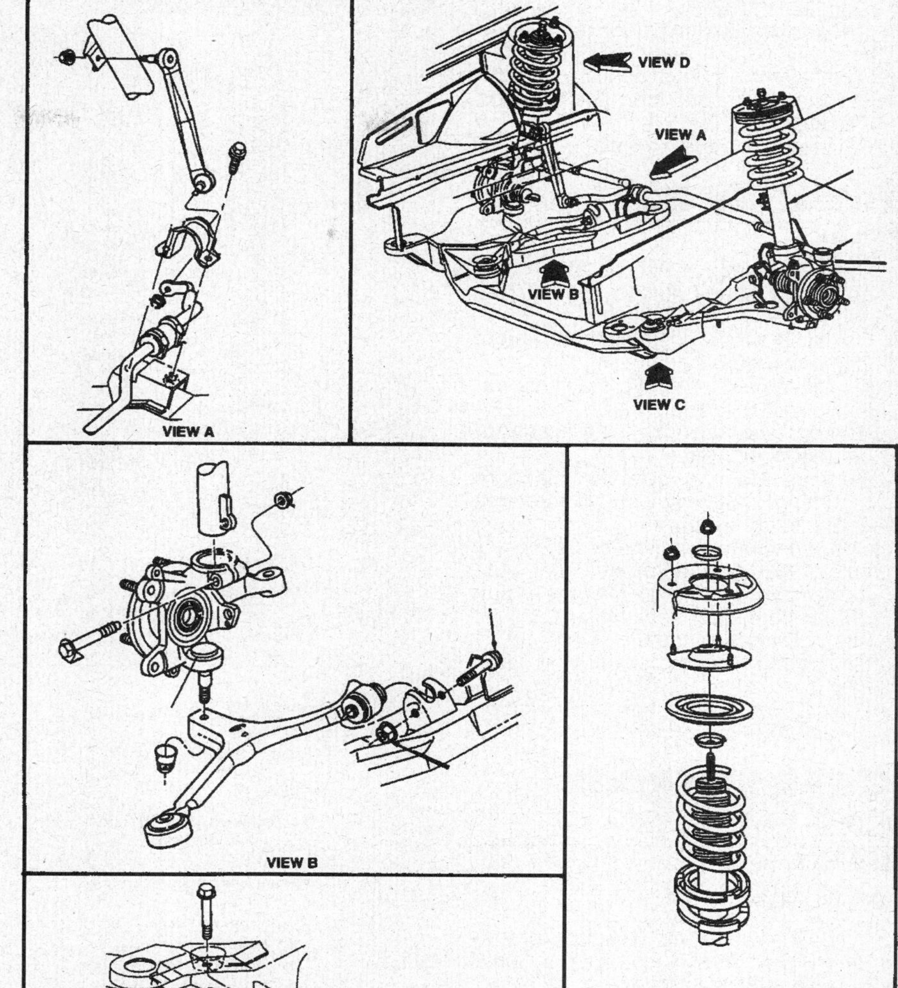

Fig. 1 Front suspension assembly

STEERING KNUCKLE

REPLACE

1998–99

1. Place ignition switch in Off position and ensure steering wheel is unlocked.
2. Remove hub nut and loosen three strut mounting nuts.
3. Raise and support vehicle. **Do not raise vehicle with lower control arm.**
4. Remove wheel and tire assembly.
5. **On SHO models,** disconnect height sensor wiring connector.
6. **On all models,** remove brake caliper and wire it aside.
7. Remove brake rotor and tie rod end.
8. Remove nut and stabilizer bar link from strut.
9. Remove lower control arm to steering knuckle pinch nut and bolt, and slightly spread joint and remove lower control arm.
10. Using suitable hub remover/installer, press axle from hub. Wire axle shaft to body to maintain level position. **Do not allow axle shaft to move outward. Overextension of constant velocity (CV) joint could result in separation of internal parts, which could cause CV joint failure.**
11. Remove rotor splash shield.
12. Remove strut to steering knuckle pinch bolt, spread joint slightly, and remove steering knuckle and hub assembly.
13. Reverse procedure to install, noting the following:
    a. Tighten all fastener to specifications in following order: strut to steering knuckle pinch bolt, lower control arm to steering knuckle pinch bolt, stabilizer bar assembly to strut, tie rod end mounting nut, and strut mounting nuts.
    b. With vehicle on ground, tighten hub nut to specifications.

2000–02

Wheel hub retainer is a torque prevailing design and cannot be reused. If loosened, retainer must be replaced.

1. Ensure steering wheel in an unlocked position.
2. Remove hub cap or wheel cover, wheel hub retainer and washer, discard retainer.
3. Using suitable joint removal tool, remove tie rod end from steering knuckle.
4. Remove anti-lock brake sensor.
5. Unclip ABS sensor wire retainer and position sensor out of way.
6. Remove knuckle to shock mounting bolt and nut, discard nut.
7. Using suitable joint removal tool, disconnect ball joint from lower arm.
8. Using a pry bar, push lower arm down until ball joint is free from arm.

9. Using front wheel hub installation tool No. T81P-1104–C, or equivalent, press halfshaft from wheel bearing and hub.
10. Wire halfshaft in level position.
11. Remove flag bolt, then the steering knuckle.
12. Reverse procedure to install.

STABILIZER BAR

REPLACE

1. Raise and support vehicle on a hoist, and place safety stands behind front subframe.
2. **On SHO models,** disconnect height sensor wiring connector.
3. **On all models,** remove stabilizer bar link to strut mounting nuts.
4. Remove stabilizer bar link to stabilizer bar mounting nuts.
5. Remove steering gear to subframe mounting bolts and move steering gear off subframe.
6. Support subframe with a second set of safety stands and remove rear subframe mounting bolts. Lower rear part of subframe to gain access to stabilizer bar mounting brackets.
7. Remove mounting brackets and stabilizer bar.
8. Reverse procedure to install. Tighten all fasteners to specifications.

POWER STEERING GEAR

REPLACE

1998–99

1. Working inside of vehicle, remove steering column tube boot to cowl panel mounting screws.
2. Remove steering column intermediate shaft coupling to steering column lower yoke mounting bolt.
3. Position steering column tube boot out of way and remove steering column intermediate shaft coupling to power steering rack pinch bolt.
4. Remove steering column intermediate shaft coupling.
5. Raise and support vehicle on a twin post hoist. Remove front tire and wheel assemblies.
6. Disconnect exhaust system at dual converter Y-pipe attachment and remove dual converter Y-pipe.
7. Support vehicle with jackstands under rear edge of front subframe.
8. Remove tie rod cotter pins and nuts, and separate tie rod end from wheel knuckles.
9. Remove tie rod from front wheel spindle tie rod. Mark position of jam nut to maintain alignment.
10. Remove nuts from steering gear to front subframe bolts.
11. Remove rear subframe to body mounting bolts.
12. Lower front twin post carefully until rear subframe separates from body, approximately four inches.
13. Remove heat shield push-pin retainers from power steering hose bracket.

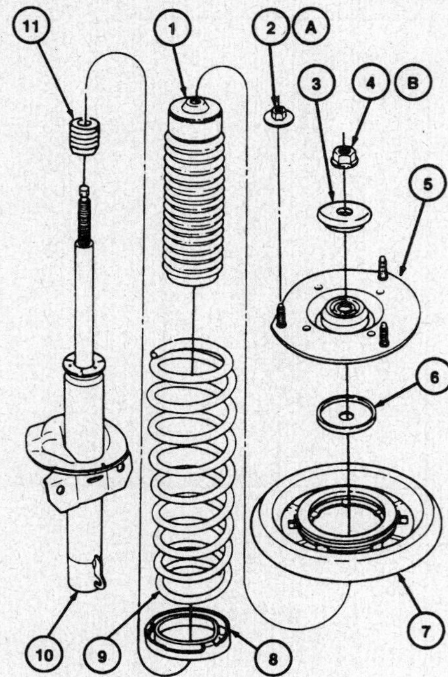

Item	Description
1	Dust Boot
2	Nut (3 Req'd)
3	Washer
4	Nut
5	Front Shock Absorber Mounting Bracket
6	Washer
7	Front Suspension Bearing and Seal
8	Front Spring Insulator
9	Front Coil Spring
10	Front Spring and Shock
11	Jounce Bumper
A	Tighten to 30-40 N·m (23-29 Lb-Ft)
B	Tighten to 53-72 N·m (40-53 Lb-Ft)

FM2029500087000X

Fig. 2 McPherson strut assembly

14. Remove steering shaft U-joint shield.
15. Remove screw and power steering lefthand turn pressure hose from power steering hose bracket.
16. Remove mounting screws and power steering hose bracket.
17. Remove lefthand stabilizer bar link and disconnect VAPS electrical connectors from power steering auxiliary actuator.
18. Rotate power steering short rack to clear bolts from front subframe and pull left to ease line fitting removal.
19. Place drain pan under vehicle and remove hydraulic power steering pressure hose and power steering return hose from fittings on power steering short rack.
20. Remove stabilizer bar links.
21. Remove power steering short rack assembly through lefthand wheelwell.
22. Reverse procedure to install.

2000–02

VIN U, 1 & 2 Engines

1. Turn steering wheel ½ turn to right, then turn ignition switch to Off position.
2. Remove air cleaner outlet pipe.
3. Remove power steering pressure hose, discard seals.
4. Remove intermediate shaft pinch bolt, discard bolt.
5. Center steering wheel and turn ignition switch to Off position.
6. **Do not allow steering wheel to rotate while steering column intermediate shaft is disconnected or damage to air bag clockspring will result.**
7. Disconnect intermediate shaft from steering gear.
8. Remove front wheel and tire assemblies.
9. Loosen tie rod jam nuts, remove and discard tie rod end cotter pins and nuts, then remove tie rod ends from steering knuckle using suitable joint removal tool.
10. For assembly reference, count and record number of turns required to remove tie rod ends, then remove tie rod ends.
11. Remove nuts and disconnect both stabilizer bar links from stabilizer bar.
12. Remove catalytic converter.
13. Remove and discard steering gear mounting nuts.
14. Remove remaining brackets and pipes from steering gear.
15. Support rear of front subframe with suitable jack stands, then remove bolts and lower subframe approximately 4 inches.
16. Remove steering gear through left fender well.
17. Reverse procedure to install

VIN S Engines

1. Turn steering wheel ¼ turn, then turn ignition switch to Off position.
2. Remove both front wheel and tire assemblies.
3. Loosen tie rod end jam nuts, remove and discard tie rod end cotter pins and nuts, then remove tie rod ends from steering knuckle with suitable joint removal tool.
4. For assembly reference, count number of turns required to remove tie rod ends from steering gear, then remove tie rod ends.
5. Remove nuts and disconnect both stabilizer bar links from stabilizer bar.
6. Remove bolt and disconnect intermediate shaft coupling.
7. **Do not allow steering wheel to rotate while steering column intermediate shaft is disconnected or damage to air bag clockspring will occur.**
8. Remove catalytic converter.
9. Remove and discard both steering gear mounting nuts.
10. Remove bolts and lower rear of front

subframe approximately 4 inches.

11. Disconnect power steering pressure switch, then remove power steering pressure hose.
12. Remove bracket/heat shield.
13. Remove power steering lines from steering gear.
14. Remove any remaining brackets or pipes, then remove steering gear through left fender well.
15. Reverse procedure to install.

POWER STEERING PUMP

REPLACE

These models use three different power steering pumps. Type CII appears on 3.0L (VIN U, 1 and 2) engines. Type CIII is used on 3.0L (VIN S) engines. The 3.4L engine uses pump type ZUA. **All three types are replaced only as complete assemblies. They have no serviceable components.**

VIN U, 1 & 2 ENGINES

1. Remove drive belt and alternator.
2. Drain and remove coolant recovery reservoir.
3. Remove power steering return hose from pump and drain fluid into clean container.
4. Remove idler pulley from power steering pump support.
5. Remove power steering bracket mounting bolt from under tensioner mounting.
6. Remove power steering pump support with pump still attached.
7. Remove pulley using pump pulley remover tool No. T69L-10300-B, or equivalent.
8. Reverse procedure to install. Tighten all fasteners to specifications.

VIN S ENGINE

1. Drain and remove coolant recovery reservoir.
2. Remove drive belt.
3. Remove power steering reservoir pump hose from between pump and reservoir. Drain fluid into clean container.
4. Remove pulley using pump pulley remover tool No. T69L-10300-B, or equivalent.
5. Disconnect power steering lefthand turn pressure hose from pump.
6. Remove three pump mounting bolts and pump.
7. Reverse procedure to install. Tighten all fasteners to specifications.

3.4L ENGINE

1. Remove drive belt.
2. Disconnect power steering lefthand turn pressure hose from pump. Drain fluid into clean container.
3. Remove power steering reservoir pump hose from between pump and reservoir.
4. Remove three pump mounting bolts and pump.
5. Remove mounting nut and pulley.
6. Reverse procedure to install. Tighten all fasteners to specifications.

TIGHTENING SPECIFICATIONS

Year	Component	Torque/Ft. Lbs.
1998–2002	Control Arm Pivot Bolt	72–97
	Control Arm To Knuckle	①
	Control Arm To Subframe	72–97
	Hub Nut	170–202
	Power Steering High pressure Hose	①
	Power Steering return Hose	①
	Stabilizer Bar Bracket To Subframe	22–39
	Stabilizer Bar Link Assembly To Stabilizer Bar	35–48
	Stabilizer Bar Link Assembly To Shock Strut	57–75
	Steering Gear mounting Nuts	85–100
	Strut Top Mount To Body	30–40
	Strut To Top Mount	39–53
	Strut To Knuckle	72–97
	Tension Strut To Control Arm	70–95
	Tension Strut To Subframe	70–95
	Tie Rod End To Steering Knuckle	35–46
	Wheel Lug	85–105

① — 1998 Models.

Wheel Alignment

NOTE: Prior To Performing Any Service Operations Listed In This Section, Consult The "Technical Service Bulletins" Section For Related Information.

INDEX

PRELIMINARY INSPECTION

1. Ensure all tires are inflated to proper pressure.
2. Inspect tires for wear patterns that may indicate improper wheel alignment, tire imbalance or damage due to bulges or separations.
3. Inspect suspension for modifications such as trailer towing equipment or heavy duty handling components.
4. Inspect vehicle for signs of overloading or sagging: ensure luggage compartment does not contain heavy objects.
5. Road test vehicle to isolate area of concern.

FRONT WHEEL ALIGNMENT

CASTER & CAMBER

Caster is not adjustable. If inspection shows caster to not be within specifications, inspect vehicle for suspension component damage, deteriorated bushings or distorted body mounting points.

1. Loosen subframe to body mounting bolts.
2. Install a ¾ inch outside diameter pipe or similar tool into lefthand front subframe and body alignment holes, **Fig. 1.**
3. Align lefthand front subframe and body alignment holes, and slightly tighten lefthand front subframe mounting bolt.
4. Repeat previous alignment steps on righthand front alignment holes and inspect lefthand front alignment again.
5. Tighten subframe mounting bolts to specifications.
6. Center punch spot welds on both strut alignment plates and loosen strut mounting nuts, **Fig. 2.**
7. Using Rotunda Spot-Eze, or equivalent, remove spot welds. **Do not drill deeper than thickness of alignment plates.**
8. Remove strut mounting nuts and alignment plates.
9. Remove burrs from strut towers and alignment plates, and paint all exposed metal on strut towers and alignment plates.

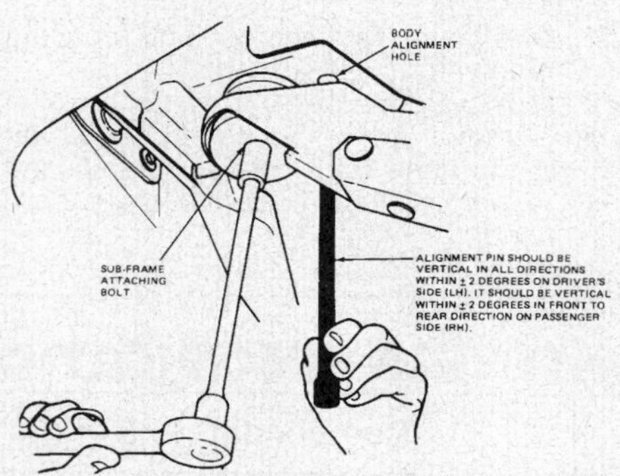

Fig. 1 Front suspension alignment

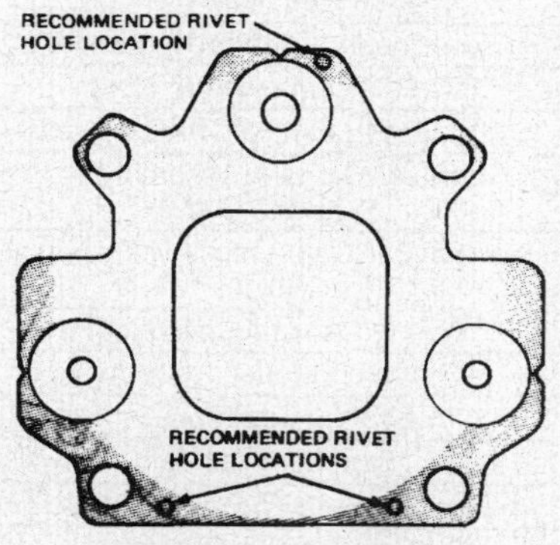

Fig. 3 Rivet hole location

10. Install alignment plates and loosely install strut mounting nuts.
11. Align front end and tighten strut mounting nuts to specifications.
12. Drill three ⅛ inch holes as indicated in **Fig. 3,** through alignment plates and strut towers, and paint exposed metal. **Do not drill deeper than ⅜ inch into strut tower.**
13. Install three ⅛ inch diameter pop rivets with a grip range of ¼ inch into alignment plate/strut tower.

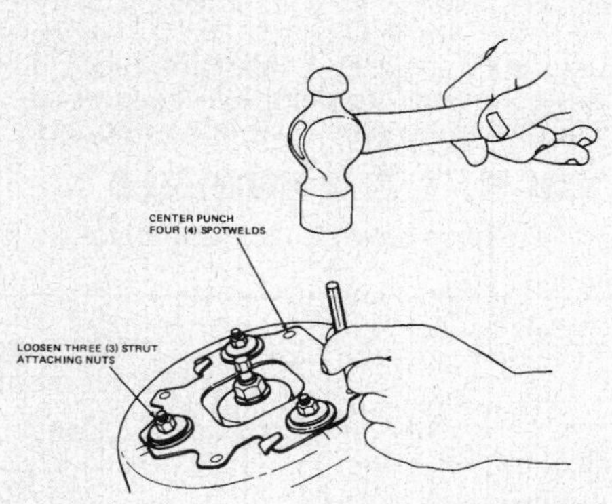

Fig. 2 Alignment plate loosening

TOE-IN

1. Lock steering wheel in straight ahead position using suitable steering wheel holder.
2. Loosen and slide off small outer clamps from steering boot to prevent boot from twisting during adjustment procedure.
3. Loosen tie rod adjusting, and adjust lefthand and righthand tie rods until each wheel has half the desired total toe specification.
4. Tighten tie rod adjusting nuts and install clamps.
5. Remove steering wheel holding tool.

REAR WHEEL ALIGNMENT

CASTER & CAMBER

The caster and camber angles are factory set and cannot be adjusted. However, rear camber adjustment kit part No. E7DZ-5K751-B, or an equivalent, may be installed to allow for adjustment.

TOE-IN

On sedan models, toe-in is adjusted by rotating the cams located inside the rear inner lower control arm bushings.

On wagon models, toe-in is adjusted by rotating the cams located inside the outer lower control arm bushings.

FOCUS

NOTE: Refer To The Rear Of This Manual For Manufacturer's Special Service Tool Suppliers.

INDEX OF SERVICE OPERATIONS

Specifications

GENERAL ENGINE SPECIFICATIONS

Year	Engine		Fuel System	Bore x Stroke, Inches	Comp. Ratio	Net HP @ RPM	Maximum Torque, Ft. Lbs. @ RPM	Oil Pressure, psi
	Liter	VIN Code①						
2000–01	2.0L (DOHC)	3	SFI	3.39 x 3.52	9.6:1	130	135	②
	2.0L (SOHC)	P	SFI	3.39 x 3.52	9.35:1	110	125	③

SFI–Sequential Electronic Fuel Injection.

① — The eighth digit of the VIN denotes engine code.

② — Pressure at normal operating temperature should be 19–36 psi @ 800–850 RPM and 54–80 psi @ 4000 RPM.

③ — Pressure at normal operating temperature should be 35–65 psi @ 2000 RPM.

TUNE UP SPECIFICATIONS

Year	Engine/VIN①	Spark Plug Gap, Inch	Firing Order, Fig.	Curb Idle Speed	Fuel Pump Pressure, psi	Valve Clearance, Inch	
						Intake	Exhaust
2000–01	2.0L (DOHC)/3	.054	1–3–4–2	②	35–55③	.004–.007	.010–.013
	2.0L (SOHC)/P	.054	1–3–4–2	②	35–55③	—	—

① — The eighth digit of the VIN denotes engine code.

② — Idle speed is electronically controlled and is non adjustable.

③ — Key on, engine off.

FRONT WHEEL ALIGNMENT SPECIFICATIONS

Year	Vehicle	Caster Angle, Degrees		Camber Angle, Degrees		Toe-In, Degrees
		Limits	Desired	Limits	Desired	
2000–01	Sedan	+1.93 to +3.93	+2.93	-1.85 to +.6	-.6	–.25 to +.25
	Wagon	+1.44 to +3.5	+2.47	-1.87 to +.63	-.62	–.25 to +.25

REAR WHEEL ALIGNMENT SPECIFICATIONS

Year	Vehicle	Camber, Degrees		Toe-In, Degrees	
		Limits	Desired	Limits	Desired
2000–01	Sedan	-2.18 to +.27	-.93	+.16 to +.84	+.5
	Wagon	-1.86 to +.64	-.61	0 to +.68	+.34

FLUID CAPACITIES & COOLING SYSTEM DATA

Year	Engine/ VIN①	Coolant Capacity, Qts.	Coolant Type	Radiator Cap Relief Pressure, Lbs.	Thermo. Opening Temp.	Fuel Tank, Gals.	Engine Oil Refill, Qts.②	Transmission Fluid	
								Man. Trans., Qts.	Auto. Trans., Qts.
2000–01	2.0L (DOHC)/ 3	5.2–6.1	Ethylene Glycol	20	197°F	13.2	4.5	2	7
	2.0L (SOHC)/ P	—	Ethylene Glycol	20	190°F	13.2	4	2.4	7

① — The eighth digit of the VIN denotes engine code.

② — Including oil filter.

LUBRICANT DATA

Year	Lubricant Type					
	Transmission			Power Steering	Brake System	Hydraulic Clutch Fluid
	Manual		Automatic			
	IB5	MTX 75				
2000–01	①	②	Mercon V XT-5-QM	③	DOT 3	DOT 4

① — Transaxle fluid meeting Ford specification WSD-M2C200–C.

② — Transaxle fluid meeting Ford specification ESD-M2C186–A.

③ — Power steering fluid meeting Ford specification WSA-M2C195–A.

Electrical

NOTE: On Air Bag Equipped Models, Refer To "Air Bag System Precautions" Located In The Front Of This Manual For System Disarming & Arming Procedures.

NOTE: Refer To "Computer Relearn Procedures" Located In The Front Of This Manual When Battery Power To The Computer Has Been Interrupted.

INDEX

PRECAUTIONS

AIR BAG SYSTEMS

Refer to "Air Bag System Precautions" in the front of this manual for system disarming and arming procedures.

BATTERY GROUND CABLE

Prior to service, disconnect battery ground cable and isolate as required.

ELECTROSTATIC DISCHARGE

Electronic modules are sensitive to electrical charges. Ensure modules are not exposed to these charges or damage may result.

FUSE PANEL & FLASHER LOCATION

The central junction box is located in the lefthand side footwell, **Fig. 1.**

The fuse box is located under the lefthand side of instrument panel, **Fig. 2.**

FUEL PUMP RELAY LOCATION

The fuel pump relay is located in the battery junction box in the engine compartment, **Fig. 3.**

STARTER

REPLACE

DOHC ENGINE

1. Raise and support vehicle.
2. Disconnect starter motor electrical connector.
3. Remove mounting bolts and starter motor.
4. Reverse procedure to install, noting the following:
    a. **Torque** mounting bolts to 26 ft. lbs.
    b. **Torque** electrical connector nut to 106 inch lbs.

SOHC ENGINE

1. Remove air cleaner outlet tube.
2. Remove starter motor mounting bolts.
3. Raise and support vehicle.
4. Disconnect starter motor electrical connector.
5. Remove starter motor.
6. Reverse procedure to install, noting the following:
    a. **Torque** mounting bolts to 26 ft. lbs.
    b. **Torque** electrical connector nut to 106 inch lbs.

ALTERNATOR

REPLACE

DOHC ENGINE

1. Remove drive belt.
2. Remove cover and disconnect electrical connectors.
3. Remove mounting bolt and secure coolant expansion tank to one side.
4. Secure power steering reservoir to one side.
5. Remove mounting bolt and secure engine wiring loom bracket to one side.
6. Disconnect ground cable.
7. Remove mounting nuts and secure evaporative emission canister purge valve to one side.
8. Remove righthand mounting bolt and fully loosen lefthand bolt. Lefthand bolt cannot be remove at this time.
9. Remove alternator.
10. Reverse procedure to install, noting the following:
    a. **Torque** mounting bolts to 18 ft. lbs.
    b. **Torque** electrical connector nut to 71 inch lbs.

SOHC ENGINE

1. Remove drive belt.
2. Remove power steering pipe support brackets.
3. Remove exhaust manifold heat shield.
4. Raise and support vehicle.
5. Disconnect alternator electrical connectors.
6. Remove mounting bolts and alternator.
7. Reverse procedure to install, nothing the following:
    a. **Torque** mounting bolts to 35 ft. lbs.
    b. **Torque** electrical connector nut to 71 inch lbs.

IGNITION COIL

REPLACE

DOHC ENGINE

1. Disconnect spark plug wires and electrical connectors from ignition coil.
2. Remove mounting bolts, then the ignition coil.
3. Reverse procedure to install. **Torque** mounting bolts to 53 inch lbs.

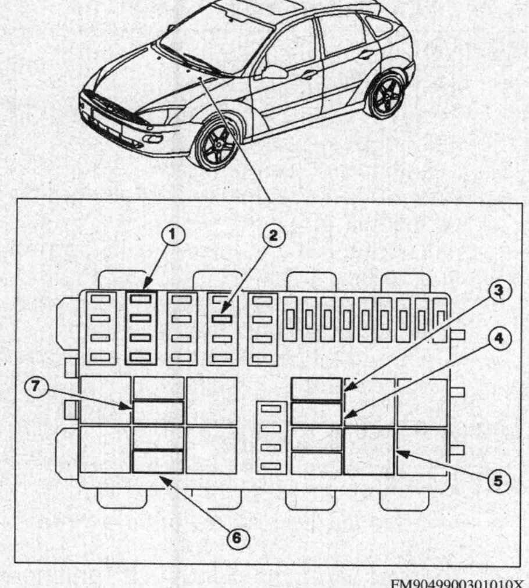

Fig. 1 Central junction box (Part 1 of 2)

SOHC ENGINE

1. Disconnect spark plug wires and electrical connectors from ignition coil.
2. Remove mounting bolts, ignition coil, capacitor and bracket.
3. Remove mounting bolts, then the ignition coil and capacitor from bracket.
4. Reverse procedure to install. **Torque** mounting bolts to 88 inch lbs.

IGNITION LOCK

REPLACE

1. Remove mounting screws, fastener and instrument panel lower panel.
2. Disconnect steering column upper shroud using a suitable thin bladed screwdriver to release clip on each side.
3. Remove audio control switch using a suitable thin bladed screwdriver to release locking tang and disconnecting electrical connector.
4. Release locking lever, then remove mounting screws and steering column lower shroud.
5. Disconnect electrical connector, then remove mounting screw and passive anti-theft system transceiver.
6. Insert and turn ignition key to accessory position No. 1.
7. Depress detent using a suitable thin bladed screwdriver.
8. Remove lock cylinder.
9. Reverse procedure to install.

IGNITION SWITCH

REPLACE

1. Remove mounting screws, fastener and instrument panel lower panel.
2. Disconnect steering column upper shroud using a suitable thin bladed screwdriver to release clip on each side.
3. Release locking lever, then remove mounting screws and steering column lower shroud.
4. Release clips and remove ignition switch.
5. Reverse procedure to install.

NEUTRAL SAFETY SWITCH

REPLACE

1. Disconnect Transmission Range (TR) sensor electrical connector and selector lever cable.
2. Remove manual control lever. **Shift lever must be held while loosening manual shaft lever.**
3. Remove mounting bolts and TR sensor.
4. Reverse procedure to install, noting the following:
   a. Align TR sensor with alignment tool No. 307-415, or equivalent.
   b. **Torque** mounting bolts to 88 inch lbs.

HEADLAMP SWITCH

REPLACE

1. Remove driver's side lower footwell trim.
2. Remove mounting screws and disconnect lamp switch bezel.
3. Remove mounting screws, disconnect electrical connectors and remove lamp switch.
4. Reverse procedure to install.

AIR BAG MODULE

REPLACE

DRIVER'S

1. Disarm air bag system as outlined under "Passive Restraint Systems"
2. Turn steering wheel to access and remove mounting bolts.
3. Disconnect electrical connector from air bag module and sliding contact.
4. Remove air bag module.
5. Disconnect contact plate left and right-hand electrical connectors.
6. Reverse procedure to install. **Torque** mounting bolts to 44 inch lbs.

STEERING WHEEL

REPLACE

1. Remove air bag module as outlined under "Passive Restraint Systems."
2. Ensure steering wheel is centered.
3. Remove ignition key to lock steering in position.
4. Disconnect speed control electrical connector.
5. Remove mounting bolt and steering wheel.
6. Reverse procedure to install, noting the following:
   a. Ensure air bag sliding contact is centralized.
   b. **Torque** mounting bolt to 37 ft. lbs.
   c. Turn steering wheel counterclockwise to check location.

Item	Description
1	Fuse F16 (10 A) for dipped beam, left
2	Fuse F17 (10 A) for dipped beam, right
3	Fuse F26 (10 A) main beam, left
4	Fuse F27 (10 A) main beam, right
5	Fuse F22 (15 A) - Dipped beam /daytime running lights
6	Main beam relay
7	Dipped beam relay
8	Headlamp washer system relay
9	Brake light relay
10	Daytime running lights relay

FM9049900301020X

Fig. 1 Central junction box (Part 2 of 2)

STEERING COLUMN

REPLACE

1. Disarm air bag module as outlined under "Passive Restraint Systems."
2. Center steering wheel, then remove key to lock steering in position.
3. Remove mounting screws and fasteners, then disconnect instrument panel lower panel.
4. Disconnect hood release cable and data link electrical connector.
5. Remove instrument panel lower panel.
6. Remove steering column upper shroud under suitable thin bladed screwdriver to release clips.
7. Release steering column locking lever, then remove mounting screws and steering column lower shroud.
8. Disconnect passive anti-theft system transceiver, wiper/washer switch and air bag sliding contact/speed control electrical connectors.
9. Disconnect ignition switch and turn signal/flash-to-pass switch electrical connectors.
10. Release locating pin and wiring harness, then disconnect wiring harness from steering column.
11. Remove mounting bolt and disconnect steering column pinion shaft extension.
12. Remove mounting nuts, Torx bolt and steering column.
13. Reverse procedure to install, noting the following:
    a. **Torque** mounting bolt and nuts to 115 inch lbs.
    b. **Torque** steering column pinion shaft extension mounting bolt to 21 ft. lbs.
    c. **Torque** hood release cable nut to 15 ft. lbs.

INSTRUMENT CLUSTER

REPLACE

1. Disconnect instrument cluster bezel.
2. Disconnect luggage compartment release switch electrical connector and remove instrument cluster bezel.
3. Remove instrument cluster mounting screws.
4. Release locking tang and disconnect electrical connector.
5. Remove instrument cluster. **Instrument cluster must be kept upright to avoid allowing leaking silicone liquid to leak from gauges.**
6. Reverse procedure to install.

RADIO

REPLACE

1. Install radio remover tools No. T87P-19061-A, or equivalent, into locating holes until they click into place.
2. Pull tools gently left and right until locking tangs release.
3. Slide radio out of instrument panel.
4. Disconnect electrical connectors and remove radio.
5. Reverse procedure to install.

WIPER MOTOR

REPLACE

FRONT

1. Ensure wiper motor is in park position.
2. Lift plastic caps and loosen wiper arm mounting nuts approximately two turns.
3. Lift and release wiper arms from taper, then move to one side.
4. Remove mounting nuts and wiper arms.
5. Remove caps, mounting bolts and air cowl grille.
6. Remove wiper motor protective cap and disconnect electrical connector.
7. Remove mounting bolts, wiper motor and linkage.
8. Mark lever position in relation to assembly plate for installation alignment.
9. Remove mounting nut, bolts and wiper motor from plate and lever.
10. Reverse procedure to install, noting the following:
    a. Ensure wiper motor is in park position.
    b. **Torque** wiper motor mounting bolts to 71 inch lbs.
    c. **Torque** linkage bolt to 15 ft. lbs.
    d. Fit guide pins before fitting mounting bolts when installing wiper linkage.
    e. Ensure wiper blades do not touch air cowl griller or molding.

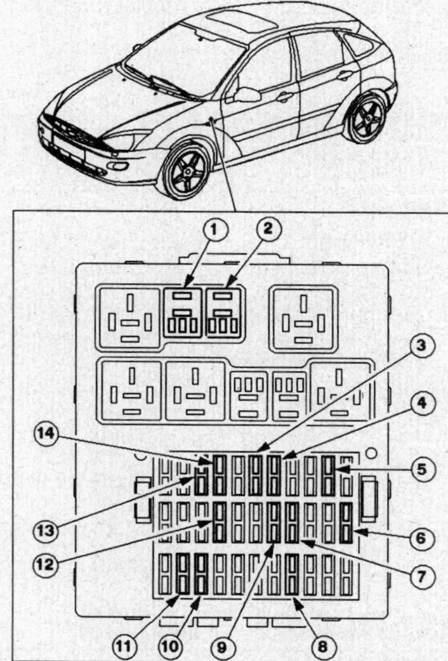

Fig. 2 Fuse box (Part 1 of 2)

    f. Check wiper operation.

REAR

1. Ensure wiper motor is in park position.
2. Lift plastic caps and loosen wiper arm mounting nuts approximately two turns.
3. Lift and release wiper arms from taper, then move to one side.
4. Remove mounting nuts and wiper arms.
5. Remove two mounting bolts and 10 clips, then the cover.
6. Disconnect wiper motor electrical connector and ground lead.
7. Remove mounting bolts and wiper motor from bracket.
    a. Ensure wiper motor is in park position.
    b. **Torque** wiper motor mounting bolts to 71 inch lbs.
    c. Check wiper operation.

BLOWER MOTOR

REPLACE

1. Remove passenger side footwell lower trim.
2. Disconnect floor level ventilation hose.
3. Disconnect electrical connect.
4. Remove mounting screws and blower motor.
5. Reverse procedure to install.

CABIN AIR FILTER

REPLACE

1. Position wipers vertically.
2. Remove caps, mounting screws and passenger side of air cowl grille.
3. Open flap and remove filter.
4. Reverse procedure to install, noting the following:
    a. Ensure filter is installed in correct direction flow.
    b. Clean grille rubber edging between wiper motor and filter housing.
    c. Ensure air cowl grille gasket is seated correctly.

HEATER CORE

REPLACE

1. Remove audio unit as outlined previously.
2. Recover A/C refrigerant as outlined under "Air Conditioning."
3. Drain cooling system into suitable container.
4. Remove instrument panel as outlined under "Dash Panel Service" in Volume 2 of this manual.
5. Disconnect coolant hoses from heat exchanger take off connection.
6. Disconnect refrigerant lines from evaporator using suitable A/C fitting removal tool.
7. Remove cross vehicle beam as follows:
    a. Remove cap, then the bolt behind cap, **Fig. 4.**
    b. Unclip and remove ventilation hoses, remove screws and disconnect wiring harnesses from beam, **Fig. 5.**
    c. Unclip and remove ventilation hoses, remove screws, then detach junction box from cross vehicle beam, **Fig. 6.**
    d. Remove ventilation hose, unclip wiring harnesses from beam, remove cross vehicle beam bracket, then the cross vehicle beam, **Fig. 7.**
8. Remove rear footwell ventilation hoses, **Fig. 8.**
9. Unclip wiring harnesses from heater housing.
10. Remove heater housing mounting nuts from inside of vehicle and from engine compartment area of vehicle.
11. Remove heater housing.
12. Reverse procedure to install.

EVAPORATOR CORE

REPLACE

Refer to"Heater Core, Replace" for evaporator core replacement.

Item	Description
1	Rear wiper relay
2	Windscreen wiper relay
3	Fuse F35 (7,5 A) - Interior lights
4	Fuse F36 (7,5 A) - Interior lights
5	Fuse F39 (10A) - reversing lights
8	Fuse F59 (7,5 A) - Direction indicators, electronic module
9	Fuse F47 (7,5A) - left-hand side lights
10	Fuse F54 (15 A) - Brake light
11	Fuse F53 (10A) - reversing lights
12	Fuse F44 (20 A) - Fog lamps
13	Fuse F32 (10 A) for instrument cluster illumination
14	Fuse F33 (15 A) - Hazard warning lights switch

FM9049900302020X

Fig. 2 Fuse box (Part 2 of 2)

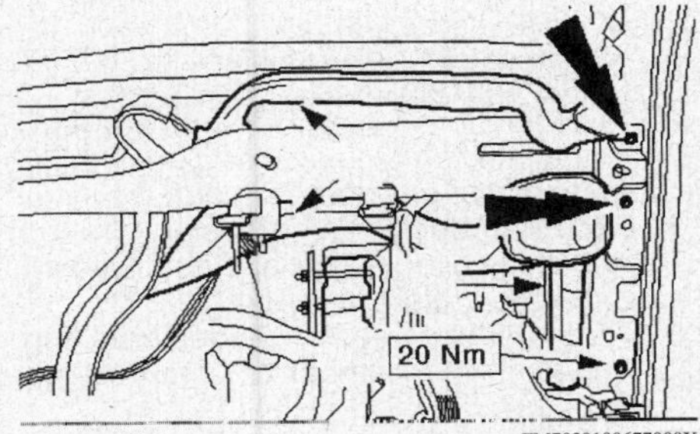

Fig. 5 Ventilation hoses and wiring harness locations

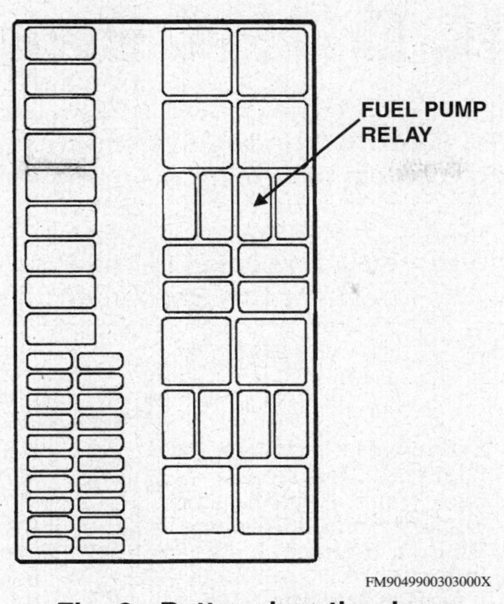

Fig. 3 Battery junction box

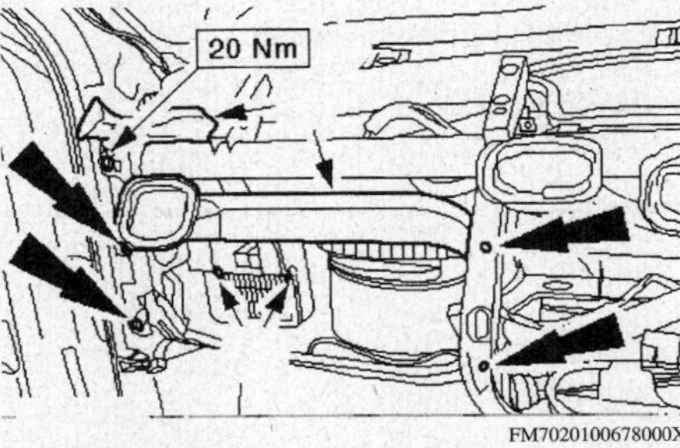

Fig. 6 Central junction box and ventilation hose locations

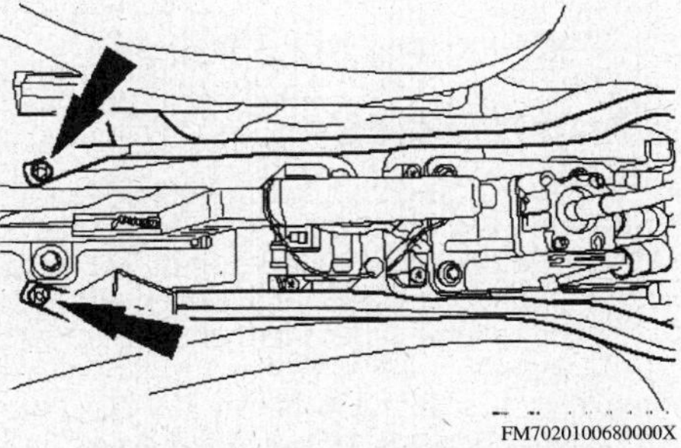

Fig. 8 Rear footwell ventilation hoses

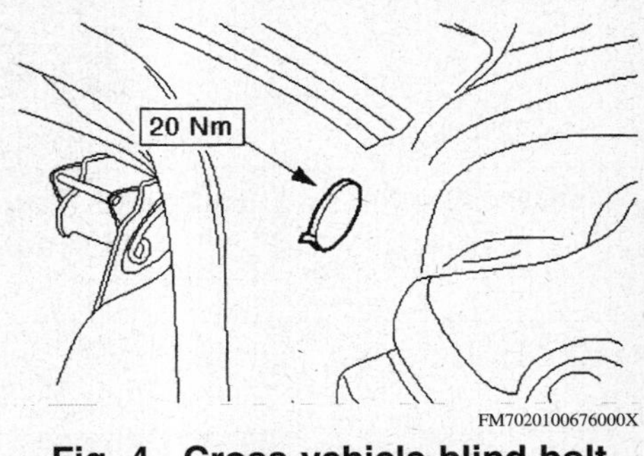

Fig. 4 Cross vehicle blind bolt location

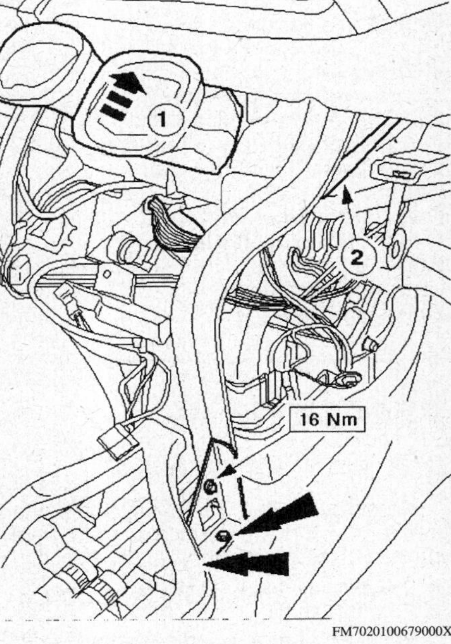

Fig. 7 Cross vehicle beam removal

2.0L DOHC Engine

NOTE: On Air Bag Equipped Models, Refer To "Air Bag System Precautions" Located In The Front Of This Manual For System Disarming & Arming Procedures.

NOTE: Refer To "Computer Relearn Procedures" Located In The Front Of This Manual When Battery Power To The Computer Has Been Interrupted.

INDEX

PRECAUTIONS

AIR BAG SYSTEMS

Refer to "Air Bag System Precautions" in the front of this manual for system disarming and arming procedures.

BATTERY GROUND CABLE

Prior to service, disconnect battery ground cable and isolate as required.

FUEL SYSTEM PRESSURE RELIEF

1. Remove fuel pump fuse.
2. Start and run engine until it stalls.
3. Crank engine for approximately five seconds to ensure fuel supply manifold pressure has been relieved.
4. Install fuel pump fuse.

QUICK DISCONNECT HOSES

R-CLIP

When working with R-clip type connections, **Fig. 1,** do not use tools to disconnect. Use of tools may deform clip components and could cause leaks.

To disconnect, bend shipping tab downward, **Fig. 1.** Spread R-clip and push clip into fitting. Separate fitting from tube.

To install, first inspect fitting and tube for damage and ensure connections are clean. Apply a light coat of clean 5W–30 motor oil to male end of tube. Insert R-clip into fitting. Align tube and fitting, then insert tube into fitting and push together until a click is heard. Pull on connection to ensure it is fully engaged.

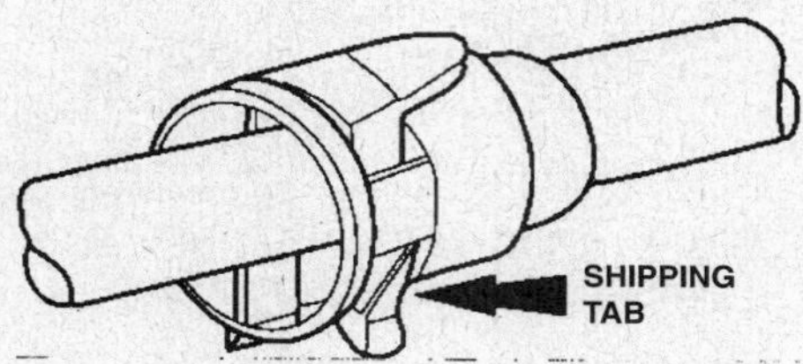

Fig. 1 R-clip connection

SPRING LOCK

When working with spring lock type connections, **Fig. 2,** spring lock tool set No. T84L-19623-B, or equivalent, must be used to disconnect fittings. When connecting spring lock type fittings, inspect and clean both coupling ends. Lubricate fuel line O-ring seals with clean 5W-30 motor oil. When connection is made, pull on line to ensure it is fully engaged.

VAPOR TUBE

To disconnect vapor tube connections, squeeze fitting (1) and disconnect vapor tube from fitting (2), **Fig. 3.** To connect, ensure fittings are clean and free from damage. Push tube onto fitting until it snaps into place. Pull on connection to verify fitting is secure.

COMPRESSION PRESSURE

Before performing compression test, ensure the following conditions are met: crankcase oil is of correct viscosity and at correct level, ensure battery is fully charged and engine is at normal operating temperature.

1. Turn ignition switch to off position.
2. Remove all spark plugs.
3. Set throttle plates to wide open position.
4. Install a suitable compression gauge in No. 1 cylinder.
5. Install an auxiliary starter switch in starting circuit.
6. With ignition switch off, use auxiliary starter switch to crank engine a minimum of five compression strokes.
7. Note number of compression strokes necessary to reach highest reading and record highest reading.
8. Repeat test on each cylinder, cranking engine same number of compression strokes.
9. Indicated compression pressures are considered within specifications if lowest reading cylinder is within 75 percent of highest reading.

ENGINE

REPLACE

1. Relieve fuel system pressure as outlined under "Precautions."
2. Ensure engine is cool, then open coolant expansion tank.
3. Remove battery, then the battery tray and ground cable.
4. Disconnect MAF sensor and PCV hose from air cleaner housing.
5. Remove air cleaner housing.
6. Disconnect all body ground cables as required.
7. Remove air cleaner intake hose from core support.
8. Drain engine coolant into a suitable container.
9. Loosen right and left suspension strut

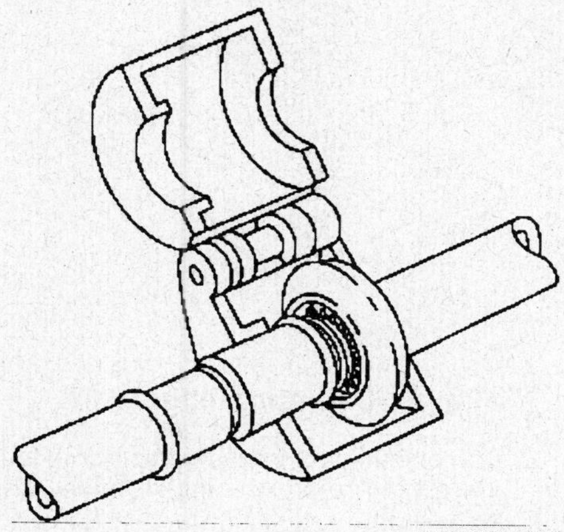

Fig. 2 Spring lock connection

center nuts five turns. Use a suitable Allen key to prevent strut piston rod from turning.

10. Loosen right and left front wheel nuts.
11. **On models equipped with manual transaxle,** move shift lever to neutral position, then remove shift lever cover and attach gearshift alignment tool No. T97P-7025-A, or equivalent, to gearshift lever.
12. **On all models,** disconnect speed control and accelerator cables.
13. Disconnect the following connectors:
    a. Ignition coil.
    b. Radio interference filter.
    c. Heated oxygen sensor.
    d. Cooling fan.
    e. Fuel injector wiring.
    f. Alternator and engine harness.
14. **On models equipped with manual transaxle,** disconnect reverse lamp switch, then the high pressure line from clutch slave cylinder.
15. **On all models,** disconnect vehicle speed sensor and CKP sensor.
16. Remove air deflector and cooling fan.
17. Disconnect engine vacuum hoses.
18. Disconnect fuel lines, then the heater hoses.
19. **On models equipped with automatic transaxle,** proceed as follows:
    a. Disconnect selector lever cable from transaxle.
    b. Remove selector cable bracket.
    c. Mark location of transaxle cooling lines, then remove.
20. **On models equipped with manual transaxle,** proceed as follows:
    a. Disconnect shift cable from gear lever.
    b. Pretension the abutment collars by turning counterclockwise and remove cable assembly from bracket.
    c. Disconnect selector cable from selector lever.
    d. Pretension abutment collars by turning counterclockwise and remove cable assembly from bracket.
    e. Release adjustment mechanism by pressing inward.
21. **On all models,** raise and support vehicle.
22. Remove drive belt cover.
23. Disconnect power steering pressure switch, then remove accessory drive belt.
24. **On models equipped with A/C** remove compressor from mounting bracket, then attach to radiator crossmember.
25. **On all models,** disconnect coolant hose, then remove power steering pump attaching bolts.
26. Lower vehicle, then disconnect power steering high pressure line.
27. Remove power steering pump, then the coolant expansion tank and position aside.
28. Remove power steering reservoir and position aside.
29. Raise and support vehicle.
30. Remove flexible exhaust pipe.
31. Remove engine roll restrictor.
32. Remove front wheels.
33. Remove lower ball joint attaching bolts, then disconnect lower ball joint from steering knuckle.
34. Disconnect intermediate shaft bearing cap and discard nuts and bearing cap. **Ensure inner joint is not bent more than 18° and outer joint is not bent more than 45°.**
35. Pull intermediate shaft with front halfshaft from transmission and support using suitable mechanics wire.
36. Remove lefthand driveshaft from transaxle and support using suitable mechanics wire.
37. Install differential plug tool No. 205–164, or equivalent, to both sides of differential.
38. Place assembly table with wooden blocks under vehicle, then lower vehicle until engine and transmission assembly is on assembly stand.
39. Secure engine and transmission assembly to assembly stand using a suitable safety strap.
40. Remove rear engine mount, then the front engine mount.
41. Raise and support vehicle.
42. Install engine lift brackets tool No. T70P-6000 and spreader bar tool No. D93P-6001-A3, or equivalents to engine.
43. Attaching a suitable lifting crane to spreader bar.
44. Remove starter motor and ground cable.
45. Remove engine to transmission attaching bolts, then separate engine from transmission.
46. Reverse procedure to install noting the following:
    a. When installing front driveshafts, use new snap rings, center bearing caps and bolts. Right halfshaft should be installed first, then the left.
    b. **On models equipped with manual transaxle,** bleed hydraulic clutch system.
    c. **On all models,** fill all fluids to proper level and inspect for leaks.

INTAKE MANIFOLD

REPLACE

1. Relieve fuel system pressure as outlined under "Precautions."

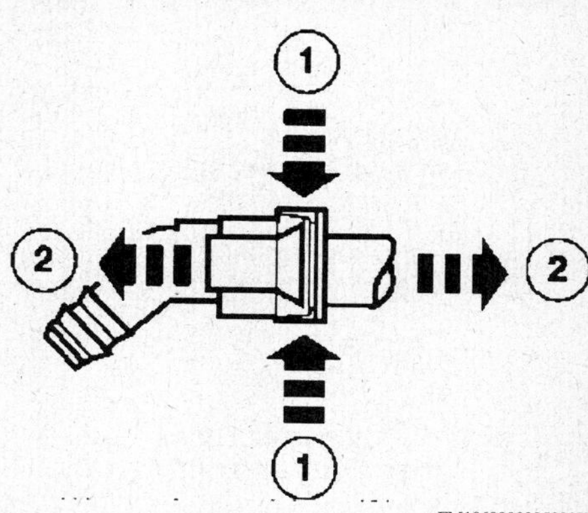

Fig. 3 Vapor tube connection

2. Disconnect MAF sensor electrical connector, crankcase ventilation hose and air intake hose from air cleaner housing.
3. Remove air cleaner housing from engine compartment.
4. Disconnect accelerator cable and speed control cable from throttle body.
5. Remove EGR valve and EGR pipe bracket.
6. Disconnect vacuum hoses from throttle body.
7. Disconnect fuel injector and Camshaft Position (CMP) sensor electrical connectors.
8. Remove fuel line from throttle body.
9. Remove intake manifold studs from front of engine.
10. Remove intake manifold attaching bolts and nuts, then the intake manifold.
11. Reverse procedure to install. Tighten bolts, nuts and studs to specification.

EXHAUST MANIFOLD

REPLACE

1. Raise and support vehicle.
2. Remove exhaust manifold bracket, then disconnect heated oxygen sensor electrical connectors.
3. Lower vehicle and remove heat shield from side of engine.
4. Remove air cleaner housing and air inlet hose.
5. Remove catalytic converter to exhaust manifold attaching bolts.
6. Remove exhaust manifold to cylinder head attaching bolts, then the exhaust manifold.
7. Reverse procedure to install.

CYLINDER HEAD

REPLACE

When cleaning cylinder head surfaces, do not use metal scrapers, wires brushes, power abrasive discs or other abrasive methods to clean sealing surfaces. Use only a plastic scraping tool to remove all traces of gasket material.

Cylinder head bolts are of torque to yield style and must be replaced when removed.

1. Raise and support vehicle, then drain cooling system.

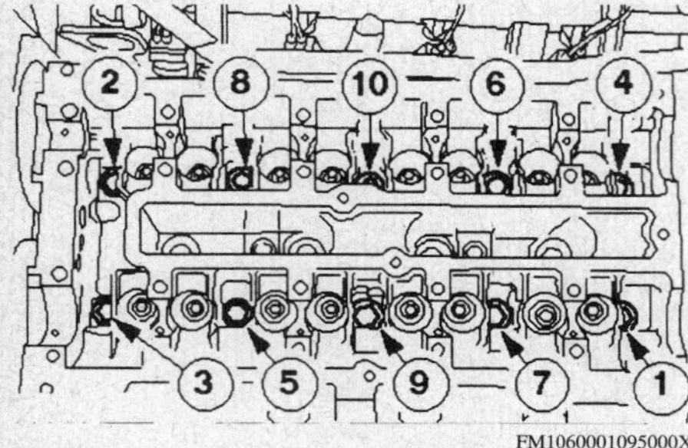

Fig. 4 Cylinder head bolt loosening sequence

2. Disconnect brake booster pipe from intake manifold, then the oil pressure switch connector.
3. Lower vehicle and remove intake manifold as outlined under "Intake Manifold, Replace."
4. Remove exhaust manifold heat shield, then the catalytic converter to exhaust manifold attaching bolts.
5. Remove thermostat housing attaching bolts, then the thermostat housing.
6. Remove power steering pipe bracket and oil level indicator tube.
7. Remove timing belt as outlined under "Timing Belt, Replace."
8. Remove camshafts as outlined under "Camshaft, Replace."
9. Remove power steering pump from its bracket and position aside.
10. Remove alternator from bracket and position aside.
11. Remove upper bolt from alternator bracket.
12. Remove cylinder head attaching bolts in sequence, **Fig. 4.**
13. Remove cylinder head.
14. Reverse procedure to install, noting the following:
    a. Ensure sealing surface and bolt holes are clean.
    b. Using sequence shown in **Fig. 5,** tighten cylinder head bolts in three steps. First step, **torque** bolts to 15 ft. lbs.; second step, **torque** bolts to 30 ft. lbs.; third step, tighten bolts an additional 90.°

VALVE COVER

REPLACE

1. Remove air inlet hose from throttle body and air cleaner housing.
2. Remove timing belt upper cover attaching bolts, then the upper cover.
3. Disconnect spark plug connectors and the crankcase ventilation hose.
4. Remove valve cover attaching bolts, then the valve cover.
5. Reverse procedure to install.

VALVE CLEARANCE SPECIFICATIONS

Valve	Clearance, Inches
Intake	.004–.007
Exhaust	.010–.013

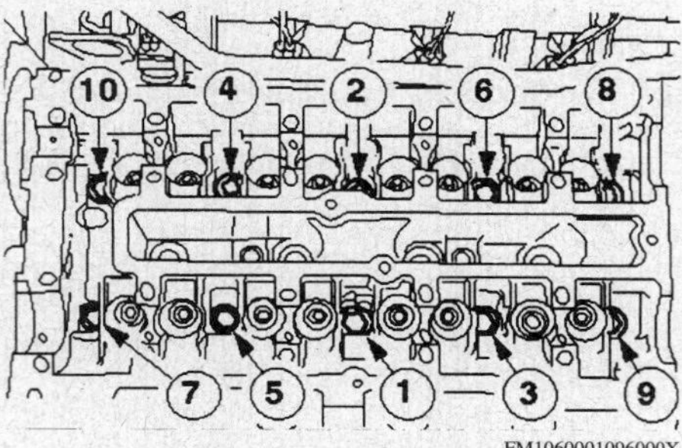

Fig. 5 Cylinder head bolt tightening sequence

VALVE ADJUSTMENT

1. Remove valve cover as outlined under "Valve Cover, Replace."
2. Turn crankshaft to TDC on No. 1 cylinder.
3. Measure valve clearance on No. 1 cylinder, using a suitable feeler gauge.
4. Rotate engine 180°, then measure valve clearance on No. 3 cylinder.
5. Rotate engine 180°, then measure valve clearance on No. 4 cylinder.
6. Rotate engine 180°, then measure valve clearance on No. 2 cylinder.
7. If valve adjustment is necessary, remove camshafts as outlined under "Camshaft, Replace."
8. Each tappet is marked with a number that indicates its thickness in millimeters.
9. To determine correct size tappet needed add tappet size to measured clearance.
10. Select and install a tappet that will bring clearance within specifications, refer to "Valve Clearance Specifications."
11. Install camshafts as outlined under "Camshaft, Replace."

CRANKSHAFT DAMPER

REPLACE

1. Raise and support vehicle.
2. Remove serpentine drive belt as outlined under "Serpentine Drive Belt."
3. Remove crankshaft pulley/vibration damper.
4. Reverse procedure to install.

TIMING BELT

REPLACE

REMOVAL

1. Raise and support vehicle.
2. Remove serpentine drive belt as outlined under "Serpentine Drive Belt."
3. Remove crankshaft pulley/vibration damper.
4. Remove lower timing belt cover.
5. Lower vehicle, then remove coolant expansion tank and position aside.
6. Remove power steering fluid reservoir and position aside.
7. Position a suitable jack with a wooden block under the oil pan, then raise engine enough to remove load from front engine mount.

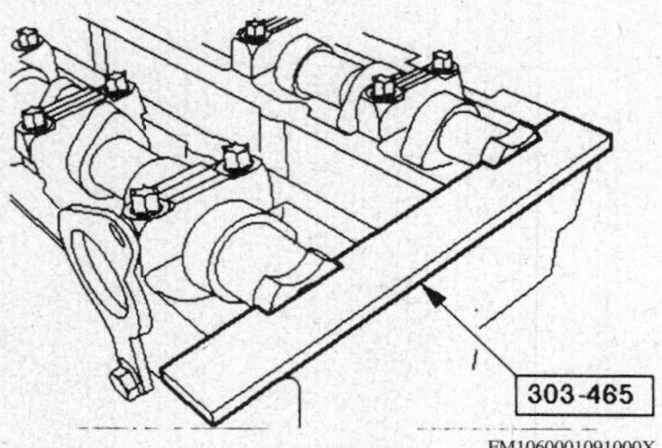

Fig. 6 Camshaft alignment

8. Mark position of front engine mount for installation reference, then remove engine mount.
9. Remove timing belt upper cover attaching bolts. **Do not remove upper cover at this time.**
10. Remove timing belt center cover and front engine mounting bracket.
11. Remove timing belt upper cover.
12. Disconnect spark plug wire connectors, then the PCV hose.
13. Remove cylinder head cover, then the spark plugs.
14. Turn crankshaft until cylinder No. 1 is at TDC.
15. Loosen timing belt tensioner attaching bolt by turning clockwise, then turn bolt four turns and unhook timing belt tensioner.
16. Remove timing belt.
17. To prevent camshaft pulley from turning, attach camshaft pulley remover tool No. T74P-6256-B, or equivalent, to camshaft pulley.
18. Loosen camshaft pulley attaching bolts.

INSTALLATION

1. Turn camshafts to ignition position on No. 1 cylinder, then insert camshaft alignment plate tool No. 303–465, or equivalent, **Fig. 6.**
2. Position crankshaft to TDC on No. 1 cylinder, **Fig. 7.**
3. Remove blanking plug and install crankshaft TDC timing peg tool No. T97-P6000-A, or equivalent, **Fig. 8.**
4. Starting from crankshaft timing pulley and working counterclockwise, install timing belt. Pull belt tight while installing.
5. Hook belt tensioner into pressed steel cover. Loosely install tensioner bolt.
6. Tension belt by turning tensioner counterclockwise until arrow points at mark, **Fig. 9.**
7. To prevent camshaft pulley from turning, attach camshaft pulley remover tool No. T74P-6256-B, or equivalent, to camshaft pulley.
8. Tighten camshaft pulley attaching bolts to specifications.
9. Remove crankshaft TDC timing peg and camshaft alignment plate tools.
10. Turn crankshaft two complete revolutions in normal direction of rotation, then check for correct valve timing as follows:
    a. Install crankshaft TDC timing peg

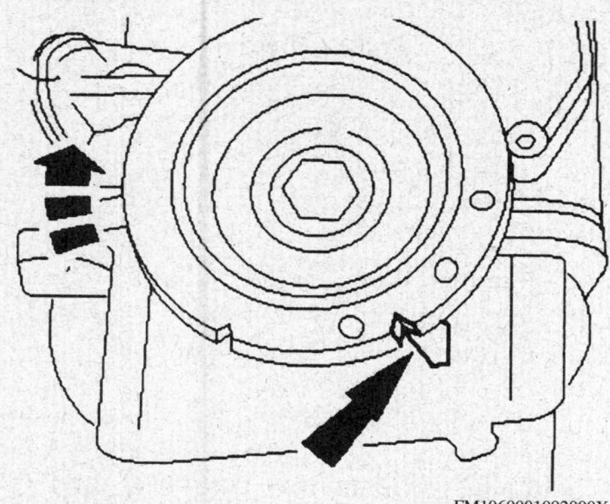

Fig. 7 Crankshaft timing mark alignment

tool No. T97-P6000-A, or equivalent, ensure crankshaft is touching tool.
   b. Insert camshaft alignment plate tool No. 303–465, or equivalent, if necessary, loosen pulleys to correct camshaft alignment.
   c. Remove crankshaft TDC timing peg and camshaft alignment plate tools.
11. Install blanking plug and tighten to specifications.
12. Install cylinder head cover and spark plugs.
13. Coat inside of spark plug connectors with suitable silicone sealant, then connect to spark plugs.
14. Place center and upper timing belt covers into position.
15. Install center cover and front engine mounting bracket attaching bolts and tighten to specification.
16. Ensure upper timing belt cover and gasket are properly aligned, then install upper cover attaching bolts and tighten to specification.
17. Install front engine mount, power steering reservoir and coolant expansion tank.
18. Remove jack and wooden block from under oil pan.
19. Raise and support vehicle, then install lower timing belt cover.
20. Install crankshaft pulley.
21. Install serpentine belt and drive belt cover.
22. Lower vehicle.

CAMSHAFT

REPLACE

REMOVAL

1. Remove intake manifold as outlined under "Intake Manifold, Replace."
2. Remove timing belt as outlined under "Timing Belt, Replace."
3. To prevent camshaft pulley from turning, attach camshaft pulley remover tool No. T74P-6256-B, or equivalent, to camshaft pulley.
4. Remove camshaft pulley retaining bolt, then the camshaft pulley.
5. Using loosening sequence shown in **Fig. 10,** remove camshaft bearing cap attaching bolts in several steps.

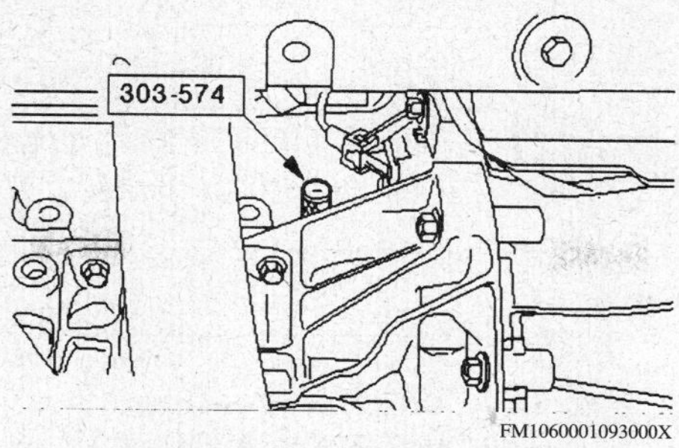

Fig. 8 Crankshaft TDC timing peg installation

6. Remove oil seals and camshafts.

INSTALLATION

1. Camshaft bearing caps have identification numbers stamped on the outer face. Apply a suitable sealant to bearing caps marked "0" and "5" as shown in **Fig. 11.**
2. Turn crankshaft to approximately 60° BTDC on No. 1 cylinder.
3. Lubricate camshafts and bearing caps with clean engine oil, then place camshafts into position so that none of the cams are at full lift.
4. Install and tighten camshaft bearing cap bolts as follows:
   a. Using tightening sequence shown in **Fig. 12,** install and tighten camshaft bearing cap bolts evenly ½ turn at a time.
   b. **Torque** bolts to 88 inch lbs. in sequence
   c. **Torque** bolts to 14 ft. lbs. in sequence.
5. Lubricate camshaft and new camshaft oil seal lip with clean engine oil, then install oil seal.
6. Install camshaft timing pulleys. **Do not tighten pulley bolts fully at this time. Pulleys must be able to turn freely on the camshafts.**
7. Install timing belt as outlined under "Timing Belt, Replace."
8. Install intake manifold as outlined under "Intake Manifold, Replace."
9. Install valve cover as outlined under "Valve Cover, Replace."

CRANKSHAFT SEAL

REPLACE

1. Remove crankshaft timing belt as outlined under "Timing Belt, Replace."
2. Pull off crankshaft pulley hub.
3. Remove timing belt thrust washer. Note position of thrust washer for installation reference.
4. Remove crankshaft front oil seal using oil seal remover tool No. 303-49, or equivalent.
5. Reverse procedure to install. Lubricate new oil seal with clean engine oil.

CRANKSHAFT REAR OIL SEAL

REPLACE

1. Remove transaxle to engine attaching bolts, then remove transaxle.

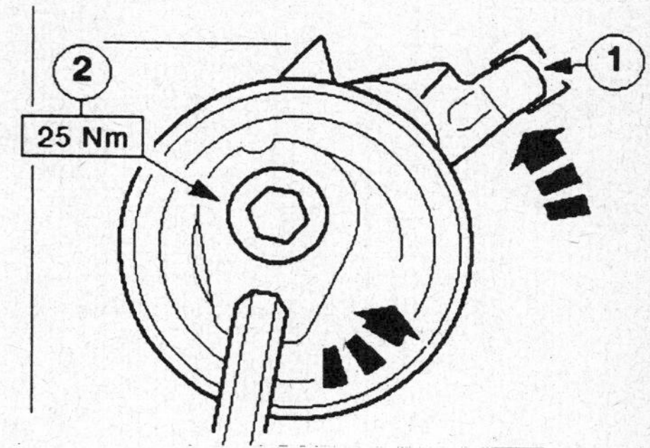

Fig. 9 Timing belt tensioner alignment

2. **On models equipped with manual transaxle,** attach flywheel locking device tool No. T74P-6375-A, or equivalent, to flywheel, then remove clutch pressure plate, clutch disk and flywheel.
3. **On models equipped with automatic transaxle,** attach flywheel locking device tool No. T74P-6375-A, or equivalent, to driveplate, then remove driveplate attaching bolts and the driveplate.
4. **On all models,** remove crankshaft rear seal using seal remover tool No. T92C-6700-CH, or equivalent.
5. Reverse procedure to install.

OIL PAN

REPLACE

1. Raise and support vehicle, then drain engine oil into suitable container.
2. Remove oil pan attaching bolts.
3. Separate oil pan from lower crankcase with a suitable sharp tool.
4. Reverse procedure to install, noting the following:
   a. Install ten M6 X 20 studs into dead end bores shown in **Fig. 13. Always use studs. Sealer in dead end bores may cause damage to ladder frame.**
   b. Apply suitable sealant to oil pan mating surface. Install oil pan within ten minutes of applying sealant.
   c. Using sequence shown in **Fig. 14,** tighten oil pan bolts in two steps: first step, **torque** bolts to 53 inch lbs.; second step, **torque** bolts to 89 inch lbs.

SERPENTINE DRIVE BELT

ROUTING

Refer to **Figs. 15 and 16** for serpentine belt routing.

REPLACE

1. Raise and support vehicle.
2. Remove splash shield.
3. Rotate belt tensioner counterclockwise, then remove belt.
4. Reverse procedure to install.

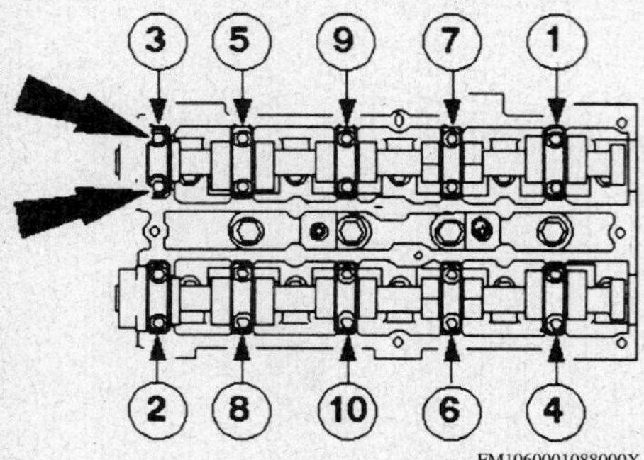

Fig. 10 Camshaft bearing cap bolt loosening sequence

COOLING SYSTEM BLEED

When releasing system pressure, cover the expansion tank cap with a thick cloth to prevent the possibility of scalding.

When draining the engine coolant or changing coolant system components, do not allow coolant to come into contact with the timing belt or accessory drive belt. Contamination of belts may result in premature failure.

1. Relieve cooling system pressure by turning expansion tank cap 1/4 turn, remove cap when pressure has been released.
2. Raise and support vehicle.
3. Drain coolant into suitable container.
4. Close radiator drain valve when all coolant has been drained from system.
5. Lower vehicle.
6. Disconnect heater supply hose from engine.
7. Using a suitable funnel, fill cooling system through the supply hose until coolant starts to trickle from engine.
8. Reconnect heater supply hose.
9. Set heater temperature control to HOT position and heater blower motor switch to OFF position. Ensure A/C is switched OFF.
10. Refill coolant expansion tank to MAX mark.
11. Install expansion tank cap.
12. Warm engine up at 2750 RPM for two fan cycles.
13. Allow engine to cool, then check coolant level and top up to MAX mark as necessary

THERMOSTAT

REPLACE

1. Drain engine cooling system into suitable container.
2. Disconnect coolant hoses from thermostat housing.

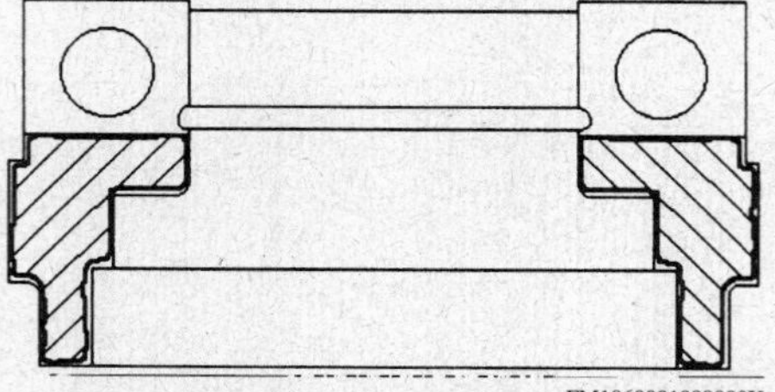

Fig. 11 Camshaft bearing cap sealant application

3. Remove thermostat housing bolts, then the housing.
4. Remove thermostat and gasket.
5. Reverse procedure to install.

WATER PUMP

REPLACE

1. Drain engine cooling system into suitable container.
2. Loosen water pump pulley attaching bolts.
3. Remove drive belt as outlined under "Serpentine Drive Belt."
4. Remove water pump pulley.
5. Remove timing belt as outlined under "Timing Belt, Replace."
6. Remove timing belt idler pulley.
7. Disconnect water pump hose.
8. Remove water pump lower and lower bolts, then the water pump.
9. Remove and discard water pump sealing ring.
10. Reverse procedure to install.

RADIATOR

REPLACE

1. Remove cooling fan motor and shroud.
2. Drain coolant into suitable container.
3. Raise and support vehicle.
4. Remove 4-pin type retainers from radiator air deflector.
5. Lower vehicle, then disconnect upper radiator hose.
6. Raise and support vehicle.
7. **On models equipped with A/C,** support condenser and transaxle fluid cooler.
8. **On all models,** disconnect lower radiator hoses.
9. Disconnect horn electrical connector.
10. Remove radiator support bracket bolts, then bracket.
11. Remove radiator from vehicle.
12. Reverse procedure to install, noting the following:
    a. **Torque** radiator bracket bolts to 19 ft. lbs.
    b. Fill, then bleed coolant system as outlined under "Coolant System, Bleed."

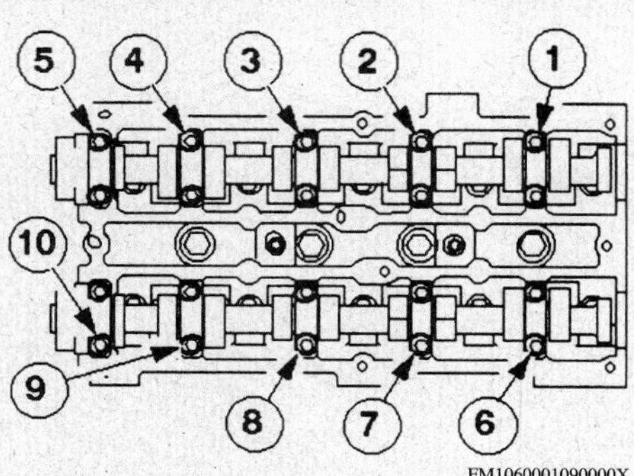

Fig. 12 Camshaft bearing cap bolt tightening sequence

FUEL PUMP

REPLACE

1. Relieve fuel system pressure as outlined under "Precautions."
2. Drain fuel tank into a suitable container.
3. Disconnect exhaust pipe from rear hanger.
4. Disconnect center muffler from hanger.
5. Disconnect exhaust pipe from remaining hangers, then position aside.
6. Remove heat shield.
7. Disconnect fuel tank vent and filler pipes.
8. Disconnect inline fuel coupling as outlined under "Precautions."
9. Disconnect evaporative emission pipe, then the rollover valve connector.
10. Place a suitable jack under fuel tank, then remove fuel tank support strap bolt.
11. Partially lower tank and disconnect fuel pump electrical connector.
12. Disconnect fuel pressure sensor electrical connector.
13. Remove fuel tank from vehicle.
14. Remove fuel pump module from fuel tank using fuel tank sender unit wrench tool No. 310-069, or equivalent.
15. Reverse procedure to install.

FUEL FILTER

REPLACE

1. Relieve fuel system pressure as outlined under "Precautions."
2. Raise and support vehicle.
3. Disconnect evaporative emission pipe.
4. Remove fuel filter outlet pipe, then disconnect fuel filter inlet pipe.
5. Remove fuel filter and bracket pipe.
6. Separate fuel filter from bracket.
7. Reverse procedure to install.

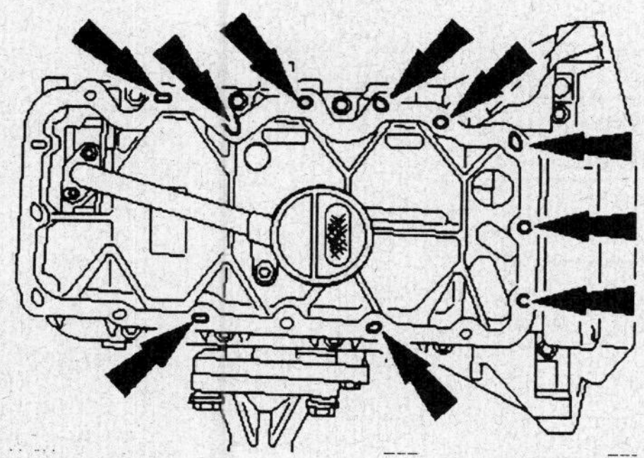

FM1060001097000X

Fig. 13 Lower crankcase dead end bore stud installation

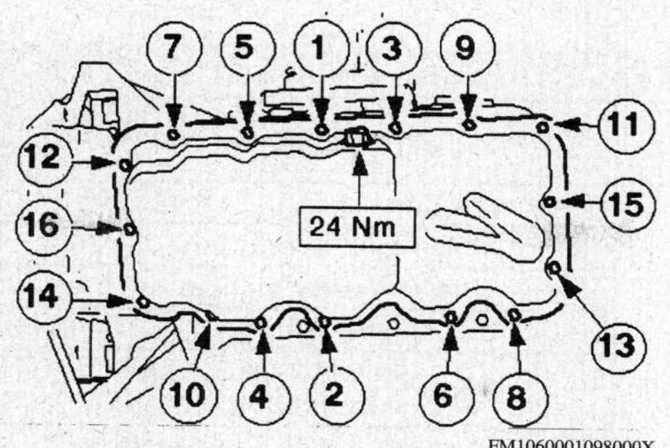

FM1060001098000X

Fig. 14 Oil pan bolt tightening sequence

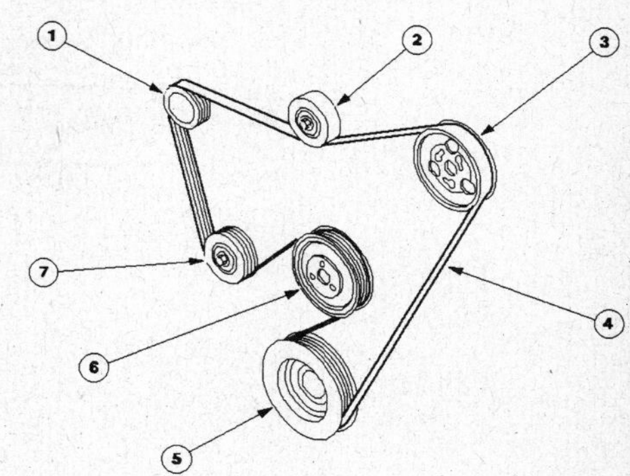

Item	Description
1	Generator pulley
2	Belt idler pulley
3	Power steering pump pulley
4	Accesory drive belt
5	Crankshaft pulley
6	Water pump pulley
7	Belt tensioner

FM1060001106000X

Fig. 15 Serpentine drive belt routing. Less A/C

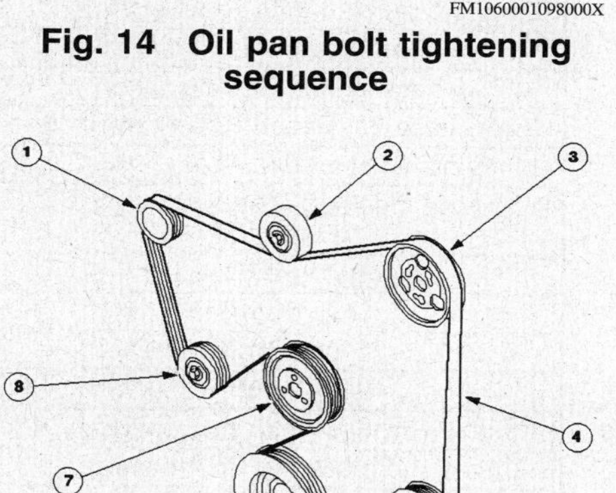

Item	Description
1	Generator pulley
2	Belt idler pulley
3	Power steering pump pulley
4	Accessory drive belt
5	A/C compressor pulley
6	Crankshaft pulley
7	Water pump pulley
8	Belt tensioner

FM1060001107000X

Fig. 16 Serpentine drive belt routing. With A/C

TIGHTENING SPECIFICATIONS

Year	Component	Torque, Ft. Lbs.
2000–01	Alternator Bracket To Cylinder Block	48
	Alternator To Bracket	18
	Camshaft Bearing Cap	③
	Camshaft Pulleys	50
	Catalytic Converter To Exhaust Manifold	35
	Catalytic Converter To Exhaust Pipe	35
	Clutch Pressure Plate	21
	Connecting Rod Bearing Cap	②
	Crankcase Ventilation Pipe Bracket	17
	Crankshaft Belt Pulley	85
	Cylinder Block Oil Gallery Blanking Plugs	17
	Drive Belt Idler Pulley	30
	Driveplate	83
	EGR Pipe to Ignition Coil Bracket	53①
	EGR Valve	18
	Engine Roll Restrictor To Subframe	35
	Engine Roll Restrictor To Transaxle	35
	Exhaust Manifold Heat Shield	89①
	Exhaust Manifold Nuts	12
	Exhaust Manifold Studs	44①
	Flywheel	83
	Front Engine Lifting Eye	35
	Front Engine Mounting To Engine	59
	Fuel Pump Module	59
	Fuel Rail	89①
	Idler Pulley	17
	Ignition Coil Bracket To	15
	Intake Manifold Bolts & Nuts	13
	Intake Manifold Studs	44①
	Lower Crankcase to Cylinder Block	16
	Main Bearing Bolts	⑤
	Oil Drain Plug	18
	Oil Intake Pipe To Oil Pump	89①
	Oil Pan	④
	Oil Pressure Switch	20
	Oil Pump	96①
	Power Steering Pump To Bracket	18
	Rear Crankshaft Oil Seal Carrier	13
	Rear Engine Lifting Eye	35
	Rear Engine Mounting To Body	35
	Spark Plugs	11
	Starter Motor To Transmission	26
	Thermostat Housing	15
	Timing Belt Cover (Upper)	89①
	Timing Belt Tensioner	18
	Transaxle Oil Drain Plug	33
	Valve Cover	62①
	Water Pump Pulley	18
	Wheel Lug Nuts	63

① — Inch lbs.
② — First step, torque to 26 ft. lbs.; second step, an additional 90.°
③ — Refer to "Camshaft, Replace" for tightening procedure.
④ — Refer to "Oil Pan, Replace" for tightening procedure.
⑤ — First step, torque to 18 ft. lbs.; second step, an additional 60.°

2.0L SOHC Engine

NOTE: On Air Bag Equipped Models, Refer To "Air Bag System Precautions" Located In The Front Of This Manual For System Disarming & Arming Procedures.

NOTE: Refer To "Computer Relearn Procedures" Located In The Front Of This Manual When Battery Power To The Computer Has Been Interrupted.

INDEX

PRECAUTIONS

AIR BAG SYSTEMS

Refer to "Air Bag System Precautions" in the front of this manual for system disarming and arming procedures.

BATTERY GROUND CABLE

Prior to service, disconnect battery ground cable and isolate as required.

FUEL SYSTEM PRESSURE RELIEF

1. Remove fuel pump fuse.
2. Start engine and allow to idle until engine stalls.
3. Crank engine for approximately five seconds to ensure fuel supply manifold pressure has been relieved.
4. Install fuel pump fuse into battery junction box.

QUICK DISCONNECT HOSES

R-CLIP

When working with R-clip type connections, **Fig. 1,** do not use tools to disconnect. Use of tools may deform clip components and could cause leaks.

To disconnect, bend shipping tab downward, **Fig. 1.** Spread R-clip and push clip into fitting. Separate fitting from tube.

To install, first inspect fitting and tube for damage and ensure connections are clean. Apply a light coat of clean 5W–30 motor oil to male end of tube. Insert R-clip into fitting. Align tube and fitting, then insert tube into fitting and push together until a click is heard. Pull on connection to ensure it is fully engaged.

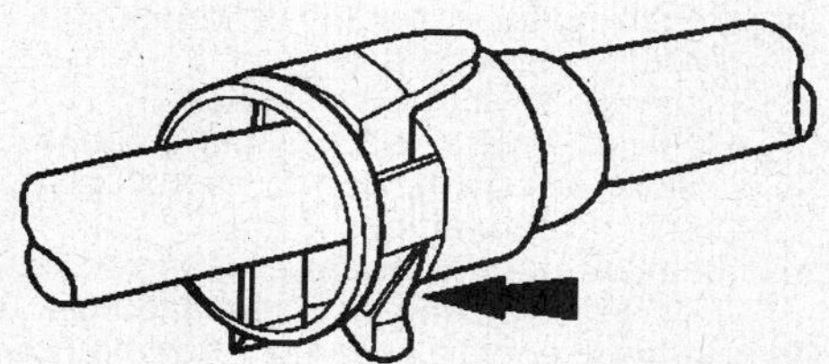

Fig. 1 R-clip connection

SPRING LOCK

When working with spring lock type connections, **Fig. 2,** spring lock tool set No. T84L-19623-B or equivalent, must be used to disconnect fittings. When connecting spring lock type fittings, inspect and clean both coupling ends. Lubricate fuel line O-ring seals with clean 5W-30 motor oil. When connection is made, pull on line to ensure it is fully engaged.

VAPOR TUBE

To disconnect vapor tube connections, squeeze fitting (1) and disconnect vapor tube from fitting (2), **Fig. 3.** To connect, ensure fittings are clean and free from damage. Push tube onto fitting until it snaps into place. Pull on connection to verify fitting is secure.

COMPRESSION PRESSURE

Before performing compression test, ensure the following conditions are met: crankcase oil is of correct viscosity and at correct level, ensure battery is fully charged and engine is at normal operating temperature.

1. Turn ignition switch to OFF position.
2. Remove all spark plugs.
3. Set throttle plates to wide open position.
4. Install a suitable compression gauge in No. 1 cylinder.
5. Install an auxiliary starter switch in starting circuit.
6. With ignition switch off, use auxiliary starter switch to crank engine a minimum of five compression strokes.
7. Note number of compression strokes necessary to reach highest reading and record highest reading.
8. Repeat test on each cylinder, cranking engine same number of compression strokes.
9. Indicated compression pressures are considered within specifications if lowest reading cylinder is within 75 percent of highest reading.

ENGINE

REPLACE

AUTOMATIC TRANSAXLE

1. Relieve fuel system pressure as outlined under "Precautions."
2. Open coolant expansion tank.
3. Disconnect ground lead from battery tray assembly, then remove tray.
4. Disconnect ground cable from chassis.
5. Drain coolant into suitable container.

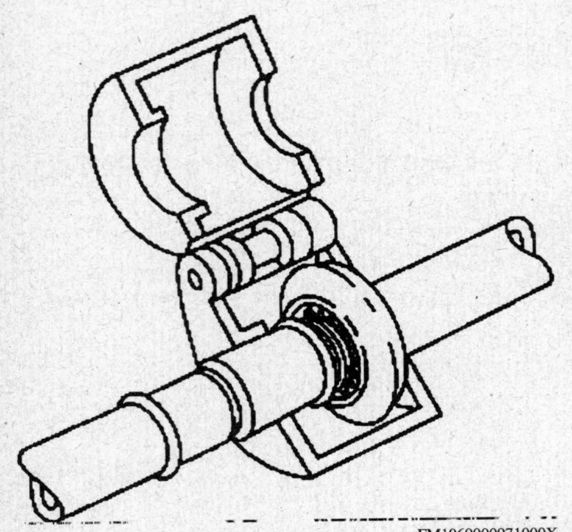

Fig. 2 Spring lock connection

6. Using a suitable Allen wrench to prevent strut piston rod from turning, loosen strut nuts by five turns on both sides.
7. Disconnect mass air flow sensor electrical connector, intake air hose, then remove air cleaner housing from rubber bushing.
8. Remove air cleaner intake pipe, accelerator cable and speed control cable.
9. Disconnect electrical connectors from power steering pump pressure switch, alternator and heated oxygen sensor.
10. Disconnect both powertrain control module connectors.
11. Remove vacuum hoses from EVAP, Brake Servo, Delta Pressure Feedback Electronic System Sensor and EGR valve.
12. Disconnect vacuum hoses from intake manifold.
13. Disconnect fuel hose and drain excess fuel into suitable container.
14. Disconnect coolant hose from intake manifold.
15. Remove coolant hoses from water pump and coolant pipe, then disconnect coolant expansion tank and set aside.
16. Remove PAS reservoir and lay to one side.
17. Remove radiator fan assembly.
18. Remove upper starter motor bolts.
19. Remove accessory drive belt.
20. Remove power steering high pressure pipe, then remove power steering pump and position to one side.
21. Remove alternator and alternator bracket, **Fig. 4.**
22. Disconnect both lower suspension arms.
23. Disconnect oxygen sensor electrical connectors, then remove drive belt cover.
24. **On models equipped with air conditioning,** remove A/C compressor and tie to radiator cross member.
25. **On all models,** disconnect exhaust pipe.
26. Remove torque converter cover bolts, then disconnect torque converter from engine drive plate.
27. Remove transaxle lower flange bolts, **Fig. 5.**

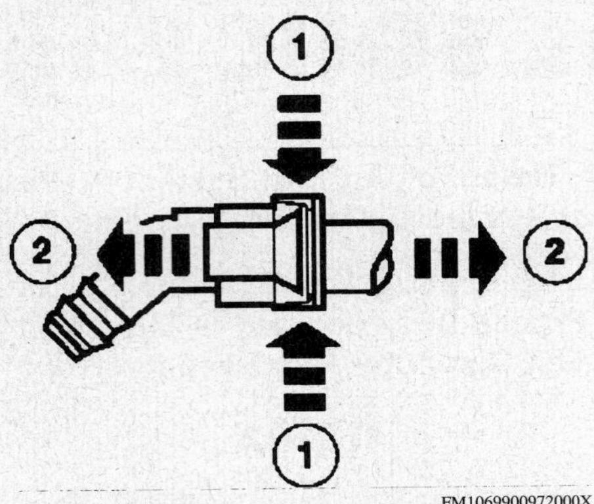

Fig. 3 Vapor tube connection

28. Disconnect righthand front drive halfshaft from intermediate shaft.
29. Remove lefthand front drive halfshaft from tripod housing.
30. Remove intermediate shaft and secure out of way with cable tie.
31. Disconnect starter motor electrical connectors, then remove starter motor.
32. Remove crankshaft pulley, righthand engine support insulator and lefthand and righthand transaxle flange bolts.
33. Disconnect fuel line, drain excess fuel into suitable container.
34. Attach suitable engine lifting device, then raise engine slightly to relieve pressure on support insulators.
35. Remove engine front mounting, **Fig. 6.**
36. Disconnect crankshaft position sensor electrical connector.
37. Remove upper transaxle flange bolts, then separate engine from transaxle.
38. Remove engine assembly from top of vehicle.
39. Use torque converter holding tool No. 307-346, or equivalent, to hold torque converter in transaxle assembly.
40. Reverse procedure to install.

MANUAL TRANSMISSION

1. Relieve fuel system pressure as outlined under "Precautions."
2. Open coolant expansion tank.
3. Remove battery ground cable from battery tray assembly, then remove tray from vehicle.
4. Disconnect ground cable from vehicle chassis.
5. Drain coolant into suitable container.
6. Using a suitable Allen wrench to prevent strut piston rods from turning, loosen both strut nut approximately five turns.
7. Disconnect mass air flow sensor electrical connector, remove air intake hose, then remove air cleaner housing from rubber bushing.
8. Remove air cleaner air intake pipe.
9. Remove accelerator and speed control cables and lay to one side.
10. Disconnect electrical connectors from power steering pressure switch, alternator and heated oxygen sensor.
11. Disconnect both powertrain control modules.
12. Disconnect vehicle speed sensor and reverse lamp switch electrical connectors.
13. Remove high pressure pipe from clutch slave cylinder.
14. Remove vacuum hoses from EVAP, brake servo, Delta Pressure Feedback Electronic System Sensor and EGR valve.
15. Remove any remaining vacuum hoses from intake manifold.
16. Disconnect fuel line and drain excess fuel into suitable container.
17. Remove coolant hoses from intake manifold, water pump and coolant pipes.
18. Remove coolant expansion tank and position to one side.
19. Remove accessory drive belt.
20. Remove power steering high pressure pipe, then remove power steering pump and position to one side.
21. Remove PA reservoir and position to one side.
22. Remove radiator fan, catalytic converter, flexible exhaust pipe and drive belt cover.
23. Remove shift cable and selector cable cover, then the cables.
24. **On models equipped with air conditioning,** remove air conditioning compressor and secure it to radiator crossmember.
25. **On all models,** remove righthand engine support insulator, **Fig. 7.**
26. Remove both lower suspension arms.
27. Remove righthand front drive halfshaft from intermediate shaft. **Inner joint must not be bent at more than 18°, outer joint must not be bent at more than 45°.**
28. Remove lefthand front drive halfshaft from tripod housing.
29. Position engine assembly stand with wooden blocks on it under vehicle.
30. Carefully lower vehicle until engine and transaxle assembly is on engine stand.
31. Remove engine rear mount, **Fig. 8.**
32. Remove front engine mount, **Fig. 6.**
33. Secure engine and transaxle assembly with restraining strap to assembly table.
34. Carefully raise vehicle, then pull assembly stand forward with engine and transaxle assembly.
35. Use a suitable lifting device to separate engine from transaxle.
36. Reverse procedure to install.

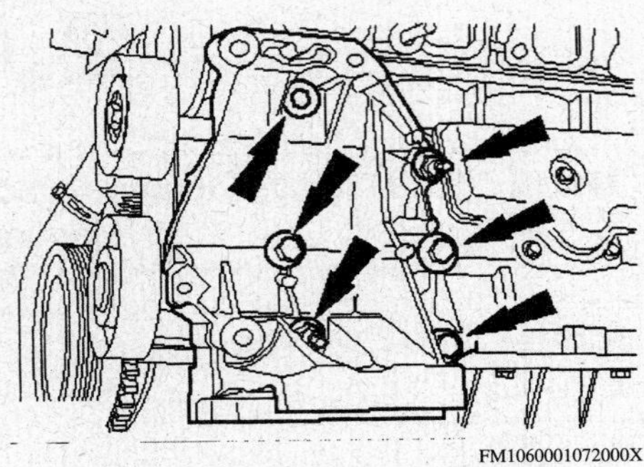

Fig. 4 Alternator bracket

Fig. 5 Transaxle lower flange bolts

INTAKE MANIFOLD

REPLACE

1. Raise and support vehicle.
2. Remove intake manifold bracket, **Fig. 9.**
3. Disconnect electrical connector of mass air flow sensor, remove intake hose, then remove air cleaner housing from rubber bushing.
4. Unhook accelerator and speed control cables, pull off plastic clips and position cables to one side.
5. Remove vacuum hoses from EVAP system, brake servo, Delta Pressure Feedback Electronic System Sensor and EGR valve.
6. Disconnect and remove EGR valve.
7. Clamp coolant hoses to prevent leakage and remove from intake manifold.
8. Disconnect throttle position sensor and idle air control valve.
9. Remove oil level indicator tube.
10. Remove any remaining vacuum hoses or electrical connectors from intake manifold.
11. Remove intake manifold mounting bolts, then the manifold.
12. Reverse procedure to install, noting the following:
    a. Replace intake manifold gasket.
    b. Install intake manifold bolts and tighten to specification.

EXHAUST MANIFOLD

REPLACE

1. Remove air cleaner housing from rubber bushing.
2. Disconnect heated oxygen sensor electrical connector.
3. Remove exhaust manifold heat shield.
4. Remove EGR tube at exhaust manifold, then loosen tube nut approximately three turns at valve.
5. Remove catalytic converter.
6. Remove exhaust manifold attaching nuts, then the manifold.
7. Reverse procedure to install.

CYLINDER HEAD

REPLACE

When cleaning cylinder head surfaces, do not use metal scrapers, wires brushes, power abrasive discs or other abrasive methods to clean sealing surfaces. Use only a plastic scraping tool to remove all traces of gasket material.

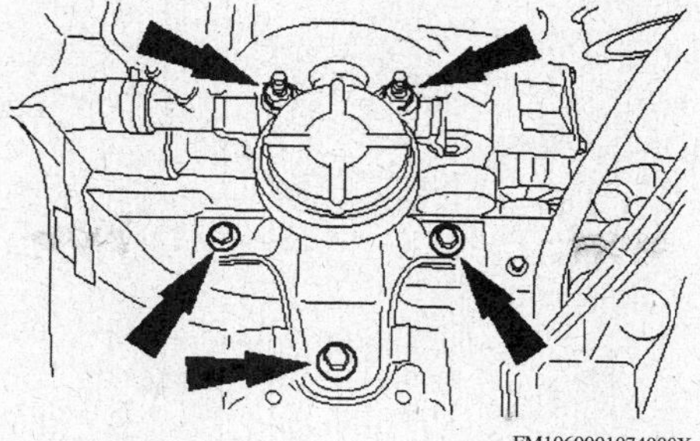

Fig. 6 Engine front mounting

Cylinder head bolts are of torque to yield style and must be replaced when removed.

1. Disconnect mass air flow sensor, detach intake air hose, then remove air cleaner housing from rubber bushing.
2. Detach battery ground cable from battery tray, then remove battery tray.
3. Unhook accelerator and speed control cables, pull off plastic clips and position cables to one side.
4. Disconnect both powertrain control module connectors.
5. Disconnect heated oxygen sensor electrical connector.
6. Detach vacuum hoses from EVAP, brake servo, Delta Pressure Feedback Electronic System Sensor and EGR valve.
7. Remove oil level indicator tube.
8. Drain coolant into suitable container and remove coolant hoses from thermostat housing.
9. Disconnect fuel line, drain excess fuel into suitable container.
10. Raise and support vehicle.
11. Disconnect knock sensor and oil pressure sensor electrical connectors, **Fig. 10.**
12. Remove intake manifold bracket.
13. Disconnect and remove catalyst monitor sensor electrical connector.
14. Lower vehicle.
15. Remove exhaust manifold heat shield.
16. Remove catalytic converter from exhaust manifold.
17. Remove timing belt as outlined in "Timing Belt, Replace."
18. Disconnect crankshaft position sensor electrical connector.
19. Loosen cylinder head bolts in sequence, **Fig. 11,** then remove cylinder head.
20. Reverse procedure to install, noting the following:
    a. Lubricate cylinder head bolts with Super Premium 5W 30 SAE X0-5W 30-QSP, or equivalent, meeting Ford specification WSS-M2C153-G prior to installation.
    b. Install cylinder head and **torque** cylinder head bolts in sequence, **Fig. 12,** to 37 ft. lbs.
    c. Back all bolts off one half turn (180°).
    d. **Torque** all bolts in sequence to 37 ft. lbs.
    e. Rotate all bolts in sequence, 90°.
    f. Rotate all bolts a final time, in sequence, 90°.

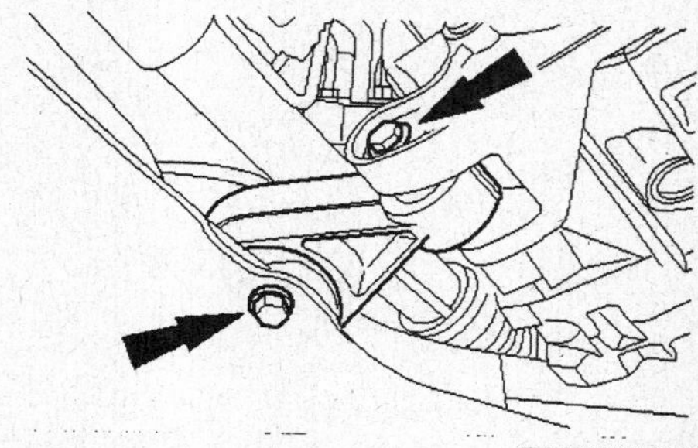

Fig. 7 Right hand engine support insulator

CAMSHAFT OIL SEAL

REPLACE

1. Remove timing belt as outlined under "Timing Belt, Replace."
2. Using wrench tool No. 303-098, or equivalent, remove camshaft sprocket.
3. Using seal remover tool No. 303-409, or equivalent, remove and discard camshaft oil seal.
4. Reverse procedure to install, noting the following:
    a. Lubricate new camshaft seal and camshaft running face with clean 5W-30 engine oil.
    b. Using seal installer tool No. 303-160, or equivalent, install new seal. Draw seal into place with timing belt sprocket bolt.
    c. Use wrench tool No. 303-098, or equivalent, to hold sprocket in place while tightening bolt.
    d. Tighten all fasteners to specifications.
    e. Start engine, then inspect for and correct any leakage.

VALVE ADJUSTMENT

Valve clearance is hydraulically controlled and is not adjustable.

TIMING BELT

REPLACE

1. Remove coolant reservoir mounting bolt, then position reservoir aside.
2. Disconnect power steering fluid reservoir and position aside.
3. Using a suitable ⅜ inch drive breaker bar, rotate serpentine belt tensioner to relieve tension, then remove the belt.
4. Raise and support vehicle.
5. Remove timing belt upper cover.
6. Remove crankshaft pulley retaining bolt, then the pulley.
7. Lower the vehicle.
8. Disconnect spark plug wires at the plugs.
9. Remove spark plug wire separators at valve cover.
10. Remove spark plugs.
11. Support engine using a suitable floor jack and a wooden block under oil pan.
12. Slowly raise engine until tension is relieved from its front mount.
13. Remove engine front mount.
14. Remove timing belt cover.

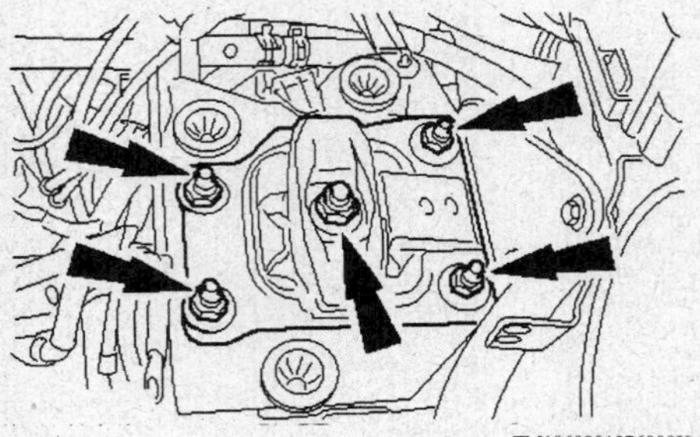

Fig. 8 Rear engine mount

15. Remove engine front mount bracket.
16. Rotate engine in normal rotation direction until timing marks are properly aligned, **Fig. 13.**
17. Using a suitable 8MM hex wrench, rotate timing belt tensioner counterclockwise ¼ turn, then insert a ⅛ inch drill bit to lock tensioner in place.
18. Remove timing belt.
19. Reverse procedure to install, noting the following:
    a. Route the new timing belt over pulleys in a counterclockwise direction, starting at crankshaft. Keep tension on belt span from crankshaft to camshaft while routing belt over camshaft.
    b. Remove drill bit from tensioner.
    c. Rotate crankshaft at least two turns clockwise to position No. 1 piston at TDC.
    d. Ensure timing marks are properly aligned, **Fig. 13.** Repeat previous steps if marks are not aligned as illustrated.
    e. Tighten all fasteners to specifications.

CAMSHAFT

REPLACE

1. Disconnect battery ground cable from battery tray, then remove tray from vehicle.
2. Disconnect mass air flow sensor and air cleaner outlet pipe, then remove air cleaner assembly from rubber bushing.
3. Remove air cleaner intake pipe.
4. Disconnect and remove ignition coil.
5. Disconnect PCV hoses.
6. Remove valve cover and rocker arms.
7. Remove valve tappet guide plate retainers, valve guide tappet plates, then the valve tappets. Keep tappets in order for reassembly.
8. Remove timing belt as outlined under "Timing Belt, Replace."
9. Remove camshaft oil seal.
10. Support engine with a suitable engine lifting device.
11. Remove rear engine mount, **Fig. 8.**
12. Remove camshaft thrust plate, **Fig. 14.**
13. Remove and discard blanking plug from rear of cylinder head.
14. Remove camshaft from rear of cylinder head.
15. Reverse procedure to install, noting the following:
    a. Coat cylinder head bore with Super Premium 5W30 SAE motor oil, or equivalent, meeting Ford specification prior to camshaft installation.
    b. Install camshaft through rear of cylinder head.
    c. Tighten all fasteners to specification.

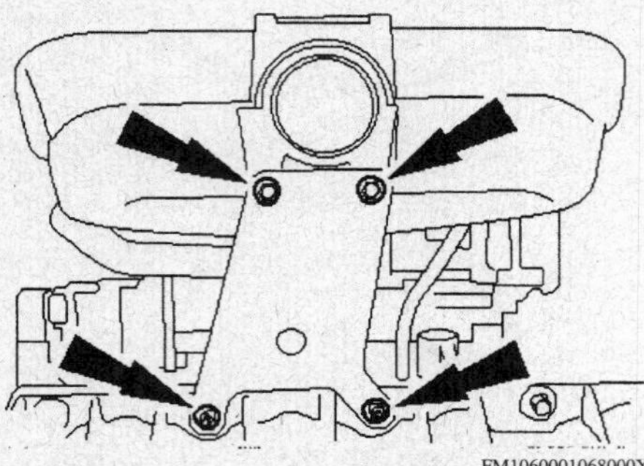

Fig. 9 Intake manifold bracket

CRANKSHAFT FRONT OIL SEAL

REPLACE

1. Remove timing belt as outlined under "Timing Belt, Replace."
2. Support engine using a suitable floor jack and a wooden block under oil pan.
3. Install engine support tool Nos. 303-290, 303-050, 303-290-01 and 303-290-03, or their equivalents.
4. Remove floor jack.
5. Raise and support vehicle.
6. Remove crankshaft timing belt pulley.
7. Using seal remover tool No. 303-409, or equivalent, remove and discard crankshaft seal.
8. Reverse procedure to install, noting the following:
    a. Lubricate new crankshaft seal and the crankshaft surface with clean 5W-30 engine oil.
    b. Using seal installer tool No. 303-164, or equivalent, install crankshaft front seal.
    c. Start engine, then inspect for and correct any leakage.

CRANKSHAFT REAR OIL SEAL

REPLACE

1. Remove transaxle assembly.
2. Remove flywheel.
3. Using seal removal tool No. 303–409, or equivalent, carefully pry out seal.
4. Inspect rear seal area of crankshaft for damage or excessive wear.
5. Reverse procedure to install.

OIL PAN

REPLACE

1. Remove three way catalytic converter.
2. Remove bolts and two brackets, **Fig. 15.**
3. Remove intake manifold bracket bolts and the bracket, **Fig. 16.**

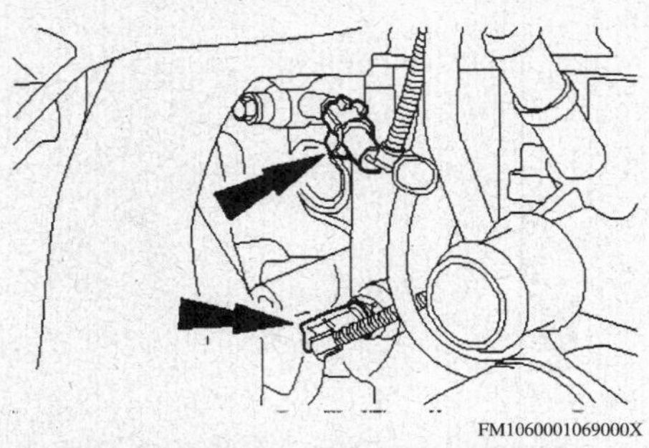

Fig. 10 Knock sensor & oil pressure switch connectors

4. Remove axle shaft bracket clamp bolts and the clamp, **Fig. 17.**
5. Remove axle shaft bracket bolts and the bracket, **Fig. 18.**
6. Remove coolant tube bolt.
7. Drain engine oil into an approved container.
8. Note locations of oil pan stud bolts, **Fig. 19.**
9. Remove oil pan attaching fasteners, then the oil pan. Discard the gasket.
10. Reverse procedure to install, noting the following:
    a. **Do not use abrasive grinding discs when removing gasket material. Use plastic scrapers. Avoid gouging or scratching aluminum sealing surfaces.**
    b. Use a suitable solvent to clean gasket sealing surfaces.
    c. Apply a .12 inch wide bead of silicone gasket sealant meeting Ford specification WSE-M4G323-A6, or equivalent, at oil pump to block joints and crankshaft rear seal retainer to block joints. **Oil pan must be installed within 10 minutes of sealant application.**
    d. Ensure press fit tabs fully engage in oil pan gasket channel.
    e. Tighten oil pan fasteners to specifications in sequence outlined in **Fig. 20.**
    f. Fill engine with proper engine oil.
    g. Start engine, then inspect for and correct any leakage.

SERPENTINE DRIVE BELT TENSIONER

REPLACE

1. Raise and support vehicle.
2. Remove serpentine belt splash shield.
3. Using a suitable ⅜ inch drive breaker bar, rotate tensioner clockwise, then remove belt.
4. Remove power steering pipe to exhaust manifold bracket nuts, then position pipe aside.
5. Remove exhaust manifold heat shield fasteners, then the shield.
6. Remove serpentine drive belt tensioner mounting fasteners, then the tensioner.
7. Reverse procedure to install. Tighten all fasteners to specifications.

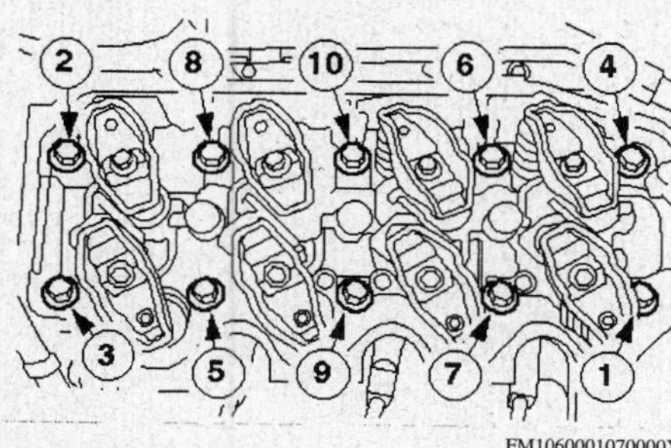

Fig. 11 Cylinder head bolt loosening sequence

OIL PUMP

REPLACE

1. Remove timing belt as outlined in "Timing Belt, Replace."
2. Install suitable engine support fixture.
3. Remove crankshaft timing belt pulley, oil pan and crankshaft position sensor.
4. Remove two bolts, then the oil pump screen cover and tube. Discard gasket
5. Remove oil pump bolts, **Fig. 21,** then the oil pump. Discard gasket, remove oil pump seal.
6. Reverse procedure to install.

SERPENTINE DRIVE BELT ROUTING

Refer to **Figs. 22 and 23,** for serpentine accessory drive belt routing.

COOLING SYSTEM BLEED

When releasing system pressure, cover the expansion tank cap with a thick cloth to prevent the possibility of scalding.

When draining the engine coolant or changing coolant system components, do not allow coolant to come into contact with the timing belt or accessory drive belt. Contamination of belts may result in premature failure.

1. Relieve cooling system pressure by turning expansion tank cap a quarter of a turn, remove cap when pressure has been released.
2. Raise and support vehicle.
3. Drain coolant into suitable container.
4. Close radiator drain valve when all coolant has been drained from system.
5. Lower vehicle.
6. Disconnect heater supply hose from engine.
7. Using a suitable funnel, fill cooling system through the supply hose until coolant starts to trickle from engine.
8. Reconnect heater supply hose.
9. Set heater temperature control to HOT position and heater blower motor switch to OFF position. Ensure A/C is switched OFF.
10. Refill coolant expansion tank to MAX mark.
11. Install expansion tank cap.
12. Warm engine up at 2750 RPM for two fan cycles.
13. Allow engine to cool, then check coolant level and top up to MAX mark as necessary

THERMOSTAT

REPLACE

1. Drain coolant into suitable container.
2. Remove thermostat housing bolts, then the housing.
3. Remove thermostat.
4. Remove and discard O-ring seals.
5. Reverse procedure to install, noting the following:
   a. Install new thermostat with new O-ring seals.
   b. Tighten thermostat housing bolts to specifications.
   c. Fill and bleed cooling system as outlined under "Cooling System Bleed."
   d. Inspect for and correct any leakage.

WATER PUMP

REPLACE

1. Drain cooling system into suitable container.
2. Remove timing belt and timing belt tensioner as outlined in "Timing Belt, Replace."
3. Disconnect coolant hoses.
4. Remove water pump.
5. Reverse procedure to install.

RADIATOR

REPLACE

1. Raise and support vehicle.
2. Remove cooling fan motor and shroud.
3. Drain coolant into suitable container.
4. Remove four pin type retainers from radiator air deflector.
5. Lower vehicle.
6. Disconnect upper radiator hose.
7. Raise and support vehicle.
8. **On models equipped with air conditioning,** support condenser and transaxle cooler.
9. **On all models,** disconnect upper coolant hose, radiator lower coolant hoses and horn electrical connectors.
10. Remove radiator support bracket bolts, then the bracket.
11. Remove radiator from vehicle.
12. Reverse procedure to instal.

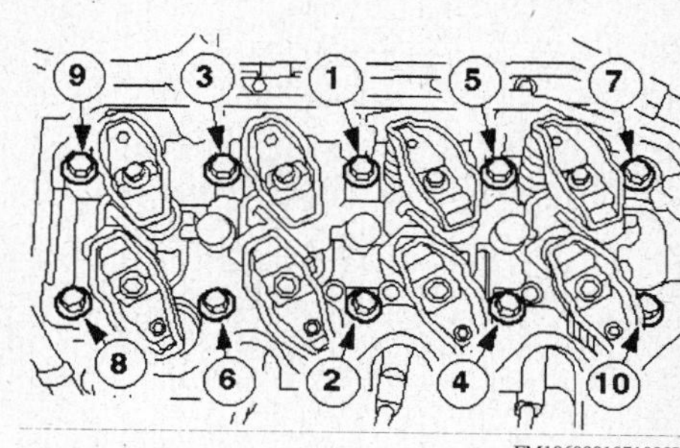

Fig. 12 Cylinder head bolt tightening sequence

FUEL PUMP

REPLACE

1. Relieve fuel pressure as outlined in "Precautions."
2. Drain fuel tank into suitable container.
3. Disconnect exhaust pipe from hanger insulators.
4. Disconnect center muffler from exhaust insulator.
5. Disconnect exhaust pipe and secure to frame with wire.
6. Remove heat shield.
7. Make a note of position of fuel vent and filler pipe retaining clamps and clip for installation reference.
8. Disconnect fuel tank vent and filer pipes.
9. Disconnect inline fuel coupling.
10. Disconnect evaporative emission pipe and rollover valve.
11. Place a suitable jack or lifting device under fuel tank.
12. Remove fuel tank support strap bolt, then partially lower fuel tank.
13. Disconnect fuel pump electrical connector and fuel tank pressure sensor electrical connector, then lower tank from vehicle.
14. Disconnect fuel supply line from fuel pump module.
15. Using fuel tank sender wrench No. 310–069, or equivalent, remove lockring.
16. Rotate fuel pump module counterclockwise and lift from tank.
17. Reverse procedure to install.

FUEL FILTER

REPLACE

1. Relieve fuel pressure as outlined in "Precautions."
2. Raise and support vehicle.
3. Disconnect evaporative emission pipe, **Fig. 24.**
4. Remove fuel filter outlet pipe.
5. Disconnect fuel filter inlet pipe.
6. Remove fuel filter and bracket, then remove fuel filter from bracket.
7. Reverse procedure to install.

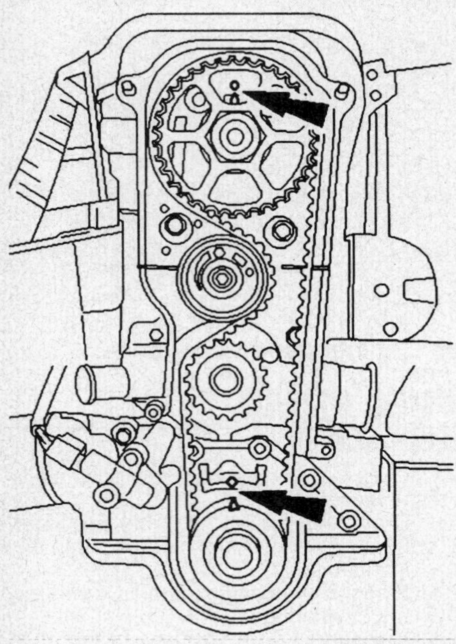

Fig. 13 Timing mark alignment

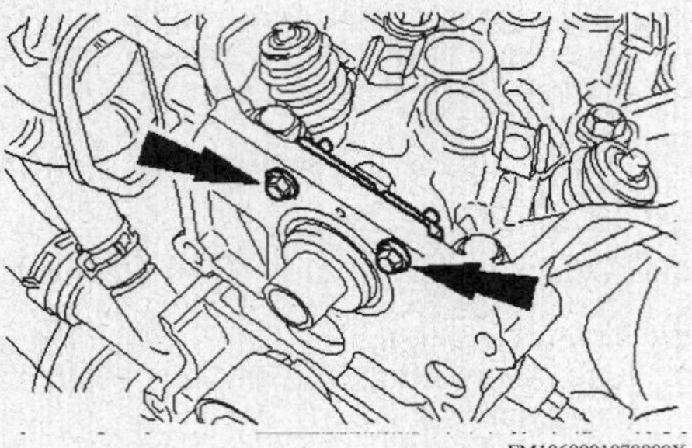

Fig. 14 Camshaft thrust plate

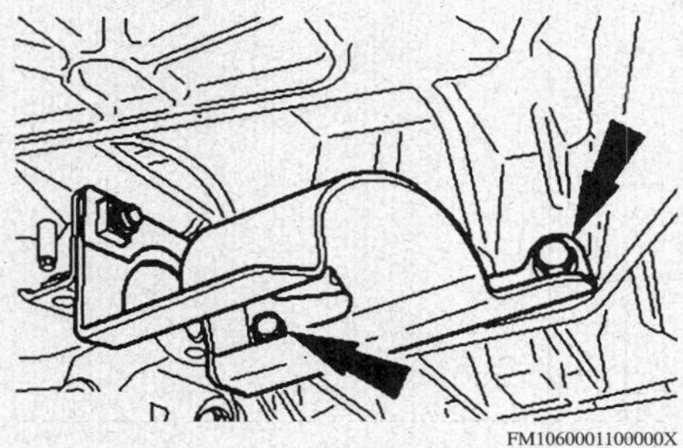

Fig. 15 Bolt & bracket locations

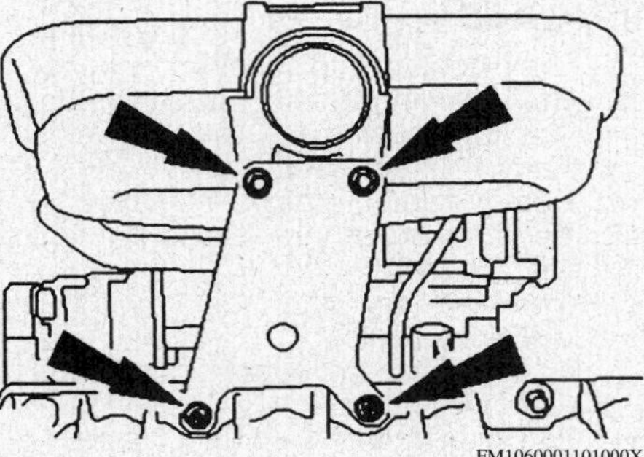

Fig. 16 Intake manifold bracket removal

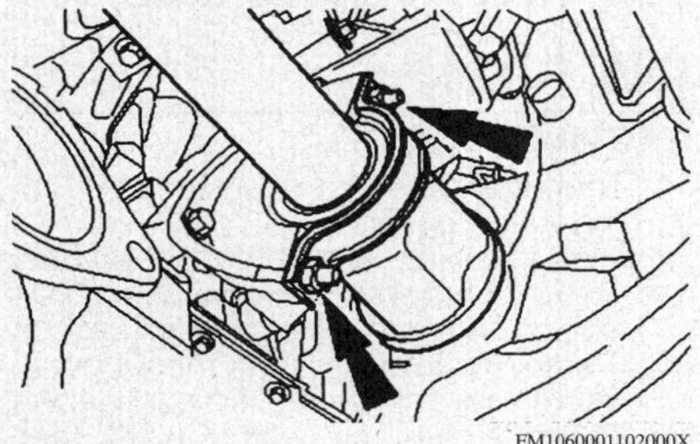

Fig. 17 Axle shaft bracket clamp removal

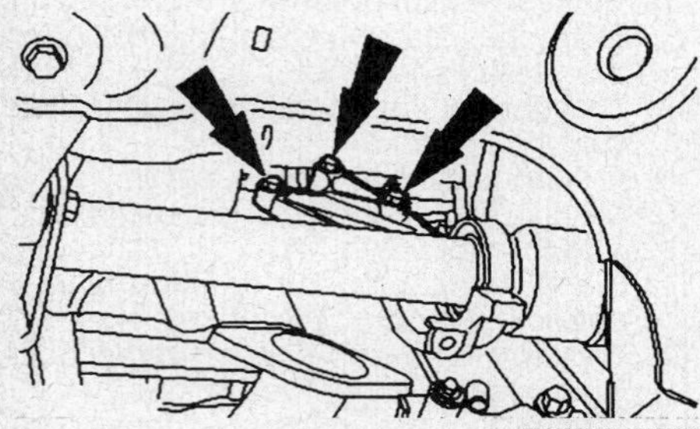

Fig. 18 Axle shaft bracket removal

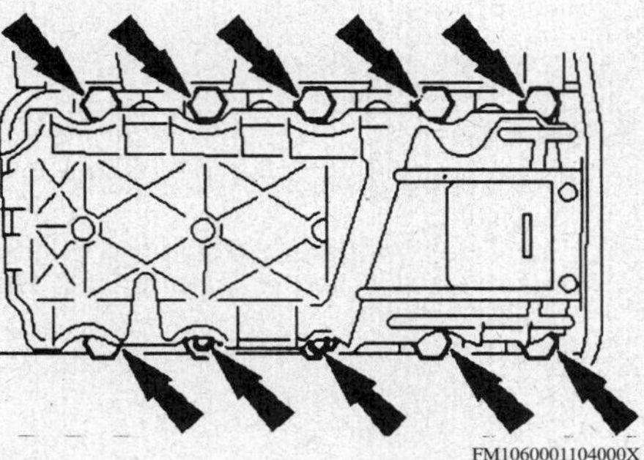

Fig. 19 Oil pan stud bolt locations

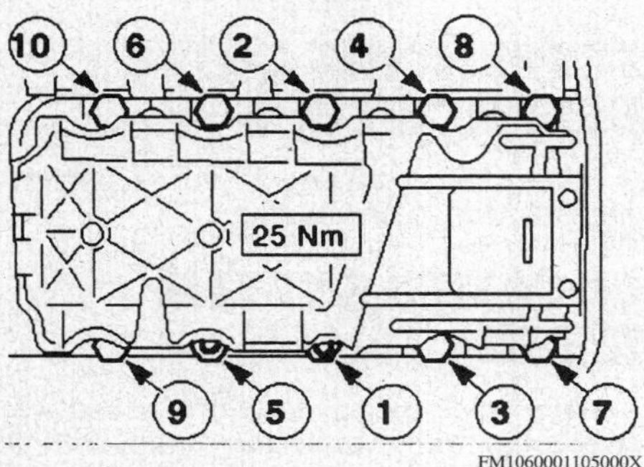

Fig. 20 Oil pan fastener tightening sequence

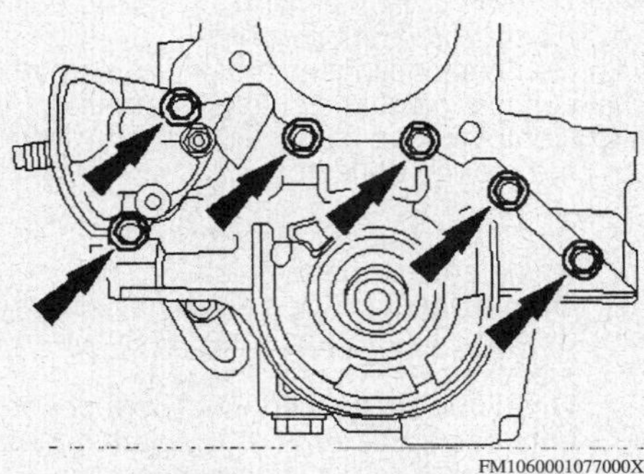

Fig. 21 Oil pump replacement

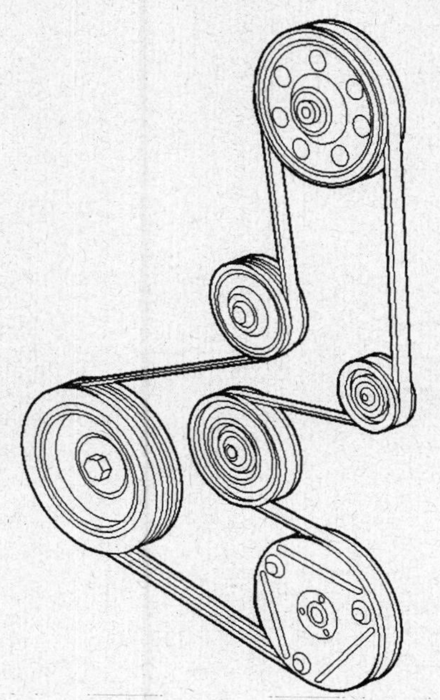

FM1060001079000X

Fig. 22 Serpentine belt routing. With A/C

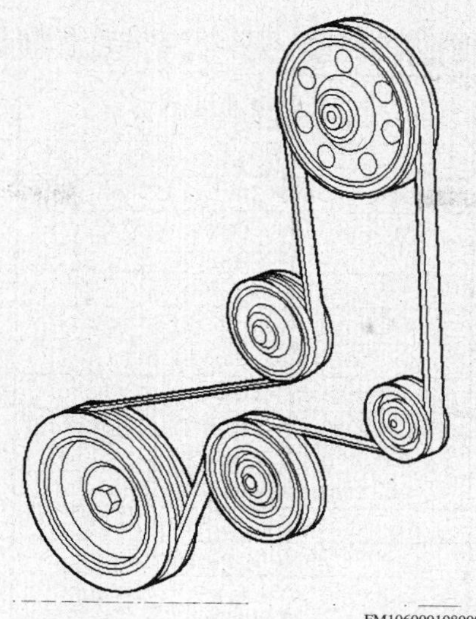

FM1060001080000X

Fig. 23 Serpentine belt routing. Less A/C

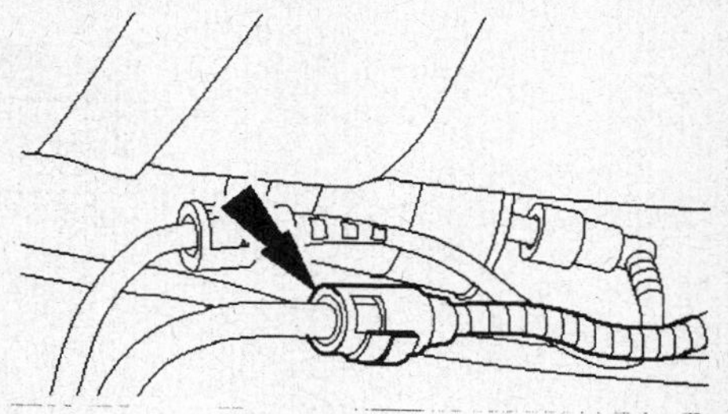

FM1060001083000X

Fig. 24 Evaporative emission pipe

TIGHTENING SPECIFICATIONS

Year	Component	Torque/Ft. Lbs.
2000–01	A/C Compressor Bolts	18
	Accessory Drive Bracket Bolts & Nuts	35
	Alternator Mounting Bolts (Lower & Upper)	35
	Battery Tray	18
	Camshaft Position Sensor	18
	Camshaft Pulley Bolt	77
	Camshaft Thrust Plate Bolts	89②
	Catalytic Converter To Exhaust Manifold Bolts	30
	Crankshaft Position Sensor	53②
	Crankshaft Pulley	89
	Cylinder Head Bolts	①
	EGR Manifold Tube To Exhaust Manifold	53②
	EGR Valve To EGR Manifold Tube	18
	EGR Valve To Intake Manifold	53②
	Engine Oil Drain Plug	18
	Engine Roll Restrictor To Subframe	35
	Engine Roll Restrictor To Transaxle	35
	Exhaust Manifold Nuts	20
	Flexible Exhaust Pipe	35
	Front Engine Mounting To Body	35
	Front Engine Mounting To Engine	59
	Intake Manifold Bracket Nuts & Bolts	89②
	Intake Manifold Nuts	③
	Intermediate Shaft Bracket	35
	Knock Sensor	10
	Lefthand Transaxle Flange Bolts	35
	Lower Ball Joint To Spindle Carrier	35
	Lower Transaxle Flange Bolts	35
	Oil Intake Pipe To Oil Pump	89②
	Oil Pan Baffle	18
	Oil Pan To Crankcase	18
	Oil Pump	10
	Oil Pump Tube	89②
	Power Steering Pump	17
	Rear Crankshaft Oil Seal Retainer	18
	Rear Engine Mounting (Nut On Transaxle Mounting Bracket)	98
	Rear Engine Mounting To Body	35
	Rocker Arms	18
	Starter Motor To Transaxle	26
	Thermostat Housing	10
	Timing Belt Cover (Lower)	89②
	Timing Belt Cover (Upper)	35
	Timing Belt Tensioner	18
	Upper Transaxle Flange Bolts	35
	Valve Cover Bolts	80②
	Water Pump	18
	Wheel Lug Nuts	63

①— Refer to procedure outlined in “Cylinder Head, Replace”
②— Inch Lbs.
③— 89 Inch Lbs. plus 180°.

Clutch & Manual Transaxle

NOTE: On Air Bag Equipped Models, Refer To "Air Bag System Precautions" Located In The Front Of This Manual For System Disarming & Arming Procedures.

NOTE: Refer To "Computer Relearn Procedures" Located In The Front Of This Manual When Battery Power To The Computer Has Been Interrupted.

INDEX

PRECAUTIONS

AIR BAG SYSTEMS

Refer to "Air Bag System Precautions" in the front of this manual for system disarming and arming procedures.

BATTERY GROUND CABLE

Prior to service, disconnect battery ground cable and isolate as required.

DESCRIPTION

This model is equipped with a hydraulic clutch system with both the IB5 and MTX75 transaxles.

ADJUSTMENTS

SHIFT LINKAGE

IB5 Transaxle

1. Shift transaxle into neutral, then remove gearshift lever cover.
2. Insert 3 mm drill bit **Fig. 1,** then raise and support vehicle.
3. Open shift and selector cable cover.
4. Unlock selector cable by depressing colored insert, then move selector to center position **Fig. 2.**
5. Move gearshift lever to righthand or lefthand stop position to engage 3rd or 4th gear, then lock selector cable **Fig. 3.**
6. Close shift and selector cable cover, then lower vehicle.
7. Remove drill bit, then install shift lever cover.

HYDRAULIC SYSTEM SERVICE

CLUTCH SYSTEM BLEED

IB5 Transaxle

1. Disconnect MAF sensor electrical connector then remove air intake pipe.

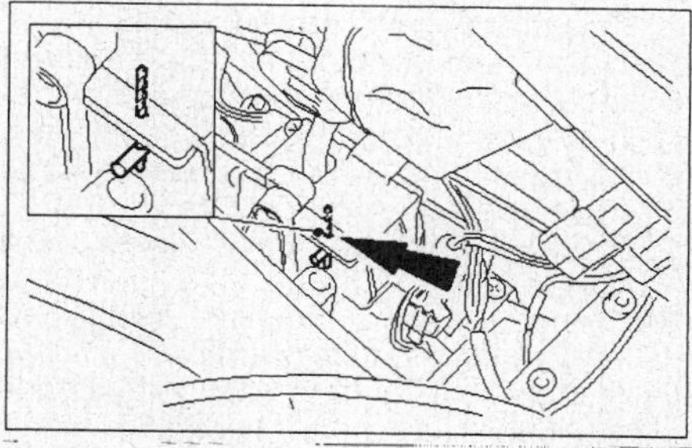

Fig. 1 3mm drill bit placement

2. Drain brake fluid reservoir to MIN mark using suitable suction device.
3. Fill reservoir of vacuum pump tool No. 416–D002, or equivalent, with Super DOT 4 brake fluid to approximately 100 ml.
4. Install vacuum pump, **reservoir must be below bleed nipple.**
5. Open bleed nipple and pump approximately 80 ml of brake fluid into clutch control system.
6. Tighten bleeder screw, then remove vacuum pump.
7. Bleed clutch control system by depressing clutch pedal 4–5 times ensuring full travel is reached.
8. Install air intake pipe, then connect MAF sensor.
9. Check brake fluid level and fill with Super DOT 4 brake fluid if level is below MIN mark.
10. Start engine and carefully engage reverse after 2 seconds, if abnormal noises are heard depress clutch pedal 4–5 times ensuring full travel is reached. If abnormal noises are still heard, repeat steps 1–9.

MTX75 Transaxle

1. Fill brake fluid reservoir to top edge with Super DOT 4 brake fluid.
2. Remove protective cap from bleed nipple, then install a suitable transparent hose.
3. Place hose in a suitable container, then depress clutch pedal slowly several times and hold at bottom of its travel.
4. Open bleed nipple until brake fluid flows through bleed hose, then tighten bleed nipple.
5. Release clutch pedal and repeat steps 3 and 4 until brake fluid which flows into container is clear and free of bubbles.
6. Install protective cap, then depress clutch pedal ten times and check its operation.
7. Fill brake fluid reservoir with Super DOT 4 brake fluid if level is below MIN mark.

CLUTCH MASTER CYLINDER

1. Drain brake fluid reservoir.
2. Disconnect MAF sensor, then remove air cleaner assembly.
3. Remove central junction box.
4. Remove lines from clutch master cylinder.
5. Remove lower instrument panel cover, then footwell insulation panel.
6. Remove clutch master cylinder clip and mounting bolts
7. Remove clutch master cylinder from pedal mount, then pull piston rod from clutch pedal.
8. Reverse procedure to install, bleed clutch system as outlined under "Clutch System Bleed."

SLAVE CYLINDER REPLACE

1. Remove Transaxle as outlined under "Transaxle, Replace."
2. Remove slave cylinder bolts, then slave cylinder.
3. Reverse procedure to install noting the following:
   a. **On MTX75 transaxles,** use new slave cylinder and seal ring.
   b. **On all transaxles,** bleed clutch system as outlined under "Clutch System Bleed."

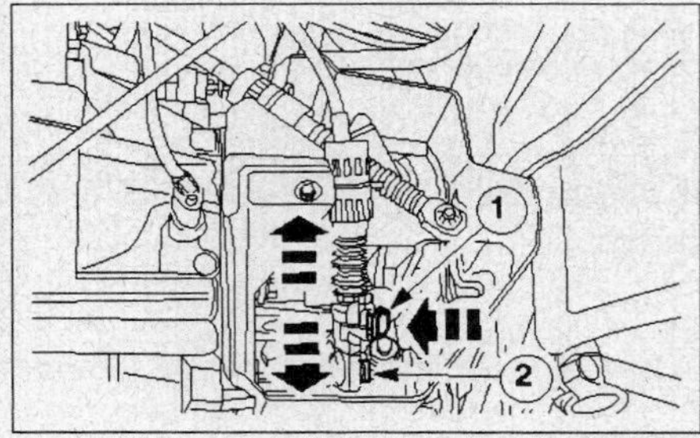

Fig. 2 Shift linkage adjustment

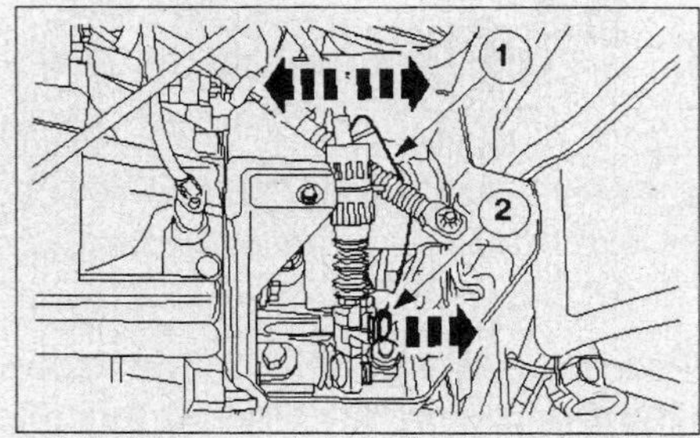

Fig. 3 3rd or 4th gear adjustment

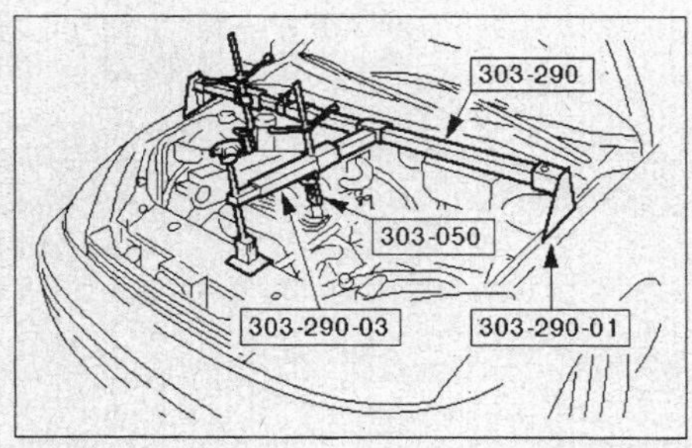

Fig. 4 Engine support fixture

CLUTCH

REPLACE

1. Remove transaxle as outlined under "Transaxle, Replace."
2. Remove pressure plate bolts evenly loosening a maximum of two turns working in a diagonal pattern.
3. Remove pressure plate and clutch disc.
4. Reverse procedure to install noting the following:
   a. Use clutch disc alignment tool No. 308–020, or equivalent, to center clutch disc to locating pins on flywheel.
   b. Using new bolts, tighten bolts a maximum of two turns working in a diagonal pattern to specifications.
   c. Ensure input shaft of transaxle aligns squarely into hub of clutch disc.

TRANSAXLE

REPLACE

IB5 TRANSAXLE

1. Remove battery, then battery tray.
2. Using an Allen key to prevent piston rod from rotating, loosen left and right strut nuts five turns.
3. Disconnect MAF sensor, then remove air cleaner assembly and intake pipe.
4. Remove high pressure line from clutch slave cylinder.
5. Disconnect vacuum hoses, VSS connector and reverse light switch connector.
6. Install engine support fixture tool Nos. 303–050, 303–290, 303–290–01 and 303–290–03, or equivalents **Fig. 4.**
7. Remove rear engine mount, then mounting bracket.
8. Using engine support, lower engine/transaxle.
9. Raise and support vehicle. then open cover on shift and selector cable.
10. Remove shift and selector cable end fittings from shift and selector lever.
11. Remove shift and selector cable from bracket by turning lower part of abutment clockwise and upper part counter clockwise.
12. Remove right and left lower suspension arm ball joints.
13. Remove righthand halfshaft intermediate bearing mounting bracket.
14. Remove righthand and lefthand halfshafts and secure, **ensure inner joints do not bend more than 18° and outer joints more than 45°.**
15. Disconnect front exhaust pipe and detach from rubber insulators, then remove roll resistor **Fig. 5.**
16. Using engine support lower engine/transaxle as far as possible.
17. Remove drive belt cover, then lower flange bolts.
18. Using suitable wooden block, tilt engine/transaxle forward.
19. Remove starter motor flange bolt, then position starter motor aside.
20. Support transaxle using suitable transaxle jack, then remove flange bolts and lower transaxle.
21. Reverse procedure to install tightening to specifications.

MTX75 TRANSAXLE

1. Remove battery, then battery tray.
2. Disconnect MAF sensor, crankcase ventilation hose and intake hose, then remove air cleaner assembly.
3. Disconnect ground lead.
4. Using an Allen key to prevent piston rod from rotating, loosen right and left strut nuts five turns.
5. Shift transaxle into neutral and remove gearshift lever cover, then install gearshift lever aligner tool No. 308–273, or equivalent, **Fig. 6.**
6. Remove intake tube, then air cleaner intake with resonator.
7. Remove shift cable from gear lever, then turn abutment collar counter clockwise and remove cable from bracket.
8. Remove selector cable from selector lever, then turn abutment collar counter clockwise and remove cable from bracket.
9. Raise and support vehicle, then remove flexible exhaust pipe.
10. Remove roll restrictor **Fig. 5.**
11. Remove righthand and lefthand suspension arms.
12. Loosen righthand driveshaft together with intermediate shaft.
13. Remove intermediate shaft bearing cap and discard cap and nuts.
14. Remove intermediate shaft from transaxle together with driveshaft and secure, **ensure inner joint does not bend more than 18° and outer joint more than 45°.**
15. Using driveshaft removal tool Nos. 100–001 and 205–241 or equivalent, **Fig. 7,** loosen driveshaft from transaxle.
16. Remove lefthand driveshaft from transaxle and secure, **ensure inner joint does not bend more than 18° and outer joint more than 45°.** Plug transaxle opening.
17. Remove drive belt cover, then lower vehicle.
18. Remove clutch slave cylinder high pressure line, then secure using suitable ties.
19. Disconnect reverse light switch connector.
20. Install engine support fixture tool Nos. 303–290A, 303–290–01, 303–290–02 and 303–290–03A, or equivalents **Fig. 8.**
21. Remove rear engine mount.
22. Using engine support lower engine/transaxle assembly slightly.
23. Remove rear engine mount bracket, then two upper flange bolts.
24. Remove starter motor bolts, then position and secure starter motor aside.
25. Raise and support vehicle, then disconnect VSS connector.
26. Push engine/transaxle assembly forward, then install suitable wooden block between engine and subframe.
27. Support transaxle using suitable transaxle jack, then remove lower flange bolts.
28. Lower transaxle from vehicle.
29. Reverse procedure to install tightening to specifications.

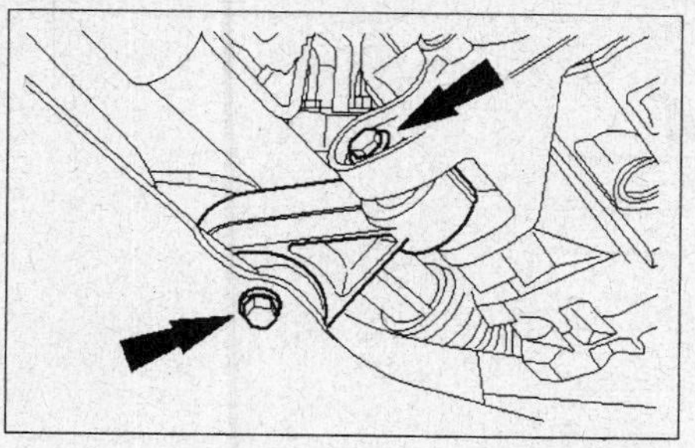
FM5049900110000X

Fig. 5 Roll restrictor

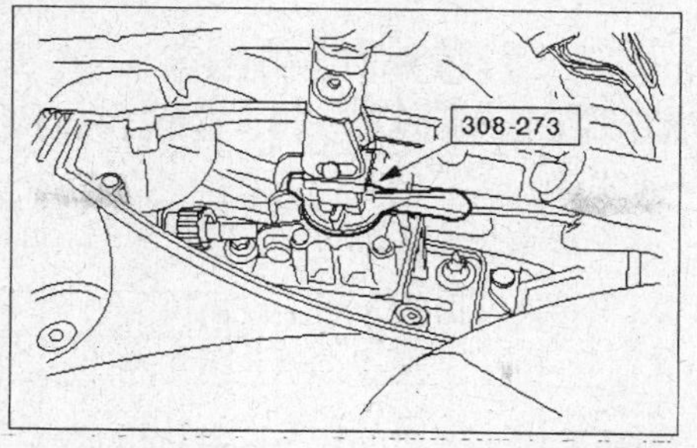

FM5049900111000X

Fig. 6 Gearshift lever aligner tool

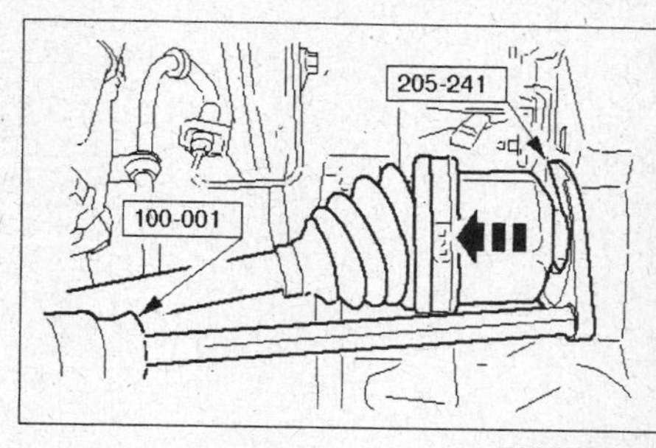

FM5049900112000X

Fig. 7 Lefthand driveshaft removal

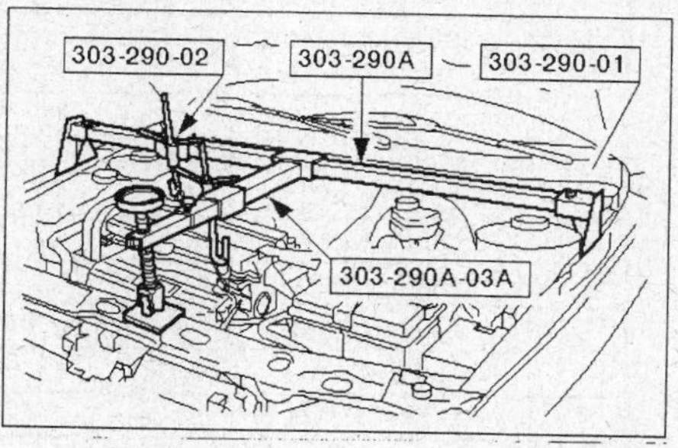

FM5049900113000X

Fig. 8 Engine support fixture

TIGHTENING SPECIFICATIONS

Year	Component	Torque, Ft. Lbs.
IB5 TRANSAXLE		
2000–01	Battery Box	18
	Bleed Nipple	89①
	Clutch Slave Cylinder	89①
	Engine Roll Restrictor To Engine	35
	Engine Roll Restrictor To Subframe	35
	Flange Bolts Transaxle To Engine	35
	Front Exhaust Pipe	35
	Gearshift Cable Bracket	15
	Gearshift Cable Cover	44①
	Lower Suspension Arm To Spindle Carrier	35
	Pressure Plate	21
	Rear Engine Mount	35
	Rear Engine Mount Bracket	59
	Rear Engine Mount Strut	89①
	Reverse Lamp Switch	13
	Selector Finger	13
	Selector Gate	16
	Selector Lever To Selector Shaft	18
	Slave Cylinder High Pressure Line Bracket	21
	Suspension Strut Nut Top	35
	Transaxle Fluid Filler Plug	26
	Transaxle Housing	17
	Transaxle Housing Final Cover	10

Continued

TIGHTENING SPECIFICATIONS—Continued

MTX75 TRANSAXLE

2000–01	Ball Joint To Selector Lever Shaft	11
	Bleed Nipple	10
	Catalytic Convertor To Exhaust	35
	Clutch Slave Cylinder To Transaxle	89①
	Flange Bolts	35
	Gearshift Lever To Gearshift Lever Shaft	22
	Gearshift Lever To Selector Shaft	30
	Lower Suspension Arm Ball Joint To Spindle Carrier	35
	Pressure Plate	21
	Rear Engine Mount Bracket To Transaxle	59
	Rear Engine Mount Central Nut	98
	Rear Engine Mount Four Nuts	35
	Reverse Gear Idler Shaft Mount	25
	Reverse Light Actuating Pin	18
	Reverse Light Switch	89①
	Righthand Halfshaft Center Bearing To Bracket	18
	Roll Restrictor To Subframe	35
	Roll Restrictor To Transaxle	35
	Selector Gate To Housing	89①
	Selector Finger To Selector Shaft	21
	Starter Motor To Transaxle Housing	26
	Suspension Strut Nut	35
	Transaxle End Housing To Clutch End Hosing Section	24
	Transaxle Fluid Drain Plug	33
	Transaxle Fluid Fill Plug	33

① — Inch lbs.

Rear Suspension

NOTE: On Air Bag Equipped Models, Refer To "Air Bag System Precautions" Located In The Front Of This Manual For System Disarming & Arming Procedures.

NOTE: Refer To "Computer Relearn Procedures" Located In The Front Of This Manual When Battery Power To The Computer Has Been Interrupted.

INDEX

PRECAUTIONS

AIR BAG SYSTEMS

Refer to "Air Bag System Precautions" in the front of this manual for system disarming and arming procedures.

BATTERY GROUND CABLE

Prior to service, disconnect battery ground cable and isolate as required.

DESCRIPTION

Refer to **Figs. 1 and 2** when removing rear suspension components.

HUB & BEARING

REPLACE

1. Raise and support vehicle, then remove wheel.
2. Remove dust cap, if dust cap is damaged on removal a new dust cap must be used on installation.
3. Remove hub retaining nut, **Fig. 3.**
4. Remove hub assembly.
5. Remove and discard ABS sensor ring.
6. Remove circlip, then using a suitable drift, press out the bearing, **Fig. 4.**
7. Reverse procedures to install. Tighten new retainer and wheel lug nuts to specifications.

WHEEL BEARING INSPECTION

1. Raise and support vehicle and check loose bearing by rocking wheels at top and bottom.
2. Spin wheel quickly by hand and ensure wheel turns smoothly without noise.
3. Position Dial Indicator Gauge Bracket Tool No. 100–D004 and Dial Indicator Gauge Tool No. 100–D005, or equivalent, against wheel hub, then push and pull wheel hub, **Fig. 5.**
4. Push and pull wheel by hand in an axial direction and measure end play.
5. If end play exceeds specifications, check and adjust rear axle wheel hub retainer, replace bearing as necessary.

REAR WHEEL SPINDLE

REPLACE

1. Release parking brake adjustment.
2. Loosen wheel nuts, raise and support vehicle, then remove wheel.
3. **On models equipped with anti-lock brakes,** detach wheel speed sensor, **Fig. 6.**
4. **On all models,** remove dust cap, if dust cap is damaged during removal, replace with new cap, **Fig. 7.**
5. Remove hub retaining nut, then brake drum. CAUTION: Use a socket to remove hub retaining nut to prevent damage. Ensure ABS ring is not knocked or damaged and is kept free from metallic fragments when removing brake drum.
6. Remove wheel spindle, **Fig. 8.**
7. Reverse procedures to install noting the following:
   a. Tighten parking brake adjustment.
   b. CAUTION: Use a socket to install hub retaining nut to prevent damage. Ensure ABS ring is not knocked or damaged and is kept free from metallic fragments when installing brake drum.

SHOCK ABSORBER

REPLACE

1. **On 3–door models,** remove luggage compartment interior trim panel, then remove shock absorber top mounting nut, **Fig. 9.**
2. **On all models,** raise and support vehicle.
3. Remove lower shock absorber bolt.
4. Remove upper shock absorber bolt, then remove shock absorber, **Figs. 10 and 11.**
5. Reverse procedure to install noting the following:
   a. Final tightening of suspension components must be performed with vehicle weight on road wheels.
   b. Tighten lower mounting bolt to specifications.

CONTROL ARM

REPLACE

REAR LOWER ARM

1. Loosen wheel nuts, then raise and support vehicle.
2. Set suspension to design height.
3. Remove rear wheel.
4. Remove stabilizer bar link from lower arm, **Fig. 12.**
5. Using suitable coil spring compressor, remove rear lower arm, **Fig. 13.**
6. Reverse procedure to install lower arm.

FRONT LOWER ARM

1. Set suspension to design height.
2. Remove mounting bolts, then remove front lower arm, **Fig. 14.**
3. Reverse procedures to install.

UPPER ARM

1. Loosen wheel nuts, then set suspension to design height.
2. Remove wheel and outer bolt, **Fig. 15.**
3. Remove inner bolt, then remove upper arm, **Fig. 16.**
4. Reverse procedures to install.

COIL SPRING

Refer to "Control Arm, Replace" when removing coil spring.

TIE-BAR

REPLACE

1. Remove brake backing plate.
2. Detach parking brake sleeve, then detach parking brake cable, **Fig. 17.**

3. Detach cable guide, then pull cable and guide through tie-bar.
4. Detach rear brake flex hose, disconnecting pipe at union, **Fig. 18.**
5. Set suspension to design height.
6. Remove shock absorber lower bolt, front lower arm outer bolt, then remove.
7. Using suitable coil spring compressor, remove rear lower arm bolts, **Fig. 19.**
8. Remove spring.
9. Detach and remove upper arm.
10. Remove tie-bar front mounting bolts, then tie-bar.
11. Reverse procedures to install noting the following:
    a. Bleed brake system.
    b. Check rear wheel alignment.

REAR CROSSMEMBER

REPLACE

1. Raise and support vehicle.
2. Remove stabilizer bar as described under "Stabilizer Bar, Replace."
3. Remove rear lower arms, front lower arms and upper arms as described under "Control Arm, Replace." Ensure wheel knuckles are supported before removing arms.
4. Support exhaust system, then remove exhaust system bracket.
5. **On 3–door models,** disconnect EVAP, emission canister vent solenoid electrical connector **Fig. 20.**
6. Remove vent pipes, then emission canister, **Fig. 21.**
7. **On all models,** support rear crossmember with suitable jack, then remove three retaining bolts from either side, **Fig. 22.**
8. Lower and remove crossmember.
9. Reverse procedures to install noting the following:
    a. Do not lower suspension from design height.
    b. Check rear wheel alignment.

STABILIZER BAR

REPLACE

1. Set suspension to design height.
2. Detach stabilizer bar link from rear lower arms, **Fig. 12.**
3. Remove stabilizer bar from both sides, **Fig. 23.**
4. Reverse procedures to install noting the following:
    a. Verify bushing nipple is on the left-hand side when installing onto stabilizer bar in either side, **Fig. 24.**
    b. Apply water to clamp to assist installation.

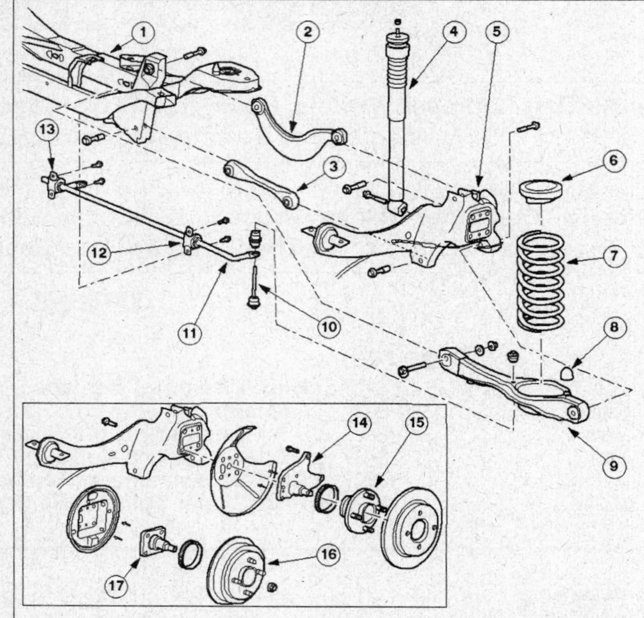

Item	Description
1	Crossmember
2	Upper arm
3	Front lower arm
4	Shock absorber assembly
5	Tie-bar and knuckle
6	Spring pad
7	Spring
8	Bump stop
9	Rear lower arm
10	Stabilizer bar link
11	Stabilizer bar
12	Stabilizer bar bushing
13	Stabilizer bar bushing clamp
14	Wheel spindle (disc brakes)
15	Wheel hub (disc brakes)
16	Drum and hub assembly (drum brakes)
17	Wheel spindle (drum brakes)

FM2039900095000X

Fig. 1 Rear suspension. Except Wagon

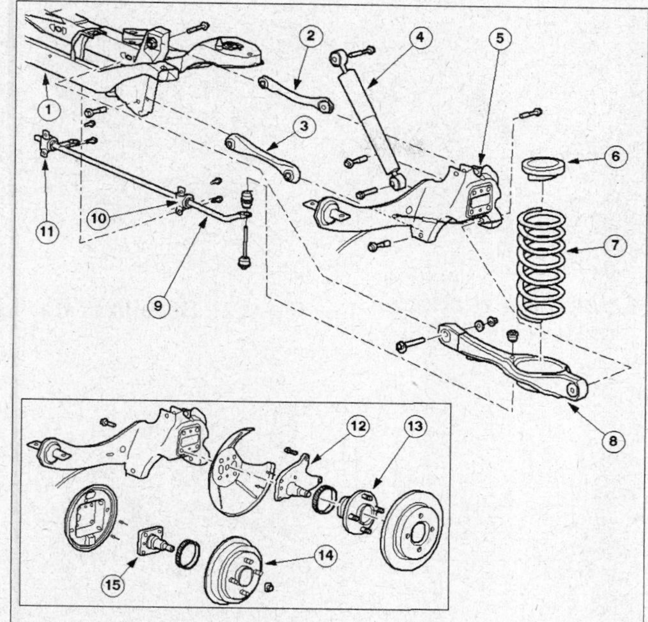

Item	Description
1	Crossmember
2	Upper arm
3	Front lower arm
4	Shock absorber
5	Tie-bar and knuckle
6	Spring pad
7	Spring
8	Rear lower arm
9	Stabilizer bar
10	Stabilizer bar bushing
11	Stabilizer bar bushing clamp
12	Wheel spindle (disc brakes)
13	Wheel hub (disc brakes)
14	Drum and hub assembly (drum brakes)
15	Wheel spindle (drum brakes)

FM2039900096000X

Fig. 2 Rear suspension. Wagon

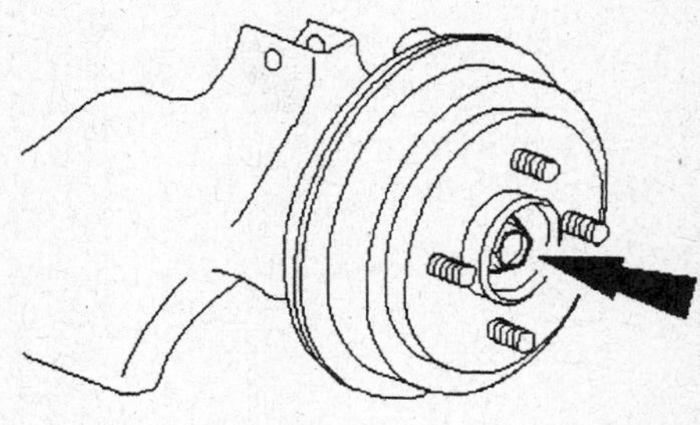

FM2039900097000X

Fig. 3 Hub nut removal

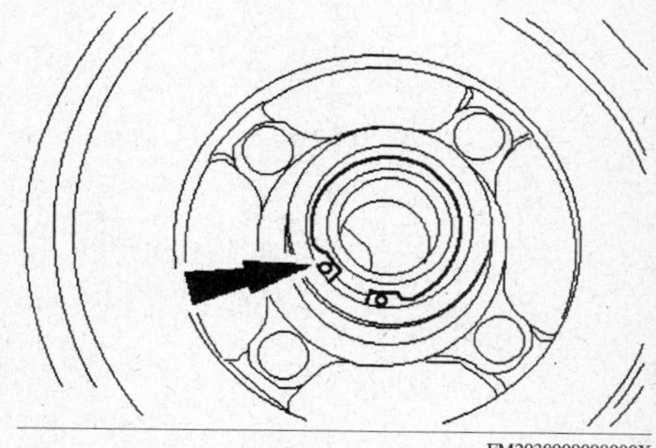

FM2039900098000X

Fig. 4 Circlip removal

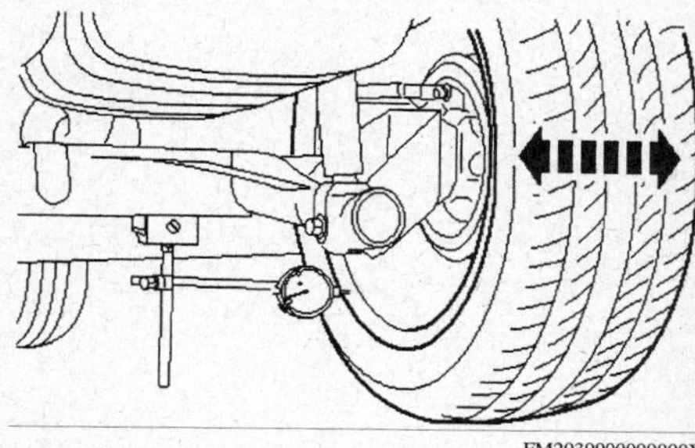

FM2039900099000X

Fig. 5 Wheel bearing inspection

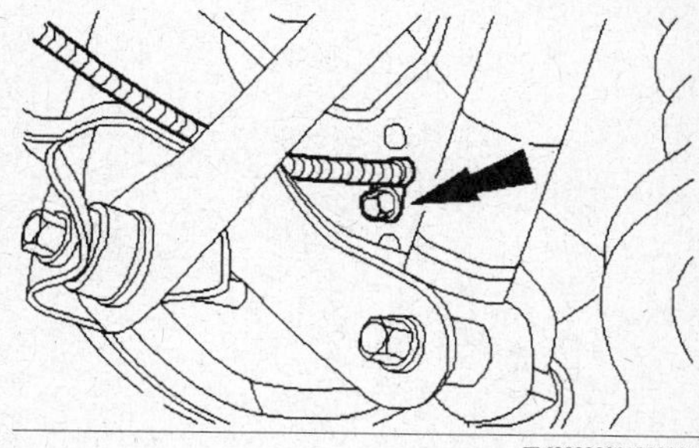

FM2039900100000X

Fig. 6 Wheel speed sensor removal

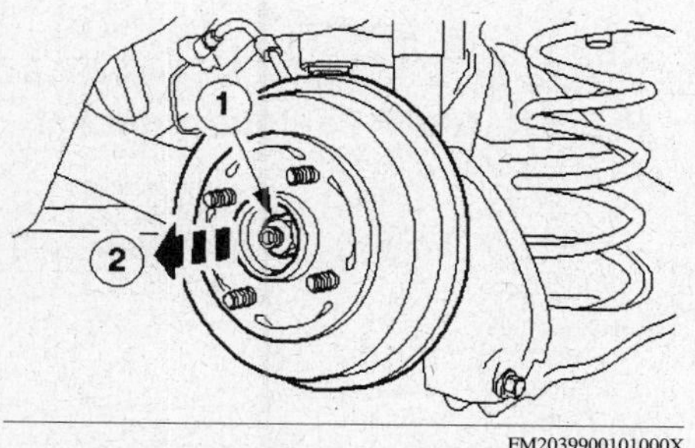

FM2039900101000X

Fig. 7 Hub nut & cap removal

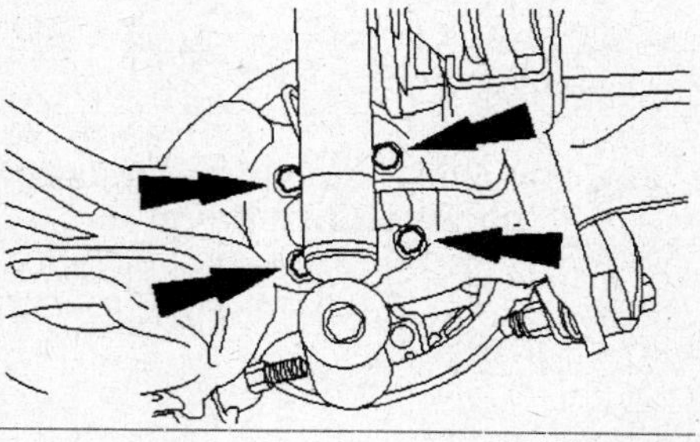

FM2039900102000X

Fig. 8 Spindle removal

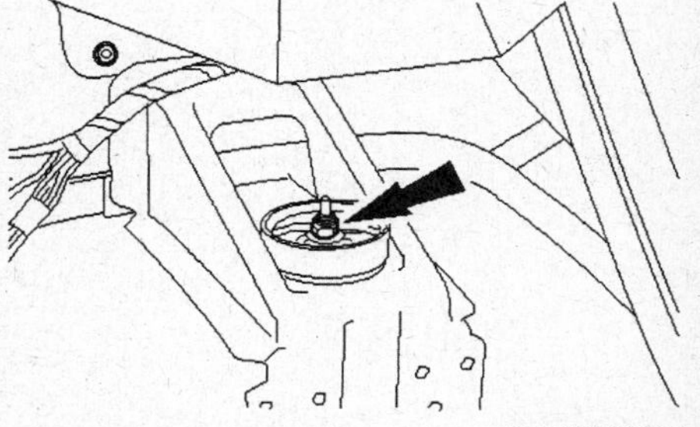

FM2039900103000X

Fig. 9 Shock absorber removal (3-door)

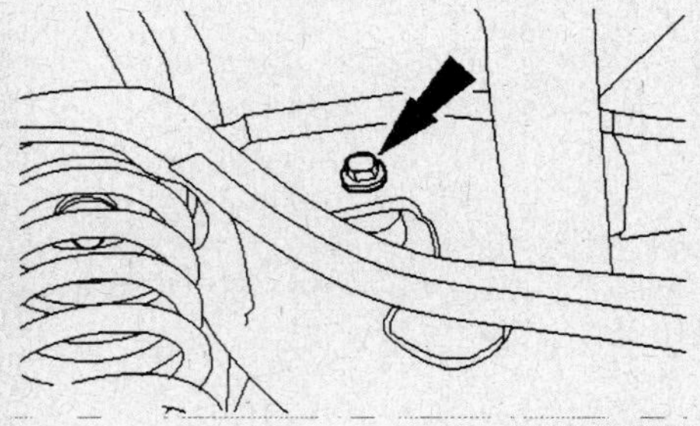

Fig. 10 Upper bolt removal

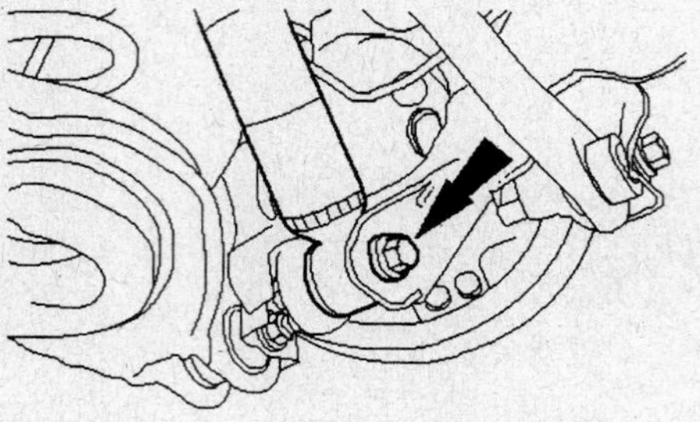

Fig. 11 Lower bolt & shock removal

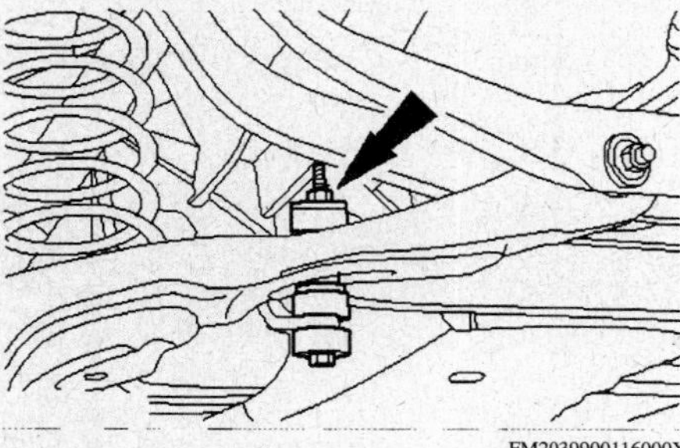

Fig. 12 Stabilizer bar link removal

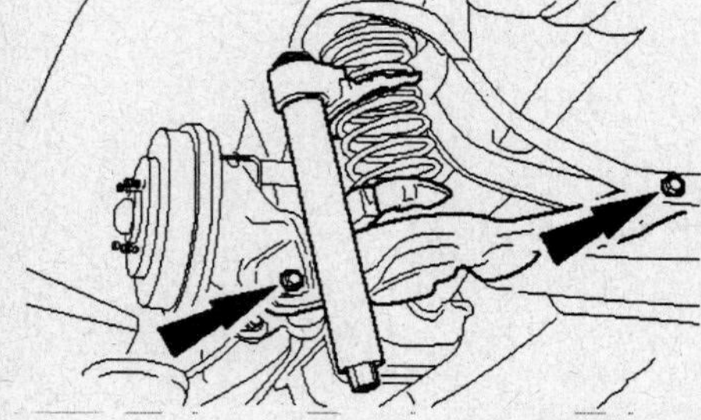

Fig. 13 Rear lower arm removal

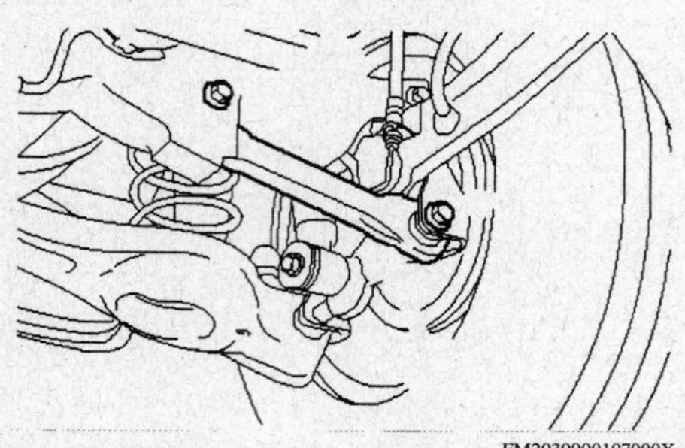

Fig. 14 Front lower arm removal

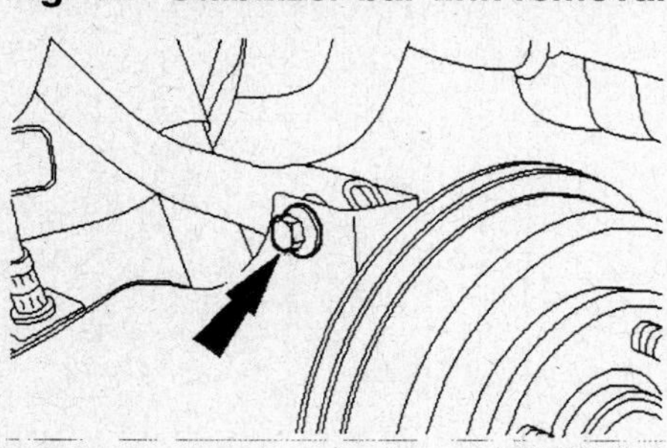

Fig. 15 Upper arm bolt removal

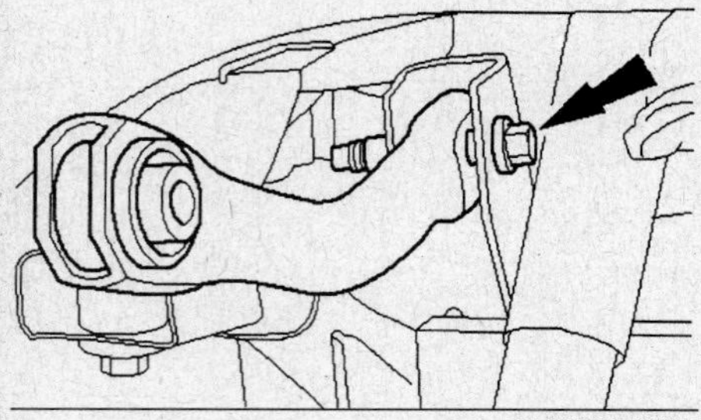

Fig. 16 Upper arm removal

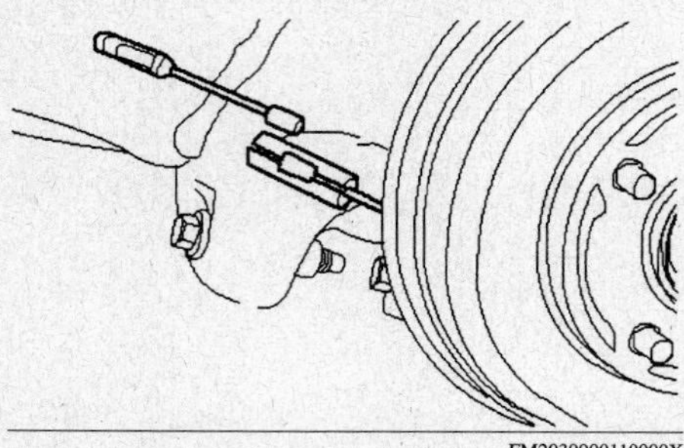

Fig. 17 Parking brake cable removal

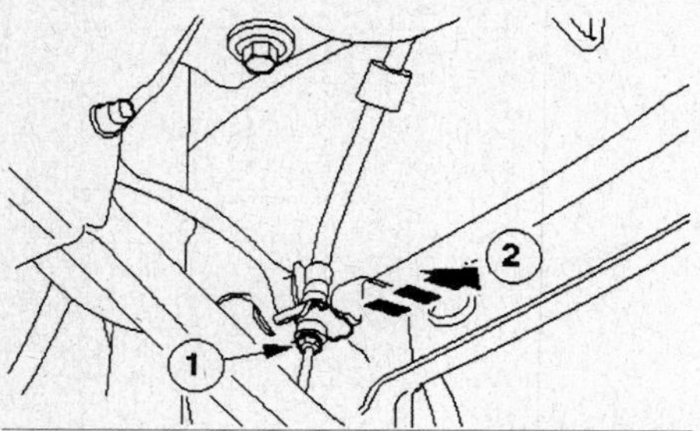

Fig. 18 Brake pipe union removal

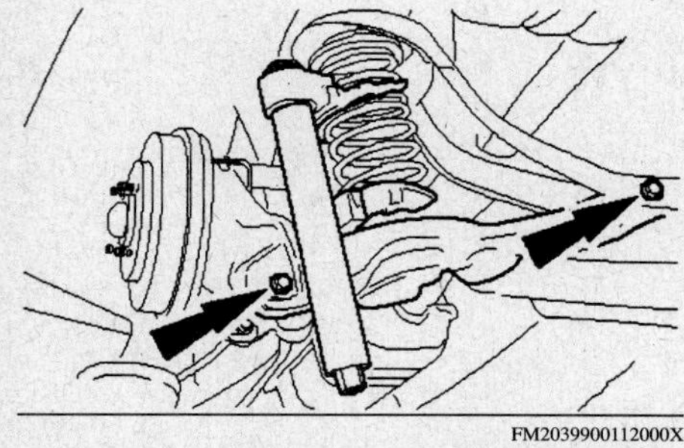

Fig. 19 Spring & lower arm bolt removal

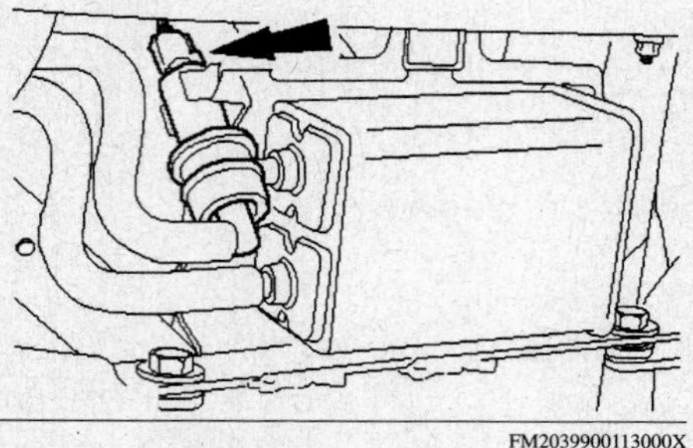

Fig. 20 EVAP emission canister connector removal

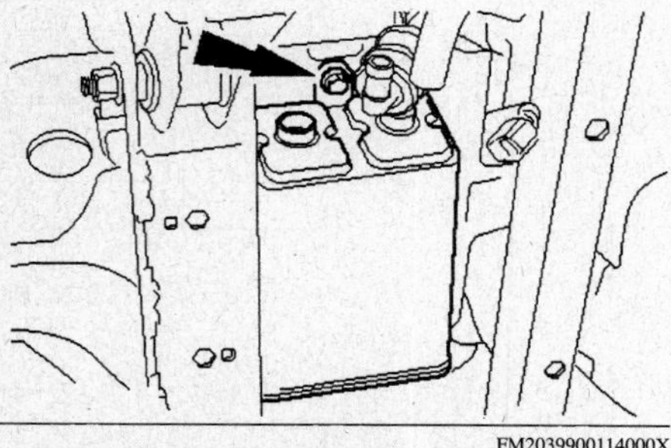

Fig. 21 EVAP canister removal

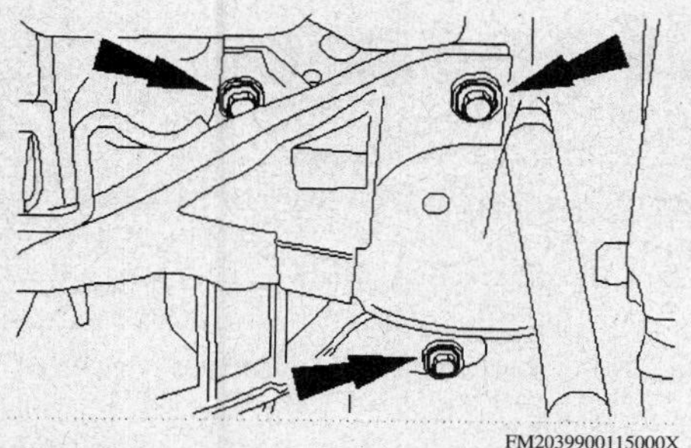

Fig. 22 Crossmember removal

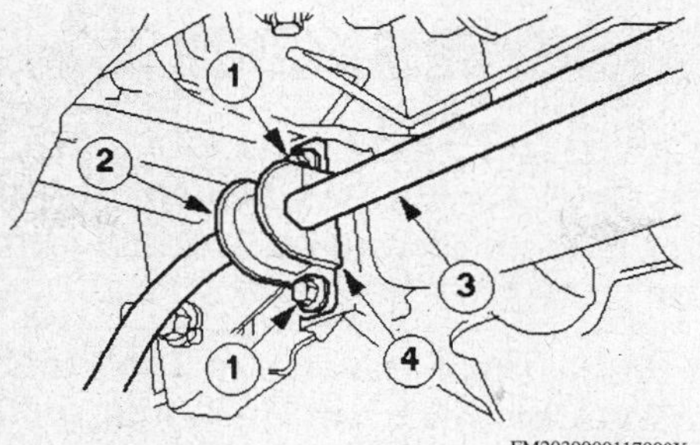

Fig. 23 Stabilizer bar removal

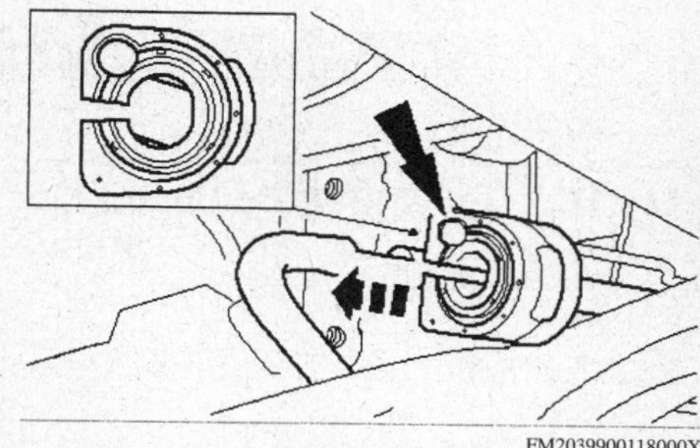
Fig. 24 Stabilizer bushing

TIGHTENING SPECIFICATIONS

Year	Component	Torque, Ft. Lbs
2000–01	Crossmember Retaining Bolt	85
	EVAP Canister Bolt	84①
	Front Lower Arm Bolt	85
	Inside Rear Lower Arm Bolt	84①
	Lower Arm Bolt	85
	Lower Shock Bolt	85
	Lug Nut	94
	Outside Rear Lower Arm Bolt	85
	Spindle Bolt	49
	Stabilizer Bar Link	11
	Stabilizer Bracket Bolt	35
	Tie Bar Mounting Bolt	85
	Top Shock Mounting Bolt	13
	Upper Arm Bolt	85
	Upper Shock Bolt	85
	Wheel Hub Nut	173
	Wheel Speed Sensor	84①

① — Inch lbs.

Front Suspension & Steering

NOTE: On Air Bag Equipped Models, Refer To "Air Bag System Precautions" Located In The Front Of This Manual For System Disarming & Arming Procedures.

NOTE: Refer To "Computer Relearn Procedures" Located In The Front Of This Manual When Battery Power To The Computer Has Been Interrupted.

INDEX

PRECAUTIONS

AIR BAG SYSTEMS

Refer to "Air Bag System Precautions" in the front of this manual for system disarming and arming procedures.

BATTERY GROUND CABLE

Prior to service, disconnect battery ground cable and isolate as required.

DESCRIPTION

Refer to **Fig. 1** for exploded view of front suspension.

HUB & BEARING

REPLACE

1. Remove knuckle as outlined under "Steering Knuckle, Replace."
2. Using bearing puller No. 205–D064, or equivalent, and suitable drift, remove wheel hub and outer bearing race, **Fig. 2.**
3. Remove bearing circlip.
4. Using suitable drift, remove inner bearing.
5. Using bearing cup installer No. 205–139, or equivalent, and suitable drift, install new bearing.
6. Install bearing circlip.
7. Install wheel hub.
8. Install knuckle.

WHEEL BEARING INSPECTION

The wheel bearing cannot be adjusted. Replacement is required if inspection fails.

1. Road test vehicle on smooth road. Make several right and left turns.
2. Replace left bearing if noise is heard on right turns.
3. Replace right bearing if noise is heard on left turns.
4. If noise is heard on right and left turns, inspect side that is louder first.
5. Inspect bearing as follows:
   a. Raise and support vehicle. rock wheels at top and bottom to check for bearing looseness.
   b. Spin wheel quickly by hand. Ensure wheel turns smoothly without noise from bearing.
   c. Remove wheel and tire assembly, then brake caliper anchor plate.
   d. Position dial indicator gauge bracket and gauge Nos. 100–D004 & 100–D005, or equivalent, against wheel hub, then push and pull wheel hub.
   e. Measure end play.
   f. Replace bearing if end play exists.

BALL JOINT

REPLACE

Refer to "Control Arm, Replace" when servicing the ball joint.

STRUT

REPLACE

1. Raise and support vehicle, then remove wheel and tire assembly.
2. Remove knuckle as outlined under "Steering Knuckle, Replace."
3. Remove strut tower nuts, then strut and spring assembly from vehicle.
4. Reverse procedure to install.

COIL SPRING & STRUT SERVICE

1. Using suitable coil spring compressor, compress spring.
2. Use suitable Allen key to prevent piston rod rotation, then remove thrust bearing nut.
3. Disassemble strut and spring assembly as shown, **Fig. 3.**
4. Reverse procedure to assemble.

CONTROL ARM

REPLACE

1. Raise and support vehicle, then remove wheel and tire assembly.
2. Remove ball joint bolt, then ball joint from knuckle, **Fig. 4.**
3. Remove lower arm bolts, **Fig. 5.**
4. Remove lower arm from vehicle.
5. Install lower arm. New nuts, bolts and washers must be used.
6. Referring to **Fig. 6,** tighten bolts and nuts as follows:
   a. **Torque** nut 1 to 74 ft. lbs.
   b. Tighten nut 1 an additional 60°.
   c. **Torque** nut 2 to 89 ft. lbs.
   d. **Torque** bolt 3 to 89 ft. lbs.
   e. Tighten bolt 3 an additional 90°. Ensure bolt 3 torque is 125–170 ft. lbs.

STEERING KNUCKLE

REPLACE

1. Loosen strut tower nuts at least 5 turns.
2. Raise and support vehicle, then remove wheel and tire assembly.
3. Disconnect brake hose from support bracket.
4. Disconnect wheel speed sensor, then remove and secure brake caliper.
5. Remove brake rotor.
6. Remove tie rod end using tie rod end remover No. 211–001, or equivalent.
7. Remove ball joint from knuckle.
8. Remove hub retaining nut, then using suitable puller, separate wheel hub from half shaft.
9. Remove knuckle pinch bolt from strut.

10. Remove knuckle from strut, then vehicle.
11. Reverse procedure to install. Refer to **Fig. 7** when installing halfshaft.

HALFSHAFT

REPLACE

1. Loosen strut lock nut 5 rotations. Use Allen key to prevent piston from rotating.
2. Raise and support vehicle, then remove wheel and tire assembly.
3. Disconnect ball joint from knuckle.
4. Remove hub nut.
5. Using puller No. 204–069 and stud extension tool No. 204–085, or equivalents, **Fig. 8,** separate halfshaft from wheel hub.
6. **On right side,** remove intermediate shaft bearing mounting nuts.
7. **On either side,** remove halfshaft from transaxle using puller No. 205–241 and handle No. 100–001, or equivalents.
8. Allow fluid to drain into suitable container.
9. Reverse procedure to install. Ensure halfshaft is fully seated into transaxle.

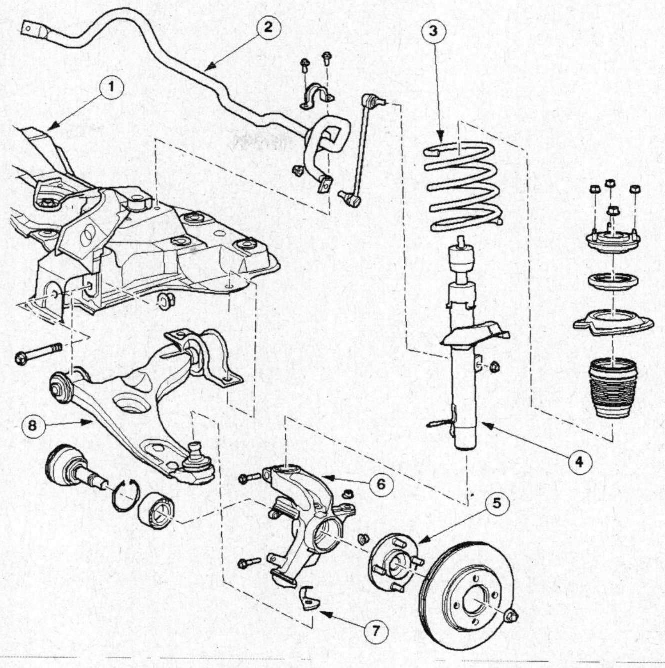

Fig. 1 Exploded view of front suspension (Part 1 of 2)

STABILIZER BAR

REPLACE

1. Center steering wheel , then lock in position.
2. Disconnect steering column shaft from pinion extension, **Fig. 9.**
3. Raise and support vehicle, then remove wheel and tire assemblies.
4. Remove tie rod end nuts, then using tie rod end remover No. 211–001, or equivalent, detach tie rod ends from knuckles.
5. Disconnect stabilizer bar links.
6. Remove ball joints from knuckles.
7. Remove support insulator to transaxle center bolt, **Fig. 10.**
8. Using suitable transmission jack, support crossmember.
9. Remove six crossmember bolts, **Fig. 11.**
10. Lower crossmember.
11. Remove clamp bolts and clamps.
12. Remove stabilizer bar.
13. Install bushings onto stabilizer bar. **Do not use lubricant.**
14. Set and support stabilizer bar to design height, **Fig. 12.**
15. Install clamps and clamp bolts.
16. Referring to **Fig. 13,** tighten bolts in sequence as follows:
    a. **Torque** bolts to 37 ft. lbs.
    b. **Torque** bolts to 52 ft. lbs.
17. Remove stabilizer supports.
18. Using alignment tool No. 502–002, or equivalent, align crossmember as follows:
    a. Insert guide pins through alignment holes, **Fig. 14.**
    b. Slide locking plates into grooves and tighten guide pin sleeve.
    c. Raise crossmember, engaging guide pins into chassis aligning holes.
19. Install crossmember bolts, then remove transmission jack and alignment pins.
20. Reverse remaining procedure to install.

TIE ROD

REPLACE

1. Remove steering gear as outlined under "Power Steering Gear, Replace."
2. Remove tie rod end and locknut.
3. Remove boot from steering gear.
4. Rotate pinion to expose rack gear teeth.
5. Secure steering gear in suitable vise.
6. Remove tie rod using suitable pipe wrench, **Fig. 15.**
7. Remove all traces of thread locking compound.
8. Reverse procedure to install. Apply thread locking compound to inner threads of new tie rod.

TIE ROD END

REPLACE

1. Raise and support vehicle, then remove wheel and tire assembly.
2. Loosen tie rod end lock nut, then remove retaining nut.
3. Using tie rod end remover No. 211–001, or equivalent, release tie rod end from knuckle.
4. Note number of turns required to remove tie rod end.
5. Remove tie rod end and lock nut.
6. Reverse procedure to install. Inspect toe adjustment after installation.

POWER STEERING GEAR

REPLACE

Refer to **Fig. 16** for power steering system components.

1. Center steering wheel, then lock into position.
2. Remove instrument panel lower cover.
3. Disconnect steering column shaft from pinion extension.
4. Raise and support vehicle, then remove front wheel and tire assemblies.
5. Using tie rod end removal tool No. 211–001, or equivalent, remove tie rod ends from knuckles.
6. Disconnect stabilizer bar links from struts.
7. Using coupling tool No. 310–041, or equivalent, disconnect fluid cooler hose and allow fluid to drain into suitable container.
8. Remove support insulator to transaxle center bolt, **Fig. 17.**
9. Remove steering gear heat shield.
10. Disconnect hose support clamp, then remove power steering hoses from steering gear. Allow fluid to drain into suitable container.
11. Using suitable transmission jack, support crossmember.
12. Remove 6 crossmember bolts, **Fig. 18.**
13. Lower crossmember.
14. Remove steering column coupling shaft and floor seal.
15. Move floor seal upwards.
16. Remove bolts, then steering gear.
17. Inspect and replace O-rings as required.
18. Install steering column coupling shaft

Item	Description
1	Crossmember
2	Stabilizer bar
3	Spring
4	Strut
5	Wheel hub
6	Wheel knuckle
7	Lower arm ball joint heat shield
8	Lower arm

FM2020000172020X

Fig. 1 Exploded view of front suspension (Part 2 of 2)

and floor seal.

19. Using alignment tool No. 502–002, or equivalent, align crossmember as follows:
    a. Insert guide pins through alignment holes, **Fig. 19.**
    b. Slide locking plates into grooves and tighten guide pin sleeve.
    c. Raise crossmember, engaging guide pins into chassis aligning holes.
20. Install crossmember bolts, then remove alignment pins.
21. Reverse remaining procedure to complete installation. Fill and bleed power steering system as outlined under "Power Steering System Bleed."

POWER STEERING PUMP

REPLACE

1. Remove accessory drive belt, then raise and support vehicle.
2. Using coupling tool No. 310–041, or equivalent, disconnect fluid cooler hose and allow fluid to drain into suitable container.
3. Lower vehicle, then detach pressure line support brackets.
4. Detach speed control cable as required.
5. Disconnect PSP switch electrical connector.
6. Cover alternator to prevent fluid contamination, then disconnect low pressure hose.
7. Disconnect pressure line union, then allow fluid to drain into suitable container.

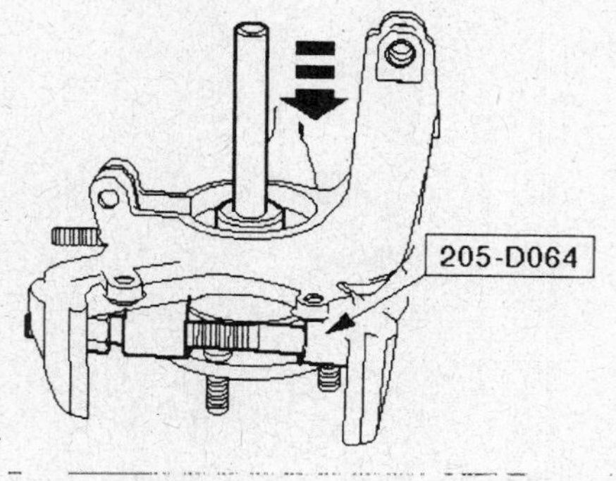

FM2020000168000X

Fig. 2 Hub & outer race removal

8. Remove four pump bolts, then pump from vehicle.
9. Remove PSP switch and pressure hose union from pump.
10. Reverse procedure to install, noting the following:
    a. Using installer No. 211–D027, or equivalent, install new O-ring seal onto pressure line.
    b. Fill and bleed system as outlined under "Power Steering System Bleed."

POWER STEERING PUMP PULLEY

REPLACE

1. Remove accessory drive belt.
2. Using remover No. 211–185, or equivalent, remove power steering pump pulley. Ensure pulley is flush with end of pump shaft.
3. Reverse procedure to install.

POWER STEERING SYSTEM BLEED

1. Fill power steering fluid reservoir to MAX mark with fresh power steering fluid.
2. Start engine and slowly turn wheel from lock to lock once. Ensure fluid level does not fall below MIN mark as air could enter system.
3. Stop engine and inspect system for leaks.
4. Check and fill reservoir as required.
5. Using vacuum tool No. 416–D002, or equivalent, maintain a vacuum of 15 in.-Hg. If vacuum decreases more than 2 in.-Hg in 5 minutes, check for leaks.
6. Start engine and turn wheel from lock to lock once, then turn to the right just off the lock stop.

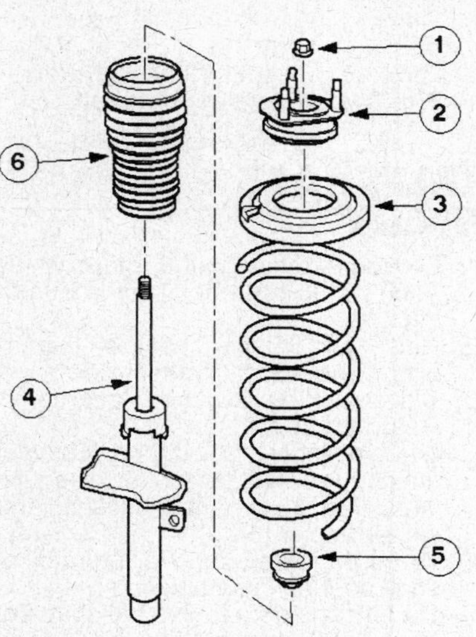

FM2020000180000X

Fig. 3 Strut & spring service

7. Stop engine and apply a vacuum of 15 in.-Hg. Maintain vacuum for 5 minutes until air is evacuated from the system.
8. Release vacuum, then repeat steps 6 and 7, turning wheel to the left, just off the stop lock.
9. Remove vacuum tool and fill reservoir as required.
10. Start engine and turn wheel from lock to lock. If excessive noise is apparent, repeat procedure.
11. If noise level is still unacceptable, allow vehicle to stand overnight and repeat procedure.

POWER STEERING FLUID COOLER

REPLACE

1. Disconnect coolant expansion tank and position aside.
2. Remove hose from power steering fluid reservoir and allow fluid to drain into suitable container.
3. Detach hose from bracket, then raise and support vehicle.
4. Remove radiator splash shield.
5. Using coupling tool No. 310–041, or equivalent, disconnect fluid cooler hose and allow fluid to drain into suitable container.
6. Remove fluid cooler from vehicle.
7. Reverse procedure to install. Fill and bleed power steering system as outlined under "Power Steering System Bleed."

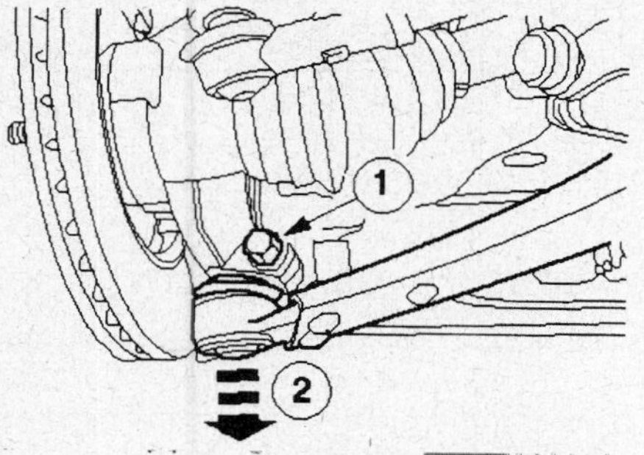

Fig. 4 Ball joint removal

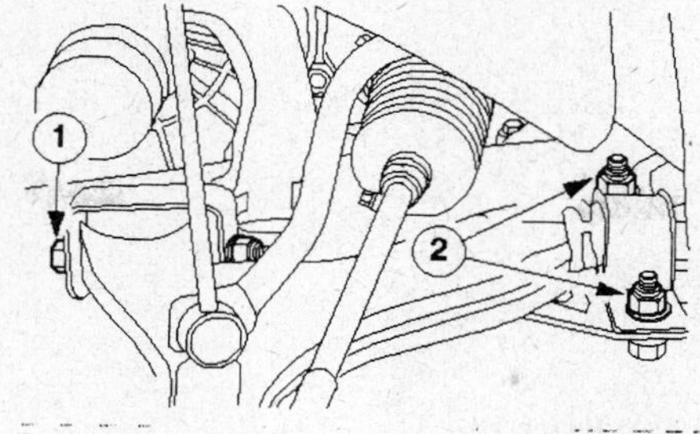

Fig. 5 Lower arm removal

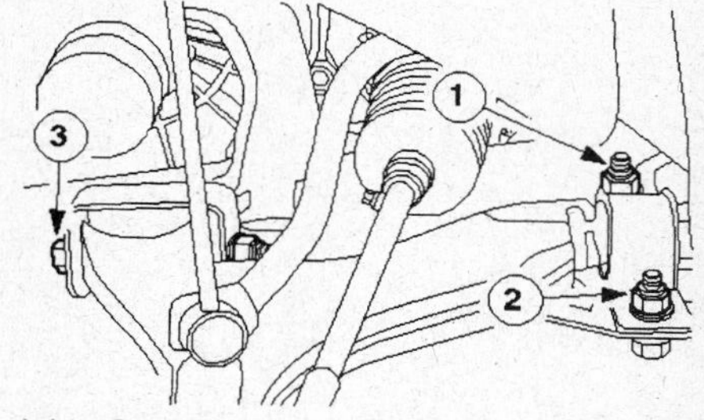

Fig. 6 Lower arm tightening sequence

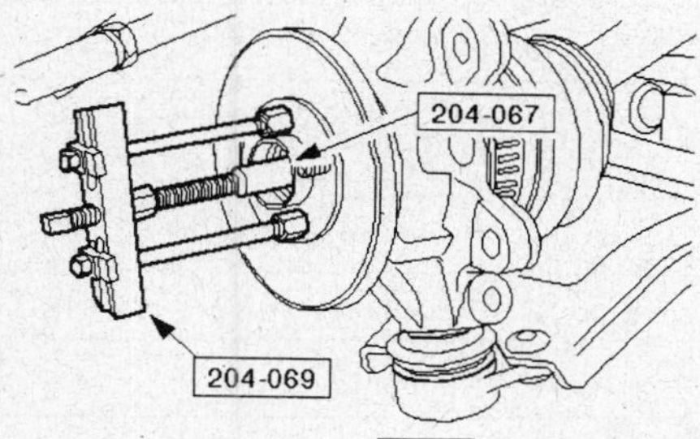

Fig. 7 Halfshaft installation

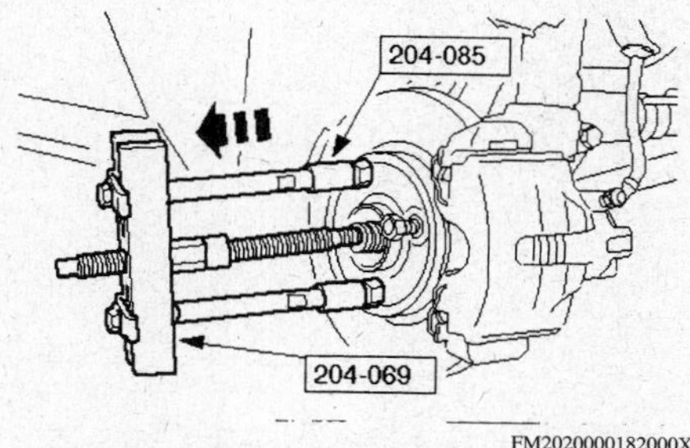

Fig. 8 Halfshaft separation

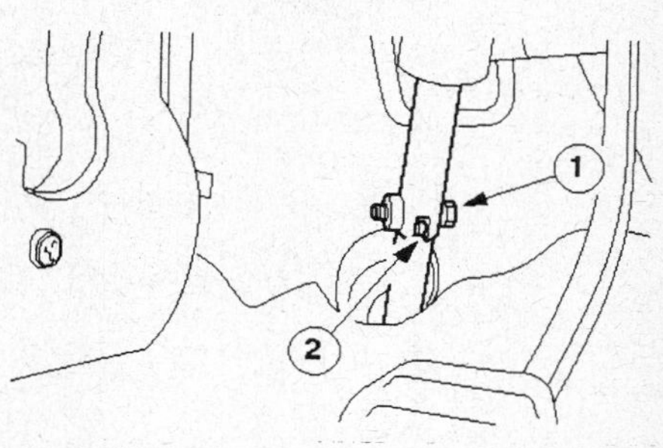

Fig. 9 Column shaft removal

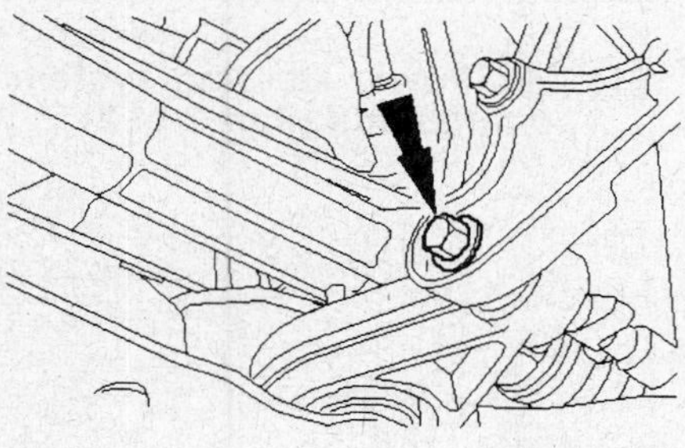

Fig. 10 Support insulator bolt removal

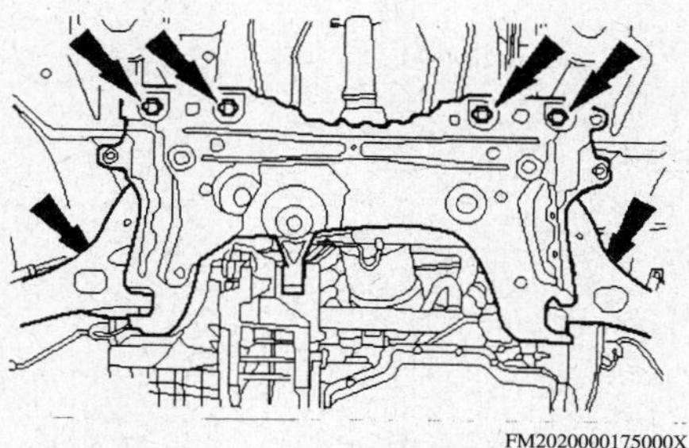

Fig. 11 Crossmember removal

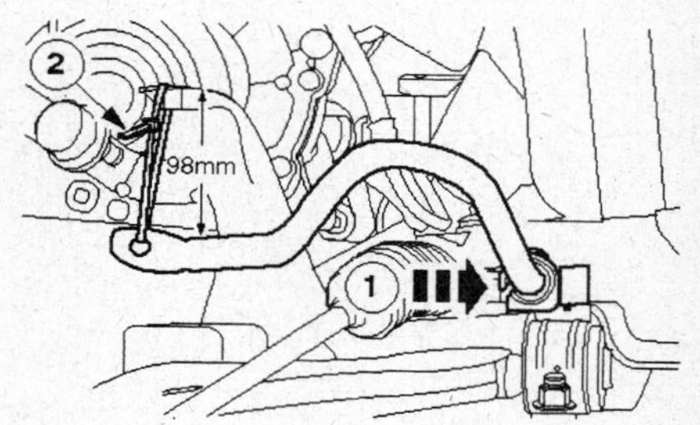

Fig. 12 Stabilizer bar design height setting

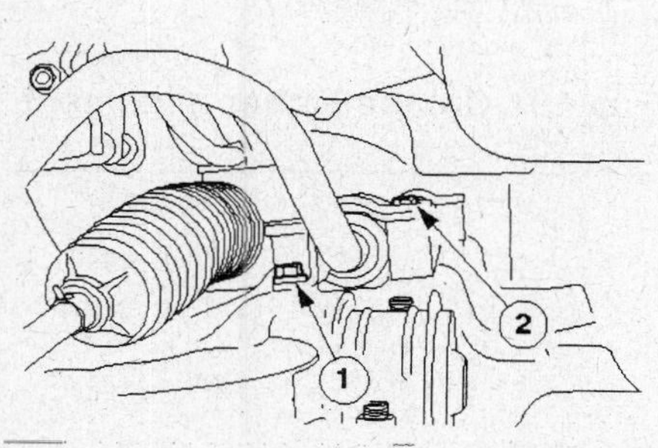

Fig. 13 Clamp tightening sequence

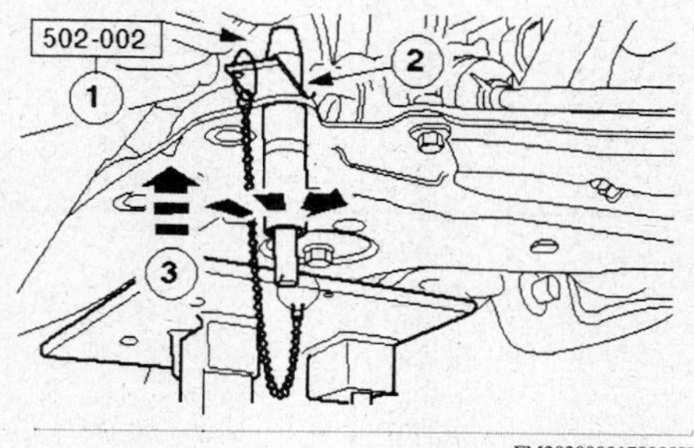

Fig. 14 Crossmember alignment

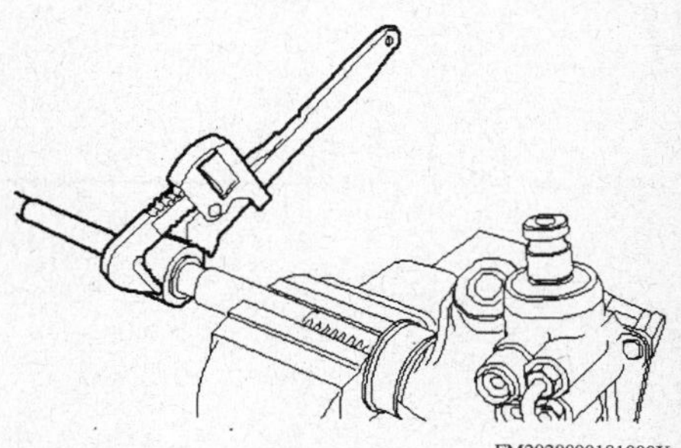

Fig. 15 Tie rod removal

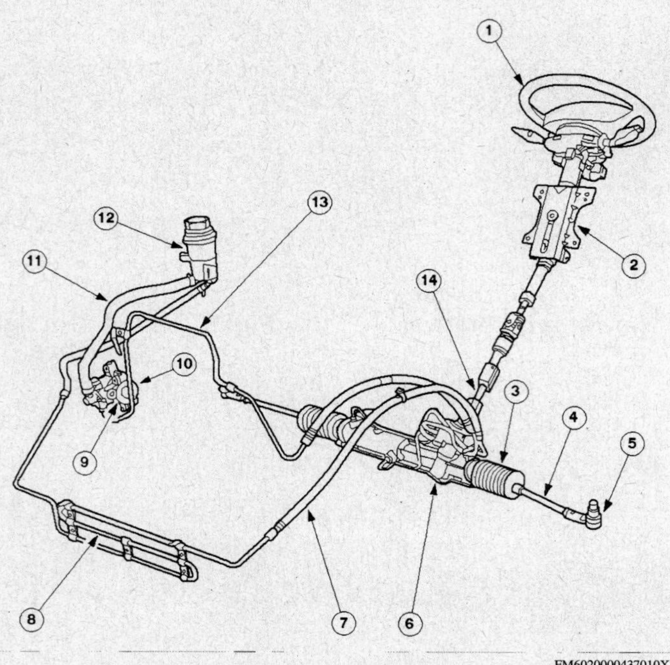

Fig. 16 Power steering system components (Part 1 of 2)

Item	Description
1	Steering wheel
2	Steering column
3	Boot
4	Tie-rod
5	Tie-rod end
6	Steering gear
7	Steering gear to fluid cooler hose
8	Fluid cooler
9	Power steering pressure (PSP) switch
10	Power steering pump
11	Fluid supply hose
12	Fluid reservoir
13	Pump to steering gear hose
14	Steering column shaft coupling

FM6020000437020X

Fig. 16 Power steering system components (Part 2 of 2)

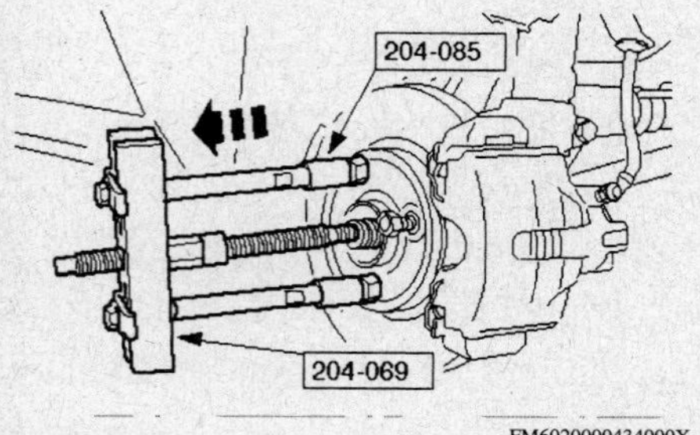

Fig. 17 Support bolt removal

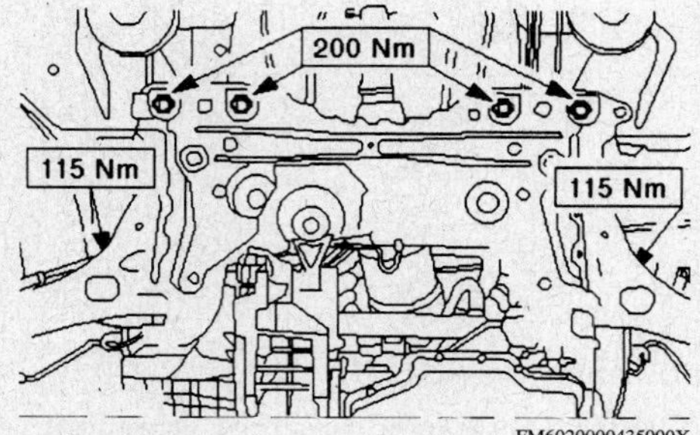

Fig. 18 Crossmember mounting bolts

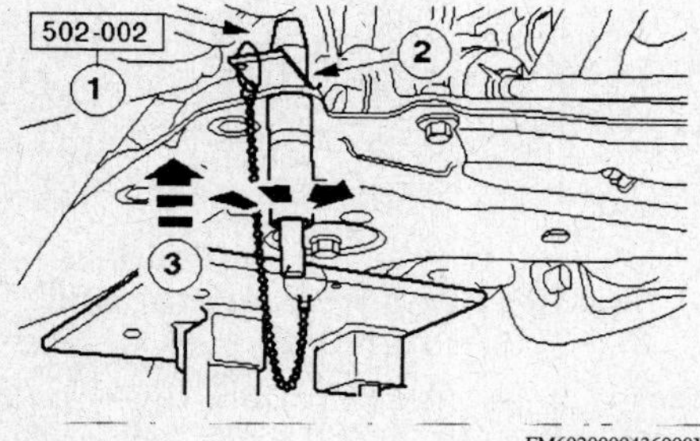

Fig. 19 Crossmember alignment

TIGHTENING SPECIFICATIONS

Year	Component	Torque, Ft. Lbs.
2000–01	Caliper To Knuckle Bolts	21
	Column Shaft To Pinion Bolt	26
	Crossmember Front Bolts	85
	Crossmember Rear Bolts	148
	Fluid Cooler Bolts	44①
	Hose Clamps	17
	Hub Nut	233
	Knuckle To Strut Pinch Bolt	66
	Lower Arm To Knuckle Pinch Bolt	37
	Pressure Line To Pump Union	48
	Pressure Line Support Bracket	②
	Pump Bolts	17
	PSP Switch	15
	Speed Sensor Bolt	80①
	Stabilizer Bar Link Nuts	37
	Steering Gear Bolts	59
	Steering Gear Heat Shield	53①
	Strut Mounting Nuts	18
	Strut Thrust Bearing Nut	35
	Support Insulator Center Bolt	37
	Tie Rod End Retaining Nuts	35
	Wheel Lug Nuts	63

① — Inch lbs.
② — DOHC engine, 18 ft. lbs. SOHC engine, 44 inch lbs.

Wheel Alignment

INDEX

PRELIMINARY INSPECTION

This procedure should be performed on a suitable flat surface in accordance with the equipment manufacturers directions.

1. Inspect all suspension components for damage or wear and replace as required.
2. Inflate all tires to specifications.
3. Ensure vehicle is at curb weight.
4. The spare tire, jack and all vehicle tools must be in their proper locations.
5. Remove all luggage and additional items from vehicle.
6. Jounce vehicle to bring suspension to normal design height setting.

SUSPENSION DESIGN HEIGHT SETTING

The final suspension tightening procedures must be done only at the design height setting.

1. Raise and safely support vehicle.
2. **On sedan models,** proceed as follows:
   a. Fabricate a .787 inch wide by 4.45 inch long spacer.
   b. Compress suspension coil spring (2) using a suitable coil spring compressor until rear lower arm (3) contacts spacer (1), **Fig. 1,** then position spacer as illustrated and raise rear lower control arm.
   c. Remove jounce bumper (1), **Fig. 2,** then install spacer (2) between rear lower arm and crossmember, ensuring it is in a vertical plane.
3. **On wagon models,** proceed as follows:
   a. Fabricate a .787 inch wide by 6.18 inch long spacer.
   b. Compress suspension using a suitable coil spring compressor until rear lower arm contacts spacer, **Fig. 1,** then position spacer as illustrated and raise rear lower control arm.
   c. Install spacer between rear lower arm and crossmember, ensuring it is in a vertical plane, **Fig. 3.**

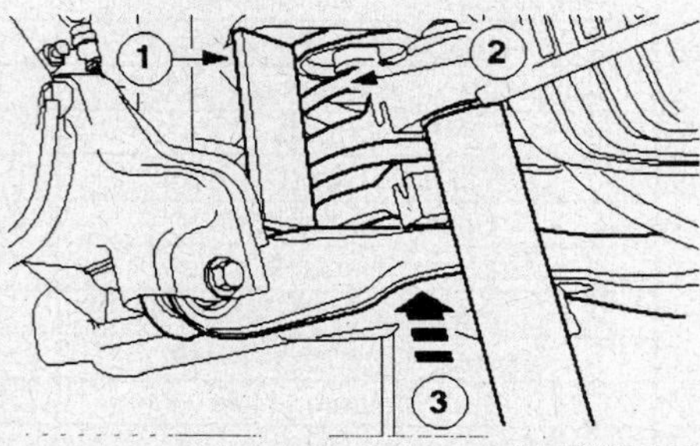

Fig. 1 Suspension design height setting

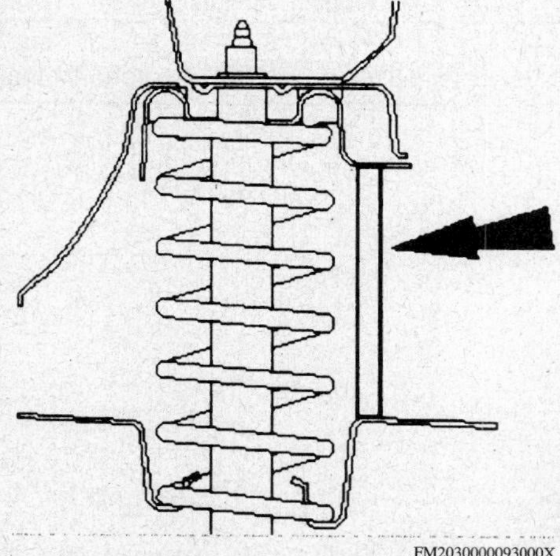

Fig. 3 Spacer installation. Wagon

FRONT WHEEL ALIGNMENT

CASTER & CAMBER

On these models, caster and camber are not adjustable.

TOE

1. Perform "Preliminary Inspection" as outlined in this section.
2. Inspect toe setting using suitable equipment.

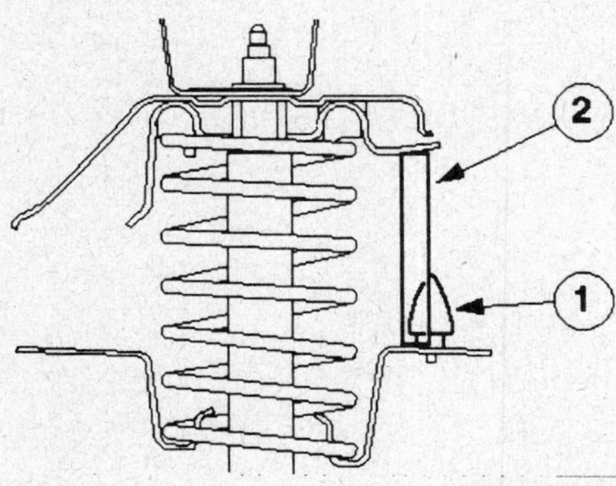

Fig. 2 Spacer installation. Sedan

3. Center the steering wheel, then lock it in position and remove ignition key.
4. Loosen both tie rod end locknuts.
5. Remove tie rod boot outer clamps.
6. Rotate each tie rod in equal clockwise or counterclockwise amounts to adjust toe setting.
7. **Torque** tie rod end locknuts to 46 ft. lbs.
8. Install boot outer clamps.
9. Inspect toe setting again and adjust if required.

REAR WHEEL ALIGNMENT

CASTER & CAMBER

On these models, caster and camber are not adjustable.

TOE

1. Perform "Preliminary Inspection" as outlined in this section.
2. Inspect toe setting using suitable equipment.
3. Loosen rear lower arm cam bolt nut.
4. Rotate bolt and eccentric until proper toe setting is reached.
5. **Torque** cam bolt nut to 85 ft. lbs.
6. Inspect toe setting again and adjust if required.

AIR CONDITIONING

TABLE OF CONTENTS

System Testing

NOTE: On Air Bag Equipped Models, Refer To "Air Bag System Precautions" Located In The Front Of This Manual For System Disarming & Arming Procedures.

NOTE: Refer To "Computer Relearn Procedures" Located In The Front Of This Manual When Battery Power To The Computer Has Been Interrupted.

INDEX

PRECAUTIONS

BATTERY GROUND CABLE

Prior to service, disconnect battery ground cable and isolate as required.

SAFETY

Protective goggles should be worn when opening any refrigerant lines. A bottle of sterile mineral oil and a quantity of weak boric acid solution must always be kept nearby when servicing air conditioning system. **If liquid coolant does touch eyes, immediately use a few drops of sterile mineral oil to wash them out, then wash eyes clean with weak boric acid solution. Seek a doctor's aid immediately even though irritation may have ceased.**

Freon refrigerant used in vehicle A/C systems will usually be in a vapor state when being handled in a repair shop. But if a portion of liquid coolant should come in contact with hands or face, note that its temperature momentarily will be at least 22° below zero.

When checking a system for leaks with a torch type leak detector, do not breathe vapors coming from flame. Do not recover refrigerant in area of a live flame. A poisonous phosgene gas is produced when refrigerant is burned. While a small amount of this gas produced by a leak detector is not harmful unless inhaled directly at flame.

Never allow temperature of refrigerant drums to exceed 125°F. Resultant increase in temperature will cause a corresponding increase in pressure which may cause safety plug to release or drum to burst.

If it is necessary to heat a drum of refrigerant when charging a system, drum should be placed in water that is no hotter than 125°F. Never use a blowtorch, or other open flame. If possible, a pressure release mechanism should be attached before drum is heated.

CLEANLINESS

Air conditioning systems are extremely sensitive to moisture and dirt. Importance of clean working conditions is extremely important, as smallest particle of foreign matter in an air conditioning system will contaminate refrigerant, causing rust, ice or damage to compressor. For this reason, all replacement parts are sold in vacuum sealed containers and should not be opened until they are to be installed in system. If, for any reason, a part has been removed from its container for any length of time, part must be completely flushed remove any dust or moisture that may have accumulated during storage. In cases of collision repairs where system has been open for any length of time, entire system must be purged completely and a new receiver-drier must be installed because element of existing unit will have become saturated and unable to remove any moisture from system once system is recharged.

When making gauge connections, purge gauge lines first by cracking charging valve and allowing a small amount of refrigerant to flow through lines, then connect lines immediately.

Cleanliness is especially important when servicing compressors because of very close tolerances used in these units. Consequently, repairs to compressor itself should not be attempted unless all proper tools are at hand and a virtually spotless work area is provided.

GENERAL SERVICE

Use care when disconnecting or connecting refrigerant lines; always use a back-up wrench and be careful not to overtighten any connection. Overtightening may result in a line or flare seat distortion and a system leak.

When making pressure checks on systems having service valves, ensure valve is in intermediate position. If turned in too far, hose connection will be closed, a position used for isolating compressor. When closing gauge port, do not overtighten valve or damage to seat will result.

After disconnecting gauge lines, check valve areas to ensure service valves are correctly seated and Schraeder valves, if used, are not leaking.

DESCRIPTION

Major components of R-134a air conditioning systems are similar to those used previously on R-12 fixed orifice tube type systems. R-12 and R-134a components are similar in design and function. As a result, all diagnosis and testing procedures for R-12 components can be used for R-134a system components. However, it should be noted that R-134a system components can only be replaced with other R-134a components. R-134a components cannot be replaced with components used with R-12 systems. Same rule applies for R-12 components, they cannot be replaced with R-134a components.

To identify which type of air conditioning system a particular vehicle has, visually inspect system for identification tags located on major components. R-134a system components have yellow R-134a NON-CFC tags. These systems can also be identified by a gold colored air conditioning compressor clutch and green colored O-rings used throughout system.

EXERCISE SYSTEM

An important fact most car owners ignore is that A/C system must be used periodically. Car manufacturers caution that when air conditioner is not used regularly, particularly during cold months, it should be turned on for a few minutes once every two or three weeks while engine is running. This keeps system in good operating condition.

Checking out system for effects of disuse before onset of summer is one of most important aspects of A/C system servicing.

First clean out condenser core, mounted in most cases at front of vehicle's radiator. All obstructions, such as leaves, bugs, and dirt, must be removed, as they will reduce heat transfer and impair efficiency of system. Ensure space between condenser and radiator also is free of foreign matter.

Ensure evaporator water drain is open. Evaporator cools and dehumidifies air before it enters car.

PERFORMANCE TEST

R-134a systems require use of special service equipment designed specifically for R-134a systems. R-12 servicing equipment cannot be used on R-134a systems.

EXCEPT ESCORT, TRACER & ZX2

Refrigerant system problems are diagnosed by checking refrigerant pressures and clutch cycle rate and times. Compare pressures and cycle time to charts shown in **Fig. 1.** Conditional requirements for refrigerant system tests must be satisfied to obtain accurate pressure readings. If findings do not fall between lines on respective charts, refer to **Fig. 2** to determine specific cause of improper readings.

After necessary repairs have been performed, take pressure readings while meeting conditional requirements to ensure problem has been corrected.

Visual inspection of system may determine problems with refrigerant system. By making a visual inspection, some of following problems can be diagnosed: obstructed air passages, broken belts, disconnected or broken wires, loose or broken mounting brackets and refrigerant leaks.

A refrigerant leak will usually appear as an oily residue at leakage point in system.

ESCORT, TRACER & ZX2

1. Connect manifold gauge set to system.
2. Start engine and turn on A/C system.
3. As soon as system is stabilized, record high and low pressures as shown by manifold gauges.
4. Low side pressure should be 35–50 psi. High side pressure should be 178–235 psi. As low pressure drops, high pressure should rise.
5. When clutch disengages, low side pressure should rise and high side pressure should drop.
6. Determine A/C clutch cycle rate per minute (one cycle is A/C clutch On time plus Off time).
7. Record A/C Off time in seconds.
8. Record A/C On time in seconds.

IMPORTANT — TEST REQUIREMENTS

The following test conditions must be established to obtain accurate pressure readings:

- Run engine at 1500 rpm for 10 minutes.
- Operate A/C system on max A/C (recirculating air).
- Run blower at max speed.
- Stabilize in car temperature @ 70°F to 80°F (21°C to 22°C).

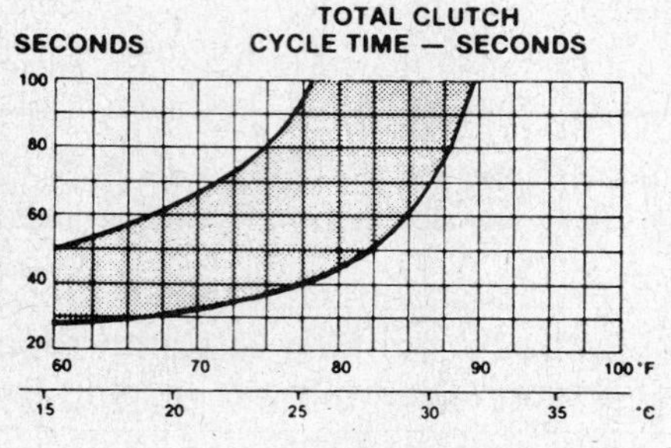

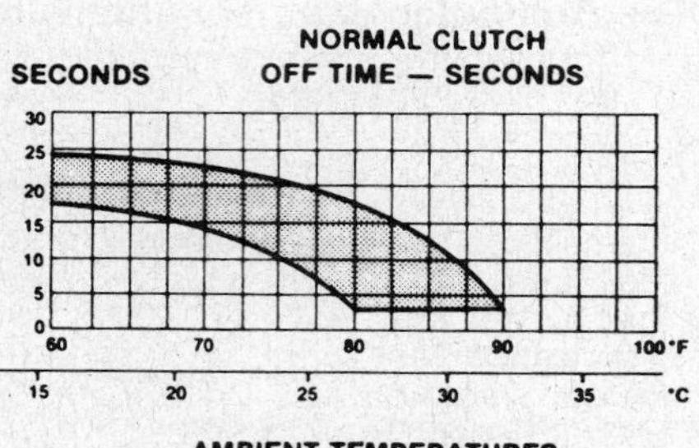

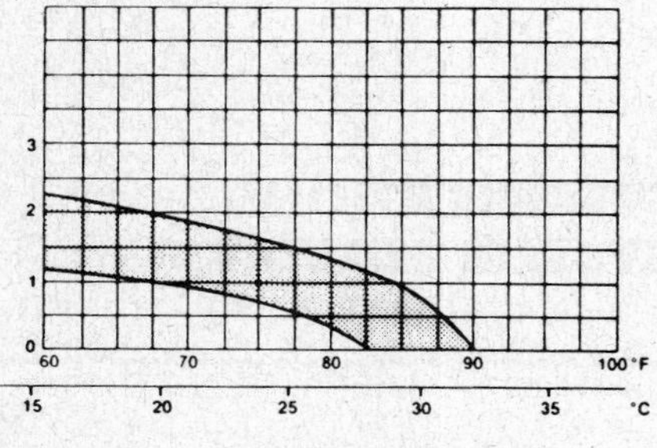

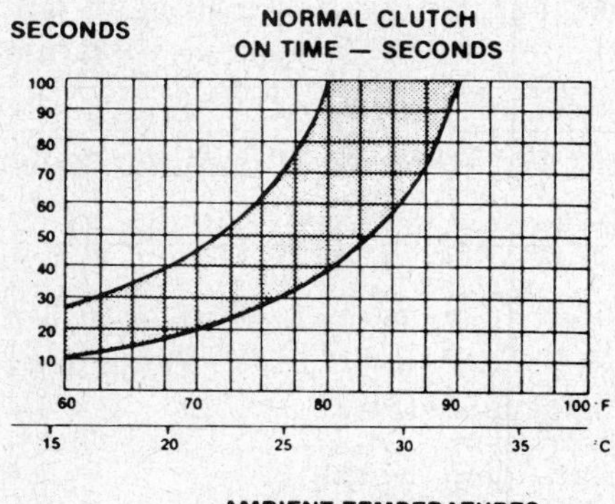

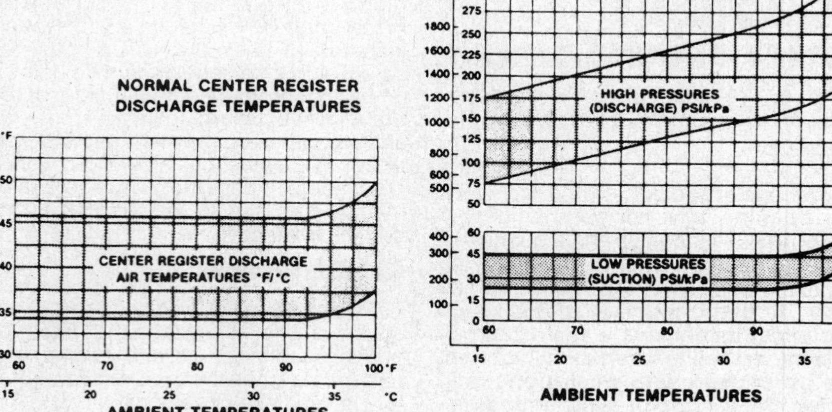

Fig. 1 Refrigerant pressure & temperature charts.

9. Record center duct temperature.
10. Determine and record ambient temperature.
11. Compare test readings with applicable chart, **Fig. 1.**

LEAK TEST

R-134a systems require use of special service equipment designed specifically for R-134a systems. R-12 servicing equipment cannot be used on R-134a systems.

Testing refrigerant system for leaks is one of most important phases of troubleshooting. One or more of methods outlined will prove useful in detecting leaks or checking connections if service work is performed. Before beginning any leak test, attach a manifold gauge set and note pressure. If little or no pressure is indicated, a partial charge must be installed. Check all connections, compressor head gasket, oil filler plug and compressor shaft seal for leaks.

ELECTRONIC DETECTORS

There are a number of electronic leak detectors available to perform leak tests. Refer to operating instructions for unit being used and observe these general procedures:

1. Move detector probe one inch per second in areas of suspected leaks.
2. Position probe below test point, as refrigerant gas is heavier than air.
3. Ensure to check service access gauge port valve fittings, particularly when valve caps are missing, as dirt accumulations can destroy sealing area of valve core when manifold gauge set is attached. Replace missing valve caps after cleaning valve core area. **Valve caps should only be finger tightened. Using pliers to tighten valve caps may distort sealing surface of valve.**
4. Check for leaks in manifold gauge set and hoses, as well as rest of system.

FLAME-TYPE (HALIDE) DETECTORS

When using flame-type detectors, avoid inhaling fumes produced by burning refrigerant. Do not use this type detector where concentrations of combustible or explosive gases, dusts or vapors may exist.

1. Adjust detector flame as low as possible to obtain maximum sensitivity. Ensure copper element is cherry red and not burned away. Flame will be almost colorless.
2. Slowly move detector along areas of suspected leaks. A slight leak will cause flame to change to a bright yellow-green color. A significant leak will be indicated by a brilliant blue flame. Position detector under areas being tested as refrigerant gas is heavier than air. **Presence of dust in pickup hose may cause a change in color of flame. If not recognized, a false diagnosis could be made. Store leak detector in a clean place and ensure hose is free of dust before leak testing.**
3. Check for leaks in manifold gauge set and hoses, as well as rest of system.
4. Use a small fan to ventilate areas where leak detector indicates refrigerant constantly. These areas are contaminated with refrigerant and must be ventilated before leak can be pinpointed.

NOTE: System test requirements must be met to obtain accurate test readings for evaluation. Refer to the normal refrigerant system pressure/temperature and the normal clutch cycle ratio and times charts.

High (Discharge) Pressure	Low (Suction) Pressure	Clutch Cycle Time			Component — Causes
		Rate	On	Off	
High	High	Continuous Run			Condenser — Inadequate Airflow
High	Normal to High				Engine Overheating
Normal to High	Normal				Air in Refrigerant Refrigerant Overcharge (a) Humidity or Ambient Temp Very High (b)
Normal	High				Fixed Orifice Tube — Missing O Rings Leaking/Missing
Normal	High	Slow	Long	Long	Clutch Cycling Switch — High Cut In
Normal	Normal	Slow or No Cycle	Long or Continuous	Normal or No Cycle	Moisture in Refrigerant System Excessive Refrigerant Oil
		Fast	Short	Short	Clutch Cycling Switch — Low Cut In or High Cut Out
Normal	Low	Slow	Long	Long	Clutch Cycling Switch — Low Cut Out
Normal to Low	High	Continuous Run			Compressor — Low Performance
Normal to Low	Normal to High				A/C Suction Line — Partially Restricted or Plugged (c)
Normal to Low	Normal	Fast	Short	Normal	Evaporator — Restricted Airflow
			Short to Very Short	Normal to Long	Condenser fixed orifice Tube or A/C Liquid Line — Partically Restricted or Plugged
			Short to Very Short	Short to Very Short	Low Refrigerant Charge
			Short to Very Short	Long	Evaporator Core — Partially Restricted or Plugged
Normal to Low	Low	Continuous Run			A/C Suction Line — Partially Restricted or Plugged (d) Clutch Cycling Switch — Sticking Closed
Low	Normal	Very Fast	Very Short	Very Short	Clutch Cycling Switch — Cycling Range Too Close
Erratic Operation or Compressor Not Running		—	—	—	Clutch Cycling Switch — Dirty Contacts or Sticking Open Poor Connection at A/C Clutch Connector or Clutch Cycling Switch Connector A/C Electrical Circuit Erratic
Additional Possible Cause Components Associated with Inadequate Compressor Operation					
• Compressor Drive Belt — Loose • Compressor Clutch — Slipping • Clutch Coil Open — Shorted or Loose Mounting • Control Assembly Switch — Dirty Contacts or Sticking Open • Clutch Wiring Circuit — High Resistance Open or Blown Fuse					
Additional Possible Cause Components Associated with a Damaged Compressor					
• Compressor Clutch — Seized • Clutch Cycling Switch — Sticking Closed • Suction Accumulator Drier — Refrigerant Oil Bleed Hole Plugged • Refrigerant Leaks					

(a) Compressor may make noise on initial run. This is slugging condition caused by excessive liquid refrigerant.
(b) Compressor clutch may not cycle in ambient temperatures above 80°F depending on humidity conditions.
(c) Low pressure reading will be normal to high if pressure is taken at accumulator and if restriction is downstream of service access valve.
(d) Low pressure reading will be low if pressure is taken near the compressor and restriction is upstream of service access valve.

FM7029100028000X

Fig. 2 Refrigerant system pressure evaluation chart. Except Escort, Tracer & ZX2

FLUID LEAK DETECTORS

Apply leak detector solution around joints to be tested. A cluster of bubbles will form immediately if there is a leak. A white foam that forms after a short while will indicate an extremely small leak. In some confined areas such as sections of evaporator and condenser, electronic leak detectors will be more useful.

TRACER DYE

R-134a fluorescent tracer dye has been added to the A/C systems of new vehicles. Leak checking can be performed with an ultraviolet lamp and is an acceptable alternative to using an electronic leak detector. The fluorescent lifespan of the leak tracer dye is 500 hours of A/C system use, after which another injection of dye is required. A/C system pressure must be above 80 psi for the operation. Scan all components, fittings and lines of the A/C system with Rotunda Ultraviolet Lamp 164–R0721, or equivalent, the exact location of the leak or leaks can be pinpointed by the bright yellow-green glow of the tracer dye. Since more than one leak may exist in the system, always inspect each component.

After the leak is serviced, the traces of dye can be removed from the previously leaking areas by using any general purpose oil solvent. Verify the service by operation the A/C system for a short while and reinspecting the system with the UV lamp. Rotunda Fluoro-Lite for R-134a/PAG A/C Systems 164–R3712, or equivalent, may be introduced into the A/C system using Rotunda R-134a Fluorescent Tracer Dye Injector 164–R2610, or equivalent. Inject the dye while charging the system and check for leaks as follows:

1. Adjust quick disconnect valve on dye injector to maximum counterclockwise (closed) position.
2. Remove plug from end of dye injector reservoir and fill reservoir with ¼ ounces of Rotunda Fluoro-Lite for R-134a/PAG A/C Systems 164-R3712, or equivalent.
3. Replace plug, then tighten securely.
4. Attach low-side quick disconnect from

either the manifold gauge set or the charging station to the plug on the dye injector.

5. Install dye injector quick disconnect valve to high-pressure service port on vehicle.
6. Adjust all quick disconnect valves to maximum clockwise (open) position.
7. Charge vehicle with required amount of refrigerant , then flow of refrigerant through dye injector will inject dye into vehicle system.
8. When vehicle charging is complete, close dye injector and high-side quick disconnect valves and remove quick disconnects from vehicle.
9. Recover refrigerant from dye injector and close low-side quick disconnect valve.
10. Remove dye injector from low-side quick disconnect valve. The dye injector should only be connected to charging/recovery station when dye is to be injected. The dye injector has a one-way check valve that will prevent system refrigerant recovery and evacuation.
11. Using Rotunda Ultraviolet Lamp 164–R0721 or equivalent, check system for leaks.

DISCHARGING SYSTEM

R-134a systems require use of special service equipment designed specifically for R-134a systems. R-12 servicing equipment cannot be used on R-134a systems.

R-12 recovery stations cannot be used on R-134a systems. A separate recovery station must be used on R-134a systems. Refrigerants are not compatible and will contaminate R-12 recovery station.

Use of refrigerant recovery and recycling stations allows recovery and reuse of refrigerant after contaminants and moisture have been removed.

When using a recovery or recycling station, follow manufacturer's operating instructions, noting following:

1. **Use extreme caution and observe all safety and service precautions related to use of refrigerants.**
2. Connect refrigerant recycling station hose(s) to vehicle A/C service port(s) and recovery station inlet fitting. Hoses used should have shutoff devices or check valves within 12 inches of hose ends to minimize introduction of air into recycling station and to minimize amount of refrigerant released when hose(s) is disconnected.
3. Turn recycling station On to start recovery process. Allow recycling station to pump refrigerant from A/C system until station pressure gauge indicates vacuum.
4. After vehicle A/C system has been evacuated, close station inlet valve, if equipped.
5. Turn station Off. On some stations pump will automatically be turned Off by a low pressure switch.
6. Allow vehicle A/C system to remain closed for approximately two minutes. Observe vacuum level indicated on gauge. If pressure does not rise, disconnect recycling station hose(s).
7. If system pressure rises, repeat steps 3 through 6 until vacuum level remains stable for two minutes.
8. Service A/C system as necessary, then evacuate and recharge A/C system.

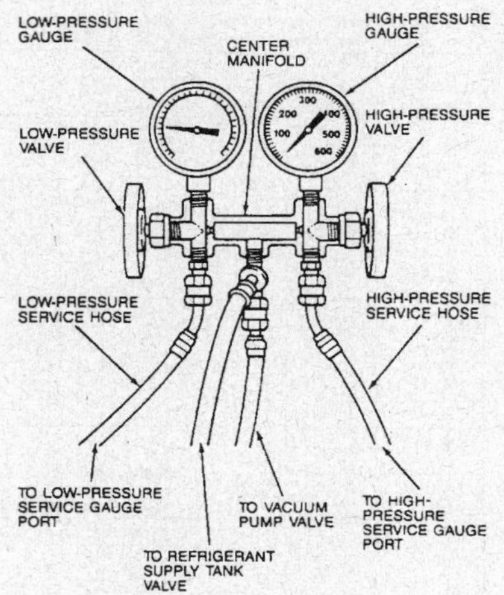

Fig. 3 Refrigerant system service connections

SYSTEM EVACUATION

R-134a systems require use of special service equipment designed specifically for R-134a systems. R-12 servicing equipment cannot be used on R-134a systems.

Vacuum pumps suitable for removing air and moisture from A/C systems are commercially available. A specification for system pump down used here is 28–29½ inches vacuum. This reading can be attained at or near sea level only. For each 1000 feet of altitude, reading will be one inch of vacuum less than standard specification given. For example, at 5000 feet elevation, only 23–24½ inches of vacuum can be obtained. **System must be completely discharged before it can be evacuated. Damage to vacuum pump will result if pressurized refrigerant is allowed to enter pump assembly.**

1. Connect vacuum pump to gauge manifold. With gauges connected into system, remove cap from vacuum hose connector. Install center hose from gauge manifold to vacuum pump connector. Mid position high and low side compressor service valve (if used). Open high and low side gauge manifold hand valves.
2. Operate vacuum pump a minimum of 30 minutes for air and moisture removal. Watch compound gauge to see that system pumps down into a vacuum. System will reach 28–29½ inches Hg vacuum in a maximum of five minutes. If system does not pump down, check all connections and leak test if necessary.
3. Close gauge manifold hand valves and shutoff vacuum pump.
4. Check ability of system to hold vacuum. Watch compound gauge to see that gauge does not rise at a faster rate than one inch vacuum every four or five minutes. If compound gauge rises at too rapid a rate, install partial charge and leak test. Then discharge system as outlined above.
5. If system holds vacuum, charge system with refrigerant.

CHARGING SYSTEM

R-134a systems require use of special service equipment designed specifically for R-134a systems. R-12 servicing equipment cannot be used on R-134a systems.

Refer to "A/C Specifications" for refrigerant capacities.

When charging from small cans, do not open manifold gauge set high pressure (discharge) gauge valve, as this can cause containers to explode.

1. Connect manifold gauge set **Fig. 3,** then set valves closed to center hose, disconnect vacuum pump from manifold gauge set.
2. Connect center hose of manifold gauge set to refrigerant supply.
3. Purge air from center hose by loosening hose at manifold gauge set and open refrigerant drum valve. When refrigerant escapes from hose, tighten center hose connection at manifold gauge set.
4. On vehicles so equipped, disconnect wire harness connector at clutch cycling pressure switch. Install jumper wire across terminals of connector.
5. On all models, open manifold gauge set low side valve and allow refrigerant to enter system. Refrigerant can must be kept upright if vehicle low pressure service gauge port is not on suction accumulator/drier or suction accumulator fitting.
6. When system stops drawing refrigerant in, start engine and set control lever to A/C position and blower switch to Hi position to draw remaining refrigerant into system.
7. When specified weight of refrigerant is in system, close gauge set low pressure valve and refrigerant supply valve.
8. On vehicles so equipped, remove jumper wire from clutch cycling pressure switch connector and connect connector to pressure switch.
9. On all models, operate system until pressures stabilize to check operation and system pressures. During high ambient temperatures, a high volume fan may be necessary to blow air through radiator and condenser to cool engine and prevent excessive refrigerant system pressures.
10. When charging is complete and system operating pressures are normal, disconnect manifold gauge set from vehicle and install protective caps on service gauge port valves.

System Service

NOTE: On Air Bag Equipped Models, Refer To "Air Bag System Precautions" Located In The Front Of This Manual For System Disarming & Arming Procedures.

NOTE: Refer To "Computer Relearn Procedures" Located In The Front Of This Manual When Battery Power To The Computer Has Been Interrupted.

INDEX

OIL CHARGE

Refrigerant oil required for R-134a air conditioning systems is a polyalkylene glycol (PAG) oil. Ford specification part No. WSH-M1C231-B, or equivalent. This type of refrigerant oil is designed specifically for R-134a systems and is not suitable for use in R-12 systems. Never use an R-134a refrigerant oil in R-12 systems. Never use R-12 refrigerant oil YN-9 in R-134a systems.

FORD FS-10 SWASH PLATE 10 CYLINDER COMPRESSOR

A new service replacement compressor contains 7 oz. of refrigerant oil.

1. Drain and measure oil from old compressor.
2. Drain oil from new compressor into clean measuring device.
3. If 3–5 oz. were drained from old compressor, add equal amount plus 1 oz. of new oil to new compressor.
4. If more than 5 oz. were drained from old compressor, add equal amount of new oil to new compressor.
5. If less then 3 oz. was drained from old compressor, add 3 oz. to new compressor.
6. When other air conditioning system components are replaced, add the following quantities of refrigerant oil:
   a. Accumulator, same amount drained from old accumulator plus 2 oz.
   b. Evaporator core, 3 oz.
   c. Condenser, 1 oz.
7. Add 2 oz. of new oil after replacing other system components such as hoses, evaporator core orifice, cycling switch, compressor pressure relief valve and pressure cutoff switch, or following minor repairs such O-ring, port, compressor shaft seal and hose leaks.

FORD SC-90V VARIABLE SCROLL COMPRESSOR

A new service replacement compressor contains 7 oz. of refrigerant oil.

1. Drain and measure oil from old compressor.
2. Drain oil from new compressor into clean measuring device.
3. If 3–5 oz. were drained from old compressor, add equal amount plus 1 oz. of new oil to new compressor.
4. If more than 5 oz. were drained from old compressor, add equal amount of new oil to new compressor.
5. If less then 3 oz. was drained from old compressor, add 3 oz. to new compressor.
6. When other air conditioning system components are replaced, add the following quantities of refrigerant oil:
   a. Accumulator, same amount drained from old accumulator plus 2 oz.
   b. Evaporator core, 1oz.
   c. Condenser, 1 oz.
7. Add .75 oz. of new oil after replacing other system components such as hoses, evaporator core orifice, cycling switch, compressor pressure relief valve and pressure cutoff switch, or following minor repairs such O-ring, port, compressor shaft seal and hose leaks.

FORD VS-90

Refer to "Ford FS-10 Swash Plate 10 Cylinder Compressor."

NIPPONDENSO 10P15 SERIES COMPRESSORS

A new service replacement compressor contains 8 oz. of refrigerant oil.

1. Drain and measure oil from old compressor.
2. Drain oil from new compressor into clean measuring device.
3. If 3–5 oz. were drained from old compressor, install equal amount plus 1 oz. of new oil to new compressor.
4. If more than 5 oz. were drained from old compressor, install equal amount of new oil to new compressor.
5. If less then 3 oz. was removed from old compressor, install 3 oz. in new compressor.
6. When other air conditioning system components are replaced, add the following quantities of refrigerant oil:
   a. Accumulator, same amount drained from old accumulator plus 2 oz.
   b. Evaporator core, 3 oz.
   c. Condenser, 1 oz.
7. Replacement of other components such as valves or hoses does not require any additional refrigerant oil. However, if a hose bursts with a fully charged system, an additional 2 oz. is recommended and accumulator should be replaced.

PANASONIC COMPRESSOR

When replacing system components, add or drain the following quantities of refrigerant oil: compressor, drain 1.7 oz.; condenser, add one oz.; receiver-drier, add amount drained from old drier plus .34 oz.

1. Drain and measure oil from old compressor.
2. Drain oil from new compressor into clean measuring device.
3. Install equal amount plus .676 oz. of new oil to compressor.
4. When other air conditioning system components are replaced, add the following quantities of refrigerant oil:
   a. Accumulator, same amount drained from old accumulator plus 1 oz.
   b. Evaporator core, 3 oz.
   c. Condenser, 1 oz.

OIL LEVEL CHECK

Oil level of these compressors should be checked whenever refrigerant has been lost due to leakage or through normal system servicing.

Specifications

INDEX

A/C SPECIFICATIONS

Year	Compressor Model	Refrigerant		Refrigerant Oil		Compressor Clutch Air Gap, Inch
		Type	Capacity, Lbs.	Viscosity	Total System Capacity, Oz. ①	
CONTINENTAL						
1998–2002	Ford FS-10	R-134a	2.13	②	7	.014–.033
CONTOUR						
1998–2000	Ford FS-10	R-134a	1.63	②	7	.014–.033
COUGAR						
1998	Ford FS-10	R-134a	2.25	②	7	.014–.033
1999–2002	Ford FS-10	R-134a	③	②	④	.014–.033
CROWN VICTORIA						
1998–2000	Ford FS-10	R-134a	2.13	②	7.5	.014–.030
ESCORT						
1998–2002	Ford FS-10	R-134a	1.75	②	6.6	.014–.030
FOCUS						
2000–01	Ford FS-10	R-134a	③	②	④	.014–.033
	FVS 090	R-134a	③	②	④	.014–.033
GRAND MARQUIS						
1998–2002	Ford FS-10	R-134a	2.13	②	7.5	.014–.030
LS						
2000–01	Ford VS-90	R-134a	1.75	②	7	.014–030
2002	Ford SC-90V	R-134a	1.75	②	7	.014–030
MARK VIII						
1998	Ford FS-10	R-134a	2.13	②	7	.014–.033
MUSTANG						
1998–2002	Ford FS-10	R-134a	2.13	②	8.6	.014–.030
MYSTIQUE						
1998–2000	Ford FS-10	R-134a	1.63	②	7	.014–.033
SABLE						
1998–99	Ford FS-10	R-134a	2.13	②	7	.014–.030
2000–02	Ford FS-10	R-134a	2.13	②	6.6	.014–.033
TAURUS						
1998–2002	Ford FS-10	R-134a	2.13	②	6.6	.014–.030
TAURUS SHO						
1998–99	Sanden	R-134a	2.13	②	7	.016–.027
THUNDERBIRD						
2002	Ford SC-90V	R-134a	1.75	②	7	.014–.033
TOWN CAR						
1998–2002	Ford FS-10	R-134a	2.13	②	7.5	.014–.030
TRACER						
1998–99	Ford FS-10	R-134a	1.75	②	7	.014–.033
ZX2						
1998–2000	Ford FS-10	R-134a	1.75	②	7	.014–.033

① — Oil level inches cannot be checked.
② — Motorcraft YN-12c PAG (Polyalkaline Glycol), or equivalent.
③ — See label on vehicle.
④ — Transfer the oil from the accumulator/dehydrator being renewed to a measuring cylinder.

Fill the new accumulator/dehydrator w/the same quantity of fresh oil plus 90 ml.

CHARGING VALVE LOCATION

Model	High Pressure Fitting	Low Pressure Fitting
Continental	High Pressure Line From Compressor	Accumulator
Cougar	High Pressure Line From Compressor	Low Pressure Line From Compressor
Contour	High Pressure Line From Compressor	Low Pressure Line From Compressor
Crown Victoria	High Pressure Line From Compressor	Accumulator
Escort	High Pressure Line From Compressor	Low Pressure Line From Compressor
Focus	High Pressure Line From Compressor	Low Pressure Line Form Compressor
Grand Marquis	High Pressure Line From Compressor	Accumulator
LS	High Pressure Line From Compressor	Accumulator
Mark VIII	High Pressure Line From Compressor	Low Pressure Line From Compressor
Mystique	High Pressure Line From Compressor	Low Pressure Line From Compressor
Sable	High Pressure Line From Compressor	Accumulator
Taurus	High Pressure Line From Compressor	Accumulator
Thunderbird	High Pressure Line From Compressor	Accumulator
Town Car	High Pressure Line From Compressor	Accumulator
Tracer	High Pressure Line From Compressor	Low Pressure Line From Compressor
ZX2	High Pressure Line From Compressor	Low Pressure Line From Compressor

BELT TENSION

Engine	New, Lbs.	Used, Lbs.
2.0L④	①	①
2.5L④	①	①
3.0L	②	③
3.0L⑤	②	③
3.4L SHO	①	①
3.8L	①	①
3.9L	①	①
4.6L	①	①

① — Drive belt tension is not adjustable. Drive belt tensioner automatically adjusts tensioner.
② — 5-rib belt, 140–160 lbs.; 6-rib belt, belt tension is not adjustable; drive belt tensioner automatically adjusts tensioner.
③ — 5-rib belt, 110–130 lbs.; 6-rib belt, belt tension is not adjustable; drive belt tensioner automatically adjusts tensioner.
④ — Contour, Escort, Focus, Mystique, Tracer, ZX2 & 1999–2002 Cougar.
⑤ — LS.

COOLING FANS

TABLE OF CONTENTS

Electric Cooling Fans

NOTE: On Air Bag Equipped Models, Refer To "Air Bag System Precautions" Located In The Front Of This Manual For System Disarming & Arming Procedures.

NOTE: Refer To "Computer Relearn Procedures" Located In The Front Of This Manual When Battery Power To The Computer Has Been Interrupted.

NOTE: "Wire Color Code Identification And Symbol Identification" Located At The Front Of This Manual Can Be Used As An Aid When Using Wiring Circuits Found In This Section.

INDEX

PRECAUTIONS

AIR BAG SYSTEMS

Refer to "Air Bag System Precautions" in the front of this manual for system disarming and arming procedures.

BATTERY GROUND CABLE

Prior to service, disconnect battery ground cable and isolate as required.

DESCRIPTION

CONTINENTAL

The electric drive cooling fan system consists of a fan and a two-speed electric motor. The fan motor will only run when ignition switch is in Run position.

Cooling fan is controlled during engine operation by the Integrated Relay Control Module (IRCM) and EEC module. These controls activate the fan at low speed when engine temperature reaches approximately 215°F, or when A/C is on and vehicle does not provide enough air flow. Fan will continue to run until engine temperature drops to approximately 210°F.

Cooling fan will run at high speed when fan has been operating at low speed, but engine temperature is still above 230°F, or during idle when engine temperature has reached approximately 236°F. Cooling fan will begin to operate at low speed when engine temperature drops to approximately 224°F. Cooling fan does not cycle with A/C.

CONTOUR, MYSTIQUE & COUGAR

The cooling fan system consists of a fan blade with a two-speed cooling fan motor. Vehicles with the 2.0L engine have a single cooling fan motor and fan blade system, vehicles with the 2.5L engine have dual cooling fan motors and fan blades.

The cooling fan motors operate only when the ignition switch is in the Run position, preventing cooling fan motor operation after the ignition switch is turned to the Off position.

CROWN VICTORIA, GRAND MARQUIS & TOWN CAR

Auxiliary cooling fan motor runs continuously when air conditioning is on and does not cycle on/off with A/C clutch. Fan will shut off at speeds above 45 mph when coolant temperature is less than 220°F. Auxiliary cooling fan will also operate when temperatures are above 220°F even with A/C off.

ESCORT, TRACER & ZX2

The cooling fan is controlled by a Constant Control Relay Module (CCRM), Powertrain Control Module (PCM) and Engine Coolant Temperature (ECT) sensor. The fan comes on when engine temperature is at 221°F and when the air conditioning is turned on.

FOCUS

The cooling fan is controlled by the engine management system and an increase in coolant temperature may cause the fan to operate even with the ignition in the Off position.

MARK VIII

Variable Control Relay Module (VCRM) is used to control engine cooling fan operation speed and A/C clutch operation in addition to other non-A/C functions. VCRM control fan operation when required will increase and decrease fan speed as necessary depending on refrigerant system high side pressure. VCRM also can turn the A/C clutch circuit off if high side pressure exceeds 425 psi.

The VCRM stops fan control operation at vehicle speeds in excess of approximately 45 mph. Fan operation will resume when vehicle speed drops to approximately 42 mph. Fan control will not shut off when AC high side pressure is above 300 psi. In event of an ACP sensor failure, fan control will continue to operate.

MUSTANG

This system consists of a dual-speed fan, which operates only when ignition switch is in the run position. Cooling fan is controlled during vehicle operation by the Constant Control Relay Module (CCRM) and Powertrain Control Module (PCM). Cooling fan operates when coolant temperature reaches 221°F, or with air conditioning on and vehicle speed below 43 mph. Fan will continue to run until coolant temperature drops to 200°F, or vehicle speed reaches at least 48 mph.

SABLE & TAURUS

Electric cooling fan system consists of two electrical fans, CCRM, PCM, A/C cycling switch and A/C clutch coil circuit. The cooling fan motors operate only when ignition switch is in the RUN position, preventing cooling fan from operating after the ignition switch is turned Off. **The electric cooling fan may come on at any time without warning with ignition switch in the RUN position, even if the motor is not running.**

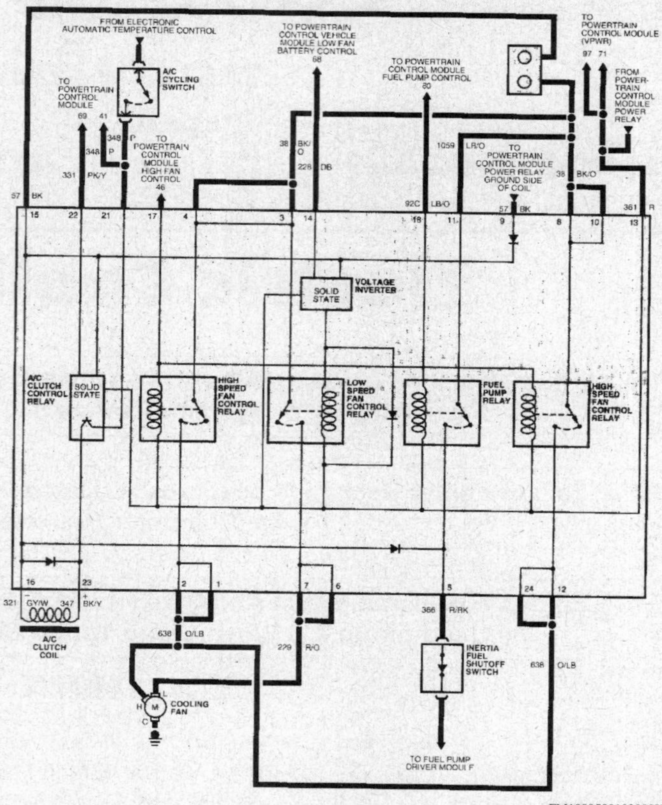

Fig. 1 Cooling fan wiring diagram. 1998 Continental

SYSTEM DIAGNOSIS & TESTING

Cooling fan systems used on models not listed in this section are controlled by the Powertrain Control Module. Refer to **MOTOR's "Domestic Engine Performance & Driveability Manual"** for Powertrain Control (EEC) diagnostic procedures and testing on these models.

Perform visual inspection prior to performing any diagnosis and testing procedures.

1. Check coolant level and condition.
2. Check condition of radiator, thermostat and hoses.
3. Check for fan blade interference.
4. Check for proper mounting of fan motor.
5. Check for proper fan blade attachment to motor.
6. Check for blown fuses.
7. Check wiring harnesses for damaged wires and poor or corroded connectors.
8. Ensure battery is fully charged.

WIRING DIAGRAMS

Refer to **Figs. 1 through 35** for wiring diagrams.

DIAGNOSTIC TESTS

CONTINENTAL, MARK VIII & 1998 MUSTANG

Refer to **Fig. 36 and 37** for symptom chart and **Figs. 38 through 41** for diagnostic charts.

CONTOUR & MYSTIQUE

Refer to **Fig. 42** for symptom chart and **Figs. 43 through 46** for diagnostic charts.

COUGAR

Refer to **Fig. 47** for symptom chart and **Figs. 48 through 51** diagnostic charts.

1998 CROWN VICTORIA, GRAND MARQUIS & TOWN CAR

Refer to **Fig. 52** for symptom chart and **Figs. 53 through 56** for diagnostic charts.

1999–2002 CROWN VICTORIA & GRAND MARQUIS

Refer to **Fig. 57** for symptom chart and **Figs. 58 through 61** for diagnostic charts.

ESCORT, TRACER & ZX2

Refer to **Fig. 62** for symptom chart and **Figs. 63 through 69** for diagnostic charts.

FOCUS

Refer to **Fig. 70** for symptom chart and **Figs. 71 through 73** for diagnostic chart.

MUSTANG

1998

Refer to "Continental, Mark VIII & Thunderbird."

1999–2002

Refer to **Fig. 74** for symptom chart and **Figs. 75 through 78** for diagnostic charts.

1998–99 SABLE & TAURUS

Refer to **Figs. 79** for symptom charts and **Figs. 80 through 82** for diagnostic charts.

2000–02 SABLE & TAURUS

Refer to **Figs. 83** for symptom charts and **Figs. 84 through 87** for diagnostic charts.

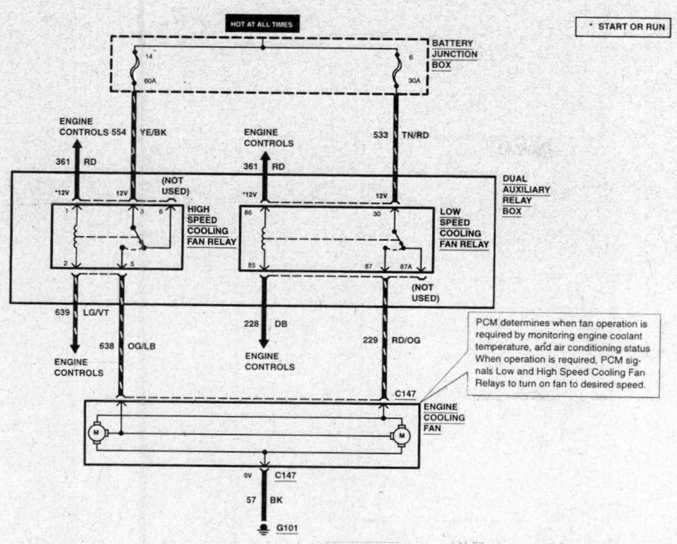

FM9040000587000X

Fig. 2 Cooling fan wiring diagram. 1999–2001 Continental

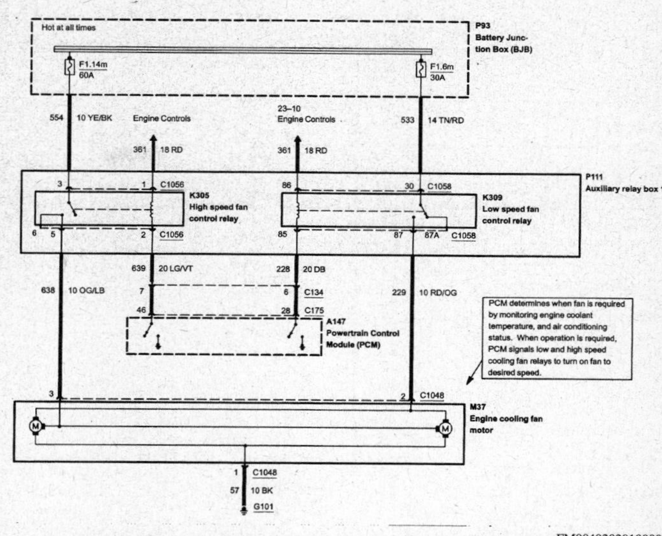

FM9040202018000X

Fig. 3 Cooling fan wiring diagram. 2002 Continental

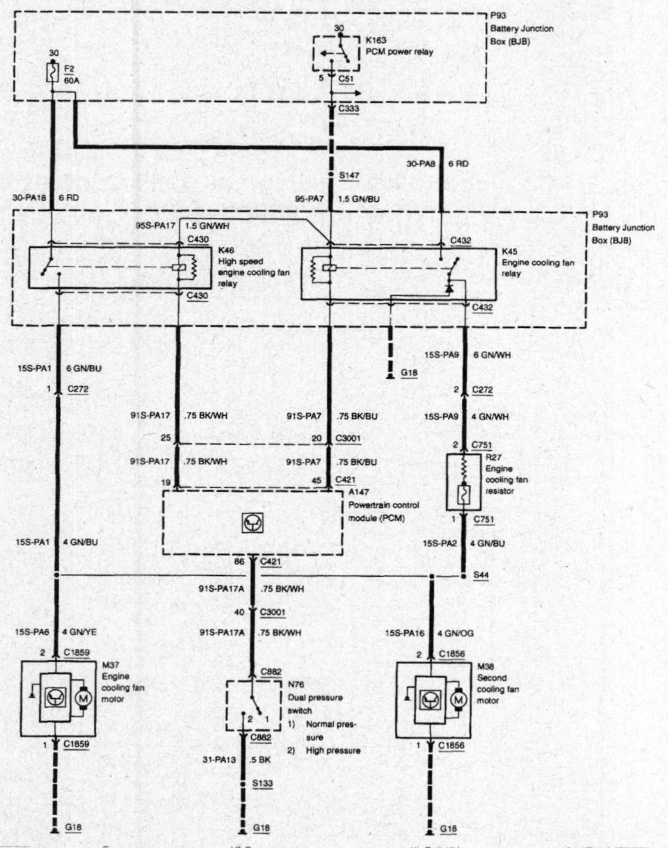

FM1049800032000X

Fig. 4 Cooling fan wiring diagram. 1998 Contour & Mystique

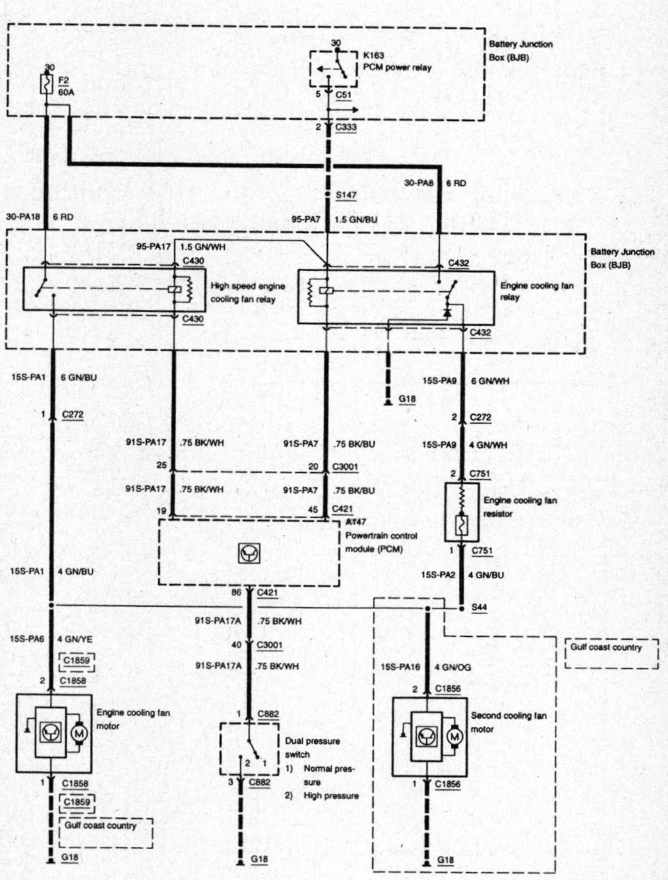

FM1049900422000X

Fig. 5 Cooling Fan wiring diagram. 1999 Contour & Mystique w/2.0L engine & A/C

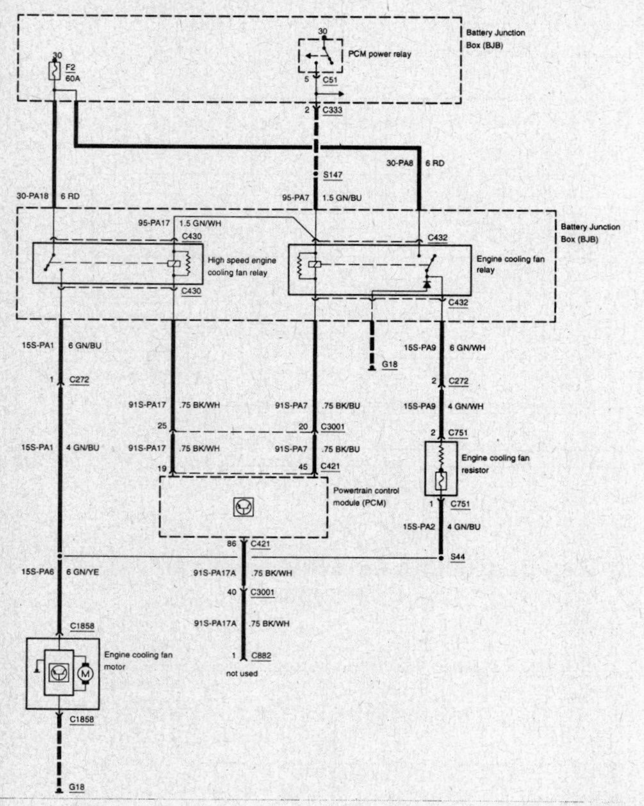

Fig. 6 Cooling fan wiring diagram. 1999 Contour & Mystique w/2.0L engine less A/C

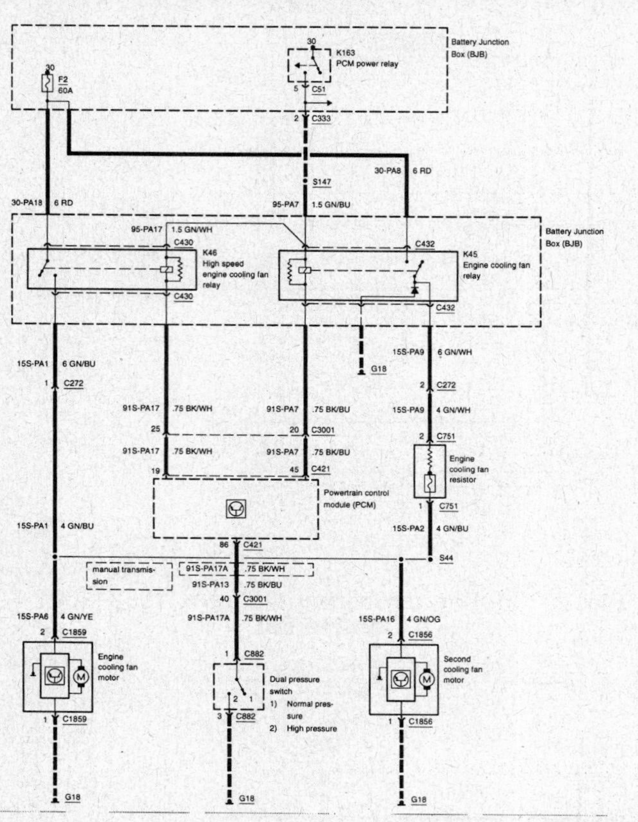

Fig. 7 Cooling fan wiring diagram. 1999 Contour & Mystique w/2.5L engine & A/C

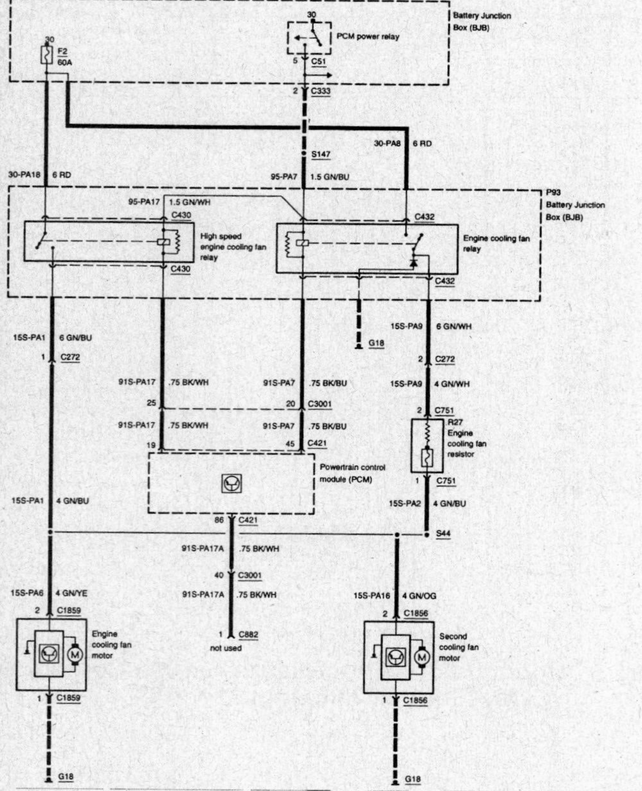

Fig. 8 Cooling fan wiring diagram. 1999 Contour & Mystique w/2.5L engine less A/C

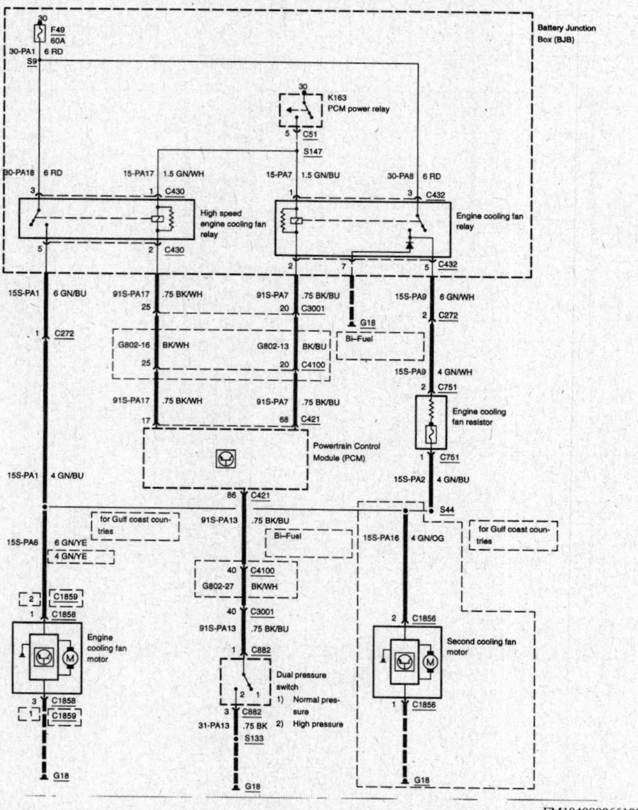

Fig. 9 Cooling fan wiring diagram. 2000 Contour & Mystique w/2.0L engine & A/C

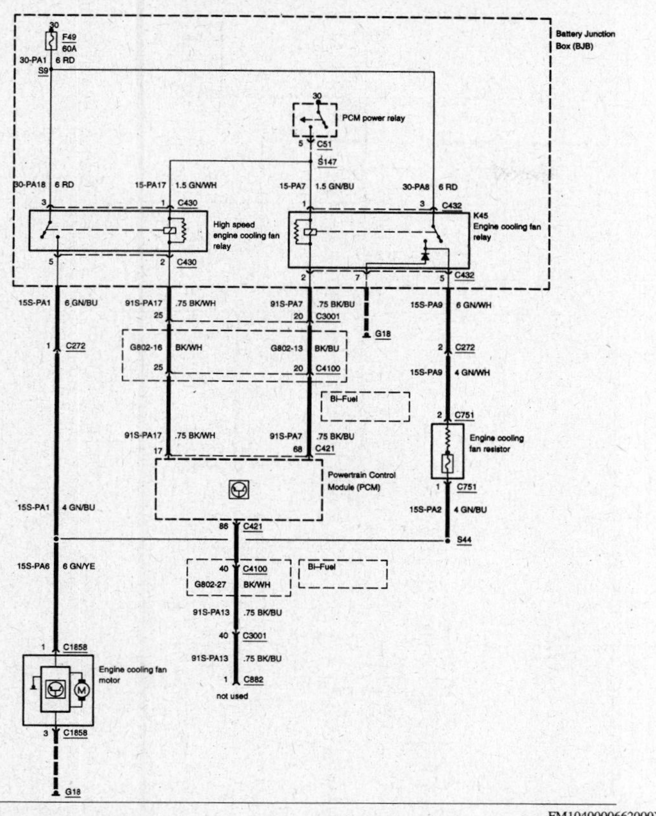

FM1040000662000X

Fig. 10 Cooling fan wiring diagram. 2000 Contour Mystique w/2.0L engine less A/C

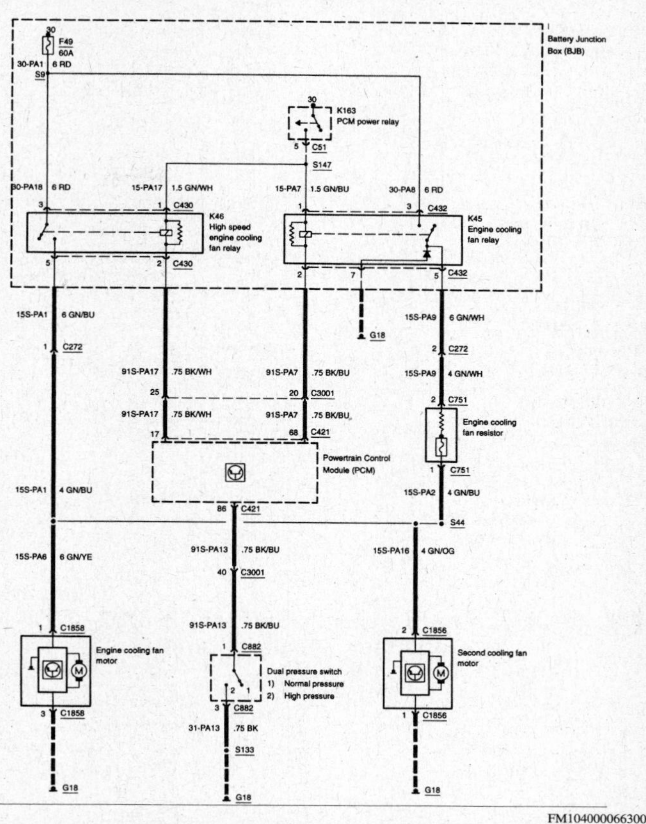

FM1040000663000X

Fig. 11 Cooling fan wiring diagram. 2000 Contour & Mystique w/2.5L engine & A/C

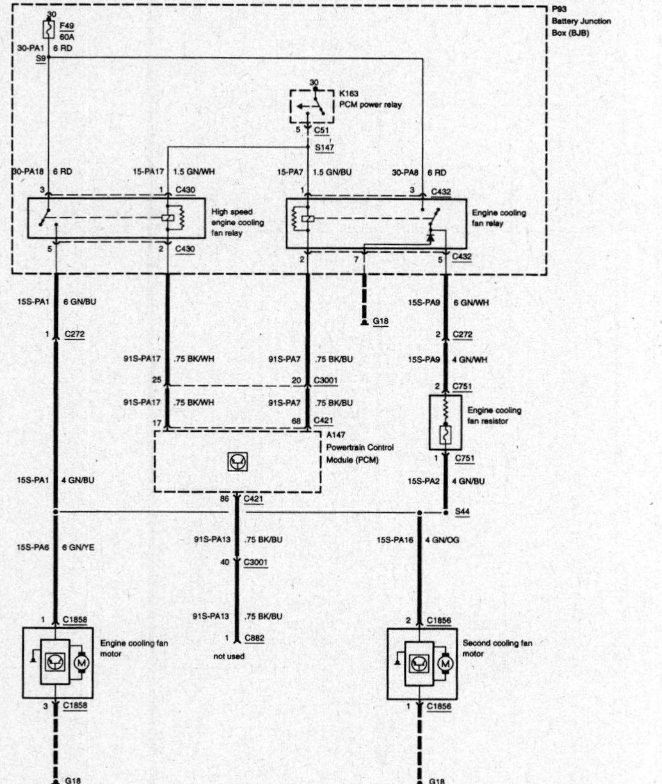

FM1040000664000X

Fig. 12 Cooling fan wiring diagram. 2000 Contour & Mystique w/2.5L engine less A/C

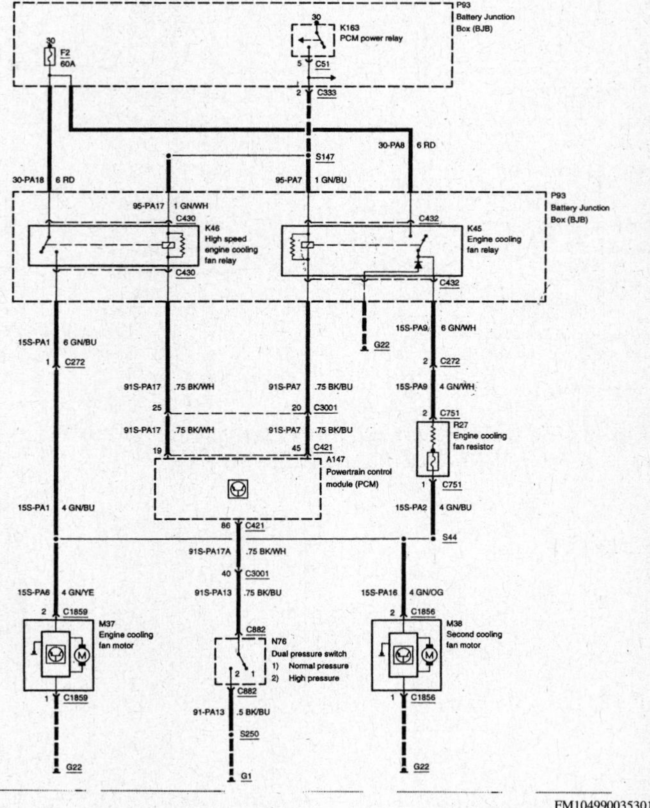

FM1049900353010X

Fig. 13 Cooling fan wiring diagram (Part 1 of 2). 1999 Cougar w/2.0L engine

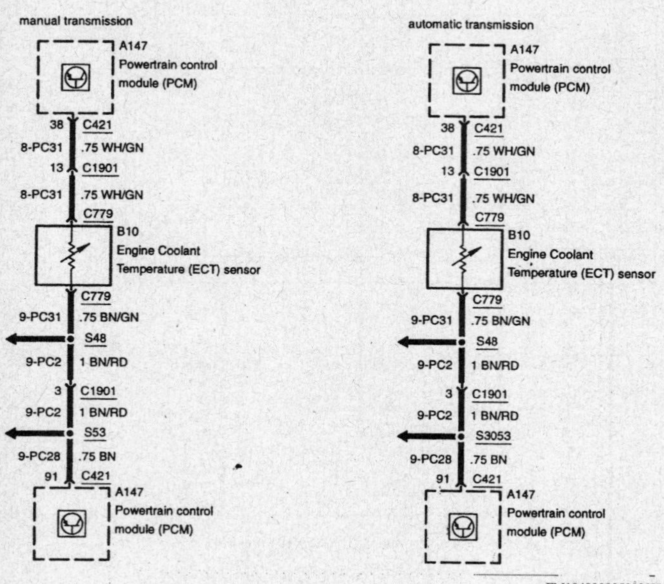

Fig. 13 Cooling fan wiring diagram (Part 2 of 2). 1999 Cougar w/2.0L engine

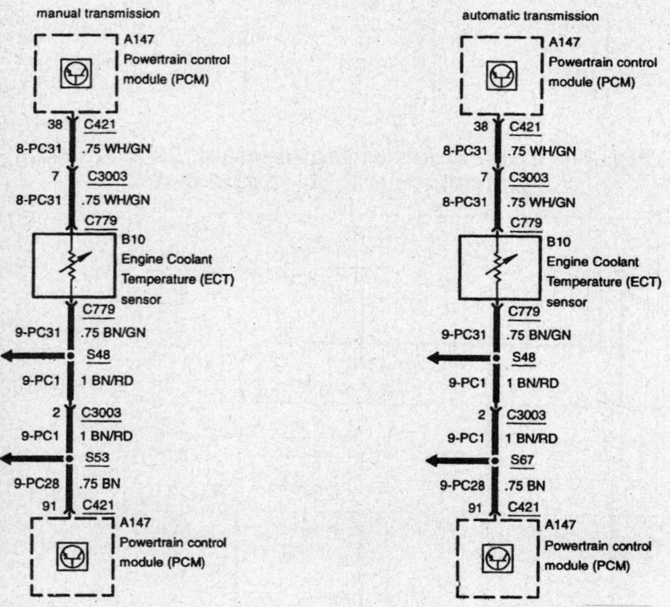

Fig. 14 Cooling fan wiring diagram (Part 2 of 2). 1999 Cougar w/2.5L engine

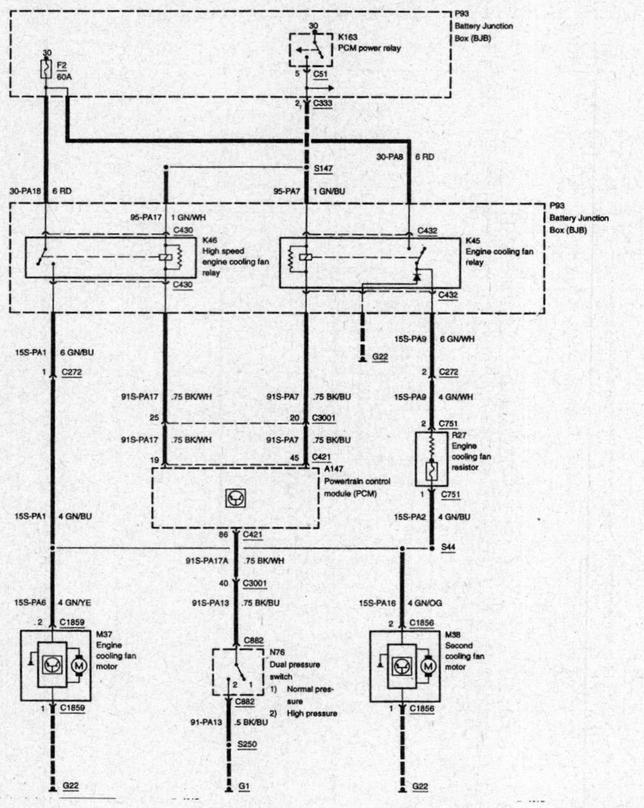

Fig. 14 Cooling fan wiring diagram (Part 1 of 2). 1999 Cougar w/2.5L engine

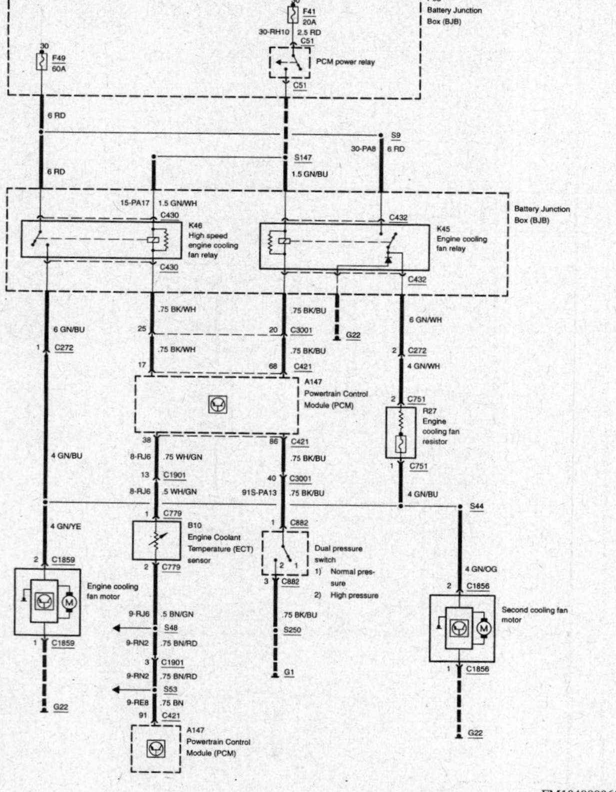

Fig. 15 Cooling fan wiring diagram. 2000–01 Cougar w/2.0L engine

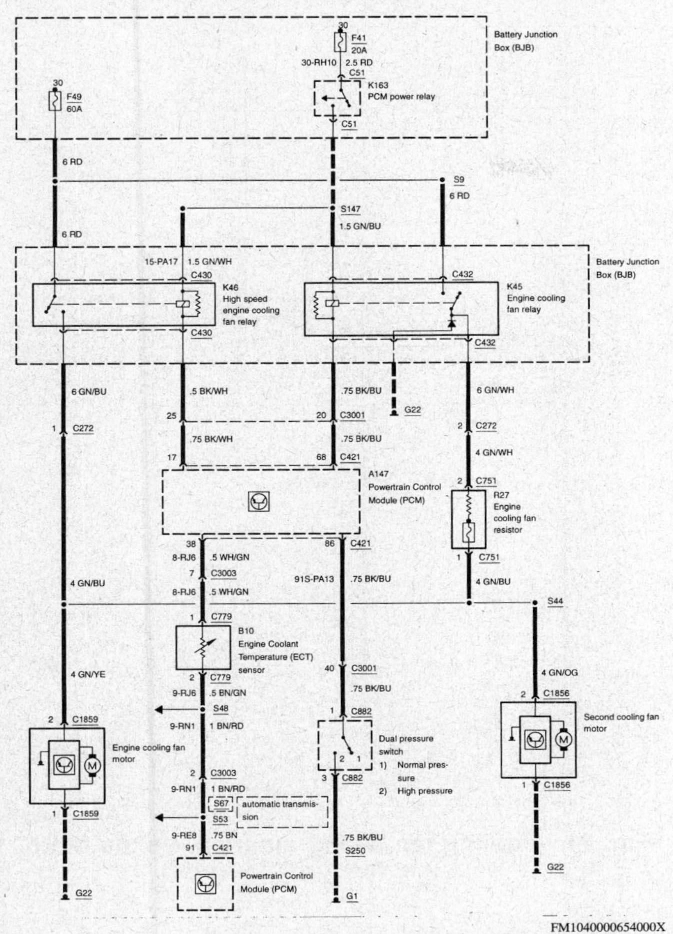

Fig. 16 Cooling fan wiring diagram. 2000–01 Cougar w/2.5L engine

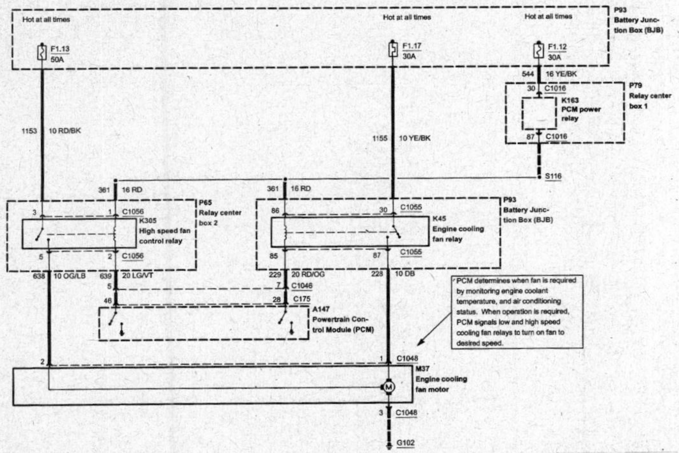

Fig. 18 Cooling fan wiring diagram. 2002 Crown Victoria & Grand Marquis

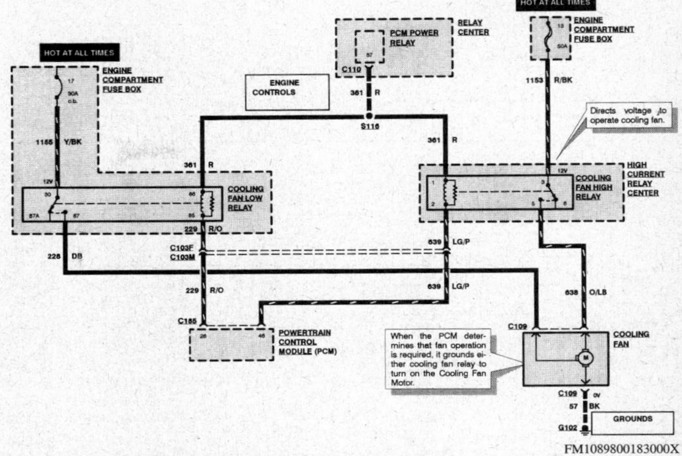

Fig. 17 Cooling fan wiring diagram. 1998–2001 Crown Victoria & Grand Marquis

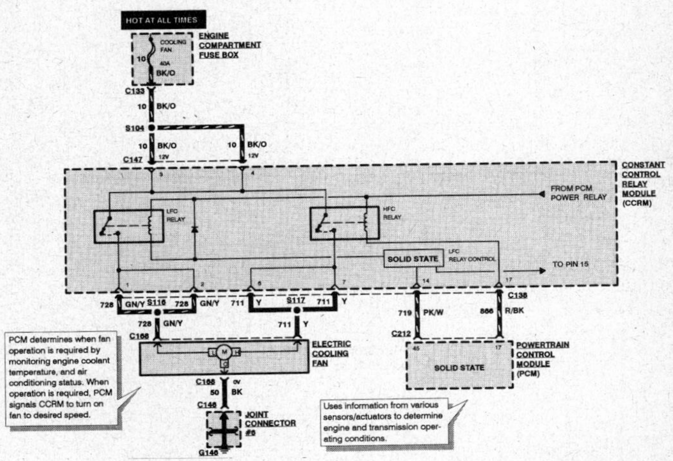

Fig. 19 Cooling fan wiring diagram (Part 1 of 2). 1998–2001 Escort, 1998–99 Tracer & 1998–2000 ZX2

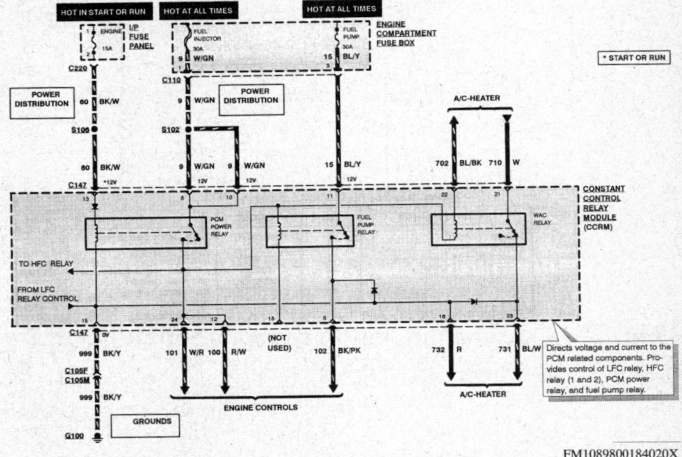

Fig. 19 Cooling fan wiring diagram (Part 2 of 2). 1998–2001 Escort & 1998–99 Tracer & 1998–2000 ZX2

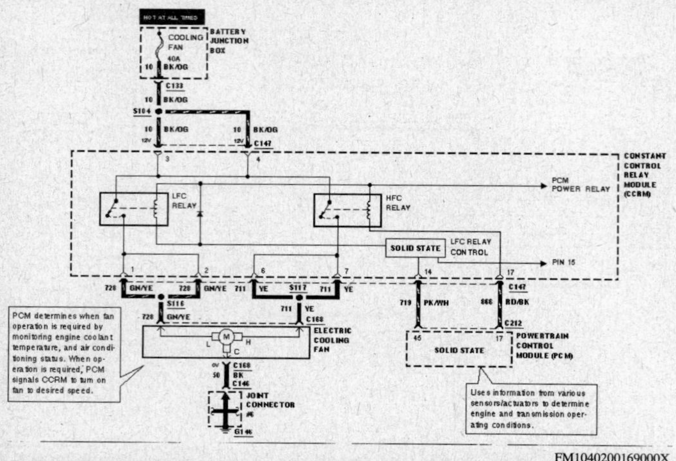

Fig. 20 Cooling Fan Wiring Diagram. 2002 Escort

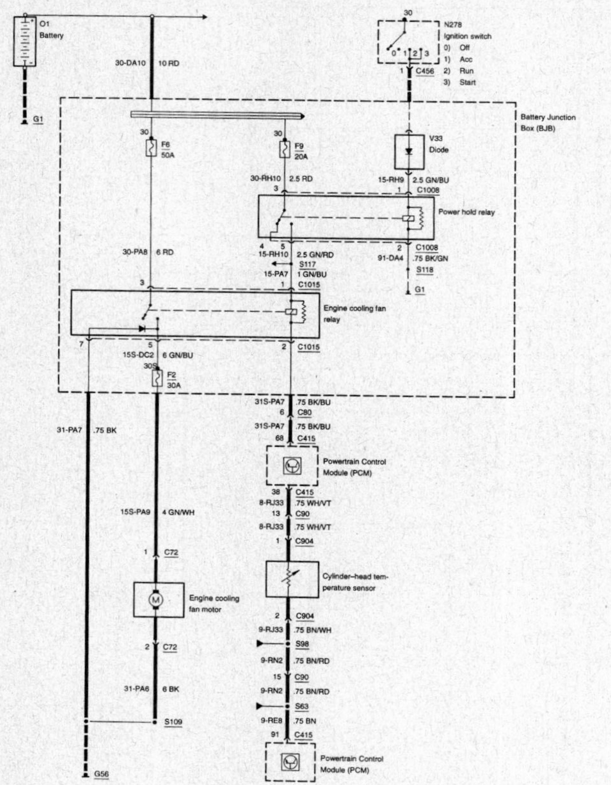

Fig. 21 Cooling fan wiring diagram. Focus DOHC less A/C

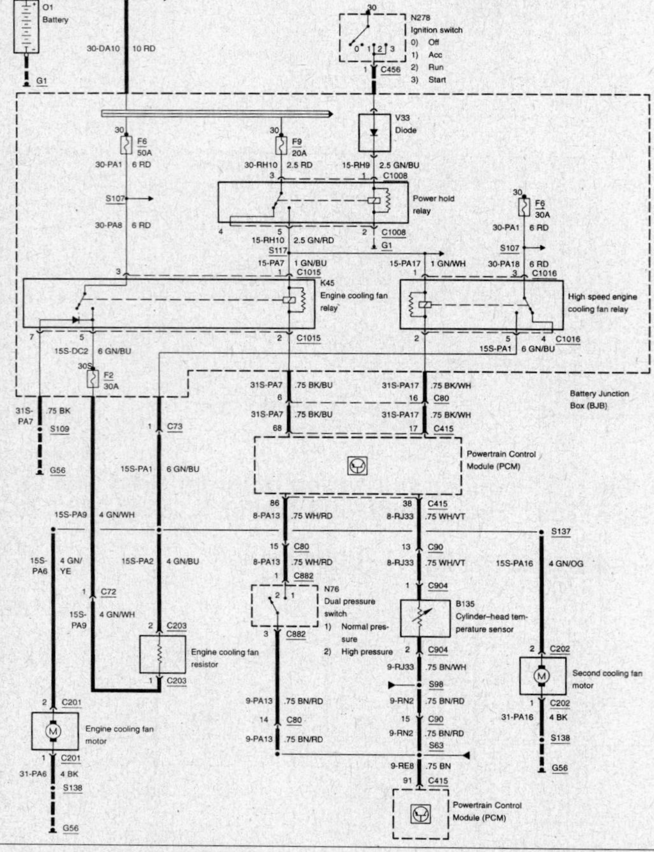

Fig. 22 Cooling fan wiring diagram. Focus DOHC with A/C

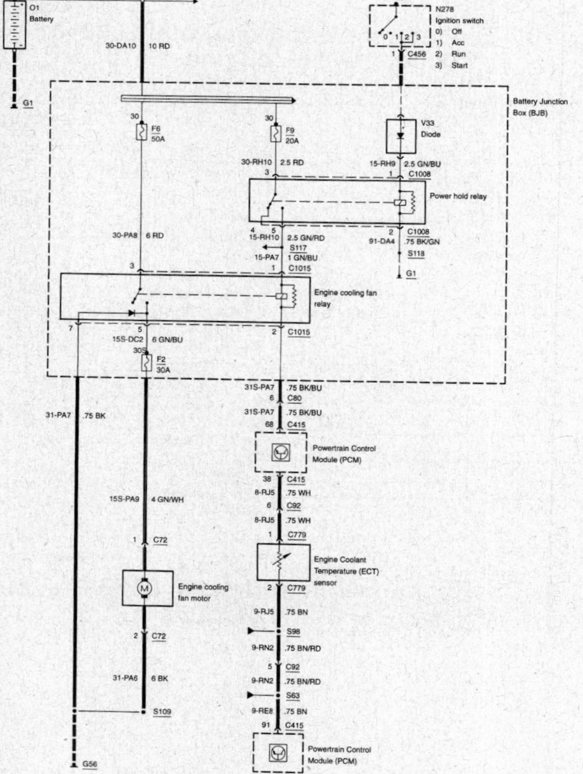

Fig. 23 Cooling fan wiring diagram. Focus SOHC less A/C

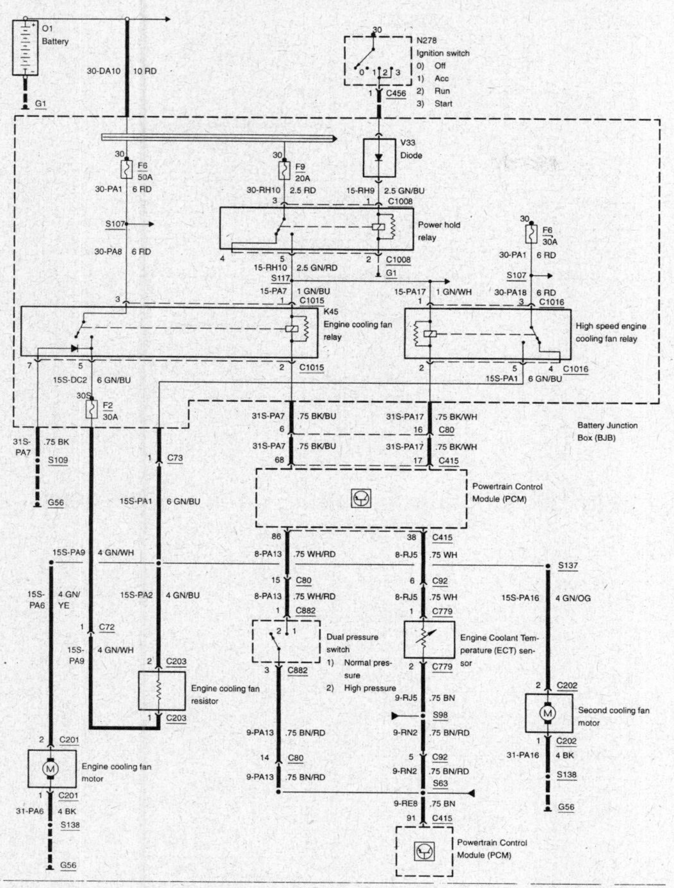

Fig. 24 Cooling fan wiring diagram. Focus SOHC with A/C

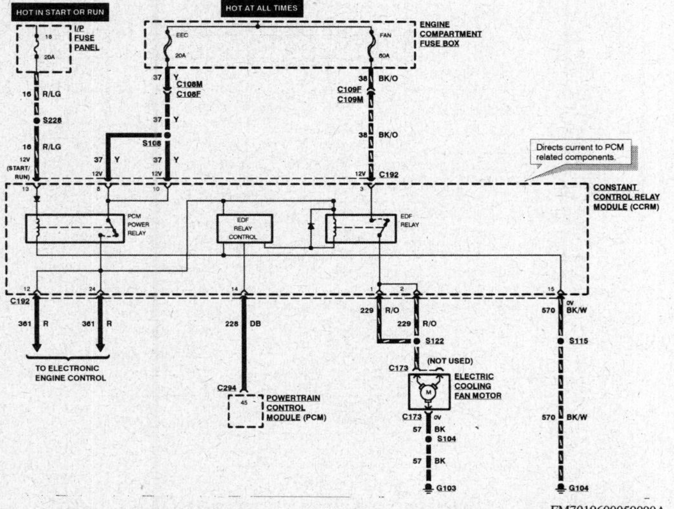

Fig. 26 Cooling fan wiring circuit. 1998 Mustang w/3.8L engine

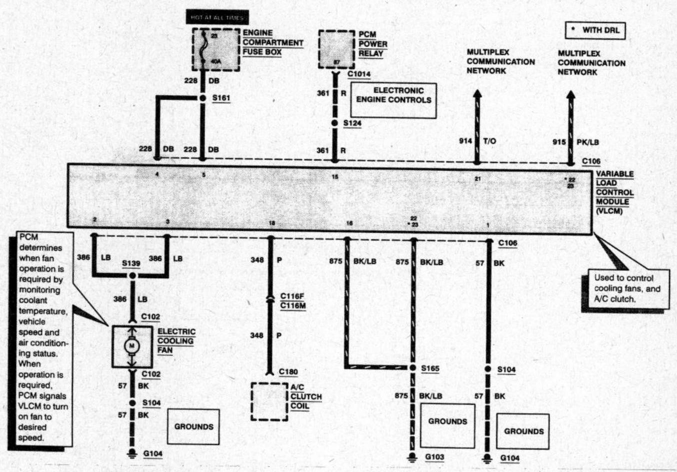

Fig. 25 Cooling fan wiring diagram. Mark VIII

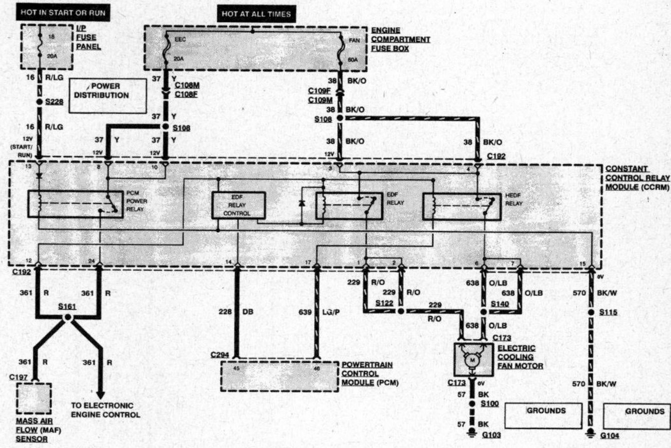

Fig. 27 Cooling fan wiring circuit. 1998 Mustang w/4.6L engine

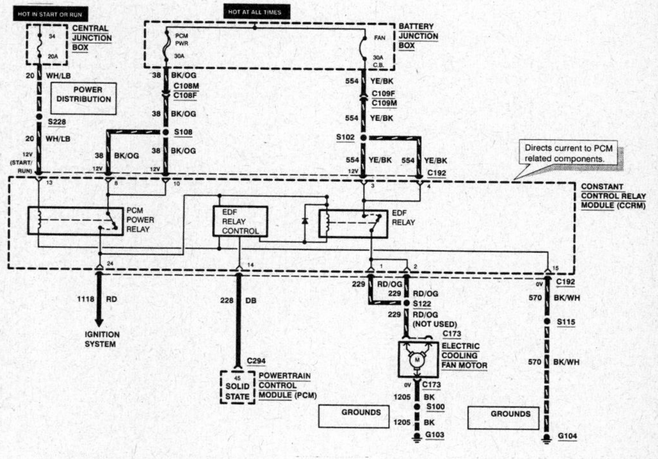

Fig. 28 Cooling fan wiring circuit. 1999–2001 Mustang w/3.8L engine

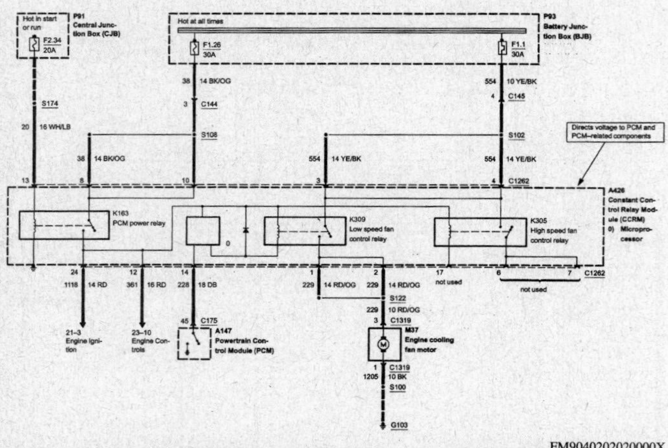

FM9040202020000X

Fig. 29 Cooling fan wiring diagram. 2002 Mustang w/3.8L engine

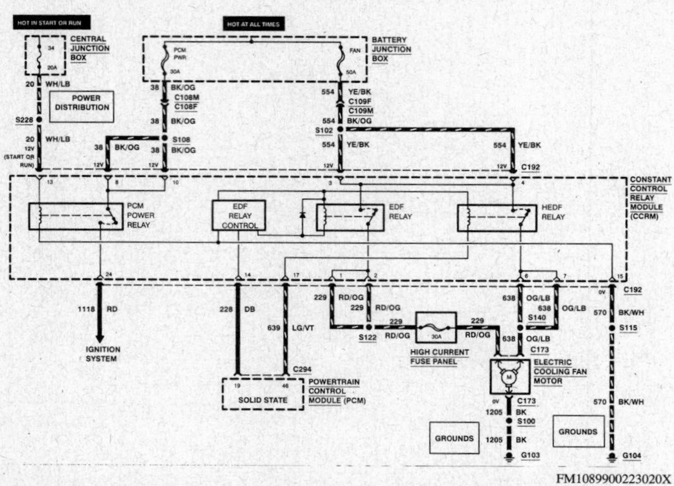

FM1089900223020X

Fig. 30 Cooling fan wiring circuit. 1999–2001 Mustang w/4.6L engine

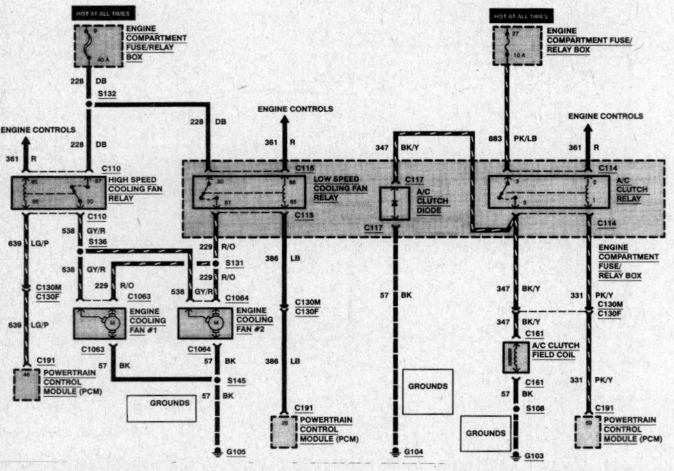

FM1089800182000X

Fig. 31 Cooling fan wiring diagram. 1998–99 Sable & Taurus

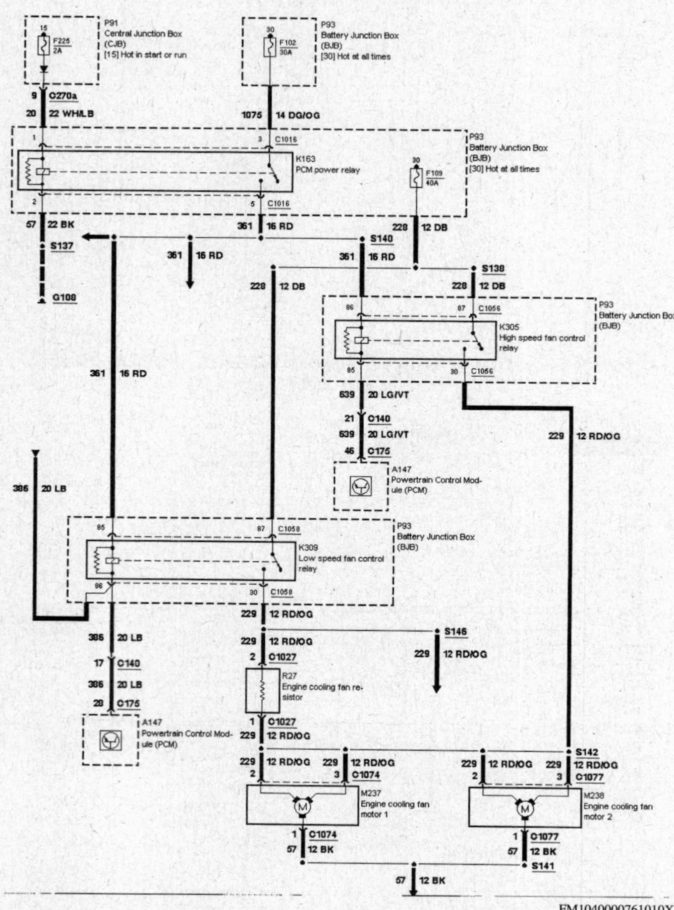

FM1040000761010X

Fig. 32 Cooling fan wiring diagram (Part 1 of 3). 2000–01 Sable & Taurus

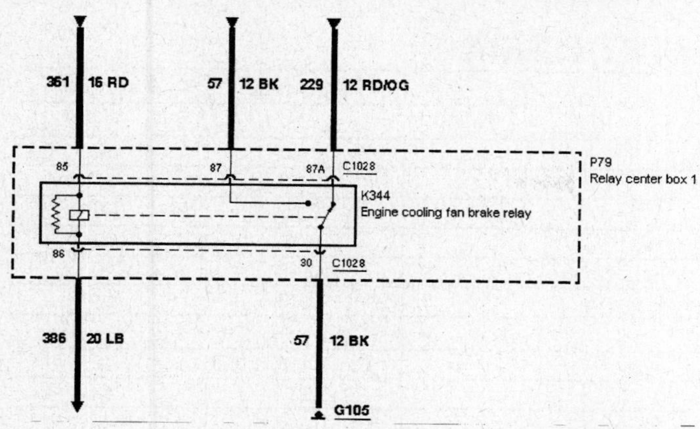

Fig. 32 Cooling fan wiring diagram (Part 2 of 3). 2000–01 Sable & Taurus

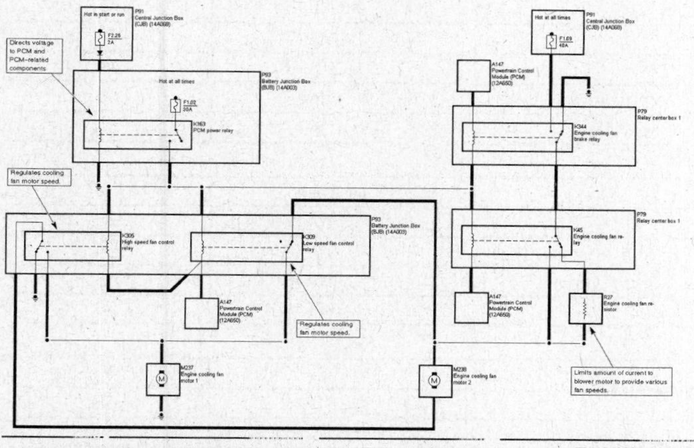

Fig. 33 Cooling Fan Wiring Diagram. 2002 Sable & Taurus

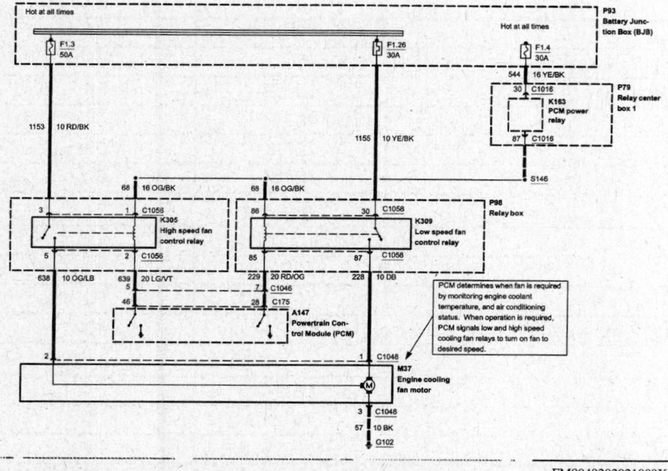

Fig. 35 Cooling fan wiring diagram. 2002 Town Car

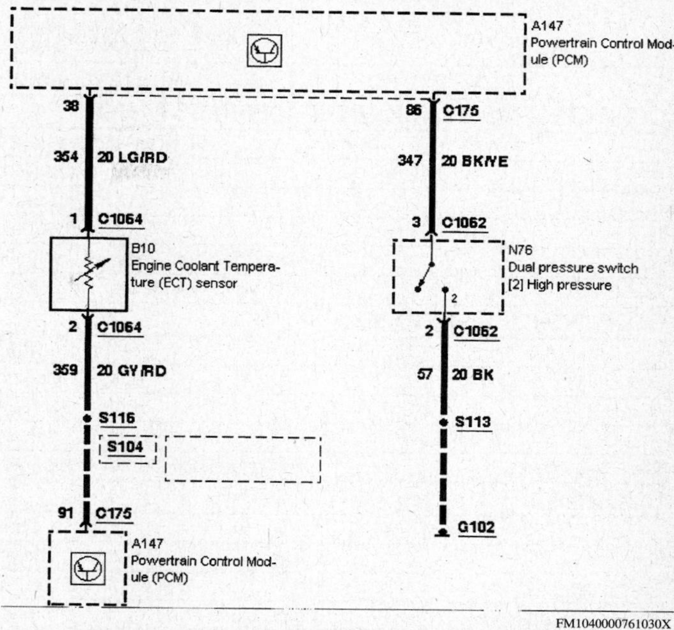

Fig. 32 Cooling fan wiring diagram (Part 3 of 3). 2000–01 Sable & Taurus

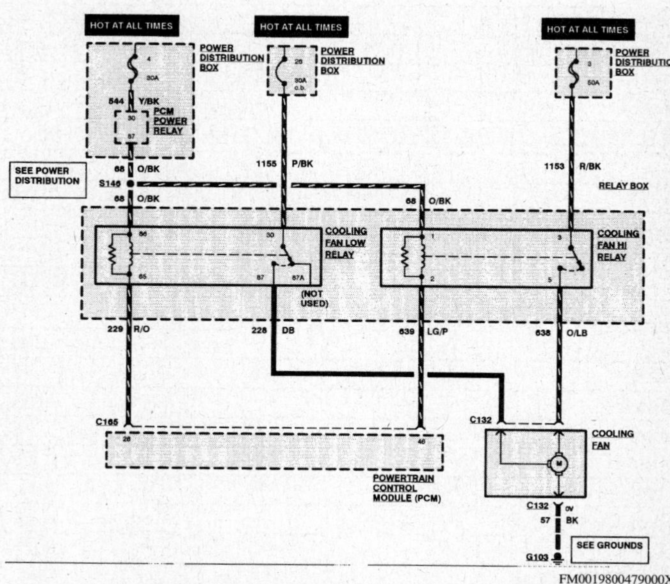

Fig. 34 Cooling fan wiring diagram. 1998–2001 Town Car

DIAGNOSTIC CHART INDEX

Test	Description	Page No.	Fig. No.
CONTINENTAL, MARK VIII & 1998 MUSTANG			
—	Symptom Chart (1998–99)	10-13	36
—	Symptom Chart (2000–02)	10-13	37
Test A	Loss Of Coolant	10-13	38
Test B	Engine Overheats	10-14	39
Test C	Engine Does Not Reach Normal Operating Temperature	10-15	40
Test D	Engine Block Heater Does Not Operate Properly	10-15	41
CONTOUR & MYSTIQUE			
—	Symptom Chart	10-16	42
Test A	Loss Of Coolant	10-16	43
Test B	Engine Overheats	10-16	44
Test C	Engine Does Not Reach Normal Operating Temperature	10-16	45
Test D	Engine Block Heater Does Not Operate Properly	10-16	46
COUGAR			
—	Symptom Chart	10-16	47
Test A	Loss Of Coolant	10-17	48
Test B	Engine Overheats	10-17	49
Test C	Engine Does Not Reach Normal Operating Temperature	10-17	50
Test D	Engine Block Heater Does Not Operate Correctly	10-17	51
1998 CROWN VICTORIA, GRAND MARQUIS & TOWN CAR			
—	Symptom Chart	10-17	52
Test A	Loss Of Coolant	10-17	53
Test B	Engine Overheats	10-18	54
Test C	Engine Does Not Reach Normal Operating Temperature	10-18	55
Test D	Block Heater Does Not Operate Properly	10-18	56
1999-2002 CROWN VICTORIA & GRAND MARQUIS			
—	Symptom Chart	10-19	57
Test A	Loss Of Coolant	10-19	58
Test B	Engine Overheats	10-20	59
Test C	Engine Does Not Reach Normal Operating Temperature	10-21	60
Test D	Block Heater Does Not Operate Properly	10-21	61
ESCORT, TRACER & ZX2			
—	Symptom Chart	10-21	62
Test A	Loss Of Coolant	10-21	63
Test B	Engine Overheats	10-21	64
Test C	Engine Does Not Reach Normal Operating Temperature	10-21	65
Test D	Block Heater Does Not Operate Properly	10-22	66
Test A	Loss Of Coolant	10-22	67
Test B	Engine Overheats	10-23	68
Test C	Engine Does Not Reach Normal Operating Temperature	10-23	69
FOCUS			
—	Symptom Chart	10-23	70
Test A	Loss Of Coolant	10-24	71
Test B	Engine Overheats	10-24	72
Test C	Engine Does Not Reach Normal Operating Temperature	10-24	73
1999–2002 MUSTANG			
—	Symptom Chart	10-24	74
Test A	Loss Of Coolant	10-24	75
Test B	Engine Overheats	10-25	76
Test C	Engine Does Not Reach Normal Operating Temperature	10-26	77
Test D	Block Heater Does Not Operate Correctly	10-26	78
1998–99 SABLE & TAURUS			
—	Symptom Chart	10-26	79
Test A	Loss Of Coolant	10-26	80
Test B	Engine Overheats	10-27	81
Test C	Block Heater Does Not Operate Properly	10-27	82

Continued

DIAGNOSTIC CHART INDEX—Continued

Condition	Possible Source	Action
• Loss of Engine Coolant	• Radiator. • Water pump seal. • Radiator hoses. • Heater hoses. • Heater core. • Engine gaskets. • Degas bottle.	• GO to Pinpoint Test A.
• The Engine (6007) Overheats	• Water thermostat (8575). • Water pump. • Internal engine coolant leak. • Radiator. • Heater core. • Cooling fan. • Pressure relief cap.	• GO to Pinpoint Test B.

FM1089800298010X

Fig. 36 Symptom Chart (Part 1 of 2). 1998-99 Continental, Mark VIII & 1998 Mustang

Condition	Possible Source	Action
• Loss of engine coolant	• Radiator. • Thermostat housing assembly. • Heater control valve. • Oil cooler. • PCV heater system. • Throttle body adapter heating. • Water pump seal. • Radiator hoses. • Heater hoses. • Heater core. • Engine gaskets. • Degas bottle.	• GO to Pinpoint Test A.
• The engine overheats	• Water thermostat. • Airlock in the system. • Water pump. • Internal engine coolant leak. • Radiator. • Radiator airflow obstruction • Heater core. • Cooling fan. • Pressure relief cap.	• GO to Pinpoint Test B.
• The engine does not reach normal operating temperature	• Water thermostat.	• GO to Pinpoint Test C.
• The block heater does not operate correctly	• Block heater power cable. • Block heater.	• GO to Pinpoint Test D.

FM1080000303000X

Fig. 37 Symptom Chart. 2000-02 Continental

Condition	Possible Source	Action
• The Engine Does Not Reach Normal Operating Temperature	• Water thermostat.	• GO to Pinpoint Test C.
• The Cooling Fan Operates Continuously	• Circuit. • Variable load control module. • Powertrain control module (PCM) (12A650). • Engine coolant temperature sensor.	• REFER to the Powertrain Control/Emissions Diagnosis Manual [1].
• The Cooling Fan Is Inoperative	• Circuit. • Variable load control module. • Powertrain control module. • Cooling fan motor.	• REFER to the Powertrain Control/Emissions Diagnosis Manual [1].
• The Cooling Fan Runs With No Low Speed	• Circuit. • Variable load control module. • Powertrain control module. • Cooling fan motor.	• REFER to the Powertrain Control/Emissions Diagnosis Manual [1].
• The Cooling Fan Runs With No High Speed	• Circuit. • Variable load control module. • Powertrain control module. • Cooling fan motor.	• REFER to the Powertrain Control/Emissions Diagnosis Manual [1].

FM1089800298020X

Fig. 36 Symptom Chart (Part 2 of 2). 1998-99 Continental, Mark VIII & 1998 Mustang

TEST CONDITIONS	TEST DETAILS/RESULTS/ACTIONS
A1 CHECK THE ENGINE COOLANT LEVEL	
NOTE: Allow the engine to cool before checking the engine coolant level.	
1 	2 Visually check the engine coolant level at the degas bottle. • Is the engine coolant level within specification? → **Yes** GO to **A2**. → **No** REFILL the engine coolant as necessary. GO to **A6**.

FM1089800299010X

Fig. 38 Test A: Loss Of Coolant (Part 1 of 4). 1998-99 Continental, Mark VIII & 1998 Mustang

TEST CONDITIONS	TEST DETAILS/RESULTS/ACTIONS
A2 CHECK THE PRESSURE RELIEF CAP	
	[1] Perform the pressure relief cap test; • Is pressure relief cap OK? → **Yes** GO to **A3**. → **No** REPLACE the damaged pressure relief cap. TEST the system for normal operation.
A3 CHECK THE ENGINE COOLANT FOR INTERNAL LEAK	
[1] 	[2] Inspect the engine coolant in degas bottle for signs of transmission fluid or engine oil. • Is oil or transmission fluid evident in coolant? → **Yes** If engine oil is evident, REPAIR engine as necessary. If transmission fluid is evident, INSTALL a new radiator as necessary. → **No** GO to **A4**.
A4 CHECK THE ENGINE AND THE TRANSMISSION FOR COOLANT	
	[1] Remove the oil level dipsticks (6750) from the engine and the transmission. • Is coolant evident in oil or transmission fluid? → **Yes** If coolant is in engine, REPAIR engine as necessary. If coolant is in transmission, REPAIR or REPLACE the radiator as necessary. → **No** GO to **A5**.

FM1089800299020X

Fig. 38 Test A: Loss Of Coolant (Part 2 of 4). Continental, Mark VIII & 1998 Mustang

TEST CONDITIONS	TEST DETAILS/RESULTS/ACTIONS
A5 PRESSURE TEST THE ENGINE COOLING SYSTEM	
	[1] Pressure test the engine cooling system; refer to the Component Tests in this section. • Does the engine cooling system leak? → **Yes** REPAIR or REPLACE leaking components. TEST the system for normal operation. → **No** The cooling system is operational. RETURN to the Symptom Chart.
A6 CHECK THE COOLANT RECOVERY SYSTEM	
	[1] **WARNING: Never remove the pressure relief cap under any conditions while the engine is operating. Failure to follow these instructions could result in damage to the cooling system or engine and/or personal injury. To avoid having scalding hot coolant or steam blow out of the cooling system, use extreme care when removing the pressure relief cap from a hot degas bottle. Wait until the engine has cooled, then wrap a thick cloth around the pressure relief cap and turn it slowly one turn (counterclockwise). Step back while the pressure is released from the cooling system. When certain all the pressure has been released, remove the pressure relief cap (still with a cloth).** Allow the engine to cool. [2] Remove the pressure relief cap. [3] Inspect the pressure relief cap for foreign material between the sealing gasket and the diaphragm. • Is the pressure relief cap OK? → **Yes** GO to **A7**. → **No** CLEAN or REPLACE the pressure relief cap. TEST the system for normal operation. GO to **A1**.

FM1089800299030X

Fig. 38 Test A: Loss Of Coolant (Part 3 of 4). Continental, Mark VIII & 1998 Mustang

TEST CONDITIONS	TEST DETAILS/RESULTS/ACTIONS
A7 CHECK THE DEGAS BOTTLE	
	[1] **NOTE:** The engine must be cool when coolant is added to the degas bottle. Add coolant to the degas bottle until fluid is between the coolant fill level marks. • Does the degas bottle leak? → **Yes** REPLACE the degas bottle. TEST the system for normal operation. → **No** PERFORM Pressure Test in this section; REPAIR as necessary. TEST the system for normal operation.

FM1089800299040X

Fig. 38 Test A: Loss Of Coolant (Part 4 of 4). Continental, Mark VIII & 1998 Mustang

TEST CONDITIONS	TEST DETAILS/RESULTS/ACTIONS
B1 CHECK THE ENGINE COOLANT LEVEL	
NOTE: If the engine is hot, allow the engine to cool before proceeding.	
[1] 	[1] **WARNING: Never remove the pressure relief cap under any conditions while the engine is operating. Failure to follow these instructions could result in damage to the cooling system or engine and/or personal injury. To avoid having scalding hot coolant or steam blow out of the cooling system, use extreme care when removing the pressure relief cap from a hot degas bottle. Wait until the engine has cooled, then wrap a thick cloth around the pressure relief cap and turn it slowly one turn (counterclockwise). Step back while the pressure is released from the cooling system. When certain all the pressure has been released, remove the pressure relief cap (still with a cloth).** [2] Check the engine coolant level at the degas bottle. • Is the engine coolant OK? → **Yes** GO to **B2**. → **No** REFILL the engine coolant at the degas bottle. GO to Pinpoint Test A.

FM1089800300010X

Fig. 39 Test B: Engine Overheats (Part 1 of 3). Continental, Mark VIII & 1998 Mustang

TEST CONDITIONS	TEST DETAILS/RESULTS/ACTIONS
B2 CHECK THE COOLANT CONDITION	
	1 Check the coolant for contaminants such as rust, corrosion, or discoloration. • Is the coolant condition OK? → **Yes** GO to **B3**. → **No** FLUSH the engine cooling system; TEST the system for normal operation.
B3 CHECK FOR AN AIRFLOW OBSTRUCTION	
	1 Inspect the A/C condenser core (19712) and radiator for obstructions such as leaves or dirt. • Is there an obstruction? → **Yes** REMOVE the obstruction. CLEAN the A/C condenser core and radiator. TEST the system for normal operation. → **No** GO to **B4**.
B4 CHECK THE HEATER CORE OPERATION	
1 2	1 Install the pressure relief cap.

FM1089800300020X

Fig. 39 Test B: Engine Overheats (Part 2 of 3). Continental, Mark VIII & 1998 Mustang

TEST CONDITIONS	TEST DETAILS/RESULTS/ACTIONS
B4 CHECK THE HEATER CORE OPERATION (Continued)	
	3 As the engine starts to heat up, feel the inlet and outlet heater water hoses (18472). They should feel approximately the same after three or four minutes. • Is the heater water hose approximately the same temperature as the inlet heater water hose ? → **Yes** GO to **B5**. → **No** TURN the engine off. REPAIR or REPLACE heater core. the system for normal operation.
B5 CHECK THE WATER THERMOSTAT OPERATION	
1	1 Start the engine and allow the engine to run for ten minutes.
	2 Feel the inlet and outlet heater water hoses and the underside of the upper radiator hose (8260). • Are the upper radiator hose and the heater water hoses cold? → **Yes** REPLACE the water thermostat; TEST the system for normal operation. → **No** GO to **B6**.
B6 CHECK THE COOLING FAN OPERATION	
1	1 Perform the Electric Coolant Fan Test in the Powertrain Control/Emissions Diagnosis Manual [2]. • Is the cooling fan operation OK? → **Yes** GO to Section 303-00 for diagnosis and testing of the engine. → **No** REPLACE the fan component determined; TEST the system for normal operation.

FM1089800300030X

Fig. 39 Test B: Engine Overheats (Part 3 of 3). Continental, Mark VIII & 1998 Mustang

	Test Step	Result	Action to Take
C1	CHECK ENGINE TEMPERATURE		
	• Start engine and allow to RUN for 10 minutes. • Feel inlet and outlet heater water hoses and underside of upper radiator hose. • **Are upper radiator hose and heater water hoses cold?**	Yes No	▶ REPLACE water thermostat RETEST system. ▶ Diagnose instrument cluster.

FM1089600159000X

Fig. 40 Test C: Engine Does Not Reach Normal Operating Temperature. Continental, Mark VIII & 1998 Mustang

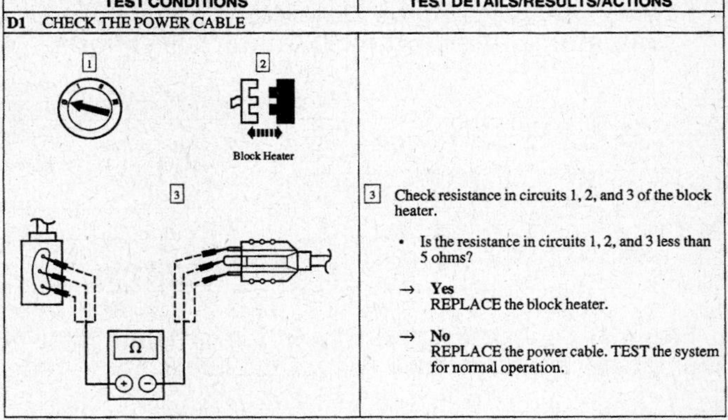

TEST CONDITIONS	TEST DETAILS/RESULTS/ACTIONS
D1 CHECK THE POWER CABLE	
1 2 3	3 Check resistance in circuits 1, 2, and 3 of the block heater. • Is the resistance in circuits 1, 2, and 3 less than 5 ohms? → **Yes** REPLACE the block heater. → **No** REPLACE the power cable. TEST the system for normal operation.

FM1089800302000X

Fig. 41 Test D: Block Heater Does Not Operate Properly. Continental, Mark VIII & 1998 Mustang

Condition	Possible Source	Action
• Loss of Coolant	• Damaged radiator. • Damaged water pump. • Loose / damaged radiator hoses. • Loose / damaged heater hoses. • Damaged heater core. • Damaged engine gaskets. • Damaged radiator coolant recovery reservoir.	• GO to Pinpoint Test A.

FM1089600147010X

Fig. 42 Symptom Chart (Part 1 of 2). Contour & Mystique

Test Step		Result	Action to Take
A1	CHECK ENGINE COOLANT LEVEL		
	NOTE: If engine is hot, allow engine to cool down before proceeding. • Check engine coolant level at radiator coolant recovery reservoir. • **Is engine coolant level OK?**	Yes ▶ No ▶	System OK. REFILL. GO to **A2**.
A2	CHECK FOR VISIBLE LEAKAGE		
	• Engine coolant has an added dye color that makes the coolant an excellent leak detector. • Check entire cooling system for visible leakage. • **Is there visible leakage?**	Yes ▶ No ▶	SERVICE. RETEST system. GO to **A3**.
A3	CHECK PRESSURE RELIEF CAP		
	• Using Rotunda Radiator / Heater Core Pressure Tester 014-R1052 or equivalent, test pressure relief cap. • **Did pressure relief cap test OK?**	Yes ▶ No ▶	GO to **A4**. REPLACE damaged pressure relief cap. RETEST system.
A4	CHECK COOLANT FOR INTERNAL LEAKAGE		
	• Inspect coolant in radiator coolant recovery reservoir for signs of transmission fluid or engine oil. • **Is oil evident in coolant?**	Yes ▶ No ▶	Locate & Repair source of contamination. GO to **A5**.
A5	CHECK ENGINE AND TRANSAXLE FOR COOLANT		
	• Remove oil level dipsticks from engine and transaxle. • Carefully inspect oil level dipsticks for evidence of coolant. • **Is coolant evident?**	Yes ▶ No ▶	Locate & Repair source of contamination. GO to **A6**.
A6	PRESSURE TEST COOLING SYSTEM		
	• Using Rotunda Radiator / Heater Core Pressure Tester 014-R1052 or equivalent, pressurize cooling system. • Check for any signs of visible leakage. • NOTE: Check inside vehicle for possible heater core leakage. • **Is there leakage?**	Yes ▶ No ▶	SERVICE. RETEST system. Cooling system is operational at this time. RETEST system.

FM1089600148000X

Fig. 43 Test A: Loss Of Coolant. Contour & Mystique

Test Step		Result	Action to Take
C1	CHECK ENGINE TEMPERATURE		
	• Start engine and allow to RUN for 15 minutes. • Feel inlet and outlet heater water hoses and underside of upper radiator hose. • **Are upper radiator hose and heater water hoses cold?**	Yes ▶ No ▶	TEST water thermostat. RETEST system. Engine coolant temperature gauge testing procedure.

FM1089600150000X

Fig. 45 Test C: Engine Does Not Reach Normal Operating Temperature. Contour & Mystique

Test Step		Result	Action to Take
D3	CHECK HEATER SHORT TO GROUND		
	• Measure resistance from terminal 1 of power cable to engine block. • Measure resistance from terminal 3 of power cable to engine block. • **Does resistance equal 1,000,000 ohms or more?**	Yes ▶ No ▶	GO to **D4**. REPLACE block heater. RESTORE vehicle. RETEST system.
D4	CHECK HEATER ELEMENT RESISTANCE		
	• Measure resistance from terminal 1 of power cable to terminal 3 of power cable. • **Does resistance measure between 30 ohms and 40 ohms?**	Yes ▶ No ▶	SERVICE AC power source. Block heater OK. REPLACE block heater. Heater element either open or shorted.

FM1089600151020X

Fig. 46 Test D: Engine Block Heater Does Not Operate Properly (Part 2 of 2). Contour & Mystique

Condition	Possible Sources	Action
•Loss of coolant	•Hoses. •Hose connections. •Radiator. •Water pump. •Heater core. •Gaskets. •Engine casting cracks. •Engine block core plugs.	•GO to Pinpoint Test A.

FM1080000263010X

Fig. 47 Symptom Chart (Part 1 of 2). Cougar

Condition	Possible Source	Action
• Engine Overheats	• Damaged water thermostat. • Damaged water pump. • Internal engine coolant leak. • Cooling fan inoperative. • Plugged radiator. • Plugged heater core.	• GO to Pinpoint Test B.
• Engine Does Not Reach Normal Operating Temperature	• Damaged water thermostat. • Cooling fan. • Low engine coolant.	• GO to Pinpoint Test C.
• Engine Block Heater Does Not Operate Properly	• Block heater power cable. • Block heater.	• GO to Pinpoint Test D.
• Low Speed Fan Inoperative	• Low speed relay. • Cooling fan resistor. • Powertrain control module.	• Diagnose circuit as necessary.
• High Speed Fan Inoperative	• High speed relay. • A/C pressure cut-off switch. • Powertrain control module.	• Diagnose circuit as necessary.

FM1089600147020X

Fig. 42 Symptom Chart (Part 2 of 2). Contour & Mystique

Test Step		Result	Action to Take
B1	CHECK ENGINE COOLANT LEVEL		
	NOTE: If engine is hot, allow engine to cool down before proceeding. • Check engine coolant level at radiator coolant recovery reservoir. • **Is engine coolant level OK?**	Yes ▶ No ▶	GO to **B2**. REFILL. GO to Pinpoint Test A.
B2	CHECK COOLANT CONDITION		
	• Check coolant for contaminants such as rust or corrosion. Also check for discolorization. • Check with hydrometer for protection level between -34 to -43°C (-30 to -45°F). • **Is coolant condition OK?**	Yes ▶ No ▶	GO to **B3**. FLUSH system. RETEST system.
B3	CHECK FOR AIR FLOW OBSTRUCTION		
	• Inspect A/C condenser core and radiator for obstructions such as leaves or bugs. • **Is there any obstruction?**	Yes ▶ No ▶	REMOVE obstruction and CLEAN A/C condenser core and radiator. RETEST system. GO to **B4**.
B4	CHECK HEATER CORE OPERATION		
	• Install pressure relief cap. • Start engine and allow to run. • As engine starts to warm up, feel the inlet and outlet heater water hoses. They should be the same temperature after three or four minutes. • **Is outlet heater water hose the same temperature as the inlet heater water hose?**	Yes ▶ No ▶	GO to **B5**. TURN engine OFF before it overheats. SERVICE heater core. RETEST system.
B5	CHECK WATER THERMOSTAT OPERATION		
	• Allow engine to run for 10 minutes. • Feel the inlet and outlet heater water hoses and the underside of the upper radiator hose. • **Are the upper radiator hose and heater water hoses cold?**	Yes ▶ No ▶	REPLACE water thermostat. RETEST system. LEAVE engine RUNNING. GO to **B6**.
B6	CHECK COOLING FAN(S)		
	• Check engine coolant temperature gauge at instrument cluster. Allow engine to RUN until high side of normal range is attained. • Check for cooling fan operation. • **Did cooling fan(s) operate OK?**	Yes ▶ No ▶	Diagnose engine operation. Diagnose climate control.

FM1089600149000X

Fig. 44 Test B: Engine Overheats. Contour & Mystique

Test Step		Result	Action to Take
D1	CHECK ENGINE BLOCK HEATER POWER CABLE		
	• Check continuity of Circuits 1, 2 and 3 in engine block heater power cable using Rotunda Digital Volt Ohmmeter 014-00407 or equivalent. • **Is there continuity in Circuits 1, 2 and 3?**	Yes ▶ No ▶	GO to **D2**. REPLACE block heater power cable. RETEST system.
D2	CHECK GROUND		
	• Install power cable to block heater. • Measure resistance from ground terminal of power cable, Pin 2, to engine block. • **Does resistance equal 1 ohm or less?**	Yes ▶ No ▶	GO to **D3**. REPLACE block heater. RESTORE vehicle. RETEST system.

FM1089600151010X

Fig. 46 Test D: Engine Block Heater Does Not Operate Properly (Part 1 of 2). Contour & Mystique

Condition	Possible Sources	Action
•The engine overheats	•Engine coolant. •Thermostat. •Fuse. •Circuit. •Fan motor. •Engine coolant temperature (ECT) sensor. •Powertrain control module (PCM).	•GO to Pinpoint Test B.
•The engine does not reach normal operating temperature	•Thermostat. •Electric fans.	•GO to Pinpoint Test C.
•Engine block heater does not operate properly	•Block heater power cable. •Block heater.	•GO to Pinpoint Test D.

FM1080000263020X

Fig. 47 Symptom Chart (Part 2 of 2). Cougar

CONDITIONS	DETAILS/RESULTS/ACTIONS
A1: VISUAL INSPECTION	
	1 Visually inspect for loss of coolant. • Is the engine cooling system leaking? → **Yes** REPAIR the components in question. → **No** CARRY OUT the Pressure Test.

FM1080000264000X

Fig. 48 Test A: Loss Of Coolant. Cougar

CONDITIONS	DETAILS/RESULTS/ACTIONS
	1 Inspect the coolant level and condition. • Is the coolant OK? → **Yes** GO TO **B2** → **No** If coolant is weak or contaminated, FLUSH and REFILL with new coolant as necessary. If the coolant is low, REFILL the system and CARRY OUT the Component Test.
B2: CHECK THERMOSTAT	
	1 Carry out the component test in this section. • Is the thermostat OK? → **Yes** Diagnose cooling system. → **No** INSTALL a new thermostat.

FM1080000265020X

Fig. 49 Test B: Engine Overheats (Part 2 of 2). Cougar

CONDITIONS	DETAILS/RESULTS/ACTIONS
D1: CHECK ELECTRICAL CONNECTOR AND WIRE	
1	2 Check for corroded terminals on the electrical connector.

FM1080000267010X

Fig. 51 Test D: Engine Block Heater Does Not Operate Correctly (Part 1 of 2). Cougar

Condition	Possible Source	Action
• Loss of Coolant	• Damaged radiator. • Loose/damaged radiator hoses. • Loose/damaged heater hoses. • Damaged heater core. • Damaged engine gaskets. • Damaged degas bottle. • Damaged fluid cooler (police/trailer tow only).	• GO to Pinpoint Test A.
• Engine Overheats	• Damaged water thermostat. • Damaged water pump. • Internal engine coolant leak. • Cooling fan inoperative. • Plugged radiator, interior or exterior. • Plugged heater core. • Electro-Drive cooling fan operating in reverse.	• GO to Pinpoint Test B.
• Engine Does Not Reach Normal Operating Temperature	• Damaged water thermostat. • Cooling fans.	• GO to Pinpoint Test C.
• Block Heater Does Not Operate Properly	• Block heater. • Block heater power cable.	• GO to Pinpoint Test D.
• Auxiliary Electric Cooling Fan Runs Continuously	• Circuit. • Powertrain control module. • Engine coolant temperature sensor.	• Diagnose circuit as necessary.

FM1089600161000X

Fig. 52 Symptom Chart. 1998 Crown Victoria, Grand Marquis & Town Car

CONDITIONS	DETAILS/RESULTS/ACTIONS
B1: CHECK COOLANT	

WARNING: Never remove the expansion tank cap under any circumstances while the engine is operating. Failure to follow these instructions may result in damage to the cooling system of the engine and/or personal injury. To avoid having scalding hot water or steam blow out of the cooling system, use extreme care when removing the expansion tank cap from a hot cooling system. Wait until the engine has cooled, then wrap a thick cloth around the expansion tank cap and turn it slowly until the pressure begins to release, step back while the pressure is released from the cooling system. When certain all the pressure has been released (still with a cloth) turn and remove the expansion tank cap. Failure to follow these instructions may result in personal injury.

FM1080000265010X

Fig. 49 Test B: Engine Overheats (Part 1 of 2). Cougar

CONDITIONS	DETAILS/RESULTS/ACTIONS
C1: CHECK THERMOSTAT	
	1 Carry out the component test in this section. • Is the thermostat OK? → **Yes** Diagnose cooling system. → **No** INSTALL a new thermostat.

FM1080000266000X

Fig. 50 Test C: Engine Does Not Reach Normal Operating Temperature. Cougar

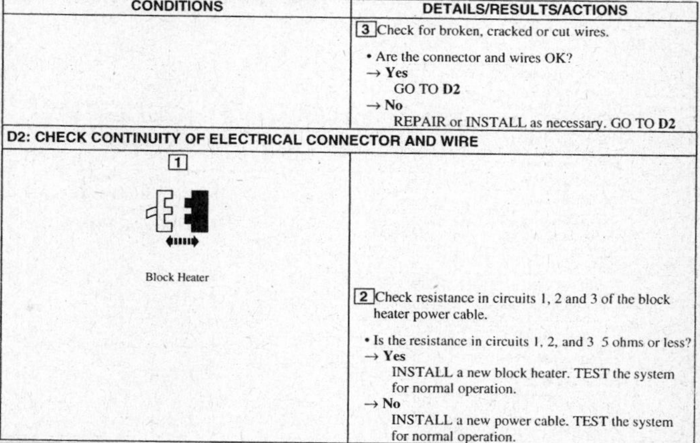

CONDITIONS	DETAILS/RESULTS/ACTIONS
	3 Check for broken, cracked or cut wires. • Are the connector and wires OK? → **Yes** GO TO **D2** → **No** REPAIR or INSTALL as necessary. GO TO **D2**
D2: CHECK CONTINUITY OF ELECTRICAL CONNECTOR AND WIRE	
1 Block Heater	2 Check resistance in circuits 1, 2 and 3 of the block heater power cable. • Is the resistance in circuits 1, 2, and 3 5 ohms or less? → **Yes** INSTALL a new block heater. TEST the system for normal operation. → **No** INSTALL a new power cable. TEST the system for normal operation.

FM1080000267020X

Fig. 51 Test D: Engine Block Heater Does Not Operate Correctly (Part 2 of 2). Cougar

	Test Step	Result		Action to Take
A1	CHECK ENGINE COOLANT LEVEL			
	NOTE: If engine is hot, allow engine to cool down before proceeding. • Check engine coolant level at degas bottle. • **Is coolant level OK?**	Yes No	▶ ▶	GO to **A2**. REFILL. GO to **A7**.
A2	CHECK FOR VISIBLE LEAKAGE			
	• Engine coolant has an added dye color that makes the coolant an excellent leak detector. • Check entire cooling system for visible leakage. • **Is there visible leakage?**	Yes No	▶ ▶	SERVICE. RETEST system. GO to **A3**.
A3	CHECK PRESSURE RELIEF CAP			
	• Using Rotunda Radiator/Heater Core Pressure Tester 014-R1069 or equivalent, test pressure relief cap. • **Did pressure relief cap test OK?**	Yes No	▶ ▶	GO to **A4**. REPLACE damaged pressure relief cap. RETEST system.
A4	CHECK COOLANT FOR INTERNAL LEAKAGE			
	• Inspect coolant in degas bottle for signs of transmission fluid or engine oil. • **Is oil evident in coolant?**	Yes No	▶ ▶	**Locate & Repair source of contamination.** GO to **A5**.

FM1089600162010X

Fig. 53 Test A: Loss Of Coolant (Part 1 of 2). 1998 Crown Victoria, Grand Marquis & Town Car

	Test Step	Result ▶	Action to Take
A5	CHECK ENGINE AND TRANSMISSION FOR COOLANT		
	• Remove oil level dipsticks from engine and transmission. • Carefully inspect oil level dipsticks for evidence of coolant. • **Is coolant evident?**	Yes ▶	If coolant is in engine oil, CHECK for leak in engine head gasket or cracked engine block. If coolant is in transmission fluid, SERVICE for transmission fluid leakage.
		No ▶	GO to **A6**.
A6	PRESSURE TEST COOLING SYSTEM		
	• Using Rotunda Radiator/Heater Core Pressure Tester 014-R1069 or equivalent, pressurize cooling system • Check for any signs of visible leakage. NOTE: Check inside vehicle for possible heater core leakage. • **Is there leakage?**	Yes ▶ No ▶	SERVICE. RETEST system. GO to **A7**.
A7	CHECK COOLANT RECOVERY		
	• Allow engine to cool. Remove pressure relief cap and inspect cap for foreign material between sealing gasket and diaphragm. • **Is cap OK?**	Yes ▶ No ▶	GO to **A8**. SERVICE
A8	CHECK DEGAS HOSE		
	• Remove degas hose. • Inspect hose for obstruction, cracks or cuts. • **Is hose condition OK?**	Yes ▶ No ▶	GO to **A9**. SERVICE degas hose as required. RESTORE vehicle.
A9	CHECK DEGAS BOTTLE		
	• Replenish coolant in degas bottle to FULL COLD level as described. • Inspect degas bottle for leaks. • **Is there leakage at degas bottle?**	Yes ▶ No ▶	REPLACE degas bottle. RESTORE vehicle. Pressure Test, Component Tests. SERVICE as required.

FM1089600162020X

Fig. 53 Test A: Loss Of Coolant (Part 2 of 2). 1998 Crown Victoria, Grand Marquis & Town Car

	Test Step	Result ▶	Action to Take
B1	CHECK ENGINE COOLANT LEVEL		
	NOTE: If engine is hot, allow engine to cool down before proceeding. • Remove pressure relief cap and check engine coolant level at degas bottle. • **Is engine coolant level OK?**	Yes ▶ No ▶	GO to **B2**. REFILL. GO to Pinpoint Test A.
B2	CHECK COOLANT CONDITION		
	• Check coolant for contaminants such as rust or corrosion. Also check for color discoloration. • **Is coolant condition OK?**	Yes ▶ No ▶	GO to **B3**. FLUSH system. RETEST system.
B3	CHECK FOR AIR FLOW OBSTRUCTION		
	• Inspect A/C condenser core and radiator for obstructions such as leaves or bugs. • **Is there any obstruction?**	Yes ▶	REMOVE obstruction and CLEAN A/C condenser core and radiator RETEST system.
		No ▶	GO to **B4**.

FM1089600163010X

Fig. 54 Test B: Engine Overheats (Part 1 of 2). 1998 Crown Victoria, Grand Marquis & Town Car

	Test Step	Result ▶	Action to Take
C1	CHECK ENGINE TEMPERATURE		
	• Start engine and allow to run for 15 minutes. • Feel inlet and outlet heater water hoses and underside of upper radiator hose. • **Are upper radiator hose and heater water hoses cold?**	Yes ▶ No ▶	REPLACE water thermostat RETEST system. Diagnose instrument cluster.

FM1089600164000X

Fig. 55 Test C: Engine Does Not Reach Normal Operating Temperature. 1998 Crown Victoria, Grand Marquis & Town Car

	Test Step	Result ▶	Action to Take
B4	CHECK HEATER CORE OPERATION		
	• Install pressure relief cap. • Start engine and allow to run. • As engine starts to warm up, feel the inlet and outlet heater water hoses. They should feel the same after three or four minutes. • **Is outlet heater water hose the same temperature as the inlet heater water hose?**	Yes ▶ No ▶	GO to **B5**. TURN engine OFF before it overheats. SERVICE heater core RETEST system.
B5	CHECK WATER THERMOSTAT OPERATION		
	• Allow engine to run for 10 minutes. • Feel the inlet and outlet heater water hoses and the underside of the upper radiator hose. • **Are the upper radiator hose and heater water hoses cold?**	Yes ▶ No ▶	REPLACE water thermostat RETEST system. LEAVE engine RUNNING. GO to **B6**.
B6	CHECK COOLING FAN CLUTCH		
	• Check for proper cooling fan clutch operation • **Is cooling fan clutch operating correctly?**	Yes ▶ No ▶	GO to **B7**. REPLACE fan clutch. RETEST system.
B7	CHECK AUXILIARY ELECTRIC COOLING FAN		
	• Connect Rotunda New Generation Star (NGS) Tester 007-00500 or equivalent to vehicle. • Key on, engine off. • Output Test Mode accessed on tester. • Command cooling fan on. • **Does auxiliary electric cooling fan come on rotating in the proper direction?**	Yes ▶ No ▶	Diagnose engine operation. GO to **B8**.
B8	CHECK FOR POWER AND GROUND TO AUXILIARY ELECTRIC COOLING FAN		
	• Still in output test mode (OTM) with cooling fan commanded ON. • Measure voltage at Circuit 228 (DB) and ground at the cooling fan vehicle harness connector. • **Is voltage greater than 10.5 volts?**	Yes ▶	Turn ignition switch OFF. CHECK Circuit 229 (DB) and ground Circuit 57 (BK) are not reversed to the fan motor. If circuits are OK, REPLACE cooling fan. RESTORE vehicle. RETEST system.
		No ▶	REMAIN in Output Test Mode (OTM). GO to **B9**.
B9	CHECK GROUND CIRCUIT TO AUXILIARY ELECTRIC COOLING FAN		
	• Still in output test mode (OTM) with cooling fan commanded ON. • Cooling fan disconnected. • Measure voltage between the battery negative terminal and Circuit 228 (DB) at the cooling fan vehicle harness connector. • **Is voltage now greater than 10.5 volts?**	Yes ▶	TURN ignition switch OFF. SERVICE open ground Circuit 57 (BK) to cooling fan. RECONNECT cooling fan. RESTORE vehicle. RETEST system.
		No ▶	TURN ignition switch OFF. GO to **B10**.
B10	CHECK FOR B+ TO AUXILIARY ELECTRIC COOLING FAN RELAY		
	• Turn ignition switch OFF. • Disconnect cooling fan relay. • Measure voltage between the B+ Circuit 37 (Y) at the cooling fan relay and the battery negative post. • **Is voltage greater than 10.5 volts?**	Yes ▶ No ▶	GO to **B11**. SERVICE open B+ circuit to cooling fan relay. RESTORE vehicle. RETEST system.
B11	CHECK POWER-TO-FAN CIRCUIT CONTINUITY		
	• Turn ignition switch OFF. • Cooling fan disconnected. • Cooling fan relay disconnected. • Measure resistance between the cooling fan relay power Circuit 37 (Y) and fan power Circuit 228 (DB) vehicle harness connector. • **Is resistance less than 5.0 ohms?**	Yes ▶	REPLACE cooling fan relay. RESTORE vehicle. RETEST system.
		No ▶	SERVICE open in Circuit 228 (DB) between cooling fan relay and cooling fan connector. RESTORE vehicle. RETEST system.

FM1089600163020X

Fig. 54 Test B: Engine Overheats (Part 2 of 2). 1998 Crown Victoria, Grand Marquis & Town Car

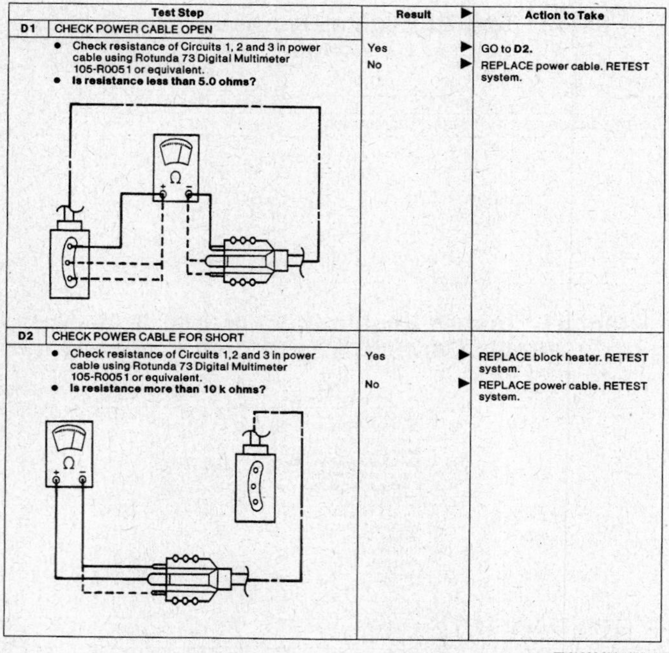

	Test Step	Result ▶	Action to Take
D1	CHECK POWER CABLE OPEN		
	• Check resistance of Circuits 1, 2 and 3 in power cable using Rotunda 73 Digital Multimeter 105-R0051 or equivalent. • **Is resistance less than 5.0 ohms?**	Yes ▶ No ▶	GO to **D2**. REPLACE power cable. RETEST system.
D2	CHECK POWER CABLE FOR SHORT		
	• Check resistance of Circuits 1,2 and 3 in power cable using Rotunda 73 Digital Multimeter 105-R0051 or equivalent. • **Is resistance more than 10 k ohms?**	Yes ▶ No ▶	REPLACE block heater. RETEST system. REPLACE power cable. RETEST system.

FM1089600165000X

Fig. 56 Test D: Block Heater Does Not Operate Properly. 1998 Crown Victoria, Grand Marquis & Town Car

Condition	Possible Source	Action
• Loss of Engine Coolant	• Radiator. • Water pump seal. • Radiator hoses. • Heater hoses. • Heater core. • Engine gaskets. • Degas bottle.	• GO to Pinpoint Test A.
• The Engine Overheats	• Water thermostat. • Water pump. • Internal engine coolant leak. • Radiator. • Heater core. • Cooling fan. • Pressure relief cap.	• GO to Pinpoint Test B.
• The Engine Does Not Reach Normal Operating Temperature	• Water thermostat.	• GO to Pinpoint Test C.
• The Block Heater Does Not Operate Properly	• Block heater power cable. • Block heater.	• GO to Pinpoint Test D.

FM1089900304000X

Fig. 57 Symptom Chart. 1999-2002 Crown Victoria & Grand Marquis

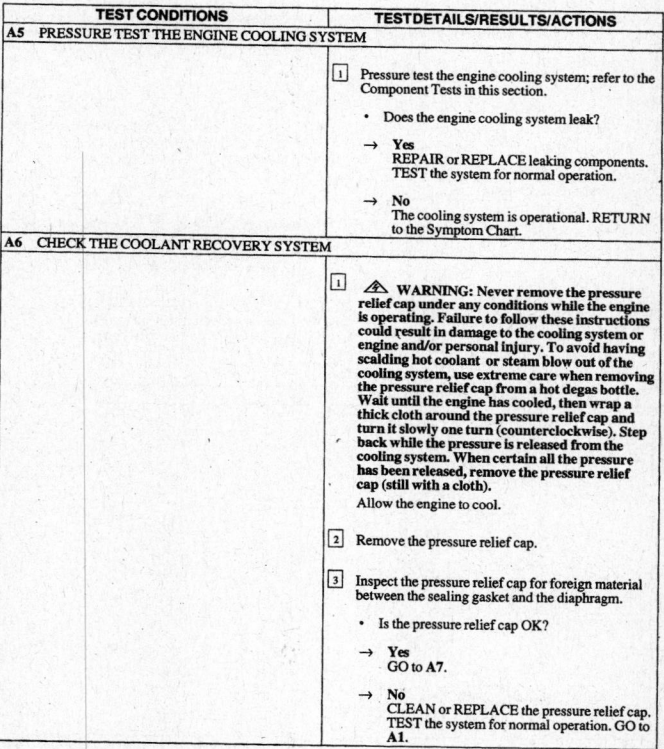

TEST CONDITIONS	TEST DETAILS/RESULTS/ACTIONS
A2 CHECK THE PRESSURE RELIEF CAP	
	1 Perform the pressure relief cap test; refer to the Component Tests in this section. • Is pressure relief cap OK? → **Yes** GO to **A3**. → **No** REPLACE the damaged pressure relief cap. TEST the system for normal operation.
A3 CHECK THE ENGINE COOLANT FOR INTERNAL LEAK	
1	2 Inspect the engine coolant in degas bottle for signs of transmission fluid or engine oil. • Is oil or transmission fluid evident in coolant? → **Yes** If engine oil is evident, REPAIR engine as necessary. If transmission fluid is evident, REPAIR or REPLACE the radiator as necessary. → **No** GO to **A4**.
A4 CHECK THE ENGINE AND THE TRANSMISSION FOR COOLANT	
	1 Remove the oil level dipsticks from the engine and the transmission. • Is coolant evident in oil or transmission fluid? → **Yes** If coolant is in engine, REPAIR engine as necessary. If coolant is in transmission, REPAIR or REPLACE the radiator as necessary. → **No** GO to **A5**.

FM1089900305020X

Fig. 58 Test A: Loss Of Coolant (Part 2 of 4). 1999-2002 Crown Victoria & Grand Marquis

TEST CONDITIONS	TEST DETAILS/RESULTS/ACTIONS
A1 CHECK THE ENGINE COOLANT LEVEL	
NOTE: Allow the engine to cool before checking the engine coolant level.	
1	2 Visually check the engine coolant level at the degas bottle. • Is the engine coolant level within specification? → **Yes** GO to **A2**. → **No** REFILL the engine coolant as necessary. GO to **A6**.

FM1089900305010X

Fig. 58 Test A: Loss Of Coolant (Part 1 of 4). 1999-2002 Crown Victoria & Grand Marquis

TEST CONDITIONS	TEST DETAILS/RESULTS/ACTIONS
A5 PRESSURE TEST THE ENGINE COOLING SYSTEM	
	1 Pressure test the engine cooling system; refer to the Component Tests in this section. • Does the engine cooling system leak? → **Yes** REPAIR or REPLACE leaking components. TEST the system for normal operation. → **No** The cooling system is operational. RETURN to the Symptom Chart.
A6 CHECK THE COOLANT RECOVERY SYSTEM	
	1 **WARNING: Never remove the pressure relief cap under any conditions while the engine is operating. Failure to follow these instructions could result in damage to the cooling system or engine and/or personal injury. To avoid having scalding hot coolant or steam blow out of the cooling system, use extreme care when removing the pressure relief cap from a hot degas bottle. Wait until the engine has cooled, then wrap a thick cloth around the pressure relief cap and turn it slowly one turn (counterclockwise). Step back while the pressure is released from the cooling system. When certain all the pressure has been released, remove the pressure relief cap (still with a cloth).** Allow the engine to cool. 2 Remove the pressure relief cap. 3 Inspect the pressure relief cap for foreign material between the sealing gasket and the diaphragm. • Is the pressure relief cap OK? → **Yes** GO to **A7**. → **No** CLEAN or REPLACE the pressure relief cap. TEST the system for normal operation. GO to **A1**.

FM1089900305030X

Fig. 58 Test A: Loss Of Coolant (Part 3 of 4). 1999-2002 Crown Victoria & Grand Marquis

TEST CONDITIONS	TEST DETAILS/RESULTS/ACTIONS
A7 CHECK THE DEGAS BOTTLE	
	1 **NOTE:** The engine must be cool when coolant is added to the degas bottle. Add coolant to the degas bottle until fluid is between the coolant fill level marks. • Does the degas bottle leak? → **Yes** REPLACE the degas bottle. TEST the system for normal operation. → **No** PERFORM the cooling system pressure test; REPAIR as necessary. TEST the system for normal operation.

FM1089900305040X

Fig. 58 Test A: Loss Of Coolant (Part 4 of 4). 1999-2002 Crown Victoria & Grand Marquis

TEST CONDITIONS	TEST DETAILS/RESULTS/ACTIONS
B2 CHECK THE COOLANT CONDITION	
	1 Check the coolant for contaminants such as rust, corrosion, or discoloration. • Is the coolant condition OK? → **Yes** GO to **B3**. → **No** FLUSH the engine cooling system; TEST the system for normal operation.
B3 CHECK FOR AN AIRFLOW OBSTRUCTION	
	1 Inspect the A/C condenser core and radiator for obstructions such as leaves or dirt. • Is there an obstruction? → **Yes** REMOVE the obstruction. CLEAN the A/C condenser core and radiator. TEST the system for normal operation. → **No** GO to **B4**.
B4 CHECK THE HEATER CORE OPERATION	
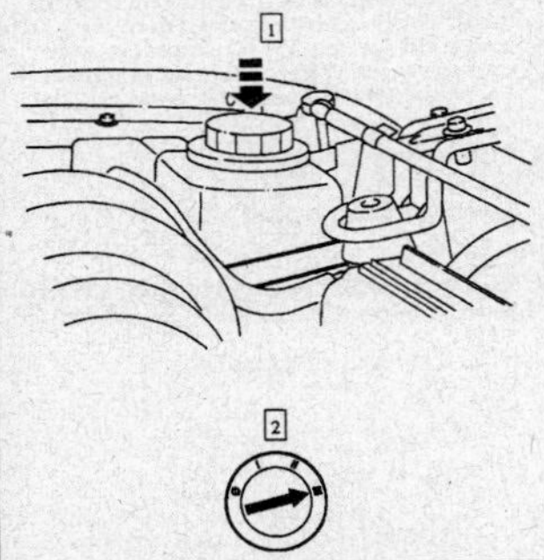 1 2	1 Install the pressure relief cap.

FM1089900306020X

Fig. 59 Test B: Engine Overheats (Part 2 of 3). 1999-2002 Crown Victoria & Grand Marquis

TEST CONDITIONS	TEST DETAILS/RESULTS/ACTIONS
B1 CHECK THE ENGINE COOLANT LEVEL	
NOTE: If the engine is hot, allow the engine to cool before proceeding.	
 1	1 **WARNING: Never remove the pressure relief cap under any conditions while the engine is operating. Failure to follow these instructions could result in damage to the cooling system or engine and/or personal injury. To avoid having scalding hot coolant or steam blow out of the cooling system, use extreme care when removing the pressure relief cap from a hot degas bottle. Wait until the engine has cooled, then wrap a thick cloth around the pressure relief cap and turn it slowly one turn (counterclockwise). Step back while the pressure is released from the cooling system. When certain all the pressure has been released, remove the pressure relief cap (still with a cloth).** 2 Check the engine coolant level at the degas bottle. • Is the engine coolant OK? → **Yes** GO to **B2**. → **No** REFILL the engine coolant at the degas bottle. GO to Pinpoint Test A.

FM1089900306010X

Fig. 59 Test B: Engine Overheats (Part 1 of 3). 1999-2002 Crown Victoria & Grand Marquis

TEST CONDITIONS	TEST DETAILS/RESULTS/ACTIONS
B4 CHECK THE HEATER CORE OPERATION (Continued)	
	3 As the engine starts to heat up, feel the inlet and outlet heater water hoses. They should feel approximately the same after three or four minutes. • Is the heater water hose approximately the same temperature as the inlet heater water hose? → **Yes** GO to **B5**. → **No** TURN the engine off. REPAIR or REPLACE heater core. TEST the system for normal operation.
B5 CHECK THE WATER THERMOSTAT OPERATION	
 1	1 Start the engine and allow the engine to run for ten minutes. 2 Feel the inlet and outlet heater water hoses and the underside of the upper radiator hose. • Are the upper radiator hose and the heater water hoses cold? → **Yes** REPLACE the water thermostat. TEST the system for normal operation. → **No** GO to **B6**.
B6 CHECK THE COOLING FAN OPERATION	
 1	1 Perform the cooling fan component tests; refer to the Component Tests in this section. • Is the cooling fan operation OK? → **Yes** GO to diagnosis and testing of the engine. → **No** REPLACE the fan component determined; TEST the system for normal operation.

FM1089900306030X

Fig. 59 Test B: Engine Overheats (Part 3 of 3). 1999-2002 Crown Victoria & Grand Marquis

TEST CONDITIONS	TEST DETAILS/RESULTS/ACTIONS
C1 CHECK THE ENGINE TEMPERATURE	
1	1 Start the engine and allow the engine to idle for ten minutes.
2	2 Feel the inlet and heater water hoses and the underside of the upper radiator hose. • Are the upper radiator hose and the heater water hoses cold? → **Yes** REPLACE the water thermostat; TEST the system for normal operation. → **No** GO to diagnosis and testing of the engine coolant temperature gauge.

FM1089900307000X

Fig. 60 Test C: Engine Does Not Reach Normal Operating Temperature. 1999-2002 Crown Victoria & Grand Marquis

Condition	Possible Source	Action
• Loss of Coolant	• Hoses and hose connections. • Radiator. • Water pump. • Heater core. • Gaskets. • Engine casting cracks. • Engine block core plugs.	• GO to Pinpoint Test A.
• Engine Overheats	• Engine coolant weak, contaminated or low. • Thermostat. • Fuse. • Constant control relay module. • Circuit. • Fan motor. • Engine coolant temperature sensor. • Powertrain control module.	• GO to Pinpoint Test B.
• Engine Does Not Reach Normal Operating Temperature	• Thermostat.	• REPLACE the thermostat.
• Engine Block Heater Does Not Operate Properly	• Power cord. • Engine block heater.	• REPLACE the power cord. • REPLACE the engine block heater.
• Engine Cooling Fan Operates Continuously	• Constant control relay module. • Circuit. • Powertrain control module.	• Diagnose circuit as necessary.
• Engine Cooling Fan Low Speed Inoperative	• Constant control relay module. • Circuit. • Powertrain control module. • Fan motor.	• Diagnose circuit as necessary.
• Engine Cooling Fan High Speed Inoperative	• Constant control relay module. • Circuit. • Powertrain control module. • Fan motor.	• Diagnose circuit as necessary.

FM1089600130000A

Fig. 62 Symptom Chart. Escort, Tracer & ZX2

TEST CONDITIONS	TEST DETAILS/RESULTS/ACTIONS
B1 CHECK COOLANT	
	1 Inspect the coolant level and quality. • Is the coolant OK? → **Yes** GO to **B2**. → **No** If coolant is weak or contaminated, FLUSH and REPLACE as necessary. If the coolant is low, REFILL the system and PERFORM the Pressure Test.

FM1089600132010X

Fig. 64 Test B: Engine Overheats (Part 1 of 2). 1998–2000 Escort, Tracer & ZX2

TEST CONDITIONS	TEST DETAILS/RESULTS/ACTIONS
D1 CHECK THE POWER CABLE	
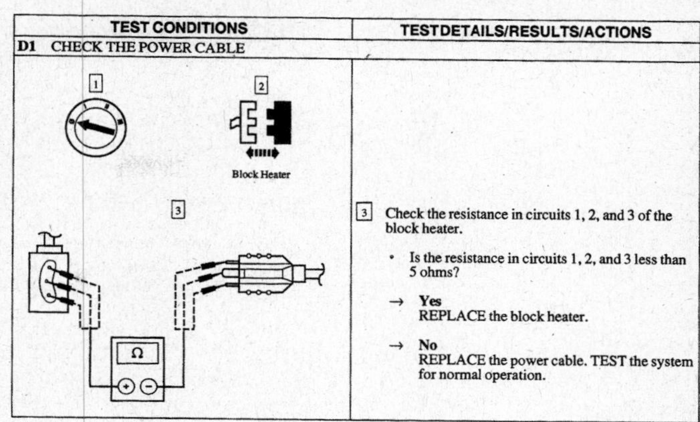	3 Check the resistance in circuits 1, 2, and 3 of the block heater. • Is the resistance in circuits 1, 2, and 3 less than 5 ohms? → **Yes** REPLACE the block heater. → **No** REPLACE the power cable. TEST the system for normal operation.

FM1089900308000X

Fig. 61 Test D: Block Heater Does Not Operate Properly. 1999-2002 Crown Victoria & Grand Marquis

TEST CONDITIONS	TEST DETAILS/RESULTS/ACTIONS
A1 VISUAL INSPECTION	
1	2 Visually inspect for evidence of coolant leakage. • Is (are) there any visible coolant leak(s)? → **Yes** REPAIR the component(s) in question. REFER to the appropriate section. → **No** PERFORM the Pressure Test.

FM1089600131000X

Fig. 63 Test A: Loss Of Coolant. 1998–2000 Escort, Tracer & ZX2

TEST CONDITIONS	TEST DETAILS/RESULTS/ACTIONS
B2 CHECK THERMOSTAT	
	1 Perform the thermostat operation component test • Is the thermostat OK? → **Yes** → **No** REPLACE the thermostat.

FM1089600132020X

Fig. 64 Test B: Engine Overheats (Part 2 of 2). 1998–2000 Escort, Tracer & ZX2

TEST CONDITIONS	TEST DETAILS/RESULTS/ACTIONS
C1 CHECK ENGINE TEMPERATURE	
1	1 **Test Thermostat** • Is the thermostat OK? → **Yes** REFER to the Symptom Chart in this section. → **No** REPLACE the water thermostat. TEST for normal operation.

FM1089700175000X

Fig. 65 Test C: Engine Does Not Reach Normal Operating Temperature. 1998–2000 Escort, Tracer & ZX2

TEST CONDITIONS	TEST DETAILS/RESULTS/ACTIONS
D1 CHECK POWER CABLE	
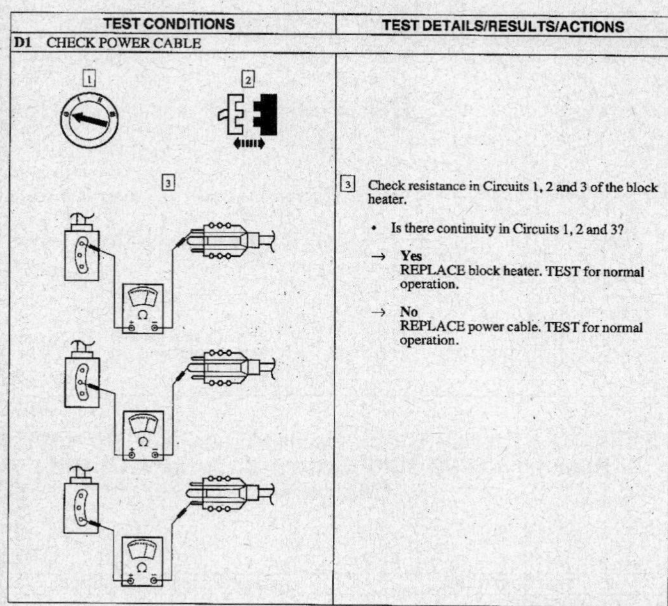	3 Check resistance in Circuits 1, 2 and 3 of the block heater. • Is there continuity in Circuits 1, 2 and 3? → Yes REPLACE block heater. TEST for normal operation. → No REPLACE power cable. TEST for normal operation.

FM1089700176000X

Fig. 66 Test D: Block Heater Does Not Operate Properly. 1998–2000 Escort, Tracer & ZX2

A2 TEST THE DEGAS BOTTLE PRESSURE RELIEF CAP

1 **WARNING:**
To avoid personal injury, do not unscrew the coolant pressure relief cap while the engine is operating or hot. The cooling system is under pressure; steam and hot liquid can release forcefully when the cap is loosened slightly.

Allow the engine to cool.

2 Remove the pressure relief cap.

3 Inspect the pressure relief cap for foreign material between the sealing gasket and the diaphragm.

- **Is the pressure relief cap OK?**

→ **Yes**

REFER to Component Tests Pressure Test.

→ **No**

CLEAN or INSTALL a new pressure relief cap. TEST the system for normal operation. Go to «A3».

FM1080000268020X

Fig. 67 Test A: Loss Of Coolant (Part 2 of 6). 2001–02 Escort

A4 CHECK THE ENGINE FOR COOLANT

1 Remove the oil level indicators from the engine.

- **Is coolant evident in the oil?**

→ **Yes**

If coolant is in the engine, diagnose engine cooling.

→ **No**

Go to «A5».

FM1080000268040X

Fig. 67 Test A: Loss Of Coolant (Part 4 of 6). 2001–02 Escort

A1 VISUAL INSPECTION

WARNING:
To avoid personal injury, do not unscrew the coolant pressure relief cap while the engine is operating or hot. The cooling system is under pressure; steam and hot liquid can release forcefully when the cap is loosened slightly.

1

2 Visually inspect for evidence of coolant leakage.

- **Is (are) there any visible coolant leak(s)?**

→ **Yes**

REPAIR the component(s) in question.

→ **No**

Go to «A2».

FM1080000268010X

Fig. 67 Test A: Loss Of Coolant (Part 1 of 6). 2001–02 Escort

A3 CHECK THE ENGINE COOLANT FOR INTERNAL LEAK

WARNING:
To avoid personal injury, do not unscrew the coolant pressure relief cap while the engine is operating or hot. The cooling system is under pressure; steam and hot liquid can release forcefully when the cap is loosened slightly.

1

2 Inspect the engine coolant in the degas bottle for signs of engine oil.

- **Is oil evident in the coolant?**

→ **Yes**

If engine oil is evident, diagnose engine cooling.

→ **No**

Go to «A4».

FM1080000268030X

Fig. 67 Test A: Loss Of Coolant (Part 3 of 6). 2001–02 Escort

A5 CHECK THE DEGAS BOTTLE

WARNING:
To avoid personal injury, do not unscrew the coolant pressure relief cap while the engine is operating or hot. The cooling system is under pressure; steam and hot liquid can release forcefully when the cap is loosened slightly.

1 **Note:**
The engine must be cool when coolant is added to the degas bottle.

Add coolant to the degas bottle until fluid is between the coolant fill level marks.

- **Does the degas bottle leak?**

→ **Yes**

INSTALL a new degas bottle. TEST the system for normal operation.

→ **No**

Go to «A6».

FM1080000268050X

Fig. 67 Test A: Loss Of Coolant (Part 5 of 6). 2001–02 Escort

A6 PRESSURE TEST THE ENGINE COOLING SYSTEM

1 Pressure test the engine cooling system.

- **Does the engine cooling system leak?**

➔ **Yes**

REPAIR or INSTALL new components. TEST the system for normal operation.

➔ **No**

The cooling system is operational. RETURN to the Symptom Chart.

FM1080000268060X

Fig. 67 Test A: Loss Of Coolant (Part 6 of 6). 2001–02 Escort

B2 CHECK THE COOLANT CONDITION

1 Check the coolant for dirt, rust or contamination.

- **Is the coolant condition OK?**

➔ **Yes**

Go to «B3».

➔ **No**

FLUSH the engine cooling system.
TEST the system for normal operation.

FM1080000269020X

Fig. 68 Test B: Engine Overheats (Part 2 of 4). 2001–02 Escort

B4 CHECK THERMOSTAT

1 Carry out the thermostat mechanical component test

- **Is the thermostat OK?**

➔ **Yes**

REFER to the Symptom Chart and diagnose engine cooling.

➔ **No**

INSTALL a new thermostat.

FM1080000269040X

Fig. 68 Test B: Engine Overheats (Part 4 of 4). 2001–02 Escort

Condition	Possible Sources	Action
•Loss of coolant	•Hoses. •Hose connections. •Radiator. •Water pump. •Coolant expansion tank. •Heater core. •Gaskets. •Engine casting cracks. •Engine block core plugs.	•GO to Pinpoint Test A.
•The engine overheats	•Engine coolant loss. •Towingweight exceeded. •System restriction. •Blocked radiator grille. •Thermostat. •Fuse. •Circuit. •Fan motor. •Water pump. •Accessory drive belt. •Cylinder head temperature (CHT) sensor. •Powertrain control module (PCM).	•GO to Pinpoint Test B.

FM1080000271010X

Fig. 70 Symptom Chart (Part 1 of 2). Focus

B1 CHECK COOLANT

⚠ **WARNING:**
Never remove the pressure relief cap while the engine is operating or when the cooling system is hot. Failure to follow these instructions can result in damage to the cooling system or engine or personal injury. To avoid having scalding hot coolant or steam blow out of the degas bottle when removing the pressure relief cap, wait until the engine has cooled, then wrap a thick cloth around the pressure relief cap and turn it slowly. Step back while the pressure is released from the cooling system. When you are sure all the pressure has been released (still with a cloth) turn and remove the pressure relief cap.

1 Inspect the coolant level and quality.

- **Is the coolant OK?**

➔ **Yes**

Go to «B2».

➔ **No**

If coolant is weak or contaminated, FLUSH and REPLACE as necessary.

If the coolant is low, REFILL the system and PERFORM the Pressure Test.

FM1080000269010X

Fig. 68 Test B: Engine Overheats (Part 1 of 4). 2001–02 Escort

B3 CHECK FOR AN AIRFLOW OBSTRUCTION

1 Inspect the A/C condenser core and radiator for obstructions such as leaves and dirt.

- **Is there an obstruction?**

➔ **Yes**

REMOVE the obstruction. CLEAN the A/C condenser core and radiator. TEST the system for normal operation.

➔ **No**

Go to «B4».

FM1080000269030X

Fig. 68 Test B: Engine Overheats (Part 3 of 4). 2001–02 Escort

C1 CHECK ENGINE TEMPERATURE

1

Carry out the Thermostat Mechanical and Electrical Component Test

- **Is the thermostat OK?**

➔ **Yes**

REFER to the Symptom Chart in this section.

➔ **No**

INSTALL a new water thermostat. TEST for normal operation.

FM1080000270000X

Fig. 69 Test C: Engine Does Not Reach Normal Operating Temperature. 2001–02 Escort

Condition	Possible Sources	Action
•The engine does not reach normal operating temperature	•Thermostat. •Electric fans.	•GO to Pinpoint Test C.

FM1080000271020X

Fig. 70 Symptom Chart (Part 2 of 2). Focus

CONDITIONS	DETAILS/RESULTS/ACTIONS
A1: CHECK FOR COOLANT LEAKS	
	1 Visually inspect for loss of coolant. • Is the engine cooling system leaking? → Yes REPAIR the components in question. → No CARRY OUT the Pressure Test.

FM1080000272000X

Fig. 71 Test A: Loss Of Coolant. Focus

CONDITIONS	DETAILS/RESULTS/ACTIONS
B2: CHECK THERMOSTAT	
	1 Carry out the component test • Is the thermostat OK? → Yes Diagnose cooling system. → No INSTALL a new thermostat.

FM1080000273020X

Fig. 72 Test B: Engine Overheats (Part 2 of 2). Focus

Condition	Possible Source	Action
• Loss of coolant	• Radiator. • Water pump seal. • Radiator hoses. • Heater hoses. • Heater core. • Engine gaskets. • Degas bottle or coolant expansion tank.	• GO to Pinpoint Test A.
• The engine overheats	• Water thermostat. • Water pump. • Internal engine coolant leak. • Radiator. • Heater core. • Cooling fan. • Pressure relief cap or radiator cap.	• GO to Pinpoint Test B.
• The engine does not reach normal operating temperature	• Water thermostat.	• GO to Pinpoint Test C.
• The block heater does not operate correctly	• Block heater power cable. • Block heater.	• GO to Pinpoint Test D.

FM1089900203000X

Fig. 74 Symptom Chart. 1999–2001 Mustang

TEST CONDITIONS	TESTDETAILS/RESULTS/ACTIONS
A1 CHECK THE ENGINE COOLANT LEVEL	
Note: Allow the engine to cool before checking the engine coolant level.	
1	2 Visually check the engine coolant level at the degas bottle or coolant expansion tank. • Is the engine coolant level within specification? → Yes GO to **A2**. → No REFILL the engine coolant as necessary. GO to **A6**.

FM1089900204010X

Fig. 75 Test A: Loss Of Coolant (Part 1 of 4). 1999–2002 Mustang

CONDITIONS	DETAILS/RESULTS/ACTIONS
B1: CHECK COOLANT	
WARNING: Never remove the expansion tank cap under any circumstances while the engine is operating. Failure to follow these instructions may result in damage to the cooling system of the engine and may cause personal injury. To avoid having scalding hot water or steam blow out of the cooling system, use extreme care when removing the expansion tank cap from a hot cooling system. Wait until the engine has returned to outside air temperature, then wrap a thick cloth around the expansion tank cap and turn it slowly until the pressure begins to release, step back while the pressure is released from the cooling system. When certain all the pressure has been released (still with a cloth) turn and remove the expansion tank cap. Failure to follow these instructions may result in personal injury.	
	1 Inspect the coolant level and condition. • Is the coolant OK? → Yes GO TO **B2** → No If coolant is weak or contaminated, FLUSH and REFILL with new coolant as necessary. If the coolant is low, REFILL the system and CARRY OUT the Component Test.

FM1080000273010X

Fig. 72 Test B: Engine Overheats (Part 1 of 2). Focus

CONDITIONS	DETAILS/RESULTS/ACTIONS
C1: CHECK THERMOSTAT	
	1 Carry out the component test in this section. • Is the thermostat OK? → Yes Diagnose cooling system. → No INSTALL a new thermostat.

FM1080000274000X

Fig. 73 Test C: Engine Does Not Reach Normal Operating Temperature. Focus

TEST CONDITIONS	TESTDETAILS/RESULTS/ACTIONS
A2 CHECK THE PRESSURE RELIEF CAP	
	1 Carry out the Cap—3.8L or Cap—4.6L test. • Is pressure relief cap/radiator cap OK? → Yes GO to **A3**. → No INSTALL a new pressure relief cap/radiator cap. TEST the system for normal operation.
A3 CHECK THE ENGINE COOLANT FOR INTERNAL LEAK	
1	2 Inspect the engine coolant in degas bottle/coolant expansion tank for signs of transmission fluid or engine oil. • Is oil or transmission fluid evident in the coolant? → Yes If engine oil is evident If transmission fluid is evident, REPAIR or INSTALL a new radiator as necessary. → No GO to **A4**.
A4 CHECK THE ENGINE AND THE TRANSMISSION FOR COOLANT	
	1 Remove the oil level dipstick from the engine and the transmission. • Is coolant evident in the oil or transmission fluid? → Yes If coolant is in engine If coolant is in transmission, REPAIR or INSTALL a new radiator as necessary. → No GO to **A5**.

FM1089900204020X

Fig. 75 Test A: Loss Of Coolant (Part 2 of 4). 1999–2002 Mustang

TEST CONDITIONS	TEST DETAILS/RESULTS/ACTIONS
A5 PRESSURE TEST THE ENGINE COOLING SYSTEM	
	[1] Pressure test the engine cooling system; go to Component Tests in this section. • Does the engine cooling system leak? → **Yes** REPAIR or install new components. TEST the system for normal operation. → **No** The cooling system is operational. RETURN to the Symptom Chart.
A6 CHECK THE COOLANT RECOVERY SYSTEM	
	[1] **WARNING: Never remove the pressure relief cap/radiator cap under any conditions while the engine is operating. Failure to follow these instructions could result in damage to the cooling system or engine and/or personal injury. To avoid having scalding hot coolant or steam blow out of the cooling system, use extreme care when removing the pressure relief cap from a hot degas bottle or the radiator cap from the radiator. Wait until the engine has cooled, then wrap a thick cloth around the pressure relief cap and turn it slowly one turn (counterclockwise) or with a thick cloth around the radiator cap turn the radiator cap (counterclockwise) slowly to the first pressure stop, step back while the pressure is released from the cooling system. When certain all the pressure has been released, remove the pressure relief cap/radiator cap (still with a cloth).** Allow the engine to cool. [2] Remove the pressure relief cap/radiator cap. [3] Inspect the pressure relief cap/radiator cap for foreign material between the sealing gasket and the diaphragm. • Is the pressure relief cap/radiator cap OK? → **Yes** GO to **A7**. → **No** CLEAN the pressure relief cap/radiator cap or INSTALL a new cap. TEST the system for normal operation. GO to **A1**.

FM1089900204030X

Fig. 75 Test A: Loss Of Coolant (Part 3 of 4). 1999–2002 Mustang

TEST CONDITIONS	TEST DETAILS/RESULTS/ACTIONS
B1 CHECK THE ENGINE COOLANT LEVEL	
Note: If the engine is hot, allow the engine to cool before proceeding.	
[1] 	[1] **WARNING: Never remove the pressure relief cap/radiator cap under any conditions while the engine is operating. Failure to follow these instructions could result in damage to the cooling system or engine and/or personal injury. To avoid having scalding hot coolant or steam blow out of the cooling system, use extreme care when removing the pressure relief cap from a hot degas bottle or the radiator cap from the radiator. Wait until the engine has cooled, then wrap a thick cloth around the pressure relief cap and turn it slowly one turn (counterclockwise) or with a thick cloth around the radiator cap turn the radiator cap (counterclockwise) slowly to the first pressure stop. Step back while the pressure is released from the cooling system. When certain all the pressure has been released, remove the pressure relief cap/radiator cap (still with a cloth).** [2] Check the engine coolant level at the degas bottle/coolant expansion tank. • Is the engine coolant OK? → **Yes** GO to **B2**. → **No** REFILL the engine coolant at the degas bottle/coolant expansion tank. GO to Pinpoint Test A.
B2 CHECK THE COOLANT CONDITION	
	[1] Check the coolant for contaminants such as rust, corrosion, or discoloration. • Is the coolant condition OK? → **Yes** GO to **B3**. → **No** FLUSH the engine cooling system; TEST the system for normal operation.

FM1089900205010X

Fig. 76 Test B: Engine Overheats (Part 1 of 3). 1999–2002 Mustang

TEST CONDITIONS	TEST DETAILS/RESULTS/ACTIONS
A7 CHECK THE DEGAS BOTTLE/COOLANT EXPANSION TANK	
	[1] **Note:** The engine must be cool when coolant is added to the degas bottle/coolant expansion tank. Add coolant to the degas bottle/coolant expansion tank until the fluid is between the coolant fill level marks. • Does the degas bottle/coolant expansion tank leak? → **Yes** INSTALL a new degas bottle/coolant expansion tank. TEST the system for normal operation. → **No** CARRY out the cooling system pressure test; REPAIR as necessary. TEST the system for normal operation.

FM1089900204040X

Fig. 75 Test A: Loss Of Coolant (Part 4 of 4). 1999–2002 Mustang

TEST CONDITIONS	TEST DETAILS/RESULTS/ACTIONS
B3 CHECK FOR AN AIRFLOW OBSTRUCTION	
	[1] Inspect the A/C condenser core and radiator for obstructions such as leaves or dirt. • Is there an obstruction? → **Yes** REMOVE the obstruction. CLEAN the A/C condenser core and radiator. TEST the system for normal operation. → **No** GO to **B4**.
B4 CHECK THE HEATER CORE OPERATION	
[2] 	[1] Install the pressure relief cap/radiator cap. [3] As the engine starts to heat up, feel the inlet and outlet heater water hoses. They should feel approximately the same after three or four minutes. • Is the outlet heater water hose approximately the same temperature as the inlet heater water hose? → **Yes** GO to **B5**. → **No** TURN the engine off. REPAIR or INSTALL a new heater core. TEST the system for normal operation.
B5 CHECK THE WATER THERMOSTAT OPERATION	
[1] 	[1] Start the engine and allow the engine to run for ten minutes.

FM1089900205020X

Fig. 76 Test B: Engine Overheats (Part 2 of 3). 1999–2002 Mustang

TEST CONDITIONS	TEST DETAILS/RESULTS/ACTIONS
B5 CHECK THE WATER THERMOSTAT OPERATION (Continued)	
	2 Feel the inlet and outlet heater water hoses and the underside of the upper radiator hose. • Are the upper radiator hose and the heater water hoses cold? → **Yes** INSTALL a new water thermostat; TEST the system for normal operation. → **No** GO to **B6**.
B6 CHECK THE COOLING FAN OPERATION	
1	1 Carry out the cooling fan component tests; go to Component Tests. • Is the cooling fan operation OK? → **Yes** TEST the system for normal operation. → **No** INSTALL a new fan component determined; TEST the system for normal operation.

FM1089900205030X

Fig. 76 Test B: Engine Overheats (Part 3 of 3). 1999–2002 Mustang

TEST CONDITIONS	TEST DETAILS/RESULTS/ACTIONS
D1 CHECK THE POWER CABLE	
1 2 Block Heater	
3	3 Check the resistance in circuits 1, 2, and 3 of the block heater. • Is the resistance in circuits 1, 2, and 3 less than 5 ohms? → **Yes** INSTALL a new block heater. → **No** INSTALL a new power cable. TEST the system for normal operation.

FM1089900207000X

Fig. 78 Test D: Block Heater Does Not Operate Correctly. 1999–2002 Mustang

TEST CONDITIONS	TEST DETAILS/RESULTS/ACTIONS
C1 CHECK THE ENGINE TEMPERATURE	
1	1 Start the engine and allow the engine to idle for ten minutes.

FM1089900206010X

Fig. 77 Test C: Engine Does Not Reach Normal Operating Temperature (Part 1 of 2). 1999–2002 Mustang

TEST CONDITIONS	TEST DETAILS/RESULTS/ACTIONS
C1 CHECK THE ENGINE TEMPERATURE (Continued)	
2	2 Feel the inlet and heater water hoses and the underside of the upper radiator hose. • Are the upper radiator hose and the heater water hoses cold? → **Yes** INSTALL a new water thermostat; TEST the system for normal operation. → **No** For diagnosis and testing of the engine coolant temperature gauge

FM1089900206020X

Fig. 77 Test C: Engine Does Not Reach Normal Operating Temperature (Part 2 of 2). 1999–2002 Mustang

Condition	Possible Source	Action
• Loss of Coolant	• Damaged radiator. • Damaged water pump. • Loose / damaged radiator hoses. • Loose / damaged heater water hoses. • Loose / damaged degas bottle supply hose (engine and radiator). • Loose / damaged coolant reservoir pressure relief cap. • Damaged heater core. • Damaged engine gaskets / O-rings. • Damaged / incorrectly installed thermostat O-ring. • Damaged cylinder head. • Damaged cylinder block.	• GO to Pinpoint Test A.
• Engine Overheats	• Low coolant level. • Incorrect coolant mixture. • Loose / damaged degas bottle pressure relief cap. • Damaged water thermostat. • Damaged water pump. • Internal engine coolant leak. • Cooling fan inoperative. • Plugged radiator. • Plugged heater core. • Collapsed lower radiator hose. • Plugged internal engine coolant passage.	• GO to Pinpoint Test B.
• Engine Does Not Reach Normal Operating Temperature	• Damaged water thermostat. • Cooling fan. • Low engine coolant.	• Diagnose circuit as necessary.
• Engine Block Heater Does Not Operate Properly	• Block heater power cable. • Block heater.	• GO to Pinpoint Test C.
• Cooling Fan Runs Continuously	• Circuit. • Constant control relay module (CCRM). • Powertrain control module. • Engine coolant temperature sensor.	• Diagnose circuit as necessary.
• Cooling Fan Runs, No Low Speed	• Circuit. • Constant control relay module (CCRM). • Fan dropping resistor damaged. • Powertrain control module. • Cooling fan motor.	• Diagnose circuit as necessary.
• Cooling Fan Runs, No High Speed	• Circuit. • Constant control relay module (CCRM). • Powertrain control module. • Cooling fan motor.	• Diagnose circuit as necessary.

FM1089600152000X

Fig. 79 Symptom Chart. 1998–99 Sable & Taurus

Test Step		Result ▶	Action to Take
A1	CHECK ENGINE COOLANT LEVEL		
	NOTE: If engine is hot, allow engine to cool down before proceeding. • Check engine coolant level at degas bottle. • **Is engine coolant level OK?**	Yes ▶ No ▶	GO to **A2**. REFILL. GO to **A7**.

FM1089600153010X

Fig. 80 Test A: Loss Of Coolant (Part 1 of 2). 1998–99 Sable & Taurus

	Test Step	Result	Action to Take
A2	CHECK FOR VISIBLE LEAKAGE		
	• Engine coolant has an added dye color that makes the coolant an excellent leak detector. • Check entire cooling system for visible leakage. • **Is there visible leakage?**	Yes No	SERVICE. RETEST system. GO to **A3**.
A3	CHECK PRESSURE RELIEF CAP		
	• Using Rotunda Radiator/Heater Core Pressure Tester 014-R1072 or equivalent, test pressure relief cap. • **Did pressure relief cap test OK?**	Yes No	GO to **A4**. REPLACE damaged radiator cap. RETEST system.
A4	CHECK COOLANT FOR INTERNAL LEAKAGE		
	• Inspect coolant in degas bottle for signs of transmission fluid or engine oil. • **Is oil evident in coolant?**	Yes No	Locate & Repair source of contamination. GO to **A5**.
A5	CHECK ENGINE AND TRANSAXLE FOR COOLANT		
	• Remove oil level dipstick from engine and transaxle. • Carefully inspect oil level dipstick for evidence of coolant. • **Is coolant evident?**	Yes No	Locate & Repair source of contamination. GO to **A6**.
A6	PRESSURE TEST COOLING SYSTEM		
	• Using Rotunda Radiator/Heater Core Pressure Tester 014-R1072 or equivalent, pressurize cooling system. • Check for any signs of visible leakage. NOTE: Check inside vehicle for possible heater core leakage. • **Is there leakage?**	Yes No	RETEST system. Cooling system is operational at this time. RETEST system.
A7	CHECK COOLANT RECOVERY		
	• Allow engine to cool. Remove pressure relief cap, inspect cap for foreign material between sealing gasket and diaphragm. • **Is cap OK?**	Yes No	GO to **A8**. SERVICE.
A8	CHECK RADIATOR OVERFLOW HOSE		
	• Remove radiator overflow hose. • Inspect hose for obstructions, cracks or cuts. • **Is hose condition OK?**	Yes No	GO to **A9**. SERVICE radiator overflow hose as required.
A9	CHECK RESERVOIR		
	• Replenish coolant in degas bottle to top of cold fill range. • Inspect reservoir for leaks. • **Is there leakage at reservoir?**	Yes No	REPLACE degas bottle. REFER to Pressure Test. SERVICE as required.

FM1089600153020X

Fig. 80 Test A: Loss Of Coolant (Part 2 of 2). 1998–99 Sable & Taurus

	Test Step	Result	Action to Take
C1	CHECK POWER CABLE OPEN		
	• Check resistance of Circuits 1, 2 and 3 in power cable using Rotunda 73 Digital Multimeter 105-R0051 or equivalent. • **Is resistance less than 5 ohms?**	Yes No	GO to **C2**. REPLACE power cable. RETEST system.

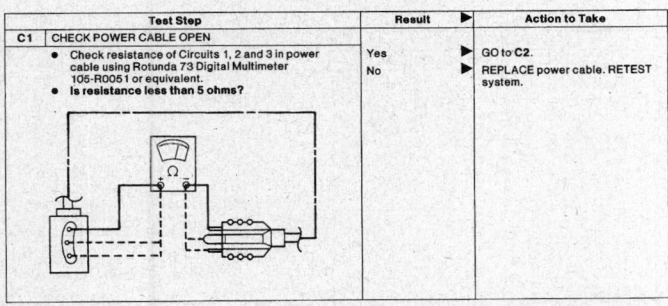

FM1089600155010X

Fig. 82 Test C: Block Heater Does Not Operate Properly (Part 1 of 2). 1998–99 Sable & Taurus

Condition	Possible Source	Action
• Loss of engine coolant	• Radiator. • Thermostat housing assembly. • Heater control valve. • Oil cooler. • PCV heater system. • Throttle body adapter heating. • Water pump seal. • Radiator hoses. • Heater hoses. • Heater core. • Engine gaskets. • Degas bottle.	• GO to Pinpoint Test A.

FM1080000275010X

Fig. 83 Symptom Chart (Part 1 of 2). 2000–02 Sable & Taurus

Condition	Possible Source	Action
• The engine overheats	• Water thermostat. • Airlock in the system. • Water pump. • Internal engine coolant leak. • Radiator. • Radiator airflow obstruction. • Heater core. • Cooling fan. • Pressure relief cap.	• GO to Pinpoint Test B.
• The engine does not reach normal operating temperature	• Water thermostat.	• GO to Pinpoint Test C.
• The block heater does not operate correctly	• Block heater power cable. • Block heater.	• GO to Pinpoint Test D.

FM1080000275020X

Fig. 83 Symptom Chart (Part 2 of 2). 2000–02 Sable & Taurus

	Test Step	Result	Action to Take
B1	CHECK ENGINE COOLANT LEVEL		
	NOTE: If engine is hot, allow engine to cool down before proceeding. • Remove pressure relief cap and check engine coolant level at pressure relief cap and degas bottle. • **Is engine coolant level OK?**	Yes No	GO to **B2**. REFILL as described. GO to Pinpoint Test A.

FM1089600154010X

Fig. 81 Test B: Engine Overheats (Part 1 of 2). 1998–99 Sable & Taurus

	Test Step	Result	Action to Take
B2	CHECK COOLANT CONDITION		
	• Check coolant for contaminants such as rust or corrosion. Also check for fluid discoloration. • Check coolant concentration for proper 50/50 mixture. • **Is coolant condition OK?**	Yes No	GO to **B3**. FLUSH system RETEST system.
B3	CHECK FOR AIR FLOW OBSTRUCTION		
	• Inspect A/C condenser core and radiator for obstructions such as leaves or bugs. • **Is there any obstruction?**	Yes No	REMOVE obstruction and CLEAN A/C condenser core and radiator RETEST system. GO to **B4**.
B4	CHECK HEATER CORE OPERATION		
	• Install pressure relief cap. • Start engine and allow to run. • As engine starts to warm up, feel the inlet and outlet heater water hoses. They should feel the same after three or four minutes. • **Is outlet heater water hose the same temperature as the inlet heater water hose?**	Yes No	GO to **B5**. TURN engine OFF before it overheats. SERVICE heater core. RETEST system.
B5	CHECK WATER THERMOSTAT OPERATION		
	• Allow engine to run for 10 minutes. • Feel the inlet and outlet heater water hoses and the underside of the upper radiator hose. • **Are the upper radiator hose and heater water hoses cold?**	Yes No	REPLACE water thermostat RETEST system. LEAVE engine RUNNING. GO to **B6**.
B6	CHECK COOLING FAN		
	• Check temperature gauge at instrument cluster. Allow engine to RUN until high side of normal range is attained. • Check for cooling fan operation. • **Did cooling fan operate OK?**	Yes No	Diagnose engine operation. Diagnose circuit as necessary.

FM1089600154020X

Fig. 81 Test B: Engine Overheats (Part 2 of 2). 1998–99 Sable & Taurus

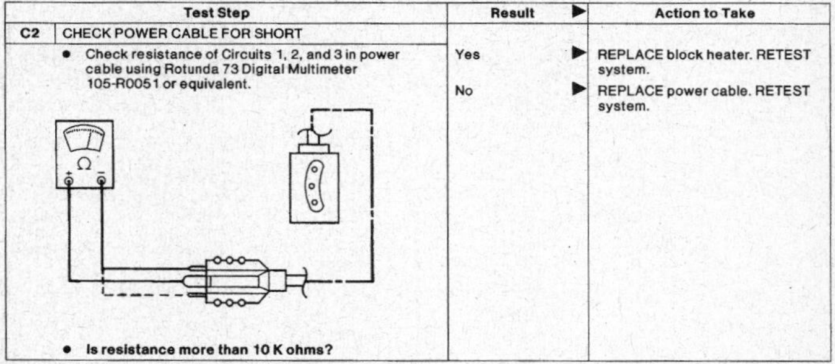

	Test Step	Result	Action to Take
C2	CHECK POWER CABLE FOR SHORT		
	• Check resistance of Circuits 1, 2, and 3 in power cable using Rotunda 73 Digital Multimeter 105-R0051 or equivalent. • **Is resistance more than 10 K ohms?**	Yes No	REPLACE block heater. RETEST system. REPLACE power cable. RETEST system.

FM1089600155020X

Fig. 82 Test C: Block Heater Does Not Operate Properly (Part 2 of 2). 1998–99 Sable & Taurus

TEST CONDITIONS	TEST DETAILS/RESULTS/ACTIONS
A1 CHECK THE ENGINE COOLANT LEVEL	
Note: Allow the engine to cool before checking the engine coolant level.	
1	2 Visually check the engine coolant level at the degas bottle. • Is the engine coolant level within specification? → **Yes** GO to **A2**. → **No** REFILL the engine coolant as necessary. GO to **A6**.

FM1080000276010X

Fig. 84 Test A: Loss Of Coolant (Part 1 of 3). 2000–02 Sable & Taurus

TEST CONDITIONS	TEST DETAILS/RESULTS/ACTIONS
A2 TEST THE DEGAS BOTTLE PRESSURE RELIEF CAP	
	1 ⚠ **WARNING: To avoid personal injury, do not unscrew the coolant pressure relief cap while the engine is on or hot. The cooling system is under pressure; steam and hot liquid can come out forcefully when the cap is loosened slightly.** Allow the engine to cool.
	2 Remove the pressure relief cap.
	3 Inspect the pressure relief cap for foreign material between the sealing gasket and the diaphragm. • Is the pressure relief cap OK? → **Yes** REFER to Component Tests Pressure Test. → **No** CLEAN or INSTALL a new pressure relief cap. TEST the system for normal operation. GO to **A1**.
A3 CHECK THE ENGINE COOLANT FOR INTERNAL LEAK	
1 	
	2 Inspect the engine coolant in the degas bottle for signs of engine oil. • Is oil evident in the coolant? → **Yes** If engine oil is evident, diagnose engine. → **No** GO to **A4**.

FM1080000276020X

Fig. 84 Test A: Loss Of Coolant (Part 2 of 3). 2000–02 Sable & Taurus

TEST CONDITIONS	TEST DETAILS/RESULTS/ACTIONS
A4 CHECK THE ENGINE FOR COOLANT	
	1 Remove the oil level dipsticks from the engine. • Is coolant evident in the oil? → **Yes** If coolant is in the engine, diagnose engine. → **No** GO to **A5**.
A5 PRESSURE TEST THE ENGINE COOLING SYSTEM	
	1 Pressure test the engine cooling system. • Does the engine cooling system leak? → **Yes** REPAIR or INSTALL new components. TEST the system for normal operation. → **No** The cooling system is operational. RETURN to the Symptom Chart.
A6 CHECK THE DEGAS BOTTLE	
	1 **Note:** The engine must be cool when coolant is added to the degas bottle. Add coolant to the degas bottle until fluid is between the coolant fill level marks. • Does the degas bottle leak? → **Yes** INSTALL a new degas bottle. TEST the system for normal operation. → **No** Carry out the cooling system pressure test. REFER to the Component Tests REPAIR as necessary. TEST the system for normal operation.

FM1080000276030X

Fig. 84 Test A: Loss Of Coolant (Part 3 of 3). 2000–02 Sable & Taurus

TEST CONDITIONS	TEST DETAILS/RESULTS/ACTIONS
B1 CHECK THE ENGINE COOLANT LEVEL	
Note: If the engine is hot, allow the engine to cool before proceeding.	
1 	1 ⚠ **WARNING: To avoid personal injury, do not unscrew the coolant pressure relief cap while the engine is operating or hot. The cooling system is under pressure; steam and hot liquid can come out forcefully when the cap is loosened slightly.** Check the engine coolant level at the degas bottle. • Is the engine coolant OK? → **Yes** GO to **B2**. → **No** REFILL the engine coolant at the degas bottle. GO to Pinpoint Test A.
B2 CHECK THE COOLANT CONDITION	
	1 Check the coolant for contaminants such as rust, corrosion, or discoloration. • Is the coolant condition OK? → **Yes** GO to **B3**. → **No** FLUSH the engine cooling system. TEST the system for normal operation.
B3 CHECK FOR AN AIRFLOW OBSTRUCTION	
	1 Inspect the A/C condenser core and radiator for obstructions such as leaves or dirt. • Is there an obstruction? → **Yes** REMOVE the obstruction. CLEAN the A/C condenser core and radiator. TEST the system for normal operation. → **No** GO to **B4**.

FM1080000277010X

Fig. 85 Test B: Engine Overheats (Part 1 of 3). 2000–02 Sable & Taurus

TEST CONDITIONS	TEST DETAILS/RESULTS/ACTIONS
B4 CHECK THE HEATER CORE OPERATION	
1 	1 Start the engine.
	2 As the engine starts to heat up, feel the inlet and outlet heater water hoses. They should feel approximately the same after three or four minutes. • Is the outlet heater water hose approximately the same temperature as the inlet heater water hose? → **Yes** GO to **B5**. → **No** TURN the engine off. REPAIR or INSTALL a new heater core. TEST the system for normal operation.
B5 CHECK THE WATER THERMOSTAT OPERATION	
1 	1 Start the engine and allow the engine to run for 10 minutes.
2 	2 Turn the engine off.
	3 Feel the upper and lower radiator hose. • Are the upper and lower radiator hoses cold? → **Yes** CARRY OUT thermostat component tests. → **No** GO to **B6**.

FM1080000277020X

Fig. 85 Test B: Engine Overheats (Part 2 of 3). 2000–02 Sable & Taurus

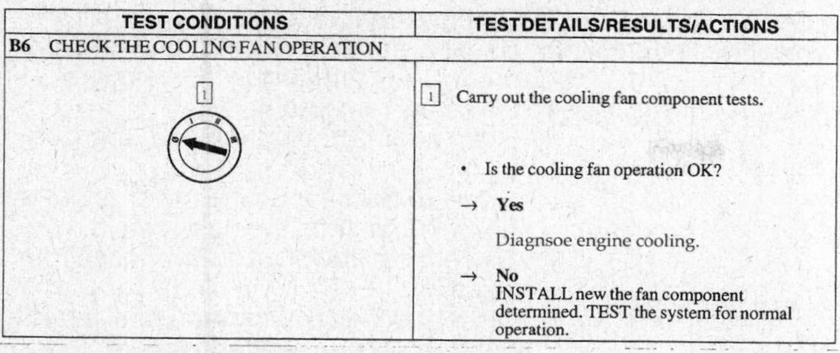

TEST CONDITIONS	TESTDETAILS/RESULTS/ACTIONS
B6 CHECK THE COOLING FAN OPERATION	
1	1 Carry out the cooling fan component tests. • Is the cooling fan operation OK? → Yes Diagnsoe engine cooling. → No INSTALL new the fan component determined. TEST the system for normal operation.

FM1080000277030X

Fig. 85 Test B: Engine Overheats (Part 3 of 3). 2000–02 Sable & Taurus

TEST CONDITIONS	TESTDETAILS/RESULTS/ACTIONS
C1 CHECK THE ENGINE TEMPERATURE	
1	1 Start the engine and allow the engine to idle for 10 minutes.
2	2 Feel the upper and lower radiator hoses. • Are the upper and lower radiator hoses cold? → Yes CARRY OUT thermostat component tests. → No INSPECT engine coolant temperature gauge.

FM1080000278000X

Fig. 86 Test C: Engine Does Not Reach Normal Operating Temperature. 2000–02 Sable & Taurus

TEST CONDITIONS	TESTDETAILS/RESULTS/ACTIONS
D1 CHECK THE POWER CABLE	
1 2 Block Heater	

FM1080000279010X

Fig. 87 Test D: Block Heater Does Not Operate Correctly (Part 1 of 2). 2000–02 Sable & Taurus

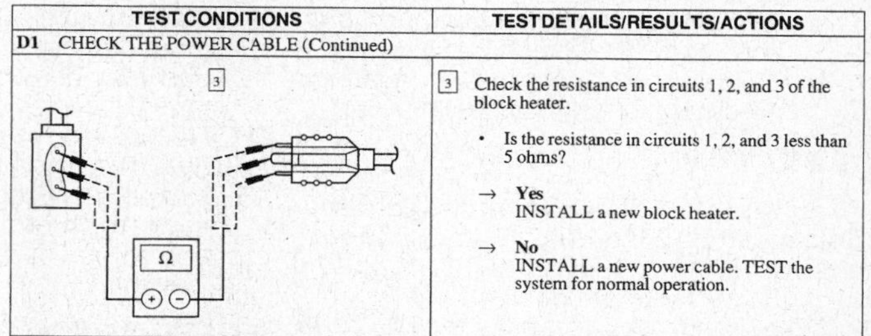

TEST CONDITIONS	TESTDETAILS/RESULTS/ACTIONS
D1 CHECK THE POWER CABLE (Continued)	
3	3 Check the resistance in circuits 1, 2, and 3 of the block heater. • Is the resistance in circuits 1, 2, and 3 less than 5 ohms? → Yes INSTALL a new block heater. → No INSTALL a new power cable. TEST the system for normal operation.

FM1080000279020X

Fig. 87 Test D: Block Heater Does Not Operate Correctly (Part 2 of 2). 2000–02 Sable & Taurus

COMPONENT REPLACEMENT

CCRM/IRCM

CONTINENTAL

Refer to "Cooling Fan Motor."

MUSTANG

1. **On models equipped with 3.8L engine,** remove right inner fender splash shield.
2. **On all models,** disconnect CCRM and remove CCRM mounting nuts.
3. Reverse procedure to install, noting the following:
   a. **On models equipped with 3.8L engine, torque** CCRM mounting nuts to 12–17 inch lbs.
   b. **On models equipped with 4.6L engine, torque** CCRM mounting nuts to 36 inch lbs.

SABLE & TAURUS

1. Disconnect engine control sensor wiring from module connector
2. Release clips and module from battery tray.
3. Reverse procedure to install. **Torque** engine control sensor connector to 12–18 inch lbs.

COOLING FAN RELAY

CONTOUR & MYSTIQUE

1. Locate fan control relay in engine compartment power distribution box, then remove relay.
2. Reverse procedure to install.

COOLING FAN MOTOR

CONTINENTAL

1. Remove radiators as described under "Radiator, Replace."
2. Remove fan shroud mounting bolts, cooling fan motor/blade/shroud assembly.
3. Remove fan blade mounting clips and blades.
4. Remove motor mounting screws and motors.
5. If necessary, remove Constant Control Relay Module (CCRM).
6. Reverse procedure to install. **Torque** CCRM mounting screws to 40–56 inch lbs. and shroud mounting bolts to 24–48 ft. lbs.

CONTOUR & MYSTIQUE

1998

1. Disconnect wiring connectors and mounting clips.
2. Remove cooling fan ground cable from RH front fender apron.
3. Remove shroud screws and position for access to fan motor.
4. Remove cooling fan motor.
5. Reverse procedure to install.

1999–2000 w/2.0L Engine

1. Remove battery, then raise and support vehicle.
2. Remove lower radiator splash shield.
3. Remove air conditioning accumulator bolts and place to one side.
4. Disconnect fan resistor connector.
5. Lower vehicle.
6. Disconnect fan motor connectors and remove wiring harness from fan shroud.
7. Remove motors, fans, and shroud assembly.
8. Reverse procedure to install.

1999–2000 w/2.5L Engine

1. Drain cooling system into a suitable container.
2. Remove steel coolant pipe connecting bottom hose to water pump hose.
3. Disconnect hoses and remove pipe.
4. Raise and support vehicle.
5. Disconnect fan resistor and motor connectors.
6. Remove fan wiring harness from fan shroud.
7. Remove motor, fan and shroud assembly.
8. Reverse procedure to install.

COUGAR

2.0L Engine

1. Raise and support vehicle.
2. Remove lower radiator splash shield.
3. Disconnect fan motor connector.
4. Disconnect fan resistor connector and wiring harness.
5. Remove air conditioning accumulator bolts and place to one side.
6. Lower vehicle.
7. Disconnect air conditioning compressor connector.
8. Disconnect heated oxygen sensor connector and wiring harness.
9. Disconnect air conditioning tube from mounting bracket.
10. Remove fan shroud nut, then the fan shroud.
11. Reverse procedure to install.

2.5L Engine

1. Drain coolant into suitable container.
2. Remove radiator.
3. Raise and support vehicle.
4. Disconnect cooling fan connector and wiring harness.
5. Disconnect all remaining electrical connectors and remaining harnesses.

6. Remove fan assembly.
7. Reverse procedure to install.

CROWN VICTORIA, GRAND MARQUIS & TOWN CAR

1998

1. Disconnect cooling fan motor wiring connector.
2. Remove fan shroud.
3. Remove radiator upper sight shield.
4. Loosen fan shroud from radiator mounting and remove lower radiator hose from supports on fan shroud.
5. Lift shroud out of vehicle.
6. Remove cooling fan motor assembly from fan shroud.
7. Reverse procedure to install noting following:
   a. **Torque** cooling fan motor mounting screws to 27–53 inch lbs.
   b. **Torque** fan shroud mounting screws to 24–48 inch lbs.

1999–2002

Caution: Do not mix standard (green) coolant with Extended Life (orange) coolant.

1. Drain coolant from degas bottle.
2. Disconnect degas bottle supply and overflow hoses.
3. Remove mounting bolt, then the degas bottle.
4. Disconnect fan motor connector.
5. Remove two bolts, then the fan blade, fan motor and fan shroud assembly.
6. Reverse procedure to install.

ESCORT, TRACER & ZX2

Fan motor, blade and shroud are not serviced separately.

1. Remove air cleaner outlet tube.
2. Disconnect fan motor electrical connector, then upstream heated oxygen sensor electrical connector.
3. Remove shroud bolts, then fan blade and shroud as assembly.
4. Reverse procedure to install.

FOCUS

1. Disconnect cooling fan electrical connectors, then two pin type retainers.
2. Raise and support vehicle.
3. Remove cooling fan motor, then fan shroud.
4. Reverse procedure to install.

MARK VIII

1. Loosen fan shroud from radiator, then remove lower hose from shroud.
2. Lift fan motor assembly and shroud out from vehicle, then disconnect fan motor electrical connector.
3. Remove mounting bolts, then separate fan from shroud.
4. Reverse procedure to install.

MUSTANG

1998

1. Remove fan wiring harness from routing clips.
2. Disconnect wiring harness from fan motor connector (pull up on single lock finger to separate connector).
3. Remove shroud mounting screws, then the fan assembly.
4. Remove mounting clip from end of motor shaft, then the fan. A small metal burr may be present on motor after mounting clip is removed. Removal of burr may be necessary prior to fan removal.
5. Remove fan motor to shroud mounting nuts, then the fan motor.
6. Reverse procedure to install. **Torque** motor to shroud nuts to 48–62 inch lbs. and shroud to radiator screws to 72–96 inch lbs.

1999–2002

1. Remove degas bottle or coolant expansion tank.
2. Disconnect electrical connector and separate fan harness from shroud.
3. Remove mounting bolts, fan, motor and shroud.
4. Reverse procedure to install. **Torque** mounting bolts to 89 inch lbs.

SABLE & TAURUS

1998

1. Disconnect cooling fan motor wiring connector.
2. Remove cooling fan motor from shroud.
3. Reverse procedure to install. **Torque** fan mounting bolts to 71–106 inch lbs.

1999

Do not mix Standard (green) Coolant with Extended Life Coolant (orange). If mixing occurs, drain engine cooling system and refill with originally equipped coolant type. If this contamination occurs, the service change interval on Extended Life Coolant will be reduced from 6 years/150,000 miles to 3 years/30,000 miles.

1. Remove engine air cleaner assembly.
2. Remove battery and battery tray.
3. Using a suitable AC recovery station, recover AC refrigerant from system.
4. Raise and support vehicle.
5. Drain engine coolant into suitable container.
6. Remove bolts mounting lower radiator hose shield, then the hose shield.
7. Disconnect lower radiator hose from radiator.
8. Disconnect A/C evaporator muffler and hoses from A/C condenser core.
9. Disconnect lower transmission oil cooler tube from radiator using tool No. No. 310-S039 (3/8 inch fuel line disconnect tool), or equivalent.
10. Remove screws from the lower transmission oil cooler tube and allow transmission oil cooler tube to hang.
11. Remove both transmission oil cooler tubes from left end of power steering/ transmission oil cooler.
12. Remove lower radiator mounts.
13. Lower vehicle.
14. Remove four bolts hood latch support and position hood latch support aside.
15. Remove front bumper cover.
16. Remove upper radiator support.
17. Disconnect radiator overflow hose from radiator.
18. Remove power distribution box and harness and bracket and position power distribution box and harness aside.
19. Disconnect fan motor from engine control sensor wiring.
20. Remove six screws mounting engine control sensor wiring and position engine control sensor wiring aside.
21. Disconnect power steering fluid cooler from power steering pump.
22. Support fan blade and fan shroud assembly.
23. Remove bolts from cooling fan motor, fan blade and fan shroud assembly brackets to sub-frame.
24. Lift cooling fan motor, fan blade and fan shroud assembly out of vehicle.
25. Reverse procedure to install.

2000–02

1. Drain engine coolant into a suitable container.
2. Remove distribution box, then set aside and disconnect cooling fan electrical connectors.
3. Remove retainers, then cooling fan.
4. Reverse procedure to install.

Hydraulic Cooling Fans

NOTE: On Air Bag Equipped Models, Refer To "Air Bag System Precautions" Located In The Front Of This Manual For System Disarming & Arming Procedures.

NOTE: Refer To "Computer Relearn Procedures" Located In The Front Of This Manual When Battery Power To The Computer Has Been Interrupted.

INDEX

PRECAUTIONS

AIR BAG SYSTEMS

Refer to "Air Bag System Precautions" in the front of this manual for system disarming and arming procedures.

BATTERY GROUND CABLE

Prior to service, disconnect battery ground cable and isolate as required.

DESCRIPTION

The hydraulic cooling fan is controlled by the Powertrain Control Module (PCM) via the hydraulic fan solenoid. The fan motor operates only when the engine is running.

The cooling fan operates at 2200–2400 RPM. Operating pressure is 900 psi, with a maximum pressure of 1200 psi. The fans operating flow rate is 3.75–4.25 gallons per minute.

SYSTEM DIAGNOSIS & TESTING

The hydraulic cooling fan system is controlled by the Powertrain Control Module. Refer to **MOTOR's "Domestic Engine Performance & Driveability Manual"** for powertrain control diagnostic procedures and testing.

Perform visual inspection prior to performing any diagnosis and testing procedures. Inspect the following:

1. Leaks.
2. Restricted airflow through condenser/radiator.
3. Damaged hoses.
4. Loose/damaged hose clamps.
5. Damaged water gasket.
6. Damaged head gaskets.
7. Damaged water pump.
8. Damaged radiator.
9. Damaged degas bottle.
10. Damaged heater core.
11. Hydraulic cooling fan system:
    a. Fluid level.
    b. Hydraulic line or joint leaks.
    c. Kinked hydraulic lines.
12. Damaged cylinder head temperature sensor.
13. Damaged wiring.
14. Hydraulic cooling fan pump solenoid/solenoid wiring.

WIRING DIAGRAMS

Refer to **Fig. 1** for wiring diagram.

DIAGNOSTIC TESTS

Refer to **Fig. 2** for symptom chart and to **Figs. 3 through 6** for diagnostic charts.

COMPONENT REPLACEMENT

COOLING FAN MOTOR

1. Drain engine cooling system into suitable container.
2. Remove upper radiator sight shield.
3. Remove air cleaner outlet tube.
4. Remove mounting bolts and radiator support brackets, **Fig. 7.**
5. Remove upper radiator hose.
6. Remove mounting bolt and position receiver drier out of way.
7. **On models equipped with 3.9L engine,** remove mounting bolt and position electric water pump out of way, **Fig. 8.**
8. **On all models,** disconnect high pressure cooling fan line, **Fig. 9.**
9. Disconnect return hose, **Fig. 10.**
10. Separate return hose from fan shroud and position out of way, **Fig. 11.**
11. Remove mounting bolts and fan shroud assembly, **Fig. 12.**
12. Support A/C condenser with suitable mechanics wire.
13. Raise and support vehicle.
14. Remove mounting screws, then right and lefthand splash shields.
15. Remove radiator air deflector.
16. Disconnect lower radiator hose.
17. Remove radiator condenser mounting bolts.
18. Remove mounting bolts and condenser support brackets.
19. Remove radiator from vehicle bottom.
20. Reverse procedure to install, noting the following:
    a. **Torque** radiator condenser mounting bolts to 89 inch lbs.
    b. **Torque** lower radiator hose clamp to 10 ft. lbs.
    c. **Torque** cooling fan high pressure line mounting bolt to 15 ft. lbs.
    d. **Torque** cooling fan high pressure line bracket mounting bolt to 71 inch lbs.
    e. **Torque** electric water pump mounting bolt to 89 inch lbs.
    f. **Torque** receiver drier mounting bolt 96 inch lbs.
    g. **Torque** upper radiator support mounting bolts to 89 inch lbs.

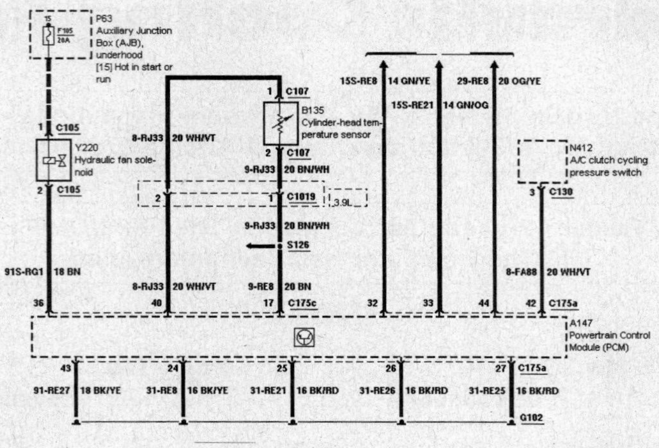

Fig. 1 Wiring diagram. LS

Condition	Possible Source	Action
Loss Of Engine Coolant	Auxiliary Water Pump (3.9L Engine Only)	Go To Pinpoint Test A
	Degas Bottle	
	Engine Gaskets	
	Heater Control Valve	
	Heater Core	
	Heater Hoses	
	Oil Cooler	
	PCV Heater System	
	Radiator	
	Radiator Hoses	
	Thermostat Housing Assembly	
	Throttle Body Adapter Heating (3.9L Engine)	
	Water Pump Seal	
Engine Overheats	Airlock In The System	Go To Pinpoint Test B
	Cooling Fan	
	Heater Core	
	Internal Engine Coolant Leak	
	Pressure Relief Cap	
	Radiator	
	Radiator Airflow Obstruction	
	Water Pump	
	Water Thermostat	
Engine Does Not Reach Normal Operating Temperature	Water Thermostat	Go To Pinpoint Test C
Block Heater Does Not Operate Correctly	Block Heater	Go To Pinpoint Test D
	Block Heater Power Cable	
Noisy Cooling Fan Operation	Blocked Reservoir Screen	Refill Fluid To Specified Level. Install A New Line. Check For Leaks & Retest. Retest & Check For Leaks.
	Hydraulic Motor	
	Hydraulic Pump	
	Incorrect Fluid Level	
	Kinked Or Leaking Line	

Fig. 2 Symptom Chart

A1	CHECK THE ENGINE COOLANT LEVEL

Note:
Allow the engine to cool before checking the engine coolant level.

1

2 Visually check the engine coolant level at the degas bottle.

- **Is the engine coolant level within specification?**

→ **Yes**

Go to «A2».

→ **No**

REFILL the engine coolant as necessary. Go to «A6».

FM1089900209010X

Fig. 3 Test A: Loss Of Coolant (Part 1 of 6)

A2	DEGAS BOTTLE PRESSURE RELIEF CAP

1 **⚠ WARNING:**
Never remove the pressure relief cap under any conditions while the engine is operating. Failure to follow these instructions could result in damage to the cooling system or engine and/or personal injury. To avoid having scalding hot coolant or steam blow out of the cooling system, use extreme care when removing the pressure relief cap from a hot degas bottle. Wait until the engine has cooled, then wrap a thick cloth around the pressure relief cap and turn it slowly one turn (counterclockwise). Step back while the pressure is released from the cooling system. When certain all the pressure has been released, remove the pressure relief cap (still with a cloth).

Allow the engine to cool.

2 Remove the pressure relief cap.

3 Inspect the pressure relief cap for foreign material between the sealing gasket and the diaphragm.

- **Is the pressure relief cap OK?**

→ **Yes**

REFER to Component Tests.

→ **No**

CLEAN or INSTALL a new pressure relief cap. TEST the system for normal operation. Go to «A1».

FM1089900209020X

Fig. 3 Test A: Loss Of Coolant (Part 2 of 6)

A3	CHECK THE ENGINE COOLANT FOR INTERNAL LEAK

1

2 Inspect the engine coolant in the degas bottle for signs of engine oil.

- **Is oil evident in the coolant?**

→ **Yes**

If engine oil is evident, inspect engine.

→ **No**

Go to «A4».

FM1089900209030X

Fig. 3 Test A: Loss Of Coolant (Part 3 of 6)

A4	CHECK THE ENGINE FOR COOLANT

1 Remove the oil level indicator from the engine.

- **Is coolant evident in the oil?**

→ **Yes**

If coolant is in the engine, inspect engine.

→ **No**

Go to «A5».

FM1089900209040X

Fig. 3 Test A: Loss Of Coolant (Part 4 of 6)

A5	PRESSURE TEST THE ENGINE COOLING SYSTEM

1 Pressure test the engine cooling system

- **Does the engine cooling system leak?**

→ **Yes**

REPAIR or INSTALL new components. TEST the system for normal operation.

→ **No**

The cooling system is operational. RETURN to the Symptom Chart.

FM1089900209050X

Fig. 3 Test A: Loss Of Coolant (Part 5 of 6)

A6	CHECK THE DEGAS BOTTLE

1 **Note:**
The engine must be cool when coolant is added to the degas bottle.

Add coolant to the degas bottle until fluid is between the coolant fill level marks.

- **Does the degas bottle leak?**

→ **Yes**

INSTALL a new degas bottle. TEST the system for normal operation.

→ **No**

CARRY OUT the cooling system pressure test.
REPAIR as necessary. TEST the system for normal operation.

FM1089900209060X

Fig. 3 Test A: Loss Of Coolant (Part 6 of 6)

B1 CHECK THE ENGINE COOLANT LEVEL

Note:
If the engine is hot, allow the engine to cool before proceeding.

1

⚠ **WARNING:**
Never remove the pressure relief cap under any conditions while the engine is operating. Failure to follow these instructions could result in damage to the cooling system or engine and/or personal injury. To avoid having scalding hot coolant or steam blow out of the cooling system, use extreme care when removing the pressure relief cap from a hot degas bottle. Wait until the engine has cooled, then wrap a thick cloth around the pressure relief cap and turn it slowly one turn (counterclockwise). Step back while the pressure is released from the cooling system. When certain all the pressure has been released, remove the pressure relief cap (still with a cloth).

2 Check the engine coolant level at the degas bottle.

- **Is the engine coolant OK?**

→ **Yes**

Go to «B2».

→ **No**

REFILL the engine coolant at the degas bottle. GO to «Pinpoint Test A».

FM1089900210010X

Fig. 4 Test B: Engine Overheats (Part 1 of 6)

B3 CHECK FOR AN AIRFLOW OBSTRUCTION

1 Inspect the A/C condenser core and radiator for obstructions such as leaves or dirt.

- **Is there an obstruction?**

→ **Yes**

REMOVE the obstruction. CLEAN the A/C condenser core and radiator. TEST the system for normal operation.

→ **No**

Go to «B4».

FM1089900210030X

Fig. 4 Test B: Engine Overheats (Part 3 of 6)

B5 CHECK THE WATER THERMOSTAT OPERATION

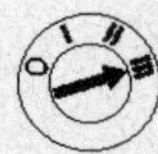

1

Start the engine and allow the engine to run for 10 minutes.

2

3 Feel the upper and lower radiator hoses.

- **Are the upper and lower radiator hoses cold?**

→ **Yes**

INSTALL a new water thermostat. TEST the system for normal operation.

→ **No**

Go to «B6».

FM1089900210050X

Fig. 4 Test B: Engine Overheats (Part 5 of 6)

B2 CHECK THE COOLANT CONDITION

1 Check the coolant for contaminants such as rust, corrosion, or discoloration.

- **Is the coolant condition OK?**

→ **Yes**

Go to «B3».

→ **No**

FLUSH the engine cooling system.
TEST the system for normal operation.

FM1089900210020X

Fig. 4 Test B: Engine Overheats (Part 2 of 6)

B4 CHECK THE HEATER CORE OPERATION

1 Install the pressure relief cap.

2

3 As the engine starts to heat up, feel the inlet and outlet heater water hoses. They should feel approximately the same after three or four minutes.

- **Is the outlet heater water hose approximately the same temperature as the inlet heater water hose?**

→ **Yes**

Go to «B5».

→ **No**

TURN the engine off. REPAIR or INSTALL a new heater core.
TEST the system for normal operation.

FM1089900210040X

Fig. 4 Test B: Engine Overheats (Part 4 of 6)

B6 CHECK THE COOLING FAN OPERATION

1

Carry out the cooling fan component tests

- **Is the cooling fan operation OK?**

→ **Yes**

Refer to MOTOR's "DOMESTIC ENGINE PERFORMANCE & DRIVEABILITY MANUAL."

→ **No**

INSTALL a new fan component as necessary. TEST the system for normal operation.

FM1089900210060X

Fig. 4 Test B: Engine Overheats (Part 6 of 6)

C1	CHECK THE ENGINE TEMPERATURE

1

Start the engine and allow the engine to idle for 10 minutes.

2

Feel the upper and lower radiator hoses.

- **Are the upper and lower radiator hoses cold?**

→ **Yes**

INSTALL a new water thermostat. TEST the system for normal operation.

→ **No**

Diagnose and test the engine coolant temperature gauge.

FM1089900211000X

Fig. 5 Test C: Check Engine Temperature

D1	CHECK THE POWER CABLE

1

2 *Block Heater*

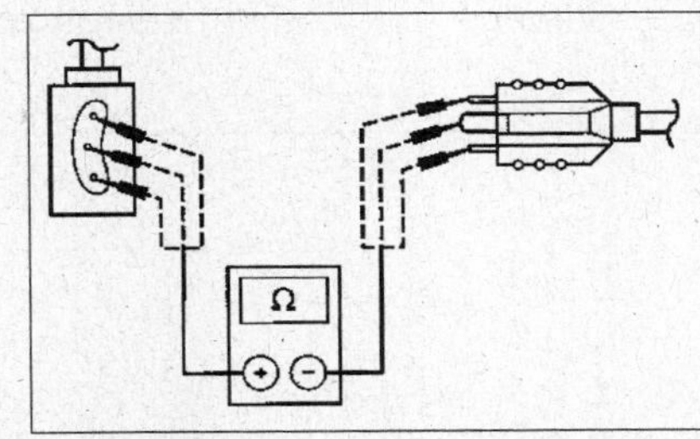

3

Check the resistance in circuits 1, 2, and 3 of the block heater.

- **Are the resistances in circuits 1, 2, and 3 less than 5 ohms?**

→ **Yes**

INSTALL a new block heater. TEST the system for normal operation.

→ **No**

INSTALL a new power cable. TEST the system for normal operation.

FM1089900212000X

Fig. 6 Test D: Check Power Cable

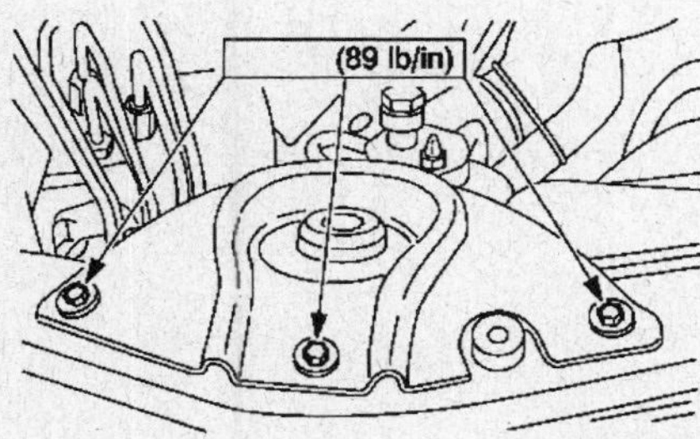

FM1089900213000X

Fig. 7 Radiator support brackets replacement. LS & Thunderbird

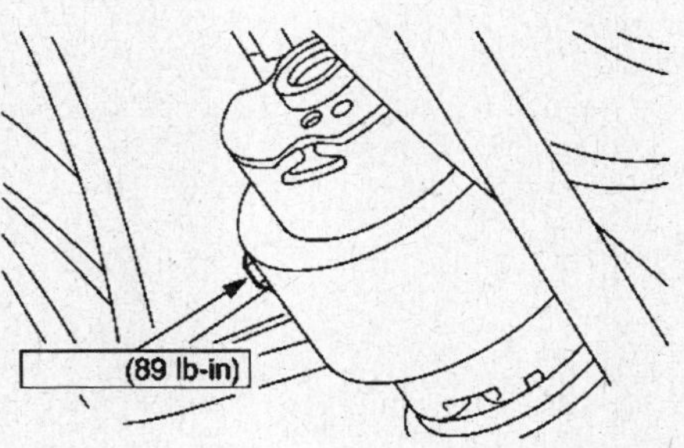

FM1089900214000X

Fig. 8 Electric water pump replacement. LS equipped w/3.9L engine & Thunderbird

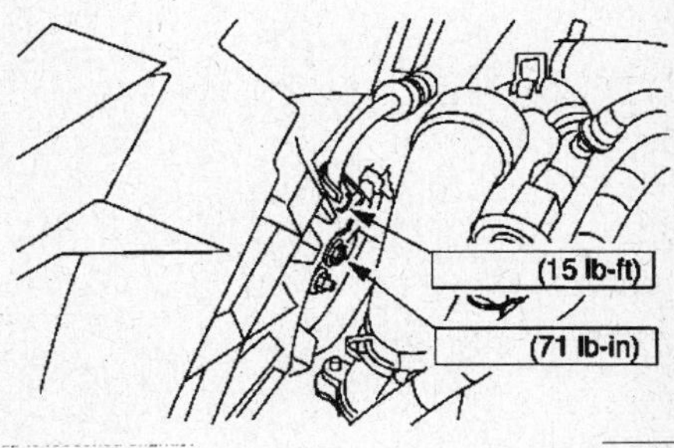

FM1089900215000X

Fig. 9 Cooling fan high pressure line replacement. LS & Thunderbird

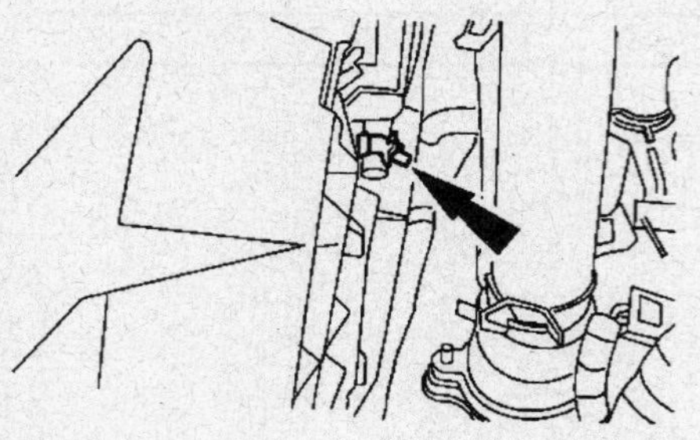

Fig. 10 Return line replacement. LS & Thunderbird

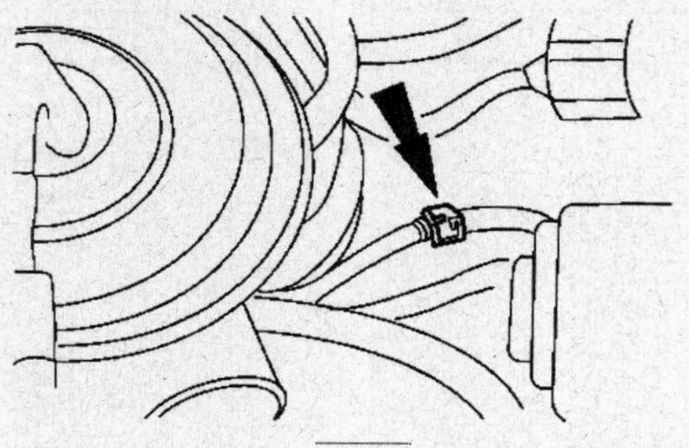

Fig. 11 Fan shroud return line separation. LS & Thunderbird

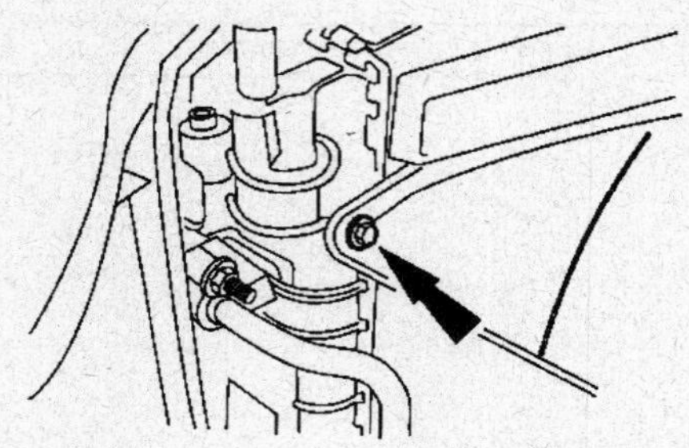

Fig. 12 Fan shroud mounting bolts replacement. LS & Thunderbird

STARTER MOTORS
Ford Motorcraft Starters

NOTE: On Air Bag Equipped Models, Refer To "Air Bag System Precautions" Located In The Front Of This Manual For System Disarming & Arming Procedures.

NOTE: Refer To "Computer Relearn Procedures" Located In The Front Of This Manual When Battery Power To The Computer Has Been Interrupted.

NOTE: "Electrical Symbol & Wire Color Code Identification" Located In The Front Of This Manual May Be Used As An Aid When Using Wiring Circuits Found In This Section.

INDEX

APPLICATION CHART

Model	Year
Continental	1998–2002
Contour	1998–2000
Cougar	1999–2002
Crown Victoria	1998–2002
Escort	1998–2002
Focus	2000–02
Grand Marquis	1998–2002
LS	2000–02
Mark VIII	1998
Mustang	1998–2002
Mystique	1998–2000
Sable	1998–2002
Taurus	1998–2002
Thunderbird	2002
Town Car	1998–2002
Tracer	1998–1999
ZX2	1998–2000

GENERAL INFORMATION

SOLENOID SWITCHES

The solenoid switch on a cranking motor not only closes the circuit between the battery and the cranking motor but also shifts the drive pinion into mesh with the engine flywheel ring gear. This is done by means of a linkage between the solenoid switch plunger and the shift lever on the cranking motor.

There are two windings in the solenoid; a pull-in winding and a hold-in winding. Both windings are energized when the external control switch is closed. They produce a magnetic field which pulls the plunger in so that the drive pinion is shifted into mesh, and the main contacts in the solenoid switch are closed to connect the battery directly to the cranking motor. Closing the main switch contacts shorts out the pull-in winding since this winding is connected across the main contacts. The magnetism produced by the hold-in winding is sufficient to hold the plunger in, and shorting out the pull-in winding reduces drain on the battery. When the control switch is opened, it disconnects the hold-in winding from the battery. When the hold-in winding is disconnected from the battery, the shift lever spring withdraws the plunger from the solenoid, opening the solenoid switch contacts and at the same time withdrawing the drive pinion from mesh. Proper operation of the switch depends on maintaining a definite balance between the magnetic strength of the pull-in and hold-in windings.

This balance is established in the design by the size of the wire and the number of turns specified. An open circuit in the hold-in winding or attempts to crank with a discharged battery will cause the switch to chatter.

STARTER MOTOR SERVICE

To obtain full performance data on a starting motor or to determine the cause of abnormal operation, the starting motor should be submitted to a no-load and torque test. These tests are best performed with the starter mounted on a starter bench tester.

From a practical standpoint, however, a simple torque test may be made quickly with the starter in the car. Ensure the battery is fully charged and that the starter circuit wires and terminals are in good condition, then operate the starter to see if the engine turns over normally. If it does not, the torque developed is below standard and the starter should be removed for further checking.

DESCRIPTION

FORD MOTORCRAFT STARTER w/PERMANENT MAGNET & GEAR REDUCTION

This type of starter motor, **Fig. 1,** has the starter solenoid mounted on the starter housing. The starter relay connects battery power to the starter solenoid, causing it to energize. On models equipped with manual transmission, a clutch switch in the starter control circuit prevents operation unless the clutch pedal is depressed. On models equipped with automatic transmission, a neutral safety switch in the starter control circuit prevents operation of the starter unless the selector lever is in the Neutral or Park position.

When the starter solenoid is energized, a magnetic field is created in the solenoid windings. The plunger core is drawn to the solenoid coil and a lever connected to the drive assembly engages the drive pinion gear into the flywheel ring gear. When the plunger is all the way in, its contact disc closes the circuit between the battery and the motor feed terminals. This sends current to the motor and the drive pinion gear cranks the flywheel to start the engine. When the current flows to the engine, the solenoid pull-in coil is bypassed and the hold-in coil keeps the drive pinion gear engaged with the flywheel until the ignition switch is released from the On position.

TROUBLESHOOTING

STARTER SYSTEM DIAGNOSIS

Refer to **Figs. 2 through 19** for starter system diagnostic troubleshooting charts.

DIAGNOSIS & TESTING

Motor Feed Circuit Voltage Drop Test

1. Ensure battery is fully charged.
2. Disconnect inertia fuel shutoff switch.
3. Connect a remote starter switch between starter solenoid S terminal and battery positive.
4. Connect a suitable multi-meter positive lead to battery positive post, connect negative lead to starter M terminal, **Fig. 20.**
5. Engage remote starter switch and note voltage.
6. Reading should be approximately .5 volts.
7. If reading is .5 volts or less, refer to "Motor Ground Circuit Component Test."
8. If voltage reading is greater than .5 volts, indicating excessive resistance, move multi-meter negative lead to starter solenoid B terminal and repeat test.
9. If voltage reading at B terminal is less than .5 volt, inspect starter solenoid connections or solenoid contacts.
10. Remove cables from B, S and M terminals, clean, re-install and perform voltage drop test again.
11. If voltage drop reading is still greater than .5 volts when checked at M terminal or less than .5 volts when checked at B terminal, replace starter.
12. If voltage drop reading is still greater than .5 volts at B terminal after terminal cleaning, replace positive battery cable.

Motor Ground Circuit Voltage Drop Test

1. Disconnect inertia fuel cutoff switch.

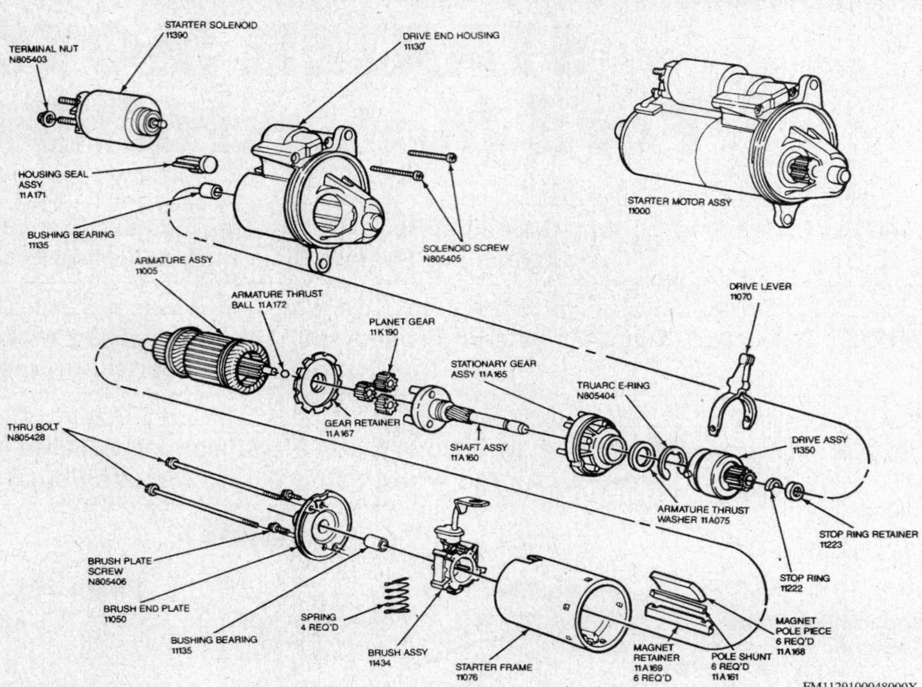

Fig. 1 Exploded view of Ford Motorcraft gear reduced permanent magnet starter motor

Condition	Possible Source	Action
• The Engine Does Not Crank or the Relay Clicks	• Battery. • Starter motor (11002). • Starter motor relay. • Ignition switch. • Damaged fuse. • Anti-theft system. • Circuitry.	• GO to Pinpoint Test A.
• The Engine Cranks Slowly	• Battery. • Starter motor. • Circuitry.	• PERFORM the Starter Motor—Voltage Drop Test
• Unusual Starter Noise	• Starter mounting. • Flywheel/ring gear. • Starter motor.	• GO to Pinpoint Test B.

FM1120100592010X

Fig. 2 Starting system troubleshooting chart (Part 1 of 2). Continental

2. Connect a remote starter switch between starter solenoid S terminal and battery positive terminal.
3. Connect suitable multi-meter positive lead to starter motor housing, connect negative lead to negative battery terminal, **Fig. 21.**
4. Engage remote starter switch and crank engine.
5. Read and record voltage reading, reading should be approximately .2 volts or less.
6. If voltage drop is more than .2 volts, clean negative cable connections at battery and body connections and retest.
7. If voltage drop is greater than .2 volts, determine which way the current is flowing in cable, then connect multimeter positive cable to end nearest battery positive.
8. Connect multi-meter negative lead to terminal at other end of cable.
9. Crank engine and note voltage reading. Voltage reading should be approximately .2 volts or lower.
10. If voltage drop is too high, clean terminal ends and perform test again.
11. If voltage drop reading is still too high, replace cable.
12. If voltage reading is less than .2 volts and engine cranks slowly, replace starter motor.

Load Test

1. Ensure battery is fully charged before performing this test.
2. Set parking brake and shift transmission into neutral.
3. Disconnect ignition coil electrical connector.
4. Connect suitable starter, alternator, battery regulator electrical tester.
5. Connect remote starter switch across starter relay S terminal and battery terminal.
6. Turn ignition key to Run position.
7. Crank engine with remote starter switch and note reading on voltmeter.
8. Stop cranking engine and turn carbon pile rheostat until voltmeter indicates same reading as obtained in previous step.
9. The ammeter will indicate starter current draw under load.
10. Compare amperage indicated with

Condition	Possible Source	Action
• The Starter Spins But The Engine Does Not Crank	• Starter motor • Damaged flywheel/ring gear teeth.	• INSPECT the starter motor mounting and engagement. REPLACE the starter motor. • INSPECT the flywheel/ring gear for damaged, missing or worn teeth. REPAIR as required.

FM1120100592020X

Fig. 2 Starting system troubleshooting chart (Part 2 of 2). Continental

Condition	Possible Sources	Action
• The Engine Does Not Crank and The Relay Clicks	• Battery. • Circuitry. • Starter motor.	• GO to Pinpoint Test A.
• The Engine Cranks Slowly	• Battery. • Circuitry. • Starter motor.	• GO to Pinpoint Test B.
• Unusual Starter Noise	• Starter motor. • Ring gear.	• GO to Pinpoint Test C.
• Starter Motor Spins but the Engine Does Not Crank	• Solenoid	• GO to Pinpoint Test D.
• The Engine Does Not Crank and PATS LED Does Not Prove Out Normally	• PATS control module. • Circuitry. • Encode ignition key.	• Diagnose PATS.

FM1120100642000X

Fig. 3 Starting system troubleshooting chart. 1998 Contour & Mystique

Condition(s):

☐ The Engine Does Not Crank and the Relay Clicks - but PATS LED Proves Out Normally.

Possible Source(s):

- Battery.
- Circuitry.
- Starter motor.

Action(s) to take:

- GO to «Pinpoint Test A».

☐ The Engine Cranks Slowly

Possible Source(s):

- Battery.
- Circuitry.
- Starter motor.

Action(s) to take:

- GO to «Pinpoint Test B».

☐ Unusual Starter Noise

Possible Source(s):

- Starter motor.
- Ring gear.

Action(s) to take:

- GO to «Pinpoint Test C».

FM1120100651010X

Fig. 4 Starting system troubleshooting chart (Part 1 of 2). 1999–2000 Contour & Mystique

☐ Starter Motor Spins but the Engine Does Not Crank

Possible Source(s):

- Solenoid

Action(s) to take:

- GO to «Pinpoint Test D».

☐ The Engine Does Not Crank and PATS LED Does Not Prove Out Normally

Possible Source(s):

- PATS control module.
- Circuitry.
- Encode ignition key.

Action(s) to take:

- Diagnose PATS System

FM1120100651020X

Fig. 4 Starting system troubleshooting chart (Part 2 of 2). 1999–2000 Contour & Mystique

specifications listed in "Starter Specifications" chart.

No Load Test

1. Remove starter motor.
2. Connect suitable battery, alternator battery regulator electrical tester to a fully charged battery and a remote starter switch to starter motor.
3. Engage remote starter switch and ensure pinion shifts to crank position and that starter motor operates smoothly.
4. While starter motor is operating, check voltmeter and ammeter readings.
5. Voltmeter should read approximately 11 volts and amperage should be no more than 70 amps.
6. If voltage is lower than specified or amperage is higher than specified, refer to "Starter Motor No Load Test Results", **Fig. 22** for corrective actions.

Diagnostic Pinpoint Test

CONTINENTAL

Refer to **Figs. 23 and 24** for starting system pinpoint tests.

CONTOUR & MYSTIQUE

1998

Refer to **Figs. 25 through 28** for starting system pinpoint tests.

1999–2000

Refer to **Figs. 29 through 32** for starting system pinpoint tests.

COUGAR

Refer to **Figs. 33 through 35** for starting system pinpoint tests.

CROWN VICTORIA & GRAND MARQUIS

1998

Refer to **Figs. 36 through 38** for starting system pinpoint tests.

1999–2002

Refer to **Figs. 39 and 40** for starting system pinpoint tests.

ESCORT, TRACER & ZX2

1998

Refer to **Figs. 41 through 44** for starting system pinpoint tests.

1999–2002

Refer to **Figs. 45 and 46** for starting system pinpoint tests.

FOCUS

Refer to **Figs. 47 through 49** for starting system pinpoint tests.

LS & THUNDERBIRD

Refer to **Figs. 50 and 51** for starting system pinpoint tests.

MARK VIII

Refer to **Figs. 52 through 55** for starting system pinpoint tests.

MUSTANG

1998

Refer to **Figs. 56 through 58** for starting system pinpoint tests.

1999–2002

Refer to **Figs. 59 and 60** for starting system pinpoint tests.

SABLE & TAURUS

1998

Refer to **Figs. 61 through 64** for starting system pinpoint tests

1999

Refer to **Figs. 65 through 68** for starting system pinpoint tests.

2000–02

Refer to **Figs. 69 and 70** for starting system pinpoint tests.

TOWN CAR

1998

Refer to **Figs. 71 and 72** for starting system pinpoint tests

1999–2002

Refer to **Figs. 73 and 74** for starting system pinpoint tests.

Condition	Possible Sources	Action
•Engine does not crank but relay clicks	•Battery. •Starter motor •Relay. •Circuit	•GO to Pinpoint Test A.
•Engine does not crank and relay does not click	•Battery. •Fuse. •Relay. •Circuit. •Starter motor. •Ignition switch.	•GO to Pinpoint Test B.
•Engine cranks slowly	•Battery. •Circuitry. •Starter motor.	•GO to Pinpoint Test C.
•Unusual starter motor noise	•Starter motor. •Flywheel ring gear.	•CHECK flywheel ring gear. •INSPECT starter motor for alignment, cracked case. Make sure the mounting bolts are tightened. If necessary, INSTALL a new starter motor.
•The starter spins but the engine does not crank	•Starter motor.	•INSPECT the flywheel ring gear for missing teeth. CHECK starter motor for correct mounting. If concern persists, INSTALL a new starter motor.

FM1120100600000X

Fig. 5 Starting system troubleshooting chart. 1999–2002 Cougar

Condition	Possible Source	Action
• The Engine Does Not Crank	• Battery. • Starter motor. • Starter motor solenoid relay switch. • Starter motor relay. • Ignition switch (11572). • Damaged fuse. • Anti-theft system. • Circuitry.	• GO to Pinpoint Test A.
• The Engine Cranks in Reverse and Other Forward Gears	• Shift linkage (Adjustment). • Digital Transmission Range (TR) Sensor.	
• The Engine Cranks Slowly	• Battery. • Starter motor. • Circuitry.	• PERFORM the Starter Motor—Voltage Drop Test REFER to Starter Motor—Voltage Drop

FM1120100612010X

Fig. 7 Starting system troubleshooting chart (Part 1 of 2). 1999–2002 Crown Victoria & Grand Marquis

Condition	Possible Source	Action
• The Engine Cranks Slowly	• Battery. • Starter motor. • Circuitry.	• CARRY OUT the starter motor-motor feed circuit and/or the starter motor-ground circuit test.
• The Engine Does Not Crank or the Relay Clicks	• Battery. • Starter motor. • Circuitry.	• GO to Pinpoint Test A.
• Unusual Starter Noise	• Starter mounting. • Starter motor. • Improper starter drive engagement.	• GO to Pinpoint Test B.

FM1120100635010X

Fig. 9 Starting system troubleshooting chart (Part 1 of 2). 1999–2002 Escort, Tracer & ZX2

Condition	Possible Sources	Action
•Engine does not crank but relay clicks	•Battery. •Starter motor •Relay. •Circuit.	•GO to Pinpoint Test A.
•Engine does not crank and relay does not click	•PATS. •Battery. •Fuse. •Relay. •Circuit. •Starter motor. •Ignition switch. •Ignition switch (manual transaxle only)	•GO to Pinpoint Test B.
•Engine cranks slowly	•Battery. •Circuit. •Starter motor.	•GO to Pinpoint Test C.
•Unusual starter motor noise	•Starter motor. •Flywheel ring gear.	•CHECK flywheel ring gear. •INSPECT starter motor for alignment, cracked case. Make sure the mounting bolts are tightened. If necessary, INSTALL a new starter motor.

FM1120100685010X

Fig. 10 Starting system troubleshooting chart (Part 1 of 2). 2000–01 Focus

Condition	Possible Source	Action
• Engine Cranks Slowly	• Discharged battery (open circuit voltage under 12.2 volts). • Low battery capacity (charged battery with less than 9.6 cranking volts). • High resistance in cranking circuit (starter draw may be higher than normal). • Starter motor (worn bushings/bearings, shorted windings). • Engine mechanical concerns.	• GO to Pinpoint Test A.
• Engine Does Not Crank	• Low battery. • Open fuse. • Open ignition switch. • Shorts to ground. • Engine system. • Inoperative starter motor. • Starter interrupt relay (if incorporated). • High resistance in battery feed to starter solenoid B+ or S terminals or ground circuit.	• GO to Pinpoint Test B.
• Unusual Starter Noise	• Starter motor. • Worn or damaged flywheel ring gear tooth damage or excessive ring gear runout. • Inoperative components.	• GO to Pinpoint Test C.

FM1120100611000X

Fig. 6 Starting system troubleshooting chart. 1998 Crown Victoria & Grand Marquis

Condition	Possible Source	Action
• Unusual Starter Noise	• Starter mounting. • Flywheel/ring gear. • Starter motor.	• GO to Pinpoint Test B.
• The Starter Spins But the Engine Does Not Crank	• Starter motor. • Damaged flywheel/ring gear teeth.	• INSPECT the starter motor mounting and engagement. REPAIR as required. • INSPECT the flywheel/ring gear for damaged, missing or worn teeth. REPAIR as required.

FM1120100612020X

Fig. 7 Starting system troubleshooting chart (Part 2 of 2). 1999–2002 Crown Victoria & Grand Marquis

Condition	Possible Source	Action
• The Engine Does Not Crank or the Relay Does Click	• Battery. • Starter motor. • Circuit.	• GO to Pinpoint Test A.
• The Engine Cranks Slowly	• Battery. • Starter motor. • Circuit.	• GO to Pinpoint Test B.
• Unusual Starter Noise	• Starter mounting. • Starter motor. • Improper starter drive engagement.	• GO to Pinpoint Test C.
• Starter Spins but Engine Does Not Crank	• Drive pinion/overrunning clutch. • Starter solenoid. • Drive lever and pin.	• Replace the starter frame and magnet.
• Engine Cranks With Clutch Pedal Not Applied (Manual)	• Starter clutch pedal position switch.	• REPLACE the starter clutch pedal position switch.

FM1120100631000X

Fig. 8 Starting system troubleshooting chart. 1998 Escort, Tracer & ZX2

Condition	Possible Source	Action
• Starter Spins but Engine Does Not Crank	• Starter motor. • Damaged flywheel/ring gear teeth.	• INSPECT the starter motor mounting and engagement. REPAIR as necessary. • INSPECT the flywheel/ring gear for damaged, missing or worn teeth. REPAIR as necessary.
• Engine Cranks With Clutch Pedal Not Applied (Manual)	• Starter clutch pedal position switch.	• REPLACE the starter clutch pedal position switch.

FM1120100635020X

Fig. 9 Starting system troubleshooting chart (Part 2 of 2). 1999–2002 Escort, Tracer & ZX2

Condition	Possible Sources	Action
•The starter spins but the engine does not crank	•Starter motor.	•INSPECT the flywheel ring gear for missing teeth. CHECK starter motor for correct mounting. If concern persists, INSTALL a new starter motor.

FM1120100685020X

Fig. 10 Starting system troubleshooting chart (Part 2 of 2). 2000–01 Focus

Condition	Possible Source	Action
• The engine cranks slowly	• Battery. • Ignition switch. • Starter motor. • Circuitry.	• CARRY OUT the starter motor-motor feed circuit and/or the starter motor-ground circuit test.
• The engine does not crank	• Battery. • Central junction box (CJB) fuse F201 (5A). • Auxiliary junction box (AJB) fuse F121 (30A). • Battery junction box (BJB) fuse F422 (20A). • Ignition switch. • Starter relay. • Anti-theft system. • Circuitry.	• GO to Pinpoint Test A.
• Unusual starter noise	• Starter motor. • Starter motor mounting. • Incorrect starter motor drive engagements.	• GO to Pinpoint Test B.
• The starter spins but the engine does not crank	• Starter motor. • Broken flywheel/ring gear teeth.	• INSPECT the starter motor mounting and engagement. • INSPECT the flywheel/ring gear for broke, missing or worn teeth. REPAIR as necessary.
• Engine cranks with clutch pedal not applied (manual transmission)	• Starter clutch pedal position (CPP) switch.	• INSTALL a new clutch pedal position (CPP) switch.

FM1120100652000X

Fig. 11 Starting system troubleshooting chart. 2000–02 LS & Thunderbird

Condition	Possible Source	Action
• No Communication With The Steering Column/Ignition/Lighting (SCIL) Control Module	• Steering column/ignition/lighting control module. • Circuitry.	• GO to Pinpoint Test A.
• The Engine Does Not Crank or The Relay Does Click	• Low battery. • Open fuse. • Open ignition switch. • Shorts to ground. • Engine system. • Inoperative starter motor. • High resistance in battery feed to starter solenoid B+ or S terminals or ground circuit. • Starter interrupt relay, if incorporated.	• GO to Pinpoint Test B.
• The Engine Cranks Slowly	• Low battery. • Ground not secure. • Connections loose. • Inoperative starter motor. • Shorted fuse or ignition switch. • High resistance in battery feed to starter solenoid B+ or ground circuit. • Ring gear runout is excessive.	• GO to Pinpoint Test C.
• Unusual Starter Noise	• Starter motor. • Worn or damaged flywheel ring gear tooth, damage or excessive ring gear runout. • Inoperative components.	• GO to Pinpoint Test D.

FM1120100615000X

Fig. 12 Starting system troubleshooting chart. Mark VIII

Condition	Possible Source	Action
• Engine Cranks Slowly	• Discharged battery (open circuit voltage under 12.2 volts). • Low battery capacity (charged battery with less than 9.6 cranking volts). • High resistance in cranking circuit (starter draw may be higher than normal). • Starter motor (worn bushings/bearings, shorted windings). • Engine mechanical concerns.	• GO to Pinpoint Test A.
• Engine Does Not Crank	• Low battery. • Open fuse. • Open ignition switch. • Shorts to ground. • Engine system. • Inoperative starter motor. • High resistance in battery cables. • High resistance in circuit to S terminal on starter. • Open start interrupt relay.	• GO to Pinpoint Test B.
• Unusual Starter Noise	• Flywheel ring gear tooth damage or excessive ring gear runout. • Starter motor worn or damaged. • Inoperative components.	• GO to Pinpoint Test C.

FM1120100655000X

Fig. 13 Starting system troubleshooting chart. 1998 Mustang

Condition	Possible Source	Action
• The engine does not crank	• Battery. • BJB fuse ignition switch (40A) • CJB Fuse 6 (20A). • Starter motor (11002). • Ignition switch (11572). • Circuitry. • Starter motor relay. • Clutch pedal position (CPP) switch.	• GO to Pinpoint Test A.
• The engine cranks slowly	• Battery. • Starter motor. • Ignition switch. • Circuitry.	• CARRY OUT The Starter Motor-Voltage Drop Test Component Test.
• Unusual starter noise	• Starter motor mounting. • Starter motor. • Incorrect starter drive engagement.	• GO to Pinpoint Test B.
• The starter spins but the engine does not crank	• Starter Motor • Damaged flywheel/ring gear teeth.	• INSPECT the starter motor mounting and engagement. REPAIR as necessary. • INSPECT the flywheel/ring gear for damaged, missing or worn teeth. REPAIR as necessary.

FM1120100659000X

Fig. 14 Starting system troubleshooting chart. 1999–2002 Mustang

Condition	Possible Source	Action
• Starter Motor Cranks Engine Slowly or No Cranking With Relay/Solenoid Clicking or Chattering	• Discharged battery (open circuit voltage under 12.2 volts). • Low battery capacity (charged battery with less than 9.6 cranking volts). • High resistance in cranking circuit (starter draw may be higher than normal). • Starter motor (worn bushings/bearings, shorted windings). • Engine mechanical concerns.	GO to Pinpoint Test A.
• Starter Motor Does Not Crank Engine	• Low battery. • Open fuse. • Open ignition switch. • Shorts to ground. • Engine system. • Inoperative starter motor. • High resistance in battery feed to starter solenoid B+ or S terminals or ground circuits. • Open starter relay (if incorporated).	• GO to Pinpoint Test B for 3.0L (2V). • GO to Pinpoint Test C for 3.0L (4V) and 3.4L (4V).
• Unusual Starter Motor Noise During Starter Overrun	• Worn or damaged starter motor. • Flywheel ring gear tooth damage or excessive ring gear runout. • Inoperative components.	• GO to Pinpoint Test D.

FM1120100662000X

Fig. 15 Starting system troubleshooting chart. 1998 Sable & Taurus

Condition	Possible Source	Action
• Starter Motor Cranks Engine Slowly or No Cranking With Relay/Solenoid Clicking or Chattering	• Discharged battery (open circuit voltage under 12.2 volts). • Low battery capacity (charged battery with less than 9.6 cranking volts). • High resistance in cranking circuit (starter draw may be higher than normal). • Starter motor (worn bushings/bearings, shorted windings). • Engine mechanical concerns.	GO to Pinpoint Test A.
• Starter Motor Does Not Crank Engine	• Low battery. • Open fuse. • Open ignition switch. • Shorts to ground. • Engine system. • Inoperative starter motor. • High resistance in battery feed to starter solenoid B+ or S terminals or ground circuits. • Open starter relay (if incorporated).	• GO to Pinpoint Test B for 3.0L (2V). • GO to Pinpoint Test C for 3.0L (4V) and 3.4L (4V).
• Unusual Starter Motor Noise During Starter Overrun	• Worn or damaged starter motor. • Flywheel ring gear tooth damage or excessive ring gear runout. • Inoperative components.	• GO to Pinpoint Test D.

FM1120100667000X

Fig. 16 Starting system troubleshooting chart. 1999 Sable & Taurus

Condition	Possible Source	Action
• The engine does not crank	• Battery. • Open fuse. • Starter motor. • Ignition switch. • Digital transmission range (TR) sensor. • Circuitry. • Starter motor relay. • Anti-theft system.	• GO to Pinpoint Test A.
• The engine cranks slowly	• Battery. • Starter motor. • Ignition switch. • Circuitry.	• CARRY OUT the starter motor component test.
• Unusual starter noise	• Starter motor mounting. • Starter motor. • Incorrect starter drive engagement.	• GO to Pinpoint Test B.
• The starter spins but the engine does not crank	• Starter motor. • Damaged flywheel/ring gear teeth.	• INSPECT the starter motor mounting and engagement. • INSPECT the flywheel/ring gear for damaged, missing or worn teeth. REPAIR as necessary.

FM1120100672000X

Fig. 17 Starting system troubleshooting chart. 2000–02 Sable & Taurus

Condition	Possible Source	Action
• The Engine Does Not Crank	• Battery. • Starter motor. • Starter motor solenoid relay switch. • Starter motor relay. • Ignition switch (11572). • Damaged fuse. • Anti-theft system. • Circuitry.	• GO to Pinpoint Test A.
• The Engine Cranks in Reverse and Other Forward Gears	• Shift linkage (Adjustment). • Digital Transmission Range (TR) Sensor.	• **Diagnose transmission shift linkage & digital sensor**
• The Engine Cranks Slowly	• Battery. • Starter motor. • Circuitry.	• PERFORM the Starter Motor—Voltage Drop Test Component Test.

FM1120100682010X

Fig. 19 Starting system troubleshooting chart (Part 1 of 2). 1999–2002 Town Car

Condition	Possible Source	Action
• The Engine Does Not Crank	• Battery. • Starter motor. • Starter motor solenoid relay switch. • Starter motor relay. • Ignition switch. • Damaged fuse. • Anti-theft system. • Circuitry.	• GO to Pinpoint Test A.
• The Engine Cranks Slowly	• Battery. • Starter motor. • Circuitry.	• PERFORM the Starter Motor—Voltage Drop Test Component

FM1120100679010X

Fig. 18 Starting system troubleshooting chart (Part 1 of 2). 1998 Town Car

Condition	Possible Source	Action
• Unusual Starter Noise	• Starter mounting. • Flywheel/ring gear. • Starter motor.	• GO to Pinpoint Test B.
• The Starter Spins But the Engine Does Not Crank	• Starter motor. • Damaged flywheel/ring gear teeth.	• INSPECT the starter motor mounting and engagement. REPAIR as required. • INSPECT the flywheel/ring gear for damaged, missing or worn teeth. REPAIR as required.

FM1120100679020X

Fig. 18 Starting system troubleshooting chart (Part 2 of 2). 1998 Town Car

Condition	Possible Source	Action
• Unusual Starter Noise	• Starter mounting. • Flywheel/ring gear. • Starter motor.	• GO to Pinpoint Test B.
• The Starter Spins But the Engine Does Not Crank	• Starter motor. • Damaged flywheel/ring gear teeth.	• INSPECT the starter motor mounting and engagement. REPAIR as required. • INSPECT the flywheel/ring gear for damaged, missing or worn teeth. REPAIR as required.

FM1120100682020X

Fig. 19 Starting system troubleshooting chart (Part 2 of 2). 1999–2002 Town Car

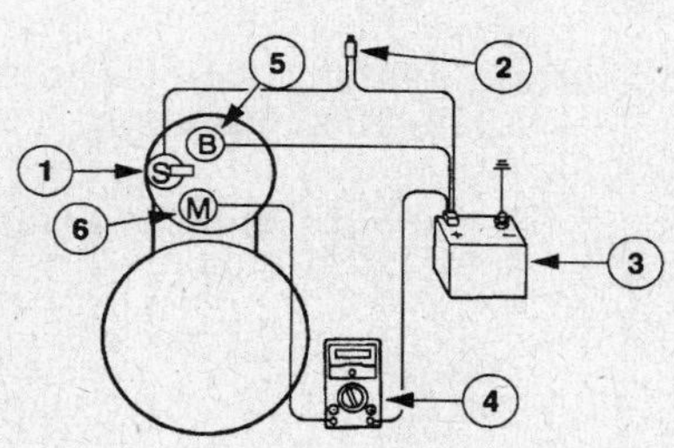

Item	Part Number	Description
1	—	S-Terminal
2	—	Remote Starter Switch
3	10653	Battery
4	—	Rotunda 73 Digital Multimeter
5	—	B-Terminal
6	—	M-Terminal

FM1120100598000X

Fig. 20 Starter motor feed circuit voltage drop test

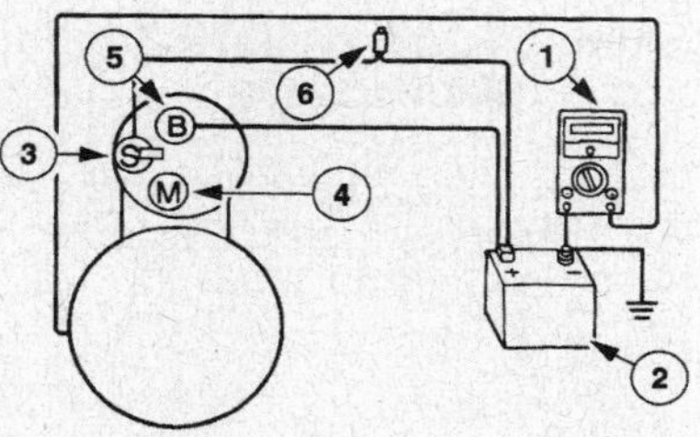

Item	Part Number	Description
1	—	Rotunda 73 Digital Multimeter
2	10653	Battery
3	—	S-Terminal
4	—	M-Terminal
5	—	B-Terminal
6	—	Remote Starter Switch

FM1120100599000X

Fig. 21 Starter motor ground circuit voltage drop test

Condition	Possible Sources	Action
•Normal current and speed	•Battery. •Switches. •Wiring.	•RECHECK battery, switches and wiring, including voltage drop tests, if cranking starter motor operation on engine is slow or sluggish.
•Current flow with test circuit switch open	•Solenoid contacts.	•TEST and, if necessary, INSTALL a new solenoid assembly.
•Failure to operate with very little or no current	•Solenoid winding.	•INSPECT and TEST solenoid assembly.
	•Field circuit.	•INSPECT and TEST frame and field coil assembly.
	•Armature coil or commutator bars.	•INSPECT armature.
	•Brush springs or brushes.	•INSPECT brushes and brush springs.
•Failure to operate with high current	•Bearing or drivetrain.	•INSPECT bearing, armature, driveshaft and related drive parts.

FM1120100604010X

Fig. 22 Starter motor no load test results (Part 1 of 2)

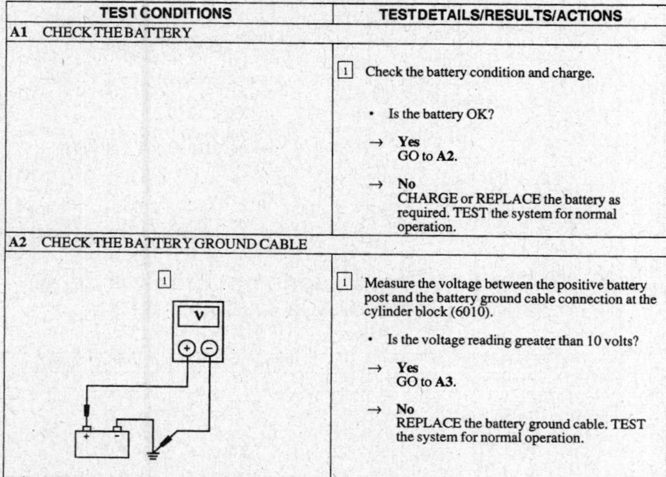

TEST CONDITIONS	TESTDETAILS/RESULTS/ACTIONS
A1 CHECK THE BATTERY	
	1 Check the battery condition and charge. • Is the battery OK? → **Yes** GO to **A2**. → **No** CHARGE or REPLACE the battery as required. TEST the system for normal operation.
A2 CHECK THE BATTERY GROUND CABLE	
1	1 Measure the voltage between the positive battery post and the battery ground cable connection at the cylinder block (6010). • Is the voltage reading greater than 10 volts? → **Yes** GO to **A3**. → **No** REPLACE the battery ground cable. TEST the system for normal operation.

FM1120100596010X

Fig. 23 Test A: Engine does not crank or relay clicks (Part 1 of 10). Continental

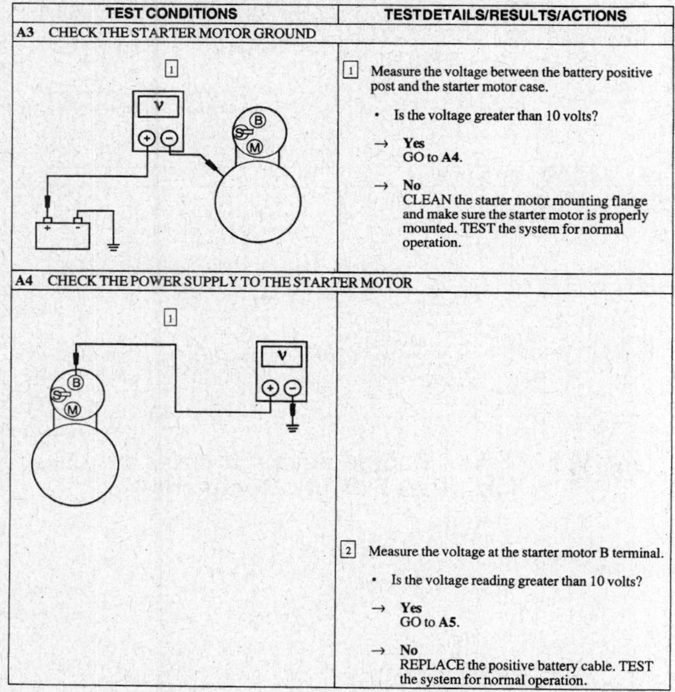

TEST CONDITIONS	TESTDETAILS/RESULTS/ACTIONS
A3 CHECK THE STARTER MOTOR GROUND	
1	1 Measure the voltage between the battery positive post and the starter motor case. • Is the voltage greater than 10 volts? → **Yes** GO to **A4**. → **No** CLEAN the starter motor mounting flange and make sure the starter motor is properly mounted. TEST the system for normal operation.
A4 CHECK THE POWER SUPPLY TO THE STARTER MOTOR	
1	2 Measure the voltage at the starter motor B terminal. • Is the voltage reading greater than 10 volts? → **Yes** GO to **A5**. → **No** REPLACE the positive battery cable. TEST the system for normal operation.

FM1120100596020X

Fig. 23 Test A: Engine does not crank or relay clicks (Part 2 of 10). Continental

Condition	Possible Sources	Action
	•Terminals or fields.	•INSPECT and TEST frame and field coil assembly, solenoid assembly and brush installations for shorts.
•Low speed with high current	•Bushings, gear reduction unit, armature shaft, pole shoe or driveshaft.	•INSPECT bearing, armature, driveshaft and gear reduction gears.
	•Armature.	•INSPECT and TEST armature.
	•Armature or fields.	•INSPECT and TEST frame and field coil assembly and armature.
•Low speed with normal or low current	•Connections, leads or commutator.	•INSPECT internal wiring, electrical connections and armature commutator.
	•Solenoid winding.	•INSPECT and TEST solenoid assembly.
	•Field circuit.	•INSPECT and TEST frame and field coil assembly.
	•Armature coils or commutator bars.	•INSPECT armature.
	•Brush springs or brushes.	•INSPECT brushes and brush springs.
•High speed with high current	•Fields.	•INSPECT and TEST field and frame assembly.

FM1120100604020X

Fig. 22 Starter motor no load test results (Part 2 of 2)

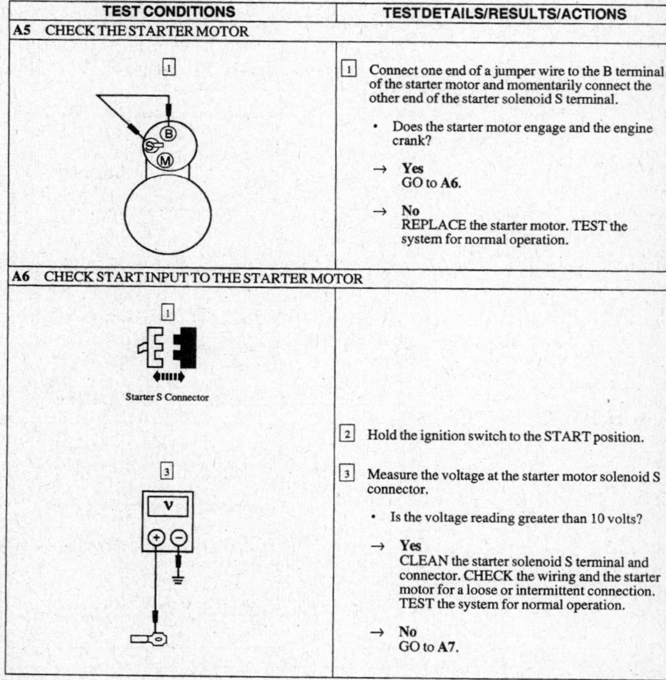

TEST CONDITIONS	TESTDETAILS/RESULTS/ACTIONS
A5 CHECK THE STARTER MOTOR	
1	1 Connect one end of a jumper wire to the B terminal of the starter motor and momentarily connect the other end of the starter solenoid S terminal. • Does the starter motor engage and the engine crank? → **Yes** GO to **A6**. → **No** REPLACE the starter motor. TEST the system for normal operation.
A6 CHECK START INPUT TO THE STARTER MOTOR	
1 Starter S Connector	
	2 Hold the ignition switch to the START position.
3	3 Measure the voltage at the starter motor solenoid S connector. • Is the voltage reading greater than 10 volts? → **Yes** CLEAN the starter solenoid S terminal and connector. CHECK the wiring and the starter motor for a loose or intermittent connection. TEST the system for normal operation. → **No** GO to **A7**.

FM1120100596030X

Fig. 23 Test A: Engine does not crank or relay clicks (Part 3 of 10). Continental

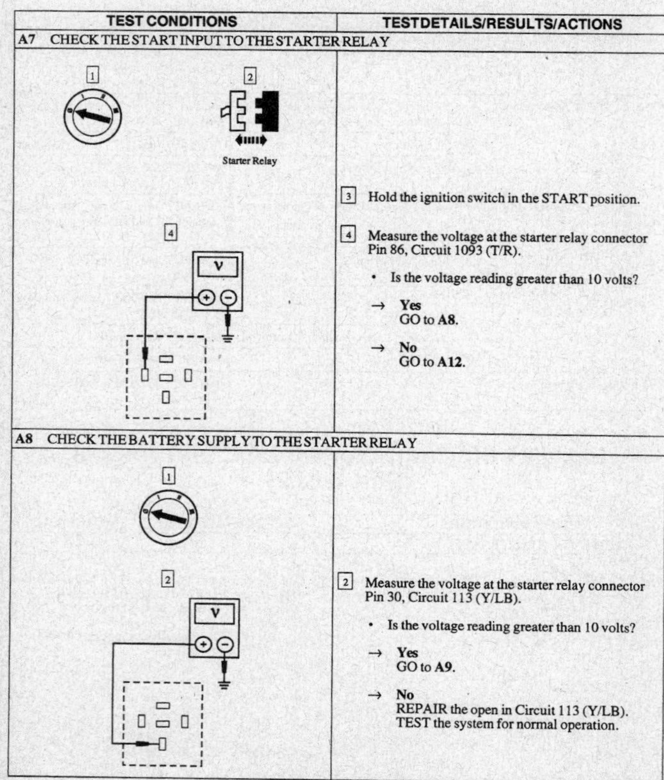

TEST CONDITIONS	TEST DETAILS/RESULTS/ACTIONS
A7 CHECK THE START INPUT TO THE STARTER RELAY	
1 2 Starter Relay 4	3 Hold the ignition switch in the START position. 4 Measure the voltage at the starter relay connector Pin 86, Circuit 1093 (T/R). • Is the voltage reading greater than 10 volts? → **Yes** GO to **A8.** → **No** GO to **A12.**
A8 CHECK THE BATTERY SUPPLY TO THE STARTER RELAY	
1 2	2 Measure the voltage at the starter relay connector Pin 30, Circuit 113 (Y/LB). • Is the voltage reading greater than 10 volts? → **Yes** GO to **A9.** → **No** REPAIR the open in Circuit 113 (Y/LB). TEST the system for normal operation.

FM1120100596040X

Fig. 23 Test A: Engine does not crank or relay clicks (Part 4 of 10). Continental

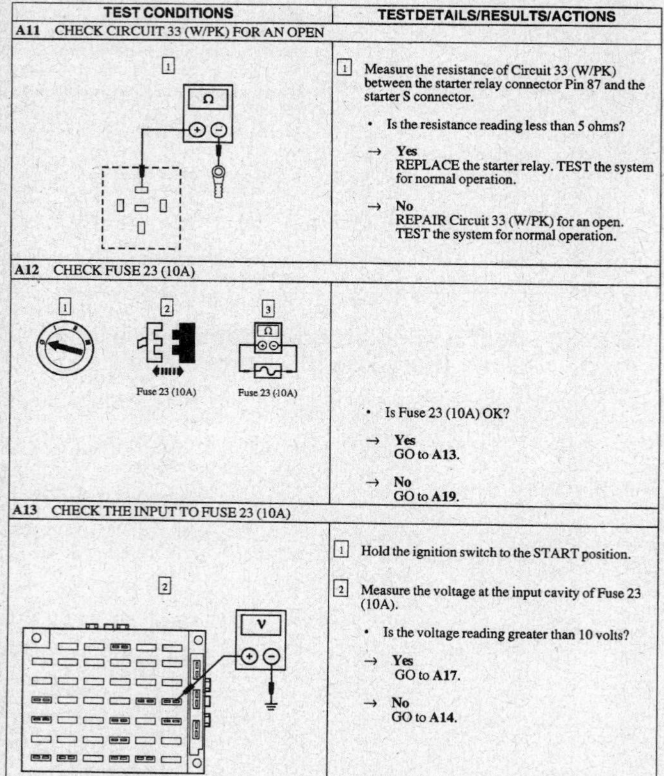

TEST CONDITIONS	TEST DETAILS/RESULTS/ACTIONS
A11 CHECK CIRCUIT 33 (W/PK) FOR AN OPEN	
1	1 Measure the resistance of Circuit 33 (W/PK) between the starter relay connector Pin 87 and the starter S connector. • Is the resistance reading less than 5 ohms? → **Yes** REPLACE the starter relay. TEST the system for normal operation. → **No** REPAIR Circuit 33 (W/PK) for an open. TEST the system for normal operation.
A12 CHECK FUSE 23 (10A)	
1 2 Fuse 23 (10A) 3 Fuse 23 (10A)	• Is Fuse 23 (10A) OK? → **Yes** GO to **A13.** → **No** GO to **A19.**
A13 CHECK THE INPUT TO FUSE 23 (10A)	
2	1 Hold the ignition switch to the START position. 2 Measure the voltage at the input cavity of Fuse 23 (10A). • Is the voltage reading greater than 10 volts? → **Yes** GO to **A17.** → **No** GO to **A14.**

FM1120100596060X

Fig. 23 Test A: Engine does not crank or relay clicks (Part 6 of 10). Continental

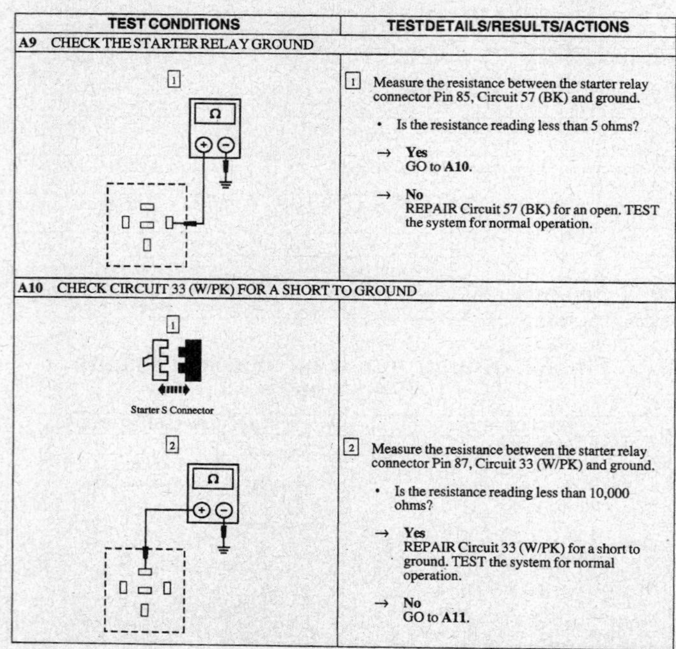

TEST CONDITIONS	TEST DETAILS/RESULTS/ACTIONS
A9 CHECK THE STARTER RELAY GROUND	
1	1 Measure the resistance between the starter relay connector Pin 85, Circuit 57 (BK) and ground. • Is the resistance reading less than 5 ohms? → **Yes** GO to **A10.** → **No** REPAIR Circuit 57 (BK) for an open. TEST the system for normal operation.
A10 CHECK CIRCUIT 33 (W/PK) FOR A SHORT TO GROUND	
1 Starter S Connector 2	2 Measure the resistance between the starter relay connector Pin 87, Circuit 33 (W/PK) and ground. • Is the resistance reading less than 10,000 ohms? → **Yes** REPAIR Circuit 33 (W/PK) for a short to ground. TEST the system for normal operation. → **No** GO to **A11.**

FM1120100596050X

Fig. 23 Test A: Engine does not crank or relay clicks (Part 5 of 10). Continental

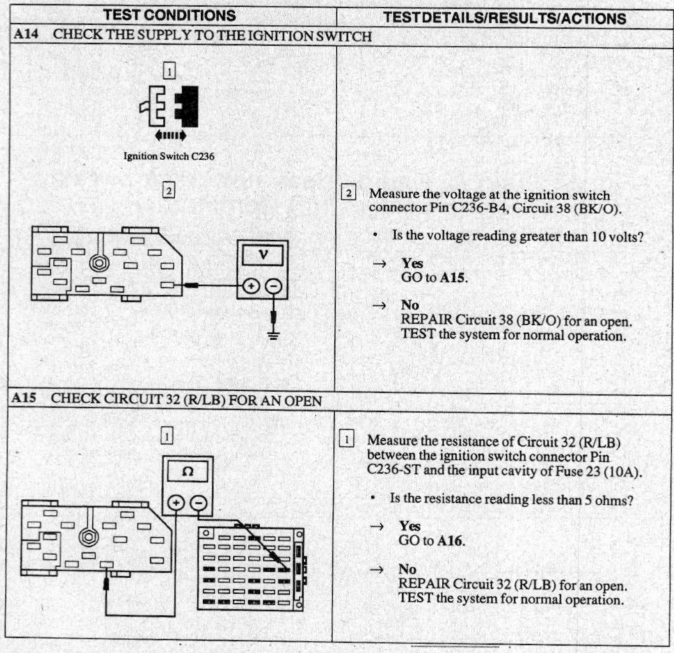

TEST CONDITIONS	TEST DETAILS/RESULTS/ACTIONS
A14 CHECK THE SUPPLY TO THE IGNITION SWITCH	
1 Ignition Switch C236 2	2 Measure the voltage at the ignition switch connector Pin C236-B4, Circuit 38 (BK/O). • Is the voltage reading greater than 10 volts? → **Yes** GO to **A15.** → **No** REPAIR Circuit 38 (BK/O) for an open. TEST the system for normal operation.
A15 CHECK CIRCUIT 32 (R/LB) FOR AN OPEN	
1	1 Measure the resistance of Circuit 32 (R/LB) between the ignition switch connector Pin C236-ST and the input cavity of Fuse 23 (10A). • Is the resistance reading less than 5 ohms? → **Yes** GO to **A16.** → **No** REPAIR Circuit 32 (R/LB) for an open. TEST the system for normal operation.

FM1120100596070X

Fig. 23 Test A: Engine does not crank or relay clicks (Part 7 of 10). Continental

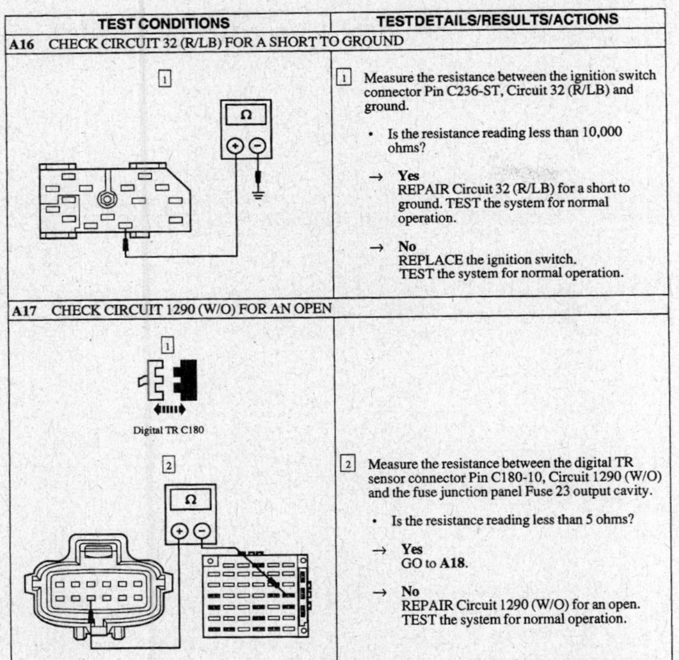

TEST CONDITIONS	TEST DETAILS/RESULTS/ACTIONS
A16 CHECK CIRCUIT 32 (R/LB) FOR A SHORT TO GROUND	
1	1 Measure the resistance between the ignition switch connector Pin C236-ST, Circuit 32 (R/LB) and ground. • Is the resistance reading less than 10,000 ohms? → **Yes** REPAIR Circuit 32 (R/LB) for a short to ground. TEST the system for normal operation. → **No** REPLACE the ignition switch. TEST the system for normal operation.
A17 CHECK CIRCUIT 1290 (W/O) FOR AN OPEN	
1 Digital TR C180	
2	2 Measure the resistance between the digital TR sensor connector Pin C180-10, Circuit 1290 (W/O) and the fuse junction panel Fuse 23 output cavity. • Is the resistance reading less than 5 ohms? → **Yes** GO to **A18**. → **No** REPAIR Circuit 1290 (W/O) for an open. TEST the system for normal operation.

FM1120100596080X

Fig. 23 Test A: Engine does not crank or relay clicks (Part 8 of 10). Continental

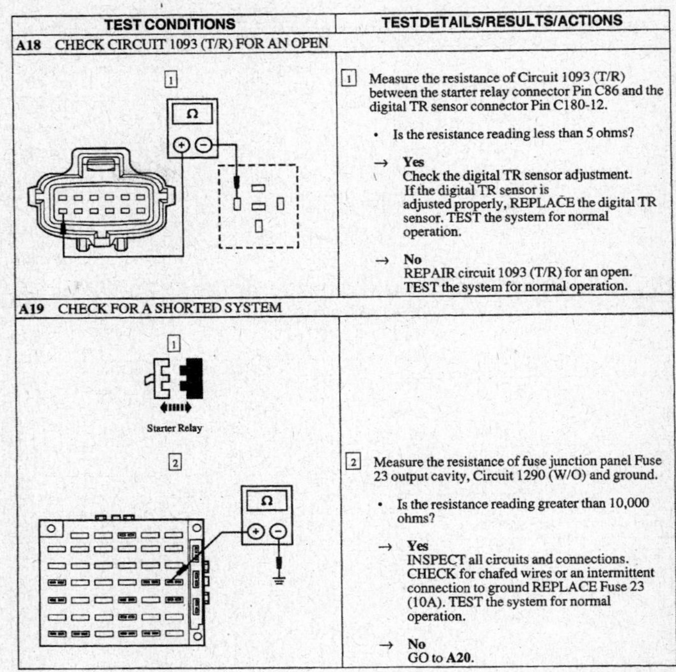

TEST CONDITIONS	TEST DETAILS/RESULTS/ACTIONS
A18 CHECK CIRCUIT 1093 (T/R) FOR AN OPEN	
1	1 Measure the resistance of Circuit 1093 (T/R) between the starter relay connector Pin C86 and the digital TR sensor connector Pin C180-12. • Is the resistance reading less than 5 ohms? → **Yes** Check the digital TR sensor adjustment. If the digital TR sensor is adjusted properly, REPLACE the digital TR sensor. TEST the system for normal operation. → **No** REPAIR circuit 1093 (T/R) for an open. TEST the system for normal operation.
A19 CHECK FOR A SHORTED SYSTEM	
1 Starter Relay	
2	2 Measure the resistance of fuse junction panel Fuse 23 output cavity, Circuit 1290 (W/O) and ground. • Is the resistance reading greater than 10,000 ohms? → **Yes** INSPECT all circuits and connections. CHECK for chafed wires or an intermittent connection to ground REPLACE Fuse 23 (10A). TEST the system for normal operation. → **No** GO to **A20**.

FM1120100596090X

Fig. 23 Test A: Engine does not crank or relay clicks (Part 9 of 10). Continental

TEST CONDITIONS	TEST DETAILS/RESULTS/ACTIONS
A20 CHECK FOR A SHORTED DIGITAL TRANSMISSION RANGE (TR) SENSOR	
1 Digital TR C180	
2	2 Measure the resistance between the digital TR sensor connector Pin C180-10, Circuit 1290 (W/O) and ground. • Is the resistance reading greater than 10,000 ohms? → **Yes** GO to **A21**. → **No** REPAIR Circuit 1290 (W/O) for a short to ground. TEST the system for normal operation.
A21 CHECK CIRCUIT 1093 (T/R) FOR A SHORT TO GROUND	
1	1 Measure the resistance between the digital TR sensor connector Pin C180-12, Circuit 1093 (T/R) and ground. • Is the resistance reading greater than 10,000 ohms? → **Yes** CHECK the digital TR sensor adjustment. If the digital TR sensor is adjusted properly, REPLACE the digital TR sensor. TEST the system for normal operation. → **No** REPAIR circuit 1093 (T/R) for a short to ground. TEST the system for normal operation.

FM1120100596100X

Fig. 23 Test A: Engine does not crank or relay clicks (Part 10 of 10). Continental

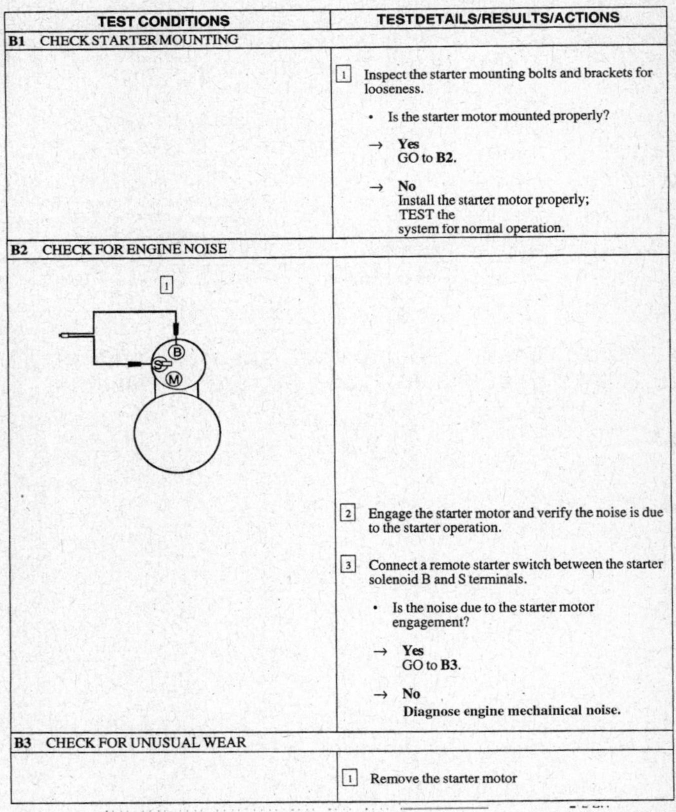

TEST CONDITIONS	TEST DETAILS/RESULTS/ACTIONS
B1 CHECK STARTER MOUNTING	
	1 Inspect the starter mounting bolts and brackets for looseness. • Is the starter motor mounted properly? → **Yes** GO to **B2**. → **No** Install the starter motor properly; TEST the system for normal operation.
B2 CHECK FOR ENGINE NOISE	
1	2 Engage the starter motor and verify the noise is due to the starter operation. 3 Connect a remote starter switch between the starter solenoid B and S terminals. • Is the noise due to the starter motor engagement? → **Yes** GO to **B3**. → **No** Diagnose engine mechainical noise.
B3 CHECK FOR UNUSUAL WEAR	
	1 Remove the starter motor

FM1120100597010X

Fig. 24 Test B: Unusual starter noises (Part 1 of 2). Continental

TEST CONDITIONS	TEST DETAILS/RESULTS/ACTIONS
B3 CHECK FOR UNUSUAL WEAR (Continued)	
	[2] Inspect the ring gear for damaged or worn teeth. • Is the noise due to ring gear tooth damage? → **Yes** REPLACE the ring gear. EXAMINE the starter pinion teeth. If damaged, REPLACE the starter motor. TEST the system for normal operation. → **No** REPLACE the starter motor. TEST the system for normal operation.

FM1120100597020X

Fig. 24 Test B: Unusual starter noises (Part 2 of 2). Continental

CONDITIONS	DETAILS/RESULTS/ACTIONS
	• Is the voltage greater than 10 volts? → **Yes** GO to **A3**. → **No** GO to **A5**.
A3 CHECK THE VOLTAGE TO THE STARTER MOTOR	
NOTE: Both wires coming from the battery are black, make note of which wire is coming from the positive battery terminal before making measurements.	
[1] [2]	[2] Measure the voltage between starter motor C973a-30, circuit 30 (RD) and ground. • Is the voltage greater than 10 volts? → **Yes** GO to **A4**. → **No** REPAIR the BK circuit from the positive battery terminal. TEST the system for normal operation.
A4 CHECK THE STARTER MOTOR GROUND	
NOTE: Both wires coming from the battery are black, make note of which wire is coming from the positive battery terminal before making measurements.	

FM1120100643020X

Fig. 25 Test A: Engine does not crank and relay clicks (Part 2 of 19). 1998 Contour & Mystique

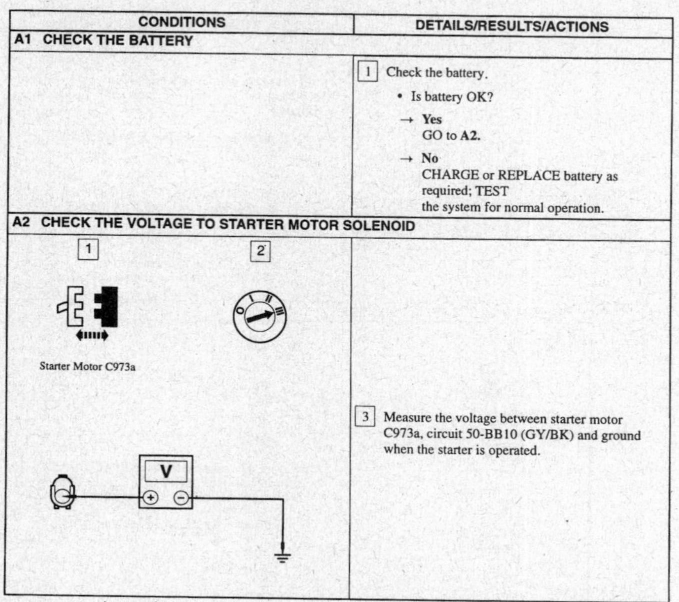

CONDITIONS	DETAILS/RESULTS/ACTIONS
A1 CHECK THE BATTERY	
	[1] Check the battery. • Is battery OK? → **Yes** GO to **A2**. → **No** CHARGE or REPLACE battery as required; TEST the system for normal operation.
A2 CHECK THE VOLTAGE TO STARTER MOTOR SOLENOID	
[1] [2] Starter Motor C973a	[3] Measure the voltage between starter motor C973a, circuit 50-BB10 (GY/BK) and ground when the starter is operated.

FM1120100643010X

Fig. 25 Test A: Engine does not crank and relay clicks (Part 1 of 19). 1998 Contour & Mystique

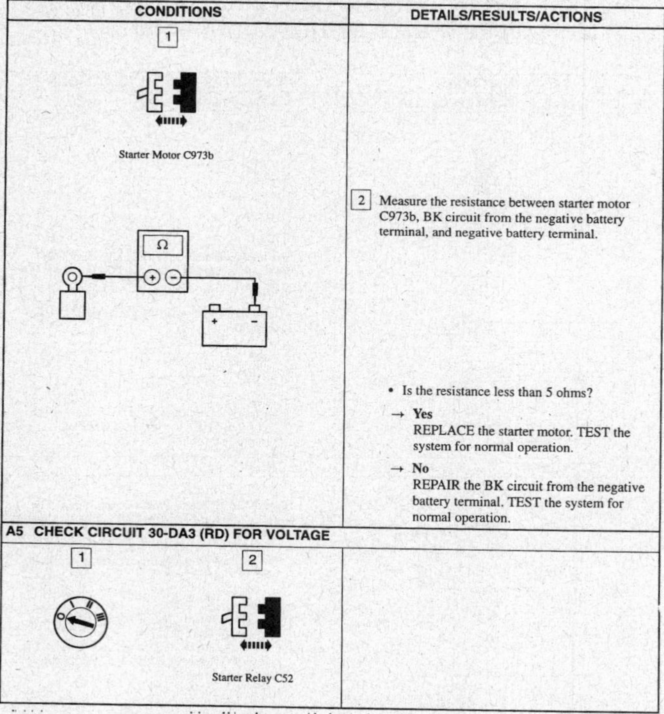

CONDITIONS	DETAILS/RESULTS/ACTIONS
[1] Starter Motor C973b	[2] Measure the resistance between starter motor C973b, BK circuit from the negative battery terminal, and negative battery terminal. • Is the resistance less than 5 ohms? → **Yes** REPLACE the starter motor. TEST the system for normal operation. → **No** REPAIR the BK circuit from the negative battery terminal. TEST the system for normal operation.
A5 CHECK CIRCUIT 30-DA3 (RD) FOR VOLTAGE	
[1] [2] Starter Relay C52	

FM1120100643030X

Fig. 25 Test A: Engine does not crank and relay clicks (Part 3 of 19). 1998 Contour & Mystique

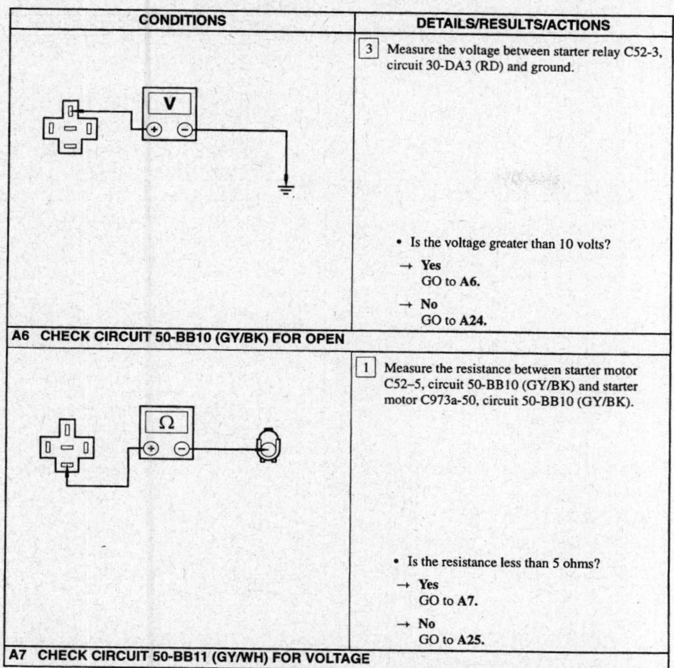

CONDITIONS	DETAILS/RESULTS/ACTIONS
	3 Measure the voltage between starter relay C52-3, circuit 30-DA3 (RD) and ground. • Is the voltage greater than 10 volts? → **Yes** GO to **A6.** → **No** GO to **A24.**
A6 CHECK CIRCUIT 50-BB10 (GY/BK) FOR OPEN	
	1 Measure the resistance between starter motor C52-5, circuit 50-BB10 (GY/BK) and starter motor C973a-50, circuit 50-BB10 (GY/BK). • Is the resistance less than 5 ohms? → **Yes** GO to **A7.** → **No** GO to **A25.**
A7 CHECK CIRCUIT 50-BB11 (GY/WH) FOR VOLTAGE	

FM1120100643040X

Fig. 25 Test A: Engine does not crank and relay clicks (Part 4 of 19). 1998 Contour & Mystique

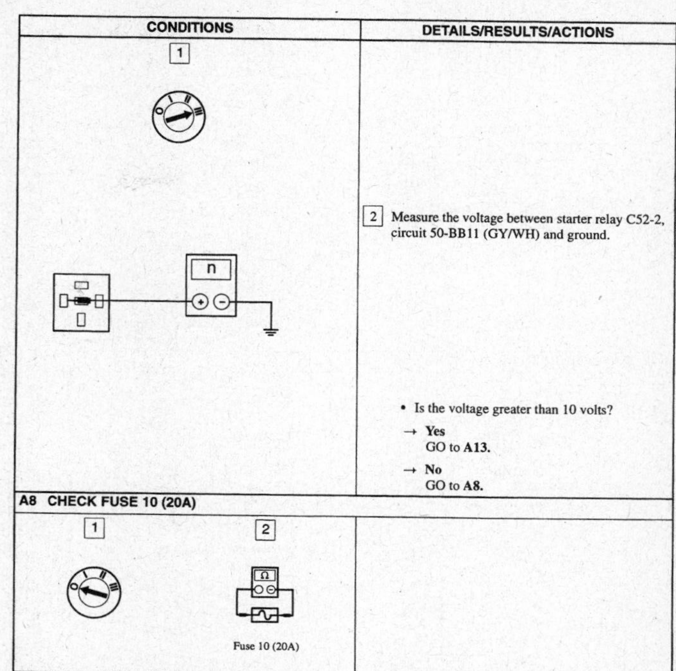

CONDITIONS	DETAILS/RESULTS/ACTIONS
1	
	2 Measure the voltage between starter relay C52-2, circuit 50-BB11 (GY/WH) and ground. • Is the voltage greater than 10 volts? → **Yes** GO to **A13.** → **No** GO to **A8.**
A8 CHECK FUSE 10 (20A)	
1 2 Fuse 10 (20A)	

FM1120100643050X

Fig. 25 Test A: Engine does not crank and relay clicks (Part 5 of 19). 1998 Contour & Mystique

CONDITIONS	DETAILS/RESULTS/ACTIONS
	• Is the fuse OK? → **Yes** GO to **A9.** → **No** REPLACE the fuse 10 (20A). TEST the system for normal operation. If fuse fails again, CHECK for short to ground, REPAIR as necessary.
A9 CHECK CIRCUIT 30-BB9 (RD) FOR OPEN	
1 Ignition Switch C456 2 Fuse 10 (20A) TIV2601021	3 Measure the resistance between fuse 10 (20A) load side, circuit 30-BB9 (RD) and ignition switch C456-1, circuit 30-BB9 (RD). • Is the resistance less than 5 ohms? → **Yes** GO to **A10.** → **No** REPAIR circuit 30-BB9 (RD). TEST the system for normal operation.
A10 CHECK THE IGNITION SWITCH	

FM1120100643060X

Fig. 25 Test A: Engine does not crank and relay clicks (Part 6 of 19). 1998 Contour & Mystique

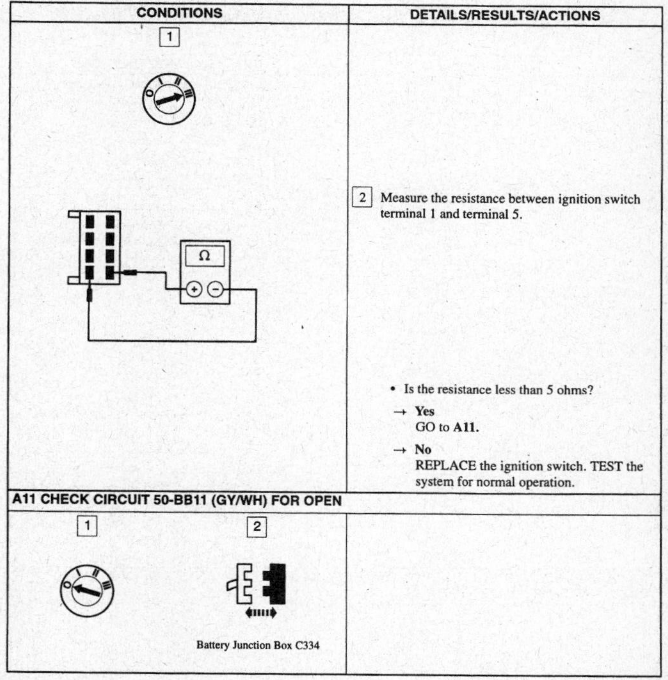

CONDITIONS	DETAILS/RESULTS/ACTIONS
1	
	2 Measure the resistance between ignition switch terminal 1 and terminal 5. • Is the resistance less than 5 ohms? → **Yes** GO to **A11.** → **No** REPLACE the ignition switch. TEST the system for normal operation.
A11 CHECK CIRCUIT 50-BB11 (GY/WH) FOR OPEN	
1 2 Battery Junction Box C334	

FM1120100643070X

Fig. 25 Test A: Engine does not crank and relay clicks (Part 7 of 19). 1998 Contour & Mystique

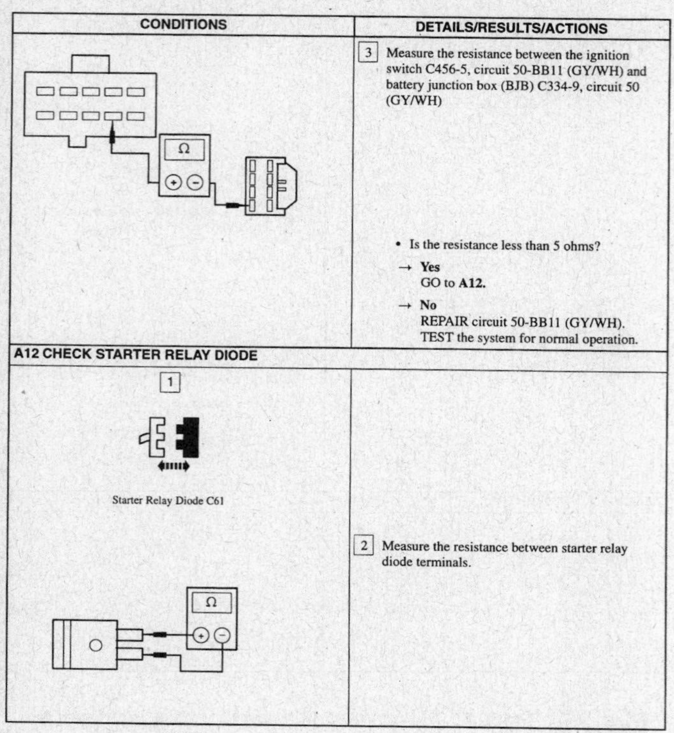

CONDITIONS	DETAILS/RESULTS/ACTIONS
	3 Measure the resistance between the ignition switch C456-5, circuit 50-BB11 (GY/WH) and battery junction box (BJB) C334-9, circuit 50 (GY/WH) • Is the resistance less than 5 ohms? → **Yes** GO to **A12.** → **No** REPAIR circuit 50-BB11 (GY/WH). TEST the system for normal operation.
A12 CHECK STARTER RELAY DIODE	
1 Starter Relay Diode C61	
	2 Measure the resistance between starter relay diode terminals.

FM1120100643080X

Fig. 25 Test A: Engine does not crank and relay clicks (Part 8 of 19). 1998 Contour & Mystique

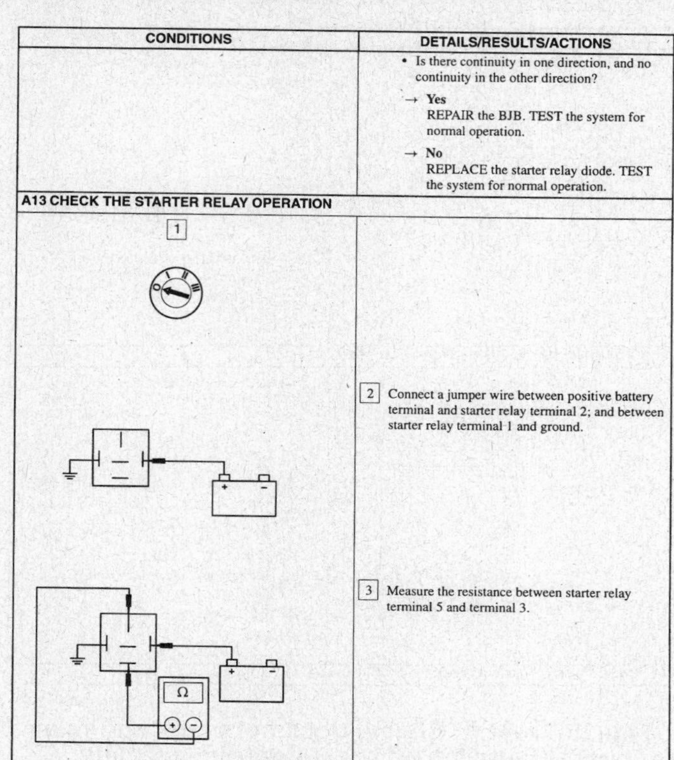

CONDITIONS	DETAILS/RESULTS/ACTIONS
	• Is there continuity in one direction, and no continuity in the other direction? → **Yes** REPAIR the BJB. TEST the system for normal operation. → **No** REPLACE the starter relay diode. TEST the system for normal operation.
A13 CHECK THE STARTER RELAY OPERATION	
1	
	2 Connect a jumper wire between positive battery terminal and starter relay terminal 2; and between starter relay terminal 1 and ground.
	3 Measure the resistance between starter relay terminal 5 and terminal 3.

FM1120100643090X

Fig. 25 Test A: Engine does not crank and relay clicks (Part 9 of 19). 1998 Contour & Mystique

CONDITIONS	DETAILS/RESULTS/ACTIONS
	• Is the resistance less than 5 ohms? → **Yes** GO to **A14.** → **No** REPLACE the starter relay. TEST the system for normal operation.
A14 CHECK CIRCUIT 50-BB10 (GY/BK) FOR SHORT TO GROUND	
	1 Measure the resistance between the starter relay C52-5, circuit 50-BB10 (GY/BK) and ground. • Is the resistance greater than 10,000 ohms? → **Yes** If equipped with manual transmission, GO to **A15.** If equipped with automatic transmission, GO to **A16.** → **No** REPAIR circuit 50 (GY/BK). TEST the system for normal operation.
A15 CHECK CIRCUIT 31S-BB12 (BK/YE) BETWEEN CLUTCH PEDAL POSITION (CPP) SWITCH AND STARTER RELAY FOR OPEN	
1 Clutch Pedal Position (CPP) Switch C1919	

FM1120100643100X

Fig. 25 Test A: Engine does not crank and relay clicks (Part 10 of 19). 1998 Contour & Mystique

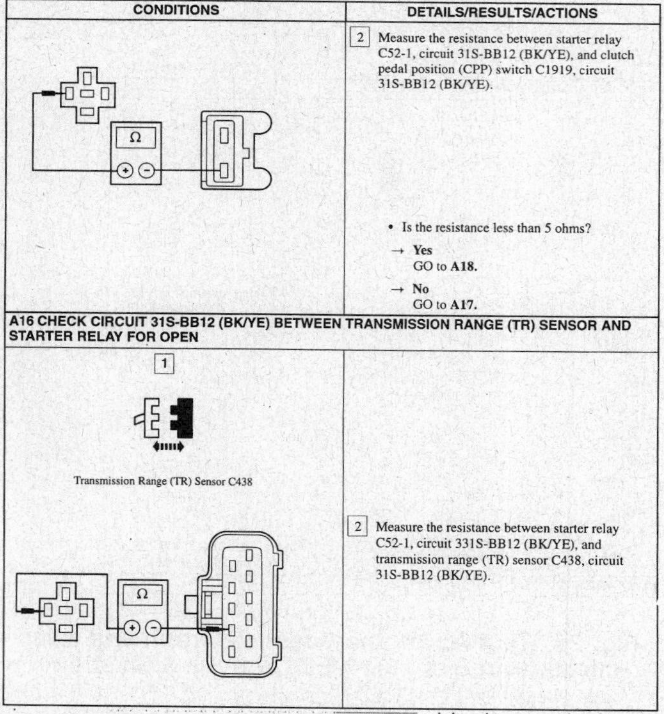

CONDITIONS	DETAILS/RESULTS/ACTIONS
	2 Measure the resistance between starter relay C52-1, circuit 31S-BB12 (BK/YE), and clutch pedal position (CPP) switch C1919, circuit 31S-BB12 (BK/YE). • Is the resistance less than 5 ohms? → **Yes** GO to **A18.** → **No** GO to **A17.**
A16 CHECK CIRCUIT 31S-BB12 (BK/YE) BETWEEN TRANSMISSION RANGE (TR) SENSOR AND STARTER RELAY FOR OPEN	
1 Transmission Range (TR) Sensor C438	
	2 Measure the resistance between starter relay C52-1, circuit 331S-BB12 (BK/YE), and transmission range (TR) sensor C438, circuit 31S-BB12 (BK/YE).

FM1120100643110X

Fig. 25 Test A: Engine does not crank and relay clicks (Part 11 of 19). 1998 Contour & Mystique

CONDITIONS	DETAILS/RESULTS/ACTIONS
	• Is the resistance less than 5 ohms? → **Yes** GO to **A19.** → **No** GO to **A17.**
A17 CHECK BATTERY JUNCTION BOX (BJB) FOR OPEN	
1 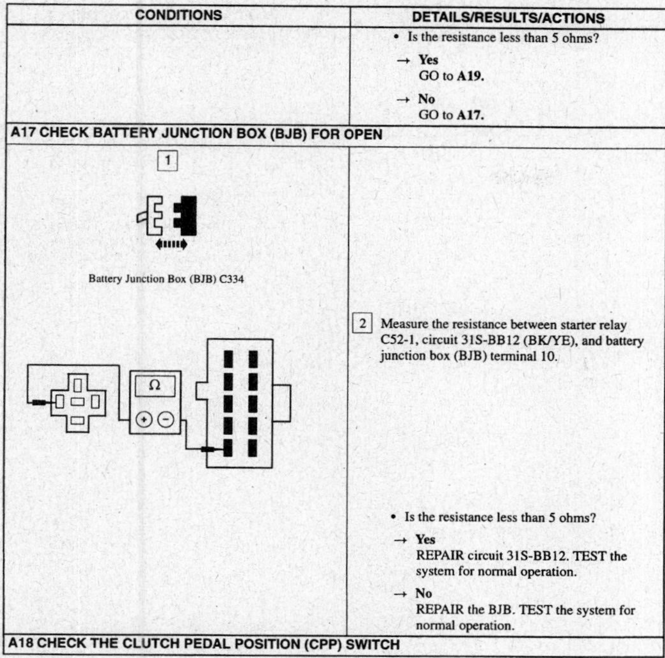 	2 Measure the resistance between starter relay C52-1, circuit 31S-BB12 (BK/YE), and battery junction box (BJB) terminal 10. • Is the resistance less than 5 ohms? → **Yes** REPAIR circuit 31S-BB12. TEST the system for normal operation. → **No** REPAIR the BJB. TEST the system for normal operation.
A18 CHECK THE CLUTCH PEDAL POSITION (CPP) SWITCH	

FM1120100643120X

Fig. 25 Test A: Engine does not crank and relay clicks (Part 12 of 19). 1998 Contour & Mystique

CONDITIONS	DETAILS/RESULTS/ACTIONS
	• Is the vehicle equipped with PATS control module? → **Yes** GO to **A21.** → **No** If built for Mexico, GO to **A22.** If equipped with anti-theft, GO to **A23.** If not equipped with anti-theft, REPAIR circuit 31-BB6 (BK) [manual transmission], or circuit 31S-PF9 (BK) [automatic transmission]. TEST the system for normal operation.
A21 CHECK THE CIRCUIT BETWEEN ANTI-THEFT/CENTRAL LOCKING MODULE AND THE CPP/TR SENSOR FOR OPEN	
1 Anti-Theft/Central Locking Module C451a	

FM1120100643140X

Fig. 25 Test A: Engine does not crank and relay clicks (Part 14 of 19). 1998 Contour & Mystique

CONDITIONS	DETAILS/RESULTS/ACTIONS
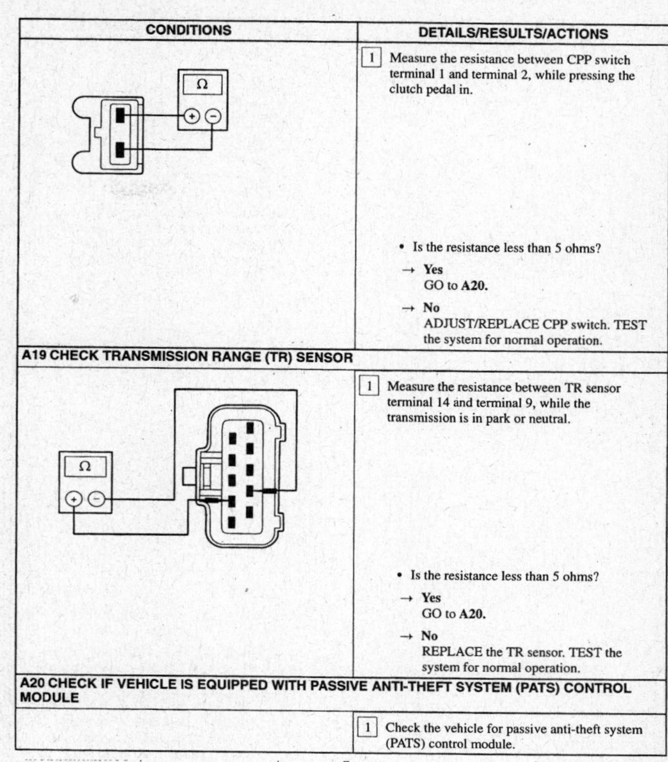 	1 Measure the resistance between CPP switch terminal 1 and terminal 2, while pressing the clutch pedal in. • Is the resistance less than 5 ohms? → **Yes** GO to **A20.** → **No** ADJUST/REPLACE CPP switch. TEST the system for normal operation.
A19 CHECK TRANSMISSION RANGE (TR) SENSOR	
	1 Measure the resistance between TR sensor terminal 14 and terminal 9, while the transmission is in park or neutral. • Is the resistance less than 5 ohms? → **Yes** GO to **A20.** → **No** REPLACE the TR sensor. TEST the system for normal operation.
A20 CHECK IF VEHICLE IS EQUIPPED WITH PASSIVE ANTI-THEFT SYSTEM (PATS) CONTROL MODULE	
	1 Check the vehicle for passive anti-theft system (PATS) control module.

FM1120100643130X

Fig. 25 Test A: Engine does not crank and relay clicks (Part 13 of 19). 1998 Contour & Mystique

CONDITIONS	DETAILS/RESULTS/ACTIONS
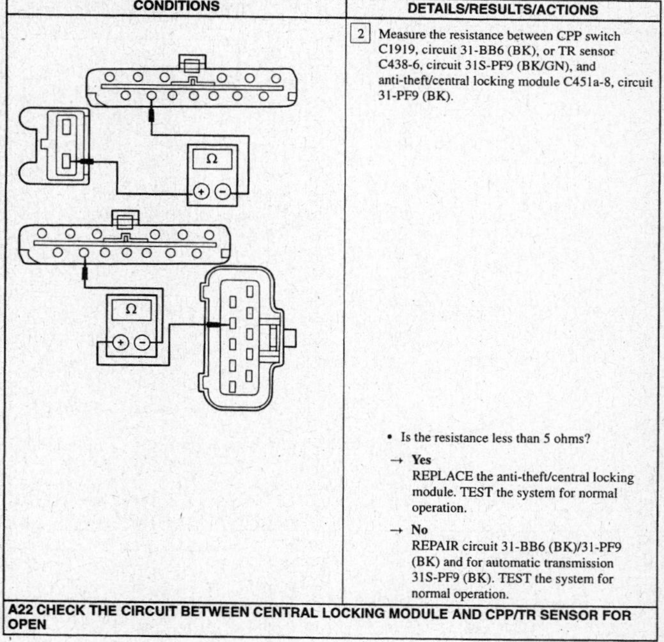 	2 Measure the resistance between CPP switch C1919, circuit 31-BB6 (BK), or TR sensor C438-6, circuit 31S-PF9 (BK/GN), and anti-theft/central locking module C451a-8, circuit 31-PF9 (BK). • Is the resistance less than 5 ohms? → **Yes** REPLACE the anti-theft/central locking module. TEST the system for normal operation. → **No** REPAIR circuit 31-BB6 (BK)/31-PF9 (BK) and for automatic transmission 31S-PF9 (BK). TEST the system for normal operation.
A22 CHECK THE CIRCUIT BETWEEN CENTRAL LOCKING MODULE AND CPP/TR SENSOR FOR OPEN	

FM1120100643150X

Fig. 25 Test A: Engine does not crank and relay clicks (Part 15 of 19). 1998 Contour & Mystique

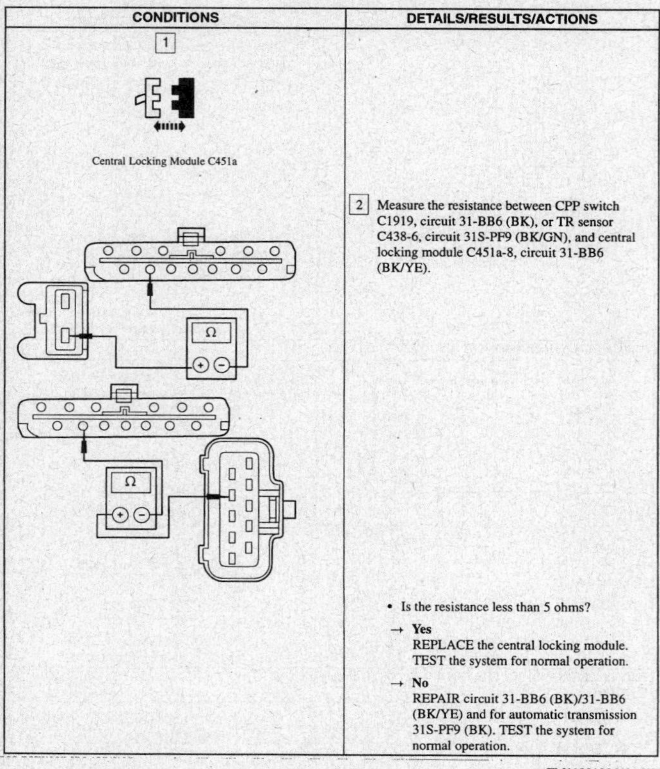

CONDITIONS	DETAILS/RESULTS/ACTIONS
1 Central Locking Module C451a	
	2 Measure the resistance between CPP switch C1919, circuit 31-BB6 (BK), or TR sensor C438-6, circuit 31S-PF9 (BK/GN), and central locking module C451a-8, circuit 31-BB6 (BK/YE). • Is the resistance less than 5 ohms? → **Yes** REPLACE the central locking module. TEST the system for normal operation. → **No** REPAIR circuit 31-BB6 (BK)/31-BB6 (BK/YE) and for automatic transmission 31S-PF9 (BK). TEST the system for normal operation.

FM1120100643160X

Fig. 25 Test A: Engine does not crank and relay clicks (Part 16 of 19). 1998 Contour & Mystique

CONDITIONS	DETAILS/RESULTS/ACTIONS
A24 CHECK CIRCUIT 30-DA3 (RD) FOR OPEN	
1 BJB C330	
	2 Measure the voltage between BJB C330, circuit 30-DA3 (RD), and ground. • Is the voltage greater than 10 volts? → **Yes** REPAIR the BJB. TEST the system for normal operation. → **No** REPAIR circuit 30-DA3 (RD). TEST the system for normal operation.
A25 CHECK THE BJB FOR OPEN	
1 BJB C332	

FM1120100643180X

Fig. 25 Test A: Engine does not crank and relay clicks (Part 18 of 19). 1998 Contour & Mystique

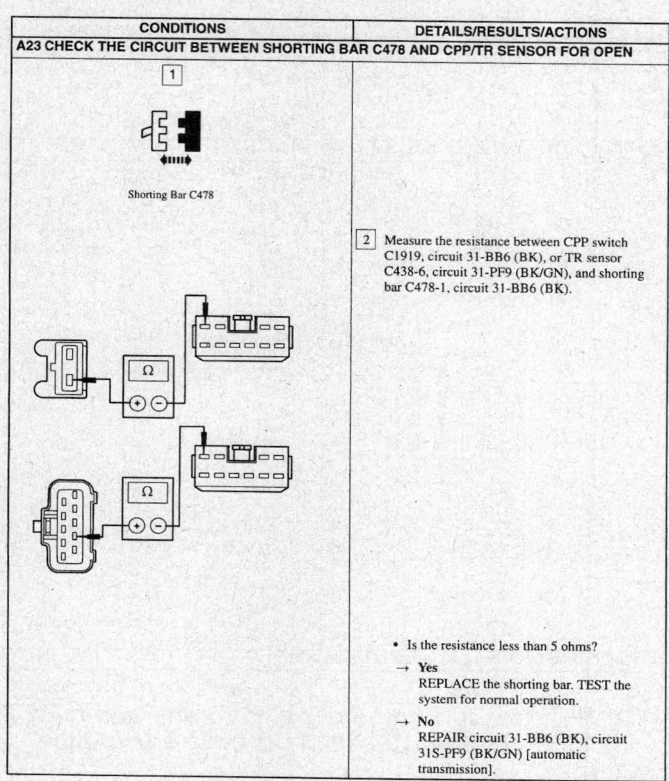

CONDITIONS	DETAILS/RESULTS/ACTIONS
A23 CHECK THE CIRCUIT BETWEEN SHORTING BAR C478 AND CPP/TR SENSOR FOR OPEN	
1 Shorting Bar C478	
	2 Measure the resistance between CPP switch C1919, circuit 31-BB6 (BK), or TR sensor C438-6, circuit 31-PF9 (BK/GN), and shorting bar C478-1, circuit 31-BB6 (BK). • Is the resistance less than 5 ohms? → **Yes** REPLACE the shorting bar. TEST the system for normal operation. → **No** REPAIR circuit 31-BB6 (BK), circuit 31S-PF9 (BK/GN) [automatic transmission].

FM1120100643170X

Fig. 25 Test A: Engine does not crank and relay clicks (Part 17 of 19). 1998 Contour & Mystique

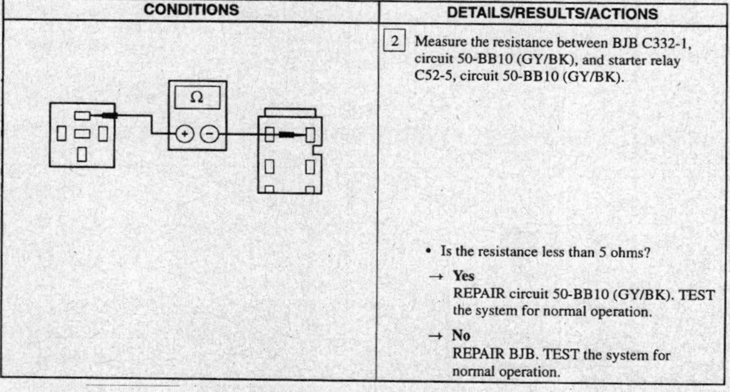

CONDITIONS	DETAILS/RESULTS/ACTIONS
	2 Measure the resistance between BJB C332-1, circuit 50-BB10 (GY/BK), and starter relay C52-5, circuit 50-BB10 (GY/BK). • Is the resistance less than 5 ohms? → **Yes** REPAIR circuit 50-BB10 (GY/BK). TEST the system for normal operation. → **No** REPAIR BJB. TEST the system for normal operation.

FM1120100643190X

Fig. 25 Test A: Engine does not crank and relay clicks (Part 19 of 19). 1998 Contour & Mystique

CONDITIONS	DETAILS/RESULTS/ACTIONS
B1 CHECK THE STARTER MOTOR LOAD	
	1 Perform the Starter Motor Load Component Test on the starter motor. • Is the starter motor OK? → **Yes** GO to **B3.** → **No** GO to **B2.**
B2 CHECK THE BATTERY	
	1 Check the battery.

FM1120100644010X

Fig. 26 Test B: Engine cranks slowly (Part 1 of 2). 1998 Contour & Mystique

CONDITIONS	DETAILS/RESULTS/ACTIONS
	• Is the battery OK? → **Yes** GO to **B4.** → **No** CHARGE or REPLACE the battery. TEST the system for normal operation.
B3 CHECK THE VOLTAGE DROP ON THE STARTER MOTOR	
	1 Perform the Starter Motor – Voltage Drop Component Test on the starter motor • Is the starter motor OK? → **Yes** GO to **B4.** → **No** CLEAN circuit connections as necessary. TEST the system for normal operation.
B4 PERFORM STARTER MOTOR NO-LOAD TEST	
	1 Perform the Starter Motor-No-Load Component Test on the starter motor. • Is the starter motor OK? → **Yes** Diagnose engine mechanical components. → **No** REPAIR or REPLACE the starter motor. TEST the system for normal operation.

FM1120100644020X

Fig. 26 Test B: Engine cranks slowly (Part 2 of 2). 1998 Contour & Mystique

CONDITIONS	DETAILS/RESULTS/ACTIONS
	• Is the starter motor mounted correctly? → **Yes** GO to **C2.** → **No** CORRECTLY INSTALL the starter motor TEST the system for normal operation.
C2 CHECK THE STARTER DRIVE	
1 Starter Motor	2 Inspect the ring gear for damage and wear. • Is the ring gear damaged? → **Yes** REPAIR ring gear as required. TEST the system for normal operation. → **No** REPLACE the starter motor. TEST the system for normal operation.

FM1120100645020X

Fig. 27 Test C: Unusual starter noise (Part 2 of 2). 1998 Contour & Mystique

A1 CHECK THE BATTERY

1 Check the battery;

- **Is battery OK?**

→ **Yes**

Go to «A2».

→ **No**

RECHARGE or INSTALL a new battery as required

FM1120100647010X

Fig. 29 Test A: Engine does not crank & relay clicks (Part 1 of 23). 1999–2000 Contour & Mystique

CONDITIONS	DETAILS/RESULTS/ACTIONS
C1 CHECK THE STARTER MOTOR MOUNTING	
	1 Check the starter motor and mounting brackets for correct alignment, cracks, and looseness.

FM1120100645010X

Fig. 27 Test C: Unusual starter noise (Part 1 of 2). 1998 Contour & Mystique

CONDITIONS	DETAILS/RESULTS/ACTIONS
D1 CHECK STARTER SOLENOID	
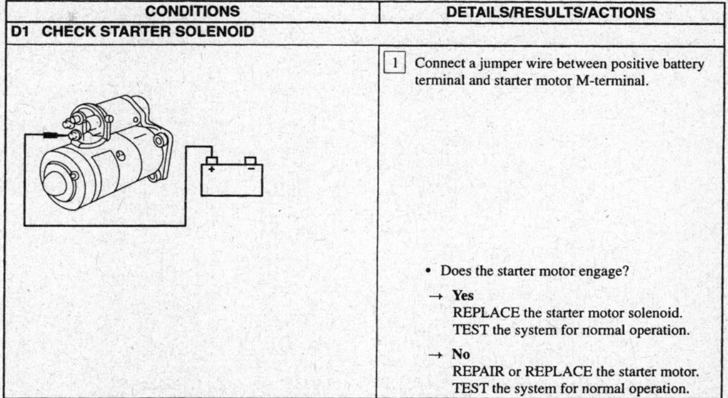	1 Connect a jumper wire between positive battery terminal and starter motor M-terminal. • Does the starter motor engage? → **Yes** REPLACE the starter motor solenoid. TEST the system for normal operation. → **No** REPAIR or REPLACE the starter motor. TEST the system for normal operation.

FM1120100646000X

Fig. 28 Test D: Starter spins but engine does not crank. 1998 Contour & Mystique

A2 CHECK THE VOLTAGE TO STARTER MOTOR SOLENOID

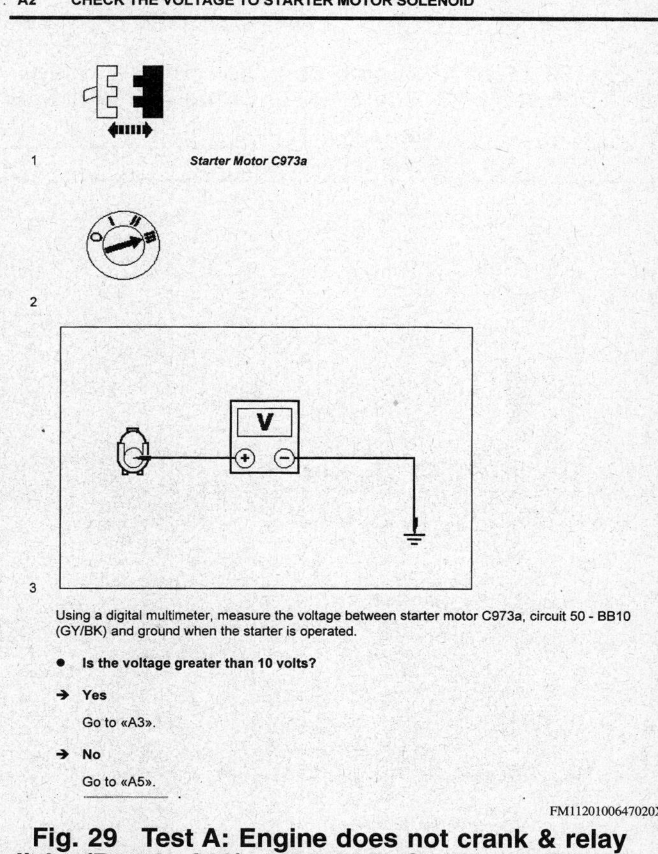

Using a digital multimeter, measure the voltage between starter motor C973a, circuit 50 - BB10 (GY/BK) and ground when the starter is operated.

- **Is the voltage greater than 10 volts?**

→ **Yes**

Go to «A3».

→ **No**

Go to «A5».

FM1120100647020X

Fig. 29 Test A: Engine does not crank & relay clicks (Part 2 of 23). 1999–2000 Contour & Mystique

A3 CHECK THE VOLTAGE TO THE STARTER MOTOR

Note:
Both wires coming from the battery are black, make a note of which wire is coming from the positive battery terminal before making measurements.

1

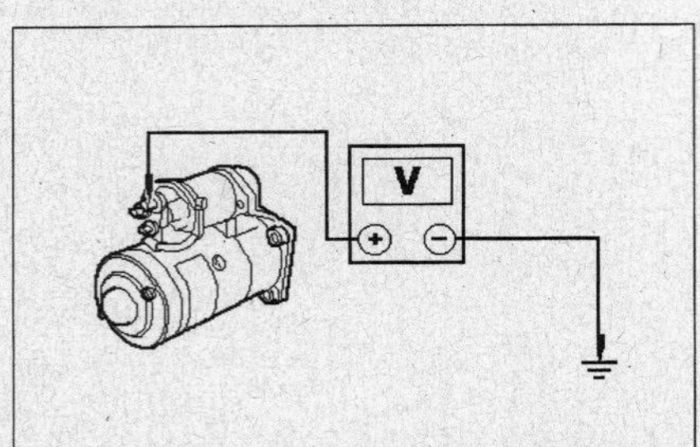

2

Using a digital multimeter, measure the voltage between starter motor C973a pin 30, circuit 30 (RD) and ground.

- **Is the voltage greater than 10 volts?**

➔ **Yes**

Go to «A4».

➔ **No**

REPAIR the BK circuit from the positive battery terminal. TEST the system for normal operation.

FM1120100647030X

Fig. 29 Test A: Engine does not crank & relay clicks (Part 3 of 23). 1999–2000 Contour & Mystique

A4 CHECK THE STARTER MOTOR GROUND

Note:
Both wires coming from the battery are black, make a note of which wire is coming from the positive battery terminal before making measurements.

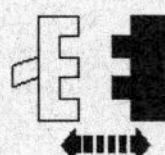

1 *Starter Motor C973b*

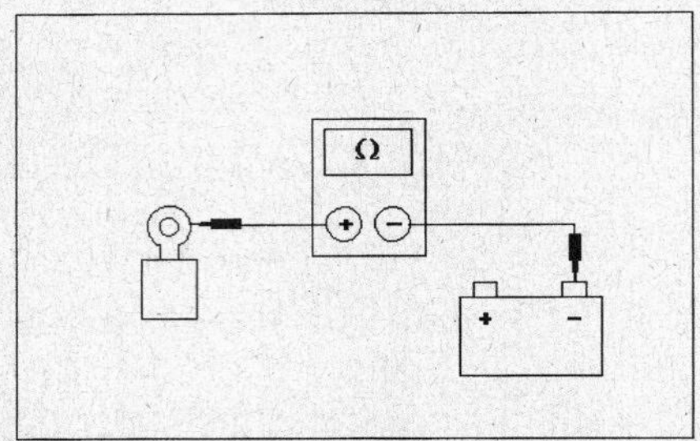

2

Using a digital multimeter, measure the resistance between starter motor C973b, BK circuit from the negative battery terminal, and negative battery terminal.

- **Is the resistance less than 5 ohms?**

➔ **Yes**

INSTALL a new starter motor. TEST the system for normal operation.

➔ **No**

REPAIR the BK circuit from the negative battery terminal. TEST the system for normal operation.

FM1120100647040X

Fig. 29 Test A: Engine does not crank & relay clicks (Part 4 of 23). 1999–2000 Contour & Mystique

A5 CHECK CIRCUIT 30 - DA3 (RD) FOR VOLTAGE

1

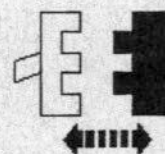

2 *Starter Relay C52*

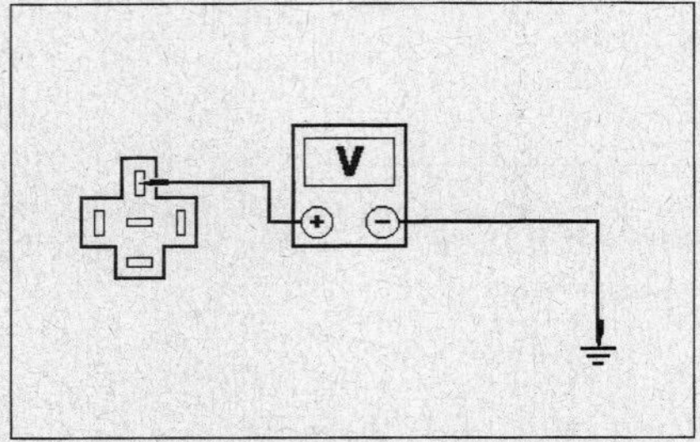

3

Using a digital multimeter, measure the voltage between starter relay C52 pin 3, circuit 30 - DA3 (RD) and ground.

- **Is the voltage greater than 10 volts?**

➔ **Yes**

Go to «A6».

➔ **No**

Go to «A22».

FM1120100647050X

Fig. 29 Test A: Engine does not crank & relay clicks (Part 5 of 23). 1999–2000 Contour & Mystique

A6 CHECK CIRCUIT 50 - BB10 (GY/BK) FOR OPEN

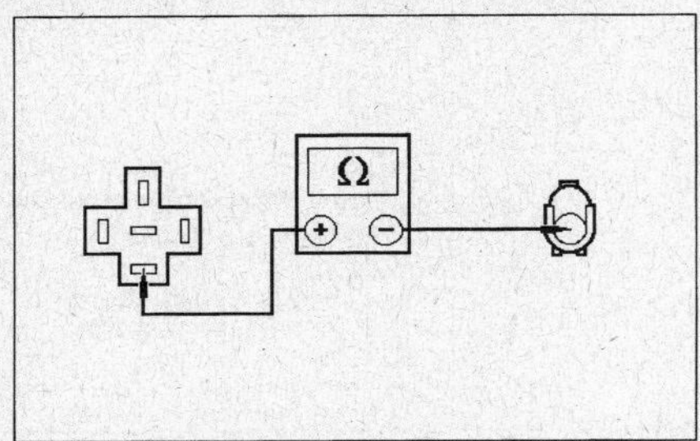

1

Using a digital multimeter, measure the resistance between starter motor C52 pin 5, circuit 50 - BB10 (GY/BK) and starter motor C973a pin 50, circuit 50 - BB10 (GY/BK).

- **Is the resistance less than 5 ohms?**

➔ **Yes**

Go to «A7».

➔ **No**

Go to «A23».

FM1120100647060X

Fig. 29 Test A: Engine does not crank & relay clicks (Part 6 of 23). 1999–2000 Contour & Mystique

A7 CHECK CIRCUIT 50 - BB11 (GY/WH) FOR VOLTAGE

1

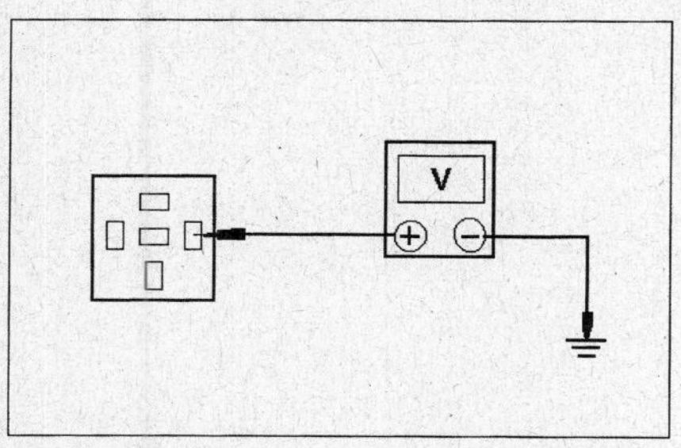

2

Using a digital multimeter, measure the voltage between starter relay C52 pin 1, circuit 50 - BB11 (GY/WH) and ground.

- **Is the voltage greater than 10 volts?**

➔ **Yes**

Go to «A13».

➔ **No**

Go to «A8».

FM1120100647070X

Fig. 29 Test A: Engine does not crank & relay clicks (Part 7 of 23). 1999–2000 Contour & Mystique

A9 CHECK CIRCUIT 30 - BB9 (RD) FOR OPEN

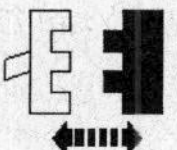

1 *Ignition Switch C456*

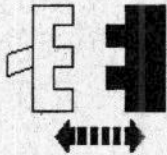

2 *Fuse 10 (20A)*

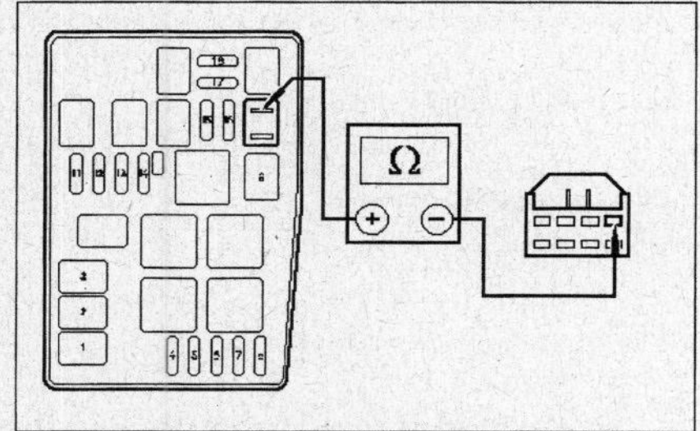

3

Using a digital multimeter, measure the resistance between fuse 10 (20A) load side, circuit 30 - BB9 (RD) and ignition switch C456 pin 1, circuit 30 - BB9 (RD).

- **Is the resistance less than 5 ohms?**

➔ **Yes**

Go to «A10».

➔ **No**

REPAIR circuit 30 - BB9 (RD). TEST the system for normal operation.

FM1120100647090X

Fig. 29 Test A: Engine does not crank & relay clicks (Part 9 of 23). 1999–2000 Contour & Mystique

A8 CHECK FUSE 10 (20A)

1

2 *Fuse 10 (20A)*

- **Is the fuse OK?**

➔ **Yes**

Go to «A9».

➔ **No**

INSTALL a new fuse 10 (20A). TEST the system for normal operation. If fuse fails again, CHECK for short to ground, REPAIR as necessary.

FM1120100647080X

Fig. 29 Test A: Engine does not crank & relay clicks (Part 8 of 23). 1999–2000 Contour & Mystique

A10 CHECK THE IGNITION SWITCH

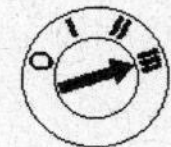

1

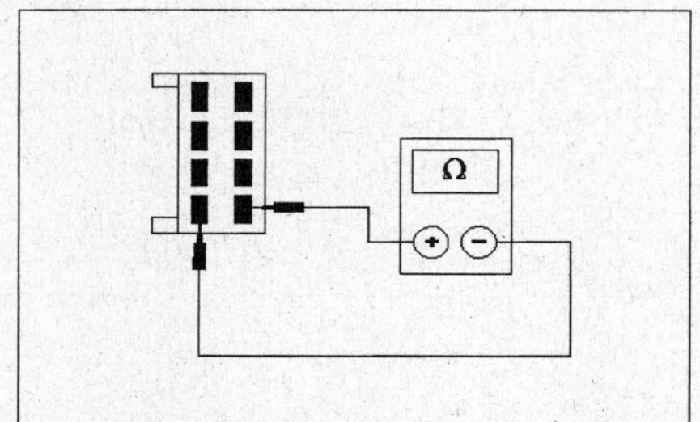

2

Using a digital multimeter, measure the resistance between ignition switch pin 1 and pin 5.

- **Is the resistance less than 5 ohms?**

➔ **Yes**

Go to «A11».

➔ **No**

INSTALL a new ignition switch. TEST the system for normal operation.

FM1120100647100X

Fig. 29 Test A: Engine does not crank & relay clicks (Part 10 of 23). 1999–2000 Contour & Mystique

A11	CHECK CIRCUIT 50 - BB11 (GY/WH) FOR OPEN

1

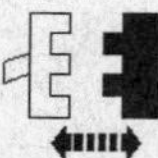

2 *Battery Junction Box C334*

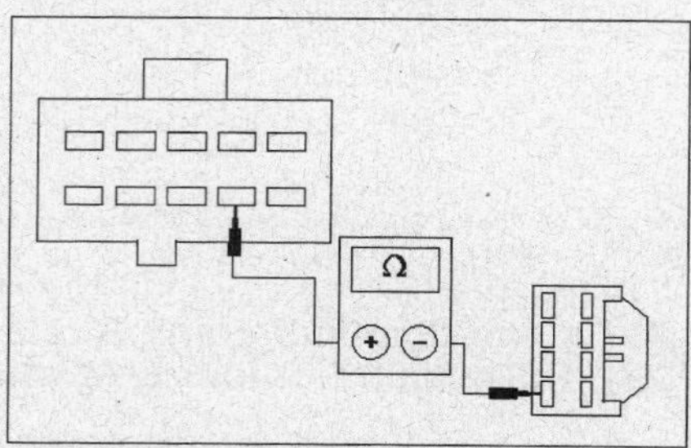

3

Using a digital multimeter, measure the resistance between the ignition switch C456 pin 5, circuit 50 - BB11 (GY/WH) and battery junction box (BJB) C334 pin 9, circuit 50 (GY/WH)

- **Is the resistance less than 5 ohms?**

➔ **Yes**

Go to «A12».

➔ **No**

REPAIR circuit 50 - BB11 (GY/WH). TEST the system for normal operation.

FM1120100647110X

Fig. 29 Test A: Engine does not crank & relay clicks (Part 11 of 23). 1999–2000 Contour & Mystique

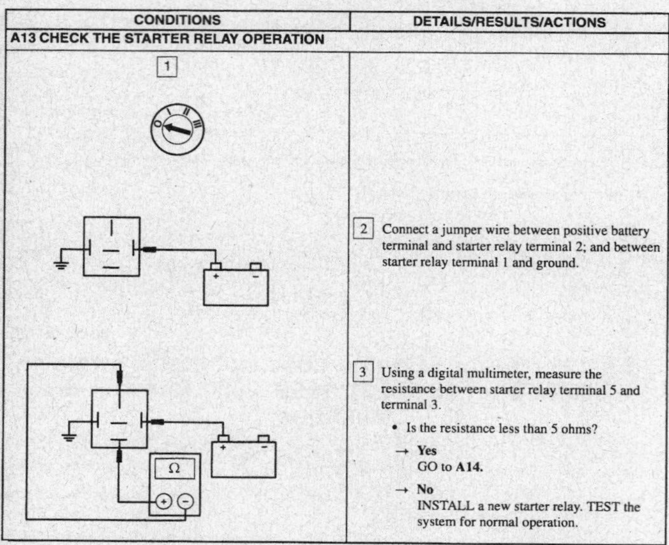

CONDITIONS	DETAILS/RESULTS/ACTIONS
A13 CHECK THE STARTER RELAY OPERATION	
1	
	2 Connect a jumper wire between positive battery terminal and starter relay terminal 2; and between starter relay terminal 1 and ground.
	3 Using a digital multimeter, measure the resistance between starter relay terminal 5 and terminal 3. • Is the resistance less than 5 ohms? → **Yes** GO to **A14.** → **No** INSTALL a new starter relay. TEST the system for normal operation.

FM1120100647130X

Fig. 29 Test A: Engine does not crank & relay clicks (Part 13 of 23). 1999–2000 Contour & Mystique

A12	CHECK STARTER RELAY DIODE

1 *Starter Relay Diode C61*

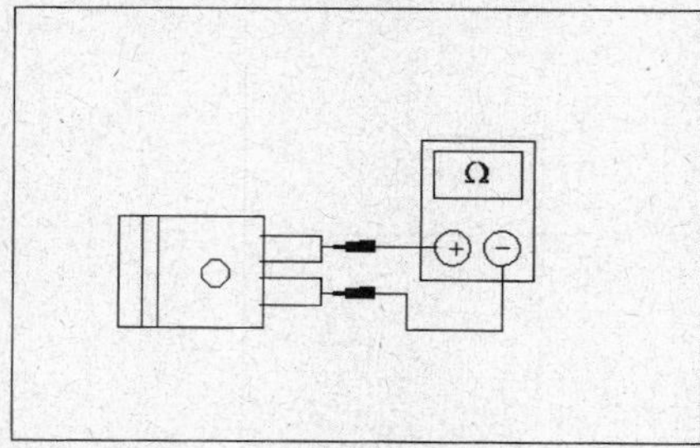

2

Using a digital multimeter, measure the resistance between starter relay diode terminals.

- **Is there continuity in one direction, and no continuity in the other direction?**

➔ **Yes**

REPAIR the BJB. TEST the system for normal operation.

➔ **No**

INSTALL a new starter relay diode. TEST the system for normal operation.

FM1120100647120X

Fig. 29 Test A: Engine does not crank & relay clicks (Part 12 of 23). 1999–2000 Contour & Mystique

A14	CHECK CIRCUIT 50 - BB10 (GY/BK) FOR SHORT TO GROUND

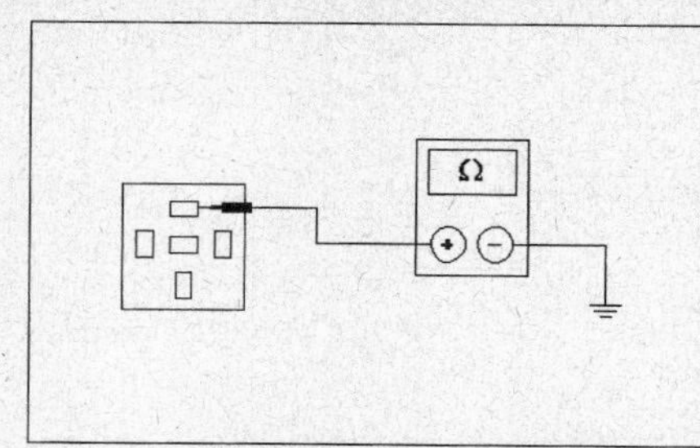

1

Using a digital multimeter, measure the resistance between the starter relay C52 pin 5, circuit 50 - BB10 (GY/BK) and ground.

- **Is the resistance greater than 10,000 ohms?**

➔ **Yes**

If equipped with manual transmission, Go to «A15».

If equipped with automatic transmission, Go to «A16».

➔ **No**

REPAIR circuit 50 (GY/BK). TEST the system for normal operation.

FM1120100647140X

Fig. 29 Test A: Engine does not crank & relay clicks (Part 14 of 23). 1999–2000 Contour & Mystique

A15 CHECK CIRCUIT 31S - BB12 (BK/YE) BETWEEN CLUTCH PEDAL POSITION (CPP) SWITCH AND STARTER RELAY FOR OPEN

1 *Clutch Pedal Position (CPP) Switch C1919*

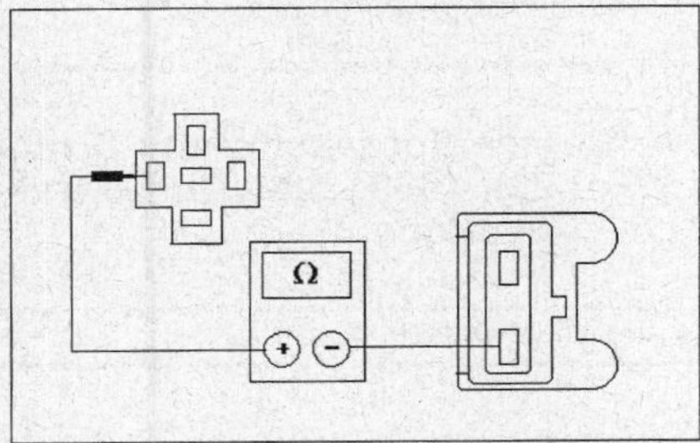

2

Using a digital multimeter, measure the resistance between starter relay C52 terminal 1, circuit 31S - BB12 (BK/YE), and clutch pedal position (CPP) switch C1919 pin 2, circuit 31S - BB12 (BK/YE).

- **Is the resistance less than 5 ohms?**

→ **Yes**

Go to «A18».

→ **No**

Go to «A17».

FM1120100647150X

Fig. 29 Test A: Engine does not crank & relay clicks (Part 15 of 23). 1999–2000 Contour & Mystique

A17 CHECK BATTERY JUNCTION BOX (BJB) FOR OPEN

1 *Battery Junction Box (BJB) C334*

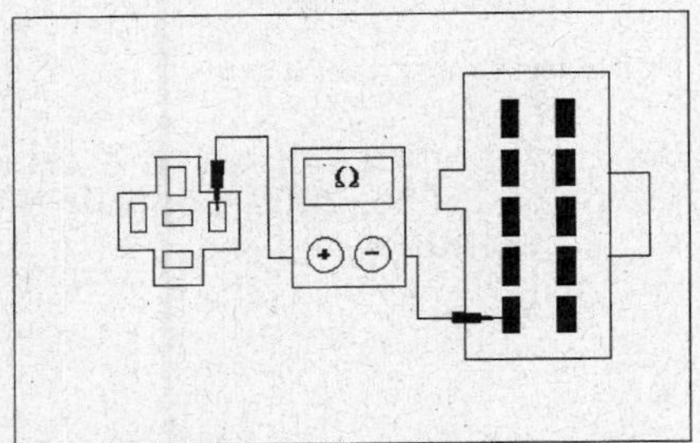

2

Using a digital multimeter, measure the resistance between starter relay C52 terminal 2, circuit 31S - BB12 (BK/YE), and battery junction box (BJB) terminal 10.

- **Is the resistance less than 5 ohms?**

→ **Yes**

REPAIR circuit 31S - BB12. TEST the system for normal operation.

→ **No**

REPAIR the BJB. TEST the system for normal operation.

FM1120100647170X

Fig. 29 Test A: Engine does not crank & relay clicks (Part 17 of 23). 1999–2000 Contour & Mystique

A16 CHECK CIRCUIT 31S - BB12 (BK/YE) BETWEEN TRANSMISSION RANGE (TR) SENSOR AND STARTER RELAY FOR OPEN

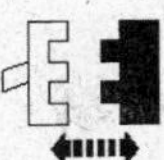

1 *Transmission Range (TR) Sensor C1942*

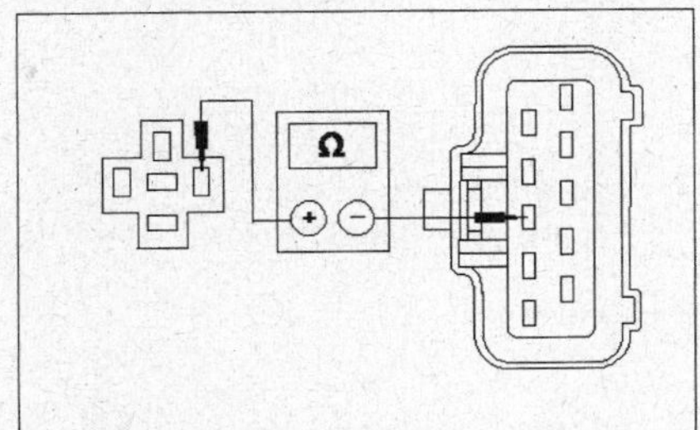

2

Using a digital multimeter, measure the resistance between starter relay C52 terminal 2, circuit 31S - BB12 (BK/YE), and transmission range (TR) sensor C1942, pin 3 circuit 31S - BB12 (BK/YE).

- **Is the resistance less than 5 ohms?**

→ **Yes**

Go to «A19».

→ **No**

Go to «A17».

FM1120100647160X

Fig. 29 Test A: Engine does not crank & relay clicks (Part 16 of 23). 1999–2000 Contour & Mystique

A18 CHECK THE CLUTCH PEDAL POSITION (CPP) SWITCH

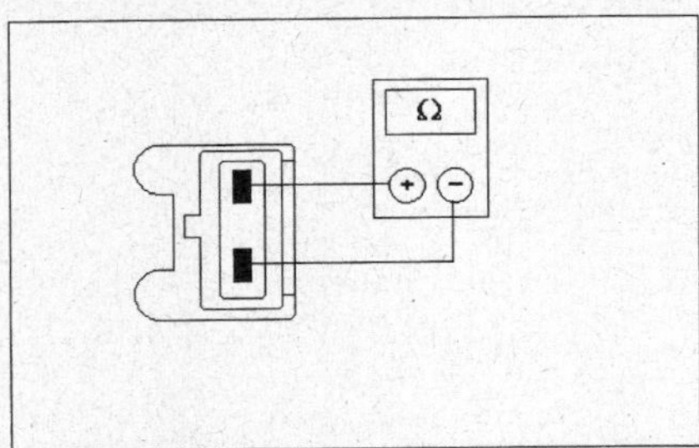

1

Using a digital multimeter, measure the resistance between CPP switch pin 1 and pin 2, while pressing the clutch pedal in.

- **Is the resistance less than 5 ohms?**

→ **Yes**

Go to «A20».

→ **No**

ADJUST/INSTALL a new CPP switch. TEST the system for normal operation.

FM1120100647180X

Fig. 29 Test A: Engine does not crank & relay clicks (Part 18 of 23). 1999–2000 Contour & Mystique

A19	CHECK TRANSMISSION RANGE (TR) SENSOR

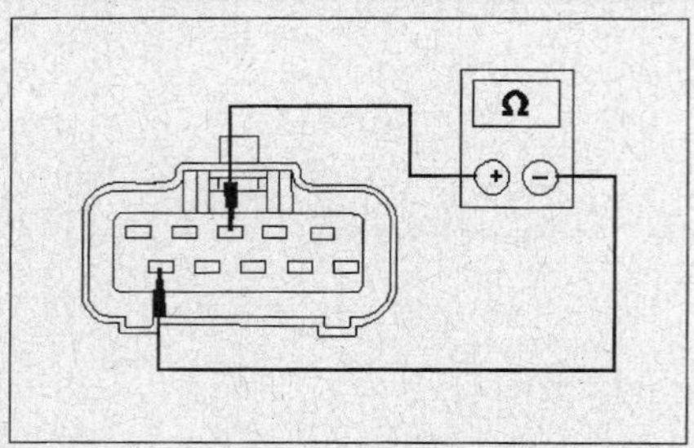

1

Using a digital multimeter, measure the resistance between TR sensor pin 3 and pin 6, while the transmission is in park or neutral.

- **Is the resistance less than 5 ohms?**

➔ **Yes**

Go to «A20».

➔ **No**

INSTALL a new TR sensor. TEST the system for normal operation.

FM1120100647190X

Fig. 29 Test A: Engine does not crank & relay clicks (Part 19 of 23). 1999–2000 Contour & Mystique

A21	CHECK THE CIRCUIT BETWEEN POWERTRAIN CONTROL MODULE (PCM) AND THE CPP/TR SENSOR FOR OPEN

1 *PCM C421*

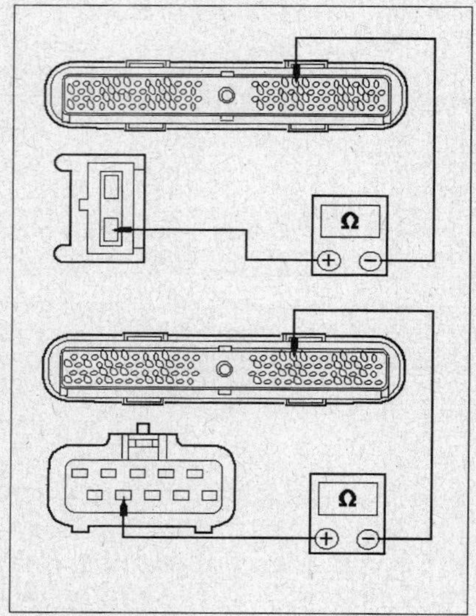

2

Using a digital multimeter, measure the resistance between CPP switch C1919 pin 1, circuit 31 - BB6 (BK), or TR sensor C1942 pin 6, circuit 31S - PF9 (BK/GN), and PCM C421 pin 18, circuit 31 - PF9 (BK).

- **Is the resistance less than 5 ohms?**

➔ **Yes**

Diagnose PATS system.

➔ **No**

REPAIR circuit 31 - BB6 (BK)/31 - PF9 (BK) and for automatic transmission 31S - PF9 (BK). TEST the system for normal operation.

FM1120100647210X

Fig. 29 Test A: Engine does not crank & relay clicks (Part 21 of 23). 1999–2000 Contour & Mystique

A20	CHECK IF VEHICLE IS EQUIPPED WITH PASSIVE ANTI - THEFT SYSTEM (PATS)

1 Check the vehicle for PATS system.

- **Is the vehicle equipped with PATS?**

➔ **Yes**

Go to «A21».

➔ **No**

If not equipped with PATS, REPAIR circuit 31 - BB6 (BK) [manual transmission], or circuit 31S - PF9 (BK) [automatic transmission]. TEST the system for normal operation.

FM1120100647200X

Fig. 29 Test A: Engine does not crank & relay clicks (Part 20 of 23). 1999–2000 Contour & Mystique

A22	CHECK CIRCUIT 30 - DA3 (RD) FOR OPEN

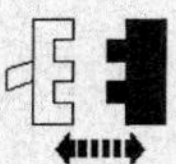

1 *BJB C330*

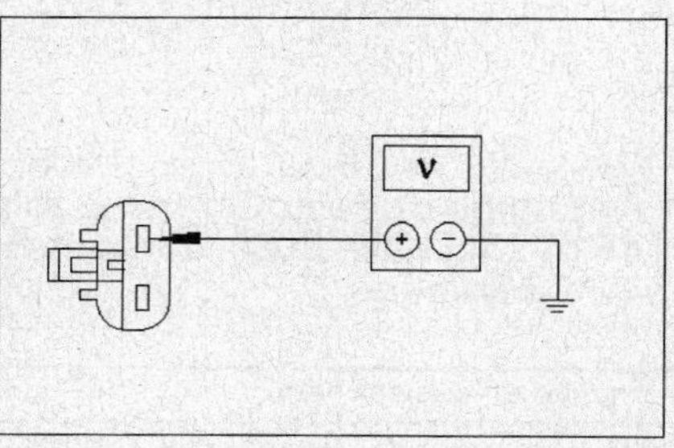

2

Using a digital multimeter, measure the voltage between BJB C330, circuit 30 - DA3 (RD), and ground.

- **Is the voltage greater than 10 volts?**

➔ **Yes**

REPAIR the BJB. TEST the system for normal operation.

➔ **No**

REPAIR circuit 30 - DA3 (RD). TEST the system for normal operation.

FM1120100647220X

Fig. 29 Test A: Engine does not crank & relay clicks (Part 22 of 23). 1999–2000 Contour & Mystique

A23 CHECK THE BJB FOR OPEN

1 BJB C332

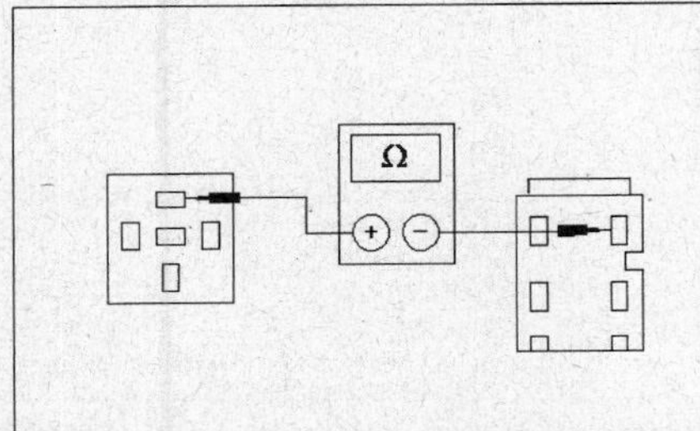

2

Using a digital multimeter, measure the resistance between BJB C332 pin 1, circuit 50 - BB10 (GY/BK), and starter relay C52 terminal 5, circuit 50 - BB10 (GY/BK).

- **Is the resistance less than 5 ohms?**

➔ **Yes**

REPAIR circuit 50 - BB10 (GY/BK). TEST the system for normal operation.

➔ **No**

REPAIR BJB. TEST the system for normal operation.

FM1120100647230X

Fig. 29 Test A: Engine does not crank & relay clicks (Part 23 of 23). 1999–2000 Contour & Mystique

B2 CHECK THE BATTERY

1 Check the battery

- **Is the battery OK?**

➔ **Yes**

Go to «B4».

➔ **No**

CHARGE or INSTALL a new battery. TEST the system for normal operation.

FM1120100648020X

Fig. 30 Test B: Engine cranks slowly (Part 2 of 4). 1999–2000 Contour & Mystique

B4 CARRY OUT STARTER MOTOR NO - LOAD TEST

1 Carry out the Starter Motor No - Load Component Test on the starter motor

- **Is the starter motor OK?**

➔ **Yes**

For engine diagnosis and testing; Diagnose engine mechanical components.

➔ **No**

REPAIR or INSTALL a new starter motor. TEST the system for normal operation.

FM1120100648040X

Fig. 30 Test B: Engine cranks slowly (Part 4 of 4). 1999–2000 Contour & Mystique

B1 CHECK THE STARTER MOTOR LOAD

1 Carry out the Starter Motor Load Component Test on the starter motor;

- **Is the starter motor OK?**

➔ **Yes**

Go to «B3».

➔ **No**

Go to «B2».

FM1120100648010X

Fig. 30 Test B: Engine cranks slowly (Part 1 of 4). 1999–2000 Contour & Mystique

B3 CHECK THE VOLTAGE DROP ON THE STARTER MOTOR

1 Perform the Starter Motor - Voltage Drop Component Test on the starter motor;

- **Is the starter motor OK?**

➔ **Yes**

Go to «B4».

➔ **No**

CLEAN circuit connections as necessary. TEST the system for normal operation.

FM1120100648030X

Fig. 30 Test B: Engine cranks slowly (Part 3 of 4). 1999–2000 Contour & Mystique

C1 CHECK THE STARTER MOTOR MOUNTING

1 Check the starter motor and mounting brackets for correct alignment, cracks, and looseness.

- **Is the starter motor mounted correctly?**

➔ **Yes**

Go to «C2».

➔ **No**

CORRECTLY INSTALL the starter motor; TEST the system for normal operation.

FM1120100649010X

Fig. 31 Test C: Unusual starter noise (Part 1 of 2). 1999–2000 Contour & Mystique

C2 CHECK THE STARTER DRIVE

1 *Starter Motor*

2 Inspect the ring gear for damage and wear.

- **Is the ring gear damaged?**

➔ **Yes**

REPAIR ring gear as required. TEST the system for normal operation.

➔ **No**

INSTALL a new starter motor. TEST the system for normal operation.

FM1120100649020X

Fig. 31 Test C: Unusual starter noise (Part 2 of 2). 1999–2000 Contour & Mystique

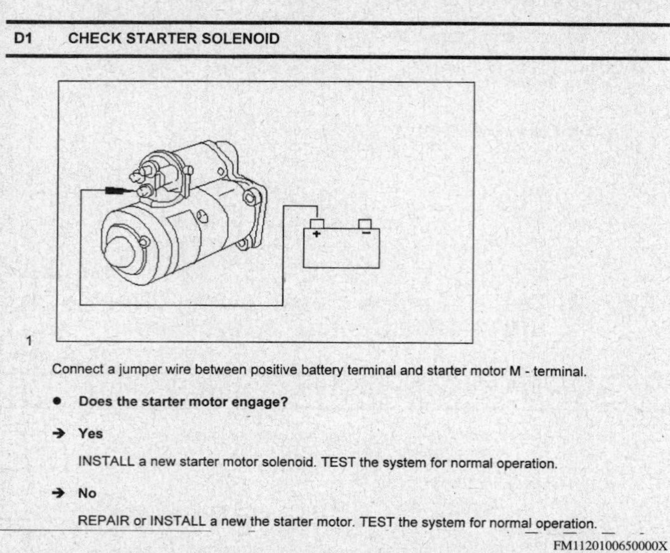

D1 CHECK STARTER SOLENOID

1

Connect a jumper wire between positive battery terminal and starter motor M - terminal.

- Does the starter motor engage?

→ Yes

INSTALL a new starter motor solenoid. TEST the system for normal operation.

→ No

REPAIR or INSTALL a new the starter motor. TEST the system for normal operation.

FM1120100650000X

Fig. 32 Test D: Starter spins but engine does not crank. 1999–2000 Contour & Mystique

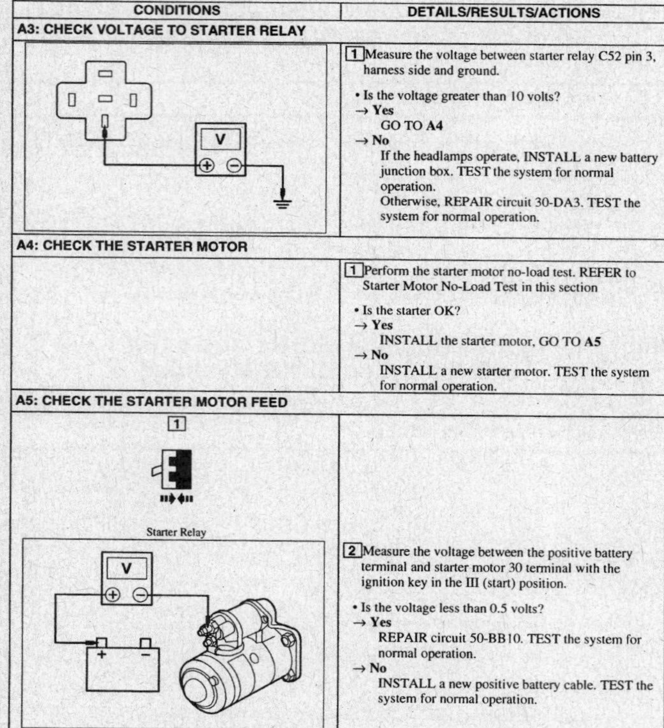

CONDITIONS	DETAILS/RESULTS/ACTIONS
A3: CHECK VOLTAGE TO STARTER RELAY	
	1 Measure the voltage between starter relay C52 pin 3, harness side and ground. • Is the voltage greater than 10 volts? → **Yes** GO TO **A4** → **No** If the headlamps operate, INSTALL a new battery junction box. TEST the system for normal operation. Otherwise, REPAIR circuit 30-DA3. TEST the system for normal operation.
A4: CHECK THE STARTER MOTOR	
	1 Perform the starter motor no-load test. REFER to Starter Motor No-Load Test in this section • Is the starter OK? → **Yes** INSTALL the starter motor, GO TO **A5** → **No** INSTALL a new starter motor. TEST the system for normal operation.
A5: CHECK THE STARTER MOTOR FEED	
1 Starter Relay	
	2 Measure the voltage between the positive battery terminal and starter motor 30 terminal with the ignition key in the III (start) position. • Is the voltage less than 0.5 volts? → **Yes** REPAIR circuit 50-BB10. TEST the system for normal operation. → **No** INSTALL a new positive battery cable. TEST the system for normal operation.

FM1120100601020X

Fig. 33 Test A: Engine does not crank & relay clicks (Part 2 of 2). Cougar

CONDITIONS	DETAILS/RESULTS/ACTIONS
A1: CHECK THE BATTERY	
	1 Check the battery. • Is the battery OK? → **Yes** GO TO **A2** → **No** INSTALL a new battery. TEST the system for normal operation.
A2: CHECK THE STARTER RELAY	
1 Starter Relay	
	2 Carry out the ISO mini relay component test. • Is the relay OK? → **Yes** GO TO **A3** → **No** INSTALL a new starter relay. TEST the system for normal operation.

FM1120100601010X

Fig. 33 Test A: Engine does not crank & relay clicks (Part 1 of 2). Cougar

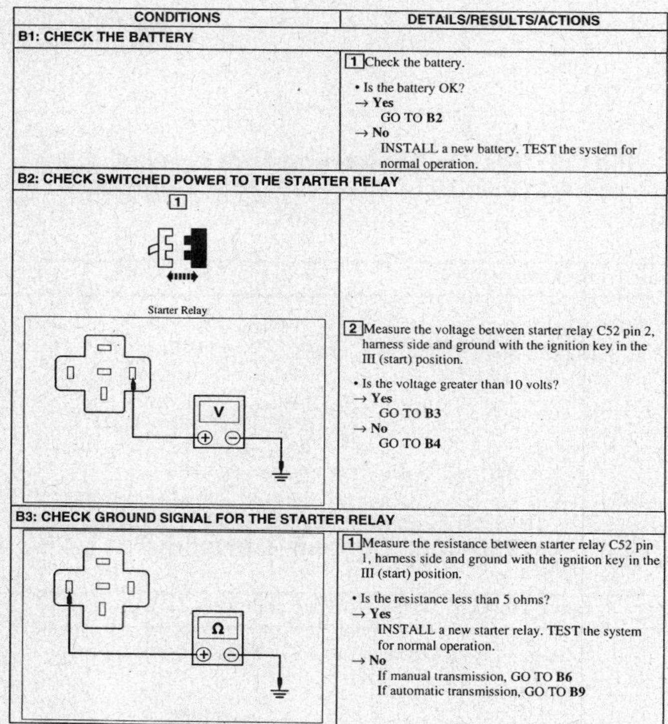

CONDITIONS	DETAILS/RESULTS/ACTIONS
B1: CHECK THE BATTERY	
	1 Check the battery. • Is the battery OK? → **Yes** GO TO **B2** → **No** INSTALL a new battery. TEST the system for normal operation.
B2: CHECK SWITCHED POWER TO THE STARTER RELAY	
1 Starter Relay	
	2 Measure the voltage between starter relay C52 pin 2, harness side and ground with the ignition key in the III (start) position. • Is the voltage greater than 10 volts? → **Yes** GO TO **B3** → **No** GO TO **B4**
B3: CHECK GROUND SIGNAL FOR THE STARTER RELAY	
	1 Measure the resistance between starter relay C52 pin 1, harness side and ground with the ignition key in the III (start) position. • Is the resistance less than 5 ohms? → **Yes** INSTALL a new starter relay. TEST the system for normal operation. → **No** If manual transmission, GO TO **B6** If automatic transmission, GO TO **B9**

FM1120100602010X

Fig. 34 Test B: Engine does not crank & relay does not click (Part 1 of 5). Cougar

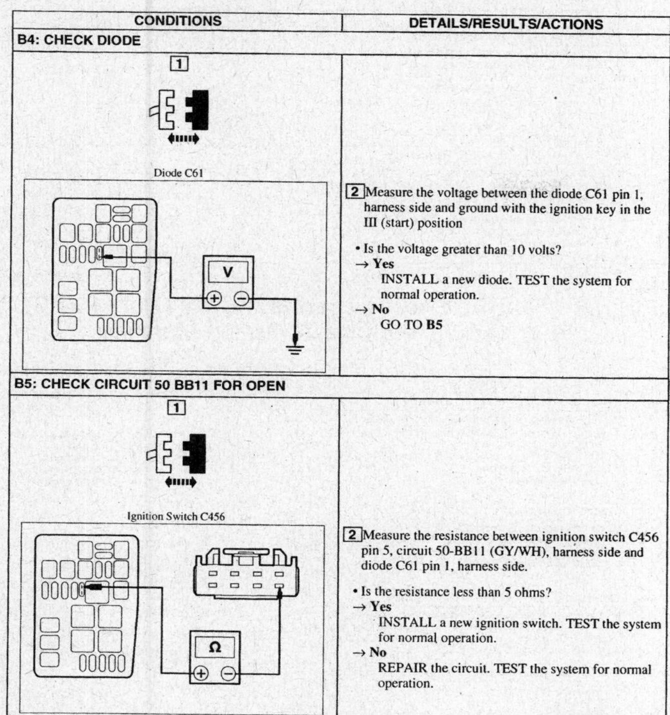

CONDITIONS	DETAILS/RESULTS/ACTIONS
B4: CHECK DIODE	
1 Diode C61	2 Measure the voltage between the diode C61 pin 1, harness side and ground with the ignition key in the III (start) position • Is the voltage greater than 10 volts? → **Yes** INSTALL a new diode. TEST the system for normal operation. → **No** GO TO **B5**
B5: CHECK CIRCUIT 50 BB11 FOR OPEN	
1 Ignition Switch C456	2 Measure the resistance between ignition switch C456 pin 5, circuit 50-BB11 (GY/WH), harness side and diode C61 pin 1, harness side. • Is the resistance less than 5 ohms? → **Yes** INSTALL a new ignition switch. TEST the system for normal operation. → **No** REPAIR the circuit. TEST the system for normal operation.

FM1120100602020X

Fig. 34 Test B: Engine does not crank & relay does not click (Part 2 of 5). Cougar

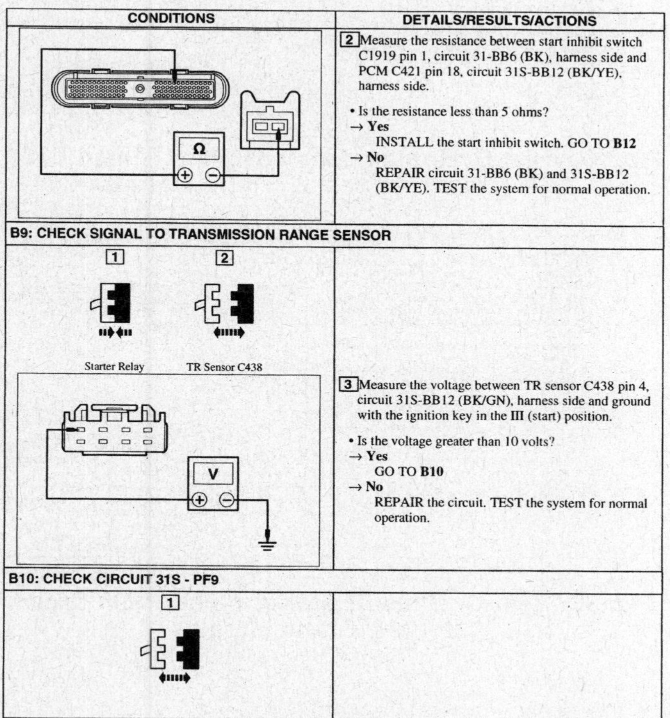

CONDITIONS	DETAILS/RESULTS/ACTIONS
	2 Measure the resistance between start inhibit switch C1919 pin 1, circuit 31-BB6 (BK), harness side and PCM C421 pin 18, circuit 31S-BB12 (BK/YE), harness side. • Is the resistance less than 5 ohms? → **Yes** INSTALL the start inhibit switch. GO TO **B12** → **No** REPAIR circuit 31-BB6 (BK) and 31S-BB12 (BK/YE). TEST the system for normal operation.
B9: CHECK SIGNAL TO TRANSMISSION RANGE SENSOR	
1 Starter Relay 2 TR Sensor C438	3 Measure the voltage between TR sensor C438 pin 4, circuit 31S-BB12 (BK/GN), harness side and ground with the ignition key in the III (start) position. • Is the voltage greater than 10 volts? → **Yes** GO TO **B10** → **No** REPAIR the circuit. TEST the system for normal operation.
B10: CHECK CIRCUIT 31S - PF9	
1	

FM1120100602040X

Fig. 34 Test B: Engine does not crank & relay does not click (Part 4 of 5). Cougar

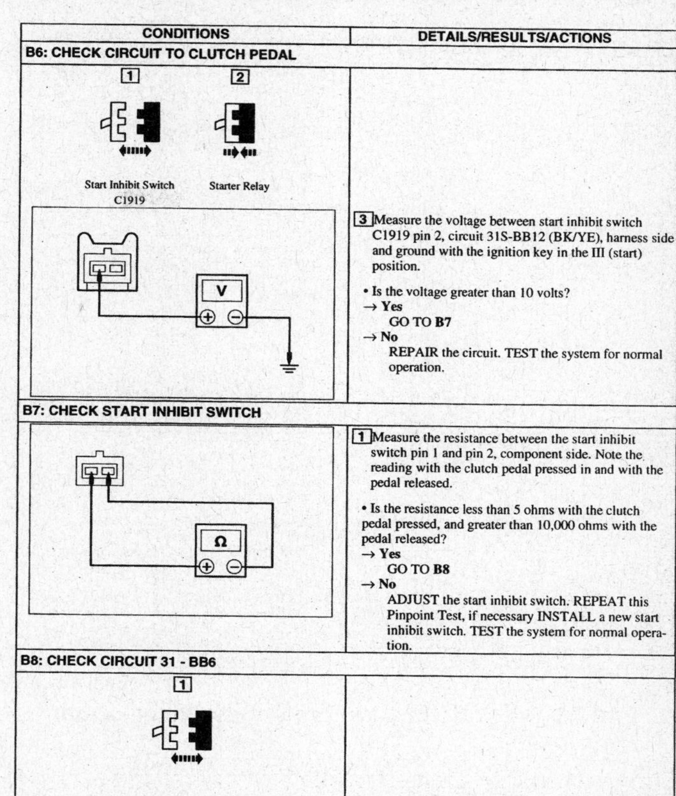

CONDITIONS	DETAILS/RESULTS/ACTIONS
B6: CHECK CIRCUIT TO CLUTCH PEDAL	
1 Start Inhibit Switch C1919 2 Starter Relay	3 Measure the voltage between start inhibit switch C1919 pin 2, circuit 31S-BB12 (BK/YE), harness side and ground with the ignition key in the III (start) position. • Is the voltage greater than 10 volts? → **Yes** GO TO **B7** → **No** REPAIR the circuit. TEST the system for normal operation.
B7: CHECK START INHIBIT SWITCH	
	1 Measure the resistance between the start inhibit switch pin 1 and pin 2, component side. Note the reading with the clutch pedal pressed in and with the pedal released. • Is the resistance less than 5 ohms with the clutch pedal pressed, and greater than 10,000 ohms with the pedal released? → **Yes** GO TO **B8** → **No** ADJUST the start inhibit switch. REPEAT this Pinpoint Test, if necessary INSTALL a new start inhibit switch. TEST the system for normal operation.
B8: CHECK CIRCUIT 31 - BB6	
1	

FM1120100602030X

Fig. 34 Test B: Engine does not crank & relay does not click (Part 3 of 5). Cougar

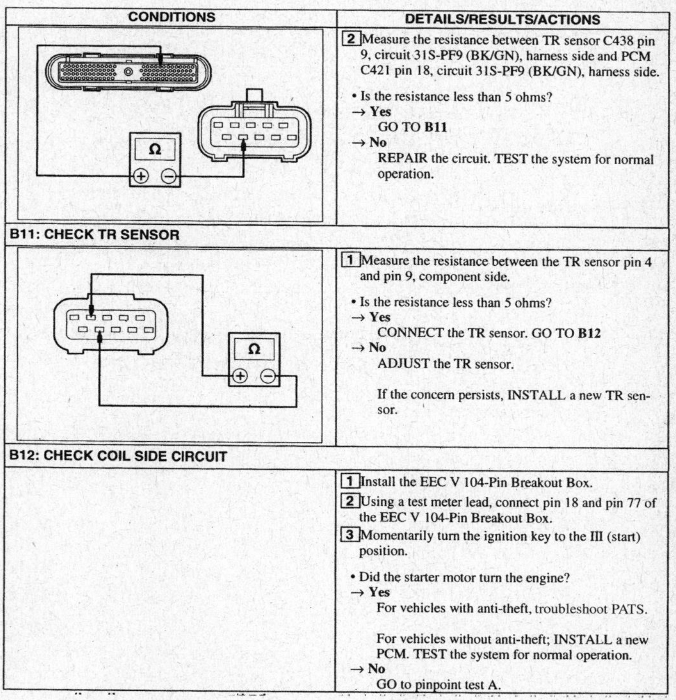

CONDITIONS	DETAILS/RESULTS/ACTIONS
	2 Measure the resistance between TR sensor C438 pin 9, circuit 31S-PF9 (BK/GN), harness side and PCM C421 pin 18, circuit 31S-PF9 (BK/GN), harness side. • Is the resistance less than 5 ohms? → **Yes** GO TO **B11** → **No** REPAIR the circuit. TEST the system for normal operation.
B11: CHECK TR SENSOR	
	1 Measure the resistance between the TR sensor pin 4 and pin 9, component side. • Is the resistance less than 5 ohms? → **Yes** CONNECT the TR sensor. GO TO **B12** → **No** ADJUST the TR sensor. If the concern persists, INSTALL a new TR sensor.
B12: CHECK COIL SIDE CIRCUIT	
	1 Install the EEC V 104-Pin Breakout Box. 2 Using a test meter lead, connect pin 18 and pin 77 of the EEC V 104-Pin Breakout Box. 3 Momentarily turn the ignition key to the III (start) position. • Did the starter motor turn the engine? → **Yes** For vehicles with anti-theft, troubleshoot PATS. For vehicles without anti-theft; INSTALL a new PCM. TEST the system for normal operation. → **No** GO to pinpoint test A.

FM1120100602050X

Fig. 34 Test B: Engine does not crank & relay does not click (Part 5 of 5). Cougar

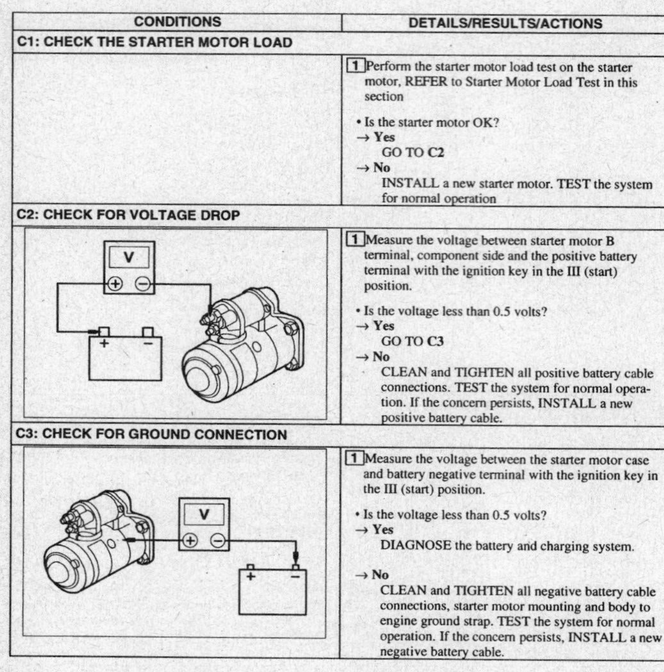

CONDITIONS	DETAILS/RESULTS/ACTIONS
C1: CHECK THE STARTER MOTOR LOAD	
	1 Perform the starter motor load test on the starter motor, REFER to Starter Motor Load Test in this section • Is the starter motor OK? → **Yes** GO TO C2 → **No** INSTALL a new starter motor. TEST the system for normal operation
C2: CHECK FOR VOLTAGE DROP	
	1 Measure the voltage between starter motor B terminal, component side and the positive battery terminal with the ignition key in the III (start) position. • Is the voltage less than 0.5 volts? → **Yes** GO TO C3 → **No** CLEAN and TIGHTEN all positive battery cable connections. TEST the system for normal operation. If the concern persists, INSTALL a new positive battery cable.
C3: CHECK FOR GROUND CONNECTION	
	1 Measure the voltage between the starter motor case and battery negative terminal with the ignition key in the III (start) position. • Is the voltage less than 0.5 volts? → **Yes** DIAGNOSE the battery and charging system. → **No** CLEAN and TIGHTEN all negative battery cable connections, starter motor mounting and body to engine ground strap. TEST the system for normal operation. If the concern persists, INSTALL a new negative battery cable.

FM1120100603000X

Fig. 35 Test C: Engine cranks slowly. Cougar

	Test Step	Result	Action to Take
A3	CHECK STARTER GROUND CIRCUIT RESISTANCE		
	• Connect voltmeter positive lead to the starter motor housing. • Connect voltmeter negative lead to battery negative terminal. • Disconnect inertia fuel shutoff switch electrical connector to prevent engine from starting. • Crank engine and record voltmeter reading during engine cranking. • **Is voltage more than 0.3 volt?**	Yes ▶ No ▶	SERVICE connections between battery negative terminal and engine block and starter motor-to-transaxle housing connection. GO to **A4**.
A4	CHECK STARTER CURRENT DRAW		
	• Perform Starter Motor Test as described. • **Is starter motor OK?**	Yes ▶ No ▶	Diagnose engine mechanical components. SERVICE starter motor as required.

FM1120100608020X

Fig. 36 Test A: Engine cranks slowly (Part 2 of 2). 1998 Crown Victoria & Grand Marquis

	Test Step	Result	Action to Take
B7	MANUALLY CRANK STARTER		
	• Ignition switch OFF. Transmission in PARK or NEUTRAL. • Connect one end of a jumper wire to the starter B+ terminal and momentarily touch the other end to the S terminal. • **Does starter motor crank?**	Yes ▶ No ▶	System operating properly. REPLACE starter motor as described. RETEST new starter motor.

FM1120100609020X

Fig. 37 Test B: Engine does not crank (Part 2 of 2). 1998 Crown Victoria & Grand Marquis

	Test Step	Result	Action to Take
A1	CHECK BATTERY STATE OF CHARGE		
	NOTE: To perform an accurate base circuit voltage reading, remove the surface charge by turning on the headlamps (10 seconds maximum). Read base circuit voltage after battery voltage stabilizes. • Connect voltmeter to battery positive and negative terminals. • Measure open circuit voltage. • **Is voltage 12.4 volts or higher?**	Yes ▶ No ▶	GO to **A2**. SERVICE battery and charging system as required.
A2	CHECK STARTER B+ CURRENT RESISTANCE		
	• Connect voltmeter positive lead to battery positive terminal and voltmeter negative lead to the starter Solenoid B+ terminal. • Disconnect inertia fuel shutoff switch electrical connector to prevent engine from starting. • Crank engine and record voltmeter reading during engine cranking. • **Is voltage more than 0.6 volt?**	Yes ▶ No ▶	SERVICE connections between battery positive terminal and starter solenoid B+ connection. GO to **A3**.

FM1120100608010X

Fig. 36 Test A: Engine cranks slowly (Part 1 of 2). 1998 Crown Victoria & Grand Marquis

	Test Step	Result	Action to Take
B1	CHECK BATTERY VOLTAGE TO STARTER		
	NOTE: Remove plastic safety cap on starter solenoid. • Ignition switch OFF. Transmission in PARK or NEUTRAL. • Check for voltage from starter B+ terminal to starter drive end housing (ground). • **Does voltmeter indicate B+?**	Yes ▶ No ▶	GO to **B2**. CHECK wire connections between battery and starter solenoid. CHECK ground connection at battery to ground and starter solenoid to ground for open or short.
B2	CHECK VOLTAGE TO IGNITION SWITCH		
	• Disconnect connector C292. Connect positive lead of voltmeter to Circuit 37 (Y) and negative lead to ground. • **Does voltmeter indicate B+?**	Yes ▶ No ▶	GO to **B3**. CHECK MAXI fuse starter/generator or Circuit 37 (Y). RESTORE vehicle. RETEST system.
B3	CHECK VOLTAGE THROUGH IGNITION SWITCH		
	• Connect connector C292. With ignition switch in START position, back-probe Circuit 33 (W/P) with a voltmeter positive lead and negative lead to ground. • **Does voltmeter indicate B+?**	Yes ▶ No ▶	GO to **B4**. REPLACE ignition switch. RESTORE vehicle. RETEST system.
B4	CHECK VOLTAGE TO TRANSMISSION RANGE SENSOR		
	• Disconnect transmission range sensor connector C168. • With ignition switch in START, connect voltmeter positive lead to Pin C168-4, Circuit 33 (W/PK) and negative lead to ground. • **Does voltmeter indicate B+?**	Yes ▶ No ▶	GO to **B5**. CHECK Circuit 33 (W/PK) for open or short. RESTORE vehicle. RETEST system.
B5	CHECK VOLTAGE THROUGH TRANSMISSION RANGE SENSOR		
	• Connect connector C168. With transmission in PARK or NEUTRAL and ignition switch in START, back-probe Pin C168-1, Circuit 32 (R/LB) at transmission range sensor connector. • **Does voltmeter indicate B+?**	Yes ▶ No ▶	GO to **B6**. REPLACE transmission range sensor. RESTORE vehicle. RETEST system.
B6	CHECK IGNITION VOLTAGE TO STARTER		
	• Disconnect Circuit 32 (R/LB) from starter motor. • Connect positive lead of voltmeter to Pin C168-1Circuit 32 (R/LB) and negative lead to ground. Place transmission in PARK and ignition switch in START. • **Does voltmeter indicate B+?**	Yes ▶ No ▶	GO to **B7**. CHECK Circuit 32 (R/LB). RESTORE vehicle. RETEST system.

FM1120100609010X

Fig. 37 Test B: Engine does not crank (Part 1 of 2). 1998 Crown Victoria & Grand Marquis

	Test Step	Result	Action to Take
C1	CHECK STARTER MOUNTING		
	• Check that starter motor mounting is flushed (not cocked). Check that all connections are secure. • Check that other necessary components related to the starting system are securely mounted ignition switch, distributor, battery and transmission switches. • Check wiring connections for damage or shorting due to corrosion or stray wires. • **Are the starting system components and wiring secure and undamaged?**	Yes ▶ No ▶	GO to **C2**. SERVICE or REPLACE wiring or component mountings as required. RETEST starting system for noises.
C2	CRANK ENGINE		
	• Put ignition switch in START then RUN position. As engine is starting, listen to individual components for noise due to gear tooth damage, shorting, sparking or knocking. • Pinpoint noise to component. • **Is noise due to ring gear tooth damage?**	Yes ▶ No ▶	REPLACE flywheel ring gear. EXAMINE starter pinion teeth. If damaged, REPLACE starter motor or starter drive. If noise sounds like shorting or sparking, check grounded feeds to battery or starter motor. If noise sounds like knocking, diagnose engine mechanical components.

FM1120100610000X

Fig. 38 Test C: Unusual starter noise. 1998 Crown Victoria & Grand Marquis

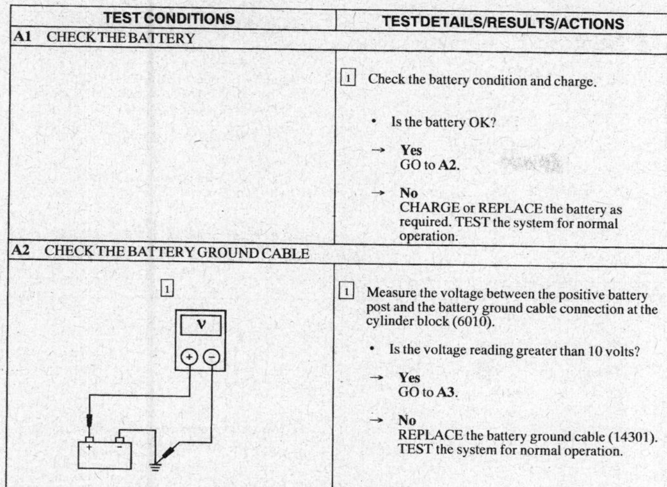

TEST CONDITIONS	TEST DETAILS/RESULTS/ACTIONS
A1 CHECK THE BATTERY	
	1 Check the battery condition and charge. • Is the battery OK? → **Yes** GO to **A2**. → **No** CHARGE or REPLACE the battery as required. TEST the system for normal operation.
A2 CHECK THE BATTERY GROUND CABLE	
1	1 Measure the voltage between the positive battery post and the battery ground cable connection at the cylinder block (6010). • Is the voltage reading greater than 10 volts? → **Yes** GO to **A3**. → **No** REPLACE the battery ground cable (14301). TEST the system for normal operation.

FM1120100613010X

Fig. 39 Test A: Engine does not crank (Part 1 of 13). 1999–2002 Crown Victoria & Grand marquis

TEST CONDITIONS	TEST DETAILS/RESULTS/ACTIONS
A5 CHECK THE STARTER MOTOR	
1	1 Connect one end of a jumper wire to the starter motor solenoid B terminal of the starter motor and momentarily connect the other end to the starter motor solenoid S-terminal. • Does the starter motor engage and the engine crank? → **Yes** GO to **A6**. → **No** REPLACE the starter motor. TEST the system for normal operation.
A6 CHECK START INPUT TO THE STARTER MOTOR	
1 Starter S Connector	1 Disconnect the starter motor solenoid S-terminal.
	2 Hold the ignition switch to the START position.
3	3 Measure the voltage at the starter motor solenoid S connector. • Is the voltage reading greater than 10 volts? → **Yes** CLEAN the starter motor solenoid S-terminal stud and connector. CHECK the wiring and the starter motor for a loose or intermittent connection. TEST the system for normal operation. → **No** GO to **A7**.

FM1120100613030X

Fig. 39 Test A: Engine does not crank (Part 3 of 13). 1999–2002 Crown Victoria & Grand Marquis

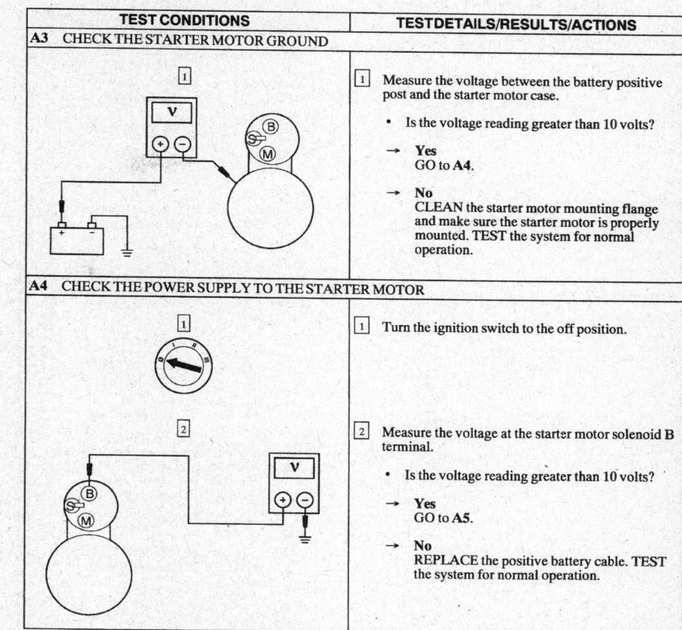

TEST CONDITIONS	TEST DETAILS/RESULTS/ACTIONS
A3 CHECK THE STARTER MOTOR GROUND	
1	1 Measure the voltage between the battery positive post and the starter motor case. • Is the voltage reading greater than 10 volts? → **Yes** GO to **A4**. → **No** CLEAN the starter motor mounting flange and make sure the starter motor is properly mounted. TEST the system for normal operation.
A4 CHECK THE POWER SUPPLY TO THE STARTER MOTOR	
1	1 Turn the ignition switch to the off position.
2	2 Measure the voltage at the starter motor solenoid B terminal. • Is the voltage reading greater than 10 volts? → **Yes** GO to **A5**. → **No** REPLACE the positive battery cable. TEST the system for normal operation.

FM1120100613020X

Fig. 39 Test A: Engine does not crank (Part 2 of 13). 1999–2002 Crown Victoria & Grand Marquis

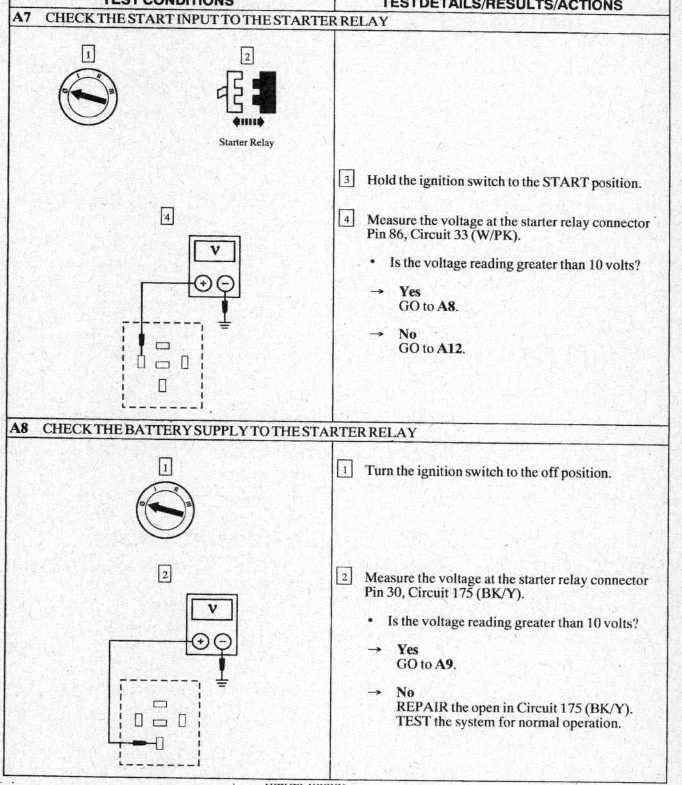

TEST CONDITIONS	TEST DETAILS/RESULTS/ACTIONS
A7 CHECK THE START INPUT TO THE STARTER RELAY	
1 2 Starter Relay	
	3 Hold the ignition switch to the START position.
4	4 Measure the voltage at the starter relay connector Pin 86, Circuit 33 (W/PK). • Is the voltage reading greater than 10 volts? → **Yes** GO to **A8**. → **No** GO to **A12**.
A8 CHECK THE BATTERY SUPPLY TO THE STARTER RELAY	
1	1 Turn the ignition switch to the off position.
2	2 Measure the voltage at the starter relay connector Pin 30, Circuit 175 (BK/Y). • Is the voltage reading greater than 10 volts? → **Yes** GO to **A9**. → **No** REPAIR the open in Circuit 175 (BK/Y). TEST the system for normal operation.

FM1120100613040X

Fig. 39 Test A: Engine does not crank (Part 4 of 13). 1999–2002 Crown Victoria & Grand Marquis

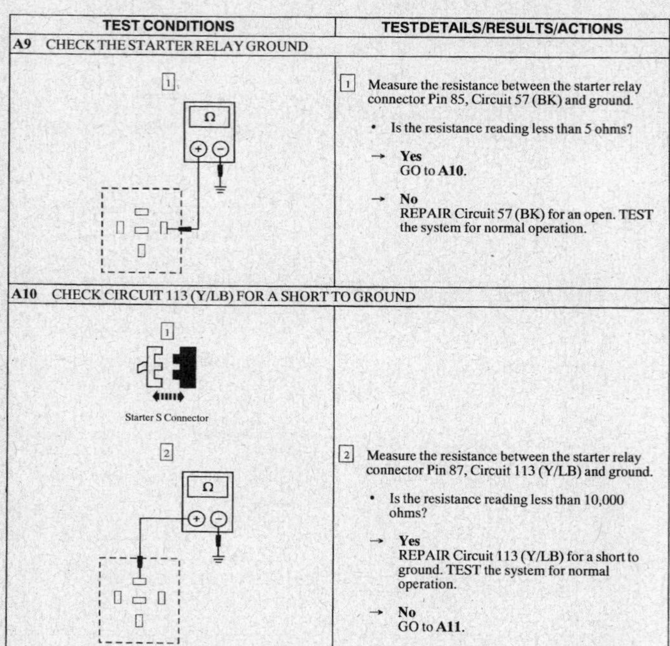

TEST CONDITIONS	TEST DETAILS/RESULTS/ACTIONS
A9 CHECK THE STARTER RELAY GROUND	
1	1 Measure the resistance between the starter relay connector Pin 85, Circuit 57 (BK) and ground. • Is the resistance reading less than 5 ohms? → **Yes** GO to **A10**. → **No** REPAIR Circuit 57 (BK) for an open. TEST the system for normal operation.
A10 CHECK CIRCUIT 113 (Y/LB) FOR A SHORT TO GROUND	
1 Starter S Connector	
2	2 Measure the resistance between the starter relay connector Pin 87, Circuit 113 (Y/LB) and ground. • Is the resistance reading less than 10,000 ohms? → **Yes** REPAIR Circuit 113 (Y/LB) for a short to ground. TEST the system for normal operation. → **No** GO to **A11**.

FM1120100613050X

Fig. 39 Test A: Engine does not crank (Part 5 of 13). 1999–2002 Crown Victoria & Grand Marquis

TEST CONDITIONS	TEST DETAILS/RESULTS/ACTIONS
A13 CHECK THE INPUT TO FUSE 26 (5A) (Continued)	
2	2 Measure the voltage at the input cavity of Fuse 26 (5A). • Is the voltage reading greater than 10 volts? → **Yes** GO to **A17**. → **No** GO to **A14**.

FM1120100613070X

Fig. 39 Test A: Engine does not crank (Part 7 of 13). 1999–2002 Crown Victoria & Grand Marquis

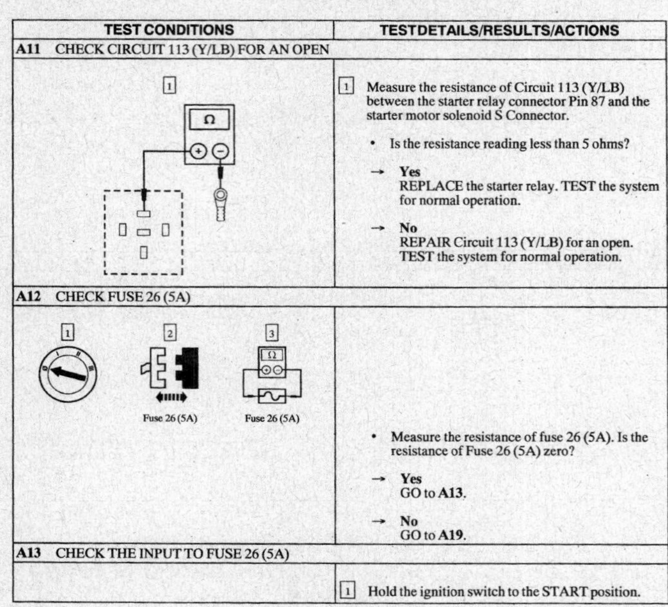

TEST CONDITIONS	TEST DETAILS/RESULTS/ACTIONS
A11 CHECK CIRCUIT 113 (Y/LB) FOR AN OPEN	
1	1 Measure the resistance of Circuit 113 (Y/LB) between the starter relay connector Pin 87 and the starter motor solenoid S Connector. • Is the resistance reading less than 5 ohms? → **Yes** REPLACE the starter relay. TEST the system for normal operation. → **No** REPAIR Circuit 113 (Y/LB) for an open. TEST the system for normal operation.
A12 CHECK FUSE 26 (5A)	
1 2 Fuse 26 (5A) 3 Fuse 26 (5A)	• Measure the resistance of fuse 26 (5A). Is the resistance of Fuse 26 (5A) zero? → **Yes** GO to **A13**. → **No** GO to **A19**.
A13 CHECK THE INPUT TO FUSE 26 (5A)	
	1 Hold the ignition switch to the START position.

FM1120100613060X

Fig. 39 Test A: Engine does not crank (Part 6 of 13). 1999–2002 Crown Victoria & Grand Marquis

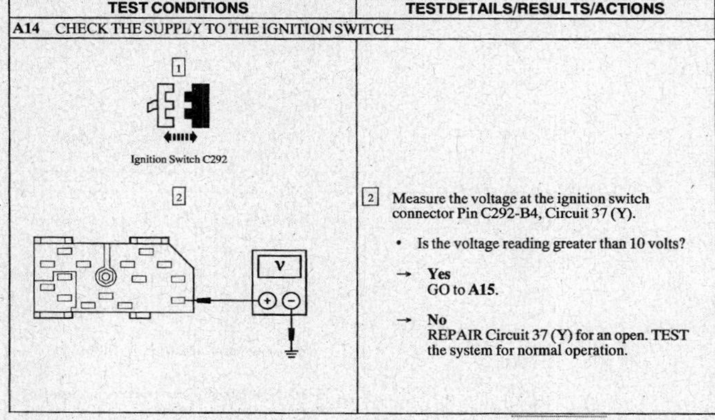

TEST CONDITIONS	TEST DETAILS/RESULTS/ACTIONS
A14 CHECK THE SUPPLY TO THE IGNITION SWITCH	
1 Ignition Switch C292	
2	2 Measure the voltage at the ignition switch connector Pin C292-B4, Circuit 37 (Y). • Is the voltage reading greater than 10 volts? → **Yes** GO to **A15**. → **No** REPAIR Circuit 37 (Y) for an open. TEST the system for normal operation.

FM1120100613080X

Fig. 39 Test A: Engine does not crank (Part 8 of 13). 1999–2002 Crown Victoria & Grand Marquis

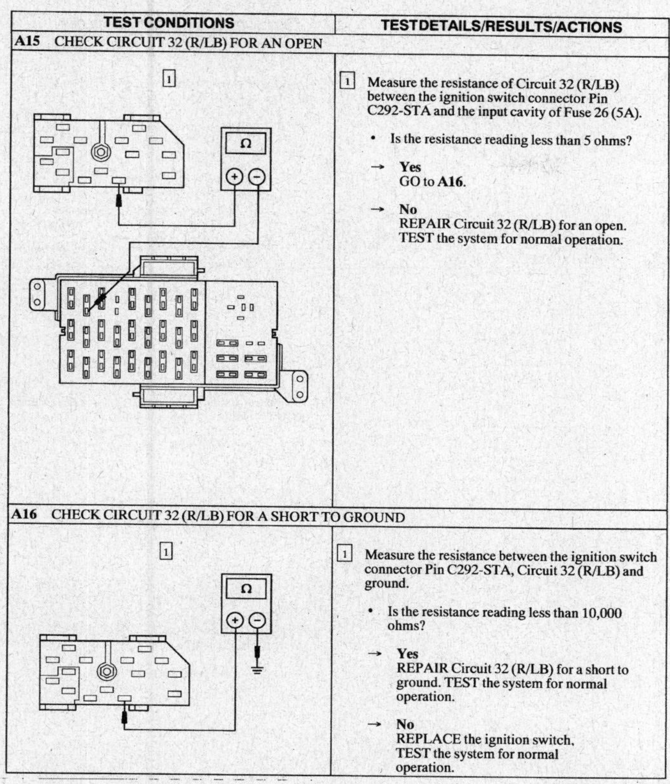

TEST CONDITIONS	TEST DETAILS/RESULTS/ACTIONS
A15 CHECK CIRCUIT 32 (R/LB) FOR AN OPEN	
1	1 Measure the resistance of Circuit 32 (R/LB) between the ignition switch connector Pin C292-STA and the input cavity of Fuse 26 (5A). • Is the resistance reading less than 5 ohms? → **Yes** GO to **A16**. → **No** REPAIR Circuit 32 (R/LB) for an open. TEST the system for normal operation.

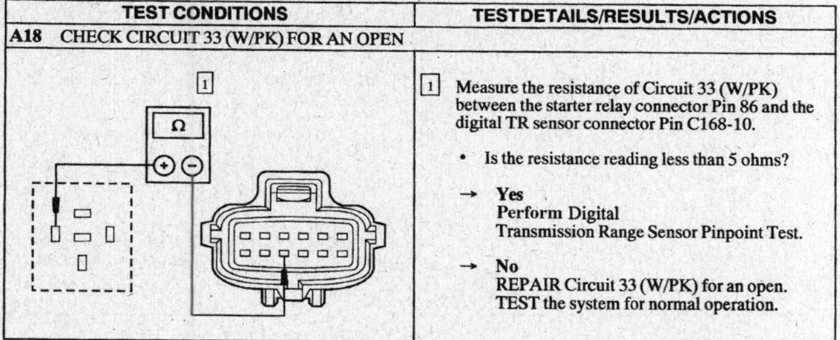

TEST CONDITIONS	TEST DETAILS/RESULTS/ACTIONS
A16 CHECK CIRCUIT 32 (R/LB) FOR A SHORT TO GROUND	
1	1 Measure the resistance between the ignition switch connector Pin C292-STA, Circuit 32 (R/LB) and ground. • Is the resistance reading less than 10,000 ohms? → **Yes** REPAIR Circuit 32 (R/LB) for a short to ground. TEST the system for normal operation. → **No** REPLACE the ignition switch. TEST the system for normal operation.

FM1120100613090X

Fig. 39 Test A: Engine does not crank (Part 9 of 13). 1999–2002 Crown Victoria & Grand Marquis

TEST CONDITIONS	TEST DETAILS/RESULTS/ACTIONS
A18 CHECK CIRCUIT 33 (W/PK) FOR AN OPEN	
1	1 Measure the resistance of Circuit 33 (W/PK) between the starter relay connector Pin 86 and the digital TR sensor connector Pin C168-10. • Is the resistance reading less than 5 ohms? → **Yes** Perform Digital Transmission Range Sensor Pinpoint Test. → **No** REPAIR Circuit 33 (W/PK) for an open. TEST the system for normal operation.

FM1120100613110X

Fig. 39 Test A: Engine does not crank (Part 11 of 13). 1999–2002 Crown Victoria & Grand Marquis

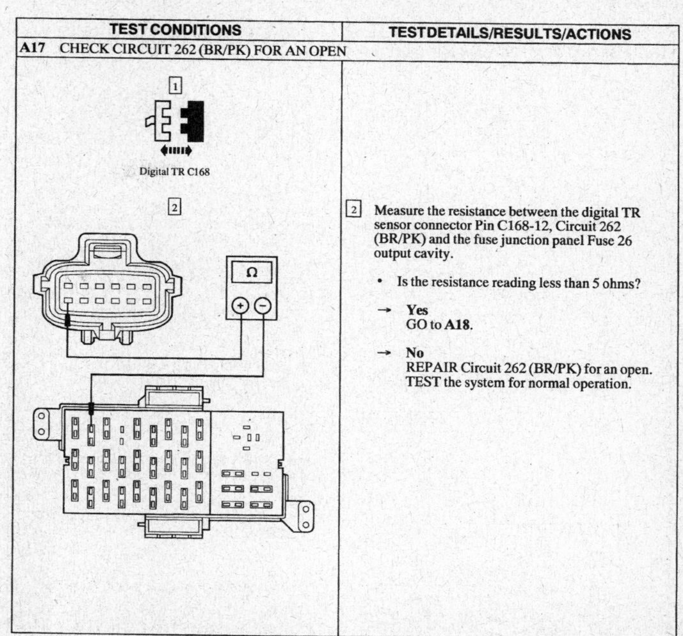

TEST CONDITIONS	TEST DETAILS/RESULTS/ACTIONS
A17 CHECK CIRCUIT 262 (BR/PK) FOR AN OPEN	
1 Digital TR C168 2	2 Measure the resistance between the digital TR sensor connector Pin C168-12, Circuit 262 (BR/PK) and the fuse junction panel Fuse 26 output cavity. • Is the resistance reading less than 5 ohms? → **Yes** GO to **A18**. → **No** REPAIR Circuit 262 (BR/PK) for an open. TEST the system for normal operation.

FM1120100613100X

Fig. 39 Test A: Engine does not crank (Part 10 of 13). 1999–2002 Crown Victoria & Grand Marquis

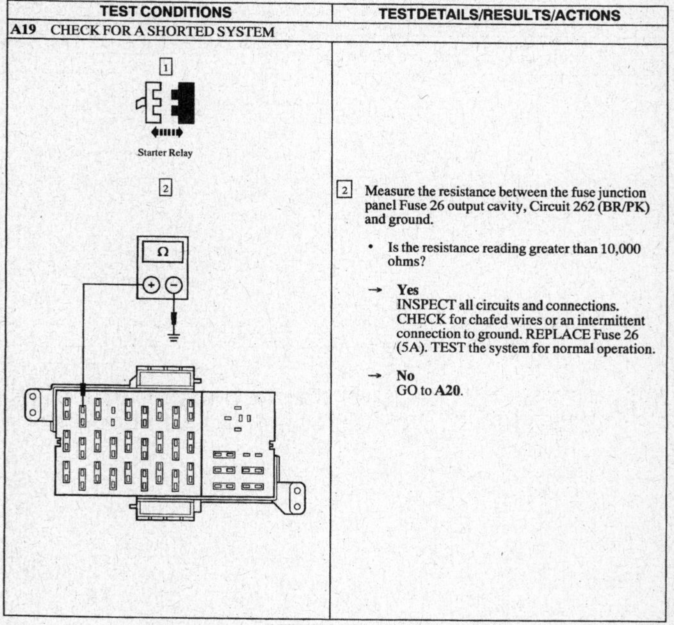

TEST CONDITIONS	TEST DETAILS/RESULTS/ACTIONS
A19 CHECK FOR A SHORTED SYSTEM	
1 Starter Relay 2	2 Measure the resistance between the fuse junction panel Fuse 26 output cavity, Circuit 262 (BR/PK) and ground. • Is the resistance reading greater than 10,000 ohms? → **Yes** INSPECT all circuits and connections. CHECK for chafed wires or an intermittent connection to ground. REPLACE Fuse 26 (5A). TEST the system for normal operation. → **No** GO to **A20**.

FM1120100613120X

Fig. 39 Test A: Engine does not crank (Part 12 of 13). 1999–2002 Crown Victoria & Grand Marquis

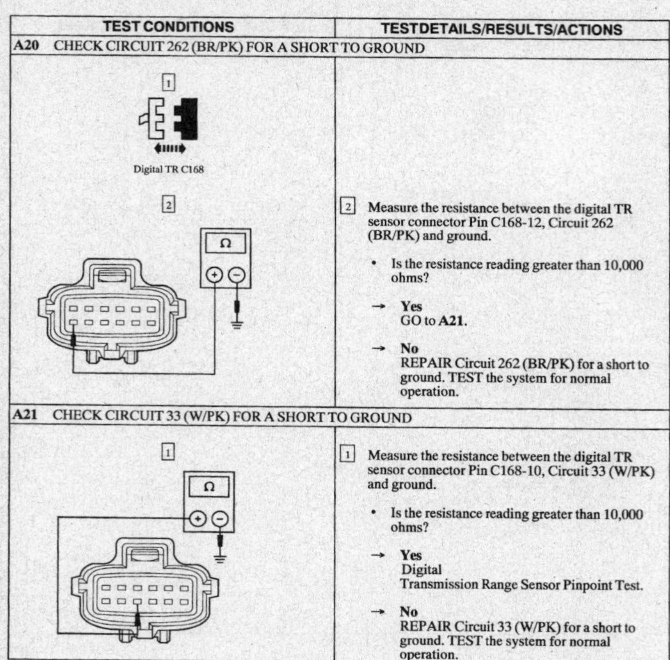

TEST CONDITIONS	TEST DETAILS/RESULTS/ACTIONS
A20 CHECK CIRCUIT 262 (BR/PK) FOR A SHORT TO GROUND	
1 Digital TR C168	
2	2 Measure the resistance between the digital TR sensor connector Pin C168-12, Circuit 262 (BR/PK) and ground. • Is the resistance reading greater than 10,000 ohms? → **Yes** GO to **A21**. → **No** REPAIR Circuit 262 (BR/PK) for a short to ground. TEST the system for normal operation.
A21 CHECK CIRCUIT 33 (W/PK) FOR A SHORT TO GROUND	
1	1 Measure the resistance between the digital TR sensor connector Pin C168-10, Circuit 33 (W/PK) and ground. • Is the resistance reading greater than 10,000 ohms? → **Yes** Digital Transmission Range Sensor Pinpoint Test. → **No** REPAIR Circuit 33 (W/PK) for a short to ground. TEST the system for normal operation.

FM1120100613130X

Fig. 39 Test A: Engine does not crank (Part 13 of 13). 1999–2002 Crown Victoria & Grand Marquis

TEST CONDITIONS	TEST DETAILS/RESULTS/ACTIONS
B3 CHECK FOR UNUSUAL WEAR	
	1 Remove the starter motor. 2 Inspect the ring gear for damaged or worn teeth. • Is the noise due to flywheel ring gear (6384) tooth damage? → **Yes** REPLACE the flywheel ring gear. EXAMINE the starter pinion teeth. If damaged, REPLACE the starter motor. TEST the system for normal operation. → **No** REPLACE the starter motor. TEST the system for normal operation.

FM1120100614020X

Fig. 40 Test B: Unusual starter noise (Part 2 of 2). 1999–2002 Crown Victoria & Grand Marquis

TEST CONDITIONS	TEST DETAILS/RESULTS/ACTIONS
B1 CHECK THE STARTER MOUNTING	
	1 Inspect the starter motor mounting bolts and brackets for looseness. • Is the starter motor mounted properly? → **Yes** GO to **B2**. → **No** INSTALL the starter motor properly; TEST the system for normal operation.
B2 CHECK FOR ENGINE NOISE	
1	
2	2 Connect a remote starter switch between the starter motor solenoid B and S terminals.
	3 Engage the starter motor and verify the noise is due to the starter operation. • Is the noise due to the starter motor engagement? → **Yes** GO to **B3**. → **No** Diagnose engine mechanical components.

FM1120100614010X

Fig. 40 Test B: Unusual starter noise (Part 1 of 2). 1999–2002 Crown Victoria & Grand Marquis

TEST CONDITIONS	TEST DETAILS/RESULTS/ACTIONS
A1 CHECK THE BATTERY CONNECTIONS	
	1 Inspect the battery terminals for loose or corroded connections. • Are the battery terminals clean and tight? → **Yes** GO to **A2**. → **No** CLEAN and TIGHTEN the battery cable connections. TEST the system for normal operation.
A2 CHECK THE BATTERY	
	1 Check the battery. • Is the battery OK? → **Yes** GO to **A3**. → **No** CHARGE or REPLACE the battery.

FM1120100631010X

Fig. 41 Test A: Engine does not crank or relay clicks (Part 1 of 8). 1998 Escort, Tracer & ZX2

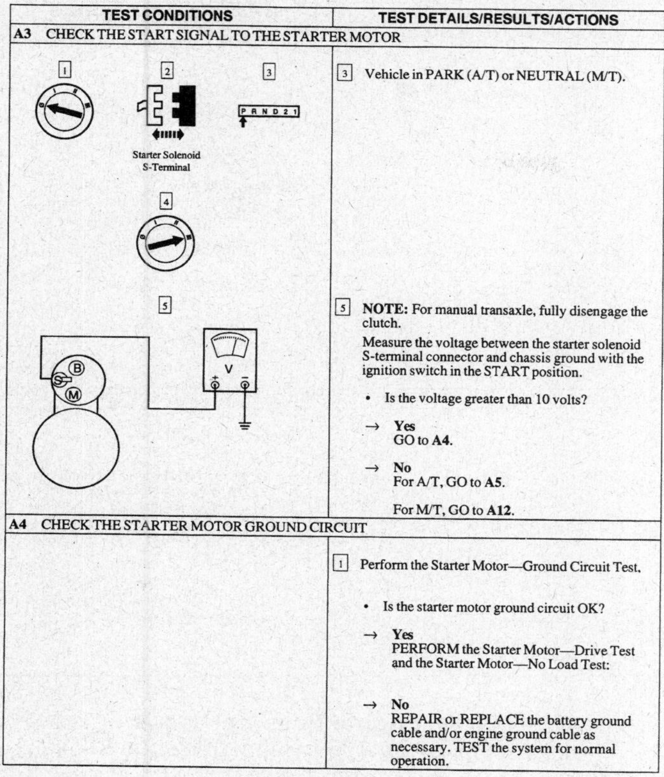

TEST CONDITIONS	TEST DETAILS/RESULTS/ACTIONS
A3 CHECK THE START SIGNAL TO THE STARTER MOTOR	
1 2 3 Starter Solenoid S-Terminal; P R N D 2 1	3 Vehicle in PARK (A/T) or NEUTRAL (M/T).
4	
5	5 **NOTE:** For manual transaxle, fully disengage the clutch. Measure the voltage between the starter solenoid S-terminal connector and chassis ground with the ignition switch in the START position. • Is the voltage greater than 10 volts? → **Yes** GO to **A4.** → **No** For A/T, GO to **A5.** For M/T, GO to **A12.**
A4 CHECK THE STARTER MOTOR GROUND CIRCUIT	
	1 Perform the Starter Motor—Ground Circuit Test. • Is the starter motor ground circuit OK? → **Yes** PERFORM the Starter Motor—Drive Test and the Starter Motor—No Load Test: → **No** REPAIR or REPLACE the battery ground cable and/or engine ground cable as necessary. TEST the system for normal operation.

FM1120100631020X

Fig. 41 Test A: Engine does not crank or relay clicks (Part 2 of 8). 1998 Escort, Tracer & ZX2

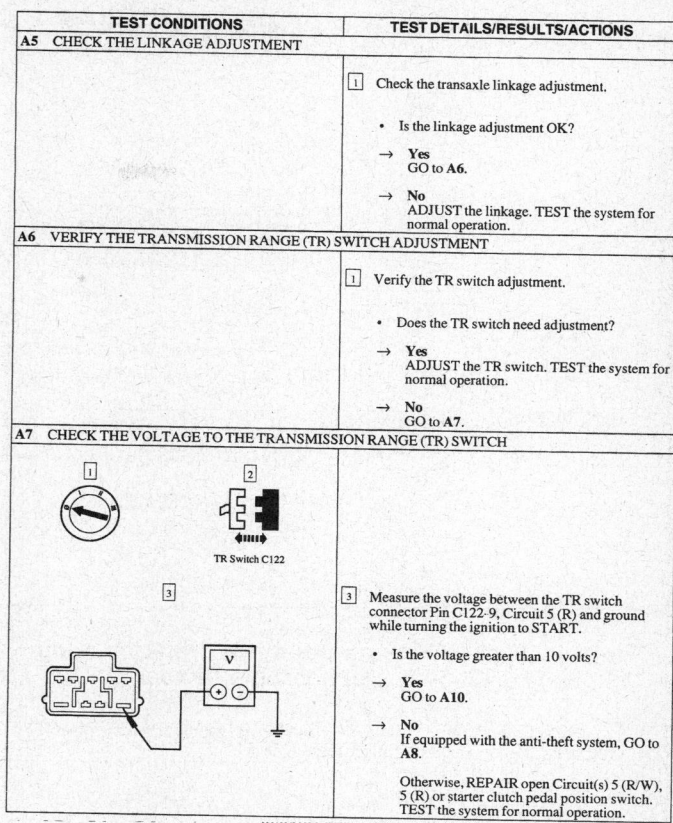

TEST CONDITIONS	TEST DETAILS/RESULTS/ACTIONS
A8 CHECK THE ANTI-THEFT SYSTEM OPERATION	
	1 Verify the proper operation of the starter cut relay. • Is the starter cut relay OK? → **Yes** GO to **A9.** → **No** REPAIR anti-theft system. TEST the system for normal operation.
A9 CHECK THE VOLTAGE AT THE STARTER CUT RELAY	
1 2 Starter Cut Relay	
3	3 Measure the voltage between the starter cut relay connector C179-30, circuit 5 (R/W) and the ground while turning the ignition to START. • Is the voltage greater than 10 volts? → **Yes** REPAIR open Circuit 5 (R), or starter clutch pedal position switch. → **No** REPAIR circuit 5 (R/W).

FM1120100631040X

Fig. 41 Test A: Engine does not crank or relay clicks (Part 4 of 8). 1998 Escort, Tracer & ZX2

TEST CONDITIONS	TEST DETAILS/RESULTS/ACTIONS
A5 CHECK THE LINKAGE ADJUSTMENT	
	1 Check the transaxle linkage adjustment. • Is the linkage adjustment OK? → **Yes** GO to **A6.** → **No** ADJUST the linkage. TEST the system for normal operation.
A6 VERIFY THE TRANSMISSION RANGE (TR) SWITCH ADJUSTMENT	
	1 Verify the TR switch adjustment. • Does the TR switch need adjustment? → **Yes** ADJUST the TR switch. TEST the system for normal operation. → **No** GO to **A7.**
A7 CHECK THE VOLTAGE TO THE TRANSMISSION RANGE (TR) SWITCH	
1 2 TR Switch C122	
3	3 Measure the voltage between the TR switch connector Pin C122-9, Circuit 5 (R) and ground while turning the ignition to START. • Is the voltage greater than 10 volts? → **Yes** GO to **A10.** → **No** If equipped with the anti-theft system, GO to **A8.** Otherwise, REPAIR open Circuit(s) 5 (R/W), 5 (R) or starter clutch pedal position switch. TEST the system for normal operation.

FM1120100631030X

Fig. 41 Test A: Engine does not crank or relay clicks (Part 3 of 8). 1998 Escort, Tracer & ZX2

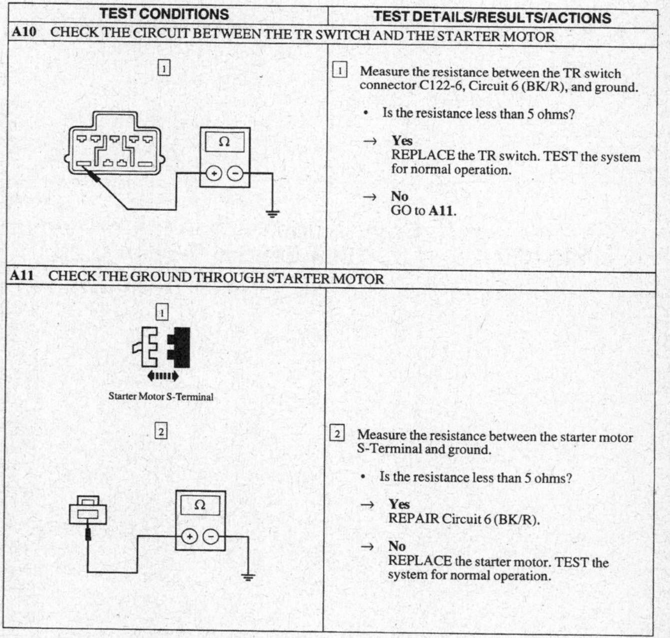

TEST CONDITIONS	TEST DETAILS/RESULTS/ACTIONS
A10 CHECK THE CIRCUIT BETWEEN THE TR SWITCH AND THE STARTER MOTOR	
1	1 Measure the resistance between the TR switch connector C122-6, Circuit 6 (BK/R), and ground. • Is the resistance less than 5 ohms? → **Yes** REPLACE the TR switch. TEST the system for normal operation. → **No** GO to **A11.**
A11 CHECK THE GROUND THROUGH STARTER MOTOR	
1 Starter Motor S-Terminal	
2	2 Measure the resistance between the starter motor S-Terminal and ground. • Is the resistance less than 5 ohms? → **Yes** REPAIR Circuit 6 (BK/R). → **No** REPLACE the starter motor. TEST the system for normal operation.

FM1120100631050X

Fig. 41 Test A: Engine does not crank or relay clicks (Part 5 of 8). 1998 Escort, Tracer & ZX2

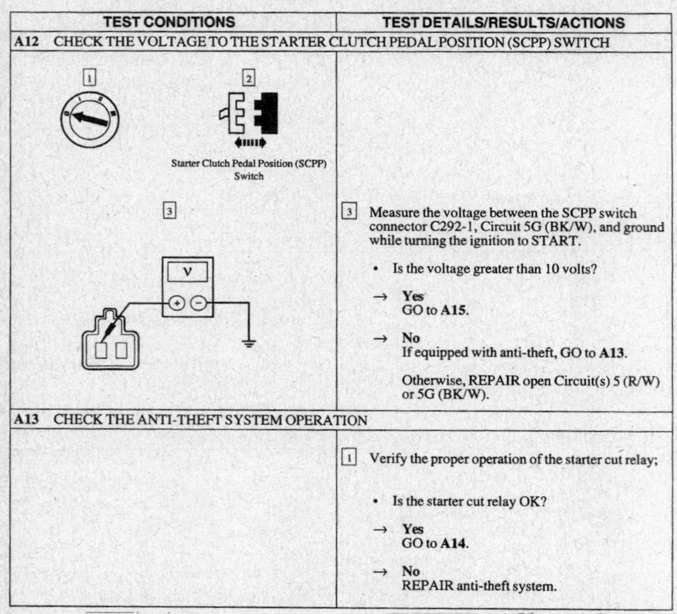

TEST CONDITIONS	TEST DETAILS/RESULTS/ACTIONS
A12 CHECK THE VOLTAGE TO THE STARTER CLUTCH PEDAL POSITION (SCPP) SWITCH	
1 2 Starter Clutch Pedal Position (SCPP) Switch 3 V	3 Measure the voltage between the SCPP switch connector C292-1, Circuit 5G (BK/W), and ground while turning the ignition to START. • Is the voltage greater than 10 volts? → **Yes** GO to **A15**. → **No** If equipped with anti-theft, GO to **A13**. Otherwise, REPAIR open Circuit(s) 5 (R/W) or 5G (BK/W).
A13 CHECK THE ANTI-THEFT SYSTEM OPERATION	
	1 Verify the proper operation of the starter cut relay; • Is the starter cut relay OK? → **Yes** GO to **A14**. → **No** REPAIR anti-theft system.

FM1120100631060X

Fig. 41 Test A: Engine does not crank or relay clicks (Part 6 of 8). 1998 Escort, Tracer & ZX2

TEST CONDITIONS	TEST DETAILS/RESULTS/ACTIONS
A16 CHECK THE GROUND THROUGH THE STARTER MOTOR	
1 Starter Motor S-Terminal 2 Ω	2 Measure the resistance between starter motor S-Terminal and ground. • Is the resistance less than 5 ohms? → **Yes** REPAIR Circuit 6 (BK/R), 5 (R) or TR jumper for open. → **No** REPLACE the starter motor. TEST the system for normal operation.

FM1120100631080X

Fig. 41 Test A: Engine does not crank or relay clicks (Part 8 of 8). 1998 Escort, Tracer & ZX2

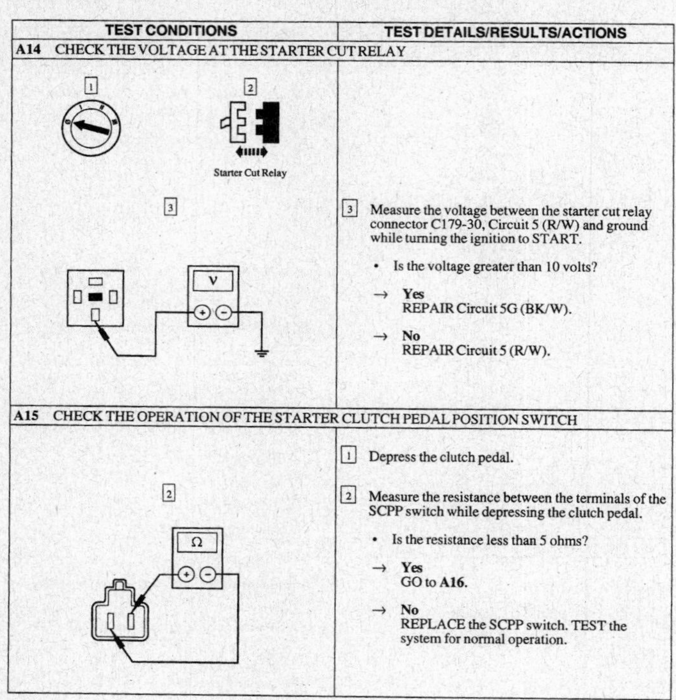

TEST CONDITIONS	TEST DETAILS/RESULTS/ACTIONS
A14 CHECK THE VOLTAGE AT THE STARTER CUT RELAY	
1 2 Starter Cut Relay 3 V	3 Measure the voltage between the starter cut relay connector C179-30, Circuit 5 (R/W) and ground while turning the ignition to START. • Is the voltage greater than 10 volts? → **Yes** REPAIR Circuit 5G (BK/W). → **No** REPAIR Circuit 5 (R/W).
A15 CHECK THE OPERATION OF THE STARTER CLUTCH PEDAL POSITION SWITCH	
2 Ω	1 Depress the clutch pedal. 2 Measure the resistance between the terminals of the SCPP switch while depressing the clutch pedal. • Is the resistance less than 5 ohms? → **Yes** GO to **A16**. → **No** REPLACE the SCPP switch. TEST the system for normal operation.

FM1120100631070X

Fig. 41 Test A: Engine does not crank or relay clicks (Part 7 of 8). 1998 Escort, Tracer & ZX2

TEST CONDITIONS	TEST DETAILS/RESULTS/ACTIONS
A1 CHECK THE BATTERY CONNECTIONS	
	1 Inspect the battery terminals for loose or corroded connections. • Are the battery terminals clean and tight? → **Yes** GO to **A2**. → **No** CLEAN and TIGHTEN the battery cable connections. TEST the system for normal operation.
A2 CHECK THE BATTERY	
	1 Check the battery. • Is the battery OK? → **Yes** GO to **A3**. → **No** CHARGE or REPLACE the battery.

FM1120100632010X

Fig. 42 Test B: Engine cranks slowly (Part 1 of 2). 1998 Escort, Tracer & ZX2

TEST CONDITIONS	TEST DETAILS/RESULTS/ACTIONS
B2 CHECK THE BATTERY	
	1 Check the battery. • Is the battery OK? → **Yes** GO to **B3**. → **No** CHARGE or REPLACE the battery. TEST the system for normal operation.
B3 CHECK THE STARTER MOTOR CONNECTIONS	
	1 Inspect the starter motor terminals for loose or corroded connections. • Are the starter motor terminal connections clean and tight? → **Yes** GO to **B4**. → **No** CLEAN and TIGHTEN the starter motor connections. TEST the system for normal operation.
B4 CHECK THE STARTER MOTOR	
	1 Perform the Starter Motor-Load Test Component Test. • Is the starter motor OK? → **Yes** Diagnose engine mechanical components. → **No** REPLACE the starter motor. TEST the system for normal operation.

FM1120100632020X

Fig. 42 Test B: Engine cranks slowly (Part 2 of 2). 1998 Escort, Tracer & ZX2

TEST CONDITIONS	TEST DETAILS/RESULTS/ACTIONS
C1 CHECK THE STARTER MOTOR MOUNTING (Continued)	
	2 Check the starter motor for proper alignment. • Is the starter motor mounted properly? → **Yes** GO to **C2**. → **No** REINSTALL the starter motor properly. TEST the system for normal operation.
C2 INSPECT THE STARTER MOTOR	
	1 Remove the starter motor 2 Inspect the starter motor for damage. • Is the starter motor damaged? → **Yes** REPLACE the starter motor. → **No** Diagnose engine mechanical components.

FM1120100633020X

Fig. 43 Test C: Unusual starter noise (Part 2 of 2). 1998 Escort, Tracer & ZX2

TEST CONDITIONS	TEST DETAILS/RESULTS/ACTIONS
C1 CHECK THE STARTER MOTOR MOUNTING	
	1 Check the starter motor mounting bolts for looseness.

FM1120100633010X

Fig. 43 Test C: Unusual starter noise (Part 1 of 2). 1998 Escort, Tracer & ZX2

TEST CONDITIONS	TEST DETAILS/RESULTS/ACTIONS
D1 CHECK BATTERY	
	1 Check the battery. • Is the battery OK? → **Yes** GO to **D2**. → **No** CHARGE or REPLACE the battery; TEST the system for normal operation.

FM1120100634010X

Fig. 44 Test D: Starter motor spins but does not crank (Part 1 of 2). 1998 Escort, Tracer & ZX2

TEST CONDITIONS	TEST DETAILS/RESULTS/ACTIONS
D2 CHECK FLYWHEEL RING GEAR	
	1 Remove the starter motor. • Is the flywheel ring gear OK? → **Yes** GO to **D3**. → **No** REPLACE the flywheel.
D3 CHECK STARTER DRIVE, OUTPUT SHAFT AND STARTER MOTOR	
	1 Inspect starter drive and output shaft for proper operation. • Is the starter drive OK? → **Yes** CLEAN and TIGHTEN battery and starter motor connections. → **No** REPLACE the starter motor. TEST the system for normal operation.

FM1120100634020X

Fig. 44 Test D: Starter motor spins but does not crank (Part 2 of 2). 1998 Escort, Tracer & ZX2

TEST CONDITIONS	TEST DETAILS/RESULTS/ACTIONS
A1 CHECK THE BATTERY CONNECTIONS	
	1 Inspect the battery terminals for loose or corroded connections. • Are the battery terminals clean and tight? → **Yes** GO to **A2**. → **No** CLEAN and TIGHTEN the battery cable connections. TEST the system for normal operation.
A2 CHECK THE BATTERY	
	1 Check the battery. • Is the battery OK? → **Yes** GO to **A3**. → **No** CHARGE or REPLACE the battery.
A3 CHECK THE START SIGNAL TO THE STARTER MOTOR	
1 2 3 P R N D 2 1 Starter Solenoid C121	3 Vehicle in PARK (A/T) or NEUTRAL (M/T).

FM1120100636010X

Fig. 45 Test A: Engine does not start or relay clicks (Part 1 of 6). 1999–2002 Escort, Tracer & ZX2

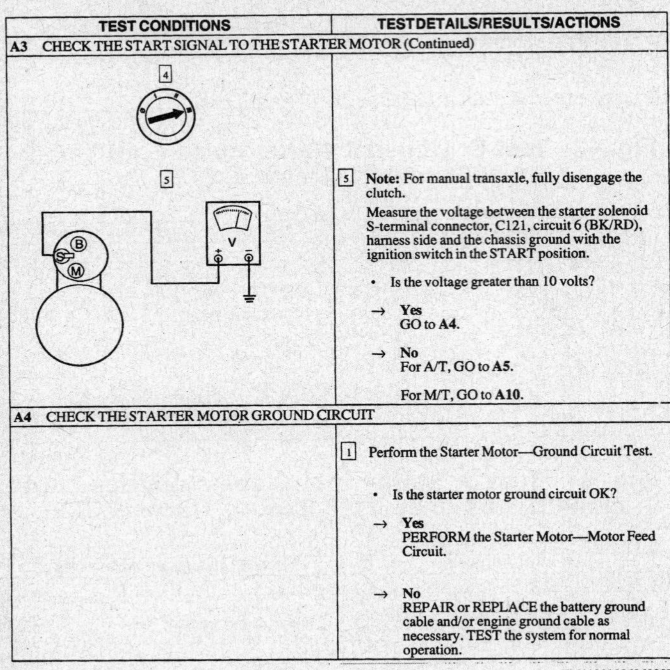

TEST CONDITIONS	TEST DETAILS/RESULTS/ACTIONS
A3 CHECK THE START SIGNAL TO THE STARTER MOTOR (Continued)	
4	
5	5 **Note:** For manual transaxle, fully disengage the clutch. Measure the voltage between the starter solenoid S-terminal connector, C121, circuit 6 (BK/RD), harness side and the chassis ground with the ignition switch in the START position. • Is the voltage greater than 10 volts? → **Yes** GO to **A4**. → **No** For A/T, GO to **A5**. For M/T, GO to **A10**.
A4 CHECK THE STARTER MOTOR GROUND CIRCUIT	
	1 Perform the Starter Motor—Ground Circuit Test. • Is the starter motor ground circuit OK? → **Yes** PERFORM the Starter Motor—Motor Feed Circuit. → **No** REPAIR or REPLACE the battery ground cable and/or engine ground cable as necessary. TEST the system for normal operation.

FM1120100636020X

Fig. 45 Test A: Engine does not start or relay clicks (Part 2 of 6). 1999–2002 Escort, Tracer & ZX2

TEST CONDITIONS	TEST DETAILS/RESULTS/ACTIONS
A8 CHECK THE CIRCUIT BETWEEN THE TR SWITCH AND THE STARTER MOTOR	
1	1 Measure the resistance between the TR switch connector C122 pin 6, Circuit 6 (BK/RD), harness side and ground. • Is the resistance less than 5 ohms? → **Yes** REPLACE the TR switch. TEST the system for normal operation. → **No** GO to **A9**.
A9 CHECK THE GROUND THROUGH THE STARTER MOTOR	
1 Starter Motor S-Terminal	
2	2 Measure the resistance between the starter motor S-Terminal and ground. • Is the resistance less than 5 ohms? → **Yes** REPAIR circuit 6 (BK/RD). TEST the system for normal operation. → **No** REPLACE the starter motor. TEST the system for normal operation.

FM1120100636040X

Fig. 45 Test A: Engine does not start or relay clicks (Part 4 of 6). 1999–2002 Escort, Tracer & ZX2

TEST CONDITIONS	TEST DETAILS/RESULTS/ACTIONS
A5 CHECK THE LINKAGE ADJUSTMENT	
	1 Check the transaxle linkage adjustment. • Is the linkage adjustment OK? → **Yes** GO to **A6**. → **No** ADJUST the linkage. TEST the system for normal operation.
A6 VERIFY THE TRANSMISSION RANGE (TR) SWITCH ADJUSTMENT	
	1 Verify the transmission range (TR) switch adjustment. • Does the TR switch need adjustment? → **Yes** ADJUST the TR switch. TEST the system for normal operation. → **No** GO to **A7**.
A7 CHECK THE VOLTAGE TO THE TR SWITCH	
1 2 TR Switch C122	
3	3 Measure the voltage between the TR switch connector C122 pin 9, circuit 5 (RD), harness side and ground while turning the ignition to START. • Is the voltage greater than 10 volts? → **Yes** GO to **A8**. → **No** REPAIR the circuit or the starter clutch pedal position (SCPP) switch. TEST the system for normal operation.

FM1120100636030X

Fig. 45 Test A: Engine does not start or relay clicks (Part 3 of 6). 1999–2002 Escort, Tracer & ZX2

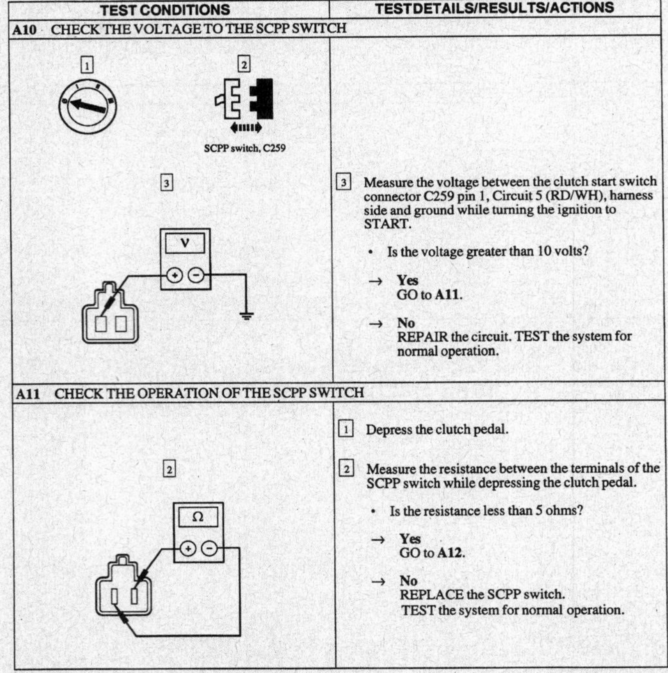

TEST CONDITIONS	TEST DETAILS/RESULTS/ACTIONS
A10 CHECK THE VOLTAGE TO THE SCPP SWITCH	
1 2 SCPP switch, C259	
3	3 Measure the voltage between the clutch start switch connector C259 pin 1, Circuit 5 (RD/WH), harness side and ground while turning the ignition to START. • Is the voltage greater than 10 volts? → **Yes** GO to **A11**. → **No** REPAIR the circuit. TEST the system for normal operation.
A11 CHECK THE OPERATION OF THE SCPP SWITCH	
	1 Depress the clutch pedal.
2	2 Measure the resistance between the terminals of the SCPP switch while depressing the clutch pedal. • Is the resistance less than 5 ohms? → **Yes** GO to **A12**. → **No** REPLACE the SCPP switch. TEST the system for normal operation.

FM1120100636050X

Fig. 45 Test A: Engine does not start or relay clicks (Part 5 of 6). 1999–2002 Escort, Tracer & ZX2

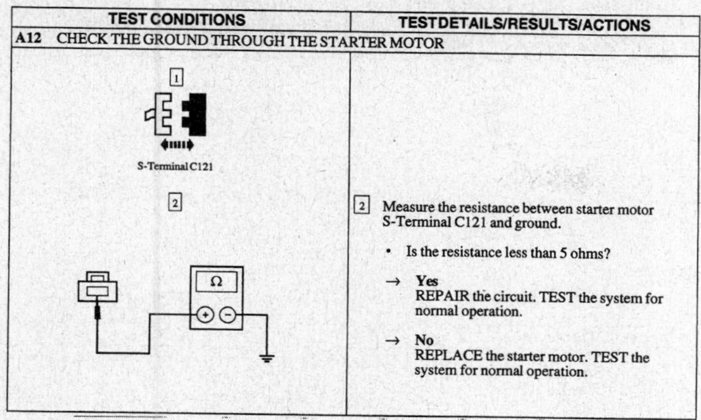

TEST CONDITIONS	TEST DETAILS/RESULTS/ACTIONS
A12 CHECK THE GROUND THROUGH THE STARTER MOTOR	
1 S-Terminal C121	
2	2 Measure the resistance between starter motor S-Terminal C121 and ground. • Is the resistance less than 5 ohms? → **Yes** REPAIR the circuit. TEST the system for normal operation. → **No** REPLACE the starter motor. TEST the system for normal operation.

FM1120100636060X

Fig. 45 Test A: Engine does not start or relay clicks (Part 6 of 6). 1999–2002 Escort, Tracer & ZX2

TEST CONDITIONS	TEST DETAILS/RESULTS/ACTIONS
B2 INSPECT THE STARTER MOTOR (Continued)	
	2 Inspect the starter motor for damage. • Is the starter motor damaged? → **Yes** REPLACE the starter motor. TEST the system for normal operation. → **No** Diagnose engine mechanical components.

FM1120100637020X

Fig. 46 Test B: Unusual starter noise (Part 2 of 2). 1999–2002 Escort, Tracer & ZX2

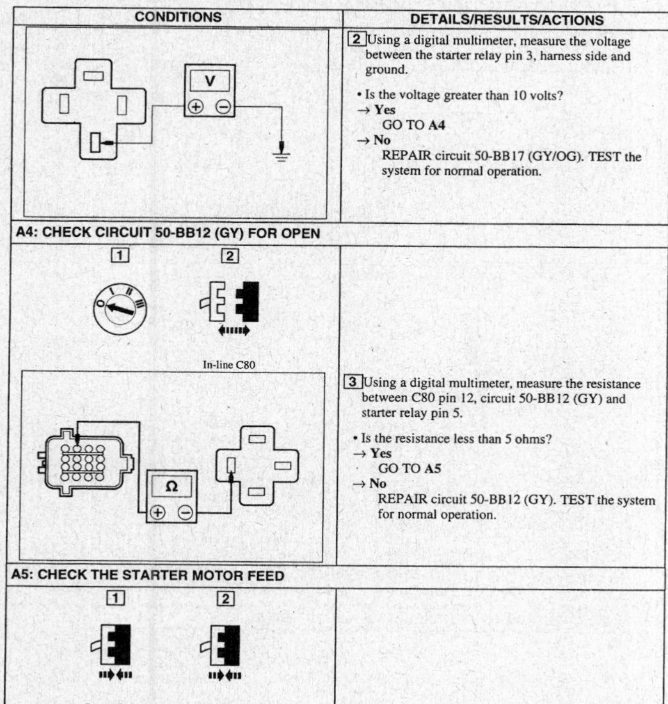

CONDITIONS	DETAILS/RESULTS/ACTIONS
	2 Using a digital multimeter, measure the voltage between the starter relay pin 3, harness side and ground. • Is the voltage greater than 10 volts? → **Yes** GO TO **A4** → **No** REPAIR circuit 50-BB17 (GY/OG). TEST the system for normal operation.
A4: CHECK CIRCUIT 50-BB12 (GY) FOR OPEN	
1 2 In-line C80	3 Using a digital multimeter, measure the resistance between C80 pin 12, circuit 50-BB12 (GY) and starter relay pin 5. • Is the resistance less than 5 ohms? → **Yes** GO TO **A5** → **No** REPAIR circuit 50-BB12 (GY). TEST the system for normal operation.
A5: CHECK THE STARTER MOTOR FEED	
1 Starter Relay 2 In-line C80	

FM1120100686020X

Fig. 47 Test A: Engine does not crank and relay clicks (Part 2 of 3). Focus

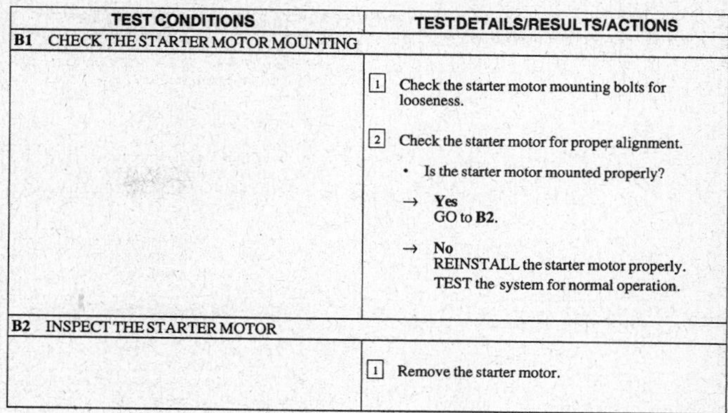

TEST CONDITIONS	TEST DETAILS/RESULTS/ACTIONS
B1 CHECK THE STARTER MOTOR MOUNTING	
	1 Check the starter motor mounting bolts for looseness. 2 Check the starter motor for proper alignment. • Is the starter motor mounted properly? → **Yes** GO to **B2**. → **No** REINSTALL the starter motor properly. TEST the system for normal operation.
B2 INSPECT THE STARTER MOTOR	
	1 Remove the starter motor.

FM1120100637010X

Fig. 46 Test B: Unusual starter noise (Part 1 of 2). 1999–2002 Escort, Tracer & ZX2

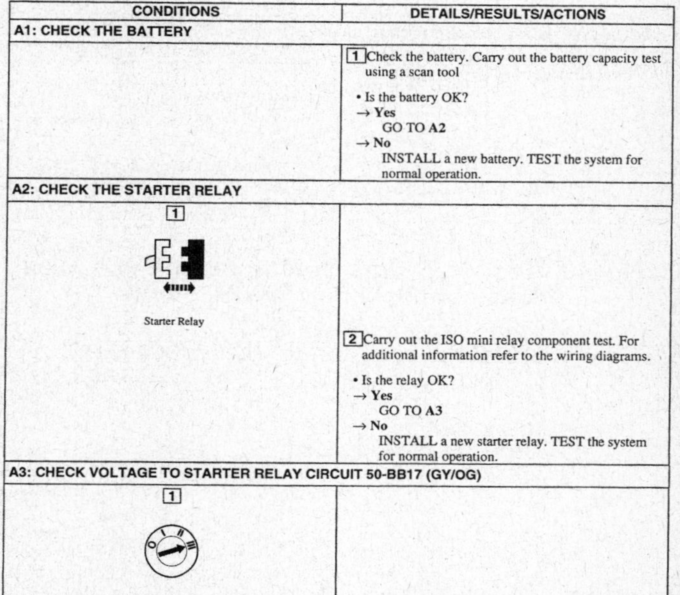

CONDITIONS	DETAILS/RESULTS/ACTIONS
A1: CHECK THE BATTERY	
	1 Check the battery. Carry out the battery capacity test using a scan tool • Is the battery OK? → **Yes** GO TO **A2** → **No** INSTALL a new battery. TEST the system for normal operation.
A2: CHECK THE STARTER RELAY	
1 Starter Relay	2 Carry out the ISO mini relay component test. For additional information refer to the wiring diagrams. • Is the relay OK? → **Yes** GO TO **A3** → **No** INSTALL a new starter relay. TEST the system for normal operation.
A3: CHECK VOLTAGE TO STARTER RELAY CIRCUIT 50-BB17 (GY/OG)	
1	

FM1120100686010X

Fig. 47 Test A: Engine does not crank and relay clicks (Part 1 of 3). Focus

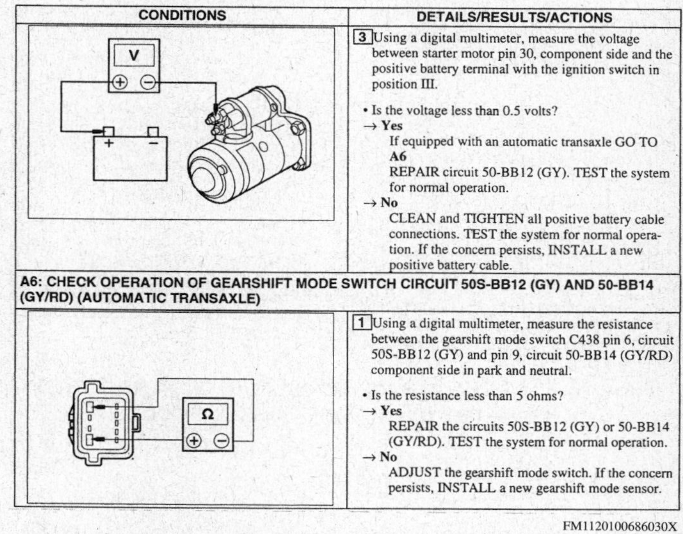

CONDITIONS	DETAILS/RESULTS/ACTIONS
	3 Using a digital multimeter, measure the voltage between starter motor pin 30, component side and the positive battery terminal with the ignition switch in position III. • Is the voltage less than 0.5 volts? → **Yes** If equipped with an automatic transaxle GO TO **A6** REPAIR circuit 50-BB12 (GY). TEST the system for normal operation. → **No** CLEAN and TIGHTEN all positive battery cable connections. TEST the system for normal operation. If the concern persists, INSTALL a new positive battery cable.
A6: CHECK OPERATION OF GEARSHIFT MODE SWITCH CIRCUIT 50S-BB12 (GY) AND 50-BB14 (GY/RD) (AUTOMATIC TRANSAXLE)	
	1 Using a digital multimeter, measure the resistance between the gearshift mode switch C438 pin 6, circuit 50S-BB12 (GY) and pin 9, circuit 50-BB14 (GY/RD) component side in park and neutral. • Is the resistance less than 5 ohms? → **Yes** REPAIR the circuits 50S-BB12 (GY) or 50-BB14 (GY/RD). TEST the system for normal operation. → **No** ADJUST the gearshift mode switch. If the concern persists, INSTALL a new gearshift mode sensor.

FM1120100686030X

Fig. 47 Test A: Engine does not crank and relay clicks (Part 3 of 3). Focus

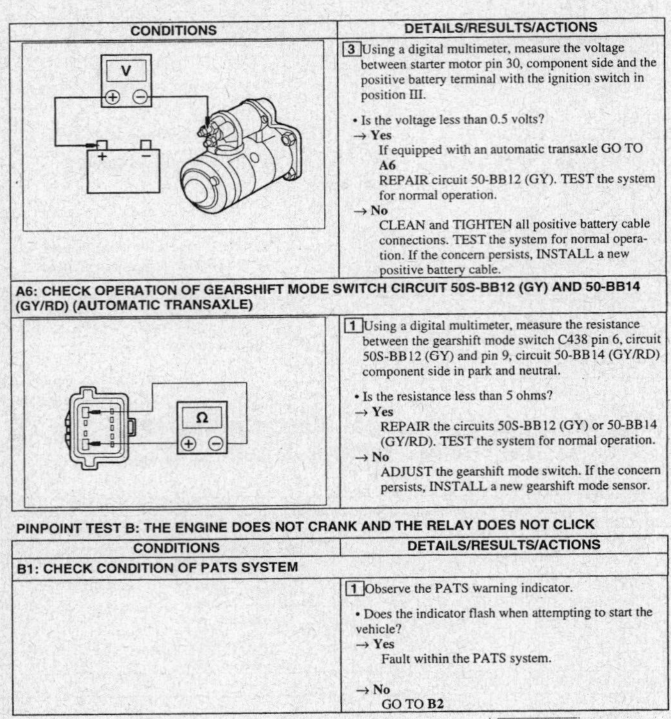

CONDITIONS	DETAILS/RESULTS/ACTIONS
	3 Using a digital multimeter, measure the voltage between starter motor pin 30, component side and the positive battery terminal with the ignition switch in position III. • Is the voltage less than 0.5 volts? → Yes If equipped with an automatic transaxle GO TO **A6** REPAIR circuit 50-BB12 (GY). TEST the system for normal operation. → No CLEAN and TIGHTEN all positive battery cable connections. TEST the system for normal operation. If the concern persists, INSTALL a new positive battery cable.
A6: CHECK OPERATION OF GEARSHIFT MODE SWITCH CIRCUIT 50S-BB12 (GY) AND 50-BB14 (GY/RD) (AUTOMATIC TRANSAXLE)	
	1 Using a digital multimeter, measure the resistance between the gearshift mode switch C438 pin 6, circuit 50S-BB12 (GY) and pin 9, circuit 50-BB14 (GY/RD) component side in park and neutral. • Is the resistance less than 5 ohms? → Yes REPAIR the circuits 50S-BB12 (GY) or 50-BB14 (GY/RD). TEST the system for normal operation. → No ADJUST the gearshift mode switch. If the concern persists, INSTALL a new gearshift mode sensor.

PINPOINT TEST B: THE ENGINE DOES NOT CRANK AND THE RELAY DOES NOT CLICK

CONDITIONS	DETAILS/RESULTS/ACTIONS
B1: CHECK CONDITION OF PATS SYSTEM	
	1 Observe the PATS warning indicator. • Does the indicator flash when attempting to start the vehicle? → Yes Fault within the PATS system. → No GO TO **B2**

FM1120100687010X

Fig. 48 Test B: Engine does not crank and relay does not click (Part 1 of 5). Focus

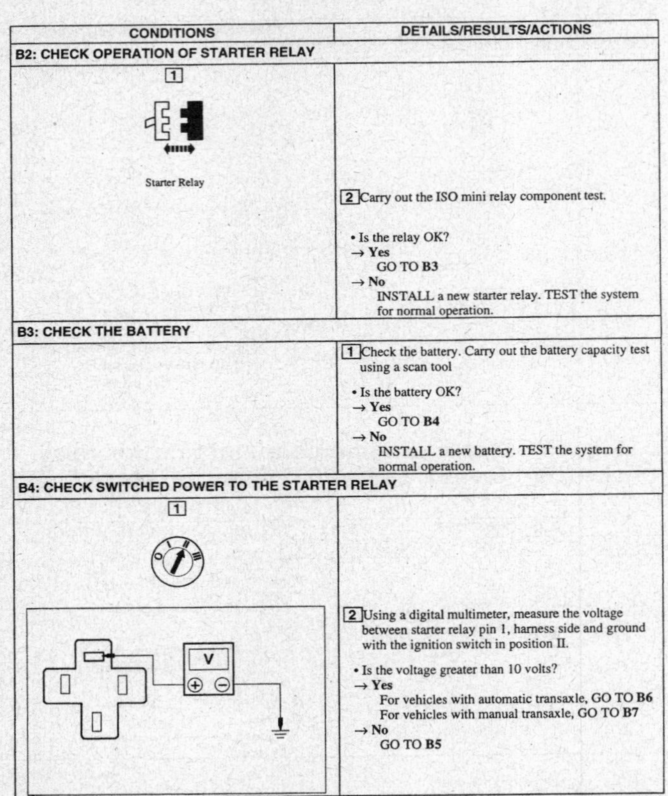

CONDITIONS	DETAILS/RESULTS/ACTIONS
B2: CHECK OPERATION OF STARTER RELAY	
1 Starter Relay	2 Carry out the ISO mini relay component test. • Is the relay OK? → Yes GO TO **B3** → No INSTALL a new starter relay. TEST the system for normal operation.
B3: CHECK THE BATTERY	
	1 Check the battery. Carry out the battery capacity test using a scan tool • Is the battery OK? → Yes GO TO **B4** → No INSTALL a new battery. TEST the system for normal operation.
B4: CHECK SWITCHED POWER TO THE STARTER RELAY	
1	2 Using a digital multimeter, measure the voltage between starter relay pin 1, harness side and ground with the ignition switch in position II. • Is the voltage greater than 10 volts? → Yes For vehicles with automatic transaxle, GO TO **B6** For vehicles with manual transaxle, GO TO **B7** → No GO TO **B5**

FM1120100687020X

Fig. 48 Test B: Engine does not crank and relay does not click (Part 2 of 5). Focus

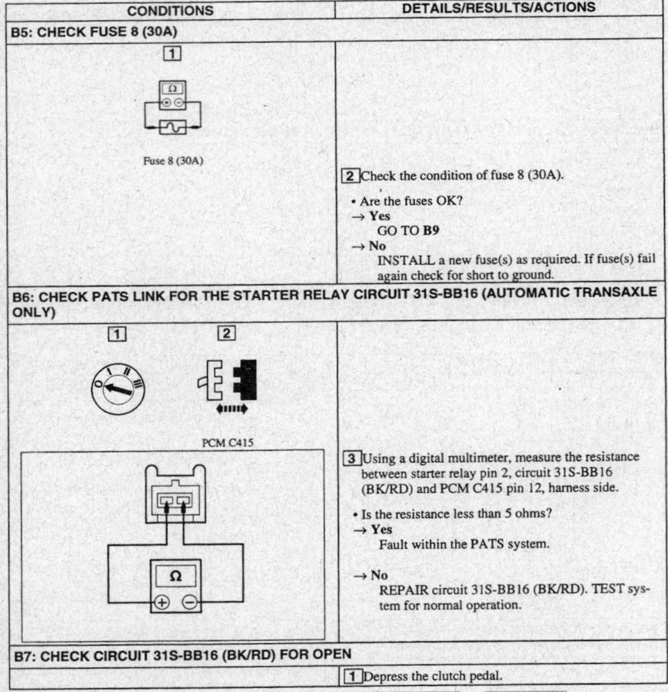

CONDITIONS	DETAILS/RESULTS/ACTIONS
B5: CHECK FUSE 8 (30A)	
1 Fuse 8 (30A)	2 Check the condition of fuse 8 (30A). • Are the fuses OK? → Yes GO TO **B9** → No INSTALL a new fuse(s) as required. If fuse(s) fail again check for short to ground.
B6: CHECK PATS LINK FOR THE STARTER RELAY CIRCUIT 31S-BB16 (AUTOMATIC TRANSAXLE ONLY)	
1 2 PCM C415	3 Using a digital multimeter, measure the resistance between starter relay pin 2, circuit 31S-BB16 (BK/RD) and PCM C415 pin 12, harness side. • Is the resistance less than 5 ohms? → Yes Fault within the PATS system. → No REPAIR circuit 31S-BB16 (BK/RD). TEST system for normal operation.
B7: CHECK CIRCUIT 31S-BB16 (BK/RD) FOR OPEN	
	1 Depress the clutch pedal.

FM1120100687030X

Fig. 48 Test B: Engine does not crank and relay does not click (Part 3 of 5). Focus

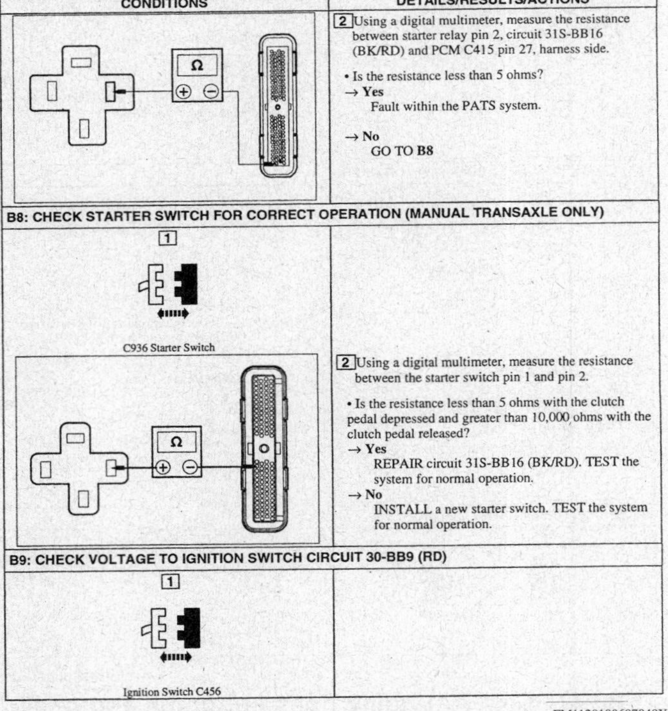

CONDITIONS	DETAILS/RESULTS/ACTIONS
	2 Using a digital multimeter, measure the resistance between starter relay pin 2, circuit 31S-BB16 (BK/RD) and PCM C415 pin 27, harness side. • Is the resistance less than 5 ohms? → Yes Fault within the PATS system. → No GO TO **B8**
B8: CHECK STARTER SWITCH FOR CORRECT OPERATION (MANUAL TRANSAXLE ONLY)	
1 C936 Starter Switch	2 Using a digital multimeter, measure the resistance between the starter switch pin 1 and pin 2. • Is the resistance less than 5 ohms with the clutch pedal depressed and greater than 10,000 ohms with the clutch pedal released? → Yes REPAIR circuit 31S-BB16 (BK/RD). TEST the system for normal operation. → No INSTALL a new starter switch. TEST the system for normal operation.
B9: CHECK VOLTAGE TO IGNITION SWITCH CIRCUIT 30-BB9 (RD)	
1 Ignition Switch C456	

FM1120100687040X

Fig. 48 Test B: Engine does not crank and relay does not click (Part 4 of 5). Focus

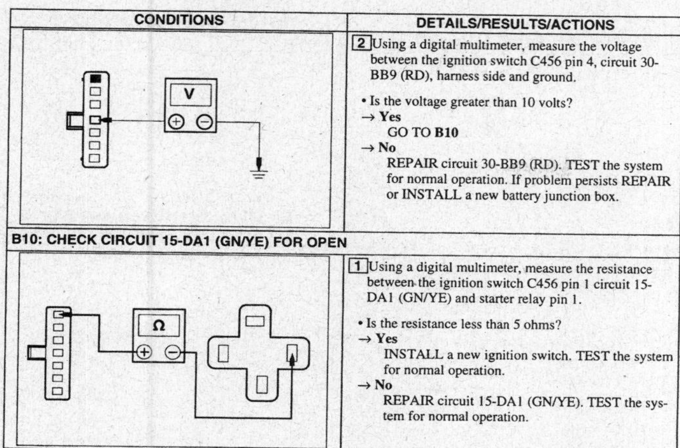

CONDITIONS	DETAILS/RESULTS/ACTIONS
	2 Using a digital multimeter, measure the voltage between the ignition switch C456 pin 4, circuit 30-BB9 (RD), harness side and ground. • Is the voltage greater than 10 volts? → **Yes** GO TO **B10** → **No** REPAIR circuit 30-BB9 (RD). TEST the system for normal operation. If problem persists REPAIR or INSTALL a new battery junction box.
B10: CHECK CIRCUIT 15-DA1 (GN/YE) FOR OPEN	
	1 Using a digital multimeter, measure the resistance between the ignition switch C456 pin 1 circuit 15-DA1 (GN/YE) and starter relay pin 1. • Is the resistance less than 5 ohms? → **Yes** INSTALL a new ignition switch. TEST the system for normal operation. → **No** REPAIR circuit 15-DA1 (GN/YE). TEST the system for normal operation.

FM1120100687050X

Fig. 48 Test B: Engine does not crank and relay does not click (Part 5 of 5). Focus

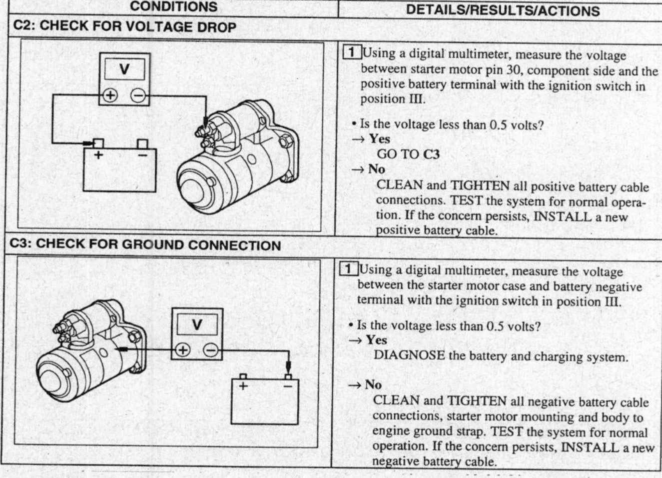

CONDITIONS	DETAILS/RESULTS/ACTIONS
C2: CHECK FOR VOLTAGE DROP	
	1 Using a digital multimeter, measure the voltage between starter motor pin 30, component side and the positive battery terminal with the ignition switch in position III. • Is the voltage less than 0.5 volts? → **Yes** GO TO **C3** → **No** CLEAN and TIGHTEN all positive battery cable connections. TEST the system for normal operation. If the concern persists, INSTALL a new positive battery cable.
C3: CHECK FOR GROUND CONNECTION	
	1 Using a digital multimeter, measure the voltage between the starter motor case and battery negative terminal with the ignition switch in position III. • Is the voltage less than 0.5 volts? → **Yes** DIAGNOSE the battery and charging system. → **No** CLEAN and TIGHTEN all negative battery cable connections, starter motor mounting and body to engine ground strap. TEST the system for normal operation. If the concern persists, INSTALL a new negative battery cable.

FM1120100688020X

Fig. 49 Test C: Engine cranks slowly (Part 2 of 2). Focus

CONDITIONS	DETAILS/RESULTS/ACTIONS
C1: CHECK THE STARTER MOTOR LOAD	
	1 Carry out the starter motor load test on the starter motor. • Is the starter motor OK? → **Yes** GO TO **C2** → **No** INSTALL a new starter motor. TEST the system for normal operation

FM1120100688010X

Fig. 49 Test C: Engine cranks slowly (Part 1 of 2). Focus

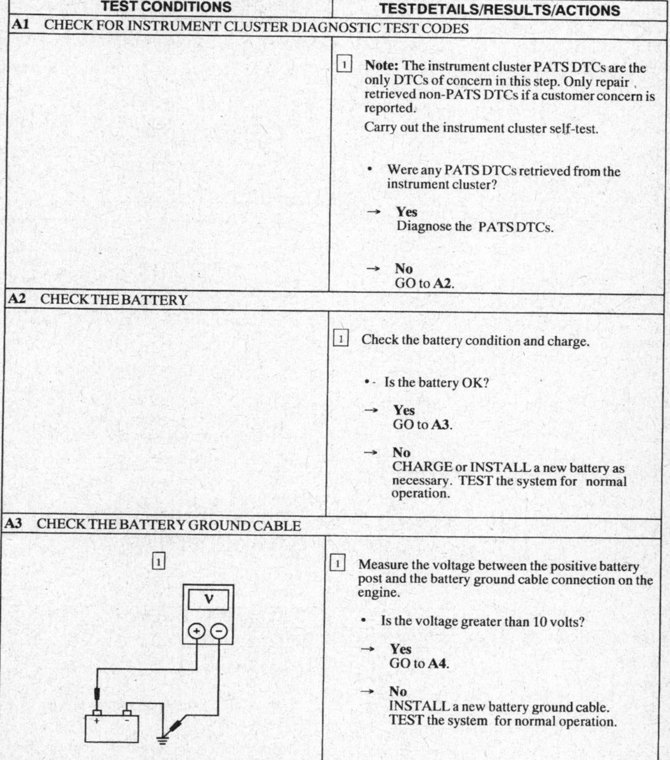

TEST CONDITIONS	TESTDETAILS/RESULTS/ACTIONS
A1 CHECK FOR INSTRUMENT CLUSTER DIAGNOSTIC TEST CODES	
	1 **Note:** The instrument cluster PATS DTCs are the only DTCs of concern in this step. Only repair retrieved non-PATS DTCs if a customer concern is reported. Carry out the instrument cluster self-test. • Were any PATS DTCs retrieved from the instrument cluster? → **Yes** Diagnose the PATS DTCs. → **No** GO to **A2**.
A2 CHECK THE BATTERY	
	1 Check the battery condition and charge. • Is the battery OK? → **Yes** GO to **A3**. → **No** CHARGE or INSTALL a new battery as necessary. TEST the system for normal operation.
A3 CHECK THE BATTERY GROUND CABLE	
1	1 Measure the voltage between the positive battery post and the battery ground cable connection on the engine. • Is the voltage greater than 10 volts? → **Yes** GO to **A4**. → **No** INSTALL a new battery ground cable. TEST the system for normal operation.

FM1120100653010X

Fig. 50 Test A: Engine does not crank (Part 1 of 17). LS & Thunderbird

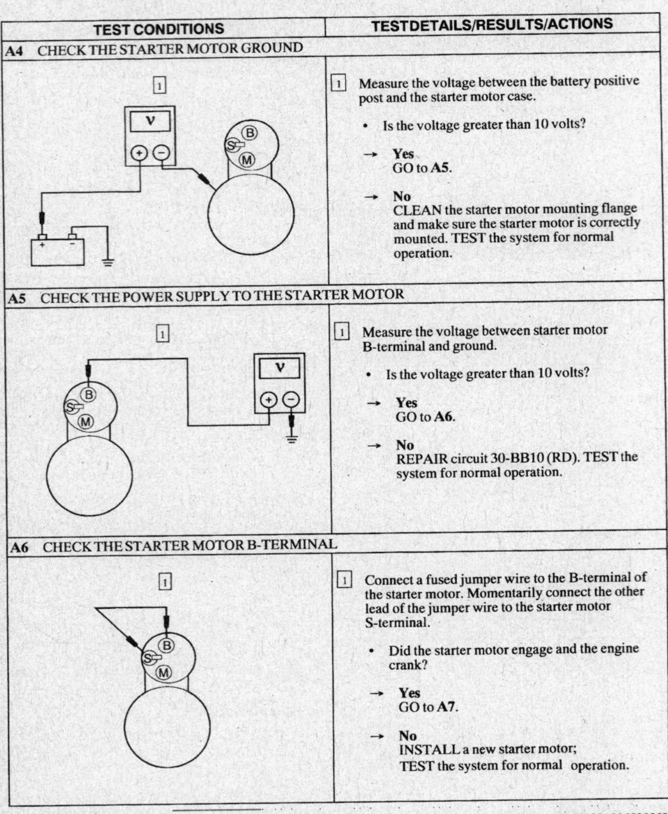

TEST CONDITIONS	TEST DETAILS/RESULTS/ACTIONS
A4 CHECK THE STARTER MOTOR GROUND	
1	1 Measure the voltage between the battery positive post and the starter motor case. • Is the voltage greater than 10 volts? → **Yes** GO to **A5**. → **No** CLEAN the starter motor mounting flange and make sure the starter motor is correctly mounted. TEST the system for normal operation.
A5 CHECK THE POWER SUPPLY TO THE STARTER MOTOR	
1	1 Measure the voltage between starter motor B-terminal and ground. • Is the voltage greater than 10 volts? → **Yes** GO to **A6**. → **No** REPAIR circuit 30-BB10 (RD). TEST the system for normal operation.
A6 CHECK THE STARTER MOTOR B-TERMINAL	
1	1 Connect a fused jumper wire to the B-terminal of the starter motor. Momentarily connect the other lead of the jumper wire to the starter motor S-terminal. • Did the starter motor engage and the engine crank? → **Yes** GO to **A7**. → **No** INSTALL a new starter motor; TEST the system for normal operation.

FM1120100653020X

Fig. 50 Test A: Engine does not crank (Part 2 of 17). LS & Thunderbird

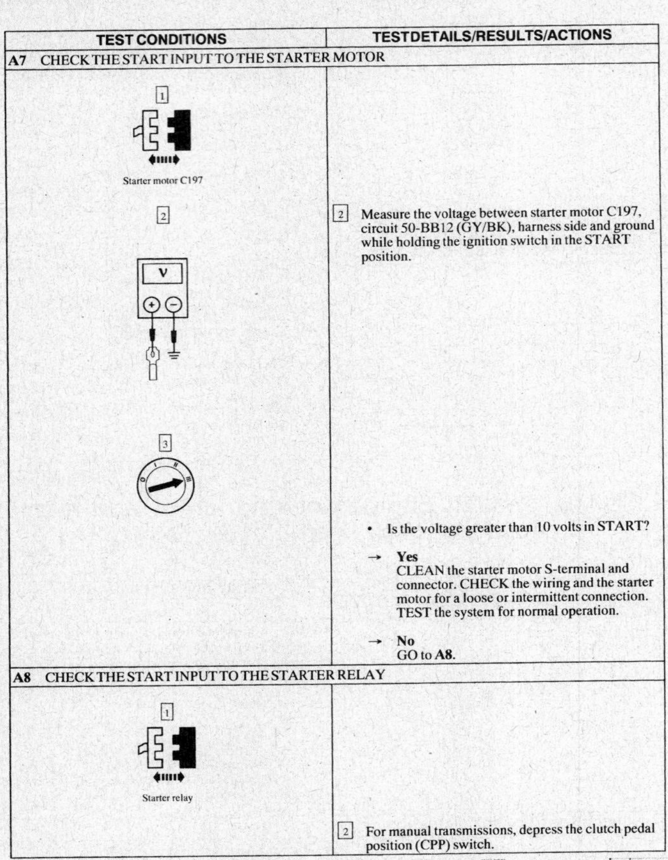

TEST CONDITIONS	TEST DETAILS/RESULTS/ACTIONS
A7 CHECK THE START INPUT TO THE STARTER MOTOR	
1 Starter motor C197 2 3	2 Measure the voltage between starter motor C197, circuit 50-BB12 (GY/BK), harness side and ground while holding the ignition switch in the START position. • Is the voltage greater than 10 volts in START? → **Yes** CLEAN the starter motor S-terminal and connector. CHECK the wiring and the starter motor for a loose or intermittent connection. TEST the system for normal operation. → **No** GO to **A8**.
A8 CHECK THE START INPUT TO THE STARTER RELAY	
1 Starter relay	2 For manual transmissions, depress the clutch pedal position (CPP) switch.

FM1120100653030X

Fig. 50 Test A: Engine does not crank (Part 3 of 17). LS & Thunderbird

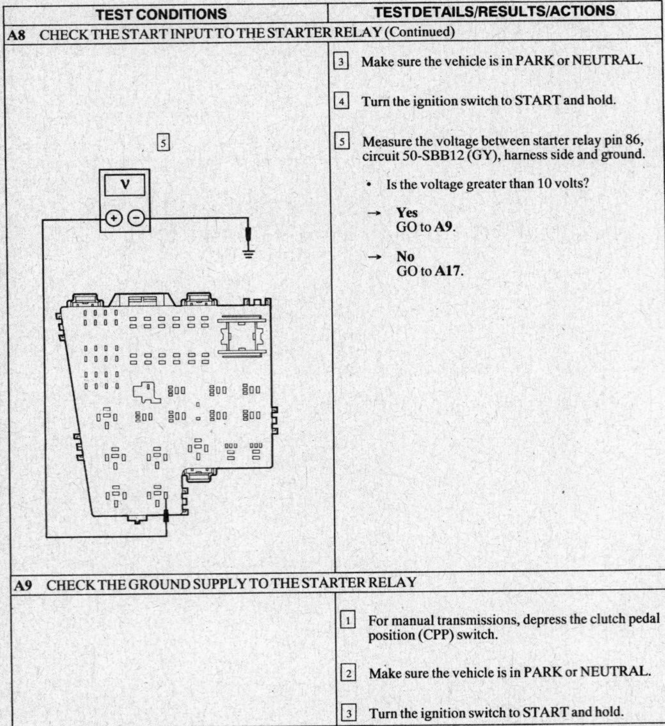

TEST CONDITIONS	TEST DETAILS/RESULTS/ACTIONS
A8 CHECK THE START INPUT TO THE STARTER RELAY (Continued)	
5	3 Make sure the vehicle is in PARK or NEUTRAL. 4 Turn the ignition switch to START and hold. 5 Measure the voltage between starter relay pin 86, circuit 50-SBB12 (GY), harness side and ground. • Is the voltage greater than 10 volts? → **Yes** GO to **A9**. → **No** GO to **A17**.
A9 CHECK THE GROUND SUPPLY TO THE STARTER RELAY	
	1 For manual transmissions, depress the clutch pedal position (CPP) switch. 2 Make sure the vehicle is in PARK or NEUTRAL. 3 Turn the ignition switch to START and hold.

FM1120100653040X

Fig. 50 Test A: Engine does not crank (Part 4 of 17). LS & Thunderbird

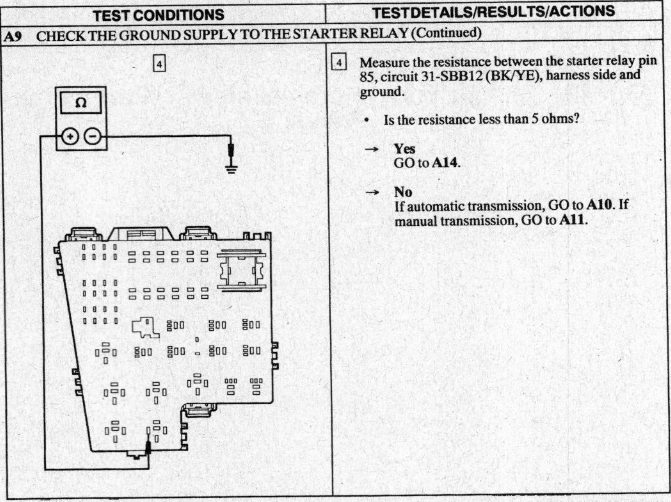

TEST CONDITIONS	TEST DETAILS/RESULTS/ACTIONS
A9 CHECK THE GROUND SUPPLY TO THE STARTER RELAY (Continued)	
4	4 **Measure the resistance between the starter relay pin 85, circuit 31-SBB12 (BK/YE), harness side and ground.** • Is the resistance less than 5 ohms? → **Yes** GO to **A14**. → **No** If automatic transmission, GO to **A10**. If manual transmission, GO to **A11**.

FM1120100653050X

Fig. 50 Test A: Engine does not crank (Part 5 of 17). LS & Thunderbird

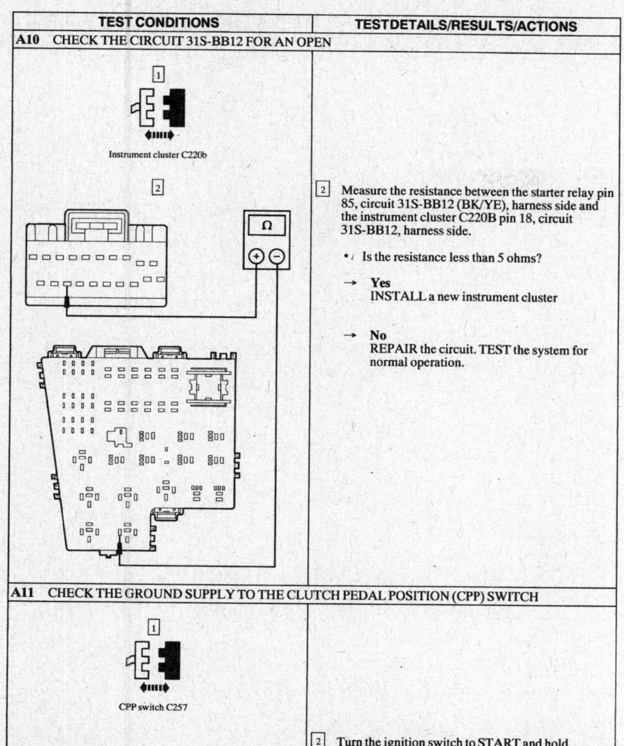

TEST CONDITIONS	TESTDETAILS/RESULTS/ACTIONS
A10 CHECK THE CIRCUIT 31S-BB12 FOR AN OPEN	
1 Instrument cluster C220b	
2	2 Measure the resistance between the starter relay pin 85, circuit 31S-BB12 (BK/YE), harness side and the instrument cluster C220B pin 18, circuit 31S-BB12, harness side. • Is the resistance less than 5 ohms? → **Yes** INSTALL a new instrument cluster → **No** REPAIR the circuit. TEST the system for normal operation.
A11 CHECK THE GROUND SUPPLY TO THE CLUTCH PEDAL POSITION (CPP) SWITCH	
1 CPP switch C257	
	2 Turn the ignition switch to START and hold.

FM1120100653060X

Fig. 50 Test A: Engine does not crank (Part 6 of 17). LS & Thunderbird

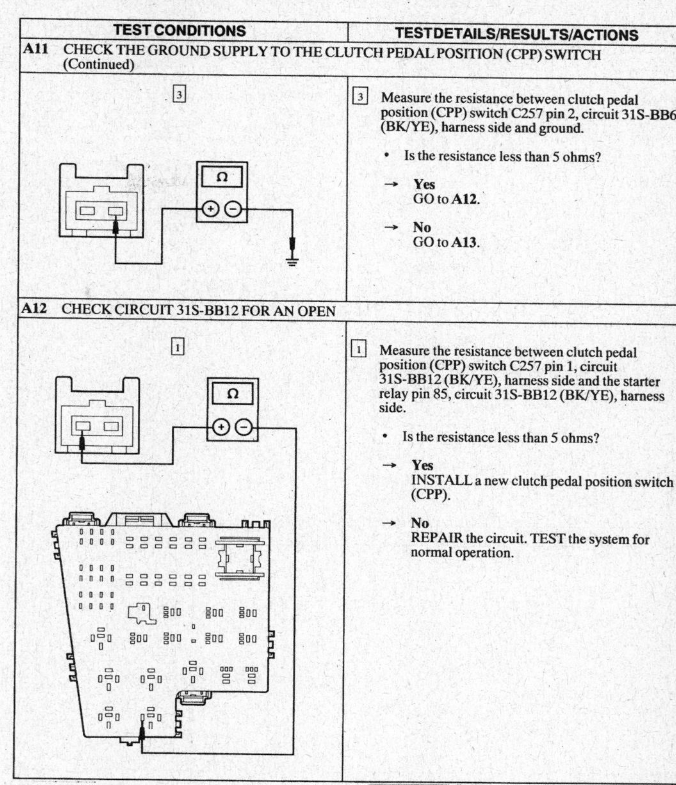

TEST CONDITIONS	TESTDETAILS/RESULTS/ACTIONS
A11 CHECK THE GROUND SUPPLY TO THE CLUTCH PEDAL POSITION (CPP) SWITCH (Continued)	
3	3 Measure the resistance between clutch pedal position (CPP) switch C257 pin 2, circuit 31S-BB6 (BK/YE), harness side and ground. • Is the resistance less than 5 ohms? → **Yes** GO to **A12**. → **No** GO to **A13**.
A12 CHECK CIRCUIT 31S-BB12 FOR AN OPEN	
1	1 Measure the resistance between clutch pedal position (CPP) switch C257 pin 1, circuit 31S-BB12 (BK/YE), harness side and the starter relay pin 85, circuit 31S-BB12 (BK/YE), harness side. • Is the resistance less than 5 ohms? → **Yes** INSTALL a new clutch pedal position switch (CPP). → **No** REPAIR the circuit. TEST the system for normal operation.

FM1120100653070X

Fig. 50 Test A: Engine does not crank (Part 7 of 17). LS & Thunderbird

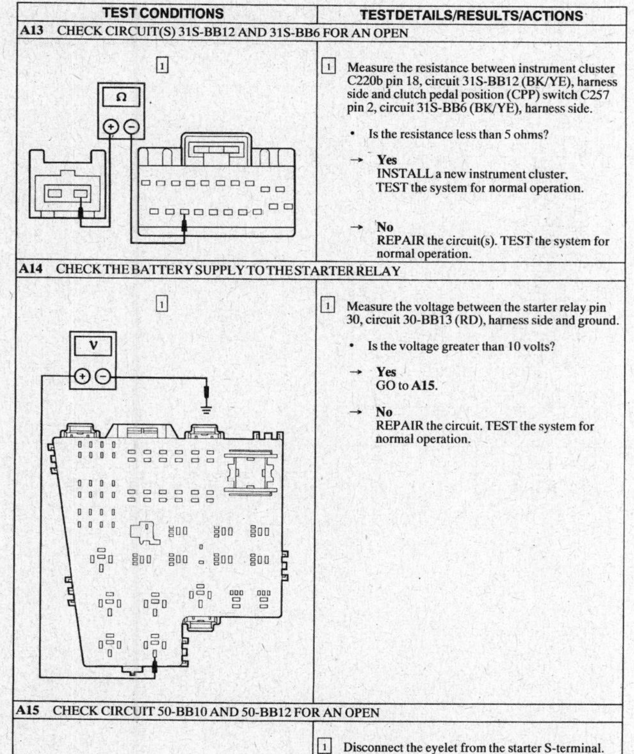

TEST CONDITIONS	TESTDETAILS/RESULTS/ACTIONS
A13 CHECK CIRCUIT(S) 31S-BB12 AND 31S-BB6 FOR AN OPEN	
1	1 Measure the resistance between instrument cluster C220b pin 18, circuit 31S-BB12 (BK/YE), harness side and clutch pedal position (CPP) switch C257 pin 2, circuit 31S-BB6 (BK/YE), harness side. • Is the resistance less than 5 ohms? → **Yes** INSTALL a new instrument cluster. TEST the system for normal operation. → **No** REPAIR the circuit(s). TEST the system for normal operation.
A14 CHECK THE BATTERY SUPPLY TO THE STARTER RELAY	
1	1 Measure the voltage between the starter relay pin 30, circuit 30-BB13 (RD), harness side and ground. • Is the voltage greater than 10 volts? → **Yes** GO to **A15**. → **No** REPAIR the circuit. TEST the system for normal operation.
A15 CHECK CIRCUIT 50-BB10 AND 50-BB12 FOR AN OPEN	
	1 Disconnect the eyelet from the starter S-terminal.

FM1120100653080X

Fig. 50 Test A: Engine does not crank (Part 8 of 17). LS & Thunderbird

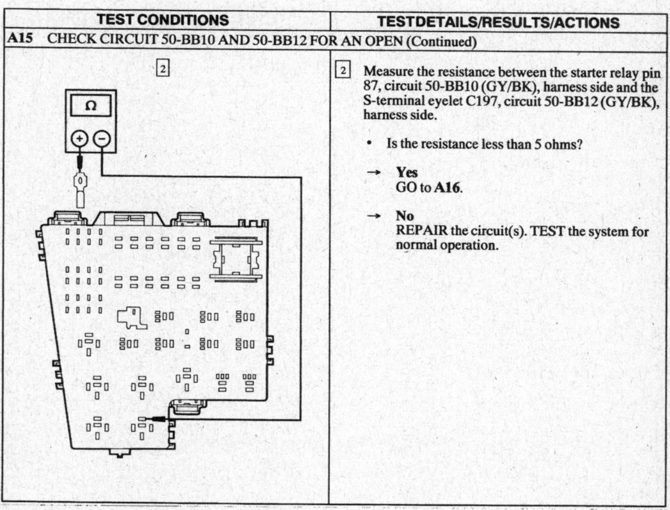

TEST CONDITIONS	TESTDETAILS/RESULTS/ACTIONS
A15 CHECK CIRCUIT 50-BB10 AND 50-BB12 FOR AN OPEN (Continued)	
2	2 Measure the resistance between the starter relay pin 87, circuit 50-BB10 (GY/BK), harness side and the S-terminal eyelet C197, circuit 50-BB12 (GY/BK), harness side. • Is the resistance less than 5 ohms? → **Yes** GO to **A16**. → **No** REPAIR the circuit(s). TEST the system for normal operation.

FM1120100653090X

Fig. 50 Test A: Engine does not crank (Part 9 of 17). LS & Thunderbird

TEST CONDITIONS	TEST DETAILS/RESULTS/ACTIONS
A16 CHECK CIRCUIT 50-BB10 AND 50-BB12 FOR A SHORT TO GROUND	
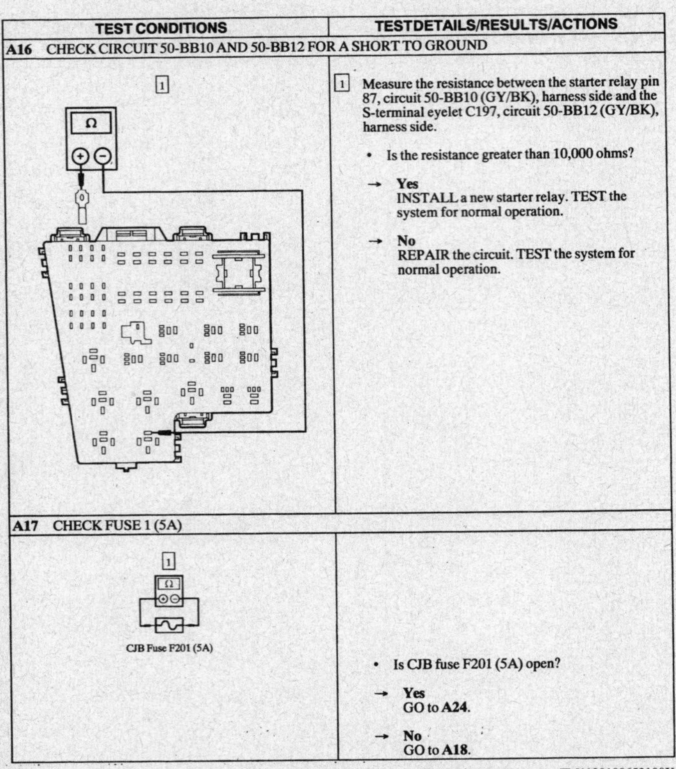	1 Measure the resistance between the starter relay pin 87, circuit 50-BB10 (GY/BK), harness side and the S-terminal eyelet C197, circuit 50-BB12 (GY/BK), harness side. • Is the resistance greater than 10,000 ohms? → **Yes** INSTALL a new starter relay. TEST the system for normal operation. → **No** REPAIR the circuit. TEST the system for normal operation.
A17 CHECK FUSE 1 (5A)	
1 CJB Fuse F201 (5A)	• Is CJB fuse F201 (5A) open? → **Yes** GO to **A24**. → **No** GO to **A18**.

FM1120100653100X

Fig. 50 Test A: Engine does not crank (Part 10 of 17). LS & Thunderbird

TEST CONDITIONS	TEST DETAILS/RESULTS/ACTIONS
A19 CHECK THE BATTERY INPUT TO THE IGNITION SWITCH	
1 Ignition switch C250 2	2 Measure the voltage between ignition switch C250 pin 1, circuit 30-BB9 (RD), harness side and ground. • Is the voltage greater than 10 volts? → **Yes** GO to **A20**. → **No** REPAIR the circuit. TEST the system for normal operation.

FM1120100653120X

Fig. 50 Test A: Engine does not crank (Part 12 of 17). LS & Thunderbird

TEST CONDITIONS	TEST DETAILS/RESULTS/ACTIONS
A18 CHECK THE START INPUT TO FUSE 1	
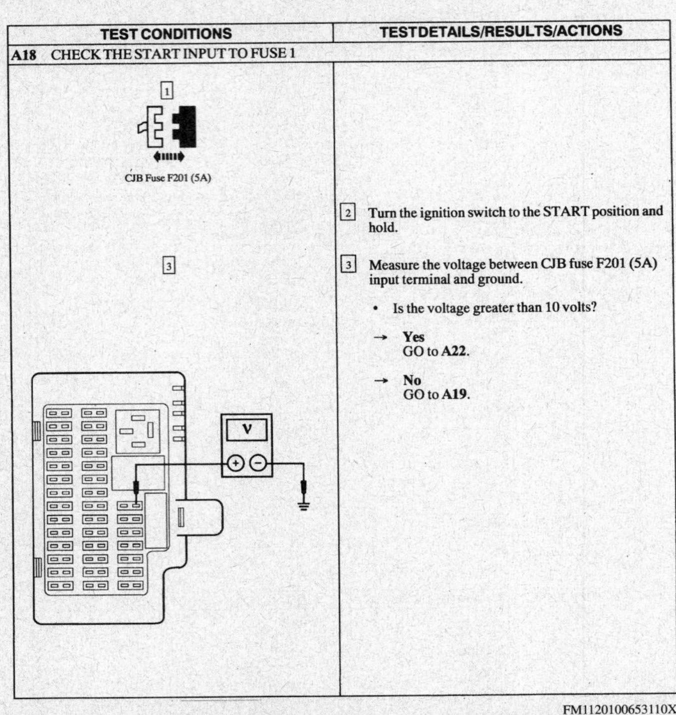	2 Turn the ignition switch to the START position and hold. 3 Measure the voltage between CJB fuse F201 (5A) input terminal and ground. • Is the voltage greater than 10 volts? → **Yes** GO to **A22**. → **No** GO to **A19**.

FM1120100653110X

Fig. 50 Test A: Engine does not crank (Part 11 of 17). LS & Thunderbird

TEST CONDITIONS	TEST DETAILS/RESULTS/ACTIONS
A20 CHECK CIRCUIT 50-DD5 FOR AN OPEN	
1 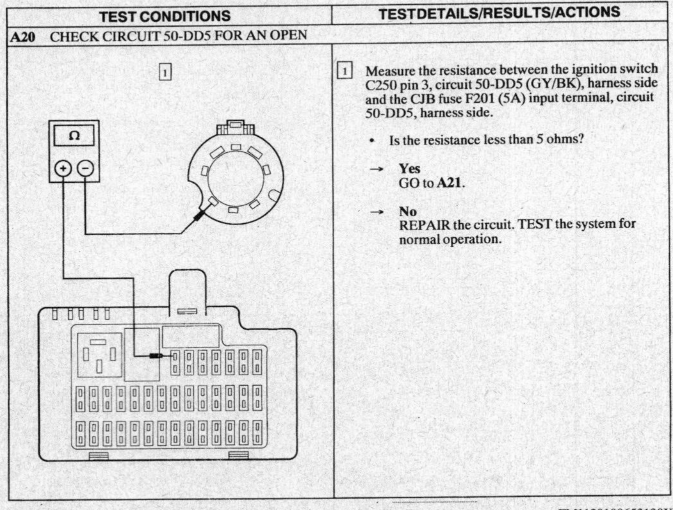	1 Measure the resistance between the ignition switch C250 pin 3, circuit 50-DD5 (GY/BK), harness side and the CJB fuse F201 (5A) input terminal, circuit 50-DD5, harness side. • Is the resistance less than 5 ohms? → **Yes** GO to **A21**. → **No** REPAIR the circuit. TEST the system for normal operation.

FM1120100653130X

Fig. 50 Test A: Engine does not crank (Part 13 of 17). LS & Thunderbird

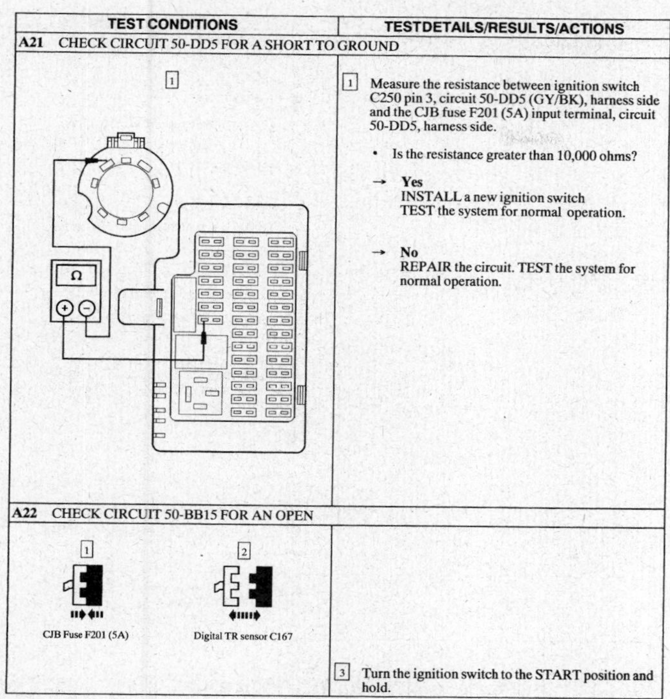

TEST CONDITIONS	TEST DETAILS/RESULTS/ACTIONS
A21 CHECK CIRCUIT 50-DD5 FOR A SHORT TO GROUND	
1	1 Measure the resistance between ignition switch C250 pin 3, circuit 50-DD5 (GY/BK), harness side and the CJB fuse F201 (5A) input terminal, circuit 50-DD5, harness side. • Is the resistance greater than 10,000 ohms? → **Yes** INSTALL a new ignition switch TEST the system for normal operation. → **No** REPAIR the circuit. TEST the system for normal operation.
A22 CHECK CIRCUIT 50-BB15 FOR AN OPEN	
1 CJB Fuse F201 (5A) 2 Digital TR sensor C167	3 Turn the ignition switch to the START position and hold.

FM1120100653140X

Fig. 50 Test A: Engine does not crank (Part 14 of 17). LS & Thunderbird

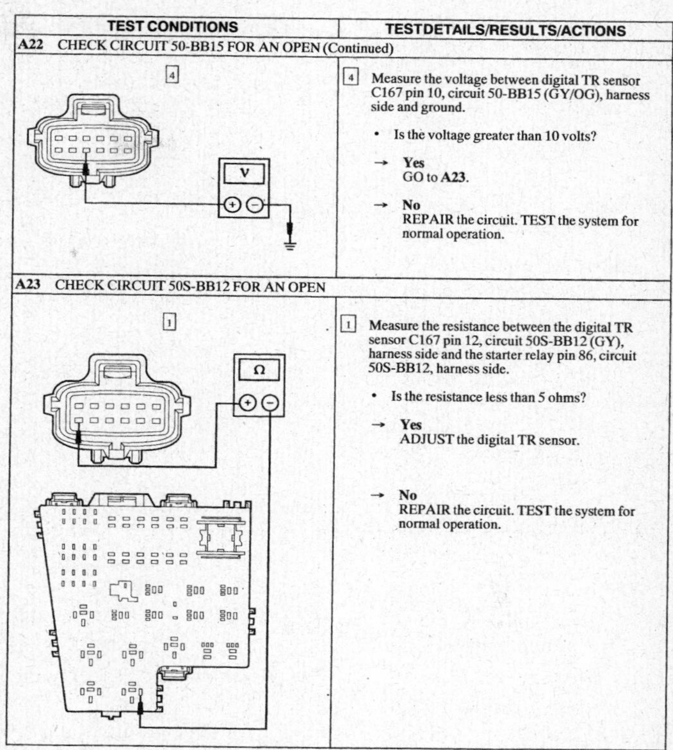

TEST CONDITIONS	TEST DETAILS/RESULTS/ACTIONS
A22 CHECK CIRCUIT 50-BB15 FOR AN OPEN (Continued)	
4	4 Measure the voltage between digital TR sensor C167 pin 10, circuit 50-BB15 (GY/OG), harness side and ground. • Is the voltage greater than 10 volts? → **Yes** GO to **A23**. → **No** REPAIR the circuit. TEST the system for normal operation.
A23 CHECK CIRCUIT 50S-BB12 FOR AN OPEN	
1	1 Measure the resistance between the digital TR sensor C167 pin 12, circuit 50S-BB12 (GY), harness side and the starter relay pin 86, circuit 50S-BB12, harness side. • Is the resistance less than 5 ohms? → **Yes** ADJUST the digital TR sensor. → **No** REPAIR the circuit. TEST the system for normal operation.

FM1120100653150X

Fig. 50 Test A: Engine does not crank (Part 15 of 17). LS & Thunderbird

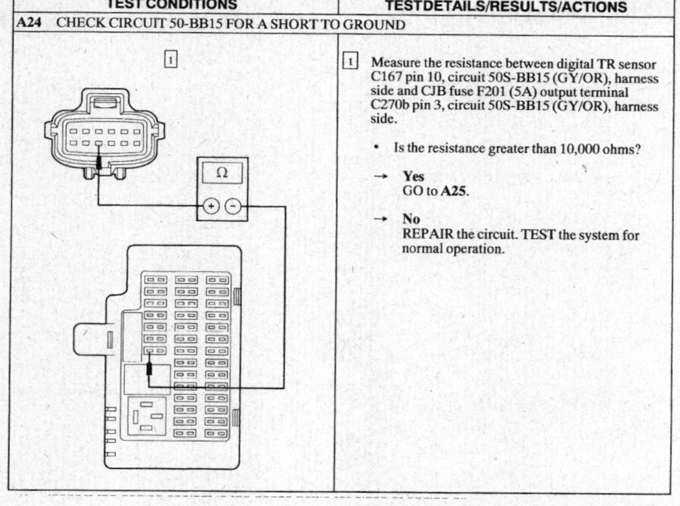

TEST CONDITIONS	TEST DETAILS/RESULTS/ACTIONS
A24 CHECK CIRCUIT 50-BB15 FOR A SHORT TO GROUND	
1	1 Measure the resistance between digital TR sensor C167 pin 10, circuit 50S-BB15 (GY/OR), harness side and CJB fuse F201 (5A) output terminal C270b pin 3, circuit 50S-BB15 (GY/OR), harness side. • Is the resistance greater than 10,000 ohms? → **Yes** GO to **A25**. → **No** REPAIR the circuit. TEST the system for normal operation.

FM1120100653160X

Fig. 50 Test A: Engine does not crank (Part 16 of 17). LS & Thunderbird

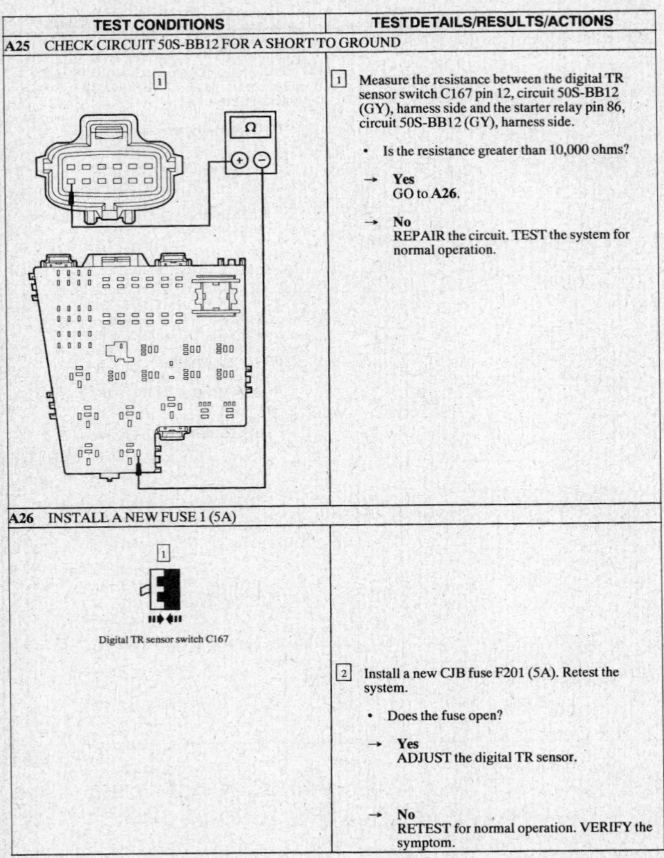

TEST CONDITIONS	TEST DETAILS/RESULTS/ACTIONS
A25 CHECK CIRCUIT 50S-BB12 FOR A SHORT TO GROUND	
1	1 Measure the resistance between the digital TR sensor switch C167 pin 12, circuit 50S-BB12 (GY), harness side and the starter relay pin 86, circuit 50S-BB12 (GY), harness side. • Is the resistance greater than 10,000 ohms? → **Yes** GO to **A26**. → **No** REPAIR the circuit. TEST the system for normal operation.
A26 INSTALL A NEW FUSE 1 (5A)	
1 Digital TR sensor switch C167	
	2 Install a new CJB fuse F201 (5A). Retest the system. • Does the fuse open? → **Yes** ADJUST the digital TR sensor. → **No** RETEST for normal operation. VERIFY the symptom.

FM1120100653170X

Fig. 50 Test A: Engine does not crank (Part 17 of 17). LS & Thunderbird

TEST CONDITIONS	TEST DETAILS/RESULTS/ACTIONS
B3 CHECK FOR UNUSUAL WEAR (Continued)	
	2 Inspect the ring gear for damaged or worn teeth. • Is the noise due to flywheel ring gear tooth damage? → **Yes** INSTALL a new flywheel ring gear. EXAMINE the starter pinion teeth. If damaged, INSTALL a new starter motor. TEST the system for normal operation. → **No** INSTALL a new starter motor. TEST the system for normal operation.

FM1120100654020X

Fig. 51 Test B: Unusual starter noise (Part 2 of 2). LS & Thunderbird

TEST CONDITIONS	TEST DETAILS/RESULTS/ACTIONS
B1 CHECK THE STARTER MOUNTING	
	1 Inspect the starter motor mounting bolts and brackets for looseness. • Is the starter motor mounted correctly? → **Yes** GO to **B2**. → **No** INSTALL the starter motor correctly. TEST the system for normal operation.
B2 CHECK FOR ENGINE NOISE	
	1 Turn the ignition switch to the OFF position. 2 Connect a fused jumper wire from the B-terminal to the S-terminal of the starter motor. Engage the starter motor and verify the noise is due to the starter operation. • Is the noise due to the starter motor engagement? → **Yes** GO to **B3**. → **No** **Diagnose Engine Mechanical Components**
B3 CHECK FOR UNUSUAL WEAR	
	1 Remove the starter motor.

FM1120100654010X

Fig. 51 Test B: Unusual starter noise (Part 1 of 2). LS & Thunderbird

TEST CONDITIONS	TEST DETAILS/RESULTS/ACTIONS
A1 CHECK CIRCUIT 875 (BK/LB) FOR AN OPEN	
1 Steering Column/Ignition/Lighting Control Module Connector C288	
2	2 Connect an ohmmeter between the steering column/ignition/lighting control module connector Pin C288-14, Circuit 875 (BK/LB) and ground. • Is the resistance reading 5 ohms or less? → **Yes** GO to **A2**. → **No** REPAIR Circuit 875 (BK/LB) for an open. RESTORE the vehicle. REPEAT the steering column/ignition/lighting control module self test.
A2 CHECK CIRCUIT 57 (BK) FOR AN OPEN	
1 Steering Column/Ignition/Lighting Control Module Connector C287	
2	2 Connect an ohmmeter between the steering column/ignition/lighting control module connector Pin C287-7, Circuit 57 (BK) and ground. • Is the resistance reading 5 ohms or less? → **Yes** GO to **A3**. → **No** REPAIR Circuit 57 (BK) for an open. RESTORE the vehicle. REPEAT the steering column/ignition/lighting control module self test.

FM1120100616010X

Fig. 52 Test A: No communication with steering column/ignition/lighting control module (Part 1 of 3). Mark VIII

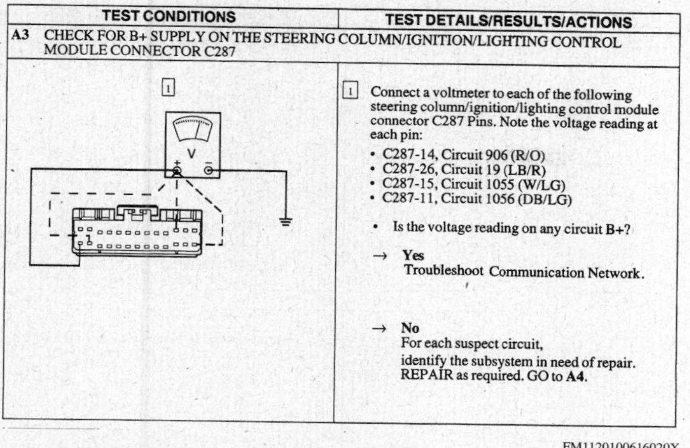

TEST CONDITIONS	TEST DETAILS/RESULTS/ACTIONS
A3 CHECK FOR B+ SUPPLY ON THE STEERING COLUMN/IGNITION/LIGHTING CONTROL MODULE CONNECTOR C287	
1	1 Connect a voltmeter to each of the following steering column/ignition/lighting control module connector C287 Pins. Note the voltage reading at each pin: • C287-14, Circuit 906 (R/O) • C287-26, Circuit 19 (LB/R) • C287-15, Circuit 1055 (W/LG) • C287-11, Circuit 1056 (DB/LG) • Is the voltage reading on any circuit B+? → **Yes** Troubleshoot Communication Network. → **No** For each suspect circuit, identify the subsystem in need of repair. REPAIR as required. GO to **A4**.

FM1120100616020X

Fig. 52 Test A: No communication with steering column/ignition/lighting control module (Part 2 of 3). Mark VIII

TEST CONDITIONS	TEST DETAILS/RESULTS/ACTIONS
B1 CHECK FOR VOLTAGE AT STARTER	
1 2 P R N D	3 Raise the vehicle on hoist.

FM1120100617010X

Fig. 53 Test B: Engine does not crank or relay clicks (Part 1 of 10). Mark VIII

TEST CONDITIONS	TEST DETAILS/RESULTS/ACTIONS
B1 CHECK FOR VOLTAGE AT STARTER (Continued)	
4	4 **NOTE:** Remove plastic safety cap on starter solenoid and connector at starter solenoid S terminal. Connect a voltmeter to starter B+ terminal. • Is voltage 11 volts or more? → **Yes** GO to **B2**. → **No** CHECK the wire connections between battery and starter solenoid. If no concerns are noticed, CHECK battery charging system.
B2 MANUALLY CRANK STARTER	
1	1 Connect a jumper wire to the B+ starter terminal and momentarily touch the other end to starter solenoid S terminal. • Does the starter motor crank and crank quickly? → **Yes** RESTORE the starter connections. GO to **B3**. → **No** REPLACE the starter motor. TEST the system for normal operation.
B3 CHECK THE STEERING COLUMN/IGNITION LIGHTING CONTROL MODULE FOR START INPUT	
1 New Generation Star (NGS) Tester 2 Read Steering Column/Ignition/Lighting Control Module PID IGN__SCI 3	• Does PID IGN__SCI read START? → **Yes** GO to **B4**. → **No** **Diagnose iginition switch circuits & components.**TEST the starter system.

FM1120100617020X

Fig. 53 Test B: Engine does not crank or relay clicks (Part 2 of 10). Mark VIII

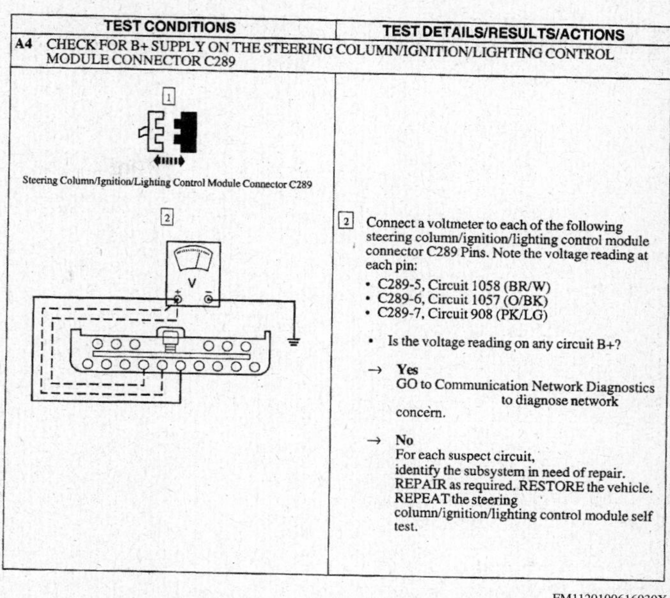

TEST CONDITIONS	TEST DETAILS/RESULTS/ACTIONS
A4 CHECK FOR B+ SUPPLY ON THE STEERING COLUMN/IGNITION/LIGHTING CONTROL MODULE CONNECTOR C289	
1 Steering Column/Ignition/Lighting Control Module Connector C289	
2	2 Connect a voltmeter to each of the following steering column/ignition/lighting control module connector C289 Pins. Note the voltage reading at each pin: • C289-5, Circuit 1058 (BR/W) • C289-6, Circuit 1057 (O/BK) • C289-7, Circuit 908 (PK/LG) • Is the voltage reading on any circuit B+? → **Yes** GO to Communication Network Diagnostics to diagnose network concern. → **No** For each suspect circuit, identify the subsystem in need of repair. REPAIR as required. RESTORE the vehicle. REPEAT the steering column/ignition/lighting control module self test.

FM1120100616030X

Fig. 52 Test A: No communication with steering column/ignition/lighting control module (Part 3 of 3). Mark VIII

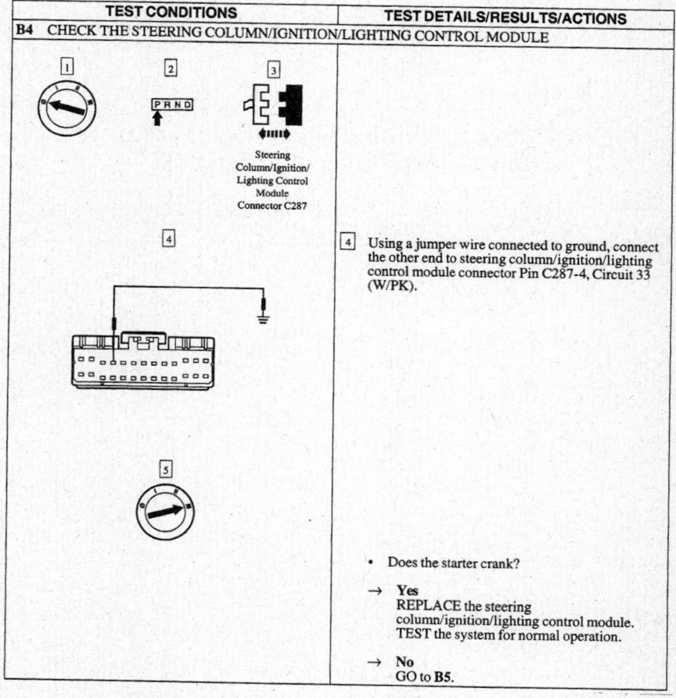

TEST CONDITIONS	TEST DETAILS/RESULTS/ACTIONS
B4 CHECK THE STEERING COLUMN/IGNITION/LIGHTING CONTROL MODULE	
1 2 P R N D 3 Steering Column/Ignition/ Lighting Control Module Connector C287	
4	4 Using a jumper wire connected to ground, connect the other end to steering column/ignition/lighting control module connector Pin C287-4, Circuit 33 (W/PK).
5	• Does the starter crank? → **Yes** REPLACE the steering column/ignition/lighting control module. TEST the system for normal operation. → **No** GO to **B5**.

FM1120100617030X

Fig. 53 Test B: Engine does not crank or relay clicks (Part 3 of 10). Mark VIII

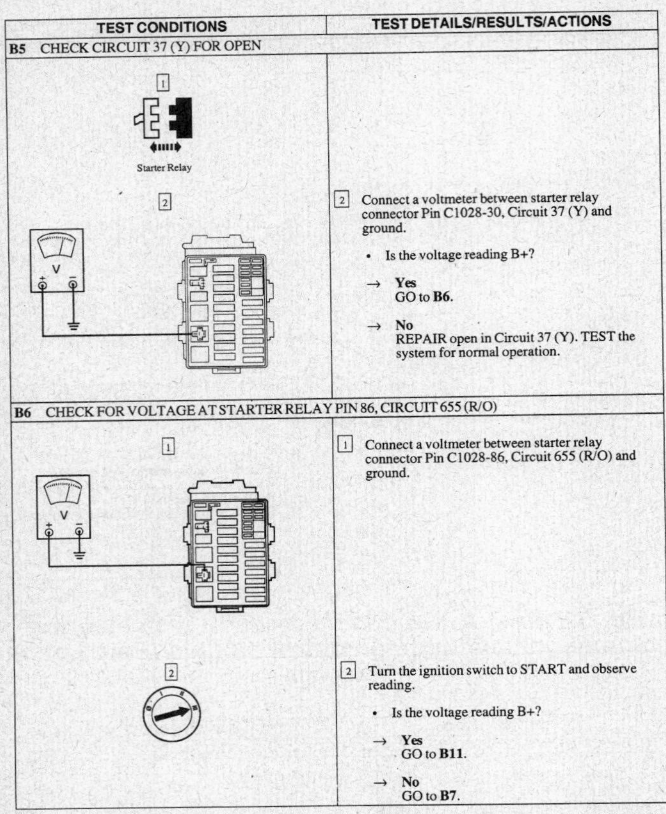

TEST CONDITIONS	TEST DETAILS/RESULTS/ACTIONS
B5 CHECK CIRCUIT 37 (Y) FOR OPEN	
1 Starter Relay 2	2 Connect a voltmeter between starter relay connector Pin C1028-30, Circuit 37 (Y) and ground. • Is the voltage reading B+? → **Yes** GO to **B6**. → **No** REPAIR open in Circuit 37 (Y). TEST the system for normal operation.
B6 CHECK FOR VOLTAGE AT STARTER RELAY PIN 86, CIRCUIT 655 (R/O)	
1	1 Connect a voltmeter between starter relay connector Pin C1028-86, Circuit 655 (R/O) and ground.
2	2 Turn the ignition switch to START and observe reading. • Is the voltage reading B+? → **Yes** GO to **B11**. → **No** GO to **B7**.

FM1120100617040X

Fig. 53 Test B: Engine does not crank or relay clicks (Part 4 of 10). Mark VIII

TEST CONDITIONS	TEST DETAILS/RESULTS/ACTIONS
B8 CHECK FUSE 6 (10A) INPUT (Continued)	
3	• Is the voltage reading B+? → **Yes** REPAIR Circuit 655 (R/O) for open. TEST the system for normal operation. → **No** GO to **B9**.

FM1120100617060X

Fig. 53 Test B: Engine does not crank or relay clicks (Part 6 of 10). Mark VIII

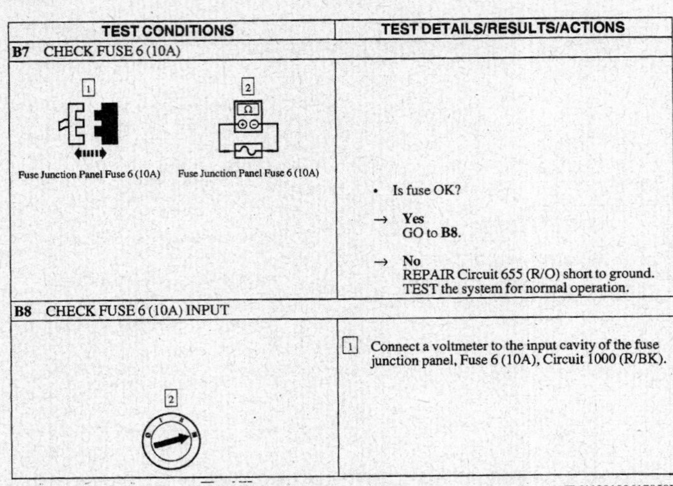

TEST CONDITIONS	TEST DETAILS/RESULTS/ACTIONS
B7 CHECK FUSE 6 (10A)	
1 Fuse Junction Panel Fuse 6 (10A) 2 Fuse Junction Panel Fuse 6 (10A)	• Is fuse OK? → **Yes** GO to **B8**. → **No** REPAIR Circuit 655 (R/O) short to ground. TEST the system for normal operation.
B8 CHECK FUSE 6 (10A) INPUT	
2	1 Connect a voltmeter to the input cavity of the fuse junction panel, Fuse 6 (10A), Circuit 1000 (R/BK).

FM1120100617050X

Fig. 53 Test B: Engine does not crank or relay clicks (Part 5 of 10). Mark VIII

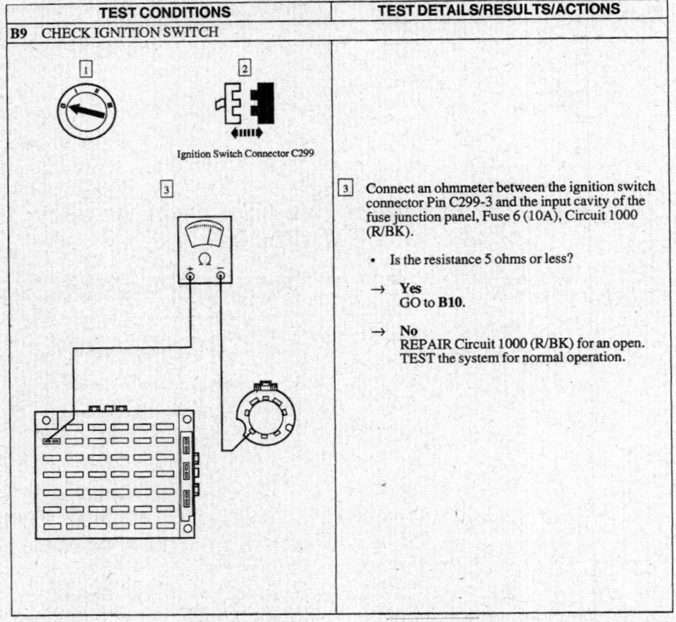

TEST CONDITIONS	TEST DETAILS/RESULTS/ACTIONS
B9 CHECK IGNITION SWITCH	
1 2 Ignition Switch Connector C299 3	3 Connect an ohmmeter between the ignition switch connector Pin C299-3 and the input cavity of the fuse junction panel, Fuse 6 (10A), Circuit 1000 (R/BK). • Is the resistance 5 ohms or less? → **Yes** GO to **B10**. → **No** REPAIR Circuit 1000 (R/BK) for an open. TEST the system for normal operation.

FM1120100617070X

Fig. 53 Test B: Engine does not crank or relay clicks (Part 7 of 10). Mark VIII

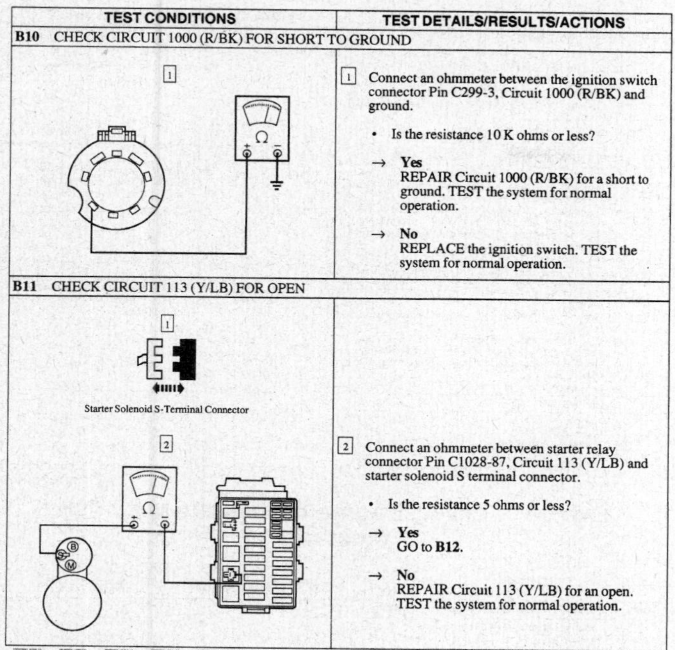

TEST CONDITIONS	TEST DETAILS/RESULTS/ACTIONS
B10 CHECK CIRCUIT 1000 (R/BK) FOR SHORT TO GROUND	
1	1 Connect an ohmmeter between the ignition switch connector Pin C299-3, Circuit 1000 (R/BK) and ground. • Is the resistance 10 K ohms or less? → **Yes** REPAIR Circuit 1000 (R/BK) for a short to ground. TEST the system for normal operation. → **No** REPLACE the ignition switch. TEST the system for normal operation.
B11 CHECK CIRCUIT 113 (Y/LB) FOR OPEN	
1 Starter Solenoid S-Terminal Connector	
2	2 Connect an ohmmeter between starter relay connector Pin C1028-87, Circuit 113 (Y/LB) and starter solenoid S terminal connector. • Is the resistance 5 ohms or less? → **Yes** GO to **B12**. → **No** REPAIR Circuit 113 (Y/LB) for an open. TEST the system for normal operation.

FM1120100617080X

Fig. 53 Test B: Engine does not crank or relay clicks (Part 8 of 10). Mark VIII

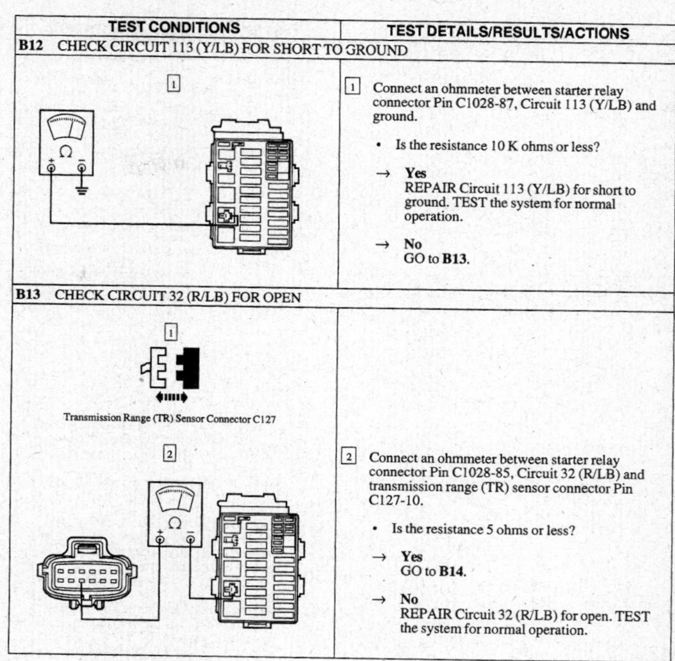

TEST CONDITIONS	TEST DETAILS/RESULTS/ACTIONS
B12 CHECK CIRCUIT 113 (Y/LB) FOR SHORT TO GROUND	
1	1 Connect an ohmmeter between starter relay connector Pin C1028-87, Circuit 113 (Y/LB) and ground. • Is the resistance 10 K ohms or less? → **Yes** REPAIR Circuit 113 (Y/LB) for short to ground. TEST the system for normal operation. → **No** GO to **B13**.
B13 CHECK CIRCUIT 32 (R/LB) FOR OPEN	
1 Transmission Range (TR) Sensor Connector C127	
2	2 Connect an ohmmeter between starter relay connector Pin C1028-85, Circuit 32 (R/LB) and transmission range (TR) sensor connector Pin C127-10. • Is the resistance 5 ohms or less? → **Yes** GO to **B14**. → **No** REPAIR Circuit 32 (R/LB) for open. TEST the system for normal operation.

FM1120100617090X

Fig. 53 Test B: Engine does not crank or relay clicks (Part 9 of 10). Mark VIII

TEST CONDITIONS	TEST DETAILS/RESULTS/ACTIONS
B14 CHECK CIRCUIT 33 (W/PK) FOR OPEN	
1 Steering Column/Ignition/Lighting Control (SCIL) C287	
2	2 Connect an ohmmeter between steering column/ignition/lighting control module connector Pin C287-4 and transmission range (TR) sensor connector Pin C127-12. • Is the resistance 5 ohms or less? → **Yes** REPLACE the transmission range (TR) sensor. TEST the system for normal operation. → **No** REPAIR Circuit 33 (W/PK) for open. TEST the system for normal operation.

FM1120100617100X

Fig. 53 Test B: Engine does not crank or relay clicks (Part 10 of 10). Mark VIII

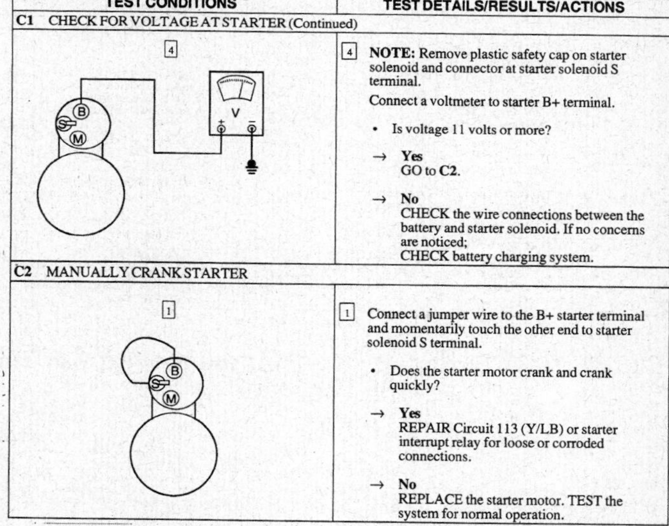

TEST CONDITIONS	TEST DETAILS/RESULTS/ACTIONS
C1 CHECK FOR VOLTAGE AT STARTER (Continued)	
4	4 **NOTE:** Remove plastic safety cap on starter solenoid and connector at starter solenoid S terminal. Connect a voltmeter to starter B+ terminal. • Is voltage 11 volts or more? → **Yes** GO to **C2**. → **No** CHECK the wire connections between the battery and starter solenoid. If no concerns are noticed; CHECK battery charging system.
C2 MANUALLY CRANK STARTER	
1	1 Connect a jumper wire to the B+ starter terminal and momentarily touch the other end to starter solenoid S terminal. • Does the starter motor crank and crank quickly? → **Yes** REPAIR Circuit 113 (Y/LB) or starter interrupt relay for loose or corroded connections. → **No** REPLACE the starter motor. TEST the system for normal operation.

FM1120100618000X

Fig. 54 Test C: Engine cranks slowly. Mark VIII

TEST CONDITIONS	TEST DETAILS/RESULTS/ACTIONS
D1 CHECK STARTER MOUNTING	
	1 Check that starter is properly mounted.
	2 Check that all the connections are secure.

FM1120100619010X

Fig. 55 Test D: Unusual starter noise (Part 1 of 2). Mark VIII

TEST CONDITIONS	TEST DETAILS/RESULTS/ACTIONS
D1 CHECK STARTER MOUNTING (Continued)	
	[3] Check other starter system components for proper mounting and connection, starter relay, battery, digital transmission range (TR) sensor and steering column/ignition/lighting control module. • Are the starting system components and wiring secure and undamaged? → **Yes** GO to **D2**. → **No** REPAIR as required. TEST the system for normal operation.
D2 CRANK ENGINE	
[1] [2]	[3] As engine is starting listen to individual components for noise due to gear tooth damage, shorting, sparking or knocking. • Is the noise due to ring gear tooth damage? → **Yes** REPLACE the ring gear. EXAMINE the starter pinion teeth. If damaged, REPLACE the starter motor or starter drive. TEST the system for normal operation. → **No** If noise sounds like shorting or sparking CHECK the ground feeds to battery or starter motor. If noise sounds like knocking, **Diagnose engine mechanical components.**

FM1120100619020X

Fig. 55 Test D: Unusual starter noise (Part 2 of 2). Mark VIII

	Test Step	Result ▶	Action to Take
B1	CHECK BATTERY VOLTAGE TO STARTER		
	NOTE: Remove plastic safety cap on starter solenoid. • Ignition switch OFF. Transmission in PARK or NEUTRAL. • Check for voltage from starter B+ terminal to starter drive end housing (ground). • **Does voltmeter indicate B+?**	Yes No	▶ GO to **B2**. ▶ SERVICE wire connection between battery and starter solenoid. CHECK ground connection at battery to ground and starter solenoid to ground for an open or short.
B2	MANUALLY CRANK STARTER		
	• Ignition switch OFF. Transmission in PARK or NEUTRAL. • Connect one end of a jumper wire to the starter B+ terminal and momentarily touch the other end to the S-terminal. • **Does starter motor crank?**	Yes No	▶ GO to **B3**. ▶ REPLACE starter motor as described. RETEST new starter motor.
B3	CHECK VOLTAGE TO IGNITION SWITCH		
	• Disconnect ignition switch connector C209, connect positive lead of voltmeter to Circuit 37 (Y) and negative lead to ground. • **Does voltmeter indicate B+?**	Yes No	▶ GO to **B4**. ▶ SERVICE fuse IGN SW (40A) or Circuit 37 (Y). RESTORE vehicle and RETEST system.

FM1120100657010X

Fig. 57 Test B: Engine does not crank (Part 1 of 2). 1998 Mustang

	Test Step	Result ▶	Action to Take
A1	CHECK BATTERY STATE OF CHARGE		
	NOTE: To perform an accurate base circuit voltage reading, remove the surface charge by turning on the headlamps (10 seconds maximum). Read base circuit voltage after battery voltage stabilizes. • Connect voltmeter to battery positive and negative terminals. • Measure open circuit voltage. • **Is voltage 12.4 volts or higher?**	Yes No	▶ GO to **A2**. ▶ SERVICE battery and charging system as required.
A2	CHECK STARTER B+ CIRCUIT RESISTANCE		
	• Connect voltmeter positive lead to battery positive terminal and voltmeter negative lead to the starter solenoid B+ terminal. • Disconnect inertia fuel shutoff switch electrical connector C417 to prevent engine from starting. • Crank engine and record voltmeter reading during engine cranking. • **Is voltage more than 6 volts?**	Yes No	▶ SERVICE connections between battery positive solenoid B+ terminal and connection. ▶ GO to **A3**.
A3	CHECK STARTER GROUND CIRCUIT RESISTANCE		
	• Connect voltmeter positive lead to the starter motor housing. • Connect voltmeter negative lead to battery negative terminal. • Disconnect inertia fuel shutoff switch electrical connector C417 to prevent engine from starting. • Crank engine and record voltmeter reading during engine cranking. • **Is voltage more than 0.3 volt?**	Yes No	▶ SERVICE connections between battery negative terminal and engine block. ▶ GO to **A4**.
A4	CHECK STARTER CURRENT DRAW		
	• Perform Starter Motor Component Test as described. • **Is starter motor OK?**	Yes No	▶ Troubleshoot for engine mechanical concerns. ▶ SERVICE starter motor as required.

FM1120100656000X

Fig. 56 Test A: Engine cranks slowly. 1998 Mustang

	Test Step	Result ▶	Action to Take
B4	CHECK VOLTAGE THROUGH IGNITION SWITCH		
	• Connect ignition switch connector C209, with ignition switch in START position, back-probe Circuit 33 (W/PK) with a voltmeter positive lead and negative lead to ground. • **Does voltmeter indicate B+?**	Yes No	▶ GO to **B5**. ▶ SERVICE ignition switch. RESTORE vehicle. RETEST system.
B5	CHECK VOLTAGE TO TRANSMISSION RANGE SENSOR OR CLUTCH PEDAL POSITION SWITCH		
	• Disconnect transmission range (TR) sensor connector C110 or clutch pedal position (CPP) switch connector C255. • Turn ignition switch to START. • Connect voltmeter positive lead to TR sensor connector Pin C110-4, Circuit 33 (W/PK) or CPP switch connector C255, Circuit 33 (W/PK) and negative lead to ground. • **Does voltmeter indicate B+?**	Yes No	▶ GO to **B6**. ▶ SERVICE Circuit 33 (W/PK) for open or short. RESTORE vehicle. RETEST system.
B6	CHECK VOLTAGE THROUGH TRANSMISSION RANGE SENSOR OR CLUTCH PEDAL POSITION SWITCH		
	• Connect connector C110 or C255. With transmission in PARK or NEUTRAL and ignition switch in START, back-probe Circuit 32 (R/LB) at TR sensor connector Pin C110-1, Circuit 32 (R/LB) or CPP switch connector C255, Circuit 32 (R/LB). • **Does voltmeter indicate B+?**	Yes No	▶ GO to **B7**. ▶ REPLACE TR or CPP switch sensor. RESTORE vehicle and RETEST system.
B7	CHECK IGNITION VOLTAGE TO STARTER		
	• Disconnect Circuit 33 (W/PK) from starter motor. • Connect positive lead of voltmeter to Circuit 33 (W/PK) and negative lead to ground. Place transmission in PARK or NEUTRAL. Press clutch pedal to floor and turn ignition switch to START. • **Does voltmeter indicate B+?**	Yes No	▶ CHECK and SERVICE "S" terminal connection to starter. ▶ SERVICE Circuit 33 (W/PK). RESTORE vehicle and RETEST system.

FM1120100657020X

Fig. 57 Test B: Engine does not crank (Part 2 of 2). 1998 Mustang

	Test Step	Result ▶	Action to Take
C1	CHECK STARTER MOUNTING		
	• Check starter motor mounting to be flush (not cocked). Check that all connections are secure. Refer to Removal and Installation for starter motor mounting information. • Check other necessary components related to the starting system to be securely mounted. Ignition switch, battery and transmission switches. • Check wiring connections for damage or shorting due to corrosion or stray wires. • **Are the starting system components and wiring secure and undamaged?**	Yes No	▶ GO to **C2**. ▶ SERVICE or REPLACE wiring or component mountings as required. RETEST starting system for noises.
C2	CRANK ENGINE		
	• Put ignition switch in START then RUN. As engine is starting, listen to individual components for noise due to gear tooth damage, shorting, sparking or knocking. • Pinpoint noise to component. • **Is noise due to ring gear tooth damage?**	Yes No	▶ REPLACE flywheel ring gear assembly. ▶ If noise sounds like shorting or sparking, CHECK grounded feeds to battery or starter motor. Diagnose engine Mechanical components

FM1120100658000X

Fig. 58 Test C: Unusual starter noise. 1998 Mustang

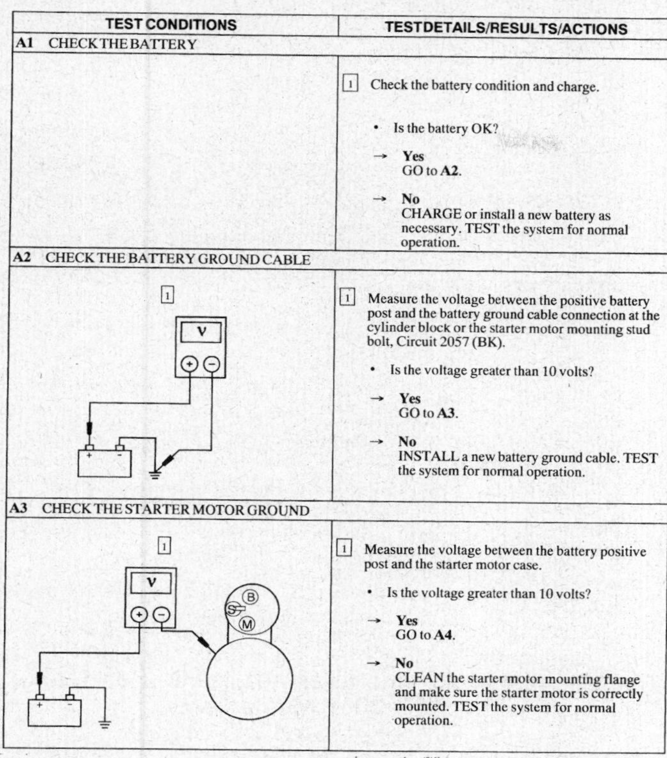

TEST CONDITIONS	TEST DETAILS/RESULTS/ACTIONS
A1 CHECK THE BATTERY	
	1 Check the battery condition and charge. • Is the battery OK? → **Yes** GO to **A2**. → **No** CHARGE or install a new battery as necessary. TEST the system for normal operation.
A2 CHECK THE BATTERY GROUND CABLE	
1	1 Measure the voltage between the positive battery post and the battery ground cable connection at the cylinder block or the starter motor mounting stud bolt, Circuit 2057 (BK). • Is the voltage greater than 10 volts? → **Yes** GO to **A3**. → **No** INSTALL a new battery ground cable. TEST the system for normal operation.
A3 CHECK THE STARTER MOTOR GROUND	
1	1 Measure the voltage between the battery positive post and the starter motor case. • Is the voltage greater than 10 volts? → **Yes** GO to **A4**. → **No** CLEAN the starter motor mounting flange and make sure the starter motor is correctly mounted. TEST the system for normal operation.

FM1120100660010X

Fig. 59 Test A: Engine does not crank (Part 1 of 9). 1999–2002 Mustang

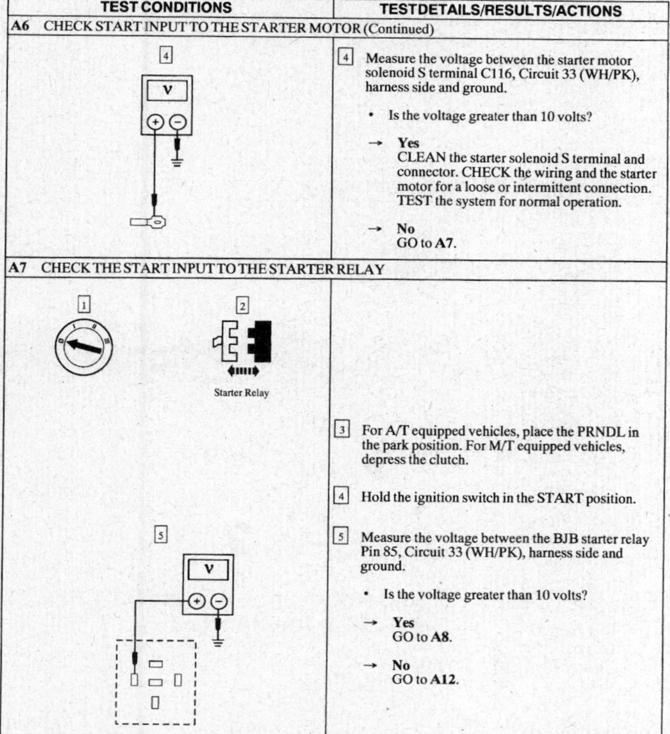

TEST CONDITIONS	TEST DETAILS/RESULTS/ACTIONS
A6 CHECK START INPUT TO THE STARTER MOTOR (Continued)	
4	4 Measure the voltage between the starter motor solenoid S terminal C116, Circuit 33 (WH/PK), harness side and ground. • Is the voltage greater than 10 volts? → **Yes** CLEAN the starter solenoid S terminal and connector. CHECK the wiring and the starter motor for a loose or intermittent connection. TEST the system for normal operation. → **No** GO to **A7**.
A7 CHECK THE START INPUT TO THE STARTER RELAY	
1 2 Starter Relay	3 For A/T equipped vehicles, place the PRNDL in the park position. For M/T equipped vehicles, depress the clutch. 4 Hold the ignition switch in the START position.
5	5 Measure the voltage between the BJB starter relay Pin 85, Circuit 33 (WH/PK), harness side and ground. • Is the voltage greater than 10 volts? → **Yes** GO to **A8**. → **No** GO to **A12**.

FM1120100660030X

Fig. 59 Test A: Engine does not crank (Part 3 of 9). 1999–2002 Mustang

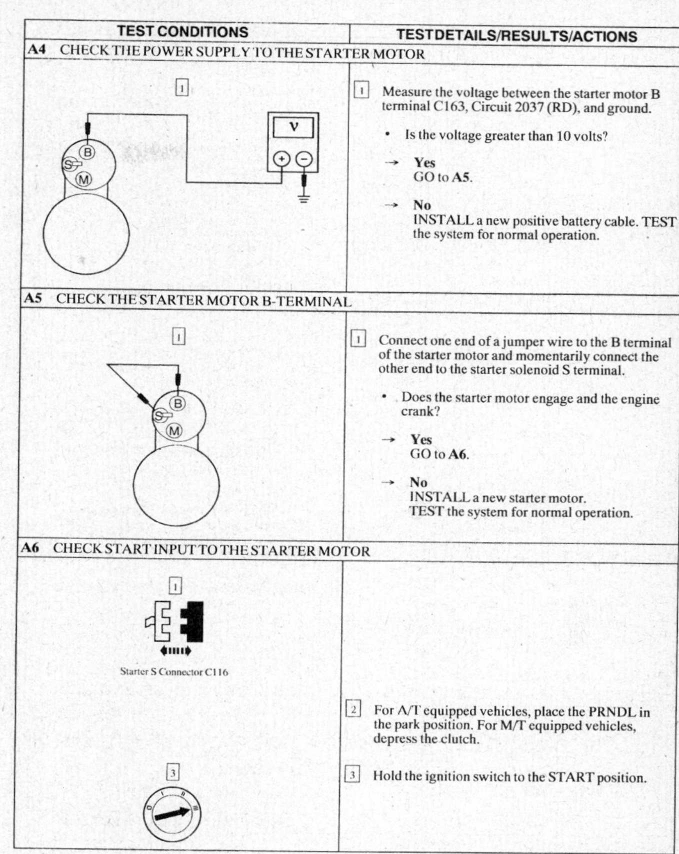

TEST CONDITIONS	TEST DETAILS/RESULTS/ACTIONS
A4 CHECK THE POWER SUPPLY TO THE STARTER MOTOR	
1	1 Measure the voltage between the starter motor B terminal C163, Circuit 2037 (RD), and ground. • Is the voltage greater than 10 volts? → **Yes** GO to **A5**. → **No** INSTALL a new positive battery cable. TEST the system for normal operation.
A5 CHECK THE STARTER MOTOR B-TERMINAL	
1	1 Connect one end of a jumper wire to the B terminal of the starter motor and momentarily connect the other end to the starter solenoid S terminal. • Does the starter motor engage and the engine crank? → **Yes** GO to **A6**. → **No** INSTALL a new starter motor. TEST the system for normal operation.
A6 CHECK START INPUT TO THE STARTER MOTOR	
1 Starter S Connector C116	2 For A/T equipped vehicles, place the PRNDL in the park position. For M/T equipped vehicles, depress the clutch.
3	3 Hold the ignition switch to the START position.

FM1120100660020X

Fig. 59 Test A: Engine does not crank (Part 2 of 9). 1999–2002 Mustang

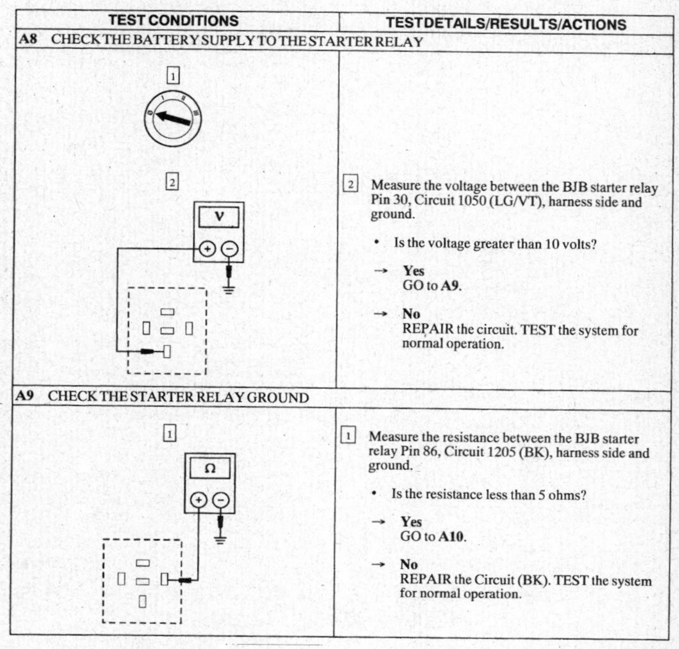

TEST CONDITIONS	TEST DETAILS/RESULTS/ACTIONS
A8 CHECK THE BATTERY SUPPLY TO THE STARTER RELAY	
1	
2	2 Measure the voltage between the BJB starter relay Pin 30, Circuit 1050 (LG/VT), harness side and ground. • Is the voltage greater than 10 volts? → **Yes** GO to **A9**. → **No** REPAIR the circuit. TEST the system for normal operation.
A9 CHECK THE STARTER RELAY GROUND	
1	1 Measure the resistance between the BJB starter relay Pin 86, Circuit 1205 (BK), harness side and ground. • Is the resistance less than 5 ohms? → **Yes** GO to **A10**. → **No** REPAIR the Circuit (BK). TEST the system for normal operation.

FM1120100660040X

Fig. 59 Test A: Engine does not crank (Part 4 of 9). 1999–2002 Mustang

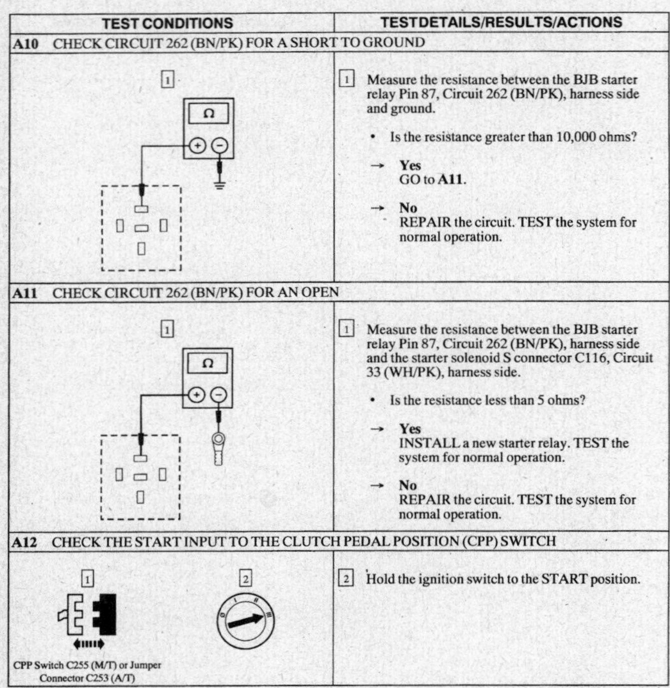

TEST CONDITIONS	TEST DETAILS/RESULTS/ACTIONS
A10 CHECK CIRCUIT 262 (BN/PK) FOR A SHORT TO GROUND	
1	1 Measure the resistance between the BJB starter relay Pin 87, Circuit 262 (BN/PK), harness side and ground. • Is the resistance greater than 10,000 ohms? → **Yes** GO to **A11**. → **No** REPAIR the circuit. TEST the system for normal operation.
A11 CHECK CIRCUIT 262 (BN/PK) FOR AN OPEN	
1	1 Measure the resistance between the BJB starter relay Pin 87, Circuit 262 (BN/PK), harness side and the starter solenoid S connector C116, Circuit 33 (WH/PK), harness side. • Is the resistance less than 5 ohms? → **Yes** INSTALL a new starter relay. TEST the system for normal operation. → **No** REPAIR the circuit. TEST the system for normal operation.
A12 CHECK THE START INPUT TO THE CLUTCH PEDAL POSITION (CPP) SWITCH	
1 2 CPP Switch C255 (M/T) or Jumper Connector C253 (A/T)	2 Hold the ignition switch to the START position.

FM1120100660050X

Fig. 59 Test A: Engine does not crank (Part 5 of 9). 1999–2002 Mustang

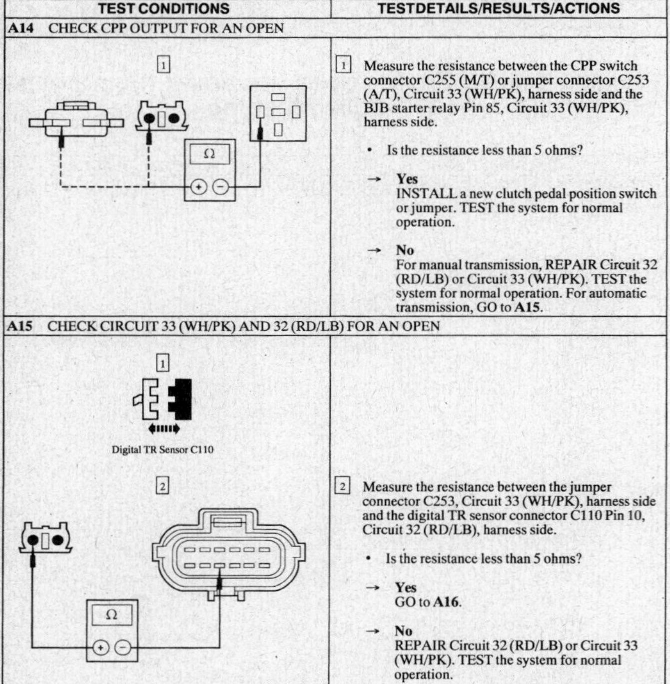

TEST CONDITIONS	TEST DETAILS/RESULTS/ACTIONS
A14 CHECK CPP OUTPUT FOR AN OPEN	
1	1 Measure the resistance between the CPP switch connector C255 (M/T) or jumper connector C253 (A/T), Circuit 33 (WH/PK), harness side and the BJB starter relay Pin 85, Circuit 33 (WH/PK), harness side. • Is the resistance less than 5 ohms? → **Yes** INSTALL a new clutch pedal position switch or jumper. TEST the system for normal operation. → **No** For manual transmission, REPAIR Circuit 32 (RD/LB) or Circuit 33 (WH/PK). TEST the system for normal operation. For automatic transmission, GO to **A15**.
A15 CHECK CIRCUIT 33 (WH/PK) AND 32 (RD/LB) FOR AN OPEN	
1 Digital TR Sensor C110	
2	2 Measure the resistance between the jumper connector C253, Circuit 33 (WH/PK), harness side and the digital TR sensor connector C110 Pin 10, Circuit 32 (RD/LB), harness side. • Is the resistance less than 5 ohms? → **Yes** GO to **A16**. → **No** REPAIR Circuit 32 (RD/LB) or Circuit 33 (WH/PK). TEST the system for normal operation.

FM1120100660070X

Fig. 59 Test A: Engine does not crank (Part 7 of 9). 1999–2002 Mustang

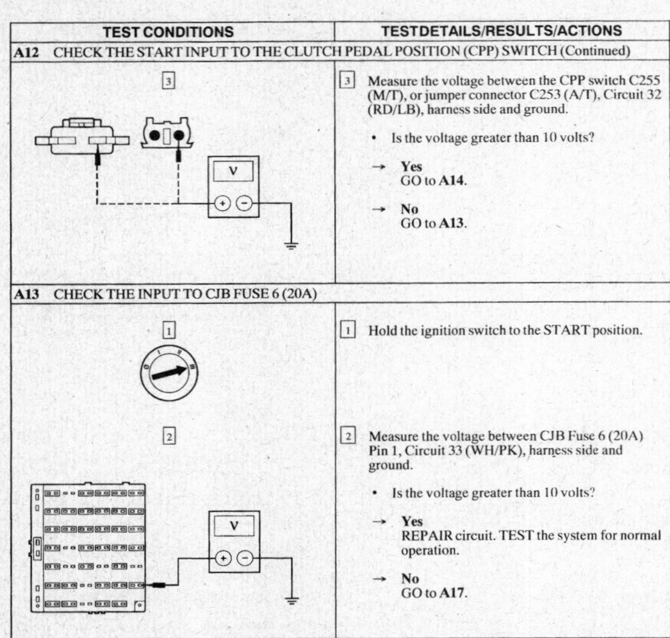

TEST CONDITIONS	TEST DETAILS/RESULTS/ACTIONS
A12 CHECK THE START INPUT TO THE CLUTCH PEDAL POSITION (CPP) SWITCH (Continued)	
3	3 Measure the voltage between the CPP switch C255 (M/T), or jumper connector C253 (A/T), Circuit 32 (RD/LB), harness side and ground. • Is the voltage greater than 10 volts? → **Yes** GO to **A14**. → **No** GO to **A13**.
A13 CHECK THE INPUT TO CJB FUSE 6 (20A)	
1	1 Hold the ignition switch to the START position.
2	2 Measure the voltage between CJB Fuse 6 (20A) Pin 1, Circuit 33 (WH/PK), harness side and ground. • Is the voltage greater than 10 volts? → **Yes** REPAIR circuit. TEST the system for normal operation. → **No** GO to **A17**.

FM1120100660060X

Fig. 59 Test A: Engine does not crank (Part 6 of 9). 1999–2002 Mustang

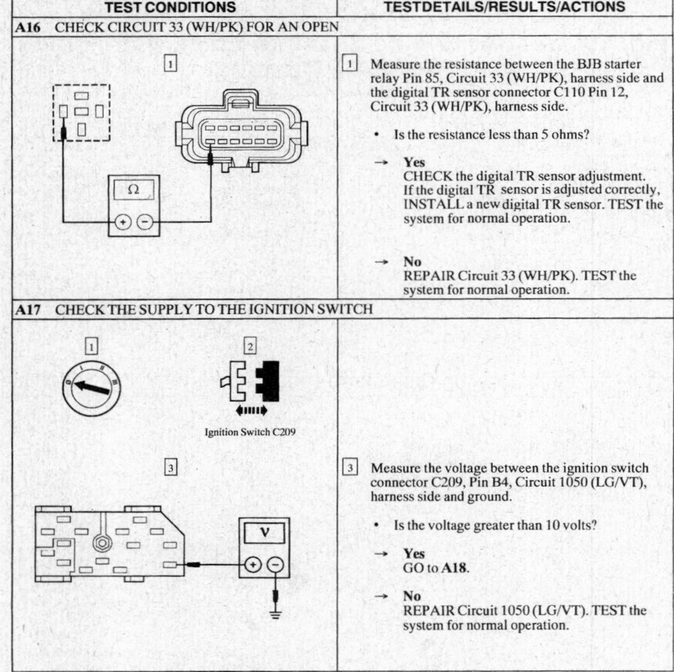

TEST CONDITIONS	TEST DETAILS/RESULTS/ACTIONS
A16 CHECK CIRCUIT 33 (WH/PK) FOR AN OPEN	
1	1 Measure the resistance between the BJB starter relay Pin 85, Circuit 33 (WH/PK), harness side and the digital TR sensor connector C110 Pin 12, Circuit 33 (WH/PK), harness side. • Is the resistance less than 5 ohms? → **Yes** CHECK the digital TR sensor adjustment. If the digital TR sensor is adjusted correctly, INSTALL a new digital TR sensor. TEST the system for normal operation. → **No** REPAIR Circuit 33 (WH/PK). TEST the system for normal operation.
A17 CHECK THE SUPPLY TO THE IGNITION SWITCH	
1 2 Ignition Switch C209	
3	3 Measure the voltage between the ignition switch connector C209, Pin B4, Circuit 1050 (LG/VT), harness side and ground. • Is the voltage greater than 10 volts? → **Yes** GO to **A18**. → **No** REPAIR Circuit 1050 (LG/VT). TEST the system for normal operation.

FM1120100660080X

Fig. 59 Test A: Engine does not crank (Part 8 of 9). 1999–2002 Mustang

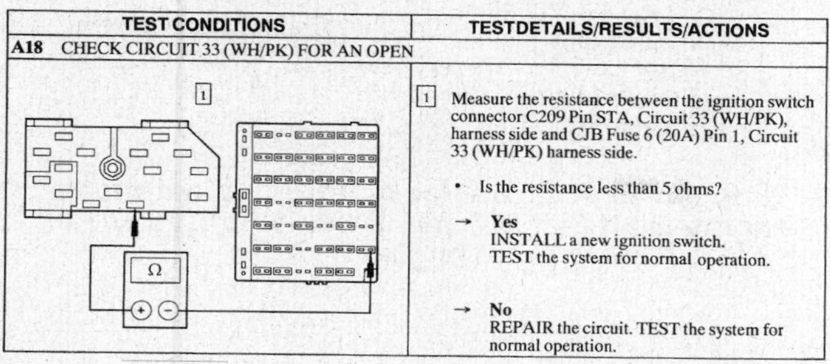

TEST CONDITIONS	TEST DETAILS/RESULTS/ACTIONS
A18 CHECK CIRCUIT 33 (WH/PK) FOR AN OPEN	
1	1 Measure the resistance between the ignition switch connector C209 Pin STA, Circuit 33 (WH/PK), harness side and CJB Fuse 6 (20A) Pin 1, Circuit 33 (WH/PK) harness side. • Is the resistance less than 5 ohms? → **Yes** INSTALL a new ignition switch. TEST the system for normal operation. → **No** REPAIR the circuit. TEST the system for normal operation.

FM1120100660090X

Fig. 59 Test A: Engine does not crank (Part 9 of 9). 1999–2002 Mustang

TEST CONDITIONS	TEST DETAILS/RESULTS/ACTIONS
B2 CHECK FOR ENGINE NOISE	
1	
2	2 Connect a remote starter switch between the starter solenoid B and S terminals.
	3 Engage the starter motor and verify the noise is due to the starter operation. • Is the noise due to the starter motor engagement? → **Yes** GO to **B3**. → **No** continue the diagnosis.
B3 CHECK FOR UNUSUAL WEAR	
	1 Remove the starter motor.

FM1120100661020X

Fig. 60 Test B: Unusual starter noise (Part 2 of 3). 1999–2002 Mustang

Test Step		Result	►	Action to Take
A1	CHECK BATTERY STATE OF CHARGE			
	NOTE: To perform an accurate base voltage reading, remove the surface charge by turning on the headlamps (10 seconds maximum). Read base voltage after battery voltage stabilizes. • Connect voltmeter to battery positive and negative terminals. • Measure open circuit voltage. • **Is voltage 12.4 volts or higher?**	Yes No	► ►	GO to **A2.** SERVICE battery and charging system as required.
A2	CHECK STARTER B+ CURRENT RESISTANCE			
	• Connect voltmeter positive lead to battery positive terminal and voltmeter negative lead to the battery starter solenoid B+ terminal. • Disconnect inertia fuel shutoff switch electrical connector to prevent engine from starting. • Crank engine and record voltmeter reading during engine cranking. • **Is voltage more than 0.6 volts ?**	Yes No	► ►	GO to **A3.** SERVICE connections between battery positive terminal and starter solenoid B+ connection.

FM1120100663010X

Fig. 61 Test A: Starter motor cranks engine slowly or no cranking with relay/solenoid clicking or chattering (Part 1 of 2). 1998 Sable & Taurus

TEST CONDITIONS	TEST DETAILS/RESULTS/ACTIONS
B1 CHECK STARTER MOUNTING	
	1 Inspect the starter mounting bolts and brackets for looseness. • Is the starter motor mounted correctly? → **Yes** GO to **B2**. → **No** INSTALL the starter motor correctly. TEST the system for normal operation.

FM1120100661010X

Fig. 60 Test B: Unusual starter noise (Part 1 of 3). 1999–2002 Mustang

TEST CONDITIONS	TEST DETAILS/RESULTS/ACTIONS
B3 CHECK FOR UNUSUAL WEAR (Continued)	
	2 Inspect the ring gear. • Is the noise due to ring gear tooth damage? → **Yes** INSTALL a new ring gear. EXAMINE the starter pinion teeth. If damaged, INSTALL a new starter motor. normal operation. → **No** INSTALL a new starter motor. TEST the system for normal operation.

FM1120100661030X

Fig. 60 Test B: Unusual starter noise (Part 3 of 3). 1999–2002 Mustang

Test Step		Result	►	Action to Take
A3	CHECK STARTER GROUND CIRCUIT RESISTANCE			
	• Connect voltmeter positive lead to the starter motor housing. • Connect voltmeter negative lead to battery negative terminal. • Disconnect inertia fuel shutoff switch electrical connector to prevent engine from starting. • Crank engine and record voltmeter reading during engine cranking. • **Is voltage more than 0.3 volts?**	Yes No	► ►	SERVICE connections between battery negative terminal and engine block and starter motor-to-transaxle housing connection. GO to **A4.**
A4	CHECK STARTER CURRENT DRAW			
	• Perform starter testing as described. • **Is starter motor OK?**	Yes No	► ►	Diagnose engine Mechanical Components SERVICE starter motor as required.

FM1120100663020X

Fig. 61 Test A: Starter motor cranks engine slowly or no cranking with relay/solenoid clicking or chattering (Part 2 of 2). 1998 Sable & Taurus

Test Step		Result	Action to Take
B1	CHECK BATTERY VOLTAGE TO STARTER		
	NOTE: Remove plastic safety cap on starter solenoid. • Ignition switch OFF. Transaxle in PARK or NEUTRAL. • Check for voltage from starter B+ terminal to starter drive end housing (ground). • **Does voltmeter indicate B+?**	Yes No	GO to **B2**. SERVICE wire connection between battery and starter solenoid. CHECK ground connection at battery to ground and starter solenoid to ground for open or short.
B2	CHECK VOLTAGE TO IGNITION SWITCH		
	• Disconnect connector C299, connect positive lead of voltmeter to Circuit 37 (Y) and negative lead to ground. • **Does voltmeter indicate B+?**	Yes No	GO to **B3**. SERVICE Fuse 5 (40A) or Circuit 37 (Y). RESTORE vehicle. RETEST system.
B3	CHECK VOLTAGE THROUGH IGNITION SWITCH		
	• Connect connector C299. With ignition switch in START, back-probe Circuit 32 (R/LB) with a voltmeter positive lead and negative lead to ground. • **Does voltmeter indicate B+?**	Yes No	GO to **B4**. SERVICE ignition switch. RESTORE vehicle. RETEST system.
B4	CHECK VOLTAGE TO TRANSMISSION RANGE SENSOR		
	• Disconnect transmission range sensor connector C171. • With ignition switch in START. • Connect voltmeter positive lead to Pin C171-8, Circuit 32 (R/LB) and negative lead to ground. • **Does voltmeter indicate B+?**	Yes No	GO to **B5**. SERVICE Circuit 32 (R/LB) for open or short. RESTORE vehicle. RETEST system.
B5	CHECK VOLTAGE THROUGH TRANSMISSION RANGE SENSOR		
	• Connect connector C171. With transaxle in PARK or NEUTRAL and ignition switch in START, back-probe Pin C171-5, Circuit 33 (W/PK) at transmission range sensor connector. • **Does voltmeter indicate B+?**	Yes No	GO to **B6**. REPLACE transmission range (TR) sensor. RESTORE vehicle. RETEST system.
B6	CHECK IGNITION VOLTAGE TO STARTER		
	• Disconnect C148, Circuit 33 (W/PK) from starter motor. • Connect positive lead of voltmeter to Circuit 33 (W/PK) and negative lead to ground. Place transaxle in PARK and ignition switch in START. • **Does voltmeter indicate B+?**	Yes No	GO to **B7**. SERVICE Circuit 33 (W/PK). RESTORE vehicle. RETEST system.

FM1120100664010X

Fig. 62 Test B: Starter motor does not crank engine (Part 1 of 2). 1998 Sable & Taurus w/3.0L engine

Test Step		Result	Action to Take
C1	CHECK BATTERY VOLTAGE TO STARTER		
	NOTE: Remove plastic safety cap on starter solenoid. • Ignition switch OFF, transaxle in PARK or NEUTRAL. • Check for voltage from starter B+ terminal to starter drive end housing (ground). • **Does voltmeter indicate B+?**	Yes No	GO to **C2**. SERVICE wire connection between battery and starter solenoid. CHECK ground connection at battery to ground and starter solenoid to ground for open or short.
C2	CHECK VOLTAGE TO IGNITION SWITCH		
	• Disconnect connector C299, connect positive lead of voltmeter to Circuit 37 (Y) and negative lead to ground. • **Does voltmeter indicate B+?**	Yes No	GO to **C3**. SERVICE Fuse 5 (40A) or Circuit 37 (Y). RESTORE vehicle. RETEST system.
C3	CHECK VOLTAGE THROUGH IGNITION SWITCH		
	• Connect connector C299. With ignition switch in START, back-probe Circuit 32 (R/LB) with a voltmeter positive lead and negative lead to ground. • **Does voltmeter indicate B+?**	Yes No	GO to **C4**. SERVICE ignition switch. RESTORE vehicle. RETEST system.
C4	CHECK VOLTAGE THROUGH FUSE PANEL		
	• Disconnect connector C235. • With ignition switch in START position, connect voltmeter positive lead to Pin C235-34, Circuit 32 (R/LB) and negative lead to ground. • **Does voltmeter indicate B+?**	Yes No	GO to **C5**. SERVICE Circuit 32 (R/LB) for open or short. RESTORE vehicle. RETEST system.
C5	CHECK VOLTAGE TO TRANSMISSION RANGE SENSOR		
	• Reconnect connector C235. • Disconnect transmission range sensor Connector C107. • Place ignition switch in START. • Connect voltmeter positive lead to Pin C107-10, Circuit 262 (BR/PK) and negative lead to ground. • **Does voltmeter indicate B+?**	Yes No	GO to **C6**. SERVICE Circuit 262 (BR/PK) for open or short, or CHECK Fuse 20 (10A) in fuse panel. RESTORE vehicle. RETEST system.
C6	CHECK VOLTAGE THROUGH TRANSMISSION RANGE SENSOR		
	• Connect connector C107. With transaxle in PARK or NEUTRAL and ignition switch in START, back-probe Pin C107-12, Circuit 1093 (T/R) at transmission range sensor connector. • **Does voltmeter indicate B+?**	Yes No	GO to **C7**. REPLACE transmission range sensor. RESTORE vehicle. RETEST system.
C7	CHECK VOLTAGE SUPPLY TO STARTER RELAY		
	• Disconnect connector C121. • Remove starter relay. • Connect positive lead of voltmeter to Pin C121-86 and negative lead to ground. Place transaxle in PARK and ignition switch in START. • **Does voltmeter indicate B+?**	Yes No	GO to **C8**. SERVICE Circuit 1093 (T/R). RESTORE vehicle. RETEST system.

FM1120100665010X

Fig. 63 Test C: Starter motor does not crank engine (Part 1 of 2). 1998 Sable & Taurus w/3.0L & 3.4L engines

Test Step		Result	Action to Take
B7	MANUALLY CRANK STARTER		
	• Ignition switch OFF, transaxle in PARK or NEUTRAL. • Connect one end of a jumper wire to the starter B+ terminal and momentarily touch the other end to the S-terminal. • **Does starter motor crank?**	Yes No	System operating properly. REPLACE starter motor as described. RETEST new starter motor.

FM1120100664020X

Fig. 62 Test B: Starter motor does not crank engine (Part 2 of 2). 1998 Sable & Taurus w/3.0L engine

Test Step		Result	Action to Take
C8	CHECK VOLTAGE SUPPLY TO STARTER RELAY		
	• Reconnect connector C121. • Remove starter relay. • Connect positive lead of voltmeter to Pin C121-30 and negative lead to ground. Place transaxle in PARK or NEUTRAL and ignition switch in START. • **Does voltmeter indicate B+?**	Yes No	GO to **C9**. SERVICE Circuit 1050 (LG/P) or SERVICE MAXI ignition Fuse (40A). RESTORE vehicle. RETEST system.
C9	CHECK IGNITION VOLTAGE TO STARTER		
	• Disconnect Circuit 33 (W/PK) from starter motor. • Connect a fused jumper wire from C121-30 to C121-87. • Connect positive lead of voltmeter to Circuit 33 (W/PK) and negative lead to ground. • **Does voltmeter indicate B+?**	Yes No	GO to **C10**. SERVICE Circuit 33 (W/PK). RESTORE vehicle. RETEST system.
C10	MANUALLY CRANK STARTER		
	• Ignition switch OFF. Transaxle in PARK or NEUTRAL. • Connect one end of a jumper wire to the starter B+ terminal and momentarily touch the other end to the S-terminal. • **Does starter motor crank?**	Yes No	System operating properly. REPLACE starter motor as described. RETEST new starter motor.

FM1120100665020X

Fig. 63 Test C: Starter motor does not crank engine (Part 2 of 2). 1998 Sable & Taurus w/3.0L & 3.4L engines

Test Step		Result	Action to Take
D1	CHECK STARTER MOUNTING		
	• Check that starter motor mounting is flush (not cocked). Check that all connections are secure. Refer to Removal and Installation for mounting information. • Check other necessary components related to the starting system to be securely mounted: ignition switch, distributor, battery and transaxle switches. • Check wiring connections for damage or shorting due to corrosion or stray wires. • **Are the starting system components and wiring secure and undamaged?**	Yes No	GO to **D2**. SERVICE or REPLACE wiring or component mountings as required. RETEST starting system for noises.
D2	CRANK ENGINE		
	• Turn ignition switch in START then RUN position. As engine is starting, listen to individual components for noise due to gear tooth damage, shorting, sparking or knocking. • Pinpoint noise to component. • **Is noise due to ring gear tooth damage?**	Yes No	REPLACE ring gear. EXAMINE starter drive pinion. If damaged, REPLACE starter motor or starter drive. If noise sounds like shorting or sparking, CHECK grounded feeds to battery or starter motor. If noise sounds like knocking, Diagnose engine mechanical components

FM1120100666000X

Fig. 64 Test D: Unusual starter noise during starter overrun. 1998 Sable & Taurus

Test Step		Result	Action to Take
A1	CHECK BATTERY STATE OF CHARGE		
	NOTE: To perform an accurate base voltage reading, remove the surface charge by turning on the headlamps (10 seconds maximum). Read base voltage after battery voltage stabilizes. • Connect voltmeter to battery positive and negative terminals. • Measure open circuit voltage. • **Is voltage 12.4 volts or higher?**	Yes No	GO to **A2**. SERVICE battery and charging system as required.
A2	CHECK STARTER B+ CURRENT RESISTANCE		
	• Connect voltmeter positive lead to battery positive terminal and voltmeter negative lead to the battery starter solenoid B+ terminal. • Disconnect inertia fuel shutoff switch electrical connector to prevent engine from starting. • Crank engine and record voltmeter reading during engine cranking. • **Is voltage more than 0.6 volts ?**	Yes No	GO to **A3**. SERVICE connections between battery positive terminal and starter solenoid B+ connection.

FM1120100668010X

Fig. 65 Test A: Starter motor cranks engine slowly or no cranking with relay/solenoid clicking or chattering (Part 1 of 2). 1999 Sable & Taurus

Test Step		Result	Action to Take
A3	CHECK STARTER GROUND CIRCUIT RESISTANCE		
	• Connect voltmeter positive lead to the starter motor housing. • Connect voltmeter negative lead to battery negative terminal. • Disconnect inertia fuel shutoff switch electrical connector to prevent engine from starting. • Crank engine and record voltmeter reading during engine cranking. • **Is voltage more than 0.3 volts?**	Yes No	SERVICE connections between battery negative terminal and engine block and starter motor-to-transaxle housing connection. GO to **A4**.
A4	CHECK STARTER CURRENT DRAW		
	• Perform starter testing as described. • **Is starter motor OK?**	Yes No	Diagnose engine mechanical components SERVICE starter motor as required.

FM1120100668020X

Fig. 65 Test A: Starter motor cranks engine slowly or no cranking with relay/solenoid clicking or chattering (Part 2 of 2). 1999 Sable & Taurus

Test Step		Result	Action to Take
B7	CHECK THE START INPUT TO THE STARTER RELAY		
	• Disconnect starter relay C148. • Make sure the vehicle is in PARK or NEUTRAL. • Measure the voltage between starter relay C121-86, Circuit 1093 (TN/RD), and ground. • Turn ignition switch to START. • **Is the voltage greater than 10 volts?**	Yes No	GO to **B8**. GO to **B11**.
B8	CHECK THE BATTERY SUPPLY TO THE STARTER RELAY		
	• Measure the voltage between starter relay C121-30, Circuit 1050 (LG/VT), harness side and ground. • **Is the voltage greater than 10 volts?**	Yes No	GO to **B9**. REPAIR Circuit 1050 (LG/VT) or Fuse 3 (40A). TEST the system for normal operation.
B9	CHECK THE STARTER RELAY GROUND		
	• Measure the resistance between starter relay C121-85, Circuit 57 (BK), harness side and ground. • **Is resistance less than 5 ohms?**	Yes No	GO to **B10**. REPAIR Circuit 57 (BK). TEST the system for normal operation.
B10	CHECK CIRCUIT 33 (WH/PK) FOR AN OPEN		
	• Measure the resistance between starter relay C121-87, Circuit 33 (WH/PK), harness side and starter motor C148, Circuit 33 (WH/PK), harness side. • **Is the resistance less than 5 ohms?**	Yes No	INSTALL a new starter relay. TEST the system for normal operation. REPAIR Circuit 33 (WH/PK). TEST the system for normal operation.
B11	CHECK THE VOLTAGE TO THE IGNITION SWITCH		
	• Disconnect ignition switch C299. • Measure the voltage between ignition switch C299-B4, Circuit 1050 (LG/VT), harness side and ground. • **Is the voltage greater than 10 volts?**	Yes No	GO to **B12**. REPAIR Circuit 1050 (LG/VT) or Fuse 3 (40A). TEST the system for normal operation.
B12	CHECK THE IGNITION SWITCH OUTPUT		
	• Reconnect ignition switch C299. • Remove fuse junction panel Fuse 7 (10A). • Measure the voltage between fuse junction panel Fuse 7 (10A) input cavity, Circuit 32 (RD/LB) and ground. • Hold the ignition switch to START. • **Is the voltage greater than 10 volts?**	Yes No	GO to **B14**. GO to **B13**.
B13	CHECK THE IGNITION SWITCH		
	• Carry out the ignition switch component test. Refer to the Wiring Diagram manual. • **Did the ignition switch pass?**	Yes No	REPAIR Circuit 32 (RD/LB) for an open or short. TEST the system for normal operation. INSTALL a new ignition switch. TEST the system for normal operation.
B14	CHECK THE VOLTAGE TO THE TRANSMISSION RANGE (TR) SENSOR		
	• Install Fuse 7 (10A) • Disconnect TR sensor C171. • Measure the voltage between TR sensor C171-10, Circuit 262 (BN/PK), harness side and ground. • Turn the ignition switch to START. • **Is the voltage greater than 10 volts?**	Yes No	GO to **B15**. REPAIR Circuit 262 (BN/PK) for an open or short. TEST the system for normal operation.

FM1120100669020X

Fig. 66 Test B: Starter motor does not crank engine (Part 2 of 3). 1999 Sable & Taurus w/3.0 (2V) engine

Test Step		Result	Action to Take
B1	CHECK THE BATTERY		
	• Check the battery condition and charge. Refer to Section 14-00. • **Is the battery OK?**	Yes No	GO to **B2**. CHARGE or INSTALL a new battery as necessary. TEST the system for normal operation.
B2	CHECK THE BATTERY GROUND CABLE		
	• Measure the voltage between the positive post of the battery and the battery ground cable connection on the engine. • **Is the voltage greater than 10 volts?**	Yes No	GO to **B3**. INSTALL a new battery ground cable. TEST the system for normal operation.
B3	CHECK THE STARTER MOTOR GROUND		
	• Measure the voltage between the battery positive post and the starter motor case. • **Is the voltage greater than 10 volts?**	Yes No	GO to **B4**. CLEAN the starter motor mounting flange and make sure the starter motor is properly mounted. TEST the system for normal operation.
B4	CHECK BATTERY VOLTAGE TO STARTER		
	NOTE: Remove the plastic safety cap on the starter solenoid. • Turn the ignition switch to OFF and make sure the transaxle is in PARK or NEUTRAL. • Measure the voltage between the starter motor B terminal and ground. • **Is the voltage greater than 10 volts?**	Yes No	GO to **B5**. INSTALL a new positive battery cable. TEST the system for normal operation.
B5	CHECK THE STARTER MOTOR B- TERMINAL		
	• Connect one end of a jumper wire to the starter motor B- terminal, momentarily connect the other end to the starter motor S-terminal. • **Did the starter motor engage and the engine crank?**	Yes No	GO to **B6**. INSTALL a new starter motor. TEST the system for normal operation.
B6	CHECK THE START INPUT TO THE STARTER MOTOR		
	• Disconnect starter motor C148. • Measure the voltage between starter motor C148, Circuit 33 (WH/PK), harness side and ground. • Turn the ignition switch to START. • **Is the voltage greater than 10 volts?**	Yes No	CLEAN the starter motor S-terminal and connector. CHECK the wiring and the starter motor for a loose or intermittent connection. TEST the system for normal operation. GO to **B7**.

FM1120100669010X

Fig. 66 Test B: Starter motor does not crank engine (Part 1 of 3). 1999 Sable & Taurus

Test Step		Result	Action to Take
B15	CHECK CIRCUIT 1093 (TN/RD) FOR AN OPEN		
	• Measure the resistance between starter relay C121-86, Circuit 1093 (TN/RD), harness side and TR sensor C171-12, Circuit 1093 (TN/RD), harness side. • **Is the resistance less than 5 ohms?**	Yes No	CHECK the TR sensor adjustment. IF the TR sensor is adjusted properly, INSTALL a new TR sensor. TEST the system for normal operation. REPAIR Circuit 1093 (TN/RD). TEST the system for normal operation.

FM1120100669030X

Fig. 66 Test B: Starter motor does not crank engine (Part 3 of 3). 1999 Sable & Taurus w/3.0L (2V) engine

Test Step		Result	Action to Take
C1	CHECK FOR PATS DTCS		
	• Check the PATS module for DTCs. • **Are any PATS DTCs retrieved?**	Yes No	Repair the PATS system before proceeding with this test. GO to **C2**.
C2	CHECK THE BATTERY		
	• Check the battery condition and charge. • **Is the battery OK?**	Yes No	GO to **C3**. CHARGE or INSTALL a new battery as necessary. TEST the system for normal operation.
C3	CHECK THE BATTERY GROUND CABLE		
	• Measure the voltage between the positive post of the battery and the battery ground cable connection on the engine. • **Is the voltage greater than 10 volts?**	Yes No	GO to **C4**. INSTALL a new battery ground cable. TEST the system for normal operation.
C4	CHECK THE STARTER MOTOR GROUND		
	• Measure the voltage between the battery positive post and the starter motor case. • **Is the voltage greater than 10 volts?**	Yes No	GO to **C5**. CLEAN the starter motor mounting flange and make sure the starter motor is properly mounted. TEST the system for normal operation.
C5	CHECK THE BATTERY VOLTAGE TO STARTER		
	NOTE: Remove the plastic safety cap on the starter solenoid. • Turn the ignition switch to OFF and make sure the transaxle is in PARK or NEUTRAL. • Measure the voltage between the starter motor B terminal and ground. • **Is the voltage greater than 10 volts?**	Yes No	GO to **C6**. INSTALL a new positive battery cable. TEST the system for normal operation.
C6	CHECK THE STARTER MOTOR B-TERMINAL		
	• Connect one end of a jumper wire to the starter motor B- terminal, momentarily connect the other end to the starter motor S-terminal. • **Did the starter motor engage and the engine crank?**	Yes No	GO to **C7**. INSTALL a new starter motor. TEST the system for normal operation.
C7	CHECK THE START INPUT TO THE STARTER MOTOR		
	• Disconnect starter motor C148. • Measure the voltage between starter motor C148, Circuit 33 (WH/PK), harness side and ground. • Turn the ignition switch to START. • **Is the voltage greater than 10 volts?**	Yes No	CLEAN the starter motor S-terminal and connector. CHECK the wiring and the starter motor for a loose or intermittent connection. TEST the system for normal operation. GO to **C8**.

FM1120100670010X

Fig. 67 Test C: Starter motor does not start engine (Part 1 of 3). 1999 Sable & Taurus w/3.0L (4V) & 3.4L (4V) engines

Test Step	Result ▶	Action to Take
C8 CHECK THE START INPUT TO THE STARTER RELAY		
• Disconnect starter relay C121. • Make sure the vehicle is in PARK or NEUTRAL. • Measure the voltage between starter relay C121-86, Circuit 1093 (TN/RD), and ground. • Turn the ignition switch to START. • **Is the voltage greater than 10 volts?**	Yes ▶ No ▶	GO to **C9**. GO to **C13**.
C9 CHECK THE BATTERY SUPPLY TO THE STARTER RELAY		
• Measure the voltage between starter relay C121-30, Circuit 1050 (LG/VT), harness side and ground. • **Is the voltage greater than 10 volts?**	Yes ▶ No ▶	GO to **C10**. REPAIR Circuit 1050 (LG/VT) or Fuse 3 (40A). TEST the system for normal operation.
C10 CHECK THE STARTER RELAY GROUND SIGNAL		
• Measure the resistance between starter relay C121-85, Circuit 329 (PK), harness side and ground. • Turn the ignition switch to START. • **Is the resistance less than 5 ohms?**	Yes ▶ No ▶	GO to **C12**. GO to **C11**.
C11 CHECK CIRCUIT 329 (PK) FOR AN OPEN		
• Disconnect the PATS module C242. • Measure the resistance between PATS module C242-1, Circuit 329 (PK), harness side and starter relay C121-85, Circuit 329 (PK), harness side. • **Is the resistance less than 5 ohms?**	Yes ▶ No ▶	INSTALL a new PATS module. TEST the system for normal operation. REPAIR Circuit 329 (PK). TEST the system for normal operation.
C12 CHECK CIRCUIT 33 (WH/PK) FOR AN OPEN		
• Measure the resistance between starter relay C121-87, Circuit 33 (WH/PK), harness side and starter motor C148, Circuit 33 (WH/PK), harness side. • **Is the resistance less than 5 ohms?**	Yes ▶ No ▶	INSTALL a new starter relay. TEST the system for normal operation. REPAIR Circuit 33 (WH/PK). TEST the system for normal operation.
C13 CHECK THE VOLTAGE TO THE IGNITION SWITCH		
• Disconnect ignition switch C299. • Measure the voltage between ignition switch C299-B4, Circuit 1050 (LG/VT), harness side and ground. • **Is the voltage greater than 10 volts?**	Yes ▶ No ▶	GO to **C14**. REPAIR Circuit 1050 (LG/VT) or Fuse 3 (40A). TEST the system for normal operation.
C14 CHECK THE IGNITION SWITCH OUTPUT		
• Reconnect ignition switch C299. • Remove fuse junction panel fuse 7 (10A). • Measure the voltage between fuse junction panel fuse 7 (10A) input cavity, Circuit 32 (RD/LB) and ground. • Hold the ignition switch to START. • **Is the voltage greater than 10 volts?**	Yes ▶ No ▶	GO to **C16**. GO to **C15**.
C15 CHECK THE IGNITION SWITCH		
• Carry out the ignition switch component test. Refer to the Wiring Diagram manual. • **Did the ignition switch pass?**	Yes ▶ No ▶	REPAIR Circuit 32 (RD/LB) for an open or short. TEST the system for normal operation. INSTALL a new ignition switch. TEST the system for normal operation.
C16 CHECK THE VOLTAGE TO THE TRANSMISSION RANGE (TR) SENSOR		
• Install Fuse 7 (10A). • Disconnect TR sensor C107-10. • Measure the voltage between TR sensor C107-10, Circuit 262 (BN/PK), harness side and ground. • Turn the ignition switch to START. • **Is the voltage greater than 10 volts?**	Yes ▶ No ▶	GO to **C17**. REPAIR Circuit 262 (BN/PK) for an open or short. TEST the system for normal operation.

FM1120100670020X

Fig. 67 Test C: Starter motor does not start engine (Part 2 of 3). 1999 Sable & Taurus w/3.0L (4V) & 3.4L (4V) engines

Test Step	Result ▶	Action to Take
D1 CHECK STARTER MOUNTING		
• Check that starter motor mounting is flush (not cocked). Check that all connections are secure. Refer to Removal and Installation for mounting information. • Check other necessary components related to the starting system to be securely mounted: ignition switch, distributor, battery and transaxle switches. • Check wiring connections for damage or shorting due to corrosion or stray wires. • **Are the starting system components and wiring secure and undamaged?**	Yes ▶ No ▶	GO to **D2**. SERVICE or REPLACE wiring or component mountings as required. RETEST starting system for noises.
D2 CRANK ENGINE		
• Turn ignition switch in START then RUN position. As engine is starting, listen to individual components for noise due to gear tooth damage, shorting, sparking or knocking. • Pinpoint noise to component. • **Is noise due to ring gear tooth damage?**	Yes ▶ No ▶	REPLACE ring gear. EXAMINE starter drive pinion. If damaged, REPLACE starter motor or starter drive. If noise sounds like shorting or sparking, CHECK grounded feeds to battery or starter motor. If noise sounds like knocking Diagnose engine mechanical components

FM1120100671000X

Fig. 68 Test D: Unusual starter motor noise during starter overrun. 1999 Sable & Taurus

Test Step	Result ▶	Action to Take
C17 CHECK CIRCUIT 1093 (TN/RD) FOR AN OPEN		
• Measure the resistance between starter relay C121-86, Circuit 1093 (TN/RD), harness side and TR sensor C107-12, Circuit 1093 (TN/RD), harness side. • **Is resistance less than 5 ohms?**	Yes ▶ No ▶	CHECK the TR sensor adjustment. If the TR sensor is adjusted properly, INSTALL a new TR sensor. TEST the system for normal operation. REPAIR Circuit 1093 (TN/RD). TEST the system for normal operation.

FM1120100670030X

Fig. 67 Test C: Starter motor does not start engine (Part 3 of 3). 1999 Sable & Taurus w/3.0L (4V) & 3.4L (4V) engines

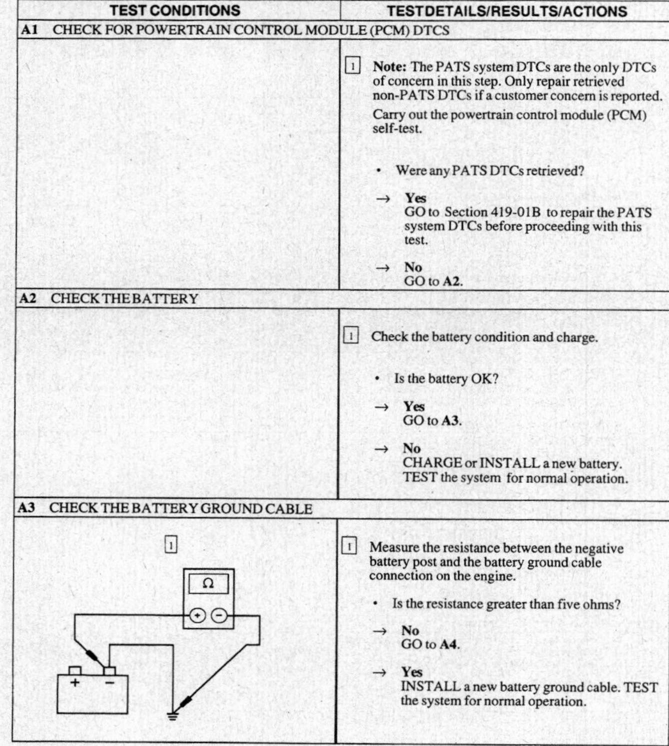

TEST CONDITIONS	TESTDETAILS/RESULTS/ACTIONS
A1 CHECK FOR POWERTRAIN CONTROL MODULE (PCM) DTCS	
	1 **Note:** The PATS system DTCs are the only DTCs of concern in this step. Only repair retrieved non-PATS DTCs if a customer concern is reported. Carry out the powertrain control module (PCM) self-test. • Were any PATS DTCs retrieved? → **Yes** GO to Section 419-01B to repair the PATS system DTCs before proceeding with this test. → **No** GO to **A2**.
A2 CHECK THE BATTERY	
	1 Check the battery condition and charge. • Is the battery OK? → **Yes** GO to **A3**. → **No** CHARGE or INSTALL a new battery. TEST the system for normal operation.
A3 CHECK THE BATTERY GROUND CABLE	
1	1 Measure the resistance between the negative battery post and the battery ground cable connection on the engine. • Is the resistance greater than five ohms? → **No** GO to **A4**. → **Yes** INSTALL a new battery ground cable. TEST the system for normal operation.

FM1120100673010X

Fig. 69 Test A: Engine does not crank (Part 1 of 8). 2000–02 Sable & Taurus

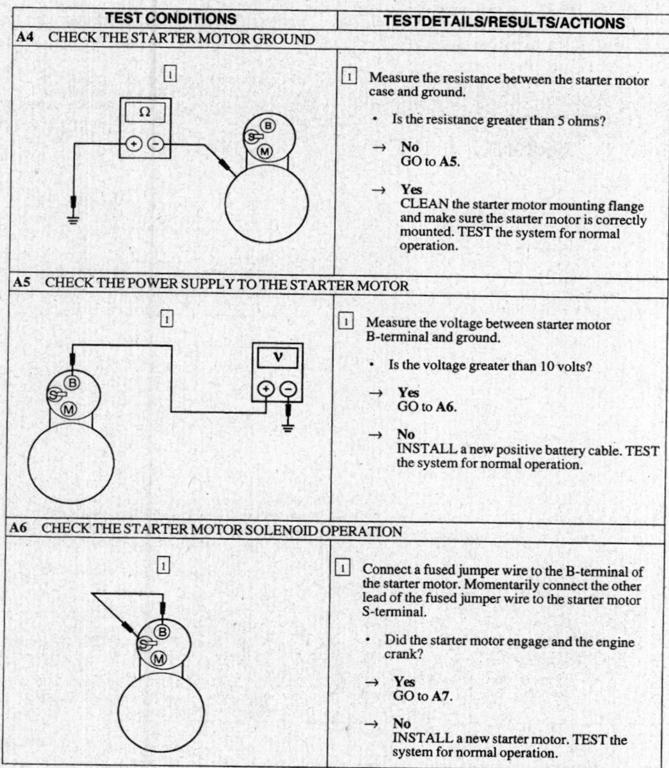

TEST CONDITIONS	TEST DETAILS/RESULTS/ACTIONS
A4 CHECK THE STARTER MOTOR GROUND	
1	1 Measure the resistance between the starter motor case and ground. • Is the resistance greater than 5 ohms? → **No** GO to **A5**. → **Yes** CLEAN the starter motor mounting flange and make sure the starter motor is correctly mounted. TEST the system for normal operation.
A5 CHECK THE POWER SUPPLY TO THE STARTER MOTOR	
1	1 Measure the voltage between starter motor B-terminal and ground. • Is the voltage greater than 10 volts? → **Yes** GO to **A6**. → **No** INSTALL a new positive battery cable. TEST the system for normal operation.
A6 CHECK THE STARTER MOTOR SOLENOID OPERATION	
1	1 Connect a fused jumper wire to the B-terminal of the starter motor. Momentarily connect the other lead of the fused jumper wire to the starter motor S-terminal. • Did the starter motor engage and the engine crank? → **Yes** GO to **A7**. → **No** INSTALL a new starter motor. TEST the system for normal operation.

FM1120100673020X

Fig. 69 Test A: Engine does not crank (Part 2 of 8). 2000–02 Sable & Taurus

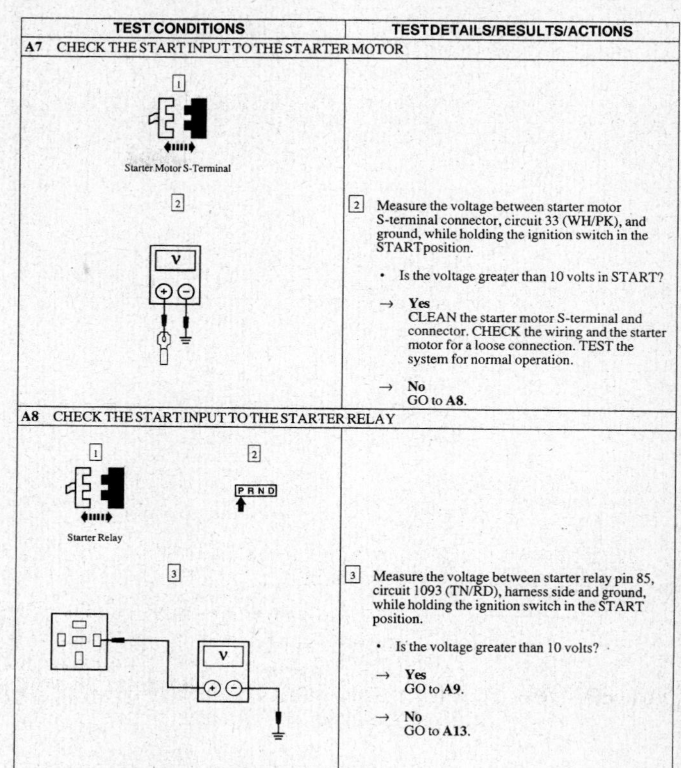

TEST CONDITIONS	TEST DETAILS/RESULTS/ACTIONS
A7 CHECK THE START INPUT TO THE STARTER MOTOR	
1 Starter Motor S-Terminal	
2	2 Measure the voltage between starter motor S-terminal connector, circuit 33 (WH/PK), and ground, while holding the ignition switch in the START position. • Is the voltage greater than 10 volts in START? → **Yes** CLEAN the starter motor S-terminal and connector. CHECK the wiring and the starter motor for a loose connection. TEST the system for normal operation. → **No** GO to **A8**.
A8 CHECK THE START INPUT TO THE STARTER RELAY	
1 Starter Relay 2 PRND	
3	3 Measure the voltage between starter relay pin 85, circuit 1093 (TN/RD), harness side and ground, while holding the ignition switch in the START position. • Is the voltage greater than 10 volts? → **Yes** GO to **A9**. → **No** GO to **A13**.

FM1120100673030X

Fig. 69 Test A: Engine does not crank (Part 3 of 8). 2000–02 Sable & Taurus

TEST CONDITIONS	TEST DETAILS/RESULTS/ACTIONS
A9 CHECK THE BATTERY SUPPLY TO THE STARTER RELAY	
1	1 Measure the voltage between starter relay pin 87, circuit 1050 (LG/VT), harness side and ground. • Is the voltage greater than 10 volts? → **Yes** GO to **A10**. → **No** REPAIR the circuit in question. TEST the system for normal operation.
A10 CHECK THE GROUND SIGNAL TO THE STARTER RELAY	
1	1 Measure the resistance between starter relay pin 86, circuit 329 (PK), harness side and ground, while holding the ignition switch in the START position. • Is the resistance less than 5 ohms? → **Yes** GO to **A12**. → **No** GO to **A11**.
A11 CHECK CIRCUIT 329 (PK) FOR AN OPEN	
1 PCM C175	

FM1120100673040X

Fig. 69 Test A: Engine does not crank (Part 4 of 8). 2000–02 Sable & Taurus

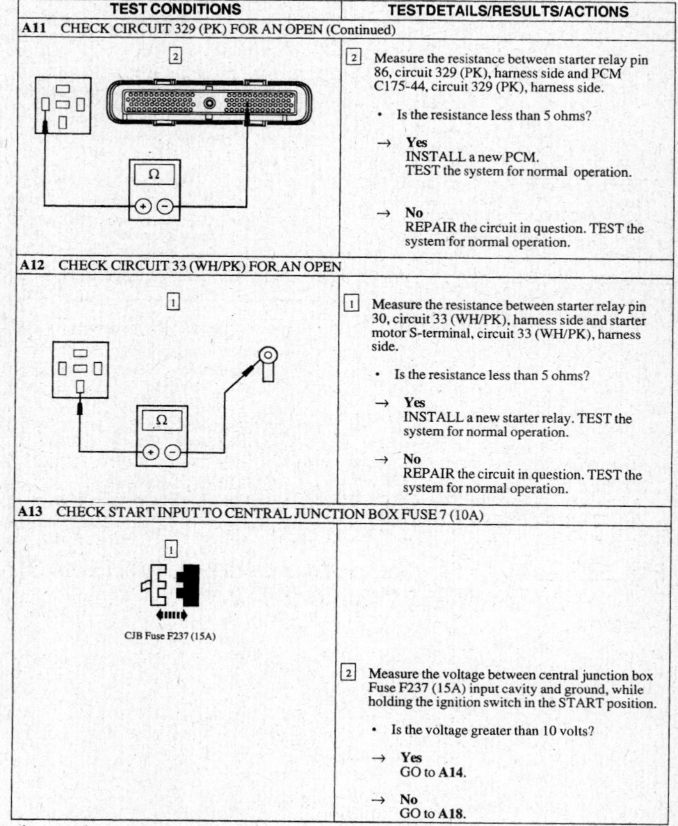

TEST CONDITIONS	TEST DETAILS/RESULTS/ACTIONS
A11 CHECK CIRCUIT 329 (PK) FOR AN OPEN (Continued)	
2	2 Measure the resistance between starter relay pin 86, circuit 329 (PK), harness side and PCM C175-44, circuit 329 (PK), harness side. • Is the resistance less than 5 ohms? → **Yes** INSTALL a new PCM. TEST the system for normal operation. → **No** REPAIR the circuit in question. TEST the system for normal operation.
A12 CHECK CIRCUIT 33 (WH/PK) FOR AN OPEN	
1	1 Measure the resistance between starter relay pin 30, circuit 33 (WH/PK), harness side and starter motor S-terminal, circuit 33 (WH/PK), harness side. • Is the resistance less than 5 ohms? → **Yes** INSTALL a new starter relay. TEST the system for normal operation. → **No** REPAIR the circuit in question. TEST the system for normal operation.
A13 CHECK START INPUT TO CENTRAL JUNCTION BOX FUSE 7 (10A)	
1 CJB Fuse F237 (15A)	
	2 Measure the voltage between central junction box Fuse F237 (15A) input cavity and ground, while holding the ignition switch in the START position. • Is the voltage greater than 10 volts? → **Yes** GO to **A14**. → **No** GO to **A18**.

FM1120100673050X

Fig. 69 Test A: Engine does not crank (Part 5 of 8). 2000–02 Sable & Taurus

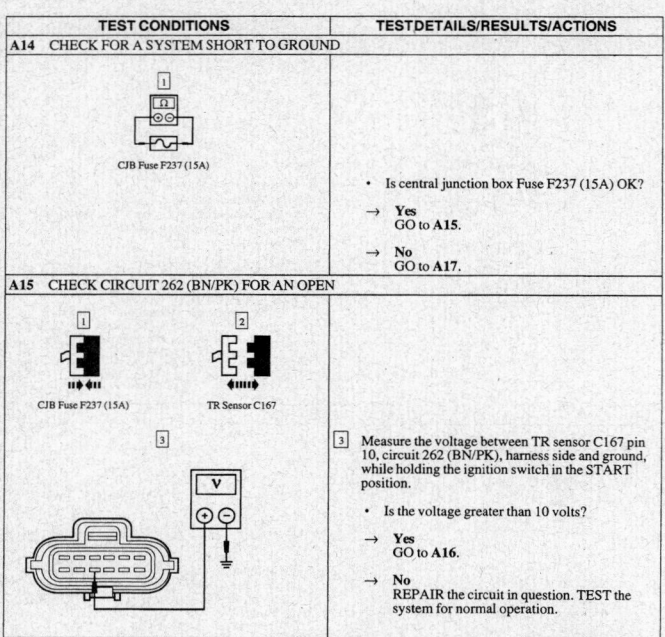

TEST CONDITIONS	TEST DETAILS/RESULTS/ACTIONS
A14 CHECK FOR A SYSTEM SHORT TO GROUND	
1 CJB Fuse F237 (15A)	• Is central junction box Fuse F237 (15A) OK? → **Yes** GO to **A15**. → **No** GO to **A17**.
A15 CHECK CIRCUIT 262 (BN/PK) FOR AN OPEN	
1 CJB Fuse F237 (15A) 2 TR Sensor C167	
3	3 Measure the voltage between TR sensor C167 pin 10, circuit 262 (BN/PK), harness side and ground, while holding the ignition switch in the START position. • Is the voltage greater than 10 volts? → **Yes** GO to **A16**. → **No** REPAIR the circuit in question. TEST the system for normal operation.

FM1120100673060X

Fig. 69 Test A: Engine does not crank (Part 6 of 8). 2000–02 Sable & Taurus

TEST CONDITIONS	TEST DETAILS/RESULTS/ACTIONS
A18 CHECK THE POWER SUPPLY TO THE IGNITION SWITCH	
1 Ignition Switch C250	
2	2 Measure the voltage between ignition switch C250 pin B4, circuit 1050 (LG/VT), harness side and ground. • Is the voltage greater than 10 volts? → **Yes** GO to **A19**. → **No** REPAIR the circuit in question. TEST the system for normal operation.
A19 CHECK THE IGNITION SWITCH	
	1 Carry out the ignition switch component test. • Did the ignition switch pass the component test? → **Yes** REPAIR circuit 32 (RD/LB). TEST the system for normal operation. → **No** INSTALL a new ignition switch. TEST the system for normal operation.

FM1120100673080X

Fig. 69 Test A: Engine does not crank (Part 8 of 8). 2000–02 Sable & Taurus

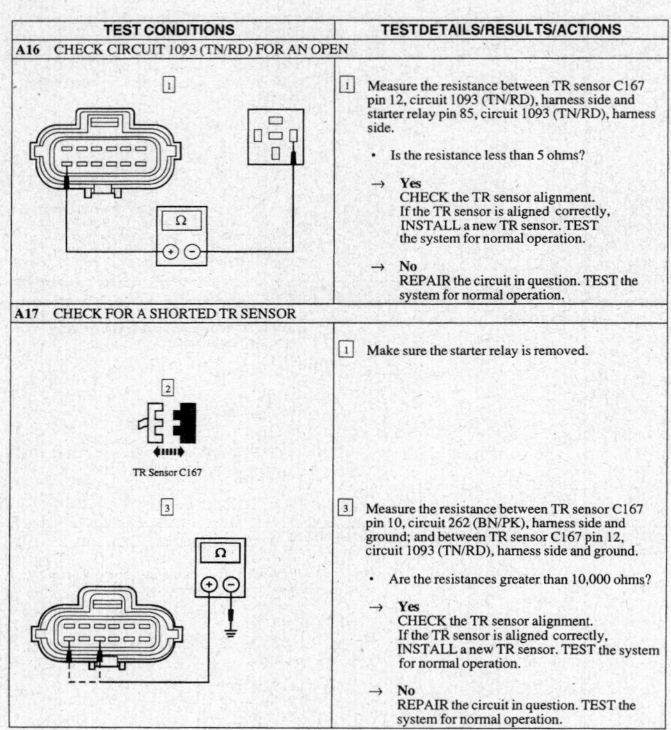

TEST CONDITIONS	TEST DETAILS/RESULTS/ACTIONS
A16 CHECK CIRCUIT 1093 (TN/RD) FOR AN OPEN	
1	1 Measure the resistance between TR sensor C167 pin 12, circuit 1093 (TN/RD), harness side and starter relay pin 85, circuit 1093 (TN/RD), harness side. • Is the resistance less than 5 ohms? → **Yes** CHECK the TR sensor alignment. If the TR sensor is aligned correctly, INSTALL a new TR sensor. TEST the system for normal operation. → **No** REPAIR the circuit in question. TEST the system for normal operation.
A17 CHECK FOR A SHORTED TR SENSOR	
	1 Make sure the starter relay is removed.
2 TR Sensor C167	
3	3 Measure the resistance between TR sensor C167 pin 10, circuit 262 (BN/PK), harness side and ground; and between TR sensor C167 pin 12, circuit 1093 (TN/RD), harness side and ground. • Are the resistances greater than 10,000 ohms? → **Yes** CHECK the TR sensor alignment. If the TR sensor is aligned correctly, INSTALL a new TR sensor. TEST the system for normal operation. → **No** REPAIR the circuit in question. TEST the system for normal operation.

FM1120100673070X

Fig. 69 Test A: Engine does not crank (Part 7 of 8). 2000–02 Sable & Taurus

TEST CONDITIONS	TEST DETAILS/RESULTS/ACTIONS
B1 CHECK STARTER MOUNTING	
	1 Inspect the starter mounting bolts and brackets for looseness. • Is the starter motor mounted correctly? → **Yes** GO to **B2**. → **No** INSTALL the starter motor correctly. TEST the system for normal operation.
B2 CHECK FOR ENGINE NOISE	
1	
2 B S M	2 Connect a remote starter switch between the starter solenoid B and S terminals.
	3 Engage the starter motor and verify the noise is due to the starter operation. • Is the noise due to the starter motor engagement? → **Yes** GO to **B3**. → **No** Diagnose engine mechanical components

FM1120100674010X

Fig. 70 Test B: Unusual starter noise (Part 1 of 2). 2000–02 Sable & Taurus

TEST CONDITIONS	TEST DETAILS/RESULTS/ACTIONS
B3 CHECK FOR UNUSUAL WEAR	
	1 Remove the starter motor.
	2 Inspect the ring gear for damaged or worn teeth. • Is the noise due to ring gear tooth damage? → **Yes** INSTALL a new ring gear. EXAMINE the starter pinion teeth. If damaged, INSTALL a new starter motor. TEST the system for normal operation. → **No** INSTALL a new starter motor. system for normal operation.

FM1120100674020X

Fig. 70 Test B: Unusual starter noise (Part 2 of 2). 2000–02 Sable & Taurus

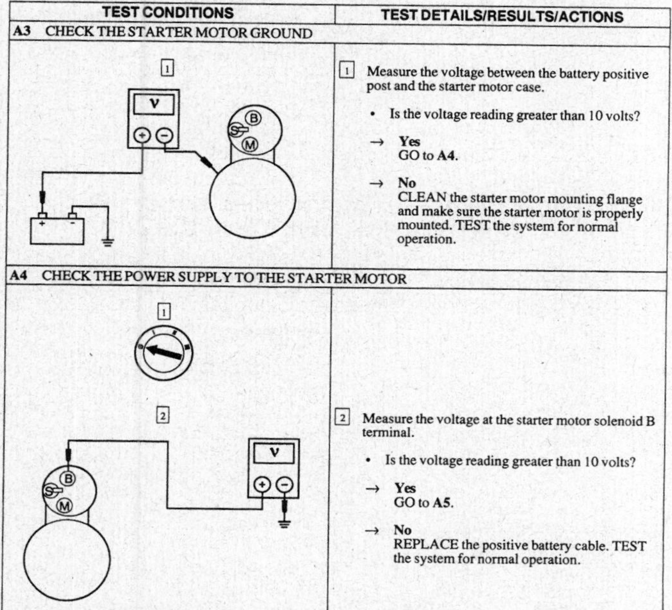

TEST CONDITIONS	TEST DETAILS/RESULTS/ACTIONS
A3 CHECK THE STARTER MOTOR GROUND	
1	1 Measure the voltage between the battery positive post and the starter motor case. • Is the voltage reading greater than 10 volts? → **Yes** GO to **A4**. → **No** CLEAN the starter motor mounting flange and make sure the starter motor is properly mounted. TEST the system for normal operation.
A4 CHECK THE POWER SUPPLY TO THE STARTER MOTOR	
1	
2	2 Measure the voltage at the starter motor solenoid B terminal. • Is the voltage reading greater than 10 volts? → **Yes** GO to **A5**. → **No** REPLACE the positive battery cable. TEST the system for normal operation.

FM1120100680020X

Fig. 71 Test A: Engine does not crank (Part 2 of 13). 1998 Town Car

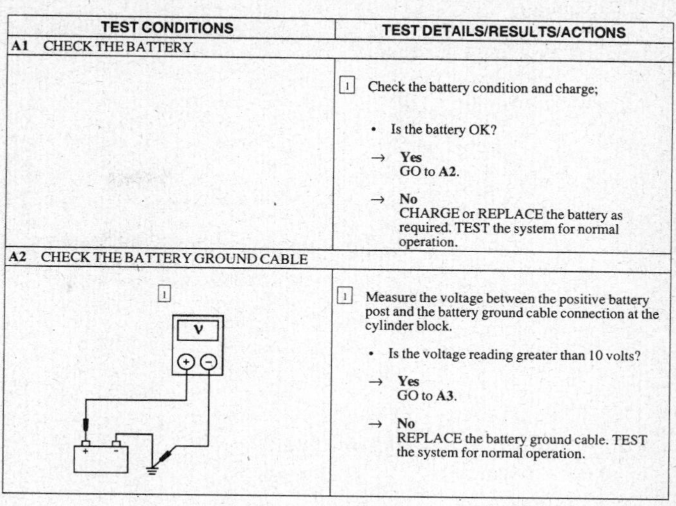

TEST CONDITIONS	TEST DETAILS/RESULTS/ACTIONS
A1 CHECK THE BATTERY	
	1 Check the battery condition and charge; • Is the battery OK? → **Yes** GO to **A2**. → **No** CHARGE or REPLACE the battery as required. TEST the system for normal operation.
A2 CHECK THE BATTERY GROUND CABLE	
1	1 Measure the voltage between the positive battery post and the battery ground cable connection at the cylinder block. • Is the voltage reading greater than 10 volts? → **Yes** GO to **A3**. → **No** REPLACE the battery ground cable. TEST the system for normal operation.

FM1120100680010X

Fig. 71 Test A: Engine does not crank (Part 1 of 13). 1998 Town Car

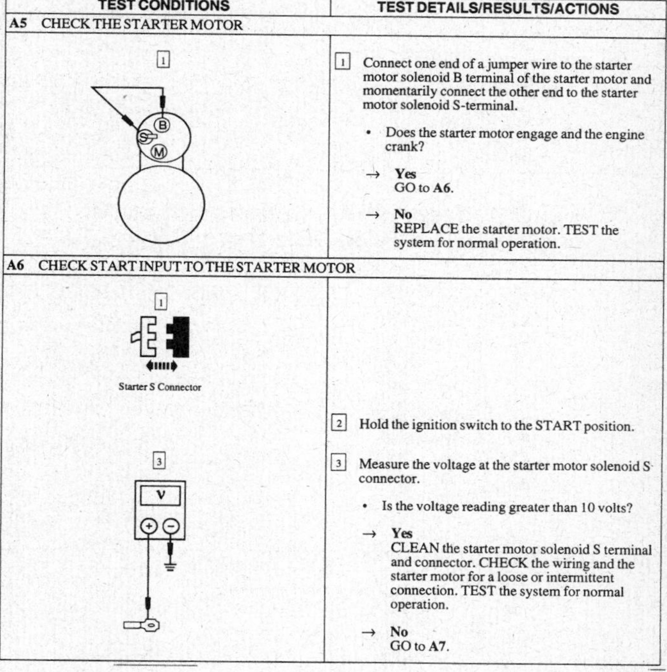

TEST CONDITIONS	TEST DETAILS/RESULTS/ACTIONS
A5 CHECK THE STARTER MOTOR	
1	1 Connect one end of a jumper wire to the starter motor solenoid B terminal of the starter motor and momentarily connect the other end to the starter motor solenoid S-terminal. • Does the starter motor engage and the engine crank? → **Yes** GO to **A6**. → **No** REPLACE the starter motor. TEST the system for normal operation.
A6 CHECK START INPUT TO THE STARTER MOTOR	
1 Starter S Connector	
	2 Hold the ignition switch to the START position.
3	3 Measure the voltage at the starter motor solenoid S connector. • Is the voltage reading greater than 10 volts? → **Yes** CLEAN the starter motor solenoid S terminal and connector. CHECK the wiring and the starter motor for a loose or intermittent connection. TEST the system for normal operation. → **No** GO to **A7**.

FM1120100680030X

Fig. 71 Test A: Engine does not crank (Part 3 of 13). 1998 Town Car

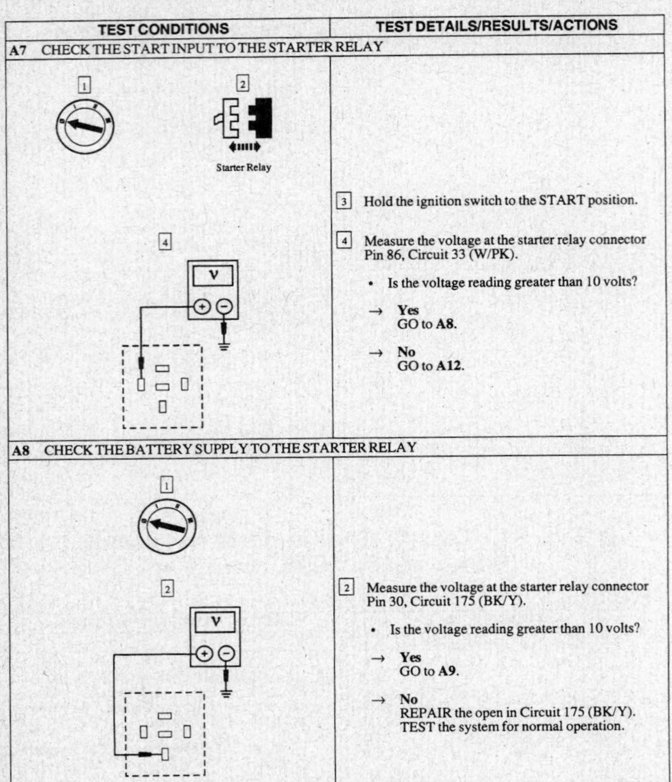

TEST CONDITIONS	TEST DETAILS/RESULTS/ACTIONS
A7 CHECK THE START INPUT TO THE STARTER RELAY	
1 2 Starter Relay	3 Hold the ignition switch to the START position.
4	4 Measure the voltage at the starter relay connector Pin 86, Circuit 33 (W/PK). • Is the voltage reading greater than 10 volts? → **Yes** GO to **A8**. → **No** GO to **A12**.
A8 CHECK THE BATTERY SUPPLY TO THE STARTER RELAY	
1	
2	2 Measure the voltage at the starter relay connector Pin 30, Circuit 175 (BK/Y). • Is the voltage reading greater than 10 volts? → **Yes** GO to **A9**. → **No** REPAIR the open in Circuit 175 (BK/Y). TEST the system for normal operation.

FM1120100680040X

Fig. 71 Test A: Engine does not crank (Part 4 of 13). 1998 Town Car

TEST CONDITIONS	TEST DETAILS/RESULTS/ACTIONS
A11 CHECK CIRCUIT 113 (Y/LB) FOR AN OPEN	
1	1 Measure the resistance of Circuit 113 (Y/LB) between the starter relay connector Pin 87 and the starter motor solenoid S Connector. • Is the resistance reading less than 5 ohms? → **Yes** REPLACE the starter relay. TEST the system for normal operation. → **No** REPAIR Circuit 113 (Y/LB) for an open. TEST the system for normal operation.
A12 CHECK FUSE 26 (5A)	
1 2 3 Fuse 26 (5A) Fuse 26 (5A)	• Is Fuse 26 (5A) OK? → **Yes** GO to **A13**. → **No** GO to **A19**.
A13 CHECK THE INPUT TO FUSE 26 (5A)	
	1 Hold the ignition switch to the START position.

FM1120100680060X

Fig. 71 Test A: Engine does not crank (Part 6 of 13). 1998 Town Car

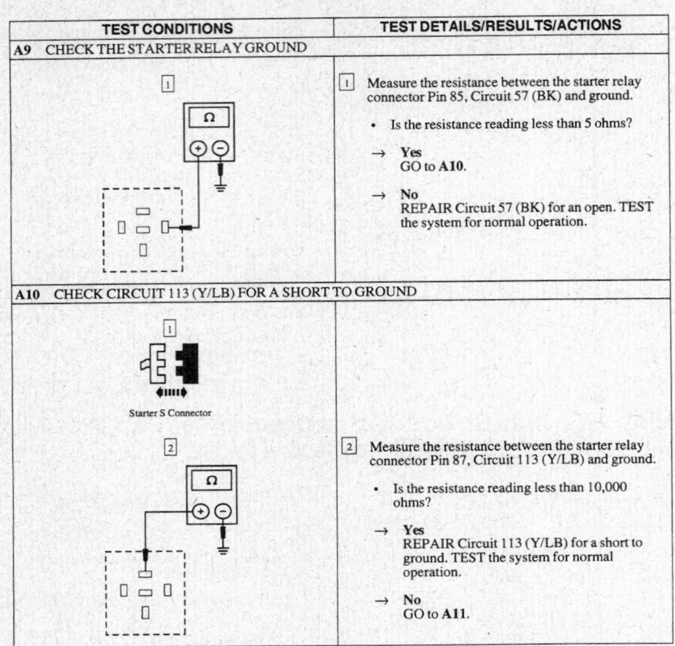

TEST CONDITIONS	TEST DETAILS/RESULTS/ACTIONS
A9 CHECK THE STARTER RELAY GROUND	
1	1 Measure the resistance between the starter relay connector Pin 85, Circuit 57 (BK) and ground. • Is the resistance reading less than 5 ohms? → **Yes** GO to **A10**. → **No** REPAIR Circuit 57 (BK) for an open. TEST the system for normal operation.
A10 CHECK CIRCUIT 113 (Y/LB) FOR A SHORT TO GROUND	
1 Starter S Connector	
2	2 Measure the resistance between the starter relay connector Pin 87, Circuit 113 (Y/LB) and ground. • Is the resistance reading less than 10,000 ohms? → **Yes** REPAIR Circuit 113 (Y/LB) for a short to ground. TEST the system for normal operation. → **No** GO to **A11**.

FM1120100680050X

Fig. 71 Test A: Engine does not crank (Part 5 of 13). 1998 Town Car

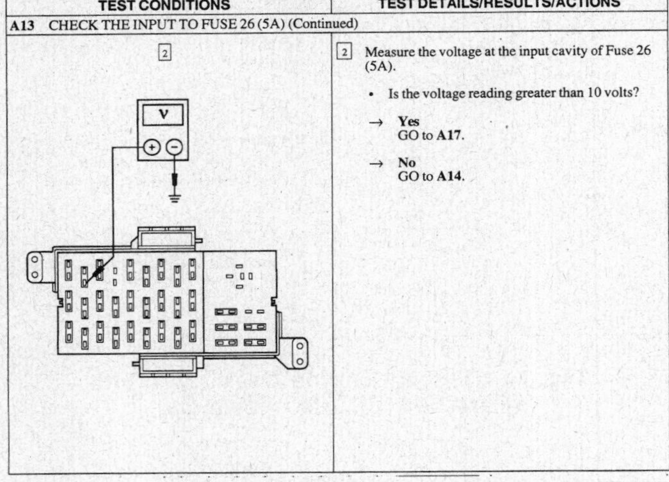

TEST CONDITIONS	TEST DETAILS/RESULTS/ACTIONS
A13 CHECK THE INPUT TO FUSE 26 (5A) (Continued)	
2	2 Measure the voltage at the input cavity of Fuse 26 (5A). • Is the voltage reading greater than 10 volts? → **Yes** GO to **A17**. → **No** GO to **A14**.

FM1120100680070X

Fig. 71 Test A: Engine does not crank (Part 7 of 13). 1998 Town Car

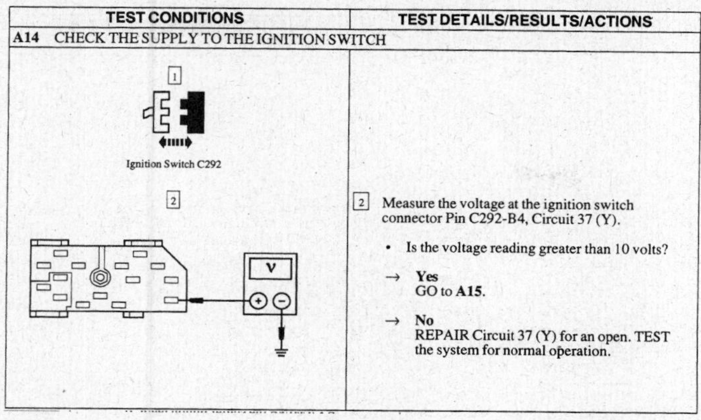

TEST CONDITIONS	TEST DETAILS/RESULTS/ACTIONS
A14 CHECK THE SUPPLY TO THE IGNITION SWITCH	
1 Ignition Switch C292	
2	2 Measure the voltage at the ignition switch connector Pin C292-B4, Circuit 37 (Y). • Is the voltage reading greater than 10 volts? → **Yes** GO to **A15**. → **No** REPAIR Circuit 37 (Y) for an open. TEST the system for normal operation.

FM1120100680080X

Fig. 71 Test A: Engine does not crank (Part 8 of 13). 1998 Town Car

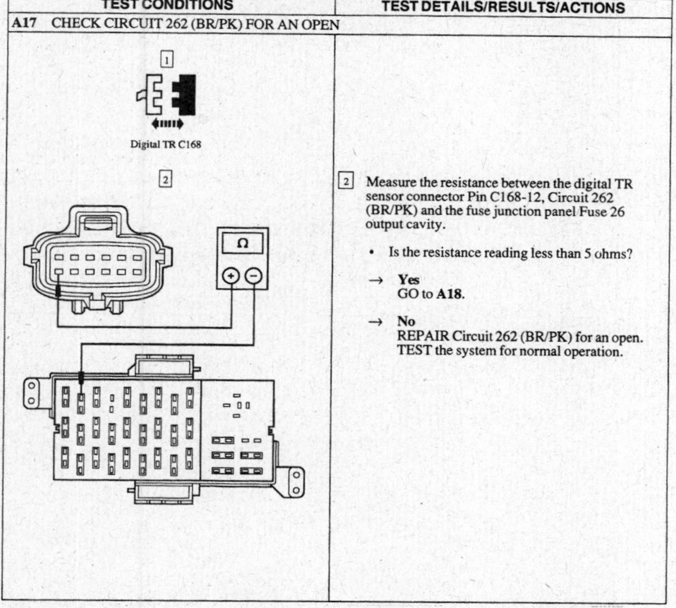

TEST CONDITIONS	TEST DETAILS/RESULTS/ACTIONS
A17 CHECK CIRCUIT 262 (BR/PK) FOR AN OPEN	
1 Digital TR C168	
2	2 Measure the resistance between the digital TR sensor connector Pin C168-12, Circuit 262 (BR/PK) and the fuse junction panel Fuse 26 output cavity. • Is the resistance reading less than 5 ohms? → **Yes** GO to **A18**. → **No** REPAIR Circuit 262 (BR/PK) for an open. TEST the system for normal operation.

FM1120100680100X

Fig. 71 Test A: Engine does not crank (Part 10 of 13). 1998 Town Car

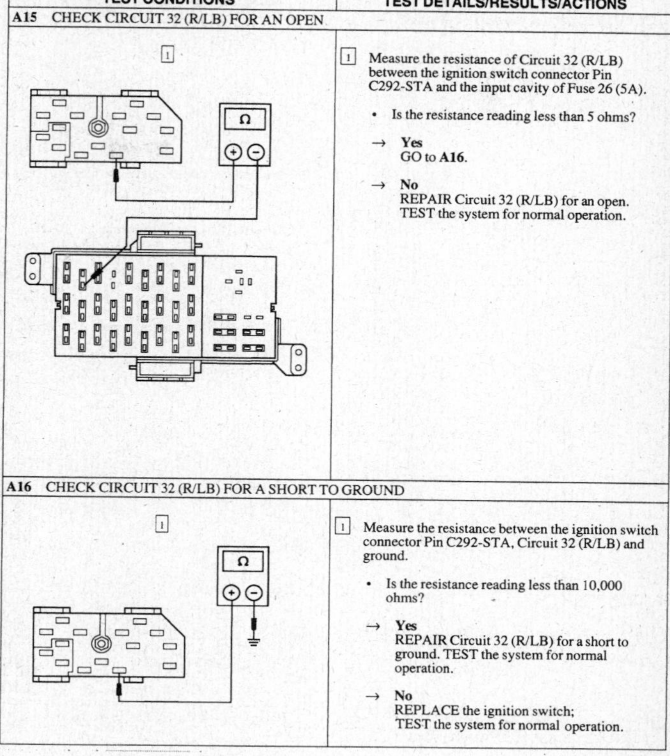

TEST CONDITIONS	TEST DETAILS/RESULTS/ACTIONS
A15 CHECK CIRCUIT 32 (R/LB) FOR AN OPEN	
1	1 Measure the resistance of Circuit 32 (R/LB) between the ignition switch connector Pin C292-STA and the input cavity of Fuse 26 (5A). • Is the resistance reading less than 5 ohms? → **Yes** GO to **A16**. → **No** REPAIR Circuit 32 (R/LB) for an open. TEST the system for normal operation.
A16 CHECK CIRCUIT 32 (R/LB) FOR A SHORT TO GROUND	
1	1 Measure the resistance between the ignition switch connector Pin C292-STA, Circuit 32 (R/LB) and ground. • Is the resistance reading less than 10,000 ohms? → **Yes** REPAIR Circuit 32 (R/LB) for a short to ground. TEST the system for normal operation. → **No** REPLACE the ignition switch; TEST the system for normal operation.

FM1120100680090X

Fig. 71 Test A: Engine does not crank (Part 9 of 13). 1998 Town Car

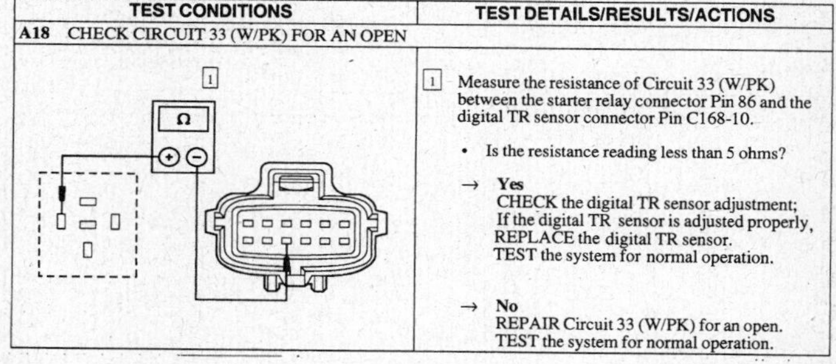

TEST CONDITIONS	TEST DETAILS/RESULTS/ACTIONS
A18 CHECK CIRCUIT 33 (W/PK) FOR AN OPEN	
1	1 Measure the resistance of Circuit 33 (W/PK) between the starter relay connector Pin 86 and the digital TR sensor connector Pin C168-10. • Is the resistance reading less than 5 ohms? → **Yes** CHECK the digital TR sensor adjustment; If the digital TR sensor is adjusted properly, REPLACE the digital TR sensor. TEST the system for normal operation. → **No** REPAIR Circuit 33 (W/PK) for an open. TEST the system for normal operation.

FM1120100680110X

Fig. 71 Test A: Engine does not crank (Part 11 of 13). 1998 Town Car

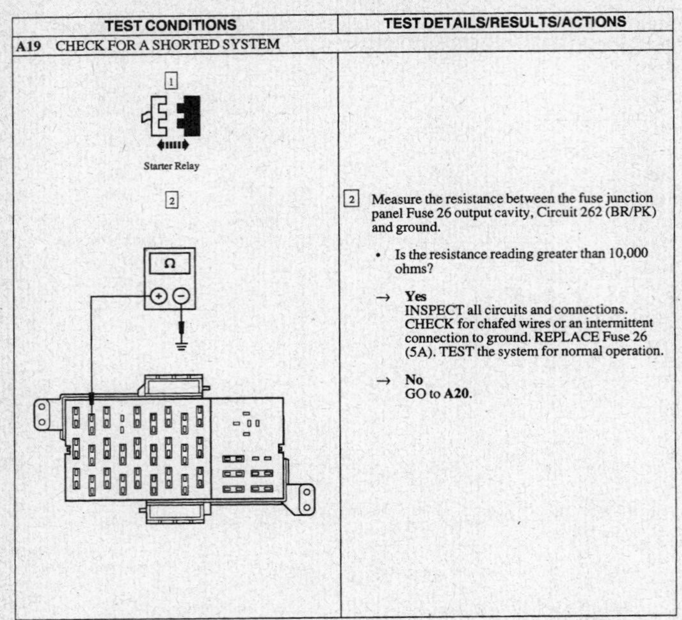

TEST CONDITIONS	TEST DETAILS/RESULTS/ACTIONS
A19 CHECK FOR A SHORTED SYSTEM	
1 Starter Relay	
2	2 Measure the resistance between the fuse junction panel Fuse 26 output cavity, Circuit 262 (BR/PK) and ground. • Is the resistance reading greater than 10,000 ohms? → **Yes** INSPECT all circuits and connections. CHECK for chafed wires or an intermittent connection to ground. REPLACE Fuse 26 (5A). TEST the system for normal operation. → **No** GO to **A20**.

FM1120100680120X

Fig. 71 Test A: Engine does not crank (Part 12 of 13). 1998 Town Car

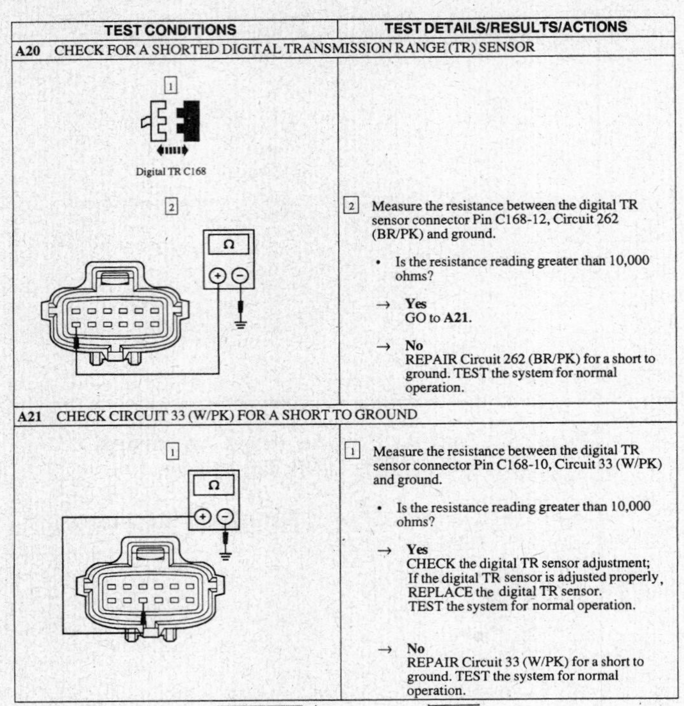

TEST CONDITIONS	TEST DETAILS/RESULTS/ACTIONS
A20 CHECK FOR A SHORTED DIGITAL TRANSMISSION RANGE (TR) SENSOR	
1 Digital TR C168	
2	2 Measure the resistance between the digital TR sensor connector Pin C168-12, Circuit 262 (BR/PK) and ground. • Is the resistance reading greater than 10,000 ohms? → **Yes** GO to **A21**. → **No** REPAIR Circuit 262 (BR/PK) for a short to ground. TEST the system for normal operation.
A21 CHECK CIRCUIT 33 (W/PK) FOR A SHORT TO GROUND	
1	1 Measure the resistance between the digital TR sensor connector Pin C168-10, Circuit 33 (W/PK) and ground. • Is the resistance reading greater than 10,000 ohms? → **Yes** CHECK the digital TR sensor adjustment; If the digital TR sensor is adjusted properly, REPLACE the digital TR sensor. TEST the system for normal operation. → **No** REPAIR Circuit 33 (W/PK) for a short to ground. TEST the system for normal operation.

FM1120100680130X

Fig. 71 Test A: Engine does not crank (Part 13 of 13). 1998 Town Car

TEST CONDITIONS	TEST DETAILS/RESULTS/ACTIONS
B1 CHECK THE STARTER MOUNTING	
	1 Inspect the starter motor mounting bolts and brackets for looseness. • Is the starter motor mounted properly? → **Yes** GO to **B2**. → **No** INSTALL the starter motor properly; TEST the system for normal operation.
B2 CHECK FOR ENGINE NOISE	
1	
2	2 Connect a remote starter switch between the starter motor solenoid B and S terminals.
	3 Engage the starter motorand verify the noise is due to the starter operation. • Is the noise due to the starter motor engagement? → **Yes** GO to **B3**. → **No** **Diagnose engine mechanical components**

FM1120100681010X

Fig. 72 Test B: Engine does not crank (Part 1 of 2). 1998 Town Car

TEST CONDITIONS	TEST DETAILS/RESULTS/ACTIONS
B3 CHECK FOR UNUSUAL WEAR	
	1 Remove the starter motor.
	2 Inspect the ring gear for damaged or worn teeth. • Is the noise due to flywheel ring gear tooth damage? → **Yes** REPLACE the flywheel ring gear. EXAMINE the starter pinion teeth. If damaged, REPLACE the starter motor. TEST the system for normal operation. → **No** REPLACE the starter motor. TEST the system for normal operation.

FM1120100681020X

Fig. 72 Test B: Engine does not crank (Part 2 of 2). 1998 Town Car

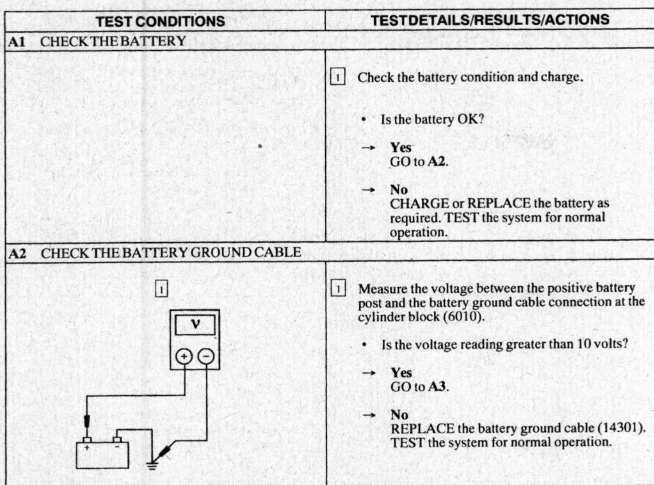

TEST CONDITIONS	TEST DETAILS/RESULTS/ACTIONS
A1 CHECK THE BATTERY	
	1 Check the battery condition and charge. • Is the battery OK? → **Yes** GO to **A2**. → **No** CHARGE or REPLACE the battery as required. TEST the system for normal operation.
A2 CHECK THE BATTERY GROUND CABLE	
1	1 Measure the voltage between the positive battery post and the battery ground cable connection at the cylinder block (6010). • Is the voltage reading greater than 10 volts? → **Yes** GO to **A3**. → **No** REPLACE the battery ground cable (14301). TEST the system for normal operation.

FM1120100683010X

Fig. 73 Test A: Engine does not crank (Part 1 of 12). 1999–2002 Town Car

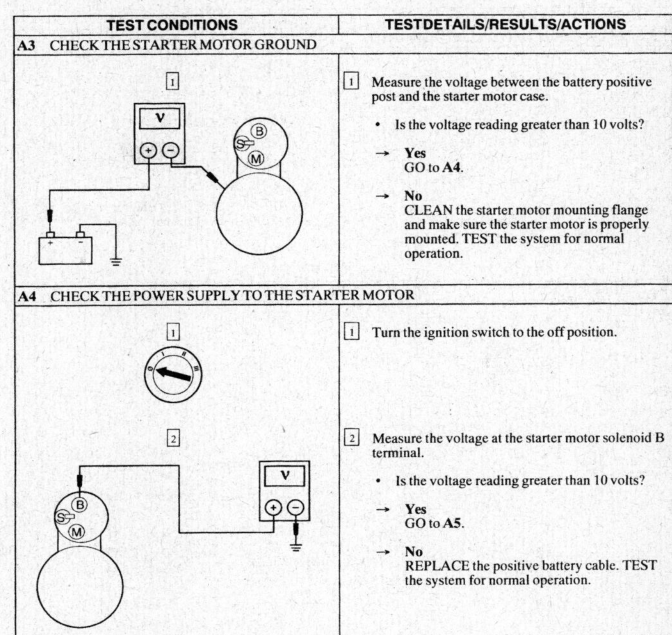

TEST CONDITIONS	TEST DETAILS/RESULTS/ACTIONS
A3 CHECK THE STARTER MOTOR GROUND	
1	1 Measure the voltage between the battery positive post and the starter motor case. • Is the voltage reading greater than 10 volts? → **Yes** GO to **A4**. → **No** CLEAN the starter motor mounting flange and make sure the starter motor is properly mounted. TEST the system for normal operation.
A4 CHECK THE POWER SUPPLY TO THE STARTER MOTOR	
1	1 Turn the ignition switch to the off position.
2	2 Measure the voltage at the starter motor solenoid B terminal. • Is the voltage reading greater than 10 volts? → **Yes** GO to **A5**. → **No** REPLACE the positive battery cable. TEST the system for normal operation.

FM1120100683020X

Fig. 73 Test A: Engine does not crank (Part 2 of 12). 1999–2002 Town Car

TEST CONDITIONS	TEST DETAILS/RESULTS/ACTIONS
A5 CHECK THE STARTER MOTOR	
1	1 Connect one end of a jumper wire to the starter motor solenoid B terminal of the starter motor and momentarily connect the other end to the starter motor solenoid S-terminal. • Does the starter motor engage and the engine crank? → **Yes** GO to **A6**. → **No** REPLACE the starter motor. TEST the system for normal operation.
A6 CHECK START INPUT TO THE STARTER MOTOR	
1 Starter S Connector	1 Disconnect the starter motor solenoid S-terminal.
	2 Hold the ignition switch to the START position.
3	3 Measure the voltage at the starter motor solenoid S connector. • Is the voltage reading greater than 10 volts? → **Yes** CLEAN the starter motor solenoid S-terminal stud and connector. CHECK the wiring and the starter motor for a loose or intermittent connection. TEST the system for normal operation. → **No** GO to **A7**.

FM1120100683030X

Fig. 73 Test A: Engine does not crank (Part 3 of 12). 1999–2002 Town Car

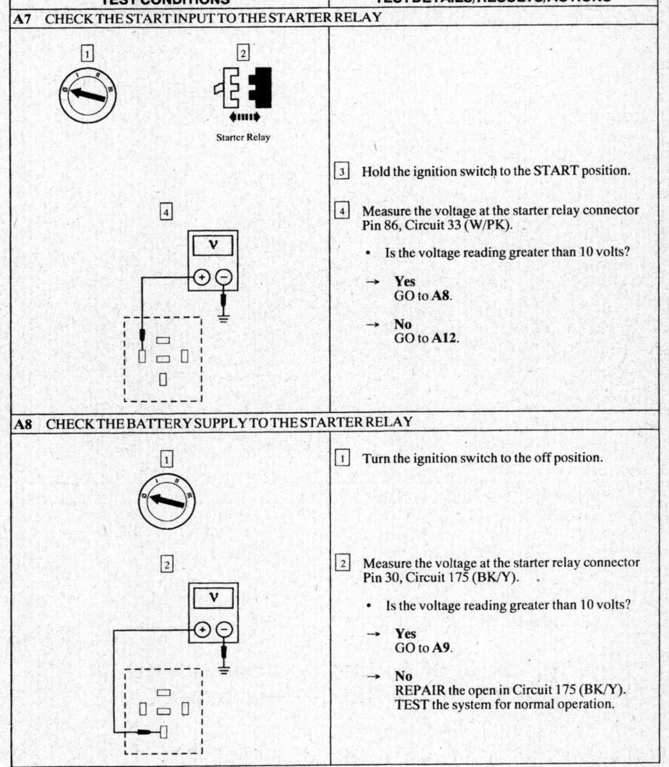

TEST CONDITIONS	TEST DETAILS/RESULTS/ACTIONS
A7 CHECK THE START INPUT TO THE STARTER RELAY	
1 2 Starter Relay	
	3 Hold the ignition switch to the START position.
4	4 Measure the voltage at the starter relay connector Pin 86, Circuit 33 (W/PK). • Is the voltage reading greater than 10 volts? → **Yes** GO to **A8**. → **No** GO to **A12**.
A8 CHECK THE BATTERY SUPPLY TO THE STARTER RELAY	
1	1 Turn the ignition switch to the off position.
2	2 Measure the voltage at the starter relay connector Pin 30, Circuit 175 (BK/Y). • Is the voltage reading greater than 10 volts? → **Yes** GO to **A9**. → **No** REPAIR the open in Circuit 175 (BK/Y). TEST the system for normal operation.

FM1120100683040X

Fig. 73 Test A: Engine does not crank (Part 4 of 12). 1999–2002 Town Car

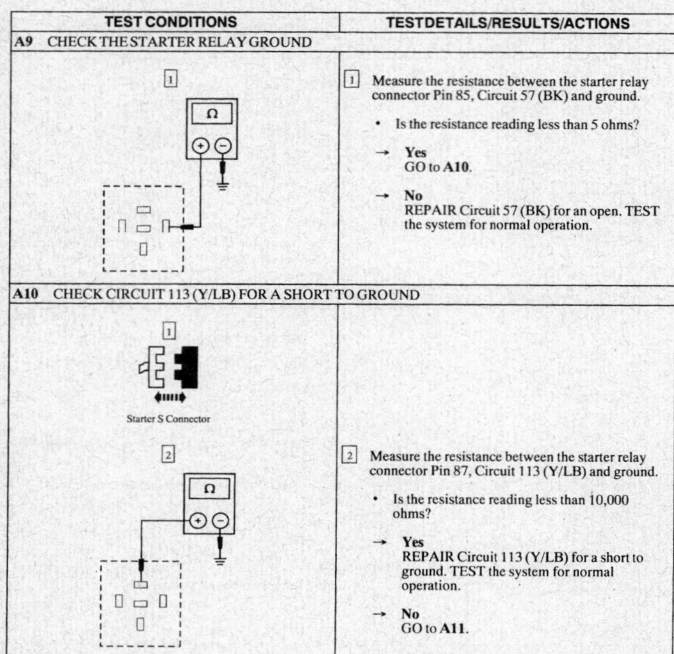

TEST CONDITIONS	TEST DETAILS/RESULTS/ACTIONS
A9 CHECK THE STARTER RELAY GROUND	
1	1 Measure the resistance between the starter relay connector Pin 85, Circuit 57 (BK) and ground. • Is the resistance reading less than 5 ohms? → **Yes** GO to **A10**. → **No** REPAIR Circuit 57 (BK) for an open. TEST the system for normal operation.
A10 CHECK CIRCUIT 113 (Y/LB) FOR A SHORT TO GROUND	
1 Starter S Connector	
2	2 Measure the resistance between the starter relay connector Pin 87, Circuit 113 (Y/LB) and ground. • Is the resistance reading less than 10,000 ohms? → **Yes** REPAIR Circuit 113 (Y/LB) for a short to ground. TEST the system for normal operation. → **No** GO to **A11**.

FM1120100683050X

Fig. 73 Test A: Engine does not crank (Part 5 of 12). 1999–2002 Town Car

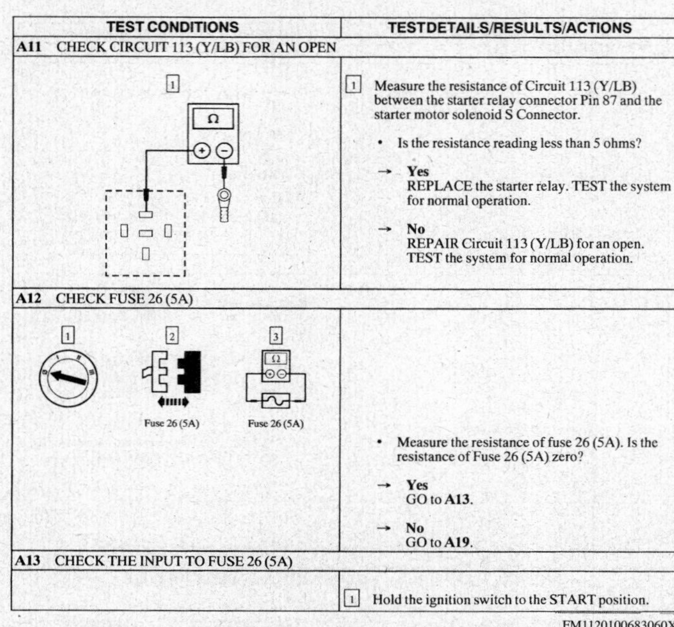

TEST CONDITIONS	TEST DETAILS/RESULTS/ACTIONS
A11 CHECK CIRCUIT 113 (Y/LB) FOR AN OPEN	
1	1 Measure the resistance of Circuit 113 (Y/LB) between the starter relay connector Pin 87 and the starter motor solenoid S Connector. • Is the resistance reading less than 5 ohms? → **Yes** REPLACE the starter relay. TEST the system for normal operation. → **No** REPAIR Circuit 113 (Y/LB) for an open. TEST the system for normal operation.
A12 CHECK FUSE 26 (5A)	
1 2 Fuse 26 (5A) 3 Fuse 26 (5A)	• Measure the resistance of fuse 26 (5A). Is the resistance of Fuse 26 (5A) zero? → **Yes** GO to **A13**. → **No** GO to **A19**.
A13 CHECK THE INPUT TO FUSE 26 (5A)	
	1 Hold the ignition switch to the START position.

FM1120100683060X

Fig. 73 Test A: Engine does not crank (Part 6 of 12). 1999–2002 Town Car

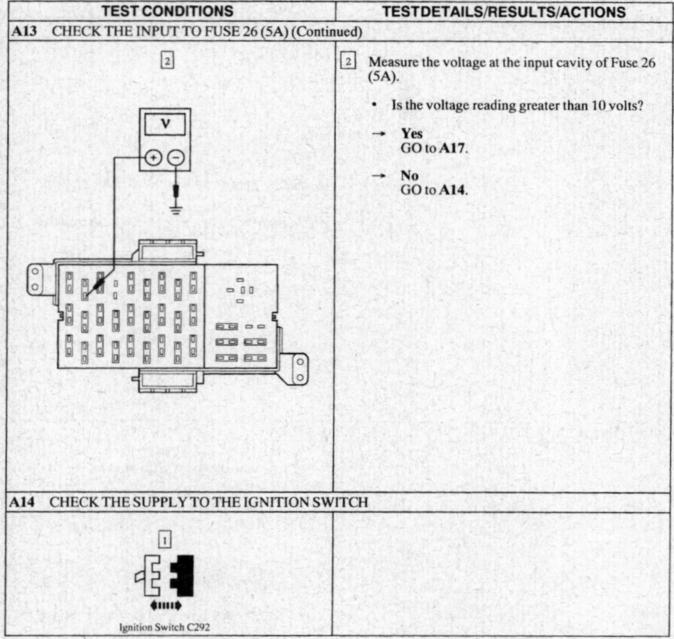

TEST CONDITIONS	TEST DETAILS/RESULTS/ACTIONS
A13 CHECK THE INPUT TO FUSE 26 (5A) (Continued)	
2	2 Measure the voltage at the input cavity of Fuse 26 (5A). • Is the voltage reading greater than 10 volts? → **Yes** GO to **A17**. → **No** GO to **A14**.
A14 CHECK THE SUPPLY TO THE IGNITION SWITCH	
1 Ignition Switch C292	

FM1120100683070X

Fig. 73 Test A: Engine does not crank (Part 7 of 12). 1999–2002 Town Car

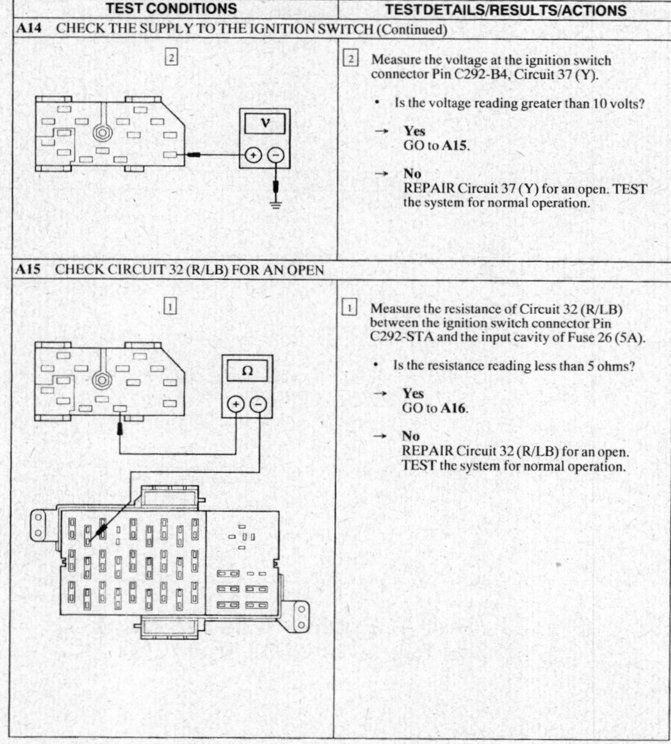

TEST CONDITIONS	TEST DETAILS/RESULTS/ACTIONS
A14 CHECK THE SUPPLY TO THE IGNITION SWITCH (Continued)	
2	2 Measure the voltage at the ignition switch connector Pin C292-B4, Circuit 37 (Y). • Is the voltage reading greater than 10 volts? → **Yes** GO to **A15**. → **No** REPAIR Circuit 37 (Y) for an open. TEST the system for normal operation.
A15 CHECK CIRCUIT 32 (R/LB) FOR AN OPEN	
1	1 Measure the resistance of Circuit 32 (R/LB) between the ignition switch connector Pin C292-STA and the input cavity of Fuse 26 (5A). • Is the resistance reading less than 5 ohms? → **Yes** GO to **A16**. → **No** REPAIR Circuit 32 (R/LB) for an open. TEST the system for normal operation.

FM1120100683080X

Fig. 73 Test A: Engine does not crank (Part 8 of 12). 1999–2002 Town Car

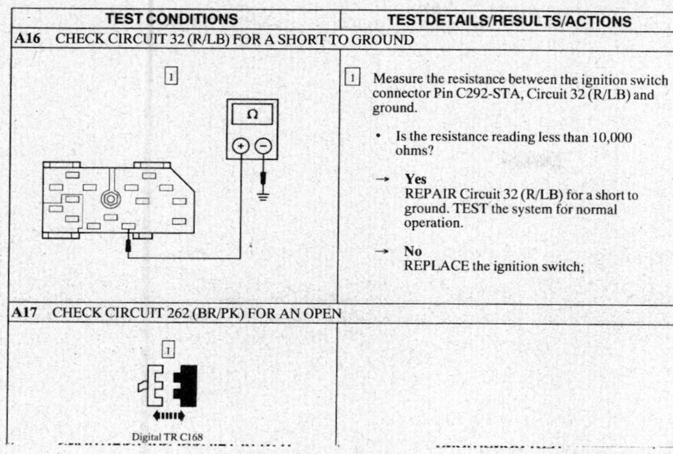

TEST CONDITIONS	TEST DETAILS/RESULTS/ACTIONS
A16 CHECK CIRCUIT 32 (R/LB) FOR A SHORT TO GROUND	
1	1 Measure the resistance between the ignition switch connector Pin C292-STA, Circuit 32 (R/LB) and ground. • Is the resistance reading less than 10,000 ohms? → **Yes** REPAIR Circuit 32 (R/LB) for a short to ground. TEST the system for normal operation. → **No** REPLACE the ignition switch;
A17 CHECK CIRCUIT 262 (BR/PK) FOR AN OPEN	
1 Digital TR C168	

FM1120100683090X

Fig. 73 Test A: Engine does not crank (Part 9 of 12). 1999–2002 Town Car

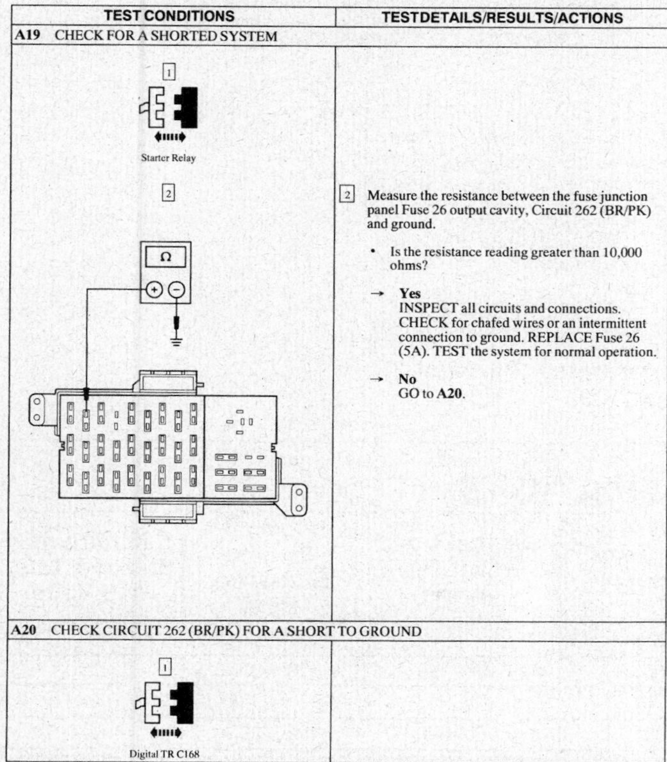

TEST CONDITIONS	TEST DETAILS/RESULTS/ACTIONS
A19 CHECK FOR A SHORTED SYSTEM	
1 Starter Relay 2	2 Measure the resistance between the fuse junction panel Fuse 26 output cavity, Circuit 262 (BR/PK) and ground. • Is the resistance reading greater than 10,000 ohms? → **Yes** INSPECT all circuits and connections. CHECK for chafed wires or an intermittent connection to ground. REPLACE Fuse 26 (5A). TEST the system for normal operation. → **No** GO to **A20**.
A20 CHECK CIRCUIT 262 (BR/PK) FOR A SHORT TO GROUND	
1 Digital TR C168	

FM1120100683110X

Fig. 73 Test A: Engine does not crank (Part 11 of 12). 1999–2002 Town Car

TEST CONDITIONS	TEST DETAILS/RESULTS/ACTIONS
B1 CHECK THE STARTER MOUNTING	
	1 Inspect the starter motor mounting bolts and brackets for looseness. • Is the starter motor mounted properly? → **Yes** GO to **B2**. → **No** INSTALL the starter motor properly; TEST the system for normal operation.

FM1120100684010X

Fig. 74 Test B: Unusual starter noise (Part 1 of 2). 1999–2002 Town Car

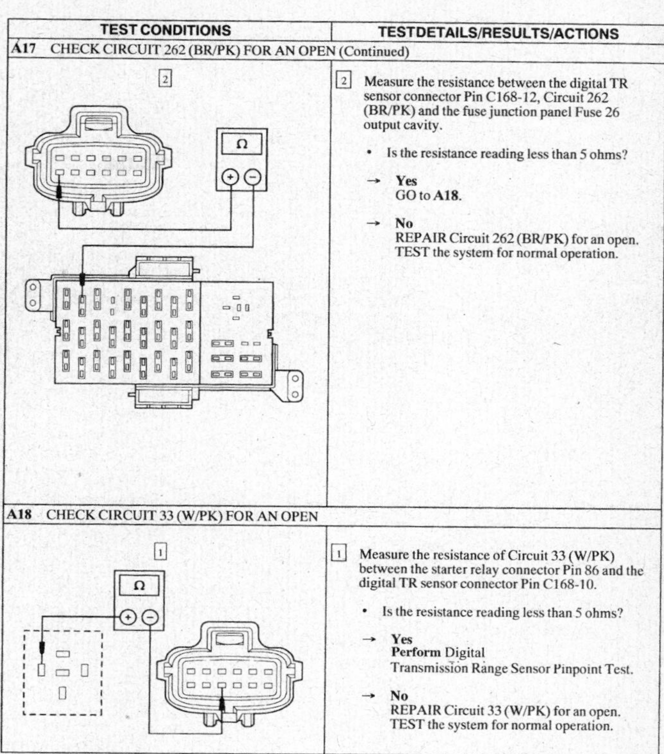

TEST CONDITIONS	TEST DETAILS/RESULTS/ACTIONS
A17 CHECK CIRCUIT 262 (BR/PK) FOR AN OPEN (Continued)	
2	2 Measure the resistance between the digital TR sensor connector Pin C168-12, Circuit 262 (BR/PK) and the fuse junction panel Fuse 26 output cavity. • Is the resistance reading less than 5 ohms? → **Yes** GO to **A18**. → **No** REPAIR Circuit 262 (BR/PK) for an open. TEST the system for normal operation.
A18 CHECK CIRCUIT 33 (W/PK) FOR AN OPEN	
1	1 Measure the resistance of Circuit 33 (W/PK) between the starter relay connector Pin 86 and the digital TR sensor connector Pin C168-10. • Is the resistance reading less than 5 ohms? → **Yes** **Perform** Digital Transmission Range Sensor Pinpoint Test. → **No** REPAIR Circuit 33 (W/PK) for an open. TEST the system for normal operation.

FM1120100683100X

Fig. 73 Test A: Engine does not crank (Part 10 of 12). 1999–2002 Town Car

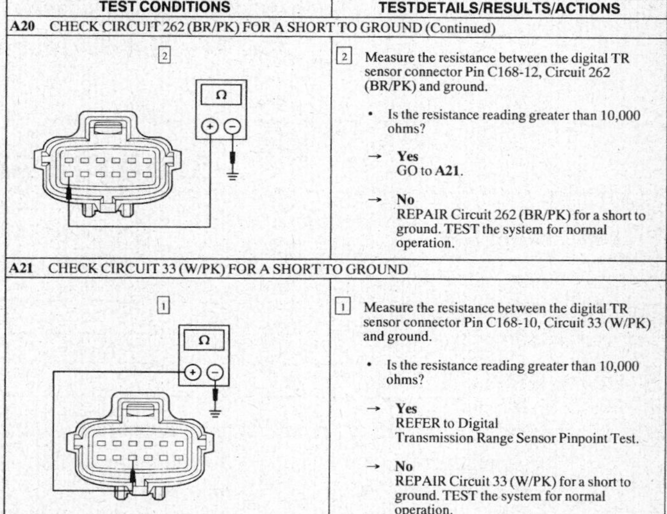

TEST CONDITIONS	TEST DETAILS/RESULTS/ACTIONS
A20 CHECK CIRCUIT 262 (BR/PK) FOR A SHORT TO GROUND (Continued)	
2	2 Measure the resistance between the digital TR sensor connector Pin C168-12, Circuit 262 (BR/PK) and ground. • Is the resistance reading greater than 10,000 ohms? → **Yes** GO to **A21**. → **No** REPAIR Circuit 262 (BR/PK) for a short to ground. TEST the system for normal operation.
A21 CHECK CIRCUIT 33 (W/PK) FOR A SHORT TO GROUND	
1	1 Measure the resistance between the digital TR sensor connector Pin C168-10, Circuit 33 (W/PK) and ground. • Is the resistance reading greater than 10,000 ohms? → **Yes** REFER to Digital Transmission Range Sensor Pinpoint Test. → **No** REPAIR Circuit 33 (W/PK) for a short to ground. TEST the system for normal operation.

FM1120100683120X

Fig. 73 Test A: Engine does not crank (Part 12 of 12). 1999–2002 Town Car

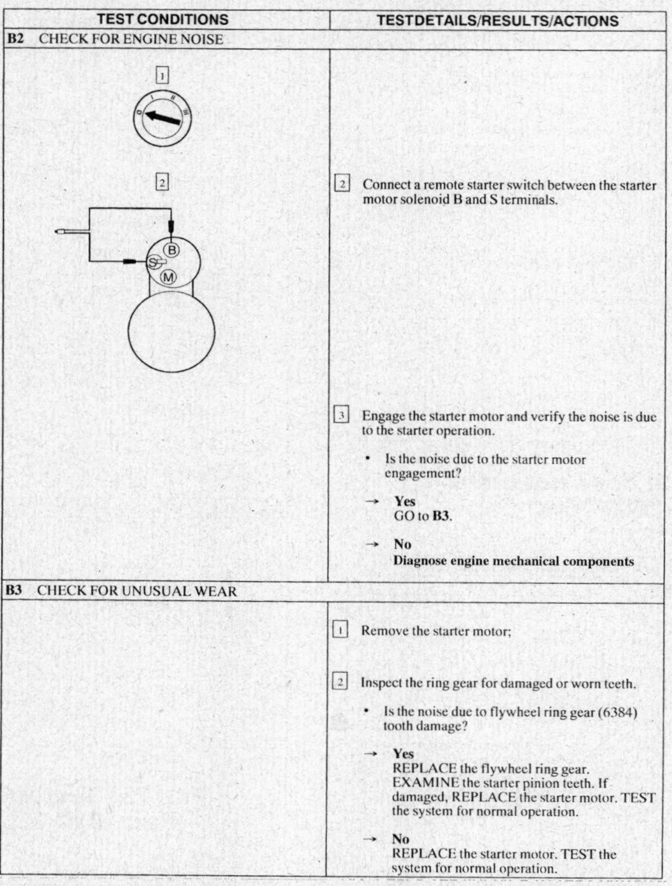

TEST CONDITIONS	TESTDETAILS/RESULTS/ACTIONS
B2 CHECK FOR ENGINE NOISE	
1	
2	2 Connect a remote starter switch between the starter motor solenoid B and S terminals.
	3 Engage the starter motor and verify the noise is due to the starter operation. • Is the noise due to the starter motor engagement? → **Yes** GO to **B3**. → **No** **Diagnose engine mechanical components**
B3 CHECK FOR UNUSUAL WEAR	
	1 Remove the starter motor; 2 Inspect the ring gear for damaged or worn teeth. • Is the noise due to flywheel ring gear (6384) tooth damage? → **Yes** REPLACE the flywheel ring gear. EXAMINE the starter pinion teeth. If damaged, REPLACE the starter motor. TEST the system for normal operation. → **No** REPLACE the starter motor. TEST the system for normal operation.

FM1120100684020X

Fig. 74 Test B: Unusual starter noise (Part 2 of 2). 1999–2002 Town Car

STARTER SPECIFICATIONS

Starter Frame Dia., Inch	Brush Spring Tension, Ounces	No Load, Amps	Max Load, Amps	Normal Load Current Draw, Amps	Normal Engine Cranking, RPM	Minimum Stall, Ft. Lbs. @ 5 Volts
ESCORT, TRACER & ZX2						
3.0	64	60–80	800	130–190	200–250	10
EXCEPT ESCORT, TRACER & ZX2						
3.0	64	60–80	800	130–220	140–220	14.7

ALTERNATORS

TABLE OF CONTENTS

Ford Motorcraft Alternator

NOTE: On Air Bag Equipped Models, Refer To "Air Bag System Precautions" Located In The Front Of This Manual For System Disarming & Arming Procedures.

NOTE: Refer To "Computer Relearn Procedures" Located In The Front Of This Manual When Battery Power To The Computer Has Been Interrupted.

NOTE: "Electrical Symbol & Wire Color Code Identification" Located In The Front Of This Manual May Be Used As An Aid When Using Wiring Circuits Found In This Section.

INDEX

APPLICATION CHART

Model	Year
Continental	1998–2002
Contour	1998–2000
Cougar	1999–2002
Crown Victoria	1998–2002
Escort	1998–2002
Focus	2000–01
Grand Marquis	1998–2002
LS	2000–02
Mustang	1998–2002
Mystique	1998–2000
Sable	1998–2002
Taurus	1998–2002

Continued

APPLICATION CHART—Continued

Model	Year
Thunderbird	2002
Town Car	1998–2002
Tracer	1998–99
ZX2	1998–2002

PRECAUTIONS

AIR BAG SYSTEMS

Refer to "Air Bag System Precautions" in the front of this manual for system disarming and arming procedures.

BATTERY GROUND CABLE

Prior to service, disconnect battery ground cable and isolate as required.

GENERAL

1. Ensure proper battery polarity when servicing units. Reversed polarity will damage rectifiers and regulators.
2. If booster battery is used for starting, ensure proper polarity.
3. When a fast charger is used to charge a vehicle battery, vehicle battery cables should be disconnected unless fast charger is equipped with a special alternator protector, in which case vehicle battery cables need not be disconnected. A fast charger should never be used to start a vehicle as damage to rectifiers will result.
4. Unless system includes a load relay or field relay, grounding alternator output terminal will damage alternator and/or circuits. This is true even when system is not in operation since a circuit breaker is not used and battery voltage is applied to the alternator output terminal at all times. The field or load relay acts as a circuit breaker in that it is controlled by ignition switch.
5. Before starting any on vehicle tests of alternator or regulator, battery should be inspected and circuit inspected for faulty wiring or insulation, loose or corroded connections and poor ground circuits.
6. Ensure alternator belt tension is tight enough to prevent slipping under load.
7. To prevent damage to the system, ignition should be Off and battery ground cable disconnected before making any test connections.
8. Vehicle battery must be fully charged or a fully charged battery may be installed for test purposes.

DESCRIPTION

The electrical charging system is a negative ground system consisting of an integral alternator/voltage regulator (IGR), charge indicator, storage battery and required wiring and cables.

The "I" circuit, or ignition circuit is used to turn on the alternator regulator. This circuit is powered up with the ignition in the Run position. The circuit also turns the indicator lamp on if there is a fault in the charging system.

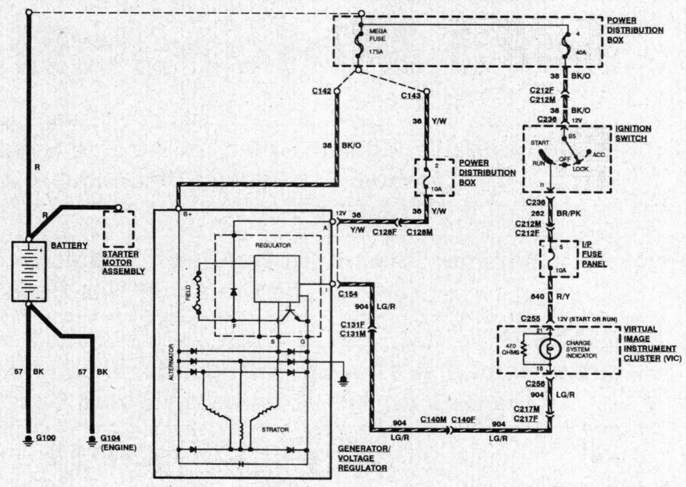

Fig. 1 Wiring diagram. 1998–2001 Continental

The "A" circuit, or the battery sense circuit, is used to sense battery voltage. This circuit also supplies power to the alternator stator and coil. With the system functioning normally, alternator output current is determined by voltage at the "A" circuit (battery sense voltage). The "A" circuit voltage is compared to a set voltage inside the regulator to maintain the proper alternator output. The set voltage will vary with temperature and is typically higher in the winter than in the summer, allowing for better battery recharge in the winter and reducing the chance of overcharging the battery in the summer.

The "S" circuit, or stator and coil circuit, is used to feed back a voltage signal from the alternator to the regulator. This voltage is typically ½ battery voltage and is used by the regulator to turn off the indicator.

If an ammeter is used in the charging system, the regulator 1 terminal and the alternator stator terminal are not used. When the ignition is turned On, the field relay closes and electrical current passes through the regulator "A" terminal and is metered to the alternator field. When the engine is started, the alternator field rotates causing the alternator to operate.

Closing the ignition switch energizes the warning lamp or ammeter and turns on the regulator output stage. The alternator receives maximum field current and is ready to generate an output voltage. As the alternator rotor speed increases, the output and stator terminal voltages increase from zero to the system regulation level determined by the regulator setting. When the ignition is turned Off, the solid state relay circuit turns the output stage off, interrupting the current flow through the regulator so there is no current drain on the battery.

DIAGNOSIS & TESTING

Wiring Diagrams

CONTINENTAL

Refer to **Fig. 1 and 2** for charging system wiring diagram.

CONTOUR & MYSTIQUE

Refer to **Figs. 3 through 5** for charging system wiring diagrams.

COUGAR

Refer to **Figs. 6 through 10** for charging system wiring diagrams.

CROWN VICTORIA & GRAND MARQUIS

Refer to **Figs. 11 and 12** for charging system wiring diagram.

ESCORT, TRACER & ZX2

Refer to **Fig. 13** for charging system wiring diagram.

FOCUS

Refer to **Figs. 14 and 15** for charging system wiring diagrams.

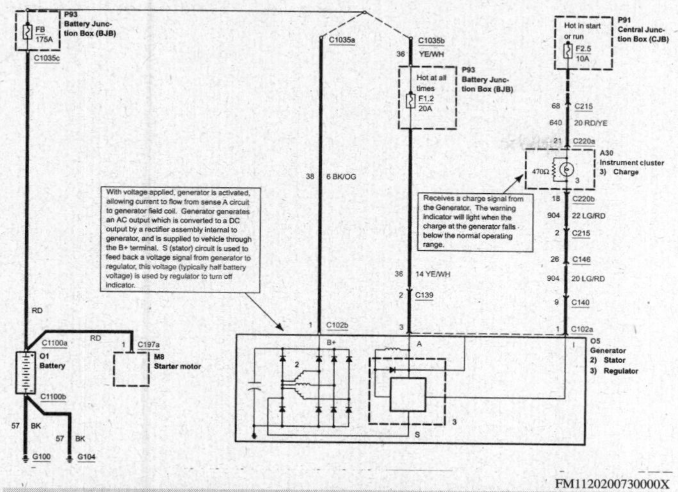

Fig. 2 Wiring diagram. 2002 Continental

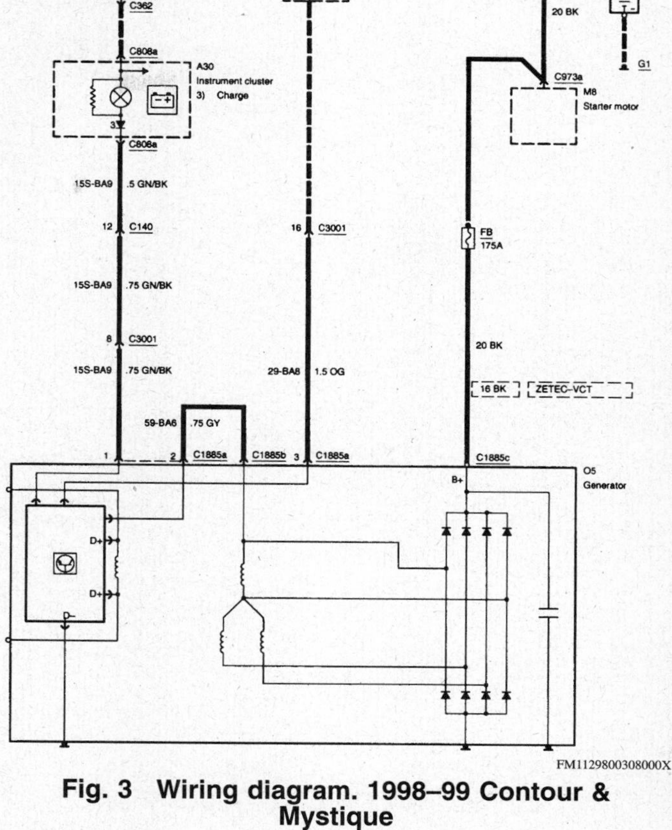

Fig. 3 Wiring diagram. 1998–99 Contour & Mystique

LS

Refer to **Fig. 16** for charging system wiring diagram.

MUSTANG

Refer to **Figs. 17 through 20** for charging system wiring diagrams.

SABLE & TAURUS

Refer to **Figs. 21 through 24** for charging system wiring diagrams.

THUNDERBIRD

Refer to **Figs. 26** for charging system wiring diagrams.

TOWN CAR

Refer to **Figs. 27 through 29** for charging system wiring diagrams.

Diagnostic Tests

CONTINENTAL

Refer to **Fig. 30 and 31** for symptom charts and **Figs. 32 through 51** for diagnostic tests.

CONTOUR & MYSTIQUE

Refer to **Fig. 52** for symptom charts and **Figs. 53 through 60** for diagnostic tests.

COUGAR

DIAGNOSIS BY SYMPTOM

Charging System Warning Indicator Is On, Intermittent Or Flickers w/Engine Running

1. Possible sources are as follows:
   a. Accessory drive belt.
   b. Fuse No. 7 (20A).
   c. Wiring circuit.
   d. Alternator.

Refer to "Pinpoint test A."

Charging System Warning Indicator Is Off w/Ignition In Run Position & Engine Off

1. Possible sources are as follows:
   a. Bulb.
   b. Circuit.
   c. Alternator.

Radio Interference

1. Possible sources are as follows:
   a. Circuit.
   b. Alternator.

Refer to "Pinpoint Test B: Radio Interference."

System Overcharges

1. Possible sources are as follows:
   a. Alternator.

PINPOINT TEST A: CHARGING SYSTEM WARNING INDICATOR IS ON w/ENGINE RUNNING

Test A1: Inspect Battery

1. Inspect battery capacity.
2. If battery capacity is not at normal operating range, replace battery.
3. Inspect system once again.

Test A2: Inspect Charging System

1. Perform load test as described in this section.
2. If alternator output is not as specified, refer to "Test A3: Inspect For A Good Ground."

Test A3: Inspect For A Good Ground

1. Measure voltage between alternator case and battery ground terminal.
2. If voltage is less than .5 volts, refer to "Test A4: Inspect Battery Cable."
3. If voltage is more than .5 volts, clean and tighten alternator mounting bolts, engine to body ground strap and battery round cable.
4. Inspect system again for normal operation.
5. If voltage is still not as specified, replace battery ground cable.

Test A4: Inspect Battery Cable

1. Measure voltage between alternator B+ terminal and battery positive terminal. Voltage should be less than .5 volts.
2. If voltage is as specified, refer to "Test A5: Inspect Battery Feed To The Alternator."

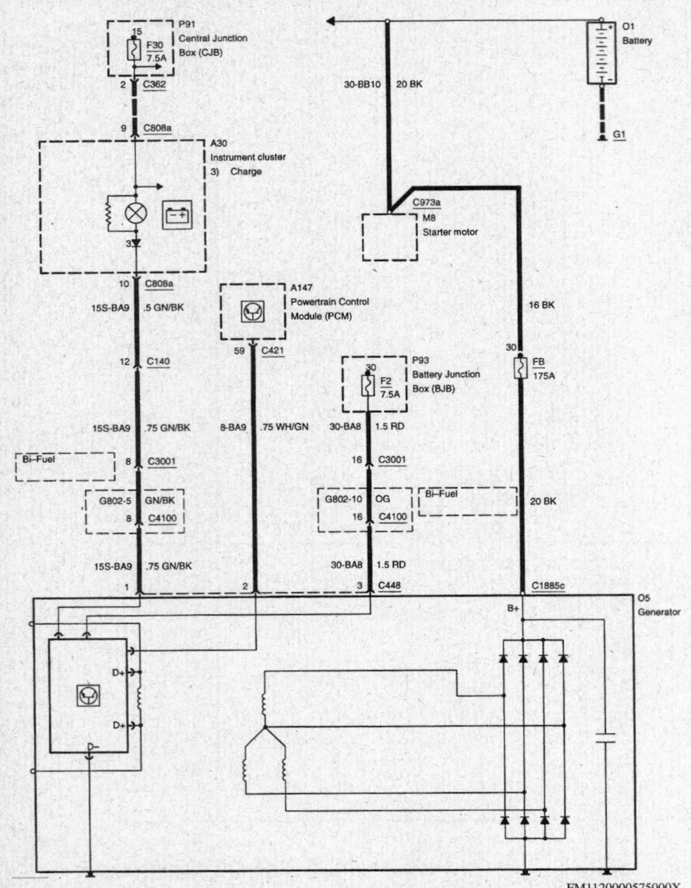

Fig. 4 Wiring diagram. 2000 Contour & Mystique w/2.0L engine

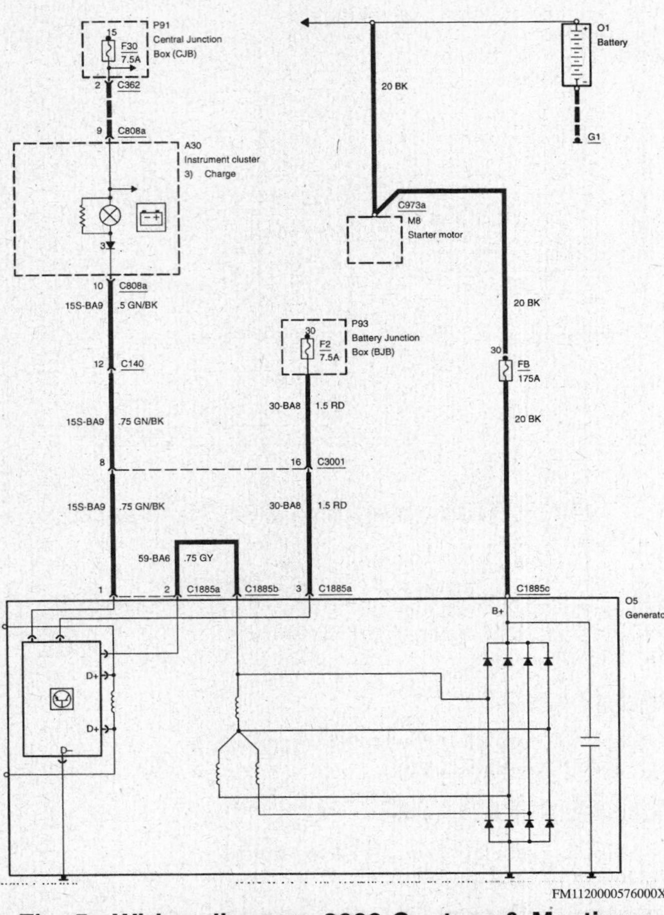

Fig. 5 Wiring diagram. 2000 Contour & Mystique w/2.5L engine

3. If voltage is not as specified, clean and tighten battery positive cable connections.
4. Inspect system operation. If voltage is still not as specified, replace battery positive cable.

Test A5: Inspect Battery Feed To The Alternator

1. Measure voltage between alternator B+ terminal and ground. Battery voltage should be present.
2. If voltage is as specified, refer to "Test A6: Inspect Power To The Voltage Regulator."
3. If voltage is not as specified, inspect fusible link FB 175A.
4. Inspect system operation again. If voltage is not as specified, repair battery positive cable.

Test A6: Inspect Power To Voltage Regulator

1. Measure voltage between alternator connector pin No. 3 harness side and ground. There should be 10 volts or more present.
2. If voltage is as specified, proceed as follows:
   a. **On models with 2.0L engine,** replace alternator and inspect system once again.
   b. **On models with 2.5L engine,** refer to "Test A7: Charging System Warning Indicator Is On w/The Engine Running."

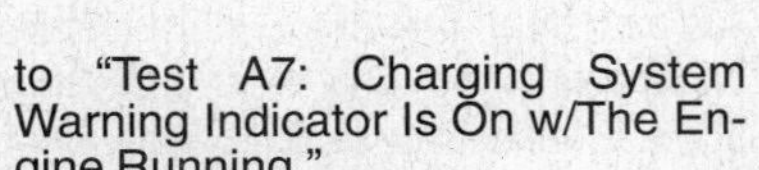

3. **On all models,** if voltage is not as specified, inspect fuse No. F7 and charging system once again.

Inspect Output Feedback To Regulator

1. Measure resistance between alternator connector pin No. 2 harness side and pin No. 1 harness side. Resistance should be less than 5 ohms.
2. If resistance is as specified, replace alternator and inspect system once again.
3. If resistance is not as specified, repair circuit and inspect system once again.

PINPOINT TEST B: RADIO INTERFERENCE

Test B1: Isolate The Alternator

1. Remove accessory drive belt.
2. Run engine for a few seconds with radio turned on.
3. If radio interference is still present, inspect audio entertainment system for malfunctions.
4. If radio interference is not present, clean and tighten battery clamps and alternator mounting bolts.
5. If interference is still present, replace alternator.

CROWN VICTORIA & GRAND MARQUIS

Refer to **Figs. 61 and 62** for symptom charts and **Figs. 63 through 86** for diagnostic tests.

ESCORT & TRACER

Refer to **Fig. 87** for symptom chart and **Figs. 88 through 94** for diagnostic tests.

FOCUS

DIAGNOSIS BY SYMPTOM

Charging System Warning Indicator Is On w/Engine Running

1. Possible sources are as follows:
   a. Accessory drive belt.
   b. Battery junction box fuse No. 10 (10A).
   c. Wiring circuit.
   d. Alternator.

   Refer to "Pinpoint test A."

Charging System Warning Indicator Is Off w/Ignition On & Engine Off

1. Possible sources are as follows:

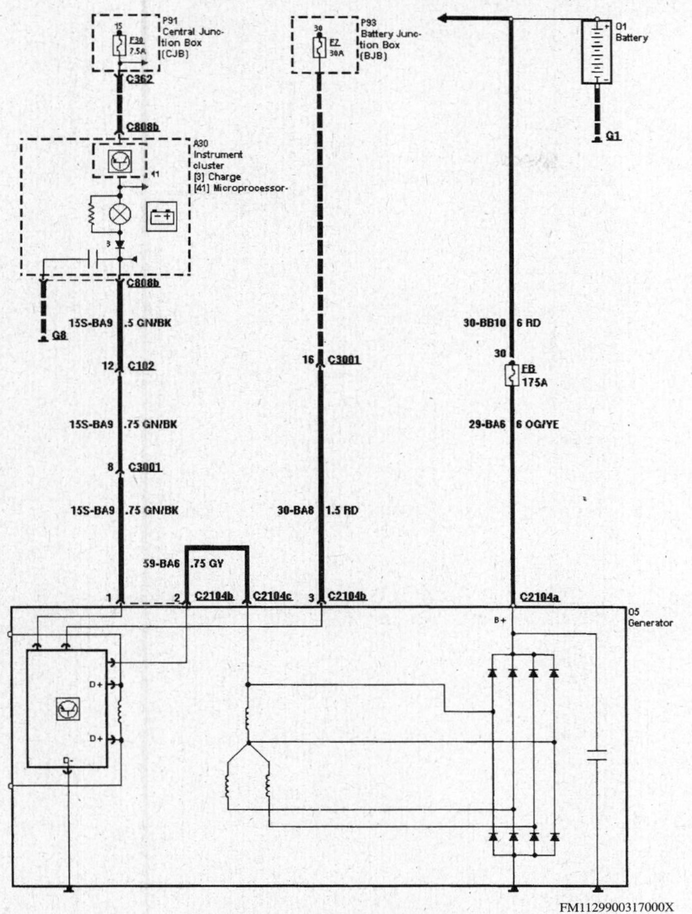

Fig. 6 Wiring diagram. 1999 Cougar

FM1120000574000X

Fig. 7 Wiring diagram. 2000 Cougar w/2.0L engine

 a. Bulb.
 b. Circuit.
 c. Alternator.

Radio Interference

1. Possible sources are as follows:
 a. Circuit.
 b. Alternator.

Refer to "Pinpoint Test B."

System Overcharges

1. Possible sources are as follows:
 a. Alternator.

PINPOINT TEST A: CHARGING SYSTEM WARNING INDICATOR IS ON w/ENGINE RUNNING

Test A1: Inspect Battery

1. Inspect battery capacity.
2. If battery capacity is not at normal operating range, replace battery.
3. Inspect system once again.

Test A2: Inspect Charging System

1. Perform load test as outlined in this section.
2. If alternator output is not as specified, refer to "Test A3: Inspect For A Good Ground."

Test A3: Inspect For A Good Ground

1. Measure voltage between alternator case and battery ground terminal.
2. If voltage is less than .5 volts, refer to "Test A4: Inspect Battery Cable."
3. If voltage is more than .5 volts, clean and tighten alternator mounting bolts, engine to body ground strap and battery ground cable.
4. Inspect system again for normal operation.
5. If voltage is still not as specified, replace battery ground cable.

Test A4: Inspect Battery Cable

1. Measure voltage between alternator B+ terminal and battery positive terminal. Voltage should be less than .5 volts.
2. If voltage is as specified, refer to "Test A5: Inspect Battery Feed To Alternator."
3. If voltage is not as specified, clean and tighten battery positive cable connections.
4. Inspect system operation. If voltage is still not as specified, replace battery positive cable.

Test A5: Inspect Battery Feed To Alternator

1. Measure voltage between alternator B+ terminal and ground. Battery voltage should be present.
2. If voltage is as specified, refer to "Test A6: Inspect Power To Voltage Regulator."
3. If voltage is not as specified, inspect fusible links and fuses and replace as required.
4. Inspect system operation again. If voltage is not as specified, repair battery positive cable.

Test A6: Inspect Power To Voltage Regulator

1. Measure voltage between alternator connector pin No. 3 harness side and ground. Battery voltage should be present.
2. If voltage is as specified, replace alternator and inspect system once again.
3. If voltage is not as specified, inspect fuse No. F10 and repair circuit 30-BA10.

PINPOINT TEST B: RADIO INTERFERENCE

Test B1: Isolate The Alternator

1. Remove accessory drive belt.
2. Run engine for a few seconds with radio turned on.
3. If radio interference is still present, inspect audio entertainment system for malfunctions.

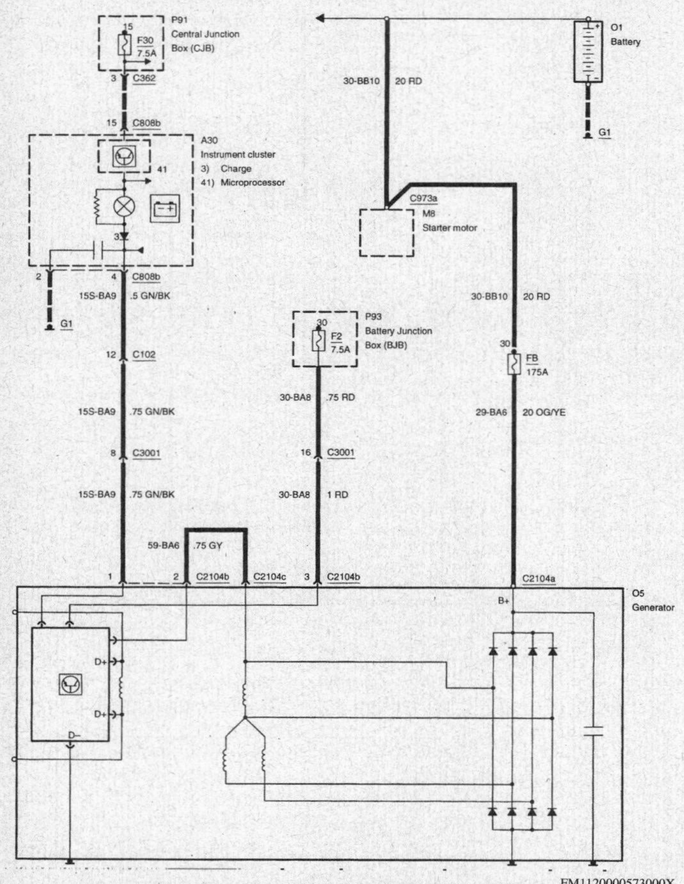

Fig. 8 Wiring diagram. 2000 Cougar w/2.5L engine

Fig. 9 Wiring diagram. 2001 Cougar w/2.0L engine

4. If radio interference is not present, clean and tighten battery clamps and alternator mounting bolts.
5. If interference is still present, replace alternator.

LS & THUNDERBIRD

Refer to **Figs. 95** for symptom chart and **Figs. 96 through 103** for diagnostic tests.

MUSTANG

Refer to **Figs. 104 through 107** for symptom charts and **Figs. 108 through 138** for diagnostic tests.

SABLE & TAURUS

Refer to **Fig. 139 through 140** for symptom chart and **Figs. 141 through 163** for diagnostic tests.

TOWN CAR

Refer to **Fig. 164 through 165** for symptom charts and **Figs. 166 through 185** for diagnostic tests.

No-Load Test

EXCEPT CONTINENTAL, SABLE, TAURUS & TOWN CAR

1. Connect voltmeter leads across battery terminals.
2. Read and record voltage. This value is the base voltage.
3. Start engine and monitor engine speed.
4. Run engine at 1500 RPM with no electrical load.
5. Read voltage, noting the following:
   a. Voltage should be 14.1–15.1 volts.
   b. If voltage increase is less than 2.5 volts over base voltage, refer to "Load Test" in this section.
   c. If there is no voltage increase or voltage increase is greater than 2.5 volts, refer to "Diagnostic Tests" in this section.

CONTINENTAL, SABLE, TAURUS & TOWN CAR

To inspect charging system, use Rotunda alternator tester tool No. 010-00725, or equivalent.

1. Switch Rotunda alternator tester to voltmeter function.
2. Connect voltmeter positive lead to alternator B+ terminal and negative lead to ground.
3. Turn all electrical accessories off.
4. With engine running at 2000 RPM, measure alternator output voltage, which should be between 13 and 15 volts. If voltage is not as specified, refer to "Diagnostic Tests" in this section.

Load Test

EXCEPT CONTINENTAL & TOWN CAR

1. Connect leads of voltmeter across battery terminals.
2. Read and record voltage. This value is the base voltage.
3. With engine running, turn on air conditioner, set blower motor to high speed and headlamps to high beam position.
4. Increase engine speed to approximately 2000 RPM, noting the following:
   a. Voltage should increase a minimum of .5 volts above base voltage.
   b. If voltage does not increase, refer to "Diagnostic Tests" in this section.
   c. If voltage increases as specified, charging system is operating properly.

CONTINENTAL & TOWN CAR

To inspect charging system, use Rotunda alternator tester tool No. 010-00725, or equivalent.

1. Turn off all lamps and electrical components.

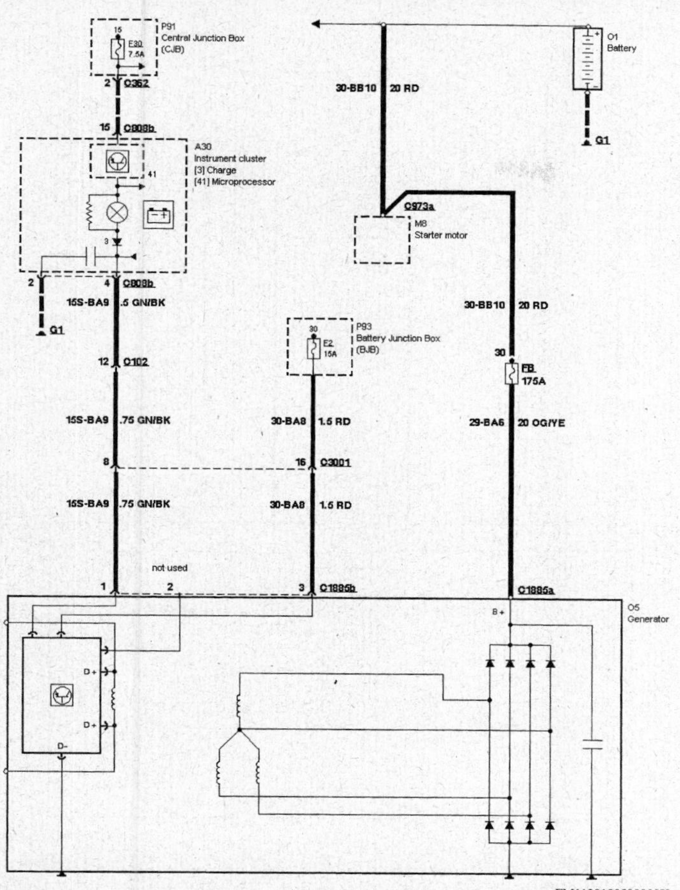

Fig. 10 Wiring diagram. 2001 Cougar w/2.5L engine

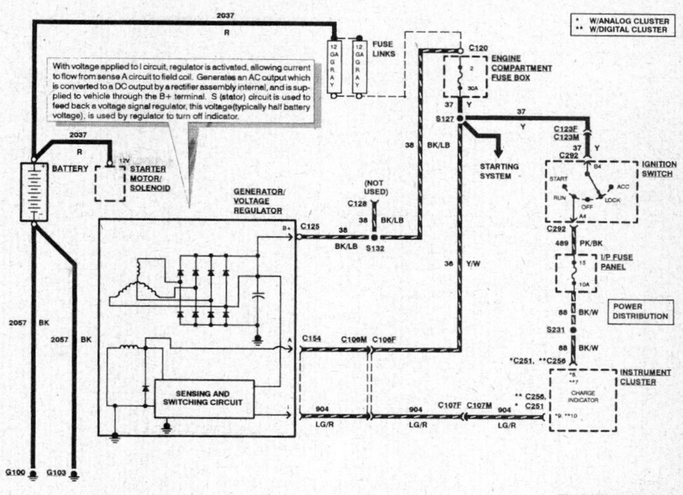

Fig. 11 Wiring diagram. 1998–2001 Crown Victoria & Grand Marquis

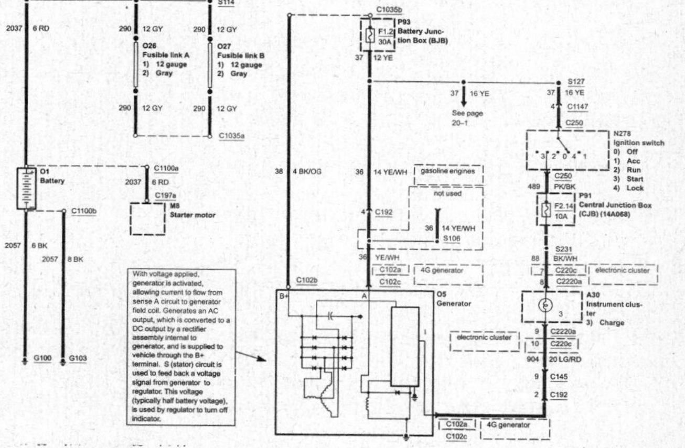

Fig. 12 Wiring diagram. 2002 Crown Victoria & Grand Marquis

2. Apply parking brake, then place transmission in Neutral position.
3. Switch alternator tester to ammeter function.
4. Connect tester positive and negative leads to battery.
5. Connect current probe to alternator B+ output lead.
6. With engine running at 2000 RPM, adjust tester load bank to determine output of alternator, noting the following:
   a. **On 1998–2002 Continental,** alternator output should be greater than 87 amps at 2000 RPM.
   b. **On 1998 Town Car,** alternator output should be greater than 107 amps at 2000 RPM.
   c. **On all models,** if alternator output is not as specified, refer to "Diagnostic Tests" in this section.

Drain Test

A periodic pulsing of up to 80 mA (0.080 amp) is caused by the integrated control panel (ICP) and is considered normal, but no production vehicle should have a continuous draw of more than 50 mA (0.050 amp).

Inspect for current drains on battery in excess of 50 milliamperes with all the electrical accessories off and the vehicle at rest. This test can be performed in three ways. **Do not perform these tests on a recently recharged lead-acid battery. Explosive gases can cause personal injury.**

CLAMP ON DC AMMETER TEST

1. Connect a 12 volt test lamp in series with battery positive terminal. If test lamp glows, a drain exists.
2. Use a clamp type current probe to battery positive or ground terminal. Ensure probe is properly calibrated to prevent false readings.
3. Connect an inline ammeter between battery positive or ground post and its respective cable.
4. Turn ignition Off.
5. Ensure all electrical loads are off.
6. Ensure engine compartment lamp operates properly, then disconnect lamp.
7. Clamp meter clip securely around positive or negative battery cable. **Do not start vehicle with clip on cable.**
8. Record current reading, noting the following:
   a. Current reading should be less than .05 amp.
   b. If current reading exceeds .05 amps, it indicates a constant drain which could cause a discharged battery.
   c. Possible sources of current drain are vehicle lamps such as engine compartment lamp, glove compartment lamp or luggage compartment lamp.
9. If drain is not caused by vehicle lamps, remove fuses one at a time until cause of drain is located.
10. If drain is still undetermined, disconnect leads at starter relay one at a time to find offending circuit.

INLINE MULTIMETER TEST

This test will require a digital volt amp ohmmeter with an appropriate ampere scale.

1. Drive vehicle at least five minutes over 30 mph to turn on and exercise all vehicle systems.
2. Turn ignition Off.
3. Allow vehicle to sit with key off at least 40 minutes. This will allow modules to time out and power down.

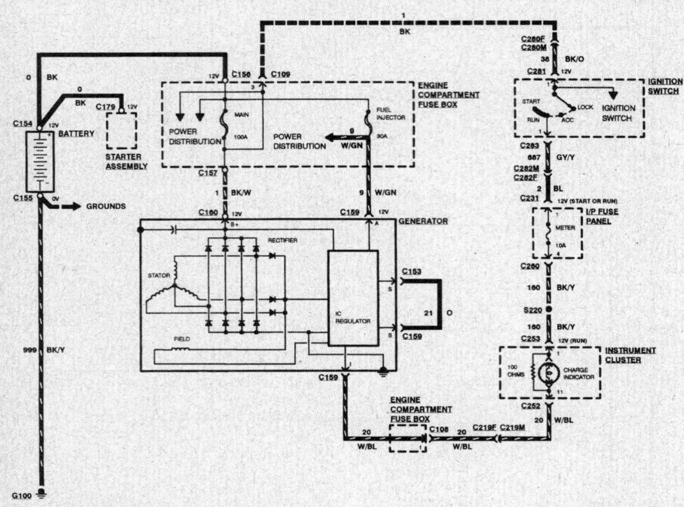

Fig. 13 Wiring diagram. Escort, Tracer & ZX2

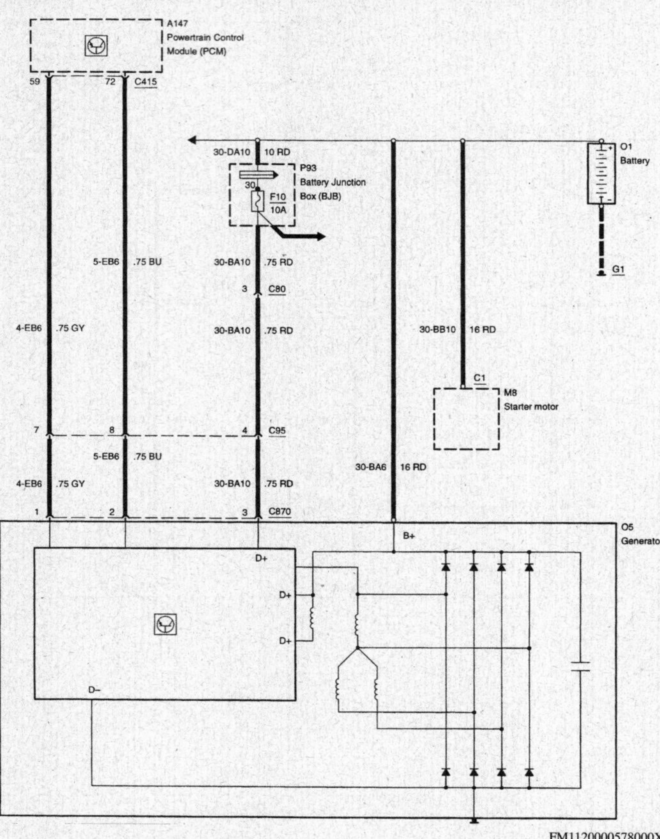

Fig. 14 Wiring diagram. Focus w/2.0L SPI engine

4. Ensure all electrical loads are turned off.
5. Connect a fused jumper wire between battery ground cable and negative battery post to prevent modules from resetting and to catch capacitive drains.
6. Disconnect battery ground cable from post without breaking jumper wire connection.
7. Ensure engine compartment lamp operates properly, then disconnect lamp.
8. Measure battery voltage, and if less than 11.5 volts, charge battery to above 11.5 volts.
9. **Do not crank engine with ammeter connected.** Set ammeter to DC amperage scale, noting the following:
   a. Current reading should be less than .05 amp.
   b. If reading is between .2 and .9 amp, a drain may be present.
   c. Possible sources of current drain are vehicle lamps such as engine compartment lamp, glove compartment lamp or luggage compartment lamp.
10. If drain is not caused by vehicle lamps, remove fuses one at a time until cause is located.
11. If cause of drain is still undetermined, disconnect leads at starter relay one at a time to find offending circuit.

ELECTRONIC DRAINS WHICH SHUT OFF w/BATTERY CABLE DISCONNECTED TEST

1. Perform "Inline Multimeter Test" as outlined previously.
2. Ensure all doors are closed and accessories are turned off.
3. Turn ignition to Run for a moment without starting engine, then turn ignition Off.
4. **On models equipped with Illuminated Entry Lamps,** wait a few minutes for those lamps to turn off.
5. **On all models,** connect ammeter and note amperage drain.
6. Current drain reading should not exceed 50 mA (0.05 amp). If drain exceeds specifications after a few minutes, and if this drain did not appear in previous tests, it is most likely due to an inoperative electronic component. Remove fuses from battery/central junction box one at a time as in previous tests to locate offending circuit.

BATTERY CABLE DISCONNECTED TEST

1. Connect a 12 volt test lamp in series with battery positive terminal. If test lamp glows, a drain exists.
2. Use a clamp type current probe to battery positive or ground terminal. Ensure probe is properly calibrated to prevent false readings.
3. Connect an inline ammeter between battery positive or ground post and its respective cable.
4. Without starting engine, turn ignition On for a few seconds, then Off.
5. **On models equipped with Illuminated Entry Lamps,** wait one minute for those lamps to turn off.
6. **On all models,** connect ammeter and read amperage, noting the following:
   a. Current reading should be less than .05 amp.
   b. If reading exceeds .05 amp after a few minutes and drain did not show up in previous tests, drain is most likely caused by a faulty electronic component.
7. Remove fuses and disconnect starter leads one at a time to locate offending circuit.

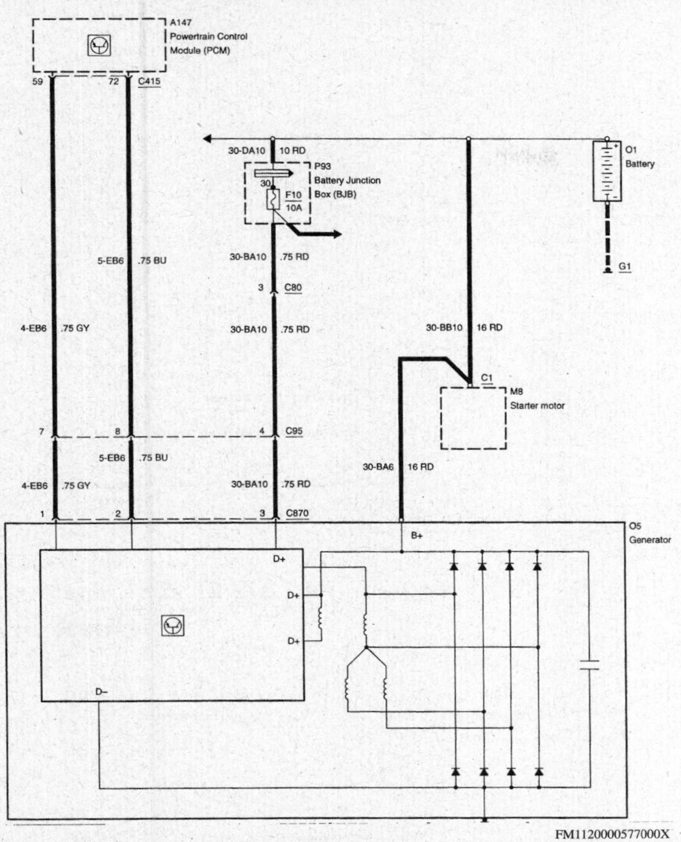

Fig. 15 Wiring diagram. Focus w/2.0L Zetec engine

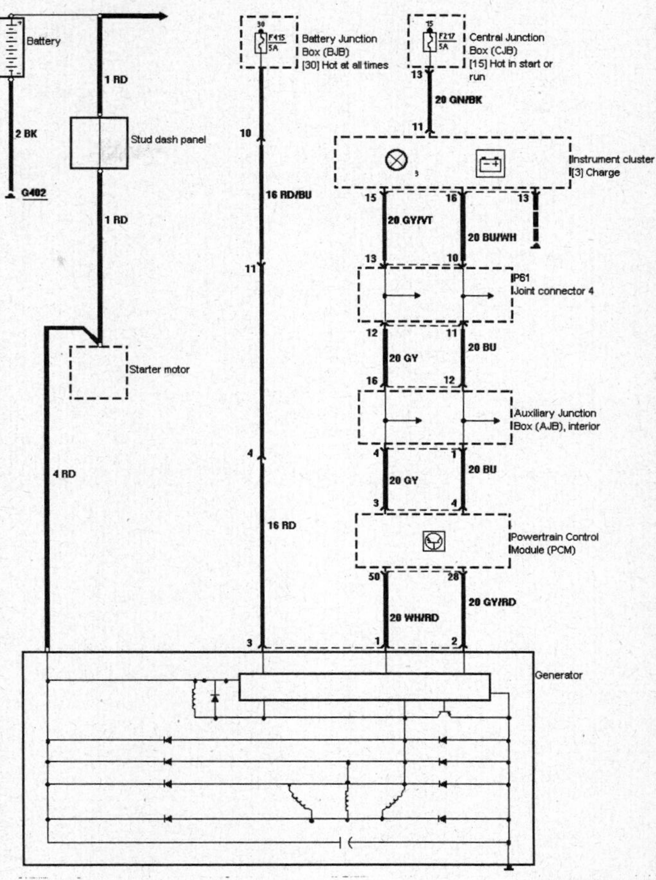

Fig. 16 Wiring diagram. LS

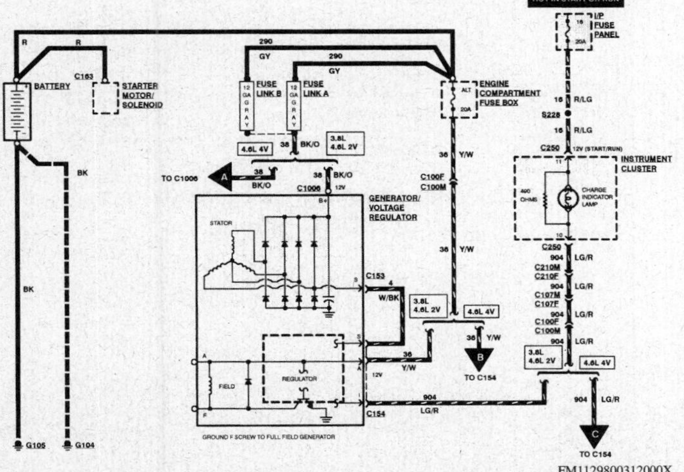

Fig. 17 Wiring diagram. 1998 Mustang

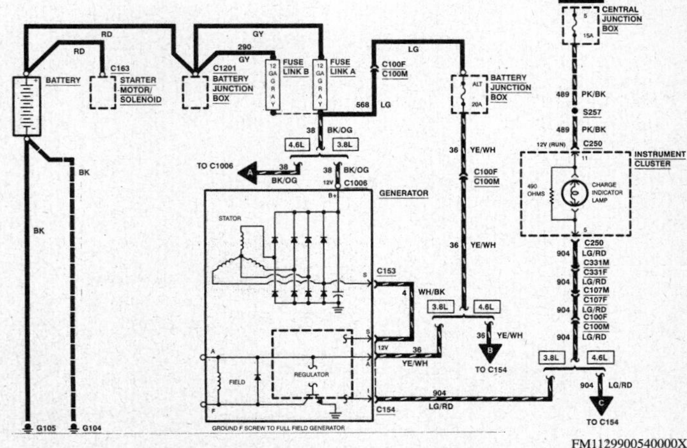

Fig. 18 Wiring diagram. 1999–2000 Mustang

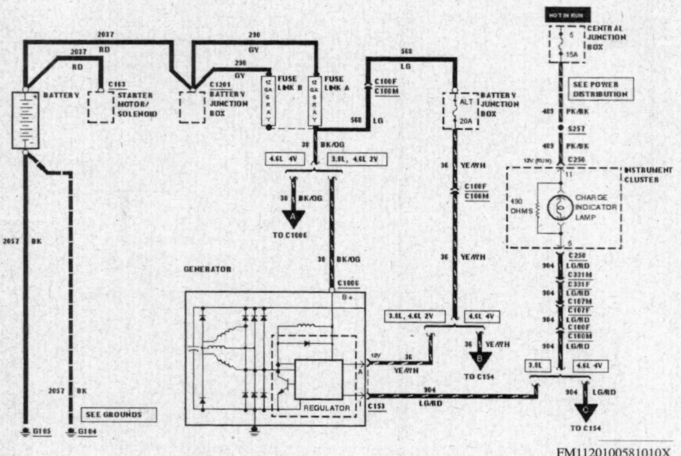

FM1120100581010X

Fig. 19 Wiring diagram (Part 1 of 2). 2001 Mustang

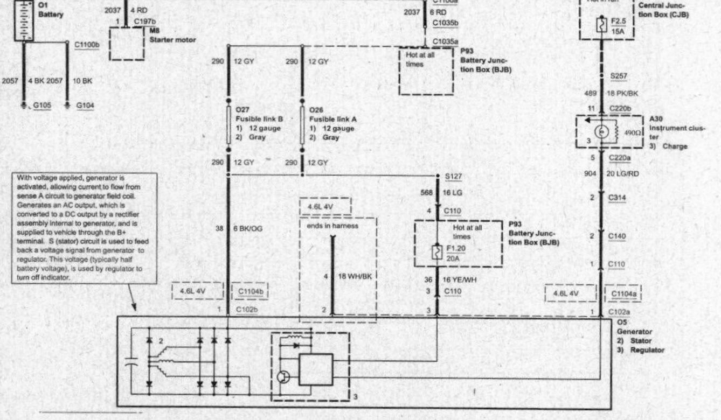

FM1120200728000X

Fig. 20 Wiring diagram. 2002 Mustang

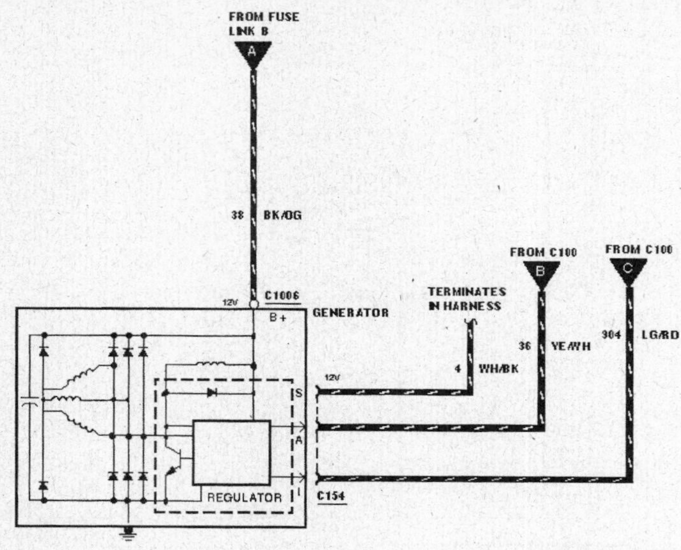

FM1120100581020X

Fig. 19 Wiring diagram (Part 2 of 2). 2001 Mustang

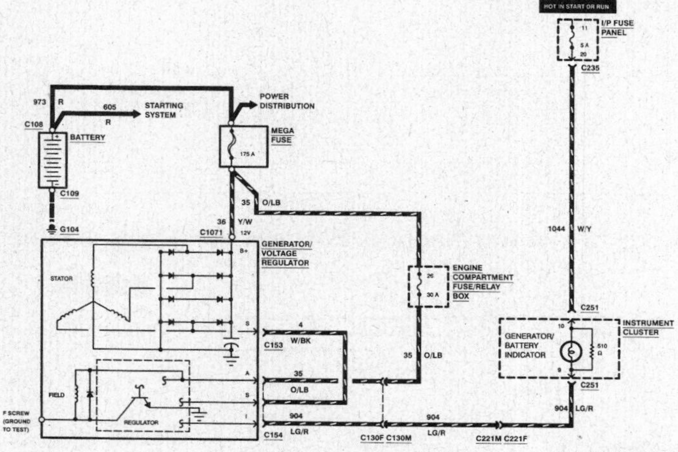

FM1129800309000X

Fig. 21 Wiring diagram. 1998–99 Sable & Taurus w/3.0L SOHC engine

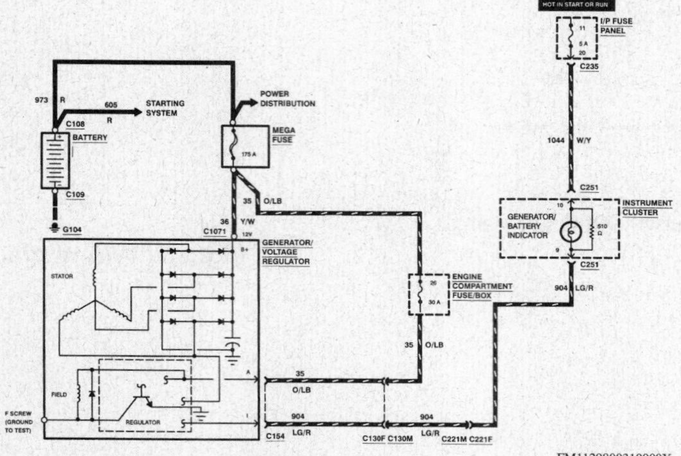

FM1129800310000X

Fig. 22 Wiring diagram. 1998–99 Sable & Taurus w/3.0L DOHC & 3.4L engines

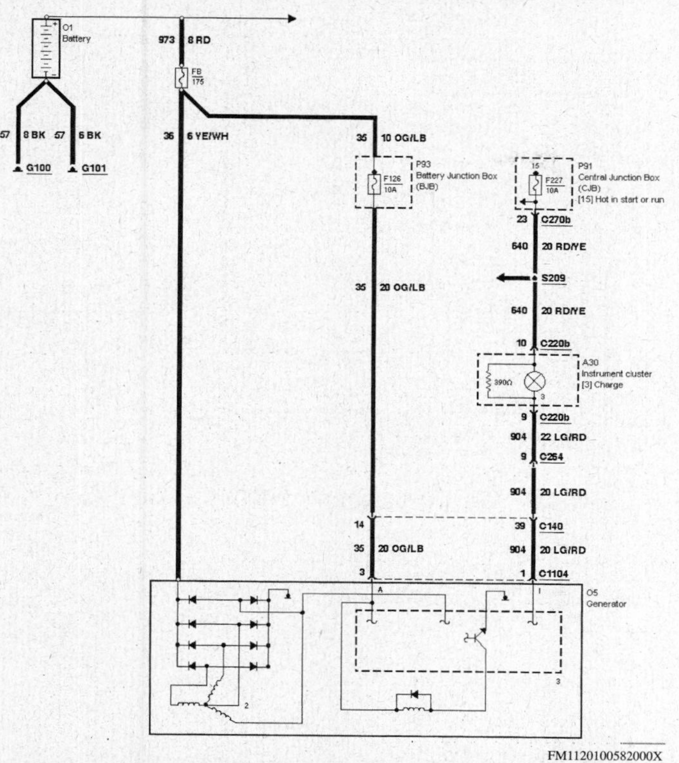

Fig. 23 Wiring diagram. 2000–01 Sable & Taurus w/3.0L SOHC engine

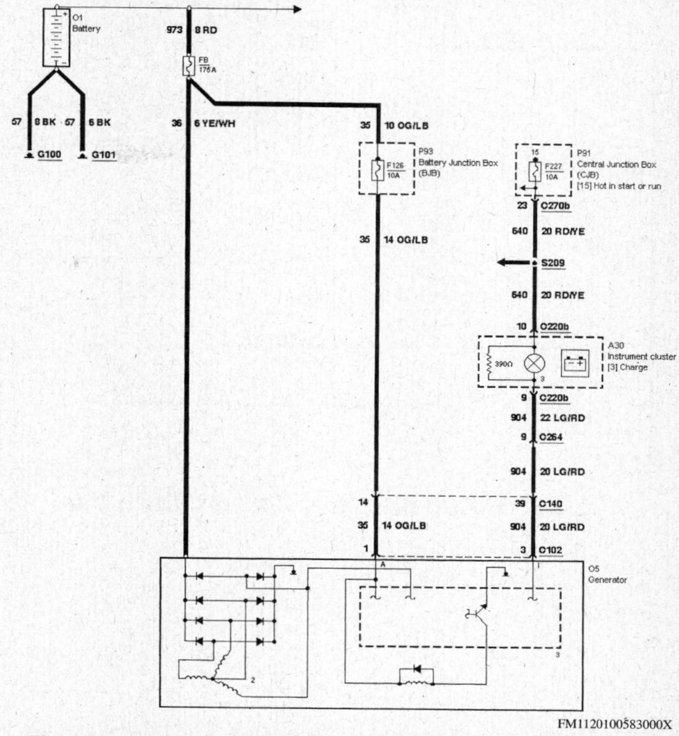

Fig. 24 Wiring diagram. 2000–01 Sable & Taurus w/3.0L DOHC engine

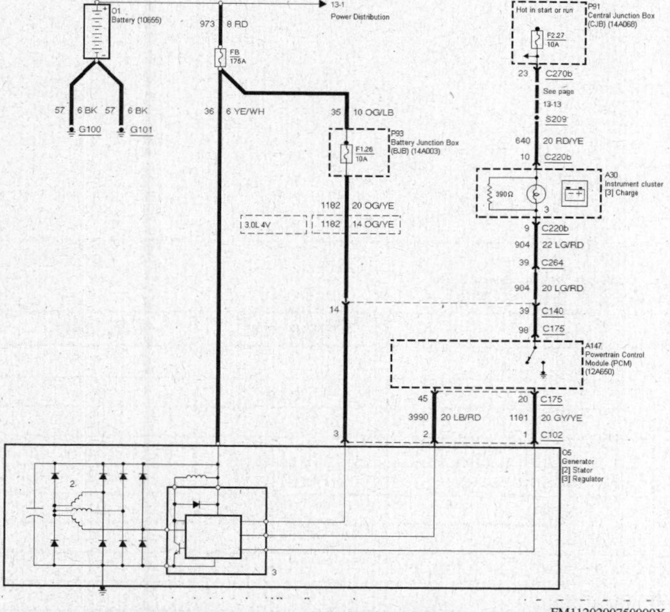

Fig. 25 Wiring Diagram. 2002 Sable & Taurus

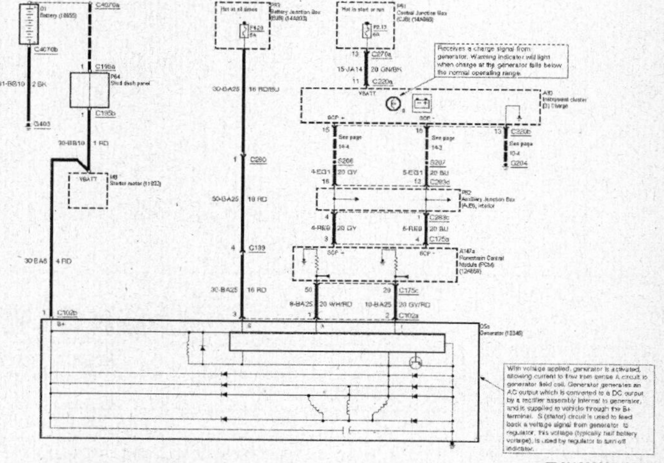

Fig. 26 Wiring Diagram. Thunderbird

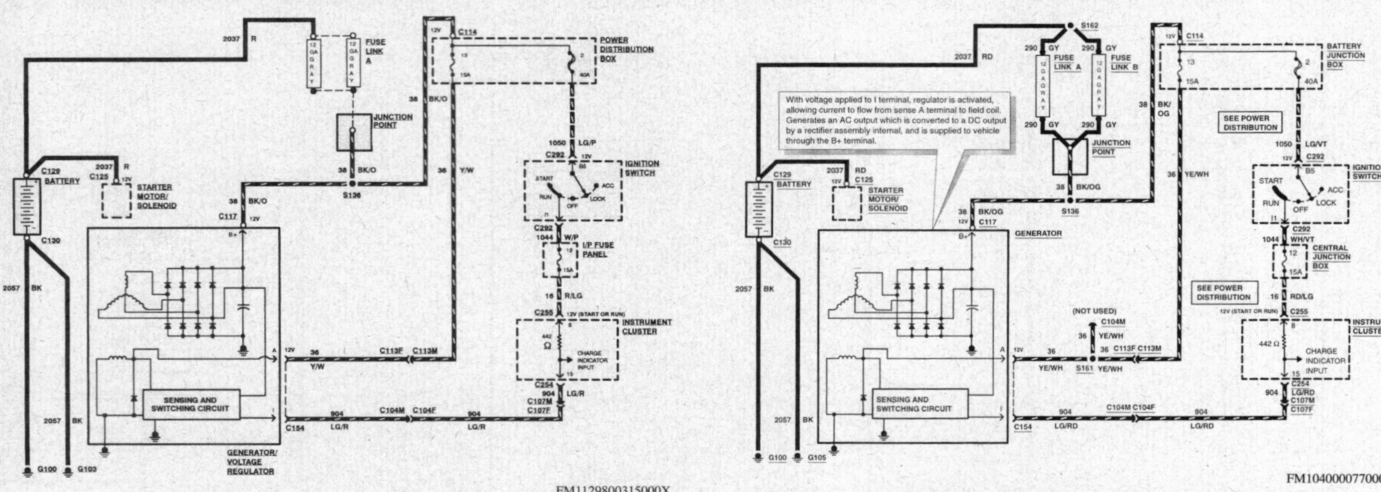

Fig. 27 Wiring diagram. 1998–99 Town Car

Fig. 28 Wiring diagram. 2000–01 Town Car

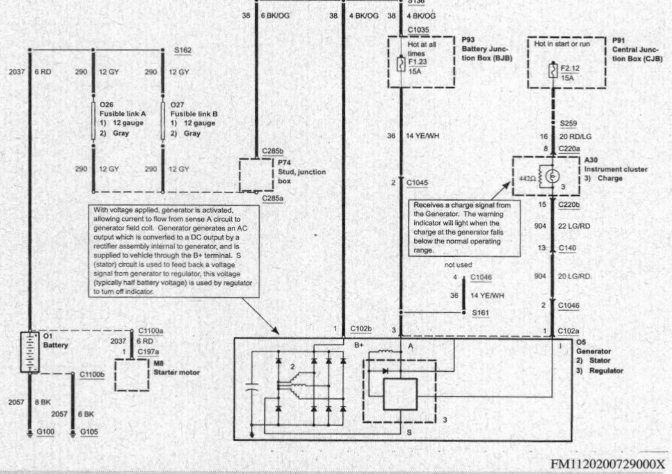

Fig. 29 Wiring diagram. 2002 Town Car

DIAGNOSTIC CHART INDEX

Test	Description	Page No.	Fig. No.
1998–2001 CONTINENTAL			
—	Symptom Chart	12-16	30
Test A	Warning Indicator Is On, Engine Running	12-16	32
Test B	Warning Indicator Is Off w/Ignition In Run Position & Engine Off	12-17	33
Test C	Warning Indicator Is On w/Engine Running & Battery Voltage Increases	12-18	34
Test D	Warning Indicator Is Off w/Ignition In Run Position & Engine Off	12-18	35
Test E	Warning Indicator Operates Properly But Battery Voltage Does Not Increase	12-18	36
Test F	Battery Is Dead Or Will Not Stay Charged Or Low Battery Or Alternator Voltage	12-18	37
Test G	Warning Indicator Flickers/Intermittent	12-19	38
Test H	System Overcharges, Battery Voltage Greater Than 15	12-19	39
Test J	Battery Leakage Or Damage	12-20	40
Test K	Voltage Gauge Reads High Or Low	12-20	41
Test L	Alternator Is Noisy	12-20	42
Test M	Radio Interference	12-21	43
2002 CONTINENTAL			
—	Symptom Chart	12-16	31
Test A	Battery is discharged or voltage is low	12-21	44
Test B	Charging System Warning Indicator Is On With The Engine Running(System Voltage Does Not Increase)	12-21	45

Continued

DIAGNOSTIC CHART INDEX—Continued

Test	Description	Page No.	Fig. No.
2002 CONTINENTAL			
Test C	System Overcharges (Battery Voltage Is Greater Than 15.5 Volts)	12-22	46
Test D	Charging System Warning Indicator Is On With The Engine Running And The System Increases Voltage.	12-22	47
Test E	Charging System Warning Indicator Is Off With The Ignition Switch In The Run Position And The Engine Off.	12-22	48
Test F	Charging System Warning Indicator Lamp Flickers Or Is Intermittent	12-23	49
Test G	Generator Is Noisy	12-23	50
Test H	Radio Interference	12-23	51
1998–2000 CONTOUR & MYSTIQUE			
—	Symptom Chart	12-24	52
Test A	System Does Not Charge	12-24	53
Test B	System Overcharges	12-26	54
Test C	Warning Indicator Stays On	12-26	55
Test D	Warning Indicator Is Inoperative	12-26	56
Test E	Warning Indicator Flickers/Intermittent	12-27	57
Test F	Alternator Is Noisy	12-28	58
Test G	Radio Interference	12-28	59
Test H	Battery Does Not Hold A Charge	12-28	60
1998–99 CROWN VICTORIA & GRAND MARQUIS			
—	Symptom Chart	12-29	61
Test A	System Does Not Charge	12-29	63
Test B	System Overcharges	12-29	64
Test C	Indicator Lamp Stays On, Engine Running	12-30	65
Test D	Indicator Lamp Stays On, Ignition Off	12-30	66
Test E	Indicator Lamp Does Not Light	12-30	67
Test F	Indicator Lamp Flickers/Intermittent	12-30	68
Test G	Alternator Is Noisy	12-30	69
Test H	Radio Interference	12-30	70
2000–01 CROWN VICTORIA & GRAND MARQUIS			
—	Symptom Chart	12-29	62
Test A	Battery Discharged or Voltage Low	12-30	71
Test B	Indicator Stays On, Engine Running	12-31	72
Test C	System Overcharges	12-31	73
Test D	Indicator Stays On, Engine Running	12-32	74
Test E	Indicator Off, Key On	12-32	75
Test F	Indicator Flickers Or Intermittent	12-32	76
Test G	Alternator Is Noisy	12-32	77
Test H	Radio Interference	12-33	78
2002 CROWN VICTORIA & GRAND MARQUIS			
—	Symptom Chart	12-29	62
Test A	Battery Is Discharged Or Voltage Is Low	12-33	79
Test B	Charging System Warning Indicator Is On With The Engine Running (The Engine Voltage Does Not Increase)	12-33	80
Test C	System Overcharges (Battery Voltage Is Greater Than 15.5 Volts)	12-34	81
Test D	Charging System Warning Indicator Is On With The Engine Running And The System Increases Voltage	12-34	82
Test E	Charging System Warning Indicator Is Off With The Ignition Switch In The Run Position And The Engine Off	12-34	83
Test F	Charging System Warning Indicator Flickers Or Is Intermittent	12-35	84
Test G	Generator Is Noisy	12-35	85
Test H	Radio Interference	12-35	86
ESCORT, TRACER & ZX2			
—	Symptom Chart	12-36	87
Test A	System Overcharges	12-36	88
Test B	Warning Indicator Stays On	12-36	89
Test C	Warning Indicator Flickers/Intermittent	12-37	90

Continued

DIAGNOSTIC CHART INDEX—Continued

Test	Description	Page No.	Fig. No.
ESCORT, TRACER & ZX2			
Test D	Alternator Is Noisy	12-37	91
Test E	Radio Interference	12-38	92
Test F	Battery Does Not Hold A Charge	12-38	93
Test G	System Does Not Charge	12-38	94
LS & THUNDERBIRD			
—	Symptom Chart	12-38	95
Test A	Battery Is Discharged Or Battery Voltage Is Low	12-39	96
Test B	Charging System Warning IndicatorIs On With The Engine Running (The Charging System Voltage Does Not Increase)	12-39	97
Test C	Charging System Overcharges (Battery Voltage Is Greater Than 15.5 Volts)	12-40	98
Test D	Charging System Warning Indicator Is On With The Engine Running And The Battery Increases Voltage	12-41	99
Test E	Charging System Warning Indicator Is Off With The Ignition Switch In The Run Position And The Engine Is Off	12-42	100
Test F	Charging System Warning Indicator Flickers Or Is Intermittent	12-43	101
Test G	Alternator Is Noisy	12-44	102
Test H	Radio Interference	12-45	103
1998 MUSTANG			
—	Symptom Chart	12-45	104
Test A	System Does Not Charge	12-46	108
Test B	System Overcharges	12-46	109
Test C	Indicator Lamp Stays On, Engine Running	12-46	110
Test D	Indicator Lamps Stay On, Ignition Off	12-47	111
Test E	Indicator Lamp Does Not Light	12-47	112
Test F	Indicator Lamp Flickers/Intermittent	12-47	113
Test G	Alternator Is Noisy	12-47	114
Test H	Radio Interference	12-47	115
1999–2001 MUSTANG w/3.8L ENGINE			
—	Symptom Chart	12-45	105
Test A	System Does Not Charge	12-47	116
Test B	System Overcharging	12-48	117
Test C	Indicator Lamp Remains Lit w/Engine Running	12-48	118
Test D	Indicator Lamp Does Not Light	12-48	119
Test E	Indicator Lamp Flickers Or Lights Intermittently	12-49	120
Test F	Alternator Noisy	12-49	121
Test G	Radio Interference	12-50	122
1999–2001 MUSTANG w/4.6L ENGINE			
—	Symptom Chart	12-45	106
Test H	System Does Not Charge	12-50	123
Test I	System Overcharging	12-50	124
Test J	Indicator Lamp Lights, Engine Running	12-50	125
Test K	Indicator Lamp Does Not Light	12-51	126
Test L	Indicator Lamp Flickers or Lights Intermittently	12-51	127
Test M	Alternator is Noisy	12-51	128
Test N	Radio Interference	12-52	129
Test O	Battery Discharged or Voltage Low	12-52	130
2002 MUSTANG			
—	Symptom Chart	12-46	107
Test A	Battery Is Charged Or Voltage Is Low	12-52	131
Test B	Charging System Warning Indicator Is On With The Engine Running (The Battery Voltage Does Not Increase)	12-53	132
Test C	System Overcharges (Battery Voltage Is Greater Than 15.5 Volts)	12-54	133
Test D	Charging System Warning Indicator Is On With The Engine Runnning And The Battery Increases Voltage	12-54	134
Test E	Charging System Warning Indicator Is Off With The Ignition Switch In the Run Position And The Engine Off	12-54	135

Continued

DIAGNOSTIC CHART INDEX—Continued

Test	Description	Page No.	Fig. No.
2002 MUSTANG			
Test F	Charging System Warning Indicator Lamp Flickers Or Is Intermittent	12-55	136
Test G	Generator Is Noisy	12-55	137
Test H	Radio Interference	12-56	138
1998–99 SABLE & TAURUS			
—	Symptom Chart	12-56	139
Test A	System Does Not Charge	12-57	141
Test B	System Overcharges	12-57	142
Test C	Indicator Lamp Stays On, Engine Running	12-57	143
Test D	Indicator Lamp Stays On, Ignition Off	12-57	144
Test E	Indicator Lamp Does Not Light	12-57	145
Test F	Indicator Lamp Flickers/Intermittent	12-57	146
Test G	Alternator Is Noisy	12-57	147
Test H	Radio Interference	12-58	148
2000–01 SABLE & TAURUS			
—	Symptom Chart	12-56	139
Test A	Battery Is Discharged Or Voltage Is Low	12-58	149
Test B	Charge Indicator Lights w/Engine Running, System Voltage Does Not Increase	12-58	150
Test C	System Overcharges	12-59	151
Test D	Charge Indicator Lights w/Engine Running, System Voltage Increases	12-60	152
Test E	Charge Indicator Off w/Ignition In Run Position & Engine Off	12-60	153
Test F	Indicator Flickers/Intermittent	12-60	154
Test G	Alternator Is Noisy	12-57	147
Test H	Radio Interference	12-61	155
2002 SABLE & TAURUS			
—	Symptom Chart	12-56	140
Test A	Battery Is Discharged Or Voltage Is Low	12-61	156
Test B	Charging System Warning Indicator Is On With The Engine Running (System Voltage Does Not Increase)	12-62	157
Test C	System Overcharges (Battery Voltage Greater Than 15 Volts)	12-62	158
Test D	Charging System Warning Indicator Is On With The Engine Running (The System Increases Voltage)	12-63	159
Test E	Charging System Warning Indicator Is Off With The Ignition Switch In The Run Position And The Engine Off	12-64	160
Test F	Charging System Warning Indicator Lamp Flickers Or Is Intermittent	12-64	161
Test G	Alternator Is Noisy	12-65	162
Test H	Radio Interference	12-65	163
1998–2001 TOWN CAR			
—	Symptom Chart	12-66	164
Test A	Warning Indicator Lights w/Engine Running, Battery Voltage Does Not Increase	12-66	166
Test B	Warning Indicator Is Off w/Ignition In Run Position & Engine Off	12-67	167
Test C	Warning Indicator Is On w/Engine Running & Battery Voltage Increase	12-67	168
Test D	Warning Indicator Off w/Ignition In Run Position & Engine Off	12-67	169
Test E	Warning Indicator Operates Properly But Battery Voltage Does Not Increase	12-67	170
Test F	Battery Is Dead Or Will Not Stay Charged Or Low Battery Or Alternator Voltage	12-68	171
Test G	Warning Indicator Flickers Or Is Intermittent	12-68	172
Test H	System Overcharges, Battery Voltage Greater Than 15	12-68	173
Test J	Battery Leakage Or Damage	12-69	174
Test K	Voltage Gauge Reads High Or Low	12-70	175
Test L	Alternator Is Noisy	12-70	176
Test M	Radio Interference	12-70	177
2002 TOWN CAR			
—	Symptom Chart	12-66	165
Test A	Battery Is Discharged Or Voltage Is Low	12-70	178
Test B	Charging System Warning Indicator Is On With The Engine Running (System Voltage Does Not Increase)	12-71	179
Test C	System Overcharges (Battery Voltage Is Greater Than 15.5 Volts)	12-72	180

Continued

DIAGNOSTIC CHART INDEX—Continued

Condition	Possible Source	Action
• The Charging System Warning Indicator is ON with the Engine Running (The Battery Voltage Does Not Increase)	• A Circuit 35 (O/LB). • A Circuit in-line mini-fuse. • B+ Circuit 36 (Y/W). • B+ mega fuse. • I Circuit 904 (LG/R) • Voltage regulator. • Generator	• GO to Pinpoint Test A.
• The Charging System Warning Indicator is OFF with the Ignition Switch in the RUN Position and the Engine OFF (Battery Voltage Does Not Increase)	• Voltage regulator connector. • I Circuit 904 (LG/R). • Fuse 19 (10A). • Voltage regulator. • Loose or damaged generator. • Harness connector.	• GO to Pinpoint Test B.
• The Charging System Warning Indicator is ON with the Engine Running and the Battery Voltage Increases	• Generator. • Voltage regulator.	• GO to Pinpoint Test C.

FM1129800244010X

Fig. 30 Symptom chart (Part 1 of 2). 1998–2001 Continental

Condition	Possible Source	Action
• The Charging System Warning Indicator is OFF with the Ignition Switch in the RUN Position and the Engine OFF (Battery Voltage Increases)	• Charging system warning indicator lamp bulb. • Instrument cluster. • Generator. • Voltage regulator.	• GO to Pinpoint Test D.
• The Charging System Warning Indicator Operates Correctly but the Battery Voltage Does Not Increase	• B+ Circuit 36 (Y/W). • B+ mega fuse. • Loose or damaged harness connector. • Battery cables. • Generator. • Voltage regulator.	• GO to Pinpoint Test E.
• The Battery is Dead or Will Not Stay Charged or Low Battery or Generator Voltage	• Corroded terminal(s). • Loose connection(s). • High key-off load. • Generator. • Voltage regulator.	• GO to Pinpoint Test F.
• The Charging System Warning Indicator Flickers/Is Intermittent	• Loose connection(s). • In-line mini-fuse A Circuit loose. • Fuse 19 (10A) I Circuit loose. • Generator. • Voltage regulator.	• GO to Pinpoint Test G.
• The System Overcharges (Battery Voltage Greater Than 15.5 Volts)	• A Circuit 35 (O/LB). • Generator (low output). • Voltage regulator. • I Circuit 904 (LG/R).	• GO to Pinpoint Test H.
• Battery Leakage or Damage	• A Circuit 35 (O/LB). • Generator. • Voltage regulator. • Battery.	• GO to Pinpoint Test J.
• The Voltage Gauge Reads High or Low	• Generator (low output) • Voltage regulator. • Voltage gauge. • Instrument cluster/wiring.	• GO to Pinpoint Test K.
• The Generator is Noisy	• Loose bolts/brackets. • Drive belt. • Generator/Pulley.	• GO to Pinpoint Test L.
• Radio Interference	• Generator. • Wiring/routing. • In-vehicle entertainment system.	• GO to Pinpoint Test M.

FM1129800244020X

Fig. 30 Symptom chart (Part 2 of 2). 1998–2001 Continental

Condition	Possible Sources	Action
• Battery is discharged or voltage is low	• Corroded terminal(s). • Loose connection(s). • High key-off current drain(s). • Battery. • Generator.	• GO to Pinpoint Test A.
• The charging system warning indicator is on with the engine running (the system voltage does not increase)	• Circuitry. • Voltage regulator. • Generator.	• GO to Pinpoint Test B.
• The system overcharges (battery voltage greater than 15.5 volts)	• Circuitry. • Voltage regulator. • Generator.	• GO to Pinpoint Test C.
• The charging system warning indicator is on with the engine running and the system increases voltage	• Circuitry. • Instrument cluster. • Voltage regulator. • Generator.	• GO to Pinpoint Test D.

FM1120200731010X

Fig. 31 Symptom Chart (Part 1 of 2). 2002 Continental

Condition	Possible Sources	Action
• The charging system warning indicator is off with the ignition switch in the RUN position and the engine off	• Bulb. • Circuitry. • Instrument cluster. • Voltage regulator. • Generator.	• GO to Pinpoint Test E.
• The charging system warning indicator flickers or is intermittent	• Corroded terminal(s). • Fuse(s). • Circuitry. • Voltage regulator. • Generator.	• GO to Pinpoint Test F.
• The generator is noisy	• Bolts or brackets. • Drive belt. • Generator or pulley.	• GO to Pinpoint Test G.
• Radio interference	• Generator. • Circuitry. • In-vehicle entertainment system.	• GO to Pinpoint Test H.

FM1120200731020X

Fig. 31 Symptom Chart (Part 2 of 2). 2002 Continental

TEST CONDITIONS	TEST DETAILS/RESULTS/ACTIONS
A1 CHECK A CIRCUIT FUSE 20 (15A)	
1 2 Fuse 20 (15A)	2 Check the A circuit Fuse 20 (15A) in the Power Distribution Box. • Is the fuse OK? → **Yes** GO to **A2**. → **No** REPLACE Fuse 20 (15A). Test the system for normal operation.
A2 CHECK THE DRIVE BELT TENSION	
1 V	1 Measure the voltage between the B+ terminal at the generator circuit 38 (BK/O). • Is the voltage equal to battery positive voltage (B+)? → **Yes** GO to A3. → **No** REPAIR Circuit 38 (BK/O). TEST the system for normal operation.

FM1129800245010X

Fig. 32 Test A: Warning Indicator Is On, Engine Running (Part 1 of 3). 1998–2001 Continental

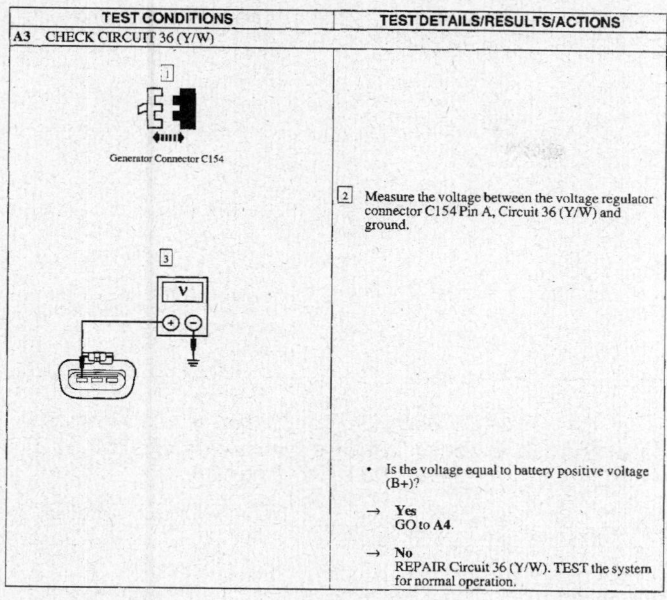

TEST CONDITIONS	TEST DETAILS/RESULTS/ACTIONS
A3 CHECK CIRCUIT 36 (Y/W)	
1 Generator Connector C154	
3	2 Measure the voltage between the voltage regulator connector C154 Pin A, Circuit 36 (Y/W) and ground.
	• Is the voltage equal to battery positive voltage (B+)? → **Yes** GO to **A4**. → **No** REPAIR Circuit 36 (Y/W). TEST the system for normal operation.

FM1129800224502OX

Fig. 32 Test A: Warning Indicator Is On, Engine Running (Part 2 of 3). 1998–2001 Continental

TEST CONDITIONS	TEST DETAILS/RESULTS/ACTIONS
B1 CHECK GENERATOR CONNECTOR C154	
1 Generator Connector C154	2 Check the generator connector C154 for bent or damaged pins. • Is the connector OK? → **Yes** GO to **B2**. → **No** REPAIR connector C154 as necessary. TEST the system for normal operation.
B2 CHECK GENERATOR GROUNDS	
	1 Check all ground connections between the generator, voltage regulator, and battery. • Are the ground connections OK? → **Yes** GO to **B3**. → **No** REPAIR connections as necessary. TEST the system for normal operation.

FM1129800246010X

Fig. 33 Test B: Warning Indicator Is Off w/Ignition In Run Position & Engine Off (Part 1 of 2). 1998–2001 Continental

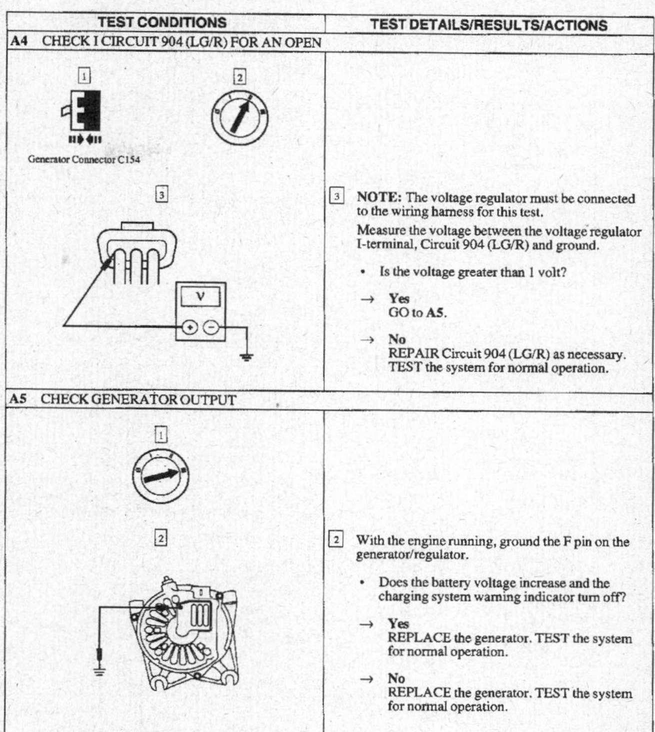

TEST CONDITIONS	TEST DETAILS/RESULTS/ACTIONS
A4 CHECK I CIRCUIT 904 (LG/R) FOR AN OPEN	
1 Generator Connector C154 2	
3	3 **NOTE:** The voltage regulator must be connected to the wiring harness for this test. Measure the voltage between the voltage regulator I-terminal, Circuit 904 (LG/R) and ground. • Is the voltage greater than 1 volt? → **Yes** GO to **A5**. → **No** REPAIR Circuit 904 (LG/R) as necessary. TEST the system for normal operation.
A5 CHECK GENERATOR OUTPUT	
1	
2	2 With the engine running, ground the F pin on the generator/regulator. • Does the battery voltage increase and the charging system warning indicator turn off? → **Yes** REPLACE the generator. TEST the system for normal operation. → **No** REPLACE the generator. TEST the system for normal operation.

FM1129800245030X

Fig. 32 Test A: Warning Indicator Is On, Engine Running (Part 3 of 3). 1998–2001 Continental

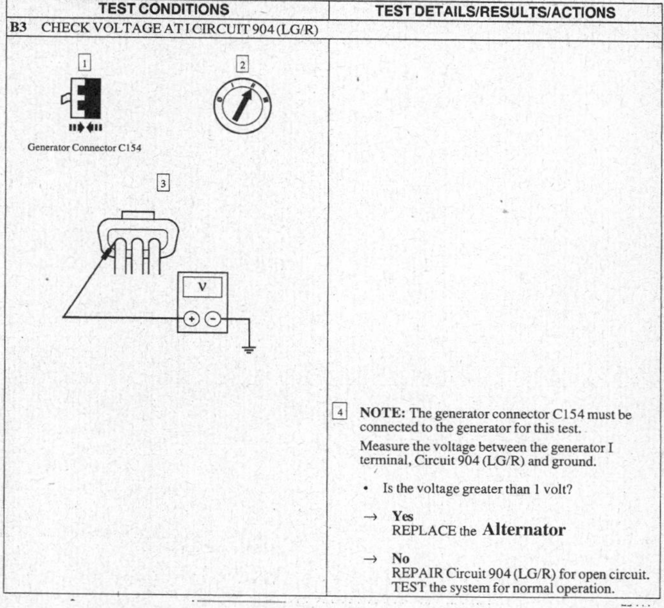

TEST CONDITIONS	TEST DETAILS/RESULTS/ACTIONS
B3 CHECK VOLTAGE AT I CIRCUIT 904 (LG/R)	
1 Generator Connector C154 2	
3	
	4 **NOTE:** The generator connector C154 must be connected to the generator for this test. Measure the voltage between the generator I terminal, Circuit 904 (LG/R) and ground. • Is the voltage greater than 1 volt? → **Yes** REPLACE the Alternator → **No** REPAIR Circuit 904 (LG/R) for open circuit. TEST the system for normal operation.

FM1129800246020X

Fig. 33 Test B: Warning Indicator Is Off w/Ignition In Run Position & Engine Off (Part 2 of 2). 1998–2001 Continental

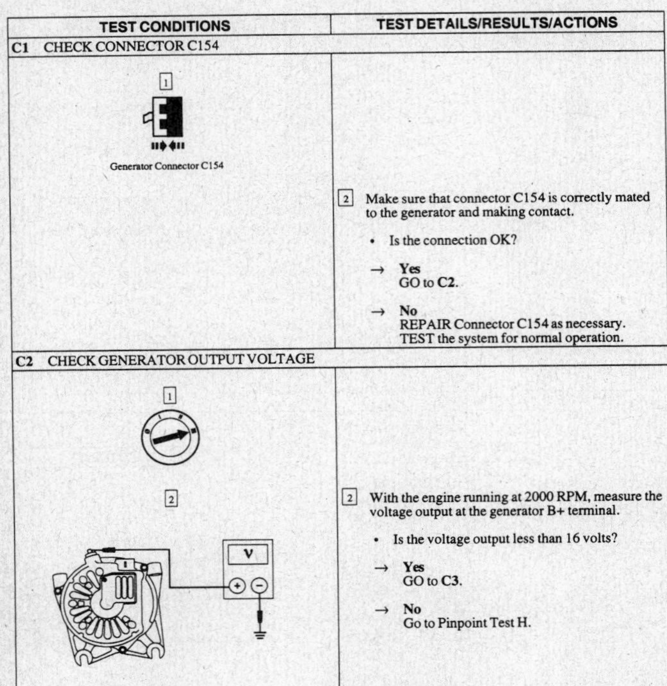

TEST CONDITIONS	TEST DETAILS/RESULTS/ACTIONS
C1 CHECK CONNECTOR C154	
1 Generator Connector C154	2 Make sure that connector C154 is correctly mated to the generator and making contact. • Is the connection OK? → **Yes** GO to **C2**. → **No** REPAIR Connector C154 as necessary. TEST the system for normal operation.
C2 CHECK GENERATOR OUTPUT VOLTAGE	
1 2 V	2 With the engine running at 2000 RPM, measure the voltage output at the generator B+ terminal. • Is the voltage output less than 16 volts? → **Yes** GO to **C3**. → **No** Go to Pinpoint Test H.

FM1129800247010X

Fig. 34 Test C: Warning Indicator Is On w/Engine Running & Battery Voltage Increases (Part 1 of 2). 1998–2001 Continental

TEST CONDITIONS	TEST DETAILS/RESULTS/ACTIONS
E1 CHECK CIRCUIT 36 (Y/W) VOLTAGE	
1 2 V	2 Check for voltage at generator B+ connector with the key ON and the engine OFF. • Is the voltage equal to battery positive voltage (B+)? → **Yes** GO to **E2**. → **No** REPAIR Circuit 36 (Y/W) as necessary. TEST the system for normal operation.
E2 CHECK GENERATOR CONNECTORS	
1 Generator Connector C154	2 Check the battery and generator connector C154 for corrosion and tightness. • Are the connectors clean and tight? → **Yes** REFER to Component Tests—Generator On-Vehicle Tests. → **No** REPAIR the connectors as necessary. TEST the system for normal operation.

FM1129800249000X

Fig. 36 Test E: Warning Indicator Operates Properly But Battery Voltage Does Not Increase. 1998–2001 Continental

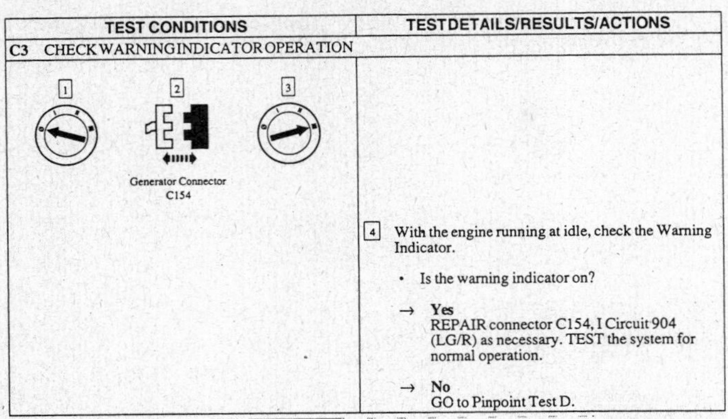

TEST CONDITIONS	TEST DETAILS/RESULTS/ACTIONS
C3 CHECK WARNING INDICATOR OPERATION	
1 2 3 Generator Connector C154	4 With the engine running at idle, check the Warning Indicator. • Is the warning indicator on? → **Yes** REPAIR connector C154, I Circuit 904 (LG/R) as necessary. TEST the system for normal operation. → **No** GO to Pinpoint Test D.

FM1129800247020X

Fig. 34 Test C: Warning Indicator Is On w/Engine Running & Battery Voltage Increases (Part 2 of 2). 1998–2001 Continental

TEST CONDITIONS	TEST DETAILS/RESULTS/ACTIONS
D1 CHECK CHARGING SYSTEM WARNING INDICATOR OPERATION	
1 2 3	3 Ground the generator connector C154 I circuit with the key ON and the engine OFF. • Is the warning indicator on? → **Yes** REPLACE the generator. TEST for normal operation. → **No** REPAIR connector C154 I Circuit 904 (LG/R) as necessary. TEST for normal operation.

FM1129800248000X

Fig. 35 Test D: Warning Indicator Is Off w/Ignition In Run Position & Engine Off. 1998–2001 Continental

TEST CONDITIONS	TEST DETAILS/RESULTS/ACTIONS
F1 CHECK BATTERY DRAIN	
	1 Make sure that all interior lights and switches are off and all doors are closed. Perform battery drain test. • Is the drain greater than 0.5 amps? → **Yes** Go to Component Tests, Battery—Drain Testing. → **No** GO to **F2**.
F2 CHECK GENERATOR OUTPUT	
	1 Check generator output. • Is the generator OK? → **Yes** GO to **F3**. → **No** REPLACE the generator. TEST the system for normal operation.
F3 CHECK BATTERY CONDITION	
	1 Check the battery capacity. • Is the battery OK? → **Yes** GO to **F4**. → **No** REPLACE the battery. TEST the system for normal operation.

FM1129800250010X

Fig. 37 Test F: Battery Is Dead Or Will Not Stay Charged Or Low Battery Or Alternator Voltage (Part 1 of 2). 1998–2001 Continental

TEST CONDITIONS	TEST DETAILS/RESULTS/ACTIONS
F4 CHECK OTHER SYSTEMS FOR DRAINS	
	1 Check for drains from electronic modules. • Are electronic modules OK? → **Yes** RECHARGE the battery. TEST the system for normal operation. → **No** REPLACE the defective module as necessary. TEST the system for normal operation.

FM1129800250020X

Fig. 37 Test F: Battery Is Dead Or Will Not Stay Charged Or Low Battery Or Alternator Voltage (Part 2 of 2). 1998–2001 Continental

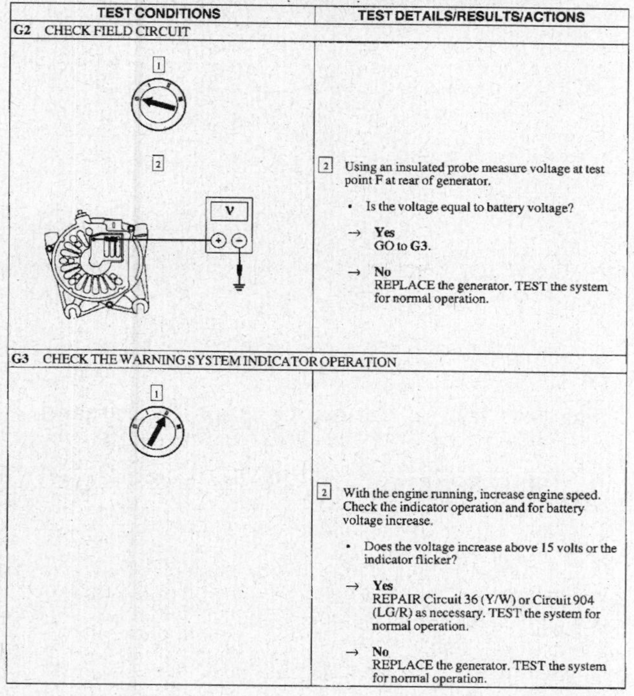

TEST CONDITIONS	TEST DETAILS/RESULTS/ACTIONS
G2 CHECK FIELD CIRCUIT	
1 2	2 Using an insulated probe measure voltage at test point F at rear of generator. • Is the voltage equal to battery voltage? → **Yes** GO to **G3**. → **No** REPLACE the generator. TEST the system for normal operation.
G3 CHECK THE WARNING SYSTEM INDICATOR OPERATION	
1	2 With the engine running, increase engine speed. Check the indicator operation and for battery voltage increase. • Does the voltage increase above 15 volts or the indicator flicker? → **Yes** REPAIR Circuit 36 (Y/W) or Circuit 904 (LG/R) as necessary. TEST the system for normal operation. → **No** REPLACE the generator. TEST the system for normal operation.

FM1129800251020X

Fig. 38 Test G: Warning Indicator Flickers/ Intermittent (Part 2 of 2). 1998–2001 Continental

TEST CONDITIONS	TEST DETAILS/RESULTS/ACTIONS
H2 CHECK BATTERY VOLTAGE	
1 2	3 With the engine running turn off all accessories. Increase the engine speed and monitor the voltage at the battery. • Does battery voltage remain less than 15 volts? → **Yes** GO to **H3**. → **No** GO to **H5**.

FM1129800252020X

Fig. 39 Test H: System Overcharges, Battery Voltage Greater Than 15.5 Volts (Part 2 of 4). 1998–2001 Continental

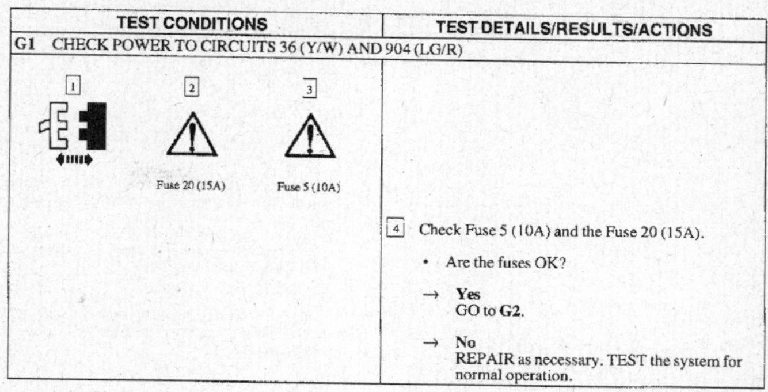

TEST CONDITIONS	TEST DETAILS/RESULTS/ACTIONS
G1 CHECK POWER TO CIRCUITS 36 (Y/W) AND 904 (LG/R)	
1 2 3 Fuse 20 (15A) Fuse 5 (10A)	4 Check Fuse 5 (10A) and the Fuse 20 (15A). • Are the fuses OK? → **Yes** GO to **G2**. → **No** REPAIR as necessary. TEST the system for normal operation.

FM1129800251010X

Fig. 38 Test G: Warning Indicator Flickers/ Intermittent (Part 1 of 2). 1998–2001 Continental

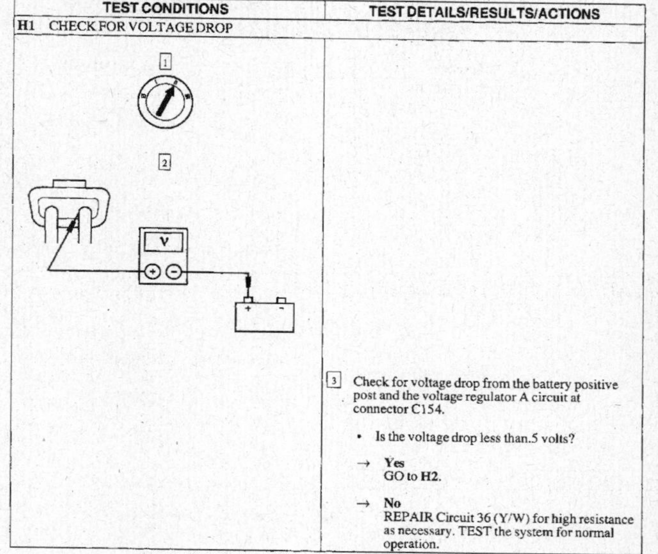

TEST CONDITIONS	TEST DETAILS/RESULTS/ACTIONS
H1 CHECK FOR VOLTAGE DROP	
1 2	3 Check for voltage drop from the battery positive post and the voltage regulator A circuit at connector C154. • Is the voltage drop less than.5 volts? → **Yes** GO to **H2**. → **No** REPAIR Circuit 36 (Y/W) for high resistance as necessary. TEST the system for normal operation.

FM1129800252010X

Fig. 39 Test H: System Overcharges, Battery Voltage Greater Than 15.5 Volts (Part 1 of 4). 1998–2001 Continental

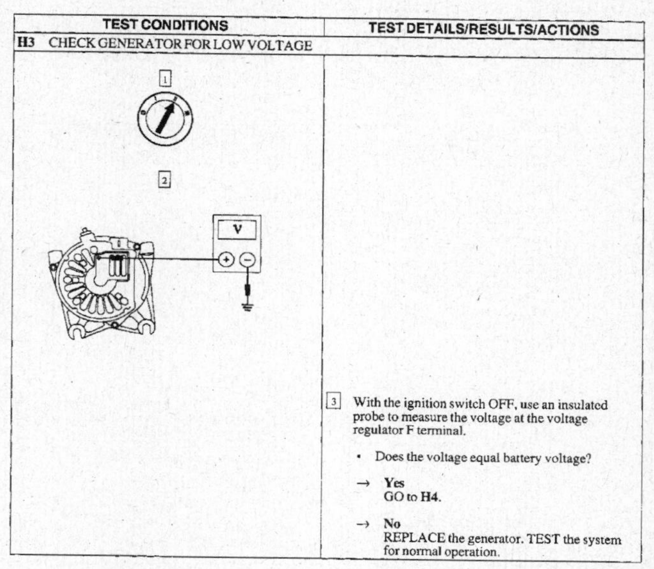

TEST CONDITIONS	TEST DETAILS/RESULTS/ACTIONS
H3 CHECK GENERATOR FOR LOW VOLTAGE	
1 2	3 With the ignition switch OFF, use an insulated probe to measure the voltage at the voltage regulator F terminal. • Does the voltage equal battery voltage? → **Yes** GO to **H4**. → **No** REPLACE the generator. TEST the system for normal operation.

FM1129800252030X

Fig. 39 Test H: System Overcharges, Battery Voltage Greater Than 15.5 Volts (Part 3 of 4). 1998–2001 Continental

H4 CHECK THE WARNING SYSTEM INDICATOR OPERATION	
1	2 With the engine running, increase engine speed and check the indicator operation and for battery voltage increase. • Does the voltage increase above 15 volts or the indicator flicker? → **Yes** REPAIR Circuit 36 (Y/W) or Circuit 904 (LG/R) as necessary. TEST the system for normal operation. → **No** REPLACE the generator. TEST the system for normal operation.

FM1129800252040X

Fig. 39 Test H: System Overcharges, Battery Voltage Greater Than 15.5 Volts (Part 4 of 4). 1998–2001 Continental

TEST CONDITIONS	TEST DETAILS/RESULTS/ACTIONS
J1 CHECK FOR ACID LEAKAGE DAMAGE	
	1 Check for Acid damage to vehicle harness and to the body. • REPAIR damaged areas as necessary. → **Yes** REPAIR damaged areas as necessary. → **No** GO to **J2**.
J2 CHECK CHARGING SYSTEM FOR OVERCHARGING	
1 2 V	3 With the engine running turn off all accessories. Increase the engine speed and monitor the voltage at the battery. • Does battery voltage increase more than 15 volts? → **Yes** Go to Pinpoint Test H. → **No** GO to **J3**.

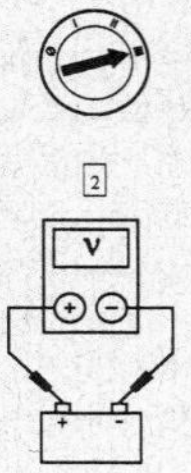

FM1129800253010X

Fig. 40 Test J: Battery Leakage Or Damage (Part 1 of 2). 1998–2001 Continental

TEST CONDITIONS	TEST DETAILS/RESULTS/ACTIONS
J3 CHECK BATTERY MOUNTING	
	1 Make sure the battery is properly mounted and level in the battery tray. • Is the battery properly mounted? → **Yes** GO to **J4**. → **No** REPAIR as necessary. TEST the system for normal operation.
J4 CHECK FOR BATTERY CONTACT	
	1 Make sure that there are no fasteners or other parts contacting the battery case causing excess pressure. • Is there anything contacting the battery case? → **Yes** REPAIR as necessary. TEST the system for normal operation. → **No** GO to **J5**.
J5 CHECK BATTERY CASE FOR DAMAGE	
	1 Check the battery case for defects such as cracks or poor seals. • Is the battery OK? → **Yes** System is OK. Test the system for normal operation. → **No** REPLACE the battery. TEST the system for normal operation.

FM1129800253020X

Fig. 40 Test J: Battery Leakage Or Damage (Part 2 of 2). 1998–2001 Continental

TEST CONDITIONS	TEST DETAILS/RESULTS/ACTIONS
K1 CHECK BATTERY VOLTAGE	
1 2 V	3 With the engine running turn off all accessories. Increase the engine speed and monitor the voltage at the battery. • Is the battery voltage more than 15 volts? → **Yes** Go to Pinpoint Test H. → **No** GO to **K2**.

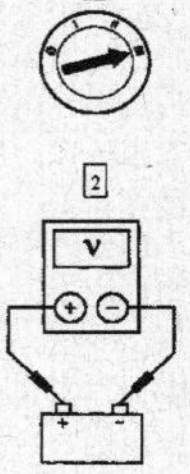

FM1129800254010X

Fig. 41 Test K: Voltage Gauge Reads High Or Low (Part 1 of 2). 1998–2001 Continental

TEST CONDITIONS	TEST DETAILS/RESULTS/ACTIONS
K2 CHECK VOLTAGE GAUGE OPERATION	
1 V	2 With the engine running monitor the voltage gauge reading and the battery voltage. • Are the voltage readings consistent? → **Yes** System is operating normally. → **No** Inspect instrument cluster.

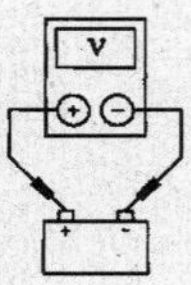

FM1129800254020X

Fig. 41 Test K: Voltage Gauge Reads High Or Low (Part 2 of 2). 1998–2001 Continental

TEST CONDITIONS	TEST DETAILS/RESULTS/ACTIONS
L1 CHECK FOR ACCESSORY DRIVE NOISE	
	1 Check the drive belt to make sure it is properly installed and aligned. • Is the drive belt OK? → **Yes** GO to **L2**. → **No** REPAIR the accessory drive belt as required. RETEST the system.

FM1129800255010X

Fig. 42 Test L: Alternator Is Noisy (Part 1 of 2). 1998–2001 Continental

TEST CONDITIONS	TEST DETAILS/RESULTS/ACTIONS
L2 CHECK THE GENERATOR MOUNTING	
	1 Check the generator and generator mounting brackets for loose bolts or misalignment. • Is the generator mounted correctly? → **Yes** REPLACE the generator. RETEST the system. → **No** INSTALL the generator to specifications. RETEST the system.

FM1129800255020X

Fig. 42 Test L: Alternator Is Noisy (Part 2 of 2). 1998–2001 Continental

CONDITIONS	DETAILS/RESULTS/ACTIONS
A1 CHECK BATTERY CONDITION	
	1 Carry out the Battery — Condition Test to determine if the battery can hold a charge and is OK for use. • Is the battery OK? → **Yes** GO to **A2**. → **No** INSTALL a new battery. TEST the system for normal operation.

FM1120200732010X

Fig. 44 Test A: Battery Is Discharged Or Voltage Is Low (Part 1 of 2). 2002 Continental

CONDITIONS	DETAILS/RESULTS/ACTIONS
A2 CHECK FOR GENERATOR OUTPUT	
	1 Carry out the Generator On-Vehicle Load/No-Load Tests. • Is the generator OK? → **Yes** GO to **A3**. → **No** GO to Pinpoint Test B.
A3 CHECK FOR CURRENT DRAINS	
	1 Carry out the Battery — Drain Test. • Are there any excessive current drains? → **Yes** REPAIR as necessary. TEST the system for normal operation. → **No** GO to **A4**.
A4 CHECK FOR CURRENT DRAINS WHICH SHUT OFF WHEN THE BATTERY IS DISCONNECTED	
	1 Carry out the Battery — Electronic Drains Which Shut Off When the Battery Cable is Disconnected Test. • Are there any current drains which shut off when the battery is disconnected? → **Yes** REPAIR as necessary. TEST the system for normal operation. → **No** GO to Pinpoint Test B.

FM1120200732020X

Fig. 44 Test A: Battery Is Discharged Or Voltage Is Low (Part 2 of 2). 2002 Continental

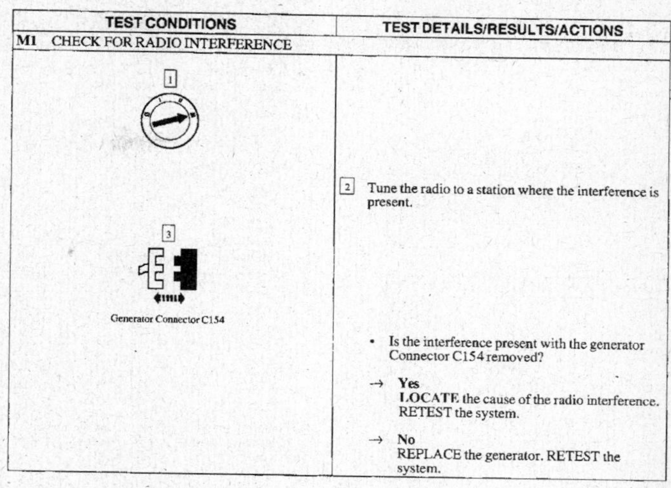

TEST CONDITIONS	TEST DETAILS/RESULTS/ACTIONS
M1 CHECK FOR RADIO INTERFERENCE	
1 3 Generator Connector C154	2 Tune the radio to a station where the interference is present. • Is the interference present with the generator Connector C154 removed? → **Yes** LOCATE the cause of the radio interference. RETEST the system. → **No** REPLACE the generator. RETEST the system.

FM1129800256000X

Fig. 43 Test M: Radio Interference. 1998–2001 Continental

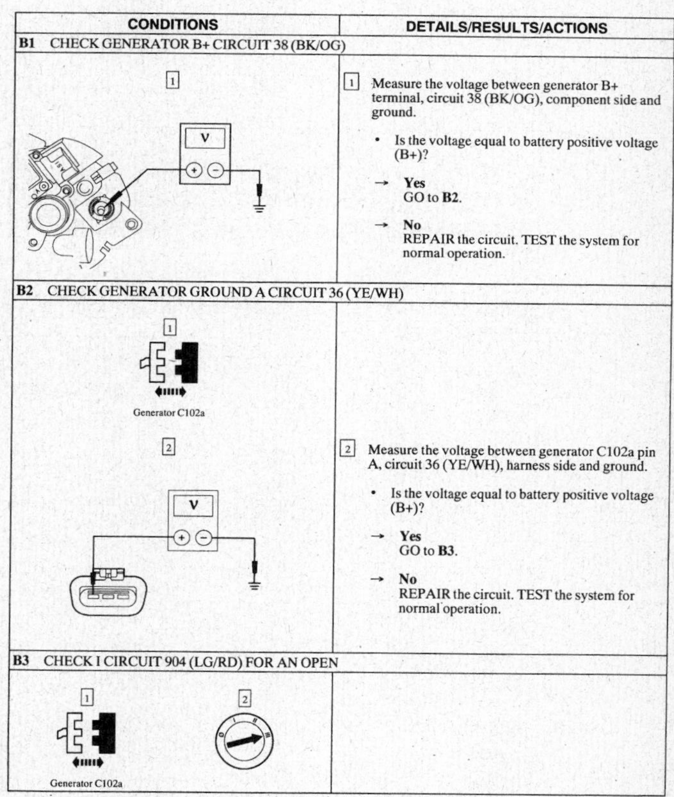

CONDITIONS	DETAILS/RESULTS/ACTIONS
B1 CHECK GENERATOR B+ CIRCUIT 38 (BK/OG)	
1 V	1 Measure the voltage between generator B+ terminal, circuit 38 (BK/OG), component side and ground. • Is the voltage equal to battery positive voltage (B+)? → **Yes** GO to **B2**. → **No** REPAIR the circuit. TEST the system for normal operation.
B2 CHECK GENERATOR GROUND A CIRCUIT 36 (YE/WH)	
1 Generator C102a 2 V	2 Measure the voltage between generator C102a pin A, circuit 36 (YE/WH), harness side and ground. • Is the voltage equal to battery positive voltage (B+)? → **Yes** GO to **B3**. → **No** REPAIR the circuit. TEST the system for normal operation.
B3 CHECK I CIRCUIT 904 (LG/RD) FOR AN OPEN	
1 2 Generator C102a	

FM1120200733010X

Fig. 45 Test B: Charging System Warning Indicator Is On With The Engine Running (System Voltage Does Not Increase) (Part 1 of 2). 2002 Continental

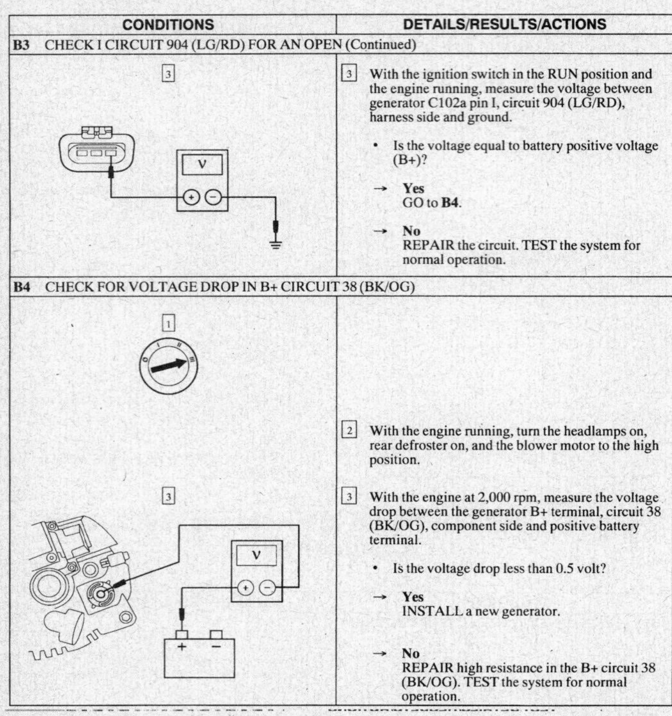

CONDITIONS	DETAILS/RESULTS/ACTIONS
B3 CHECK I CIRCUIT 904 (LG/RD) FOR AN OPEN (Continued)	
3	3 With the ignition switch in the RUN position and the engine running, measure the voltage between generator C102a pin I, circuit 904 (LG/RD), harness side and ground. • Is the voltage equal to battery positive voltage (B+)? → **Yes** GO to **B4**. → **No** REPAIR the circuit. TEST the system for normal operation.
B4 CHECK FOR VOLTAGE DROP IN B+ CIRCUIT 38 (BK/OG)	
1	
	2 With the engine running, turn the headlamps on, rear defroster on, and the blower motor to the high position.
3	3 With the engine at 2,000 rpm, measure the voltage drop between the generator B+ terminal, circuit 38 (BK/OG), component side and positive battery terminal. • Is the voltage drop less than 0.5 volt? → **Yes** INSTALL a new generator. → **No** REPAIR high resistance in the B+ circuit 38 (BK/OG). TEST the system for normal operation.

FM1120200733020X

Fig. 45 Test B: Charging System Warning Indicator Is On With The Engine Running (System Voltage Does Not Increase) (Part 2 of 2). 2002 Continental

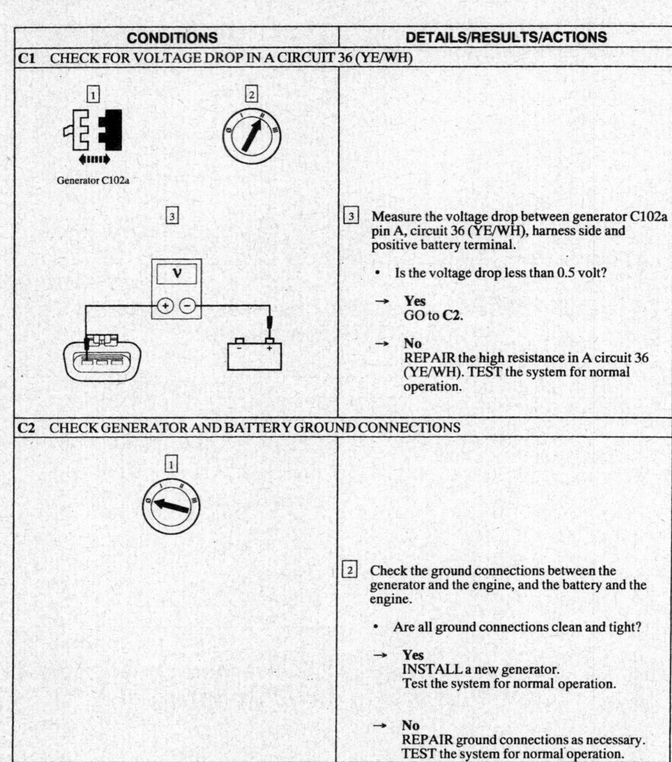

CONDITIONS	DETAILS/RESULTS/ACTIONS
C1 CHECK FOR VOLTAGE DROP IN A CIRCUIT 36 (YE/WH)	
1 2 Generator C102a	
3	3 Measure the voltage drop between generator C102a pin A, circuit 36 (YE/WH), harness side and positive battery terminal. • Is the voltage drop less than 0.5 volt? → **Yes** GO to **C2**. → **No** REPAIR the high resistance in A circuit 36 (YE/WH). TEST the system for normal operation.
C2 CHECK GENERATOR AND BATTERY GROUND CONNECTIONS	
1	
	2 Check the ground connections between the generator and the engine, and the battery and the engine. • Are all ground connections clean and tight? → **Yes** INSTALL a new generator. Test the system for normal operation. → **No** REPAIR ground connections as necessary. TEST the system for normal operation.

FM1120200734000X

Fig. 46 Test C: System Overcharges (Battery Voltage Is Greater Than 15.5 Volts). 2002 Continental

CONDITIONS	DETAILS/RESULTS/ACTIONS
E1 CHECK THE CHARGING SYSTEM WARNING INDICATOR LAMP	
1 Generator C102a	
2	2 With the engine off, connect a fused (15A) jumper wire between the generator C102a pin I, circuit 904 (LG/RD), harness side and ground.
3	

FM1120200736010X

Fig. 48 Test E: Charging System Warning Indicator Is Off With The Ignition Switch In The Run Position And The Engine Off (Part 1 of 2). 2002 Continental

CONDITIONS	DETAILS/RESULTS/ACTIONS
D1 CHECK I CIRCUIT 904 (LG/RD) FOR SHORT TO GROUND	
1 2 Generator C102a	2 With the ignition switch in the RUN position, check the charging system warning indicator. • Is the charging system warning indicator illuminated? → **Yes** REPAIR generator I circuit 904 (LG/RD) for a short to ground. TEST the system for normal operation. → **No** INSTALL a new generator. TEST the system for normal operation.

FM1120200735000X

Fig. 47 Test D: Charging System Warning Indicator Is On With The Engine Running And The System Increases Voltage. 2002 Continental

CONDITIONS	DETAILS/RESULTS/ACTIONS
E1 CHECK THE CHARGING SYSTEM WARNING INDICATOR LAMP (Continued)	
	• Is the charging system warning indicator lamp illuminated? → **Yes** INSTALL a new generator. TEST the system for normal operation. → **No** Diagnosis and test the instrument cluster.

FM1120200736020X

Fig. 48 Test E: Charging System Warning Indicator Is Off With The Ignition Switch In The Run Position And The Engine Off (Part 2 of 2). 2002 Continental

CONDITIONS	DETAILS/RESULTS/ACTIONS
F1 CHECK FOR LOOSE CONNECTIONS	
	1 Check all generator, battery, and power distribution connections for looseness, corrosion, loose or bent terminals, or loose eyelets. • Are all connections clean and tight? → **Yes** GO to **F2**. → **No** REPAIR as necessary. TEST the system for normal operation.
F2 CHECK FUSE CONNECTIONS	
1	1 With the engine running, check BJB fuse 13 (15A) in A circuit 36 (YE/WH) and the CJB fuse 12 (15A) in I circuit 904 (LG/RD) for looseness by wiggling the fuse and noting the charging system warning indicator lamp operation. • Does the charging system warning indicator flicker? → **Yes** REPAIR loose fuse connection(s) as necessary. TEST the system for normal operation. → **No** GO to **F3**.

FM1120200737010X

Fig. 49 Test F: Charging System Warning Indicator Lamp Flickers Or Is Intermittent (Part 1 of 2). 2002 Continental

CONDITIONS	DETAILS/RESULTS/ACTIONS
G1 CHECK FOR ACCESSORY DRIVE NOISE	
	1 Check the accessory drive belt for damage and correct installation. Check the accessory mounting brackets and generator pulley for looseness or misalignment. • Is the accessory drive OK? → **Yes** GO to **G2**. → **No** REPAIR as necessary. TEST the system for normal operation.
G2 CHECK GENERATOR MOUNTING	
	1 Check the generator mounting for loose bolts or misalignment. • Is the generator mounted correctly? → **Yes** GO to **G3**. → **No** REPAIR as necessary. TEST the system for normal operation.
G3 CHECK GENERATOR FOR ELECTRICAL NOISE	
1 Generator C102a 2	3 With the engine running, turn the headlamps on, rear defroster on, and the blower motor to the high position. • Is the noise still present? → **Yes** GO to **G4**. → **No** INSTALL a new generator. TEST the system for normal operation.

FM1120200738010X

Fig. 50 Test G: Generator Is Noisy (Part 1 of 2). 2002 Continental

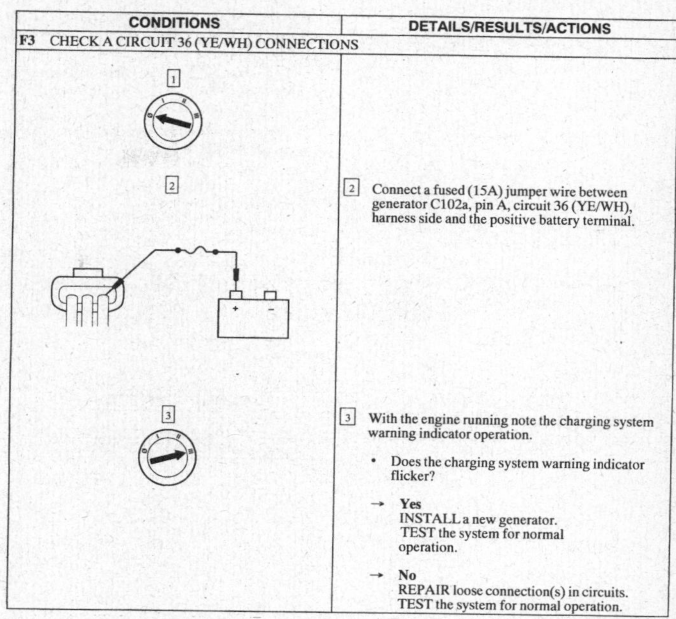

CONDITIONS	DETAILS/RESULTS/ACTIONS
F3 CHECK A CIRCUIT 36 (YE/WH) CONNECTIONS	
1	
2	2 Connect a fused (15A) jumper wire between generator C102a, pin A, circuit 36 (YE/WH), harness side and the positive battery terminal.
3	3 With the engine running note the charging system warning indicator operation. • Does the charging system warning indicator flicker? → **Yes** INSTALL a new generator. TEST the system for normal operation. → **No** REPAIR loose connection(s) in circuits. TEST the system for normal operation.

FM1120200737020X

Fig. 49 Test F: Charging System Warning Indicator Lamp Flickers Or Is Intermittent (Part 2 of 2). 2002 Continental

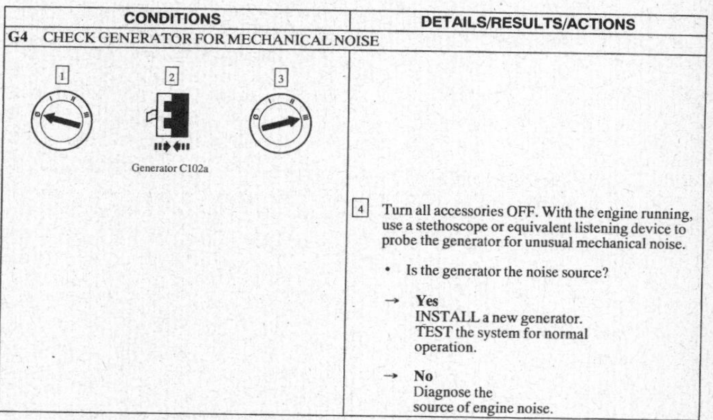

CONDITIONS	DETAILS/RESULTS/ACTIONS
G4 CHECK GENERATOR FOR MECHANICAL NOISE	
1 2 Generator C102a 3	4 Turn all accessories OFF. With the engine running, use a stethoscope or equivalent listening device to probe the generator for unusual mechanical noise. • Is the generator the noise source? → **Yes** INSTALL a new generator. TEST the system for normal operation. → **No** Diagnose the source of engine noise.

FM1120200738020X

Fig. 50 Test G: Generator Is Noisy (Part 2 of 2). 2002 Continental

CONDITIONS	DETAILS/RESULTS/ACTIONS
H1 VERIFY GENERATOR IS SOURCE OF RADIO INTERFERENCE	
1	1 With the engine running, tune the radio to a station where the interference is present.
	2 Tune the radio to a station where the interference is present.
3 4 Generator C102a 5	

FM1120200739010X

Fig. 51 Test H: Radio Interference (Part 1 of 2). 2002 Continental

CONDITIONS	DETAILS/RESULTS/ACTIONS
H1 VERIFY GENERATOR IS SOURCE OF RADIO INTERFERENCE (Continued)	
	• Is the interference present with the generator disconnected? → **Yes** Diagnose and test in-vehicle entertainment system. → **No** INSTALL a new generator. TEST the system for normal operation.

FM1120200739020X

Fig. 51 Test H: Radio Interference (Part 2 of 2). 2002 Continental

CONDITIONS	DETAILS/RESULTS/ACTIONS
A1 CHECK FOR POOR GROUNDS	
1	2 Measure the voltage between generator casing and negative (-) battery terminal. • Is the voltage less than 0.25 volts? → **Yes** GO to **A2**. → **No** CLEAN and REPAIR grounds as required. TEST the system for normal operation.
A2 CHECK FOR OPEN 'B+' CIRCUIT – CIRCUIT 20 (BK)	
	1 Measure the voltage between generator 'B+' terminal, circuit 20 (BK) and ground. • Is the voltage equal to battery voltage? → **Yes** GO to **A3**. → **No** REPAIR circuit 20 (BK). TEST the system for normal operation.

FM1129800298010X

Fig. 53 Test A: System Does Not Charge (Part 1 of 6). 1998–2000 Contour & Mystique

Condition	Possible Sources	Action
• The System Does Not Charge	• Circuitry. • Voltage regulator. • Generator.	• GO to Pinpoint Test A.
• The System Overcharges	• Voltage regulator. • Circuitry. • Generator.	• GO to Pinpoint Test B.
• The Charging System Warning Indicator Stays On	• Circuitry. • Voltage regulator. • Generator. • Instrument cluster.	• GO to Pinpoint Test C.

FM1129800297010X

Fig. 52 Symptom chart (Part 1 of 2). 1998–2000 Contour & Mystique

Condition	Possible Sources	Action
• The Charging System Warning Indicator Is Inoperative	• Circuitry. • Lamp. • Voltage regulator. • Generator.	• GO to Pinpoint Test D.
• The Charging System Warning Indicator Flickers / Is Intermittent	• Circuitry. • Voltage regulator. • Generator.	• GO to Pinpoint Test E.
• The Generator Is Noisy	• Accessory drive belt. • Accessory brackets. • Pulley. • Generator.	• GO to Pinpoint Test F.
• Radio Interference	• Voltage regulator. • Generator.	• GO to Pinpoint Test G.
• The Battery Does Not Hold A Charge	• Battery. • Voltage regulator. • Generator.	• GO to Pinpoint Test H.

FM1129800297020X

Fig. 52 Symptom chart (Part 2 of 2). 1998–2000 Contour & Mystique

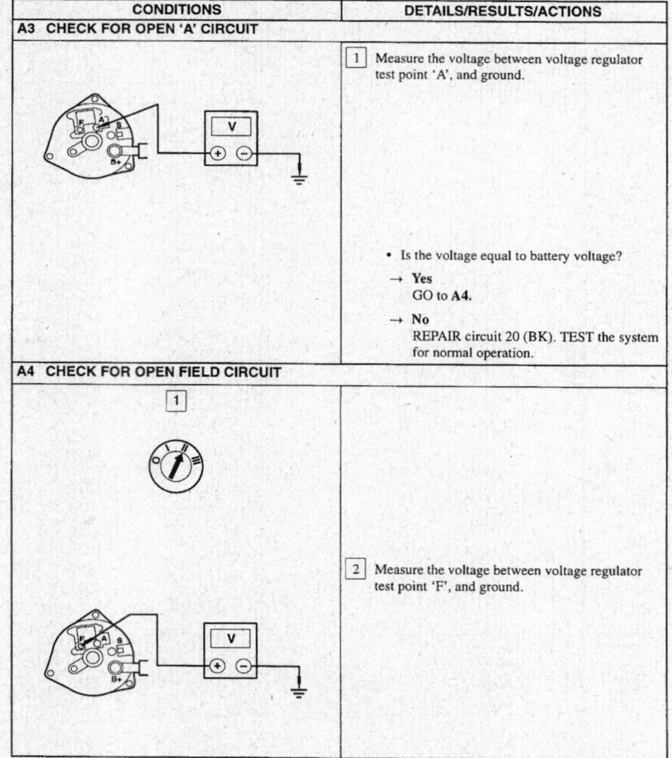

CONDITIONS	DETAILS/RESULTS/ACTIONS
A3 CHECK FOR OPEN 'A' CIRCUIT	
	1 Measure the voltage between voltage regulator test point 'A', and ground. • Is the voltage equal to battery voltage? → **Yes** GO to **A4**. → **No** REPAIR circuit 20 (BK). TEST the system for normal operation.
A4 CHECK FOR OPEN FIELD CIRCUIT	
1	2 Measure the voltage between voltage regulator test point 'F', and ground.

FM1129800298020X

Fig. 53 Test A: System Does Not Charge (Part 2 of 6). 1998–2000 Contour & Mystique

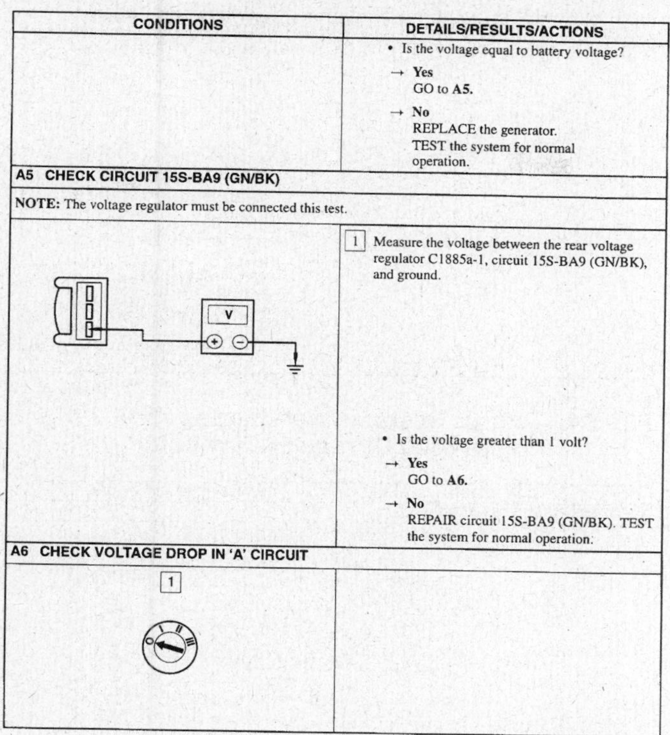

CONDITIONS	DETAILS/RESULTS/ACTIONS
	• Is the voltage equal to battery voltage? → **Yes** GO to **A5.** → **No** REPLACE the generator. TEST the system for normal operation.
A5 CHECK CIRCUIT 15S-BA9 (GN/BK)	
NOTE: The voltage regulator must be connected this test.	
	1 Measure the voltage between the rear voltage regulator C1885a-1, circuit 15S-BA9 (GN/BK), and ground. • Is the voltage greater than 1 volt? → **Yes** GO to **A6.** → **No** REPAIR circuit 15S-BA9 (GN/BK). TEST the system for normal operation.
A6 CHECK VOLTAGE DROP IN 'A' CIRCUIT	
1	

FM1129800298030X

Fig. 53 Test A: System Does Not Charge (Part 3 of 6). 1998–2000 Contour & Mystique

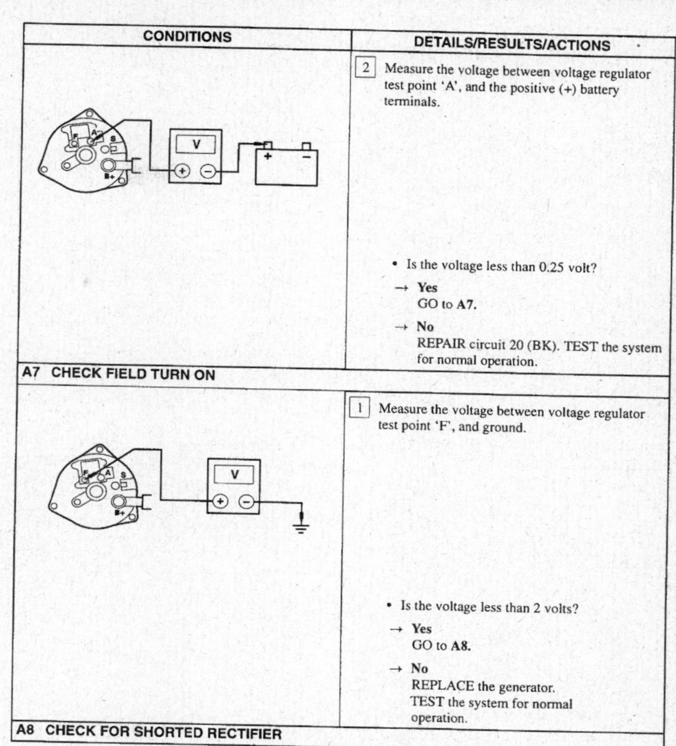

CONDITIONS	DETAILS/RESULTS/ACTIONS
	2 Measure the voltage between voltage regulator test point 'A', and the positive (+) battery terminals. • Is the voltage less than 0.25 volt? → **Yes** GO to **A7.** → **No** REPAIR circuit 20 (BK). TEST the system for normal operation.
A7 CHECK FIELD TURN ON	
	1 Measure the voltage between voltage regulator test point 'F', and ground. • Is the voltage less than 2 volts? → **Yes** GO to **A8.** → **No** REPLACE the generator. TEST the system for normal operation.
A8 CHECK FOR SHORTED RECTIFIER	

FM1129800298040X

Fig. 53 Test A: System Does Not Charge (Part 4 of 6). 1998–2000 Contour & Mystique

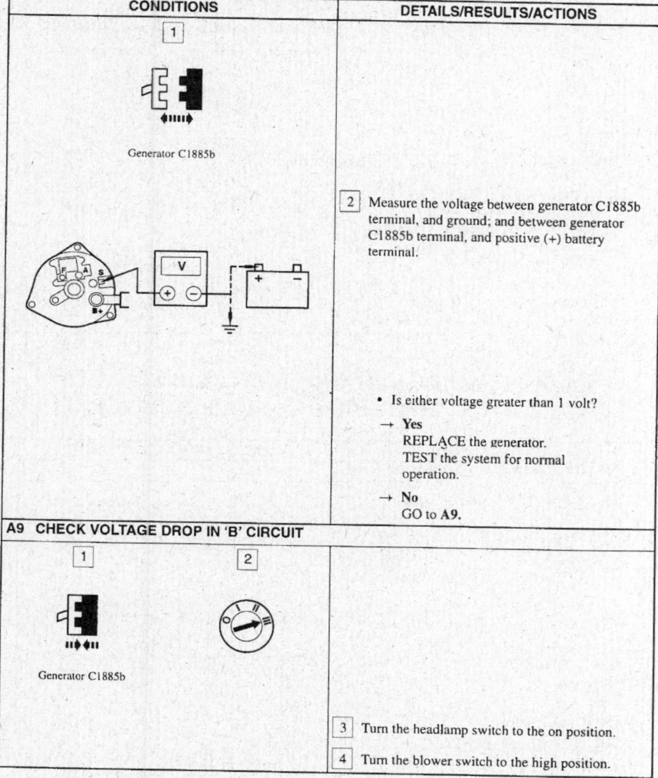

CONDITIONS	DETAILS/RESULTS/ACTIONS
1 Generator C1885b	
	2 Measure the voltage between generator C1885b terminal, and ground; and between generator C1885b terminal, and positive (+) battery terminal. • Is either voltage greater than 1 volt? → **Yes** REPLACE the generator. TEST the system for normal operation. → **No** GO to **A9.**
A9 CHECK VOLTAGE DROP IN 'B' CIRCUIT	
1 2 Generator C1885b	3 Turn the headlamp switch to the on position. 4 Turn the blower switch to the high position.

FM1129800298050X

Fig. 53 Test A: System Does Not Charge (Part 5 of 6). 1998–2000 Contour & Mystique

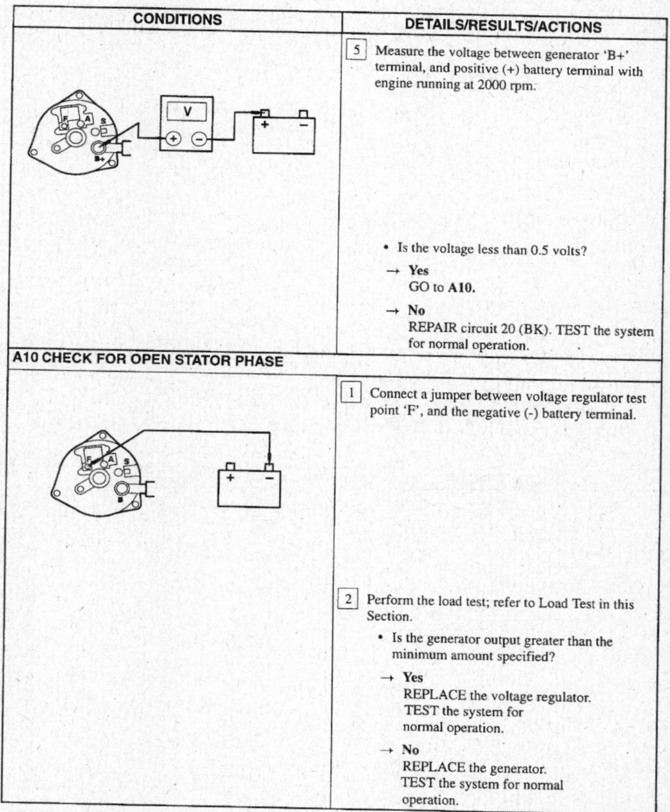

CONDITIONS	DETAILS/RESULTS/ACTIONS
	5 Measure the voltage between generator 'B+' terminal, and positive (+) battery terminal with engine running at 2000 rpm. • Is the voltage less than 0.5 volts? → **Yes** GO to **A10.** → **No** REPAIR circuit 20 (BK). TEST the system for normal operation.
A10 CHECK FOR OPEN STATOR PHASE	
	1 Connect a jumper between voltage regulator test point 'F', and the negative (-) battery terminal. 2 Perform the load test; refer to Load Test in this Section. • Is the generator output greater than the minimum amount specified? → **Yes** REPLACE the voltage regulator. TEST the system for normal operation. → **No** REPLACE the generator. TEST the system for normal operation.

FM1129800298060X

Fig. 53 Test A: System Does Not Charge (Part 6 of 6). 1998–2000 Contour & Mystique

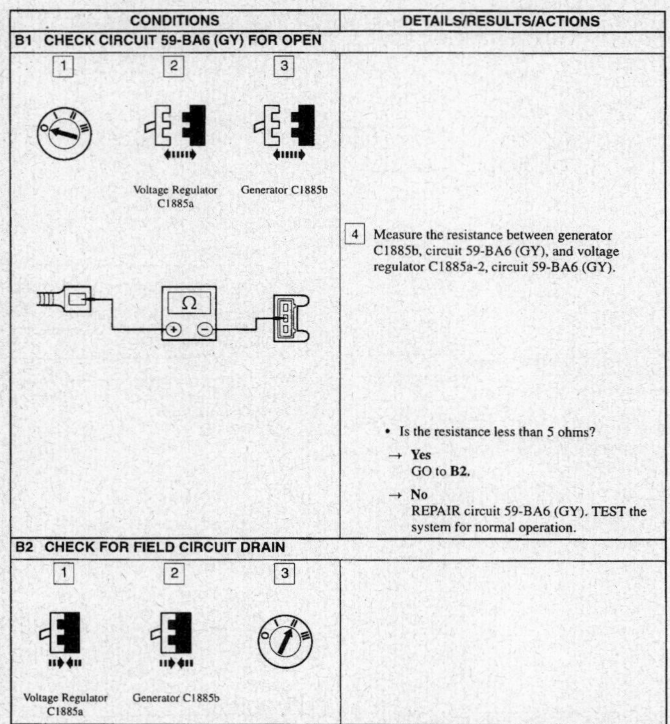

CONDITIONS	DETAILS/RESULTS/ACTIONS
B1 CHECK CIRCUIT 59-BA6 (GY) FOR OPEN	
1 2 3 Voltage Regulator C1885a; Generator C1885b	4 Measure the resistance between generator C1885b, circuit 59-BA6 (GY), and voltage regulator C1885a-2, circuit 59-BA6 (GY). • Is the resistance less than 5 ohms? → **Yes** GO to **B2.** → **No** REPAIR circuit 59-BA6 (GY). TEST the system for normal operation.
B2 CHECK FOR FIELD CIRCUIT DRAIN	
1 2 3 Voltage Regulator C1885a; Generator C1885b	

FM1129800299010X

Fig. 54 Test B: System Overcharges (Part 1 of 2). 1998–2000 Contour & Mystique

CONDITIONS	DETAILS/RESULTS/ACTIONS
C1 CHECK FOR OPEN 'A' CIRCUIT	
	1 Measure the voltage between voltage regulator test point 'A', and ground. • Is the voltage equal to the battery voltage? → **Yes** GO to **C2.** → **No** REPAIR circuit 20 (BK). TEST the system for normal operation.

FM1129800300010X

Fig. 55 Test C: Warning Indicator Stays On (Part 1 of 3). 1998–2000 Contour & Mystique

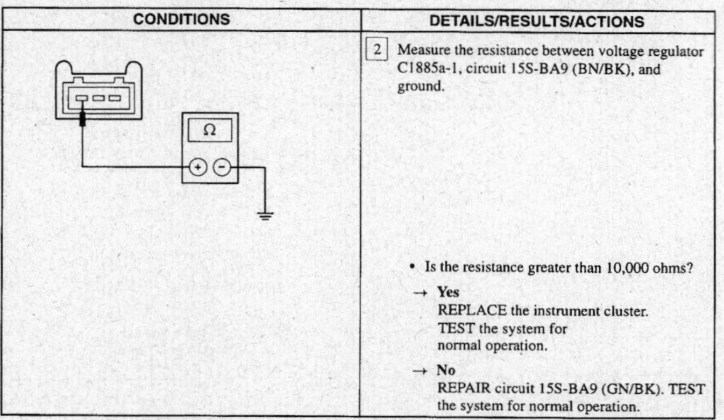

CONDITIONS	DETAILS/RESULTS/ACTIONS
	2 Measure the resistance between voltage regulator C1885a-1, circuit 15S-BA9 (BN/BK), and ground. • Is the resistance greater than 10,000 ohms? → **Yes** REPLACE the instrument cluster. TEST the system for normal operation. → **No** REPAIR circuit 15S-BA9 (GN/BK). TEST the system for normal operation.

FM1129800300030X

Fig. 55 Test C: Warning Indicator Stays On (Part 3 of 3). 1998–2000 Contour & Mystique

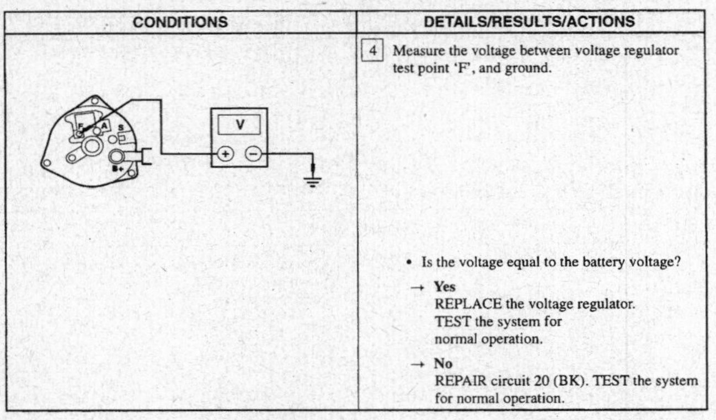

CONDITIONS	DETAILS/RESULTS/ACTIONS
	4 Measure the voltage between voltage regulator test point 'F', and ground. • Is the voltage equal to the battery voltage? → **Yes** REPLACE the voltage regulator. TEST the system for normal operation. → **No** REPAIR circuit 20 (BK). TEST the system for normal operation.

FM1129800299020X

Fig. 54 Test B: System Overcharges (Part 2 of 2). 1998–2000 Contour & Mystique

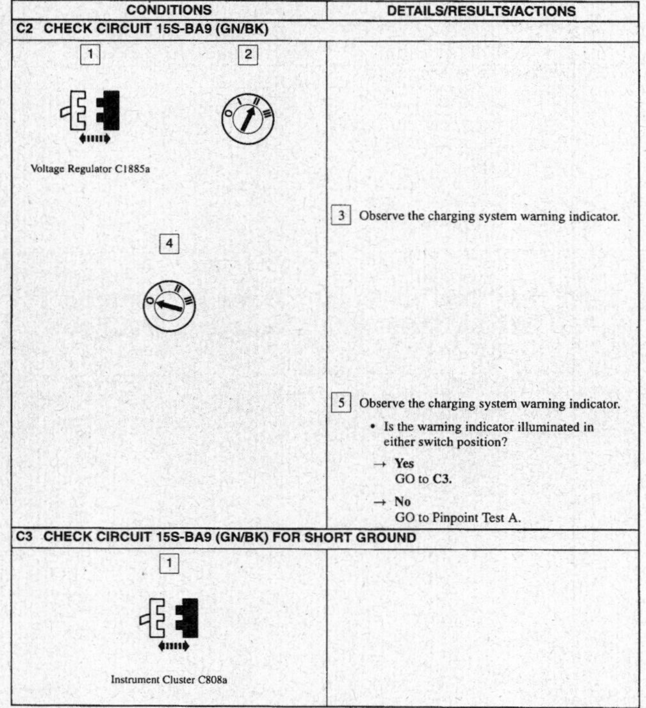

CONDITIONS	DETAILS/RESULTS/ACTIONS
C2 CHECK CIRCUIT 15S-BA9 (GN/BK)	
1 2 Voltage Regulator C1885a	3 Observe the charging system warning indicator.
4	5 Observe the charging system warning indicator. • Is the warning indicator illuminated in either switch position? → **Yes** GO to **C3.** → **No** GO to Pinpoint Test A.
C3 CHECK CIRCUIT 15S-BA9 (GN/BK) FOR SHORT GROUND	
1 Instrument Cluster C808a	

FM1129800300020X

Fig. 55 Test C: Warning Indicator Stays On (Part 2 of 3). 1998–2000 Contour & Mystique

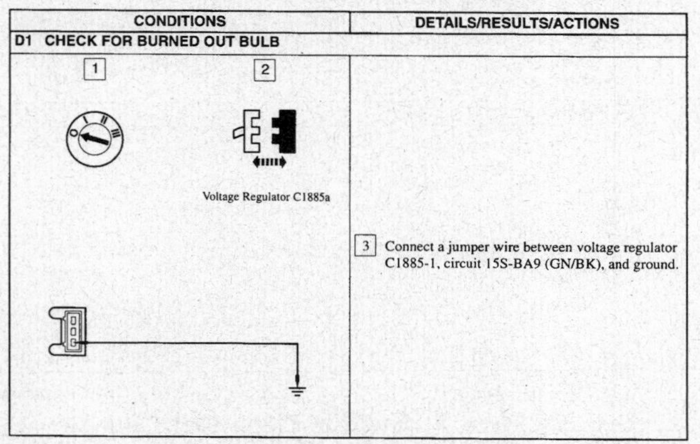

CONDITIONS	DETAILS/RESULTS/ACTIONS
D1 CHECK FOR BURNED OUT BULB	
1 2 Voltage Regulator C1885a	3 Connect a jumper wire between voltage regulator C1885-1, circuit 15S-BA9 (GN/BK), and ground.

FM1129800301010X

Fig. 56 Test D: Warning Indicator Is Inoperative (Part 1 of 4). 1998–2000 Contour & Mystique

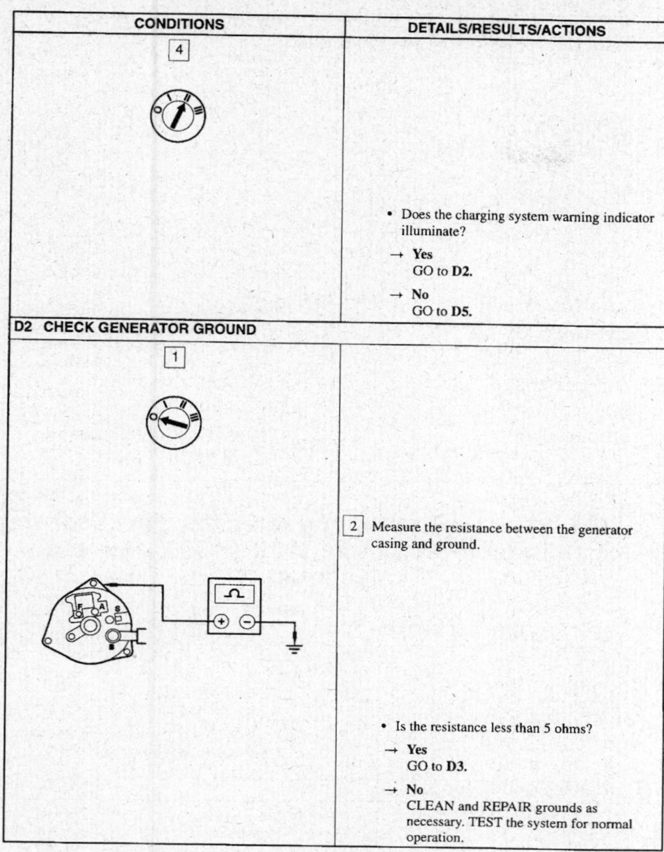

CONDITIONS	DETAILS/RESULTS/ACTIONS
4	• Does the charging system warning indicator illuminate? → Yes GO to **D2.** → No GO to **D5.**
D2 CHECK GENERATOR GROUND	
1	
	2 Measure the resistance between the generator casing and ground.
	• Is the resistance less than 5 ohms? → Yes GO to **D3.** → No CLEAN and REPAIR grounds as necessary. TEST the system for normal operation.

FM1129800301020X

Fig. 56 Test D: Warning Indicator Is Inoperative (Part 2 of 4). 1998–2000 Contour & Mystique

CONDITIONS	DETAILS/RESULTS/ACTIONS
	• Is the voltage greater than 1 volt? → Yes REPLACE the generator. TEST the system for normal operation. → No REPLACE the voltage regulator. TEST the system for normal operation.
D5 CHECK CIRCUIT 15S-BA9 (GN/BK) FOR OPEN	
1 2 Instrument Cluster C808a	
	3 Measure the resistance between voltage regulator C1885a-1, circuit 15S-BA9 (GN/BK), and instrument cluster C808a-3, circuit 15S-BA9 (GN/BK).
	• Is the resistance less than 5 ohms? → Yes REPLACE the instrument cluster. TEST the system for normal operation. → No REPAIR circuit 15S-BA9. TEST the system for normal operation.

FM1129800301040X

Fig. 56 Test D: Warning Indicator Is Inoperative (Part 4 of 4). 1998–2000 Contour & Mystique

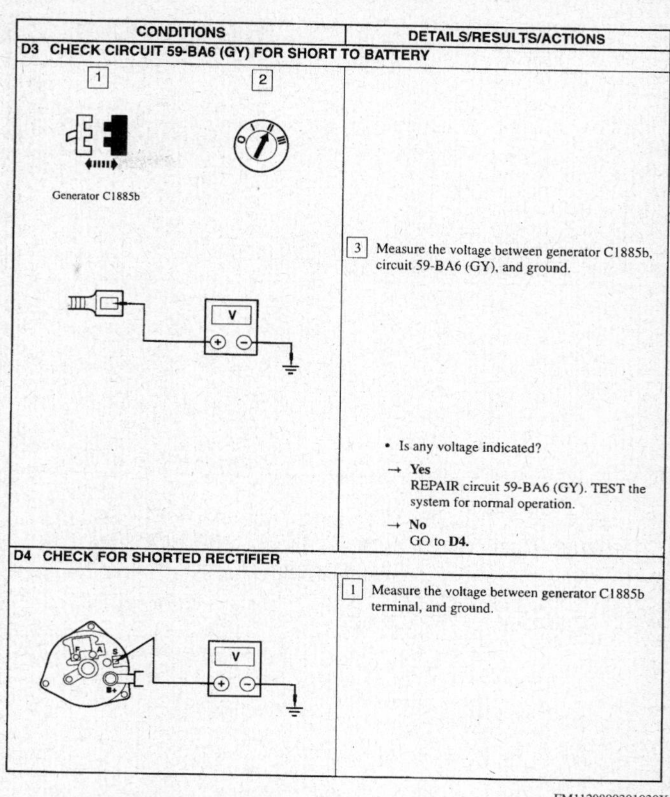

CONDITIONS	DETAILS/RESULTS/ACTIONS
D3 CHECK CIRCUIT 59-BA6 (GY) FOR SHORT TO BATTERY	
1 2 Generator C1885b	
	3 Measure the voltage between generator C1885b, circuit 59-BA6 (GY), and ground.
	• Is any voltage indicated? → Yes REPAIR circuit 59-BA6 (GY). TEST the system for normal operation. → No GO to **D4.**
D4 CHECK FOR SHORTED RECTIFIER	
	1 Measure the voltage between generator C1885b terminal, and ground.

FM1129800301030X

Fig. 56 Test D: Warning Indicator Is Inoperative (Part 3 of 4). 1998–2000 Contour & Mystique

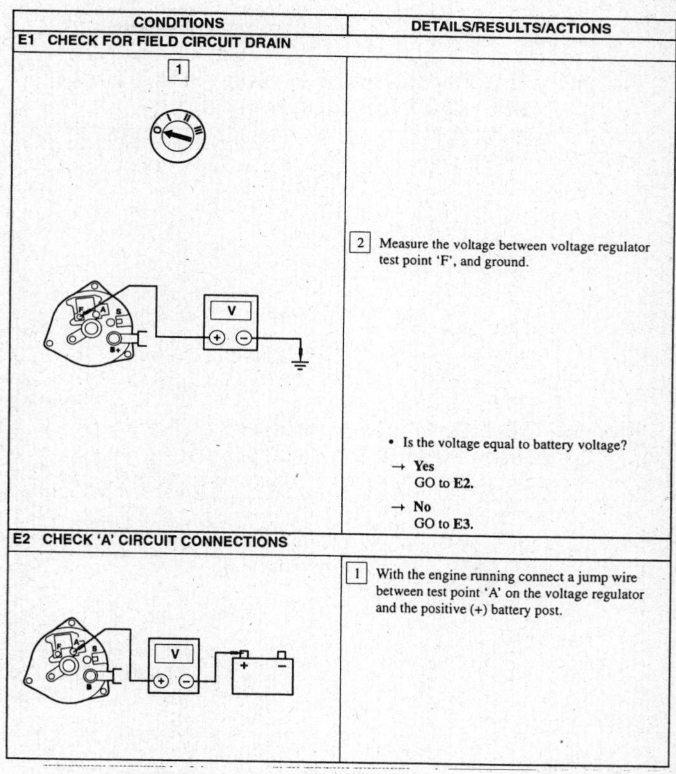

CONDITIONS	DETAILS/RESULTS/ACTIONS
E1 CHECK FOR FIELD CIRCUIT DRAIN	
1	
	2 Measure the voltage between voltage regulator test point 'F', and ground.
	• Is the voltage equal to battery voltage? → Yes GO to **E2.** → No GO to **E3.**
E2 CHECK 'A' CIRCUIT CONNECTIONS	
	1 With the engine running connect a jump wire between test point 'A' on the voltage regulator and the positive (+) battery post.

FM1129800302010X

Fig. 57 Test E: Warning Indicator Flickers/ Intermittent (Part 1 of 3). 1998–2000 Contour & Mystique

CONDITIONS	DETAILS/RESULTS/ACTIONS
	• Does the charging system warning indicator flicker? → **Yes** REPLACE the voltage regulator. TEST the system for normal operation. If concern still exits, REPLACE the generator. TEST the system for normal operation. → **No** REPAIR circuit 20 (BK) TEST the system for normal operation.
E3 CHECK FOR LOOSE BRUSH HOLDER SCREWS	
	1 Remove the generator. 2 Check the brush holder screws located on voltage regulator test points 'A' and 'F'. • Are the brush holder screws tight? → **Yes** GO to **E4.** → **No** TIGHTEN the screws to 3.0 Nm. TEST the system for normal operation.

FM1129800302020X

Fig. 57 Test E: Warning Indicator Flickers/ Intermittent (Part 2 of 3). 1998–2000 Contour & Mystique

CONDITIONS	DETAILS/RESULTS/ACTIONS
F1 CHECK FOR ACCESSORY DRIVE NOISE	
	1 Check the accessory drive for the following: – Correct drive belt installation. – Damaged pulley. • Is the accessory drive OK? → **Yes** GO to **F2.** → **No** REPAIR as required.TEST the system for normal operation.
F2 CHECK GENERATOR FOR PROPER INSTALLATION	
	1 Check generator and mounting brackets for proper alignment and installation.

FM1129800303010X

Fig. 58 Test F: Alternator Is Noisy (Part 1 of 2). 1998–2000 Contour & Mystique

CONDITIONS	DETAILS/RESULTS/ACTIONS
G1 VERIFY RADIO INTERFERENCE	
1	2 Tune the radio to a station where interference is present.

FM1129800304010X

Fig. 59 Test G: Radio Interference (Part 1 of 2). 1998–2000 Contour & Mystique

CONDITIONS	DETAILS/RESULTS/ACTIONS
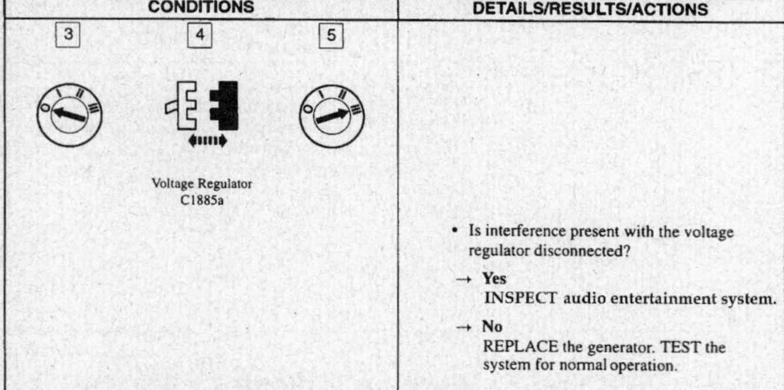	• Is interference present with the voltage regulator disconnected? → **Yes** INSPECT audio entertainment system. → **No** REPLACE the generator. TEST the system for normal operation.

FM1129800304020X

Fig. 59 Test G: Radio Interference (Part 2 of 2). 1998–2000 Contour & Mystique

CONDITIONS	DETAILS/RESULTS/ACTIONS
E4 CHECK THE SLIP RINGS FOR SHORT TO GROUND	
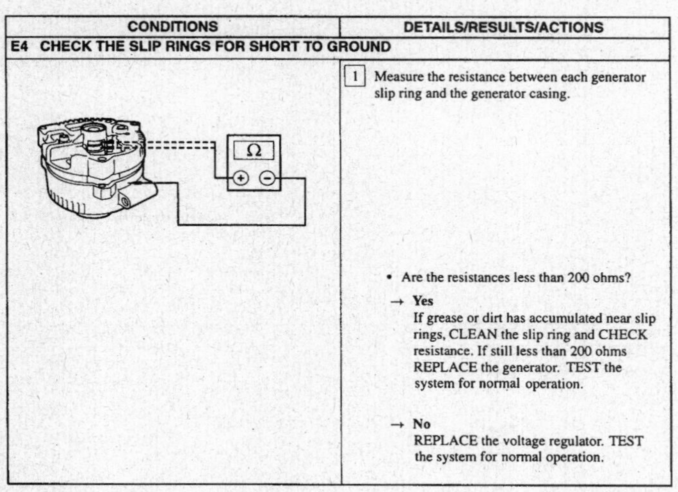	1 Measure the resistance between each generator slip ring and the generator casing. • Are the resistances less than 200 ohms? → **Yes** If grease or dirt has accumulated near slip rings, CLEAN the slip ring and CHECK resistance. If still less than 200 ohms REPLACE the generator. TEST the system for normal operation. → **No** REPLACE the voltage regulator. TEST the system for normal operation.

FM1129800302030X

Fig. 57 Test E: Warning Indicator Flickers/ Intermittent (Part 3 of 3). 1998–2000 Contour & Mystique

CONDITIONS	DETAILS/RESULTS/ACTIONS
	• Is the generator installed properly? → **Yes** GO to **F3.** → **No** INSTALL the generator correctly. TEST the system for normal operation.
F3 CHECK GENERATOR PULLEY	
	1 Check the generator pulley for damage and correct alignment. • Is the generator pulley OK? → **Yes** REPLACE the generator. TEST the ection system for normal operation. → **No** REPLACE the generator pulley. TEST the system for normal operation.

FM1129800303020X

Fig. 58 Test F: Alternator Is Noisy (Part 2 of 2). 1998–2000 Contour & Mystique

CONDITIONS	DETAILS/RESULTS/ACTIONS
H1 CHECK BATTERY CAPACITY	
	1 Perform battery capacity test. • Is the battery capacity OK? → **Yes** GO to **H2.** → **No** REPLACE the battery. TEST the system for normal operation.
H2 CHECK FOR KEY-OFF CURRENT DRAIN	
	1 Perform the battery drain component test. • Is the current drain OK? → **Yes** GO to **H3.** → **No** RETURN to the component tests to find the cause of key-off battery drain. TEST the system for normal operation.

FM1129800305010X

Fig. 60 Test H: Battery Does Not Hold A Charge (Part 1 of 2). 1998–2000 Contour & Mystique

CONDITIONS	DETAILS/RESULTS/ACTIONS
H3 CHECK THE GENERATOR	
	1 Perform the generator base voltage and no-load test. • Is the generator output voltage within the specified range? → Yes REPLACE the battery. TEST the system for normal operation. → No GO to Pinpoint Test A.

FM1129800305020X

Fig. 60 Test H: Battery Does Not Hold A Charge (Part 2 of 2). 1998–2000 Contour & Mystique

Condition	Possible Source	Action
• Battery is discharged or voltage is low	• Corroded terminal(s). • Loose connection(s). • High key-off current drain(s). • Battery. • Generator.	• GO to Pinpoint Test A.
• The charging system warning indicator is on with the engine running (the system voltage does not increase)	• Circuitry. • Voltage regulator. • Generator.	• GO to Pinpoint Test B.
• The system overcharges (battery voltage greater than 15.5 volts)	• Circuitry. • Voltage regulator. • Generator.	• GO to Pinpoint Test C.
• The charging system warning indicator is on with the engine running and the system increases voltage	• Circuitry. • Instrument cluster. • Voltage regulator. • Generator.	• GO to Pinpoint Test D.
• The charging system warning indicator is off with the ignition switch in the RUN position and the engine off	• Bulb. • Circuitry. • Instrument cluster. • Voltage regulator. • Generator.	• GO to Pinpoint Test E.
• The charging system warning indicator flickers or is intermittent	• Corroded terminal(s). • Fuse(s). • Circuitry. • Voltage regulator. • Generator.	• GO to Pinpoint Test F.
• The generator is noisy	• Bolts or brackets. • Drive belt. • Generator or pulley.	• GO to Pinpoint Test G.
• Radio interference	• Generator. • Circuitry. • In-vehicle entertainment system.	• GO to Pinpoint Test H.

FM1120000541000X

Fig. 62 Symptom chart. 2000–02 Crown Victoria & Grand Marquis

Test Step		Result ▶	Action to Take
A5	CHECK BATTERY		
	• Perform Battery Capacity Testing • **Is the battery capacity OK?**	Yes ▶ No ▶	GO to **A6.** REPLACE battery.
A6	CHECK FOR KEY-OFF DRAIN		
	• Perform Battery Drain Testing as described. • **Is current drain less than 50 mA (or test lamp off)?**	Yes ▶ No ▶	GO to **A7.** GO to Drain Testing in Component Tests to find cause of ignition switch-OFF battery drain.
A7	CHECK FOR OPEN B+ CIRCUIT		
	• Measure voltage at B+ terminal on back of generator, Circuit 38 (BK / O). • **Is voltage at B+ terminal equal to battery voltage?**	Yes ▶ No ▶	GO to **A8.** SERVICE open in Circuit 38 (BK / O).
A8	CHECK FOR OPEN A CIRCUIT		
	• Measure voltage at test point A on voltage regulator. • **Is voltage at test point A equal to battery voltage?**	Yes ▶ No ▶	GO to **A9.** CHECK power distribution box Fuse STR / ALT (30A) in Circuit 36 (Y / W) and REPLACE if required. If OK, SERVICE open in Circuit 36 (Y / W).
A9	CHECK FOR OPEN I CIRCUIT		
	NOTE: Voltage regulator must be connected to wiring harness for this test. • Turn ignition switch to RUN position. • Measure voltage at wiring harness I terminal, Circuit 904 (LG / R) at connector C154. • **Is voltage greater than 1 V?**	Yes ▶ No ▶	GO to **A10.** SERVICE open or high resistance in Circuit 904 (LG / R).
A10	CHECK VOLTAGE DROP IN A CIRCUIT		
	• Measure voltage drop between test point A on the voltage regulator and positive (+) battery post. • **Is voltage drop less than 0.25 V?**	Yes ▶ No ▶	GO to **A11.** SERVICE excess voltage drop in Circuit 36 (Y / W). CHECK fuse and connectors in Circuit 36 (Y / W) and SERVICE as required.
A11	CHECK FOR SHORTED RECTIFIER		
	• Remove one-pin S connector C153 from generator. • Measure voltage between the S terminal on back of generator and ground. • Measure voltage between positive (+) battery terminal and S terminal on back of generator. • **Is either voltage reading greater than 1 V?**	Yes ▶ No ▶	REPLACE generator. GO to **A12.**
A12	CHECK VOLTAGE DROP IN B+ CIRCUIT		
	• Install S connector C153. • Turn ignition switch to RUN. • Turn headlamps ON and set blower on HIGH. • With engine running at 2000 rpm, measure voltage drop between B+ terminal on back of generator and positive (+) battery post. • **Is voltage drop less than 0.5 V?**	Yes ▶ No ▶	GO to **A13.** SERVICE excess voltage drop in Circuit 38 (BK / O). CHECK fuse link in Circuit 38 and connections between battery and power distribution box.
A13	CHECK FOR OPEN / SHORTED FIELD		
	• Remove generator from vehicle. • Remove voltage regulator. • Measure resistance between the generator slip rings. • **Is resistance greater than 10 ohms OR less than 1 ohm?**	Yes ▶ No ▶	REPLACE generator. REPLACE voltage regulator. RETEST system.

FM1129800267020X

Fig. 63 Test A: System Does Not Charge (Part 2 of 2). 1998–99 Crown Victoria & Grand Marquis

Condition	Possible Source	Action
• System Does Not Charge	• Ignition switch OFF battery drain. • Circuitry. • Voltage regulator. • Generator. • Battery. • Battery connections. • Drive belt.	• GO to Pinpoint Test A.
• System Overcharges (Battery Boils Over)	• Circuitry. • Poor ground. • Voltage regulator. • Generator.	• GO to Pinpoint Test B.
• Indicator Lamp Stays ON, Engine Running	• Circuitry. • Voltage regulator. • Generator.	• GO to Pinpoint Test C.
• Indicator Lamp Stays ON, Ignition Switch OFF	• Circuitry. • Improper lamp circuit wiring. • Instrument cluster.	• GO to Pinpoint Test D.
• Indicator Lamp Does Not Come On	• Burned out lamp. • Circuitry. • Poor ground. • Voltage regulator. • Generator.	• GO to Pinpoint Test E.
• Indicator Lamp Flickers / Intermittent	• Loose connection to generator, voltage regulator or power distribution box. • Circuitry. • Loose brush holder screw. • Voltage regulator. • Generator.	• GO to Pinpoint Test F.
• Generator Noisy	• Accessory drive belt. • Accessory brackets. • Bent pulley. • Generator. • Other accessories.	• GO to Pinpoint Test G.
• Radio Interference	• Voltage regulator. • Generator. • Other components.	• GO to Pinpoint Test H.

FM1129800266000X

Fig. 61 Symptom chart. 1998–99 Crown Victoria & Grand Marquis

Test Step		Result ▶	Action to Take
A1	CHECK BATTERY CONNECTIONS		
	• Inspect battery cables for loose or corroded connections. • Inspect battery for corrosion. • **Are battery cables clean, tight and free from corrosion?**	Yes ▶ No ▶	GO to **A2.** SERVICE battery and cables as necessary. RESTORE vehicle. RETEST system.
A2	CHECK DRIVE BELT TENSION		
	• Perform drive belt adjustment procedure. • **Is the drive belt adjusted properly?**	Yes ▶ No ▶	GO to **A3.** ADJUST or REPLACE drive belt.
A3	LOOSE BATTERY POST		
	• Check for loose battery posts. • **Are posts OK?**	Yes ▶ No ▶	GO to **A4.** REPLACE battery.
A4	CRACKED BATTERY COVER		
	• Remove battery hold down clamps and shields. • Check for broken / cracked case or battery cover. • **Are case and cover OK?**	Yes ▶ No ▶	GO to **A5.** REPLACE battery.

FM1129800267010X

Fig. 63 Test A: System Does Not Charge (Part 1 of 2). 1998–99 Crown Victoria & Grand Marquis

Test Step		Result ▶	Action to Take
B1	CHECK VOLTAGE DROP IN A CIRCUIT		
	• Turn ignition switch to RUN position. • Measure voltage between test point A on voltage regulator connector C154 and positive (+) battery post. • **Is voltage drop less than 0.25 V?**	Yes ▶ No ▶	GO to **B2.** SERVICE excess voltage drop in Circuit 36 (Y / W). CHECK power distribution box Fuse STR / ALT (30A) and connectors in Circuit 36 (Y / W). SERVICE as required.
B2	CHECK VOLTAGE DROP IN I CIRCUIT		
	NOTE: Voltage regulator must be connected to wiring harness for this test. • Measure voltage at wiring harness I terminal connector C154, Circuit 904 (LG / R). • **Is voltage greater than 1 V?**	Yes ▶ No ▶	GO to **B3.** SERVICE high resistance in Circuit 904 (LG / R).
B3	CHECK FOR POOR GROUNDS		
	• Check for poor ground connections between voltage regulator and generator, battery and engine, or engine and battery. • **Are all ground connections clean and tight?**	Yes ▶ No ▶	GO to **B4.** CLEAN or SERVICE grounds as required.
B4	CHECK FOR GROUNDED SLIP RING		
	• Remove generator from vehicle. • Remove voltage regulator. • Measure resistance from each generator slip ring to the generator housing. • **Is resistance from either slip ring to housing less than 200 ohms?**	Yes ▶ No ▶	If grease or dirt has accumulated near slip rings, CLEAN slip rings and RECHECK resistance. If still less than 200 ohms, REPLACE generator. REPLACE voltage regulator.

FM1129800268000X

Fig. 64 Test B: System Overcharges. 1998–99 Crown Victoria & Grand Marquis

	Test Step	Result	Action to Take
C1	CHECK FOR OPEN A CIRCUIT		
	• Measure voltage at test point A on the voltage regulator. • **Is voltage at test point A equal to battery voltage?**	Yes	▶ GO to **C2**.
		No	▶ CHECK power distribution box Fuse STR/ALT (30A) in Circuit 36 (Y/W) and REPLACE if required. If OK, SERVICE open in Circuit 36 (Y/W).
C2	CHECK FOR SHORTED I CIRCUIT		
	• Remove three-pin voltage regulator connector C154. • Turn ignition switch to RUN position. • **Is indicator lamp on?**	Yes	▶ SERVICE short to ground in Circuit 904 (LG/R).
		No	▶ GO to **C3**.
C3	CHECK S CIRCUIT FUNCTION		
	• Install voltage regulator connector C154. • Remove one-pin S connector C153. • Connect wiring harness S terminal, Circuit 4 (W/BK) to positive (+) battery post using a jumper wire. • **Is indicator lamp on?**	Yes	▶ REMOVE jumper wire. GO to **C4**.
		No	▶ REMOVE jumper wire. GO to **C5**.
C4	CHECK FOR OPEN S CIRCUIT		
	• Remove three-pin voltage regulator connector C154. • Measure wiring resistance between the one-pin S connector and the S (center) pin of the voltage regulator connector. • **Is resistance greater than 1 ohm?**	Yes	▶ SERVICE open or excess resistance in Circuit 4 (W/BK).
		No	▶ CHECK for loose or bent pin in voltage regulator or connector. If OK, REPLACE voltage regulator.
C5	CHECK STATOR OUTPUT VOLTAGE		
	• Start engine. • Measure voltage at S terminal on back of generator. • **Is voltage at least 1/2 of battery voltage?**	Yes	▶ GO to **C6**.
		No	▶ GO to Pinpoint Test A to find the cause of low generator output.
C6	CHECK GENERATOR OUTPUT VOLTAGE		
	• Measure voltage at the B+ terminal on back of generator with engine running at 2000 rpm and all accessories turned OFF. • **Is voltage greater than 15.5 V?**	Yes	▶ GO to Pinpoint Test B to find cause of high output voltage.
		No	▶ REPLACE voltage regulator.

FM1129800269000X

Fig. 65 Test C: Indicator Lamp Stays On, Engine Running. 1998–99 Crown Victoria & Grand Marquis

	Test Step	Result	Action to Take
F1	CHECK FOR LOOSE CONNECTIONS		
	• Check these connections for corrosion, loose or bent pins, or loose eyelets: — Three-pin voltage regulator connector C154. — One-pin S connector C153. — Generator B+ eyelet. — Power distribution box eyelets. — Battery cables. • **Are all connections clean and tight?**	Yes	▶ GO to **F2**.
		No	▶ CLEAN or SERVICE connections as required.
F2	CHECK FOR LOOSE A CIRCUIT FUSE		
	• Turn ignition switch to RUN. • Check power distribution box Fuse STR/ALT (30A) for a loose connection by wiggling fuse with engine running. • **Does indicator lamp flicker?**	Yes	▶ SERVICE loose fuse connection.
		No	▶ GO to **F3**.
F3	CHECK A CIRCUIT CONNECTIONS		
	• With engine running, connect test point A on voltage regulator to the positive (+) battery post using a jumper wire. • **Does indicator lamp flicker?**	Yes	▶ GO to **F4**.
		No	▶ SERVICE poor connection in Circuit 36 (Y/W).
F4	CHECK BRUSH HOLDER SCREWS		
	• Remove generator from vehicle. • Check brush holder screws, located on voltage regulator. • **Are the brush holder screws tight?**	Yes	▶ GO to **F5**.
		No	▶ TIGHTEN screws.
F5	CHECK FOR GROUNDED SLIP RING		
	• Remove voltage regulator. • Measure resistance from each generator slip ring to generator housing. • **Is resistance from either slip ring to housing less than 200 ohms?**	Yes	▶ If grease or dirt has accumulated near slip rings, CLEAN slip rings and RECHECK resistance. If still less than 200 ohms, REPLACE generator.
		No	▶ REPLACE voltage regulator.

FM1129800272000X

Fig. 68 Test F: Indicator Lamp Flickers/Intermittent. 1998–99 Crown Victoria & Grand Marquis

	Test Step	Result	Action to Take
H1	VERIFY RADIO INTERFERENCE		
	• Start engine. • Tune radio to a station where interference is present. • Remove three-pin voltage regulator connectorC154. • **Is interference present with connector removed?**	Yes	▶ LOCATE cause of the radio interference.
		No	▶ REPLACE generator.

FM1129800274000X

Fig. 70 Test H: Radio Interference. 1998–99 Crown Victoria & Grand Marquis

	Test Step	Result	Action to Take
D1	CHECK LAMP CIRCUIT WIRING		
	• Turn ignition switch to OFF position. • Remove three-pin voltage regulator connector C154. • **Measure voltage at wiring harness I terminal, Circuit 904 (LG/R).** • **Is voltage greater than 0 V?**	Yes	▶ SERVICE Circuit 904 (LG/R). Circuit should be HOT in RUN position only.
		No	▶ SERVICE instrument cluster.

FM1129800270000X

Fig. 66 Test D: Indicator Lamp Stays On, Ignition Off. 1998–99 Crown Victoria & Grand Marquis

	Test Step	Result	Action to Take
E1	CHECK FOR OPEN I CIRCUIT		
	• Remove three-pin voltage regulator connectorC154. • Turn ignition switch to RUN position. • Measure voltage at wiring harness I terminal, Circuit 904 (LG/R). • **Is voltage equal to B+?**	Yes	▶ GO to **E2**.
		No	▶ SERVICE open in Circuit 904 (LG/R).
E2	CHECK FOR BURNED OUT BULB		
	• Connect wiring harness I terminal, Circuit 904 (LG/R) to ground with a jumper wire. • **Is indicator lamp on?**	Yes	▶ REMOVE jumper wire. GO to **E3**.
		No	▶ REPLACE lamp or SERVICE high resistance in lamp socket or Circuit 904 (LG/R).
E3	CHECK FOR POOR GROUNDS		
	• Check for poor ground connections between voltage regulator and generator, battery and engine, or engine and battery. • **Are all ground connections clean and tight?**	Yes	▶ GO to **E4**.
		No	▶ CLEAN or SERVICE grounds as required.
E4	CHECK S CIRCUIT WIRING		
	• Remove one-pin S connector C153 from generator. • Measure voltage at wiring harness S terminal, Circuit 4 (W/BK). • **Is voltage greater than 0 V?**	Yes	▶ SERVICE Circuit 4 (W/BK). Circuit should be HOT only when engine is running.
		No	▶ GO to **E5**.
E5	CHECK FOR SHORTED RECTIFIER		
	• Measure voltage at the S terminal on the back of generator. • **Is voltage greater than 1 V?**	Yes	▶ If lamp is on with one-pin S connector removed, REPLACE generator.
		No	▶ REPLACE voltage regulator.

FM1129800271000X

Fig. 67 Test E: Indicator Lamp Does Not Light. 1998–99 Crown Victoria & Grand Marquis

	Test Step	Result	Action to Take
G1	CHECK FOR ACCESSORY DRIVE NOISE		
	• Check drive belt to make sure that it is installed properly and is not damaged. • **Is drive belt OK?**	Yes	▶ GO to **G2**.
		No	▶ and SERVICE accessory drive belt as required.
G2	CHECK GENERATOR MOUNTING		
	• Check generator and generator mounting bracket for loose bolts or misalignment condition. • **Is generator mounted correctly?**	Yes	▶ GO to **G3**.
		No	▶ INSTALL generator to specification.
G3	CHECK GENERATOR PULLEY		
	• Check generator pulley for damage (bent) or a misalignment condition. • **Is pulley OK?**	Yes	▶ If noise is still present REPLACE generator.
		No	▶ REPLACE generator pulley.

FM1129800273000X

Fig. 69 Test G: Alternator Is Noisy. 1998–99 Crown Victoria & Grand Marquis

TEST CONDITIONS	TEST DETAILS/RESULTS/ACTIONS
A1 CHECK BATTERY CONDITION	
	☐ Carry out the Battery — Condition Test to determine if the battery can hold a charge and is OK for use. • Is the battery OK? → **Yes** GO to **A2**. → **No** INSTALL a new battery. TEST the system for normal operation.
A2 CHECK FOR GENERATOR OUTPUT	
	☐ Carry out the On-Vehicle Generator Load/No-Load Tests. • Is the generator OK? → **Yes** GO to **A3**. → **No** GO to Pinpoint Test B.
A3 CHECK FOR CURRENT DRAINS	
	☐ Carry out the Battery — Drain Test. • Are there any excessive current drains? → **Yes** REPAIR as necessary. TEST the system for normal operation. → **No** GO to **A4**.

FM1120000542010X

Fig. 71 Test A: Battery Discharged or Voltage Low (Part 1 of 2). 2000–01 Crown Victoria & Grand Marquis

TEST CONDITIONS	TEST DETAILS/RESULTS/ACTIONS
A4 CHECK FOR CURRENT DRAINS WHICH SHUT OFF WHEN THE BATTERY IS DISCONNECTED	
	1 Carry out the Battery — Electronic Drains Which Shut Off When the Battery Cable is Disconnected Test. • Are there any current drains which shut off when the battery is disconnected? → **Yes** REPAIR as necessary. TEST the system for normal operation. → **No** GO to Pinpoint Test B.

FM1120000542020X

Fig. 71 Test A: Battery Discharged or Voltage Low (Part 2 of 2). 2000–01 Crown Victoria & Grand Marquis

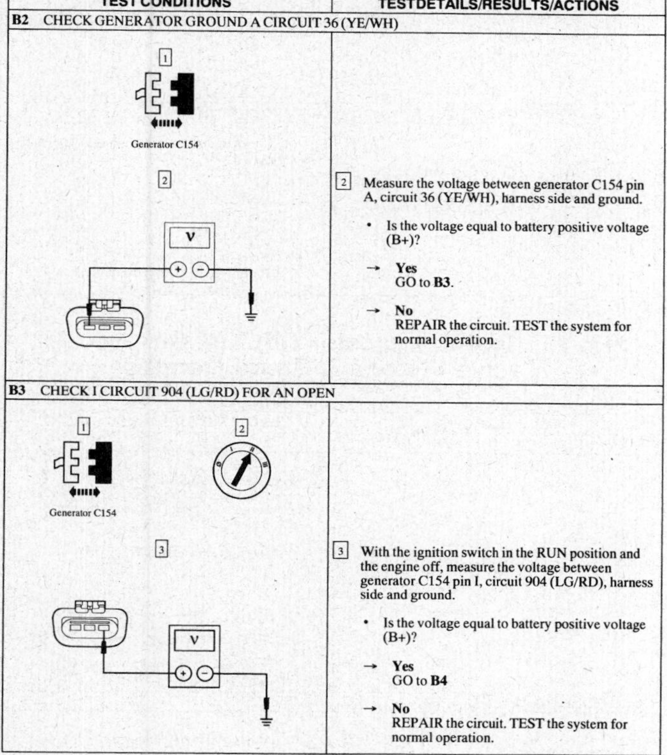

TEST CONDITIONS	TEST DETAILS/RESULTS/ACTIONS
B2 CHECK GENERATOR GROUND A CIRCUIT 36 (YE/WH)	
1 Generator C154	
2	2 Measure the voltage between generator C154 pin A, circuit 36 (YE/WH), harness side and ground. • Is the voltage equal to battery positive voltage (B+)? → **Yes** GO to **B3**. → **No** REPAIR the circuit. TEST the system for normal operation.
B3 CHECK I CIRCUIT 904 (LG/RD) FOR AN OPEN	
1 Generator C154 2	
3	3 With the ignition switch in the RUN position and the engine off, measure the voltage between generator C154 pin I, circuit 904 (LG/RD), harness side and ground. • Is the voltage equal to battery positive voltage (B+)? → **Yes** GO to **B4** → **No** REPAIR the circuit. TEST the system for normal operation.

FM1120000543020X

Fig. 72 Test B: Indicator Stays On, Engine Running (Part 2 of 3). 2000–01 Crown Victoria & Grand Marquis

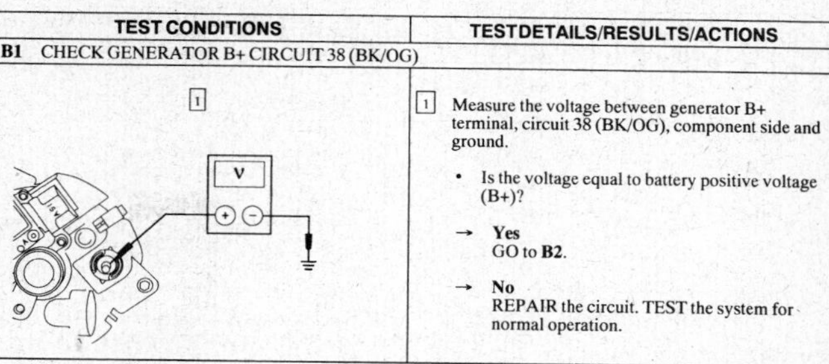

TEST CONDITIONS	TEST DETAILS/RESULTS/ACTIONS
B1 CHECK GENERATOR B+ CIRCUIT 38 (BK/OG)	
1	1 Measure the voltage between generator B+ terminal, circuit 38 (BK/OG), component side and ground. • Is the voltage equal to battery positive voltage (B+)? → **Yes** GO to **B2**. → **No** REPAIR the circuit. TEST the system for normal operation.

FM1120000543010X

Fig. 72 Test B: Indicator Stays On, Engine Running (Part 1 of 3). 2000–01 Crown Victoria & Grand Marquis

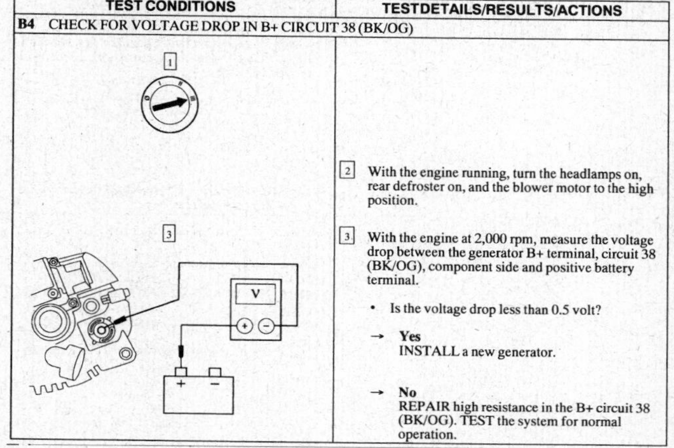

TEST CONDITIONS	TEST DETAILS/RESULTS/ACTIONS
B4 CHECK FOR VOLTAGE DROP IN B+ CIRCUIT 38 (BK/OG)	
1	
	2 With the engine running, turn the headlamps on, rear defroster on, and the blower motor to the high position.
3	3 With the engine at 2,000 rpm, measure the voltage drop between the generator B+ terminal, circuit 38 (BK/OG), component side and positive battery terminal. • Is the voltage drop less than 0.5 volt? → **Yes** INSTALL a new generator. → **No** REPAIR high resistance in the B+ circuit 38 (BK/OG). TEST the system for normal operation.

FM1120000543030X

Fig. 72 Test B: Indicator Stays On, Engine Running (Part 3 of 3). 2000–01 Crown Victoria & Grand Marquis

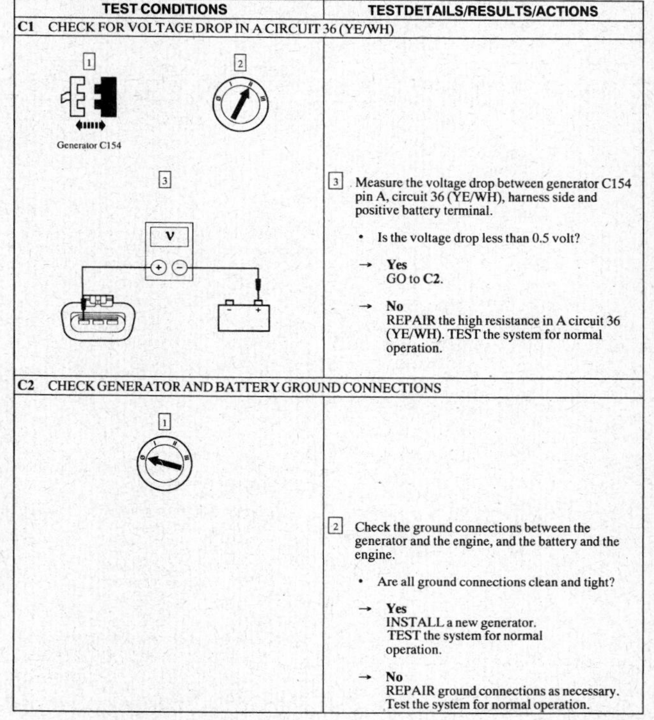

TEST CONDITIONS	TEST DETAILS/RESULTS/ACTIONS
C1 CHECK FOR VOLTAGE DROP IN A CIRCUIT 36 (YE/WH)	
1 Generator C154 2	
3	3 Measure the voltage drop between generator C154 pin A, circuit 36 (YE/WH), harness side and positive battery terminal. • Is the voltage drop less than 0.5 volt? → **Yes** GO to **C2**. → **No** REPAIR the high resistance in A circuit 36 (YE/WH). TEST the system for normal operation.
C2 CHECK GENERATOR AND BATTERY GROUND CONNECTIONS	
1	
	2 Check the ground connections between the generator and the engine, and the battery and the engine. • Are all ground connections clean and tight? → **Yes** INSTALL a new generator. TEST the system for normal operation. → **No** REPAIR ground connections as necessary. Test the system for normal operation.

FM1120000544000X

Fig. 73 Test C: System Overcharges. 2000–01 Crown Victoria & Grand Marquis

TEST CONDITIONS	TEST DETAILS/RESULTS/ACTIONS
D1 CHECK I CIRCUIT 904 (LG/RD) FOR SHORT TO GROUND	
1 Generator C154 2	2 With the ignition switch in the RUN position, check the charging system warning indicator. • Is the charging system warning indicator illuminated? → **Yes** REPAIR generator I circuit 904 (LG/RD) for a short to ground. TEST the system for normal operation. → **No** INSTALL a new generator. TEST the system for normal operation.

FM1120000545000X

Fig. 74 Test D: Indicator Stays On, Engine Running. 2000–01 Crown Victoria & Grand Marquis

TEST CONDITIONS	TEST DETAILS/RESULTS/ACTIONS
F1 CHECK FOR LOOSE CONNECTIONS	
	1 Check all generator, battery, and power distribution connections for looseness, corrosion, loose or bent terminals, or loose eyelets. • Are all connections clean and tight? → **Yes** GO to **F2**. → **No** REPAIR as necessary. TEST the system for normal operation.
F2 CHECK FUSE CONNECTIONS	
1	1 With the engine running, check BJB fuse 2 (30A) in A circuit 36 (YE/WH) and the CJB fuse 15 (10A) in I circuit 904 (LG/RD) for looseness by wiggling the fuse and noting the charging system warning indicator lamp operation. • Does the charging system warning indicator flicker? → **Yes** REPAIR loose fuse connection(s) as necessary. TEST the system for normal operation. → **No** GO to **F3**.

FM1120000547010X

Fig. 76 Test F: Indicator Flickers or Intermittent (Part 1 of 2). 2000–01 Crown Victoria & Grand Marquis

TEST CONDITIONS	TEST DETAILS/RESULTS/ACTIONS
F3 CHECK A CIRCUIT 36 (YE/WH) CONNECTIONS	
1	
2	2 Connect a fused (15A) jumper wire between generator C154, pin A, circuit 36 (YE/WH), harness side and the positive battery terminal.
3	3 With the engine running note the charging system warning indicator operation. • Does the charging system warning indicator flicker? → **Yes** INSTALL a new generator. TEST the system for normal operation. → **No** REPAIR loose connection(s) in circuits. TEST the system for normal operation.

FM1120000547020X

Fig. 76 Test F: Indicator Flickers or Intermittent (Part 2 of 2). 2000–01 Crown Victoria & Grand Marquis

TEST CONDITIONS	TEST DETAILS/RESULTS/ACTIONS
E1 CHECK THE CHARGING SYSTEM WARNING INDICATOR LAMP	
1 Generator C154	
2	2 With the engine off, connect a fused (15A) jumper wire between the generator C154 pin I, circuit 904 (LG/RD), harness side and ground.
3	
E1 CHECK THE CHARGING SYSTEM WARNING INDICATOR LAMP (Continued)	
	• Is the charging system warning indicator lamp illuminated? → **Yes** INSTALL a new generator. TEST the system for normal operation. → **No** INSPECT the instrument cluster.

FM1120000546000X

Fig. 75 Test E: Indicator Off, Key On. 2000–01 Crown Victoria & Grand Marquis

TEST CONDITIONS	TEST DETAILS/RESULTS/ACTIONS
G1 CHECK FOR ACCESSORY DRIVE NOISE	
	1 Check the accessory drive belt for damage and correct installation. Check the accessory mounting brackets and generator pulley for looseness or misalignment. • Is the accessory drive OK? → **Yes** GO to **G2**. → **No** REPAIR as necessary. TEST the system for normal operation.
G2 CHECK GENERATOR MOUNTING	
	1 Check the generator mounting for loose bolts or misalignment. • Is the generator mounted correctly? → **Yes** GO to **G3**. → **No** REPAIR as necessary. TEST the system for normal operation.
G3 CHECK GENERATOR FOR ELECTRICAL NOISE	
1 Generator C154 2	3 With the engine running, turn the headlamps on, rear defroster on, and the blower motor to the high position. • Is the noise still present? → **Yes** GO to **G4**. → **No** INSTALL a new generator. TEST the system for normal operation.

FM1120000548010X

Fig. 77 Test G: Alternator Is Noisy (Part 1 of 2). 2000–01 Crown Victoria & Grand Marquis

TEST CONDITIONS	TEST DETAILS/RESULTS/ACTIONS
G4 CHECK GENERATOR FOR MECHANICAL NOISE	
1 2 3 Generator C154	
	4 Turn all accessories OFF. With the engine running, use a stethoscope or equivalent listening device to probe the generator for unusual mechanical noise. • Is the generator the noise source? → **Yes** INSTALL a new generator. TEST the system for normal operation. → **No** INSPECT for source of engine noise.

FM1120000548020X

Fig. 77 Test G: Alternator Is Noisy (Part 2 of 2). 2000–01 Crown Victoria & Grand Marquis

CONDITIONS	DETAILS/RESULTS/ACTIONS
A1 CHECK BATTERY CONDITION	
	1 Carry out the Battery — Condition Test to determine if the battery can hold a charge and is OK for use. • Is the battery OK? → **Yes** GO to **A2**. → **No** INSTALL a new battery. TEST the system for normal operation.

FM1120200740010X

Fig. 79 Test A: Battery Is Discharged Or Voltage Is Low (Part 1 of 2). 2002 Crown Victoria & Grand Marquis

CONDITIONS	DETAILS/RESULTS/ACTIONS
A2 CHECK FOR GENERATOR OUTPUT	
	1 Carry out the On-Vehicle Generator Load/No-Load Tests. • Is the generator OK? → **Yes** GO to **A3**. → **No** GO to Pinpoint Test B.
A3 CHECK FOR CURRENT DRAINS	
	1 Carry out the Battery — Drain Test. • Are there any excessive current drains? → **Yes** REPAIR as necessary. TEST the system for normal operation. → **No** GO to **A4**.
A4 CHECK FOR CURRENT DRAINS WHICH SHUT OFF WHEN THE BATTERY IS DISCONNECTED	
	1 Carry out the Battery — Electronic Drains Which Shut Off When the Battery Cable is Disconnected Test. Refer to Component Tests in this section. • Are there any current drains which shut off when the battery is disconnected? → **Yes** REPAIR as necessary. TEST the system for normal operation. → **No** GO to Pinpoint Test B.

FM1120200740020X

Fig. 79 Test A: Battery Is Discharged Or Voltage Is Low (Part 2 of 2). 2002 Crown Victoria & Grand Marquis

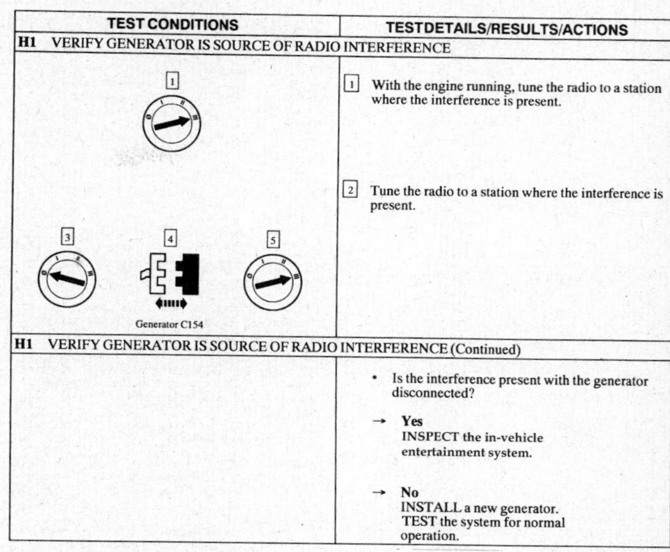

TEST CONDITIONS	TEST DETAILS/RESULTS/ACTIONS
H1 VERIFY GENERATOR IS SOURCE OF RADIO INTERFERENCE	
1	1 With the engine running, tune the radio to a station where the interference is present.
3 4 5 Generator C154	2 Tune the radio to a station where the interference is present.
H1 VERIFY GENERATOR IS SOURCE OF RADIO INTERFERENCE (Continued)	
	• Is the interference present with the generator disconnected? → **Yes** INSPECT the in-vehicle entertainment system. → **No** INSTALL a new generator. TEST the system for normal operation.

FM1120000549000X

Fig. 78 Test H: Radio Interference. 2000–01 Crown Victoria & Grand Marquis

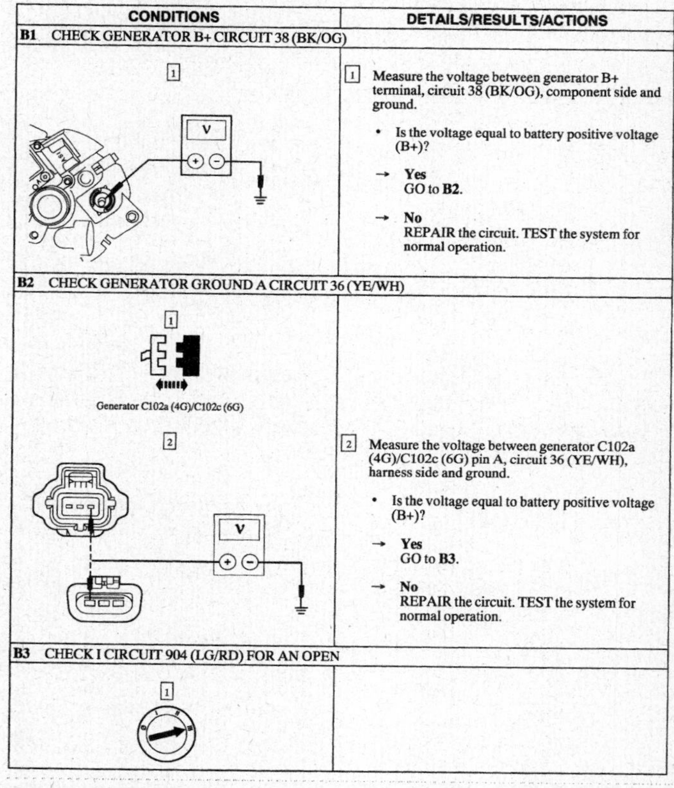

CONDITIONS	DETAILS/RESULTS/ACTIONS
B1 CHECK GENERATOR B+ CIRCUIT 38 (BK/OG)	
1	1 Measure the voltage between generator B+ terminal, circuit 38 (BK/OG), component side and ground. • Is the voltage equal to battery positive voltage (B+)? → **Yes** GO to **B2**. → **No** REPAIR the circuit. TEST the system for normal operation.
B2 CHECK GENERATOR GROUND A CIRCUIT 36 (YE/WH)	
1 Generator C102a (4G)/C102c (6G)	
2	2 Measure the voltage between generator C102a (4G)/C102c (6G) pin A, circuit 36 (YE/WH), harness side and ground. • Is the voltage equal to battery positive voltage (B+)? → **Yes** GO to **B3**. → **No** REPAIR the circuit. TEST the system for normal operation.
B3 CHECK I CIRCUIT 904 (LG/RD) FOR AN OPEN	
1	

FM1120200741010X

Fig. 80 Test B: Charging System Warning Indicator Is On With The Engine Running (The Engine Voltage Does Not Increase) (Part 1 of 2). 2002 Crown Victoria & Grand Marquis

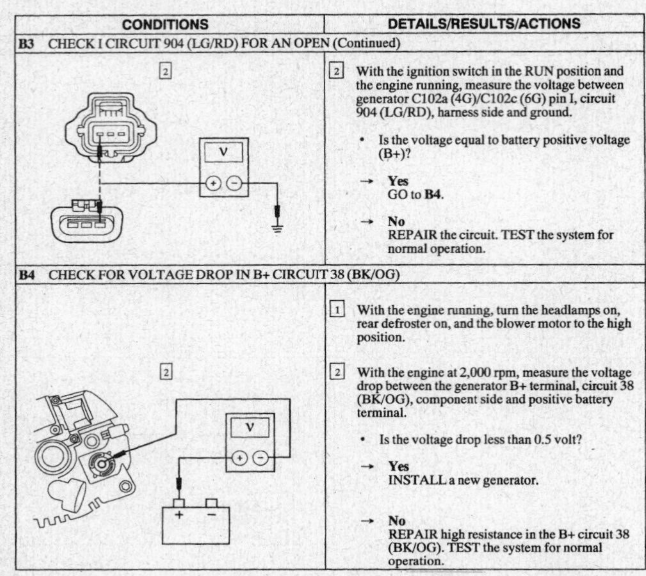

CONDITIONS	DETAILS/RESULTS/ACTIONS
B3 CHECK I CIRCUIT 904 (LG/RD) FOR AN OPEN (Continued)	
2	2 With the ignition switch in the RUN position and the engine running, measure the voltage between generator C102a (4G)/C102c (6G) pin I, circuit 904 (LG/RD), harness side and ground. • Is the voltage equal to battery positive voltage (B+)? → **Yes** GO to **B4**. → **No** REPAIR the circuit. TEST the system for normal operation.
B4 CHECK FOR VOLTAGE DROP IN B+ CIRCUIT 38 (BK/OG)	
2	1 With the engine running, turn the headlamps on, rear defroster on, and the blower motor to the high position. 2 With the engine at 2,000 rpm, measure the voltage drop between the generator B+ terminal, circuit 38 (BK/OG), component side and positive battery terminal. • Is the voltage drop less than 0.5 volt? → **Yes** INSTALL a new generator. → **No** REPAIR high resistance in the B+ circuit 38 (BK/OG). TEST the system for normal operation.

FM1120200741020X

Fig. 80 Test B: Charging System Warning Indicator Is On With The Engine Running (The Engine Voltage Does Not Increase) (Part 2 of 2). 2002 Crown Victoria & Grand Marquis

CONDITIONS	DETAILS/RESULTS/ACTIONS
D1 CHECK I CIRCUIT 904 (LG/RD) FOR SHORT TO GROUND	
1 2	2 With the ignition switch in the RUN position, check the charging system warning indicator. • Is the charging system warning indicator illuminated? → **Yes** REPAIR generator I circuit 904 (LG/RD) for a short to ground. TEST the system for normal operation. → **No** INSTALL a new generator. TEST the system for normal operation.

FM1120200743000X

Fig. 82 Test D: Charging System Warning Indicator Is On With The Engine Running And The System Increases Voltage. 2002 Crown Victoria & Grand Marquis

CONDITIONS	DETAILS/RESULTS/ACTIONS
E1 CHECK THE CHARGING SYSTEM WARNING INDICATOR LAMP	
1 2 3	2 With the engine off, connect a fused (15A) jumper wire between the generator C102a (4G)/C102c (6G) pin I, circuit 904 (LG/RD), harness side and ground.

FM1120200744010X

Fig. 83 Test E: Charging System Warning Indicator Is Off With The Ignition Switch In The Run Position And The Engine Off (Part 1 of 2). 2002 Crown Victoria & Grand Marquis

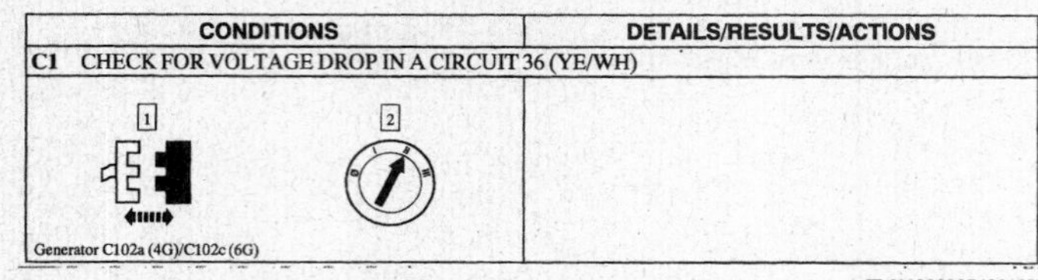

CONDITIONS	DETAILS/RESULTS/ACTIONS
C1 CHECK FOR VOLTAGE DROP IN A CIRCUIT 36 (YE/WH)	
1 2 Generator C102a (4G)/C102c (6G)	

FM1120200742010X

Fig. 81 Test C: System Overcharges (Battery Voltage Is Greater Than 15.5 Volts) (Part 1 of 2). 2002 Crown Victoria & Grand Marquis

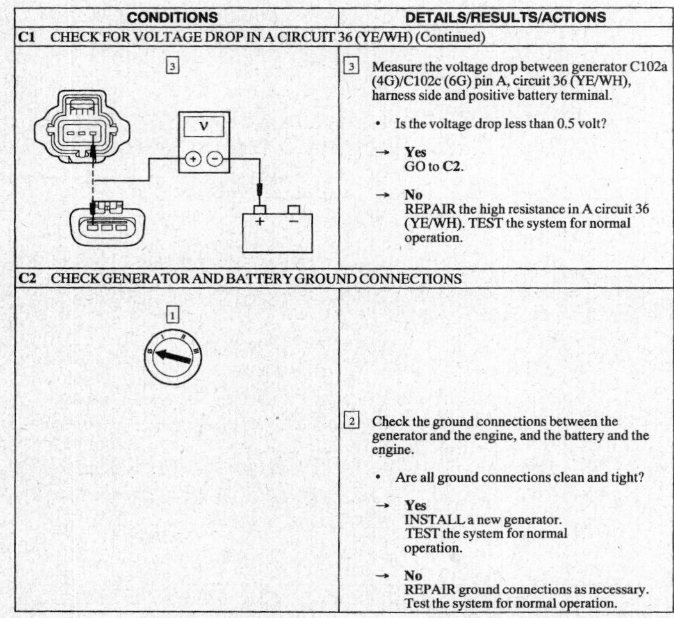

CONDITIONS	DETAILS/RESULTS/ACTIONS
C1 CHECK FOR VOLTAGE DROP IN A CIRCUIT 36 (YE/WH) (Continued)	
3	3 Measure the voltage drop between generator C102a (4G)/C102c (6G) pin A, circuit 36 (YE/WH), harness side and positive battery terminal. • Is the voltage drop less than 0.5 volt? → **Yes** GO to **C2**. → **No** REPAIR the high resistance in A circuit 36 (YE/WH). TEST the system for normal operation.
C2 CHECK GENERATOR AND BATTERY GROUND CONNECTIONS	
1	2 Check the ground connections between the generator and the engine, and the battery and the engine. • Are all ground connections clean and tight? → **Yes** INSTALL a new generator. TEST the system for normal operation. → **No** REPAIR ground connections as necessary. Test the system for normal operation.

FM1120200742020X

Fig. 81 Test C: System Overcharges (Battery Voltage Is Greater Than 15.5 Volts) (Part 2 of 2). 2002 Crown Victoria & Grand Marquis

CONDITIONS	DETAILS/RESULTS/ACTIONS
E1 CHECK THE CHARGING SYSTEM WARNING INDICATOR LAMP (Continued)	
	• Is the charging system warning indicator lamp illuminated? → **Yes** INSTALL a new generator. TEST the system for normal operation. → **No** Test the instrument cluster.

FM1120200744020X

Fig. 83 Test E: Charging System Warning Indicator Is Off With The Ignition Switch In The Run Position And The Engine Off (Part 2 of 2). 2002 Crown Victoria & Grand Marquis

CONDITIONS	DETAILS/RESULTS/ACTIONS
F1 CHECK FOR LOOSE CONNECTIONS	
	1 Check all generator, battery, and power distribution connections for looseness, corrosion, loose or bent terminals, or loose eyelets. • Are all connections clean and tight? → **Yes** GO to **F2**. → **No** REPAIR as necessary. TEST the system for normal operation.
F2 CHECK FUSE CONNECTIONS	
1	1 With the engine running, check BJB fuse 2 (30A) in A circuit 36 (YE/WH) and the CJB fuse 14 (10A) in I circuit 904 (LG/RD) for looseness by wiggling the fuse and noting the charging system warning indicator lamp operation. • Does the charging system warning indicator flicker? → **Yes** REPAIR loose fuse connection(s) as necessary. TEST the system for normal operation. → **No** GO to **F3**.

FM1120200745010X

Fig. 84 Test F: Charging System Warning Indicator Flickers Or Is Intermittent (Part 1 of 2). 2002 Crown Victoria & Grand Marquis

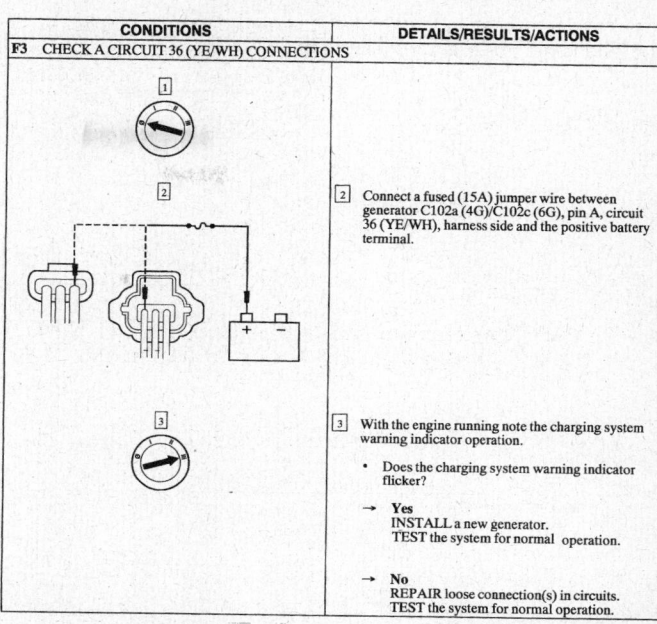

CONDITIONS	DETAILS/RESULTS/ACTIONS
F3 CHECK A CIRCUIT 36 (YE/WH) CONNECTIONS	
1	
2 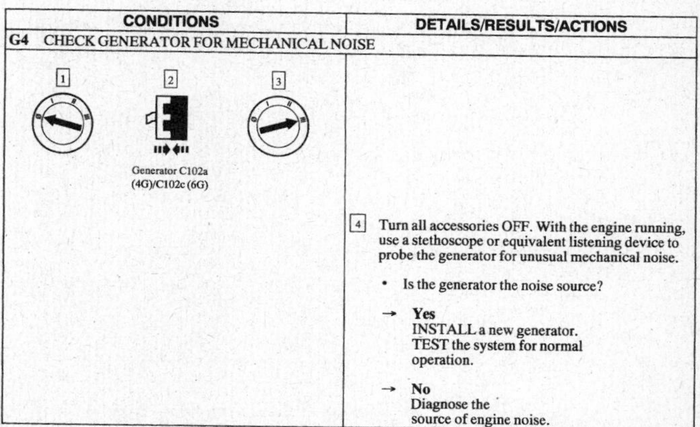	2 Connect a fused (15A) jumper wire between generator C102a (4G)/C102c (6G), pin A, circuit 36 (YE/WH), harness side and the positive battery terminal.
3	3 With the engine running note the charging system warning indicator operation. • Does the charging system warning indicator flicker? → **Yes** INSTALL a new generator. TEST the system for normal operation. → **No** REPAIR loose connection(s) in circuits. TEST the system for normal operation.

FM1120200745020X

Fig. 84 Test F: Charging System Warning Indicator Flickers Or Is Intermittent (Part 2 of 2). 2002 Crown Victoria & Grand Marquis

CONDITIONS	DETAILS/RESULTS/ACTIONS
G1 CHECK FOR ACCESSORY DRIVE NOISE	
	1 Check the accessory drive belt for damage and correct installation. Check the accessory mounting brackets and generator pulley for looseness or misalignment. • Is the accessory drive OK? → **Yes** GO to **G2**. → **No** REPAIR as necessary. TEST the system for normal operation.
G2 CHECK GENERATOR MOUNTING	
	1 Check the generator mounting for loose bolts or misalignment. • Is the generator mounted correctly? → **Yes** GO to **G3**. → **No** REPAIR as necessary. TEST the system for normal operation.
G3 CHECK GENERATOR FOR ELECTRICAL NOISE	
1 2 Generator C102a (4G)/C102c (6G)	3 With the engine running, listen for the concern. Use a stethoscope or equivalent listening device, if necessary. • Is the noise still present? → **Yes** GO to **G4**. → **No** INSTALL a new generator. TEST the system for normal operation.

FM1120200746010X

Fig. 85 Test G: Generator Is Noisy (Part 1 of 2). 2002 Crown Victoria & Grand Marquis

CONDITIONS	DETAILS/RESULTS/ACTIONS
G4 CHECK GENERATOR FOR MECHANICAL NOISE	
1 2 3 Generator C102a (4G)/C102c (6G)	4 Turn all accessories OFF. With the engine running, use a stethoscope or equivalent listening device to probe the generator for unusual mechanical noise. • Is the generator the noise source? → **Yes** INSTALL a new generator. TEST the system for normal operation. → **No** Diagnose the source of engine noise.

FM1120200746020X

Fig. 85 Test G: Generator Is Noisy (Part 2 of 2). 2002 Crown Victoria & Grand Marquis

CONDITIONS	DETAILS/RESULTS/ACTIONS
H1 VERIFY GENERATOR IS SOURCE OF RADIO INTERFERENCE	
1	2 With the engine running, tune the radio to a station where the interference is present.
3 4 5	

FM1120200747010X

Fig. 86 Test H: Radio Interference (Part 1 of 2). 2002 Crown Victoria & Grand Marquis

CONDITIONS	DETAILS/RESULTS/ACTIONS
H1 VERIFY GENERATOR IS SOURCE OF RADIO INTERFERENCE (Continued)	
	6 Tune the radio to a station where the interference is present, with the engine running. • Is the interference present with the generator disconnected? → **Yes** Test the in-vehicle entertainment system. → **No** INSTALL a new generator. TEST the system for normal operation.

FM1120200747020X

Fig. 86 Test H: Radio Interference (Part 2 of 2). 2002 Crown Victoria & Grand Marquis

Condition	Possible Source	Action
• Radio Interference	• Generator. • Regulator. • Other components.	• GO to Pinpoint Test E.
• The Battery Does Not Hold a Charge	• Battery drain. • Circuitry. • Regulator. • Generator. • Battery.	• GO to Pinpoint Test F.
• The System Does Not Charge	• Drive Belt. • Generator. • Circuitry.	• GO to Pinpoint Test G.

FM1129800227020X

Fig. 87 Symptom chart (Part 2 of 2). Escort, Tracer & ZX2

TEST CONDITIONS	TEST DETAILS/RESULTS/ACTIONS
A2 CHECK CIRCUIT 21 (O) FOR OPEN	
1 2 3 Voltage Regulator C159 Generator C153 4	4 Measure the resistance between voltage regulator C159-S, circuit 21 (O), and generator C153. • Is the resistance less than 5 ohms? → **Yes** GO to **A3**. → **No** REPAIR circuit 21 (O). TEST the system for normal operation.
A3 CHECK FOR POOR GROUNDS	
	1 Check for poor ground connections between the voltage regulator and the generator, the generator and the engine, or the engine and the battery. • Are all ground connections clean and tight? → **Yes** REPLACE the voltage regulator. TEST the system for normal operation. → **No** CLEAN and REPAIR the ground(s) as required. TEST the system for normal operation.

FM1129800228020X

Fig. 88 Test A: System Overcharges (Part 2 of 2). Escort, Tracer & ZX2

Condition	Possible Source	Action
• The System Overcharges	• Voltage drop in circuit A. • Generator. • Regulator.	• GO to Pinpoint Test A.
• The Charging System Warning Indicator Stays On	• Open A circuit. • Shorted I circuit. • Open/high resistance S circuit. • Regulator. • Generator.	• GO to Pinpoint Test B.
• The Charging System Warning Indicator Is Inoperative	• Circuitry. • Instrument cluster.	• INSPECT Instrument Cluster & Panel Lighting.
• The Charging System Warning Indicator Flickers/Is Intermittent	• Circuitry. • Generator.	• GO to Pinpoint Test C.
• Generator Is Noisy	• Drive belt. • Generator. • Related components.	• GO to Pinpoint Test D.

FM1129800227010X

Fig. 87 Symptom chart (Part 1 of 2). Escort, Tracer & ZX2

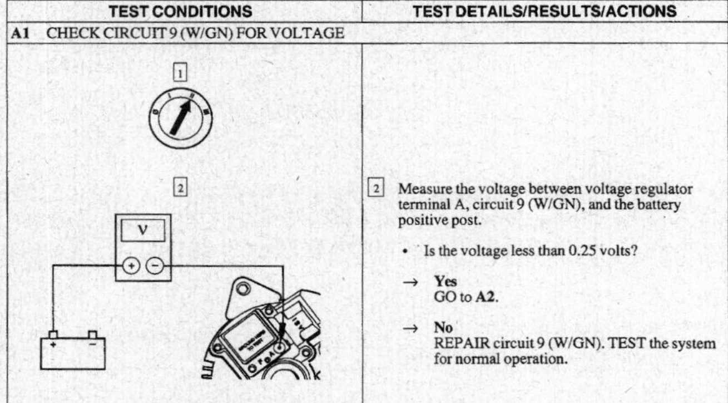

TEST CONDITIONS	TEST DETAILS/RESULTS/ACTIONS
A1 CHECK CIRCUIT 9 (W/GN) FOR VOLTAGE	
1 2	2 Measure the voltage between voltage regulator terminal A, circuit 9 (W/GN), and the battery positive post. • Is the voltage less than 0.25 volts? → **Yes** GO to **A2**. → **No** REPAIR circuit 9 (W/GN). TEST the system for normal operation.

FM1129800228010X

Fig. 88 Test A: System Overcharges (Part 1 of 2). Escort, Tracer & ZX2

TEST CONDITIONS	TEST DETAILS/RESULTS/ACTIONS
B1 CHECK SYSTEM VOLTAGE	
	1 Perform No-Load Test in this section. • Is the system voltage below the specified range (undercharging)? → **Yes** GO to **B2**. → **No** REPAIR circuit 20 (W/BL) for short to ground. TEST the system for normal operation.
B2 CHECK CIRCUIT 9 (W/GN) FOR OPEN	
1 2	2 Measure the voltage between voltage regulator terminal A and ground. • Is the voltage equal to battery voltage? → **Yes** GO to **B3**. → **No** REPAIR circuit 9 (W/GN). TEST the system for normal operation.

FM1129800229010X

Fig. 89 Test B: Warning Indicator Stays On (Part 1 of 4). Escort, Tracer & ZX2

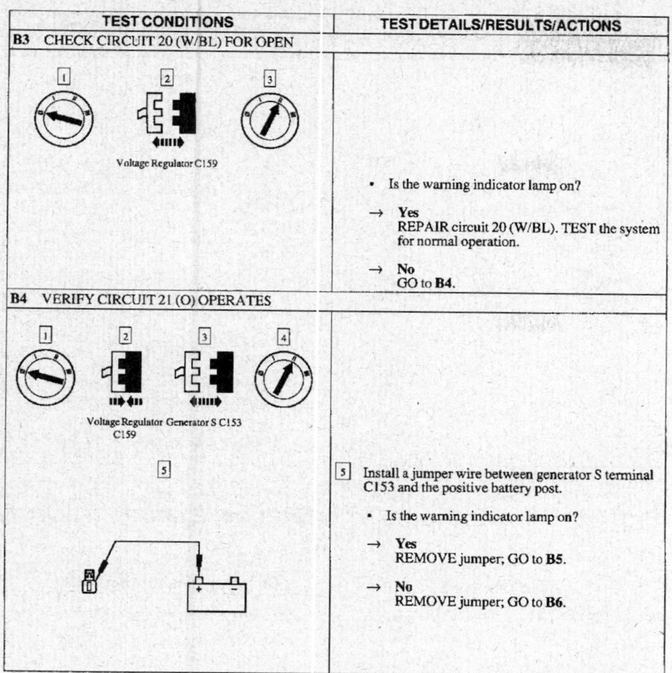

TEST CONDITIONS	TEST DETAILS/RESULTS/ACTIONS
B3 CHECK CIRCUIT 20 (W/BL) FOR OPEN	
1 2 3 Voltage Regulator C159	• Is the warning indicator lamp on? → **Yes** REPAIR circuit 20 (W/BL). TEST the system for normal operation. → **No** GO to **B4**.
B4 VERIFY CIRCUIT 21 (O) OPERATES	
1 2 3 4 Voltage Regulator C159 Generator S C153	
5	5 Install a jumper wire between generator S terminal C153 and the positive battery post. • Is the warning indicator lamp on? → **Yes** REMOVE jumper; GO to **B5**. → **No** REMOVE jumper; GO to **B6**.

FM1129800229020X

Fig. 89 Test B: Warning Indicator Stays On (Part 2 of 4). Escort, Tracer & ZX2

TEST CONDITIONS	TEST DETAILS/RESULTS/ACTIONS
B7 CHECK GENERATOR OUTPUT VOLTAGE	
1	
2	2 Measure the voltage between generator B+ terminal and ground with the engine running at 1500 rpm and all accessories off. • Is the voltage 14.1 volts or greater? → **Yes** GO to Pinpoint Test A. → **No** REPLACE the voltage regulator. TEST the system for normal operation.

FM1129800229040X

Fig. 89 Test B: Warning Indicator Stays On (Part 4 of 4). Escort, Tracer & ZX2

TEST CONDITIONS	TEST DETAILS/RESULTS/ACTIONS
C1 CHECK FOR LOOSE CONNECTIONS	
1	
	2 Check the following connections for corrosion, loose or bent pins and/or terminals, or loose eyelets: — Voltage regulator connector. — Generator S terminal connector. — Generator B+ eyelet. — Power distribution box eyelets. — Battery cables. • Are all connections clean and tight? → **Yes** GO to **C2**. → **No** REPAIR or CLEAN connections as required. TEST the system for normal operation.

FM1129800230010X

Fig. 90 Test C: Warning Indicator Flickers/ Intermittent (Part 1 of 2). Escort, Tracer & ZX2

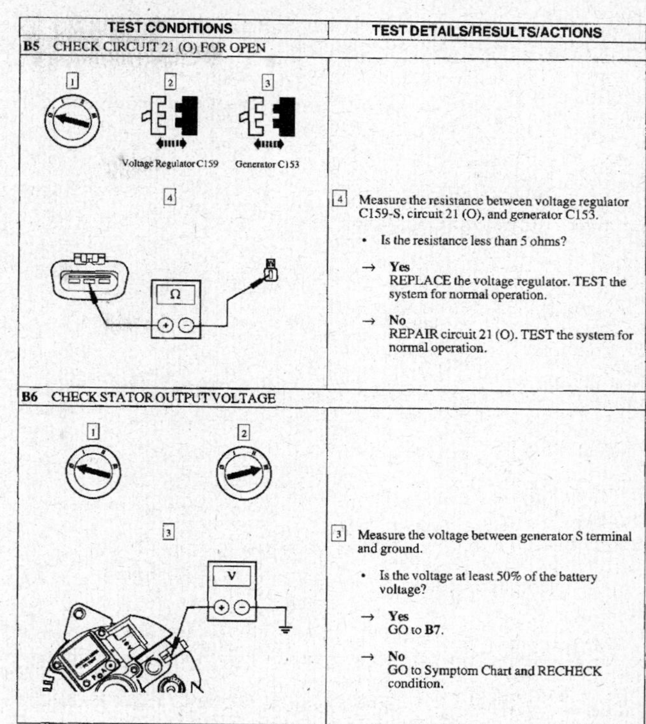

TEST CONDITIONS	TEST DETAILS/RESULTS/ACTIONS
B5 CHECK CIRCUIT 21 (O) FOR OPEN	
1 2 3 Voltage Regulator C159 Generator C153	
4	4 Measure the resistance between voltage regulator C159-S, circuit 21 (O), and generator C153. • Is the resistance less than 5 ohms? → **Yes** REPLACE the voltage regulator. TEST the system for normal operation. → **No** REPAIR circuit 21 (O). TEST the system for normal operation.
B6 CHECK STATOR OUTPUT VOLTAGE	
1 2	
3	3 Measure the voltage between generator S terminal and ground. • Is the voltage at least 50% of the battery voltage? → **Yes** GO to **B7**. → **No** GO to Symptom Chart and RECHECK condition.

FM1129800229030X

Fig. 89 Test B: Warning Indicator Stays On (Part 3 of 4). Escort, Tracer & ZX2

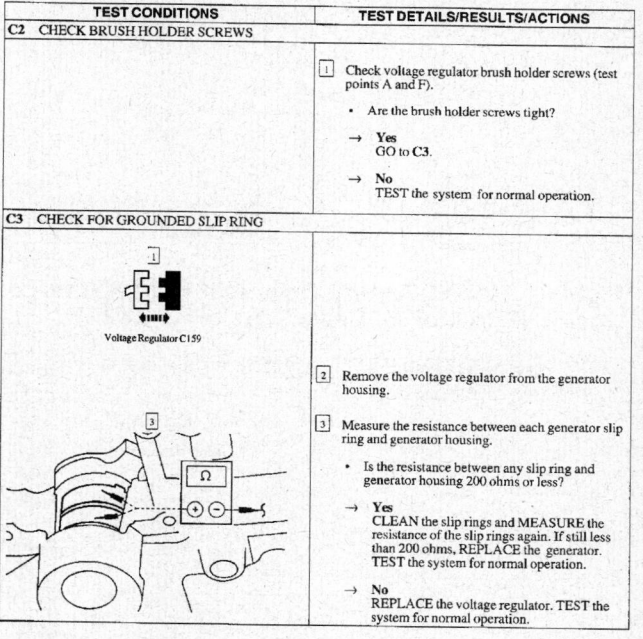

TEST CONDITIONS	TEST DETAILS/RESULTS/ACTIONS
C2 CHECK BRUSH HOLDER SCREWS	
	1 Check voltage regulator brush holder screws (test points A and F). • Are the brush holder screws tight? → **Yes** GO to **C3**. → **No** TEST the system for normal operation.
C3 CHECK FOR GROUNDED SLIP RING	
1 Voltage Regulator C159	2 Remove the voltage regulator from the generator housing.
3	3 Measure the resistance between each generator slip ring and generator housing. • Is the resistance between any slip ring and generator housing 200 ohms or less? → **Yes** CLEAN the slip rings and MEASURE the resistance of the slip rings again. If still less than 200 ohms, REPLACE the generator. TEST the system for normal operation. → **No** REPLACE the voltage regulator. TEST the system for normal operation.

FM1129800230020X

Fig. 90 Test C: Warning Indicator Flickers/ Intermittent (Part 2 of 2). Escort, Tracer & ZX2

TEST CONDITIONS	TEST DETAILS/RESULTS/ACTIONS
D1 CHECK FOR ACCESSORY DRIVE NOISE	
	1 Check the drive belt for damage and verify correct installation
	2 Check the accessory mounting brackets for loose bolts or misalignment.

FM1129800231010X

Fig. 91 Test D: Alternator Is Noisy (Part 1 of 2). Escort, Tracer & ZX2

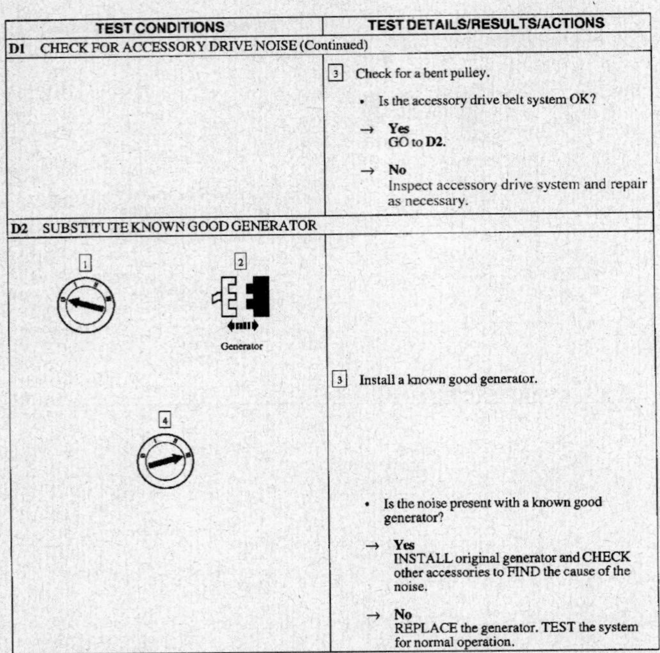

TEST CONDITIONS	TEST DETAILS/RESULTS/ACTIONS
D1 CHECK FOR ACCESSORY DRIVE NOISE (Continued)	
	3 Check for a bent pulley. • Is the accessory drive belt system OK? → **Yes** GO to **D2**. → **No** Inspect accessory drive system and repair as necessary.
D2 SUBSTITUTE KNOWN GOOD GENERATOR	
1 2 4 Generator	3 Install a known good generator. • Is the noise present with a known good generator? → **Yes** INSTALL original generator and CHECK other accessories to FIND the cause of the noise. → **No** REPLACE the generator. TEST the system for normal operation.

FM1129800231020X

Fig. 91 Test D: Alternator Is Noisy (Part 2 of 2). Escort, Tracer & ZX2

TEST CONDITIONS	TEST DETAILS/RESULTS/ACTIONS
F1 CHECK BATTERY	
1	2 Inspect condition of battery. • Is the battery OK? → **Yes** GO to **F2**. → **No** REPLACE the battery. TEST the system for normal operation.

FM1129800233010X

Fig. 93 Test F: Battery Does Not Hold A Charge (Part 1 of 2). Escort, Tracer & ZX2

TEST CONDITIONS	TEST DETAILS/RESULTS/ACTIONS
G1 CHECK DRIVE BELT TENSION	
	1 Inspect the drive belt tension • Is the drive belt tension correct? → **Yes** GO to **G2**. → **No** REPLACE the drive belt or drive belt tensioner. TEST the system for normal operation.
G2 CHECK SYSTEM VOLTAGE	
	1 Perform No-Load Test. • Is the system voltage below the specified range (undercharging)? → **Yes** GO to Pinpoint Test B. → **No** Perform Drain Testing in this section. REPAIR the system in question. TEST the system for normal operation.

FM1129800234000X

Fig. 94 Test G: System Does Not Charge. Escort, Tracer & ZX2

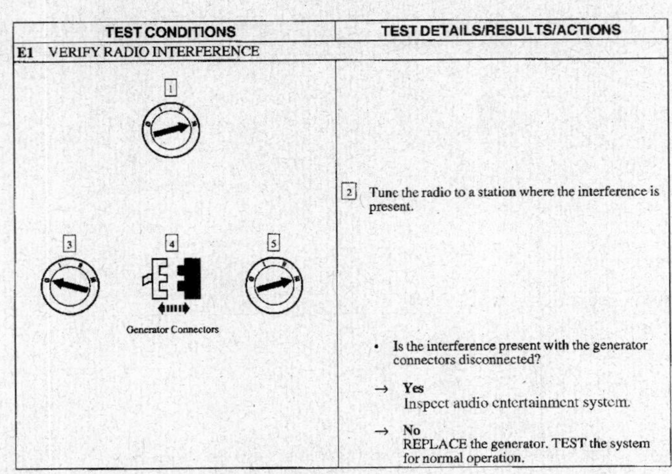

TEST CONDITIONS	TEST DETAILS/RESULTS/ACTIONS
E1 VERIFY RADIO INTERFERENCE	
1 3 4 5 Generator Connectors	2 Tune the radio to a station where the interference is present. • Is the interference present with the generator connectors disconnected? → **Yes** Inspect audio entertainment system. → **No** REPLACE the generator. TEST the system for normal operation.

FM1129800232000X

Fig. 92 Test E: Radio Interference. Escort, Tracer & ZX2

TEST CONDITIONS	TEST DETAILS/RESULTS/ACTIONS
F2 CHECK FOR KEY-OFF DRAIN	
	1 Perform the Drain Testing. • Is the drain less than 0.05 amps? → **Yes** GO to Pinpoint Test G. → **No** REPAIR the system in question. TEST the system for normal operation.

FM1129800233020X

Fig. 93 Test F: Battery Does Not Hold A Charge (Part 2 of 2). Escort, Tracer & ZX2

Condition	Possible Sources	Action
• The battery is discharged or battery voltage is low	• Circuitry. • High key-off current drain(s). • Battery. • Generator.	• GO to Pinpoint Test A .
• The charging system warning indicator is on with the engine running (the charging system voltage does not increase)	• Generator. • Rear battery junction box (BJB) fuse 20 (5A) • Circuitry.	• GO to Pinpoint Test B .
• The charging system overcharges (battery voltage is greater than 15.5 volts)	• Rear BJB fuse 20 (5A). • Circuitry. • Generator.	• GO to Pinpoint Test C .
• The charging system warning indicator is on with the engine running and the battery increases voltage	• Rear BJB fuse 20 (5A). • Generator. • Instrument cluster. • Powertrain control module(PCM). • Circuitry.	• GO to Pinpoint Test D .
• The charging system warning indicator is off with the ignition switch in the RUN position and the engine off	• Generator connector unplugged C102a. • Battery. • Circuitry. • Instrument cluster. • PCM.	• GO to Pinpoint Test E .
• The charging system warning indicator flickers or is intermittent	• Rear BJB fuse 20 (5A). • Generator connector unplugged (C102a). • Circuitry. • Generator.	• GO to Pinpoint Test F .
• The generator is noisy	• Loose bolts/brackets. • Drive belt. • Generator/pulley.	• GO to Pinpoint Test G .
• Radio interference	• Generator. • Wiring/routing. • In-vehicle entertainment system.	• GO to Pinpoint Test H .

FM1120200791000X

Fig. 95 Symptom Chart. LS & Thunderbird

CONDITIONS	DETAILS/RESULTS/ACTIONS
A1 CHECK THE GENERATOR OUTPUT	
	1 Carry out the On-Vehicle Generator Load/No Load Tests. • **Is the generator OK?** → **Yes** GO to A2 . → **No** GO to Pinpoint Test B .
A2 CHECK FOR CURRENT DRAINS	
	1 Carry out the Battery — Drain Test. • **Are there any excessive current drains?** → **Yes** REPAIR as necessary. TEST the system for normal operation. → **No** GO to A3 .
A3 CHECK FOR CURRENT DRAINS WHICH SHUT OFF WHEN THE BATTERY IS DISCONNECTED	
	1 Carry out the Battery — Electronic Drains Which Shut Off When the Battery Cable is Disconnected Test. • **Are there any current drains which shut off when the battery is disconnected?** → **Yes** REPAIR as necessary. TEST the system for normal operation. → **No** GO to Pinpoint Test B .

FM1120200792000X

Fig. 96 Test A: Battery Is Discharged Or Battery Voltage Is Low. LS & Thunderbird

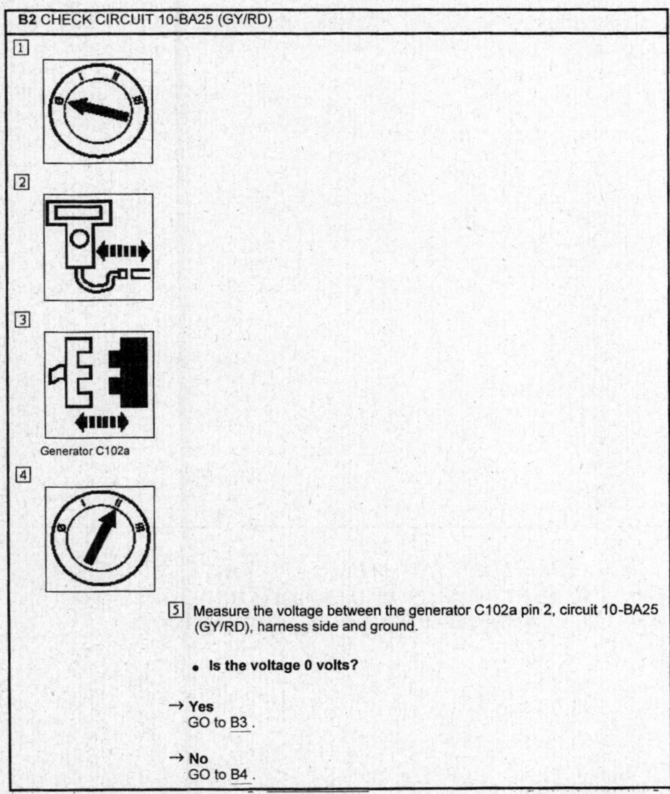
B2 CHECK CIRCUIT 10-BA25 (GY/RD)

1

2

3

Generator C102a

4

5 Measure the voltage between the generator C102a pin 2, circuit 10-BA25 (GY/RD), harness side and ground.

• **Is the voltage 0 volts?**

→ **Yes**
GO to B3 .

→ **No**
GO to B4 .

FM1120200793020X

Fig. 97 Test B: Charging System Warning Indicator Is On With The Engine Running/The Charging System Voltage Does Not Increase (Part 2 of 5). LS & Thunderbird

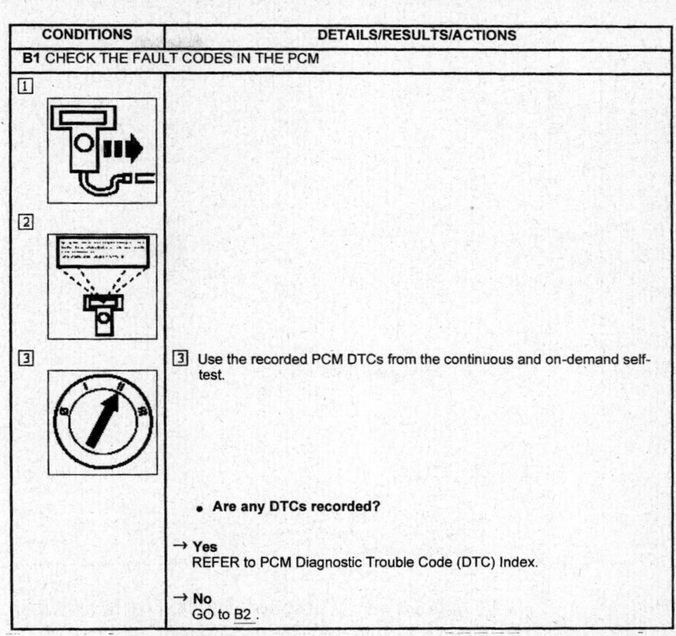

CONDITIONS	DETAILS/RESULTS/ACTIONS
B1 CHECK THE FAULT CODES IN THE PCM	
1	
2	
3	3 Use the recorded PCM DTCs from the continuous and on-demand self-test. • **Are any DTCs recorded?** → **Yes** REFER to PCM Diagnostic Trouble Code (DTC) Index. → **No** GO to B2 .

FM1120200793010X

Fig. 97 Test B: Charging System Warning Indicator Is On With The Engine Running/The Charging System Voltage Does Not Increase (Part 1 of 5). LS & Thunderbird

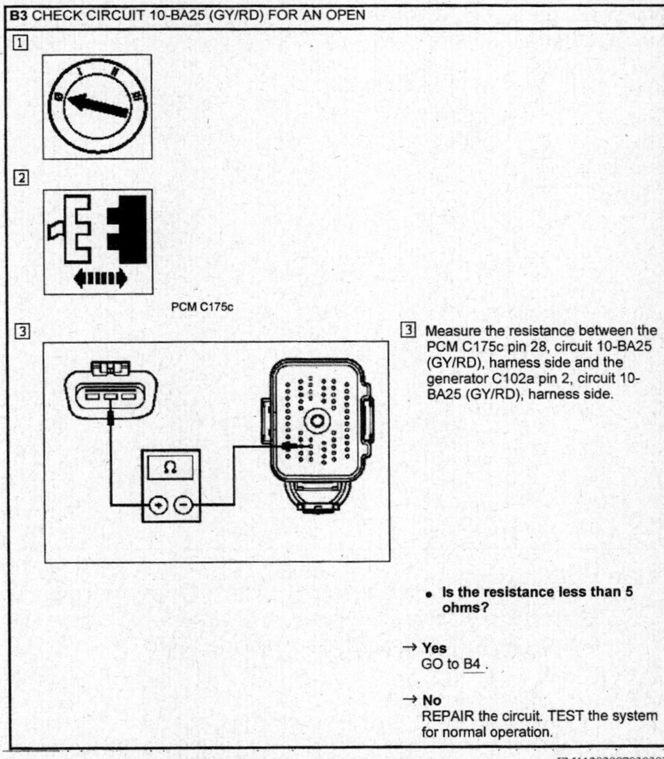
B3 CHECK CIRCUIT 10-BA25 (GY/RD) FOR AN OPEN

1

2

PCM C175c

3

3 Measure the resistance between the PCM C175c pin 28, circuit 10-BA25 (GY/RD), harness side and the generator C102a pin 2, circuit 10-BA25 (GY/RD), harness side.

• **Is the resistance less than 5 ohms?**

→ **Yes**
GO to B4 .

→ **No**
REPAIR the circuit. TEST the system for normal operation.

FM1120200793030X

Fig. 97 Test B: Charging System Warning Indicator Is On With The Engine Running/The Charging System Voltage Does Not Increase (Part 3 of 5). LS & Thunderbird

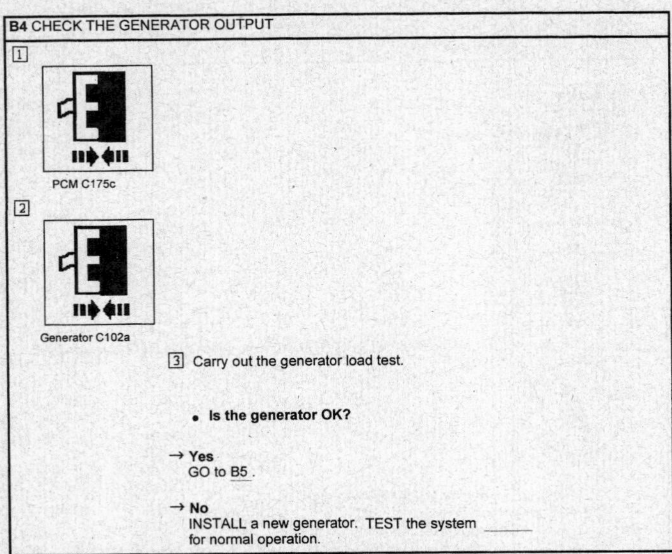

B4 CHECK THE GENERATOR OUTPUT
1
PCM C175c
2
Generator C102a
3 Carry out the generator load test.
• Is the generator OK?
→ Yes
GO to B5 .
→ No
INSTALL a new generator. TEST the system for normal operation.

FM1120200793040X

Fig. 97 Test B: Charging System Warning Indicator Is On With The Engine Running/The Charging System Voltage Does Not Increase (Part 4 of 5). LS & Thunderbird

B5 CHECK FOR CORRECT MODULE OPERATION
1 Check for: • corrosion • pushed-out pins 2 Connect any disconnected connectors. 3 Make sure all other system connectors are fully seated. 4 Operate the system and verify the concern is still present. • **Is the concern still present?** → **Yes** INSTALL a new PCM. REPEAT the PCM self-test. → **No** The system is operating correctly at this time. Concern may have been caused by a loose or corroded connector. CLEAR the DTCs. REPEAT the self-test.

FM1120200793050X

Fig. 97 Test B: Charging System Warning Indicator Is On With The Engine Running/The Charging System Voltage Does Not Increase (Part 5 of 5). LS & Thunderbird

CONDITIONS	DETAILS/RESULTS/ACTIONS
C1 CHECK THE FAULT CODES IN THE PCM	
1 2 3	3 Use the recorded PCM DTCs from the continuous and on-demand self-test. • **Are any DTCs recorded?** → **Yes** → **No** GO to C2 .

FM1120200794010X

Fig. 98 Test C: Charging System Overcharges /Battery Voltage Is Greater Than 15.5 Volts (Part 1 of 3). LS & Thunderbird

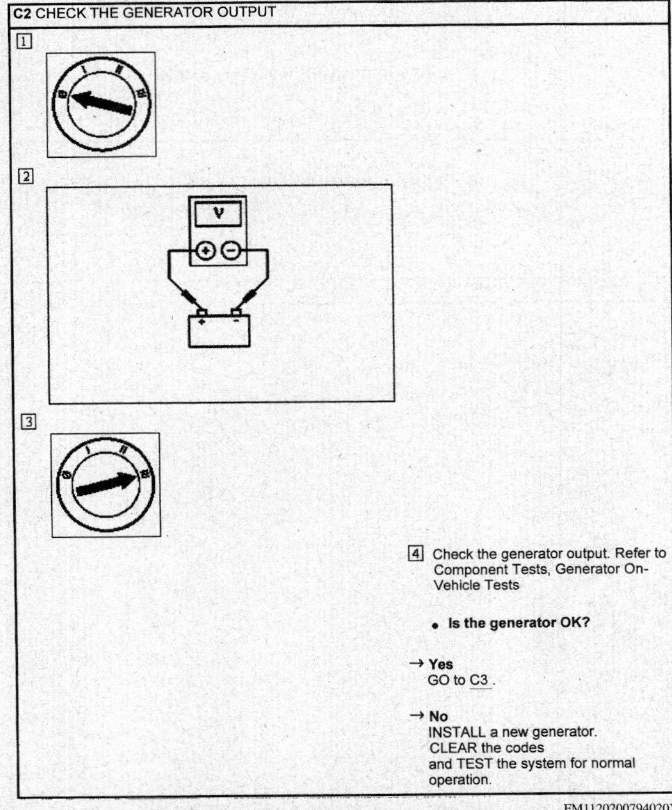

C2 CHECK THE GENERATOR OUTPUT
1
2
V
3
4 Check the generator output. Refer to Component Tests, Generator On-Vehicle Tests
• Is the generator OK?
→ Yes
GO to C3 .
→ No
INSTALL a new generator.
CLEAR the codes
and TEST the system for normal operation.

FM1120200794020X

Fig. 98 Test C: Charging System Overcharges /Battery Voltage Is Greater Than 15.5 Volts (Part 2 of 3). LS & Thunderbird

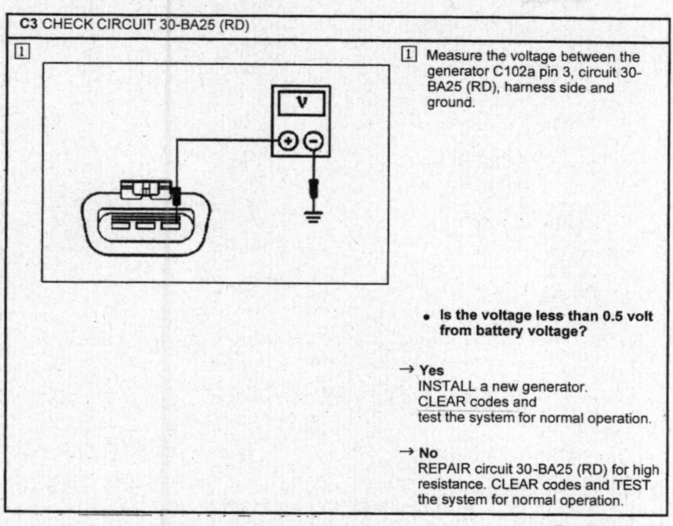

C3 CHECK CIRCUIT 30-BA25 (RD)
1
1 Measure the voltage between the generator C102a pin 3, circuit 30-BA25 (RD), harness side and ground.
V
• Is the voltage less than 0.5 volt from battery voltage?
→ Yes
INSTALL a new generator. CLEAR codes and test the system for normal operation.
→ No
REPAIR circuit 30-BA25 (RD) for high resistance. CLEAR codes and TEST the system for normal operation.
FM1120200794030X

Fig. 98 Test C: Charging System Overcharges /Battery Voltage Is Greater Than 15.5 Volts (Part 3 of 3). LS & Thunderbird

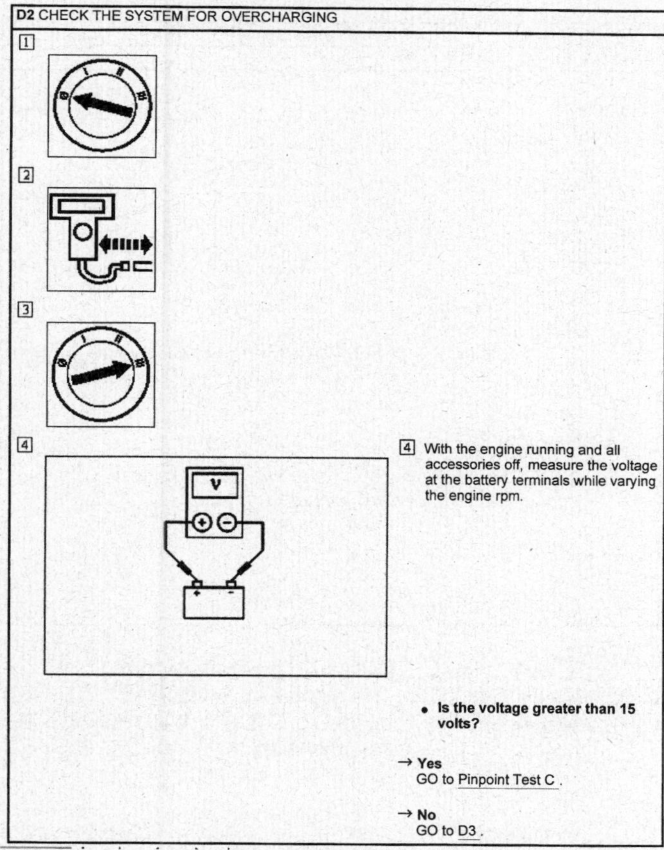

D2 CHECK THE SYSTEM FOR OVERCHARGING
1
2
3
4
V
4 With the engine running and all accessories off, measure the voltage at the battery terminals while varying the engine rpm.
• Is the voltage greater than 15 volts?
→ Yes
GO to Pinpoint Test C .
→ No
GO to D3 .
FM1120200795020X

Fig. 99 Test D: Charging System Warning Indicator Is On With The Engine Running And The Battery Increases Voltage (Part 2 of 6). LS & Thunderbird

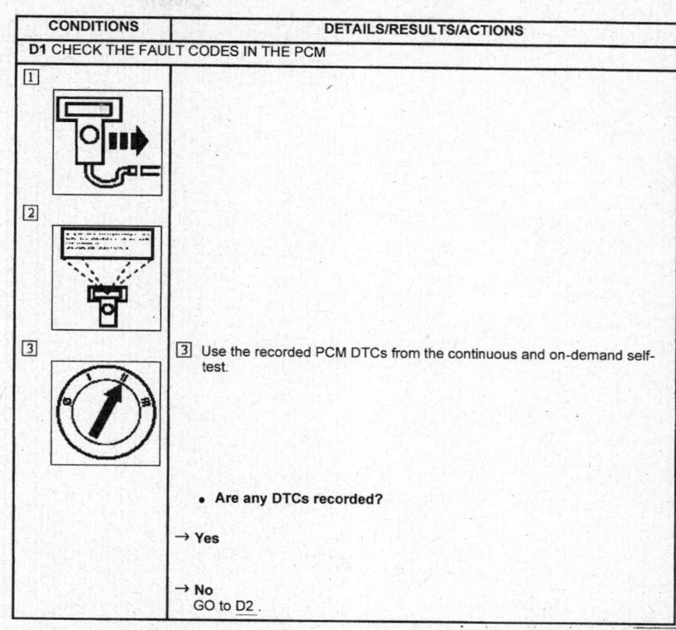

Fig. 99 Test D: Charging System Warning Indicator Is On With The Engine Running And The Battery Increases Voltage (Part 1 of 6). LS & Thunderbird

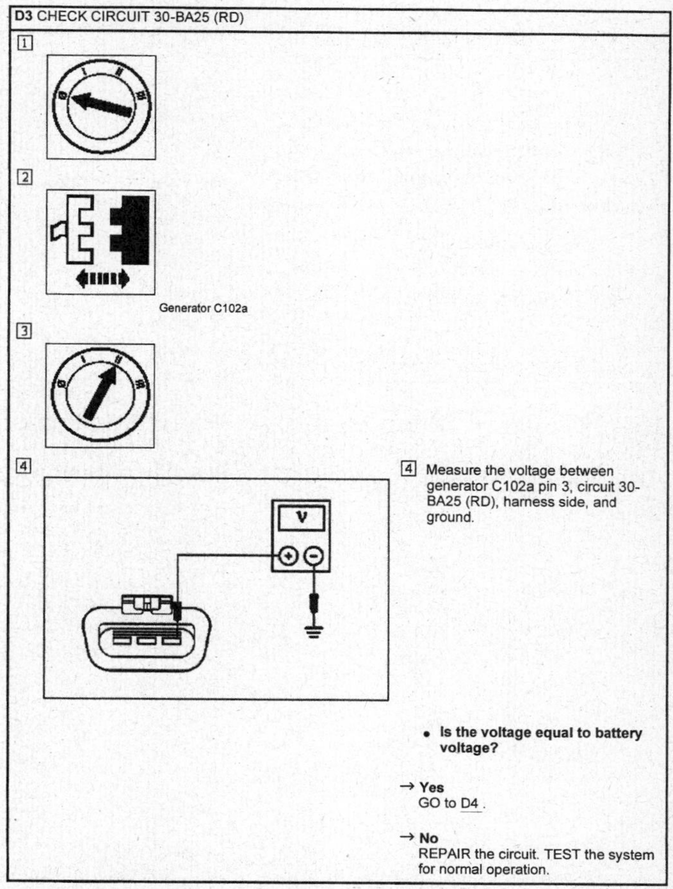

D3 CHECK CIRCUIT 30-BA25 (RD)
1
2
Generator C102a
3
4
V
4 Measure the voltage between generator C102a pin 3, circuit 30-BA25 (RD), harness side, and ground.
• Is the voltage equal to battery voltage?
→ Yes
GO to D4 .
→ No
REPAIR the circuit. TEST the system for normal operation.
FM1120200795030X

Fig. 99 Test D: Charging System Warning Indicator Is On With The Engine Running And The Battery Increases Voltage (Part 3 of 6). LS & Thunderbird

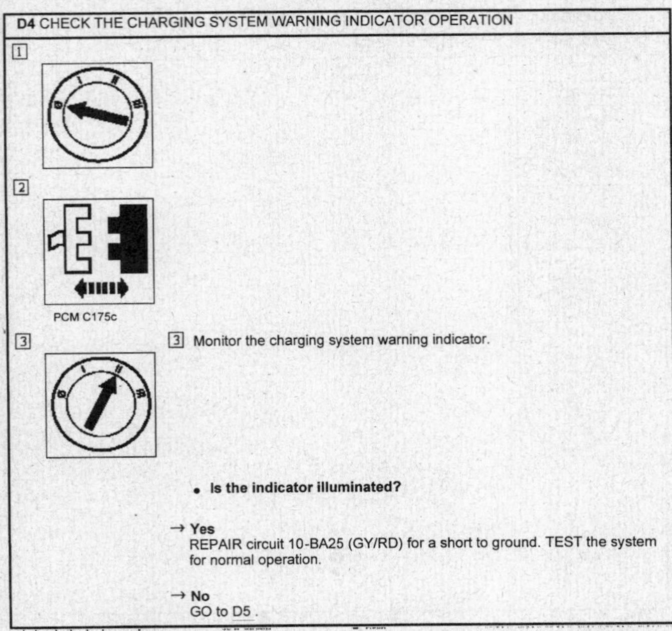
D4 CHECK THE CHARGING SYSTEM WARNING INDICATOR OPERATION

1

2

PCM C175c

3

3 Monitor the charging system warning indicator.

- Is the indicator illuminated?

→ Yes
REPAIR circuit 10-BA25 (GY/RD) for a short to ground. TEST the system for normal operation.

→ No
GO to D5 .

FM1120200795040X

Fig. 99 Test D: Charging System Warning Indicator Is On With The Engine Running And The Battery Increases Voltage (Part 4 of 6). LS & Thunderbird

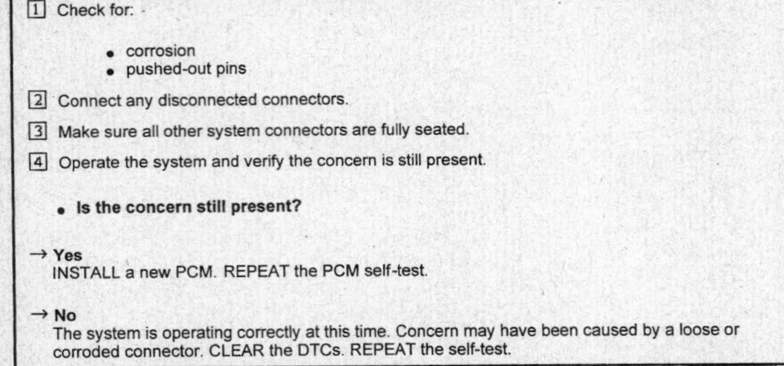
D6 CHECK FOR CORRECT MODULE OPERATION

1 Check for:

- corrosion
- pushed-out pins

2 Connect any disconnected connectors.

3 Make sure all other system connectors are fully seated.

4 Operate the system and verify the concern is still present.

- Is the concern still present?

→ Yes
INSTALL a new PCM. REPEAT the PCM self-test.

→ No
The system is operating correctly at this time. Concern may have been caused by a loose or corroded connector. CLEAR the DTCs. REPEAT the self-test.

FM1120200795060X

Fig. 99 Test D: Charging System Warning Indicator Is On With The Engine Running And The Battery Increases Voltage (Part 6 of 6). LS & Thunderbird

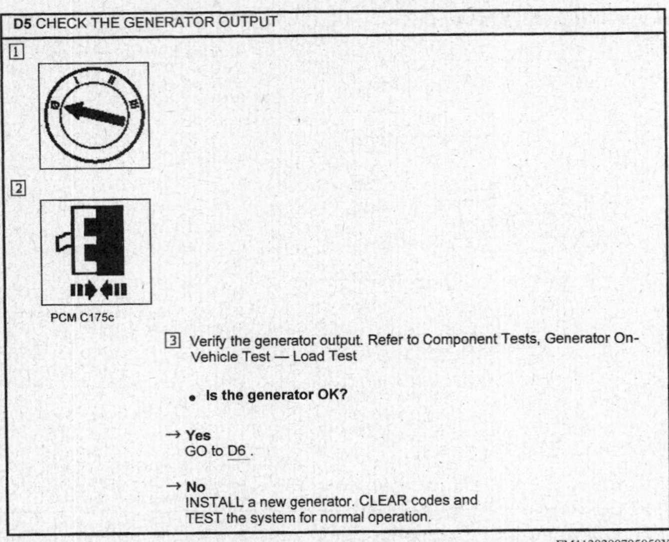
D5 CHECK THE GENERATOR OUTPUT

1

2

PCM C175c

3 Verify the generator output. Refer to Component Tests, Generator On-Vehicle Test — Load Test

- Is the generator OK?

→ Yes
GO to D6 .

→ No
INSTALL a new generator. CLEAR codes and TEST the system for normal operation.

FM1120200795050X

Fig. 99 Test D: Charging System Warning Indicator Is On With The Engine Running And The Battery Increases Voltage (Part 5 of 6). LS & Thunderbird

CONDITIONS	DETAILS/RESULTS/ACTIONS
E1 CHECK THE FAULT CODES IN THE PCM	
1	
2	
3	3 Use the recorded PCM DTCs from the continuous and on-demand self-test. • Are any DTCs recorded? → Yes → No GO to E2 .

FM1120200796010X

Fig. 100 Test E: Charging System Warning Indicator Is Off With The Ignition Switch In The Run Position And The Engine Is Off (Part 1 of 3). LS & Thunderbird

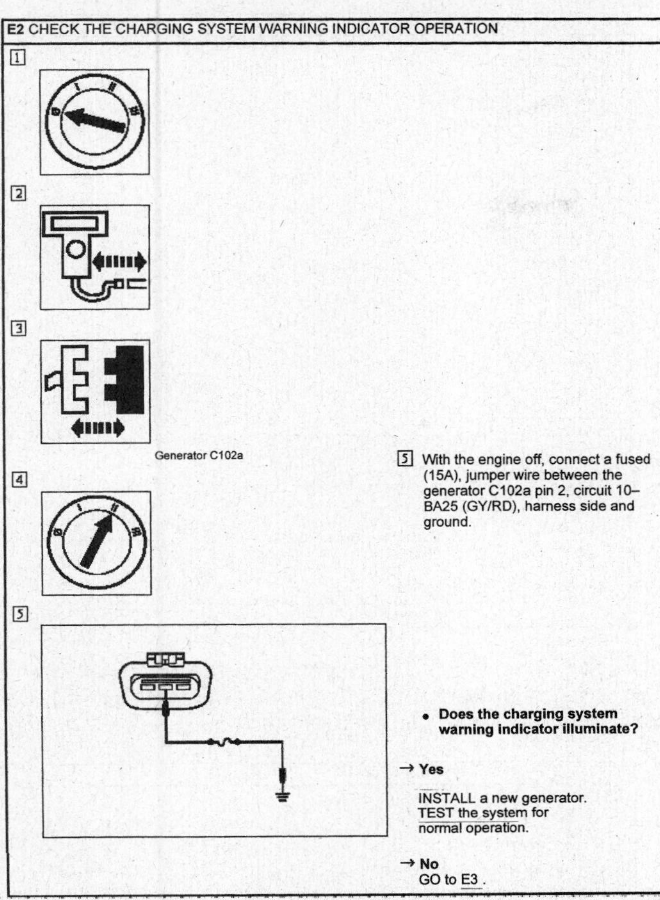
E2 CHECK THE CHARGING SYSTEM WARNING INDICATOR OPERATION

1

2

3

Generator C102a

4

5 With the engine off, connect a fused (15A), jumper wire between the generator C102a pin 2, circuit 10–BA25 (GY/RD), harness side and ground.

5

- **Does the charging system warning indicator illuminate?**

→ **Yes**
INSTALL a new generator. TEST the system for normal operation.

→ **No**
GO to E3 .

FM1120200796020X

Fig. 100 Test E: Charging System Warning Indicator Is Off With The Ignition Switch In The Run Position And The Engine Is Off (Part 2 of 3). LS & Thunderbird

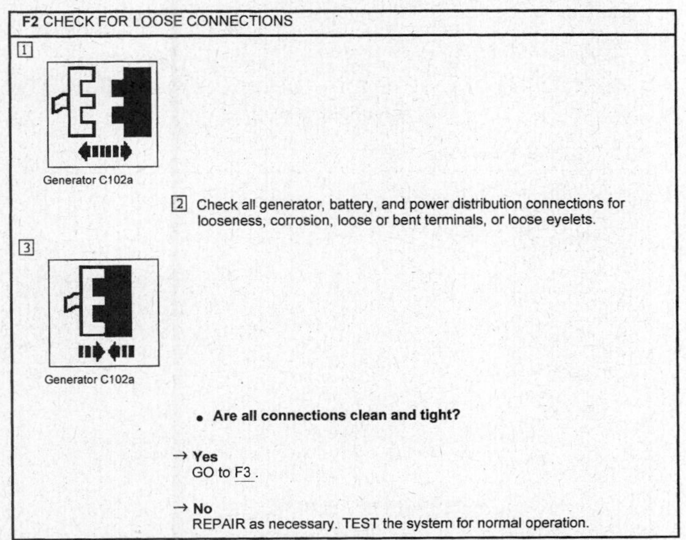
F2 CHECK FOR LOOSE CONNECTIONS

1

Generator C102a

2 Check all generator, battery, and power distribution connections for looseness, corrosion, loose or bent terminals, or loose eyelets.

3

Generator C102a

- **Are all connections clean and tight?**

→ **Yes**
GO to F3 .

→ **No**
REPAIR as necessary. TEST the system for normal operation.

FM1120200797020X

Fig. 101 Test F: Charging System Warning Indicator Flickers Or Is Intermittent (Part 2 of 6). LS & Thunderbird

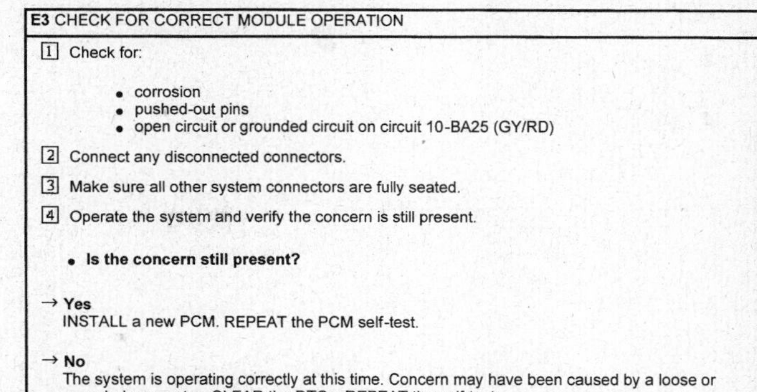
E3 CHECK FOR CORRECT MODULE OPERATION

1 Check for:

- corrosion
- pushed-out pins
- open circuit or grounded circuit on circuit 10-BA25 (GY/RD)

2 Connect any disconnected connectors.

3 Make sure all other system connectors are fully seated.

4 Operate the system and verify the concern is still present.

- **Is the concern still present?**

→ **Yes**
INSTALL a new PCM. REPEAT the PCM self-test.

→ **No**
The system is operating correctly at this time. Concern may have been caused by a loose or corroded connector. CLEAR the DTCs. REPEAT the self-test.

FM1120200796030X

Fig. 100 Test E: Charging System Warning Indicator Is Off With The Ignition Switch In The Run Position And The Engine Is Off (Part 3 of 3). LS & Thunderbird

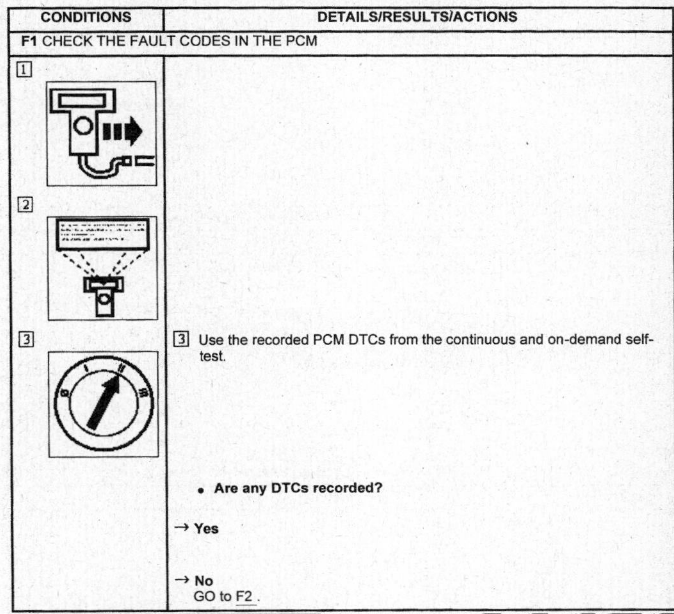
CONDITIONS	DETAILS/RESULTS/ACTIONS
F1 CHECK THE FAULT CODES IN THE PCM	
1	
2	
3	3 Use the recorded PCM DTCs from the continuous and on-demand self-test. • **Are any DTCs recorded?** → **Yes** → **No** GO to F2 .

FM1120200797010X

Fig. 101 Test F: Charging System Warning Indicator Flickers Or Is Intermittent (Part 1 of 6). LS & Thunderbird

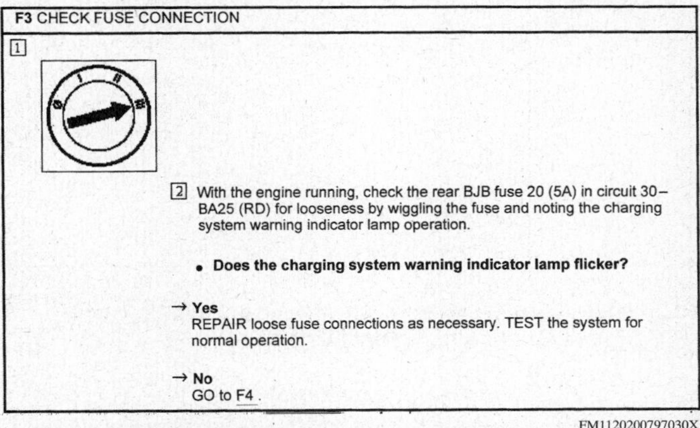
F3 CHECK FUSE CONNECTION

1

2 With the engine running, check the rear BJB fuse 20 (5A) in circuit 30–BA25 (RD) for looseness by wiggling the fuse and noting the charging system warning indicator lamp operation.

- **Does the charging system warning indicator lamp flicker?**

→ **Yes**
REPAIR loose fuse connections as necessary. TEST the system for normal operation.

→ **No**
GO to F4 .

FM1120200797030X

Fig. 101 Test F: Charging System Warning Indicator Flickers Or Is Intermittent (Part 3 of 6). LS & Thunderbird

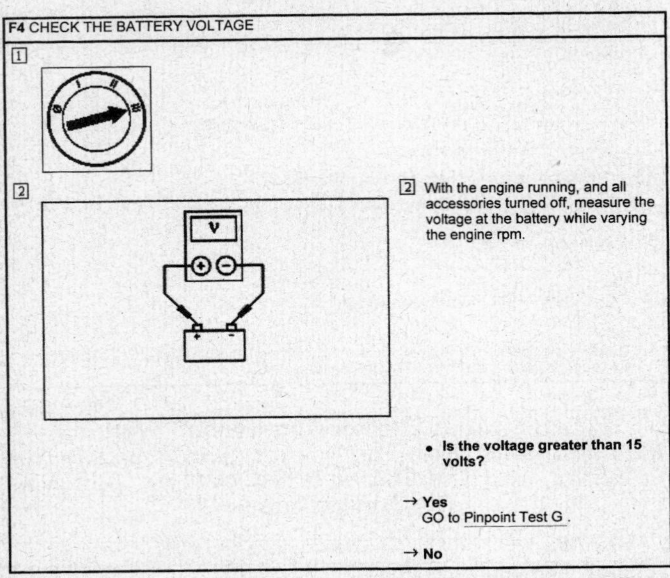

F4 CHECK THE BATTERY VOLTAGE

1

2

2 With the engine running, and all accessories turned off, measure the voltage at the battery while varying the engine rpm.

- **Is the voltage greater than 15 volts?**

→ **Yes**
GO to Pinpoint Test G .

→ **No**

FM1120200797040X

Fig. 101 Test F: Charging System Warning Indicator Flickers Or Is Intermittent (Part 4 of 6). LS & Thunderbird

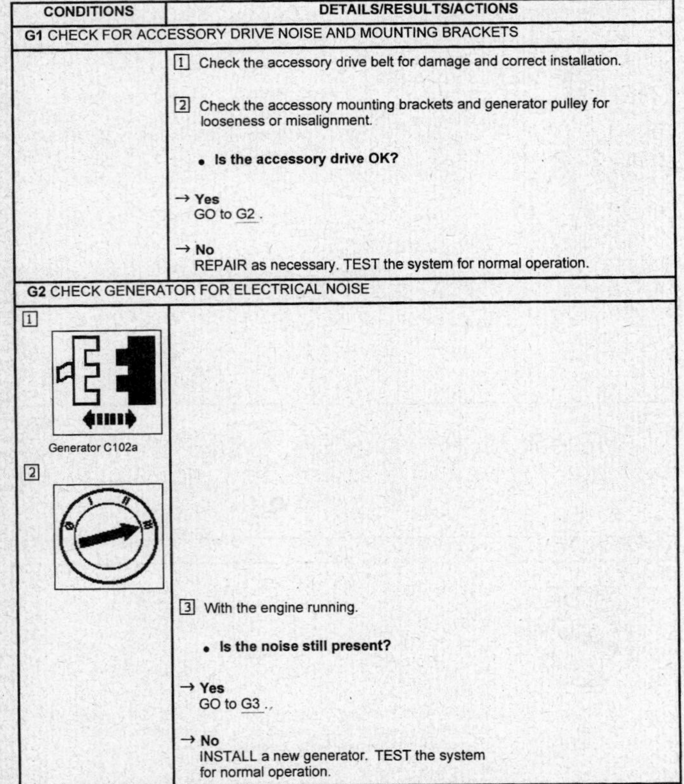

CONDITIONS	DETAILS/RESULTS/ACTIONS
G1 CHECK FOR ACCESSORY DRIVE NOISE AND MOUNTING BRACKETS	
	1 Check the accessory drive belt for damage and correct installation. 2 Check the accessory mounting brackets and generator pulley for looseness or misalignment. • **Is the accessory drive OK?** → **Yes** GO to G2 . → **No** REPAIR as necessary. TEST the system for normal operation.
G2 CHECK GENERATOR FOR ELECTRICAL NOISE	
1 Generator C102a 2	3 With the engine running. • **Is the noise still present?** → **Yes** GO to G3 . → **No** INSTALL a new generator. TEST the system for normal operation.

FM1120200798010X

Fig. 102 Test G: Alternator Is Noisy (Part 1 of 2). LS & Thunderbird

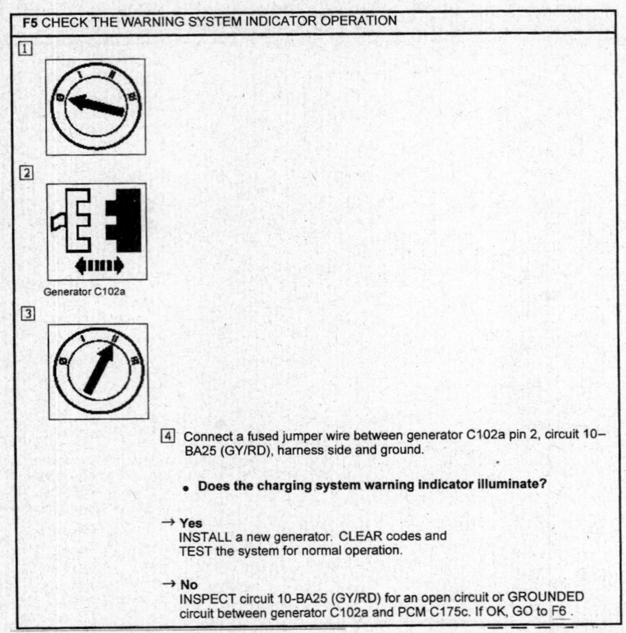

F5 CHECK THE WARNING SYSTEM INDICATOR OPERATION

1

2

Generator C102a

3

4 Connect a fused jumper wire between generator C102a pin 2, circuit 10–BA25 (GY/RD), harness side and ground.

- **Does the charging system warning indicator illuminate?**

→ **Yes**
INSTALL a new generator. CLEAR codes and TEST the system for normal operation.

→ **No**
INSPECT circuit 10-BA25 (GY/RD) for an open circuit or GROUNDED circuit between generator C102a and PCM C175c. If OK, GO to F6 .

FM1120200797050X

Fig. 101 Test F: Charging System Warning Indicator Flickers Or Is Intermittent (Part 5 of 6). LS & Thunderbird

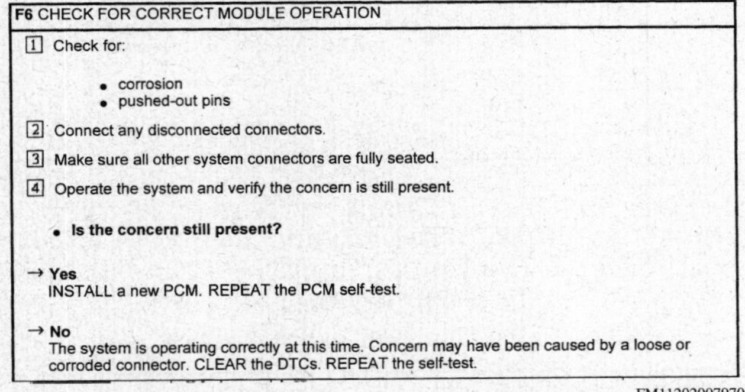

F6 CHECK FOR CORRECT MODULE OPERATION

1 Check for:

- corrosion
- pushed-out pins

2 Connect any disconnected connectors.

3 Make sure all other system connectors are fully seated.

4 Operate the system and verify the concern is still present.

- **Is the concern still present?**

→ **Yes**
INSTALL a new PCM. REPEAT the PCM self-test.

→ **No**
The system is operating correctly at this time. Concern may have been caused by a loose or corroded connector. CLEAR the DTCs. REPEAT the self-test.

FM1120200797060X

Fig. 101 Test F: Charging System Warning Indicator Flickers Or Is Intermittent (Part 6 of 6). LS & Thunderbird

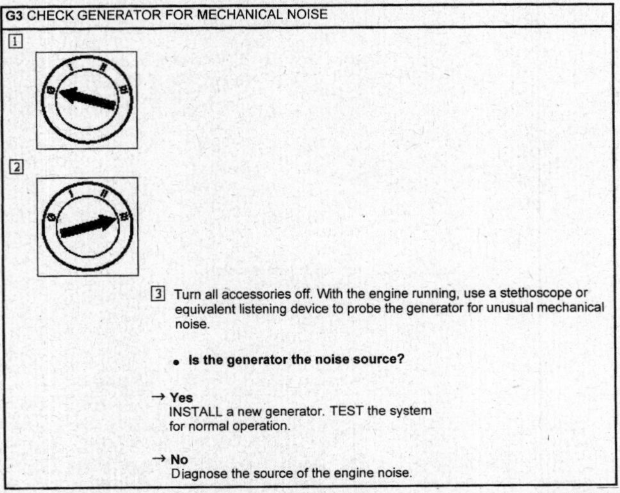

G3 CHECK GENERATOR FOR MECHANICAL NOISE

1

2

3 Turn all accessories off. With the engine running, use a stethoscope or equivalent listening device to probe the generator for unusual mechanical noise.

- **Is the generator the noise source?**

→ **Yes**
INSTALL a new generator. TEST the system for normal operation.

→ **No**
Diagnose the source of the engine noise.

FM1120200798020X

Fig. 102 Test G: Alternator Is Noisy (Part 2 of 2). LS & Thunderbird

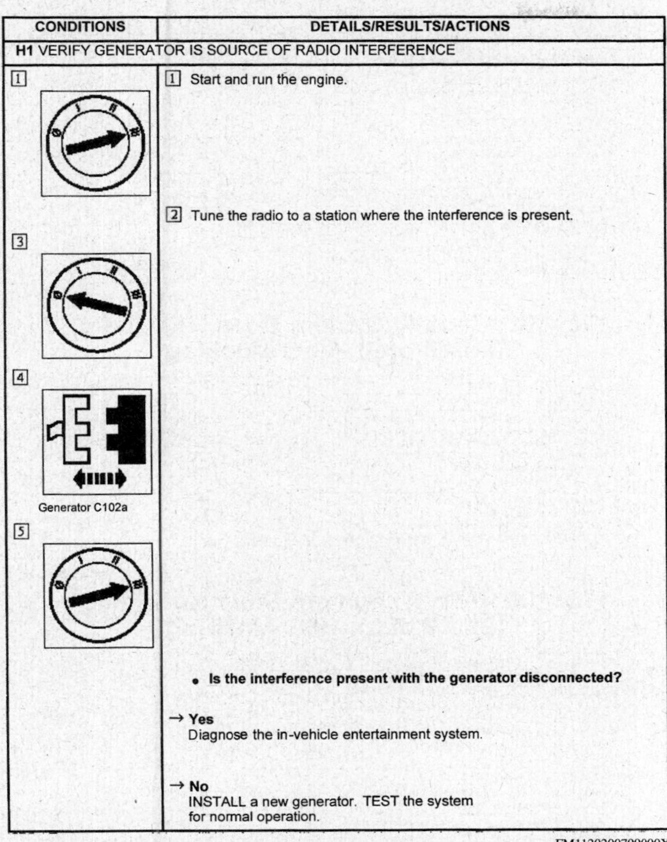

CONDITIONS	DETAILS/RESULTS/ACTIONS
H1 VERIFY GENERATOR IS SOURCE OF RADIO INTERFERENCE	
1	1 Start and run the engine.
3	2 Tune the radio to a station where the interference is present.
4 Generator C102a	
5	• **Is the interference present with the generator disconnected?** → **Yes** Diagnose the in-vehicle entertainment system. → **No** INSTALL a new generator. TEST the system for normal operation.

FM1120200799000X

Fig. 103 Test H: Radio Interference. LS & Thunderbird

Condition	Possible Source	Action
• The battery is not being charged by generator	• Voltage regulator connector. • Charging system warning indicator lamp bulb. • Voltage regulator. • Generator. • Connections.	• GO to Pinpoint Test A.
• Battery overcharging (voltage is greater than 15.5 volts)	• S Circuit 4 (WH/BK). • Generator. • Voltage regulator.	• GO to Pinpoint Test B.
• The charging system warning indicator is on with the engine running (system is charging)	• I Circuit 904 (LG/RD). • Instrument cluster. • S Circuit 4 (WH/BK). • Generator. • Voltage regulator.	• GO to Pinpoint Test C.
• The charging system indicator lamp does not come on	• I Circuit 904 (LG/RD). • Connections. • Battery cables. • Generator. • Voltage regulator. • Instrument panel. • Indicator lamp.	• GO to Pinpoint Test D.
• The charging system warning indicator flickers or is intermittent	• Connections. • I Circuit fuse loose CJB Fuse 5 (15A). • A Circuit fuse loose. • Generator. • Voltage regulator.	• GO to Pinpoint Test E.
• The generator is noisy	• Bolts or brackets. • Drive belt. • Generator or pulley.	• GO to Pinpoint Test F.

FM1120000550010X

Fig. 105 Symptom chart (Part 1 of 2). 1999–2001 Mustang w/3.8L engine

Condition	Possible Source	Action
• System Does Not Charge	• Circuitry. • Voltage regulator. • Generator. • Battery. • Battery connections. • Drive belt.	• GO to Pinpoint Test A.
• System Overcharges (Battery Boils Over)	• Circuitry. • Poor ground. • Voltage regulator. • Generator.	• GO to Pinpoint Test B.
• Indicator Lamp Stays ON, Engine Running	• Circuitry. • Voltage regulator. • Generator.	• GO to Pinpoint Test C.
• Indicator Lamp Stays ON, Ignition Switch OFF	• Circuitry. • Improper lamp circuit wiring. • Instrument cluster.	• GO to Pinpoint Test D.
• Indicator Lamp Does Not Come On	• Circuitry. • Burned out lamp. • Poor ground. • Voltage regulator. • Generator.	• GO to Pinpoint Test E.
• Indicator Lamp Flickers / Intermittent	• Loose connection to generator, voltage regulator or power distribution box. • Circuitry. • Loose brush holder screw. • Voltage regulator. • Generator.	• GO to Pinpoint Test F.
• Generator Noisy	• Accessory drive belt. • Accessory brackets. • Bent pulley. • Generator. • Other accessories.	• GO to Pinpoint Test G.
• Radio Interference	• Voltage regulator. • Generator. • Other components.	• GO to Pinpoint Test H.

FM1129700209000X

Fig. 104 Symptom chart. 1998 Mustang

Condition	Possible Source	Action
• Radio interference	• Generator. • Wiring or routing. • In-vehicle entertainment system.	• GO to Pinpoint Test G.
• The voltage gauge (if equipped) is inaccurate	• Generator. • Voltage regulator. • Voltage gauge. • Instrument cluster. • Wiring.	• Repair as required.
• Battery is discharged or voltage is low	• Corroded terminal(s). • Loose connection(s). • High key-off current drains. • Battery. • Generator.	• GO to Pinpoint Test O.

FM1120000550020X

Fig. 105 Symptom chart (Part 2 of 2). 1999–2001 Mustang w/3.8L engine

Condition	Possible Source	Action
• The battery is not being charged by the generator	• Fuse links. • I Circuit 904 (LG/RD). • I Circuit fuse (20A). • Generator. • Charging system warning indicator lamp bulb. • Harness connector.	• GO to Pinpoint Test H.
• Battery overcharging (voltage greater than 15.5 volts)	• Generator.	• GO to Pinpoint Test I.
• The charging system warning indicator lamp is on with the engine running (system is charging)	• I Circuit 904 (LG/RD). • Instrument cluster. • Generator.	• GO to Pinpoint Test J.
• The charging system warning indicator lamp does not come on	• Lamp bulb. • Instrument cluster. • I Circuit 904 (LG/RD). • Harness connector. • Generator.	• GO to Pinpoint Test K.

FM1120000551010X

Fig. 106 Symptom chart (Part 1 of 2). 1999–2001 Mustang w/4.6L engine

Condition	Possible Source	Action
• The charging system warning indicator lamp flickers or is intermittent	• Corroded terminals. • Connections. • Fuses. • Generator.	• GO to Pinpoint Test L.
• The generator is noisy	• Bolts or brackets. • Drive belt. • Generator or pulley.	• GO to Pinpoint Test M.
• Radio interference	• Harness routing. • In-vehicle entertainment system. • A Circuit 36 (YE/WH). • Generator.	• GO to Pinpoint Test N.
• Voltage gauge (if equipped) is inaccurate.	• Generator. • Voltage regulator. • Voltage gauges. • Instrument cluster. • Wiring.	• REPAIR as required.
• Battery is discharged or voltage is low	• Corroded terminal(s). • Loose connection(s). • High key-off current drains. • Battery. • Generator.	• GO to Pinpoint Test O.

FM1120000551020X

Fig. 106 Symptom chart (Part 2 of 2). 1999–2001 Mustang w/4.6L engine

Condition	Possible Sources	Action
• Battery is discharged or voltage is low	• Circuitry. • High key-off current drain(s). • Battery. • Generator.	• GO to Pinpoint Test A .
• The charging system warning indicator is on with the engine running (the system voltage does not increase)	• Circuitry. • Voltage regulator. • Generator.	• GO to Pinpoint Test B .
• The system overcharges (the battery voltage is greater than 15.5 volts)	• Circuitry. • Voltage regulator. • Generator.	• GO to Pinpoint Test C .
• The charging system warning indicator is on with the engine running and the battery increases voltage	• Circuitry. • Instrument cluster. • Voltage regulator. • Generator.	• GO to Pinpoint Test D .
• The charging system warning indicator is off with the ignition switch in the RUN position and the engine off	• Bulb. • Circuitry. • Instrument cluster. • Voltage regulator. • Generator.	• GO to Pinpoint Test E .
• The charging system warning indicator flickers or is intermittent	• Central junction box (CJB) fuse 5 (15A). • Generator connector unplugged (C102a). • Circuitry. • Generator.	• GO to Pinpoint Test F .
• The generator is noisy	• Bolts or brackets. • Drive belt. • Generator or pulley.	• GO to Pinpoint Test G .
• Radio interference	• Generator. • Circuitry. • In-vehicle entertainment system.	• GO to Pinpoint Test H .

FM1120200761000X

Fig. 107 Symptom Chart. 2002 Mustang

	Test Step	Result	Action to Take
A5	CHECK BATTERY		
	• Perform Battery Capacity Testing. • **Is the battery OK?**	Yes No	GO to **A6**. REPLACE battery.
A6	CHECK FOR KEY-OFF DRAIN		
	• Perform Battery Drain Testing as described. • **Is current drain less than 50 mA (or test lamp off)?**	Yes No	GO to **A7**. GO to Drain Testing to find cause of ignition switch-OFF battery drain.
A7	CHECK FOR OPEN B+ CIRCUIT		
	• Measure voltage at B+ terminal at generator connector C1006. • **Is voltage at B+ terminal equal to battery voltage?**	Yes No	GO to **A8**. SERVICE open in Circuit 38 (BK/O).
A8	CHECK FOR OPEN A CIRCUIT		
	• Measure voltage at A circuit on the voltage regulator connector C154. • **Is voltage at A circuit equal to battery voltage?**	Yes No	GO to **A9** on 3.8L and 4.6L (2V). GO to **A10** for 4.6L (4V). CHECK power distribution box Fuse ALT (20A) in Circuit 36 (Y/W) and REPLACE if required. If OK, SERVICE open in Circuit 36 (Y/W).
A9	CHECK FOR OPEN FIELD CIRCUIT		
	• Measure voltage at test point F on voltage regulator. • **Is voltage at test point F equal to battery voltage?**	Yes No	GO to **A10**. GO to **A16**.
A10	CHECK FOR OPEN I CIRCUIT		
	• Turn ignition switch to RUN position. • NOTE: Voltage regulator must be connected to wiring harness for this test. Measure voltage at wiring harness I terminal of connector C154, Circuit 904 (LG/R). • **Is voltage greater than 1 V?**	Yes No	GO to **A11**. SERVICE open or high resistance in Circuit 904 (LG/R).
A11	CHECK VOLTAGE DROP IN A CIRCUIT		
	• Measure voltage drop between A Circuit on voltage regulator and positive (+) battery post. • **Is voltage drop less than 0.25 V?**	Yes No	GO to **A12** on 3.8L and 4.6L (2V). On 4.6L (4V), GO to **A14**. SERVICE excess voltage drop in Circuit 36 (Y/W). CHECK fuse and connectors in Circuit 36 (Y/W) and SERVICE as required.
A12	CHECK FIELD TURN-ON		
	• Measure voltage at test point F on voltage regulator. • **Is voltage at test point F less than 2 V?**	Yes No	GO to **A13**. GO to **A16**.
A13	CHECK FOR SHORTED RECTIFIER		
	• Remove one-pin S connector C153 from generator. • Measure voltage between S terminal on back of generator and ground. • Measure voltage between positive (+) battery terminal and S terminal on back of generator. • **Is either voltage reading greater than 1 V?**	Yes No	REPLACE generator. GO to **A14**.
A14	CHECK VOLTAGE DROP IN B+ CIRCUIT		
	• Turn ignition switch to RUN position. • Turn headlamps ON and set blower on HIGH. • With engine running at 2000 rpm, measure voltage drop between the B+ terminal on back of generator and positive (+) battery post. • **Is voltage drop less than 0.5 V?**	Yes No	GO to **A15** on 3.8L and 4.6L (2V). On 4.6L (4V), REPLACE generator. SERVICE excess voltage drop in Circuit 38 (BK/O). CHECK fuse link in Circuit 38 (BK/O) and the connections between the battery and power distribution box.

FM1129700210020X

Fig. 108 Test A: System Does Not Charge (Part 2 of 3). 1998 Mustang

	Test Step	Result	Action to Take
A1	CHECK BATTERY CONNECTIONS		
	• Inspect battery cables for loose or corroded connections. • Inspect battery for corrosion. • **Are battery cables clean, tight and free from corrosion?**	Yes No	GO to **A2**. CLEAN and TIGHTEN battery cables.
A2	CHECK DRIVE BELT TENSION		
	• Perform drive belt adjustment procedure. • **Is the drive belt adjusted properly?**	Yes No	GO to **A3**. ADJUST or REPLACE drive belt.
A3	LOOSE BATTERY POST		
	• Check for loose battery posts. • **Are posts OK?**	Yes No	GO to **A4**. REPLACE battery.
A4	CRACKED BATTERY COVER		
	• Remove battery hold down clamps and shields. • Check for broken/cracked case or battery cover. • **Are case and cover OK?**	Yes No	GO to **A5**. REPLACE battery.

FM1129700210010X

Fig. 108 Test A: System Does Not Charge (Part 1 of 3). 1998 Mustang

	Test Step	Result	Action to Take
A15	CHECK FOR OPEN STATOR PHASE		
	• Connect test point F on the voltage regulator to negative (-) battery post using a jumper wire. • Perform Generator Load Test as described. • **Is generator output current greater than minimum output specified?**	Yes No	REPLACE voltage regulator. REPLACE generator.
A16	CHECK FOR OPEN/SHORTED FIELD		
	• Remove generator from vehicle. • Remove voltage regulator. • Measure resistance between generator slip rings. • **Is resistance greater than 10 ohms OR less than 1 ohm?**	Yes No	REPLACE generator. REPLACE voltage regulator. RETEST system.

FM1129700210030X

Fig. 108 Test A: System Does Not Charge (Part 3 of 3). 1998 Mustang

	Test Step	Result	Action to Take
B1	CHECK VOLTAGE DROP IN A CIRCUIT		
	• Turn ignition switch to ON. • Measure voltage between A circuit on voltage regulator and positive (+) battery post. • **Is voltage drop less than 0.25 V?**	Yes No	GO to **B2**. SERVICE excess voltage drop in Circuit 36 (Y/W). CHECK power distribution box Fuse ALT (20A) and connectors in Circuit 36 (Y/W) and SERVICE as required.
B2	CHECK VOLTAGE DROP IN I CIRCUIT		
	• NOTE: Voltage regulator must be connected to wiring harness for this test. Measure voltage at wiring harness I terminal connector C154, Circuit 904 (LG/R). • **Is voltage greater than 1 V?**	Yes No	GO to **B3**. SERVICE high resistance in Circuit 904 (LG/R).
B3	CHECK FOR POOR GROUNDS		
	• Check for poor ground connections between voltage regulator and generator, generator and engine, or engine and battery. • **Are all ground connections clean and tight?**	Yes No	GO to **B4** on 3.8L and 4.6L (2V). REPLACE generator on 4.6L (4V). CLEAN or SERVICE grounds as required.
B4	CHECK FOR FIELD CIRCUIT DRAIN		
	• Turn ignition switch to OFF position. • Measure voltage at test point F on voltage regulator. • **Is voltage at test point F equal to battery voltage?**	Yes No	Generator is OK. REPLACE voltage regulator. GO to **B5**.
B5	CHECK FOR GROUNDED SLIP RING		
	• Remove generator from vehicle. • Remove voltage regulator. • Measure resistance from each generator slip ring to the generator housing. • **Is resistance from either slip ring to housing less than 200 ohms?**	Yes No	If grease or dirt has accumulated near slip rings, CLEAN slip rings and RECHECK resistance. If still less than 200 ohms, REPLACE generator. REPLACE voltage regulator.

FM1129700211000X

Fig. 109 Test B: System Overcharges. 1998 Mustang

	Test Step	Result	Action to Take
C1	CHECK FOR OPEN A CIRCUIT		
	• Measure voltage at A circuit on voltage regulator. • **Is voltage at A circuit equal to battery voltage?**	Yes No	GO to **C2**. CHECK fuse in Circuit 36 (Y/W) and REPLACE if required. If OK, SERVICE open in Circuit 36 (Y/W).
C2	CHECK FOR SHORTED I CIRCUIT		
	• Remove voltage regulator connector C154. • Turn ignition switch to RUN. • **Is indicator lamp on?**	Yes No	SERVICE short to ground in Circuit 904 (LG/R). GO to **C3** on 3.8L and 4.6L (2V). GO to **C6** on 4.6L (4V).
C3	CHECK S CIRCUIT FUNCTION		
	• Install voltage regulator connector C154. • Remove one-pin S connector. • Connect wiring harness S terminal, Circuit 4 (W/BK) to positive (+) battery post using a jumper wire. • **Is indicator lamp on?**	Yes No	REMOVE jumper wire. GO to **C4**. REMOVE jumper wire. GO to **C5**.
C4	CHECK FOR OPEN S CIRCUIT		
	• Remove three-pin voltage regulator connector C154. • Measure wiring resistance between one-pin S connector C153and S (center) pin of voltage regulator connector. • **Is resistance greater than 1 ohm?**	Yes No	SERVICE open or excess resistance in Circuit 4 (W/BK). CHECK for loose or bent pin in voltage regulator or connector. If OK, REPLACE voltage regulator.
C5	CHECK STATOR OUTPUT VOLTAGE		
	• Turn ignition switch to RUN. • Measure voltage at S terminal on back of generator. • **Is voltage at least 1/2 of battery voltage?**	Yes No	GO to **C6**. GO to Pinpoint Test A to find the cause of low generator output.
C6	CHECK GENERATOR OUTPUT VOLTAGE		
	• Measure voltage at B+ terminal at connector C1006 on the back of generator with engine running at 2000 rpm and all accessories turned OFF. • **Is voltage greater than 15.5 V?**	Yes No	GO to Pinpoint Test B to find the cause of high output voltage. REPLACE voltage regulator on 3.8L and 4.6L (2V). REPLACE generator on 4.6L (4V).

FM1129700212000X

Fig. 110 Test C: Indicator Lamp Stays On, Engine Running. 1998 Mustang

Test Step		Result		Action to Take
D1	CHECK LAMP CIRCUIT WIRING			
	• Turn ignition switch to OFF position. • Disconnect voltage regulator connector C154. • Measure voltage at wiring harness I terminal, Circuit 904 (LG/R). • **Is voltage greater than zero V?**	Yes	▶	SERVICE Circuit 16 (R/LG). Circuit should be HOT in ignition switch START or RUN only.
		No	▶	SERVICE instrument cluster.

FM1129700213000X

Fig. 111 Test D: Indicator Lamps Stay On, Ignition Off. 1998 Mustang

Test Step		Result		Action to Take
E4	CHECK S CIRCUIT WIRING			
	• Remove one-pin S connector from generator C153. • Measure voltage at wiring harness S terminal, Circuit 4 (W/BK). • **Is voltage greater than zero V?**	Yes	▶	SERVICE Circuit 4 (W/BK). Circuit should be HOT only when engine is running.
		No	▶	GO to **E5**.
E5	CHECK FOR SHORTED RECTIFIER			
	• Measure voltage at the S terminal on the back of generator. • **Is voltage greater than 1 V?**	Yes	▶	If lamp is on with one-pin S connector removed, REPLACE generator.
		No	▶	REPLACE voltage regulator.

FM1129700214020X

Fig. 112 Test E: Indicator Lamp Does Not Light (Part 2 of 2). 1998 Mustang

Test Step		Result		Action to Take
G1	CHECK FOR ACCESSORY DRIVE NOISE			
	• Check the drive belt to make sure that it is installed properly and is not damaged. • **Is drive belt OK?**	Yes	▶	GO to **G2**.
		No	▶	SERVICE accessory drive belt as required.
G2	CHECK GENERATOR MOUNTING			
	• Check generator and generator mounting bracket for loose bolts or misalignment condition. • **Is generator mounted correctly?**	Yes	▶	GO to **G3**.
		No	▶	INSTALL generator to specification.
G3	CHECK GENERATOR PULLEY			
	• Check generator pulley for damage (bent) or a misalignment condition. • **Is pulley OK?**	Yes	▶	REPLACE generator.
		No	▶	REPLACE generator pulley.

FM1129700216000X

Fig. 114 Test G: Alternator Is Noisy. 1998 Mustang

Test Step		Result		Action to Take
H1	VERIFY RADIO INTERFERENCE			
	• Turn ignition switch to RUN position. • Tune radio to a station where interference is present. • Remove voltage regulator connector C154. • **Is interference present with connector removed?**	Yes	▶	Locate cause of radio interference.
		No	▶	REPLACE generator.

FM1129700217000X

Fig. 115 Test H: Radio Interference. 1998 Mustang

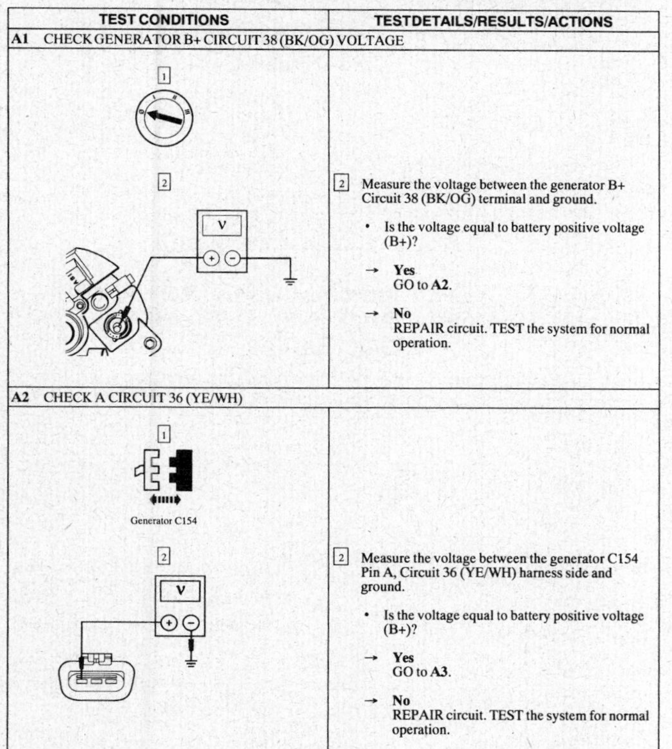

TEST CONDITIONS	TESTDETAILS/RESULTS/ACTIONS
A1 CHECK GENERATOR B+ CIRCUIT 38 (BK/OG) VOLTAGE	
1	
2	2 Measure the voltage between the generator B+ Circuit 38 (BK/OG) terminal and ground. • Is the voltage equal to battery positive voltage (B+)? → **Yes** GO to **A2**. → **No** REPAIR circuit. TEST the system for normal operation.
A2 CHECK A CIRCUIT 36 (YE/WH)	
1 Generator C154	
2	2 Measure the voltage between the generator C154 Pin A, Circuit 36 (YE/WH) harness side and ground. • Is the voltage equal to battery positive voltage (B+)? → **Yes** GO to **A3**. → **No** REPAIR circuit. TEST the system for normal operation.

FM1120000552010X

Fig. 116 Test A: System Does Not Charge (Part 1 of 3). 1999–2001 Mustang w/3.8L Engine

Test Step		Result		Action to Take
E1	CHECK FOR OPEN I CIRCUIT			
	• Remove voltage regulator connector C154. • Turn ignition switch to RUN. • Measure voltage at wiring harness I terminal, Circuit 904 (LG/R). • **Is voltage equal to B+?**	Yes	▶	GO to **E2**.
		No	▶	SERVICE open in Circuit 904 (LG/R).
E2	CHECK FOR BURNED OUT BULB			
	• Connect wiring harness I terminal, Circuit 904 (LG/R) to ground with a jumper wire. • **Is indicator lamp on?**	Yes	▶	REMOVE jumper wire. GO to **E3**.
		No	▶	REPLACE lamp or SERVICE high resistance in lamp socket or Circuit 904 (LG/R).
E3	CHECK FOR POOR GROUNDS			
	• Check for poor ground connections between voltage regulator and generator, generator and engine, or engine and battery. • **Are all ground connections clean and tight?**	Yes	▶	GO to **E4** on 3.8L and 4.6L (2V). REPLACE generator on 4.6L (2V).
		No	▶	CLEAN or SERVICE grounds as required.

FM1129700214010X

Fig. 112 Test E: Indicator Lamp Does Not Light (Part 1 of 2). 1998 Mustang

Test Step		Result		Action to Take
F1	CHECK FOR LOOSE CONNECTIONS			
	• Check these connections for corrosion, loose or bent pins, or loose eyelets: — voltage regulator connector C154 — one-pin S connector C153 3.8L and 4.6L (2V) only — generator B+ eyelet — power distribution box eyelets — battery cables • **Are all connections clean and tight?**	Yes	▶	GO to **F2** on 3.8L and 4.6L (2V). GO to **F3** on 4.6L (2V).
		No	▶	CLEAN or SERVICE connections as required.
F2	CHECK FOR FIELD CIRCUIT DRAIN			
	• Turn ignition switch to OFF position. • Measure voltage at test point F on voltage regulator. • **Is voltage at test point F equal to battery voltage?**	Yes	▶	GO to **F3**.
		No	▶	GO to **F5**.
F3	CHECK FOR LOOSE A CIRCUIT FUSE			
	• Turn ignition switch to RUN. • Check the power distribution box ALT Fuse (20A) for a loose connection by wiggling fuse with engine running. • **Does indicator lamp flicker?**	Yes	▶	SERVICE loose fuse connection.
		No	▶	GO to **F4**.
F4	CHECK A CIRCUIT CONNECTIONS			
	• With engine running, connect A circuit on voltage regulator to positive (+) battery post using a jumper wire. • **Does indicator lamp flicker?**	Yes	▶	REPLACE voltage regulator. If concern still exists, REPLACE generator on 3.8L and 4.6L (2V). REPLACE generator on 4.6L (2V).
		No	▶	SERVICE poor connection in Circuit 36 (Y/W).
F5	CHECK BRUSH HOLDER SCREWS			
	• Remove generator from vehicle. • Check the brush holder screws, located on the voltage regulator (test points F and A). • **Are the brush holder screws tight?**	Yes	▶	GO to **F6**.
		No	▶	TIGHTEN screws to 2.8-4.0 N-m (25-35 lb-in).
F6	CHECK FOR GROUNDED SLIP RING			
	• Remove voltage regulator. • Measure resistance from each generator slip ring to the generator housing. • **Is resistance from either slip ring to housing less than 200 ohms?**	Yes	▶	If grease or dirt has accumulated near slip rings, CLEAN slip rings and RECHECK resistance. If still less than 200 ohms, REPLACE generator.
		No	▶	REPLACE voltage regulator.

FM1129700215000X

Fig. 113 Test F: Indicator Lamp Flickers/Intermittent. 1998 Mustang

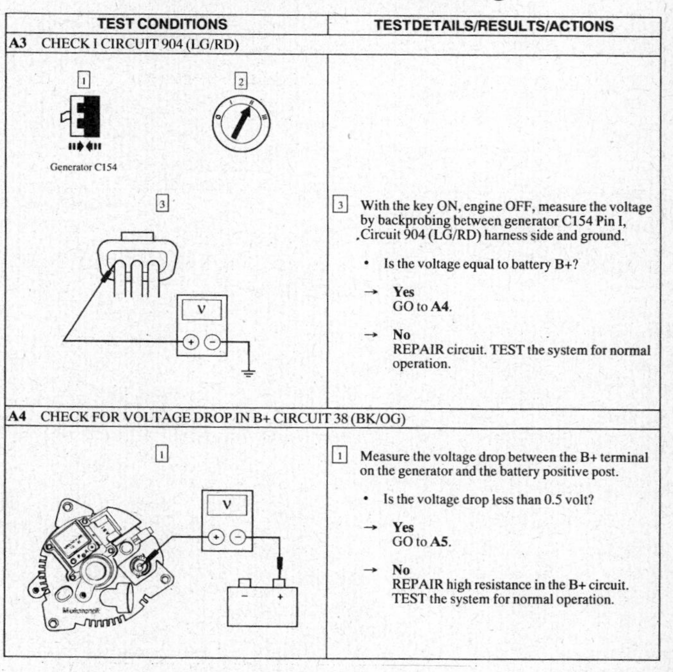

TEST CONDITIONS	TESTDETAILS/RESULTS/ACTIONS
A3 CHECK I CIRCUIT 904 (LG/RD)	
1 Generator C154 2	
3	3 With the key ON, engine OFF, measure the voltage by backprobing between generator C154 Pin I, Circuit 904 (LG/RD) harness side and ground. • Is the voltage equal to battery B+? → **Yes** GO to **A4**. → **No** REPAIR circuit. TEST the system for normal operation.
A4 CHECK FOR VOLTAGE DROP IN B+ CIRCUIT 38 (BK/OG)	
1	1 Measure the voltage drop between the B+ terminal on the generator and the battery positive post. • Is the voltage drop less than 0.5 volt? → **Yes** GO to **A5**. → **No** REPAIR high resistance in the B+ circuit. TEST the system for normal operation.

FM1120000552020X

Fig. 116 Test A: System Does Not Charge (Part 2 of 3). 1999–2001 Mustang w/3.8L Engine

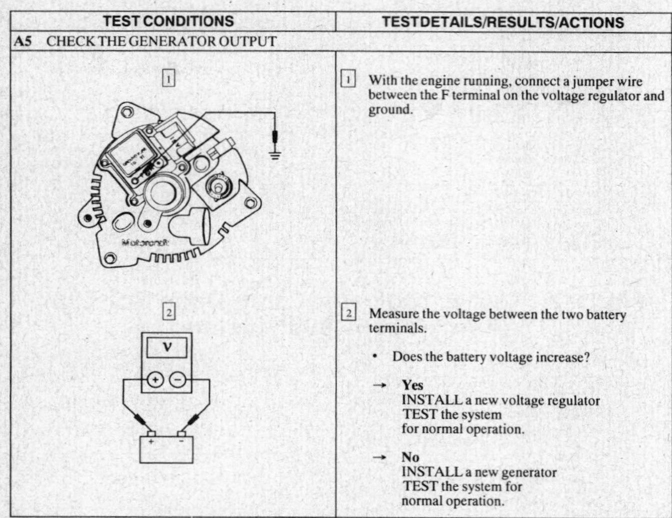

TEST CONDITIONS	TEST DETAILS/RESULTS/ACTIONS
A5 CHECK THE GENERATOR OUTPUT	
1	1 With the engine running, connect a jumper wire between the F terminal on the voltage regulator and ground.
2	2 Measure the voltage between the two battery terminals. • Does the battery voltage increase? → **Yes** INSTALL a new voltage regulator TEST the system for normal operation. → **No** INSTALL a new generator TEST the system for normal operation.

FM1120000552030X

Fig. 116 Test A: System Does Not Charge (Part 3 of 3). 1999–2001 Mustang w/3.8L Engine

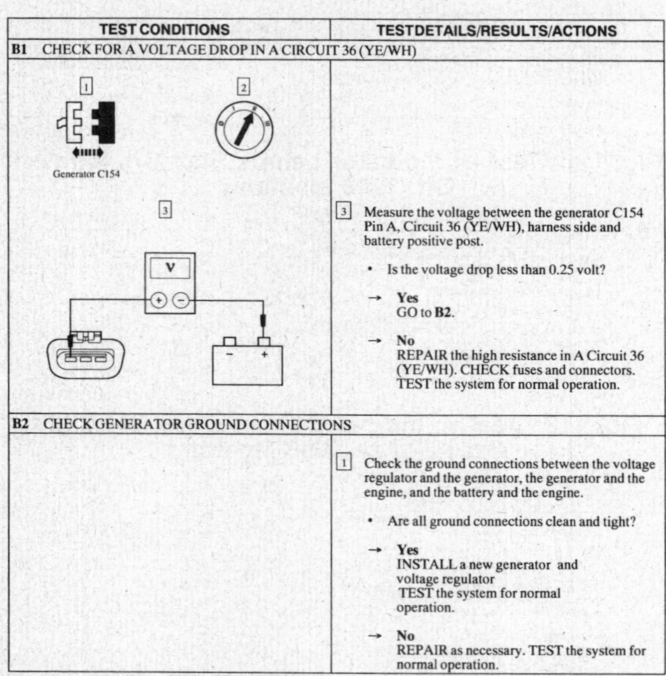

TEST CONDITIONS	TEST DETAILS/RESULTS/ACTIONS
B1 CHECK FOR A VOLTAGE DROP IN A CIRCUIT 36 (YE/WH)	
1 2 Generator C154	
3	3 Measure the voltage between the generator C154 Pin A, Circuit 36 (YE/WH), harness side and battery positive post. • Is the voltage drop less than 0.25 volt? → **Yes** GO to **B2**. → **No** REPAIR the high resistance in A Circuit 36 (YE/WH). CHECK fuses and connectors. TEST the system for normal operation.
B2 CHECK GENERATOR GROUND CONNECTIONS	
	1 Check the ground connections between the voltage regulator and the generator, the generator and the engine, and the battery and the engine. • Are all ground connections clean and tight? → **Yes** INSTALL a new generator and voltage regulator TEST the system for normal operation. → **No** REPAIR as necessary. TEST the system for normal operation.

FM1120000553000X

Fig. 117 Test B: System Overcharging. 1999–2001 Mustang w/3.8L Engine

TEST CONDITIONS	TEST DETAILS/RESULTS/ACTIONS
C1 CHECK I CIRCUIT 904 (LG/RD) FOR SHORT TO GROUND	
1 2 Generator C154	
	3 Turn the key ON, engine OFF. • Is the charging system warning indicator lamp on? → **Yes** REPAIR the short to ground in I Circuit 904 (LG/RD). TEST the system for normal operation. → **No** GO to **C2**.
C2 INSPECT GENERATOR S C153	
	1 Inspect generator C153 to make sure it is correctly mated to the generator and making contact with the S terminal. • Is the generator C153 OK? → **Yes** GO to **C3**. → **No** REPAIR as necessary. TEST the system for normal operation.

FM1120000554010X

Fig. 118 Test C: Indicator Lamp Remains Lit w/Engine Running (Part 1 of 2). 1999–2001 Mustang w/3.8L Engine

TEST CONDITIONS	TEST DETAILS/RESULTS/ACTIONS
C3 CHECK GENERATOR FOR LOW VOLTAGE	
1 Generator C153	
2	2 With the engine running at 2,000 rpm, measure the voltage between generator C153, Circuit 4 (WH/BK), harness side and ground. • Is the voltage greater than 5 volts? → **Yes** INSTALL a new voltage regulator TEST the system for normal operation. → **No** INSTALL a new generator TEST the system for normal operation.

FM1120000554020X

Fig. 118 Test C: Indicator Lamp Remains Lit w/Engine Running (Part 2 of 2). 1999–2001 Mustang w/3.8L Engine

TEST CONDITIONS	TEST DETAILS/RESULTS/ACTIONS
D1 CHECK CHARGING SYSTEM WARNING INDICATOR LAMP	
1 2 Generator C154	
3	3 With the engine OFF, connect a fused 15A jumper wire between generator C154 Pin I, Circuit 904 (LG/RD), harness side and ground. • Is the charging system warning indicator lamp on? → **Yes** INSTALL a new voltage regulator TEST the system for normal operation. → **No** INSPECT lamp as required.

FM1120000555000X

Fig. 119 Test D: Indicator Lamp Does Not Light. 1999–2001 Mustang w/3.8L Engine

TEST CONDITIONS	TEST DETAILS/RESULTS/ACTIONS
E1 CHECK FOR LOOSE CONNECTIONS	
	1 Check all generator, battery, and power distribution connections for looseness, corrosion, loose or bent terminals, or loose eyelets. • Are all connections clean and tight? → **Yes** GO to **E2**. → **No** REPAIR as necessary. TEST the system for normal operation.
E2 CHECK FUSES/FUSE LINKS	
1	1 With the engine running, check fuses in A Circuit 36 (YE/WH) and I Circuit 904 (LG/RD), and fuse links, Circuit 38 (GY), for looseness by wiggling the fuse and noting the charging system warning indicator lamp. • Did the charging system warning indicator lamp flicker? → **Yes** REPAIR loose fuse connections as necessary. TEST the system for normal operation. → **No** GO to **E3**.
E3 CHECK A CIRCUIT 36 (YE/WH) CONNECTIONS	
1	1 Connect a fused 20A jumper wire by back probing between generator C154 Pin A, Circuit 36 (YE/WH) and battery positive post.

FM1120000556010X

Fig. 120 Test E: Indicator Lamp Flickers Or Lights Intermittently (Part 1 of 3). 1999–2001 Mustang w/3.8L Engine

TEST CONDITIONS	TEST DETAILS/RESULTS/ACTIONS
F1 CHECK FOR ACCESSORY DRIVE NOISE	
	1 Check the accessory drive belt for damage and correct installation. Check the accessory mounting brackets and generator pulley for looseness or misalignment. • Is the accessory drive OK? → **Yes** GO to **F2**. → **No** REPAIR as necessary. TEST the system for normal operation.
F2 CHECK GENERATOR MOUNTING	
	1 Check the generator mounting for loose bolts or misalignment. • Is the generator mounted correctly? → **Yes** GO to **F3**. → **No** REPAIR as necessary. TEST the system for normal operation.
F3 CHECK GENERATOR FOR ELECTRICAL NOISE	
1 2 Generator C154	3 With the engine running, turn the headlights ON, rear defroster ON, and the blower motor to HI. • Is the noise still present? → **Yes** GO to **F4**. → **No** INSTALL a new generator (10346). TEST the system for normal operation.

FM1120000557010X

Fig. 121 Test F: Alternator Noisy (Part 1 of 2). 1999–2001 Mustang w/3.8L Engine

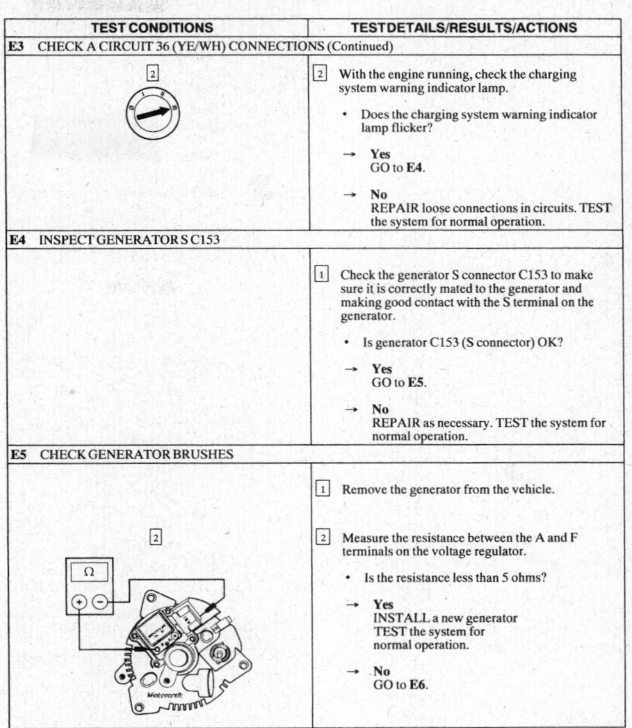

TEST CONDITIONS	TEST DETAILS/RESULTS/ACTIONS
E3 CHECK A CIRCUIT 36 (YE/WH) CONNECTIONS (Continued)	
2	2 With the engine running, check the charging system warning indicator lamp. • Does the charging system warning indicator lamp flicker? → **Yes** GO to **E4**. → **No** REPAIR loose connections in circuits. TEST the system for normal operation.
E4 INSPECT GENERATOR S C153	
	1 Check the generator S connector C153 to make sure it is correctly mated to the generator and making good contact with the S terminal on the generator. • Is generator C153 (S connector) OK? → **Yes** GO to **E5**. → **No** REPAIR as necessary. TEST the system for normal operation.
E5 CHECK GENERATOR BRUSHES	
	1 Remove the generator from the vehicle.
2	2 Measure the resistance between the A and F terminals on the voltage regulator. • Is the resistance less than 5 ohms? → **Yes** INSTALL a new generator TEST the system for normal operation. → **No** GO to **E6**.

FM1120000556020X

Fig. 120 Test E: Indicator Lamp Flickers Or Lights Intermittently (Part 2 of 3). 1999–2001 Mustang w/3.8L Engine

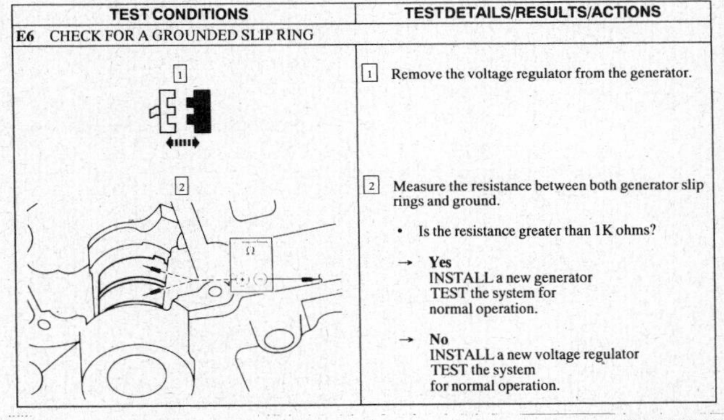

TEST CONDITIONS	TEST DETAILS/RESULTS/ACTIONS
E6 CHECK FOR A GROUNDED SLIP RING	
1	1 Remove the voltage regulator from the generator.
2	2 Measure the resistance between both generator slip rings and ground. • Is the resistance greater than 1K ohms? → **Yes** INSTALL a new generator TEST the system for normal operation. → **No** INSTALL a new voltage regulator TEST the system for normal operation.

FM1120000556030X

Fig. 120 Test E: Indicator Lamp Flickers Or Lights Intermittently (Part 3 of 3). 1999–2001 Mustang w/3.8L Engine

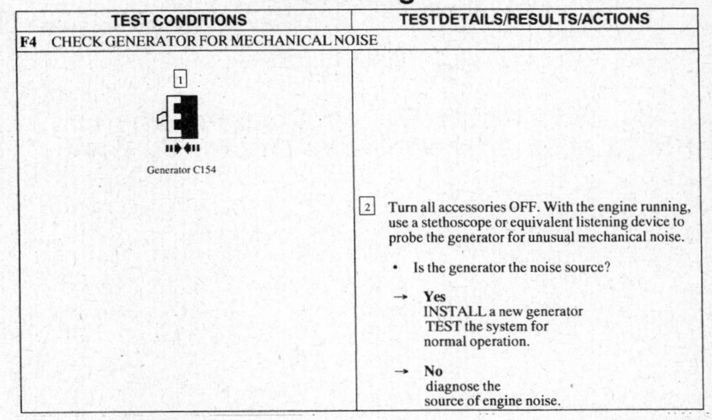

TEST CONDITIONS	TEST DETAILS/RESULTS/ACTIONS
F4 CHECK GENERATOR FOR MECHANICAL NOISE	
1 Generator C154	2 Turn all accessories OFF. With the engine running, use a stethoscope or equivalent listening device to probe the generator for unusual mechanical noise. • Is the generator the noise source? → **Yes** INSTALL a new generator TEST the system for normal operation. → **No** diagnose the source of engine noise.

FM1120000557020X

Fig. 121 Test F: Alternator Noisy (Part 2 of 2). 1999–2001 Mustang w/3.8L Engine

TEST CONDITIONS	TESTDETAILS/RESULTS/ACTIONS
G1 VERIFY GENERATOR IS SOURCE OF RADIO INTERFERENCE	
1	1 Start and run the engine.
2	2 Tune the radio to a station where the interference is present.
3 4 5 Generator C154	
	• Is the interference present with the generator disconnected? → **Yes** INSPECT the in-vehicle entertainment system. → **No** INSTALL a new generator (10346). TEST the system for normal operation.

FM1120000558000X

Fig. 122 Test G: Radio Interference. 1999–2001 Mustang w/3.8L Engine

TEST CONDITIONS	TESTDETAILS/RESULTS/ACTIONS
H3 CHECK I CIRCUIT 904 (LG/RD)	
1 Generator C154 2	
3	3 **Note:** The generator (GEN) must be connected to the wiring harness for this test. Measure the voltage between generator C154 pin I, circuit 904 (LG/RD), harness side and ground. • Is the voltage equal to B+? → **Yes** GO to **H4**. → **No** REPAIR circuit. TEST the system for normal operation.
H4 CHECK FOR VOLTAGE DROP IN THE B+ CIRCUIT	
1	
2	2 With the engine running, headlights ON, defroster ON, blower on HI, measure the voltage drop between the B+ terminal on generator and the battery positive post. • Is the voltage drop less than .5 volt? → **Yes** INSTALL a new generator TEST the system for normal operation. → **No** REPAIR the high resistance in the B+ circuit as necessary. TEST the system for normal operation.

FM1120000559020X

Fig. 123 Test H: System Does Not Charge (Part 2 of 2). 1999–2001 Mustang w/4.6L Engine

TEST CONDITIONS	TESTDETAILS/RESULTS/ACTIONS
H1 CHECK GENERATOR B+ CIRCUIT 38 (BK/OG) VOLTAGE	
1	1 Measure the voltage between the generator B+ terminal, harness side and ground. • Is the voltage equal to battery positive voltage (B+)? → **Yes** GO to **H2**. → **No** REPAIR generator B+ circuit as necessary. TEST the system for normal operation.
H2 CHECK A CIRCUIT 36 (YE/WH)	
1 Generator C154	
2	2 Measure the voltage between the generator C154 pin A, circuit 36 (YE/WH) harness side, and ground. • Is the voltage equal to battery positive voltage (B+)? → **Yes** GO to **H3**. → **No** REPAIR circuit. TEST the system for normal operation.

FM1120000559010X

Fig. 123 Test H: System Does Not Charge (Part 1 of 2). 1999–2001 Mustang w/4.6L Engine

TEST CONDITIONS	TESTDETAILS/RESULTS/ACTIONS
I1 CHECK FOR A VOLTAGE DROP IN A CIRCUIT 36 (YE/WH)	
1 Generator C154 2	
	3 With the key ON, engine OFF, measure the voltage between generator C154, pin A, circuit 36 (YE/WH), harness side and battery positive post. • Is the voltage drop less than 0.25 volt? → **Yes** GO to **I2**. → **No** REPAIR circuit. TEST the system for normal operation.
I2 CHECK GROUND CONNECTIONS	
	1 Check ground connections between the generator and the engine, and the battery and the engine. • Are all ground connections clean and tight? → **Yes** INSTALL a new generator TEST the system for normal operation. → **No** REPAIR as necessary. TEST the system for normal operation.

FM1120000560000X

Fig. 124 Test I: System Overcharging. 1999–2001 Mustang w/4.6L Engine

TEST CONDITIONS	TESTDETAILS/RESULTS/ACTIONS
J1 CHECK FOR SHORTED I CIRCUIT	
1 2 Generator C154	• Is the charging system warning indicator lamp on? → **Yes** REPAIR generator I circuit 904 (LG/RD) for a short to ground as necessary. TEST the system for normal operation. → **No** INSTALL a new generator TEST the system for normal operation.

FM1120000561000X

Fig. 125 Test J: Indicator Lamp Lights, Engine Running. 1999–2001 Mustang w/4.6L Engine

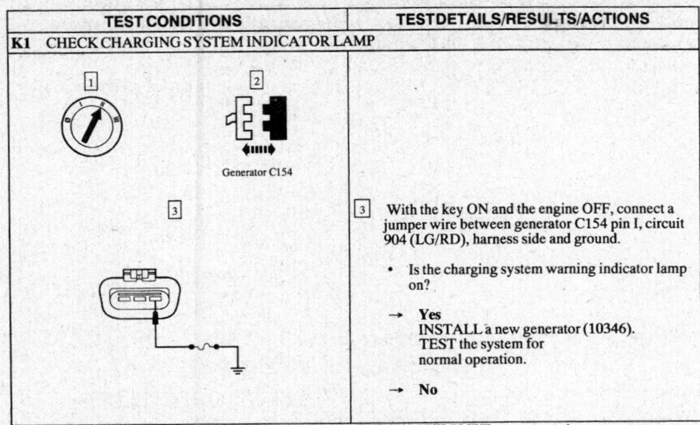

TEST CONDITIONS	TESTDETAILS/RESULTS/ACTIONS
K1 CHECK CHARGING SYSTEM INDICATOR LAMP	
1	
2 Generator C154	
3	3 With the key ON and the engine OFF, connect a jumper wire between generator C154 pin I, circuit 904 (LG/RD), harness side and ground. • Is the charging system warning indicator lamp on? → **Yes** INSTALL a new generator (10346). TEST the system for normal operation. → **No**

FM1120000562000X

Fig. 126 Test K: Indicator Lamp Does Not Light. 1999–2001 Mustang w/4.6L Engine

TEST CONDITIONS	TESTDETAILS/RESULTS/ACTIONS
L3 CHECK A CIRCUIT 36 (YE/WH) CONNECTIONS	
1	
2	2 Connect a jumper wire between the generator C154, pin A, circuit 36 (YE/WH), harness side and battery positive post.
3	3 Start and run the engine. • Does the charging system warning indicator lamp flicker? → **Yes** INSTALL a new generator TEST the system for normal operation. → **No** REPAIR loose connections in circuits. TEST the system for normal operation.

FM1120000563020X

Fig. 127 Test L: Indicator Lamp Flickers or Lights Intermittently (Part 2 of 2). 1999–2001 Mustang w/4.6L Engine

TEST CONDITIONS	TESTDETAILS/RESULTS/ACTIONS
L1 CHECK FOR LOOSE CONNECTIONS	
	1 Check all generator, battery, and power distribution connections for looseness, corrosion, loose or bent terminals, or loose eyelets. • Are all connections clean and tight? → **Yes** GO to **L2**. → **No** TEST the system for normal operation.
L2 CHECK FUSES AND FUSE LINKS	
	1 With the engine running, check the fuses for A circuit 36 (YE/WH) and I circuit 904 (LG/RD), and circuit 38 (GY) fuse links for looseness by wiggling the fuse/fuse link and noting the charging system warning indicator lamp operation. • Did the charging system warning indicator lamp flicker? → **Yes** REPAIR loose fuse connections as necessary. TEST the system for normal operation. → **No** GO to **L3**.

FM1120000563010X

Fig. 127 Test L: Indicator Lamp Flickers or Lights Intermittently (Part 1 of 2). 1999–2001 Mustang w/4.6L Engine

TEST CONDITIONS	TESTDETAILS/RESULTS/ACTIONS
M1 CHECK FOR ACCESSORY DRIVE NOISE	
	1 Check the accessory drive (serpentine) belt for damage and to verify correct installation. Check the accessory mounting brackets for loose bolts or misalignment. Check for a bent generator pulley. • Is the accessory drive OK? → **Yes** GO to **M2**. → **No** continue diagnosis and testing of the accessory drive system or REPAIR as necessary. TEST the system for normal operation.
M2 CHECK GENERATOR MOUNTING	
	1 Check the generator mounting for loose bolts or misalignment. • Is the generator mounted correctly? → **Yes** GO to **M3**. → **No** REPAIR as necessary. TEST the system for normal operation.
M3 CHECK GENERATOR FOR ELECTRICAL NOISE	
1	
	2 With the engine running, turn the headlights ON, rear defroster ON, and blower motor to HI.
3 Generator C154	

FM1120000564010X

Fig. 128 Test M: Alternator is Noisy (Part 1 of 2). 1999–2001 Mustang w/4.6L Engine

TEST CONDITIONS	TESTDETAILS/RESULTS/ACTIONS
M3 CHECK GENERATOR FOR ELECTRICAL NOISE (Continued)	
	• Is the noise still present with the generator disconnected? → **Yes** GO to **M4**. → **No** INSTALL a new generator TEST the system for normal operation.
M4 CHECK GENERATOR FOR MECHANICAL NOISE	
1 Generator C154	2 Turn all accessories OFF. With the engine running, use a stethoscope or other listening device, to listen to the generator for unusual mechanical noise. • Is the generator the noise source? → **Yes** INSTALL a new generator TEST the system for normal operation. → **No** diagnose the source of engine noise.

FM1120000564020X

Fig. 128 Test M: Alternator is Noisy (Part 2 of 2). 1999–2001 Mustang w/4.6L Engine

TEST CONDITIONS	TESTDETAILS/RESULTS/ACTIONS
O1 CHECK BATTERY CONDITION	
	1 Carry out the Battery — Condition Test to determine if the battery can hold a charge and is OK for use. • Is the battery OK? → **Yes** GO to **O2**. → **No** INSTALL a new battery. TEST the system for normal operation.
O2 CHECK FOR GENERATOR OUTPUT	
	1 Carry out the On-Vehicle Generator Load/No-Load Test. • Is the generator OK? → **Yes** GO to **O3**. → **No** GO to Pinpoint Test B.
O3 CHECK FOR CURRENT DRAINS	
	1 Carry out the Battery — Drain Test. • Are there any excessive current drains? → **Yes** REPAIR as necessary. TEST the system for normal operation. → **No** GO to **O4**.

FM1120000566010X

Fig. 130 Test O: Battery Discharged or Voltage Low (Part 1 of 2). 1999–2001 Mustang w/4.6L Engine

TEST CONDITIONS	TESTDETAILS/RESULTS/ACTIONS
N1 VERIFY GENERATOR FOR SOURCE OF RADIO INTERFERENCE	
	1 With the engine running, tune the radio to station where interference is present and disconnect generator C154. • Is radio interference still present with the generator C154 disconnected? → **Yes** diagnose the cause of the radio interference. → **No** INSTALL a new generator TEST the system for normal operation.

FM1120000565000X

Fig. 129 Test N: Radio Interference. 1999–2001 Mustang w/4.6L Engine

TEST CONDITIONS	TESTDETAILS/RESULTS/ACTIONS
O4 CHECK FOR CURRENT DRAINS WHICH SHUT OFF WHEN THE BATTERY IS DISCONNECTED	
	1 Carry out the Battery — Electronic Drains Which Shut Off When the Battery Cable is Disconnected Test. • Are there any current drains which shut off when the battery is disconnected? → **Yes** REPAIR as necessary. TEST the system for normal operation. → **No** If 3G generator, GO to Pinpoint Test A. If 4G or 6G generator, GO to Pinpoint Test H.

FM1120000566020X

Fig. 130 Test O: Battery Discharged or Voltage Low (Part 2 of 2). 1999–2001 Mustang w/4.6L Engine

CONDITIONS	DETAILS/RESULTS/ACTIONS
A1 CHECK BATTERY CONDITION	
	1 Carry out the Battery—Condition Test to determine if the battery can hold a charge and is OK for use. • **Is the battery OK?** → **Yes** GO to A2 . → **No** INSTALL a new battery. TEST the system for normal operation.
A2 CHECK THE GENERATOR OUTPUT	
	1 Carry out the On-Vehicle Generator Load/No Load Test. • **Is the generator OK?** → **Yes** GO to A3 . → **No** GO to Pinpoint Test B .
A3 CHECK FOR CURRENT DRAINS	
	1 Carry out the Battery—Drain Test. • **Are there any excessive current drains?** → **Yes** REPAIR as necessary. TEST the system for normal operation. → **No** GO to A4 .
A4 CHECK FOR CURRENT DRAINS WHICH SHUT OFF WHEN THE BATTERY IS DISCONNECTED	
	1 Carry out the Battery—Electronic Drains Which Shut Off When the Battery Cable is Disconnected Test. Refer or Component Tests • **Are there any current drains which shut off when the battery is disconnected?** → **Yes** REPAIR as necessary. TEST the system for normal operation. → **No** GO to Pinpoint Test B .

FM1120200762000X

Fig. 131 Test A: Battery Is Charged Or Voltage Is Low. 2002 Mustang

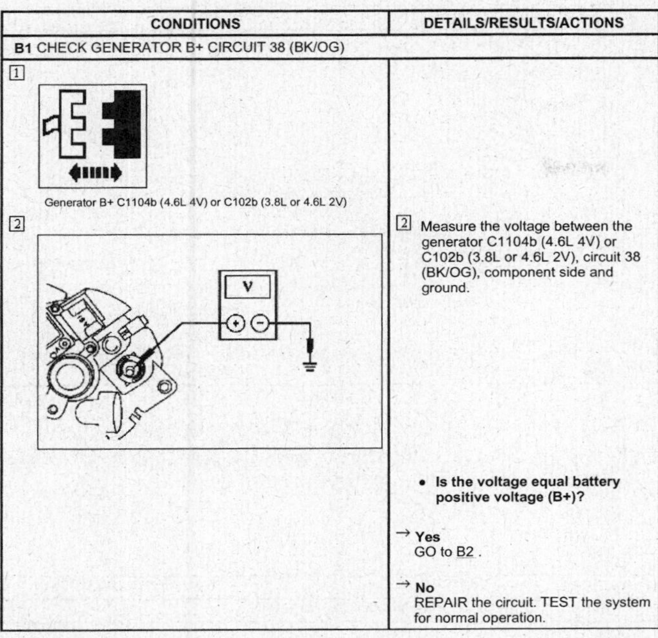

CONDITIONS	DETAILS/RESULTS/ACTIONS
B1 CHECK GENERATOR B+ CIRCUIT 38 (BK/OG)	
1 Generator B+ C1104b (4.6L 4V) or C102b (3.8L or 4.6L 2V)	
2	2 Measure the voltage between the generator C1104b (4.6L 4V) or C102b (3.8L or 4.6L 2V), circuit 38 (BK/OG), component side and ground. • **Is the voltage equal battery positive voltage (B+)?** → **Yes** GO to B2 . → **No** REPAIR the circuit. TEST the system for normal operation.

FM1120200763010X

Fig. 132 Test B: Charging System Warning Indicator Is On With The Engine Running/The Battery Voltage Does Not Increase (Part 1 of 4). 2002 Mustang

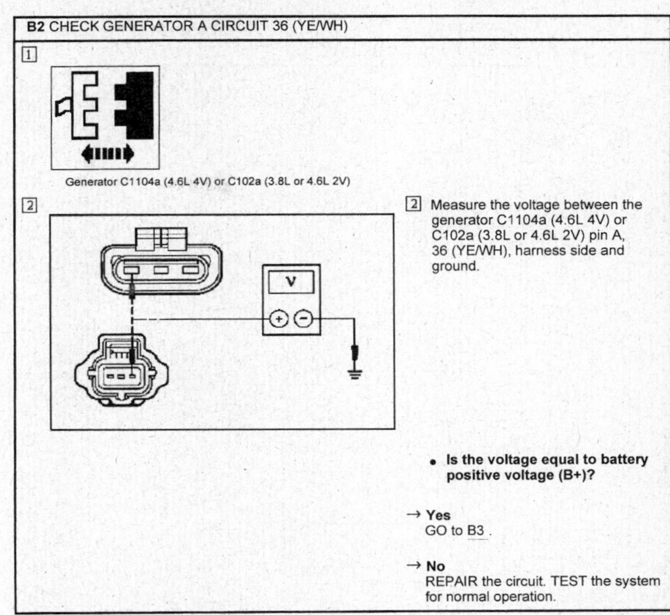

B2 CHECK GENERATOR A CIRCUIT 36 (YE/WH)

1 Generator C1104a (4.6L 4V) or C102a (3.8L or 4.6L 2V)

2 Measure the voltage between the generator C1104a (4.6L 4V) or C102a (3.8L or 4.6L 2V) pin A, 36 (YE/WH), harness side and ground.

• **Is the voltage equal to battery positive voltage (B+)?**

→ **Yes** GO to B3 .

→ **No** REPAIR the circuit. TEST the system for normal operation.

FM1120200763020X

Fig. 132 Test B: Charging System Warning Indicator Is On With The Engine Running/The Battery Voltage Does Not Increase (Part 2 of 4). 2002 Mustang

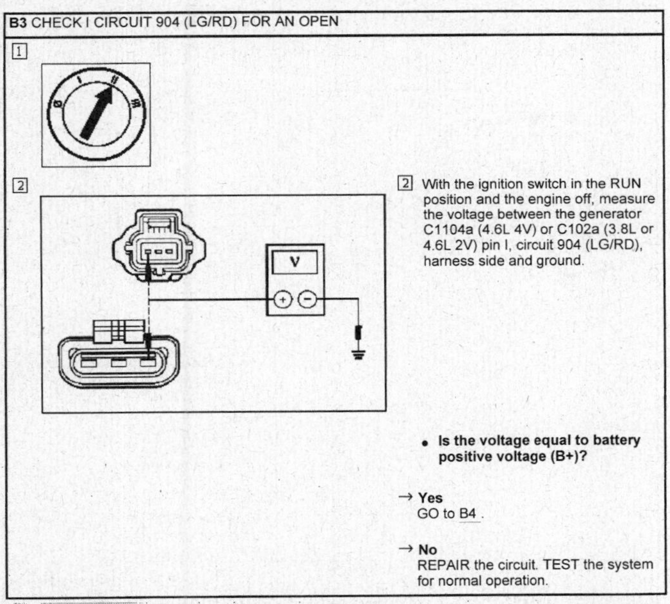

B3 CHECK I CIRCUIT 904 (LG/RD) FOR AN OPEN

1

2 With the ignition switch in the RUN position and the engine off, measure the voltage between the generator C1104a (4.6L 4V) or C102a (3.8L or 4.6L 2V) pin I, circuit 904 (LG/RD), harness side and ground.

• **Is the voltage equal to battery positive voltage (B+)?**

→ **Yes** GO to B4 .

→ **No** REPAIR the circuit. TEST the system for normal operation.

FM1120200763030X

Fig. 132 Test B: Charging System Warning Indicator Is On With The Engine Running/The Battery Voltage Does Not Increase (Part 3 of 4). 2002 Mustang

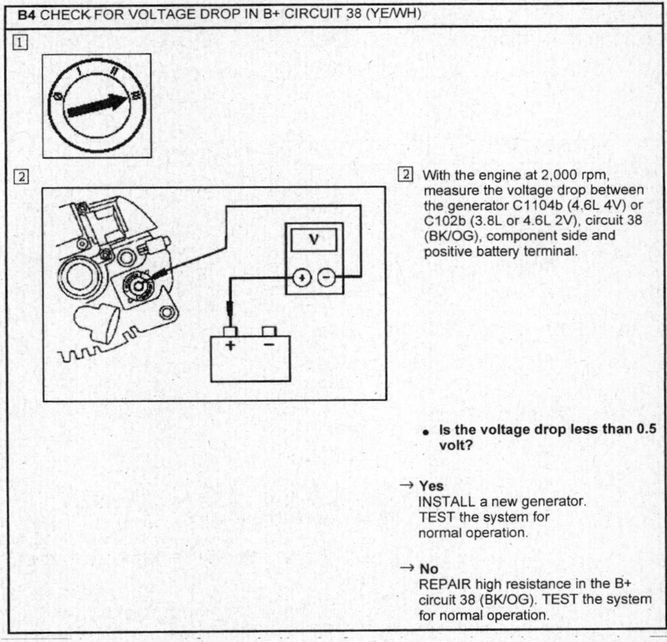

B4 CHECK FOR VOLTAGE DROP IN B+ CIRCUIT 38 (YE/WH)

1

2 With the engine at 2,000 rpm, measure the voltage drop between the generator C1104b (4.6L 4V) or C102b (3.8L or 4.6L 2V), circuit 38 (BK/OG), component side and positive battery terminal.

• **Is the voltage drop less than 0.5 volt?**

→ **Yes** INSTALL a new generator. TEST the system for normal operation.

→ **No** REPAIR high resistance in the B+ circuit 38 (BK/OG). TEST the system for normal operation.

FM1120200763040X

Fig. 132 Test B: Charging System Warning Indicator Is On With The Engine Running/The Battery Voltage Does Not Increase (Part 4 of 4). 2002 Mustang

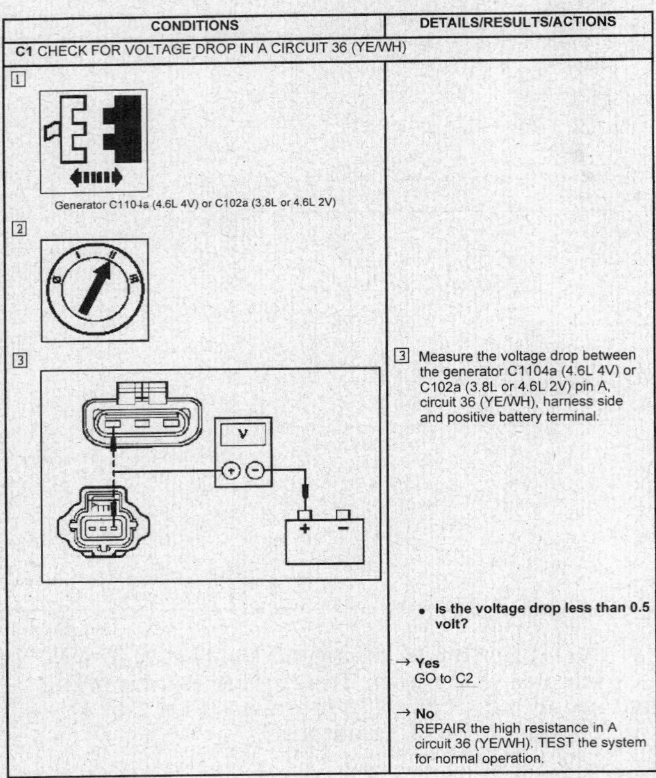

CONDITIONS	DETAILS/RESULTS/ACTIONS
C1 CHECK FOR VOLTAGE DROP IN A CIRCUIT 36 (YE/WH)	
1 Generator C1104a (4.6L 4V) or C102a (3.8L or 4.6L 2V)	
2	
3	3 Measure the voltage drop between the generator C1104a (4.6L 4V) or C102a (3.8L or 4.6L 2V) pin A, circuit 36 (YE/WH), harness side and positive battery terminal. • **Is the voltage drop less than 0.5 volt?** → **Yes** GO to C2 . → **No** REPAIR the high resistance in A circuit 36 (YE/WH). TEST the system for normal operation.

FM1120200764010X

Fig. 133 Test C: System Overcharges/Battery Voltage Is Greater Than 15.5 Volts (Part 1 of 2). 2002 Mustang

CONDITIONS	DETAILS/RESULTS/ACTIONS
D1 CHECK I CIRCUIT 904 (LG/RD) FOR A SHORT TO GROUND	
1 Generator C1104a (4.6L 4V) or C102a (3.8L or 4.6L 2V)	
2	
	3 With the ignition switch in the RUN position, check the charging system warning indicator. • **Is the charging system warning indicator illuminated?** → **Yes** REPAIR I circuit 904 (LG/RD) for a short to ground. TEST the system for normal operation. → **No** INSTALL a new generator. TEST the system for normal operation.

FM1120200765000X

Fig. 134 Test D: Charging System Warning Indicator Is On With The Engine Running And The Battery Increases Voltage. 2002 Mustang

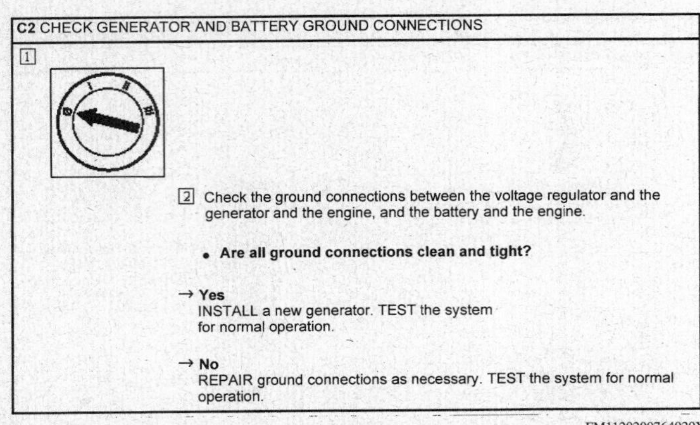

C2 CHECK GENERATOR AND BATTERY GROUND CONNECTIONS

1

2 Check the ground connections between the voltage regulator and the generator and the engine, and the battery and the engine.

- **Are all ground connections clean and tight?**

→ **Yes**
INSTALL a new generator. TEST the system for normal operation.

→ **No**
REPAIR ground connections as necessary. TEST the system for normal operation.

FM1120200764020X

Fig. 133 Test C: System Overcharges/Battery Voltage Is Greater Than 15.5 Volts (Part 2 of 2). 2002 Mustang

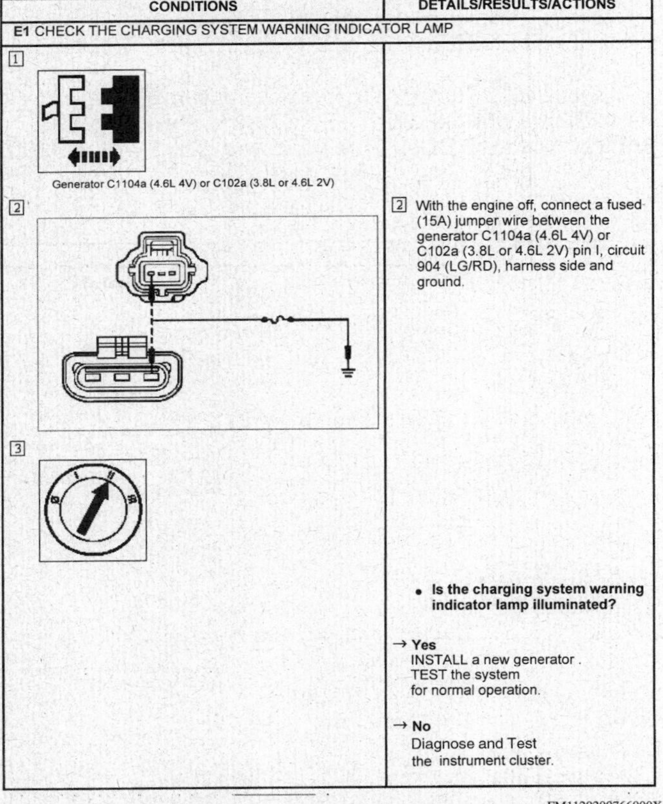

CONDITIONS	DETAILS/RESULTS/ACTIONS
E1 CHECK THE CHARGING SYSTEM WARNING INDICATOR LAMP	
1 Generator C1104a (4.6L 4V) or C102a (3.8L or 4.6L 2V)	
2	2 With the engine off, connect a fused (15A) jumper wire between the generator C1104a (4.6L 4V) or C102a (3.8L or 4.6L 2V) pin I, circuit 904 (LG/RD), harness side and ground.
3	• **Is the charging system warning indicator lamp illuminated?** → **Yes** INSTALL a new generator . TEST the system for normal operation. → **No** Diagnose and Test the instrument cluster.

FM1120200766000X

Fig. 135 Test E: Charging System Warning Indicator Is Off With The Ignition Switch In the Run Position And The Engine Off. 2002 Mustang

CONDITIONS	DETAILS/RESULTS/ACTIONS
F1 CHECK FOR LOOSE CONNECTIONS	
	1 Check all generator, battery, and power distribution connections for looseness, corrosion, loose or bent terminals, or loose eyelets. • **Are all connections clean and tight?** → **Yes** GO to F2 . → **No** REPAIR as necessary. TEST the system for normal operation.
F2 CHECK FUSE	
1	2 With the engine running, check battery junction box (BJB) fuse 20 (20A) in A circuit 36 (YE/WH) for looseness by wiggling the fuse and noting the charging system warning indicator lamp operation. • **Does the charging system warning indicator lamp flicker?** → **Yes** REPAIR loose fuse connections as necessary. TEST the system for normal operation. → **No** GO to F3 .

FM1120200767010X

Fig. 136 Test F: Charging System Warning Indicator Lamp Flickers Or Is Intermittent (Part 1 of 2). 2002 Mustang

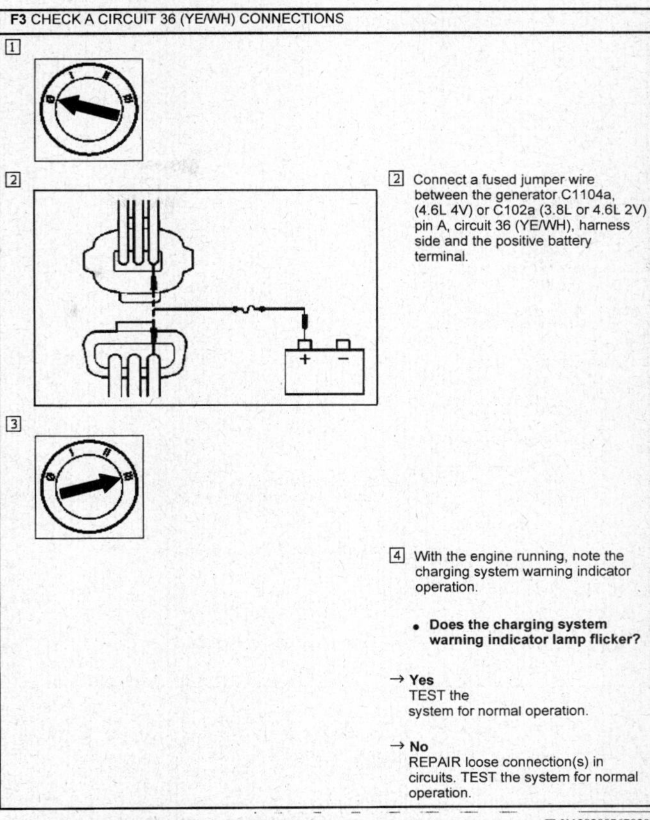

F3 CHECK A CIRCUIT 36 (YE/WH) CONNECTIONS

1

2 Connect a fused jumper wire between the generator C1104a, (4.6L 4V) or C102a (3.8L or 4.6L 2V) pin A, circuit 36 (YE/WH), harness side and the positive battery terminal.

3

4 With the engine running, note the charging system warning indicator operation.

• **Does the charging system warning indicator lamp flicker?**

→ **Yes**
TEST the system for normal operation.

→ **No**
REPAIR loose connection(s) in circuits. TEST the system for normal operation.

FM1120200767020X

Fig. 136 Test F: Charging System Warning Indicator Lamp Flickers Or Is Intermittent (Part 2 of 2). 2002 Mustang

CONDITIONS	DETAILS/RESULTS/ACTIONS
G1 CHECK FOR ACCESSORY DRIVE NOISE	
	1 Check the accessory drive belt for damage and correct installation. Check the accessory mounting brackets and generator pulley for looseness or misalignment. • **Is the accessory drive OK?** → **Yes** GO to G2 . → **No** REPAIR as necessary. TEST the system for normal operation.
G2 CHECK GENERATOR MOUNTING	
	1 Check the generator mounting for loose bolts or misalignment. • **Is the generator mounted correctly?** → **Yes** GO to G3 . → **No** REPAIR as necessary. TEST the system for normal operation.

FM1120200768010X

Fig. 137 Test G: Generator Is Noisy (Part 1 of 3). 2002 Mustang

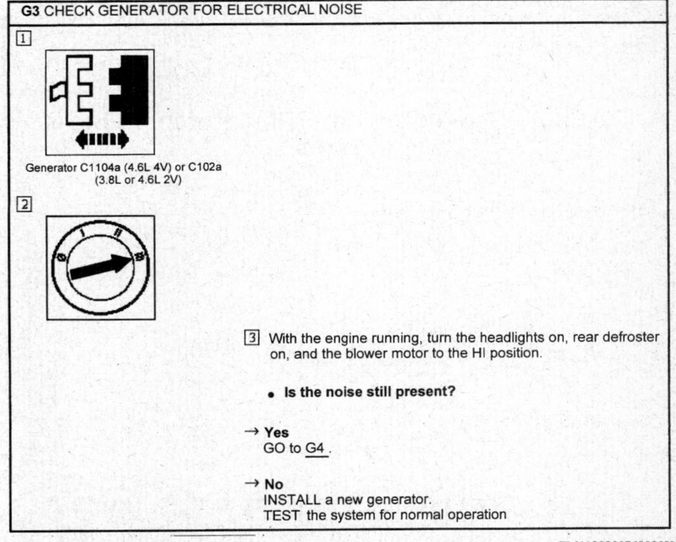

G3 CHECK GENERATOR FOR ELECTRICAL NOISE

1

2

3 With the engine running, turn the headlights on, rear defroster on, and the blower motor to the HI position.

• **Is the noise still present?**

→ **Yes**
GO to G4 .

→ **No**
INSTALL a new generator.
TEST the system for normal operation

FM1120200768020X

Fig. 137 Test G: Generator Is Noisy (Part 2 of 3). 2002 Mustang

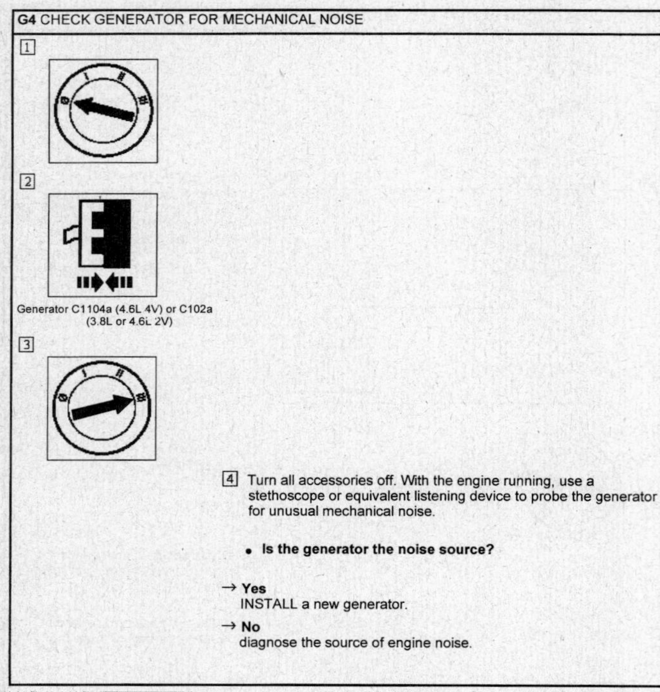

G4 CHECK GENERATOR FOR MECHANICAL NOISE

1

2

Generator C1104a (4.6L 4V) or C102a (3.8L or 4.6L 2V)

3

4 Turn all accessories off. With the engine running, use a stethoscope or equivalent listening device to probe the generator for unusual mechanical noise.

- **Is the generator the noise source?**

→ **Yes**
INSTALL a new generator.

→ **No**
diagnose the source of engine noise.

FM1120200768030X

Fig. 137 Test G: Generator Is Noisy (Part 3 of 3). 2002 Mustang

Condition	Possible Source	Action
• System Does Not Charge	• Ignition switch OFF battery drain. • Circuitry. • Voltage regulator. • Generator. • Battery. • Battery connections. • Drive belt.	• GO to Pinpoint Test A.
• System Overcharges (Battery Boils Over)	• Circuitry. • Poor ground. • Voltage regulator. • Generator.	• GO to Pinpoint Test B.
• Indicator Lamp Stays On, Engine Running	• Circuitry. • Voltage regulator. • Generator.	• GO to Pinpoint Test C.
• Indicator Lamp Stays On, Ignition Switch OFF	• Circuitry. • Improper lamp circuit wiring. • Instrument cluster.	• GO to Pinpoint Test D.

FM1129800218010X

Fig. 139 Symptom chart (Part 1 of 2). Sable & Taurus

Condition	Possible Source	Action
• Indicator Lamp Does Not Come On	• Circuitry. • Burned out indicator bulb. • Poor ground. • Voltage regulator. • Generator.	• GO to Pinpoint Test E.
• Indicator Lamp Flickers/Intermittent	• Loose connection to generator, voltage regulator or power distribution box. • Circuitry. • Loose brush holder screw. • Voltage regulator. • Generator.	• GO to Pinpoint Test F.
• Generator Noisy	• Accessory drive belt. • Accessory brackets. • Bent pulley. • Generator. • Other accessories.	• GO to Pinpoint Test G.
• Radio Interference	• Voltage regulator. • Generator. • Other components.	• GO to Pinpoint Test H.

FM1129800218020X

Fig. 139 Symptom chart (Part 2 of 2). Sable & Taurus

CONDITIONS	DETAILS/RESULTS/ACTIONS
H1 VERIFY GENERATOR IS SOURCE OF RADIO INTERFERENCE	
1	
	2 With the engine running, tune the radio to a station where the interference is present.
3	
4 Generator C1104a (4.6L 4V) or C102a (3.8L or 4.6L 2V)	
5	
	6 With the engine running, note any radio interference. • **Is the interference present with the generator disconnected?** → **Yes** Diagnos and test the in-vehicle entertainment system. → **No** INSTALL a new generator. TEST the system for normal operation.

FM1120200769000X

Fig. 138 Test H: Radio Interference. 2002 Mustang

Condition	Possible Sources	Action
• Battery is discharged or voltage is low	• Circuitry. • High key-off current drain(s). • Battery. • Generator.	• GO to Pinpoint Test A.
• The charging system warning indicator is on with the engine running (the system voltage does not increase)	• Generator. • BJB fuse 2 (10A) • Circuitry.	• GO to Pinpoint Test B.
• The system overcharges (battery voltage greater than 15 volts)	• BJB fuse 2 (10A). • Circuitry. • Generator.	• GO to Pinpoint Test C.
• The charging system warning indicator is on with the engine running (the system increases voltage)	• BJB fuse 2 (10A). • Generator. • Instrument cluster. • PCM. • Circuitry.	• GO to Pinpoint Test D.
• The charging system warning indicator is off with the ignition switch in the RUN position and the engine off	• Generator connector unplugged (C102). • Battery. • Circuitry. • Instrument cluster. • PCM.	• GO to Pinpoint Test E.
• The charging system warning indicator flickers or is intermittent	• BJB fuse 2 (10A). • Generator connector unplugged (C102). • Circuitry. • Generator.	• GO to Pinpoint Test F.
• The generator is noisy	• Loose bolts/brackets. • Drive belt. • Generator/pulley.	• GO to Pinpoint Test G.
• Radio interference	• Generator. • Wiring/routing. • In-vehicle entertainment system.	• GO to Pinpoint Test H.

FM1120200770000X

Fig. 140 Symptom Chart. 2002 Sable & Taurus

	Test Step	Result	Action to Take
A1	CHECK DRIVE BELT TENSIONER		
	• Check the automatic drive belt tensioner. • **Is the drive belt adjusted properly?**	Yes ▶ No ▶	GO to **A2.** REPLACE the drive belt.
A2	CHECK BATTERY CONNECTIONS		
	• Inspect the battery cables for loose or corroded connections. • Inspect battery for corrosion. • **Are the battery cables clean, tight and free from corrosion?**	Yes ▶ No ▶	GO to **A3.** SERVICE battery and cables as necessary. RESTORE vehicle. RETEST system.
A3	LOOSE BATTERY POST		
	• Check for loose battery posts. • **Are posts OK?**	Yes ▶ No ▶	GO to **A4.** REPLACE battery. RETEST system.
A4	CRACKED BATTERY COVER		
	• Remove battery hold down clamps and shields. • Check for broken/cracked case or battery cover. • **Are case and cover OK?**	Yes ▶ No ▶	GO to **A5.** REPLACE battery.
A5	CHECK FOR KEY-OFF DRAIN		
	• Perform battery Drain Testing as described. • **Is current drain less than 50 mA (or test lamp off)?**	Yes ▶ No ▶	GO to **A6.** SERVICE the cause of ignition switch OFF battery drain. RETEST system.
A6	CHECK BATTERY		
	• Perform the battery Capacity Testing as described in Component Tests. • **Is the battery capacity OK?**	Yes ▶ No ▶	GO to **A7.** REPLACE battery. RETEST system.
A7	CHECK FOR OPEN B+ CIRCUIT		
	• Measure voltage at B+ terminal on the back of the generator. • **Is voltage at B+ terminal equal to battery voltage?**	Yes ▶ No ▶	GO to **A8.** SERVICE open in B+ Circuit. RETEST system.

FM1129800219010X

Fig. 141 Test A: System Does Not Charge (Part 1 of 2). 1998–99 Sable & Taurus

	Test Step	Result	Action to Take
B1	CHECK VOLTAGE DROP IN A CIRCUIT		
	• Turn ignition switch to RUN. • Measure voltage between A terminal on the voltage regulator and the positive (+) battery post. • **Is voltage drop less than 0.25 V?**	Yes ▶ No ▶	GO to **B2.** SERVICE excess voltage drop in Circuit 35 (O/LB). CHECK Alternator Fuse (30A) and connectors in Circuit 35 (O/LB) and SERVICE as required. RETEST system.
B2	CHECK VOLTAGE DROP IN I CIRCUIT		
	• NOTE: Voltage regulator must be connected to wiring harness for this test. Measure voltage at connector C154 I terminal, Circuit 904 (LG/R). • **Is voltage greater than 1 V?**	Yes ▶ No ▶	GO to **B3.** SERVICE high resistance in Circuit 904 (LG/R). RETEST system.
B3	CHECK FOR POOR GROUNDS		
	• Check for poor ground connections between voltage regulator and generator, generator and engine, or engine and battery. • **Are all ground connections clean and tight?**	Yes ▶ No ▶	REPLACE generator. RETEST system. CLEAN or SERVICE grounds as required. RETEST system.

FM1129800220000X

Fig. 142 Test B: System Overcharges. 1998–99 Sable & Taurus

	Test Step	Result	Action to Take
D1	CHECK LAMP CIRCUIT WIRING		
	• Turn ignition switch to OFF position. • Disconnect voltage regulator connector C154. • Measure voltage at C154 I terminal, Circuit 904 (LG/R). • **Is voltage greater than zero V?**	Yes ▶ No ▶	SERVICE Circuit 1044 (W/Y). Circuit should be HOT in RUN or START position only. RETEST system. SERVICE instrument cluster. RETEST system.

FM1129800222000X

Fig. 144 Test D: Indicator Lamp Stays On, Ignition Off. 1998–99 Sable & Taurus

	Test Step	Result	Action to Take
F1	CHECK FOR LOOSE CONNECTIONS		
	• Check these connections for corrosion, loose or bent pins, or loose eyelets: — Voltage regulator connector C154. — One-pin S connector C153 (3.0L (2V) only). — Generator B+ eyelet. — Power distribution box eyelets. — Battery cables. • **Are all connections clean and tight?**	Yes ▶ No ▶	GO to **F2.** CLEAN or SERVICE connections as required. RETEST system.
F2	CHECK FOR LOOSE A CIRCUIT FUSE		
	• Start engine. • Check the Alternator Fuse (30A) in the power distribution box for a loose connection by wiggling the fuse with the engine running. • **Does indicator lamp flicker?**	Yes ▶ No ▶	SERVICE loose fuse connection. RETEST system. GO to F3.
F3	CHECK A CIRCUIT CONNECTIONS		
	• With engine running, connect Circuit A on the voltage regulator to the positive (+) battery post using a jumper wire. • **Does indicator lamp flicker?**	Yes ▶ No ▶	REPLACE voltage regulator, if concern still exists REPLACE generator. RETEST system. SERVICE poor connection in Circuit 35 (O/LB). RETEST system.

FM1129800224000X

Fig. 146 Test F: Indicator Lamp Flickers/ Intermittent. 1998–99 Sable & Taurus

	Test Step	Result	Action to Take
A8	CHECK FOR OPEN A CIRCUIT		
	• Measure voltage at A circuit on the voltage regulator. • **Is voltage at test point A equal to battery voltage?**	Yes ▶ No ▶	GO to **A9.** CHECK Alternator Fuse (30A) in Circuit 35 (O/LB) and REPLACE if required. If OK, SERVICE open in Circuit 35 (O/LB). RETEST system.
A9	CHECK FOR OPEN I CIRCUIT		
	NOTE: Voltage regulator must be connected to wiring harness for this test. • Turn ignition switch to RUN position. • Measure voltage at connector C154 I terminal, Circuit 904 (LG/R). • **Is voltage greater than 1 V?**	Yes ▶ No ▶	GO to **A10.** SERVICE open or high resistance in Circuit 904 (LG/R). RETEST system.
A10	CHECK VOLTAGE DROP IN A CIRCUIT		
	• Measure voltage drop between test point A on the voltage regulator and the positive (+) battery post. • **Is voltage drop less than 0.25 V?**	Yes ▶ No ▶	GO to **A11.** SERVICE excess voltage drop in Circuit 35 (O/LB). CHECK Alternator Fuse (30A) and connectors in Circuit 35 (O/LB) and SERVICE as required. RETEST system.
A11	CHECK VOLTAGE DROP IN B+ CIRCUIT		
	• Start engine. • Turn headlamps on and set blower on HIGH. • With engine running at 2000 rpm, measure voltage drop between the B+ terminal on the back of the generator and the positive (+) battery post. • **Is voltage drop less than 0.5 V?**	Yes ▶ No ▶	GO to **A12.** SERVICE excess voltage drop in B+ Circuit. CHECK the connections between the battery and power distribution box. RETEST system.
A12	CHECK FOR OPEN/SHORTED FIELD		
	• Remove generator from vehicle. • Remove voltage regulator. • Measure resistance between the generator slip rings. • **Is resistance greater than 10 ohms OR less than 1 ohm?**	Yes ▶ No ▶	REPLACE generator. RETEST system. REPLACE voltage regulator. RETEST system.

FM1129800219020X

Fig. 141 Test A: System Does Not Charge (Part 2 of 2). 1998–99 Sable & Taurus

	Test Step	Result	Action to Take
C1	CHECK FOR OPEN A CIRCUIT		
	• Measure voltage at terminal A on the voltage regulator. • **Is voltage at test point A equal to battery voltage?**	Yes ▶ No ▶	GO to **C2.** CHECK Alternator Fuse (30A) in Circuit 35 (O/LB) and REPLACE if required. If OK, SERVICE open in Circuit 35 (O/LB). RETEST system.
C2	CHECK FOR SHORTED I CIRCUIT		
	• Disconnect voltage regulator connector C154. • Turn ignition switch to RUN position. • **Is indicator lamp on?**	Yes ▶ No ▶	SERVICE short to ground in Circuit 904 (LG/R). RETEST system. GO to **C3.**
C3	CHECK GENERATOR OUTPUT VOLTAGE		
	• Measure voltage at the B+ terminal on the back of the generator with the engine running at 2000 rpm and all accessories turned OFF. • **Is voltage greater than 15.5 V?**	Yes ▶ No ▶	GO to Pinpoint Test B to find the cause of high output voltage. RETEST system. REPLACE voltage regulator. RETEST system.

FM1129800221000X

Fig. 143 Test C: Indicator Lamp Stays On, Engine Running. 1998–99 Sable & Taurus

	Test Step	Result	Action to Take
E1	CHECK INSTRUMENT CLUSTER OPERATION		
	• Turn ignition switch to RUN. • **Are all other warning lamps and instrument cluster lit for a short time?**	Yes ▶ No ▶	GO to **E2.** SERVICE instrument cluster.
E2	CHECK FOR OPEN I CIRCUIT		
	• Disconnect voltage regulator connector C154. • Turn ignition switch to RUN. • Measure voltage at C154 I terminal, Circuit 904 (LG/R). • **Is voltage equal to B+?**	Yes ▶ No ▶	GO to **E3.** SERVICE open in Circuit 904 (LG/R). RETEST system.
E3	CHECK FOR BURNED OUT BULB		
	• Connect C154 I-terminal, Circuit 904 (LG/R) to ground with a jumper wire. • **Is indicator lamp on?**	Yes ▶ No ▶	REMOVE jumper wire. GO to **E4.** REPLACE lamp or SERVICE high resistance in lamp socket or Circuit 904 (LG/R). RETEST system.
E4	CHECK FOR POOR GROUNDS		
	• Check for poor ground connections between voltage regulator and generator, generator and engine, or engine and battery. • **Are all ground connections clean and tight?**	Yes ▶ No ▶	REPLACE generator. CLEAN or SERVICE grounds as required. RETEST system.

FM1129800223000X

Fig. 145 Test E: Indicator Lamp Does Not Light. 1998–99 Sable & Taurus

	Test Step	Result	Action to Take
G1	CHECK FOR ACCESSORY DRIVE BELT NOISE		
	• Check the drive belt to make sure that it is installed properly and is not damaged. • **Is drive belt OK?**	Yes ▶ No ▶	GO to **G2.** SERVICE accessory drive belt as required. RETEST system.
G2	CHECK GENERATOR MOUNTING		
	• Check the generator and generator mounting bracket for loose bolts or misalignment condition. • **Is generator mounted correctly?**	Yes ▶ No ▶	If noise is still present, REPLACE generator. RETEST system. INSTALL generator to specifications. RETEST system.

FM1129800225000X

Fig. 147 Test G: Alternator Is Noisy. Sable & Taurus

	Test Step	Result		Action to Take
H1	CHECK RADIO INTERFERENCE WITH REGULATOR DISCONNECTED			
	• Start engine. • Tune radio to a station where interference is present. • Remove voltage regulator connector C154. • **Is interference present with connector removed?**	Yes	▶	Locate cause of radio interference.
		No	▶	REPLACE generator. RETEST system.

FM1129800226000X

Fig. 148 Test H: Radio Interference. 1998–99 Sable & Taurus

A2 CHECK THE GENERATOR OUTPUT

1 Carry out the On — Vehicle Generator Load/No Load Test.

- **Is the generator OK?**

→ **Yes**

Go to «A3».

→ **No**

GO to «Pinpoint Test B».

FM1120100584020X

Fig. 149 Test A: Battery Is Discharged Or Voltage Is Low (Part 2 of 4). 2000–01 Sable & Taurus

A4 CHECK FOR CURRENT DRAINS WHICH SHUT OFF WHEN THE BATTERY IS DISCONNECTED

1 Carry out the Battery — Electronic Drains Which Shut Off When the Battery Cable is Disconnected Test.

- **Are there any current drains which shut off when the battery is disconnected?**

→ **Yes**

REPAIR as necessary. TEST the system for normal operation.

→ **No**

GO to «Pinpoint Test B».

FM1120100584040X

Fig. 149 Test A: Battery Is Discharged Or Voltage Is Low (Part 4 of 4). 2000–01 Sable & Taurus

B1 CHECK GENERATOR B+ CIRCUIT 36 (YE/WH)

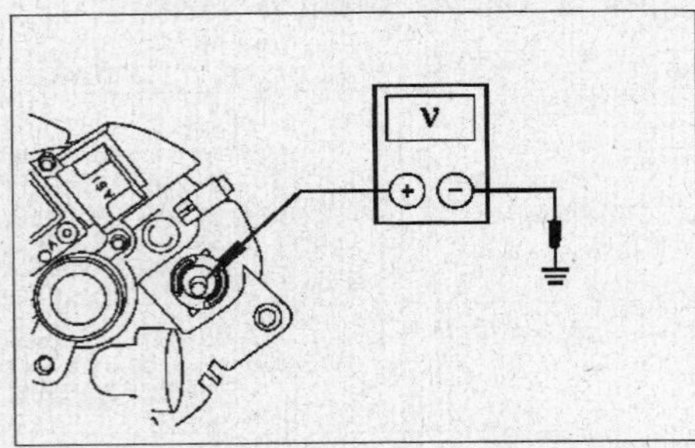

1

Measure the voltage between generator B+ terminal, circuit 36 (YE/WH), component side and ground.

- **Is the voltage equal to battery positive voltage (B+)?**

→ **Yes**

Go to «B2».

→ **No**

REPAIR the circuit. TEST the system for normal operation.

FM1120100585010X

Fig. 150 Test B: Charge Indicator Lights w/Engine Running, System Voltage Does Not Increase (Part 1 of 5). 2000–01 Sable & Taurus

A1 CHECK THE BATTERY CONDITION

1 Carry out the Battery - Capacity Test to determine if the battery can hold a charge and is OK for use.

- **Is the battery OK?**

→ **Yes**

Go to «A2».

→ **No**

INSTALL a new battery. TEST the system for normal operation.

FM1120100584010X

Fig. 149 Test A: Battery Is Discharged Or Voltage Is Low (Part 1 of 4). 2000–01 Sable & Taurus

A3 CHECK FOR CURRENT DRAINS

1 Carry out the Battery - Drain Test.

- **Are there any excessive current drains?**

→ **Yes**

REPAIR as necessary. TEST the system for normal operation.

→ **No**

Go to «A4».

FM1120100584030X

Fig. 149 Test A: Battery Is Discharged Or Voltage Is Low (Part 3 of 4). 2000–01 Sable & Taurus

B2 CHECK GENERATOR A CIRCUIT 35 (OG/LB)

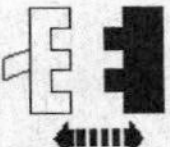

1 *Generator C102a (4V) or C1104 (2V)*

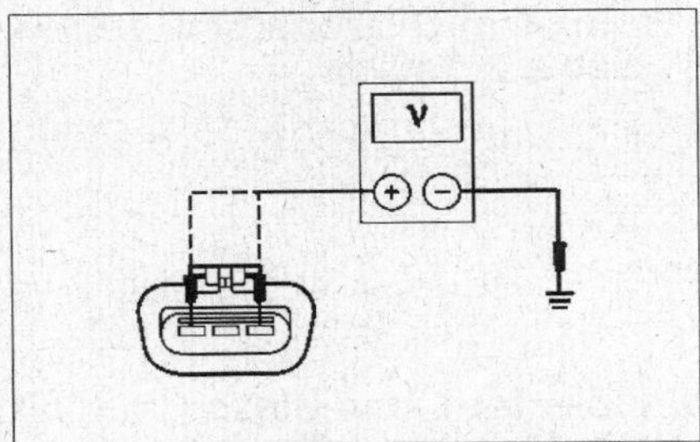

2

Measure the voltage between generator C102a (4V) or C1104 (2V) pin A, circuit 35 (OG/LB), harness side and ground.

- **Is the voltage equal to battery positive voltage (B+)?**

→ **Yes**

Go to «B3».

→ **No**

Repair the circuit. Test system for normal operation.

FM1120100585020X

Fig. 150 Test B: Charge Indicator Lights w/Engine Running, System Voltage Does Not Increase (Part 2 of 5). 2000–01 Sable & Taurus

B3	CHECK I CIRCUIT 904 (LG/RD) FOR AN OPEN

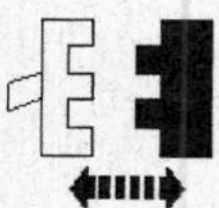

1 *Generator C102a (4V) or C1104 (2V)*

2

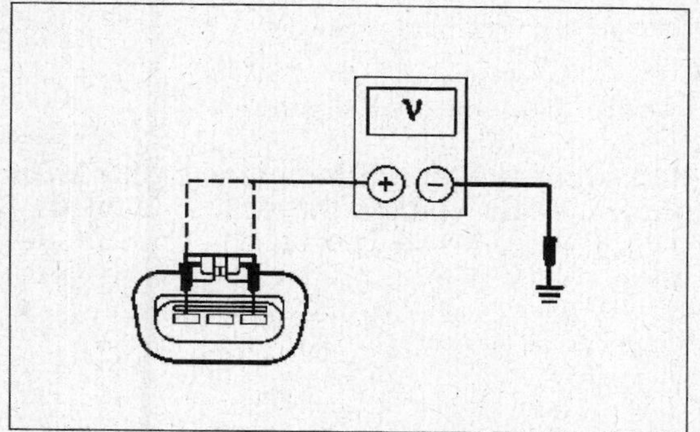

3

FM1120100585030X

Fig. 150 Test B: Charge Indicator Lights w/Engine Running, System Voltage Does Not Increase (Part 3 of 5). 2000–01 Sable & Taurus

B4	CHECK FOR VOLTAGE DROP IN B+ CIRCUIT 36 (YE/WH)

1

2 With the engine running, turn the headlamps on, rear defroster on, and the blower motor to the high position.

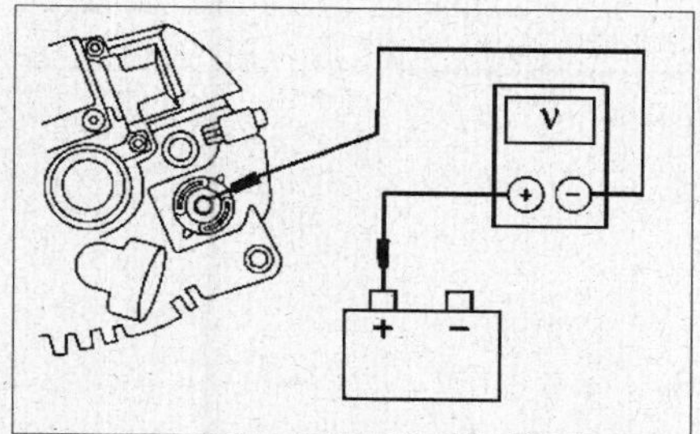

3

With the engine at 2,000 rpm, measure the voltage drop between the generator B+ terminal, circuit 36 (YE/WH), component side and positive battery terminal.

- **Is the voltage drop less than 0.5 volt?**

→ **Yes**

INSTALL a new generator. TEST the system for normal operation.

→ **No**

REPAIR high resistance in the B+ circuit 36 (YE/WH). TEST the system for normal operation.

FM1120100585050X

Fig. 150 Test B: Charge Indicator Lights w/Engine Running, System Voltage Does Not Increase (Part 5 of 5). 2000–01 Sable & Taurus

With the ignition switch in the RUN position and the engine running, measure the voltage between generator C102a (4V) or C1104 (2V) pin I, circuit 904 (LG/RD), harness side and ground.

- **Is the voltage equal to battery positive voltage (B+)?**

→ **Yes**

Go to «B4».

→ **No**

REPAIR the circuit. TEST the system for normal operation.

FM1120100585040X

Fig. 150 Test B: Charge Indicator Lights w/Engine Running, System Voltage Does Not Increase (Part 4 of 5). 2000–01 Sable & Taurus

C1	CHECK FOR VOLTAGE DROP IN A CIRCUIT 35 (OG/LB)

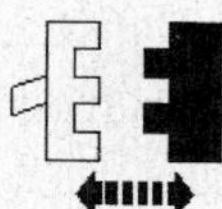

1 *Generator C102a (4V) or C1104 (2V)*

2

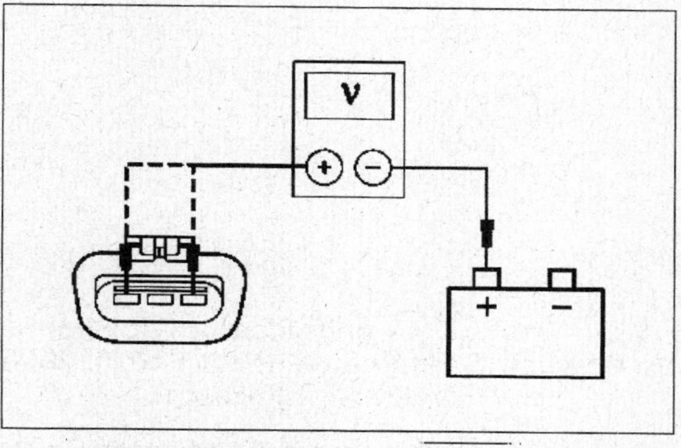

3

FM1120100586010X

Fig. 151 Test C: System Overcharges (Part 1 of 3). 2000–01 Sable & Taurus

Measure the voltage drop between generator C102a (4V) or C1104 (2V) pin A, circuit 35 (OG/LB), harness side and positive battery terminal.

- **Is the voltage drop less than 0.5 volt?**

→ **Yes**

Go to «C2».

→ **No**

REPAIR the high resistance in A circuit 35 (OG/LB). TEST the system for normal operation.

FM1120100586020X

Fig. 151 Test C: System Overcharges (Part 2 of 3). 2000–01 Sable & Taurus

C2	CHECK GENERATOR AND BATTERY GROUND CONNECTIONS

1

2 Check the ground connections between the voltage regulator and the generator (3.0L 2V engine only), the generator and the engine, and the battery and the engine.

- **Are all ground connections clean and tight?**

→ **Yes**

INSTALL a new generator. TEST the system for normal operation.

→ **No**

REPAIR ground connections as necessary. TEST the system for normal operation.

FM1120100586030X

Fig. 151 Test C: System Overcharges (Part 3 of 3). 2000–01 Sable & Taurus

E1	CHECK THE CHARGING SYSTEM WARNING INDICATOR LAMP

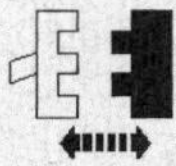

1 *Generator C102a (4V) or C1104 (2V)*

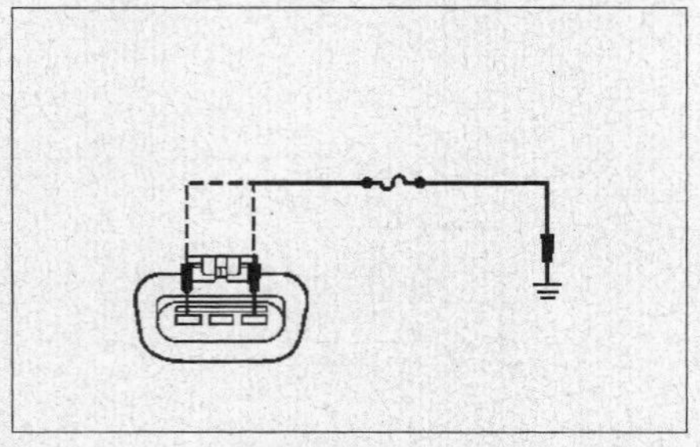

2

With the engine off, connect a fused (15A) jumper wire between the generator C102a (4V) or C1104 (2V) pin I, circuit 904 (LG/RD), harness side and ground.

FM1120100588010X

Fig. 153 Test E: Charge Indicator Off w/Ignition In Run Position & Engine Off (Part 1 of 2). 2000–01 Sable & Taurus

F1	CHECK FOR LOOSE CONNECTIONS

1 Check all generator, battery, and power distribution connections for looseness, corrosion, loose or bent terminals, or loose eyelets.

- **Are all connections clean and tight?**

→ **Yes**

Go to «F2».

→ **No**

REPAIR as necessary. TEST the system for normal operation.

FM1120100589010X

Fig. 154 Test F: Indicator Flickers/Intermittent (Part 1 of 4). 2000–01 Sable & Taurus

D1	CHECK I CIRCUIT 904 (LG/RD) FOR SHORT TO GROUND

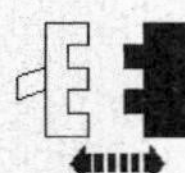

1 *Generator C102a (4V) or C1104 (2V)*

2

3 With the ignition switch in the RUN position, check the charging system warning indicator.

- **Is the charging system warning indicator illuminated?**

→ **Yes**

REPAIR I circuit 904 (LG/RD) for a short to ground. TEST the system for normal operation.

→ **No**

INSTALL a new generator; TEST the system for normal operation.

FM1120100587000X

Fig. 152 Test D: Charge Indicator Lights w/Engine Running, System Voltage Increases. 2000–01 Sable & Taurus

3

- **Is the charging system warning indicator lamp illuminated?**

→ **Yes**

INSTALL a new generator. TEST the system for normal operation.

→ **No**

Diagnose instrument cluster fault condition.

FM1120100588020X

Fig. 153 Test E: Charge Indicator Off w/Ignition In Run Position & Engine Off (Part 2 of 2). 2000–01 Sable & Taurus

F2	CHECK FUSE CONNECTIONS

1

With the engine running, check the BJB fuse F126 (30A) in A circuit 35 (OG/LB) and the CJB fuse F227 (10A) in I circuit 904 (LG/RD) for looseness by wiggling the fuse and noting the charging system warning indicator operation.

- **Does the charging system warning indicator flicker?**

→ **Yes**

REPAIR loose fuse connection(s) as necessary. TEST the system for normal operation.

→ **No**

Go to «F3».

FM1120100589020X

Fig. 154 Test F: Indicator Flickers/Intermittent (Part 2 of 4). 2000–01 Sable & Taurus

F3	CHECK A CIRCUIT 35 (OG/LB) CONNECTIONS

1

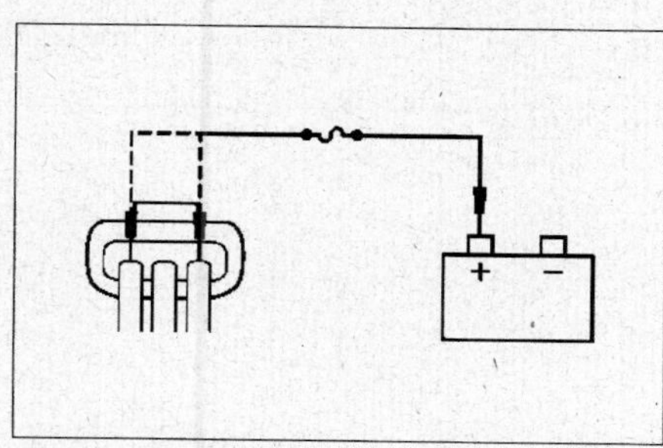

2

Connect a fused (15A) jumper wire between generator C102a (4V) or C1104 (2V) pin A, circuit 35 (OG/LB) and the positive battery terminal.

FM1120100589030X

Fig. 154 Test F: Indicator Flickers/Intermittent (Part 3 of 4). 2000–01 Sable & Taurus

H1	VERIFY GENERATOR IS SOURCE OF RADIO INTERFERENCE

1

2 With the engine running, tune the radio to a station where the interference is present.

3

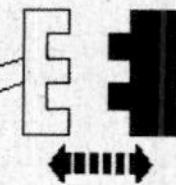

4 *Generator C102a (4V) or C1104 (2V)*

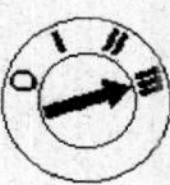

5

FM1120100590010X

Fig. 155 Test H: Radio Interference (Part 1 of 2). 2000–01 Sable & Taurus

3

With the engine running, note the charging system warning indicator operation.

- **Does the charging system warning indicator flicker?**

➔ **Yes**

INSTALL a new generator. TEST the system for normal operation.

➔ **No**

REPAIR loose connection(s) in circuits. TEST the system for normal operation.

FM1120100589040X

Fig. 154 Test F: Indicator Flickers/Intermittent (Part 4 of 4). 2000–01 Sable & Taurus

6 With the engine running, note any radio interference.

- **Is the radio interference present with the generator disconnected?**

➔ **Yes**

TEST the in-vehicle entertainment system.

➔ **No**

INSTALL a new generator. TEST the system for normal operation.

FM1120100590020X

Fig. 155 Test H: Radio Interference (Part 2 of 2). 2000–01 Sable & Taurus

CONDITIONS	DETAILS/RESULTS/ACTIONS
A1 CHECK THE GENERATOR OUTPUT	
	[1] Carry out the On-Vehicle Generator Load/No Load Tests. • Is the generator OK? → **Yes** GO to **A2**. → **No** GO to Pinpoint Test B.
A2 CHECK FOR CURRENT DRAINS	
	[1] Carry out the Battery — Drain Test. • Are there any excessive current drains? → **Yes** REPAIR as necessary. TEST the system for normal operation. → **No** GO to **A3**.
A3 CHECK FOR CURRENT DRAINS WHICH SHUT OFF WHEN THE BATTERY IS DISCONNECTED	
	[1] Carry out the Battery — Electronic Drains Which Shut Off When the Battery Cable is Disconnected Test. • Are there any current drains which shut off when the battery is disconnected? → **Yes** REPAIR as necessary. TEST the system for normal operation. → **No** GO to Pinpoint Test B.

FM1120200771000X

Fig. 156 Test A: Battery Is Discharged Or Voltage Is Low. 2002 Sable & Taurus

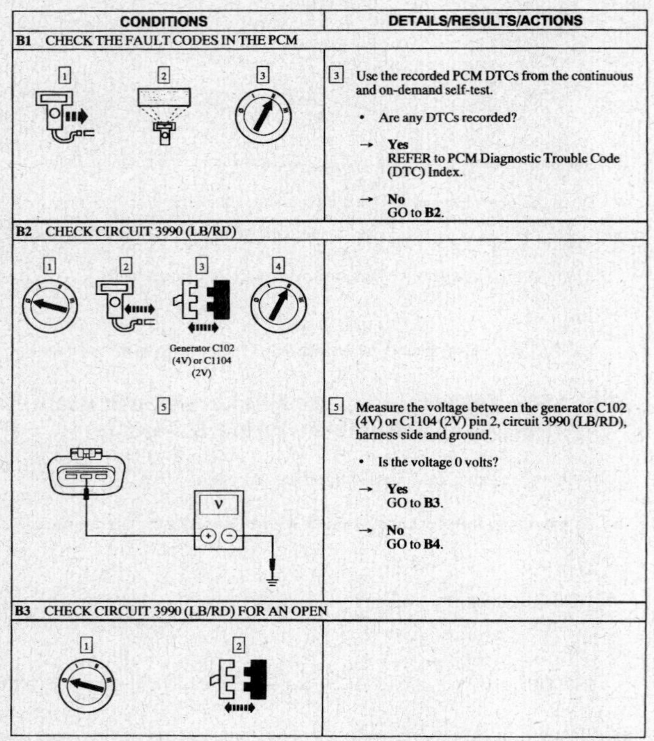

CONDITIONS	DETAILS/RESULTS/ACTIONS
B1 CHECK THE FAULT CODES IN THE PCM	
1 2 3	3 Use the recorded PCM DTCs from the continuous and on-demand self-test. • Are any DTCs recorded? → **Yes** REFER to PCM Diagnostic Trouble Code (DTC) Index. → **No** GO to **B2**.
B2 CHECK CIRCUIT 3990 (LB/RD)	
1 2 3 4 Generator C102 (4V) or C1104 (2V) 5 V	5 Measure the voltage between the generator C102 (4V) or C1104 (2V) pin 2, circuit 3990 (LB/RD), harness side and ground. • Is the voltage 0 volts? → **Yes** GO to **B3**. → **No** GO to **B4**.
B3 CHECK CIRCUIT 3990 (LB/RD) FOR AN OPEN	
1 2	

FM1120200772010X

Fig. 157 Test B: Charging System Warning Indicator Is On With The Engine Running/System Voltage Does Not Increase (Part 1 of 3). 2002 Sable & Taurus

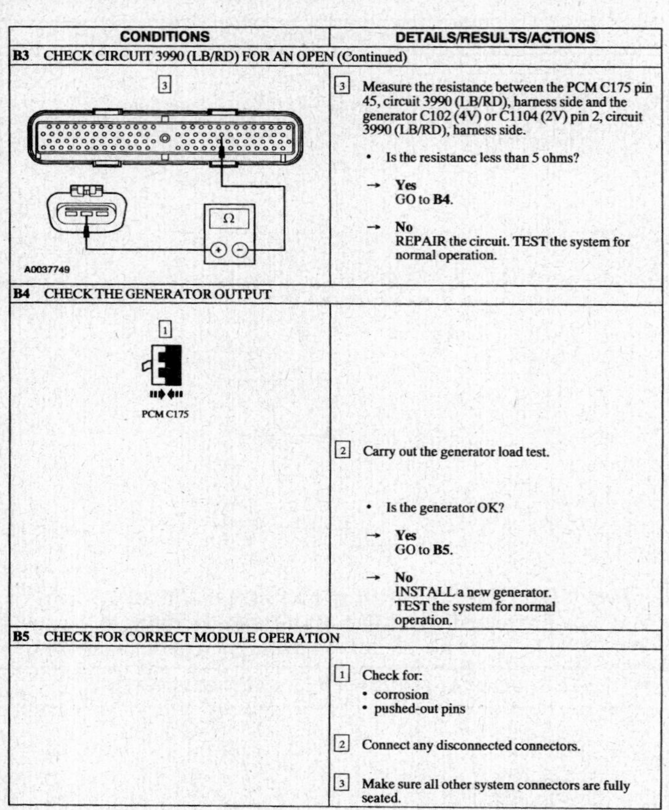

CONDITIONS	DETAILS/RESULTS/ACTIONS
B3 CHECK CIRCUIT 3990 (LB/RD) FOR AN OPEN (Continued)	
3 Ω A0037749	3 Measure the resistance between the PCM C175 pin 45, circuit 3990 (LB/RD), harness side and the generator C102 (4V) or C1104 (2V) pin 2, circuit 3990 (LB/RD), harness side. • Is the resistance less than 5 ohms? → **Yes** GO to **B4**. → **No** REPAIR the circuit. TEST the system for normal operation.
B4 CHECK THE GENERATOR OUTPUT	
1 PCM C175	2 Carry out the generator load test. • Is the generator OK? → **Yes** GO to **B5**. → **No** INSTALL a new generator. TEST the system for normal operation.
B5 CHECK FOR CORRECT MODULE OPERATION	
	1 Check for: • corrosion • pushed-out pins 2 Connect any disconnected connectors. 3 Make sure all other system connectors are fully seated.

FM1120200772020X

Fig. 157 Test B: Charging System Warning Indicator Is On With The Engine Running/System Voltage Does Not Increase (Part 2 of 3). 2002 Sable & Taurus

CONDITIONS	DETAILS/RESULTS/ACTIONS
B5 CHECK FOR CORRECT MODULE OPERATION (Continued)	
	4 Operate the system and verify the concern is still present. • Is the concern still present? → **Yes** INSTALL a new PCM. CLEAR the DTCs. REPEAT the PCM self-test. → **No** The system is operating correctly at this time. Concern may have been caused by a loose or corroded connector. CLEAR the DTCs. REPEAT the self-test.

FM1120200772030X

Fig. 157 Test B: Charging System Warning Indicator Is On With The Engine Running/System Voltage Does Not Increase (Part 3 of 3). 2002 Sable & Taurus

CONDITIONS	DETAILS/RESULTS/ACTIONS
C1 CHECK THE FAULT CODES IN THE PCM	
1 2 3	3 Use the recorded PCM DTCs from the continuous and on-demand self-test. • Are any DTCs recorded? → **Yes** REFER to PCM Diagnostic Trouble Code (DTC) Index. → **No** GO to **C2**.
C2 CHECK THE BATTERY VOLTAGE	
1 2 3	

FM1120200773010X

Fig. 158 Test C: System Overcharges/Battery Voltage Greater Than 15 Volts (Part 1 of 3). 2002 Sable & Taurus

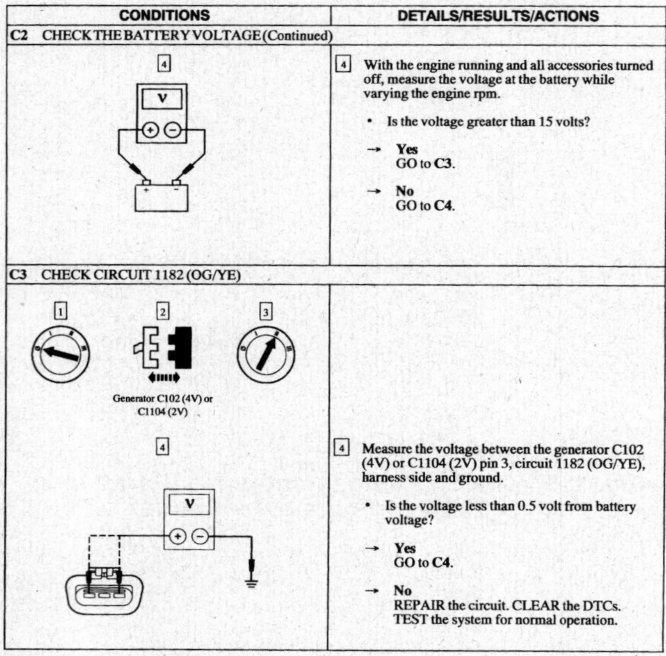

CONDITIONS	DETAILS/RESULTS/ACTIONS
C2 CHECK THE BATTERY VOLTAGE (Continued)	
4 V	4 With the engine running and all accessories turned off, measure the voltage at the battery while varying the engine rpm. • Is the voltage greater than 15 volts? → **Yes** GO to **C3**. → **No** GO to **C4**.
C3 CHECK CIRCUIT 1182 (OG/YE)	
1 2 3 Generator C102 (4V) or C1104 (2V) 4 V	4 Measure the voltage between the generator C102 (4V) or C1104 (2V) pin 3, circuit 1182 (OG/YE), harness side and ground. • Is the voltage less than 0.5 volt from battery voltage? → **Yes** GO to **C4**. → **No** REPAIR the circuit. CLEAR the DTCs. TEST the system for normal operation.

FM1120200773020X

Fig. 158 Test C: System Overcharges/Battery Voltage Greater Than 15 Volts (Part 2 of 3). 2002 Sable & Taurus

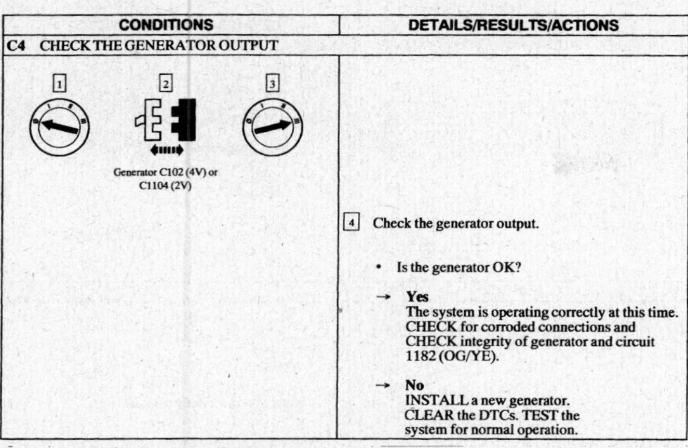

CONDITIONS	DETAILS/RESULTS/ACTIONS
C4 CHECK THE GENERATOR OUTPUT	
1 2 3 Generator C102 (4V) or C1104 (2V)	4 Check the generator output. • Is the generator OK? → **Yes** The system is operating correctly at this time. CHECK for corroded connections and CHECK integrity of generator and circuit 1182 (OG/YE). → **No** INSTALL a new generator. CLEAR the DTCs. TEST the system for normal operation.

FM1120200773030X

Fig. 158 Test C: System Overcharges/Battery Voltage Greater Than 15 Volts (Part 3 of 3). 2002 Sable & Taurus

CONDITIONS	DETAILS/RESULTS/ACTIONS
D2 CHECK THE SYSTEM FOR OVERCHARGING (Continued)	
4	4 With the engine running and all accessories off, measure the voltage at the battery terminals while varying the engine rpm. • Is the voltage greater than 15 volts? → **Yes** GO to Pinpoint Test C. → **No** GO to **D3**.
D3 CHECK CIRCUIT 1182 (OG/YE)	
1 2 3 4	4 Measure the voltage between generator C102 (4V) or C1104 (2V) pin 3, circuit 1182 (OG/YE), harness side, and ground. • Is the voltage equal to battery voltage? → **Yes** GO to **D4**. → **No** REPAIR the circuit. TEST the system for normal operation.
D4 CHECK THE CHARGING SYSTEM WARNING INDICATOR OPERATION	
1 2 3	3 Monitor the charging system warning indicator. • Is the indicator illuminated? → **Yes** REPAIR circuit 3990 (LB/RD). TEST the system for normal operation. → **No** GO to **D5**.

FM1120200774020X

Fig. 159 Test D: Charging System Warning Indicator Is On With The Engine Running/The System Increases Voltage (Part 2 of 3). 2002 Sable & Taurus

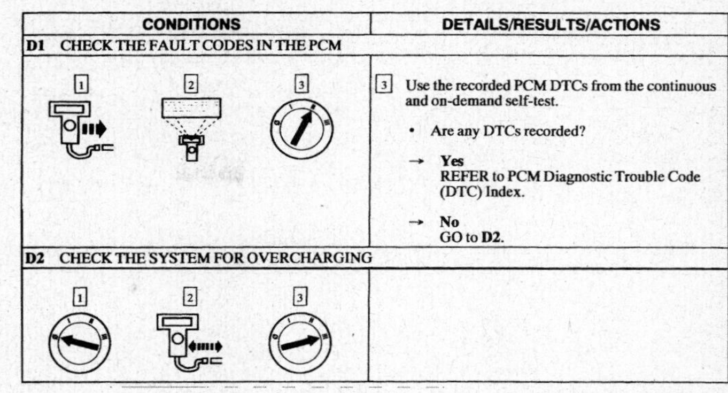

CONDITIONS	DETAILS/RESULTS/ACTIONS
D1 CHECK THE FAULT CODES IN THE PCM	
1 2 3	3 Use the recorded PCM DTCs from the continuous and on-demand self-test. • Are any DTCs recorded? → **Yes** REFER to PCM Diagnostic Trouble Code (DTC) Index. → **No** GO to **D2**.
D2 CHECK THE SYSTEM FOR OVERCHARGING	
1 2 3	

FM1120200774010X

Fig. 159 Test D: Charging System Warning Indicator Is On With The Engine Running/The System Increases Voltage (Part 1 of 3). 2002 Sable & Taurus

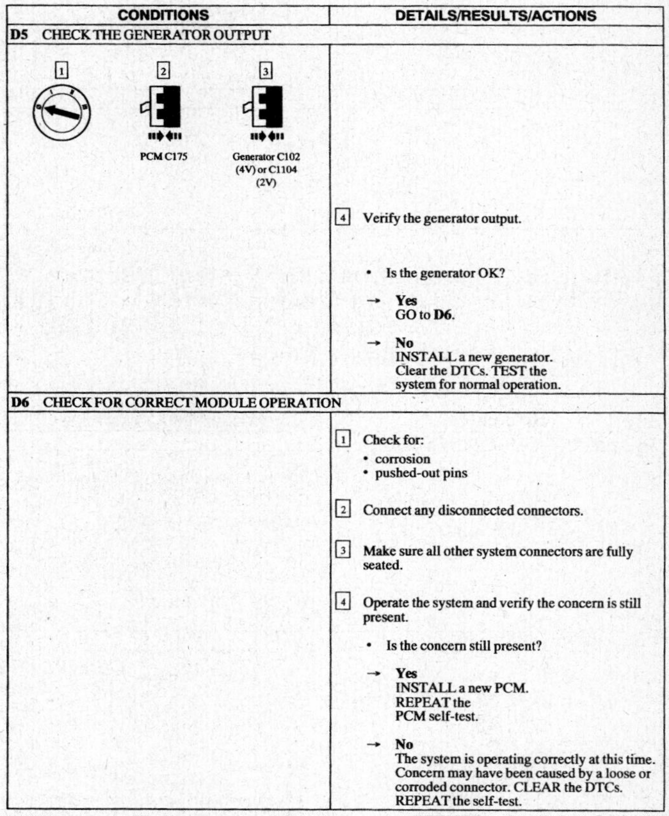

CONDITIONS	DETAILS/RESULTS/ACTIONS
D5 CHECK THE GENERATOR OUTPUT	
1 2 3 PCM C175 Generator C102 (4V) or C1104 (2V)	4 Verify the generator output. • Is the generator OK? → **Yes** GO to **D6**. → **No** INSTALL a new generator. Clear the DTCs. TEST the system for normal operation.
D6 CHECK FOR CORRECT MODULE OPERATION	
	1 Check for: • corrosion • pushed-out pins 2 Connect any disconnected connectors. 3 Make sure all other system connectors are fully seated. 4 Operate the system and verify the concern is still present. • Is the concern still present? → **Yes** INSTALL a new PCM. REPEAT the PCM self-test. → **No** The system is operating correctly at this time. Concern may have been caused by a loose or corroded connector. CLEAR the DTCs. REPEAT the self-test.

FM1120200774030X

Fig. 159 Test D: Charging System Warning Indicator Is On With The Engine Running/The System Increases Voltage (Part 3 of 3). 2002 Sable & Taurus

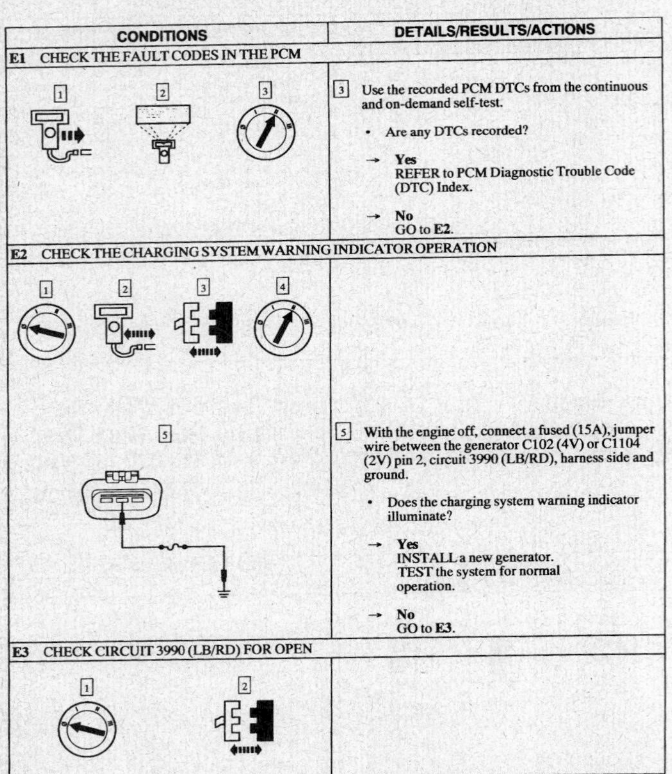

CONDITIONS	DETAILS/RESULTS/ACTIONS
E1 CHECK THE FAULT CODES IN THE PCM	
1 2 3	3 Use the recorded PCM DTCs from the continuous and on-demand self-test. • Are any DTCs recorded? → **Yes** REFER to PCM Diagnostic Trouble Code (DTC) Index. → **No** GO to **E2**.
E2 CHECK THE CHARGING SYSTEM WARNING INDICATOR OPERATION	
1 2 3 4 5	5 With the engine off, connect a fused (15A), jumper wire between the generator C102 (4V) or C1104 (2V) pin 2, circuit 3990 (LB/RD), harness side and ground. • Does the charging system warning indicator illuminate? → **Yes** INSTALL a new generator. TEST the system for normal operation. → **No** GO to **E3**.
E3 CHECK CIRCUIT 3990 (LB/RD) FOR OPEN	
1 2	

FM1120200775010X

Fig. 160 Test E: Charging System Warning Indicator Is Off With The Ignition Switch In The Run Position And The Engine Off (Part 1 of 2). 2002 Sable & Taurus

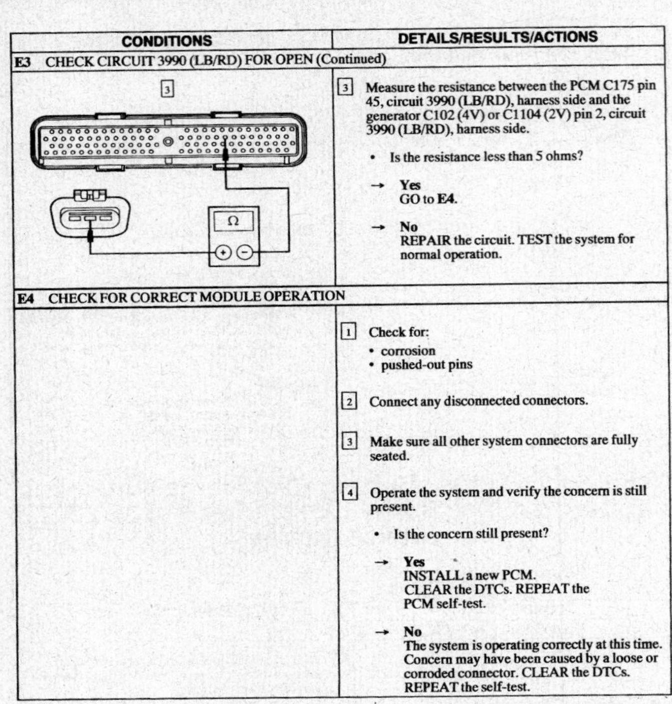

CONDITIONS	DETAILS/RESULTS/ACTIONS
E3 CHECK CIRCUIT 3990 (LB/RD) FOR OPEN (Continued)	
3	3 Measure the resistance between the PCM C175 pin 45, circuit 3990 (LB/RD), harness side and the generator C102 (4V) or C1104 (2V) pin 2, circuit 3990 (LB/RD), harness side. • Is the resistance less than 5 ohms? → **Yes** GO to **E4**. → **No** REPAIR the circuit. TEST the system for normal operation.
E4 CHECK FOR CORRECT MODULE OPERATION	
	1 Check for: • corrosion • pushed-out pins 2 Connect any disconnected connectors. 3 Make sure all other system connectors are fully seated. 4 Operate the system and verify the concern is still present. • Is the concern still present? → **Yes** INSTALL a new PCM. CLEAR the DTCs. REPEAT the PCM self-test. → **No** The system is operating correctly at this time. Concern may have been caused by a loose or corroded connector. CLEAR the DTCs. REPEAT the self-test.

FM1120200775020X

Fig. 160 Test E: Charging System Warning Indicator Is Off With The Ignition Switch In The Run Position And The Engine Off (Part 2 of 2). 2002 Sable & Taurus

CONDITIONS	DETAILS/RESULTS/ACTIONS
F1 CHECK THE FAULT CODES IN THE PCM	
1 2 3	3 Use the recorded PCM DTCs from the continuous and on-demand self-test. • Are any DTCs recorded? → **Yes** Diagnose Trouble Code → **No** GO to **F2**.
F2 CHECK FOR LOOSE CONNECTIONS	
1 Generator C102 (4V) or C1104 (2V) 3 Generator C102 (4V) or C1104 (2V)	2 Check all generator, battery, and power distribution connections for looseness, corrosion, loose or bent terminals, or loose eyelets. • Are all connections clean and tight? → **Yes** GO to **F3**. → **No** REPAIR as necessary. TEST the system for normal operation.

FM1120200776010X

Fig. 161 Test F: Charging System Warning Indicator Lamp Flickers Or Is Intermittent (Part 1 of 4). 2002 Sable & Taurus

CONDITIONS	DETAILS/RESULTS/ACTIONS
F3 CHECK FUSE CONNECTION	
1	2 With the engine running, check BJB fuse 2 (10A) in circuit 1182 (OG/YE) for looseness by wiggling the fuse and noting the charging system warning indicator lamp operation. • Does the charging system warning indicator lamp flicker? → **Yes** REPAIR loose fuse connections as necessary. TEST the system for normal operation. → **No** GO to **F4**.
F4 CHECK THE BATTERY VOLTAGE	
1 2 V	2 With the engine running, and all accessories turned off, measure the voltage at the battery while varying the engine rpm. • Is the voltage greater than 15 volts? → **Yes** GO to Pinpoint Test C. → **No** GO to **F5**.

FM1120200776020X

Fig. 161 Test F: Charging System Warning Indicator Lamp Flickers Or Is Intermittent (Part 2 of 4). 2002 Sable & Taurus

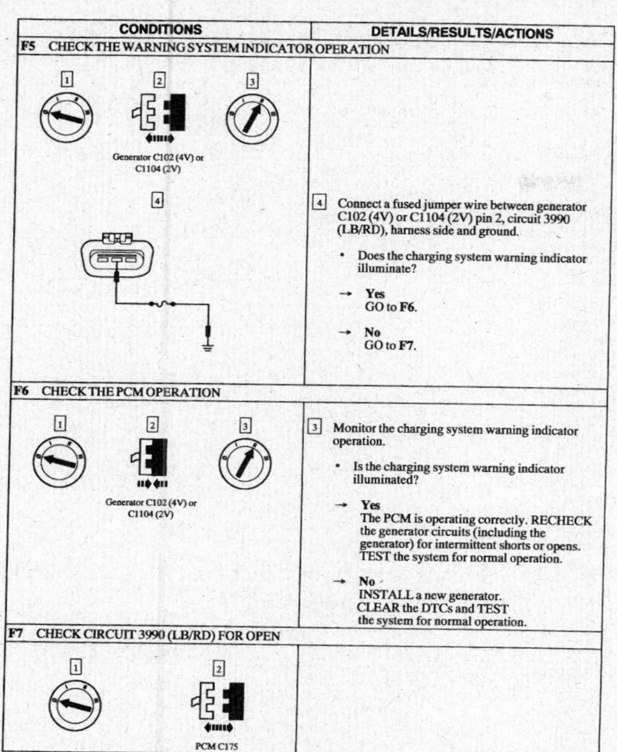

CONDITIONS	DETAILS/RESULTS/ACTIONS
F5 CHECK THE WARNING SYSTEM INDICATOR OPERATION	
1 2 3 Generator C102 (4V) or C1104 (2V)	
4	4 Connect a fused jumper wire between generator C102 (4V) or C1104 (2V) pin 2, circuit 3990 (LB/RD), harness side and ground. • Does the charging system warning indicator illuminate? → **Yes** GO to **F6**. → **No** GO to **F7**.
F6 CHECK THE PCM OPERATION	
1 2 3 Generator C102 (4V) or C1104 (2V)	3 Monitor the charging system warning indicator operation. • Is the charging system warning indicator illuminated? → **Yes** The PCM is operating correctly. RECHECK the generator circuits (including the generator) for intermittent shorts or opens. TEST the system for normal operation. → **No** INSTALL a new generator. CLEAR the DTCs and TEST the system for normal operation.
F7 CHECK CIRCUIT 3990 (LB/RD) FOR OPEN	
1 2 PCM C175	

FM1120200776030X

Fig. 161 Test F: Charging System Warning Indicator Lamp Flickers Or Is Intermittent (Part 3 of 4). 2002 Sable & Taurus

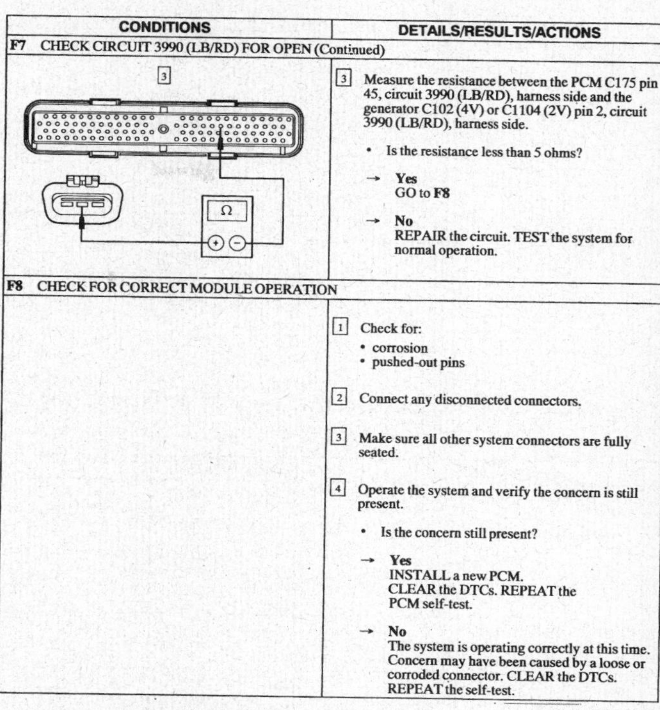

CONDITIONS	DETAILS/RESULTS/ACTIONS
F7 CHECK CIRCUIT 3990 (LB/RD) FOR OPEN (Continued)	
3	3 Measure the resistance between the PCM C175 pin 45, circuit 3990 (LB/RD), harness side and the generator C102 (4V) or C1104 (2V) pin 2, circuit 3990 (LB/RD), harness side. • Is the resistance less than 5 ohms? → **Yes** GO to **F8** → **No** REPAIR the circuit. TEST the system for normal operation.
F8 CHECK FOR CORRECT MODULE OPERATION	
	1 Check for: • corrosion • pushed-out pins 2 Connect any disconnected connectors. 3 Make sure all other system connectors are fully seated. 4 Operate the system and verify the concern is still present. • Is the concern still present? → **Yes** INSTALL a new PCM. CLEAR the DTCs. REPEAT the PCM self-test. → **No** The system is operating correctly at this time. Concern may have been caused by a loose or corroded connector. CLEAR the DTCs. REPEAT the self-test.

FM1120200776040X

Fig. 161 Test F: Charging System Warning Indicator Lamp Flickers Or Is Intermittent (Part 4 of 4). 2002 Sable & Taurus

CONDITIONS	DETAILS/RESULTS/ACTIONS
G1 CHECK FOR ACCESSORY DRIVE NOISE AND MOUNTING BRACKETS	
	1 Check the accessory drive belt for damage and correct installation

FM1120200777010X

Fig. 162 Test G: Alternator Is Noisy (Part 1 of 2). 2002 Sable & Taurus

CONDITIONS	DETAILS/RESULTS/ACTIONS
G1 CHECK FOR ACCESSORY DRIVE NOISE AND MOUNTING BRACKETS (Continued)	
	2 Check the accessory mounting brackets and generator pulley for looseness or misalignment. • Is the accessory drive OK? → **Yes** GO to **G2**. → **No** REPAIR as necessary. TEST the system for normal operation.
G2 CHECK GENERATOR FOR ELECTRICAL NOISE	
1 2 Generator C102 (4V) or C1104 (2V)	• Is the noise still present? → **Yes** GO to **G3**. → **No** INSTALL a new generator. TEST the system for normal operation.
G3 CHECK GENERATOR FOR MECHANICAL NOISE	
1 2	3 Turn all accessories off. With the engine running, use a stethoscope or equivalent listening device to probe the generator for unusual mechanical noise. • Is the generator the noise source? → **Yes** INSTALL a new generator. TEST the system for normal operation. → **No** Diagnose source of engine noise.

FM1120200777020X

Fig. 162 Test G: Alternator Is Noisy (Part 2 of 2). 2002 Sable & Taurus

CONDITIONS	DETAILS/RESULTS/ACTIONS
H1 VERIFY GENERATOR IS SOURCE OF RADIO INTERFERENCE	
1	1 Start and run the engine.
	2 Tune the radio to a station where the interference is present.
3 4 5 Generator C102 (4V) or C1104 (2V)	• Is the interference present with the generator disconnected? → **Yes** Diagnosis and test the in-vehicle entertainment system. → **No** INSTALL a new generator. TEST the system for normal operation.

FM1120200778000X

Fig. 163 Test H: Radio Interference. 2002 Sable & Taurus

Condition	Possible Source	Action
• The Charging System Warning Indicator is ON with the Engine Running (The Battery Voltage Does Not Increase)	• A Circuit. • A Circuit in-line mini-fuse. • B+ Circuit 38 (B/O). • B+ fuse links. • I Circuit 904 (LG/R) • Generator	• GO to Pinpoint Test A.
• The Charging System Warning Indicator is OFF with the Ignition Switch in RUN and the Engine OFF (Battery Voltage Does Not Increase When the Engine is Running).	• Voltage regulator connector. • I Circuit 904 (LG/R). • I Circuit fuse(s). • Charging system warning indicator lamp bulb. • Loose or damaged generator. • Harness connector.	• GO to Pinpoint Test B.
• The Charging System Warning Indicator is ON with the Engine Running and the Battery Voltage Increases	• Generator.	• GO to Pinpoint Test C.
• The Charging System Warning Indicator is OFF with the Ignition Switch in RUN and the Engine OFF (Battery Voltage Increases When the Engine is Running).	• Charging system warning indicator lamp bulb. • Instrument cluster. • Generator.	• GO to Pinpoint Test D.

FM1129800284010X

Fig. 164 Symptom chart (Part 1 of 2). 1998–2001 Town Car

Condition	Possible Sources	Action
• Battery is discharged or voltage is low	• Corroded terminal (s). • Loose connection (s). • High key-off current drain(s). • Battery. • Generator.	• GO to Pinpoint Test A .
• The charging system warning indicator is on with the engine running (the system voltage does not increase)	• Circuitry. • Voltage regulator. • Generator.	• GO to Pinpoint Test B .
• The system overcharges (battery voltage greater than 15.5 volts)	• Circuitry. • Voltage regulator. • Generator.	• GO to Pinpoint Test C .
• The charging system warning indicator is on with the engine running and the system increases voltage	• Circuitry. • Instrument cluster. • Voltage regulator. • Generator.	• GO to Pinpoint Test D .
• The charging system warning indicator is off with the ignition switch in the RUN position and the engine off	• Bulb. • Circuitry. • Instrument cluster. • Voltage regulator. • Generator.	• GO to Pinpoint Test E .
• The charging system warning indicator flickers or is intermittent	• Corroded terminal (s). • Fuse(s). • Circuitry. • Voltage regulator. • Generator.	• GO to Pinpoint Test F .
• The generator is noisy	• Bolts or brackets. • Drive belt. • Generator or pulley.	• GO to Pinpoint Test G .
• Radio interference	• Generator. • Circuitry. • In-vehicle entertainment system.	• GO to Pinpoint Test H .

FM1120200779000X

Fig. 165 Symptom Chart. 2002 Town Car

TEST CONDITIONS	TEST DETAILS/RESULTS/ACTIONS
A1 CHECK A CIRCUIT GENERATOR (10A) MINI FUSE	
1 2 Generator Mini Fuse (10A)	2 Check the generator (10A) A Circuit Mini Fuse in the power distribution box. • Is the fuse OK? → **Yes** GO to **A2**. → **No** REPLACE the Generator Mini Fuse (10A). TEST the system for normal operation.
A2 CHECK GENERATOR OUTPUT CIRCUIT	
1	1 Measure the voltage at the B+ terminal of the generator, Circuit 38 (BK/O). • Is the voltage equal to battery positive voltage (B+)? → **Yes** GO to **A3**. → **No** REPAIR generator output Circuit 38 (BK/O) or fusible links Circuit 290 (GY). TEST the system for normal operation.

FM1129800285010X

Fig. 166 Test A: Warning Indicator Lights w/Engine Running, Battery Voltage Does Not Increase (Part 1 of 3). 1998–2001 Town Car

Condition	Possible Source	Action
• The Charging System Warning Indicator Operates Correctly but the Battery Voltage Does Not Increase	• B+ Circuit 38 (B/O). • B+ fuse links. • Loose or damaged harness connector. • Battery cables. • Generator. • Voltage regulator.	• GO to Pinpoint Test E.
• The Battery is Dead or Will Not Stay Charged or Low Battery or Generator Voltage	• Corroded terminal(s). • Loose connection(s). • High key-off load. • Generator.	• GO to Pinpoint Test F.
• The Charging System Warning Indicator Flickers or Is Intermittent	• Loose connection(s). • In-line mini-fuse A Circuit loose. • I Circuit fuse(s). • Generator.	• GO to Pinpoint Test G.
• The System Overcharges (Battery Voltage Greater Than 15.5 Volts)	• A Circuit. • Generator. • I Circuit.	• GO to Pinpoint Test H.
• Battery Leakage or Damage	• A Circuit. • Generator. • Battery.	• GO to Pinpoint Test J.
• The Voltage Gauge Reads High or Low	• Generator. • Voltage gauge. • Instrument cluster/wiring.	• GO to Pinpoint Test K.
• The Generator is Noisy	• Loose bolts/brackets. • Drive belt. • Generator/Pulley.	• GO to Pinpoint Test L.
• Radio Interference	• Generator. • Wiring/routing. • In-vehicle entertainment system.	• GO to Pinpoint Test M.

FM1129800284020X

Fig. 164 Symptom chart (Part 2 of 2). 1998–2001 Town Car

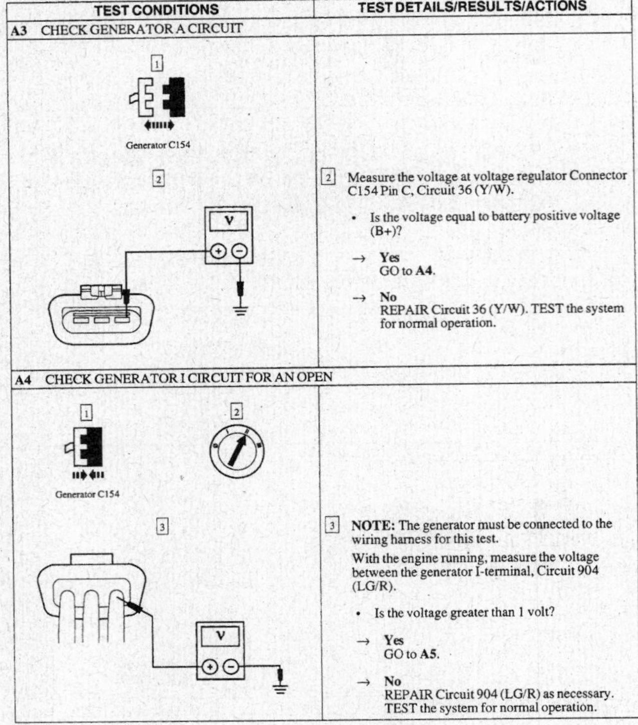

TEST CONDITIONS	TEST DETAILS/RESULTS/ACTIONS
A3 CHECK GENERATOR A CIRCUIT	
1 Generator C154	
2	2 Measure the voltage at voltage regulator Connector C154 Pin C, Circuit 36 (Y/W). • Is the voltage equal to battery positive voltage (B+)? → **Yes** GO to **A4**. → **No** REPAIR Circuit 36 (Y/W). TEST the system for normal operation.
A4 CHECK GENERATOR I CIRCUIT FOR AN OPEN	
1 2 Generator C154	
3	3 **NOTE:** The generator must be connected to the wiring harness for this test. With the engine running, measure the voltage between the generator I-terminal, Circuit 904 (LG/R). • Is the voltage greater than 1 volt? → **Yes** GO to **A5**. → **No** REPAIR Circuit 904 (LG/R) as necessary. TEST the system for normal operation.

FM1129800285020X

Fig. 166 Test A: Warning Indicator Lights w/Engine Running, Battery Voltage Does Not Increase (Part 2 of 3). 1998–2001 Town Car

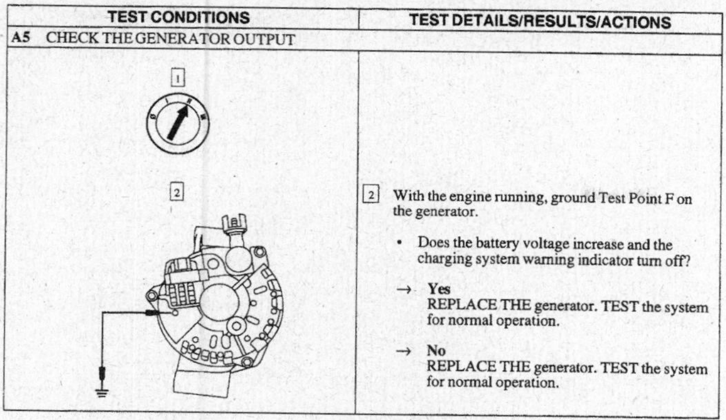

TEST CONDITIONS	TEST DETAILS/RESULTS/ACTIONS
A5 CHECK THE GENERATOR OUTPUT	
1	
2	2 With the engine running, ground Test Point F on the generator. • Does the battery voltage increase and the charging system warning indicator turn off? → **Yes** REPLACE THE generator. TEST the system for normal operation. → **No** REPLACE THE generator. TEST the system for normal operation.

FM1129800285030X

Fig. 166 Test A: Warning Indicator Lights w/Engine Running, Battery Voltage Does Not Increase (Part 3 of 3). 1998–2001 Town Car

TEST CONDITIONS	TEST DETAILS/RESULTS/ACTIONS
B2 CHECK THE GENERATOR GROUNDS	
	1 Check all the ground connections between the generator and the battery. • Are all the ground connections OK? → **Yes** GO to **B3**. → **No** REPAIR the connections as necessary. TEST the system for normal operation.
B3 CHECK THE VOLTAGE AT THE GENERATOR I CIRCUIT	
1 Generator C154 2 3	3 **NOTE:** The generator Connector C154 must be connected to the generator test. With engine running, measure the voltage at the generator I terminal, Circuit 904 (LG/R). • Is the voltage greater than 1 volt? → **Yes** REPLACE the generator. → **No** REPAIR Circuit 904 (LG/R) for an open circuit. TEST the system for normal operation.

FM1129800286020X

Fig. 167 Test B: Warning Indicator Is Off w/Ignition In Run Position & Engine Off (Part 2 of 2). 1998–2001 Town Car

TEST CONDITIONS	TEST DETAILS/RESULTS/ACTIONS
D1 CHECK THE CHARGING SYSTEM WARNING INDICATOR OPERATION	
1 2 Generator Connector C154 3	3 Ground the generator Connector C154 I Circuit with the key ON and the engine OFF. • Is the warning indicator on? → **Yes** REPLACE the generator. TEST the system for normal operation. → **No** REPAIR Connector C154, I Circuit 904 (LG/R) as necessary. TEST the system for normal operation.

FM1129800288000X

Fig. 169 Test D: Warning Indicator Off w/Ignition In Run Position & Engine Off. 1998–2001 Town Car

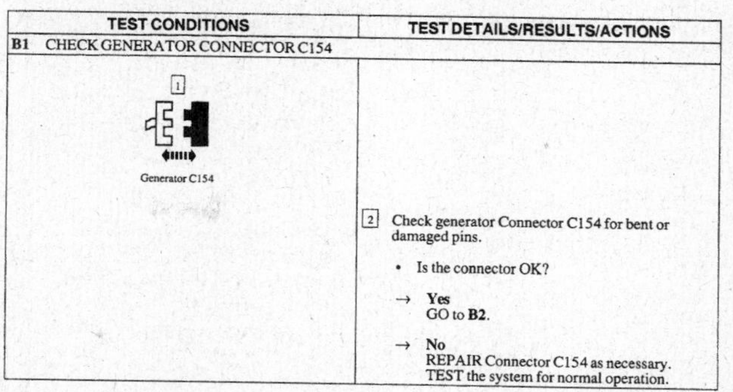

TEST CONDITIONS	TEST DETAILS/RESULTS/ACTIONS
B1 CHECK GENERATOR CONNECTOR C154	
1 Generator C154	2 Check generator Connector C154 for bent or damaged pins. • Is the connector OK? → **Yes** GO to **B2**. → **No** REPAIR Connector C154 as necessary. TEST the system for normal operation.

FM1129800286010X

Fig. 167 Test B: Warning Indicator Is Off w/Ignition In Run Position & Engine Off (Part 1 of 2). 1998–2001 Town Car

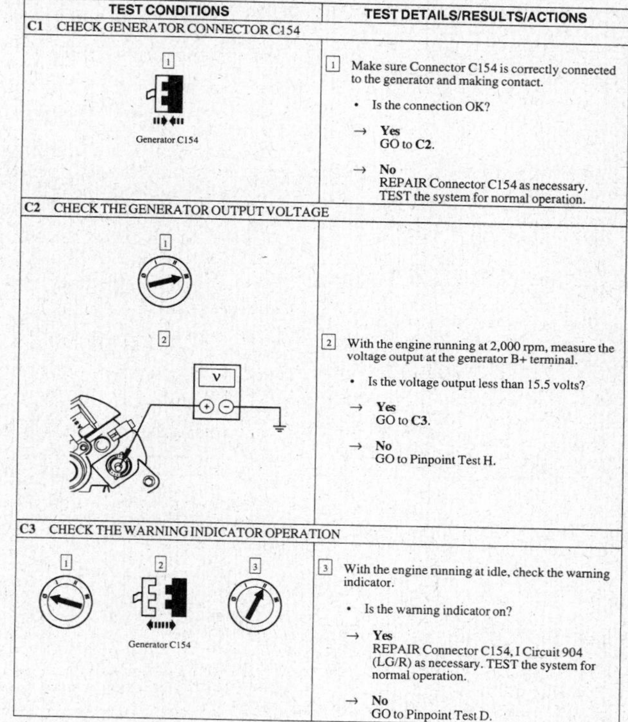

TEST CONDITIONS	TEST DETAILS/RESULTS/ACTIONS
C1 CHECK GENERATOR CONNECTOR C154	
1 Generator C154	1 Make sure Connector C154 is correctly connected to the generator and making contact. • Is the connection OK? → **Yes** GO to **C2**. → **No** REPAIR Connector C154 as necessary. TEST the system for normal operation.
C2 CHECK THE GENERATOR OUTPUT VOLTAGE	
1 2	2 With the engine running at 2,000 rpm, measure the voltage output at the generator B+ terminal. • Is the voltage output less than 15.5 volts? → **Yes** GO to **C3**. → **No** GO to Pinpoint Test H.
C3 CHECK THE WARNING INDICATOR OPERATION	
1 2 Generator C154 3	3 With the engine running at idle, check the warning indicator. • Is the warning indicator on? → **Yes** REPAIR Connector C154, I Circuit 904 (LG/R) as necessary. TEST the system for normal operation. → **No** GO to Pinpoint Test D.

FM1129800287000X

Fig. 168 Test C: Warning Indicator Is On w/Engine Running & Battery Voltage Increase. 1998–2001 Town Car

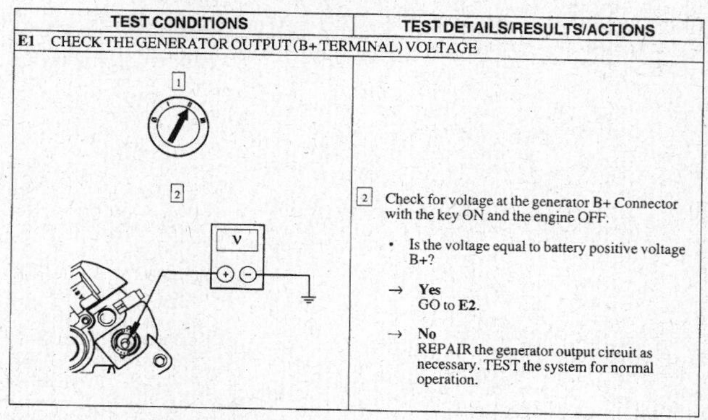

TEST CONDITIONS	TEST DETAILS/RESULTS/ACTIONS
E1 CHECK THE GENERATOR OUTPUT (B+ TERMINAL) VOLTAGE	
1 2	2 Check for voltage at the generator B+ Connector with the key ON and the engine OFF. • Is the voltage equal to battery positive voltage B+? → **Yes** GO to **E2**. → **No** REPAIR the generator output circuit as necessary. TEST the system for normal operation.

FM1129800289010X

Fig. 170 Test E: Warning Indicator Operates Properly But Battery Voltage Does Not Increase (Part 1 of 2). 1998–2001 Town Car

TEST CONDITIONS	TEST DETAILS/RESULTS/ACTIONS
E2 CHECK THE GENERATOR CONNECTORS	
1 Generator C154 2 Generator C154	3 Check the battery connections and generator Connector C154 for corrosion and tightness. • Are the connectors clean and tight? → **Yes** REFER to Lead and No Lead Tests in this section. → **No** REPAIR the connectors as necessary. TEST the system for normal operation.

FM1129800289020X

Fig. 170 Test E: Warning Indicator Operates Properly But Battery Voltage Does Not Increase (Part 2 of 2). 1998–2001 Town Car

TEST CONDITIONS	TEST DETAILS/RESULTS/ACTIONS
F2 CHECK THE GENERATOR OUTPUT	
	1 Check the generator output; refer to Component Tests, Alternator On-Vehicle Tests in this section. • Is the generator OK? → **Yes** GO to **F3**. → **No** REPLACE the generator. TEST the system for normal operation.
F3 CHECK THE BATTERY CONDITION	
	1 Check the battery capacity • Is the battery OK? → **Yes** GO to **F4**. → **No** REPLACE the battery. TEST the system for normal operation.
F4 CHECK OTHER SYSTEMS FOR DRAINS	
	1 Check for drains from the electronic modules; refer to Component Test, Battery—Electronic Drains Which Shut Off When the Battery Cable is Disconnected • Are all the electronic modules OK? → **Yes** RECHARGE the battery. TEST the system for normal operation. → **No** REPLACE the damaged module as necessary. TEST the system for normal operation.

FM1129800290020X

Fig. 171 Test F: Battery Is Dead Or Will Not Stay Charged Or Low Battery Or Alternator Voltage (Part 2 of 2). 1998–2001 Town Car

TEST CONDITIONS	TEST DETAILS/RESULTS/ACTIONS
G3 CHECK THE SYSTEM WARNING INDICATOR OPERATION	
1	2 With the engine running, increase engine speed to 2000 rpm and check the indicator operation for battery voltage increase. • Does the voltage reading increase above 15.5 volts or the warning indicator flicker? → **Yes** REPLACE the generator. TEST the system for normal operation. → **No** REPAIR Circuit 36 (Y/W) or Circuit 904 (LG/R) as necessary. TEST the system for normal operation.

FM1129800291020X

Fig. 172 Test G: Warning Indicator Flickers Or Is Intermittent (Part 2 of 2). 1998–2001 Town Car

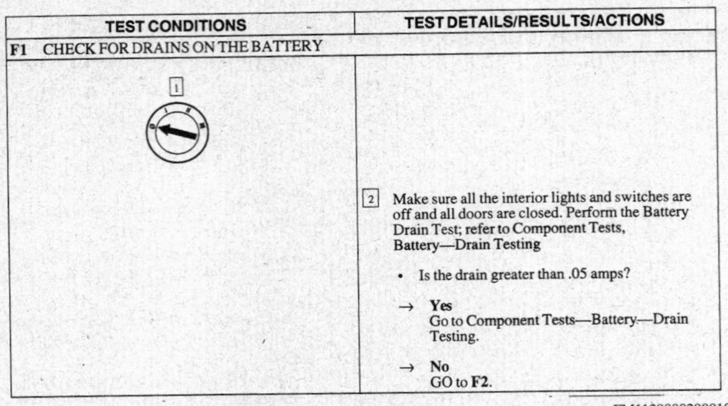

TEST CONDITIONS	TEST DETAILS/RESULTS/ACTIONS
F1 CHECK FOR DRAINS ON THE BATTERY	
1	2 Make sure all the interior lights and switches are off and all doors are closed. Perform the Battery Drain Test; refer to Component Tests, Battery—Drain Testing • Is the drain greater than .05 amps? → **Yes** Go to Component Tests—Battery—Drain Testing. → **No** GO to **F2**.

FM1129800290010X

Fig. 171 Test F: Battery Is Dead Or Will Not Stay Charged Or Low Battery Or Alternator Voltage (Part 1 of 2). 1998–2001 Town Car

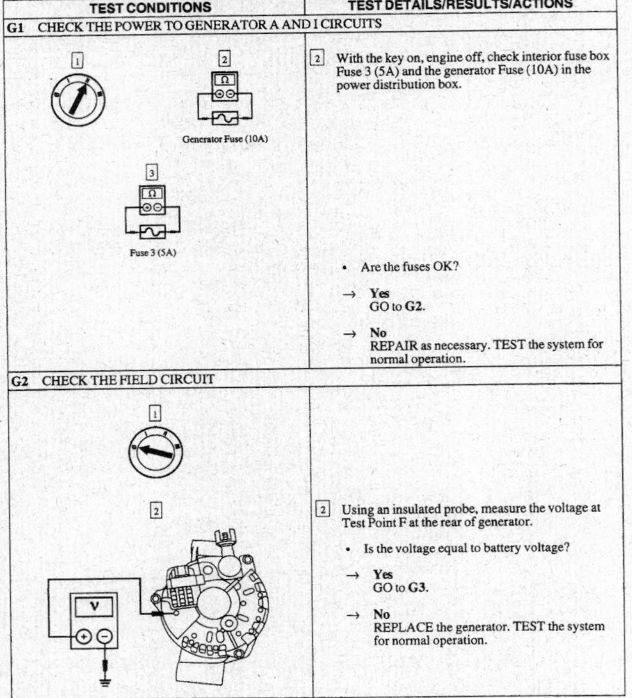

TEST CONDITIONS	TEST DETAILS/RESULTS/ACTIONS
G1 CHECK THE POWER TO GENERATOR A AND I CIRCUITS	
1 2 Generator Fuse (10A) 3 Fuse 3 (5A)	2 With the key on, engine off, check interior fuse box Fuse 3 (5A) and the generator Fuse (10A) in the power distribution box. • Are the fuses OK? → **Yes** GO to **G2**. → **No** REPAIR as necessary. TEST the system for normal operation.
G2 CHECK THE FIELD CIRCUIT	
1 2	2 Using an insulated probe, measure the voltage at Test Point F at the rear of generator. • Is the voltage equal to battery voltage? → **Yes** GO to **G3**. → **No** REPLACE the generator. TEST the system for normal operation.

FM1129800291010X

Fig. 172 Test G: Warning Indicator Flickers Or Is Intermittent (Part 1 of 2). 1998–2001 Town Car

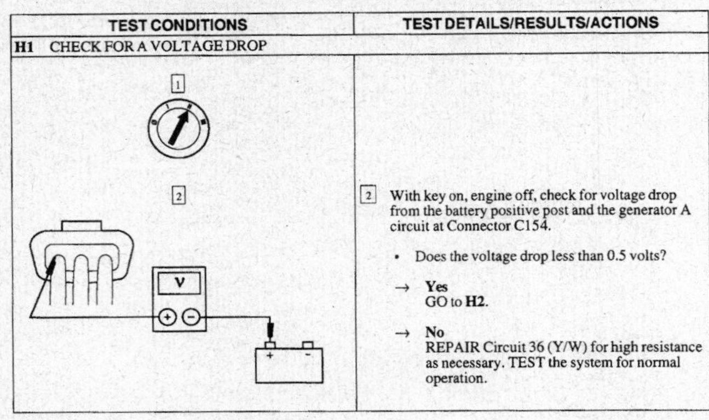

TEST CONDITIONS	TEST DETAILS/RESULTS/ACTIONS
H1 CHECK FOR A VOLTAGE DROP	
1 2	2 With key on, engine off, check for voltage drop from the battery positive post and the generator A circuit at Connector C154. • Does the voltage drop less than 0.5 volts? → **Yes** GO to **H2**. → **No** REPAIR Circuit 36 (Y/W) for high resistance as necessary. TEST the system for normal operation.

FM1129800292010X

Fig. 173 Test H: System Overcharges, Battery Voltage Greater Than 15.5 Volts (Part 1 of 4). 1998–2001 Town Car

TEST CONDITIONS	TEST DETAILS/RESULTS/ACTIONS
H2 CHECK THE BATTERY VOLTAGE	
1 2	3 With the engine running, turn off all the accessories. Increase the engine speed and monitor the voltage at the battery. • Does battery voltage remain less than 15 volts? → **Yes** GO to **H3**. → **No** GO to **H5**.

FM1129800292020X

Fig. 173 Test H: System Overcharges, Battery Voltage Greater Than 15.5 Volts (Part 2 of 4). 1998–2001 Town Car

TEST CONDITIONS	TEST DETAILS/RESULTS/ACTIONS
H5 CHECK THE VOLTAGE REGULATOR OPERATION	
1	1 With the engine running, use an insulated probe to monitor the voltage at Test Point F while increasing the engine speed. • Does the voltage reading at Pin F increase with higher engine speed? → **Yes** REPLACE the generator. TEST the system for normal operation. → **No** REPLACE the generator. TEST the system for normal operation.

FM1129800292040X

Fig. 173 Test H: System Overcharges, Battery Voltage Greater Than 15.5 Volts (Part 4 of 4). 1998–2001 Town Car

TEST CONDITIONS	TEST DETAILS/RESULTS/ACTIONS
J1 CHECK FOR ACID LEAKAGE DAMAGE	
	1 Check for acid damage to the vehicle harnesses and to the body. • Is there acid damage? → **Yes** REPAIR the damaged areas as necessary. → **No** GO to **J2**.
J2 CHECK THE CHARGING SYSTEM FOR OVERCHARGING	
1	1 With the engine running, turn off all the accessories. Increase the engine speed and monitor the voltage at the battery.

FM1129800293010X

Fig. 174 Test J: Battery Leakage Or Damage (Part 1 of 3). 1998–2001 Town Car

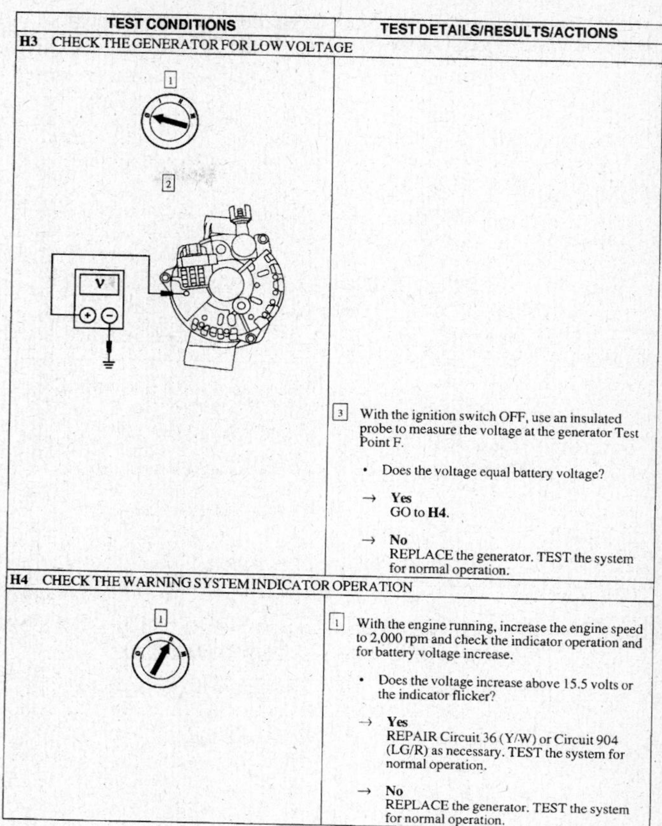

TEST CONDITIONS	TEST DETAILS/RESULTS/ACTIONS
H3 CHECK THE GENERATOR FOR LOW VOLTAGE	
1 2	3 With the ignition switch OFF, use an insulated probe to measure the voltage at the generator Test Point F. • Does the voltage equal battery voltage? → **Yes** GO to **H4**. → **No** REPLACE the generator. TEST the system for normal operation.
H4 CHECK THE WARNING SYSTEM INDICATOR OPERATION	
1	1 With the engine running, increase the engine speed to 2,000 rpm and check the indicator operation and for battery voltage increase. • Does the voltage increase above 15.5 volts or the indicator flicker? → **Yes** REPAIR Circuit 36 (Y/W) or Circuit 904 (LG/R) as necessary. TEST the system for normal operation. → **No** REPLACE the generator. TEST the system for normal operation.

FM1129800292030X

Fig. 173 Test H: System Overcharges, Battery Voltage Greater Than 15.5 Volts (Part 3 of 4). 1998–2001 Town Car

TEST CONDITIONS	TEST DETAILS/RESULTS/ACTIONS
J2 CHECK THE CHARGING SYSTEM FOR OVERCHARGING (Continued)	
2	• Does battery voltage increase more than 15.5 volts? → **Yes** GO to Pinpoint Test H. → **No** GO to **J3**.
J3 CHECK THE BATTERY MOUNTING	
	1 Make sure the battery is properly mounted and level in the battery tray. • Is the battery properly mounted? → **Yes** GO to **J4**. → **No** REPAIR as necessary. TEST the system for normal operation.
J4 CHECK FOR BATTERY CONTACT	
	1 Make sure there are no fasteners or other parts contacting the battery case causing excess pressure. • Is there anything contacting the battery case? → **Yes** REPAIR as necessary. TEST the system for normal operation. → **No** GO to **J5**.

FM1129800293020X

Fig. 174 Test J: Battery Leakage Or Damage (Part 2 of 3). 1998–2001 Town Car

TEST CONDITIONS	TEST DETAILS/RESULTS/ACTIONS
J5 CHECK THE BATTERY CASE FOR DAMAGE	
	1 Check the battery case for defects such as cracks or poor seals. • Is the battery OK? → **Yes** The system is OK. TEST the system for normal operation. → **No** REPLACE the battery. TEST the system for normal operation.

FM1129800293030X

Fig. 174 Test J: Battery Leakage Or Damage (Part 3 of 3). 1998–2001 Town Car

TEST CONDITIONS	TEST DETAILS/RESULTS/ACTIONS
K2 CHECK THE VOLTAGE GAUGE OPERATION	
1	1 With the engine running, monitor the voltage gauge reading and the battery voltage. • Are the voltage readings consistent? → **Yes** The system is operating normally. → **No** The voltage gauge is inaccurate.

FM1129800294020X

Fig. 175 Test K: Voltage Gauge Reads High Or Low (Part 2 of 2). 1998–2001 Town Car

TEST CONDITIONS	TEST DETAILS/RESULTS/ACTIONS
M1 VERIFY THERE IS RADIO INTERFERENCE	
1	1 Start and run the engine.
	2 Tune the radio to a station where the interference is present.
3	3 Turn the engine off.
4	4 Disconnect the generator Connector C176.
5	5 Start and run the engine. • Is the interference present with the generator disconnected? → **Yes** INSPECT the in-vehicle entertainment system. → **No** GO to **M2**.
M2 SUBSTITUTE A KNOWN GOOD GENERATOR	
1	1 Turn the engine off.
	2 Install a known good generator.

FM1129800296010X

Fig. 177 Test M: Radio Interference (Part 1 of 2). 1998–2001 Town Car

TEST CONDITIONS	TEST DETAILS/RESULTS/ACTIONS
M2 SUBSTITUTE A KNOWN GOOD GENERATOR (Continued)	
3	3 Start and run the engine. • Is there radio interference with a known good generator? → **Yes** INSTALL the original generator and INSPECT the in-vehicle entertainment system. → **No** REPLACE the generator. TEST the system for normal operation.

FM1129800296020X

Fig. 177 Test M: Radio Interference (Part 2 of 2). 1998–2001 Town Car

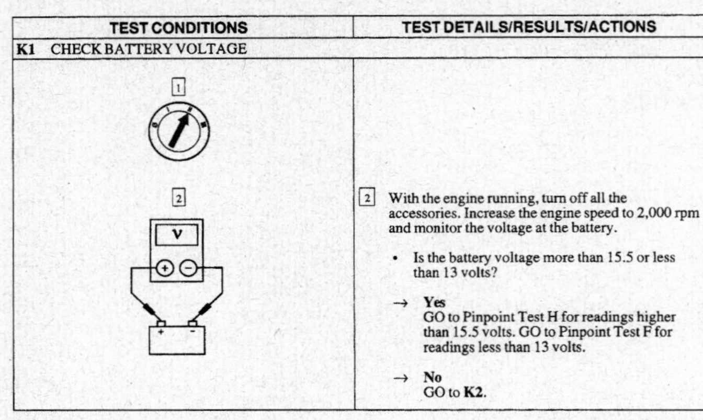

TEST CONDITIONS	TEST DETAILS/RESULTS/ACTIONS
K1 CHECK BATTERY VOLTAGE	
1	
2	2 With the engine running, turn off all the accessories. Increase the engine speed to 2,000 rpm and monitor the voltage at the battery. • Is the battery voltage more than 15.5 or less than 13 volts? → **Yes** GO to Pinpoint Test H for readings higher than 15.5 volts. GO to Pinpoint Test F for readings less than 13 volts. → **No** GO to **K2**.

FM1129800294010X

Fig. 175 Test K: Voltage Gauge Reads High Or Low (Part 1 of 2). 1998–2001 Town Car

TEST CONDITIONS	TEST DETAILS/RESULTS/ACTIONS
L1 CHECK FOR ACCESSORY DRIVE NOISE	
	1 Check the drive belt for damage and verify installation
	2 Check the accessory mounting brackets for loose bolts or misalignment.
	3 Check for a bent generator pulley.
	4 Check other accessories for a bent, misaligned or loose pulley. • Is the accessory drive OK? → **Yes** REPLACE the generator. TEST the system for normal operation. → **No** INSPECT the accessory drive system.

FM1129800295000X

Fig. 176 Test L: Alternator Is Noisy. 1998–2001 Town Car

CONDITIONS	DETAILS/RESULTS/ACTIONS
A1 CHECK BATTERY CONDITION	
	1 Carry out the Battery — Condition Test to determine if the battery can hold a charge and is OK for use. • **Is the battery OK?** → **Yes** GO to A2 . → **No** INSTALL a new battery. TEST the system for normal operation.
A2 CHECK FOR GENERATOR OUTPUT	
	1 Carry out the Generator On-Vehicle Load/No-Load Tests. • **Is the generator OK?** → **Yes** GO to A3 . → **No** GO to Pinpoint Test B .
A3 CHECK FOR CURRENT DRAINS	
	1 Carry out the Battery — Drain Test. • **Are there any excessive current drains?** → **Yes** REPAIR as necessary. TEST the system for normal operation. → **No** GO to A4 .

FM1120200780010X

Fig. 178 Test A: Battery Is Discharged Or Voltage Is Low (Part 1 of 2). 2002 Town Car

A4 CHECK FOR CURRENT DRAINS WHICH SHUT OFF WHEN THE BATTERY IS DISCONNECTED
1 Carry out the Battery — Electronic Drains Which Shut Off When the Battery Cable is Disconnected Test. • **Are there any current drains which shut off when the battery is disconnected?** → **Yes** REPAIR as necessary. TEST the system for normal operation. → **No** GO to Pinpoint Test B .

FM1120200780020X

Fig. 178 Test A: Battery Is Discharged Or Voltage Is Low (Part 2 of 2). 2002 Town Car

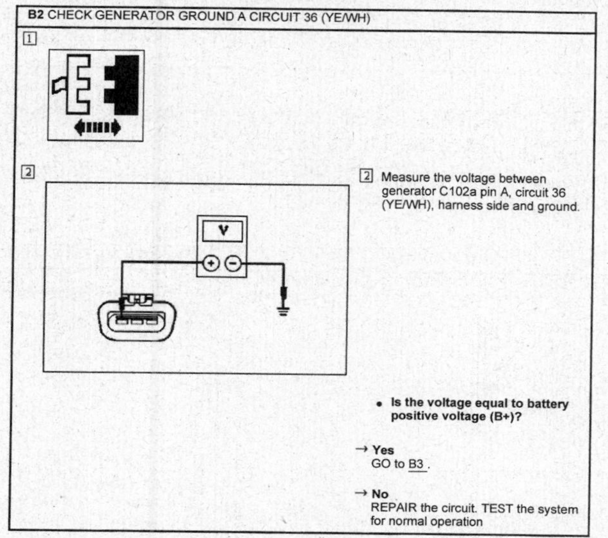
B2 CHECK GENERATOR GROUND A CIRCUIT 36 (YE/WH)

1

2

2 Measure the voltage between generator C102a pin A, circuit 36 (YE/WH), harness side and ground.

• **Is the voltage equal to battery positive voltage (B+)?**

→ **Yes**
GO to B3 .

→ **No**
REPAIR the circuit. TEST the system for normal operation

FM1120200781020X

Fig. 179 Test B: Charging System Warning Indicator Is On With The Engine Running/System Voltage Does Not Increase (Part 2 of 4). 2002 Town Car

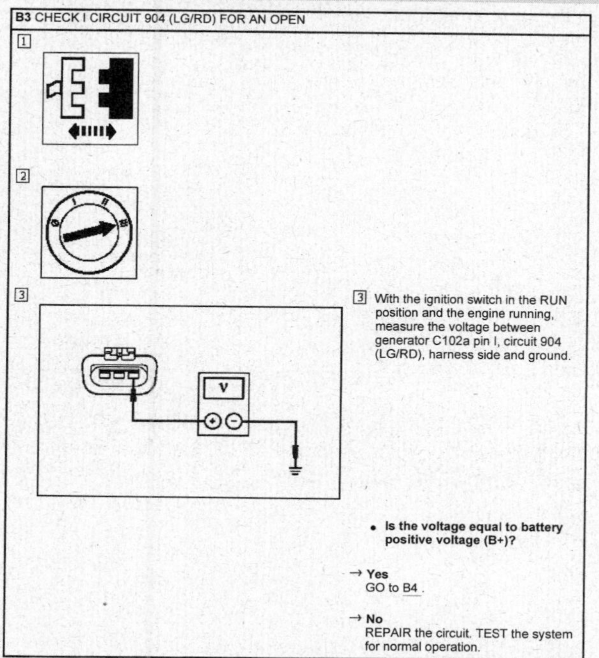
B3 CHECK I CIRCUIT 904 (LG/RD) FOR AN OPEN

1

2

3

3 With the ignition switch in the RUN position and the engine running, measure the voltage between generator C102a pin I, circuit 904 (LG/RD), harness side and ground.

• **Is the voltage equal to battery positive voltage (B+)?**

→ **Yes**
GO to B4 .

→ **No**
REPAIR the circuit. TEST the system for normal operation.

FM1120200781030X

Fig. 179 Test B: Charging System Warning Indicator Is On With The Engine Running/System Voltage Does Not Increase (Part 3 of 4). 2002 Town Car

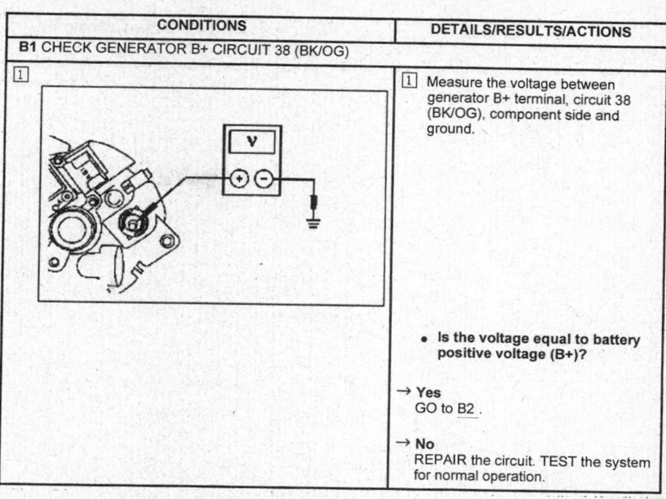
CONDITIONS	DETAILS/RESULTS/ACTIONS
B1 CHECK GENERATOR B+ CIRCUIT 38 (BK/OG)	
1	1 Measure the voltage between generator B+ terminal, circuit 38 (BK/OG), component side and ground. • **Is the voltage equal to battery positive voltage (B+)?** → **Yes** GO to B2 . → **No** REPAIR the circuit. TEST the system for normal operation.

FM1120200781010X

Fig. 179 Test B: Charging System Warning Indicator Is On With The Engine Running/System Voltage Does Not Increase (Part 1 of 4). 2002 Town Car

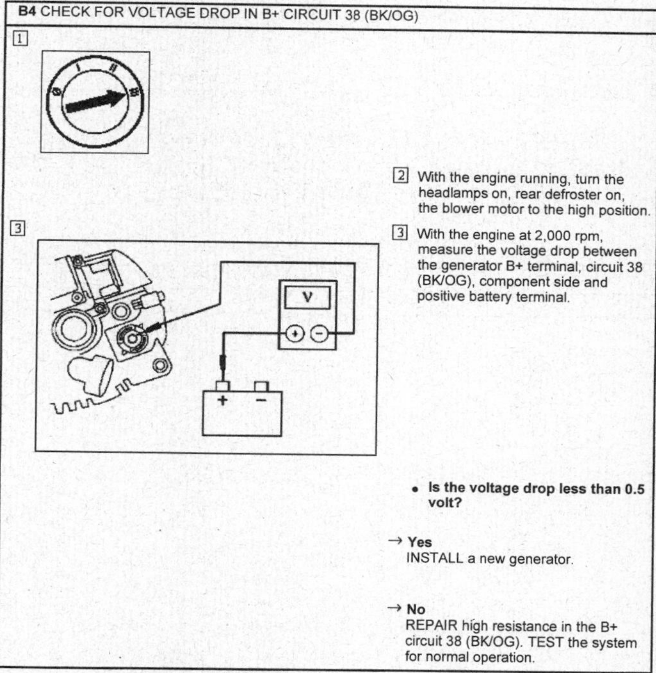
B4 CHECK FOR VOLTAGE DROP IN B+ CIRCUIT 38 (BK/OG)

1

2 With the engine running, turn the headlamps on, rear defroster on, the blower motor to the high position.

3

3 With the engine at 2,000 rpm, measure the voltage drop between the generator B+ terminal, circuit 38 (BK/OG), component side and positive battery terminal.

• **Is the voltage drop less than 0.5 volt?**

→ **Yes**
INSTALL a new generator.

→ **No**
REPAIR high resistance in the B+ circuit 38 (BK/OG). TEST the system for normal operation.

FM1120200781040X

Fig. 179 Test B: Charging System Warning Indicator Is On With The Engine Running/System Voltage Does Not Increase (Part 4 of 4). 2002 Town Car

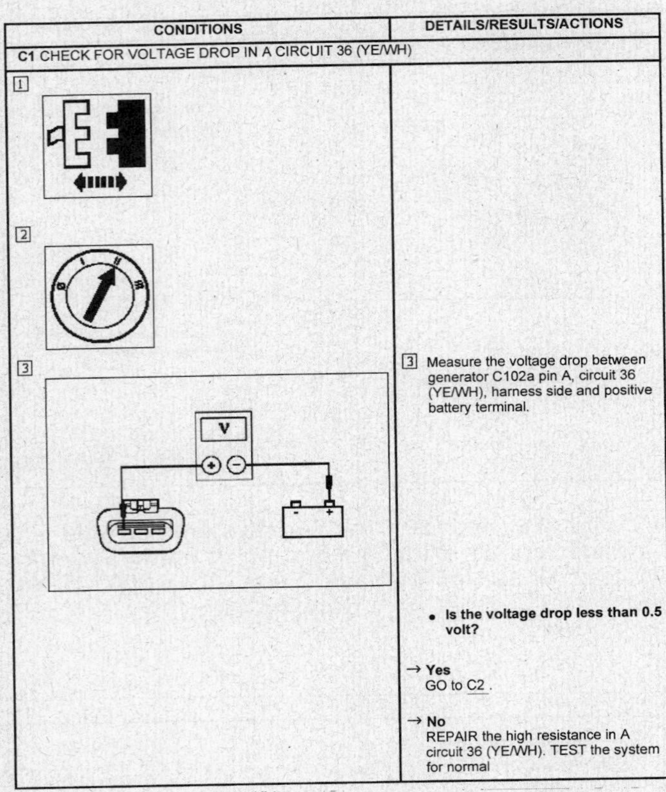

CONDITIONS	DETAILS/RESULTS/ACTIONS
C1 CHECK FOR VOLTAGE DROP IN A CIRCUIT 36 (YE/WH)	
1	
2	
3	3 Measure the voltage drop between generator C102a pin A, circuit 36 (YE/WH), harness side and positive battery terminal. • **Is the voltage drop less than 0.5 volt?** → **Yes** GO to C2 . → **No** REPAIR the high resistance in A circuit 36 (YE/WH). TEST the system for normal

FM1120200782010X

Fig. 180 Test C: System Overcharges/Battery Voltage Is Greater Than 15.5 Volts (Part 1 of 2). 2002 Town Car

CONDITIONS	DETAILS/RESULTS/ACTIONS
D1 CHECK I CIRCUIT 904 (LG/RD) FOR SHORT TO GROUND	
1 Generator C102a	
2	2 With the ignition switch in the RUN position, check the charging system warning indicator. • **Is the charging system warning indicator illuminated?** → **Yes** REPAIR generator I circuit 904 (LG/RD) for a short to ground. TEST the system for normal operation. → **No** INSTALL a new generator. TEST the system for normal operation.

FM1120200783000X

Fig. 181 Test D: Charging System Warning Indicator Is On With The Engine Running And The System Increases Voltage. 2002 Town Car

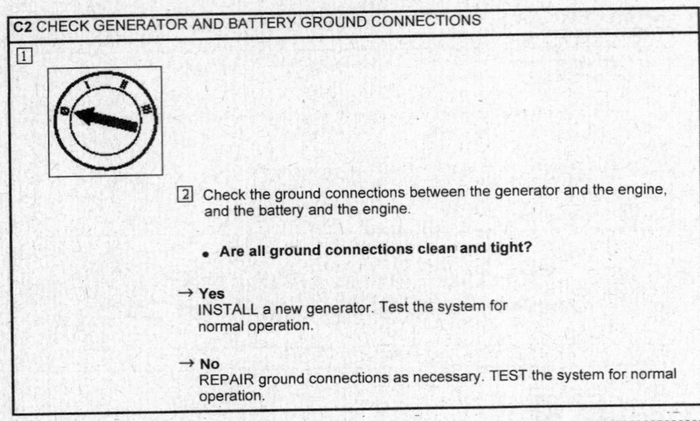

C2 CHECK GENERATOR AND BATTERY GROUND CONNECTIONS

1

2 Check the ground connections between the generator and the engine, and the battery and the engine.

• **Are all ground connections clean and tight?**

→ **Yes**
INSTALL a new generator. Test the system for normal operation.

→ **No**
REPAIR ground connections as necessary. TEST the system for normal operation.

FM1120200782020X

Fig. 180 Test C: System Overcharges/Battery Voltage Is Greater Than 15.5 Volts (Part 2 of 2). 2002 Town Car

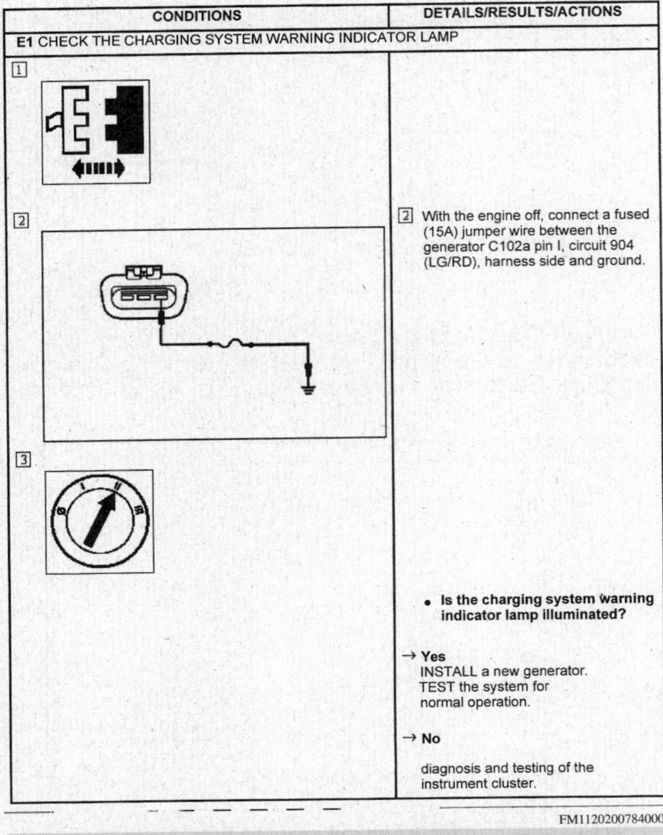

CONDITIONS	DETAILS/RESULTS/ACTIONS
E1 CHECK THE CHARGING SYSTEM WARNING INDICATOR LAMP	
1	
2	2 With the engine off, connect a fused (15A) jumper wire between the generator C102a pin I, circuit 904 (LG/RD), harness side and ground.
3	• **Is the charging system warning indicator lamp illuminated?** → **Yes** INSTALL a new generator. TEST the system for normal operation. → **No** diagnosis and testing of the instrument cluster.

FM1120200784000X

Fig. 182 Test E: Charging System Warning Indicator Is Off With The Ignition Switch In The Run Position And The Engine Off. 2002 Town Car

CONDITIONS	DETAILS/RESULTS/ACTIONS
F1 CHECK FOR LOOSE CONNECTIONS	
	1 Check all generator, battery, and power distribution connections for looseness, corrosion, loose or bent terminals, or loose eyelets. • **Are all connections clean and tight?** → **Yes** GO to F2 . → **No** REPAIR as necessary. TEST the system for normal operation.

FM1120200785010X

Fig. 183 Test F: Charging System Warning Indicator Lamp Flickers Or Is Intermittent (Part 1 of 3). 2002 Town Car

F3 CHECK A CIRCUIT 36 (YE/WH) CONNECTIONS

1

2 Connect a fused (15A) jumper wire between generator C102a, pin A, circuit 36 (YE/WH), harness side and the positive battery terminal.

3 With the engine running note the charging system warning indicator operation.

• **Does the charging system warning indicator flicker?**

→ **Yes**
INSTALL a new generator. TEST the system for normal operation.

→ **No**
REPAIR loose connection(s) in circuits. TEST the system for normal operation.

FM1120200785030X

Fig. 183 Test F: Charging System Warning Indicator Lamp Flickers Or Is Intermittent (Part 3 of 3). 2002 Town Car

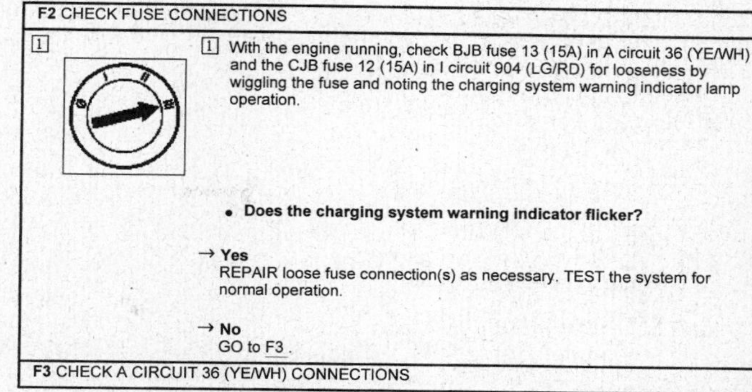

F2 CHECK FUSE CONNECTIONS

1 With the engine running, check BJB fuse 13 (15A) in A circuit 36 (YE/WH) and the CJB fuse 12 (15A) in I circuit 904 (LG/RD) for looseness by wiggling the fuse and noting the charging system warning indicator lamp operation.

• **Does the charging system warning indicator flicker?**

→ **Yes**
REPAIR loose fuse connection(s) as necessary. TEST the system for normal operation.

→ **No**
GO to F3 .

F3 CHECK A CIRCUIT 36 (YE/WH) CONNECTIONS

FM1120200785020X

Fig. 183 Test F: Charging System Warning Indicator Lamp Flickers Or Is Intermittent (Part 2 of 3). 2002 Town Car

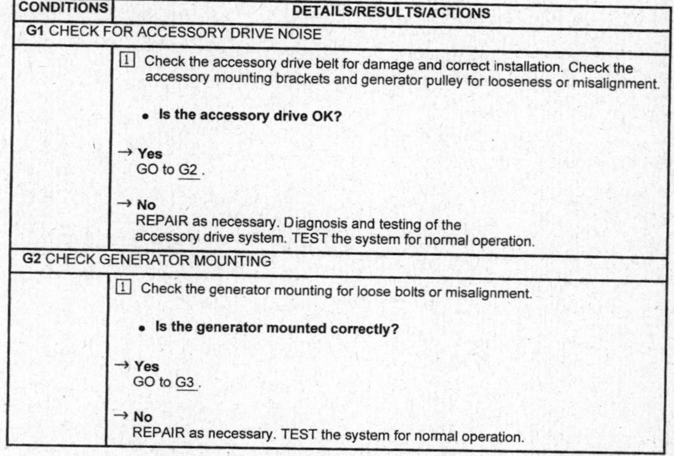

CONDITIONS	DETAILS/RESULTS/ACTIONS
G1 CHECK FOR ACCESSORY DRIVE NOISE	
	1 Check the accessory drive belt for damage and correct installation. Check the accessory mounting brackets and generator pulley for looseness or misalignment. • **Is the accessory drive OK?** → **Yes** GO to G2 . → **No** REPAIR as necessary. Diagnosis and testing of the accessory drive system. TEST the system for normal operation.
G2 CHECK GENERATOR MOUNTING	
	1 Check the generator mounting for loose bolts or misalignment. • **Is the generator mounted correctly?** → **Yes** GO to G3 . → **No** REPAIR as necessary. TEST the system for normal operation.

FM1120200786010X

Fig. 184 Test G: Alternator Is Noisy (Part 1 of 3). 2002 Town Car

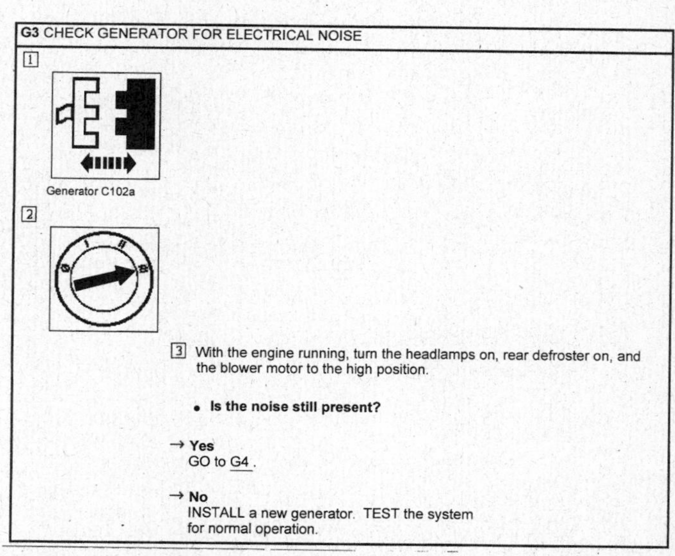

G3 CHECK GENERATOR FOR ELECTRICAL NOISE

1

Generator C102a

2

3 With the engine running, turn the headlamps on, rear defroster on, and the blower motor to the high position.

• **Is the noise still present?**

→ **Yes**
GO to G4 .

→ **No**
INSTALL a new generator. TEST the system for normal operation.

FM1120200786020X

Fig. 184 Test G: Alternator Is Noisy (Part 2 of 3). 2002 Town Car

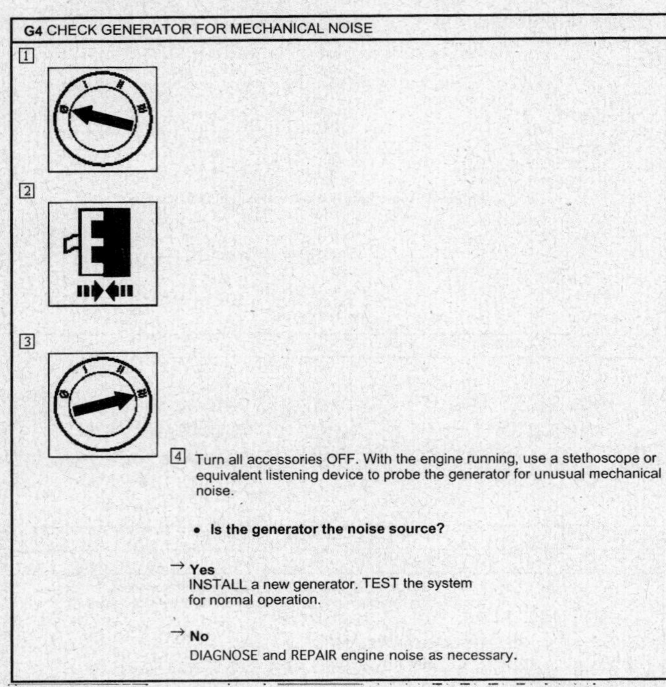

Fig. 184 Test G: Alternator Is Noisy (Part 3 of 3). 2002 Town Car

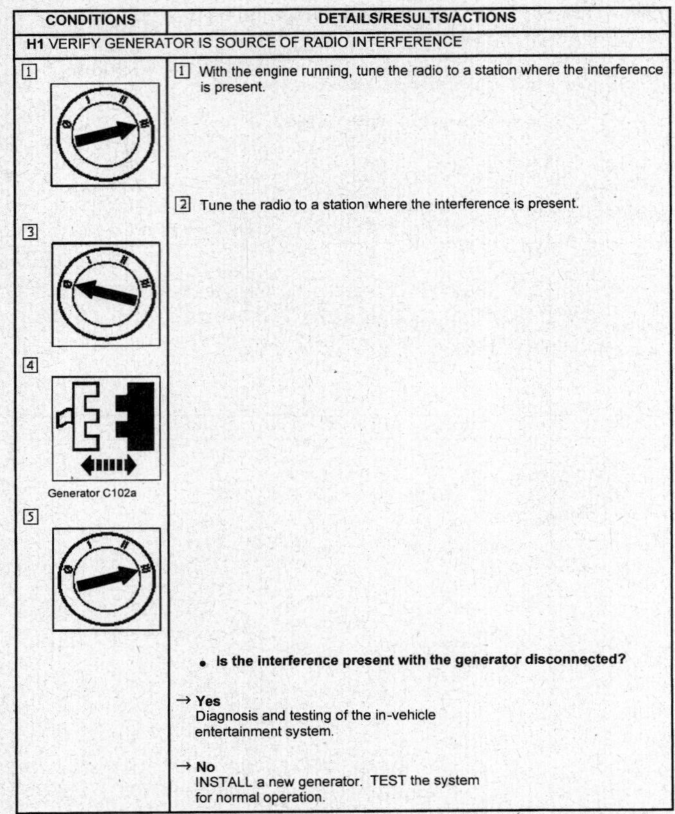

Fig. 185 Test H: Radio Interference . 2002 Town Car

ALTERNATOR SPECIFICATIONS

Model	Year	Model	Amp Rating
Continental	1998–2002	F8OU-CA	130
Contour	1998–2000	—	130
Cougar	1999–2002	—	—
Crown Victoria	1998–99	F6AU	130
	2000–02	F6LU-CA	130
Escort	1998–99	F5OU-AA	75
	2000–02	—	⑤
Focus	2000–02	—	—
Grand Marquis	1998–99	F6AU	130
	2000–02	F6LU-CA	130
LS	2000–02	④	105
Mustang	1998–99	②	130
	2000	⑥	⑦
	2001–02	⑧	⑨
Mystique	1998–2000	—	130
Sable	1998–2000	F6DU-F	130
	2001	①	③
Taurus	1998–2000	F6DU-F	130
	2001	①	③
Thunderbird	2002	XR8U-CD	105
Town Car	1998–2002	F6LU-CA	130
Tracer	1998–99	F5OU-AA	130
ZX2	1998–99	F1DU-A	95
	2000–02	—	⑤

① — 3.0L SOHC engine, XF2V-AB; 3.0L DOHC engine, XF2V-BC.
② — 3.8L & 4.6L SOHC engines, F6AU; 4.6L DOHC engine, F6ZU-BC.
③ — 3.0L SOHC engine, 110 MPS; 3.0L DOHC engine, 125 amps.
④ — 3.0L engine, XR8U-AC. 3.9L engine, XR8U-CD.
⑤ — SPI engine, 75 amps.; Zetec engine, 95 amps.
⑥ — 3.8L engine, F8ZU-AA; 4.6L SOHC engine, XR3U-AB; 4.6L DOHC engine, F6ZU-BE.
⑦ — 3.8L engine, 115 amps; 4.6L SOHC engine, 110 amps; 4.6L DOHC engine, 120 amps.
⑧ — 3.8L engine, 1R3U-BA; 4.6L SOHC engine, XR3U-AB; 4.6L DOHC engine, F6ZU-BE.
⑨ — 3.8L & 4.6L SOHC engines, 110 amps; 4.6L DOHC engine, 120 amps.

Melco Alternators

NOTE: On Air Bag Equipped Models, Refer To "Air Bag System Precautions" Located In The Front Of This Manual For System Disarming & Arming Procedures.

NOTE: Refer To "Computer Relearn Procedures" Located In The Front Of This Manual When Battery Power To The Computer Has Been Interrupted.

NOTE: "Electrical Symbol & Wire Color Code Identification" Located In The Front Of This Manual May Be Used As An Aid When Using Wiring Circuits Found In This Section.

INDEX

APPLICATION CHART

Model	Year	Alternator
Mark VIII	1998	Melco

PRECAUTIONS

AIR BAG SYSTEMS

Refer to "Air Bag System Precautions" in the front of this manual for system disarming and arming procedures.

BATTERY GROUND CABLE

Prior to service, disconnect battery ground cable and isolate as required.

GENERAL

1. Ensure proper battery polarity when servicing units. Reversed battery polarity will damage rectifiers and regulators.
2. If booster battery is used for starting, ensure proper polarity.
3. When a fast charger is used to charge a vehicle battery, vehicle battery cables should be disconnected unless fast charger is equipped with a special alternator protector, in which case vehicle battery cables need not be disconnected. A fast charger should never be used to start a vehicle as damage to rectifiers will result.
4. Unless system includes a load relay or field relay, grounding alternator output terminal will damage alternator and/or circuits. This is true even when system is not in operation since a circuit breaker is not used and battery voltage is applied to the alternator output terminal at all times. The field or load relay acts as a circuit breaker in that it is controlled by ignition switch.
5. Before starting any on vehicle tests of alternator or regulator, battery should be inspected and circuit inspected for faulty wiring or insulation, loose or corroded connections and poor ground circuits.
6. Ensure alternator belt tension is tight enough to prevent slipping under load.
7. To prevent damage to the system, Ignition should be off and battery ground cable disconnected before making any test connections.
8. Vehicle battery must be fully charged or a fully charged battery may be installed for test purposes.

DESCRIPTION

The charging system is a negative ground system consisting of an alternator with a integral rectifier and regulator, **Fig. 1** .

The "B" terminal is connected internally to the rectifier bridge output. Externally, the cable connected to the "B" terminal supplies Direct Current (DC) output to the electrical system to charge the battery and operate the vehicle accessories while the engine is running.

The "L" terminal is connected internally (through a network of integrated circuits) to the field coil. When the ignition is turned On, the field coil is energized to "turn on" the regulator power transistor.

The "S" terminal is connected internally to the voltage regulator sensing circuit. Externally, the "S" terminal is connected to the ignition side of the ignition switch. The "S" circuit is used to tell the voltage regulator how much alternator output is required.

The Integrated Circuit (IC) electronic voltage regulator is part of the rotor, brush, and brush holder assembly. There is no voltage adjustment. The IC regulator automatically reduces regulated voltage when ambient temperature increases, so that battery charging voltage is maintained at the proper level.

DIAGNOSIS & TESTING

Wiring Diagrams

MARK VIII

Refer to **Fig. 2** for charging system wiring diagram.

Diagnostic Tests

MARK VIII

Refer to **Fig. 3** for symptom chart and **Figs. 4 through 15** for diagnostic tests.

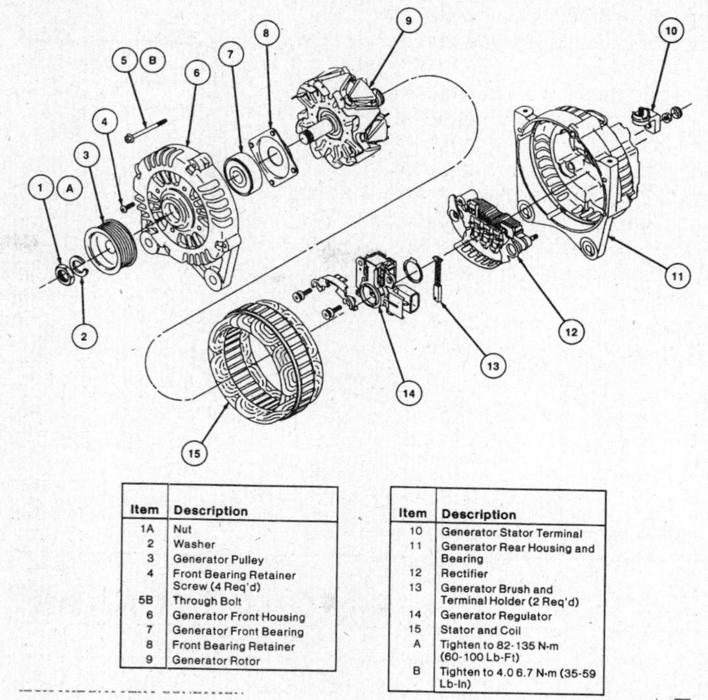

Item	Description
1A	Nut
2	Washer
3	Generator Pulley
4	Front Bearing Retainer Screw (4 Req'd)
5B	Through Bolt
6	Generator Front Housing
7	Generator Front Bearing
8	Front Bearing Retainer
9	Generator Rotor

Item	Description
10	Generator Stator Terminal
11	Generator Rear Housing and Bearing
12	Rectifier
13	Generator Brush and Terminal Holder (2 Req'd)
14	Generator Regulator
15	Stator and Coil
A	Tighten to 82-135 N·m (60-100 Lb-Ft)
B	Tighten to 4.0 6.7 N·m (35-59 Lb-In)

Fig. 1 Exploded view of Melco alternator. Mark VIII

No-Load Test

Prior to testing, turn headlamps on for 10–15 seconds to remove battery surface charge. Wait until voltage stabilizes before performing test.

1. Connect Rotunda 88 Digital Multimeter tool No. 105-00053, or equivalent.
2. Connect Rotunda 73 Digital Multimeter tool No. 105-00051, or equivalent across battery terminals and record base voltage.
3. Start engine and run at 1500 RPM with no electrical load.
4. Voltage should be 14.1–14.7 volts.
5. If voltage increases but less than 2.5 volts, perform "Load Test."
6. If voltage does not increase, or increases more than 2.5 volts, perform "Output Test."

Load Test

1. With engine running, turn headlamps on and blower motor to high. If equipped, turn on air conditioning.
2. Increase engine speed to 2000 RPM.
3. Voltage should increase at least .5 volts above base voltage.
4. If voltage does not increase as specified, perform "Output Test."

Output Test

VAT-40 TESTER

1. Connect Rotunda VAT-40 tool No. 078-00005, or equivalent's leads to vehicle and turn all accessories off.
2. Turn ignition On and read discharge rate on ammeter.
3. Start engine and run at 1500–2000 RPM.
4. Slowly increase load control knob of Rotunda VAT-40 until highest amp reading is obtained, then turn load control knob off.
5. Add discharge rate to highest amp reading for total alternator output.
6. Alternator is functioning properly if total alternator output is more than specified, **Fig. 16.**
7. If amperage is below specifications, refer to "Voltage Test."

ARBST TESTER

1. Switch Alternator, Regulator, Battery and Starter Tester (ARBST) tool No. 010-00725, or equivalent to ammeter function, then connect positive and negative leads to battery.
2. Connect current probe to alternator "B+" output lead.
3. With engine running at 2000 RPM, adjust ARBST load bank to determine alternator output.
4. Alternator is functioning properly if total alternator output is more than specified, **Fig. 16.**
5. If amperage is below specifications, refer to "Voltage Test."

Stator & Coil Grounded Test

Alternator must be disassembled to conduct this tests.

1. Use Rotunda 73 Digital Multimeter tool No. 105-00051, or equivalent to inspect three stator and coil leads, and stator and coil core continuity.
2. If there is continuity, replace stator and coil.

Stator & Coil Open Test

Alternator must be disassembled to conduct this test.

1. Inspect stator and coil laminations for overheating.
2. If burn spots are evident, replace stator and coil.
3. Use Rotunda 73 Digital Multimeter tool No. 105-00051, or equivalent to inspect stator and coil leads for continuity.
4. If there is no continuity, replace stator.

Alternator Rotor Open Or Short Test

Alternator must be disassembled to conduct this test.

1. Use Rotunda 73 Digital Multimeter tool No. 105-00051, or equivalent to measure resistance between two slip rings.
2. If resistance is not 3.5–4.5 ohms, replace rotor.
3. Inspect for continuity between each slip ring and rotor core.
4. If there is continuity, replace rotor.
5. Inspect slip ring color and condition.
6. If rings are dark, clean them with fine sandpaper.
7. If rings are grooved, refinish them on a lathe.

Brush Test

Alternator must be disassembled to inspect brushes.

1. Inspect bushes for wear.
2. If brushes are worn down to wear line, replace.
3. Using a suitable spring pressure gauge, push each brush into its holder until tip of brush projects .079 inch out of its holder.
4. Measure brush pressure, and if not 5.6–15.5 oz., replace brush spring.

Rectifier Test

Alternator must be disassembled to inspect rectifier.

1. Using Rotunda 73 Digital Multimeter tool No. 105-00051, or equivalent, inspect for continuity between diode positive leads and heat sink.

2. If no continuity exists for any positive diode lead to heat sink, replace rectifier.
3. Reverse ohmmeter leads and inspect continuity between diode negative leads and heat sink.
4. If continuity exists from any negative diode lead to heat sink, replace rectifier.
5. Inspect diode trio (smaller diodes between main diode leads) for continuity in both directions.
6. If any diode does not show continuity in one direction only, replace diode trio.

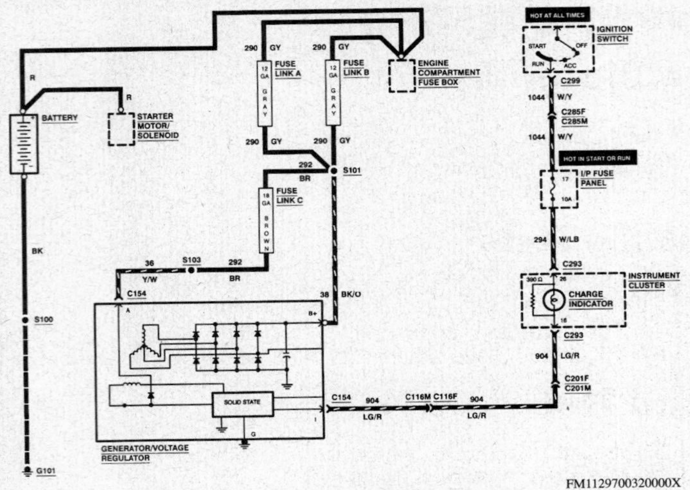

Fig. 2 Wiring diagram. Mark VIII

DIAGNOSTIC CHART INDEX

Test	Description	Page No.	Fig. No.
MARK VIII			
—	Diagnostic Symptom Chart	12-79	3
Test A	Charging System Warning Indicator Is On w/The Engine Running (Battery Voltage Does Not Increase)	12-79	4
Test B	Charging System Warning Indicator Is Off w/Ignition In Run Position & Engine Off (Battery Voltage Does Not Increase)	12-79	5
Test C	Charging System Warning Indicator Is On w/Engine Running & Battery Voltage Increases	12-80	6
Test D	Charging System Warning Indicator Is Off w/Ignition In Run Position & Engine Off (Battery Voltage Increases)	12-80	7
Test E	Charging System Warning indicator Operates Properly But Battery Voltage Does Not Increase	12-80	8
Test F	Battery Dead Or Will Not Stay Charged Or Low Battery Or Alternator Voltage	12-81	9
Test G	Charging System Warning Indicator Flickers	12-81	10
Test H	System Overcharges (Battery Voltage Greater Than 15.5 Volts)	12-81	11
Test J	Battery Leakage Or Damage	12-82	12
Test K	Voltage Gauge Reads High Or Low	12-82	13
Test L	Alternator Is Noisy	12-83	14
Test M	Radio Interference	12-83	15

Condition	Possible Source	Action
• The Charging System Warning Indicator is ON with the Engine Running (The Battery Voltage Does Not Increase)	• A Circuit 35 (O/LB). • A Circuit in-line mini-fuse. • B+ Circuit 36 (Y/W). • B+ mega fuse. • I Circuit 904 (LG/R). • Voltage regulator. • Generator.	• GO to Pinpoint Test A.
• The Charging System Warning Indicator is OFF with the Ignition Switch in the RUN Position and the Engine OFF (Battery Voltage Does Not Increase)	• Voltage regulator connector. • I Circuit 905 (LG/R). • Fuse 19 (10A). • Voltage regulator. • Loose or damaged generator. • Harness connector.	• GO to Pinpoint Test B.
• The Charging System Warning Indicator Stays ON with the Engine Running and the Battery Voltage Increases	• Generator. • Voltage regulator.	• GO to Pinpoint Test C.
• The Charging System Warning Indicator is OFF with the Ignition Switch in the RUN Position and the Engine OFF (Battery Voltage Increases)	• Charging system warning indicator lamp bulb. • Instrument cluster. • Generator. • Voltage regulator.	• GO to Pinpoint Test D.

FM1129700167010X

Fig. 3 Diagnostic symptom chart (Part 1 of 2). Mark VIII

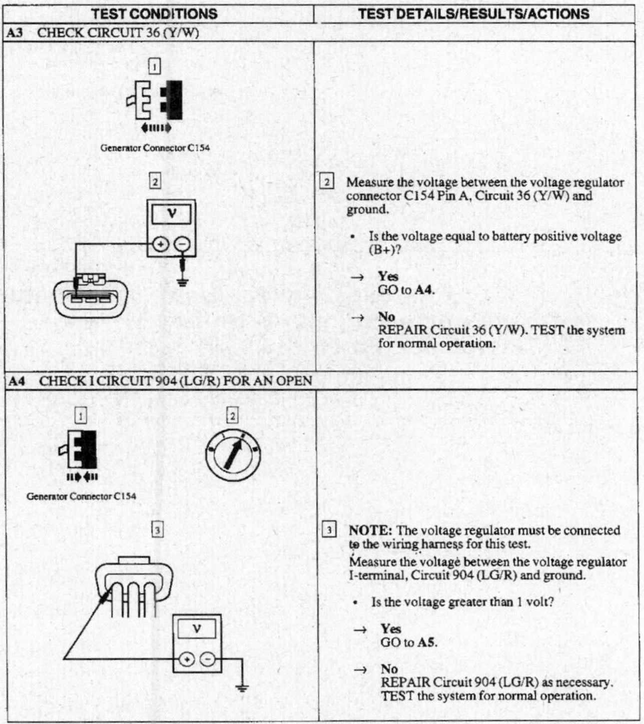

TEST CONDITIONS	TEST DETAILS/RESULTS/ACTIONS
A3 CHECK CIRCUIT 36 (Y/W)	
1 Generator Connector C154	
2	2 Measure the voltage between the voltage regulator connector C154 Pin A, Circuit 36 (Y/W) and ground. • Is the voltage equal to battery positive voltage (B+)? → **Yes** GO to **A4**. → **No** REPAIR Circuit 36 (Y/W). TEST the system for normal operation.
A4 CHECK I CIRCUIT 904 (LG/R) FOR AN OPEN	
1 Generator Connector C154 2	
3	3 **NOTE:** The voltage regulator must be connected to the wiring harness for this test. Measure the voltage between the voltage regulator I-terminal, Circuit 904 (LG/R) and ground. • Is the voltage greater than 1 volt? → **Yes** GO to **A5**. → **No** REPAIR Circuit 904 (LG/R) as necessary. TEST the system for normal operation.

FM1129700168020X

Fig. 4 Test A: Charging System Warning Indicator Is On w/The Engine Running (Battery Voltage Does Not Increase, Part 2 of 3). Mark VIII

TEST CONDITIONS	TEST DETAILS/RESULTS/ACTIONS
A5 CHECK GENERATOR OUTPUT	
1	
2	2 With the engine running, ground the F pin on the generator/regulator. • Does the battery voltage increase and the charging system warning indicator turn off? → **Yes** REPLACE the generator. TEST the system for normal operation. → **No** REPLACE the generator. TEST the system for normal operation.

FM1129700168030X

Fig. 4 Test A: Charging System Warning Indicator Is On w/The Engine Running (Battery Voltage Does Not Increase, Part 3 of 3). Mark VIII

Condition	Possible Source	Action
• The Charging System Warning Indicator Operates Correctly but the Battery Voltage Does Not Increase	• B+ Circuit 36 (Y/W). • B+ mega fuse. • Loose or damaged harness connector. • Battery cables. • Generator. • Voltage regulator.	• GO to Pinpoint Test E.
• The Battery is Dead or Will Not Stay Charged or Low Battery or Generator Voltage	• Corroded terminal(s). • Loose connection(s). • High key-off load. • Generator. • Voltage regulator.	• GO to Pinpoint Test F.
• The Charging System Warning Indicator Flickers/Is Intermittent	• Loose connection(s). • In-line mini-fuse A Circuit loose. • Fuse 19 (10A) I Circuit loose. • Generator. • Voltage regulator.	• GO to Pinpoint Test G.
• The System Overcharges (Battery Voltage Greater Than 15.5 Volts)	• A Circuit 35 (O/LB). • Generator (low output). • Voltage regulator. • I Circuit 904 (LG/R).	• GO to Pinpoint Test H.
• Battery Leakage or Damage	• A Circuit 35 (O/LB). • Voltage regulator. • Voltage gauge. • Instrument cluster/wiring.	• GO to Pinpoint Test J.
• The Voltage Gauge Reads High or Low	• Generator (low output). • Voltage regulator. • Voltage gauge. • Instrument cluster/wiring.	• GO to Pinpoint Test K.
• The Generator is Noisy	• Loose bolts/brackets. • Drive belt. • Generator/Pulley.	• GO to Pinpoint Test L.
• Radio Interference	• Generator. • Wiring/routing.. • In-vehicle entertainment system.	• GO to Pinpoint Test M.

FM1129700167020X

Fig. 3 Diagnostic symptom chart (Part 2 of 2). Mark VIII

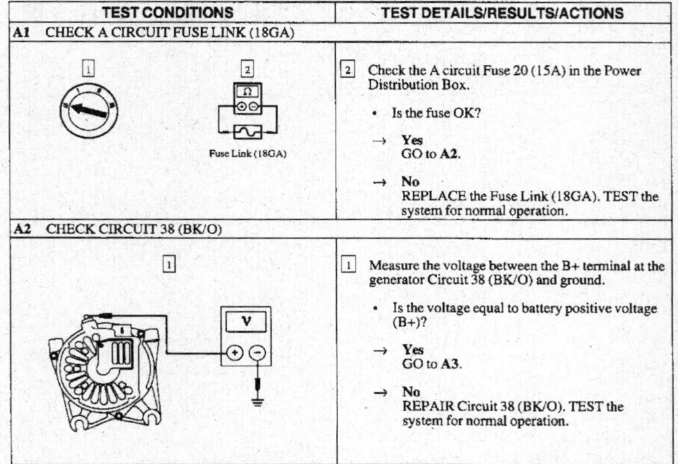

TEST CONDITIONS	TEST DETAILS/RESULTS/ACTIONS
A1 CHECK A CIRCUIT FUSE LINK (18GA)	
1 2 Fuse Link (18GA)	2 Check the A circuit Fuse 20 (15A) in the Power Distribution Box. • Is the fuse OK? → **Yes** GO to **A2**. → **No** REPLACE the Fuse Link (18GA). TEST the system for normal operation.
A2 CHECK CIRCUIT 38 (BK/O)	
1	1 Measure the voltage between the B+ terminal at the generator Circuit 38 (BK/O) and ground. • Is the voltage equal to battery positive voltage (B+)? → **Yes** GO to **A3**. → **No** REPAIR Circuit 38 (BK/O). TEST the system for normal operation.

FM1129700168010X

Fig. 4 Test A: Charging System Warning Indicator Is On w/The Engine Running (Battery Voltage Does Not Increase, Part 1 of 3). Mark VIII

TEST CONDITIONS	TEST DETAILS/RESULTS/ACTIONS
B1 CHECK GENERATOR CONNECTOR C154	
1 Generator Connector C154	
	2 Check generator connector C154 for bent, or damaged pins. • Is the connector OK? → **Yes** GO to **B2**. → **No** REPAIR connector C154 as necessary. TEST the system for normal operation.

FM1129700169010X

Fig. 5 Test B: Charging System Warning Indicator Is Off w/Ignition In Run & Engine Off (Battery Voltage Does Not Increase, Part 1 of 2). Mark VIII

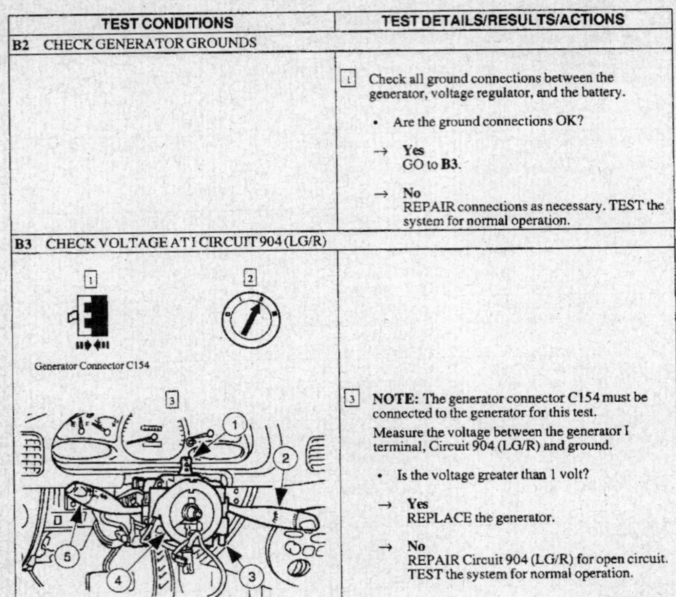

TEST CONDITIONS	TEST DETAILS/RESULTS/ACTIONS
B2 CHECK GENERATOR GROUNDS	
	1 Check all ground connections between the generator, voltage regulator, and the battery. • Are the ground connections OK? → **Yes** GO to **B3**. → **No** REPAIR connections as necessary. TEST the system for normal operation.
B3 CHECK VOLTAGE AT I CIRCUIT 904 (LG/R)	
1 2 Generator Connector C154 3	3 **NOTE:** The generator connector C154 must be connected to the generator for this test. Measure the voltage between the generator I terminal, Circuit 904 (LG/R) and ground. • Is the voltage greater than 1 volt? → **Yes** REPLACE the generator. → **No** REPAIR Circuit 904 (LG/R) for open circuit. TEST the system for normal operation.

FM1129700169020X

Fig. 5 Test B: Charging System Warning Indicator Is Off w/Ignition In Run & Engine Off (Battery Voltage Does Not Increase, Part 2 of 2). Mark VIII

TEST CONDITIONS	TEST DETAILS/RESULTS/ACTIONS
C3 CHECK WARNING INDICATOR OPERATION	
1 2 3 Generator Connector C154	4 With the engine running at idle, check the Warning Indicator. • Is the Warning Indicator on? → **Yes** REPAIR connector C154, I circuit 904 (LG/R) as necessary. TEST the system for normal operation. → **No** GO to Pinpoint Test D.

FM1129700170020X

Fig. 6 Test C: Charging System Warning Indicator Is On w/Engine Running & Battery Voltage Increases (Part 2 of 2). Mark VIII

TEST CONDITIONS	TEST DETAILS/RESULTS/ACTIONS
D1 CHECK CHARGING SYSTEM WARNING INDICATOR OPERATION	
1 2 Generator Connector C154 3	3 Ground the generator connector C154 I circuit with the key ON and the engine OFF. • Is the warning indicator on? → **Yes** REPLACE the generator. TEST the system for normal operation. → **No** REPAIR connector C154 I circuit 904 (LG/R) as necessary. TEST the system for normal operation.

FM1129700171000X

Fig. 7 Test D: Charging System Warning Indicator Is Off w/Ignition In Run & Engine Off (Battery Voltage Increases). Mark VIII

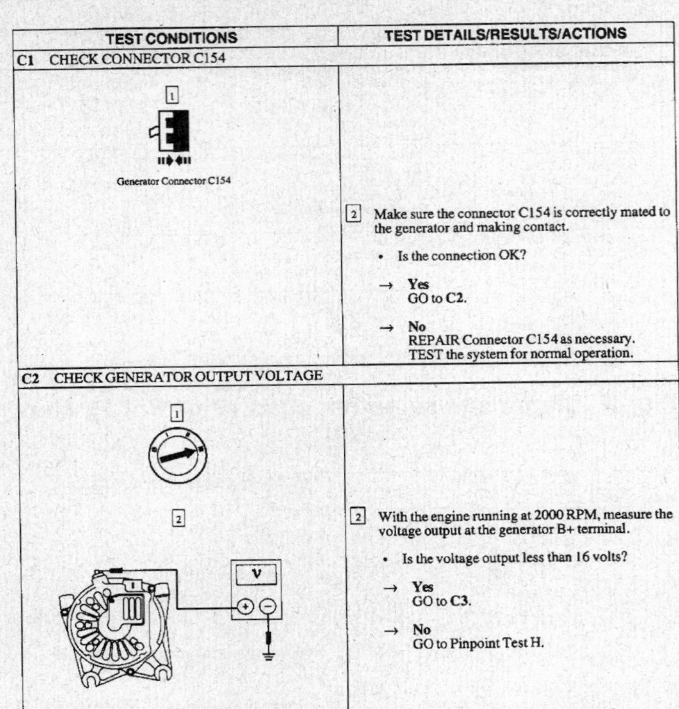

TEST CONDITIONS	TEST DETAILS/RESULTS/ACTIONS
C1 CHECK CONNECTOR C154	
1 Generator Connector C154	2 Make sure the connector C154 is correctly mated to the generator and making contact. • Is the connection OK? → **Yes** GO to **C2**. → **No** REPAIR Connector C154 as necessary. TEST the system for normal operation.
C2 CHECK GENERATOR OUTPUT VOLTAGE	
1 2	2 With the engine running at 2000 RPM, measure the voltage output at the generator B+ terminal. • Is the voltage output less than 16 volts? → **Yes** GO to **C3**. → **No** GO to Pinpoint Test H.

FM1129700170010X

Fig. 6 Test C: Charging System Warning Indicator Is On w/Engine Running & Battery Voltage Increases (Part 1 of 2). Mark VIII

TEST CONDITIONS	TEST DETAILS/RESULTS/ACTIONS
E1 CHECK CIRCUIT 38 (BK/O) VOLTAGE	
1 2	2 Check for voltage at generator B+ connector with the key ON and the engine OFF. • Is the voltage equal to battery positive voltage (B+)? → **Yes** GO to **E2**. → **No** SERVICE Circuit 38 (BK/O) as necessary. TEST the system for normal operation.
E2 CHECK GENERATOR CONNECTORS	
1 Generator Connector C154	2 Check the battery and generator connector C154 for corrosion and tightness. • Are the connectors clean and tight? → **Yes** Diagnose system. → **No** SERVICE the connectors as necessary. TEST the system for normal operation.

FM1129700172000X

Fig. 8 Test E: Charging System Warning indicator Operates Properly But Battery Voltage Does Not Increase. Mark VIII

TEST CONDITIONS	TEST DETAILS/RESULTS/ACTIONS
F1 CHECK BATTERY DRAIN	
1	2 Make sure that all interior lights and switches are off and all doors are closed. Perform batterv drain test • Is the drain greater than 0.5 amps? → **Yes** GO to Component Tests—Battery—Drain Testing → **No** GO to **F2**.
F2 CHECK GENERATOR OUTPUT	
	1 Check generator output. • Is the generator OK? → **Yes** GO to **F3**. → **No** REPLACE the generator. TEST the system for normal operation.
F3 CHECK BATTERY CONDITION	
	1 Check the battery capacity. • Is the battery OK? → **Yes** GO to **F4**. → **No** REPLACE the battery. TEST the system for normal operation.

FM1129700173010X

Fig. 9 Test F: Battery Dead Or Will Not Stay Charged Or Low Battery Or Alternator Voltage (Part 1 of 2). Mark VIII

TEST CONDITIONS	TEST DETAILS/RESULTS/ACTIONS
G2 CHECK FIELD CIRCUIT	
1 2	2 Using an insulated probe measure voltage at test point F at rear of generator. • Is the voltage equal to battery voltage? → **Yes** GO to **G3**. → **No** REPLACE generator. TEST the system for normal operation.
G3 CHECK THE WARNING SYSTEM INDICATOR OPERATION	
1	2 With the engine running, increase engine speed. Check the indicator operation and for battery voltage increase. • Does the voltage increase above 15 volts or the indicator flicker? → **Yes** SERVICE Circuit 36 (Y/W) or Circuit 904 (LG/R) as necessary. TEST the system for normal operation. → **No** REPLACE the generator. TEST the system for normal operation.

FM1129700174020X

Fig. 10 Test G: Charging System Warning Indicator Flickers (Part 2 of 2). Mark VIII

TEST CONDITIONS	TEST DETAILS/RESULTS/ACTIONS
F4 CHECK OTHER SYSTEMS FOR DRAINS	
	1 Check for drains from electronic modules. • Are electronic modules OK? → **Yes** RECHARGE the battery. TEST the system for normal operation. → **No** REPLACE the defective module as necessary. TEST the system for normal operation.

FM1129700173020X

Fig. 9 Test F: Battery Dead Or Will Not Stay Charged Or Low Battery Or Alternator Voltage (Part 2 of 2). Mark VIII

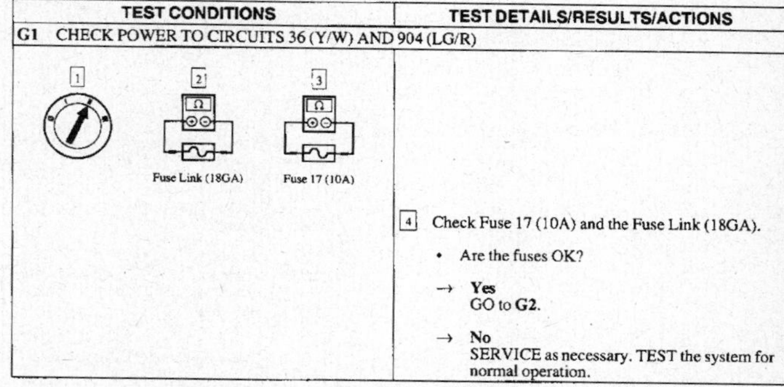

TEST CONDITIONS	TEST DETAILS/RESULTS/ACTIONS
G1 CHECK POWER TO CIRCUITS 36 (Y/W) AND 904 (LG/R)	
1 2 3 Fuse Link (18GA) Fuse 17 (10A)	4 Check Fuse 17 (10A) and the Fuse Link (18GA). • Are the fuses OK? → **Yes** GO to **G2**. → **No** SERVICE as necessary. TEST the system for normal operation.

FM1129700174010X

Fig. 10 Test G: Charging System Warning Indicator Flickers (Part 1 of 2). Mark VIII

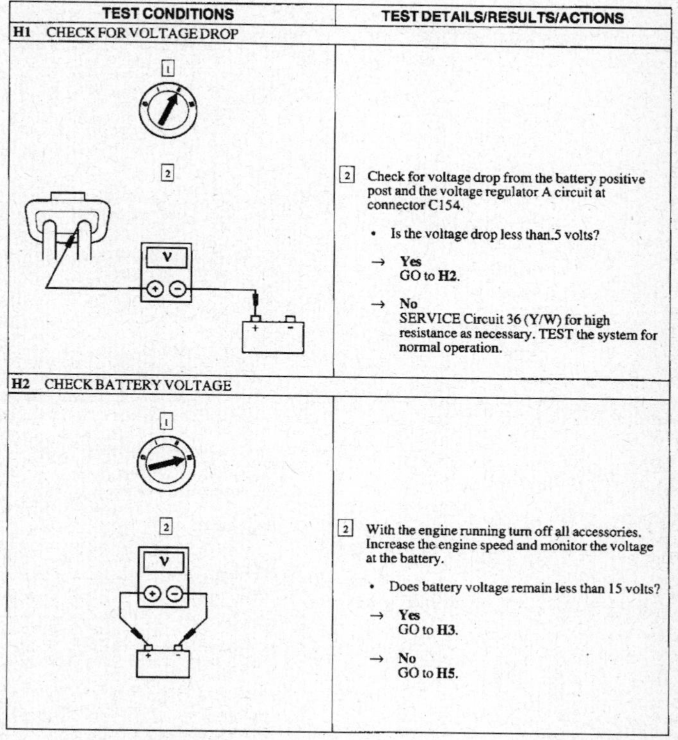

TEST CONDITIONS	TEST DETAILS/RESULTS/ACTIONS
H1 CHECK FOR VOLTAGE DROP	
1 2	2 Check for voltage drop from the battery positive post and the voltage regulator A circuit at connector C154. • Is the voltage drop less than.5 volts? → **Yes** GO to **H2**. → **No** SERVICE Circuit 36 (Y/W) for high resistance as necessary. TEST the system for normal operation.
H2 CHECK BATTERY VOLTAGE	
1 2	2 With the engine running turn off all accessories. Increase the engine speed and monitor the voltage at the battery. • Does battery voltage remain less than 15 volts? → **Yes** GO to **H3**. → **No** GO to **H5**.

FM1129700175010X

Fig. 11 Test H: System Overcharges (Battery Voltage Greater Than 15.5 Volts, Part 1 of 3). Mark VIII

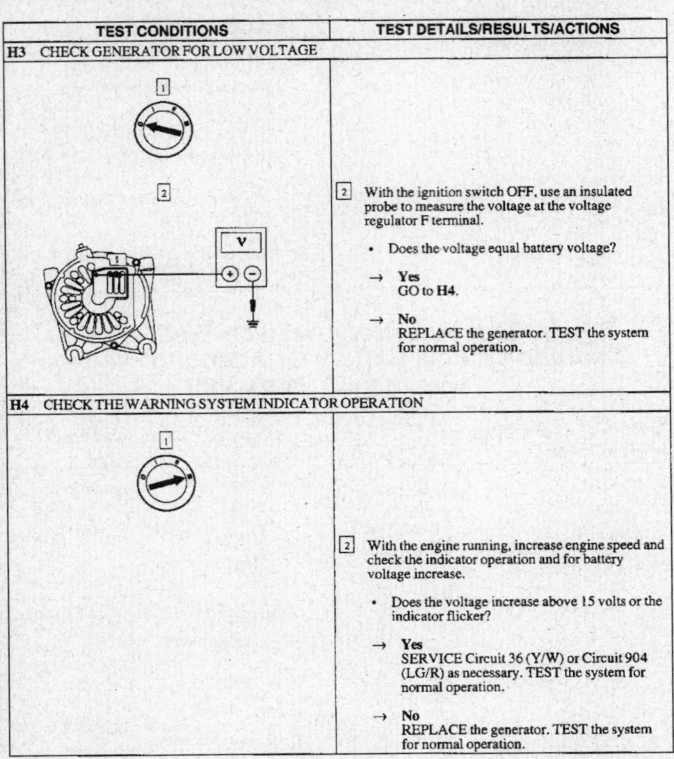

TEST CONDITIONS	TEST DETAILS/RESULTS/ACTIONS
H3 CHECK GENERATOR FOR LOW VOLTAGE	
1	
2	2 With the ignition switch OFF, use an insulated probe to measure the voltage at the voltage regulator F terminal. • Does the voltage equal battery voltage? → **Yes** GO to **H4**. → **No** REPLACE the generator. TEST the system for normal operation.
H4 CHECK THE WARNING SYSTEM INDICATOR OPERATION	
1	
	2 With the engine running, increase engine speed and check the indicator operation and for battery voltage increase. • Does the voltage increase above 15 volts or the indicator flicker? → **Yes** SERVICE Circuit 36 (Y/W) or Circuit 904 (LG/R) as necessary. TEST the system for normal operation. → **No** REPLACE the generator. TEST the system for normal operation.

FM1129700175020X

Fig. 11 Test H: System Overcharges (Battery Voltage Greater Than 15.5 Volts, Part 2 of 3). Mark VIII

TEST CONDITIONS	TEST DETAILS/RESULTS/ACTIONS
J2 CHECK CHARGING SYSTEM FOR OVERCHARGING	
1	
2	2 With the engine running turn off all accessories. Increase the engine speed and monitor the voltage at the battery. • Does battery voltage increase more than 15 volts? → **Yes** GO to Pinpoint Test H. → **No** GO to **J3**.
J3 CHECK BATTERY MOUNTING	
	1 Make sure the battery is properly mounted and level in the battery tray. • Is the battery properly mounted? → **Yes** GO to **J4**. → **No** SERVICE as necessary. TEST the system for normal operation.
J4 CHECK FOR BATTERY CONTACT	
	1 Make sure that there are no fasteners or other parts contacting the battery case causing excess pressure. • Is there anything contacting the battery case? → **Yes** SERVICE as necessary. TEST the system for normal operation. → **No** GO to **J5**.

FM1129700176020X

Fig. 12 Test J: Battery Leakage Or Damage (Part 2 of 3). Mark VIII

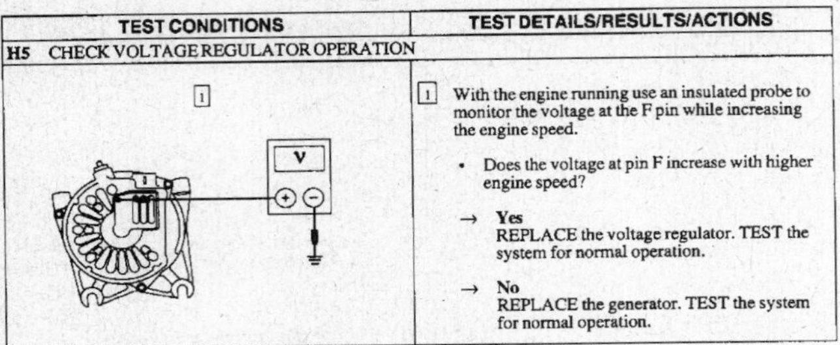

TEST CONDITIONS	TEST DETAILS/RESULTS/ACTIONS
H5 CHECK VOLTAGE REGULATOR OPERATION	
1	1 With the engine running use an insulated probe to monitor the voltage at the F pin while increasing the engine speed. • Does the voltage at pin F increase with higher engine speed? → **Yes** REPLACE the voltage regulator. TEST the system for normal operation. → **No** REPLACE the generator. TEST the system for normal operation.

FM1129700175030X

Fig. 11 Test H: System Overcharges (Battery Voltage Greater Than 15.5 Volts, Part 3 of 3). Mark VIII

TEST CONDITIONS	TEST DETAILS/RESULTS/ACTIONS
J1 CHECK FOR ACID LEAKAGE DAMAGE	
	1 Check for acid damage to vehicle harnesses and to the body. • Is there acid damage? → **Yes** SERVICE damaged areas as necessary. → **No** GO to **J2**.

FM1129700176010X

Fig. 12 Test J: Battery Leakage Or Damage (Part 1 of 3). Mark VIII

TEST CONDITIONS	TEST DETAILS/RESULTS/ACTIONS
J5 CHECK BATTERY CASE FOR DAMAGE	
	1 Check the battery case for defects such as cracks, or poor seals. • Is the battery OK? → **Yes** System is OK. TEST the system for normal operation. → **No** REPLACE the battery. TEST the system for normal operation.

FM1129700176030X

Fig. 12 Test J: Battery Leakage Or Damage (Part 3 of 3). Mark VIII

TEST CONDITIONS	TEST DETAILS/RESULTS/ACTIONS
K1 CHECK BATTERY VOLTAGE	
1	
2	2 With the engine running turn off all accessories. Increase the engine speed and monitor the voltage at the battery. • Is the battery voltage more than 15 volts? → **Yes** GO to Pinpoint Test H. → **No** GO to **K2**.

FM1129700177010X

Fig. 13 Test K: Voltage Gauge Reads High Or Low (Part 1 of 2). Mark VIII

TEST CONDITIONS	TEST DETAILS/RESULTS/ACTIONS
K2 CHECK VOLTAGE GAUGE OPERATION	
1	1 With the engine running monitor the voltage gauge reading and the battery voltage. • Are the voltage readings consistent? → **Yes** System is operating normally. → **No** Diagnose instrument cluster.

FM1129700177020X

Fig. 13 Test K: Voltage Gauge Reads High Or Low (Part 2 of 2). Mark VIII

TEST CONDITIONS	TEST DETAILS/RESULTS/ACTIONS
L1 CHECK FOR ACCESSORY DRIVE NOISE	
	[1] Check the drive belt to make sure it is properly installed and aligned. • Is the drive belt OK? → **Yes** GO to **L2**. → **No** SERVICE the accessory drive system as required. TEST the system for normal operation.
L2 CHECK THE GENERATOR MOUNTING	
	[1] Check the generator and the generator mounting brackets for loose bolts or misalignment. • Is the generator mounted correctly? → **Yes** REPLACE the generator. TEST the system for normal operation. → **No** INSTALL the generator to specifications. TEST the system for normal operation.

FM1129700178000X

Fig. 14 Test L: Alternator Is Noisy. Mark VIII

TEST CONDITIONS	TEST DETAILS/RESULTS/ACTIONS
M1 CHECK FOR RADIO INTERFERENCE	
[1] 	
	[2] Tune the radio to a station where the interference is present.
[3]  Generator Connector C154	
	• Is the interference present with the generator connector C154 disconnected? → **Yes** find the cause of the radio interference. TEST the system for normal operation. → **No** REPLACE the generator. TEST the system for normal operation.

FM1129700179000X

Fig. 15 Test M: Radio Interference. Mark VIII

Year	Amp Rating	Min. Amps @ 2000
MARK VIII		
1998	130	87

Fig. 16 Total alternator output specifications

ALTERNATOR SPECIFICATIONS

Model	Year	Model	Amp Rating
Mark VIII	1998	F6LU-CA	130

STEERING COLUMNS

NOTE: On Air Bag Equipped Models, Refer To "Air Bag System Precautions" Located In The Front Of This Manual For System Disarming & Arming Procedures.

NOTE: Refer To "Computer Relearn Procedures" Located In The Front Of This Manual When Battery Power To The Computer Has Been Interrupted.

NOTE: Models Equipped With "Automatic Ride Control System" Utilize A Steering Sensor Located On The Steering Column Assembly. For Sensor Replacement, Refer To "Automatic Ride Control System" In The "Active Suspension" Section.

INDEX

PRECAUTIONS

AIR BAG SYSTEMS

Refer to "Air Bag System Precautions" in the front of this manual for system disarming and arming procedures.

BATTERY GROUND CABLE

Prior to service, disconnect battery ground cable and isolate as required. Allow one minute for back-up power supply to be depleted.

DESCRIPTION

The steering column used on models equipped with air bags is of a modular construction and features easy to service electrical switches. The washer/wiper switch and the combination turn signal/hazard/horn/flash-to-pass/dimmer switch are attached with self-tapping screws.

These models are equipped with either a brush type or a clockspring type slip ring. Removal and installation procedures for the two types are the same except where noted.

Fasteners used on steering column components must be replaced after removal. The fasteners are coated with an epoxy adhesive and cannot be used again.

Whenever the steering column is removed or is separated from the steering gear, the steering column must be in locked position to prevent the steering wheel from being rotated accidentally and damaging the air bag slip ring.

The Thunderbird and Lincoln LS models are equipped with a power tilt/telescopic steering column of modular construction. It has easy-to-service electrical switches. This column is equipped with an electric tilt and telescopic mechanism that allows the steering wheel angle and length to be adjusted to suit the driver.

On models equipped with the memory package, the steering wheel position is stored in memory the same way as driver seat position and retrieved as a personality feature. The steering column is controlled by the instrument cluster module.

STEERING COLUMN

REPLACE

CONTINENTAL

1. Ensure wheels are in straight-ahead position.
2. Remove steering wheel as outlined in "Electrical" section of "Continental, Mark VIII & Town Car" chapter.
3. Remove instrument panel lower trim cover and air bag sliding contact as outlined in "Passive Restraint Systems" chapter.
4. Remove tilt wheel handle and shank by unscrewing it from column and removing mounting screws.
5. Rotate ignition switch lock cylinder to run position, press lock cylinder retaining pin through access hole and remove lock cylinder.
6. Remove four upper and lower steering column shrouds.
7. Remove instrument panel reinforcement brace.
8. Disconnect shift cable and bracket from steering column, then the transaxle shift cable loop from shift tube hook.
9. Remove multi-function switch mounting screws, then position switch aside.
10. Remove ignition switch mounting screw and disconnect wiring.
11. Remove front mounting nuts and steering column impact absorber.
12. Remove steering column lower yoke pinch bolt.
13. Remove and discard rear column mounting nuts, then carefully lower and support the column.
14. Disconnect parking brake release vacuum hose extensions at parking brake release switch or remove vacuum release assembly.
15. Disconnect shift cable and bracket from selector lever pivot.
16. Remove shift cable and bracket from lower column mounting.
17. Remove shift lock actuator mounting screws and shift lock actuator.
18. Reverse procedure to install.

CONTOUR & MYSTIQUE

Do not remove steering wheel and driver's air bag module as an assembly unless the column is locked or the steering column gear input shaft coupling is secured to keep it from turning. This will avoid damage to the air bag sliding contact assembly.

1. Ensure wheels are in straight-ahead position.
2. Remove steering column opening finish panel.

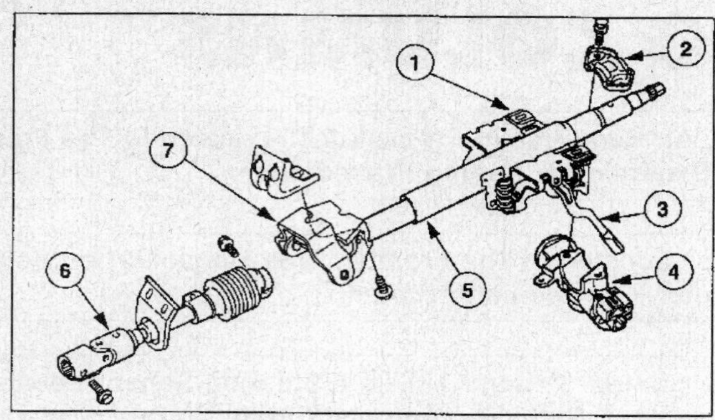

Item	Description
1	Steering Column Upper Mounting Bracket
2	Ignition Switch Lock Cylinder Bracket
3	Tilt Lever (If Equipped)
4	Lock Cylinder
5	Steering Column
6	Steering Column Intermediate Shaft Coupling
7	Steering Column Support Bracket

FM6049700096000X

Fig. 1 Exploded view of steering column. Escort, Tracer, ZX2 & 2001 Focus

3. Remove upper and lower steering column shrouds.
4. Remove and discard pinch bolt at lower steering column shaft, then disengage shaft from steering gear.
5. Disconnect steering column switches' wiring harness electrical connectors.
6. Remove mounting bolts, then lower and remove steering column.
7. Reverse procedure to install.

COUGAR

1. Remove driver's side instrument panel lower cover.
2. Center and lock steering wheel.
3. Remove steering column upper and lower shrouds.
4. Disconnect flexible coupling. Discard pinch bolt.
5. Disconnect electrical connectors on righthand and lefthand sides of steering column.
6. Cut cable tie and disconnect air bag control module electrical connector.
7. Unclip wiring harnesses, unbolt steering column and slide outwards to disengage retaining tab.
8. Reverse procedure to install.

CROWN VICTORIA, GRAND MARQUIS & TOWN CAR

1. Ensure wheels are in straight-ahead position.
2. Remove air bag sliding contact.
3. Disconnect multi-function switch electrical connectors.
4. Remove mounting screws and multi-function switch.
5. Remove instrument panel reinforcement brace.
6. Disconnect ignition switch electrical connector.
7. Disconnect brake shift interlock solenoid connector.
8. Remove passive anti-theft system (PATS) sensor ring.
9. Disconnect, then remove shift cable and bracket from steering column.
10. Remove and discard lower steering column shaft pinch bolt.
11. Disconnect lower steering column shaft from steering column lower yoke.
12. Remove and discard steering column mounting nuts, then lower the steering column to floor.
13. Disconnect parking brake release vacuum hose extension from parking brake release switch.
14. Disconnect and position shift cable and bracket aside.
15. Remove steering column.
16. Reverse procedure to install.

ESCORT, TRACER & ZX2

1. Remove steering wheel as outlined in "Electrical" section of appropriate chassis chapter.
2. Remove mounting screws, then the upper and lower steering column shrouds.
3. Loosen mounting nut, then remove hood latch control handle and cable. Position aside.
4. Remove mounting screws and release instrument panel steering column cover.
5. Disconnect headlamp switch electrical connector and remove instrument panel steering column cover.
6. Disconnect steering column electrical connectors and remove retainer plate.
7. Remove mounting bolts and lower steering column tube.
8. Remove steering column input shaft coupling to steering gear input shaft pinch bolt. Discard bolt.
9. Remove steering column support bracket mounting nuts, then the column.
10. Reverse procedure to install.

FOCUS

1. Ensure wheels are in straight-ahead position.
2. Remove ignition key.
3. Remove mounting screws, release fastener and disconnect instrument panel lower panel.
4. Disconnect hood release cable and data link electrical connector, then remove instrument panel lower panel.
5. Remove steering column upper shroud using suitable thin bladed screwdriver to release clips on each side.
6. Release steering column locking lever, then remove mounting screws and steering column lower shroud.
7. Disconnect passive anti-theft system (PATS) transceiver, wiper/washer switch and air bag sliding contact/ speed control on the righthand side of steering column.
8. Disconnect ignition switch and turn signal/flash-to-pass switch electrical connectors on lefthand side of steering column.
9. Disconnect steering column wiring harness by releasing locating pin.
10. Remove mounting bolt and disconnect steering column shaft from steering gear pinion extension.
11. Remove mounting bolts and steering column.
12. Reverse procedure to install.

LS & THUNDERBIRD

1. Ensure wheels are in straight-ahead position.
2. Remove driver's air bag module and air bag sliding contact as outlined in "Passive Restraint Systems" section.
3. Remove steering wheel as outlined in "Electrical" section of "LS" chapter.
4. Remove steering column shaft pinch bolt and separate intermediate shaft from steering column yoke. Discard pinch bolt.
5. Disconnect electronic steering sensor and steering column release motor electrical connectors.
6. **On models equipped with automatic transmission,** remove and discard locknuts while supporting steering column.
7. **On models equipped with manual transmission,** remove and discard locknuts while supporting steering column. Lower the steering column and disconnect lock actuator electrical connector.
8. **On all models,** remove steering column.
9. Reverse procedure to install.

MARK VIII

1. Remove driver's air bag module and air bag sliding contact as outlined in "Passive Restraint Systems" section.
2. Remove steering wheel as outlined in "Electrical" section of "Continental, Mark VIII & Town Car" chapter.
3. Remove lower instrument panel insulator mounting screws and courtesy lamp, then position aside.

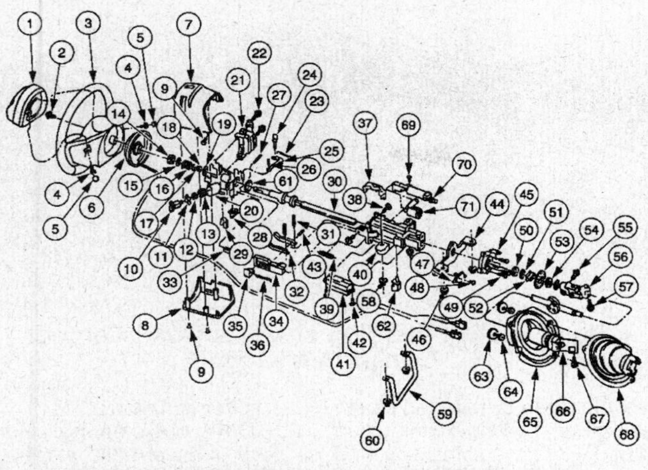

Item	Part Number	Description
1	043B13	Driver Air Bag Module
2	N804385-S100	Steering Wheel Bolt
3	3600	Steering Wheel
4	N808324-S424	Air Bag Module Retaining Screws
5	3L518	Steering Wheel Spoke Cover
6	14A664	Air Bag Sliding Contact – Assy
7	3530	Steering Column Shroud – (Upper)
8	3530	Steering Column Shroud – (Lower)
9	55929	Shroud Retaining Screws
10	11582	Ignition Switch Lock Cylinder
11	3C610	Bearing Retainer
12	3E700	Steering Column Lock Housing Bearing
13	3E717	Steering Column Lock Gear
14	13318	Turn Indicator Cancel Cam
15	3C610	Snap Ring
16	3520	Steering Column Upper Bearing Spring
17	3518	Steering Column Bearing Sleeve

FM6049900123010X

Fig. 2 Exploded view of steering column (Part 1 of 3). Continental

Item	Part Number	Description
18	3L539	Steering Column Bearing Tolerance Ring
19	3517	Steering Column Bearing – (Small)
20	3511	Steering Column Lock Cylinder Housing
21	13K359	Multi-Function Switch
22	390345-S36	Screws
23	3D655	Steering Column Position Spring
24	3F609	Tilt Wheel Handle and Shank
25	3D544	Steering Column Release Lever
26	N805857	Steering Column Lock Actuator Lever Pin
27	N806157	Pin-Lock Cam Pivot
28	3E695	Steering Column Lock Cam
29	14A163	Wiring Harness Retainer – (Upper)
30	3524	Steering Shaft Assy
31	3B664	Steering Column Locking Lever Spring
32	3B661 (RH), 3D653 (LH)	Steering Column Locking Lever
33	3E715	Steering Column Lock Lever Actuator – (Upper)
34	3E715	Steering Column Lock Lever Actuator – (Lower)
35	3E691	Steering Column Lock Pawl – (Shaft)
36	3E696	Steering Column Lock Spring – (Shaft)
37	14A099	Wiring Shield
38	N806582	Tilt Pivot Screws
39	3D655	Steering Column Position Spring
40	3F723	Steering Actuator Housing
41	11572	Ignition Switch
42	N805858	Screws
43	3F530	Steering Column Lock Actuator Lever Pin
44	3668	Steering Column Lower Mounting Bracket
45	3D681	Steering Column Lower Bearing Retainer
46	N806423-S56	Column Mounting Nuts
47	14A206	Wire Connector Bracket
48	N804409	Screw
49	N805859	Lower Bearing Housing Retaining Screws
50	3518	Steering Column Bearing Sleeve – (Lower)
51	3517	Steering Column Bearing – (Lower)
52	3L539	Steering Column Bearing Tolerance Ring
53	3C131	Suspension Height Sensor Control Ring

FM6049900123020X

Fig. 2 Exploded view of steering column (Part 2 of 3). Continental

4. Remove mounting screws and position steering column cover aside.
5. Remove instrument panel reinforcement to instrument panel mounting bolts, then position reinforcement aside.
6. Remove air conditioning duct and disconnect junction box electrical connectors.
7. Disconnect electrical connector at bottom of steering column.
8. Remove steering column lower yoke pinch bolt.
9. Slide intermediate shaft into lower steering shaft.
10. While supporting steering column, remove and discard steering column mounting nuts.
11. Remove steering column.
12. Reverse procedure to install.

MUSTANG

1. Remove steering wheel as outlined in "Electrical" section of "Mustang" chapter.
2. Remove steering column lower yoke to lower steering column shaft mounting bolt.
3. Remove ignition switch lock cylinder as outlined in "Electrical" section of "Mustang" chapter.
4. Remove steering column opening cover, reinforcement and instrument panel cross brace.
5. Remove upper and lower steering column shrouds.
6. Disconnect ignition switch and key warning buzzer electrical connectors.
7. Remove multi-function switch mounting screws and position aside.
8. Remove nuts mounting steering shaft tube boot to dash panel.
9. Remove steering column to instrument panel mounting nuts and lower column to clear mounting bolts.
10. **On models equipped with automatic transmission,** remove ignition/shifter interlock cable.
11. **On all models,** remove steering column.
12. Reverse procedure to install.

SABLE & TAURUS

Do not remove steering wheel or air bag module as an assembly unless the column is locked or the steering column gear input shaft coupling is secured to keep it from turning. This will avoid damage to the air bag sliding contact assembly.

1. Ensure wheels are in straight-ahead position.
2. Remove steering wheel as outlined in "Electrical" section of "Sable & Taurus" chapter.
3. Remove steering column intermediate shaft coupling to steering column lower yoke mounting bolt.
4. Remove lower instrument panel steering column cover.
5. Push in on release pin by inserting suitable tool into access hole located in bottom of lower steering column

54	3520	Steering Column Upper Bearing Spring
55	N803942-S100	Bolt — Flange Yoke
56	3N725	Steering Column Lower Yoke
57	N803942	Bolt
58	N806423-S56	Upper Column Mounting Nuts
59	3E644	Steering Column Absorber
60	N801555	Nuts
61	3517	Steering Column Bearing — (Large)
62	14A163	Wiring Harness Retainer — (Lower)
63	N804326	Nut (2 Req'd)
64	N804795-S2	Nut (3 Req'd)
65	3513	Steering Column Opening Weather Seal
66	3A525	Steering Column Intermediate Shaft Coupling
67	N806349-S100	Bolt
68	3513	Steering Column Opening Weather Seal — (Secondary)
69	N806038-S2	Screw
70	3F719	Ignition/Shifter Interlock Cable
71	7H178	Bracket

FM6049900123030X

Fig. 2 Exploded view of steering column (Part 3 of 3). Continental

shroud, then rotate ignition cylinder clockwise to Run position and remove cylinder.

6. Remove lower and upper steering column shrouds.
7. Remove PATS transmitter retaining screws, then position transmitter aside.
8. **On models equipped with column shift,** unsnap and slide shift control selector lever boot toward end of control lever. Remove control lever by removing retaining pin.
9. **On models equipped with overdrive lock-out switch on column lever,** disconnect wiring connector at bottom of steering column and remove wiring from column with control lever.
10. **On all models,** disconnect wiring connectors for ignition switch, horn, speed control, interlock switch and air bag module.
11. Remove mounting screws and position multi-function switch aside.
12. Remove shift indicator cable from shifter tube.
13. Remove shifter indicator retainer mounting screw from column adjustment cable.
14. Remove nuts securing steering column to instrument panel support bracket and carefully lower steering column.
15. **On models equipped with console shift,** disconnect BTSI electrical connector.
16. **On all models,** remove steering column.
17. Reverse procedure to install. Adjust shift indicator cable as required.

STEERING COLUMN SERVICE

ESCORT, TRACER, ZX2 & 2001 FOCUS

The steering column is serviced as a unit. If service other than the air bag clockspring, combination switch or ignition switch assembly is required, the steering column must be replaced, **Fig. 1.**

CONTINENTAL

1. Remove steering column as outlined under "Steering Column, Replace."
2. **Record steering column lock gear, bearing and retainer position prior to removal.**
3. Remove bearing retainer, lock housing bearing and lock gear, **Fig. 2.**
4. Disconnect electrical connector, then remove screws and shock absorber electronic steering sensor.
5. Remove steering column lower bearing spring and sensor ring.
6. Remove steering column bearing tolerance ring from column shaft.
7. Remove mounting bolts and ignition switch.
8. Remove lock cylinder housing pivot screws.
9. **Steering column position spring is under tension and may come out with great force.**
10. Pry up on steering column locking levers using fabricated tool and remove column position spring.
11. Remove turn signal cancel cam and snap ring.
12. Remove steering column upper bearing spring and sleeve.
13. Slide steering column shaft in toward steering column lock cylinder housing and out.
14. Slide steering column bearing tolerance ring off steering column shaft.
15. Remove column bearing from steering column lock cylinder housing using suitable punch, .
16. Remove mounting screws and parking brake release switch.
17. Remove mounting bolts, brake shift interlock solenoid.
18. Remove mounting bolts, clamps and shift tube.
19. Remove mounting bolts, transaxle selector lever arm and support.
20. Remove gearshift selector tube spring and drive out shift tube gearshift lever pin.
21. Remove gearshift lever and column shift selector lever plunger. Replace lever plunger if it is bent.
22. Remove gearshift lever socket bushings and transaxle control selector lever spring clip.
23. Drive out steering column lock lever pin and remove steering column lock pawl.
24. Remove lower steering column bearing and sleeve.
25. Remove mounting bolts and steering column lower bearing retainer.
26. Remove upper and lower steering column actuators.
27. Reverse procedure to assemble.

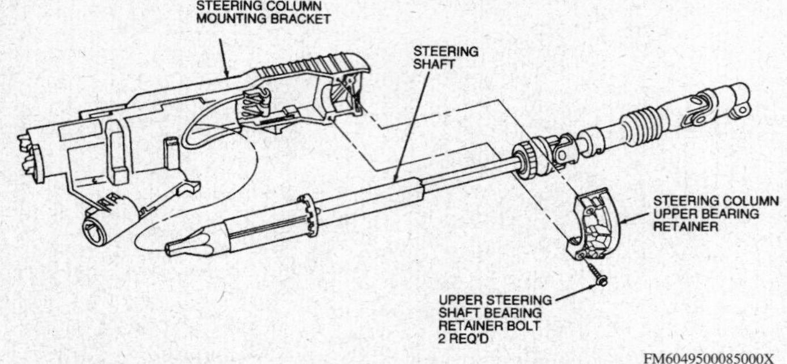

Fig. 3 Lower steering shaft removal. Contour, Cougar & Mystique

CONTOUR & MYSTIQUE

1. Remove mounting screws and air bag module.
2. Disconnect wiring harness connectors for air bag module and speed control.
3. Remove steering wheel mounting bolt.
4. Remove steering wheel. **Do not damage air bag sliding contact harness during removal.**
5. Apply tape across air bag sliding contact stator and rotor to prevent accidental rotation.
6. Remove lock cylinder, ignition switch and combination switch as outlined in "Electrical" section of "Contour, Cougar Mystique" chapter.
7. Remove lower steering shaft bearing retainer, **Fig. 3.**
8. Remove lower steering shaft.
9. Reverse procedure to install.

COUGAR

Refer to "Contour & Mystique."

CROWN VICTORIA, GRAND MARQUIS & TOWN CAR

1. Remove steering column as outlined under "Steering Column, Replace."
2. **Record positions of column lock gear, bearing and retainer prior to removal.**
3. Remove bearing retainer, lock housing bearing and lock gear, **Fig. 4.**
4. Disconnect electrical connector, then remove screws and shock absorber electronic steering sensor.
5. Remove steering column lower bearing spring and sensor ring.
6. Remove steering column bearing tolerance ring from column shaft.
7. Remove mounting bolts and ignition switch.
8. Remove lock cylinder housing pivot screws.
9. **Steering column position spring is under tension and may come out**

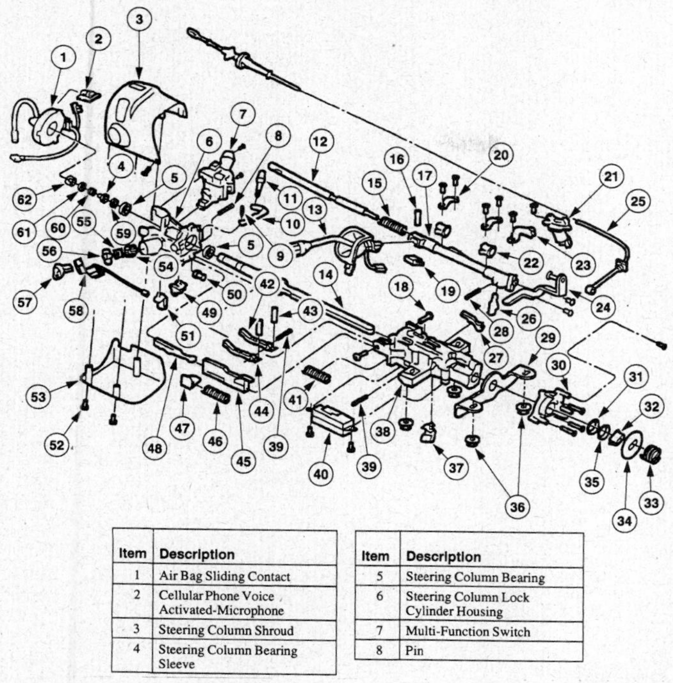

Item	Description
1	Air Bag Sliding Contact
2	Cellular Phone Voice Activated-Microphone
3	Steering Column Shroud
4	Steering Column Bearing Sleeve

Item	Description
5	Steering Column Bearing
6	Steering Column Lock Cylinder Housing
7	Multi-Function Switch
8	Pin

FM6049900124010X

Fig. 4 Exploded view of steering column (Part 1 of 2). Crown Victoria, Grand Marquis & Town Car

Item	Description
9	Steering Column Release Lever Pin
10	Steering Column Release Lever
11	Tilt Wheel Handle and Shank
12	Column Shift Selector Lever Plunger
13	Gearshift Lever
14	Steering Column Shaft
15	Transmission Control Selector Lever Plunger Spring
16	Gearshift Lever Pin
17	Transmission Column Shift Selector Tube
18	Tilt Column Pivot Screw
19	Transmission Control Selector Lever Spring Clip
20	Gearshift Tube Bushing Clamp
21	Brake Shift Interlock Solenoid
22	Gearshift Lever Socket Bushing
23	Transmission Shift Selector Position Insert
24	Transmission Selector Lever Arm and Support
25	Shift Cable and Bracket
26	Gearshift Lever
27	Steering Column Lock Pawl
28	Gearshift Lever Pin
29	Steering Column Instrument Panel Bracket
30	Steering Column Lower Bearing Retainer
31	Steering Column Bearing Sleeve
32	Steering Column Bearing Tolerance Ring
33	Steering Column Bearing Spring
34	Suspension Height Sensor Control Ring

Item	Description
35	Steering Column Bearing
36	Steering Column Retaining Nuts
37	Wiring Harness Retainer
38	Steering Actuator Housing
39	Steering Column Lock Lever Pin
40	Ignition Switch
41	Steering Column Position Spring
42	Steering Column Lock Lever
43	Steering Column Position Lock Spring
44	Steering Column Locking Lever
45	Steering Column Lock Lever Actuator
46	Steering Column Lock Spring
47	Steering Column Lock Pawl
48	Steering Column Lock Actuator
49	Steering Column Lock Cam
50	Steering Column Tilt Flange Bumper
51	Wiring Harness Retainer
52	Shroud Screws
53	Steering Column Shroud
54	Steering Column Lock Gear
55	Steering Column Lock Housing Bearing
56	Bearing Retainer
57	Ignition Switch Lock Cylinder
58	Passive Anti-Theft System (PATS) Sensor Ring
59	Steering Column Bearing Tolerance Ring
60	Steering Column Upper Bearing Spring
61	Bearing Retainer
62	Turn Indicator Cancel Cam

FM6049900124020X

Fig. 4 Exploded view of steering column (Part 2 of 2). Crown Victoria, Grand Marquis & Town Car

with great force.

10. Pry up on steering column locking levers using fabricated tool and remove column position spring.
11. Remove turn signal cancel cam and snap ring.
12. Remove steering column upper bearing spring and sleeve.
13. Slide steering column shaft in toward steering column lock cylinder housing and out.
14. Slide steering column bearing tolerance ring off steering column shaft.
15. Remove column bearing from steering column lock cylinder housing using suitable punch.
16. Remove mounting screws and parking brake release switch.
17. Remove mounting bolts, brake shift interlock solenoid.
18. Remove mounting bolts, clamps and shift tube.
19. Remove mounting bolts, transaxle selector lever arm and support.
20. Remove gearshift selector tube spring and drive out shift tube gearshift lever pin.
21. Remove gearshift lever and column shift selector lever plunger. Replace lever plunger if it is bent.
22. Remove gearshift lever socket bushings and transaxle control selector lever spring clip.
23. Drive out steering column lock lever pin and remove steering column lock pawl.
24. Remove lower steering column bearing and sleeve.
25. Remove mounting bolts and steering column lower bearing retainer.
26. Remove upper and lower steering column actuators.
27. Reverse procedure to assemble.

LS & THUNDERBIRD

DISASSEMBLY

1. Remove steering column as outlined under "Steering Column, Replace."
2. Place steering column in suitable vise.
3. **On models equipped with manual transmission,** proceed as follows:
   a. Remove shear bolts' heads using suitable drill motor with ⅜ inch drill bit.
   b. Remove steering wheel lock actuator. **Do not damage actuator.**
   c. Remove steering column upper shaft assembly shear bolts using suitable locking pliers.
4. **On all models,** remove electronic steering sensor, **Fig. 5.**
5. **Do not telescope steering column manually or by any means except for those outlined in this procedure. Failure to do so can result in damage to steering column potentiometer and actuator. Ensure overtravel of potentiometer does not occur while operating it with battery charger to avoid damage and electrical failures.**
6. Disconnect steering column release motor (telescopic) electrical connector.
7. Connect telescopic release motor electrical terminals using suitable 1 amp 12 volt battery charger and telescope column out until it is fully extended.
8. Connect steering column release motor (telescopic) electrical connector.
9. Replace steering column release motor if it is damaged or inoperable before installing telescoping steering column.
10. **Do not disconnect steering column release motors' harness electrical connectors.**
11. Remove mounting screws and steering column release motors.
12. Remove mounting bolts, steering column outer housing cover plate, outer housing and column track.
13. Remove steering column connector link.
14. Install spring compressor tool No. 211-201 (T97P-3D655-A), or equivalent, on steering column position spring and tighten by hand.
15. Remove spring mounting bolts.
16. Release spring tension using spring compressor tool, then remove spring and tool.
17. Separate front and rear halves of steering column upper shaft and column inner housing. The upper shaft sensor ring and coupler are serviced as an assembly.
18. Remove rear half of steering column upper shaft from support.
19. **Curl strap on steering column actuator (16) must not be bent or altered under any circumstance.**
20. Remove steering column telescopic actuator. Replace steering column telescopic actuator if curl strap is damaged.
21. Remove column track from support and potentiometer.

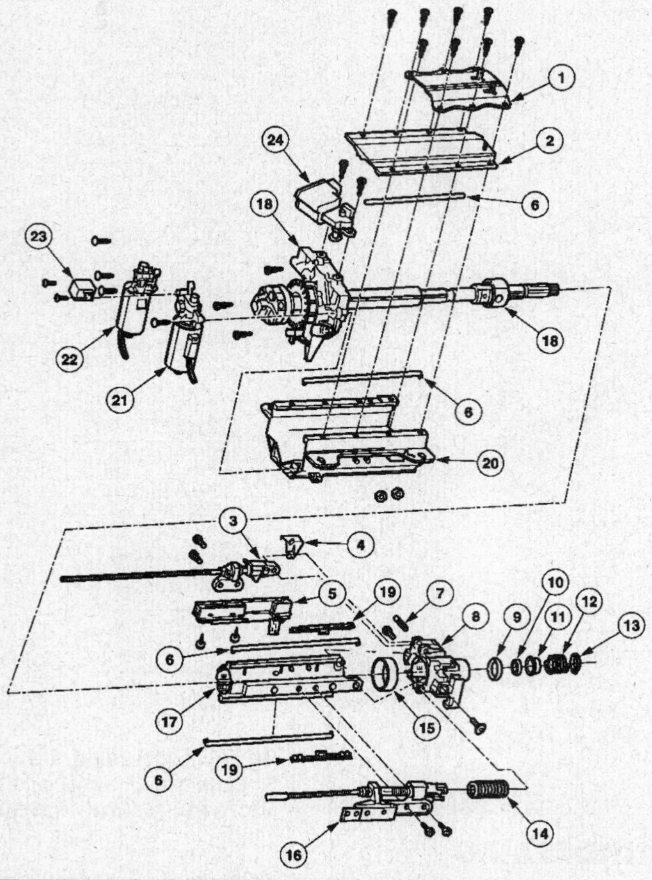

Item	Part Number	Description
1	3F790	Steering column outer housing plate
2	3F789	Steering column outer housing
3	3F797	Steering column actuator assembly (tilt)

FM6049900122010X

Fig. 5 Exploded view of steering column (Part 1 of 2). LS & Thunderbird

Item	Part Number	Description
4	3A517	Steering column connector link
5	14A605	Steering column potentiometer assembly
6	3B628	Steering column track
7	3D545	Steering column release pin
8	3511	Steering column tube flange
9	3517	Steering column tube bearing assembly
10	3L539	Steering column upper bearing tolerance ring
11	3518	Steering column bearing sleeve
12	3520	Steering column upper bearing spring
13	97663	Steering column upper bearing retainer
14	3D655	Steering column position spring
15	3517	Steering column tube bearing assembly
16	3F797	Steering column actuator assembly (telescopic)
17	3F791	Steering column inner housing
18	3524	Steering column upper shaft assembly
19	3F795	Steering column inner track bearing retainer assembly
20	3B718	Steering column support assembly
21	3D538	Steering column release motor assembly (telescopic)
22	3D538	Steering column release motor assembly (tilt)
23	18B015	Steering wheel absorber electronic steering sensor
24	3K772	Steering wheel lock actuator (manual transmission only)

FM6049900122020X

Fig. 5 Exploded view of steering column (Part 2 of 2). LS & Thunderbird

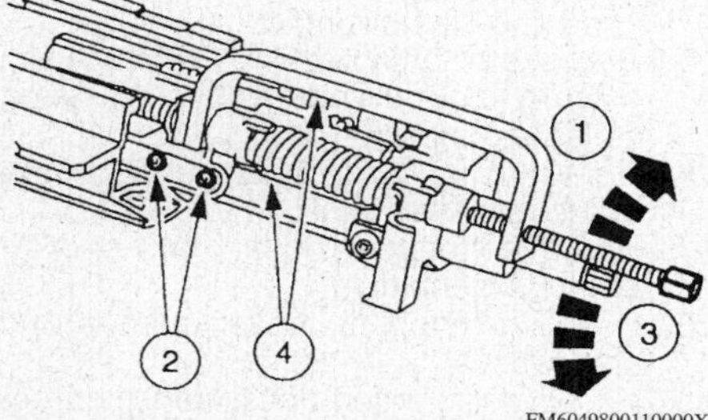

FM6049800110000X

Fig. 6 Tilt spring removal. Mark VIII

22. Remove steering column release pin and place inner housing in suitable vise.
23. Remove steering column tilt actuator , inner track bearing retainers and column tracks.
24. Remove steering column tube flange and column upper bearing retainer.
25. Remove column upper bearing spring and bearing sleeve.
26. Spread out steering column upper bearing tolerance ring using suitable flat blade screwdriver and slide it out of column upper shaft.
27. Remove front half of steering column upper shaft.
28. Drive out small and large steering column tube bearing assemblies using suitable brass drifts.

ASSEMBLY

1. Install large and small steering column tube bearings using suitable bearing installer tools.
2. Slide steering shaft into tilt housing and install steering column upper bearing tolerance ring.
3. Install column bearing sleeve and upper bearing spring.
4. Install steering column upper bearing retainer, tube flange and mounting bolts.
5. Position steering column tilt actuator and install mounting bolts.
6. Install steering column release pin, potentiometer and mounting screws.
7. Install steering column telescopic actuator and mounting nuts.
8. Install steering column track on support. Apply Premium Long-Life Grease part No. XG-1-C, or equivalent, to steering column track bearing surface.
9. **Staging of steering column inner track bearings is critical. They must be installed against rear column inner housing track bearing retaining end. Inner housing must be installed in fully extended (out) position.**
10. Attach steering column tracks and inner track bearings to steering column inner housing.

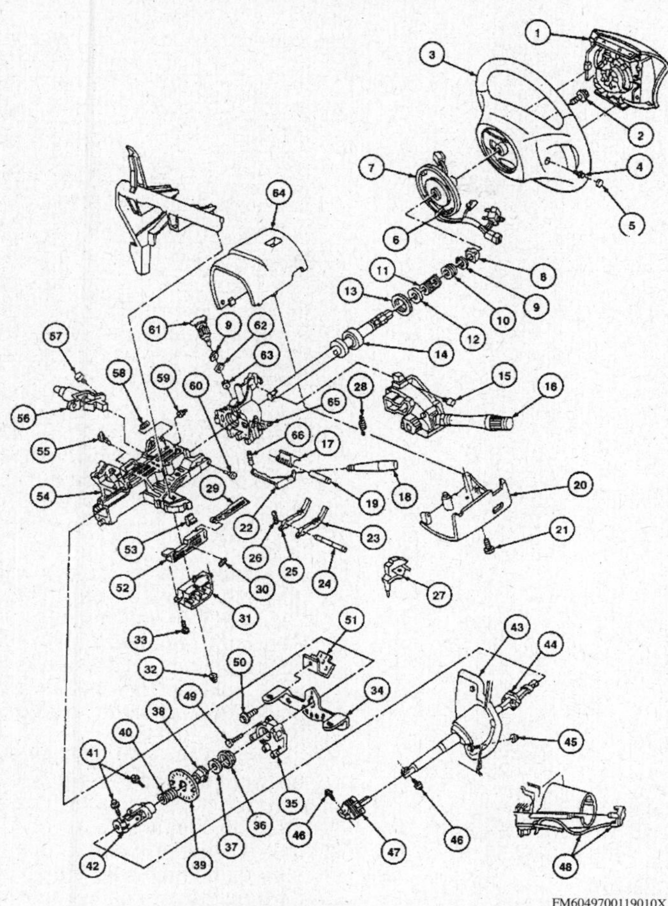

Fig. 7 Exploded view of steering column (Part 1 of 2). Mustang

Item	Description
1	Driver Air Bag Module
2	Steering Wheel Bolt
3	Steering Wheel
4	Air Bag Module Retaining Screws (2 Req'd)
5	Steering Wheel Spoke Cover (2 Req'd)
6	Locking Tabs
7	Air Bag Sliding Contact
8	Turn Indicator Cancel Cam
9	Snap Ring
10	Steering Column Upper Bearing Spring
11	Steering Column Bearing Sleeve (Upper)
12	Steering Column Bearing (Upper)(Small)
13	Steering Column Bearing (Large)
14	Steering Shaft Assy
15	Screw
16	Multi-Function Switch
17	Steering Column Lock Cam
18	Tilt Wheel Handle and Shank
19	Pin - Lock Cam Pivot
20	Steering Column Shroud (Lower)
21	Shroud Retaining Screws
22	Steering Column Release Lever
23	Steering Column Lock RH Lever
24	Steering Column Lock Actuator Lever Pin
25	Steering Column Lock Left Hand Lever
26	Steering Column Locking Lever Spring
27	Wiring Shield
28	Steering Column Position Spring
29	Steering Column Lock Lever Actuator
30	Steering Column Lock Spring (Shaft)
31	Ignition Switch
32	Lower Column Mounting Nuts
33	Screw
34	Steering Column Mounting Bracket
35	Steering Column Lower Bearing Retainer
36	Steering Column Bearing Sleeve
37	Steering Column Bearing (Lower)
38	Steering Column Bearing Tolerance Ring (Lower)
39	Suspension Height Sensor Control Ring
40	Steering Column Upper Bearing Spring
41	Bolt - Flange Yoke
42	Steering Column Lower Yoke
43	Steering Column Tube Boot
44	Lower Steering Column Shaft
45	Nut
46	Bolt
47	Steering Column Intermediate Shaft Coupling
48	Ignition Key Warning Switch Terminal and Wire
49	Lower Bearing Housing Retaining Screw
50	Screw
51	Wire Connector Bracket
52	Steering Column Lock Lever Actuator (Lower)
53	Steering Column Lock Pawl
54	Steering Actuator Housing
55	Steering Column Lock Actuator Cover
56	Ignition / Shifter Interlock Cable
57	Screw
58	Steering Column Position Spring
59	Steering Column Tilt Flange Bumper
60	Tilt Pivot Screws
61	Ignition Switch Lock Cylinder
62	Steering Column Lock Housing Bearing
63	Steering Column Lock Gear
64	Steering Column Shroud (Upper)
65	Steering Column Lock Cylinder Housing
66	Steering Column Lock Actuator Lever Pin

FM6049700119020X

Fig. 7 Exploded view of steering column (Part 2 of 2). Mustang

11. Apply Premium Long-Life Grease to column track bearings and steering column tracks' bearing surface.
12. Install rear half of steering column upper shaft into steering column support and mounting bolts.
13. Join front and rear halves of steering column upper shaft and steering column inner housing in column support housing.
14. Position steering column spring.
15. Compress spring until actuator telescopic assembly bolt using compressor tool No. 211-201 (T97P-3D655-A), or equivalent, until holes align. Install mounting bolts, then remove tool.
16. Install steering column connector link and column track on outer housing. Apply grease to bearing surface of steering column track.
17. Ensure steering column inner track bearing retainers are properly staged.
18. Install steering column outer housing and housing cover plate. Hand tighten loosely.
19. Ensure steering column inner track bearings are properly staged. Adjust as required.
20. Apply Threadlock 262 part No. E2FZ-19554-B, or equivalent, to bolt threads, then tighten mounting bolts to specifications.
21. Install steering column release motors and mounting screws.
22. Disconnect steering column telescopic release motor electrical connector.
23. Connect motor electrical connector terminals to a suitable 1 amp 12 volt battery charger and test column for normal operation.
24. Connect steering column telescopic release motor electrical connector.
25. Disconnect steering column tilt release motor electrical connector.
26. Connect motor electrical connector terminals to battery charger and test column for normal operation.
27. Connect steering column tilt release motor electrical connector.
28. Install electronic steering sensor with screws.
29. **On models equipped with manual transmission,** install steering wheel lock actuator and new shear bolts.
30. **On all models,** remove steering column from vise.
31. Install steering column as outlined under "Steering Column, Replace."

MARK VIII

1. Remove shock absorber electronic steering sensor.
2. Remove tilt and telescope motors, then the housing cover.
3. Remove potentiometer link.
4. Install tilt spring compressor tool No. T97P-3D655-A, or equivalent, **Fig. 6.**
5. Remove telescoping actuator mounting bolts.
6. Slowly turn tilt spring compressor bolt counterclockwise to release spring tension.
7. Remove tilt spring compressor and tilt spring.
8. Separate front and rear halves of steering column shaft. **Scribe mark on steering shaft tube to show location of steering shaft flat.**
9. Remove potentiometer and telescope actuator.
10. Separate front steering shaft from support housing.
11. Remove tilt actuator pivot pin, mounting bolts and tilt actuator.
12. Remove tilt pivot bolts.
13. Remove retaining ring and press out rear steering shaft.
14. Drive out steering column small and large rear bearings using suitable brass drift.
15. Reverse procedure to assemble.

MUSTANG

DISASSEMBLY

1. Remove steering column as outlined under "Steering Column, Replace."
2. Remove steering column lower yoke, steering column upper bearing spring, suspension height sensor control ring and steering column upper bearing tolerance ring, **Fig. 7.**
3. Remove turn indicator cancel cam by pushing up with suitable flat-bladed

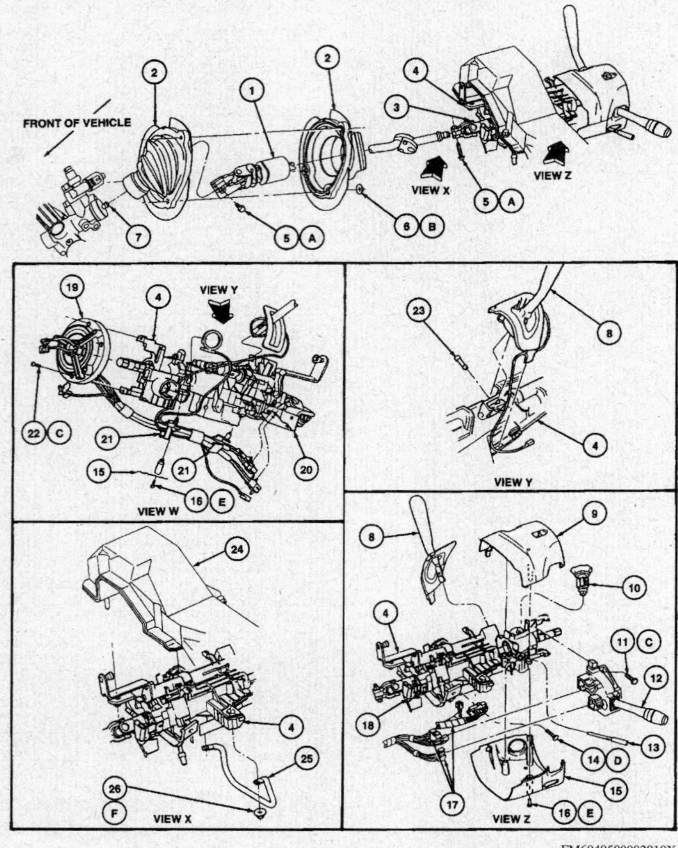

FM6049500082010X

Fig. 8 Exploded view of steering column (Part 1 of 2). 1998–99 Sable & Taurus w/column shift

Item	Description
1	Steering Column Intermediate Shaft Coupling
2	Steering Column Opening Weather Seal (2 Req'd)
3	Steering Column Lower Yoke
4	Steering Column Tube
5	Bolt (2 Req'd)
6	Nut (3 Req'd)
7	Steering Gear
8	Steering Column Intermediate Shaft Coupling
9	Steering Column Shroud
10	Ignition Switch Lock Cylinder
11	Bolt (2 Req'd)
12	Multi-Function Switch
13	Tilt Wheel Handle and Shank
14	Screw (Part of 14401)
15	Steering Column Shroud
16	Screw (3 Req'd)
17	Main Wiring
18	Steering Column Lower Bearing Retainer

Item	Description
19	Air Bag Sliding Contact
20	Wire Connector Bracket
21	Wiring Harness Retainer (2 Req'd)
22	Screw (3 Req'd)
23	Gearshift Lever Pin
24	Part of Instrument Panel Brace
25	Steering Column Absorber
26	Nut (4 Req'd)
A	Tighten to 22-28 N·m (16-21 Lb-Ft)
B	Tighten to 5-6 N·m (40-56 Lb-In)
C	Tighten to 2-3 N·m (19-25 Lb-In)
D	Tighten to 0.9-1.3 N·m (8-10 Lb-In)
E	Tighten to 0.7-1.0 N·m (6-8 Lb-In)
F	Tighten to 13-17 N·m (10-12 Lb-Ft)

FM6049500082020X

Fig. 8 Exploded view of steering column (Part 2 of 2). 1998–99 Sable & Taurus w/column shift

screwdriver. **Record flush surface direction.**

4. Remove ignition switch, steering column bearing retainer and spring.
5. Remove steel steering column upper bearing tolerance ring and tube bearing sleeve.
6. Remove ignition switch bore plastic steering column upper bearing retainer.
7. Remove metal steering column lock housing bearing from ignition switch bore and steering column lock gear.
8. Remove pivot bolts and lock cylinder housing. **Steering column position spring will release when bolts are removed.**
9. Remove steering gear input worm gear and rack from steering column tube.
10. Remove steering column lock lever actuator and steering actuator housing.
11. Remove lower steering column tube bearing and steering column lower bearing retainer.
12. Remove tilt position lever using suitable drift.
13. Remove steering column lock lefthand lever and steering column locking lever springs.

ASSEMBLY

1. Install steering gear input worm gear and rack into steering actuator housing.
2. Install lower steering column tube bearing and steering column instrument panel clamp. Tighten mounting nuts and bolts to specifications.
3. Install suspension height sensor control ring, steering column upper bearing tolerance ring, steering column upper bearing spring and steering column lower yoke to steering gear input worm gear and rack. Tighten mounting nuts and bolts to specifications.
4. Position steering column lock lever actuator and steering actuator housing in lock cylinder housing.
5. Spray actuators with multi-purpose grease part No. DOAZ-19584-AA, or equivalent.
6. Position actuator cam in lock cylinder housing and install cam pivot pin with small hammer. Tap pin in until flush with lock cylinder housing.
7. Install one steering column locking lever spring and righthand steering column locking lever with steering column lock actuator lever pin.
8. Tap steering column lock actuator lever pin into place while driving out drift.
9. Support steering actuator housing in vise and drive steering column lock actuator lever pin flush with steering actuator housing.
10. Place two nuts or spacers to hold steering column lock lefthand lever/righthand steering column locking lever away from steering actuator housing.
11. Lubricate pivot bolts with multi-purpose grease part No. DOAZ-19584-AA, or equivalent.
12. Position steering column position spring on lock cylinder housing and install lock cylinder housing and pivot bolts. Tighten pivot bolts to specifications.
13. Install steel steering column upper bearing tolerance ring and steering column tube bearing sleeve over steering column.
14. Install steering column upper bearing spring and new steering column upper bearing retainer on top side of steering column upper bearing spring using 3/4 inch by 2/3 inch PVC pipe.
15. Install turn indicator cancel cam, flush surface facing up.
16. Install ignition switch.
17. Align pin from ignition switch with slot in lock/column and position slot in lock/column with index mark on casting. Tighten mounting screws to specifications.
18. Install steering column lock gear and coat lock gear with multi-purpose grease part No. DOAZ-19584-AA, or equivalent.
19. Install metal steering column lock housing bearing and coat lock gear with multi-purpose grease.
20. Install steering column upper bearing retainer.
21. Install steering column as outlined under "Steering Column, Replace."

SABLE & TAURUS

1998–99

1. Remove steering column as outlined under "Steering Column, Replace."
2. Remove steering column lower yoke, bearing spring, suspension height sensor control ring and steering column bearing tolerance ring.
3. Remove turn indicator cancel cam by pushing up with suitable flat bladed screwdriver. **Record direction of flush surface.**
4. Remove mounting bolts and ignition switch, **Figs. 8 and 9.**

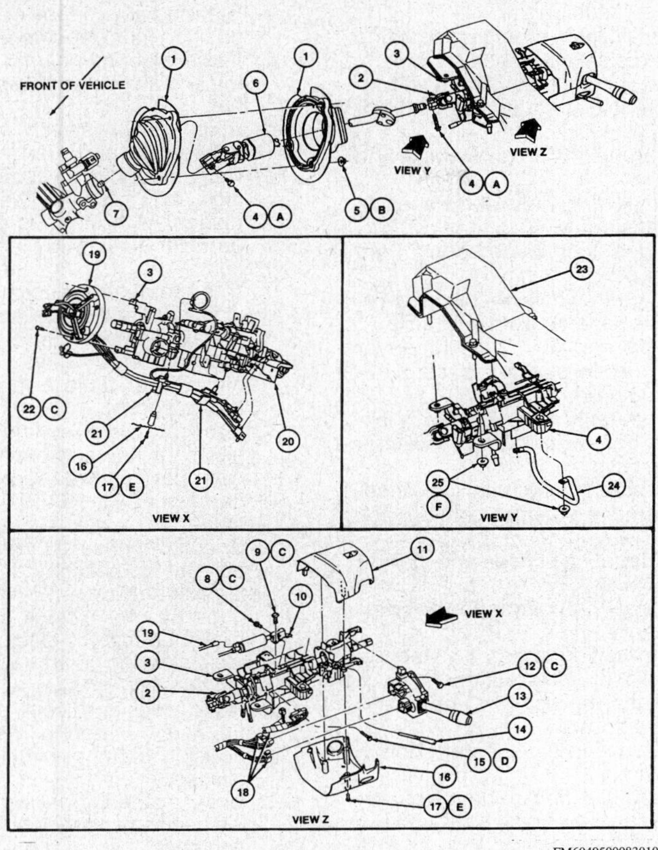

FM6049500083010X

Fig. 9 Exploded view of steering column (Part 1 of 2). 1998–99 Sable & Taurus w/console shift

Item	Description
1	Steering Column Opening Weather Seal (2 Req'd)
2	Steering Column Lower Yoke
3	Steering Column Tube
4	Bolt (2 Req'd)
5	Nut (3 Req'd)
6	Steering Column Intermediate Shaft Coupling
7	Steering Gear
8	Bolt (1 Req'd)
9	Bolt (1 Req'd)
10	Ignition / Shifter Interlock Cable
11	Steering Column Shroud
12	Bolt (2 Req'd)
13	Multi-Function Switch
14	Tilt Wheel Handle and Shank
15	Screw (Part of 14401)
16	Steering Column Shroud
17	Screw (3 Req'd)

Item	Description
18	Main Wiring
19	Air Bag Sliding Contact
20	Wire Connector Bracket
21	Wiring Harness Retainer (2 Req'd)
22	Screw (3 Req'd)
23	Part of Instrument Panel Bace
24	Steering Column Absorber
25	Nut (4 Req'd)
A	Tighten to 22-28 N·m (16-21 Lb-Ft)
B	Tighten to 5-6 N·m (40-56 Lb-In)
C	Tighten to 2-3 N·m (1925 Lb-In)
D	Tighten to 0.9-1.3 N·m (8-11 Lb-In)
E	Tighten to 0.7-1.0 N·m (6-8 Lb-In)
F	Tighten to 13-17 N·m (10-12 Lb-Ft)

FM6049500083020X

Fig. 9 Exploded view of steering column (Part 2 of 2). 1998–99 Sable & Taurus w/console shift

5. Remove bearing retainer and steering column upper bearing spring.
6. Remove steel steering column bearing tolerance ring and bearing sleeve.
7. Remove ignition switch lock cylinder bore plastic bearing and metal steering column lock housing bearing.
8. Remove steering column lock gear and tilt pivot bolts. **Steering column position spring will release when bolts are removed.**
9. Remove steering column lock cylinder housing and steering shaft.
10. **On models equipped with column shift,** proceed as follows:
    a. Remove shift lock actuator and transaxle shift selector insert.
    b. Remove transaxle column shift selector tube mounting screws.
    c. Remove pin retaining steering column lock pawl from steering actuator housing, then the lock pawl.
11. **On all models,** remove steering column lock lever actuator from steering actuator housing.
12. Remove retainer mounting screws and steering column lower bearing.
13. Remove steering column mounting bracket and lock actuator lever pin.
14. Remove steering column locking lever, lock lefthand lever and locking lever springs.
15. Reverse procedure to assemble.

2000–02

Console Shift

1. Remove steering column as outlined under "Steering Column, Replace."
2. Remove mounting screws and ignition switch.
3. Record steering column lock gear, bearing and retainer positions for installation alignment, **Fig. 10.**
4. Remove bearing retainer, lock housing bearing and lock gear.
5. Remove lower bearing spring and sensor ring.
6. Remove lower bearing tolerance ring from shaft.
7. Remove tilt pivot mounting screws.
8. Remove lock cylinder housing and shaft assembly from actuator housing by prying up on lock actuator lever using suitable fabricated too, **Fig. 11.**
9. Remove position spring.**Steering column position spring is under tension and can come out with great force.**
10. Remove turn indicator cancel cam.
11. Remove snap ring, upper bearing spring and sleeve.
12. Slide steering column shaft in toward lock cylinder housing and steering column bearing tolerance ring from steering column shaft, then remove shaft.
13. Remove lower bearing from lock cylinder housing using suitable punch.
14. Remove lock cylinder housing bearing using suitable punch
15. Remove lower bearing and sleeve.
16. Remove mounting bolts and lower bearing retainer.
17. Remove upper and lower lock lever actuators.
18. Remove ignition lock cylinder lockout lever and lock actuator lever return spring.
19. Remove pin and lock actuator lever, then the pin and locking lever cam using suitable pin punch.
20. Remove pin, tilt locking levers and springs using suitable pin punch. **Do not remove tilt lock levers if not required.**
21. Reverse procedure to install, noting the following:
    a. Lock lever with two teeth is installed on lefthand side.
    b. Lubricate lock lever actuator with ignition lock grease part No. F0AZ-19584-A, or equivalent.
    c. Lower bearing UP position must face forward.
    d. Install steering column bearing so inner race is visible using suitable bearing installer tool or socket.
    e. Lubricate tilt pivot bushings and mounting screws with ignition lock grease.
    f. Ensure upper and lower lock actuators are aligned.
    g. Align ignition switch with actuator housing slot and index mark.
    h. Ensure narrow section of lock gear keyhole is in 1 o'clock position with tab inboard at 3 o'clock position.
    i. Coat lock gear with ignition lock grease.
    j. Lubricate lock housing bearing with ignition lock grease and rotate counterclockwise.
    k. Ensure upper bearing retainer firmly engages lock housing retention tabs

Column Shift

1. Remove steering column as outlined under "Steering Column, Replace."
2. Unclip steering column opening gearshift lever seal, then remove retaining pin and gearshift lever.
3. Record steering column lock gear,

bearing and retainer prior positions for installation alignment, **Fig. 12.**

4. Remove steering column lock housing bearing and gear.
5. **On models equipped with fixed steering column,** remove steering column shaft bottom snap ring.
6. **On models equipped with tilt steering column,** remove steering column lower bearing spring and sensor ring.
7. **On all models,** remove steering column bearing tolerance ring.
8. Remove lock cylinder housing pivot mounting screws.
9. Pry up steering column locking levers using suitable fabricated tool, **Fig. 11.**
10. Remove lock cylinder housing and steering column shaft from steering actuator housing.
11. **On models equipped with tilt steering column,** remove the steering column position spring. **Steering column position spring is under tension and can come out with great force.**
12. **On all models,** remove turn indicator cancel cam by prying up flush surface using suitable flat-blade screwdriver.
13. Remove snap ring, steering column upper bearing spring and sleeve.
14. Slide steering column shaft in toward steering column lock cylinder housing, then remove bearing tolerance ring and shaft.
15. Remove steering column upper bearing from lock cylinder housing using suitable punch.
16. **On models equipped with tilt steering column,** remove steering column lower bearing from lock cylinder housing using suitable punch.
17. **On all models,** remove mounting screws and plastic harness retainer.
18. Remove mounting bolts, brake shift interlock solenoid and transaxle shift position insert.
19. Remove mounting bolts, clamps and shift tube.
20. Remove mounting bolts and transaxle shift arm assembly.
21. Remove gearshift lever spring from shift tube.
22. Drive out gearshift lever pin and remove gearshift lever from shift tube.
23. Remove column shift selector lever plunger. If lever plunger is bent, replace as required.
24. Remove gearshift lever socket bushings and transaxle control selector lever spring clip.
25. Drive out steering column lock lever pin and remove steering column lock pawl.
26. Remove mounting screws and ignition switch.
27. Remove steering column lower bearing and sleeve.
28. Remove mounting bolts and steering column lower bearing retainer.
29. Remove steering column upper and lower lock actuator.
30. Reverse procedure to install, noting the following:
    a. Lubricate steering column lock actuators, and coat lock pawl and pin surfaces with ignition lock grease part No. F0AZ-19584-A, or equivalent.
    b. Steering column lower bearing UP position must face engine.
    c. Install steering column lower bearing and sleeve so inner race is visible.
    d. Align ignition switch with steering column slot and index mark.
    e. Coat gearshift lever socket bushings and column shift selector plunger with steering gear grease part No. C3AZ-19578-A, or equivalent.
    f. Coat gearshift selector tube spring with steering gear grease.
    g. Install upper and large steering column bearings so inner race is visible with suitable bearing installer tool or socket.
    h. Lubricate lock cylinder housing bushings and mounting screws with rust penetrant and inhibitor part No. F2AZ-19A501-A, or equivalent.
    i. Ensure upper and lower steering column lock actuators are aligned.
    j. Narrow section of lock gear keyhole must be in 1 o'clock position with tab inboard at 3 o'clock position.
    k. Coat steering column lock gear with ignition lock grease.
    l. Rotate lock gear counterclockwise.
    m. Lubricate steering column lock housing bearing with ignition lock grease.
    n. Ensure steering column lock housing bearing engages housing retention tabs.

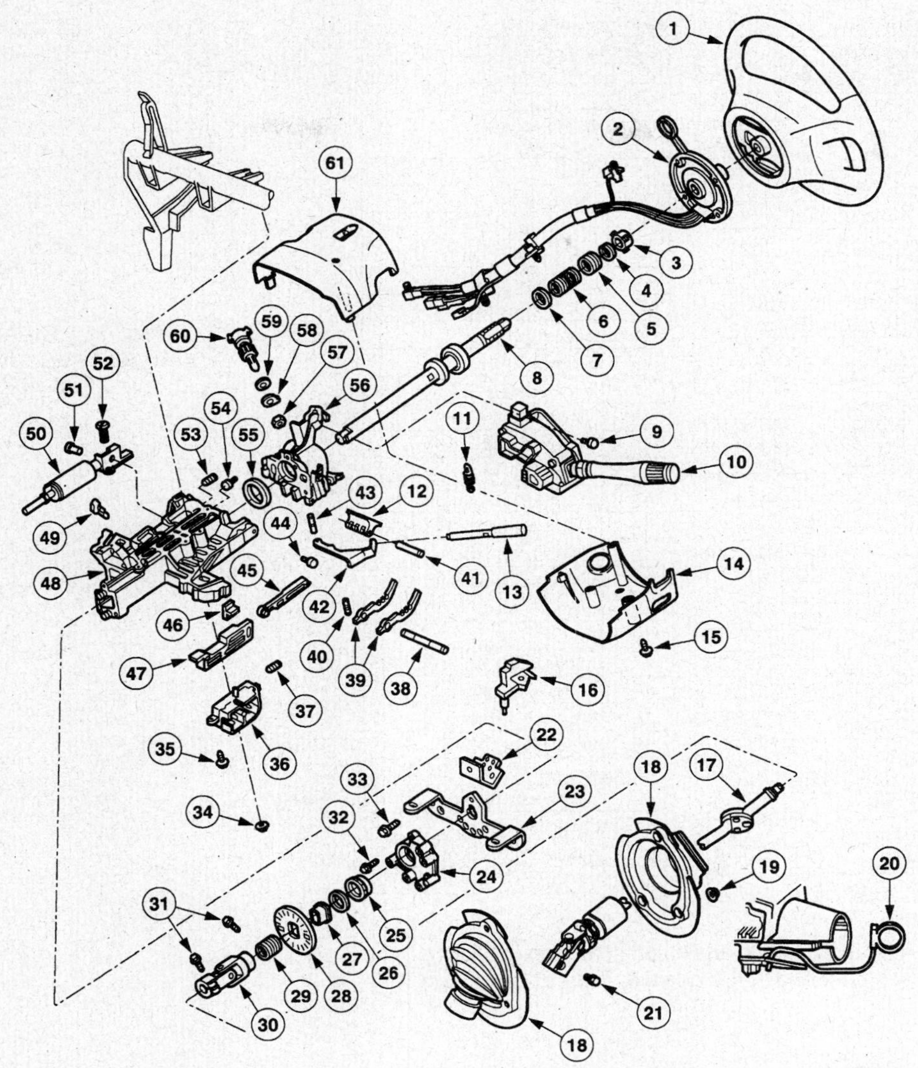

Fig. 10 Exploded view of steering column (Part 1 of 2). 2000–02 Sable & Taurus w/console shift

Item	Description
1	Steering wheel
2	Air bag sliding contact
3	Turn indicator cancel cam
4	Snap ring
5	Bearing spring
6	Upper bearing sleeve
7	Upper bearing (small)
8	Shaft assembly
9	Screw
10	Multi-function switch
11	Lock lever spring return
12	Lock cam
13	Tilt wheel handle
14	Lower shroud
15	Shroud retaining screws
16	Wiring shield
17	Intermediate shaft
18	Tube boot
19	Nut
20	Perimeter anti-theft system (PATS)sensor
21	Bolt
22	Wire connector bracket
23	Mounting bracket
24	Bearing retaining
25	Bearing sleeve
26	Lower bearing
27	Lower bearing tolerance ring
28	Sensor ring
29	Bearing spring
30	Coupling
31	Bolt — flange yoke

Item	Description
32	Bearing housing retaining screw
33	Screw
34	Steering column mounting lower nuts
35	Screw
36	Ignition switch
37	Lock spring (shaft)
38	Lock actuator lever pin
39	Lock actuator lever
40	Lock lever spring (2 req'd)
41	Lock cam pivot pin
42	Release lever
43	Lock actuator lever pin
44	Tilt pivot screws
45	Lock lever upper actuator
46	Lock pawl
47	Lock lever lower actuator
48	Actuator housing
49	Lock actuator cover
50	Ignition/shifter interlock cable
51	Screw
52	Screw
53	Position spring
54	Tilt flange bumper
55	Lower bearing (large)
56	Lock cylinder housing
57	Lock gear
58	Lock housing bearing
59	Bearing retainer
60	Ignition switch lock cylinder
61	Upper shroud

FM6040000131020X

Fig. 10 Exploded view of steering column (Part 2 of 2). 2000–02 Sable & Taurus w/console shift

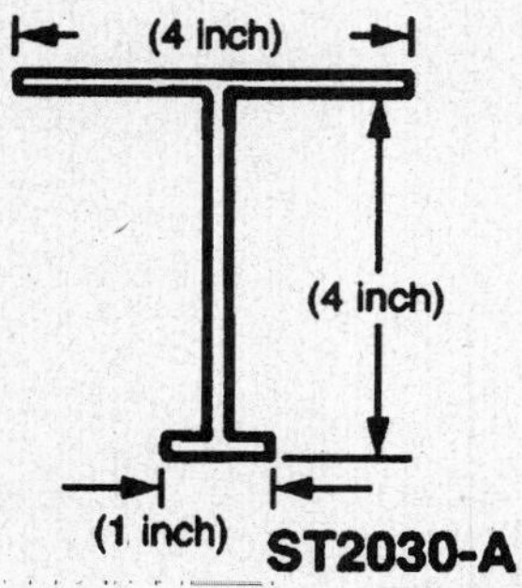

FM6040000133000X

Fig. 11 Steering column locking lever fabricated tool dimensions. 2000–02 Sable & Taurus

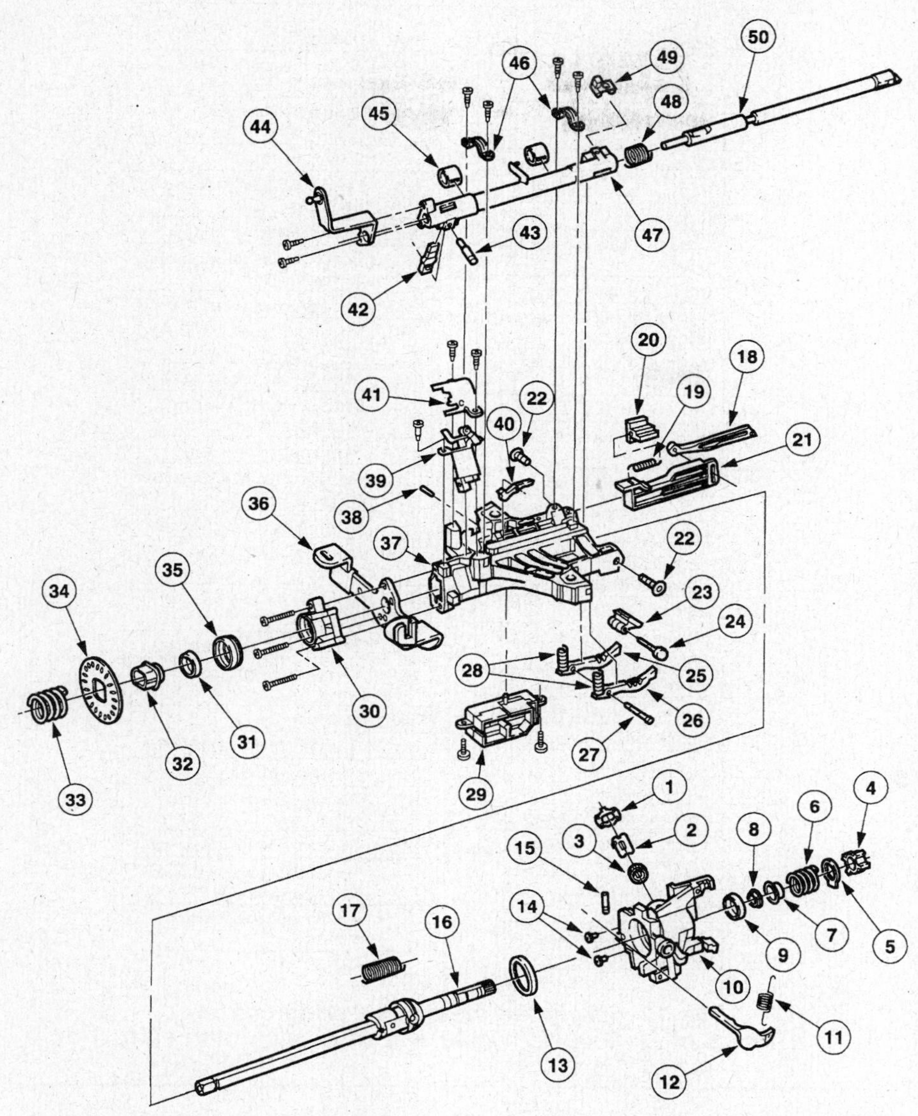

Fig. 12 Exploded view of steering column (Part 1 of 2). 2000–02 Sable & Taurus w/column shift

Item	Description
1	Steering column upper bearing retainer
2	Steering column lock housing bearing
3	Steering column lock gear
4	Turn indicator cancel cam
5	Snap ring
6	Steering column upper bearing spring
7	Steering column bearing sleeve
8	Steering column upper bearing tolerance ring
9	Upper steering column bearing (small)
10	Lock cylinder housing
11	Steering column release lever spring
12	Steering column release lever
13	Upper steering column bearing (large)
14	Lock cylinder housing bumper
15	Tilt release lever pivot pin
16	Steering shaft assy
17	Steering column position spring
18	Upper lock actuator assy
19	Steering column lock spring
20	Steering column lock pawl
21	Lower lock actuator assy
22	Tilt pivot screws
23	Steering column lock cam
24	Steering column lock cam pivot pin
25	Steering column locking lever (RH)
26	Steering column locking lever (LH)

Item	Description
27	Steering column lock lever actuator pin
28	Steering column locking lever spring
29	Ignition switch
30	Steering column lower bearing retainer
31	Steering column bearing
32	Lower steering column bearing tolerance ring
33	Steering column bearing spring
34	Suspension height sensor control ring
35	Steering column bearing sleeve
36	Steering column lower mounting bracket
37	Steering actuator housing
38	Steering column lock lever pin (shifter)
39	Brake shift interlock solenoid
40	Steering column lock pawl (shifter)
41	Transmission shift selector position insert
42	Transmission gearshift lever
43	Transmission gearshift lever pin
44	Shift arm assy
45	Gearshift lever socket bushing
46	Gearshift tube bushing clamp
47	Transmission column shift selector tube
48	Gearshift selector tube spring
49	Transmission control selector lever spring clip
50	Column shift selector lever plunger

FM6040000132020X

Fig. 12 Exploded view of steering column (Part 2 of 2). 2000–02 Sable & Taurus w/column shift

TIGHTENING SPECIFICATIONS

Year	Component	Torque/Ft. Lbs.
CONTINENTAL		
1998–2002	Clockspring Screws	18–26①
	Driver's Air Bag Module (1998)	90–122①
	Driver's Air Bag Module (1999–2002)	108①
	Ignition Switch	47–64①
	Lower Column Bearing	62–97①
	Multi-Function Switch	18–26①
	Shift Cable & Bracket	62–97①
	Shift Selector Tube	62–97①
	Steering Actuator Housing Pivot	14–19
	Steering Column Boot	45–53①
	Steering Column Impact Absorber	10–14
	Steering Column	10–12
	Steering Column Trim Shroud	6–8①
	Steering Column Yoke	19–25
	Steering Wheel (1998–99)	25–34
	Steering Wheel (2000–02)	23–25

Continued

TIGHTENING SPECIFICATIONS—Continued

Year	Component	Torque/Ft. Lbs.
CONTOUR & MYSTIQUE		
1998–2000	Air Bag Module	96–120①
	Flexible Coupling To Steering Column	18
	Flexible Coupling To Steering Gear	14
	Lower Bearing Retainer Collar	17
	Steering Column	18
	Steering Wheel	37
COUGAR		
1999–2002	Driver's Air Bag Module	44①
	Flexible Coupling To Steering Column	18
	Flexible Coupling To Steering Gear	14
	Lower Bearing Retainer Collar	17
	Steering Column	18
	Steering Wheel	37
CROWN VICTORIA & GRAND MARQUIS		
1998	Air Bag Module	16–53①
	Air Bag Sliding Contact	18–26①
	Column Shift Selector Tube	62–97①
	Ignition Switch	45–61
	Lock Housing	14–19
	Lower Steering Column Shaft	19–25
	Multi-Function Switch	18–26①
	Shift Cable & Bracket	62–97①
	Steering Boot	45–61①
	Steering Column Gear Input Shaft Coupling	19–25
	Steering Column Lower Bearing	62–97①
	Steering Column Lower Yoke To Steering Gear Input	19–25
	Steering Column Shroud	6–10①
	Steering Column Support Bracket	10–12
	Steering Wheel	25–33
1999–2002	Brake Shift Interlock Solenoid	80①
	Driver's Air Bag Module	108①
	Ignition Switch	53①
	Lock Cylinder Housing	16
	Lower Steering Column Shaft, Lower	35
	Lower Steering Column Shaft, Upper	22
	Parking Brake Release Switch	27①
	Shift Tube	80①
	Shock Absorber Electronic Steering Sensor	9①
	Steering Column Lower Bearing	80①
	Steering Column Support	11
	Steering Wheel	30
	Transmission Range Indicator	27①
	Transmission Selector Lever Arm & Support	11

Continued

TIGHTENING SPECIFICATIONS—Continued

Year	Component	Torque/Ft. Lbs.
ESCORT, TRACER & ZX2		
1998–2002	Driver's Air Bag Module	70–103①
	Ignition/Shifter Interlock Cable Mounting Bracket	35–53①
	Steering Column Input Shaft Coupling To Steering Gear Input Shaft	30–36
	Steering Column Shaft To Steering Column Gear Input Shaft Coupling	30–36
	Steering Column Support Bracket	89–106①
	Steering Column Upper Mounting Bracket	80–124①
	Steering Wheel	34–46
FOCUS		
2000–01	Air Bag Module	44①
	Hood Release Cable	15
	Steering Column	10
	Steering Column Shaft	21
	Steering Wheel	37
LS		
2000–02	Driver's Air Bag Module	108①
	Electronic Steering Sensor	27①
	Steering Column	13
	Steering Column Actuator Telescopic Bolt	11
	Steering Column Actuator Telescopic Nut	13
	Steering Column Actuator Tilt, Bolt	11
	Steering Column Actuator Tilt, Nut	13
	Steering Column Outer Housing Cover Plate	10
	Steering Column Release Motor	27①
	Steering Column Tube Flange Pivot Bolts	17
	Steering Column Upper Shaft	10
	Steering Shaft Pinch Bolt	22
	Steering Wheel (2000–01)	30
	Steering Wheel (2002)	38
	Steering Wheel Lock Actuator Mounting	108①
MARK VIII		
1998	Air Bag Module	89–123①
	Bearing Housing Pivot	14–19
	Front Steering Shaft End Plate	107–132①
	Housing Cover	107–132①
	Ignition Switch	14–16①
	Instrument Panel Reinforcement Brace	25–38
	Potentiometer	26①
	Shift Interlock Solenoid	14–16①
	Steering Column Shaft To Steering Gear	31–41
	Steering Column Shaft To Lower Yoke	31–41
	Steering Column Mount	24–34
	Steering Shaft Yoke	22–30
	Steering Wheel	23–35

Continued

TIGHTENING SPECIFICATIONS—Continued

Year	Component	Torque/Ft. Lbs.
MARK VIII		
1998	Telescope Actuator, Bolt	10–12
	Telescope Actuator, Nut	7–10
	Telescope/Tilt Motors	18–25①
	Tilt Actuator	10–12
MUSTANG		
1998–2002	Air Bag Sliding Contact	18–26
	Air Bag Sliding Contact	18–26
	Driver's Air Bag Module	36–53①
	Ignition Switch	45–61①
	Interlock Cable	14–17①
	Intermediate Shaft Coupler	19
	Lock Cylinder	17
	Steering Column Gear Input Shaft Coupling To Column Shaft	30–40
	Steering Column Gear Input Shaft Coupling To Gear Pinch	19–25
	Steering Column Lower Bearing	80①
	Steering Column Lower Mount	62–97①
	Steering Column Mount	10–12
	Steering Column Pivot	14–19
	Steering Column Tube Boot	71–88①
	Steering Wheel	23–32
SABLE & TAURUS		
1998–99	Air Bag Module	89–123①
	Air Bag Sliding Contact	18–26①
	Ignition Switch	45–61①
	Interlock Cable	14–17①
	Lower Shroud	7–8①
	Steering Column	10–12
	Steering Column Gear Input Shaft Coupling	16–20
	Steering Column Lower Yoke	17–20
	Steering Column Mounting Bracket	62–97①
	Steering Column Tube	14–53①
	Steering Column Tube Flange	14–19
	Steering Wheel	25–33
	Wiring Harness	8–11①
2000–02	Brake Shift Interlock Solenoid	80①
	Ignition Switch	54①
	Instrument Panel Opening Cover Support	11
	Lock Cylinder Housing	17
	Shift Tube	80①
	Steering Column	11
	Steering Column Coupler	18
	Steering Column Finish Panel	62①
	Steering Column Lower Bearing	80①
	Steering Column Shaft	36
	Steering Wheel Pinion Shaft	13
	Transaxle Selector Lever Arm & Support	11

Continued

TIGHTENING SPECIFICATIONS—Continued

Year	Component	Torque/Ft. Lbs.
THUNDERBIRD		
2002	Driver's Air Bag Module	108①
	Electronic Steering Sensor	27①
	Steering Column	13
	Steering Column Actuator Telescopic Bolt	11
	Steering Column Actuator Telescopic Nut	13
	Steering Column Actuator Tilt, Bolt	11
	Steering Column Actuator Tilt, Nut	13
	Steering Column Outer Housing Cover Plate	10
	Steering Column Release Motor	27①
	Steering Column Tube Flange Pivot Bolts	17
	Steering Column Upper Shaft	10
	Steering Shaft Pinch Bolt	22
	Steering Wheel	38
	Steering Wheel Lock Actuator Mounting	108①
TOWN CAR		
1998–2000	Brake Shift Interlock Solenoid	62–97①
	Ignition Switch	47–64①
	Lock Cylinder Housing	14–19
	Parking Brake Release Switch	18–26①
	Shift Tube	62–97①
	Shock Absorber Electronic Steering Sensor	10–13①
	Steering Column Lower Bearing	63–98①
	Steering Column Support	10–13
	Steering Wheel	25–34
	Transmission Range Indicator	62–97①
	Transmission Selector Lever Arm & Support	10–13
	Upper Intermediate Shaft To Lower Intermediate Shaft	19–25
	Upper Intermediate Steering Shaft To Steering Column Shaft	19–25
2001–02	Brake Shift Interlock Solenoid	80①
	Ignition Switch	62①
	Lock Cylinder Housing	16
	Parking Brake Release Switch	27①
	Shift Tube	80①
	Shock Absorber Electronic Steering Sensor	13①
	Steering Column Lower Bearing	80①
	Steering Column Support	11
	Steering Wheel	30
	Transmission Range Indicator	80①
	Transmission Selector Arm & Support	11
	Upper Intermediate Shaft To Lower Intermediate Shaft	22
	Upper Intermediate Steering Shaft To Steering Column Shaft	22

① — Inch lbs.

POWER STEERING

TABLE OF CONTENTS

Power Steering Pressure Specifications

Year	Vehicle	Engine	Minimum Flow①②	Minimum Relief Pressure, psi	Maximum Relief Pressure, psi	Pump Model③	Maximum Free Flow @ 1500 RPM①
1998	Continental	4.6L	1.70	1300	1480	HBD-AX	2.7
	Contour	2.0L & 2.5L	1.15	—	1380	HBD-AE	2.4
	Crown Victoria	4.6L	1.40	1200	1380	CIII	3.2④
	Escort	2.0L	1.15	1117	1247	CIII	2.4
	Grand Marquis	4.6L	1.40	1200	1380	CIII	3.2④
	Mark VIII	4.6L	1.40	1200	1380	HBD-AN	2.7
	Mustang	3.8L	0.90	1050	1230	HBC-KC	–
		4.6L	1.25	1200	1380	HBD-CA	–
	Mystique	2.0L & 2.5L	1.15	—	1380	HBD-AE	2.4
	Sable	3.0L (2V)	0.90	1300	1480	HBC-LC	2.3
		3.0L (4V)	0.90	1300	1480	HBC-BM	2.3
	Taurus	3.0L (2V)	0.90	1300	1480	HBC-LC	2.3
		3.0L (4V)	0.90	1300	1480	HBC-BM	2.3
		3.4L	2.00	1470	1590	ZUA	2.6
	Town Car	4.6L	1.40	1200	1380	CIII	3.2④
	Tracer	2.0L	1.15	1117	1247	CIII	2.4
	ZX2	2.0L	1.15	1117	1247	CIII	2.4
1999	Continental	4.6L	1.70	1300	1480	HBD-AX	2.7
	Contour & Mystique	2.0L & 2.5L	1.15	—	1380	HBD-AE	2.4
	Crown Victoria	4.6L	1.40	1200	1380	CIII	3.2④
	Cougar	2.0L & 2.5L	1.13	1200	1380	HBD-AE	2.4④
	Escort & ZX2	2.0L	1.15	1117	1247	CIII	2.4
	Mustang	3.8L	0.90	1050	1230	CII	2.6
		4.6L	1.25	1200	1380	CIII	2.6
	Sable	3.0L (2V)	0.90	1300	1480	CII	2.3
		3.0L (4V)	0.90	1300	1480	CIII	2.3
	Taurus	3.0L (2V)	0.90	1300	1480	CII	2.3
		3.0L (4V)	0.90	1300	1480	CIII	2.3
		3.4L	2.00	1470	1590	ZUA	2.6
	Town Car	4.6L	1.40	1200	1380	CIII	3.2④
	Tracer	2.0L	1.15	1117	1247	CIII	2.4
2000	Continental	4.6L	1.70	1300	1480	HBD-AX	2.7
	Contour & Mystique	2.0L & 2.5L	1.15	—	1380	HBD-AE	2.4
	Cougar	2.0L & 2.5L	1.13	1200	1380	HBD-AE	2.4④
	Crown Victoria	4.6L	1.40	1200	1380	CIII	3.2④
	Escort & ZX2	2.0L	1.15	1117	1247	CIII	2.4
	Grand Marquis	4.6L	1.40	1200	1380	CIII	3.2④
	Focus	2.0L	—	—	—	—	—
	LS	3.0L	1.40	1400	1530	—	2.4
		3.9L	1.40	1400	1530	—	2.4
	Mustang	3.8L	0.90	1050	1230	CII	2.6
		4.6L	1.25	1200	1380	CIII	2.6
	Sable & Taurus	3.0L (2V)	1.15	1400	1530	CII	2.8
		3.0L (4V)	1.15	1400	1530	CIII	2.8
	Town Car	4.6L	1.40	1200	1380	CIII	3.2④

Continued

Year	Vehicle	Engine	Minimum Flow①②	Minimum Relief Pressure, psi	Maximum Relief Pressure, psi	Pump Model③	Maximum Free Flow @ 1500 RPM①
2001	Continental	4.6L	1.70	1200	1380	HBD-BM	2.7④
	Cougar	2.0L & 2.5L	1.13	1200	1380	HBD-AE	2.4④
	Crown Victoria	4.6L	1.40	1200	1380	HBC-CS	3.2④
	Escort & ZX2	2.0L	1.15	1117	1247	CIII	2.4
	Focus	2.0L	—	—	—	—	—
	Grand Marquis	4.6L	1.40	1200	1380	HBC-CS	3.2④
	LS	3.0L	1.40	1400	1530	—	2.6
		3.9L	1.40	1400	1530	—	2.6
	Mustang	3.8L	0.90	1050	1230	CII	2.6
		4.6L	1.25	1200	1380	CIII	2.6
	Sable & Taurus	3.0L (2V)	1.15	1400	1530	CII	2.8
		3.0L (4V)	1.15	1400	1530	CIII	2.8
	Town Car	4.6L	1.40	1200	1380	CIII	3.2④
2002	Continental	4.6L	1.70	1200	1380	HBD-BM	2.7④
	Cougar	2.0L & 2.5L	1.13	1200	1380	HBD-AE	2.4④
	Crown Victoria	4.6L	1.40	1200	1380	HBC-CS	3.2④
	Escort & ZX2	2.0L	1.15	1117	1247	CIII	2.4
	Grand Marquis	4.6L	1.40	1200	1380	HBC-CS	3.2④
	LS	3.0L	1.40	1400	1530	—	2.6
		3.9L	1.40	1400	1530	—	2.6
	Mustang	3.8L	0.90	1050	1230	CII	2.6
		4.6L	1.25	1200	1380	CIII	2.6
	Sable & Taurus	3.0L (2V)	1.15	1400	1530	CII	2.8
		3.0L (4V)	1.15	1400	1530	CIII	2.8
	Thunderbird	3.9L	1.40	1400	1530	—	2.6
	Town Car	4.6L	1.40	1200	1380	CIII	3.2④

① — Gallons per minute.
② — Flow is dependent on pump model, engine RPM & pulley ratio. Engine idle speed must be within specifications when measuring minimum flow.
③ — Power steering pump identification tag is located on the reservoir body.
④ — At 2500 RPM.

Power Steering Pump Application Chart

Year	Model	Type	Page No.
1998	Continental	2	14-8
	Contour	5	14-12
	Crown Victoria	6	14-12
	Escort & ZX2	6	14-12
	Grand Marquis	6	14-12
	Mark VIII	5	14-12
	Mustang w/3.8L	2	14-8
	Mustang w/4.6L	5	14-12
	Mystique	5	14-12
	Sable w/3.0L (2V)	2	14-8
	Sable w/3.0L (4V)	5	14-12
	Taurus w/3.0L (2V)	2	14-8
	Taurus w/3.0L (4V)	5	14-12
	Taurus SHO	1	14-8
	Town Car	6	14-12
	Tracer	6	14-12
1999	Continental	2	14-8
	Contour & Mystique	5	14-12
	Cougar	5	14-12
	Crown Victoria	2	14–8
	Escort & ZX2	6	14-12
	Grand Marquis	2	14-8
	Mustang w/3.8L	2	14-8
	Mustang w/4.6L	6	14-12
	Sable w/3.0L (2V)	2	14-8
	Sable w/3.0L (4V)	5	14-12
	Taurus w/3.0L (2V)	2	14-8
	Taurus w/3.0L (4V)	5	14-12
	Taurus w/3.4L	1	14-8
	Town Car	6	14-12
2000	Continental	2	14-8
	Contour & Mystique	5	14-12
	Cougar	5	14-12
	Crown Victoria	2	14-8
	Escort & ZX2	6	14-12
	Focus SOHC	4	14-12
	Focus DOHC	6	14-12
	Grand Marquis	2	14–8
	LS	2	14–8
	Mustang w/3.8L	2	14-8
	Mustang w/4.6L	6	14-12
	Sable & Taurus w/3.0L (2V)	2	14-8
	Sable & Taurus w/3.0L (4V)	5	14-12
	Town Car	6	14-12

Continued

Year	Model	Type	Page No.
2001	Continental	2	14-8
	Cougar	5	14-12
	Crown Victoria	2	14-8
	Escort & ZX2	6	14-12
	Focus SOHC	4	14-
	Focus DOHC	6	14-12
	Grand Marquis	2	14-8
	LS	2	14–8
	Mustang w/3.8L	2	14-8
	Mustang w/4.6L	6	14-12
	Sable & Taurus w/3.0L (2V)	2	14-8
	Sable & Taurus w/3.0L (4V)	5	14-12
	Town Car	6	14-12
2002	Continental	2	14-8
	Cougar	5	14-12
	Crown Victoria	2	14-8
	Escort & ZX2	6	14-12
	Grand Marquis	2	14-8
	LS	2	14-8
	Mustang w/3.8L	2	14-8
	Mustang w/4.6L	6	14-12
	Sable & Taurus w/3.0L (2V)	2	14-8
	Sable & Taurus w/3.0L (4V)	5	14-12
	Thunderbird	2	14-8
	Town Car	6	14-12

Power Steering Gear Application Chart

Year	Model	Type	Page No.
1998	Continental	2①	14-12
	Contour	2	14-12
	Crown Victoria	3	14-20
	Escort & ZX2	2	14-12
	Grand Marquis	3	14-20
	Mark VIII	2①	14-12
	Mustang	2	14-12
	Mystique	2	14-12
	Sable	2①	14-12
	Taurus	2①	14-12
	Tracer	2	14-12
1999	Continental	2①	14-12
	Contour & Mystique	2	14-12
	Cougar	2	14-12
	Crown Victoria	3	14-20
	Escort & ZX2	2	14-12
	Grand Marquis	2	14-12
	Mustang	2	14-12
	Sable	2	14-12
	Taurus	2	14-12
2000	Continental	2①	14-12
	Contour & Mystique	2	14-12
	Cougar	2	14-12
	Crown Victoria	3	14-20
	Escort & ZX2	2	14-12
	Focus	5	14-24
	Grand Marquis	3	14-20
	LS	2	14-12
	Mustang	2	14-12
	Sable	2	14-12
	Taurus	2	14-12
2001	Continental	2①	14-12
	Cougar	2	14-12
	Crown Victoria	3	14-20
	Escort & ZX2	2	14-12
	Focus	4	14-24
	Grand Marquis	3	14-20
	LS	2	14-12
	Mustang	2	14-12
	Sable	2	14-12
	Taurus	2	14-12
2002	Continental	2①	14-12
	Cougar	2	14-12
	Crown Victoria	3	14-20
	Escort & ZX2	2	14-12
	Focus	4	14-24
	Grand Marquis	3	14-20
	LS	2	14-12
	Mustang	2	14-12
	Sable	2	14-12
	Taurus	2	14-12
	Thunderbird	2	14–12

① — Refer to "Power Steering Assist Systems."

Power Steering Assist System Application Chart

Year	Model	Type	Page No.
1998	Crown Victoria	1	14-27
	Grand Marquis	1	14-27
	Mark VIII	1	14-27
	Sable	2	14-52
	Taurus	2	14-52
	Thunderbird	1	14-27
	Town Car	1	14-27
1999–2002	Crown Victoria	1	14-27
	Grand Marquis	1	14-27
	LS	3	14–58
	Thunderbird	3	14–58
	Town Car	1	14-27

Type 1-ZUA Vane-Type Pump

NOTE: These Pumps Are Not Serviceable. If Service Is Required, Pump Must Be Replaced.

Type 2-Ford Model CII Slipper-Type Pump

NOTE: On Air Bag Equipped Models, Refer To "Air Bag System Precautions" Located In The Front Of This Manual For System Disarming & Arming Procedures.

NOTE: Refer To "Computer Relearn Procedures" Located In The Front Of This Manual When Battery Power To The Computer Has Been Interrupted.

INDEX

PRECAUTIONS

AIR BAG SYSTEMS

Refer to "Air Bag System Precautions" in the front of this manual for system disarming and arming procedures.

BATTERY GROUND CABLE

Prior to service, disconnect battery ground cable and isolate as required.

DESCRIPTION

The Ford model CII power steering pump is a belt driven 10-slipper type pump incorporating a fiberglass filled nylon reservoir. The reservoir is attached to the rear side of the aluminum pump housing assembly. The pump body is encased within the housing and reservoir assembly. The pump design incorporates a pump pressure fitting which allows the pump pressure line to swivel. A pressure sensitive identification tag is attached to the reservoir body. This tag indicates the basic model number and the suffix.

TROUBLESHOOTING

POWER STEERING PUMP LEAKS

1. Excessive fluid fill.
2. Dipstick missing, loose, damaged or missing O-ring.
3. Broken or cracked fluid reservoir.
4. Loose or damaged hose fittings.
5. Shaft seal not pressed flush with housing surface.
6. Shaft seal damage.
7. Rotor shaft damage, helical grooving or OD has an axial scratch.
8. Shaft bushing worn.
9. Plugged drainback hole.
10. Damaged or missing reservoir O-ring.
11. Damaged or missing outlet fitting O-rings.
12. Excessive pump assembly bracket vibration.
13. Plate and bushing reservoir seal groove damage, metal chips or foreign material in seal groove.
14. Faulty outlet fitting.

POWER STEERING PUMP NOISE, MOAN OR WHINE

1. Fluid aeration.
2. Low fluid.
3. Hose grounded.
4. Steering column grounded.
5. Valve cover O-ring or baffle missing or damaged.
6. Interference between components in pumping elements.
7. Loose or poor bracket alignment.
8. Cam contour damaged.

COMPONENT SERVICE

DISASSEMBLE

1. Remove pulley from pump, **Fig. 1.**
2. Remove outlet fitting, flow control valve and flow control valve spring from pump, then remove reservoir.
3. Place a suitable C-clamp in a vise.
4. Position lower support plate tool No. T78P-3733-A2 or equivalent over pump rotor shaft.
5. Install upper compressor plate tool No. T78P-3733-A1 or equivalent into upper portion of C-clamp.
6. While holding compressor tool, place pump assembly into C-clamp with rotor shaft facing downward, **Fig. 2.**
7. Tighten C-clamp until a slight bottoming of valve cover is observed.
8. Through small hole located on side of pump housing, insert a suitable drift and push inward on valve cover snap ring. While pushing inward on snap ring, place a screwdriver under snap ring edge and remove ring from housing, **Fig. 3.**
9. Loosen C-clamp and remove lower support plate tool, then remove pump assembly.
10. Remove pump valve cover and O-ring.
11. Remove rotor shaft, upper plate, cam and rotor assembly and two dowel pins.
12. Remove lower plate and spring, by tapping housing on a flat surface.
13. Using a suitable screwdriver, remove rotor shaft seal.

ASSEMBLE

1. Position rotor on rotor shaft splines with triangle detent on rotor counterbore facing upward, **Fig. 1.**
2. Install snap ring into groove on end of rotor shaft.
3. Position insert cam over rotor. Ensure recessed notch on insert cam is facing upward.

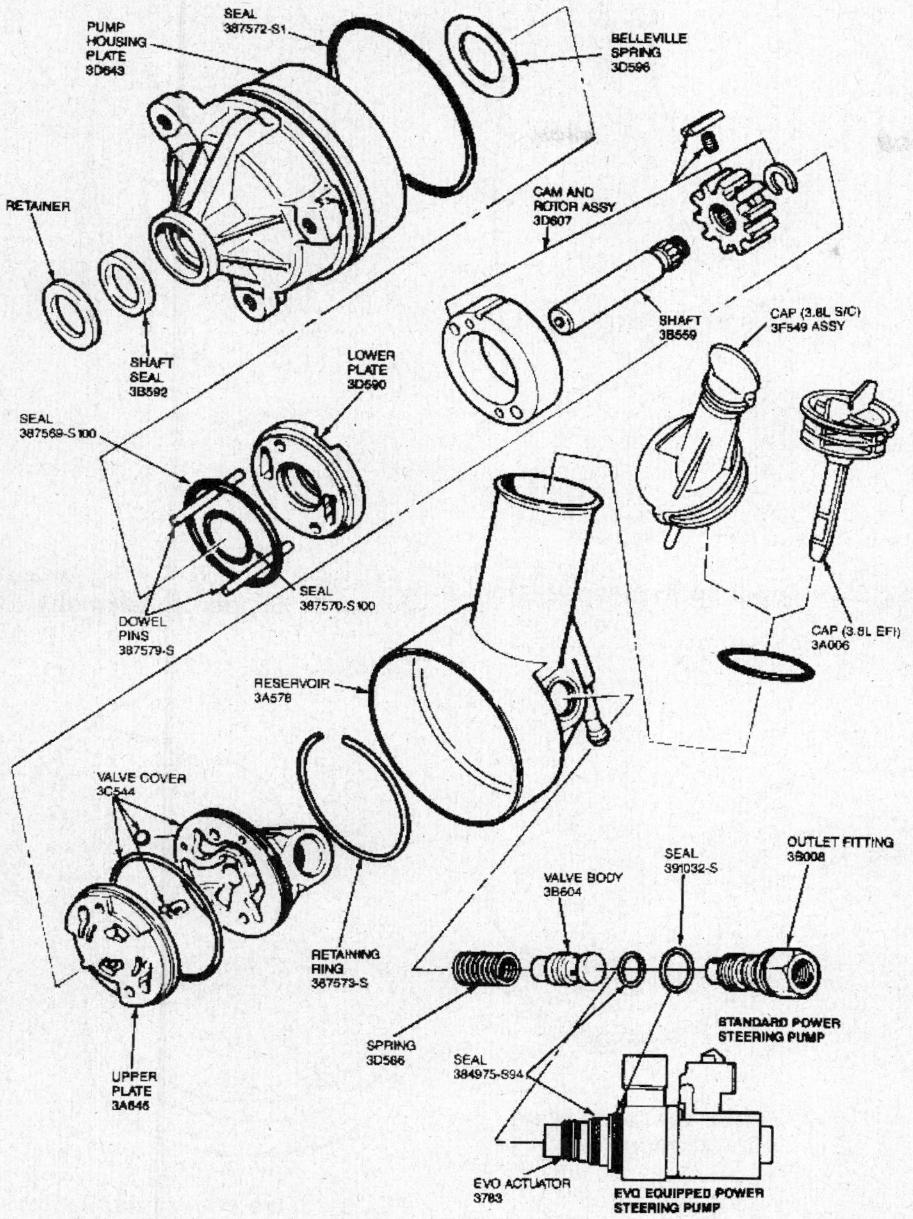

FM6029100059000X

Fig. 1 Exploded view of Ford Model CII power steering pump

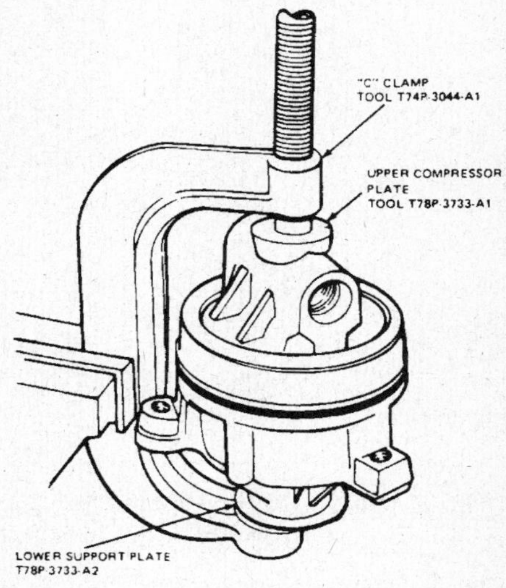

FM6029100060000X

Fig. 2 Positioning pump in C-clamp

4. With rotor extended upward approximately half out of cam, insert spring into rotor pocket, **Fig. 4.**
5. Use a slipper to compress spring, then install slipper with groove facing cam, **Fig. 5.**
6. Perform steps 4 and 5 on slipper cavity beneath opposite inlet recess.
7. While holding cam stationary, index rotor left or right one space and install another spring and slipper until all ten rotor cavities have been filled. Ensure when turning rotor that springs and slippers remain in position.
8. Apply Loctite No. 242 or 271 adhesive, or equivalents to outside diameter of seal and Locquic NF or T primer, or equivalent to seal bore in housing. Install rotor shaft seal using seal driver tool No. T78P-3733-A3 or equivalent. Using a plastic mallet, drive seal into bore until properly seated.
9. Position pump plate on flat surface with pulley side facing downward.
10. Install two dowel pins and spring into housing. **Spring must be inserted with dished surface facing upward.**
11. Lubricate inner and outer O-ring seals with power steering fluid, then install seals on lower pressure plate.
12. Install lower pressure plate into housing and over dowel pin with O-ring seals facing toward front of pump. Position assembly on C-clamp. Place seal driver tool No. T78P-3733-A3 or equivalent, into rotor shaft hole and press on lower plate lightly until it bottoms in pump housing. This will seat the outer O-ring seal.
13. Install cam, rotor and slippers and rotor shaft assembly into pump housing over dowel pins. When installing assembly into pump housing, stepped holes must be used for dowel pins and notch in cam insert must be toward reservoir and approximately 180° opposite square mounting lug on housing, **Fig. 6.**
14. Position upper pressure plate over dowel pins with recess directly over recessed notch on cam insert and approximately 180° opposite square mounting lug, **Fig. 7.**
15. Lubricate O-ring seal with power steering fluid, then position O-ring on valve cover. Ensure plastic baffle is securely in position on valve cover. A coat of petroleum jelly may be used to hold baffle in position.
16. Insert valve cover over dowel pins. Ensure outlet fitting hole in valve cover is aligned with square mounting lug on housing, **Fig. 8.**
17. Place assembly in C-clamp and compress valve cover into pump housing until snap ring groove on housing is exposed.
18. Install valve cover snap ring in pump housing. Ensure snap ring ends are near access hole in pump housing.
19. Remove pump assembly from C-clamp.
20. Lubricate O-ring seal with power steering fluid, then place seal on pump housing.
21. Install reservoir on pump housing.
22. Install flow control valve and spring into valve cover.
23. Lubricate O-ring seals with power steering fluid, then place seals on outlet fitting.
24. Install outlet fitting on valve cover. Tighten outlet fitting to specifications. Use care not to cock flow control valve when installing. Do not force valve forward otherwise damage to housing may result.

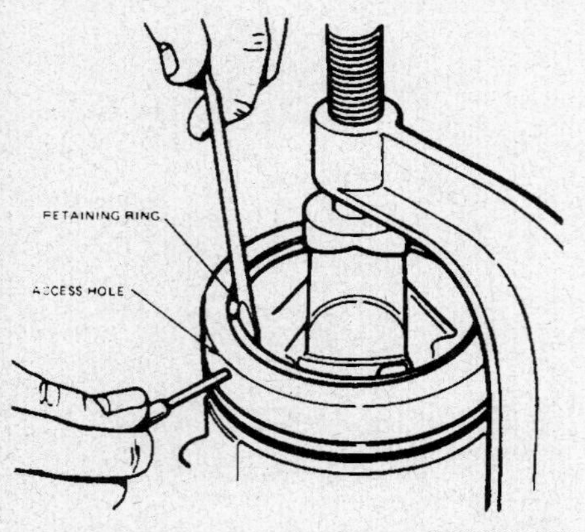

FM6029100061000X

Fig. 3 Valve cover retaining ring removal

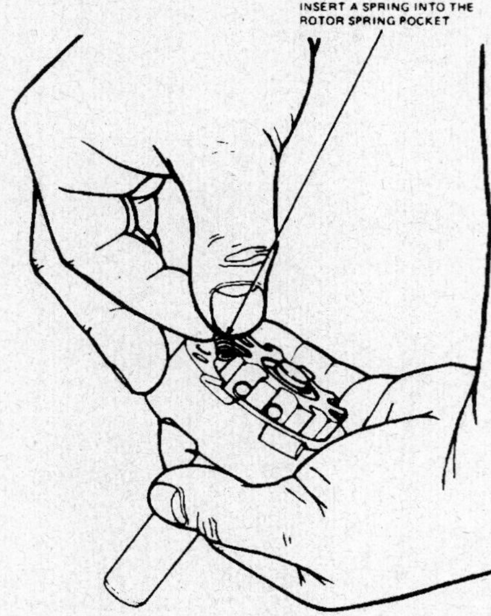

FM6029100062000X

Fig. 4 Slipper springs installation

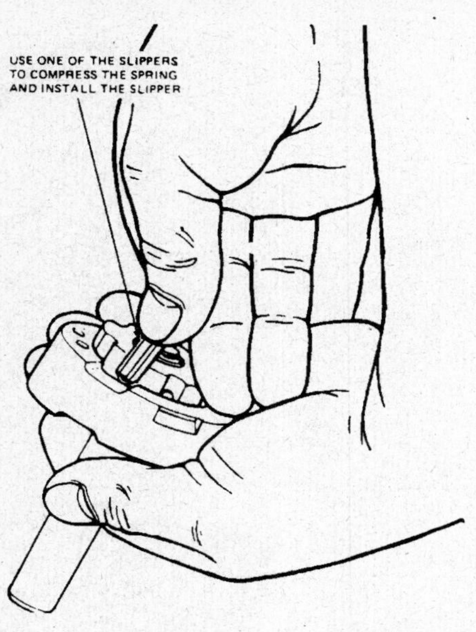

FM6029100063000X

Fig. 5 Slipper installation

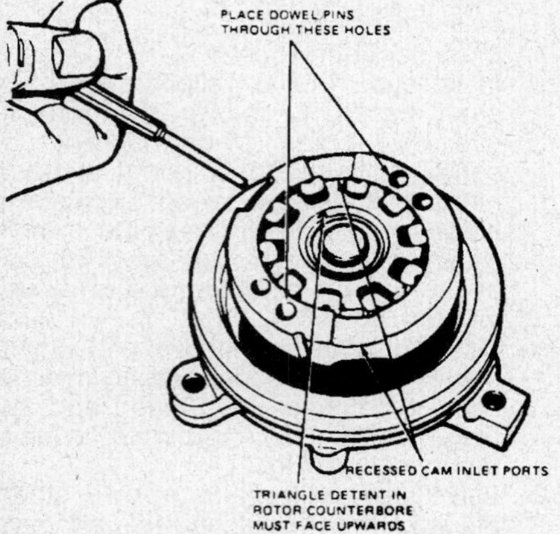

FM6029100064000X

Fig. 6 Assembling cam, slippers & rotor

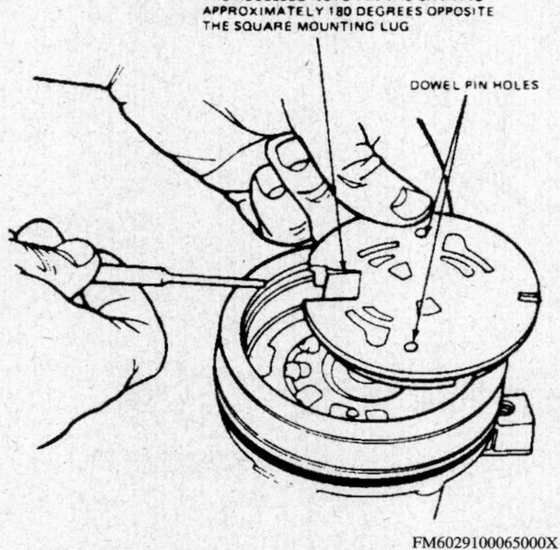

FM6029100065000X

Fig. 7 Upper pressure plate installation

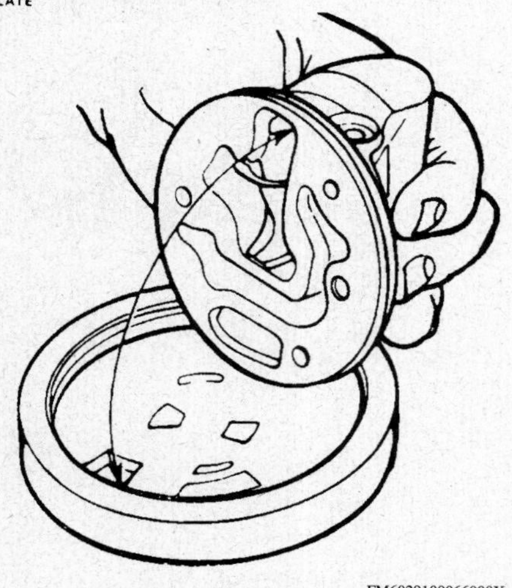

FM6029100066000X

Fig. 8 Valve cover installation

TIGHTENING SPECIFICATIONS

CONTINENTAL

Year	Component	Torque/Ft. Lbs.
1998–2002	Pressure Hose Fitting	31–39
	Reservoir Bolts	54–61①
	Return Hose Fitting	31–39
	Steering Pump To Engine Bolts	15–22

① — Inch lbs.

MUSTANG

Year	Component	Torque/Ft. Lbs.
1998	Front Bolts To Support Bracket	30–45
	Outlet Fitting To Reservoir & Valve Cover	25–34
	Pivot Bolt	30–45
	Pressure Hose Tube Nut To Pump Pressure Fitting	10–25
	Pump Bracket To Rear Support	①
	Pump To Bracket	30–45
	Rear Support To Engine Head	30–45
	Return Hose To Pump (Hose Clamp)	12–24②
	Support Bracket To Engine	30–45
	Support Bracket To Water Pump Housing	30–45
1999–2002	Power Steering Pump Mounting Bolts	38
	Pressure Line Fitting At Pump	30

① — Less A/C, 30–45 ft. lbs., w/A/C, 18–24 ft. lbs.
② — Inch lbs.

SABLE & TAURUS

Year	Component	Torque/Ft. Lbs.
1998–99	Hose Bracket	84–96①
	Pressure Hose Fitting	24–30
	Return Hose Fitting	24–30
	Support Bracket	17–24
2000–02	Hose Bracket	89①
	Pressure Hose Fitting	27
	Return Line	27
	Support Bracket	35

① — Inch lbs.

Type 4-Focus Power Steering Pump

NOTE: These Pumps Are Not Serviceable. If Service Is Required, Pump Must Be Replaced.

Type 5-Atsugi Vane-Type Pump

NOTE: These Pumps Are Not Serviceable. If Service Is Required, Pump Must Be Replaced.

Type 6-Ford CIII Vane-Type Pump

NOTE: These Pumps Are Not Serviceable. If Service Is Required, Pump Must Be Replaced.

Type 2-Ford Integral Rack & Pinion Steering Gear

NOTE: On Air Bag Equipped Models, Refer To "Air Bag System Precautions" Located In The Front Of This Manual For System Disarming & Arming Procedures.

NOTE: Refer To "Computer Relearn Procedures" Located In The Front Of This Manual When Battery Power To The Computer Has Been Interrupted.

NOTE: Also Refer To "Type 1-Ford Variable Assist Electronic Variable Orifice (EVO) System" For Mark VIII, & Cougar Models Equipped With EVO System.

INDEX

PRECAUTIONS

AIR BAG SYSTEMS

Refer to "Air Bag System Precautions" in the front of this manual for system disarming and arming procedures.

BATTERY GROUND CABLE

Prior to service, disconnect battery ground cable and isolate as required.

DESCRIPTION

These power rack and pinion steering gears, **Figs. 1 through 3,** are hydraulic-mechanical units, using an integral piston and rack to provide power assisted steering control. Internal valve controls pump flow and pressure as required during operation. The unit consists of a rotary hydraulic control valve connected to the input shaft and a boost cylinder integral with the rack.

OPERATION

The rotary control valve utilizes the relative rotational position of the input shaft and valve sleeve to control fluid flow. As the steering wheel is turned, the resistance of the wheels and weight of the vehicle cause a torsion bar to deflect, **Figs. 1 through 3.** This deflection changes position of rotary valve and sleeve ports, thereby directing fluid under pressure to the proper end of the power cylinder. The pressure differential acting on the piston attached to the rack provides the power assist.

The control valve is forced back to a centered position by the torsion bar when steering effort is removed. Pressure is then equalized on each side of the piston and the front wheels tend to return to a straight ahead position.

TROUBLESHOOTING

Refer to **Fig. 4** for troubleshooting procedure.

DIAGNOSIS & TESTING

POWER STEERING PRESSURE TEST

During the following procedure, power steering system pressure may exceed 1200 psi. Confirm proper tool fit prior to performing test. Exercise extreme caution or damage or personal injury may result.

1. Prior to performing pump flow and pressure tests, ensure following conditions exist:
   a. Proper pump reservoir fluid level.
   b. Proper tire air pressure.
   c. Proper pump belt tension.
   d. Proper model and vehicle pump application.
   e. Proper size pulleys on pump and engine.
   f. Ensure system is not damaged or leaking, repair as required.
2. The following test equipment is required:
   a. Engine tachometer.
   b. Thermometer: 0–300°F.
   c. **On all models except SHO,** power steering system analyzer tool No.78L-33610–A or equivalent.
   d. **On all models,** a set of adapter fittings.
3. The test procedure used in conjunction with the power steering system analyzer can be used to determine:
   a. System backpressure.
   b. Pump flow.
   c. Steering gear internal leakage.
   d. Pump relief pressure.
4. The readouts from step 3 can be used to determine which of the following conditions or components may be faulty:
   a. Hose or fitting restriction.
   b. Sticking gear valve.
   c. Insufficient pump capacity.
   d. Sticking relief valve.
   e. Suspension system binding.
5. Disconnect pump high pressure line, then connect suitable analyzer hose adapter, **Figs. 5 through 8.**
6. **On all models except SHO,** thread other analyzer adapter to pump.
7. **On all models,** connect analyzer hose to adapters, tighten both connections to 15 ft. lbs. maximum.
8. If required, add power steering fluid, start engine and allow to run about two minutes. Ensure idle is set to specifications.
9. With engine at idle, record the following:
   a. Flow, gallons per minute at 165–175°F.
   b. Pressure, psi at 165–175°F, at idle with gate fully open.
   c. If gallon per minute flow is below specifications, pump may require service. However, continue the test, measuring flow and relief pressure.
   d. If pressure is above 150 psi, inspect hoses for restrictions.
10. Partially close gate valve to build up 740 psi, observe and record flow at 165–175°F:

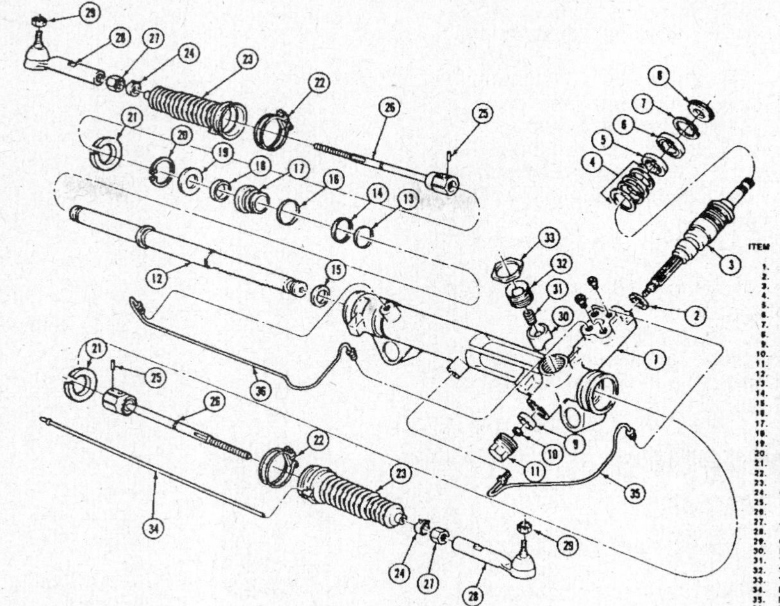

Fig. 1 Exploded view of steering gear. Cougar, Mark VIII & Mustang

   a. **On all models except SHO,** if flow drops lower than .9 gallons per minute, disassemble pump and replace cam pack. if pressure plates are cracked or worn, replace as required.
11. **On all models,** completely close and partially open gate valve three times. **Do not allow valve to remain closed for more than five seconds.** Observe and record pressure.
12. **On all models except SHO,** if pressure is lower than specifications, replace pump flow control valve.
13. If pressure is above specifications, pump flow control valve should be removed and cleaned or replaced.
14. **On all models,** fully open gate valve and increase engine speed to about 2500 RPM, then observe and record flow.
15. **On all models except SHO,** if flow exceeds maximum per-minute free flow, pump flow control valve should be removed and cleaned or replaced.
16. **On all models,** inspect idle speed. With engine at idle, turn steering wheel to lefthand and righthand stops, then record pressure and flow at stops.
17. Pressure at both stops should be about the same as maximum pump output pressure, flow should drop below .5 gallons per minute.
18. If pressure is not within specifications, excessive internal leakage is indicated, remove and disassemble steering gear, replace worn or damaged components and inspect rack piston and valve seals for damage.
19. While watching pressure gauge, turn steering wheel slightly in both directions and quickly release wheel. The gauge needle should move from normal backpressure and snap back as the wheel is released. If needle returns slowly or sticks, the steering gear rotary valve is sticking.
20. Flush power steering system as outlined under "Power Steering System Service."
21. If fault condition still exists, inspect ball joint and linkage.
22. Disconnect and remove analyzer, then connect lines.

POWER STEERING SYSTEM SERVICE

Power Steering System Bleed

1. Air trapped in power steering system may be removed with power steering pump air evacuator assembly vacuum tester tool No. 021-00014, or equivalent.
2. **Do not use engine vacuum to purge power steering system.**
3. Remove reservoir cap.
4. Inspect and fill reservoir to cold fill mark with suitable fluid.
5. Disconnect ignition coil wire, then raise and support front wheels.
6. Crank engine with starter motor, then inspect fluid level. **Do not turn steering wheel.**
7. If fluid level has dropped, fill reservoir to cold fill mark, crank engine with starter motor while turning steering wheel lock to lock, then inspect fluid level.
8. Install air evacuator rubber stopper tightly to pump reservoir, then connect coil wire.
9. With engine at idle, apply 15 inches maximum vacuum to pump reservoir for a minimum of three minutes. As air purges from system, vacuum will decrease. Maintain adequate vacuum.

10. Release vacuum, then remove vacuum source. If fluid level has dropped, fill to "cold fill" mark.
11. With engine at idle, apply 15 inches maximum vacuum to pump reservoir, then turn steering wheel from lock to lock every 30 seconds for about five minutes. **Do not hold steering wheel on stops when turning.** Maintain adequate vacuum.
12. Release vacuum, then remove vacuum equipment.
13. Add power steering fluid if required, then install cap.
14. Start engine, turn steering wheel, inspect connections for oil leaks.
15. If severe aeration is indicated, repeat steps 7 through 14.

Power Steering System Flush

1. Disconnect power steering return hose.
2. Place return line in suitable container, then plug reservoir return line at reservoir.
3. Fill reservoir using Motorcraft Dexron II part No. ESW-M2C33-F or equivalent.
4. Disconnect coil wire, then raise and support front wheels.
5. While adding about two quarts of fluid, turn ignition to start position (using ignition key), then crank engine with starter and turn steering wheel right to left.
6. When all the fluid is added, turn ignition Off and connect coil wire.
7. Remove reservoir return line plug, then connect line to reservoir.
8. Fill reservoir to specified level.
9. Lower vehicle, then start engine, slowly turn steering wheel several times lock to lock, then inspect fluid level, adding fluid as required.

Adjustments

STEERING GEAR

CONTINENTAL, MARK VIII, MUSTANG, SABLE AND TAURUS

Rack yoke bearing preload is the only service adjustment required. This adjustment is performed with the steering gear removed from the vehicle. Refer to the individual vehicle chapters for steering gear removal.

1. Clean steering gear's exterior, then install two long bolts and washers through bushings and attach to bench fixture tool No. T57L-500-B or equivalent.
2. Do not remove external pressure lines unless damaged or leaking. Drain power steering fluid by rotating input shaft from lock to lock two times using pinion shaft torque adapter tool No. T74P-3504-R or equivalent. Cover ports on valve housing with a clean shop cloth while draining gear.
3. Position an inch pound torque wrench and pinion shaft adapter tool on input shaft splines.

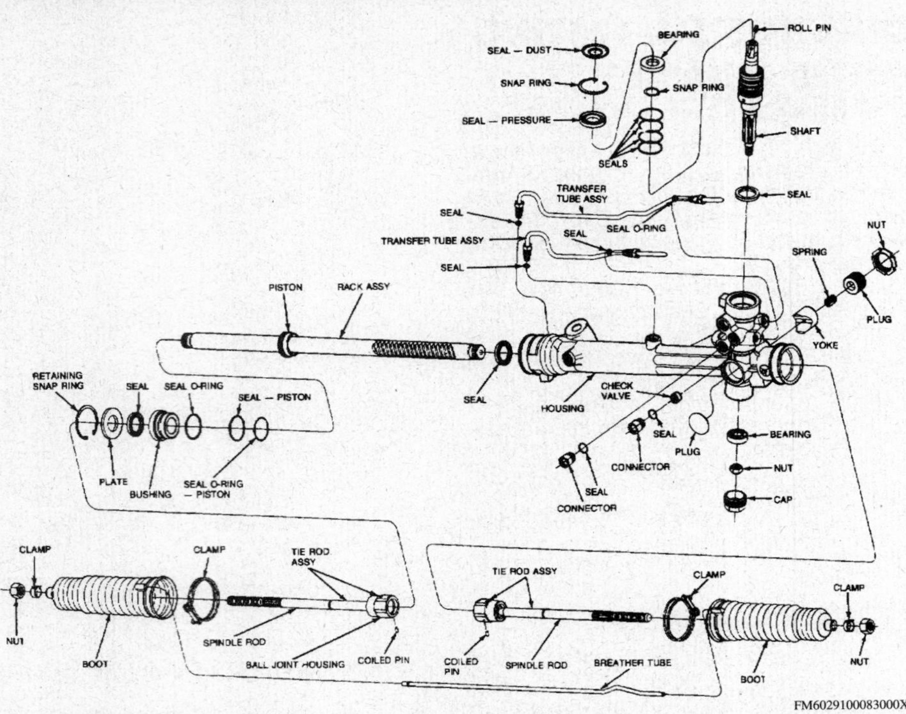

Fig. 2 Exploded view of steering gear. Continental, Sable & Taurus

4. Loosen yoke plug locknut using pinion housing yoke locknut wrench tool No. T78P-3504-H or equivalent, then loosen yoke plug using a ¾ inch socket wrench, **Fig. 9.**
5. Clean yoke plug threads then, with rack at center of travel, **torque** yoke plug to 40–50 inch lbs.
6. Back off yoke plug approximately ⅛ turn until torque required to rotate input shaft is 7–18 inch lbs.
7. While holding yoke plug in position, tighten locknut to specifications. Using pinion housing yoke locknut wrench tool No. T78P-3504-H or equivalent, measure input shaft rotating torque after tightening locknut.
8. If the external pressure lines were removed in Step 2, they must be replaced with new ones. Remove the copper seals from the pressure ports prior to installing new lines.
9. Remove steering gear from holding fixture, then install external pressure lines. Tighten pump to gear and return line fittings and valve and power cylinder (gear housing) fittings to specifications.

Component Service

CONTINENTAL, MARK VIII, MUSTANG, SABLE AND TAURUS

TIE ROD ENDS, BELLOWS & BALL JOINT SOCKETS

Disassemble

1. Install two long bolts and washers through bushings and attach gear to holding fixture tool No. T57L-500-B or equivalent.
2. Loosen jam nuts on outer ends of tie rods, then remove tie rod ends and jam nuts.
3. Remove four clamps attaching bellows to tie rods and gear housing.
4. Drain power steering fluid, then remove bellows with breather tube. Use care not to damage bellows.
5. If pinion is to be removed, remove pinion before proceeding.
6. Thread point of roll pin remover tool No. T78P-3504-N or equivalent, into roll pin on ball socket and tighten finger tight. Remove roll pins, **Fig. 10.**
7. if pinion was not removed, remove gear housing from holding fixture and place on bench to prevent damage to gear teeth.
8. Position rack so that several teeth are exposed. Hold rack using an adjustable wrench on end teeth while loosening ball sockets with nut wrench tool No. T74P-3504-U or equivalent, **Fig. 11.**

Assemble

This procedure has been modified by a technical service bulletin.

1. **On models equipped with tie rods retained by a rivet or pin,** proceed as follows:
   a. Install tie rod and ball socket assemblies onto rack. Hold one ball socket with 1 5⁄16 inch wrench while tightening other ball socket to specifications, using nut wrench tool No. T74P3504-U or equivalent. Both ball socket assemblies will be torqued simultaneously using this method. **If pinion was not removed from housing, this step**

must be performed with the steering gear removed from the holding fixture and positioned on bench to prevent damage to gear teeth.

b. Support ball housing using a wooden block, then install roll pins by tapping lightly with a plastic mallet.
c. If pinion was removed, install pinion as described under "Input Shaft and Valve Assembly."
d. Thoroughly clean rack and housing bore.
e. Apply lubricant to bellows clamp under cut on tie rod, then install bellows and breather tube.
f. Install clamps retaining bellows to steering gear. Use tool No. T63P-9171-A or equivalent to secure clamp to gear.
g. Install clamps retaining bellows to tie rods, then the jam nuts and tie rod ends.

2. **On models equipped with tie rods not retained by a rivet or pin,** proceed as follows:
   a. Turn rack to lefthand stop, then place suitable adjustable wrench on rack to prevent turning during tightening procedures.
   b. Using a suitable wrench, tighten tie rod to rack to specifications.
   c. Install rack boots, then secure to rack body and tie rod using suitable clamps. Tighten to specifications.
   d. Install tie rod end jam nuts and tie rod ends to tie rods, then tighten to specifications after final adjustment.

STEERING GEAR

The steering gear on these models is not serviceable and must be replaced as an assembly.

CONTOUR, COUGAR, LS, MYSTIQUE & THUNDERBIRD

TIE ROD ENDS, BELLOWS & BALL JOINT SOCKETS

1. Secure steering gear in holding fixture tool No. T57L-500-B or equivalent.
2. Loosen tie rod end jam nuts, then remove tie rod ends and jam nuts from tie rods. Record turns required to remove tie rod ends.
3. Remove rack boot clamps, then the rack boots.
4. Place a suitable adjustable wrench only on rack end teeth, then, using a suitable pipe wrench, loosen and remove tie rods. Do not allow rack to turn in gear.
5. Reverse procedure to install. Tighten to specifications.

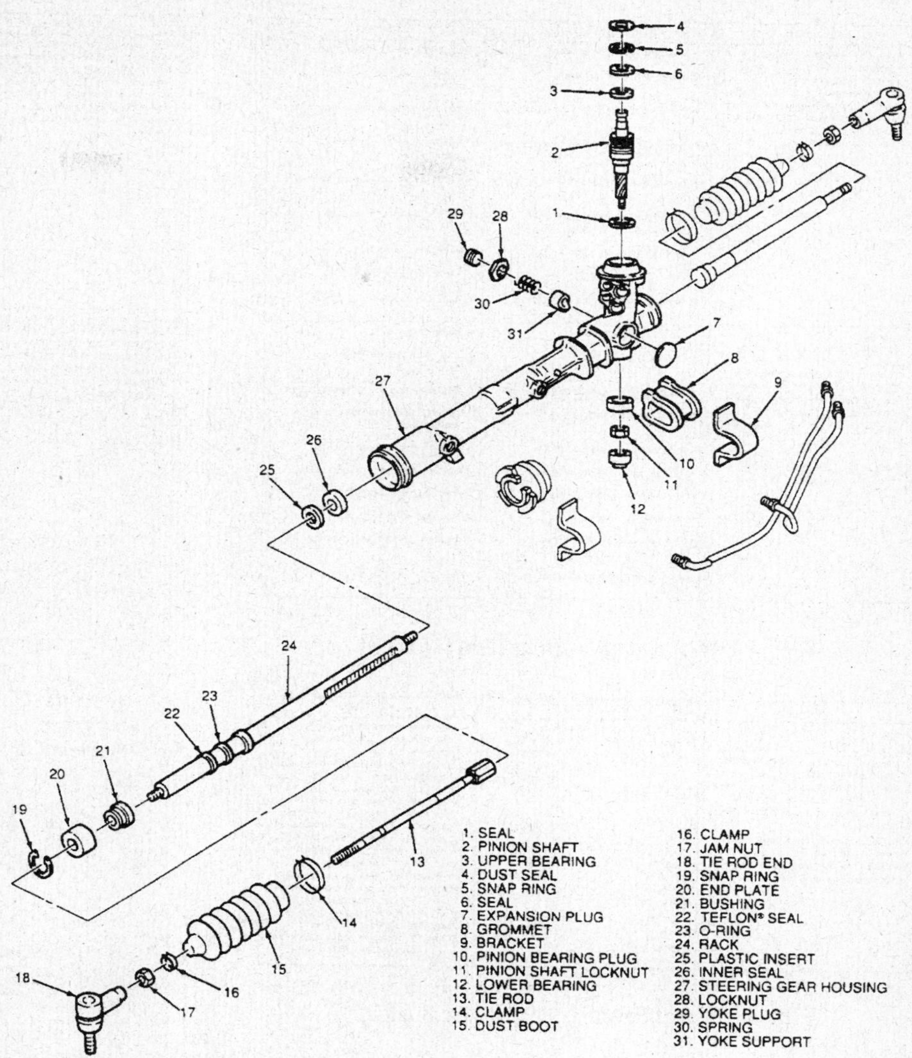

Fig. 3 Exploded view of steering gear. Escort & Tracer

STEERING GEAR

The steering gear on these models is not serviceable and must be replaced as an assembly.

ESCORT, TRACER & ZX2

TIE ROD ENDS, BELLOWS & BALL JOINT SOCKETS

1. Raise and support vehicle, then disconnect tie rod ends from knuckle using separator tool No. T85M-3395-A or equivalent.
2. Loosen tie rod end jam nuts, then remove tie rod ends and jam nuts from tie rods. **Record turns required to remove tie rod ends.**
3. Remove rack boot clamps, then the rack boots.
4. Place a 20 MM crowfoot wrench, or equivalent, on end of rack, then, using tie rod socket tool No. C3AZ-19578-A or equivalent, loosen and remove tie rods. **Do not allow rack to turn in gear.**
5. Reverse procedure to install. Tighten nuts and bolts to specifications.

STEERING GEAR

The steering gear on these models is not serviceable and must be replaced as an assembly.

CONDITION	POSSIBLE SOURCE	ACTION
• Wander — Vehicle wander is a condition where the vehicle wanders side to side on the roadway when it is driven straight ahead while the steering wheel is held in a firm position. Evaluation should be conducted on a level road (little road crown).	• Improper wheel alignment.	• Set alignment to specification.
	• Loose outer tie rod ends.	• Replace outer tie rod end assemblies.
	• Inner tie rod ball housing loose or worn.	• Replace inner tie rod assemblies.
	• Gear assembly mounting loose.	• Tighten mounting bolts to specification.
	• Loose suspension struts or ball joints.	• Adjust or replace as required.
	• Column intermediate shaft connecting bolts loose.	• Tighten bolts to specification.
	• Loose wheel bearings.	• Service as required.
	• Column intermediate shaft joints loose or worn.	• Replace intermediate shaft.
• Feedback — (Rattle, chuckle, knocking noises in the steering gear). Feedback is a condition where roughness is felt in the steering wheel by the driver when the vehicle is driven over rough pavement.	• Column U-joints loose.	• Replace if bad.
	• Loose outer tie rod ends.	• Replace outer tie rod end assemblies.
	• Loose/worn inner tie rod ball.	• Replace inner tie rod assemblies.
	• Gear assembly mounting loose.	• Tighten mounting bolts to specification.
	• Loose pinion bearing cap.	• Tighten cap to specification.
	• Loose pinion bearing locknut.	• Tighten locknut to specification.
	• Piston disengaged or loose on rack.	• Replace rack assembly.
	• Steering gear yoke worn.	• Replace yoke assembly.
	• Column intermediate shaft connecting bolts loose.	• Tighten bolts to specification.
	• Loose suspension struts on ball joints.	• Adjust or replace as necessary.

FM6029100087010X

Fig. 4 Troubleshooting (Part 1 of 3)

CONDITION	POSSIBLE SOURCE	ACTION
• Hissing Sound There is some noise in all power steering systems. One of the most common is a hissing sound most evident at standstill parking. There is no relationship between this noise and the performance of the steering gear. **CAUTION: Do not hold steering wheel at full lock more than five seconds, as damage to power steering pump may result.**	• Hiss may be expected when the steering wheel is at the end of travel or when turning at standstill.	• Hiss is a normal characteristic of rotary steering gears and in no way affects steering. Do not replace the rack assembly unless the hiss is extremely objectionable. A replacement rack will also exhibit a slight noise and is not always a cure for the condition. Investigate for a grounded column or a loose boot at the dash panel. Any metal-to-metal contact will transmit valve hiss into the passenger compartment through the steering column. Verify clearance between flexible coupling components. Ensure steering column shaft and gear are aligned so flexible coupling rotates in a flat plane and is not distorted as shaft rotates.

FM6029100087030X

Fig. 4 Troubleshooting (Part 3 of 3)

CONDITION	POSSIBLE SOURCE	ACTION
• Poor Returnability — Sticky Feel — Poor returnability is noticed when the steering fails to return to center following a turn without manual effort from the driver. In addition, when the driver returns the steering to center, it may have a sticky or catchy feel.	• Misaligned steering column or column flange rubbing steering wheel and/or flange.	• Align column.
	• Check rotational torque of intermediate shaft joints.	• If binding, replace intermediate shaft.
	• Improper wheel alignment.	• Set to specification.
	• Tight inner tie rod ball joints.	• Replace inner tie rod as required.
	• Binding in valve assembly	• Replace input shaft valve assembly.
	• Bent or damaged rack.	• Replace rack assembly.
	• Bent or damaged sub-frame.	• Replace as necessary.
	• Column bearing binding.	• Replace bearing.
	• Tight suspension struts or lower control arm ball joints.	• Adjust or replace as required.
	• Contamination in system.	• Flush power steering system.
	• Deformed engine mounts.	• Replace as required.
• Heavy Steering Efforts (Poor or loss of assist) — A heavy effort and poor assist condition is recognized by the driver while turning corners and especially while parking. A road test will verify this condition.	• Leakage/loss of fluid.	• external leakage service.
	• Low pump fluid.	• Fill as necessary.
	• Pump external leakage.	• Service
	• Improper drive belt tension.	• Readjust belt tension.
	• Hose or cooler external leakage.	• Replace as necessary.
	• Improper engine idle speed.	• Readjust idle.
	• Pulley loose or warped.	• Replace pulley.
	• Pump/flow pressure not to specification.	
	• Hose/cooler line restrictions.	• Clear or replace as required.
	• Valve plastic ring cut or twisted.	• Replace ring.
	• Damaged/worn plastic piston ring.	• Replace ring.
	• Loose/missing rubber backup piston O-ring.	• Replace/install O-ring.
	• Loose rack piston.	• Replace rack assembly.
	• Gear assembly oil passages restricted.	• Clear/service as required.
	• Bent/damaged rack assembly.	• Replace rack assembly.

FM6029100087020X

Fig. 4 Troubleshooting (Part 2 of 3)

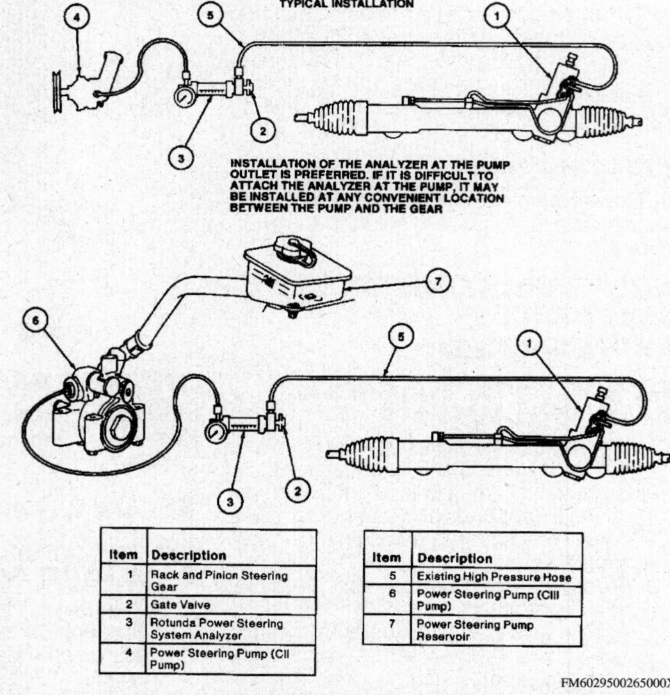

Item	Description
1	Rack and Pinion Steering Gear
2	Gate Valve
3	Rotunda Power Steering System Analyzer
4	Power Steering Pump (CII Pump)

Item	Description
5	Existing High Pressure Hose
6	Power Steering Pump (CIII Pump)
7	Power Steering Pump Reservoir

FM6029500265000X

Fig. 5 Pressure test connections. Mark VIII & Mustang

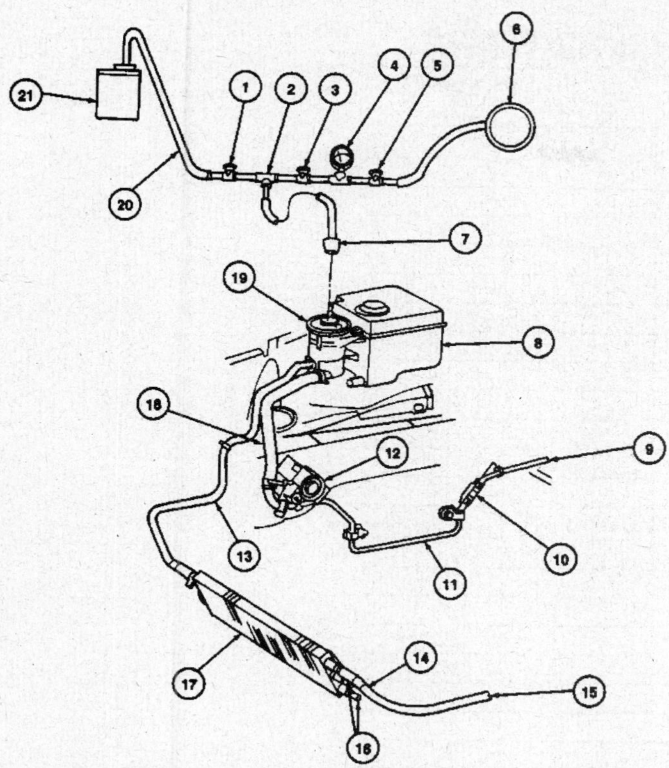

Item	Description
1	Valve No. 1
2	Tee
3	Valve No. 2
4	0 to 30 Inch Vacuum Gauge
5	Valve No. 3
6	Vacuum Source
7	No. 7 Stopper
8	Radiator Coolant Recovery Reservoir
9	Power Steering Left Turn Pressure Hose (To Auxiliary Actuator)
10	Intermediate Connection

Item	Description
11	Power Steering Pressure Hose
12	Power Steering Pump
13	Oil Cooler-To-Reservoir Hose
14	Power Steering Return Hose
15	From Power Steering Gear
16	Transmission Fluid Cooler Ports
17	Combination Power Steering and Automatic Transmission Fluid Cooler
18	Power Steering Reservoir Pump Hose

FM6029500266000X

Fig. 6 Pressure test connections. Continental

POWER STEERING ANALYZER 014-00207
PRESSURE LINE ASSY
RETURN LINE ASSY
STEERING GEAR

FM6029100090000X

Fig. 7 Pressure test connections. Sable & Taurus, except SHO

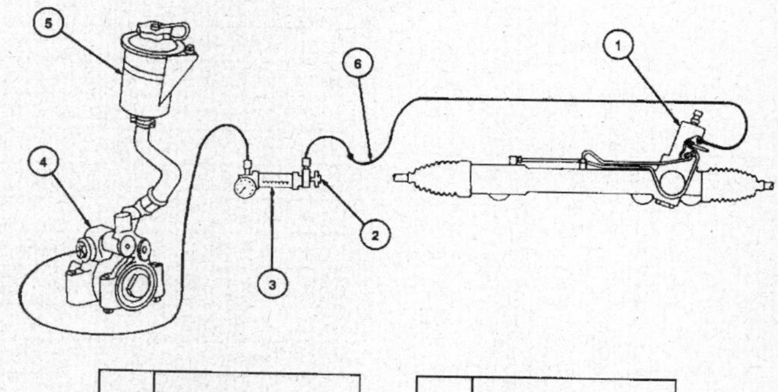

Item	Description
1	Steering Gear
2	Gate Valve
3	Rotunda Power Steering System Analyzer

Item	Description
4	Power Steering Pump
5	Power Steering Pump Auxiliary Reservoir
6	Existing High Pressure Hose

FM6029400202000X

Fig. 8 Pressure test connections. Contour, Cougar & Mystique

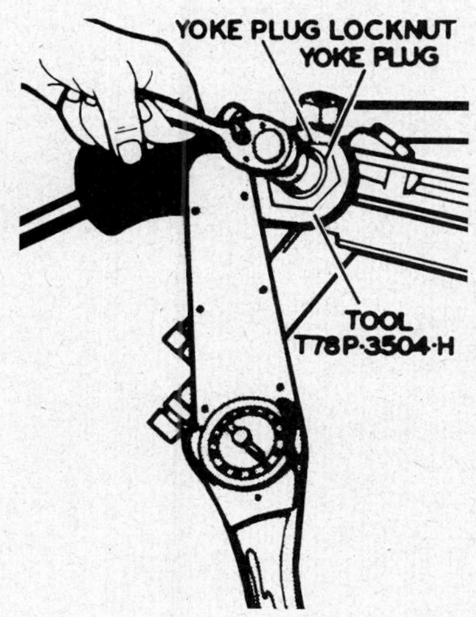

FM6029100092000X

Fig. 9 Yoke plug locknut removal. Continental, Mark VIII, Mustang, Sable and Taurus

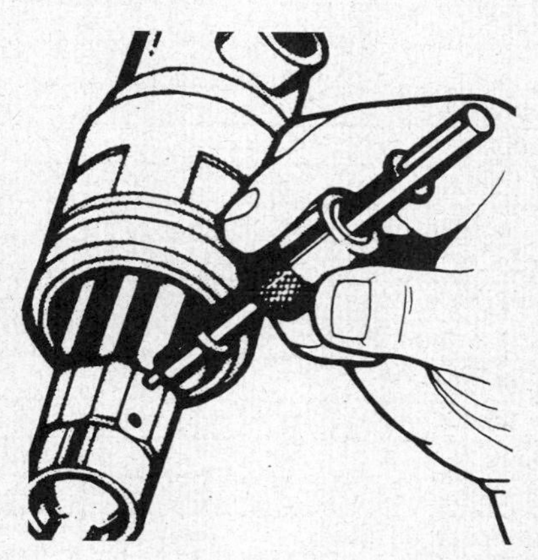

FM6029100093000X

Fig. 10 Roll pin removal from ball socket. Continental, Mark VIII, Mustang, Sable & Taurus

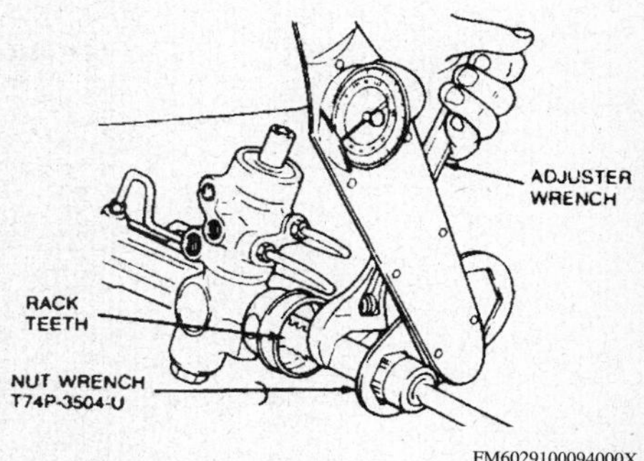

FM6029100094000X

Fig. 11 Tie rod & ball socket removal. Continental, Mark VIII, Mustang, Sable & Taurus

TIGHTENING SPECIFICATIONS

Component	Torque/Ft. Lbs.
CONTINENTAL	
Bellows Clamp Screw	20–30①
Gear Hose Fittings	24–30
Gear Housing Return Line	20–25
Gear To Crossmember	100–144
Intermediate Shaft To Steering Column	15–24
Intermediate Shaft To Steering Gear	30–38
Pressure Line Fitting To Actuator Banjo Bolt	22–28
Pump Pressure Line Fitting	42–54
Tie Rod Ball Socket To Rack	②
Tie Rod End Jam Nut	35–48
Tie Rod End To Spindle Arm	35–47
VAPS Actuator	24–30
CONTOUR, MYSTIQUE & COUGAR	
Bellows Clamp Screw	25①
Flexible Coupling Pinch Bolt	21
Gear Hose Fittings	23
Gear Housing Return Line	23
Gear Cover Plate Bolts	37
Gear To Crossmember	101
Pump Pressure Line Fitting	48
Tie Rod End Jam Nut	45
Tie Rod End To Spindle Arm	21
ESCORT, TRACER & ZX2	
A/C Compressor	15–22
High Pressure Line To Housing Flare Nut	21–25
Return Line To Housing Flare Nut	21–25
Tie Rod End Jam Nuts	25–37
Tie Rod To Rack	40–50
LS & THUNDERBIRD	
Hose Bracket To Steering Gear Bolt	89①
Steering Gear To Frame Nuts	46①
Steering Grear Fluid Lines	23
Steering Shaft To Gear Pinch Bolt	26
Tie Rod To Steering Knuckle	74
Tie Rod To Rack	88
MARK VIII	
Bellows Clamp Screw	20–30①
Gear Hose Fittings	20–25
Gear To Crossmember	100–144
Steering Flex Coupling Bolt	20–30
Tie Rod End Jam Nut	35–46
Tie Rod End To Spindle Arm	35–49
Tie Rod Socket Assembly To Rack	②
1998 MUSTANG	
Bellows Clamp Screw	20–30①
Gear Hose Fittings	20–25
Gear To Crossmember	30–40
Pump Pressure Hose Fitting	26–33
Steering Flex Coupling Bolt	20–30
Tie Rod End Jam Nut	35–50
Tie Rod End To Spindle Arm	35–47
Tie Rod Socket Assembly To Rack	②

Continued

TIGHTENING SPECIFICATIONS—Continued

Component	Torque/Ft. Lbs.
1999–2002 MUSTANG	
Front Wheel Spindle Tie Rod	74
Pressure Line Fitting	48
Steering Gear Mounting Nut	35
Steering Intermediate Shaft Coupling Pinch Bolt	25
Tie Rod End Castellated Nut	11
Tie Rod End Jam Nut	41
SABLE & TAURUS	
Bellows Clamp Screw	20–30①
Gear Hose Fittings	15–25
Gear Housing Return Line	24–30
Gear To Crossmember	85–100
Intermediate Shaft To Steering Column	15–25
Intermediate Shaft To Steering Gear	30–38
Pressure Line Fitting To Actuator Banjo Bolt	22–28
Pump Pressure Line Fitting	42–54
Tie Rod Ball Socket To Rack	66–81
Tie Rod End Jam Nut	35–50
Tie Rod End To Spindle Arm	35–47
VAPS Actuator	24–30

①— Inch lbs.
②— Tie rod retained w/pin or rivet, 55–65 ft. lbs., tie rod not retained by a pin or rivet, 68–81 ft. lbs.

Type 3-Ford Torsion Bar Power Steering Gear

NOTE: On Air Bag Equipped Models, Refer To "Air Bag System Precautions" Located In The Front Of This Manual For System Disarming & Arming Procedures.

NOTE: Refer To "Computer Relearn Procedures" Located In The Front Of This Manual When Battery Power To The Computer Has Been Interrupted.

NOTE: Also Refer To "Type 1-Ford Variable Assist Electronic Variable Orifice (EVO) System," For Models Equipped With EVO System.

INDEX

PRECAUTIONS

AIR BAG SYSTEMS

Refer to "Air Bag System Precautions" in the front of this manual for system disarming and arming procedures.

BATTERY GROUND CABLE

Prior to service, disconnect battery ground cable and isolate as required.

DESCRIPTION

The power steering unit, **Fig. 1,** is a torsion bar type of hydraulic-assisted system. This system furnishes power to reduce the amount of turning effort required at the steering wheel. It also reduces road shock and vibrations.

The unit includes a worm and one piece rack-piston which is meshed to the gear teeth on the steering sector shaft. The unit also includes a hydraulic valve, valve actuator, input shaft and torsion bar assembly which are mounted on the end of the worm shaft and operated by a twisting action of the torsion bar.

The gear unit is designed with the one piece rack-piston, worm and sector shaft in the one housing and the valve spool in an attaching housing. This makes internal fluid passages possible between valve and cylinder, thus eliminating all external lines and hoses except the pressure and return hoses between pump and gear.

The power cylinder is an integral part of the gear housing. The piston is double acting in that fluid pressure may be applied to either of its sides.

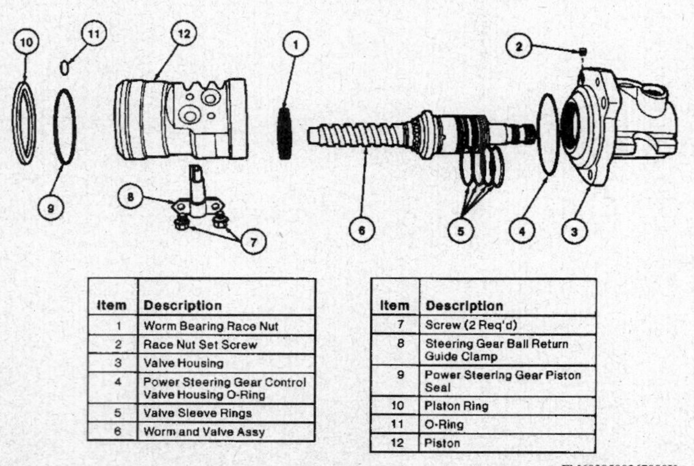

Item	Description
1	Worm Bearing Race Nut
2	Race Nut Set Screw
3	Valve Housing
4	Power Steering Gear Control Valve Housing O-Ring
5	Valve Sleeve Rings
6	Worm and Valve Assy

Item	Description
7	Screw (2 Req'd)
8	Steering Gear Ball Return Guide Clamp
9	Power Steering Gear Piston Seal
10	Piston Ring
11	O-Ring
12	Piston

Fig. 1 Exploded view of Ford power steering gear

OPERATION

The operation of the hydraulic control valve spool is governed by the twisting of a torsion bar. All effort applied to the steering wheel is transmitted directly through the input shaft and torsion bar to the worm and piston. Any resistance to the turning of the front wheels results in twisting of the bar. The twisting of the bar increases as the front wheel turning effort increases. The control valve spool, actuated by the twisting of the torsion bar, directs fluid to the side of the piston where hydraulic assistance is required.

As the torsion bar twists, its radial motion is transferred into axial motion by three helical threads. Thus, the valve is moved off center, and fluid is directed to one side of the piston or the other.

TROUBLESHOOTING

STEERING DRIFT/WANDER

1. Tire size and pressure.

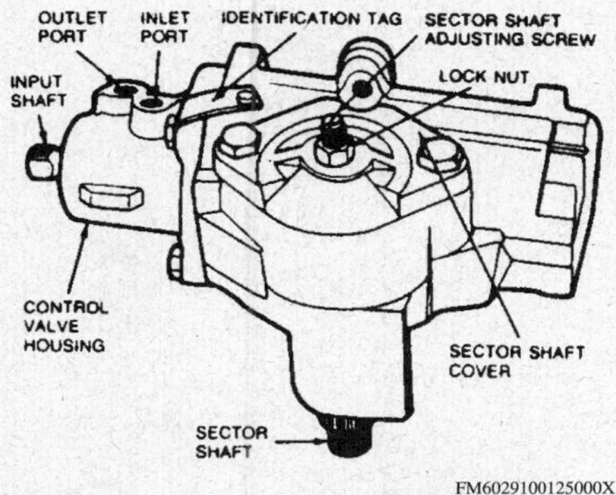

Fig. 2 Mesh load adjustment

2. Loose or worn tie rod ends or ball joints.
3. Steering gear mounting insulators or retaining bolts loose or damaged.
4. Loose front suspension lower arm struts.
5. Steering column gear input shaft coupling connecting bolts loose.
6. Steering gear input shaft coupling joints lose or worn.
7. Improper wheel alignment.
8. Excessive toe-in.
9. Excessive friction between components.

PULLS TO ONE SIDE

1. Improper tire pressure.
2. Improper tire size or type.
3. Vehicle is unevenly loaded.
4. Improper wheel alignment.
5. Damaged front or rear suspension components.
6. Steering gear valve effort out of adjustment.
7. Front or rear brakes operating improperly.
8. Bent rear axle housing, damaged or sagging front coil springs or damaged or worn rear suspension component.
9. loose or damaged rear suspension retaining fasteners.

FEEDBACK (RATTLE, CHUCKLE OR KNOCKING NOISES FROM STEERING GEAR)

1. Steering column gear input shaft coupling joints loose or worn.
2. Loose tie rod ends.
3. Steering gear retaining bolts loose or damaged.
4. Loose suspension bushings, fasteners or ball joints.
5. Improper steering gear adjustment.

POOR RETURNABILITY, STICKY FEEL

1. Improper tire pressure, tire size or tire type.
2. Misaligned steering column or column flange.
3. Steering column gear input shaft universal joints binding.
4. Steering column tube boot tears.
5. Binding or damaged tie rod ends.
6. Damaged or worn front suspension components.
7. Improper wheel alignment.
8. Column bearing binding.
9. Contamination in system.
10. Improper steering gear adjustment.

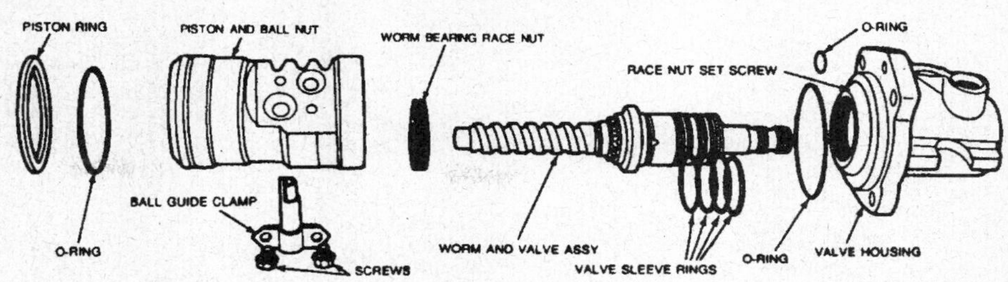

Fig. 3 Exploded view of ball nut & valve housing

HEAVY STEERING EFFORT, POOR ASSIST OR LOSS OF ASSIST

1. Contamination of system by foreign objects in power steering oil reservoir or metallic particles in fluid being generated by cam pack discrepancies.
2. Low power steering fluid.
3. Steering gear assembly internal or external leak.
4. Improper drive belt tension.
5. Hose or cooler external leak or internal restriction.
6. Improper engine idle speed.
7. Power steering pump pulley loose or warped.
8. Power steering pump flow or pressure not to specifications.
9. Improper steering gear adjustments.
10. System contamination.
11. EVO power steering control valve actuator sticking.

POWER STEERING PUMP LEAKS AT EVO CONTROL VALVE ACTUATOR

1. Damaged power steering control valve actuator ring.
2. EVO power steering control valve actuator electrical connector damaged.
3. EVO power steering control valve actuator damaged.

NOISY PUMP

Swish Type Noise

A swish type noise may be created by the flow of excessive fluid into the bypass port of the pump valve housing with temperatures below 130.° This is a normal condition and will diminish when fluid temperature increases.

1. Low fluid level and possible leak.

Clicking Type Noise

1. Excessive power steering pump wear.

Moan or Whine Type Noise

1. Fluid aeration.
2. Power steering pump loose or misaligned with engine.
3. Low fluid.
4. Hose or steering column grounded.
5. Damaged internal components.

POWER STEERING SYSTEM SERVICE

Adjustments

MESH LOAD

1998

During vehicle break-in period, some factory adjustments may change. These changes will not necessarily affect operation of the steering gear, but should excessive steering lash be encountered, a mesh load adjustment may be required.

1. Disconnect steering gear sector shaft arm form steering gear sector shaft.
2. Disconnect fluid return line at reservoir and cap reservoir return line pipe.
3. Place end of return line in a clean container and cycle steering wheel in both directions as required to discharge fluid from gear.
4. Remove ornamental cover from wheel hub and turn steering wheel 45° from lefthand stop.
5. Using an inch lb. torque wrench on steering wheel nut, determine torque required to rotate shaft slowly through an approximate ¼ turn from the 45° position.
6. Turn steering gear back to center, then determine torque required to rotate shaft back and forth across center position.
7. Loosen adjuster nut and turn adjusting screw, **Fig. 2,** until reading is as follows:
   a. **On models with 0–5000 miles,** reset if total mesh load over mechanical center if not 15–24 inch lbs. Set torque rocking across center to a value 11–15 inch lbs. greater than that measured 45° from righthand stop.
   b. **On models with more than 5000 miles,** reset if mesh load measured while rocking input shaft over center is less than 10 inch lbs. greater than torque 45° from righthand stop. Set torque measured rocking across center to a value of 10–14 inch lbs. greater than that measured 45° from righthand stop.
8. **On all models,** inspect readings, then replace Pitman arm and steering wheel.
9. Connect fluid return line and replenish reservoir.

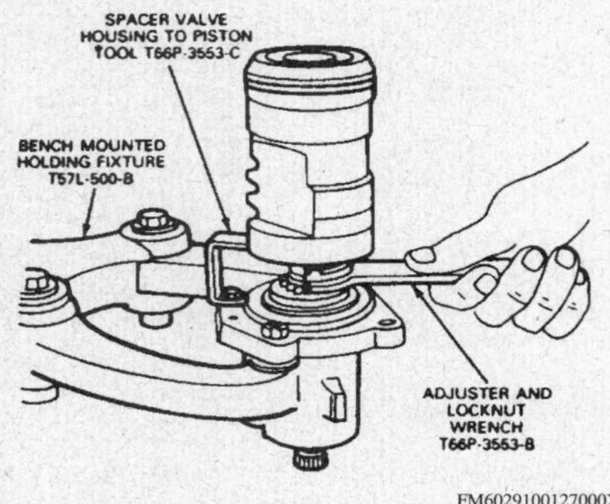

Fig. 4 Input shaft removal

1999-2002

Perform the following adjustment with the steering gear and fluid lines disconnected from the vehicles steering system components.

1. Rotate input shaft either right or left to the stop.
2. Rotate the shaft in the opposite direction and count the number of turns.
3. Rotate the shaft back one half the number of turns counted.
4. Using a suitable inch lb. torque wrench, measure the torque required to rotate the input shaft 45° either side of center. If torque reading is not 12–16 inch lbs., turn sector shaft adjusting screw to adjust mesh load.

Component Service

OVERHAUL

GEAR

Disassemble

1. Hold steering gear over drain pan in an inverted position and cycle input shaft six times to drain remaining fluid from gear.
2. Using suitable mounting pads for support, install gear in bench mounting fixture tool No. T57L-500-B or equivalent.
3. Remove locknut from adjusting screw.
4. Turn input shaft to either stop, then turn it back approximately 1 5/8 turns to center the gear. **Input shaft spline indexing flat should be facing downward.**
5. Remove sector shaft cover bolts.
6. Tap lower end of sector shaft with a soft-faced hammer to loosen it, then lift cover and shaft from housing as a unit. Discard O-ring.
7. Turn sector shaft cover counterclockwise off adjuster screw.
8. Remove valve housing attaching bolts. Lift valve housing from gear housing while holding piston to prevent it from rotating off worm shaft. Remove valve housing and lube passage O-rings and discard.
9. Remove valve housing attaching bolts and ID tag, while holding piston separate valve housing from housing, remove and discard O-rings.
10. With piston held, remove ball clamp screws and guide clamp, **Fig. 3.**
11. With finger over ball guide opening,

Fig. 5 Piston assembly on worm shaft

turn piston so ball guide faces downward over clean container, then allow guide tubes to drop to container.
12. Rotate input shaft from stop to stop, until all balls fall from piston, then remove valve assembly from piston. **Ensure all balls have been removed. Worm may no longer be removed from piston.**
13. Install valve body to bench mounting fixture tool No. T57L-500-B or equivalent, then loosen valve housing race nut lockscrew. Using adjuster locknut wrench tool No. T66P-3553-B and spacer valve housing tool No. T66P-3553-C or equivalents, remove worm bearing race.
14. Slide input shaft, worm and valve assembly from valve housing, **Fig. 4.**

Assemble

1. Install worm and valve in housing.
2. Install retaining nut in housing, then tighten nut using Adjuster and locknut wrench tool No. T66P-3553 or equivalent. Because length of tool required to tighten nut will affect torque wrench reading, the following formula for determining torque must be used: torque (using tool T66P-3553-B or equivalent) equals (length of torque wrench × 72 ft. lbs. length of torque wrench + 5.5 inches).
3. Install race nut screw and tighten to specifications.
4. Place piston on bench with ball guide holes facing up. Insert worm shaft into piston so that first groove is in alignment with hole nearest to center of piston, **Fig. 5.**
5. Place ball guide into piston. Place balls in guide (27 minimum), turning worm clockwise (viewed from input end of shaft). If all balls have not been fed into guide upon reaching righthand stop, rotate input shaft in one direction and then in the other while installing balls. After balls have been installed, do not rotate input shaft or piston more than 3½ turns off the righthand stop. This is to prevent balls from falling out of circuit.
6. Secure guides to ball nut with clamp and tighten to specifications.
7. Apply petroleum jelly to piston seal.
8. Place a new O-ring on valve housing.
9. Slide piston and valve into gear housing, being careful not to damage seal.
10. Align lube passage in valve housing with one in gear housing, place O-ring

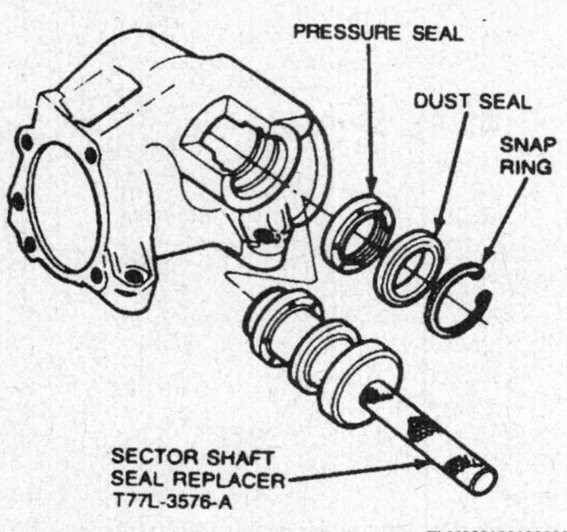

Fig. 6 Exploded view of steering gear housing

in gear housing oil passage hole, then identification tag and install but do not tighten attaching bolts at this time.
11. Rotate ball nut so that teeth are in same plane as sector teeth. Tighten valve housing attaching bolts.
12. Position sector shaft cover O-ring in gear housing. Turn input shaft as required to center piston.
13. Apply petroleum jelly to sector shaft journal, then position sector shaft and cover into gear housing. Install air conditioner line mounting bracket, if equipped, and two sector shaft cover bolts, then tighten to specifications.
14. Attach an inch pound torque wrench to input shaft and adjust mesh load as outlined previously.

GEAR HOUSING

1. Remove lower end housing snap ring, **Fig. 6.**
2. Using puller attachment tool No. T58L-101-B or equivalent, remove and discard dust and pressure seals. **Bearing is not serviceable and must be replaced as an assembly.**
3. Using suitable multi purpose grease, lubricate new pressure, dust seal and sector shaft seal bore.
4. Install dust seal on sector shaft, using seal replacer tool No. T77L-3576-A or equivalent with seal raised lip toward tool, then install pressure seal with lip away from tool. Pressure seal flat side should be against flat side of dust deal.
5. Install tool to sector shaft bore, then drive tool until seals clear snap ring grooves. **Do not bottom the seal against bearing or seals will not function properly.**
6. Install snap ring in housing groove.

REPLACEMENT

VALVE HOUSING

1. Using puller attachment tool No. T58L-101-B or equivalent, remove and discard dust seal, **Fig. 7.**
2. Remove snap ring from valve housing, then turn fixture so valve housing is upside down.
3. Install bearing remover tool No. T65P-3524-A2 and installer tool No. T65P-3524-A3 or equivalents to valve body opposite the oil seal, then gently tap

bearing and seal from housing. Discard seal. **Exercise care when inserting and removing tool to prevent damage to valve bore in housing.**

4. If damaged, remove oil inlet and outlet tube seats with rack bushing holding tool No. T74P-3504-L or equivalent.
5. Coat tube seats with petroleum jelly and position them in housing. Install and tighten tube nuts to press seats to proper location using brass tube seat replacer tool No. T74P-3504-M or equivalent.
6. Coat bearing and seal surface in housing with a film of petroleum jelly.
7. Install bearing with metal side that covers rollers facing downward then, using bearing installer tool No. T65P-3524-A or equivalent, seat bearing. Inspect for smooth bearing operation.
8. Dip new oil seal in premium power steering fluid or equivalent, then place it in housing with metal side of seal facing outward. Drive seal into housing until outer edge of seal does not quite clear snap ring.
9. Place snap ring in housing, then drive on ring until snap ring seats in its groove to properly locate seal.
10. Apply coating of suitable multipurpose grease between seals.
11. Place dust seal in housing with dished side (rubber side) facing outward. Drive dust seal in place so that it is located behind undercut in input shaft when it is installed.

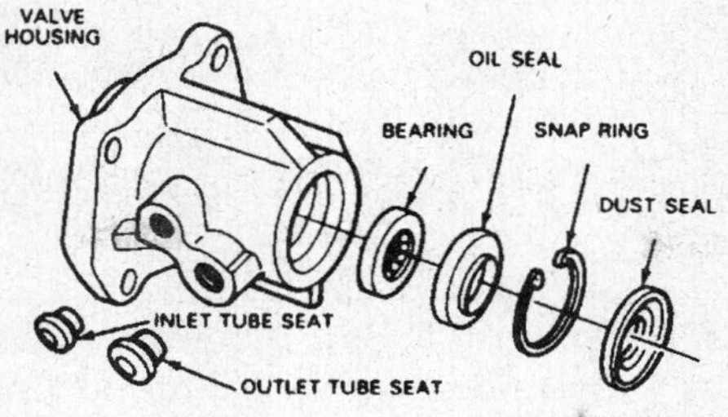

Fig. 7 Exploded view of valve housing

WORM & VALVE SLEEVES

1. Cut valve sleeve rings from valve sleeve, then position worm end of assembly in soft jawed vice.
2. Using Tool Kit No. T75L-3517-A1 or equivalent, install four valve sleeve rings. Ensure they turn freely in grooves after installation.

PISTON & BALL NUT

1. Remove plastic ring and O-ring from piston and ball nut, **Fig. 3.**
2. Dip a new O-ring in premium power steering fluid, or equivalent, then lubricate and install on piston and ball nut.
3. Install new Teflon ring on piston and ball nut, being careful not to stretch it any more than required.

INSPECTION

VALVE SPOOL CENTERING INSPECTION

The "out of car" procedure for valve centering inspection is the same as for the "in car" equivalent except the torque and simultaneous pressure reading must be made at the righthand and lefthand stops instead of either side of center.

1. Install a 2000 psi pressure gauge in pressure line between pump outlet port and steering gear inlet port. Ensure valve on gauge is in fully open position.
2. Inspect fluid level in reservoir and replenish as required.
3. Start engine and cycle steering wheel from stop to stop to bring steering lubricant up to normal operating temperature. Stop engine and inspect reservoir. Add fluid as required.
4. With engine running at a fast idle speed (1000 RPM) and steering wheel centered, attach an inch pound torque wrench to steering wheel retaining nut. Apply sufficient torque to wrench in each direction (either side of center) to get a gauge reading of 250 psi.
5. The torque reading should be the same in both directions. If the difference between readings exceed 4 inch lbs., the shaft and control assemblies must be replaced.

TIGHTENING SPECIFICATIONS

Year	Component	Torque/Ft. Lbs.
1998–2002	Ball Return Guide Clamp Screw	42–70①
	Flex Coupling To Gear Input Shaft Bolt	20–30
	Gear To Side Rail Bolts	50–65
	Hose Clamps	12–24①
	Mesh Load Adjusting Screw Locknut	35–45
	Piston End Cap	70–110
	Pitman Arm To Sector Shaft Nut	200–250
	Pressure Hose To Gear	16–25
	Race Nut Setscrew	15–25①
	Race Retaining Nut	②
	Return Hose To Gear	16–25
	Sector Shaft Cover Bolts	55–70
	Valve Housing To Gear Housing	30–45

① — Inch lbs.

② — Refer to "Component Service."

Type 4-Focus Rack & Pinion Steering Gear

NOTE: On Air Bag Equipped Models, Refer To "Air Bag System Precautions" Located In The Front Of This Manual For System Disarming & Arming Procedures.

NOTE: Refer To "Computer Relearn Procedures" Located In The Front Of This Manual When Battery Power To The Computer Has Been Interrupted.

INDEX

PRECAUTIONS

AIR BAG SYSTEMS

Refer to "Air Bag System Precautions" in the front of this manual for system disarming and arming procedures.

BATTERY GROUND CABLE

Prior to service, disconnect battery ground cable and isolate as required.

DESCRIPTION

The steering gear is operated and controlled by the hydraulic fluid supplied by the power steering pump.

The rack and pinion is held in position by two mounting brackets and rubber bushings. The gear uses an integral piston and rack design to provide power assisted steering control.

POWER STEERING SYSTEM SERVICE

Component Service

POWER STEERING PUMP, REPLACE

SOHC Engine

1. Mark running direction of serpentine belt with suitable chalk or felt tip marker.
2. Using a suitable ½ inch square drive breaker bar, rotate serpentine belt tensioner clockwise and remove the belt.
3. Use flange holding tool No. 205-126 (T78P-4851-A) or equivalent to prevent power steering pump pulley from rotating.
4. Remove pump pulley retaining nut.
5. Disconnect power steering fluid reservoir hose from pump. Allow fluid to drain into an approved container.
6. Disconnect power steering fluid pressure hose from pump.
7. Remove steering fluid reservoir to pump hose union. Discard O-ring.
8. Reverse procedure to install, noting the following:
   a. Using Teflon seal expander tool No. D90P-3517-A or equivalent, push a new O-ring onto tool.
   b. Locate tool onto union and install O-ring.
   c. Ensure serpentine belt is installed in proper running direction.
   d. Tighten all fasteners to specifications.
   e. Fill and bleed power steering system as outlined in this section.

DOHC Engine

1. Mark running direction of serpentine belt with suitable chalk or felt tip marker.
2. Remove serpentine belt.
3. Using spring lock coupling disconnector tool No. T90T-9550-C or equivalent, disconnect power steering fluid cooler hose. Allow fluid to drain into an approved container.
4. Lower the vehicle to floor.
5. **On models equipped with speed control,** disconnect speed control cable.
6. **On all models,** disconnect power steering pressure (PSP) switch electrical connector.
7. Disconnect power steering fluid supply hose.
8. Disconnect pressure line union from power steering pump.
9. Remove four power steering pump mounting bolts, then the pump.
10. Remove PSP switch.
11. Reverse procedure to install, noting the following:
   a. If installing a new power steering pump, remove unions that are supplied with it and retain for future use.
   b. Using Teflon seal expander tool No. D90P-3517-A or equivalent, push a new O-ring onto tool.
   c. Locate tool onto union and install O-ring.
   d. Ensure serpentine belt is installed in proper running direction.
   e. Tighten all fasteners to specifications.
   f. Fill and bleed power steering system as outlined in this section.

POWER STEERING PUMP TO GEAR PRESSURE LINE, REPLACE

1. Raise and safely support vehicle.
2. Using spring lock coupling disconnector tool No. T90T-9550-C or equivalent, disconnect power steering fluid cooler hose. Drain fluid into an approved container.
3. Remove hose support clamp.
4. Disconnect hoses from steering gear.
5. Lower the vehicle to floor.
6. **On models equipped with DOHC engine,** proceed as follows:
   a. Disconnect pressure line support brackets.
   b. Disconnect speed control cable, if equipped.
7. **On models equipped with SOHC engine,** disconnect pressure line support brackets.

8. **On all models,** disconnect pressure line union from power steering pump.
9. Remove pressure line. Discard O-rings.
10. Reverse procedure to install, noting the following:
    a. If a new pressure line is being installed, push new line into new union.
    b. Using Teflon seal expander tool No. D90P-3517-A or equivalent, push a new O-ring onto tool.
    c. Locate tool onto union and install O-ring.
    d. Tighten all fasteners to specifications.
    e. Fill and bleed power steering system as outlined in this section.

POWER STEERING FLUID COOLER, REPLACE

1. Remove coolant expansion tank mounting bolts, then position tank aside.
2. Disconnect hose from power steering fluid reservoir. Allow fluid to drain into an approved container.
3. Disconnect reservoir hose from bracket.
4. Raise and safely support vehicle.
5. Remove radiator splash shield.
6. Using spring lock coupling disconnector tool No. T90T-9550-C or equivalent, disconnect power steering fluid cooler hose. Drain fluid into an approved container.
7. Remove power steering fluid cooler.
8. Reverse procedure to install, noting the following:
    a. Tighten all fasteners to specifications.
    b. Fill and bleed power steering system as outlined in this section.

STEERING GEAR, REPLACE

Removal

1. Ensure front wheels are in straight-ahead position and steering wheel is centered.
2. Remove instrument panel lower panel.
3. Disconnect steering column shaft from steering gear pinion extension.
4. Loosen front wheel lug nuts.
5. Raise and safely support vehicle.
6. Remove front wheels and tires.
7. Remove and discard tie rod end retaining nuts.
8. Ball joint seals must be wrapped in cloth to protect them as tie rod ends are disconnected from knuckles.
9. Using tie rod end remover tool No. 3290-D or equivalent, separate tie rod ends from knuckles.
10. Using spring lock coupling disconnector tool No. T90T-9550-C or equivalent, disconnect power steering fluid cooler hose. Drain fluid into an approved container.
11. Remove support insulator to transaxle center bolt.
12. Remove steering gear heat shield.
13. Remove hose support clamp.
14. Disconnect power steering hoses from steering gear.
15. Using a suitable jack, safely support

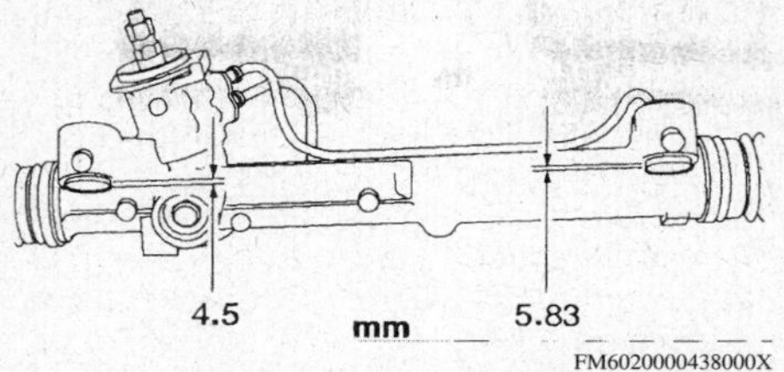

Fig. 1 Steering gear bushing installation depths

the crossmember.

16. Remove six crossmember mounting bolts, then lower the crossmember.
17. Remove steering column coupling shaft and floor seal.
18. Remove steering gear from vehicle.

Installation

1. Inspect O-rings and replace as required.
2. Ensure pressure valve is properly located in valve body.
3. Install steering gear.
4. Inspect floor seal before installation. Ensure its sealing surface is clean and not damaged. Foam portion should be between .79–98 inch.
5. Install steering column coupling shaft and floor seal.
6. Install crossmember as follows:
    a. Using subframe alignment pins tool No. T94P-2100-AH or equivalent, insert guide pins through crossmember aligning holes.
    b. Slide locking plates into grooves, then tighten guide pin sleeve.
    c. Raise crossmember, engaging guide pins into chassis alignment holes.
    d. Install crossmember mounting bolts.
    e. Remove transmission jack and alignment pins.
7. Install power steering hoses.
8. Install steering gear heat shield.
9. Install support insulator to transaxle center bolt.
10. Connect fluid cooler hose.
11. Install stabilizer bar links to strut and spring assemblies.
12. Install tie rod ends with new retaining nuts.
13. Install tires and wheels.
14. **Ensure steering wheel is still centered.**
15. Lower the vehicle to floor.
16. Connect steering column coupling shaft to steering gear pinion extension. **Install a new clamp bolt.**
17. Install instrument panel lower panel.
18. Fill power steering fluid system as outlined in this section.
19. If a new steering gear has been installed, inspect and adjust toe as required.

STEERING GEAR BUSHING, REPLACE

1. Remove steering gear as outlined in this section.
2. Using bushing remover and installer tool No. 205-297 and wheel hub installer tool No. 204-148, or equivalents, remove insulator bushings.
3. Thoroughly clean bushing housing and inspect for signs of damage. If the housing is damaged, replace steering gear.
4. Reverse procedure to install, noting the following:
    a. Lubricate new bushings with a suitable rubber lubricant.
    b. Using bushing and hub installer tools, install new bushings to proper depth, **Fig. 1.**
    c. Tighten all fasteners to specifications.

POWER STEERING SYSTEM FILL

1. When filling reservoir, ensure fluid is clean and not agitated prior to use. Fluid should be poured slowly to minimize chances of aeration.
2. Fill reservoir to "MAX" mark with proper power steering fluid.
3. Using hand vacuum pump tool No. D95L-7559-A or equivalent, apply 25–30 inches of vacuum for 30 seconds.
4. Observe vacuum gauge reading, and if it decreases by more than two inches in five minutes, inspect power steering system for leaks.
5. Remove vacuum pump tool.
6. Fill reservoir to "MAX" mark with proper power steering fluid. Inspect the level when fluid is cold.

POWER STEERING SYSTEM FLUSH

1. Disconnect CKP sensor electrical connector.
2. Disconnect return line from power steering fluid reservoir and drain fluid into an approved container.
3. Cap the reservoir with a suitable portion of hose.
4. Place end of return line into a suitable container.
5. Fill reservoir to "MAX" mark with proper power steering fluid. When filling, ensure fluid is clean and not agitated prior to use. Fluid should be poured slowly to minimize chances of aeration.
6. Crank engine while adding ½ gallon of power steering fluid. **Do not crank continuously for more than 30 seconds.**
7. Turn ignition Off when all fluid has been used up.
8. Connect return line to reservoir.
9. Fill reservoir to "MAX" mark with proper power steering fluid. Inspect the level when fluid is cold.
10. Connect CKP sensor electrical connector.

Power Steering System Bleed

1. Fill reservoir to "MAX" mark with proper power steering fluid. Inspect the level when fluid is cold.
2. Ensure fluid in reservoir does not drop below "MIN" mark to prevent air from

entering system.
3. Start engine and slowly turn steering wheel once from lock to lock.
4. Stop engine and examine all hose connections, steering gear boots, valve body and steering pump for external leaks.
5. Inspect power steering fluid reservoir fluid level and refill as required.
6. Using hand vacuum pump tool No. D95L-7559-A or equivalent, apply 15 inches of vacuum.
7. Observe vacuum gauge reading, and if it decreases by more than two inches in five minutes, inspect power steering system for leaks.
8. Start engine and slowly turn steering wheel from lock to lock once, then turn to the right, but just off the lock stop.
9. Stop engine and apply 15 inches of vacuum for a minimum of five minutes until air is evacuated from system.
10. Release vacuum at pump tool.
11. Repeat bleed procedure, but this time turn steering wheel to the left, just off the lock stop.
12. Remove vacuum pump and refill reservoir as required.
13. Start engine, then turn steering wheel from lock to lock.
14. Repeat bleed procedure if excessive noise is present.
15. If noise level is still excessive, allow vehicle to sit overnight, then repeat bleed procedure the next day.

POWER STEERING SYSTEM PURGE

1. Park vehicle on an even surface, then apply parking brake.
2. Raise and safely support vehicle so front tire clear the ground.
3. Disconnect CKP sensor electrical connector.
4. When filling reservoir, ensure fluid is clean and not agitated prior to use. Fluid should be poured slowly to minimize chances of aeration.
5. Fill reservoir to "MAX" mark with proper power steering fluid.
6. Crank engine and continue adding fluid to reservoir until level remains constant. **Do not crank continuously for more than 30 seconds.**
7. While cranking engine for 30 seconds, turn steering wheel from lock to lock.
8. Turn ignition Off.
9. Inspect reservoir fluid level and add fluid as required.
10. Connect CKP sensor electrical connector.
11. Start engine and allow it to run for several minutes.
12. Turn ignition Off.
13. Inspect reservoir fluid level and add fluid as required. **Make final inspection when fluid is cold.**
14. If air is still present, bleed power steering system as outlined in this section.

TIE ROD END INSPECTION

1. Raise and safely support vehicle.
2. Visually inspect steering linkage and front suspension components for signs of loose retainers, nut or bolts, worn or damaged front suspension, steering gear bushings or boots.
3. Grab a road wheel and apply a rocking motion to it, inspecting for any freeplay in wheel bearings or suspension components. Replace faulty components as required.
4. To isolate steering gear design clearance, inspect righthand linkage with steering gear held against the righthand lock stop, then the lefthand linkage with steering held against lefthand lock stop.
5. With an assistant holding steering firmly against lock stops, grab road wheel and apply a rocking motion to it, looking for any freeplay in steering linkage.
6. If any freeplay is discovered, establish where it originates by compressing the boot and feeling for play in tie rod inner joint while continuing to rock road wheel.
7. Replace tie rod if play is apparent in its inner ball joint.
8. If no freeplay is discovered within tie rod inner ball joint, install a new tie rod end.

TIGHTENING SPECIFICATIONS

Year	Component	Torque/Ft. Lbs.
2000–02	Crossmember Front Bolts	85
	Crossmember Rear Bolts	148
	Fluid Cooler Bolts	44①
	Power Steering Pressure (PSP) Switch	15
	Pressure Line To Pump Union	48
	Power Steering Gear Hose Clamps	17
	Power Steering Pump Bolts	17
	Pressure Line Support Bracket (DOHC Engine)	18
	Pressure Line Support Bracket (SOHC Engine)	44①
	Stabilizer Bar Link Nuts	37
	Steering Column Shaft Coupling	18
	Steering Column Shaft To Pinion Bolt	26
	Steering Gear Bolts	59
	Steering Gear Heat Shield Bolts	53①
	Support Insulator Center Bolt	37
	Tie Rod End Retaining Nuts	35
	Wheel Lug Nuts	63

① — Inch lbs.

Type 1-Ford Variable Assist Electronic Variable Orifice (EVO) System

NOTE: On Air Bag Equipped Models, Refer To "Air Bag System Precautions" Located In The Front Of This Manual For System Disarming & Arming Procedures.

NOTE: Refer To "Computer Relearn Procedures" Located In The Front Of This Manual When Battery Power To The Computer Has Been Interrupted.

NOTE: "Electrical Symbol & Wire Color Code Identification" Located In The Front Of This Manual May Be Used As An Aid When Using Wiring Circuits Found In This Section.

INDEX

PRECAUTIONS

AIR BAG SYSTEMS

Refer to "Air Bag System Precautions" in the front of this manual for system disarming and arming procedures.

BATTERY GROUND CABLE

Prior to service, disconnect battery ground cable and isolate as required.

DESCRIPTION

The electronic variable orifice system, **Fig. 1** is designed to vary the flow from the power steering pump based on vehicle speed and the rate of steering wheel rotation. The system provides full assist at low speed for light parking effort and minimum assist at high speed for good road feel and directional stability. In the event of system failure, full assist is provided.

TROUBLESHOOTING

CROWN VICTORIA, GRAND MARQUIS & TOWN CAR

Refer to symptom charts, **Figs. 2 and 3**, for troubleshooting procedures.

MARK VIII

Refer to symptom charts, **Figs. 4 and 5**, for troubleshooting procedures.

DIAGNOSIS & TESTING

Wiring Diagrams

CROWN VICTORIA & GRAND MARQUIS

Refer to **Figs. 6 and 7** for wiring diagrams.

MARK VIII

Refer to **Fig. 8** for wiring diagram.

TOWN CAR

Refer to **Fig. 9** for wiring diagrams.

Pinpoint Tests

CROWN VICTORIA & GRAND MARQUIS

1998

Diagnosis and testing requires the use of a Super Star II hand held diagnostic tester, Rotunda model No. 007-0041A or equivalent, and a suitable digital volt-ohm meter.

Refer to **Fig. 10** for symptom chart and **Figs. 11 through 21** for system diagnosis and testing.

1999–2002

If vehicle is equipped with air suspension, perform the procedure as outlined in "Auto Test."

Refer to **Fig. 22** for symptom chart and **Figs. 23 through 35** for system diagnosis and testing.

MARK VIII

Refer to **Fig. 36** for symptom chart and **Figs. 37 through 40** for system diagnosis and testing.

TOWN CAR

Refer to **Fig. 41** for symptom chart and **Figs. 42 through 47** for pinpoint tests.

Auto Test

CROWN VICTORIA & GRAND MARQUIS

1999–2002

Open luggage compartment, then connect New Generation Star (NGS) Tester to air suspension/steering test connector. Select "Air Suspension Auto Test." At the beginning of the automatic portion of the test,

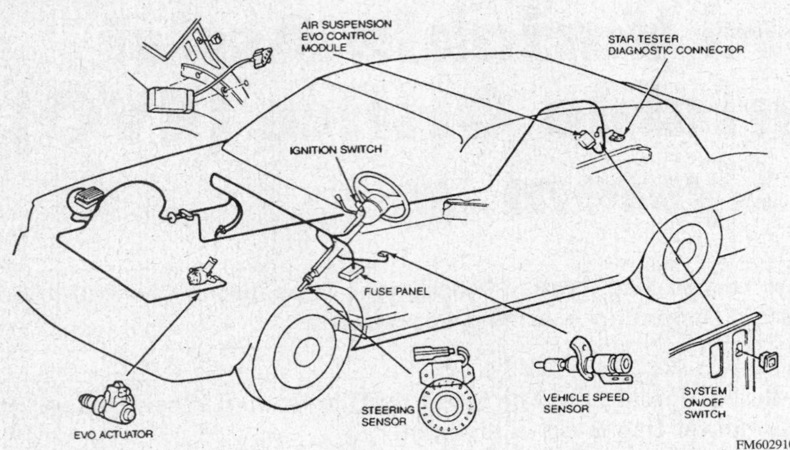

Fig. 1 Electronic variable orifice system component locations

the air suspension module inspects for a damaged air suspension control module, for unstable battery voltage, then for shorted or open circuits that would create DTCs 39–46 and DTCs 68–71. If shorts or opens are detected, the automatic portion of the test is ended and a DTC 13 is displayed on the Star Tester. If no shorts or opens are detected, the automatic portion of the test continues. The air suspension control module attempts to raise and lower the vehicle to verify that all three air suspension height sensor states (trim, high and low) can be reached. A properly functioning vehicle will be at trim height at the end of the Auto Test procedure. If all three states are not reached, the Auto Test will end and the Star Tester will display a DTC 13. If all systems are functional, a DTC 12 will be displayed. If all systems are functional, perform the manual input portion of the test by following the prompts on the display of the Star Tester.

After the Auto Test and the manual test have been performed, the DTCs will be displayed automatically. Each DTC detected will be displayed for approximately 15 seconds. The code display will continue until all DTCs have been displayed and will repeat until the Star tester button is released.

MARK VIII

1. Open hood and locate air suspension/steering test connector on righthand front shock tower. Install battery charger to power vehicle during testing.
2. Open luggage compartment, then connect New Generation Star (NGS) Tester to air suspension/steering test connector. Select air suspension auto test.
3. Ensure both doors are closed, turn air suspension switch to OFF, then to ON.
4. Turn ignition from Off to Run, then press trigger button to begin auto test.
5. **Do not lean on vehicle or open doors while DTC 10 is displayed. This will introduce false errors into the test results.**
6. DTC 10 is displayed while the auto test is running. Any faults discovered by the auto test will halt test and the DTCs will be displayed.
7. When DTC 12 is displayed, open driver door, turn steering wheel a minimum of ¼ turn in both directions, exit vehicle and close the driver door, then open and close the passenger door and press trigger to continue test.
8. Read displayed DTCs. DTC 11 means vehicle has passed auto test. Other DTCs retrieved indicate faults that must be repaired.
9. If vehicle passes auto test, exit diagnostics by turning ignition Off and disconnecting New Generation Star (NGS) Tester.

POWER STEERING SYSTEM SERVICE

Component Service

CONTROL MODULE, REPLACE

Crown Victoria, Grand Marquis & Town Car

The EVO control module and air suspension modules are one unit. Turn air suspension switch off, then proceed as follows:

1. **On 1998 models,** remove glove compartment, then detach control module from snap in fingers on bracket behind glove compartment.
2. **On 1999–2002 models,** remove lower dash panel, disconnect lamp from panel, disconnect wiring, then remove screws from module.
3. **On all models,** pull module out to access connectors.
4. Disconnect each connector by pushing connector release button and pulling connector from module.
5. Reverse procedure to install. **Torque** attaching nuts to 60–84 inch lbs.

CONTROL VALVE ACTUATOR, REPLACE

1998

1. Disconnect EVO wiring harness connector from EVO actuator.
2. Disconnect return hose, then pressure hose from the power steering pump. Plug all openings.
3. Disconnect belt from pulley, then remove pump and pulley assembly.
4. Place power steering pump in a vise and remove EVO actuator assembly from power steering pump using a 6 MM Allen hex from the back side of the actuator.
5. Install actuator assembly to pump housing, then **torque** to 10–15 ft. lbs.
6. Install pump and pulley assembly to engine. **Torque** four pump retaining bolts to 15–22 ft. lbs.
7. Remove plugs and connect return and pressure hoses to power steering pump.
8. Connect EVO wiring harness to EVO actuator assembly.
9. Purge power steering system of air.

1999–2002

1. Raise and support vehicle.
2. Remove engine oil filter.
3. Disconnect power steering auxiliary actuator electrical connector.
4. Remove screw, then the power steering auxiliary actuator.
5. Reverse procedure to install.

STEERING SENSOR, REPLACE

1. **On 1999–2002 models,** remove sound panel, finish panel and knee bolster and bracket from under steering column.
2. **On all models,** disconnect sensor electrical connector.
3. Remove sensor electrical connector from bracket under instrument panel.
4. Remove two sensor retaining screws, then the sensor, **Fig. 48.**
5. Reverse procedure to install.

STEERING SENSOR RING, REPLACE

1. Remove steering column as outlined under "Steering Column Section."
2. Remove steering shaft from steering column, then the sensor ring.
3. Reverse procedure to install.

SPEED SENSOR, REPLACE

1. Raise and support vehicle.
2. Remove speed sensor mounting clip retaining bolt.
3. Remove speed sensor and driven gear from transmission.
4. Disconnect electrical connector from speed sensor.
5. Remove driven gear retainer, then the driven gear.
6. Reverse procedure to install. Ensure internal O-ring is seated in sensor housing.

Condition	Possible Source	Action
• NOTE: Evaluation should be conducted on a level road (little road crown) Steering Drift / Wander — Condition Where the Vehicle Wanders Side-To-Side on the Roadway When it is Driven Straight Ahead While the Steering Wheel is Held in a Firm Position	• Check tire size and pressure. • Check if vehicle is unevenly loaded or overloaded. • Loose / worn tie rod ends or ball socket. • Steering gear mounting insulators and / or retaining bolts loose or damaged. • Loose front suspension lower arm struts or ball joint(s). • Steering column gear input shaft coupling connecting bolts loose. • Steering column gear input shaft coupling joints loose / worn. • Improper wheel alignment. • Excessive friction between components. • Excessive toe-in.	• Be sure tire sizes are correct and ADJUST tire pressures. • ADJUST load. • REPLACE tie rod end assembly as necessary. • REPLACE bolts. • REPLACE arm and ball joint assembly. • TIGHTEN at gear and at column. • REPLACE steering column intermediate shaft coupling assembly. • ADJUST as required. • REFER to Sensitive Steering Diagnostic and Service Procedure. • CHECK alignment.
• Pulls to One Side — A Condition Where the Vehicle Tends to Pull to One Side When Driven on a Level Surface	• Improper tire pressure. • Improper tire size or different type. • Vehicle is unevenly or excessively loaded. • Improper wheel alignment. • Damaged front suspension components. • Damaged rear suspension components. • Steering gear valve effort out of balance. • Check front and rear brakes for proper operation. • Check for bent rear axle housing and for damaged or sagging front coil springs in the front and / or rear suspension. • Check for damaged air spring in the front and / or rear suspension. • Check rear suspension for loose / worn rear shock absorber struts, suspension arm retaining fasteners.	• ADJUST tire pressure. • REPLACE as required. • ADJUST load. • ADJUST as required. • REFER to front suspension replacement. • REFER to rear suspension replacement. • PLACE transmission in NEUTRAL while driving and TURN engine off (coasting). If vehicle does not pull with the engine off, REPLACE the steering gear valve assembly. If vehicle does drift with engine off CROSS switch front tire / wheel assemblies. —If vehicle pulls to opposite side, CROSS switch tire / wheel assemblies that were on the rear to same side on the front. —If vehicle pull direction is not changed, CHECK front suspension components and wheel alignment. • ADJUST if necessary. • REPLACE if necessary. • REPLACE if necessary. • TIGHTEN all retaining fasteners.

FM6029600224020X

Fig. 2 Steering systems symptom chart (Part 1 of 3). Crown Victoria, Grand Marquis & Town Car

Condition	Possible Source	Action
• Feedback (Rattle, Chuckle, Knocking Noises in Steering Gear) — Condition Where Roughness is Felt in the Steering Wheel by the Driver When the Vehicle is Driven Over Rough Pavement	• Steering column gear input shaft coupling joints loose / worn. • Loose tie rod ends. • Steering gear retaining bolts loose or damaged. • Steering column gear input shaft coupling connecting bolts loose. • Loose suspension bushings / fasteners or ball joints. • Check steering gear adjustments. • Check steering column conditions.	• REPLACE steering column intermediate shaft coupling assembly. • REPLACE tie rod ends. • REPLACE retaining bolts and tighten. • TIGHTEN bolts to specification at steering gear and at steering column intermediate shaft coupling. • TIGHTEN suspension fasteners, REPLACE worn bushings, or REPLACE ball joints.
• Poor Returnability, Sticky Feel — Condition Noticed When the Steering Fails to Return to Center Following a Turn Without Manual Effort From the Driver. In Addition, When the Driver Returns the Steering Wheel to Center, it May Have a Sticky or Catchy Feel	• Improper tire pressure. • Improper tire size or incorrect type. • Misaligned steering column or column flange rubbing steering wheel and / or flange. • Steering column gear input shaft coupling universal joints binding. • Check for steering column tube boot tears and / or evidence of binding or damage to tie rod ends. • Damaged / worn front suspension components. • Improper wheel alignment. • Column bearing binding. • Contamination in system. • Check steering gear adjustments.	• ADJUST tire pressures. • REPLACE as required. • ALIGN steering column. • REPLACE steering column intermediate shaft coupling assembly. • REPLACE as necessary. • INSPECT control arm ball joints. • ADJUST toe as required. • REPLACE bearing. • FLUSH power steering system as outlined under Cleaning and Inspection.
• Light Steering Efforts at All Vehicle Speeds	• Electronic variable orifice (EVO actuator).	• Vehicles with air suspension, GO to Pinpoint Test B1. Vehicles without air suspension, GO to Pinpoint Test DTC 28.
• Excessive Steering Effort While Making Quick Maneuvers at High Speed	• Steering sensor.	• Vehicles with air suspension, GO to Pinpoint Test B. Vehicles without air suspension, GO to Pinpoint Test DTC 33.

FM6029600224030X

Fig. 2 Steering systems symptom chart (Part 2 of 3). Crown Victoria, Grand Marquis & Town Car

Condition	Possible Source	Action
• Heavy Steering Efforts, Poor Assist or Loss of Assist — Condition Recognized by the Driver While Turning Corners and During Parking Maneuvers	• Low power steering pump fluid. • Steering gear assembly external or internal leak. • Power steering pump external leak. • Improper drive belt tension. • Hose or cooler external leak. • Improper engine idle speed. • Power steering pump pulley loose or warped. • Power steering pump flow / pressure not to specifications. • Hose or cooler line restriction. • Check steering gear adjustments. • System contamination. • EVO power steering control valve actuator sticking.	• FILL as required and CHECK for system leaks. • REPLACE power steering pump. • ADJUST drive belt tension. • SERVICE / REPLACE as necessary. • ADJUST idle. • REPLACE power steering pump pulley. • CLEAN or REPLACE as necessary. • INSPECT system for foreign objects, kinked hose, etc. —FLUSH system. • Vehicles with air suspension, GO to Pinpoint Test B. • Vehicles without air suspension, GO to Pinpoint Test A.
• Fluid Leakage	• Overfilled system. • Component leak.	• CORRECT fluid level as required. • LOCATE suspect component, and
• Power Steering Pump Leaks, EVO Power Steering Control Valve Actuator	• Damaged EVO power steering control valve actuator ring. • EVO power steering control valve actuator electrical connector damaged. • EVO power steering control valve actuator damaged.	• Vehicles without air suspension, GO to Pinpoint Test A. Vehicles with air suspension, GO to Pinpoint Test B.

FM6029600224040X

Fig. 2 Steering systems symptom chart (Part 3 of 3). Crown Victoria, Grand Marquis & Town Car

Condition	Possible Source	Action
• Drive Belt Squeal (Particularly at Full Steering Wheel Travel and Stand Still Parking)	• Loose drive belt.	• ADJUST drive belt tension to specification.
• Chirp Noise in Steering Pump	• Loose or worn drive belt.	• ADJUST drive belt tension to specification or REPLACE drive belt.
• Power Steering Pump Noisy	• Low fluid level and possible leak.	• REFILL to specified level. PURGE air from system. CHECK for leaks. SERVICE as required.
• Swish Type Noise	• A noise created by the flow of excessive fluid into the bypass port of the pump valve housing (with temperature below 55°C (130°F). The shearing effect of the cooler (heavier) fluid is not detrimental to power steering pump operation.	• A normal condition. Noise will diminish with fluid temperature increase.
• Clicking Type Noise	• Excessive power steering pump wear.	• REPLACE power steering pump.

FM6029600225010X

Fig. 3 Power steering pump noise symptom chart (Part 1 of 2). Crown Victoria, Grand Marquis & Town Car

Condition	Possible Source	Action
• Power Steering Pump / Remote Power Steering Oil Reservoir Leaks	• Excessive fluid fill. • Fluid cap missing, loose, damaged or missing O-ring. • Loose or damaged hose fittings. • Leakage at shaft seal or any visible point on pump.	• ADJUST fluid to proper level. • SERVICE or REPLACE, if required. • SERVICE or REPLACE. • REPLACE power steering pump.
• Power Steering Pump — No or Poor Assist	• Contamination can be caused by foreign objects in the power steering oil reservoir or power steering pump or metallic particles being generated by cam pack discrepancies.	• Thoroughly flush system when installing a serviced or new power steering pump.
• Moan or Whine Type Noise	• Fluid aeration. • Power steering pump loose or misaligned on engine. • Low fluid. • Hose grounded. • Steering column grounded. • Damaged internal components.	• PURGE the power steering system to reduce aeration noise. • TIGHTEN or ALIGN as required. • CHECK fluid level. • CHECK for hose being grounded. • CHECK steering column tube alignment. • REPLACE power steering pump.

FM6029600225020X

Fig. 3 Power steering pump noise symptom chart (Part 2 of 2). Crown Victoria, Grand Marquis & Town Car

CONDITION	POSSIBLE SOURCE	ACTION
• NOTE: Evaluation should be conducted on a level road (little road crown). Wander — Condition Where Vehicle Wanders Side-To-Side on Roadway When it is Driven Straight Ahead While Steering Wheel is Held in a Firm Position	• Check tire size and pressure. • Check if vehicle is unevenly loaded or overloaded. • Loose / worn front wheel spindle tie rods or ball socket. • Steering gear mounting insulators and / or retaining bolts loose or damaged. • Loose front suspension lower arm struts or ball joint(s). • Steering column gear input shaft coupling connecting bolts loose. • Steering column gear input shaft coupling joints loose / worn. • Improper wheel alignment.	• Be sure tire sizes are correct and ADJUST tire pressures. • ADJUST load. • REPLACE front wheel spindle tie rod or tie rod assembly as necessary. • REPLACE bolts. • REPLACE arm and ball joint assembly. • TIGHTEN at power steering short rack and at steering column. • REPLACE steering column gear input shaft coupling assembly. • ADJUST as required.

FM6029500238010X

Fig. 4 Steering systems symptom chart (Part 1 of 4). Mark VIII

CONDITION	POSSIBLE SOURCE	ACTION
• Poor Returnability, Sticky Feel — Condition Noticed When the Steering Fails to Return to Center Following a Turn Without Manual Effort From the Driver. In Addition, When the Driver Returns the Steering Wheel to Center, it May Have a Sticky or Catchy Feel	• Improper tire pressure. • Improper tire size or different type. • Misaligned steering column or column flange rubbing steering wheel and / or flange. • Steering column gear input shaft universal joints binding. • Check for steering column tube boot tears and / or evidence of binding or damage to front wheel spindle tie rods or ball joints. • Damaged / worn front suspension components. • Improper wheel alignment. • Column bearing binding. • Contamination in system.	• ADJUST tire pressures. • REPLACE as required. • ALIGN steering column. • REPLACE steering column gear input shaft coupling assembly. • REPLACE as necessary. • INSPECT control arm ball joints. • ADJUST toe as required. • REPLACE steering column tube bearing. • FLUSH power steering system.
• Light Steering Efforts at All Vehicle Speeds	• Variable assist (EVO).	• REFER to Pinpoint Test B.
• Excessive Steering Effort While Making Quick Maneuvers at High Speed	• Variable assist (EVO).	• REFER to Pinpoint Test C.
• Heavy Steering Efforts, Poor Assist or Loss of Assist — Condition Recognized by the Driver While Turning Corners and During Parking Maneuvers	• Low power steering pump fluid. • Power steering short rack assembly external or internal leak. • Power steering pump external leak. • Improper drive belt tension • Hose or cooler external leak. • Improper engine idle speed. • Power steering pump pulley loose or warped. • Power steering pump flow / pressure not to specifications. • Hose or cooler line restricted. • Check steering gear adjustments. • System contaminated. • EVO power steering control valve actuator sticking.	• FILL as required and CHECK for system leaks. • REPLACE power steering pump. • CHECK drive belt tensioner. • SERVICE / REPLACE as necessary. • REPLACE power steering pump pulley. • CLEAN or REPLACE as necessary. • INSPECT system for foreign objects, kinked hose, etc. —FLUSH system. • GO to Pinpoint Test A.
• Fluid Leakage	• Overfilled system. • Component leak.	• CORRECT fluid level as required. • LOCATE suspect component, and
• Drive Belt Squeal	• Check drive belt for proper tension or glazing.	• CHECK automatic tensioner or REPLACE drive belt as required.
• Power Steering Pump Noisy	• Low fluid level and possible leak.	• REFILL to specified level. PURGE air from system. CHECK for leaks. SERVICE as required.
• Swish Type Noise	• Fluid flow into the bypass valve of the pump valve housing with fluid temperature below 54°C (130°F).	• Normal noise.

FM6029500238030X

Fig. 4 Steering systems symptom chart (Part 3 of 4). Mark VIII

CONDITION	POSSIBLE SOURCE	ACTION
• Pulls to One Side — A Condition Where Vehicle Tends to Pull to One Side When Driven on a Level Surface	• Improper tire pressure. • Improper tire size or different type. • Vehicle is unevenly or excessively loaded. • Improper wheel alignment. • Damaged front suspension components. • Damaged rear suspension components. • Steering gear valve effort out of balance. • Check front and rear brakes for proper operation. • Check for damaged air spring in the front and / or rear suspension. • Check rear suspension for loose / worn rear shock absorber struts, rear suspension arm and bushing retaining fasteners.	• ADJUST tire pressure. • REPLACE as required. • ADJUST load. • ADJUST as required. • PLACE transmission in NEUTRAL while driving and TURN engine off (coasting). If vehicle does not pull with the engine off, REPLACE the power steering short rack assembly. • If vehicle does drift with engine off: — CROSS-SWITCH front tire / wheel assemblies. — If vehicle pulls to opposite side, CROSS-SWITCH tire / wheel assemblies that were on the rear to same side on the front. — If vehicle pull direction is not changed, CHECK front suspension components and wheel alignment. • ADJUST if necessary. • REPLACE if necessary. • TIGHTEN all retaining fasteners.
• Feedback (Rattle, Chuckle, Knocking Noises in Power Steering Short Rack — Condition Where Roughness is Felt in the Steering Wheel By the Driver When the Vehicle is Driven Over Rough Pavement	• Steering column gear input shaft coupling loose / worn. • Loose front wheel spindle tie rods and / or tie rod inner ball joints. • Steering gear mounting insulators and / or retaining bolts loose or damaged. • Steering column gear input shaft coupling connecting bolts loose. • Loose suspension bushings / fasteners or ball joints. • Check steering column conditions.	• REPLACE steering column gear input shaft coupling assembly. • REPLACE front wheel spindle tie rods. • REPLACE retaining bolts. • TIGHTEN bolts at power steering short rack to flex coupling and flex coupling to intermediate shaft. • TIGHTEN suspension fasteners, REPLACE worn bushings, or REPLACE ball joints.

FM6029500238020X

Fig. 4 Steering systems symptom chart (Part 2 of 4). Mark VIII

CONDITION	POSSIBLE SOURCE	ACTION
• Whine Type Noise	• Aerated fluid, vacuum leak in system.	• PURGE system of air.
• Clicking Type Noise	• Excessive power steering pump wear.	• REPLACE power steering pump.
• Power Steering Pump / Remote Reservoir Leaks	• Excessive fluid fill. • Loose or damaged hose fittings. • Leak at shaft seal: — Seal damage. — Rotor shaft damage, such as helical grooving or the OD has an axial scratch. — Shaft bushing worn. • Damaged or missing outlet fitting O-rings. • Loose outlet fitting. • Outlet fitting, damaged. • Remote reservoir cracked / damaged.	• ADJUST fluid to proper level. • SERVICE or REPLACE. • REPLACE power steering pump. • REPLACE O-rings. • TIGHTEN as required. • REPLACE outlet fitting. • REPLACE remote reservoir.
• Power Steering Pump Leaks, EVO Power Steering Control Valve Actuator	• Damaged EVO actuator O-rings. • EVO actuator electrical connector damaged. • EVO power steering control valve actuator damaged.	• REPLACE power steering control valve actuator. • REPLACE power steering control valve actuator. • REPLACE power steering control valve actuator.

FM6029500238040X

Fig. 4 Steering systems symptom chart (Part 4 of 4). Mark VIII

CONDITION	POSSIBLE SOURCE	ACTION
• Drive Belt Squeal (Particularly at Full Wheel Travel and Stand Still Parking)	• Loose drive belt.	• CHECK automatic tensioner.
• Chirp Noise in Power Steering Pump	• Loose or worn drive belt.	• CHECK automatic tensioner or REPLACE drive belt.
• Swish Type Noise	• A noise created by the flow of excessive fluid into the bypass port of the pump valve housing (with temperature below 130°). The shearing effect of the cooler (heavier) oil is not detrimental to power steering pump operation.	• A normal condition. Noise will diminish with fluid temperature increase.
• Power Steering Pump — No or Poor Assist	• Contamination can be caused by foreign objects in the power steering oil reservoir or power steering pump, or metallic particles being generated by cam pack discrepancies.	• System must be flushed thoroughly when installing a serviced or new power steering pump.
• Moan or Whine Type Noise	• Fluid aeration. • Power steering pump loose. • Low fluid. • Hose grounded. • Steering column grounded. • Damaged internal components.	• PURGE the power steering system to reduce aeration noise. • TIGHTEN as required. • CHECK fluid level. • CHECK for hose being grounded. • CHECK steering column alignment. • REPLACE power steering pump.

FM6029500239010X

Fig. 5 Power steering pump noise symptom chart (Part 1 of 2). Mark VIII

CONDITION	POSSIBLE SOURCE	ACTION
• Steering Gear Hiss	• Check steering column gear input shaft coupling and steering gear for alignment and binding. • Check for grounded or loose boot at dash panel. • Input shaft and valve assembly.	• ADJUST steering column and/or steering column gear input shaft coupling. • ALIGN boot or TIGHTEN fasteners as required. • REPLACE—Only if noise is extremely objectionable.
• Noise/Rattle (Steering Column)	• Loose bolts/attaching brackets. • Looseness of ball bearings or insufficient lube. • Steering shaft insulators cracked or dry. • Flex coupling compressed or extended.	• TIGHTEN. • LUBE or REPLACE bearings. • REPLACE or LUBE insulators as required. • REPOSITION shaft assembly to flatten flex coupling.
• Noise/Squeak or Cracks (Steering Column)	• Dry bushings. • Loose or mispositioned shrouds. • Steering wheel rubbing against shrouds. • Dry shift lever grommets. • Insufficient lube on speed control slip ring. • Upper or lower bearing sleeve out of position.	• LUBE shaft seal and shift tube seal. • TIGHTEN or REPOSITION shrouds as required. • REPLACE shroud(s) or steering wheel or REPOSITION shrouds as required. • LUBE grommets. • LUBE slip ring. • REPOSITION bearing sleeve.
• Excessive Travel of Shift Lever Out of Park Detent with Steering Column Locked	• Shift cane spacer clip too small or missing.	• REPLACE or ADD spacer clip.
• Ignition Lock Cylinder Binds in Lock and/or Accessory Position	• Shift cane spacer clip too large.	• REPLACE spacer clip.
• Other Causes of Noise	• Improper assembly of pump rotating group. • Imperfections on inside diameter or power steering pump CAM surface. • Damaged power steering pump rotor splines. • Hairline crack on cam inner surface. • Interference between power steering pump rotor and cam. • Excessively worn or scored pumping elements and power steering pump pressure plates. • Internal damage or component imperfection.	• REPLACE power steering pump as required. • REPLACE power steering pump. • REPLACE power steering pump. • REPLACE power steering pump. • REPLACE power steering pump. • REPLACE power steering pump. • REPLACE power steering pump.

FM6029500239020X

Fig. 5 Power steering pump noise symptom chart (Part 2 of 2). Mark VIII

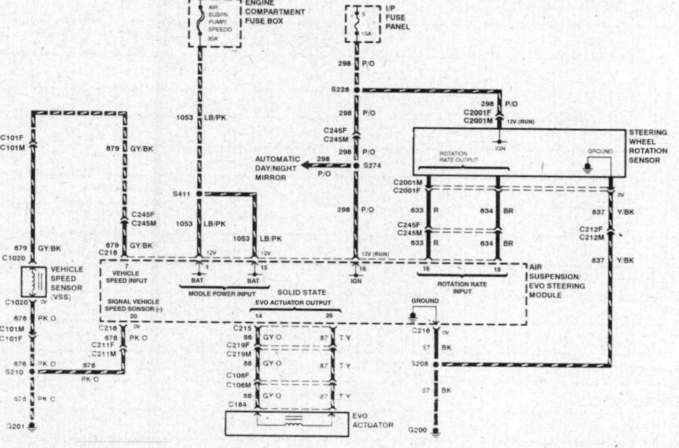

FM6029700284000X

Fig. 7 Wiring diagram. Crown Victoria & Grand Marquis w/air suspension

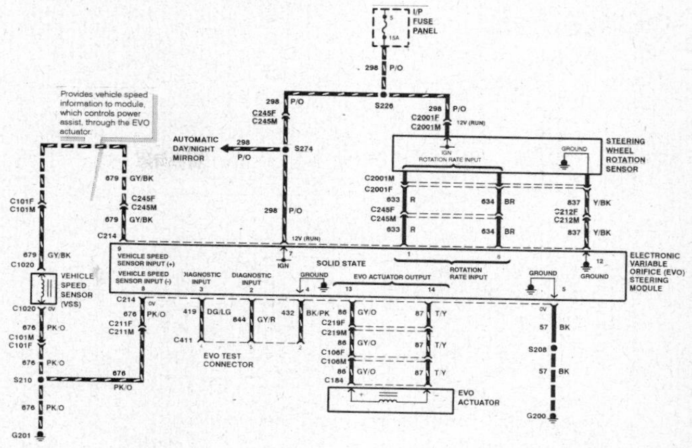

FM6029700283000X

Fig. 6 Wiring diagram. Crown Victoria & Grand Marquis less air suspension

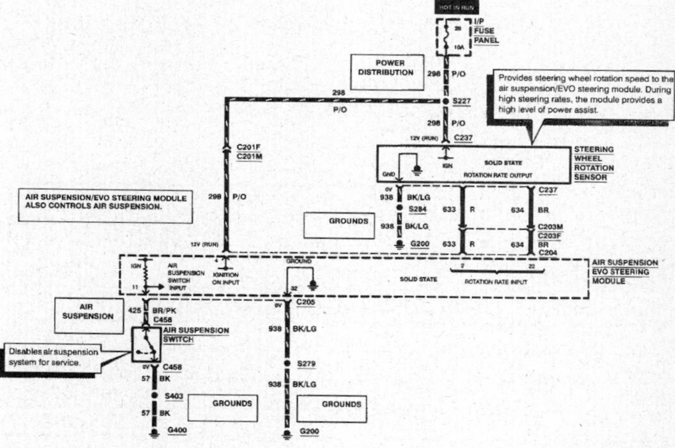

FM6029700273010X

Fig. 8 Wiring diagram (Part 1 of 2). Mark VIII

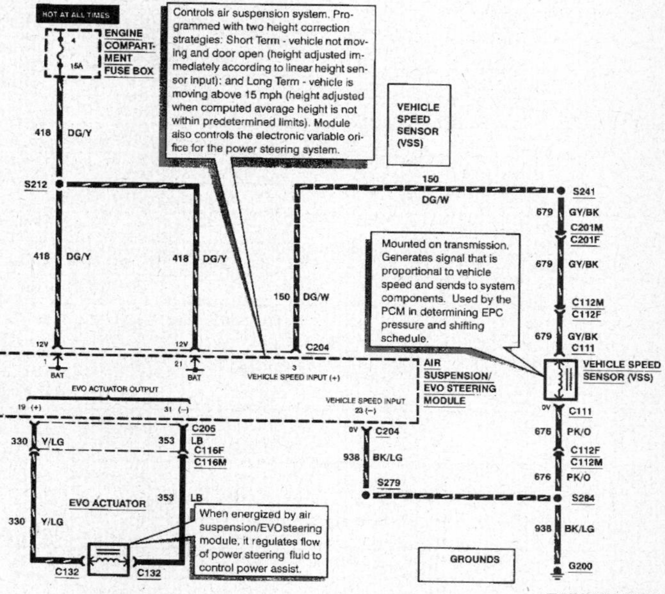

FM6029700273020X

Fig. 8 Wiring diagram (Part 2 of 2). Mark VIII

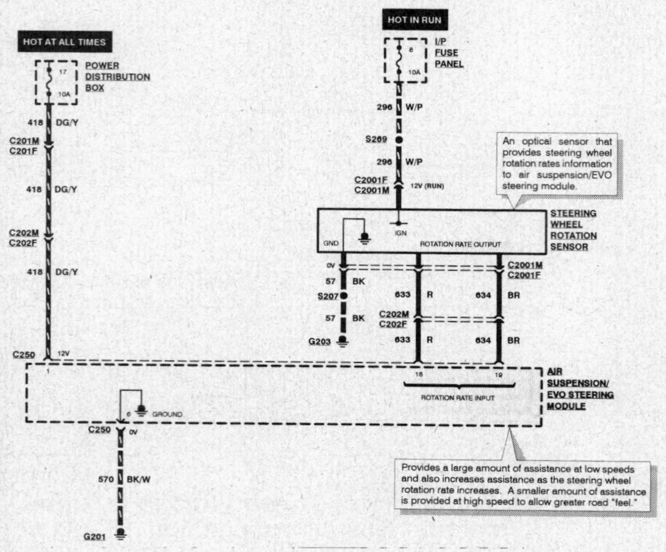

Fig. 9 Wiring diagram (Part 1 of 2). Town Car

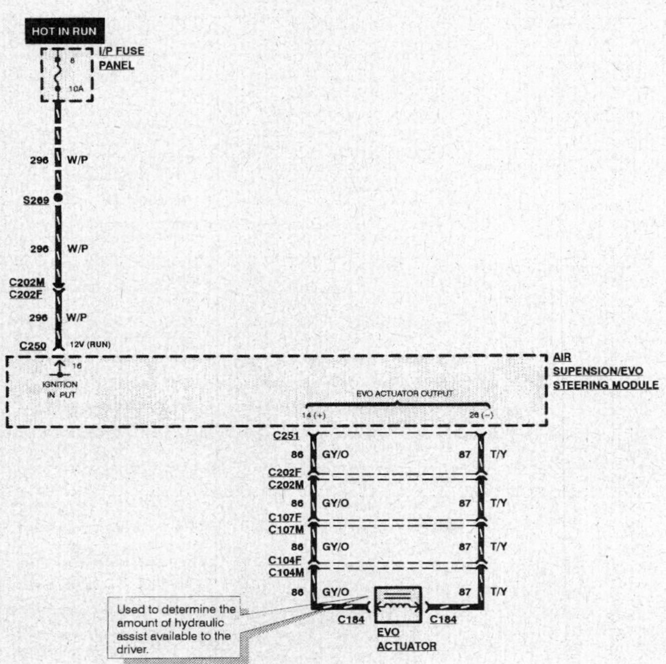

Fig. 9 Wiring diagram (Part 2 of 2). Town Car

DIAGNOSTIC CHART INDEX

Code/Test	Description	Page No.	Fig. No.
1998 CROWN VICTORIA & GRAND MARQUIS			
—	Symptom Chart	14-33	10
Code 16	Steering Very Difficult or Very Easy	14-35	21
Code 17	Steering Very Difficult or Very Easy	14-36	21
Code 18	Steering Very Difficult or Very Easy	14-36	21
Code 27	Actuator Circuit Open	14-33	11
Code 28	Actuator Circuit Shorted	14-34	12
Code 29	Actuator High Side Short To Ground	14-34	13
Code 30	Actuator Circuit Shorted To Battery	14-34	14
Code 31	Actuator Circuit Low Side Shorted To Ground	14-34	15
Code 33	Steering Wheel Rotation Not Detected	14-34	16
Code 35	Vehicle Speed Above 15 mph Not Detected	14-34	17
Code 55	Steering Does Not Vary w/Vehicle Speed	14-34	18
Code 74	Steering Wheel Rotation Not Detected	14-35	19
Test A	Steering Diagnostics Can Not Be Entered	14-35	20
Test B	Steering Very Difficult or Very Easy	14-35	21
1999–2002 CROWN VICTORIA & GRAND MARQUIS			
—	Symptom chart	14-36	22
Code 16	EVO Actuator Shorted; EVO Actuator Shorted or Open; EVO Actuator Resistance Out Of Range	14-38	27
Code 17	EVO Actuator Shorted; EVO Actuator Shorted or Open; EVO Actuator Resistance Out Of Range	14-38	27
Code 18	EVO Actuator Shorted; EVO Actuator Shorted or Open; EVO Actuator Resistance Out Of Range	14-38	27
DTC 27	EVO Actuator Circuit Open	14-39	28
DTC 28	EVO Actuator Circuit Shorted	14-39	29
DTC 29	EVO Actuator Circuit High Side Shorted To Ground	14-40	30
DTC 30	EVO Actuator Circuit Shorted To Battery	14-40	31
DTC 31	EVO Actuator Circuit Low Side Shorted	14-40	32
DTC 33	Steering Rotation Not Detected	14-41	33
DTC 35	Vehicle Speed Above 15 mph Not Detected	14-41	34

Continued

DIAGNOSTIC CHART INDEX—Continued

Condition	Possible Source	Action
• Steering Very Difficult / Very Easy DTC 16, 17 or 18	• Power steering pump actuator valve. • Circuitry open / shorted. • EVO control module. • Computer controlled suspension.	• GO to EVO Steering Diagnosis. PERFORM Actuator Output Circuit Test, Steering Wheel Sensor Test and Vehicle Speed Sensor Test as outlined. PERFORM Pinpoint Test B
• Engine Stalls with High Wheel Rotation	• Inoperative idle speed control circuit.	
• Steering Does Not Vary with Increased Wheel Rotation Speed	• Steering wheel rotation sensor inoperative. • Open / shorted circuitry.	• GO to EVO Steering Diagnosis. PERFORM Steering Wheel Sensor Test as outlined. PERFORM Pinpoint Test B (vehicles with Computer Controlled Suspension System).
• Steering Does Not Vary With Vehicle Speed DTC 55 or DTC 35	• Vehicle speed sensor. • Circuitry open / shorted. • EVO control module.	• GO to EVO Steering Diagnosis. PERFORM Vehicle Speed Sensor Test as outlined (DTC 35) for vehicles without computer controlled suspension. PERFORM Pinpoint Test DTC 55 (vehicles with Computer Controlled Suspension System).
• Steering Diagnostics Can Not Be Entered	• Circuitry open / shorted. • EVO control module. • Computer controlled suspension.	• GO to Pinpoint Test A (vehicle without Computer Controlled Suspension).

FM6029600224010X

Fig. 10 Symptom chart. 1998 Crown Victoria & Grand Marquis

Test Step		Result ▶	Action to Take
27-1	CHECK EVO ACTUATOR CONNECTION		
	• Ignition switch OFF. • Access EVO actuator. • Check actuator harness connector. • **Is actuator harness connector firmly plugged into actuator?**	Yes ▶ No ▶	GO to **27-2**. INSTALL actuator harness connector correctly. REPEAT Actuator Output Circuit Test.
27-2	CHECK HIGH SIDE CIRCUIT CONTINUITY		
	• Access EVO control module. • Disconnect control module connector. • Access EVO actuator. • Disconnect actuator connector. • Measure resistance between Pin 13, Circuit 86 (GY / O) of control module and Circuit 86 (GY / O) at actuator. • **Is resistance less than 5 ohms?**	Yes ▶ No ▶	GO to **27-3**. SERVICE open high side circuit. GO to Pinpoint Test A.
27-3	CHECK LOW SIDE CIRCUIT CONTINUITY		
	• Measure resistance between Pin 14, Circuit 87 (T/Y) of control module and Circuit 87 (T/Y) at actuator. • **Is resistance less than 5 ohms?**	Yes ▶ No ▶	REPLACE EVO actuator. RESTORE vehicle. REPEAT Actuator Output Test. SERVICE open low side circuit. RESTORE vehicle. REPEAT Actuator Output Test.

FM6029600226000X

Fig. 11 Code 27: Actuator Circuit Open. 1998 Crown Victoria & Grand Marquis

Test Step	Result	Action to Take
28-1 CHECK CIRCUIT RESISTANCE		
• Ignition switch OFF. • Access EVO control module. • Disconnect harness connector. • Access EVO actuator. • Disconnect actuator connector. • Measure resistance between Pin 13, Circuit 86 (GY/O) and Pin 14, Circuit 87 (T/Y) of control module connector. • **Is resistance less than 100K ohms?**	Yes	SERVICE short between Circuit 86 (GY/O) and Circuit 87 (T/Y). RESTORE vehicle. REPEAT Actuator Output Test.
	No	GO to **28-2**.
28-2 CHECK ACTUATOR RESISTANCE		
• Measure resistance of EVO actuator. • **Is resistance less than 5 ohms?**	Yes	REPLACE EVO actuator. RESTORE vehicle. REPEAT Actuator Output Test.
	No	REPLACE control module. RESTORE vehicle. REPEAT Actuator Output Test.

FM6029600227000X

Fig. 12 Code 28: Actuator Circuit Shorted. 1998 Crown Victoria & Grand Marquis

Test Step	Result	Action to Take
29-2 CHECK ACTUATOR		
• Reconnect EVO actuator. • Measure resistance between Pin 13, Circuit 86 (GY/O) and Pin 5, Circuit 57 (BK). • **Is resistance less than 100K ohms?**	Yes	REPLACE EVO actuator. RESTORE vehicle. REPEAT Actuator Output Test.
	No	REPLACE EVO control module. RESTORE vehicle. REPEAT Actuator Output Test.

FM6029600228020X

Fig. 13 Code 29: Actuator High Side Short To Ground (Part 2 of 2). 1998 Crown Victoria & Grand Marquis

Test Step	Result	Action to Take
31-1 CHECK CIRCUIT 87 (T/Y)		
• Ignition switch OFF. • Access EVO actuator and disconnect harness connector. • Access EVO control module and disconnect harness connector. • Measure resistance between Pin 14, Circuit 87 (T/Y) and Pin 5, Circuit 57 (BK). • **Is resistance less than 10K ohms?**	Yes	SERVICE Circuit 87 (T/Y) for short to ground. RESTORE vehicle. REPEAT Actuator Output Test.
	No	GO to **31-2**.
31-2 CHECK ACTUATOR		
• Reconnect EVO actuator. • Measure resistance between Pin 14, Circuit 87 (T/Y) and Pin 5, Circuit 57 (BK). • **Is resistance less than 10K ohms?**	Yes	REPLACE EVO actuator. RESTORE vehicle. REPEAT Actuator Output Test.
	No	REPLACE control module. RESTORE vehicle. REPEAT Actuator Output Test.

FM6029600230000X

Fig. 15 Code 31: Actuator Circuit Low Side Shorted To Ground. 1998 Crown Victoria & Grand Marquis

Test Step	Result	Action to Take
33-2 CHECK STEERING WHEEL ROTATION SENSOR SUPPLY		
• Turn ignition switch to RUN. • Measure voltage at steering wheel rotation sensor Circuit 298 (P/O). • **Is B+ present?**	Yes	REPLACE sensor. RESTORE vehicle. REPEAT steering wheel sensor test.
	No	SERVICE Circuit 298 (P/O) between Fuse 17 (15A) of fuse junction panel and sensor. RESTORE vehicle. REPEAT Steering Wheel Sensor Test.

FM6029600231020X

Fig. 16 Code 33: Steering Wheel Rotation Not Detected (Part 2 of 2). 1998 Crown Victoria & Grand Marquis

Test Step	Result	Action to Take
55-1 CHECK SPEED SENSOR CONNECTION (DTC 55 CONCERN)		
• Make sure harness connection on vehicle speed sensor (located on the transmission) is properly seated. • **Is connector properly seated?**	Yes	GO to **55-2**.
	No	MAKE proper connection. GO to Pinpoint Test Step **B1**.
55-2 SPEED SENSOR CHECK		
• Turn ignition switch to the OFF position. • Disconnect electrical connectors from the EVO module (located in luggage compartment). • Make sure there is no damage to harness and that: — Circuit 679 (GY/BK) is in Pin 7. — Circuit 676 (PK/O) is in Pin 20. • **Are wires damaged or crossed?**	Yes	SERVICE wires. GO to Pinpoint Test Step **B1**.
	No	GO to **55-3**.
55-3 TEST SPEED SENSOR GROUND CIRCUIT		
• Test continuity of speed sensor ground Circuit 676 (PK/O) from Pin 20 to Pin 6. • **Is there continuity?**	Yes	GO to **55-4**.
	No	SERVICE wire or ground eyelet as necessary. GO to Pinpoint Test Step **B1**.

FM6029600233010X

Fig. 18 Code 55: Steering Does Not Vary w/Vehicle Speed (Part 1 of 2). 1998 Crown Victoria & Grand Marquis

Test Step	Result	Action to Take
29-1 CHECK CIRCUIT 86 (GY/O)		
• Ignition switch OFF. • Access EVO actuator and disconnect harness connector. • Access EVO control module and disconnect harness connector. • Measure resistance between Pin 13, Circuit 86 (GY/O) and Pin 5, Circuit 57 (BK). • **Is resistance less than 100K ohms?**	Yes	SERVICE Circuit 86 (GY/O) and/or Circuit 86 (GY/O) for short to ground. RESTORE vehicle. REPEAT Actuator Output Test.
	No	GO to **29-2**.

FM6029600228010X

Fig. 13 Code 29: Actuator High Side Short To Ground (Part 1 of 2). 1998 Crown Victoria & Grand Marquis

Test Step	Result	Action to Take
30-1 CHECK ACTUATOR CIRCUIT 86 (GY/O)		
• Ignition switch OFF. • Access EVO control module. • Disconnect harness connector. • Disconnect EVO actuator. • Measure voltage between Pin 13, Circuit 86 (GY/O) and Pin 5, Circuit 57 (BK). • **Is B+ present?**	Yes	SERVICE Circuit 86 (GY/O) for short to B+. RESTORE vehicle. REPEAT Actuator Output Test.
	No	GO to **30-2**.
30-2 CHECK ACTUATOR CIRCUIT 87 (T/Y)		
• Measure voltage between Pin 14, Circuit 87 (T/Y) and Pin 5, Circuit 57 (BK). • **Is B+ present?**	Yes	SERVICE Circuit 87 (T/Y) for short to B+. RESTORE vehicle. REPEAT Actuator Output Test.
	No	REPLACE EVO control module. RESTORE vehicle. REPEAT Actuator Output Test.

FM6029600229000X

Fig. 14 Code 30: Actuator Circuit Shorted To Battery. 1998 Crown Victoria & Grand Marquis

Test Step	Result	Action to Take
33-1 CHECK CIRCUIT CONTINUITY		
• Ignition switch OFF. • Access EVO control module and disconnect harness connector. • Access steering wheel rotation sensor and disconnect harness connector. • Measure resistance of Circuit 633 (R/Y), 634 (BR) and 837 (Y/BK) between steering wheel rotation sensor connector and EVO control module connector. • **Is resistance less than 5 ohms?**	Yes	GO to **33-2**.
	No	SERVICE open or high resistance circuits. RESTORE vehicle. REPEAT Steering Wheel Sensor Test.

FM6029600231010X

Fig. 16 Code 33: Steering Wheel Rotation Not Detected (Part 1 of 2). 1998 Crown Victoria & Grand Marquis

Test Step	Result	Action to Take
35-1 CHECK SPEEDOMETER OPERATION		
• Check for proper speedometer operation. • **Does speedometer indicate vehicle speeds above 24 km/h (15 mph)?**	Yes	GO to **35-2**.
	No	SERVICE Circuits 679 (GY/BK) and/or 676 (PK/O) or vehicle speed sensor.
35-2 CHECK CIRCUIT 679 (GY/BK)		
• Ignition switch OFF. • Access instrument cluster connector C2 and disconnect harness connector. • Access EVO control module and disconnect harness connector • Measure resistance between instrument cluster Pin C2-14 and EVO control module Pin 9. • **Is resistance 5 ohms or less?**	Yes	GO to **35-3**.
	No	SERVICE open in Circuit 679 (GY/BK) between instrument cluster and EVO control module. RESTORE vehicle. REPEAT Vehicle Speed Sensor Test.
35-3 CHECK CIRCUIT 676 (PK/O)		
• Measure resistance between EVO control module Pin 8 and Pin 5. • **Is resistance 5 ohms or less?**	Yes	REPLACE EVO control module. RESTORE vehicle. REPEAT Vehicle Speed Sensor Test.
	No	SERVICE open Circuit 676 (PK/O). RESTORE vehicle. REPEAT Vehicle Speed Sensor Test.

FM6029600232000X

Fig. 17 Code 35: Vehicle Speed Above 15 mph Not Detected. 1998 Crown Victoria & Grand Marquis

Test Step	Result	Action to Take
55-4 TEST VEHICLE SPEED SENSOR		
• Turn ignition switch to RUN position. • Perform Speedometer/Odometer Reads Inaccurately Test. • **Are concerns found?**	Yes	GO to Pinpoint Test Step
	No	GO to **55-5**.
55-5 EVO CONTROL MODULE CHECK		
• Turn ignition switch to OFF position. • Make sure harness connectors are properly connected to module. • Check air suspension switch connection. • Check if the air suspension switch is turned on. • **Is connector properly seated?**	Yes	GO to **55-6**.
	No	SECURE connection. GO to **55-6**.
55-6 CHECK POWER FEED		
• Turn ignition switch to the OFF position. • Disconnect EVO control module connectors C1 and C2. • Turn ignition switch to RUN position. • Using Rotunda Digital Volt-Ohmmeter 014-00407 or equivalent, measure voltage from Pin 16, Circuit 295 (LB/PK) Town Car, Circuit 298 (P/O) Crown Victoria, Grand Marquis (ignition-run only) to Pin 6, Circuit 57 (BK) (ground) at pin connectors. • Measure voltage from Pin 1 to Pin 6. • If 12 volts from Pin 1 to Pin 6 connect, test light between Pins 1 and 6. • **Are there 12 volts with bright light?**	Yes	REPLACE EVO control module. RESTORE vehicle. RETEST system.
	No	SERVICE short to ground, high resistance or open in Circuit 298 (P/O), 295 (LB/PK) or 1053 (LB/PK) as necessary. GO to Pinpoint Test Step **B1**.

FM6029600233020X

Fig. 18 Code 55: Steering Does Not Vary w/Vehicle Speed (Part 2 of 2). 1998 Crown Victoria & Grand Marquis

Test Step		Result	Action to Take
74-1	CHECK CIRCUIT RESISTANCE		
	• Ignition switch OFF. • Access EVO control module and disconnect harness Connector C216. • Access steering wheel rotation sensor and disconnect harness Connector C2001. • Measure resistance of Circuit 633 (R/Y) and 634 (BR) between steering wheel rotation sensor Connector C2001 and EVO control module Connector C216. • **Is resistance less than 5 ohms?**	Yes	GO to **74-2**.
		No	SERVICE open or high resistance circuits. RESTORE vehicle. REPEAT Steering Wheel Sensor Test.
74-2	CHECK STEERING WHEEL ROTATION SENSOR SUPPLY		
	• Turn ignition switch to RUN. • Measure voltage at steering wheel rotation sensor Circuit 298 (P/O). • **Is B+ present?**	Yes	REPLACE sensor. RESTORE vehicle. REPEAT steering wheel sensor test.
		No	SERVICE Circuit 298 (P/O) between Fuse 5 (15A) of fuse junction panel and sensor. RESTORE vehicle. REPEAT Steering Wheel Sensor Test.

FM6029700279000X

Fig. 19 Code 74: Steering Wheel Rotation Not Detected. 1998 Crown Victoria & Grand Marquis

Test Step		Result	Action to Take
A5	CHECK GROUND		
	• Measure resistance from Pin 5, Circuit 57 (BK) to a known good ground. • **Is resistance 5 ohms or less?**	Yes	SERVICE Circuit 298 (P/O) for open. RESTORE vehicle. REPEAT Entering EVO Diagnostics.
		No	SERVICE Circuit 57 (BK) for open. RESTORE vehicle. REPEAT Entering EVO Diagnostics.

FM6029600234020X

Fig. 20 Test A: Steering Diagnostics Can Not Be Entered (Part 2 of 2). 1998 Crown Victoria & Grand Marquis

Test Step		Result	Action to Take
B1	DETERMINE REQUIRED TEST STEP (DTC 16, 17 AND 18)		
	• Enter EVO Steering Diagnosis as outlined. • Read and record displayed DTC(s). • Each DTC must be addressed individually. If more than one DTC is detected, perform the test step required for each DTC. • **Is DTC 16, 17 or 18 displayed?**	Yes	GO to **B6**.
		No	GO to **B2**.
B2	DETERMINE REQUIRED TEST STEP (DTC 74)		
	• Read and record displayed DTC(s). • Each DTC must be addressed individually. If more than one DTC is detected, perform the test step required for each DTC. • **Is DTC 74 displayed?**	Yes	GO to **B22**.
		No	GO to **B3**.
B3	DETERMINE REQUIRED TEST STEP (DTC 55)		
	NOTE: Code 55 is only generated in drive cycle test. • Cycle ignition on, then off. • Turn Star tester on with button raised. • Depress button. • Read and record displayed DTC(s). • Each DTC must be addressed individually. If more than one DTC is detected, perform the test step required for each DTC. • **Is DTC 55 displayed?**	Yes	GO to Pinpoint Test DTC 55.
		No	GO to **B4**.
B4	DETERMINE REQUIRED TEST STEP (DTC 11/15)		
	• Read and record displayed DTC(s). • Each DTC must be addressed individually. If more than one DTC is detected, perform the test step required for each DTC. • **Is DTC 11 or 15 displayed?**	Yes	REFER to Pump Flow and Pressure Tests as outlined in Service Procedures.
		No	GO to **B5**.
B5	DETERMINE REQUIRED TEST STEP (OTHER DTCs)		
	• Read and record displayed DTC(s). • Each DTC must be addressed individually. If more than one DTC is detected, perform the test step required for each DTC. • **Are DTCs other than 11, 15, 16, 17, 18, 55 or 74 detected?**	Yes	suspension diagnostics.
		No	GO to **B6**.
B6	EVO ACTUATOR VALVE CHECK (SHORT TO GROUND OR AN OPEN CIRCUIT) (DTC 16, 17 AND 18 CONCERN)		
	• Turn ignition switch to OFF position. • Verify harness connection on the EVO power steering control valve actuator on power steering pump is properly seated. • **Is connector properly seated?**	Yes	GO to **B7**.
		No	MAKE proper connection. GO to **B1**.
B7	DTC 16: EVO ACTUATOR VALVE CHECK (SHORT TO GROUND)		
	• Turn ignition switch to OFF position. • Read all DTCs. • **Is DTC 16 displayed?**	Yes	GO to **B13**.
		No	GO to **B8**.

FM6029600235010X

Fig. 21 Test B: Codes 16, 17 or 18: Steering Very Difficult or Very Easy (Part 1 of 5). 1998 Crown Victoria & Grand Marquis

Test Step		Result	Action to Take
A1	DIAGNOSTIC LAMP CHECK		
	• Test the Rotunda Super Star II Tester 007-0041B or equivalent in another vehicle to see if the equipment is functional. • Check connection of tool to data link connector. • **Are concerns found?**	Yes	REPLACE tester.
		No	GO to **A2**.
A2	RETEST CONTROL MODULE		
	• Turn ignition switch to OFF position. • Connect Rotunda Super Star II Tester 007-0041B or equivalent to data link connector. • Start engine. • Latch HOLD/TEST button down. • **Does DTC 20 appear?**	Yes	GO to Entering EVO Diagnostics.
		No	GO to **A3**.
A3	EVO CONTROL MODULE CHECK		
	• Turn ignition switch to OFF position. • Make sure connector is properly connected to module. • **Is connection properly secured?**	Yes	GO to **A4**.
		No	SECURE connection. GO to Entering EVO Diagnostics.
A4	CHECK POWER FEED		
	• Turn ignition switch to the OFF position. • Disconnect EVO control module connector. • Turn ignition switch to RUN position. • Using Rotunda Digital Volt-Ohmmeter 014-00407 or equivalent, measure voltage from Pin 7, Circuit 298 (P/O) to Pin 5, Circuit 57 (BK) at harness connector. • **Are there 12 volts?**	Yes	REPLACE EVO control module. RESTORE vehicle. RETEST system.
		No	GO to **A5**.

FM6029600234010X

Fig. 20 Test A: Steering Diagnostics Can Not Be Entered (Part 1 of 2). 1998 Crown Victoria & Grand Marquis

Test Step		Result	Action to Take
B8	DTC 17: EVO ACTUATOR VALVE CHECK (SHORT TO GROUND OR AN OPEN CIRCUIT)		
	• Turn ignition switch to the OFF position. • Read all DTCs. • **Is DTC 17 displayed?**	Yes	GO to **B10**.
		No	GO to **B9**.
B9	DTC 18: EVO ACTUATOR VALVE CHECK (BAD VALVE INDUCTANCE)		
	• Turn ignition switch to OFF position. • Read all DTCs. • **Is DTC 18 displayed?**	Yes	REPLACE EVO valve. RESTORE vehicle. RETEST system.
		No	GO to **B10**.
B10	CHECK RESISTANCE ACROSS ACTUATOR VALVE		
	• Ignition switch in OFF position. • Locate the control module behind glove compartment. Harness connector can be disconnected from module without removing module. • Using an ohmmeter, measure resistance across Pin 14 and Pin 26 of harness connector. Resistance should be 7-18 ohms. If the resistance is greater than 1000 ohms, the circuit is open. • **Is resistance between 7-18 ohms?**	Yes	GO to **B11**.
		No	GO to **B12**.
B11	CHECK CONTINUITY OF WIRING		
	• Ignition switch in OFF position. • Disconnect EVO harness connector from EVO actuator valve located on power steering pump. • Test continuity of Circuits 86 (GY/O) and 87 (T/Y) from the actuator connector to the EVO control module connector. • **Is there continuity?**	Yes	GO to **B12**.
		No	SERVICE wires as necessary. GO to **B1**.
B12	CHECK EVO ACTUATOR VALVE		
	• Disconnect EVO harness connector from EVO power steering control valve actuator located on power steering pump. • Using an ohmmeter, measure resistance across the two actuator valve connector pins. • **Is resistance greater than 20 ohms or less than 5 ohms?**	Yes	REPLACE EVO valve. RESTORE vehicle. RETEST system.
		No	GO to **B14**.
B13	CHECK EVO ACTUATOR VALVE RESISTANCE		
	• Disconnect EVO harness connector from EVO power steering control valve actuator located on power steering pump. • Using an ohmmeter, measure resistance across the two actuator valve connector pins. • **Is resistance between 5-20 ohms?**	Yes	GO to **B14**.
		No	GO to **B17**.
B14	CHECK WIRE HARNESS		
	• Ignition switch in OFF position. • EVO harness disconnected from EVO power steering control valve actuator. • Disconnect EVO control module from the connector behind glove compartment. • **Was module not connected properly?**	Yes	MAKE proper connection. RESTORE vehicle. RETEST system.
		No	GO to **B15**.
B15	CHECK WIRE HARNESS FOR SHORT TO GROUND (PIN 14 RESISTANCE OVER 1000 OHMS)		
	• Using an ohmmeter, measure resistance between Pin 6 (ground) and Pin 14 of harness connector. • **Is resistance over 1000 ohms?**	Yes	GO to **B17**.
		No	GO to **B16**.

FM6029600235020X

Fig. 21 Test B: Codes 16, 17 or 18: Steering Very Difficult or Very Easy (Part 2 of 5). 1998 Crown Victoria & Grand Marquis

Step	Test Step	Result	Action to Take
B16	CHECK WIRE HARNESS FOR SHORT TO GROUND (PIN 14 RESISTANCE LESS THAN 10 OHMS)		
	• Using an ohmmeter, measure resistance between Pin 6 (ground) and Pin 14 of harness connector. • **Is resistance less than 10 ohms?**	Yes ▶ No ▶	SERVICE harness. RESTORE vehicle. RETEST system. GO to **B19.**
B17	CHECK WIRE HARNESS FOR SHORT TO GROUND (PIN 26 RESISTANCE LESS THAN 10 OHMS)		
	• Using an ohmmeter, measure resistance between Pin 6 (ground) and Pin 26 of harness connector. • **Is resistance less than 10 ohms?**	Yes ▶ No ▶	SERVICE harness. RESTORE vehicle. RETEST system. GO to **B18.**
B18	CHECK WIRE HARNESS FOR SHORT TO GROUND (PIN 26 RESISTANCE OVER 1000 OHMS)		
	• Using an ohmmeter, measure resistance between Pin 6 (ground) and Pin 26 of harness connector. • **Is resistance over 1000 ohms?**	Yes ▶ No ▶	GO to **B19.** GO to **B20.**
B19	CHECK HARNESS FOR SHORT TO B+		
	• Ignition switch in RUN position. • EVO harness disconnected from EVO power steering control valve actuator on power steering pump. • Using a voltmeter, measure the voltage across — Pin 14 and Pin 6 — Pin 26 and Pin 6 • **Is either voltage greater than 5 volts?**	Yes ▶ No ▶	SERVICE wires. GO to **B1.** GO to **B20.**
B20	CHECK FOR SHORT ACROSS CIRCUITS 86 (GY/O) AND 87 (T/Y) (RESISTANCE LESS THAN 10 OHMS)		
	• Ignition switch in OFF position. • EVO harness disconnected from EVO power steering control valve actuator on power steering pump. • Using an ohmmeter, measure resistance across Pin 14 and Pin 26 on harness connector. • **Is resistance less than 10 ohms?**	Yes ▶ No ▶	SERVICE wires. GO to **B1.** GO to **B21.**
B21	CHECK FOR SHORT ACROSS CIRCUITS 86 (GY/O) AND 87 (T/Y) (RESISTANCE OVER 1000 OHMS)		
	• Ignition switch in OFF position. • EVO harness disconnected from EVO power steering control valve actuator on power steering pump. • Using an ohmmeter, measure resistance across Pin 14 and Pin 26 on harness connector. • **Is resistance over 1000 ohms?**	Yes ▶ No ▶	REPLACE EVO control module. RESTORE vehicle. RETEST system. GO to DTC 55-5.
B22	CHECK STEERING WHEEL SENSOR CONNECTION (DTC 74 CONCERN)		
	• Verify harness connection on steering wheel rotation sensor (located on lower portion of steering column) is properly seated. • **Is connector properly seated?**	Yes ▶ No ▶	GO to **B23.** MAKE proper connection. GO to **B1.**

FM6029600235030X

Fig. 21 Test B: Codes 16, 17 or 18: Steering Very Difficult or Very Easy (Part 3 of 5). 1998 Crown Victoria & Grand Marquis

Step	Test Step	Result	Action to Take
B27	CHECK FOR SHORT ACROSS CIRCUITS 834 (R/Y) AND 835 (R/W) (RESISTANCE LESS THAN 10 OHMS)		
	• Turn ignition switch to the OFF position. • Steering sensor disconnected. • Disconnect pin connectors. • Measure resistance between: — Pin 18 and Pin 19. — Pin 18 and Pin 6. — Pin 19 and Pin 6 of the harness connectors (in luggage compartment). • **Is resistance less than 10 ohms?**	Yes ▶ No ▶	SERVICE wires as necessary. GO to **B1.** GO to **B28.**
B28	TEST STEERING SENSOR POWER CIRCUIT		
	• Turn ignition switch to RUN position. • Using a voltmeter, measure the voltage between Circuits 295 (LB/PK) and 57 (BK) (Town Car) and 298 (P/O) and 837 (Y/BK) (Crown Victoria, Grand Marquis) at the steering sensor connector. • **Are there 12 volts?**	Yes ▶ No ▶	REPLACE steering sensor. RESTORE vehicle. RETEST system. SERVICE Circuit 295 (LB/PK) (Town Car), Circuit 298 (P/O) (Crown Victoria, Grand Marquis). CHECK/REPLACE Fuse 17 (15A), Crown Victoria, Grand Marquis, 7 (15A), Town Car. GO to **B1.**

FM6029600235050X

Fig. 21 Test B: Codes 16, 17 or 18: Steering Very Difficult or Very Easy (Part 5 of 5). 1998 Crown Victoria & Grand Marquis

Condition	Possible Source	Action
• No communication with the EVO control module	• CJB Fuse: — 5 (15A). • Battery junction box (BJB) Fuse: — 8 (30A). • Circuitry. • EVO control module.	• GO to Pinpoint Test A.
• No communication with the air suspension control module	• CJB Fuse: — 5 (15A). • BJB Fuse: — 8 (30A). • Circuitry. • Air suspension control module.	• GO to Pinpoint Test B.
• Unable to enter auto test — EVO control module	• CJB Fuse: — 5 (15A). • BJB Fuse: — 8 (30A). • Circuitry. • EVO control module.	• GO to Pinpoint Test C.
• Unable to enter auto test — air suspension control module	• CJB Fuse: — 5 (15A). • BJB Fuse: — 8 (30A). • Circuitry. • Air suspension control module.	• GO to Pinpoint Test D.
• Steering very difficult/very easy	• Power steering pump actuator valve. • Circuitry open/shorted. • EVO control module. • Air suspension module.	• PERFORM actuator output test and steering wheel sensor test. PERFORM Pinpoint Test E (with air suspension).
• Steering does not vary with increased wheel rotation	• Steering wheel rotation sensor inoperative. • Open/shorted circuitry.	• PERFORM Steering Wheel Sensor Test. PERFORM Pinpoint Test E (with air suspension).

FM6029900334000X

Fig. 22 Symptom chart. 1999–2002 Crown Victoria & Grand Marquis

Step	Test Step	Result	Action to Take
B23	STEERING WHEEL ROTATION SENSOR CHECK		
	• Ignition switch in OFF position. • Disconnect EVO control module and leave connectors mated. • Examine wiring harness, verify that there is no damage and: • **Crown Victoria, Grand Marquis** — Circuit 633 (R) is in Pin 18. — Circuit 634 (BR) is in Pin 19. — Circuit 837 (Y/BK) is connected to Circuit 57 (BK). — Circuit 57 (BK) is in Pin 6 (ground). — Circuit 298 (P/O) is connected to steering sensor, supplying B+ with ignition switch in RUN. • **Town Car** — Circuit 633 (R) is in Pin 18. — Circuit 634 (BR) is in Pin 19. — Circuit 57 (BK) is in Pin 6 (ground). — Circuit 295 (LB/PK) is connected to steering sensor, B+ 12 volts with ignition switch in RUN. • **Are wires damaged or crossed?**	Yes ▶ No ▶	SERVICE wires as necessary. GO to **B1.** GO to **B24.**
B24	TEST STEERING WHEEL ROTATION SENSOR SIGNALS		
	• Start engine. • NOTE: The resistance values will vary between meters, but the needle on all meters should swing from a low to a higher resistance and back approximately every nine degrees of steering wheel rotation. While rotating the steering wheel slowly, and using an analog ohmmeter such as, Rotunda Inductive Dwell-Tach-Volt Ohmmeter 164-R0254 or equivalent, set to the 1K scale, measure the resistance from: — Pin 18 to Pin 6. — Pin 19 to Pin 6. • **Does meter needle swing for both circuits?**	Yes ▶ No ▶	SHUT OFF engine. REPLACE EVO control module. RESTORE vehicle. RETEST system. GO to **B25.**
B25	STEERING WHEEL ROTATION SENSOR WIRE CHECK		
	• Disconnect EVO control module from connectors C1 and C2 located under dash. • Turn ignition switch to OFF position. • Disconnect steering sensor (located on lower steering column). • Check wires at steering sensor connector for damage and/or incorrect location. • Test continuity of Circuits 633 (R), 634 (BR) and 57 (BK) from steering sensor to EVO control module connector. (Refer to Electrical Schematic). • Test continuity from Circuit 837 (Y/BK) to 57 (BK) (Crown Victoria, Grand Marquis). • **Is there continuity?**	Yes ▶ No ▶	GO to **B26.** SERVICE wires as necessary. GO to **B1.**
B26	CHECK FOR SHORT ACROSS CIRCUITS 834 (R/Y) AND 835 (R/W) (RESISTANCE OVER 1000 OHMS)		
	• Turn ignition switch to OFF position. • Steering sensor disconnected. • Disconnect pin connectors. Measure resistance between: — Pin 18 and Pin 19. — Pin 18 and Pin 6. — Pin 19 and Pin 6 of the pin connectors (in luggage compartment). • **Is resistance over 1000 ohms?**	Yes ▶ No ▶	GO to **B28.** GO to **B27.**

FM6029600235040X

Fig. 21 Test B: Codes 16, 17 or 18: Steering Very Difficult or Very Easy (Part 4 of 5). 1998 Crown Victoria & Grand Marquis

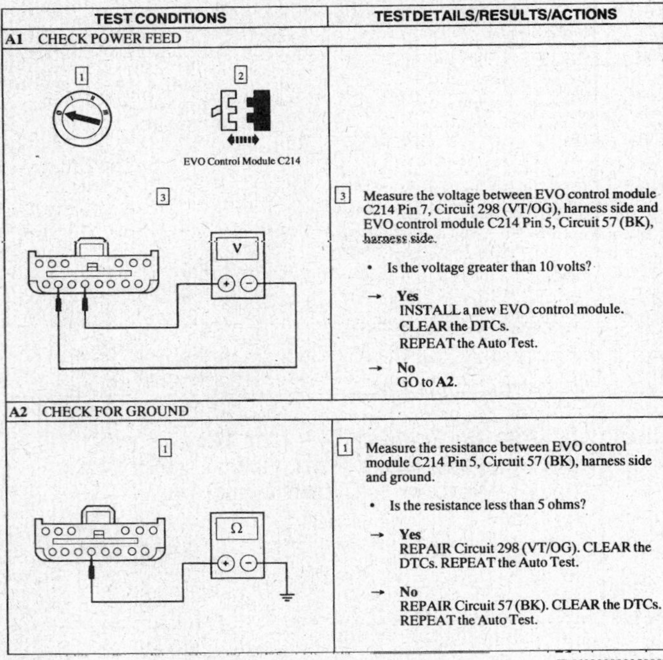

TEST CONDITIONS	TESTDETAILS/RESULTS/ACTIONS
A1 CHECK POWER FEED	
1 2 3	3 Measure the voltage between EVO control module C214 Pin 7, Circuit 298 (VT/OG), harness side and EVO control module C214 Pin 5, Circuit 57 (BK), harness side. • Is the voltage greater than 10 volts? → **Yes** INSTALL a new EVO control module. CLEAR the DTCs. REPEAT the Auto Test. → **No** GO to **A2.**
A2 CHECK FOR GROUND	
1	1 Measure the resistance between EVO control module C214 Pin 5, Circuit 57 (BK), harness side and ground. • Is the resistance less than 5 ohms? → **Yes** REPAIR Circuit 298 (VT/OG). CLEAR the DTCs. REPEAT the Auto Test. → **No** REPAIR Circuit 57 (BK). CLEAR the DTCs. REPEAT the Auto Test.

FM6029900335000X

Fig. 23 Test A: No Communication w/EVO Control Module. 1999–2002 Crown Victoria & Grand Marquis

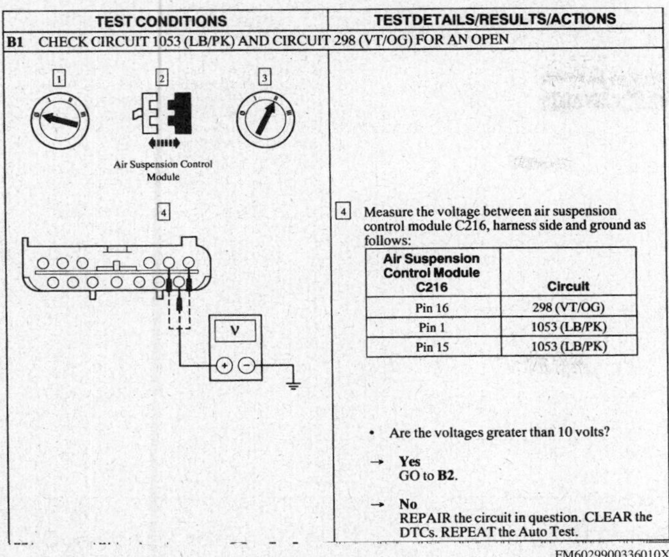

TEST CONDITIONS	TEST DETAILS/RESULTS/ACTIONS
B1 CHECK CIRCUIT 1053 (LB/PK) AND CIRCUIT 298 (VT/OG) FOR AN OPEN	
1 2 3 4	4 Measure the voltage between air suspension control module C216, harness side and ground as follows:

Air Suspension Control Module C216	Circuit
Pin 16	298 (VT/OG)
Pin 1	1053 (LB/PK)
Pin 15	1053 (LB/PK)

- Are the voltages greater than 10 volts?

→ **Yes**
GO to **B2**.

→ **No**
REPAIR the circuit in question. CLEAR the DTCs. REPEAT the Auto Test.

FM6029900336010X

Fig. 24 Test B: No Communication w/Air Suspension Control Module. (Part 1 of 4). 1999–2002 Crown Victoria & Grand Marquis

TEST CONDITIONS	TEST DETAILS/RESULTS/ACTIONS
B4 CHECK CIRCUIT 419 (DG/LG) FOR VOLTAGE AT THE AIR SUSPENSION TEST CONNECTOR	
1	1 Measure the voltage between air suspension test connector C459 Pin 4, Circuit 419 (DG/LG), harness side and ground. • Is the voltage greater than 10 volts? → **Yes** GO to **B5**. → **No** REPAIR the circuit. CLEAR the DTCs. REPEAT the Auto Test.
B5 CHECK CIRCUIT 844 (GY/RD)	
1	1 Measure the resistance between air suspension control module C215 Pin 9, Circuit 844 (GY/RD), harness side and air suspension test connector C459 Pin 5, Circuit 844 (GY/RD), harness side; and between air suspension control module C215 Pin 9, Circuit 844 (GY/RD), harness side and ground. • Is the resistance less than 5 ohms between air suspension control module and air suspension test connector; and greater than 10,000 ohms between air suspension control module and ground? → **Yes** GO to **B6**. → **No** REPAIR the circuit. CLEAR the DTCs. REPEAT the Auto Test.

FM6029900336030X

Fig. 24 Test B: No Communication w/Air Suspension Control Module. (Part 3 of 4). 1999–2002 Crown Victoria & Grand Marquis

TEST CONDITIONS	TEST DETAILS/RESULTS/ACTIONS
C1 CHECK COMMUNICATION TO THE EVO CONTROL MODULE	
	1 Check communication between the Super Star II Tester and the EVO control module. • Does the Super Star II Tester communicate? → **Yes** INSTALL a new EVO control module. REPEAT the Auto Test. → **No** GO to Pinpoint Test A.

FM6029900337000X

Fig. 25 Test C: Unable To Enter Auto Test-EVO Control Module. 1999–2002 Crown Victoria & Grand Marquis

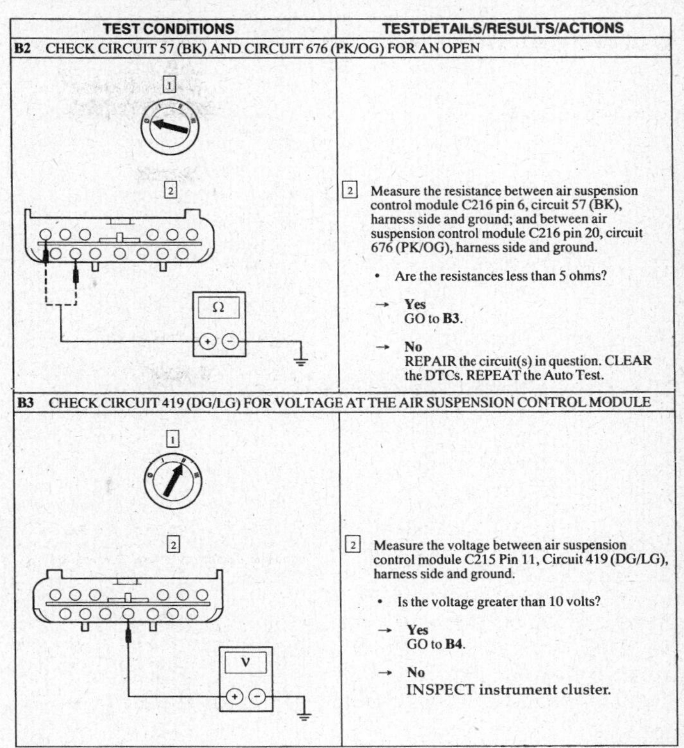

TEST CONDITIONS	TEST DETAILS/RESULTS/ACTIONS
B2 CHECK CIRCUIT 57 (BK) AND CIRCUIT 676 (PK/OG) FOR AN OPEN	
1 2	2 Measure the resistance between air suspension control module C216 pin 6, circuit 57 (BK), harness side and ground; and between air suspension control module C216 pin 20, circuit 676 (PK/OG), harness side and ground. • Are the resistances less than 5 ohms? → **Yes** GO to **B3**. → **No** REPAIR the circuit(s) in question. CLEAR the DTCs. REPEAT the Auto Test.
B3 CHECK CIRCUIT 419 (DG/LG) FOR VOLTAGE AT THE AIR SUSPENSION CONTROL MODULE	
1 2	2 Measure the voltage between air suspension control module C215 Pin 11, Circuit 419 (DG/LG), harness side and ground. • Is the voltage greater than 10 volts? → **Yes** GO to **B4**. → **No** INSPECT instrument cluster.

FM6029900336020X

Fig. 24 Test B: No Communication w/Air Suspension Control Module. (Part 2 of 4). 1999–2002 Crown Victoria & Grand Marquis

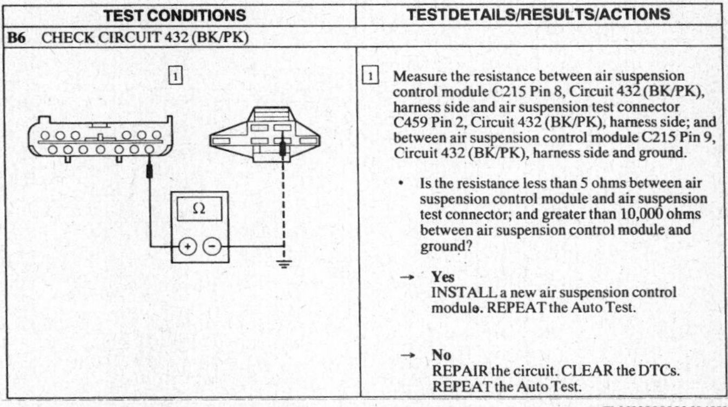

TEST CONDITIONS	TEST DETAILS/RESULTS/ACTIONS
B6 CHECK CIRCUIT 432 (BK/PK)	
1	1 Measure the resistance between air suspension control module C215 Pin 8, Circuit 432 (BK/PK), harness side and air suspension test connector C459 Pin 2, Circuit 432 (BK/PK), harness side; and between air suspension control module C215 Pin 9, Circuit 432 (BK/PK), harness side and ground. • Is the resistance less than 5 ohms between air suspension control module and air suspension test connector; and greater than 10,000 ohms between air suspension control module and ground? → **Yes** INSTALL a new air suspension control module. REPEAT the Auto Test. → **No** REPAIR the circuit. CLEAR the DTCs. REPEAT the Auto Test.

FM6029900336040X

Fig. 24 Test B: No Communication w/Air Suspension Control Module. (Part 4 of 4). 1999–2002 Crown Victoria & Grand Marquis

TEST CONDITIONS	TEST DETAILS/RESULTS/ACTIONS
D1 CHECK COMMUNICATION TO THE AIR SUSPENSION CONTROL MODULE	
	1 Check communication between the Super Star II Tester and the air suspension control module. • Does the Super Star II Tester communicate? → **Yes** INSTALL a new air suspension control module. REPEAT the Auto Test. → **No** GO to Pinpoint Test B.

FM6029900338000X

Fig. 26 Test D: Unable To Enter Auto Test-Air Suspension Control Module. 1999–2002 Crown Victoria & Grand Marquis

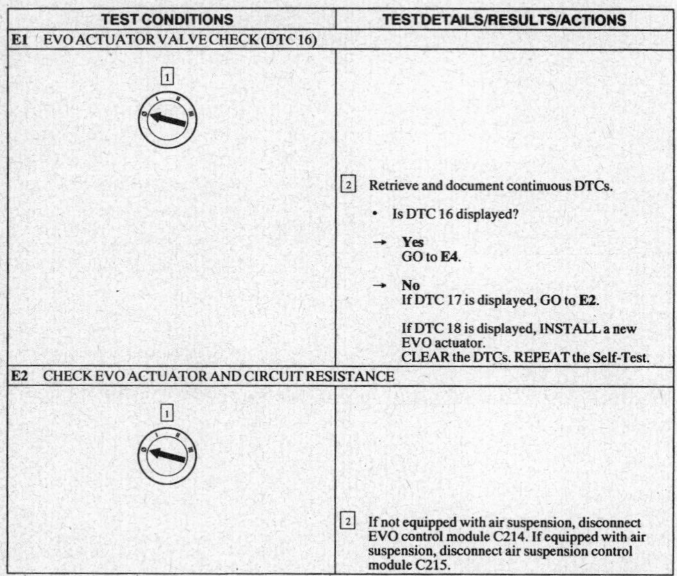

TEST CONDITIONS	TEST DETAILS/RESULTS/ACTIONS
E1 EVO ACTUATOR VALVE CHECK (DTC 16)	
1	2 Retrieve and document continuous DTCs. • Is DTC 16 displayed? → **Yes** GO to **E4**. → **No** If DTC 17 is displayed, GO to **E2**. If DTC 18 is displayed, INSTALL a new EVO actuator. CLEAR the DTCs. REPEAT the Self-Test.
E2 CHECK EVO ACTUATOR AND CIRCUIT RESISTANCE	
1	2 If not equipped with air suspension, disconnect EVO control module C214. If equipped with air suspension, disconnect air suspension control module C215.

FM6029900339010X

Fig. 27 DTC 16: EVO Actuator Shorted; DTC 17: EVO Actuator Shorted or Open; DTC 18: EVO Actuator Resistance Out Of Range (Part 1 of 6). 1999–2002 Crown Victoria & Grand Marquis

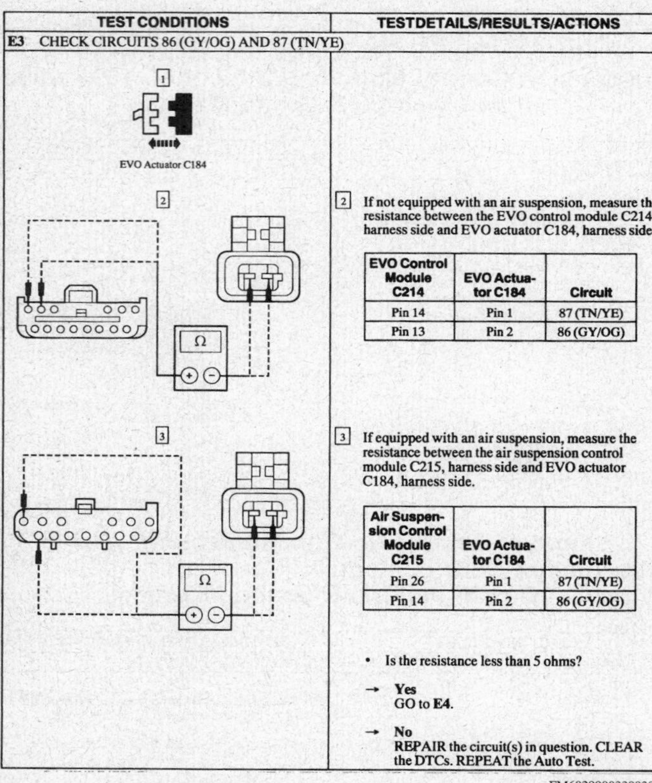

TEST CONDITIONS	TEST DETAILS/RESULTS/ACTIONS
E3 CHECK CIRCUITS 86 (GY/OG) AND 87 (TN/YE)	
1	
2	2 If not equipped with an air suspension, measure the resistance between the EVO control module C214, harness side and EVO actuator C184, harness side.

EVO Control Module C214	EVO Actuator C184	Circuit
Pin 14	Pin 1	87 (TN/YE)
Pin 13	Pin 2	86 (GY/OG)

3 If equipped with an air suspension, measure the resistance between the air suspension control module C215, harness side and EVO actuator C184, harness side.

Air Suspension Control Module C215	EVO Actuator C184	Circuit
Pin 26	Pin 1	87 (TN/YE)
Pin 14	Pin 2	86 (GY/OG)

• Is the resistance less than 5 ohms?

→ **Yes** GO to **E4**.

→ **No** REPAIR the circuit(s) in question. CLEAR the DTCs. REPEAT the Auto Test.

FM6029900339030X

Fig. 27 Test E-DTC 16: EVO Actuator Shorted; DTC 17: EVO Actuator Shorted or Open; DTC 18: EVO Actuator Resistance Out Of Range (Part 3 of 6). 1999–2002 Crown Victoria & Grand Marquis

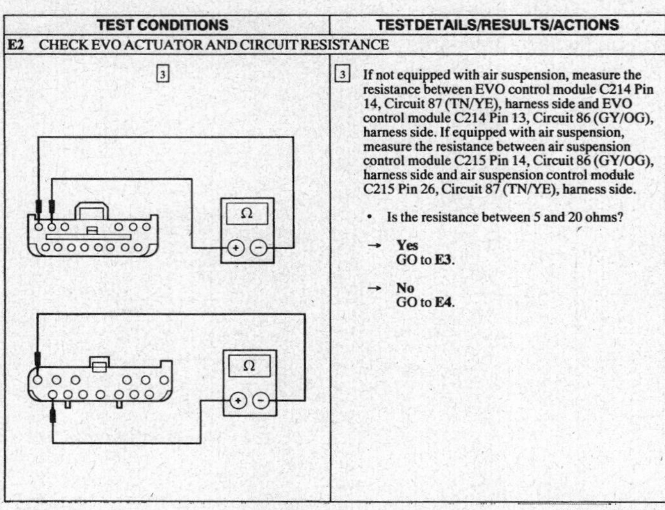

TEST CONDITIONS	TEST DETAILS/RESULTS/ACTIONS
E2 CHECK EVO ACTUATOR AND CIRCUIT RESISTANCE	
3	3 If not equipped with air suspension, measure the resistance between EVO control module C214 Pin 14, Circuit 87 (TN/YE), harness side and EVO control module C214 Pin 13, Circuit 86 (GY/OG), harness side. If equipped with air suspension, measure the resistance between air suspension control module C215 Pin 14, Circuit 86 (GY/OG), harness side and air suspension control module C215 Pin 26, Circuit 87 (TN/YE), harness side. • Is the resistance between 5 and 20 ohms? → **Yes** GO to **E3**. → **No** GO to **E4**.

FM6029900339020X

Fig. 27 Test E-DTC 16: EVO Actuator Shorted; DTC 17: EVO Actuator Shorted or Open; DTC 18: EVO Actuator Resistance Out Of Range (Part 2 of 6). 1999–2002 Crown Victoria & Grand Marquis

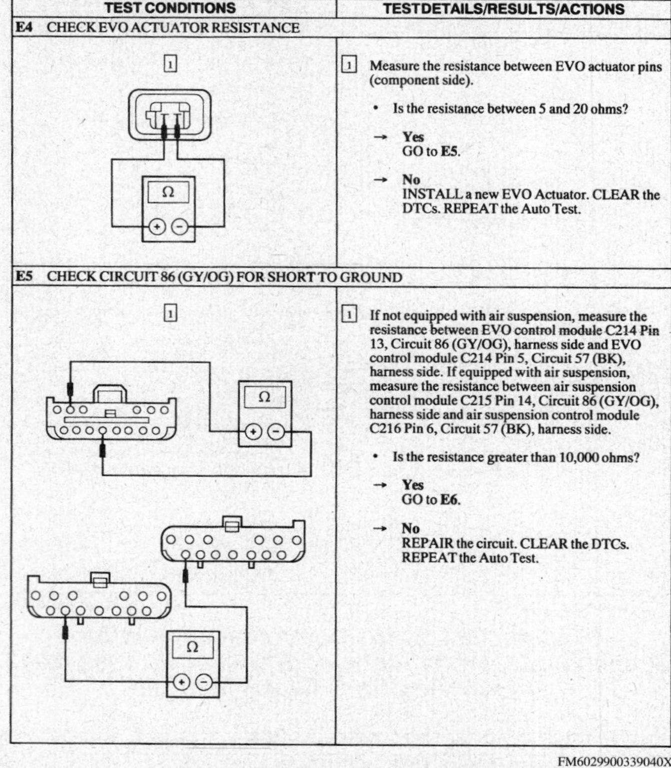

TEST CONDITIONS	TEST DETAILS/RESULTS/ACTIONS
E4 CHECK EVO ACTUATOR RESISTANCE	
1	1 Measure the resistance between EVO actuator pins (component side). • Is the resistance between 5 and 20 ohms? → **Yes** GO to **E5**. → **No** INSTALL a new EVO Actuator. CLEAR the DTCs. REPEAT the Auto Test.
E5 CHECK CIRCUIT 86 (GY/OG) FOR SHORT TO GROUND	
1	1 If not equipped with air suspension, measure the resistance between EVO control module C214 Pin 13, Circuit 86 (GY/OG), harness side and EVO control module C214 Pin 5, Circuit 57 (BK), harness side. If equipped with air suspension, measure the resistance between air suspension control module C215 Pin 14, Circuit 86 (GY/OG), harness side and air suspension control module C216 Pin 6, Circuit 57 (BK), harness side. • Is the resistance greater than 10,000 ohms? → **Yes** GO to **E6**. → **No** REPAIR the circuit. CLEAR the DTCs. REPEAT the Auto Test.

FM6029900339040X

Fig. 27 Test E-DTC 16: EVO Actuator Shorted; DTC 17: EVO Actuator Shorted or Open; DTC 18: EVO Actuator Resistance Out Of Range (Part 4 of 6). 1999–2002 Crown Victoria & Grand Marquis

TEST CONDITIONS	TESTDETAILS/RESULTS/ACTIONS
E6 CHECK CIRCUIT 87 (TN/YE) FOR SHORT TO GROUND	
1 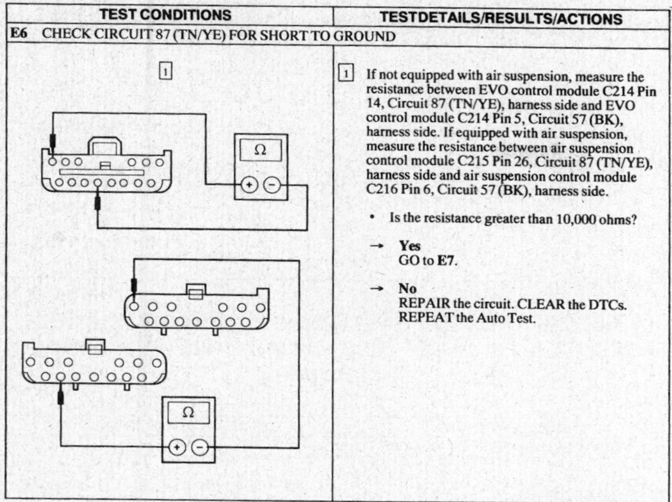	1 If not equipped with air suspension, measure the resistance between EVO control module C214 Pin 14, Circuit 87 (TN/YE), harness side and EVO control module C214 Pin 5, Circuit 57 (BK), harness side. If equipped with air suspension, measure the resistance between air suspension control module C215 Pin 26, Circuit 87 (TN/YE), harness side and air suspension control module C216 Pin 6, Circuit 57 (BK), harness side. • Is the resistance greater than 10,000 ohms? → **Yes** GO to **E7**. → **No** REPAIR the circuit. CLEAR the DTCs. REPEAT the Auto Test.

FM6029900339050X

Fig. 27 Test E-DTC 16: EVO Actuator Shorted; DTC 17: EVO Actuator Shorted or Open; DTC 18: EVO Actuator Resistance Out Of Range (Part 5 of 6). 1999–2002 Crown Victoria & Grand Marquis

TEST CONDITIONS	TESTDETAILS/RESULTS/ACTIONS
F1 CHECK EVO ACTUATOR FOR AN OPEN	
1 2 EVO Actuator C184	
3	3 Measure the resistance between EVO actuator pins (component side). • Is the resistance between 5 and 20 ohms? → **Yes** GO to **F2**. → **No** INSTALL a new EVO actuator. CLEAR the DTCs. REPEAT the Auto Test.
F2 CHECK CIRCUIT 86 (GY/OG) FOR AN OPEN	
1 2 EVO Control Module C214	
3	3 Measure the resistance between EVO control module C214 Pin 13, Circuit 86 (GY/OG), harness side and EVO actuator C184 Pin 2, Circuit 86 (GY/OG), harness side. • Is the resistance less than 5 ohms? → **Yes** GO to **F3**. → **No** REPAIR the circuit. CLEAR the DTCs. REPEAT the Auto Test.

FM6029900340010X

Fig. 28 DTC 27: EVO Actuator Circuit Open (Part 1 of 2). 1999–2002 Crown Victoria & Grand Marquis

TEST CONDITIONS	TESTDETAILS/RESULTS/ACTIONS
E7 CHECK FOR SHORT TO BATTERY	
1 2 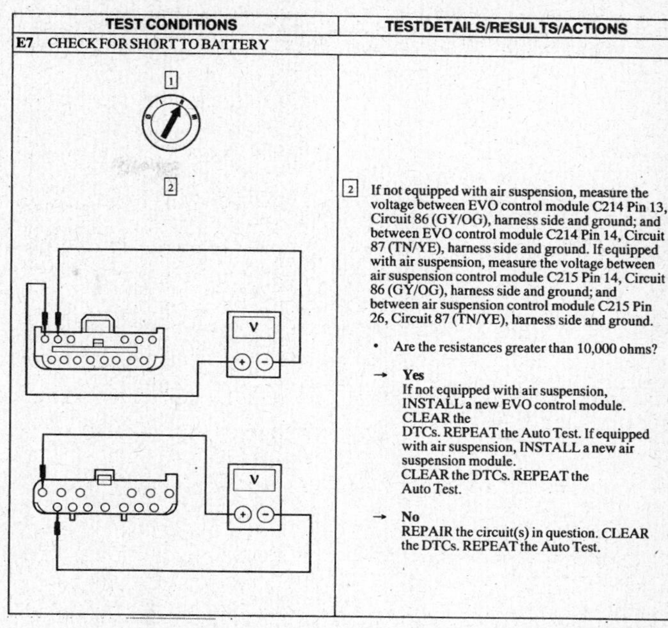	2 If not equipped with air suspension, measure the voltage between EVO control module C214 Pin 13, Circuit 86 (GY/OG), harness side and ground; and between EVO control module C214 Pin 14, Circuit 87 (TN/YE), harness side and ground. If equipped with air suspension, measure the voltage between air suspension control module C215 Pin 14, Circuit 86 (GY/OG), harness side and ground; and between air suspension control module C215 Pin 26, Circuit 87 (TN/YE), harness side and ground. • Are the resistances greater than 10,000 ohms? → **Yes** If not equipped with air suspension, INSTALL a new EVO control module. CLEAR the DTCs. REPEAT the Auto Test. If equipped with air suspension, INSTALL a new air suspension module. CLEAR the DTCs. REPEAT the Auto Test. → **No** REPAIR the circuit(s) in question. CLEAR the DTCs. REPEAT the Auto Test.

FM6029900339060X

Fig. 27 Test E-DTC 16: EVO Actuator Shorted; DTC 17: EVO Actuator Shorted or Open; DTC 18: EVO Actuator Resistance Out Of Range (Part 6 of 6). 1999–2002 Crown Victoria & Grand Marquis

TEST CONDITIONS	TESTDETAILS/RESULTS/ACTIONS
F3 CHECK CIRCUIT 87 (TN/YE) FOR AN OPEN	
1 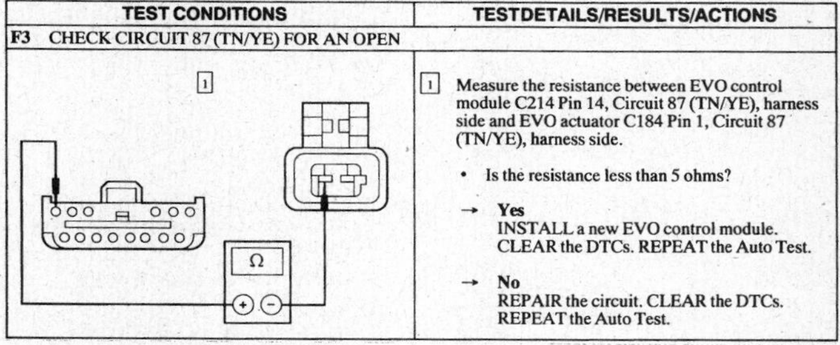	1 Measure the resistance between EVO control module C214 Pin 14, Circuit 87 (TN/YE), harness side and EVO actuator C184 Pin 1, Circuit 87 (TN/YE), harness side. • Is the resistance less than 5 ohms? → **Yes** INSTALL a new EVO control module. CLEAR the DTCs. REPEAT the Auto Test. → **No** REPAIR the circuit. CLEAR the DTCs. REPEAT the Auto Test.

FM6029900340020X

Fig. 28 DTC 27: EVO Actuator Circuit Open (Part 2 of 2). 1999–2002 Crown Victoria & Grand Marquis

TEST CONDITIONS	TESTDETAILS/RESULTS/ACTIONS
G1 CHECK EVO ACTUATOR FOR A SHORT	
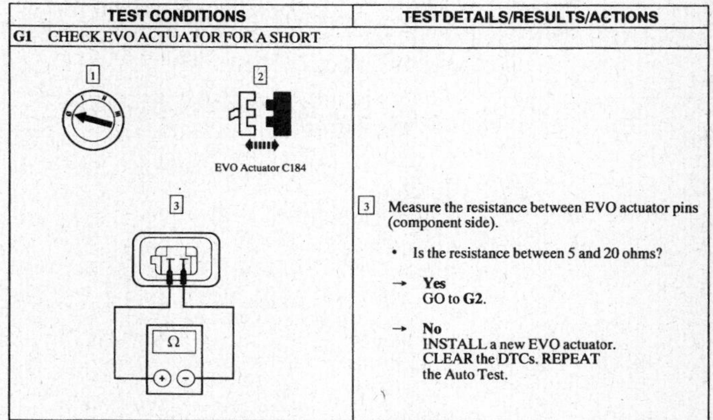	3 Measure the resistance between EVO actuator pins (component side). • Is the resistance between 5 and 20 ohms? → **Yes** GO to **G2**. → **No** INSTALL a new EVO actuator. CLEAR the DTCs. REPEAT the Auto Test.

FM6029900341010X

Fig. 29 DTC 28: EVO Actuator Circuit Shorted (Part 1 of 3). 1999–2002 Crown Victoria & Grand Marquis

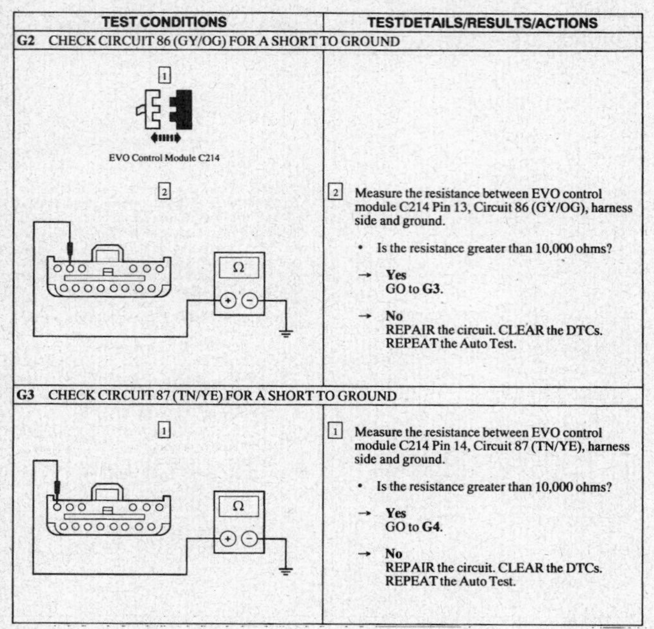

TEST CONDITIONS	TESTDETAILS/RESULTS/ACTIONS
G2 CHECK CIRCUIT 86 (GY/OG) FOR A SHORT TO GROUND	
1 EVO Control Module C214	
2	2 Measure the resistance between EVO control module C214 Pin 13, Circuit 86 (GY/OG), harness side and ground. • Is the resistance greater than 10,000 ohms? → **Yes** GO to **G3**. → **No** REPAIR the circuit. CLEAR the DTCs. REPEAT the Auto Test.
G3 CHECK CIRCUIT 87 (TN/YE) FOR A SHORT TO GROUND	
1	1 Measure the resistance between EVO control module C214 Pin 14, Circuit 87 (TN/YE), harness side and ground. • Is the resistance greater than 10,000 ohms? → **Yes** GO to **G4**. → **No** REPAIR the circuit. CLEAR the DTCs. REPEAT the Auto Test.

FM6029900341020X

Fig. 29 DTC 28: EVO Actuator Circuit Shorted (Part 2 of 3). 1999–2002 Crown Victoria & Grand Marquis

TEST CONDITIONS	TESTDETAILS/RESULTS/ACTIONS
H1 CHECK CIRCUIT 86 (GY/OG) FOR SHORT TO GROUND	
1 2 3 EVO Actuator C184 EVO Control Module C214	
4	4 Measure the resistance between EVO control module C214 Pin 13, Circuit 86 (GY/OG), harness side and ground. • Is the resistance less than 10,000 ohms? → **Yes** REPAIR the circuit. CLEAR the DTCs. REPEAT the Auto Test. → **No** GO to **H2**.

FM6029900342010X

Fig. 30 DTC 29: EVO Actuator Circuit High Side Shorted To Ground (Part 1 of 2). 1999–2002 Crown Victoria & Grand Marquis

TEST CONDITIONS	TESTDETAILS/RESULTS/ACTIONS
I1 CHECK CIRCUIT 86 (GY/OG) FOR SHORT TO BATTERY	
1 2 3 EVO Actuator C184 EVO Control Module C214	
4	4 Measure the voltage between EVO control module C214 Pin 13, Circuit 86 (GY/OG), harness side and ground. • Is voltage present? → **Yes** REPAIR the circuit. CLEAR the DTCs. REPEAT the Auto Test. → **No** GO to **I2**.

FM6029900343010X

Fig. 31 DTC 30: EVO Actuator Circuit Shorted To Battery (Part 1 of 2). 1999–2002 Crown Victoria & Grand Marquis

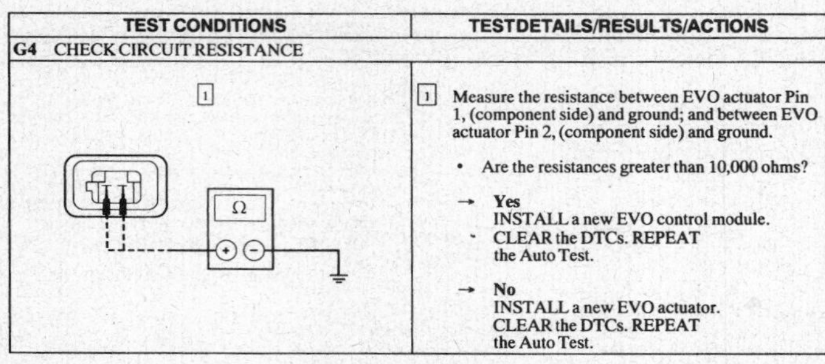

TEST CONDITIONS	TESTDETAILS/RESULTS/ACTIONS
G4 CHECK CIRCUIT RESISTANCE	
1	1 Measure the resistance between EVO actuator Pin 1, (component side) and ground; and between EVO actuator Pin 2, (component side) and ground. • Are the resistances greater than 10,000 ohms? → **Yes** INSTALL a new EVO control module. CLEAR the DTCs. REPEAT the Auto Test. → **No** INSTALL a new EVO actuator. CLEAR the DTCs. REPEAT the Auto Test.

FM6029900341030X

Fig. 29 DTC 28: EVO Actuator Circuit Shorted (Part 3 of 3). 1999–2002 Crown Victoria & Grand Marquis

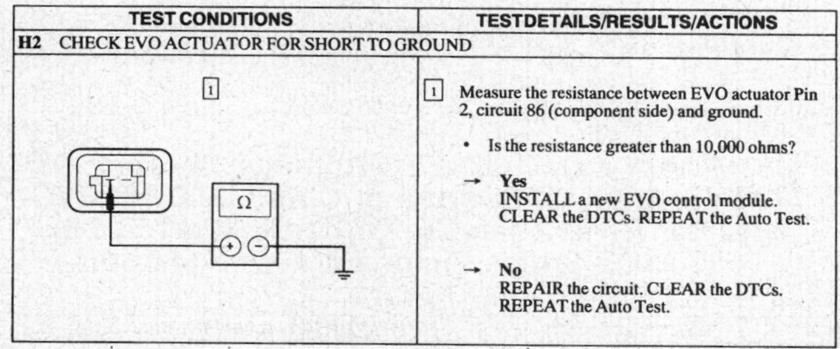

TEST CONDITIONS	TESTDETAILS/RESULTS/ACTIONS
H2 CHECK EVO ACTUATOR FOR SHORT TO GROUND	
1	1 Measure the resistance between EVO actuator Pin 2, circuit 86 (component side) and ground. • Is the resistance greater than 10,000 ohms? → **Yes** INSTALL a new EVO control module. CLEAR the DTCs. REPEAT the Auto Test. → **No** REPAIR the circuit. CLEAR the DTCs. REPEAT the Auto Test.

FM6029900342020X

Fig. 30 DTC 29: EVO Actuator Circuit High Side Shorted To Ground (Part 2 of 2). 1999–2002 Crown Victoria & Grand Marquis

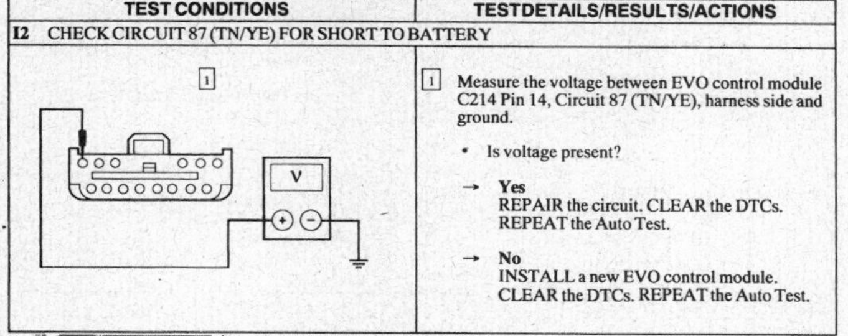

TEST CONDITIONS	TESTDETAILS/RESULTS/ACTIONS
I2 CHECK CIRCUIT 87 (TN/YE) FOR SHORT TO BATTERY	
1	1 Measure the voltage between EVO control module C214 Pin 14, Circuit 87 (TN/YE), harness side and ground. • Is voltage present? → **Yes** REPAIR the circuit. CLEAR the DTCs. REPEAT the Auto Test. → **No** INSTALL a new EVO control module. CLEAR the DTCs. REPEAT the Auto Test.

FM6029900343020X

Fig. 31 DTC 30: EVO Actuator Circuit Shorted To Battery (Part 2 of 2). 1999–2002 Crown Victoria & Grand Marquis

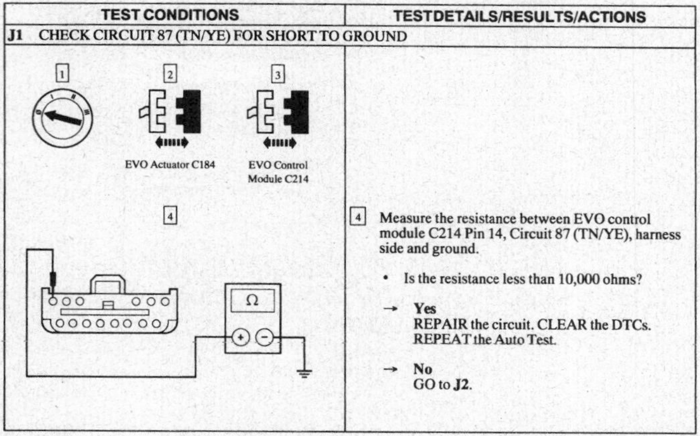

TEST CONDITIONS	TESTDETAILS/RESULTS/ACTIONS
J1 CHECK CIRCUIT 87 (TN/YE) FOR SHORT TO GROUND	
1 2 3 EVO Actuator C184 EVO Control Module C214	
4	4 Measure the resistance between EVO control module C214 Pin 14, Circuit 87 (TN/YE), harness side and ground. • Is the resistance less than 10,000 ohms? → **Yes** REPAIR the circuit. CLEAR the DTCs. REPEAT the Auto Test. → **No** GO to **J2**.

FM6029900344010X

Fig. 32 DTC 31: EVO Actuator Circuit Low Side Shorted To Ground (Part 1 of 2). 1999–2002 Crown Victoria & Grand Marquis

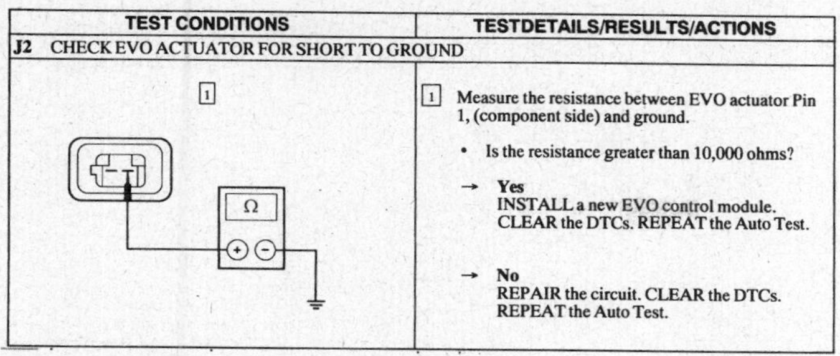

TEST CONDITIONS	TEST DETAILS/RESULTS/ACTIONS
J2 CHECK EVO ACTUATOR FOR SHORT TO GROUND	
1	1 Measure the resistance between EVO actuator Pin 1, (component side) and ground. • Is the resistance greater than 10,000 ohms? → **Yes** INSTALL a new EVO control module. CLEAR the DTCs. REPEAT the Auto Test. → **No** REPAIR the circuit. CLEAR the DTCs. REPEAT the Auto Test.

FM6029900344020X

Fig. 32 DTC 31: EVO Actuator Circuit Low Side Shorted To Ground (Part 2 of 2). 1999–2002 Crown Victoria & Grand Marquis

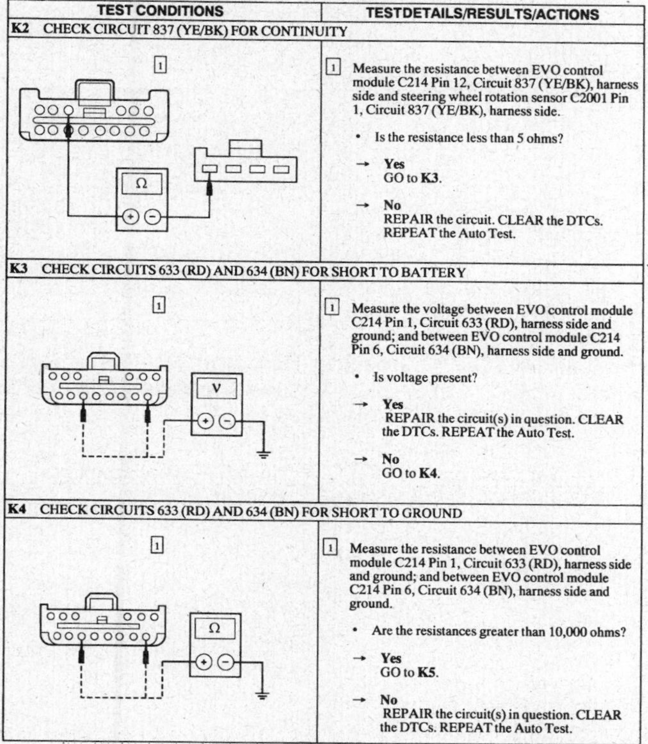

TEST CONDITIONS	TEST DETAILS/RESULTS/ACTIONS
K2 CHECK CIRCUIT 837 (YE/BK) FOR CONTINUITY	
1	1 Measure the resistance between EVO control module C214 Pin 12, Circuit 837 (YE/BK), harness side and steering wheel rotation sensor C2001 Pin 1, Circuit 837 (YE/BK), harness side. • Is the resistance less than 5 ohms? → **Yes** GO to **K3**. → **No** REPAIR the circuit. CLEAR the DTCs. REPEAT the Auto Test.
K3 CHECK CIRCUITS 633 (RD) AND 634 (BN) FOR SHORT TO BATTERY	
1	1 Measure the voltage between EVO control module C214 Pin 1, Circuit 633 (RD), harness side and ground; and between EVO control module C214 Pin 6, Circuit 634 (BN), harness side and ground. • Is voltage present? → **Yes** REPAIR the circuit(s) in question. CLEAR the DTCs. REPEAT the Auto Test. → **No** GO to **K4**.
K4 CHECK CIRCUITS 633 (RD) AND 634 (BN) FOR SHORT TO GROUND	
1	1 Measure the resistance between EVO control module C214 Pin 1, Circuit 633 (RD), harness side and ground; and between EVO control module C214 Pin 6, Circuit 634 (BN), harness side and ground. • Are the resistances greater than 10,000 ohms? → **Yes** GO to **K5**. → **No** REPAIR the circuit(s) in question. CLEAR the DTCs. REPEAT the Auto Test.

FM6029900345020X

Fig. 33 DTC 33: Steering Rotation Not Detected (Part 2 of 4). 1999–2002 Crown Victoria & Grand Marquis

TEST CONDITIONS	TEST DETAILS/RESULTS/ACTIONS
K6 CHECK STEERING WHEEL ROTATION SENSOR	
5	5 **Note:** Touch 73 Digital Multimeter leads together to be sure the audio (beep) function is operational. **Note:** The 73 Digital Multimeter should beep several times while rotating the steering wheel. Connect 73 Digital Multimeter leads between EVO control module C214 Pin 1, Circuit 633 (RD), harness side and ground; and between EVO control module C214 Pin 6, Circuit 634 (BN), harness side and ground. Listen for an audible beep while turning the steering wheel one quarter turn in each direction. • Does 73 Digital Multimeter beep multiple times in each direction? → **Yes** INSTALL a new EVO control module. CLEAR the DTCs. REPEAT the Auto Test. → **No** INSTALL a new steering wheel rotation sensor. CLEAR the DTCs. REPEAT the Auto Test.

FM6029900345040X

Fig. 33 DTC 33: Steering Rotation Not Detected (Part 4 of 4). 1999–2002 Crown Victoria & Grand Marquis

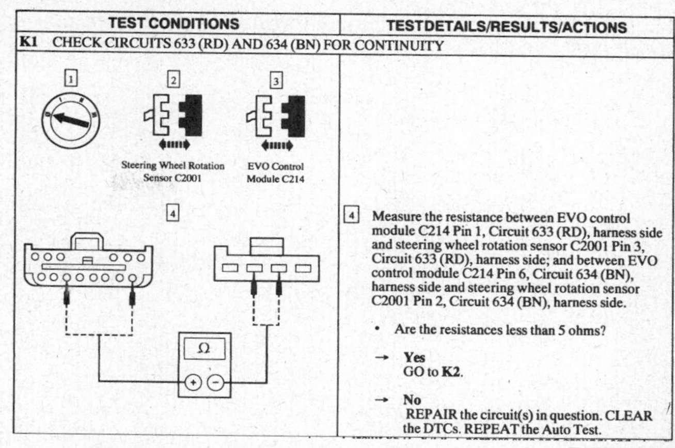

TEST CONDITIONS	TEST DETAILS/RESULTS/ACTIONS
K1 CHECK CIRCUITS 633 (RD) AND 634 (BN) FOR CONTINUITY	
1 2 3 Steering Wheel Rotation Sensor C2001 EVO Control Module C214 4	4 Measure the resistance between EVO control module C214 Pin 1, Circuit 633 (RD), harness side and steering wheel rotation sensor C2001 Pin 3, Circuit 633 (RD), harness side; and between EVO control module C214 Pin 6, Circuit 634 (BN), harness side and steering wheel rotation sensor C2001 Pin 2, Circuit 634 (BN), harness side. • Are the resistances less than 5 ohms? → **Yes** GO to **K2**. → **No** REPAIR the circuit(s) in question. CLEAR the DTCs. REPEAT the Auto Test.

FM6029900345010X

Fig. 33 DTC 33: Steering Rotation Not Detected (Part 1 of 4). 1999–2002 Crown Victoria & Grand Marquis

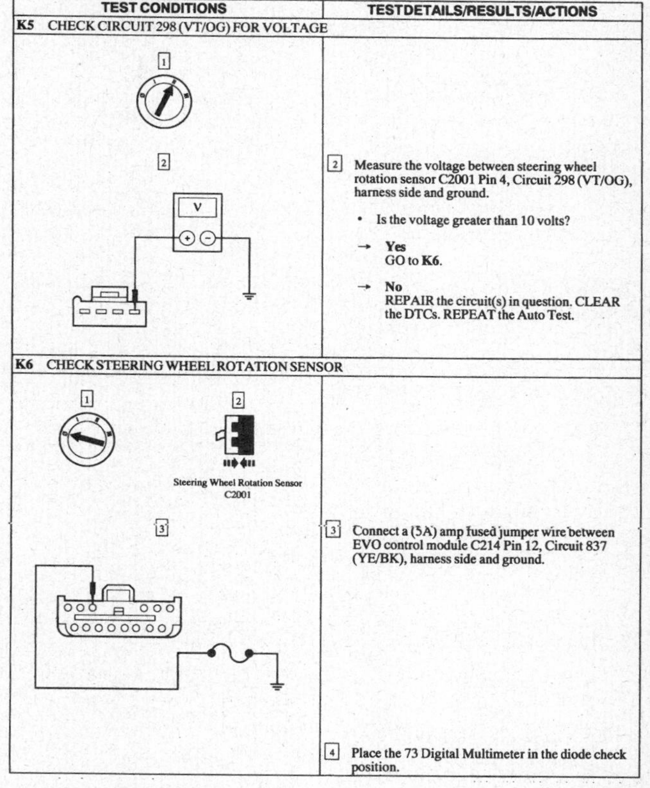

TEST CONDITIONS	TEST DETAILS/RESULTS/ACTIONS
K5 CHECK CIRCUIT 298 (VT/OG) FOR VOLTAGE	
1 2	2 Measure the voltage between steering wheel rotation sensor C2001 Pin 4, Circuit 298 (VT/OG), harness side and ground. • Is the voltage greater than 10 volts? → **Yes** GO to **K6**. → **No** REPAIR the circuit(s) in question. CLEAR the DTCs. REPEAT the Auto Test.
K6 CHECK STEERING WHEEL ROTATION SENSOR	
1 2 Steering Wheel Rotation Sensor C2001 3	3 Connect a (5A) amp fused jumper wire between EVO control module C214 Pin 12, Circuit 837 (YE/BK), harness side and ground.
	4 Place the 73 Digital Multimeter in the diode check position.

FM6029900345030X

Fig. 33 DTC 33: Steering Rotation Not Detected (Part 3 of 4). 1999–2002 Crown Victoria & Grand Marquis

TEST CONDITIONS	TEST DETAILS/RESULTS/ACTIONS
L1 CHECK SPEEDOMETER OPERATION	
	1 Drive the vehicle and check for correct speedometer operation. • Does the speedometer indicate vehicle speeds above 24 km/h (15 mph)? → **Yes** GO to **L2**. → **No** INSPECT instrument cluster. CLEAR the DTCs. REPEAT the Auto Test.

FM6029900346010X

Fig. 34 DTC 35: Vehicle Speed Above 15 mph Not Detected (Part 1 of 2). 1999–2002 Crown Victoria & Grand Marquis

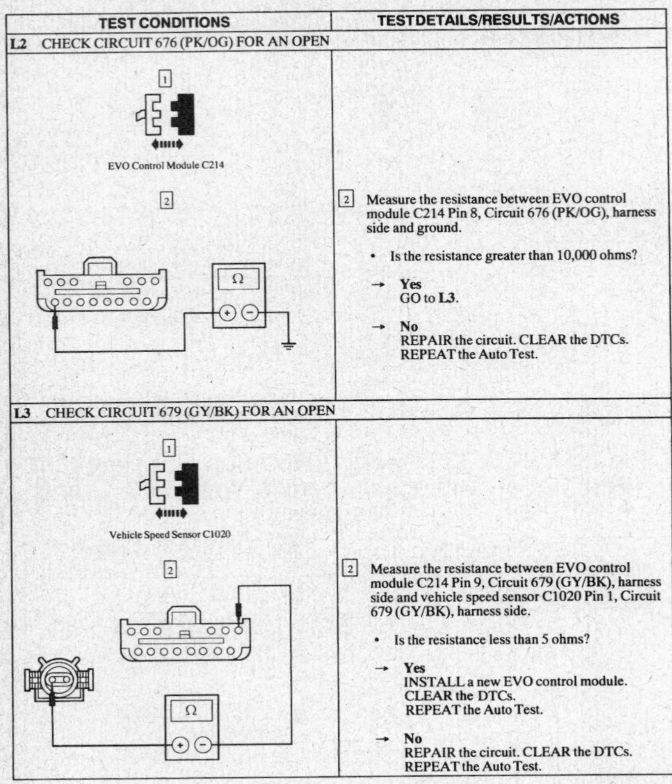

TEST CONDITIONS	TEST DETAILS/RESULTS/ACTIONS
L2 CHECK CIRCUIT 676 (PK/OG) FOR AN OPEN	
1 EVO Control Module C214	
2	2 Measure the resistance between EVO control module C214 Pin 8, Circuit 676 (PK/OG), harness side and ground. • Is the resistance greater than 10,000 ohms? → **Yes** GO to **L3**. → **No** REPAIR the circuit. CLEAR the DTCs. REPEAT the Auto Test.
L3 CHECK CIRCUIT 679 (GY/BK) FOR AN OPEN	
1 Vehicle Speed Sensor C1020	
2	2 Measure the resistance between EVO control module C214 Pin 9, Circuit 679 (GY/BK), harness side and vehicle speed sensor C1020 Pin 1, Circuit 679 (GY/BK), harness side. • Is the resistance less than 5 ohms? → **Yes** INSTALL a new EVO control module. CLEAR the DTCs. REPEAT the Auto Test. → **No** REPAIR the circuit. CLEAR the DTCs. REPEAT the Auto Test.

FM6029900346020X

Fig. 34 DTC 35: Vehicle Speed Above 15 mph Not Detected (Part 2 of 2). 1999–2002 Crown Victoria & Grand Marquis

TEST CONDITIONS	TEST DETAILS/RESULTS/ACTIONS
M3 CHECK CIRCUIT 837 (YE/BK) FOR GROUND	
1	1 Measure the resistance between steering wheel rotation sensor C2001 Pin 1, Circuit 837 (YE/BK), harness side and ground. • Is the resistance greater than 10,000 ohms? → **Yes** GO to **M4**. → **No** REPAIR the circuit. CLEAR the DTCs. REPEAT the Auto Test.
M4 CHECK CIRCUITS 633 (RD) AND 634 (BN) FOR SHORT TO BATTERY	
1	1 Measure the voltage between air suspension control module C216 Pin 18, Circuit 633 (RD), harness side and ground; and between air suspension control module C216 pin 19, circuit 634 (BN), harness side and ground. • Is voltage present? → **Yes** REPAIR the circuit(s) in question. CLEAR the DTCs. REPEAT the Auto Test. → **No** GO to **M5**.
M5 CHECK CIRCUITS 633 (RD) AND 634 (BN) FOR SHORT TO GROUND	
1	1 Measure the resistance between air suspension control module C216 Pin 18, Circuit 633 (RD), harness side and ground; and between air suspension control module C216 Pin 19, Circuit 634 (BN), harness side and ground. • Are the resistances greater than 10,000 ohms? → **Yes** GO to **M6**. → **No** REPAIR the circuit(s) in question. CLEAR the DTCs. REPEAT the Auto Test.

FM6029900347020X

Fig. 35 DTC 74: Steering Rotation Not Detected (Part 2 of 4). 1999–2002 Crown Victoria & Grand Marquis

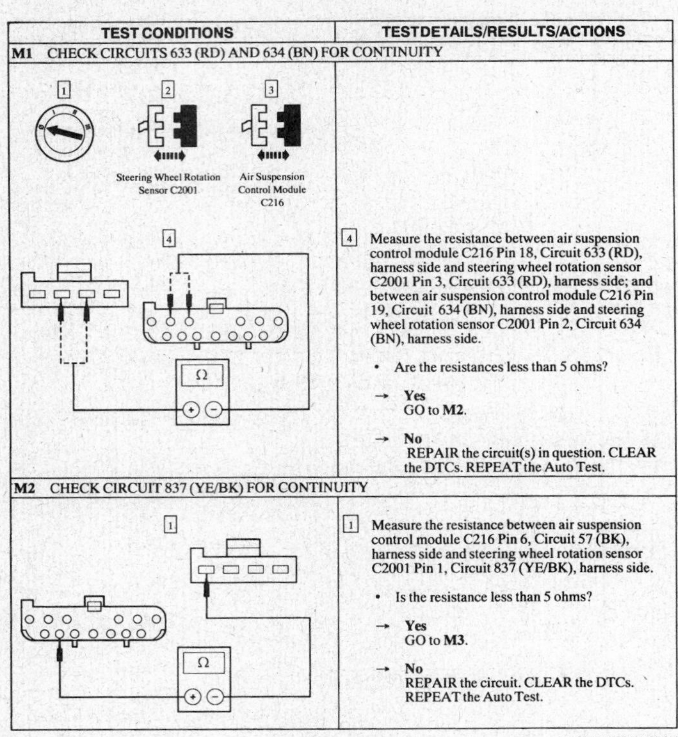

TEST CONDITIONS	TEST DETAILS/RESULTS/ACTIONS
M1 CHECK CIRCUITS 633 (RD) AND 634 (BN) FOR CONTINUITY	
1 2 Steering Wheel Rotation Sensor C2001 3 Air Suspension Control Module C216	
4	4 Measure the resistance between air suspension control module C216 Pin 18, Circuit 633 (RD), harness side and steering wheel rotation sensor C2001 Pin 3, Circuit 633 (RD), harness side; and between air suspension control module C216 Pin 19, Circuit 634 (BN), harness side and steering wheel rotation sensor C2001 Pin 2, Circuit 634 (BN), harness side. • Are the resistances less than 5 ohms? → **Yes** GO to **M2**. → **No** REPAIR the circuit(s) in question. CLEAR the DTCs. REPEAT the Auto Test.
M2 CHECK CIRCUIT 837 (YE/BK) FOR CONTINUITY	
1	1 Measure the resistance between air suspension control module C216 Pin 6, Circuit 57 (BK), harness side and steering wheel rotation sensor C2001 Pin 1, Circuit 837 (YE/BK), harness side. • Is the resistance less than 5 ohms? → **Yes** GO to **M3**. → **No** REPAIR the circuit. CLEAR the DTCs. REPEAT the Auto Test.

FM6029900347010X

Fig. 35 DTC 74: Steering Rotation Not Detected (Part 1 of 4). 1999–2002 Crown Victoria & Grand Marquis

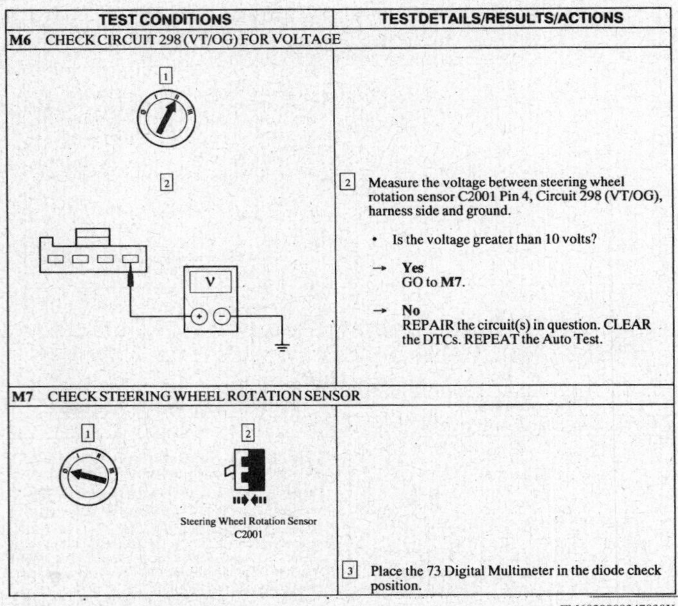

TEST CONDITIONS	TEST DETAILS/RESULTS/ACTIONS
M6 CHECK CIRCUIT 298 (VT/OG) FOR VOLTAGE	
1	
2	2 Measure the voltage between steering wheel rotation sensor C2001 Pin 4, Circuit 298 (VT/OG), harness side and ground. • Is the voltage greater than 10 volts? → **Yes** GO to **M7**. → **No** REPAIR the circuit(s) in question. CLEAR the DTCs. REPEAT the Auto Test.
M7 CHECK STEERING WHEEL ROTATION SENSOR	
1 2 Steering Wheel Rotation Sensor C2001	3 Place the 73 Digital Multimeter in the diode check position.

FM6029900347030X

Fig. 35 DTC 74: Steering Rotation Not Detected (Part 3 of 4). 1999–2002 Crown Victoria & Grand Marquis

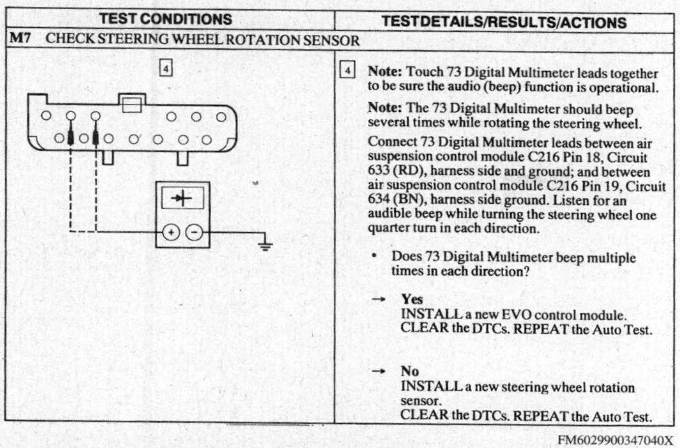

TEST CONDITIONS	TEST DETAILS/RESULTS/ACTIONS
M7 CHECK STEERING WHEEL ROTATION SENSOR	
4	4 **Note:** Touch 73 Digital Multimeter leads together to be sure the audio (beep) function is operational. **Note:** The 73 Digital Multimeter should beep several times while rotating the steering wheel. Connect 73 Digital Multimeter leads between air suspension control module C216 Pin 18, Circuit 633 (RD), harness side and ground; and between air suspension control module C216 Pin 19, Circuit 634 (BN), harness side ground. Listen for an audible beep while turning the steering wheel one quarter turn in each direction. • Does 73 Digital Multimeter beep multiple times in each direction? → **Yes** INSTALL a new EVO control module. CLEAR the DTCs. REPEAT the Auto Test. → **No** INSTALL a new steering wheel rotation sensor. CLEAR the DTCs. REPEAT the Auto Test.

FM6029900347040X

Fig. 35 DTC 74: Steering Rotation Not Detected (Part 4 of 4). 1999–2002 Crown Victoria & Grand Marquis

• Steering Diagnostics Cannot Be Entered	• Circuitry open/shorted. • Control module.	• GO to Pinpoint Test C.
• Steering Does Not Vary With Vehicle Speed	• Vehicle speed sensor. • Circuitry open/shorted. • Control module.	• GO to Pinpoint Test D.

FM6029700274020X

Fig. 36 Symptom chart (Part 2 of 2). Mark VIII

TEST CONDITIONS	TEST DETAILS/RESULTS/ACTIONS
A1 CHECK EVO POWER STEERING CONTROL VALVE ACTUATOR	
1 2 EVO Actuator Connector C132	
3	3 Connect an ohmmeter between the EVO actuator connector C132, Circuit 353 (LB) and Circuit 330 (Y/LG). • Is the resistance less than 8 ohms or more than 16 ohms? → **Yes** REPLACE the EVO power steering control valve actuator. REPEAT the Auto Test. → **No** GO to **A2**.
A2 CHECK THE HARNESS FOR SHORT TO B+	
1 2 Air Suspension/Electronic Variable Orifice (EVO) Control Module Connector C205	
3	3 Connect a voltmeter to the air suspension/electronic variable orifice (EVO) control module connector Pin C205-19, Circuit 330 (Y/LG). Note the reading.

FM6029700275010X

Fig. 37 Test A: DTC 35, EVO Power Steering Control Valve Actuator Concern (Part 1 of 3). Mark VIII

Code	Description	Error Handling	Generated	Validation
10	Auto test in progress		Auto Test	
11	Auto test passed		Auto Test	
12	Perform manual tests		Auto Test	
15	No faults stored in memory		Auto Test	
18	Control Module Detects Low Battery Voltage	Disable air suspension and EVO until senses more than 13 volts for 1 second	Auto Test	Less than 11 volts for 1 second continuous
19	Control Module Detects High Battery Voltage	Disable Air Suspension and EVO until senses less than 17.5 volts for 1 second	Auto Test	More than 19 volts for 1 second continuous
20	Control Module Memory Error 2	Disable Air Suspension	Drive Cycle Auto Test	More than 19 volts for 1 second continuous
25	Air Suspension Height Sensor Supply Not 5 Volts	Disable Air Suspension	Drive Cycle Auto Test	
29	Two Door Cycles Not Detected During Test		Auto Test	
35	EVO Power Steering Control Valve Actuator Concern	Air suspention normal, EVO full assist	Drive Cycle Auto Test	Fault after 1 second continuous GO to Pinpoint Test A
45	Steering Rotation Not Detected		Auto Test	GO to Pinpoint Test B
50	LH Front Air Suspension Height Sensor Signal Out Of Range	Disable Air Suspension	Drive Cycle Auto Test	Fault after 1 second continuous
55	RH Front Air Suspension Height Sensor Signal Out Of Range	Disable Air Suspension	Drive Cycle Auto Test	Fault after 1 second continuous
60	LH Rear Air Suspension Height Sensor Signal Out Of Range	Disable Air Suspension	Drive Cycle Auto Test	Fault after 1 second continuous
70	Vent Solenoid Valve	Disable Air Suspension	Drive Cycle Auto Test	Fault after 1 second continuous
75	Compressor Relay Control Circuit	Disable Air Suspension	Drive Cycle Auto Test	Fault after 1 second continuous

FM6029700274010X

Fig. 36 Symptom chart (Part 1 of 2). Mark VIII

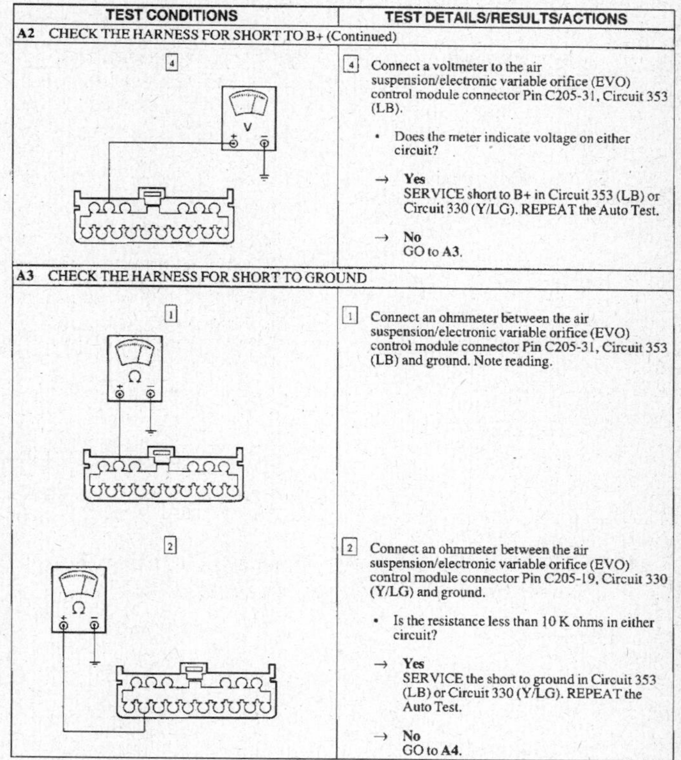

TEST CONDITIONS	TEST DETAILS/RESULTS/ACTIONS
A2 CHECK THE HARNESS FOR SHORT TO B+ (Continued)	
4	4 Connect a voltmeter to the air suspension/electronic variable orifice (EVO) control module connector Pin C205-31, Circuit 353 (LB). • Does the meter indicate voltage on either circuit? → **Yes** SERVICE short to B+ in Circuit 353 (LB) or Circuit 330 (Y/LG). REPEAT the Auto Test. → **No** GO to **A3**.
A3 CHECK THE HARNESS FOR SHORT TO GROUND	
1	1 Connect an ohmmeter between the air suspension/electronic variable orifice (EVO) control module connector Pin C205-31, Circuit 353 (LB) and ground. Note reading.
2	2 Connect an ohmmeter between the air suspension/electronic variable orifice (EVO) control module connector Pin C205-19, Circuit 330 (Y/LG) and ground. • Is the resistance less than 10 K ohms in either circuit? → **Yes** SERVICE the short to ground in Circuit 353 (LB) or Circuit 330 (Y/LG). REPEAT the Auto Test. → **No** GO to **A4**.

FM6029700275020X

Fig. 37 Test A: DTC 35, EVO Power Steering Control Valve Actuator Concern (Part 2 of 3). Mark VIII

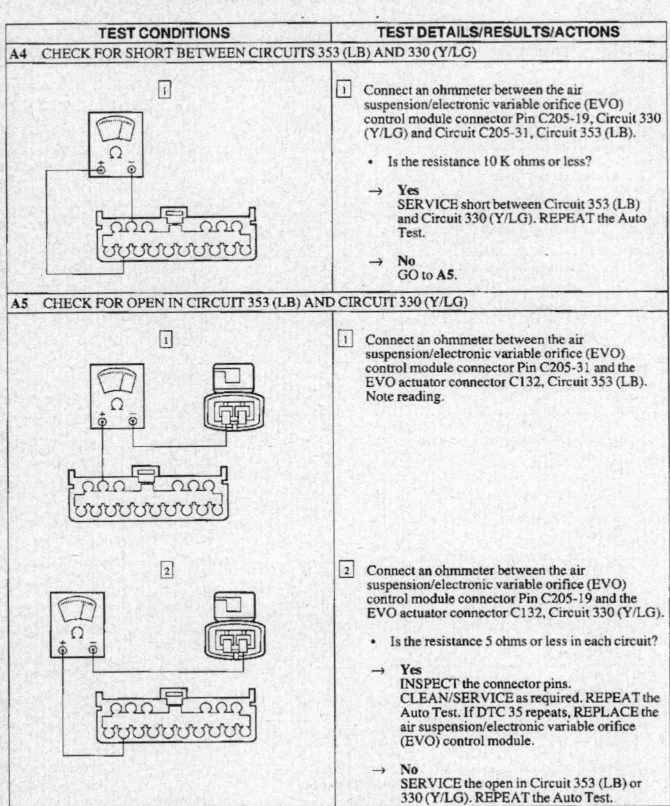

TEST CONDITIONS	TEST DETAILS/RESULTS/ACTIONS
A4 CHECK FOR SHORT BETWEEN CIRCUITS 353 (LB) AND 330 (Y/LG)	
1	1 Connect an ohmmeter between the air suspension/electronic variable orifice (EVO) control module connector Pin C205-19, Circuit 330 (Y/LG) and Circuit C205-31, Circuit 353 (LB). • Is the resistance 10 K ohms or less? → **Yes** SERVICE short between Circuit 353 (LB) and Circuit 330 (Y/LG). REPEAT the Auto Test. → **No** GO to **A5**.
A5 CHECK FOR OPEN IN CIRCUIT 353 (LB) AND CIRCUIT 330 (Y/LG)	
1	1 Connect an ohmmeter between the air suspension/electronic variable orifice (EVO) control module connector Pin C205-31 and the EVO actuator connector C132, Circuit 353 (LB). Note reading.
2	2 Connect an ohmmeter between the air suspension/electronic variable orifice (EVO) control module connector Pin C205-19 and the EVO actuator connector C132, Circuit 330 (Y/LG). • Is the resistance 5 ohms or less in each circuit? → **Yes** INSPECT the connector pins. CLEAN/SERVICE as required. REPEAT the Auto Test. If DTC 35 repeats, REPLACE the air suspension/electronic variable orifice (EVO) control module. → **No** SERVICE the open in Circuit 353 (LB) or 330 (Y/LG). REPEAT the Auto Test.

FM6029700275030X

Fig. 37 Test A: DTC 35, EVO Power Steering Control Valve Actuator Concern (Part 3 of 3). Mark VIII

TEST CONDITIONS	TEST DETAILS/RESULTS/ACTIONS
B3 CHECK CIRCUITS 633 (R) AND 634 (BR) FOR CHANGING VOLTAGE AT CONTROL MODULE	
1 Shock Absorber Electronic Steering Sensor Connector C237 2 Air Suspension/Electronic Variable Orifice (EVO) Control Module Connector C204	
3	3 **NOTE:** The meter reading should change between 5 volts and zero volts several times while rotating the steering wheel. Connect a voltmeter to the air suspension/electronic variable orifice (EVO) control module connector Pin C204-2, Circuit 633 (R).
	4 Slowly rotate the steering wheel one quarter of a turn while observing the meter reading.

FM6029700276020X

Fig. 38 Test B: DTC 45, Steering Rotation Not Detected (Part 2 of 6). Mark VIII

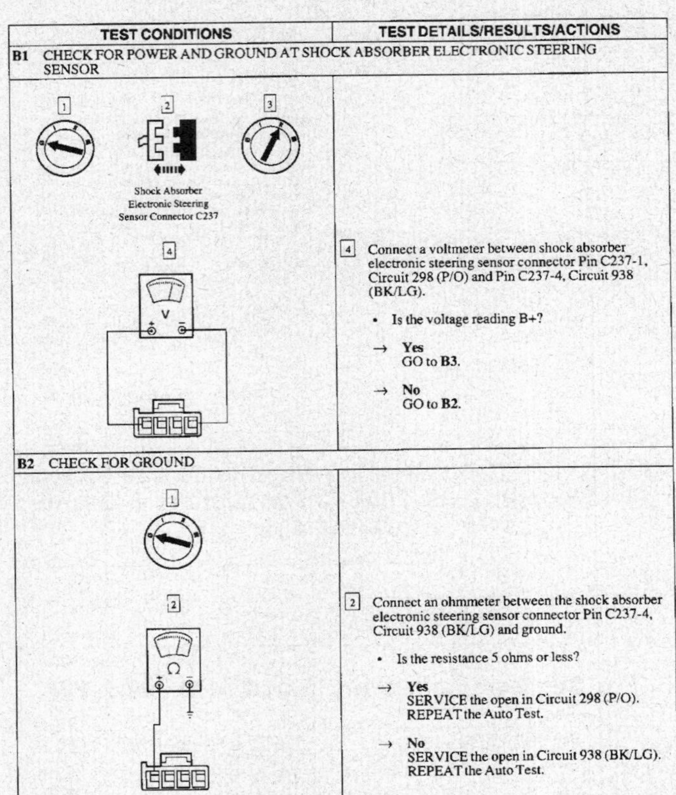

TEST CONDITIONS	TEST DETAILS/RESULTS/ACTIONS
B1 CHECK FOR POWER AND GROUND AT SHOCK ABSORBER ELECTRONIC STEERING SENSOR	
1 2 3 Shock Absorber Electronic Steering Sensor Connector C237	
4	4 Connect a voltmeter between shock absorber electronic steering sensor connector Pin C237-1, Circuit 298 (P/O) and Pin C237-4, Circuit 938 (BK/LG). • Is the voltage reading B+? → **Yes** GO to **B3**. → **No** GO to **B2**.
B2 CHECK FOR GROUND	
1	
2	2 Connect an ohmmeter between the shock absorber electronic steering sensor connector Pin C237-4, Circuit 938 (BK/LG) and ground. • Is the resistance 5 ohms or less? → **Yes** SERVICE the open in Circuit 298 (P/O). REPEAT the Auto Test. → **No** SERVICE the open in Circuit 938 (BK/LG). REPEAT the Auto Test.

FM6029700276010X

Fig. 38 Test B: DTC 45, Steering Rotation Not Detected (Part 1 of 6). Mark VIII

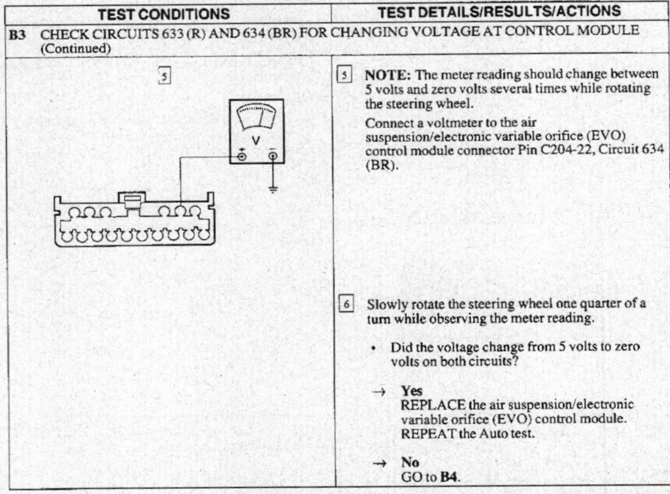

TEST CONDITIONS	TEST DETAILS/RESULTS/ACTIONS
B3 CHECK CIRCUITS 633 (R) AND 634 (BR) FOR CHANGING VOLTAGE AT CONTROL MODULE (Continued)	
5	5 **NOTE:** The meter reading should change between 5 volts and zero volts several times while rotating the steering wheel. Connect a voltmeter to the air suspension/electronic variable orifice (EVO) control module connector Pin C204-22, Circuit 634 (BR).
	6 Slowly rotate the steering wheel one quarter of a turn while observing the meter reading. • Did the voltage change from 5 volts to zero volts on both circuits? → **Yes** REPLACE the air suspension/electronic variable orifice (EVO) control module. REPEAT the Auto test. → **No** GO to **B4**.

FM6029700276030X

Fig. 38 Test B: DTC 45, Steering Rotation Not Detected (Part 3 of 6). Mark VIII

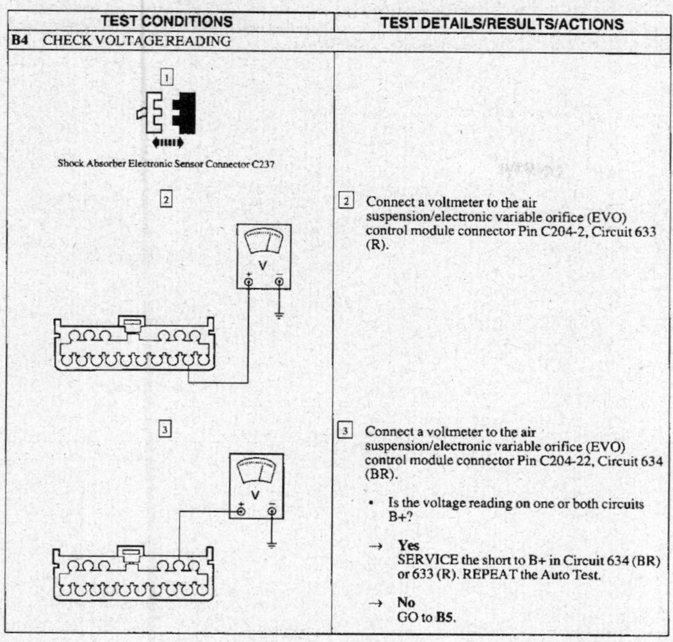

TEST CONDITIONS	TEST DETAILS/RESULTS/ACTIONS
B4 CHECK VOLTAGE READING	
1 Shock Absorber Electronic Sensor Connector C237	
2	2 Connect a voltmeter to the air suspension/electronic variable orifice (EVO) control module connector Pin C204-2, Circuit 633 (R).
3	3 Connect a voltmeter to the air suspension/electronic variable orifice (EVO) control module connector Pin C204-22, Circuit 634 (BR). • Is the voltage reading on one or both circuits B+? → **Yes** SERVICE the short to B+ in Circuit 634 (BR) or 633 (R). REPEAT the Auto Test. → **No** GO to **B5**.

FM6029700276040X

Fig. 38 Test B: DTC 45, Steering Rotation Not Detected (Part 4 of 6). Mark VIII

TEST CONDITIONS	TEST DETAILS/RESULTS/ACTIONS
B6 CHECK FOR OPEN CIRCUIT ON 633 (R) OR 634 (BR) (Continued)	
2	2 Connect an ohmmeter between the air suspension/electronic variable orifice (EVO) control module connector Pin C204-22 and shock absorber electronic steering sensor connector Pin C237-3, Circuit 634 (BR). • Is the resistance 5 ohms or less in each circuit? → **Yes** REPLACE the shock absorber electronic steering sensor. REPEAT the Auto Test. → **No** SERVICE Circuit 633 (R) or 634 (BR) for an open. REPEAT the Auto Test.

FM6029700276060X

Fig. 38 Test B: DTC 45, Steering Rotation Not Detected (Part 6 of 6). Mark VIII

TEST CONDITIONS	TEST DETAILS/RESULTS/ACTIONS
C1 RECHECK AUTO TEST	
2 Auto Test	1 Make sure the air suspension service switch is ON. 2 If the function test codes 211 through 228 are continuously displayed Pin C2-11, Circuit 425 (BR/PK) is not at ground. Possibly caused by the air suspension switch or involved circuitry. • Are DTCs 211 through 228 displayed? → **Yes** GO to **C11**. → **No** GO to **C2**.
C2 CHECK FOR DTC	
1 Auto Test	1 Perform the Auto Test and check for DTCs. • Are any DTCs retrieved? → **Yes** GO to the Air Suspension/Electronic Variable Orifice (EVO) Control Module Diagnostic Trouble Code Index. → **No** GO to C3.

FM6029700277010X

Fig. 39 Test C: Steering Diagnostics Cannot Be Entered (Part 1 of 7). Mark VIII

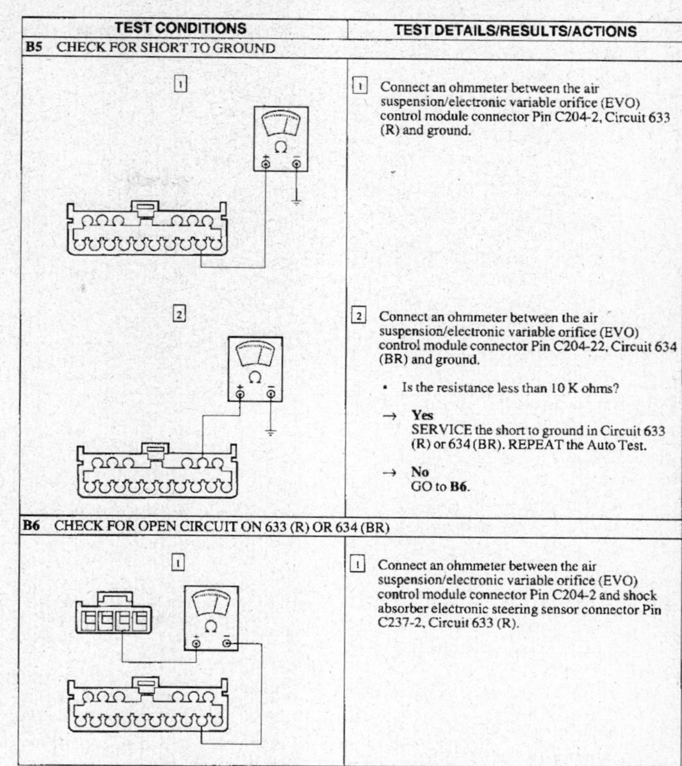

TEST CONDITIONS	TEST DETAILS/RESULTS/ACTIONS
B5 CHECK FOR SHORT TO GROUND	
1	1 Connect an ohmmeter between the air suspension/electronic variable orifice (EVO) control module connector Pin C204-2, Circuit 633 (R) and ground.
2	2 Connect an ohmmeter between the air suspension/electronic variable orifice (EVO) control module connector Pin C204-22, Circuit 634 (BR) and ground. • Is the resistance less than 10 K ohms? → **Yes** SERVICE the short to ground in Circuit 633 (R) or 634 (BR). REPEAT the Auto Test. → **No** GO to **B6**.
B6 CHECK FOR OPEN CIRCUIT ON 633 (R) OR 634 (BR)	
1	1 Connect an ohmmeter between the air suspension/electronic variable orifice (EVO) control module connector Pin C204-2 and shock absorber electronic steering sensor connector Pin C237-2, Circuit 633 (R).

FM6029700276050X

Fig. 38 Test B: DTC 45, Steering Rotation Not Detected (Part 5 of 6). Mark VIII

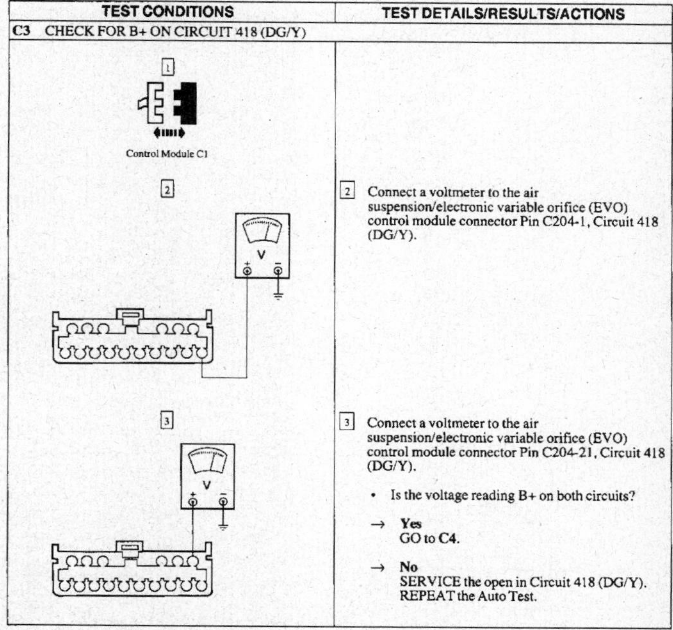

TEST CONDITIONS	TEST DETAILS/RESULTS/ACTIONS
C3 CHECK FOR B+ ON CIRCUIT 418 (DG/Y)	
1 Control Module C1	
2	2 Connect a voltmeter to the air suspension/electronic variable orifice (EVO) control module connector Pin C204-1, Circuit 418 (DG/Y).
3	3 Connect a voltmeter to the air suspension/electronic variable orifice (EVO) control module connector Pin C204-21, Circuit 418 (DG/Y). • Is the voltage reading B+ on both circuits? → **Yes** GO to **C4**. → **No** SERVICE the open in Circuit 418 (DG/Y). REPEAT the Auto Test.

FM6029700277020X

Fig. 39 Test C: Steering Diagnostics Cannot Be Entered (Part 2 of 7). Mark VIII

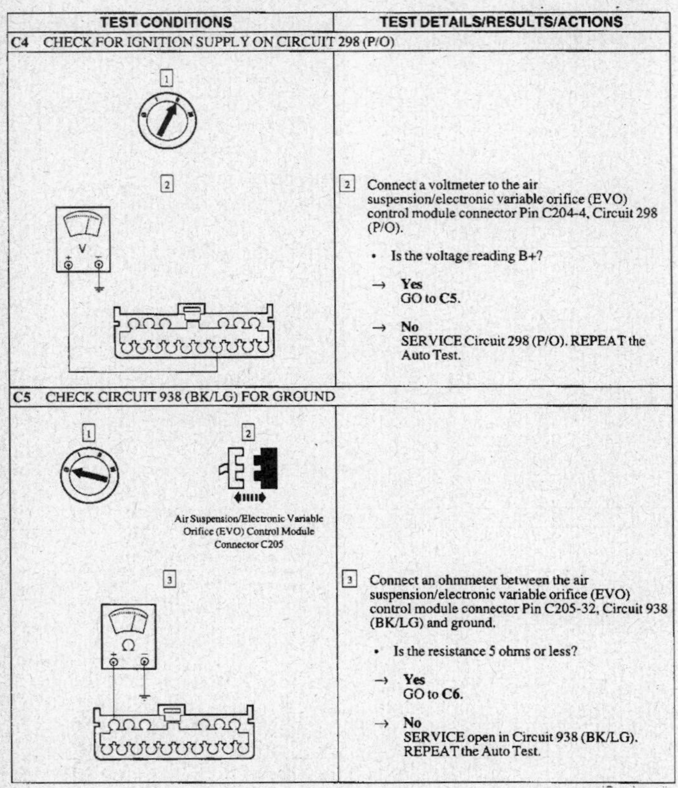

TEST CONDITIONS	TEST DETAILS/RESULTS/ACTIONS
C4 CHECK FOR IGNITION SUPPLY ON CIRCUIT 298 (P/O)	
1	
2	2 Connect a voltmeter to the air suspension/electronic variable orifice (EVO) control module connector Pin C204-4, Circuit 298 (P/O). • Is the voltage reading B+? → **Yes** GO to **C5**. → **No** SERVICE Circuit 298 (P/O). REPEAT the Auto Test.
C5 CHECK CIRCUIT 938 (BK/LG) FOR GROUND	
1 2 Air Suspension/Electronic Variable Orifice (EVO) Control Module Connector C205	
3	3 Connect an ohmmeter between the air suspension/electronic variable orifice (EVO) control module connector Pin C205-32, Circuit 938 (BK/LG) and ground. • Is the resistance 5 ohms or less? → **Yes** GO to **C6**. → **No** SERVICE open in Circuit 938 (BK/LG). REPEAT the Auto Test.

FM6029700277030X

Fig. 39 Test C: Steering Diagnostics Cannot Be Entered (Part 3 of 7). Mark VIII

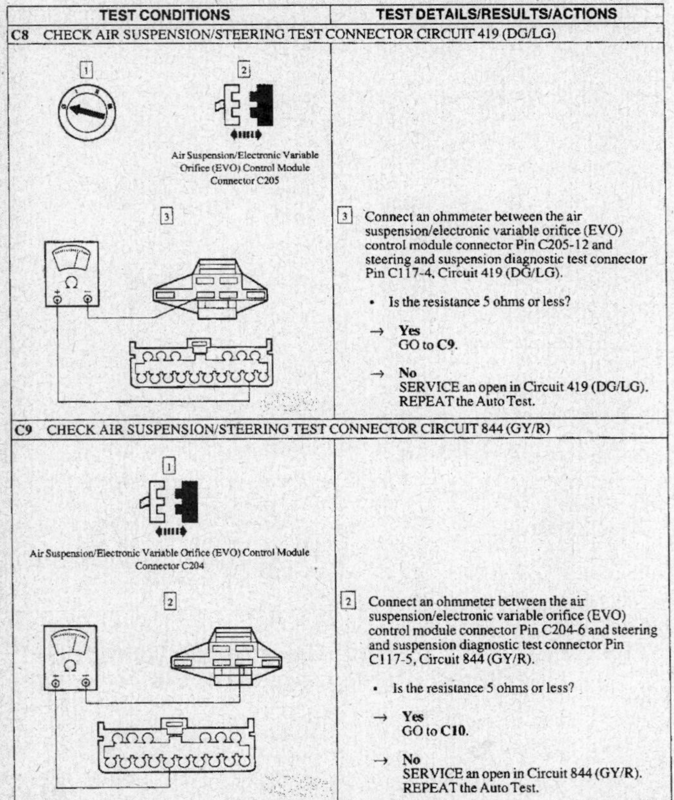

TEST CONDITIONS	TEST DETAILS/RESULTS/ACTIONS
C8 CHECK AIR SUSPENSION/STEERING TEST CONNECTOR CIRCUIT 419 (DG/LG)	
1 2 Air Suspension/Electronic Variable Orifice (EVO) Control Module Connector C205	
3	3 Connect an ohmmeter between the air suspension/electronic variable orifice (EVO) control module connector Pin C205-12 and steering and suspension diagnostic test connector Pin C117-4, Circuit 419 (DG/LG). • Is the resistance 5 ohms or less? → **Yes** GO to **C9**. → **No** SERVICE an open in Circuit 419 (DG/LG). REPEAT the Auto Test.
C9 CHECK AIR SUSPENSION/STEERING TEST CONNECTOR CIRCUIT 844 (GY/R)	
1 Air Suspension/Electronic Variable Orifice (EVO) Control Module Connector C204	
2	2 Connect an ohmmeter between the air suspension/electronic variable orifice (EVO) control module connector Pin C204-6 and steering and suspension diagnostic test connector Pin C117-5, Circuit 844 (GY/R). • Is the resistance 5 ohms or less? → **Yes** GO to **C10**. → **No** SERVICE an open in Circuit 844 (GY/R). REPEAT the Auto Test.

FM6029700277050X

Fig. 39 Test C: Steering Diagnostics Cannot Be Entered (Part 5 of 7). Mark VIII

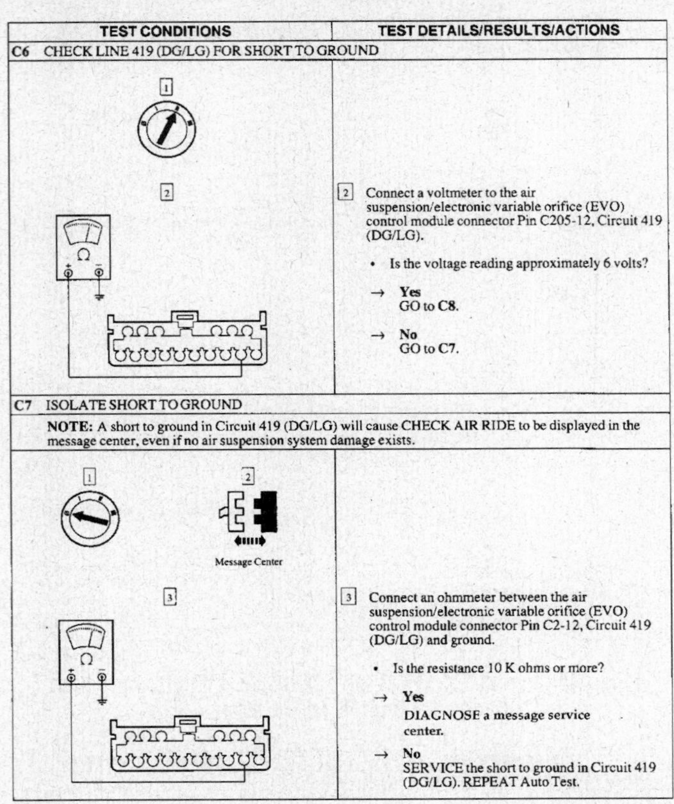

TEST CONDITIONS	TEST DETAILS/RESULTS/ACTIONS
C6 CHECK LINE 419 (DG/LG) FOR SHORT TO GROUND	
1	
2	2 Connect a voltmeter to the air suspension/electronic variable orifice (EVO) control module connector Pin C205-12, Circuit 419 (DG/LG). • Is the voltage reading approximately 6 volts? → **Yes** GO to **C8**. → **No** GO to C7.
C7 ISOLATE SHORT TO GROUND	
NOTE: A short to ground in Circuit 419 (DG/LG) will cause CHECK AIR RIDE to be displayed in the message center, even if no air suspension system damage exists.	
1 2 Message Center	
3	3 Connect an ohmmeter between the air suspension/electronic variable orifice (EVO) control module connector Pin C2-12, Circuit 419 (DG/LG) and ground. • Is the resistance 10 K ohms or more? → **Yes** DIAGNOSE a message service center. → **No** SERVICE the short to ground in Circuit 419 (DG/LG). REPEAT Auto Test.

FM6029700277040X

Fig. 39 Test C: Steering Diagnostics Cannot Be Entered (Part 4 of 7). Mark VIII

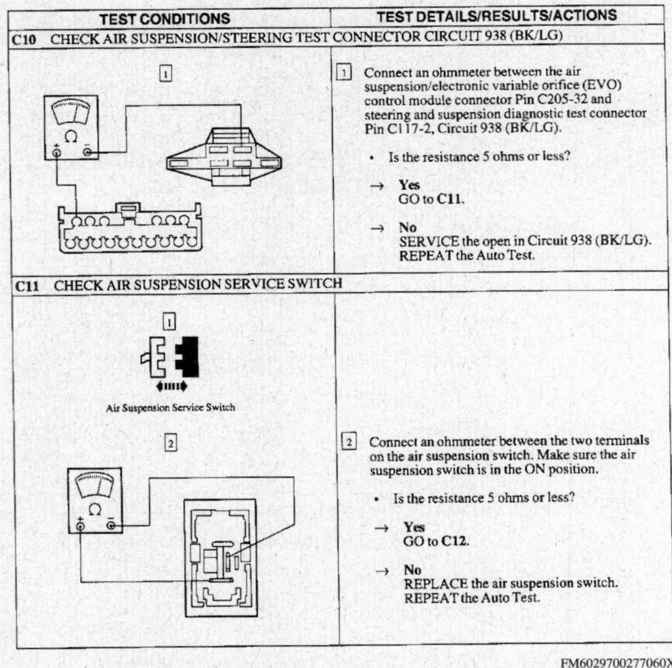

TEST CONDITIONS	TEST DETAILS/RESULTS/ACTIONS
C10 CHECK AIR SUSPENSION/STEERING TEST CONNECTOR CIRCUIT 938 (BK/LG)	
1	1 Connect an ohmmeter between the air suspension/electronic variable orifice (EVO) control module connector Pin C205-32 and steering and suspension diagnostic test connector Pin C117-2, Circuit 938 (BK/LG). • Is the resistance 5 ohms or less? → **Yes** GO to **C11**. → **No** SERVICE the open in Circuit 938 (BK/LG). REPEAT the Auto Test.
C11 CHECK AIR SUSPENSION SERVICE SWITCH	
1 Air Suspension Service Switch	
2	2 Connect an ohmmeter between the two terminals on the air suspension switch. Make sure the air suspension switch is in the ON position. • Is the resistance 5 ohms or less? → **Yes** GO to **C12**. → **No** REPLACE the air suspension switch. REPEAT the Auto Test.

FM6029700277060X

Fig. 39 Test C: Steering Diagnostics Cannot Be Entered (Part 6 of 7). Mark VIII

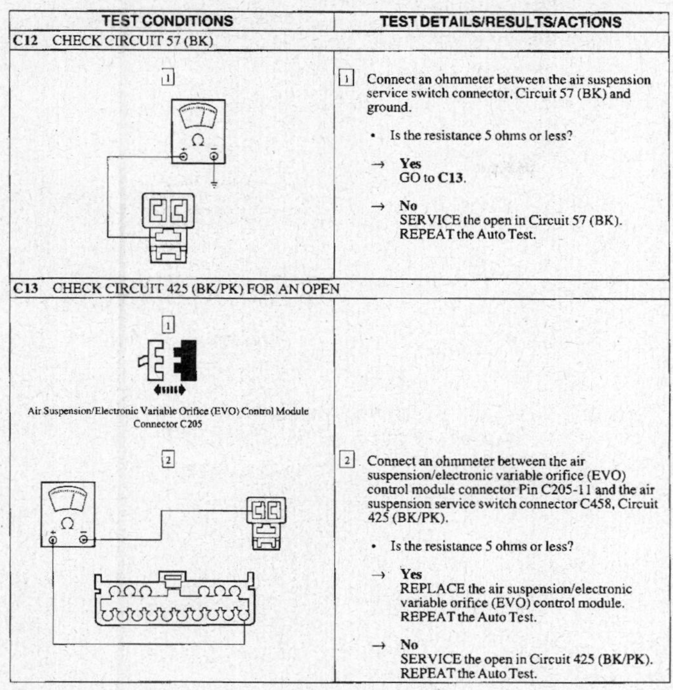

TEST CONDITIONS	TEST DETAILS/RESULTS/ACTIONS
C12 CHECK CIRCUIT 57 (BK)	
1	1 Connect an ohmmeter between the air suspension service switch connector, Circuit 57 (BK) and ground. • Is the resistance 5 ohms or less? → **Yes** GO to **C13**. → **No** SERVICE the open in Circuit 57 (BK). REPEAT the Auto Test.
C13 CHECK CIRCUIT 425 (BK/PK) FOR AN OPEN	
1 Air Suspension/Electronic Variable Orifice (EVO) Control Module Connector C205 2	2 Connect an ohmmeter between the air suspension/electronic variable orifice (EVO) control module connector Pin C205-11 and the air suspension service switch connector C458, Circuit 425 (BK/PK). • Is the resistance 5 ohms or less? → **Yes** REPLACE the air suspension/electronic variable orifice (EVO) control module. REPEAT the Auto Test. → **No** SERVICE the open in Circuit 425 (BK/PK). REPEAT the Auto Test.

FM6029700277070X

Fig. 39 Test C: Steering Diagnostics Cannot Be Entered (Part 7 of 7). Mark VIII

TEST CONDITIONS	TEST DETAILS/RESULTS/ACTIONS
D3 CHECK CONNECTOR WIRING	
1 2 Air Suspension/Electronic Variable Orifice (EVO) Control Module Connector C204	3 Check the wiring for damage and make sure Pin C204-3 is Circuit 150 (DG/W) and Pin C204-23 is Circuit 938 (BK/LG). • Are the wires damaged or crossed? → **Yes** SERVICE the wires. REPEAT Step D2. → **No** GO to **D4**.
D4 CHECK VEHICLE SPEED SENSOR CIRCUIT RESISTANCE	
1	1 Connect an ohmmeter between the air suspension/electronic variable orifice (EVO) control module connector Pin C204-3, Circuit 150 (DG/W) and Pin C204-23, Circuit 938 (BK/LG). • Is the resistance between 180 ohms and 240 ohms? → **Yes** INSPECT the connector pins. CLEAN and SERVICE as needed. If the connector pins do not need service REPLACE the air suspension/electronic variable orifice (EVO) control module. RETEST the system. → **No** GO to **D5**.

FM6029700278020X

Fig. 40 Test D: Steering Does Not Vary w/Vehicle Speed (Part 2 of 5). Mark VIII

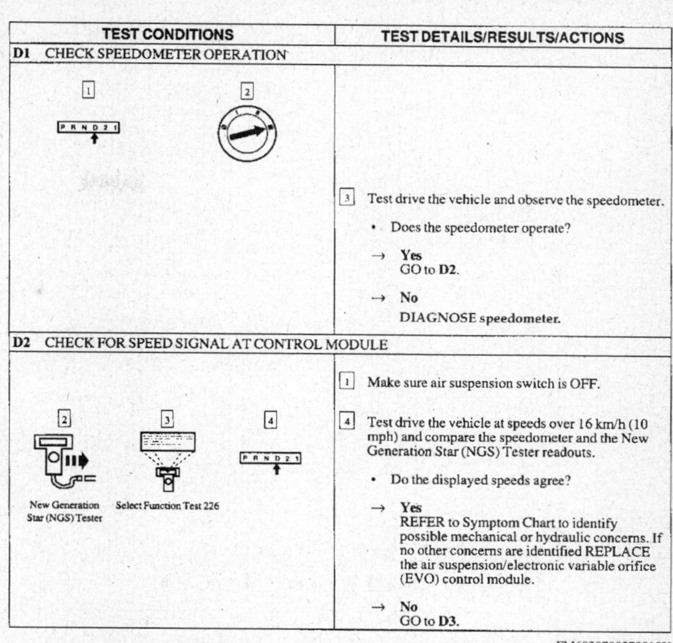

TEST CONDITIONS	TEST DETAILS/RESULTS/ACTIONS
D1 CHECK SPEEDOMETER OPERATION	
1 P R N D 2 1 2	3 Test drive the vehicle and observe the speedometer. • Does the speedometer operate? → **Yes** GO to **D2**. → **No** DIAGNOSE speedometer.
D2 CHECK FOR SPEED SIGNAL AT CONTROL MODULE	
2 New Generation Star (NGS) Tester 3 Select Function Test 226 4 P R N D 2 1	1 Make sure air suspension switch is OFF. 4 Test drive the vehicle at speeds over 16 km/h (10 mph) and compare the speedometer and the New Generation Star (NGS) Tester readouts. • Do the displayed speeds agree? → **Yes** REFER to Symptom Chart to identify possible mechanical or hydraulic concerns. If no other concerns are identified REPLACE the air suspension/electronic variable orifice (EVO) control module. → **No** GO to **D3**.

FM6029700278010X

Fig. 40 Test D: Steering Does Not Vary w/Vehicle Speed (Part 1 of 5). Mark VIII

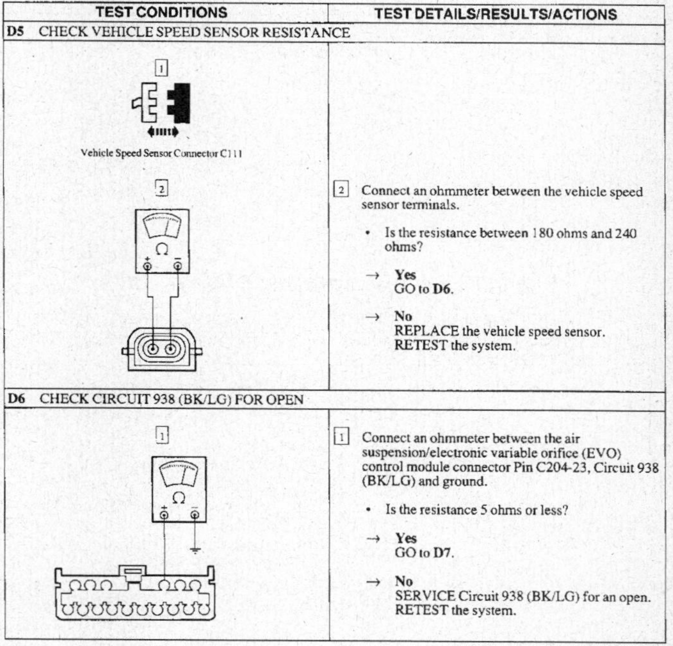

TEST CONDITIONS	TEST DETAILS/RESULTS/ACTIONS
D5 CHECK VEHICLE SPEED SENSOR RESISTANCE	
1 Vehicle Speed Sensor Connector C111 2	2 Connect an ohmmeter between the vehicle speed sensor terminals. • Is the resistance between 180 ohms and 240 ohms? → **Yes** GO to **D6**. → **No** REPLACE the vehicle speed sensor. RETEST the system.
D6 CHECK CIRCUIT 938 (BK/LG) FOR OPEN	
1	1 Connect an ohmmeter between the air suspension/electronic variable orifice (EVO) control module connector Pin C204-23, Circuit 938 (BK/LG) and ground. • Is the resistance 5 ohms or less? → **Yes** GO to **D7**. → **No** SERVICE Circuit 938 (BK/LG) for an open. RETEST the system.

FM6029700278030X

Fig. 40 Test D: Steering Does Not Vary w/Vehicle Speed (Part 3 of 5). Mark VIII

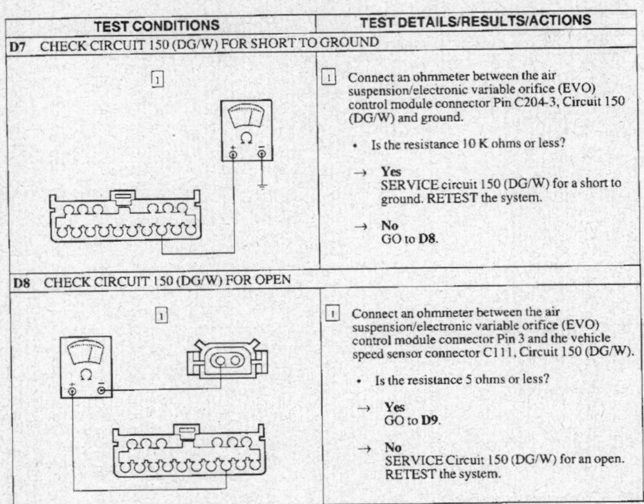

TEST CONDITIONS	TEST DETAILS/RESULTS/ACTIONS
D7 CHECK CIRCUIT 150 (DG/W) FOR SHORT TO GROUND	
1	1 Connect an ohmmeter between the air suspension/electronic variable orifice (EVO) control module connector Pin C204-3, Circuit 150 (DG/W) and ground. • Is the resistance 10 K ohms or less? → **Yes** SERVICE circuit 150 (DG/W) for a short to ground. RETEST the system. → **No** GO to **D8**.
D8 CHECK CIRCUIT 150 (DG/W) FOR OPEN	
1	1 Connect an ohmmeter between the air suspension/electronic variable orifice (EVO) control module connector Pin 3 and the vehicle speed sensor connector C111, Circuit 150 (DG/W). • Is the resistance 5 ohms or less? → **Yes** GO to **D9**. → **No** SERVICE Circuit 150 (DG/W) for an open. RETEST the system.

FM6029700278040X

Fig. 40 Test D: Steering Does Not Vary w/Vehicle Speed (Part 4 of 5). Mark VIII

Condition	Possible Source	Action
• Steering Is Very Difficult/Very Easy	• Power steering pump. • Power steering linkage. • Steering gear.	• GO to Pinpoint Test C.
• Steering Does Not Vary With Increased Wheel Rotation	• Power steering pump. • Power steering hose(s).	• GO to Pinpoint Test D.
• Steering Does Not Vary With Vehicle Speed	• Circuitry. • Rear Air suspension control module.	• GO to Pinpoint Test E.
• No Communication With The Module — Rear Air Suspension Control Module	• Fuse. • Circuitry. • Rear Air suspension control module.	• GO to Pinpoint Test F.
• Power Steering Pump Noisy	• Low fluid level and possible leakage. • Plugged reservoir filter. • Power steering pump.	• REFILL to specified level. Refer to Final Fill. CHECK for leaks. REPAIR and/or REPLACE as necessary. • REPLACE the reservoir • REPLACE the power steering pump
• System Back Pressure	• Power steering pump. • Power steering gear. • Hoses or fittings. • Power steering pump.	• REFER to Pump Flow And Pressure Test.

FM6029800289000X

Fig. 41 Symptom chart. Town Car

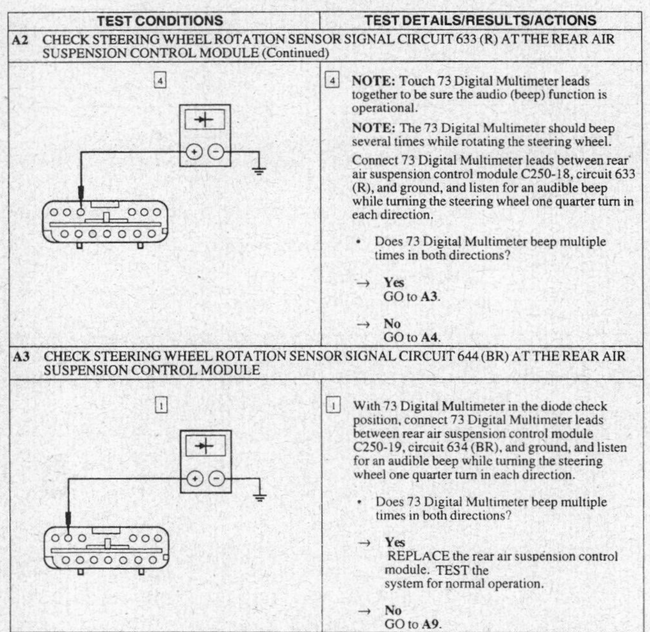

TEST CONDITIONS	TEST DETAILS/RESULTS/ACTIONS
A2 CHECK STEERING WHEEL ROTATION SENSOR SIGNAL CIRCUIT 633 (R) AT THE REAR AIR SUSPENSION CONTROL MODULE (Continued)	
4	4 **NOTE:** Touch 73 Digital Multimeter leads together to be sure the audio (beep) function is operational. **NOTE:** The 73 Digital Multimeter should beep several times while rotating the steering wheel. Connect 73 Digital Multimeter leads between rear air suspension control module C250-18, circuit 633 (R), and ground, and listen for an audible beep while turning the steering wheel one quarter turn in each direction. • Does 73 Digital Multimeter beep multiple times in both directions? → **Yes** GO to **A3**. → **No** GO to **A4**.
A3 CHECK STEERING WHEEL ROTATION SENSOR SIGNAL CIRCUIT 644 (BR) AT THE REAR AIR SUSPENSION CONTROL MODULE	
1	1 With 73 Digital Multimeter in the diode check position, connect 73 Digital Multimeter leads between rear air suspension control module C250-19, circuit 634 (BR), and ground, and listen for an audible beep while turning the steering wheel one quarter turn in each direction. • Does 73 Digital Multimeter beep multiple times in both directions? → **Yes** REPLACE the rear air suspension control module. TEST the system for normal operation. → **No** GO to **A9**.

FM6029800290020X

Fig. 42 Pinpoint test A: DTC C1441, C1442, Steering Sensor Circuit Failure (Part 2 of 5). Town Car

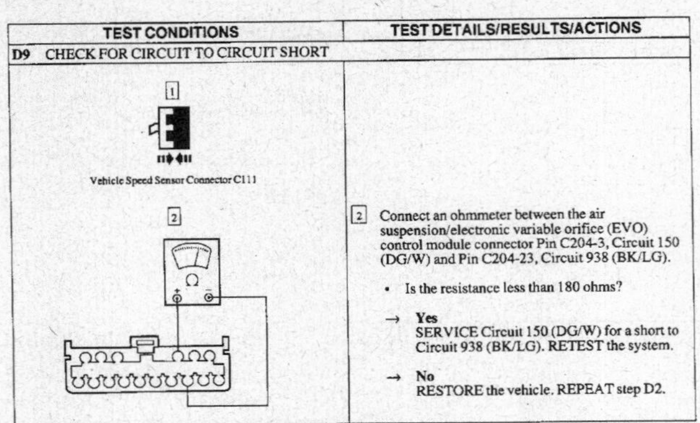

TEST CONDITIONS	TEST DETAILS/RESULTS/ACTIONS
D9 CHECK FOR CIRCUIT TO CIRCUIT SHORT	
1 Vehicle Speed Sensor Connector C111 2	2 Connect an ohmmeter between the air suspension/electronic variable orifice (EVO) control module connector Pin C204-3, Circuit 150 (DG/W) and Pin C204-23, Circuit 938 (BK/LG). • Is the resistance less than 180 ohms? → **Yes** SERVICE Circuit 150 (DG/W) for a short to Circuit 938 (BK/LG). RETEST the system. → **No** RESTORE the vehicle. REPEAT step D2.

FM6029700278050X

Fig. 40 Test D: Steering Does Not Vary w/Vehicle Speed (Part 5 of 5). Mark VIII

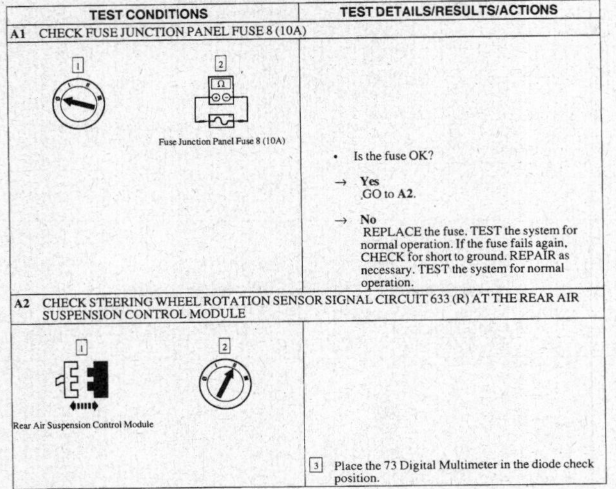

TEST CONDITIONS	TEST DETAILS/RESULTS/ACTIONS
A1 CHECK FUSE JUNCTION PANEL FUSE 8 (10A)	
1 2 Fuse Junction Panel Fuse 8 (10A)	• Is the fuse OK? → **Yes** GO to **A2**. → **No** REPLACE the fuse. TEST the system for normal operation. If the fuse fails again, CHECK for short to ground. REPAIR as necessary. TEST the system for normal operation.
A2 CHECK STEERING WHEEL ROTATION SENSOR SIGNAL CIRCUIT 633 (R) AT THE REAR AIR SUSPENSION CONTROL MODULE	
1 2 Rear Air Suspension Control Module	3 Place the 73 Digital Multimeter in the diode check position.

FM6029800290010X

Fig. 42 Pinpoint test A: DTC C1441, C1442, Steering Sensor Circuit Failure (Part 1 of 5). Town Car

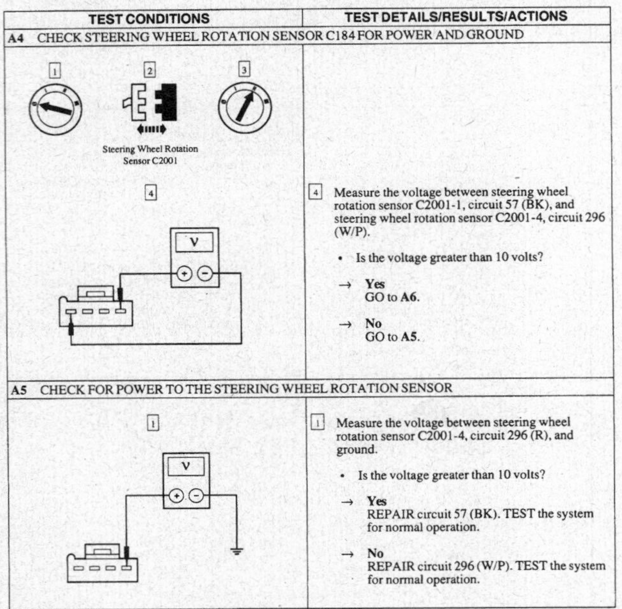

TEST CONDITIONS	TEST DETAILS/RESULTS/ACTIONS
A4 CHECK STEERING WHEEL ROTATION SENSOR C184 FOR POWER AND GROUND	
1 2 3 Steering Wheel Rotation Sensor C2001 4	4 Measure the voltage between steering wheel rotation sensor C2001-1, circuit 57 (BK), and steering wheel rotation sensor C2001-4, circuit 296 (W/P). • Is the voltage greater than 10 volts? → **Yes** GO to **A6**. → **No** GO to **A5**.
A5 CHECK FOR POWER TO THE STEERING WHEEL ROTATION SENSOR	
1	1 Measure the voltage between steering wheel rotation sensor C2001-4, circuit 296 (R), and ground. • Is the voltage greater than 10 volts? → **Yes** REPAIR circuit 57 (BK). TEST the system for normal operation. → **No** REPAIR circuit 296 (W/P). TEST the system for normal operation.

FM6029800290030X

Fig. 42 Pinpoint test A: DTC C1441, C1442, Steering Sensor Circuit Failure (Part 3 of 5). Town Car

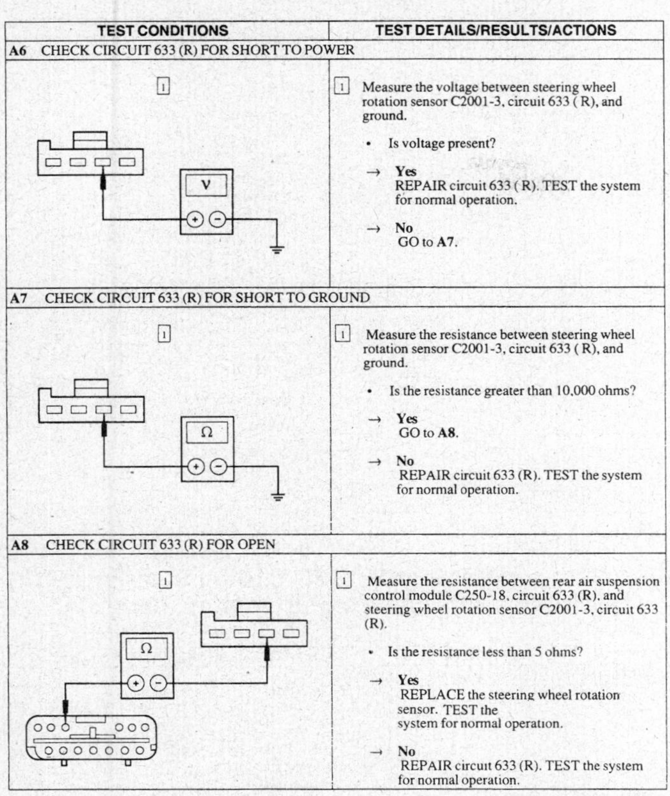

TEST CONDITIONS	TEST DETAILS/RESULTS/ACTIONS
A6 CHECK CIRCUIT 633 (R) FOR SHORT TO POWER	
1	1 Measure the voltage between steering wheel rotation sensor C2001-3, circuit 633 (R), and ground. • Is voltage present? → **Yes** REPAIR circuit 633 (R). TEST the system for normal operation. → **No** GO to **A7**.
A7 CHECK CIRCUIT 633 (R) FOR SHORT TO GROUND	
1	1 Measure the resistance between steering wheel rotation sensor C2001-3, circuit 633 (R), and ground. • Is the resistance greater than 10,000 ohms? → **Yes** GO to **A8**. → **No** REPAIR circuit 633 (R). TEST the system for normal operation.
A8 CHECK CIRCUIT 633 (R) FOR OPEN	
1	1 Measure the resistance between rear air suspension control module C250-18, circuit 633 (R), and steering wheel rotation sensor C2001-3, circuit 633 (R). • Is the resistance less than 5 ohms? → **Yes** REPLACE the steering wheel rotation sensor. TEST the system for normal operation. → **No** REPAIR circuit 633 (R). TEST the system for normal operation.

FM6029800290040X

Fig. 42 Pinpoint test A: DTC C1441, C1442, Steering Sensor Circuit failure (Part 4 of 5). Town Car

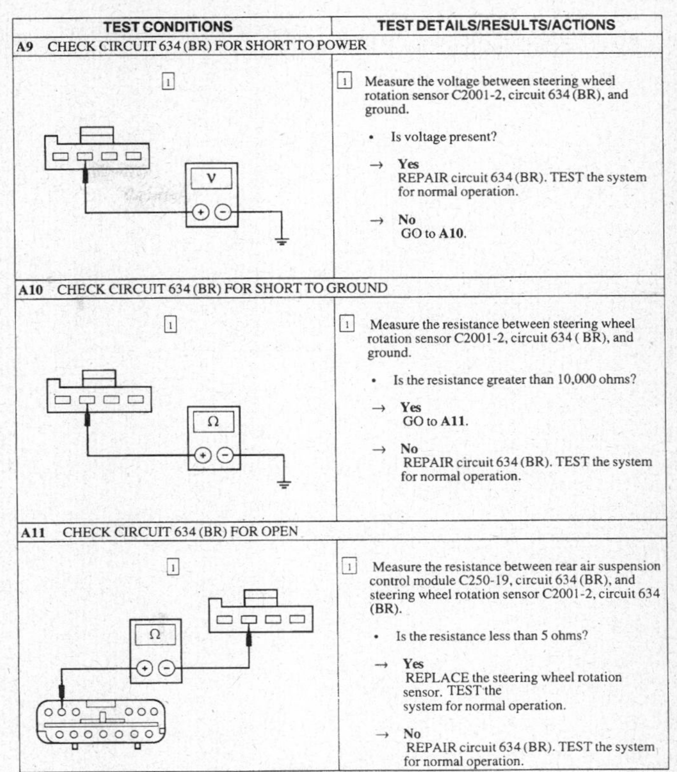

TEST CONDITIONS	TEST DETAILS/RESULTS/ACTIONS
A9 CHECK CIRCUIT 634 (BR) FOR SHORT TO POWER	
1	1 Measure the voltage between steering wheel rotation sensor C2001-2, circuit 634 (BR), and ground. • Is voltage present? → **Yes** REPAIR circuit 634 (BR). TEST the system for normal operation. → **No** GO to **A10**.
A10 CHECK CIRCUIT 634 (BR) FOR SHORT TO GROUND	
1	1 Measure the resistance between steering wheel rotation sensor C2001-2, circuit 634 (BR), and ground. • Is the resistance greater than 10,000 ohms? → **Yes** GO to **A11**. → **No** REPAIR circuit 634 (BR). TEST the system for normal operation.
A11 CHECK CIRCUIT 634 (BR) FOR OPEN	
1	1 Measure the resistance between rear air suspension control module C250-19, circuit 634 (BR), and steering wheel rotation sensor C2001-2, circuit 634 (BR). • Is the resistance less than 5 ohms? → **Yes** REPLACE the steering wheel rotation sensor. TEST the system for normal operation. → **No** REPAIR circuit 634 (BR). TEST the system for normal operation.

FM6029800290050X

Fig. 42 Pinpoint test A: DTC C1441, C1442, Steering Sensor Circuit Failure (Part 5 of 5). Town Car

TEST CONDITIONS	TEST DETAILS/RESULTS/ACTIONS
B1 CHECK THE POWER STEERING CONTROL VALVE ACTUATOR	
1 2 Power Steering Control Valve Actuator C184	3 Check the power steering control valve actuator C184 for damaged pigtail, bent pins, dirt, or corrosion. • Are the connector and pigtail OK? → **Yes** GO to **B2**. → **No** REPAIR as necessary. TEST the system for normal operation.
B2 CHECK THE POWER STEERING CONTROL VALVE ACTUATOR FOR SHORT TO GROUND	
1	1 Measure the resistance between power steering control valve actuator terminal (component side), and ground. • Is the resistance greater than 10,000 ohms? → **Yes** GO to **B3**. → **No** REPLACE the power steering control valve actuator. TEST the system for normal operation.

FM6029800291010X

Fig. 43 Pinpoint test B: DTC C1897, Steering VAPS II Circuit Loop Failure (Part 1 of 4). Town Car

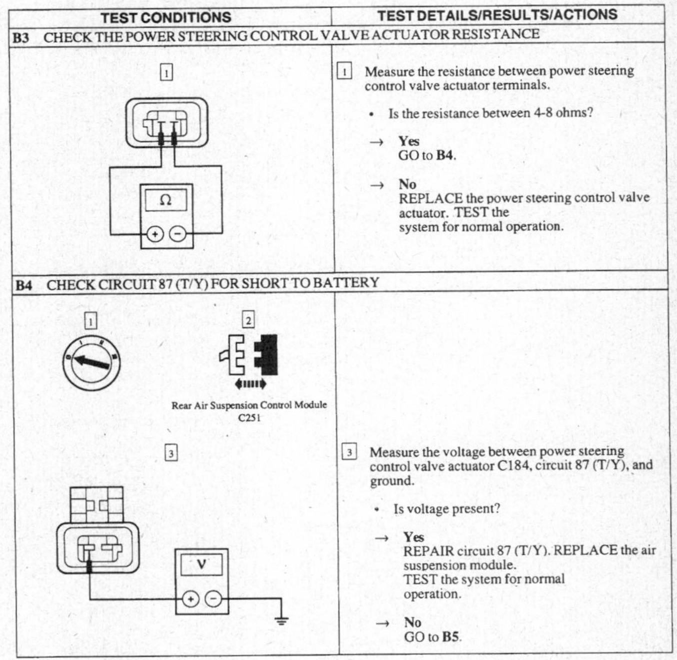

TEST CONDITIONS	TEST DETAILS/RESULTS/ACTIONS
B3 CHECK THE POWER STEERING CONTROL VALVE ACTUATOR RESISTANCE	
1	1 Measure the resistance between power steering control valve actuator terminals. • Is the resistance between 4-8 ohms? → **Yes** GO to **B4**. → **No** REPLACE the power steering control valve actuator. TEST the system for normal operation.
B4 CHECK CIRCUIT 87 (T/Y) FOR SHORT TO BATTERY	
1 2 Rear Air Suspension Control Module C251 3	3 Measure the voltage between power steering control valve actuator C184, circuit 87 (T/Y), and ground. • Is voltage present? → **Yes** REPAIR circuit 87 (T/Y). REPLACE the air suspension module. TEST the system for normal operation. → **No** GO to **B5**.

FM6029800291020X

Fig. 43 Pinpoint test B: DTC C1897, Steering VAPS II Circuit Loop Failure (Part 2 of 4). Town Car

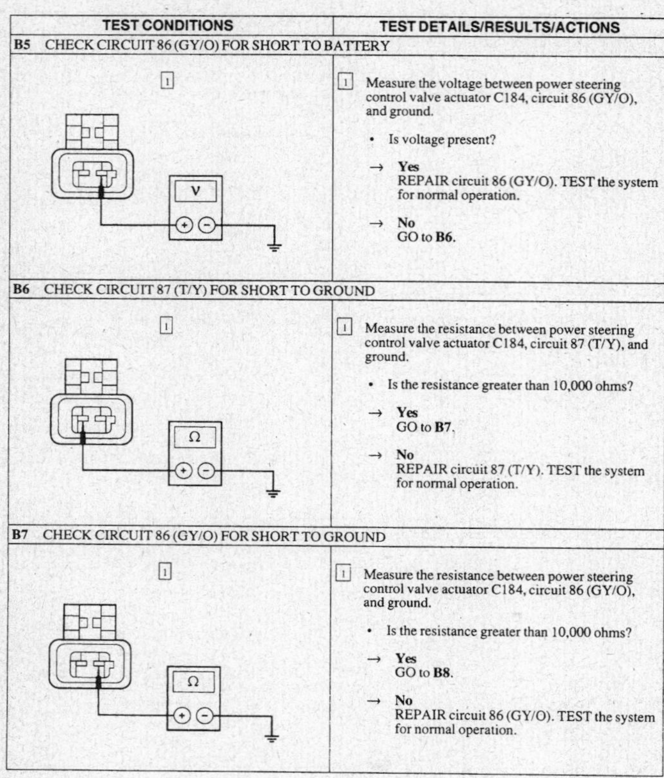

TEST CONDITIONS	TEST DETAILS/RESULTS/ACTIONS
B5 CHECK CIRCUIT 86 (GY/O) FOR SHORT TO BATTERY	
1	1 Measure the voltage between power steering control valve actuator C184, circuit 86 (GY/O), and ground. • Is voltage present? → **Yes** REPAIR circuit 86 (GY/O). TEST the system for normal operation. → **No** GO to **B6**.
B6 CHECK CIRCUIT 87 (T/Y) FOR SHORT TO GROUND	
1	1 Measure the resistance between power steering control valve actuator C184, circuit 87 (T/Y), and ground. • Is the resistance greater than 10,000 ohms? → **Yes** GO to **B7**. → **No** REPAIR circuit 87 (T/Y). TEST the system for normal operation.
B7 CHECK CIRCUIT 86 (GY/O) FOR SHORT TO GROUND	
1	1 Measure the resistance between power steering control valve actuator C184, circuit 86 (GY/O), and ground. • Is the resistance greater than 10,000 ohms? → **Yes** GO to **B8**. → **No** REPAIR circuit 86 (GY/O). TEST the system for normal operation.

FM6029800291030X

Fig. 43 Pinpoint test B: DTC C1897, Steering VAPS II Circuit Loop Failure (Part 3 of 4). Town Car

TEST CONDITIONS	TEST DETAILS/RESULTS/ACTIONS
C1 CHECK THE POWER STEERING PUMP (Continued)	
1 **Ignition ON, Engine Running** 2 **Check power steering pump for leaks by turning steering Wheel and observing pump**	3 Perform the Pump Flow and Pressure Test; go to Component Tests. • Is the power steering pump OK? → **Yes** GO to **C2**. → **No** REPLACE the power steering pump TEST the system for normal operation.
C2 CHECK THE STEERING LINKAGE	
	1 Visually check the steering linkage while an assistant rotates the steering wheel from stop to stop. • Does the steering linkage move smoothly from stop to stop? → **Yes** GO to **C3**. → **No** REPLACE the damaged steering linkage component(s) TEST the system for normal operation.
C3 CHECK THE STEERING ASSEMBLY	
	1 Check the ball joints for worn surfaces. • Are the ball joints OK ? → **Yes** GO to **C4**. → **No** REPLACE worn ball joints. TEST the system for normal operation.
C4 CHECK THE STEERING GEAR	
	1 Visually check the steering gear operation while an assistant rotates the steering wheel from stop to stop.

FM6029800292010X

Fig. 44 Pinpoint test C: Steering Is Very Difficult/ Very Easy (Part 1 of 2). Town Car

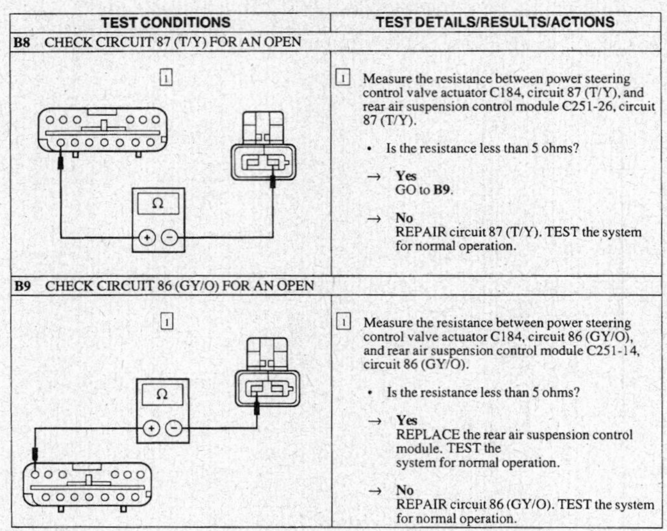

TEST CONDITIONS	TEST DETAILS/RESULTS/ACTIONS
B8 CHECK CIRCUIT 87 (T/Y) FOR AN OPEN	
1	1 Measure the resistance between power steering control valve actuator C184, circuit 87 (T/Y), and rear air suspension control module C251-26, circuit 87 (T/Y). • Is the resistance less than 5 ohms? → **Yes** GO to **B9**. → **No** REPAIR circuit 87 (T/Y). TEST the system for normal operation.
B9 CHECK CIRCUIT 86 (GY/O) FOR AN OPEN	
1	1 Measure the resistance between power steering control valve actuator C184, circuit 86 (GY/O), and rear air suspension control module C251-14, circuit 86 (GY/O). • Is the resistance less than 5 ohms? → **Yes** REPLACE the rear air suspension control module. TEST the system for normal operation. → **No** REPAIR circuit 86 (GY/O). TEST the system for normal operation.

FM6029800291040X

Fig. 43 Pinpoint test B: DTC C1897, Steering VAPS II Circuit Loop Failure (Part 4 of 4). Town Car

TEST CONDITIONS	TEST DETAILS/RESULTS/ACTIONS
C4 CHECK THE STEERING GEAR (Continued)	
	2 Check the steering gear mounting fasteners for loose bolts. • Is the steering gear OK? → **Yes** If condition still exists, GO to the Symptom Chart. → **No** TIGHTEN and/or REPLACE the steering gear; TEST the system for normal operation.

FM6029800292020X

Fig. 44 Pinpoint test C: Steering Is Very Difficult/ Very Easy (Part 2 of 2). Town Car

TEST CONDITIONS	TEST DETAILS/RESULTS/ACTIONS
D1 CHECK THE POWER STEERING PUMP	
1	2 Check the power steering pump for leaks by rotating the steering wheel while watching the power steering pump. 3 Perform the Pump Flow and Pressure Test; go to Component Tests. • Is the power steering pump OK? → **Yes** INSPECT for kinked lines or hoses from the power steering pump. REPLACE lines or hoses as necessary. TEST the system for normal operation. → **No** REPLACE the power steering pump. TEST the system for normal operation.

FM6029800293000X

Fig. 45 Pinpoint test D: Steering Does Not Vary w/Increased Wheel Rotation. Town Car

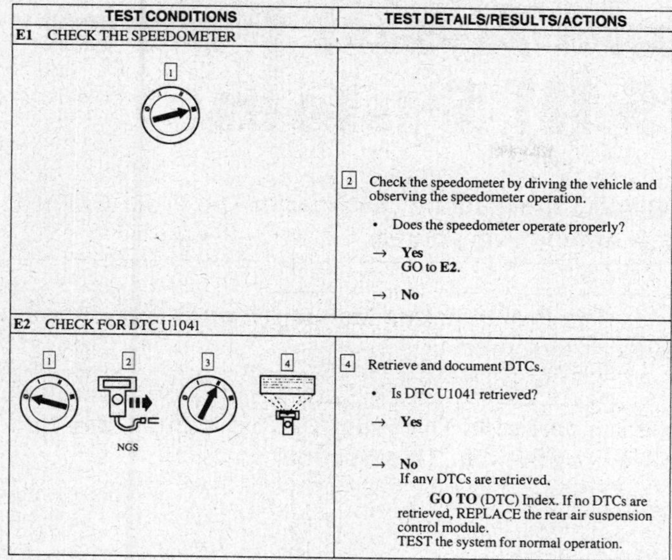

TEST CONDITIONS	TEST DETAILS/RESULTS/ACTIONS
E1 CHECK THE SPEEDOMETER	
1	2 Check the speedometer by driving the vehicle and observing the speedometer operation. • Does the speedometer operate properly? → **Yes** GO to **E2**. → **No**
E2 CHECK FOR DTC U1041	
1 2 3 4 NGS	4 Retrieve and document DTCs. • Is DTC U1041 retrieved? → **Yes** → **No** If any DTCs are retrieved, **GO TO** (DTC) Index. If no DTCs are retrieved, REPLACE the rear air suspension control module. TEST the system for normal operation.

FM6029800294000X

Fig. 46 Pinpoint test E: Steering Does Not Vary w/Vehicle Speed. Town Car

TEST CONDITIONS	TEST DETAILS/RESULTS/ACTIONS
F3 CHECK CIRCUIT 418 (DG/Y) FOR AN OPEN	
1 V	1 Measure the voltage between rear air suspension control module C250-1, circuit 418 (DG/Y), and ground. • Is the voltage greater than 10 volts? → **Yes** GO to **F4**. → **No** REPAIR circuit 418 (DG/Y). TEST the system for normal operation.
F4 CHECK CIRCUIT 57 (BK) FOR AN OPEN	
1 2 Ω	2 Measure the resistance between rear air suspension control module C250-6, circuit 57 (BK), and ground. • Is the resistance less than 5 ohms? → **Yes** → **No** REPAIR circuit 57 (BK). TEST the system for normal operation.

FM6029800295020X

Fig. 47 Pinpoint test F: No Communication w/Rear Air Suspension Control Module (Part 2 of 2). Town Car

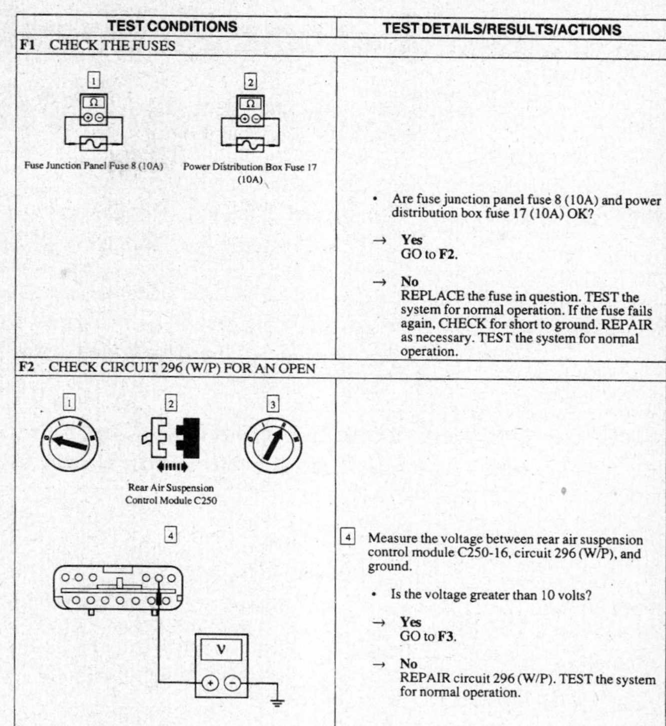

TEST CONDITIONS	TEST DETAILS/RESULTS/ACTIONS
F1 CHECK THE FUSES	
1 2 Fuse Junction Panel Fuse 8 (10A) Power Distribution Box Fuse 17 (10A)	• Are fuse junction panel fuse 8 (10A) and power distribution box fuse 17 (10A) OK? → **Yes** GO to **F2**. → **No** REPLACE the fuse in question. TEST the system for normal operation. If the fuse fails again, CHECK for short to ground. REPAIR as necessary. TEST the system for normal operation.
F2 CHECK CIRCUIT 296 (W/P) FOR AN OPEN	
1 2 3 Rear Air Suspension Control Module C250 4 V	4 Measure the voltage between rear air suspension control module C250-16, circuit 296 (W/P), and ground. • Is the voltage greater than 10 volts? → **Yes** GO to **F3**. → **No** REPAIR circuit 296 (W/P). TEST the system for normal operation.

FM6029800295010X

Fig. 47 Pinpoint test F: No Communication w/Rear Air Suspension Control Module (Part 1 of 2). Town Car

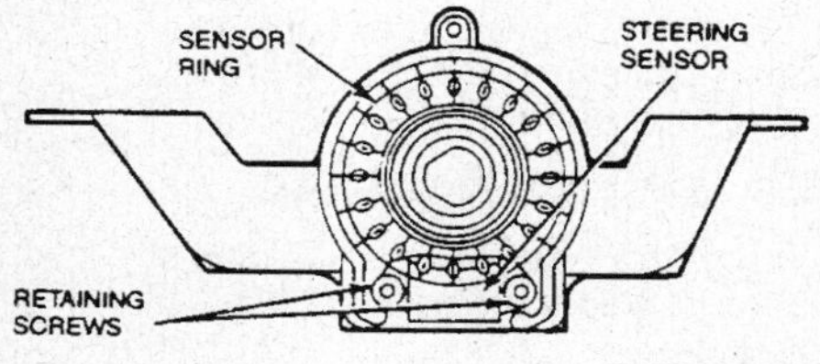

FM6029100190000X

Fig. 48 Steering sensor removal

Type 2-Ford Variable Assist Power Steering (VAPS II) System

NOTE: On Air Bag Equipped Models, Refer To "Air Bag System Precautions" Located In The Front Of This Manual For System Disarming & Arming Procedures.

NOTE: Refer To "Computer Relearn Procedures" Located In The Front Of This Manual When Battery Power To The Computer Has Been Interrupted.

NOTE: "Electrical Symbol & Wire Color Code Identification" Located In The Front Of This Manual May Be Used As An Aid When Using Wiring Circuits Found In This Section.

INDEX

PRECAUTIONS

AIR BAG SYSTEMS

Refer to "Air Bag System Precautions" in the front of this manual for system disarming and arming procedures.

BATTERY GROUND CABLE

Prior to service, disconnect battery ground cable and isolate as required.

DESCRIPTION

The Variable Assist Power Steering (VAPS II) System uses the Generic Electronics Module (GEM) to improve steering characteristics. The VAPS II system begins operation as soon as the ignition is turned to Run, and maintains control as long as the ignition is in the Run position.

The level of assist provided by the VAPS II system depends on vehicle speed. The faster the vehicle speed, the less assist provided by the VAPS II system. Vehicle speed is determined by the GEM based on signals received from the Vehicle Speed Sensor (VSS).

Condition	Possible Source	Action
NOTE: Discolored Steering Fluid in a Rack-and-Pinion Steering System Should Not be Misdiagnosed as a Functional or Noise Concern When Steering Very Difficult / Very Easy. • High (Excessive) Power Steering Efforts at All Vehicle Speeds is Recognized While Turning Corners and During Low Speed Maneuvers and Especially While Parking. The Assist Concerns May Occur in Both Directions or Only in One Direction, They May be Intermittent, or Consistent	• Low power steering pump fluid. • Power rack and pinion steering gear assembly external or internal leak. • Power steering pump external leak. • Power steering pump pressure and flow improper. • Improper drive belt tension. • Hose external leak. • Hose restriction. • Power steering pump pulley loose / warped. • Power steering pump drive belt loose / glazed / broken or water on drive belt. • Engine idle too low. • Tires not properly inflated. • Suspension bent or interference. • System contaminated. • Flex coupling rubbing against housing face. • Steering column misaligned or binding.	• FILL as required and CHECK for system leaks. • REPLACE power rack and pinion steering gear. • PERFORM Pump Flow and Pressure Tests SERVICE as required. • CHECK for proper drive belt tension. • SERVICE or REPLACE as necessary. • CLEAN and REPLACE as necessary. • REPLACE power steering pump pulley. • INSPECT, CHECK drive belt tension or REPLACE as required. • ADJUST idle. REFER to Powertrain Control / Emissions Diagnosis • INFLATE. • INSPECT, SERVICE or REPLACE as necessary. • INSPECT system for foreign object, kinked hose, etc. — FLUSH system. • REPOSITION flex coupling. • ALIGN steering column assembly.
• Engine Stalls With High Wheel Rotation	• Inoperative idle speed control circuit. • Pressure switch or pressure hose blocked.	• REFER to Powertrain Control / Emissions Diagnosis
• No Communications With Generic Electronic Module	• Generic electronic module. • Circuits.	• GO to Pinpoint Test A.
• Steering Does Not Vary With Vehicle Speed	• Damaged vehicle speed sensor. • Power steering control valve actuator inoperative.	• GO to Pinpoint Test B.

FM6029400210010X

Fig. 1 Symptom troubleshooting chart (Part 1 of 7)

TROUBLESHOOTING

Refer to **Fig. 1** for troubleshooting procedures.

DIAGNOSIS & TESTING

ACCESSING DIAGNOSTIC TROUBLE CODES

Using Rotunda New Generation Star Tester No. 007-00500, or equivalent, perform diagnostic tests for GEM. The Diagnostic Link Connector (DLC) is located on the LH side of the steering wheel, under the instrument panel. The Generic Electronic Module (GEM) is located at the LH rear of the engine compartment.

DIAGNOSTIC TROUBLE CODE INTERPRETATION

Refer to **Fig. 2** for diagnostic trouble code interpretation.

WIRING DIAGRAM

Refer to **Figs. 3 and 4** for wiring diagrams.

PINPOINT TESTS

Refer to **Figs. 5 through 13** for pinpoint tests.

Condition	Possible Source	Action
NOTE: Clean Off the Steering Gear Before Performing ANY Steering Gear External Leakage Checks. • External Leakage	• Leaks between power steering control valve actuator and steering gear.	• NOTE: The only serviceable components on the VAPS power rack and pinion steering gear are the tie rod bellows, front wheel spindle tie rods, power steering control valve actuator, and actuator bolts and seals. All external leaks, which cannot be serviced by tightening tube fittings, are to be serviced by installing a power steering short rack assembly.
		• TIGHTEN actuator bolts.
	• Leaks between power steering control valve actuator and actuator bolts.	• TIGHTEN actuator bolts.
		• REPLACE two upper actuator seals.
	• Power rack and pinion steering gear fittings loose, cross threaded or stripped.	• INSPECT and TIGHTEN or REPLACE power steering short rack assembly
	• Leaks from power rack and pinion steering gear seals (input shaft, pinion or either rack seals).	• REPLACE power steering short rack assembly.
	• Steering gear housing cracked or leaking (due to a porous condition).	• REPLACE power steering short rack assembly.
NOTE: This Condition Should be Checked on Center Only. The Loose Condition Can be Detected With Greater Reliability With the Engine off and Steering Wheel Straight Ahead. A Very Light Touch on the Steering Wheel Should be Used in Checking for This Condition. • Loose On Center	• Power rack and pinion steering gear mounting bolts loose.	• TIGHTEN retaining nuts to specification.
	• Steering column intermediate shaft coupling connecting bolt loose.	• TIGHTEN.
	• Intermediate shaft spring loaded U-bolt distorted.	• REPLACE U-bolt.
	• Flex coupling clamp bolt loose.	• TIGHTEN.
	• Gear front wheel spindle tie rod inner ball socket loose.	• REPLACE gear front wheel spindle tie rod.
	• Steering column intermediate shaft coupling joints loose or worn.	• REPLACE steering column intermediate shaft coupling assembly.
	• Steering column clips missing or broken.	• REPLACE as required.
	• Flex coupling fractured.	• REPLACE as required.
	• Front wheel spindle tie rod loose or worn.	• TIGHTEN or REPLACE as required.
	• Wheel loose or worn.	• REPLACE as required.
	• Loose lug nuts.	• TIGHTEN.
• Steering Wheel Not Centered Properly NOTE: Groove on Steel Hub of Steering Wheel Must be in Line With Mark on Top End of Steering Shaft With Front Wheels in Straight Ahead Position to Line Up Steering Wheel Spokes Properly. Steering Wheel Centerline Should be Within 10 Degrees of Vertical Plane After Toe-In is Adjusted.	• Incorrect toe setting.	• SET front end alignment.
	• Flex coupling clamp bolts loose/missing.	• REPLACE and TIGHTEN.
	• Pinion installed in rack off location.	• REPLACE power steering short rack assembly.
	• Improperly installed steering wheel.	• REPOSITION steering wheel.
	• Power rack and pinion steering gear loose on front sub-frame.	• TIGHTEN.
	• Steering column intermediate shaft coupling installed off location in column shaft V-block.	• INDEX shaft to correct position.

FM6029400210020X

Fig. 1 Symptom troubleshooting chart (Part 2 of 7)

Condition	Possible Source	Action
NOTE: Perform the Following Test to Determine if Concern is Related to Power Rack and Pinion Steering Gear or Vehicle System: • Uneven Drive Efforts, Pulls or Leads to One Side—Condition Recognized by the Driver While Turning the Steering Wheel in a Left or Right Turn. This Condition Will Reveal Lighter Efforts in One Direction, Very Noticeable to the Driver. Vehicle Pulls or Leads to One Side. Keep in Mind Road Conditions and Wind. Pulls or Leads Refers to the Tendency of a Vehicle to Drift Consistently to One Side on a Reasonably Flat Road. It May or May Not be Accompanied by Unequal Effort Requirements at the Steering Wheel. At 24-88 km/h (15-55 mph) on a Flat Straight Surface, Set Vehicle in a Straight Line, Place Shift Selector in NEUTRAL Position and Turn Off Ignition. If the Vehicle Continues to Pull or Drift in the Same Direction as the Original Concern, Then the Power Rack and Pinion Steering Gear is Not the Cause. If the Vehicle Does Not Pull, but Remains on a Straight Line This Indicates a Power Rack and Pinion Steering Gear Concern and Steering Efforts Should Also be Noticeably Light in Direction of Pull. This Condition is Normally Due to an Unbalanced Power Rack and Pinion Steering Gear Valve Assembly.	• Radial tires (misaligned belts).	• REPLACE as necessary.
	• Front or rear end misaligned.	• ALIGN.
	• Steering gear valve efforts unbalanced. (Efforts will be lighter in one direction.)	• REPLACE power steering short rack assembly.
	• Front suspension components damaged.	• REPLACE as required.
	• Low tire pressure or incorrect front to rear.	• CHECK pressure and INFLATE/DEFLATE as necessary.
	• Incorrect tire size or incorrect type.	• CORRECT as required.
	• Check front and rear brakes for proper operation.	• ADJUST if necessary.
	• Check rear axle housing for damaged or sagging front coil springs in the front or rear suspension.	• REPLACE if necessary.
	• Check rear suspension for loose or worn rear shock absorber, suspension arm retaining fasteners.	• TIGHTEN all retaining fasteners.
	• Vehicle unevenly loaded.	• CORRECT as required.
	• Front wheel bearing or rear wheel bearing worn.	
	• Power rack and pinion steering gear retaining bolts loose or damaged.	• TIGHTEN.
	• Steering column misaligned or binding.	• ALIGN steering column assembly.
	• Halfshaft or CV joint bind.	• REPLACE CV joints.

FM6029400210040X

Fig. 1 Symptom troubleshooting chart (Part 4 of 7)

Condition	Possible Source	Action
NOTE: Discolored Steering Fluid in Rack-and-Pinion Steering System Should Not Be Misdiagnosed as a Functional or Noise Concern. • Smoothness/Sticky Feeling—Condition of Momentary Build Up, Hitch, Lump or Hesitation in Steering Efforts, Usually Occurring Just as the Turn is Begun. It May Occur Right or Left, and in Rare Cases, Occur in Both Directions. It May be Noticed During Parking, Low Speed Turns or at Road Speeds. If This Condition is Detected During Parking Maneuvers, It May Also be Noticed During Higher Speed Driving	• Loose or worn drive belt.	• TIGHTEN or REPLACE.
	• Front suspension lower arm (LH)/front suspension lower arm (RH) ball joint worn.	• REPLACE front suspension lower arm (LH)/ front suspension lower arm (RH) assembly.
	• Column trim rubbing steering wheel.	• REPOSITION trim on column.
	• Binding in steering gear control valve assembly.	• REPLACE power steering short rack assembly.
	• Water or oil on drive belt.	• CLEAN or REPLACE.
	• Steering column misaligned or binding.	• ALIGN steering column.
	• Flex coupling distorted or fractured.	• ALIGN or REPLACE as required.
	• Flex housing rubbing against housing face.	• ALIGN or REPOSITION flex coupling.
	• Steering column intermediate shaft coupling loose, worn or binding.	• REPLACE as required.
	• Steering column intermediate shaft coupling connecting bolt loose.	• TIGHTEN.
	• Steering linkage, front spring and shocks are loose, worn or binding.	• LUBRICATE, ADJUST or REPLACE as necessary.
	• Tight steering column bearings.	• LUBRICATE or REPLACE as required.
	• Steering column clips missing or damaged.	• SERVICE as required.
	• Steering gear retaining bolts loose or damaged.	• TIGHTEN.
	• Front wheel bearing loose or worn.	• REPLACE as required.
	• Loose lug nuts.	• TIGHTEN.
	• Bent or damaged power rack and pinion steering gear assembly.	• REPLACE power steering short rack assembly.
	• Low tire pressure.	• INFLATE.
	• Improper front end alignment.	• ALIGN front end.

FM6029400210030X

Fig. 1 Symptom troubleshooting chart (Part 3 of 7)

Condition	Possible Source	Action
NOTE: The Following Condition is Accompanied By a Momentary Build Up, Hitch, Lump, or Hesitation, in Steering Efforts Usually Occurring Just Off Center Either in One Direction or Both. Concern Occurs Only During Driving, and Not During Parking Maneuvers. • Poor Returnability is a Condition Noticed When the Vehicle Fails to Return to a Nearly Straight Ahead Position After a Corner Maneuver. The Steering Wheel Should Return Within a Reasonable Period of Time Without Undue Help From the Driver. Returnability Concerns May Occur From Both Directions or Only From One Direction.	• Column trim rubbing steering wheel.	• REPOSITION trim ring in steering column tube assembly slots.
	• Front suspension lower arm (LH)/front suspension lower arm (RH) worn.	• REPLACE front suspension lower arm (LH)/front suspension lower arm (RH).
	• Brinelled or binding upper strut bearing.	• REPLACE bearing.
	• Tight front wheel spindle tie rod and/or tie rod end ball joints.	• REPLACE front wheel spindle tie rod and/or tie rod ends.
	• Steering valve assembly off balance. Efforts will be light in one direction and return will be poor in light direction.	• REPLACE power steering short rack assembly.
	• Improper front end alignment.	• ALIGN front end.
	• Steering linkage, front spring and shocks, loose, worn or binding.	• LUBRICATE, ADJUST or REPLACE as necessary.
	• Tilt column bearing sideloaded by spring.	• REMOVE spring. If improved, REPLACE tilt yoke, shaft or steering wheel.
	• Steering column intermediate shaft coupling joints binding.	• REPLACE steering column intermediate shaft coupling assembly.
	• Bent or damaged front crossmember.	• REPLACE as necessary.
	• Steering column bearing binding.	• REPLACE as necessary.
	• Steering column misaligned or binding.	• ALIGN steering column assembly.
	• Low tire pressure or incorrect pressure front to rear.	• CHECK pressure and INFLATE/DEFLATE as necessary.
	• Steering wheel clear vision off location.	• ADJUST as required.
	• Incorrect tire size or incorrect type.	• REPLACE as required.

FM6029400210050X

Fig. 1 Symptom troubleshooting chart (Part 5 of 7)

CONDITION	POSSIBLE SOURCE	ACTION
• NOTE: A Common Noise in the Rack-and-Pinion Power Steering Short Rack is a Hissing Sound. The Sound is Most Evident at Static Position or During Parking Maneuvers. There is no Relationship Between This Noise and Performance of the Steering. "Hiss" May Occur at end of Steering Wheel Travel or When Slowly Turning at Stand Still, or at a Particular Position.	• Steering column gear input shaft coupling connecting bolt loose.	• TIGHTEN.
	• Column trim rubbing steering wheel.	• REPOSITION trim on steering column.
	• Loose or worn pump drive belt.	• ADJUST or REPLACE as required.
	• Front suspension lower arm (LH)/front suspension lower arm (RH) worn or binding.	• REPLACE as required.
	• Brinelled or binding upper strut bearing.	• REPLACE strut bearing.
	• Flex coupling distorted.	• ALIGN flex coupling.
Noise/Rattle/Clicks/Pops/Squeaks/Creaks/Clunk/Squawk/Hiss There are Many System Noises Which Can be Misdiagnosed as Originating From the Power Power Steering Short Rack. Most System Noises are RPM Sensitive. Therefore, Turning the Steering Wheel Will Vary the RPM and Consequently the Noise Pitch. Careful Diagnosis is Necessary to Prevent Unnecessary Services. Disconnecting of Belts and Re-evaluation is Essential in Many Cases, as is Partially Cycling the Steering Wheel With the Engine in OFF.	• Flex coupling clamp bolt loose.	• TIGHTEN.
	• Power steering pump support loose or misaligned.	• TIGHTEN and ALIGN.
	• Lack of lubricant where horn brush contacts rub steering wheel plate.	• LUBRICATE or ADJUST as required.
	• Column shaft clips missing.	• REPLACE as required.
	• Column U-joints loose.	• REPLACE if necessary.
	• Loose tie rod ends or ball joints.	• REPLACE tie rod assembly.
	• Power steering short rack assembly loose on frame.	• TIGHTEN.
	• Loose suspension struts.	• ADJUST or REPLACE as required.
	• Flex coupling fractured.	• REPLACE as required.
	• Loose lug nuts.	• TIGHTEN.
	• Pressure hose grounded against front fender or vacuum canister.	• REPOSITION pressure hoses.
	• Front wheel bearing loose or worn.	• REPLACE front wheel bearing.
	• Steering column misaligned or lower steering column tube bearing out of position.	• CORRECT as necessary.
	• Steering shaft insulators cracked or dry.	• REPLACE or LUBRICATE as required.
	• Kinked pressure hoses.	• REPOSITION pressure hoses.
	• Power steering short rack or power steering pump external leak.	• INSPECT and REPLACE or SERVICE as required.
	• Power steering pump pulley loose or warped.	• REPLACE power steering pump pulley assembly.
	• Aerated fluid.	• PURGE and EVACUATE system.
	• Water in steering fluid.	• PURGE and EVACUATE system.

FM6029400210060X

Fig. 1 Symptom troubleshooting chart (Part 6 of 7)

Condition	Possible Source	Action
NOTE: Pointing Characteristics are Normal with the Rack-and-Pinion Steering System Up to 10 Degrees Off-Center. • Wandering/Darting/Pointing— Condition Noticed When the Vehicle is Driven in a Straight Ahead Position With the Steering Wheel Held in a Firm Position, and the Vehicle Wanders to Either Side. Darting Refers to Down the Road Steering Feel, It is Not Smooth and Seems to be Sticky and the Driver Cannot Make Minor Correction With Ease. Pointing Refers to the Inability of the Vehicle to Return to a Straight Ahead Position After a Moderate to Higher Speed Lane Change.	• Power rack and pinion steering gear retaining bolts loose or damaged.	• TIGHTEN.
	• Improper front or rear end alignment.	• ALIGN.
	• Front lower control arm ball joint(s) worn.	• REPLACE as required.
	• Brinelled or binding strut upper bearing.	• REPLACE bearing.
	• Steering wheel clear vision off location.	• CORRECT as required.
	• Column trim rubbing steering wheel.	• REPOSITION trim on steering column assembly.
	• Loose suspension struts or ball joints binding.	• ADJUST or REPLACE as required.
	• Loose front wheel spindle tie rods.	• REPLACE front wheel spindle tie rods.
	• Steering column intermediate shaft coupling joint loose or worn.	• REPLACE steering column intermediate shaft coupling.
	• Steering column misaligned or binding.	• ALIGN steering column assembly.
	• Tie rod inner ball joint loose or worn.	• REPLACE front wheel spindle tie rod.
	• Steering column intermediate shaft coupling connecting bolt loose.	• TIGHTEN.
	• Low tire pressure or incorrect pressure front to rear.	• CHECK tire pressure and INFLATE/DEFLATE as necessary.
	• Incorrect tire size or incorrect type.	• CORRECT as required.
	• Radial tires (misaligned belts).	• REPLACE as required.
	• Front wheel bearing and/or rear wheel bearing loose or worn.	
	• Loose or worn rear suspension.	• TIGHTEN or REPLACE as necessary.
	• Loose flex coupling bolt.	• TIGHTEN.
	• Improper brake operation or adjustment.	• INSPECT and ADJUST. CORRECT as required.
	• Vehicle unevenly loaded.	• CORRECT as required.

FM6029400210070X

Fig. 1 Symptom troubleshooting chart (Part 7 of 7)

DTC	Description
B1301	Power Door Lock Circuit Failure
B1302	Delayed Accessory Relay Coil Circuit Failure
B1304	Delayed Accessory Relay Coil Circuit Short To Battery
B1309	All Door Lock Sense Circuit Short To Ground
B1310	Power Door Unlock Circuit Failure
B1314	Battery Saver Relay Coil Circuit Open
B1315	Battery Saver Relay Coil Circuit Short to Battery
B1316	Battery Saver Relay Coil Circuit Short to Ground
B1317	Battery Voltage High
B1318	Battery Voltage Low
B1322	Door Ajar LF Circuit Short to Ground
B1323	Door Ajar Lamp Circuit Failure
B1325	Door Ajar Lamp Circuit Short to Ground
B1330	Door Ajar RF Circuit Short to Ground
B1334	Liftgate/Decklid Ajar Circuit Short To Ground
B1338	Door Ajar RR Circuit Short to Ground
B1345	Heated Rear Window Switch Input Short to Ground
B1347	Heated Rear Window Switch Input Short to Ground
B1349	Heated Rear Window Relay Output Circuit Short to Battery
B1352	Ignition Key-In Circuit Failure
B1359	Ignition RUN/ACC Circuit Failure
B1365	Ignition Start Circuit Short to Battery
B1371	Illuminated Entry Relay Coil Circuit Failure
B1373	Illuminated Entry Relay Short to Battery
B1397	Power Door Unlock Circuit Short to Battery
B1398	LF Power Window One Touch Window Relay Circuit Failure

FM6029400211010X

Fig. 2 GEM DTC Index (Part 1 of 3)

DTC	Description
B1400	LF Power Window One Touch Window Relay Circuit Short to Battery
B1405	LF Power Window Down Input Short to Battery
B1408	LF Power Window Up Input Short to Battery
B1410	LF Power Window Motor Circuit Failure
B1426	Safety Belt Lamp Circuit Short to Battery
B1428	Safety Belt Lamp Circuit Failure
B1432	Wiper Brake/Run Relay Circuit Short to Battery
B1433	Wiper Brake/Run Relay Circuit Short to Ground
B1434	Wiper HI/LO Speed Relay Coil Circuit Failure
B1436	Wiper HI/LO Speed Relay Coil Circuit Short to Battery
B1438	Wiper Mode Select Switch Circuit Failure
B1441	Wiper Front Mode Select Switch Circuit Short To Ground
B1445	Door Handle Switch Circuit Short to Ground
B1446	Wiper Front Park Sense Circuit Failure
B1448	Wiper Front Park Sense Circuit Short to Battery
B1450	Wiper Wash/Delay Switch Circuit Failure
B1453	Wiper Wash/Delay Switch Circuit Short to Ground
B1458	Wiper Washer Pump Motor Relay Circuit Failure
B1460	Wiper Washer Pump Motor Relay Coil Circuit Short to Battery
B1462	Safety Belt Switch Circuit Failure
B1465	Wiper Run Relay Coil Circuit Open
B1466	Wiper HI/LO Speed Not Switching
B1473	Wiper Low Speed Motor Circuit Failure
B1474	Battery Saver Relay Power Output Circuit Short to Battery

FM6029400211020X

Fig. 2 GEM DTC Index (Part 2 of 3)

DTC	Description
B1475	Delayed Accessory Relay Contact Short to Battery
B1476	Wiper High Speed Motor Circuit Failure
B1555	Ignition RUN/START Circuit Failure
B1574	Door Ajar LR Circuit Short to Ground
B1577	Park Lamp Input Circuit Short to Battery
B1610	Illuminated Entry Input Circuit Short to Ground
B1833	Door Unlock/Disarm Switch Circuit Short to Ground
B1834	Door Unlock/Disarm Output Circuit Failure
B1836	Door Unlock/Disarm Output Circuit Short to Battery
B1838	Battery Saver Relay Power Circuit Failure
B1840	Wiper Front Power Circuit Failure
C1899	VAPS Circuit Short to Battery
C1928	VAPS Solenoid Actuator Return Circuit Short to Ground
P1882	Engine Coolant Level Switch Short to Ground
P1883	Engine Coolant Level Lamp Circuit Failure
P1884	Engine Coolant Level Lamp Short to Battery

FM6029400211030X

Fig. 2 GEM DTC Index (Part 3 of 3)

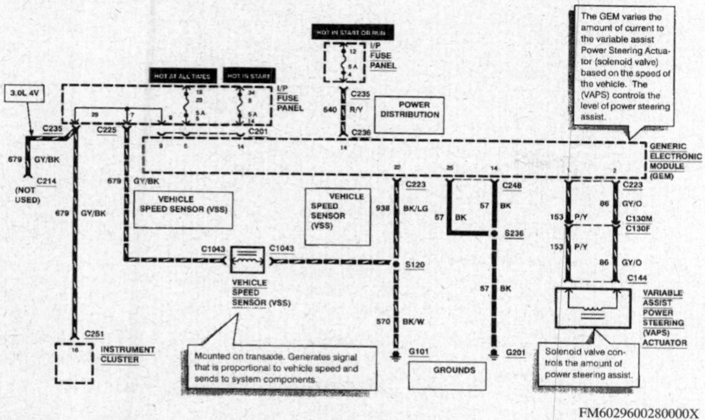

Fig. 3 VAPS wiring diagram. Sable & Taurus except SHO

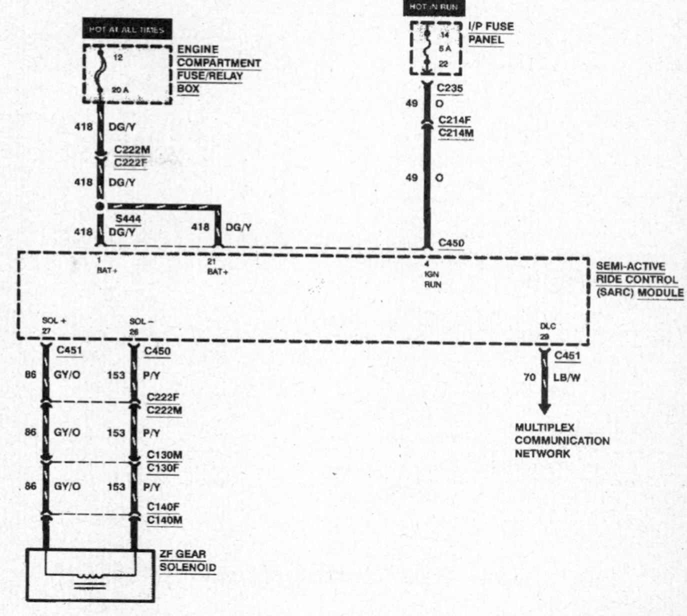

Fig. 4 VAPS wiring diagram (Part 1 of 2). Taurus SHO

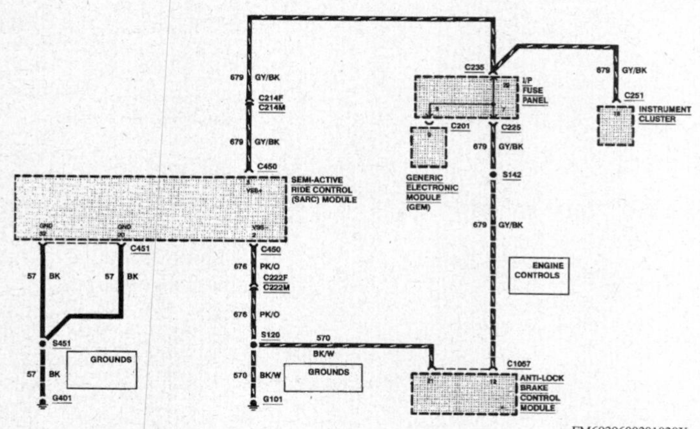

Fig. 4 VAPS wiring diagram (Part 2 of 2). Taurus SHO

DIAGNOSTIC CHART INDEX

	Test Step	Result	Action to Take
A1	CHECK THE FUSES		
	• Check the following I/P fuse panel fuses: fuse 23 (5A), fuse 20 (5A), and fuse 8 (5A). • **Are the resistances less than 5 ohms?**	Yes No	▶ GO to **A2**. ▶ REPLACE the fuse(s). RETEST system. If the fuse(s) fail(s) again, CHECK for short to ground. REPAIR as necessary.
A2	CHECK CIRCUIT 640 (R/Y) FOR OPEN		
	• Key OFF. • Disconnect generic electronic module (GEM) C236. • Key ON. • Measure the voltage between GEM C236-14, circuit 640 (R/Y), and ground. • **Is the voltage greater than 10 volts?**	Yes No	▶ GO to **A3**. ▶ REPAIR circuit 640 (R/Y). TEST the system for normal operation.
A3	CHECK THE I/P FUSE PANEL FOR VOLTAGE		
	• Key OFF. • Disconnect I/P fuse panel C201. • Key ON. • Measure the voltage between I/P panel terminal 5 and ground; and between terminal 15 and ground. • Measure the voltage between I/P fuse panel terminal 14 while holding the key in the start position. • **Are the voltages greater than 10 volts?**	Yes No	▶ GO to **A4**. ▶ REPLACE the I/P fuse panel. TEST the system for normal operation.
A4	CHECK CIRCUIT 57 (BK) FOR OPEN		
	• Key OFF. • Disconnect GEM C248. • Measure the resistance between GEM C248-14, and C248-25, circuit 57 (BK), and ground. • **Is the resistance less than 5 ohms?**	Yes No	▶ GO to **A5**. ▶ REPAIR circuit 57 (BK). TEST the system for normal operation.
A5	CHECK CIRCUIT 570 (BK/W) FOR OPEN		
	• Disconnect GEM C223. • Measure the resistance between GEM C223-12, circuit 570 (BK/W), and ground. • **Is the resistance less than 5 ohms?**	Yes No	▶ GO to **A6**. ▶ REPAIR circuit 570 (BK/W). TEST the system for normal operation.
A6	CHECK CIRCUIT 938 (BK/LG) FOR OPEN		
	• Measure the resistance between GEM C223-22, circuit 938 (BK/LG), and ground. • **Is the resistance less than 5 ohm?**	Yes No	▶ DIAGNOSE communication network. ▶ REPAIR circuit 938 (BK/LG). TEST the system for normal operation.

FM6029800282000X

Fig. 5 Test A: No Communication w/GEM

	Test Step	Result	Action to Take
B1	CHECK GEM VEHICLE SPEED PID		
	• NGS installed. • Access GEM PID VSS__GEM. • Drive vehicle while observing VSS__GEM PID. • **Does PID change and reflect vehicle speed when compared to speedometer?**	Yes No	▶ PERFORM on board diagnostic self test. SERVICE any DTC retrieved. REPEAT self test and test drive to confirm service. If symptom still present, condition is mechanical. GO to mechanical diagnostic procedures. ▶ TURN vehicle OFF. GO to **B2**.
B2	CHECK CIRCUIT 679 (GY/BK) FOR OPEN		
	• Disconnect vehicle speed sensor connector. • Disconnect fuse junction panel connector C3. • Using ohmmeter, measure resistance between fuse junction panel Pin C3-7, Circuit 679 (GY/BK) and vehicle speed sensor connector Circuit 679 (GY/BK). • **Is resistance 5 ohms or less?**	Yes No	▶ GO to **B3**. ▶ SERVICE Circuit 679 (GY/BK) for open circuit. RESTORE vehicle. REPEAT B1.

FM6029400213010X

Fig. 7 Test B: Steering Does Not Vary w/Vehicle Speed (Part 1 of 2)

	Test Step	Result	Action to Take
B1	CONFIRM VEHICLE SPEED SIGNAL FUNCTION		
	• Drive vehicle at normal city/highway speeds and observe speedometer. • **Is speedometer displaying correct speed?**	Yes No	▶ GO to **B2**. ▶ **Diagnose Speedometer**
B2	CHECK CONTINUITY IN CIRCUIT 676 (PK/O) AND CIRCUIT 570 (BK/W)		
	• Disconnect module connector C450. • Using an ohmmeter, measure resistance between module connector Pin C450-2, Circuit 676 (PK/O), and ground. • **Is resistance less than 5 ohms?**	Yes No	▶ LEAVE module disconnected. GO to **B3**. ▶ REPAIR Circuit 676 (PK/O), and Circuit 570 (BK/W). REPEAT self-test.
B3	CHECK CIRCUIT 679 (GY/BK) FOR AN OPEN		
	• Disconnect the anti-lock brake control module C1057. • Using an ohmmeter, measure resistance between module connector Pin C450-3, Circuit 679 (GY/BK), and anti-lock brake control module connector Pin C1057-12, Circuit 679 (GY/BK). • **Is resistance less than 5 ohms?**	Yes No	▶ REPLACE module. REPEAT self-test. ▶ REPAIR Circuit 679 (GY/BK). REPEAT self-test.

FM6029900308000X

Fig. 8 Test B: Vehicle Speed Signal Failure

	Test Step	Result	Action to Take
B1342-1	CHECK FOR DTC B1342		
	• Clear stored DTCs from memory by cycling ignition switch to OFF, starting engine, and performing the "Clear Continuous DTCs" function under the DIAGNOSTIC TEST MODES menu on the NGS or equivalent. • Repeat ON-DEMAND SELF TEST under DIAGNOSTIC TEST MODES on the NGS or equivalent. • **Is DTC B1342 present?**	Yes No	▶ REPLACE module. RESTORE vehicle. RETEST system. ▶ Diagnosis complete. RESTORE vehicle. RETEST system.

FM6029900307000X

Fig. 10 Code B1342: ECU Internal Failure

	Test Step	Result	Action to Take
A1	CHECK FOR BATTERY VOLTAGE		
	• Disconnect battery charger. • Measure voltage across battery terminals. • **Is the voltage greater than 11 volts?**	Yes No	▶ GO to **A2**. ▶ REPAIR the charging system.
A2	CHECK CIRCUIT 57 (BK) RESISTANCE		
	• Turn ignition switch OFF. • Disconnect module from vehicle harness connectors C450 and C451. • Measure resistance between module Pin C451-32, C451-20, Circuit 57 (BK) and ground. • **Is resistance less than 5 ohms?**	Yes No	▶ GO to **A3**. ▶ REPAIR Circuit 57 (BK). REPEAT On-Demand Self-Test.
A3	CHECK CIRCUIT 418 (DG/Y) RESISTANCE		
	• Remove power distribution box Fuse 12 (20A). • Check resistance from output side of Fuse 12 (20A) Circuit 418 (DG/Y) to Pin C450-1, Circuit 418 (DG/Y) module connector. • **Is resistance less than 5 ohms?**	Yes No	▶ GO to **A4**. ▶ REPAIR Circuit 418 (DG/Y). REPEAT On-Demand Self Test.
A4	CHECK CIRCUIT 49 (O) RESISTANCE		
	• Remove fuse junction panel Fuse 14 (5A). • Check resistance from output side of Fuse 14 (5A) to Pin C450-4, Circuit 49 (O). • **Is resistance less than 5 ohms?**	Yes No	▶ **Diagnose Module Communications network.** ▶ REPAIR Circuit 49 (O). REPEAT On-Demand Self-Test.

FM6029900310000X

Fig. 6 Test A: No Communication w/Module

	Test Step	Result	Action to Take
B3	CHECK CIRCUIT 679 (GY/BK) FOR SHORT TO GROUND		
	• Using ohmmeter, measure resistance from Pin C3-7, Circuit 679 (GY/BK) to a known ground. • **Is resistance 10,000 ohms or more?**	Yes No	▶ GO to **B4**. ▶ SERVICE Circuit 679 (GY/BK) for short to ground. RESTORE vehicle. REPEAT **B1**.
B4	CHECK CIRCUIT 679 (GY/BK) FOR SHORT TO BATTERY		
	• Using voltmeter connected to a known ground, measure voltage at Pin C3-7, Circuit 679 (GY/BK). • **Is B+ voltage present?**	Yes No	▶ SERVICE Circuit 679 (GY/BK) for short to battery. RESTORE vehicle. REPEAT **B1**. ▶ GO to **B5**.
B5	CHECK FUSE JUNCTION PANEL FOR OPEN CIRCUIT		
	• Disconnect GEM fuse junction panel connector C1. • Using ohmmeter, measure resistance between C1-9 and C3-7. • **Is resistance 5 ohms or less?**	Yes No	▶ GO to **B6**. ▶ REPLACE fuse junction panel. RESTORE vehicle. REPEAT **B1**.
B6	CHECK FUSE JUNCTION PANEL FOR INTERNAL SHORT TO BATTERY		
	• Disconnect GEM from fuse junction panel. • Turn ignition switch to RUN. • Measure voltage between GEM fuse junction panel connector Pin C1-9 and a known ground. • **Is B+ voltage present?**	Yes No	▶ REPLACE internally shorted fuse junction panel. RESTORE vehicle. REPEAT **B1**. ▶ GO to **B7**.
B7	CHECK FUSE JUNCTION PANEL FOR INTERNAL OPEN CIRCUIT		
	• Using ohmmeter connected to known ground, measure resistance at Pin C1-9. • **Is resistance less than 10,000 ohms?**	Yes No	▶ REPLACE grounded fuse junction panel. RESTORE vehicle. REPEAT B1. ▶ REPLACE vehicle speed sensor. RESTORE vehicle. REPEAT **B1**.

FM6029400213020X

Fig. 7 Test B: Steering Does Not Vary w/Vehicle Speed (Part 2 of 2)

	Test Step	Result	Action to Take
B1318-1	CHECK CHARGING SYSTEM OPERATION		
	• Have engine running. • Make sure lights, radio, and accessories are OFF. • Measure voltage between battery terminals. • **Is voltage less than 12.5 volts?**	Yes No	▶ REPAIR charging system. ▶ GO to **B1318-2**.
B1318-2	CHECK CONTROL MODULE SUPPLY		
	• Have engine running. • Make sure lights, radio, and accessories are OFF. • Disconnect module from harness. • Measure voltage between module connector Pins C450-1 and C450-21, Circuit 418 (DG/Y), and ground. • **Are the voltages greater than 10 volts?**	Yes No	▶ GO to **B1318-3**. ▶ REPAIR circuit 418 (DG/Y) and/or REPLACE the Power Distribution Box Fuse 12 (20A).
B1318-3	CHECK CIRCUIT RESISTANCE		
	• Measure resistance between module C451-20, and C451-32, Circuit 57 (BK), and ground. • **Are the resistances more than 5 ohms?**	Yes No	▶ REPAIR Circuit 57 (BK). RETEST system. ▶ If DTC B1318 is a continuous DTC and not encountered during self-test, CLEAR DTCs and REPEAT self-test. If DTC B1318 is a self-test DTC, REPLACE module. REPEAT self-test.

FM6029900306000X

Fig. 9 Code B1318: Battery Voltage Low

	Test Step	Result	Action to Take
C1897-1	CHECK STEERING SOLENOID CIRCUITS		
	• Disconnect module connectors C450 and C451. • Using an ohmmeter, measure the resistance between Pin C450-26, Circuit 153 (P/Y) and Pin C451-27, Circuit 86 (GY/O). • **Is resistance between 5 and 9 ohms?**	Yes No	▶ GO to **C1897-3**. ▶ GO to **C1897-2**.
C1897-2	CHECK RESISTANCE OF STEERING SOLENOID		
	• Disconnect steering solenoid 2-pin connector C140. • Using an ohmmeter, measure resistance of steering solenoid. • **Is resistance between 5 and 9 ohms?**	Yes No	▶ REPAIR Circuit 86 (GY/O), Circuit 153 (P/Y). REPEAT self-test. ▶ REPLACE steering solenoid. REPEAT self-test.
C1897-3	CHECK CIRCUIT 86 (GY/O) FOR SHORT		
	• Using an ohmmeter, measure resistance between module Pin C451-32, Circuit 57 (BK) and C451-27, Circuit 86 (GY/O). • **Is resistance greater than 10,000 ohms?**	Yes No	▶ GO to **C1897-4**. ▶ REPAIR Circuit 86 (GY/O). REPEAT self-test.
C1897-4	CHECK CIRCUIT 153 (P/Y) FOR SHORT		
	• Using an ohmmeter, measure resistance between module Pins C450-26, Circuit 153 (P/Y), C451-32, Circuit 57 (BK). • **Is resistance 10,000 ohms or more?**	Yes No	▶ GO to **C1897-5**. ▶ REPAIR Circuit 153 (P/Y). RETEST system.

FM6029900309010X

Fig. 11 Code C1897: Variable Assist Power Steering Circuit Loop Failure (Part 1 of 2)

Test Step		Result	Action to Take
C1897-5	CHECK STEERING SOLENOID FOR SHORT TO BATTERY		
	• Using an ohmmeter, measure resistance between module Pins C450-26, Circuit 153 (P / Y), C451-27, Circuit 86 (GY / O) and Pin C450-1, Circuit 418 (DG / Y). • **Is resistance 10,000 ohms or more?**	Yes No	GO to **C1897-6**. REPAIR Circuit 153 (P / Y) or Circuit 86 (GY / O). RETEST system.
C1897-6	CHECK FOR DAMAGED / CORRODED PINS		
	• Carefully inspect all connector pins for damage or corrosion. • **Are pins damaged or corroded?**	Yes No	REPAIR / CLEAN pins as necessary. REPEAT self test. REPLACE module. REPEAT self test.

FM6029900309020X

Fig. 11 Code C1897: Variable Assist Power Steering Circuit Loop Failure (Part 2 of 2)

Test Step		Result	Action to Take
C1899-1	CHECK PID		
	• NGS installed. • Start engine. • Access GEM PID VAPSOUT. • Drive vehicle at various speeds. • Read VAPSOUT valve. • **Is PID VAPSOUT value constant at 100%?**	Yes No	TURN engine OFF. GO to **C1899-2**. GO to **C1899-4**.
C1899-2	CHECK CIRCUIT 86 (GY / O)		
	• Disconnect GEM connector C4. • Using voltmeter attached to a known ground, measure voltage on Pin C4-2, Circuit 86 (GY / O). • **Is B+ present?**	Yes No	SERVICE Circuit 86 (GY / O) for short to battery. GO to **C1899-3**.
C1899-3	READ PID WITH CIRCUIT OPEN		
	• Reconnect GEM connector C4. • Disconnect variable assist power steering actuator. • Start engine. • Access VAPSOUT PID. • **Is VAPSOUT value 100%?**	Yes No	REPLACE GEM. RESTORE vehicle. REPEAT self-test. GO to **C1899-4**.
C1899-4	PERFORM WIGGLE TEST		
	• Reconnect variable assist power steering actuator. • Access GEM wiggle test. Follow directions displayed on NGS. • Tap actuators, connectors and flex harness from variable assist power steering actuator and GEM. • **Is DTC C1899 retrieved during wiggle test?**	Yes	NOTE: Both Circuit 153 (P / Y) and Circuit 86 (GY / O0 must be serviced. SERVICE connector, actuator or harness being agitated when DTC C1899 was recorded for short to battery. RESTORE vehicle. REPEAT self test.
		No	REPEAT on-board diagnostic self test. If DTC C1899 retrieved, REPLACE GEM. RESTORE vehicle. REPEAT self test.

FM6029400214000X

Fig. 12 Code C1899: VAPSII Circuit Short To Battery

Test Step		Result	Action to Take
C1928-1	ELIMINATE ACTUATOR		
	• Turn engine OFF. • Disconnect variable assist power steering actuator from harness. • Start engine. • Read VAPS__IN PID. • **Is PID VAPS__IN value 0?**	Yes No	GO to **C1928-2**. REPLACE variable assist power steering actuator. (Actuator has internal short to ground.) RESTORE vehicle. REPEAT on demand self test.
C1928-2	CHECK CIRCUIT 153 (P / Y) FOR SHORT TO GROUND		
	• Ignition switch OFF. • Disconnect GEM connector C4. • Using ohmmeter attached to a known ground, measure resistance at Pin C4-1, Circuit 153 (P / Y). • **Is resistance less than 10,000 ohms?**	Yes No	SERVICE Circuit 153 (P / Y) for short to ground. RESTORE vehicle. REPEAT on demand self test. REPLACE GEM. RESTORE vehicle. REPEAT on demand self test.

FM6029400215000X

Fig. 13 Code C1928: VAPSII Solenoid Actuator Return Circuit Short To Ground

Type 3-Ford Variable Assist Power Steering (VAPS) System

NOTE: On Air Bag Equipped Models, Refer To "Air Bag System Precautions" Located In The Front Of This Manual For System Disarming & Arming Procedures.

NOTE: Refer To "Computer Relearn Procedures" Located In The Front Of This Manual When Battery Power To The Computer Has Been Interrupted.

NOTE: "Electrical Symbol & Wire Color Code Identification" Located In The Front Of This Manual May Be Used As An Aid When Using Wiring Circuits Found In This Section.

INDEX

PRECAUTIONS

AIR BAG SYSTEMS

Refer to "Air Bag System Precautions" in the front of this manual for system disarming and arming procedures.

BATTERY GROUND CABLE

Prior to service, disconnect battery ground cable and isolate as required.

DESCRIPTION

The Variable Assist Power Steering (VAPS) System uses the Front Electronics Module (FEM) to improve steering characteristics. The VAPS system begins operation when engine speed exceeds 100 rpm.

The level of assist provided by the VAPS system depends on vehicle speed. The faster the vehicle speed, the less assist provided by the VAPS system. Vehicle speed is determined by the FEM and is based on Pulse Width Modulated (PWM) current sent to the control valve actuator.

Engine rpm is provided to the FEM by the Powetrain Control Module (PCM) through the Standard Corporate Protocol (SCP). Vehicle speed is provided through the ABS system.

TROUBLESHOOTING

NO COMMUNICATION w/FRONT ELECTRONICS MODULE (FEM)

Refer to pinpoint test C; "Front electronics module does not respond to diagnostic tool"

HARD STEERING OR LACK OF ASSIST

1. Seized lower steering column shaft U-joint.
2. Damaged or fractured steering column bearings.
3. Power steering pump.
4. Suspension components.
5. Steering gear internal leakage.

EXCESSIVE STEERING PUMP NOISE

Power steering pump failure.

EXCESSIVE STEERING WHEEL PLAY

1. Damaged, loose or worn tie-rod.
2. Damaged or worn steering gear.
3. Loose, worn or damaged steering column bearings.
4. Loose, worn or damaged lower steering column shaft U-joint.

STEERING WANDER

1. Unevenly loaded or overloaded vehicle.
2. Loose, worn or damaged tie-rod.
3. Loose or damaged steering gear mounting bolts.
4. Loose lower steering column shaft U-joint bolts or joints.
5. Loose, worn or damaged steering column bearings.
6. Suspension components.

DRIFT/PULL

1. Unevenly loaded or overloaded vehicle.
2. Loose, worn or damaged tie-rod.
3. Wheel alignment.
4. Suspension components.
5. Steering gear valve effort out of balance.
6. Check brake system for correct operation.
7. Incorrect frame or underbody alignment.

FEEDBACK

1. Loose, worn or damaged tie-rod.
2. Loose, worn or damaged steering gear insulators or bolts.
3. Loose lower steering column shaft U-joint bolts.
4. Loose suspension bushings, fasteners or ball joints.
5. Worn or damaged steering column bearings.

POOR RETURNABILITY/ STICKY STEERING

1. Binding lower steering column shaft U-joints.
2. Loose, worn or damaged tie-rod ends.
3. Suspension components

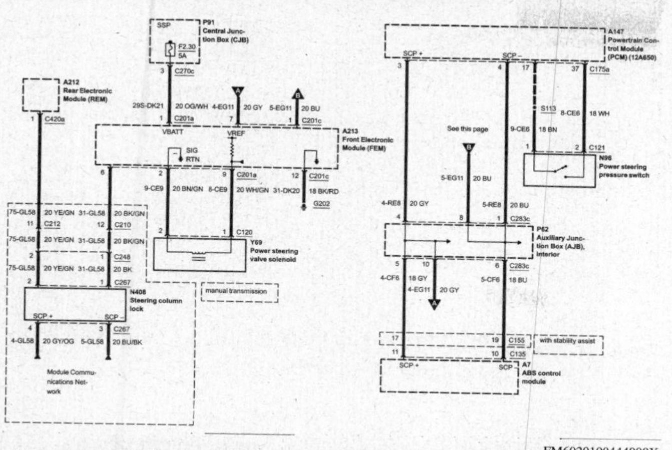

FM6020100444000X

Fig. 1 VAPS wiring diagram. LS & Thunderbird

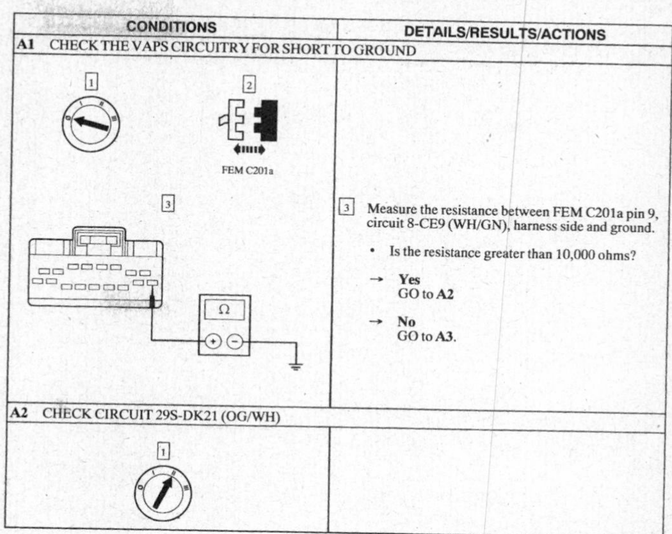

CONDITIONS	DETAILS/RESULTS/ACTIONS
A1 CHECK THE VAPS CIRCUITRY FOR SHORT TO GROUND	
1 2 FEM C201a 3	3 Measure the resistance between FEM C201a pin 9, circuit 8-CE9 (WH/GN), harness side and ground. • Is the resistance greater than 10,000 ohms? → **Yes** GO to **A2** → **No** GO to **A3**.
A2 CHECK CIRCUIT 29S-DK21 (OG/WH)	
1	

FM6020100446010X

Fig. 2 Test A: DTC C1924 VAPS solenoid actuator output circuit short to ground (Part 1 of 2)

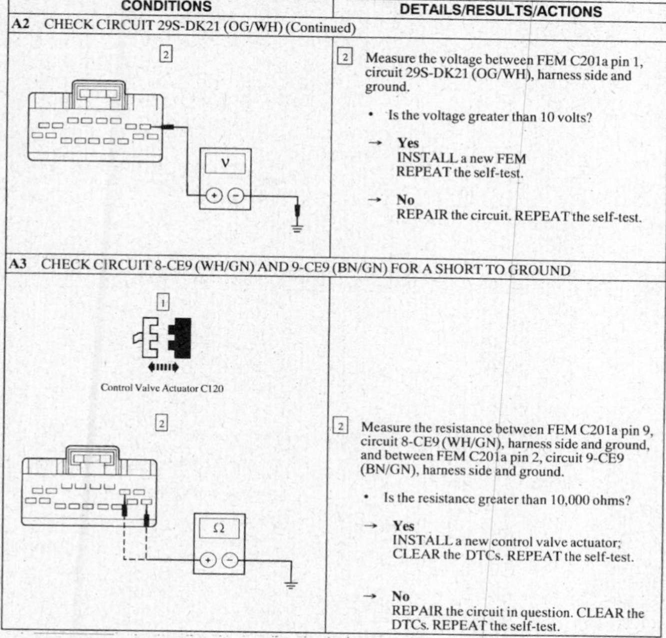

CONDITIONS	DETAILS/RESULTS/ACTIONS
A2 CHECK CIRCUIT 29S-DK21 (OG/WH) (Continued)	
2	2 Measure the voltage between FEM C201a pin 1, circuit 29S-DK21 (OG/WH), harness side and ground. • Is the voltage greater than 10 volts? → **Yes** INSTALL a new FEM REPEAT the self-test. → **No** REPAIR the circuit. REPEAT the self-test.
A3 CHECK CIRCUIT 8-CE9 (WH/GN) AND 9-CE9 (BN/GN) FOR A SHORT TO GROUND	
1 Control Valve Actuator C120 2	2 Measure the resistance between FEM C201a pin 9, circuit 8-CE9 (WH/GN), harness side and ground, and between FEM C201a pin 2, circuit 9-CE9 (BN/GN), harness side and ground. • Is the resistance greater than 10,000 ohms? → **Yes** INSTALL a new control valve actuator; CLEAR the DTCs. REPEAT the self-test. → **No** REPAIR the circuit in question. CLEAR the DTCs. REPEAT the self-test.

FM6020100446020X

Fig. 2 Test A: DTC C1924 VAPS solenoid actuator output circuit short to ground (Part 2 of 2)

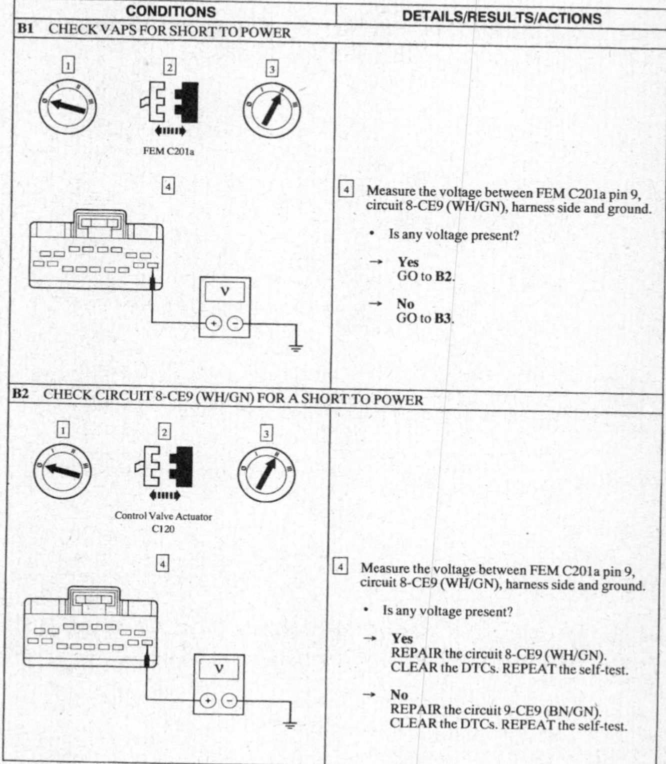

CONDITIONS	DETAILS/RESULTS/ACTIONS
B1 CHECK VAPS FOR SHORT TO POWER	
1 2 FEM C201a 3 4	4 Measure the voltage between FEM C201a pin 9, circuit 8-CE9 (WH/GN), harness side and ground. • Is any voltage present? → **Yes** GO to **B2**. → **No** GO to **B3**.
B2 CHECK CIRCUIT 8-CE9 (WH/GN) FOR A SHORT TO POWER	
1 2 Control Valve Actuator C120 3 4	4 Measure the voltage between FEM C201a pin 9, circuit 8-CE9 (WH/GN), harness side and ground. • Is any voltage present? → **Yes** REPAIR the circuit 8-CE9 (WH/GN). CLEAR the DTCs. REPEAT the self-test. → **No** REPAIR the circuit 9-CE9 (BN/GN). CLEAR the DTCs. REPEAT the self-test.

FM6020100447010X

Fig. 3 Test B: DTC C1925 VAPS solenoid actuator return circuit failure (Part 1 of 3)

4. Binding steering column bearings.

SHIMMY

1. Loose, worn or damaged tie-rod.
2. Suspension components.

POWER STEERING PUMP NOISY

1. Low fluid level and possible leakage.
2. Plugged reservoir.
3. Power steering pump.

DIAGNOSIS & TESTING

ACCESSING DIAGNOSTIC TROUBLE CODES

Diagnosing and testing requires the use of a New Generation Star (NGS) scan tool No. 418–F052 or equivalent and a suitable digital volt-ohm meter. The Data Link Connector (DLC) is located under the instrument panel, between the steering column and radio.

WIRING DIAGRAM

Refer to **Fig. 1** for wiring diagram.

PINPOINT TESTS

Refer to **Figs. 2 through 4** for pinpoint tests.

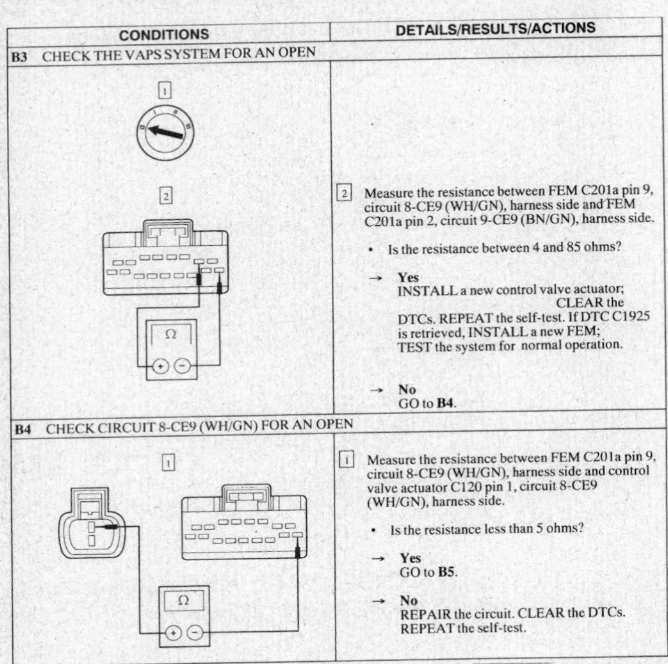

CONDITIONS	DETAILS/RESULTS/ACTIONS
B3 CHECK THE VAPS SYSTEM FOR AN OPEN	
1 2	2 Measure the resistance between FEM C201a pin 9, circuit 8-CE9 (WH/GN), harness side and FEM C201a pin 2, circuit 9-CE9 (BN/GN), harness side. • Is the resistance between 4 and 85 ohms? → **Yes** INSTALL a new control valve actuator; CLEAR the DTCs. REPEAT the self-test. If DTC C1925 is retrieved, INSTALL a new FEM; TEST the system for normal operation. → **No** GO to **B4**.
B4 CHECK CIRCUIT 8-CE9 (WH/GN) FOR AN OPEN	
1	1 Measure the resistance between FEM C201a pin 9, circuit 8-CE9 (WH/GN), harness side and control valve actuator C120 pin 1, circuit 8-CE9 (WH/GN), harness side. • Is the resistance less than 5 ohms? → **Yes** GO to **B5**. → **No** REPAIR the circuit. CLEAR the DTCs. REPEAT the self-test.

FM6020100447020X

Fig. 3 Test B: DTC C1925 VAPS solenoid actuator return circuit failure (Part 2 of 3)

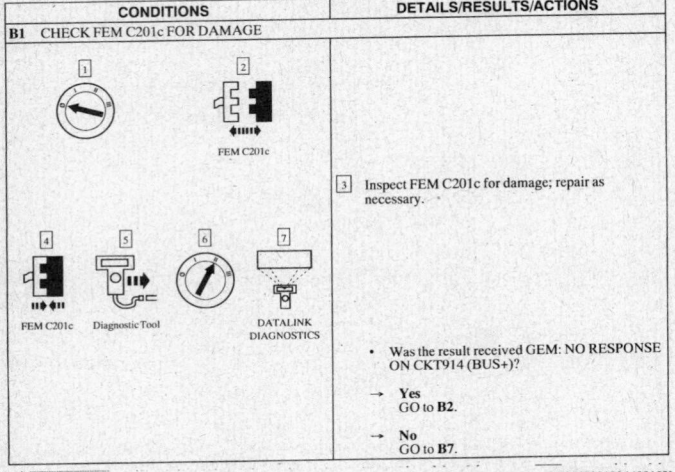

CONDITIONS	DETAILS/RESULTS/ACTIONS
B1 CHECK FEM C201c FOR DAMAGE	
1 2 FEM C201c	3 Inspect FEM C201c for damage; repair as necessary.
4 FEM C201c 5 Diagnostic Tool 6 7 DATALINK DIAGNOSTICS	• Was the result received GEM: NO RESPONSE ON CKT914 (BUS+)? → **Yes** GO to **B2**. → **No** GO to **B7**.

FM6020100448010X

Fig. 4 Test C: Front electronics module does not respond to diagnostic tool (Part 1 of 6)

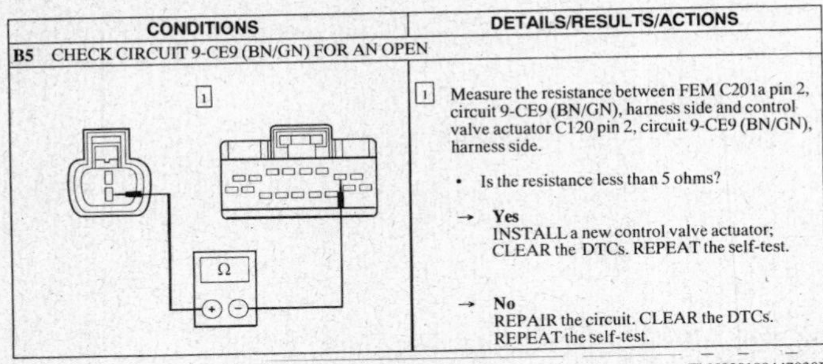

CONDITIONS	DETAILS/RESULTS/ACTIONS
B5 CHECK CIRCUIT 9-CE9 (BN/GN) FOR AN OPEN	
1	1 Measure the resistance between FEM C201a pin 2, circuit 9-CE9 (BN/GN), harness side and control valve actuator C120 pin 2, circuit 9-CE9 (BN/GN), harness side. • Is the resistance less than 5 ohms? → **Yes** INSTALL a new control valve actuator; CLEAR the DTCs. REPEAT the self-test. → **No** REPAIR the circuit. CLEAR the DTCs. REPEAT the self-test.

FM6020100447030X

Fig. 3 Test B: DTC C1925 VAPS solenoid actuator return circuit failure (Part 3 of 3))

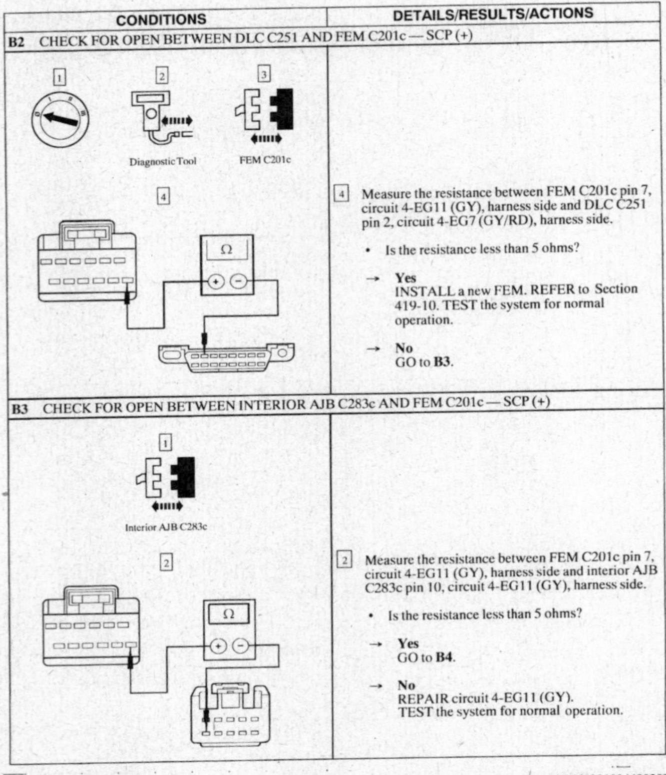

CONDITIONS	DETAILS/RESULTS/ACTIONS
B2 CHECK FOR OPEN BETWEEN DLC C251 AND FEM C201c — SCP (+)	
1 2 Diagnostic Tool 3 FEM C201c 4	4 Measure the resistance between FEM C201c pin 7, circuit 4-EG11 (GY), harness side and DLC C251 pin 2, circuit 4-EG7 (GY/RD), harness side. • Is the resistance less than 5 ohms? → **Yes** INSTALL a new FEM. REFER to Section 419-10. TEST the system for normal operation. → **No** GO to **B3**.
B3 CHECK FOR OPEN BETWEEN INTERIOR AJB C283c AND FEM C201c — SCP (+)	
1 Interior AJB C283c 2	2 Measure the resistance between FEM C201c pin 7, circuit 4-EG11 (GY), harness side and interior AJB C283c pin 10, circuit 4-EG11 (GY), harness side. • Is the resistance less than 5 ohms? → **Yes** GO to **B4**. → **No** REPAIR circuit 4-EG11 (GY). TEST the system for normal operation.

FM6020100448020X

Fig. 4 Test C: Front electronics module does not respond to diagnostic tool (Part 2 of 6)

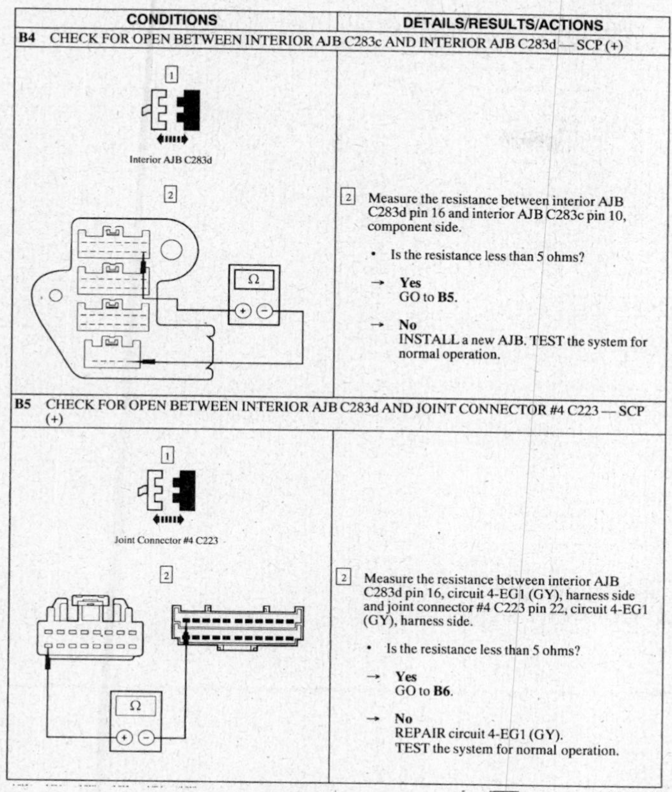

CONDITIONS	DETAILS/RESULTS/ACTIONS
B4 CHECK FOR OPEN BETWEEN INTERIOR AJB C283c AND INTERIOR AJB C283d — SCP (+)	
1 Interior AJB C283d	
2	2 Measure the resistance between interior AJB C283d pin 16 and interior AJB C283c pin 10, component side. • Is the resistance less than 5 ohms? → **Yes** GO to **B5**. → **No** INSTALL a new AJB. TEST the system for normal operation.
B5 CHECK FOR OPEN BETWEEN INTERIOR AJB C283d AND JOINT CONNECTOR #4 C223 — SCP (+)	
1 Joint Connector #4 C223	
2	2 Measure the resistance between interior AJB C283d pin 16, circuit 4-EG1 (GY), harness side and joint connector #4 C223 pin 22, circuit 4-EG1 (GY), harness side. • Is the resistance less than 5 ohms? → **Yes** GO to **B6**. → **No** REPAIR circuit 4-EG1 (GY). TEST the system for normal operation.

FM6020100448030X

Fig. 4 Test C: Front electronics module does not respond to diagnostic tool (Part 3 of 6)

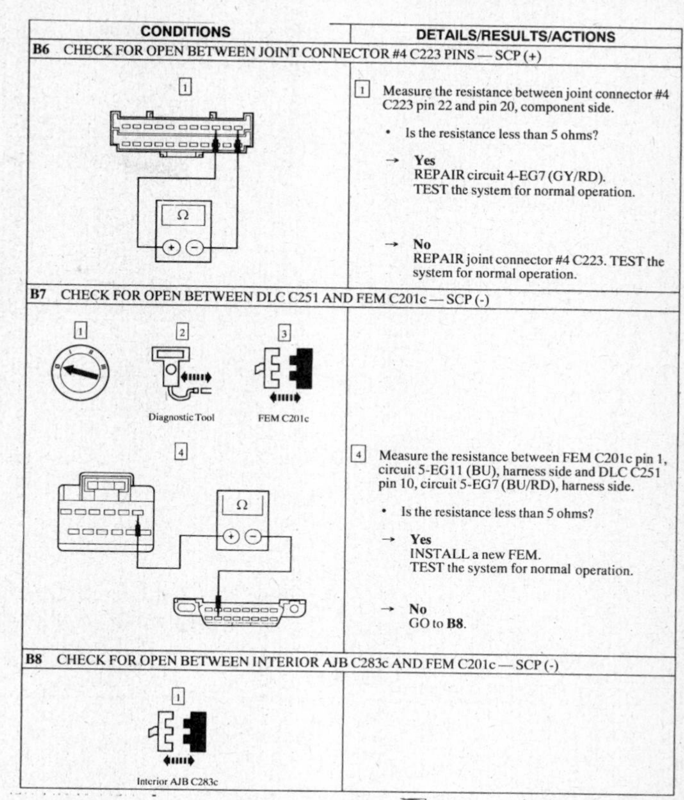

CONDITIONS	DETAILS/RESULTS/ACTIONS
B6 CHECK FOR OPEN BETWEEN JOINT CONNECTOR #4 C223 PINS — SCP (+)	
1	1 Measure the resistance between joint connector #4 C223 pin 22 and pin 20, component side. • Is the resistance less than 5 ohms? → **Yes** REPAIR circuit 4-EG7 (GY/RD). TEST the system for normal operation. → **No** REPAIR joint connector #4 C223. TEST the system for normal operation.
B7 CHECK FOR OPEN BETWEEN DLC C251 AND FEM C201c — SCP (-)	
1 2 Diagnostic Tool 3 FEM C201c	
4	4 Measure the resistance between FEM C201c pin 1, circuit 5-EG11 (BU), harness side and DLC C251 pin 10, circuit 5-EG7 (BU/RD), harness side. • Is the resistance less than 5 ohms? → **Yes** INSTALL a new FEM. TEST the system for normal operation. → **No** GO to **B8**.
B8 CHECK FOR OPEN BETWEEN INTERIOR AJB C283c AND FEM C201c — SCP (-)	
1 Interior AJB C283c	

FM6020100448040X

Fig. 4 Test C: Front electronics module does not respond to diagnostic tool (Part 4 of 6)

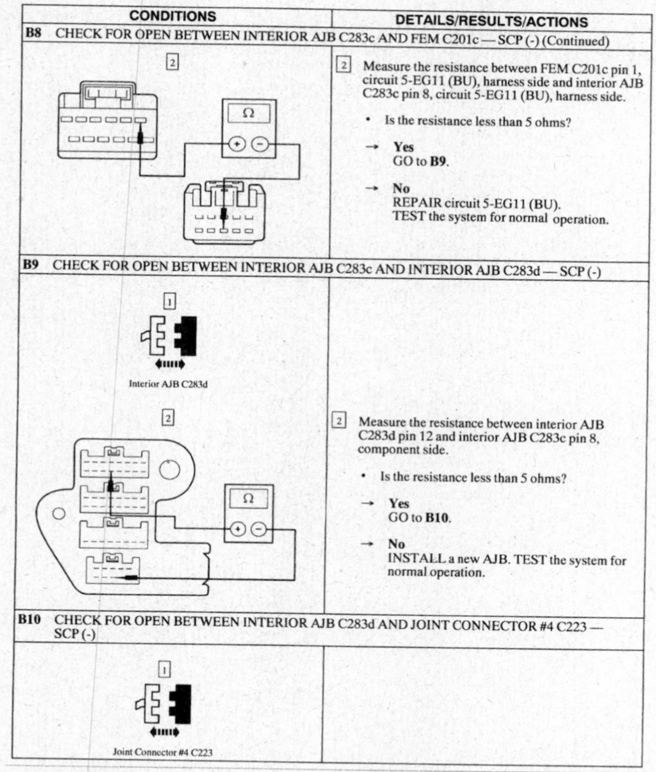

CONDITIONS	DETAILS/RESULTS/ACTIONS
B8 CHECK FOR OPEN BETWEEN INTERIOR AJB C283c AND FEM C201c — SCP (-) (Continued)	
2	2 Measure the resistance between FEM C201c pin 1, circuit 5-EG11 (BU), harness side and interior AJB C283c pin 8, circuit 5-EG11 (BU), harness side. • Is the resistance less than 5 ohms? → **Yes** GO to **B9**. → **No** REPAIR circuit 5-EG11 (BU). TEST the system for normal operation.
B9 CHECK FOR OPEN BETWEEN INTERIOR AJB C283c AND INTERIOR AJB C283d — SCP (-)	
1 Interior AJB C283d	
2	2 Measure the resistance between interior AJB C283d pin 12 and interior AJB C283c pin 8, component side. • Is the resistance less than 5 ohms? → **Yes** GO to **B10**. → **No** INSTALL a new AJB. TEST the system for normal operation.
B10 CHECK FOR OPEN BETWEEN INTERIOR AJB C283d AND JOINT CONNECTOR #4 C223 — SCP (-)	
1 Joint Connector #4 C223	

FM6020100448050X

Fig. 4 Test C: Front electronics module does not respond to diagnostic tool (Part 5 of 6)

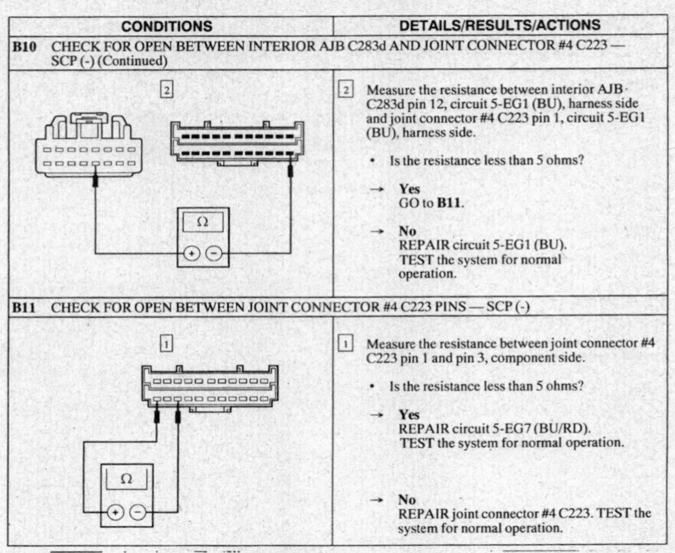

CONDITIONS	DETAILS/RESULTS/ACTIONS
B10 CHECK FOR OPEN BETWEEN INTERIOR AJB C283d AND JOINT CONNECTOR #4 C223 — SCP (-) (Continued)	
2	2 Measure the resistance between interior AJB C283d pin 12, circuit 5-EG1 (BU), harness side and joint connector #4 C223 pin 1, circuit 5-EG1 (BU), harness side. • Is the resistance less than 5 ohms? → **Yes** GO to **B11**. → **No** REPAIR circuit 5-EG1 (BU). TEST the system for normal operation.
B11 CHECK FOR OPEN BETWEEN JOINT CONNECTOR #4 C223 PINS — SCP (-)	
1	1 Measure the resistance between joint connector #4 C223 pin 1 and pin 3, component side. • Is the resistance less than 5 ohms? → **Yes** REPAIR circuit 5-EG7 (BU/RD). TEST the system for normal operation. → **No** REPAIR joint connector #4 C223. TEST the system for normal operation.

FM6020100448060X

Fig. 4 Test C: Front electronics module does not respond to diagnostic tool (Part 6 of 6)

DISC BRAKES

TABLE OF CONTENTS

Front Disc Brakes

NOTE: On Air Bag Equipped Models, Refer To "Air Bag System Precautions" Located In The Front Of This Manual For System Disarming & Arming Procedures.

NOTE: Refer To "Computer Relearn Procedures" Located In The Front Of This Manual When Battery Power To The Computer Has Been Interrupted.

NOTE: Prior to Performing Any Service Operations Listed In This Section, Consult The "Technical Service Bulletins" Section For Related Information.

INDEX

PRECAUTIONS

AIR BAG SYSTEMS

Refer to "Air Bag System Precautions" in the front of this manual for system disarming and arming procedures.

BATTERY GROUND CABLE

Prior to service, disconnect battery ground cable and isolate as required.

SYSTEM DEPRESSURIZING

On models equipped with anti-lock brakes, hydraulic system must be depressurized prior to disconnecting any hydraulic lines or fittings, by pumping the brake pedal a minimum of 25 times with ignition in Off position.

DESCRIPTION

SINGLE PISTON CALIPERS

The caliper assembly consists of a pin sliding caliper housing, inner and outer shoe and lining assemblies and a single piston, **Figs. 1 and 2.** The caliper slides on two pins which also act as attaching bolts between caliper and the combination anchor plate and spindle. The outer brake shoe and lining assembly is longer than the inner brake shoe and lining assembly. Inner and outer shoe and lining assemblies are attached to the caliper by spring clips riveted to the shoe surfaces. The inner shoe is attached to the caliper by installing the spring clip to the inside of the caliper piston. The outer shoe clips directly to the caliper housing. A wear indicator is incorporated, which emits a noise when the lining is worn to a point for required replacement. Lefthand and righthand inner and outer shoes are not interchangeable.

DUAL PISTON CALIPERS

The caliper assembly consists of a sliding bridge type caliper housing with dual pistons, caliper mounting frame and inner and outer friction pad assemblies, **Figs. 3 and 4.** The caliper is located into and slides on the anchor frame by its thrust face and a locating pin and clip. The friction pads are retained into the anchor frame by the caliper sliding bridge assembly and use an anti-rattle spring clip to reduce brake noise. The friction pads are retained into the sliding bridge assembly by clips located on the back of the friction pad.

Righthand and lefthand caliper and inner and outer righthand and lefthand friction pads are unique and cannot be interchanged. When servicing this system, mark all components with location marks for later reference and assembly.

TROUBLESHOOTING

BRAKE ROUGHNESS

Thickness Variation

If roughness or vibration is encountered during highway operation or if pedal pumping is experienced at low speeds, the disc may have excessive thickness variation. Measure the disc at 12 points with a micrometer at a radius approximately one inch from edge of disc. If thickness measurements vary by more than .0005 inch, replace the disk.

Lateral Runout

Excessive lateral runout of braking disc may cause a "knocking back" of the pistons, possibly creating increased pedal travel and vibration when brakes are applied.

Wheel Bearing Looseness

Adjust the wheel bearings as outlined under "Front Steering & Suspension" before measuring lateral runout. The readjustment is important and will be required at the completion of the test to prevent bearing failure.

BRAKE BOOSTER OPERATION TEST

1. Inspect hydraulic system for leaks or insufficient fluid.
2. With transmission in park, stop engine.
3. Apply brakes several times to release all vacuum in system.
4. Depress brake pedal and hold in applied position.
5. Start engine and note whether brake pedal moves downward under constant foot pressure.
6. If no pedal movement is felt, brake booster system is inoperative.
7. Remove vacuum hose from power brake booster valve.
8. Inspect for vacuum at valve end of hose with engine at idle speed and transmission in neutral.
9. Ensure all unused vacuum ports are properly capped, and vacuum hoses are not cracked or deteriorated.
10. If manifold vacuum is present, and no pedal movement is noted during testing, replace power brake booster.
11. Operate engine a minimum of ten seconds at fast idle. Stop engine and let vehicle stand for ten minutes.
12. Apply brake pedal with approximately 20 ft. lbs., of force.
13. The pedal feel should be the same as that noted with engine operating.
14. If the bake pedal feels hard (no power assist), replace check valve and repeat test.
15. If brake pedal still feels hard after check valve replacement, replace power brake booster.

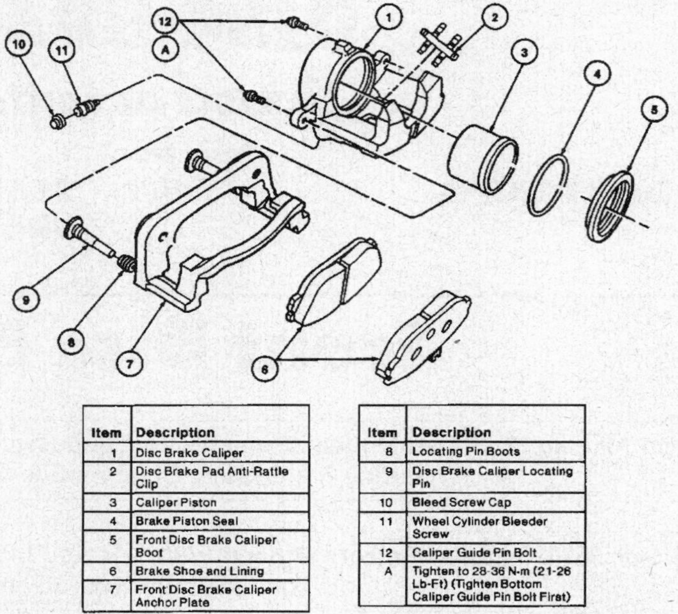

Item	Description
1	Disc Brake Caliper
2	Disc Brake Pad Anti-Rattle Clip
3	Caliper Piston
4	Brake Piston Seal
5	Front Disc Brake Caliper Boot
6	Brake Shoe and Lining
7	Front Disc Brake Caliper Anchor Plate

Item	Description
8	Locating Pin Boots
9	Disc Brake Caliper Locating Pin
10	Bleed Screw Cap
11	Wheel Cylinder Bleeder Screw
12	Caliper Guide Pin Bolt
A	Tighten to 28-36 N-m (21-26 Lb-Ft) (Tighten Bottom Caliper Guide Pin Bolt First)

Fig. 1 Exploded view of single piston disc brake caliper. Continental, Contour, Cougar, Mark VIII, Mustang (except Cobra), Mystique, Sable & Taurus

16. If pedal movement feels spongy, bleed hydraulic system to remove air from system.

BRAKE MASTER CYLINDER

Normal Conditions

The following conditions are considered normal and are not indications the brake master cylinder is malfunctioning:

1. A slight turbulence in brake master cylinder reservoir fluid occurring when the brake pedal is released. Turbulence occurs as brake fluid returns to master cylinder after releasing brakes.
2. A trace of brake fluid on booster shell below master cylinder mounting flange. This condition results from the lubricating action of the master cylinder wiping seal.

Abnormal Conditions

Prior to performing any diagnosis, ensure brake system warning indicator is functional.

Diagnostic procedures in this section use brake pedal feel, warning indicator illumination, and brake fluid level indicators in diagnosing brake system problems. The following conditions are considered abnormal:

1. **Brake pedal goes down fast.** Inspect for external or internal leak.
2. **Brake pedal eases down slowly.** Inspect for internal or external leak.
3. **Brake pedal is low or feels spongy.**
   a. Inspect fluid level in brake master cylinder reservoir.
   b. Inspect brake master cylinder reservoir cap vent holes for clogging.
   c. Inspect rear brake adjustment.
   d. Inspect for air in hydraulic system.
4. **Brake pedal effort is excessive.** Inspect for binding or obstructed brake pedal linkage or insufficient power brake booster vacuum.
5. **Rear brakes lock up during light brake pedal application.** Inspect for wrong tire pressure, worn tires, grease or fluid on brake linings, damaged linings, improperly adjusted parking brakes or damaged brake pressure control valve.
6. **Brake pedal effort is erratic.** Inspect for power brake booster malfunction, extreme caliper piston knock back or improperly installed disc brake shoe or lining.
7. **Brake warning indicator is on.** Inspect for low fluid level, ignition wire routing too close to fluid level indicator or float assembly damage.

Bypass Condition Inspection

1. Inspect fluid level in brake master cylinder reservoir. Fill if required.
2. Observe fluid level in brake master cylinder. If, after several brake applications the fluid level remains the same, measure wheel turning torque required to rotate wheels with brakes applied as follows:
   a. Place transmission in neutral.
   b. Raise vehicle on hoist.
   c. Apply brakes slowly to a minimum of 100 ft. lbs., and hold for approximately 15 seconds.
   d. With brakes still applied, exert 75 ft. lbs., of torque on one front wheel and one rear wheel.
   e. If either wheel rotates, inspect internal components of brake master cylinder.
   f. Repair or replace as required.

Non-Pressure Leaks

An empty brake master cylinder reservoir condition may be caused by either of the following non-pressure external leaks:

1. Inspect for an external leak that may occur at the brake master cylinder reservoir cap due to improper positioning of gasket and cap.
2. Inspect for a leak at the brake master cylinder reservoir mounting grommets. Install new grommets if required.

BRAKE SYSTEM BLEED

Pressure bleeding is recommended for all hydraulic disc brake systems.

Do not reuse brake fluid drained from the hydraulic system when bleeding the brakes. Ensure disc brake pistons are returned to their normal positions and the shoe and lining assemblies are properly seated.

Do not shake the pressure bleeder tank while air is being added or after it has been pressurized. This will prevent air from the tank getting into the lines. Do not move the tank during the bleeding operation. The tank should be kept at least one third full.

On models equipped with power brakes, exhaust the vacuum in the power unit by pumping the brake pedal several times with the engine Off.

On vehicles equipped with disc brakes and master cylinders without proportioners or pressure control valves located in the master cylinder outlet port, the brake metering valve or combination valve must be held in position using a suitable tool.

On vehicles equipped with plastic reservoirs, do not exceed 25 psi bleeding pressure.

When bleeding without pressure, open the bleed valve three quarters of a turn, depress the pedal a full stroke, close the bleeder and allow the pedal to return slowly to its released position. Repeat until no more air is visible in fluid.

Discard drained or bled brake fluid. Do not spill fluid on vehicle surfaces, brake fluid will damage painted finishes.

Flushing is essential if there is water, mineral oil or other contaminants in the lines, and whenever new components are installed in the hydraulic system. Fluid contamination is usually indicated by swollen and deteriorated cups and other rubber components.

If air has entered system due to low fluid levels, or removal of master cylinder brake lines, all four wheels will require bleeding. If a line is disconnected at only one cylinder, then only that cylinder needs to be bled.

Master cylinders equipped with bleeder valves should be bled first before the wheel cylinders are bled. In all cases where a master cylinder has been overhauled, it must be bled. Where there is no bleeder valve, leave the lines loose, then actuate the brake pedal to expel the air. Tighten lines and repeat until no air is visible in expelled fluid.

SYSTEM PRIMING

When a new master cylinder is installed or if the brake system has been partially or completely emptied, fluid may not flow from the bleeder screws during normal bleeding. It may be required to prime the system using the following procedure:

1. Remove brake lines from master cylinder.
2. Install short brake lines in master cylinder and position them back into the reservoir. Ensure short brake line ends are submerged in reservoir brake fluid.
3. Fill reservoir with recommended brake fluid, then cover master cylinder fluid reservoir with shop towel.
4. Pump brakes until clear, bubble-free fluid comes out of both brake lines. If any brake fluid spills on paint, wash it off immediately with water.
5. Remove short brake lines, then install original brake lines.
6. Bleed each brake line at master cylinder using the following procedure:
   a. Have assistant pump brake pedal 10 times, then hold firm pressure on pedal.
   b. Open rearmost brake line fittings until stream of brake fluid comes out. Have assistant maintain pressure on brake pedal until brake line fitting is tightened.
   c. Repeat this operation until clear, bubble-free fluid comes out from around tube fitting.
   d. Repeat bleeding operation at front brake line fitting.
7. If any of brake lines or calipers have been removed, it may be required to prime system by gravity bleeding. Gravity bleed system after master cylinder is primed and bled. To prime system using gravity method, proceed as follows:
   a. Fill master cylinder with manufacturer recommended brake fluid or equivalent.
   b. Loosen both rear bleeder screws and leave open until clear brake fluid flows out. **Inspect reservoir fluid level frequently. Do not allow fluid level to drop below halfway.**
   c. Tighten rear bleeder screws.
   d. Loosen bleeder screw on front caliper and leave open until clear fluid flows out. **Bleed front calipers one side at a time.**
8. After master cylinder has been primed, lines bled at master cylinder and brake system primed, resume normal brake system bleeding at each wheel.

WHEEL BLEEDING SEQUENCE

Rear Wheel Drive .....RR-LR-RF-LF
Front Wheel Drive ....RR-LF-LR-RF

INSPECTION

Remove wheels and inspect brake disc, caliper and linings. Inspect wheel bearings and repack if required.

If the caliper is cracked or fluid leakage through the casting is evident, it must be replaced as a unit.

If caliper is removed when installing new components, clean all components in alcohol, then wipe dry using lint-free cloths. Blow out drilled passages and bores with compressed air. Inspect dust boots for punctures or tears, replace as required.

Inspect piston bores in both housings for scoring or pitting. Bores showing light scratches or corrosion can be cleaned with crocus cloth. Bores with deep scratches or scoring may be honed, provided the diameter of the bore is not increased more than .002 inch. If the bore does not clean up within this specification, replace the caliper.

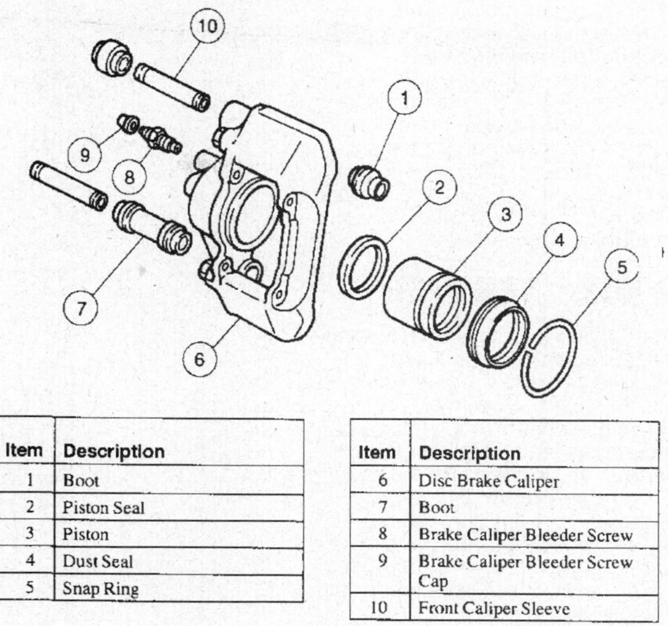

Item	Description
1	Boot
2	Piston Seal
3	Piston
4	Dust Seal
5	Snap Ring

Item	Description
6	Disc Brake Caliper
7	Boot
8	Brake Caliper Bleeder Screw
9	Brake Caliper Bleeder Screw Cap
10	Front Caliper Sleeve

FM4079500074000X

Fig. 2 Exploded view of single piston disc brake caliper. Escort, Tracer & ZX2

Black stains on the bore walls are caused by piston seals and do not adversely affect caliper performance.

When using a hone, install the hone baffle before honing the bore. The baffle is used to protect the hone stones from damage. Use extreme care in cleaning the caliper after honing. Remove all dust and grit by flushing the caliper with alcohol. Wipe the caliper dry with a clean lint-free cloth, then repeat cleaning procedure.

BRAKE DISC SERVICE

Disc brake service is critical due to the close tolerances required in machining the brake disc to ensure proper brake operation.

Maintaining close control of the shape of the rubbing surfaces is required to prevent brake roughness. In addition, the surface finish must be non-directional and maintained at a micro-inch finish. This is required to avoid pulls and erratic performance, and to promote long lining life and equal lining wear of both the lefthand and righthand brakes.

Do not attempt to refinish the rubbing surfaces unless precision equipment, capable of measuring in micro inches (millionths of an inch), is available.

To inspect the disc lateral runout, mount a dial indicator, so the indicator's plunger contacts the disc one inch from the outer edge, **Fig. 5.** If the total indicated runout exceeds specifications, install a new disc.

To inspect parallelism (thickness variation), mount dial indicators, **Fig. 6,** so the plunger contacts the rotor approximately one inch from the outer edge. If parallelism exceeds specifications, replace the rotor.

BRAKE PAD SERVICE

On models with anti-lock brakes, the brake hydraulic system must be depressurized before disconnecting any hydraulic lines or fittings. Depressurize the system by pumping the brake pedal a minimum of 25 times with the ignition in the Off position.

CONTINENTAL, COUGAR, CROWN VICTORIA, GRAND MARQUIS, LS, MARK VIII, MUSTANG (EXCEPT COBRA), SABLE, TAURUS, THUNDERBIRD & TOWN CAR

Removal

1. Remove brake fluid until reservoir is half full.
2. **On models equipped with air suspension,** turn air suspension service switch to Off position.
3. **On all models,** raise and support front of vehicle, then remove wheel and tire assembly.
4. Remove two caliper anchor bracket mounting bolts and discard.
5. Lift front disc brake caliper anchor plate away from rotor using a rotating motion.

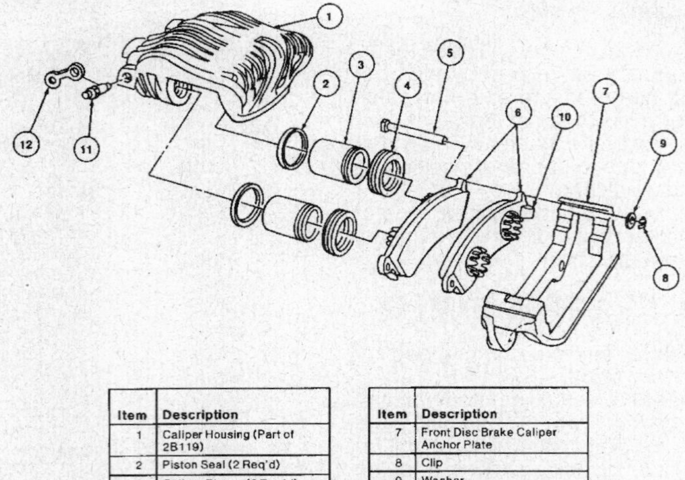

Item	Description
1	Caliper Housing (Part of 2B119)
2	Piston Seal (2 Req'd)
3	Caliper Piston (2 Req'd)
4	Dust Boot (2 Req'd)
5	Front Brake Locating Pin
6	Brake Shoe and Lining

Item	Description
7	Front Disc Brake Caliper Anchor Plate
8	Clip
9	Washer
10	Anti-Rattle Clip and Insulator
11	Wheel Cylinder Bleeder Screw
12	Cover

FM4079500073000X

Fig. 3 Exploded view of dual piston disc brake caliper. Mustang Cobra

6. Remove outer brake shoe from disc brake caliper assembly by sliding brake shoe away from outer leg to disengage it from anchor plate.
7. Remove inner brake shoe and lining assembly by sliding brake shoe away from piston disengaging it from the caliper anchor plate.
8. Suspend caliper from inner fender housing with wire to avoid damaging brake hose.

Installation

1. Using a suitable C-clamp and block of wood 2¾ x 1 inch and approximately ¾ inch thick, seat caliper piston in bore, then remove C-clamp and wooden block. Some models have pistons made of phenolic material. Do not seat these pistons in bore by applying C-clamp directly to piston. Use extra care during this procedure to prevent damage to the piston. Metal or sharp objects should not come into direct contact with the piston or damage may result.
2. Install caliper anchor plate with caliper guide pin bolts. Tighten lower bolt first, then upper bolt to specifications.
3. Ensure anti-rattle spring and anti-rattle clip are seated in caliper lining inspection opening. Anti-rattle clips must be installed from lining side.
4. Engage brake shoe and lining in anchor plate by first engaging the side opposite anti-rattle clip. Press other end of brake shoe and lining to compress disc brake pad anti-rattle clip, then engage brake shoe lining in front anchor plate.
5. Inspect caliper and anchor plate assembly to ensure brake shoes and linings are properly installed.
6. Position caliper and anchor plate assembly over rotor. Install two new caliper anchor bracket bolts. Tighten mounting bolt to specifications.
7. Inspect caliper locating pin and pin boots. If caliper locating pin is binding, remove and clean.
8. Install wheel and tire assembly, then lower vehicle.
9. **On models equipped with air suspension,** turn air suspension service switch to On position.
10. **On all models,** fill master cylinder, then pump brake pedal several times to position brake linings before moving vehicle.

CONTOUR & MYSTIQUE

1. Raise and support vehicle.
2. Remove wheels.
3. Remove brake pad retaining clip.
4. Disconnect and detach brake pad wear sensor connector (if equipped).
5. Remove bolt covers and bolts, then the caliper.
6. Secure caliper out of way to prevent damage to flexible brake hose.
7. Remove outer and inner brake pads.
8. Reverse procedure to install.

ESCORT, TRACER & ZX2

Removal

1. Raise and support vehicle, then remove wheel and tire assembly.
2. Remove springs and brake pad retaining pins, **Fig. 7.**
3. Remove brake pads and shims from caliper assembly.

Installation

1. Push piston fully back into caliper bore.
2. Apply grease between shims and brake pad guide plates, then position brake pads and shims into caliper.
3. Install springs, two brake pad retaining pins, then wheel and tire assembly.

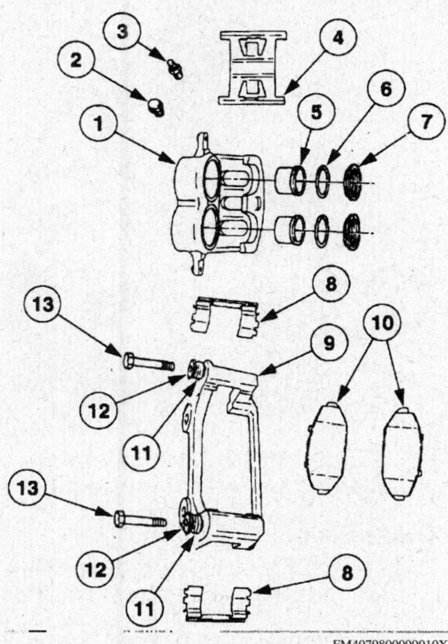

Fig. 4 Exploded view of dual piston disc brake caliper (Part 1 of 2). Crown Victoria, Grand Marquis, LS, Thunderbird & Town Car

FOCUS

Removal

1. Raise and support vehicle.
2. Remove front wheels.
3. Disconnect brake hose from support bracket on front strut.
4. Remove outer brake pad retaining clip.
5. Remove bolt covers and bolts, then pull caliper outwards to release piston.
6. Support brake caliper from wire hook, do not allow caliper to hang from brake hose.
7. Lift outer pad retaining clip over spring retaining lugs, then remove outer and inner brake pads.

Installation

1. Fully retract caliper piston into caliper.
2. Install inner then outer brake pads.
3. Push outer retaining clip over spring retaining lugs.
4. Install caliper, then the bolts and covers.
5. Install brake hose onto support bracket.
6. Install outer pad retaining clip.
7. Install wheels and inspect brake fluid level.

MUSTANG COBRA

Removal

Brake components are not interchangeable. Ensure each component is installed back in it's original location.

1. Remove approximately ½ of brake fluid from master cylinder reservoir.
2. Raise and support vehicle.
3. Remove wheel assemblies. **Use caution not to damage disc brake shields or bleeder screws.**
4. Remove clip and washer from caliper locating pin, then remove pin.
5. Lift caliper with pads from anchor frame.
6. Secure assembly out of way with wire or tie wrap.
7. Mark inner and outer friction pads for later reference, then remove pads.

Inspection

Inspect caliper piston and caliper pin boots for damage, replace boots as required.

Inspect rotor for wear and runout. Minor glazing of surfaces can be removed by hand sanding with a medium grit sandpaper.

Installation

1. Clean sliding and contact surfaces of brake components.
2. Remove protective paper from adhesive insulator material on friction pads. **Do not to contaminate adhesive surface.**
3. Install friction pads into caliper, ensure correct pad is fully seated into proper position of caliper.
4. Use a suitable C-clamp to compress pistons into caliper. Ensure sufficient clearance exists to allow pads to fit over rotor.
5. Place caliper into position on anchor frame, then install locating pin, washer and clip.
6. Install wheel assemblies, tighten lug nuts to specifications. **Use caution not to damage brake shields or bleeder screws.**
7. Lower vehicle, then pump brake pedal until a firm pedal is achieved. Inspect and adjust brake fluid level as needed.

CALIPER SERVICE

REPLACEMENT

On models with anti-lock brakes, the brake booster system must be depressurized before disconnecting any hydraulic lines or fittings. Depressurize the system by pumping the brake pedal a minimum of 25 times with the ignition in the Off position.

CONTINENTAL, COUGAR, CROWN VICTORIA, GRAND MARQUIS, LS, MARK VIII, MUSTANG (EXCEPT COBRA), SABLE, TAURUS, THUNDERBIRD & TOWN CAR

Before removing calipers, mark lefthand and righthand calipers so they can be installed in the same position.

1. **On models equipped with air suspension,** turn air suspension service switch to Off position.
2. **On all models,** raise and support front of vehicle, then remove wheel and tire assembly.
3. Loosen brake tube fitting connecting brake tube to fitting on frame. Plug brake tube.

Item	Part Number	Description
1	2B120	Disc brake caliper
2	2L126	Bleeder screw cap
3	2208	Bleeder screw
4	2B164	Anti-rattle spring
5	2196	Caliper piston
6	2B115	Piston seal
7	2207	Piston dust boot
8	2L200	Shoe slipper
9	2B292	Front disc brake caliper anchor plate
10	2001	Brake pads
11	2A492	Guide pin boot
12	2B296	Guide pin
13	2N386	Caliper bolt

FM4079800099020X

Fig. 4 Exploded view of dual piston disc brake caliper (Part 2 of 2). Crown Victoria, Grand Marquis, LS, Thunderbird & Town Car

4. Remove retaining clip from brake hose and bracket, then disconnect brake hose from caliper.
5. Remove caliper locating pins.
6. Lift caliper from rotor and spindle anchor plate assembly.
7. **On models equipped with phenolic caliper piston,** do not pry directly against the piston or damage may result.
8. **On all models,** reverse procedure to install, noting the following:
   a. Install caliper assembly over rotor with outer shoe against rotor braking surface to prevent pinching piston boot between inner brake shoe and piston. **Ensure calipers are installed in proper position.**
   b. Bleed brake system as outlined under "Brake System Bleed."
   c. Pump brake pedal several times to position brake shoes before moving vehicle.
9. Turn air suspension switch to ON position.

CONTOUR & MYSTIQUE

1. Raise and support vehicle.
2. Remove wheel and tire assembly.
3. Disconnect and detach brake pad wear sensor connector (if equipped).
4. Loosen brake hose union.
5. Remove brake pad retaining clip.
6. Remove bolt covers and bolts, then the caliper.
7. Remove outer and inner brake pad.
8. Disconnect and plug brake hose from caliper.
9. Reverse procedure to install.

ESCORT, TRACER & ZX2

1. Raise and support vehicle, then remove brake pads as outlined under "Brake Pad Service."
2. Using suitable needle nose vise grips, clamp center of brake flex hose to prevent brake fluid leakage.
3. Remove banjo bolt retaining brake flex hose to caliper.
4. Disconnect brake hose from caliper

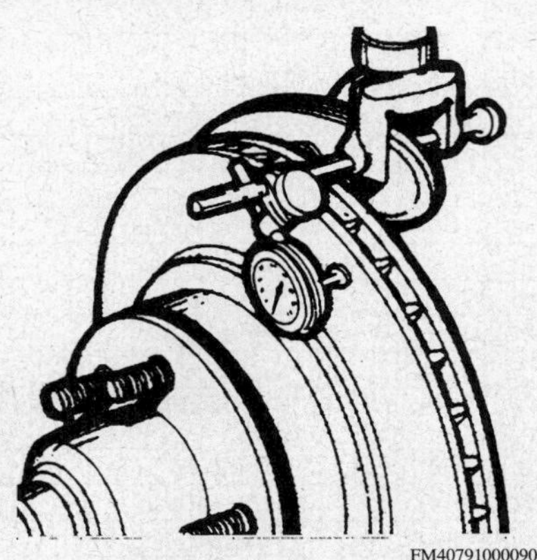

Fig. 5 Rotor lateral runout inspection

and discard two copper washers.
5. Remove two caliper bolts, then the caliper.
6. Reverse procedure to install, noting the following:
   a. Use new copper sealing washers.
   b. Bleed brakes as outlined under "Brake System Bleed."

FOCUS

1. Raise and support vehicle.
2. Remove front wheels.
3. Disconnect brake hose from support bracket on front strut.
4. Loosen brake hose fitting on caliper.
5. Remove front brake pads as outlined under "Brake Pad Service."
6. Disconnect front caliper from brake hose. Cap brake hose to prevent contamination.
7. Reverse procedure to install, bleed brakes as outlined under "Brake System Bleed."

MUSTANG COBRA

Brake components are unique, and are not interchangeable. Ensure each component is installed back in it's original location.

1. Remove brake pads as outlined under "Brake Pad Service."
2. Remove brake flex hose from caliper and discard copper sealing washers.
3. If required, remove two caliper anchor frame bolts, then lift caliper/anchor frame assembly off rotor.
4. Reverse procedure to install, noting the following:
   a. Use new copper sealing washers.
   b. Bleed brakes as outlined under "Brake System Bleed."

OVERHAUL

CONTINENTAL, COUGAR, CROWN VICTORIA, GRAND MARQUIS, LS, MARK VIII, MUSTANG (EXCEPT COBRA), SABLE, TAURUS, THUNDERBIRD & TOWN CAR

Disassemble

1. Remove caliper assembly from vehicle as outlined under "Caliper Service."
2. Position fiber block and shop towels between caliper piston and caliper housing, then apply compressed air to caliper brake line fitting bore to force piston from caliper.
3. Remove dust boot from caliper assembly, **Fig. 1.**
4. Remove piston seal from cylinder and discard.

Inspection

1. Inspect piston for scratches, scoring or damage. Replace if required.
2. Inspect caliper bore for scratches, scoring or corrosion. Light scratches or slight corrosion can be polished out using crocus cloth.
3. Ensure bleeder screw and bleeder screw bore hole in caliper are fully open.
4. Inspect caliper bushings for corrosion and dust boot retaining ring for damage or tension loss. Replace components as required.

Assemble

1. Lubricate piston seal with clean brake fluid, then install seal in caliper bore. **Ensure seal is firmly seated in groove.**
2. Install new dust boot in outer groove of caliper bore, **Fig. 1.**
3. Coat piston with clean brake fluid and install piston in caliper bore.
4. Spread dust boot over piston as it is installed, then seat dust boot in piston groove.
5. Install caliper assembly as described previously.
6. **On models equipped with air suspension,** turn air suspension service switch to On position.

ESCORT, TRACER & ZX2

Disassemble

1. Remove front caliper as described previously.
2. Remove front caliper sleeves and dust boots.
3. Remove caliper bleed screw cap and screw.
4. Remove snap ring from caliper piston dust seal, then the seal.
5. Position wood block or shop towels between caliper and piston, then apply air pressure to brake hose fitting to remove piston from caliper. Use only enough air pressure to ease piston from caliper bore. **Keep hands and fingers away from piston, as personal injury may result.**

Inspection

1. Inspect piston for scratches, scoring or damage. Replace if required.
2. Inspect caliper bore for scratches, scoring or corrosion. Light scratches or slight corrosion can be polished out using crocus cloth.
3. Ensure bleeder screw and bleeder screw bore hole in caliper are fully open.
4. Inspect caliper bushings for corrosion and dust boot retaining ring for damage or tension loss. Replace components as required.

Fig. 6 Rotor parallelism (thickness variation) inspection

Assemble

1. Lubricate piston seal with brake fluid, then position seal in caliper bore groove.
2. Lubricate piston and caliper bore with brake fluid.
3. Install caliper assembly as outlined under "Caliper Service."

FOCUS

Disassemble

1. Remove brake caliper as described previously.
2. Place a block of wood or some shop towels between brake caliper piston and housing.
3. Extract caliper piston using compressed air applied to caliper.
4. Remove and discard caliper dust seal and piston seal.
5. Inspect caliper piston and piston bore for pitting or scoring.
6. Replace damaged or scored components as required.

Assemble

1. Lubricate piston bore, piston seal and caliper piston with DOT 3 brake fluid meeting Ford specifications.
2. Install new caliper seal into machined groove in piston bore.
3. Install new dust seal onto caliper piston.
4. Install caliper piston into caliper bore.
5. Seat dust seal and install caliper.
6. Bleed brake system as outlined under "Brake System Bleed."

MUSTANG COBRA

Disassemble

1. Remove caliper assembly from vehicle.
2. Drain any remaining brake fluid from caliper.
3. Position fiber block and shop towels between caliper pistons and caliper housing, then apply compressed air to caliper brake line fitting bore to force pistons from caliper.
4. Remove dust boots from caliper assembly.

5. Remove piston seals from cylinder and discard.

Inspection

1. Inspect pistons for scratches, scoring or damage. Replace if required.
2. Inspect caliper bores for scratches, scoring or corrosion. Light scratches or slight corrosion can be polished out using crocus cloth.
3. Ensure bleeder screw and bleeder screw bore hole in caliper are fully open.

Assemble

1. Lubricate piston seals with clean brake fluid, then install seals in caliper bore. **Ensure seals are firmly seated in groove.**
2. Install new dust boots in outer groove of caliper bore.
3. Coat pistons with clean brake fluid and install pistons in caliper bore.
4. Install dust boots over piston as they are installed, then seat dust boots in piston groove.
5. Install caliper assembly.

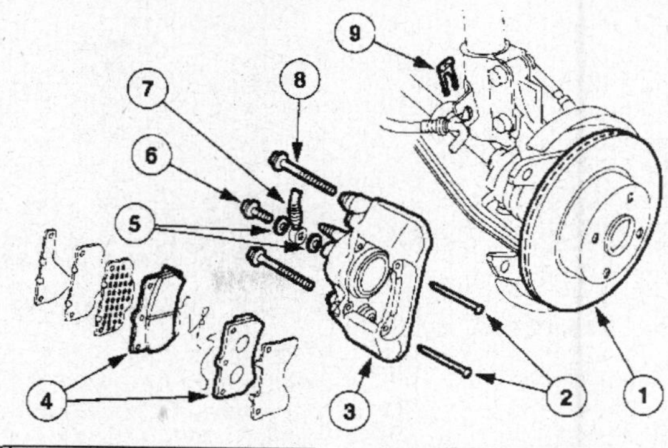

Item	Description
1	Front Disc Brake Rotor
2	Disc Brake Caliper Locating Pin
3	Disc Brake Caliper
4	Brake Pads

Item	Description
5	Copper Washers (2 Req'd)
6	Banjo Bolt
7	Front Brake Hose
8	Brake Caliper Bolt (2 Req'd)
9	Brake Hose Clip

FM4079500075000X

Fig. 7 Front disc brake assembly. Escort, Tracer & ZX2

ROTOR

REPLACE

If caliper does not require servicing, do not disconnect brake hose or remove caliper from vehicle. Position caliper aside with wire or tie straps to avoid damaging caliper or hose.

If excessive force must be used to remove the rotor, then it should be inspected for lateral runout before installation.

REMOVAL

1. **On models equipped with air suspension,** turn service switch Off.
2. **On all models,** raise and support vehicle, then remove wheel and tire assembly. **Use care to avoid damage or interference with caliper bleeder screw fitting and brake rotor shield.**
3. Remove caliper anchor bracket bolts. Position caliper aside and support with wire or tie straps to avoid damaging caliper and hose. **Use care to prevent deformation of rotor and nicking, scratching or contaminating brake lining and rotor surfaces.**
4. Remove front rotor from hub assembly by pulling it off hub studs, noting the following:
   a. If excessive force is required to remove rotor, inspect rotor for lateral runout prior to installation.
   b. If additional force is required to remove front disc brake rotor, apply suitable rust penetrant and inhibitor on front and rear rotor/hub mating surfaces.
   c. Strike rotor between studs with plastic hammer. If rotor still will not come off, install three-jaw puller tool No. D80L-1013-A, or equivalent, and remove rotor.

INSTALLATION

Failure to clean rust and foreign material from rotor and hub mounting surfaces when installing new or old rotors will result in high rotor lateral runout, which will speed up the development of brake roughness, shudder or vibration.

1. If front disc brake rotor is being replaced, remove protective coating from new rotor with suitable carburetor cleaner.
2. If original rotor is being installed, ensure rotor braking and mounting surfaces are clean.
3. Apply suitable lubricant to pilot diameter of front disc brake rotor, then install rotor on wheel hub assembly.
4. Install caliper and caliper anchor bracket bolts on rotor. Tighten caliper anchor bracket bolts to specifications.
5. Install wheel and tire assembly, then tighten wheel hub bolt nuts to specifications. **Failure to tighten wheel hub bolt nuts with torque wrench in star pattern may result in high rotor runout, which will speed development of brake roughness, shudder and vibration.**
6. Lower vehicle, then pump brake pedal to position brake linings prior to moving vehicle.
7. Turn air suspension service switch On.
8. Road test vehicle.

TECHNICAL SERVICE BULLETINS

CLICKING DURING BRAKING AFTER DIRECTION CHANGE

1998–99 Escort, Tracer & ZX2

On some of these models, the front brakes may click during application after changing direction.

This condition may be caused by excessive clearance between caliper bracket and inned brake pad. To correct this condition, proceed as follows:

1. Raise and support vehicle, then remove front wheel and tire assemblies.
2. Measure clearance between steel inner brake pad and steering knuckle while pushing brake pad to extreme side of knuckle. Clearance should be .016–.037 inch.
3. If clearance is more than .037 inch, proceed as follows:
   a. Remove caliper and inspect for missing guide plates between steering knuckle ears.
   b. If missing, install new guide plates.
   c. Measure gap as previously described. If clearance is more than .028, proceed to next step.
4. If clearance is more than .028 inch, proceed as follows:
   a. Remove caliper.
   b. Break all four tabs off new guide plate (part No. F5CZ-2B164-AA). Ensure to break tabs off to bottom of bend relief holes.
   c. Install revised guide plate inside another new guide plate.
   d. Install guide plates over steering knuckle ear. Outer guide plate can be slightly bent inward to improve retention.
   e. Install another new guide plate on outer ear. This plate may also be bent as long as assembled dimension does not become less than .016 inch.
   f. Remove inner brake pads and shims.
   g. Clean shims and inner pad mating surfaces with suitable brake cleaner.
   h. Apply silicone brake caliper grease and dielectric compound (part No. D7AZ-19A331-A, or equivalent) to inner brake pad back. Grease should entirely cover shim/inner pad interface, but not bleed out excessively when shims are pressed to inner pad back.

i. Assemble caliper and inner pads/ shims.
j. Ensure gap is not less than .016 inch.

GRINDING NOISE, PULL AND/OR DRAG AND UNEVEN FONT BRAKE PAD WEAR

1998-99 Escort, Tracer & ZX2

A grinding noise, brake pull, brake drag and/or uneven front brake pad wear may occur on some vehicles. This may be caused by an accumulation of corrosion on the caliper slide pins. This condition will only occur in the "rust belt" areas or where high-levels of salt are used to melt roadway ice. To address this concern, remove corrosion from brake caliper slide bores, then replace guide pins, guide pin seals and front brake pads.

GROANING DURING CITY DRIVING

1998-99 Contour & Mystique & 1999 Cougar

On some of these models the front brakes may groan during city driving.

This condition may be caused by front brake pads' damping rate. To correct this condition, install revised pads (less pad wear warning, part No. XS8Z-2001-CA; with pad wear warning part, No. XS6Z-2001-DA).

SQUEALING OR MOANING/GROANING

1998 Continental

On some of these models, the front brakes may have a high frequency squealing or a moaning/groaning under moderate braking. This noise is not to be confused with intermittent squeals or groans during first few brake applications in morning or while braking in reverse.

This condition may be caused by high frequency response between the lining, caliper and rotor. To correct this condition, install revised front brake pads (part No. F3Z-2001-CB).

COMPOSITE ROTORS

Continental, Sable & Taurus

The disc rotor is a hat section-type of composite steel and cast iron. A Rotunda Rotor Mounting Adapter tool No. 054-00032, or equivalent, is required for use on the brake lathe for refinishing. **Failure to use the adapter will result in gouging the brake disc, making it unfit for use.**

A new design full-cast front disc brake rotor is now available for service use. If service is required, install the new full cast front disc rotors, part No. F10Y-1125-B **in pairs only. Never install a full cast rotor on one side of the vehicle with a composite rotor on the other side.**

IMPROVED BRAKE CALIPER SLIDE GREASE

When performing any disc brake service, lubricate all required components with silicone brake caliper grease and dielectric compound, part No. D7AZ-19A331-A, also known as Motorcraft WA-10. If this is not available, an equivalent meeting Ford specification ESE-M1C171-A should be used.

DISC BRAKE SPECIFICATIONS

Refer to "Rear Disc Brakes & Parking Brakes" for specification charts.

TIGHTENING SPECIFICATIONS

Year/ Model	Component	Torque/Ft. Lbs.
CONTINENTAL		
1998–2002	Brake Hose Bolts	16–44
	Front Brake Master Cylinder Tube Fitting	18
	Front Caliper Bleeder Screw	84①
	Locating Pins	18–25
	Rear Brake Master Cylinder Tube Fitting	13
	Rear Caliper Bleeder Screw	84①
	Wheel Caliper Bleeder Screw	71①
	Wheel Lug Nuts	65–88
COUGAR		
1999–2002	Brake Hose To Caliper Union	11
	Caliper To Knuckle Bolts	21
	Wheel Lug Nuts	94
CROWN VICTORIA, GRAND MARQUIS & TOWN CAR		
1998–2002	Brake Hose Bolts	16–44
	Locating Pins	40–60
	Wheel Lug Nuts	65–88
ESCORT, TRACER & ZX2		
1998–2002	Brake Hose Bolts	16–44
	Caliper Bolts	36–43
	Locating Pins	18–25
	Wheel Lug Nuts	74–100
FOCUS		
2000–02	Brake Hose To Caliper Union	11
	Caliper To Knuckle Bolts	21
	Wheel Lug Nuts	94
LS		
2000–02	Brake Hose Bolts	16–44
	Wheel Lug Nuts	100
MUSTANG		
1998–2002	Brake Hose Bolts	16–44
	Locating Pins	45–65
	Wheel Lug Nuts	85–105
SABLE & TAURUS		
1998–2002	Brake Hose Bolts	16–44
	Locating Pins	18–25
	Wheel Lug Nuts	85–104

① — Inch lbs.

Rear Disc & Parking Brakes

NOTE: On Air Bag Equipped Models, Refer To "Air Bag System Precautions" Located In The Front Of This Manual For System Disarming & Arming Procedures.

NOTE: Refer To "Computer Relearn Procedures" Located In The Front Of This Manual When Battery Power To The Computer Has Been Interrupted.

INDEX

PRECAUTIONS

AIR BAG SYSTEMS

Refer to "Air Bag System Precautions" in the front of this manual for system disarming and arming procedures.

BATTERY GROUND CABLE

Prior to service, disconnect battery ground cable and isolate as required.

SYSTEM DEPRESSURIZING

On models equipped with anti-lock brakes, hydraulic system must be depressurized prior to disconnecting any hydraulic lines or fittings, by pumping the brake pedal a minimum of 25 times with ignition in Off position.

DESCRIPTION

CONTINENTAL, COUGAR, LS, MARK VIII, MUSTANG, SABLE & TAURUS

Sliding caliper rear disc brakes are used on these models. The caliper is basically the same as the larger front wheel caliper. However, a parking brake mechanism and a larger inner brake shoe anti-rattle spring have been added.

The parking brake lever, located at the rear of the caliper, is actuated by a cable system similar to rear drum brake applications. When the parking brake is applied, the cable rotates the lever and operating shaft, driving the caliper piston and brake shoe assembly against the rotor. An automatic adjuster in the assembly compensates for lining wear and maintains proper clearance in the parking brake mechanism.

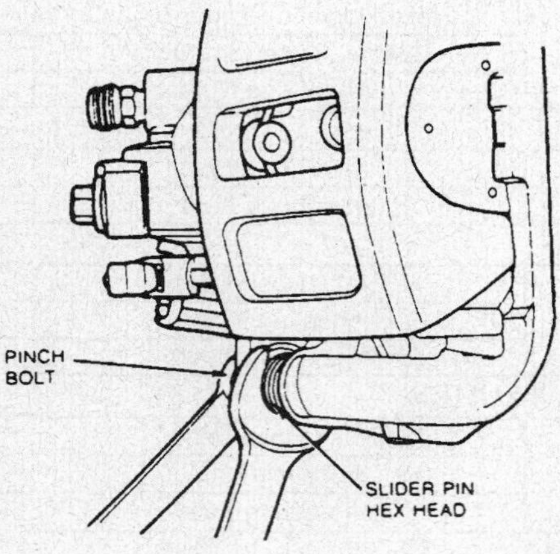

Fig. 1 Slider pin removal. Continental, Cougar, Mark VIII, Mustang, Sable & Taurus

The cast iron rotors are ventilated by curved fins located between the braking surfaces and are designed to cause the rotor to act as an air pump when the vehicle is traveling forward. The rotors are not interchangeable and are identified by a "Right or Left" marking cast inside the hat section of the rotor. The rotor is secured to the axle flange in the same manner as a rear brake drum. A splash shield is bolted to a forged axle adapter to protect the inboard rotor surface.

CONTOUR & MYSTIQUE

During normal operation, hydraulic pressure from the master cylinder pushes the piston, forward and applies pressure on the inboard brake pad. This pressure also causes the caliper to slide inward on the guide pins. As the brakes are applied, the square cut piston seal distorts. When the brake pedal is released, the square cut seal returns the piston to its normal position. If the piston moves no further than the square cut deformation limit, no self-adjustment takes place. If piston movement is greater than the deformation limit of the square cut seal, the piston and sleeve nut will travel on the threads of the spindle. When the brake pedal is released, the piston returns the amount the square cut seal was deformed but it does not return to its original position. The tightened adjuster spring does not allow the sleeve nut to rotate and travel on the thread. The piston can adjust outward from the caliper housing but it cannot move inward.

The parking brake cable is attached to the caliper at the operating lever. When the parking brake is applied, the operating lever pushes the connecting link against the piston which forces application of the brake pads. When the parking brake is released, pressure against the piston is released and the brake pads return to their normal position.

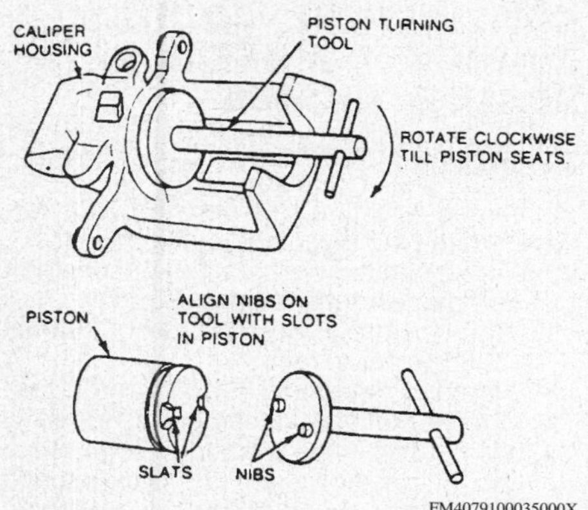

Fig. 2 Caliper piston seating. Continental, Cougar, Mark VIII, Mustang, Sable & Taurus

CROWN VICTORIA, GRAND MARQUIS & TOWN CAR

The rear disc brake system uses a pin slider-type caliper assembly, and a cast iron rotor bolted to the rear axle shaft flange. The caliper has a phenolic piston with a seal and a press-in type dust boot.

The inner pads are interchangeable left to right and use a three-finger clip fit inside the caliper piston. The outer pads are interchangeable left to right and use a dual-purpose clip which holds the brake pads on the caliper housing and also prevents caliper rattle.

The flanges on both inner and outer pads slide on a machined surfaces of the brake adapter.

ESCORT, TRACER & ZX2

The self-adjusting rear disc brake system consists of a disc rotor and a single piston caliper. The brake pads are held in position between the caliper and the rotor by two guides, two shims and an anti rattle spring. It is not required to remove the caliper completely to replace the brake pads; they can be removed simply by pivoting the caliper on its mounting bracket. **On some models it may be required to disconnect the parking brake cable to allow full caliper rotation.**

During normal operation, hydraulic pressure from the master cylinder pushes the piston forward and applies pressure on the inboard brake pad. This pressure also causes the caliper to slide inward on the guide pins. As the brakes are applied, the square cut piston seal distorts. When the brake pedal is released, The square cut seal returns the piston to its normal position. If the piston moves no further than the square cut deformation limit, no self-adjustment takes place. If piston movement is greater than the deformation limit of the square cut seal, the piston and sleeve nut will travel on the threads of the spindle. This is because the loosened adjuster spring allows the sleeve nut to rotate. When the brake pedal is released, the piston returns the amount the square cut seal was deformed but it does not return to its original position. This is because the tightened adjuster spring does not allow the sleeve nut to rotate and travel on the thread. The piston can adjust outward from the caliper housing but it cannot move inward.

The parking brake cable is attached to the caliper at the operating lever. When the parking brake is applied, the operating lever pushes the connecting link against the piston which forces application of the brake pads. When the parking brake is released, pressure against the piston is released and the brake pads return to their normal position.

TROUBLESHOOTING

BRAKE ROUGHNESS

If roughness or vibration is encountered during highway operation or if pedal pumping is experienced at low speeds, the disc may have excessive thickness variation. Measure the disc at 12 points with a micrometer at a radius approximately one inch from the edge of the disc. If thickness measurements vary by more than .0005 inch, replace the rotor.

Excessive lateral runout of braking disc may cause a "knocking back" of the pistons, possibly creating increased pedal travel and vibration when brakes are applied.

Adjust the wheel bearings before inspecting the runout. The readjustment is very important and will be required at the completion of the test to prevent bearing failure. Adjust the wheel bearings as outlined under "Front Suspension & Steering."

BRAKE SYSTEM BLEED

Pressure bleeding is recommended for all hydraulic disc brake systems.

Do not use brake fluid drained from the hydraulic system when bleeding the brakes. Ensure disc brake pistons are returned to their normal positions and the shoe and lining assemblies are properly seated. Before driving the vehicle, inspect the brake operation.

Do not shake the pressure bleeder tank while air is being added or after it has been pressurized. This will prevent air from the tank getting into the lines. Set the tank in the required location, then bring the air hose to the tank. Do not move the tank during the bleeding operation. The tank should be kept at least one third full.

On models equipped with power brakes, exhaust the vacuum in the power unit by pumping the brake pedal several times with the engine Off before starting to bleed the system.

On vehicles equipped with disc brakes and master cylinders without proportioners or pressure control valves located in the master cylinder outlet port, the brake metering valve or combination valve must be held in position using a suitable tool.

On vehicles equipped with plastic reservoirs, do not exceed 25 psi bleeding pressure.

When bleeding without pressure, open the bleed valve three quarters of a turn, depress the brake pedal a full stroke, then close the bleeder valve and allow the pedal to return slowly to its released position. Repeat as required until fluid is free of air bubbles.

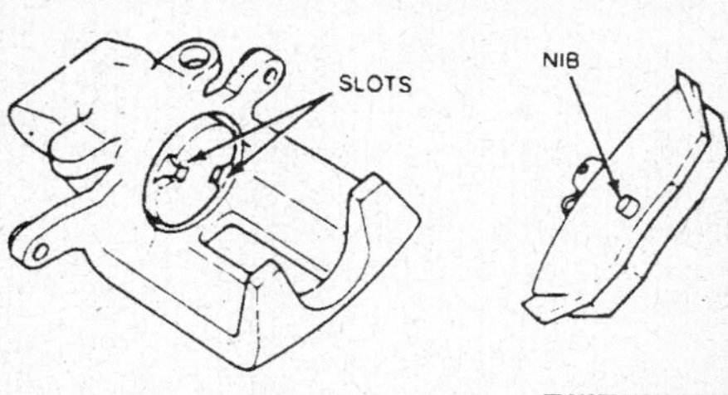

Fig. 3 Caliper piston to brake pad nib positioning. Continental, Cougar, Mark VIII, Mustang, Sable & Taurus

Discard drained or bled brake fluid. Brake fluid will damage painted finishes. Do not spill fluid on vehicle surfaces.

Flushing is essential if there is water, mineral oil or other contaminants in the lines, and whenever new components are installed in the hydraulic system. Fluid contamination is usually indicated by swollen and deteriorated cups and other rubber components.

Bleeding is required on all four wheels if air has entered the system because of low fluid level or the line or lines have been disconnected. If a line is disconnected at any one wheel cylinder, only that cylinder needs to be bled.

Master cylinders equipped with bleeder valves should be bled first before the wheel cylinders are bled. In all cases where a master cylinder has been overhauled, it must be bled. Where there is no bleeder valve, this can be done by leaving the lines loose, actuating the brake pedal to expel the air then tightening the lines.

After overhauling a dual master cylinder used in conjunction with disc brakes, air may be trapped between the master cylinder pistons. Bleed the cylinder before installing it on the vehicle.

SYSTEM PRIMING

When a new master cylinder is installed or the brake system is partially or completely emptied, fluid may not flow from the bleeder screws during normal bleeding. If required, prime the system using the following procedure:

1. Remove brake lines from master cylinder.
2. Install short brake lines in master cylinder and position them back into the reservoir. Ensure short brake line ends are submerged in reservoir brake fluid.
3. Fill reservoir with recommended brake fluid, then cover master cylinder fluid reservoir with shop towel.
4. Pump brakes until clear, bubble-free fluid comes out of both brake lines. **If any brake fluid spills on paint, wash it off immediately with water.**
5. Remove short brake lines, then reinstall original brake lines.
6. Bleed each brake line at master cylinder as follows:
   a. Have assistant pump brake pedal

10 times, then hold firm pressure on pedal.

b. Open rearmost brake line fittings with tubing wrench until stream of brake fluid comes out. Have assistant maintain pressure on brake pedal until brake line fitting is tightened.

c. Repeat until clear, bubble-free fluid comes out from around tube fitting.

d. Repeat bleeding operation at front brake line fitting.

7. If any of brake lines or calipers have been removed, it may be helpful to prime system by gravity bleeding. This should be done after master cylinder is primed and bled. To prime system using gravity method, use following procedure:

   a. Fill master cylinder with manufacturer's recommended brake fluid, or equivalent.

   b. Loosen both rear bleeder screws and leave open until clear brake fluid flows out. **Inspect reservoir fluid level frequently. Do not allow fluid level to drop below halfway.**

   c. Tighten rear bleeder screws.

   d. Loosen bleeder screw on front caliper and leave open until clear fluid flows out. **Bleed front calipers one side at a time.**

8. After master cylinder has been primed, lines bled at master cylinder and brake system primed, resume normal brake system bleeding at each wheel.

WHEEL BLEEDING SEQUENCE

Rear Wheel Drive.....RR-LR-RF-LF
Front Wheel Drive....RR-LF-LR-RF

INSPECTION

Remove wheels and inspect brake disc, calipers and linings. Inspect and repack wheel bearings if required.

If the caliper is cracked or fluid leakage through the casting is evident, it must be replaced as a unit.

If caliper was removed when installing new components, clean all components in alcohol, then wipe dry using lint-free cloths. Using an air hose, blow out drilled passages and bores. Inspect dust boots for punctures or tears. If punctures or tears are evident, install new boots during assembly.

Inspect piston bores in both housings for scoring or pitting. Bores showing light scratches or corrosion can usually be cleaned with crocus cloth. Bores with deep scratches or scoring may be honed, provided the diameter of the bore is not increased more than .002 inch. If the bore does not clean up within this specification, a new caliper housing should be installed. Black stains on the bore walls are caused by piston seals and will not adversely affect caliper performance.

When using a hone, install the hone baffle before honing the bore. The baffle is used to protect the hone stones from damage. Use extreme care in cleaning the caliper after honing. Remove all dust and grit

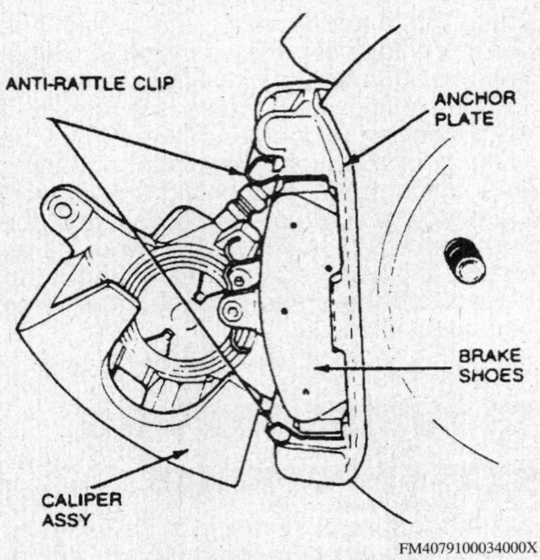

Fig. 4 Anti-rattle clip positioning. Continental, Cougar, Mark VIII, Mustang, Sable & Taurus

by flushing the caliper with alcohol. Wipe the caliper dry with a clean lint-free cloth, then repeat cleaning procedure.

BRAKE DISC SERVICE

Disc brake service is critical due to the close tolerances required in machining the brake disc to ensure proper brake operation.

Maintaining close control of the shape of the rubbing surfaces is required to prevent brake roughness. In addition, the surface finish must be non-directional and maintained at a micro-inch finish. This is required to avoid pulls and erratic performance and promote long lining life and equal lining wear of both the lefthand and righthand brakes.

Do not attempt to refinish the rubbing surfaces unless precision equipment, capable of measuring in micro inches (millionths of an inch) is available.

To inspect the disc lateral runout, mount a dial indicator on a convenient part, such as a steering knuckle, tie rod, or caliper housing, so the indicator's plunger contacts the disc one inch from the outer edge. If the total indicated runout exceeds specifications, install a new disc.

To inspect parallelism (thickness variation), mount dial indicators so the plunger contacts the rotor approximately one inch from the outer edge. If parallelism exceeds specifications, replace the rotor.

BRAKE PAD SERVICE

On models with anti-lock brakes, the brake system power booster must be depressurized before disconnecting any hydraulic lines or fittings. Depressurize the system by pumping the brake pedal a minimum of 25 times with the ignition in the Off position.

After performing any service work, obtain a firm brake pedal before moving the vehicle.

CONTINENTAL, COUGAR, MARK VIII, MUSTANG, SABLE & TAURUS

Removal

On models with air suspension, turn service switch Off before beginning repairs.

1. Raise and support rear of vehicle, then remove wheel and tire assembly.
2. Remove brake hose bracket to shock unit bracket screw.
3. Remove retaining clip, then disconnect parking brake cable from lever.
4. Using open end wrench to hold slider pin in position, remove upper pinch bolt, **Fig. 1.** Loosen, but do not lower, slider pin pinch bolt.
5. Carefully rotate caliper away from rotor, then remover inner and outer brake pads and anti-rattle springs from anchor plate.

Installation

1. Using rear caliper piston adjuster tool No. T87P-2588-A, or equivalent, rotate caliper piston clockwise until fully seated, **Fig. 2.** Position one of two piston slots so it will engage nib on rear of brake pad, **Fig. 3.**
2. Position inner and outer brake pads on anchor plate, then install anti-rattle springs.
3. Carefully rotate caliper assembly over brake rotor. Ensure brake pads and anti-rattle springs are properly positioned, **Fig. 4.**
4. Apply suitable thread sealer and locking compound to pinch bolt threads. Install and tighten pinch bolts to specification, while holding slider pin in position with suitable open end wrench.
5. Position parking brake cable to lever, then install retaining clip.
6. Position brake hose and bracket to shock unit bracket and install attaching bolt.
7. Install wheel and tire assembly, then lower vehicle.
8. **On models equipped with air suspension,** turn service switch On.
9. **On all models,** cycle brake pedal several times to position brake pads and caliper piston.

CONTOUR & MYSTIQUE

Removal

1. Remove a sufficient amount of fluid from brake fluid reservoir to prevent an overflow when retracting caliper pistons.
2. Raise and support vehicle.
3. Remove wheel and tire assemblies.
4. Remove guide pin, **Fig. 5.**
5. Remove caliper locating pin cover, then caliper locating pin.
6. Lift caliper from friction pads and anchor frame assembly.

Installation

1. Using rear caliper piston adjuster tool No. T87P-2588-A, or equivalent, rotate

caliper piston clockwise until fully seated, **Fig. 2.** Position one piston slot so it will engage nib on rear of brake pad, **Fig. 3.**
2. Ensure all locating pin, guide pin, caliper and anchor frame mounting and sliding surfaces are clean.
3. Place inner and outer pads into position on anchor frame.
4. Place caliper into position on anchor frame.
5. Apply a suitable thread lock compound to mounting threads of locating pin, then apply a suitable brake lubricant to sliding surface of locating pin.
6. Install and tighten locating pin to specifications.
7. Install guide pin, then lock into place with suitable cotter pin.
8. Install wheel and tire assemblies, lower vehicle, then tighten lug nuts to specifications.
9. Apply brake pedal and parking brake several times to adjust rear brakes, adjust parking brake cable if required as outlined under "Parking Brake Service."

CROWN VICTORIA, GRAND MARQUIS & TOWN CAR

Replacement

1. **On models equipped with air suspension,** turn service switch Off before beginning repairs.
2. **On all models,** remove master cylinder cap and inspect fluid level in reservoir. Remove brake fluid until reservoir is half full.
3. Raise and support vehicle, then remove wheel and tire assembly.
4. Remove caliper as previously described.
5. Remove inner and outer brake linings.
6. Inspect both rotor braking surfaces. Minor scoring or buildup of lining material does not require machining or replacement of the rotor assembly. Hand sand glaze from both rotor braking surfaces using garnet paper 100-A (medium grit) or aluminum oxide 150-J (medium).
7. Suspend caliper inside fender housing with wire or tie straps. Use care not to damage caliper or stretch brake hose.
8. **Use care to prevent damaging plastic piston. Metal or sharp objects should not come in direct contact with piston surface or damage will result.** Using a suitable C-clamp and wood block approximately 2¾ inch x 1 inch and at least ¾ inch thick, seat caliper piston in piston bore. **This procedure must be done to provide clearance for caliper assembly to fit over rotor.**
9. Remove all rust buildup from inside of caliper legs (outer shoe contact area).
10. Install inner shoe and lining assembly in caliper piston(s). Do not bend shoe clips during installation in piston or distortion and rattles may occur.
11. Install outer pad in caliper assembly. Ensure clips are properly seated.
12. Install caliper assembly as previously described.

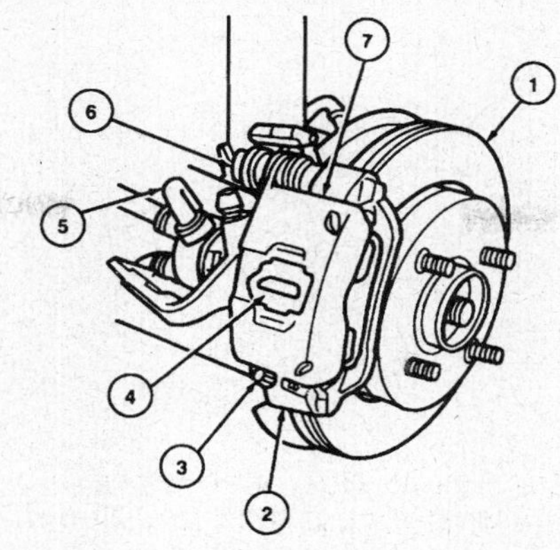

Item		Description
1		Rear Disc Brake Rotor
2		Rear Disc Brake Caliper Anchor Plate
3		Guide Pin
4		Anti-Rattle Clip
5		Parking Brake Lever
6		Disc Brake Caliper Locating Pin
7		Rear Disc Brake Caliper

FM4079300071000X

Fig. 5 Brake pad replacement. Contour & Mystique

13. Install wheels, and lower vehicle.
14. **On models equipped with air suspension,** turn service switch On.

ESCORT, TRACER & ZX2

Removal

1. Remove approximately two thirds of brake fluid from master cylinder.
2. Raise and support vehicle, then remove wheel and tire assembly.
3. Loosen parking brake cable housing adjusting nut, then remove cable housing from bracket and parking lever.
4. Turn brake adjuster screw counterclockwise with suitable Allen wrench to pull caliper piston inward, **Fig. 6.** Turn brake adjuster screw until it stops, this will fully retract caliper piston.
5. Remove lower caliper retaining bolt, then pivot caliper to clear brake pads. If required, pry caliper outward, **Fig. 7.**
6. If required remove caliper, then support caliper with wire from strut assembly.
7. Remove anti-rattle springs from disc pads, then the disc pads, anti-rattle shims and retaining clips. If disc pads and anti-rattle shims are to be used again, they must be installed in their original positions, **Figs. 8.**
8. If required, remove and resurface rotor at this time. **Rotor must be machined while it is bolted to hub. Rotor and hub are mounted as an assembly on lathe to decrease possibility of rotor runout.**

Installation

1. Install disc pad retaining clips, then position anti-rattle shims on disc pads.
2. Position disc pads into caliper anchor bracket.
3. Install anti-rattle springs into disc pads.
4. Lubricate guide pin bushings with high temperature grease part No. D7AZ-19590-A, or equivalent.
5. Install caliper on guide pin if caliper was removed, then pivot caliper over brake disc pads.
6. Install caliper retaining bolt, then tighten to specifications.
7. Bleed brake system.
8. Position parking brake cable into parking brake lever and bracket.
9. Adjust parking brake cable so there is no clearance between cable end and parking brake lever.
10. Tighten parking brake cable locknut to specification.
11. Install wheel and tire assembly.

LS & THUNDERBIRD

1. Raise and support vehicle, then remove wheel and tire assembly.
2. Remove mounting bolts and caliper. **Do not allow caliper to hang from brake hose.**
3. Remove brake pads.
4. Measure brake disc and resurface as required. **Use hub-mount brake lathe if required to machine brake disc.** Install new brake disc if beyond specification.
5. Compress disc brake piston and adjuster into the disc brake caliper using rear caliper piston adjuster tool No. T87P-2588-A, or equivalent.
6. Reverse procedure to install.

CALIPER SERVICE

REPLACEMENT

CONTINENTAL, COUGAR, MARK VIII, MUSTANG, SABLE & TAURUS

Removal

1. Raise and support rear of vehicle, then remove wheel and tire assembly.
2. Disconnect brake hose from caliper assembly.
3. Remove retaining clip, then disconnect parking brake cable from lever arm.
4. Using open end wrench to hold slider pin in position, remove pinch bolts, **Fig. 1.**
5. Lift caliper assembly from anchor plate, then remove slider pins and boots.

Installation

1. Apply suitable silicone dielectric compound to slider pins and inside of boots.
2. Place slider pins and boots on anchor plate, then position caliper assembly on anchor plate. Ensure brake pads and anti-rattle springs are properly positioned, **Fig. 4.**
3. Apply suitable sealer and thread locking compound to pinch bolt threads, then install pinch bolts.
4. Using open end wrench to hold slider pin in position, tighten pinch bolts to specifications.

5. Attach parking brake cable to lever arm, then install retaining clip.
6. Using replacement washers, connect brake hose to caliper. Tighten retaining bolt to specifications.
7. Bleed brake system as outlined under "Brake System Bleed," then install wheel and tire assembly.
8. Cycle brake pedal several times to position brake pads and caliper piston.

CONTOUR & MYSTIQUE

Removal

1. Raise and support vehicle.
2. Remove wheel and tire assemblies.
3. Disconnect and remove parking brake cable from caliper.
4. Remove brake hose banjo bolt, discard sealing washers.
5. Remove guide pin, **Fig. 5.**
6. Remove caliper locating pin cover, then caliper locating pin.
7. Lift caliper from friction pads and anchor frame assembly.

Installation

1. Using rear caliper piston adjuster tool No. T87P-2588-A, or equivalent, position one piston slot so it will engage nib on rear of brake pad, **Fig. 3.**
2. Ensure all locating pin, guide pin, caliper and anchor frame mounting and sliding surfaces are clean and free of residues.
3. Place inner and outer pads into position on anchor frame.
4. Place caliper into position on anchor frame.
5. Apply a suitable thread lock compound to mounting threads of locating pin, then apply a suitable brake lubricant to sliding surface of locating pin.
6. Install and tighten locating pin to specifications.
7. Install guide pin, lock into place with suitable cotter pin.
8. Install parking brake cable.
9. Install brake hose using new sealing washers, then bleed brakes as outlined under "Brake System Bleed."
10. Install wheel and tire assemblies, lower vehicle, then tighten lug nuts to specifications.
11. Apply brake pedal and parking brake several times to adjust rear brakes, adjust parking brake cable if required as outlined under "Parking Brake Service."

CROWN VICTORIA, GRAND MARQUIS & TOWN CAR

Visually inspect caliper. If the caliper housing is leaking, it should be replaced. If a seal is leaking, the caliper must be disassembled and new seals and dust boot installed. If a piston is seized in the bore, replace caliper. Care must be taken when removing plastic piston.

Removal

1. **On models equipped with air suspension,** turn service switch Off before beginning repairs.
2. **On all models,** raise and support vehicle, then remove wheel and tire assembly.

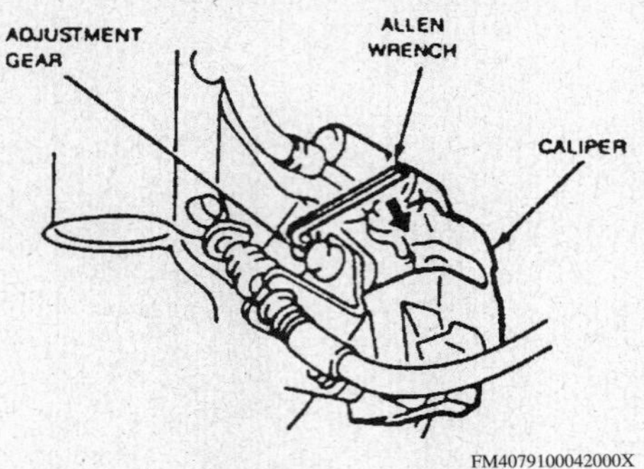

Fig. 6 Rear disc brake adjustment gear location. Escort, Tracer & ZX2

3. Remove flexible brake hose retaining bolt from caliper, then plug hose and caliper fitting.
4. Using Tore drive bit tool No. D79P-2100-T40, or equivalent, remove caliper locating pins.
5. Lift caliper off rotor and anchor plate using rotating motion. **Do not pry directly against plastic piston or piston damage will result.**

Installation

1. Retract piston fully into piston bore and position caliper assembly above rotor with anti-rattle spring located on lower adapter support arm.
2. Install caliper over rotor with rotating motion. Ensure inner shoe is properly positioned.
3. Install caliper locating pins. **Caliper locating pins must be inserted and started by hand.**
4. Tighten locating pins to specifications.
5. Remove plugs from caliper fittings, then install flexible brake hose on caliper with new gasket on each side of fitting outlet.
6. Insert retaining bolt through washers and fittings. Tighten bolt to specifications.
7. Bleed brake system as outlined under "Brake System Bleed."
8. Pump brake pedal to position brake linings before moving vehicle.
9. **On models equipped with air suspension,** turn service switch On.

ESCORT, TRACER & ZX2

Removal

1. Remove wheel and tire assembly, then the brake pads as outlined under "Brake Pad Service."
2. Remove brake flex hose clip from strut assembly bracket.
3. Remove brake flex hose to caliper banjo bolt.
4. Remove and discard two copper washers sealing flex hose banjo fitting.
5. Remove lower caliper bolt.
6. Using cold chisel, remove upper caliper guide pin dust cap to gain access to Allen head guide pin.
7. Using Allen wrench, loosen and remove upper caliper guide pin.
8. Lift caliper off rotor.

Installation

Before installation, remove upper and lower guide pin bushings and lubricate with high temperature grease D7AZ-19590-A, or equivalent.

1. Install brake pads and shims as outlined under "Brake Pad Service."
2. Position caliper over rotor, then install caliper retaining bolts and tighten to specifications.
3. Install two new copper washers, then the banjo bolt on flex hose banjo fitting.
4. Position flex hose on caliper and install banjo bolt. Tighten bolt to specifications.
5. Bleed brake system as outlined under "Brake System Bleed," then install wheel and tire assembly.

LS & THUNDERBIRD

1. Raise and support vehicle, then remove wheel and tire assembly.
2. Disengage parking brake cable end from parking brake lever arm.
3. Remove parking brake cable and conduit.
4. Remove caliper bolts, caliper flow bolt and caliper.
5. Discard copper washers.
6. Reverse procedure to install using new copper washers.
7. Bleed brake system as previously described.

OVERHAUL

CONTINENTAL, COUGAR, MARK VIII, MUSTANG, SABLE & TAURUS

Disassemble

1. Remove caliper assembly from vehicle as described previously.
2. Position caliper assembly in soft-jawed vise.
3. Using tool No. T75P-2588-B, or equivalent, rotate caliper piston counterclockwise to remove from caliper bore, **Fig. 2.**
4. Remove piston dust boot and seal from caliper piston bore.
5. Remove snap ring retaining pushrod to caliper. Use care when removing, snap ring and spring cover are under spring load.
6. Remove spring cover, spring, washer, key plate and pushrod and strut pin from caliper.
7. Remove O-ring from pushrod.
8. Remove parking brake lever return spring, then the brake lever stop bolt and pull lever from caliper.

Cleaning & Inspection

1. Clean all metal components with isopropyl alcohol.
2. Use compressed air to clean out passages and grooves.
3. Inspect caliper bore for damage and excessive wear.
4. Inspect caliper piston for pitting, scoring or worn plating and replace as required.

Assemble

1. Apply light coating of silicone dielectric compound to parking brake lever bore and parking brake lever seal, then position seal into caliper bore.
2. Apply silicone dielectric compound to parking brake lever shaft, then insert shaft into caliper housing bore.
3. Install O-ring into groove on pushrod, then apply silicone dielectric compound to recesses in pushrod.
4. Place strut pin into caliper housing and into recess of parking brake lever shaft.
5. Position pushrod into caliper housing bore, ensure strut pin is properly located between shaft recesses and recess at end of pushrod.
6. Position key plate over pushrod, so washer nib is located in hole in caliper housing.
7. Install flat washer, spring and spring cage into caliper bore.
8. Install snap ring using rear caliper spring compressor set No. T87P-2588-P, or equivalent. Ensure snap ring is properly seated in recess.
9. Lubricate replacement piston seal with clean brake fluid, then install seal into caliper bore groove.
10. Lubricate piston and dust boot with clean brake fluid, then install dust boot into caliper bore.
11. Position piston into dust boot, seating dust boot in piston groove.
12. Using rear caliper spring compressor set No. T75P-2588-B, or equivalent, turn piston in clockwise direction until piston is fully seated in caliper bore, **Fig. 2.**
13. Position one of two slots on piston so it will engage nib on rear of disc pad when caliper is installed, **Fig. 3.**
14. Install caliper assembly as described previously.

CONTOUR & MYSTIQUE

Disassemble

1. Remove caliper as described previously, then drain fluid from caliper.
2. Using rear caliper piston adjuster tool No. T87P-2588-A, or equivalent, rotate caliper piston counterclockwise to remove piston and adjuster from caliper and adjuster spindle, **Fig. 2.**
3. Remove and discard caliper piston dust seal and piston seal.
4. Remove bleeder screw, then locating pin, pin dust seals and bushings.
5. Cut tie-wrap, then remove cover and dust seals from parking brake actuator.
6. Mount caliper in a suitable vice with soft jaws, positioned to access parking brake actuator.
7. Compress actuator spring, then remove parking brake actuator arm and cam.
8. Remove cup washer and adjuster springs from adjuster spindle, note position of components for later assembly.
9. Remove adjuster spindle and seal from caliper, then remove seal from spindle.

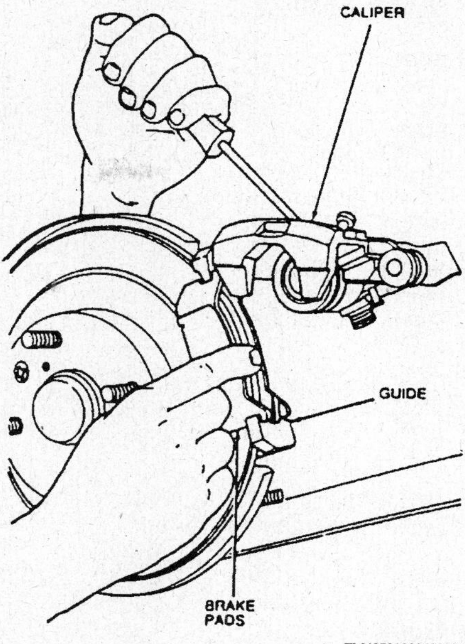

Fig. 7 Rear caliper rotating into position for brake pad replacement. Escort, Tracer & ZX2

Cleaning & Inspection

1. Clean all metal components with isopropyl alcohol.
2. Use compressed air to clean out passages and grooves.
3. Inspect caliper bore for damage and excessive wear.
4. Inspect parking brake and adjuster components for damage and excessive wear.
5. Inspect caliper piston for pitting, scoring or worn plating and replace as required.

Assemble

1. Position caliper housing in a suitable vice with soft jaws.
2. Install a new seal to adjuster spindle, then install spindle into caliper.
3. Install adjuster springs and cup washer onto spindle in order of disassembly.
4. Compress cup washer and spring, then install parking brake actuator cam and arm.
5. Install parking brake actuator dust boot and cover, and secure with a suitable tie-wrap.
6. Replace any removed locating pin, bushings and seals, then lubricate with a suitable brake grease.
7. Install bleeder screw.
8. Install new caliper piston seal into groove, lubricate with clean brake fluid.
9. Install new piston dust seal onto piston, then pack seal with a suitable disc brake slide grease. Lubricate piston surfaces with clean brake fluid.
10. Using rear caliper piston adjuster tool No. T87P-2588-A, or equivalent, rotate caliper piston clockwise to install piston into caliper and onto adjuster spindle.
11. Seat piston dust seal into caliper.
12. Install caliper into vehicle as described previously.

CROWN VICTORIA, GRAND MARQUIS & TOWN CAR

Visually inspect caliper. If the caliper housing is leaking, it should be replaced. If a seal is leaking, the caliper must be disassembled and new seals and dust boot installed. If a piston is seized in the bore, replace the caliper. Care must be taken when removing the plastic piston.

Disassemble

On models with air suspension, turn service switch Off before beginning repairs.

1. Remove caliper from caliper mounting bracket.
2. Remove outer pad by slipping down caliper leg until clip is disengaged, then inner pad by pulling it straight out of piston.
3. Place shop towels between the caliper piston and caliper bridge. Do not place fingers between these areas. Two methods can be used to remove the piston from the caliper bore: one method is using low volume air pressure, the other is with hydraulic pressure. If air pressure is not available, slowly apply brake pedal until caliper piston is forced from bore. This method can only be done one caliper at a time. If air pressure is to be used, use following procedure:
   a. Disconnect flexible hose from caliper assembly, then remove caliper from vehicle.
   b. Using air nozzle, apply light air pressure to brake hose inlet until piston is free from caliper. **Do not use shop pressure if it cannot be adjusted down to a safe level (15–30 psi), or personal injury**

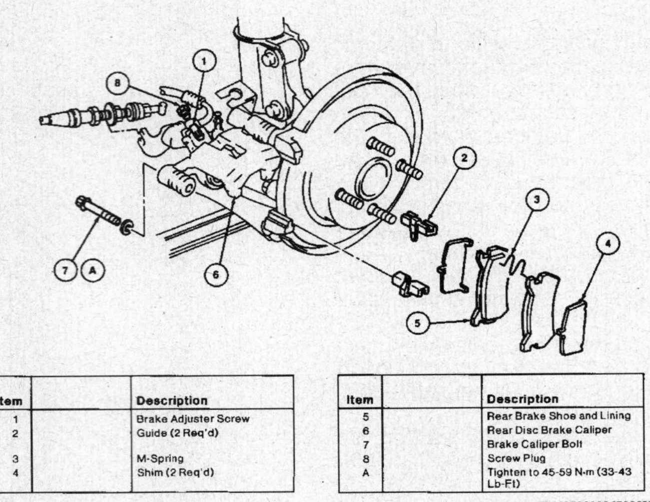

Item		Description
1		Brake Adjuster Screw
2		Guide (2 Req'd)
3		M-Spring
4		Shim (2 Req'd)

Item		Description
5		Rear Brake Shoe and Lining
6		Rear Disc Brake Caliper
7		Brake Caliper Bolt
8		Screw Plug
A		Tighten to 45-59 N·m (33-43 Lb-Ft)

FM4079300067000X

Fig. 8 Rear brake pad replacement. Escort, Tracer & ZX2

and/or damage to components could result.

4. Remove seal and dust boot from caliper assembly.

Cleaning & Inspection

Clean all metal components with Isopropyl alcohol. Dry grooves and passageways with compressed air. Ensure caliper bore and component components are cleaned thoroughly. Inspect cylinder bore and piston for damage or excessive wear.

Examine piston for surface irregularities or small chips and cracks. Minor surface imperfections are allowable, provided they do not enter the dust boot groove area. Replace piston if damaged.

Assemble

1. Coat new seal and dust boot with clean brake fluid, then install in caliper assembly.
2. Coat piston with clean brake fluid, then place piston in caliper assembly and push firmly into caliper bore.
3. With piston seated, completely seat piston using a suitable C-clamp and a block of wood approximately 2¾ inch x 1 inch x ¾ inch thick.
4. Ensure dust boot is tight in boot groove on piston and in caliper.
5. Install brake pads as outlined under "Brake Pad Service," then the caliper assembly.

ESCORT, TRACER & ZX2

Disassemble

1. Remove caliper as previously described.
2. Open bleeder screw and drain brake fluid from caliper through brake flex hose fitting. After draining fluid, close bleeder screw.
3. Remove caliper guide bushing and dust boots.
4. Pry retaining spring off dust boot with screwdriver, then remove piston.
5. Remove and discard dust boot.
6. Remove piston seal from caliper and discard. **Use plastic or wooden pick to remove seal. Metal tools can scratch or nick seal groove, resulting in a possible seal leak.**
7. Remove stopper snap ring.
8. Remove adjusting spindle, stopper and connecting link. Separate adjuster spindle and stopper.
9. Remove Oaring from adjuster spindle, then discard Oaring.
10. Remove parking brake return spring, then operating lever nut and lockjaws.
11. Mark relationship between operating lever and shaft, then remove lever from shaft.
12. Remove seal from caliper housing.
13. Remove shaft from caliper housing, then the needle bearings.

Inspection

1. Inspect caliper bore, piston seal groove and piston for cuts, deep scratches and pitting. Piston and piston bore may be lightly polished with crocus cloth. If deep scratches cannot be removed, replace caliper assembly.
2. Caliper seal groove must be free of deep scratches which would prevent seal from operating properly.
3. Inspect upper guide pin and lower guide pin bushing for wear.
4. Inspect bushing dust boots for damage or poor sealing.

Assemble

1. Lubricate needle bearings with orange grease included in caliper rebuilding kit part No. FOJY-2221-A.
2. Align opening in bearing with bore in caliper housing, then install needle bearings.
3. Install operating shaft into caliper housing.
4. Install operating lever. Align marks made during removal.
5. Install lockjaws nut.
6. Install connecting link into operating shaft.
7. Install O-ring onto adjuster spindle, then position stopper onto adjuster spindle so pin will align with caliper housing.
8. Install adjuster spindle in caliper by aligning adjuster spindle pins with caliper holes.
9. Install parking brake return spring.
10. Lubricate new piston seal with brake fluid and install in caliper groove, then lubricate caliper bore and caliper piston with brake fluid.
11. Install dust boot in caliper bore.
12. Install piston in caliper bore by rotating piston until seated.
13. Install upper guide pin dust boot, then the lower guide pin bushing dust boot.
14. Install caliper upper guide pin, then the lower guide pin bushing.
15. Install caliper as outlined under "Caliper Service."

LS & THUNDERBIRD

1. Remove brake caliper as previously described.
2. Drain brake fluid from caliper.
3. Secure brake caliper in suitable vise.
4. Turn brake piston counterclockwise with rear caliper piston adjuster tool No. T87P-2588-A, or equivalent.
5. Remove brake piston from caliper bore.
6. Remove and discard piston dust boot and piston seal from caliper bore.
7. Reverse procedure to assemble, noting the following:
   a. Install new seals and dust boots.
   b. Use new brake fluid when assembling and bleeding the brake system.

ROTOR

REPLACE

CONTINENTAL, COUGAR, MARK VIII, MUSTANG, SABLE & TAURUS

Removal

1. Remove rear disc brake caliper assembly as outlined under "Caliper Service." Do not disconnect flexible hose unless caliper requires service. Support caliper with wire or tie strap so flexible hose is not stretched or twisted.
2. Remove rear disc support bracket to wheel knuckle bolts, then the rear disc support bracket and brake shoes and linings.
3. Remove two nuts, then the rotor from rear hub.

Installation

1. If installing new rotor, remove protective coating from rotor with suitable carburetor cleaner.
2. Lubricate rear hub pilot diameter with suitable grease.
3. Install rotors on axle shaft flange, then the two nuts.
4. Install inner and outer brake shoes and linings in rear disc support bracket.
5. Install rear disc support bracket as follows:

a. Clean rear disc support bracket and bolt threads, then add one drop of suitable sealer to each bolt.
b. Install caliper/rear support bracket assembly to rear wheel knuckle.
c. Install bolts, then tighten to specifications.
6. Install inner and outer brake shoes and linings as outlined under "Brake Pad Service."
7. Install rear disc brake caliper as outlined under "Caliper Service."

CONTOUR & MYSTIQUE

1. Remove caliper and friction pads as outlined under "Brake Pad Service."
2. Remove two bolts retaining caliper anchor frame, then the frame.
3. Remove rotor to hub retainers, then the rotor.
4. Reverse procedures to install, noting the following:
   a. Ensure rotor and mounting surfaces are clean and free of rust, fluids and Protestants.
   b. Lubricate hub pilot boss with a suitable brake grease.
   c. Tighten fasteners to specification.

ESCORT, TRACER & ZX2

1. Raise and support vehicle, then remove wheel and tire assembly.
2. Remove rear brake shoe and lining as outlined under "Brake Pad Service."
3. Remove two rear disc brake rotor screws.
4. Using screwdriver, pivot rear disc brake caliper on rear disc support bracket and remove rotor.
5. Reverse procedure to install.

CROWN VICTORIA, GRAND MARQUIS & TOWN CAR

Removal

1. Raise and support vehicle, then remove wheel and tire assembly.
2. Remove rear disc brake caliper assembly as outlined under "Caliper Service." Do not disconnect flexible hose unless caliper requires service. Position caliper aside and support wire or tie strap to avoid damaging caliper.
3. Remove rotor push nuts, then the disc brake rotor. If additional force is required, use following procedure:
   a. Apply rust penetrant and inhibitor part No. D7AZ-19A501-AA or equivalent to rotor/flange mating surface.
   b. Install three-jaw puller tool No. D80L-1013-A, or equivalent, then remove rear disc brake rotor. **If excessive force is required to remove rotor, it should be inspected for lateral runout prior to installation.**

Installation

1. If installing new rotor, remove protective coating with suitable carburetor cleaner. If installing original rotor, ensure rotor braking and mounting surfaces are clean.
2. Install rotor and push nuts.
3. Install caliper as outlined under "Caliper Service."
4. Install wheel and tire assembly, then lower vehicle and tighten wheel hub bolt nuts to specifications.
5. Pump brake pedal to position brake shoes and linings before moving vehicle and road testing.

LS & THUNDERBIRD

1. Remove support bracket.
2. Remove and discard the pushups, if equipped.
3. Remove brake disc.
4. Reverse procedure to install.

PARKING BRAKE SERVICE

PARKING BRAKE LININGS, REPLACE

CROWN VICTORIA, GRAND MARQUIS & TOWN CAR

1. Remove tire and wheel assembly.
2. Remove brake rotor.
3. Remove brake shoe adjusting screw spring, then the brake shoe adjusting screw.
4. Remove brake shoe hold down springs.
5. Remove parking bake shoe and linings.
6. Reverse procedure to install noting the following:
   a. Lubricate brake shoe contact point before installation with silicone brake caliper grease and dielectric compound part No. D7AZ-19A331-A or equivalent.
   b. Use a brake adjusting gauge to set the rear brake shoe and lining diameter to .020 inch less than the inside diameter of drum portion of rear brake.
   c. Adjust parking brake cable tension.

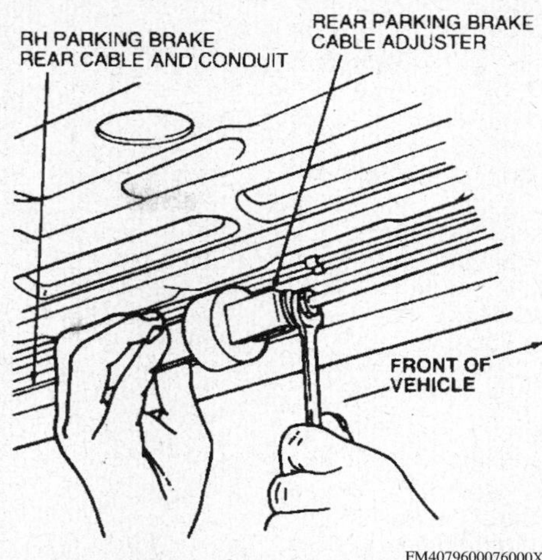

Fig. 9 Park brake adjustment. Sable & Taurus

ADJUSTMENTS

PARKING BRAKE

Cougar, Crown Victoria, Grand Marquis & Town Car

1. Apply parking brake control fully with 100 lbs., foot pedal effort, then release brake control.
2. Place transmission in Neutral, then raise and support vehicle.
3. With parking brake control in Off position, grasp pensioner around housing. Using an hook tool place end into rounded end of clip between clip and housing. Unlock clip by pulling downward with tool and support pensioner.
4. The pensioner spring will take up cable slack and reload cables, while holding pensioner, lock clip by pushing up on bottom of clip. If clip does not slide up move assembly slightly to align closest groove on adjuster rod to clip.
5. Examine pensioner for remaining cable take up capability. If none is present, inspect all cables, parking brake control and brackets for possible damage or deflection.

Continental & Mark VIII

1. Fully release parking brake control, then raise and support vehicle.
2. Pull parking brake cable adjuster clip downward. The pensioner spring will take up cable slack and reload the cables.
3. Push up on bottom of clip to lock adjustment. If clip does not slide up, move assembly slightly to align closest groove on parking brake cable adjuster rod with clip.
4. Apply 157 lbs. of force to parking brake control, apply force for 20 minutes.
5. Repeat steps 2 and 3, then lower vehicle and verify operation of parking brake.

Contour & Mystique

The parking brake is self-adjusting. After brake system service, operate parking brake several times to adjust system.

Escort, Tracer & ZX2

1. Start engine and shift into Reverse position.
2. With vehicle moving in Reverse, depress brake pedal several times.
3. Shift into Park position, then stop engine.
4. Remove parking brake console.
5. Turn adjusting nut until parking brake lever stroke is five to seven notches when pulled with force of 22 lbs.
6. Install parking brake console.

Sable & Taurus

1. Ensure parking brake control is fully released, then raise and support vehicle.
2. Using Rotunda cable tension gauge tool No. 014–R1056, or equivalent, tighten adjusting nut against rear parking brake cable adjuster until cable tension is 34–46 lbs., **Fig. 9.**
3. Apply parking brake control fully, then release.
4. Verify cable tension is still within specification and their is no drag on rear brakes.
5. Lower vehicle and verify operation of parking brake.

Mustang

If any parking brake system component requires service or if the rear axle housing is removed, the cable tension must be released as follows:

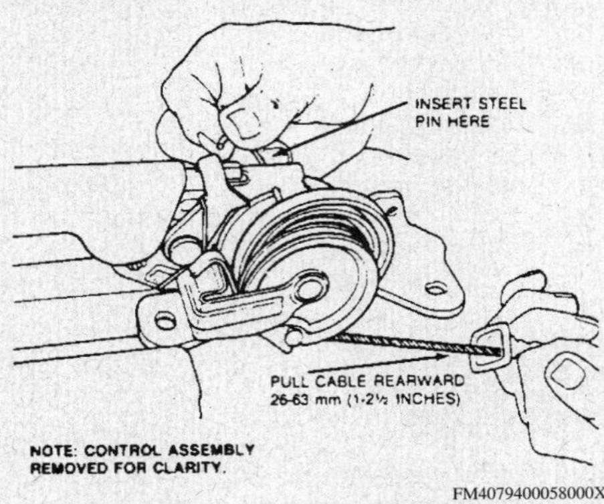

Fig. 10 Self-adjuster reel rotation. Mustang

1. Place parking brake control in released position.
2. Remove console top panel as follows:
   a. Carefully pry finish panel up from retaining clips, then disconnect electrical connectors.
3. Raise and support vehicle with assistant inside.
4. Have another assistant pull parking brake cable and equalizer rearward approximately 1–2 ½ inches, **Fig. 10,** to rotate self-adjuster reel backward.
5. Insert steel locking through holes in lever and parking brake control assembly to lock ratchet wheel in cable-released position. **Do not remove steel locking until rear cable and conduit are connected to parking brake cable and equalizer. Pin removal releases the tension in the ratchet wheel, causing spring to unwind and release tension. If pin is removed without rear cable and conduit attached, entire assembly must be removed to reset spring tension.**

DISC BRAKE SPECIFICATIONS

ROTOR SPECIFICATIONS

Model	Year	Front Disc Brake						Rear Disc Brake					
			Rotor						Rotor				
		Brake Lining Wear Limit, Inch①	Thickness, Inch			Thickness Variation Parallelism Inch	Lateral Run Out (T.I.R.) Inch	Brake Lining Wear Limit, Inch②	Thickness, Inch			Thickness Variation Parallelism Inch	Lateral Run-Out (T.I.R.) Inch
			Nominal	Min. Refinish	Discard Limit③				Nominal	Min. Refinish	Discard Limit③		
Continental	1998–2002	.039	1.024	—	.974	.00035	.0030	.039	.550	—	.502	.00040	.004
Contour & Mystique	1998–2000	.125	.950	—	.870	.00060	.0060	.125	.790	—	.710	.00060	.006
Cougar	1999–2002	—	.950	—	.870	.00060	.0030	—	.790	—	.710	.00060	.003
Crown Victoria & Grand Marquis	1998	.039	1.100	—	1.010	.00035	.0020	.039	.550	—	.510	.00040	.002
	1999–2002	.039	1.120	—	1.030	.00035	.0020	.039	.560	—	.520	—	.002
Escort, Tracer & ZX2	1998–2002	.080	.870	.820	.790	—	.0020	.040	.350	—	.280	—	.002
Focus	2000–02	.059	.870	—	.790	.00080	.0020	—	—	—	—	—	—
LS	2000–02	.079	1.181	—	1.120	.00040	.0040	.039	.787	—	.740	.00040	.004
Mark VIII	1998	.039	1.024	—	.974	.00035	.0030	.039	—	—	.657	.00035	.003
Mustang	1998	.040	1.030	—	.970	.00040	.0014	.040	.550	—	.500	.00030	.002
	1999–2002	.080	1.063	—	1.010	.00035	.0020	.039	.550	—	.510	.00040	.002
Sable & Taurus	1998–99	.039	1.020	—	.974	.00040	.0024	.039	.550	—	.500	.00040	.0004
	2000–02	.039	1.063	—	1.010	.00040	.0020	.039	.550	—	.502	.00040	.004
Thunderbird	2002	.040	1.120	1.030	1.010	.00035	.0020	.039	.560	—	.510	—	.003
Town Car	1998	.039	1.063	—	1.010	.00035	.0020	.039	.550	—	.510	.00040	.002
	1999–2002	.039	1.120	—	1.010	.00035	.0020	.039	.560	—	.520	—	.002

① — With 16 inch wheels.

② — Above rivet head or backing plate. Original equipment type brake lining.

③ — Discard thickness is stamped on rotor.

CALIPER SPECIFICATIONS

Model	Year	Caliper Bore Diameter Inch
FRONT		
Continental	1998–2002	③
Contour & Mystique	1998–2000	2.360
Cougar	1999–2002	③
Crown Victoria & Grand Marquis	1998	1.89
	1999–2002	③
Escort, Tracer & ZX2	1998–2002	2.120③
Focus	2000–02	③
LS	2000	②
	2001–02	③
Mark VIII	1998	2.598
Mustang	1998–2000	①
	2001–02	③
Sable & Taurus	1998–2000	2.598
	2001–02	③
Thunderbird	2002	③
Town Car	1998	2.599
	1999–2002	③
REAR		
Continental	1998–2000	1.690
	2001–02	③
Contour & Mystique	1998	1.420
	1999–2000	1.69
Cougar	1999–2002	③
Crown Victoria & Grand Marquis	1998–2000	1.890
	2001–02	③
Escort, Tracer & ZX2	1998–2002	1.190③
LS	2000–02	③
Mark VIII	1998	1.790
Mustang	1998–2000	1.500
	2001–02	③
Sable & Taurus	1998–2000	1.690
	2001–02	③
Thunderbird	2002	③
Town Car	1998–2002	③

① — Except Mustang Cobra, 2.60 inches; Mustang Cobra w/dual pistons, 1.50 inches.
② — One piston is 1.492 inches; the other is 1.772 inches.
③ — It is required to replace brake caliper if scoring or damage to caliper cylinder. Do not hone cylinder.

TIGHTENING SPECIFICATIONS

Year/ Model	Component	Torque/Ft. Lbs.
CONTINENTAL		
1998–2002	Anchor Plate Bolt	64–88
	Brake Adapter Retaining Bolt	44–60
	Brake Hose Bracket To Shock	8–11
	Brake Hose To Caliper (Banjo) Bolt	30–40
	Brake Pin Retaining Bolt	23–26
	Disc Brake Caliper Bolts	23–28
	Disc Brake Shield	80–106①
	Rear Caliper Bleeder Screw	12–18
CONTOUR & MYSTIQUE		
1998–2000	Anchor Plate Bolts	43
	Brake Hose To Caliper (Banjo) Bolt	17–21
	Caliper Retaining Bolts	20
	Disc Brake Shield	60–84①
	Wheel Lug	62
COUGAR		
1999–2002	Anchor Plate Bolts	89
	Backing Plate Bolts	37
	Caliper Brake Hose Union	120①
	Caliper Locating Bolt	30
	Rear Brake Cylinder Brake Tube Union	10
	Rear Wheel Cylinder Bolts	108①
	Rear Hub Nut	214
	Shield Bolts	17
CROWN VICTORIA, GRAND MARQUIS & TOWN CAR		
1998–2002	Anchor Plate To Spindle	125–169
	Brake Hose To Caliper (Banjo) Bolt	30–44
	Caliper Bleed Screw	80–106①
	Caliper Locating Pin	22–30
	Hydraulic Tube Connections	9–11
	Rear Caliper Anchor Plate Mounting Nuts	45–55
	Wheel Lug	85–104
ESCORT, TRACER & ZX2		
1998–2002	Brake Hose To Caliper (Banjo) Bolt	16–22
	Brake Caliper Bolts	33–43
	Parking Brake Cable Lockout	14–21
	Screw Plug	9–12
	Wheel Lug	74–100
LS & THUNDERBIRD		
2000–02	Anchor Plate	76
	Axle Shaft	221
	Caliper	26
	Caliper Bleeder Screw	60–120①
	Caliper Flow Bolt	35
	Master Cylinder Tube Fitting	11–15
	Support Bracket	36
	Wheel Lug	100
MARK VIII		
1998	Anchor Plate Bolt	64–88
	Axle Nut	188–254
	Brake Hose To Caliper (Banjo) Bolt	30–45
	Brake Pin Retainer	23–26
	Disc Shield Retaining Bolt	22–37
	Parking Brake Lever Limiting Bolt	60–84①

Continued

TIGHTENING SPECIFICATIONS—Continued

Year/ Model	Component	Torque/Ft. Lbs.
MARK VIII		
	Wheel Lug	85–105
MUSTANG		
1998–2002	Anchor Plate Nut	64–88
	Brake Hose To Axle Bolt	18–24
	Brake Hose To Caliper (Banjo) Bolt	20–30
	Brake Pin Retainer	30–35
	Disc Brake Adapter Retaining Bolt	30–40
	Limiting Bolt	60–84①
	Parking Brake Cable To Axle Bracket	23–26
	Rear Disc Shield	80–106①
	Rear Disc Shield Support Bracket	64–88
	Wheel Lug	85–105
SABLE & TAURUS		
1998–2002	Anchor Plate Bolt	64–88
	Axle Nut	188–254
	Brake Adapter Retaining Bolt	44–60
	Brake Hose Bracket To Shock	8–11
	Brake Hose To Caliper (Banjo) Bolt	30–40
	Brake Pin Retaining Bolt	23–26
	Disc Brake Shield	72–108①
	Hub Nut	188–254
	Park Brake Lever Limit Bolt	60–84①
	Rear Anti-Lock Sensor	36–60①

① — Inch lbs.

DRUM BRAKES

TABLE OF CONTENTS

Contour, Cougar, Mystique, Sable & Taurus

NOTE: On Air Bag Equipped Models, Refer To "Air Bag System Precautions" Located In The Front Of This Manual For System Disarming & Arming Procedures.

NOTE: Refer To "Computer Relearn Procedures" Located In The Front Of This Manual When Battery Power To The Computer Has Been Interrupted.

INDEX

PRECAUTIONS

AIR BAG SYSTEMS

Refer to "Air Bag System Precautions" in the front of this manual for system disarming and arming procedures.

BATTERY GROUND CABLE

Prior to service, disconnect battery ground cable and isolate as required.

SAFETY PRECAUTIONS

When working on or around brake assemblies, care must be taken to prevent breathing asbestos dust, as many manufacturers incorporate asbestos fibers in the production of brake linings. During routine service operations the amount of asbestos dust from brake lining wear is at a low level, due to a chemical breakdown during use. A few precautions will minimize exposure. **Do not sand or grind brake linings unless suitable local exhaust ventilation equipment is used to prevent excessive asbestos exposure.**

1. Wear suitable respirator approved for asbestos dust use during all repair procedures.
2. When cleaning brake dust from brake parts, use vacuum cleaner with highly efficient filter system. If suitable vacuum cleaner is not available, use water-soaked rag. **Do not use compressed air or dry brush to clean brake parts.**
3. Keep work area clean, using same equipment as for cleaning brake parts.
4. Properly dispose of rags and vacuum cleaner bags by placing them in plastic bags.
5. **Never use gasoline, kerosene, alcohol, motor oil, transmission fluid, or any fluid containing mineral oil to clean brake system components. These fluids will damage rubber caps and seals. If system contamination is suspected, inspect brake fluid in reservoir for dirt, discoloration, or separation (breakdown) of brake fluid into distinct layers. Drain and flush hydraulic system with clean brake fluid if contamination is suspected.**

INSPECTION

1. Inspect components for damage and unusual wear. Replace as necessary.
2. Inspect wheel cylinders. Boots which are torn, cut, or heat damaged indicate need for wheel cylinder replacement. Fluid spilling from boot center hole, or wetness around wheel cylinder ends indicates cup leakage and need for wheel cylinder replacement. **A small amount of fluid is always present and is considered normal, acting as lubricant for cylinder pistons.**
3. Inspect backing plate for evidence of seal leakage. If leakage exists, refer to "Contour, Cougar & Mystique" or "Sable & Taurus" chassis chapters for axle seal replacement procedure.
4. Inspect backing plate bolts and ensure they are tight.
5. Inspect adjuster screw operation. If satisfactory, lightly lubricate adjusting screw and washer with suitable brake lubricant. If operation is unsatisfactory, replace.
6. Using fine emery cloth or other suitable abrasive, clean rust and dirt from shoe contact surfaces on backing plate.

BRAKE SERVICE

REMOVAL

1. Raise and support rear of vehicle, then remove tire and wheel assembly.
2. Remove drum retainer push nuts, then slide drum off hub, **Fig. 1.**
3. If drum is stuck to hub, use suitable hammer to lightly tap on face of drum in flange mounting area to release.
4. If brake lining is dragging on brake

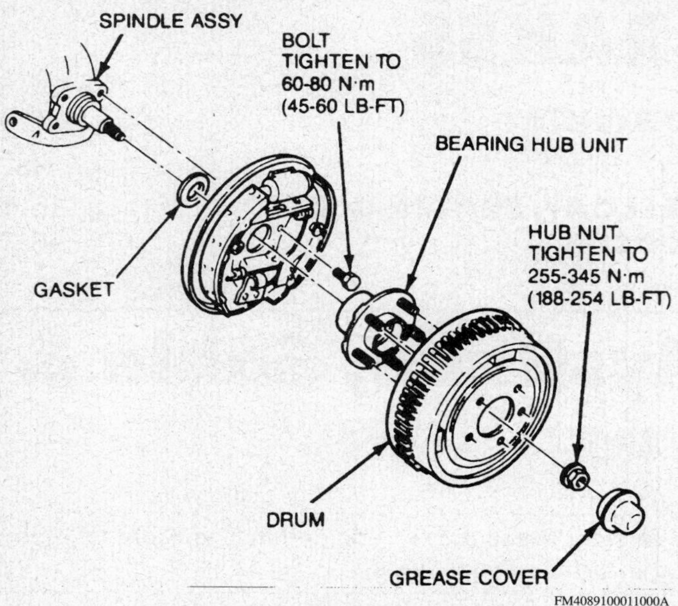

Fig. 1 Drum & hub assembly

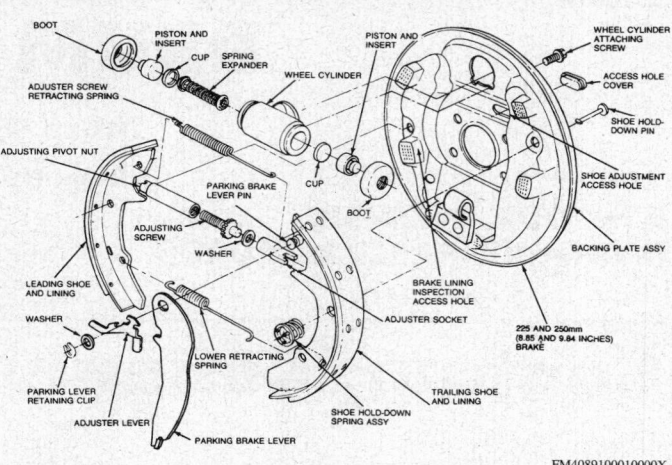

drum, back off brake adjustment by holding adjustment lever off star wheel, then loosen star wheel, **Fig. 2.**

5. Remove hub nut cover and discard.
6. Remove hub nut and discard, then slide hub and one-piece bearing assembly off spindle.
7. Install suitable wheel cylinder piston retainer tool.
8. Using suitable tool, remove shoe hold-down springs and pins.
9. Lift shoes, springs and adjuster assembly off backing plate and wheel cylinder assembly, being careful not to bend adjusting lever.
10. Remove parking brake cable from parking brake lever.
11. Remove retracting springs from lower shoe attachments and upper shoe to adjusting lever attachment points, then separate shoes and disengage adjuster mechanism.
12. Clean dirt from drum, backing plate and all other components. **Do not use compressed air or dry brush to clean brake parts. Many brake parts contain asbestos fibers which, if inhaled, can cause serious injury. Clean brake parts with water-soaked rag or suitable vacuum cleaner to minimize airborne dust.**

INSTALLATION

1. Lightly lubricate backing plate shoe contact surfaces with suitable brake lubrication.
2. Apply thin uniform coat of suitable brake lubricant to adjuster screw threads and socket end of adjusting screw.
3. Install stainless steel washer over socket end of adjusting screw and install socket, then turn adjusting screw fully into adjusting pivot nut and back off ½ turn.
4. Assemble parking brake lever to trailing shoe and lining assembly by installing spring washer and a new horseshoe retaining clip. Crimp clip until it securely retains lever to shoe.
5. Attach parking brake cable to parking brake lever.
6. Attach lower shoe retracting spring to leading and trailing shoe assemblies and install on backing plate. It will be necessary to stretch retracting spring as shoes are installed downward over anchor plate to inside of shoe retaining plate.
7. Install adjuster screw assembly between leading shoe slot and the slot in trailing shoe and parking brake lever. Adjuster socket end slot must fit into the trailing shoe and parking brake lever. **Adjuster socket blade is marked "R" or "L" for righthand and lefthand brake assemblies. The R or L adjuster blade must be installed with letter R or L in upright position (facing wheel cylinder) on proper side to ensure deeper of two slots in adjuster sockets fits into parking brake lever.**
8. Assemble adjuster lever in groove located in parking brake lever pin and into slot of adjuster socket that fits into trailing shoe web.
9. Attach upper retracting spring to leading shoe slot and, using suitable tool, stretch other end of spring into notch on adjuster lever. **If adjuster lever does not contact star wheel after installing spring, adjuster socket may be improperly installed.**
10. Install hub to spindle, then tighten new hub nut to specifications.
11. Install new hub nut cover.
12. Install brake drum to hub, then install drum retainer push nuts.
13. Install tire and wheel assembly.

FM4089100010000X

Fig. 2 Drum brake assembly

14. If any hydraulic connections have been opened, bleed system as described in "Hydraulic Brake System."
15. Adjust parking brake as described under "Adjustments."
16. Inspect all hydraulic lines and connections for leakage, repairing as necessary.
17. Inspect master cylinder fluid level and replenish as necessary.
18. Inspect brake pedal for proper feel and return.
19. Lower vehicle and road test. **Do not severely apply brakes immediately after installation of new linings or permanent damage may occur to linings, and/or drums may become scored. Brakes must be used moderately during first several hundred miles of operation to ensure proper burnishing of linings.**

ADJUSTMENTS

SERVICE BRAKES

Although the brakes are self-adjusting, an initial adjustment will be required after a brake repair. This adjustment is performed as follows:

1. Determine inside diameter of brake drum surface using brake shoe gauge tool No. D81L-1103-A, or equivalent. Adjust brake shoe diameter to fit gauge. Hold automatic adjusting lever out of engagement while rotating adjusting screw and ensure screw rotates freely.
2. Install brake drum, **Fig. 1,** then the tire and wheel assembly.

PARKING BRAKE

1. Ensure parking brake lever is released.
2. With transmission in Neutral, raise and support vehicle.
3. Tighten parking brake nut against brake equalizer until rear brakes drag, then loosen nut until rear brakes are fully released.
4. Lower vehicle, then inspect parking brake operation.

DRUM BRAKE SPECIFICATIONS

Year	Model	Brake Drum		
		Inside Dia., Inch	Inside Diameter Limit (Max.), Inch①	Max. Runout, Inch
CONTOUR, COUGAR & MYSTIQUE				
1998–2002	—	9.00	9.04	—
SABLE & TAURUS				
1998–2002	—	8.86	8.92	—

① — For reference only. Always use specifications found on component.

TIGHTENING SPECIFICATIONS

Year	Component	Torque/Ft. Lbs.
CONTOUR, COUGAR & MYSTIQUE		
1998–2002	ABS Sensor	120①
	Axle Nut	214
	Backing Plate Bolts	37
	Brake Hose	10
	Hub Nut	214
	Wheel Cylinder Bolts	108①
	Wheel Lug Nuts	94
SABLE & TAURUS		
1998–2002	ABS Sensor	72–96①
	Axle Nut	188–254
	Brake Backing Plate To Spindle Bolt	45–59
	Brake Hose	12–14
	Hub Nut	188–254
	Parking Brake Stop Bolt	96–108①
	Wheel Cylinder Attaching Bolts	9–13
	Wheel Lug Nuts	85–104

① — Inch lbs.

Escort, Tracer & ZX2

NOTE: On Air Bag Equipped Models, Refer To "Air Bag System Precautions" Located In The Front Of This Manual For System Disarming & Arming Procedures.

NOTE: Refer To "Computer Relearn Procedures" Located In The Front Of This Manual When Battery Power To The Computer Has Been Interrupted.

INDEX

PRECAUTIONS

AIR BAG SYSTEMS

Refer to "Air Bag System Precautions" in the front of this manual for system disarming and arming procedures.

BATTERY GROUND CABLE

Prior to service, disconnect battery ground cable and isolate as required.

SAFETY PRECAUTIONS

When working on or around brake assemblies, care must be taken to prevent breathing asbestos dust. Many manufacturers incorporate asbestos fibers in the production of brake linings. During routine service operations, the amount of asbestos dust from brake lining wear is at a low level due to a chemical breakdown during use. **Do not sand or grind brake linings unless suitable local exhaust ventilation equipment is used to prevent excessive asbestos exposure.**

1. Wear suitable respirator approved for asbestos dust use during all repair procedures.
2. When cleaning brake dust from brake parts, use vacuum cleaner with highly efficient filter system. If suitable vacuum cleaner is not available, use water-soaked rag. **Do not use compressed air or dry brush to clean brake parts.**
3. Keep work area clean, using same equipment as for cleaning brake parts.
4. Properly dispose of rags and vacuum cleaner bags by placing them in plastic bags.
5. **Never use gasoline, kerosene, alcohol, motor oil, transmission fluid, or any fluid containing mineral oil to clean brake system components. These fluids will damage rubber caps and seals. If system contamination is suspected, inspect brake fluid in reservoir for dirt, discoloration, or separation (breakdown) of brake fluid into distinct layers. Drain and flush hydraulic system with clean brake fluid if contamination is suspected.**

INSPECTION

1. Inspect components for damage and unusual wear. Replace as necessary.
2. Inspect wheel cylinders. Boots which are torn, cut, or heat damaged indicate need for wheel cylinder replacement. Fluid spilling from boot center hole, or wetness around wheel cylinder ends indicates cup leakage and need for wheel cylinder replacement. **A small amount of fluid is always present and is considered normal, acting as lubricant for cylinder pistons.**
3. Inspect backing plate for evidence of seal leakage. If leakage exists, refer to "Escort, Tracer & ZX2" chassis chapters for axle seal replacement procedure.
4. Inspect backing plate bolts and ensure tightness.
5. Inspect adjuster screw operation. If satisfactory, lightly lubricate adjusting screw and washer with suitable brake lubricant. If operation is unsatisfactory, replace.
6. Using fine emery cloth or other suitable abrasive, clean rust and dirt from shoe contact surfaces on backing plate.

BRAKE SERVICE

REMOVAL

1. Raise and support vehicle, then remove wheel and tire assembly.
2. Remove brake drum screws, then the brake drum.
3. Remove wheel hub as described in "Escort, Tracer & ZX2" chassis chapter.
4. Remove brake shoe retracting springs, **Fig. 1,** using screwdriver to push in and twist spring to disengage it from pin.
5. Remove righthand anti-rattle spring.
6. Push and turn brake shoe hold down springs, then remove them.
7. Remove primary rear shoe and lining from backing plate, then the secondary shoe and lining.

INSTALLATION

1. If rear shoes and linings are to be used again, inspect them to ensure they meet specifications.
2. Clean backing plate with suitable brake vacuum, then lubricate shoe and lining contact points and areas where shoes and linings ride with suitable lubricant, such as Motorcraft WA-10.
3. Tighten wheel cylinder bolts to specifications.
4. If new shoes and linings are being installed, resurface drums to remove glazing and ensure an equal friction surface from side to side. Resurfacing will also correct out-of-round and bell conditions.
5. Position secondary rear shoe and lining on backing plate, then install one shoe hold-down spring.
6. Position primary rear shoe and lining on backing plate, then install other shoe hold-down spring.
7. Install righthand anti-rattle spring, then the upper and lower shoe retracting springs.
8. Measure drum, shoes and linings with brake adjustment gauge tool No. D81L-1103-A, or equivalent, **Fig. 2.**
9. Inset screwdriver into knurled quadrant of rear quad operating lever stopper, **Fig. 1,** then adjust shoes and linings to same measurement of drum.
10. Install wheel hub as described in "Escort, Tracer & ZX2" chassis section.
11. Install drum, then the drum screws. Tighten screws to specifications.
12. Install wheel and tire assembly.

ADJUSTMENTS

PARKING BRAKE

1. Start engine and move shift control selector lever into Reverse position.
2. With vehicle moving in Reverse, press and release brake pedal several times.

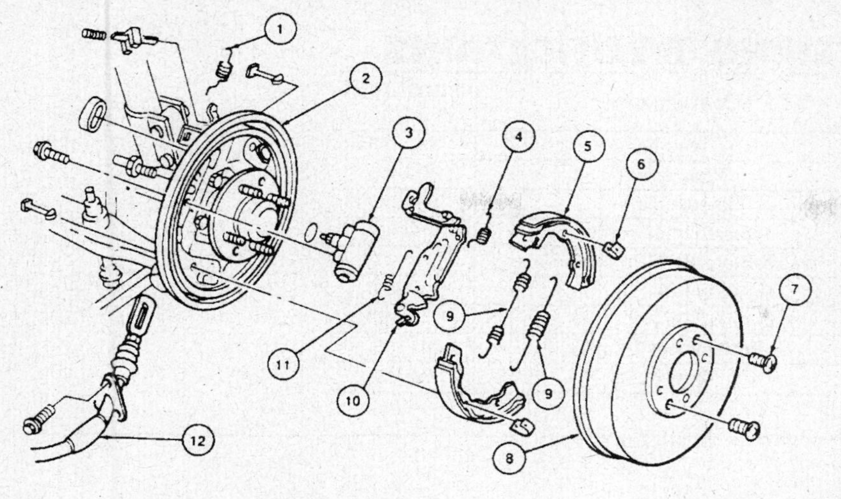

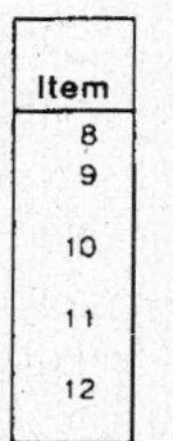

Item	Description	Item	Description
1	Parking Brake Link Spring	8	Brake Drum
2	Brake Backing Plate	9	Brake Shoe Retracting Spring
3	Rear Wheel Cylinder	10	Parking Brake Actuating Lever
4	Right Hand Anti-Rattle Spring	11	Rear Brake Adjusting Quadrant Spring
5	Rear Brake Shoe and Lining	12	Parking Brake Rear Cable and Conduit
6	Brake Shoe Hold Down Spring		
7	Screw		

FM4089400016000X

Fig. 1 Exploded view of drum brake

3. Move shift control selector lever into Park position, then stop engine.
4. Position both front seats to rearmost position, then remove front console screws.
5. Recline both front seats, then remove rear console screws.
6. Unbuckle safety belts, then, with parking brake control engaged, remove console.
7. Turn adjusting nut, **Fig. 3,** until control stroke is five to seven notches when pulled with 22 lbs. of force.
8. Feed safety belt ends through proper holes in console, then install console over parking brake control.
9. Install console screws, then return both seats to original positions.

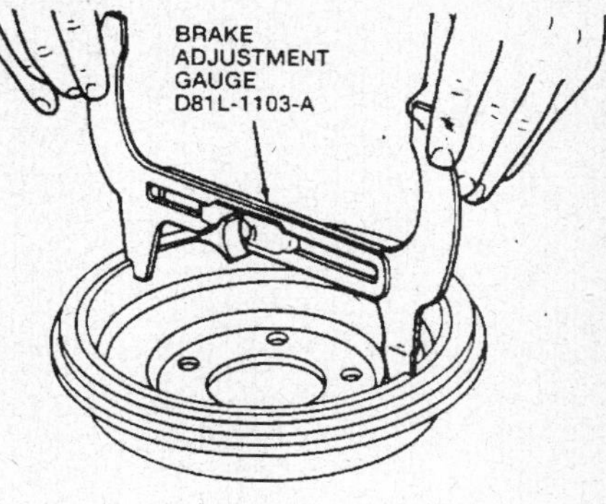

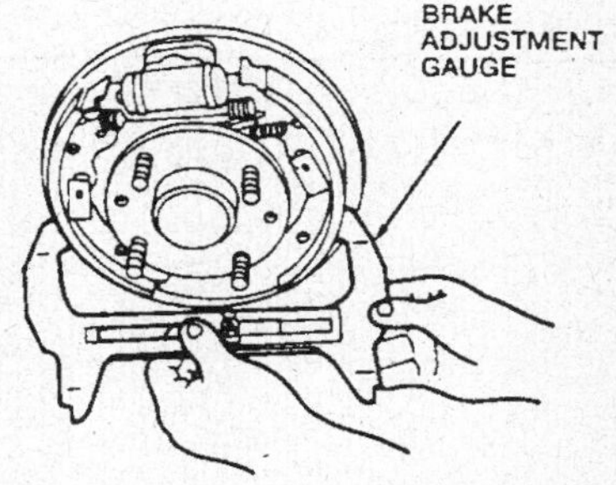

FM4089400017000X

Fig. 2 Drum brake & shoe lining measurements

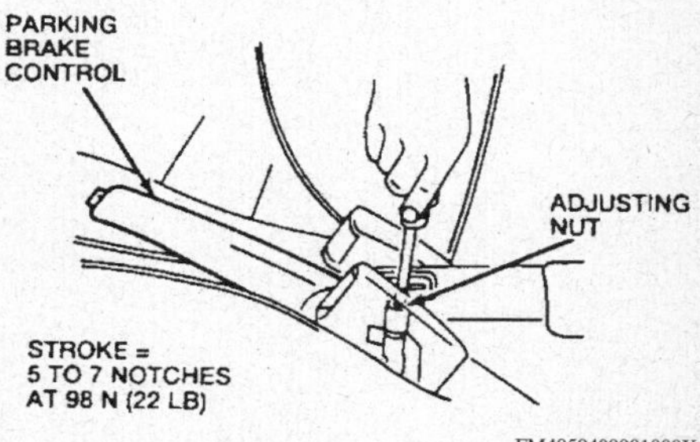

FM4059400001000X

Fig. 3 Parking brake adjustment

DRUM BRAKE SPECIFICATIONS

Year	Brake Drum		
	Inside Dia (Nominal) ., Inch	Inner Dia. Limit (Max.), Inch①	Max. Runout, Inch
1998–2002	9.00	9.04	—

① — For reference only. Always use specifications found on component.

TIGHTENING SPECIFICATIONS

Year	Component	Torque/Ft. Lbs.
1998–2002	Axle Nut	130–174
	Backing Plate	33–43
	Bleeder Screws	53–77①
	Brake Drum Screws	84–120①
	Cable Bracket To Backing Plate	14–19
	Hose	12–16
	Hub Nut	130–174
	Rear Wheel Cylinder	84–108①
	Wheel Lug	74–100

① — Inch lbs.

Focus

NOTE: On Air Bag Equipped Models, Refer To "Air Bag System Precautions" Located In The Front Of This Manual For System Disarming & Arming Procedures.

NOTE: Refer To "Computer Relearn Procedures" Located In The Front Of This Manual When Battery Power To The Computer Has Been Interrupted.

INDEX

PRECAUTIONS

AIR BAG SYSTEMS

Refer to "Air Bag System Precautions" in the front of this manual for system disarming and arming procedures.

BATTERY GROUND CABLE

Prior to service, disconnect battery ground cable and isolate as required.

SAFETY PRECAUTIONS

When working on or around brake assemblies, care must be taken to prevent breathing asbestos dust. Many manufacturers incorporate asbestos fibers in the production of brake linings. During routine service operations, the amount of asbestos dust from brake lining wear is at a low level due to a chemical breakdown during use. **Do not sand or grind brake linings unless suitable local exhaust ventilation equipment is used to prevent excessive asbestos exposure.**

1. Wear suitable respirator approved for asbestos dust use during all repair procedures.
2. When cleaning brake dust from brake parts, use vacuum cleaner with highly efficient filter system. If suitable vacuum cleaner is not available, use water-soaked rag. **Do not use compressed air or dry brush to clean brake parts.**
3. Keep work area clean, using same equipment as for cleaning brake parts.
4. Properly dispose of rags and vacuum cleaner bags by placing them in plastic bags.
5. **Never use gasoline, kerosene, alcohol, motor oil, transmission fluid, or any fluid containing mineral oil to clean brake system components. These fluids will damage rubber caps and seals. If system contamination is suspected, inspect brake fluid in reservoir for dirt, discoloration, or separation (breakdown) of brake fluid into distinct layers. Drain and flush hydraulic system with clean brake fluid if contamination is suspected.**

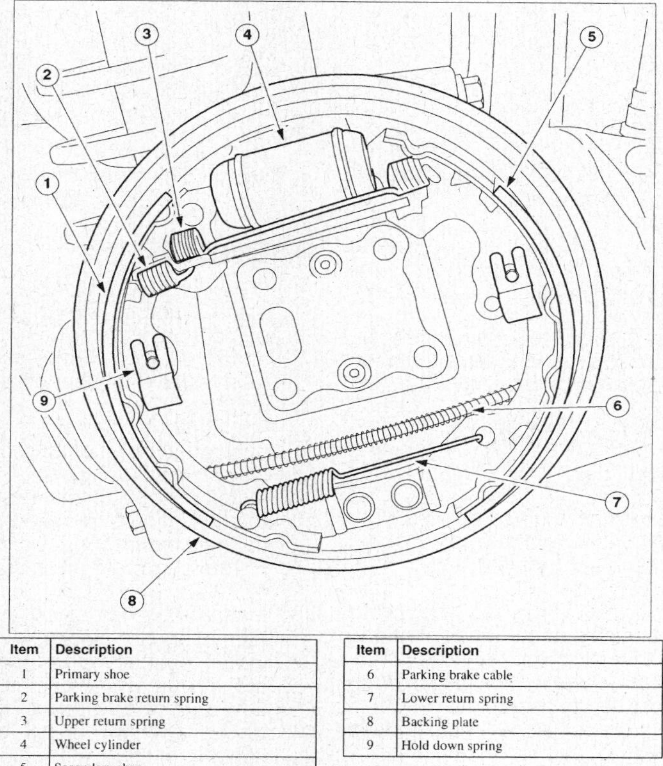

Item	Description
1	Primary shoe
2	Parking brake return spring
3	Upper return spring
4	Wheel cylinder
5	Secondary shoe
6	Parking brake cable
7	Lower return spring
8	Backing plate
9	Hold down spring

FM4080100043000X

Fig. 1 Rear brake spring locations

INSPECTION

1. Inspect components for damage and unusual wear. Replace as necessary.
2. Inspect wheel cylinders. Boots which are torn, cut, or heat damaged indicate need for wheel cylinder replacement. Fluid spilling from boot center hole or wetness around wheel cylinder ends indicates cup leakage and need for wheel cylinder replacement. **A small amount of fluid is always present and is considered normal, acting as lubricant for cylinder pistons.**
3. Inspect backing plate for evidence of seal leakage. If leakage exists, refer to "Focus" chassis chapters for axle seal replacement procedure.
4. Inspect backing plate bolts and ensure they are tight.
5. Inspect adjuster screw operation. If

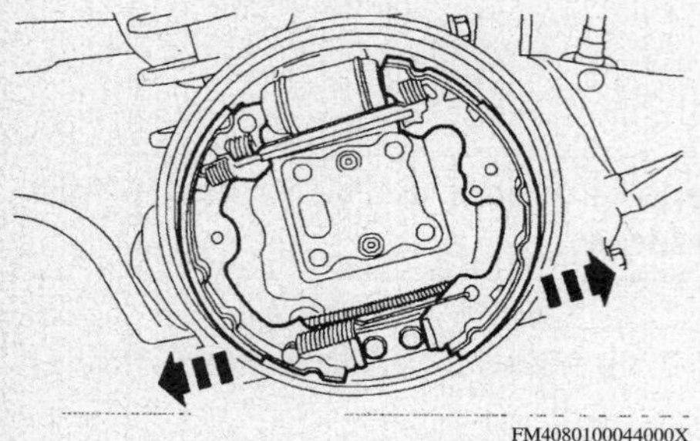

Fig. 2 Brake shoe removal

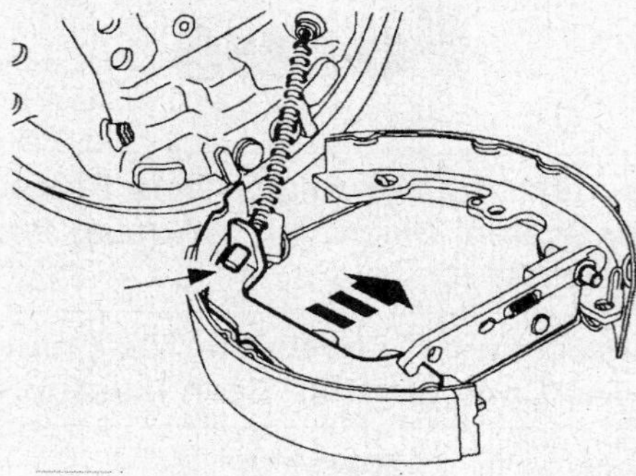

Fig. 3 Parking brake cable removal

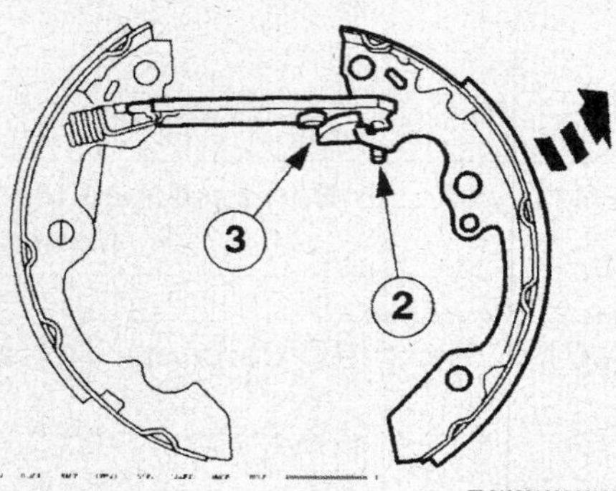

Fig. 4 Primary brake shoe removal

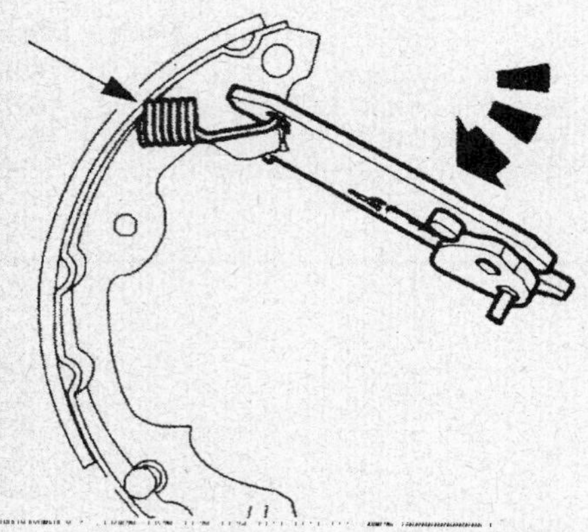

Fig. 5 Secondary brake shoe removal

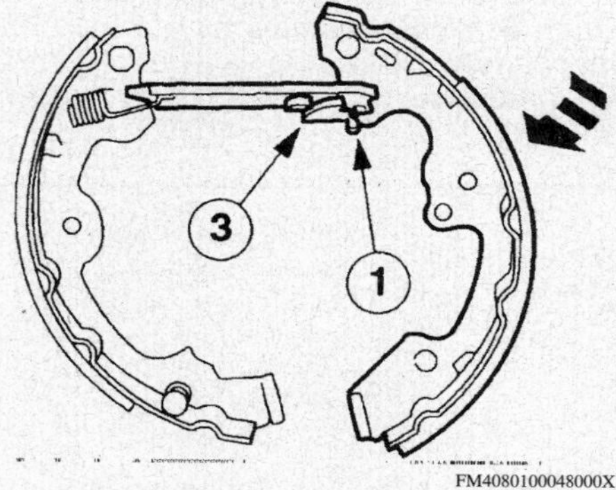

Fig. 6 Primary brake shoe to strut assembly

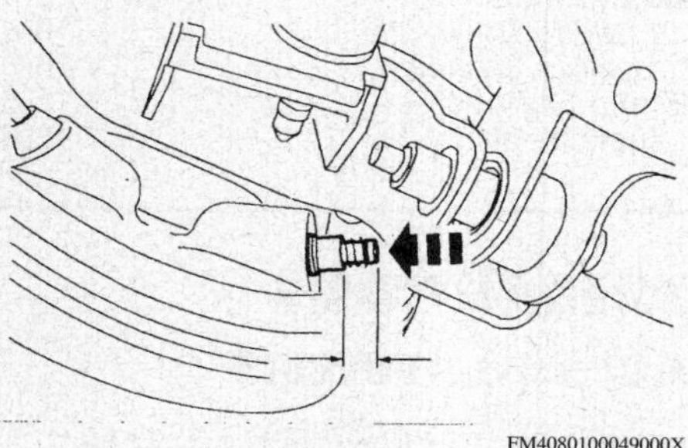

Fig. 7 Parking brake cable plunger inspection

satisfactory, lightly lubricate adjusting screw and washer with suitable brake lubricant. If operation is unsatisfactory, replace.

6. Using fine emery cloth or other suitable abrasive, clean rust and dirt from shoe contact surfaces on backing plate.

BRAKE SERVICE

REMOVAL

1. Remove brake drum as follows:
   a. Release parking brake.
   b. Raise and support vehicle, then remove wheels.
   c. **On models equipped with anti-lock brakes,** remove wheel speed sensor.
   d. **On all models,** remove brake drum and wheel hub assembly.
2. Remove brake shoe hold down springs, **Fig. 1,** and pins.
3. Disconnect brake shoes from wheel cylinders. Hold wheel cylinder pistons in place with rubber bands.
4. Remove shoes from anchor block, **Fig. 2.**
5. Push parking brake lever inward, then remove cable, **Fig. 3.**
6. Remove lower return spring, then the upper return spring.
7. Remove primary shoe from strut and brake shoe adjuster, **Fig. 4.**
8. Remove secondary shoe from support. Support spring is under pressure, **Fig. 5.**
9. Remove parking brake return spring.

INSTALLATION

1. Clean, check and apply Silicone dielectric compound to backing plate contact points.
2. Install parking brake return spring, then install strut support and move upward.
3. Install strut to primary brake shoe, push shoe inwards and rotate adjuster fully clockwise, **Fig. 6.**
4. Install upper and lower return springs.
5. Push parking brake lever inward, then connect parking brake cable.
6. Remove rubber band holding wheel cylinders in place.
7. Install brake shoes to wheel cylinder then to anchor block.
8. Install hold down springs, then the brake drum and wheel hub assembly.
9. **On models equipped with anti-lock brake system,** install wheel speed sensor.
10. **On all models,** install wheels and tighten to specification.
11. Operate brake pedal to achieve automatic brake adjustment.

ADJUSTMENTS

SERVICE BRAKES

These models are equipped with self adjusting brake mechanisms and require no adjustment. The brakes are adjusted as necessary whenever the service brakes are applied.

PARKING BRAKE

1. Remove parking brake boot clip, then the boot.
2. Ensure rear brakes are not hot when adjusting.
3. Release parking brake to its lowest position.
4. Remove clip, then loosen parking brake cable adjustment nut until there is no tension in cable.
5. Apply and release brake pedal to ensure brakes are adjusted correctly.
6. Raise and support vehicle.
7. Ensure parking brake cable is correctly routed in its clips.
8. Lower vehicle.
9. Raise parking brake control lever up four notches.
10. Tighten parking brake cable adjustment nut until increased torque is noted.
11. Apply and release handbrake lever several times with sufficient force to settle parking brake system.
12. Release parking brake lever to it's lowest position.
13. Inspect movement of plunger in right and left backing plates while moving lever up and down, **Fig. 7.**
14. Total movement of both right and left hand plungers added together should be .039–.315 inch.
15. If further adjustment is necessary, adjust cable using parking brake cable adjustment nut.
16. Install parking brake adjustment nut clip, then the control lever boot.

DRUM BRAKE SPECIFICATIONS

Year	Brake Drum		
	Inside Dia., Inch	Inside Diameter Limit (Max.), Inch	Max. Runout, Inch
2000–01	7.99	8.03①	—.

① — For reference only. Always use specifications found on component.

TIGHTENING SPECIFICATIONS

Year	Component	Torque/Ft. Lbs.
2000–01	Brake Drum & Wheel Hub Nuts	49
	Brake Pipe To Wheel Cylinder	71①
	Wheel Cylinder To Backing Plate	108①
	Wheel Speed Sensor	80①
	Wheel Lug Nuts	94

① — Inch lbs.

HYDRAULIC BRAKE SYSTEMS

NOTE: On Air Bag Equipped Models, Refer To "Air Bag System Precautions" Located In The Front Of This Manual For System Disarming & Arming Procedures.

NOTE: Refer To "Computer Relearn Procedures" Located In The Front Of This Manual When Battery Power To The Computer Has Been Interrupted.

INDEX

PRECAUTIONS

AIR BAG SYSTEMS

Refer to "Air Bag System Precautions" in the front of this manual for system disarming and arming procedures.

BATTERY GROUND CABLE

Prior to service, disconnect battery ground cable and isolate as required.

DESCRIPTION

This system operates on the same principles as conventional front and rear split systems using primary and secondary master cylinders moving simultaneously to exert hydraulic pressure on their respective systems, **Fig. 1.**

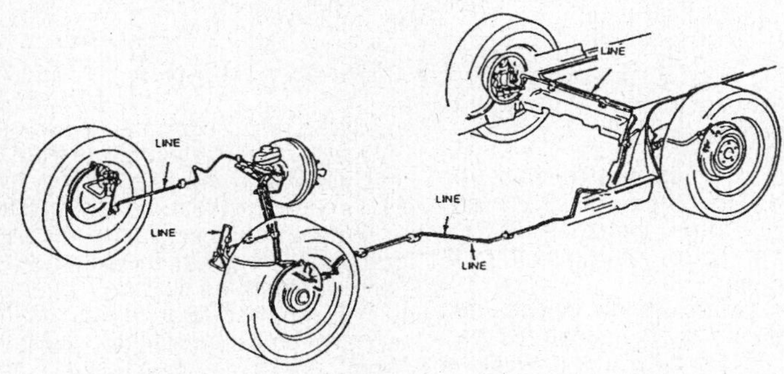

Fig. 1 Diagonally split brake system

The hydraulic brake lines on this system, however, have been diagonally split front to rear (left front to right rear and right front to left rear) in place of separate lines to the front and rear wheels.

In the event of a system failure this would cause the remaining good system to do all the braking on one front wheel and the opposite rear wheel, thus maintaining 50% of the total braking force. The hydraulic pressure loss would result in a pressure differential in the system and cause a warning light on the dashboard to glow as in front and rear split systems.

BRAKE WARNING LIGHT SYSTEMS

When a pressure differential occurs between the front and rear brake systems, the valves will shuttle toward the side with the low pressure. Movement of the differential valve forces the switch plunger upward over the tapered shoulder of the valve to close the switch contacts and light the dual brake warning lamp, signaling a brake system failure.

The valve assembly consists of two valves in a common bore that are spring loaded toward the centered position. The spring-loaded switch contact plunger rests on top of the valves in the centered position. When a pressure differential occurs between the front and rear brake systems, the valves will shuttle toward the side with the low pressure. The spring-loaded switch plunger is triggered and the ground circuit for the warning light is completed, lighting the lamp.

As pressure falls in one system, the other system's normal pressure forces the piston to the inoperative side, contacting the switch terminal, causing the warning light on the instrument panel to glow.

On front wheel drive models, a fluid level indicator replaces the pressure differential valve used in previous brake systems. It is contained inside the body of the master cylinder plastic reservoir and activates the brake warning light when fluid level is low.

Testing Warning Light Systems

If the parking brake light is connected into the service brake warning light system, the brake warning light will flash only when the parking brake is applied with the ignition turned ON. The same light will also glow should one of the two service brake systems fail when the brake pedal is applied.

To test the system, turn the ignition on and apply the parking brake. If the lamp fails to light, inspect for a burned out bulb, disconnected socket, a broken or disconnected wire at the switch.

To test the brake warning system, raise the car and open a wheel bleeder valve while a helper depresses the brake pedal and observes the warning light on the instrument panel. If the bulb fails to light, inspect for a burned out bulb, disconnected socket, or a broken or disconnected wire at the switch. If the bulb is not burned out, and wire continuity is proven, replace the brake warning switch.

COMBINATION VALVE

The combination valve is a metering valve, failure warning switch, and a proportioner in one assembly and is used on disc brake applications. The metering valve delays front disc braking until the rear drum brake shoes contact the drum. The failure warning switch is actuated in event of front or rear brake system failure, in turn activating a dash warning lamp. The proportioner balances front to rear braking action during rapid deceleration.

Combination valves used on diagonally split brake systems do not use metering valves instead two proportioning valves are used.

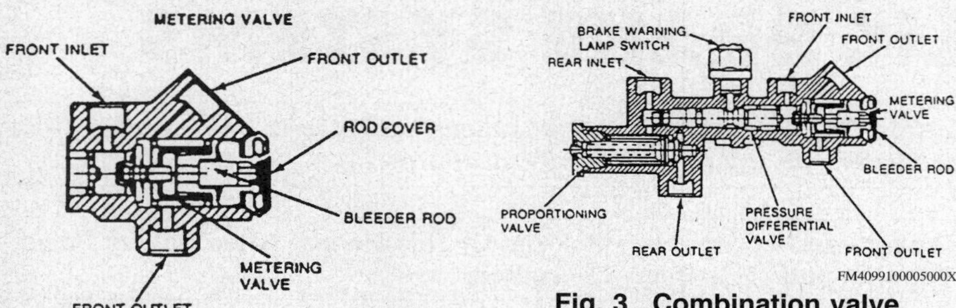

Fig. 2 Metering valve

Fig. 3 Combination valve

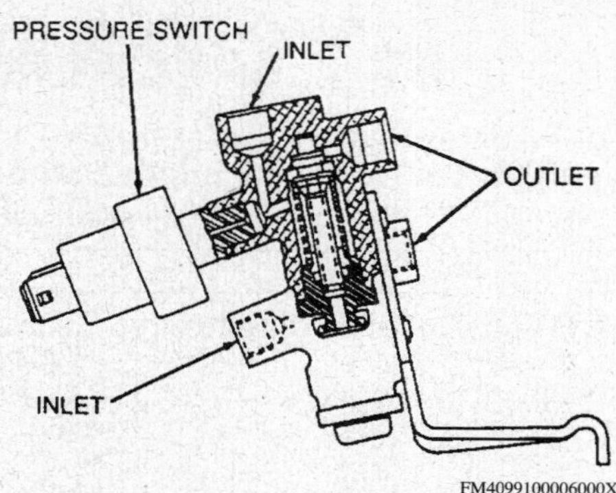

Fig. 4 Pressure control valve

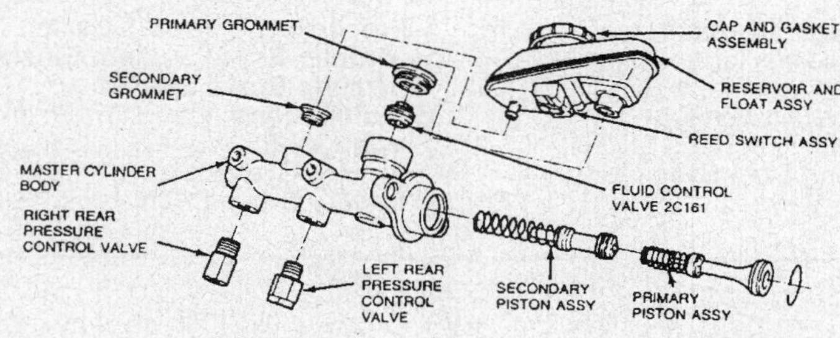

Fig. 5 Exploded view of master cylinder

Metering Valve

When the brakes are not applied, the metering valve, **Fig. 2,** permits the brake fluid to flow through the valve, thus allowing the fluid to expand and contract with temperature changes.

When the brakes are initially applied, the metering valve, stem moves to the left, preventing fluid to flow through the valve to the front disc brakes. This is accomplished by the smooth end of the metering valve stem contacting the metering valve seal lip at 4–30 psi. The metering valve spring holds the retainer against the seal until a predetermined pressure is produced at the valve inlet port which overcomes the spring pressure and permits hydraulic pressure to actuate the front disc brakes. The increased pressure into the valve is metered through the valve seal, to the front disc brakes, producing an increased force on the diaphragm. The diaphragm then pulls the pin, in turn pulling the retainer and reduces the spring pressure on the metering valve seal. Eventually, the pressure reaches a point at which the spring is pulled away by the diaphragm pin and retainer, leaving the metering valve unrestricted, permitting full pressure to pass through the metering valve.

On some applications, two-way or three-way combination valves are used. The three-way combination valve consists of a metering valve, failure warning switch and a proportioner mounted in an aluminum body, **Fig. 3.** The two-way combination valve consists of a failure warning switch and a proportioner. On models equipped with metering valves, the metering valve release rod must be pushed in during bleeding operations on the front wheels.

Failure Warning Switch

If the rear brake system fails, the front system pressure forces the switch piston to one side. The switch pin is then forced up into the switch, completing the electrical circuit and activates the dash warning lamp.

When repairs are made and pressure returns to the system, the piston moves to the left, resetting the switch. The detent on the piston requires approximately 100–450 psi to permit full reset of the piston. In event of front brake system failure, the piston moves to the left and the same sequence of events is followed as for rear system failure except the piston resets to the right.

Proportioner Or Pressure Control Valve

During rapid deceleration, a portion of vehicle weight is transferred to the front wheels. This resultant loss of weight at rear wheels must be compensated for to avoid early rear wheel skid. The proportioner or pressure control valve, **Fig. 4,** reduces rear brake system pressure, delaying rear wheel skid. When the proportioner or pressure control valve is incorporated in the combination valve assembly, pressure developed within the valve acts against the large end of the piston, overcoming the spring pressure, moving the piston. The piston then contacts the stem seat and restricts line pressure through the valve.

During normal braking operation, the proportioner or pressure control valve is not functional. Brake fluid flows into the proportioner or pressure control valve between the piston center hole and the valve stem, through the stop plate and to the rear brakes. Spring pressure loads the piston during normal braking, causing it to rest against the stop plate.

On diagonally split brake systems, two proportioners or pressure control valves are used. One controls the left rear brake, the other the right rear brake. On front wheel drive models less power brakes, the proportioners or pressure control valves are located in the combination valve. On front wheel drive models with power brakes, the proportioners or pressure control valves are installed in the master cylinder rear brake outlet ports, **Fig. 5.**

BRAKE DISTRIBUTION VALVE & SWITCH

This switch assembly which is used on some diagonally split brake systems, is connected to the outlet ports of the master cylinder and also to the brake warning light that warns the driver if either the primary or secondary brake system has failed.

When hydraulic pressure is equal in both primary and secondary brake systems, the switch remains centered. If pressure fails in one of the systems, hydraulic pressure moves the piston toward the inoperative side. The shoulder of the piston contacts the switch terminal, providing a ground and lighting the warning lamp.

PROPORTIONING VALVE & SWITCH

Description

The proportioning valve (when used), **Fig. 6,** provides balanced braking action between front and rear brakes under a wide range of braking conditions. The valve regulates the hydraulic pressure applied to the rear wheel cylinders, thus limiting rear braking action when high pressures are required at the front brakes. In this manner, premature rear wheel skid is prevented.

Testing

When a premature rear wheel slide is obtained on a brake application, it usually is an indication that the fluid pressure to the rear wheels is above the 50% reduction ratio for the rear line pressure and that malfunction has occurred within the proportioning valve.

To test the valve, install gauge set shown in **Fig. 6,** in brake line between master cylinder and proportioning valve, and at output end of proportioning valve and brake line as shown. Ensure all joints are fluid tight.

Have a helper exert pressure on brake pedal (holding pressure). Obtain a reading on master cylinder output of approximately 700 psi. While pressure is being held as above, reading on valve outlet should be

550–610 psi. If the pressure readings do not meet these specifications, the valve should be removed and a new valve installed.

COMPONENT REPLACEMENT

MASTER CYLINDER

CONTINENTAL, CROWN VICTORIA, GRAND MARQUIS, MARK VIII, MUSTANG & TOWN CAR

1. **On models equipped with ABS,** depress brake pedal several times to exhaust all vacuum in the system.
2. **On all models,** disconnect brake lines from master cylinder, then all necessary electrical connectors.
3. **On models equipped with ABS,** disconnect hydraulic control unit supply hose at master cylinder. Secure hose in a position to prevent brake fluid loss.
4. **On models equipped with ABS and traction control,** remove two bolts which attach proportioning valve bracket to brake master cylinder. Secure proportioning valve and tubes in a position to prevent damage or loss of brake fluid.
5. **On all models,** remove nuts retaining master cylinder to brake booster.
6. Remove master cylinder.
7. Reverse procedure to install. After installation is complete, fill master cylinder with manufacturer recommended brake fluid and bleed brakes.

CONTOUR, COUGAR & MYSTIQUE

1. Apply brake pedal several times to exhaust all vacuum in system.
2. Disconnect brake warning switch, then remove brake tubes from primary and secondary outlet ports of master cylinder.
3. **On models equipped with manual transaxle,** disconnect hose to hydraulic clutch master cylinder, then drain brake fluid into a suitable container.
4. **On all models,** remove brake lines.
5. Remove two nuts and master cylinder.
6. Reverse procedure to install. After installation is complete, fill master cylinder with manufacturer recommended brake fluid and bleed brakes.

ESCORT, TRACER & ZX2

1. **On 1998 models,** remove air cleaner assembly.
2. **On models equipped with manual transaxle,** disconnect clutch master cylinder hose from brake master cylinder reservoir.
3. **On all models,** disconnect master cylinder fluid level sensor and brake tubes from master cylinder.
4. Cap brake tubes and master cylinder ports.
5. Remove two master cylinder to power booster nuts and master cylinder.
6. Reverse procedure to install. After installation is complete, fill master cylinder with manufacturer recommended brake fluid and bleed brakes.

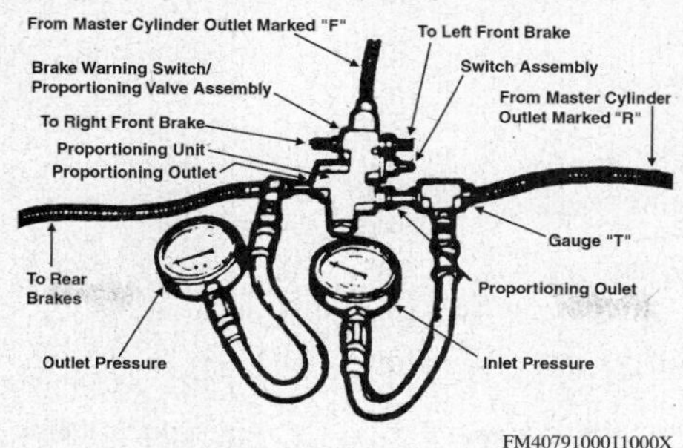

Fig. 6 Proportioning valve test gauge connection

LS & THUNDERBIRD

1. Disconnect fluid level sensor connector.
2. Remove vapor management valve (VMV) nuts.
3. Remove VMV hose and position valve aside.
4. Disconnect brake tubes.
5. Disconnect brake master cylinder IVD solenoid electrical connector.
6. Remove brake master cylinder mounting nuts.
7. Unclip fuel line and vapor management hose from fastener, then position aside.
8. Remove brake master cylinder.
9. Reverse procedure to install. Bleed brake system.

SABLE & TAURUS

1998–99

1. Apply brake several times to exhaust all vacuum in the system.
2. Remove brake tubes from primary and secondary outlet ports of brake master cylinder.
3. Disconnect brake fluid level warning switch connector.
4. Remove nut retaining cowl top inner panel tube to brake master cylinder.
5. Disconnect cowl top inner panel tube from cowl and remove.
6. Remove two nuts retaining brake master cylinder to power brake booster assembly.
7. Slide brake master cylinder forward and upward from vehicle.
8. Reverse procedure to install. After installation is complete, fill master cylinder with manufacturer recommended brake fluid and bleed brakes.

2000–02

1. Disconnect brake fluid level sensor electrical connector.
2. Loosen fittings and disconnect brake tubes from master cylinder.
3. Remove master cylinder bolts, then the master cylinder.
4. Reverse procedure to install noting the following:
   a. If installing a new master cylinder it must be primed before installing.
   b. After installation is complete, fill master cylinder with manufacturer recommended brake fluid and bleed brakes.

WHEEL CYLINDERS

REMOVAL

1. Remove wheel, drum and brake shoes.
2. Disconnect hydraulic line at wheel cylinder. Do not pull metal line away from cylinder as the cylinder connection will bend metal line and make installation difficult. Line will separate from cylinder when cylinder is moved away from brake backing plate.
3. Remove screws holding cylinder to brake plate and remove cylinder.

INSTALLATION

1. Wipe end of hydraulic line to remove any foreign matter.
2. Place hydraulic cylinder in position. Enter tubing into cylinder and start connecting fitting.
3. Secure cylinder to backing plate and then complete tightening of tubing fitting.
4. Install brake shoes, drum and wheel.
5. Bleed system as outlined under "Brake System Bleed" and adjust brakes.

COMPONENT SERVICE

MASTER CYLINDER OVERHAUL

DISASSEMBLE

1. Clean outside of master cylinder thoroughly. Drain brake fluid from master cylinder.
2. Remove stop bolt and pressure control valves, if equipped.
3. Using a screwdriver, carefully pry up on reservoir and remove it from master cylinder body.
4. Remove fluid control valve, if equipped.
5. Depress primary piston and remove snap ring from retaining groove at open end of bore.
6. Remove primary and secondary piston assemblies from master cylinder. If secondary piston does not come out, apply air pressure to secondary outlet port to remove.

INSPECTION

When disassembled, wash all parts in clean brake fluid only. Use an air hose to blow out all passages, orifices and valve holes. Air dry and place parts on clean paper or lint-free cloth. Inspect master cylinder bore for scoring, rust, pitting or etching. Any of these conditions will require replacement of the housing. Inspect master cylinder pistons for scoring, pitting or distortion. Replace piston if any of these conditions exist.

If either master cylinder housing or piston is replaced, clean new parts with clean brake fluid and blow out all passages with air hose.

Examine reservoirs for foreign matter and check all passages for restrictions. If there is any suspicion of contamination or evidence of corrosion, completely flush hydraulic system as outlined below.

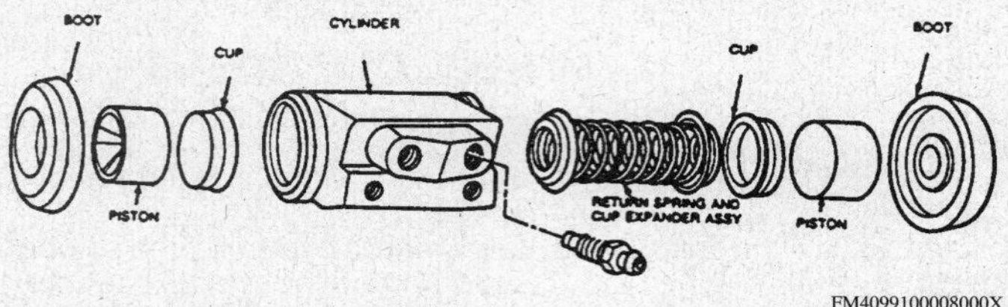

Fig. 7 Exploded view of typical wheel cylinder

When overhauling a master cylinder, use all parts contained in repair kit. Before starting reassembly, dip all cups, seals, pistons, springs, check valves and retainers in clean brake fluid and place in a clean pan or on clean paper. Wash hands with soap and water only to prevent contamination of rubber parts from oil, kerosene or gasoline. During assembly, dip all parts in clean brake fluid.

Inspect through side outlet of dual master cylinder housing to make certain cup lips do not hang up on edge of hole or turn back, which would result in faulty operation. A piece of $3/16$ inch rod with an end rounded off will be helpful in guiding cups past hole.

When overhauling aluminum master cylinders, carefully inspect master cylinder bore for corrosion. If corroded, replace master cylinder. Do not hone or use abrasives on the bore of these cylinders.

ASSEMBLE

1. Coat replacement piston assemblies in clean heavy duty DOT 3 brake fluid before assembly.
2. Install secondary piston assembly into bore, spring end first.
3. Install primary piston assembly, spring end first.
4. Depress primary piston and install snap ring.
5. **On models except Escort, Tracer and ZX2,** install fluid control valve and **torque** to 96–120 inch lbs.
6. **On Escort, Tracer and ZX2 models,** install fluid control valve and **torque** to 33–39 ft. lbs.
7. **On all models,** install stop bolt and pressure control valves, if equipped.
8. Lubricate new reservoir grommets with brake fluid and install in master cylinder body.
9. Install reservoir into new grommets.
10. Fill and bench bleed master cylinder.

WHEEL CYLINDERS

Overhaul

1. Refer to **Fig. 7** as a guide, then remove boots, pistons, springs and cups from cylinder.
2. Place all parts, except cylinder casting in clean brake fluid. Wipe cylinder walls with clean brake fluid.
3. Examine cylinder bore. A scored bore may be honed providing the diameter is not increased more than .005 inch. Replace worn or damaged parts from the repair kit.
4. Before assembling, wash hands with soap and water only, as oil, kerosene or gasoline will contaminate rubber parts.
5. Lubricate cylinder wall and rubber cups with brake fluid.
6. Install springs, cups, pistons and boots in housing.

BRAKE SYSTEM BLEED

Pressure bleeding is recommended for all hydraulic brake systems. Ensure all dirt and contaminants are removed from master cylinder area prior to removing reservoir cap.

To prevent air from the pressure tank getting into the lines, do not shake the tank while air is being added to the tank or after it has been pressurized. Set the tank in the required location, bring the air hose to the tank, and do not move it during the bleeding operation. The tank should be kept at least one-third full.

On vehicles equipped with disc brakes and master cylinders without proportioners or pressure control valves located in the master cylinder outlet port, the brake metering valve or combination valve must be held in position using a suitable tool.

If air does get into the fluid, releasing the pressure will cause the bubbles to increase in size, rise to the top of the fluid, and escape. Pressure should not be greater than about 35 psi.

On vehicles equipped with plastic reservoirs, do not exceed 25 psi during bleeding pressure.

When bleeding without pressure, open the bleed valve three-quarters of a turn, depress the pedal a full stroke, then allow the pedal to return slowly to its released position. It is suggested that after the pedal has been depressed to the end of its stroke, the bleeder valve should be closed before the start of the return stroke. On models with power brakes, first reduce the vacuum in the power unit to zero by pumping the brake pedal several times with the engine off before starting to bleed the system.

Pressure bleeding eliminates the need for pedal pumping.

Discard drained or bled brake fluid. Care should be taken not to spill brake fluid, since this can damage the finish of the car.

Flushing is essential if there is water, mineral oil or other contaminants in the lines, and whenever new parts are installed in the hydraulic system. Fluid contamination is usually indicated by swollen and deteriorated cups and other rubber parts.

Wheel cylinders on disc brakes are equipped with bleeder valves, and are bled in the same manner as wheel cylinders for drum brakes.

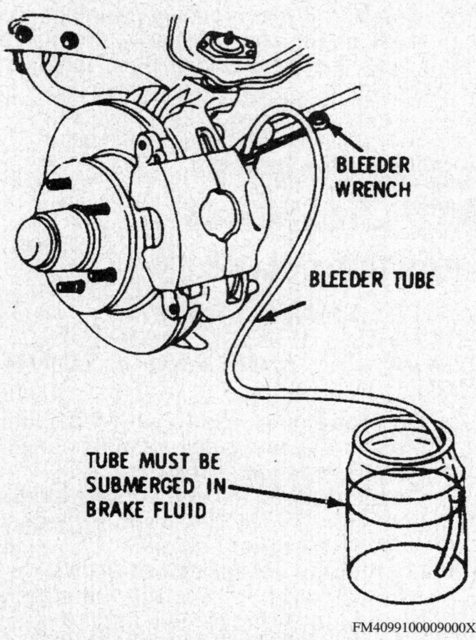

Fig. 8 Hydraulic brake system flushing

Bleeding is necessary on all four wheels if air has entered the system because of low fluid level, or the line or lines have been disconnected. If a line is disconnected at any one wheel cylinder, that cylinder only need be bled. On brake reline jobs, bleeding is advisable to remove any air or contaminants.

Master cylinders equipped with bleeder valves should be bled first before the wheel cylinders are bled. In all cases where a master cylinder has been overhauled, it must be bled. Where there is no bleeder valve, this can be done by leaving the lines loose, actuating the brake pedal to expel the air and then tightening the lines.

After overhauling a dual master cylinder used in conjunction with disc brakes, it is advisable to bleed the cylinder before installing it on the car. The reason for this recommendation is that air may be trapped between the master cylinder pistons because there is only one residual pressure valve (check valve) used in these units.

SYSTEM PRIMING

When a new master cylinder has been installed or the brake system emptied or partially emptied, fluid may not flow from the bleeder screws during normal bleeding. It may be necessary to prime the system using the following procedure:

1. Using a tubing wrench, remove the brake lines from the master cylinder.
2. Install short brake lines in the master cylinder and position them back into the reservoir, ensure the short brake line ends are submerged in the reservoir brake fluid.
3. Fill the reservoir with recommended brake fluid, then cover master cylinder fluid reservoir with shop towel.
4. Pump the brakes until clear, bubble free fluid comes out of both brake lines. **If any brake fluid spills on paint, wash it off immediately with water.**

5. Remove the short brake lines, then re-install original brake lines.
6. Bleed each brake line at the master cylinder using the following procedure:
   a. Have assistant pump brake pedal ten times, then hold firm pressure on the pedal.
   b. Open the rearmost brake line fittings with a tubing wrench until a stream of brake fluid comes out. Have assistant maintain pressure on the brake pedal until the brake line fitting is tightened again.
   c. Repeat this operation until clear, bubble free fluid comes out from around tube fitting.
   d. Repeat this bleeding operation at the front brake line fitting.
7. If any of the brake lines or calipers have been removed, it may be helpful to prime the system by gravity bleeding. this should be done after the master cylinder is primed and bled. To prime the system using the gravity method, proceed as follows:
   a. Fill the master cylinder with recommended brake fluid.
   b. Loosen both rear bleeder screws and leave them open until clear brake fluid flows out. **Check reservoir fluid level frequently; do not allow fluid level to drop below half full.**
   c. Tighten rear bleeder screws.
   d. Loosen bleeder screw on front caliper, leave open until clear fluid flows out. **Bleed front calipers one side at a time.**
8. After the master cylinder has been primed, the lines bled at the master cylinder and the brake system primed, normal brake system bleeding can be resumed at each wheel.

WHEEL BLEEDING SEQUENCE

Rear Wheel Drive .....RR-LR-RF-LF
Front Wheel Drive ....RR-LF-LR-RF

HYDRAULIC BRAKE SYSTEM FLUSH

Whenever new brake components are installed in the hydraulic system, it is recommended that the entire hydraulic system be thoroughly flushed with clean brake fluid.

It may sometime become necessary to flush out the system due to the presence of mineral oil, kerosene, gasoline, etc., which will cause swelling of rubber piston cups and valves and render them inoperative.

Flushing is performed at each wheel in the same manner as the bleeding operation except that the bleeder valve is opened 1½ turns and the fluid is forced through the lines and bleeder valve until it emerges clear in color, **Fig. 8.** Approximately one quart of clean brake fluid is required to flush the hydraulic system. After completing the flushing operation at all bleeder valves, check to ensure the master cylinder is filled to the proper level.

HYDRAULIC BRAKE SYSTEM SPECIFICATIONS

Year	Model	Master Cylinder Bore Dia., Inch
1998–2002	Continental	—
	Contour & Mystique	—
	Cougar	—
	Crown Victoria & Grand Marquis	—
	Escort & Tracer	—
	LS	—
	Mark VIII	—
	Mustang	①
	Sable & Taurus	—
	Thunderbird	—
	Town Car	—
	ZX2	—

① — 3.8L engine 1.06 inch, 4.6L engines 1.00 inch.

POWER BRAKE UNITS

NOTE: On Models Equipped With Anti-Lock Brakes, Refer To "Anti-Lock Brake" Section.

NOTE: On Air Bag Equipped Models, Refer To "Air Bag System Precautions" Located In The Front Of This Manual For System Disarming & Arming Procedures.

NOTE: Refer To "Computer Relearn Procedures" Located In The Front Of This Manual When Battery Power To The Computer Has Been Interrupted.

NOTE: Prior To Performing Any Service Operations Listed In This Section, Consult The "Technical Service Bulletins" Section For Related Information.

INDEX

APPLICATION CHART

Model	Year	Power Brake Booster Type
Continental	1998–2002	Dual Diaphragm
Contour	1998–2000	Single Diaphragm
Cougar	1999–2002	Single Diaphragm
Crown Victoria	1998–2002	Bendix Tandem Diaphragm
Escort	1998–2002	Single Diaphragm
Focus	2000–01	Single Diaphragm
Grand Marquis	1998–2002	Bendix Tandem Diaphragm
LS	2000–02	Dual Diaphragm
Mark VIII	1998	Bendix Tandem Diaphragm
Mustang	1998–2002	①
Mystique	1998–2000	Single Diaphragm
Sable	1998–2002	Bendix Single Diaphragm
Taurus	1998–2002	Bendix Single Diaphragm
Thunderbird	2002	Dual Diaphragm
Town Car	1998–2002	Bendix Tandem Diaphragm
Tracer	1998–99	Single Diaphragm
ZX2	1998–2002	Single Diaphragm

① — 3.8L engine, Bendix Tandem Diaphragm. 4.6L engine, Bendix Hydro-Boost system.

PRECAUTIONS

AIR BAG SYSTEMS

Refer to "Air Bag System Precautions" in the front of this manual for system disarming and arming procedures.

BATTERY GROUND CABLE

Prior to service, disconnect battery ground cable and isolate as required.

DESCRIPTION

VACUUM ASSIST DIAPHRAGM TYPE

The vacuum assist diaphragm assembly multiplies the force exerted on the master cylinder piston in order to increase the hydraulic pressure delivered to the wheel cylinders while decreasing the effort necessary to obtain acceptable stopping performance.

Vacuum assist units get their energy by opposing engine vacuum to atmospheric pressure. A piston, cylinder and flexible diaphragm utilize this energy to provide brake assistance. The diaphragm is balanced with engine vacuum until the brake pedal is depressed, allowing atmospheric pressure to unbalance the unit and apply force to the brake system.

Brakes will operate even if the power unit fails. This means the conventional brake system and the power assist system are completely separate. Troubleshooting conventional and power assist systems are exactly the same until the power unit is reached. As with conventional hydraulic brakes, a spongy pedal still means air is trapped in the hydraulic system. Power brakes give higher line pressure, making leaks more critical.

BENDIX DIAPHRAGM TYPES

These units are of the vacuum suspended type. Some units are of the single diaphragm type, while others are of the tandem diaphragm type. Both single piston and double piston or split system type master cylinders are used.

The vacuum suspended diaphragm type units utilize engine manifold vacuum and atmospheric pressure for its power. It consists of three basic elements combined into a single power unit. The three basic elements of the single diaphragm type are:

1. A vacuum power section which includes a front and rear shell, a power diaphragm, a return spring and a pushrod.
2. A control valve, built integral with the power diaphragm and connected through a valve rod to the brake pedal, controls the degree of brake application or release in accordance with the pressure applied to the brake pedal.
3. A hydraulic master cylinder, attached to the vacuum power section which contains all the elements of the conventional brake master cylinder except for the pushrod, supplies fluid under pressure to the wheel brakes in proportion to the pressure applied to the brake pedal.

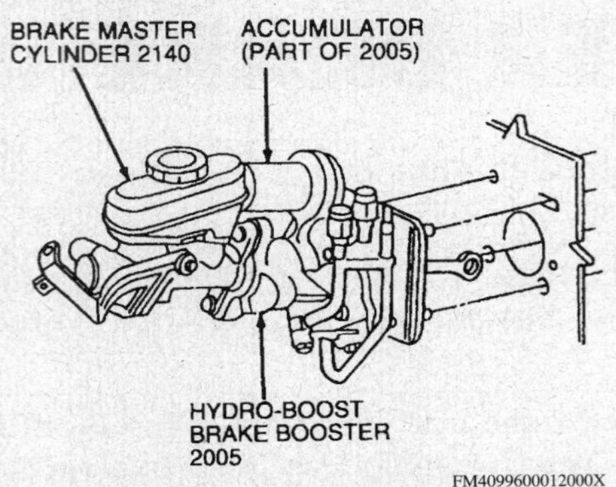

Fig. 1 Bendix Hydro-Boost

Operation

Upon application of the brakes, the valve rod and plunger move to the lefthand in the power diaphragm to close the vacuum port and open the atmospheric port to admit air through the air cleaner and valve at the rear diaphragm chamber. With vacuum present in the rear chamber, a force is developed to move the power diaphragm, hydraulic pushrod and hydraulic piston or pistons to close the compensating port or ports and force fluid under pressure through the residual check valve or valves and lines into the front and rear wheel cylinders to actuate the brakes.

As pressure is developed within the master cylinder a counter force acting through the hydraulic pushrod and reaction disc against the vacuum power diaphragm and valve plunger sets up a reaction force opposing the force applied to the valve rod and plunger. This reaction force tends to close the atmospheric port and reopen the vacuum port. Since this force is in opposition to the force applied to the brake pedal by the driver it gives the driver a "feel" of the amount of brake applied. The proportion of reactive force applied to the valve plunger through the reaction disc is designed into the Master-Vac to ensure maximum power consistent with maintaining pedal feel. The reaction force is in direct proportion to the hydraulic pressure developed within the brake system.

BENDIX HYDRO-BOOST SYSTEM

The Bendix Hydro-Boost System, **Fig. 1**, is a hydraulically operated booster with fluid provided by the power steering pump. If power steering fluid flow is interrupted, a reserve accumulator system stores enough fluid under pressure to provide at least two power-assisted stops. Manual brake application is permitted if the reserve system is depleted.

The Hydro-Boost booster, power steering pump and hydraulic hoses are all serviced separately. If the booster becomes inoperative or is damaged, it must be replaced as an assembly.

TROUBLESHOOTING

Complaints about power brake operation should be handled as if two separate systems exist. Inspect for faults in the hydraulic system first. If it is satisfactory, start inspecting the power brake circuit. For a quick inspection of proper power unit operation, press the brake pedal firmly and then start the engine. The pedal should fall away slightly and less pressure should be needed to maintain the pedal in any position.

Another inspection begins with installation of a suitable pressure gauge in the brake hydraulic system. Take a reading with the engine Off and the power unit not operating. Maintaining the same pedal height, start the engine and take another reading. There should be a substantial pressure increase in the second reading.

Pedal free travel and total travel are critical on models equipped with power brakes. Pedal travel should be kept strictly to specifications.

Take a manifold vacuum reading or inspect operation of the external vacuum pump if the power unit is not giving enough assistance. Remember, though, on currently produced emission controlled engines, manifold vacuum readings may be less than 15 inches Hg at idle. If manifold vacuum is abnormally low, tune the engine and then inspect the power brakes again. Naturally, loose vacuum lines and clogged air intake filters will cut down brake efficiency. Most units have a check valve that retains some vacuum in the system when the engine is Off. A vacuum gauge inspection of this valve will tell when it is restricted, stuck open or closed.

Failure of the brakes to release in most instances is caused by a tight or misaligned connection between the power unit and the brake linkage. If this connection is free, look for a broken piston, diaphragm or bellows and return spring.

A simple hydraulic system inspection should be made before proceeding. Loosen the connection between the master cylinder and the brake booster. If the brakes release, the trouble is in the power unit; if the brakes still will not release, look for a restricted brake line or similar difficulties in the regular hydraulic circuit.

A residual pressure check valve is usually included immediately under the brake line connection on hydraulic assist power brakes. This valve maintains a slight hydraulic pressure within the brake lines and wheel cylinders to give better pedal response. If it is sticking, the brakes may not release.

Power brakes that have a hard pedal are usually suffering from a milder form of the same ills that cause complete power unit failure. Collapsed or leaking vacuum lines or insufficient manifold vacuum, as well as punctured diaphragms or bellows and leaky piston seals, all lead to weak power unit operation. A steady hiss when the brake is held down means a vacuum leak that will cause poor power unit operation.

Do not immediately condemn the power unit if the brakes grab. First look for all the usual causes, such as greasy linings, scored rotors or drums. Then investigate the power unit. When the trouble has been traced to the power unit, inspect for a damaged reaction control. The reaction control is usually made up of a diaphragm, spring and valves that tends to resist pedal action. It is put in the system to give the pedal "feel."

On models equipped with the Bendix Hydro-Boost system, ensure engine is in Off position, then pressing and releasing the brake pedal several times to relieve all hydraulic pressure from the booster. Depress and hold the pedal with light pressure. Start engine and note pedal reaction. If it does not fall slightly and hold, press and release the pedal several times, then depress and hold with medium foot pressure. If the pedal now moves toward the floor, inspect for brake fluid leakage at master cylinder, brake hoses and all connections, **Fig. 2.**

To inspect the Hydro-Boost unit for leakage, idle the engine, then depress and hold the brake pedal for no more than five seconds with heavy foot pressure. If the booster shows any signs of fluid leakage, it must be replaced.

An accumulator reserve retention inspection requires operating the engine at idle, then depressing and holding the brake pedal for no more than five seconds with heavy foot pressure, or holding the steering wheel at full stop. Turn the ignition Off, then wait 8–12 hours. Depress the brake pedal and inspect for reserve. If no reserve is present, the booster is defective and must be replaced.

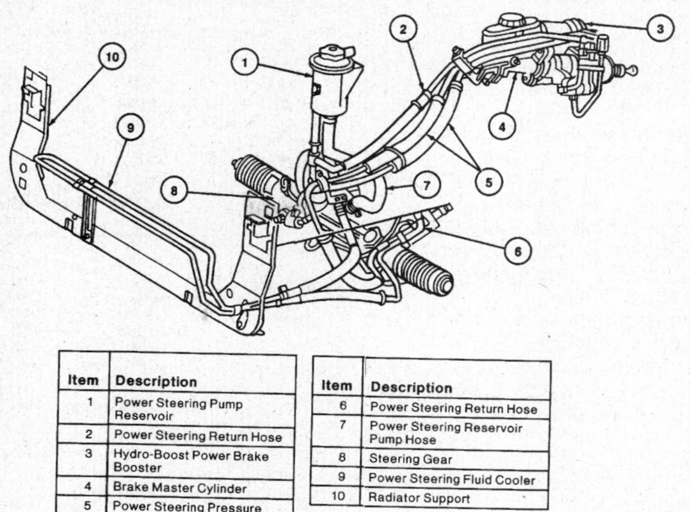

Item	Description	Item	Description
1	Power Steering Pump Reservoir	6	Power Steering Return Hose
2	Power Steering Return Hose	7	Power Steering Reservoir Pump Hose
3	Hydro-Boost Power Brake Booster	8	Steering Gear
4	Brake Master Cylinder	9	Power Steering Fluid Cooler
5	Power Steering Pressure Hose	10	Radiator Support

FM4099600013000X

Fig. 2 Hydro-Boost system fluid distribution. Mustang w/4.6L engine

BENDIX DIAPHRAGM TYPES

Hard Pedal Or No Assist

1. Air cleaner element clogged.
2. Control valve faulty.
3. Defective diaphragm.
4. Worn or distorted reaction plate or levers.
5. Cracked or broken power piston or levers.
6. Internal or external leaks.

Brakes Grab

1. Control valve defective or sticking.
2. Bind in linkage.
3. Reaction diaphragm leaking.
4. Worn or distorted levers or plate.

No Or Slow Release

1. Pushrod adjustment improper.
2. Linkage binding.
3. Return spring defective.

BENDIX HYDRO-BOOST TYPE

No Power Assist

1. Power steering pump drive belt slipping or worn.
2. Power steering pump fluid level improper.
3. Linkage binding.
4. Hydro-Boost unit failure.

Erratic Booster Operation, Binding, Grabbing Or Sticking

1. Supply hose leakage or obstructions.
2. Hydro-Boost unit seal leakage.

ADJUSTMENTS

PUSHROD

Proper adjustment of the master cylinder pushrod is necessary to ensure proper operation of the power brake system. A pushrod that is too long will prevent the master cylinder piston from completely releasing hydraulic pressure, eventually causing the brakes to drag. A pushrod that is too short will cause excessive brake pedal travel and cause groaning noises to come from the booster when the brakes are applied. A properly adjusted pushrod that remains assembled to the booster with which is was matched during production should not require service adjustment. However, if the booster, master cylinder or pushrod are serviced, the pushrod may require adjustment.

If the power unit pushrod requires an adjustment the Power Unit Repair Kit for the unit being serviced includes a gauge. The gauge measures from the end of the pushrod to the power unit shell.

ESCORT, TRACER & ZX2

Refer to "Hydraulic Brake Systems" section for adjustment procedure.

EXCEPT ESCORT, TRACER & ZX2

Bendix Type

1. Disconnect master cylinder from booster leaving brake lines connected, and secure cylinder to prevent lines from being damaged.
2. Start engine and operate engine at idle speed.
3. With engine running, position gauge over pushrod. Gauge should bottom against booster housing with a force of approximately 5 lbs. applied to pushrod, **Fig. 3.**
4. If force required to seat gauge exceeds 5 lbs., shorten length of pushrod. If force required to seat gauge is less than 5 lbs., lengthen pushrod. **Ensure pushrod is properly seated in booster when performing gauge inspection.**
5. Install master cylinder, then remove reservoir cover.
6. With engine running, observe fluid surface in reservoir when brakes are applied and released rapidly. If no movement is observed on fluid surface, pushrod is adjusted too long.

Single Diaphragm Booster

1. Remove master cylinder as previously outlined.
2. Position master cylinder gauge T87C-2500-A, or equivalent, on end of master cylinder.
3. Loosen setscrew and push gauge plunger against bottom of primary piston.
4. While holding gauge in position, tighten setscrew.
5. Invert gauge and place over brake booster pushrod. Reading should be zero.
6. If clearance is not zero, loosen pushrod locknut and adjust pushrod.
7. Reverse procedure to install.

POWER BRAKE UNIT SERVICE

POWER BOOSTER, REPLACE

CONTINENTAL

1. Remove battery, then disconnect speed control actuator electrical connector.
2. Remove two retaining nuts and speed control actuator cable and position aside.

3. Remove two strut tower brace nuts and brace.
4. Remove windshield wiper motor, then rubber grommet from lower cowl panel.
5. Remove lower cowl panel nut and bolts, then lower cowl panel.
6. Disconnect power brake booster check valve, then master cylinder.
7. Remove retaining nut and evaporative emission canister purge valve.
8. Disconnect EVAP electrical connector, then vacuum hoses.
9. Remove instrument close out panel pushpins and the panel.
10. Remove stoplight switch retaining pin, then slide stoplight switch and booster push rod from brake pedal pin.
11. Remove retaining nuts and power brake booster.
12. Reverse procedure to install, noting the following:
    a. Ensure proper clearance between pushrod and master cylinder exists as described under "Adjustments."
    b. Bleed brake system as described in "Hydraulic Brake Systems" section.
    c. **Torque** booster to dash panel retaining nuts to 19–25 ft. lbs.

CONTOUR & MYSTIQUE

Pump brake pedal several times to exhaust any vacuum in the booster.

1. Disconnect brake fluid level indicator.
2. **On models equipped with 2.0L engine,** remove mass air flow sensor and air cleaner cover.
3. **On all models,** disconnect vacuum hose from booster unit.
4. Remove master cylinder.
5. Remove booster mounting bolts, then while an assistant holds and guides booster unit out of panel, remove brake booster pushrod retainer from rod.
6. Remove booster from vehicle.
7. Reverse procedure to install, noting the following:
    a. Ensure proper clearance between pushrod and master cylinder exists as described under "Adjustments."
    b. Bleed brake system as described in the "Hydraulic Brake Systems" section.
    c. **Torque** booster to dash panel retaining nuts to 29 ft. lbs.
    d. **Torque** master cylinder to booster locking nuts to 15–28 ft. lbs.

CROWN VICTORIA, GRAND MARQUIS & TOWN CAR

1. Disconnect fluid level sensor connector.
2. Position speed control cable out of way.
3. Disconnect power brake booster check valve.
4. Remove brake master cylinder nuts.
5. Remove wiring harness bracket and position aside.
6. Remove brake master cylinder and position aside.
7. Remove instrument close-out panel pushpins, then the panel.
8. Remove stoplight switch retaining pin.
9. Slide stoplight switch and booster push rod off brake pedal pin.
10. Remove brake booster retaining nuts, then the power brake booster.
11. Reverse procedure to install. **Torque** retaining nuts to 16–21 ft. lbs.

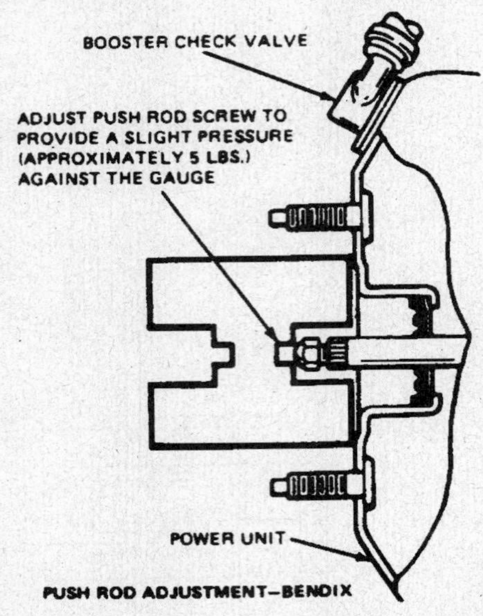

Fig. 3 Master cylinder pushrod adjustment. Bendix type vacuum booster

ESCORT, TRACER & ZX2

Pump brake pedal several times to exhaust any vacuum in the booster.

1. Remove master cylinder as described in the "Hydraulic Brake Systems" section.
2. Disconnect rubber hose connecting intake manifold to power brake unit.
3. **On Escort, Tracer and ZX2 models,** remove instrument panel steering column cover.
4. **On all models,** remove spring clip in brake pedal clevis pin.
5. Remove brake pedal clevis pin, then brake pedal pushrod from brake pedal.
6. Remove power brake unit attaching nuts, then power brake unit from vehicle.
7. Reverse procedure to install, noting the following:
    a. Ensure proper clearance between pushrod and master cylinder exists as described under "Adjustments."
    b. **Torque** booster to dash panel retaining nuts to 14–19 ft. lbs.
    c. **Torque** master cylinder retaining nuts to 8–12 ft. lbs.

FOCUS

If fluid is spilled on paintwork, it must be immediately rinsed off with cold water.

1. Remove master cylinder as outlined under "Hydraulic Brake Systems."
2. **On models equipped with speed control,** disconnect speed control unit electrical connector then remove speed control unit.
3. **On all models,** remove brake tubes from bulkhead retainers.
4. Disconnect hydraulic control unit electrical connector.
5. Disconnect brake lines from hydraulic control unit, cap all fittings to prevent contamination.
6. Remove brake booster actuating rod from brake pedal.
7. Remove brake booster retaining nuts from inside of vehicle, then remove brake booster.
8. Reverse procedure to install.

LS & THUNDERBIRD

Removal

1. Remove wiper arm nuts and remove wiper arms, then disconnect washer hose.
2. Remove pushpins, rubber trim and cowl cover.
3. Remove vacuum hose bracket nut and position bracket aside.
4. Remove cowl brace center and end bolts, then the bracket.
5. Disconnect coolant reservoir return hose.
6. Remove brake master cylinder.
7. Disconnect power brake booster check valve and electrical connector.
8. Remove coolant reservoir bolts and disconnect hose.
9. Remove coolant reservoir.
10. Remove clip and brake pedal pin.
11. Remove mounting nuts and power brake booster.

Installation

1. Install power brake booster and mounting nuts.
2. Install brake pedal pin and clip.
3. Install radiator coolant recovery reservoir mounting bolts and hose.
4. Connect power brake booster electrical connector and check valve.
5. Connect coolant reservoir return hose.
6. Install brake master cylinder.
7. Install cowl brace end and center bolts.
8. Install vacuum hose bracket nut.
9. Install cowl cover, rubber trim and pushpins.
10. Connect washer hose and install wiper arm nuts.
11. Bleed brake system.

MARK VIII

1. Remove windshield wiper motor.
2. Disconnect power brake booster check valve.
3. Disconnect fluid level sensor connector.
4. Remove nut retaining wire harness support bracket, then the bracket.
5. Remove nuts retaining brake master cylinder to power brake booster.
6. Position brake master cylinder out of the way.
7. Disconnect harness connectors.
8. Working inside vehicle below the instrument panel, remove retaining clip from the powertrain control module.
9. Remove power brake booster push rod from brake pedal.
10. Disconnect electrical connector from stoplight switch.
11. Remove hairpin retainer and push rod spacer.
12. Remove push rod, stoplight switch and

push rod bushing.
13. Remove processor bracket to brake booster retaining nuts. Position bracket to the side.
14. Remove brake pedal support bracket to booster studs retaining nuts.
15. From inside the engine compartment, move power brake booster forward until booster studs clear the instrument panel.
16. Rotate front of power brake booster toward engine, then remove power brake booster.
17. Reverse procedures to install, noting the following:
    a. **Torque** power brake booster-to-instrument panel retaining nut to 16–21 ft. lbs.
    b. **Torque** break master cylinder-to-power brake booster locking nuts to 16–21 ft. lbs.
    c. **Torque** pedal support bracket-to-cowl bolt to 16–21 ft. lbs.
    d. **Torque** master cylinder brake tube fittings 13–17 ft. lbs.

MUSTANG

Vacuum Type System

Pump brake pedal several times to exhaust any vacuum in the booster.

1. Remove air cleaner assembly.
2. Disconnect manifold vacuum hose from power booster check valve.
3. Disconnect hydraulic lines from master cylinder and cap open lines and ports.
4. Remove master cylinder retaining nuts and master cylinder.
5. **On models equipped with manual transmission,** remove clutch cable routing bracket and position cable aside.
6. **On all models,** disconnect accelerator cable at dash panel and accelerator pedal and shaft, then reposition to gain maneuvering room for brake booster.
7. Working under instrument panel, disconnect electrical connector from stop lamp switch.
8. Remove hairpin type retainer. Slide stop lamp switch off brake pedal pin just far enough for the switch outer hole to clear the pin, then lower switch away from pin.
9. Slide brake master cylinder pushrod bushing off of brake pedal pin.
10. Remove booster-to-dash panel attaching nuts.
11. **On models equipped with speed control,** unfasten control amplifier from lower outboard booster stud and position aside.
12. **On all models,** work from engine compartment and move booster forward until booster studs clear the dash panel, then raise front of unit and remove from vehicle.
13. Reverse procedure to install, noting the following:
    a. Ensure proper clearance between pushrod and master cylinder exists as described under "Adjustments."
    b. Bleed brake system as described in the "Hydraulic Brake Systems" section.
    c. **Torque** booster to dash panel retaining nuts and master cylinder to booster locking nuts to 15–23 ft. lbs.

Hydro-Boost System

The booster should not be carried by the accumulator, nor should it be dropped on this portion. The accumulator contains high pressure nitrogen gas and can be dangerous if mishandled.

If the accumulator is ready for disposal, it must be kept clear of excessive heat, fire or incineration. Before disposal, drill a 1⁄16 inch diameter hole in the accumulator can's end to relieve the gas pressure. Be sure to use wear safety glasses while performing this operation.

Do not activate the booster when the master cylinder has been removed.

1. Apply brake pedal several times to discharge accumulator.
2. Remove brake lines from proportioning valve's primary and secondary ports.
3. Disconnect fluid level sensor.
4. **On models equipped with automatic transmission,** disconnect shift interlock cable.
5. **On models equipped with manual transmission,** disconnect clutch cable from master cylinder routing bracket.
6. **On all models,** remove hose routing bracket from master cylinder.
7. Disconnect power steering pressure hoses and return line from Hydro-Boost unit. Move hoses out of the way.
8. Remove electrical connector from brake lamp switch.
9. Loosen four booster retaining nuts and brake pedal support bracket to cowl bolt.
10. Remove hairpin type retainer. Slide stop lamp switch off brake pedal pin just far enough for switch outer arm to clear pin, then remove switch.
11. Slide brake master cylinder pushrod bushing off brake pedal pin.
12. Remove booster to firewall attaching nuts.
13. Move booster and master cylinder forward and upward until booster's studs clear firewall. Remove unit from vehicle.
14. Reverse procedure to install, noting the following:
    a. **Torque** booster to firewall nuts to 16–21 ft. lbs.
    b. **Torque** brake pedal support bracket to cowl bolt to 14–19 ft. lbs.
    c. **Torque** brake line fittings in ports to 11–17 ft. lbs.
    d. **Torque** power steering pressure hoses and return line to booster tubes to 10–15 ft. lbs., **Fig. 2.**
    e. Bleed brake system. Check power brake operation and bleed booster of air if necessary.

SABLE & TAURUS

1998–99

Pump brake pedal several times to exhaust any vacuum in the booster.

1. Disconnect vacuum hose from booster unit.
2. Disconnect air cleaner cover and position aside.
3. Remove speed control actuator nuts, then position actuator aside.
4. Disconnect brake fluid level sensor from master cylinder.
5. Remove nut holding cowl top inner panel tube to master cylinder mounting stud, then remove master cylinder.
6. Working under instrument panel, disconnect electrical connector from stop lamp switch.
7. Remove stop lamp switch retaining pin and white nylon washer. Slide switch off brake pedal pin enough so outer plate of switch clears the pin, then remove switch from pin.
8. Remove brake booster-to-dash panel attaching nuts, then slide booster pushrod and pushrod bushing off brake pedal pin.
9. Slide booster out of panel.
10. Reverse procedure to install, noting the following:
    a. Ensure proper clearance between pushrod and master cylinder exists as described under "Adjustments."
    b. Bleed brake system as described in the "Hydraulic Brake Systems" section.
    c. **Torque** booster to dash panel retaining nuts and cowl top inner panel tube nut to 16–21 ft. lbs.
    d. **Torque** master cylinder to booster locking nuts to 19–28 ft. lbs.

2000

1. Remove brake master cylinder as outlined under "Hydraulic Brake Systems."
2. Remove cowl vent screen.
3. Disconnect speed control mounting nuts and electrical connector and position out of way.
4. Disconnect vacuum check valve from brake booster.
5. Remove heater hose retainer and position out of way.
6. Disconnect electrical connector retainers and position wiring harness out of way.
7. Remove steering column opening cover.
8. Disconnect electrical connector, remove push rod retainer, then slide push rod off pin and remove stop light switch, washer and bushing.
9. Remove and discard brake booster nuts.
10. Remove brake booster from vehicle.
11. Reverse procedure to install, noting the following:
    a. Perform push rod adjustment as outlined in this section.
    b. Use new nuts when mounting brake booster.

2001–02

1. Disconnect mass air flow sensor and breather tubes.
2. Disconnect outlet tube from throttle body.
3. Remove engine air cleaner housing

cover and position aside.

4. Remove wiper mounting arm and pivot shaft.
5. Remove brake master cylinder as outlined under "Hydraulic Brake Systems."
6. Disconnect electrical connector, remove mounting nuts and position speed control module and bracket out of way.
7. Disconnect manual control lever cable from transmission range sensor and remove manual cable bracket and nut.
8. Remove manual cable bracket bolts and position bracket out of way.
9. Remove vacuum outlet manifold assembly.
10. Disconnect vacuum check valve from brake booster.
11. Remove heater hose retainer strap and position hose out of way.
12. Remove wiring harnesses and connectors from brake booster.
13. Remove steering column opening cover.
14. Disconnect stoplight switch electrical connector, remove push rod retainer, then push rod off of pin.
15. Remove stoplight switch, washer and bushing.
16. Remove and discard brake booster mounting nuts.
17. Remove brake booster.
18. Reverse procedure to install, noting the following:
    a. Perform pushrod adjustment as outlined in this section.
    b. Use new nuts when mounting brake booster.

1999–2002 COUGAR

2.0L Engine

1. Remove air cleaner and mass air flow sensor.
2. Remove air cleaner outlet tube.
3. Disconnect engine wiring harness electrical connector.
4. **On models equipped with automatic transaxle,** remove automatic transaxle fluid dipstick.
5. **On all models,** remove master cylinder.
6. Remove brake booster actuator rod retaining clip.
7. Disconnect vacuum hose from brake booster. **Do not pull on accelerator speed control cable.**
8. Remove brake booster.
9. Reverse procedure to install, noting the following:
    a. Bleed brake system.
    b. Ensure that brake booster connecting rod is correctly positioned through bulkhead rubber boot.

2.5L Engine

1. Remove air cleaner and air cleaner outlet tube.
2. Remove master cylinder as outlined under "Hydraulic Brake Systems."
3. Disconnect vacuum hose from brake booster.
4. Remove brake booster actuator rod retaining clip.
5. **On models equipped with automatic transaxle,** remove automatic transaxle fluid dipstick.
6. **On all models,** remove brake booster nuts.
7. Follow master cylinder brake lines back and remove from control unit.
8. Disconnect electrical connectors from booster.
9. **On models equipped with automatic transaxle,** disconnect gear selector cable and bracket.
10. **On all models,** disconnect starter motor power cable.
11. Depressurize fuel system as outlined under "Precautions" in "2.0L or 2.5L Engine" sections in this manual.
12. Disconnect fuel flow and return lines.
13. Remove brake booster from vehicle.
14. Reverse procedure to install.

OVERHAUL

Overhaul is not required. If it has been determined that the brake booster is defective, replace power brake unit as an assembly. In some instances, the only service required is replacement of the check valve and grommet and pushrod adjustment.

TECHNICAL SERVICE BULLETINS

LONGER THAN EXPECTED PEDAL TRAVEL WITHOUT ADDITIONAL PEDAL EFFORT/REDUCED POWER BRAKE ASSIST DURING RAPID, REPEATED BRAKE APPLICATIONS DURING HIGH ALTITUDE OPERATION

2000 LS

This bulletin applies to 2000 LS models built from 3/1/1999 through 8/9/1999 with V-6 engine.

Customers may encounter one or both of the following:

Reduced power brake assist during rapid repeated brake applications when operating at high altitudes.

Longer than expected brake pedal travel without additional pedal effort when vehicle is stopped and engine is running.

A revised brake supply vacuum manifold is available to address this concern.

AUTOMATIC TRANSMISSIONS/ TRANSAXLES

TABLE OF CONTENTS

Application Chart

Model	Year	Engine	Transmission/ Transaxle
Continental	1998–2000	All	AX4N
	2001–02	All	4F50N
Contour	1998–2000	All	CD4E
Cougar	1999–2002	All	CD4E
Crown Victoria	1998–2002	All	4R70W
Escort	1998–2002	All	F4E-III
Focus	2000–01	All	4F27E
Grand Marquis	1998–2002	All	4R70W
LS	2000–02	All	5R55N
Mark VIII	1998	All	4R70W
Mustang	1998–2002	All	4R70W
Mystique	1998–2000	All	CD4E
Sable	1998–2000	3.0L	AX4N or AX4S
	2001	All	AX4N or AX4S
	2002	All	AX4N or 4F50N
Taurus	1998–99	3.0L	AX4N or AX4S
		3.4L	AX4N
	2000–01	All	AX4S
	2000–02	All	AX4N or 4F50N
Thunderbird	2002	All	5R55N
Tracer	1998–99	All	F4E-III
Town Car	1998–2002	All	4R70W
ZX2	1998–2002	All	F4E-III

AX4S (AXOD-E) Automatic Overdrive Transaxle

NOTE: On Air Bag Equipped Models, Refer To "Air Bag System Precautions" Located In The Front Of This Manual For System Disarming & Arming Procedures.

NOTE: Refer To "Computer Relearn Procedures" Located In The Front Of This Manual When Battery Power To The Computer Has Been Interrupted.

NOTE: "Electrical Symbol & Wire Color Code Identification" Located In The Front Of This Manual May Be Used As An Aid When Using Wiring Circuits Found In This Section.

NOTE: Prior To Performing Any Service Operations Listed In This Section, Consult "Technical Service Bulletins" Section For Related Information.

INDEX

PRECAUTIONS

AIR BAG SYSTEMS

Refer to "Air Bag System Precautions" in front of this manual for system disarming and arming procedures.

BATTERY GROUND CABLE

Prior to service, disconnect battery ground cable and isolate as required.

IDENTIFICATION

Identification tags located on top of converter housing, includes transaxle assembly number, serial number and build date, **Fig. 1.**

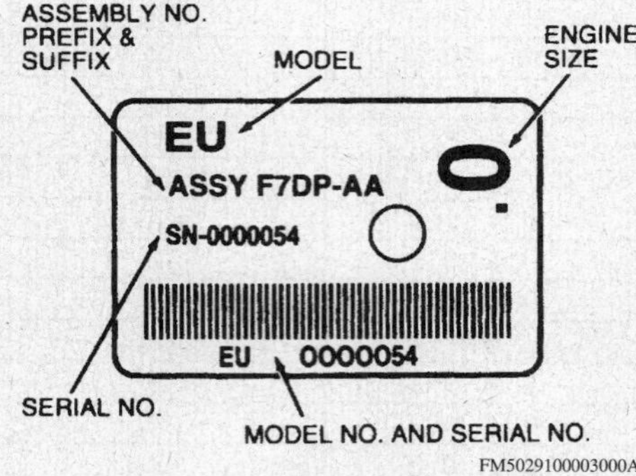

Fig. 1 Identification tag

DESCRIPTION

This automatic overdrive transaxle is fully automatic with four forward speeds and one Reverse in addition to Neutral and Park, **Fig. 2.**

AX4S (AXOD-E) transaxle has two planetary gear sets and a combination planetary/differential gear set. Four multiple plate clutches, two band assemblies and two one-way clutches.

A lock-up torque converter is coupled to engine crankshaft and transmits engine power to gear train by means of a drive link assembly (chain) that connects drive and driven sprockets. Converter clutch application is controlled through an electronic control integrated in on-board EEC-IV system, **Fig. 3.** These controls, along with hydraulic controls in valve body, operate a piston plate clutch in torque converter to provide improved fuel economy by eliminating converter slip when applied.

TORQUE CONVERTER

Converter

Torque converter couples engine to turbine shaft. It also provides torque multiplication and absorbs engine shock of gear shifting.

Piston Plate Clutch & Damper

Piston plate clutch and damper transmit engine power to turbine from converter cover during lock-up.

Converter Cover

Converter cover transmits power from engine into converter. Also, oil pump driveshaft is splined to converter cover.

Turbine

Turbine is splined to drive sprocket turbine shaft and driven by fluid by impeller.

Impeller

Impeller is driven by converter cover. Together with reactor it supplies torque multiplication.

Reactor

Reactor, also called stator, contains a one-way clutch to hold it stationary only when reaction is required. It also causes hydraulic reaction during torque multiplication.

GEAR TRAIN

Forward Clutch

Forward clutch locks driven sprocket to low one-way clutch.

Low One-Way Clutch

Low one-way clutch transmits torque from driven sprocket to sun gear of forward planetary gear set in first gear. It also provides engine braking in third gear in connection with forward clutch.

Overdrive Band

Overdrive band holds sun gear of forward planetary gear set stationary in fourth gear (overdrive).

Direct Clutch

Direct clutch locks sun gear of planetary of forward planetary gear set to direct one-way clutch in third gear.

Direct One-Way Clutch

Direct one-way clutch transmits torque from driven sprocket to sun gear of forward planetary gear set in third gear and provides engine braking in manual low.

Intermediate Clutch

Intermediate clutch locks driven sprocket to planetary of forward planetary gear set in second and third gear.

Reverse Clutch

Reverse clutch holds planetary of forward planetary gear set and ring gear of rear planetary gear set stationary in reverse gear.

Planetary Gears

Two planetary gear sets are used to provide four forward speeds, including reverse, depending upon clutch and/or band applications.

Parking Gear

Parking gear allows output (axle) shaft to be mechanically locked by parking pawl anchored in case.

Low Intermediate Band

Low intermediate band holds sun gear of rear planetary gear set stationary in low, first and second gears.

Final Drive Sun Gear

Final drive sun gear transfers torque from transaxle output to final drive planetary.

Final Drive Planet

Final drive planet drives differential.

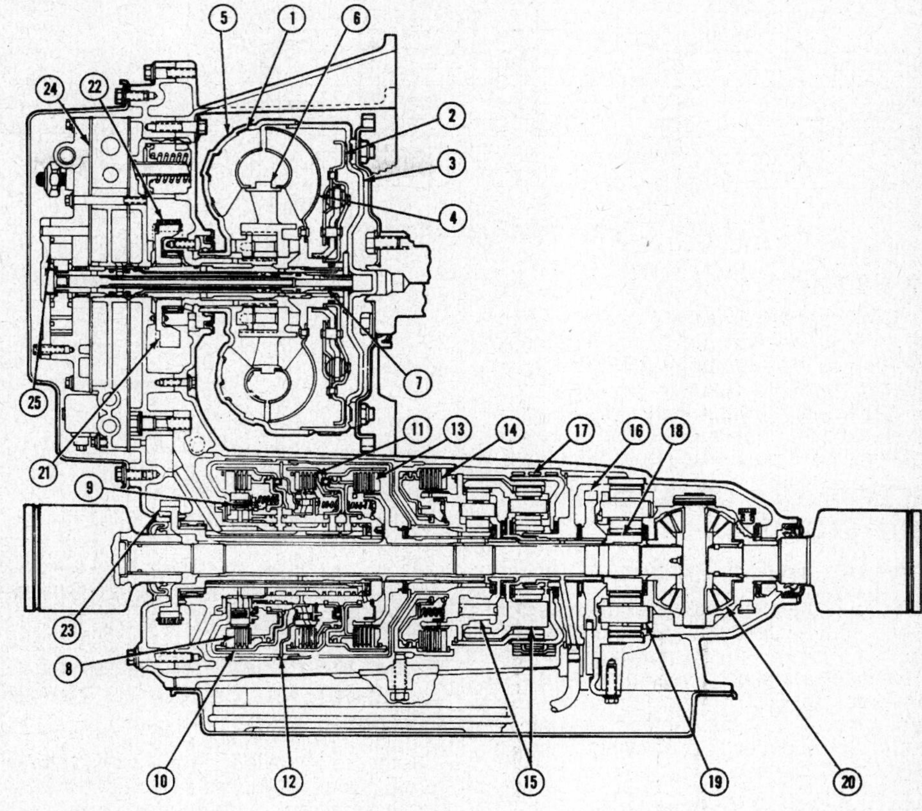

1. TORQUE CONVERTER
2. CONVERTER CLUTCH (PISTON PLATE CLUTCH AND DAMPER ASSEMBLY)
3. CONVERTER COVER
4. TURBINE
5. IMPELLER
6. REACTOR
7. OIL PUMP DRIVESHAFT
8. FORWARD CLUTCH
9. LOW ONE-WAY CLUTCH
10. OVERDRIVE BAND
11. DIRECT CLUTCH
12. DIRECT ONE-WAY CLUTCH
13. INTERMEDIATE CLUTCH
14. REVERSE CLUTCH
15. PLANETARY GEARS
16. PARKING GEAR
17. LOW-INTERMEDIATE BAND
18. FINAL DRIVE SUN GEAR
19. FINAL DRIVE PLANET
20. DIFFERENTIAL ASSEMBLY
21. DRIVE SPROCKET
22. DRIVE LINK ASSEMBLY (CHAIN)
23. DRIVEN SPROCKET
24. VALVE BODY (MAIN CONTROL ASSEMBLY)
25. OIL PUMP

FM5028800007000X

Fig. 2 Cross-sectional view of transaxle

Differential

Differential drives front axle shafts and provides differential action if driving wheels are turning at different speeds.

TORQUE CONVERTER & GEAR TRAIN

Drive Sprocket

Drive sprocket transmits power from converter to drive link (chain).

Drive Link (Chain)

Drive link transmits converter power to gear train.

Driven Sprocket

Driven sprocket transmits converter power to gear train.

HYDRAULIC SYSTEM

Valve Body

Valve body or main control directs fluid (oil) under pressure to torque converter, band servos, clutches and governor to control transaxle operation.

Oil Pump

Oil pump provides a supply of fluid (oil) under pressure to operate, lubricate and cool transaxle. Pump is a variable capacity vane and rotor pump with output flow proportional to demand. It is located within transaxle control valve and pump.

Overdrive Servo

Overdrive servo applies overdrive band in fourth gear.

Low-Intermediate Servo

Low-intermediate servo applies low-intermediate band in manual, low, first and second gears.

Governor

Governor provides a road speed signal to hydraulic control system for shift control and is driven by a gear on differential.

Gear	Low-Int Band	Overdrive Band	Forward Clutch	Intermediate Clutch	Direct Clutch	Reverse Clutch	Low One-Way Clutch	Direct One-Way Clutch
1st Gear Manual Low	Applied		Applied		Applied		Holding	
1st Gear (Drive)	Applied		Applied				Holding	
2nd Gear (Drive)	Applied		Applied	Applied			Overrunning	
3rd Gear (Drive)			Applied	Applied	Applied			Holding
4th Gear (Overdrive)		Applied		Applied	Applied			Overrunning
Reverse (R)			Applied			Applied	Holding	
Neutral (N)			Applied					
Park (P)			Applied					

FM5029501137000X

Fig. 3 Clutch & band application chart

Reservoir

Two reservoir areas are used to control oil level, dependent on fluid temperature. Along with lower sump, a fluid reservoir is located in lower section of valve body cover. As fluid temperature in reservoir increases, a thermostatic element closes, retaining fluid in upper reservoir.

ELECTRICAL COMPONENT FUNCTION

Turbine Speed Sensor

Turbine speed sensor is a variable reluctance sensor used with vehicle electronic control system. Sensor, along with a rotating exciter wheel on driven sprocket, sends a signal to EEC microprocessor. EEC reads this signal and reacts to speed information it transmits by controlling clutch application.

Shift Control Solenoid

Shift control solenoids provide proper operating gear selection and are controlled by EEC. There are three shift control solenoids in this transaxle. They are three port, normally open feed to control flow of oil to a hydraulic spool valve.

Transaxle Oil Temperature Sensor

Transaxle oil temperature sensor informs EEC of transaxle oil temperature. It is a thermostat whose resistance varies according to temperature.

Variable Force Solenoid

Variable force solenoid is an analog pressure regulator that varies transaxle line pressure as directed by microprocessor.

Modulated Lock-Up Solenoid Or Modulated Converter Clutch Control

Solenoid receives an electronic signal from EEC microprocessor and uses this information to vary pressure which sets slip in converter clutch.

DOWNSHIFTS

Under certain conditions transaxle will automatically downshift to a lower gear range without moving shift selector lever. There are three different types of downshift categories:

Coastdown

Coastdown downshift occurs when vehicle is coasting down to a stop.

Torque Demand

Torque demand downshift occurs during part throttle acceleration when demand for torque is greater than engine can provide at that gear ratio. Transaxle will disengage converter clutch to provide added acceleration, if applied.

Kickdown

Kickdown downshift occurs when accelerator pedal is depressed fully to floor. A forced downshift into second gear is possible less than 55 mph. Less than approximately 25 mph a forced kickdown to first gear will occur. All shift speed specifications will vary because of tire size and engine calibration requirements.

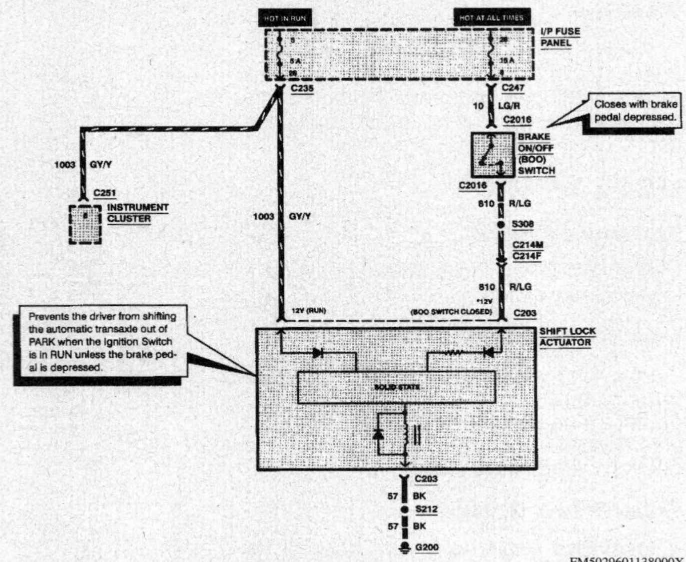

FM5029601138000X

Fig. 4 Brake-shift interlock system wiring circuit. 1998–99

TROUBLESHOOTING

BRAKE-SHIFT INTERLOCK SYSTEM

Refer to wiring diagrams **Figs. 4 and 5**, and troubleshooting charts **Figs. 6 and 7.**

TRANSAXLE

Refer to troubleshooting charts **Figs. 8 through 38.**

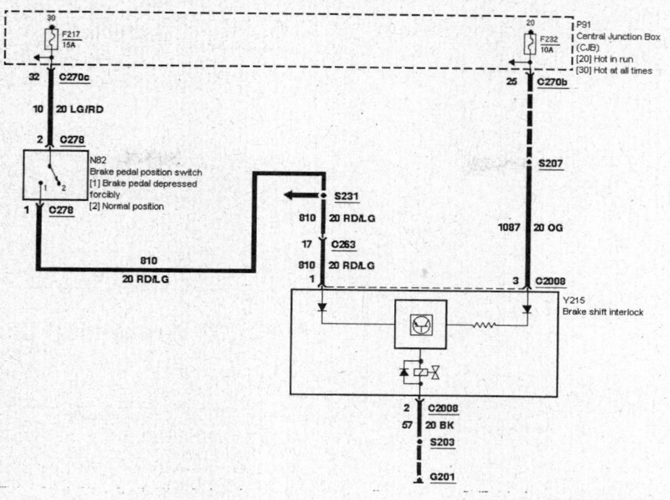

Fig. 5 Brake-shift interlock system wiring circuit. 2000–01

TROUBLESHOOTING TEST INDEX

Test	Description	Page No.	Fig. No.
—	Brake-Shift Interlock System Troubleshooting Chart (1998–99)	19-6	6
—	Brake-Shift Interlock System Troubleshooting Chart (2000–01)	19-6	7
201/301	No Forward Engagement	19-6	8
202/302	No Reverse Engagement	19-6	9
203/303	Harsh Reverse Engagement	19-7	10
204/304	Harsh Forward Engagement	19-7	11
205/305	Delayed/Soft Reverse Engagement	19-7	12
206/306	Delayed/Soft Forward Engagement	19-7	13
210/310	Some Or All Shifts Missing	19-8	14
211/311	Shift Timing Is Early/Late	19-8	15
212/312	Shift Timing Is Erratic/Hunting	19-8	16
213/313	Shift Feel Is Soft/Slipping	19-8	17
214/314	Shift Feel Is Harsh	19-9	18
215/315	No 1st Gear, Engages Higher Gear	19-9	19
216/316	No Manual 1st Gear	19-9	20
220/320	No Automatic 1–2 Shift	19-9	21
221/321	No Automatic 2–3 Shift	19-10	22
222/322	No Automatic 3–4 Shift	19-10	23
223/323	No Automatic 4–3 Shift	19-10	24
224/324	No Automatic 3–2 Shift	19-11	25
225/325	No Automatic 2–1 Shift	19-11	26
240/340	No Torque Converter Apply	19-11	27
241/341	Torque Converter Always Applied/Stalls Vehicle	19-11	28
242/342	Torque Converter Cycling/Shudder/Chatter	19-11	29
249/349	No Engine Braking In 3rd Gear D Position	19-12	30
250/350	No Engine Braking In 1st Gear Manual	19-12	31
251/351	Shift Lever Efforts High	19-12	32
252/352	External Leaks	19-12	33
253/353	Poor Vehicle Performance	19-12	34
254/354	Noise/Vibration In Forward/Reverse	19-12	35
255/355	Engine Will Not Crank	19-12	36
256/356	No Park Range	19-12	37
257/357	Transaxle Overheating	19-13	38

	Test Step	Result		Action to Take
A1	CHECK ELECTRON IGN FUSE			
	• Check Fuse 5 (5A) located in fuse junction panel. • **Is fuse OK?**	Yes No	▶ ▶	GO to **A3**. GO to **A2**
A2	CHECK FOR SHORT TO GROUND			
	• Turn ignition switch OFF. • Remove Fuse 5 (5A). • Disconnect shift-lock actuator connector C203 located to the right of steering column. • Measure resistance of the Circuit 1003 (GY/Y) between the correct terminal of Fuse 5 (5A) and ground. • **Is resistance greater than 10,000 ohms?**	Yes No	▶ ▶	REPLACE Fuse 5 (5A). GO to **A3.** SERVICE Circuit 1003 (GY/Y) wire between fuse junction panel and shift-lock actuator.
A3	CHECK POWER SUPPLY FROM FUSE 5 (5A)			
	• Reinstall Fuse 5 (5A). • Turn ignition switch to RUN. • Measure voltage on Circuit 1003 (GY/Y) wire and ground. • **Is voltage greater than 10 volts?**	Yes No	▶ ▶	GO to **A4.** SERVICE Circuit 1003 (GY/Y) wire between interior fuse panel and shift-lock actuator.
A4	CHECK POWER SUPPLY FROM FUSE 28 (15A)			
	• Turn ignition switch OFF. • Disconnect connector C2016. • Turn ignition switch ON. • Measure voltage on Circuit 10 (LG/R) and ground. • **Is voltage B+?**	Yes No	▶ ▶	GO to **A5.** SERVICE Circuit 10 (LG/R) for open. RESTORE vehicle and TEST system for normal operation.
A5	CHECK WIRE BETWEEN STOPLIGHT SWITCH AND SHIFT-LOCK ACTUATOR			
	• Turn ignition switch OFF. • Disconnect shift-lock actuator connector C203. • Apply brake pedal. • Measure voltage on Circuit 810 (R/LG) wire and ground. • **Is voltage greater than 10 volts with brake pedal applied and less than 1 volt with brake pedal released?**	Yes No	▶ ▶	GO to **A6.** SERVICE Circuit 810 (R/LG) wire between stoplight switch and shift-lock actuator.
A6	CHECK SHIFT-LOCK ACTUATOR GROUND			
	• Measure resistance of Circuit 57 (BK) and ground. • **Is resistance less than 5 ohms?**	Yes No	▶ ▶	REPLACE shift-lock actuator. SERVICE BK wire.

FM5029601139000X

Fig. 6 Brake-shift interlock system troubleshooting chart. 1998–99

Possible Component	Reference/Action
201 — ELECTRICAL ROUTINE	
Powertrain Control System	
• Electrical Inputs/Outputs, Vehicle Wiring Harnesses, powertrain control module.	• Run On-Board Diagnostics. Refer to MOTOR's Domestic Transmission Manual for diagnosis. Using the Rotunda Transmission Tester 007-00130 with AX4S Cable and Overlay 007-00087 or equivalent, perform transmission voltage tests. If DTC P1700 is present, check for a low transaxle fluid level. Then, continue to Hydraulic/Mechanical Routines.
301 — HYDRAULIC/MECHANICAL ROUTINE	
Fluid • Improper level, low	• Adjust fluid to proper level.
Driveshafts • Worn, damaged, misassembled	• Inspect for damage. Service as required.
Shift Linkage • Damaged, out of adjustment	• Inspect and service as required. Verify linkage adjustment After servicing linkage, verify Transmission Range sensor is properly adjusted.

FM5029801571010X

Fig. 8 Routines 201 & 301: No Forward Engagement (Part 1 of 2)

Possible Component	Reference/Action
Improper Pressures • Low Forward Clutch pressure, Low Line pressure, Low Intermediate Clutch pressure, Low EPC pressure	• Check pressure at line and EPC taps. Perform line pressures and stall speed tests. If pressures are low, check the following possible components: — fluid filter and fluid screen ring, — main control valve body, — pump assembly, — reverse clutch assembly, — low intermediate band servo, and — intermediate clutch assembly.
Fluid Filter and Fluid Filter Seal • Plugged, damaged • Fluid Filter Seal damaged	• Replace fluid filter and fluid filter seal.
Main Control Valve Body • Forward Clutch Pressure Tap Plug—damaged, loose or missing • Bolts out of torque specifications • Gaskets—damaged, off location • Pump assembly shaft—broken • 3-4 Shift Valve, Main Regulator Valve, Forward Clutch Control Valve, Manual Control Valve, 2-3 Servo Regulator Valve—stuck, damaged	• Inspect. Service as required. • Tighten bolts to specifications. • Inspect gasket for damage. Replace as required. • Service/replace as required. • Inspect. Service as required.
Pump Assembly • Bolts out of torque specification • Gaskets damaged, off location • Porosity/cross leaks and ball missing or leaking • Components damaged	• Tighten bolts to specification. • Inspect for damage. Replace as required. • Inspect for porosity and leaks. Replace as required. • Inspect for damage. Replace as required.
Support Assembly—Driven Sprocket • Bolts out of torque specifications • Seals—missing, damaged • Seal grooves damaged	• Tighten bolts to specifications. Use sealant on two external chain cover bolts. • Inspect seals. Replace as required. • Inspect for damage. Service as required.
Forward Clutch Assembly • Seals, Piston • Check balls • Piston cracked • Friction Elements—damaged or worn	• Perform Air Pressure Tests • Inspect seals for damage and replace as required. • Inspect for mislocation, poor seating damage. Replace cylinder as required. • Inspect piston. Replace as required. • Check for abnormal wear, damage. Replace as required.
Low One-Way Clutch Assembly • Worn, damaged or misassembled	• Inspect for damage. Service as required.
Low Intermediate Servo Assembly • • Seals, Piston • Fluid Transfer Tubes, Band, Anchor Pins—worn, damaged, loose, leaking • Apply Rod—incorrect length	• Perform Air Pressure Tests • Inspect. Replace as required. • Inspect. Service as required. • Replace as required.
Output Shaft • Splines damaged	• Inspect for damage. Service as required.

FM5029801571020X

Fig. 8 Routines 201 & 301: No Forward Engagement (Part 2 of 2)

Condition	Possible Source
• Shift Interlock System Does Not Release/Lock Correctly	• Circuitry open/shorted. • Fuse(s). • Stoplight switch. • Ignition/shifter interlock cable. • Shift lock actuator.
• Shift Control Linkage is Out of Correct Gear Relationship	• Damaged ignition/shifter interlock cable. • Loose ignition/shifter interlock cable. • Loose bracket. • Shift linkage out of adjustment.

FM5020002253000X

Fig. 7 Brake-shift interlock system troubleshooting chart. 2000–01

Possible Component	Reference/Action
202 — ELECTRICAL ROUTINE	
Powertrain Control System	
• Electrical Inputs/Outputs, Vehicle Wiring Harnesses, powertrain control module.	• Run On-Board Diagnostics. Refer to MOTOR's Domestic Transmission Manual for diagnosis. Using the Rotunda Transmission Tester 007-00130 with AX4S cable and overlay 007-00087 or equivalent, perform transmission voltage tests. If DTC P1700 is present, check for a low transaxle fluid level. Then, continue to Hydraulic/Mechanical Routines.
302 — HYDRAULIC/MECHANICAL ROUTINE	
Fluid • Improper level	• Adjust fluid to proper level.
Halfshafts • Worn, damaged, misassembled	• Inspect for damage. Service as required.
Shift Linkage • Damaged or out of adjustment	• Inspect and service as required. Verify linkage adjustment. After servicing linkage, verify that the Transmission Range sensor is properly adjusted.
Improper Pressures • Low Reverse Clutch pressure, Low Line pressure, Low Forward Clutch pressure, Low EPC pressure	• Check pressure at line and EPC taps. Perform Line Pressure and Stall Speed Tests. If pressures are low, check the following possible components: — fluid filter and fluid screen ring, — main control valve body, — pump assembly, — reverse clutch assembly.
Fluid Filter and Fluid Filter Seal • Plugged or damaged	• Replace fluid filter and fluid filter seal.
Main Control Valve Body • Forward Clutch Pressure Tap Plug—damaged, loose, missing • Bolts out of torque specification. • Gasket—damaged, off location • Pump Assembly Shaft—broken • Forward Clutch Control Valve, Manual Control Valve, Main Regulator Valve, Springs—stuck, damaged	• Inspect. Service as required. • Tighten bolts to specification. • Inspect for damage. Replace as required. • Inspect. Service/replace as required. • Inspect for damage. Service as required.
Pump Assembly • Bolts out of torque specification. • Gasket damaged, off location • Porosity/cross leaks/ball missing or leaking, plugged hole • Components damaged	• Tighten bolts to specification. • Inspect for damage and replace as required. • Replace pump assembly. • Inspect for damage and replace as required.
Support Assembly—Driven Sprocket • Bolts out of torque specification • Seals missing or damaged • Seal grooves damaged	• Tighten bolts to specification. Use sealant on two external chain cover bolts. • Inspect seals. Replace as required. • Inspect for damage. Service as required.
Forward Clutch Assembly • Seals, Piston • Check Balls • Piston—cracked • Friction Elements—worn, damaged	• Perform Air Pressure Tests • Inspect seals for damage. Replace as required. • Inspect for mislocation, poor seating, and damage. Replace cylinder as required. • Inspect piston. Replace as required. • Check for abnormal wear, damage. Replace as required.

FM5029801572010X

Fig. 9 Routines 202 & 302: No Reverse Engagement (Part 1 of 2)

Possible Component	Reference/Action
Low-One-Way Clutch Assembly • Worn, damaged, misassembled or Code P1784 present	• Inspect for damage. Service as required.
Reverse Clutch Assembly • Seals, Piston • Check Ball • Friction Elements damaged or worn • Reverse Clutch Apply Fluid Transfer Tube leaking or improperly installed	• Perform Air Pressure Tests • Inspect for damage. Service as required. • Inspect. Service as required.
Output Shaft • Splines damaged	• Inspect for damage. Service as required.

FM5029801572020X

Fig. 9 Routines 202 & 302: No Reverse Engagement (Part 2 of 2)

Possible Component	Reference/Action
203 — ELECTRICAL ROUTINE	
Powertrain Control System • Electrical Inputs/Outputs, Vehicle Wiring Harnesses, Powertrain Control Module, EPC Solenoid, TFT, TSS, TR, PSP, TPS, MAF, VSS, IAT, ISC	• Run On-Board Diagnostic. Refer to MOTOR's Domestic Transmission Manual for diagnosis. Perform Pinpoint Tests A, B, D and F using the Rotunda Transmission Tester 007-00130 with AX4S cable and overlay 007-00087 and Transmission Range (TR) Sensor Cable (MLP-B Cable) (007-00127) or equivalents as described. Service as required. Clear codes. Road Test and rerun On-Board Diagnostic.
303 — HYDRAULIC/MECHANICAL ROUTINE	
Fluid • Improper level • Condition	• Adjust fluid to proper level. • Inspect Fluid Level and Condition.
Shift Linkage • Damaged or out of adjustment	• Inspect and service as required. Verify linkage adjustment. After servicing linkage, verify that the Transmission Range sensor is properly adjusted.
Improper Pressures • High Line pressure, High EPC pressure	• Check pressure at line and EPC pressure taps. Perform Line Pressure and Stall Speed Tests. If high, check the following possible components: Main Control Valve Body, Fluid Filter and Fluid Screen Ring.
Fluid Filter and Fluid Filter Seal • Plugged or damaged • Fluid Filter Seal damaged	• Replace fluid filter and fluid filter seal.
Main Control Valve Body • Bolts out of torque specification • Gasket—damaged, off location • B1 Check Ball, Pressure Failsafe Valve, Manual Control Valve, Main Regulator Valve—stuck, damaged	• Tighten bolts to specification. • Inspect for damage. Replace as required. • Inspect for damage. Service as required.
Pump Assembly • Bolts out of torque specification • Gasket damaged, off location • Porosity/cross leaks • Components damaged	• Tighten bolts to specification. • Inspect for damage and replace as required. • Replace pump assembly. • Inspect for damage and replace as required.

FM5029801573010X

Fig. 10 Routines 203 & 303: Harsh Reverse Engagement (Part 1 of 2)

Possible Component	Reference/Action
204 — ELECTRICAL ROUTINE	
Powertrain Control System • Electrical Inputs/Outputs, Vehicle Wiring Harnesses, Powertrain Control Module, EPC Solenoid, TFT, TSS, TR, PSP, TPS, MAF, IAT, ISC	• Run On-Board Diagnostic. Refer to MOTOR's Domestic Transmission Manual for diagnosis. Perform Pinpoint Tests A, B, D and F using the Rotunda Transmission Tester 007-00130 with AX4S cable and overlay 007-00087 and Transmission Range (TR) Sensor Cable (MLP-B Cable) 007-00127 or equivalents. Service as required. Clear codes. Road Test and rerun On-Board Diagnostic.
304 — HYDRAULIC/MECHANICAL ROUTINE	
Fluid • Improper level • Condition	• Adjust fluid to proper level. • Inspect Fluid Level and Condition.
Shift Linkage • Damaged, out of adjustment	• Inspect. Service as required. Verify linkage adjustment. After servicing linkage, verify that the Transmission Range sensor is properly adjusted.
Improper Pressures • High Forward Clutch pressure, High Line pressure, High EPC pressure	• Check pressure at line, EPC and forward clutch pressure taps. Perform Line Pressure and Stall Speed Tests. If pressures are high, check the following possible components: Main Control Valve Body, Pump Assembly.
Main Controls • Bolts out of torque specification • Gaskets—damaged, off location • Main Regulator Valve, Backout Valve, Pressure Failsafe Valve • EPC Solenoid—stuck, damaged • 2-3 Servo Regulator Valve, Engagement Valve, B3 or B2 Check Ball—missing, damaged	• Tighten bolts to specification. • Inspect for damage. Replace as required. • Inspect. Service as required. • Inspect for damage and contamination. Service as required. • Inspect for damage and contamination. Service as required.
Pump Assembly • Bolts out of specification • Porosity/cross leaks • Gaskets damaged, off location	• Tighten bolts to specification. • Inspect for porosity/leaks. Replace pump assembly. • Inspect for damage and replace as required.
Low and Intermediate Servo • Seals, Piston • Fluid Tubes—damaged, loose, leaking, misassembled • Band, Anchor Pins • Apply Rod—incorrect length	• Perform Air Pressure Tests as described. • Inspect for damage. Replace as required. • Inspect for damage. Replace as required. • Inspect for damage. Replace as required. • Replace as required.

FM5029801574010X

Fig. 11 Routines 204 & 304: Harsh Forward Engagement (Part 1 of 2)

Possible Component	Reference/Action
Support Assembly—Driven Sprocket • Bolts out of torque specification • Seals missing or damaged • Seal grooves damaged	• Tighten bolts to specification. Use sealant on two external chain cover bolts. • Inspect seals. Replace as required. • Inspect for damage. Service as required.
Neutral to Drive Accumulator • Piston or seals damaged	• Inspect for damage. Service as required.
Forward Clutch Assembly • Seals, Piston • Check Ball • Piston cracked • Friction Elements—damaged, worn	• Perform Air Pressure Tests • Inspect seals for damage. Service as required. • Inspect for mislocation, poor seating and damage. Replace cylinder as required. • Inspect piston. Replace as required. • Check for abnormal wear, damage. Replace as required.
Reverse Clutch Assembly • Seals, Piston • Check Ball • Friction Elements damaged or worn • Support and Spring and Piston damaged or worn • Reverse Clutch Apply Fluid Transfer Tube leaking or improperly installed	• Perform Air Pressure Tests • Inspect for damage. Service as required. • Inspect for damage. Service as required. • Inspect for damage. Service as required. • Inspect for damage. Service as required. • Inspect. Service as required.

FM5029801575020X

Fig. 12 Routines 205 & 305: Delayed/Soft Reverse Engagement (Part 2 of 2)

Possible Component	Reference/Action
Reverse Clutch Assembly • Seals, Piston • Friction Elements damaged, worn • Return Spring Piston damaged, worn • Reverse Clutch Apply Fluid Transfer Tube leaking or improperly installed	• Perform Air Pressure Tests • Inspect for damage. Service as required.

FM5029801573020X

Fig. 10 Routines 203 & 303: Harsh Reverse Engagement (Part 2 of 2)

Possible Component	Reference/Action
Neutral to Drive Accumulator • Piston stuck, seals or springs—damaged, missing	• Check for damage. Replace as required.
Forward Clutch Assembly • Check Ball • Friction Element damaged or worn • Spring, Rear Clutch Pressure damaged • Forward Clutch Return Spring damaged	• Perform Air Pressure Tests • Inspect for mislocation, poor seating, damage. Replace front clutch cylinder. • Check for wear or damage, replace as required. • Check for damage, replace as required. • Check for damage, replace as required.
Low and Intermediate Band/Rear Sun Gear and Drum • Friction Elements—damaged, worn • Drum damaged	• Check for damage. Replace as required.

FM5029801574020X

Fig. 11 Routines 204 & 304: Harsh Forward Engagement (Part 2 of 2)

Possible Component	Reference/Action
205 — ELECTRICAL ROUTINE	
Powertrain Control System • Electrical Inputs/Outputs, Vehicle Wiring Harnesses, Powertrain Control Module, EPC Solenoid, TFT Sensor	• Run On-Board Diagnostic. Refer to MOTOR's Domestic Transmission Manual for diagnosis. Perform Pinpoint Tests B and E using the Rotunda Transmission Tester 007-00130 with AX4S cable and overlay 007-00087 or equivalent. Service as required. Clear codes. Road Test and rerun On-Board Diagnostic.
305 — HYDRAULIC/MECHANICAL ROUTINE	
Fluid • Improper level • Condition	• Adjust fluid to proper level. • Inspect as described under Fluid Check
Shift Linkage • Damaged, out of adjustment	• Inspect and service as required. Verify linkage adjustment. After servicing linkage, verify that the Transmission Range sensor is properly adjusted.
Improper Pressures • Low Reverse Clutch pressure, Low Line pressure, Low EPC pressure	• Check pressure at line and EPC taps. Perform Line Pressure and Stall Speed Tests. If pressures are low, check the following possible components: Main Control Valve Body, Pump Assembly, Reverse Clutch Assembly.
Fluid Filter and Fluid Filter Seal • Plugged or damaged • Fluid Filter Seal damaged	• Replace fluid filter and fluid filter seal.
Main Controls • Bolts out of torque specification • Gaskets—damaged, off location • Seals, Manual Control Valve, Main Regulator Valve, B5 Check Ball, Converter Drain Back Valve, Springs—missing, damaged or misassembled • EPC Solenoid stuck, damaged • Failsafe Valve (Zero EPC Pressure Only) stuck, damaged	• Tighten bolts to specification. • Inspect for damage. Replace as required. • Inspect for damage. Service as required. • Inspect for damage. Service as required. • Inspect for damage. Service as required.
Pump Assembly • Bolts out of torque specification • Porosity/cross leaks/ball missing or leaking • Gaskets damaged, off location • Components damaged	• Tighten bolts to specification. • Replace pump assembly. • Inspect for damage and replace as required. • Inspect for damage and replace as required.

FM5029801575010X

Fig. 12 Routines 205 & 305: Delayed/Soft Reverse Engagement (Part 1 of 2)

Possible Component	Reference/Action
206 — ELECTRICAL ROUTINE	
Powertrain Control System • Electrical Inputs/Outputs, Vehicle Wiring Harnesses, Powertrain Control Module, EPC Solenoid, TFT Sensor	• Run On-Board Diagnostic. Refer to MOTOR's Domestic Transmission Manual for diagnosis. Perform Pinpoint Tests B and E using the Rotunda Transmission Tester 007-00130 with AX4S cable and overlay 007-00087 or equivalent as described. Service as required. Clear codes. Road Test and rerun On-Board Diagnostic.
306 — HYDRAULIC/MECHANICAL ROUTINE	
Fluid • Improper level • Condition	• Adjust fluid to proper level. • Inspect as described under Fluid Check.
Shift Linkage • Damaged, out of adjustment	• Inspect and service as required. Verify linkage adjustment. After servicing linkage, verify that the Transmission Range sensor is properly adjusted.
Improper Pressures • Low Forward Clutch pressure, Low Line pressure, Low EPC pressure	• Check pressure at line and EPC taps. Perform Line Pressure and Stall Speed Tests. If pressures are low, check the following possible components: Fluid Filter and Fluid Screen Ring, Main Control Valve Body and Pump Assembly.
Fluid Filter and Fluid Filter Seal • Plugged or damaged • Fluid Filter Seal damaged	• Replace fluid filter and fluid filter seal.

FM5029801576010X

Fig. 13 Routines 206 & 306: Delayed/Soft Forward Engagement (Part 1 of 2)

Possible Component	Reference/Action
Main Control Valve Body	
• Bolts out of torque specification	• Tighten bolts to specification.
• Gaskets—damaged, off location	• Inspect for damage. Replace.
• 3-4 Shift Valve, Backout Valve, Main Regulator Valve, Manual Control Valve, 2-3 Servo Regulator Valve, Engagement Valve, B5 Check Ball —stuck, damaged, missing	• Inspect. Service as required.
• EPC Solenoid—stuck, damaged	• Inspect for damage and contamination. Service as required.
• Pressure Failsafe Valve stuck or damaged	• Inspect for damage. Service as required.
Pump Assembly	
• Bolts out of torque specification	• Tighten bolts to specification.
• Porosity/cross leaks	• Inspect for porosity and leaks. Replace as required.
• Gaskets damaged, off location	• Inspect for damage and replace as required.
• Components damaged	• Inspect for damage and replace as required.
Low Intermediate Servo Assembly	
	• Perform Air Pressure Tests
• Seals, Piston	• Inspect seals and piston for damage. Replace as required.
• Fluid Transfer Tubes—damaged, loose, leaking	• Inspect for damage. Service as required.
• Band, Anchor Pins—damaged	• Inspect for damage. Service as required.
• Apply Rod—incorrect length	• Replace as required.
Neutral to Drive Accumulator	
• Seals, Bore—damaged, stuck	• Inspect for damage. Replace.
Support Assembly—Driven Sprocket	
• Bolts out of torque specification	• Tighten bolts to specification. Use sealant on two external chain cover bolts.
• Seals missing or damaged	• Inspect seals. Replace as required.
• Seal grooves damaged	• Inspect for damage. Service as required.
Forward Clutch Assembly	
	• Perform Air Pressure Tests
• Seals, Piston, front support	• Inspect seals for damage and replace as required.
• Check Balls	• Inspect for incorrect location, poor seating damage. Replace cylinder as required.
• Friction Elements—damaged or worn	• Check for abnormal wear or damage. Replace as required.
Low and Intermediate Band/Rear Sun Gear and Drum	
• Friction Elements—damaged, worn	• Inspect for damage. Service as required.
• Drum damaged	

FM5029801576020X

Fig. 13 Routines 206 & 306: Delayed/Soft Forward Engagement (Part 2 of 2)

Possible Component	Reference/Action
211 — ELECTRICAL ROUTINE	
Powertrain Control System	
• Electrical Inputs/Outputs, Vehicle Wiring Harnesses, Powertrain Control Module, Shift Solenoids, TFT, TP, MAF, VSS, IAT, ECT	• Perform Shift Point Road Test and Torque Converter Clutch Operation Test. • Run On-Board Diagnostic. Refer to MOTOR's Domestic Transmission Manual for diagnosis. Perform Pinpoint Tests A and B using the Rotunda Transmission Tester 007-00130 with AX4S cable and overlay 007-00087 or equivalents. Service as required. Clear codes. Road Test and rerun On-Board Diagnostic.
311 — HYDRAULIC/MECHANICAL ROUTINE	
Other	
• Tire size change, Chain ratio change, Speedometer Gear	• Refer to the specification decal and verify vehicle has original equipment. Changes in tire size and chain ratio will affect shift timing.
Fluid	
• Improper level	• Adjust fluid to proper level.
Main Control Valve Body	
• Bolts out of torque specification	• Tighten bolts to specification.
• Gaskets—damaged, off location	• Inspect for damage. Replace.
• Valves, Accumulators, Seals, Springs, Clips—damaged, missing, misassembled	• Inspect for damage and contamination. Service as required.
	• Refer to the appropriate shift routine(s) for further diagnosis: **Shift 1-2, Routine** 220/320 **Shift 2-3, Routine** 221/321 **Shift 3-4, Routine** 222/322 **Shift 4-3, Routine** 223/323 **Shift 3-2, Routine** 224/324 **Shift 2-1, Routine** 225/325

FM5029801578000X

Fig. 15 Routines 211 & 311: Shift Timing Is Early/Late

Possible Component	Reference/Action
213 — ELECTRICAL ROUTINE	
Powertrain Control System	
• Electrical Inputs/Outputs, Vehicle Wiring Harnesses, Powertrain Control Module, EPC Solenoid, TFT, ECT, TP, MAF	• Perform Shift Point Road Test • Run On-Board Diagnostic. Refer to MOTOR'S Diagnostic Transmission Manual for diagnosis. Perform Pinpoint Tests B and E using the Rotunda Transmission Tester 007-00130 with AX4S cable and overlay 007-00087 or equivalents. Service as required. Clear codes. Road Test and rerun On-Board Diagnostic.
313 — HYDRAULIC/MECHANICAL ROUTINE	
Fluid	
• Improper level	• Adjust fluid to proper level.
• Condition	• Inspect Fluid Level and Condition.

FM5029801580010X

Fig. 17 Routines 213 & 313: Shift Feel Is Soft/Slipping (Part 1 of 2)

Possible Component	Reference/Action
210 — ELECTRICAL ROUTINE	
Powertrain Control System	
• Electrical Inputs/Outputs, Vehicle Wiring Harnesses, Powertrain Control Module, Shift Solenoids, TR Sensor, TP, MAF, VSS	• Run On-Board Diagnostic. Refer to MOTOR's Domestic Transmission Manual for diagnosis. Perform Pinpoint Tests A and D using the Rotunda Transmission Tester 007-00130 with AX4S cable and overlay 007-00087 and Transmission Range (TR) Sensor Cable (MLP-B Cable) 007-00127 or equivalents. Service as required. Clear codes. Road Test and rerun On-Board Diagnostic. If DTC P1700 is present, check for a low transaxle fluid level. Then, continue.
310 — HYDRAULIC/MECHANICAL ROUTINE	
Fluid	
• Improper level	• Adjust fluid to proper level.
• Condition	• Inspect Fluid Condition and Condition.

FM5029801577010X

Fig. 14 Routines 210 & 310: Some Or All Shifts Missing (Part 1 of 2)

Possible Component	Reference/Action
Shift Linkage	
• Damaged, out of adjustment	• Inspect and service as required. Verify linkage adjustment. After servicing linkage, verify that the TR sensor is properly adjusted.
Vehicle Speed Input	
• Speedometer Gear—DRIVE—damaged	• Inspect gears.
• Speedometer Gear—DRIVEN—Gear and Shaft Assembly	
• Differential Assembly—damaged or missing	
• Speedometer DRIVE GEAR—damaged	
Go to Reference/Action to diagnose specific missing shifts	
• Shift Concern: 1-2 Shift (Automatic)	• Routine 220/320
• Shift Concern: 2-3 Shift (Automatic)	• Routine 221/321
• Shift Concern: 3-4 Shift (Automatic)	• Routine 222/322
• Shift Concern: 4-3 Shift (Automatic)	• Routine 223/323
• Shift Concern: 3-2 Shift (Automatic)	• Routine 224/324
• Shift Concern: 2-1 Shift (Automatic)	• Routine 225/325

FM5029801577020X

Fig. 14 Routines 210 & 310: Some Or All Shifts Missing (Part 2 of 2)

Possible Component	Reference/Action
212 — ELECTRICAL ROUTINE	
Powertrain Control System	
• Electrical Inputs/Outputs, Vehicle Wiring Harnesses, Powertrain Control Module, Shift Solenoids, TR, TCC, TSS and TFT Sensor, TP, VSS, ECT, IAT, MAF	• Perform Shift Point Road Test and Torque Converter Clutch Operation Test. • Run On-Board Diagnostic. Refer to MOTOR's Domestic Transmission Manual for diagnosis. Perform Pinpoint Tests A, B, C, D and F using the Rotunda Transmission Tester 007-00130 with AX4S cable and overlay 007-00087 and Transmission Range (TR) Sensor Cable (MLP-B Cable) 007-00127 or equivalents. Service as required. Clear codes. Road Test and rerun On-Board Diagnostic.
312 — HYDRAULIC/MECHANICAL ROUTINE	
Fluid	
• Improper level	• Adjust fluid to proper level.
Main Control Valve Body	
• Bolts out of torque specifications	• Tighten bolts to specifications.
• Gaskets—damaged, off location	• Inspect for damage. Replace as required
• Valves, Accumulators, Seals, Clips, Intermediate Clutch Shuttle Valve —stuck, damaged	• Inspect for damage. Service as required.
Vehicle Speed Input	
• Speedometer Gear—DRIVE—damaged	• Inspect gears.
• Speedometer Gear—DRIVEN—Gear and Shaft Assembly	
• Differential Assembly—damaged or missing	
• Speedometer DRIVE GEAR—damaged	
Torque Converter Clutch (TCC)	• Refer to Routine 342, converter cycling.
Go to Reference/Action to diagnose specific missing shifts	
• Shift Concern: 1-2 Shift (Automatic)	• Routine 220/320
• Shift Concern: 2-3 Shift (Automatic)	• Routine 221/321
• Shift Concern: 3-4 Shift (Automatic)	• Routine 222/322
• Shift Concern: 4-3 Shift (Automatic)	• Routine 223/323
• Shift Concern: 3-2 Shift (Automatic)	• Routine 224/324
• Shift Concern: 2-1 Shift (Automatic)	• Routine 225/325

FM5029801579000X

Fig. 16 Routines 212 & 312: Shift Timing Is Erratic/Hunting

Possible Component	Reference/Action
Shift Linkage	
• Damaged, out of adjustment	• Inspect. Service as required. Verify linkage adjustment After servicing linkage, verify that the transmission range sensor is properly adjusted.
Improper Pressures	
• Low Line pressure, Low EPC pressure	• Check pressures at line and EPC taps. Perform Line Pressure and Stall Speed Tests If pressures are low or all shifts are soft/slipping, go to Main Control Valve Body. • If pressures are OK and a specific shift is soft/slipping, refer to the appropriate routine(s) for additional diagnosis. **Shift 1-2, Routine** 220/320 **Shift 2-3, Routine** 221/321 **Shift 3-4, Routine** 222/322 **Shift 4-3, Routine** 223/323 **Shift 3-2, Routine** 224/324 **Shift 2-1, Routine** 225/325
Main Control Valve Body	
• Bolts out of torque specifications	• Tighten bolts to specifications.
• Gaskets—damaged, off location	• Inspect for damage. Service as required.
• 1-2 Capacity Modulator Valve, Accumulator/Regulator Valve, Main Regulator Valve, 2-3 Servo Regulator Valve, Check Balls, 3-2 Shift Timing Valve, Clips, Springs—damaged, misassembled, missing	• Inspect. Service as required.
• EPC Solenoid—stuck, damaged	• Inspect for damage and contamination. Service as required.
• Pressure Failsafe Valve (Zero EPC Pressure Only) stuck, damaged	• Inspect for damage. Service as required.

FM5029801580020X

Fig. 17 Routines 213 & 313: Shift Feel Is Soft/Slipping (Part 2 of 2)

Possible Component	Reference/Action
214 — ELECTRICAL ROUTINE	
Powertrain Control System	
• Electrical Inputs/Outputs, Vehicle Wiring Harnesses, Powertrain Control Module, EPC Solenoid, TFT, TR Sensor and Shift Solenoid No. 3, MAF, TP, VSS, A/C, ECT, IAT, PSP	• Run On-Board Diagnostic. Refer to MOTOR'S Domestic Transmission Manual. for diagnosis. Perform Pinpoint Tests A, B, D and E using the Rotunda Transmission Tester 007-00130 with AX4S cable and overlay 007-00087 and Transmission Range (TR) Sensor Cable (MLP-B Cable) 007-00127 or equivalents Service as required. Clear codes. Road Test and rerun On-Board Diagnostic.
314 — HYDRAULIC/MECHANICAL ROUTINE	
Fluid	
• Improper level	• Adjust fluid to proper level.
Improper Pressures	
• High Line pressure High EPC pressure	• Check pressures at line and EPC taps. Perform Line Pressure Test. If pressures are high or all shifts are harsh, go to Main Control Valve Body. • If pressures are OK and a specific shift is harsh, refer to the appropriate shift routine in the following chart: **Shift** 1-2, **Routine** 220/320 **Shift** 2-3, **Routine** 221/321 **Shift** 3-4, **Routine** 222/322 **Shift** 4-3, **Routine** 223/323 **Shift** 3-2, **Routine** 224/324 **Shift** 2-1, **Routine** 225/325

FM5029801581010X

Fig. 18 Routines 214 & 314: Shift Feel Is Harsh (Part 1 of 2)

Possible Component	Reference/Action
216 — ELECTRICAL ROUTINE	
Powertrain Control System	
• Electrical Inputs/Outputs, Vehicle Wiring Harnesses, Powertrain Control Module and Shift Solenoids, Transaxle Internal Wiring Harness	• Run On-Board Diagnostic. MOTOR'S Domestic Transmission Manual for diagnosis. Perform Pinpoint Test A using the Rotunda Transmission Tester 007-00130 with AX4S cable and overlay 007-00087 or equivalent as described. Service as required. Clear codes. Road Test and rerun On-Board Diagnostic. If DTC P1700 is present, check for a low transaxle fluid level. Then, continue to Hydraulic/Mechanical Routines.

FM5029801583010X

Fig. 20 Routines 216 & 316: No Manual 1st Gear (Part 1 of 2)

Possible Component	Reference/Action
316 — HYDRAULIC/MECHANICAL ROUTINE	
Shift Linkage	
• Damaged or out of adjustment	• Inspect and service as required. Verify linkage adjustment After servicing linkage, verify that the Transmission Range sensor is properly adjusted.
Improper Pressures	
• Low Direct Clutch pressure, Low Line pressure, Low EPC pressure	• Check pressure at line and EPC pressure taps. Perform Line Pressure Test If pressures are low, check the following possible components: Main Control Valve Body, Support Assembly, Driven Sprocket, Direct Clutch Assembly.
Main Control Valve Body	
• Bolts out of torque specifications	• Tighten bolts to specifications.
• Gaskets—damaged, off location	• Inspect for damage. Replace as required.
• Manual Control Valve, Manual Low Relief Valve and Spring, Springs, Clips—stuck, damaged, missing	• Inspect for damage. Service as required.
Support Assembly—Driven Sprocket	
• Bolts out of torque specifications	• Tighten bolts to specifications. Use sealant on two external chain cover bolts.
• Seals missing or damaged	• Inspect seals. Replace as required.
• Seal grooves damaged	• Inspect for damage. Service as required.
Direct Clutch	
	• Perform Air Pressure Tests
• Check Ball, Piston, Piston Seals, Plates	• Inspect for damage. Service as required.
• Friction Elements—damaged, worn	• Inspect for damage. Service as required.
Low One-Way Clutch Assembly	
• Not Overrunning, damaged	• Inspect for damage. Service as required.
Low Intermediate Band	
• Damaged, worn, burned out or missassembled	• Inspect for damage. Service as required.
Forward Clutch Assembly	
	• Perform Air Pressure Tests
• Seals, Piston	• Inspect seals for damage. Service as required.
• Check Ball	• Inspect for mislocation, poor seating and damage. Replace cylinder as required.
• Piston cracked	• Inspect piston. Replace as required.
• Friction Elements—damaged, worn	• Check for abnormal wear, damage. Replace as required.

FM5029801583020X

Fig. 20 Routines 216 & 316: No Manual 1st Gear (Part 2 of 2)

Possible Component	Reference/Action
220 — ELECTRICAL ROUTINE	
Powertrain Control System	
• Electrical Inputs/Outputs, Vehicle Wiring Harnesses, Powertrain Control Module, Shift Solenoids, TR, TFT and EPC, TP, MAF	• Run On-Board Diagnostic. Refer to MOTOR'S Domestic Transmission Manual. for diagnosis. Perform Pinpoint Tests A, B, D and E using the Rotunda Transmission Tester 007-00130 with AX4S cable and overlay 007-00087 and Transmission Range (TR) Sensor Cable (MLP-B Cable) 007-00127 or equivalents If DTC P1700 is present, check for a low transaxle fluid level, then continue to Hydraulic/Mechanical Routine. Service as required. Clear codes. Road Test and rerun On-Board Diagnostic.

FM5029801584010X

Fig. 21 Routines 220 & 320: No Automatic 1–2 Shift (Part 1 of 2)

Possible Component	Reference/Action
Main Control Valve Body	
• Bolts out of torque specifications	• Tighten bolts to specifications.
• Gaskets—damaged, off location	• Inspect for damage. Replace as required.
• 1-2 Capacity Modulator Valve, Accumulator Regulator Valve, Main Regulator Valve, 2-3 Servo Regulator Valve, 3-2 Timing Valve, Springs, Clips, Check Balls—stuck, damaged, misassembled	• Inspect. Service as required.
• EPC Solenoid, Shift Solenoid 3—stuck or damaged	• Inspect for damage, contamination. Service as required.

FM5029801581020X

Fig. 18 Routines 214 & 314: Shift Feel Is Harsh (Part 2 of 2)

Possible Component	Reference/Action
215 — ELECTRICAL ROUTINE	
Powertrain Control System	
• Electrical Inputs/Outputs, Vehicle Wiring Harnesses, Powertrain Control Module, Shift Solenoids, TR Sensor, VSS	• Run On-Board Diagnostic. Refer to MOTOR'S Domestic Transmission Manual. for diagnosis. Perform Pinpoint Tests A and D using the Rotunda Transmission Tester 007-00130 with AX4S cable and overlay 007-00087 and Transmission Range (TR) Sensor Cable (MLP-B Cable) 007-00127 or equivalents. Service as required. Clear codes. Road Test and rerun On-Board Diagnostic. If DTC P1700 is present, check for a low transaxle fluid level. Then, continue to Hydraulic/Mechanical Routines.
315 — HYDRAULIC/MECHANICAL ROUTINE	
Shift Linkage	
• Damaged or out of adjustment	• Inspect and service as required. Verify linkage adjustment After servicing linkage, verify that the Transmission Range sensor is properly adjusted.
Main Control Valve Body	
• Bolts out of torque specifications	• Tighten to specifications.
• Gaskets—damaged, off location	• Inspect for damage. Replace as required.
• Shift Valves, Intermediate Clutch Shuttle Valve, Forward Clutch Control Valve, Springs, Clips—stuck, damaged, misassembled	• Inspect. Service as required.
• For diagnosis related to a specific gear, use the Transmission Tester to determine gear	• Refer to the following routines: **Shift** 1-2, **Routine** 220/320 **Shift** 2-3, **Routine** 221/321 **Shift** 3-4, **Routine** 222/322
Mechanical	
• Bands, clutches or seals damaged or worn	• Refer to Transaxle Disassembly and Assembly.

FM5029801582000X

Fig. 19 Routines 215 & 315: No 1st Gear, Engages Higher Gear

Possible Component	Reference/Action
320 — HYDRAULIC/MECHANICAL ROUTINE	
Shift Linkage	
• Damaged or out of adjustment	• Inspect and service as required. Verify linkage adjustment After servicing linkage, verify that the Transmission Range sensor is properly adjusted.
Speedometer Gear—Drive	
• Damaged	• Inspect for damage. Service as required.
Speedometer Gear—Driven	
• Damaged	• Inspect for damage. Service as required.
Improper Pressures	
• Intermediate Clutch pressure, Line pressure, EPC pressure	• Check pressure at line, EPC and intermediate clutch taps. Perform Line Pressure Test If not OK, check Main Control Valve Body.
Main Control Valve Body	
• Bolts out of torque specification	• Tighten bolts to specification.
• Gaskets—damaged, off location	• Inspect for damage. Replace as required.
• Intermediate Clutch Tap—loose, missing	• Inspect. Service as required.
• 1-2 Shift Valve, Accumulator Regulator Valve, 1-2 Capacity Modulator Valve, Main Regulator Valve, Intermediate Shuttle Valve, Springs, B10 Check Ball, Clips—loose, missing, stuck, misassembled	• Inspect. Service as required.
• SS1 not functioning properly	• Activate solenoid using NGS. If solenoid operation cannot be felt when placing hand on solenoid, replace solenoid. Inspect O-rings for damage. Service as required.
1-2 Accumulator Assembly	
	• Perform Air Pressure Tests
• Piston Seals, Springs—damaged, missing	• Inspect for damage. Service as required.
Support Assembly—Driven Sprocket	
• Seals—damaged, missing • Holes blocked	• Inspect for damage, missing or blockage. Service as required.
Pump Assembly	
• Porosity/cross leak	• Inspect and replace as required.
• Gasket damaged, off location	• Inspect for damage. Replace as required.
• Components damaged	• Inspect for damage or missing ball. Replace pump assembly if required.
Low One-Way Clutch Assembly	
• Not overrunning, damaged	• Inspect for damage. Replace as required.
Intermediate Clutch Assembly	
	• Perform Air Pressure Tests
• Seals—damaged	• Inspect for damage. Replace as required.
• Piston—damaged	• Inspect for damage. Replace as required.
• Friction—damaged, worn	• Inspect for damage. Replace as required.
• Check Ball—missing, damaged	• Inspect for damage. Service or replace as required.
Front Planet Carrier	
• Damaged	• Inspect for weld damage. Service as required.
Differential Assembly	
• Damaged or missing	• Inspect for damage. Service as required.
Speedometer Drive Gear	
• Damaged or missing	• Inspect for damage. Service as required.

FM5029801584020X

Fig. 21 Routines 220 & 320: No Automatic 1–2 Shift (Part 2 of 2)

Possible Component	Reference/Action
221 — ELECTRICAL ROUTINE	
Powertrain Control System • Electrical Inputs/Outputs, Vehicle Wiring Harnesses, Powertrain Control Module, Shift Solenoids, TFT, EPC, TP, MAF	• Run On-Board Diagnostic. Refer to MOTOR'S Domestic Transmission Manual. for diagnosis. Perform Pinpoint Tests A, B and E using the Rotunda Transmission Tester 007-00130 with AX4S cable and overlay 007-00087 and Transmission Range (TR) Sensor Cable (MLP-B Cable) 007-00127 or equivalents as described. Service as required. Clear codes. Road Test and rerun On-Board Diagnostic.
321 — HYDRAULIC/MECHANICAL ROUTINE	
Shift Linkage • Damaged or out of adjustment	• Inspect and service as required. Verify linkage adjustment After servicing linkage, verify that the Transmission Range sensor is properly adjusted.
Speedometer Gear—Drive • Damaged	• Inspect for damage. Service as required.
Speedometer Gear—Driven • Damaged	• Inspect for damage. Service as required.
Improper Pressures • Direct Clutch pressure, EPC pressure	• Check pressure at EPC and line taps. Perform Line Pressure Test If not OK, check the Main Control Valve Body.
Main Control Valve Body • Bolts out of torque specification • Gaskets—damaged, off location • 1-2 Shift Valve, 2-3 Shift Valve, 2-3 Servo Regulator Valve/Spring —stuck, damaged • B3, B8, B9, B10, B11 Check Balls—damaged, missing • SS1, SS2, SS3 not functioning properly	• Tighten bolts to specification. • Inspect for damage. Replace as required. • Inspect. Service as required. • Inspect for damage. Service as required. • Activate solenoid using NGS. If solenoid operation cannot be felt when placing hand on solenoid, replace solenoid. Inspect O-rings for damage. Service as required.
Low Intermediate Servo Assembly • Wrong Apply Rod, Servo Bore or Piston damaged, Piston Seals damaged or missing, Return Spring or Retaining Clip missing, broken	• Perform Air Pressure Tests • Inspect for damage. Service as required.
Support Assembly—Driven Sprocket • Seals—damaged, missing, holes blocked	• Inspect for damage. Service as required.
Direct One-Way Clutch • Not holding, damaged	• Perform Air Pressure Tests • Inspect for damage. Replace as required.
Direct Clutch Assembly • Seals • Piston • Friction damaged or worn • Check Ball not seating • Return Spring Assembly	• Perform Air Pressure Tests • Inspect for damage. Replace as required. • Inspect for damage. Replace as required. • Inspect for damage. Replace as required. • Inspect for damage. Replace as required. • Inspect for damage. Replace as required.
Case • Servo Release Passage blocked • Servo Release Tube—leaking, loose	• Inspect for damage. Replace case if damaged.

FM5029801585010X

Fig. 22 Routines 221 & 321: No Automatic 2–3 Shift (Part 1 of 2)

Possible Component	Reference/Action
222 — ELECTRICAL ROUTINE	
Powertrain Control System • Electrical Inputs/Outputs, Vehicle Wiring Harnesses, Powertrain Control Module, Shift Solenoids, TR Sensor, EPC Solenoid, VSS	• Run On-Board Diagnostic. Refer to MOTOR'S Domestic Transmission Manual for diagnosis. Perform Pinpoint Tests A, D and E using the Rotunda Transmission Tester 007-00130 with AX4S cable and overlay 007-00087 and Transmission Range (TR) Sensor Cable (MLP-B Cable) 007-00127 or equivalents. Service as required. Clear codes. Road Test and rerun On-Board Diagnostic.
322 — HYDRAULIC/MECHANICAL ROUTINE	
Shift Linkage • Damaged or out of adjustment	• Inspect and service as required. Verify linkage adjustment After servicing linkage, verify that the TR sensor is properly adjusted.
Speedometer Gear—Drive • Damaged	• Inspect for damage. Service as required.
Speedometer Gear—Driven • Damaged	• Inspect for damage. Service as required.
Overdrive Servo Assembly • Wrong Apply Rod • Servo Bore or Piston damaged • Piston Seals—damaged, missing • Return Spring Retaining Clip—missing, broken	• Perform Air Pressure Tests • Inspect. Replace if incorrect. • Inspect for damage. Service as required. • Inspect for damage. Service as required. • Inspect for damage. Service as required.
Main Control Valve Body • Bolts out of torque specification • Gaskets—damaged, off location • 3-4 Shift Valve, 1-2 Shift Valve, Accumulator Regulator Valve, Forward Clutch Control Valve—stuck, damaged • SS3 not functioning properly • EPC Solenoid stuck, damaged • B4, B11 Check Balls	• Tighten bolts to specification. • Inspect for damage. Replace as required. • Inspect. Service as required. • Activate solenoid using NGS. If solenoid operation cannot be felt when placing hand on solenoid, replace solenoid. Inspect O-rings for damage. Service as required. • Inspect for damage. Service as required. • Inspect for damage. Replace as required.
3-4 Accumulator Assembly • Accumulator Piston—stuck, damaged • Piston Seals—missing, damaged • Springs—missing, damaged, holes blocked	• Perform Air Pressure Tests • Inspect for damage. Service as required. • Inspect for damage. Service as required. • Inspect for damage. Service as required.
Support Assembly—Driven Sprocket • Seals—damaged, missing, holes blocked	• Inspect for damage, missing or blockage. Service as required.
OD Band • OD Band—damaged, worn, misassembled • Direct Overrunning Clutch Assembly damaged	• Inspect for damage. Replace as required. • Inspect for damage. Replace as required.

FM5029801586010X

Fig. 23 Routines 222 & 322: No Automatic 3–4 Shift (Part 1 of 2)

Possible Component	Reference/Action
Direct/Intermediate Clutch Hub • Seals damaged, missing or holes blocked	• Inspect for damage. Service as required.
Speedometer Drive Gear • Damaged	• Inspect for damage. Service as required.

FM5029801585020X

Fig. 22 Routines 221 & 321: No Automatic 2–3 Shift (Part 2 of 2)

Possible Component	Reference/Action
Differential Assembly • Damaged or missing	• Inspect for damage. Service as required.
Speedometer Drive Gear • Damaged	• Inspect for damage. Service as required.

FM5029801586020X

Fig. 23 Routines 222 & 322: No Automatic 3–4 Shift (Part 2 of 2)

Possible Component	Reference/Action
223 — ELECTRICAL ROUTINE	
Powertrain Control System • Electrical Inputs/Outputs, Vehicle Wiring Harnesses, Powertrain Control Module, Shift Solenoids, TR sensor, TSS, EPC Solenoid, VSS	• Perform Torque Converter Clutch Operation Test • Run On-Board Diagnostic. Refer to MOTOR'S Domestic Transmission Manual for diagnosis. Perform Pinpoint Tests A, D, E and F using the Rotunda Transmission Tester 007-00130 with AX4S cable and overlay 007-00087 and Transmission Range (TR) Sensor Cable (MLP-B Cable) 007-00127 or equivalents. Service as required. Clear codes. Road Test and rerun On-Board Diagnostic.
323 — HYDRAULIC/MECHANICAL ROUTINE	
Speedometer Gear—Drive • Damaged	• Inspect for damage. Service as required.
Speedometer Gear—Driven • Damaged	• Inspect for damage. Service as required.
Main Control Valve Body • Bolts out of torque specification • Gaskets—damaged, off location • 1-2 Shift Valve, 3-4 Shift Valve, Accumulator Regulator Valve—stuck, damaged • SS1 not functioning properly • EPC Solenoid—stuck, damaged • B4, B11 Check Balls—damaged, missing	• Tighten bolts to specification. • Inspect for damage. Replace as required. • Inspect. Service as required. • Activate solenoid using NGS. If solenoid operation cannot be felt when placing hand on solenoid, replace solenoid. Inspect O-rings for damage. Service as required. • Inspect for damage. Perform Pinpoint Test E. • Inspect for damage. Service as required.
Overdrive Band • Overdrive Band—damaged, worn, misassembled • Direct One-Way Clutch Assembly damaged	• Inspect for damage. Replace as required. • Inspect for damage. Service as required.
Overdrive Servo Assembly • Servo Cover, Seal, Rod and Piston Cushion Spring—damaged • Apply Rod wrong • Servo Bore or Piston damaged • Piston Seals—damaged, missing • Return Spring Retaining Clip—missing, broken	• Perform Air Pressure Tests • Inspect for damage. Service as required. • Inspect Rod as described under Transaxle, Assembly. • Inspect for damage. Service as required. • Inspect for damage. Service as required. • Inspect for damage. Service as required.
Torque Converter Clutch • Not releasing	• See: Converter Always Applied Diagnostic Routine 241/341.
Differential Assembly • Damaged	• Inspect for damage. Service as required.
Speedometer Drive Gear • Wrong or missing	• Inspect for damage. Service as required.

FM5029801587000X

Fig. 24 Routines 223 & 323: No Automatic 4–3 Shift

Possible Component	Reference/Action
224 — ELECTRICAL ROUTINE	
Powertrain Control System • Electrical Inputs/Outputs, Vehicle Wiring Harnesses, Powertrain Control Module, Shift Solenoids, TR Sensor, PSP, VSS	• Run On-Board Diagnostic. Refer to MOTOR'S Domestic Transmission Manual for diagnosis. Perform Pinpoint Tests A and D using the Rotunda Transmission Tester 007-00130 with AX4S cable and overlay 007-00087 and Transmission Range (TR) Sensor Cable (MLP-B Cable) 007-00127. Service as required. Clear codes. Road Test and rerun On-Board Diagnostic.
324 — HYDRAULIC/MECHANICAL ROUTINE	
• Improper Pressures — Direct Clutch — EPC pressure — Forward Clutch — Line pressure	• Check pressure at line, direct clutch and EPC taps. Perform Line Pressure and Stall Speed Tests if not within specification, check main control valve body.
Speedometer Gear—Drive • Damaged	• Inspect for damage. Service as required.
Speedometer Gear—Driven • Damaged	• Inspect for damage. Service as required.
Main Control Valve Body • Bolts out of torque specification • Gaskets—damaged, off location • 3-2 Shift Timing Valve, Backout Valve, Forward Clutch Control, 1-2, 2-3 Shift Valves—stuck, damaged • 3-2 Shift Timing Spring Clip—damaged, missing • B5 Check Ball • SS1, SS2 or SS3 not functioning properly	• Tighten bolts to specification. • Inspect for damage. Replace as required. • Inspect. Service as required. • Inspect for damage. Service as required. • Inspect. Service as required. • Activate solenoid using NGS. If solenoid operation cannot be felt when placing hand on solenoid, replace solenoid. Inspect O-rings for damage. Service as required.
Low/Intermediate Servo Assembly • Spring, Bore, Piston—damaged, missing • Incorrect Servo Apply Rod length	• Perform Air Pressure Tests • Inspect for damage. Replace as required. • Replace as required.
Support Assembly—Driven Sprocket • Seals—damaged, missing, holes blocked	• Inspect for damage, missing or blockage. Service as required.
Low One-Way Clutch Assembly • Not Overrunning—damaged	• Inspect for damage. Replace as required.
Forward Clutch Assembly • Return Spring damaged • Friction Elements damaged • Seals/Piston damaged • Check Ball damaged, stuck or missing	• Perform Air Pressure Tests • Inspect for damage. Service as required. • Inspect for damage. Service as required. • Inspect for damage. Service as required. • Inspect for damage. Service as required.
Direct Clutch Assembly • Support and Spring damaged • Support and Spring Retaining Ring out of position • Check Ball not functioning	• Perform Air Pressure Tests • Inspect for damage. Replace as required. • Inspect for damage. Replace as required. • Inspect for damage. Replace as required.
Low/Intermediate Band • Damaged, worn, burnt, misassembled	• Inspect for damage. Replace as required.
Differential Assembly • Damaged	• Inspect for damage. Service as required.
Speedometer Drive Gear • Damaged	• Inspect for damage. Service as required.

FM5029801588000X

Fig. 25 Routines 224 & 324: No Automatic 3–2 Shift

Possible Component	Reference/Action
240 — ELECTRICAL ROUTINE	
Powertrain Control System • Electrical Inputs/Outputs, Vehicle Wiring Harnesses, Powertrain Control Module, TFT, TSS, TR, TCC, VSS, TP, ECT	• Perform Torque Converter Clutch Operation Test • Run On-Board Diagnostic. Refer to MOTOR'S Domestic Transmission Manual for diagnosis. Perform Pinpoint Tests B, C, D and F using the Rotunda Transmission Tester 007-00130 with AX4S cable and overlay 007-00087 and Transmission Range (TR) Sensor Cable (MLP-B Cable) 007-00127 or equivalents. Service as required. Clear codes. Road Test and rerun On-Board Diagnostic.
340 — HYDRAULIC/MECHANICAL ROUTINE	
Improper Pressures • Low Line pressure, Low EPC	• Check pressure at line and EPC taps. Perform Line Pressure and Stall Speed Tests If low, check main control valve body.

FM5029801590010X

Fig. 27 Routines 240 & 340: No Torque Converter Apply (Part 1 of 2)

Possible Component	Reference/Action
241 — ELECTRICAL ROUTINE	
Powertrain Control System • Electrical Inputs/Outputs, Vehicle Wiring Harnesses, Powertrain Control Module, TFT, TSS, TCC, TR, ECT, MAF	• Perform Torque Converter Clutch Operation Test • Run On-Board Diagnostic. Refer to MOTOR'S Domestic Transmission Manual for diagnosis. Perform Pinpoint Tests B, C and F using the Rotunda Transmission Tester 007-00130 with AX4S cable and overlay 007-00087 or equivalents. Service as required. Clear codes. Road Test and rerun On-Board Diagnostic.
341 — HYDRAULIC/MECHANICAL ROUTINE	
Main Control Valve Body • Bolts out of torque specification • Gaskets—damaged, off location • Torque Converter Clutch Control Valve or Plunger—stuck, damaged • TCC Solenoid not functioning properly	• Tighten bolts to specification. • Inspect gaskets. Service as required. • Inspect. Service as required. • Activate solenoid using NGS. If solenoid operation cannot be felt when placing hand on solenoid, replace solenoid.
Torque Converter • No end clearance • Piston Plate damaged/stuck to cover	• Inspect and replace as required. • If cover is heat stained, replace converter.

FM5029801591000X

Fig. 28 Routines 241 & 341: Torque Converter Always Applied/Stalls Vehicle

Possible Component	Reference/Action
225 — ELECTRICAL ROUTINE	
Powertrain Control System • Electrical Inputs/Outputs, Vehicle Wiring Harnesses, Powertrain Control Module, Shift Solenoids, TR Sensor, VSS, IAC, PSP	• Run On-Board Diagnostic. Refer to MOTOR'S Domestic Transmission manual for diagnosis. Perform Pinpoint Tests A and D using the Rotunda Transmission Tester 007-00130 with AX4S cable and overlay 007-00087 and Transmission Range (TR) Sensor Cable (MLP-B Cable) 007-00127. Service as required. Clear codes. Road Test and rerun On-Board Diagnostic.
325 — HYDRAULIC/MECHANICAL ROUTINE	
Speedometer Gear—Drive • Damaged	• Inspect for damage. Service as required.
Speedometer Gear—Driven • Damaged	• Inspect for damage. Service as required.
Main Control Valve Body • Bolts out of torque specification • Gaskets—damaged, off location • 1-2 Shift Valve, Backout Valve, Intermediate Clutch Shuttle Valve, Main Regulator Valve • SS1 not functioning properly • B10 Check Ball—missing, damaged	• Tighten bolts to specification. • Inspect for damage. Replace as required. • Inspect. Service as required. • Activate solenoid using transmission tester. If solenoid operation cannot be felt when placing hand on solenoid, replace solenoid. Inspect O-rings for damage. Service as required. • Inspect for damage. Service as required.
Intermediate Clutch Assembly • Support and Spring—damaged, misassembled • Friction Element—damaged, worn • Check Ball damaged	• Perform Air Pressure Tests • Inspect for damage. Replace as required. • Inspect for damage. Replace as required. • Inspect. Service as required.
Low One-Way Clutch Assembly • Not Holding, damaged	• Inspect for damage. Replace as required.
Differential Assembly • Damaged	• Inspect for damage. Service as required.
Speedometer Drive Gear • Damaged	• Inspect for damage. Service as required.

FM5029801589000X

Fig. 26 Routines 225 & 325: No Automatic 2–1 Shift

Possible Component	Reference/Action
Main Control Valve Body • Bolts out of torque specification • Gaskets—damaged, off location • Valve Body Pilot Sleeve—damaged, misaligned. Manual Shift Valve, Torque Converter Clutch Control Valve and/or Plunger, Converter Regulator Valve, Springs, Solenoid Regulator Valve—stuck, damaged • TCC Solenoid not functioning properly	• Tighten bolts to specification. • Inspect gaskets. Service as required. • Inspect. Service as required. • Activate solenoid using NGS. If solenoid operation cannot be felt when placing hand on solenoid, replace solenoid. Inspect O-rings for damage. Service as required.
Turbine Shaft • Seals—damaged, missing	• Inspect for damage. Replace as required.
Pump Assembly Shaft • Seals—damaged, missing	• Inspect seals for damage. Service as required
Torque Converter • Leakage, Friction Material, Internal Seals	• Inspect and replace as required.

FM5029801590020X

Fig. 27 Routines 240 & 340: No Torque Converter Apply (Part 2 of 2)

Possible Component	Reference/Action
242 — ELECTRICAL ROUTINE	
Powertrain Control System • Electrical Inputs/Outputs, Vehicle Wiring Harnesses, Powertrain Control Module, TCC, TR Sensor, TFT, TSS, TP, ECT, VSS	• Perform Torque Converter Clutch Operation Test • Run On-Board Diagnostic. Refer to MOTOR'S Domestic Transmission Manual for diagnosis. Perform Pinpoint Tests C and D using the Rotunda Transmission Tester 007-00130 with AX4S cable and overlay 007-00087 and Transmission Range (TR) Sensor Cable (MLP-B Cable) 007-00127. Service as required. Clear codes. Road Test and rerun On-Board Diagnostic.

FM5029801592010X

Fig. 29 Routines 242 & 342: Torque Converter Cycling/Shudder/Chatter (Part 1 of 2)

Possible Component	Reference/Action
342 — HYDRAULIC/MECHANICAL ROUTINE	
Fluid Condition	• Inspect fluid condition. If burnt, drain fluid and converter. Replace fluid and fluid filter assembly. Bring vehicle to normal operating temperature. Perform Drive Cycle NGS. Perform On-Board Diagnostic. If condition still exists, continue diagnostics.
Improper Pressures • Low Line pressure, Low EPC	• Check pressure at line and EPC taps. Perform Line Pressure and Stall Speed Tests • If not OK, check the Main Control Valve Body.
Main Control Valve Body • Bolts out of torque specification • Gaskets—damaged, off location • Valve Body Pilot Sleeve—damaged, misaligned Manual Shift Valve, Torque Clutch Control Valve and Plunger, Converter Regulator Valve—stuck, damaged • TCC Solenoid not functioning properly	• Tighten bolts to specification. • Inspect for damage. Replace as required. • Inspect. Service as required. • Activate solenoid using NGS. If solenoid operation cannot be felt when placing hand on solenoid, replace solenoid. Inspect O-rings for damage. Service as required.
Turbine Shaft • Seals—damaged, missing	• Inspect for damage. Replace as required.
Pump Assembly Shaft • Seals—damaged, missing	• Inspect seals for damage. Service as required.
Torque Converter • End Clearance—excessive • Leakage, Friction Materials, Internal Seals	• Inspect as described. Replace as required. • Inspect as described. Replace as required.

FM5029801592020X

Fig. 29 Routine 242 & 342: Torque Converter Cycling/Shudder/Chatter (Part 2 of 2)

Possible Component	Reference/Action
249 — ELECTRICAL ROUTINE	
Powertrain Control System • Electrical Inputs/Outputs, Vehicle Wiring Harnesses, Powertrain Control Module, Shift Solenoid No. 3 (SS-3)	• Run On-Board Diagnostic. • **Refer to MOTOR'S Domestic Transmission Manual** for diagnosis. Perform Pinpoint Test A using the Rotunda Transmission Tester 007-00130 with AX4S cable and overlay 007-00087 . Service as required. Clear codes. Road Test and rerun On-Board Diagnostic.
349 — HYDRAULIC/MECHANICAL ROUTINE	
Shift Linkage Cable • TR Sensor—damaged, out of adjustment	• Inspect for damage. Service as required. Verify linkage adjustment . After servicing the linkage, verify that the transmission range sensor is properly adjusted.
Improper Pressures • Forward Clutch Pressure, Line Pressure	• Check pressure at line tap. Perform Line Pressure and Stall Speed Tests If not OK, check the following components: Main Controls and Forward Clutch Assembly.
Main Control Valve Body • Bolts out of torque specification • Gaskets—damaged, off location • Shift Valves, Forward Clutch Control Valve damaged, stuck or misassembled.	• Tighten bolts to specification. • Inspect for damage. Replace gaskets. • Inspect for damage. Service as required.

FM5029801593010X

Fig. 30 Routines 249 & 349: No Engine Braking In 3rd Gear D Position (Part 1 of 2)

Possible Component	Reference/Action
250 — ELECTRICAL ROUTINE	
• No Electrical Concerns	• No action required
350 — HYDRAULIC/MECHANICAL ROUTINE	
Shift Linkage • Damaged or out of adjustment	• Inspect and service as required. Verify linkage adjustment After servicing linkage, verify that the TR sensor is properly adjusted.
Improper Pressures • Direct Clutch pressure	• Check pressure at direct clutch tap. Perform Line Pressure Test If not OK, check Main Control Valve Body and Direct Clutch Assembly.
Main Control Valve Body • Bolts out of torque specification • Gaskets—damaged, off location • Manual Low Relief Valve, 1-2 Shift Valve, Pull-In Valve—stuck, damaged or misassembled	• Tighten bolts to specification. • Inspect for damage. Replace as required. • Inspect. Clean or service as required.
Direct Clutch Assembly • Seals • Piston • Friction Damaged or worn • Check Ball Not Seating • Return Spring Assembly	• Inspect. Service or replace as required. • Inspect. Service or replace as required. • Inspect. Service or replace as required. • Inspect. Service or replace as required. • Inspect. Service or replace as required.
Direct One-Way Clutch • Damaged	• Inspect for damage. Service as required.

FM5029801594000X

Fig. 31 Routines 250 & 350: No Engine Braking In 1st Gear Manual

Possible Component	Reference/Action
253 — ELECTRICAL ROUTINE	
Powertrain Control System • Electrical Inputs/Outputs, Vehicle Wiring Harnesses, Powertrain Control Module, TCC Solenoid	• Perform Shift Point Road Test and Torque Converter Clutch Operation Test • Run On-Board Diagnostic. **Refer to MOTOR'S Domestic Transmission Manual** for diagnosis. Perform Pinpoint Test C using the Rotunda Transmission Tester 007-00130 with AX4S cable and overlay 007-00087 or equivalents . Service as required. Clear codes. Road test and rerun On-Board Diagnostic.
353 — HYDRAULIC/MECHANICAL ROUTINE	
Verify proper shift scheduling and engagements	• Go to the appropriate Diagnostic Routines.
Torque Converter Clutch always applied	• Go to Routine 341.
Torque Converter Clutch • Damaged	• Replace converter if damaged.

FM5029801596000X

Fig. 34 Routines 253 & 353: Poor Vehicle Performance

Possible Component	Reference/Action
354 — HYDRAULIC/MECHANICAL ROUTINE	
For Noises/Vibrations That Change With Engine Speed: • Converter components • Fluid level (low) — Pump cavitation • Pump Assembly • Engine drive accessories • Cooler Inlet and Outlet Tubes grounding out • Flywheel	• Locate source of disturbance and service as required.
For Noises/Vibrations That Change With Vehicle Speed: • Engine Mounts — loose or damaged • Driveline concerns — Driveshaft shudder — Driveshaft Joint — Suspension — Modifications • Output/Driveshaft Splines worn or damaged	• Locate source of disturbance and service as required.
Other Noises/Vibrations: • Main Controls — Valve resonance • Cooler Inlet and Outlet Tubes grounding • Anti-Lock (ABS) Brake System • Power Steering Pump	• Locate source of disturbance and service as required. • Locate source of disturbance and service as required. • **Refer to ABS.** • **Refer to Power Steering**

FM5029801597020X

Fig. 35 Routines 254 & 354: Noise/Vibration In Forward/Reverse (Part 2 of 2)

Possible Component	Reference/Action
• SS-3 damaged, stuck	• Perform Pinpoint Test A.
Forward Clutch Assembly • Return Spring, Piston, Seals, Friction Elements, Check Ball —stuck, damaged, misassembled	• Perform Air Pressure Tests • Inspect for damage. Service as required.
Low One-Way Clutch Assembly • Not Overrunning, damaged	• Inspect for damage. Service as required.

FM5029801593020X

Fig. 30 Routines 249 & 349: No Engine Braking In 3rd Gear D Position (Part 2 of 2)

Possible Component	Reference/Action
251 — ELECTRICAL ROUTINE	
• No Electrical Concerns	• No action required
351 — HYDRAULIC/MECHANICAL ROUTINE	
Shift Linkage • Damaged or out of adjustment	• Inspect and service as required. Verify linkage adjustment After servicing linkage, verify that the transmission range sensor is properly adjusted.
Manual Control Lever • Retaining Pin damaged, Nut loose, Detent Spring—bent, damaged or Park Mechanism damaged	• Inspect and service as required.

FM5029801595010X

Fig. 32 Routines 251 & 351: Shift Lever Efforts High (Part 1 of 2)

Possible Component	Reference/Action
Main Control Valve Body • Manual Shift Valve stuck • Bolts out of torque specification	• Inspect and service or replace as necessary. • Tighten bolts to specification.
Brake Shift Interlock	

FM5029801595020X

Fig. 32 Routines 251 & 351: Shift Lever Efforts High (Part 2 of 2)

Possible Component	Reference/Action
252 — ELECTRICAL ROUTINE	
Engine Components • Vehicle Speed Sensor, Seals	• Inspect and service as required.
Transaxle Components • Transaxle Connector, TSS Seals	• Inspect and service as required.
352 — HYDRAULIC/MECHANICAL ROUTINE	
Seals/Gaskets • Converter, TSS, Pan, Extension Housing — Gasket/Seal, Manual Control Lever, Fluid Level Indicator, Servo Covers, Driveshaft Axles	• Locate source and service as required.
Other • Cooler Fitting, Pressure Taps, Transaxle Connectors, Speedometer Cover, Cooler Inlet and Outlet Tubes, Case Porosity, Case cracked • Vent blocked or damaged	• Locate source and service as required. • Check vent for damage or blockage; service as required.

FM5029801601000X

Fig. 33 Routines 252 & 352: External Leaks

Possible Component	Reference/Action
254 — ELECTRICAL ROUTINE	
• No electrical concerns	• No action required

FM5029801597010X

Fig. 35 Routines 254 & 354: Noise/Vibration In Forward/Reverse (Part 1 of 2)

Possible Component	Reference/Action
255 — ELECTRICAL ROUTINE	
Powertrain Control System • Electrical Inputs/Outputs, Vehicle Wiring Harnesses, Powertrain Control Module, TR Sensor	• Perform Torque Converter Clutch Operation Test Run On-Board Diagnostic. **Refer to MOTOR'S Domestic Transmission Manual** for diagnosis. Perform Pinpoint Test D using the Rotunda Transmission Tester 007-00130 with AX4S cable and overlay 007-00087 and Transmission Range (TR) Sensor Cable (MLP-B Cable) 007-00127 . Service as required. Clear codes. Road Test and rerun On-Board Diagnostic.
355 — HYDRAULIC/MECHANICAL ROUTINE	
Shift Linkage/Cable, TR Sensor • Damaged or out of adjustment	• Inspect and service as required. Verify linkage adjustment After servicing linkage, verify that the transmission range sensor is properly adjusted.

FM5029801598000X

Fig. 36 Routines 255 & 355: Engine Will Not Crank

Possible Component	Reference/Action
256 — ELECTRICAL ROUTINE	
• No Electrical Concerns	• No action required

FM5029801599010X

Fig. 37 Routines 256 & 356: No Park Range (Part 1 of 2)

Possible Component	Reference/Action
356 — HYDRAULIC/MECHANICAL ROUTINE	
Shift Linkage • Damaged or out of adjustment	• Inspect and service as required. Verify linkage adjustment After servicing linkage, verify that the transmission range sensor is properly adjusted.
Park Mechanism • Parking Pawl, Parking Pawl Return Spring, Park Rod Guide Cup, Parking Pawl Shaft, Parking Lever Actuating Rod, Manual Control Lever, Manual Lever Detent Spring—damaged	• Inspect and service as required.

FM5029801599020X

Fig. 37 Routines 256 & 356: No Park Range (Part 2 of 2)

Possible Component	Reference/Action
257 — ELECTRICAL ROUTINE	
Refer to Electrical Routine 240, Torque Converter Not Applying	• Refer to Electrical Routine 240, Torque Converter - No Applying
357 — HYDRAULIC/MECHANICAL ROUTINE	
Fluid • Improper level • Condition	• Adjust fluid to proper level. • Inspect. Fluid Level and Condition.
Cooler Lines • Damaged, blocked or reversed	• Inspect and service as required.
Auxiliary Cooler • Damaged, blocked or restricted, improperly installed	• Inspect and service as required.
Vehicle Concerns Causing Engine Overheating	• **Refer to appropriate chassis manual.**
Main Control Valve Body • Torque Converter Clutch Control Valve and Plunger, Converter Regulator Valve stuck or damaged	• Inspect and service as required.
Torque Converter Clutch Not Applying • Seized Torque Converter Clutch	• See Routine 240/340. Inspect. Service as required.
Excessive Towing Loads	• Check gross vehicle weight.
Incorrect Idle or Performance	• Refer to MOTOR'S Auto Engine Performance & Driveability Manual.
Improper Clutch or Band Application or Fluid Pressure Control System	• Inspect. Service as required.

FM5029801600000X

Fig. 38 Routines 257 & 357: Transaxle Overheating

MAINTENANCE

Refer to "Lubricant Data" chart in the appropriate chassis chapter of this manual for transmission fluid specifications.

FLUID INSPECTION

1. Start engine and allow to reach normal operating temperature.
2. Move transaxle selector lever through each range, allowing enough time in each range for transaxle to engage. Return selector lever to Park position and apply parking brake. **Do not turn off engine during fluid level inspection.**
3. Clean all dirt from transaxle fluid dipstick cap before removing dipstick from filler tube.
4. Remove dipstick from tube, wipe it clean and push it all way back into tube. Ensure dipstick is fully seated.
5. Pull dipstick out of tube and inspect fluid level. Fluid should be between arrows.
6. If vehicle has been operating for extended period at high speed or in city traffic in hot weather or vehicle is being used to tow trailer, transaxle fluid must be allowed to cool for approximately 30 minutes after engine has been turned off for accurate reading to be obtained.

FLUID CHANGE

Normal maintenance and lubrication requirements do not necessitate periodic fluid change. If vehicle is operated under abnormal conditions, fluid should be changed every 30,000 miles. If major failure has occurred in transaxle, it will have to be removed for service. At this time converter should be thoroughly flushed to remove any foreign matter.

1. Raise and support vehicle.
2. Disconnect inlet line from radiator fitting or top auxiliary cooler fitting.
3. Install 5/16 or 3/8 inch I.D. hose over end of cooler line and put opposite end into drain pan.
4. Lower vehicle, then start engine with transaxle in Park.
5. Run engine between idle and 1500 RPM from approximately four minutes or until transaxle fluid is no longer being pumped out of hose.
6. Shut engine off as soon as fluid has stopped being pumped out to prevent damage to transaxle
7. Connect hoses and fill transaxle to specifications.

ADJUSTMENTS

SHIFT CONTROL LINKAGE

1. Place gearshift lever in Overdrive position.
2. Hang a three pound weight on gearshift lever to ensure lever is located firmly on Overdrive detent.
3. Loosen manual control lever-to-control cable mounting nut.
4. Move transaxle manual control lever to Overdrive position, second detent from most rearward position.
5. Tighten mounting nut to specifications.
6. Inspect operation of transaxle in each range position. Ensure park mechanism and transaxle range sensor are functioning properly.

IN-VEHICLE REPAIRS

VALVE BODY, REPLACE

Oil pump and valve body are removed as an assembly.

Removal

1. Remove air cleaner, battery and battery tray.
2. Disconnect digital transaxle range sensor and transaxle harness electrical connectors and position engine wire harness.
3. Place digital TR sensor manual lever in Park position.
4. Install three-bar engine support tool No. D88L-6000-A with engine lifting brackets tool No. T70P-6000, or equivalents, and support engine.
5. Remove main control cover upper mounting bolts, then raise and support vehicle.
6. Remove lefthand front wheel assembly and lefthand front fender splash shield.
7. Remove lefthand engine support and insulator.
8. Position drain pan under transaxle main control cover and remove remaining lower transaxle main control cover bolts, transaxle main control cover and gasket.
9. Disconnect transaxle fluid temperature sensor from main control valve body and solenoid electrical connectors.
10. Remove transaxle wiring harness from chain cover.
11. Remove main control valve body mounting bolts in sequence, **Fig. 39.**
12. Disconnect manual linkage, then carefully slide pump and main control valve body off of pump shaft.

Installation

1. Carefully slide pump and main control valve body over pump shaft and onto chain cover.
2. **On models equipped with ABS,** hydraulic modulator may not afford enough clearance to be able to rotate pump and main control valve body to complete engagement between pump shaft and pump. It may be necessary to rotate crankshaft using 7/8 inch deep well socket on crankshaft pulley to complete. Engagement pump shaft with pump.
3. **On models less ABS,** remove manual shift valve from main control valve body.
4. **On all models,** rotate main control valve body as required to allow engagement between pump shaft and pump. Main control valve body should slide flush onto chain cover with little effort.
5. Align main control valve body to installation position and install manual shift valve.
6. Rotate pump and main control valve body clockwise and connect manual valve link with manual shift valve.
7. Position main control valve body and install pump using valve body guide pin tool No. T86P-70100-C, or equivalent. Tighten mounting bolts to specifications in sequence, **Fig. 40.**
8. Install transaxle wiring harness into chain cover, then connect transaxle fluid temperature sensor and solenoid electrical connectors to solenoids and main control valve body.
9. Install main control cover with new gasket to chain cover and tighten side pan bolts to specifications.
10. Install lefthand engine support and insulator, then the lefthand front fender splash shield and tire assembly.
11. Lower vehicle, then remove three-bar engine support and engine lifting brackets.
12. Connect Transaxle Range (TR) sensor

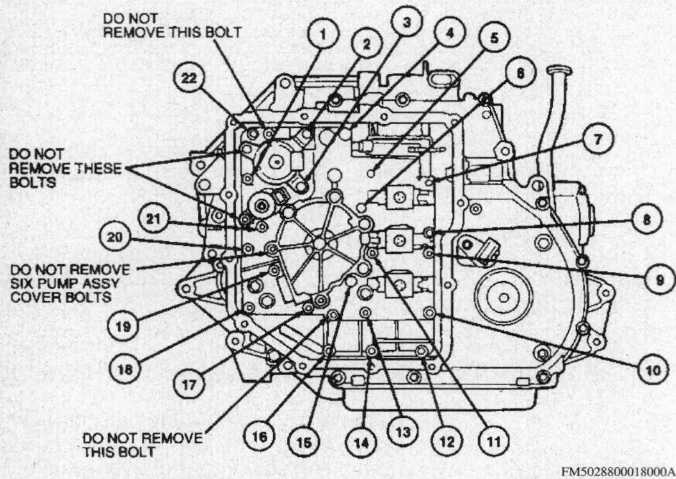

Fig. 39 Oil pump & valve body bolt removal

FM5028800019000X

Fig. 40 Oil pump & valve body bolt tightening sequence

and transaxle harness electrical connectors and position engine wire harness.

13. Install battery tray, battery and air cleaner.
14. Fill transaxle with specified transaxle fluid.
15. Start engine, move transaxle selector lever through all ranges, inspecting pump and valve body cover for leakage.

BRAKE-SHIFT INTERLOCK ACTUATOR/SOLENOID, REPLACE

1. Remove lower steering column shroud.
2. Remove steering column mounting nuts and lower steering column to floor.
3. Disconnect actuator/solenoid electrical connector.
4. Remove ignition/shifter interlock cable to steering column mounting screws.
5. Remove solenoid from solenoid retainer bracket.
6. Reverse procedure to install.

BRAKE-SHIFT INTERLOCK ACTUATOR, REPLACE

Column Shift

1. Remove mounting screws and upper steering column shroud.
2. Insert scratch awl into access hole located in bottom of lower steering column shroud.
3. Push in on ignition lock cylinder release pin and rotate ignition lock cylinder clockwise to Run position.
4. Remove ignition lock cylinder from steering column.
5. Remove lower shroud, then mounting screws and knee bolster from instrument panel.
6. Loosen shift indicator adjustment mechanism.
7. Disconnect shift indicator cable and adjustment mechanism from steering column lever.
8. Rotate shift indicator adjustment wheel clockwise until enough slack exists to disconnect shift indicator cable from steering column lever. Disconnect cable.
9. Rotate shift indicator adjustment wheel clockwise until shift indicator cable can be pulled through adjustment wheel and adjustment mechanism can fall away from steering column tube.
10. Remove mounting nuts and steering column absorber.
11. Remove mounting nuts and lower steering column and disconnect ignition/shifter interlock actuator electrical connector.
12. Remove Torx head screws and ignition/shifter interlock actuator from steering column tube.
13. Reverse procedure to install. Tighten Torx head bolts and steering column nuts to specifications.

Floor Shift

The ignition/shifter interlock actuator on floor shift vehicles is only serviced with ignition/shifter interlock cable. If ignition/shifter interlock actuator replacement on vehicles equipped with floor shift becomes necessary, ignition/shifter interlock cable must be replaced as an assembly.

BRAKE-SHIFT INTERLOCK CABLE, REPLACE

1. Unsnap and remove upper console bezels.
2. Disconnect ignition/shifter interlock cable conduit from bracket and pull cable from pink cam on transaxle range selector lever and housing.
3. Remove mounting screws and upper steering column shroud.
4. Insert scratch awl into access hole located in bottom of lower steering column shroud and push in on ignition lock cylinder release pin.
5. Rotate ignition lock cylinder clockwise to Run position and remove ignition lock cylinder from steering column tube.
6. Remove lower steering column shroud, then the mounting screws and knee bolster from instrument panel.
7. Remove steering column absorber mounting nuts, then the steering column nuts and lower steering column.
8. Remove ignition/shifter interlock actuator mounting screws and ignition/shifter interlock cable, **Fig. 41.**
9. Reverse procedure to install.

TRANSAXLE

REPLACE

1. Remove battery and tray.
2. Remove air cleaner.
3. Disconnect transaxle harness and transaxle range sensor electrical connectors.
4. Remove shift actuator cable fitting, then disconnect transaxle shift cable from shift cable bracket and transaxle.
5. Disconnect fluid cooler lines from transaxle.
6. Remove upper transaxle to engine bolts and transaxle to engine stud.
7. Install two engine lifting eyes from engine lift bracket tool set No. 014-00796, or equivalent, to front and rear locations on engine.
8. Install three-bar engine support tool No. D88L-6000-A, or equivalent, and support engine.
9. Raise and support vehicle.
10. Place suitable drain pan under transaxle.
11. Loosen lower transaxle pan mounting bolts and drain fluid from transaxle.
12. When fluid is drained to level of transaxle pan flange, remove remaining transaxle pan bolts gradually, allowing fluid to drain.
13. Remove transaxle oil pan.
14. When transaxle fluid has completely drained, install transaxle pan.
15. Raise and support vehicle, then remove front wheels.
16. Remove and discard front axle retainer nut and washer.
17. Remove nut from stabilizer bar link at shock absorber end, then the link from shock and position aside.
18. Remove nut from lower ball joint and loosen ball joint in lower control arm using suitable pitman arm type puller.
19. Place suitable pry bar through opening

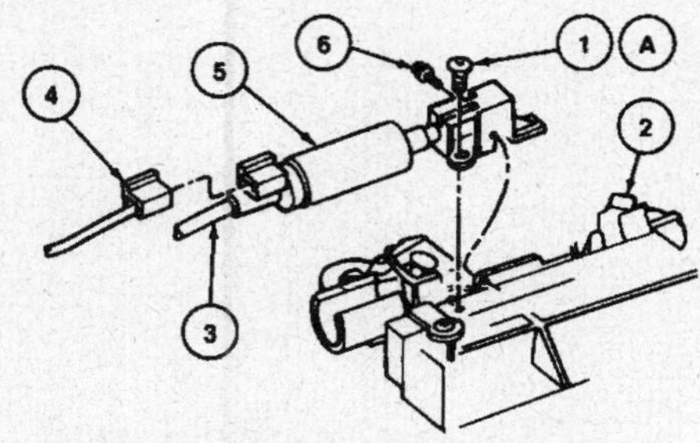

Item	Description
1	Screw
2	Steering Column Tube
3	Ignition / Shifter Interlock Cable
4	Ignition / Shifter Interlock Actuator Electrical Connector
5	Ignition / Shifter Interlock Actuator
6	Screw
A	Tighten to 2.0 N·m (17 Lb-In)

FM5029601140000X

Fig. 41 Brake-shift interlock cable replacement

in lower control arm and under frame and pry down on control arm to release lower ball joint

20. Remove outer CV joint from hub.
21. **Do not use hammer to drive joint from hub.**
22. **Do not allow driveshaft to hang from inner joint.**
23. Remove inner joint from transaxle.
24. Repeat procedure to remove other driveshaft
25. Disconnect heated oxygen sensor electrical connectors.
26. Remove bolts, nuts and Y-pipe.
27. Disconnect starter motor electrical connectors.
28. Remove bolt, stud and starter motor.
29. Remove transaxle housing cover.
30. Position high-lift transmission jack tool No. 014-00210, or equivalent, under transaxle and support transaxle.
31. Remove lower transaxle to engine mounting bolt.
32. Remove flexplate to torque converter mounting nuts.
33. Remove mounting bolts, nuts and rear engine support from transaxle.
34. Remove transaxle.
35. Reverse procedure to install, noting following:
    a. Tighten mounting bolts and nuts to specifications.
    b. Install new front axle retainer nut.
    c. Install new driveshaft bearing retainer circlip.
    d. Install new halfshaft ball joint nut.
    e. When installing driveshaft joints into transaxle use care not to damage seal.
    f. Inspect for proper engagement of lefthand driveshaft inner joint spline into transaxle side gears.
    g. Ensure proper engagement of transaxle shaft spline into righthand inner CV joint.
    h. Ensure bearing retainer circlips is properly seated.

Year	Engine	Engineering Part No.	Model No.	Service Part No.
1998	3.0L	F8DP-7000-AA	PNA-EV & EV1	N/A

Fig. 42 Transaxle application data. 1998 Sable & Taurus

TECHNICAL SERVICE BULLETINS

HARSH 3-2 DOWNSHIFT OR SHUDDER

Sable & Taurus

On some of these models there may be a harsh 3–2 downshift when coasting around a corner then accelerating away. There may also be a shudder on turns if the throttle is held to accelerate through the turn.

This condition may be caused by air entering the fluid filler pickup because of low fluid level.

To correct this condition, ensure the fluid level is at the top of dipstick hash marks.

HARSH SHIFTS & ENGAGEMENTS AFTER TRANSAXLE EXCHANGE

1998 Sable & Taurus

On these models, there may be harsh shifts and engagements after transaxle has been replaced. Diagnostic Trouble Codes (DTCs) 628, P0741 and/or P1744 may be stored.

This condition may be caused by improper transaxle being installed.

To correct this condition, replace transaxle with proper unit, **Fig. 42.**

TIGHTENING SPECIFICATIONS

Year	Component	Torque/Ft. Lbs.
1998–2000	Bracket Tubes To Case	84–108①
	Brake Hose Routing Clip	96①
	Brake-Shift Interlock Actuator	17①
	Case To Chain Cover (10 MM)	84–108①
	Case To Chain Cover (13 MM)	24–26
	Case To Reverse Clutch	25–35
	Case To Reverse Clutch	84–108①
	Case To Stator Support	84–108①
	Chain Cover To Case (10 MM)	19–20
	Chain Cover To Case (13 MM)	25–35
	Chain Cover To Front Support (7 MM)	25–35
	Chain Cover To Front Support (13 MM)	20–22
	Control Arm To Knuckle	36–44
	Detent Spring To Chain Cover	84–108①
	Differential Brace To Case	26–37
	Dust Cover To Case	84–108①
	Dust Cover	15–21
	Engine To Case	41–50
	Filler Tube To Case	84–108①
	Governor Cover To Case	84–108①
	Insulator Bracket To Frame	40–50
	Insulator Mount To Transmission	25–33
	Insulator To Bracket	55–70
	Low/Intermediate Servo Cover To Case	84–108①
	Main Control Cover To Chain Cover	10–12
	Manual Cable Bracket	10–20
	Manual Lever To Manual Shaft	12–16
	Neutral Start Switch To Case	84–108①
	Oil Pan To Case	10–12
	Oil Pump To Main Control	84–108①
	Overdrive Servo Cover To Case	84–108①
	Park Abutment To Case	20–22
	Pressure Switch To Pump Body	9–13
	Pressure Tap Plug For Chain Cover & Pump Body	9–13
	Pump Body To Chain Cover	84–108①
	Pump Cover To Pump Body	84–108①②
	Separator Plate To Main Control	84–108①
	Separator Plate To Pump Body	84–108①
	Shift Control Lever	13–17
	Solenoid To Main Control	84–108①
	Stabilizer To Control Arm	98–125
	Stabilizer U-Clamp To Bracket	60–70
	Starter	16–21
	Steering Column	10–21
	Tie Rod To Knuckle	23–35①
	Torque Converter To Flexplate	20–34
	Transaxle To Engine	39–53
	Valve Body/Solenoid To Chain Cover	84–108①

① — Tighten to minimum specified torque, then continue rotating to nearest cotter pin slot.
② — Refer to "Valve Body, Replace" for tightening sequence.

CD4E Automatic Transaxle

NOTE: On Air Bag Equipped Models, Refer To "Air Bag System Precautions" Located In The Front Of This Manual For System Disarming & Arming Procedures.

NOTE: Refer To "Computer Relearn Procedures" Located In The Front Of This Manual When Battery Power To The Computer Has Been Interrupted.

NOTE: "Electrical Symbol & Wire Color Code Identification" Located In The Front Of This Manual May Be Used As An Aid When Using Wiring Circuits Found In This Section.

NOTE: Prior To Performing Any Service Operations Listed In This Section, Consult "Technical Service Bulletins" Section For Related Information.

INDEX

PRECAUTIONS

AIR BAG SYSTEMS

Refer to "Air Bag System Precautions" in front of this manual for system disarming and arming procedures.

BATTERY GROUND CABLE

Prior to service, disconnect battery ground cable and isolate as required.

IDENTIFICATION

The CD4E automatic transaxle may be identified by a tag located at rear of transaxle case, on bottom of main control cover, **Fig. 1.**

DESCRIPTION

The CD4E transaxle is a four-speed, front wheel drive automatic overdrive unit with a three element torque converter and torque converter clutch. Its gear train consists of a compound planetary gearset, pinion and side gear differential, chain drive and planetary gearset final drive.

Both electronic and hydraulic control systems are employed by CD4E. Electronic functions include shift scheduling, 3-2 shift timing, coast braking, Electronic Pressure Control (EPC, for shift quality) and Torque Converter Clutch (TCC) control. Hydraulic functions include modification of line pressure and shift valve position for optimal shift feel and scheduling, modulated application of TCC, 3-2 shift timing and engine braking.

In addition, a control switch is provided which allows driver to prevent a shift into 4th (Overdrive) gear and uses engine braking to help slow vehicle.

TROUBLESHOOTING

SHIFT INTERLOCK SYSTEM

Refer to wiring diagram, **Fig. 2,** and troubleshooting charts, **Fig. 3.**

TRANSAXLE

Refer to troubleshooting charts **Figs. 4 through 41.**

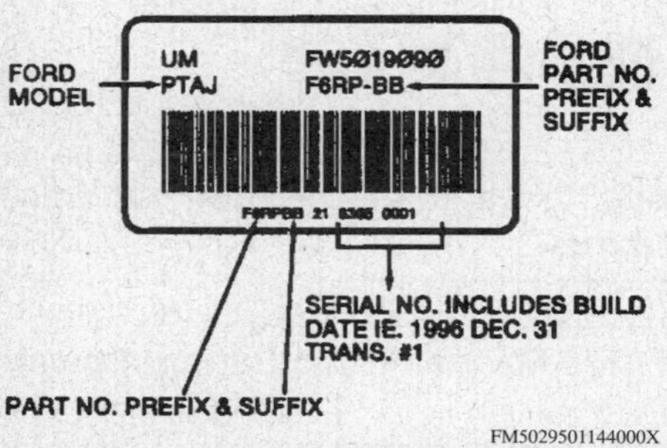

Fig. 1 CD4E identification tag

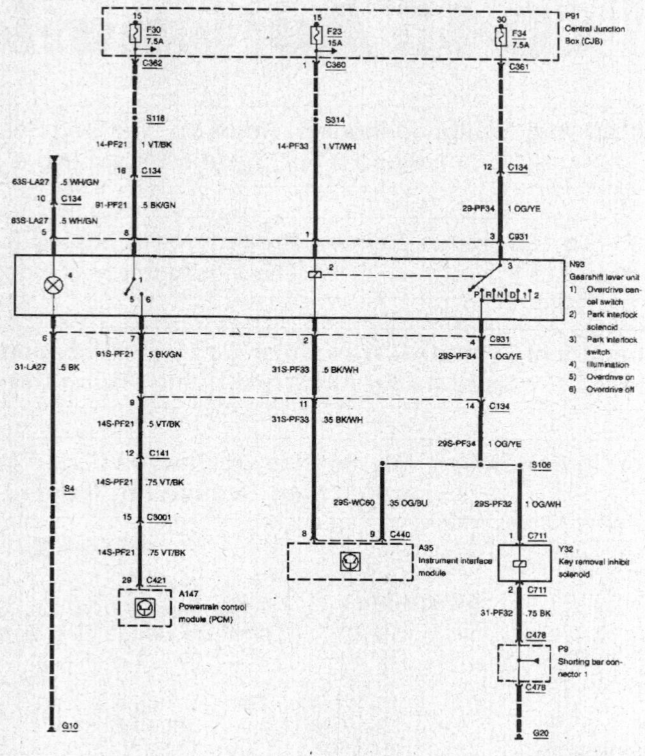

Fig. 2 Shift interlock system wiring diagram

TROUBLESHOOTING TEST INDEX

Test	Description	Page No.	Fig. No.
—	Shift Interlock System Troubleshooting Chart	19-19	3
201/301	No Forward Engagement	19-22	4
202/302	No Reverse Engagement	19-22	5
203/303	Harsh Reverse Or Forward Engagement	19-22	6
205/304	Delayed/Soft Reverse Or Forward Engagement	19-23	7
207/307	No Forward & No Reverse Engagement	19-23	8
210/310	Some Or All Shifts Missing	19-23	9
211/311	Shift Timing Is Early/Late	19-23	10
212/312	Shift Timing Is Erratic/Hunting	19-24	11
213/313	Shift Feel Is Soft/Slipping	19-24	12
214/314	Shift Feel Is Harsh	19-24	13
215/315	No 1st Gear, Engages In Higher Gear	19-24	14
216/316	No Manual 1st Gear	19-25	15
220/320	No Automatic 1–2 Shift	19-25	16
221/321	No Automatic 2–3 Shift	19-25	17
222/322	No Automatic 3–4 Shift	19-25	18
226/326	Soft/Slipping 1–2 Only Shift	19-26	19
227/327	Soft/Slipping 2–3 Only Shift	19-26	20
228/328	Soft/Slipping 3–4 Only Shift	19-26	21
229/329	Soft/Slipping 4–3 Only Shift	19-26	22
230/330	Soft/Slipping 3–2 Only Shift	19-27	23
231/331	Soft/Slipping 2–1 Only Shift	19-27	24
232/332	Harsh 1–2 Shift Only	19-27	25
233/333	Harsh 2–3 Shift Only	19-27	26
234/334	Harsh 3–4 Shift Only	19-27	27
235/335	Harsh 4–3 Shift Only	19-28	28
236/336	Harsh 3–2 Shift Only	19-28	29
240/340	No Torque Converter Apply	19-28	30

Continued

TROUBLESHOOTING TEST INDEX—Continued

CONDITIONS	DETAILS/RESULTS/ACTIONS
A1 CHECK INTERIOR PANEL FUSE 23 (15A)	
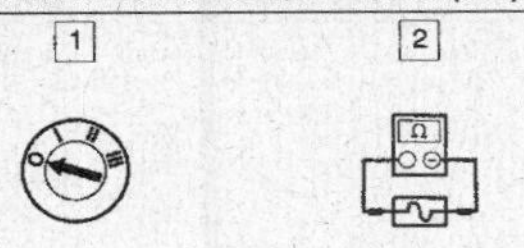 1 2 I/P Fuse 23 (15A)	

FM5019800707010X

Fig. 3 Shift Interlock System Troubleshooting Chart (Part 1 of 10)

CONDITIONS	DETAILS/RESULTS/ACTIONS
	• Is fuse OK? → **Yes** RECONNECT fuse. GO to **A2**. → **No** REPLACE fuse. If fuse fails again, CHECK circuit for short to ground. TEST the system for normal operation.
A2 CHECK INTERIOR PANEL FUSE 34 (7.5A)	
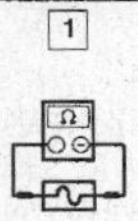 1 I/P Fuse 34 (7.5A)	• Is fuse OK? → **Yes** RECONNECT fuse. GO to **A3**. → **No** REPLACE fuse. ATTEMPT to shift gearshift lever. If fuse fails again, CHECK circuit for short to ground. TEST the system for normal operation.
A3 CHECK INTERIOR PANEL FUSE 30 (7.5A)	
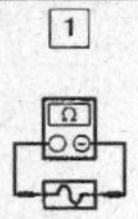 1 I/P Fuse 30 (7.5A)	

FM5019800707020X

Fig. 3 Shift Interlock System Troubleshooting Chart (Part 2 of 10)

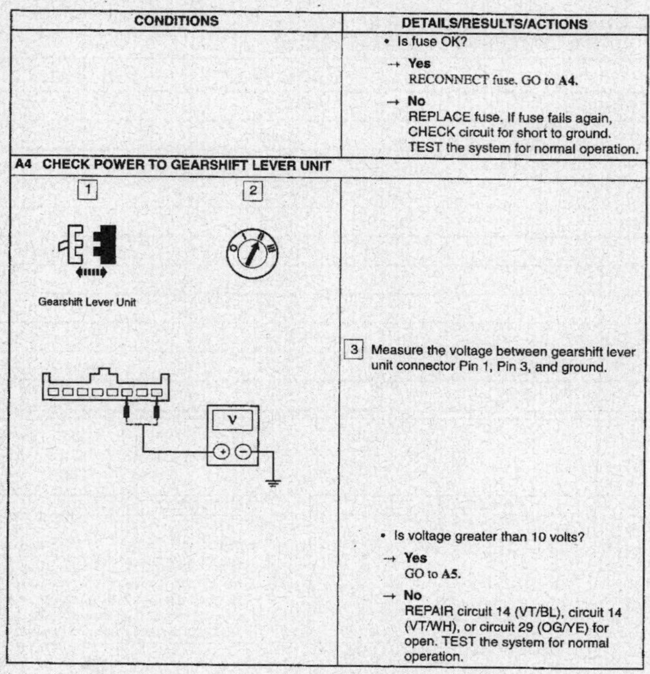

CONDITIONS	DETAILS/RESULTS/ACTIONS
	• Is fuse OK? → **Yes** RECONNECT fuse. GO to **A4**. → **No** REPLACE fuse. If fuse fails again, CHECK circuit for short to ground. TEST the system for normal operation.
A4 CHECK POWER TO GEARSHIFT LEVER UNIT	
1 2 Gearshift Lever Unit	3 Measure the voltage between gearshift lever unit connector Pin 1, Pin 3, and ground. • Is voltage greater than 10 volts? → **Yes** GO to **A5**. → **No** REPAIR circuit 14 (VT/BL), circuit 14 (VT/WH), or circuit 29 (OG/YE) for open. TEST the system for normal operation.

FM5019800707030X

Fig. 3 Shift Interlock System Troubleshooting Chart (Part 3 of 10)

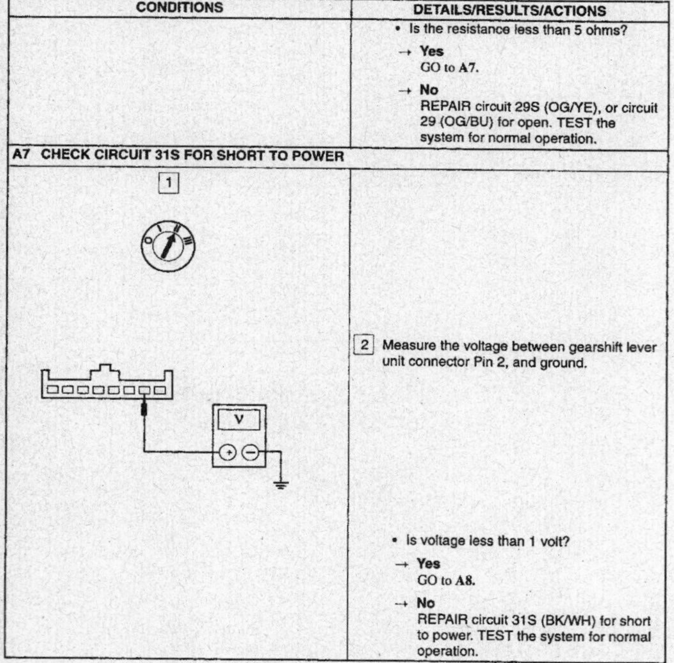

CONDITIONS	DETAILS/RESULTS/ACTIONS
	• Is the resistance less than 5 ohms? → **Yes** GO to **A7**. → **No** REPAIR circuit 29S (OG/YE), or circuit 29 (OG/BU) for open. TEST the system for normal operation.
A7 CHECK CIRCUIT 31S FOR SHORT TO POWER	
1	2 Measure the voltage between gearshift lever unit connector Pin 2, and ground. • Is voltage less than 1 volt? → **Yes** GO to **A8**. → **No** REPAIR circuit 31S (BK/WH) for short to power. TEST the system for normal operation.

FM5019800707050X

Fig. 3 Shift Interlock System Troubleshooting Chart (Part 5 of 10)

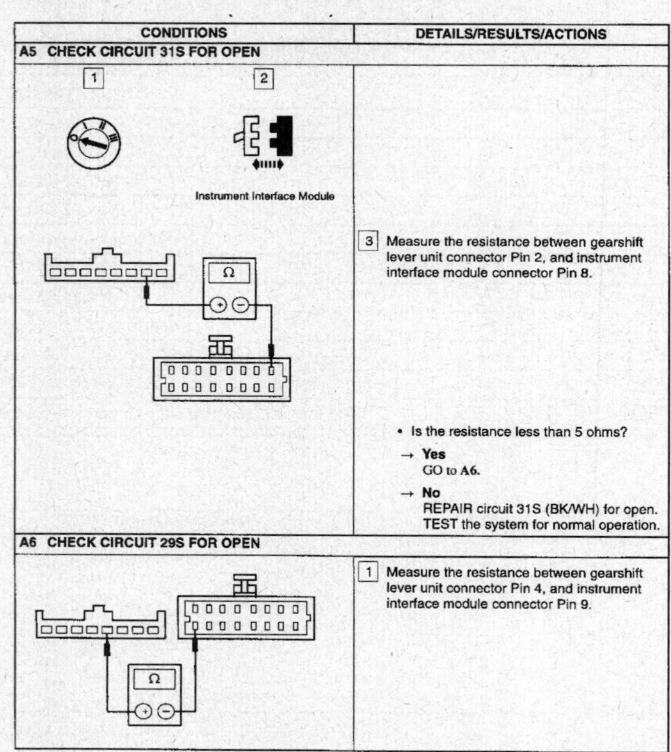

CONDITIONS	DETAILS/RESULTS/ACTIONS
A5 CHECK CIRCUIT 31S FOR OPEN	
1 2 Instrument Interface Module	3 Measure the resistance between gearshift lever unit connector Pin 2, and instrument interface module connector Pin 8. • Is the resistance less than 5 ohms? → **Yes** GO to **A6**. → **No** REPAIR circuit 31S (BK/WH) for open. TEST the system for normal operation.
A6 CHECK CIRCUIT 29S FOR OPEN	
	1 Measure the resistance between gearshift lever unit connector Pin 4, and instrument interface module connector Pin 9.

FM5019800707040X

Fig. 3 Shift Interlock System Troubleshooting Chart (Part 4 of 10)

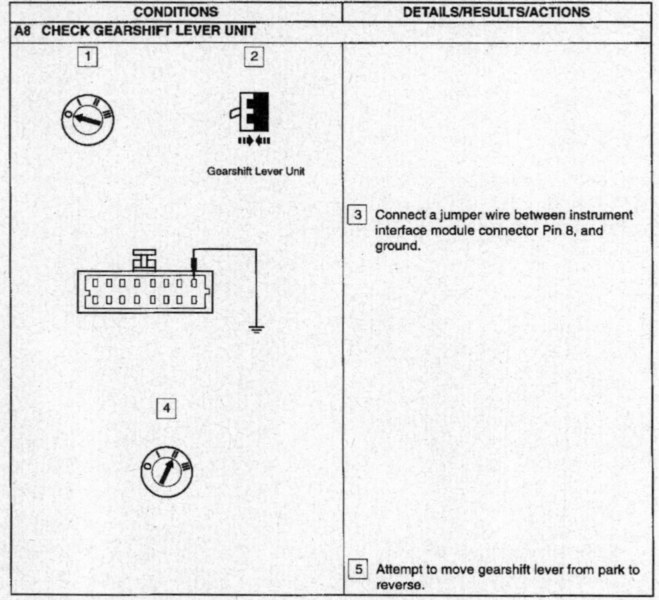

CONDITIONS	DETAILS/RESULTS/ACTIONS
A8 CHECK GEARSHIFT LEVER UNIT	
1 2 Gearshift Lever Unit 4	3 Connect a jumper wire between instrument interface module connector Pin 8, and ground. 5 Attempt to move gearshift lever from park to reverse.

FM5019800707060X

Fig. 3 Shift Interlock System Troubleshooting Chart (Part 6 of 10)

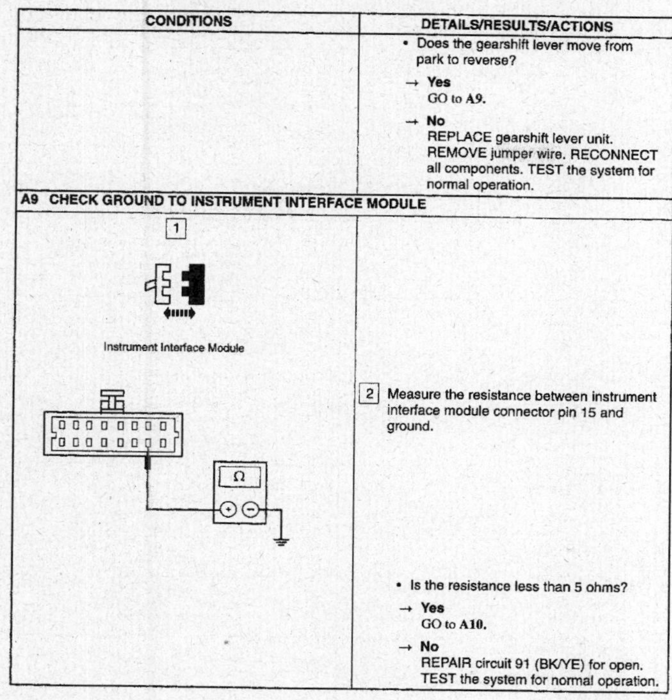

CONDITIONS	DETAILS/RESULTS/ACTIONS
	• Does the gearshift lever move from park to reverse? → **Yes** GO to **A9.** → **No** REPLACE gearshift lever unit. REMOVE jumper wire. RECONNECT all components. TEST the system for normal operation.
A9 CHECK GROUND TO INSTRUMENT INTERFACE MODULE	
1 Instrument Interface Module	
	2 Measure the resistance between instrument interface module connector pin 15 and ground.
	• Is the resistance less than 5 ohms? → **Yes** GO to **A10.** → **No** REPAIR circuit 91 (BK/YE) for open. TEST the system for normal operation.

FM5019800707070X

Fig. 3 Shift Interlock System Troubleshooting Chart (Part 7 of 10)

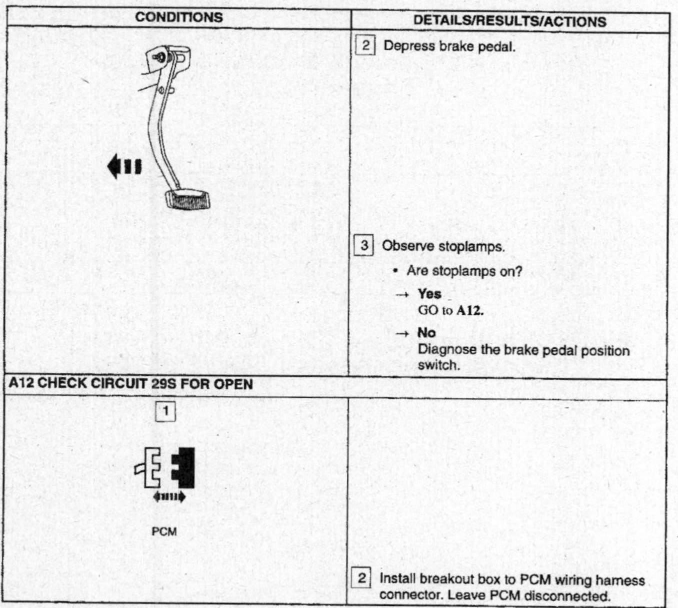

CONDITIONS	DETAILS/RESULTS/ACTIONS
	2 Depress brake pedal.
	3 Observe stoplamps. • Are stoplamps on? → **Yes** GO to **A12.** → **No** Diagnose the brake pedal position switch.
A12 CHECK CIRCUIT 29S FOR OPEN	
1 PCM	
	2 Install breakout box to PCM wiring harness connector. Leave PCM disconnected.

FM5019800707090X

Fig. 3 Shift Interlock System Troubleshooting Chart (Part 9 of 10)

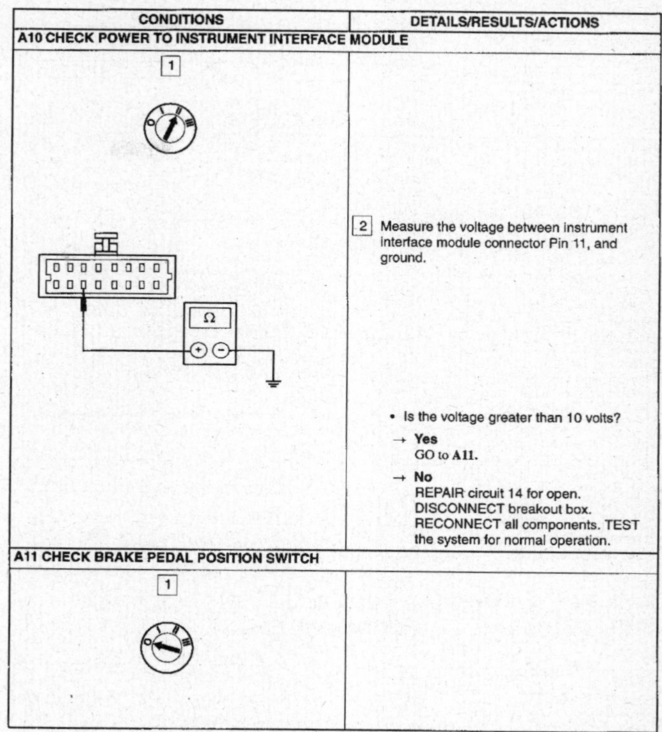

CONDITIONS	DETAILS/RESULTS/ACTIONS
A10 CHECK POWER TO INSTRUMENT INTERFACE MODULE	
1	
	2 Measure the voltage between instrument interface module connector Pin 11, and ground.
	• Is the voltage greater than 10 volts? → **Yes** GO to **A11.** → **No** REPAIR circuit 14 for open. DISCONNECT breakout box. RECONNECT all components. TEST the system for normal operation.
A11 CHECK BRAKE PEDAL POSITION SWITCH	
1	

FM5019800707080X

Fig. 3 Shift Interlock System Troubleshooting Chart (Part 8 of 10)

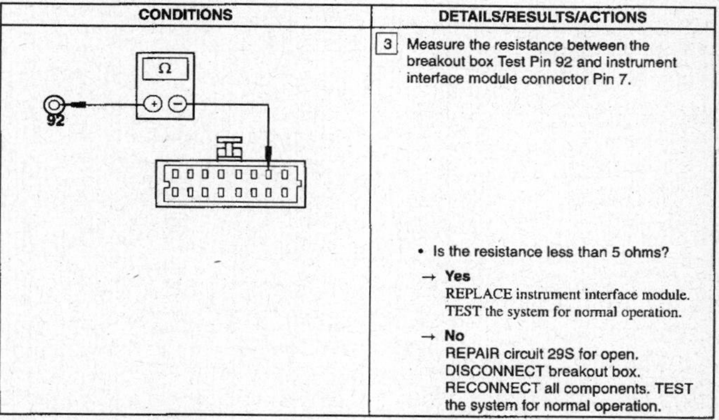

CONDITIONS	DETAILS/RESULTS/ACTIONS
92	3 Measure the resistance between the breakout box Test Pin 92 and instrument interface module connector Pin 7.
	• Is the resistance less than 5 ohms? → **Yes** REPLACE instrument interface module. TEST the system for normal operation. → **No** REPAIR circuit 29S for open. DISCONNECT breakout box. RECONNECT all components. TEST the system for normal operation.

FM5019800707100X

Fig. 3 Shift Interlock System Troubleshooting Chart (Part 10 of 10)

Possible Component	Reference/Action
201 — ELECTRICAL ROUTINE	
No Electrical Concerns	
301 — HYDRAULIC/MECHANICAL ROUTINE	
Internal or External Shift Linkages • Damaged, misadjusted, misassembled	• INSPECT and SERVICE as required. ADJUST linkage. After servicing linkage, VERIFY that the transmission range (TR) sensor is properly adjusted.
Pump Assembly • Bolts out of torque specifications • Gaskets damaged • Porosity/cross leaks and/or ball plug missing or leaking, or a plugged hole • Pump Support Seal Rings, No. 3 or No. 4, damaged	• RETORQUE bolts to specifications. • INSPECT for damage and replace. • INSPECT for porosity and leaks. REPLACE as required. • INSPECT for damage. SERVICE as required.
Main Controls • Bolts out of torque specifications • Gaskets damaged or leaking • Pressure Tap Plate/Gasket leaking or damaged • Separator Plates damaged • Hydraulic Passages damaged • Main Regulator Valve stuck, damaged or misassembled • Forward Accumulator leaking	• RETORQUE bolts to specifications. • INSPECT for damage. SERVICE as required. • INSPECT for damage. SERVICE as required. • INSPECT for damage. SERVICE as required. • INSPECT for damage. SERVICE as required. • INSPECT for damage. SERVICE as required. • INSPECT for damage. SERVICE as required.
Forward Clutch and Coast Clutch Assembly • Seals or Pistons damaged • Forward Clutch Return Spring damaged • Ball Check Valve damaged • Friction Elements severely damaged or worn • Forward/Coast/Direct clutch cylinder damaged, leaking, misassembled or binding • Cylinder to Hub Weld broken or Splines damaged	• PERFORM air pressure check. • INSPECT for damage. SERVICE as required. • INSPECT for damage. SERVICE as required. • INSPECT for mislocation, poor seating damage. REPLACE piston as required. • CHECK for abnormal wear, damage. SERVICE as required. • INSPECT for damage. SERVICE as required. • INSPECT for damage. SERVICE as required.
Low OWC Assembly • Worn, damaged, misassembled	• INSPECT for damage. SERVICE as required.
Forward OWC Assembly • Worn, damaged, misassembled	• INSPECT for damage. SERVICE as required.
Low Intermediate Carrier • Damaged, misassembled	• INSPECT for damage. SERVICE as required.

FM5029801535000X

Fig. 4 Routines 201 & 302: No Forward Engagement

Possible Component	Reference/Action
203 — ELECTRICAL ROUTINE	
Powertrain Control System • Electrical Inputs/Outputs, Vehicle Wiring Harnesses, Powertrain Control Module, EPC Solenoid, Transmission Fluid Temperature Sensor	• RUN OBD Tests. REFER to MOTOR's Domestic Transmission Manual for diagnosis. PERFORM Service Manual Pinpoint Tests "E and B" and the Engagement Test routine using the Transmission Tester (007-00130 and CD4E Update Kit 007-00088). SERVICE as required. CLEAR codes, ROAD TEST and RERUN OBD Tests.
303 — HYDRAULIC/MECHANICAL ROUTINE	
Fluid • Level • Condition	• ADJUST fluid to proper level. • INSPECT per Service Manual instructions under Fluid Condition Check.
CV Joints/Front Wheel Driveshaft and Joint • Splines damaged	• INSPECT for damage. SERVICE as required.
Powertrain Mounts • Loose, broken, missing or misaligned • Powertrain contacting with other vehicle components	• INSPECT mounts per Service Manual procedures. SERVICE as required. • INSPECT for contact. SERVICE as required.
External Shift Linkage • Damaged, misadjusted	• INSPECT and SERVICE as required. ADJUST to linkage After servicing linkage, VERIFY that the transmission range (TR) sensor is properly adjusted.
Improper Pressures • Improper Line Pressure	• CHECK pressure at Line tap. PERFORM Control Pressure and Stall Speed Tests. If high, VERIFY Engagements at Minimum EPC using the Transmission Tester. If Line remains HIGH, CHECK the following component: Main Controls.
Internal Shift Linkages • Damaged, misadjusted	• INSPECT and SERVICE as required. ADJUST linkage. After servicing linkage, VERIFY that the TR sensor is properly adjusted.
Oil Filter and Seal Assembly • Filter/Seal damaged, plugged • Recirc Seal damaged, plugged or out of position	• REPLACE filter and seal assembly. • REPLACE Recirculation Seal.
Main Controls • Bolts out of torque specifications • Gaskets damaged • Low/Reverse Accumulator Piston and Spring (Reverse), Main Regulator Valve, Forward Accumulator Piston and Spring misassembled, stuck or damaged • EPC Solenoid stuck or damaged	• RETORQUE bolts to specifications. • INSPECT for damage and REPLACE as required. • INSPECT for damage. SERVICE as required. • INSPECT for damage, contamination. ACTIVATE solenoid using transmission tester. SERVICE as required.
Forward Cl. Assembly (Forward Only) • Forward Clutch Cylinder damaged • Piston Bore damaged • Friction Elements damaged, worn • Forward Clutch Return Spring damaged or missing • Ball Check damaged • Piston or Seals damaged	• PERFORM Air Pressure Test. • INSPECT for damage. SERVICE as required. • INSPECT for damage. SERVICE as required. • INSPECT for damage. SERVICE as required. • INSPECT for damage. SERVICE as required. • INSPECT for damage. SERVICE as required. • INSPECT for damage. SERVICE as required.
Reverse Cl. Assembly (Reverse Only) • Seals or Piston damaged • Reverse Piston damaged • Friction Elements damaged, worn, misassembled	• PERFORM Air Pressure Test. • INSPECT for damage. SERVICE as required. • INSPECT for damage. SERVICE as required. • INSPECT for damage. SERVICE as required.

FM5029801537010X

Fig. 6 Routines 203 & 303: Harsh Reverse Or Forward Engagement (Part 1 of 2)

Possible Component	Reference/Action
202 — ELECTRICAL ROUTINE	
Powertrain Control System • Electrical Inputs/Outputs, Vehicle Wiring Harnesses, Powertrain Control Module, Shift Solenoid No. 1 (ON), transmission range (TR) sensor	• RUN OBD Tests. REFER to MOTOR's Domestic Transmission Manual for diagnosis. PERFORM Service Manual pinpoint tests "A and D" and the Engagement Test routine using the Transmission Tester (007-00130), CD4E Update Kit (007-00088) and TR Sensor Cable (007-0086A). SERVICE as required. CLEAR codes, ROAD TEST and RERUN OBD Tests.
302 — HYDRAULIC/MECHANICAL ROUTINE	
External Shift Linkage • Damaged, misadjusted	• INSPECT and SERVICE as required. After servicing linkage, VERIFY that the TR sensor is properly adjusted.
Improper Pressures • Low Line Pressure	• CHECK pressure at Line pressure tap. PERFORM Control Pressure and Stall Speed Tests. If pressure is low, CHECK the following possible components: Main Control, Oil Pump Assembly, Rev. Cl. Assembly, Low/Reverse Cl. Assembly.
Internal Shift Linkage • Damaged, misadjusted	• INSPECT and SERVICE as required. ADJUST linkage After servicing linkage, VERIFY that the TR sensor is properly adjusted.
Main Controls • Bolts out of torque specifications • Gasket damaged • 1-2 Shift Valve, SS1, Main Regulator Valve, Low/Reverse Modulator Valve, Low/Reverse Accumulator Piston, Pressure Tap Plate damaged, missing, stuck, misassembled • Separator Plates damaged • Hydraulic Passages damaged	• RETORQUE bolts to specifications. • INSPECT for damage and REPLACE as required. • INSPECT for damage. SERVICE as required. • INSPECT for damage. SERVICE as required. • INSPECT for damage. SERVICE as required.
Oil Pump Assembly • Bolts out of torque specifications • Gasket damaged • Porosity/cross leaks/ball plug missing or leaking, plugged hole • Pump Support Seal Rings, No. 6 or No. 7, damaged	• RETORQUE bolts to specifications. • INSPECT for damage and REPLACE as required. • REPLACE oil pump assembly. • INSPECT for damage. SERVICE as required.
Reverse Clutch Assembly • Seals - Piston damaged • Ball Check Valve damaged • Friction Elements worn, severely damaged or misassembled • Piston Return Spring damaged • Reverse Clutch Hub to Forward/Coast/Direct Hub Splines damaged	• PERFORM Air Pressure Test • INSPECT for damage. SERVICE as required. • INSPECT for damage. SERVICE as required. • INSPECT for damage. SERVICE as required. • INSPECT for damage. SERVICE as required. • INSPECT for damage. SERVICE as required.
Low/Reverse Clutch Assembly • Seals or piston damaged • Friction elements worn or severely damaged • Piston Return Spring damaged • Wave Spring missing • Piston Bore damaged	• PERFORM Air Pressure Test. • INSPECT for damage. SERVICE as required. • INSPECT for damage. SERVICE as required. • INSPECT for damage. SERVICE as required. • INSPECT for spring. SERVICE as required. • INSPECT for damage. SERVICE as required.
Forward/Coast/Direct Clutch Cylinder • Reverse Seal Rings damaged, missing, misassembled	• INSPECT for damage. SERVICE as required.
Case • Reverse to Low/Reverse Clutch feeds have severe cross leakage or porosity	• PERFORM Air Pressure Test. • INSPECT for damage. SERVICE as required.
Reverse/Overdrive Gear Set • Damaged	• INSPECT for damage. SERVICE as required.

FM5029801536000X

Fig. 5 Routines 202 & 302: No Reverse Engagement

Possible Component	Reference/Action
• Return Spring Assembly damaged, worn • Ball Check damaged, missing	• INSPECT for damage. SERVICE as required. • INSPECT for damage. SERVICE as required.
Low/Reverse Cl. Assembly (Reverse Only) • Seals or Reverse Clutch Piston damaged • Wave Spring damaged • Friction Elements damaged, worn, misassembled • Return Spring Assembly damaged, worn or misassembled • Piston Bore damaged	• PERFORM Air Pressure Test. • INSPECT for damage. SERVICE as required. • INSPECT for damage. SERVICE as required. • INSPECT for damage. SERVICE as required. • INSPECT for damage. SERVICE as required. • INSPECT for damage. SERVICE as required.
Direct Clutch Assembly (Reverse Only) • Friction Elements Severely damaged	• PERFORM Air Pressure Test. • INSPECT for damage. SERVICE as required.

FM5029801537020X

Fig. 6 Routines 203 & 303: Harsh Reverse Or Forward Engagement (Part 2 of 2)

Possible Component	Reference/Action
205 — ELECTRICAL ROUTINE	
No Electrical Concerns	
305 — HYDRAULIC/MECHANICAL ROUTINE	
Fluid • Improper level • Condition	• ADJUST fluid to proper level. • INSPECT per Service Manual instructions under Fluid Condition Check.
External Shift Linkages • Damaged, misadjusted or misassembled	• INSPECT and SERVICE as required. ADJUST linkage. After servicing linkage, VERIFY that the transmission range (TR) sensor is properly adjusted.
Improper Pressures • Low Line Pressure	• CHECK pressure at line tap. PERFORM Control Pressure and Stall Speed Tests. If pressure is low, CHECK the following possible components: Main Control, Oil Pump Assembly, Clutch Assemblies, Oil Filter and Seal Assembly, Recirculating Seal.
Internal Shift Linkages • Damaged, misadjusted or misassembled	• INSPECT and SERVICE as required. ADJUST linkage. After servicing linkage, VERIFY that the TR sensor is properly adjusted.
Oil Pump Assembly • Bolts out of torque specifications • Gaskets damaged • Porosity/cross leaks/ball plug missing or leaking, or passage blockage • Pump Support Seal Rings, No. 3 or No. 4 (Forward), or No. 6 or No. 7 (Reverse), damaged • Pump Gear/Pocket damaged • Separator Plate damaged	• RETORQUE bolts to specifications. • INSPECT for damage and REPLACE as required. • REPLACE oil pump assembly. • INSPECT for damage. SERVICE as required. • INSPECT for damage. SERVICE as required. • INSPECT for damage. SERVICE as required.
Oil Filter and Seal Assembly • Filter/Seal damaged, plugged • Recirculating Seal damage or out of position	• REPLACE filter and seal assembly. • REPLACE/RESEAT Recirculating Seal.
Main Controls • Bolts out of torque specifications • Gaskets damaged • Manual Valve, Main Regulator Valve, Low/Reverse Modulator Valve stuck, damaged or misassembled • Separator Plates damaged • Pressure Tap Plate/Gasket leaks, damaged, misassembled	• RETORQUE bolts to specifications. • INSPECT for damage and REPLACE as required. • INSPECT for damage. SERVICE as required. • INSPECT for damage. SERVICE as required. • INSPECT for damage. SERVICE as required.
Low/Reverse Cl. Assembly (Reverse Only)	• PERFORM Air Pressure Check.

FM5029801538010X

Fig. 7 Routines 205 & 305: Delayed/Soft Reverse Or Forward Engagement (Part 1 of 2)

Possible Component	Reference/Action
• Piston or Seals damaged • Friction Elements damaged, worn • Return Spring damaged • Piston Bore damaged • Excessive Cl. Pack End Clearance	• INSPECT for damage. SERVICE as required. • INSPECT for damage. SERVICE as required. • INSPECT for damage. SERVICE as required. • INSPECT for damage. SERVICE as required. • SERVICE as required.
Reverse Cl. Assembly (Reverse Only) • Seals or Piston damaged • Check Ball damaged • Friction Elements damaged, worn • Return Spring worn, damaged • Piston Bore damaged • Excessive Cl. Pack End Clearance	• PERFORM Air Pressure Check. • INSPECT for damage. SERVICE as required. • INSPECT for damage. SERVICE as required. • INSPECT for damage. SERVICE as required. • INSPECT for damage. SERVICE as required. • INSPECT for damage. SERVICE as required. • INSPECT. SERVICE as required.
Forward Clutch Assembly (Forward Only) • Seals or Piston damaged • Ball check damaged, missing or not sealing properly • Friction Elements damaged, worn or excessive end clearance	• PERFORM Air Pressure Check. • INSPECT for damage. SERVICE as required. • INSPECT for damage, proper seating or missing. REPLACE cylinder as required. • INSPECT for damage and end clearance. SERVICE as required.
Forward/Coast/Direct Clutch Cylinder Assembly • Reverse Seal Ring damaged or missing • Cylinder damaged or leaking	• INSPECT for damage. SERVICE as required. • INSPECT for damage. SERVICE as required.

FM5029801538020X

Fig. 7 Routines 205 & 305: Delayed/Soft Reverse Or Forward Engagement (Part 2 of 2)

Possible Component	Reference/Action
207 — ELECTRICAL ROUTINE	
No Electrical Concerns	
307 — HYDRAULIC/MECHANICAL ROUTINE	
Fluid • Improper level	• ADJUST fluid to proper level.
External Shift Linkages • Damaged, misadjusted or misassembled	• INSPECT and SERVICE as required. ADJUST linkage. After servicing linkage, VERIFY that the transmission range (TR) sensor is properly adjusted.
Improper Pressures • Low/No Line Pressure	• CHECK pressure at Line tap. PERFORM Control Pressure and Stall Speed Tests. If pressure is low, CHECK the following possible components: Oil Filter and Seal Assembly, Main Controls, Oil Pump Assembly. If OK, PROCEED to Turbine Shaft. • CHECK Flex Plate. • CHECK Torque Converter Pump Shaft and Assembly.
Internal Shift Linkages • Damaged, misadjusted or misassembled	• INSPECT and SERVICE as required. ADJUST linkage After servicing linkage, VERIFY that the TR sensor is properly adjusted
Pump Assembly • Bolts out of torque specifications • Gasket damaged, missing • Porosity/cross leaks or passage(s) blocked • Pump Support Seal Rings missing • Pump Shaft broken, damaged	• RETORQUE bolts to specifications. • INSPECT for damage and REPLACE as required. • INSPECT for porosity, leaks, blockage. REPLACE pump as required. • INSPECT for damage. SERVICE as required. • INSPECT for damage. SERVICE as required.
Filter and Seal Assembly • Filter/Seal damaged, plugged, or missing	• REPLACE filter and seal assembly per Service Manual procedures.

FM5029801539010X

Fig. 8 Routines 207 & 307: No Forward & No Reverse Engagement (Part 1 of 2)

Possible Component	Reference/Action
• Recirculating Seal damaged or out of position	• REPLACE/RESEAT Recirculating Seal.
Main Controls • Bolts out of torque specifications • Gaskets damaged • Pressure Plate/Gasket damaged or missing • Main Regulator Valve, Manual Valve stuck, damaged, plugged, missing, "Z" Link not connected	• RETORQUE bolts to specifications. • INSPECT for damage and REPLACE as required. • INSPECT for damage. SERVICE as required. • INSPECT for damage. SERVICE as required.
Flywheel (Starter Gear) • Damaged, broken	• INSPECT for damage. SERVICE as required.
Torque Converter Assembly • Pump Drive Shaft Insert damaged • Studs broken or damaged • Splines damaged • Internal Blades damaged, broken	• INSPECT for damage. SERVICE as required. • INSPECT torque converter. If damaged, REPLACE.
Turbine Shaft to Forward/Coast/Direct Clutch Cylinder Hsg. • Splines damaged	• INSPECT for damage. SERVICE as required.
Chain and Sprocket Assembly • Broken, damaged	• INSPECT for damage. SERVICE as required.
Park Mechanism • Parking Pawl Return Spring damaged, missing or misassembled	• INSPECT for damage. SERVICE as required.
Front Wheel Drive Shafts and Joints • Broken or splines damaged	• INSPECT for damage. SERVICE as required.
Final Drive and Differential Assembly • Splines damaged • Gearset damaged	• INSPECT for damage. SERVICE as required. • INSPECT for damage. SERVICE as required.
Planetary Gearsets • Gear Teeth, Carriers, Splines damaged, or broken	• INSPECT for damage. SERVICE as required.

FM5029801539020X

Fig. 8 Routines 207 & 307: No Forward & No Reverse Engagement (Part 2 of 2)

Possible Component	Reference/Action
210 — ELECTRICAL ROUTINE	
Powertrain Control System • Electrical Inputs/Outputs, Vehicle Wiring Harnesses, Powertrain Control Module, Shift Solenoids, Transmission Range (TR) sensor, throttle position sensor, VSS, TCS	• PERFORM Shift Point Test. • RUN OBD Tests. REFER to MOTOR's Domestic Transmission Manual for diagnosis. PERFORM Service Manual Pinpoint Tests "A and D" using Transmission Tester (007-00130 CD4E cable 007-00125) and the TR Sensor Cable (007-0086A). SERVICE as required. CLEAR codes, ROAD TEST and RERUN OBD Tests.
310 — HYDRAULIC/MECHANICAL ROUTINE	
Fluid • Improper level	• ADJUST fluid to proper level.
Internal and External Shift Linkages • Damaged, misadjusted or misassembled	• INSPECT and SERVICE as required. ADJUST linkage After servicing linkage, VERIFY that the TR sensor is properly adjusted.
Speedo Input • Speedometer Drive Gear damaged • Speedometer Gear damaged • Speedometer Driven Gear Retainer damaged or missing	• INSPECT for damage. SERVICE as required. • INSPECT for damage. SERVICE as required. • INSPECT for damage. SERVICE as required.
Go to Reference/Action to diagnose specific missing shifts • Shift Concern: No 1-2 Shift • Shift Concern: No 2-3 Shift • Shift Concern: No 3-4 Shift	• Routine 220/320 • Routine 221/321 • Routine 222/322

FM5029801540000X

Fig. 9 Routines 210 & 310: Some Or All Shifts Missing

Possible Component	Reference/Action
211 — ELECTRICAL ROUTINE	
Powertrain Control System • Electrical Inputs/Outputs, Vehicle Wiring Harnesses, Powertrain Control Module, Throttle Position Sensor, Vehicle Speed Sensor, Transmission Fluid Temperature Sensor	• PERFORM Shift Point Test. • RUN OBD Tests. REFER to MOTOR's Domestic Transmission Manual for diagnosis. PERFORM Service Manual Pinpoint Tests "B" using the Transmission Tester (007-00130 and CD4E cable 007-00125) SERVICE as required. CLEAR codes, ROAD TEST and RERUN OBD Tests.
311 — HYDRAULIC/MECHANICAL ROUTINE	
Other • Tire Size change • Speedometer Gear broken or incorrect • Speedometer Drive Gear damaged	• REFER to the spec. decal on door panel and VERIFY that vehicle has original equipment. Changes in tire size or speedometer gear will affect shift timing. • INSPECT for damage. SERVICE as required. • INSPECT for damage. SERVICE as required.

FM5029801541000X

Fig. 10 Routines 211 & 311: Shift Timing Is Early/Late

Possible Component	Reference/Action
212 — ELECTRICAL ROUTINE	
Powertrain Control System	
• Engine Concerns	• REFER to MOTOR'S AEP & DM to diagnose erratic engine operations. • PERFORM Shift Point Test.
• Electrical Inputs/Outputs, Vehicle Wiring Harnesses, Powertrain Control Module, Shift Solenoids, Transmission Range (TR) Sensor, Brake On/Off Switch, TCC Solenoid, Vehicle Speed Sensor, Throttle Position Sensor, TSS, EPC, 3-2T/CCS	• RUN OBD Tests. REFER to MOTOR's Domestic Transmission Manual for diagnosis. PERFORM Service Manual Pinpoint Tests "A,C,D,F and G" using Transmission Tester (007-00130 and CD4E cable 007-00125) and the TR Sensor Cable (007-0086A). SERVICE as required. CLEAR codes, ROAD TEST and RERUN OBD Tests.
312 — HYDRAULIC/MECHANICAL ROUTINE	
Fluid	
• Improper level	• ADJUST fluid to proper level.
• Condition	• INSPECT Fluid Condition.
Vehicle Speed Input	
• Speedometer Drive Gear damaged	• INSPECT for damage. SERVICE as required.
• Speedometer Gear damaged	• INSPECT for damage. SERVICE as required.
Main Control	
• Bolts out of torque specifications	• RETORQUE bolts to specifications.
• Gaskets damaged	• INSPECT for damage and REPLACE as required.
• 3-2 Timing Valve, Pull-in Valve, 2-4 Accumulator, Servo Release Shuttle Valve, 3-2 Control Valve stuck, damaged, misassembled	• INSPECT for damage. SERVICE as required.
• Solenoid Screen blocked	• CLEAN or REPLACE screen.
• Separator Plates damaged, blocked	• INSPECT for damage. SERVICE as required.
• Pressure Tap Plate/Gasket damaged	• INSPECT for damage. SERVICE as required.
• SS1, SS2, 3-2T/CCS Solenoid malfunction, stuck, damaged	• ACTIVATE solenoids with tester. INSPECT for damage. SERVICE as required.
Go to Reference/Action to diagnose specific shift concern	
• Shift Concern: No 1-2 Shift	• Routine 220/320
• Shift Concern: No 2-3 Shift	• Routine 221/321
• Shift Concern: No 3-4 Shift	• Routine 222/322
• Shift Concern: Soft/Slip 1-2 Shift	• Routine 226/326
• Shift Concern: Soft/Slip 2-3 Shift	• Routine 227/327
• Shift Concern: Soft/Slip 3-4 Shift	• Routine 228/328
• Shift Concern: Soft/Slip 4-3 Shift	• Routine 229/329
• Shift Concern: Soft/Slip 3-2 Shift	• Routine 230/330
• Shift Concern: Soft/Slip 2-1 Shift	• Routine 231/331

FM5029801542010X

Fig. 11 Routines 212 & 312: Shift Timing Is Erratic/Hunting (Part 1 of 2)

Possible Component	Reference/Action
• Porosity/cross leaks	• INSPECT for porosity. SERVICE as required.
Oil Filter/Seal Assembly	
• Filter/Seal damaged, plugged or missing	• REPLACE filter and seal assembly.
• Recirculating Seal damaged or out of position	• REPLACE Recirculating Seal.

FM5029801543020X

Fig. 12 Routines 213 & 313: Shift Feel Is Soft/Slipping (Part 2 of 2)

Possible Component	Reference/Action
214 — ELECTRICAL ROUTINE	
Powertrain Control System	
• Electrical Inputs/Outputs, Vehicle Wiring Harnesses, Powertrain Control Module, EPC Solenoid, Transmission Fluid Temperature Sensor, TSS, Throttle Position Sensor, Vehicle Speed Sensor, Mass Air Flow Sensor, TCC Solenoid, Transmission Range (TR) Sensor, 3-2T/CCS	• PERFORM Torque Converter Clutch Operation Test. • RUN OBD Tests. REFER to MOTOR's Domestic Transmission Manual for diagnosis. PERFORM Service Manual Pinpoint Tests "B, C, D, E, F and G" using Transmission Tester (007-00130 and CD4E cable 007-00125) and TR Sensor Cable (007-0086A). SERVICE as required. CLEAR codes, ROAD TEST and RERUN OBD Tests.
314 — HYDRAULIC/MECHANICAL ROUTINE	
Fluid	
• Improper level	• ADJUST fluid to proper level.
• Condition	• Inspect Fluid Condition.
CV Joint/Front Wheel Driveshafts and Joints	
• Damaged, loose, splines damaged	• INSPECT for damage. SERVICE as required.
Powertrain Mounts	
• Damaged, loose, missing	• INSPECT for damage. SERVICE as required.
Improper Pressures	
• High Line Pressure	• CHECK pressure at Line tap. PERFORM Control Pressure Test and Stall Speed Tests. If pressures are high or all shifts are harsh, GO to Main Control. • If pressures are OK and a specific shift is harsh. **Shift** 1-2, **Routine** 232/332 **Shift** 2-3, **Routine** 233/333 **Shift** 3-4, **Routine** 234/334 **Shift** 4-3, **Routine** 235/335 **Shift** 3-2, **Routine** 236/336 **Shift** 2-1, **Routine** 237/337
Main Controls	
• Bolts out of torque specifications	• RETORQUE bolts to specifications.
• Gaskets damaged	• INSPECT for damage. SERVICE as required.
• Main Regulator Valve, By-Pass Valve, Line Modulator Valve stuck damaged or misassembled. Springs tangled, missing, damaged	• INSPECT for damage. SERVICE as required.
• EPC Solenoid stuck or damaged	• INSPECT for damage, contamination. ACTIVATE solenoid using transmission tester. SERVICE as required.
• Hydraulic Passages damaged	• INSPECT for damage. SERVICE as required.
• Separator Plate damaged, blocked	• INSPECT for damage. SERVICE as required.
Torque Converter Assembly NOTE: If TCC Applied during shifts	
• Piston damaged	• INSPECT for damage. SERVICE as required.
• Pump Support Seal No. 1 (CBY circuit) leaking, missing or damaged	• INSPECT for damage. SERVICE as required.
• Case leakage	• INSPECT for damage. SERVICE as required.
• Converter Assembly damaged	• If heat stained, REPLACE converter.

FM5029801544000X

Fig. 13 Routines 214 & 314: Shift Feel Is Harsh

Possible Component	Reference/Action
• Shift Concern: Harsh 1-2 Shift	• Routine 232/332
• Shift Concern: Harsh 2-3 Shift	• Routine 233/333
• Shift Concern: Harsh 3-4 Shift	• Routine 234/334
• Shift Concern: Harsh 4-3 Shift	• Routine 235/335
• Shift Concern: Harsh 3-2 Shift	• Routine 236/336

FM5029801542020X

Fig. 11 Routines 212 7 312: Shift Timing Is Erratic/Hunting (Part 2 of 2)

Possible Component	Reference/Action
213 — ELECTRICAL ROUTINE	
Powertrain Control System • Electrical Inputs/Outputs, Vehicle Wiring Harnesses, Powertrain Control Module, EPC Solenoid, Transmission Fluid Temperature Sensor, Throttle Position Sensor, Mass Air Flow Sensor	• PERFORM Shift Point Test. • RUN OBD Tests. REFER to MOTOR's Domestic Transmission Manual for diagnosis. PERFORM Service Manual Pinpoint Tests "B and E" using the Transmission Tester (007-00130 and CD4E cable 007-00125). SERVICE as required. CLEAR codes. ROAD TEST and RERUN OBD Tests.
313 — HYDRAULIC/MECHANICAL ROUTINE	
Fluid	
• Improper level	• ADJUST fluid to proper level.
• Condition	• INSPECT Fluid Condition.
External Shift Linkage	
• Damaged, misadjusted or misassembled	• INSPECT and SERVICE as required. ADJUST linkage. After servicing linkage, VERIFY that the transmission range (TR) Sensor is properly adjusted.
Improper Pressures	
• Low Line Pressure	• CHECK pressures at Line tap. PERFORM Control Pressure Tests. If pressures are low or all shifts are soft/slipping, GO to Main Control, Oil Pump Assembly, Oil Filter/Seal Assembly. If pressures are OK and a specific shift is soft/slipping, REFER to the appropriate routine(s) for additional diagnosis. **Shift** 1-2, **Routine** 226/326 **Shift** 2-3, **Routine** 227/327 **Shift** 3-4, **Routine** 228/328 **Shift** 4-3, **Routine** 229/329 **Shift** 3-2, **Routine** 230/330 **Shift** 2-1, **Routine** 231/331
Internal Shift Linkage	
• Damaged, misadjusted or misassembled	• INSPECT and SERVICE as required. ADJUST linkage. After servicing linkage, VERIFY that the TR Sensor is properly adjusted.
Main Controls	
• Bolts out of torque specifications	• RETORQUE bolts to specifications.
• Gaskets damaged	• INSPECT gaskets and REPLACE as required.
• Main Regulator Valve, Line Modulator Valve stuck, damage or misassembled or springs missing, tangled or damaged	• INSPECT for damage. SERVICE as required.
• EPC Solenoid stuck or damaged	• INSPECT for damage, contamination. ACTIVATE solenoid using the trans tester. SERVICE as required.
• Separator Plates damaged, blocked	• INSPECT for damage. SERVICE as required.
• Pressure Tap Plate/Gasket damaged or missing	• INSPECT for damage. SERVICE as required.
Oil Pump Assembly	
• Bolts out of torque specifications	• RETORQUE bolts to specifications.
• Gaskets damaged	• INSPECT for damage and REPLACE as required.

FM5029801543010X

Fig. 12 Routines 213 & 313: Shift Feel Is Soft/Slipping (Part 1 of 2)

Possible Component	Reference/Action
215 — ELECTRICAL ROUTINE	
Powertrain Control System • Electrical Inputs/Outputs, Vehicle Wiring Harnesses, Powertrain Control Module, Shift Solenoids, Transmission Range (TR) Sensor	• RUN OBD Tests. REFER to MOTOR's Domestic Transmission Manual for diagnosis. PERFORM Service Manual Pinpoint Tests "A and D" using the Transmission Tester (007-00130 and CD4E cable 007-00125) and the TR Sensor Cable (007-0086A). SERVICE as required. CLEAR codes, ROAD TEST and RERUN OBD Tests.
315 — HYDRAULIC/MECHANICAL ROUTINE	
External Shift Linkages	
• Damaged, misadjusted or misassembled	• INSPECT for proper adjustment. SERVICE as required. ADJUST After servicing linkage, VERIFY that the TR Sensor is properly adjusted.
Main Controls	
• Bolts out of torque specifications	• RETORQUE bolts to specifications.
• Gaskets damaged	• INSPECT for damage and REPLACE as required.
• Pull In Valve, Solenoid Regulator Valve, Shift Valves stuck, damaged, misassembled	• INSPECT for damage. SERVICE as required.
• Solenoid Filter Gasket damaged or misassembled	• INSPECT for damage. SERVICE as required.
• Hydraulic Passages damaged	• INSPECT for damage. SERVICE as required.
• SS1, SS2 Solenoid malfunction	• ACTIVATE solenoid with transmission tester. SERVICE as required.
For diagnosis related to a specific gear, use Transmission Tester (007-00130) to determine gear	• REFER to the following routines: **Shift** 1-2, **Routine** 220/320 **Shift** 2-3, **Routine** 221/321 **Shift** 3-4, **Routine** 222/322
Mechanical	
• Seals, Clutches damaged, worn • Direct Clutch, 2/4 Band, 2/4 Servo damaged, stuck on	• SERVICE as required.

FM5029801545000X

Fig. 14 Routines 215 & 315: No 1st Gear, Engages In Higher Gear

Possible Component	Reference/Action
216 — ELECTRICAL ROUTINE	
Powertrain Control System	
• Electrical Inputs/Outputs, Vehicle Wiring Harnesses, Powertrain Control Module, Shift Solenoids, Transmission Range (TR) Sensor	• RUN OBD Tests. REFER to MOTOR's Domestic Transmission Manual for diagnosis. PERFORM Service Manual Pinpoint Tests "A and D" using the Transmission Tester (007-00130 and CD4E cable 007-00125) and the TR Sensor Cable (007-0086A). SERVICE as required. CLEAR codes, ROAD TEST and RERUN OBD Tests.
316 — HYDRAULIC/MECHANICAL ROUTINE	
Internal and External Shift Linkages	
• Damaged, misadjusted or misassembled	• INSPECT and SERVICE as required. ADJUST linkage After servicing linkage, VERIFY that the TR sensor is properly adjusted. REFER to Disassembly/Assembly procedures
Main Controls	
• Bolts out of torque specifications	• RETORQUE bolts to specifications.
• Gaskets damaged	• INSPECT for damage and REPLACE as required.
• Pull-in Valve stuck, damaged	• INSPECT for damage. SERVICE as required.
• SS2 stuck "ON"	• ACTIVATE solenoid using transmission tester. SERVICE as required.
• Hydraulic Passages damaged	• INSPECT for damage. SERVICE as required.
• Separator Plates damaged, blocked	• INSPECT for damage. SERVICE as required.

FM5029801546000X

Fig. 15 Routines 216 & 316: No Manual 1st Gear

Possible Component	Reference/Action
221 — ELECTRICAL ROUTINE	
Powertrain Control System	
• Electrical Inputs/Outputs, Vehicle Wiring Harnesses, Powertrain Control Module, Shift Solenoids, Transmission Range (TR) Sensor	• RUN OBD Tests. REFER to MOTOR's Domestic Transmission Manual for diagnosis. PERFORM Service Manual Pinpoint Tests "A and D" using the Transmission Tester (007-00130 and CD4E cable and overlay 007-00125) and the TR Sensor Cable (007-0086A) as outlined in this manual. SERVICE as required. CLEAR codes, ROAD TEST and RERUN OBD Tests.
321 — HYDRAULIC/MECHANICAL ROUTINE	
Improper Pressures	

FM5029801548010X

Fig. 17 Routines 221 & 321: No Automatic 2–3 Shift (Part 1 of 2)

Possible Component	Reference/Action
222 — ELECTRICAL ROUTINE	
Powertrain Control System	
• Electrical Inputs/Outputs, Vehicle Wiring Harnesses, Powertrain Control Module, Shift Solenoids, Transmission Range (TR) Sensor, Transmission Control Switch (TCS).	• RUN OBD Tests. REFER to MOTOR's Domestic Transmission Manual for diagnosis. PERFORM Service Manual Pinpoint Tests "A and D" using the Transmission Tester (007-00130 and CD4E cable and overlay 007-00125) and the TR Sensor Cable (007-0086A) SERVICE as required. CLEAR codes, ROAD TEST and RERUN OBD Tests.
322 — HYDRAULIC/MECHANICAL ROUTINE	
Improper Pressures	
• Line pressure	• CHECK pressure at Line tap. PERFORM Control Pressure Tests. If out of specification CHECK Main Control.
Main Control	
• Bolts out of torque specifications	• RETORQUE bolts to specifications.
• Gasket leaks	• INSPECT for damage and REPLACE as required.
• 3-4 Shift Valve, Main Regulator Valve stuck, damaged or misassembled	• INSPECT for damage. SERVICE as required.
• SS1 malfunction (also No 1st)	• ACTIVATE solenoid using transmission tester. SERVICE as required.

FM5029801549010X

Fig. 18 Routines 222 & 322: No Automatic 3–4 Shift (Part 1 of 2)

Possible Component	Reference/Action
220 — ELECTRICAL ROUTINE	
Powertrain Control System	
• Electrical Inputs/Outputs, Vehicle Wiring Harnesses, Powertrain Control Module, Shift Solenoids, Transmission Range (TR) Sensor	• RUN OBD Tests. REFER to MOTOR's Domestic Transmission Manual for diagnosis. PERFORM Service Manual Pinpoint Tests "A and D" using the Transmission Tester (007-00130 and CD4E cable and overlay 007-00125) and the TR Sensor Cable (007-0086A). SERVICE as required. CLEAR codes, ROAD TEST and RERUN OBD Tests.
320 — HYDRAULIC/MECHANICAL ROUTINE	
Improper Pressures	
• Line Pressure	• CHECK pressure at Line tap. PERFORM Control Pressure and Stall Speed Tests. If not OK, CHECK the following possible components: Main Control.
Main Control	
• Bolts out of torque specifications	• RETORQUE bolts to specifications.
• Gaskets damaged	• INSPECT for damage and REPLACE as required.
• 1-2 Shift Valve, 2-4 Accumulator, Main Regulator Valve stuck, damaged, or misassembled	• INSPECT for damage. SERVICE as required.
• SS1 malfunction	• INSPECT for damage. ACTIVATE solenoid by using transmission tester.
• Pressure Tap Plate/Gasket damaged	• INSPECT for damage. SERVICE as required.
• Separator Plates damaged	• INSPECT for damage. SERVICE as required.
• Hydraulic Passages damaged	• INSPECT for damage. SERVICE as required.
Int/OD Band and Servo Assembly	
NOTE: Also No 4th gear	
• Seals damaged, missing	• INSPECT for damage. SERVICE as required.
• Piston damaged	• INSPECT for damage. SERVICE as required.
• Band damaged, worn	• INSPECT for damage. SERVICE as required.
• Springs damaged	• INSPECT for damage. SERVICE as required.
• Servo Rod or Rod Bore damaged	• INSPECT for damage. SERVICE as required.
Low OWC Assembly	
• Damaged	• INSPECT for damage. SERVICE as required.
OD/Reverse Sun Gear and Shell	
• Damaged, weld broken • Lugs damaged	• INSPECT for damage. SERVICE as required.
Case	
• Low and Intermediate Band Anchor Area damaged	• INSPECT for damage. If damaged REPLACE the case.
• Porosity/leakage in Servo Apply, Servo Release circuits	• INSPECT case for leakage/porosity. PERFORM Air Pressure Tests. REPLACE case as required.

FM5029801547000X

Fig. 16 Routines 220 & 320: No Automatic 1–2 Shift

Possible Component	Reference/Action
• Line Pressure	• CHECK pressure at Line pressure tap. PERFORM Control Pressure Tests. If NOT OK, CHECK the following possible component: Main Control.
Main Control	
• Bolts out of torque specifications	• RETORQUE bolts to specifications.
• Gasket leaks	• INSPECT for damage and REPLACE as required.
• 2-3 Shift Valve (also No 4th), Main Regulator Valve stuck, damaged, misassembled	• INSPECT for damage. SERVICE as required.
• SS2 malfunction (also no 4th)	• INSPECT for damage. ACTIVATE solenoid by using transmission tester.
• Separator Plates damaged	• INSPECT for damage. SERVICE as required.
• Pressure Tap Plate/Gasket leaks	• INSPECT for damage. SERVICE as required.
• Hydraulic Passages damaged	• INSPECT for damage. SERVICE as required.
Oil Pump Assembly	
• Bolts out of torque specifications	• RETORQUE bolts to specifications.
• Gaskets damaged	• INSPECT for damage and REPLACE as required.
• Porosity/cross leaks	• INSPECT for damage. SERVICE as required.
• Pump Support Seal Rings, No. 4 or No. 5, damaged	• INSPECT for damage. SERVICE as required.
Direct Clutch Assembly	• PERFORM Air Pressure Check.
• Seals or Piston damaged	• INSPECT for damage. SERVICE as required.
• Piston Bore damaged	• INSPECT for damage. SERVICE as required.
• Friction severely damaged, worn	• INSPECT for damage. SERVICE as required.
• Ball Check not seating properly	• INSPECT for damage. SERVICE as required.
• Return Spring Assembly damaged	• INSPECT for damage. SERVICE as required.
• Cylinder Bore/Splines damaged	• INSPECT for damage. SERVICE as required.
• Shell/Hub damaged	• INSPECT for damage. SERVICE as required.
INT/OD Servo	
• Piston or Piston Bore damaged	• INSPECT for damage. SERVICE as required.
• Rod Bore or Rod damaged, leaking	• INSPECT for damage. SERVICE as required.
Case	
• Leakage in the Servo Apply, Servo Release or Direct Clutch Circuits	• INSPECT case for damage. PERFORM Air Pressure Tests. SERVICE or REPLACE case as required.

FM5029801548020X

Fig. 17 Routines 221 & 321: No Automatic 2–3 Shift (Part 2 of 2)

Possible Component	Reference/Action
• Separator Plates damaged or Orifice blocked	• INSPECT for damage. SERVICE as required.
INT/OD Band and Servo Assembly	
NOTE: Also No 2nd gear	
• INT/OD Band damaged, worn	• INSPECT for damage. SERVICE as required.
• Servo Rod or Rod Bore damaged	• INSPECT for damage. SERVICE as required.
• Servo Piston or Cover damaged or leaking	• INSPECT for damage. SERVICE as required.
• Springs damaged	• INSPECT for damage. SERVICE as required.
Coast Clutch Assembly	
• Seals damaged, missing	• INSPECT for damage. SERVICE as required.
• Piston damaged	• INSPECT for damage. SERVICE as required.
• Friction severely damaged, worn	• INSPECT for damage. SERVICE as required.
• Check ball severely damaged	• INSPECT for damage. SERVICE as required.
Forward OWC Assembly	
• Damaged	• INSPECT for damage. SERVICE as required.
Case (Also No 2nd gear)	
• Band anchor damaged	• INSPECT for damage. PERFORM Air Pressure Checks. SERVICE as required.
• Servo Apply and Servo Release circuits leaking	• INSPECT for damage. SERVICE as required.

FM5029801549020X

Fig. 18 Routines 222 & 322: No Automatic 3–4 Shift (Part 2 of 2)

Possible Component	Reference/Action
226 — ELECTRICAL ROUTINE	
Powertrain Control System	
• Electrical Inputs/Outputs, Vehicle Wiring Harnesses, Powertrain Control Module, EPC Solenoid, Transmission Fluid Temperature Sensor	• RUN OBD Tests. PERFORM Stall Speed Tests. PERFORM Pinpoint Tests "B and E" using the Transmission Tester (007-00130 and CD4E cable and overlay 007-00125) and the TR Sensor (MLP Sensor) Cable (007-0086A). SERVICE as required. CLEAR codes, ROAD TEST and RERUN OBD Tests.
326 — HYDRAULIC/MECHANICAL ROUTINE	
Main Control	
• Bolts out of torque specifications	• RETORQUE bolts to specifications.
• Gaskets damaged	• INSPECT for damage and REPLACE as required.
• 2-4 Accumulator Piston Plug and Seal (also soft 3-4 shift), Main Regulator Valve, Line Modulator Valve (also soft 3-4 shift) stuck, damaged or misassembled	• INSPECT for damage. SERVICE as required.
• Hydraulic Passages damaged	• INSPECT for damage. SERVICE as required.
• Pressure Tap Plate/Gasket damaged	• INSPECT for damage. SERVICE as required.
• Separator Plates damaged	• INSPECT for damage. SERVICE as required.
INT/OD Band and Servo Assembly	
• Piston, Seals or Piston Bore damaged, missing	• INSPECT for damage. SERVICE as required.
• Servo Rod or Rod Bore damaged	• INSPECT for damage. SERVICE as required.
• Intermediate/Overdrive Band and/or Reverse Clutch Drum Assembly worn, damaged or misassembled	• INSPECT for damage. SERVICE as required.
• Springs damaged	• INSPECT for damage. SERVICE as required.
• Servo Cover and Seal damaged	• INSPECT for damage. SERVICE as required.
Forward OWC Assembly (slips in 1st)	
• Not holding or damaged	• INSPECT for damage. SERVICE as required.
Forward Clutch Assembly (slips in 1st)	• PERFORM Air Pressure Check.
• Seals damaged	• INSPECT for damage. SERVICE as required.
• Return Spring damaged	• INSPECT for damage. SERVICE as required.
• Friction elements damaged	• INSPECT for damage. SERVICE as required.
• Pump Supports Seals No. 3, No. 4 damaged	• INSPECT for damage. SERVICE as required.
Low OWC Assembly	

FM5029801550010X

Fig. 19 Routines 226 & 326: Soft/Slipping 1–2 Only Shift (Part 1 of 2)

Possible Component	Reference/Action
228 — ELECTRICAL ROUTINE	
Powertrain Control System	

FM5029801552010X

Fig. 21 Routines 228 & 328: Soft/Slipping 3–4 Only Shift (Part 1 of 2)

Possible Component	Reference/Action
• Electrical Inputs/Outputs, Vehicle Wiring Harnesses, Powertrain Control Module, EPC Solenoids, Transmission Fluid Temperature Sensor	• RUN OBD Tests. REFER to MOTOR's Domestic Transmission Manual for diagnosis. PERFORM Service Manual Pinpoint Tests "B and E" using the Transmission Tester (007-00130 and CD4E cable and overlay 007-00125). SERVICE as required. CLEAR codes, ROAD TEST and RERUN OBD Tests.
328 — HYDRAULIC/MECHANICAL ROUTINE	
Main Control	
• Bolts out of torque specifications	• RETORQUE bolts to specifications.
• Gasket Leaks	• INSPECT for damage and REPLACE as required.
• Line Modulator Valve, 2-4 Accumulator Valve Plug and Seal (also soft 1-2 shift), stuck, damaged or misassembled	• INSPECT for damage. SERVICE as required.
• Pressure Tap Plate/Gasket leaks	• INSPECT for damage. SERVICE as required.
• Hydraulic passages damaged	• INSPECT for damage. SERVICE as required.
• Separator Plates damaged or Orifice blocked	• INSPECT for damage. SERVICE as required.
INT/OD Band and Servo Assembly	
• INT/OD Band and/or Reverse Clutch Drum Assembly worn, damaged or misassembled	• INSPECT for damage. SERVICE as required.
• Piston, Seals or Piston Bore damaged, missing	• INSPECT for damage. SERVICE as required.
• Servo Cover or Seal damaged	• PERFORM Air Pressure Check. INSPECT for damage. SERVICE as required.
• Servo Rod or Rod Bore damaged	• INSPECT for damage. SERVICE as required.
• Springs damaged	• INSPECT for damage. SERVICE as required.
Direct Clutch Assembly	
NOTE: May also have 3rd gear slip	• PERFORM Air Pressure Check.
• Seals damaged, missing	• INSPECT for damage. SERVICE as required.
• Piston damaged	• INSPECT for damage. SERVICE as required.
• Check Ball damaged, missing or leaking	• INSPECT for damage. SERVICE as required.
• Return Spring damaged	• INSPECT for damage. SERVICE as required.
• Friction elements damaged	• INSPECT for damage. SERVICE as required.
Case	
• Band anchor damaged	• INSPECT for damage. SERVICE as required.
• Servo apply and servo release circuits leaking	• INSPECT for damage. PERFORM Air Pressure Check. SERVICE as required.

FM5029801552020X

Fig. 21 Routines 228 & 328: Soft/Slipping 3–4 Only Shift (Part 2 of 2)

Possible Component	Reference/Action
• Not overrunning, damaged	• INSPECT for damage. SERVICE as required.
Low Reverse Clutch Assembly	
• Friction elements severely damaged	• INSPECT for damage. SERVICE as required.
Case	
• Band Anchor damaged	• INSPECT for damage. If damaged REPLACE the case.
• Porosity/Leakage in Servo Apply, Servo Release circuits	• INSPECT case for leakage/porosity. PERFORM Air Pressure checks. REPLACE case as required.

FM5029801550020X

Fig. 19 Routines 226 & 326: Soft/Slipping 1–2 Only Shift (Part 2 of 2)

Possible Component	Reference/Action
227 — ELECTRICAL ROUTINE	
Powertrain Control System	
• Electrical Inputs/Outputs, Vehicle Wiring Harnesses, Powertrain Control Module, EPC Solenoid, Transmission Fluid Temperature Sensor	• RUN OBD Tests. REFER to MOTOR's Domestic Transmission Manual for diagnosis. PERFORM Service Manual Pinpoint Tests "B and E" using the Transmission Tester (007-00130 and CD4E cable and overlay 007-00125). SERVICE as required. CLEAR codes, ROAD TEST and RERUN OBD Tests. PERFORM Stall Speed Test.
327 — HYDRAULIC/MECHANICAL ROUTINE	
Oil Pump Assembly	
• Bolts out of torque specifications	• RETORQUE bolts to specifications.
• Gaskets damaged	• INSPECT for damage and REPLACE as required.
• Pump support seals No. 4 or No. 5 damaged, missing	• INSPECT for damage. SERVICE as required.
Main Control	
• Bolts out of torque specifications	• RETORQUE bolts to specifications.
• Gasket Leaks	• INSPECT for damage and REPLACE as required.
• Line Modulator Valve (also soft 1-2 and 3-4 shifts), Servo Release Shuttle Valve stuck damaged or misassembled	• INSPECT for damage. SERVICE as required.
• Hydraulic passages damaged	• INSPECT for damage. SERVICE as required.
• Separator Plates damaged	• INSPECT for damage. SERVICE as required.
• Pressure Tap Plate/Gasket leaks	• INSPECT for damage. SERVICE as required.
Direct Clutch Assembly	• PERFORM Air Pressure Check.
• Seals or Piston damaged	• INSPECT for damage. SERVICE as required.
• Piston bore damaged	• INSPECT for damage. SERVICE as required.
• Friction element damaged, worn or excessive end clearance	• INSPECT for damage. CHECK end clearance. SERVICE as required.
• Check ball not seating properly	• INSPECT for damage. SERVICE as required.
• Return Spring Assembly damaged	• INSPECT for damage. SERVICE as required.
INT/OD Servo	
• Piston or piston bore damaged	• INSPECT for damage. SERVICE as required.
• Servo rod or rod bore damaged	• INSPECT for damage. SERVICE as required.
Case	
• Leakage in the Servo Apply, Servo Release or Direct Clutch circuits	• INSPECT case for damage. PERFORM Air Pressure Checks. SERVICE or REPLACE case as required.
Forward OWC Assembly	
• Not holding, damaged	• INSPECT for damage. SERVICE as required.

FM5029801551000X

Fig. 20 Routines 227 & 327: Soft/Slipping 2–3 Only Shift

Possible Component	Reference/Action
229 — ELECTRICAL ROUTINE	
Powertrain Control System	
• Electrical Inputs/Outputs, Vehicle Wiring Harnesses, Powertrain Control Module, EPC Solenoid, Vehicle Speed Sensor, Mass Air Flow Sensor, Throttle Position Sensor	• RUN OBD Tests. REFER to MOTOR's Domestic Transmission Manual for diagnosis. PERFORM Service Manual Pinpoint Test "E" using the Transmission Tester (007-00130 and CD4E cable and overlay 007-00125). SERVICE as required. CLEAR codes, ROAD TEST and RERUN OBD Tests.
329 — HYDRAULIC/MECHANICAL ROUTINE	
Main Control	
• Bolts out of torque specifications	• RETORQUE bolts to specifications.
• Gasket Leaks	• INSPECT for damage and REPLACE as required.
• Servo Release Shuttle Valve, Main Regulator Valve stuck, damaged, or misassembled	• INSPECT for damage. SERVICE as required.
• Hydraulic passages damaged	• INSPECT for damage. SERVICE as required.
• Pressure Tap Plate/Gasket leaks, or damaged	• INSPECT for damage. SERVICE as required.
• Separator Plates damaged, blocked	• INSPECT for damage. SERVICE as required.
INT/OD Band and Servo Assembly	
• INT/OD Band and Reverse Clutch Drum Assembly worn, damaged or misassembled	• INSPECT for damage. SERVICE as required.

FM5029801553010X

Fig. 22 Routines 229 & 329: Soft/Slipping 4–3 Only Shift (Part 1 of 2)

Possible Component	Reference/Action
• Servo Return Spring broken	• INSPECT for damage. SERVICE as required.
• Servo Rod damaged	• INSPECT for damage. SERVICE as required.
• Piston seal damaged	• INSPECT for damage. SERVICE as required.
Direct Clutch Assembly	• PERFORM Air Pressure Check.
• Seals damaged, missing	• INSPECT for damage. SERVICE as required.
• Piston damaged	• INSPECT for damage. SERVICE as required.
• Check Ball damaged, missing or leaking	• INSPECT for damage. SERVICE as required.
• Return Spring damaged	• INSPECT for damage. SERVICE as required.
• Friction elements damaged	• INSPECT for damage. SERVICE as required.
Forward/Coast Clutch Assembly	• PERFORM Air Pressure Check.
• Seals damaged, missing	• INSPECT for damage. SERVICE as required.
• Piston damaged	• INSPECT for damage. SERVICE as required.
• Friction Elements worn, damaged	• INSPECT for damage. SERVICE as required.
• Check Ball not functioning	• INSPECT for damage. SERVICE as required.
• Forward Clutch Piston and Return Spring damaged	• INSPECT for damage. SERVICE as required.
Case	
• Porosity/cross leaks in Servo Apply, Servo Release, Direct Clutch circuits	• INSPECT for damage. PERFORM Air Pressure Check. SERVICE as required.

FM5029801553020X

Fig. 22 Routines 229 & 329: Soft/Slipping 4–3 Only Shift (Part 2 of 2)

Possible Component	Reference/Action
230 — ELECTRICAL ROUTINE	
Powertrain Control System	
• Electrical Inputs/Outputs, Vehicle Wiring Harnesses, Powertrain Control Module, EPC Solenoid, Throttle Position Sensor, Vehicle Speed Sensor, Mass Air Flow Sensor, 3-2 Timing/Coast Clutch Solenoid (3-2T/CCS)	• RUN OBD Tests. REFER to MOTOR's Domestic Transmission Manual for diagnosis. PERFORM Service Manual Pinpoint Tests "E and G" using the Transmission Tester (007-00130 and CD4E cable and overlay 007-00125. SERVICE as required. CLEAR codes, ROAD TEST and RERUN OBD Tests.
330 — HYDRAULIC/MECHANICAL ROUTINE	
Main Control	
• Bolts out of torque specifications	• RETORQUE bolts to specifications.
• Gasket damaged	• INSPECT for damage and REPLACE as required.
• 3-2 Timing Valve, Solenoid Regulator Valve, 3-2 Control Valve stuck, damaged or misassembled	• INSPECT for damage. SERVICE as required.
• 3-2T/CCS Solenoid malfunction	• ACTIVATE solenoid using Transmission Tester (007-00130 and CD4E cable and overlay 007-00125). SERVICE as required.
• Pressure Tap Plate/Gasket leaks or damaged	• INSPECT for damage. SERVICE as required.
• Separator Plates damaged, blocked	• INSPECT for damage. SERVICE as required.
Direct Clutch Assembly	• PERFORM Air Pressure Check.
• Return Spring damaged, broken	• INSPECT for damage. SERVICE as required.
• Friction elements damaged, worn	• INSPECT for damage. SERVICE as required.
• Ball check not releasing	• INSPECT for damage. SERVICE as required.
• Piston or seal damaged	• INSPECT for damage. SERVICE as required.
INT/OD Band and Servo Assembly	
• INT/OD Band and/or Reverse Clutch Drum Assembly worn, damaged or misassembled	• INSPECT for damage. SERVICE as required.
• Servo piston damaged	• INSPECT for damage. SERVICE as required.
• Servo Return and Cushion Springs damaged, misassembled	• INSPECT for damage. SERVICE as required.
• Springs damaged, misassembled	• INSPECT for damage. SERVICE as required.
• Servo rod bent, damaged	• INSPECT for damage. SERVICE as required.
Oil Pump Assembly	
• Bolts out of torque specifications	• RETORQUE bolts to specifications.
• Gaskets damaged	• INSPECT for damage and REPLACE as required.
• Porosity/cross leaks	• INSPECT for porosity, leaks. REPLACE pump as required.

FM5029801554010X

Fig. 23 Routines 230 & 330: Soft/Slipping 3–2 Only Shift (Part 1 of 2)

Possible Component	Reference/Action
231 — ELECTRICAL ROUTINE	
Powertrain Control System	
• Electrical Inputs/Outputs, Vehicle Wiring Harnesses, Powertrain Control Module, EPC Solenoid, Transmission Fluid Temperature Sensor, Throttle Position Sensor, Mass Air Flow Sensor	• RUN OBD Tests. REFER to MOTOR's Domestic Transmission Manual for diagnosis. PERFORM Service Manual Pinpoint Tests "B and E" using the Transmission Tester (007-00130 and CD4E cable and overlay 007-001215). SERVICE as required. CLEAR codes, ROAD TEST and RERUN OBD Tests.
331 — HYDRAULIC/MECHANICAL ROUTINE	
Pump	
• Gaskets damaged	• INSPECT for damage and REPLACE as required.
• Porosity/cross leaks	• INSPECT for leak/porosity. REPLACE as required.
• Pump support seals No. 3 or 4 leaking, misassembled, damaged	• INSPECT for damage. SERVICE as required.
Intermediate OD Servo and Band Assembly	
• Servo Piston damaged	• INSPECT for damage. SERVICE as required.
• Servo Piston Return Spring damaged	• INSPECT for damage. SERVICE as required.
Forward Clutch Assembly	• PERFORM Air Pressure Check.
• Piston or Seals damaged	• INSPECT for damage. SERVICE as required.
• Friction Elements damaged	• INSPECT for damage. SERVICE as required.
Low OWC	
• Damaged, not holding	• INSPECT for damage. SERVICE as required.

FM5029801555000X

Fig. 24 Routines 231 & 331: Soft/Slipping 2–1 Only Shift

Possible Component	Reference/Action
233 — ELECTRICAL ROUTINE	
Powertrain Control System	
• Electrical Inputs/Outputs, Vehicle Wiring Harnesses, Powertrain Control Module, EPC Solenoid, Transmission Range (TR) Sensor, Vehicle Speed Sensor, Transmission Fluid Temperature Sensor, Mass Air Flow Sensor, TCC solenoid, TSS	• RUN OBD Tests. REFER to MOTOR's Domestic Transmission Manual for diagnosis. PERFORM Service Manual Pinpoint Tests "B, C, D, E and F" with Transmission Tester (007-00130 and CD4E Update kit 007-00088) and the TR Sensor (MLP Sensor) Cable. SERVICE as required. CLEAR codes, ROAD TEST and RERUN OBD Tests.
333 — HYDRAULIC/MECHANICAL ROUTINE	
Main Control	
• Bolts out of torque specifications	• RETORQUE bolts to specifications.
• Gasket leaks	• INSPECT for damage and REPLACE as required.
• Line Modulator Valve (also 1-2 and 3-4 harsh shift), Servo Release Shuttle Valve stuck, damaged or misassembled	• INSPECT for damage. SERVICE as required.
• Separator plates damaged	• INSPECT for damage. SERVICE as required.
• Hydraulic passages damaged	• INSPECT for damage. SERVICE as required.
Pump	
• Bolts out of torque specifications	• RETORQUE bolts to specifications.
• Gasket damaged	• INSPECT for damage and REPLACE as required.
• Porosity/cross leaks	• INSPECT for damage. SERVICE as required.
• Pump support seal rings No. 4 or No. 5 damaged	• INSPECT for damage and REPLACE as required.
Direct Clutch Assembly	• PERFORM Air Pressure Check.
• Piston or piston bore damaged	• INSPECT for damage. SERVICE as required.
• Friction elements damaged, worn	• INSPECT for damage. SERVICE as required.
• Ball check not seating properly	• INSPECT for damage. SERVICE as required.
• Return Spring damaged	• INSPECT for damage. SERVICE as required.
• Clutch cylinder splines damaged	• INSPECT for damage. SERVICE as required.
INT/OD Servo	
• Servo Piston or Piston Bore damaged	• INSPECT for damage. SERVICE as required.
• Servo rod damaged	• INSPECT for damage. SERVICE as required.
Case	
• Leakage in the Servo Apply, Servo Release or Direct Clutch circuits	• INSPECT case for damage. PERFORM Air Pressure Check. SERVICE or REPLACE case as required.
• Servo Rod Bore damaged	• INSPECT for damage. SERVICE as required.

FM5029801557000X

Fig. 26 Routines 233 & 333: Harsh 2–3 Shift Only

Possible Component	Reference/Action
• Pump Support seal rings No. 4, 5, 6 damaged or misassembled	• INSPECT for damage. SERVICE as required.
• Forward to direct passage leaks	• INSPECT for damage. SERVICE as required.
Case	
• Band Anchor damaged	• INSPECT for damage. SERVICE as required.
• Leakage in servo apply/release circuits	• INSPECT for leaks. PERFORM Air Pressure Check. SERVICE as required.
• Case bore damaged (Servo Rod)	• INSPECT for damage. SERVICE as required.

FM5029801554020X

Fig. 23 Routine 230 & 330: Soft/Slipping 3–2 Only Shift (Part 2 of 2)

Possible Component	Reference/Action
232 — ELECTRICAL ROUTINE	
Powertrain Control System	
• Electrical Inputs/Outputs, Vehicle Wiring Harnesses, Powertrain Control Module, EPC Solenoids, Transmission Fluid Temperature Sensor, Vehicle Speed Sensor, TSS, Throttle Position Sensor, Mass Air Flow Sensor, TCC solenoid, Transmission Range (TR) Sensor	• RUN OBD Tests. REFER to MOTOR's Domestic Transmission Manual for diagnosis. PERFORM Service Manual Pinpoint Tests "B, C, D, E and F" with Transmission Tester (007-00130 and CD4E cable and overlay 007-00125) and the TR Sensor Cable. SERVICE as required. CLEAR codes, ROAD TEST and RERUN OBD Tests. PERFORM Stall Speed Tests.
332 — HYDRAULIC/MECHANICAL ROUTINE	
Main Control	
• Bolts out of torque specifications	• RETORQUE bolts to specifications.
• Gasket leaks	• INSPECT for damage and REPLACE as required.
• 2-4 Accumulator Valve, 3-2 Control Valve (also harsh 3-4 shift) stuck, damaged or misassembled	• INSPECT for damage. SERVICE as required.
• Separator plates damaged	• INSPECT for damage. SERVICE as required.
• Hydraulic passages damaged	• INSPECT for damage. SERVICE as required.
Pump	
• Bolts out of torque specifications	• RETORQUE bolts to specifications.
• Gasket damaged	• INSPECT for damage and REPLACE as required.
• Pump support seal rings No. 3 or No. 4 damaged	• INSPECT for damage. SERVICE as required.
• Porosity/cross leaks	• INSPECT for damage. SERVICE as required.

FM5029801556010X

Fig. 25 Routines 232 & 332: Harsh 1–2 Shift Only (Part 1 of 2)

Possible Component	Reference/Action
INT/OD Band and Servo Assembly	
• Cushion return springs damaged	• INSPECT for damage. SERVICE as required.
• INT/OD Band damaged, worn	• INSPECT for damage. SERVICE as required.
• INT/OD Band and/or Reverse Clutch Drum Assembly worn, damaged or misassembled	• INSPECT for damage. SERVICE as required.
Forward Clutch Assembly	• PERFORM Air Pressure Check.
• Seals damaged	• INSPECT for damage. SERVICE as required.
• Return Spring damaged	• INSPECT for damage. SERVICE as required.
• Friction elements damaged	• INSPECT for damage. SERVICE as required.
Case	
• Band Anchor Area damaged	• INSPECT for damage. If damaged, REPLACE the case.

FM5029801556020X

Fig. 25 Routines 232 & 332: Harsh 1–2 Shift Only (Part 2 of 2)

Possible Component	Reference/Action
234 — ELECTRICAL ROUTINE	
Powertrain Control System	

FM5029801558010X

Fig. 27 Routines 234 & 334: Harsh 3–4 Shift Only (Part 1 of 2)

Possible Component	Reference/Action
• Electrical Inputs/Outputs, Vehicle Wiring Harnesses, Powertrain Control Module, EPC Solenoid, Vehicle Speed Sensor, 3-2T/CCS, Transmission Range (TR) Sensor, Transmission Fluid Temperature Sensor, TSS, Throttle Position Sensor, Mass Air Flow Sensor, TCC solenoid	• RUN OBD Tests. REFER to MOTOR's Domestic Transmission Manual for diagnosis. PERFORM Service Manual Pinpoint Tests "B, C, D, E, F and G" with Transmission Tester (007-00130 and CD4E cable and overlay 007-00125) and the TR Sensor Cable as outlined in this manual. SERVICE as required. CLEAR codes, ROAD TEST and RERUN OBD Tests.
334 — HYDRAULIC/MECHANICAL ROUTINE	
Main Control	
• Bolts out of torque specifications	• RETORQUE bolts to specifications.
• Gasket leaks	• INSPECT for damage and REPLACE as required.
• Line Modulator Valve (also 1-2 and 2-3 harsh shift), 3-2 Control Valve, 2-4 Accumulator Valve, Coast Clutch Valve, stuck, damaged or misassembled	• INSPECT for damage. SERVICE as required.
• Hydraulic passages damaged	• INSPECT for damage. SERVICE as required.
• Separator plates damaged, blocked	• INSPECT for damage. SERVICE as required.
Pump	
• Bolts out of torque specifications	• RETORQUE bolts to specifications.
• Gasket damaged	• INSPECT for damage and REPLACE as required.
• Porosity/cross leaks	• INSPECT for damage. SERVICE as required.
• Coast Clutch Teflon seals damaged	• INSPECT for damage and REPLACE as required.
INT/OD Band and Servo Assembly	
• INT/OD Band and Reverse Clutch Drum Assembly, damaged, worn, misassembled	• INSPECT for damage. SERVICE as required.
• Servo Piston or Cover damaged or leaking	• INSPECT for damage. SERVICE as required.
• Springs damaged	• INSPECT for damage. SERVICE as required.
Coast Clutch Assembly	
• Piston or Seals damaged, missing	• INSPECT for damage. SERVICE as required.
• Friction elements damaged, worn	• INSPECT for damage. SERVICE as required.
• Check Ball not functioning	• INSPECT for damage. SERVICE as required.
Direct Clutch Assembly	• PERFORM Air Pressure Check.
• Piston or seals damaged, missing	• INSPECT for damage. SERVICE as required.
• Check Ball damaged, missing or leaking	• INSPECT for damage. SERVICE as required.
• Return Spring damaged	• INSPECT for damage. SERVICE as required.
• Friction elements damaged	• INSPECT for damage. SERVICE as required.
• Clutch Cylinder splines damaged	• INSPECT for damage. SERVICE as required.
Case	
• Band Anchor damaged	• INSPECT for damage. SERVICE as required.

FM5029801558020X

Fig. 27 Routines 234 & 334: Harsh 3–4 Shift Only (Part 2 of 2)

Possible Component	Reference/Action
235 — ELECTRICAL ROUTINE	
Powertrain Control System	
• Electrical Inputs/Outputs, Vehicle Wiring Harnesses, Powertrain Control Module, EPC Solenoid, Transmission Range (TR) Sensor, Vehicle Speed Sensor, 3-2T/CCS, Transmission Fluid Temperature Sensor, TSS, Throttle Position Sensor, Mass Air Flow Sensor, TCC solenoid	• RUN OBD Tests. Refer to MOTOR'S Domestic Transmission Manual. PERFORM Service Manual Pinpoint Tests "B, C, D, E, F and G" with Transmission Tester (007-00130 and CD4E cable and overlav 007-00125) and the TR Sensor Cable SERVICE as required. CLEAR codes, ROAD TEST and RERUN OBD Tests.
335 — HYDRAULIC/MECHANICAL ROUTINE	
Main Control	
• Bolts out of torque specifications	• RETORQUE bolts to specifications.
• Gasket leaks	• INSPECT for damage and REPLACE as required.
• Servo Release Shuttle Valve, 3-2 Timing/Coast Clutch Valve stuck, damaged or misassembled	• INSPECT for damage. SERVICE as required.
• Hydraulic passages damaged	• INSPECT for damage. SERVICE as required.

FM5029801559010X

Fig. 28 Routines 235 & 335: Harsh 4–3 Shift Only (Part 1 of 2)

Possible Component	Reference/Action
236 — ELECTRICAL ROUTINE	
Powertrain Control System	
• Electrical Inputs/Outputs, Vehicle Wiring Harnesses, Powertrain Control Module, EPC Solenoid, Transmission Range (TR) Sensor, Vehicle Speed Sensor, 3-2T/CCS, Transmission Fluid Temperature Sensor, TSS, throttle position sensor, Mass Air Flow Sensor, TCC solenoid	• RUN OBD Tests. REFER to MOTOR's Domestic Transmission Manual for diagnosis. PERFORM Service Manual Pinpoint Tests "B, C, D, E, F and G" with Transmission Tester (007-00130 and CD4E cable and overlay 007-00125) and the TR Sensor Cable. SERVICE as required. CLEAR codes, ROAD TEST and RERUN OBD Tests.
336 — HYDRAULIC/MECHANICAL ROUTINE	
Main Control	
• Bolts out of torque specifications	• RETORQUE bolts to specifications.
• Gasket damaged	• INSPECT for damage and REPLACE as required.
• 3-2 Timing Valve, Solenoid Regulator Valve, 3-2 Control Valve stuck, damaged, misassembled	• INSPECT for damage. SERVICE as required.
• Hydraulic passages damaged	• INSPECT for damage and REPLACE as required.
• Separator plates damaged or blocked	• INSPECT for damage. SERVICE as required.
• 3-2T/CCS Solenoid malfunction	• ACTIVATE solenoid using Transmission Tester. If Coast Clutch operation is OK PROCEED to Direct Clutch Assembly.
Direct Clutch Assembly	• PERFORM Air Pressure Check.
• Return Spring damaged, broken	• INSPECT for damage. SERVICE as required.
• Friction Elements damaged, worn	• INSPECT for damage. SERVICE as required.
• Check Ball not exhausting	• INSPECT for damage. SERVICE as required.
INT/OD Band and Servo Assembly	
• INT/OD Band and/or Reverse Clutch Drum Assembly damaged, worn or misassembled	• INSPECT for damage. SERVICE as required.
• Servo Piston damaged	• INSPECT for damage. SERVICE as required.
• Servo Return and Cushion Springs damaged, misassembled	• INSPECT for damage. SERVICE as required.
• Springs damaged, misassembled	• INSPECT for damage. SERVICE as required.
• Servo Rod bent or damaged	• INSPECT for damage. SERVICE as required.
Oil Pump Assembly	
• Bolts out of torque specifications	• RETORQUE bolts to specifications.
• Gaskets damaged	• INSPECT for damage and REPLACE as required.

FM5029801560010X

Fig. 29 Routines 236 & 336: Harsh 3–2 Shift Only (Part 1 of 2)

Possible Component	Reference/Action
240 — ELECTRICAL ROUTINE	
Powertrain Control System	
• Electrical Inputs/Outputs, Vehicle Wiring Harnesses, Powertrain Control Module, Transmission Fluid Temperature Sensor, TCC solenoid, Brake On/Off (BOO) Switch, TSS	• PERFORM Torque Converter Control Operation Tests. RUN OBD Tests. Refer to MOTOR'S Domestic Transmission Manual. PERFORM Service Manual Pinpoint Tests "B, C and F" with Transmission Tester (007-00130 and CD4E cable and overlay 007-00125) SERVICE as required. CLEAR codes, ROAD TEST and RERUN OBD Tests.
340 — HYDRAULIC/MECHANICAL ROUTINE	
Main Control	
• Bolts out of torque specifications	• RETORQUE bolts to specifications.
• Gasket damaged	• INSPECT for damage and REPLACE as required.
• Solenoid Pressure Regulator Valve, Bypass Clutch Control Valve and Plunger, Converter Regulator Valve stuck, damaged, misassembled	• INSPECT for damage. SERVICE as required.
• TCC Solenoid malfunction	• ACTIVATE solenoid using Transmission Tester. SERVICE as required.
• Hydraulic passages damaged	• INSPECT for damage and REPLACE as required.
• Separator plates damaged or blocked	• INSPECT for damage. SERVICE as required.
Torque Converter Assembly	
• Leakage, Internal damage	• INSPECT for damage and leakage. PERFORM Converter checks REPLACE as required

FM5029801561000X

Fig. 30 Routines 240 & 340: No Torque Converter Apply

Possible Component	Reference/Action
251 — ELECTRICAL ROUTINE	
No Electrical Concerns	
351 — HYDRAULIC/MECHANICAL ROUTINE	
Brake Shift Interlock	• REFER to "Troubleshooting" in this section.
Internal and External Shift Linkages	
• Damaged, misadjusted or misassembled	• INSPECT and SERVICE as required. ADJUST linkage as outlined in Service Manual. After servicing linkage, VERIFY that the transmission range (TR) sensor is properly adjusted.
• Manual Control Lever damaged, park mechanism damaged, Shaft bent, Detent Lever Shaft Bore (in case) damaged, Detent Spring bent/damaged, Nut Loose	• INSPECT for damage. SERVICE as required.
Main Control	
• Bolts out of torque specifications	• RETORQUE bolts to specifications.
• Manual Valve stuck, damaged	• INSPECT for damage. SERVICE as required.

FM5029801563000X

Fig. 32 Routines 251 & 351: Shift Lever Efforts High

Possible Component	Reference/Action
• Separator plates damaged, blocked	• INSPECT for damage. SERVICE as required.
Pump	
• Bolts out of torque specifications	• RETORQUE bolts to specifications.
• Porosity/cross leaks, Seal Rings damaged, missing or leaking ball plug	• INSPECT pump for damage. SERVICE or REPLACE pump as required.
• Gasket damaged	• INSPECT for damage and REPLACE as required.
• Pump Support Seal Rings No. 2, 3, 4, or No. 5 (Coast and Direct Clutch circuits) damaged	• INSPECT for damage. SERVICE as required.
INT/OD Band and Servo Assembly	
• Servo Rod bent, damaged	• INSPECT for damage. SERVICE as required.
• Servo Return Spring Broken	• INSPECT for damage. SERVICE as required.
Coast Clutch Assembly	
• Seals damaged, missing	• INSPECT for damage. SERVICE as required.
• Piston damaged	• INSPECT for damage. SERVICE as required.
• Friction elements worn, damaged	• INSPECT for damage. SERVICE as required.
• Check Ball not functioning	• INSPECT for damage. SERVICE as required.
• Forward clutch piston and Return Spring damaged	• INSPECT for damage. SERVICE as required.
Case	
• Porosity/cross leaks in servo apply, servo release, direct clutch, coast clutch circuits	• INSPECT for damage. PERFORM Air Pressure Check. SERVICE as required.

FM5029801559020X

Fig. 28 Routines 235 & 335: Harsh 4–3 Shift Only (Part 2 of 2)

Possible Component	Reference/Action
• Porosity/cross leaks	• INSPECT for porosity, leaks. REPLACE as required.
• Pump Support Seal Rings damaged or misassembled	• INSPECT for damage. SERVICE as required.
Case	
• Band Anchor damaged	• INSPECT for damage. SERVICE as required.
• Servo Rod Bore damaged	• INSPECT for damage. SERVICE as required.

FM5029801560020X

Fig. 29 Routines 236 & 336: Harsh 3–2 Shift Only (Part 2 of 2)

Possible Component	Reference/Action
240 — ELECTRICAL ROUTINE	
Powertrain Control System	
• Electrical Inputs/Outputs, Vehicle Wiring Harnesses, Powertrain Control Module, Transmission Fluid Temperature Sensor, TCC solenoid, Brake On/Off (BOO) Switch, TSS	• PERFORM Torque Converter Control Operation Tests. RUN OBD Tests. REFER to MOTOR Domestic Transmission Manual for diagnosis. PERFORM Service Manual Pinpoint Tests "B, C and F" with Transmission Tester (007-00130 and CD4E cable and overlay 007-00125) SERVICE as required. CLEAR codes, ROAD TEST and RERUN OBD Tests.
340 — HYDRAULIC/MECHANICAL ROUTINE	
Main Control	
• Bolts out of torque specifications	• RETORQUE bolts to specifications.
• Gasket damaged	• INSPECT for damage and REPLACE as required.
• Solenoid Pressure Regulator Valve, Bypass Clutch Control Valve and Plunger, Converter Regulator Valve stuck, damaged, misassembled	• INSPECT for damage. SERVICE as required.
• TCC Solenoid malfunction	• ACTIVATE solenoid using Transmission Tester. SERVICE as required.
• Hydraulic passages damaged	• INSPECT for damage and REPLACE as required.
• Separator plates damaged or blocked	• INSPECT for damage. SERVICE as required.
Torque Converter Assembly	
• Leakage, Internal damage	• INSPECT for damage and leakage. PERFORM Converter checks as outlined in this manual. REPLACE as required.

FM5029801562010X

Fig. 31 Routines 241 & 341: Torque Converter Always Applied/Stalls Vehicle (Part 1 of 2)

Possible Component	Reference/Action
• Pump Support No. 1 Seal Ring damaged, missing, misassembled	• INSPECT for damage. SERVICE as required.
Torque Converter Assembly	
• Internal Seals damaged	• INSPECT. SERVICE as required.
• Piston Plate damage/stuck to Cover	• If cover is heat stained, REPLACE converter.
Case	
• Porosity/cross leaks from the CBY circuit	• INSPECT for porosity/leaks. SERVICE or REPLACE case as required.

FM5029801562020X

Fig. 31 Routines 241 & 341: Torque Converter Always Applied/Stalls Vehicle (Part 2 of 2)

Possible Component	Reference/Action
252 — ELECTRICAL ROUTINE	
No Electrical Concerns	
352 — HYDRAULIC/MECHANICAL ROUTINE	
Fluid	
• Improper level	• ADJUST fluid to proper level.
Seals/Gaskets	
• Differential Seals, Speedometer Gear, Retainer Seal, Pump, Main Control Cover, Servo Cover, Split Flange Gasket, Converter Impeller Hub, Manual Lever Shaft Seal, Oil Level Indicator Tube.	• LOCATE source of leak. SERVICE as required. If Differential Seal or Converter Impeller Hub is leaking, INSPECT drain back holes in Case/Converter Housing, INSPECT surface of linkshaft or front wheel driveshaft and joint for a rough surface. Rough surface may cause seal leakage. SERVICE as required.
Other	
• Oil Tube Fitting, Line Pressure Tap, Pressure Port Plugs, Drain Plug, Fluid Cooler Tubes, Case porosity, Case cracked	• LOCATE source of leak. SERVICE as required.
• Vent blocked or damaged	• CHECK vent for damage or blockage. SERVICE as required.
• Bolts at Split Flange or Main Control Cover leaking	• INSPECT for leaks. SERVICE as required.
Sensors/Connectors	
• Transmission Connector, Transmission Range (TR) Sensor, TSS or Seal	• LOCATE source of leak. SERVICE as required.

FM5029801564000X

Fig. 33 Routines 252 & 352: External Leaks

Possible Component	Reference/Action
253 — ELECTRICAL ROUTINE	
Powertrain Control System • Base Engine Concerns.	• REFER to MOTOR's Auto Engine Performance & Driveability Manual.

FM5029801565010X

Fig. 34 Routines 253 & 353: Poor Vehicle Performance (Part 1 of 2)

Possible Component	Reference/Action
254 — ELECTRICAL ROUTINE	
No Electrical Concerns	
354 — HYDRAULIC/MECHANICAL ROUTINE	
For Noises/Vibrations that Change with Engine Speed: • Torque Converter Components • Fluid Level (Low) Pump cavitation • Oil Pump Assembly • Engine Drive Accessories • Fluid Cooler Tubes grounding out • Flywheel • Inspection Cover	• LOCATE source of disturbance. SERVICE as required.
For Noises/Vibrations that Change with Vehicle Speed: • Powertrain Mounts Loose, Damaged • Tires • Driveline Concerns: Front Wheel Driveshaft and Joint or Linkshaft, Differential: Final Drive/Chain, Suspension, Modifications • Planetary Gear Sets	• LOCATE source of disturbance. SERVICE as required. For Specific Shifts or Torque Converter concerns,
• Chain grounding to Chain Pan • FWD OWC • Torque Converter Assembly	• INSPECT Chain Pan for signs of damage or misinstallation. SERVICE as required.
• LH and RH Front Wheel Driveshaft and Joint Splines worn, damaged • Speedometer Cable or Gears	• INSPECT for damage. SERVICE as required.
Other Noises/Vibrations: • Shift Cable and Bracket Vibration, Grounding. • Cooler Lines Grounding	• LOCATE source of disturbance. SERVICE as required.

FM5029801566000X

Fig. 35 Routines 254 & 354: Noise/Vibration In Forward/Reverse

Possible Component	Reference/Action
• Electrical Inputs/Outputs, Vehicle Wiring Harnesses, Powertrain Control Module, Transmission Range (TR) Sensor (damaged/misadjusted)	• RUN OBD Tests. REFER to MOTOR's Domestic Transmission Manual for diagnosis. PERFORM Pinpoint Test "D" using the TR Sensor Cable. SERVICE as required. CLEAR codes, ROAD TEST and RERUN OBD Tests.
355 — HYDRAULIC/MECHANICAL ROUTINE	
Starter/Flywheel • Damaged or misassembled	• INSPECT for damage, misassembly. SERVICE as required.
Internal and External Shift Linkages or TR Sensor • Damaged, misadjusted or misassembled	• ADJUST linkage. After servicing linkage, VERIFY that the transmission range (TR) sensor is properly adjusted.

FM5029801567020X

Fig. 36 Routines 255 & 355: Engine Will Not Crank (Part 2 of 2)

Possible Component	Reference/Action
257 — ELECTRICAL ROUTINE	
Powertrain Control System • Electrical Inputs/Outputs, Vehicle Wiring Harnesses, Powertrain Control Module, TCC Solenoid, Transmission Fluid Temperature Sensor, TSS	• RUN OBD Tests. PERFORM Pinpoint Tests "B, C and F" using the Transmission Tester (007-00130 and CD4E cable and overlay 007-00125). SERVICE as required. CLEAR codes, ROAD TEST and RERUN OBD Tests.
357 — HYDRAULIC/MECHANICAL ROUTINE	
Vehicle Concerns Causing Engine Overheating	• REFER to Engine diagnosis.
Fluid • Improper level • Condition	• ADJUST fluid to proper level. • INSPECT Fluid Condition If fluid is aerated, CHECK Thermo Valve and Filter Seals. SERVICE as required.
Oil Cooler Tubes • Damaged, blocked, reversed	• INSPECT for damage. SERVICE as required.
Intake Cooler • Damaged, blocked, restricted or leaking	• INSPECT for damage. SERVICE as required.
Auxiliary Cooler (If equipped) • Damaged, blocked, restricted, improperly installed	• INSPECT for damage or improper installation. SERVICE as required.
Main Control • Bolts out of torque specifications	• RETORQUE bolts to specifications.

FM5029801569010X

Fig. 38 Routines 257 & 357: Transaxle Overheating (Part 1 of 2)

Possible Component	Reference/Action
• Electrical Inputs/Outputs, Vehicle Wiring Harnesses, Powertrain Control Module, Transmission Fluid Temperature Sensor, TCC Solenoid, Transmission Range (TR) Sensor, Throttle Position Sensor	• PERFORM Torque Converter Clutch Operation Test. RUN OBD Tests. REFER to MOTOR's Domestic Transmission Manual for diagnosis. PERFORM Service Manual Pinpoint Tests "B, C, D" using the Transmission Tester (007-00130 and CD4E cable and overlay 007-00125) and the TR Sensor Cable (007-0086A). CLEAR codes, ROAD TEST and RERUN OBD Tests.
353 — HYDRAULIC/MECHANICAL ROUTINE	
Internal and External Shift Linkages or TR Sensor • Damaged, misadjusted or misassembled	• INSPECT and SERVICE as required. ADJUST linkage as outlined in Service Manual. After servicing linkage, VERIFY that the TR Sensor is properly adjusted.
Verify Proper Shift Scheduling and Engagements	• GO to the appropriate Diagnostic Routines per Index.
Torque Converter Clutch Always Applied	• GO to Routine No. 341.
Torque Converter OWC Clutch • Damaged	• PERFORM Service Manual inspection procedures. SERVICE or REPLACE as required.

FM5029801565020X

Fig. 34 Routines 253 & 353: Poor Vehicle Performance (Part 2 of 2)

Possible Component	Reference/Action
255 — ELECTRICAL ROUTINE	
Powertrain Control System • Base Engine Concerns	• REFER to MOTOR's Domestic Engine Performance & Driveability Manual.

FM5029801567010X

Fig. 36 Routines 255 & 355: Engine Will Not Crank (Part 1 of 2)

Possible Component	Reference/Action
256 — ELECTRICAL ROUTINE	
No Electrical Concerns	
356 — HYDRAULIC/MECHANICAL ROUTINE	
Internal or External Shift Linkages • Damaged, misadjusted or misassembled	• INSPECT and SERVICE as required. ADJUST linkage as outlined in Service Manual. After servicing linkage, VERIFY that the transmission range (TR) sensor is properly adjusted.
Park Mechanism • Park Gear on Driven Sprocket Assembly, Parking Pawl Return Spring, Park Pawl Ratcheting Springs, Parking Pawl Shaft, Manual Control Lever, Cam Apply Lever, Manual Lever Detent Spring, TR Sensor, Parking Pawl Apply Cam, Manual Shaft nut damaged, missing or misassembled	• INSPECT for damage. SERVICE as required.

FM5029801568000X

Fig. 37 Routines 256 & 356: No Park Range

Possible Component	Reference/Action
• Main Regulator Valve, Bypass Clutch Control Valve, Converter Regulator Valve stuck, damaged, misassembled • Hydraulic Passages damaged • Separator Plates/Gaskets damaged • TCC Solenoid malfunction (OFF)	• INSPECT for damage. SERVICE as required. • INSPECT for damage. SERVICE as required. • INSPECT for damage. SERVICE as required. • ACTIVATE solenoid using Transmission Tester. SERVICE as required.
Torque Converter Clutch - No Apply	• SEE Routine No. 240/340.
Oil Pump Assembly • Gasket damaged • Rear Lube Passage blocked	• INSPECT for damage and REPLACE as required. • INSPECT for damage. SERVICE as required.
Chain Pan • Missing	• INSPECT for missing pan. INSTALL pan if missing.
Thermostatic Oil Level Control Valve • Stuck open or damaged • Gasket damaged or missing • Bolt or bracket damaged, missing, or improperly installed	• INSPECT for damage. SERVICE as required. • INSPECT for damage and REPLACE as required. • INSPECT for damage. SERVICE as required.
Case/Converter Housing/Stator Support • Front Lube Passage blocked or restricted	• INSPECT passages. SERVICE as required.

FM5029801569020X

Fig. 38 Routines 257 & 357: Transaxle Overheating (Part 2 of 2)

Possible Component	Reference/Action
258 — ELECTRICAL ROUTINE	
Powertrain Control System • Electrical Inputs/Outputs, Vehicle Wiring Harnesses, Powertrain Control Module, 3-2 Timing/Coast Clutch Solenoid	• RUN OBD Tests. REFER to MOTOR's Domestic Transmission Manual for diagnosis. PERFORM Service Manual Pinpoint Test "G" using the Transmission Tester (007-00130 and CD4E cable and overlay 007-00125). SERVICE. CLEAR codes, ROAD TEST and RERUN OBD Tests. PERFORM Stall Speed Tests.
358 — HYDRAULIC/MECHANICAL ROUTINE	
Main Controls • Bolts out of torque specifications • Gaskets damaged • Low/Reverse Modulator Valve, Coast Clutch Valve stuck damaged or misassembled • 3-2 Timing/Coast Clutch Solenoid stuck or damaged • Hydraulic Passages damaged • Pressure Tap Plate/Gasket damaged • Separator Plate/Gasket damaged	• RETORQUE bolts to specifications. • INSPECT for damage and REPLACE as required. • INSPECT for damage. SERVICE as required. • INSPECT for damage, contamination. ACTIVATE solenoid with Transmission Tester. SERVICE as required. • INSPECT for damage. SERVICE as required. • INSPECT for damage. SERVICE as required. • INSPECT for damage. SERVICE as required.
Coast Clutch Assembly • Assembly misassembled, damaged • Forward Clutch Hub Seal damaged • Piston or Seals damaged • Ball check damaged, missing	• INSPECT for damage. SERVICE as required. • INSPECT for damage. SERVICE as required. • INSPECT for damage. SERVICE as required. • INSPECT for damage. SERVICE as required.
Low/Reverse Clutch Assembly • Assembly misassembled, damaged • Piston or Seals damaged	• PERFORM Air Pressure Check. • INSPECT for damage. SERVICE as required. • INSPECT for damage. SERVICE as required.
Oil Pump Assembly • Pump Support No. 2 or No. 3 Seal Rings for the Coast Clutch circuit damaged, missing	• INSPECT for damage. SERVICE as required.

FM5029801570000X

Fig. 39 Routines 258 & 358: No Engine Braking In 1st Gear Manual Only

Possible Component	Reference/Action
259 — ELECTRICAL ROUTINE	
Powertrain Control System • Electrical Inputs/Outputs, Vehicle Wiring Harnesses, Powertrain Control Module, 3-2 Timing/Coast Clutch Solenoid	• RUN OBD Tests. REFER to MOTOR's Domestic Transmission Manual for diagnosis. PERFORM Service Manual Pinpoint Test "G" using the Transmission Tester (007-00130 and CD4E cable and overlay 007-00125). SERVICE as required. CLEAR codes, ROAD TEST and RERUN OBD Tests. PERFORM Stall Speed Tests.
359 — HYDRAULIC/MECHANICAL ROUTINE	
Internal or External Shift Linkages • Damaged, misadjusted or misassembled	• INSPECT and SERVICE as required. ADJUST linkage. After servicing linkage, VERIFY that the transmission range (TR) sensor is properly adjusted.
Main Controls • 3-4 Shift Valve, 1-2 Shift Valve, Pull-in Valve, Coast Clutch Control Valve stuck, damaged • 3-2 Timing/Coast Clutch Solenoid stuck or damaged	• INSPECT for damage. SERVICE as required. • INSPECT for damage, contamination. ACTIVATE solenoid with Transmission Tester. SERVICE as required.
Forward OWC Assembly • Damaged, misassembled	• INSPECT for damage. SERVICE as required.
Coast Clutch Assembly • Assembly misassembled, damaged • Forward Clutch hub Seal damaged • Piston or Seals damaged • Ball check damaged, missing	• INSPECT for damage. SERVICE as required. • INSPECT for damage. SERVICE as required. • INSPECT for damage. SERVICE as required. • INSPECT for damage. SERVICE as required.
Pump Assembly • Pump Support No. 2 or No. 3 Seal Rings for the Coast Clutch circuit damaged, missing	• INSPECT for damage. SERVICE as required.

FM5029801647000X

Fig. 40 Routines 259 & 359: No Engine Braking In Drive w/TCS On Or Manual 2nd Position

Possible Component	Reference/Action
262 — ELECTRICAL ROUTINE	
No Electrical Concerns	
362 — HYDRAULIC/MECHANICAL ROUTINE	
Internal or External Shift Linkages • Damaged, misadjusted or misassembled	• INSPECT and SERVICE as required. ADJUST linkage. After servicing linkage, VERIFY that the transmission range (TR) sensor is properly adjusted.
Oil Pump Assembly • Gaskets severely damaged • Pump Support Seal Ring No. 2, leakage from Lube Circuit into FC Circuit	• INSPECT for damage and REPLACE as required. • INSPECT for damage. SERVICE as required.
Forward/Coast Clutch Assembly • Friction plates severely damaged • Return Spring damaged • Ball Check damaged, missing	• INSPECT for damage. SERVICE as required. • INSPECT for damage. SERVICE as required. • INSPECT for damage. SERVICE as required.

FM5029801648000X

Fig. 41 Routines 262 & 362: Vehicle Movement w/Transaxle Range Selector In N Position

MAINTENANCE

Refer to "Lubricant Data" chart in the appropriate chassis chapter of this manual for transmission fluid specifications.

FLUID INSPECTION

Under ordinary circumstances, transaxle fluid level need not be inspected. However, if transaxle is not functioning properly or if external fluid leakage is indicated, inspect fluid as follows:

1. With vehicle on level surface, start engine and move selector lever through all gear ranges. Allow each gear to engage completely.
2. Place selector lever in Park position and lock parking brake.
3. With engine still running, remove dipstick from tube and wipe end clean.
4. Slide dipstick back in tube. Ensure it seats properly.
5. Remove dipstick from tube and note fluid level. **If level is below bottom hole on dipstick and outside temperature is more than 50°F, vehicle should not be driven.**
6. If vehicle has been driven until reaching normal operating temperature, fluid level should be within cross-hatched hot area on dipstick. If vehicle has not been driven and outside temperature is more than 50°F, fluid level should be above bottom hole on dipstick.
7. Inspect fluid condition as follows:
   a. Observe fluid color and inspect for burned odor. If fluid is dark brown or black, or if odor is detected, overheating or component failure is indicated.
   b. Wipe dipstick and examine stain for solid particles, gum or varnish. If these are present, change and inspect fluid.

FLUID CHANGE

Automatic transaxle fluid should be changed every 30,000 miles if vehicle operates for prolonged periods at idle or less than 30°F, is driven regularly in dusty conditions or on salted, muddy or rough road surfaces or if contamination is suspected.

1. Raise and support vehicle, then place suitable container under transaxle drain plug.
2. Remove plug and allow fluid to drain. **If internal transaxle problem is suspected, drain fluid through suitable paper filter. While small accumulation of metal or friction particles may indicate normal wear, excessive amount warrants further internal transaxle service.**
3. Clean drain plug threads and apply thin coat of Teflon pipe sealant part No. D8AZ-19554-A, or equivalent. Install drain plug and tighten to specifications.
4. Lower vehicle and add six quarts of Mercon ATF, or equivalent, to transaxle.
5. Start engine and move selector lever through all gear ranges. Inspect fluid level as outlined under "Fluid Inspection." Adjust as required.

ADJUSTMENTS

SHIFT CONTROL LINKAGE

1. Ensure transaxle is in D position by viewing TR sensor. Alignment marks will be aligned with D arrow on TR sensor body when transaxle is in full Drive position.
2. Have someone hold shift lever in D position, then raise and support vehicle.
3. Remove transaxle shift cable from shift arm using suitable screwdriver.
4. Depress two locking tabs on adjustment lock cylinder and rotate adjustment lock cylinder, **Fig. 42,** shift cable is now unlocked and free to slide in retainer.
5. Ensure assistant is holding gearshift lever so indicator is centered on D.
6. Grasp cable forward of adjustment lock cylinder and move as required to align cable eye with pin on shift arm.
7. Install shift cable end to shift arm by pressing on by hand. Rotate adjustment lock cylinder clockwise until it snaps into place.
8. Lower vehicle and shift transaxle through all transaxle ranges.
9. Ensure shift control linkage operation is proper and indicator is properly aligned.

TRANSAXLE RANGE SENSOR

1. Turn manual control lever to Neutral.
2. Remove engine air intake resonator and mass air flow sensor.
3. Loosen transaxle range sensor mounting bolts.
4. Align sensor slots using transaxle range sensor adjustment tool No. T94P-70010-AH, or equivalent.
5. Tighten mounting bolts to specifications.

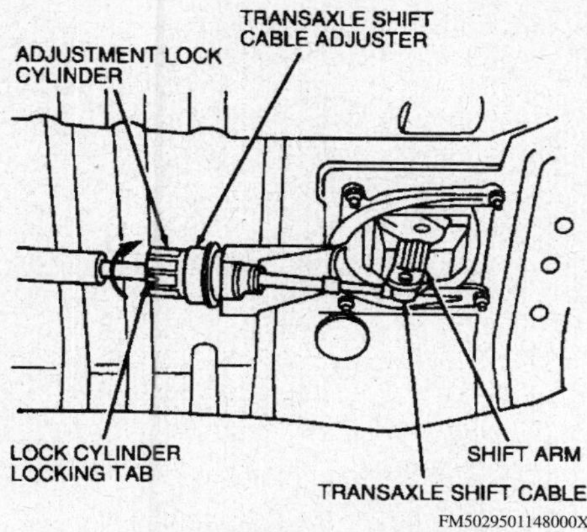

Fig. 42 Shift control linkage adjustment

6. Install air intake resonator and mass air flow sensor.
7. Inspect for proper operation with parking brake control engaged. Engine should start in Park or Neutral only and backup lamps should activate only in Reverse.

IN-VEHICLE REPAIRS

SELECTOR LEVER & HOUSING, REPLACE

1. Raise and support vehicle.
2. Remove center underbody heat shield mounting nuts.
3. Disconnect shift cable and bracket from transaxle range selector lever stud.
4. Remove four bracket mounting nuts.
5. Remove bracket with transaxle shift cable connected and position aside.
6. Lower vehicle.
7. Pry bezel from console using suitable screwdriver.
8. Lift gearshift lever out of console to access transaxle control switch wiring harness connector.
9. Disconnect transaxle control switch wiring harness connector and remove gearshift lever.
10. Reverse procedure to install.

SHIFT CABLE & BRACKET, REPLACE

1. Raise and support vehicle.
2. Remove center underbody heat shield mounting nuts.
3. Remove front underbody heat shield mounting nuts.
4. Disconnect shift cable and bracket from transaxle range selector lever stud.
5. Pull transaxle shift cable and bracket plastic snap retainer from bracket.
6. Lower vehicle, then disconnect shift cable and bracket from manual control lever stud on transaxle.
7. Remove shift cable and bracket to transaxle case mounting bolts.
8. Remove shift cable and bracket by guiding out through engine compartment.
9. Reverse procedure to install.

DIFFERENTIAL OIL SEALS, REPLACE

1. Raise and support vehicle, then remove front wheels and drain transaxle fluid into suitable container.
2. Remove front wheel driveshaft and joint.
3. Remove differential oil seal using converter seal remover tool No. T94P-77000-B and impact slide hammer tool No. T50T-100-A, or equivalents.
4. Reverse procedure to install, noting following:
   a. Apply thin film of petroleum jelly to outer diameter and lip of new oil seal.
   b. Tap seal into place using output seal replacement tool No. T86P-1177-B, or equivalent.
   c. Fill transaxle with suitable ATF.

TRANSAXLE RANGE (TR) SENSOR, REPLACE

1. Place manual control lever in Neutral.
2. Remove engine air intake resonator and mass air flow sensor.
3. Disconnect electrical harness from TR sensor.
4. Remove mounting bolts and range sensor.
5. Reverse procedure to install.

TURBINE SHAFT SPEED (TSS) SENSOR, REPLACE

1. Raise and support vehicle.
2. Place suitable drain pan under TSS sensor, then disconnect electrical connector.
3. Remove mounting bolt and TSS.
4. Reverse procedure to install, noting following:
   a. Replace TSS O-ring if damaged or worn.
   b. Apply thin film of suitable petroleum jelly to O-ring before installation.
   c. Tighten TSS bolt to specifications.
   d. Inspect and adjust transmission fluid as required.

INTERMEDIATE & OVERDRIVE SERVO, REPLACE

Servicing intermediate and overdrive servo in vehicle is only recommended in event of a leak. If servicing is required because of a servo condition, it will be necessary to disassemble transaxle to inspect overdrive band assembly and direct clutch for damage.

1. Raise and support vehicle.
2. Install servo cover replacement tool No. T94P-77000-L, or equivalent, and compress servo cover, **Fig. 43. Servo cover is under high spring pressure.**
3. Remove servo cover retaining ring and slowly release tension on cover.
4. Releasing all servo cover tension and remove tool.
5. Remove servo cover, intermediate and overdrive servo piston and return spring.
6. Inspect intermediate and overdrive servo piston and servo cover for nicks or cuts. Replace as required.

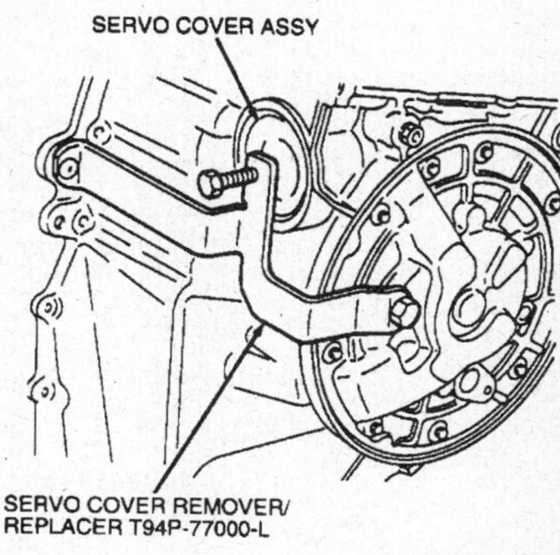

Fig. 43 Servo cover replacement tool installation

7. Reverse procedure to install. Lubricate intermediate and overdrive servo and servo cover with light coat of transmission fluid.

CONTROL VALVE, REPLACE

REMOVAL

1. Remove battery and air cleaner.
2. Remove power distribution box bolt and position aside.
3. Remove seven bolts and battery tray.
4. Remove two screws from air conditioning accumulator bracket and position air conditioning suction accumulator/dryer out of way. **Use extreme care not to place excessive pressure on air conditioning lines and fittings.**
5. Disconnect connector, then remove mounting bolts and TR sensor.
6. Disconnect transaxle harness electrical connector and place suitable drain pan under main control cover.
7. Disconnect transaxle cooler inlet line from transaxle and position aside.
8. Remove control cover bolts, cover and gasket from transaxle.
9. Remove wire harness clip from main control valve body.
10. Remove main control valve body bolts.
11. **Do not damage manual valve when disconnecting manual valve from manual valve link.**
12. Carefully lift main control valve body away from case while disconnecting manual valve link.
13. Squeeze retaining tabs on solenoid valve body harness connector and push solenoid valve body connector down through transaxle case.
14. Remove main control valve body.

INSTALLATION

1. Apply thin film of petroleum jelly to new O-ring and install on solenoid electrical connector.
2. Position main control slightly away from transaxle case and push electrical connector into its bore until tabs lock in place.
3. Connect manual valve link to manual

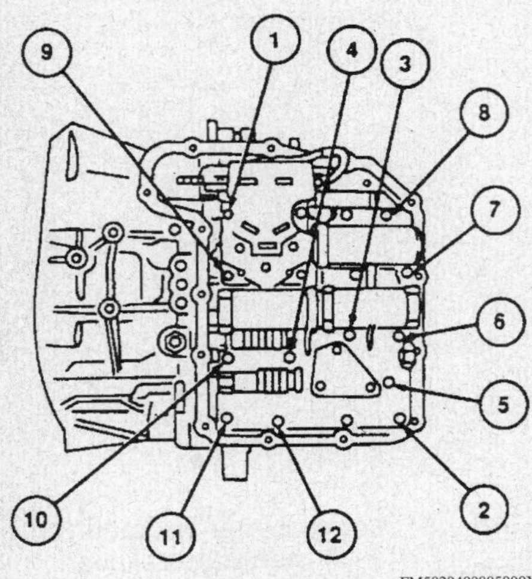

Fig. 44 Main control valve body bolt tightening sequence

valve and carefully position main control valve body to transaxle case.
4. Install main control valve body bolts hand tight and tighten to specifications in sequence, **Fig. 44.**
5. Loosen ball stud on manual valve detent lever.
6. Disconnect shift cable from manual control lever, then remove manual lever mounting bolt and manual lever from manual shaft.
7. Install shifter shaft alignment tool No. T94-77000-H, or equivalent, on manual control shaft.
8. Rotate manual control shaft until tool alignment pin fits into case hole.
9. Rotate manual valve detent lever to D position and initially tighten manual valve detent lever ball stud.
10. Remove shifter shaft alignment tool from main control shaft and rotate manual valve detent lever until socket can be placed on manual valve detent lever ball stud. Tighten manual valve detent lever ball stud nut to specifications.
11. Rotate manual valve detent lever to N position.
12. Install manual control lever on manual control shaft and secure with manual control lever mounting bolt. Tighten to specifications.
13. Connect shift cable to manual control lever and install wire harness clip to main control valve body.
14. Position gasket on main control cover and install cover on transaxle case. Tighten bolts to specifications in sequence, **Fig. 45.**
15. Connect transaxle cooler inlet line to transaxle and tighten to specifications.
16. Remove drain pan from under main control cover and connect transaxle harness connector.
17. Install transaxle range sensor and tighten to specifications.
18. Connect TR sensor connector, position air conditioning suction accumulator/dyer on front subframe and tighten mounting bolts to specifications.
19. Install battery tray, then position power distribution box and tighten mounting bolts to specifications.
20. Install air cleaner.
21. Fill transaxle fluid with suitable fluid.
22. Start vehicle and shift transaxle through all gear ranges.
23. Inspect and add fluid as required.

VEHICLE SPEED SENSOR, REPLACE

1. Raise and support vehicle.
2. Disconnect vehicle speed sensor (VSS) connector.
3. Remove speedometer cable from VSS.
4. Remove driven gear retainer and driven gear, then inspect driven gear retainer O-ring for nicks and cuts. Replace as required.
5. Reverse procedure to install.

VEHICLE SPEED SENSOR & SPEEDOMETER DRIVEN GEAR, REPLACE

1. Raise and support vehicle.
2. Disconnect Vehicle Speed Sensor (VSS) electrical connector.
3. Remove speedometer cable from VSS.
4. Remove VSS, then driven gear retainer and driven gear.
5. Inspect driven gear retainer O-ring for nicks or cuts. Replace as required.
6. Reverse procedure to install.

SHIFT INTERLOCK ACTUATOR, REPLACE

1. Remove gearshift lever as outlined under “Selector Lever & Housing, Replace.”
2. Remove wiring harness connector from gearshift lever and shift lock actuator to gearshift lever mounting screws.
3. Remove shift lock actuator.
4. Reverse procedure to install.

TRANSAXLE

REPLACE

REMOVAL

1. Place selector lever in D position and remove battery.
2. Secure radiator in position on both side.
3. Remove air cleaner.
4. Loosen left and righthand strut locknuts five turns. Use suitable Allen wrench to stop piston rod from turning.
5. Remove both front wheels' lug nuts.
6. Disconnect ground cable, automatic transaxle control electrical connector, Transaxle Range (TR) switch electrical connector and wiring harness retaining clip.
7. **On models equipped with 2.5L engine,** proceed as follows:
   a. Disconnect engine coolant hose.
   b. Remove mounting bolts and water pump cover.
   c. Disconnect starter motor and re-

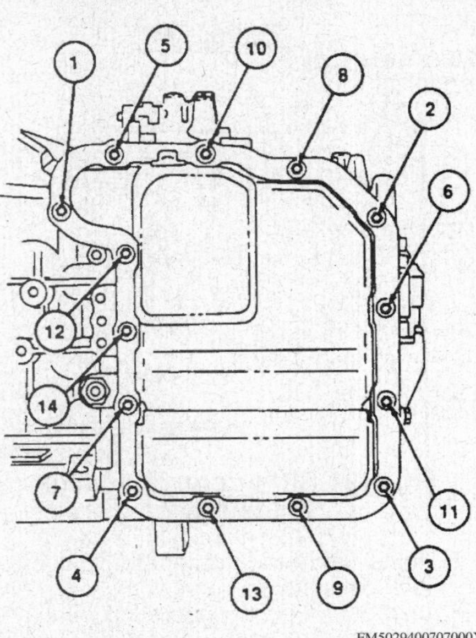

Fig. 45 Main control cover bolt loosening/tightening sequence

move starter motor bracket. Starter will remain in vehicle.
8. **On all models,** install three-bar engine support tool No. D88L-6000-A, or equivalent.
9. Remove rear transaxle mount bracket.
10. Remove upper bellhousing mounting bolts.
11. Disconnect Turbine Shaft Speed (TSS) sensor electrical connector.
12. Disconnect bracket and selector lever selector cable.
13. Raise and support vehicle.
14. Drain transmission fluid into suitable container. Tighten drain plug to specifications.
15. Remove bolts and clips, then the radiator splash shield.
16. Remove righthand fender splash shields.
17. Rotate bumper brackets forward and remove.
18. Remove air conditioning suction/ accumulator drier bracket mounting bolts.
19. Disconnect HO_2S electrical connector.
20. Remove front exhaust pipe and Three-Way Catalytic Converter (TWC).
21. Remove transaxle cooler line bracket to front subframe mounting bolt.
22. Disconnect lower suspension arm ball joints and stabilizer link rods.
23. Disconnect ABS wiring harness bracket from strut.
24. Raise transaxle slight using suitable transmission jack.
25. Remove nuts and center bolt, then disconnect lefthand engine mount.
26. Disconnect righthand engine mount.
27. Remove steering gear heat shield.
28. Remove mounting bolts using steering gear wrench tool No. T97P-3504-A, or equivalent.
29. Tie steering gear up and out of way using suitable wire or rope.
30. Disconnect power steering hoses from subframe.

31. Position accumulator out of way remove transaxle cooler line brackets.
32. Secure wood blocks approximately 40 inches in length to powertrain lift tool No. 014-0076, or equivalent, then position lift under subframe.
33. Remove mounting bolts and subframe.
34. Remove rear mount through-bolt.
35. Remove transaxle cooler lines. **Do not loosen transaxle cooler inlet connector.**
36. Unclip transaxle cooler line from hold-down.
37. Disconnect lefthand halfshaft using halfshaft remover tool No. T86P-3511-A and slide hammer tool No. T50T-100-A, or equivalents.
38. Pull lefthand halfshaft out and support up and out of way. **Do not bend inner halfshaft joint more than 18° or outer joint more than 45.°**
39. Remove righthand halfshaft and intermediate shaft, then support righthand halfshaft out of way.
40. Remove rubber inspection cover from transaxle to engine spacer plate located at righthand rear corner of engine.
41. Remove rubber cover and torque converter mounting nuts.
42. Install suitable high-lift transmission jack with CD4E adapter.
43. Remove lower, then front bellhousing bolts.
44. Open clamp and disconnect main control cover vent tube.
45. **On models equipped with 2.0L engine,** remove mounting bolts and starter motor.
46. **On all models,** secure torque converter with converter holding tool No. T97T-7902-A, or equivalent.
47. Lower transaxle.

Item Description	Replacing (New) Part Number	Replacing (New) Identification	Replacing (New) Rod Length	Replaced (Old) Part Number	Replaced (Old) Identification	Replaced (Old) Rod Length
Servo Return Spring	F3RZ-7H073-A	Plain	--	F7RZ-7H073-AA	Green	--
Servo Rod Assembly	F4RZ-7H188-D	2-Grooves	101.67mm (4.00")	F7RZ-7H188-AA	2-Grooves	101.77mm (4.01")
	F4RZ-7H188-E*	1-Groove	102.87mm (4.05")	F7RZ-7H188-BA	1-Groove	102.99mm (4.05")
	F4RZ-7H188-F	0-Groove	103.87mm (4.09")	F7RZ-7H188-CA	0-Groove	104.23mm (4.10")
Servo Cover And Seal	F4RZ-7D027-A#	--	--	F4RZ-7D027-A	--	--

FMA059800093000X

Fig. 46 CD4E servo components listing. 1998 Contour & Mystique & 1999 Cougar

INSTALLATION

1. Secure torque converter in place with torque converter holding tool No. T97T-7902-A, or equivalent.
2. Lay steel straightedge on transaxle flange and measure depth between flange and torque converter centering spigot.
3. If distance is not at least .472, torque converter hub is not fully engaging oil pump drive gear. Correct condition as required.
4. Apply thin layer of suitable high temperature grease to centering spigot bore.
5. Raise and position transaxle using suitable high-lift transmission jack and adapter.
6. Remove holding tool.
7. Install transaxle mounting bolts and tighten to specifications.
8. Install torque converter mounting nuts and tighten to specifications.
9. Install inspection cover.
10. **Do not bend inner halfshaft joint more than 18° or outer more than 45.°**
11. Install righthand halfshaft and intermediate shaft. **Do not damage oil seal.**
12. Install new snap ring and ensure it engages properly.
13. Install lefthand halfshaft and new snap ring.
14. Install upper and lower oil cooler lines. Tighten to specifications.
15. Install rear mount through-bolt. **Do not tighten just yet.**
16. **On models equipped with 2.0L engine,** install starter motor, ground cable and electrical connector.
17. **On all models,** install transaxle wiring harness and connect VSS electrical connector.
18. Place wooden block approximately 40 inches long on powertrain lift tool No. 014-000765, or equivalent.
19. Secure subframe to lift and raise into position. **Do not tighten mounting bolts just yet.**
20. Install transaxle cooler line brackets and mounting bolt.
21. Install power steering hose with mounting nut and bolts.
22. Install steering gear using steering gear wrench tool No. T97P-3504-A, or equivalent.
23. Install steering gear heat shield and tighten bolts to specifications.
24. Align subframe with body locating holes using powertrain alignment pins tool No. T94P-2100-AH, or equivalent.
25. Tighten subframe mounting bolts diagonally to specifications.
26. Remove lefthand mount and install powertrain alignment gauge tool No. T94P-6000-AH, or equivalent, and align subframe.
27. Install mounting and through-bolts.
28. Lower vehicle. **Do not twist or strain rear engine mounting brackets.**
29. Tighten rear engine mount bracket nuts to specifications.
30. Raise and support vehicle.
31. Install righthand mount and tighten mounting bolts to specifications.
32. Tighten rear mount through-bolt to specifications.
33. Remove alignment tools, then install lefthand mount. Tighten mounting bolts to specifications.
34. Connect lower suspension arm ball joints and stabilizer link rods.
35. Attach ABS wiring harness bracket to strut.
36. Install front exhaust pipe and TWC with new gaskets.
37. Connect HO_2S electrical connector.
38. Install accumulator bracket bolts.
39. Install bumper brackets.
40. Install righthand fender and radiator splash shields.
41. Install front wheels.
42. Connect selector lever selector cable and bracket.
43. Connect TSS sensor electrical connector.
44. Install upper bellhousing bolts and tighten to specifications.
45. Remove three-bar engine support.
46. **On models equipped with 2.5L engine,** proceed as follows:
    a. Connect starter motor and install bracket.
    b. Install water pump cover.
    c. Connect engine coolant hose.
47. **On all models,** connect ground cable, automatic transaxle control electrical connector, TR switch electrical connector and wiring harness retaining clip.
48. Tighten strut locknuts, then tighten to specifications.
49. Remove radiator supports.
50. Fill transaxle with suitable ATF.

TECHNICAL SERVICE BULLETINS

HARSH SHIFT ON HEAVY ACCELERATION

1998 Contour & Mystique w/2.0L Engine

On some of these models there may be harsh shifts during heavy acceleration.

This condition may be caused by Mass Air Flow (MAF) sensor deterioration.

To correct this condition, perform MAF sensor diagnostics as outlined under "Electronic Engine Control System V" section (Test DC) in **MOTOR's** "Domestic Engine Performance & Driveability Manual."

ATF LEAK ON MAIN CONTROL

Contour & Mystique w/2.0L Engine

On these models, automatic transmission fluid may be leaking down main control cover.

This condition may be caused by seeping from grommet-style vent assembly.

To correct this condition, install remote vent kit part No. F6RZ-7034-AA. Follow kit instructions, noting the following:

1. When installing new design main control cover and/or new design tube assembly, fully seat tube straight end onto main control cover fitting and mount clamp securely onto brazed fitting.

2. Route tube assembly toward battery rear.
3. Attach clip to battery hold-down bracket bolt.
4. Ensure 90° tube end is routed downward.

PRNDL INDICATOR BEZEL BREAKS

1998 Contour & Mystique

On these models, built through December 4, 1998, the PRNDL indicator bezel may break.

This condition may be caused by bezel material incompatibility with cleaning products.

To correct this condition, install revised bezel part No. F8RZ-7D443-AA.

RECALIBRATION CROSS REFERENCE			
Old Calibration	Old Part Number (-12A650-)	New Calibration	New Part Number (-12A650-)
8-04A-R10	97BB-CD	8-04A-R10	97BB-BGA
8-04A-R12	98BB-BMB	8-04A-R12	98BB-CSA
8-04P-R10	97BB-DD	8-04P-R10	97BB-BHA
8-04P-R12	98BB-BNB	8-04P-R12	98BB-CTA
8-12B-R10	97BB-WE	8-12B-R10	97BB-BJA
8-12T-R10	97BB-XE	8-12T-R10	97BB-BKA
8-12B-R10	97BB-AHE	8-12B-R10	97BB-BLA
9EQA-AAF	98BB-AXF	9EQA-ASG	98BB-BXA
9EQA-BAF	98BB-AYF	9EQA-BSG	98BB-BYA
9LCA-AAE	98BB-ALE	9LCA-ASF	98BB-BZA
9LCA-BAE	98BB-AME	9LCA-BSG	98BB-CAB
9LCA-AAE	98BB-ANE	9LCA-ASF	98BB-CBA
9LCA-ABE	98BB-ASE	9LCA-ATF	98BB-CEA
9LCA-BBE	98BB-ATE	9LCA-BTG	98BB-CFA

FMA059800094000X

Fig. 47 PCM programming. 1998 Contour & Mystique & 1999 Cougar

HARSH 1-2 UPSHIFT OR 3-2 DOWNSHIFT

1998 Contour & Mystique & 1999 Cougar

On Contour and Mystique models built through May 31, 1998, and Cougar models built through June 11, 1998, there may be harsh shifts. Under light throttle there may be harsh 1–2 upshifts. After a 1–3 upshift, there may be a harsh 3–2 downshift.

These conditions may be caused by transaxle band being applied for 2nd gear without hydraulic servo pressure.

To correct this condition, proceed as follows:

1. Remove servo cover.
2. Replace servo rod with cushion spring part No. F4RZ-7H188-A based on servo components listing, **Fig. 46,** and having same number of identification grooves as removed servo rod.
3. Program Powertrain Control Module (PCM) according to **Fig. 47.**

TIGHTENING SPECIFICATIONS

Year	Component	Torque, Ft. Lbs.
CONTOUR & MYSTIQUE		
1998–2000	ABS Wire Loom	35
	Air Conditioning Suction Accumulator/ Dryer Bracket	48–72①
	Battery Tray	72–84①
	Bumper Bracket	84①
	Cooler Lines	17
	Drain Plug	19–21
	Engine Mount Bracket, Righthand	35
	Lower Radiator Support Brackets	20
	Main Control Valve Body	84–96①
	Mount Through-Bolt	87
	Power Steering Hydraulic Line	56–76
	Shift Cable Mounting Bracket	15–19
	Steering Gear	96
	Steering Gear Heat Shield	18
	Starter Motor (2.0L Engine)	15–20
	Starter Motor (2.5L Engine)	43–58
	Strut Upper Mounting	34
	Sub-Frame	96
	Suspension Arm To Knuckle Pinch Bolts	61
	Tie Rod End To Front Knuckle	23–35
	Torque Converter To Flexplate	23–29
	Transaxle Cooler Inlet Line Fitting	17
	Transaxle Range Sensor	108①
	Transaxle (2.0L Engine)	30
	Transaxle (2.5L Engine)	35
	Turbine Shaft Speed (TSS) Sensor	108–120①
	Vehicle Speed Sensor (VSS)	43–53①
	Wheel Lug Nuts (1998)	62
	Wheel Lug Nuts (1999)	92
	Wheel Lug Nuts (2000)	94

Continued

TIGHTENING SPECIFICATIONS—Continued

Year	Component	Torque, Ft. Lbs.
COUGAR		
1999–2002	A/C Suction Accumulator/Dryer Bracket	62①
	Accumulator Body Transfer Plate Bolts	108①
	Cooler Lines	30
	Drain Plug	20
	Main Control Valve Body Cover Bolts	12
	Power Steering Hydraulic Line	56–76
	Rear Engine Support Isolator Through-Bolt	89
	Shift Cable Bolts To Control Lever	17
	Steering Gear	101
	Steering Gear Heat Shield	18
	Starter Motor	18
	Strut Upper Mounting	34
	Subframe Bolts	96
	Suspension Arm To Knuckle Pinch Bolts	61
	Tie Rod End To Front Knuckle	23–35
	Torque Converter To Flexplate	27
	Transaxle Cooler Inlet Line Fitting	17
	Transaxle Range Sensor	108①
	Transaxle Case To Engine	35
	Turbine Shaft Speed (TSS) Sensor	10
	Transaxle Support Brackets	35
	Vehicle Speed Sensor (VSS)	44①
	Wheel Lug Nuts	94

① — Inch labs.

F4E-III Automatic Transaxle

NOTE: On Air Bag Equipped Models, Refer To "Air Bag System Precautions" Located In The Front Of This Manual For System Disarming & Arming Procedures.

NOTE: Refer To "Computer Relearn Procedures" Located In The Front Of This Manual When Battery Power To The Computer Has Been Interrupted.

NOTE: "Electrical Symbol & Wire Color Code Identification" Located In The Front Of This Manual May Be Used As An Aid When Using Wiring Circuits Found In This Section.

NOTE: Prior To Performing Any Service Operations Listed In This Section, Consult "Technical Service Bulletins" Section For Related Information.

INDEX

PRECAUTIONS

AIR BAG SYSTEMS

Refer to "Air Bag System Precautions" in front of this manual for system disarming and arming procedures.

BATTERY GROUND CABLE

Prior to service, disconnect battery ground cable and isolate as required.

IDENTIFICATION

The F4E-III automatic transaxle can be identified by a tag located on top of transaxle case, **Fig. 1.**

Fig. 1 Identification tag

DESCRIPTION

The F4E-III automatic transaxle is a four-speed transaxle using a combination of electronic, hydraulic and mechanical systems to control forward and reverse gear shifting, torque converter lock-up and self-diagnosis, **Fig. 2.**

TROUBLESHOOTING

BRAKE-SHIFT INTERLOCK SYSTEM

Refer to wiring diagram, **Fig. 3** and troubleshooting chart, **Fig. 4.**

TRANSAXLE

Refer to troubleshooting charts, **Figs. 5 through 8.**

MAINTENANCE

Refer to "Lubricant Data" chart in the appropriate chassis chapter of this manual for transmission fluid specifications.

FLUID INSPECTION

If vehicle has been operated for an extended period at high speeds, in city traffic, in hot weather or pulling a trailer, allow ATF to cool for approximately 30 minutes after engine has been turned off to obtain accurate reading.

1. Park vehicle on level surface, apply parking brake and block wheels.
2. Start engine, depress brake pedal and move gearshift lever through each range, allowing each range to engage, then return to Park.
3. Allow ATF to reach normal operating temperature. Do not turn engine off while inspecting level.
4. Clean dirt from transaxle fluid level indicator cap, then pull dip stick from filler tube, wipe clean and push back into tube until seated.
5. Pull dip stick from filler tube and inspect fluid level.
6. If fluid is low, add ATF in ½ pint increments to avoid over filling.

FLUID CHANGE

Normal maintenance and lubrication requirements do not require periodic automatic transaxle fluid change. If a major repair is required, such as clutch band, bearing, etc., transaxle will have to be removed for service. Torque converter, oil pan, fluid cooler and fluid cooler tubes must be thoroughly flushed to remove any contamination.

1. Remove fluid level indicator, then raise and support vehicle.
2. Place suitable drain pan under transaxle, remove drain plug and washer. Discard washer. **It may be useful to**

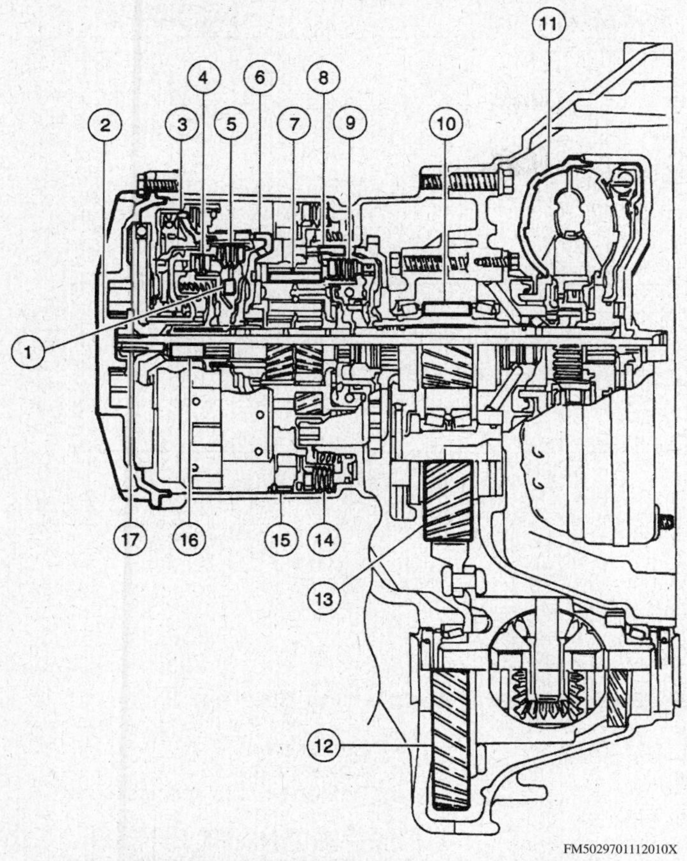

Fig. 2 Cross-sectional view of transaxle (Part 1 of 2)

Item	Description
1	One-Way Clutch
2	Oil Pump
3	Reverse Clutch
4	Coasting Clutch
5	Forward Clutch
6	2-4 Band
7	Front Planet
8	Front Sun Shell
9	3-4 Clutch

Item	Description
10	Output Gear
11	Torque Converter
12	Differential
13	Idler Gear
14	Low/Reverse Clutch
15	One-Way Clutch
16	Turbine Shaft
17	Oil Pump Shaft

FM5029701112020X

Fig. 2 Cross-sectional view of transaxle (Part 2 of 2)

measure amount of ATF drained from transaxle.

3. Install new washer and drain plug, then lower vehicle.
4. Fill transaxle with approximately same amount of ATF drained.
5. Inspect fluid level.

ADJUSTMENTS

SHIFT CABLE & BRACKET

1. With gearshift lever in Park position, loosen transaxle range switch cable nut.
2. Move shift cable toward rear as far as possible.
3. Inspect cable for tension or movement restriction, then tighten to specifications.

TRANSAXLE CONTROL SELECTOR DIAL BEZEL

1. Place gearshift lever in Park.
2. Loosen transaxle control selector dial bezel screws.
3. Place stiff wire in slider panel and position slider panel pointer to align with P. position on transaxle control selector dial bezel.
4. Tighten screws to specifications.

THROTTLE VALVE CONTROL ACTUATOR CABLE

1. Remove square head plug L and install transmission test adapter No. D87C-77000-A, or equivalent, and suitable pressure gauge.
2. With all accessories off, shift gearshift lever to Park and warm engine to normal operating temperature.
3. Ensure transaxle fluid is 140–160°F using NGS tester, or equivalent.
4. Apply parking brake and ensure idle is 670–730 RPM.
5. Loosen bolt 1 and 2, **Fig. 9.**
6. Ensure throttle plate is fully closed, then tighten bolt 1 to specifications.
7. Pull cable conduit until line pressure slightly exceeds 81 psi, then push cable until line pressure decreases to 71 psi with engine at idle.
8. Tighten bolt 2 to specifications.
9. Ensure all slack is removed from cable by apply slight downward pressure on cable.
10. Turn engine off and ensure throttle valve control actuating cable moves smoothly.
11. Start engine, press accelerator slightly and return engine to idle.
12. Ensure line pressure is 62–81 psi.
13. Turn ignition Off.
14. Remove pressure gauge and adapter, then install new square head plug and tighten to specifications.

TRANSAXLE RANGE (TR) SWITCH

1. Remove air cleaner.
2. Remove shift cable and bracket nut, then control cable front clamp.
3. Rotate manual control lever to neutral position and loosen TR switch bolts.
4. Disconnect TR switch electrical connector.
5. Connect suitable ohmmeter between TR switch terminals A and H, then adjust TR switch until there is no continuity by rotating housing on manual control lever.
6. While holding switch in place, tighten TR switch bolts to specifications.
7. Install shift cable and bracket, then tighten nut to specifications.
8. Install air cleaner.

IN-VEHICLE REPAIRS

SHIFT LOCK ACTUATOR, REPLACE

1. Remove shift console.
2. Remove righthand and front gearshift lever knob screws, then the knob.
3. Remove transaxle control selector dial bezel mounting screws, then disconnect miniature bulb from bezel.
4. Disconnect shift lock actuator and park range switch electrical connectors, then screws and shift lock actuator.
5. Revere procedure to install, noting following:
   a. Apply threadlock and sealer part No. EOAZ-19554-AA, or equivalent, to gearshift lever knob screws.
   b. Adjust transaxle control selector dial bezel.
   c. Tighten nuts, bolts and screws to specifications.

SHIFT CABLE & BRACKET

1. Remove Powertrain Control Module (PCM), then the air bag diagnostic monitor and bracket.
2. Remove rear air bag safing sensor and bracket.
3. Remove shift console.
4. Remove righthand and front gearshift lever knob screws, then the knob.
5. Remove transaxle control selector dial bezel mounting screws, then bezel.
6. Remove gearshift lever cable nut, cable floor pan bracket bolts and cable bulkhead bracket nuts.
7. Remove transaxle range switch cable

nut and control cable front clamp, then shift cable and bracket.

8. Reverse procedure to install, noting following:
   a. Apply threadlock and sealer part No. EOAZ-19554-AA, or equivalent, on gearshift lever knob screws.
   b. Adjust shift cable and bracket.
   c. Adjust transaxle control selector dial bezel.
   d. Tighten mounting bolts and nuts to specifications.

GEARSHIFT LEVER

1. Remove shift console.
2. Remove righthand and front gearshift lever knob screws, then the knob.
3. Remove transaxle control selector dial bezel mounting screws, then bezel.
4. Disconnect shift lock actuator and park range switch electrical connectors.
5. Remove screws and shift lock actuator.
6. Remove gearshift lever cable nut and cable floor pan bracket bolts. **Do not kink shift cable and bracket.**
7. Loosen ignition/shift interlock cable locknut B, **Fig. 10. Do not loosen locknut A from factory setting. Do not kink cable.**
8. Remove gearshift lever nuts, then gearshift lever.
9. Reverse procedure to install, noting following:
   a. Apply threadlock and sealer part No. EOAZ-19554-AA, or equivalent, to gearshift lever knob screws.
   b. Adjust shift cable and bracket.
   c. Adjust transaxle control selector dial bezel.
   d. Tighten mounting bolts and nuts to specifications.

IGNITION/SHIFTER INTERLOCK CABLE

1. Remove shift console.
2. Remove righthand and front gearshift lever knob screws, then the knob.
3. Remove transaxle control selector dial bezel mounting screws, then bezel.
4. Loosen ignition/shift interlock cable locknut B, **Fig. 10. Do not loosen locknut A from factory setting. Do not kink cable.**
5. Remove steering column shroud screws and shroud.
6. Remove hood latch control handle nut, then position cable aside.
7. Remove instrument panel steering column cover screw and cover.
8. Remove ignition/shifter interlock cable bracket nut and cable.
9. Reverse procedure to install, noting following:
   a. Apply threadlock and sealer part No. EOAZ-19554-AA, or equivalent, to gearshift lever knob screws.
   b. Adjust shift cable and bracket.
   c. Adjust transaxle control selector dial bezel.
   d. Tighten mounting bolts and nuts to specifications.

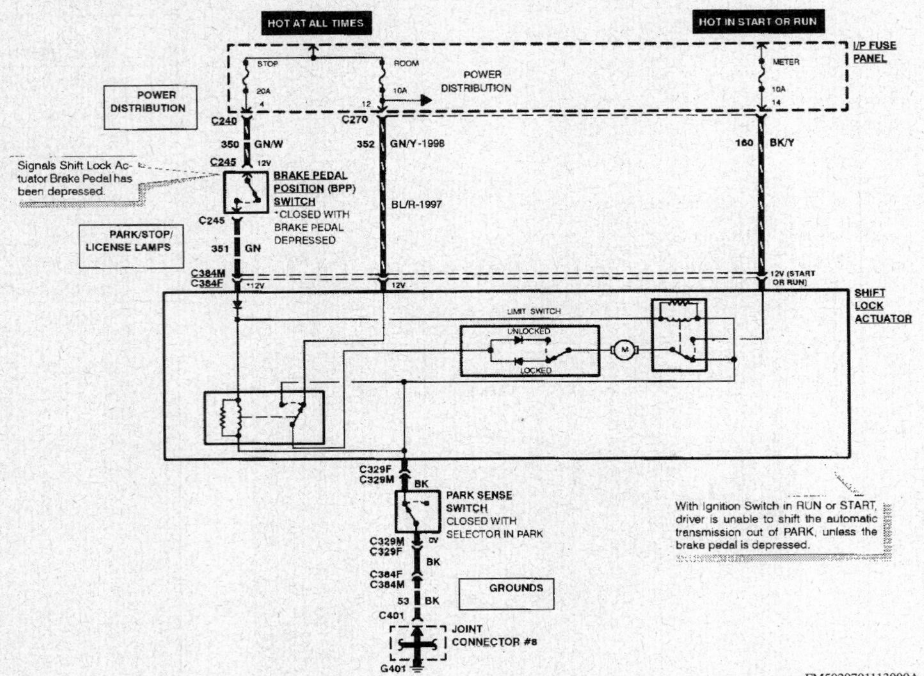

Fig. 3 Brake-shift interlock wiring diagram

MAIN CONTROL VALVE BODY, REPLACE

1. Raise and support vehicle.
2. Position suitable drain pan under transaxle, then remove plug and washer.
3. Place suitable drain pan under transaxle oil pan.
4. Remove all pan bolts except corner bolts.
5. Remove two rear corner bolts and allow fluid to drain.
6. Remove remaining bolts and oil pan.
7. Remove and discard case gasket.
8. Remove bolts holding wire retainers to main control valve body, then disconnect solenoid electrical connectors.
9. Remove remaining valve body bolts, then carefully remove valve body.
10. Reverse procedure to install, noting following:
    a. Position main control valve body into transaxle case, ensuring manual valve aligns with detent lever pin.
    b. Install valve body bolts, ensure those in locations A are 1.18 inches long below head, while those in C are 1.97 inches, **Fig. 11.**

TRANSAXLE RANGE (TR) SWITCH, REPLACE

1. Remove air cleaner outlet tube.
2. Remove shift cable and bracket nut, then the control cable front clamp.
3. Remove manual lever control nut and shift outer lever, then disconnect TR switch electrical connector.
4. Remove switch bolts and switch.
5. Reverse procedure to install, noting following:
   a. Ensure transaxle is in Neutral.
   b. Align TR switch mark with manual control lever.
   c. Adjust switch.
   d. Tighten bolts to specifications.

TURBINE SHAFT SPEED (TSS) SENSOR, REPLACE

1. Remove air cleaner outlet tube and air cleaner, then the battery tray.
2. Remove TSS sensor bolt and sensor.
3. Reverse procedure to install. Install new O-ring.

VEHICLE SPEED SENSOR

1. Raise and support vehicle.
2. Disconnect vehicle speed sensor electrical connector.
3. Unclip HO_2S wire clip from VSS bracket.
4. Remove VSS bolt, then gently pry VSS out of transaxle case.
5. Reverse procedure to install.

DIFFERENTIAL OIL SEALS, REPLACE

1. Install three-bar engine support tool No. D88L-6000-A, or equivalent, then raise and support vehicle.
2. Remove front tires and wheels.
3. Remove lefthand splash shield.
4. Remove transaxle case plug and washer, then drain ATF into suitable container.
5. Remove front wheel driveshaft and joints. Refer to "Front Wheel Drive Axles" chapter.
6. Carefully pry differential seal from case.
7. Reverse procedure to install. Tap in new seals using differential seal replacer No. T87C-7700-H, or equivalent.

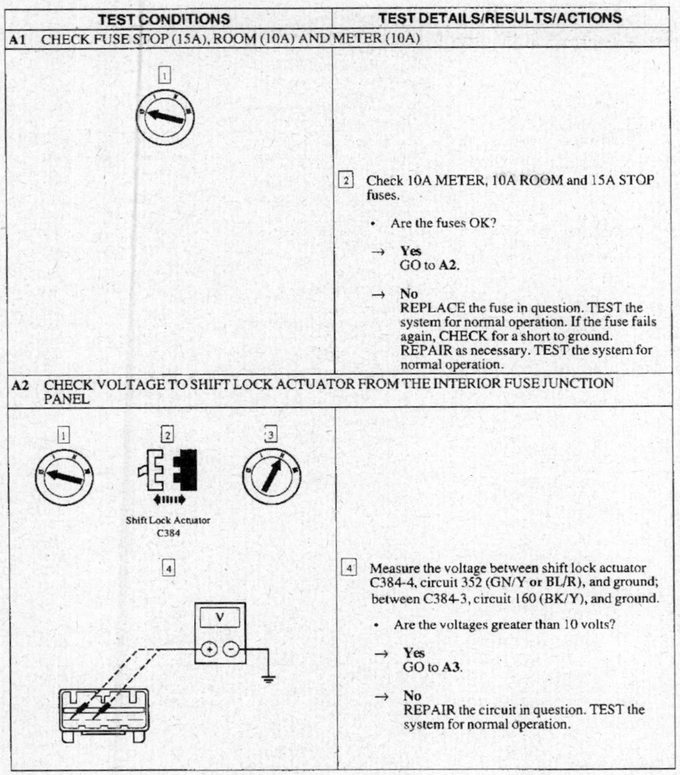

TEST CONDITIONS	TEST DETAILS/RESULTS/ACTIONS
A1 CHECK FUSE STOP (15A), ROOM (10A) AND METER (10A)	
1	2 Check 10A METER, 10A ROOM and 15A STOP fuses. • Are the fuses OK? → **Yes** GO to **A2**. → **No** REPLACE the fuse in question. TEST the system for normal operation. If the fuse fails again, CHECK for a short to ground. REPAIR as necessary. TEST the system for normal operation.
A2 CHECK VOLTAGE TO SHIFT LOCK ACTUATOR FROM THE INTERIOR FUSE JUNCTION PANEL	
1 2 3 Shift Lock Actuator C384 4	4 Measure the voltage between shift lock actuator C384-4, circuit 352 (GN/Y or BL/R), and ground; between C384-3, circuit 160 (BK/Y), and ground. • Are the voltages greater than 10 volts? → **Yes** GO to **A3**. → **No** REPAIR the circuit in question. TEST the system for normal operation.

FM5029701115010A

Fig. 4 Shift Interlock System Does Not Release Or Lock Properly (Part 1 of 3)

THROTTLE VALVE CONTROL ACTUATING CABLE, REPLACE

1. Loosen throttle valve control actuating nuts, then remove cable from throttle control lever.
2. Remove cable bolt from transaxle.
3. Remove main control valve body as outlined under "Valve Body, Replace."
4. Remove cable from throttle control lever, then the cable from vehicle.
5. Reverse procedure to install.

TRANSAXLE

REPLACE

1. Remove battery tray, air cleaner outlet tub and air cleaner.
2. Disconnect Computer Control Relay Module (CCRM) electrical connector.
3. Remove bracket bolt and nut, then CCRM and bracket.
4. Remove shift cable and bracket nut from manual control shift outer lever, then shift cable and bracket clip.
5. Disconnect Transaxle Range (TR) switch, transaxle solenoid, turbine shaft speed (TSS) sensor, HO_2S and vehicle speed sensor (VSS) electrical connectors.
6. Remove starter motor.
7. Install three-bar engine support tool No. D88L-6000-A, or equivalent.
8. Place suitable drain pan under transaxle, then disconnect fluid cooler lines from transaxle.
9. Remove lefthand engine support insulator nuts and washers, then two upper transaxle to engine bolts.
10. Raise and support vehicle, then remove front tires and wheels.
11. Remove lefthand splash shields.
12. Remove case plug, then drain transaxle fluid.
13. Remove front wheel driveshaft and joints as outlined in "Front Wheel Drive Axles" chapter.
14. Install two transaxle plugs tool No. T88C-7025-AH, or equivalent, into transaxle to hold differential side gears. **Failure to install transaxle plugs may cause gears to become improperly positioned.**
15. Disconnect heated oxygen sensor wire clip.
16. Remove front engine crossmember bolts and crossmember.
17. Disconnect air conditioning line from retainer on front engine crossmember.
18. Remove engine support crossmember bolts and nuts, then lefthand engine mount and transaxle mount nuts.
19. Remove transaxle housing cover bolts and cover.
20. Remove four flexplate to converter mounting nuts.
21. Remove lower transaxle to engine bolts.
22. Remove upper front transaxle to engine bolt. Bolt remains in block.
23. Position high-lift transaxle jack tool No. 014-00210, or equivalent, and secure transaxle to jack.

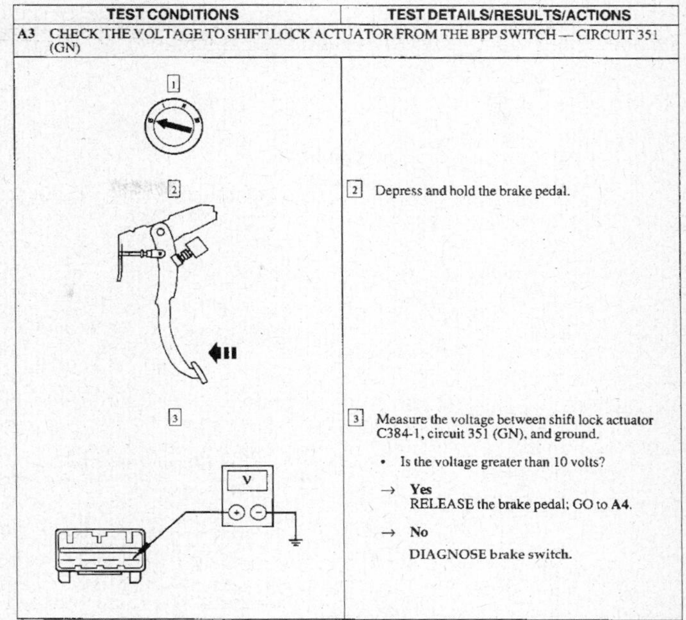

TEST CONDITIONS	TEST DETAILS/RESULTS/ACTIONS
A3 CHECK THE VOLTAGE TO SHIFT LOCK ACTUATOR FROM THE BPP SWITCH — CIRCUIT 351 (GN)	
1 2	2 Depress and hold the brake pedal.
3	3 Measure the voltage between shift lock actuator C384-1, circuit 351 (GN), and ground. • Is the voltage greater than 10 volts? → **Yes** RELEASE the brake pedal; GO to **A4**. → **No** DIAGNOSE brake switch.

FM5029701115020A

Fig. 4 Shift Interlock System Does Not Release Or Lock Properly (Part 2 of 3)

24. Remove middle transaxle to engine bolts, then carefully lower transaxle.
25. Reverse procedure to install, noting following:
    a. Lubricate torque converter pilot hub with multi-purpose grease part No. DOAZ-19584-AA, or equivalent.
    b. Align torque converter studs to flexplate.
    c. To ease installation, loosen front transaxle support insulator through-bolt and transaxle insulator bolt.
    d. Tighten nuts and bolts to specifications.

TECHNICAL SERVICE BULLETINS

ERRATIC SHIFT WITH DTC P0712

1998 Escort & Tracer

On some of these models, the transaxle may have erratic shifts with Diagnostic Trouble Code (DTC) P0712.

This condition may be caused by the Transmission Fluid Temperature (TFT) wire being pinched on the valve body spring clip.

To correct this condition, proceed as follows:

1. Remove transaxle pan.
2. Remove TFT sensor retaining clip and inspect wire for chaffing or breaks.
3. Repair wire and install ¼ or ⅜ inch plastic conduit around affected area.
4. Install clip being careful not to pinch wire.
5. Install transaxle pan.

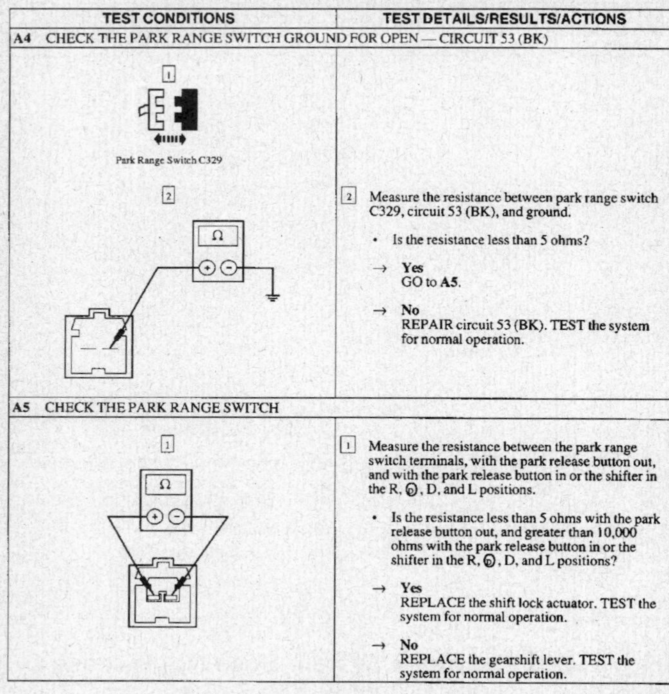

TEST CONDITIONS	TEST DETAILS/RESULTS/ACTIONS
A4 CHECK THE PARK RANGE SWITCH GROUND FOR OPEN — CIRCUIT 53 (BK)	
1 Park Range Switch C329	
2	2 Measure the resistance between park range switch C329, circuit 53 (BK), and ground. • Is the resistance less than 5 ohms? → **Yes** GO to **A5**. → **No** REPAIR circuit 53 (BK). TEST the system for normal operation.
A5 CHECK THE PARK RANGE SWITCH	
1	1 Measure the resistance between the park range switch terminals, with the park release button out, and with the park release button in or the shifter in the R, Ⓞ, D, and L positions. • Is the resistance less than 5 ohms with the park release button out, and greater than 10,000 ohms with the park release button in or the shifter in the R, Ⓞ, D, and L positions? → **Yes** REPLACE the shift lock actuator. TEST the system for normal operation. → **No** REPLACE the gearshift lever. TEST the system for normal operation.

FM5029701115030A

Fig. 4 Shift Interlock System Does Not Release Or Lock Properly (Part 3 of 3)

Condition	Possible Source	Action
• Vehicle Does Not Move in Reverse (R), but Forward Positions Are OK	• Reverse clutch worn or damaged. • LOW and REVERSE clutch slipping or damaged.	• INSPECT reverse clutch. • INSPECT the LOW and REVERSE clutch pack clearance.
• Noise Severe Under Acceleration or Deceleration, but OK in Park (P), Neutral (N), or at a Steady Speed	• Engine mounts grounding out. • Torque converter failure. • Gear or reverse clutch failure. • Selector cable grounding out.	• REPLACE the engine mounts; • EXAMINE/REPLACE. • EXAMINE/REPLACE. • INSTALL and ROUTE the cable as specified.
• Noise in Park (P) or Neutral (N) — Does Not Stop in Drive (D)	• Loose flex plate-to-converter nuts. • Oil pump worn. • Torque converter failure.	• TIGHTEN to specification. • EXAMINE/REPLACE the oil pump. • EXAMINE/REPLACE the torque converter.
• Noise in All Gears — Changes Acceleration to Deceleration	• ATF level. • Front wheel driveshaft and joint. • Final drive gear set worn.	• CHECK ATF level and FILL as necessary. • REPLACE as required. • EXAMINE/SERVICE the final drive gear set.
• Noise in All Gears — Does Not Change Acceleration to Deceleration	• Defective vehicle speed sensor (VSS). • Bearings worn or damaged. • Front planet worn.	• EXAMINE/REPLACE the VSS. • EXAMINE/REPLACE the bearings. • REPLACE the front planet.
• Harsh Shifts (Any Gears)	• Throttle valve control actuating cable out of adjustment. • Idle air control valve sticking. • Engine mounts loose. • Front wheel driveshaft and joint. • Line pressure incorrect. • Band adjustment. • Main control valve body. • 2-4 band. • Sticking accumulator piston.	• CHECK the throttle valve control actuating cable adjustment. • INSPECT the idle air control valve. • REPLACE as required; • REPLACE as required; • CHECK the band adjustment. • INSPECT the main control valve body. • INSPECT the 2-4 band. • INSPECT the accumulator piston.

FM5029701118020X

Fig. 5 Automatic Concerns (Part 2 of 5)

Condition	Possible Source	Action
• Engine Does Not Crank in Park (P) and/or Neutral (N)	• Gearshift lever and linkage out of adjustment. • Transmission range (TR) switch does not operate or is disconnected. • TR switch not correctly aligned to the transaxle.	• CONFIRM the selector or linkage adjustment and operation. • ADJUST the TR switch.
• Engine Starts in Gearshift Lever Positions Other Than Park (P) or Neutral (N)	• Gearshift lever or linkage damaged or out of adjustment. • TR switch damaged or out of adjustment.	• CONFIRM the gearshift lever or linkage adjustment and operation. • CONFIRM the TR switch adjustment and operation.
• Vehicle Moves in Park (P) Range or Transaxle Stays in Park (P) When not in Park (P) Range	• Gearshift lever and linkage out of adjustment. • Parking pawl is damaged.	• CONFIRM the gearshift lever or linkage adjustment and operation. • INSPECT the parking pawl;
• Vehicle Moves in Neutral (N)	• Gearshift lever and linkage out of adjustment. • Control valve damaged. • Torque converter damaged. • Forward clutch damaged.	• CONFIRM the gearshift lever or linkage adjustment and operation. • INSPECT the control valve. REPAIR or REPLACE as required. • INSPECT the forward clutch. REPAIR or REPLACE as required.
• Vehicle Does Not Move in Overdrive Ⓞ, Drive (D), Low (L) and Reverse (R)	• Transmission shift cable damaged. • Control valves. • Automatic transmission fluid (ATF) level. • Oil pump dirty, broken, or damaged seals. • Torque converter damaged.	• INSPECT the transaxle shift cable. REPAIR or REPLACE as required. • INSPECT the control valves. • CHECK ATF level and FILL as necessary. • INSPECT the oil pump. REPAIR or REPLACE as required. • INSPECT the torque converter. REPAIR or REPLACE as required.
• Vehicle Does Not Move in Any Forward Gearshift Lever Position, but Reverse (R) Is OK	• Control valves. • Forward clutch worn or damaged. • One-way clutch No. 1 worn or damaged. • Oil flow to forward clutch blocked.	• INSPECT the control valves. • INSPECT the clutch. • INSPECT the one-way clutch.

FM5029701118010X

Fig. 5 Automatic Concerns (Part 1 of 5)

Condition	Possible Source	Action
• Soft Shifts (Any Gears)	• ATF level. • Throttle valve control actuating cable out of adjustment. • Idle air control valve sticking. • Line pressure. • Band adjustment. • Band servo. • Pressure regulator damaged. • Main control valve body. • Sticking accumulator piston. • Internal ATF leakage. • Oil pump worn.	• CHECK ATF level and FILL as necessary. • CHECK the throttle valve control actuating cable adjustment. • INSPECT the idle air control valve. • CHECK the band adjustment. • INSPECT the band servo. • INSPECT the pressure regulator. • INSPECT the main control valve body. • INSPECT the accumulator piston. • INSPECT the automatic transaxle. • INSPECT the oil pump.
• Erratic Shifting, Incorrect Shift Points, Incorrect Shift Sequence	• ATF level and quality. • Throttle valve control actuating cable out of adjustment. • Throttle position sensor (TP sensor) out of range. • Line pressure. • 2-4 band adjustment. • Control valves. • Clutches slipping.	• CHECK ATF level and condition and FILL as necessary. • CHECK the throttle valve control actuating cable adjustment. • INSPECT throttle position sensor signal. • CHECK the band adjustment. • INSPECT the control valves. • INSPECT the clutches.
• Improper Lockup	• Throttle position sensor out of range. • Control valves. • Torque converter.	• INSPECT throttle position sensor signal. • INSPECT the control valves. • INSPECT, REPLACE the torque converter.
• Skipping Gears (For Example, Shift 1st to 3rd, or 2nd to Overdrive Ⓞ)	• Transmission fluid temperature sensor. • Main control valve body. • Control valves. • 2-4 band.	• EXAMINE/REPLACE the transmission fluid temperature sensor. • INSPECT the main control valve body. • INSPECT the control valves. • CHECK the 2-4 band adjustment.

FM5029701118030X

Fig. 5 Automatic Concerns (Part 3 of 5)

Condition	Possible Source	Action
• **NOTE:** Excessive overheating may cause damage to the internal components. Always retest the automatic transaxle for other symptoms after the overheating problem is resolved and the burnt fluid is replaced. Transaxle Overheating	• ATF level. • Poor engine performance. • Restriction in oil cooler lines. • Worn clutch, incorrect band application, or poor oil pressure control.	• CHECK ATF level and FILL as necessary. • ADJUST according to specifications. REPAIR or REPLACE the oil cooler lines.
• Drags in Reverse (R) as if Parking Brake Is Applied	• Brakes partially applied. • 2-4 band adjustment incorrect.	• INSPECT the 2-4 band adjustment.
• Drags in Forward Gears as if Parking Brake Is Applied	• Brakes partially applied. • 2-4 band adjustment incorrect.	• INSPECT the 2-4 band adjustment.
• Engine Runaway or Flare-up on Upshift	• Transmission fluid temperature sensor. • ATF level low. • Main control valve body damaged or sticking valves. • Oil pump pressure inadequate. • Clutches slipping.	• INSPECT the transmission fluid temperature sensor. • CHECK ATF level. • INSPECT the main control valve body and solenoid valves. • INSPECT the clutches.
• Engine Runaway or Flare-up on Downshift	• ATF level low. • Oil pump pressure inadequate. • Clutches slipping.	• CHECK ATF level and FILL as necessary. • INSPECT the clutches.
• Excessive Creep	• Ignition timing and idle speed. • Throttle valve control actuating cable out of adjustment. • Manual valve misadjusted.	• CHECK and ADJUST as necessary. • INSPECT the throttle valve control actuating cable adjustment. • ADJUST the manual valve.

FM5029701118040X

Fig. 5 Automatic Concerns (Part 4 of 5)

Condition	Possible Source	Action
• Shift Shock in All Ranges	• Low fluid. • Throttle valve control actuating cable out of adjustment. • Idle air control valve sticking or damaged. • Front wheel driveshaft and joint or engine mounts. • 2-4 band and servo. • Pressure regulator sticking or damaged. • Control valves. • Coasting clutch. • Accumulator piston. • Low/Reverse clutch. • 3-4 clutch.	• CHECK fluid level. • INSPECT the cable adjustment. • CLEAN, REPAIR or REPLACE the throttle valve. • REPAIR or REPLACE front wheel driveshaft and joint or engine mounts. • CHECK the adjustment. • CLEAN, REPAIR, or REPLACE. • CHECK for clogging, blockage; REPAIR as required. • CHECK for wear; REPLACE coasting clutch. • CLEAN, REPAIR, or REPLACE. • CHECK for adjustment, wear, and damage; REPAIR as required. • INSPECT, REPAIR, or REPLACE.
• Harsh 1-2 Shift	• Throttle valve control actuating cable broken or out of adjustment. • 1-2 accumulator piston sticking or damaged. • Idle speed.	• CHECK the throttle valve control actuating cable adjustment. • INSPECT and REPAIR or REPLACE.
• Harsh Engagement NEUTRAL-REVERSE	• NEUTRAL-REVERSE accumulator sticking or damaged. • Idle speed.	• INSPECT, REPAIR or REPLACE.
• Harsh Engagement NEUTRAL-OVERDRIVE (D)	• N-D accumulator sticking or damaged.	• INSPECT, REPAIR or REPLACE.
• 2-3 Shift Shock	• 2-3 accumulator piston sticking or damaged.	• INSPECT and REPAIR or REPLACE.
• Erratic Shifts	• Throttle valve control actuating cable broken or out of adjustment. • Main control valve body.	• INSPECT the throttle valve control actuating cable adjustment. • INSPECT the main control valve body and solenoid valves.
• Soft Shift in All Ranges	• Low fluid. • Throttle valve control actuating cable broken or out of adjustment. • Idle air control valve sticking or damaged. • Pressure regulator valve sticking or damaged. • Main control valve body.	• CHECK fluid level. • INSPECT the cable adjustment. • CLEAN, REPAIR, or REPLACE. • CLEAN, REPAIR, or REPLACE. • INSPECT the main control valve body and solenoid valves.

FM5029701119010X

Fig. 6 Shift Feel Concerns (Part 1 of 2)

Condition	Possible Source	Action
• No Creep	• Parking brakes partially applied. • ATF level and condition. • Throttle valve control actuating cable out of adjustment. • Gearshift lever and linkage out of adjustment. • Ignition timing idle speed. • Main control valve body. • Control valves. • Forward clutch. • Reverse clutch. • Oil pump.	• INSPECT the brake adjustment. • CHECK ATF level and condition and FILL as necessary. • INSPECT the throttle valve control actuating cable adjustment. • CONFIRM the gearshift lever and linkage adjustment and operation. • INSPECT the main control valve body. • INSPECT the control valves. • INSPECT the clutch. • INSPECT the reverse clutch. • INSPECT the oil pump.
• Engine Stalls When Put Into Gear	• Main control valve body. • Timing idle speed. • Control valves. • Torque converter. • Oil pump.	• INSPECT the main control valve body. • INSPECT the control valves. • INSPECT, REPLACE torque converter. • INSPECT the oil pump.
• No Kickdown	• Main control valve body.	• INSPECT main control valve body.
• Poor Fuel Economy	• Brake on/off (BOO) switch. • Torque converter clutch (TCC) solenoid. • Engine performance.	• INSPECT BOO switch. • INSPECT TCC solenoid.
• Lack of Power	• Engine performance. • Torque converter. • Forward clutch.	• INSPECT forward clutch.
• Surges While Cruising	• TCC solenoid. • Main control valve body.	• INSPECT TCC solenoid. • INSPECT main control valve body.
• Poor Acceleration	• Engine performance. • TCC solenoid. • Main control valve body. • Torque converter.	• INSPECT TCC solenoid. • INSPECT main control valve body. • INSPECT/REPLACE torque converter.

FM5029701118050X

Fig. 5 Automatic Concerns (Part 5 of 5)

Condition	Possible Source	Action
• 1-2 Soft Shift	• 2-4 band is too loose. • Main control valve body.	• INSPECT the adjustment. • INSPECT the main control valve body and solenoid valves.
• 2-3 Soft Shift	• 2-3 accumulator sticking or damaged. • Main control valve body.	• INSPECT, CLEAN, REPAIR, or REPLACE. • INSPECT the main control valve body and solenoid valves.
• Neutral (N)-Reverse (R) Soft Shift	• N-D accumulator piston sticking or damaged.	• INSPECT, CLEAN, REPAIR, or REPLACE.
• No Lockup	• Lockup valve sticking or damaged. • Torque converter.	• INSPECT, CLEAN, REPAIR, or REPLACE. • INSPECT the torque converter.
• Drags in REVERSE as if Parking Brake Is Applied	• 2-4 band is too tight.	• CHECK adjustment.
• Slow to Engage in REVERSE	• Reverse clutch. • LOW and REVERSE clutch.	• INSPECT for damage or wear; REPAIR or REPLACE. • INSPECT for damage or wear; REPAIR or REPLACE.

FM5029701119020X

Fig. 6 Shift Feel Concerns (Part 2 of 2)

Condition	Possible Source	Action
• Engine Has Momentary Runaway During 3-2 Downshift	• 2-4 band damaged or misadjusted.	• INSPECT for adjustment or damage; REPAIR or REPLACE.
• Hesitation in 3-2 Shift	• Main control valve body.	• INSPECT the main control valve body and solenoid valves. REPLACE as required.
• No Engine Braking (D) to DRIVE	• Fluid blockage to coasting clutch or failed coasting clutch. • Main control valve body.	• CHECK for blockage and coasting clutch condition. • INSPECT the main control valve body and solenoid valves. REPLACE as required.
• No Engine Braking DRIVE to LOW	• Fluid blockage to coasting clutch or failed coasting clutch. • 2-4 band. • Main control valve body. • Control valve.	• INSPECT coasting clutch for blockage or damage. • CHECK adjustment and INSPECT condition. • INSPECT the main control valve body and solenoid valves. REPLACE as required. • INSPECT, CLEAN or REPAIR.

FM5029701120000X

Fig. 7 Downshift Concerns

Condition	Possible Source	Action
• No 2-3 Upshift	• 3-4 clutch damaged. • Main control valve body.	• CHECK clutch adjustment for damage. • INSPECT the main control valve body and solenoid valves. REPLACE as required.
• No 2nd Gear (Transaxle Shifts 1-3)	• Loose 2-4 band. • Main control valve body.	• ADJUST 2-4 band. • INSPECT the main control valve body and solenoid valves. REPLACE as required.
• No Lockup	• Torque converter clutch (TCC) solenoid not functioning. • Torque converter.	• INSPECT the TCC solenoid and related hydraulic circuit. • INSPECT the torque converter.
• Shift Points Incorrect	• 2-4 band out of adjustment. • Main control valve body.	• CHECK 2-4 band adjustments. • INSPECT the main control valve body and solenoid valves. REPLACE as required.
• Engine Runaway When Upshifting	• Park/neutral position switch. • Main control valve body. • One-way clutch. • 2-4 band and servo. • 3-4 clutch.	• CHECK the adjustment and condition. • CLEAN, INSPECT, REPAIR or REPLACE. • INSPECT, REPAIR or REPLACE. • CHECK the adjustment and condition. • CHECK the condition and REPAIR.
• No Upshift Into Overdrive	• One-way clutch. • Main control valve body.	• CHECK one-way clutch. • CHECK orifices, solenoid valves and main control valve body.
• Delayed 1-2 Shift	• 2-4 band damaged or misadjusted. • Main control valve body.	• INSPECT for damage or misadjustment. REPAIR or REPLACE. • INSPECT valve body and solenoid valves. REPLACE as required.

FM5029701121000X

Fig. 8 Upshift Concerns

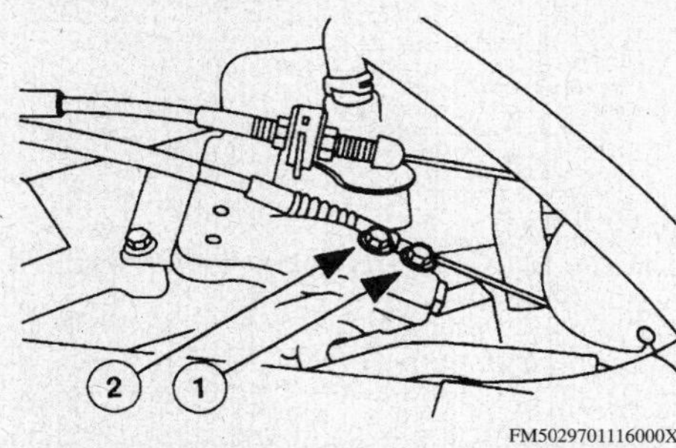

Fig. 9 Throttle valve control actuator cable adjustment

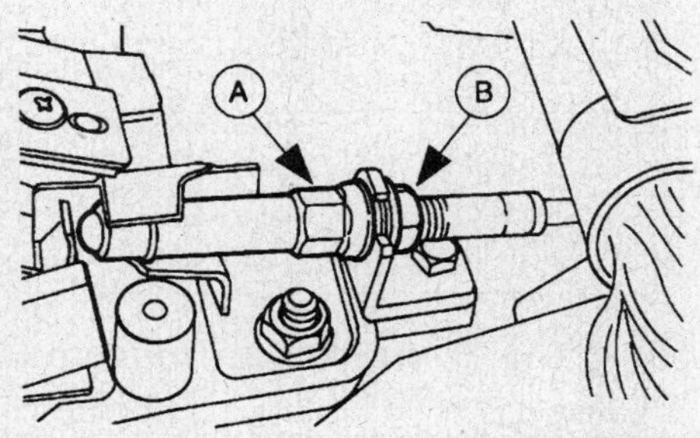

Fig. 10 Interlock cable removal

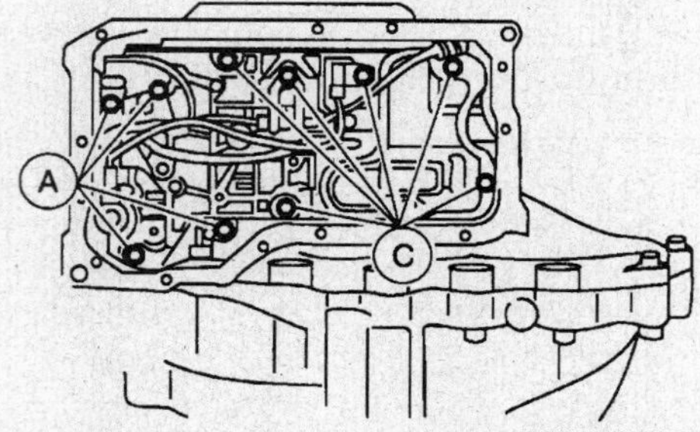

Fig. 11 Valve body installation

TIGHTENING SPECIFICATIONS

Year	Component	Torque/Ft. Lbs.
1998–2002	Bearing Housing Bolts	14–18
	Drain Plug	29–39
	Engine Mount	50–68
	Engine Support Crossmember	69–97
	Fluid Cooler Line	24–35
	Front Engine Crossmember	69–97
	Front Engine Mount Nuts	28–37
	Gearshift Lever	12–16
	Gearshift Lever Knob	18–26①
	Lefthand Engine Mount	28–37
	Oil Pan	74–95①
	Pressure Port Plug	44–86①
	Shift Cable	72–96①
	Shift Cable Bracket Nut	12–16
	Shift Solenoid Bolts	70–95
	Shifter Interlock Cable	7–11①
	Shifter Interlock Cable Bracket	38–54①
	Shift Lock Actuator	12–16①
	Throttle Cable	60–84①
	Transaxle Case To Converter Housing	28–38
	Transaxle Mount	28–38
	Transaxle To Engine	40–58
	Transmission Control Selector Dial Bezel	18–26①
	Transmission Range Sensor	70–95①
	Transmission Range Switch Cable	12–16
	Transmission Range Switch Manual Control Lever	33–47
	Turbine Shaft Speed Sensor	70–95①
	Valve Body	70–95①
	Vehicle Speed Sensor	70–95①
	Wheel Lug Nuts	66–87

① — Inch lbs.

4F27E Automatic Transaxle

NOTE: On Air Bag Equipped Models, Refer To "Air Bag System Precautions" Located In The Front Of This Manual For System Disarming & Arming Procedures.

NOTE: Refer To "Computer Relearn Procedures" Located In The Front Of This Manual When Battery Power To The Computer Has Been Interrupted.

INDEX

PRECAUTIONS

AIR BAG SYSTEMS

Refer to "Air Bag System Precautions" in the front of this manual for system disarming and arming procedures.

BATTERY GROUND CABLE

Prior to service, disconnect battery ground cable and isolate as required.

IDENTIFICATION

The transaxle can be identified by the vehicle certification (VC) label, **Fig. 1.**

DESCRIPTION

The 4F27E is a four-speed, front wheel drive electronically controlled transaxle with a maximum input torque after torque converter of 270 ft. lbs., **Fig. 2.** Gear ratios are attained through two planetary gear sets connected one behind the other. The planetary gear sets are driven or locked by a combination of three multi-plate clutches, a multi-plate brake, a brake band and a one-way roller clutch. Torque is transmitted to the final drive through an intermediate gear stage.

The electrical and hydraulic operations of the 4F27E transaxle are controlled by the EEC V PCM. Also incorporated into the transaxle electronics is an overdrive cancel switch which can be used in the D gear range to prevent a 3–4 shift or to command a 4–3 shift. The TCC is used in 3rd and 4th gears, depending on throttle position and vehicle speed. The transaxle also incorporates Electronic Synchronous Shift Control (ESSC) which allows for smooth gear shifting for the life on transaxle.

If a critical electrical component fails, the PCM will initiate a hydraulic emergency operating program which will maintain limited transaxle operation. Electronic testing of the transaxle is accomplished through the vehicle DLC and by use of the Worldwide Diagnostic System (WDS) tool No. 418-F224, or equivalent.

TROUBLESHOOTING

Brake Shift Interlock

Refer to troubleshooting chart **Fig. 3.**

Transaxle

DELAYED FORWARD AND REVERSE ENGAGEMENT

1. Powertrain control system.
2. Shift solenoids "C" and "D."
3. TR sensor and TFT sensor.
4. Poor fluid quality.
5. Improper fluid level.
6. Improper line pressures.
7. Valve body:

MFD. BY FORD MOTOR CO. IN U.S.A.

DATE: XXXXX GVWR: XXXXXXXXXXXXXX
FRONT GAWR: XXXXXXX XXXXXXX
REAR GAWR: XXXXXXX XXXXXXX

THIS VEHICLE CONFORMS TO ALL APPLICABLE FEDERAL MOTOR VEHICLE SAFETY, BUMPER, AND THEFT PREVENTION STANDARDS IN EFFECT ON THE DATE OF MANUFACTURE SHOWN ABOVE.

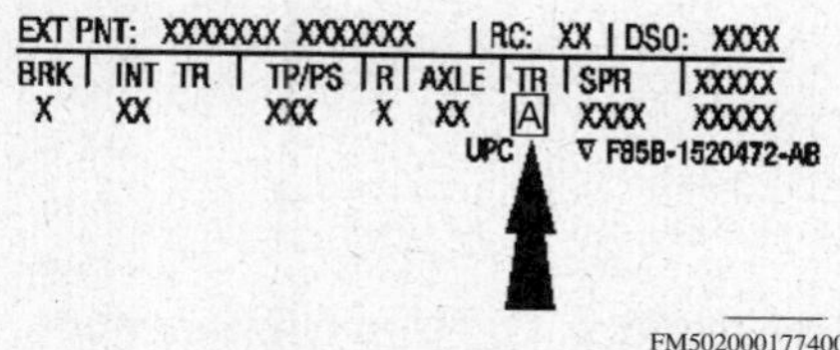

FM5020001774000X

Fig. 1 Transaxle identification

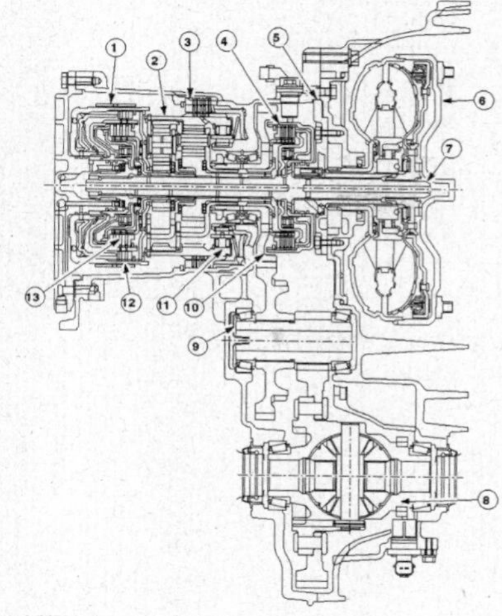

Item	Description
1	2nd/4th gear brake band
2	Planetary gear sets
3	Low/reverse gear brake
4	Forward gear clutch
5	Fluid pump and stator support
6	Torque converter
7	Transmission input shaft
8	Differential
9	Intermediate gear stage
10	Transmission output gear
11	1st gear one-way clutch
12	Reverse gear clutch
13	3rd/4th gear clutch

FM5020001775000X

Fig. 2 Cross-sectional view of transaxle

   a. Not tightened to specifications.
   b. Separator plate damaged.
   c. Contamination.
   d. Valves or springs damaged, improperly assembled, missing, stuck or damaged.
8. Fluid pump:
   a. Not tightened to specifications.
   b. Damaged gasket.
   c. Porosity, cross leaks, ball missing or plugged fluid passages.

DELAYED/SOFT FORWARD ENGAGEMENT

1. Powertrain control system.
2. Shift solenoid "C."
3. Pressure control solenoid "A"
4. Improper line pressures.
5. Valve body:
   a. Not tightened to specifications.
   b. Separator plate damaged.
   c. Contamination.
   d. Valves or springs damaged, improperly assembled, missing, stuck or damaged.
6. Forward clutch:
   a. Damaged piston seals.
   b. Damaged clutch piston balance.
   c. Worn friction components.
   d. Damaged return springs.

DELAYED/SOFT REVERSE ENGAGEMENT

1. Powertrain control system.
2. Shift solenoid "D."
3. Pressure control solenoid "A."
4. Improper line pressures.
5. Valve body:
   a. Not tightened to specifications.
   b. Separator plate damaged.
   c. Contamination.
   d. Valves or springs damaged, improperly assembled, missing, stuck or damaged.
6. Low/reverse clutch:
   a. Damaged piston seals.
   b. Damaged clutch piston balance.
   c. Worn friction components.
   d. Damaged return springs.

EARLY OR LATE SHIFT

1. Powertrain control system.
2. Shift solenoids "A," "B," "C," "D" and "E."
3. VSS, VFS or TSS.
4. Poor fluid quality.
5. Improper fluid level.
6. Valve body:
   a. Not tightened to specifications.
   b. Separator plate damaged.
   c. Contamination.
   d. Valves or springs damaged, improperly assembled, missing, stuck or damaged.
7. Servo seals or retaining ring damage.
8. Band:
   a. Damaged band.
   b. Servo worn or damaged.
   c. Improper adjustment.
   d. Anchor bolt damaged or worn.

ENGINE WILL NOT CRANK

1. Powertrain control system.
2. Shift cable or TR sensor damaged or misaligned.
3. Flexplate or adapter plate damaged.

ERRATIC SHIFT OR HUNTING

1. Powertrain control system.
2. VSS or IAT sensor.
3. Poor fluid quality.
4. Improper fluid level.
5. Valve body:
   a. Not tightened to specifications.
   b. Separator plate damaged.
   c. Contamination.
   d. Valves or springs damaged, improperly assembled, missing, stuck or damaged.

EXTERNAL LEAKS

1. Powertrain control system.
2. Transaxle wiring harness.
3. Improper fluid level.
4. Damaged transaxle case.
5. Leakage at seals or gaskets.

FLUID VENTING OR FOAMING

1. Improper fluid level.
2. Poor fluid quality.
3. Fluid pump:
   a. Not tightened to specifications.
   b. Damaged gasket.
   c. Porosity, cross leaks, ball missing or plugged fluid passages.
4. Case vent damaged.
5. Transaxle overheating.

HARSH FORWARD & REVERSE ENGAGEMENT

1. Powertrain control system.
2. Shift solenoids "C" and "D."
3. TR sensor or TFT sensor.
4. Poor fluid quality.
5. Improper fluid level.
6. Improper line pressures.
7. Valve body:
   a. Not tightened to specifications.
   b. Separator plate damaged.
   c. Contamination.
   d. Valves or springs damaged, improperly assembled, missing, stuck or damaged.
8. Forward clutch:
   a. Damaged piston seals.
   b. Damaged clutch piston balance.
   c. Worn friction components.
   d. Damaged return springs.
9. Reverse and low/reverse clutch:
   a. Damaged piston seals.
   b. Damaged clutch piston balance.
   c. Worn friction components.
   d. Damaged return springs.

HARSH MANUAL 1ST GEAR ENGAGEMENT

1. Powertrain control system.
2. Shift solenoid "C."
3. Improper fluid pressures.
4. Turbine shaft speed sensor.
5. Valve body:
   a. Not tightened to specifications.
   b. Separator plate damaged.
   c. Contamination.

A1	CHECK IF STOPLAMPS LIGHT

1 Switch ON ignition. Depress brake pedal.

- **Are the stoplamps ON?**

→ **Yes**

Go to «A3».

→ **No**

Go to «A2».

FM5020001785010X

Fig. 3 Test A: Shift Interlock System Inoperative (Part 1 of 13)

d. Valves or springs damaged, improperly assembled, missing, stuck or damaged.

6. Forward clutch:
   a. Damaged piston seals.
   b. Damaged clutch piston balance.
   c. Worn friction components.
   d. Damaged return springs.

HARSH REVERSE ENGAGEMENT

1. Powertrain control system.
2. Shift solenoid "D."
3. Improper line pressures.
4. Valve body:
   a. Not tightened to specifications.
   b. Separator plate damaged.
   c. Contamination.
   d. Valves or springs damaged, improperly assembled, missing, stuck or damaged.
5. Reverse and low/reverse clutch:
   a. Damaged piston seals.
   b. Damaged clutch piston balance.
   c. Worn friction components.
   d. Damaged return springs.

HARSH SHIFT, ALL GEARS

1. Powertrain control system.
2. Shift solenoids "A," "B," "C," "D" or "E."
3. TR, TFT, IAT or VSS.
4. Pressure control solenoid "A."
5. Improper line pressures.
6. Valve body:
   a. Not tightened to specifications.
   b. Separator plate damaged.
   c. Contamination.
   d. Valves or springs damaged, improperly assembled, missing, stuck or damaged.
7. Input shaft damage.
8. Servo seals or retaining ring damaged.
9. Band:
   a. Damaged band.
   b. Servo worn or damaged.
   c. Improper adjustment.
   d. Anchor bolt damaged or worn.
10. Forward clutch:
    a. Damaged piston seals.
    b. Damaged clutch piston balance.
    c. Worn friction components.
    d. Damaged return springs.
11. Final drive gear and differential damage.
12. Damage to transaxle case.

HARSH 1-2 SHIFT

1. Powertrain control system.
2. Shift solenoid "D."
3. TSS, TR sensor or TFT.
4. Improper line pressures.
5. Valve body:
   a. Not tightened to specifications.
   b. Separator plate damaged.
   c. Contamination.
   d. Valves or springs damaged, improperly assembled, missing, stuck or damaged.
6. Servo piston, seals or cover damaged.
7. Band:
   a. Damaged band.
   b. Servo worn or damaged.
   c. Improper adjustment.
   d. Anchor bolt damaged or worn.

HARSH 2-1 SHIFT

1. Powertrain control system.
2. Shift solenoid "D."
3. TSS, TR sensor or TFT.
4. Improper line pressures.
5. Valve body:
   a. Not tightened to specifications.
   b. Separator plate damaged.
   c. Contamination.
   d. Valves or springs damaged, improperly assembled, missing, stuck or damaged.
6. One-way clutch worn, damaged or improperly assembled.
7. Servo piston, seals or cover damaged.
8. Band:
   a. Damaged band.
   b. Servo worn or damaged.
   c. Improper adjustment.
   d. Anchor bolt damaged or worn.

HARSH 2-3 SHIFT

1. Powertrain control system.
2. Shift solenoid "E."
3. TSS, TR sensor or TFT.
4. Improper line pressures.
5. Valve body:
   a. Not tightened to specifications.
   b. Separator plate damaged.
   c. Contamination.
   d. Valves or springs damaged, improperly assembled, missing, stuck or damaged.
6. Direct clutch:
   a. Damaged piston seals.
   b. Damaged clutch piston balance.

A2	CHECK FUSE 54 IN CJB

1

2

F54 (15 A)

- **Is fuse F54 OK?**

→ **Yes**

Diagnose exterior lighting concern.

→ **No**

INSTALL a new fuse. RECHECK system.

FM5020001785020X

Fig. 3 Test A: Shift Interlock System Inoperative (Part 2 of 13)

c. Worn friction components.
d. Damaged return springs.

7. Servo piston, seals or cover damaged.
8. Band:
   a. Damaged band.
   b. Servo worn or damaged.
   c. Improper adjustment.
   d. Anchor bolt damaged or worn.

HARSH 3-2 SHIFT

1. Powertrain control system.
2. Shift solenoid "E."
3. TSS, TR sensor or TFT.
4. Improper line pressures.
5. Valve body:
   a. Not tightened to specifications.
   b. Separator plate damaged.
   c. Contamination.
   d. Valves or springs damaged, improperly assembled, missing, stuck or damaged.
6. Servo piston, seals or cover damaged.
7. Band:
   a. Damaged band.
   b. Servo worn or damaged.
   c. Improper adjustment.
   d. Anchor bolt damaged or worn.
8. Direct clutch:
   a. Damaged piston seals.
   b. Damaged clutch piston balance.
   c. Worn friction components.
   d. Damaged return springs.

HARSH 3-4 SHIFT

1. Powertrain control system.
2. Shift solenoid "A" and "C."
3. TR sensor or TFT.
4. Improper line pressures.
5. Valve body:
   a. Not tightened to specifications.
   b. Separator plate damaged.
   c. Contamination.
   d. Valves or springs damaged, improperly assembled, missing, stuck or damaged.
6. Forward or direct clutch:
   a. Damaged piston seals.
   b. Damaged clutch piston balance.
   c. Worn friction components.
   d. Damaged return springs.

A3 CHECK KEY REMOVAL INHIBIT CIRCUIT

1 Turn ignition ON, gear selection in "P" (PARK) position.

- **Can ignition switch be turned into position "0" and can key be removed only when gear selector in "P"?**

→ **Yes**

Go to «A4».

→ **No**

Go to «A8».

FM5020001785030X

Fig. 3 Test A: Shift Interlock System Inoperative (Part 3 of 13)

A4 CHECK VOLTAGE TO PARK INTERLOCK SOLENOID

1 *Gearshift lever unit (C931)*

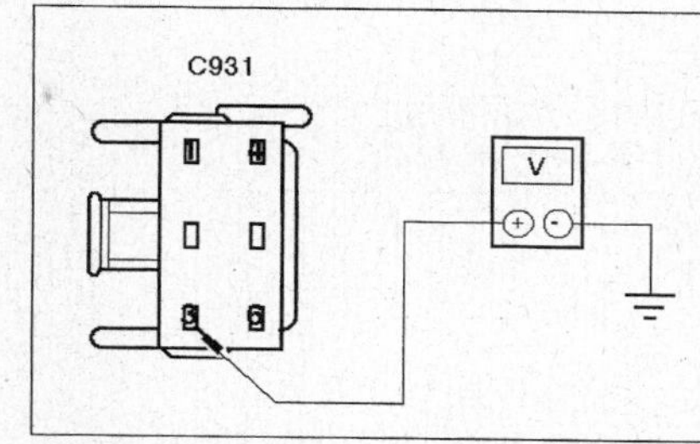

2

Measure the voltage between C931 pin 3 (GN/WH) and ground.

- **Is the voltage 0 V when brake pedal is not depressed, and is battery voltage indicated when brake pedal is depressed?**

→ **Yes**

Go to «A5».

→ **No**

REPAIR circuit 15S-TA33 between C444 (stoplamp switch), Pin 1 and C931, pin 3 for open.

FM5020001785040X

Fig. 3 Test A: Shift Interlock System Inoperative (Part 4 of 13)

HARSH 4-3 SHIFT

1. Powertrain control system.
2. Shift solenoids "A" and "C."
3. TR sensor or TFT.
4. Improper line pressures.
5. Valve body:
   a. Not tightened to specifications.
   b. Separator plate damaged.
   c. Contamination.
   d. Valves or springs damaged, improperly assembled, missing, stuck or damaged.
6. Forward clutch:
   a. Damaged piston seals.
   b. Damaged clutch piston balance.
   c. Worn friction components.
   d. Damaged return springs.
7. Servo piston, seals or cover damaged.
8. Band:
   a. Damaged band.
   b. Servo worn or damaged.
   c. Improper adjustment.
   d. Anchor bolt damaged or worn.

HIGH SHIFT LEVER EFFORT

1. Powertrain control system.
2. Shift cable or TR sensor damaged or not aligned.
3. Valve body:
   a. Not tightened to specifications.
   b. Separator plate damaged.
   c. Contamination.
   d. Valves or springs damaged, improperly assembled, missing, stuck or damaged.
4. Manual shift components inside case damaged.

NO FORWARD ENGAGEMENT IN ANY GEAR

1. Powertrain control system.
2. Shift solenoids "C," "D" and "E."
3. Valve body:
   a. Not tightened to specifications.
   b. Separator plate damaged.
   c. Contamination.
   d. Valves or springs damaged, improperly assembled, missing, stuck or damaged.
4. Forward clutch:
   a. Damaged piston seals.
   b. Damaged clutch piston balance.
   c. Worn friction components.
   d. Damaged return springs.
5. Forward planetary damage.
6. Low one-way clutch worn, damaged or assembled improperly.

NO FORWARD IN O/D ONLY

1. Powertrain control system.
2. Shift solenoid "C."
3. Poor fluid quality.
4. Improper fluid level.
5. Forward clutch:
   a. Damaged piston seals.
   b. Damaged clutch piston balance.
   c. Worn friction components.
   d. Damaged return springs.
6. Servo piston and cover damage.
7. Band:
   a. Damaged band.
   b. Servo worn or damaged.
   c. Improper adjustment.
   d. Anchor bolt damaged or worn.
8. Damage to transaxle case.

NO ENGINE BRAKING IN ANY GEAR

1. Powertrain control system.
2. Shift solenoid "D."

NO ENGINE BRAKING IN MANUAL 1ST

1. Powertrain control system.
2. Shift solenoid "D."
3. Improper fluid level.
4. Improper line pressures.
5. Fluid pump:
   a. Not tightened to specifications.
   b. Damaged gasket.
   c. Porosity, cross leaks, ball missing or plugged fluid passages.
6. Low/reverse clutch:
   a. Damaged piston seals.
   b. Damaged clutch piston balance.
   c. Worn friction components.
   d. Damaged return springs.

NO FORWARD & REVERSE

1. Powertrain control system. If there is no electrical activity, transaxle will default to 3rd gear.
2. Poor fluid quality.
3. Improper fluid level.
4. Shift cable or TR sensor damaged or misaligned.
5. Valve body:
   a. Not tightened to specifications.
   b. Separator plate damaged.
   c. Contamination.
   d. Valves or springs damaged, improperly assembled, missing, stuck or damaged.
6. Turbine shaft damaged.
7. Fluid pump:
   a. Not tightened to specifications.
   b. Gasket damaged.
   c. Porosity, cross leaks, ball missing or plugged fluid passages.
8. Forward or rear planetary damage.
9. Forward clutch:
   a. Damaged piston seals.
   b. Damaged clutch piston balance.
   c. Worn friction components.
   d. Damaged return springs.
10. Final drive gearset and differential damage.
11. Damaged flexplate or adapter plate.
12. Damaged torque converter impeller or turbine hub.
13. Low one-way clutch worn, damaged or improperly assembled.

NO MANUAL 2ND GEAR

1. Powertrain control system.
2. Shift solenoid "D."
3. Improper fluid pressures.
4. Valve body:
   a. Not tightened to specifications.

A5 CHECK GROUND TO PARK INTERLOCK SOLENOID

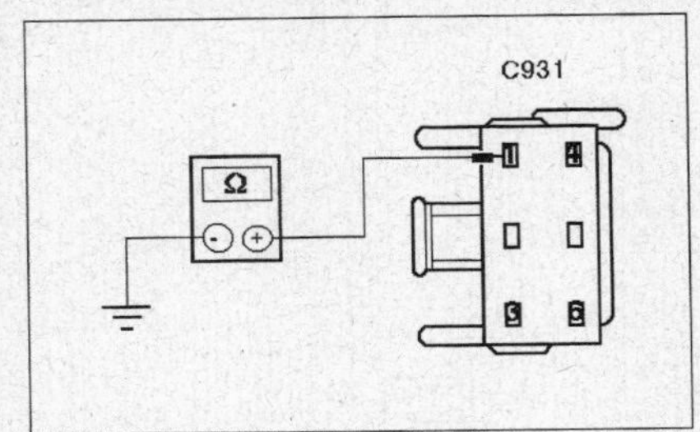

1 Measure resistance between C931, pin 1 (BK) and ground.

- **Is resistance less than 5 ohms?**

→ **Yes**

Go to «A6».

→ **No**

REPAIR circuit 31-TA34 between C931, pin 1 and ground for open.

FM5020001785050X

Fig. 3 Test A: Shift Interlock System Inoperative (Part 5 of 13)

A6 CHECK SELECTOR LEVER CIRCUIT

1 Measure resistance at the connector of the gearshift lever unit (C931), between pins 3 and 1. Gearshift lever in position "P".

- **Is resistance less than 10 ohms?**

→ **Yes**

Go to «A7».

→ **No**

REPLACE park interlock solenoid.

FM5020001785060X

Fig. 3 Test A: Shift Interlock System Inoperative (Part 6 of 13)

A7 CHECK FUNCTION OF PARK INTERLOCK SOLENOID

1 Position gearshift lever into positions "R", "N", "D", "1" and "2".
— If necessary, release mechanically as described in this section.

- **Is resistance greater than 10 ohms in all mentioned positions?**

→ **Yes**

Park interlock solenoid is electrically OK, CHECK for mechanical fault.

→ **No**

REPLACE park interlock solenoid.

FM5020001785070X

Fig. 3 Test A: Shift Interlock System Inoperative (Part 7 of 13)

   b. Separator plate damaged.
   c. Contamination.
   d. Valves or springs damaged, improperly assembled, missing, stuck or damaged.
5. Servo seal or retaining ring damage.
6. Band:
   a. Damaged band.
   b. Servo worn or damaged.
   c. Improper adjustment.
   d. Anchor bolt damaged or worn.
7. Direct one-way clutch worn, damaged or improperly assembled.

NO PARK ENGAGEMENT

1. Shift cable or TR sensor damaged or misaligned.
2. Park system components inside transaxle case damaged.

NO REVERSE

1. Powertrain control system.
2. Shift solenoids "C," "D" and "E."
3. Valve body:
   a. Not tightened to specifications.
   b. Separator plate damaged.
   c. Contamination.
   d. Valves or springs damaged, improperly assembled, missing, stuck or damaged.
4. Reverse and low/reverse clutch:
   a. Damaged piston seals.
   b. Worn friction components.
   c. Damaged clutch piston balance.
   d. Damaged return springs.

NO 1ST GEAR, ENGAGES IN HIGHER GEAR

1. Powertrain control system.
2. TR sensor.
3. Shift solenoid "C."
4. Improper line pressures.
5. Valve body:
   a. Not tightened to specifications.
   b. Separator plate damaged.
   c. Contamination.
   d. Valves or springs damaged, improperly assembled, missing, stuck or damaged.
6. Low one-way clutch improperly assembled, worn or damaged.

NO 1ST GEAR IN MANUAL 1ST

1. Powertrain control system.
2. Improper line pressures.
3. Valve body:
   a. Not tightened to specifications.
   b. Separator plate damaged.
   c. Contamination.
   d. Valves or springs damaged, improperly assembled, missing, stuck or damaged.
4. Low/reverse clutch:
   a. Damaged piston seals.
   b. Damaged clutch piston balance.
   c. Worn friction components.
   d. Damaged return springs.
5. Overdrive planetary damage.

NO 1-2 SHIFT

1. Powertrain control system.
2. Shift solenoid "D."
3. VSS, TR or TSS.
4. Improper fluid level.
5. Valve body:
   a. Not tightened to specifications.
   b. Separator plate damaged.
   c. Contamination.
   d. Valves or springs damaged, improperly assembled, missing, stuck or damaged.
6. Servo seals damaged.
7. Band:
   a. Damaged band.
   b. Servo worn or damaged.
   c. Improper adjustment.
   d. Anchor bolt damaged or worn.
8. Overdrive planetary damaged.
9. Forward clutch:
   a. Damaged piston seals.
   b. Damaged clutch piston balance.
   c. Worn friction components.
   d. Damaged return springs.

NO 2-1 SHIFT

1. Powertrain control system.
2. Shift solenoid "D."
3. TR or VSS.
4. Improper line pressures.
5. Valve body:
   a. Not tightened to specifications.
   b. Separator plate damaged.
   c. Contamination.
   d. Valves or springs damaged, improperly assembled, missing, stuck or damaged.
6. One-way clutch or band damaged.

NO 2-3 SHIFT

1. Powertrain control system.
2. Shift solenoids "D" and "E."
3. TR or VSS.
4. Improper line pressures.
5. Valve body:
   a. Not tightened to specifications.
   b. Separator plate damaged.
   c. Contamination.
   d. Valves or springs damaged, improperly assembled, missing, stuck or damaged.
6. Damaged servo seals.
7. Forward or intermediate clutch:
   a. Damaged piston seals.
   b. Damaged clutch piston balance.
   c. Worn friction components.
   d. Damaged return springs.

NO 3-4 OR 4-3 SHIFT

1. Powertrain control system.
2. Shift solenoids "A" and "C."
3. TR or VSS.
4. Improper line pressures.
5. Valve body:
   a. Not tightened to specifications.
   b. Separator plate damaged.
   c. Contamination.
   d. Valves or springs damaged, improperly assembled, missing, stuck or damaged.

A8 CHECK FUSE F8 IN CJB

1 F8 (30 A)

- **Is the fuse F8 OK?**

→ **Yes**

Go to «A9».

→ **No**

INSTALL a new fuse. RECHECK the system.

FM5020001785080X

Fig. 3 Test A: Shift Interlock System Inoperative (Part 8 of 13)

A9 CHECK PARK INTERLOCK SWITCH

1 Gearshift lever unit (C931)

2 Connect a jumper wire between C931, pin 2 (BK/YE) and ground.
— Be sure that only pin 2 and not another pin is grounded.

- **Can ignition key be removed when jumper wire is connected?**

→ **Yes**

Go to «A10».

→ **No**

Go to «A11».

FM5020001785090X

Fig. 3 Test A: Shift Interlock System Inoperative (Part 9 of 13)

6. Forward clutch:
   a. Damaged piston seals.
   b. Damaged clutch piston balance.
   c. Worn friction components.
   d. Damaged return springs.
7. Servo or band damage.

NO 3-2 SHIFT

1. Powertrain control system.
2. Shift solenoid "E."
3. TR sensor or VSS.
4. Improper fluid pressures.
5. Valve body:
   a. Not tightened to specifications.
   b. Separator plate damaged.
   c. Contamination.
   d. Valves or springs damaged, improperly assembled, missing, stuck or damaged.
6. Servo seals damaged.
7. Band:
   a. Damaged band.
   b. Servo worn or damaged.
   c. Improper adjustment.
   d. Anchor bolt damaged or worn.
8. Direct clutch:
   a. Damaged piston seals.
   b. Damaged clutch piston balance.
   c. Worn friction components.
   d. Damaged return springs.

NOISE OR VIBRATION IN FORWARD OR REVERSE

1. Powertrain control system.
2. Shift solenoids "A," "B," "C," "D" or "E."
3. Pressure control solenoid "A."
4. Fluid pump:
   a. Not tightened to specifications.
   b. Damaged gasket.
   c. Porosity, cross leaks, ball missing or plugged fluid passages.
5. Flexplate or adapter plate damaged.
6. Adapter plate aligned improperly.

POOR TRANSAXLE PERFORMANCE

1. Powertrain control system.
2. VSS, TSS or TFT.
3. Shift solenoid "A," "B," "C," "D" or "E."
4. Pressure control solenoid "A."
5. Improper fluid level.
6. Input shaft damaged.
7. Forward clutch:
   a. Damaged piston seals.
   b. Damaged clutch piston balance.
   c. Worn friction components.
   d. Damaged return springs.
8. Torque converter one-way clutch slipping.
9. Improper torque converter used to rebuild.

SLIP/CHATTER IN MANUAL 1ST

1. Powertrain control system.
2. Shift solenoid "C."
3. Poor fluid quality.
4. Improper fluid level.
5. Improper line pressures.
6. Valve body:
   a. Not tightened to specifications.
   b. Separator plate damaged.
   c. Contamination.
   d. Valves or springs damaged, improperly assembled, missing, stuck or damaged.
7. Fluid pump:
   a. Not tightened to specifications.
   b. Damaged gasket.
   c. Porosity, cross leaks, ball missing or plugged fluid passages.
8. Forward clutch:
   a. Damaged piston seals.
   b. Damaged clutch piston balance.
   c. Worn friction components.
   d. Damaged return springs.
9. Low one-way clutch worn, damaged or improperly assembled.

SLIP/CHATTER IN MANUAL 2ND

1. Powertrain control system.
2. Shift solenoid "D."
3. Poor fluid quality.
4. Improper fluid level.
5. Improper line pressures.
6. Valve body:
   a. Not tightened to specifications.
   b. Separator plate damaged.
   c. Contamination.
   d. Valves or springs damaged, improperly assembled, missing, stuck or damaged.
7. Fluid pump:
   a. Not tightened to specifications.
   b. Damaged gasket.
   c. Porosity, cross leaks, ball missing or plugged fluid passages.
8. Servo piston, seals or cover damage.
9. Band:
   a. Damaged band.
   b. Servo worn or damaged.
   c. Improper adjustment.
   d. Anchor bolt damaged or worn.
10. Overdrive planetary damage.
11. Forward clutch:
    a. Damaged piston seals.
    b. Damaged clutch piston balance.
    c. Worn friction components.
    d. Damaged return springs.

SLIP/CHATTER IN MANUAL 3RD

1. Improper fluid level.
2. Poor fluid quality.
3. Improper fluid pressures.
4. Fluid pump:
   a. Not tightened to specifications.
   b. Damaged gasket.
   c. Porosity, cross leaks, ball missing or plugged fluid passages.
5. Forward clutch:
   a. Damaged piston seals.
   b. Damaged clutch piston balance.
   c. Worn friction components.
   d. Damaged return springs.

SOFT OR SLIPPING SHIFT, ALL GEARS

1. Powertrain control system.
2. Shift solenoids "A," "B," "C," "D" or "E."
3. TFT, IAT, VFS or VSS.
4. Pressure control solenoid "A."
5. Poor fluid quality.
6. Improper fluid level.
7. Improper line pressures.
8. Valve body:
   a. Not tightened to specifications.
   b. Separator plate damaged.
   c. Contamination.
   d. Valves or springs damaged, improperly assembled, missing, stuck or damaged.
9. Fluid pump:
   a. Not tightened to specifications.
   b. Damaged gasket.
   c. Porosity, cross leaks, ball missing or plugged fluid passages.
10. Intermediate servo seal or retaining ring damaged.
11. Intermediate band:
    a. Damaged band.
    b. Servo worn or damaged.

A10 CHECK GROUND TO SELECTOR LEVER UNIT

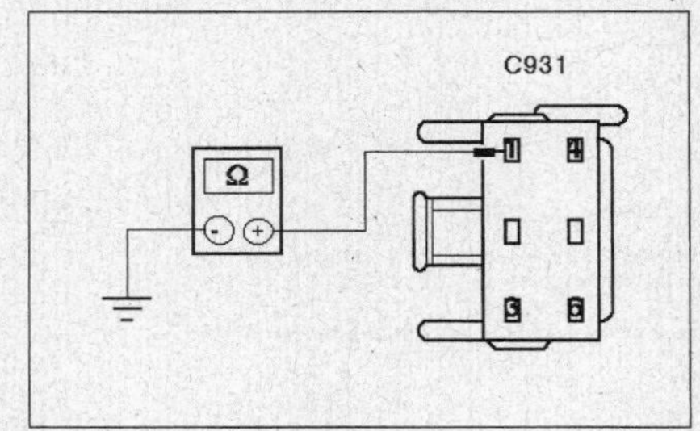

1 Measure resistance between C931, pin 1 (BK) and ground.

- **Is resistance less than 5 ohms?**

→ **Yes**

REPLACE the gearshift lever unit.

→ **No**

REPAIR circuit 31-TA34 between C931, pin 1 and ground for open.

FM5020001785100X

Fig. 3 Test A: Shift Interlock System Inoperative (Part 10 of 13)

A11 CHECK VOLTAGE AT FUSE F8

1 Measure voltage at fuse F8 (30A).

- **Is battery voltage indicated?**

→ **Yes**

Go to «A12».

→ **No**

REPAIR supply circuit to F8 for open.

FM5020001785110X

Fig. 3 Test A: Shift Interlock System Inoperative (Part 11 of 13)

c. Improper adjustment.
d. Anchor bolt damaged or worn.

12. Forward clutch or direct clutch:
    a. Damaged piston seals.
    b. Damaged clutch piston balance.
    c. Worn friction components.
    d. Damaged return springs.
13. Damage to transaxle case.

SOFT/SLIPPING 1-2 SHIFT

1. Powertrain control system.
2. Shift solenoid "D."
3. TSS, VSS or TFT.
4. Poor fluid quality.
5. Improper fluid level.
6. Improper fluid pressures.
7. Valve body:
    a. Not tightened to specifications.
    b. Separator plate damaged.
    c. Contamination.
    d. Valves or springs damaged, improperly assembled, missing, stuck or damaged.
8. Servo seals, piston or cover damage.
9. Band:
    a. Damaged band.
    b. Servo worn or damaged.
    c. Improper adjustment.
    d. Anchor bolt damaged or worn.

SOFT/SLIPPING 2-1 SHIFT

1. Powertrain control system.
2. Shift solenoid "D."
3. VSS, TFT, TSS or TR sensor.
4. Improper line pressures.
5. Valve body:
    a. Not tightened to specifications.
    b. Separator plate damaged.
    c. Contamination.
    d. Valves or springs damaged, improperly assembled, missing, stuck or damaged.
6. Servo piston, seals or cover damaged.
7. Band:
    a. Damaged band.
    b. Servo worn or damaged.
    c. Improper adjustment.
    d. Anchor bolt damaged or worn.

SOFT/SLIPPING 2-3 SHIFT

1. Powertrain control system.
2. Shift solenoid "E."
3. TSS or TFT.
4. Improper line pressures.
5. Valve body:
    a. Not tightened to specifications.
    b. Separator plate damaged.
    c. Contamination.
    d. Valves or springs damaged, improperly assembled, missing, stuck or damaged.
6. Servo seal, piston or cover damage.
7. Band:
    a. Damaged band.
    b. Servo worn or damaged.
    c. Improper adjustment.
    d. Anchor bolt damaged or worn.
8. Direct clutch:
    a. Damaged piston seals.
    b. Damaged clutch piston balance.
    c. Worn friction components.
    d. Damaged return springs.

SOFT/SLIPPING 3-2 SHIFT

1. Powertrain control system.
2. Shift solenoid "E."
3. TFT sensor.
4. Improper line pressures.
5. Valve body:
    a. Not tightened to specifications.
    b. Separator plate damaged.
    c. Contamination.
    d. Valves or springs damaged, improperly assembled, missing, stuck or damaged.
6. Servo piston, seals or cover damaged.
7. Band:
    a. Damaged band.
    b. Servo worn or damaged.
    c. Improper adjustment.
    d. Anchor bolt damaged or worn.

SOFT/SLIPPING 3-4 SHIFT

1. Powertrain control system.
2. Shift solenoids "A" and "C."
3. TFT sensor.
4. Improper fluid pressures.
5. Valve body:
    a. Not tightened to specifications.
    b. Separator plate damaged.
    c. Contamination.
    d. Valves or springs damaged, improperly assembled, missing, stuck or damaged.
6. Forward clutch:
    a. Damaged piston seals.
    b. Damaged clutch piston balance.
    c. Worn friction components.
    d. Damaged return springs.
7. Servo piston, seal or cover damage.
8. Band:
    a. Damaged band.
    b. Servo worn or damaged.
    c. Improper adjustment.
    d. Anchor bolt damaged or worn.

SOFT/SLIPPING 4-3 SHIFT

1. Powertrain control system.
2. Shift solenoids "A" and "C."
3. TFT sensor.
4. Improper fluid pressures.
5. Valve body:
    a. Not tightened to specifications.
    b. Separator plate damaged.
    c. Contamination.
    d. Valves or springs damaged, improperly assembled, missing, stuck or damaged.
6. Forward clutch:
    a. Damaged piston seals.
    b. Damaged clutch piston balance.
    c. Worn friction components.
    d. Damaged return springs.
7. Servo piston, seal or cover damage.

SOME OR ALL SHIFTS MISSING

1. Powertrain control system.
2. Shift solenoids "A," "B," "C," "D" and "E."
3. Pressure control solenoid "A."
4. Poor fluid quality.
5. Improper fluid level.
6. Shift cable or TR sensor damaged or misaligned.
7. Improper line pressures.
8. Valve body:
    a. Not tightened to specifications.
    b. Separator plate damaged.
    c. Contamination.
    d. Valves or springs damaged, improperly assembled, missing, stuck or damaged.
9. Fluid pump:
    a. Not tightened to specifications.
    b. Damaged gasket.
    c. Porosity, cross leaks, ball missing or plugged fluid passages.

A12 CHECK VOLTAGE AT IGNITION SWITCH

1 Ignition switch (C456)

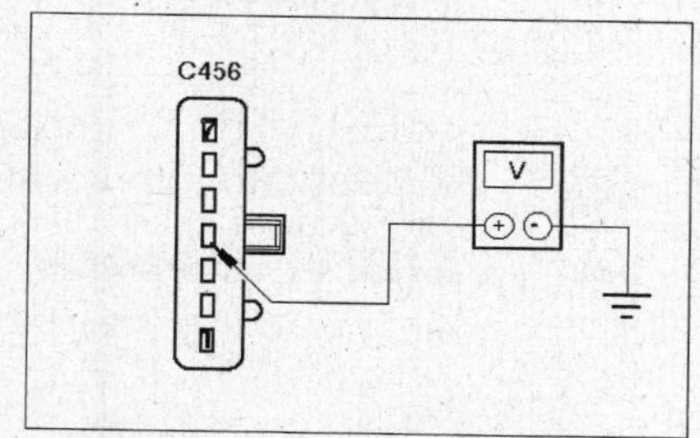

2

Measure the voltage between C456, pin 4 (RD) and ground.

- **Is battery voltage indicated?**

→ **Yes**

Go to «A13».

→ **No**

REPAIR circuit between fuse F8 (30 A) and C456, pin 4 for open.

FM5020001785120X

Fig. 3 Test A: Shift Interlock System Inoperative (Part 12 of 13)

A13 CHECK CIRCUIT 31S-TA34

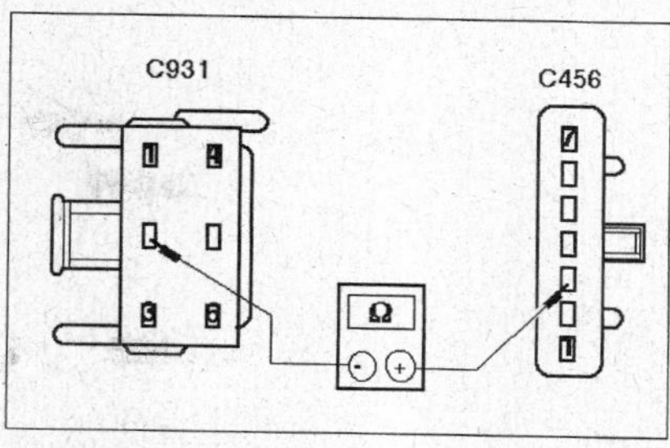

1

Measure resistance between C456, pin 3 (BK/WH) and C931, pin 2 (BK/YE).

- **Is resistance less than 1 ohm?**

→ **Yes**

REPLACE key removal inhibit solenoid.

→ **No**

REPAIR circuit 31S-TA34 between C456, pin 3 and C931, pin 2 for open.

FM5020001785130X

Fig. 3 Test A: Shift Interlock System Inoperative (Part 13 of 13)

10. Direct or forward clutch:
    a. Damaged piston seals.
    b. Damaged clutch piston balance.
    c. Worn friction components.
    d. Damaged return springs.
11. One way clutch worn, damaged or improperly assembled.
12. Servo damage.

TCC ALWAYS APPLIED, STALLS VEHICLE

1. Powertrain control system.
2. Shift solenoids "B" and "C."
3. Valve body:
    a. Not tightened to specifications.
    b. Separator plate damaged.
    c. Contamination.
    d. Valves or springs damaged, improperly assembled, missing, stuck or damaged.
4. Low one-way clutch worn, damaged or assembled improperly.
5. Torque converter internal failure.

TCC CYCLING, SHUDDER OR CHATTER

1. Powertrain control system.
2. Shift solenoids "B" and "C."
3. Poor fluid quality.
4. Valve body:
    a. Not tightened to specifications.
    b. Separator plate damaged.
    c. Contamination.
    d. Valves or springs damaged, improperly assembled, missing, stuck or damaged.
5. Torque converter internal failure.

TCC DOES NOT APPLY

1. Powertrain control system.
2. Shift solenoids "B" and "C."
3. TFT sensor.
4. Improper line pressures.
5. Valve body:
    a. Not tightened to specifications.
    b. Separator plate damaged.
    c. Contamination.
    d. Valves or springs damaged, improperly assembled, missing, stuck or damaged.
6. Fluid pump:
    a. Not tightened to specifications.
    b. Damaged gasket.
    c. Porosity, cross leaks, ball missing or plugged fluid passages.
7. Torque converter internal failure.

TRANSAXLE OVERHEATS

1. Powertrain control system.
2. TFT sensor.
3. Shift solenoid "B."
4. Improper fluid level.
5. Improper line pressures.
6. Valve body:
    a. Not tightened to specifications.
    b. Separator plate damaged.
    c. Contamination.
    d. Valves or springs damaged, improperly assembled, missing, stuck or damaged.
7. Fluid pump:
    a. Not tightened to specifications.
    b. Damaged gasket.
    c. Porosity, cross leaks, ball missing or plugged fluid passages.
8. Case vent damaged.
9. Torque converter internal failure.
10. Restriction in transaxle cooling system.
11. Excessive trailer tow load.
12. Poor engine performance.

MAINTENANCE

Refer to "Lubricant Data" chart in the appropriate chassis chapter of this manual for transmission fluid specifications.

FLUID INSPECTION

If vehicle has been operated at high speed for extended periods of time, in city traffic during hot weather or used to pull a trailer, allow transaxle fluid to cool for 30 minutes before inspecting.

1. Operate vehicle until operating temperature is achieved.
2. Park vehicle on level surface and apply parking brake.
3. Start engine and apply brakes.
4. Move gear selector through each gear range allow transaxle to engage in each gear.
5. Place gear selector in Park position and leave engine running.
6. Remove dipstick and wipe clean.
7. Install dipstick ensuring it is fully seated to filler tube.
8. Remove dipstick and inspect fluid level.
9. Fluid level should appear approximately halfway between MIN and MAX lines on dipstick.

FLUID CHANGE

1. Raise and support vehicle.
2. Position suitable drain pan under transaxle pan.
3. Remove transaxle pan mounting bolts.
4. Separate pan from transaxle case using oil pan separator tool No. 21-179, or equivalent.
5. Clean silicone gasket material from gasket surfaces using Ford Metal Surface Cleaner, or equivalent.
6. Apply .059 inch thick bead of Loctite 5699, or equivalent, around transaxle pan.
7. Install fluid pan and tighten mounting bolts to specifications.

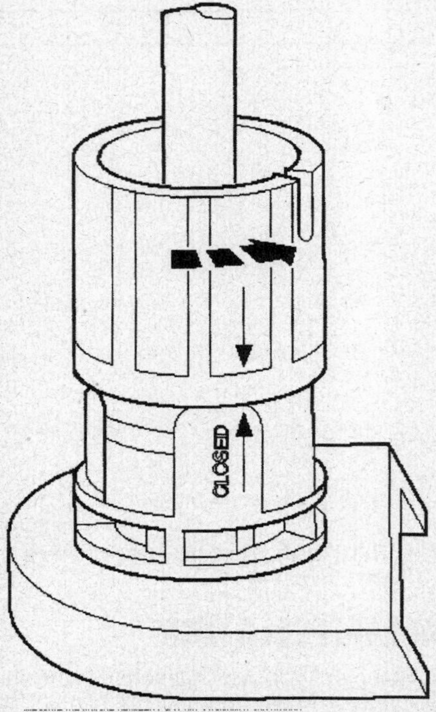

Fig. 4 Selector lever locking sleeve

ADJUSTMENTS

MANUAL LINKAGE INSPECTION

Inspect for improperly adjusted shift linkage. This is done by matching the detents in the shift lever with those in the transaxle. If they match and shift indicator indicates improper gear position, the indicator on the console is improperly adjusted.

SHIFT LINKAGE, ADJUST

1. Apply parking brake.
2. Place shift lever to D position.
3. Raise and support vehicle.
4. Open selector lever locking mechanism by turning counterclockwise, **Fig. 4.** Ensure outer sleeve moves freely after unlocking.
5. Ensure Transaxle Range (TR) sensor alignment mark is in line with selector lever, **Fig. 5.**
6. Close selector lever cable outer sleeve by turning locking mechanism clockwise.
7. Lower vehicle and ensure proper cable adjustment.

IN-VEHICLE REPAIRS

SHIFT CABLE, REPLACE

1. Raise and support vehicle.
2. Support flexible exhaust pipe using suitable mechanics wire.
3. Disconnect front exhaust pipe and disconnect from hanger insulator, **Fig. 6.**
4. Disconnect O_2S2 and remove wiring protection, **Fig. 7.**

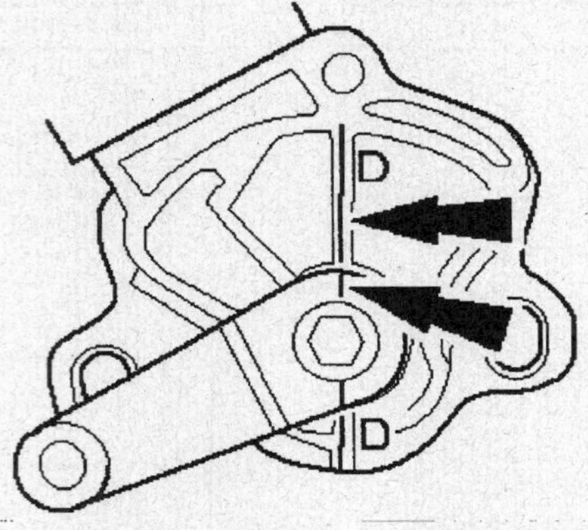

Fig. 5 TR sensor alignment

5. Remove mounting bolts and heat shield.
6. Unclip shift cable.
7. Open cable adjuster by turning cable outer sleeve counterclockwise.
8. Disconnect and remove cable from TR sensor bracket.
9. Lower vehicle and remove floor console as outlined under "Brake Shift Interlock Actuator, Replace."
10. Place shift lever in Park position.
11. Remove shift cable from shift lever and bracket.
12. Remove footwell heater channel.
13. Remove center console front cover.
14. Unclip, remove mounting screws and heater housing cover, **Fig. 8.**
15. Pull carpet and insulation back to access shift cable as required.
16. Attach suitable piece of mechanic's wire to transaxle end of shift cable.
17. Remove shift cable and grommet, **Fig. 9.**
18. Reverse procedure to install. Adjust cable as outlined under "Shift Linkage, Adjust" in "Adjustments" section.

FLEXPLATE, REPLACE

1. Remove transaxle as outlined under "Transaxle, Replace."
2. Hold flexplate in place by installing flexplate locking tool No. T74P-6375-A, or equivalent.
3. Remove mounting bolts and flexplate.
4. If rear crankshaft seal requires replacement, proceed as follows:
   a. Remove crankshaft rear seal using seal removal tool No. T92C-6700-CH, or equivalent.
   b. Ensure crankshaft seal area is free of damage.
   c. Install new oil seal using seal installer tool No. T88P-6701-B1, or equivalent.
5. Reverse procedure to install flexplate. Tighten mounting bolts to specifications.

FLEXPLATE INSPECTION

Inspect flexplate ring gear for damaged, worn or missing teeth, signs of heat damage, distortion or cracking. Replace as required.

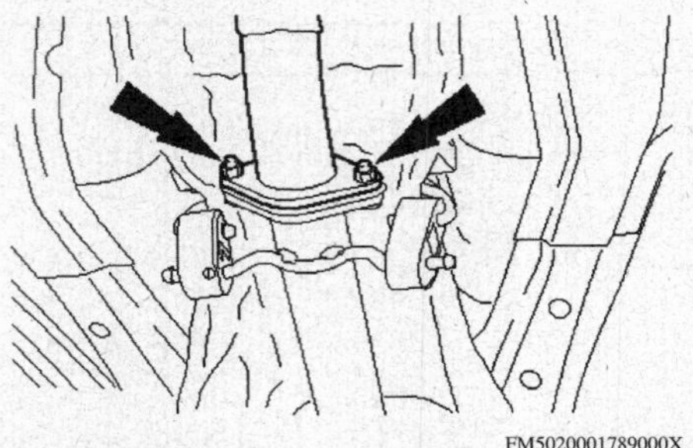

Fig. 6 Exhaust pipe replacement

VALVE BODY, REPLACE

1. Drain transaxle fluid into suitable container as outlined under "Fluid Change."
2. Remove TFT sensor and filter.
3. Remove ground wire bolt, then disconnect and remove solenoid harness, **Fig. 10.**
4. Remove mounting bolts and valve body.
5. Place identification marks on accumulators and springs for installation reference.
6. Remove accumulator pistons and springs.
7. Reverse procedure to install noting the following:
   a. Thinner and longer springs are used for neutral/drive accumulator.
   b. Ensure manual valve is installed to manual control valve shift lever.
   c. Tighten mounting bolts to specifications.

DIGITAL TRANSAXLE RANGE (TR) SENSOR, REPLACE

Removal

1. Disconnect TR sensor and shift cable.
2. Remove manual control lever and TR sensor.

Installation

1. Install TR sensor and align using TR sensor alignment tool No. 307-415, or equivalent.
2. Install manual control lever and tighten mounting bolt to specifications.
3. Place manual control lever to D (3), **Fig. 11.**
4. Ensure marks on manual control lever are aligned with TR sensor alignment marks.
5. Connect shift cable and TR sensor electrical connector.

BRAKE SHIFT INTERLOCK ACTUATOR, REPLACE

1. Remove floor console front cupholders.
2. Remove front console mounting screws.
3. Remove rear cupholder and console mounting nuts.
4. Remove parking brake shroud from parking brake handle.
5. Raise parking brake lever.
6. Place shift lever in neutral position and

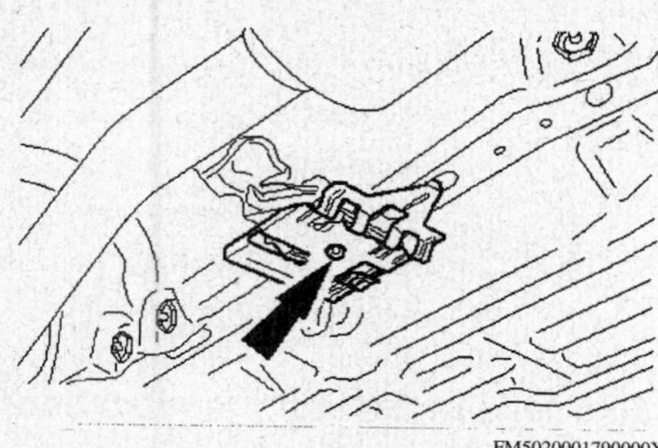

Fig. 7 O_2S2 wiring insulator

remove floor console.
7. Disconnect overdrive cancel switch.
8. Remove shift handle bolt (1) and shift handle (2), **Fig. 12.**
9. Remove shift interlock actuator (3), **Fig. 12.**
10. Reverse procedure to install

TRANSAXLE FLUID COOLER, REPLACE

1. Secure radiator using suitable tie-strap, **Fig. 13.**
2. Remove radiator splash shield.
3. Disconnect horn electrical connector.
4. Remove radiator bracket, **Fig. 14.**
5. Mark position of transaxle feed and return hoses for installation reference.
6. Ensure transaxle fluid is not hot before removing cooler hoses.
7. Disconnect cooler hoses. Plug open ends.
8. **On models equipped with air conditioning,** remove condenser bracket and position condenser aside.
9. **On all models,** remove transaxle fluid cooler.
10. Reverse procedure to install. Ensure transaxle fluid is at proper level.

HALFSHAFT OIL SEAL, REPLACE

1. Hold center strut shaft using suitable hex key, then loosen strut center nuts five turns.
2. Raise and support vehicle.
3. Remove front wheels.
4. Remove tie rod to knuckle nuts.
5. Disconnect tie rod from steering knuckle using separator tool No. 211-001, or equivalent.
6. Disconnect lower suspension arms from steering knuckles.
7. Remove intermediate bearing bracket from righthand halfshaft, **Fig. 15.**
8. Remove left and righthand halfshafts from transaxle using halfshaft removal tool No. T86P-3541-A, or equivalent, noting the following:
   a. Support halfshaft using suitable mechanics wire.
   b. Ensure inner CV joint does not bend more than 18.°
   c. Outer CV joint should not bend more than 45.°
   d. Install suitable plugs into transaxle.
9. Remove seals using seal removal tool No. T94P-77000-B and slide hammer tool No. T50T-100-A, or equivalents.
10. Reverse procedure to install, noting the following:
    a. Install new halfshaft snap rings.
    b. Install new seals using seal installer tool No. T86P-1177-B, or equivalent.
    c. Install new nuts and new intermediate bearing cap.
    d. Tighten to mounting bolts, nuts and screws specifications.
    e. Ensure transaxle fluid is at proper level.

OUTPUT SHAFT SPEED SENSOR (OSS), REPLACE

1. Raise and support vehicle.
2. Disconnect OSS sensor and remove mounting bolt, **Fig. 16.**
3. Remove OSS and allow fluid to drain into suitable container.
4. Inspect OSS bore and O-ring. Service as required.
5. Reverse procedure to install, noting the following:
   a. Lubricate O-ring using suitable petroleum jelly.
   b. Tighten to mounting bolt to specifications.

TURBINE SHAFT SPEED SENSOR (TSS), REPLACE

1. Remove battery and tray.
2. Remove air cleaner and intake tube with resonator.
3. Remove TSS sensor, **Fig. 17.**
4. Inspect OSS bore and O-ring. Service as required.
5. Reverse procedure to install, noting the following:
   a. Lubricate O-ring using suitable petroleum jelly.
   b. Tighten mounting bolt to specifications.

TRANSAXLE

REPLACE

1. Remove battery and tray.
2. Remove air cleaner, intake tube and resonator
3. Disconnect vacuum hoses and position aside, as required.
4. Hold center strut shaft using suitable hex key and loosen strut center nuts five turns.
5. Disconnect TSS, TR sensor and transaxle harness connector
6. Remove two upper starter motor bolts and two upper bellhousing bolts.
7. Support engine using engine support bar and adapters tool No. 303-290, or equivalent.
8. Remove oil filler tube and selector lever cable bracket.
9. Raise and support vehicle, then remove front wheels.
10. Disconnect front exhaust pipe and bracket.
11. Disconnect starter motor electrical connectors.

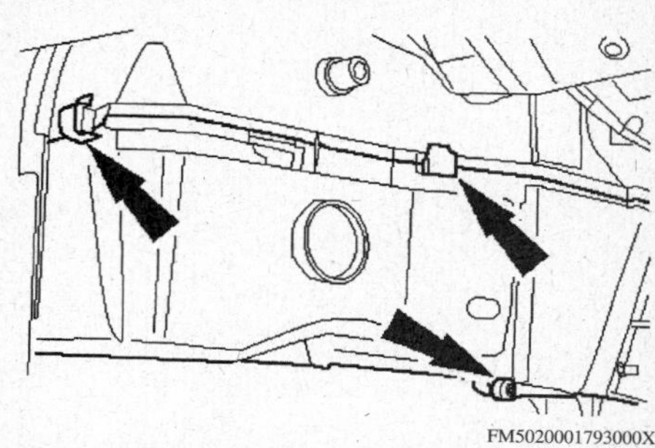

Fig. 8 Heater cover replacement

12. Remove starter motor lower bolt and righthand engine support insulator, **Fig. 18.**
13. Remove tie rod to steering knuckle nuts.
14. Disconnect tie rods from steering knuckles using separator tool No. 211-001, or equivalent.
15. Disconnect lower suspension arms from steering knuckles.
16. Remove righthand halfshaft intermediate bearing cap, **Fig. 15.**
17. Remove left and righthand halfshafts from transaxle using halfshaft removal tool No. T86P-3541-A, or equivalent, noting the following:
    a. Support halfshaft using suitable mechanics wire.
    b. Ensure inner CV joint does not bend more than 18.°
    c. Outer CV joint should not bend more than 45.°
18. Install suitable plugs into transaxle.
19. Disconnect output shaft speed sensor.
20. Mark oil cooler lines for installation reference and remove.
21. Remove torque converter cover.
22. Remove torque converter to flexplate nuts.
23. Remove four upper transaxle to engine mounting bolts. Record bolt locations for installation reference.
24. Remove rear engine mount, **Fig. 19.**
25. Lower engine and transaxle using engine support bar.
26. Remove rear engine mount bracket and oil filler tube.
27. Support transaxle using suitable transmission jack and retaining strap.
28. Remove remaining transaxle to engine mounting bolts. Record bolt locations for installation reference.
29. Separate from engine, lower and remove transaxle.
30. Install torque converter retaining tool No. T97T-7902-A, or equivalent, to bellhousing.
31. Reverse procedure to install noting the following:
    a. Install new self locking nuts.
    b. Install new righthand halfshaft intermediate bearing cap and nuts.
    c. Install new halfshaft snap rings.
    d. Tighten mounting bolts and nuts to specifications.

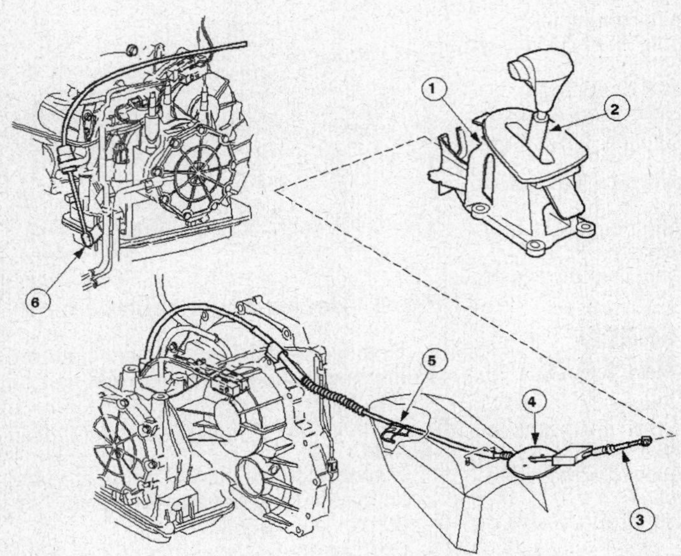

Item	Description
1	Selector lever assembly
2	Selector lever
3	Selector lever cable
4	Selector lever cable grommet
5	Selector lever cable clip
6	Shift shaft lever

FM5020001794000X

Fig. 9 Shift cable components

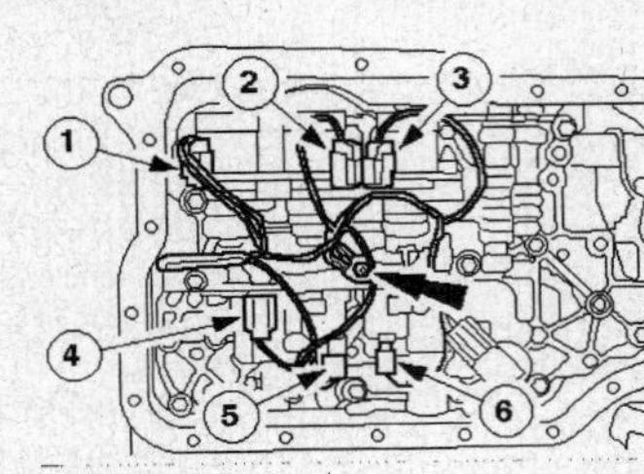

1) Solenoid SSC; Color N (Neutral/White)
2) Solenoid SSE; Color G (Green)
3) Solenoid SSD; Color L (Blue)
4) Solenoid EPC; Color B (Black)
5) Solenoid SSA; Color N (Neutral)
6) Solenoid SSB; Color B (Black)

FM5020001802000X

Fig. 10 Solenoid harness connector identification

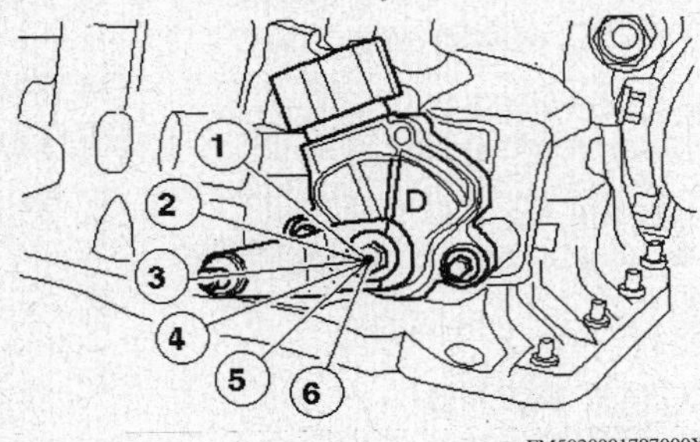

FM5020001797000X

Fig. 11 TR sensor installation

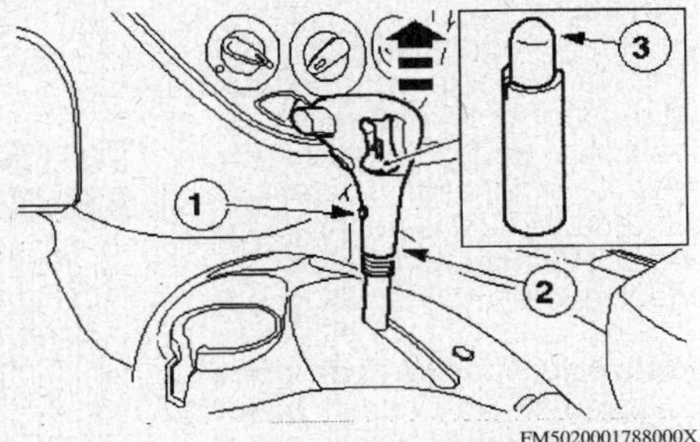

FM5020001788000X

Fig. 12 Brake shift interlock actuator

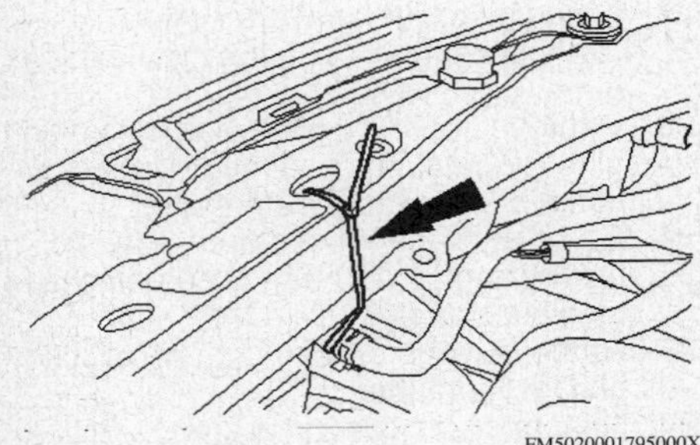

FM5020001795000X

Fig. 13 Radiator support location

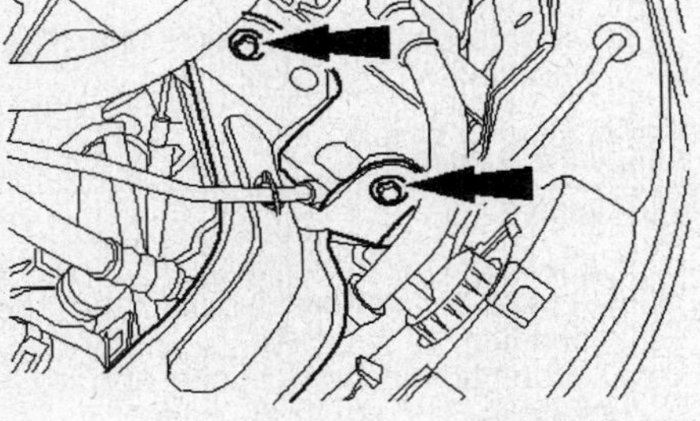

FM5020001796000X

Fig. 14 Radiator bracket location

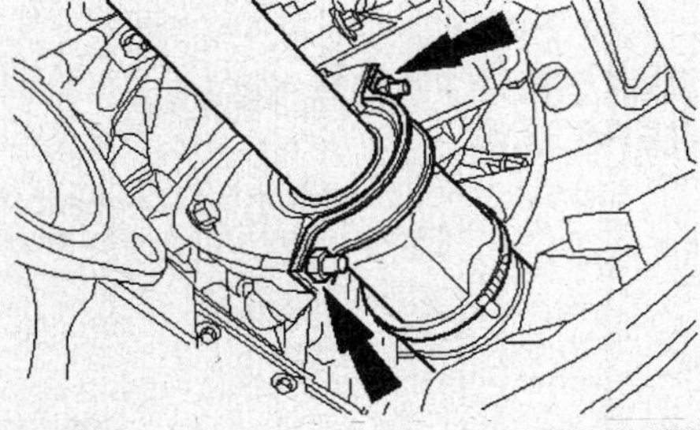

FM5020001798000X

Fig. 15 Intermediate bearing cap removal

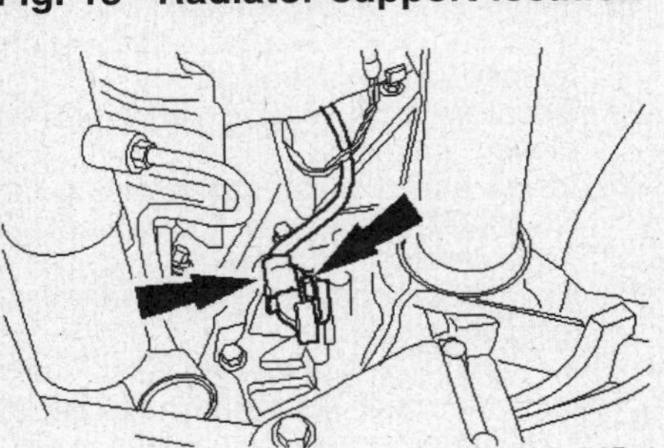

FM5020001799000X

Fig. 16 OSS removal

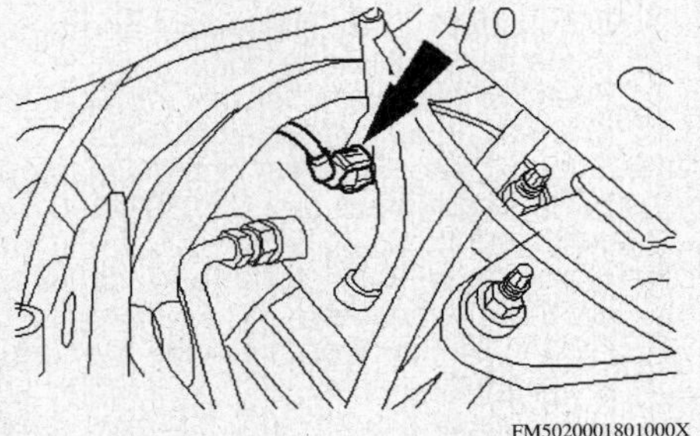

FM5020001801000X

Fig. 17 TSS replacement

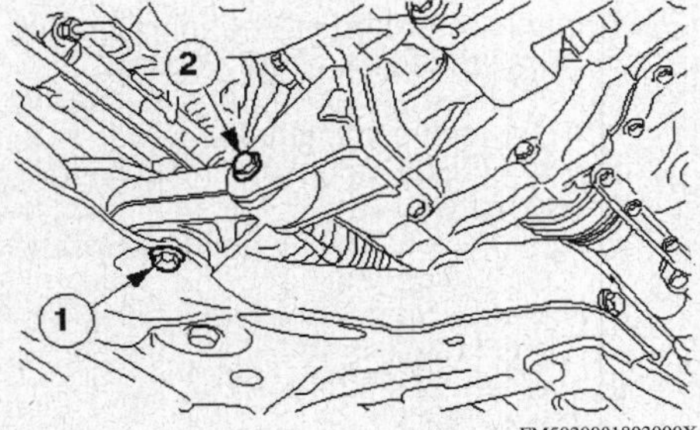

FM5020001803000X

Fig. 18 Righthand engine support insulator replacement

FM5020001804000X

Fig. 19 Rear engine mount replacement

TIGHTENING SPECIFICATIONS

Year	Component	Torque/Ft. Lbs.
2000–01	Converter Housing To Transaxle Case	16
	Cooler Lines	18
	End Cover	16
	Engine Support Insulator, Righthand	35
	Engine To Transaxle	35
	Exhaust Pipe Flange	35
	Final Drive Input Gear Bearing Retainer	332
	Halfshaft Center Bearing, Righthand	18
	Lower Suspension Arm	37
	Manual Control Lever	89①
	Oil Filler Tube	80①
	Oil Pan	62①
	Oil Pump	16
	Oil Pump Case	10
	Output Shaft Speed (OSS) Sensor	89①
	Parking Pawl Cover	10
	Rear Engine Mount	35
	Rear Engine Mount Center	98
	Rear Engine Mounting Bracket	59
	Shifter	10
	Solenoid Body	80①
	Starter Motor	26
	Suspension Strut	35
	Tie Rod End	35
	Torque Converter To Flexplate	27
	Transaxle Range (TR) Sensor	89①
	Turbine Shaft Speed (TSS) Sensor	89①
	Valve Body	80①
	Wiring Harness	89①

① — Inch lbs.

4F50N (AX4N) Automatic Transaxle

NOTE: On Air Bag Equipped Models, Refer To "Air Bag System Precautions" Located In The Front Of This Manual For System Disarming & Arming Procedures.

NOTE: Refer To "Computer Relearn Procedures" Located In The Front Of This Manual When Battery Power To The Computer Has Been Interrupted.

NOTE: Prior To Performing Any Service Operations Listed In This Section, Consult "Technical Service Bulletins" Section For Related Information.

INDEX

PRECAUTIONS

AIR BAG SYSTEMS

Refer to "Air Bag System Precautions" in front of this manual for system disarming and arming procedures.

BATTERY GROUND CABLE

Prior to service, disconnect battery ground cable and isolate as required.

IDENTIFICATION

Transaxle identification tag is located on top of converter housing, **Fig. 1.**

Fig. 1 Transaxle identification tag

DESCRIPTION

The 4F50N (AX4N) automatic transaxle is a four-speed unit with automatic shift control, **Fig. 2.** All upshifting, downshifting, line pressure and torque converter clutch operations are controlled by EEC-V electronic engine control system. transaxle control is separate from engine control strategy in PCM, although some input signals are shared.

TROUBLESHOOTING

BRAKE-SHIFT INTERLOCK SYSTEM

Refer to "AX4S (AXOD-E) Automatic Overdrive Transaxle."

TRANSAXLE

Refer to troubleshooting charts **Figs. 3 through 47.**

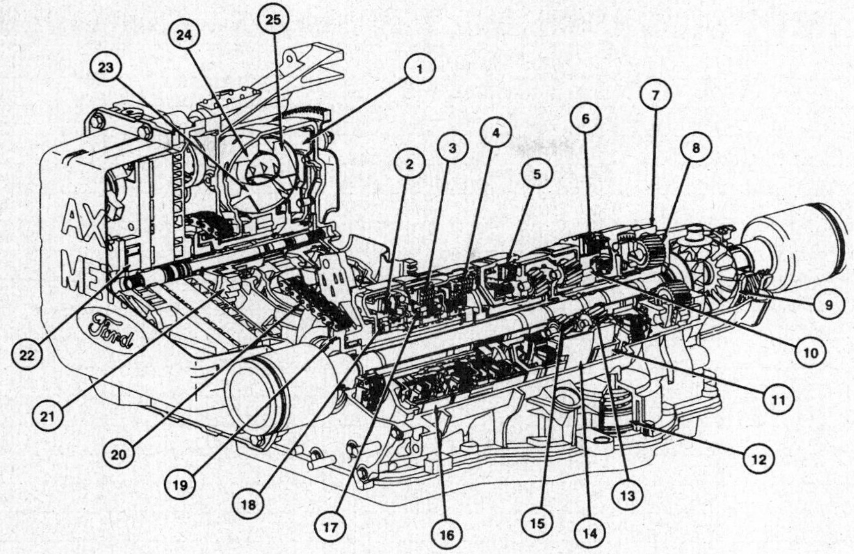

Item	Description
1	Torque Converter
2	Forward Clutch Assy
3	Direct Clutch Assy
4	Intermediate Clutch Assy
5	Reverse Clutch Assy
6	Low/Intermediate Clutch Assy
7	Final Drive Ring Gear
8	Final Drive Gearset
9	Differential Assy
10	Low/Intermediate One-Way Roller Clutch Assy
11	Coast Band
12	Coast Servo Piston

Item	Description
13	Rear Planetary Gearset
14	Rear Planetary Ring Gear
15	Front Planetary Gearset
16	Overdrive Band
17	Direct One-Way Roller Clutch Assy
18	Low One-Way Sprag Clutch
19	Driven Sprocket
20	Drive Chain
21	Drive Sprocket
22	Pump Assy
23	Reactor
24	Impeller
25	Turbine

FM5029601058000X

Fig. 2 Cross-sectional view of transaxle

TROUBLESHOOTING TEST INDEX

Test	Description	Page No.	Fig. No.
201/301	No Forward Engagement	19-58	3
202/302	No Reverse Engagement	19-58	4
203/303	Harsh Reverse Engagement	19-59	5
204/304	Harsh Forward Engagement	19-59	6
205/305	Delayed/Soft Reverse Engagement	19-59	7
206/306	Delayed/Soft Forward Engagement	19-59	8
207/307	No Forward & No Reverse Engagement	19-60	9
208/308	Harsh Forward & Reverse Engagement	19-60	10
209/309	Delayed/Soft Forward & Reverse Engagement	19-60	11
210/310	Some Or All Shifts Missing	19-61	12
211/311	Shift Timing Is Early/Late	19-61	13
212/312	Shift Timing Is Erratic/Hunting	19-61	14
213/313	Shift Feel Is Soft/Slipping	19-62	15
214/314	Shift Feel Is Harsh	19-62	16
215/315	No 1st Gear, Engages In Higher Gear	19-62	17
216/316	No Manual 1st Gear	19-62	18
220/320	No 1–2 Automatic Shift	19-63	19
221/321	No 2–3 Automatic Shift	19-63	20
222/322	No 3–4 Automatic Shift	19-63	21
223/323	No 4–3 Automatic Shift	19-64	22

Continued

TROUBLESHOOTING TEST INDEX—Continued

Test	Description	Page No.	Fig. No.
224/324	No 3–2 Automatic Shift	19-64	23
225/325	No 2–1 Automatic Shift	19-64	24
226/326	Soft/Slipping 1–2 Shift	19-64	25
227/327	Soft/Slipping 2–3 Shift	19-64	26
228/328	Soft/Slipping 3–4 Shift	19-64	27
229/329	Soft/Slipping 4–3 Shift	19-65	28
230/330	Soft/Slipping 3–2 Shift	19-65	29
231/331	Soft/Slipping 2–1 Shift	19-65	30
232/332	Harsh 1–2 Shift	19-65	31
233/333	Harsh 2–3 Shift	19-65	32
234/334	Harsh 3–4 Shift	19-65	33
235/335	Harsh 4–3 Shift	19-65	34
236/336	Harsh 3–2 Shift	19-65	35
237/337	Harsh 2–1 Shift	19-66	36
240/340	No Torque Converter Apply	19-66	37
241/341	Torque Converter Always Applied/Stalls Vehicle	19-66	38
242/342	Torque Converter Cycling/Shudder/Chatter	19-66	39
250/350	No Engine Braking In 1st Gear Manual	19-66	40
251/351	Shift Lever Efforts High	19-67	41
252/352	External Leaks	19-67	42
253/353	Poor Vehicle Performance	19-67	43
254/354	Noise/Vibration In Forward/Reverse	19-67	44
255/355	Engine Will Not Crank	19-67	45
256/356	No Park Range	19-67	46
257/357	Transaxle Overheating	19-67	47

Possible Component	Reference/Action
201 — ELECTRICAL ROUTINE	
Powertrain Control System • Electrical Inputs/Outputs, Vehicle Wiring Harnesses, Powertrain Control Module	• Run On-Board Diagnostics. **Refer to MOTOR'S Domestic Transmission Manual** for diagnosis. Using Rotunda Transmission Tester 007-00130 and Rotunda AX4N Cable and Overlay 007-00117 or equivalent, perform transmission voltage tests If DTC P1700 is present, check for low transaxle fluid level. Then, continue to Hydraulic/Mechanical Routines.
301 — HYDRAULIC/MECHANICAL ROUTINE	
Shift Linkage • Damaged, out of adjustment	• Inspect and service as required. Verify linkage adjustment After servicing linkage, verify TR sensor is properly adjusted.

FM5029801602010X

Fig. 3 Routines 201 & 301: No Forward Engagement (Part 1 of 2)

Possible Component	Reference/Action
Improper Pressures • Low Forward Clutch pressure, low line pressure, low EPC pressure	• Check pressure at line and EPC taps. Perform line pressures and stall speed tests. If pressures are low, check the following possible components: — main control valve body, — pump assembly, — low intermediate clutch assembly, — low intermediate apply tube and seal, N-D accumulator assembly.
Main Control Valve Body • Bolts out of torque specification • Gaskets and separator plate damaged, off location • Manual Control Valve damaged	• Tighten bolts to specification. • Inspect gasket for damage. Replace as required. • Inspect. Service as required.
Fluid Pump Assembly • Bolts out of torque specification • Gaskets and Separator Plate damaged, off location • Porosity/cross leaks/ball missing or leaking • Components damaged	• Tighten bolts to specification. • Inspect for damage. Replace as required. • Inspect for porosity and leaks. Replace as required. • Inspect for damage. Replace as required.
Low Intermediate One-Way Clutch Assembly • DTC P1700 present • Worn, damaged, misassembled • Roller—damaged • Case—damaged • Springs—damaged • Inner/Outer races—damaged	 • Inspect for damage. Service as required. • Inspect for damage. Service as required. • Inspect for damage. Service as required. • Inspect for damage. Service as required. • Inspect for damage. Service as required.
Low Intermediate Clutch Assembly • Seals, Piston—damaged • Fluid Tubes and Seals, Band, Anchor Pin—worn, damaged, loose, leaking • Friction elements—damaged, clearance check incorrect • Wave Spring—damaged, missing	 • Perform Air Pressure Tests • Inspect. Replace as required. • Inspect. Service as required. • Inspect. Service as required.
Low/Intermediate Accumulator Assembly • Piston Seals—damaged, leaking • Shaft or Bore—damaged, leaking	 • Inspect for damage. Service as required. • Inspect for damage. Service as required.

FM5029801602020X

Fig. 3 Routines 201 & 301: No Forward Engagement (Part 2 of 2)

Possible Component	Reference/Action
202 — ELECTRICAL ROUTINE	
Powertrain Control System • Electrical Inputs/Outputs, Vehicle Wiring Harnesses, Powertrain Control Module	• Run On-Board Diagnostics. **Refer to MOTOR'S Domestic Transmission Manual** for diagnosis. Using Rotunda Transmission Tester 007-00130 and Rotunda AX4N Cable and Overlay 007-00117 or equivalent, perform transmission voltage tests. If DTC P1700 is present, check for low transaxle fluid level. Then, continue to Hydraulic/Mechanical Routines.
302 — HYDRAULIC/MECHANICAL ROUTINE	
Shift Linkage (Internal/External) • Damaged or out of adjustment	• Inspect and service as required. Verify linkage adjustment. After servicing linkage, verify that the TR sensor is properly adjusted.

FM5029801603010X

Fig. 4 Routines 202 & 302: No Reverse Engagement (Part 1 of 2)

Possible Component	Reference/Action
Improper Pressures • Low line pressure, low EPC pressure	• Perform Line Pressure and Stall Speed Tests **Check pressure at line and EPC taps.** 401 for specifications. If pressures are low, check the following possible components: — main control valve body, — pump assembly, — reverse clutch assembly, — reverse apply tube and seal, N-R accumulator assembly.
Main Control Valve Body • Bolts out of torque specification • Gasket and Separator Plate—damaged, off location • Manual Control Valve, Springs—stuck, damaged	• Tighten bolts to specification. • Inspect for damage. Replace as required. • Inspect for damage. Service as required.
Pump Assembly • Bolts out of torque specification • Gasket damaged • Porosity/cross leaks, pump assembly leaking, plugged hole • Components damaged	• Tighten bolts to specification. • Inspect for damage and replace as required. • Replace pump assembly. • Inspect for damage and replace as required.
Reverse Clutch Assembly • Seals, Piston, Springs damaged • Clearance Check out of specification • Friction Elements damaged or worn • Reverse Apply Tube and Seal leaking or incorrectly installed	• Perform Air Pressure Tests • Inspect for damage. Service as required. • Inspect. Perform clearance checks. • Inspect for damage. Service as required. • Inspect. Service as required.
N-R Accumulator Assembly • Seals, Piston—damaged, leaking • Shaft or Bore—damaged, leaking	• Inspect for damage. Service as required. • Inspect for damage. Service as required.

FM5029801603020X

Fig. 4 Routines 202 & 302: No Reverse Engagement (Part 2 of 2)

Possible Component	Reference/Action
• EPC Solenoid—stuck, damaged	• Inspect for damage. Perform Pinpoint Test E. **Refer to MOTOR'S Domestic Transmission Manual.** Service as required. Activate solenoid using Rotunda Transmission Tester 007-00130 and Rotunda AX4N Cable and Overlay 007-00117 or equivalent. If solenoid operation cannot be felt when placing hand on solenoid, replace solenoid. Inspect O-rings for damage. Service as required.
Reverse Clutch Assembly • Piston damaged, stuck • Friction Elements damaged, worn • Return Spring Piston damaged, worn, stuck • Reverse Apply Tube leaking or incorrectly installed • Wave Spring—damaged, worn	• Perform Air Pressure Tests • Inspect for damage. Service as required. • Inspect for damage. Service as required. • Inspect for damage. Service as required. • Inspect for damage. Service as required. • Inspect for damage. Service as required.
N-R Accumulator Assembly • Stuck, damaged, components missing • Shaft or Bore—damaged	• Inspect for damage. Service as required. • Inspect for damage. Service as required.

FM5029801604020X

Fig. 5 Routines 203 & 303: Harsh Reverse Engagement (Part 2 of 2)

Possible Component	Reference/Action
205 — ELECTRICAL ROUTINE	
Powertrain Control System • Electrical Inputs/Outputs, Vehicle Wiring Harnesses, Powertrain Control Module (PCM), EPC Solenoid, TFT, TR Sensor, Internal Harness	• Run On-Board Diagnostic. Refer to MOTOR's "Domestic Transmission Manual" for diagnosis. Perform Pinpoint Tests B, D and E using the Rotunda Transmission Tester 007-00130 and Rotunda AX4N Cable and Overlay 007-00117 and Rotunda Transmission Range (TR) Sensor Cable (MLP-B Cable) 007-00127 or (TRS-E Cable) 007-00111 or equivalent. Service as required. Clear codes. Road Test and rerun On-Board Diagnostic.
305 — HYDRAULIC/MECHANICAL ROUTINE	
Shift Linkage (Internal/External) • Damaged, out of adjustment	• Inspect and service as required. Verify linkage adjustment. After servicing linkage, verify that the TR sensor is properly adjusted.
Improper Pressures • Low line pressure, low EPC pressure	• Check pressure at line and EPC taps. Perform line pressure and stall speed tests. If pressures are low, check the following possible components: Main Control Valve Body, Pump Assembly, Reverse Clutch Assembly, Reverse Clutch Tube
Main Controls • Bolts out of torque specification • Gaskets and Separator Plate—damaged, off location • Manual Control Valve, Main Regulator Valve, Converter Drain Back Valve, Springs—missing, damaged, misassembled	• Tighten bolts to specification. • Inspect for damage. Replace as required. • Inspect for damage. Service as required.
Pump Assembly • Bolts out of torque specification • Porosity/cross leaks, oil pump leaking • Gaskets damaged, off location • EPC Solenoid—stuck, damaged • Components damaged	• Tighten bolts to specification. • Replace pump assembly. • Inspect for damage and replace as required. • Inspect for damage. Perform Pinpoint Test E. Service as required. Activate solenoid using Rotunda Transmission Tester 007-00130 and Rotunda AX4N Cable and Overlay 007-00117 or equivalent. If solenoid operation cannot be felt when placing hand on solenoid, replace solenoid. Inspect O-rings for damage. Service as required. • Inspect for damage and replace as required.
Reverse Clutch Assembly • Seals, Piston, worn, damaged • Wave Spring damaged • Friction elements damaged or worn • Return Spring and Piston damaged or worn • Reverse Apply Tube or Seal leaking	• Perform Air Pressure Tests • Inspect for damage. Service as required. • Inspect for damage. Service as required. • Inspect for damage. Service as required. • Inspect for damage. Service as required. • Inspect. Service as required.
Neutral-Drive Accumulator • Piston, Seals damaged, leaking	• Inspect for damage. Service as required.

FM5029801606000X

Fig. 7 Routines 205 & 305: Delayed/Soft Reverse Engagement

Possible Component	Reference/Action
203 — ELECTRICAL ROUTINE	
Powertrain Control System • Electrical Inputs/Outputs, Vehicle Wiring Harnesses, Powertrain Control Module (PCM), EPC Solenoid, TFT, TSS, TP Sensor, MAF Sensor, VSS, IAT Sensor, ISC and PSP sensor, Engine rpm.	• Run On-Board Diagnostic. **Refer to MOTOR'S Domestic Transmission Manual** for diagnosis. Perform Pinpoint Tests B, E, and F using the Rotunda Transmission Tester 007-00130 and Rotunda AX4N Cable and Overlay 007-00117 or equivalent. Service as required. Clear codes. Road Test and rerun On-Board Diagnostic.
303 — HYDRAULIC/MECHANICAL ROUTINE	
Improper Pressures • High line pressure, high EPC pressure	• Perform Line Pressure and Stall Speed Tests Check pressure at line and EPC pressure taps. If high, check the following possible components: Main Control Valve Body, Fluid Filter and Fluid Pan Screen Ring.
Main Control • Bolts out of torque specification • Gasket and Separator Plate—damaged, off location • B1 Check Ball, Pressure Failsafe Valve, Main Regulator Valve—stuck, damaged	• Tighten bolts to specification. • Inspect for damage. Replace as required. • Inspect for damage. Service as required.
Pump Assembly • Bolts out of torque specification • Gasket damaged, off location • Components damaged	• Tighten bolts to specification. • Inspect for damage and replace as required. • Inspect for damage and replace as required.

FM5029801604010X

Fig. 5 Routines 203 & 303: Harsh Reverse Engagement (Part 1 of 2)

Possible Component	Reference/Action
204 — ELECTRICAL ROUTINE	
Powertrain Control System • Electrical Inputs/Outputs, Vehicle Wiring Harnesses, Powertrain Control Module (PCM), TP, MAF, IAT, ISC, VSS, PSP, EPC, TFT, TSS, Internal Harness	• Run On-Board Diagnostic. Refer to MOTOR Domestic Transmission Manual[18] for diagnosis. Perform Pinpoint Tests B, E and F using the Rotunda Transmission Tester 007-00130 and Rotunda AX4N Cable and Overlay 007-00117 or equivalent. Service as required. Clear codes, road test and rerun On-Board Diagnostic.
304 — HYDRAULIC/MECHANICAL ROUTINE	
Improper Pressures • High line pressure, high EPC pressure • Check pressure at line and EPC pressure taps. If pressures are high, check the following possible components: Main Controls, Pump Assembly.	• Perform Line Pressure Tests
Main Controls • Bolts out of torque specification • Gaskets and Separator Plate—damaged, off location • Main Regulator Valve, Pressure Failsafe Valve • B3 Check Ball—damaged, missing	• Tighten bolts to specification. • Inspect for damage. Replace as required. • Inspect. Service as required. • Inspect for damage and contamination. Service as required.
Pump Assembly • Bolts out of torque specification • Gaskets and Separator—damaged, off location • EPC Solenoid—stuck, damaged	• Tighten bolts to specification. • Inspect for damage. Replace as required. • Inspect for damage and contamination. Service as required. Activate solenoid using transmission tester. If solenoid operation cannot be felt when placing hard on solenoid, replace solenoid. Inspect O-rings for damage. Service as required.
Low Intermediate Clutch Assembly • Seals, Piston—worn, damaged • Friction element—damaged • Wave Spring—damaged	• Perform Air Pressure Tests • Inspect for damage. Replace as required. • Inspect for damage. Replace as required.
Neutral-to-Drive Accumulator • Piston stuck, seals or springs, missing, damaged	• Check for damage. Replace as required.

FM5029801605000X

Fig. 6 Routines 204 & 304: Harsh Forward Engagement

Possible Component	Reference/Action
206 — ELECTRICAL ROUTINE	
Powertrain Control System • Electrical Inputs/Outputs, Vehicle Wiring Harnesses, Powertrain Control Module (PCM), EPC Solenoid, TFT, TR Sensor, Internal Harness	• Run On-Board Diagnostic. Refer to MOTOR's "Domestic Transmission Manual" for diagnosis. Perform Service Manual Pinpoint Tests B, D and E using the Rotunda Transmission Tester 007-00130 and Rotunda AX4N Cable and Overlay 007-00117 and Rotunda Transmission Range (TR) Sensor Cable (MLP-B Cable) 007-00127 or (TRS-E Cable) 007-00111 or equivalent. Service as required. Clear codes. Road Test and rerun On-Board Diagnostic.
306 — HYDRAULIC/MECHANICAL ROUTINE	
Shift Linkage • Damaged, out of adjustment	• Inspect and service as required. Verify linkage adjustment. After servicing linkage, verify that the TR sensor is properly adjusted.
Improper Pressures • Low line pressure, low EPC pressure	• Check pressure at line and EPC taps. Perform line pressure and stall speed tests. If pressures are low, check the following possible components: Main Control Valve Body and Pump Assembly, Low/Intermediate Clutch.
Main Control Valve Body • Bolts out of torque specification • Gaskets and Separator Plate—damaged, off location • Main Regulator Valve—stuck, damaged, missing	• Tighten bolts to specification. • Inspect for damage. Replace. • Inspect. Service as required.
Pump Assembly • Bolts out of torque specification • Porosity/cross leaks • Gaskets damaged, off location • Components damaged • EPC Solenoid—stuck, damaged	• Tighten bolts to specification. • Inspect for porosity and leaks. Replace as required. • Inspect for damage and replace as required. • Inspect for damage and replace as required. • Inspect for damage. Perform Pinpoint Test E. Refer to MOTOR'S Domestic Transmission Manual. Service as required. Activate solenoid using Rotunda Transmission Tester 007-00130 and Rotunda AX4N Cable and Overlay 007-00117 or equivalent. If solenoid operation cannot be felt when placing hand on solenoid, replace solenoid. Inspect O-rings for damage. Service as required.
Low/Intermediate Clutch Assembly Perform Air Pressure Tests as described. • Seals, Piston—worn, damaged • Low/Intermediate Fluid Tubes and Seals—damaged, loose, leaking • Band, Anchor Pins—damaged • Wave Spring—damaged	• Inspect seals and piston for damage. Replace as required. • Inspect for damage. Service as required. • Inspect for damage. Service as required. • Inspect for damage. Service as required.
Neutral-Drive Accumulator • Seals, Bore—damaged, stuck, leaking	• Inspect for damage. Service as required.

FM5029801607000X

Fig. 8 Routines 206 & 307: Delayed/Soft Forward Engagement

Possible Component	Reference/Action
207—ELECTRICAL ROUTINE	
No Electrical Concerns	
307—HYDRAULIC/MECHANICAL ROUTINE	
Fluid	
• Improper level—low	• Adjust fluid to proper level.
Halfshaft	
• Splines—worn, damaged	• Inspect for damage. Service as required.
• Shaft—misassembled, incorrect	
Shift Linkage (Internal/External)	
• Damaged, out of adjustment, misassembled	• Inspect. Service as required. Verify linkage adjustment. After servicing linkage, verify that the TR sensor is properly adjusted.
Improper Pressures	
• Low line pressure, low EPC pressure	• Perform Line Pressure and Stall Tests
•	• Check pressure at line pressure and EPC tap. If pressures are low, check the following possible components: Fluid Filter and Seal Assembly, Main Control, Pump Assembly, Reverse Clutch Assembly, Forward Clutch Assembly.
Fluid Filter and Seal Assembly	
• Plugged, damaged	• Replace filter and seal assembly.
Main Controls	
• Bolts out of torque specification	• Tighten bolts to specification.
• Gaskets and Separator Plate—damaged, off location	• Inspect for damage. Replace as required.
• Pump Shaft—broken	• Inspect. Service/replace as required.
• Forward Clutch Control Valve, Manual Valve, Springs—stuck, damaged	• Inspect for damage. Service as required.
• Main Regulator Valve (only if line pressure is out of specification)—damaged	• Inspect for damage. Service as required.
• Components—damaged	• Inspect for damage. Service as required.
Pump Assembly	
• Bolts out of torque specification	• Tighten bolts to specification.
• Gaskets—damaged, off location	• Inspect for damage. Replace as required.
• Porosity/cross leaks—leaking, plugged hole	• Replace pump assembly.
• Components damaged	• Inspect for damage. Replace as required.
Support Assembly—Driven Sprocket	
• Bolts out of torque specification	• Tighten bolts to specification.
• Seals missing or damaged	• Inspect seals. Replace as required.
• Seal grooves damaged	• Inspect for damage. Service as required.
Forward Clutch Assembly	
• Seals, Piston and Seal Assembly	• Perform Air Pressure Tests
•	• Inspect for damage. Service as required.
• Wave Spring—missing	• Inspect for spring. Service as required.
• Check Balls	• Inspect for mislocation, poor seating and damage. Replace cylinder as required.
• Piston—cracked	• Inspect piston. Replace as required.
• Friction elements—worn, damaged	• Check for abnormal wear, damage. Replace as required.
• Retaining Ring missing	• Inspect for ring/damage. Service as required.

FM5029801608010X

Fig. 9 Routines 207 & 307: No Forward & No Reverse Engagement (Part 1 of 2)

Possible Component	Reference/Action
208—ELECTRICAL ROUTINE	
Powertrain Control System	
• Electrical inputs/outputs, vehicle wiring harnesses, Powertrain Control Module (PCM), TP, MAF, VSS, IAT, PSP, TFT, TR sensor, internal harness, EPC solenoid, engine rpm, ISC.	• Run On-Board Diagnostics. Refer to MOTOR's "Domestic Transmission Manual" for diagnosis. Perform Pinpoint Tests B, D and E using Rotunda Transmission Tester 007-00130 and Rotunda AX4N Cable and Overlay 007-00117 and Rotunda Transmission Range (TR) Sensor Cable (MLP-B Cable) 007-00127 or (TRS-E Cable) 007-00111 or equivalent. Service as required. Clear codes, road test and rerun On-Board Diagnostics.
308—HYDRAULIC/MECHANICAL ROUTINE	
Fluid	
• Improper level	• Adjust fluid to proper level.
Improper Pressures	
• High line pressure, high EPC pressure	• Perform Line Pressure Tests.
•	• Check pressure at line and EPC pressure taps. If high, check the following possible components: Main Controls, Fluid Filter and Seal.
Main Controls	
• Bolts out of torque specification	• Tighten bolts to specification.
• Gaskets and Separator—damaged, off location	• Inspect for damage. Replace as required.
• B1, B4 Check Ball, Pressure Failsafe Valve, Main Regulator Valve—stuck, damaged, missing	• Inspect for damage. Service as required.
• Line Modulator Valve—stuck open	• Inspect for damage. Service as required.
Pump Assembly	
• Bolts out of torque specification	• Tighten bolts to specification.
• Gaskets—damaged, off location	• Inspect for damage. Replace as required.
• Components—damaged	• Inspect for damage. Replace as required.
• EPC Solenoid—stuck, damaged	• Inspect for damage and contamination. Service as required. Activate solenoid using transmission tester. If solenoid operation cannot be felt when placing hand on solenoid, replace solenoid. Inspect O-rings for damage. Service as required.
Forward Clutch Assembly	
• Seals, Piston—worn, damaged	• Inspect for damage. Service as required.
• Friction elements—damaged, worn	• Inspect for damage. Service as required.
• Return Spring Piston—damaged, worn	• Inspect for damage. Service as required.
• Check Ball—missing	• Inspect for damage. Service as required.
• Wave Spring—damaged	• Inspect for damage. Service as required.

FM5029801609000X

Fig. 10 Routines 208 & 308: Harsh Forward & Reverse Engagement

Possible Component	Reference/Action
Low One-Way Clutch Assembly	
• Worn, damaged, misassembled	• Inspect for damage. Service as required.
Output Shaft	
• Splines damaged	• Inspect for damage. Service as required.
Other Possible Components	
• Turbine Shafts	• Inspect for damage. Service as required.
• Chain	• Inspect for damage. Service as required.
• Flywheel	• Inspect for damage. Service as required.
• Sprockets	• Inspect for damage. Service as required.
• Front Sun Gear and Shell Assembly	• Inspect for damage. Service as required.
• Front or Rear Planetaries	• Inspect for damage. Service as required.
• Rear Sun Drum and Race Assembly	• Inspect for damage. Service as required.
• Final Drive Assembly	• Inspect for damage. Service as required.
• Oil Pump Shaft Assembly	• Inspect for damage. Service as required.

FM5029801608020X

Fig. 9 Routines 207 & 307: No Forward & No Reverse Engagement (Part 2 of 2)

Possible Component	Reference/Action
209—ELECTRICAL ROUTINE	
Powertrain Control System	
• Electrical inputs/outputs, vehicle wiring harnesses, Powertrain Control Module (PCM), TFT, TR Sensor, internal harness, EPC solenoid.	• Run ON-Board Diagnostics. Refer to MOTOR's "Domestic Transmission Manual" for diagnosis. Perform Pinpoint Tests B, D and E using Rotunda Transmission Tester 007-00130 and Rotunda AX4N Cable and Overlay 007-00117 and Rotunda Transmission Range (TR) Sensor Cable (MLP-B Cable) 007-00127 or (TRS-E Cable) 007-00111 or equivalent. Service as required. Clear codes, road test and rerun On-Board Diagnostics.
309—HYDRAULIC/MECHANICAL ROUTINE	
Fluid	
• Improper level	• Adjust fluid to proper level.
• Condition	• Inspect. Service as required.
Shift Linkage (Internal/External)	
• Damaged, out of adjustment	• Inspect. Service as required. Verify linkage adjustment. After servicing linkage, verify that the TR sensor is properly adjusted.
Improper Pressures	
• Low line pressure, low EPC pressure	• Perform Line Pressure and Stall Tests.
•	• Check pressure at line and EPC tap. If pressures are low, check the following possible components: Main Control, Pump Assembly.
Fluid Filter and Seal Assembly	
• Plugged—damaged, not properly seated	• Replace filter and seal assembly.
• Filter Seal—damaged	
Main Controls	
• Bolts out of torque specification	• Tighten bolts to specification.
• Gaskets and Separator Plate—damaged, off location	• Inspect for damage. Replace as required.
• Seals, Manual Valve, Main Regulator Valve, Line Modulator Valve, Springs—missing, damaged or misassembled	• Inspect for damage. Service as required.
Pump Assembly	
• Bolts out of torque specification	• Tighten bolts to specification.
• Gaskets—damaged, off location	• Inspect for damage. Replace as required.
• Porosity/Cross Leaks—leaking	• Replace pump assembly.
• Components damaged	• Inspect for damage. Replace as required.
• EPC Solenoid—stuck, damaged	• Inspect for damage. Replace as required. Activate solenoid using Rotunda Transmission Tester 007-00130 and Rotunda AX4N Cable and Overlay 007-00117. If solenoid operation cannot be felt when placing hand on solenoid, replace solenoid. Inspect O-rings for damage. Service as required.
Forward Clutch Assembly	
• Assembly	• Perform Air Pressure Tests.
• Seals, Piston—damaged, worn	• Inspect seals for damage. Service as required.
• Check Ball—missing, damaged	• Inspect for mislocation, poor seating and damage. Replace cylinder as required.
• Piston—cracked	• Inspect piston. Replace as required.
• Friction elements—damaged, worn	• Check for abnormal wear, damage. Replace as required.

FM5029801610000X

Fig. 11 Routines 209 & 309: Delayed/Soft Forward & Reverse Engagement

Possible Component	Reference/Action
210 — ELECTRICAL ROUTINE	
Powertrain Control System • Electrical Inputs/Outputs, Vehicle Wiring Harnesses, Powertrain Control Module (PCM), Shift Solenoids, (SS1, SS2, SS3), TP, MAF, VSS, TR Sensor, Internal Wiring Harness.	• Run On-Board Diagnostic. Refer to MOTOR's "Domestic Transmission Manual" for diagnosis. Perform Service Manual Pinpoint Tests A and D using the Rotunda Transmission Tester 007-00130 and Rotunda AX4N Cable and Overlay 007-00117 and the Rotunda Transmission Range (TR) Sensor Cable (MLP-B Cable) 007-00127 or (TRS-E Cable) 007-00111 or equivalent. Service as required. Clear codes. Road Test and rerun On-Board Diagnostic. If DTC P1700 is present, check for low transmission fluid level.
310 — HYDRAULIC/MECHANICAL ROUTINE	
Fluid • Improper level • Condition	• Adjust fluid to proper level. • Inspect Fluid Condition.
Shift Linkage (Internal/External) • Damaged, out of adjustment	• Inspect and service as required. Verify linkage adjustment. After servicing linkage, verify that the TR sensor is properly adjusted.
Vehicle Speed Input • Speedometer Gear—DRIVE—damaged • Speedometer Gear—DRIVEN—Gear and Shaft Assembly—damaged • Differential Assembly—damaged or missing • Speedometer DRIVE GEAR—damaged	• Refer to Disassembly and Assembly for teardown information on these gears. Also refer to the appropriate shift routines as described at the end of this routine.
Filter and Seal Assembly • Plugged, missing	• Inspect. Service as required.
Apply and Release Fluid Tubes • Damaged, missing • Seal or O-ring—damaged	• Inspect for damage. Service as required. • Inspect for damage. Service as required.
Forward Support—Driven Sprocket • Seals—damaged • Holes—blocked	• Inspect for damage. Service as required. • Inspect for damage. Service as required.
Planetary Gear Sets • Damaged	• Inspect for damage. Service as required.
One-Way Clutch Assembly • Damaged	• Inspect for damage. Service as required.
Other Components • Clutches • Output Shafts (Differential) • Overdrive Band • Powerflow Components	• Inspect for damage. Service as required. • Inspect for damage. Service as required. • Inspect for damage. Service as required. • Inspect for damage. Service as required.
Go to Reference/Action • Shift Concern: No 1-2 • Shift Concern: No 2-3 • Shift Concern: No 3-4 • Shift Concern: No 4-3 • Shift Concern: No 3-2 • Shift Concern: No 2-1	• For further diagnosis, refer to the appropriate shift routine(s): • Routine 220/320 • Routine 221/321 • Routine 222/322 • Routine 223/323 • Routine 224/324 • Routine 225/325

FM5029801611000X

Fig. 12 Routines 210 & 310: Some Or All Shifts Missing

Possible Component	Reference/Action
Filter and Seal Assembly • Plugged, missing	• Inspect. Service as required.
Apply and Release Fluid Tubes • Damaged, missing • Seal or O-ring—damaged	• Inspect for damage. Service as required. • Inspect for damage. Service as required.

FM5029801612020X

Fig. 13 Routines: 211 & 311: Shift Timing Is Early/Late (Part 2 of 2)

Possible Component	Reference/Action
211 — ELECTRICAL ROUTINE	
Powertrain Control System • Electrical Inputs/Outputs, Vehicle Wiring Harnesses, Powertrain Control Module (PCM), Shift Solenoids (SS1, SS2, SS3), TP, MAF, VSS, IAT, ECT, TFT, Internal Wire Harness, EPC Solenoid	• Perform Shift Point Road Test and Torque Converter Clutch Operation Test. • Run On-Board Diagnostic. Refer to MOTOR's "Domestic Transmission Manual" for diagnosis. Perform Pinpoint Tests A, B and E using the Rotunda Transmission Tester 007-00130 and Rotunda AX4N Cable and Overlay 007-00117 or equivalent. Service as required. Clear codes. Road Test and rerun On-Board Diagnostic.
311 — HYDRAULIC/MECHANICAL ROUTINE	
Other • Tire size or chain ratio—change, Speedometer Gear	• Refer to the specification decal and verify vehicle has original equipment. Changes in tire size and chain ratio will affect shift timing.
Fluid • Improper level	• Adjust fluid to proper level.
Shift Linkage • Damaged, out of adjustment	• Inspect. Service as required. Verify linkage adjustment. After servicing linkage, verify that the TR sensor is properly adjusted.
Main Controls • Bolts out of torque specification • Gaskets and Separator Plate—damaged, off location • Valves, Accumulators, Seals, Springs, Clips—damaged, missing, misassembled	• Tighten bolts to specification. • Inspect for damage. Replace. • Inspect for damage and contamination. Service as required. • Refer to the appropriate shift for further diagnosis: • Shift Concern: Soft/Slipping 1-2 Routine 226/326 • Shift Concern: Soft/Slipping 2-3 Routine 227/327 • Shift Concern: Soft/Slipping 3-4 Routine 228/328 • Shift Concern: Soft/Slipping 4-3 Routine 229/329 • Shift Concern: Soft/Slipping 3-2 Routine 230/330 • Shift Concern: Soft/Slipping 2-1 Routine 231/331
Front Support—Driven Sprocket • Seals—damaged • Holes—blocked	• Inspect for damage. Service as required. • Inspect for damage. Service as required.
Planetary Gear Sets • Damaged	• Inspect for damage. Service as required.
One-Way Clutch Assembly • Damaged	• Inspect for damage. Service as required.
Other Components • Clutches • Output Shaft (differential) • Overdrive Band • Powerflow Components	• Inspect for damage. Service as required. • Inspect for damage. Service as required. • Inspect for damage. Service as required. • Inspect for damage. Service as required.
Vehicle Speed Input • Speedometer Gear—DRIVE—damaged • Speedometer Gear—DRIVEN—Gear and Shaft Assembly, damaged • Differential Assembly—damaged • Speedometer DRIVE GEAR—damaged	• Refer to Disassembly for teardown information on these gears. Also refer to the appropriate shift routines as noted under Main Controls.

FM5029801612010X

Fig. 13 Routines 211 & 311: Shift Timing Is Early/Late (Part 1 of 2)

Possible Component	Reference/Action
212 — ELECTRICAL ROUTINE	
Powertrain Control System • Electrical Inputs/Outputs, Vehicle Wiring Harnesses, Powertrain Control Module (PCM), TCC and Shift Solenoids (SS1, SS2, SS3), TP, VSS, ECT, IAT, MAF, TR, TFT Sensors, Internal Wire Harness.	• Perform Shift Point Road Test and Torque Converter Clutch Operation Test. • Run On-Board Diagnostic. Refer to MOTOR's "Domestic Transmission Manual" for diagnosis. Perform Service Manual Pinpoint Tests A, B, C, D and F using the Rotunda Transmission Tester 007-00130 and Rotunda AX4N Cable and Overlay 007-00117 and the Rotunda Transmission Range (TR) Sensor Cable (MLP-B Cable) 007-00127 or (TRS-E Cable) 007-00111 or equivalent. Service as required. Clear codes. Road Test and rerun On-Board Diagnostic.
312 — HYDRAULIC/MECHANICAL ROUTINE	
Fluid • Improper level • Condition	• Adjust fluid to proper level. • Inspect. Service as required.
Shift Linkage (Internal/External) • Damaged, out of adjustment	• Inspect. Service as required. Verify linkage adjustment. After servicing linkage, verify that the TR sensor is properly adjusted.
Main Control Valve Body • Bolts out of torque specification • Gaskets and Separator Plate—damaged, off location • Valves, Accumulators, Seals, Clips, Check Ball—stuck, damaged, contaminated	• Tighten bolts to specification. • Inspect for damage. Replace as required. • Inspect for damage. Service as required.
Vehicle Speed Input • Speedometer Gear—DRIVE—damaged • Speedometer Gear—DRIVEN—Gear and Shaft Assembly, damage • Differential Assembly—damaged or missing • Speedometer DRIVE GEAR—damaged	• Refer to Disassembly and Assembly for teardown information on these gears. Also refer to the appropriate shift routines as noted below.
Torque Converter Clutch •	• Refer to Torque Converter Cycling (Routine 242/342).
Front Support—Driven Sprocket • Seals—damaged • Holes—blocked	• Inspect for damage. Service as required. • Inspect for damage. Service as required.
Planetary Gear Sets • Damaged	• Inspect for damage. Service as required.
One-Way Clutch Assembly • Damaged	• Inspect for damage. Service as required.
Other Components • Clutches • Output Shaft (differential) • Overdrive Band • Powerflow Components	• Inspect for damage. Service as required. • Inspect for damage. Service as required. • Inspect for damage. Service as required. • Inspect for damage. Service as required.

FM5029801613010X

Fig. 14 Routines 212 & 312: Shift Timing Is Erratic/Hunting (Part 1 of 2)

Possible Component	Reference/Action
Filter and Seal Assembly • Plugged, missing	• Inspect. Service as required.
Apply and Release Oil Tubes • Damaged, missing • Seal or O-ring—damaged	• Inspect for damage. Service as required. • Inspect for damage. Service as required.
For Diagnosis Related to a Specific Shift • Shift Concern: No 1-2 • Shift Concern: No 2-3 • Shift Concern: No 3-4 • Shift Concern: No 4-3 • Shift Concern: No 3-2 • Shift Concern: No 2-1 • Shift Concern: Soft/Slip 1-2 • Shift Concern: Soft/Slip 2-3 • Shift Concern: Soft/Slip 3-4 • Shift Concern: Soft/Slip 4-3 • Shift Concern: Soft/Slip 3-2 • Shift Concern: Soft/Slip 2-1 • Shift Concern: Harsh 1-2 • Shift Concern: Harsh 2-3 • Shift Concern: Harsh 3-4 • Shift Concern: Harsh 4-3 • Shift Concern: Harsh 3-2 • Shift Concern: Harsh 2-1	• Refer to the appropriate routine for further diagnosis: • Routine 220/320 • Routine 221/321 • Routine 222/322 • Routine 223/323 • Routine 224/324 • Routine 225/325 • Routine 226/326 • Routine 227/327 • Routine 228/328 • Routine 229/329 • Routine 230/330 • Routine 231/331 • Routine 232/332 • Routine 233/333 • Routine 234/334 • Routine 235/335 • Routine 236/336 • Routine 237/337

FM5029801613020X

Fig. 14 Routines 212 & 312: Shift Timing Is Erratic/ Hunting (Part 2 of 2)

Possible Component	Reference/Action
213 — ELECTRICAL ROUTINE	
Powertrain Control System • Electrical Inputs/Outputs, Vehicle Wiring Harnesses, Powertrain Control Module (PCM), EPC Solenoid, MAF, TP, ECT, IAT, TFT, Internal Harness, TSS.	• Perform Shift Point Road Test as described under Road Test Vehicle. • Run On-Board Diagnostic. Refer to MOTOR's "Domestic Transmission Manual" for diagnosis. Perform Service Manual Pinpoint Tests B, E and F using the Transmission Tester 007-00130 and Rotunda AX4N Cable and Overlay 007-00117 or equivalent. Service as required. Clear codes. Road Test and rerun On-Board Diagnostic.
313 — HYDRAULIC/MECHANICAL ROUTINE	
Fluid • Improper level • Condition	• Adjust fluid to proper level. • Inspect Fluid Condition.
Filter and Seal Assembly • Damaged, partially plugged	• Inspect for damage. Service as required.
Shift Linkage (Internal/External) • Damaged, out of adjustment	• Inspect. Service as required. Verify linkage adjustment. After servicing linkage, verify that the TR sensor is properly adjusted.
Improper Pressures • Low line pressure, low EPC pressure	• Check pressures at line and EPC taps. If pressures are low or all shifts are soft/slipping, go to Main Control.

FM5029801614010X

Fig. 15 Routines 213 & 313: Shift Feel Is Soft/ Slipping (Part 1 of 2)

Possible Component	Reference/Action
	• If pressures are OK and a specific shift is soft/slipping, refer to the following chart. **Soft/Slipping Shift** 1-2, **Routine** 226/326 **Soft/Slipping Shift** 2-3, **Routine** 227/327 **Soft/Slipping Shift** 3-4, **Routine** 228/328 **Soft/Slipping Shift** 4-3, **Routine** 229/329 **Soft/Slipping Shift** 3-2, **Routine** 230/330 **Soft/Slipping Shift** 2-1, **Routine** 231/331
Main Controls • Bolts out of torque specification • Gaskets and Separator Plate—damaged, off location • Line Modulator Valve, 2-3 Capacity Modulator Valve, Accumulator/Regulator Valve, Main Regulator Valve, Check Balls, 3-2 Shift Timing Valve, Clips, Springs—damaged, missing	• Tighten bolts to specification. • Inspect for damage. Replace as required. • Inspect. Service as required.
Pump Assembly • Bolts out of torque specification • Gaskets and Separator—damaged, off location • EPC Solenoid—stuck, damaged	• Tighten bolts to specification. • Inspect for damage. Replace as required. • Inspect for damage and contamination. Service as required. Activate solenoid using Rotunda Transmission Tester 007-00130 and Rotunda AX4N Cable and Overlay 007-00117 or equivalent. If solenoid operation cannot be felt when placing hand on solenoid, replace solenoid. Inspect O-rings for damage. Service as required.
Front Support Assembly—Drive • Damaged	• Inspect for damage. Service as required.
Apply and Release Oil Supply Tubes • Damaged, blocked • Seal—leaking	• Inspect for damage. Service as required. • Inspect for damage. Service as required.

FM5029801614020X

Fig. 15 Routines 213 & 313: Shift Feel Is Soft/ Slipping (Part 2 of 2)

Possible Component	Reference/Action
214 — ELECTRICAL ROUTINE	
Powertrain Control System • Electrical Inputs/Outputs, Vehicle Wiring Harnesses, Powertrain Control Module (PCM), EPC Solenoid, MAF, TP, VSS, ECT, IAT, PSP, TFT, TR Sensor, Internal Wire Harness and Shift Solenoid No. 3 (SS3), A/C	• Run On-Board Diagnostic. Refer to MOTOR's "Domestic Transmission Manual" for diagnosis. Perform Pinpoint Tests A, B, D and E using the Rotunda Transmission Tester 007-00130 and Rotunda AX4N Cable and Overlay 007-00117 and Rotunda Transmission Range (TR) Sensor Cable (MLP-B Cable) 007-00127 or (TRS-E Cable) 007-00111 or equivalent. Service as required. Clear codes. Road Test and rerun On-Board Diagnostic.
314 — HYDRAULIC/MECHANICAL ROUTINE	
Fluid • Improper level	• Adjust fluid to proper level.
Improper Pressures • High line pressure High EPC pressure	• Check pressures at line and EPC taps. Perform Line Pressure Test. If pressures are high or all shifts are harsh, go to Main Control Valve Body. • If pressures are OK and a specific shift is harsh, refer to the appropriate shift routine in the following chart: **Harsh Shift** 1-2, **Routine** 232/332 **Harsh Shift** 2-3, **Routine** 233/333 **Harsh Shift** 3-4, **Routine** 234/334 **Harsh Shift** 4-3, **Routine** 235/335 **Harsh Shift** 3-2, **Routine** 236/336 **Harsh Shift** 2-1, **Routine** 237/337

FM5029801615010X

Fig. 16 Routines 214 & 314: Shift Feel Is Harsh (Part 1 of 2)

Possible Component	Reference/Action
Main Control Valve Body • Bolts out of torque specification • Gaskets and Separator Plate—damaged, off location • 2-3 Capacity Modulator Valve, Main Regulator Valve, Line Modulator Valve, 3-2 Timing Valve, Springs, Clips, Check Balls—stuck, damaged	• Tighten bolts to specification. • Inspect for damage. Replace as required. • Inspect. Service as required.
Pump Assembly • Bolts out of torque specification • Gaskets and Separator—damaged, off location • EPC Solenoid—stuck or damaged	• Tighten bolts to specification. • Inspect for damage. Replace as required. • Inspect for damage, contamination. Service as required. Activate solenoid using Rotunda Transmission Tester 007-00130 and Rotunda AX4N Cable and Overlay 007-00117. If solenoid operation cannot be felt when placing hand on solenoid, replace solenoid. Inspect O-rings for damage. Service as required.

FM5029801615020X

Fig. 16 Routines: 214 & 314: Shift Feel Is Harsh (Part 2 of 2)

Possible Component	Reference/Action
215 — ELECTRICAL ROUTINE	
Powertrain Control System • Electrical Inputs/Outputs, Vehicle Wiring Harnesses, Powertrain Control Module (PCM), Shift Solenoids, (SS1, SS2, SS3), VSS Sensor, Internal Wire Harness	• Run On-Board Diagnostic. Refer to MOTOR's "Domestic Transmission Manual" for diagnosis. Perform Service Manual Pinpoint Tests A using the Rotunda Transmission Tester 007-00130 and Rotunda AX4N Cable and Overlay 007-00117 or equivalent. Service as required. If DTC P1700 is present, check for low transmission fluid level, Then, continue to Hydraulic/Mechanical Routines. Clear codes. Road test and rerun on-board diagnostic.
315 — HYDRAULIC/MECHANICAL ROUTINE	
Main Control Valve Body • Bolts out of torque specification • Gaskets and Separator Plate—damaged, off location • Shift Valves, Forward Clutch Control Valve, Springs, Clips—stuck, damaged, missing, misassembled • Shift Solenoid—stuck, damaged • For diagnosis related to a specific gear, use the Transmission Tester to determine gear.	• Tighten bolts to specification. • Inspect for damage. Replace as required. • Inspect. Service as required. • Inspect for damage. Perform Pinpoint Test A. Service as required. Activate solenoid using transmission tester. If solenoid operation cannot be felt when placing hand on solenoid, replace solenoid. Inspect O-rings for damage. Service as required. • Refer to the following routines: **No Shift** 1-2, **Routine** 220/320 **No Shift** 2-3, **Routine** 221/321 **No Shift** 3-4, **Routine** 222/322
Mechanical • Fluid tubes—damaged • Bands, clutches or seals damaged or worn	• Inspect. Service as required. • Inspect. Service as required.

FM5029801616000X

Fig. 17 Routines 215 & 315: No 1st Gear, Engages In Higher Gear

Possible Component	Reference/Action
216 — ELECTRICAL ROUTINE	
Powertrain Control System • Electrical Inputs/Outputs, Vehicle Wiring Harnesses, Powertrain Control Module	• Run On-Board Diagnostics. Refer to MOTOR's "Domestic Transmission Manual" for diagnosis. Using Rotunda Transmission Tester 007-00130 and Rotunda AX4N Cable and Overlay 007-00117 or equivalent, perform transmission functional tests. If DTC P1700 is present, check for low transaxle fluid level. Then, continue to Hydraulic/Mechanical Routines.

FM5029801617010X

Fig. 18 Routines 216 & 316: No Manual 1st Gear (Part 1 of 2)

Possible Component	Reference/Action
316 — HYDRAULIC/MECHANICAL ROUTINE	
Shift Linkage (Internal/External)	
• Damaged or out of adjustment	• Inspect and service as required. Verify linkage adjustment. After servicing linkage, verify that the TR sensor is properly adjusted.
Improper Pressures	
• Low line pressure, low EPC pressure	• Check pressure at line and EPC pressure taps. Perform Line Pressure Test If pressures are low, check the following possible components: Main Control Valve Body.
Main Control Valve Body	
• Bolts out of torque specification	• Tighten bolts to specification.
• Gaskets and Separator Plate—damaged, off location	• Inspect for damage. Replace as required.
• Manual Control Valve, Manual Downshift Valve, Springs, Shift Valves, Clips—stuck, damaged, missing	• Inspect for damage. Service as required.
• B8 Check Ball damaged, missing	• Inspect for damage. Service as required.
Low/Intermediate One-Way Clutch Assembly	
• DTCs P1784, P1785 present	
• Worn, damaged, misassembled	• Inspect for damage. Service as required.
• Roller—damaged	• Inspect for damage. Service as required.
• Case—damaged	• Inspect for damage. Service as required.
• Springs—damaged	• Inspect for damage. Service as required.
• Inner/Outer races—damaged	• Inspect for damage. Service as required.

FM5029801617020X

Fig. 18 Routines 216 & 316: No Manual 1st Gear (Part 2 of 2)

Possible Component	Reference/Action
Pump Assy	
• Porosity/Cross Leaks	• Inspect. Replace as required.
• Gasket damaged—off location	• Inspect for damaged. Replace as required.
• Component damaged	• Inspect for damage, missing ball. Replace pump assembly if required.
1-2 Accumulator Assembly	
	• Perform Air Pressure Tests
• Piston Seals, Springs—damaged, missing	• Inspect for damage. Service as required.
Support Assembly—Driven Sprocket	
• Seals—damaged, missing • Holes blocked	• Inspect for damage, missing or blockage. Service as required.
Low One-Way Clutch Assembly	
• Not overrunning, damaged	• Inspect for damage. Replace as required.
Intermediate Clutch Assembly	
	• Perform Air Pressure Tests
• Seals—damaged	• Inspect for damage. Replace as required.
• Piston—damaged	• Inspect for damage. Replace as required.
• Check ball missing, damaged	• Inspect for damage. Replace as required.
• Friction—damaged, worn	• Inspect for damage. Replace as required.
• Cylinder Hub Lube Grooves—blocked, damaged	• Inspect for damage. Replace as required.
• Return Spring Assembly—damaged	• Inspect for damage. Replace as required.
Front Planet Carrier	
• Damaged	• Inspect for damage. Service as required.

FM5029801618020X

Fig. 19 Routines 220 & 320: No 1–2 Automatic Shift (Part 2 of 2)

Possible Component	Reference/Action
Support Assembly—Driven Sprocket	
• Seals—damaged, missing, holes blocked	• Inspect for damage. Service as required.
Direct One-Way Clutch	
• Not holding, damaged	• Inspect for damage. Replace as required.
Direct Clutch Assembly	
	• Perform Air Pressure Tests.
• Seals—damaged	• Inspect for damage. Replace as required.
• Piston—damaged	• Inspect for damage. Replace as required.
• Friction plates damaged or worn	• Inspect for damage. Replace as required.
• Check Ball not seating	• Inspect for damage. Replace as required.
• Return Spring Assembly—damaged	• Inspect for damage. Replace as required.
2-3 Accumulator	
• Pistons, Seals—leaking, damaged	• Inspect for damage. Service as required.
• Rod or Bore, Spring—damaged	• Inspect for damage. Service as required.

FM5029801619020X

Fig. 20 Routines 221 & 321: No 2–3 Automatic Shift (Part 2 of 2)

Possible Component	Reference/Action
220 — ELECTRICAL ROUTINE	
Powertrain Control System	
• Electrical Inputs/Outputs, Vehicle Wiring Harnesses, Powertrain Control Module (PCM), Shift Solenoids, (SS1, SS2), TR Sensor, Internal Wire Harness NOTE: If SS1 is ON, it equals a third gear start.	• Run On-Board Diagnostic. Refer to MOTOR's "Domestic Transmission Manual" for diagnosis. Perform Pinpoint Tests A and D using the Rotunda Transmission Tester 007-00130 and Rotunda AX4N Cable and Overlay 007-00117 and Rotunda Transmission Range (TR) Sensor Cable (MLP-B Cable) 007-00127 or (TRS-E Cable) 007-00111 or equivalent as described. If DTC P1700 is present, check for low transaxle fluid level. Then, continue to Hydraulic/Mechanical Routines and service. Clear codes. Road Test and rerun On-Board Diagnostic.
320 — HYDRAULIC/MECHANICAL ROUTINE	
Improper Pressures	
• Line pressure, EPC pressure	• Check pressure at line, EPC and intermediate clutch taps. Perform Line Pressure Test. If not OK, check Main Control Valve Body.
Main Control Valve Body	
• Bolts out of torque specification	• Tighten bolts to specification.
• Gaskets and Separator Plate—damaged, off location	• Inspect for damage. Replace as required.
• 1-2 Shift Valve, Springs, Clips—loose, stuck, missing, misassembled	• Inspect. Service as required.
• SS1 and SS2 not functioning properly	• Activate solenoid using Rotunda Transmission Tester 007-00130 and Rotunda AX4N Cable and Overlay 007-00117. If solenoid operation cannot be felt when placing hand on solenoid, replace solenoid. Inspect O-rings for damage. Service as required.

FM5029801618010X

Fig. 19 Routines 220 & 320: No 1–2 Automatic Shift (Part 1 of 2)

Possible Component	Reference/Action
221 — ELECTRICAL ROUTINE	
Powertrain Control System	
• Electrical Inputs/Outputs, Vehicle Wiring Harnesses, Powertrain Control Module (PCM), Shift Solenoid (SS1), Internal Wire Harness	• Run On-Board Diagnostic. Refer to MOTOR's "Domestic Transmission Manual" for diagnosis. Perform Pinpoint Test A, using the Rotunda Transmission Tester 007-00130 and Rotunda AX4N Cable and Overlay 007-00117 or equivalent. Service as required. Clear codes. Road Test and rerun On-Board Diagnostic.
321 — HYDRAULIC/MECHANICAL ROUTINE	
Improper Pressures	
• Line pressure, EPC pressure	• Check pressure at EPC and line taps. Perform Line Pressure Test. If not OK, check the Main Control Valve Body.
Main Control Valve Body	
• Bolts out of torque specification	• Tighten bolts to specification.
• Gaskets and Separator Plate—damaged, off location	• Inspect for damage. Replace as required.
• 1-2 Shift Valve, 2-3 Shift Valve, 2-3 Capacity Modulator Valve—stuck, damaged	• Inspect. Service as required.
• B8 Check Ball—damaged, missing	• Inspect for damage. Service as required.
• SS1 damaged	• Activate solenoid using Rotunda Transmission Tester 007-00130 and Rotunda AX4N Cable and Overlay 007-00117 or equivalent. If solenoid operation cannot be felt when placing hand on solenoid, replace solenoid. Inspect O-rings for damage. Service as required.
Low Intermediate Servo Assembly	
• Wrong Apply Rod, Servo Bore or Piston damaged, Piston Seals damaged, Return Spring or Retaining Clip damaged, missing	• Inspect for damage. Service as required.

FM5029801619010X

Fig. 20 Routines 221 & 321: No 2–3 Automatic Shift (Part 1 of 2)

Possible Component	Reference/Action
222 — ELECTRICAL ROUTINE	
Powertrain Control System	
• Electrical Inputs/Outputs, Vehicle Wiring Harnesses, Powertrain Control Module (PCM), Shift Solenoid SS3, TR Sensor, Internal Wire Harness, VSS	• Run On-Board Diagnostic. Refer to MOTOR's "Domestic TRansmission Manual" for diagnosis. Perform Pinpoint Tests A and D using the Rotunda Transmission Tester 007-00130 and Rotunda AX4N Cable and Overlay 007-00117 and Rotunda Transmission Range (TR) Sensor Cable (MLP-B Cable) 007-00127 or (TRS-E Cable) 007-00111 or equivalent. Service as required. Clear codes. Road Test and rerun On-Board Diagnostic.
322 — HYDRAULIC/MECHANICAL ROUTINE	
Overdrive Servo Assembly	
	• Perform Air Pressure Tests.
• Apply Rod incorrect	• Inspect. Replace if incorrect.
• Servo Bore or Piston damaged, incorrect	• Inspect for damage. Service as required.
• Piston Seals—damaged, missing	• Inspect for damage. Service as required.
• Return Spring Retaining Clip—broken, missing	• Inspect for damage. Service as required.
• Wave Spring—damaged	• Inspect for damage. Service as required.
Main Control Valve Body	
• Bolts out of torque specification	• Tighten bolts to specification.
• Gaskets and Separator Plate—damaged, off location	• Inspect for damage. Replace as required.
• 3-4 Shift Valve, Line Modulator Valve, Forward Clutch Control Valve—stuck, damaged	• Inspect. Service as required.
• SS3 not functioning properly	• Activate solenoid using Rotunda Transmission Tester 007-00130 and Rotunda AX4N Cable and Overlay 007-00117 or equivalent. If solenoid operation cannot be felt when placing hand on solenoid, replace solenoid. Inspect O-rings for damage. Service as required.
3-4 Accumulator Assembly	
	• Perform Air Pressure Tests.
• Accumulator Piston—damaged	• Inspect for damage. Service as required.
• Piston Seals—missing, damaged	• Inspect for damage. Service as required.
• Springs—damaged	• Inspect for damage. Service as required.
• Rod or Bore—damaged	• Inspect for damage. Service as required.
OD Band	
• OD Band—damaged, worn, misassembled	• Inspect for damage. Replace as required.
• Direct One-Way Clutch Assembly damaged	• Inspect for damage. Replace as required.

FM5029801620000X

Fig. 21 Routines 222 & 322: No 3–4 Automatic Shift

Possible Component	Reference/Action
223 — ELECTRICAL ROUTINE	
Powertrain Control System Perform Torque Converter Clutch Operation Test as described under • Electrical Inputs/Outputs, Vehicle Wiring Harnesses, Powertrain Control Module (PCM), Shift Solenoid (SS3), TR sensor, Internal Wiring Harness, VSS	• Run On-Board Diagnostic. Refer to MOTOR's "Domestic Transmission Manual" for diagnosis. Perform Pinpoint Tests A and D using the Rotunda Transmission Tester 007-00130 and Rotunda AX4N Cable and Overlay 007-00117 and Rotunda Transmission Range (TR) Sensor Cable (MLP-B Cable) 007-00127 or (TRS-E Cable) 007-00111 or equivalent. Service as required. Clear codes. Road Test and rerun On-Board Diagnostic.
323 — HYDRAULIC/MECHANICAL ROUTINE	
Component Special Note •	• Perform manual 4-3 pull in. If OK, Go to overdrive servo assembly in this routine. If not OK, Go to Main Control in this routine.
Main Control • Bolts out of torque specification • Gaskets and Separator Plate—damaged, off location • 3-4 Shift Valve—stuck, damaged • SS3—damaged	• Tighten bolts to specification. • Inspect for damage. Replace. • Inspect. Service as required. • Inspect for damage and contamination. Service as required. Activate solenoid using Rotunda Transmission Tester 007-00130 and Rotunda AX4N Cable and Overlay 007-00117 or equivalent. If solenoid operation cannot be felt when placing hand on solenoid, replace solenoid. Inspect O-rings for damage. Service as required.
OD Band • OD Band—damaged, worn, misassembled	• Inspect for damage. Replace as required.
Overdrive Servo Assembly • Apply Rod—incorrect • Servo Bore or Piston—damaged • Piston Seals—damaged, missing • Return Spring Retaining Clip—broken, missing	• Inspect Rod. • Inspect for damage. Service as required. • Inspect for damage. Service as required. • Inspect for damage. Service as required.

FM5029801621000X

Fig. 22 Routines 223 & 323: No 4–3 Automatic Shift

Possible Component	Reference/Action
Low One-Way Clutch Assembly • Not Overrunning—damaged	• Inspect for damage. Replace as required.
Forward Clutch Assembly • Check Ball leaking	• Inspect for damage. Service as required.
Intermediate Clutch Assembly • Damaged, burnt • Check Ball damaged • Seals, damaged	• Inspect for damage. Service as required. • Inspect for damage. Service as required. • Inspect for damage. Service as required.

FM5029801622020X

Fig. 23 Routines 224 & 324: No 3–2 Automatic Shift (Part 2 of 2)

Possible Component	Reference/Action
226 — ELECTRICAL ROUTINE	
No Electrical Concerns	
326 — HYDRAULIC/MECHANICAL ROUTINE	
Improper Pressures • Line pressure, EPC pressure •	• Perform Line Pressure and Stall Speed Test. • Check pressure at line and EPC taps. If not OK, check the following possible component: Main Control
Main Control • Bolts out of torque specification • Gaskets and Separator Plate—damaged, off location • 1-2 Shift Valve, Springs, Clips—loose, stuck, missing, misassembled	• Tighten bolts to specification. • Inspect gaskets for damage. Replace. • Inspect. Service as required.

FM5029801624010X

Fig. 25 Routines 226 & 326: Soft/Slipping 1–2 Shift (Part 1 of 2)

Possible Component	Reference/Action
227 — ELECTRICAL ROUTINE	
No Electrical Concerns	
327 — HYDRAULIC/MECHANICAL ROUTINE	
Improper Pressures • Line pressure, EPC pressure •	• Perform Line Pressure and Stall Speed Tests. • Check pressure at EPC and line taps. If not OK, check the following possible component: Main Control
Main Control • Bolts out of torque specification • Gaskets and Separator Plate—damaged, off location • 1-2 Shift Valve, 2-3 Shift Valve, Line Modulator Valve, 2-3 Capacity Modulator Valve, Spring—stuck, damaged • B8 Check Ball—damaged, missing or hole damaged	• Tighten bolts to specification. • Inspect gaskets and replace. • Inspect. Service as required. • Inspect for damage. Service as required.
Support Assembly—Drive Sprocket • Seals—damaged, missing, holes partially blocked	• Inspect for damage. Service as required.
Direct Clutch Assembly • Seals—damaged, worn • Piston—damaged, worn • Friction—damaged, worn • Check Ball—not seating • Return Spring Assembly—damaged, worn	• Inspect for damage. Replace as required. • Inspect for damage. Replace as required. • Inspect for damage. Replace as required. • Inspect for damage. Replace as required. • Inspect for damage. Replace as required.
Direct/Intermediate Clutch Hub • Damaged or holes partially blocked	• Inspect for damage. Service as required.
2-3 Accumulator Assembly • Piston, Seals, Spring, Rod or Bore—damaged	• Inspect for damage. Service as required.

FM5029801625000X

Fig. 26 Routines 227 & 327: Soft/Slipping 2–3 Shift

Possible Component	Reference/Action
224 — ELECTRICAL ROUTINE	
• No Electrical Concerns	• No action required.
324 — HYDRAULIC/MECHANICAL ROUTINE	
Improper Pressures • EPC pressure • Line pressure	• Perform Line Pressure Tests. • Check pressure at line and EPC taps. If not within specification, check main control valve body.
Speedometer Gear—Drive • Damaged	• Inspect for damage. Service as required.
Speedometer Gear—Driven • Damaged	• Inspect for damage. Service as required.
Main Control Valve Body • Bolts out of torque specification • Gaskets and Separator Plate—damaged, off location • 2-3 Shift Valves, 2-3 Capacity Modulator Valve—stuck, damaged	• Tighten bolts to specification. • Inspect for damage. Replace as required. • Inspect. Service as required.

FM5029801622010X

Fig. 23 Routines 224 & 324: No 3–2 Automatic Shift (Part 1 of 2)

Possible Component	Reference/Action
225 — ELECTRICAL ROUTINE	
Powertrain Control System • Electrical Inputs/Outputs, Vehicle Wiring Harnesses, Powertrain Control Module (PCM), Shift Solenoids (SS1, SS2), VSS, TR Sensor	• Run On-Board Diagnostic. Refer to MOTOR's "Domestic Transmission Manual" for diagnosis. Perform Service Manual Pinpoint Tests A and D using the Rotunda Transmission Tester 007-00130 and Rotunda AX4N Cable and Overlay 007-00117 and Rotunda Transmission Range (TR) Sensor Cable (MLP-B Cable) 007-00127 or (TRS-E Cable) 007-00111 or equivalent. Service as required. Clear codes. Road Test and rerun On-Board Diagnostic.
325 — HYDRAULIC/MECHANICAL ROUTINE	
Main Control Valve Body • Bolts out of torque specification • Gaskets and Separator Plate—damaged, off location • 1-2 Shift Valve • SS1, SS2 damaged	• Tighten bolts to specification. • Inspect for damage. Replace as required. • Inspect. Service as required. • Activate solenoid using transmission tester. If solenoid operation cannot be felt when placing hand on solenoid, replace solenoid. Inspect O-rings for damage. Service as required.
Intermediate Clutch Assembly • Return Spring—damaged, misassembled • Piston and Seal—damaged • Balance Dam—damaged • Friction element—damaged, worn	• Perform Air Pressure Tests. • Inspect for damage. Replace as required. • Inspect for damage. Replace as required. • Inspect for damage. Replace as required. • Inspect for damage. Replace as required.
Low One-Way Clutch Assembly • Not holding, damaged	• Inspect for damage. Replace as required.

FM5029801623000X

Fig. 24 Routines 225 & 325: No 2–1 Automatic Shift

Possible Component	Reference/Action
Pump Assembly • Porosity/Cross Leak • Gaskets—damaged, off location • Components—damaged	• Inspect. Replace as required. • Inspect for damage. Replace as required. • Inspect for damage, missing ball. Replace pump assembly if required.
1-2 Accumulator Assembly • Piston Seals, Springs—damaged, missing	• Inspect for damage. Service as required.
Support Assembly—Driven Sprocket • Seals—damaged, missing • Holes—partially blocked	• Inspect for damage, missing or blockage. Service as required.
Intermediate Clutch Assembly • Seals—damaged, leaking • Piston—damaged • Friction—damaged, worn • Cylinder Hub Lube Groove—restricted	• Inspect for damage. Replace as required. • Inspect for damage. Replace as required. • Inspect for damage. Replace as required. • Inspect for restriction. Service as required.

FM5029801624020X

Fig. 25 Routines 226 & 326: Soft/Slipping 1–2 Shift (Part 2 of 2)

Possible Component	Reference/Action
228 — ELECTRICAL ROUTINE	
No Electrical Concerns	
328 — HYDRAULIC/MECHANICAL ROUTINE	
Overdrive Servo Assembly • Apply Rod—damaged • Servo Bore or Piston—damaged • Piston Seals—damaged, missing	• Inspect rod. Replace if incorrect. • Inspect for damage. Service as required. • Inspect for damage. Service as required.
Main Control • Bolts out of torque specification • Gaskets and Separator Plate—damaged, off location • 3-4 Shift Valve, Line Modulator Valve, Forward Clutch Control Valve—stuck, damaged	• Tighten bolts to specification. • Inspect gaskets for damage. Replace. • Inspect. Service as required.
3-4 Accumulator Assembly • Accumulator Piston—stuck, damaged • Piston Seals—damaged, missing • Springs—damaged • Rod or Bore—damaged	• Inspect for damage. Service as required. • Inspect for damage. Service as required. • Inspect for damage. Service as required. • Inspect for damage. Service as required.
OD Band • OD Band—damaged, worn, misassembled	• Inspect for damage. Replace as required.

FM5029801626000X

Fig. 27 Routines 228 & 328: Soft/Slipping 3–4 Shift

Possible Component	Reference/Action
229 — ELECTRICAL ROUTINE	
No Electrical Concerns	
329 — HYDRAULIC/MECHANICAL ROUTINE	
Main Control • Bolts out of torque specification • Gaskets and Separator Plate—damaged, off location • 3-4 Shift Valve, Line Modulator Valve—stuck, damaged	• Tighten bolts to specification. • Inspect for damage. Replace. • Inspect. Service as required.
OD Band • OD Band—damaged, worn, misassembled	• Inspect for damage. Replace as required.
Overdrive Servo Assembly • Apply Rod—incorrect • Servo Bore or Piston—damaged • Piston Seals—damaged, missing • Return Spring Retaining Clip—damaged, missing	• Inspect. Replace if incorrect. • Inspect for damage. Service as required. • Inspect for damage. Service as required. • Inspect for damage. Service as required.
Direct Clutch Assembly • Direct Clutch assembly • Damaged • Check Ball—damaged	• Perform Air Pressure Tests • Inspect for damage. Service as required. • Inspect for damage. Service as required.
Support Assembly—Drive Sprocket • Seals—damaged, holes partially blocked	• Inspect for damage. Service as required.

FM5029801627000X

Fig. 28 Routines 229 & 329: Soft/Slipping 4–3 Shift

Possible Component	Reference/Action
231 — ELECTRICAL ROUTINE	
No Electrical Concerns	
331 — HYDRAULIC/MECHANICAL ROUTINE	
Main Control • Bolts out of torque specification • Gaskets and Separator Plate—damaged, off location • 1-2 Shift Valve, Line Modulator Valve, 3-2 Timing Valve—stuck, damaged	• Tighten bolts to specification. • Inspect for damage. Replace. • Inspect. Service as required.
Low One-Way Clutch Assembly • Clutch Assembly—damaged	• Inspect for damage. Service as required.
Support Assembly—Drive Sprocket • Seals—damaged, leaking, hole partially blocked	• Inspect for damage. Service as required.
Forward Clutch Assembly • Forward Clutch assembly • Check Ball—damaged, missing • Clutch Assembly—damaged • Friction—damaged	• Perform Air Pressure Tests • Inspect for damage. Service as required. • Inspect for damage. Service as required. • Inspect for damage. Service as required.

FM5029801629000X

Fig. 30 Routines 231 & 331: Soft/Slipping 2–1 Shift

Possible Component	Reference/Action
Main Control • Bolts out of torque specification • Gaskets and Separator Plate—damaged, off location • 1-2 Shift Valve, Springs, B10 Check Ball, Clips—stuck, missing, misassembled	• Tighten bolts to specification. • Inspect gaskets for damage. Replace. • Inspect. Service as required.
Pump Assembly • Porosity/cross leak • Gaskets—damaged, off location • Components—damaged	• Inspect. Replace as required. • Inspect for damage. Replace as required. • Inspect for damage, missing ball. Replace pump assembly if required.
1-2 Accumulator Assembly • Piston Seals, Springs—damaged, missing • Piston or Rod—stuck, damaged	• Inspect for damage. Service as required. • Inspect for damage. Service as required.
Intermediate Clutch Assembly • Seals—damaged • Piston—damaged • Friction Plates—damaged, worn • Return Spring—damaged, broken	• Inspect for damage. Replace as required. • Inspect for damage. Replace as required. • Inspect for damage. Replace as required. • Inspect for damage. Service as required.

FM5029801630020X

Fig. 31 Routines 232 & 323: Harsh 1–2 Shift (Part 2 of 2)

Possible Component	Reference/Action
234 — ELECTRICAL ROUTINE	
No Electrical Concerns	
334 — HYDRAULIC/MECHANICAL ROUTINE	
Overdrive Servo Assembly • Apply Rod—incorrect • Return Spring Retaining Clip—broken, missing	• Inspect rod. Replace if incorrect. • Inspect for damage. Service as required.

FM5029801632010X

Fig. 33 Routines 234 & 334: Harsh 3–4 Shift (Part 1 of 2)

Possible Component	Reference/Action
235 — ELECTRICAL ROUTINE	
No Electrical Concerns	
335 — HYDRAULIC/MECHANICAL ROUTINE	
Main Control • Bolts out of torque specification • Gaskets and Separator Plate—damaged, off location • 3-4 Shift Valve, Line Modulator Valve.—stuck, damaged	• Tighten bolts to specification. • Inspect for damage. Replace. • Inspect. Service as required.
OD Band • OD Band—damaged, worn, misassembled	• Inspect for damage. Replace as required.
Overdrive Servo Assembly • Apply Rod—incorrect • Servo Bore or Piston—damaged • Piston Seals—damaged, missing • Return Spring Retaining Clip—damaged, missing	• Inspect rod. Service as required. • Inspect for damage. Service as required. • Inspect for damage. Service as required. • Inspect for damage. Service as required.
Direct Clutch Assembly • Direct Clutch assembly • Damaged • Check Ball—damaged	• Perform Air Pressure Tests as described. • Inspect for damage. Service as required. • Inspect for damage. Service as required.
Support Assembly—Drive Sprocket • Seals—damaged, holes partially blocked	• Inspect for damage. Service as required.

FM5029801633000X

Fig. 34 Routines 235 & 335: Harsh 4–3 Shift

Possible Component	Reference/Action
230 — ELECTRICAL ROUTINE	
No Electrical Concerns	
330 — HYDRAULIC/MECHANICAL ROUTINE	
Main Control • Bolts out of torque specification • Gaskets and Separator Plate—damaged, off location • 1-2 Shift Valve, 3-4 Shift Valve, Line Modulator Valve, 3-2 Timing Valve—stuck, damaged	• Tighten bolts to specification. • Inspect for damage. Replace. • Inspect. Service as required.
Intermediate Clutch Assembly • Clutch Assembly—damaged • Seals—leaking	• Perform Air Pressure Tests • Inspect for damage. Service as required.
Support Assembly—Driven • Seals—damaged, leaking, hole partially blocked	• Inspect for damage. Service as required.
Forward Clutch Assembly • • Check Ball—damaged, missing • Clutch Assembly—damaged • Friction Plates—damaged	• Perform Air Pressure Tests • Inspect for damage. Service as required. • Inspect for damage. Service as required. • Inspect for damage. Service as required.

FM5029801628000X

Fig. 29 Routines 230 & 330: Soft/Slipping 3–2 Shift

Possible Component	Reference/Action
232 — ELECTRICAL ROUTINE	
No Electrical Concerns	
332 — HYDRAULIC/MECHANICAL ROUTINE	
Improper Pressures • Line pressure, EPC pressure •	• Perform Line Pressure test • Check pressure at EPC and line taps. If not OK, check the following possible component: Main Control

FM5029801630010X

Fig. 31 Routines 232 & 323: Harsh 1–2 Shift (Part 1 of 2)

Possible Component	Reference/Action
233 — ELECTRICAL ROUTINE	
No Electrical Concerns	
333 — HYDRAULIC/MECHANICAL ROUTINE	
Improper Pressures • Line Pressure, EPC pressure •	• Perform Line Pressure. • Check pressure at EPC and line taps. If not OK, check the following possible component: Main Control
Main Control • Bolts out of torque specification • Gaskets and Separator Plate—damaged, off location • 2-3 Shift Valve, 2-3 Capacity Modulator Valve/Spring—stuck, damaged • Line Modulator or Capacity Modulator Check Valves/Springs—damaged, missing	• Tighten bolts to specification. • Inspect gaskets and replace. • Inspect. Service as required. • Inspect for damage. Service as required.
Direct Clutch Assembly • • Seals—damaged, worn • Piston—damaged, worn • Friction—damaged, worn • Return Spring Assembly—damaged, worn	• Perform Air Pressure Tests. • Inspect for damage. Replace as required. • Inspect for damage. Replace as required. • Inspect for damage. Replace as required. • Inspect for damage. Replace as required.
2-3 Accumulator Assembly • Piston, Seals, Rod or Bore—damaged, stuck	• Inspect for damage. Replace as required.

FM5029801631000X

Fig. 32 Routines 233 & 333: Harsh 2–3 Shift

Possible Component	Reference/Action
Main Control • Bolts out of torque specification • Gaskets and Separator Plate—damaged, off location • 3-4 Shift Valve, Line Modulator Valve, Forward Clutch Control Valve—stuck, damaged	• Tighten bolts to specification. • Inspect for damage. Replace. • Inspect. Service as required.
3-4 Accumulator Assembly • Accumulator Piston—stuck, damaged • Piston Seals—damaged • Springs—damaged, missing • Rod or Bore—damaged	• Inspect for damage. Service as required. • Inspect for damage. Service as required. • Inspect for damage. Service as required. • Inspect for damage. Service as required.
OD Band • OD Band—damaged, worn, misassembled	• Inspect for damage. Replace as required.

FM5029801632020X

Fig. 33 Routines 234 & 334: Harsh 3–4 Shift (Part 2 of 2)

Possible Component	Reference/Action
236 — ELECTRICAL ROUTINE	
No Electrical Concerns	
336 — HYDRAULIC/MECHANICAL ROUTINE	
Main Control • Bolts out of torque specification • Gaskets and Separator Plate—damaged, off location • 3-2 Shift Timing Valve, Line Modulator Valve, 1-2, 3-4 Shift Valves,—stuck, damaged	• Tighten bolts to specification. • Inspect for damage. Service as required. • Inspect. Service as required.
Intermediate Clutch Assembly • Clutch Assembly—damaged • Seals—leaking	• Inspect for damage. Replace as required. • Inspect for damage. Service as required.

FM5029801634010X

Fig. 35 Routines 236 & 336: Harsh 3–2 Shift (Part 1 of 2)

Possible Component	Reference/Action
Support Assembly—Drive Sprocket • Seals—damaged, leaking, holes blocked, missing	• Inspect for damage, missing or blockage. Service as required.
Low One-Way Clutch Assembly • Not overrunning—damaged	• Inspect for damage. Replace as required.
Forward Clutch Assembly • Forward Clutch assembly • Clutch Assembly—damaged • Check Ball—not functioning, missing	• Perform Air Pressure Tests. • Inspect for damage. Replace as required. • Inspect for damage. Replace as required.

FM5029801634020X

Fig. 35 Routines 236 & 336: Harsh 3–2 Shift (Part 2 of 2)

Possible Component	Reference/Action
240 — ELECTRICAL ROUTINE	
Powertrain Control System • Electrical Inputs/Outputs, Vehicle Wiring Harnesses, Powertrain Control Module (PCM), TP, TFT, TSS Sensor, BOO Switch, TCC Solenoid, Internal Wiring Harness	• Perform Torque Converter Clutch Operation Test. • Run On-Board Diagnostic. Refer to MOTOR's "Domestic Transmission Manual" for diagnosis. Perform Service Manual Pinpoint Tests B, C and F using the Rotunda Transmission Tester 007-00130 and Rotunda AX4N Cable and Overlay 007-00117 or equivalent. Service as required. Clear codes. Road Test and rerun On-Board Diagnostic.
340 — HYDRAULIC/MECHANICAL ROUTINE	
Improper Pressures • Low line pressure, low EPC pressure •	• Perform Line Pressure. • Check pressure at EPC and line taps. If low, check main control valve body.
Main Control Valve Body • Bolts out of torque specification • Gaskets and Separator Plate—damaged, off location • Valve Body Pilot Sleeve—damaged, misaligned. Manual Valve, Converter Regulator Valve, Main Regulator Valve, Springs, Solenoid Regulator Valve, Bypass Clutch Control Valve—stuck, damaged	• Tighten bolts to specification. • Inspect gaskets. Service as required. • Inspect. Service as required.

FM5029801636010X

Fig. 37 Routines 240 & 340: No Torque Converter Apply (Part 1 of 2)

Possible Component	Reference/Action
241 — ELECTRICAL ROUTINE	
Powertrain Control System • Electrical Inputs/Outputs, Vehicle Wiring Harnesses, Powertrain Control Module (PCM), TCC Solenoid, Internal Wiring Harness	• Perform Torque Converter Clutch Operation Test. Run On-Board Diagnostic. Refer to MOTOR's "Domestic Transmission Manual" for diagnosis. Perform Pinpoint Test C using the Rotunda Transmission Tester 007-00130 and Rotunda AX4N Cable and Overlay 007-00117 or equivalent. Service as required. Clear codes. Road Test and rerun On-Board Diagnostic.
Main Controls • Bolts out of torque specification • Gaskets and Separator Plate—damaged, off location • Bypass Clutch Control Valve and Plunger, Solenoid Regulator Valve, Converter Regulator Valve—stuck, damaged • TCC Solenoid—not functioning properly	• Tighten bolts to specification. • Inspect gaskets. Service as required. • Inspect. Service as required. • Activate solenoid using Rotunda Transmission Tester 007-00130 and Rotunda AX4N Cable and Overlay 007-00117 or equivalent. If solenoid operation cannot be felt when placing hand on solenoid, replace solenoid.
Converter • No End Clearance to Turbine	• Check torque converter end play

FM5029801637000X

Fig. 38 Routine 241: Torque Converter Always Applied/Stalls Vehicle

Possible Component	Reference/Action
Improper Pressures • Low line pressure, low EPC	• Check pressure at line and EPC taps. Perform Line Pressure and Stall Speed Tests. • If not OK, check the Main Control Valve Body.
Main Control Valve Body • Bolts out of torque specification • Gaskets and Separator Plate—damaged, off location • Valve Body Pilot Sleeve—damaged, misaligned Manual Valve, Bypass Clutch Control Valve and Plunger, Converter Regulator Valve, Solenoid Regulator Valve—stuck, damaged • TCC Solenoid not functioning properly	• Tighten bolts to specification. • Inspect for damage. Replace as required. • Inspect. Service as required. • Activate solenoid using Rotunda Transmission Tester 007-00130 and Rotunda AX4N Cable and Overlay 007-00117 or equivalent. If solenoid operation cannot be felt when placing hand on solenoid, replace solenoid. Inspect O-rings for damage. Service as required.
Turbine Shaft • Seals—damaged, missing	• Inspect for damage. Replace as required.
Pump Shaft • Seals—damaged, missing	• Inspect seals for damage. Service as required.
Torque Converter • Refer to Reference/Action	• Inspect. Service as required.

FM5029801638020X

Fig. 39 Routines 242 & 342: Torque Converter Cycling/Shudder/Chatter (Part 2 of 2)

Possible Component	Reference/Action
237 — ELECTRICAL ROUTINE	
No Electrical Concerns	
337 — HYDRAULIC/MECHANICAL ROUTINE	
Main Control • Bolts out of torque specification • Gaskets and Separator Plate—damaged, off location • 1-2 Shift Valve, Line Modulator Valve, 3-2 Timing Valve—stuck, damaged	• Tighten bolts to specification. • Inspect for damage. Replace. • Inspect. Service as required.
Support Assembly—Driven • Seals—damaged, holes blocked	• Inspect for damage. Service as required.
Forward Clutch Assembly • Forward Clutch assembly • Check Ball—damaged, missing • Friction element—damaged • Support Assembly—damaged	• Perform Air Pressure Tests. • Inspect for damage. Service as required. • Inspect for damage. Service as required. • Inspect for damage. Service as required.
Low One-Way Clutch Assembly • Not holding—damaged	• Inspect for damage. Replace as required.

FM5029801635000X

Fig. 36 Routines 237 & 337: Harsh 2–1 Shift

Possible Component	Reference/Action
• TCC Solenoid not functioning properly	• Activate solenoid using Rotunda Transmission Tester 007-00130 and Rotunda AX4N Cable and Overlay 007-00117 or equivalent. If solenoid operation cannot be felt when placing hand on solenoid, replace solenoid. Inspect O-rings for damage. Service as required.
Turbine Shaft • Seals—damaged, missing • Holes—missing, plugged	• Inspect for damage. Replace as required. • Inspect for damage. Service as required.
Pump Assembly • Seals, Bearing—damaged, missing	• Inspect seals for damage. Service as required
Converter • Refer to Reference/Action	• Inspect as described. Service as required.

FM5029801636020X

Fig. 37 Routines 240 & 340: No Torque Converter Apply (Part 2 of 2)

Possible Component	Reference/Action
242 — ELECTRICAL ROUTINE	
Powertrain Control System • Electrical Inputs/Outputs, Vehicle Wiring Harnesses, Powertrain Control Module (PCM), TCC, TFT Sensor, BOO Switch, Internal Wiring Harness, TSS	• Perform Torque Converter Clutch Operation Test. Run On-Board Diagnostic. Refer to MOTOR's "Domestic Transmission Manual" for diagnosis. Perform Service Manual Pinpoint Tests B, C and F using the Rotunda Transmission Tester 007-00130 and Rotunda AX4N Cable and Overlay 007-00117 or equivalent. Service as required. Clear codes. Road Test and rerun On-Board Diagnostic.
342 — HYDRAULIC/MECHANICAL ROUTINE • Fluid condition	• Prior to performing this action, make sure all electrical diagnostics have been performed. Inspect fluid condition. If burnt, drain fluid and converter. Replace fluid and fluid filter assembly. Bring vehicle to normal operating temperature. Perform Transaxle Drive Cycle Test. Perform On-Board Diagnostic. If condition still exists, continue diagnostics.

FM5029801638010X

Fig. 39 Routines 242 & 342: Torque Converter Cycling/Shudder/Chatter (Part 1 of 2)

Possible Component	Reference/Action
250 — ELECTRICAL ROUTINE • No Electrical Concerns	• No action required.
350 — HYDRAULIC/MECHANICAL ROUTINE	
Improper Pressures • Line pressure, EPC pressure	• Perform Line Pressure Test. Check pressure at line and EPC taps. If not OK, check Main Control Valve Body and Direct Clutch Assembly.
Main Control Valve Body • Bolts out of torque specification • Gaskets and Separator Plate—damaged, off location • Shift Valve, Manual Downshift Modulator Valve, B8 Check Ball—stuck or damaged	• Tighten bolts to specification. • Inspect for damage. Replace as required. • Inspect. Clean or service as required.
Direct Clutch Assembly • Refer to Routine 321	• Inspect. Service or replace as required.
Direct One-Way Clutch • Damaged, refer to Routine 321	• Inspect for damage. Service as required.
Coast Band • Band—damaged • Friction Plates—damaged • Coast Band Apply Tube/Seal—damaged, loose • Low/Intermediate Coast Band—damaged • Apply Servo, Cover, Seals—damaged	• Inspect for damage. Service as required. • Inspect for damage. Service as required. • Inspect for damage. Service as required. • Inspect for damage. Service as required. • Inspect for damage. Service as required.

FM5029801639000X

Fig. 40 Routines 250 & 350: No Engine Braking In 1st Gear Manual

Possible Component	Reference/Action
251 — ELECTRICAL ROUTINE	
• No Electrical Concerns	• No action required.

FM5029801640010X

Fig. 41 Routines 251 & 351: Shift Lever Efforts High (Part 1 of 2)

Possible Component	Reference/Action
252 — ELECTRICAL ROUTINE	
• No Electrical Concerns	• No action required.
352 — HYDRAULIC/MECHANICAL ROUTINE	
Improper Fluid Level •	• Adjust fluid to proper level.
Seals/Gaskets • Converter, TSS, Halfshaft Axles, Gasket/Seal Manual Lever, Fluid Level Indicator, Servo Cover, Transaxle Pan, Improper Hub Seal, Chain Cover-to-Case	• Locate source. Service as required.
Other • Cooler Fitting, Pressure Taps, Transmission Connectors, Cooler Lines, Transaxle Pan, Case Porosity, Chain Cover Porosity, Case Cracked	• Locate Source. Service as required.
• Vent—blocked, damaged.	• Check vent for damage or blockage. Service as required.

FM5029801641000X

Fig. 42 Routines 252 & 352: External Leaks

Possible Component	Reference/Action
254 — ELECTRICAL ROUTINE	
• No electrical concerns	• No action required
354 — HYDRAULIC/MECHANICAL ROUTINE	
For Noises/Vibrations That Change With Engine Speed: • Converter components • Fluid level (low) — Pump cavitation • Pump Assembly • Engine drive accessories • Fluid Cooler Tubes grounding out • Flywheel	• Locate source of disturbance and service as required.
For Noises/Vibrations That Change With Vehicle Speed: • Engine Mounts — loose or damaged • Driveline concerns: — Halfshaft shudder — CV joints — Suspension — Modifications • Output/Halfshaft Splines worn or damaged	• Locate source of disturbance and service as required.
• TSS incorrectly installed	• Inspect. Service as required.
Other Noises/Vibrations: • Main Controls — Valve resonance	• Locate source of disturbance and service as required.
• Shift Cable — Vibration, Grounding	• Locate source of disturbance and service as required.
• Fluid Cooler Tubes grounding	• Locate source of disturbance and service as required.
• Anti-Lock (ABS) Brake System	• Refer to "Anti-Lock Brakes."
• Power Steering Pump	• Refer to Power Steering Pump.

FM5029801643000X

Fig. 44 Routines 254 & 354: Noise/Vibration In Forward/Reverse

Possible Component	Reference/Action
256 — ELECTRICAL ROUTINE	
• No Electrical Concerns	• No action required

FM5029801645010X

Fig. 46 Routines 256 & 356: No Park Range (Part 1 of 2)

Possible Component	Reference/Action
356 — HYDRAULIC/MECHANICAL ROUTINE	
Shift Linkage (Internal/External) • Damaged or out of adjustment	• Inspect and service as required. Verify linkage adjustment. After servicing linkage, verify that the TR sensor is properly adjusted.
Park Mechanism • Park Brake Pawl, Parking Pawl Return Spring, Park Rod Abutment, Parking Pawl Shaft, Parking Pawl Actuating Rod, Manual Lever, Manual Lever Detent Spring—damaged	• Inspect. Service as required.

FM5029801645020X

Fig. 46 Routines 256 & 356: No Park Range (Part 2 of 2)

Possible Component	Reference/Action
351 — HYDRAULIC/MECHANICAL ROUTINE	
Shift Linkage (Internal, External) • Damaged or out of adjustment	• Inspect and service as required. Verify linkage adjustment. After servicing linkage, verify that the TR sensor is properly adjusted.
Manual Lever • External Retaining Pin damaged, Nut loose, Detent Spring—bent, damaged; or Park Mechanism damaged, improper lever used	• Inspect and service/replace as required.
Main Control Valve Body • Manual Valve stuck	• Inspect and service or replace as necessary.
• Bolts out of torque specification	• Tighten bolts to specification.
Brake Shift Interlock •	• Refer to "AX4S (AXOD-E) Automatic Overdrive Transmission."

FM5029801640020X

Fig. 41 Routines 251 & 351: Shift Lever Efforts High (Part 2 of 2)

Possible Component	Reference/Action
253 — ELECTRICAL ROUTINE	
Powertrain Control System • Electrical Inputs/Outputs, Vehicle Wiring Harnesses, Powertrain Control Module (PCM), TCC Solenoid, TP, VSS, MAF, IAT Sensors, Internal Wiring Harness	• Perform Shift Point Road Test and Torque Converter Clutch Operation Test. • Run On-Board Diagnostic. Refer to MOTOR's "Domestic Transmission Manual" for diagnosis. Perform Service Manual Pinpoint Test C using the Rotunda Transmission Tester 007-00130 and Rotunda AX4N Cable and Overlay 007-00117 or equivalent. Service as required. Clear codes. Road test and rerun On-Board Diagnostic.
353 — HYDRAULIC/MECHANICAL ROUTINE	
Fluid • Low Level	• Adjust to proper level
Verify Proper Shift Scheduling, Engagements, Line Pressures and Stall Speed •	• Go to the appropriate Diagnostic Routines per Index.
Converter Clutch Always Applied •	• Go to Routine 341.

FM5029801642000X

Fig. 43 Routines 253 & 353: Poor Vehicle Performance

Possible Component	Reference/Action
255 — ELECTRICAL ROUTINE	
Powertrain Control System • Electrical Inputs/Outputs, Vehicle Wiring Harnesses, Powertrain Control Module (PCM), TR Sensor	• Run On-Board Diagnostic. Refer to MOTOR's "Domestic Transmission Manual" for diagnosis. Perform Pinpoint Test D using the Rotunda Transmission Tester 007-00130 and Rotunda AX4N Cable and Overlay 007-00117 and the Rotunda Transmission Range (TR) Sensor Cable (MLP-B Cable) 007-00127 or (TRS-E Cable) 007-00111 or equivalent. Service as required. Clear codes. Road Test and rerun On-Board Diagnostic.
355 — HYDRAULIC/MECHANICAL ROUTINE	
Shift Linkage/Cable (Internal/External) • Damaged or out of adjustment	• Inspect and service as required. Verify linkage adjustment. After servicing linkage, verify that the TR sensor is properly adjusted.

FM5029801644000X

Fig. 45 Routines 255 & 355: Engine Will Not Crank

Possible Component	Reference/Action
257 — ELECTRICAL ROUTINE	
Refer to Electrical Routine 240, 340 Torque Converter No Applying •	• Refer to Electrical Routine 240, 340 Torque Converter - No Applying
357 — HYDRAULIC/MECHANICAL ROUTINE	
Fluid • Improper level	• Adjust fluid to proper level.
• Condition	• Inspect as described under Fluid Condition Check.
Cooler Lines • Damaged, blocked, reversed, leaking	• Inspect and service as required.
Auxiliary Cooler • Damaged, blocked, restricted or improperly installed	• Inspect and service as required.
Vehicle Concerns Causing Engine Overheating	
Main Control Valve Body • By-Pass Clutch Control Valve and Plunger, Converter Regulator Valve, Cooler Bypass Valve/spring-stuck, damaged	• Inspect and service as required.
Torque Converter Not Applying • Seized Converter One-Way Clutch	• See Routine 240/340. Inspect. Service as required.
Excessive Towing Loads	• Check gross vehicle weight (GVW).
Idle or Performance Concern	• Refer to MOTOR's "Domestic Transmission Manual."
Improper Clutch or Band Application or Oil Pressure Control System	• Perform Line Pressure Tests and Shift Point Road Tests

FM5029801646000X

Fig. 47 Routines 257 & 357: Transaxle Overheating

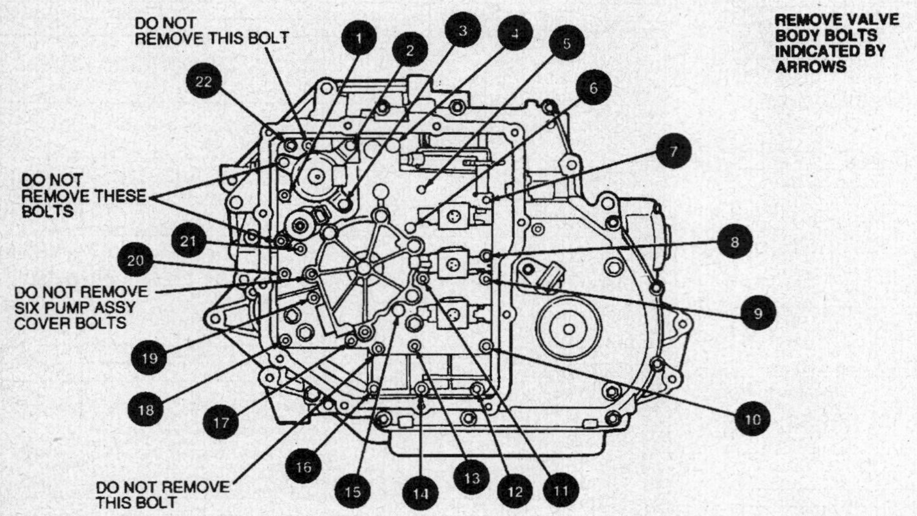

Fig. 48 Main control valve body bolt removal

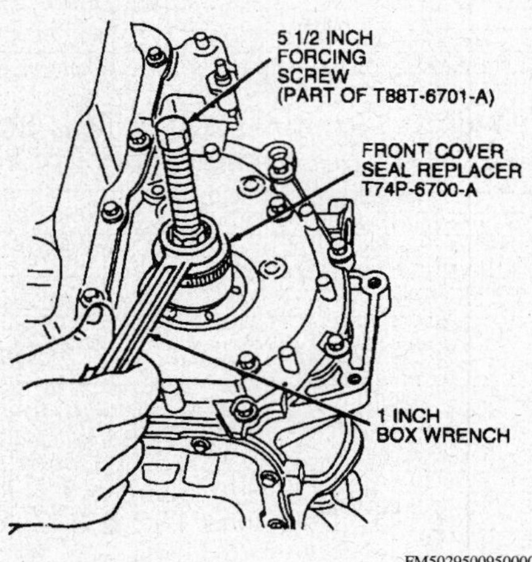

Fig. 49 Lefthand differential seal removal

MAINTENANCE

Refer to "Lubricant Data" chart in the appropriate chassis chapter of this manual for transmission fluid specifications.

FLUID INSPECTION

Fluid level should be inspected at normal operating temperature, with vehicle on a level surface.

1. Start engine and move gearshift selector through all ranges, allowing sufficient time for each position to engage.
2. Place gear selector in Park position and set parking brake.
3. With engine running, inspect fluid mark on transaxle dipstick. Fluid should be within crosshatched area of level indicator.
4. If fluid level is low, adjust fluid level as required.
5. If fluid level is too high, disconnect transaxle fluid cooler in line at cooler and drain.

FLUID CHANGE

1. Place transaxle range selector in Park and set parking brake.
2. **On models equipped with automatic air suspension,** place air suspension system switch in Off position before raising vehicle.
3. **On all models,** raise and support vehicle.
4. Remove retainer clip from lower transaxle fluid cooler line and fitting.
5. **On models equipped with 5⁄16 inch cooler lines,** disconnect transaxle cooler line using disconnection tool No. T82L-9500-AH, or equivalent.
6. **On models equipped with 3⁄8 inch cooler lines,** pinch plastic retainer tabs of push connect fitting and pull cooler line to separate it from fitting.
7. **On all models,** disconnect lower transaxle cooler line from cooler line fitting at transaxle.
8. Attach flexible hose, approximately three feet in length, to end of transaxle cooler line and gently fasten hose with clamp. Place opposite end of flexible hose into suitable container.
9. Plug transaxle cooler line fitting at transaxle.
10. Lower vehicle.
11. Place gear selector in Park and start engine.
12. Run engine at idle for approximately 40–60 seconds until steady stream of fluid stops flowing from flexible drain hose, then turn engine off.
13. Fill transaxle with 10 quarts of proper transaxle fluid and repeat previous step. This should drain 10 quarts of fluid.
14. Raise and support vehicle, then remove plug from transaxle cooler line fitting.
15. Remove flexible hose from cooler line.
16. Install cooler line into transaxle cooler fitting.
17. Install retainer clip over cooler line and fitting.
18. Lower vehicle.
19. Add two quarts of proper transaxle fluid.
20. Start engine and move gear selector through all ranges, allowing transaxle to engage in each position.
21. Inspect fluid level as outlined under "Fluid Inspection."
22. Place air suspension switch in On position, if equipped.

ADJUSTMENTS

MANUAL SHIFT LINKAGE

CONTINENTAL

Column Shifter

1. Place shift lever in OD position, then hang three pound weight on shift lever to ensure lever is firmly in OD detent.
2. Loosen adjusting nut located on top of transaxle on gearshift lever.
3. Move gearshift lever to OD position and tighten nut to specifications.
4. Inspect operation of transaxle in each transaxle range and ensure Transaxle Range (TR) sensor is functioning properly.

Console Shifter

1. Place shift lever in OD position.
2. Loosen manual control lever to transaxle shift cable mounting nut.
3. Move gearshift lever to OD position, second detent from most rearward position.
4. Tighten mounting nut to specifications.
5. Inspect operation of transaxle in each transaxle range and ensure Transaxle Range (TR) Sensor is functioning properly.

SABLE & TAURUS

Refer to "AX4S (AXOD-E) Automatic Overdrive Transaxle."

SHIFT INDICATOR CABLE

CONTINENTAL

Column Shift

1. Remove steering column tilt release lever.
2. Remove ignition switch lock cylinder as outlined under "Ignition Lock, Replace" in "Electrical" section.
3. Remove upper and lower steering column shrouds.
4. Place shift lever in OD position and hang a three pound weight on lever to ensure lever is firmly in OD detent.
5. Adjust shift cable using adjustment wheel located on shift cable until shift indicator completely covers OD indicator and calibration dots show no red.
6. Cycle shift lever through all positions and ensure shift indicator completely covers proper letter or number in each position.
7. Install steering column shrouds, ignition lock and tilt release lever.

IN-VEHICLE REPAIRS

PUMP & MAIN CONTROL VALVE BODY

1. Remove air cleaner.

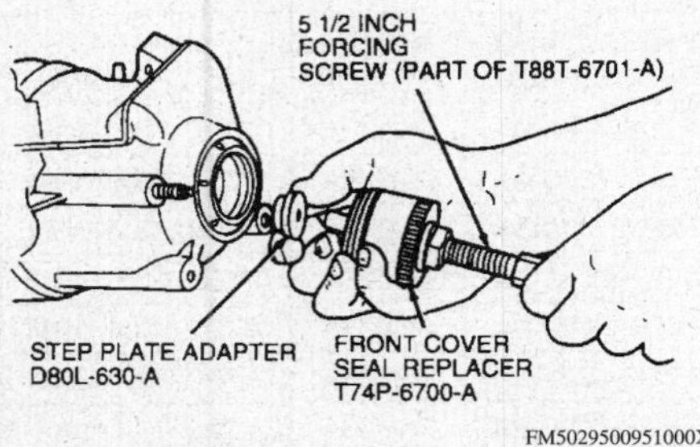

Fig. 50 Righthand differential seal removal

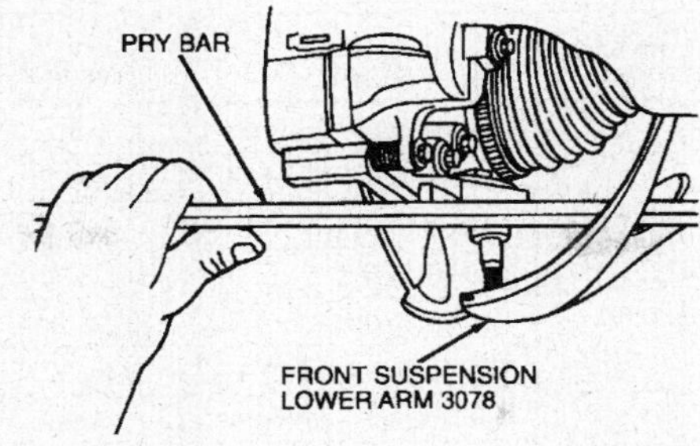

Fig. 51 Ball joint stud removal

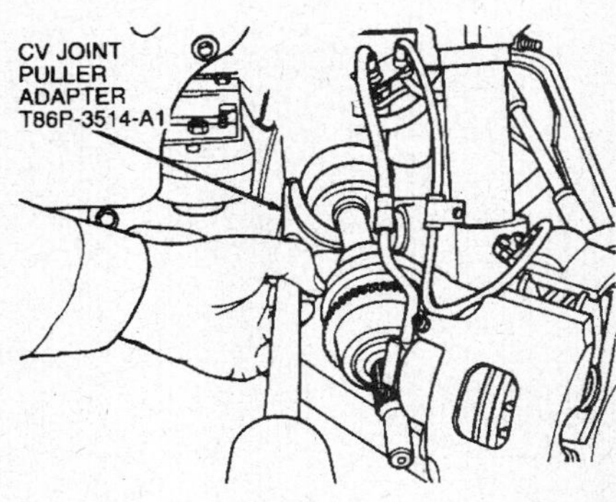

Fig. 52 CV joint puller adapter

2. Remove battery and battery tray.
3. Disconnect transaxle range sensor and transaxle harness electrical connector. Position engine wire harness out of way.
4. Place TR sensor manual lever in Park position.
5. Install Rotunda three-bar engine support tool No. D88L-6000-A with engine lift bracket set tool No. 014-00796, or equivalents, and support engine.
6. Remove transaxle side pan upper mounting bolts.
7. Raise and support vehicle.
8. Remove lefthand front tire and wheel.
9. Remove lefthand front splash shield.
10. Remove lefthand side engine support and insulator.
11. Position suitable drain pan under transaxle side pan and remove remaining lower transaxle side pan mounting bolts.
12. Remove transaxle side pan and gasket. Discard gasket.
13. Disconnect transaxle fluid temperature sensor from main control valve body and solenoid electrical connectors.
14. Remove transaxle wiring harness from chain cover.
15. Remove main control valve body mounting bolts, **Fig. 48. Do not remove pump cover bolts.**
16. Disconnect manual valve linkage and carefully slide pump and main control valve body off pump shaft and remove from transaxle.
17. Reverse procedure to install. Tighten valve body mounting bolts and transaxle side pan bolts to specifications.

TURBINE SHAFT SPEED SENSOR (TSS)

1. Remove battery and battery tray.
2. Disconnect TSS electrical connector.
3. Remove mounting bolt an TSS.
4. Reverse procedure to install.

DIFFERENTIAL OIL SEALS

Do not begin this procedure unless following components are available: new front axle hub nut, lower ball joint to lower suspension arm nut and driveshaft bearing retainer circlip. Once removed these components must not be used again. Their torque holding ability or retention capability is diminished during removal.

1. Raise and support vehicle.
2. Remove front tires and wheels.
3. Remove halfshafts as described in "Transaxle, Replace."
4. Install front cover seal replacer tool No. T74P-6700-A with 5 ½ inch forcing screw tool No. T88T-6701-A, or equivalents, into lefthand differential seal, **Fig. 49.**
5. Turn forcing screw until outer metal seal protector part of differential seal is removed. Remove outer metal seal protector from tool and discard.
6. Install seal replacer tool and forcing screw into seal portion of differential seal, then tighten forcing screw until seal portion is removed. Discard seal.
7. Install step plate adapter tool No. D80L-630-A, or equivalent, into righthand differential fluid seal opening, **Fig. 50.**
8. Turn front cover seal replacer tool No. T74P-6700-A and forcing screw T88T-6701-A, or equivalents, into metal protector portion of seal.
9. Tighten forcing screw on end of tool until metal portion of seal is removed.
10. Remove metal portion of seal from tool and discard.
11. Install seal removal tool into rubber portion of seal and tighten tool until seal is removed.
12. Reverse procedure to install. Install differential seal using output seal replacer tool No. T86P-1177-B, or equivalent.

BRAKE-SHIFT INTERLOCK ACTUATOR/SOLENOID, REPLACE

1. Remove lower steering column shroud.
2. Remove steering column mounting nuts and lower steering column to floor.
3. Disconnect actuator/solenoid electrical connector.
4. Remove ignition/shifter interlock cable to steering column mounting screws.
5. Remove solenoid from solenoid retainer bracket.
6. Reverse procedure to install.

BRAKE-SHIFT INTERLOCK CABLE, REPLACE

Console Shift

1. Remove console finish panel mounting screw.
2. Move transaxle selector lever arm and support rearward.
3. Remove transaxle gear shift opening seal.
4. Remove console panel to console panel bracket mounting screws.
5. Disconnect console electrical connectors and remove console panel.
6. Remove ignition/shifter interlock cable to shifter mounting screw and interlock/shifter cable from shifter interlock cam.
7. Remove lower steering column shroud.
8. Remove steering column mounting nuts and lower steering column to floor.
9. Disconnect actuator/solenoid electrical connector.
10. Remove ignition/shifter interlock cable to steering column mounting screws.
11. Remove solenoid from solenoid retainer bracket.
12. Pull ignition/shifter interlock cable out from under instrument panel and unhook it from retaining bracket.
13. Roll back carpet and slide cable out.
14. Reverse procedure to install, noting following:
    a. Tighten cable to steering column mounting screws to specifications.
    b. Tighten steering column mounting nuts to specifications.
    c. Inspect for proper interlock operation. Ignition key should be removable only with gearshift lever in Park. Gearshift lever should be locked in Park position with key removed.

TRANSAXLE

REPLACE

CONTINENTAL

1. Remove battery and battery tray.
2. Open luggage compartment and ensure air suspension switch is turned off.
3. Disconnect intake air temperature sensor and mass air flow sensor electrical connectors from air cleaner.
4. Disconnect hoses and tubes, then remove air cleaner.
5. Disconnect transaxle harness and range sensor electrical connectors.
6. Remove shift actuator cable fitting and nut, then disconnect cable from bracket.

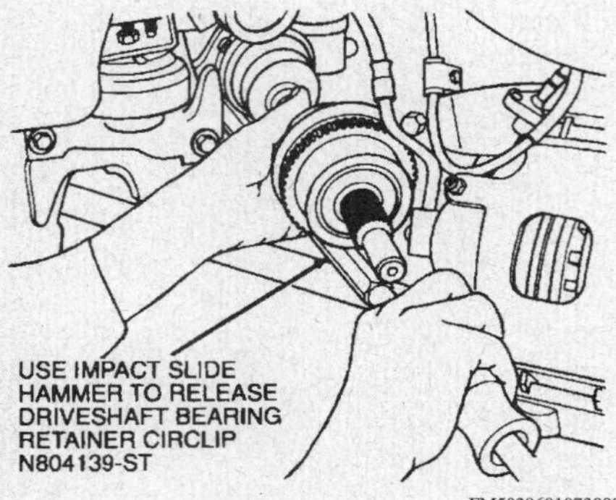
USE IMPACT SLIDE
HAMMER TO RELEASE
DRIVESHAFT BEARING
RETAINER CIRCLIP
N804139-ST
FM5029601073000X

Fig. 53 Driveshaft bearing retainer clip removal

7. Install two engine lifting eyes tool No. D81L-6001-D, or equivalent, to front and rear of engine.
8. Install three-bar engine support bracket set tool No. D88L-6000-A, or equivalent, and support engine.
9. Raise and support vehicle.
10. Place suitable drain pan under transaxle, loosen lower pan mounting bolts and drain transaxle fluid into a suitable container.
11. Remove transaxle pan bolts.
12. After fluid has completely drained from transaxle, install transaxle pan.
13. Remove front tire and wheel assemblies.
14. Depressurize air suspension system and disconnect height sensors.
15. Remove two cotter pins, two nuts and disconnect tie rod ends from steering knuckles.
16. Remove two nuts and disconnect stabilizer bar links from stabilizer bar.
17. Remove two nuts and separate lower control arm from steering knuckles.
18. Install puller tool No. T86P-3514-A1, or equivalent, between constant velocity joint and transaxle case. Turn steering hub and/or secure strut out of way using suitable wire or rope.
19. Screw extension tool No. T86P-3514-A2, or equivalent, into constant velocity joint puller and hand tighten. Screw impact slide hammer tool No. D79P-100-A, or equivalent, onto extension.
20. Remove constant velocity joint from transaxle.
21. Support end of halfshaft by suspending from conventional underbody component with suitable length or wire. **Do not allow shaft to hang unsupported. Damage to outboard constant velocity joint may result.**
22. Separate outboard constant velocity joint from hub using front hub remover tool Nos. T81P-1104-C, T83P-1104-BH, T86P-1104-A1 and T81P-1104-A, or equivalents. **Never use hammer to separate outboard constant velocity joint stub shaft from hub. Damage to constant velocity joint threads and internal components may result.**
23. Remove halfshafts.
24. Disconnect three oxygen sensor electrical connectors.

MODEL YEAR	VEHICLE	ENGINE	ENGINEERING PART NUMBER	MODEL NUMBER	SERVICE PART NUMBER
1997	Continental – Column	4.6L	F7OP-7000-BA	PNB-GA	F7OZ-7000-BRM
	Continental – Floor	4.6L	F7OP-7000-AA	PNB-CA	F7OZ-7000-ARM
	Taurus SHO	3.4L	F7DP-7000-BA	PNB-EA	F7DZ-7000-BRM
	Taurus/Sable	3.0L Vulcan	F7DP-7000-CA	PNB-FA	F7DZ-7000-CRM
	Taurus/Sable – Column	3.0L Mod	F7DP-7000-DA	PNB-DA	F7DZ-7000-DRM
	Taurus/Sable – Floor	3.0L Mod	F7DP-7000-EA	PNB-HA	F7DZ-7000-ERM
1998	Continental – Column	4.6L	F8OP-7000-BA	PNB-GA	Not Available
	Continental – Floor	4.6L	F8OP-7000-AA	PNB-CA	Not Available
	Taurus SHO	3.4L	F8DP-7000-BA	PNB-EA	Not Available
	Taurus/Sable – Column	3.0L Mod	F8DP-7000-DA	PNB-DA	Not Available
	Taurus/Sable – Floor	3.0L Mod	F8DP-7000-EA	PNB-HA	Not Available
	Taurus/Sable – Column	3.0L Vulcan	F8DP-7000-CA	PNB-FA	Not Available
	Taurus/Sable – Floor	3.0L Vulcan	F8DP-7000-FA	PNB-KA	Not Available

FMA059800091000X

Fig. 54 AX4N application data. 1998 Continental, Sable & Taurus

25. Remove mounting bolts, nuts and Y-pipe.
26. Remove splash shield from front subframe and radiator support.
27. Support power steering gear with wire, to secure power steering housing in position.
28. Remove ball joint nut from under steering knuckle and separate lower arm from steering knuckle.
29. Remove power steering gear to front subframe mounting nuts.
30. Remove power steering return hose to front subframe mounting screws and position hose of way.
31. Disconnect ride height sensor links at front suspension lower arms.
32. Remove left and righthand front engine support insulator mounting nuts.
33. Remove engine and transaxle support insulator to front subframe mounting bolts.
34. Support front subframe with adjustable jacks.
35. Remove left and righthand front subframe body insulator braces.
36. Remove front subframe to body mounting bolts.
37. With help from assistant lower subframe.
38. Remove mounting nuts and disconnect starter motor electrical connector.
39. Remove starter motor bolt, stud and starter motor.
40. Position suitable transmission jack under transaxle.
41. Remove lower engine to transaxle bolts.
42. Remove two bolts and one nut on righthand side engine mount to transaxle case.
43. Slowly lower transaxle. Ensure no obstructions exist.
44. Reverse procedure to install. Tighten mounting bolts and nuts to specifications.

SABLE & TAURUS

Removal

1. Remove battery and tray.
2. Remove air cleaner.
3. Disconnect transaxle harness electrical connector and range sensor connector.
4. Remove shift actuator cable fitting and disconnect transaxle shift cable from shift cable bracket and transaxle.
5. Disconnect fluid cooler lines from transaxle.
6. **On models equipped with 3.0L 12-valve engine,** remove one upper transaxle to engine stud.
7. **On models equipped with 3.0L 24-valve and 3.4L engines,** remove five upper transaxle to engine bolts.
8. **On all models,** remove righthand cowl and install two Rotunda engine lift bracket set tool No. 014-00796, or equivalents, to front and rear locations on engine.
9. Install three-bar engine support tool No. D88L-6000-A, or equivalent, and support engine.
10. Raise and support vehicle on hoist.
11. Place suitable drain pan under transaxle, loosen pan mounting bolt and drain.
12. When fluid level is has drained to level of transaxle pan flange, remove remaining transaxle pan bolts.
13. When transaxle fluid has completely drained, install transaxle pan.
14. Remove front tire and wheel assemblies.
15. Loosen lug nuts and remove front axle wheel hub retainer.
16. Remove stabilizer bar link top mounting nut with box end wrench while holding stud with socket.
17. Remove stabilizer bar link from front strut and position out of way.
18. Install front hub remover/replacer and two-stud adapter tool Nos. T81P-1104-C and T86P-1104-A1, or equivalents.
19. Install metric hub remover adapters and front hub replacer tool Nos. T83P-1104-BH and T81P-1104-A, or equivalents.
20. Push front wheel driveshaft joint only to point where splines are free in hub. Remove puller tool.
21. Remove and discard lower ball joint nut. Separate lower ball joint from

Application	Old Part Number (-12A650-)	Old Tear Tag	New Part Number (-12A650-)	New Tear Tag	Old Calibration	NGS/WDS Qualifier
2000 Federal CAA	YF1F-MB	GCM1	YU2Z-ASC	PRZ2	0DD14N0A05	WDS B14.14 Release or Later
2000 Federal CAA	YF1F-MC	GCM2	YU2Z-ASC	PRZ2	0DD14N0A06	WDS B14.14 Release or Later
2000 Federal CAA	YU2F-ASA	PRZ0	YU2Z-ASC	PRZ2	0DD14N0A06	WDS B14.14 Release or Later
2000 Federal CAA	YU2F-ASB	PRZ1	YU2Z-ASC	PRZ2	0DD14N0A06	WDS B14.14 Release or Later
2000 California LEV	YF1F-NB	HUK1	YU2Z-AVC	KDB2	0DD14N0B05	WDS B14.14 Release or Later
2000 California LEV	YF1F-NC	HUK2	YU2Z-AVC	KDB2	0DD14N0B05	WDS B14.14 Release or Later
2000 California LEV	YU2F-AVA	KDB0	YU2Z-AVC	KDB2	0DD14N0B05	WDS B14.14 Release or Later
2000 California LEV	YU2F-AVB	KDB1	YU2Z-AVC	KDB2	0DD14N0B06	WDS B14.14 Release or Later
2000 Federal CAA	YF1F-ADA	ALP0	YU7Z-AAB	DZD1	0DD15N0A00	WDS B14.14 Release or Later
2000 Federal CAA	YF1F-ADB	ALP1	YU7Z-AAB	DZD1	0DD15N0A05	WDS B14.14 Release or Later
2000 Federal CAA	YU7A-AAA	DZD0	YU7Z-AAB	DZD1	0DD15N0A05	WDS B14.14 Release or Later
2000 California LEV	YF1F-AEB	DNV1	YU7Z-ABB	MGN1	0DD15N0505	WDS B14.14 Release or Later
2000 California LEV	YF1F-AEC	DNV2	YU7Z-ABB	MGN1	0DD15N0506	WDS B14.14 Release or Later
2000 California LEV	YU7A-ABA	MGN0	YU7Z-ABB	MGN1	0DD15N0506	WDS B14.14 Release or Later
2001 Taurus/Sable	1F1F-GD	JQP3	1F1Z-GE	JQP4	1DD14N0507	WDS B14.14 Release or Later
2001 Taurus/Sable	1F1F-VC	PAS2	1F1Z-VD	PAS3	1DD14N0G06	WDS B14.14 Release or Later
2001 Taurus/Sable	1F1F-XC	XVH2	1F1Z-XD	XVH3	1DD14N0K06	WDS B14.14 Release or Later

FMA050100123000X

Fig. 55 PCM calibrations

Application	Old Part Number (-12A650-)	Old Tear Tag	New Part Number (-12A650-)	New Tear Tag	Old Calibration	New Calibration	NGS/WDS Qualifier
2000 Taurus/Sable 3.0L 2V Engine	YU7A-AKA	GTW0	YU7Z-AKA	GTW1	0DD12N0A10	0DD12N0A10	WDS B13.1 Release or Later
2000 Taurus/Sable 3.0L 2V Engine	YU7A-AGA	ZST0	YU7Z-AGA	ZST1	0DD13N0A05	0DD13N0A05	WDS B13.1 Release or Later
2000 Taurus/Sable 3.0L 2V Engine	YU7A-AHA	ZDF0	YU7Z-AHA	ZDF1	0DD12N0B11	0DD12N0B11	WDS B13.1 Release or Later
2000 Taurus/Sable 3.0L 2V Engine	YU7A-ALA	YOP0	YU7Z-ALA	YOP1	0DD13N0505	0DD13N0505	WDS B13.1 Release or Later
2000 Taurus/Sable 3.0L 2V Engine (FFV)	YU7A-ANB	HES1	YU7Z-ANB	HES2	ODD1ND0505	0DD1ND0505	WDS B13.1 Release or Later

FMA050100126000X

Fig. 56 PCM calibrations

lower arm using pitman arm puller tool No. T64P-3590-F, or equivalent.

22. Insert pry bar through opening in lower arm. With end of pry bar on frame rail, push down on front suspension lower arm until ball joint stud is free from front suspension lower arm. Pull hub and strut outward, remove CV joint stub shaft from hub and rest halfshaft on frame rail, **Fig. 51.**
23. Assemble CV joint puller, extension and impact slide hammer tool Nos. T86P-3514-A1, T86P-3514-A2 and D79P-100-A, or equivalents. Insert CV joint puller adapter behind inboard CV joint housing, **Fig. 52.**
24. Release driveshaft bearing retainer clip using suitable impact slide hammer, **Fig. 53.**
25. Remove halfshaft and tools.
26. Disconnect four oxygen sensor electrical connectors.
27. Remove Y-pipe.
28. Disconnect two starter motor electrical connectors.
29. Remove starter motor from transaxle.
30. **On models equipped with 3.0L 12-valve engine,** remove housing cover from transaxle.
31. **On all models,** remove front subframe.
32. Position Rotunda high-lift transmission jack tool No. 014-00210, or equivalent, under transaxle and support transaxle.
33. Remove lower engine to transaxle bolts.
34. Remove four flexplate to torque converter nuts.
35. Remove rear engine support from transaxle.
36. Remove bolt from righthand engine mount brace and slowly lower transaxle.

Installation

1. Place transaxle on Rotunda high-lift transmission jack tool No. 014-00210, or equivalent, and position under vehicle.
2. Slowly raise transaxle and align with engine block.
3. Install one bolt into righthand engine mount brace.
4. Install rear engine support to transaxle and secure with three bolts and two nuts.
5. Install torque converter to flexplate nuts.
6. **On models equipped with 3.0L 12-valve engine,** install one lower transaxle to engine bolt.
7. **On models equipped with 3.0L 24-valve and 3.4L engines,** install four lower transaxle to engine bolts.
8. **On all models,** install front subframe.
9. Remove jack from under transaxle.
10. **On models equipped with 3.0L 12-valve engine,** install transaxle housing cover and secure with one bolt.
11. **On all models,** install starter motor to transaxle.
12. Connect starter motor electrical connectors.
13. Install Y-pipe.
14. Connect oxygen sensor electrical connectors.
15. Install both halfshafts into vehicle.
16. Install front tire and wheel assemblies.
17. Lower vehicle.
18. Remove three-bar engine support.
19. Remove engine lift bracket set from engine.
20. Install upper transaxle to engine bolts.
21. Connect fluid cooler lines from transaxle.
22. Install transaxle shift cable into shift cable bracket. Connect shift cable end to TR sensor manual lever. Secure with shift actuator cable fitting and one nut.
23. Connect transaxle harness electrical connector and TR sensor connector.
24. Install air cleaner, battery and battery tray.

TECHNICAL SERVICE BULLETINS

HARSH SHIFTS & ENGAGEMENTS AFTER TRANSAXLE EXCHANGE

1998 Continental, Sable & Taurus

On these models, there may be harsh shifts and engagements after transaxle has been replaced. Diagnostic Trouble Codes (DTCs) 628, P07401 and/or P01744 may be stored.

This condition may be caused by improper transaxle being installed.

To correct this condition, replace transaxle with proper unit, **Fig. 54.**

NO 4TH GEAR

1998 Continental, Sable & Taurus

On these models, there may be no 4th gear (3–4 upshift).

This condition may be caused by broken forward clutch control valve and spring retaining clip.

To correct this condition, remove valve body and install revised retaining clip part No. F8DZ-7F194-AA.

SHUDDER, VIBRATION DURING 1ST GEAR DECELERATION, DTC P1443

2000–01 Sable & Taurus w/3.0L 24 Valve Duratec Engine

On these models, built before 10/5/2000, there may be a perceived long cold cranking time and hard starting. On 2000 models there may be an erroneous DTC P1443 and harsh coasting downshifts.

These conditions may be caused by the PCM calibration. To correct these conditions, proceed as follows:

1. Diagnose and repair any present DTCs.
2. Program PCM to latest calibration, **Fig. 55.**
3. If using a New Generation Star (NGS) tester it might ask "Would you like to modify any PCM parameters?" Reply with a "No." This will prevent changes in tire size and axle ratio. If "Yes" was entered by mistake, it may be required to key in "797" for tire size and "3.47" for final drive axle ratio.
4. Fill in Authorized Modification Decal part No. FPS 8262 and affix adjacent to VECI decal. Cover with clear plastic shield.
5. Inform vehicle owner that several drive cycles may be required to completely adapt PCM to new calibration.

SURGING SENSATION ON DOWNHILL COAST

2000 Sable & Taurus w/3.0L 2-Valve Engine

On these models there may be a closed throttle downhill surge sensation during 2–3 shifts with no vehicle speed increase, most noticeable in hilly terrain on downhill coasting with vehicle speed slowly increasing to 25 mph.

This may be caused by the PCM calibration. To correct this condition, proceed as follows:

Application	Old Part Number (-12A650-)	Old Tear Tag	New Part Number (-12A650-)	New Tear Tag	Old Calibration	New Calibration	NGS/WDS Qualifier
3.0L 2V AX4S Trans.	1F1Z-FD	VMC3	1F1Z-FE	VMC4	12S0507	12S0510	WDS B11.15 or B12.3 Release
3.0L 2V AX4N Trans.	1F1Z-ED	TYD3	1F1Z-EE	TYD4	12N0507	12N0510	WDS B11.15 or B12.3 Release
3.0L 2V Flex Fuel, AX4S Trans.	1F1Z-ZD	PKK3	1F1Z-ZE	PKK4	1FS0507	1FS0510	WDS B11.15 or B12.3 Release
3.0L 2V Flex Fuel, AX4N Trans.	1F1Z-DC	LUA3	1F1Z-DD	LUA4	1FN0507	1FN0510	WDS B11.15 or B12.3 Release
3.0L 2V, AX4N GCC Countries, Leaded Fuel	1F1Z-NC	PWF2	1F1Z-ND	PWF3	12N0G06	12N0G10	WDS B11.15 or B12.3 Release

FMA050100127000X

Fig. 57 PCM calibrations

1. Diagnose and repair any present DTCs.
2. Program PCM to latest calibration, **Fig. 56.**
3. Fill in Authorized Modification Decal part No. FPS 8262 and affix adjacent to VECI decal. Cover with clear plastic shield.

ROUGH COLD GEAR ENGAGEMENT, SURGES ON 2–3 SHIFTS

2001 Sable & Taurus w/3.0L 2-Valve Vulcan Engine

On these models, built prior to 3/1/2001, these conditions may accompany a high idle during Park to Reverse or Drive to Reverse shifts, high speed creep in Drive or Reverse when cold and engine RPM surges during a 2–3 upshift coast.

These conditions may be caused by the PCM calibrations. To correct these conditions, proceed as follows:

1. Diagnose and repair any present DTCs.
2. Program PCM to latest calibration, **Fig. 57.**
3. If using a New Generation Star (NGS) tester it might ask "Would you like to modify any PCM parameters?" Reply with a "No." This will prevent changes in tire size and axle ratio. If "Yes" was entered by mistake, it may be required to key in "797" for tire size and "3.47" for final drive axle ratio.
4. Fill in Authorized Modification Decal part No. FPS 8262 and affix adjacent to VECI decal. Cover with clear plastic shield.
5. Inform vehicle owner that several drive cycles may be required to completely adapt PCM to new calibration.

TIGHTENING SPECIFICATIONS

Year	Component	Torque/Ft. Lbs.
CONTINENTAL		
1998–2002	Battery To Starter Terminal	96–120①
	Case To Chain Cover 8 MM	108①
	Case To Chain Cover 10 MM	19
	Case To Stator Support (1998)	80–106①
	Case To Stator Support (1999–2002)	96①
	Chain Cover To Case 8 MM	96①
	Chain Cover To Case 10 MM	18
	Chain Cover To Case 13 MM	32
	Chain Cover To Case 24 MM	23
	Dust Cover To Case	89①
	Engine Mount	60–85
	Engine Mount To Support	66
	Filler Tube To Case	84–108①
	Ground Strap	13–17
	Hose Screws	20–30①
	Ignition Switch To Starter Terminal	44①
	Manual Cable Bracket	17
	Manual Lever To Manual Shaft	10
	Power Steering Line Bracket	40–50①
	Pressure Switch To Pump Body	84–108①
	Pump Body To Chain Cover (1998)	80–106①
	Pump Body To Chain Cover (1999–2002)	89①
	Rear Engine Support To Transaxle (1998)	44–60
	Rear Engine Support To Transaxle (1999–2002)	46
	Righthand Engine Mount To Transaxle Case	46
	Shaft Cable Stud	23
	Shift Cable To Manual Lever	18
	Torque Converter To Flexplate (1998)	20–34
	Torque Converter To Flexplate (1999–2002)	26
	Transaxle Cooler Line Fitting At Radiator	96–144①
	Transaxle Cooler Line Fitting At Transaxle	15
	Transaxle Cooler Line	15
	Transaxle Housing Cover (1998)	84–108①
	Transaxle Housing Cover (1999–2002)	89①
	Transaxle Pan	108①
	TSS Sensor	96①
	Upper Transaxle To Engine (1998)	25–34
	Upper Transaxle To Engine (1999–2002)	46
	Valve Body To Chain Cover (1998)	84–108①
	Valve Body To Chain Cover (1999–2002)	89①
	Valve Body To Pump (1998)	84–108①
	Valve Body To Pump (1999–2002)	89①
	Vehicle Speed Sensor	31–39①
	Wheel Hub Nut (1998)	180–200
	Wheel Hub Nut (1999–2002)	184

Continued

TIGHTENING SPECIFICATIONS—Continued

Year	Component	Torque/Ft. Lbs.
CONTINENTAL		
1998–2002	Wheel Lug Nuts (1998–99)	85–105
	Wheel Lug Nuts (2000–02)	95
	Y-Pipe	30
SABLE & TAURUS		
1998–2002	Case To Chain Cover 8 MM	108①
	Case To Chain Cover 10 MM	19
	Case To Stator Support (1998)	80–106①
	Case To Stator Support (1999–2002)	96①
	Chain Cover To Case 8 MM	96①
	Chain Cover To Case 10 MM	18
	Chain Cover To Case 13 MM	32
	Chain Cover To Case 24 MM	23
	Dust Cover To Case	89①
	Engine Mount	60–85
	Engine Mount To Support	66
	Filler Tube To Case	84–108①
	Hose Screws	20–30①
	Manual Cable Bracket	17
	Manual Lever To Manual Shaft	10
	Power Steering Line Bracket	40–50①
	Pressure Switch To Pump Body	84–108①
	Pump Body To Chain Cover (1998)	84–108①
	Pump Body To Chain Cover (1999–2002)	89①
	Shaft Cable Stud	23
	Shift Cable To Manual Lever	18
	Subframe	55–75
	Torque Converter To Flexplate (1998–99)	20–34
	Torque Converter To Flexplate (2000–02)	27
	Transaxle Cooler Line Fitting At Radiator	96–144①
	Transaxle Cooler Line Fitting At Transaxle	15
	Transaxle Cooler Line	15
	Transaxle Housing Cover (1998–99)	84–108①
	Transaxle Housing Cover (2000–02)	89①
	Transaxle Pan	108①
	Transaxle To Engine (1998)	41–50
	Transaxle To Engine, Lower (1999 3.0L 2V)	39–53
	Transaxle To Engine, Lower (1999 SHO)	25–34
	Transaxle To Engine, Lower (2000–02 3.0L 2V)	46
	Transaxle To Engine, Upper (1999–2002)	46
	TSS Sensor	96①
	Valve Body To Chain Cover (1998)	84–108①
	Valve Body To Chain Cover (1999–2002)	89①
	Valve Body To Pump (1998)	84–108①
	Valve Body To Pump (1999–2002)	89①
	Vehicle Speed Sensor	31–39①
	Wheel Hub Nut (1998–99)	180–200

Continued

TIGHTENING SPECIFICATIONS—Continued

Year	Component	Torque/Ft. Lbs.
SABLE & TAURUS		
1998–2002	Wheel Hub Nut (2000–02)	184
	Wheel Lug Nuts (1998–99)	85–105
	Wheel Lug Nuts (2000–02)	95
	Y-Pipe	30

① — Inch lbs.

4R70W (AODE-W) Automatic Overdrive Transmission

NOTE: On Air Bag Equipped Models, Refer To "Air Bag System Precautions" Located In The Front Of This Manual For System Disarming & Arming Procedures.

NOTE: Refer To "Computer Relearn Procedures" Located In The Front Of This Manual When Battery Power To The Computer Has Been Interrupted.

NOTE: "Electrical Symbol & Wire Color Code Identification" Located In The Front Of This Manual May Be Used As An Aid When Using Wiring Circuits Found In This Section.

NOTE: Prior To Performing Any Service Operations Listed In This Section, Consult "Technical Service Bulletins" Section For Related Information.

INDEX

PRECAUTIONS

AIR BAG SYSTEMS

Refer to "Air Bag System Precautions" in front of this manual for system disarming and arming procedures.

BATTERY GROUND CABLE

Prior to service, disconnect battery ground cable and isolate as required.

IDENTIFICATION

These transmissions may be identified by tag attached to upper righthand extension housing to transmission case bolt. Tags include model prefix and suffix, a service identification number and a build date code, **Fig. 1.** Service identification number indicates changes to service details which affect interchangeability when transmission model is not changed. For interpretation of this number the Ford Master Parts Catalog should be consulted.

DESCRIPTION

This unit is a four-speed automatic transmission incorporating an integral overdrive feature. With selector lever in 1 position, transmission will start and remain in first gear until selector lever is moved to another position. In 3 position, transmission will automatically shift through 1–2–3 range, but will not engage overdrive. In D position, transmission will automatically select appropriate time to shift into overdrive (4th gear). Design of transmission features a split torque path in third gear, where 40% of engine torque is transmitted hydraulically through torque converter and 60% is transmitted mechanically through solid connections (direct drive input shaft) to driveshaft. When transmission is in overdrive (4th gear), 100% of engine torque is transmitted through direct drive input shaft.

Transmission consists of a torque converter, compound planetary gear train and a hydraulic control system, **Fig. 2.** For gear control transmission has four friction clutches, two one-way roller clutches and two bands. Overdrive is accomplished by addition of a band to lock reverse sun gear while driving planet carrier. Torque converter operation is similar to other types of automatic transmission, but has an added damper and input shaft for 3rd gear and overdrive. Direct drive input shaft couples engine directly to direct clutch. This shaft is driven by torque converter cover through damper which cushions engine shock to transmission.

The 4R70W (AODE-W) transmission is an AOD-E transmission with wide ratio gears and is a four-speed rear wheel drive automatic with an electronic shift, torque converter clutch control and line pressure

I.D. TAG LOCATED ON TRANSMISSION CASE

ITEM	DESCRIPTION
1	Model Number
2	Assemble Level
3	Build Code

ITEM	DESCRIPTION
4	Serial Number
5	Build Date (YMDD)

FM5020001660000X

Fig. 1 Identification tag

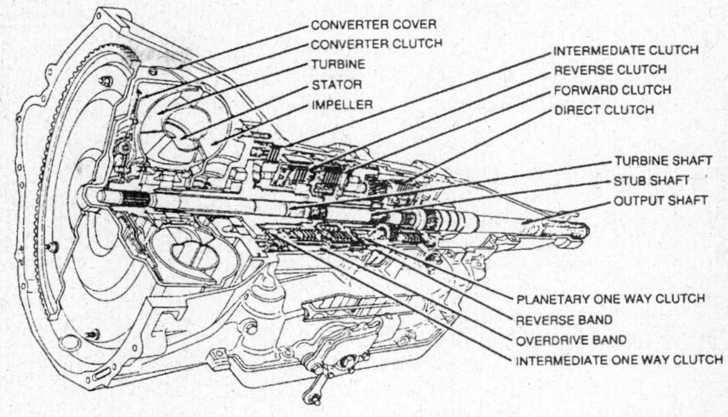

FM5029200634000X

Fig. 2 Cross-sectional view of transmission

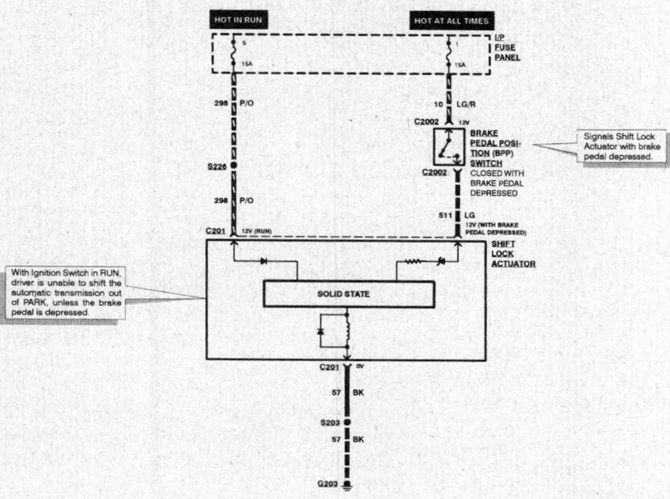

FM5029300953000A

Fig. 3 Shift interlock system wiring diagram. Crown Victoria, Grand Marquis, Mark VIII & Town Car

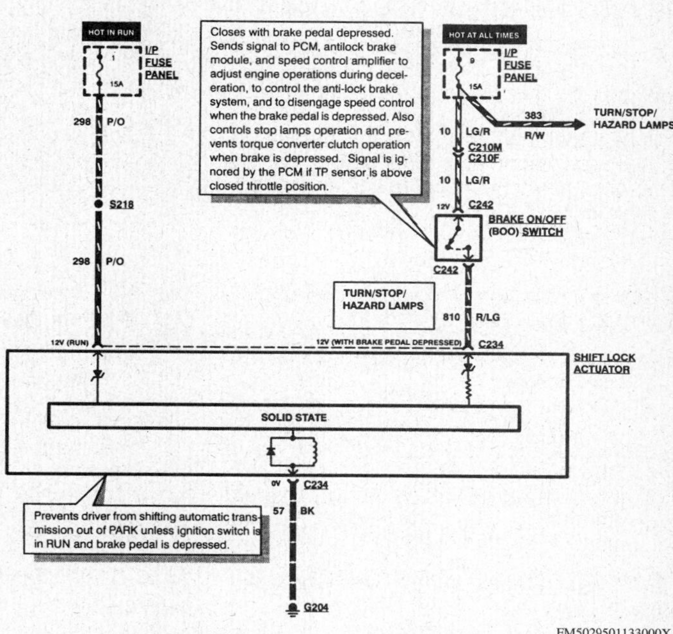

FM5029501133000X

Fig. 4 Shift interlock system wiring diagram. Mustang

controls. This transmission uses a double pinion compound gearset to produce four forward speeds and reverse. Two bands, two one-way roller clutches and four friction clutches are used to hold or drive various planetary gearset members.

For safety purposes, 4R70W also incorporates a brake shift interlock system. This prevents gear shift lever from being shifted from Park (with ignition On) unless brake pedal is applied. Brake shift interlock system includes an actuator mounted at base of steering column that runs continuously while ignition is On.

TROUBLESHOOTING

SHIFT INTERLOCK SYSTEM

CROWN VICTORIA, GRAND MARQUIS, MARK VIII, MUSTANG & TOWN CAR

Refer to wiring diagrams **Figs. 3 through 5,** and troubleshooting chart **Figs. 6 through 8.**

CROWN VICTORIA, GRAND MARQUIS & TOWN CAR

Refer to wiring diagram **Fig. 3.**

Test A1: Test Brake Lamps

1. Turn ignition On.
2. Apply brake pedal and view brake lamps.
3. If brake lamps light go to Test A7.
4. If brake lamps do not light go to Test A2.

Test A2: Test Fuse 10 (20A)

1. Turn ignition On.
2. Measure resistance of fuse 10 (20A).
3. If resistance of fuse is 5 ohms or less go to Test A4.
4. If resistance of fuse is 5 ohms or more go to Test A3.

Test A3: Test Circuit 10 (LG/R) For Short To Ground

1. Turn ignition On.
2. Disconnect Brake Pedal Position (BPP) switch connector C2002.
3. Measure resistance of circuit 10 (LG/R) at connector C2002.
4. If resistance is 10 Kohms or less, inspect circuit 10 (LG/R) for short to ground and test system for normal operation.
5. If resistance is 10 Kohms or more, go to Test A4.

Test A4: Test Circuit 10 (LG/R) For Open

1. Measure resistance between output side of fuse 10 (20A) and Brake Pedal Position (BPP) switch connector C2002, circuit 10 (LG/R).

2. If resistance is 5 ohms or less, go to Test A5.
3. If resistance is 5 ohms, or more, inspect circuit 10 (LG/R) for open and test system for normal operation.

Test A5: Test Brake Pedal Position (BPP) Switch

1. Measure resistance of BPP switch while open (Off) and closed (On).
2. If resistance of switch is greater than 10 Kohms while Off and 5 ohms or less while On, go to Test A8.
3. If resistance of switch is less than 10 Kohms while Off and 5 ohms, or more, while On, replace BPP switch and test system for normal operation.

Test A6: Inspect Circuit 810 (R/LG) For Short To Ground

1. Disconnect shift lock actuator connector C232.
2. Measure resistance of circuit 810 (R/LG) pin C232-1.
3. If resistance is 10 Kohms or less inspect circuit 810 (R/LG) for short to ground and test system for normal operation.
4. If resistance is 10 Kohms or more, go to Test A7.

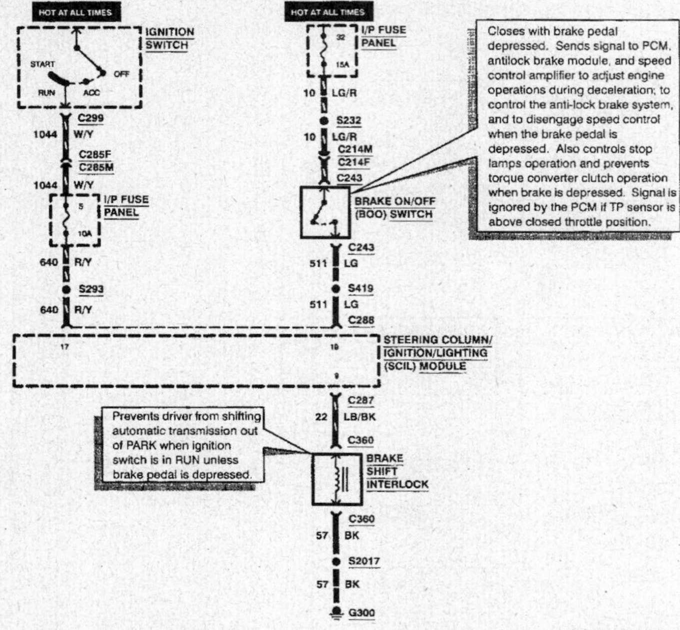

Fig. 5 Shift interlock system wiring diagram. Mark VIII

Test A7: Inspect Circuit 810 (R/LG) For Open

1. Measure resistance of circuit 810 (R/LG) between shift lock actuator pin C232-1 and brake On/Off switch connector C2002.
2. If resistance is 5 ohms or less go to Test A8.
3. If resistance is 5 ohms or more inspect circuit 810 (R/LG) for open and test system for normal operation.

Test A8: Test For B+ On Circuit 296 (W/P)

1. Measure voltage at shift lock actuator pin C298-3, circuit 296 (W/P).
2. If B+ is present, go to Test A12.
3. If B+ is not present, go to Test A9.

Test A9: Test Fuse 6 (5A)

1. Turn ignition On.
2. Measure fuse 20 (7.5A) resistance.
3. If resistance of fuse is 5 ohms or less, go to Test A11.
4. If resistance of fuse is 5 ohms, or more, go to Test A10.

Test A10: Test Circuit 296 (W/P) For Short To Ground

1. Measure resistance at Pin C232-3, circuit 296 (W/P).
2. If resistance is 10 Kohms or less, inspect circuit 296 (W/P) for short to ground, then test system for normal operation.
3. If resistance is 10 Kohms, or more, go to Test A11.

Test A11: Test Circuit 296 (W/P) For Open

1. Measure resistance of circuit 296 (W/P) between output side of fuse 20 (7.5A) and shift lock actuator pin C232-3.
2. If resistance is 5 ohms or less, go to Test A12.
3. If resistance is 5 ohms, or more, inspect circuit 296 (W/P) for open and test system for normal operation.

Test A12: Test Circuit 57 (BK) For Open

1. Measure resistance of shift lock actuator connector C232-2, circuit 57 (BK).
2. If resistance is 5 ohms or less, replace shift lock actuator and test system for normal operation.
3. If resistance is 5 ohms or more, inspect circuit 57 (BK) for open and test system for normal operation.

MUSTANG

Refer to wiring diagram, **Fig. 4.**

Test A1: Test Brake Lamps

1. Turn ignition On.
2. Apply brake pedal and view brake lamps.
3. If brake lamps light go to Test A2.
4. If brake lamps do not light inspect brake lamp circuit operation.

Test A2: Inspect Circuit 511 (LG) For Open

1. Measure voltage of circuit 511 (LG) between shift lock actuator pin C234-1 harness side and ground while pressing and releasing brake pedal.
2. If measurement is more than 10 volts with brake pedal pressed and zero volts with pedal released, go to Test A3.
3. If measurement is not more than 10 volts with brake pedal pressed and zero volts with pedal released, repair circuit.

Test A3: Test Circuit 294 (WH/LB) For Open

1. Measure voltage at shift lock actuator pin C234-3, circuit 294 (WH/LB).
2. If measurement is more than 10 volts, go to Test A4.
3. If measurement is less than 10 volts, repair circuit.

Test A4: Test Circuit 57 (BK) For Open

1. Measure resistance of shift lock actuator connector C232-2, circuit 57 (BK).
2. If resistance is 5 ohms or less, replace shift lock actuator and test system for normal operation.
3. If resistance is 5 ohms, or more, inspect circuit 57 (BK) for open and test system for normal operation.

TRANSMISSION

Refer troubleshooting charts **Figs. 9 through 39.**

TROUBLESHOOTING TEST INDEX

SHIFT INTERLOCK SYSTEM

TRANSMISSION

Continued

TRANSMISSION—Continued

	Test Step	Result	Action to Take
A1	CHECK RUN FUSE		
	• CHECK RUN Fuse (5A) located in fuse junction panel. • **Is fuse OK?**	Yes No	GO to **A3**. GO to **A2**.
A2	CHECK RESISTANCE OF CIRCUIT 298 (P/O)		
	• Turn ignition switch OFF. • Remove RUN Fuse (5A). • Disconnect shiftlock actuator connector C209. • Measure resistance of Circuit 298 (P/O) and ground. • **Is resistance greater than 10,000 ohms?**	Yes No	GO to **A3**. SERVICE Circuit 298 (P/O) for short to ground. RESTORE vehicle. RETEST system.
A3	CHECK POWER SUPPLY FROM RUN FUSE (5A)		
	• Reinstall RUN Fuse (5A). • Disconnect shiftlock actuator connector C209. • Measure voltage on Circuit 298 (P/O) and ground. • Turn ignition ON. • **Is voltage B+?**	Yes No	GO to **A4**. SERVICE Circuit 298 (P/O) for open. RESTORE vehicle. RETEST system.
A4	CHECK STOP LAMP OPERATION		
	• Press brake pedal. • **Does stoplamp operate?**	Yes No	GO to **A5**. SERVICE stoplamp circuit.
A5	CHECK POWER SUPPLY BETWEEN BRAKE PEDAL AND SHIFTLOCK ACTUATOR		
	• Apply brake pedal. • Measure voltage on Circuit 511 (LG) and ground. • **Is voltage B+ with brake pedal applied?**	Yes No	GO to **A6**. SERVICE Circuit 511 (LG) for open. RESTORE vehicle. RETEST sytsem.
A6	MEASURE RESISTANCE IN GROUND CIRCUIT		
	• With C209 disconnected, measure resistance of Circuit 57 (BK) and ground. • **Is resistance less than 5 ohms?**	Yes No	REPLACE shiftlock actuator. SERVICE Circuit 57 (BK) for open. RESTORE vehicle. RETEST system.

FM5029300954000A

Fig. 6 Shift Interlock System Troubleshooting Chart. 1998 Crown Victoria, Grand Marquis & Town Car

	Test Step	Result	Action to Take
A1	CHECK FUSE 1 (15A)		
	• Check Fuse 1 (15A) located in fuse junction panel. • **Is fuse OK?**	Yes No	GO to **A3**. GO to **A2**.
A2	CHECK RESISTANCE IN CIRCUIT 298 (P/O)		
	• Turn ignition switch OFF. • Remove Fuse 1 (15A). • Disconnect shift lock actuator connector C234. • Measure resistance of the Circuit 298 (P/O) and ground. • **Is resistance greater than 10,000 ohms?**	Yes No	GO to **A3**. SERVICE Circuit 298 (P/O) for short to ground. RESTORE vehicle. RETEST system.
A3	CHECK POWER SUPPLY FROM FUSE 1 (15A)		
	• Reinstall RUN Fuse 1 (15A). • Disconnect shift lock actuator connector C234. • Measure voltage on Circuit 298 (P/O) and ground. • Turn ignition ON. • **Is voltage B+?**	Yes No	GO to **A4**. SERVICE Circuit 298 (P/O) for open. RESTORE vehicle. RETEST system.
A4	CHECK STOPLAMP OPERATION		
	• Press brake pedal. • **Does stoplamp operate?**	Yes No	GO to **A5**. SERVICE stoplamp circuit.
A5	CHECK POWER SUPPLY BETWEEN BRAKE PEDAL AND SHIFT LOCK ACTUATOR		
	• Apply brake pedal. • Measure voltage on Circuit 810 (R/LG) and ground. • **Is voltage B+ with brake pedal applied?**	Yes No	GO to **A6**. SERVICE Circuit 810 (R/LG) for open. RESTORE vehicle. RETEST system.
A6	MEASURE RESISTANCE IN GROUND CIRCUIT		
	• With C234 disconnected, measure resistance of Circuit 57 (BK) and ground. • **Is resistance less than 5 ohms?**	Yes No	REPLACE shift lock actuator. SERVICE Circuit 57 (BK) for open. RESTORE vehicle. RETEST system.

FM5029501135000X

Fig. 7 Shift Interlock System Troubleshooting Chart. Mustang

TEST CONDITIONS	TEST DETAILS/RESULTS/ACTIONS
C1 CHECK THE BRAKE SHIFT INTERLOCK IN THE ACC POSITION	
1	
2	2 With the brake pedal released, attempt to move the transmission range selector lever to REVERSE. • Did the transmission range selector lever move to REVERSE? → **Yes** GO to **C3**. → **No** GO to **C2**.
C2 CHECK FOR THE PROPER OPERATION	
1	
2	2 Press the brake pedal.

FM5029701136010X

Fig. 8 Shift Interlock System Troubleshooting Chart (Part 1 of 6). Mark VIII

TEST CONDITIONS	TEST DETAILS/RESULTS/ACTIONS
C2 CHECK FOR THE PROPER OPERATION (Continued)	
3	3 Move the transmission range selector lever to REVERSE. • Did the transmission range selector lever move to REVERSE? → **Yes** The brake shift interlock system is operating properly. CHECK for intermittent or loose connections. CHECK the transmission range selector alignment and the adjustment. → **No** GO to **C9**.
C3 CHECK THE STEERING COLUMN ADJUSTMENT	
	1 Actuate the steering column adjustment switch to the tilt or the telescope position. • Does the steering column adjust? → **Yes** GO to **C4**. → **No** Diagnose steering column.

FM5029701136020X

Fig. 8 Shift Interlock System Troubleshooting Chart (Part 2 of 6). Mark VIII

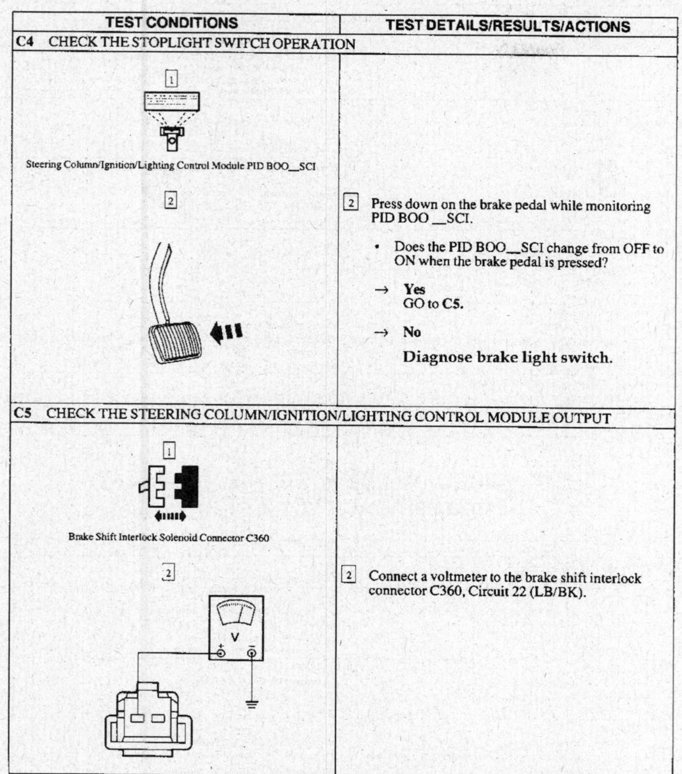

TEST CONDITIONS	TEST DETAILS/RESULTS/ACTIONS
C4 CHECK THE STOPLIGHT SWITCH OPERATION	
1 Steering Column/Ignition/Lighting Control Module PID BOO__SCI	
2	2 Press down on the brake pedal while monitoring PID BOO __SCI. • Does the PID BOO__SCI change from OFF to ON when the brake pedal is pressed? → **Yes** GO to **C5.** → **No** **Diagnose brake light switch.**
C5 CHECK THE STEERING COLUMN/IGNITION/LIGHTING CONTROL MODULE OUTPUT	
1 Brake Shift Interlock Solenoid Connector C360	
2	2 Connect a voltmeter to the brake shift interlock connector C360, Circuit 22 (LB/BK).

FM5029701136030X

Fig. 8 Shift Interlock System Troubleshooting Chart (Part 3 of 6). Mark VIII

TEST CONDITIONS	TEST DETAILS/RESULTS/ACTIONS
C5 CHECK THE STEERING COLUMN/IGNITION/LIGHTING CONTROL MODULE OUTPUT (Continued)	
3 Steering Column/Ignition/Lighting Control Module Active Command BRAKE SYSTEM 4 Trigger BRK/SHIFT On	• Is the voltage reading B+? → **Yes** GO to **C8.** → **No** GO to **C6.**
C6 CHECK CIRCUIT 22 (LB/BK) FOR A SHORT TO THE GROUND	
1 Steering Column/Ignition/Lighting Control Module Connector C287	
2	2 Connect an ohmmeter between the steering column/ignition/lighting control module connector Pin C287-9 and ground. • Is resistance reading 10 K ohms or less? → **Yes** SERVICE Circuit 22 (LB/BK) for a short to the ground. RETEST the system. → **No** GO to **C7.**

FM5029701136040X

Fig. 8 Shift Interlock System Troubleshooting Chart (Part 4 of 6). Mark VIII

TEST CONDITIONS	TEST DETAILS/RESULTS/ACTIONS
C7 CHECK CIRCUIT 22 (LB/BK) FOR AN OPEN	
1	1 Connect an ohmmeter between the steering column/ignition/lighting control module connector Pin C287-9 and the brake shift interlock solenoid connector C360, Circuit 22 (LB/BK). • Is the resistance 5 ohms or less? → **Yes** REPLACE the steering column/ignition/lighting control module. RETEST the system. → **No** SERVICE Circuit 22 (LB/BK) for an open. RETEST the system.
C8 CHECK CIRCUIT 57 (BK) FOR AN OPEN	
1	1 Connect an ohmmeter between the brake shift interlock solenoid connector C360, Circuit 57 (BK) and the ground. • Is the resistance 5 ohms or less? → **Yes** REPLACE the brake shift interlock solenoid. RETEST the system. → **No** SERVICE Circuit 57 (BK) for an open. RETEST the system.

FM5029701136050X

Fig. 8 Shift Interlock System Troubleshooting Chart (Part 5 of 6). Mark VIII

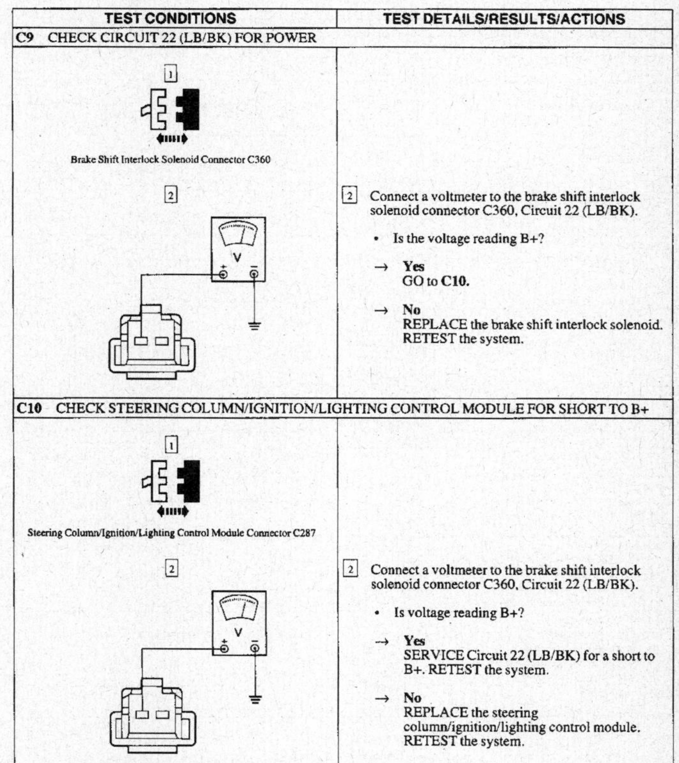

TEST CONDITIONS	TEST DETAILS/RESULTS/ACTIONS
C9 CHECK CIRCUIT 22 (LB/BK) FOR POWER	
1 Brake Shift Interlock Solenoid Connector C360	
2	2 Connect a voltmeter to the brake shift interlock solenoid connector C360, Circuit 22 (LB/BK). • Is the voltage reading B+? → **Yes** GO to **C10.** → **No** REPLACE the brake shift interlock solenoid. RETEST the system.
C10 CHECK STEERING COLUMN/IGNITION/LIGHTING CONTROL MODULE FOR SHORT TO B+	
1 Steering Column/Ignition/Lighting Control Module Connector C287	
2	2 Connect a voltmeter to the brake shift interlock solenoid connector C360, Circuit 22 (LB/BK). • Is voltage reading B+? → **Yes** SERVICE Circuit 22 (LB/BK) for a short to B+. RETEST the system. → **No** REPLACE the steering column/ignition/lighting control module. RETEST the system.

FM5029701136060X

Fig. 8 Shift Interlock System Troubleshooting Chart (Part 6 of 6). Mark VIII

Possible Component	Reference/Action
201 — ELECTRICAL ROUTINE	
• No Electrical Concerns	
301 — HYDRAULIC/MECHANICAL ROUTINE	
Fluid • Improper level • Condition	 • Adjust fluid to proper level. • Inspect Fluid Condition.
Shift Linkage • Damaged, out of adjustment	 • Inspect and service as required. Verify linkage adjustment After servicing linkage, verify Digital TR sensor is properly adjusted.

FM5029801504010X

Fig. 9 Routines 201 & 301: No Forward Engagement (Part 1 of 2)

Possible Component	Reference/Action
202 — ELECTRICAL ROUTINE	
• No Electrical Concerns	
302 — HYDRAULIC/MECHANICAL ROUTINE	
Fluid • Improper level • Condition	 • Adjust fluid to proper level. • Inspect Fluid Condition.
Shift Linkage • Damaged or out of adjustment	 • Inspect and service as required. Verify linkage adjustment. After servicing linkage, verify that the Digital TR sensor is properly adjusted.
Improper Pressures • Low reverse clutch pressure, low reverse band pressure, low line pressure	 • Check pressure at line pressure tap. If pressures are low, check the following possible components: — fluid filter and seal assembly, — main controls, — reverse servo, — pump assembly, — reverse clutch assembly.

FM5029801505010X

Fig. 10 Routines 202 & 302: No Reverse Engagement (Part 1 of 2)

Possible Component	Reference/Action
203 — ELECTRICAL ROUTINE	
Powertrain Control System • Electrical inputs/outputs, vehicle wiring harnesses, PCM, TP, MAF, EI system, EPC solenoid, TFT sensor	 • Run Self-Test. Refer to MOTOR's Domestic Transmissions for diagnosis. Perform engagement test, EPC test and Pinpoint Tests B and E using Rotunda Transmission Tester 007-00130, or equivalent. Service as required. Clear codes, road test and rerun self-test.
303 — HYDRAULIC/MECHANICAL ROUTINE	
Fluid • Improper level • Condition	 • Adjust fluid to proper level. • Inspect Fluid Condition.
Shift Linkage • Damaged or out of adjustment	 • Inspect and service as required. Verify linkage adjustment. After servicing linkage, verify that the Digital TR sensor is properly adjusted.
Improper Pressures • High line pressure, high EPC pressure	 • Check pressure at line and EPC pressure taps. Refer to Reference: If high, check the following possible components: main controls, oil filter and seal assembly.
Oil Filter and Seal Assembly • Plugged or damaged • Filter seal damaged	 • Replace filter and seal assembly.
Main Controls • No. 6 Shuttle ball, No. 5 check ball, manual valve, main regulator valve stuck, damaged or missing • Loose bolts • Gasket damaged	 • Inspect for damage. Service as required. • Tighten bolts to specification. • Inspect for damage and replace.

FM5029801506010X

Fig. 11 Routines 203 & 303: Harsh Reverse Engagement (Part 1 of 2)

Possible Component	Reference/Action
• EPC solenoid stuck or damaged	• Inspect for damage, contamination. Perform EPC test in Routine No. 203. Service as required.
Low Reverse Servo • Seals (piston and cover) damaged • Servo cover retaining ring damaged • Anchor pins (case) damaged	 • Inspect for damage. Service as required.
Pump Assembly • Loose bolts • Porosity/cross leaks • Gasket damaged • No. 1 and No. 2 seal rings damaged	 • Tighten bolts to specification. • Inspect pump assembly. Replace as required. • Inspect for damage and replace. • Inspect for damage. Service as required.
Reverse Clutch Assembly • Seals, piston damaged • Check ball missing or damaged • Friction elements damaged, worn • Return spring piston damaged, worn	 • Inspect for damage. Service as required.
Low Reverse Band • Band, servo, anchor pin damaged or worn	 • Inspect for damage. Service as required.

FM5029801506020X

Fig. 11 Routines 203 & 303: Harsh Reverse Engagement (Part 2 of 2)

Possible Component	Reference/Action
Improper Pressures • Low forward clutch pressure, low line pressure	 • Check pressure at line and forward clutch tap. If pressures are low, check the following possible components: — fluid filter and seal assembly, — main controls, pump assembly, — forward clutch assembly.
Fluid Filter and Seal Assembly • Plugged, damaged • Filter seal damaged	 • Replace fluid filter and seal assembly.
Main Controls • 3-4 shift valve, main regulator valve, manual valve stuck, damaged • Bolts out of torque specification • Gaskets damaged • 2-3 accumulator and seals damaged	 • Inspect for damage. Service as required. • Tighten bolts to specification. • Inspect gasket for damage and replace. • Inspect piston, seals and bore for damage. Service as required.
Pump Assembly • Bolts out of torque specification • Porosity/cross leaks and ball missing or leaking, plugged hole • No. 3 and No. 4 seal rings damaged • Gaskets damaged	 • Tighten bolts to specification. • Inspect for porosity and leaks. Service as required. • Inspect seals for damage. Service as required. • Inspect for damage and replace.
Forward Clutch Assembly • Seals, piston damaged • Check balls damaged, missing, mislocated, not seating properly • Friction elements damaged or worn	 • Inspect seals for damage. Service as required. • Inspect for mislocation, poor seating, damage. Replace cylinder as required. • Check for abnormal wear, damage. Service as required.
Low One-Way Clutch Assembly (Planetary) • Worn, damaged or misassembled	 • Inspect for damage. Service as required.
Output Shaft • Damaged	 • Inspect for damage. Service as required.

FM5029801504020X

Fig. 9 Routines 201 & 301: No Forward Engagement (Part 2 of 2)

Possible Component	Reference/Action
Fluid Filter and Seal Assembly • Plugged, damaged	 • Replace filter and seal assembly.
Main Controls • No. 6 shuttle ball, manual valve, main regulator valve, 1-2 accumulator seals stuck or damaged • Bolts out of torque specification • Gasket damaged	 • Inspect for damage. Service as required. • Tighten bolts to specification. • Inspect for damage and replace.
Low Reverse Servo • Seals (piston and cover) damaged • Servo cover retaining ring damaged • Anchor pins (case) damaged	 • Inspect for damage. Service as required.
Pump Assembly • Bolts out of torque specification • Porosity/cross leaks/ball missing or leaking, plugged hole • Gasket damaged • No. 1 and 2 seal rings damaged	 • Tighten bolts to specification. • Inspect pump assembly. Replace as required. • Inspect for damage and replace. • Inspect for damage. Service as required.
Reverse Clutch Assembly • Seals, piston damaged • Check ball missing or damaged • Friction elements damaged or worn	 • Inspect for damage. Service as required.
Low Reverse Band • Band, servo, anchor pins damaged or worn	 • Inspect for damage. Service as required.

FM5029801505020X

Fig. 10 Routines 202 & 302: No Reverse Engagement (Part 2 of 2)

Possible Component	Reference/Action
204 — ELECTRICAL ROUTINE	
Powertrain Control System • Electrical inputs/outputs, vehicle wiring harnesses, PCM, TFT sensor, EPC solenoid	 • Run Self-Test. Refer to MOTOR's Domestic Transmission Manual for diagnosis. Perform engagement test, EPC test and Pinpoint Tests B and E using Rotunda Transmission Tester 007-00130, or equivalent. Service as required. Clear codes, road test and rerun self-test.
304 — HYDRAULIC/MECHANICAL ROUTINE	
Fluid • Improper level • Condition	 • Adjust fluid to proper level. • Inspect as described under Fluid Condition Check.
Improper Pressures • High forward clutch pressure, high line pressure, high EPC pressure	 • Check pressure at line, EPC and forward pressure taps. If pressures are high, check the following possible components: main controls, pump assembly.
Main Controls • Main regulator valve, 2-3 backout valve, 2-3 accumulator seal/retainer stuck, damaged • Bolts out of torque specification • Gaskets damaged • EPC solenoid stuck or damaged	 • Inspect and service as required. • Tighten bolts to specification. • Inspect for damage and replace. • Inspect for damage or contamination. Perform EPC test in Routine No. 204. Service as required.
Pump Assembly • Bolts out of torque specification • Porosity/cross leaks • Gaskets damaged • No. 3 and No. 4 seal ring damage	 • Tighten bolts to specification. • Inspect for porosity/leaks. Replace pump assembly as required. • Inspect for damage and replace.
Forward Clutch Assembly • Check balls missing or damaged • Friction element damaged or worn • Forward clutch wave spring damaged • Forward clutch return spring damaged	 • Inspect for mislocation, poor seating, damage. Replace forward clutch cylinder. • Inspect for damage. Service as required. • Inspect for damage. Service as required. • Inspect for damage. Service as required.

FM5029801507000X

Fig. 12 Routines 204 & 304: Harsh Forward Engagement

Possible Component	Reference/Action
205 — ELECTRICAL ROUTINE	
• No Electrical Concerns	
305 — HYDRAULIC/MECHANICAL ROUTINE	
Fluid • Improper level • Condition	• Adjust fluid to proper level. • Inspect Fluid Condition.
Shift Linkage • Damaged, out of adjustment	• Inspect and service as required. Verify linkage adjustment. After servicing linkage, verify that the Digital TR sensor is properly adjusted.
Improper Pressures • Low reverse clutch pressure, low reverse band pressure, low line pressure	• Check pressure at line tap. If pressures are low, check the following possible components: main controls, pump assembly, reverse clutch assembly, reverse servo.
Fluid Filter and Seal Assembly • Plugged, damaged • Fluid filter seal damaged	• Replace fluid filter and seal assembly.
Main Controls • No. 6 shuttle ball, 1-2 accumulator seals, manual valve, main regulator valve stuck or damaged • Bolts out of torque specification • Gaskets damaged	• Inspect for damage. Service as required. • Tighten bolts to specification. • Inspect for damage and replace.
Low Reverse Servo • Seals (piston and cover) damaged • Servo cover retaining ring assembled wrong.	• Inspect for damage. Service as required.
Pump Assembly • Bolts out of torque specification • Porosity/cross leaks/ball missing or leaking • Gaskets damaged • No. 1 and No. 2 seal rings damaged	• Tighten bolts to specification. • Inspect pump assembly. Replace as required. • Inspect for damage and replace. • Inspect for damage. Service as required.
Reverse Clutch Assembly • Seals, piston damaged • Check ball missing or damaged • Friction elements damaged, worn • Return spring and piston damaged, worn	• Inspect for damage. Service as required.
Low Reverse Band • Damaged, worn	• Inspect for damage. Service as required.

FM5029801508000X

Fig. 13 Routines 205 & 305: Delayed/Soft Reverse Engagement

Possible Component	Reference/Action
210 — ELECTRICAL ROUTINE	
Powertrain Control System • Electrical inputs/outputs, vehicle wiring harnesses, powertrain control module, shift solenoids, output shaft speed (OSS) sensor, Digital TR sensor	• Run self-test. Refer to MOTOR's Domestic Transmission Manual for diagnosis. Perform Pinpoint Tests A, D and F using Rotunda Transmission Tester 007-00130 with Rotunda Transmission Range (TR) Sensor Cable "E" 007-00111 and Digital (TR) Sensor Overlay 007-00131, or equivalent. Service as required. Clear codes, road test and rerun self-test.
310 — HYDRAULIC/MECHANICAL ROUTINE	
Fluid • Improper level • Condition	• Adjust fluid to proper level. • Inspect as described under Fluid Condition Check.
Shift Linkage, Digital TR Sensor • Damaged, out of adjustment	• Inspect and service as required. Verify linkage adjustment. After servicing linkage, verify that the Digital TR sensor is properly adjusted. • Refer to the following shift routine(s) for further diagnosis: **Shift** 1-2, **Routine** 220/320 **Shift** 2-3, **Routine** 221/321 **Shift** 3-4, **Routine** 222/322 **Shift** 4-3, **Routine** 223/323 **Shift** 3-2, **Routine** 224/324 **Shift** 2-1, **Routine** 225/325

FM5029801510010X

Fig. 15 Routines 210 & 310: Some Or All Shifts Missing

Possible Component	Reference/Action
212 — ELECTRICAL ROUTINE	
Powertrain Control System • Electrical inputs/outputs, vehicle wiring harnesses, powertrain control module, shift solenoids, TCC solenoid, digital TR sensor, OSS	• Run self-test. Refer to MOTOR's Domestic Transmission Manual for diagnosis. Perform Pinpoint Tests A, D and F using Rotunda Transmission Tester 007-00130, with Rotunda Transmission Range (TR) Sensor Cable "E" 418-F107 (007-00111) and Digital (TR) Sensor Overlay 007-00131 or equivalent. Service as required. Clear codes, road test and rerun self-test.
312 — HYDRAULIC/MECHANICAL ROUTINE	
Fluid • Improper level • Condition	• Adjust fluid to proper level. • Inspect Fluid Condition.
Main Controls • Valves, accumulators, seals, misassembled, stuck or damaged • Gaskets damaged • Solenoid screen (in valve body) blocked or damaged	• Inspect for damage. Service as required. • Inspect for damage and replace. • Clean or replace screen.
Torque Converter Clutch • Torque converter	• Refer to Hydraulic/Mechanical Routine 342, Converter Cycling/Shudder/Chatter.

FM5029801511010X

Fig. 17 Routines 212 & 312: Shift Timing Is Erratic/Hunting (Part 1 of 2)

Possible Component	Reference/Action
206 — ELECTRICAL ROUTINE	
• No Electrical Concerns	
306 — HYDRAULIC/MECHANICAL ROUTINE	
Fluid • Improper level • Condition	• Adjust fluid to proper level. • Inspect Fluid Condition.
Shift Linkage • Damaged, out of adjustment	• Inspect and service as required. Verify linkage adjustment. After servicing linkage, verify that the Digital TR sensor is properly adjusted.

FM5029801509010X

Fig. 14 Routines 206 & 306: Delayed/Soft Forward Engagement (Part 1 of 2)

Possible Component	Reference/Action
Improper Pressures • Low forward clutch pressure, low line pressure, low EPC pressure	• Check pressure at line, forward clutch and EPC taps. If pressures are low, check the following possible components: fluid filter and seal assembly, main controls and pump assembly.
Fluid Filter and Seal Assembly • Plugged, damaged • Fluid filter seal damaged	• Replace fluid filter and seal assembly.
Main Controls • 3-4 shift valve, main regulator valve • Bolts out of torque specification • Gaskets damaged • 2-3 or 1-2 accumulator, bore damaged or stuck	• Inspect and service as required. • Tighten bolts to specification. • Inspect for damage and replace. • Inspect for damage. Service as required
Pump Assembly • Bolts out of torque specification • Porosity/cross leaks • Gaskets damaged • No. 3, No. 4 seal rings damaged	• Tighten bolts to specification. • Inspect pump assembly. Replace as required. • Inspect for damage and replace. • Inspect for damage. Service as required
Forward Clutch Assembly • Seals, piston damaged • Check balls missing, damaged • Friction elements damaged, worn	• Inspect for damage. Service as required. • Inspect for mislocation, poor seating, damage. Replace cylinder as required. • Check for damage. Service as required.

FM5029801509020X

Fig. 14 Routines 206 & 306: Delayed/Soft Forward Engagement (Part 2 of 2)

Possible Component	Reference/Action
211 — ELECTRICAL ROUTINE	
Powertrain Control System • Electrical inputs/outputs, vehicle wiring harnesses, powertrain control module, shift solenoids, EPC solenoid, TFT sensor, OSS	• Run self-test. Refer to MOTOR's Domestic Transmission Manual for diagnosis. Perform Pinpoint Tests A, B, E and F using Rotunda Transmission Tester 007-00130 or equivalent. Service as required. Clear codes, road test and rerun Self-Test.
311 — HYDRAULIC/MECHANICAL ROUTINE	
Other • Tire size change, axle ratio change	• Verify vehicle has original equipment. Refer to Certification Label and Safety Standard Certification Label. Changes in tire size, axle ratio will affect shift timing.
Fluid • Improper level • Condition	• Adjust fluid to proper level. • Inspect Fluid Condition.
Improper Pressures • Line pressure, EPC pressure	• Check pressure at line and EPC taps. If not OK, check the main controls. If OK, refer to the following shift routine(s) for further diagnosis: **Shift** 1-2, **Routine** 320 **Shift** 2-3, **Routine** 321 **Shift** 3-4, **Routine** 322 **Shift** 4-3, **Routine** 323 **Shift** 3-2, **Routine** 324 **Shift** 2-1, **Routine** 325
Main Controls • EPC solenoid, stuck or damaged hydraulically or mechanically • Valves, accumulators, seals stuck or damaged or misassembled • Gaskets damaged • Solenoid screen (in valve body) blocked or damaged	• Inspect for damage, contamination. Perform EPC tests in Routine No. 211. Service as required. • Inspect for damage. Service as required. • Inspect for damage and replace. • Clean or replace screen.

FM5029801510020X

Fig. 16 Routines 211 & 311: Some Or All Shifts Missing

Possible Component	Reference/Action
Specific Shifts	• Refer to the following shift routine(s) for further diagnosis: **Shift** 1-2, **Routine**, 320 **Shift** 2-3, **Routine**, 321 **Shift** 3-4, **Routine**, 322 **Shift** 4-3, **Routine**, 323 **Shift** 3-2, **Routine**, 324 **Shift** 2-1, **Routine**, 325

FM5029801511020X

Fig. 17 Routines 212 & 312: Shift Timing Is Erratic/Hunting (Part 2 of 2)

Possible Component	Reference/Action
213 — ELECTRICAL ROUTINE	
Powertrain Control System • Electrical inputs/outputs, vehicle wiring harnesses, powertrain control module, EPC solenoid, OSS	• Run Self-Test. Refer to MOTOR's Domestic Transmission Manual for diagnosis. Perform Pinpoint Tests E and F using Rotunda Transmission Tester 007-00130 or equivalent. Service as required. Clear codes, road test and rerun Self-Test.
313 — HYDRAULIC/MECHANICAL ROUTINE	
Fluid • Improper level • Condition	• Adjust fluid to proper level. • Inspect as described under Fluid Check.
Improper Pressures • Low line pressure, low EPC pressure	• Check pressures at line and EPC taps. If pressures are low or all shifts are soft/slipping, go to Main Controls. If pressures are OK and a specific shift is soft/slipping, refer to the following routine(s) for further diagnosis: **Shift** 1-2, **Routine**, 320 **Shift** 2-3, **Routine**, 321 **Shift** 3-4, **Routine**, 322 **Shift** 4-3, **Routine**, 323 **Shift** 3-2, **Routine**, 324 **Shift** 2-1, **Routine**, 325
Main Controls • 1-2 accumulator, 2-3 backout valve, main regulator valve, overdrive servo regulator valve stuck, damaged or misassembled • EPC solenoid stuck or damaged	• Inspect for damage. Service as required. • Inspect for damage and contamination. Perform EPC tests in Routine No. 213. Service as required.

FM5029801512000X

Fig. 18 Routines 213 & 313: Shift Feel Is Soft/ Slipping

Possible Component	Reference/Action
214 — ELECTRICAL ROUTINE	
Powertrain Control System • Electrical inputs/outputs, vehicle wiring harnesses, EPC solenoid, OSS	• Run self-test. Refer to MOTOR's Domestic Transmission Manual for diagnosis. Perform Pinpoint Tests E and F using Rotunda Transmission Tester 007-00130 or equivalent Service as required. Clear codes, road test and rerun Self-Test.
314 — HYDRAULIC/MECHANICAL ROUTINE	
Fluid • Improper level • Condition	• Adjust fluid to proper level. • Inspect Fluid Condition.

FM5029801513010X

Fig. 19 Routines 214 & 314: Shift Feel Is Harsh (Part 1 of 2)

Possible Component	Reference/Action
Improper Pressures • High line pressure, high EPC pressure	• Check pressures at line and EPC taps. If pressures are high or all shifts are harsh, go to Main Controls. If pressures are OK and a specific shift is harsh, refer to the following shift routine(s) for further diagnosis: **Shift** 1-2, **Routine**, 320 **Shift** 2-3, **Routine**, 321 **Shift** 3-4, **Routine**, 322 **Shift** 4-3, **Routine**, 323 **Shift** 3-2, **Routine**, 324 **Shift** 2-1, **Routine**, 325
Main Controls • 1-2 accumulator, 2-3 backout valve, main regulator valve, overdrive servo regulator valve stuck, damaged or misassembled • EPC solenoid stuck or damaged	• Inspect for damage. Service as required. • Inspect for damage, contamination. Perform EPC tests in Routine 214. Service as required.

FM5029801513020X

Fig. 19 Routines 214 & 314: Shift Feel Is Harsh (Part 2 of 2)

Possible Component	Reference/Action
215 — ELECTRICAL ROUTINE	
Powertrain Control System • Electrical inputs/outputs, vehicle wiring harnesses, powertrain control module, shift solenoids, digital TR sensor	• Run Self-Test. Refer to MOTOR's Domestic Transmission Manual for diagnosis. Perform Pinpoint Tests A and D using Rotunda Transmission Tester 007-00130, with Rotunda Transmission Range (TR) Sensor Cable "E" 418-F107 (007-00111) and Digital (TR) Sensor Overlay 007-00131 or equivalent. Service as required. Clear codes, road test and rerun Self-Test.
315 — HYDRAULIC/MECHANICAL ROUTINE	
Shift Linkage, Digital TR Sensor • Damaged or out of adjustment	• Inspect and service as required. Verify linkage adjustment as After servicing linkage, verify that the digital TR sensor is properly adjusted.
Improper Pressures • Low reverse clutch pressure, low reverse band pressure,low line pressure • **Forward** Off, **Intermediate**Off,**Direct** X • **Forward** Off, **Intermediate**X,**Direct** Off • **Forward** Off, **Intermediate**X,**Direct** X • **Forward** X, **Intermediate**Off, **Direct** X • **Forward** X, **Intermediate**X,**Direct** Off • **Forward** X, **Intermediate**X,**Direct** X • **Forward** X, **Intermediate**Off, **Direct** Off	• Check for which pressures are on as follows and corresponding routines • • 324, 301 • 325, 301 • 323, 324, 325, 301 • 324 • 325 • 323, 324, 325 • Refer to appropriate Mechanical Diagnosis
Mechanical • Bands, clutches or seals damaged or worn	• Refer to MOTOR's Domestic Transmission Manual.

FM5029801514000X

Fig. 20 Routines 215 & 315: No 1st Gear, Engages In Higher Gear

Possible Component	Reference/Action
216 — ELECTRICAL ROUTINE	
Powertrain Control System • Electrical inputs/outputs, vehicle wiring harnesses, PCM, shift solenoids, Digital TR sensor	• Run self-test. Refer to MOTOR's Domestic Transmission Manual for diagnosis. Perform Pinpoint Tests A and D using Rotunda Transmission Tester 007-00130 with Rotunda Transmission Range (TR) Sensor Cable "E" 007-00111 and Digital (TR) Sensor Overlay 007-00131 or equivalent. Service as required. Clear codes, road test and rerun self-test.
316 — HYDRAULIC/MECHANICAL ROUTINE	
Shift Linkage, Cable, Digital TR Sensor • Damaged or out of adjustment	• Inspect and service as required. Verify linkage adjustment. After servicing linkage, verify that the Digital TR sensor is properly adjusted.
Improper Pressures • Low reverse clutch pressure, low reverse band pressure, low line pressure, low EPC pressure	• Check pressure at line and EPC pressure taps. If pressures are low, check the following possible components: oil filter and seal assembly, main controls, reverse clutch assembly and reverse servo assembly.
Oil Filter and Seal Assembly • Plugged or damaged	• Replace filter and seal assembly.
Main Controls • No. 6 shuttle ball, manual valve, main regulator valve, low servo modulator valve stuck, damaged • Loose bolts • Gaskets damaged	• Inspect for damage. Service as required. • Tighten bolts to specification. • Inspect for damage and replace.
Low Reverse Servo • Seals (piston and cover) damaged • Servo cover retaining ring damaged • Anchor pins (case) damaged	• Inspect for damage. Service as required.

FM5029801515000X

Fig. 21 Routines 216 & 316: No Manual 1st Gear

Possible Component	Reference/Action
217 — ELECTRICAL ROUTINE	
Powertrain Control System • Electrical inputs/outputs, vehicle wiring harnesses, powertrain control module (PCM), shift solenoids, Digital TR sensor	• Run Self-Test. Refer to MOTOR's Domestic Transmission Manual for diagnosis. Perform Pinpoint Tests A and D using Rotunda Transmission Tester 007-00130 with Rotunda Transmission Range (TR) Sensor Cable "E" 007-00111 and Digital (TR) Sensor Overlay 007-00131 or equivalent Service as required. Clear codes, road test and rerun self-test.
317 — HYDRAULIC/MECHANICAL ROUTINE	
Shift Linkage, Cable, Digital TR Sensor • Damaged, out of adjustment	• Inspect and service as required. Verify linkage adjustment After servicing linkage, verify that the Digital TR sensor is properly adjusted.
Main Controls • 3-4 shift valve, 1-2 and 2-3 shift valve, 3-4 capacity modulator valve stuck, damaged or misassembled • Bolts out of torque specification • Gaskets damaged	• Inspect for damage. Service as required. • Tighten bolts to specification. • Inspect for damage and replace.

FM5029801516000X

Fig. 22 Routines 217 & 317: No Manual 2nd Gear

Possible Component	Reference/Action
220 — ELECTRICAL ROUTINE	
Powertrain Control System • Electrical inputs/outputs, vehicle wiring harnesses, PCM, MAF, TP, VSS, OSS, Digital TR sensor, shift solenoids, EI system	• Run self-test. Refer to MOTOR's Domestic Transmission Manual for diagnosis. Perform Pinpoint Tests A, D and F using Rotunda Transmission Tester 007-00130 Rotunda Transmission Range (TR) Sensor Cable "E" 007-00111 and Digital (TR) Sensor Overlay 007-00131 or equivalent. Service as required. Clear codes, road test and rerun self-test.
320 — HYDRAULIC/MECHANICAL ROUTINE	
Shift Linkage, Digital TR Sensor • Damaged or out of adjustment	• Inspect and service as required. Verify linkage adjustment After servicing linkage, verify that the Digital TR sensor is properly adjusted.
Improper Pressures • Intermediate clutch pressure, line pressure	• Check pressure at line and intermediate clutch taps. If not OK, check the Main Controls.
Main Controls • 1-2 shift valve, 1-2 accumulator valve stuck or damaged • Loose bolts • SS1 malfunction • Gasket damaged • No. 8 ball not seating	• Inspect for damage. Service as required. • Tighten bolts to specification. • Activate solenoid using transmission tester. If solenoid operation cannot be felt when placing hand on solenoid, replace solenoid. Inspect O-rings for damage. Service as required. • Inspect for damage and replace. • Inspect for damage and service as required.
Pump • Porosity/cross leaks, balls missing, damaged or leaking • Gasket damaged	• Inspect for porosity/leaks, balls missing. Replace pump as required. • Inspect for damage and replace.
Intermediate Clutch Assembly • Seals damaged • Piston damaged • Friction elements damaged or worn	• Inspect for damage. Service as required. • Inspect for damage. Service as required. • Inspect for damage. Service as required.
Intermediate One-Way Clutch Assembly • Not holding or damaged	• Inspect for damage. Service as required.
Low One-Way Clutch Assembly • Not overrunning or damaged	• Inspect for damage. Service as required.

FM5029801517000X

Fig. 23 Routines 220 & 320: No Automatic 1–2 Shift

Possible Component	Reference/Action
221 — ELECTRICAL ROUTINE	
Powertrain Control System	
• Electrical inputs/outputs, vehicle wiring harnesses, PCM, TP, MAF, VSS, OSS, Digital TR sensor, shift solenoids, EI system	• Run self-test. Refer to MOTOR's Domestic Transmission Manual for diagnosis. Perform Pinpoint Tests A, D and F using Rotunda Transmission Tester 007-00130 with Rotunda Transmission Range (TR) Sensor Cable "E" 007-00111 and Digital (TR) Sensor Overlay 007-00131 or equivalent. Service as required. Clear codes, road test and rerun self-test.
321 — HYDRAULIC/MECHANICAL ROUTINE	
Shift Linkage	
• Damaged or out of adjustment	• Inspect and service as required. Verify linkage adjustment After servicing linkage, verify that the Digital TR sensor is properly adjusted.

FM5029801533010X

Fig. 24 Routines 221 & 321: No Automatic 2–3 Shift (Part 1 of 2)

Possible Component	Reference/Action
222 — ELECTRICAL ROUTINE	
Powertrain Control System	
• Electrical inputs/outputs, vehicle wiring harnesses, PCM, TP, MAF, VSS, OSS, Digital TR sensor, TCS, shift solenoids, EI system	• Run self-test. Refer to MOTOR's Domestic Transmission Manual for diagnosis. Perform Pinpoint Tests A, D and F using Rotunda Transmission Tester 007-00130 with Rotunda Transmission Range (TR) Sensor Cable "E" 007-00111 and Digital (TR) Sensor Overlay 007-00131 or equivalent. Service as required. Clear codes, road test and rerun self-test.
322 — HYDRAULIC/MECHANICAL ROUTINE	
Shift Linkage, Digital TR Sensor	
• Damaged or out of adjustment	• Inspect and service as required. Verify linkage adjustment. After servicing linkage, verify that the Digital TR sensor is properly adjusted.
Improper Pressures	
• Forward clutch pressure, direct clutch pressure, line pressure	• Check line, direct and forward clutch pressures at appropriate taps. If pressures are out of specification, check main controls.
Main Controls	
• 3-4 shift valve, solenoid pressure regulator valve, OD servo regulator, 3-4 capacity modulator valve, 2-3 backout valve, 1-2 and 2-3 shift valves stuck, damaged	• Inspect for damaged and service as required.
• Loose bolts	• Tighten bolts to specification.

FM5029801518010X

Fig. 25 Routines 222 & 322: No Automatic 3–4 Shift (Part 1 of 2)

Possible Component	Reference/Action
223 — ELECTRICAL ROUTINE	
Powertrain Control System	
• Electrical inputs/outputs, vehicle wiring harnesses, PCM, TP, MAF, VSS, OSS, Digital TR sensor, TCS, shift solenoids, EI system.	• Run Self-Test. Refer to MOTOR's Domestic Transmission Manual for diagnosis. Perform Pinpoint Tests A, D and F using Rotunda Transmission Tester 007-00130 with Rotunda Transmission Range (TR) Sensor Cable "E" 007-00111 and Digital (TR) Sensor Overlay 007-00131 or equivalent, as described. Service as required. Clear codes, road test and rerun self test.
323 — HYDRAULIC/MECHANICAL ROUTINE	
Improper Pressures	
• Forward clutch pressure, line pressure	• Check line and forward clutch at pressure taps. If out of specification, check main controls.
Main Controls	
• 3-4 shift valve, solenoid pressure regulator valve, OD servo regulator, 3-4 capacity modulator, 2-3 backout valve, 1-2, 2-3 shift valves stuck, damaged	• Inspect for damage. Service as required.
• Check balls No. 2, No. 7, No. 9 damaged, missing or not seating properly	• Inspect for damage. Service as required.
• Loose bolts	• Tighten bolts to specification.
• SSA/SS1, malfunction	• Activate solenoid using transmission tester. If solenoid operation cannot be felt when placing hand on solenoid, replace solenoid. Inspect O-rings for damage. Service as required.
• Gaskets damaged	• Inspect for damage and replace.
• OD servo, seal, rod damaged	• Inspect for damage. Service as required.
• Solenoid screen (in main control) blocked or damaged	• Clean or replace screen.
Pump	
• Porosity/cross leaks, balls missing, damaged or leaking	• Inspect for porosity/leaks, balls missing. Replace pump as required.
• Seal rings damaged.	• Inspect for damage. Service as required.
• Gaskets damaged	• Inspect for damage and replace.

FM5029801519010X

Fig. 26 Routines 223 & 323: No Automatic 4–3 Shift (Part 1 of 2)

Possible Component	Reference/Action
Improper Pressures	
• Direct clutch pressure	• Check pressure at direct clutch tap. If not OK, check the main controls.
Main Controls	
• 2-3 shift valve, check ball No. 3 or No. 9, solenoid pressure regulator valve, 2-3 backout valve, 2-3 modulator valve, damaged or misassembled	• Inspect for damage. Service as required.
• Loose bolts	• Tighten bolts to specification.
• SS2 malfunction	• Activate solenoid using transmission tester. If solenoid operation cannot be felt when placing hand on solenoid, replace solenoid. Inspect O-rings for damage. Service as required.
• Gaskets damaged	• Inspect for damage and replace.
• Output shaft seals damaged or cup plug leaking or missing	• Inspect for damage and service as required.
• 2-3 accumulator damaged or stuck	• Inspect piston seal and bore for damage. Service as required.
• Solenoid screen (in main control) blocked or damaged	• Clean or replace screen.
Intermediate One-Way Clutch Assembly	
• Not overrunning or damaged	• Inspect for damage. Service as required.
Output Shaft	
• Seal rings damaged • Cup plug damaged or missing	• Inspect for damage. Service as required.
Direct Clutch Assembly	
• Seals or piston damaged	• Inspect for damage. Service as required.
• Friction elements worn or damaged	• Inspect for damage. Service as required.
• Check ball not seating	• Inspect for damage. Service as required.
• Return spring assembly damaged	• Inspect for damage. Service as required.
Case	
• Output shaft rear seals leaking or damaged	• Inspect for damage. Service as required. Inspect case for damaged seal area. If damaged, replace case.

FM5029801533020X

Fig. 24 Routines 221 & 321: No Automatic 2–3 Shift (Part 2 of 2)

Possible Component	Reference/Action
• SS1 or SS2 malfunction	• Activate solenoid using transmission tester. If solenoid operation cannot be felt when placing hand on solenoid, replace solenoid. Inspect O-rings for damage. Service as required.
• Gaskets damaged	• Inspect for damage and replace.
• OD servo cover, rod and piston cushion spring or seals damaged	• Inspect for damage. Service as required.
• No's 2, 4, 7, and 9 check balls damaged or missing	• Inspect for damage. Service as required.
• Solenoid screen (in main control) blocked or damaged	• Clean or replace screen.
Pump	
• Porosity/cross leaks, balls missing, damaged or leaking	• Inspect for porosity/leaks, balls missing. Replace pump as required.
• Gaskets damaged	• Inspect for damage. Replace as required.
OD Band	
• OD band and reverse clutch drum assembly damaged, worn	• Inspect for damage and service as required.
• Intermediate one-way clutch assembly damaged	• Inspect for damage. Service as required.
Forward Clutch Assembly	
• Seals or piston damaged	• Inspect for damage. Service as required.
• Friction elements worn or damaged	• Inspect for damage. Service as required.
• Check ball stuck, damaged or not seating properly	• Inspect for damage. Service as required.
Input Shaft	
• Seals damaged	• Inspect for damage. Service as required.

FM5029801518020X

Fig. 25 Routines 222 & 322: No Automatic 3–4 Shift (Part 2 of 2)

Possible Component	Reference/Action
Overdrive Band	
• OD band and reverse clutch assembly damaged, worn	• Inspect for damage. Service as required.
• Intermediate one-way clutch assembly damaged	• Inspect for damage. Service as required.
Forward Clutch Assembly	
• Seals or piston damaged	• Inspect for damage. Service as required.
• Friction elements damaged, worn	• Inspect for damage. Service as required.
• Check ball stuck, damaged or not seating properly	• Inspect for damage. Service as required.
• Forward clutch piston and return spring damaged	• Inspect for damage. Service as required.
Input Shaft	
• Seals damaged	• Inspect for damage. Service as required.

FM5029801519020X

Fig. 26 Routines 223 & 323: No Automatic 4–3 Shift (Part 2 of 2)

Possible Component	Reference/Action
224 — ELECTRICAL ROUTINE	
Powertrain Control System	
• Electrical inputs/outputs, vehicle wiring harnesses, PCM, TP, MAF, VSS, OSS, Digital TR sensor, shift solenoids, EI system.	• Run self-test. Refer to MOTOR's Domestic Transmission Manual for diagnosis. Perform Pinpoint Tests A, D and F using Rotunda Transmission Tester 007-00130 with Rotunda Transmission Range (TR) Sensor Cable "E" 007-00111 and Digital (TR) Sensor Overlay 007-00131 or equivalent. Service as required. Clear codes, road test and rerun self test.
324 — HYDRAULIC/MECHANICAL ROUTINE	
Improper Pressures	
• Direct clutch	• Check pressure at direct clutch tap. If not within specification, check Main Controls.
Main Controls	
• 2-3 shift valve stuck or damaged	• Inspect for damage. Service as required
• Check balls damaged or missing	• Inspect for damage. Service as required.
• Loose bolts	• Tighten bolts to specification.
• SSB/SS2 malfunction	• Activate solenoid using transmission tester. If solenoid operation cannot be felt when placing hand on solenoid, replace solenoid. Inspect O-rings for damage. Service as required.
• Gaskets damaged	• Inspect for damage and replace.
Intermediate One-Way Clutch	
• Not holding or damaged	• Inspect for damage. Service as required.
Direct Clutch Assembly	
• Seals or piston damaged	• Inspect for damage. Service as required.
• Friction element damaged, worn	• Inspect for damage. Service as required.
• Check ball stuck, damaged or not seating properly	• Inspect for damage. Service as required.

FM5029801520000X

Fig. 27 Routines 224 & 324: No Automatic 3–2 Shift

Possible Component	Reference/Action
225 — ELECTRICAL ROUTINE	
Powertrain Control System	
• Electrical inputs/outputs, vehicle wiring harnesses, PCM, TP, MAF, VSS, OSS, Digital TR sensor, shift solenoids, EI system.	• Run self-test. Refer to MOTOR's Domestic Transmission Manual for diagnosis. Perform Pinpoint Tests A, D and F using Rotunda Transmission Tester 007-00130 with Rotunda Transmission Range (TR) Sensor Cable "E" 007-00111 and Digital (TR) Sensor Overlay 007-00131 or equivalent. Service as required. Clear codes, road test and rerun self test.

FM5029801521010X

Fig. 28 Routines 225 & 325: No Automatic 1–2 Shift (Part 1 of 2)

Possible Component	Reference/Action
240 — ELECTRICAL ROUTINE	
Powertrain Control System	
• Electrical inputs/outputs, vehicle wiring harnesses, PCM, TP, MAF, VSS, OSS, Digital TR sensor, TFT sensor, TCC solenoids, EI system.	• Run self-test. Refer to MOTOR's Domestic Transmission Manual for diagnosis. Perform Pinpoint Tests B, D and F using Rotunda Transmission Tester 007-00130 with Rotunda Transmission Range (TR) Sensor Cable "E" 007-00111 and Digital (TR) Sensor Overlay 007-00131 or equivalent. Service as required. Clear codes, road test and rerun self test.
340 — HYDRAULIC/MECHANICAL ROUTINE	
Shift Linkage	
• Damaged, out of adjustment	• Inspect and service as required. Verify linkage adjustment. After servicing linkage, verify that the Digital TR sensor is properly adjusted.
Improper Pressures	
• Low line pressure, low EPC pressure	• Check pressure at line and EPC taps. If pressure is low, check EPC and main regulator valve. If within specification, check Main Controls.
Main Controls	
• Solenoid pressure regulator valve, manual valve, torque converter clutch control valve and plunger, converter pressure limit valve, drain back valve stuck, damaged	• Inspect for damage and service as required.
• Loose bolts	• Tighten bolts to specification.
• Solenoid screen (in valve body) blocked or damaged	• Clean or replace screen.
• TCC solenoid malfunction	• Activate solenoid using transmission tester. If solenoid operation cannot be felt when placing hand on solenoid, replace solenoid. Inspect O-rings for damage. Service as required.

FM5029801522010X

Fig. 29 Routines 240 & 340: No Torque Converter Apply (Part 1 of 2)

Possible Component	Reference/Action
241 — ELECTRICAL ROUTINE	
Powertrain Control System	
• Electrical inputs/outputs, vehicle wiring harnesses, PCM, TP, MAF, VSS, OSS, Digital TR sensor, TCS, shift solenoids, EI system.	• Run self-test. Refer to MOTOR's Domestic Transmission Manual for diagnosis. Perform Pinpoint Tests A, D and F using Rotunda Transmission Tester 007-00130 with Rotunda Transmission Range (TR) Sensor Cable "E" 007-00111 and Digital (TR) Sensor Overlay 007-00131 or equivalent. Service as required. Clear codes, road test and rerun self test.
341 — HYDRAULIC/MECHANICAL ROUTINE	
Main Controls	
• Drain back valve, torque converter clutch and plunger stuck, damaged	• Inspect for damage and service as required.
• Loose bolts	• Tighten bolts to specification.
• TCC solenoid malfunction	• Activate solenoid using transmission tester. If solenoid operation cannot be felt when placing hand on solenoid, replace solenoid. Inspect O-rings for damage. Service as required.
• No. 7 ball improper seating	• Inspect for damage. Service as required.
• Gaskets damaged	• Inspect for damage and replace.
Pump Assembly	
• Loose bolts	• Tighten bolts to specification.
• Ball missing, leaking, porosity/cross leaks	• Inspect for porosity/leaks, balls missing. Replace pump as required.
• Gaskets damaged	• Inspect for damage and replace.
Input Shaft	
• Seals damaged	• Inspect for damage. Service as required.
Torque Converter Assembly	
• No end clearance	• Inspect converter as described and replace as required.
• Piston plate damaged or stuck to cover	• If cover is heat-stained, replace converter.

FM5029801523000X

Fig. 30 Routines 241 & 341: Torque Converter Always Applied/Stalls Vehicle

Possible Component	Reference/Action
342 — HYDRAULIC/MECHANICAL ROUTINE	
Fluid	
• Condition	• Inspect fluid condition. If burnt, drain fluid and converter. Replace fluid and filter assembly. Bring vehicle to normal operating temperature. Perform Transmission Drive Cycle Test
Main Controls	
• Solenoid pressure regulator valve, No. 7 check ball, bypass clutch control valve and plunger, converter pressure limit valve stuck, damaged or misassembled	• Inspect for damage. Service as required.
• Bolts out of torque specification	• Tighten bolts to specification.
• Solenoid screen (in valve body) blocked or damaged	• Clean or replace screen.
• TCC solenoid not functioning properly	• Activate solenoid using transmission tester. If solenoid operation cannot be felt when placing hand on solenoid, replace solenoid. Inspect O-rings for damage. Service as required.
• Gaskets damaged	• Inspect for damage and replace.
Pump Assembly	
• Bolts out of torque specification	• Tighten bolts to specification.
• Porosity/cross leaks, balls missing or leaking	• Inspect for porosity/leaks or balls missing. Replace pump assembly as required.
• Gaskets damaged	• Inspect for damage and replace.
Input Shaft	
• Seals damaged	• Inspect for damage. Service as required.
Torque Converter	
• Excessive end clearance	• Inspect converter as described. Replace as required.

FM5029801524020X

Fig. 31 Routines 242 & 342: Torque Converter Cycling/Shudder/Chatter (Part 2 of 2)

Possible Component	Reference/Action
325 — HYDRAULIC/MECHANICAL ROUTINE	
Improper Pressures	
• Intermediate clutch	• Check pressure at intermediate clutch tap. If not within specifications, check Main Controls and Pump.
Main Controls	
• 1-2 shift valve, 1-2 accumulator solenoid pressure regulator valve stuck, damaged	• Inspect for damage. Service as required.
• Loose bolts	• Tighten bolts to specification.
• SS1 malfunction	• Activate solenoid using transmission tester. If solenoid operation cannot be felt when placing hand on solenoid, replace solenoid. Inspect O-rings for damage; service as required.
• Gaskets damaged	• Inspect for damage and replace.
Pump	
• Gaskets damaged	• Inspect for damage and replace.
• Porosity/cross leaks	• Inspect for leak/porosity. Replace pump as required.
Intermediate Clutch Assembly	
• Piston damaged	• Inspect for damage. Service as required.
• Friction elements damaged, worn	• Inspect for damage. Service as required.
• End clearance improper	• Inspect and correct.
Intermediate One-Way Clutch	
• Damaged	• Inspect for damage. Service as required.
Low One-Way Clutch	
• Not holding or damaged	• Inspect for damage. Service as required.

FM5029801521020X

Fig. 28 Routines 225 & 325: No Automatic 1–2 Shift (Part 2 of 2)

Possible Component	Reference/Action
• Gaskets damaged	• Inspect for damage and replace.
Pump Assembly	
• Loose bolts	• Tighten bolts to specification.
• Porosity/cross leaks, balls leaking	• Inspect for porosity/leaks, ball missing. Replace pump as required.
• Gaskets damaged	• Inspect for damage and replace.
Input Shaft	
• Seals damaged	• Inspect for damage. Service as necessary.
Torque Converter Assembly	
• Leakage, friction material damaged, internal seals damaged	• Inspect torque converter. Service or replace as required.

FM5029801522020X

Fig. 29 Routines 240 & 340: No Torque Converter Apply (Part 2 of 2)

Possible Component	Reference/Action
242 — ELECTRICAL ROUTINE	
Powertrain Control System	
• Electrical inputs/outputs, vehicle wiring harnesses, powertrain control module, torque converter clutch (TCC) solenoid, OSS	• Run Self-Test. Refer to MOTOR's Domestic Transmission Manual for diagnosis. Perform Pinpoint Test F using Rotunda Transmission Tester 007-00130 or equivalent. Service as required. Clear codes, road test and rerun Self-Test.

FM5029801524010X

Fig. 31 Routines 242 & 342: Torque Converter Cycling/Shudder/Chatter (Part 1 of 2)

Possible Component	Reference/Action
250 — ELECTRICAL ROUTINE	
• No Electrical Concerns	
350 — HYDRAULIC/MECHANICAL ROUTINE	
Shift Linkage	
• Damaged or out of adjustment	• Inspect and service as required. Verify linkage adjustment After servicing linkage, verify that the Digital TR sensor is properly adjusted.
Main Controls	
• 3-4 shift valve, 1-2 and 2-3 shift valve, gaskets, 3-4 capacity modulator valve, stuck or damaged or misassembled	• Inspect for damage. Service as required.
• OD servo assembly damaged or stuck	• Inspect cover, piston and seal for damage. Service as required.
Overdrive	
• OD band, reverse clutch drum assembly worn or damaged	• Inspect for damage. Service as required.
• Intermediate overrunning clutch assembly damaged	• Inspect for damage. Service as required.
Reverse Band (Manual 1st Only)	
• Damaged, misadjusted	• Inspect for damage. Service as required.

FM5029801525000X

Fig. 32 Routines 250 & 350: No Engine Braking In 2nd Gear, Manual 2nd Or Manual 1st

Possible Component	Reference/Action
251 — ELECTRICAL ROUTINE	
• No Electrical Concerns	

FM5029801526010X

Fig. 33 Routines 251 & 351: Shift Lever Efforts High (Part 1 of 2)

Possible Component	Reference/Action
351 — HYDRAULIC/MECHANICAL ROUTINE	
Shift Linkage, Digital TR Sensor	
• Damaged or out of adjustment	• Inspect and service as required. Verify linkage adjustment After servicing linkage, verify that the Digital TR sensor is properly adjusted.
Manual Lever	
• Retaining pin damaged, nut loose, detent spring bent or damaged or PARK mechanism damaged	• Inspect for damage. Service as required.
Main Controls	
• Manual valve stuck or damaged	• Inspect for damage. Service as required.
• Bolts out of torque specification	• Tighten bolts to specification.

FM5029801526020X

Fig. 33 Routines 251 & 351: Shift Lever Efforts High (Part 2 of 2)

Possible Component	Reference/Action
252 — ELECTRICAL ROUTINE	
Powertrain Control System • Electrical inputs/outputs, sensor seals leaking (Digital TR, OSS, VSS or transmission connector)	• Inspect for leakage and service as required.
352 — HYDRAULIC/MECHANICAL ROUTINE	
Seals, Gaskets • Torque converter, pump assembly, pan, extension housing - gasket/seal, manual lever, fluid level indicator tube	• Locate source of leak. Service as required.
Other • Cooler fitting, pressure taps, converter drain plug, band anchor pins, cooler lines, case porosity, case cracked • Vent blocked or damaged	• Locate source of leak. Service as required. • Check vent for damage or blockage. Service as required.

FM5029801527000X

Fig. 34 Routines 252 & 352: External Leaks

Possible Component	Reference/Action
254 — ELECTRICAL ROUTINE	
• No Electrical Concerns	
354 — HYDRAULIC/MECHANICAL ROUTINE	
For Noises/Vibrations That Change With Engine Speed: • Converter components • Fluid level (low) pump cavitation • Pump assembly • Engine drive accessories • Cooler lines grounding out • Flywheel	• Locate source of disturbance. Service as required.
For Noises/Vibrations That Change With Vehicle Speed: • Engine mounts loose or damaged • Driveline concerns: — u-joints — rear axle — suspension — modifications • First Gear: — low one-way clutch — gearset — friction elements • Second Gear: — intermediate one-way clutch — intermediate clutch piston bleed hole out of 12 O'clock position — friction elements • Third Gear: — torque converter — anti-clunk spring — friction elements • Fourth Gear: — gear set — friction elements — torque converter • Reverse: — gear set — friction elements • Output shaft splines worn or damaged	• Locate source of disturbance and service as required. • For specific shift or torque converter concerns, refer to the following routine(s) for further diagnosis: **Shift** 1-2,**Routine**, 320 **Shift** 2-3, **Routine**, 321 **Shift** 3-4, **Routine**, 322 **Shift** 4-3, **Routine**, 323 **Shift** 3-2, **Routine**, 324 **Shift** 2-1, **Routine**, 325 **Torque Converter Cycling** 242/342
Other Noises/Vibrations: • Main Controls, valve resonance • Shift Cable: — vibration — grounding — cooler lines — grounding	• Locate source of disturbance and service as required.

FM5029801529000X

Fig. 36 Routines 254 & 354: Noise/Vibration In Forward Or Reverse

Possible Component	Reference/Action
253 — ELECTRICAL ROUTINE	
Powertrain Control System • Electrical inputs/outputs, vehicle wiring harnesses, shift solenoids, Digital TR sensor, torque converter clutch (TCC) solenoid, transmission fluid temperature (TFT) sensor	• Run Self-Test. Refer to MOTOR's Domestic Transmission Manual for diagnosis. Perform Pinpoint Tests A, B and D using Rotunda Transmission Tester 007-00130 with Rotunda Transmission Range (TR) Sensor Cable "E" 007-00111 and Digital (TR) Sensor Overlay 007-00131,or equivalent. Service as required. Clear codes, road test and rerun Self-Test. Also refer to Routines 241/341 Torque Converter Operation Concern: Always Applied/Stalls Vehicle.
353 — HYDRAULIC/MECHANICAL ROUTINE	
Shift Linkage, Digital TR Sensor • Damaged or out of adjustment	• Inspect and service as required. Verify linkage adjustment After servicing linkage, verify that the Digital TR sensor is properly adjusted.
Verify Proper Shift Scheduling and Engagements	• Go to the appropriate Diagnostic Routines.
Torque Converter Clutch Always Applied	• Go to Hydraulic/Mechanical Routine 241/341.
Torque Converter Clutch • Damaged	• Inspect torque converter

FM5029801528000X

Fig. 35 Routines 253 & 353: Poor Vehicle Performance

Possible Component	Reference/Action
255 — ELECTRICAL ROUTINE	
Powertrain Control System • Electrical inputs/outputs, vehicle wiring harnesses, engine starting system hardware, Digital TR sensor	• Run Self-Test. Refer to MOTOR's Domestic Transmission Manual for diagnosis. Perform Pinpoint Test D using Rotunda Transmission Range (TR) Sensor Cable "E" 007-00111 and Digital (TR) Sensor Overlay 007-00131 or equivalent Service and adjust as required.
355 — HYDRAULIC/MECHANICAL ROUTINE	
Shift Linkage, Digital TR Sensor • Damaged or out of adjustment	• Inspect and service as required. Verify linkage adjustment After servicing linkage, verify that the Digital TR sensor is properly adjusted.

FM5029801530000X

Fig. 37 Routines 255 & 355: Engine Will Not Crank

Possible Component	Reference/Action
256 — ELECTRICAL ROUTINE	
• No Electrical Concerns	
356 — HYDRAULIC/MECHANICAL ROUTINE	
Shift Linkage, Digital TR Sensor • Damaged or out of adjustment	• Inspect and service as required. Verify linkage adjustment After servicing linkage, verify that the Digital TR sensor is properly adjusted.
Park Mechanism • Output shaft ring, park brake pawl, parking pawl return spring, park rod guide cup, parking pawl shaft, parking pawl actuating rod, manual lever, manual lever detent spring damaged or misassembled	• Inspect for damage or misassembly and service as required.

FM5029801531000X

Fig. 38 Routines 256 & 356: No Park Range

MAINTENANCE

Refer to "Lubricant Data" chart in the appropriate chassis chapter of this manual for transmission fluid specifications.

FLUID INSPECTION

1. Park vehicle on level surface with transmission at operating temperature.
2. Operate engine at idle speed with parking brake applied and move selector lever through each detent position. Return selector lever to Park.
3. With engine idling, remove dipstick and inspect fluid level, which should be between arrows on dipstick.
4. Add fluid as required to bring fluid to proper level.

FLUID CHANGE

Normal maintenance and lubrication requirements do not require periodic fluid changes. If vehicle accumulates 5,000 or more miles per month or it is used in continuous stop and go service, change fluid every 30,000 miles.

When filling a dry transmission and converter, install approximately 12 quarts of specified fluid. Start engine, shift selector lever through all ranges and place it at Park position. Inspect fluid level and add enough to raise level in transmission to F (full) mark on dipstick. When a partial drain and refill is required, proceed as follows:

1. Loosen oil pan bolts and allow pan to drain into suitable container.
2. Working from rear and both sides of transmission oil pan, remove bolts, allowing pan to drop and drain slowly.
3. Remove and clean pan and replace screen.
4. Place new gasket on pan and install pan and screen.
5. Add three quarts of specified fluid to transmission.
6. Run engine at fast idle until it reaches normal operating temperature.
7. Shift selector lever through all ranges and then place it in Park position.
8. Add fluid as required to bring level to full mark.

BRAKE SHIFT INTERLOCK SYSTEM

Inspection

1. With engine Off, turn ignition to Run position.
2. Place gear shift lever in Park, but do not apply brake. Ensure lever cannot be shifted from Park.
3. With brake pedal applied, ensure gear shift lever can be shifted from Park.
4. Shift to Reverse, then ensure ignition switch cannot be turned to Lock position.
5. Shift to Park, then ensure ignition switch can be turned to Lock position.

TRANSMISSION FLUID COOLER FLOW INSPECTION

Linkage, fluid and control pressure must be within specifications before performing this flow inspection.

1. Remove transmission dipstick from filler tube and place funnel in filler tube.
2. Raise and support vehicle, then remove cooler return line from its fitting in case.
3. Attach hose to cooler return line and

fasten free end of hose to funnel installed in filler tube.

4. Start engine and set idle speed at 1000 RPM with transmission in Neutral.
5. Observe fluid flow at funnel. When flow is solid, air bleeding has been completed. Flow should be liberal. If there is not liberal flow at 1000 RPM in Neutral, low pump capacity, main circuit system leakage, or cooler system restriction is indicated.
6. To separate transmission trouble from cooler system trouble, observe flow at transmission case converter outlet fitting.

Possible Component	Reference/Action
257 — ELECTRICAL ROUTINE	
Refer to Routine 240/340, Torque Converter Operation Concern: No Apply	
357 — HYDRAULIC/MECHANICAL ROUTINE	
Fluid • Improper level • Condition	• Adjust fluid to proper level. • Inspect Fluid Condition.
Cooler Lines • Damaged, blocked or reversed	• Inspect for damage and proper installation. Service as required.
Auxiliary Cooler • Damaged, blocked or restricted or improperly installed	• Inspect for damage and proper installation. Service as required.
Vehicle Concerns Causing Engine Overheating	• Inspect Cooling System.
Main Controls • Drain back valve, torque clutch control valve, converter limit valve stuck, damaged or misassembled	• Inspect for damage and service as required.
Torque Converter • No Apply	• Refer to Routine 240/340.

FM5029801532000X

Fig. 39 Routines 257 & 357: Transmission Overheating

ADJUSTMENTS

MANUAL LINKAGE

Column Shift

1. Place steering column selector lever in Overdrive and hold selector lever in position by placing three pound weight on lever.
2. Raise and support vehicle.
3. Loosen shift cable mounting nut at manual control lever.
4. Move manual control lever to Overdrive position, second detent from most forward position.
5. Tighten shift cable mounting nut to specifications.
6. Inspect shift lever for proper operation.

Floor Shift

1. Place transmission selector lever in Drive position. Hold in position with three pound rearward load.
2. Raise and support vehicle.
3. Loosen transmission shift cable and bracket to cable bracket mounting nut.
4. Move transmission manual control lever to Drive position third detent from full clockwise position.
5. Tighten mounting nut to specifications.
6. Inspect transmission operation in all selector lever positions.

IN-VEHICLE REPAIRS

BRAKE SHIFT LOCK ACTUATOR, REPLACE

CROWN VICTORIA, GRAND MARQUIS, MARK VIII & TOWN CAR

1. Remove steering column as outlined in "Steering Columns" chapter.
2. Remove mounting bolts, then insert plate and shift lock actuator.
3. Remove insert plate and discard shift lock actuator clip.
4. Reverse procedure to install.

MUSTANG

1. Remove shifter top control panel and disconnect electrical connectors.
2. Remove shifter bezel and bulb, then disconnect electrical connector.
3. Remove mounting screw and handle. **Do not pull handle too far or overdrive cancel button may be damaged.**
4. Remove brake shift interlock cable mounting clip and bolt, then disconnect cable.
5. Remove mounting screws and instrument panel steering column cover.
6. Remove mounting screws and instrument panel reinforcement.
7. Remove mounting nuts and lower steering column.
8. Remove mounting screws and brake shift cable interlock actuator.
9. Reverse proceed to install.

IGNITION/SHIFT INTERLOCK CABLE, REPLACE

MUSTANG

1. Remove console rear access covers and armrest mounting bolts.
2. Remove armrest to floor bracket mounting bolts and armrest.
3. Remove gearshift lever opening finish panel and shift knob, then slide finish panel up to remove.
4. Place emergency brake lever in up position, remove mounting screws and lift top finish panel up.
5. Disconnect electrical connectors and remove top finish panel.
6. Remove console to rear floor bracket mounting screws, insert suitable small screwdriver into notches at bottom of front upper finish panel and snap out.
7. **On models equipped with radio opening cover plate with stowage bin,** pry cover plate out of console using suitable small screwdriver.
8. **On models equipped with radio and stowage bin or radio with graphic equalizer,** proceed as follows:
   a. Install radio removal tool No. T87P-19061-A, or equivalent, into radio face plate.
   b. Push radio remover in approximately one inch to release clips.
   c. Apply light spreading force and pull radio out of instrument panel.
   d. Disconnect electrical connectors.
9. **On all models,** open glove compartment door and drop glove compartment down, then remove console to instrument panel mounting screws.
10. Remove console to bracket mounting screws and console.
11. Remove lefthand lower instrument panel trim and steering column lower shroud.
12. Remove interlock cable mounting screw and disconnect cable from shift lever cam.
13. Remove mounting nuts and lower column to floor.
14. Remove cable retaining clip and disconnect electrical connector at solenoid.
15. Remove cable mounting screw from steering column and guide interlock cable out from under console brackets.
16. Reverse procedure to install.

SHIFT LINKAGE, REPLACE

1998 CROWN VICTORIA, GRAND MARQUIS & TOWN CAR

Removal

1. Remove cable plastic terminal from gearshift lever pivot ball by prying with suitable screwdriver between cable plastic terminal and range selector lever under instrument panel.
2. Remove cable and bracket from steering column tube.
3. Raise and support vehicle.
4. Remove shift cable and bracket from transmission shift cable bracket by unlocking lock tabs and sliding cable out.
5. Remove cable to transmission manual control lever stud mounting nut and cable from stud.
6. Remove shift cable and bracket from torque converter housing and frame rail.
7. Lower vehicle.
8. Unseat cable grommet from cowl, then shift cable and bracket on engine compartment side.
9. Pull cable out of cowl.

Installation

1. Feed plastic terminal end of cable through cowl from engine compartment.
2. Pull rubber grommet on transmission range selector cable into dash panel opening and seat it securely from passenger compartment.
3. Install transmission range selector cable into steering column transmission shift cable bracket. Ensure locking tab seats fully.
4. Install shift cable and bracket to steering column casting.
5. Apply small amount of suitable grease

to column selector lever pivot ball or cable terminal.
6. Attach cable plastic terminal to shift lever pivot ball.
7. Place transmission range selector lever in Overdrive position and hang three pound weight on end.
8. Route shift cable to bracket on crossmember and through fuel rail bracket clip.
9. Insert cable clip into bracket and position cable so white band is 21 inches from ground.
10. Raise and support vehicle.
11. Install cable in shift cable bracket and clip bracket into transmission bracket. Ensure locking tabs fully seat.
12. Place transmission in Overdrive by rotating lever counterclockwise to stop, then clockwise two stops.
13. Align transmission shift cable paddle slot on manual control lever stud shoulders while tightening nut to specifications.
14. Lower vehicle and remove three pound weight.

CROWN VICTORIA, GRAND MARQUIS & TOWN CAR

1. Disconnect transmission shift cable from selector lever and support.
2. Disconnect cable from steering column instrument panel bracket.
3. Disconnect cable shift actuator cable fitting.
4. Push rubber grommet and cable through bulkhead.
5. Raise and support vehicle.
6. Disconnect shift cable from manual control lever.
7. Disconnect shift actuator cable fitting and release cable.
8. Disconnect shift cable from transmission shift cable bracket.
9. Remove mounting bolts and bracket.
10. Reverse procedure to install.

MARK VIII

1. Remove transmission control selector dial bezel.
2. Slide retaining clip and pull shift cable from lever cam.
3. Remove shift cable and shifter nut, then shift cable bracket clip.
4. Remove shift cable and bracket, then nut from transmission shift cable bracket.
5. Reverse procedure to install. Tighten mounting nuts to specifications.

MUSTANG

Removal

1. Place transmission range selector lever in Drive position.
2. Raise and support vehicle.
3. Remove shift cable and bracket mounting bolts from shifter mounted bracket.
4. Disconnect cable from shift lever ball stud.
5. Remove shift cable and bracket mounting bolts from transmission bracket.
6. Remove cable mounting nut from manual control lever and cable.

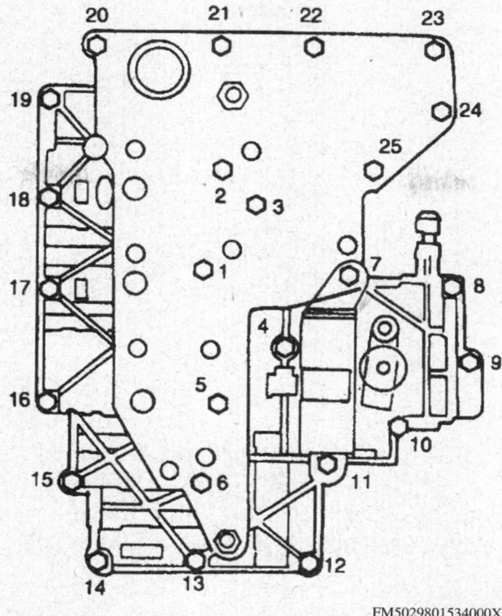

Fig. 40 Valve body tightening sequence

Installation

1. Install shift cable shifter mounted bracket and tighten mounting screws to specifications.
2. Connect shift cable and bracket to transmission range selector lever ball stud.
3. Install shift cable mounted bracket to transmission and tighten mounting nuts to specifications.
4. Place transmission manual control lever in Drive position and apply three pound rearward force to lever.
5. Connect shift cable and bracket to transmission manual control lever and tighten mounting nut to specifications.

VALVE BODY, REPLACE

REMOVAL

1. Raise and support vehicle.
2. Drain transmission fluid into suitable container.
3. Remove pan, filter and magnet.
4. Carefully pry up locking tabs, then disconnect following leads. **Do not pull on molded lead frame.**
   a. Shift solenoid SSA/SS1 and SSB/SS2.
   b. TCC solenoid.
   c. EPC solenoid.
   d. Bulkhead inter-connector.
5. Remove mounting bolts, shift and TCC solenoids.
6. Remove mounting bolts and manual control valve detent lever spring.
7. Remove mounting bolts and main control valve body. Discard pump outlet screen.

INSTALLATION

1. Position gasket and main control valve body using two alignment bolts.
2. Ensure manual valve detent lever drive pin engages manual valve properly before installing mounting bolts.
3. Loosely install mounting bolts. **Do not tighten just yet.**
4. Install manual control valve detent lever spring and mounting bolt.
5. Tighten valve body mounting bolts to specifications in sequence, **Fig. 40.**
6. Install shift, TCC solenoids and mounting bolts.
7. Connect molded lead frame inter-connector, then to EPC, TCC and shift solenoids.
8. Install filter seal.
9. If transmission is being service for contamination related failure, use new filter and seal. **Carefully remove main control bore grommet with suitable small screwdriver.**
10. Position magnet, then install gasket and pan.
11. Tighten pan mounting bolts to specifications.
12. Lower vehicle and fill transmission with suitable fluid.

EXTENSION HOUSING SEAL & GASKET, REPLACE

1. Turn air suspension switch to Off position, if equipped.
2. Raise and support vehicle.
3. Drain transmission fluid into suitable container.
4. Mark rear driveshaft yoke and axle flange alignment for assembly.
5. Remove mounting bolts and separate driveshaft from transmission.
6. Remove exhaust system as required.
7. Support transmission with suitable jack.
8. Remove transmission mounting nuts, bolts and transmission crossmember.
9. Lower transmission to access extension housing bolts.
10. Remove extension housing seal using oil seal remover tool No. T74O-77248-A, or equivalent, and suitable slide hammer.
11. Remove mounting bolts and nuts, then extension housing and gasket.
12. Reverse procedure to install, noting following:
    a. Install seal using extension housing seal replacer tool No. T61L-7657-B, or equivalent.
    b. Tighten mounting bolts and nuts to specifications.
    c. Ensure output shaft and driver shaft removal marks are properly aligned.

ELECTRONIC PRESSURE CONTROL (EPC) SOLENOID, REPLACE

1. Remove manual control lever as outlined under "Manual Control Lever Shaft & Seal, Replace."
2. Carefully pry up locking tabs, then disconnect following leads **without pulling on molded lead frame:**
   a. Shift solenoid SSA/SS1 and SSB/SS2.
   b. TCC solenoid.
   c. EPC solenoid.
   d. Bulkhead inter-connector.
3. Remove EPC solenoid.
4. Reverse procedure to install.

MANUAL CONTROL LEVER SHAFT & SEAL, REPLACE

1. Turn air suspension switch to Off position, if equipped.
2. Raise and support vehicle.
3. Drain transmission fluid into suitable container.
4. Remove pan and filter.
5. Disconnect digital Transmission Range (TR) sensor electrical connector.
6. Disconnect transmission shift linkage.
7. Remove mounting nuts and digital TR sensor.
8. Remove mounting nut and manual control valve detent lever spring.
9. Remove manual lever shaft retaining pin. Use suitable shop cloth to protect transmission case surface.
10. Remove nut and slide manual control lever shaft out.
11. Remove manual valve detent lever and parking lever actuating rod.
12. Carefully pry seal out using suitable screwdriver in seal lower edge. **Do not damage bore with prying tool.**
13. Reverse procedure to install, noting following:
    a. Install seal using oil seal replacer tool No. T74P-77498-A, or equivalent.
    b. Tighten nuts to specifications.
    c. Align digital TR sensor using alignment tool No. T97L-70010-A, or equivalent, as outlined under "Digital Transmission Range (TR) Sensor, Replace."

DIGITAL TRANSMISSION RANGE (TR) SENSOR, REPLACE

1. Position manual control lever in Neutral position.
2. Raise and support vehicle.
3. Remove mounting nut and position manual shift cable aside.
4. Remove mounting bolts, lower digital TR sensor and disconnect electrical harness.
5. Remove TR sensor.
6. Reverse procedure to install, noting following:
    a. Align digital TR sensor using digital TR sensor alignment tool No. T97L-70010-A, or equivalent.
    b. Tighten mounting nuts and bolts to specifications.

REVERSE SERVO, REPLACE

REMOVAL

1. Remove main control valve body as outlined under "Valve Body, Replace."
2. Compress servo spring using servo piston replacement tool No. T92P-70023-A, or equivalent.
3. Remove reverse band servo retaining ring.
4. Remove cover, piston and rod, and reverse band spring.

INSTALLATION

This procedure does not compensate for band wear.

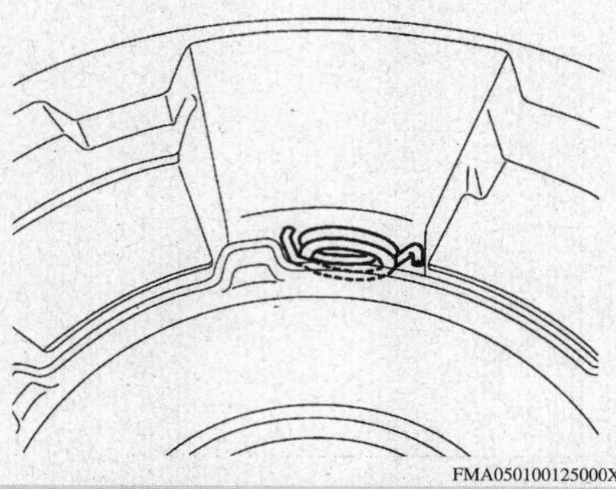

Fig. 41 Planet support spring position. 1999-2001 Crown Victoria, Grand Marquis, Mustang & Town Car

Piston rods are three different length grades. **Do not install in any transmission other than one from which they were removed.**

1. Lubricate piston seal.
2. Install reverse servo piston and return spring. **Do not install cover.**
3. Install servo piston selection tool No. T80L-77030-A, or equivalent, then tighten apply bolt to specifications.
4. Attach suitable dial indicator with bracket.
5. Position indicator stem on reverse servo piston flat portion and zero dial.
6. Loosen bolt until piston stops against tool.
7. Measure and record piston travel.
8. If piston travel is not .211–.237 inch, select proper servo to bring piston travel within specifications. Piston rod lengths are as follows:
    a. One groove pistons have rods 2.936 inches long.
    b. Two groove pistons have rods 2.989 inches long.
    c. Three groove pistons have rods 3.043 inches long.
9. Remove dial indicator and tool.
10. Install proper servo piston spring, cover and seal.
11. Compress servo spring using servo piston replacement tool No. T92P-70023-A, or equivalent.
12. Install retaining ring and main control valve body.

OVERDRIVE SERVO, REPLACE

1. Remove main control valve body as outlined under "Valve Body, Replace."
2. Compress servo spring using servo piston replacement tool No. T92P-70023-A, or equivalent.
3. Remove reverse band servo retaining ring.
4. Remove piston and return spring.
5. Reverse procedure to install.

1-2 ACCUMULATOR, REPLACE

1. Remove main control valve body as outlined under "Valve Body, Replace."
2. Compress 1–2 accumulator cover using servo piston remover/replacer tool No. T92P-70023-A, or equivalent.
3. Remove retaining ring and cover.
4. Remove lower spring, piston and upper spring.
5. Reverse procedure to install.

2-3 ACCUMULATOR, REPLACE

1. Remove main control valve body as outlined under "Valve Body, Replace."
2. Remove piston retainer.
3. Remove piston and upper spring.
4. Reverse procedure to install.

TRANSMISSION

REPLACE

CROWN VICTORIA, GRAND MARQUIS, MUSTANG & TOWN CAR

Removal

1. Raise and support vehicle.
2. Drain transmission fluid into suitable container.
3. Remove exhaust system as required.
4. Remove converter inspection cover and engine oil pan adapter plate bolts.
5. Remove flexplate to converter mounting nuts, noting following:
    a. Use suitable socket and breaker bar on crankshaft pulley mounting bolt.
    b. Rotate crankshaft clockwise as viewed from front to access each nut.
    c. **Never rotate crankshaft counterclockwise.**
6. Mark rear driveshaft yoke and axle companion flange for original position assembly.
7. Remove mounting bolts and driveshaft.
8. Disconnect transmission shift linkage and remove shift cable bracket.
9. Disconnect Output Shaft Speed (OSS) and Vehicle Speed Sensor (VSS) connectors.
10. Remove torque converter drain plug and drain fluid into suitable container.
11. Disconnect transmission wiring harness.
12. Remove mounting bolts and position starter motor out of way.
13. Raise transmission slightly with suitable jack.
14. Remove engine rear support to crossmember mounting bolts.
15. Remove crossmember mounting bolts.
16. Remove transmission support insulator, engine and transmission support and engine damper mounting body bracket.
17. Lower jack and allow transmission to hang.
18. Position suitable jack to front and raise engine to gain access to upper converter housing mounting bolts.
19. Disconnect cooler lines at transmission and plug all openings.

20. Remove lower converter housing mounting bolts.
21. Remove transmission fluid filler tube.
22. Secure transmission to suitable jack.
23. Support engine with suitable safety stand and wood block.
24. Disconnect Heated Oxygen Sensor (HO_2S) connectors.
25. Remove upper converter housing bolts.
26. Move transmission to rear to disengage dowel pins and torque converter from flexplate.
27. Install converter holding tool No. T97T-7902-A, or equivalent.
28. Lower transmission.
29. Remove holding tool and torque converter.

Installation

1. Apply multi-purpose grease part No. DOAZ-19584-AA, or equivalent, to pilot hub.
2. Tighten converter housing drain plug to specifications.
3. Install torque converter, pushing and at same time rotating through what feels like two notches or bumps.
4. Ensure converter centering spigot is approximately .4375–.5625 inch inside housing.
5. Secure transmission to suitable jack and install torque converter holding tool No. T97T-7902-A, or equivalent.
6. Ensure torque converter drive studs and housing access plug align with flexplate holes.
7. Align converter stud and flexplate bolt holes with balancing marks.
8. Move transmission and torque converter forward, squarely against flexplate.
9. Remove converter holding tool.
10. Ensure torque converter is properly seated by grasping stud, then moving back and forth. If there is no metallic clank noise and converter will not move, proceed as follows:
    a. Remove transmission.
    b. Position torque converter so impeller hub is properly engaged in pump gear.
    c. Install transmission.
11. Install converter housing mounting bolts and tighten to specifications.
12. Remove jack safety chain.
13. Connect HO_2S connectors.
14. Install fluid filler tube.
15. Install cooler lines.
16. Remove jack support from engine front.
17. Raise transmission and install transmission support insulator, engine and transmission support, and engine damper mounting body bracket.
18. Lower transmission and install rear engine crossmember nut.
19. Remove transmission jack.
20. Connect transmission wiring harness.
21. Install starter motor.
22. Install flexplate to converter mounting nuts and tighten to specifications.
23. Install inspection cover and tighten mounting bolts to specifications.
24. Install exhaust system.
25. Install vehicle speed sensor and connect wiring.
26. Install driveshaft.
27. Lower vehicle and fill transmission.

Application	Old Part Number (-12A650-)	Tear Tag	New Part Number (-12A650-)	Old Calibration	New Calibration	NGS/WDS Qualifier
ULEV (Ultra Low Emission Vehicle) A/T	1R3F-NC	N/A	1R3Z-ND	1ZE13P0506	1ZE13P0510	N/A Use WDS
ULEV (Ultra Low Emission Vehicle) M/T	1R3F-PC	N/A	1R3Z-PD	1ZE23P0506	1ZE23P0510	N/A Use WDS
LEV (Low Emission Vehicle) A/T	1R3F-BC	N/A	1R3Z-BD	1ZE13P0A06	1ZE13P0A10	N/A Use WDS
LEV (Low Emission Vehicle) M/T	1R3F-DC	N/A	1R3Z-DD	1ZE23P0A06	1ZE23P0A10	N/A Use WDS

FMA050100128000X

Fig. 42 PCM calibrations. 2001 Mustang w/3.8L engine

MARK VIII

Removal

1. Place transmission range selector in Neutral position.
2. Raise and support vehicle.
3. Disconnect transmission harness electrical connector.
4. If transmission is to be disassembled, drain fluid into suitable container.
5. Mark rear driveshaft yoke and axle companion flange for original position assembly.
6. Remove mounting bolts and position rear driveshaft yoke aside
7. Remove rear differential mounting nuts and bolts and separate driveshaft from transmission.
8. Remove mounting bolts and inspection cover.
9. Rotate crankshaft to access and remove torque converter mounting nuts.
10. Disconnect electrical connectors, then remove mounting bolts and starter motor.
11. Disconnect transmission shift linkage.
12. Disconnect transmission cooler lines.
13. Disconnect Heated Oxygen Sensor (HO_2S) connectors.
14. Position suitable jack under transmission.
15. Remove transmission to crossmember mounting bolts, bolts and crossmember.
16. Remove mounting bolts and transmission mount.
17. Remove exhaust Y-pipe.
18. Remove transmission housing mounting bolts.
19. Install torque converter holding tool No. T97T-7902-A, or equivalent.
20. Remove mounting bolt and fluid filler tube.
21. Lower and remove transmission.

Installation

1. Ensure torque converter is held securely in position with converter holding tool No. T97T-7902-A, or equivalent.
2. Raise transmission, then align converter stud and flexplate bolt holes.
3. Move transmission into position and ensure torque converter is squarely fitted to flexplate.
4. Install fluid filler tube.
5. Install transmission holding bolts and tighten to specifications.
6. Remove torque converter holding tool.
7. Install exhaust Y-pipe.
8. Position transmission mount and exhaust pipe bracket. Tighten mounting bolts to specifications.
9. Install crossmember and tighten mounting bolts to specifications.
10. Tighten transmission-to-crossmember mounting nuts to specifications.
11. Remove transmission jack.
12. Connect HO_2S electrical connectors.
13. Connect transmission cooler lines.
14. Slide transmission shift linkage into cable bracket until tabs are fully seated and connect shift cable to manual lever. Manual lever must be in Overdrive position.
15. Install starter.
16. Install torque converter mounting nuts.
17. Install transmission inspection cover.
18. Position driveshaft on transmission. Tighten rear differential nuts and bolts to specifications.
19. Position driveshaft to rear differential and tighten driveshaft bolts to specifications.
20. Lower vehicle and connect transmission harness electrical connector.

TECHNICAL SERVICE BULLETINS

VIBRATION OR EXTENSION HOUSING FLUID LEAK

Crown Victoria Police Vehicles

On some of these models there may be a vibration and/or extension housing seal leak.

This condition may be caused by extension housing bushing or seal walking or spinning out from extended high speed operation and excessive driveshaft flexing.

To correct this condition, replace extension housing part No. F5UZ-7A039-A and gasket part No. F7AZ-7086-A. Ensure vehicle has GNX level rear springs part No. F8AZ-5560-GA and that a revised Metal Matric Composite (MMC) driveshaft part No. XW7Z-4602-AA is installed.

DELAYED OR NO 2–3 UPSHIFT

Crown Victoria, Grand Marquis, Mark VIII, Mustang & Town Car

On some of these models there may a delayed or no 2–3 upshift, especially when the transmission is cold. Diagnostic Trouble Code (DTC) P0782 may be stored.

This condition may be caused by fluid pressure leakage past the 2–3 accumulator larger diameter seal.

To correct this condition, replace the 2–3 accumulator using the revised piston part No. F7AZ-7H292-AB.

1998 Crown Victoria, Grand Marquis, Mark VIII, Mustang & Town Car w/Remanufactured Transmissions

On some of these models with remanufactured transmissions (serial Nos. between R0475797–R0771887), there may a delayed or no 2–3 upshift, especially when the transmission is cold. Diagnostic Trouble Code (DTC) P0782 may be stored.

This condition may be caused by fluid pressure leakage past the 2–3 accumulator larger diameter seal.

To correct this condition, replace the 2–3 accumulator using revised piston part No. F7AZ-7H292-AB.

TRANSMISSION FLUID LEAK AT RADIATOR

1998–2000 Mustang

On some of these models there may be a transmission fluid leak at the radiator transmission oil cooler connection joint between the radiator and cooler fitting (not the cooler line into fitting).

This condition may be caused by insufficient thread sealer on the fitting.

To correct this condition, install an O-ring part No. W705181-S onto the oil cooler line fitting.

CLUNK NOISE ON 2–1 DOWNSHIFT

1999–2001 Crown Victoria, Grand Marquis, Mustang & Town Car

On these models there may be a consistent 2–1 downshift clunk noise which may be caused by an improperly positioned planet support spring.

To correct this condition, proceed as follows:

1. Determine if clunk noise is caused by transmission using Rotunda Chassis Ears tool No. 107-R2102, or equivalent.
2. If noise is not caused by transmission, continue diagnosis using Chassis Ears tool to pinpoint origin of noise and correct as required.
3. Raise and support vehicle, then inspect for and tighten loose fasteners at following locations:
   a. Driveshaft to pinion flange.
   b. Upper and lower control arms.
   c. Rear shock absorbers.
   d. Transmission mounts.
   e. Crossmember mountings.
4. Road test vehicle. If condition is still present, proceed as follows:
   a. Remove transmission as outlined under "Transmission, Replace."
   b. Disassemble transmission down to and including center support retaining ring.
   c. Note position of planet support spring, **Fig. 41.** One tang should be loaded against transmission case. The other one should be loaded against planetary gear support.
   d. If planet support spring is damaged install a replacement part No. F5AZ-7F277-AA.
   e. If planet support spring is not damaged it can be installed again.
   f. Ensure planet support spring is installed squarely with tangs loaded against transmission case on one side and against planetary gear support on the other.
   g. Install a new transmission pump gasket part No. F2VY-7A136-A.
   h. Install transmission as outlined under "Transmission, Replace."

BUMP & SLIP ON 1–2 & 2–3 SHIFTS, DTC P0442

2001 Mustang w/3.8L Engine

On these models these conditions may appear at operating temperatures and may be caused by PCM calibrations.

To correct these conditions, proceed as follows:

1. Diagnose and repair any present DTCs.
2. Program PCM to latest calibration, **Fig. 42.**
3. Fill in Authorized Modification Decal part No. FPS 8262 and affix adjacent to VECI decal. Cover with clear plastic shield.
4. Inform vehicle owner that several drive cycles may be required to completely adapt PCM to new calibration.

RPM RISE ON LIGHT THROTTLE 3–4 SHIFTS, DTC P0782

2001 Crown Victoria, Grand Marquis & Town Car

On these models there may be a 200–400 RPM rise on light throttle 3–4 shifts. The Transmission Control Indicator Lamp (TCIL) may also flash and store DTC P0782 in memory.

These conditions may be caused by the PCM calibrations. To correct these conditions, proceed as follows:

1. Diagnose and repair any present DTCs.
2. Program PCM to latest calibration, **Fig. 43. Programming will not correct conditions if particular vehicle and its axle ratio are not listed.**
3. Fill in Authorized Modification Decal part No. FPS 8262 and affix adjacent to VECI decal. Cover with clear plastic shield.

REPEATED TRANSMISSION REPAIRS

Crown Victoria, Grand Marquis, Mustang & Town Car

On these models, this condition may be caused by contamination and debris remaining in the fluid cooling system after transmission service or repairs. It must be removed by proper cleaning and flushing. Proceed as follows:

1. Clean, flush and backflush fluid cooling system using Rotunda flusher tool No. 222-00001, or equivalent. Follow tool manufacturer's instructions. Be sure to include main and auxiliary coolers, cooler lines and Cooler Bypass Valve (CBV) after each transmission overhaul or exchange.

Application	Old Part Number (-12A650-)	Tear Tag	New Part Number (-12A650-)	Old Calibration	New Calibration	NGS/WDS Qualifier
Crown Victoria/Grand Marquis - Mexico - 2.73 Axle	1W7F-FE	CTW4	1W7Z-FF	1FB1GX0M08	1FB1GX0M10	...
Crown Victoria/Grand Marquis - 2.73 Axle	1W7F-CE	RFRx	1W7Z-CF	1FB1GB0508	1FB1GB0510	1FB1GB05 CALIBRATION
Crown Victoria/Grand Marquis - Gulf Coast Countries (GCC) - 3.08 Axle	1W7F-HC	XAY2	1W7Z-HD	1FB1GX0G06	1FB1GX0G10	...
Crown Victoria - Gulf Coast Countries (GCC) Police - 3.08 Axle	1W7F-JC	GWE2	1W7Z-JD	1FB1GP0G06	1FB1GP0G10	...
Crown Victoria - Police - 3.27 Axle	1W7F-EE	BXT5	1W7Z-EG	1FBLGP0508	1FBLGP0510	1FB1GP05 CALIBRATION
Crown Victoria - Handling Package - 3.55 Axle	1W7F-DE	NHT4	1W7Z-DF	1FBLGH0508	1FBLGH0510	1FB1GH05 CALIBRATION
Town Car - 3.08 Axle	1W1F-AE	KMEx	1W1Z-AF	1VC1SB0508	1VC1SB0510	1VC1SB05 CALIBRATION
Town Car - Handling Package - 3.55 Axle	1W1F-BE	LWTx	1W1Z-BF	1VC1LH0508	1VC1LH0510	1VC1LH05 CALIBRATION
Town Car - Gulf Coast Countries (GCC) - 3.08 Axle	1W1F-CC	NNIx	1W1Z-CD	1VC1TX0G06	1VC1TX0G10	...

FMA050100129000X

Fig. 43 PCM calibrations. 2001 Crown Victoria, Grand Marquis & Town Car

2. Inspect fluid cooler flow to ensure proper fluid flow through system.
3. After confirming proper fluid flow, install a transmission fluid inline filter kit part No. XC3Z-7B155-AA in fluid cooler return line. This is line exiting cooler and entering transmission.
4. The new filter element, part No. XC3Z-7B155-BA, should be replaced every 30,000 miles.

TIGHTENING SPECIFICATIONS

Year	Component	Torque/Ft. Lbs.
1998–2002	Cooler Lines	15–19
	Crossmember	35–46
	Detent Spring	84–120①
	Digital Transmission Range Sensor	60–84①
	Driveshaft	76
	Extension Housing	19–22
	Filler Tube	28–37
	Filter	84–120①
	Front Pump Bolts (1998–2000)	15–19
	Front Pump Bolts (2001–02)	18–22
	Front Pump Support Bolts	15–19
	Governor Body Cover	20–30①
	Governor Body To Counterweight	50–60①
	Inspection Cover	23–29
	Manual Control Lever	14–19
	Manual Lever Shaft	20–27
	Neutral Start Switch	108–132①
	Oil Cooler Line	17–24
	Oil Cooler Line Fitting Jam Nut	11–14
	Oil Pan	108–132①
	Outer Throttle Lever To Shaft	12–16
	Pressure Plug	72–144①
	Push Connect Fitting	18–23
	Rear Differential Bolts & Nuts	45–59
	Rear Differential Nut, Front	57–75
	Reinforcing Plate To Valve Body (1998–2000)	84–120①
	Reinforcing Plate To Valve Body (2001–02)	89①
	Reverse Servo Selection Tool Apply Band	50①
	Shift Cable	13–17
	Shift Cable Bracket (1998)	17–23
	Shift Cable Bracket (1999–2002)	10
	Shifter Mounted Bracket	108①
	Shifter Transmission Bracket	19–25
	Stator Support	15–19
	TCC Solenoid	89①
	Torque Converter Drain Plug	21–22
	Torque Converter Housing	41–50
	Torque Converter Inspection Cover	16–22
	Torque Converter To Flexplate (1998–2001)	20–33
	Torque Converter To Flexplate (2002)	23–25
	Transmission Mount Bolts	50–68
	Transmission To Crossmember	25–34
	Transmission To Engine (1998)	40–50
	Transmission To Engine (1999–2002)	30–40
	Valve Body (1998)	84–96①
	Valve Body (1999–2002)	80–97①

① — Inch lbs.

5R55N Automatic Transmission

NOTE: On Air Bag Equipped Models, Refer To "Air Bag System Precautions" Located In The Front Of This Manual For System Disarming & Arming Procedures.

NOTE: Refer To "Computer Relearn Procedures" Located In The Front Of This Manual When Battery Power To The Computer Has Been Interrupted.

NOTE: "Electrical Symbol & Wire Color Code Identification" Located In The Front Of This Manual May Be Used As An Aid When Using Wiring Circuits Found In This Section.

NOTE: Prior To Performing Any Service Operations Listed In This Section, Consult "Technical Service Bulletins" Section For Related Information.

INDEX

PRECAUTIONS

AIR BAG SYSTEMS

Refer to "Air Bag System Precautions" in the front of this manual for system disarming and arming procedures.

BATTERY GROUND CABLE

Prior to service, disconnect battery ground cable and isolate as required.

IDENTIFICATION

Refer to **Fig. 1** for transmission identification.

Item	Description
1	Model number
2	Assemble level
3	Build code
4	Serial number
5	Build date (YMDD)

FM5020102255000X

Fig. 1 Transmission identification

DESCRIPTION

The 5R55N automatic transmission, **Fig. 2,** is a five-speed, non-synchronous transmission with the following features: five forward speeds: electronic shift, pressure and torque converter clutch controls: three compound planetary gearsets: three bands: four multi-plate clutches and three one-way clutches.

All hydraulic functions are directed by electronic solenoids to control: static engagement feel; shift feel; shift scheduling; modulated torque converter clutch (TCC) applications; engine braking utilizing the coast clutch and band and manual first and second timing.

TROUBLESHOOTING

Brake Shift Interlock

Refer to **Fig. 3** for brake shift interlock wiring diagram.

TEST D1: INSPECT DTCS

1. Retrieve Diagnostic Trouble Codes (DTCs).
2. If DTCs are present, repair as required.
3. If no DTCs are present, go to Test D2.

TEST D2: INSPECT FOR VOLTAGE ON CIRCUIT 7S-TA33 (YE/VT)

1. Turn ignition Off.
2. Disconnect brake shift interlock connector C322.
3. Turn ignition to II position.
4. Measure voltage between brake shift interlock connector C322 pin No. 2 circuit 7S-TA33 (YE/VT), harness side and ground.
5. If measurement is more than 10 volts, go to Test D5.
6. If measurement is not more than 10 volts, go to Test D3.

TEST D3: INSPECT CIRCUIT 7S-TA33 (YE/VT) FOR SHORT TO GROUND

1. Measure resistance between brake shift interlock connector C322 pin No. 2 circuit 7S-TA33 (YE/VT), harness side and ground.
2. If resistance is more than 10,000 ohms, go to Test D4.
3. If resistance is less than 10,000 ohms, repair circuit as required.

TEST D4: INSPECT CIRCUIT 7S-TA33 (YE/VT) FOR OPEN

1. Measure resistance between brake shift interlock connector C322 pin No. 2 circuit 7S-TA33 (YE/VT), harness side and Front Electrical Module (FEM) C201f pin No. 15, circuit 7S-TA33 (YE/VT), harness side.
2. If resistance is less than 5 ohms, install new FEM.
3. If resistance is more than 5 ohms, repair circuit as required.

TEST D5: INSPECT CIRCUIT 31-TA33 (BK) FOR OPEN

1. Measure resistance between brake shift interlock connector C322 pin No. 1 circuit 31-TA33 (BK), harness side and ground.
2. If resistance is less than 5 ohms, install new brake shift interlock actuator.
3. If resistance is more than 5 ohms, repair circuit as required.

Transmission

NO FORWARD IN D5 OR D4 ONLY

ELECTRICAL

PCM, vehicle wiring harnesses, pressure control solenoid "B."

HYDRAULIC/MECHANICAL

Fluid

Improper level condition.

Forward Clutch

1. Seals, piston damaged.
2. Check ball damaged, missing, not seating, off location.
3. Friction elements damaged or worn.
4. Return springs damaged.

OD Servo

1. Servo retaining ring damaged.
2. Seals (piston and cover) damaged.
3. Anchor pins in case damaged.

OD Band

1. Band damaged.
2. Servo worn or damaged.
3. Not adjusted properly.
4. Anchor pins damaged or worn.

Case

Damaged.

NO FORWARD

ELECTRICAL

PCM, vehicle wiring harnesses, pressure control solenoid "B."

HYDRAULIC/MECHANICAL

Main Control

1. Bolt not tightened to specifications.
2. Separator plate damaged.
3. Contamination.
4. Valves, springs damaged, improperly assembled, missing, stuck or bore damaged.

Center Support

1. Screw not tightened to specifications.
2. Seal rings or bearing damaged.
3. Outside diameter of case bore damage.
4. Support damaged or leaking.

Forward Clutch

1. Seals, piston damaged.
2. Check ball damaged, missing, not seating, off location.
3. Friction elements damaged or worn.
4. Return springs damaged.

Forward Planetary

Planetary damage.

Intermediate Clutch

1. Seals, piston damaged.
2. Check ball damaged, missing, not seating, off location.
3. Friction elements damaged or worn.
4. Return springs damaged.

Low One-Way Clutch

Worn, damaged or assembled improperly.

NO REVERSE

ELECTRICAL

PCM, vehicle wiring harnesses, pressure control solenoid C (PC C), shift solenoid "B" (SSB).

HYDRAULIC/MECHANICAL

Main Control

1. Bolts not tightened to specifications.
2. Separator plate damaged.
3. Contamination.
4. Valves, springs damaged, improperly assembled, missing, stuck, or bore damage.

Direct Clutch

1. Seals, piston damaged.
2. Check ball damaged, missing, not seating, off location.
3. Friction elements damaged or worn.
4. Return springs damaged.

Forward Clutch

1. Seals, piston damaged.
2. Check ball damaged, missing, not seating, off location.
3. Friction elements damaged or worn.
4. Return springs damaged.

Intermediate Clutch

1. Seals, piston damaged.
2. Check ball damaged, missing, not seating, off location.
3. Friction elements damaged or worn.
4. Return springs damaged.

Reverse Servo

1. Servo retaining ring damaged.
2. Seals (piston and cover) damaged.
3. Anchor pins in case damaged.

Reverse Band

1. Band damaged.
2. Servo worn or damaged.
3. Not adjusted properly.
4. Anchor pins damaged or worn.

Reverse Clutch

1. Seals, piston damaged.
2. Check ball damaged, missing, not seating, off location.
3. Friction elements damaged or worn.
4. Return springs damaged.

HARSH REVERSE ONLY

ELECTRICAL

PCM, vehicle wiring harnesses, pressure control solenoid C (PC C).

HYDRAULIC/MECHANICAL

Improper Pressures

High pressures.

Main Control

1. Bolts not tightened to specifications.
2. Separator plate damaged.
3. Contamination.
4. Valves, spring damaged, improperly assembled, missing, stuck or bore damaged.

Direct Clutch

1. Seals, piston damaged.
2. Check ball damaged, missing not seating, off location.
3. Friction elements damaged or worn.
4. Return springs damaged.

Forward Clutch

1. Seals, piston damaged.
2. Check ball damaged, missing, not seating, off location.
3. Friction elements damaged or worn.
4. Return springs damaged.

Intermediate Clutch

1. Seals, piston damaged.
2. Check ball damaged, missing, not seating, off location.
3. Friction elements damaged or worn.
4. Return springs damaged.

Reverse Servo

1. Servo retaining ring damaged.
2. Seals (piston and cover) damaged.
3. Anchor pins in case damaged.

Reverse Band

1. Band damaged.
2. Servo worn or damaged.
3. Not adjusted properly.
4. Anchor pins damaged or worn

Reverse Clutch

1. Seals, piston damaged.
2. Check ball damaged, missing, not seating, off location.
3. Friction elements damaged or worn.
4. Return springs damaged.

HARSH FORWARD ONLY

ELECTRICAL

PCM, vehicle wiring harnesses, Pressure Control Solenoid "A," (PC A), Pressure Control Solenoid "C" (PC C).

HYDRAULIC/MECHANICAL

Improper Pressures

High Pressures.

Main Control

1. Bolts not tightened to specifications.
2. Separator plate damaged.
3. Contamination.
4. Valves, springs damaged, improperly assembled, missing, stuck or bore damaged.

OD Servo

1. Servo retaining ring damaged.
2. Seals (piston and cover) damaged.
3. Anchor pins in case damaged.

OD Band

1. Band damaged.
2. Servo worn or damaged.
3. Not adjusted properly.

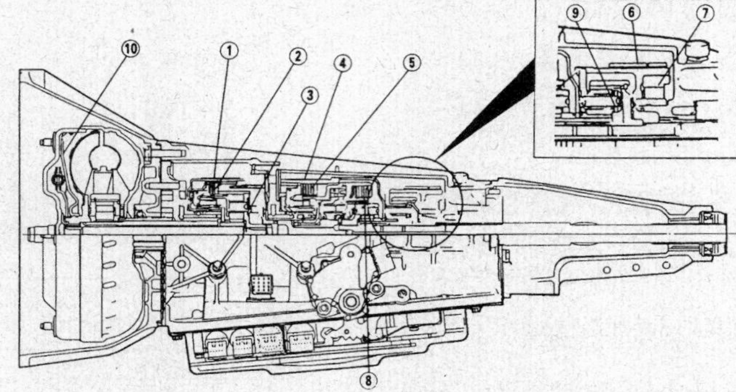

Fig. 2 Cross-sectional view of transmission

4. Anchor pins damaged or worn.

Center Support

1. Screw not tightened to specifications.
2. Seal rings or bearing damage.
3. Outside diameter of case bore damage.
4. Support damaged or leaking.

Forward Clutch

1. Seals, piston damaged.
2. Check ball damaged, missing, not seating, off location.
3. Friction elements damaged or worn.
4. Return springs damaged.

Intermediate Clutch

1. Seals, piston damaged.
2. Check ball damaged, missing, not seating, off location.
3. Friction elements damaged or worn.
4. Return springs damaged.

HARSH MANUAL 1ST GEAR ONLY

ELECTRICAL

PCM, vehicle wiring harnesses, Pressure Control Solenoid "B" (PC B), Turbine Shaft Speed (TSS) sensor.

HYDRAULIC/MECHANICAL

No hydraulic or mechanical concerns

DELAYED OR SOFT REVERSE ONLY

ELECTRICAL

PCM, vehicle wiring harnesses, Pressure Control Solenoid "C" (PC C).

HYDRAULIC/MECHANICAL

Improper pressures

Low pressure

Main Control

1. Bolts not tightened to specifications.
2. Separator plate damaged.
3. Contamination.
4. Valves, springs damaged, improperly

assembled, missing, stuck or bore damaged.

Direct Clutch

1. Seals, piston damaged.
2. Check ball damaged, missing not seating, off location.
3. Friction elements damaged or worn.
4. Return springs damaged.

Reverse Servo

1. Servo retaining ring damaged.
2. Seals (piston and cover) damaged.
3. Anchor pins in case damaged.

Reverse Band

1. Band damaged.
2. Servo worn or damaged.
3. Not adjusted properly.
4. Anchor pins damaged or worn.

DELAYED/SOFT FORWARD ONLY

ELECTRICAL

PCM, vehicle wiring harnesses, Pressure Control Solenoid "B" (PC B).

HYDRAULIC/MECHANICAL

Improper Pressures

Low pressures.

Main Control

1. Bolts not tightened to specifications.
2. Separator plate damaged.
3. Contamination.
4. Valves, spring damaged, improperly assembled, missing, stuck or bore damaged.

OD Servo

1. Servo retaining ring damaged.
2. Seals (piston and cover) damaged.
3. Anchor pins in case damaged.

OD Band

1. Band damaged.
2. Servo worn or damaged.
3. Not adjusted properly.
4. Anchor pins damaged or worn.

Center Support

1. Screw not tightened to specifications.
2. Seal rings or bearing damaged.
3. Outside diameter of case bore damage.
4. Support damaged or leaking.

Forward Clutch

1. Seals, piston damaged.
2. Check ball damaged, missing, not seating, off location.
3. Friction element damaged or worn.
4. Return springs damaged.

NO FORWARD & NO REVERSE

ELECTRICAL

PCM, vehicle wiring harnesses, Pressure Control Solenoid "B" (PC B).

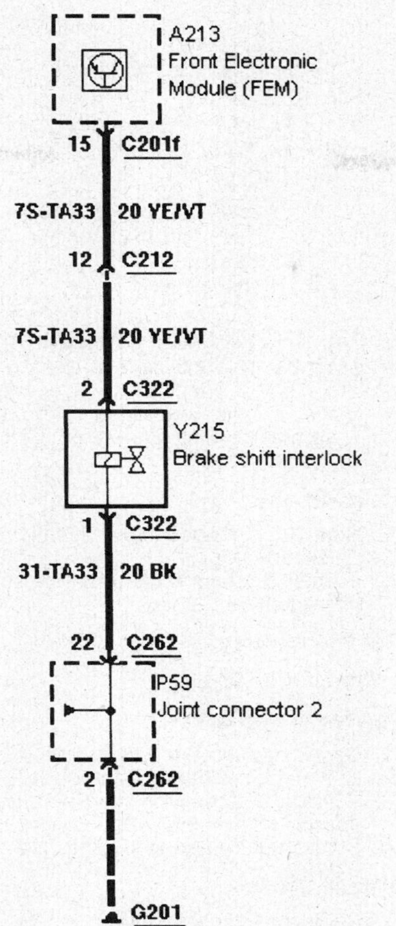

Fig. 3 Brake shift interlock wiring diagram

HYDRAULIC/MECHANICAL

Fluid

1. Improper level.
2. Condition.

Shift Cable/Digital TR Sensor

Cable system or digital TR sensor damaged, misaligned.

Main Control

1. Bolts not tightened to specifications.
2. Separator plate damaged.
3. Contamination.
4. Valve, springs damaged, improperly assembled, missing, stuck, or bore damaged.

Input Shaft

Damaged.

Fluid Pump

1. Bolts not tightened to specifications.
2. Gasket damaged.
3. Porosity, cross leaks, ball missing, plugged hole.

OD Planetary

Planetary damaged.

Center Shaft

Damaged. One-way clutch damaged

Forward Clutch

1. Seals, piston damaged.
2. Check ball damaged, missing, not seating, off location.
3. Friction elements damaged or worn.
4. Return springs damaged.

Forward Planetary

Planetary damaged.

Intermediate Clutch

1. Seals, piston damaged.
2. Check ball damaged, missing, not seating, off location.
3. Friction elements damaged or worn.
4. Return springs damaged.

Reverse Planetary

Planetary damaged.

Output Shaft

Damaged.

Torque Converter

1. Damaged flexplate or adapter plate.
2. Damaged impeller hub.
3. Damaged turbine hub.

Direct One-way Clutch

Worn, damaged or assembled improperly.

ENGAGEMENT CONCERN: HARSH FORWARD & HARSH REVERSE

ELECTRICAL

PCM, vehicle wring harnesses, digital TR sensor, Transmission Fluid (TFT) sensor.

HYDRAULIC/MECHANICAL

Fluid

1. Improper level.
2. Condition.

Improper Pressures

High pressures.

Main Control

1. Bolts not tightened to specifications.
2. Separator plate damaged.
3. Contamination.
4. Valves, springs damaged, improperly assembled, missing, stuck, or bore damaged.

Forward Clutch

1. Seals, piston damaged.
2. Check ball damaged, missing, not seating, off location.

3. Friction elements damaged or worn.
4. Return springs damaged.

Intermediate Clutch

1. Seals, piston damaged.
2. Check ball damaged, missing, not seating, off location.
3. Friction elements damaged or worn.
4. Return springs damaged.

DELAYED FORWARD & DELAYED REVERSE

ELECTRICAL

PCM, vehicle wiring harnesses, Transmission Fluid Temperature (TFT) sensor.

HYDRAULIC/MECHANICAL

Fluid

1. Improper level.
2. Condition.

Improper Pressures

High pressures

Main Control

1. Bolts not tightened to specifications.
2. Separator plate damaged.
3. Contamination.
4. Valves and springs damaged, improperly assembled, missing, stuck, or bore damaged.

Fluid Pump

1. Bolts not tightened to specifications.
2. Gasket damaged.
3. Porosity, cross leaks, ball missing, plugged hole.

SOME/ALL SHIFTS MISSING (AUTOMATIC MODE ONLY)

ELECTRICAL

PCM, vehicle wiring harnesses, Shift Solenoids A, B, C, Torque Converter Clutch (TCC) solenoid, Pressure Control Solenoids A, B, C, Output Shaft Speed (OSS) sensor, digital TR sensor, IAT sensor, VSS input.

HYDRAULIC/MECHANICAL

Some Shifts Missing ONLY

If only some shifts are missing, determine which shift(s) is missing: Refer to appropriate routine(s).

Fluid

1. Improper level.
2. Condition.

Shift Cable/Digital TR Sensor

Cable system or digital TR sensor damaged, misaligned.

Improper Pressures

High/Low pressures.

Main Control

1. Bolts not tightened to specifications.
2. Separator plate damaged.
3. Contamination.

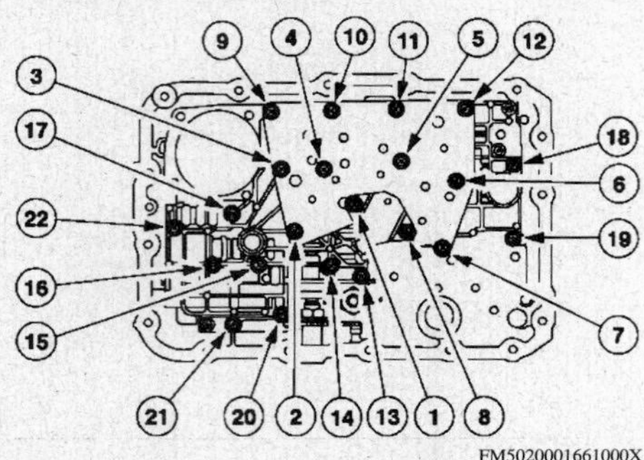

Fig. 4 Valve body mounting screws tightening sequence

4. Valve, springs damaged, improperly assembled, missing, stuck, or bore damaged.

Fluid Pump

1. Bolts not tightened to specifications.
2. Gasket damaged.
3. Porosity, cross leaks, ball missing, plugged hole.

OD Planetary

Planetary damaged.

Center Support

1. Screw not tightened to specifications.
2. Seal rings or bearing damaged.
3. Outside diameter of case bore damaged.
4. Support damaged or leaking.

Direct Clutch

1. Seals, piston damaged.
2. Check ball damaged, missing, not seating, off location.
3. Friction elements damaged or worn.
4. Return springs damaged.

Intermediate Clutch

1. Seals, piston damaged.
2. Check ball damaged, missing, not seating, off location.
3. Friction elements damaged or worn.
4. Return springs damaged.

Intermediate One-Way Clutch

Worn, damaged or assembled improperly.

EARLY/LATE TIMING

ELECTRICAL

PCM, vehicle wiring harnesses, Output Shaft Speed (OSS) sensor, IAT sensor.

HYDRAULIC/MECHANICAL

Some Shifts Early/Late Only

If only some shifts are early/late, determine which shifts are missing. Refer to appropriate condition(s).

Fluid

1. Improper level.
2. Condition.

Main Control

1. Bolts not tightened to specifications.
2. Separator plate damaged.
3. Contamination.
4. Valve, springs damaged, improperly assembled, missing, stuck, or bore damaged.

OD Servo

1. Servo retaining ring damaged.
2. Seals (piston and cover) damaged.
3. Anchor pins in case damaged.

OD Band

1. Band damaged.
2. Servo worn or damaged.
3. Not adjusted properly.
4. Anchor pins damaged or worn.

ERRATIC/HUNTING (SOME/ALL) SHIFT TIMING

ELECTRICAL

PCM, vehicle wiring harnesses, Output Shaft Speed (OSS) sensor, IAT sensor.

HYDRAULIC/MECHANICAL

Fluid

1. Improper level.
2. Condition.

Main Control

1. Bolts not tightened to specifications.
2. Separator plate damaged.
3. Contamination.
4. Valve, springs damaged, improperly assembled, missing, stuck, or bore damaged.

Further Diagnosis

For further diagnosis for timing issues, refer to appropriate condition.

SOFT/SLIPPING (SOME/ALL) ENGAGEMENT

ELECTRICAL

PCM, vehicle wiring harnesses, Shift Solenoids "A, B, C," Pressure Control Solenoids "A, B, C, D," Intermediate Shaft Speed (ISS) sensor, Transmission Fluid Temperature (TFT) sensor, IAT Sensor, VSS input.

HYDRAULIC/MECHANICAL

Some Shifts Soft/Slipping Only

If only some of the shifts are soft/slipping, determine which shift(s) is missing: Refer to appropriate condition(s).

Fluid

1. Improper level.
2. Condition.

Improper Pressures

High/Low pressures.

Main Control

1. Bolts not tightened to specifications.
2. Separator plate damaged.
3. Contamination.
4. Valves, springs damaged, improperly assembled, missing, stuck, or bore damaged.

Fluid Pump

1. Bolts not tightened to specifications.
2. Gasket damaged.
3. Porosity, cross leaks, improperly assembled ball missing, plugged hole.

Coast Clutch

1. Seals, piston damaged.
2. Check ball damaged, missing, not seating, off location.
3. Friction elements damaged or worn.
4. Return springs damaged.

Center Support

1. Screw not tightened to specifications.
2. Seal rings or bearings damaged.
3. Outside diameter of case bore damage.
4. Support damaged or leaking.

Intermediate Servo

1. Servo retaining ring damaged.
2. Seals (piston and cover) damaged.
3. Anchor pins in case damaged.

Intermediate Band

1. Band damaged.
2. Servo worn or damaged.
3. Not adjusted properly.
4. Anchor pins damaged or worn.

Direct Clutch

1. Seals, piston damaged.
2. Check ball damaged, missing, not seating, off location.
3. Friction elements damaged or worn.
4. Return springs damaged.

Forward Clutch

1. Seals, piston damaged.
2. Check ball damaged, missing, not seating, off location.
3. Friction elements damaged or worn.
4. Return springs damaged.

Intermediate Clutch

1. Seals, piston damaged.
2. Check ball damaged, missing, not seating, off location.
3. Friction elements damaged or worn.
4. Return springs damaged.

Reverse Servo

1. Servo retaining ring damaged.
2. Seals (piston and cover) damaged.
3. Anchor pins in case damaged.

Reverse Band

1. Band damaged.
2. Servo worn or damaged.
3. Not adjusted properly.
4. Anchor pins worn or damaged.

Case

Damaged.

HARSH SHIFT (SOME/ALL)

ELECTRICAL

PCM, vehicle wiring harnesses, Shift Solenoids "A, B, C," Pressure Control Solenoids "A, B, C, D," Intermediate Shaft Speed (ISS) sensor, digital TR sensor,

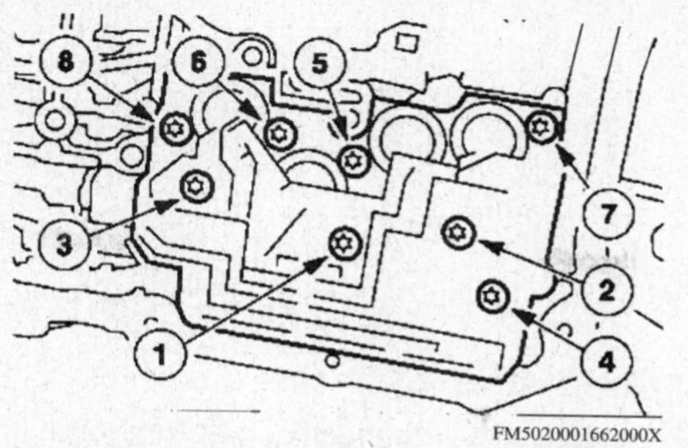

Fig. 5 Solenoid body mounting bolts tightening sequence

Transmission Fluid Temperature (TFT) sensor, IAT sensor, VSS input.

HYDRAULIC/MECHANICAL

Some Shifts Harsh Only

If only some of the shifts are harsh, determine which shift(s) is missing: Refer to appropriate routine(s).

Improper Pressures

High/Low pressures.

Main Control

1. Bolts not tightened to specifications.
2. Separator plate damaged.
3. Contamination.
4. Valves, springs damaged, improperly assembled, missing, stuck, or bore damaged.

Input Shaft

Damaged.

OD Servo

1. Servo retaining ring damaged.
2. Seals (piston and cover) damaged.
3. Anchor pins in case damaged.

OD Band

1. Band damaged.
2. Servo worn or damaged.
3. Not adjusted properly.
4. Anchor pins worn or damaged.

Center Shaft

1. Center shaft damaged.
2. One-way clutch damaged.

Intermediate Servo

1. Servo retaining ring damaged.
2. Seals (piston and cover) damaged.
3. Anchor pins in case damaged.

Intermediate Band

1. Band damaged.
2. Servo worn or damaged.
3. Not adjusted properly.
4. Anchor pins damaged or worn.

Forward Clutch

1. Seals, piston damaged.
2. Check ball damaged, missing, not seating, off location.
3. Friction elements damaged or worn.
4. Return springs damaged.

Intermediate Clutch

1. Seals, piston damaged.
2. Check ball damaged, missing, not seating, off location.
3. Friction elements damaged or worn.
4. Return springs damaged.

Reverse Servo

1. Servo retaining ring damaged.
2. Seals (piston and cover) damaged.
3. Anchor pins in case damaged.

Reverse Band

1. Band damaged.
2. Servo worn or damaged.
3. Not adjusted properly.
4. Anchor pins damaged or worn.

Output Shaft

Damaged.

Case

Damaged.

NO 1ST & 2ND GEAR IN DRIVE, ENGAGES IN HIGHER GEAR

ELECTRICAL

PCM, vehicle wiring harnesses, Shift Solenoids A, B, C, digital TR sensor.

HYDRAULIC/MECHANICAL

Improper Pressures

High/Low pressures.

Main Control

1. Bolts not tightened to specifications.
2. Separator plate damaged.
3. Contamination.
4. Valves/springs damaged, improperly assembled, missing, stuck, or bore damaged.

Intermediate Clutch

1. Seals, piston damaged.
2. Check ball damaged, missing, not seating, off location.
3. Friction elements damaged or worn.
4. Return springs damaged.

Direct One-way Clutch

Worn, damaged or assembled improperly.

Low One-Way Clutch

Worn, damaged or assembled improperly.

NO 1ST GEAR IN MANUAL 1 POSITION

ELECTRICAL

PCM, vehicle wiring harnesses, Shift Solenoids A, B, Pressure Control Solenoids B, C.

HYDRAULIC/MECHANICAL

Improper Pressures

High/Low pressures.

Main Control

1. Bolts not tightened to specifications.
2. Separator plate damaged.
3. Contamination.
4. Valves, springs damaged, improperly assembled, missing, stuck or bore damaged.

OD Planetary

Planetary damaged.

Direct One-Way Clutch

Worn, damaged or assembled improperly.

Low One-Way Clutch

Worn, damaged or assembled improperly.

NO 2ND GEAR IN MANUAL 2 POSITION

ELECTRICAL

PCM, vehicle wiring harnesses, Shift Solenoids A, B, C, Pressure Control Solenoid "B."

HYDRAULIC/MECHANICAL

Improper Pressure

High/Low pressures.

Main Control

1. Bolts not tightened to specifications.
2. Separator plate damaged.
3. Contamination.
4. Valves, springs damaged, improperly assembled, missing, stuck or bore damaged.

OD Servo

1. Servo retaining ring damaged.
2. Seals (piston and cover) damaged.
3. Not adjusted properly.
4. Anchor pins in case damage.

OD Band

1. Band damaged.
2. Servo worn or damaged.
3. Not adjusted properly.
4. Anchor pins damaged or worn.

Direct One-Way Clutch

Worn, damaged or assembled improperly.

Low One-Way Clutch

Worn, damaged or assembled improperly.

TORQUE CONVERTER DOES NOT APPLY

ELECTRICAL

PCM, vehicle wiring harnesses, Torque Converter Clutch (TCC) solenoid, Transmission Fluid Temperature (TFT) sensor.

HYDRAULIC/MECHANICAL

Improper Pressures

High/Low pressures.

Application	Tear Tag Number	NGS/SBDS Qualifier
3.0L Lincoln LS - 49S Non-Sport	BMTx	9LDA-AA CALIBRATION
3.0L Lincoln LS - 49S Sport Model	AUTx	9LDA-AC CALIBRATION
3.0L Lincoln LS - California Non-Sport	BORx	9LDA-BB CALIBRATION
3.0L Lincoln LS - California Sport Model	CAJx	9LDA-BC CALIBRATION
3.9L Lincoln LS - 50S Sport Model	WOKx	9WHA-BA CALIBRATION
3.9L Lincoln LS - California Non-Sport	NIAx, RKHx	9WHA-BB CALIBRATION

FMA050000121000X

Fig. 6 PCM calibrations. 2000 LS

Main Control

1. Bolts not tightened to specifications.
2. Separator plate damaged.
3. Contamination.
4. Valve, springs damaged, improperly assembled, missing, stuck, or bore damaged.

Fluid Pump

1. Bolts not tightened to specifications.
2. Gasket damaged.
3. Porosity, cross leaks, ball missing, plugged hole.

Torque Converter

Torque converter internal failure preventing engagement, piston application.

TORQUE CONVERTER ALWAYS APPLIED/STALLS VEHICLE

ELECTRICAL

PCM, vehicle wiring harnesses, Torque Converter Clutch (TCC) solenoid.

HYDRAULIC/MECHANICAL

Main Control

1. Bolts not tightened to specifications.
2. Separator plate damaged.
3. Contamination.
4. Valve, springs damaged, improperly assembled, missing, stuck, or bore damaged.
5. Low one-way clutch.

Torque Converter

Torque converter internal failure preventing engagement, piston release.

Low One-Way Clutch

Worn, damaged or assembled improperly.

TORQUE CONVERTER CYCLING/SHUDDER/ CHATTER

ELECTRICAL

PCM, vehicle wiring harnesses, Torque Converter Clutch (TCC) solenoid.

HYDRAULIC/MECHANICAL

Fluid

Condition—contaminated, degraded.

Main Control

1. Bolts not tightened to specifications.
2. Separator plate damaged.
3. Contamination.
4. Valve, springs damaged, improperly assembled, missing, stuck, or bore damaged.

Torque Converter

Torque converter internal leakage, clutch material damaged.

SHIFT LEVER EFFORTS HIGH

ELECTRICAL

PCM, vehicle wiring harnesses, digital TR sensor.

HYDRAULIC/MECHANICAL

Shift Cable, Digital TR sensor

Cable system or digital TR sensor damaged, misaligned.

Main Control

1. Bolts not tightened to specifications.
2. Separator plate damaged.
3. Contamination.
4. Valve/springs damaged, improperly assembled, missing, stuck, or bore damaged.

Case

1. Manual control lever assembly damage, manual valve inner lever pin bent, manual valve inner lever damaged, spring rod damaged.
2. Manual valve lever shaft retaining pin damaged.

EXTERNAL LEAKS

ELECTRICAL

Output Shaft Speed (OSS) sensor, Intermediate Shaft Speed (ISS), Turbine Shaft Speed (TSS) sensor, digital TR sensor.

HYDRAULIC/MECHANICAL

Fluid

Improper level.

Case

Case vent damaged.

Seals/Gaskets

Leakage at gaskets, seals, etc.

POOR VEHICLE PERFORMANCE

ELECTRICAL

PCM, vehicle wiring harnesses, Shift Solenoids A, B, C, Pressure Control Solenoids A, B, C, Output Shaft Speed (OSS) sensor, Turbine Shaft Speed (TSS) sensor, Transmission Fluid Temperature (TFT) sensor, digital TR sensor.

HYDRAULIC/MECHANICAL

Fluid

Improper level.

Input Shaft

Damaged.

Center Shaft

Damaged. One-way clutch damaged.

Forward Clutch

1. Seals, piston damaged.
2. Piston check ball damaged, missing, not seating, off location.
3. Friction elements damaged or worn.
4. Return springs damaged.

Intermediate Clutch

1. Seals, piston damaged.
2. Check ball damaged, missing, not seating, off location.
3. Friction elements damaged or worn.
4. Return springs damaged.

Torque Converter

1. Torque Converter one-way clutch slipping.
2. Improper torque converter used in rebuild.

NOISE/VIBRATION—FORWARD OR REVERSE

ELECTRICAL

PCM, vehicle wiring harnesses, Torque Converter Clutch (TCC) solenoid, Pressure Control Solenoids A, B, C.

HYDRAULIC/MECHANICAL

Fluid Pump

1. Bolts not tightened to specifications.
2. Gasket damaged.
3. Porosity, cross leaks, ball missing, plugged hole.

Intermediate Clutch

1. Seals, piston damaged.
2. Check ball damaged, missing, not seating, off location.
3. Friction elements damaged or worn.
4. Return springs damaged.

Low One-Way Clutch

Worn, damaged or assembled improperly.

Flexplate or Adapter Plate

1. Damaged.
2. Adapter plate not aligned properly.

ENGINE WILL NOT CRANK

ELECTRICAL

PCM, vehicle wiring harnesses, digital TR sensor.

HYDRAULIC/MECHANICAL

Shift Cable/Digital TR Sensor

Cable system or digital TR Sensor damaged, misaligned.

Application	Old Part Number (-12A650-)	Tear Tag	New Part Number (-12A650-)	Old Calibration	New Calibration	NGS/WDS Qualifier
LS - 3.0L, 5R55N	XW4F-JJ	VAV0	XU7Z-TA	9LDA-AAH	9LDA-AAH	WDS B14.3 Release
LS - 3.0L, 5R55N w/SST	XW4F-KH	DYZ0	XU7Z-SA	9LDA-ACG	9LDA-ACG	WDS B14.3 Release
LS - 3.0L, 5R55N	1U7A-JA	MSU1	1U7Z-JB	1LQ16B0507	1LQ16B0507	WDS B14.3 Release
LS - 3.0L, 5R55N w/SST	1U7A-KA	DJY1	1U7Z-KB	1LQ16S0507	1LQ16S0507	WDS B14.3 Release
LS - 3.9L, 5R55N w/SST	1U7A-HA	MFF1	1U7Z-HB	1LQ19S0506	1LQ19S0506	WDS B14.3 Release
LS - 3.9L, 5R55N w/3.31 axle	1U7A-DA	KQI1	1U7Z-DB	1LQ18B0506	1LQ18B0506	WDS B14.3 Release
LS - 3.9L, 5R55N w/3.58 axle	1U7A-GA	KSF1	1U7Z-GB	1LQ19B0506	1LQ19B0506	WDS B14.3 Release
LS - 3.9L, 5R55N 50 States w/SST	1U7A-FA	FMS1	1U7Z-FB	1LQ18S0506	1LQ18S0506	WDS B14.3 Release

FMA050100124000X

Fig. 7 PCM calibrations. 2000-01 LS

Fluid Pump

Seized.

Flexplate or Adapter Plate

Damaged.

NO PARK RANGE

ELECTRICAL

No electrical concerns.

HYDRAULIC/MECHANICAL

Shift Cable/Digital TR sensor

Able system or digital TR sensor damaged, misaligned.

Case

1. Manual control lever damage, manual valve inner lever pin bent, manual valve inner lever damaged, spring rod damaged.
2. Manual valve lever shaft retaining pin damaged.

Park System

1. Park gear, parking pawl, parking pawl return spring, park or guide plate, parking actuating rod, parking pawl shaft, manual lever, manual lever detent spring damaged or improperly assembled.
2. External linkages/brackets damaged.

TRANSMISSION OVERHEATING

ELECTRICAL

PCM, vehicle wiring harnesses, Torque Converter Clutch (TCC) solenoid, Pressure Control Solenoids A, B, C, Transmission Fluid Temperature (TFT) sensor.

HYDRAULIC/MECHANICAL

Fluid

Improper level.

Improper Pressures

High/low pressures.

Main Control

1. Bolts not tightened to specifications.
2. Separator plate damaged.
3. Contamination.
4. Valves/springs damaged, improperly assembled, missing, stuck, or bore damaged.

Fluid Pump

1. Bolts not tightened to specifications.
2. Gasket damaged.
3. Porosity, cross leaks, ball missing, plugged hole.

Case

Case vent damaged.

Torque Converter

1. Seized torque converter one-way clutch.
2. Excessive slip detected.

Transmission Cooling System

1. Restriction in the transmission cooling system.
2. Excessive trailer tow load.
3. Poor engine performance.

NO ENGINE BRAKING IN MANUAL 3RD POSITION

ELECTRICAL

PCM, vehicle wiring harnesses, shift solenoids A, B, C, Reverse Pressure (RP) switch, pressure control solenoids A, B.

HYDRAULIC/MECHANICAL

Fluid

Improper level.

Improper Pressures

High/Low pressures.

Main Control

1. Bolts not tightened to specifications.
2. Separator plate damaged.
3. Contamination.
4. Valve/springs damaged, improperly assembled, missing, stuck, or bore damaged.

Fluid Pump

1. Bolts not tightened to specifications.
2. Gasket damaged.
3. Porosity, cross leaks, ball missing, plugged hole.

Coast Clutch

1. Seals, piston damaged.
2. Check ball damaged, missing, not seating, off location.
3. Friction elements damaged or worn.
4. Return springs damaged.

Center Support

1. Screw not tightened to specifications.
2. Seals rings or bearing damaged.
3. Outside diameter of case bore damage.
4. Support damaged or leaking.

Intermediate Servo

1. Servo retaining ring damaged.
2. Seals (piston and cover) damaged.
3. Anchor pins in case damaged.

Intermediate Band

1. Band damaged.
2. Servo worn or damaged.
3. Not adjusted properly.
4. Anchor pins damaged or worn.

Intermediate Clutch

1. Seals, piston damaged.
2. Check ball damaged, missing, not seating, off location.
3. Friction elements damaged or worn.
4. Return springs damaged.

Low One-Way Clutch

Worn, damaged, or assembled improperly.

NO ENGINE BRAKING IN MANUAL 4TH (D4) POSITION

ELECTRICAL

PCM, vehicle wiring harnesses, Shift Solenoid "D," Reverse Pressure (RP) switch, Pressure Control Solenoid "B."

HYDRAULIC/MECHANICAL

Fluid

Improper level.

Main Control

1. Bolts not tightened to specifications.
2. Separator plate damaged.
3. Contamination.
4. Valve/springs damaged, improperly assembled, missing, stuck, or bore damaged.

Fluid Pump

1. Bolts not tightened to specifications.
2. Gasket damaged.
3. Porosity, cross leaks, ball missing, plugged hole.

Coast Clutch

1. Seals, piston damaged.
2. Check ball damaged, missing, not seating, off location.
3. Friction elements damaged or worn.
4. Return springs damaged.

Forward Clutch

1. Seals, piston damaged.
2. Check ball damaged, missing, not seating, off location.
3. Friction elements damaged or worn.
4. Return springs damaged.

NO ENGINE BRAKING IN MANUAL 2ND POSITION

ELECTRICAL

PCM, vehicle wiring harnesses, Shift Solenoids "A, C, D," Pressure Control Solenoid "A."

HYDRAULIC/MECHANICAL

Fluid

Improper level.

Improper Pressures

High/low pressures.

Reverse Servo

1. Servo retaining ring damaged.
2. Seals (piston and cover) damaged.
3. Anchor pins in case damaged.

Reverse Band

1. Band damaged.
2. Servo worn or damaged.
3. Not adjusted properly.
4. Anchor pins damaged or worn.

NO ENGINE BRAKING IN MANUAL 1ST POSITION

ELECTRICAL

PCM, vehicle wiring harnesses, Shift Solenoids "A, C, D," Pressure Control Solenoids A, B.

HYDRAULIC/MECHANICAL

Fluid

Improper level.

Improper pressures

High/low pressures.

Fluid Pump

1. Bolts not tightened to specifications.
2. Gasket damaged.
3. Porosity, cross leaks, ball missing, plugged hole.

Coast Clutch

1. Seals, piston damaged.
2. Check ball damaged, missing, not seating, off location.
3. Friction elements damaged or worn.
4. Return springs damaged.

Reverse Servo

1. Servo retaining ring damaged.
2. Seals (piston and cover) damaged.
3. Anchor pins in case damaged.

Reverse Band

1. Band damaged.
2. Servo worn or damaged.
3. Not adjusted properly.
4. Anchor pins damaged or worn.

FLUID VENTING/FOAMING

ELECTRICAL

No Electrical concerns.

HYDRAULIC/MECHANICAL

Fluid

1. Improper level.
2. Condition.

Fluid Pump

1. Bolts not tightened to specifications.
2. Gasket damaged.
3. Porosity, cross leaks, ball missing, plugged hole.

Intermediate Servo

1. Servo retaining ring damaged.
2. Seals (piston and cover) damaged.
3. Anchor pins in case damaged.

Intermediate Band

1. Band damaged.
2. Servo worn or damaged.
3. Not adjusted properly.
4. Anchor pins damaged or worn.

Case

Case vent damaged.

Other

Transmission overheating.

VEHICLE MOVEMENT WITH GEAR SELECTOR IN "N" POSITION

ELECTRICAL

No Electrical concerns

HYDRAULIC/MECHANICAL

Fluid

Improper level

Improper pressures

High/low pressures

SLIPS/CHATTERS IN MANUAL 1ST POSITION

ELECTRICAL

PCM, vehicle wiring harnesses, Pressure Control Solenoids A, B

HYDRAULIC/MECHANICAL

Fluid

1. Improper level.
2. Condition.

Improper Pressures

High/Low pressures

Main Control

1. Bolts not tightened to specifications.
2. Separator plate damaged.
3. Contamination.
4. Valve/springs damaged, improperly assembled, missing, stuck, or bore damaged.

Fluid Pump

1. Bolts not tightened to specifications.
2. Gasket damaged.
3. Porosity, cross leaks, ball missing, plugged hole.

Forward Clutch

1. Seals, piston damaged.
2. Check ball damaged, missing, not seating, off location.
3. Friction elements damaged or worn.
4. Return springs damaged.

Reverse Servo

1. Servo retaining ring damaged.
2. Seals (piston and cover) damaged.
3. Anchor pins in case damaged.

Reverse Band

1. Band damaged.
2. Servo worn or damaged.
3. Not adjusted properly.
4. Anchor pins damaged or worn.

Direct One-way Clutch

Worn, damaged or assembled improperly.

Low One-way Clutch

Worn, damaged or assembled improperly.

SLIPS/CHATTERS IN MANUAL 2ND POSITION

ELECTRICAL

PCM, vehicle wiring harnesses, Pressure Control Solenoids A, B.

HYDRAULIC/MECHANICAL

Fluid

1. Improper level.
2. Condition.

Improper Pressures

High/low pressures.

Fluid Pump

1. Bolts not tightened to specifications.
2. Gasket damaged.
3. Porosity, cross leaks, ball missing, plugged hole.

OD Servo

1. Servo retaining ring damaged.
2. Seals (piston and cover) damaged.
3. Anchor pins in case damaged.

OD Band

1. Band damaged.
2. Servo worn or damaged.
3. Not adjusted properly.
4. Anchor pins damaged or worn.

OD Planetary

Planetary damaged.

Forward Clutch

1. Seals, piston damaged.
2. Check ball damaged, missing, not seating, off location.
3. Friction elements damaged or worn.
4. Return springs damaged.

Reverse Servo

1. Servo retaining ring damaged.
2. Seals (piston and cover) damaged.
3. Anchor pins in case damaged.

Reverse Band

1. Band damaged.
2. Servo worn or damaged.
3. Not adjusted properly.
4. Anchor pins damaged or worn.

Low One-way Clutch

Worn, damaged or assembled improperly.

SLIP/CHATTERS IN MANUAL 3RD POSITION

ELECTRICAL

PCM, vehicle wiring harnesses, Pressure Control Solenoids A, B.

HYDRAULIC/MECHANICAL

Fluid

1. Improper level.
2. Condition.

Improper Pressures

High/Low pressures.

Fluid Pump

1. Bolts not tightened to specifications.
2. Gasket damaged.
3. Porosity, cross leaks, ball missing, plugged hole.

OD Servo

1. Servo retaining ring damaged.
2. Seals (piston and cover) damaged.
3. Anchor pins in case damaged.

OD Band

1. Band damaged.
2. Servo worn or damaged.
3. Not adjusted properly.
4. Anchor pins damaged or worn.

Intermediate Servo

1. Servo retaining ring damaged.
2. Seals (piston and cover) damaged.
3. Anchor pins in case damaged.

Intermediate Band

1. Band damaged.
2. Servo worn or damaged.
3. Not adjusted properly.
4. Anchor pins damaged or worn.

Forward Clutch

1. Seals, piston damaged.
2. Check ball damaged, missing, not seating, off location.
3. Friction elements damaged or worn.
4. Return springs damaged.

Intermediate Clutch

1. Seals, piston damaged.
2. Check ball damaged, missing, not seating, off location.
3. Friction elements damaged or worn.
4. Return springs damaged.

Direct One-way Clutch

Worn, damaged or assembled improperly.

Low One-way Clutch

Worn, damaged or assembled improperly.

ENGINE BRAKING IN ALL GEARS

ELECTRICAL

PCM, vehicle wiring harnesses, Shift Solenoid D.

HYDRAULIC/MECHANICAL

No hydraulic/mechanical concerns.

NO 2ND & 5TH GEARS

ELECTRICAL

PCM, vehicle wiring harnesses, Pressure Control Solenoids A, B.

HYDRAULIC/MECHANICAL

Intermediate Clutch

1. Seals, piston damaged.
2. Check ball damaged, missing, not seating, off location.
3. Friction elements damaged or worn.
4. Return springs damaged.

NO 3RD, 4TH & 5TH GEARS

ELECTRICAL

PCM, vehicle wiring harnesses, Pressure Control Solenoids A, B.

HYDRAULIC/MECHANICAL

Fluid Pump

1. Bolts not tightened to specifications.
2. Gasket damaged.
3. Porosity, cross leaks, ball missing, plugged hole.

OD Band

1. Band damaged.
2. Servo worn or damaged.
3. Not adjusted properly.
4. Anchor pins damaged or worn.

OD Planetary

Planetary damaged.

HARSH 1-2 SHIFT

ELECTRICAL

PCM, vehicle wiring harnesses, Shift Control Solenoid "C," Pressure Control Solenoids B, Turbine Shaft Speed (TSS) sensor, Digital TR sensor, Transmission Fluid Temperature (TFT) sensor.

HYDRAULIC/MECHANICAL

Improper Pressures

High/Low pressures

Main Control

1. Bolts not tightened to specifications.
2. Separator plate damaged.
3. Contamination.
4. Valve/springs damaged, improperly assembled, missing, stuck, or bore damaged.

OD Servo

1. Servo retaining ring damaged.
2. Seals (piston and cover) damaged.
3. Anchor pins in case damaged.

OD Band

1. Band damaged.
2. Servo worn or damaged.
3. Not adjusted properly.
4. Anchor pins damaged or worn.

Direct Clutch

1. Seals, piston damaged.
2. Check ball damaged, missing, not seating, off location.
3. Friction elements damaged or worn.
4. Return springs damaged.

Intermediate Clutch

1. Seals, piston damaged.
2. Check ball damaged, missing, not seating, off location.
3. Friction elements damaged or worn.
4. Return springs damaged.

HARSH 2-3 SHIFT

ELECTRICAL

PCM, vehicle wiring harnesses, Shift Control Solenoid "B," Pressure Control Solenoid "A," Turbine Shaft Speed (TSS) sensor, Intermediate Shaft Speed (ISS) sensor, Digital TR sensor, Transmission Fluid Temperature (TFT) sensor.

HYDRAULIC/MECHANICAL

Improper Pressures

High/Low pressures

Main Control

1. Bolts not tightened to specifications.
2. Separator plate damaged.
3. Contamination.
4. Valve/springs damaged, improperly assembled, missing, stuck, or bore damaged.

Direct Clutch

1. Seals, piston damaged.
2. Check ball damaged, missing, not seating, off location.
3. Friction elements damaged or worn.
4. Return springs damaged.

Intermediate Clutch

1. Seals, piston damaged.
2. Check ball damaged, missing, not seating, off location.
3. Friction elements damaged or worn.
4. Return springs damaged.

Direct One-Way Clutch

Worn, damaged or assembled improperly.

HARSH 3-4 SHIFT

ELECTRICAL

PCM, vehicle wiring harnesses, Shift Control Solenoid "A," Pressure Control Solenoids "C," Digital TR sensor, Transmission Fluid Temperature (TFT) sensor.

HYDRAULIC/MECHANICAL

Improper Pressures

High/low pressures.

Main Control

1. Bolts not tightened to specifications.
2. Separator plate damaged.
3. Contamination.
4. Valve/springs damaged, improperly assembled, missing, stuck, or bore damaged.

Center Support

1. Screws not tightened to specifications.
2. Seal rings or bearing damaged.
3. Outside diameter of case bore damage.
4. Support damaged or leaking.

Direct Clutch

1. Seals, piston damaged.
2. Check ball damaged, missing, not seating, off location.
3. Friction elements damaged or worn.
4. Return springs damaged.

Intermediate Clutch

1. Seals, piston damaged.
2. Check ball damaged, missing, not seating, off location.
3. Friction elements damaged or worn.
4. Return springs damaged.

HARSH 4-5 SHIFT

ELECTRICAL

PCM, vehicle wiring harnesses, Shift Solenoid "C," Pressure Control Solenoid "B," Turbine Shaft Speed (TSS) sensor, Digital TR sensor, Transmission Fluid Temperature (TFT) sensor

HYDRAULIC/MECHANICAL

Improper Pressures

High/Low pressures.

Main Control

1. Bolts not tightened to specifications.
2. Separator plate damaged.
3. Contamination.
4. Valve/springs damaged, improperly assembled, missing, stuck, or bore damaged.

OD Servo

1. Servo retaining ring damaged.
2. Seal (piston and cover) damaged.
3. Anchor pins in case damaged.

OD Band

1. Band damaged.
2. Servo worn or damaged.
3. Not adjusted properly.
4. Anchor pins damaged or worn.

HARSH 5-4 SHIFT

ELECTRICAL

PCM, vehicle wiring harnesses, Shift Control Solenoid "C," Pressure Control Solenoid "C," Turbine Shaft Speed (TSS) sensor, Digital TR sensor, Transmission Fluid Temperature (TFT) sensor.

HYDRAULIC/MECHANICAL

Improper Pressures

High/low pressures.

Main Control

1. Bolts not tightened to specifications.
2. Separator plate damaged.
3. Contamination.
4. Valve/springs damaged, improperly assembled, missing, stuck, or bore damaged.

Direct Clutch

1. Seals, piston damaged.
2. Check ball damaged, missing, not seating, off location.
3. Friction elements damaged or worn.
4. Return springs damaged.

Direct One-Way Clutch

Worn , damaged or assembled improperly.

HARSH 4-3 SHIFT

ELECTRICAL

PCM, vehicle wiring harnesses, Shift Solenoid "A," Pressure Control Solenoid "A," Digital TR sensor, Transmission Fluid Temperature (TFT) sensor.

HYDRAULIC/MECHANICAL

Improper Pressures

High/Low pressures.

Main Control

1. Bolts not tightened to specifications.
2. Separator plate damaged.
3. Contamination.
4. Valves, springs damaged, improperly assembled, missing, stuck, or bore damaged.

Direct Clutch

1. Seals, piston damaged.
2. Check ball damaged, missing, not seating, off location.
3. Friction elements damaged or worn.
4. Return springs damaged.

Intermediate Clutch

1. Seals, piston damaged.
2. Check ball damaged, missing, not seating, off location.
3. Friction elements damaged or worn.
4. Return springs damaged.

HARSH 3-2 SHIFT

ELECTRICAL

PCM, vehicle wiring harnesses, Shift Control Solenoid "C," Pressure Control Solenoid "B," Turbine Shaft Speed (TSS) sensor, Intermediate Shaft Speed (ISS) sensor, Digital TR sensor, Transmission Fluid Temperature (TFT) sensor.

HYDRAULIC/MECHANICAL

Improper Pressures

High/Low pressures.

Main Control

1. Bolts not tightened to specifications.
2. Separator plate damaged.
3. Contamination.
4. Valve/springs damaged, improperly assembled, missing, stuck, or bore damaged.

OD Servo

1. Servo retaining ring damaged.
2. Seals (piston and cover) damaged.
3. Anchor pins in case damaged.

OD Band

1. Band damaged.
2. Servo worn or damaged.
3. Not adjusted properly.
4. Anchor pins damaged or worn.

Direct Clutch

1. Seals, piston damaged.
2. Check ball damaged, missing, not seating, off location.
3. Friction elements damaged or worn.
4. Return springs damaged.

Intermediate Clutch

1. Seals, piston damaged.
2. Check ball damaged, missing, not seating, off location.
3. Friction elements damaged.
4. Return springs damaged.

HARSH 2-1 SHIFT

ELECTRICAL

PCM, vehicle wiring harnesses, Shift Control Solenoid "C," Pressure Control Solenoid "B," Turbine Shaft Speed (TSS) sensor, Digital TR sensor, Transmission Fluid Temperature (TFT) sensor.

HYDRAULIC/MECHANICAL

Improper Pressures

High/Low pressures.

Main Control

1. Bolts not tightened to specifications.
2. Separator plate damaged.
3. Contamination.
4. Valve/springs damaged, improperly assembled, missing, stuck, or bore damaged.

Direct Clutch

1. Seals, piston damaged.
2. Check ball damaged, missing, not seating, off location.
3. Friction elements damaged or worn.
4. Return springs damaged.

Intermediate Clutch

1. Seals, piston damaged.
2. Check ball damaged, missing, not seating, off location.
3. Friction elements damaged or worn.
4. Return springs damaged.

Direct Clutch One-Way Clutch

Worn, damaged or assembled improperly.

NO 1-2 SHIFT

ELECTRICAL

PCM, vehicle wiring harnesses, Shift Solenoid "C," Pressure Control Solenoid "B," Output Shaft Speed (OSS) sensor, Digital TR sensor, IAT sensor, VSS input.

HYDRAULIC/MECHANICAL

Fluid

Improper level.

Improper Pressures

High/Low pressures.

Main Control

1. Bolts not tightened to specifications.
2. Separator plate damaged.
3. Contamination.
4. Valve/springs damaged, improperly assembled, missing, stuck, or bore damaged.

OD Servo

1. Servo retaining ring damaged.
2. Seals (piston and cover) damaged.
3. Anchor pins in case damaged.

OD Band

1. Band damaged.
2. Servo worn or damaged.
3. Not adjusted properly.
4. Anchor pins damaged or worn.

OD Planetary

Planetary damaged.

Forward Clutch

1. Seals, piston damaged.
2. Check ball damaged, missing, not seating, off location.
3. Friction elements damaged or worn.
4. Return springs damaged.

Intermediate Clutch

1. Seals, piston damaged.
2. Check ball damaged, missing, not seating, off location.
3. Friction elements damaged or worn.
4. Return springs damaged.

NO 2-3 SHIFT

ELECTRICAL

PCM, vehicle wiring harnesses, Shift Solenoid "B," Torque Converter Clutch (TCC) solenoid, Pressure Control Solenoid "A," Output Shaft Speed (OSS) sensor, Digital TR sensor.

HYDRAULIC/MECHANICAL

Improper Pressures

High/low pressures.

Main Control

1. Bolts not tightened to specifications.
2. Separator plate damaged.
3. Contamination.
4. Valve/springs damaged, improperly assembled, missing, stuck, or bore damaged.

Forward Clutch

1. Seals, piston damaged.
2. Check ball, damaged, missing, not seating, off location.
3. Friction elements damaged or worn.
4. Return springs damaged.

Intermediate Clutch

1. Seals, piston damaged.
2. Check ball, damaged, missing, not seating, off location.
3. Friction elements damaged or worn.
4. Return springs damaged.

Intermediate One-Way Clutch

Worn, damaged or assembled improperly.

NO 3-4 SHIFT

ELECTRICAL

1. PCM, vehicle wiring harnesses, Shift Solenoid "A," Pressure Control Solenoid "C," Output Shaft Speed (OSS) sensor, Digital TR sensor.
2. Transmission Control Switch (TCS).

HYDRAULIC/MECHANICAL

Improper Pressures

High/Low pressures.

Main Control

1. Bolts not tightened to specifications.
2. Separator plate damaged.
3. Contamination.
4. Valve/springs damaged, improperly assembled, missing, stuck, or bore damaged.

Center Support

1. Screws not tightened to specifications.
2. Seal rings or bearing damaged.
3. Outside diameter of case bore damaged.
4. Support damaged or leaking.

Direct Clutch

1. Seals, piston damaged.
2. Check ball damaged, missing, not seating, off location.
3. Friction elements damaged or worn.
4. Return springs damaged.

Forward Clutch

1. Seals, piston damaged.
2. Check ball damaged, missing, not seating, off location.
3. Friction elements damaged or worn.
4. Return springs damaged.

Intermediate Clutch

1. Seals, piston damaged.
2. Check ball damaged, missing, not seating, off location.
3. Friction elements damaged or worn.
4. Return springs damaged.

NO 4-5 SHIFT

ELECTRICAL

1. PCM, vehicle wiring harnesses, Shift Solenoid "C," Pressure Control Solenoid "B," Output Shaft Speed (OSS) sensor, Digital TR sensor.
2. Transmission Control Switch (TCS).

HYDRAULIC/MECHANICAL

Improper Pressures

High/Low pressures.

Main Control

1. Bolts not tightened to specifications.
2. Separator plate damaged.
3. Contamination.
4. Valve/springs damaged, improperly assembled, missing, stuck, or bore damaged.

OD Servo

1. Servo retaining ring damaged.
2. Seals (piston and cover) damaged.
3. Anchor pins in case damaged.

OD Band

1. Band damaged.
2. Servo worn or damaged.
3. Not adjusted properly.
4. Anchor pins damaged or worn.

NO 5-4 SHIFT

ELECTRICAL

1. PCM, vehicle wiring harnesses, Shift Solenoid "C," Pressure Control Solenoid "C," Output Shaft Speed (OSS) sensor, Digital TR sensor.
2. Transmission Control Switch (TCS).

HYDRAULIC/MECHANICAL

Improper Pressures

High/Low pressures.

Main Control

1. Bolts not tightened to specifications.
2. Separator plate damaged.
3. Contamination.
4. Valves/springs damaged, improperly assembled, missing, stuck, or bore damaged.

Direct Clutch

1. Seals, piston damaged.
2. Check ball damaged, missing, not seating, off location.
3. Friction elements damaged or worn.
4. Return springs damaged.

NO 4-3 SHIFT

ELECTRICAL

1. PCM, vehicle wiring harnesses, Shift Solenoid "A," Pressure Control Solenoid "A," Output Shaft Speed (OSS) sensor, Digital TR sensor.
2. Transmission Control Switch (TCS).

HYDRAULIC/MECHANICAL

Improper Pressures

High/Low pressures.

Main Control

1. Bolts not tightened to specifications.
2. Separator plate damaged.
3. Contamination.
4. Valves/springs damaged, improperly assembled, missing, stuck, or bore damaged.

Forward Clutch

1. Seals, piston damaged.
2. Check ball damaged, missing, not seating, off location.
3. Friction elements damaged or worn.
4. Return springs damaged.

Intermediate Clutch

1. Seals, piston damaged.
2. Check ball damaged, missing, not seating, off location.
3. Friction elements damaged or worn.
4. Return springs damaged.

NO 3-2 SHIFT

ELECTRICAL

PCM, vehicle wiring harnesses, Shift Solenoid "C," Pressure Control Solenoid "B," Output Shaft Speed (OSS) sensor, Digital TR sensor.

HYDRAULIC/MECHANICAL

Improper Pressures

High/low pressures.

Main Control

1. Bolts not tightened to specifications.
2. Separator plate damaged.
3. Contamination.
4. Valves/springs damaged, improperly assembled, missing, stuck, or bore damaged.

OD Servo

1. Servo retaining ring damaged.
2. Seals (piston and cover) damaged.
3. Anchor pins in case damaged.

OD Band

1. Band damaged.
2. Servo worn or damaged.
3. Not adjusted properly.
4. Anchor pins damaged or worn.

Forward Clutch

1. Seals, piston damaged.
2. Check ball damaged, missing, not seating, off location.
3. Friction elements damaged or worn.
4. Return springs damaged.

Intermediate Clutch

1. Seals, piston damaged.
2. Check ball damaged, missing, not seating, off location.
3. Friction elements damaged or worn.
4. Return springs damaged.

NO 2-1 SHIFT

ELECTRICAL

PCM, vehicle wiring harnesses, Shift Solenoid C, Pressure Control Solenoid "B," Output Shaft Speed (OSS) sensor, Digital TR sensor.

HYDRAULIC/MECHANICAL

Improper Pressures

High/Low pressures.

Main Control

1. Bolts not tightened to specifications.
2. Separator plate damaged.
3. Contamination.
4. Valves/springs damaged, improperly assembled, missing, stuck, or bore damaged.

Forward Clutch

1. Seals, piston damaged.
2. Check ball damaged, missing, not seating, off location.
3. Friction elements damaged or worn.
4. Return springs damaged.

Intermediate Clutch

1. Seals, piston damaged.
2. Check ball damaged, missing, not seating, off location.
3. Friction elements damaged or worn.
4. Return springs damaged.

SOFT/SLIPPING 1-2 SHIFT

ELECTRICAL

PCM, vehicle wiring harnesses, Shift Solenoid C, Pressure Control Solenoid "B," Transmission Fluid Temperature (TFT) sensor, IAT sensor, VSS input.

HYDRAULIC/MECHANICAL

Fluid

1. Improper level.
2. Condition.

Improper Pressures

High/Low pressures.

Main Control

1. Bolts not tightened to specifications.
2. Separator plate damaged.
3. Contamination.
4. Valve/springs damaged, improperly assembled, missing, stuck, or bore damaged.

OD Servo

1. Servo retaining ring damaged.
2. Seals (piston and cover) damaged.
3. Anchor pins in case damaged.

OD Band

1. Band damaged.
2. Servo worn or damaged.
3. Not adjusted properly.
4. Anchor pins damaged or worn.

SOFT/SLIPPING 2-3 SHIFT

ELECTRICAL

PCM, vehicle wiring harnesses, Shift Solenoid "A," Pressure Control Solenoid "A," Intermediate Shaft Speed (ISS) sensor, Transmission Fluid Temperature (TFT) sensor.

HYDRAULIC/MECHANICAL

Improper Pressures

High/Low pressures.

Main Control

1. Bolts not tightened to specifications.
2. Separator plate damaged.
3. Contamination.
4. Valve/springs damaged, improperly assembled, missing, stuck, or bore damaged.

Intermediate Servo

1. Servo retaining ring damaged.
2. Seals (piston and cover) damaged.
3. Anchor pins in case damaged.

Intermediate Band

1. Band damaged.
2. Servo worn or damaged.
3. Not adjusted properly.
4. Anchor pins damaged or worn.

Intermediate Clutch

1. Seals, piston damaged.
2. Check ball damaged, missing, not seating, off location.
3. Friction elements damaged or worn.
4. Return springs damaged.

Direct One-Way Clutch

Worn, damaged or assembled improperly.

SOFT/SLIPPING 3-4 SHIFT

ELECTRICAL

PCM, vehicle wiring harnesses, Shift Solenoid "A," Pressure Control Solenoid "C," Transmission Fluid Temperature (TFT) sensor.

HYDRAULIC/MECHANICAL

Improper Pressures

High/Low pressures.

Main Control

1. Bolts not tightened to specifications.
2. Separator plate damaged.
3. Contamination.
4. Valves/springs damaged, improperly assembled, missing, stuck, or bore damaged.

Center Support

1. Screw not tightened to specifications.
2. Seal rings or bearing damaged.
3. Outside diameter of case bore damage.
4. Support damaged or leaking.

Direct Clutch

1. Seals, piston damaged.
2. Check ball damaged, missing, not seating, off location.
3. Friction elements damaged or worn.
4. Return springs damaged.

SOFT/SLIPPING 4-5 SHIFT

ELECTRICAL

PCM, vehicle wiring harnesses, Shift Solenoid C, Pressure Control Solenoid "B," Transmission Fluid Temperature (TFT) sensor.

HYDRAULIC/MECHANICAL

Improper Pressures

High/Low pressures.

Main Control

1. Bolts not tightened to specifications.
2. Separator plate damaged.
3. Contamination.
4. Valves/springs damaged, improperly assembled, missing, stuck, or bore damaged.

OD Servo

1. Servo retaining ring damaged.
2. Seals (piston and cover) damaged.
3. Anchor pins in case damaged.

OD Band

1. Band damaged.
2. Servo worn or damaged.
3. Not adjusted properly.
4. Anchor pins damaged or worn.

SOFT/SLIPPING 5-4 SHIFT

ELECTRICAL

PCM, vehicle wiring harnesses, Shift Solenoid C, Pressure Control Solenoid C, Transmission Fluid Temperature (TFT) sensor.

HYDRAULIC/MECHANICAL

Improper Pressures

High/Low pressures.

Main Control

1. Bolts not tightened to specifications.
2. Separator plate damaged.
3. Contamination.
4. Valves/springs damaged, improperly assembled, missing, stuck, or bore damaged.

Direct Clutch

1. Seals, piston damaged.
2. Check ball damaged, missing, not seating, off location.
3. Friction elements damaged or worn.
4. Return springs damaged.

Direct One-Way Clutch

Worn, damaged or assembled improperly.

SOFT/SLIPPING 4-3 SHIFT

ELECTRICAL

PCM, vehicle wiring harnesses, Shift Solenoid "A," Pressure Control Solenoid "A," Transmission Fluid Temperature (TFT) sensor.

HYDRAULIC/MECHANICAL

Improper Pressures

High/Low pressures.

Main Control

1. Bolts not tightened to specifications.
2. Separator plate damaged.
3. Contamination.
4. Valves/springs damaged, improperly assembled, missing, stuck, or bore damaged.

Intermediate Clutch

1. Seals, piston damaged.
2. Check ball damaged, missing, not seating, off location.
3. Friction elements damaged or worn.
4. Return springs damaged.

SOFT/SLIPPING 3-2 SHIFT

ELECTRICAL

PCM, vehicle wiring harnesses, Shift Solenoid C, Pressure Control "B," Intermediate Shaft Speed (ISS) sensor, Transmission Fluid Temperature (TFT) sensor.

HYDRAULIC/MECHANICAL

Improper Pressures

High/Low pressures.

Main Control

1. Bolts not tightened to specifications.
2. Separator plate damaged.
3. Contamination.
4. Valves/springs damaged, improperly assembled, missing, stuck, or bore damaged.

OD Servo

1. Servo retaining ring damaged.
2. Seals (piston and cover) damaged.
3. Anchor pins in case damaged.

OD Band

1. Band damaged.
2. Servo worn or damaged.
3. Not adjusted properly.
4. Anchor pins damaged or worn.

Direct One-Way Clutch

Worn, damaged or assembled improperly.

SOFT/SLIPPING 2-1 SHIFT

ELECTRICAL

PCM, vehicle wiring harnesses, Shift Solenoid "C," Pressure Control Solenoid "B," Transmission Fluid Temperature (TFT) sensor.

HYDRAULIC/MECHANICAL

Improper Pressures

High/Low pressures.

Main Control

1. Bolts not tightened to specifications.
2. Separator plate damaged.
3. Contamination.
4. Valves/springs damaged, improperly assembled, missing, stuck, or bore damaged.

MAINTENANCE

Ford Motor Company recommends use of Mercon V type automatic transmission fluid in this transmission. Use of a fluid other than that meeting Ford Mercon V specifications may result in transmission malfunction or failure.

FLUID LEVEL INSPECTION

1. Run engine until operating temperature is 80–120F.
2. Move selector through gears and place selector lever in Park.
3. Raise and support vehicle. Ensure vehicle is level.
4. Place suitable drain pan under transmission.
5. Remove fluid level indicator plug with transmission in Park and engine running.
6. Allow fluid to drain.
7. When fluid comes out as thin stream or drip it is at proper level.
8. If no fluid comes out hole, fluid will need to be added as follows:
   a. Remove fill plug.
   b. Fill transmission to proper fluid level.
   c. When fluid starts to drain from fluid level hole, transmission is full.
9. Install fill and fluid level indicator plug.
10. Lower vehicle, inspect transmission operation and inspect for leaks.

FLUID CHANGE

1. Run engine until operating temperature is 80–120 F.
2. Move selector through gears and place selector lever in Park.
3. Raise and support vehicle. Ensure vehicle is level.
4. Place suitable drain pan under transmission.
5. Remove drain plug and allow fluid to drain.
6. Remove converter housing plug.
7. Remove drain plug and discard.
8. Once fluid has drained, install new converter drain plug. **New converter drain plug must be used to prevent leakage.**
9. Install drain and converter housing access plugs.
10. Remove fluid level indicator and fill plugs.
11. Fill transmission to proper fluid level. When fluid starts to drain from fluid level hole, transmission is full.
12. Inspect fluid level as outlined under "Fluid Inspection."

ADJUSTMENTS

SELECTOR CABLE

1. Place selector lever in D5 position.
2. Raise and support vehicle, then disconnect selector cable from manual control lever.
3. Place control lever in D5 position, three positions from most rearward position.
4. Disconnect cable from selector lever.
5. Connect cable to manual control lever.
6. Unlock cable end adjuster.
7. Connect cable to shifter and lock end adjuster.
8. Lower vehicle.
9. Carefully move control lever from detent to detent and compare with transmission settings.
10. Ensure vehicle will start in Park or Neutral.
11. Ensure backup lamps light in Reverse.
12. If adjustments are improper, repeat procedure and adjust digital Transmission Range (TR) sensor in Neutral as outlined under "In-Vehicle Repairs."

IN-VEHICLE REPAIRS

CONTROL SWITCH, REPLACE

1. Remove center console.
2. Remove PRNDL indicator bulb and disconnect electrical connector.
3. Disconnect switches and remove harness.
4. Reverse procedure to install.

SELECTOR LEVER, REPLACE

1. Remove center console.
2. Slide cover down, then remove mounting screws, handle and cover.
3. Remove shift bezel and PRNDL indicator bulb, then the rear air conditioning air duct.
4. Remove shift interlock cable from bracket, then disconnect cable.
5. Raise and support vehicle, then disconnect transmission shift cable.
6. Lower vehicle, then remove mounting bolts and shifter.
7. Reverse procedure to install. Adjust cable as outlined in "Adjustments" section.

SHIFT CABLE, REPLACE

1. Raise and support vehicle.
2. Disconnect transmission shift cable from selector lever and bracket.
3. Remove mounting bolts and allow heat shield to rest on exhaust.
4. Remove mounting bolts and shift cable bracket and cable.
5. Reverse procedure to install. Tighten mounting bolts to specifications.
6. Adjust cable as outlined in "Adjustments" section.

BRAKE SHIFT INTERLOCK ACTUATOR, REPLACE

1. Disconnect traction control switch, if equipped.
2. Remove center console.
3. Remove PRNDL indicator bulb, rear air conditioning air duct and shifter bezel.
4. Remove shift interlock cable from bracket and disconnect cable.
5. Remove lower steering column mounting screws.
6. Remove instrument panel steering column cover.
7. Disconnect electrical connector.
8. Remove mounting screws, then position hood release cable and bracket aside.
9. Remove floor heat duct mounting screw and lower reinforcement panel.
10. Remove inner and outer instrument panel finish panels.
11. Disconnect power mirror switch and remove inner trim support panel.
12. Remove mounting screws and ignition switch.
13. Remove shift lock actuator cable mounting screws and disconnect electrical connector.
14. Remove cable from bracket.
15. Reverse procedure to install.

TRANSMISSION PAN, REPLACE

Removal

1. Raise and support vehicle.
2. Place suitable drain pan under transmission fluid pan.
3. Remove drain plug and drain fluid.
4. Remove bracket, fluid pan and gasket.
5. Remove and discard transmission fluid filter.
6. Clean and inspect transmission fluid pan and magnet.
7. Remove converter housing and drain plugs.

Installation

1. Install new converter drain plug. **New converter drain plug must be used to prevent leakage.**
2. Install converter housing access plug.
3. Lubricate fluid filter O-rings and seals with Mercon V automatic transmission fluid, then install transmission fluid filter. Ensure fluid filter O-rings are properly seated on filter.
4. Install oil pan magnet in transmission fluid pan.
5. Clean pan gasket and inspect for damage. It can be used again if in serviceable condition.
6. Install transmission fluid pan and gasket, then loosely fit mounting screws.
7. Tighten pan mounting screws to specifications in crisscross sequence.
8. Install shifter cable bracket.
9. Remove fill, drain and fluid level indicator plugs.
10. Fill transmission to proper fluid level. When fluid starts to drain from fluid level hole transmission is full.
11. Inspect fluid level as outlined under "Fluid Inspection."

VALVE BODY, REPLACE

Removal

1. Raise and support vehicle, then drain transmission fluid as outlined under "Fluid Change" in "Maintenance" section.
2. Remove converter housing and drain plugs.
3. Remove shifter cable bracket.
4. Clean area around solenoid body connector, then disconnect transmission connector.
5. Disconnect digital TR sensor connector.
6. Remove transmission fluid pan, gasket and transmission fluid filter.
7. Disconnect connector and remove reverse pressure switch and discard.
8. Remove solenoid body, valve body

cover plate and gasket. Record bolt sizes and locations for installation.
9. Remove reverse servo.
10. Remove detent spring, main control valve body, separator plate and gasket.
11. Remove intermediate clutch spring and seal. Intermediate clutch spring and seal will fall out of case.

Installation

Failure to properly seat the intermediate clutch fluid inlet tube seal and spring will cause an internal fluid leak and transmission damage. Properly install and seat the intermediate clutch fluid inlet tube seal and spring into the case using suitable drift punch.

1. Install two .248 inch valve body guide pin tools No. T95L-70010-C, or equivalent, into transmission case.
2. Install main control valve body and loosely fit mounting screws.
3. Remove guide pin tools and loosely fit remaining mounting screws.
4. Install valve body cover plate and gasket and loosely fit mounting screws.
5. Install reverse pressure switch and loosely fit mounting screws.
6. Tighten mounting screws to specifications in sequence, **Fig. 4.**
7. Install reverse servo and tighten mounting bolts in crisscross pattern.
8. Install manual control valve detent spring.
9. Install new solenoid body connector O-rings. Lubricate O-rings with clean Mercon V automatic transmission fluid.
10. Inspect transmission case bore to ensure it is free of debris and not damaged.
11. Install solenoid body and tighten mounting bolts to specifications in sequence, **Fig. 5.**
12. Connect reverse pressure switch connector.
13. Lubricate fluid filter O-rings and seals with Mercon V automatic transmission fluid, then install transmission fluid filter. Ensure fluid filter O-rings are properly seated on filter.
14. Install oil pan magnet in transmission fluid pan.
15. Install transmission fluid pan and gasket, then loosely fit mounting screws. Gasket is reusable, clean and inspect for damage.
16. Tighten pan mounting screws to specifications in crisscross sequence.
17. Install new converter drain plug. **New converter drain plug must be used to prevent leakage.**
18. Install converter housing access plug.
19. Connect digital TR sensor connector.
20. Clean area around connector to prevent contamination of solenoid body connector.
21. Lubricate new O-rings with suitable petroleum jelly and install on transmission connector.
22. Connect connector. **Do not tighten mounting screw to more than specifications.**
23. Install shift cable bracket.
24. Lower vehicle.
25. Fill transmission to proper fluid level and inspect for proper operation.

EXTENSION HOUSING SEAL, REPLACE

Removal

1. Raise and support vehicle, then remove exhaust and driveshaft.
2. Remove flange nut and discard.
3. Remove output flange using output flange remover tool No. 307-408, or equivalent.
4. Remove seal using convertor seal remover tool No. T94P-77001-BH and impact slide hammer tool No. T50T-100-A, or equivalents.

Installation

1. Install new extension housing seal using extension housing bushing replacer tool No. T74P-77052-A, or equivalent.
2. Install output flange using output shaft flange installer tool No. T307-404, or equivalent.
3. Install new flange nut and tighten to specifications.
4. Install driveshaft and exhaust.
5. Lower vehicle and adjust transmission fluid level as required.

EXTENSION HOUSING GASKET, REPLACE

Removal

1. Raise and support vehicle, then remove exhaust and driveshaft.
2. Support transmission with suitable transmission jack.
3. Remove center rear and outer mounting bolts.
4. Disconnect shift cable.
5. Remove flange nut and discard.
6. Remove output flange using output flange remover tool No. 307-408, or equivalent.
7. Remove extension housing. **Parking pawl, parking pawl return spring and parking pawl shaft may fall out during removal.**
8. Remove and discard extension housing gasket.

Installation

1. Clean extension housing and install new extension housing gasket. **Ensure park pawl is installed properly.**
2. Install the extension housing. **Ensure parking lever actuating rod is properly seated into case parking rod guide cup.**
3. Install shift cable.
4. Install rear mount and tighten mounting bolts to specifications.
5. Install output flange using output shaft flange installer tool No. T307-404, or equivalent.
6. Install new flange nut and tighten to specifications.
7. Install driveshaft and exhaust.
8. Fill transmission to proper fluid level and inspect for proper operation.

SOLENOID BODY, REPLACE

Replace solenoid body as outlined under "Valve Body, Replace."

DIGITAL TRANSMISSION RANGE (TR) SENSOR, REPLACE

Removal

1. Raise and support vehicle, then remove exhaust and driveshaft.
2. Support transmission with suitable transmission jack. **Secure transmission to transmission jack with suitable safety chain.**
3. Remove mount and lower transmission enough to gain access to digital TR sensor.
4. Disconnect shift cable.
5. Disconnect connector and remove digital TR sensor.

Installation

The digital transmission range sensor must fit flush against the boss on the case to prevent damage to the sensor.

1. Install digital TR sensor and loosely fit mounting screws.
2. Ensure manual lever is in Neutral position.
3. Align digital TR sensor using TRS alignment tool No. T97L-70010-A, or equivalent, and tighten mounting screws in alternating sequence. **Tightening one screw before other may bind or damage sensor.**
4. Connect digital TR sensor connector and shift cable.
5. Install rear mount.
6. Ensure shift cable is properly adjusted as outlined in "Adjustments" section.
7. Install driveshaft and exhaust.
8. Lower vehicle.

REVERSE SERVO, REPLACE

Replace Reverse servo as outlined under "Valve Body, Replace."

PARK SYSTEM, REPLACE

Removal

1. Raise and support vehicle, then drain transmission fluid as outlined under "Fluid Change" in "Maintenance" section.
2. Remove converter housing and drain plugs.
3. Remove shifter cable bracket.
4. Remove exhaust system as required.
5. Remove driveshaft.
6. Support transmission with suitable transmission jack. **Secure transmission to transmission jack with suitable safety chain.**
7. Remove shift cable bracket.
8. Remove transmission mount.
9. Disconnect shift cable and digital TR sensor connector.
10. Remove transmission fluid pan, gasket and transmission fluid filter.
11. Remove digital TR sensor.
12. Remove manual control valve detent spring.

13. Remove nut and manual lever shaft retaining pin. **Ensure wrench does not strike manual valve inner lever pin.**
14. Partially remove manual control lever shaft.
15. Disconnect manual valve inner lever from parking lever actuating rod.
16. Remove manual valve inner lever.
17. Remove and discard flange nut.
18. Remove output flange using output flange removal tool No. 307-408, or equivalent.
19. Remove extension housing and discard gasket. **The parking pawl, return spring and pawl shaft may fall out during extension housing removal.**
20. **If parking gear damage is found, transmission must be removed and disassembled.**
21. Inspect parking pawl, parking pawl return spring and parking pawl shaft. Discard components if damaged or worn.
22. Remove parking lever actuating rod.

Installation

1. Install parking lever actuating rod and manual control lever.
2. Assemble manual valve inner lever and parking lever actuating rod.
3. Align manual inner lever flats with manual control lever shaft flats.
4. Install manual valve inner lever and parking lever actuating rod onto manual control lever shaft.
5. Install manual valve inner lever onto manual shaft and loosely fit mounting nut.
6. Align manual control lever shaft alignment groove with manual control lever shaft spring pin bore in transmission case.
7. Install manual control lever shaft spring pin.
8. Tap manual control lever shaft spring pin into transmission case.
9. **Do not damage fluid pan rail surface when installing retaining pin.**
10. Tighten mounting nut. **Do not allow wrench to strike manual valve inner lever pin.**
11. Install manual valve detent spring.
12. Clean extension housing and install new extension housing gasket. **Ensure parking pawl is properly installed.**
13. Install extension housing. **Ensure parking lever actuating rod is properly seated into case parking rod guide cup.**
14. Lubricate fluid filter O-rings and seals with Mercon V automatic transmission fluid, then install transmission fluid filter. Ensure fluid filter O-rings are properly seated on filter.
15. Install oil pan magnet in transmission fluid pan.
16. Clean and inspect pan gasket for damage. It may be used again if in serviceable condition.
17. Install transmission fluid pan and gasket, then loosely fit mounting screws.
18. Tighten pan mounting screws to specifications in crisscross sequence.
19. Install converter housing access plug.
20. Install digital TR sensor and loosely fit mounting screws.
21. Ensure manual lever is in Neutral position.
22. Align digital TR sensor using TRS alignment tool No. T97L-70010-A, or equivalent, and tighten mounting screws in alternating sequence. **Tightening one screw before other may bind or damage sensor.**
23. Connect digital TR sensor connector.
24. Install new converter drain plug. **New converter drain plug must be used to prevent leakage.**
25. Install converter housing access plug.
26. Install shift cable.
27. Install rear mount and tighten bolts to specifications.
28. Install shift cable bracket.
29. Install output flange using output shaft flange installer tool No. T307-404, or equivalent.
30. Install new flange nut and tighten to specifications.
31. Install driveshaft and exhaust.
32. Fill transmission to proper fluid level and inspect for proper operation.

TRANSMISSION

REPLACE

REMOVAL

If the transmission is to be removed for a period of time, support the engine with suitable safety stand and wood block.

1. Raise and support vehicle, then remove exhaust.
2. If transmission disassembly is required, drain transmission fluid into suitable container as outlined under "Fluid Change."
3. Remove driveshaft.
4. Support transmission with suitable transmission jack. **Secure transmission to transmission jack with suitable safety chain.**
5. Remove mounting bolts and transmission mount.
6. Disconnect shift cable.
7. Lower transmission enough to access sensors, then disconnect TSS, OSS and ISS harness connectors.
8. Remove harness screw.
9. Disconnect transmission connector. **Clean area around connector to prevent solenoid body connector contamination.**
10. Disconnect harness retainers and remove HO_2S connector.
11. Remove shifter cable bracket and disconnect shifter cable from manual lever.
12. Disconnect digital TR sensor connector.
13. Disconnect transmission cooler line bracket and transmission cooler tubes. **Do not damage the cooler tubes.**
14. Remove access cover and apply identifying mark on nut, stud, and adapter plate for installation alignment.
15. Remove mounting nuts and bolts.
16. Lower and remove transmission.
17. Backflush and clean transmission fluid cooler.

INSTALLATION

Secure the transmission to the transmission jack with a safety chain.

1. Raise and position transmission.
2. Align flexplate to converter marks made during removal.
3. Tighten mounting bolts and nuts to specifications.
4. Install access cover.
5. Install transmission cooler tubes. **Do not bend or force cooler tubes or damage to tubes and transmission may result.**
6. Tighten cooler tube to specifications.
7. Install transmission cooler line bracket.
8. Connect digital TR sensor connector.
9. Clean area around connector to prevent contamination of solenoid body connector.
10. Lubricate new O-rings with suitable petroleum jelly and install on transmission connector.
11. Connect connector. **Do not tighten mounting screw to more than specifications.**
12. Install shift cable bracket and connect shifter cable.
13. Install HO_2S connector and connect harness retainers, then install harness mounting screw.
14. Connect TSS, OSS and ISS connectors.
15. Install rear transmission mount.
16. Install shift cable.
17. Tighten rear transmission mount mounting bolts to specifications.
18. Remove transmission jack and install driveshaft.
19. Install exhaust system.
20. Lower vehicle.
21. Inspect fluid level as outlined under "Fluid Inspection."
22. Ensure shift cable is properly adjusted as outlined in "Adjustments" section.
23. Inspect transmission operation and inspect for leaks.

TECHNICAL SERVICE BULLETINS

HARSH ENGAGEMENTS, HARSH OR DELAYED SHIFTS

2000 LS

On some of these models, built between March 15 and Dec. 1, 2000, there may be harsh engagements and/or harsh or delayed shifts.

This condition may be caused by Powertrain Control Module (PCM) calibration.

To correct this condition, program PCM with latest calibration, **Fig. 6.**

NO ENGAGEMENT

2000 LS

On some of these models built between March 15 and Nov. 11, 1999, there may be no transmission engagement or the engine may stall at idle.

This condition may be caused by the transmission fluid filter being improperly installed.

To correct this condition, proceed as follows:

1. Remove fluid pan and gasket.
2. Inspect fluid filter for proper seating.
3. If filter is improperly seated, remove and inspect seals for damage.
4. If seals are not damaged, lubricate main control bore and seals, then install filter. Ensure filter seats flush on main control.
5. If seals are damaged, replace filter.
6. **Torque** filter mounting bolts to 89 inch lbs.
7. Install gasket and pan. **Torque** mounting bolts to 96 inch lbs.

HIGH PITCHED GEAR WHINE ON COAST

2000 LS

On these models, built 3/15/1999 through 4/17/2000, this condition may appear while driving or coasting at low speeds in first or second gear and may be caused by the planetary gearset mesh.

To correct this condition, proceed as follows:

1. Diagnose and repair any present DTCs.
2. Ensure vehicle has latest PCM calibration level. Reprogram PCM as required.
3. If condition is still present, replace planetary gearset part No. YW4Z-7A398-SA.

DELAYED DRIVE OR REVERSE ENGAGEMENTS, ERRATIC & HARSH SHIFTS, DELAYED DOWNSHIFTS NEAR 20 mph

2000-01 LS

On these models, built before 10/17/2000, these conditions may be caused by PCM calibration.

To correct these conditions, proceed as follows:

1. Diagnose and repair any present DTCs.
2. Determine if conditions are caused by an internal transmission component and repair as required.
3. Clear all DTCs.
4. If fault conditions are still present, program PCM with latest calibration, **Fig. 7.**
5. After completing reprogramming procedure, proceed as follows:
   a. Monitor Transmission Fluid Temperature (TFT) until it has reached at least 130°F.
   b. Perform five Park to Reverse engagements, each five seconds apart.
   c. Perform five Drive to Reverse engagements, each five seconds apart.
   d. Perform five Reverse to Drive engagements, each five seconds apart.
   e. Perform five Neutral to Drive engagements, each five seconds apart.
   f. Fill in Authorized Modification Decal part No. FPS 8262 and affix adjacent to VECI decal. Cover with clear plastic shield.

REPEATED TRANSMISSION REPAIRS

2000-01 LS

On these models repeated transmission repairs may be caused by contamination and debris remaining in the fluid cooling system. It must be removed by proper cleaning and flushing.

1. Clean, flush and backflush fluid cooling system using Rotunda flusher tool No. 222-00001, or equivalent. Follow tool manufacturer's instructions. Be sure to include main and auxiliary coolers, cooler lines and Cooler Bypass Valve (CBV) after each transmission overhaul or exchange.
2. Inspect fluid cooler flow to ensure proper fluid flow through system.
3. After confirming proper fluid flow, install a transmission fluid inline filter kit part No. XC3Z-7B155-AA in fluid cooler return line. This is line exiting cooler and entering transmission.
4. The new filter element, part No. XC3Z-7B155-BA, should be replaced every 30,000 miles.

TIGHTENING SPECIFICATIONS

Year	Description	Torque, Ft. Lbs.
2000–02	Band Adjustment Locknut	40
	Case To Center Support	96①
	Converter Drain Plug	89①
	Digital Transmission Range (TR) Sensor	89①
	Driveshaft Bolts & Nuts	60
	Extension Housing	29
	Extension Housing Fill Plug	15
	Fluid Level Indicator Plug	89①
	Fluid Pan Drain Plug	19
	Heat Shield	89①
	Main Control	89①②
	Main Control Separator	89①
	Main Control Valve Detent Spring	89①
	Manual Control Lever	35
	Output Shaft To Flange	97
	Overdrive Band Adjustment	10
	Pressure Tap Plug	10
	Reverse Servo (2000–01)	89①
	Reverse Servo (2002)	③
	Shift Cable Bracket	18
	Shift Lock Actuator	80①
	Shifter	62①
	Solenoid Body	71①②
	Speed Sensor	89①
	Transmission Cooler Fitting	35
	Transmission Cooler Line Bracket (3.0L Engine)	89①
	Transmission Cooler Line Bracket (3.9L Engine)	13
	Transmission Cooler Tube	30
	Transmission Fluid Filter	89①
	Transmission Fluid Pan	96①
	Transmission Mount To Extension Housing Center Screw	30
	Transmission Mount To Extension Housing Screw	37
	Transmission Mount To Floor Pan	41
	Transmission To Engine	35
	Vehicle Harness	44①

① — Inch lbs.
② — Refer to "Valve Body, Replace" for tightening sequence.
③ — First stage torque to 44 inch lbs.; second stage torque to 96 inch lbs.

FRONT WHEEL DRIVE AXLES

TABLE OF CONTENTS

Continental

NOTE: On Air Bag Equipped Models, Refer To "Air Bag System Precautions" Located In The Front Of This Manual For System Disarming & Arming Procedures.

NOTE: Refer To "Computer Relearn Procedures" Located In The Front Of This Manual When Battery Power To The Computer Has Been Interrupted.

INDEX

PRECAUTIONS

AIR BAG SYSTEMS

Refer to "Air Bag System Precautions" in the front of this manual for system disarming and arming procedures.

BATTERY GROUND CABLE

Prior to service, disconnect battery ground cable and isolate as required.

DESCRIPTION

Each front wheel driveshaft employs Constant Velocity (CV) joints at both inboard (differential side) and outboard (wheel side) for vehicle operating smoothness. The CV joints are connected by an intermediate shaft which is splined at both ends and retained in the inboard and outboard CV joints by snap rings, **Fig. 1.**

Inboard CV joint is permanently retained by the intermediate driveshaft. The service components of the CV joint include the shaft and the driveshaft joint boot. The joint and outboard boot will need to be removed to replace the boot, joint or shaft.

TROUBLESHOOTING

Refer to **Fig. 2** for troubleshooting chart.

DRIVESHAFT

REPLACE

REMOVAL

If removing both righthand and left-hand driveshafts, install plugs tool No. T81P-1177B or equivalent. Failure to do so may result in dislocation of differential side gears, necessitating transaxle disassembly to align the gears again. Should the gears become misaligned, the differential will have to be removed from the transaxle for alignment.

Do not begin this procedure unless a new hub retainer nut, lower control arm to steering knuckle attaching bolt and nut and a new inboard CV joint stub shaft snap ring are available. Once removed, these components must not be reused during assembly/installation. Their torque holding ability or retention capability is diminished during removal.

1. Turn air suspension system switch Off, then discharge air from both front air springs.
2. Raise and support vehicle.
3. Remove tire and wheel assemblies.
4. Remove hub retainer nut and washer. Discard nut after removal.
5. Insert a steel pin in brake disc to prevent halfshaft from turning.
6. Remove stabilizer bar link attaching bolt at strut assembly, then position aside.
7. Remove ball joint to steering knuckle attaching nut. **Discard nut.**
8. Separate lower ball joint from steering knuckle using a suitable suspension arm puller.
9. Remove anti-lock brake sensor from steering knuckle.
10. Remove height sensor link at lower arm ball stud attachment.
11. Separate outboard CV joint from hub using front hub remover tool Nos. T81P-1104-A, T83P-1104-BH1, T86P-1104-A1 and T81P-1104-C or equivalents. **Never use a hammer to separate outboard CV joint stub shaft from hub. Damage to joint threads and internal components may result.**
12. Turn steering hub and/or wire strut assembly aside.
13. Remove CV joint from transaxle using CV joint puller tool No. T86P-3514–A2 and impact slide hammer tool No. D79P-100-A or equivalents.
14. Support end of shaft by suspending it from a conventional underbody component with a suitable length of wire. **Do not allow shaft to hang unsupported. Damage to outboard CV joint may result.**
15. Remove driveshaft assembly from vehicle.

INSTALLATION

1. Install a new snap ring onto inboard CV joint stub shaft and/or intermediate driveshaft. **Outboard CV joint stub shaft does not have a snap ring. To properly install snap ring, start one end in groove and work ring over stub shaft end and into groove. This will avoid overexpanding snap ring. The old snap ring must not be reused. A new snap ring must be installed each time inboard CV joint is installed into transaxle differential.**
2. Carefully align splines of inboard CV joint stub shaft or link shaft with splines in differential. Exerting force, push CV joint into differential until snap ring seats in differential side gear. **Use care to prevent damage to differential oil seal. A plastic hammer or equivalent may be used to aid in seating snap ring into side gear groove.**
3. Carefully align splines of outboard CV joint stub shaft with splines in hub and push shaft into hub as far as possible.
4. Temporarily attach rotor to hub with washers and two wheel lug nuts. Insert a steel rod into rotor and rotate clockwise to contact steering knuckle to prevent rotor from turning during CV joint installation.
5. Install hub nut washer and a new hub retainer nut. Manually thread retainer onto CV joint shaft as far as possible. **A new hub retainer nut must be installed.**
6. Connect control arm to steering knuckle. **A new lower ball joint to steering knuckle attaching nut must be installed.**
7. Connect stabilizer bar link to stabilizer bar.
8. Connect ride height sensor link.
9. Install anti-lock sensor link into control arm and tighten retaining bolt.
10. Install tire and wheel assembly, then lower vehicle and turn air suspension switch on.
11. Fill transaxle to operating level with proper fluid as required.

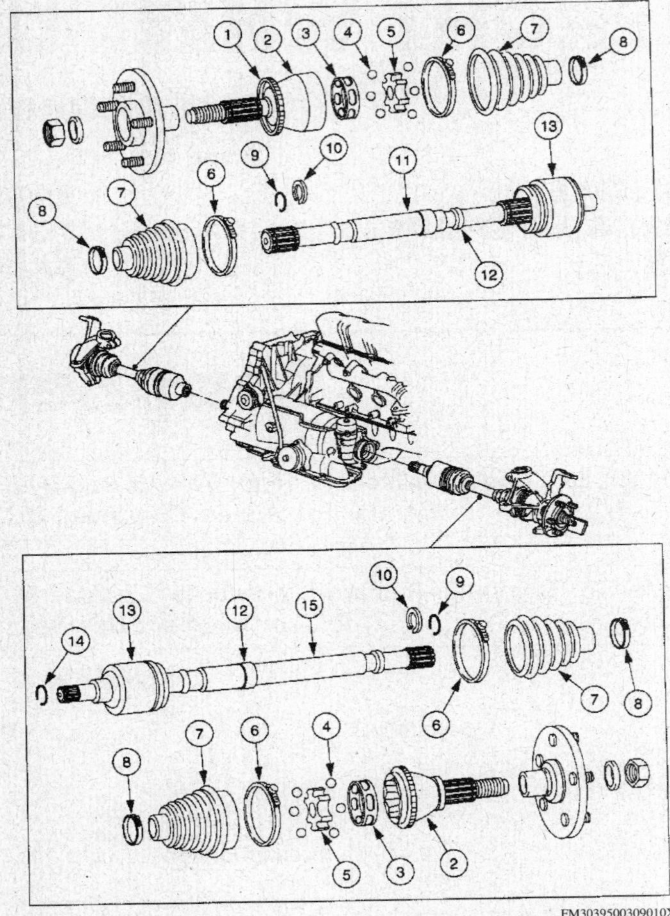

Fig. 1 Exploded view of driveshaft assemblies (Part 1 of 2)

DRIVESHAFT SERVICE

OUTBOARD JOINT

Disassemble

CV joint components are matched during manufacturing and cannot be interchanged with components from another joint. Do not intermix or substitute components between joints.

1. Clamp driveshaft into a vise. Do not allow vise jaws to contact boot or clamp.
2. Cut large boot clamp and peel away from boot.
3. Support intermediate driveshaft in a soft jaw vise and angle CV joint to expose inner bearing race.
4. Using a brass drift and hammer, give a sharp tap to inner bearing race to dislodge internal snap ring and separate CV joint from intermediate driveshaft. The boot can now be removed from shaft.
5. Inspect CV joint grease for contamination. If CV joints are operating satisfactorily, and grease does not appear to be contaminated, add grease and replace boot. If grease appears contaminated or has a gritty feeling, inspect for worn components and replace as necessary.
6. Remove snap ring located near end of shaft. Discard snap ring. A new snap ring is supplied with boot replacement kit and CV joint. **The stop ring, located just below snap ring, should only be removed if it is damaged.**
7. Clamp CV joint stub shaft in a vise with outer facing pointing upward. Care should be taken not to damage dust seal.
8. Press down on inner race until it tilts enough to allow removal of ball.
9. With cage tilted, remove ball from cage. Repeat until all six balls are removed.
10. Pivot cage and inner race assembly until it is facing straight up and down in outer race. Align cage windows with outer race lands while pivoting bearing race. With cage pivoted and aligned, lift assembly from outer race.
11. Rotate inner race up and out of cage.

Assemble

Because CV joint components are matched as a set during assembly, individual components are not available for service. If inspection determines a part to be worn or damaged, CV joint should be replaced as an assembly. Do not replace a joint if components appear polished. Shiny areas in ball races and cage spheres are normal. A CV joint should be replaced only if inspection determines a component to be cracked, broken, severely pitted, worn or otherwise unserviceable.

1. Apply a light coat of grease onto inner and outer ball races. **Use only Ford CV grease No. E43Z-19590-A or equivalent.**
2. Install inner race into bearing cage.
3. Install inner race and cage assembly into outer race.
4. Install assembly vertically and pivot 90° into position.
5. Align bearing cage and inner race with outer race.
6. Tilt inner race and cage, then install a ball. Repeat this step until all six balls are installed.
7. Lefthand and righthand intermediate driveshafts are not same end-for-end.

Item	Description
1	Front Brake Anti-Lock Sensor Indicator
2	Front Wheel Driveshaft Joint
3	Ball Cage
4	Balls (6 Req'd)
5	Race
6	Front Wheel Driveshaft Joint Boot Clamp (Large)
7	Front Wheel Driveshaft Joint Boot
8	Front Wheel Driveshaft Joint Boot Clamp (Small)

Item	Description
9	Circlip
10	Stop Ring
11	Interconnecting Shaft
12	Halfshaft Identification Label
13	Inboard CV Joint Housing
14	Circlip
15	Interconnecting Shaft

FM3039500309020X

Fig. 1 Exploded view of driveshaft assemblies (Part 2 of 2)

Condition	Possible Source
• Clicking, Popping or Grinding Noises While Turning	• Inadequate or contaminated lube in outboard front wheel driveshaft joint or inboard front wheel driveshaft joint. • Another component contacting halfshaft assembly. • Worn, damaged or improperly installed wheel bearings, brakes, suspension or steering components.
• Vibration at Highway Speeds	• Out of balance front wheels or tires. • Out of round front tires. • Improperly seated outboard front wheel driveshaft joint in front wheel hub.
• Shudder Vibration During Acceleration	• Excessively high front wheel driveshaft joint operating angles caused by improper ride height. • Excessively worn or damaged inboard front wheel driveshaft and joint or outboard front wheel driveshaft joint.
• Front Wheel Drive Shaft Joint Pullout	• Inboard driveshaft bearing retainer circlip missing or not properly seated in differential side gear. • Engine / transaxle assembly mispositioned. • Frame rail or shock tower out of position or damaged. • Front suspension components worn or damaged.

FM3039500310000X

Fig. 2 Troubleshooting chart

The outboard end is shorter from end of shaft to end of boot groove than inboard end. Take a measurement to ensure proper inboard and outboard CV joint to shaft installation, **Fig. 3.**

8. If removed, install CV joint boot after removing stop ring.
9. Ensure boot is properly seated in its groove and clamp into position.
10. If removed, install stop ring. If not removed, ensure stop ring is properly seated in groove.
11. Install a new snap ring, supplied with service kit, in groove nearest end of shaft.
12. Do not overexpand or twist snap ring during installation.
13. Before positioning boot over CV joint, pack CV joint and boot with grease supplied in service kit. Add 6.3 ounces.
14. With boot peeled back, position CV joint on shaft and tap into position. **CV joint is completely seated when snap ring locks in groove cut into CV joint inner race. Inspect for snap ring seating by trying to pull joint from shaft.**
15. Remove all excess grease from CV joint external surfaces.
16. Position boot over CV joint.
17. Ensure boot is seated in its groove and clamp in position.

DUST SEAL

Removal

Using a hammer, gently and evenly tap around dust seal until unseated.

Installation

Using seal installation tool Nos. T83T-3132-A1 and T86P-1104-A4 or equivalents, install dust seal. **Dust seal flange must face outboard.**

SPEED INDICATOR RING

Removal

1. Remove outboard CV joint as described under "Outboard Joint."
2. Position press tool No. T88P-2020-A or equivalent onto a press.
3. Position CV joint onto tool.
4. With joint in position, use press ram to apply pressure to joint and remove speed indicator ring.

Installation

1. With press tool No. T88P-2020-A or equivalent, positioned on press, place sensor ring on tool.
2. Position joint into speed indicator ring tool. Allow joint to rest on ring.
3. With joint installed on tool, place a steel plate across joint's back face. Press joint until it bottoms out in tool. Ring will be properly installed when bottomed out in tool.

INBOARD JOINT

Disassemble

Inboard CV joint is permanently retained to intermediate driveshaft. The service CV joint includes shaft and driveshaft joint boot. Joint and outboard boot will require removal to replace the boot, joint or shaft.

1. Cut and remove boot clamps, then slide boot back on shaft.
2. Remove stop ring and driveshaft bearing retainer circlip.
3. Slide boot off intermediate driveshaft.

Assemble

1. Install driveshaft boot on intermediate driveshaft, then position boot to allow for inboard joint housing installation.
2. Position boot in small boot groove.
3. Position small boot clamp and install with boot clamp replacement tool No. T95P-3514-A or equivalent. Tighten tool through bolt until tool is in closed position.
4. Fill inboard joint housing with Ford High Temperature CV Joint Grease part No. E43Z-19590-A or equivalent, meeting Ford specification ESP-M1C207-A. Spread remainder evenly inside driveshaft joint boot for a total combined fill of 16 ¾ ounces.
5. Remove all excess grease from CV joint external surfaces. Position boot over joint and move joint inward and outward as necessary to specified length **Fig. 4.** Before installing driveshaft joint boot clamp, ensure any air pressure which may have built up in boot is relieved as follows:
   a. Insert a dull tip screwdriver blade between boot and outer bearing race, allow trapped air to escape from boot.
   b. Air should be released from boot only after adjusting to specified dimension.
6. Locate clamp tabs in slots. Hand tighten clamps.
7. Ensure boot is properly seated in its groove and clamp is in position.
8. Use boot clamp replacement tool No. T95P-3514-A or equivalent, and tighten tool through bolt until tool is in closed position.
9. Work CV joint through several angles through its full travel range. Joint should compress, extend and flex smoothly.

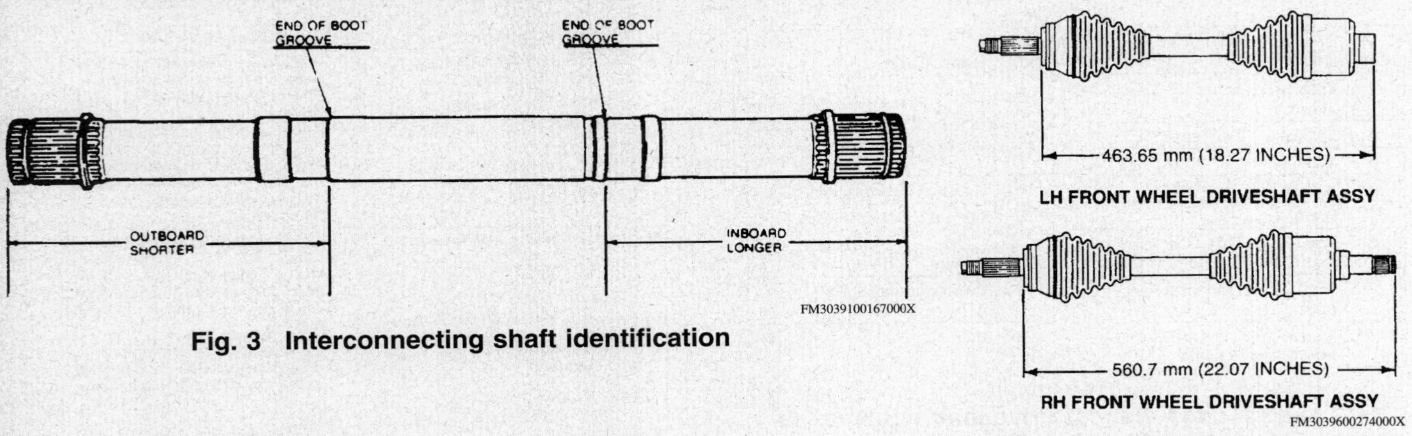

Fig. 3 Interconnecting shaft identification

Fig. 4 Driveshaft assembled lengths

TIGHTENING SPECIFICATIONS

Component	Torque/Ft. Lbs.
ABS Sensor Mounting Bolt	84①
Ball Joint Nut	46
Hub Nut	184
Stabilizer Bar Link	67
Wheel Lug Nut	95

① — Inch lbs.

Contour & Mystique

NOTE: On Air Bag Equipped Models, Refer To "Air Bag System Precautions" Located In The Front Of This Manual For System Disarming & Arming Procedures.

NOTE: Refer To "Computer Relearn Procedures" Located In The Front Of This Manual When Battery Power To The Computer Has Been Interrupted.

INDEX

PRECAUTIONS

AIR BAG SYSTEMS

Refer to "Air Bag System Precautions" in the front of this manual for system disarming and arming procedures.

BATTERY GROUND CABLE

Prior to service, disconnect battery ground cable and isolate as required.

DESCRIPTION

These models use equal length driveshafts to minimize torque steer and to provide a smooth transfer of power to the front driving wheels. An intermediate driveshaft and support bearing are used on the righthand side to compensate for transaxle offset, **Fig. 1.**

Inner CV joints are of the tripod type, while outer joints are of the ball and race type. **Outer joints contain matched components and must not be intermixed.**

TROUBLESHOOTING

Refer to **Fig. 2** for troubleshooting chart.

DRIVESHAFT

REPLACE

In all service operations the driveshaft bearing retainer circlips, **Fig. 1 must be replaced with a new part. Do not begin this procedure unless a new hub retainer nut, lower control arm to steering knuckle attaching bolt and nut, and the circlips are available. Once removed, these components must not be reused during assembly/installation. Their torque holding ability or retention capability is diminished during removal.**

LEFTHAND DRIVESHAFT

1. Raise and support vehicle, then remove front wheel assemblies.

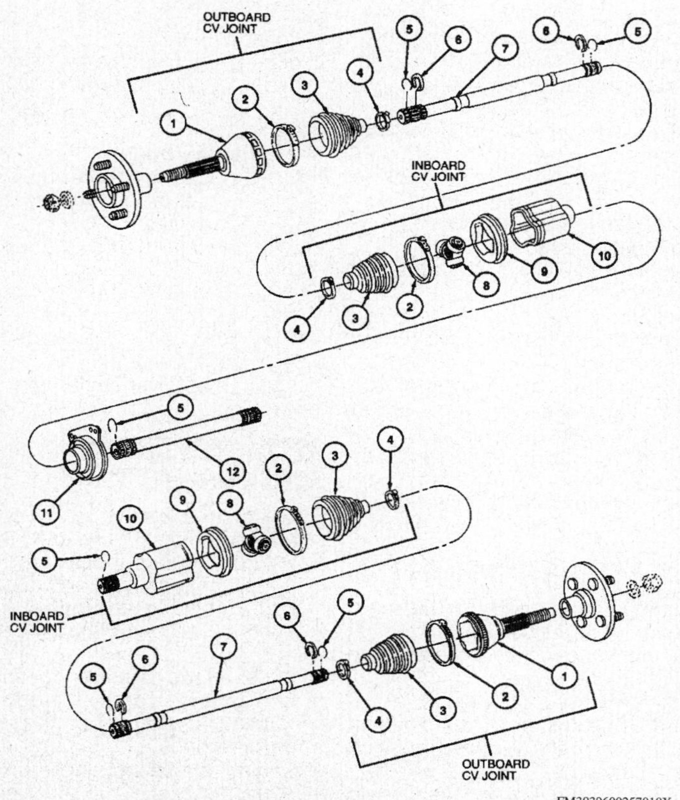

Fig. 1 Exploded view of driveshaft assemblies (Part 1 of 2)

2. Remove front axle retainer nut and washer, discard nut.
3. Remove nut from stabilizer bar link at shock absorber end, then using a suitable tie rod end puller, remove link from shock and position aside.
4. Remove nut from tie rod end, then using a suitable tie rod end puller, remove tie rod from knuckle and position aside.
5. Remove and discard lower ball joint pinch bolt, then pry lower ball joint from knuckle.
6. Remove outer joint from hub using tools shown in **Fig. 3** or their equivalents, noting the following:
   a. Do not use a hammer to drive joint from hub.
   b. Do not allow driveshaft to hang from inner joint.
7. Remove inner joint from transaxle using tools shown in **Figs. 4 and 5,** or

Item	Description
1	Front Wheel Driveshaft Joint
2	Front Wheel Driveshaft Joint Boot Clamp (Large)
3	Front Wheel Driveshaft Joint Boot
4	Front Wheel Driveshaft Joint Boot Clamp (Small)
5	Driveshaft Bearing Retainer Circlip
6	Stop Ring
7	Halfshaft
8	Tri-Pot Assembly
9	Tri-Lobe Insert
10	Inboard CV Joint Stub Shaft Pilot Bearing Housing
11	Intermediate Halfshaft Bearing
12	Intermediate Halfshaft

FM3039600257020X

Fig. 1 Exploded view of driveshaft assemblies (Part 2 of 2)

Condition	Possible Source
• Clicking, Popping or Grinding Noises While Turning	• Inadequate or contaminated lube in outboard front wheel driveshaft joint or inboard front wheel driveshaft joint. • Another component contacting driveshaft assembly. • Worn, damaged or improperly installed wheel bearings, brakes, suspension or steering components.
• Vibration at Highway Speeds	• Out-of-balance front wheels or tires. • Out-of-round front tires. • Improperly seated outboard front wheel driveshaft joint in front wheel hub.
• Shudder Vibration During Acceleration	• Excessively high CV joint operating angles caused by improper ride height. • Excessively worn or damaged inboard front wheel driveshaft joint or outboard front wheel driveshaft joint.
• Halfshaft Joint Pullout	• Inboard driveshaft bearing retainer circlip missing or not properly seated in differential side gear. • Engine / transaxle assembly mispositioned. • Frame rail or shock tower out of position or damaged. • Front suspension components worn or damaged.

FM3039500311000X

Fig. 2 Troubleshooting chart

their equivalents. **Use caution when positioning tool to avoid transaxle speed sensor damage.**

8. Remove drive axle from vehicle.
9. Reverse procedure to install, noting the following:
   a. New front axle retainer nut must be used.
   b. New driveshaft bearing retainer circlips must be used.
   c. New ball joint pinch nut and bolt must be used.
   d. Use care when installing lefthand driveshaft joint into transaxle not to damage seal.
   e. Ensure proper engagement of lefthand driveshaft inner joint spline into transaxle side gears and that bearing retainer circlip is properly seated.
   f. Check transaxle fluid, add if needed.

RIGHTHAND DRIVESHAFT

1. Raise and support vehicle, then remove front wheel assemblies.
2. Remove and discard front axle retainer nut.
3. Remove nut from stabilizer bar link at strut end, then using suitable tie rod end puller, remove link from shock and position aside.
4. Remove nut from tie rod end, then using a suitable tie rod end puller, remove tie rod from knuckle and position aside.
5. Remove and discard lower ball joint pinch bolt, then pry lower ball joint from knuckle.
6. Remove outer joint from hub using tools shown in **Fig. 3** or their equivalents, noting the following:
   a. Do not use a hammer to drive joint from hub.
   b. Do not allow driveshaft to hang from inner joint.
7. Remove inner joint from intermediate shaft using tools shown in **Fig. 4** or their equivalents.
8. Remove driveshaft from vehicle.
9. Reverse procedure to install, noting the following:
   a. New front axle retainer nut must be used.
   b. New driveshaft bearing retainer circlips must be used.
   c. New ball joint pinch nut and bolt must be used.
   d. Check transaxle fluid, add if needed.

INTERMEDIATE DRIVESHAFT

1. Remove righthand driveshaft as outlined under "Driveshaft Replace."
2. Remove intermediate driveshaft support bearing nuts and bearing shield.
3. **On models equipped with 2.0L engine,** remove exhaust clamp and two bolts.
4. **On all models,** if necessary to achieve clearance, remove intermediate driveshaft support bearing bracket and three bolts.
5. Remove intermediate driveshaft from transaxle.
6. Remove and discard driveshaft bearing retainer circlip.
7. Reverse procedure to install, noting the following:
   a. New front axle retainer nut must be used.
   b. New driveshaft bearing retainer circlip must be used.
   c. New ball joint pinch nut and bolt must be used.
   d. Use care when installing intermediate driveshaft into transaxle not to damage seal.
   e. Ensure proper engagement of intermediate driveshaft spline into transaxle side gears and that bearing retainer circlip is properly seated.

DRIVESHAFT SERVICE

INNER JOINT & BOOT

Removal

1. Remove both clamps from inner joint boot.
2. Pull inner joint outer housing out of boot and off tripod assembly.
3. Remove stop ring from groove use suitable snap ring pliers **Fig. 6,** then slide ring inward on shaft.
4. Slide tripod assembly inward on shaft splines to expose driveshaft bearing retainer circlip.
5. Remove and discard driveshaft bearing retainer circlip, then tripod assembly from shaft.
6. Remove stop ring, then inner joint boot from shaft.

Inspection

1. Clean and dry all components.
2. Inspect boot for cracks, splits and abrasion.
3. Inspect joint components for wear, cracks and broken parts.
4. Inspect shaft for worn splines and bending.

Installation

1. Place small boot clamp on shaft, then slide boot onto shaft and into position groove on shaft.
2. Place small clamp into position on boot, then using suitable boot clamp ring pliers, tighten clamp ring securely.

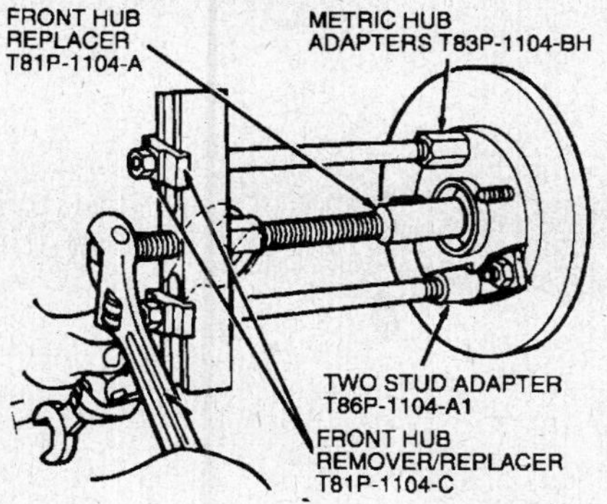

Fig. 3 Outer joint removal from hub

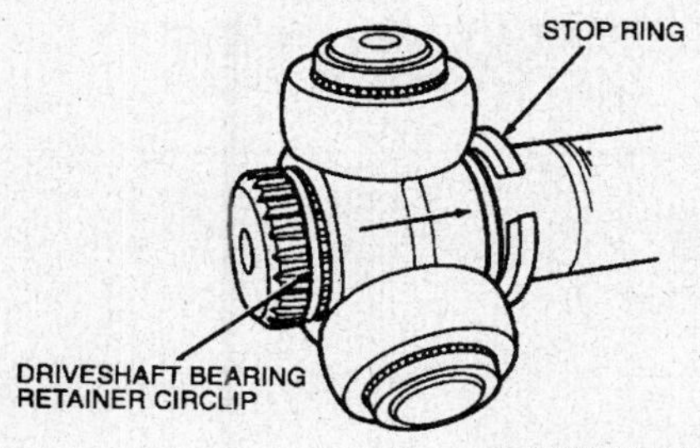

Fig. 6 Tripod removal

Use caution not to overtighten clamp ring and cut or deform boot.

3. Place stop ring onto shaft, slide stop ring past stop ring groove to allow room for installation of tripod assembly and driveshaft bearing retainer circlip.
4. Slide tripod assembly onto shaft splines, ensure chamfered side of tripod assembly is toward stop ring, **Fig. 7.**
5. Place a new driveshaft bearing retainer circlip onto shaft. **Use caution not to stretch or deform circlip during installation.**
6. Pull tripod assembly into position over driveshaft bearing retainer circlip. It may be necessary to compress driveshaft bearing retainer circlip to allow tripod assembly to move into position.
7. Place stop ring into place using suitable snap ring pliers.
8. Place trilobe boot insert into place on joint outer housing, **Fig. 8,** then fill housing and boot with suitable quantity and type CV joint grease.
9. Place joint outer housing onto tripod assembly, then position boot onto trilobe insert.
10. Ensure boot is in a relaxed position (not stretched, compressed or dimpled). If necessary, pry up edge of boot using a blunt flat tool and allow air pressure to equalize. This ensures proper joint outer housing positioning over tripod assembly.

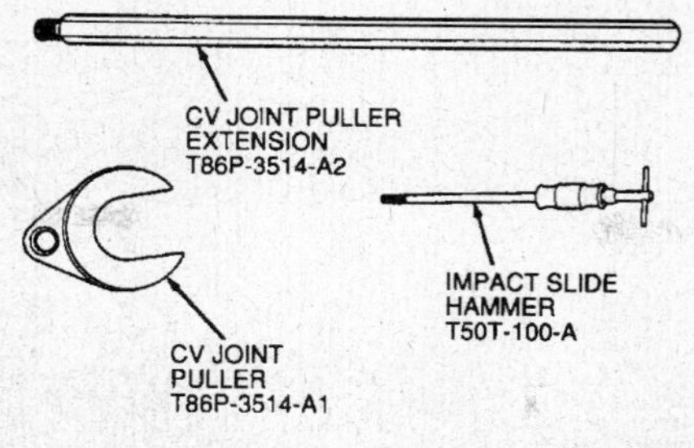

Fig. 4 Inner CV joint pulling tools

11. Clean any excess grease from outside of joint and boot.
12. Place large clamp into position on boot, then using suitable boot clamp ring pliers, tighten clamp ring securely. **Do not overtighten clamp ring, cut or deform boot.**
13. **On lefthand axle,** place a new driveshaft bearing retainer circlip onto joint housing. **Use caution not to stretch or deform circlip during installation.**
14. **On all axles,** ensure joint moves freely with no binding or excessive looseness.

OUTER JOINT & BOOT

Outer CV joint is composed of matched components. Interchanging components is not recommended.

Removal

1. Place driveshaft assembly into a suitable soft jaw vice.
2. Remove both clamps from inner joint boot.
3. Pull large end of boot back and off joint assembly.
4. Support driveshaft assembly in soft jaw vice as shown in **Fig. 9,** then tap on inner race of joint using a suitable drift punch to release driveshaft bearing retainer circlip.
5. Slide joint assembly off shaft splines to expose driveshaft bearing retainer circlip.
6. Remove and discard driveshaft bearing retainer circlip.
7. Remove joint boot from shaft.

Inspection

1. Clean and dry all components.
2. Inspect boot for cracks, splits and abrasion.
3. Inspect joint components for wear, cracks and broken parts.
4. Inspect shaft for worn splines and deformities.

Installation

1. Place small boot clamp on shaft, then slide boot onto shaft and into position groove on shaft.
2. Place small clamp into position on boot, then using suitable boot clamp ring pliers, tighten clamp ring securely. **Do not overtighten clamp ring or cut or deform boot.**

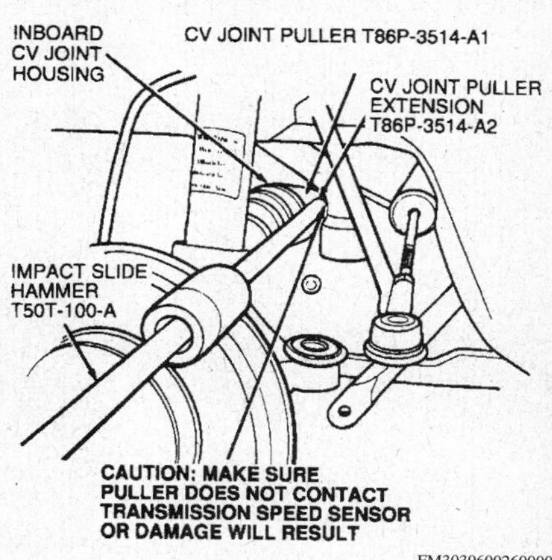

Fig. 5 Inner CV joint removal

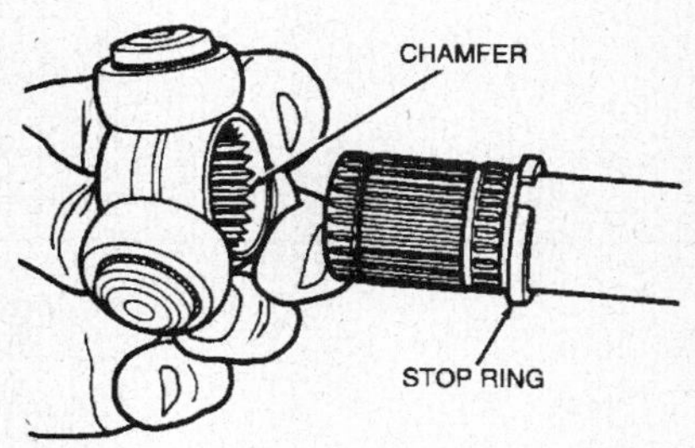

Fig. 7 Tripod installation

3. Place a new driveshaft bearing retainer circlip onto shaft. **Use caution not to stretch or deform circlip during installation.**
4. Place driveshaft in a vertical position in soft jaw vice.
5. Fill joint housing and boot with suitable quantity and type CV joint grease.
6. Place joint on driveshaft, aligning splines, then tap joint onto shaft using a soft face hammer, until driveshaft bearing retainer circlip engages joint.
7. Position boot onto outer joint.
8. Ensure boot is in a relaxed position (not stretched, compressed or dimpled). If necessary, pry up edge of boot using a blunt flat tool and allow air pressure to equalize. This ensures proper joint positioning.
9. Clean any excess grease from outside of joint and boot.
10. Place large clamp into position on boot, then using suitable boot clamp ring pliers, tighten clamp ring securely. **Do not overtighten clamp ring or cut or deform boot.**
11. Ensure joint moves freely with no binding or excessive looseness.

INTERMEDIATE DRIVESHAFT BEARING

Use suitable press and press tools to press intermediate driveshaft out of, then back into, bearing and dust shield.

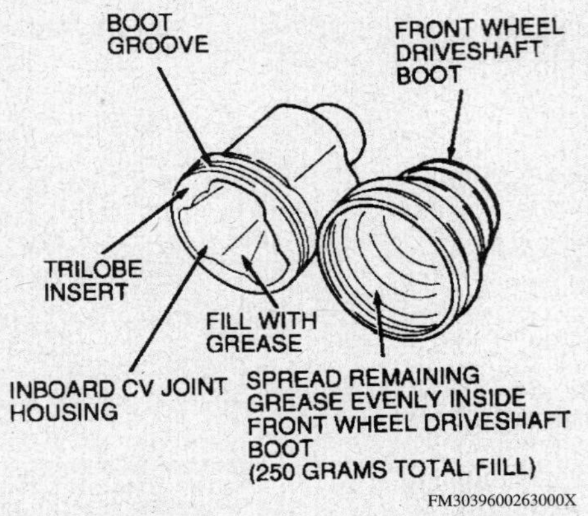

Fig. 8 Trilobe insert installation

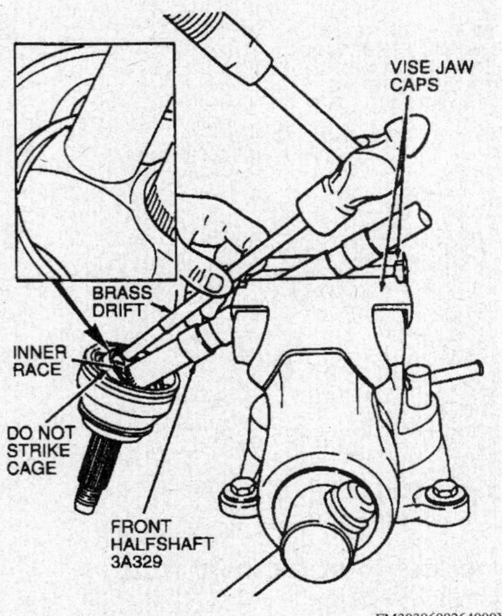

Fig. 9 Outer CV joint removal from driveshaft

TIGHTENING SPECIFICATIONS

Component	Torque/Ft. Lbs.
Ball Joint Pinch Bolt	61
Hub Nut	214
Intermediate Shaft Bracket Bolts	20
Intermediate Shaft Support Bracket Nuts	20
Stabilizer Bar Link Nut	35
Tie Rod End Nut	19
Wheel Lug Nut	95

Cougar

NOTE: On Air Bag Equipped Models, Refer To "Air Bag System Precautions" Located In The Front Of This Manual For System Disarming & Arming Procedures.

NOTE: Refer To "Computer Relearn Procedures" Located In The Front Of This Manual When Battery Power To The Computer Has Been Interrupted.

INDEX

PRECAUTIONS

AIR BAG SYSTEMS

Refer to "Air Bag System Precautions" in the front of this manual for system disarming and arming procedures.

BATTERY GROUND CABLE

Prior to service, disconnect battery ground cable and isolate as required.

DESCRIPTION

The front drive halfshafts transmit torque from the engine to the wheels. In order to allow vertical movement of the wheels and engine, the front drive halfshafts operate at varying lengths and angles. The tripod joints allow for changes in driveshaft length during axial movements.

To reduce running friction, the front drive halfshafts are fitted with constant velocity (CV) joints at both ends. Tripod joints (with tripod, running rollers and tripod housing) are fitted on the transaxle side. Fix joints (with ball star, ball cage and ball shell) are fitted on the wheel side. The lefthand tripod joint is secured in the differential with a snap ring. The intermediate shaft (righthand side) is not secured in the differential, but is secured by the intermediate shaft bearing bracket. The tripod joint of the righthand front drive halfshaft is secured in the intermediate shaft with a snap ring. The outboard constant velocity joints are attached to the wheel hubs.

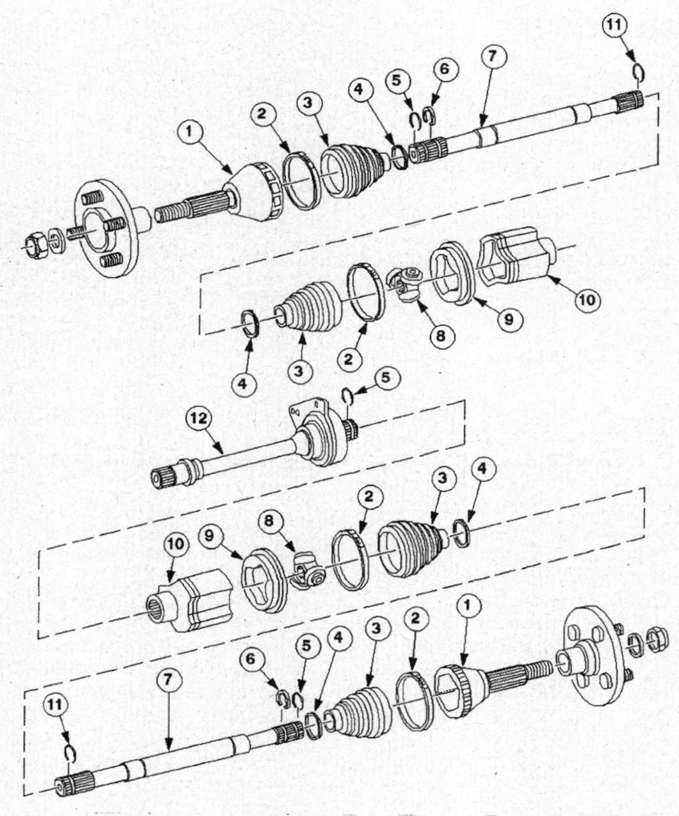

Fig. 1 Exploded view of driveshafts (Part 1 of 2)

TROUBLESHOOTING

CLICKING, POPPING OR GRINDING NOISES WHILE TURNING

1. Another component contacting halfshaft assembly.
2. Inadequate or contaminated lube in outboard/inboard front wheel halfshaft joint.
3. Inspect wheel bearings, brakes, suspension or steering components.

VIBRATION AT HIGHWAY SPEEDS

1. Out of balance front wheels or tires.
2. Out of round tires.
3. Incorrectly seated outboard front wheel halfshaft joint in front wheel hub.

SHUDDER VIBRATION DURING ACCELERATION

1. Excessively high CV joint operating angles caused by incorrect ride height.
2. Excessively worn or damaged inboard front wheel halfshaft joint or outboard front wheel halfshaft joint.

Item	Part Number	Description
1	-	Fix joint
2	-	Boot clamp (large)
3	-	Boot
4	-	Boot clamp (small)
5	-	Halfshaft joint snap ring
6	-	Snap ring
7	-	Front drive halfshaft
8	-	Tripod
9	-	Tripod housing insert
10	-	Tripod housing
11	-	Halfshaft joint snap ring
12	-	Intermediate shaft

FM3039900320020X

Fig. 1 Exploded view of driveshafts (Part 2 of 2)

HALFSHAFT JOINT PULLOUT

1. Inboard halfshaft bearing retainer circlip missing or not correctly seated in differential side gear.
2. Engine/transaxle assembly misaligned.
3. Frame rail or strut tower out of position or damaged.
4. Front suspension components worn or damaged.

DRIVESHAFT

REPLACE

In all service operations the driveshaft bearing retainer circlips must be replaced with a new part. Do not begin this procedure unless a new hub retainer nut, lower control arm to steering knuckle attaching bolt and nut, and the circlips are available. Once removed, these components must not be reused during assembly/installation. Their torque holding ability or retention capability is diminished during removal.

LEFTHAND DRIVESHAFT

1. Loosen suspension strut locknut five turns.
2. Loosen driveshaft stub nut and front wheel nuts.
3. Raise and support vehicle.
4. Remove front wheel.
5. Remove driveshaft stub nut.
6. Remove fender splash shields.
7. Remove lower ball joint to steering knuckle pinch bolt and nut, then separate ball joint from steering knuckle using a suitable pry bar.
8. Disconnect ABS wiring harness bracket from suspension strut.
9. Remove driveshaft from wheel hub using front hub removal tool No. T81P1104C or equivalent.
10. Disconnect driveshaft from transaxle using halfshaft removal tool No. T86P3514A or equivalent.
11. Insert suitable transaxle plug into driveshaft opening to prevent fluid from leaking.
12. Remove driveshaft from vehicle.
13. Reverse procedure to install.

RIGHTHAND DRIVESHAFT

1. Loosen suspension strut locknut five turns.
2. Loosen driveshaft stub nut and front wheel nuts.
3. Raise and support vehicle.
4. Remove front wheel.
5. Remove driveshaft stub nut.
6. Remove fender splash shields.
7. Remove lower ball joint to steering knuckle pinch bolt and nut, then using a suitable pry bar separate ball joint from steering knuckle.
8. Disconnect ABS wiring harness bracket from suspension strut.
9. Remove driveshaft from wheel hub using front hub removal tool No. T81P1104C or equivalent.
10. Disconnect driveshaft from intermediate driveshaft support bearing using, halfshaft removal tool No. T86P3514A or equivalent.
11. Remove driveshaft from vehicle.
12. Reverse procedure to install.

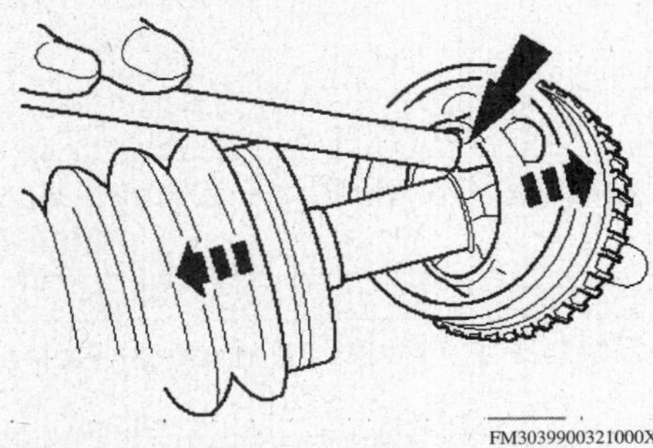

FM3039900321000X

Fig. 2 Driveshaft joint removal

INTERMEDIATE DRIVESHAFT

1. Remove righthand driveshaft as outlined under "Driveshaft Replace"
2. Remove intermediate driveshaft support bearing bracket attaching bolts. **To avoid damaging CV joint do not bend inner CV joint by more than 18°.**
3. Disconnect intermediate driveshaft from transaxle using, halfshaft removal tool No. T86P3514A or equivalent.
4. Insert suitable transaxle plug into driveshaft opening to prevent fluid from leaking.
5. Reverse procedure to install.

DRIVESHAFT SERVICE

1. Cut small and large boot clamps and discard them, **Fig. 1.**
2. Slide boot back, then pull out tripod joint.
3. Remove snap ring, then using suitable puller, pull off tripod assembly.
4. Loosen driveshaft joint at wheel end.
5. Cut boot clamps and remove.
6. Slide boot back.
7. Unseat driveshaft joint from snap ring seat using suitable brass drift, **Fig. 2.**
8. Remove driveshaft joint.
9. Remove snap ring.
10. Remove stop ring.
11. Pull off boot.
12. Reverse procedure to install noting the following:
    a. Install new snap rings and boot clamps when servicing joints.
    b. Pack tripod joint with 6 ounces of suitable high temperature Constant velocity joint grease.

TIGHTENING SPECIFICATIONS

Component	Torque/Ft. Lbs.
Ball Joint Bolt & Nut	63
Hub Nut	214
Stabilizer Link	35
Suppot Bearing Bracket Bolts	20
Tie Rod	19
Upper Strut Mount	34
Wheel Lug Nuts	95

Escort, Tracer & ZX2

NOTE: On Air Bag Equipped Models, Refer To "Air Bag System Precautions" Located In The Front Of This Manual For System Disarming & Arming Procedures.

NOTE: Refer To "Computer Relearn Procedures" Located In The Front Of This Manual When Battery Power To The Computer Has Been Interrupted.

INDEX

PRECAUTIONS

AIR BAG SYSTEMS

Refer to "Air Bag System Precautions" in the front of this manual for system disarming and arming procedures.

BATTERY GROUND CABLE

Prior to service, disconnect battery ground cable and isolate as required.

TROUBLESHOOTING

NOISE & VIBRATION ON TURNS

Clicking, popping or grinding noises while turning may be caused by the following:

1. Cut or damaged CV joint boots, resulting in contaminated lube in outboard or inboard joints.
2. Loose joint clamps.
3. Worn, damaged or improperly installed wheel bearings.
4. Halfshaft assembly connecting component.

VIBRATION AT HIGHWAY SPEEDS

1. Front wheels or tires out of balance.
2. Front tires out of round.

SHUDDER OR VIBRATION ON ACCELERATION

1. Excessively worn or damaged inboard or outboard CV joint.
2. Excessively high CV joint operating angles caused by improper ride height.

HALFSHAFT OR CV JOINT PULL-OUT

Engine Or Transaxle Misaligned

1. Inspect engine mounts for damage.

Front Suspension Components Worn Or Damaged

1. Inspect for worn bushings or bent front suspension components.

Improperly Installed Or Missing Retainers

1. Inspect for CV joint circlip missing or not properly seated in transaxle side gear.

DRIVESHAFT

REPLACE

1. Raise and support vehicle.
2. Remove front tire and wheel.
3. Raise staked portion of front axle wheel hub retainer.
4. Remove and discard front axle wheel hub retainer.
5. Remove cotter pin and tie rod end nut.
6. Separate tie rod end from steering knuckle using suitable tie rod end remover, .
7. Remove stabilizer bar as follows:
   a. Remove front stabilizer bar end nut, **Fig. 1.**
   b. Remove front stabilizer bar end bolt.
   c. Remove upper front stabilizer bar end retainer.
   d. Remove front stabilizer bar end bushing above front stabilizer bar.
   e. Remove front stabilizer bar end bushing below front stabilizer bar.
   f. Remove front stabilizer bar end bushing.
   g. Remove front stabilizer bar end bushing above front sub-frame.
   h. Remove front stabilizer bar end bushing below front sub-frame.
   i. Remove lower front stabilizer bar end retainer.
8. Remove ball joint nut and pinch bolt.
9. Separate front suspension lower arm ball joint from steering knuckle.
10. Pull driveshaft and joint from steering knuckle.
11. Insert pry bar between front wheel driveshaft and joint and transaxle case and pry outward, releasing front wheel driveshaft and joint from differential side gears.
12. **On ZX2 models with manual transaxles,** proceed as follows:
    a. Remove bolts from center support bearing.
    b. Lower driveshaft assembly and remove halfshaft from differential side gears.
    c. Separate driveshaft and joint from center support bearing and halfshaft.
13. **On all models,** reverse procedure to install.

DRIVESHAFT SERVICE

CV JOINT

Disassemble

1. Secure driveshaft in soft-jawed vise.
2. Use a punch to remove ABS sensor ring from joint housing, then discard sensor.
3. Remove boot clamps, then slide boot back to expose joint.
4. Mark joint to shaft for reference to ensure proper installation, then use soft-face hammer to separate outboard joint by gently tapping it from shaft.
5. Remove and discard bearing retainer circlip.
6. Remove snap ring from outboard side of shaft.
7. Wrap outboard shaft splines with suitable tape before sliding boot from shaft.

Assemble

1. Clean and inspect outboard bearings and cage for grit in grease or any signs of cracking or pitting. Replace if needed.
2. Lubricate outboard joint bearings with Ford CV Joint Grease part No. E43Z-19590-A or equivalent, meeting Ford specification ESP-M1C207-A.

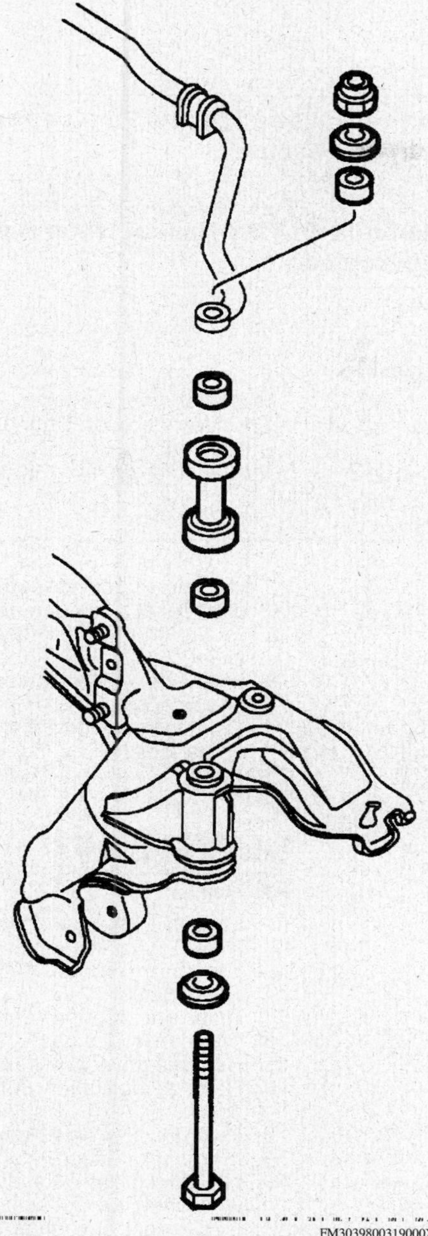

Fig. 1 Stabilizer bar removal

Transaxle	Model	Location	Length, Inches
Automatic	Except ZX2	Lefthand	24.96
		Righthand	35.93
Manual	Except ZX2	Lefthand	24.87
		Righthand	36.59
Automatic	ZX2	Lefthand	24.47
		Righthand	36.59
Manual	ZX2	Lefthand	24.49
		Righthand	24.49

Fig. 2 Halfshaft specifications

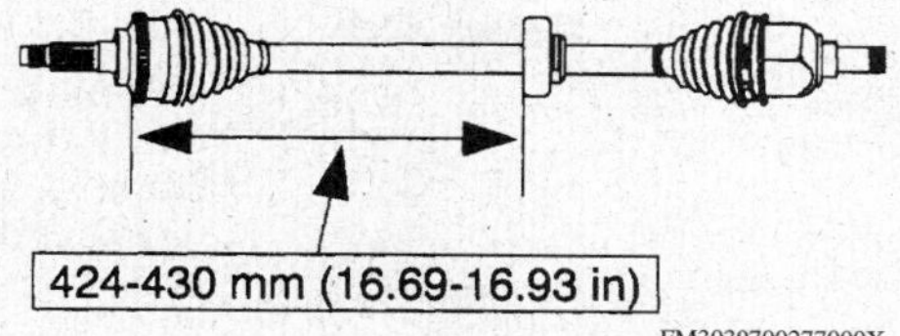

Fig. 3 Righthand damper installation

3. Wrap outboard shaft splines with suitable tape to protect joint boot from damage, then install boot on shaft.
4. Install snap ring on outboard side of shaft.
5. Install a new bearing retainer circlip.
6. Use soft-face hammer to gently install joint onto shaft.
7. Remove any excess grease on mating surfaces and slide boot forward onto joint.
8. Refer to **Fig. 2** for proper halfshaft lengths before adjusting boots and clamps.
9. After adjusting boot spacing, remove any excess air trapped in boot with a dull screwdriver.
10. Install new boot clamps with pliers tool No. D87P-1098-A or equivalent.
11. Use replacer tool No. T94P-20202-B or equivalent, to install a new ABS sensor indicator.

DYNAMIC DAMPER BEARING

1. Remove outboard driveshaft joint.
2. Remove and discard damper retaining clamp, then remove damper.
3. Install damper as shown, **Fig. 3. Use new retainer to hold band in place.**
4. Install driveshaft.

TIGHTENING SPECIFICATIONS

Component	Torque/Ft. Lbs.
Ball Joint Pinch Bolt	32–43
Center Support Bearing Bolts	32–46
Crossmember	69–93
Dynamic Damper Bearing	31–46
Hub Nut	174–235
Tie Rod End Nut	32–41
Wheel Lug Nut	74–100

Focus

NOTE: On Air Bag Equipped Models, Refer To "Air Bag System Precautions" Located In The Front Of This Manual For System Disarming & Arming Procedures.

NOTE: Refer To "Computer Relearn Procedures" Located In The Front Of This Manual When Battery Power To The Computer Has Been Interrupted.

INDEX

PRECAUTIONS

AIR BAG SYSTEMS

Refer to "Air Bag System Precautions" in the front of this manual for system disarming and arming procedures.

BATTERY GROUND CABLE

Prior to service, disconnect battery ground cable and isolate as required.

TROUBLESHOOTING

CLICKING, POPPING OR GRINDING NOISES WHILE TURNING

1. Another component contacting halfshaft assembly.
2. Inadequate or contaminated lube in outboard/inboard front wheel halfshaft joint.
3. Inspect wheel bearings, brakes, suspension or steering components.

VIBRATION AT HIGHWAY SPEEDS

1. Out of balance front wheels or tires.
2. Out of round tires.
3. Incorrectly seated outboard front wheel halfshaft joint in front wheel hub.

SHUDDER VIBRATION DURING ACCELERATION

1. Excessively high CV joint operating angles caused by incorrect ride height.
2. Excessively worn or damaged inboard front wheel halfshaft joint or outboard front wheel halfshaft joint.

HALFSHAFT JOINT PULLOUT

1. Inboard halfshaft bearing retainer circlip missing or not correctly seated in differential side gear.
2. Engine/transaxle assembly misaligned.
3. Frame rail or strut tower out of position or damaged.
4. Front suspension components worn or damaged.

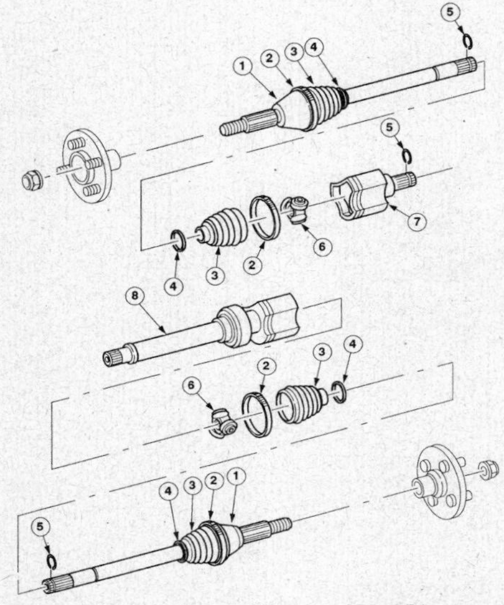

FM3030000338010X

Fig. 1 Exploded view of driveshaft (Part 1 of 2)

Item	Description
1	Fixed ball joint with front drive halfshaft
2	Clamping strap (large)
3	Boot
4	Clamping strap (small)
5	Snap-ring - CV joint, transmission end
6	Tripod star with constant velocity rollers
7	Tripode housing
8	Intermediate shaft with intermediate shaft bearing

FM3030000338020X

Fig. 1 Exploded view of driveshaft (Part 2 of 2)

DRIVESHAFT

REPLACE

1. Loosen suspension strut locknut five turns.
2. Loosen driveshaft stub nut and front wheel nuts.
3. Raise and support vehicle.
4. Remove front wheel.
5. Remove driveshaft stub nut.
6. Remove bolt, then detach lower arm ball joint.
7. **Hub nut can be re-used four times; mark nut.** Unscrew and remove hub nut, then press out halfshaft stub from wheel hub using a suitable puller.
8. Disconnect driveshaft from transaxle.
9. Remove driveshaft from vehicle.
10. Reverse procedure to install.

DRIVESHAFT SERVICE

1. Hold intermediate shaft in a vise, then separate discard clamping straps. Push back boot along shaft.
2. Pull apart tripode joint, then remove all grease and tripode snap ring **Fig. 1.**
3. Remove tripode using tool No. T81P-1104C or equivalent, then the boot.
4. Separate and discard clamping straps, then remove boot over transaxle side and accessible grease.
5. Reverse procedure to assemble.

TIGHTENING SPECIFICATIONS

Component	Torque/Ft. Lbs.
Ball Joint	63
Driveshaft Nut	214
Gaiter Clamps	15
Hub Nut	214
Suspension Strut Nut	35

Sable & Taurus

NOTE: On Air Bag Equipped Models, Refer To "Air Bag System Precautions" Located In The Front Of This Manual For System Disarming & Arming Procedures.

NOTE: Refer To "Computer Relearn Procedures" Located In The Front Of This Manual When Battery Power To The Computer Has Been Interrupted.

INDEX

PRECAUTIONS

AIR BAG SYSTEMS

Refer to "Air Bag System Precautions" in the front of this manual for system disarming and arming procedures.

BATTERY GROUND CABLE

Prior to service, disconnect battery ground cable and isolate as required.

TROUBLESHOOTING

NOISE & VIBRATION ON TURNS

Clicking, popping or grinding noises while turning may be caused by the following:

1. Cut or damaged CV joint boots, resulting in contaminated lube in outboard or inboard CV joints.
2. Loose CV joint clamps.
3. Worn, damaged or improperly installed wheel bearings.
4. Foreign object contacting driveshaft assembly.

SHUDDER OR VIBRATION ON ACCELERATION

1. Excessively worn or damaged inboard or outboard CV joint.
2. Excessively high CV joint operating angles caused by improper ride height.

VIBRATION AT HIGHWAY SPEEDS

1. Front wheels or tires out of balance.
2. Improperly seated outboard CV joint in front wheel hub.
3. Bent intermediate driveshaft.
4. Front tires out of round.

DRIVESHAFT OR CV JOINT PULL-OUT

1. Inboard CV joint circlip missing or improperly seated in transaxle side gear.
2. Engine or transaxle improperly positioned. Inspect engine mounts.
3. Frame rail or strut tower improperly positioned or damaged.
4. Front suspension components worn or damaged.

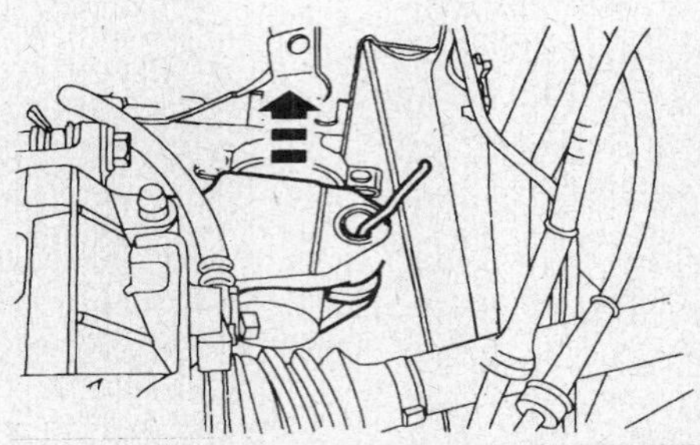

Fig. 1 Steering knuckle repositioned on strut

DRIVESHAFT

REPLACE

1. Raise and support vehicle, then remove front wheels.
2. Remove and discard front axle retainer nut and washer.
3. Remove anti-lock brake sensor wiring harness retaining clip from bracket on lower end of strut assembly, then the sensor from mounting bracket.
4. Discard nut, then position sensor aside.
5. **On SHO models,** remove wiring harness from routing clip on front strut assembly, then air suspension height sensor from height sensor ball studs.
6. **On 1998 models,** remove nut from stabilizer bar link at strut assembly lower end, then the link from strut and position aside.
7. **On 1999–2002 models,** proceed as follows:
   a. Remove lower strut to steering knuckle retaining bolt and nut, then separate steering knuckle from strut assembly.
   b. Reposition knuckle on strut body, then secure knuckle to strut using a suitable wire **Fig. 1. Failure to reposition knuckle on strut body will prevent separation of front suspension lower arm from knuckle.**
   c. Pull upward on knuckle to raise it approximately ½ inch on strut body, then secure knuckle to strut with suitable wire.
8. **On all models,** remove and discard nut from lower ball joint, then loosen ball joint in lower control arm using a suitable suspension arm puller.
9. Place a suitable pry bar through opening in lower control arm and under frame, then pry down on control arm to release lower ball joint
10. Remove outer CV joint from hub noting the following:
    a. Do not use a hammer to drive joint from hub.
    b. Separate outer CV joint from hub using a suitable front wheel hub removal tool **Fig. 2.**
    c. Do not allow driveshaft to hang from inner joint.
11. Remove inner joint from transaxle.
12. Reverse procedure to install, noting the following:
    a. New front axle retainer nut must be used.
    b. New driveshaft bearing retainer circlip must be used.
    c. New ball joint nut must be used.
    d. Use care not to damage seal when installing driveshaft joints into transaxle.
    e. Ensure proper engagement of lefthand driveshaft inner joint spline into transaxle side gears and that bearing retainer circlip is properly seated.
    f. Ensure proper engagement of transaxle shaft spline into righthand inner CV joint and that bearing retainer circlip is properly seated.

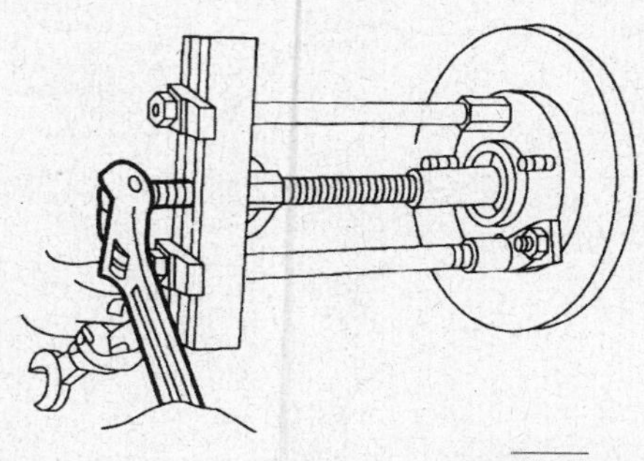

Fig. 2 Outer CV Joint removal from hub

g. Check transaxle fluid, add if necessary.

DRIVESHAFT SERVICE

OUTBOARD JOINT & BOOT

REMOVAL

CV Joint

During manufacturing, CV joint components are matched. Components cannot be interchanged with another joint's components. If a joint component is faulty, entire joint should be replaced.

1. Install soft vise jaw caps in vise to prevent damage to driveshaft, then position driveshaft in vise. Do not allow vise to contact CV joint boot or clamps.
2. Using side cutting pliers, cut large boot clamp and peel away from boot. Roll boot back over driveshaft, **Fig. 3.**
3. Turn driveshaft over in vise, then angle CV joint so that inner bearing race is exposed, **Fig. 4.** Using a brass drift and a hammer, give a sharp rap to inner bearing race to dislodge internal snap ring.
4. Separate CV joint from driveshaft.
5. Remove CV boot from shaft.
6. Inspect CV joint grease for contamination. If grease appears contaminated or has a gritty feeling, inspect for worn components and replace as necessary. If grease is not contaminated and joint was operating satisfactorily, add grease and replace boot.
7. Remove and discard circlip from end of shaft. Inspect stop ring located below circlip, if it is worn or damaged, replace it.
8. Clamp CV joint stub axle in vise with soft vise jaw caps. Be careful not to damage dust seal.
9. Push down on CV joint inner race until it tilts enough to allow ball removal, **Fig. 5. If inner race is tight, it can be tilted by tapping inner race with wooden dowel and hammer. Do not hit cage.**
10. Remove balls from cage. If balls are tight, use blunt screwdriver to pry balls from cage.
11. Pivot cage and inner race assembly until it is straight up, **Fig. 6.** Align cage windows with outer race lands while pivoting bearing cage, then lift out cage and inner race.
12. Rotate inner race up and out of cage, **Fig. 7.**

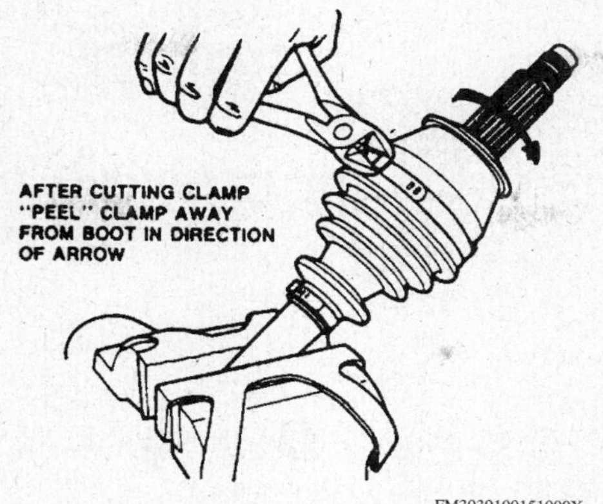

Fig. 3 Boot clamp removal

Anti-Lock Brake Sensor Wheel

1. Remove outer CV joint as outlined.
2. Place CV joint into removal tool No. T88P-20202-A **Fig. 8,** or equivalent.
3. Using a suitable press, push CV joint out of sensor wheel.
4. Use caution not to damage sensor wheel teeth.

Dust Seal

With driveshaft removed, use a light duty hammer and screwdriver to tap evenly around seal until unseated and remove seal, **Fig. 9.**

INSPECTION

During manufacturing, CV joints components are matched. Components cannot be interchanged with another joint's components. If a component is faulty, entire joint should be replaced.

Inspect all parts. If any parts are cracked, broken, severely pitted, worn or otherwise unserviceable, replace CV joint. If any parts appear polished, do not replace joint as this is a normal condition.

If anti-lock brake sensor wheel's teeth are chipped or cracked, install a replacement sensor wheel.

INSTALLATION

CV Joint

1. Apply light coating of Ford CV joint grease No. E2FZ-19590-A or equivalent on inner and outer races, then install inner race in bearing cage, **Fig. 7.**
2. Install inner race and cage assembly in outer race, **Fig. 10.**
3. Install CV joint assembly into outer race and pivot 90° into position, **Fig. 11.**
4. Align bearing cage and inner race with outer race, then tilt inner race and install a ball, followed by remaining five balls.
5. Determine which end of driveshaft is for outboard CV joint. The outboard joint side has a shorter end of boot groove to end of shaft dimension, **Fig. 12.**

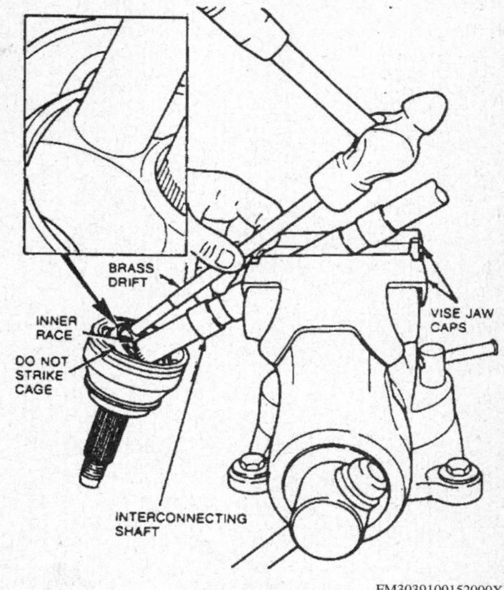

Fig. 4 Internal snap ring removal

6. Install CV joint boot and small boot clamp. If stop ring was removed, install at this time. If stop ring was not removed, ensure it is seated properly in groove.
7. Install new circlip.
8. Pack CV joint with Ford CV joint grease No. E2FZ-19590-A or equivalent. Spread any remaining grease evenly inside CV boot.
9. With boot peeled back, position CV joint on driveshaft and tap into position with a plastic hammer. Joint is properly seated when circlip locks into position. Inspect for proper retention by attempting to pull off joint.
10. Remove all excess grease from external surfaces, then position boot over joint. Ensure boot is seated in its groove, then install clamp.

Anti-Lock Brake Sensor Wheel

1. Position sensor wheel onto remover replacer tool No. T88P-20202-A or equivalent.
2. Position CV joint into sensor wheel and tool.
3. Using a suitable press, push joint into sensor wheel until joint bottoms in tool.
4. Use caution not to damage sensor wheel teeth.

Dust Seal

Install dust seal using spindle/axle seal tool No. T83T-3132-A1, and dust seal installer tool No. T83P-3425-AH or equivalents.

INBOARD JOINT & BOOT

REMOVAL

The tripod is an integral part of the intermediate driveshaft and inboard CV joint housing and are not repairable and must be replace with new components if damaged. Only the inner driveshaft boot can be replaced, **Figs. 13 and 14.**

Three types of boots and CV joints, **Fig. 15,** are used on these models. These

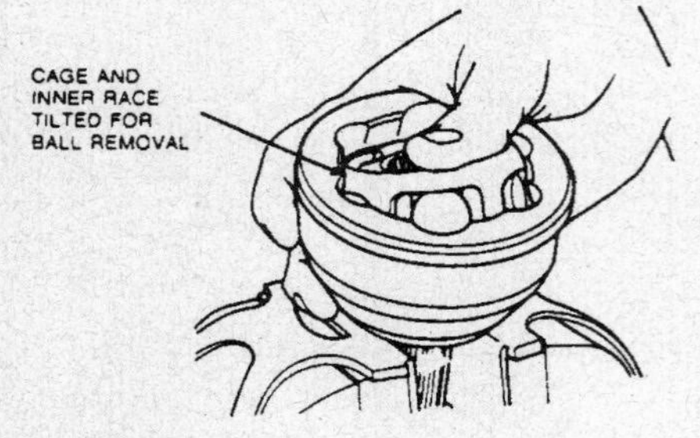

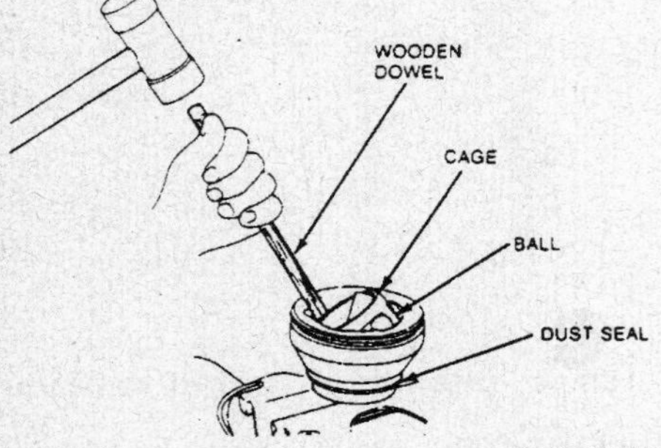

Fig. 5 CV joint ball removal

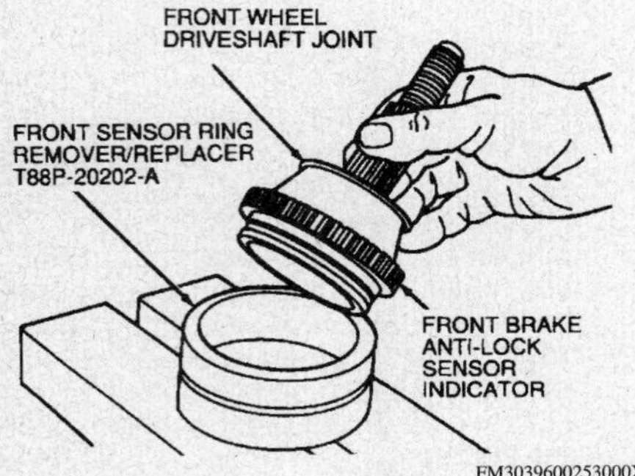

Fig. 8 Anti-Lock brake sensor wheel removal

components are not interchangeable. Always use matching type when replacing components.

1. Remove large and small boot clamp as necessary, then remove inner joint outer housing.
2. If boot replacement is necessary, remove outer CV joint as outlined under "Outboard Joint & Boot," then remove outer joint stop ring.
3. Remove old boot by sliding off outboard end of driveshaft.

INSTALLATION

1. If boot replacement is required, slide new boot onto shaft and into position groove of shaft from outer end of driveshaft.
2. Position new small boot clamp onto boot from outer end of driveshaft, then tighten clamp.

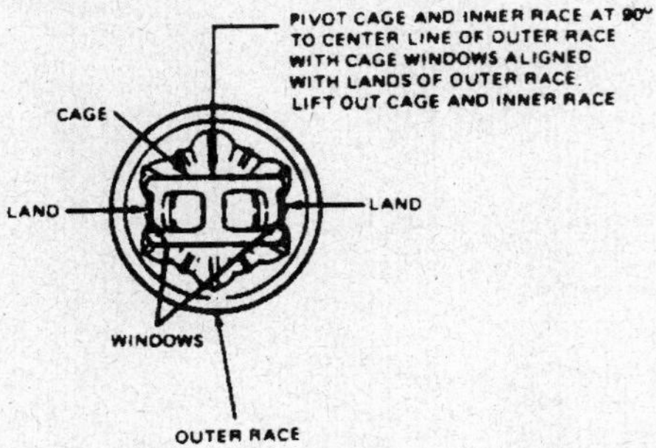

Fig. 6 Cage & inner race removal

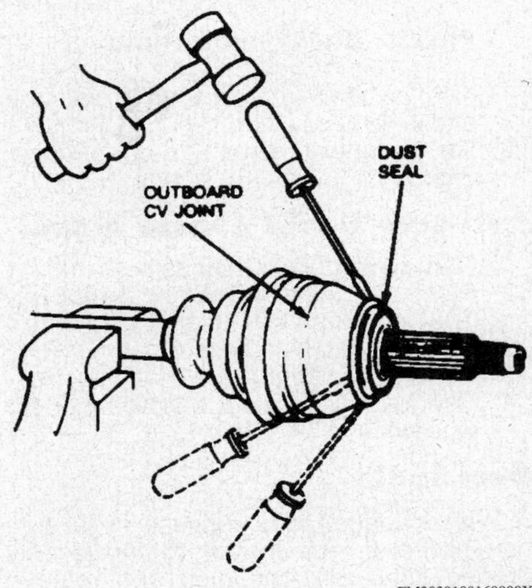

Fig. 9 Dust seal removal

3. **On models equipped with Ford CV joints** fill inner CV joint and boot with a total of 5.88 oz. of a suitable CV joint grease.
4. **On models equipped with GNK CV joints** fill inner CV joint and boot with a total of 16.75 oz. of a suitable CV joint grease.
5. If inner boot was replaced, install outer joint stop ring, then outer CV joint as outlined under "Outboard Joint & Boot."
6. Position inner joint outer housing onto tripod, then install large end of boot onto joint outer housing.
7. Ensure boot is not stretched or collapsed, if necessary use a blunt flat tool to pry up lip of boot to allow air pressure to equalize.
8. Ensure driveshaft length is proper, **Fig. 16.**
9. Clean any excess grease from outside of boot.
10. Position new large boot clamp onto boot, then tighten clamp.

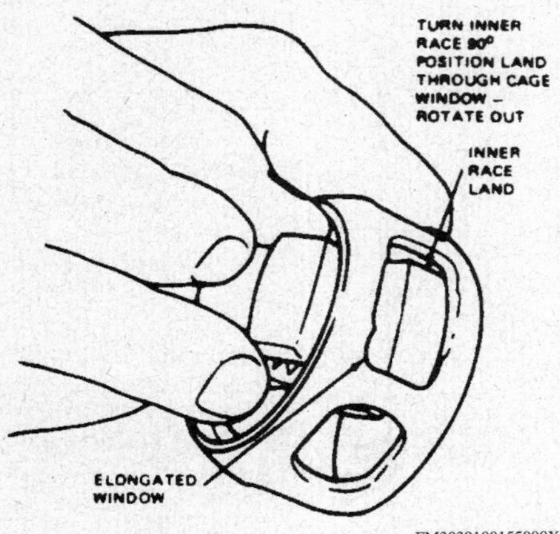

Fig. 7 Inner race replacement

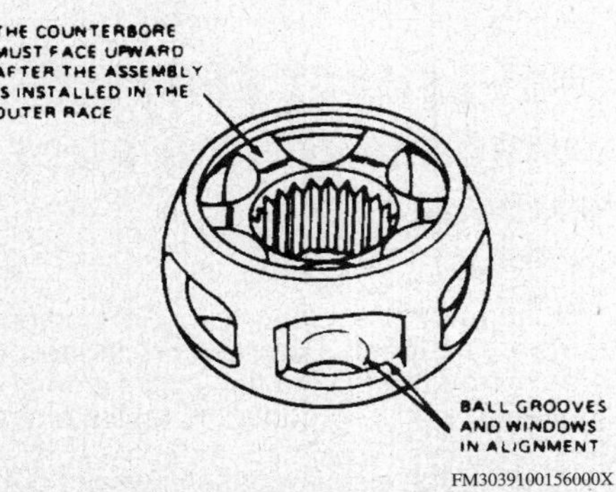

Fig. 10 Inner race & cage assembly

11. Position clamp replacement tool No. T95P-3514-A or equivalent, on clamp ear and tighten tool through bolt until tool is in closed position.

INTERMEDIATE SHAFT

DISASSEMBLE

1. Clamp Intermediate Shaft in vise with driveshaft supported on workbench. Separate Intermediate Shaft from driveshaft using puller adapter tool No. T86P-3514-A and slide hammer tool No. D79P-100-A or equivalents, **Fig. 17.**
2. Pry seal from linkshaft with screwdriver.
3. Position Intermediate Shaft in an arbor press, then press off bearing.

ASSEMBLE

1. Press on new bearing and bearing seal with arbor press.
2. Coat shaft splines with Ford CV joint grease No. E2FZ-19590-A or equivalent, then assemble Intermediate Shaft to driveshaft.

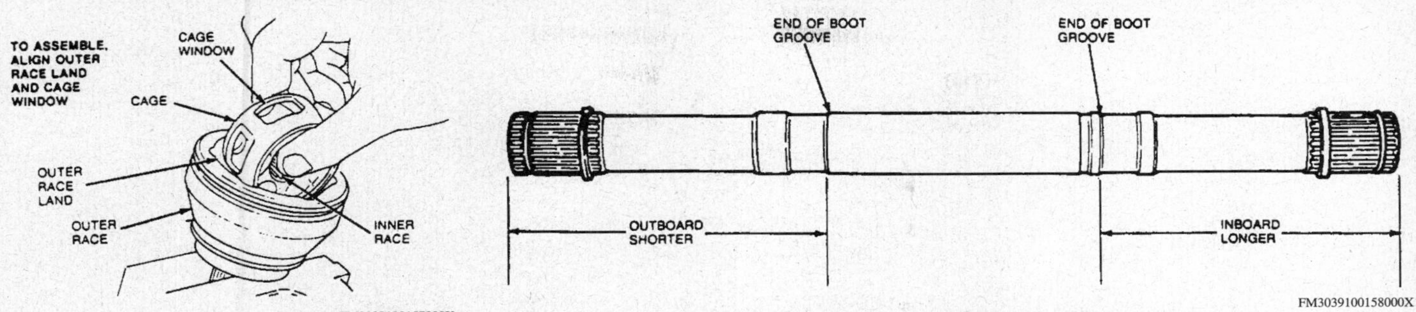

Fig. 11 CV joint assembly installation into outer race

Fig. 12 Driveshaft end identification

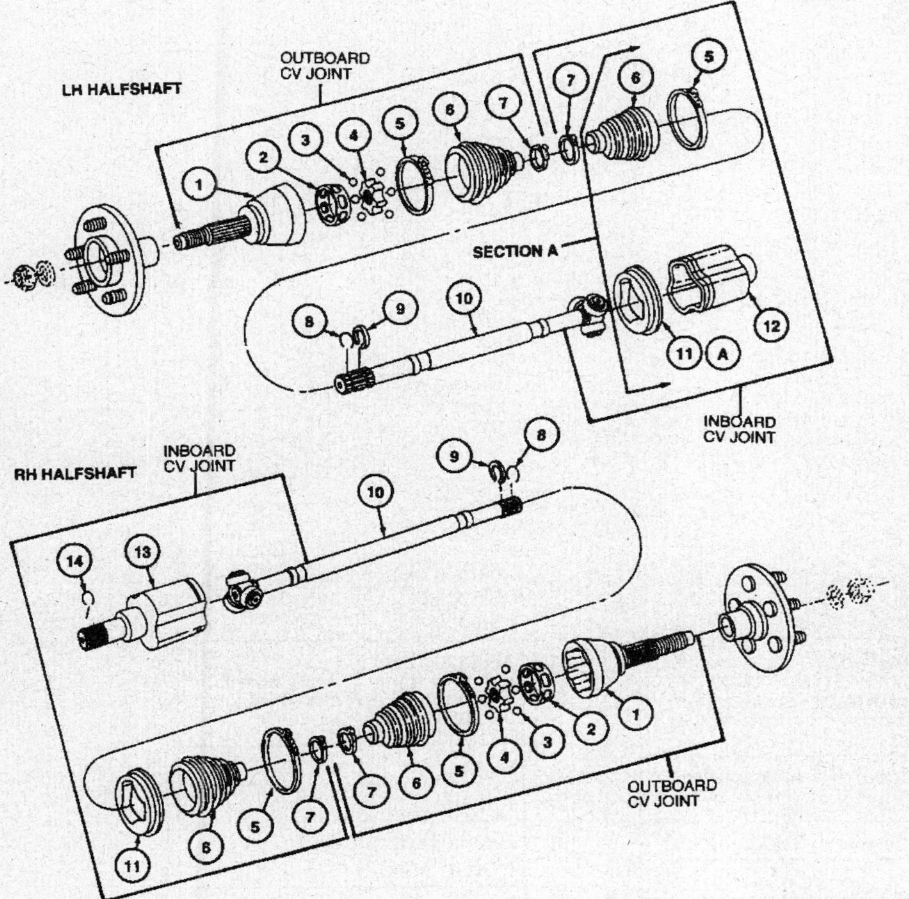

Fig. 13 Exploded view of ford driveshaft assemblies (Part 1 of 2). Ford

Item	Description
1	Front Wheel Driveshaft Joint
2	Ball Cage
3	Balls (6 required)
4	Inner Race
5	Front Wheel Driveshaft Joint Boot Clamp (Large)
6	Front Wheel Driveshaft Joint Boot
7	Front Wheel Driveshaft Joint Boot Clamp (Small)
8	Circlip
9	Stop Ring
10	Interconnecting Shaft
11	Tri-Lobe Insert
12	LH Inboard CV Joint Housing
13	RH Inboard CV Joint Housing
14	Circlip
A	Part Used Only With Ford Design Conventional Boot

FM3039600254020X

Fig. 13 Exploded view of driveshaft assemblies (Part 2 of 2). Ford

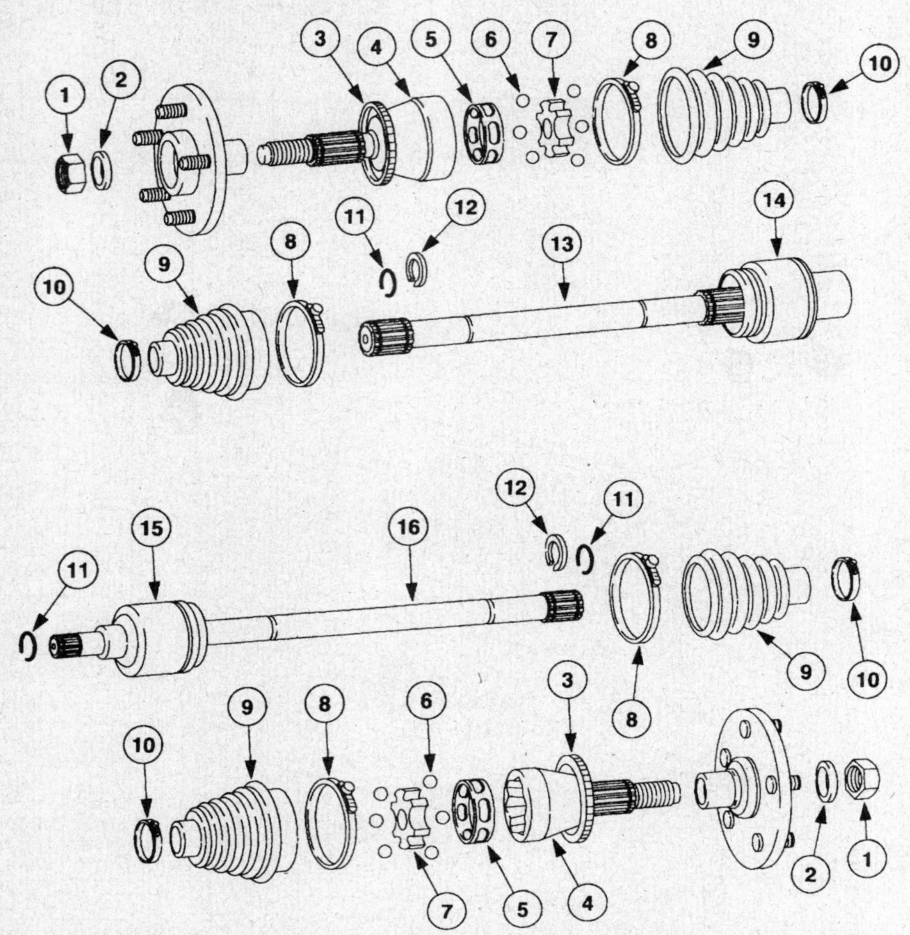

Fig. 14 Exploded view of driveshaft assemblies (Part 1 of 2). GKN

Item	Description
1	Front axle wheel hub retainer
2	Washer
3	Front brake anti-lock sensor indicator
4	Front wheel driveshaft joint
5	Ball cage (part of 3B413)
6	Balls (6 req'd) (part of 3B413)
7	Race (part of 3B413)
8	Front wheel driveshaft joint boot clamp (large)
9	Front wheel driveshaft joint boot

Item	Description
10	Front wheel driveshaft joint boot clamp (small)
11	Circlip
12	Stop ring
13	Interconnecting shaft (part of 3B437)
14	Inboard CV joint housing assembly
15	Inboard CV joint housing assembly
16	Interconnecting shaft (part of 3B436)

FM3030100394020X

Fig. 14 Exploded view of driveshaft assemblies (Part 2 of 2). GKN

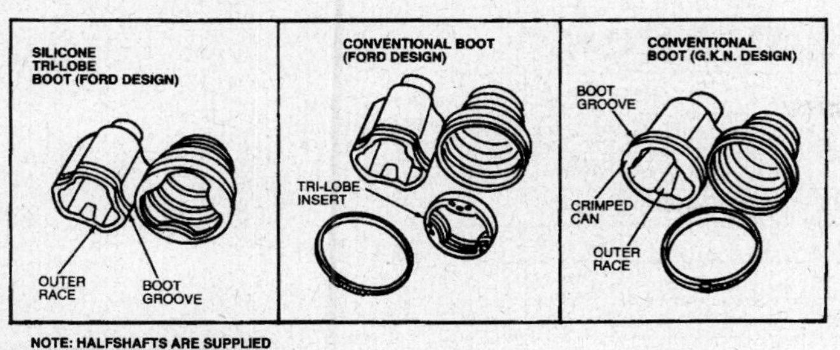

Fig. 15 CV joint & boot types

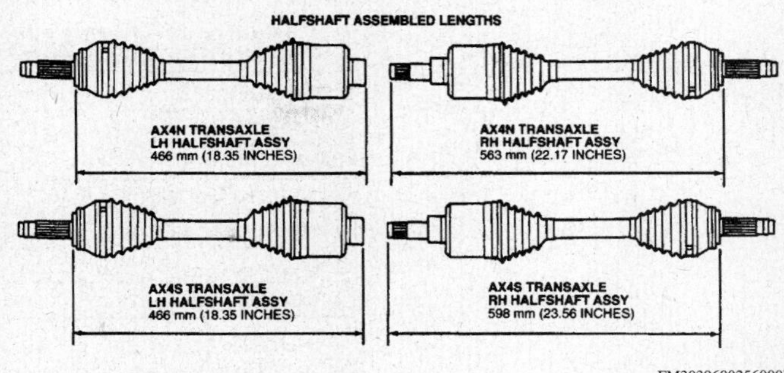

Fig. 16 Driveshaft assembled length

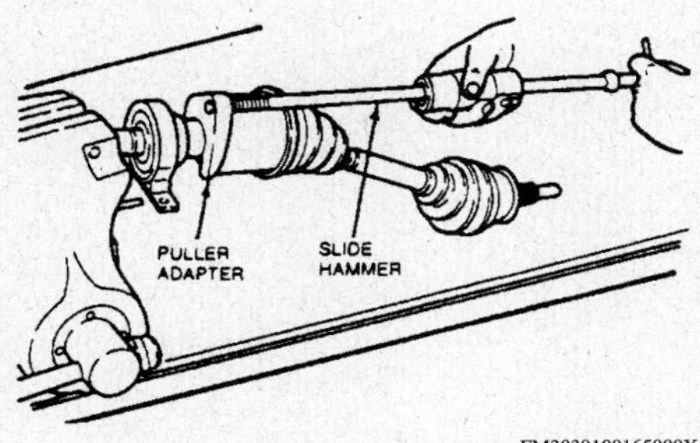

Fig. 17 Linkshaft removal

TIGHTENING SPECIFICATIONS

Component	Torque/Ft. Lbs.
Ball Joint Nut	59
Hub Nut	184②
Knuckle To Strut Bolt & Nut	108①
Lower Suspension Arm Nut	59
Stabilizer Bar Joint Nut	65
Wheel Lug Nut	85

① — Inch lbs.
② — Tighten new hub to specification in one continuous rotation. Stopping will cause nylon lock to set causing incorrect torque readings.

DRIVE AXLES

NOTE: On Air Bag Equipped Models, Refer To "Air Bag System Precautions" Located In The Front Of This Manual For System Disarming & Arming Procedures.

NOTE: Refer To "Computer Relearn Procedures" Located In The Front Of This Manual When Battery Power To The Computer Has Been Interrupted.

INDEX

IDENTIFICATION

REAR AXLE TAG

The plant code shown on the axle identification tag in **Fig. 1** is used to identify the axle assembly. The plant code will not change as long as that particular axle assembly never undergoes an external design change. If an internal design change is made to an axle during its production life and that internal change affects service parts interchangeability, a dash and numerical suffix will be added to the plant code, **Fig. 2.**

Information on axle ratio, differential type and ring gear diameter may also be found on this tag.

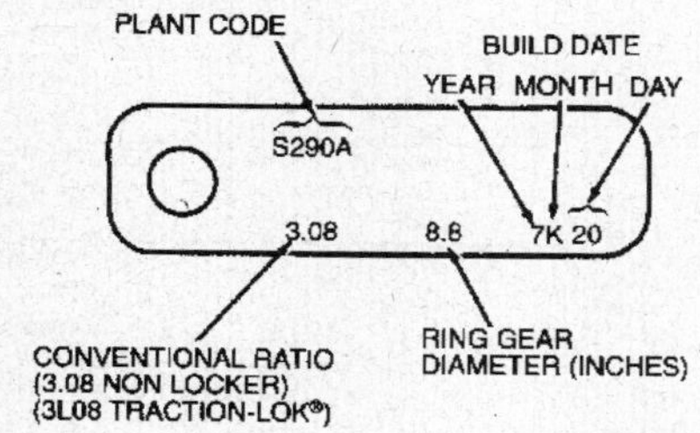

Fig. 1 Rear axle identification tag

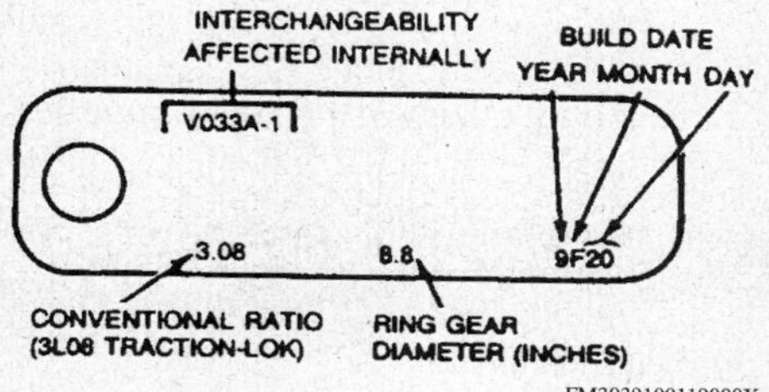

Fig. 2 Internally modified rear axle identification tag

VEHICLE CERTIFICATION LABEL

Information on axle ratio and differential type may be found on the vehicle certification label, which is affixed to the lefthand front door lock panel or door pillar. A code found in the "AX" box on the label will identify the originally installed axle. Refer to **Fig. 3** for axle identification.

TROUBLESHOOTING

Refer to troubleshooting chart, **Fig. 4,** for rear axle symptoms.

AXLE NOISE

NOISE ACCEPTABILITY

Drive axles produce a certain amount of noise, as all gear-driven parts do. Some noise is acceptable and may be audible at certain speeds or under various driving conditions, such as a newly paved blacktop road. The slight noise is in no way detrimental to rear axle operation and may be considered normal.

With Traction-Lok limited slip differential axle, slight chatter noise on slow, tight turns after extended highway driving is considered acceptable and has no detrimental effect on the axle's locking function.

GEAR NOISE

Gear noise is the typical "howling" or "whining" of the ring gear and pinion due to an improper gear pattern, gear damage or improper bearing preload. It can occur at various speeds and driving conditions or it can be continuous.

CHUCKLE

Chuckle is a particular "rattling" noise that sounds like a stick against the spokes of a bicycle wheel. It occurs while decelerating from 40 mph and can be heard all the way to a stop. The frequency varies with the vehicle's speed.

KNOCK

Knock is very similar to chuckle, though it may be louder and occurs on acceleration or deceleration.

CLUNK

Clunk may be a metallic noise heard when the automatic transmission is engaged in Reverse or Drive or it may occur when the throttle is applied or released. It is caused by backlash somewhere in the driveline or loose suspension components.

BEARING WHINE

Bearing whine is a high pitched sound similar to a whistle. It is usually caused by malfunctioning pinion bearings, which are operating at driveshaft speed. Bearing noise occurs at all driving speeds. This distinguishes it from gear whine, which usually comes and goes as speed changes.

Axle Code	Differential T ype	Gear Ratio
8	Conventional	2.73
M	Traction-Lok	2.73
Y	Conventional	3.08
Z	Traction-Lok	3.08
5	Conventional	3.27
E	Traction-Lok	3.27
F	Conventional	3.45
R	Traction-Lok	3.45
2	Conventional	3.55
K	Traction-Lok	3.55
6	Conventional	3.73
W	Traction-Lok	3.73

Fig. 3 Drive axle identification

BEARING RUMBLE

Bearing rumble sounds like marbles being tumbled. This condition is usually caused by a malfunctioning wheel bearing. The lower pitch is because the wheel bearing turns at only about one third of driveshaft speed. In addition, wheel bearing noise may be high pitched, similar to gear noise but will be evident in all four driving modes.

CHATTER ON CORNERING

Chattering noise when cornering is a condition where the whole rear end vibrates only when the vehicle is moving. The vibration is plainly felt as well as heard. In conventional axles, extra differential thrust washers cause a partial lockup condition which creates this chatter. Chatter noise on Traction-Lok axles can usually be traced to erratic movement between adjacent clutch plates and can be corrected with a lubricant change.

CLICK AT ENGAGEMENT

Click at engagement is a condition on axles of a slight noise, distinct from a "clunk" that happens in Reverse or Drive engagement. It can be corrected by installing a slinger between the companion flange and front pinion bearing.

Condition	Possible Sources	Action
• Traction-Lok® does not work in snow, mud or on ice	• Differential.	• CARRY OUT the Traction-Lok® Differential Operation Check REPAIR as necessary.
• Lubricant leaking from the pinion seal or axle shaft oil seals	• Vent.	• CLEAN the axle housing vent.
	• Damage in the seal contact area or dust slinger on the pinion flange dust shield.	• INSTALL new pinion flange and the pinion seal if damage is found.
• Differential side gears/pinion gears are scored	• Insufficient lubrication.	• INSTALL new gears. FILL the axle to specification.
	• Incorrect or contaminated lubricant type.	• INSTALL new gears. CLEAN and REFILL the axle to specification.
• Axle overheating	• Lubricant level too low.	• CHECK the lubricant level. FILL the axle to specification.
	• Incorrect or contaminated lubricant type.	• INSPECT the axle for damage. REPAIR as necessary. CLEAN and REFILL the axle to specification.
	• Bearing preload adjusted too tight.	• CHECK the ring and pinion for damage. INSPECT the ring and pinion wear pattern. ADJUST the preload as necessary.
	• Excessive gear wear.	• INSPECT all the axle gears for wear or damage. INSTALL new components as necessary.
	• Incorrect ring gear backlash.	• INSPECT the ring gear for scoring. INSPECT the ring and pinion wear pattern. ADJUST the ring gear backlash as necessary.
• Broken gear teeth on the ring gear or pinion	• Overloading the vehicle.	• INSTALL a new ring and pinion.
• Axle shaft broken	• Overloading the vehicle.	• INSTALL a new axle shaft.
	• Misaligned axle shaft tube.	• INSPECT the axle for damage. CHECK axle shaft tube alignment. INSTALL a new axle shaft.

FM3030100370000X

Fig. 4 Troubleshooting chart

LEAKAGE CONDITIONS

Most rear axle leakage conditions can be corrected without a teardown. However, it is important to clean the leaking area enough to identify the exact source of the leak.

A plugged or seized jiggle cap vent will cause excessive seal lip wear due to internal pressure buildup. When a leak occurs, inspect cap by pressing down on it with index finger. If the cap moves up and down freely, it is working properly. If it does not move freely, it must be replaced.

Inspect axle lubricant level, which should be 9⁄16 inch below bottom of filler hole.

DRIVE PINION SEAL

If the drive pinion seal leaks, it is usually because of improper installation or because of poor quality of the seal journal surface. Any damage to the seal bore, such as dings, dents and gouges, will distort the seal casing and allow leakage past the outer edge of the seal.

PINION NUT

Some models may experience oil leakage past the threads of the pinion nut. The condition can be corrected by removing the nut and applying pipe sealant with Teflon part No. D8AZ-19554-A, or equivalent, on the pinion threads and nut face. **Ensure the proper procedure for setting the bearing preload is followed when the nut is installed.**

POROUS CASTING

The differential carrier may leak through small pockets in the metal. These pockets (casting leakage) are caused by gas bubbles in the casting process.

Because the axle's sound characteristics may be changed if torn down to replace the carrier, servicing the porosity is preferable. Below are two recommended procedures that may be employed to fix a porous axle:

1. Peen a small amount of body lead into the hole, then seal the pocket with Epoxy Sealer Metallic Plastic part No. C6A7-A9554-A, or equivalent.
2. In larger pockets, drill a shallow hole and tap it for a small setscrew. Install the setscrew and seal it over with Epoxy Sealer Metallic Plastic part No. C6A7-A9554-A, or equivalent.

AXLE VENT

There have been some occurrences of lubricant leaking through the axle vent. This may be caused by a clogged or sticking axle vent cap. If this is the case, the vent assembly should be replaced. Use Stud and Bearing Mount part No. EOAZ-19554-BA, or equivalent, on vent's threads to ensure retention.

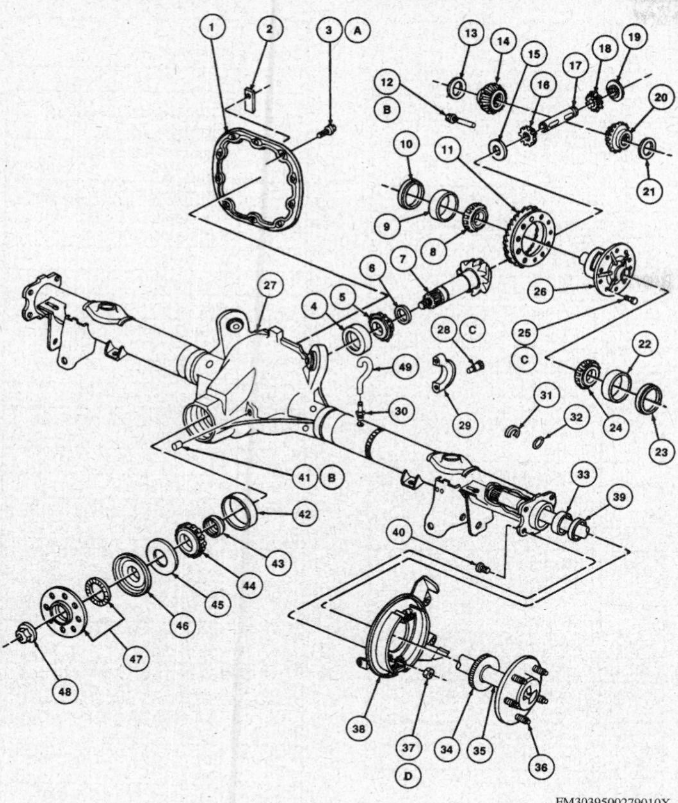

Fig. 5 Exploded view of 8.8 inch rear axles (Part 1 of 2). Crown Victoria, Grand Marquis & Town Car

Item	Description
1	Axle Housing Cover
2	I.D.Tag
3	Axle Housing Cover Bolt
4	Rear Axle Pinion Bearing Cup
5	Differential Pinion Bearing
6	Drive Pinion Bearing Adjustment Shim
7	Drive Pinion (Part of 4209)
8	Differential Bearing (RH)
9	Differential Bearing Cup
10	Differential Bearing Shim
11	Ring Gear (Part of 4209)
12	Differential Pinion Shaft Lock Pin
13	Differential Side Gear Thrust Washer
14	Differential Side Gear
15	Differential Pinion Thrust Washer
16	Differential Pinion Gear
17	Differential Pinion Shaft
18	Differential Pinion Gear
19	Differential Pinion Thrust Washer
20	Differential Side Gear
21	Differential Side Gear Thrust Washer
22	Differential Bearing
23	Differential Bearing Shim
24	Differential Bearing (LH)
25	Rear Axle Differential Gear Case Bolt
26	Differential Case
27	Rear Axle Housing

Item	Description
28	Bolt
29	Differential Bearing Cap (Part of 4010)
30	Rear Axle Housing Vent
31	U-Washer
32	Rear Axle Shaft O-Ring
33	Rear Wheel Bearing
34	Rear Brake Anti-Lock Sensor Indicator
35	Axle Shaft
36	Lug Bolt
37	Nut
38	Rear Wheel Disc Brake Adapter
39	Inner Wheel Bearing Oil Seal
40	Bolt
41	Fill Plug
42	Differential Drive Pinion Bearing Cup
43	Differential Drive Pinion Collapsible Spacer
44	Differential Pinion Bearing
45	Rear Axle Drive Pinion Shaft Oil Slinger
46	Rear Axle Drive Pinion Seal
47	Rear Axle Universal Joint Flange
48	Drive Pinion Nut
49	Formed Vent Hose
A	Tighten to 38-52 N·m (28-38 Lb-Ft)
B	Tighten to 20-41 N·m (15-30 Lb-Ft)
C	Tighten to 95-115 N·m (70-85 Lb-Ft)
D	Tighten to 27-40 N·m (20-30 Lb-Ft)

FM3039500279020X

Fig. 5 Exploded view of 8.8 inch rear axles (Part 2 of 2). Crown Victoria, Grand Marquis & Town Car

VIBRATION CONDITIONS

Few vibration conditions are caused by the axle. Most rear end vibration is caused by the tires or driveline angle.

Vehicles equipped with a Traction-Lok differential will always have both wheels driving. If, while the vehicle is being serviced, only one wheel is raised off the floor and the rear axle is driven by the engine, the wheel on the floor could drive the vehicle off the safety stand. Ensure both rear wheels are raised off the floor.

TIRES

Some vehicles are equipped with directional tires. See tire rotation arrows on tire sidewall. If a directional tire is removed for service, it must be mounted in its original location.

Do not balance the rear wheels and tires while they are mounted on the vehicle. Possible tire disintegration and/or differential failure could result, causing personal injury and/or extensive component damage. Use only an off-vehicle wheel and tire balancer.

A vibration can sometimes be corrected by properly rotating or inflating the tires. The best tires should be placed on the rear to minimize vibration, especially on vehicles with rear coil springs.

DRIVELINE ANGLE

An improper driveline (pinion) angle can often be detected by the driving condition when vibration occurs.

1. A vibration during coasting from 35–45 mph is often caused by a high pinion angle.
2. A vibration during acceleration from 35–45 mph may indicate a lower than specified pinion angle.

TRACTION-LOK DIFFERENTIAL OPERATION INSPECTION

A Traction-Lok differential can be inspected for proper operation without removing it from the axle housing using procedure outlined below:

1. Raise and support one rear wheel, then remove the wheel cover.
2. Install adapter for Traction-Lok differential tool No. T59L-4204-A, or equivalent, then connect a torque wrench of at least a 200 ft. lbs. capacity.
3. Rotate the axle shaft. **Ensure transmission is in Neutral, one wheel is on floor and other rear wheel is raised off floor.**
4. Breakaway torque required to start rotation should be at least 20 ft. lbs. The initial breakaway torque may be higher than continuous turning torque. This is considered normal.
5. Axle shaft should turn with even pressure throughout inspection without slipping or binding. If torque reading is less than specified, inspect differential for improper assembly.

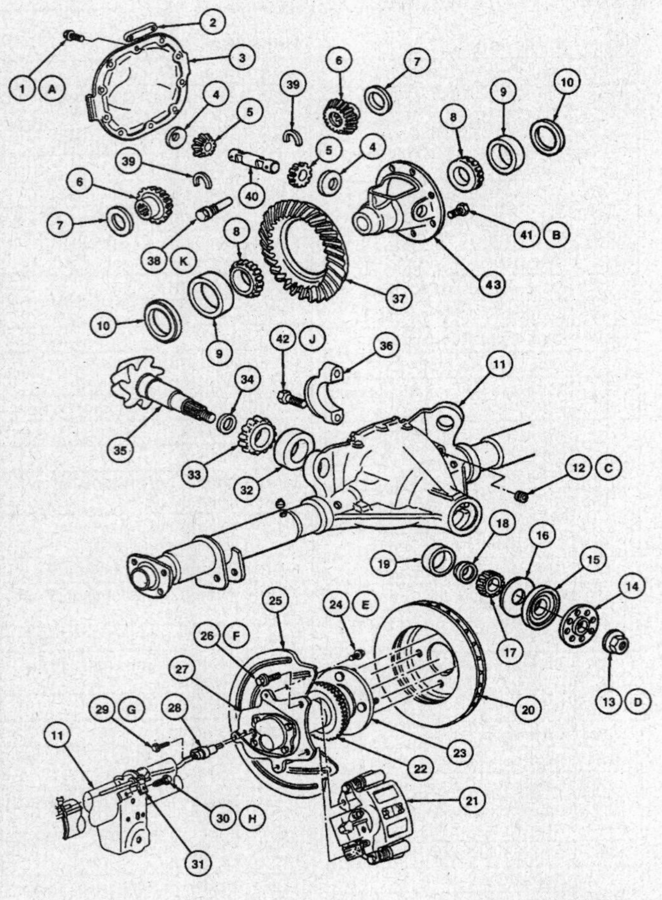

FM3039800326010X

Fig. 6 Exploded view of 7½ & 8.8 inch rear axles (Part 1 of 2). Mustang

Item	Description
1	Axle Housing Cover Bolt
2	Rear Axle Brake Line Clip
3	Axle Housing Cover
4	Differential Pinion Thrust Washer
5	Differential Pinion Gear
6	Differential Side Gear
7	Differential Side Gear Thrust Washer
8	Differential Bearing
9	Differential Bearing Cup
10	Differential Bearing Shim
11	Rear Axle Housing
12	Filler Plug
13	Pinion Nut
14	Rear Axle Universal Joint Flange
15	Rear Axle Drive Pinion Seal
16	Rear Axle Drive Pinion Shaft Oil Slinger
17	Differential Pinion Bearing
18	Differential Drive Pinion Collapsible Spacer
19	Differential Drive Pinion Bearing Cup
20	Rear Disc Brake Rotor
21	Rear Disc Brake Caliper
22	Rear Brake Anti-Lock Sensor Indicator
23	Axle Shaft Flange
24	Bolt (3 Req'd)
25	Rear Wheel Disc Brake Shield
26	Caliper Anchor Bolt
27	Left Hand Rear Disc Brake Adapter
28	Rear Brake Anti-Lock Sensor

Item	Description
29	Bolt
30	Bolt
31	Clip
32	Rear Axle Pinion Bearing Cup
33	Differential Pinion Bearing
34	Drive Pinion Bearing Adjustment Shim
35	Drive Pinion
36	Bearing Cap
37	Ring Gear
38	Differential Pinion Shaft Lock Pin
39	U-Washer
40	Differential Pinion Shaft
41	Rear Axle Differential Gear Case Bolt
42	Bearing Cap Bolt
43	Differential Case
A	Tighten to 38-52 N-m (28-38 Lb-Ft)
B	Tighten to 95-115 N-m (70-84 Lb-Ft)
C	Tighten to 20-41 N-m (15-30 Lb-Ft)
D	Tighten to 190 N-m (140 Lb-Ft)
E	Tighten to 8-12 N-m (70-106 Lb-In)
F	Tighten to 87-119 N-m (65-87 Lb-Ft)
G	Tighten to 4.5-6.8 N-m (40-60 Lb-In)
H	Tighten to 10-14 N-m (89-123 Lb-In)
J	Tighten to 102-122 N-m (76-89 Lb-Ft)
K	Tighten to 20-41 N-m (15-30 Lb-Ft)

FM3039800326020X

Fig. 6 Exploded view of 7½ & 8.8 inch rear axles (Part 2 of 2). Mustang

DISASSEMBLE

CROWN VICTORIA, GRAND MARQUIS, MUSTANG & TOWN CAR

DIFFERENTIAL CASE

1. Raise and support rear of vehicle, then loosen axle housing cover bolts and allow lubricant to drain into suitable container, **Figs. 5 and 6.**
2. Remove axle housing cover, then proceed as follows:
   a. Wipe excess lubricant from inside axle housing, then visually inspect parts for wear and/or damage.
   b. Rotate gears and inspect for roughness, indicating damaged bearings or gears.
   c. Install suitable dial indicator on axle housing cover flange, then inspect and record ring gear back face runout. Maximum back face runout is .004 inch.
3. Remove rear axles and propeller shaft. Refer to "Rear Axle & Suspension" section for procedures.
4. Scribe reference marks on differential bearing caps for assembly reference, then loosen bearing cap bolts. **Observe and record direction the arrows are facing on bearing caps. During installation, arrows must face in same direction.**
5. Using suitable tool, pry differential case, bearing cups and shims out of housing until loose in bearing caps. Remove bearing caps, then differential assembly. Mark which side cups and shims came from for reference during assembly.

DRIVE PINION

1. Scribe reference mark between drive pinion and companion flange. Hold flange with holding tool No. T78P-4851-A, or equivalent, then remove pinion nut and pinion flange.
2. Using suitable soft faced hammer, drive pinion out of front bearing cone and remove from rear of axle housing.
3. Remove oil seal and front bearing cone and roller from pinion housing.
4. Using suitable arbor press and adapters, remove rear pinion bearing.
5. Using suitable micrometer, measure and record thickness of shim which is found under rear bearing cone.
6. Remove pinion bearing cups from pinion housing with suitable brass drift. Install cups using suitable bearing cup installer. Cups are not properly installed if a .015 feeler gauge can be inserted between cup and bottom of bore at any point around the cup. **If any bearing cups are replaced, the respective cone and roller must also be replaced.**

LS & THUNDERBIRD

Extreme care must be taken not to damage aluminum rear axle housing while carrying out these procedures.

1. Remove differential housing cover.
2. Install dial indicator with bracketry tool No. 4201-G, or equivalent.
3. Measure and record ring gear runout, **Fig. 7.**
4. Attach housing spreader adapters tool No. T93P-4000-A, or equivalent, to rear axle housing with four cover bolts.
5. Attach housing spreader adapters to holding fixture tool No. T57L-500-B, or equivalent, with two ⅜ inch x 1-½ inch bolts.
6. Install differential carrier spreader tool No. T4000-E, or equivalent, onto housing spreader adapters with spreader pins aligned with housing spreader adapters holes.
7. **On models equipped with aluminum axle,** proceed as follows:
   a. Install dial indicator tool and attach

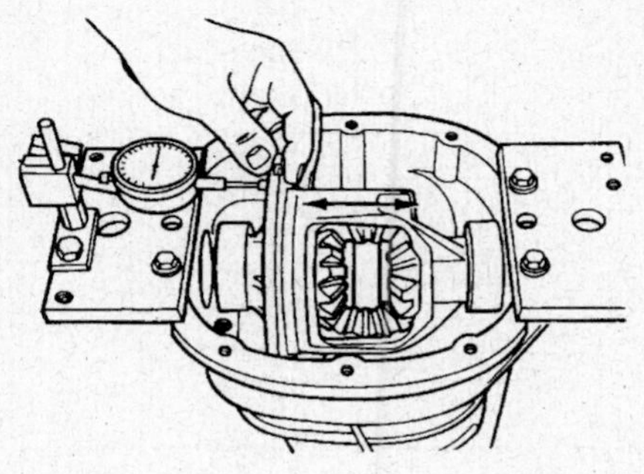

FM3039300268000X

Fig. 7 Differential case end play measurement

clutch housing alignment adapter tool No. T75L-4201-A, or equivalent to dial indicator with tip positioned in spreader adapter hole.

b. Tighten and loosen housing spreader adapter screw to normalize housing spreader adapters prior to final dial indicator reading. **Overspreading can damage rear axle housing.**
c. Adjust dial indicator to zero and tighten housing spreader screw until rear axle housing is spread to .030 inch. Remove dial indicator.

8. **On models equipped with nodular iron axle,** housing spreader adapters are used to give the rear axle housing stability. **Do not spread rear axle housing.**
9. **On all models,** mark position of bearing caps as arrows may not be visible. Bearing caps must be installed in their identical locations and positions.
10. Remove retaining bolts and bearing caps.
11. **On models equipped with aluminum axle,** proceed as follows:
    a. Position wood blocks on top and bottom of differential. **Wood blocks must be used to avoid rear axle housing damage.**
    b. Pry differential case and differential bearing shims out of rear axle housing, **Fig. 8.**
    c. Remove special tool.
12. **On models equipped with nodular iron axle,** remove differential case.
13. **On all models,** remove 10 ring gear bolts.
14. Insert suitable punch in bolt holes and drive ring gear off. **Do not damage bolt hole threads.**
15. Remove differential bearing using two-jaw puller tool No. D97L-4221-A and step plate tool No. D83T-4205-C2, or equivalents.
16. Repeat procedure on other side.
17. Remove differential lock bolt, pinion shaft, gears and side gears.
18. Install suitable torque wrench on pinion nut and record torque necessary to maintain rotation of drive pinion gear through several revolutions.
19. Install flange holding tool No. 205-478, or equivalent. **Ensure to insert cotter key in special tool.**
20. Remove pinion nut using suitable breaker bar. **After removing pinion nut, discard it. Use new nut for installation.**
21. Mark pinion flange in relation to drive pinion stem to ensure correct alignment during assembly.
22. Remove pinion flange using flange remover tool No. 307-408I, or equivalent.
23. Install pinion thread protector tool No. 205-460, or equivalent.
24. Drive pinion out of front bearing cone using suitable soft-faced hammer and remove it through rear of housing.
25. Remove rear axle drive pinion shaft oil slinger, rear axle drive pinion seal and collapsible spacer.
26. Position pinion bearing cone remover tool No. T71P-4621-B, or equivalent, under pinion bearing.
27. Remove pinion bearing using suitable press.
28. Remove front pinion bearing.
29. Measure and record thickness of drive pinion bearing adjustment shim found under differential pinion bearing.
30. Remove drive pinion bearing adjustment shim.
31. If required, remove damaged rear axle pinion bearing cups from rear axle housing using pinion outer bearing cup remover tool No. 205-482 and pinion inner bearing cup remover tool No. 205-481, or equivalents.

MARK VIII

DIFFERENTIAL CASE

1. Remove rear axle assembly as outlined under "Rear Axle & Suspension" section, then remove axle cover, **Fig. 9.**
2. Place axle carrier in holding fixture tool No. T57L-500-B, or equivalent, with housing spreader adapters tool No. T93P-4000-A and dial indicator base tool No. D78P-4201-F, or equivalents, attached.
3. Install carrier spreader tool No. T4000-E, or equivalent, to spreader adapters, then install a suitable dial gauge and brackets as shown in **Fig. 10.**
4. Zero dial gauge, then spread differential carrier .030 inch.
5. Mark differential bearing caps righthand and lefthand, noting direction of arrows cast into bearing caps.
6. Place wood blocks into differential carrier, **Fig. 8,** then pry differential case out of housing. **Wood blocks must be used to prevent damage to carrier.**
7. Place differential case into a suitable soft jaw vice, then remove ring gear bolts.
8. Use a suitable drift punch to tap ring gear from case.

DRIVE PINION

1. Remove differential case as outlined under "Differential Case Assembly."
2. If pinion shaft is to be used again, place match marks on shaft and companion flange. Use companion flange holding tool No. T78P-4851-A, or equivalent, to loosen, but not remove, pinion nut.
3. Using a suitable puller, pull companion flange loose from splines, then remove

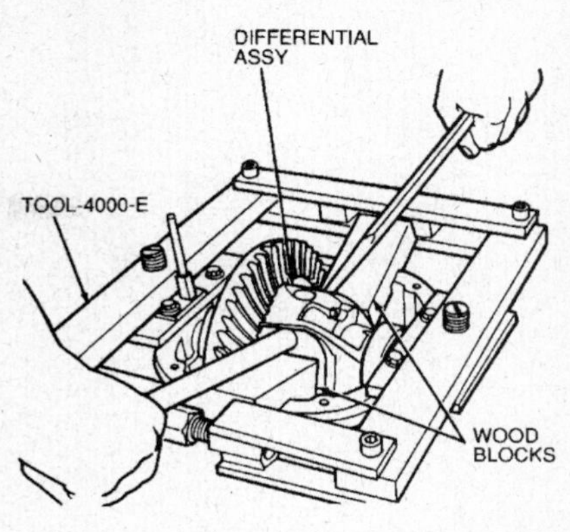

FM3039300266000X

Fig. 8 Differential case removal

flange and nut from pinion shaft.

4. Use a soft face hammer to tap pinion shaft from differential carrier.

SUBASSEMBLY SERVICE

CONVENTIONAL DIFFERENTIAL

CROWN VICTORIA, GRAND MARQUIS, MUSTANG & TOWN CAR

Differential Case Bearings

1. If differential bearings are to be replaced, remove and replace with suitable puller.
2. If ring gear backlash measured during removal exceeded .015 inch, proceed as follows:
    a. Install differential bearing cups on cones, then install differential case in rear housing with drive pinion removed.
    b. Install a .265 inch shim on lefthand side of case, then install bearing cap and tighten bolts finger-tight. Install progressively larger shims on righthand side of case until the largest shim selected can be installed with a slight drag. Install bearing cap and **torque** bolts to 70–85 ft. lbs.
3. Rotate differential several turns in either direction to ensure free rotation and to seat bearings.
4. Mount suitable dial indicator to axle housing, then inspect ring gear back face runout. Ring gear back face runout should be within .004 inch. If ring gear back face runout is within specifications, the original reading was caused by insufficient differential bearing preload. If ring gear back face runout is still not within specifications, proceed as follows:
    a. Inspect differential case runout, which should be within .004 inch.
    b. If runout is within specifications, ring gear is out of specifications and should be replaced.
    c. If runout is not within specifications,

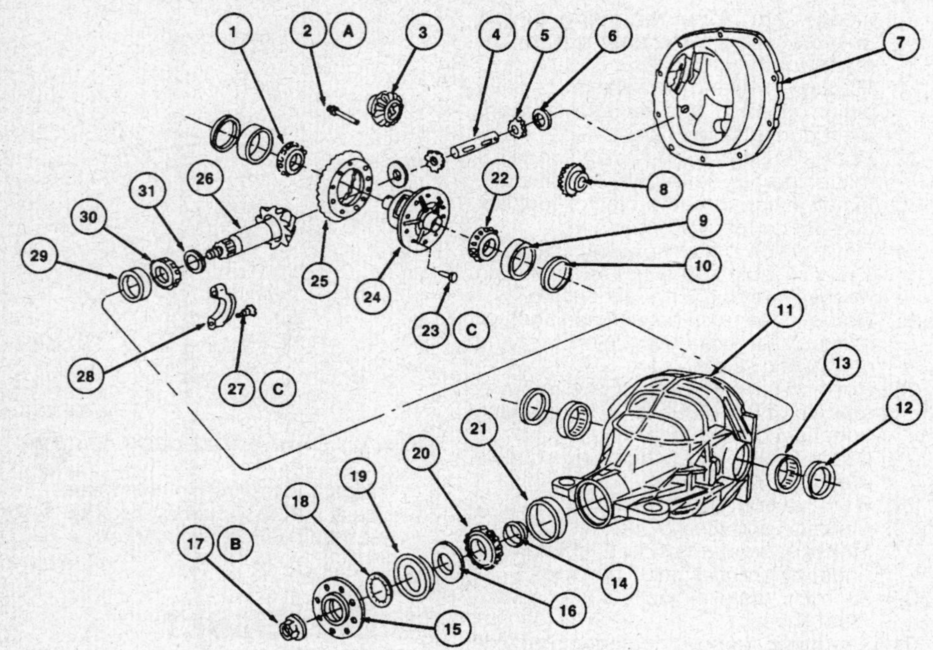

Item	Description
1	Differential Bearing (RH)
2	Differential Pinion Shaft Lock Pin
3	Differential Side Gear (RH)
4	Differential Pinion Shaft
5	Differential Pinion Gear
6	Differential Pinion Thrust Washer
7	Axle Housing Cover
8	Differential Side Gear (LH)
9	Differential Bearing Cup
10	Differential Bearing Shim
11	Rear Axle Housing
12	Inboard Cv Joint Stub Shaft Pilot Bearing Housing Seal
13	Pilot Bearing
14	Differential Drive Pinion Collapsible Spacer
15	Rear Axle Universal Joint Flange
16	Rear Axle Drive Pinion Shaft Oil Slinger
17	Pinion Nut

Item	Description
18	Drive Pinion Oil Seal Deflector
19	Rear Axle Drive Pinion Seal
20	Differential Pinion Bearing
21	Differential Drive Pinion Bearing Cup
22	Differential Bearing (LH)
23	Rear Axle Differential Gear Case Bolt
24	Differential Case
25	Ring Gear (Part of 4209)
26	Pinion (Part of 4209)
27	Bolt
28	Rear Axle Housing)
29	Rear Axle Pinion Bearing Cup
30	Differential Pinion Bearing
31	Drive Pinion Bearing Adjustment Shim
A	Tighten to 20-41 N·m(15-30 Lb-Ft)
B	Tighten to 190 N·m (140 Lb-Ft)
C	Tighten to 95-115 N·m (70-85 Lb-Ft)

FM3039500280000X

Fig. 9 Exploded view of 7 1/2 & 8.8 inch rear axles. Mark VIII

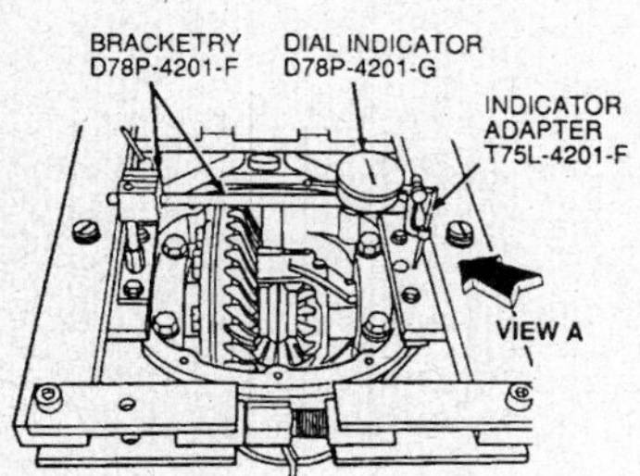

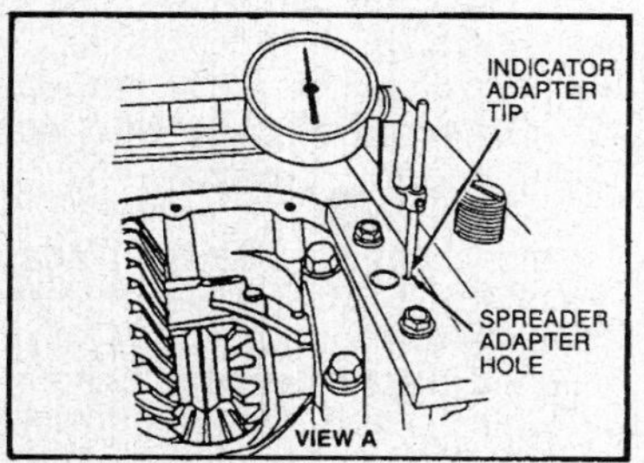

FM3039300265000X

Fig. 10 Differential carrier spreading

the differential case is damaged and should be replaced.

5. Remove differential case from axle housing, then remove ring gear. Install differential case less ring gear in housing following procedures given above.
6. Inspect differential case runout. Runout should be within .004 inch. If runout is within specifications, ring gear is out of specifications and should be replaced. If runout is not within specifications, the differential case is damaged and should be replaced.

Drive Pinion Depth Determination

Prior to determining drive pinion depth, clean pinion bearing cups and differential bearing pedestals thoroughly to ensure an accurate reading. Apply only a light oil film to bearing assemblies to avoid false readings.

1. Assemble aligning adapter, gauge disc and gauge block to tool No. T79P-4020-A, or equivalent, **Fig. 11.**
2. Place rear pinion bearing over aligning adapter, then insert tool and bearing in rear pinion bearing cup in pinion housing bore. Place front pinion bearing over screw in front pinion bearing cup and assemble tool handle onto screw. **Torque** handle to 20 inch lbs. Ensure tool is mounted securely between front and rear bearings.
3. Rotate gauge block several half turns to ensure bearings are seated properly. Rotational torque should be 20 inch lbs. with new bearings. Set gauge block at an angle approximately 45° from horizontal, **Fig. 12.**
4. Install gauge tube in differential bearing mounts, then install bearing caps and bearing cap bolts.
5. Use pinion shims to determine pinion depth by inserting shims between gauge block and gauge tube. The proper shim will fit with a slight drag. Do not attempt to force a shim between block and tube. **Do not use shims that are bent, dirty, nicked or mutilated as a gauge.**
6. Make note of proper shim size and remove tool from axle housing.
7. Using suitable arbor press and adapters, remove rear pinion bearing.
8. Install shim determined in previous step on pinion shaft, then install bearing using arbor press. **The rear pinion bearing used to determine drive pinion depth must be used in the final assembly of the axle.**

Drive Pinion Installation

1. Lubricate pinion bearings with suitable axle lubricant, then install pinion shaft and rear bearing, collapsible spacer and front bearing.
2. Install slinger (if equipped) and pinion oil seal, then insert pinion flange in seal and hold firmly in place against front bearing. From rear of housing, insert pinion shaft into flange.
3. Install pinion (yoke) nut. While holding pinion flange, tighten nut only enough to remove bearing endplay. When an increase in pinion nut turning effort is noted, stop tightening pinion nut. Rotate pinion several times in both directions to seat bearings.
4. Continue to tighten pinion nut in very small increments, then, occasionally, using suitable torque wrench, measure pinion rotational torque. The rotating torque must not exceed 20 inch lbs. **Do not exceed specified preload**

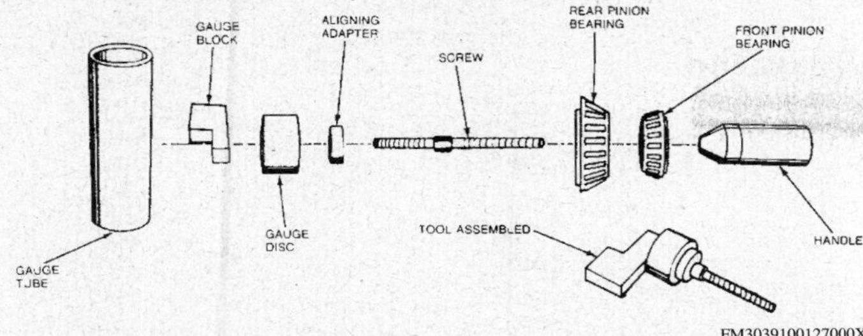

Fig. 11 Rear axle pinion depth gauge

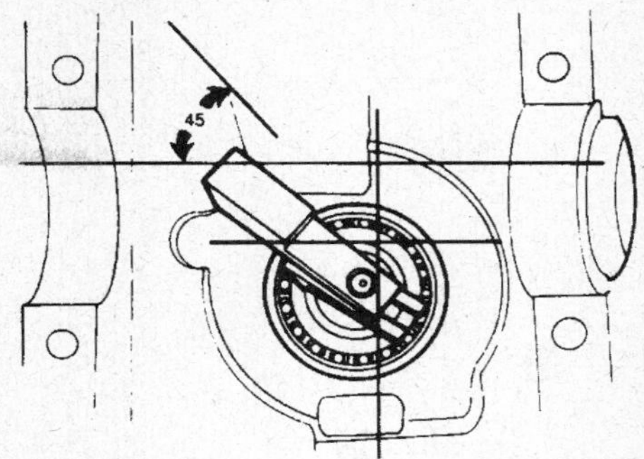

Fig. 12 Pinion depth gauge block installation

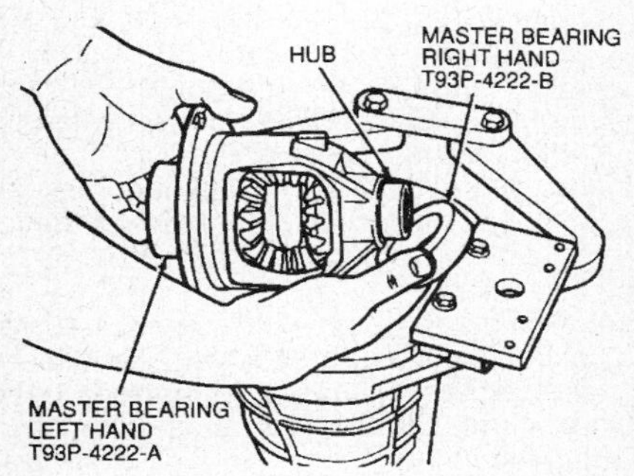

Fig. 13 Master bearing onto differential case installation

torque. Do not loosen pinion nut if preload torque is exceeded. If preload torque is exceeded, remove pinion nut, yoke, oil seal, slinger (if equipped) and collapsible spacer. Replace collapsible spacer and oil seal with new ones and repeat procedure.

LS & THUNDERBIRD

Take extreme care not to damage aluminum rear axle housing while carrying out these procedures.

1. Lubricate differential side gear thrust washers with Premium Long-Life Grease XG-1-C, or equivalent, prior to installation.
2. Install differential side gears in differential case.
3. Lubricate differential pinion thrust washers with Premium Long-Life Grease XG-1-C, or equivalent, prior to installation.
4. Install differential pinion gears with differential pinion thrust washers in differential case.
5. If new pinion shaft lock bolt is unavailable, coat threads with Threadlock and Sealer EOAZ-19554-AA, or equivalent, prior to installation.
6. Install differential pinion shaft and new differential pinion shaft lock bolt.
7. Install differential bearing on differential case using differential side bearing replacer tool No. T57L-4221-A2, or equivalent. Repeat for other side.
8. Start two of ring gear bolts through differential case and into ring gear to ensure ring gear bolt holes align with differential case bolt holes correctly then press ring gear on differential case.
9. Install the ring gear bolts. Apply Stud and Bearing Mount EOAZ-19554-BA, or equivalent, to bolts.
10. With pinion removed, place differential case/gear subassembly with differential bearing and rear axle pinion bearing cups in rear axle housing.
11. Install differential bearing shim of thickness shown on lefthand side of differential case.
12. Install lefthand bearing cap finger-tight.
13. Apply pressure toward lefthand side to fully seat differential bearing cup.
14. Install progressively larger differential bearing shims on righthand side until largest differential bearing shim selected can be assembled with slight drag feel.
15. Install righthand bearing cap and **torque** bearing caps to 77 ft. lbs.
16. Rotate differential assembly to ensure it rotates freely.
17. Install dial indicator with bracketry tool No. T4201-C, or equivalent.
18. Measure and record ring gear runout, **Fig. 7.**
19. If runout is .003 inch, original out-of-specification runout was caused by insufficient bearing preload.
20. If runout is more than .003 inch, proceed as follows:
    a. Remove differential case.
    b. Remove ring gear.
    c. Install differential case without ring gear.
    d. Rotate differential case to correctly seat differential bearings.
    e. Measure differential case flange runout using dial indicator.
    f. If runout is .003 inch, install new ring gear and pinion.
    g. If runout is more than .003 inch, ring gear is true and concern is due to either damaged differential case or differential bearings.
    h. Inspect differential bearings.
    i. If differential bearings are not damaged, install new differential case and differential bearings.
    j. Measure runout with new differential case and differential bearings.
21. Install new inner rear axle pinion bearing cup in rear axle housing using pinion inner bearing cup tool No. 205-480 and cup replacer tool No. T71P-4616-A, or equivalents.
22. Install new outer rear axle pinion bearing cup in rear axle housing using cup replacer tools.
23. Coat new rear axle pinion bearing cup with SAE 5W-30 Super Premium Motor Oil XO-5W30-QSP, or equivalent.
24. Position rear axle pinion bearing cup on handle tool No. T76P-4020-A11, screw tool No. T76P-4020-A9, pinion depth gauge aligner tool No. 205-477, pinion depth gauge disc tool No. 205-476, and gauge block tool No. T76P-4020-A10, or equivalent, **Fig. 11.**
25. Position bearing cup replacer in rear axle housing and tighten special tool to fully seat rear axle pinion bearing cup in bore.
26. Apply light film of SAE 75W140 Synthetic Rear Axle Lubricant F1TZ-19580-B, or equivalent, on front differential pinion bearing and rear differential pinion bearing assemblies.
27. Thread handle onto screw and torque to 20 inch lbs.
28. Rotate gauge block tool several half turns to correctly seat the pinion bearings, **Fig. 12. Gauge block tool must be offset to obtain an accurate reading.**
29. Position gauge tube tool No. T93P-4020-A, or equivalent, on differential bearing seat of rear axle housing.
30. Install differential bearing caps and cap bolts. Torque cap bolts to 77 ft. lbs.
31. Slight drag should be felt for correct shim selection. Remove special tool.
32. Same pinion bearings and drive pinion bearing adjustment shim used in drive pinion shim selection procedure must be used in final axle assembly.
33. Position drive pinion bearing adjustment shim, pinion bearing, and bearing/seal service plate tool No. T75L-1165-B and universal bearing puller tool No. T53T-4621-C, or equivalents, on pinion stem.
34. Firmly seat drive pinion bearing adjustment shim and pinion bearing on pinion stem using suitable press.
35. Install front pinion bearing, rear axle drive pinion shaft oil slinger and rear axle drive pinion seal.
36. Ensure pinion stem splines are free of burrs. If burrs are evident, remove using fine crocus cloth, work in rotational motion.
37. Install new drive pinion collapsible spacer on pinion stem against pinion stem shoulder.
38. Install drive pinion and drive pinion collapsible spacer into rear axle housing.

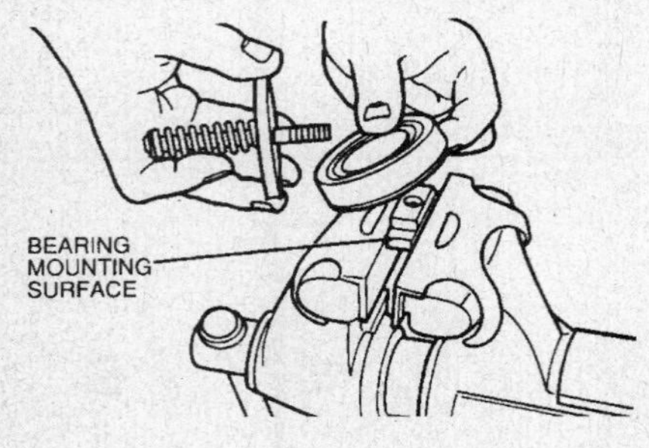

Fig. 14 Differential case bearing thickness measurement

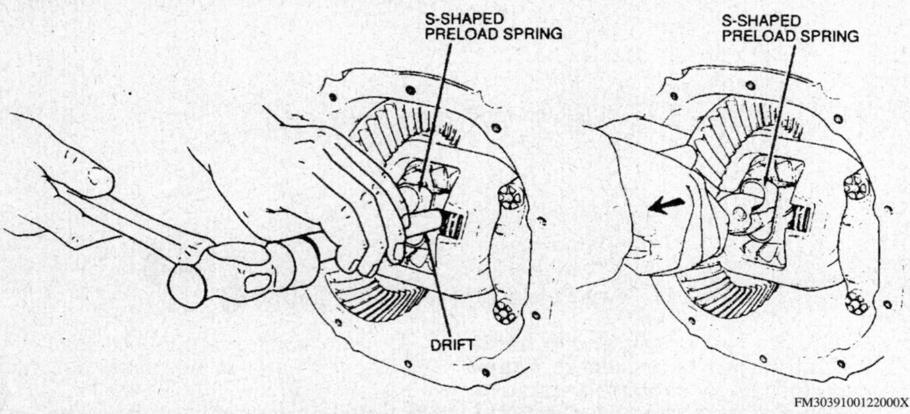

Fig. 15 C-clips "S" shaped preload spring removal. Traction-Lok

39. Master bearings are marked LH and RH.
40. Remove differential bearings and install right master bearing tool No. T93P-4222-B and left master bearing tool No. T93P-4222-A, or equivalents, on differential case.
41. Lubricate rear axle pinion flange splines using SAE 75W140 Synthetic Rear Axle Lubricant F1TZ-19580-B, or equivalent.
42. Align rear axle pinion flange with drive pinion shaft and install rear axle pinion flange. Disregard scribe marks if new rear axle pinion flange is being installed.
43. With drive pinion in place in rear axle housing, install rear axle pinion flange using pinion flange installer tool No. 205-479 and flange holding tool No. 205-478, or equivalents.
44. Tighten pinion nut using flange holding tool No. 205-478, or equivalent. **Ensure to insert cotter key in special tool.**
45. Rotate pinion occasionally to ensure differential pinion bearings seat correctly.
46. Take frequent differential pinion bearing torque preload readings by rotating pinion with suitable torque wrench. Preload **torque** should be 8–10 inch lbs. with used bearings or 16–28 inch lbs. with new bearings.
47. **Do not under any circumstance loosen pinion nut to reduce preload. If it is necessary to reduce preload, install new collapsible spacer and pinion nut.**
48. **On models equipped with aluminum axle,** proceed as follows:
    a. Place differential case and dial indicator into rear axle housing. Position dial indicator on outside mounting hole.
    b. Attach dial indicator with indicator tip positioned on machined surface of differential case flange.
    c. Move differential case to left and right as far as possible.
    d. Repeat this procedure until consistent reading is obtained.
    e. Record reading.
    f. Remove special tool and differential case from rear axle housing.

MARK VIII

Differential Case Bearings

Pinion depth and bearing preload must be determined as outlined under "Pinion Shaft Bearings," before performing this operation. The pinion must be properly installed into the carrier.

1. If differential bearings are to be replaced, remove from differential case with suitable puller.
2. Place righthand and lefthand master bearings onto differential case, **Fig. 13.**
3. Install differential case with master bearings into carrier.
4. Install a suitable dial gauge, then measure total end play **Fig. 7. Record this measurement as dimension A.**
5. Remove differential case from carrier and place in a suitable fixture or soft jaw vice for ring gear installation.
6. Use a suitable fine flat file to remove burrs on mounting surface of ring gear and differential case.
7. Place ring gear into position on differential case, then loosely install three bolts to position ring gear to differential case.
8. Place differential case with ring gear in a suitable press fixture, then press ring gear onto differential case.
9. Install remaining ring gear bolts, then **torque** bolts to 70–85 ft. lbs.
10. Place differential case, with ring gear and master bearings installed, into carrier.
11. Install a suitable dial gauge, then measure total end play between ring gear and pinion gear. **Record this measurement as dimension B.**
12. Subtract dimension B from dimension A to determine dimension C.
13. Determine thickness of new differential case bearings and their required shims as follows:
    a. Mark new bearings as righthand and lefthand.
    b. Assemble new righthand bearing into bearing preload tool No. T93P-4220-A, or equivalent, **Fig. 14,** then **torque** preload tool to 25 ft. lbs.
    c. Using a suitable depth micrometer, measure thickness of bearing. **Record this dimension as D, righthand side.**
    d. Repeat above procedure on lefthand bearing. **Record this dimension as D, lefthand side.**
14. Determine thickness of righthand bearing shim as follows:
    a. Subtract dimension D righthand side from master bearing standard thickness of .8695. **Record this measurement as dimension E, righthand side.**
    b. Add dimension E, righthand side, dimension C and preload standard of .0200. Result is righthand shim initial thickness.
    c. Round off initial shim thickness to nearest available shim thickness for final righthand side shim size.
15. Determine thickness of lefthand bearing shim as follows:
    a. Subtract dimension D, lefthand side from master bearing standard thickness of .8695. **Record this measurement as dimension E, lefthand side.**
    b. Add dimension E, lefthand side to dimension B, then subtract backlash standard of .006 to determine lefthand shim initial thickness.
    c. Round off initial shim thickness to nearest available shim thickness for final righthand side shim size.
16. Mark lefthand and righthand shims for later assembly.
17. Place righthand and lefthand differential case bearings onto their proper positions, then using a suitable press seat bearings onto differential case.

Drive Pinion Depth Determination

Refer to "Crown Victoria, Grand Marquis, Mustang & Town Car."

Drive Pinion Installation

Refer to "Crown Victoria, Grand Marquis, Mustang & Town Car."

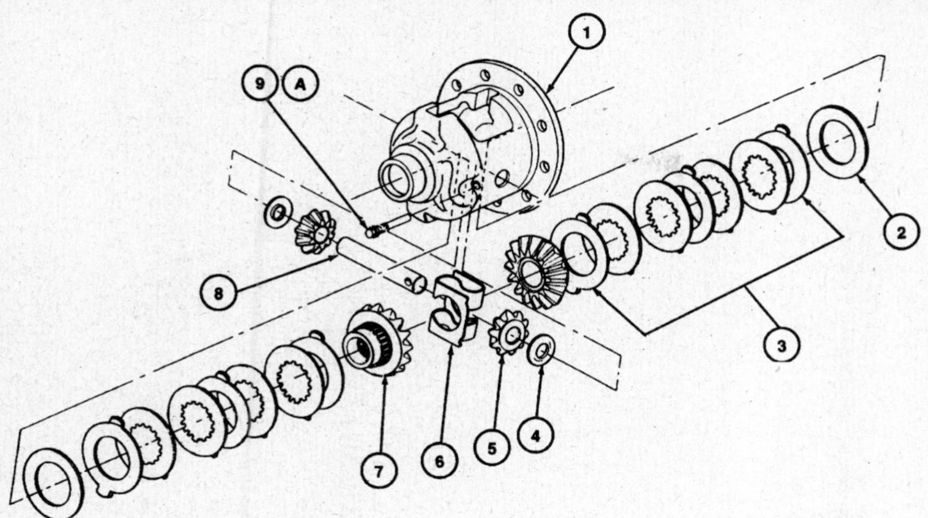

Item	Description
1	Differential Case
2	Rear Axle Differential Clutch Shim
3	Differential Clutch Pack
4	Differential Pinion Thrust Washer
5	Differential Pinion Gear

Item	Description
6	Differential Clutch Spring
7	Differential Side Gear
8	Differential Pinion Shaft
9	Differential Pinion Shaft Lock Pin
A	Tighten to 20-41 N·m (15-30 Lb-Ft)

FM3039100123000A

Fig. 16 Exploded view of Traction-Lok

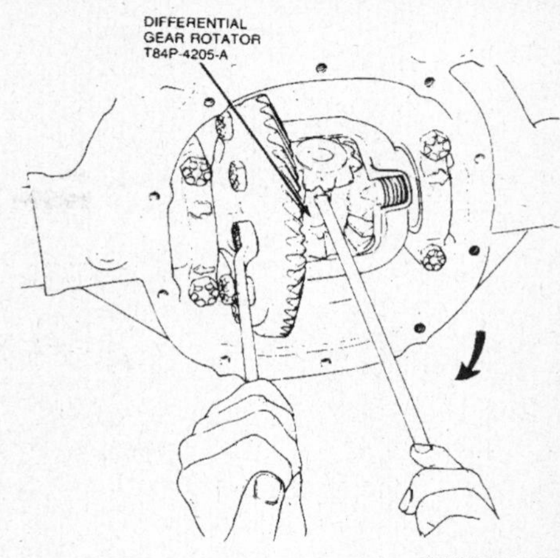

Fig. 17 Pinion gear removal & installation. Traction-Lok

TRACTION-LOK LIMITED SLIP DIFFERENTIAL

For differential case and ring gear runout inspections and differential bearing replacement, refer to "Except Traction-Lok Limited Slip Differential."

1. Remove and discard ring gear to differential case attaching bolts.
2. Tap on ring gear using a suitable mallet and remove ring gear from case.
3. Remove pinion shaft lock screw and pinion shaft.
4. Remove preloaded "S" shaped spring, **Fig. 15. Use caution when removing "S" shaped spring, since it is under tension.**
5. Rotate pinion gears and thrust washers using 12 inch socket extension inserted into pinion gear rotator tool No. T80P-4205-A, or equivalent, until they can be removed through access hole.
6. Remove lefthand and righthand side gears, clutch packs and shims, **Fig. 16.** Note order of removal and side removed from and tag for reference during assembly.
7. Apply suitable lubricant to clutch plates, then install lefthand side gear, clutch pack and new shim into differential case. Repeat procedure for righthand hand side.
8. Install pinion gears and thrust washers 180° apart and in contact with side gears.
9. Align gears with pinion shaft bore, **Fig. 17,** using 12-inch socket extension inserted in pinion shaft rotator.
10. Install "S" shaped preload spring into differential using soft faced hammer.

CLEANING & INSPECTION

CONVENTIONAL DIFFERENTIAL

Clean all parts in suitable solvent. Dry all parts except bearings with compressed air or shop towels. Allow bearings to air dry or use shop towels. Do not use compressed air to dry bearings as damage may result.

Inspect differential bearings and cups for wear, pitting, galling, flat spots or cracks. Any bearing or cup showing any signs of wear or damage must be replaced. Bearings and respective cups must be replaced as an assembly only. Do not attempt to interchange bearings and cups as bearing life will be affected.

Inspect non-machined differential case surfaces for nicks and burrs which can be removed with an oil stone or fine tooth file. Inspect pinion shaft bore to ensure it is not elongated or worn. If damage is evident, differential case must be replaced. Inspect machined differential surfaces and counterbores. They must be smooth and free of nicks, gouges, cracks and other visible damage. If damage is evident, differential case must be replaced.

Inspect pinion shaft for excessive wear, scoring or galling. Ensure shaft is smooth and concentric. If any wear or damage is evident, replace the shaft. Inspect pinion shaft lockpin for damage and to ensure it has a snug fit in the differential case. Replace lockpin or case as necessary.

Inspect pinion and ring gears for worn or chipped teeth, cracks, damaged bearing journals or attaching bolt threads. If any of the above are evident, replace ring gear and pinion as a matched set.

Inspect pinion and side gears. Gears must exhibit a uniform contact pattern without any signs of cracks, wear, scoring or galling. If any of the above are evident, replace all the gears. Inspect thrust washers for wear and replace as necessary.

Inspect pinion and ring gears for worn or chipped teeth, cracks, damaged bearing journals or attaching bolt threads. If any of the above are evident, replace ring gear and pinion as a matched set.

Inspect axle shaft C-locks (if equipped) for signs of cracks or wear and replace as necessary.

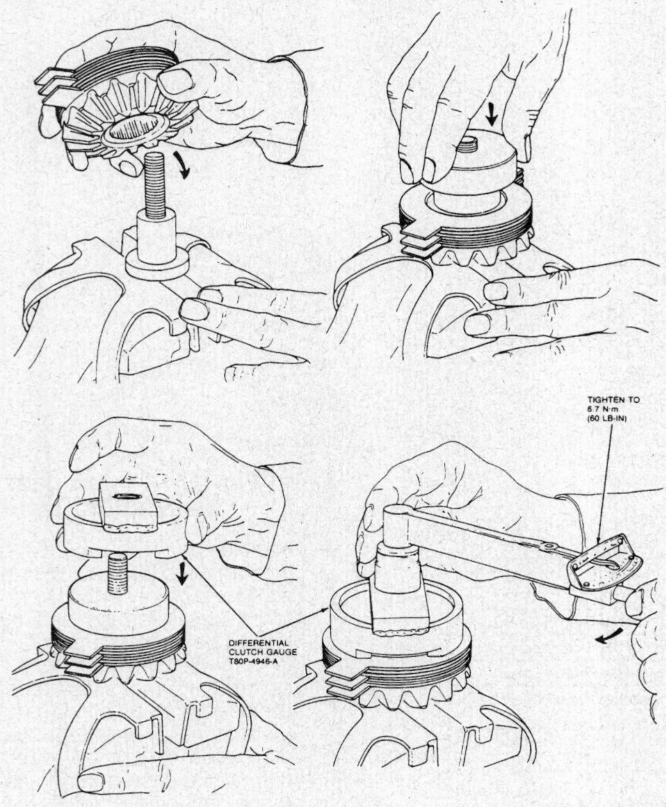

FM3039100124000X

Fig. 18 Shim thickness measuring. Traction-Lok

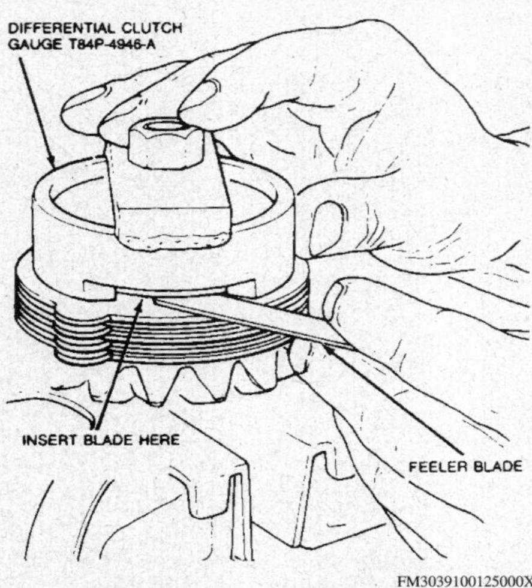

FM3039100125000X

Fig. 19 Shim thickness measurement using tool No. T80P-4946-A, or equivalent. Traction-Lok

TRACTION-LOK LIMITED SLIP DIFFERENTIAL

The cleaning and inspection of these units is the same as for conventional differentials except that cleaning solvent should not be allowed to contact the clutch plates. The clutch plates should be wiped clean only. In addition, the following steps should be performed which only apply to the Traction-Lok differential.

Visually inspect clutch packs, side gears, pinion gears and pinion shaft for damage or wear and replace as necessary.

Place each clutch pack without shims into tool No. T80P-4946-A, or equivalent, **Fig. 18. Torque** nut to 5 ft. lbs. Using feeler gauge, determine thickness of new shims by inserting thickest blade possible between clutch pack and tool, **Fig. 19,** then note size for use during assembly.

ASSEMBLE

CROWN VICTORIA, GRAND MARQUIS, MUSTANG & TOWN CAR

1. Install replacement ring gear (if removed). Apply suitable locking compound to new bolts and **torque** to 70–85 ft. lbs.
2. Apply suitable axle lubricant to differential bearing bores.
3. Place differential bearing cups on bearings, then set differential assembly in axle housing. **If ring gear and pinion gear have punch marks, assemble ring gear in carrier so marked tooth on pinion is indexed between the marked teeth of ring gear.**
4. Inspect and adjust backlash as follows:
   a. Mount suitable dial indicator on axle housing cover flange, then measure ring gear backlash. If backlash is within specifications, **Fig. 20,** proceed to step f. If backlash is not within specifications, proceed to step c. If backlash is zero, proceed to step b.
   b. If backlash measured above is zero, add .020 inch (.5 mm) to righthand side of case and subtract .020 inch (.5 mm) from lefthand side of case, then inspect backlash again. If backlash now ranges within specifications, proceed to step d.
   c. If backlash is not within specifications, correct by increasing thickness of one shim and decreasing thickness on the other shim by the same amount. Refer to **Fig. 21,** for approximate shim change.
   d. Install shims and bearing caps. **Torque** bearing cap bolts to 70–85 ft. lbs., then rotate differential case assembly several turns in both directions.
   e. Inspect backlash. If backlash is within specifications, proceed to step f. If not within specifications, repeat step c.
   f. Increase both lefthand and righthand side shims by .006 inch to provide proper differential bearing preload. Ensure shims are fully seated and the case assembly turns freely.
   g. Using suitable white marking compound applied to ring gear, inspect tooth mesh contacting pattern. **Tooth mesh contacting pattern can be improved by installing the propeller shaft and axle assemblies and rotating both tires in the drive and coast direction.**
   h. Contacting pattern should be within the primary area of the ring gear tooth surface avoiding narrow contact with the outer perimeter of tooth. Inspect pattern on the drive (pull) side of the ring gear. If serious error is determined, inspect pinion shim selection.
5. Install axle housing cover, driveshaft and axle assemblies.
6. Fill rear axle assembly with axle lubricant recommended by manufacturer. **On models equipped with 7½ inch Traction-Lok differential,** subtract 3 ounces of axle lubricant and replace with 3 ounces of Friction Modifier part No. C8AZ-19546-A, or equivalent.

LS & THUNDERBIRD

ALUMINUM

1. Draw-file differential ring gear mounting surface to remove any nicks or burrs.
2. Place ring gear onto differential case, then hand start three bolts to align ring gear holes and differential case.
3. Place differential case and ring gear onto press bed blocks with ring gear teeth facing down.
4. Press ring gear into place
5. Install remaining ring gear bolts and **torque** to 77 ft. lbs.
6. **On models equipped with aluminum axle,** proceed as follows:
   a. Place the differential case, left master bearing tool No. T93P-4222-A,

Description	inches
Maximum Runout of Backface of Ring Gear	0.004
Differential Side Gear Thrust Washer Thickness	0.030-0.032
Differential Pinion Gear Thrust Washer Thickness	0.030-0.032
Maximum Differential Case Runout	0.003
Nominal Pinion Locating Shim	0.030
Backlash Between Ring Gear and Pinion Teeth	0.008-0.015
Maximum Backlash Variation Between Teeth	0.004
Maximum Radial Runout of Companion Flange in Assembly	0.010 TIR

FM3039400281000X

Fig. 20 Rear axle specifications & tolerances

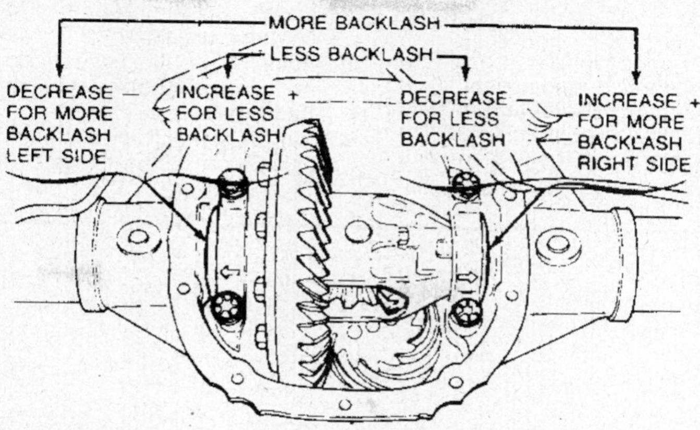

BACKLASH CHANGE REQUIRED	THICKNESS CHANGE REQUIRED	BACKLASH CHANGE REQUIRED	THICKNESS CHANGE REQUIRED
.001	.002	.009	.012
.002	.002	.010	.014
.003	.004	.011	.014
.004	.006	.012	.016
.005	.006	.013	.018
.006	.008	.014	.018
.007	.010	.015	.020
.008	.010		

FM3039100129000X

Fig. 21 Rear axle backlash adjustment

right master bearing tool No. T93P-4222-B, or equivalents, and ring gear into rear axle housing.

b. Ring gear bolt heads inside rear axle housing may interfere. If so, remove 3–5 bolts to provide clearance.
c. Attach dial indicator with the indicator tip positioned on machined surface of the case flange.
d. Rock ring gear to allow full mesh with pinion gear.
e. With gears in full mesh, set dial indicator to zero.
f. Move differential case as far as possible to the and record reading.
g. Record reading for differential bearing shim selection procedure.
h. Remove dial indicator and differential case from rear axle housing.
i. Stand height of both differential bearings must be measured prior to installation.
j. Place bearing preload tool No. T93P-4220-AR, or equivalent, base in suitable soft-jawed vise with bearing mounting surface above vise jaws.
k. Position differential bearing on bearing preload tool base.
l. Attach bolt, spring, washers and spacer, then tighten bolt.
m. Mark differential bearings left and right before measuring.
n. Invert bearing preload tool No. T93P-4220-AR, or equivalent, and clamp bolt head in suitable vise.
o. Position suitable depth micrometer flat on differential bearing.
p. Measure stand height of both differential bearings and record for differential bearing shim selection.
q. Press left and righthand differential bearing on differential case.
r. Install differential carrier spreader tool No. T4000-E, or equivalent, and dial indicator.
s. **Overspreading may damage rear axle housing.**
t. Tighten and loosen housing spreader adapter screw to normalize housing spreader adapters prior to final dial indicator reading.
u. Adjust dial indicator to zero and tighten the differential carrier spreader screw to spread rear axle housing to .030 inch.
v. Remove dial indicator.

7. **On all models,** apply light coating of Premium Long-Life Grease XG-1-C, or equivalent, to differential bearing shim to help hold in place.
8. Select correct size lefthand side differential bearing shim as follows:
   a. Add end play and bearing height.
   b. Subtract backlash.
   c. Round off initial thickness to nearest shim thickness.
9. Select correct size righthand side differential bearing shim as follows:
   a. Add end play and bearing height.
   b. Add backlash.
   c. Round off initial thickness to nearest shim thickness.
10. Install differential bearing shims in rear axle housing.
11. Position differential bearing cups on differential bearings.
12. Lower differential case in place between differential bearing shims.
13. Install bearing caps in original positions and **torque** bolts to 77 ft. lbs.
14. Tighten bearing cap bolts prior to releasing housing spreader.
15. Remove differential carrier spreader and move dial indicator to 12 o'clock position.
16. Position indicator needle centrally on drive tooth and zero indicator.
17. Turn ring gear without turning pinion gear.
18. Record indicator reading.
19. Measure ring gear backlash at four places to obtain consistent reading.
20. If backlash is not .004 inch, correct by increasing thickness of one differential bearing shim and decreasing thickness of other differential bearing shim by the same amount.
21. Ensure machined surfaces on both rear axle housing and differential housing cover are clean and free of oil before installing new silicone sealant.
22. Inside of rear axle must be covered when cleaning machined surface to prevent contamination.
23. Apply new continuous bead of Silicone Rubber D6AZ-19562-AA, or equivalent, sealant to differential housing cover.
24. Install differential housing cover.
25. Install rear axle and refill.

MARK VIII

Do not interchange righthand and lefthand side components during assembly.

1. Place differential case bearing shims into proper locations using a light film of suitable grease to hold them into place.
2. Install carrier spreader, **Fig. 10,** and spread case .030 inch.
3. Place differential case into place. **Use no force or aluminum carrier may be damaged.**
4. With carrier still spread, place differential bearing caps into place and **torque** bolts to 70–85 ft. lbs.
5. Remove carrier spreader, then install a suitable dial gauge and inspect ring gear backlash.
6. If backlash is not within specifications, **Fig. 20,** refer to **Fig. 21** for shim correction table.

ENGINE REBUILDING SPECIFICATIONS

NOTE: For Engine Tightening Specifications, Refer To The Engine Section In The Appropriate Chassis Chapter Of This Manual.

INDEX

CYLINDER HEAD, VALVE GUIDE & VALVE SEATS

All Measurements Given In Inches, Unless Otherwise Specified.

Engine Liter (VIN)①	Year	Cylinder Head Warpage Limit	Valve Guides			Valve Seats					
			Inside Diameter	Stem to Guide Clearance		Seat Angle °	Seat Width		Run-Out	Seat Insert Bore Diameter	
				Intake	Exhaust		Intake	Exhaust		Intake	Exhaust
2.0L DOHC (3)	1998–2002	②	0.2386	0.0007–0.0026	0.0007–0.0026	45	—	—	—	—	—
2.0L SOHC (P)	1998–2002	0.005	0.3170–0.3190	0.0008–0.0027	0.0018–0.0037	45.5	0.069–0.091	0.069–0.091	0.0025	1.572–1.573	1.375–1.573
2.5L DOHC (L)	1998–2002	②	—	0.0007–0.0027	0.0017–0.0037	44.75	0.043–0.055	0.055–0.066	0.0010	—	—
3.0L DOHC (S)④	1998–2002	②	—	0.0007–0.0027	0.0017–0.0037	44.75	0.043–0.055	0.055–0.066	0.0010	—	—
3.0L DOHC (S)③	2000–02	0.004	—	0.0008–0.0026	0.0010–0.0030	44.75	0.043–0.055	0.055–0.066	0.0010	—	—
3.0L SOHC (U & 2)	1998–99	0.007	0.3140–0.3150	0.0010–0.0028	0.0015–0.0033	45	0.060–0.080	0.080–0.100	0.0020	—	—
	2000–02	0.003	0.2763–0.2772	0.0010–0.0028	0.0015–0.0033	45	0.060–0.080	0.080–0.100	0.0030–0.0040	—	—
3.4L DOHC (N)	1998–99	—	—	0.0010–0.0023	0.0012–0.0025	45.0	0.039–0.055	0.039–0.055	—	—	—
3.8L OHV (4)	1998	0.007	⑤	0.0010–0.0028	0.0015–0.0033	44.47	0.060–0.080	0.060–0.080	0.0030	1.853–1.854	1.565
	1999–2002	0.007	0.2763–0.2772	0.0450–0.0900	0.0015–0.0033	44.75	0.060–0.080	0.060–0.080	0.0030	—	—
3.9L DOHC (A)	2000–02	—	—	—	—	—	—	—	—	—	—
4.6L DOHC (V)⑦	1998	—	—	0.0008–0.0027	0.0018–0.0037	45	0.071–0.086	0.071–0.086	0.0020	—	—
	1999–2002	—	—	0.0008–0.0027	0.0018	45	0.071–0.086	0.071–0.086	0.0014	—	—
4.6L DOHC (V)⑥	1998	0.004	—	0.0008–0.0027	0.0018–0.0037	45	0.075–0.083	0.075–0.083	0.0020	—	—
	1999–2002	—	—	0.0008–0.0027	0.0081–0.0037	45	0.071–0.086	0.071–0.086	0.0014	—	—
4.6L SOHC (W & 9)	1998	—	—	0.0008–0.0027	0.0018–0.0037	45	0.075–0.082	0.075–0.082	0.0020	—	—
	1999–2002	—	0.2773–0.2762	0.0008–0.0027	0.0018–0.0037	45	0.075–0.082	0.075–0.082	0.0020	—	—
4.6L SOHC (X)	1998	—	—	0.0008–0.0014	0.0018–0.0037	45	0.048–0.083	0.048–0.083	0.0020	—	—
	1999–2002	—	—	0.0008–0.0027	0.0018–0.0037	45	0.051–0.060	0.051–0.060	0.0020	—	—

DOHC — Dual Overhead Cam.
OHV — Overhead Valve.
SOHC — Single Overhead Cam.
① — Eighth digit Vehicle Identification Number (VIN) denotes engine code.
② — 0.002 inch for each six inches of length.
③ — LS.
④ — Sable & Taurus.
⑤ — Intake, 0.3415–0.3423 inch; exhaust, 0.3410–0.3418 inch.
⑥ — Mustang.
⑦ — Continental & Mark VIII.

VALVE SPRINGS

All Measurements Given In Inches, Unless Otherwise Specified.

Engine Liter (VIN)①	Year	Free Length	Installed Height	Installed Pressure Lbs @ Inches		Comp. Pressure Lbs. @ Inches		Out Of Square Limit
				Intake	Exhaust	Intake	Ex-haust	
2.0L DOHC (3)	1998–2002	1.701	1.346	33 lbs. @ 1.346	40 lbs. @ 1.346	82 lbs. @ 0.988	95 lbs. @ 1.0275	—
2.0L SOHC (P)⑤	1998–2001	1.860	1.420–1.540	95 @ 1.46	95 @ 1.46	200 @ 1.09	200 @ 1.09	⑨
2.0L SOHC (P)⑥	2001–02	2.065	1.557	⑦	⑦	⑧	⑧	⑨
2.5L DOHC (L)	1998–2002	④	—	—	—	—	—	0.064⑪
3.0L DOHC (S)②	1998–2002	1.840	1.570	51 @ 1.57	51 @ 1.57	153 @ 1.18	153 @ 1.18	⑩
3.0L DOHC (S)③	2000–02	1.740	1.315	39 @ 1.315	39 @ 1.315	90 @ 0.964	90 @ 0.964	—
3.0L SOHC (U & 2)	1998–99	1.840	1.580	65 @ 1.58	65 @ 1.58	180 @ 1.16	180 @ 1.16	—
	2000–02	1.830	1.650–1.736	64–72 @ 1.60	64–72 @ 1.60	193–217 @ 1.17	193–217 @ 1.17	—
3.4L DOHC (N)	1998–99	1.730	1.360	40 @ 1.36	40 @ 1.36	89 @ 1.00	89 @ 1.00	—
3.8L OHV (4)	1998	2.020	1.650	85 @ 1.65	85 @ 1.65	220 @ 1.18	220 @ 1.18	⑩
	1999–2002	—	1.620	79 @ 1.62	79 @ 1.62	224 @ 1.16	224 @ 1.18	⑩
3.9L DOHC (A)	2000–02	—	—	—	—	—	—	—
4.6L DOHC (V)	1998–2002	1.660	—	65 lbs. @ 1.4228	659 lbs. @ 1.4228	160 lbs. @ 1.031	160 lbs. @ 1.031	⑩
4.6L SOHC (W & 9)	1998	1.976	1.575	65 @ 1.575	65 @ 1.575	150 @ 1.103	150 @ 1.103	2.5°
	1999–2002	1.976	1.575	61 @ 1.574803	61 @ 1.574803	62 @ 1.575192	62 @ 1.575192	2.5°
4.6L SOHC (X)	1998	1.951	1.575	55 @ 1.5748	55 @ 1.5748	—	—	2°
	1999–2002	2.040–2.160	1.670–1.690	64 @ 1.68	64 @ 1.68	162 @ 1.13	162 @ 1.13	⑩

DOHC — Dual Overhead Cam.
OHV — Overhead Valve.
SOHC — Single Overhead Cam.
① — Eighth digit Vehicle Identification Number (VIN) denotes engine code.
② — Sable & Taurus.
③ — LS.
④ — Intake, 1.729 inch; exhaust, 1.847 inch.
⑤ — Escort & Tracer.
⑥ — Focus.
⑦ — Loaded, 78.7 lbs. @ 1.5575 inches.
⑧ — Unloaded, 18.7 lbs @ 1.1532 inches.
⑨ — Service limit, 5% force loss @ specified height.
⑩ — Service limit, 10% force loss @ specified height.
⑪ — Out of square limit.

VALVES

All Measurements Given In Inches, Unless Otherwise Specified.

Engine Liter (VIN)①	Year	Valves							
		Stem Diameter		Run Out	Face Angle, Degrees	Margin③		Clearance②	
		Intake	Exhaust			Int.	Exh.	Int.	Exh.
2.0L DOHC (3)	1998–2002	0.2374	0.2374	0.00138	45.0	—	—	0.0043–0.0071	0.01068–0.0134
2.0L SOHC (P)⑦	1998–2002	0.3159–0.3167	0.3149–0.3156	—	45.6	—	—	⑥	⑥
2.0L SOHC (P)⑧	2000–02	0.3159–0.3167	0.3154–0.3158	—	45.5	—	—	—	—
2.5L DOHC (L)	1998–2002	0.2350–0.2358	0.2343–0.2350	—	45.5	—	—	0.0190–0.0430	0.0190–0.0430
3.0L DOHC (S)④	1998–2002	0.2350–0.2358	0.2343–0.2350	0.00110	45.5	—	—	0.0190–0.0430	0.0190–0.0430
3.0L DOHC (S)⑤	2000–02	0.2150–0.2160	0.215	0.00110	45.5	—	—	0.00690–0.00890	0.0128–0.0148
3.0L SOHC (U & 2)	1998–99	0.3126–0.3134	0.3121–0.3129	—	44.0	—	—	0.0850–0.1850	0.0850–0.1850
	2000–02	0.2744–0.2752	0.2740–0.2748	—	45.0	—	—	0.0880–0.1890	0.0880–0.1890
3.4L DOHC (N)	1998–99	0.2346–0.2352	0.2344–0.2350	0.00100	45.5	0.020	0.020	0.0060–0.0100	0.0100–0.0140
3.8L OHV (4)	1998	0.3415–0.3423	0.3410–0.3418	0.00197	45.8	—	—	0.0890–0.1890	0.0890–0.1890
	1999–2002	0.2751–0.2738	0.2741–0.2728	0.00197	45.675	—	—	0.0890–0.1890	0.0890–0.1890
3.9L DOHC (A)	2000–01	—	—	—	—	—	—	—	—
4.6L DOHC (V)⑨	1998	0.2746–0.2754	0.2736–0.2744	0.00197	45.5	—	—	0.0315–0.0472	0.0315–0.0472
	1999–2002	0.2746–0.2754	0.2736–0.2744	—	45.5	—	—	0.0018–0.0033	0.0018–0.0033
4.6L DOHC (V)⑩	1998–2002	0.2746–0.2754	0.2736–0.2744	0.00197	45.5	—	—	0.0315–0.0472	0.0315–0.0472
4.6L SOHC (W & 9)	1998	0.2746–0.2750	0.2735–0.2744	—	45.5	—	—	0.0098–0.0256	0.0098–0.0256
	1999–2002	0.2746–0.2753	0.2736–0.2754	0.00197	45.5	—	—	0.0177–0.0335	0.0177–0.0335
4.6L SOHC (X)	1998	0.2746–0.2754	0.2736–0.2744	0.00197	45.5	—	—	0.0177–0.0335	0.0177–0.0335
	1999–2002	0.2746–0.2754	0.2746–0.2754	0.00197	45.5	—	—	0.0200–0.0300	0.0200–0.0300

DOHC — Dual Overhead Cam.
OHV — Overhead Valve.
SOHC — Single Overhead Cam.
① — Eighth digit Vehicle Identification Number (VIN) denotes engine code.
② — With cylinder @ top dead center, hold steady pressure on lifter until fully collapsed to check clearance.
③ — Minimum.
④ — Sable & Taurus.
⑤ — LS.
⑥ — Not adjustable, zero lash hydraulic lifters used.
⑦ — Escort & Tracer.
⑧ — Focus.
⑨ — Continental & Mark VIII.
⑩ — Mustang.

CAMSHAFT

All Measurements Given In Inches unless Otherwise Specified.

Engine Liter (VIN)①	Year	Camshaft Journal Diameter	Camshaft Bearing Inside Diameter	Camshaft Bearing Clearance	Camshaft Endplay	Lifter Bore Diameter	Lifter Diameter	Lifter To Bore Clearance
2.0L DOHC (3)	1998–2002	1.0221–1.0227	—	0.0008–0.0028	0.0032–0.0087	—	—	—
2.0L SOHC (P)	1998–2002	1.8007–1.8017	—	0.0013–0.0033	0.0008–0.0078	—	0.8754–0.8766	0.0009–0.0026
2.5L DOHC (L)	1998–2002	1.0600–1.0610	1.0620–1.0630	0.0010–0.0029	0.0010–0.0064	—	0.6290–0.6294	0.0007–0.0027
3.0L DOHC (S) ④	1998–2002	1.0600–1.0610	1.0620–1.0630	0.0010–0.0029	0.0075	—	0.6290–0.6294	0.0007–0.0027
3.0L DOHC (S)③	2000–02	1.0600	—	0.0010–0.0029	0.0020–0.0050	—	—	—
3.0L SOHC (U & 2)	1998–2002	2.0074–2.0084	2.0094–2.0104	0.0010–0.0030	0.0010–0.0050	0.8752–0.8767	0.8740	0.0007–0.0027
3.4L DOHC (N)	1998–99	②	—	⑤	0.0039–0.0094	—	—	—
3.8L OHV (4)	1998	2.0505–2.0515	2.0525–2.0535	0.0010–0.0030	0.0001–0.0060	0.8752–0.8767	0.8740–0.8745	0.0007–0.0027
	1999–2002	2.0670–2.0740	2.0525–2.0535	0.0010–0.0030	0.0010–0.0060	0.8752–0.8767	0.8738–0.8745	0.0007–0.0027
3.9L DOHC (A)	2000–02	—	—	—	—	—	—	—
4.6L DOHC (V)	1998–2002	1.0605–1.0615	1.0625–1.0635	0.0010–0.0030	0.0010–0.0065	—	0.6294–0.6299	0.0007–0.0027
4.6L SOHC (W & 9)	1998–2001	1.0605–1.0615	1.0625–1.0635	0.0010–0.0030	0.0011–0.0075	—	0.6294–0.6299	0.0007–0.0272
	2002	1.605–1.0615	1.0625–1.0635	0.0010–0.0030	0.0011–0.0075	—	0.6294–0.6299	0.0177–0.0334
4.6L SOHC (X)	1998–2002	1.0605–1.0615	1.0625–1.0635	0.0010–0.0030	0.0010–0.0065	—	0.6294–0.6299	0.0007–0.00272

DOHC — Dual Overhead Cam.
OHV — Overhead Valve.
SOHC — Single Overhead Cam.
① — Eighth digit Vehicle Identification Number (VIN) denotes engine code.
② — Front 1.1992–1.1998 inch, Others 0.9826–0.9833 inch.
③ — LS.
④ — Sable & Taurus.
⑤ — Front 0.0010–0.0026 inch, Others 0.0008–0.0024 inch.

CRANKSHAFT, BEARINGS & RODS

All Measurements Given In Inches, Unless Otherwise Specified.

Engine Liter (VIN)①	Year	Crankshaft				Bearing Clearance			Connecting Rods	
		Main Bearing Journal Diameter	Connecting Rod Journal Diameter	Max. Out of Round All	Max. Taper All	Main Bearings	Connecting Rod Bearings	Crankshaft Endplay	Pin Bore Diameter	Side Clearance
2.0L DOHC (3)	1998–2002	2.2827–2.2835	1.84601–1.8500	—	—	0.0004–0.0028	0.0006–0.0028	0.0035–0.0102	0.8106–0.8114	0.0006–0.0028
2.0L SOHC (P)	1998–2002	2.2827–2.2835	1.7279–1.7287	0.0003	0.0003	0.0008–0.0026	0.0008–0.0026	0.0040–0.0120	0.8098–0.8114	0.0040–0.0110⑧
2.5L DOHC (L)	1998–2002	2.4670–2.2790	1.9670–1.9680	—	—	0.0009–0.0017	0.0010–0.0025	0.0040–0.0090	0.8270–0.8280	0.0039–0.0118
3.0L DOHC (S) ②	1998–2002	2.4670–2.4790	1.9670–1.9680	0.0010	—	0.0001–0.0009	0.0010–0.0025	0.0050–0.0100	0.8270–0.8280	0.0039–0.0118
3.0L DOHC (S)⑤	2000–02	2.4670–2.4790	1.9670–1.9680	—	—	0.0001–0.0009	0.0011–0.0017	0.0040–0.0090	—	0.0039–0.0118
3.0L SOHC (U & 2)	1998–2002	2.5190–2.5198	2.1253–2.1261	0.0003	0.0003	0.0010–0.0014⑨	0.0010–0.0014⑨	0.00400–0.0080	0.9096–0.9112	0.0060–0.0140
3.4L DOHC (N)	1998–99	2.4794–2.4803	1.9675–1.9685	0.0008	0.0008	0.0004–0.0012⑦	0.0009–0.0023⑥	0.0024–0.0103	0.8274–0.8280	0.0060–0.0120④
3.8L OHV (4)	1998–2002	2.5190–2.5198	2.3103–2.3111	0.0003	0.0003	0.0010–0.0014③	0.0010–0.0014⑨	0.0040–0.0080	0.9032–0.9047	0.0047–0.0193⑧
3.9L DOHC (A)	2000–02	—	—	—	—	—	—	—	—	—
4.6L DOHC (V)	1998–2002	2.6567–2.6577	2.0856–2.0867	0.0020	—	0.00098–0.0018	0.0011–0.0027	0.0051–0.0119	0.8661–0.8671	0.0006–0.0177
4.6L SOHC (W & 9)	1998	2.6568–2.6576	2.0861–2.0867	0.0020	—	0.0011–0.0026	0.0010–0.0027	0.0051–0.0116	0.8645–0.8653	0.0006–0.0177
	1999–2002	2.6568–2.6576	2.0856–2.0867	0.0003	0.0002	0.0009–0.0026	0.0009–0.0026	0.0051–0.0119	0.8666–0.8671	0.0059–0.0177
4.6L SOHC (X)	1998	2.6568–2.6576	2.0861–2.0867	0.0020	—	0.0011–0.00256	0.0011–0.0027	0.0051–0.0116	0.8645–0.8653	0.0006–0.0177
	1999–2002	2.6600–2.6610	2.0859–2.0867	0.0020	—	0.00010–0.0020	0.0011–0.0027	0.0030–0.0150	0.8666–0.8671	0.005–0.01969

DOHC — Dual Overhead Cam.
OHV — Overhead Valve.
SOHC — Single Overhead Cam.
① — Eighth digit Vehicle Identification Number (VIN) denotes engine code.
② — Sable & Taurus.
③ — Allowable, 0.0005–0.0023 inch.
④ — Service Limit 0.0137 inch.
⑤ — LS.
⑥ — Allowable 0.0031 inch.
⑦ — Allowable 0.0024 inch.
⑧ — Service limit, 0.014 inch.
⑨ — Allowable, 0.0009–0.0027 inch.

BALANCE SHAFT

All Measurements Given In Inches, Unless Otherwise Specified.

Engine (VIN)①	Year	Balance Shaft Bore		Balance Shaft		
		Inside Bore Diameter	End Play	Journal Diameter	End Play	Runout
3.8L OHV (4)	1999–2002	2.191–2.192	0.003–0.006	2.0505–2.0515	0.003–0.008	0.001

OHV — Overhead Valve.

① — Eighth digit Vehicle Identification Number (VIN) denotes engine code.

PISTONS, PINS & RINGS

All Measurements Given In Inches, Unless Otherwise Specified.

Engine Liter (VIN)①	Year	Piston Diameter (Std.)	Piston Clearance	Piston Pin Diameter	Pin To Piston Clearance	Piston End Ring Gap④		Piston Ring Side Clearance	
						Comp.	Oil	Comp.	Oil
2.0L DOHC (3)⑬	1998–2002	㊲	0.0004–0.0012	⑤	0.0004–0.0006	⑯	0.006–0.026	㉕	⑭
2.0L DOHC (3)㊱	1998–2002	㊳	0.0004–0.0012	⑤	0.0004–0.0006	⑯	0.006–0.026	㉕	⑭
2.0L SOHC (P)	1998–2002	3.3374–3.3386	0.0008–0.0027	0.8119–0.8122	0.0003–0.0005	0.010–0.030	0.016–0.066	0.0015–0.0032	0.0015–0.0035
2.5L DOHC (L)	1998–2002	⑥	0.0005–0.0009	0.8278–0.8279	0.0001–0.0005	⑦	0.006–0.025	⑧	⑭
3.0L DOHC (S) ⑫	1998–2002	㉖㉜	0.0005–0.0009	0.8278–0.8279	0.0001–0.0007	⑦	0.006–0.026	⑧	0.0039
3.0L (S)⑨	2000–02	㉖	0.0005–0.0009	0.8272	0.0001	⑦	0.006–0.026	⑧	0.0039
3.0L SOHC (U & 2)	1998–99	⑪	0.0014–0.0022③	0.9119–0.9124	0.0002–0.0005	0.010–0.020	0.01–0.049	0.0012–0.0031	—
	2000–02	⑪	0.0012–0.0022	0.9119–0.9124	0.0002–0.0005	0.010–0.020	0.01–0.049	0.0016–0.0037	—
3.4L DOHC (N)	1998–99	③	0.0008–0.0016	0.8272–0.8273	⑩	0.008–0.014	0.008–0.028	②	0.0024–0.0059
3.8L OHV (4)	1998	⑮	0.0007–0.0017	0.9055–0.9056	0.0004–0.0007	⑱	0.006–0.026	0.0012–0.0032	—
	1999–2002	⑮	0.0007–0.0017	0.9055–0.9056	0.0004–0.0007	⑰	0.006–0.026	0.0012–0.0032	—
3.9L DOHC (A)	2000–02	—	—	—	—	—	—	—	—
4.6L DOHC (V)㉓	1998	㉚	-0.0004 to + 0.0010	0.8662–0.8663	-0.0002 – + 0.0001	㉒	0.006–0.026	㉙	⑭
	1999–2002	㉗	-0.0004 to + 0.0010	0.8662–0.8663	-0.0002 – + 0.0001	㉒	0.006–0.026	㉙	⑭
4.6L DOHC (V)㉑	1998–2002	⑲	0.0007–0.0018	0.8662–0.8663	0.0001–0.0002	㉘	0.006–0.026	㉙	⑭
4.6L SOHC (W)	1998	⑲㉞	0.0005–0.0010	0.8662–0.8663	0.0002–0.0005	㉝	0.006–0.026	㉔	0.0006
	1999–2002	⑳	—	0.8659–0.8660	0.0004–0.0006	0.002–0.006	0.006–0.012	—	—
4.6L SOHC (X)	1998	⑳	0.0005–0.0010	0.8662–0.8663	0.0002–0.0004	㉟	0.006–0.026	㉔	0.0006
	1999–2002	⑳	-0.0020 to +0.0010	0.8662–0.8663	-0.0002 – +0.005	㉛	0.006–0.022	—	—
4.6L SOHC (9)	1998	⑲㉞	0.0005–0.0010	0.8662–0.8663	0.0002–0.0005	㉝	0.006–0.026	㉔	0.0006
	1999–2002	⑳	—	0.8662–0.8663	0.0002	0.002–0.006	0.006–0.012	—	—

DOHC — Dual Overhead Cam.

OHV — Overhead Valve.

SOHC — Single Overhead Cam.

① — Eighth digit Vehicle Identification Number (VIN) denotes engine code.

② — Top ring, 0.0018–0.0031 inch; bottom, 0.0012–0.0028 inch.

③ — Coded grade 3 (brown) 3.2437–

3.2441 inch, coded grade 2 (none) 3.2433–3.2437 inch, coded grade 1 (Green) 3.2429–3.2433 inch.
④ — Minimum.
⑤ — White, 0.8120–0.8125 inch; red, 0.8120–0.8121 inch; blue, 0.8121–0.8122 inch.
⑥ — Grade 1, 3.2436–3.2444 inch; grade 2, 3.2440–3.2449 inch; grade 3, 3.2444–3.2452 inch.
⑦ — Top, 0.004–0.010 inch; bottom, 0.011–0.017 inch.
⑧ — Top, 0.0015–0.0029 inch; bottom, 0.0015–0.0033 inch.
⑨ — LS.
⑩ — Press fit, -.00024 to +.00008.
⑪ — Coded red, 3.5043–3.5053 inch; coded blue, 3.5053–3.5063 inch; coded yellow, 3.5063–3.5074 inch.
⑫ — Sable & Taurus.
⑬ — Escort & Tracer.
⑭ — Snug fit.
⑮ — Coded red, 3.8103–3.8108 inch; coded blue, 3.8108–3.8113 inch; coded yellow, 3.8113–3.8118 inch.
⑯ — Top, 0.009–0.015 inch; bottom 0.020–0.028 inch.
⑰ — Top, 0.007–0.013 inch; bottom, 0.012–0.022 inch.
⑱ — Top, 0.010–0.016 inch; bottom, 0.001–0.025 inch.
⑲ — Coded red, 3.5499–3.5504 inch; coded blue, 3.5504–3.5509 inch; coded yellow, 3.5509–3.5514 inch.
⑳ — Coded red, 3.5509–3.5515 inch; coded blue, 3.5514–3.5520 inch; coded yellow, 3.5518–3.5525 inch.
㉑ — Mustang.
㉒ — Top, 0.010–0.021 inch; bottom, 0.001–0.019 inch.
㉓ — Continental & Mark VIII.
㉔ — Top, 0.0016–0.0035 inch; bottom, 0.0012–0.0031 inch.
㉕ — Top, 0.0016–0.0028 inch; bottom, 0.0008–0.0020 inch.
㉖ — Coated: Grade 1, 3.5035–3.5043 inch; grade 2, 3.5039–3.5048 inch; grade 3, 3.5043–3.5051 inch.
㉗ — Coded red, 3.5522–3.5532 inches; coded blue, 3.5531–3.5537 inches; coded yellow, 3.5536–3.5542 inches.
㉘ — Top, 0.006–0.012 inch; bottom, 0.012–0.022 inch.
㉙ — Top, 0.0004–0.0009 inch; bottom, 0.0012–0.0032 inch.
㉚ — Coded red, 3.5512–3.5517 inches; coded blue, 3.5517–3.5520 inches; coded yellow, 3.5522–3.5527 inches.
㉛ — Top 0.005–0.011 inch; bottom, 0.018–0.022 inch.
㉜ — Uncoated Grade 1, 3.5028–3.5031 inches; grade 2, 3.5031–3.5036 inches; grade 3, 3.5043–3.5051 inches.
㉝ — Top, 0.002–0.004 inch; bottom, 0.012–0.022 inch.
㉞ — Uncoated: Grade 1, 3.5501–3.5527 inches; grade 2, 3.5512–3.5522 inches; grade 3, 3.5517–3.5527 inches.
㉟ — Top 0.005–0.011 inch; bottom, 0.012–0.022 inch.
㊱ — Contour, Cougar, Focus & Mystique.
㊲ — Class 1, 3.3373–3.3385 inch; class 2, 3.3573–3.3358 inch.
㊳ — Grade 1, 3.3392–3.3395 inch; grade 2, 3.3395–3.3399 inch; grade 3, 3.3399–3.3403 inch.

CYLINDER BLOCK

All Measurements Given In Inches, Unless Otherwise Specified.

Engine Liter (VIN)①	Year	Cylinder Bore Diameter (Std.)	Cylinder Bore Taper Max.	Cylinder Bore Out of Round Max.
2.0L DOHC (3)	1998–2002	⑦	0.0005 –0.0009	0.0010
2.0L SOHC (P)	1998–2002	3.3400	0.0005	0.0010
2.5L DOHC (L)	1998–2002	③	0.0002	0.0007
3.0L DOHC (S)⑥	1998–2002	⑤	0.0007	0.0008
3.0L DOHC (S)⑧	2000–02	④	0.0007	0.0005
3.0L SOHC (U & 2)	1998–2002	3.5040	0.0020	0.0020
3.4L DOHC (N)	1998–99	②	0.0002	0.0007
3.8L OHV (4)	1998–2002	3.8100	0.0020	0.0020
3.9L DOHC (A)	2000–02	—	—	—
4.6L SOHC (W, X & 9)	1998–2002	⑨	0.0010	0.0015

DOHC — Dual Overhead Cam.
OHV — Overhead Valve.
SOHC — Single Overhead Cam.
① — Eighth digit Vehicle Identification Number (VIN) denotes engine code.
② — Grade 1, 3.2441–3.2445 inches, grade 2, 3.2445–3.2449 inches, grade 3, 3.2449–3.2453 inches.
③ — Grade 1, 3.2465–3.2469; grade 2, 3.2469–3.2473; grade 3, 3.2473–3.2477.
④ — Grade 1, 3.5030–3.5040 inches; grade 2, 3.5040 inches; grade 3, 3.5040–3.5050 inches.
⑤ — Grade 1, 3.5039–3.5043 inches; grade 2, 3.5043–3.5047 inches; grade 3, 3.5047–3.5051 inches.
⑥ — Sable & Taurus.
⑦ — Grade 1, 3.3386–3.3390 inches; grade 2, 3.3390–3.3394 inches; grade 3, 3.3394–3.3398 inches.
⑧ — LS.
⑨ — Code red, 3.5539–3.5544 inches; blue, 3.5544–3.5549 inches; yellow, 3.5549–3.5554 inches.

OIL PUMP

All Measurements Given In Inches, Unless Otherwise Specified.

Engine Liter (VIN)①	Year	Rotor Back-lash	Rotor To Body Clear-ance	Rotor End-play⑤	Driveshaft To Pump Body Clearance	Relief Valve To Body Clearance	Relief Spring Pressure Lbs./ Inches
2.0L DOHC (3)④	1998–2002	—	—	—	—	—	—
2.0L SOHC (P)	1998–2002	—	0.0029–0.0063	0.0005–0.0035	—	0.0008–0.0031	9.3–10.3 @ 1.11
2.5L DOHC (L)④	1998–2000	—	—	—	—	—	—
3.0L DOHC (S)④	1998–2002	—	—	—	—	—	—
3.0L SOHC (U & 2)	1998–2002	0.0080–0.0012	0.0020–0.0055	0.0005–0.0055	②	0.0017–0.0029	9.1–10.1 @ 1.11
3.4L DOHC (N)	1998–99	0.0024–0.0071	0.0012–0.0035	0.0039–0.0069	0.0012–0.0035	0.0020–0.0035	52.5 @ 1.00
3.8L OHV (4)	1998–2002	0.0080–0.0012	0.0020–0.0055	0.0005–0.0055	③	0.0017–0.0029	15.2–17.1 @ 1.20
3.9L DOHC (A)④	2000–02	—	—	—	—	—	—
4.6L DOHC (V) & SOHC (W, X & 9)④	1998–2002	—	—	—	—	—	—

DOHC — Dual Overhead Cam.
OHV — Overhead Valve.
SOHC — Single Overhead Cam.
① — Eighth digit Vehicle Identification Number (VIN) denotes engine code.
② — Driver shaft to body clearance, 0.0005–0.0019 inch; idler shaft to idler clearance, 0.0005–0.0017 inch.
③ — Driver shaft to body clearance, 0.0015–0.0030 inch; idler shaft to idler clearance, 0.0005–0.0017 inch.
④ — Replace as an assembly.
⑤ — Measured between pump cover mounting surface & end of gear, using straightedge & feeler gauge.

GENERAL MOTORS CORP.

GENERAL MOTORS CORP.

ACHIEVA, ALERO, CUTLASS, GRAND AM, MALIBU & SKYLARK

NOTE: Refer To Rear Of This Manual For Vehicle Manufacturer's Special Service Tool Suppliers.

INDEX OF SERVICE OPERATIONS

Specifications

GENERAL ENGINE SPECIFICATIONS

Engine Liter/VIN Code①	Fuel Injection System	Bore & Stroke	Compression Ratio	Net H.P. @ RPM②	Maximum Torque Ft. Lbs. @ RPM	Normal Oil Pressure psi
1998						
2.4L/T	SFI	3.54 × 3.70	9.5:1	150 @ 5600	155 @ 4400	④
3.1L/M	SFI	3.50 × 3.31	9.5:1	155 @ 5200	185 @ 4000	60③
1999						
2.4L/T	SFI	3.54 × 3.70	9.5:1	150 @ 5600	155 @ 4400	④
3.1L/M	SFI	3.50 × 3.31	9.5:1	150 @ 4800	185 @ 4000	60③
3.4L/E	SFI	3.62 × 3.31	9.5:1	170 @ 5200	195 @ 4000	⑤
2000						
2.4L/T	SFI	3.54 × 3.70	9.5:1	150 @ 5600	155 @ 4400	④
3.1L/J	SFI	3.50 × 3.31	9.6:1	170 @ 5200	190 @ 4000	⑤
3.4L/E	SFI	3.62 × 3.31	9.5:1	170 @ 4800	200 @ 4000	⑤
2001						
2.4L/T	SFI	3.54 × 3.70	9.5:1	150 @ 5600	155 @ 4400	④
3.1L/J	SFI	3.51 × 3.31	9.6:1	170 @ 5200	190 @ 4000	⑤
3.4L/E	SFI	3.62 × 3.31	9.5:1	170 @ 4800	195 @ 4000	⑤
3.4L/E⑥	SFI	3.62 × 3.31	9.5:1	175 @ 5200	205 @ 4000	⑤
2002						
2.2L	SFI	3.38 x 3.72	10:1	140 @ 5600	150 @ 4000	50–80⑦
3.1L/J	SFI	3.51 × 3.31	9.6:1	170 @ 5200	190 @ 4000	⑤
3.4L/E	SFI	3.62 × 3.31	9.5:1	170 @ 4800	195 @ 4000	⑤
3.4L/E⑥	SFI	3.62 × 3.31	9.5:1	175 @ 5200	205 @ 4000	⑤

SFI — Sequential Fuel Injection
① — The eighth digit denotes engine code.
② — Ratings are as installed in vehicle.
③ — 1850 RPM w/engine at operating temperature.
④ — 10 psi minimum @ 900 RPM; 30 psi minimum @ 3000 RPM.
⑤ — 15 psi @1100 RPM.
⑥ — Ram air.
⑦ — Oil Pressure @ 1000 RPM.

TUNE UP SPECIFICATIONS

Year & Engine/VIN Code①	Spark Plug Gap, Inch	Ignition Timing, ° BTDC				Curb Idle Speed RPM③		Fast Idle Speed RPM		Fuel Pump Pressure, psi	Valve Lash
		Firing Order	Man. Trans.	Auto. Trans.	Mark Fig.	Man. Trans.	Auto. Trans.	Man. Trans.	Auto Trans.		
1998											
2.4L/T	.060	1-3-4-2	⑦	⑦	⑧	④	④	④	④	41–47⑤	⑥
3.1L/M	.060	1-2-3-4-5-6	⑦	⑦	⑧	④	④	④	④	41–47⑨	⑥
1999											
2.4L/T	.050	1-3-4-2	⑦	⑦	⑧	④	④	④	④	41–47⑤	⑥
3.1L/M	.060	1-2-3-4-5-6	⑦	⑦	⑧	④	④	④	④	41–47⑨	⑥
3.4L	.060	1-2-3-4-5-6	—	⑦	⑧	—	④	—	④	41–47②	⑥
2000–01											
2.4L/T	.050	1-3-4-2	⑦	⑦	⑧	④	④	④	④	48–55②	⑥
3.1L/J	.060	1-2-3-4-5-6	⑦	⑦	⑧	④	④	④	④	48–55②	⑥
3.4L	.060	1-2-3-4-5-6	—	⑦	⑧	—	④	—	④	48–55②	⑥
2002											
2.2L	.042	1-3-4-2	⑦	⑦	⑧	④	④	④	④	50–60	⑥
3.1L/J	.060	1-2-3-4-5-6	⑦	⑦	⑧	④	④	④	④	48–55②	⑥
3.4L	.060	1-2-3-4-5-6	—	⑦	⑧	—	④	—	④	48–55②	⑥

BTDC — Before Top Dead Center

① — The eighth digit of the Vehicle Identification Number (VIN) denotes engine code.

② — Disconnect and isolate battery ground cable. Loosen fuel filler cap. Remove fuel pressure connection cap. Wrap shop towel around fuel pressure connection while connecting pressure gauge tool No. J-34730-1A, or equivalent. Connect battery ground cable and inspect fuel pressure with ignition On, but engine not running.

③ — P: Park. When adjusting idle speed, set parking brake & block drive wheels.

④ — Idle speed is controlled by an idle air control (IAC) valve or an idle speed control (ISC) motor.

⑤ — Loosen fuel tank filler cap. Raise & support vehicle, then disconnect fuel pump electrical connector. Start engine & operate until fuel supply is depleted. Crank engine for approximately three seconds, then turn ignition Off. Connect fuel pump electrical connector and disconnect battery ground cable. Disconnect fuel line quick connect fittings and install fuel pressure test gauge tool No. J-29658-D, or a suitable equivalent. Tighten fuel tank filler cap & connect battery ground cable. Turn ignition On & inspect for leaks at gauge connections. Note fuel pressure reading with ignition turned On.

⑥ — Vehicle is equipped w/hydraulic valve lifters. No adjustment is required.

⑦ — Ignition timing is controlled by Powertrain Control Module (PCM).

⑧ — Equipped with crankshaft position sensor.

⑨ — With shop towel wrapped around fuel pressure valve to prevent fuel spillage, connect a suitable fuel pressure gauge to fuel pressure valve. Inspect fuel pressure with ignition On, but engine not running.

FRONT WHEEL ALIGNMENT SPECIFICATIONS

Model	Caster Angle, Degrees		Camber Angle, Degrees		Total Toe, Degrees	Ball Joint Wear
	Limits	Desired	Limits	Desired		
1998						
Achieva, Grand Am & Skylark	+.45 to +2.45	+1.45	−1.00 to +1.00	0	−.25 to +.25	①
Cutlass & Malibu	+3.10 to +5.10	+4.10	−1.20 to +.80	−.20	−.15 to +.35	①
1999–2002						
All	+3.10 to +5.10	+4.10	−1.20 to +.80	−.20	−.15 to +.35	①

① — Refer to “Front Suspension & Steering” section for ball joint inspection procedure.

REAR WHEEL ALIGNMENT SPECIFICATIONS

Model	Camber Angle, Degrees		Total Toe, Degrees	Thrust Angle, Degrees
	Limits	Desired		
1998				
Achieva, Grand Am & Skylark	–1.15 to +.35	–.40	–.1 to +.5	–.25 to +.25
Cutlass & Malibu	–.90 to +.10	–.20	–.26 to +.14	–.20 to +.20
1999				
Alero & Grand Am	–.70 to +.30	–.20	–.26 to +.14	–.20 to +.20
Cutlass & Malibu	–.90 to +.10	–.20	–.26 to +.14	–.20 to +.20
2000–02				
All	–.70 to +.30	–.20	–.26 to +.14	–.20 to +.20

VEHICLE RIDE HEIGHT SPECIFICATIONS

Model	Year	Body Style	Manufacturer's Original Tire Size	Measurement Points & Specifications					
				Front			Rear		
				Dim.	Specification		Dim.	Specification	
					Inches	mm		Inches	mm
Achieva	1998	All	②	A	31.5	800	B	22.31	566
				C	9.37	241	D	9.5	241
Alero	1998–2002	All	②	A	31.5	800	B	22.31	666
				C	9.37	238	D	9.56	243
Cutlass	1998–99	All	②	A	32.16	817	B	25	635
				C	9.45	240	D	9.84	250
Grand Am	1998–2002	All	②	A	31.5	800	B	22	558
				C	9.37	238	D	9.56	243
Malibu	1998–2002	All	②	C	9.33	237	D	9.62	244
Skylark	1998	All	②	A	31.5	800	B	21.4	544
				C	9.37	238	D	9.87	251

A Dim. — Measurement From Front Wheel Center to Check Point On Rocker Panel.
B Dim. — Measurement From Rear Wheel Center to Check Point On Rocker Panel.
C Dim. — Ground to Rocker Panel, Front.
D Dim. — Ground to Rocker Panel, Rear.

Dim. — Dimension.

① — ±.0.39 in (10 mm) front to rear & side to side.

② — See door sticker or inside of glove box for manufacturer's original tire size specifications. If tires on vehicle do not match manufacturer's original tire size & measurement is not within limits, it will be required refer to the Non-Standard Tire & Wheel Size Adjustment To Ride Height Specification & Tire Size Adjustment Charts.

③ — Measurement is with fuel, radiator coolant and engine oil full, spare tire, jack, hand tools and mats in designated positions and tires properly inflated.

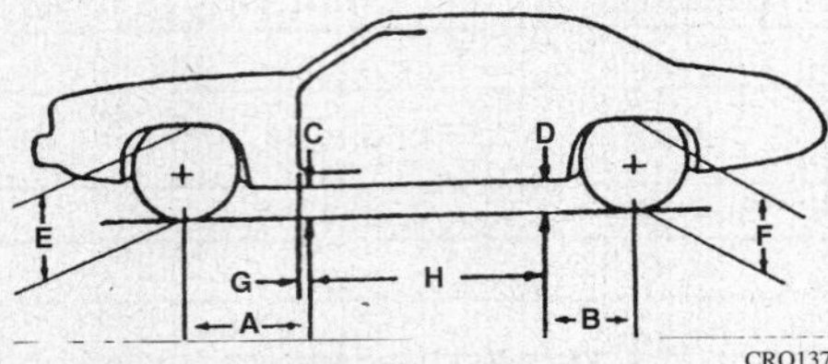

Dimensions A, B, C & D

FLUID CAPACITIES & COOLING SYSTEM DATA

Year	Engine/ VIN Code⑤	Coolant Capacity, Qts.	Coolant Type	Surge Tank Cap Relief Pressure, psi	Thermo. Opening Temp. Deg. F	Fuel Tank Gals.	Engine Oil Refill Qts.	Transaxle Oil	
								5 Speed Manual Transaxle Pts.	Auto. Transaxle Qts.①
ACHIEVA & SKYLARK									
1998	2.4L/T	10.4	Dex-Cool	15	180	15.2	4②	4	③
	3.1L/M	13.1	Dex-Cool	15	195	15.2	4②	4	④
ALERO & GRAND AM									
1998	2.4L/T	10.4	Dex-Cool	15	180	15.2	4②	4	③
	3.1L/M	13.1	Dex-Cool	15	195	15.2	4②	4	④
1999	2.4L/T	11.3	Dex-Cool	15	185	15	4	—	⑦
	3.4L/E	13.6	Dex-Cool	15	195	15	4.5	—	⑦
2000	2.4L/T	11.3	Dex-Cool	15	185	14.3	4	3.6	⑦
	3.4L/E	13.6	Dex-Cool	15	195	14.3	4.5	3.6	⑦
2001	2.4L	10.0	Dex-Cool	15	185	14.3	4	3.6	⑦
	3.4L	12.5	Dex-Cool	15	195	14.3	4	3.6	⑦
2002	2.2L	10.0	Dex-Cool	15	195	14.1	4	1.8	⑦
	3.4L	12.5	Dex-Cool	15	195	14.3	4	3.6	⑦
CUTLASS & MALIBU									
1998–99	2.4L/T	11.3	Dex-Cool	15	180	15.2	4②	—	⑥
	3.1L/M	13.6	Dex-Cool	15	195	15.2	4②	—	⑥
2000	3.1L/J	13.6	Dex-Cool	15	195	15	4.5	—	⑦
2001–02	3.1L	13.6	Dex-Cool	15	195	14.3	4.5	—	⑦

① — Approximate. Make final inspection w/dipstick.
② — When changing filter, additional oil may be required.
③ — On models w/3T40 transaxle oil pan capacity, 4 qts.; total capacity, 7 qts.; dry, 9 qts. On models w/4T60E oil pan capacity, 6 qts.; total capacity, 8 qts.; dry, 10 qts.
④ — Oil pan capacity 6 qts.; total capacity 8 qts.; dry, 10 qts.
⑤ — The eighth digit denotes engine code.
⑥ — Oil pan removal, 7.4 qts.; total capacity, 10.6 qts.
⑦ — Oil pan removal, 6.9 qts.; overhaul, 9.5 qts.; dry 12.9 qts.

LUBRICANT DATA

Year	Model	Lubricant Type				
		Transaxle		Clutch Hydraulic System	Power Steering System	Brake System
		Automatic	Manual			
1998	All	Dexron III	①	③	Power Steering Fluid ②	DOT 3
1999	All	Dexron III	①	③	Power Steering Fluid④	DOT 3
2000–02	All	Dexron III	Dexron III	DOT 3	Power Steering Fluid④	DOT 3

① — Synchromesh transaxle fluid GM P/N 12345349, or equivalent.
② — Meeting GM specification 9985010 or equivalent. In cold climates use GM P/N 12345867 or 12345866, or equivalents. System must be flushed, refilled & bled prior to installation of cold climate fluid.
③ — Hydraulic clutch fluid GM P/N 12345347, or equivalent.
④ — GM P/N 1052884 (pint), 1050017 (quart), or equivalent.

Electrical

NOTE: On Air Bag Equipped Models, Refer To "Air Bag System Precautions" Located In The Front Of This Manual For System Disarming & Arming Procedures.

NOTE: Refer To "Computer Relearn Procedures" Located In The Front Of This Manual When Battery Power To The Computer Has Been Interrupted.

INDEX

PRECAUTIONS

AIR BAG SYSTEMS

Refer to "Air Bag System Precautions" in the front of this manual for system disarming and arming procedures.

BATTERY GROUND CABLE

Prior to service, disconnect battery ground cable and isolate as required.

FUSE PANEL & FLASHER LOCATION

ACHIEVA, SKYLARK & 1998 GRAND AM

The fuse panel is located behind the lefthand side of instrument panel. The turn signal flasher is located in the convenience center next to the hazard flasher. The hazard warning flasher is located on the convenience center, behind the lefthand side of the instrument panel to the left of the steering column.

ALERO, CUTLASS, MALIBU & 1999-2002 GRAND AM

The fuse panel is located behind the lefthand side of instrument panel. The turn signal and hazard flasher is an internal component of the hazard switch located in the center of the instrument panel.

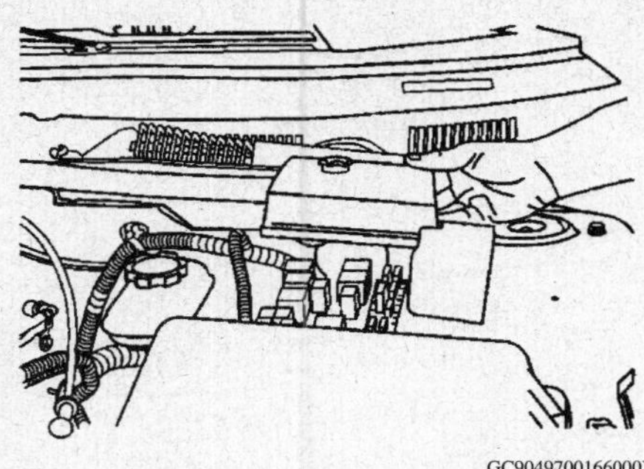

Fig. 1 Fuel pump relay location. Achieva, Alero, Grand Am & Skylark

FUEL PUMP RELAY LOCATION

ACHIEVA, ALERO, GRAND AM & SKYLARK

The fuel pump relay is located in the engine compartment relay center on the left-hand side of the engine compartment, **Fig. 1.**

CUTLASS & MALIBU

The fuel pump relay is located in the underhood bussed electrical center on the lefthand side of the engine compartment, **Fig. 2.**

RELAY CENTER LOCATION

The relay center is located on the left-hand side of the engine compartment.

STARTER

REPLACE

2.4L ENGINE

1. Remove air inlet duct from throttle body.
2. Remove starter upper mounting bolt.
3. Raise and support vehicle.
4. Remove all required shrouding and closeout panels.
5. Remove starter lower mounting bolt.
6. Position engine wiring harness aside.
7. Move starter to access solenoid wiring and remove starter electrical wiring.
8. Remove starter.
9. Reverse procedure to install, noting the following:
   a. **Torque** cable to solenoid nut to 108 inch lbs.
   b. **Torque** lower mounting bolt to 66 ft. lbs.
   c. **Torque** upper mounting bolt to 66 ft. lbs.

2.2L & 3.1L ENGINES

1. Raise and support vehicle.
2. Remove starter motor mounting bolts, then lower the starter.
3. Disconnect starter electrical connectors and remove starter.
4. Reverse procedure to install, noting the following:
   a. **On models equipped with 2.2L engine, torque** starter mounting bolts to 30 ft. lbs.
   b. **On models equipped with 3.1L engine, torque** starter mounting bolts to 37 ft. lbs.

3.4L ENGINE

Removal

1. Raise and safely support vehicle.
2. Remove flywheel inspection cover.
3. Remove all electrical connectors from starter.
4. Remove starter mounting bolts, then the starter.

Installation

1. Tighten nut next to cap on solenoid BAT terminal while starter is still on bench.
2. Secure electrical terminal on solenoid.
3. **Torque** solenoid battery terminal inside nut to 84 inch lbs.
4. Install electrical connectors to starter.
5. **Torque** solenoid battery terminal outside nut to 84 inch lbs.
6. **Torque** solenoid "S" terminal outside nut to 22 inch lbs.
7. Install starter onto engine and **torque** mounting bolts to 32 ft. lbs.
8. Install inspection cover and **torque** bolts to 84 inch lbs.

ALTERNATOR

REPLACE

2.2L & 2.4L ENGINES

1. Remove serpentine drive belt using tool No. J-37059, or equivalent to rotate tensioner.
2. Remove mounting bolts and studs.
3. Disconnect electrical leads and remove alternator.
4. Reverse procedure to install, noting the following:
   a. **On models equipped with 2.2L engine, torque** alternator mounting bolts to 15 ft. lbs.
   b. **Torque** alternator electrical connector to 13 ft. lbs.
   c. **On models equipped with 2.4L engine, torque** alternator mounting bolts to 37 ft. lbs.

3.1L ENGINE

1. Remove serpentine drive belt.
2. Disconnect alternator electrical connectors and power steering line clip.
3. Remove alternator rear brace.
4. Disconnect alternator air inlet connector.
5. Remove mounting bolts and nuts, then the alternator.
6. Reverse procedure to install. **Torque** mounting bolts to 18 ft. lbs., and nut to 37 ft. lbs.

3.4L ENGINE

1. Remove cruise control module as required.
2. Remove engine mount as required.

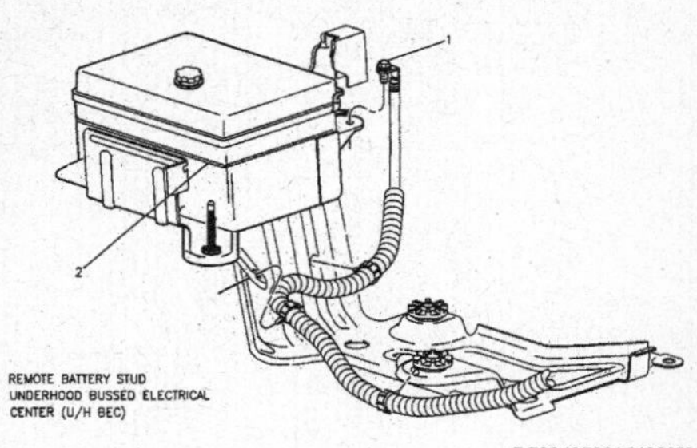

Fig. 2 Fuel pump relay location. Cutlass & Malibu

3. Using a suitable 3/8 inch breaker bar, rotate serpentine drive belt tensioner in a clockwise direction and remove belt.
4. Disconnect alternator electrical connectors and power steering line clip.
5. Remove mounting bolts and nuts, then the alternator.
6. Reverse procedure to install, noting the following:
   a. **Torque** alternator mounting bolts to 37 ft. lbs.
   b. **Torque** alternator mounting nuts to 22 ft. lbs.
   c. **Torque** engine mount to body bolt to 96 ft. lbs.
   d. **Torque** engine mount to body nut to 49 ft. lbs.
   e. **Torque** engine mount bracket support bolts to 96 ft. lbs.

COIL PACK

REPLACE

2.2L ENGINE

1. Turn ignition to Off position.
2. Disconnect Ignition Control Module (ICM) retaining screws.
3. Remove ICM from ignition coil housing assembly.
4. Reverse procedure to install, **torque** ICM retaining screws to 13 ft. lbs.

2.4L ENGINE

Removal

1. Remove accelerator and cruise control cables from their hold-down clip.
2. Remove fuel line retainer clip bolt.
3. Disconnect electronic Ignition Control Module (ICM) 11-pin electrical connector.
4. Remove ICM and coil assembly to camshaft housing bolts, **Fig. 3.**
5. If spark plug boots adhere to plugs, use remover tool No. J-36011 or equivalent to twist, then pull upward on retainers.
6. Remove coil and ICM assembly.
7. Remove housing to cover screws. Ensure ground strap remains in place.
8. Disconnect coil harness electrical connector, **Fig. 4,** then remove housing from cover.
9. Remove ignition coil(s) from housing, **Fig. 5.**
10. Disconnect coil electrical connectors.
11. Remove contact springs from housing.
12. Remove coil seals from coils.

Fig. 3 Ignition coil & control module assembly removal. 2.4L engine

Installation

1. Install new seals into ignition coils.
2. Install contact springs into housing using petroleum jelly to keep them in place.
3. Connect coil electrical connector.
4. Install coils into housing.
5. Connect ground strap if it was not done during removal.
6. Connect coil(s) electrical connector to ICM, ensuring ground strap stays in place.
7. Install housing to cover.
8. Install housing to cover screws. **Torque** to 35 inch lbs.
9. Install spark plug boots and retainers to housing.
10. Install coil and ICM assembly to engine while carefully aligning boots to plug terminals.
11. Coat coil and ICM assembly to camshaft housing bolts with GM Loctite sealant P/N 12346004 or equivalent.
12. Install bolts with isolator washer rubber sides facing down, then **torque** to 16 ft. lbs.
13. Connect ICM 11-pin electrical connector.
14. Install fuel line retainer clip bolt.
15. Install accelerator and cruise control cables into their hold-down clip.

3.1L ENGINE

1. Remove electrical connectors from ignition control module.
2. Remove spark plug wires from ignition coils.
3. Remove screws securing ignition coils to ignition module, then the coils.
4. Reverse procedure to install. **Torque** coil to module screws to 40 inch lbs.

3.4L ENGINE

1. Tag spark plug wires to ensure proper routing, then disconnect them from ignition coils.
2. Remove screws retaining ignition coils to ignition module, then the coils.

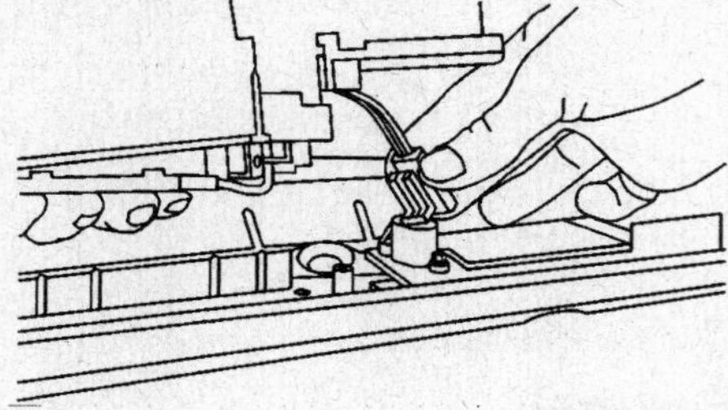

Fig. 4 Coil harness electrical connector disconnection. 2.4L engine

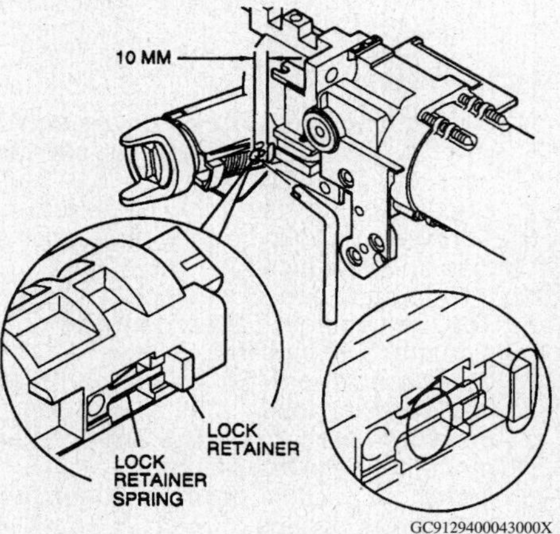

Fig. 6 Lock cylinder removal. Achieva, Skylark & 1998 Grand Am

3. Reverse procedure to install. **Torque** retaining screws to 40 inch lbs.

IGNITION LOCK

REPLACE

ACHIEVA, SKYLARK & 1998 GRAND AM

Less Ignition Key

1. Remove ignition switch assembly wiring harness and steering column.
2. Drill a 9/32 inch hole in steering column housing assembly back, **Fig. 6.**
3. Insert retainer spring tool No. J-41253, or equivalent into hole, then engage and remove lock retainer spring.
4. Hold steering column vertical and tap on housing assembly to dislodge lock retainer. It may be required to remove retainer with suitable needle nose pliers.
5. Pull lock cylinder from housing assembly, then clean metal shavings from drilled hole.
6. Reverse procedure to install.

With Ignition Key

1. Remove lower lefthand insulator panel screws and disconnect two-way yellow SIR connectors.
2. Remove tilt lever, upper and lower steering column trim covers.
3. Turn lock cylinder to Run position, push locking button on steering column back and remove lock cylinder.
4. Reverse procedure to install.

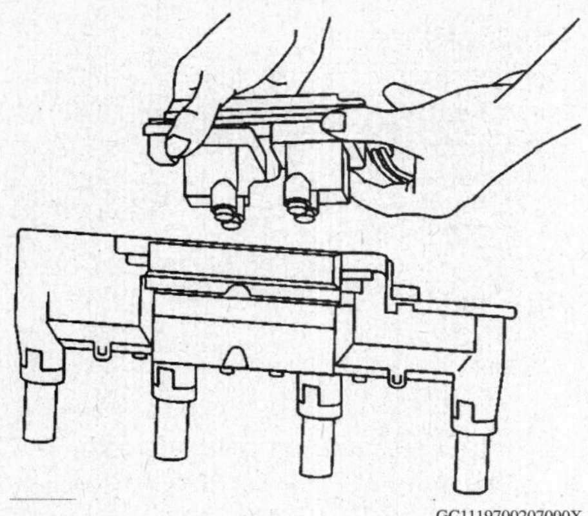

Fig. 5 Ignition coil removal. 2.4L engine

ALERO

1. Remove ignition switch bezel using suitable flatbladed screwdriver.
2. Remove radio assembly as outlined under "Radio, Replace."
3. Insert key and turn ignition switch lock cylinder to On position.
4. Remove ignition lock cylinder while rotating.
5. Reverse procedure to install.

CUTLASS, MALIBU & 1999–2002 GRAND AM

Refer to "Ignition Switch, Replace."

IGNITION SWITCH

REPLACE

ACHIEVA, SKYLARK & 1998 GRAND AM

1. Remove steering wheel and covers as outlined under "Steering Wheel, Replace."
2. Turn ignition to Off/Lock.
3. Remove ignition switch wire harness.
4. Remove tapping screws and ignition switch, **Fig. 7.**
5. Reverse procedure to install. **Torque** screws to 12 inch lbs.

ALERO

1. Remove radio assembly as outlined under "Radio, Replace."
2. Remove instrument panel cluster as outlined under "Instrument Cluster, Replace."
3. Remove bolts from ignition switch.
4. Reposition ignition switch to cluster opening for access.
5. Remove ignition switch attaching bolts to bracket, then the bracket.
6. Install key and turn lock cylinder to On position.
7. Depress transaxle park lock cable retainer to release cable.
8. Remove lock cylinder from ignition switch, depressing retaining tab and pulling cylinder out with key.

9. Disconnect pass lock electrical connector from ignition switch.
10. Disconnect electrical connectors from ignition switch.
11. Remove ignition switch through I/P cluster opening.
12. Reverse procedure to install, **torque** attaching bolts to 53 inch lbs.

CUTLASS & MALIBU

1. Remove lefthand sound insulator, ignition switch trim ring and accessory trim plates, then the instrument cluster.
2. Remove mounting bolts and electrical connectors, then the console trim plate.
3. Remove ignition lock cable from shift lever and bracket at console front.
4. Remove ignition switch.
5. Reverse procedure to install. **Torque** ignition switch mounting bolts to 18 inch lbs.

1999-2002 GRAND AM

1. Remove lefthand sound insulator.
2. Remove ignition switch trim ring.
3. Remove accessory trim plate.
4. Remove upper steering column cover.
5. Remove instrument cluster trim plate.
6. Remove instrument cluster.
7. Remove ignition switch retaining bolts, then the switch.
8. Disconnect electrical connectors.
9. Disconnect ignition lock cable from switch.
10. Insert key into ignition lock cylinder and turn to Run position.
11. Depress cylinder release plunger. This is located at four o'clock position on switch.
12. Pull on key to remove cylinder from switch.
13. Reverse procedure to install.

CLUTCH START SWITCH

REPLACE

1. Disconnect switch electrical connector.
2. Remove nuts attaching switch to mounting, then remove switch.
3. Reverse procedure to install. After installation, inspect switch for proper operation.

NEUTRAL SAFETY SWITCH

REPLACE

REMOVAL

1. Disconnect switch electrical connector.
2. Remove shift linkage retaining nut, then the linkage.
3. Remove shift linkage lever.
4. Note switch orientation and make alignment marks as required to ease installation.
5. Remove mounting screws and switch.

INSTALLATION

1. Place shift shaft in Neutral position, then align flats on shaft with those on the switch.

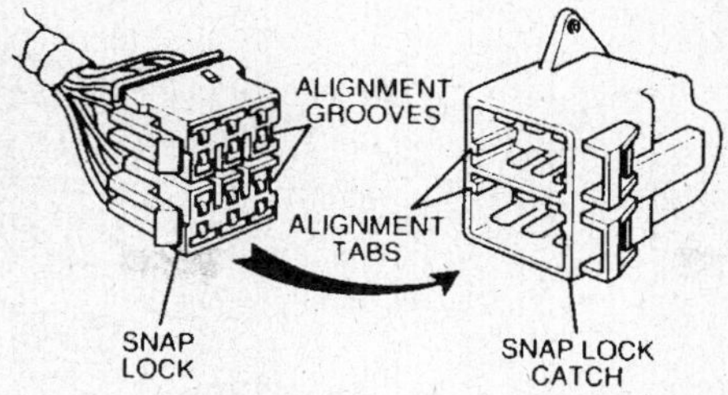

Fig. 7 Ignition switch & electrical connections. Achieva, Skylark & 1998 Grand Am

2. Loosely install switch with marks properly aligned.
3. If original switch is being installed, insert a 3/32 inch drill bit into switch adjustment hole. Move switch until drill bit drops to depth of 9/64 inch. **Torque** switch mounting screws to 18 ft. lbs., then remove drill bit.
4. New switches are pinned in Neutral position. If installation is difficult, ensure shift shaft is in Neutral. Do not rotate switch. **Torque** switch mounting screws to 18 ft. lbs.

HEADLAMP SWITCH

REPLACE

ACHIEVA, CUTLASS, MALIBU, SKYLARK & 1998 GRAND AM

1. Remove instrument cluster trim plate retaining screws, then the trim plate.
2. Disconnect headlamp switch electrical connector.
3. Remove headlamp switch from instrument panel.
4. Reverse procedure to install.

ALERO & 1999-2002 GRAND AM

1. Disarm driver's air bag module as outlined in "Air Bag System Precautions."
2. Remove steering column trim panels.
3. Remove multi-function switch retaining screws.
4. Disconnect electrical connectors at multi-function switch.
5. Remove multi-function switch from steering column.
6. Reverse procedure to install. **Torque** retaining screws to 35 inch lbs.

STOP LIGHT SWITCH

REPLACE

ACHIEVA, SKYLARK & 1998 GRAND AM

1. Disconnect electrical connectors from switch, then pull switch out of retaining clip on brake pedal support.
2. Depress brake pedal and push replacement switch into retainer until switch shoulder is bottomed against bracket.
3. Adjust switch by pulling brake pedal back against stop.
4. Ensure switch has continuity when pedal is depressed from normal rest position and stop lamps turn off when pedal returns to full rest.

ALERO, CUTLASS, MALIBU & 1999-2002 GRAND AM

Removal

1. Remove lefthand side instrument panel insulator.
2. Disconnect stop lamp switch electrical connector.
3. Remove switch retainer by grasping and turning 90° counterclockwise and pulling toward rear of vehicle.
4. Remove stop lamp switch.

Installation

1. Insert stop lamp switch into retainer until switch body has seated onto retainer.
2. Pull brake pedal upward against its internal stop.
3. Adjust switch so its plunger extends no more than .78 inch beyond threaded portion when brake pedal is fully released.
4. Rotate switch 90° clockwise until it locks into position.
5. Connect switch electrical connector.

MULTI-FUNCTION SWITCH

REPLACE

ACHIEVA, CUTLASS, MALIBU, SKYLARK & 1998 GRAND AM

1. Remove horn pad and steering wheel as outlined under "Steering Wheel, Replace."
2. Remove tilt lever from steering column, if equipped. If required, position spark plug boot or other suitable device over tilt lever (to prevent damage) and remove tilt lever using locking pliers.
3. Remove steering column upper and lower covers, then the dampener assembly.
4. Remove attaching screw and switch assembly, **Fig. 8.**
5. Reverse procedure to install.

ALERO & 1999-2002 GRAND AM

Refer to "Headlamp Switch, Replace" for replacement procedure.

TURN SIGNAL SWITCH

REPLACE

ACHIEVA, CUTLASS, MALIBU, SKYLARK & 1998 GRAND AM

Refer to "Multi-Function Switch, Replace" for replacement procedure.

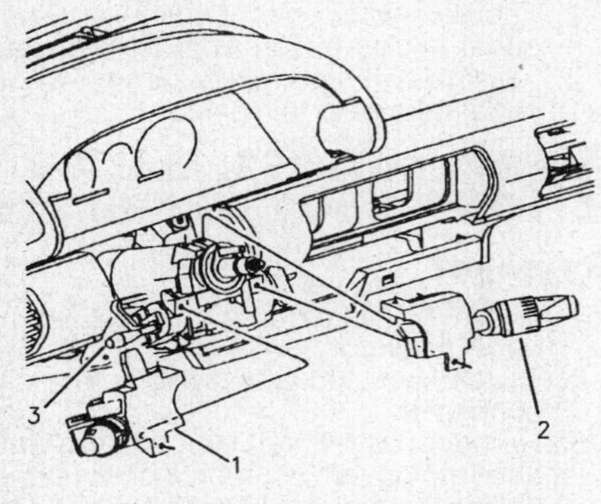

Fig. 8 Multi-function switch replacement. Achieva, Cutlass, Malibu, Skylark & 1998 Grand Am

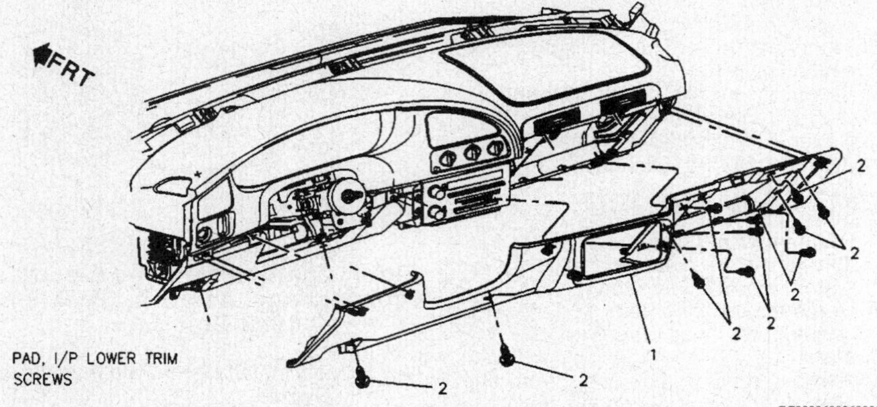

Fig. 9 Lower trim pad removal. Achieva & Skylark

ALERO & 1999-2002 GRAND AM

Refer to "Headlamp Switch, Replace" for replacement procedure.

DIMMER SWITCH

REPLACE

ACHIEVA, CUTLASS, MALIBU, SKYLARK & 1998 GRAND AM

Refer to "Multi-Function Switch, Replace" for replacement procedure.

ALERO & 1999-2002 GRAND AM

Refer to "Headlamp Switch, Replace" for replacement procedure.

STEERING WHEEL

REPLACE

1. Disarm driver's air bag module as outlined in "Air Bag System Precautions."
2. Remove attaching screws for horn pad or inflator module.
3. **On models equipped with radio controls,** remove wire protector plate connector.
4. **On all models,** remove horn pad or inflator module and horn lead, then the steering wheel retainer and nut.
5. Remove steering wheel using puller tool No. J-1859-A and legs tool No. J-42120, or equivalent.
6. Reverse procedure to install, noting the following:
   a. **Torque** steering wheel nut to 27–30 ft. lbs.
   b. Install air bag module. **Torque** screws to 89 inch lbs.

BACK-UP LAMP SWITCH

REPLACE

AUTOMATIC TRANSAXLE

Refer to "Neutral Safety Switch, Replace" for replacement procedure.

MANUAL TRANSAXLE

1. Disconnect back-up lamp switch electrical connector.
2. Using a suitable socket, remove back-up lamp switch from top of transaxle case. **Do not use an open-end wrench.**
3. Reverse procedure to install. Prior to installation, apply pipe sealant P/N 1052080, or equivalent to switch threads.

INSTRUMENT CLUSTER

REPLACE

1. Remove mounting screws, electrical connectors and instrument panel cluster trim plates.
2. Remove instrument cluster to instrument panel mounting screws.
3. Disconnect cluster electrical connectors and remove instrument cluster.
4. Reverse procedure to install.

RADIO

REPLACE

ACHIEVA & SKYLARK

1. Remove mount screws, disconnect electrical connectors and remove instrument panel cluster trim plate.
2. Twist fastener ¼ turn, remove accelerator pedal nut, courtesy lamp and left-hand sound insulator.
3. Twist fastener ¼ turn, remove courtesy lamp and righthand sound insulator.
4. Remove screws and bolts, then the lower instrument panel cluster trim pad, **Fig. 9.**
5. Remove HVAC control and radio housing attaching screws, **Fig. 10.**
6. Remove attaching nuts, then pull radio rearward.
7. Disconnect all electrical connectors and antenna lead-in, then remove radio assembly.
8. Reverse procedure to install. **Torque** radio to radio bracket attaching nuts to 17 inch lbs.

ALERO & 1999-2002 GRAND AM

1. Remove accessory trim plate.
2. Remove radio mounting screws.
3. Pull radio rearward.
4. Disconnect all electrical connectors and antenna lead-in.
5. Reverse procedure to install.

CUTLASS & MALIBU

1. Remove ignition key trim cover using a suitable flat-bladed pry tool.
2. Pull accessory trim plate to rear and remove.
3. Remove mounting screws and pull radio to rear.
4. Disconnect all electrical connectors and antenna lead-in.
5. Remove radio.
6. Reverse procedure to install.

1998 GRAND AM

1. Remove mounting screws, disconnect electrical connectors and remove instrument panel cluster trim plate, **Fig. 11.**
2. Remove HVAC control and radio housing attaching screws, **Fig. 12.**
3. Remove attaching nuts, pull radio to rear, disconnect antenna and electrical connectors and remove radio assembly.
4. Reverse procedure to install. **Torque** radio to radio bracket attaching nuts to 17 inch lbs.

WIPER MOTOR

REPLACE

ACHIEVA, CUTLASS, MALIBU, SKYLARK & 1998 GRAND AM

1. Remove wiper arm and blade assemblies.
2. Remove cowl cover assembly.

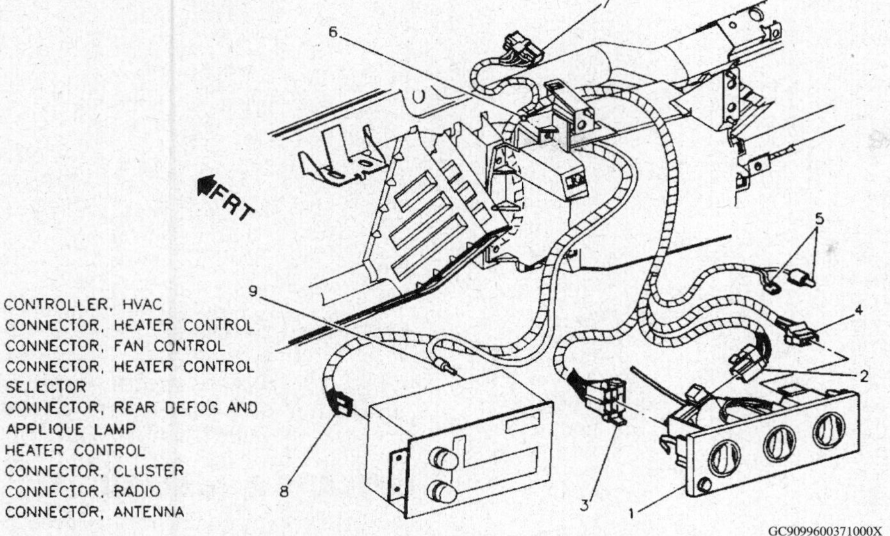

Fig. 10 HVAC control & radio removal. Achieva & Skylark

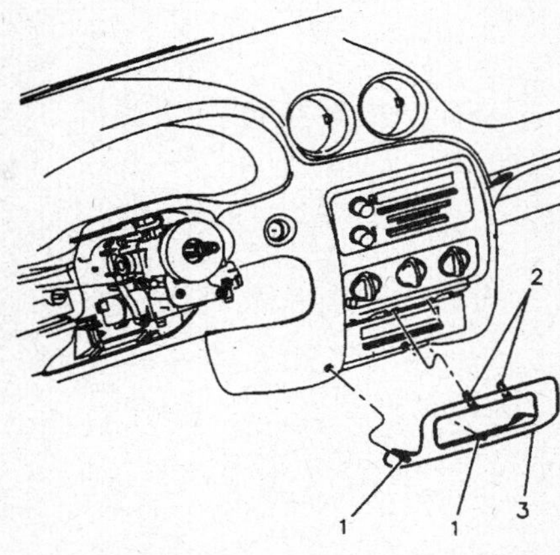

Fig. 11 Lower trim plate removal. 1998 Grand Am

3. Use wiper transmission separator tool No. J-39232, or equivalent to disconnect drive link from crank arm.
4. Disconnect wiper motor electrical connectors.
5. Remove mounting screws and wiper motor.
6. Reverse procedure to install, noting the following:
   a. **Torque** motor mounting screws to 84 inch lbs.
   b. Use wiper transmission installer tool No. J-39529, or equivalent to connect drive link to crank arm.

ALERO & 1999–2002 GRAND AM

1. Remove wiper arms from shafts.
2. Remove cowl air inlet grille.
3. Disconnect wiper motor electrical connector.
4. Remove three wiper drive system assembly to vehicle mounting screws, then the wiper assembly from vehicle.
5. Remove wiper transmission assembly from crank arm using separator tool No. J-39232, or equivalent.
6. Remove two motor to tube frame mounting screws, then the motor from frame.
7. Reverse procedure to install, noting the following:
   a. Install motor onto tube frame. **Torque** screws to 89 inch lbs.
   b. Install transmission assembly onto crank arm using installer tool No. J-39529, or equivalent.
   c. Install drive system module onto vehicle. **Torque** screws to 89 inch lbs.

WIPER SWITCH

REPLACE

1. Remove multi-function switch as outlined under "Multi-Function Switch, Replace."
2. Remove attaching screws and windshield wiper and washer switch, **Fig. 8.**
3. Reverse procedure to install.

WIPER TRANSMISSION

REPLACE

ACHIEVA, SKYLARK & 1998 GRAND AM

1. Remove wiper arm and blades assemblies.
2. Remove cowl cover assembly and disconnect drive link from crank arm using wiper transmission separator tool No. J-39232, or equivalent.
3. Remove attaching screws and guide linkage out through access hole.
4. Reverse procedure to install. **Torque** mounting screws to 72 inch lbs.

ALERO & 1999–2002 GRAND AM

1. Remove wiper arms from transmission shafts.
2. Remove air inlet screen from cowl panel.
3. Disconnect wiper motor electrical connector.
4. Remove wiper transmission retaining screws, then the transmission from the vehicle.
5. Using separator tool No. J-39232, or equivalent, disconnect motor crank arm from transmission assembly.
6. Remove transmission assembly cap.
7. Remove four screws and transmission assembly from tube frame.
8. Remove three grommets from tube frame and transmission assembly.
9. Remove motor assembly from tube frame.
10. Reverse procedure to install, noting the following:
    a. **Torque** wiper transmission to tube frame screws to 79 inch lbs.
    b. Install transmission onto crank arm using installer tool No. J-39529, or equivalent.
    c. **Torque** wiper transmission mounting screws to 79 inch lbs.

CUTLASS & MALIBU

1. Remove wiper arm and blades assemblies.
2. Remove cowl cover assembly and disconnect wiper motor connector.
3. Remove mounting screws and wiper drive system module.
4. Remove wiper motor as outlined under "Wiper Motor, Replace."
5. Remove transmission assembly caps, wiper motor grommets and transmission assembly.
6. Reverse procedure to install. **Torque** mounting screws to 72 inch lbs.

BLOWER MOTOR

REPLACE

ACHIEVA, SKYLARK & 1998 GRAND AM

1. **On models equipped with 3.1L engine,** remove serpentine belt, attaching bolts and alternator and set aside.
2. **On all models,** disconnect blower motor electrical connectors and position engine wiring harness aside.
3. Partially cut blower motor case cover, **Fig. 13.** The cutting pattern is also indicated on the blower case cover. Cover thickness is approximately 1/8 inch. Cut just through thickness of cover. Any cut deeper than thickness of cover may cause damage to cooling tube.
4. Move cut portion of cover downward and disconnect blower motor cooling tube.
5. Remove retaining screws and blower motor.
6. Reverse procedure to install. Use three retaining clips to attach cut portion of blower motor cover.

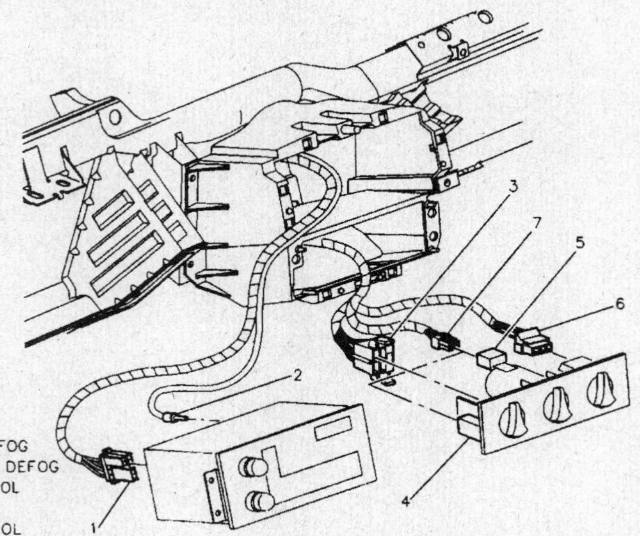

Fig. 12 HVAC control & radio removal. 1998 Grand Am

ALERO, CUTLASS, MALIBU & 1999-2002 GRAND AM

The blower motor and fan are located in the lower righthand corner of the HVAC module. The fan and motor are serviced only as a complete assembly.

1. Remove righthand closeout panel and insulator as required.
2. Position Body Control Module (BCM) aside.
3. Disconnect blower motor electrical connectors.
4. Remove blower motor attaching screws, then the motor and fan assembly.
5. Reverse procedure to install. **Torque** blower motor attaching screws to 45 inch lbs.

HEATER CORE

REPLACE

ACHIEVA, SKYLARK & 1998 GRAND AM

1. Drain coolant into an approved container.
2. Raise and support vehicle.
3. Disconnect heater hoses from heater core assembly and remove drain tube.
4. Lower vehicle, apply parking brake and block drive wheels.
5. Position transaxle shift lever in Neutral.
6. **On models equipped with automatic transaxle,** remove retaining clip and shift lever handle.
7. **On models equipped with manual transaxle,** turn shift lever handle counterclockwise to remove from lever.
8. **On all models,** carefully pry upward on outer edges of console trim plate.
9. Disconnect electrical connectors and ashtray lamp from console trim plate, then remove trim plate from console.
10. Remove attaching screws and console.
11. Remove attaching screws, then disconnect cruise control module electrical connector and lamp and remove lefthand sound insulator panel.
12. Remove attaching screws and nuts, disconnect EVO controller electrical connector and lamp and remove righthand sound insulator panel.
13. Remove attaching screws and steering column filler panel.
14. Remove floor outlet duct.
15. Remove attaching screws and heater core cover.
16. Remove mounting clamps and heater core.
17. Reverse procedure to install.

ALERO & 1999-2002 GRAND AM

1. Drain coolant into an approved container.
2. Raise and safely support vehicle.
3. Drain tube from heater case.
4. Disconnect heater hoses at heater core.
5. Lower the vehicle.
6. **On models equipped with console,** partially remove console as required.
7. **On all models,** remove righthand and lefthand closeout and insulator panels.
8. Remove steering column opening filler.
9. Remove floor air outlet duct.
10. Remove heater core cover. One mounting screw is located in a recess in center of cover.
11. Remove core mounting clamps, then the core.
12. Reverse procedure to install, noting the following:
    a. **Torque** core mounting clamps to 12 inch lbs.
    b. **Torque** cover screws to 12 inch lbs.
    c. **Torque** floor air outlet screws to 12 inch lbs.
    d. Close radiator petcock, fill cooling system and inspect for leaks.

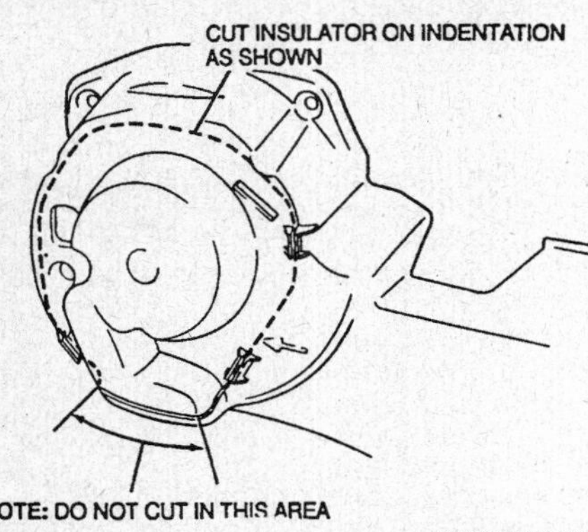

Fig. 13 Blower motor removal pattern. Achieva, Skylark & 1998 Grand Am

CUTLASS & MALIBU

1. Drain coolant into an approved container.
2. Remove heater hoses and drain tube.
3. Remove instrument panel and console as outlined in "Dash Panel Service."
4. Remove heater outlet, mounting screw and heater core cover.
5. Remove mounting clamps and heater core.
6. Reverse procedure to install.

EVAPORATOR CORE

REPLACE

ACHIEVA, SKYLARK & 1998 GRAND AM

1. Recover refrigerant charge using recycling station tool No. J-39500, or equivalent.
2. Raise and support vehicle. Remove front exhaust system heat shield.
3. Remove attaching bolts and swing cradle cross brace aside.
4. Disconnect refrigerant lines from evaporator and lower vehicle.
5. Remove righthand under dash insulator panel.
6. Disconnect heater core cover electrical connector.
7. Remove lefthand side insulator panel, steering column filler panel and center console.
8. Remove floor duct and heater core cover, then the heater shroud and straps.
9. Remove evaporator core. Use care when removing evaporator core, as heater core is only suspended by heater core pipes.
10. Reverse procedure to install. When connecting refrigerant lines, use new O-rings.

ALERO & 1999-2002 GRAND AM

1. Recover refrigerant charge using recycling station tool No. J-39500, or equivalent.
2. Raise and safely support vehicle.
3. Remove evaporator drain tube.

4. Remove lines from evaporator and discard O-rings.
5. Lower the vehicle.
6. Remove righthand and lefthand closeout and insulator panels.
7. Remove electrical junction box at heater core cover.
8. Remove steering column filler.
9. **On models equipped with console,** partially remove console to access floor duct and heater core cover.
10. **On all models,** remove floor air duct.
11. Remove heater core cover. One mounting screw is located in a recess in center of cover.
12. Remove heater core shroud and straps.
13. Remove evaporator assembly.
14. Reverse procedure to install, noting the following:
    a. **Torque** evaporator assembly screws to 12 inch lbs.
    b. **Torque** heater core shroud and straps screws to 12 inch lbs.
    c. **Torque** heater cover screws to 12 inch lbs.
    d. **Torque** floor duct screws to 12 inch lbs.
    e. **On 1999 models, torque** evaporator inlet line fitting to 14 ft. lbs., and outlet line fitting to 35 ft. lbs.
    f. **On 2000–02 models, torque** evaporator hose fitting bolt to 18 ft. lbs.
    g. **On all models,** evacuate and charge refrigerant system.

CUTLASS & MALIBU

1. Recover refrigerant charge using recycling station tool No. J-39500, or equivalent.
2. Drain coolant into an approved container.
3. Remove heater core hoses, evaporator block fitting, seal plate and moisture drain tube.
4. Remove instrument panel and console as outlined in "Dash Panel Service."
5. Remove heater outlet, mounting screw and heater core cover.
6. Remove clamps and heater core, then the mounting screw and heater core shroud.
7. Remove evaporator core.
8. Reverse procedure to install using new sealing washers. **Torque** evaporator hose to evaporator fitting nut to 18 ft. lbs.

2.2L Engine

NOTE: On Air Bag Equipped Models, Refer To "Air Bag System Precautions" Located In The Front Of This Manual For System Disarming & Arming Procedures.

NOTE: Refer To "Computer Relearn Procedures" Located In The Front Of This Manual When Battery Power To The Computer Has Been Interrupted.

INDEX

PRECAUTIONS

AIR BAG SYSTEMS

Refer to "Air Bag System Precautions" in the front of this manual for system disarming and arming procedures.

BATTERY GROUND CABLE

Prior to service, disconnect battery ground cable and isolate as required.

FUEL SYSTEM PRESSURE RELIEF

1. Disconnect battery ground cable, isolate as required.
2. Install fuel pressure gauge tool No. J34730-1A, or equivalent.
3. Install bleed hose into suitable container, then open valve to bleed system pressure.
4. Disconnect fuel pressure gauge from fuel pressure connection.

COMPRESSION PRESSURE

When inspecting cylinder compression, the engine should be at room temperature, the throttle should be open, all spark plugs removed and the battery at full charge. The lowest reading cylinder should not be less than 70% of the highest and no cylinder reading should be less than 100 psi. Turn ignition key until engine cranks through four compression cycles per cylinder. Normal compression builds up quickly and evenly to specified compression on each cylinder.

ENGINE MOUNT

REPLACE

1. Remove cruise control module.
2. Support engine with a wooden block and suitable floor jack positioned below oil pan.
3. Remove engine mount attaching nuts.
4. Remove engine mount to bracket bolts.
5. Remove engine mount.
6. Reverse procedure to install, tighten to specifications.

ENGINE

REPLACE

AUTOMATIC TRANSAXLE

1. Open and support hood. Install a protective covering over fenders. Mark upper hood hinge location to hood with a grease pencil. With an assistant, remove hood.
2. Remove air cleaner resonator to accelerator bracket bolt.
3. Remove resonator from throttle body, air cleaner intake duct and vent hose.
4. Remove accelerator cable and cruise control cable.
5. Disconnect brake booster hose from brake booster.
6. Remove power steering pump.
7. Disconnect fuel lines.
8. Drain coolant into suitable container.
9. Remove radiator inlet hose.
10. Remove surge tank to cylinder head hose.
11. Disconnect surge tank to radiator outlet hose.
12. Remove radiator outlet hose.
13. Remove inlet and outlet heater hoses.
14. Remove surge tank outlet hose attaching bolt to intake manifold.
15. Disconnect electrical connectors to engine components.
16. Remove engine electrical harness.
17. Remove upper transmission bellhousing attaching bolts.
18. Raise and support vehicle.
19. Remove engine drive belt as outlined under "Serpentine Drive Belt."
20. Remove A/C compressor.
21. Remove crankshaft balancer bolt using harmonic balancer holder tool No. J38122-A, or equivalent, to ensure crankshaft does not rotate while loosening attaching bolt.
22. Remove crankshaft balancer.
23. Disconnect alternator electrical connectors.
24. Disconnect starter motor electrical connectors.
25. Drain engine oil into suitable container.
26. Disconnect front exhaust pipe from manifold.
27. Remove starter motor as outlined under "Starter, Replace" in "Electrical" section.
28. Remove flywheel to torque converter bolts.
29. Remove lower transmission bellhousing bolts.
30. Remove transmission to engine brace.
31. Lower vehicle.
32. Install engine bracket tool No. J42451, or equivalent, to right rear side of cylinder head.
33. Install suitable engine hoist to engine.

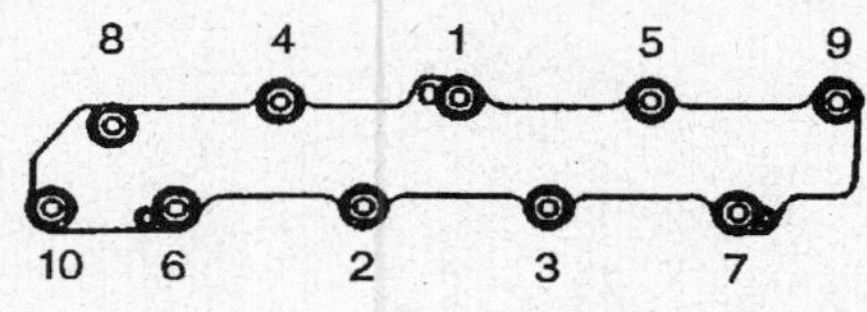

Fig. 1 Exhaust manifold tightening sequence

34. Remove engine mount as outlined under "Engine Mount, Replace."
35. Remove upper transmission bellhousing bolts.
36. Separate engine from transmission.
37. Remove engine.
38. Reverse procedure to install, tighten to specifications.

MANUAL TRANSAXLE

1. Open and support hood. Install a protective covering over fenders. Mark upper hood hinge location to hood with a grease pencil. With an assistant, remove hood.
2. Remove air cleaner resonator to accelerator bracket bolt.
3. Disconnect accelerator and cruise cables.
4. Disconnect brake booster hose.
5. Remove power steering pump.
6. Disconnect fuel lines from engine.
7. Disconnect transmission shift control cables, then from bracket.
8. Disconnect clutch actuator cylinder line.
9. Drain engine coolant into suitable container.
10. Remove radiator inlet hose from engine.
11. Remove surge tank hose from cylinder head.
12. Disconnect surge tank outlet hose to radiator.
13. Remove surge tank outlet hose to intake manifold.
14. Remove radiator outlet hose to engine.
15. Remove inlet and outlet heater hoses.
16. Disconnect electrical connectors to engine sensors and switches.
17. Remove engine harness from engine, set aside.
18. Raise and support vehicle.
19. Remove front crossmember as outlined under "Clutch & Manual Transaxle" in "Cavalier & Sunfire" chapter.
20. Remove drive axles as outlined under "Clutch & Manual Transaxle" in "Cavalier & Sunfire" chapter.
21. Remove engine drive belt as outlined under "Serpentine Drive Belt."
22. Remove A/C compressor assembly.
23. Disconnect alternator and starter electrical connectors.
24. Drain engine oil into suitable container.
25. Disconnect front exhaust pipe from manifold.
26. Support front of engine using a suitable block of wood at oil pan, lower vehicle onto engine support table.
27. Remove engine mount as outlined in "Engine Mount, Replace."
28. Remove transmission mount attaching bolts to frame.
29. Raise vehicle from engine and transmission assembly.
30. Install engine lift bracket tool No. J42451, or equivalent, to right rear of cylinder head.
31. Install suitable engine hoist to engine.
32. Remove transmission bellhousing attaching bolts.
33. Remove engine from transmission, then mount engine to suitable engine stand.
34. Reverse procedure to install, tighten to specifications.

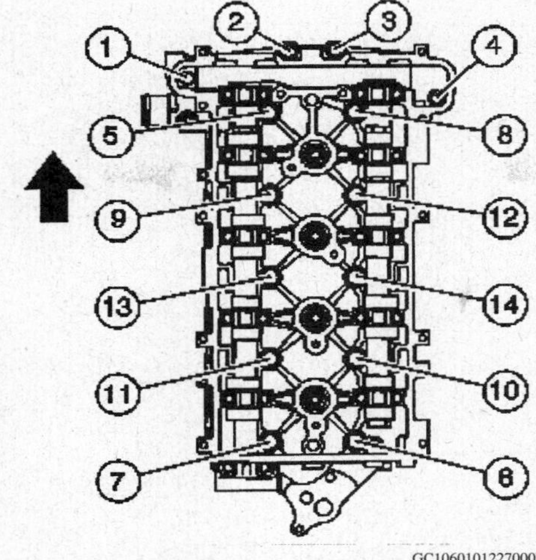

Fig. 2 Cylinder head bolt removal

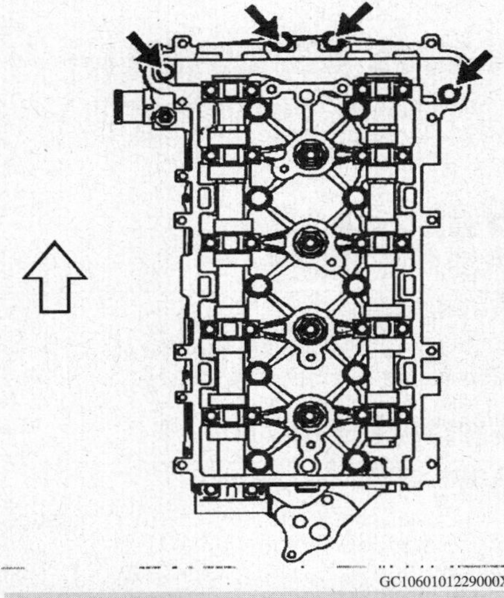

Fig. 4 Front cylinder head bolt tightening

INTAKE MANIFOLD

REPLACE

1. Remove air inlet duct and resonator.
2. Disconnect IAC, TPS and MAP sensor.
3. Disconnect EVAP and PCV hose.
4. Disconnect purge solenoid tube.
5. Disconnect brake booster hose.
6. Remove oil level indicator tube bolt.
7. Disconnect accelerator and cruise control cables.
8. Remove throttle body assembly.
9. Remove fuel rail assembly.
10. Remove KS connector from intake manifold.
11. Remove intake manifold attaching nuts and bolts, then the intake manifold.
12. Remove intake manifold gasket, replace if required.
13. Reverse procedure to install, tighten to specifications.

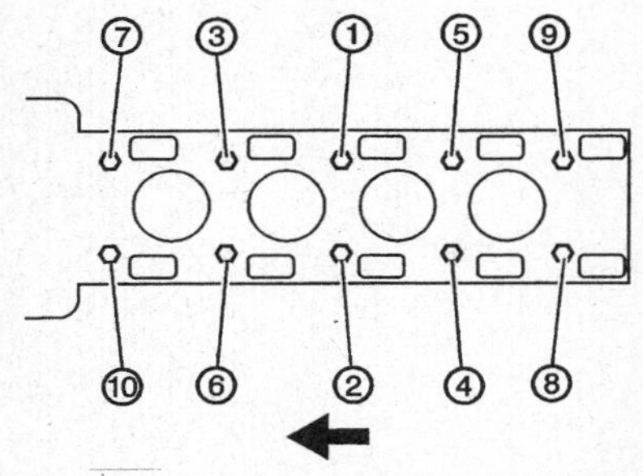

Fig. 3 Cylinder head bolt tightening sequence

EXHAUST MANIFOLD

REPLACE

1. Remove exhaust manifold heat shield.
2. Remove oxygen sensor.
3. Raise and support vehicle.
4. Remove manifold to exhaust flex decoupler attaching bolts.
5. Pull down and back on exhaust pipe in order to disengage pipe from exhaust manifold.
6. Lower vehicle.
7. Remove exhaust manifold to cylinder head retaining nuts.
8. Remove exhaust manifold, clean all sealing surfaces.
9. Reverse procedure to install, noting the following:
   a. **Torque** exhaust manifold to cylinder head retaining nuts to 106 inch lbs., in numbered sequence, **Fig. 1.**

CYLINDER HEAD

REPLACE

1. Remove intake manifold as outlined under "Intake Manifold, Replace."
2. Remove power steering pump.
3. Remove exhaust manifold as outlined under "Exhaust Manifold, Replace."
4. Remove timing chain as outlined under "Timing Chain, Replace."
5. Drain coolant system into suitable container.
6. Remove cylinder head bolts in numbered sequence, **Fig. 2,** discard bolts after removal.
7. Remove cylinder head, then the gasket cleaning all surfaces for installation.
8. Reverse procedure to install, noting the following:
   a. Install NEW cylinder head bolts.
   b. **Torque** cylinder head bolts to 22 ft.

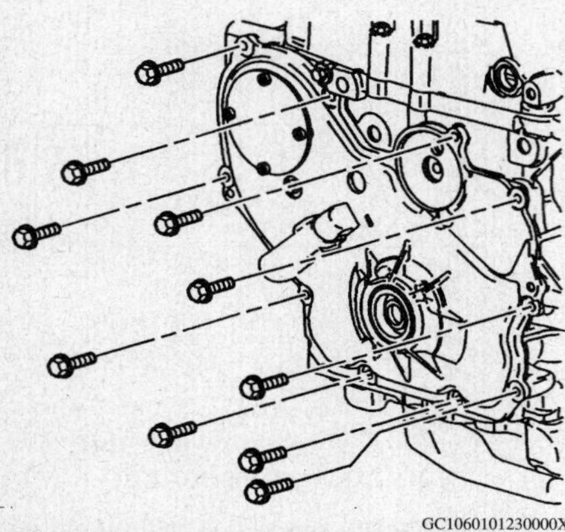

Fig. 5 Engine front cover bolt replacement

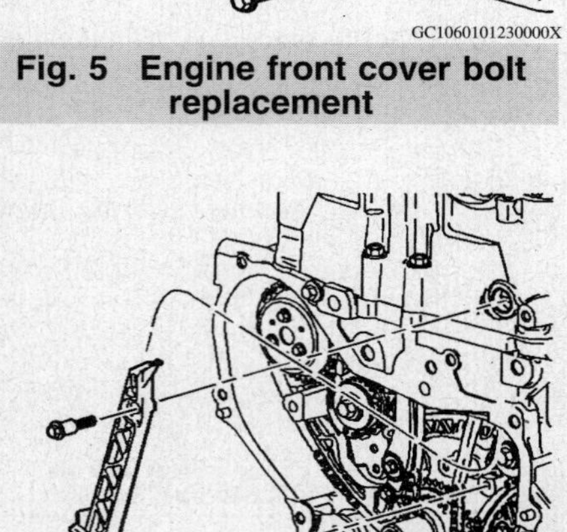

Fig. 8 Fixed timing chain guide replacement

lbs., plus 155 degrees, in numbered sequence, **Fig. 3.**

c. **Torque** front cylinder head bolts to 26 ft. lbs., **Fig. 4.**

VALVE COVER

REPLACE

1. Loosen vent hose clamp at air cleaner resonator, air cleaner intake duct clamp at air cleaner outlet resonator.
2. Loosen air cleaner outlet resonator to throttle body clamp, located forward of accelerator cable bracket. Remove air cleaner resonator to accelerator bracket bolt.
3. Remove resonator from throttle body, air cleaner intake duct and vent hose.
4. Disconnect accelerator and cruise control cables from throttle body, then the bracket.
5. Remove PCV valve.
6. Remove fuel line brackets and brake booster hose pipe from brackets.
7. Remove ignition coil and module as outlined under "Coil Pack, Replace".
8. Remove ground strap.
9. Remove camshaft cover bolts, then the camshaft cover.

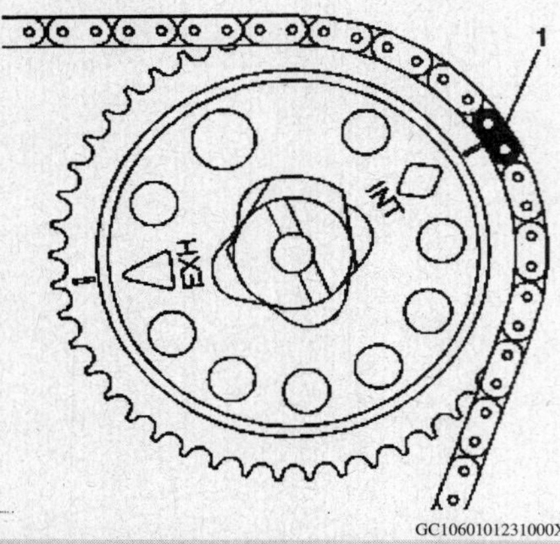

Fig. 6 Timing chain copper link alignment

10. Reverse procedure to install, tighten to specifications.

VALVE ADJUSTMENT

This engine is equipped with hydraulic valve lash adjusters. No adjustment is required.

VALVE LASH ADJUSTERS

REPLACE

Refer to "Camshaft, Replace" for valve lash adjuster replacement procedure.

FRONT COVER

REPLACE

1. Remove engine drive belt as outlined under "Serpentine Drive Belt."
2. Remove crankshaft balancer bolt using harmonic balancer holder tool No. J38122-A, or equivalent, to ensure crankshaft does not rotate while loosening attaching bolt.
3. Remove crankshaft balancer.
4. Remove engine front cover to water pump bolts, **Fig. 5.**
5. Remove remaining engine front cover attaching bolts.
6. Remove engine front cover gasket, if required.
7. Reverse procedure to install, tighten to specifications.

TIMING CHAIN

REPLACE

REMOVAL

1. Remove valve cover as outlined under "Valve Cover, Replace."
2. Raise and support vehiclet.
3. Remove front engine cover as outlined under "Front Cover, Replace,"
4. Rotate engine until crankshaft sprocket mark aligns with second silver link at five o'clock position.

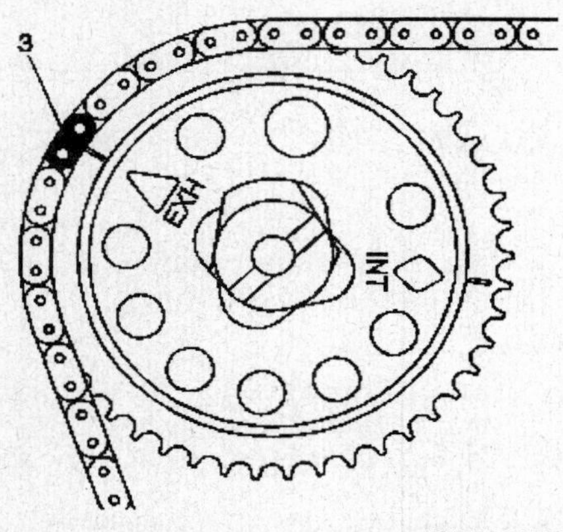

Fig. 7 Timing chain silver link alignment

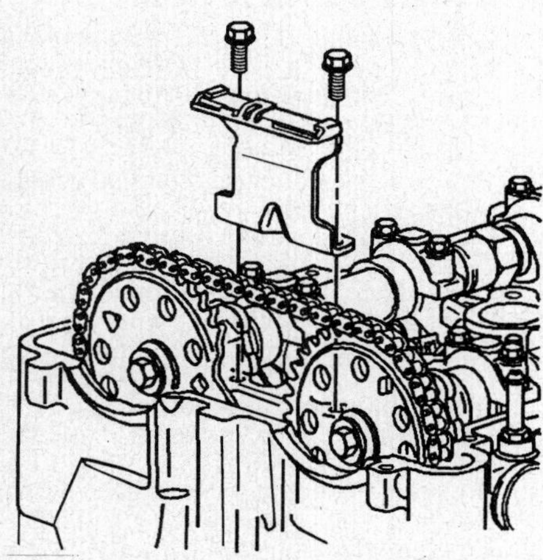

Fig. 9 Upper timing chain guide replacement

5. Lower vehicle.
6. Ensure that INT diamond on intake camshaft sprocket is aligned with copper link at two o'clock position, **Fig. 6.**
7. Ensure that EXH triangle on exhaust camshaft sprocket is aligned with silver link at ten o'clock position, **Fig. 7.**
8. Remove timing chain tensioner.
9. Remove fixed timing chain guide access plug.
10. Remove fixed timing chain guide, **Fig. 8.**
11. Remove upper timing chain guide, **Fig. 9.**
12. Install suitable 24mm wrench to hold camshafts from turning, remove exhaust camshaft sprocket bolt and camshaft sprocket, **Fig. 10,** then discard camshaft sprocket bolt.
13. Remove timing chain tensioner guide, **Fig. 11.**
14. Remove intake camshaft sprocket bolt, intake camshaft sprocket, then the timing chain through top of cylinder head, **Fig. 12.**

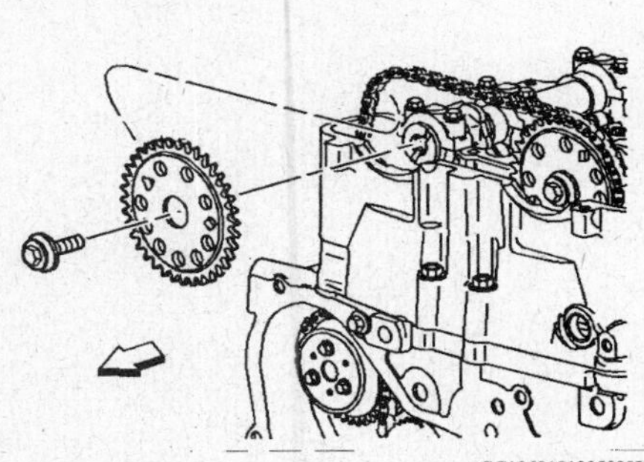

Fig. 10 Exhaust camshaft bolt & sprocket replacement

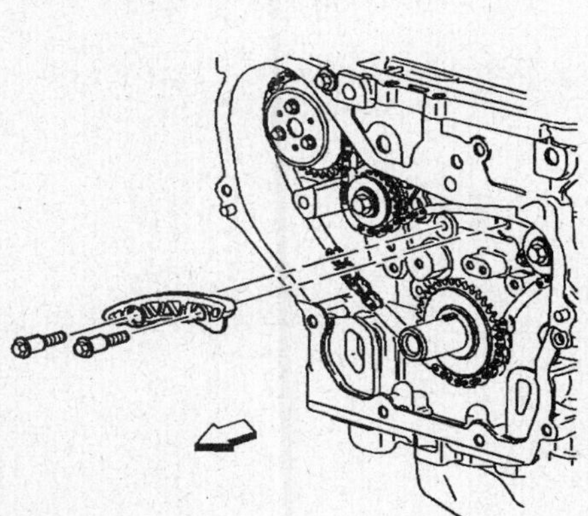

Fig. 13 Upper balance shaft drive chain guide replacement

15. Remove crankshaft sprocket, balance shaft drive chain tenstioner, then the adjustable balance shaft chain guide.
16. Remove small balance shaft drive chain guide.
17. Remove upper balance shaft drive chain guide, **Fig. 13.**
18. Remove balance shaft drive chain, **Fig. 14.**

INSTALLATION

1. Install upper balance shaft chain guide, tighten to specifications.
2. Install balance shaft drive chain with colored links lined up on marks on balance shaft drive sprockets and crankshaft sprocket, **Fig. 15.**
3. Place copper link so that it lines up with timing mark on intake side balance shaft sprocket, **Fig. 15.**
4. Move clockwise around chain, place first chrome link inline with timing mark on crankshaft drive sprocket, five o'clock position, **Fig. 15.**
5. Install chain on water pump drive sprocket, **Fig. 15.**
6. Align last chrome link with timing mark on exhaust side balance shaft drive sprocket, **Fig. 15.**
7. Install small balance shaft chain guide.
8. Tighten balance shaft chain guide bolts to specifications.
9. Install adjustable balance shaft drive chain guide, tighten to specifications.
10. Turn tensioner plunger 90 degrees in its bore and compress plunger until a paper clip can be inserted through hole in plunger body and into hole in tensioner plunger, **Fig. 16.**

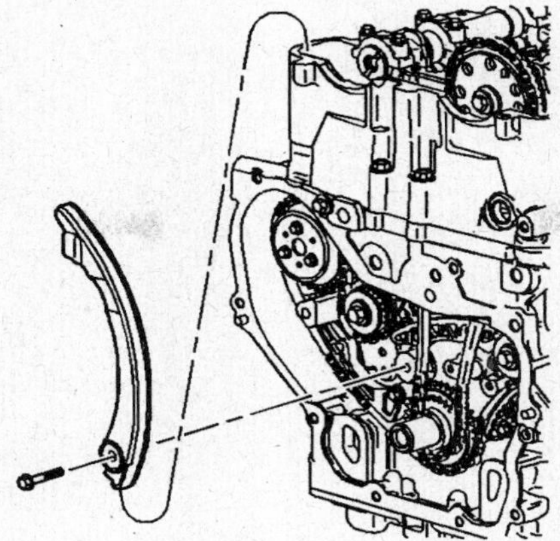

Fig. 11 Timing chain tensioner guide replacement

11. Install timing chain tensioner, tighten to specifications.
12. Remove paper clip from balance shaft drive chain tensioner.
13. Install crankshaft sprocket with timing mark at five o'clock position, **Fig. 17.**
14. Lower timing chain through opening in top of cylinder head, ensure that chain installs around both sides of cylinder block bosses.
15. Install intake camshaft sprocket with INT diamond at two o'clock position, **Fig. 6.**
16. Hand tighten new intake camshaft sprocket bolt.
17. Install timing chain around crankshaft sprocket with second silver link aligning with timing mark.
18. Install timing chain around intake camshaft sprocket with copper link aligning with INT diamond.
19. Install timing chain tensioner guide through opening in top of cylinder head, tighten to specifications.
20. Install exhaust camshaft sprocket with timing chain silver link at EXH triangle aligned ten o'clock position, **Fig. 7.**
21. Install a suitable 24mm wrench to rotate camshaft slightly, until exhaust sprocket aligns with camshaft.
22. Hand tighten new exhaust camshaft sprocket bolt.
23. Install fixed timing chain guide, tighten to specifications.
24. Apply sealant, GM P/N 12345382, or equivalent, compound to thread and install timing chain guide bolt access hole plug, tighten to specifications.
25. Install timing chain upper guide, tighten to specifications.
26. Measure timing chain tensioner when fully compressed, tensioner will measure 2.83 inch.
27. Install timing chain tensioner, tighten to specifications.
28. Install suitable rubber tipped tool, place tool down through camshaft drive to contact timing chain, release tensioner using sharp contact downwards.

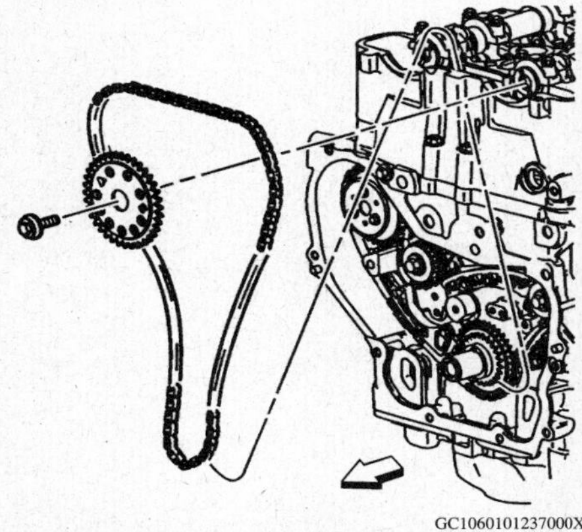

Fig. 12 Camshaft bolt, sprocket & timing chain replacement

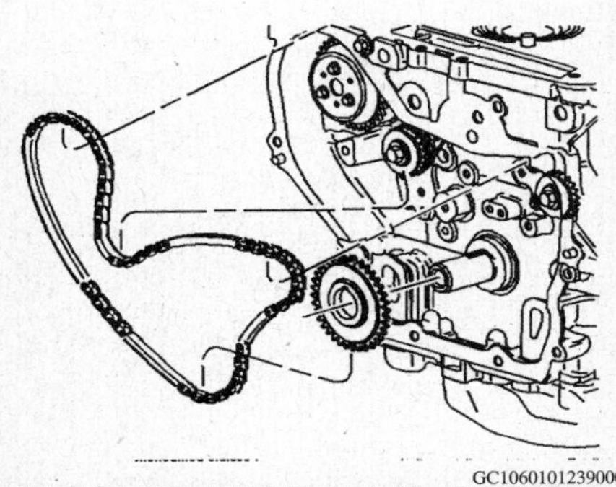

Fig. 14 Balance shaft drive chain replacement

29. Install suitable 24mm wrench to hold camshaft, **Fig. 18, torque** to 63 ft. lbs., plus 30 degrees.
30. Install valve cover.
31. Raise and support vehicle.
32. Install front engine cover as outlined under "Front Cover, Replace."
33. Lower vehicle.

CAMSHAFT

REPLACE

1. Remove valve cover as outlined under "Valve Cover, Replace."
2. Remove upper timing chain guide.
3. Install camshaft sprocket holding tool No. J43655, or equivalent, then remove both intake and exhaust camshaft sprocket bolts.
4. Slide camshaft sprockets forward.
5. **On intake side,** remove power steering pump.
6. **On both sides,** mark bearing caps for installation reference.
7. Remove bearing caps.
8. Remove exhaust and intake camshafts.
9. Remove camshaft roller followers.
10. Remove hydraulic element lash adjusters.

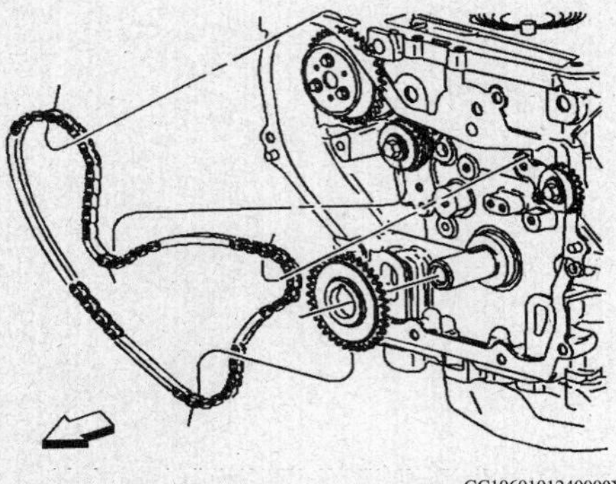
GC1060101240000X

Fig. 15 Timing chain installation

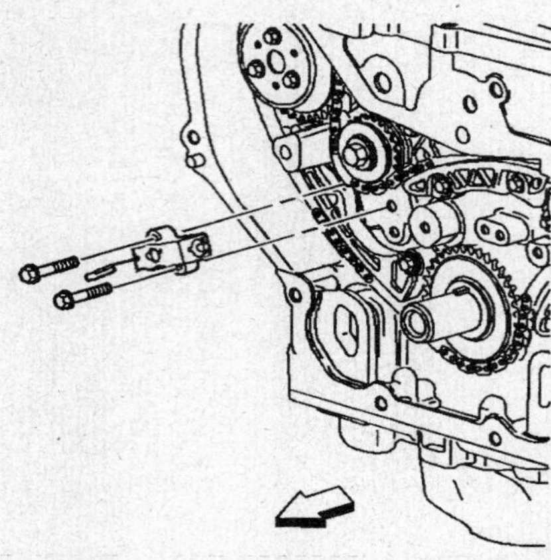
GC1060101241000X

Fig. 16 Tensioner plunger & body installation

GC1060101242000X

Fig. 17 Crankshaft sprocket timing mark

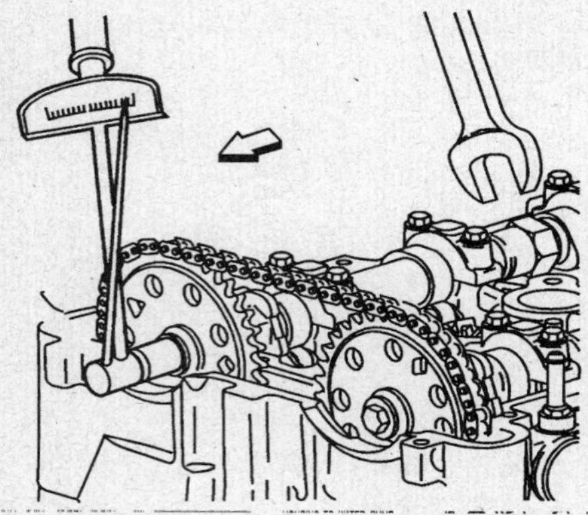
GC1060101243000X

Fig. 18 Camshaft tightening

11. Reverse procedure to install, noting the following:
    a. Lubricate valve tips using suitable lubricant.
    b. Ensure alignment notches are aligned with camshaft sprocket.
    c. **Torque** camshaft bearing cap bolts in three increments to 89 inch lbs.
    d. Apply anaerobic sealer bead, GM P/N 1052942, or equivalent, to rear intake camshaft bearing cap, tighten to specifications.
    e. **Torque** camshaft sprocket bolts to 63 ft. lbs., plus 30 degrees.

BALANCE SHAFT

REPLACE

1. Raise and support vehicle.
2. Remove front tire and wheel.
3. Remove front fender liner.
4. Remove engine drive belt as outlined under "Serpentine Drive Belt."
5. Install harmonic balancer holder tool No. J38122A, or equivalent, to prevent crankshaft from rotating while loosening crankshaft balancer bolt.
6. Remove crankshaft balancer bolt, discard bolt.
7. Remove crankshaft balancer.
8. Reverse procedure to install, tighten to specifications.

PISTON & ROD ASSEMBLY

When installing piston and rod assemblies into cylinder block, ensure arrow on top of piston faces toward front of engine. Ensure flat area on bottom of piston aligns with small dimple above connecting rod crankshaft bearing bore.

PISTONS, PINS & RINGS

Pistons and rings are available in standard size and oversize. Pistons and their pins are serviced as an assembly.

MAIN & ROD BEARINGS

Main and rod bearings are available in standard size only.

CRANKSHAFT SEAL

REPLACE

1. Remove crankshaft balancer as outlined under "Balance Shaft, Replace."
2. Remove front oil seal using suitable flat bladed tool.
3. Reverse procedure to install, using camshaft front main seal installer tool No. J35268A, or equivalent.

CRANKSHAFT REAR OIL SEAL

REPLACE

1. Remove transmission as outlined in "Automatic Transaxles/ Transmissions" or "Clutch & Manual Transaxle."
2. Remove flywheel or flexplate.
3. Remove crankshaft rear oil seal using suitable flat bladed tool.

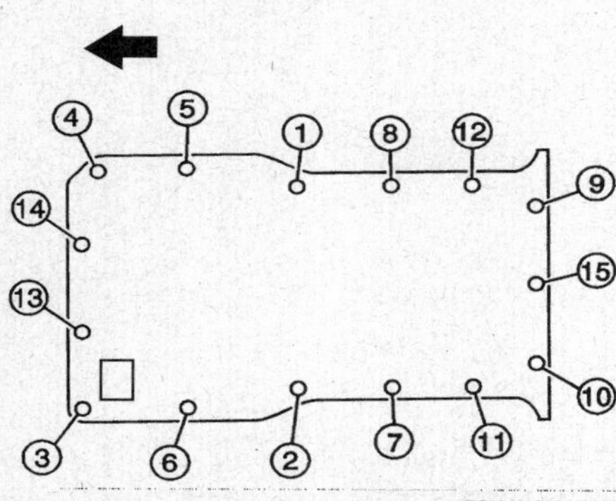

GC1060101244000X

Fig. 19 Oil pan bolt sequence

4. Reverse procedure to install, tighten to specifications.

OIL PAN

REPLACE

1. Raise and support vehicle.
2. Drain engine oil into suitable container.
3. Remove engine mount strut bracket.
4. Remove engine drive belt as outlined under "Serpentine Drive Belt."
5. Remove lower A/C compressor bolts.
6. Loosen upper A/C compressor bolts.
7. Remove oil pan bolts in numbered sequence, **Fig. 19,** then the oil pan.
8. Reverse procedure to install, tighten to specifications, in reverse numbered sequence, Fig. 19.

OIL PUMP

REPLACE

1. Remove oil pan as outlined under "Oil Pan, Replace."
2. Remove oil pump, then the drive shaft extension, **Fig. 20.**
3. Reverse procedure to install, tighten to specifications.

BELT TENSION DATA

1. Turn Off all accessories.
2. Bring engine to operating temperature.

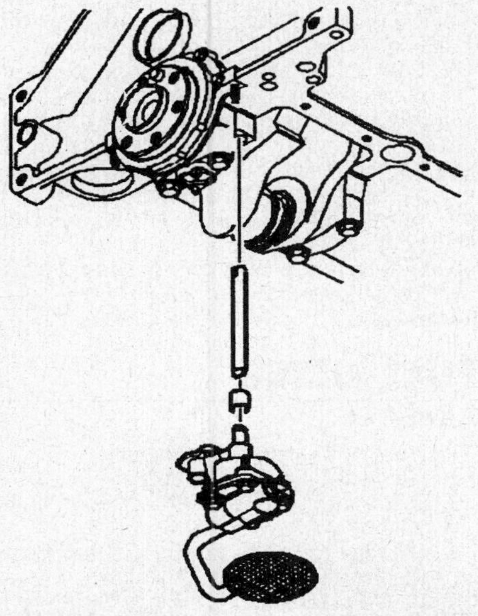

GC1060101245000X

Fig. 20 Oil pump removal

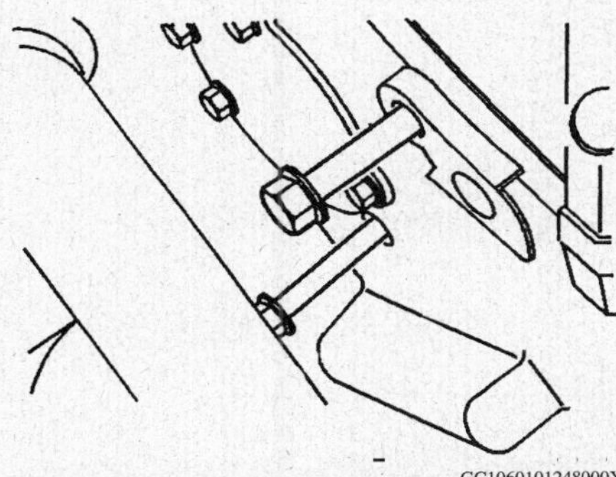

GC1060101248000X

Fig. 23 Water pump, engine block & front cover bolt removal

3. Turn engine Off.
4. Read belt tension using belt tension gauge tool No. J23600B, or equivalent, halfway between alternator and power steering pump.
5. Start engine and allow temperature to stabilize for 15 seconds.
6. Turn engine Off.
7. Install a 15mm socket, apply clockwise force to tensioner pulley bolt.
8. Release force and measure belt tension without disturbing tensioner position.
9. Install 15mm socket, apply counterclockwise force to tensioner pulley bolt and raise pulley to eliminate all tension.
10. Slowly lower pulley to belt and measure belt tension without disturbing tensioner position.
11. Average out all readings.
12. If average is less than 30–50 lbs., replace belt tensioner.

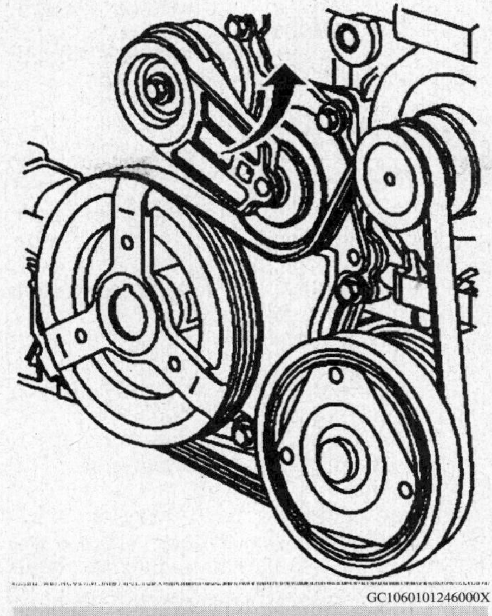

GC1060101246000X

Fig. 21 Drive belt removal

SERPENTINE DRIVE BELT

REPLACEMENT

1. Raise and support vehicle.
2. Remove front fender liner.
3. Rotate drive belt tensioner clockwise.
4. Remove drive belt, **Fig. 21.**
5. Reverse procedure to install.

COOLING SYSTEM BLEED

1. Slowly add a mixture of 50/50 DEX-COOL and clean water to cooling system until coolant level reaches and maintains top of surge tank label.
2. Install surge tank cap.
3. Start engine, run at 2000–2500 RPM until engine reaches normal operating temperature.
4. Allow engine to idle for three minutes.
5. Shut engine Off.
6. Top off coolant as required.
7. Inspect cooling system for leaks.

THERMOSTAT

REPLACE

1. **On models equipped with automatic transmission,** remove exhaust manifold as outlined under "Exhaust Manifold, Replace."
2. **On all models,** drain cooling system into suitable container.
3. Remove thermostat housing to water pump feed pipe.
4. Remove thermostat.
5. Reverse procedure to install, tighten to specifications.

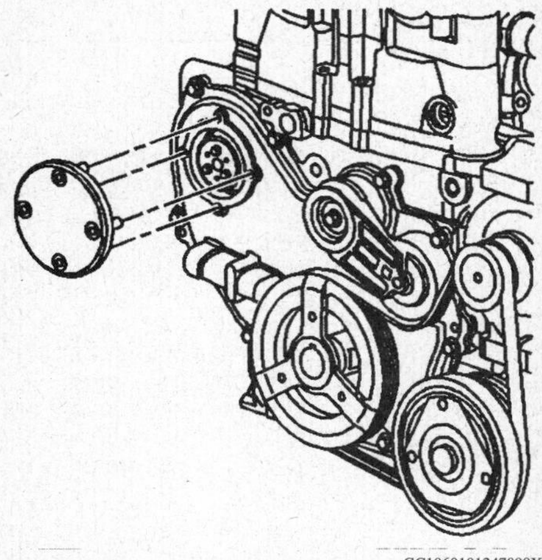

GC1060101247000X

Fig. 22 Water pump access plate removal

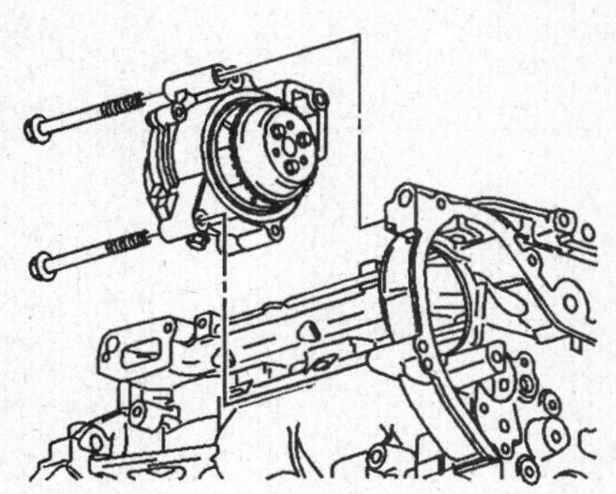

GC1060101249000X

Fig. 24 Water pump bolt removal

WATER PUMP

REPLACE

1. **On models equipped with automatic transmission,** remove exhaust manifold as outlined under "Exhaust Manifold, Replace."
2. **On all models,** drain cooling system into suitable container.
3. Raise and support vehicle.
4. Remove righthand front tire and wheel.
5. Remove front fender liner.
6. Remove access plate on water pump sprocket from timing cover, **Fig. 22.**
7. Install water pump sprocket holding tool No. J43651, or equivalent, to water pump sprocket.
8. Remove sprocket bolts to water pump.
9. Remove engine block to water pump bolt, then the engine front cover to water pump bolt, **Fig. 23.**
10. Remove feed pipes thermostat to water pump.
11. Remove water pump to engine block bolts, **Fig. 24,** then the water pump.
12. Reverse procedure to install, tighten to specifications.

RADIATOR

REPLACE

1. Remove battery and battery tray assembly.
2. Recover A/C refrigerant using suitable ACR 2000 air conditioning service center J43600, and A/C oil injectorJ45037, or equivalents.
3. Drain engine cooling system into suitable container.
4. Remove upper radiator hose.
5. Remove upper transaxle cooler line.
6. Remove coolant surge tank hose.
7. Remove condenser inlet fitting from discharge hose.
8. Disconnect cooling fan electrical connector.
9. Raise and support vehicle.
10. Remove lower cover panel.
11. Remove lower radiator hose from radiator.
12. Remove lower transaxle cooler line.
13. Remove evaporator line to condenser outlet.
14. Remove lower radiator mounting panel.
15. Remove radiator, fan and condenser as an assembly.
16. Reverse procedure to install, tighten to specifications.

FUEL PUMP

REPLACE

The fuel pump is part of the fuel sender assembly and must be replaced as a complete unit.

1. Drain fuel tank into suitable container.
2. Raise and support vehicle.
3. Disconnect the quick-connect fitting at the fuel filter.
4. Disconnect the fuel return pipe quick connect fitting.
5. Remove the rubber exhaust hangers, allow the exhaust system to rest on the rear axle.
6. Remove the exhaust heat shield.
7. Loosen the fuel filler hose clamp at the fuel tank, disconnect the fuel filler hose from the fuel tank.
8. Disconnect the evaporative emission (EVAP) vapor pipe from the EVAP canister.
9. Disconnect the electrical harness from the multi-way rear body connector and fuel strap.
10. With the aid of an assistant, support the fuel tank, disconnect the fuel tank retaining straps then lower the fuel tank.
11. Disconnect wiring harness from fuel sender and fuel tank pressure.
12. Rotate retaining ring, while pressing down on fuel sender.
13. Remove the fuel sender assembly from the tank.
14. Reverse procedure to install.

FUEL FILTER

REPLACE

1. Relieve fuel system pressure.
2. Raise and support vehicle.
3. Disconnect fuel filter fitting using suitable back-up wrench.
4. Disconnect quick connect fitting from fuel filter.
5. Remove fuel filter.
6. Reverse procedure to install, tighten to specifications.

TIGHTENING SPECIFICATIONS

Year	Component	Torque/Ft. Lbs.
2002	Accelerator & Cruise Control Cable	89①
	Accelerator Pedal Retaining Nuts	22
	Access Hole Plug	30
	Access Plate Bolts	18①
	Air Cleaner Clamps	44①
	Air Cleaner Outlet Resonator Mounting Bolt	89①
	Alternator Bolts	15
	Alternator Electrical Connecter	13
	Balance Shaft Chain Guide Bolts	89①
	Battery Terminal Nut	13
	Bell Housing Bolts	66
	Blower Motor Retaining Screw	45①
	Camshaft Bearing Cap Bolts	89①
	Camshaft Bolts	63③
	Camshaft Cover Bolts	89①
	Chain Tensioner Bolts	89①
	Condenser To Inlet Discharge Hose	18
	Condenser To Radiator Bolts	44①
	Crankshaft Balancer Bolt	74④
	Crankshaft Position Sensor Bolts	71①
	Cylinder Head Bolts	②
	Drive Belt Tensioner Bolt	33
	Engine Coolant Temperature Sensor	89①
	Engine Front Cover To Water Pump Bolts	15
	Engine Mount Nuts	49
	Engine To Transmission Brace Bolts	53
	Evaporator Core Bracket Screw	9①
	EVAP Canister Purge Valve Mounting Bracket Nut	71①
	EVAP Canister Retainer Bolt	89①
	EVAP Line Bolt	18
	Exhaust Manifold Heat Shield	18
	Exhaust Manifold Nuts	106①
	Fixed Timing Chain Guide Bolts	89①
	Flywheel Bolts	39⑤
	Front Cover Bolts	15
	Front Cover To Water Pump Bolt	15
	Fuel Filler Hose Clamp	27①
	Fuel Filler Pipe Attaching Screw	89①
	Fuel Filter Fitting	20
	Fuel Line Bracket Bolt	89①
	Fuel Pipe Mounting Bolt	53①
	Fuel Pipe Retainer Bolts	89①
	Fuel Rail Pipe Fittings	89①
	Fuel Tank Retaining Strap Bolt	26
	Ground Strap	89①
	Heated Oxygen Sensor 1	22
	Heated Oxygen Sensor 2	30
	Heater Core Bracket Screw	9①
	Heater Core Case Screw	9①
	Heater Core Cover Screw	9①
	ICM Bolts	89①

Continued

TIGHTENING SPECIFICATIONS—Continued

Year	Component	Torque/Ft. Lbs.
2002	ICM Screws	13①
	Idle Air Control Valve	27①
	Ignition Switch	53①
	Ignition Switch Bracket	53①
	Intake Manifold Nuts & Bolts	89①
	Knock Sensor	18
	Lower Radiator Mounting Panel Bolts	89①
	Manifold To Flex Decoupler	26
	Multi-Function Switch Screws	35①
	Oil Pan Bolts	18
	Park Neutral Switch Bolts	18
	Power Steering Pump Bolts	19
	Pump To Rear Bearing Cap Bolt	30
	Radiator Drain Cock	18①
	Rear Intake Camshaft Bearing Cap Bolts	18
	Spark Plugs	15①
	Starter Motor Bolts	30
	Steering Wheel Nut	27
	Throttle Body Attaching Bolts & Studs	89①
	Throttle Position Sensor Mounting Screws	18①
	Timing Chain Tensioner	55
	Timing Chain Tensioner Guide Bolt	89①
	Timing Chain Upper Guide	89①
	Transaxle Oil Cooler Line	22
	Upper Air Cleaner Cover Screws	27①
	Water Pump Drain Plug	16①
	Water Pump Feed Pipes	18①
	Water Pump Sprocket To Water Pump	89①
	Wiper Drive Module Screws	89①
	Wiper Motor Screws	89①

①— Inch lbs.
②— Refer to "Cylinder Head, Replace" procedure.
③— Tighten additional 30 degrees.
④— Tighten additional 75 degrees.
⑤— Tighten additional 25 degrees.

2.4L Engine

NOTE: On Air Bag Equipped Models, Refer To "Air Bag System Precautions" Located In The Front Of This Manual For System Disarming & Arming Procedures.

NOTE: Refer To "Computer Relearn Procedures" Located In The Front Of This Manual When Battery Power To The Computer Has Been Interrupted.

INDEX

PRECAUTIONS

AIR BAG SYSTEMS

Refer to "Air Bag System Precautions" in the front of this manual for system disarming and arming procedures.

FUEL SYSTEM PRESSURE RELIEF

Failure to relieve system pressure prior to disconnecting fuel system components may cause fire or personal injury.

1. Loosen fuel tank filler cap to relieve tank pressure.
2. Raise and safely support vehicle.
3. Disconnect fuel pump electrical connector.
4. Lower the vehicle.
5. Start and operate engine until fuel supply is consumed.
6. Crank engine for approximately three seconds to relieve remaining pressure.
7. Disconnect battery ground cable, then connect fuel pump connector.

BATTERY GROUND CABLE

Prior to service, disconnect battery ground cable and isolate as required.

COMPRESSION PRESSURE

When inspecting cylinder compression, the engine should be at room temperature, the throttle should be open, all spark plugs removed and the battery at or near full charge. The lowest reading cylinder should not be less than 70% of the highest and no cylinder reading should be less than 100 psi. Turn ignition key until engine cranks through four compression cycles. Normal compression builds up quickly and evenly to specified compression on each cylinder.

ENGINE MOUNT

REPLACE

FRONT MOUNT

1. Remove coolant recovery tank attaching bolt and position tank aside with hoses connected.
2. Install engine support tool No. J-28467-360, or equivalent then raise engine off the mount.
3. Remove mount to body attaching nuts.
4. Remove engine bracket to mount attaching bolts.
5. Remove engine mount assembly.
6. Reverse procedure to install. Tighten to specifications.

ENGINE MOUNT STRUT

1. Raise and support vehicle.
2. Remove righthand front splash shield.
3. Remove engine mount strut bolts, **Fig. 1.**
4. Remove engine mount strut.
5. Reverse procedure to install. Tighten to specifications.

ENGINE

REPLACE

ACHIEVA, MALIBU, SKYLARK & 1998 GRAND AM

1. Recover refrigerant charge using recycling station tool No. J-39500, or equivalent.
2. Drain coolant into an approved container.
3. **On models equipped with manual transaxle,** remove lefthand sound insulator and disconnect clutch push rod from pedal assembly.
4. **On all models,** disconnect heater hose at thermostat housing.
5. Disconnect radiator upper inlet hose.
6. Remove air cleaner assembly.
7. Remove coolant fan.
8. Disconnect compressor/condenser hose assembly at compressor and discard O-rings.
9. Disconnect vacuum hoses from front of engine.
10. Disconnect alternator, A/C compressor, injector harness, Idle Air Control (IAC) and Throttle Position (TP) sensors at throttle body, Manifold Air Pressure (MAP) and Intake Air Temperature (IAT) sensors, EVAP

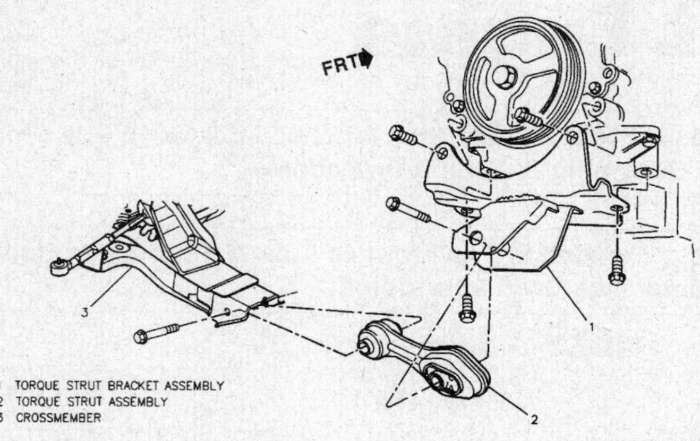

Fig. 1 Engine mount strut & bracket

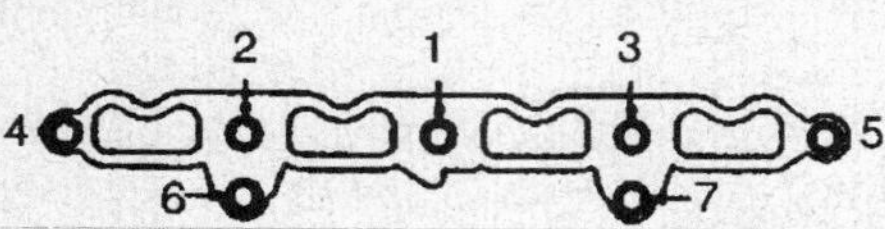

Fig. 2 Intake manifold installation & bolt tightening sequence

Canister Purge solenoid, starter solenoid and ground cables.

11. Disconnect battery ground cable from transaxle, Electronic Ignition Coil and Module ASM, two Engine Coolant Temperature sensors, oil pressure sensor/switch, oxygen sensor (O2S), Crankshaft Position (CP) sensor, backup lamp switch and camshaft position sensor.
12. Disconnect power brake vacuum hose from throttle body.
13. Disconnect throttle cable and bracket.
14. Remove power steering bolts and pump. Position pump aside with lines attached.
15. Disconnect fuel lines. Refer to "Precautions" for fuel system pressure relief.
16. Disconnect shift cables.
17. **On models equipped with manual transaxle,** disconnect clutch actuator line.
18. **On all models,** remove exhaust manifold and heat shield.
19. Disconnect radiator lower outlet hose.
20. Install engine support fixture No. J-28467-360, or equivalent.
21. Remove coolant recovery tank attaching bolt and position tank aside with hoses intact.
22. Remove engine mount assembly as outlined under "Engine Mount, Replace."
23. Raise and support vehicle.
24. Remove front wheel and tire assemblies.
25. Remove righthand splash shield.
26. Disconnect vehicle speed and sensors, starter solenoid and front ABS wheel speed sensor electrical connectors.
27. Remove engine mount strut and transaxle mount as outlined under "Engine Mount Replace."
28. Separate ball joints from steering knuckles.
29. Remove suspension supports, crossmember and stabilizer shaft as an assembly.
30. Remove heater outlet hose from radiator outlet pipe.
31. **On models equipped with manual transaxle,** disconnect axle shaft from transaxle and intermediate shaft and position aside.
32. **On all models,** remove flywheel housing cover.
33. Position suitable support below engine, then lower vehicle onto support.
34. Mark threads on support fixture hooks so setting can be duplicated when installing engine. Remove engine support fixture J-hooks.
35. Raise vehicle slowly off engine and transaxle assembly. Note that it may be required to move engine/transaxle assembly rearward to clear intake manifold.
36. Separate engine from transaxle.
37. Reverse procedure to install. Tighten to specifications. Fill all drained fluids and inspect for leaks.

ALERO & 1999–2001 GRAND AM

1. Relieve fuel system pressure as outlined under "Precautions."
2. Drain coolant into an approved container.
3. Drain engine oil using approved containers and methods.
4. Remove fuel rail assembly, then the air intake duct from air cleaner.
5. Disconnect and remove ignition coil and module assembly, then the Camshaft Position Sensor (CMP) electrical connector.
6. Remove power steering pump mounting fasteners, then position pump aside with lines and hoses intact.
7. Disconnect oil pressure sender electrical connector.
8. Remove air intake duct bracket, then the cruise control assembly and position aside.
9. Install engine support fixture tool No. J-28467-360, or equivalent.
10. Remove engine mount assembly.
11. Disconnect vacuum hose at fuel pressure regulator.
12. Raise engine using support fixture "J" hook.
13. Remove engine mount bracket, then lower the engine.
14. Raise and safely support vehicle.
15. Remove serpentine drive belt using tensioner tool No. J-36018, or equivalent.
16. Remove front tires and wheels, then the righthand front splash shield.
17. Remove harmonic balancer using puller tool No. J-24420-C, or equivalent.
18. Lower the vehicle.
19. Disconnect electrical connectors at MAP, IAT and EGR sensors, then at EVAP canister.
20. Remove alternator.
21. Remove and discard accelerator cable. **Manufacturer recommends cable replacement when engine is removed and installed.**
22. Position cruise control cable aside to avoid damage.
23. Remove accelerator cable bracket, then the starter motor.
24. Remove exhaust brace bolt from exhaust manifold, then the exhaust manifold heat shield.
25. Disconnect exhaust pipe at manifold.
26. Remove intake coolant pipe.
27. Remove torque converter bolts.
28. Raise and safely support vehicle.
29. Remove O2 sensor.
30. Remove A/C compressor bolts, then position compressor aside with lines intact.
31. Remove oil pan to bellhousing bolts.
32. Remove transaxle mount.
33. Remove transaxle to engine attaching bolts.
34. Install a suitable lifting device to engine.
35. Raise engine and separate it from transaxle.
36. If engine will be mounted onto a stand, remove flexplate mounting bolts and flexplate, then mount engine on suitable stand.
37. Reverse procedure to install, noting the following:
    a. If flexplate was removed, install it and its bolts. Tighten bolts evenly to specifications while holding flexplate in place with holder tool No. J-38122, or equivalent.
    b. Tighten to specifications.
    c. Start engine and inspect for fluid leaks.

INTAKE MANIFOLD

REPLACE

1. Remove air cleaner duct.
2. Disconnect electrical connectors at MAP, IAT and EVAP sensors and fuel injector harness.
3. Disconnect vacuum hoses from fuel regulator and EVAP canister purge solenoid to canister.
4. Remove throttle cable bracket.
5. Disconnect coolant lines from throttle body as required.
6. Remove stud-ended alternator mount bolt.
7. Remove pipe from EGR adapter.

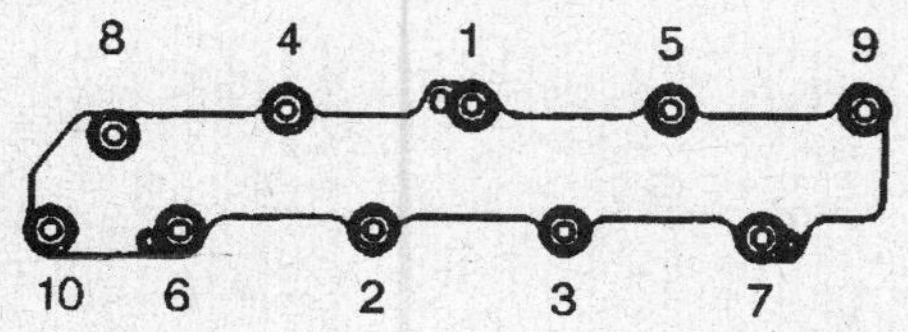

Fig. 3 Exhaust manifold installation & bolt tightening sequence

8. Raise and support vehicle.
9. Remove intake manifold support brace, then lower the vehicle.
10. Remove manifold retaining nuts, bolts, manifold and gasket, **Fig. 2.**
11. Reverse procedure to install. Tighten intake manifold bolts in sequence, **Fig. 2.**

EXHAUST MANIFOLD

REPLACE

1. Disconnect electrical connector from O2 sensor.
2. Raise and safely support vehicle.
3. Remove exhaust manifold brace to manifold bolts.
4. Remove upper heat shield.
5. Remove exhaust pipe to manifold retaining nuts, then pull down and back on pipe to disengage from manifold. **Do not bend exhaust flex coupler more than 3° in any direction.**
6. Lower the vehicle and remove exhaust manifold to cylinder head retaining nuts, manifold, seals and gaskets.
7. Reverse procedure to install. Tighten exhaust manifold attaching nuts in sequence, **Fig. 3.**

CYLINDER HEAD

REPLACE

1. Drain coolant into an approved container.
2. Remove air cleaner duct.
3. Disconnect heater inlet and throttle body hoses from coolant outlet.
4. Disconnect power brake vacuum hose.
5. Disconnect MAP, IAT, CMP sensor and EVAP canister purge solenoid electrical connectors.
6. Remove alternator stud-ended bolt.
7. Remove brace and intake manifold as outlined under "Intake Manifold, Replace."
8. Install alternator stud-ended bolt.
9. Install engine support tool No. J-28467-360, or equivalent.
10. Remove exhaust manifold as outlined under "Exhaust Manifold, Replace."
11. Remove electrical connectors, mounting bolts and ignition coil and module.
12. Remove power steering pump as outlined under "Front Suspension & Steering."
13. Remove fuel pressure regulator vacuum line and fuel injector harness connectors.
14. Remove fuel line retaining clamp and fuel rail mounting bolts on top of intake camshaft housing.

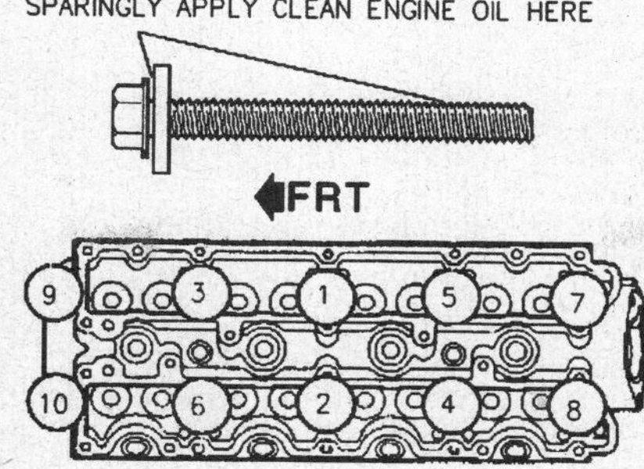

Fig. 4 Cylinder head bolt tightening sequence

15. Cover injector openings and injector nozzles.
16. Remove fuel rail with lines attached and position aside.
17. **On Alero and 1999–2001 Grand Am models,** proceed as follows:
    a. Remove timing chains as outlined under "Timing Chain, Replace."
    b. Remove timing sprockets.
    c. Remove water pump as outlined under "Water Pump, Replace."
18. **On all models except Alero and 1999–2001 Grand Am,** disconnect timing chain housing at intake camshaft housing. **Do not remove it from vehicle.**
19. **On all models,** remove intake and exhaust camshaft housings.
20. Remove valve lifters.
21. Disconnect oil pressure switch and ECT sensor electrical connectors.
22. **On models equipped with automatic transaxle,** remove transaxle fluid level indicator tube if required.
23. **On all models,** disconnect upper radiator hose and ECT sensor connectors.
24. Remove mounting bolts in reverse of tightening sequence, **Fig. 4.**
25. Reverse procedure to install. Tighten cylinder head attaching bolts using torque angle meter tool No. J-36660, or equivalent, **Fig. 4.**

CAMSHAFT LOBE LIFT SPECIFICATIONS

Engine/VIN	Int., Inch	Exh., Inch
2.4L/T	.354	.346

VALVE ADJUSTMENT

These engines are equipped with hydraulic valve lash adjusters. No adjustment is required.

VALVE GUIDES

Valve guides are an integral component

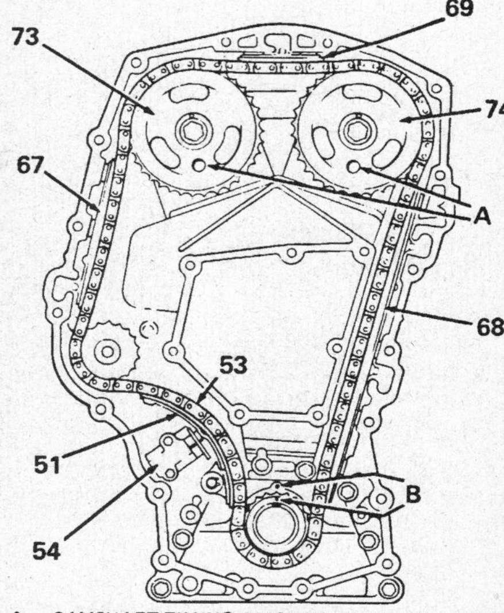

Fig. 5 Valve timing marks

of the cylinder head and are not removable. If valve stem clearance becomes excessive, the valve guide should be reamed to the next oversize and the appropriate oversize valves installed.

VALVE LASH ADJUSTERS

These engines use hydraulic valve lash adjusters. The valve lash adjusters can be replaced after the appropriate camshaft and housing are removed. Refer to "Camshaft, Replace."

FRONT COVER

REPLACE

1. Drain coolant into an approved container.
2. Remove coolant reservoir or surge tank.
3. Remove serpentine drive belt.
4. Attach engine support tool Nos. J-28467-360 and J-28467-400, or equivalents onto alternator stud-ended bolt.
5. Remove front cover upper attaching screws.
6. Remove engine mount assembly and bracket adapter. Discard adapter bolts.
7. Raise and safely support vehicle.
8. Remove righthand front wheel and tire assembly, then the righthand splash shield.
9. Using harmonic balancer tool No. J-38122, or equivalent to hold balancer in position, remove retaining bolt

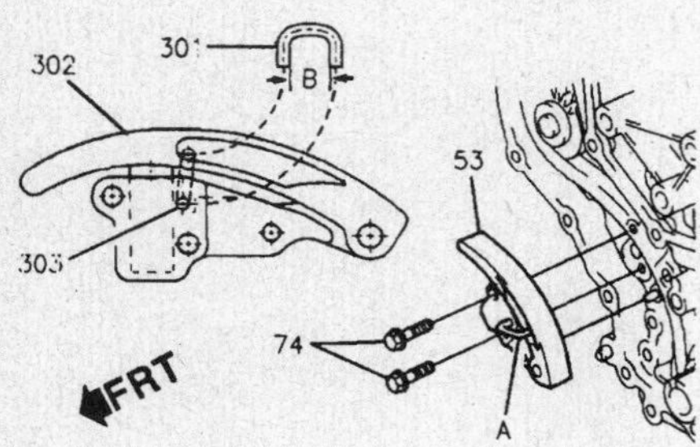

A AFTER INSTALLATION, REMOVE ANTI-RELEASE FROM TENSIONER ASM. TO RELEASE TENSIONER
B 13 mm (1/2 INCH)

53 TIMING CHAIN TENSIONER AND SHOE ASSEMBLY
74 BOLTS – 10 N m (89 LBS. IN.)
301 ANTI-RELEASE KEEPER – FABRICATED FROM HEAVY GAGE WIRE OR STEEL ROD
302 SHOE
303 RESET ACCESS HOLE

GC1069600656000X

Fig. 6 Timing chain tensioner spring & retainer

and balancer using puller tool No. J-24420-C, or equivalent.
10. Remove fasteners attaching lower portion of front cover.
11. Lower the vehicle.
12. Remove front cover and gaskets.
13. Reverse procedure to install, noting the following:
    a. Engine mount bracket adapter bolts are designed to permanently stretch when tightened. Always use proper fasteners in this particular location. Do not use stronger bolts. Components will not tighten properly if improper bolts are used.
    b. Using torque angle meter tool No. J-36660 or equivalent, **torque** engine mount bracket adapter bolts to 81 ft. lbs., then rotate an additional 90°.
    c. Tighten all remaining fasteners to specifications.

TIMING CHAIN

REPLACE

REMOVAL

1. Remove front cover as outlined under "Front Cover, Replace."
2. Rotate crankshaft in clockwise direction until camshaft sprocket timing dowel pin holes line up with timing chain housing holes, **Fig. 5.**
3. Remove timing chain guides.
4. Raise and support vehicle.
5. Ensure all timing chain slack is above tensioner, then remove tensioner, **Fig. 6.**
6. Timing chain must be disengaged from grooves in tensioner shoe to permit removal of shoe. Position a suitable screwdriver under timing chain while pulling shoe outward to disengage.
7. If removing tensioner shoe is difficult, proceed as follows:
    a. Lower the vehicle.
    b. Hold intake camshaft sprocket in

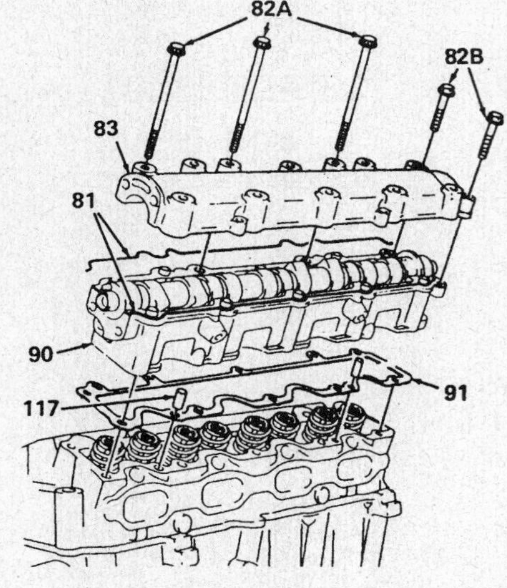

81. SEALS, CAMSHAFT HOUSING TO CAMSHAFT HOUSING COVER (EACH SEAL IS DIFFERENT)
82A. BOLT, CAMSHAFT HOUSING TO CYLINDER HEAD
82B. BOLT, CAMSHAFT HOUSING COVER TO CAMSHAFT HOUSING
83. COVER, CAMSHAFT
90. CAMSHAFT HOUSING (INTAKE SHOWN)
91. GASKET, CAMSHAFT HOUSING TO CYLINDER HEAD
117. DOWEL PIN (2)

GC1069100422000X

Fig. 7 Camshaft housing & cover

position with camshaft sprocket wrench tool No. J-39579, or equivalent.
    c. Remove sprocket bolt and washer.
    d. Remove washer and install bolt into camshaft by hand.
    e. Position a suitable three-jaw puller into intake camshaft sprocket relief holes and remove sprocket. Do not pry on camshaft sprocket as damage to sprocket or timing chain housing may result.
8. Remove mounting bolts and tensioner assembly. Use care when removing, as tensioner is spring loaded.
9. Mark timing chain and crankshaft sprocket for installation.
10. Remove timing chain.

INSTALLATION

Do not interchange timing chains between model years on this engine. There are differences in the sprockets. The links' shape matches the sprockets. Be sure the crankshaft sprocket and timing chain are assembled in the same orientation as they were removed.

1. Hold camshaft sprocket in position with camshaft sprocket tool No. J-39579, or equivalent, then install attaching bolt and washer. Use adhesive sealant compound P/N 12345493, or equivalent on bolt. Tighten to specifications.
2. Install camshaft sprocket timing alignment pin tools No. J-36800, or equivalent through holes in camshaft sprockets into timing chain housing holes to position camshafts for proper timing, **Fig. 5.**

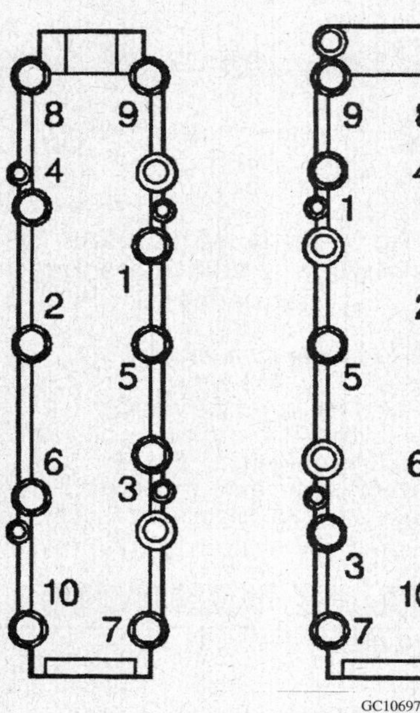

GC1069701058000X

Fig. 8 Camshaft housing bolt tightening sequence

3. If camshafts are out of position and must be rotated more than 1/8 turn, proceed as follows:
    a. Rotate crankshaft clockwise to 90° off TDC.
    b. Position camshafts and install dowels.
    c. Rotate crankshaft **counterclockwise** back to TDC. **Rotating crankshaft clockwise to TDC will damage valves and pistons.**
4. Place timing chain over exhaust camshaft sprocket, coolant pump or idler sprocket and crankshaft sprocket.
5. Remove intake camshaft timing pin and attach camshaft sprocket tool No. J-39579, or equivalent.
6. Rotate intake camshaft sprocket counterclockwise with tool until timing chain can be installed over sprocket.
7. Release tool. The timing chain tension between camshaft sprockets should tighten.
8. Timing pin should easily fit through intake camshaft sprocket timing hole into timing chain housing timing hole. If timing pin does not fit easily, repeat procedure.
9. With timing pins installed, raise and support vehicle.
10. With slack removed from timing chain between intake camshaft sprocket and crankshaft sprocket, timing marks on crankshaft and engine block should be aligned. If crankshaft timing marks are not aligned, move timing chain one tooth forward or rearward to remove slack, then align marks.
11. **On Achieva, Malibu, Skylark and 1998 Grand Am models,** proceed as follows:
    a. Load tensioner assembly to zero position by forming a keeper out of heavy gauge wire.
    b. Apply slight force on tensioner blade to compress plunger.

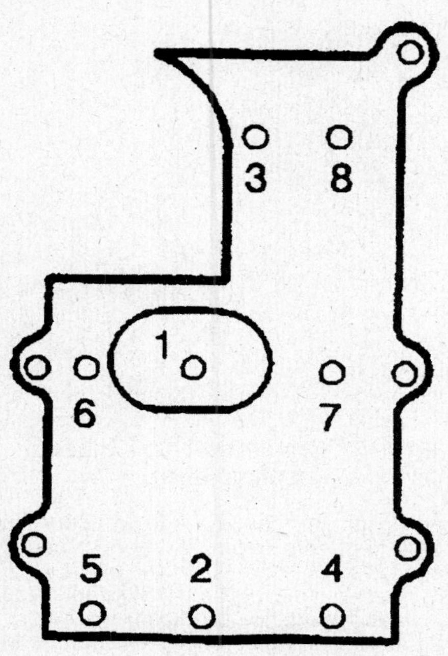

Fig. 9 Balance shaft housing bolt tightening sequence

c. Insert small screwdriver into reset access hole and pry ratchet pawl away from ratchet teeth while forcing the plunger completely in the hole.
d. Install keeper between access hole and blade.
e. Install tensioner assembly to chain housing and inspect plunger assembly installation once again, ensuring long end is toward crankshaft.
f. Tighten timing chain tensioner bolts to specifications.

12. **On Alero and 1999–2001 Grand Am models,** proceed as follows:
    a. Assemble tensioner plunger and tensioner body.
    b. With tensioner plunger fully extended, rotate tensioner with plunger down on a flat surface.
    c. Press down on tensioner body until plunger full seats in body.
    d. Install assembled tensioner onto timing chain housing.
    e. Apply hand pressure to tensioner shoe until locking tab seats into stud groove.
    f. Install tensioner bolts and **torque** to 89 inch lbs.
    g. Release plunger.
    h. Use a flat-bladed screwdriver or similar tool to press firmly against plunger's face. Press down until plunger releases against rear of tensioner shoe. **Do not damage face.**
13. **On all models,** lower vehicle enough to remove alignment dowel pins.
14. Rotate crankshaft two revolutions clockwise.
15. Align crankshaft keyway with cylinder block alignment mark and insert timing

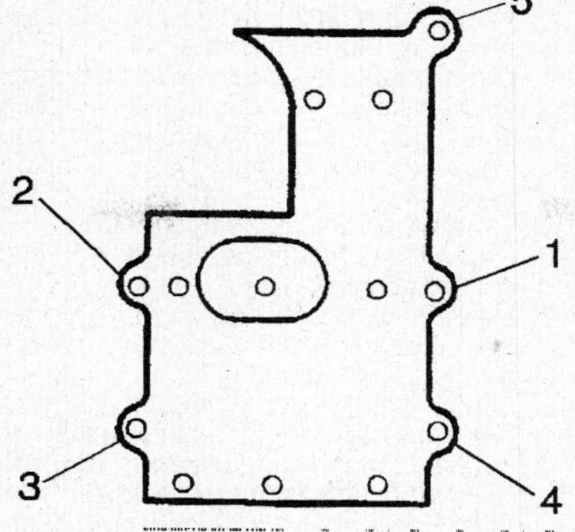

Fig. 10 Balance shaft housing to block bolt tightening sequence

pins through camshaft sprockets into timing chain housing timing holes.

16. Timing pins should slide easily through timing holes. If timing pins cannot be easily inserted, repeat procedure to properly time engine.
17. Install timing chain guides and front cover.

CAMSHAFT

REPLACE

Whenever camshaft housing to cylinder head attaching bolts are loosened, the camshaft housing to cylinder head gasket must be replaced.

INTAKE

1. Drain coolant into an approved container.
2. Disconnect ignition coil and module electrical connectors.
3. Remove mounting bolts and pull upward on ignition coil and module assembly, **Fig. 3.** If connectors are stuck to spark plugs, remove them using spark plug connector remover tool No. J-36011, or equivalent. Always pull straight upward.
4. Disconnect camshaft position electrical sensor.
5. Remove power steering pump and position aside with hoses attached.
6. Disconnect vacuum line from fuel pressure regulator and fuel injector wiring harness electrical connector.
7. Remove fuel line bracket from top of intake camshaft housing.
8. Remove fuel rail retaining bolts and fuel rail. Leave fuel lines attached and position fuel rail over master cylinder. Cover openings in cylinder head and injector nozzles.
9. Disconnect timing chain housing at intake camshaft housing. **Do not remove from vehicle.**
10. Remove front cover as outlined under "Front Cover, Replace."
11. Raise and safely support vehicle.
12. Disconnect heater hose at thermostat housing and drain cylinder block completely.

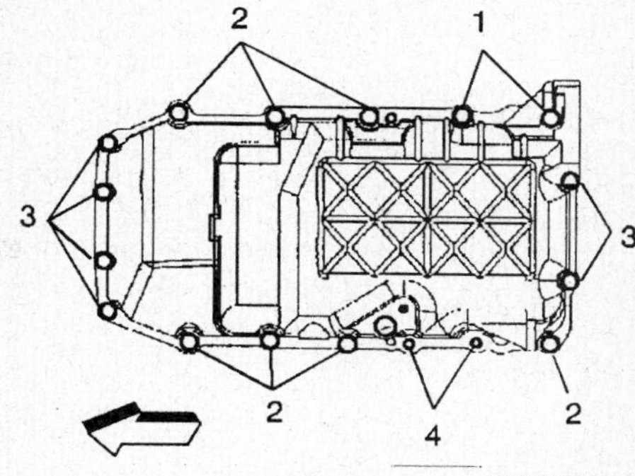

Fig. 11 Oil pan bolt identification & locations

13. Remove timing chain tensioner and timing chain as outlined under "Timing Chain, Replace."
14. Remove water pump mounting nuts as outlined under "Water Pump, Replace."
15. Remove timing chain housing to block bolts and oil pan to front cover bolts.
16. Remove lowest front cover retaining stud.
17. Lower the vehicle.
18. Remove camshaft sprocket retaining bolts and washers while holding sprockets with camshaft sprocket tool No. J-39579, or equivalent.
19. Remove camshaft sprockets. They are identical and interchangeable.
20. Remove chain housing to camshaft housing bolts. Do not remove timing chain housing.
21. Remove camshaft housing cover attaching bolts, **Fig. 7,** and note positioning of all gaskets.
22. Loosen camshaft housing to cylinder head attaching bolts in reverse order of tightening sequence, **Fig. 8.**
23. Leave two camshaft housing to cylinder head attaching bolts loosely installed. Thread four camshaft housing to cylinder head bolts into tapped camshaft housing cover holes and push cover off housing. Remove loosely installed bolts. Note positioning of all gaskets, then remove and discard gasket.
24. Loosely install one camshaft housing to cylinder head bolt to retain housing during camshaft and lifter removal.
25. Note timing chain sprocket dowel pin position for assembly and remove camshaft, using care not to damage journals.
26. Remove valve lash adjuster. Keep adjusters in order for future assembly. Store them in the upside down position on a level surface in clean engine oil to minimize lifter bleed-down.
27. Remove camshaft housing and gasket.
28. Reverse procedure to install, noting the following:
    a. Lubricate entire camshaft and valve lash adjusters with lubricant P/N 12345501, or equivalent.
    b. Apply suitable sealant to threads of camshaft housing, cover retaining, ignition coil and module assembly

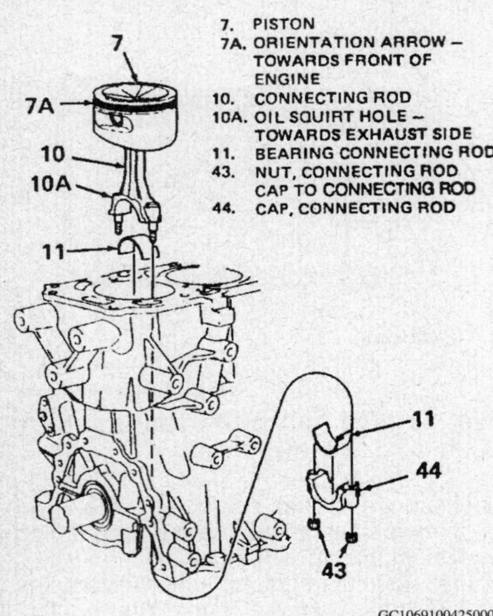

Fig. 12 Piston & rod assembly

attaching bolts.

c. install camshaft housing cover to camshaft housing, noting seal positioning is as noted during removal.
d. **Torque** camshaft housing to cylinder head bolts in sequence, **Fig. 8,** to 16 ft. lbs., then rotate an additional 90° using torque angle meter tool No. J-36660, or equivalent. **Torque** camshaft housing cover to camshaft housing bolts to 16 ft. lbs., then rotate an additional 30°.
e. Apply a ¼ inch bead of sealer P/N 12346286, or equivalent onto joint at end of camshaft housing halves before installing power steering pump and face seal.
f. Tighten timing chain housing to engine and camshaft housing fasteners to specifications.
g. Apply pipe sealant P/N 1052080, or equivalent onto ignition coil and bolts securing module cover assembly to camshaft housing.
h. If a new camshaft was installed, add engine oil supplement P/N 1052367, or equivalent to engine oil.

EXHAUST

1. Drain coolant into an approved container.
2. Disconnect ignition coil and module electrical connectors.
3. Remove mounting bolts, then pull upward on ignition coil and module assembly, **Fig. 3.** If connectors are stuck to spark plugs, use spark plug connector remover tool No. J-36011, or equivalent by pulling straight upward to remove them.
4. Disconnect oil pressure switch electrical connector.
5. Remove front cover as outlined under "Front Cover, Replace."
6. Raise and safely support vehicle.
7. Disconnect heater hose at thermostat housing and drain cylinder block completely.
8. Disconnect timing chain housing at exhaust camshaft housing, but do not remove components from vehicle.
9. **On models equipped with automatic transaxle,** remove transaxle fluid level indicator tube assembly from exhaust camshaft cover and position aside.
10. **On all models,** lower the vehicle.
11. Remove exhaust camshaft housing cover and gasket.
12. Loosen camshaft housing to cylinder head attaching bolts in reverse order of tightening sequence, **Fig. 8.**
13. Leave two camshaft housing to cylinder head attaching bolts loosely installed. Thread four camshaft housing to cylinder head bolts into tapped camshaft housing cover holes and push cover off housing. Remove loosely installed bolts, note gasket positioning, then discard gasket.
14. Loosely install one camshaft housing to cylinder head bolt to retain housing during camshaft and lifter removal.
15. Note timing chain sprocket dowel pin position for assembly and remove camshaft, using care not to damage journals.
16. Remove valve lash adjuster. Keep them in order for reassembly. Store them in the upside down position, on a level surface in clean engine oil to prevent lifter bleed-down.
17. Remove camshaft housing and gasket.
18. Reverse procedure to install, noting the following:
    a. Lubricate entire camshaft and valve lash adjusters with lubricant P/N 12345501, or equivalent.
    b. Apply suitable sealant to threads of camshaft housing, cover retaining, ignition coil and module assembly attaching bolts.
    c. When installing camshaft housing cover to camshaft housing, ensure seals are positioned as was noted during removal.
    d. **Torque** camshaft housing to cylinder head bolts in sequence, **Fig. 8,** to 11 ft. lbs., then rotate an additional 90° using torque angle meter tool No. J-36660, or equivalent. **Torque** camshaft housing cover to camshaft housing bolts to 11 ft. lbs., then rotate an additional 30°.
    e. Tighten timing chain housing to engine and camshaft housing fasteners to specifications.
    f. Apply pipe sealant P/N 1052080, or equivalent on camshaft housing and threads of cover retainer bolt.
    g. Tighten timing chain housing to engine and camshaft housing fasteners to specifications.
    h. If a new camshaft was installed, add engine oil supplement P/N 1052367, or equivalent to engine oil.

VALVE LIFTER BREAK-IN

If new lifters have been installed or if they bled down while the engine was disassembled some excessive noise might be heard when first starting up again. This is normal and no engine damage should occur. To purge trapped air from the lifters, proceed as follows:

1. Start engine and allow it to idle and warm up for five minutes.
2. Increase engine speed to 2000 RPM until lifter noise disappears.
3. Return engine to idle for another five minutes or perform a road test.

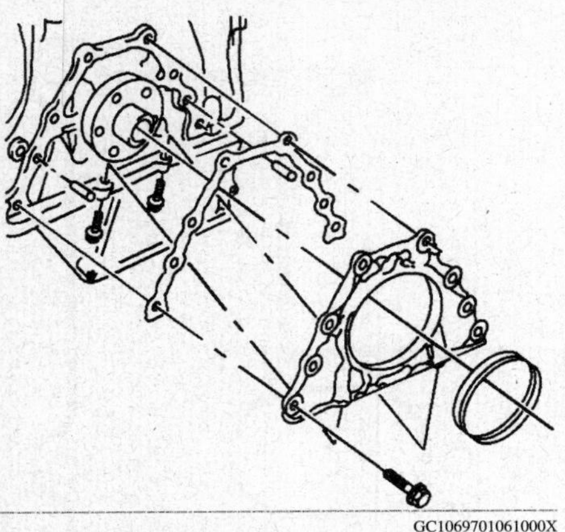

Fig. 13 Crankshaft rear oil seal replacement

BALANCE SHAFT

REPLACE

REMOVAL

1. Remove oil pan as outlined in "Oil Pan, Replace."
2. Remove mounting nut, bolt and balance shaft chain cover.
3. Loosen but do not remove balance shaft chain tensioner.
4. Remove oil pump and cover.
5. Rotate engine crankshaft until No. 1 piston is at TDC.
6. Use balance shaft holding tool No. J-41088, or equivalent to prevent balance shafts from turning while loosening bolt.
7. Mark driven sprocket's surface if it will be used again, then remove lefthand threaded driven sprocket bolt from shaft.
8. Loosen balance shaft housing bolts.
9. Remove fasteners and balance shaft housing.
10. Remove bolts and separate housing.
11. Remove balance shaft and gear subassemblies from lower housing, then the bearings, bolts and thrust plate.

INSTALLATION

1. Install thrust plate and tighten bolts to specifications.
2. Mount a suitable dial indicator and measure shaft endplay at rear side of shafts.
3. If endplay is not within .0073–.0179 inch, inspect and replace thrust plate.
4. Install balance shaft and gear subassemblies, ensuring gear timing marks are properly aligned.
5. Apply thread locker P/N 12345493, or

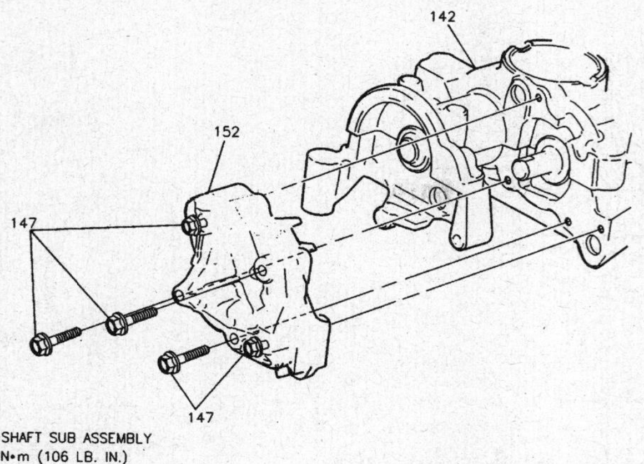

Fig. 14 Oil pump replacement

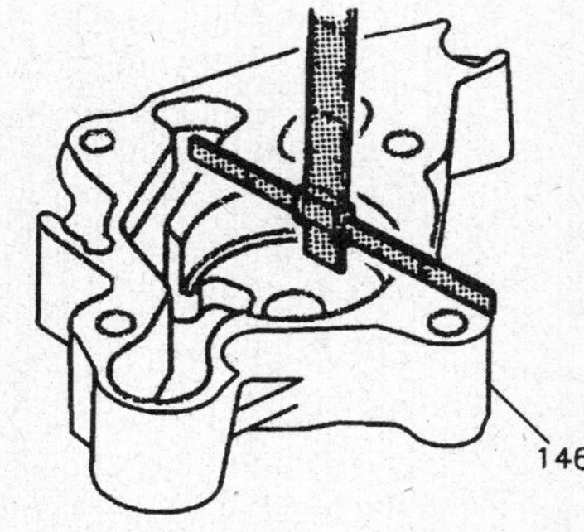

Fig. 15 Gerotor cavity depth measurement

equivalent to mounting bolts and install housing on block, then proceed as follows:
   a. **Torque** housing bolt Nos. 1, 2, 4, 5, 6 and 7, **Fig. 9,** 11 ft. lbs., then rotate an additional 40° using torque angle meter tool No. J-36660, or equivalent.
   b. **Torque** housing bolt Nos. 3 and 8 to 84 inch lbs., then rotate an additional 40°.
   c. **Torque** housing bolt Nos. 1, 2 and 4, **Fig. 10,** to 18 ft. lbs., then rotate an additional 70°.
   d. **Torque** bolt 3, **Fig. 10,** to 30 inch lbs., then rotate an additional 60°.
   e. **Torque** bolt 5, **Fig. 10,** to 39 ft. lbs.
6. Rotate balance shafts and ensure they spin freely.
7. Ensure No. 1 piston is at TDC.
8. Install balance shaft holder tool No. J-41088, or equivalent to prevent shaft rotation.
9. **Torque** balance shaft driven sprocket bolt to 22 ft. lbs., then rotate an additional 45°. **Bolt is lefthand threaded and must be tightened by rotating counterclockwise.**
10. Adjust balance shaft chain tension with three lbs. of force to .040 inch using a brass feeler gauge between guide and chain.
11. **Torque** balance shaft chain tensioner bolt to 10 ft. lbs.
12. Install balance shaft chain cover and **torque** bolt to 10 ft. lbs.
13. Install oil pan with a new gasket. Tighten fasteners to specifications, **Fig. 11.**

PISTON & ROD ASSEMBLY

Assemble piston to rod with arrow on piston toward front of engine and oil squirt hole on rod toward exhaust side of engine, **Fig. 12.**

Upon installation, use a suitable feeler gauge to measure connecting rod side clearance, which should be .0059–.0177 inch.

PISTONS, PINS & RINGS

Pistons and rings are available in standard size and oversize. Pistons and their pins are serviced as an assembly.

MAIN & ROD BEARINGS

Main and rod bearings are available in standard size only.

CRANKSHAFT REAR OIL SEAL

REPLACE

1. Remove transaxle assembly as outlined under "Transaxle, Replace."
2. **On models equipped with manual transaxle,** remove clutch as outlined under "Clutch, Replace."
3. **On all models,** remove mounting bolts and flywheel using holder tool No. J-38122, or equivalent.
4. Remove oil pan to crankshaft rear seal housing mounting bolts.
5. Remove mounting screws, crankshaft rear seal housing and gasket, **Fig. 13.**
6. Support crankshaft rear seal housing on two wooden blocks of equal thickness with crankshaft side facing upward and drive seal out through transaxle side of housing.
7. Reverse procedure to install, noting the following:
   a. If silicone strips across top of aluminum carrier oil pan, at cylinder block and at seal housing 3-way joint are damaged they can be restored to their original dimensions using silicone sealant P/N 12345739, or equivalent.
   b. Lubricate seal lips with engine oil prior to installing housing.
   c. Press replacement seal into housing using rear crankshaft seal installer No. J-36005, or equivalent.
   d. If using old flywheel to crankshaft bolts, coat their threads with adhesive sealant compound P/N 12345493, or equivalent.
   e. Tighten all fasteners to specifications.

OIL PAN

REPLACE

1. Drain crankcase and cooling system into approved containers.
2. Support engine using engine support fixture tool No. J-28467-360, or equivalent.
3. Remove flywheel housing inspection cover.
4. Remove righthand front wheel and tire assembly, then the splash shield.
5. Remove serpentine drive belt.
6. Remove A/C compressor lower mounting bolts from bracket and support with refrigerant hoses attached.
7. **On Alero and 1999–2001 Grand Am models,** remove engine to transaxle brace.
8. **On all models,** remove engine mount strut bracket bolts and position bracket aside.
9. Raise engine approximately 1½ inches.
10. Remove bolts and radiator outlet pipe.
11. Remove exhaust manifold brace.
12. Remove oil pan to flywheel cover nut and bolt.
13. **On Alero and 1999–2001 Grand Am models,** remove flywheel cover stud for clearance.
14. **On all models,** remove radiator outlet pipe from lower radiator hose and oil pan.
15. Disconnect oil level sensor electrical connector.
16. Remove mounting bolts and oil pan.
17. Reverse procedure to install, noting the following:
   a. **Torque** M8 × 1.25 × 80 bolts (1), **Fig. 11,** to 18 ft. lbs.
   b. **Torque** M8 × 1.25 × 22 bolts (2) to 18 ft. lbs.
   c. **Torque** M6 × 1.00 × 25 bolts (3) to 108 inch lbs.
   d. **Torque** bolt (4) to 19 ft. lbs.

OIL PUMP

REPLACE

1. Remove oil pan as outlined under "Oil

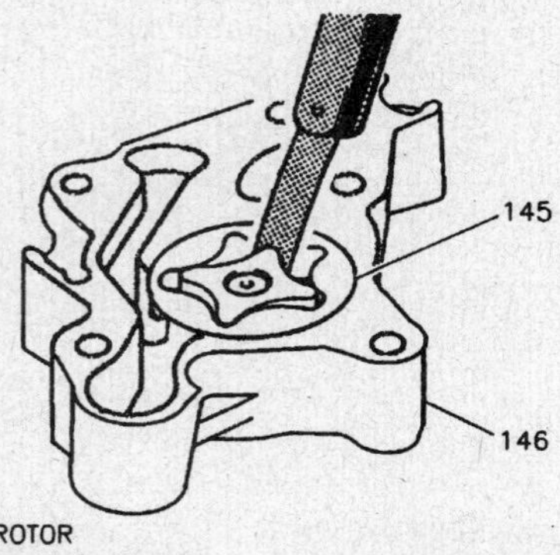

Fig. 16 Inner gear tip clearance measurement

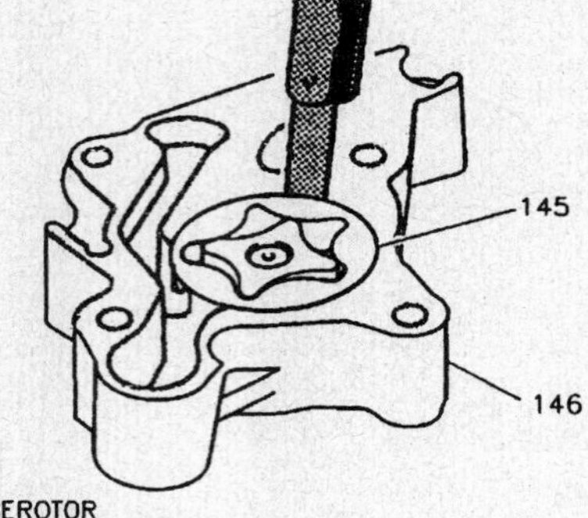

Fig. 17 Outer gerotor diameter clearance measurement

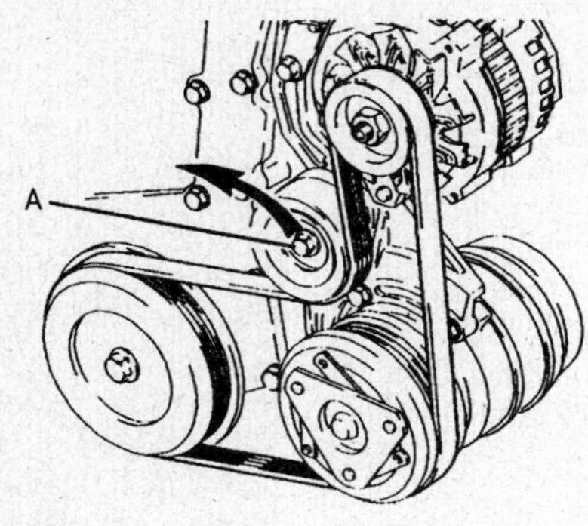

Fig. 18 Serpentine belt replacement

Pan, Replace."

2. Remove balance shaft chain cover.
3. Remove balance shaft chain tensioner assembly.
4. Remove oil pump cover, mounting bolts and pump, **Fig. 14.**
5. Reverse procedure to install, noting the following:
   a. **Torque** cover to balance shaft housing bolts to 40 ft. lbs.
   b. Adjust balance shaft tension as outlined under "Balance Shaft, Replace."
   c. Tighten remaining bolts to specifications.

OIL PUMP SERVICE

1. Remove oil pump as outlined under "Oil Pump, Replace."
2. Disassemble pump gerotor cover from housing.
3. Remove pump from balance shaft housing.
4. Disassemble pressure relief valve.
5. Remove roll pin with punch.
6. Pry out remaining bottom half of valve using suitable tool.
7. Clean all components in suitable cleaning solvent. Remove varnish, sludge and dirt.
8. Inspect pump cover and housing for cracks, scoring, porous or damaged casting, damaged threads, excessive wear or galling and replace if needed.
9. Inspect relief valve for physical damage and replace if needed.
10. Inspect gerotor for chipping, galling or excessive wear and replace if needed.
11. Measure gerotor cavity depth, **Fig. 15.**
12. Depth should be .6023–.6043 inch.
13. Measure inner gerotor tip clearance, **Fig. 16,** which should be .0059 inch maximum.
14. Measure outer gerotor diameter clearance, **Fig. 17.**
15. Diameter clearance should be .0019–.0059 inch.
16. Replace any worn component if any measurement is not within specifications.

BELT TENSION DATA

1. Turn off all accessories.
2. Bring engine to operating temperature.
3. Turn engine off.
4. Using tension gauge tool No. J-23600-B or equivalent, measure belt tension halfway between alternator and power steering pump.
5. Start engine and allow temperature to stabilize for 15 seconds.
6. Turn engine off.
7. Using a 15 mm socket, apply clockwise force to tensioner pulley bolt.
8. Release force and measure belt tension without disturbing tensioner position.
9. Using 15 mm socket, apply counterclockwise force to tensioner pulley bolt and raise pulley to eliminate all tension.
10. Slowly lower pulley to belt and measure belt tension without disturbing tensioner position.
11. Average out all three readings.
12. If average reading is less than 30–50 lbs., replace belt tensioner.

SERPENTINE DRIVE BELT

Refer to **Fig. 18,** for drive belt replacement. **Use a tight fitting 13 mm wrench at least 18 inches long.**

COOLING SYSTEM BLEED

After filling cooling system, start engine and allow it to reach operating temperature with surge tank pressure cap removed. Air will bleed through surge cap opening. Add coolant as required to bring to proper level, then install surge tank pressure cap.

THERMOSTAT

REPLACE

1. Drain coolant into an approved container until level falls below thermostat.
2. Remove exhaust manifold heat shield.
3. Remove inlet housing bolt through exhaust manifold.
4. Raise and support vehicle.
5. **On Alero and 1999–2001 Grand Am models,** proceed as follows:
   a. Remove coolant inlet housing stud from oil pan.
   b. Remove tire and wheel.
   c. Remove splash shield.
   d. Remove transaxle to engine block brace.
6. **On all models,** remove radiator outlet pipe stud.
7. Remove second coolant inlet housing bolt and inlet housing.
8. Remove thermostat, **Fig. 19.**
9. Reverse procedure to install, noting the following:
   a. **Torque** coolant inlet housing stud to oil pan to 19 ft. lbs.
   b. **Torque** coolant inlet housing bolts through exhaust manifold to 10 ft. lbs.
   c. Bring engine to operating temperature and inspect for leaks.

WATER PUMP

REPLACE

REMOVAL

1. Drain coolant into an approved container.
2. Remove drive belt as outlined under "Serpentine Drive Belt."
3. Compress tensioner and hold while removing tensioner mounting bolts and tensioner.
4. Disconnect all required electrical connectors.
5. Remove required exhaust manifold heat shields.
6. Remove heat wrap from heater hose.
7. Disconnect all required heater hoses.
8. Remove coolant inlet housing bolt through exhaust manifold.
9. Raise and safely support vehicle.
10. Remove exhaust manifold brace mounting bolt.
11. Remove exhaust pipe to manifold studs.
12. **On Alero and 1999–2001 Grand Am models,** remove heater outlet pipe bracket to transmission bolt.
13. **On all models,** pull down and back on exhaust pipe to disengage from manifold bolts. **To avoid damage do not rotate flex coupling more than 3°.**

14. **On models equipped with manual transaxle,** remove exhaust manifold brace.
15. **On all models,** remove radiator outlet pipe from oil pan and transaxle. Leave lower radiator hose attached and pull down gently on radiator outlet pipe to disengage it from water pump. Leave outlet pipe hanging.
16. Lower the vehicle and remove brake vacuum pipe from cam housing.
17. Remove mounting nuts, exhaust manifold, seals and gaskets.
18. Remove engine front cover as outlined under "Front Cover, Replace," then compress timing chain tensioner.
19. Remove cover bolts, timing chain housing nuts, water pump and cover, **Fig. 20.**

INSTALLATION

Read through this entire procedure before installing the water pump. Pay particular attention to the unusual tightening sequence.

1. Install water pump cover to pump assembly. Hand tighten bolts.
2. Install cover to block bolts hand tight.
3. Install pump to timing chain housing. Hand tighten nuts.
4. Lubricate coolant inlet pipe O-ring with clean antifreeze, then slide pipe into pump cover. Hand tighten bolts.
5. **Torque** pump assembly to timing chain housing nuts to 19 ft. lbs.
6. **Torque** pump cover to pump bolts to 10 ft. lbs.
7. **Torque** pump cover to engine block bottom bolt to 19 ft. lbs., then **torque** remaining bolts to 19 ft. lbs.
8. **Torque** coolant inlet pipe assembly to pump cover bolts to 10 ft. lbs.
9. Reverse remaining removal steps to complete installation. Tighten to specifications.

RADIATOR

REPLACE

ACHIEVA, SKYLARK & 1998 GRAND AM

1. Drain coolant into an approved container.
2. Remove air intake duct assembly.
3. Disconnect upper transaxle cooler line.
4. Disconnect upper radiator hose.
5. Lower transaxle cooler line.
6. Disconnect cooling fan electrical connector and remove cooling fan mounting bolts.
7. Remove cooling fan.
8. Remove splash guard below lower radiator hose.
9. Disconnect lower radiator hose from radiator.
10. Remove condenser line retaining clip.
11. Remove condenser to radiator attaching bolts.
12. Disconnect coolant surge tank hose.
13. Remove mounting bolts and radiator.
14. Reverse procedure to install. Tighten to specifications.

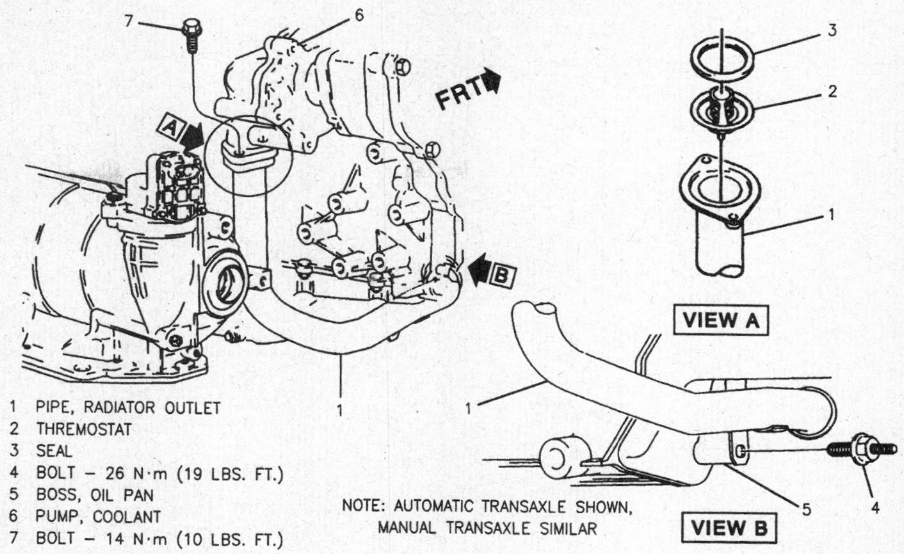

Fig. 19 Thermostat replacement

ALERO & 1999–2001 GRAND AM

1. Recover refrigerant charge using recycling station tool No. J-39500, or equivalent.
2. Drain coolant into an approved container.
3. Remove battery and battery tray.
4. Remove upper radiator hose.
5. Remove upper transaxle cooler line.
6. Remove coolant surge tank hose.
7. Remove condenser inlet fitting from discharge hose.
8. Disconnect cooling fan electrical connector.
9. Raise and safely support vehicle.
10. Remove lower closeout panel.
11. Remove lower radiator hose from radiator.
12. Remove lower transaxle cooler line.
13. Remove evaporator line from condenser outlet.
14. Remove radiator lower mounting panel.
15. Remove Condenser Radiator Fan Module (CRFM) from vehicle.
16. Remove condenser and fan shroud from radiator.
17. Reverse procedure to install, noting the following:
    a. **Torque** condenser to radiator bolt to 44 inch lbs.
    b. **Torque** radiator lower mounting panel bolts to 89 inch lbs.
    c. **Torque** condenser outlet to evaporator line bolt to 18 ft. lbs.
    d. **Torque** transaxle cooler line bolts to 22 ft. lbs.
    e. **Torque** condenser inlet fitting to discharge hose bolt to 18 ft. lbs.
    f. Close radiator petcock, fill cooling system and inspect for leaks.

CUTLASS & MALIBU

1. Recover refrigerant charge using recycling station tool No. J-39500, or equivalent.
2. Drain coolant into an approved container.
3. Remove upper radiator hose and transaxle cooler line, then the surge tank hose.
4. Remove condenser inlet fitting from discharge hose and lower transaxle cooler line.
5. Disconnect cooling fan electrical connector.
6. Raise and support vehicle.
7. Remove lower closeout panel, then the lower radiator hose and evaporator line.
8. Remove lower radiator mounting plate and condenser fan radiator module.
9. Remove condenser, fan shroud and radiator.
10. Reverse procedure to install. Tighten to specifications.

FUEL PUMP

REPLACE

The fuel pump is a component of the fuel sender assembly and must be replaced as a complete unit.

1. Relieve fuel system pressure as outlined under "Fuel System Pressure Relief."
2. Drain fuel from tank into an approved container.
3. Disconnect all required electrical connectors.
4. Remove ground wire retaining screw from underbody.
5. Disconnect hoses from tank meter assembly, tank filler and vent pipes.
6. Support fuel tank and disconnect fuel tank retaining straps.
7. Remove fuel tank from vehicle.
8. The modular fuel sender assembly might spring up from its original position. Have a shop towel ready to absorb spills because reservoir bucket is full of fuel. Tip assembly slightly to avoid float damage.
9. Using lock ring tool No. J-39765, or

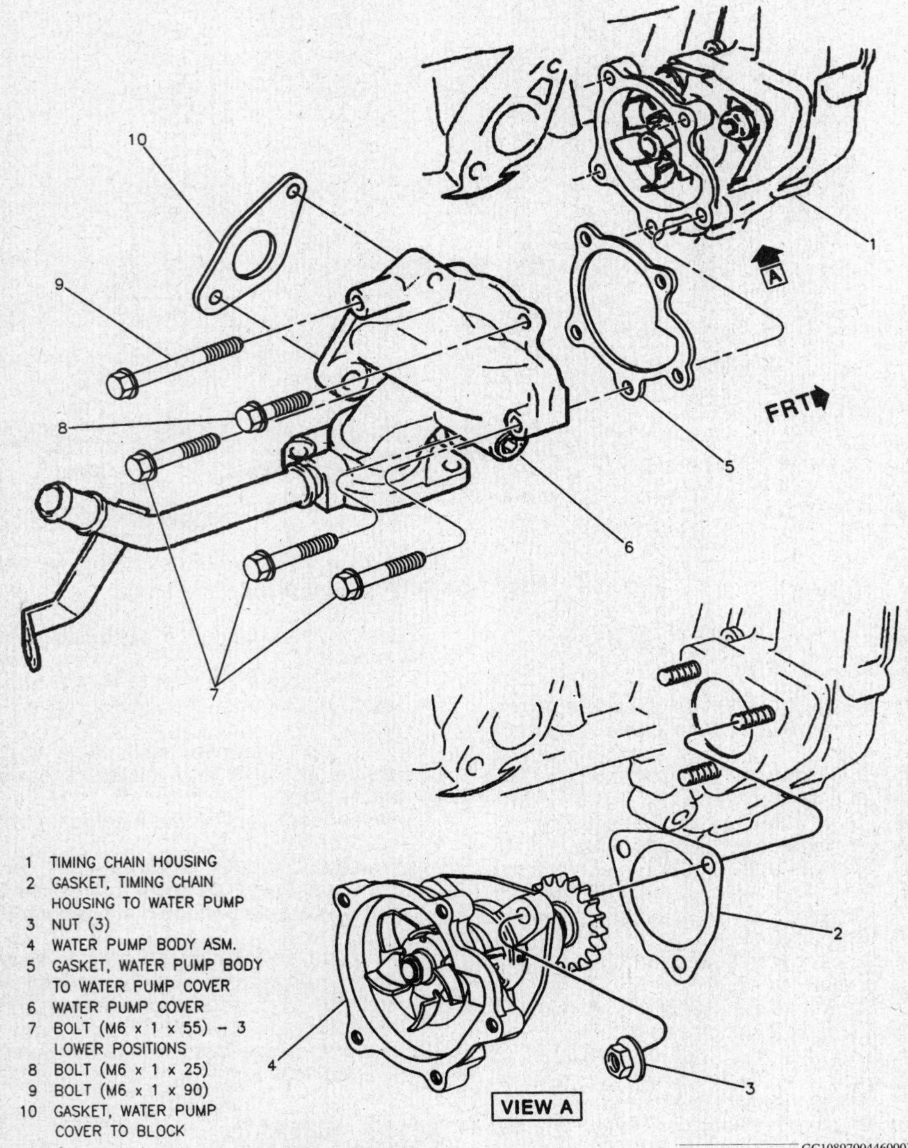

Fig. 20 Water pump replacement

equivalent, remove fuel tank sending unit and pump assembly by holding it down and removing lock ring from designated retainer slots.

10. Reverse procedure to install, noting the following:
    a. Install a new O-ring on sender tank flange.
    b. Align tab on front of fuel sender with slot on front of retainer lock ring.
    c. Slowly apply pressure to top of spring loaded sender until sender aligns flush with tank retainer.
    d. Insert lock ring into proper slots.
    e. Inspect for fuel leaks as outlined under "Fuel Leak Inspection."

FUEL LEAK INSPECTION

After fuel tank has been removed and replaced, proceed as follows:

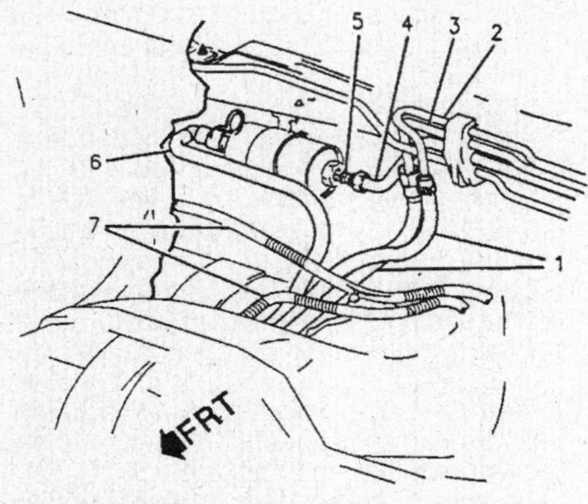

1 HOSE – PART OF FUEL SENDER
2 FUEL VAPOR PIPE
3 FUEL RETURN PIPE
4 FUEL FEED PIPE
5 FUEL FEED PIPE NUT – 27 N·m (20 LBS. FT.)
6 HOSE – PART OF FUEL SENDER
7 ABS AND FUEL SENDER HARNESS

GC1029102737000X

Fig. 21 Fuel filter replacement

1. Turn ignition On for two seconds.
2. Turn ignition Off for 10 seconds.
3. Turn ignition On.
4. Look for and correct any fuel leaks.

FUEL FILTER

REPLACE

The fuel filter is located below the rear of the vehicle, rearward of the fuel tank.

1. Relieve fuel system pressure as outlined under "Precautions."
2. Raise and support vehicle.
3. Using suitable back-up wrench, remove fuel filter fitting, **Fig. 21.**
4. Grasp filter and one nylon fuel connection line fitting, then twist quick connect fitting 1/4 turn in each direction to loosen dirt in fitting.
5. Using compressed air, clean dirt from quick connect fitting.
6. Depress quick connect fitting plastic tabs of male end connector and pull apart.
7. Remove fuel filter.
8. Reverse procedure to install, noting the following:
    a. Apply a few drops of clean engine oil to male pipe ends before connection to reduce risk of leakage and fire.
    b. Tighten to specifications.
    c. Inspect for fuel leaks as outlined under "Fuel Leak Inspection."

TIGHTENING SPECIFICATIONS

Year	Component	Torque/Ft. Lbs.
1998–2001	Balance Shaft Cover	10
	Balance Shaft Housing	⑤
	Balance Shaft Mounting	⑤
	Balance Shaft Sprocket	⑤
	Camshaft Housing & Cover	⑦
	Camshaft Position Sensor	89⑨
	Camshaft Sprocket To Cam Bolt	52
	Connecting Rod Nuts	②
	Coolant Inlet To Oil Pan	19
	Coolant Inlet To Water Pump	10
	Coolant Outlet To Cylinder Head	19
	Crankshaft Balancer To Crankshaft	129③
	Crankshaft Bearing Cap Bolts	15③
	Crankshaft Position Sensor	80⑨
	Cylinder Head Bolts	④
	Engine Mount Bracket	99
	Engine Mount To Bracket	46
	Engine Mount To Body	49
	Exhaust Camshaft Housing Rear Cover	⑦
	Exhaust Manifold Brace To Manifold Bolt	41
	Exhaust Manifold Brace To Oil Pan Nuts	19
	Exhaust Manifold Heat Shield Bolts	10
	Exhaust Manifold To Cylinder Head Nuts	41
	Exhaust Manifold To Cylinder Head Studs	11
	Exhaust Manifold To Oil Pan	19
	Exhaust Manifold Studs To Manifold	19
	Exhaust Pipe To Manifold	26
	Flexplate To Clutch Cover	22
	Flexplate To Converter	46
	Flexplate To Crankshaft	22⑥
	Front Cover To Timing Chain Housing	9
	Fuel Filter Fitting	20
	Fuel Pipe Bracket To Camshaft Housing	11①
	Fuel Pipe To Fuel Rail Nut	22
	Fuel Rail To Camshaft Housing	19
	Ignition Coil & Module Assembly To Camshaft Housing	16
	Intake Manifold Brace Bolts	19
	Intake Manifold To Cylinder Head Nuts	19
	Intake Manifold To Cylinder Head Studs	96⑨
	Knock Sensor	15
	Oil/Air Separator To Intake Manifold	19
	Oil/Air Separator To Block	19
	Oil Filter Connector To Block	21
	Oil Pan Bolts	17
	Oil Pan Bolts (Second Set)	106⑨
	Oil Pan Drain Plug	19
	Oil Pan Studs	19
	Oil Passage Plug Bolt	22
	Oil Passage Plugs, 1⁄8 × 27	89⑨
	Oil Passage Plugs, 1⁄4 × 18	15
	Oil Passage Plugs, 3⁄8 × 18	22

Continued

TIGHTENING SPECIFICATIONS—Continued

Year	Component	Torque/Ft. Lbs.
1998–2001	Oil Pump To Balance Shaft Housing, Long Bolts (Alero & 1999–2001 Grand Am)	106⑨
	Oil Pump To Balance Shaft Housing, Short Bolts (Alero & 1999–2001 Grand Am)	89⑨
	Oil Pump To Block (1998)	40
	Oil Pump Cover To Oil Pump Body (1998)	108⑨
	Oxygen Sensor To Exhaust Manifold	31
	Radiator Mounting Bolts	89⑨
	Rear Crankshaft Seal Housing To Block	108⑨
	Spark Plugs	13
	Starter	66
	Thermostat Housing	19
	Throttle Body To Intake Manifold	89⑨
	Timing Chain Housing To Block Or Camshaft Housing	19
	Timing Chain Housing To Block Stud	21
	Timing Chain Tensioner To Housing & Block	89⑨
	Transaxle To Block Bolt	44
	Transaxle To Block Nut	49
	Transaxle To Block Stud	115⑨
	Water Pump Cover	⑧
	Water Pump Cover To Block	⑧
	Water Pump To Timing Chain Housing	⑧

①— Tighten an additional 30°.
②— Tighten an additional 80°.
③— Rotate an additional 90°.
④— Refer to “Cylinder Head, Replace.”
⑤— Refer to “Balance Shaft, Replace.”
⑥— Tighten an additional 45°.
⑦— Refer to “Camshaft, Replace.”
⑧— Refer to “Water Pump, Replace.”
⑨— Inch lbs.

3.1L Engine

NOTE: On Air Bag Equipped Models, Refer To "Air Bag System Precautions" Located In The Front Of This Manual For System Disarming & Arming Procedures.

NOTE: For Procedures Not Found In This Section, Refer To "3.1L Engine" Section In The "Century, Grand Prix, Impala, Intrigue, Lumina, Monte Carlo & Regal" Chapter.

NOTE: Refer To "Computer Relearn Procedures" Located In The Front Of This Manual When Battery Power To The Computer Has Been Interrupted.

INDEX

PRECAUTIONS

AIR BAG SYSTEMS

Refer to "Air Bag System Precautions" in the front of this manual for system disarming and arming procedures.

FUEL SYSTEM PRESSURE RELIEF

Failure to relieve system pressure prior to disconnecting fuel system components may cause fire or personal injury.

1. Loosen fuel tank filler cap to relieve tank pressure.
2. Raise and safely support vehicle.
3. Disconnect fuel pump electrical connector.
4. Lower vehicle.
5. Start and operate engine until fuel supply is consumed.
6. Crank engine for approximately three seconds to relieve remaining pressure.
7. Disconnect battery ground cable and connect fuel pump connector.

BATTERY GROUND CABLE

Prior to service, disconnect battery ground cable and isolate as required.

COMPRESSION PRESSURE

When inspecting cylinder compression, the throttle should be open, all spark plugs removed and the battery at or near full charge. The lowest reading cylinder should not be less than 70% of the highest and no cylinder reading should be less than 100 psi. Turn ignition key until engine cranks through four compression cycles. Normal compression builds up quickly and evenly to specified compression on each cylinder.

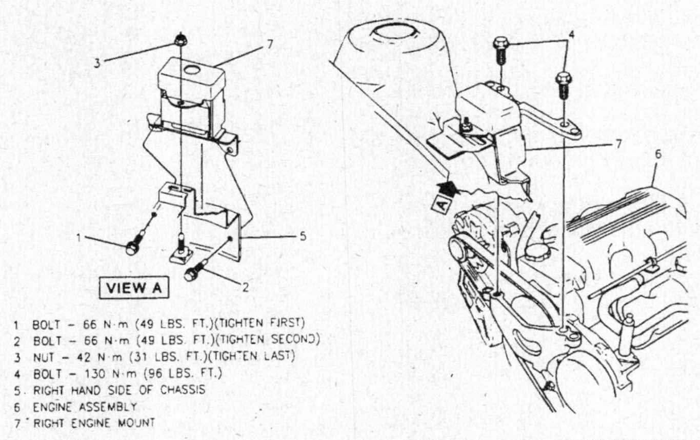

Fig. 1 Engine mount assembly

ENGINE MOUNT

REPLACE

1. Support engine by oil pan and remove engine mount assembly to engine mount bracket support bolts, **Fig. 1.**
2. Remove engine mount to body bolts and nut.
3. Remove engine mount assembly.
4. Reverse procedure to install. Tighten to specifications.

ENGINE MOUNT STRUT

REPLACE

1. Raise and support vehicle.
2. Remove righthand splash shield.
3. Remove engine mount strut bolts, **Fig. 2.**
4. Remove engine mount strut.
5. Reverse procedure to install. Tighten to specifications.

ENGINE

REPLACE

1. Relieve fuel system pressure as outlined under "Precautions."
2. Remove upper half of air cleaner assembly and throttle body duct.
3. Drain coolant into an approved container.
4. Disconnect upper radiator hose from engine and position aside.
5. Disconnect lower radiator hose from engine and position aside.
6. Disconnect coolant inlet line from surge tank.
7. Disconnect vacuum modulator, EVAP canister purge and power brake booster vacuum hoses.

8. Disconnect heater outlet hose from water pump.
9. Remove serpentine drive belt.
10. Disconnect accelerator and cruise control cable from throttle linkage.
11. Disconnect electrical connectors at electronic ignition, heated oxygen sensor, injector harness, IAC, throttle position sensor, engine coolant temperature sensor, PNP switch, transaxle shift solenoid, TCC solenoid and EGR and battery ground cable at transaxle.
12. Remove alternator as outlined under "Alternator, Replace" in "Electrical" section.
13. Disconnect power steering lines at power steering pump.
14. Disconnect fuel lines.
15. Remove cooling fan assembly.
16. Disconnect shift cable linkage and cable from mounting bracket. Transaxle should be in low gear for better accessibility.
17. Disconnect transaxle vent tube from transaxle.
18. Disconnect vacuum hose at vacuum reservoir.
19. Remove engine support fixture.
20. Loosen but do not remove upper two A/C compressor bolts.
21. Raise and support vehicle.
22. Remove front tire and wheel assemblies.
23. Remove righthand and lefthand splash shields.
24. Remove engine mount strut as outlined under "Engine Mount Strut, Replace."
25. Remove both front ABS speed sensor connectors and harness from suspension supports.
26. Remove both ball joints.
27. Remove suspension support assembly.
28. Remove drive axles from transaxle and support.
29. Remove oil filter and adapter.
30. Remove transaxle converter cover.
31. Remove starter as outlined under "Starter, Replace" in "Electrical" section.
32. Disconnect knock sensor, front crankshaft position sensor, side crankshaft position sensor, oil level sensor, VSS and transaxle ground cable.
33. Disconnect heater hoses.
34. Remove A/C compressor lower bolts and position compressor aside.
35. Remove vacuum reserve tank.
36. Remove exhaust pipe from manifold and position aside.
37. Remove engine mount strut bracket.
38. Disconnect transaxle cooling lines at radiator.
39. Remove fluid level indicator and tube.
40. Lower vehicle and engine/transaxle onto suitable table.
41. Remove transaxle mount to body bolts, **Fig. 1**.
42. Remove intermediate bracket from righthand engine mount support bracket.
43. Raise and support vehicle, leaving powertrain on table.

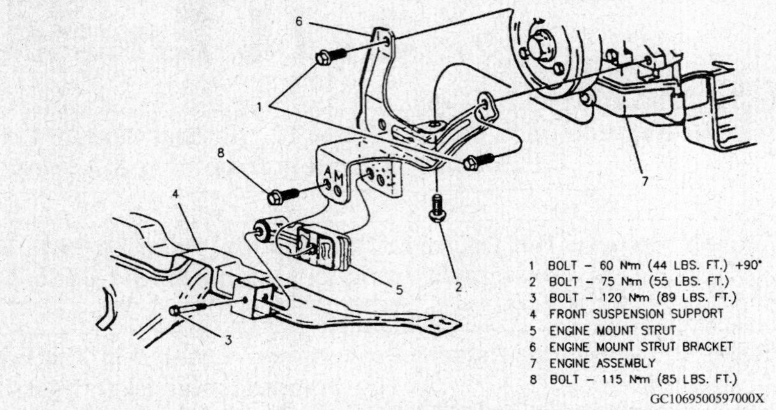

Fig. 2 Engine mount strut bolt removal

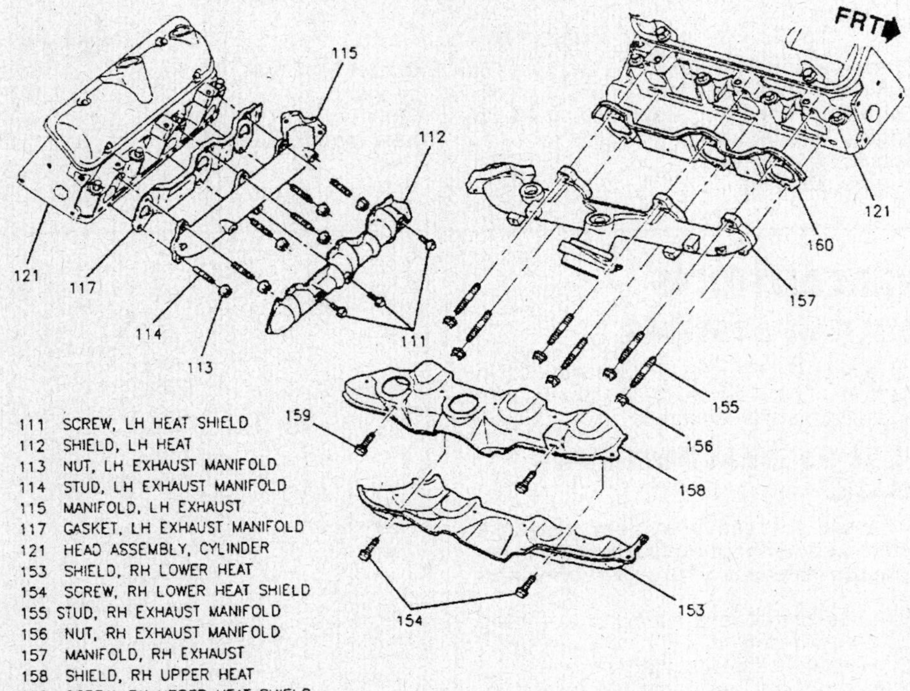

Fig. 3 Exhaust manifold assembly

44. Separate engine and transaxle assembly.
45. Reverse procedure to install, noting the following:
    a. After connecting engine to transaxle, loosely install serpentine drive belt to hold components together.
    b. Tighten to specifications.
    c. Bleed power steering system after engine installation.

INTAKE MANIFOLD

REPLACE

UPPER

1. Disconnect vacuum lines.
2. Remove electrical connector, mounting screws and MAP sensor.
3. Remove pipe, bolts, EGR valve and gaskets.
4. Remove spark plug wires.
5. Remove mounting nuts, bolts and electronic ignition control module.
6. Remove mounting nuts, studs, upper intake manifold and gasket.
7. Reverse procedure to install. Tighten to specifications.

LOWER

1. Remove fuel feed and return pipe mounting bolt and clip, then the mounting bolts and fuel injector rail assembly.
2. Remove mounting nut and heater inlet pipe.
3. Remove mounting bolts and lower intake manifold.
4. Reverse procedure to install. Tighten

to specifications.

EXHAUST MANIFOLD

REPLACE

LEFTHAND

1. Remove upper half of air cleaner assembly and throttle cable duct.
2. Partially drain coolant into an approved container and disconnect radiator hose from thermostat housing.
3. Disconnect coolant bypass pipe at coolant pump and from exhaust manifold.
4. Remove exhaust crossover heat shield.
5. Remove exhaust crossover pipe from manifold.
6. Disconnect secondary ignition wires from spark plugs.
7. Remove exhaust manifold heat shield, **Fig. 3.**
8. Remove retaining nuts and exhaust manifold.
9. Reverse procedure to install. Tighten to specifications.

RIGHTHAND

1. Remove upper half of air cleaner assembly and throttle cable duct.
2. Remove exhaust crossover heat shield.
3. Remove crossover at exhaust manifold.
4. Remove heated oxygen sensor.
5. Disconnect EGR pipe at exhaust manifold.
6. Raise and support vehicle.
7. Remove transaxle oil fill tube and level indicator assembly.
8. Remove exhaust pipe from exhaust manifold.
9. Disconnect exhaust pipe from converter flange and support converter.
10. Remove converter heat shield from body.
11. Remove exhaust manifold heat shield.
12. Remove exhaust manifold mounting nut, **Fig. 3,** then pull manifold from bottom of vehicle.
13. Reverse procedure to install.

RADIATOR

REPLACE

Refer to "2.4L Engine" section for this procedure.

TIGHTENING SPECIFICATIONS

Year	Component	Torque/Ft. Lbs.
1998-2002	Accelerator Cable Bracket Nuts & Bolts	89①
	Coolant Drain Plug	14
	Coolant Outlet Bolt	18
	Drive Belt Tensioner Bolt	37
	Engine Mount Strut Bolts	52
	Engine Mount To Body Bolts	49
	Engine Mount To Body Nut	31
	Exhaust Manifold Bolts	12
	Exhaust Manifold Heat Shield	84①
	Lower Intake Manifold Bolts	10
	Oil Filter	9–10
	Upper Intake Manifold Bolts	18
	Water Pump Bolts	89①
	Water Pump Pulley Bolts	18

① — Inch lbs.

3.4L Engine

NOTE: On Air Bag Equipped Models, Refer To "Air Bag System Precautions" Located In The Front Of This Manual For System Disarming & Arming Procedures.

NOTE: Refer To "Computer Relearn Procedures" Located In The Front Of This Manual When Battery Power To The Computer Has Been Interrupted.

INDEX

PRECAUTIONS

AIR BAG SYSTEMS

Refer to "Air Bag System Precautions" in the front of this manual for system disarming and arming procedures.

FUEL SYSTEM PRESSURE RELIEF

Failure to relieve system pressure prior to disconnecting fuel system components may cause fire or personal injury.

1. Loosen fuel tank filler cap to relieve tank pressure.
2. Raise and safely support vehicle.
3. Disconnect fuel pump electrical connector.
4. Lower the vehicle.
5. Start and operate engine until fuel supply is consumed.
6. Crank engine for approximately three seconds to relieve remaining pressure.
7. Disconnect and isolate battery ground cable, then connect fuel pump electrical connector.

BATTERY GROUND CABLE

Prior to service, disconnect battery ground cable and isolate as required.

COMPRESSION PRESSURE

When inspecting cylinder compression, the throttle should be open, all spark plugs removed and the battery at or near full charge. The lowest reading cylinder should not be less than 70% of the highest and no cylinder reading should be less than 100 psi. Crank engine until it runs through four compression cycles. Normal compression builds up quickly and evenly to specified compression on each cylinder.

ENGINE MOUNT

REPLACE

1. Support engine with a wooden block and a suitable floor jack positioned below oil pan.
2. Remove cruise control module.
3. Remove engine mount assembly to bracket support bolts.
4. Remove engine mount to body fasteners.
5. Remove engine mount assembly.
6. Reverse procedure to install, tighten to specifications.

ENGINE MOUNT STRUT

REPLACE

1. Raise and safely support vehicle.
2. Remove righthand splash shield.
3. Remove engine mount strut bolts.
4. Remove engine mount strut.
5. Reverse procedure to install. **Torque** strut bolts to 74 ft. lbs., then rotate an additional 90° using torque angle meter tool No. J-36660, or equivalent.

ENGINE

REPLACE

1. Relieve fuel system pressure as outlined under "Precautions."
2. Drain coolant into an approved container.
3. Remove engine air cleaner assembly.
4. Remove hood.
5. Remove serpentine belt.
6. Remove hoses from surge tank.
7. Remove cruise control module.
8. Remove engine wiring harness from upper side of engine and position it aside.
9. Disconnect throttle and cruise control cables. **Manufacturer recommends throttle cable replacement when engine is removed and installed.**
10. Raise and safely support vehicle.
11. Remove starter motor.
12. Remove A/C compressor with lines intact and position aside.
13. Disconnect engine lower wiring harness and position it aside.
14. Disconnect catalytic converter flange from rear exhaust manifold.
15. Remove inspection cover.

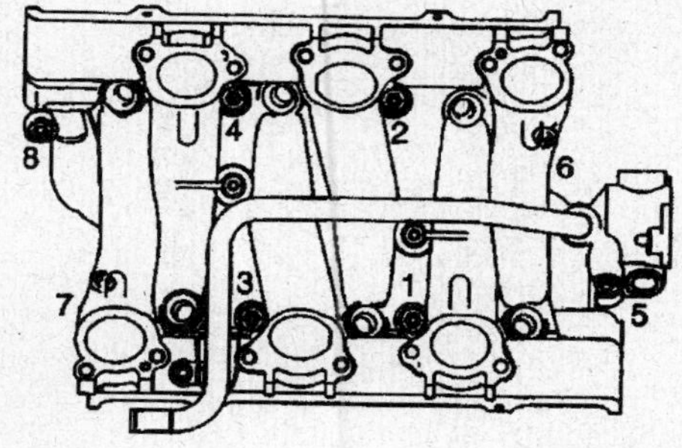

Fig. 1 Lower intake manifold bolt tightening sequence

16. Remove torque converter to flexplate bolts.
17. Remove engine splash shields.
18. Remove transaxle to engine brace.
19. Remove two outer transaxle mounting bolts.
20. Disconnect upper and lower radiator hoses.
21. Lower the vehicle.
22. Disconnect fuel lines from engine.
23. Disconnect vacuum hoses at brake booster.
24. Disconnect heater hoses.
25. Install engine support fixture tool No. J-28467-360, or equivalent.
26. Raise engine.
27. Remove engine mount and adapter.
28. Remove power steering pump.
29. Install suitable engine lifting device.
30. Remove engine support fixture.
31. Remove transaxle to engine bolts.
32. Carefully remove engine from vehicle.
33. If engine will be mounted onto a stand, remove flexplate mounting bolts and flexplate, then mount engine on suitable stand.
34. Reverse procedure to install, noting the following:
    a. If flexplate was removed, install it and its bolts. Tighten bolts evenly to specifications.
    b. Tighten to specifications.
    c. Start engine and inspect for fluid leaks.

INTAKE MANIFOLD

REPLACE

UPPER

1. Drain coolant into an approved container.
2. Remove upper half of air cleaner assembly.
3. Remove EGR valve.
4. Remove brake vacuum pipe at plenum.
5. Disconnect fuel pressure regulator vacuum hose from regulator and at PCV valve.
6. Mark and disconnect spark plug wires at plugs.
7. Remove spark plug wires from plenum harness.
8. Remove electronic ignition coil and module assembly.
9. Remove EVAP canister purge solenoid.
10. Disconnect TP and IAC sensor electrical connectors.
11. Disconnect injector harness.
12. Disconnect ECT and CMP sensor electrical connectors.
13. Disconnect vacuum modulator.
14. Disconnect MAP sensor vacuum line and electrical connector.
15. Remove MAP sensor mounting bolts, then the sensor.
16. Remove upper intake manifold mounting bolts, then the manifold with its gaskets.
17. Reverse procedure to install, tighten to specifications.

LOWER

Removal

1. Relieve fuel system pressure as outlined under "Precautions."
2. Remove upper intake manifold as outlined under "Intake Manifold, Replace."
3. Remove fuel lines at fuel rail and bracket, then the rail with injectors.
4. Remove engine mount as outlined under "Engine Mount, Replace."
5. Remove power steering pump mounting bolts, then position pump aside.
6. Remove heater inlet pipe from coolant outlet housing.
7. Remove heater bypass at coolant pump and at cylinder head.
8. Remove radiator hose at heater outlet housing.
9. Remove water outlet housing.
10. Remove valve covers as outlined under "Valve Cover, Replace."
11. Remove lower intake manifold bolts, **keeping washers in same orientation on center bolts.**
12. Remove lower intake manifold.
13. Loosen rocker arm bolts.
14. Remove pushrods, keeping them in order. Intakes have yellow stripes and are 5.75 inches long. Exhausts have green stripes and are six inches long.
15. Remove intake manifold gaskets.

Installation

1. Clean all gasket material from mating surfaces.
2. Remove excess RTV sealer from front and rear block ridges.
3. Clean sealing surfaces using a suitable degreasing compound.
4. Place a .079–.118 inch bead of RTV sealer P/N 12345739, or equivalent on each manifold-to-block contact ridge.
5. Install new manifold gaskets.
6. Coat pushrod ends with prelube P/N 1052356, or equivalent.
7. Install pushrods in proper sequence. Intakes have yellow stripes and are 5.75 inches long. Exhausts have green stripes and are six inches long.
8. Install rocker arm bolts. **Torque** to 14 ft. lbs., then rotate an additional 30° using torque angle meter tool No. J-36660, or equivalent.
9. Place lower intake manifold in position, then proceed as follows:
    a. Apply sealant P/N 12345382, or equivalent to lower intake manifold bolt threads.

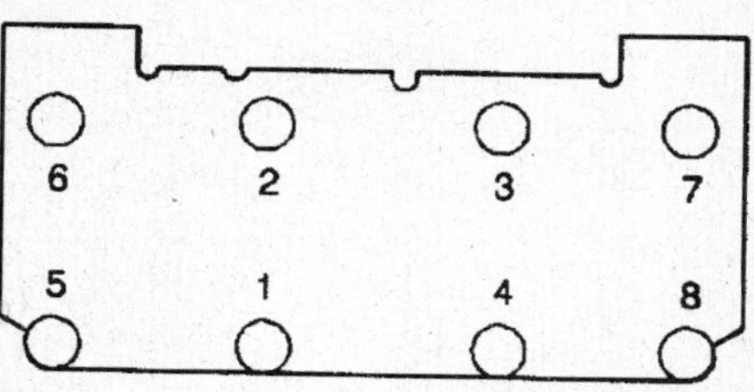

Fig. 2 Cylinder head bolt tightening sequence

    b. **Torque** vertical bolts to 10 ft. lbs. in sequence, **Fig. 1. Always tighten vertical bolts before the horizontals to avoid an oil leak.**
    c. **Torque** horizontal bolts to 10 ft. lbs. in sequence, **Fig. 1. Always tighten horizontal bolts after the verticals to avoid an oil leak.**
10. Install valve covers.
11. Install heater outlet housing.
12. Install heater inlet pipe to thermostat housing.
13. Install fuel lines to fuel rail and bracket.
14. Install upper intake manifold as outlined under "Intake Manifold, Replace."
15. Start engine and inspect for leaks.

EXHAUST MANIFOLD

REPLACE

FRONT

1. Partially drain coolant into an approved container.
2. Remove complete air cleaner assembly and TBI duct.
3. Remove exhaust crossover heat shield.
4. Remove crossover pipe at exhaust manifold.
5. Remove upper radiator hose from thermostat housing.
6. Tag and disconnect spark plug wires from front spark plugs, then position aside.
7. Remove exhaust manifold heat shield.
8. Remove exhaust manifold attaching nuts, then the manifold from bottom of vehicle. Discard manifold to head gasket.
9. Reverse procedure to install, noting the following:
    a. Clean head and manifold mating surfaces.
    b. Install a new manifold mounting gasket.
    c. Tighten to specifications.
    d. Start engine and inspect for leaks.

REAR

1. Remove complete air cleaner assembly and throttle body duct.
2. Remove O2 sensors using socket tool No. J-39194-B, or equivalent.
3. Remove exhaust crossover heat shield.
4. Disconnect EGR pipe from manifold.
5. Remove exhaust crossover pipe from manifold.
6. Remove exhaust manifold heat shield.

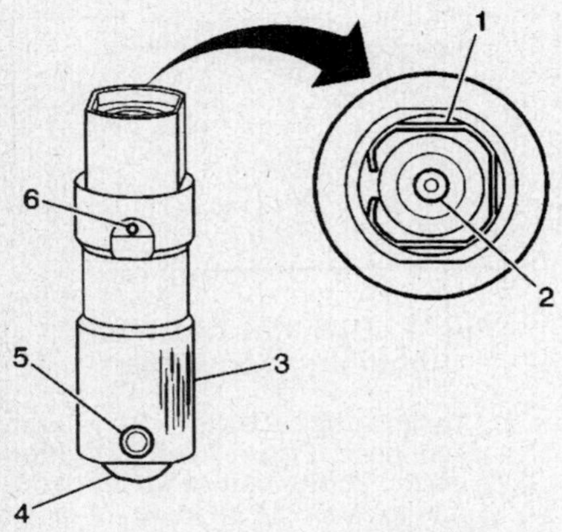

Fig. 3 Valve lifter inspection locations

7. Remove exhaust manifold attaching nuts, then the manifold.
8. Reverse procedure to install, noting the following:
   a. Clean head and manifold mating surfaces.
   b. Install a new manifold mounting gasket.
   c. Tighten to specifications.
   d. Start engine and inspect for leaks.

CYLINDER HEAD

REPLACE

FRONT

Removal

1. Relieve fuel system pressure as outlined under "Precautions."
2. Drain coolant into an approved container.
3. Remove upper half of engine air cleaner assembly.
4. Remove TBI unit duct.
5. Remove exhaust crossover.
6. Remove upper and lower intake manifolds as outlined under "Intake Manifold, Replace."
7. Remove valve cover as outlined under "Valve Cover, Replace." Use a soft rubber mallet or palm of the hand to bump cover if it will not easily budge.
8. Remove rocker arm bolts, pivot balls and arms.
9. Remove pushrods, keeping them in order. Intakes have yellow stripes and are 5.75 inches long. Exhausts have green stripes and are six inches long.
10. Remove front exhaust manifold as outlined under "Exhaust Manifold, Replace."
11. Remove cylinder head attaching bolts, then the head.

Installation

1. Clean mating surfaces of head, block and intake manifold.
2. Clean cylinder head bolts and their threads.
3. Place head gasket into position over dowel pins with "THIS SIDE UP" notice properly oriented.
4. Carefully place head into position.
5. Coat head bolt threads with sealer P/N 1052080, or equivalent.
6. Install head bolts. **Torque** to 33 ft. lbs. in sequence, **Fig. 2,** then rotate them an additional 90° using torque angle meter tool No. J-36660, or equivalent.
7. Install intake manifold gaskets.
8. Install pushrods in proper sequence. Intakes have yellow stripes and are 5.75 inches long. Exhausts have green stripes and are six inches long.
9. Install rocker arms, pivot balls and bolts. **Torque** to 14 ft. lbs., then rotate an additional 30° using torque angle meter tool No. J-36660, or equivalent.
10. Install intake manifolds as outlined under "Intake Manifold, Replace."
11. Install exhaust manifold as outlined under "Exhaust Manifold, Replace."
12. Install crossover pipe and heat shield.
13. Fill cooling system.
14. Install TBI unit duct.
15. Install upper half of air cleaner assembly.
16. Start engine and inspect for leaks.

REAR

Removal

1. Relieve fuel system pressure as outlined under "Precautions."
2. Drain coolant into an approved container.
3. Remove exhaust crossover pipe.
4. Raise and safely support vehicle.
5. Remove rear exhaust manifold as outlined under "Exhaust Manifold, Replace."
6. Lower the vehicle.
7. Remove serpentine drive belt as outlined under "Serpentine Drive Belt."
8. Remove valve cover as outlined under "Valve Cover, Replace." Use a soft rubber mallet or palm of the hand to bump cover if it will not easily budge.
9. Remove rocker arm bolts, pivot balls and arms.
10. Remove pushrods, keeping them in order. Intakes have yellow stripes and are 5.75 inches long. Exhausts have green stripes and are six inches long.
11. Remove upper and lower intake manifolds as outlined under "Intake Manifold, Replace."
12. Remove cylinder head attaching bolts, then the cylinder head.

Installation

1. Clean mating surfaces of head, block and intake manifold.
2. Clean cylinder head bolts and their threads.
3. Place head gasket into position over dowel pins with "THIS SIDE UP" notice properly oriented.
4. Carefully place head into position.
5. Coat head bolt threads with sealer P/N 1052080, or equivalent.
6. Install head bolts. **Torque** to 33 ft. lbs. in sequence, **Fig. 2,** then rotate them an additional 90° using torque angle meter tool No. J-36660, or equivalent.
7. Install intake manifold gaskets.
8. Install pushrods in proper sequence. Intakes have yellow stripes and are

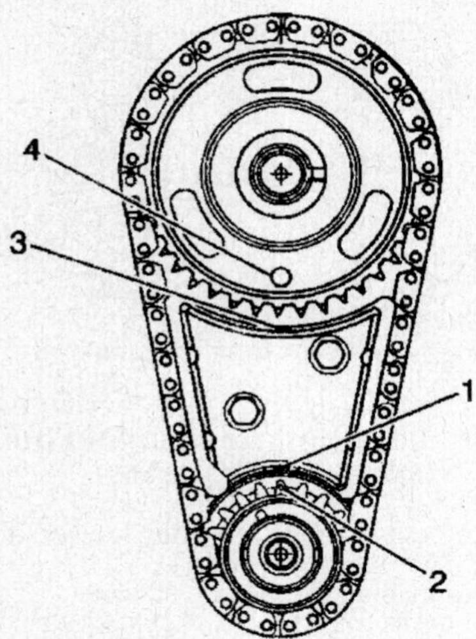

1. DAMPER LOWER TIMING MARK
2. CRANKSHAFT TIMING MARK
3. DAMPER UPPER TIMING
4. CAMSHAFT GEAR

GC1059900125000X

Fig. 4 Timing mark alignment

5.75 inches long. Exhausts have green stripes and are six inches long.

9. Install rocker arms, pivot balls and bolts. **Torque** to 14 ft. lbs., then rotate an additional 30° using torque angle meter tool No. J-36660, or equivalent.
10. Install intake manifolds as outlined under "Intake Manifold, Replace."
11. Install valve cover with a new gasket.
12. Connect spark plug wires.
13. Install serpentine belt.
14. Raise and safely support vehicle.
15. Install exhaust manifold as outlined under "Exhaust Manifold, Replace."
16. Install crossover pipe and heat shield.
17. Fill cooling system.
18. Install TBI unit duct.
19. Install upper half of air cleaner assembly.
20. Start engine and inspect for leaks.

VALVE COVER

REPLACE

FRONT

1. Partially drain coolant into an approved container.
2. Remove rear ignition wire harness and spark plug wires at spark plugs.
3. Remove heater bypass intake.
4. Disconnect PCV vacuum hose.
5. Remove valve cover retaining bolts, then the cover. If cover is stubborn, tap it lightly with palm of hand or a soft rubber mallet to break it loose.
6. Reverse procedure to install, noting the following:
   a. Install a new gasket and grommets onto cover.
   b. Apply sealer P/N 12346192, or equivalent in cover notch.
   c. Tighten to specifications.

REAR

1. Remove serpentine belt.

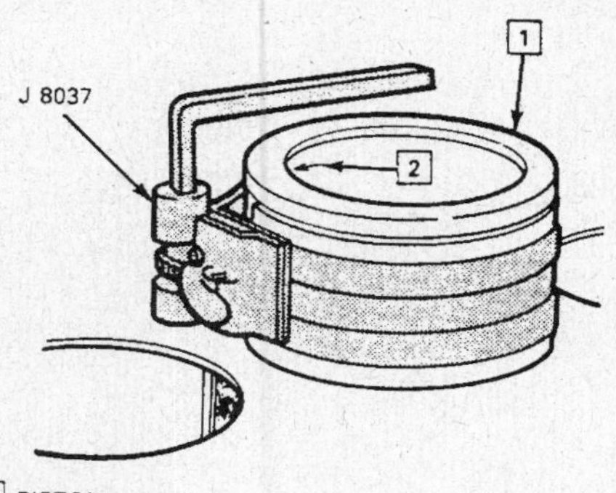

Fig. 5 Piston marking

2. Remove alternator as outlined under "Alternator, Replace" in electrical section.
3. Remove alternator bracket.
4. Remove rear bank spark plug wires.
5. Remove ignition coils and bracket.
6. Remove purge and vacuum canister solenoids.
7. Remove vacuum hose from rear bank valve cover grommet.
8. Remove serpentine belt tensioner.
9. Remove valve cover retaining bolts, then the cover. If cover is stubborn, tap it lightly with palm of hand or a soft rubber mallet to break it loose.
10. Reverse procedure to install, noting the following:
    a. Install a new gasket and grommets onto cover.
    b. Apply sealer P/N 12345739, or equivalent at cylinder head to lower intake manifold joints.
    c. Tighten to specifications.

VALVE ARRANGEMENT

FRONT TO REAR

Cowl side ....E-I-E-I-I-E
Radiator side ....E-I-I-E-I-E

VALVE LIFTERS

Roller type valve lifters, **Fig. 3,** are used in this engine and must be replaced whenever the camshaft is replaced. They must be kept in order so they will be installed in their original positions.

Inspect the lifters and look for a bent or broken clip (1), worn pushrod socket (2), scuffed or worn sides (3), flat spots on the roller (4), a loose or damaged pin, (5) a plugged oil hole (6) or worn or damaged roller bearing. Ensure the roller can rotate freely with no binding or rough operation. If the lifter show side wear the block lifter bores should also be inspected for damage or wear. Replace any lifter which does not pass these inspections.

Valve lifters must be kept in order so they will be installed in their original positions.

CAMSHAFT LOBE LIFT SPECIFICATIONS

Intake .... .2727
Exhaust .... .2727

VALVE ADJUSTMENT

These engines are equipped with hydraulic valve lash adjusters. No adjustment is required.

PUSH RODS

1. Remove rocker arm covers and rocker arms, identifying components so they will be installed in same location.
2. Remove rocker arm pivot balls and rocker arms, then the pushrods. Intakes have yellow stripes and are 5.75 inches long. Exhausts have green stripes and are six inches long.
3. Reverse procedure to install, noting the following:
    a. Ensure pushrods seat in lifters.
    b. Coat bearing surfaces of rocker arms and pivot balls with Molykote P/N 1052356, or an equivalent lubricant.
    c. Tighten to specifications.

FRONT COVER

REPLACE

1. Recover refrigerant charge using recycling station tool No. J-39500, or equivalent.
2. Drain coolant into an approved container.
3. Install engine support tool No. J-28467-360, or equivalent.
4. Remove engine mount assembly as outlined under "Engine Mount, Replace."
5. Remove engine mount bracket support.
6. Remove serpentine drive belt as outlined under "Serpentine Drive Belt."
7. Remove complete engine air cleaner assembly.
8. Remove TBI unit tube.
9. Disconnect power steering lines at power steering pump, allowing fluid to drain into a suitable container.
10. Loosen upper two A/C compressor mounting bolts.
11. Remove alternator as outlined under "Alternator, Replace."
12. Remove alternator bracket.
13. Raise and safely support vehicle.
14. Drain engine oil using approved methods and equipment.
15. Remove righthand front tire and wheel.
16. Remove righthand front splash shield.
17. Remove flexplate inspection cover.
18. Remove harmonic balancer using puller tool No. J-24420-C, or equivalent.
19. Remove serpentine belt tensioner.
20. Disconnect righthand front wheel speed sensor electrical connector and wiring harness from suspension support.
21. Remove righthand front ball joint as outlined under "Ball Joint, Replace."
22. Remove righthand stabilizer shaft from righthand suspension support and control arm.
23. Remove righthand suspension support.

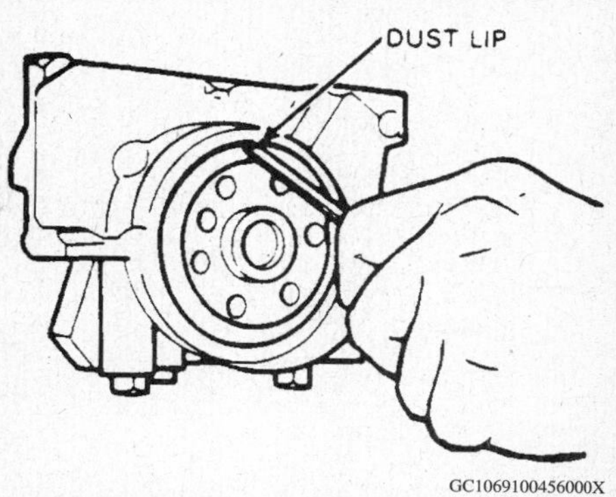

Fig. 6 Rear main seal removal

24. Separate righthand outer tie rod from knuckle if required.
25. Remove A/C compressor to oil pan bolts.
26. Remove oil filter and adapter.
27. Remove starter motor as outlined under "Starter, Replace."
28. Remove lower A/C compressor mounting bolts, then position compressor aside.
29. Remove evaporator to accumulator A/C line.
30. Remove righthand front and righthand rear engine cradle bolts.
31. Remove oil pan.
32. Remove CKP sensor.
33. Remove front cover lower bolts.
34. Lower the vehicle.
35. Remove coolant bypass to coolant pump and manifold.
36. Remove radiator hose to coolant outlet housing.
37. Remove front cover retaining bolts.
38. Carefully remove front cover.
39. Using a suitable large screwdriver or a prying tool, remove and discard front cover crankshaft oil seal.
40. Reverse procedure to install, noting the following:
    a. Clean all gasket mating surfaces using a suitable degreaser.
    b. Lubricate a new front cover crankshaft oil seal with clean engine oil.
    c. Using crankshaft seal installer and centering tool No. J-36468, or equivalent, install crankshaft oil seal with lip facing engine.
    d. Apply RTV sealer P/N 1052080, or equivalent to both sides of front cover gasket's lower tabs.
    e. Tighten to specifications.
    f. Fill cooling system, power steering reservoir and crankcase.
    g. Start engine and inspect for leaks.

FRONT COVER SEAL

REPLACE

1. Raise and safely support vehicle.
2. Remove righthand front tire and wheel.
3. Remove righthand front splash shield.
4. Using torsional dampener remover tool No. J-24420-C, or equivalent, remove crankshaft balancer.
5. Remove crankshaft key from keyway.
6. Pry out seal using suitable tool, being careful not to damage crankshaft or front cover.

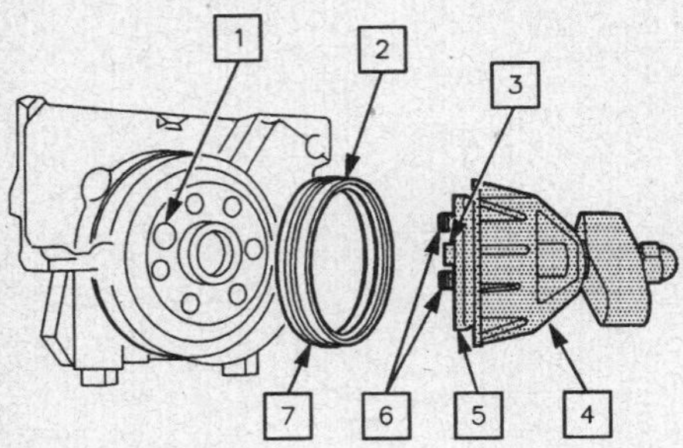

Fig. 7 Rear main seal installation

7. Reverse procedure to install, noting the following:
   a. Install a new key if old one is damaged or worn.
   b. Lubricate new seal with clean engine oil and insert in front cover with lip facing engine.
   c. Use front cover alignment and oil seal installer tool No. J-35468, or equivalent to drive seal into place.

TIMING CHAIN

REPLACE

REMOVAL

1. Remove engine front cover as outlined under "Front Cover, Replace."
2. Turn engine in normal direction of rotation until No. 1 piston reaches TDC. This is the No. 4 cylinder firing position.
3. Align camshaft gear timing mark, **Fig. 4,** with mark on top of chain damper and crankshaft gear timing mark with damper's lower mark.
4. Remove camshaft gear retaining bolt.
5. Remove camshaft gear and timing chain.
6. Remove crankshaft gear using puller tool No. J-5825-A, or equivalent. If gear is stubborn, gently tap lower edge with a plastic mallet to dislodge it.

INSTALLATION

1. Apply prelube P/N 12345501, or equivalent to crankshaft gear thrust surface.
2. Install crankshaft gear using installer tool No. J-38612, or equivalent.
3. Install timing chain damper. Tighten to specifications.
4. Ensure all timing gear and damper marks are properly aligned.
5. Hold camshaft gear with chain hanging down.
6. Install chain to crankshaft gear.
7. Align camshaft dowel with camshaft gear dowel hole.
8. Draw camshaft gear onto camshaft by tightening retaining bolt.
9. Install front cover. Tighten to specifications.
10. Fill cooling system, power steering reservoir and crankcase.
11. Start engine and inspect for leaks.

CAMSHAFT

REPLACE

1. Remove engine as outlined under "Engine, Replace."
2. Remove valve lifters.
3. Remove front cover.
4. Remove timing chain and gears.
5. Remove camshaft.
6. Reverse procedure to install, noting the following:
   a. If installing a new camshaft, also install new valve lifters. **Never use old lifters with a new camshaft.**
   b. Coat camshaft lobes with engine oil supplement P/N 12345501, or equivalent.
   c. Lubricate camshaft journals with engine oil.

PISTON & ROD ASSEMBLY

When installing piston and rod assemblies into cylinder block, ensure arrow on top of piston faces toward front of engine, **Fig. 5.** Ensure flat area on bottom of piston aligns with the small dimple above the connecting rod crankshaft bearing bore.

MAIN & ROD BEARINGS

Engine bearings are of the precision insert type. They are available for service usage in standard and various undersizes.

To determine proper replacement insert size, bearing clearance must be measured as follows:

1. Measure crankshaft journal diameter in several places, approximately 90° apart and average the measurements.
2. Measure taper and runout, which should be .0002 inch maximum.
3. Install bearing inserts and tighten rod and main bearing cap bolts to specifications, then measure I.D. with an inside micrometer. Measure connecting rod I.D. in same direction as length of rod.
4. Select a suitable set of inserts to provide specified clearance limits. **Do not mix inserts of different nominal size in same bearing bore.** If clearance limits cannot be met, crankshaft journal must be reconditioned and undersize bearing inserts installed.

CRANKSHAFT REAR OIL SEAL

REPLACE

REMOVAL

1. Using engine support fixture tool No. J-28467-360 and fixture adapters tool No. J-28467-90, or equivalents, safely support engine, then remove transaxle as outlined in "Automatic Transaxles/ Transmissions" chapter.
2. Remove flexplate.
3. Using a screwdriver or suitable tool, remove seal by inserting tool in through dust lip at an angle, **Fig. 6,** then prying seal out by moving handle of tool toward end of crankshaft pilot, repeating around circumference of seal as required. **Be careful not to damage crankshaft O.D. surface or the chamfer.**

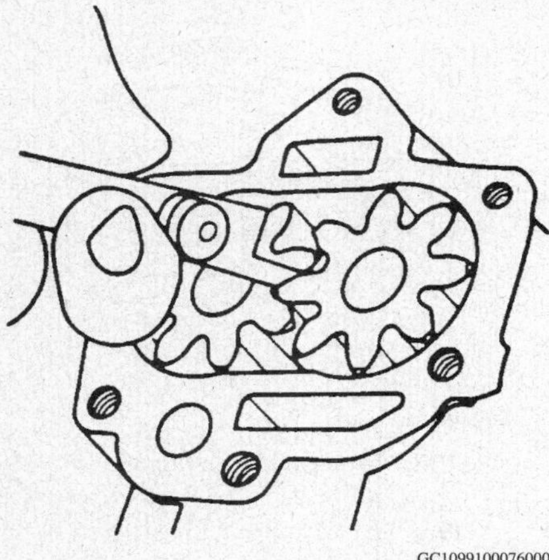

Fig. 8 Oil pump gear lash measurement

INSTALLATION

1. Inspect I.D. of bore for nicks or burrs and repair as required.
2. Inspect crankshaft for burrs or nicks on surface which contacts seal, repairing or replacing crankshaft as required.
3. Install seal as follows:
   a. Apply clean engine oil to I.D. and O.D. of new seal, then slide seal over mandrel until rear of seal bottoms squarely against collar of rear main bearing seal installer tool No. J-34686, or equivalent, **Fig. 7.**
   b. Align dowel pin of tool with dowel pin in crankshaft by hand, then **torque** attaching screws to 45 inch lbs., **Fig. 7.**
   c. Turn "T" handle of tool so collar pushes seal into bore, turning handle until collar is tight against case.
   d. Loosen "T" handle of tool until it comes to a stop, then remove attaching screws.
   e. Ensure seal is seated squarely in bore.
4. Install flexplate and transaxle.

OIL PAN

REPLACE

1. Recover refrigerant charge using recycling station tool No. J-39500, or equivalent.
2. Drain coolant into an approved container.
3. Remove serpentine belt as outlined under "Serpentine Drive Belt, Replace."

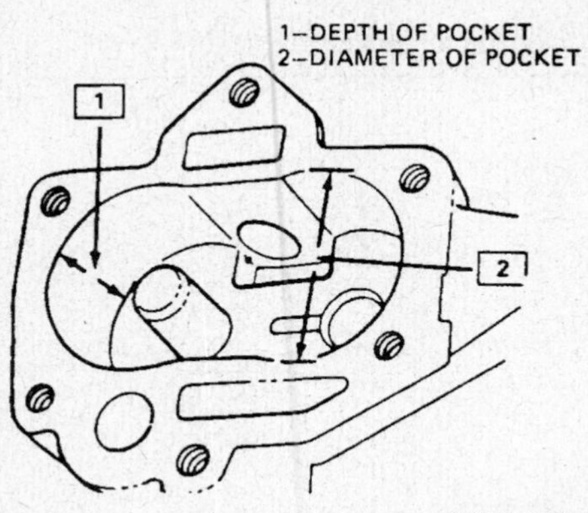

Fig. 9 Oil pump gear pocket measurement

4. Install engine support tool No. J-28467-360, or equivalent.
5. Raise and safely support vehicle.
6. Drain engine oil using approved methods and equipment.
7. Remove righthand front tire and wheel.
8. Remove righthand front splash shield.
9. Remove righthand front wheel speed sensor harness from righthand front suspension support.
10. Separate righthand front ball joint from control arm.
11. Separate righthand outer tie rod end from knuckle.
12. Remove A/C compressor and position aside with hoses intact.
13. Remove evaporator to accumulator line.
14. Remove flexplate inspection cover.
15. Remove righthand front and rear engine cradle bolts.
16. Remove harmonic balancer using puller tool No. J-24420-C, or equivalent.
17. Remove starter motor.
18. Remove all oil pan retaining and side bolts, then the oil pan.
19. Reverse procedure to install, noting the following:
    a. Clean oil pan flanges and rail, front cover, rear main cap and all bolt holes.
    b. Install a new oil pan gasket. If installing rear main cap, install sealer P/N 1052080, or equivalent on tabs that insert into cap's outer gasket grooves.
    c. Install oil pan. **Torque** retaining bolts to 18 ft. lbs. **Torque** side bolts to 37 ft. lbs.

OIL PUMP

REPLACE

1. Remove oil pan as outlined under "Oil Pan, Replace."
2. Remove oil pump mounting bolt, then the oil pump and drive shaft extension.
3. Reverse procedure to install. Tighten to specifications.

OIL PUMP SERVICE

DISASSEMBLE

1. Drain oil from pump into an approved container.
2. Remove pump driveshaft.
3. **Do not remove pickup tube from cover unless it is broken or loose.**
4. Remove pump cover and pump gears.
5. Remove pressure regulator valve and spring. If valve is stuck, soak pump housing in carburetor cleaning solvent. **Pressure regulator valve spring may be under pressure. Remove retaining pin carefully.**
6. Clean sludge, oil and varnish from all components. Varnish may be removed by soaking in carburetor cleaning solvent.

INSPECTION

1. Inspect pump housing and cover for casting imperfections, cracks or damaged threads, replacing as required. **Do not attempt to repair pump housing.** Replace spring as required.
2. Inspect idler gear shaft. If loose in housing, replace pump.
3. Inspect pressure regulator valve for scoring or sticking. Burrs may be removed with a fine oil stone.
4. Inspect pressure regulator valve spring for loss of tension or bending.
5. Inspect suction pipe and screen assembly for looseness if permanently pressed into pump body. If pipe is loose or has been removed, pump body cover must be replaced. Inspect for broken wire mesh or screen.
6. Inspect gears for chipping, galling or wear.
7. Measure gear lash in several positions, **Fig. 8,** which should be .0037–.0077 inch.
8. Measure pump housing gear pocket depth, **Fig. 9,** which should be 1.202–1.204 inches.
9. Measure pump housing gear pocket diameter, **Fig. 9.** Pump housing diameter should be 1.503–1.505 inches.
10. Measure pump gear diameters, **Fig. 10,** which should be 1.498–1.500 inches.
11. Measure pump gear side clearance, **Fig. 11,** which should be .001–.003 inch.
12. Measure oil pump end clearance, **Fig. 12,** which should be .002–.005 inch.

ASSEMBLE

1. Lubricate all internal components with clean engine oil.
2. Install pump gears.
3. Install cover and gasket. **Use only original equipment gaskets since gasket thickness is critical to proper pump operation.** Tighten to specifications.
4. Install pressure spring retaining pin, ensuring it is properly secured.
5. If installing a new pickup screen and tube, apply sealer P/N 1050026, or equivalent to tube. Drive new tube into position using plastic hammer and tube installer tool No. J-21882, or equivalent.

BELT TENSION DATA

1–LENGTH OF GEAR
2–DIAMETER OF GEAR
GC1099100078000X

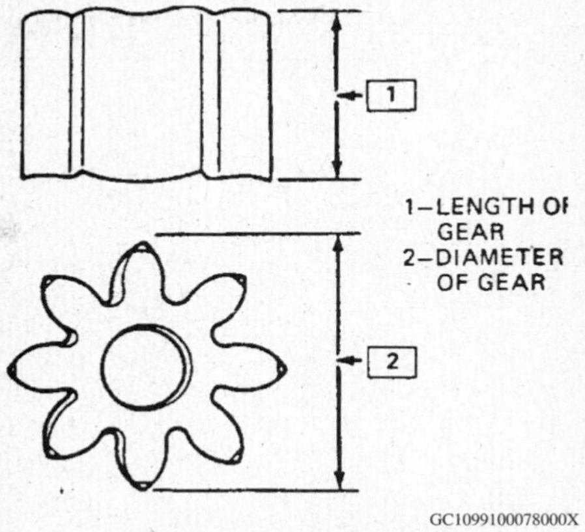

Fig. 10 Oil pump gear measurement

Belt tension is maintained automatically by a spring tensioned idler pulley. Serpentine belt adjustment is not required.

If belt slippage is indicated and belt tensioner indicator is within normal operating range, measure belt tension as follows:

1. Bring engine to operating temperature, then turn ignition Off.
2. Measure belt tension halfway between alternator and power steering pump using belt tension gauge tool No. J-23600-B, or equivalent.
3. Run engine for 15 seconds with all accessories turned Off.
4. Using a ⅜ inch breaker bar, apply clockwise force to tensioner pulley arm.
5. Release force and immediately measure belt tension without disturbing tensioner position.
6. Use breaker bar to apply a counterclockwise force to tensioner pulley arm and raise pulley arm to release all tension.
7. Slowly lower pulley to belt and measure tension without disturbing tensioner position.
8. Average out all three belt tension measurements, which should be 30–50 lbs.
9. If belt tension is not as specified, replace belt tensioner.

SERPENTINE DRIVE BELT

1. Remove cruise control module as required.
2. Remove engine mount as outlined under "Engine Mount, Replace."
3. Rotate belt tensioner in a clockwise direction using a suitable ⅜ inch breaker bar.
4. Remove serpentine belt.
5. Reverse procedure to install. Route belt around power steering pump pulley last of all.

COOLING SYSTEM BLEED

1. Close radiator petcock.

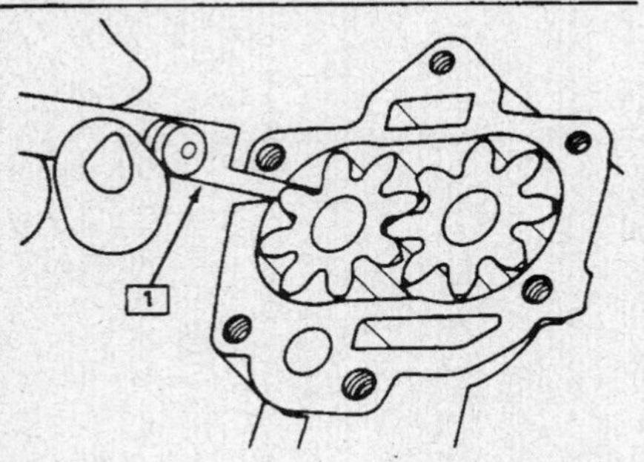
1 CHECK CLEARANCE BETWEEN GEAR TEETH AND SIDE WALL
1
GC1099100079000X

Fig. 11 Gear side clearance measurement

2. If engine block drain plugs were previously removed, coat their threads with pipe sealer P/N 12346004, or equivalent.
3. Open coolant air bleed valve located on top of thermostat bypass heater pipe assembly. **Close this valve as soon as a continuous coolant stream flows from it.**
4. Fill surge tank to base of filler neck.
5. Start engine while pressure cap is still off.
6. Operate engine until upper radiator hose starts to feel hot.
7. If surge tank coolant level is low it will need to be brought up to "full cold" line by adding proper coolant mix.
8. **On models equipped with intermittent low coolant lamp,** this lamp may occasionally light during some extreme driving conditions. This might be eliminated by removing surge tank cap and adding coolant to a level just at or above "full cold" line when system is cold.
9. **On all models,** install surge tank cap hand tight.

THERMOSTAT

REPLACE

1. Drain coolant into an approved container.
2. Remove complete engine air cleaner assembly.
3. Remove surge tank line from coolant outlet.
4. Remove coolant outlet to manifold bolts, then the outlet.
5. Remove thermostat.
6. Clean all gasket mating surfaces.
7. Reverse procedure to install. Tighten to specifications.

WATER PUMP

REPLACE

1. Drain coolant into an approved container.
2. Remove serpentine belt as outlined under "Serpentine Drive Belt."
3. Remove water pump pulley bolts, then the pulley.
4. Remove water pump to front cover bolts, then the pump.
5. Clean all gasket mating surfaces.
6. Reverse procedure to install, noting the following:
   a. Tighten water pump to front cover bolts to specifications.
   b. Tighten water pump pulley bolts to specifications.

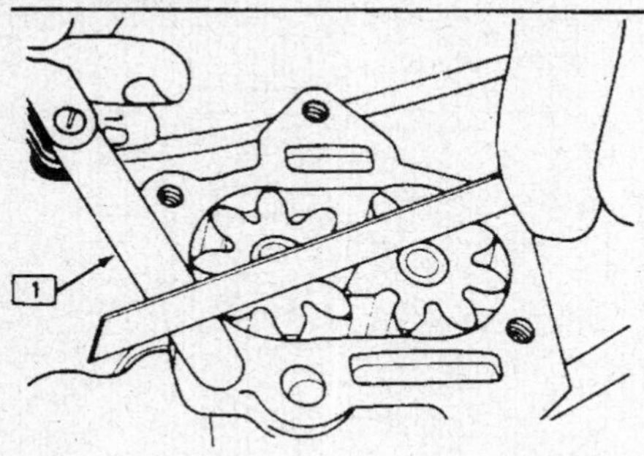
1 CHECK CLEARANCE BETWEEN STRAIGHT EDGE & GASKET
1
GC1099100080000X

Fig. 12 Oil pump end clearance measurement

   c. Fill and bleed cooling system, then inspect for leaks.

RADIATOR

REPLACE

Refer to "2.4L Engine" section for this procedure.

FUEL PUMP

REPLACE

Refer to "2.4L Engine" section for this procedure.

FUEL FILTER

REPLACE

Refer to "2.4L Engine" section for this procedure.

TIGHTENING SPECIFICATIONS

Year	Component	Torque/Ft. Lbs.
1998-2002	Accelerator Cable Bracket Nuts & Bolts	89⑤
	Alternator Bracket & Front Engine Lift Hook Bolt	37
	CKP Sensor To Front Cover Bolt	89⑤
	CKP Sensor To Block Side Bolt	96⑤
	CKP Sensor Wiring Bracket Bolt	37
	CMP Sensor Bolt	89⑤
	Camshaft Sprocket	103
	Camshaft Thrust Plate	89⑤
	Connecting Rod Bearing Cap Nuts	①
	Coolant Drain Plug	14
	Coolant Outlet Bolt	19
	Crankshaft Balancer	76
	Crankshaft Oil Deflector Nut	18
	Cylinder Head Bolts	37②
	ECT Sensor	17
	EGR Valve To Valve Pipe Bolt	18
	EGR Valve Adapter Pipe To Exhaust Manifold Nut	18
	Engine Mount Bracket Bolts	43
	Engine Mount Lower Nuts	32
	Engine Mount Strut & Lift Bracket Bolt, LH Rear Of Engine	52
	Engine Mount Upper Nut	35
	Engine Mount Strut Bolts & Nuts	35
	Engine Mount Strut Bracket Bolt At RH Vehicle Side	37
	Engine Mount Strut Bracket Bolt At Upper Radiator Support	21
	Exhaust Manifold Heat Shield	89⑤
	Exhaust Manifold Nut	12
	Exhaust Manifold Stud	13
	Exhaust Crossover Nut & Stud	18
	Flexplate Bolts	52
	Front Cover Bolts (Large)	41
	Front Cover Bolts (Medium)	35
	Front Cover Bolts (Small)	15
	Fuel Feed Pipe To Injector Rail Nut	13
	Fuel Injector Rail Bolt	89⑤
	Fuel Pipe Bracket Bolt & Stud	37
	Fuel Pipe Clip Bolt	72⑤
	Fuel Return Pipe To Fuel Injector Rail Nut	13
	HO2S	31
	Heater Inlet Pipe Nut	18
	Ignition Coil Bracket Fasteners	18
	Lower Intake Manifold Bolts	115⑤
	Upper Intake Manifold Bolts & Studs	18
	Main Bearing Cap Bolts	③
	Oil Cooler Connector	37
	Oil Cooler Hose Fitting	14
	Oil Cooler Pipe Bracket Bolt	89⑤
	Oil Filter Fitting	29
	Oil Filter	10
	Oil Gallery Plugs, ¼ Inch	14
	Oil Gallery Plugs, ⅜ Inch	24
	Oil Level Indicator Stud	18

Continued

TIGHTENING SPECIFICATIONS—Continued

Year	Component	Torque/Ft. Lbs.
1998-2002	Oil Level Sensor Bolt	89⑤
	Oil Pan	18
	Oil Pan Drain Plug	18
	Oil Pressure Indicator Switch	10
	Oil Pump To Block	30
	Oil Pump Cover	89⑤
	Oil Pump Drive Clamp Bolt	27
	Rocker Arm Bolt	④
	Rocker Arm Covers	89⑤
	Serpentine Drive Belt Shield Bolt	89⑤
	Serpentine Drive Belt Tensioner Bolt	37
	Spark Plugs	20
	Thermostat Bypass Pipe To Cylinder Head Nut	18
	Thermostat Bypass Pipe To Front Cover Bolt	108⑤
	Thermostat Bypass Pipe To TBI Unit Nut	18
	Thermostat Housing Bolt	19
	Timing Chain Damper	15
	Valve Lifter Guide Bolt	89⑤
	Water Pump To Front Cover Bolts	89⑤
	Water Pump Pulley Bolts	18

①— Tighten each bolt an additional 75°.
②— Tighten an additional 90°.
③— Tighten an additional 77°.
④— Tighten an additional 30°.
⑤— Inch lbs.

Clutch & Manual Transaxle

NOTE: For Service Procedures Refer To "Clutch & Manual Transaxle" Section In The "Cavalier & Sunfire" Chapter.

INDEX

ADJUSTMENTS

The hydraulic clutch system provides automatic clutch adjustment. There is no provision for adjustment.

CLUTCH

REPLACE

For clutch replacement procedures refer to "Clutch & Manual Transaxle" section in the "Cavalier & Sunfire" chapter.

Rear Axle & Suspension

INDEX

DESCRIPTION

ACHIEVA, SKYLARK & 1998 GRAND AM

The rear suspension, **Fig. 1,** is the semi-independent type consisting of an axle assembly with trailing arms and cross beam, coil springs and shock absorbers. A single unit hub and bearing assembly is bolted to each end of the axle assembly. The hub and bearing assembly is a sealed, non-serviceable unit and must be replaced as an assembly.

ALERO, CUTLASS, MALIBU & 1999–2002 GRAND AM

The rear suspension, **Fig. 2,** uses coil springs over struts and lightweight aluminum knuckles. Each wheel is mounted to a tri-link independent suspension system. The three links include the inverted U-channel trailing arms and front and rear stamped lateral links.

The knuckles are machined aluminum castings. **Do not use hammers or pry bars to loosen any components from them.**

REAR AXLE

REPLACE

ACHIEVA, SKYLARK & 1998 GRAND AM

1. Raise and support vehicle. Support rear suspension with suitable jack.
2. Remove rear wheel and tire assembly.
3. Disconnect brake lines from axle brackets.
4. Remove shock absorber to lower mounting bracket attaching bolts and disconnect shock absorbers from axle assembly
5. Disconnect parking brake cable.
6. Carefully lower rear axle assembly and remove coil springs and insulators.
7. Disconnect parking brake and equalizer.
8. Remove righthand tire and wheel assembly.
9. Disconnect ABS electrical connector.
10. Disconnect brake lines at wheels.
11. With assistants helping out, remove mounting bolts, then the axle assembly.
12. Reverse procedure to install, noting the following:
    a. Tighten all fasteners to specifications.
    b. Bleed brake system as outlined in "Hydraulic Brake Systems" chapter.

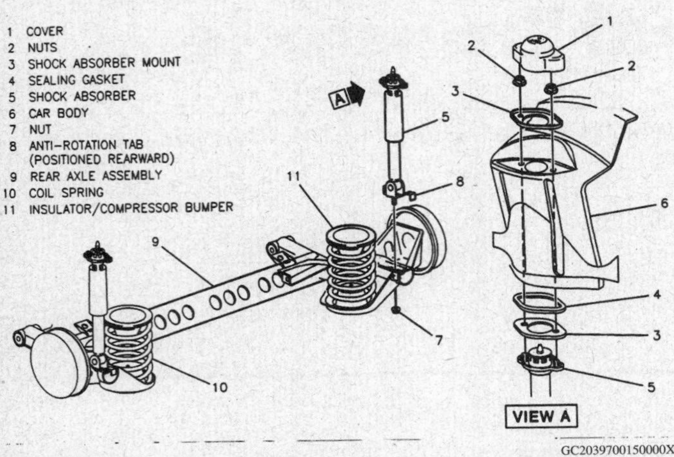

Fig. 1 Exploded view of rear suspension. Achieva, Skylark & 1998 Grand Am

(1) Link Assembly, Rear Stabilizer Shaft
(2) Stabilizer Shaft, Rear
(3) Arm, Rear Suspension Trailing
(4) Link, Lateral
(5) Bolt, Rear Suspension Support
(6) Bolt, Rear Suspension Support
(7) Bolt, Rear Suspension Support
(8) Bolt, Rear Suspension Support
(9) Bolt, Rear Suspension Support
(10) Spring, Coil
(11) Mount, Upper Strut

GC2039700141000X

Fig. 2 Exploded view of rear suspension. Alero, Cutlass, Malibu & 1999–2002 Grand Am

c. Road test vehicle to ensure proper operation.

HUB & BEARING

REPLACE

1. Raise and safely support vehicle.
2. Remove wheel and tire assembly.
3. **On models equipped with rear drum brakes,** proceed as follows:
   a. Remove brake drum. **Do not hammer on drum since damage to bearing may result.**
   b. Disconnect ABS wheel sensor electrical connector.
   c. Remove attaching bolts, then the hub and bearing assembly from axle. **Partially remove hub and bearing assembly prior to removing the upper rear hub attaching bolt.**
4. **On models equipped with rear disc brakes,** proceed as follows:
   a. Remove brake rotor as outlined in the "Disc Brakes" chapter.
   b. Disconnect parking brake cable from parking brake lever.
   c. Disconnect ABS wheel sensor electrical connector.
   d. Remove hub assembly to knuckle bolts, then the hub from knuckle.
   e. Remove Torx head bolts from rear of hub assembly, then the hub assembly from backing plate.
5. **On all models,** reverse procedure to install. Tighten all fasteners to specifications. **Avoid dropping and damaging hub and bearing assembly.**

STRUT

REPLACE

ALERO, CUTLASS, MALIBU & 1999–2002 GRAND AM

Do not hammer or pry on the machined aluminum knuckle casting or any of the components attached to it.

1. Raise and support vehicle.
2. Remove tire and wheel assembly.
3. Scribe knuckle to strut position for assembly.
4. Open luggage compartment and remove strut mount nut.
5. Remove mounting bolts from wheelwell.
6. Remove strut knuckle mounting bolts, then the strut.
7. Reverse procedure to install. Ensure scribe marks are properly aligned.

STRUT SERVICE

Refer to "Strut Service" in "Front Suspension & Steering."

SHOCK ABSORBER

REPLACE

ACHIEVA, SKYLARK & 1998 GRAND AM

If replacing both shock absorbers, remove one at a time.

1. Remove trim cover and shock absorber upper retaining nut from inside luggage compartment.
2. Raise rear of vehicle and support rear axle using a suitable jack.
3. Remove shock absorber lower attaching bolt and disconnect shock absorber from mounting bracket, **Fig. 1.**
4. Remove shock absorber from vehicle.
5. Reverse procedure to install. Tighten attaching bolt to specifications.

COIL SPRING

REPLACE

ACHIEVA, SKYLARK & 1998 GRAND AM

1. Raise and support rear of vehicle.
2. Support rear axle using a suitable jack.
3. Remove wheel and tire assemblies.
4. Remove brake line bracket attaching bolts from body and allow brake lines to hang freely.
5. Disconnect shock absorbers from axle assembly at lower mounting bracket. **Do not suspend rear axle by brake hoses since damage to hoses will result.**
6. Carefully lower rear axle assembly, then remove springs and insulators.
7. Reverse procedure to install. Upper ends of spring must be properly positioned in spring seat and within 9⁄16 inch of spring stop.

ALERO, CUTLASS, MALIBU & 1999–2002 GRAND AM

The coil spring is a component of the strut assembly. Remove the spring as outlined under "Strut Service" in the "Front Suspension & Steering" section.

CONTROL ARM BUSHING

REPLACE

ACHIEVA, SKYLARK & 1998 GRAND AM

1. Raise rear of vehicle and support rear axle under front side of spring seat using a suitable jack.
2. Remove wheel and tire assembly.
3. If righthand side bushing is to be replaced, disconnect brake line bracket from body.
4. If lefthand side bushing is to be replaced, disconnect brake line bracket from body and parking brake cable at hook guide.
5. Remove control arm to mounting bracket attaching nut, bolt and washer, then allow control arm to rotate downward.
6. Remove bushing using rear control arm bushing service set tool No. J-29376-A, long nut tool No. J-21474-18 and long bolt and bearing tool No. J-21474-19, or equivalents, **Fig. 3.**

7. Reverse procedure to install, noting the following:
   a. When installing bushing, installer arrow must align with arrow on receiver, **Fig. 3.**
   b. Tighten bolts to specifications.
   c. **Control arm attaching bolt must be tightened after vehicle is lowered to floor and is in its standing height position.**

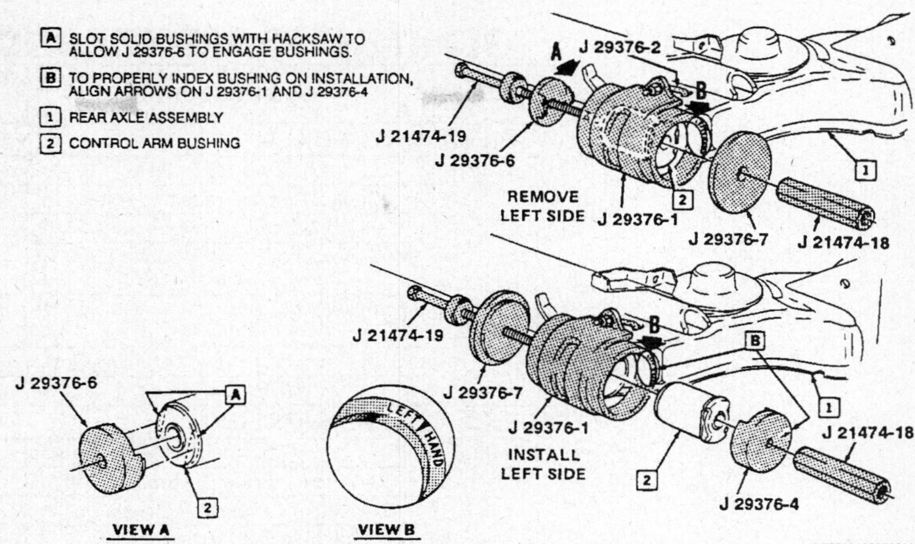

Fig. 3 Control arm bushing replacement. Achieva, Skylark & 1998 Grand Am

KNUCKLE

REPLACE

ALERO, CUTLASS, MALIBU & 1999-2002 GRAND AM

Removal

1. Raise and support vehicle, then remove tire and wheel assembly.
2. Scribe strut to knuckle position for installation reference.
3. Remove rear lateral link nut, bolt and washer, then the drum or rotor.
4. Remove ABS electrical connector and rear wheel hub.
5. Remove trailing arm from knuckle.
6. Remove strut nuts and bolts.
7. Remove knuckle.

Installation

1. Install knuckle onto vehicle.
2. Install strut to knuckle nuts and bolts. Hand tighten the bolts.
3. Install stabilizer shaft link.
4. Install trailing arm to knuckle bolt, washer and bushing. Tighten bolt to specifications.
5. Install hub assembly.
6. **On models equipped with rear disc brakes,** connect parking brake cable to parking brake lever.
7. **On all models,** install rotor or drum.
8. Install lateral links to knuckle nut, bolt and washer. Tighten nut to specifications.
9. Connect wheel speed sensor harness.
10. Tighten strut to knuckle bolts to specifications.
11. Install tire and wheel.
12. Lower the vehicle.
13. Inspect rear wheel alignment.

REAR CROSSMEMBER

REPLACE

ALERO, CUTLASS, MALIBU & 1999-2002 GRAND AM

1. Raise and support vehicle, then remove tire and wheel assemblies.
2. Remove tailpipe if required.
3. Remove brake lines and parking brake cables from crossmember.
4. Remove stabilizer shaft as outlined under "Stabilizer Shaft, Replace."
5. Disconnect rear wheel speed sensor electrical connectors, then position harness aside.
6. Remove front and rear lateral links as outlined under "Lateral Link, Replace."
7. Remove bolt from EVAP canister.
8. Support crossmember with suitable jack stands.
9. Remove mounting bolts and rear crossmember.
10. Reverse procedure to install. Tighten bolts to specifications.

TRAILING ARM

REPLACE

ALERO, CUTLASS, MALIBU & 1999-2002 GRAND AM

1. Raise and support vehicle.
2. Remove trailing arm knuckle bolt, washer and bushing.
3. Remove body bolt, then the trailing arm.
4. Reverse procedure to install. Tighten bolts to specifications.

STABILIZER SHAFT

REPLACE

ALERO, CUTLASS, MALIBU & 1999-2002 GRAND AM

1. Raise and support vehicle, then remove tire and wheel assemblies if required.
2. Remove link bolts.
3. Remove mounting nuts and insulator brackets.
4. Remove stabilizer shaft.
5. Reverse procedure to install. Tighten bolts to specifications.

LATERAL LINK

REPLACE

ALERO, CUTLASS, MALIBU & 1999-2002 GRAND AM

1. Raise and support vehicle, then remove tire and wheel assembly.
2. If removing front lateral line and trailing arm, remove ABS wire harness.
3. Remove knuckle bolt, nut and washer. Push bolt forward enough for removal clearance.
4. Remove crossmember nut and rear lateral link and trailing arm.
5. Reverse procedure to install.

TIGHTENING SPECIFICATIONS

Year	Component	Torque/Ft. Lbs.
ACHIEVA, SKYLARK		
1998	Axle To Body Bracket	68
	Control Arm To Underbody Nuts	59①
	Hub & Bearing To Axle Bolts	37
	Shock Absorber Lower Mounting Bolt To Axle	35
	Shock Absorber Upper Mounting Bolt To Body	13
	Shock Absorber Upper Mounting Nut	21
	Wheel Lug Nuts	100
ALERO, CUTLASS, MALIBU		
1998–2002	Crossmember	89
	Disc Brake Caliper To Bracket Bolt	81
	Disc Brake Caliper To Knuckle Bolt	85
	Lateral Link To Crossmember	89
	Lateral Link To Knuckle	89
	Stabilizer Shaft Bracket	39
	Stabilizer Shaft Link	51
	Strut Nut	89
	Strut To Body	18
	Strut To Knuckle	89
	Trailing Arm To Body	48①
	Trailing Arm To Knuckle	51
	Wheel Hub To Knuckle	70
	Wheel Lug Nuts	100
GRAND AM		
1998	Axle To Body Bracket	68
	Control Arm To Underbody Nuts	59①
	Hub & Bearing To Axle Bolts	37
	Shock Absorber Lower Mounting Bolt To Axle	35
	Shock Absorber Upper Mounting Bolt To Body	13
	Shock Absorber Upper Mounting Nut	21
	Wheel Lug Nuts	100
1999–2002	Crossmember	89
	Disc Brake Caliper To Bracket Bolt	81
	Disc Brake Caliper To Knuckle Bolt	85
	Lateral Link To Crossmember	89
	Lateral Link To Knuckle	89
	Stabilizer Shaft Bracket	39
	Stabilizer Shaft Link	51
	Strut Nut	89
	Strut To Body	18
	Strut To Knuckle	89
	Trailing Arm To Body	48①
	Trailing Arm To Knuckle	51
	Wheel Hub To Knuckle	70
	Wheel Lug Nuts	100

① — Tighten an additional 120°.

Front Suspension & Steering

INDEX

PRECAUTIONS

AIR BAG SYSTEMS

Refer to "Air Bag System Precautions" in the front of this manual for system disarming and arming procedures.

BATTERY GROUND CABLE

Prior to service, disconnect battery ground cable and isolate as required.

DESCRIPTION

The front suspension on these vehicles, **Fig. 1,** is of the strut and spring design. The lower control arms pivot from the lower side rails through rubber bushings. The upper end of the strut is isolated by a rubber mount incorporating a bearing for wheel turning. The tie rods connect to the steering arm on the strut, below the spring seat. The lower end of the steering knuckle pivots on a ball stud which is retained to the lower control arm by rivets and is secured to the steering knuckle with a nut and cotter pin. The sealed wheel bearings are integral with the hub and are serviced as an assembly.

WHEEL BEARING

REPLACE

1. Raise and safely support vehicle.
2. Remove wheel and tire assembly.
3. Install modified outer seal protector tool No. J-34754, or equivalent.
4. Place shop towels under outer joint to protect it from sharp edges.
5. Insert suitable drift punch into caliper and rotor to prevent turning and remove axle shaft nut and washer, **Fig. 2.**
6. Remove lower ball joint cotter pin and nut, then loosen joint from steering knuckle using joint separator tool No. J-38892, or equivalent.
7. If lefthand drive axle shaft is being remove, turn wheel to right. If righthand drive axle shaft is being removed, turn wheel left.
8. Remove ABS sensor wire and disconnect stabilizer link.
9. Position a suitable pry bar between suspension support and lower control arm and separate lower ball joint from steering knuckle.
10. Use front hub knuckle remover tool No. J-28733-B, or equivalent to separate drive axle shaft from hub and bearing assembly, **Fig. 3.**
11. When removing righthand axle shaft, use slide hammer tool No. J-2619-01 and axle shaft removal tool No. J-33008, or equivalents.
12. Separate drive axle shaft from hub and wheel bearing assembly and move strut and knuckle assembly rearward. Use wire or rope to suspend drive axle shaft from underbody. Use care not to overextend driveshaft joints.
13. Remove caliper attaching bolts and brake caliper with brake hose attached. Use wire to suspend caliper from underbody. Do not allow caliper to hang from brake hose.
14. Remove brake rotor, hub and bearing assembly attaching bolts, **Fig. 4.**
15. Remove hub and bearing assembly.
16. Reverse procedure to install, noting following:
    a. Tighten attaching fasteners to specifications.
    b. Inspect front wheel alignment and adjust as required.

BALL JOINT INSPECTION

Ball joints must be replaced if any looseness is detected in the joint or the seal is cut.

To inspect the ball joints, raise the front of the vehicle allowing the suspension to hang free. Grasp the tire at the top and bottom and move the top of tire with an in-and-out motion. Look for any horizontal movement of the steering knuckle relative to the front lower control arm.

If the ball stud is disconnected from the steering knuckle and any looseness is detected or if the ball stud can be twisted in its socket using finger pressure, replace the ball joint.

Ball stud tightness in the steering knuckle boss should also be inspected when inspecting the ball joint. This may be done by shaking the wheel and feeling for movement of the stud end or castellated nut at the knuckle boss. Inspecting the fastener torque at the castellated nut is an alternative method of inspecting for wear. A loose nut can indicate a bent stud or an opened-up hole in the knuckle boss. Worn or damaged ball joints and knuckles must be replaced.

BALL JOINT

REPLACE

1. Raise and support vehicle. Remove tire and wheel assembly.
2. Remove lower ball joint cotter pin and nut.
3. **On models equipped with ABS,** position wheel speed sensor wiring aside as required.
4. **On all models,** using ball joint separator tool No. J-43828, or equivalent, separate lower ball joint from steering knuckle, **Fig. 5.**
5. Locate center of rivet body and mark with a center punch.
6. Using a ⅛ inch drill bit, drill pilot holes completely through rivets. **Avoid damaging CV joint boots.**
7. Using a ½ inch drill bit, drill final holes through rivets to ensure proper fitting of new ball joint.
8. Remove nut attaching stabilizer shaft link.
9. Remove ball joint from knuckle and lower control arm.
10. Reverse procedure to install using bolts provided in service package. Tighten all fasteners to specifications.

STRUT

REPLACE

1. Remove strut assembly body attaching nuts and bolt.
2. Raise and support vehicle.
3. Place jack stands under front crossmember, then lower vehicle slightly so it rests on stands, not on control arms.
4. Remove wheel and tire. Install modified outer seal protector tool No. J-34754, or equivalent if required.
5. Remove tie rod end cotter pin and nut, then, using tie rod puller tool No. J-24319-01, or equivalent, disconnect tie rod from strut assembly.
6. Remove brake line bracket.

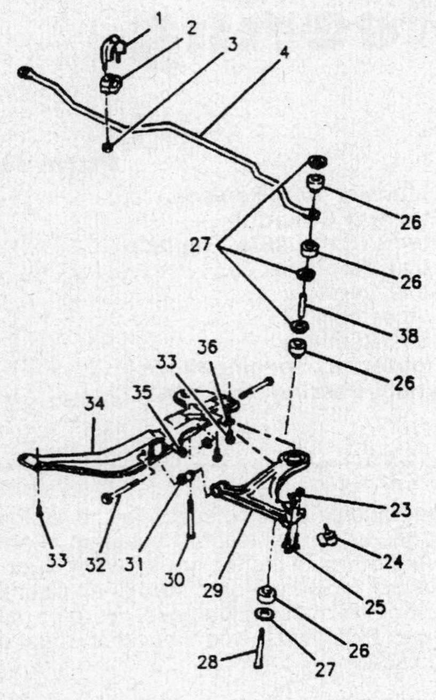

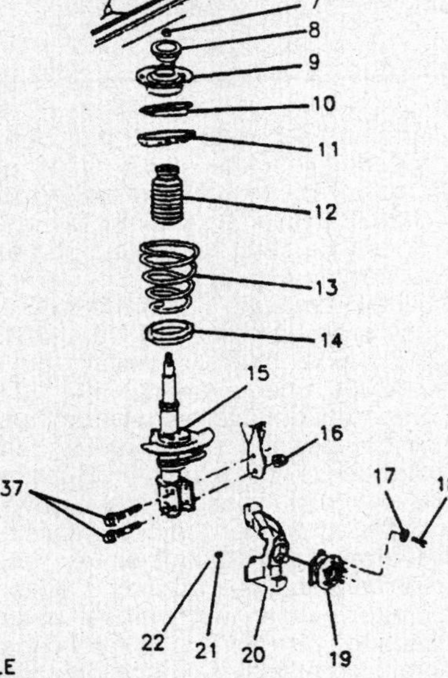

1 CLAMP, STABILIZER SHAFT
2 INSULATOR, STABILIZER SHAFT
3 NUT
4 STABILIZER SHAFT
5 BOLT
6 NUT
7 NUT, STRUT DAMPENER SHAFT
8 RATE WASHER
9 STRUT MOUNT
10 UPPER SPRING SEAT
11 UPPER SPRING INSULATOR
12 DUST TUBE ASSEMBLY
13 SPRING
14 LOWER SPRING INSULATOR
15 STRUT
16 NUT
17 WASHER
18 BOLT
19 HUB AND BEARING ASSEMBLY
20 STEERING KNUCKLE
21 NUT, BALL JOINT
22 COTTER PIN
23 NUT
24 BALL JOINT
25 BOLT
26 INSULATOR, STABILIZER LINK
27 WASHER, STABILIZER LINK
28 BOLT, STABILIZER LINK
29 CONTROL ARM
30 BOLT
31 BUSHING, CONTROL ARM
32 BOLT
33 BOLT
34 SUSPENSION SUPPORT
35 NUT
36 WASHER
37 BOLT
38 SPACER, STABILIZER LINK

GC202970027I000X

Fig. 1 Exploded view of front suspension

7. Scribe alignment marks on strut flange, **Fig. 6.**
8. Remove attaching bolts and strut, **Fig. 1.** Use care not to damage spring coating.
9. Reverse procedure to install, noting the following:
   a. Align marks on strut flange and steering knuckle made during removal.
   b. Tighten all fasteners to specifications.
   c. Inspect wheel alignment and adjust as required.

STRUT SERVICE

DISASSEMBLE

1. **On Achieva, Skylark and 1998 Grand Am models,** position strut compressor tool No. J-34013-B in holding fixture J-3289-20, or equivalent, then position strut in strut compressor. Use care not to damage spring coating.
2. **On Alero, Cutlass, Malibu and 1999–2002 Grand Am models,** position strut compressor tool No. J-34013-B in holding fixture J-3289-20 with adapter tool No. J-34013-88, or equivalents.
3. **On all models,** compress strut to approximately half of its height. Use care not to bottom spring or damper rod.
4. Remove nut from strut dampener shaft and position alignment rod tool No. J-34013-27, or equivalent on dampener shaft. Use guide rod tool to position dampener shaft down through bearing cap while compressing coil spring.
5. Remove strut components, **Figs. 7 and 8.**

1. DRIFT PUNCH
2. 6 POINT DEEP WELL SOCKET

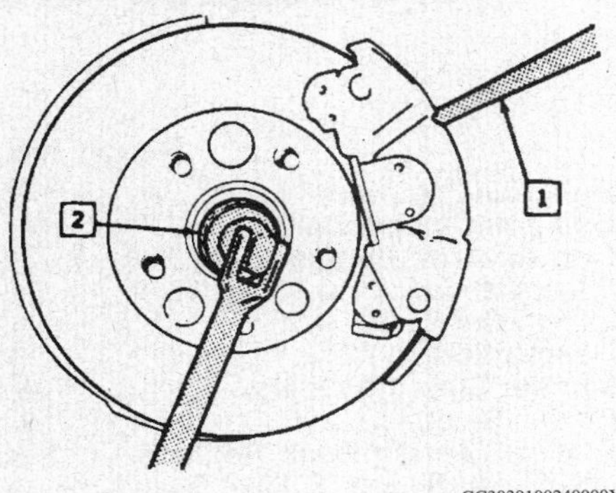

GC3039100240000X

Fig. 2 Drive axle shaft nut replacement

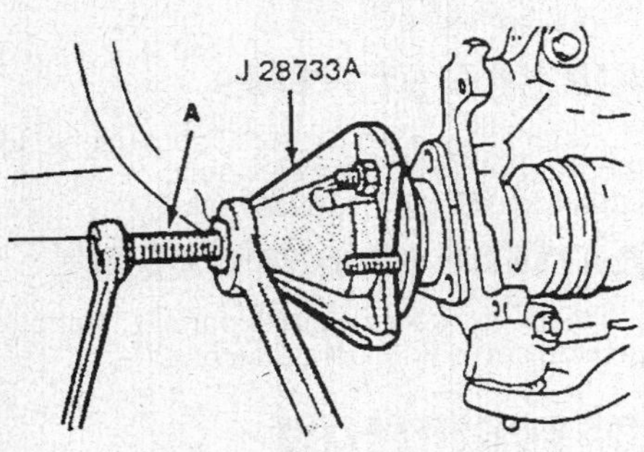

A. TURN FORCING SCREW UNTIL AXLE SPLINES ARE JUST LOOSE

GC3039100241000X

Fig. 3 Drive axle shaft removal from hub

ASSEMBLE

1. Install bearing cap.
2. Mount strut to strut compressor tool using bottom locking pin only.
3. Extend dampener shaft and install dampener rod clamp tool No. J-34013-20, or equivalent.
4. Install spring over dampener.
5. Swing strut assembly up and install upper locking pin.
6. Install upper insulator, dust shield, bumper and upper spring seat. The flat on upper spring seat should face in the same direction as centerline of strut assembly knuckle, **Fig. 9.**
7. Install guide rod tool onto dampener shaft, then compress strut unit until dampener shaft threads are visible. Remove guide rod tool and install retaining nut.
8. While holding dampener shaft in position with a suitable wrench, tighten retaining nut to specifications.
9. Remove dampener rod clamp tool.

CONTROL ARM

REPLACE

REMOVAL

1. Raise and support vehicle. Remove wheel and tire assembly.

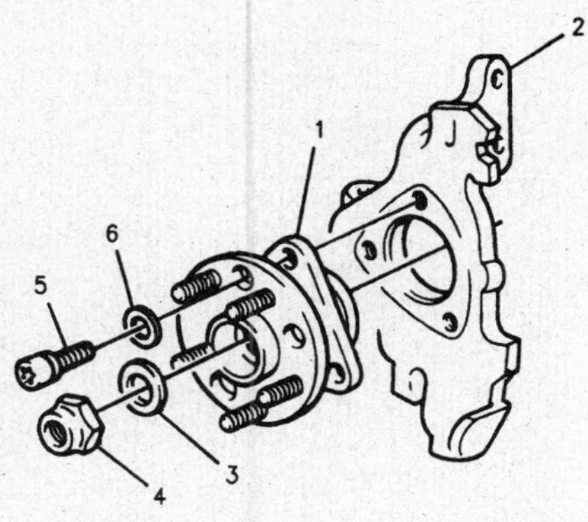

1 HUB AND BEARING ASSEMBLY
2 STEERING KNUCKLE
3 WASHER
4 DRIVE AXLE NUT
5 HUB AND BEARING RETAINING BOLT
6 WASHER

GC3039700369000X

Fig. 4 Front hub & wheel bearing replacement

2. Disconnect stabilizer bar at lower control arm and control arm support.
3. Remove ball joint cotter pin and nut.
4. Separate ball joint from steering knuckle with ball joint separator tool No. J-43828, or equivalent.
5. Remove mounting bolts, support and control arm as an assembly, **Fig. 10.**
6. **On Achieva, Skylark and 1998 Grand Am models,** separate control arm from support and use lower control arm front bushing set tool No. J-29792, or equivalent to remove bushings from control arm.

INSTALLATION

1. **On Achieva, Skylark and 1998 Grand Am models,** proceed as follows:
   a. Install control arm into position and loosely install mounting bolts.
   b. Install ball joint to knuckle nut. Tighten to specifications and install cotter pin.
   c. Install stabilizer link nut and tighten to specifications.
   d. If vehicle is sitting on a suspension contact hoist, raise vehicle slightly, then remove jack stands from under suspension supports.
   e. Install tire and wheel.
   f. Lower the vehicle to the ground, then tighten, in order, the center, front and rear suspension support mounting bolts to specifications.
   g. Tighten, in order, the control arm front and rear mounting bolts to specifications.
2. **On Alero, Cutlass, Malibu and 1999–2002 Grand Am models,** proceed as follows:
   a. Install control arm into position and hand tighten rear mounting bolt.
   b. Install and hand tighten front mounting bolt.
   c. Install stabilizer shaft link.

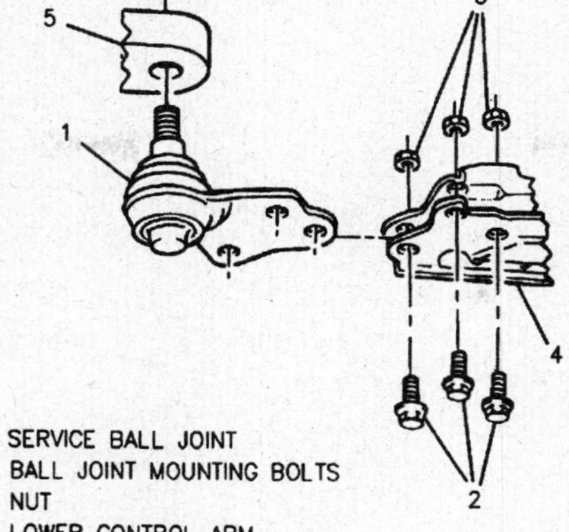

1 SERVICE BALL JOINT
2 BALL JOINT MOUNTING BOLTS
3 NUT
4 LOWER CONTROL ARM
5 STEERING KNUCKLE
6 NUT
7 PIN

GC2029700272000X

Fig. 5 Lower ball joint to lower control arm replacement

   d. Install lower ball joint to knuckle.
   e. Raise vehicle slightly, then remove jack stands from under crossmember.
   f. Install tire and wheel.
   g. Lower the vehicle to the ground, then tighten, in order, the control arm front and rear mounting bolts to specifications.
3. **On all models,** inspect front wheel alignment and adjust as required.

STEERING KNUCKLE

REPLACE

1. Raise and support vehicle. Remove wheel and tire.
2. Remove front hub and bearing as outlined under "Wheel Bearing, Replace."
3. Remove steering knuckle to strut mounting bolts, then the knuckle.
4. Reverse procedure to install. Tighten all fasteners to specifications.

STABILIZER BAR

REPLACE

1. Raise and support vehicle, allowing control arms to hang free.
2. Remove front wheels and tires.
3. **On Alero, Cutlass, Malibu and 1999–2002 Grand Am models,** proceed as follows:
   a. Remove stabilizer shaft links.
   b. Using separator tool No. J-24319-01, or equivalent, separate tie rod ends from knuckles.
   c. Remove transaxle rear mount bolt.
   d. Remove power steering line bracket from crossmember.
4. **On all models,** disconnect stabilizer bar at control arms and suspension support assemblies, **Fig. 11.**
5. Loosen front and remove rear and center bolts from suspension support assembly. Lower support enough to allow stabilizer bar removal.
6. Remove stabilizer bar with insulators.

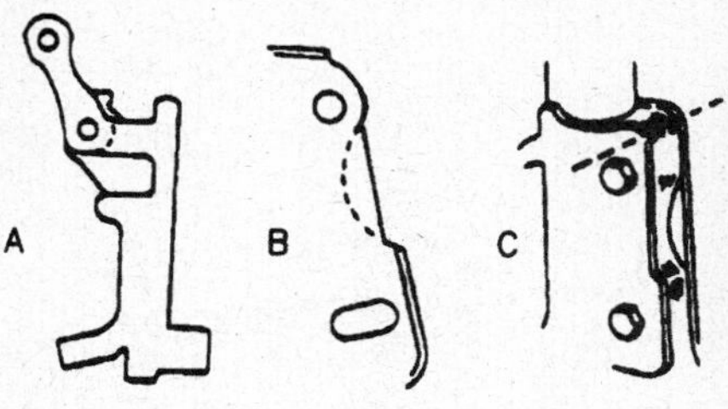

A SCRIBE KNUCKLE ALONG LOWER OUTBOARD STRUT RADIUS
B SCRIBE STRUT FLANGE ON INBOARD SIDE ALONG CURVE OF KNUCKLE
C SCRIBE ACROSS STRUT/KNUCKLE INTERFACE

GC2029700273000X

Fig. 6 Strut & knuckle alignment marks

7. Reverse procedure to install, noting the following:
   a. **On Achieva, Skylark and 1998 Grand Am models,** tighten, in order, the center, front and rear suspension support mounting bolts to specifications. Tighten, in order, the stabilizer shaft clamp nuts and control arm nuts to specifications.
   b. **On Alero, Cutlass, Malibu and 1999–2002 Grand Am models,** tighten, in order, the lefthand rear, righthand rear, lefthand front and righthand front crossmember mounting bolts to specifications.

POWER STEERING GEAR

REPLACE

ACHIEVA, SKYLARK & 1998 GRAND AM

1. Remove lefthand sound insulator and steering shaft coupling pinch bolt.
2. Remove line retainer, then the master cylinder from brake booster and position aside with lines attached.
3. Move power brake booster away from cowl and remove brake pedal pushrod from pedal.
4. Remove inner tie rod bolts, lock plates and washers.
5. Remove steering gear mounting clamps, **Fig. 12.**
6. Disconnect steering gear hydraulic lines.
7. Move steering gear slightly forward, remove lower pinch bolt from flexible coupling, detach coupling from steering gear stub shaft and remove dash seal.
8. Remove steering gear through lefthand wheel opening.
9. Reverse procedure to install, noting the following:
   a. If steering gear mounting clamp studs have backed out during removal, install studs to cowl and tighten until stud is fully seated.
   b. Torque should not exceed 15 ft. lbs.
   c. After second use of studs, thread

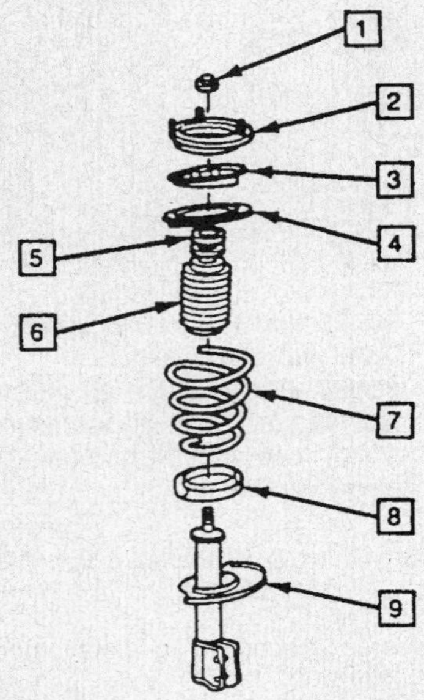

1 STRUT MOUNT NUT
2 STRUT MOUNT
3 SPRING SEAT
4 SPRING UPPER INSULATOR
5 JOUNCE BUMPER
6 STRUT DUST SHIELD
7 SPRING
8 SPRING LOWER INSULATOR
9 STRUT

GC2029100167000X

Fig. 7 Exploded view of strut assembly. Achieva, Skylark & 1998 Grand Am

locking kit No. 1052624 or equivalent must be used.

ALERO, CUTLASS, MALIBU & 1999-2002 GRAND AM

1. Carefully siphon fluid from power steering reservoir.
2. Raise and support vehicle, then remove front tires and wheels.
3. Remove stabilizer shaft links from control arms.
4. Using separator tool No. J-24319-01, or equivalent, remove tie rods from knuckles.
5. Remove intermediate shaft lower pinch bolt.
6. Support rear of crossmember with suitable jack stands.
7. Remove stabilizer shaft.
8. Remove steering gear mounting bolts.
9. **On Cutlass and Malibu models, if required,** proceed as follows:

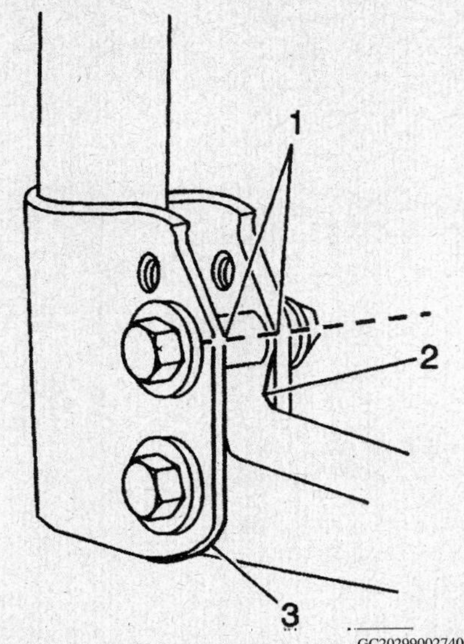

Fig. 8 Exploded view of strut assembly. Alero, Cutlass, Malibu & 1999–2002 Grand Am

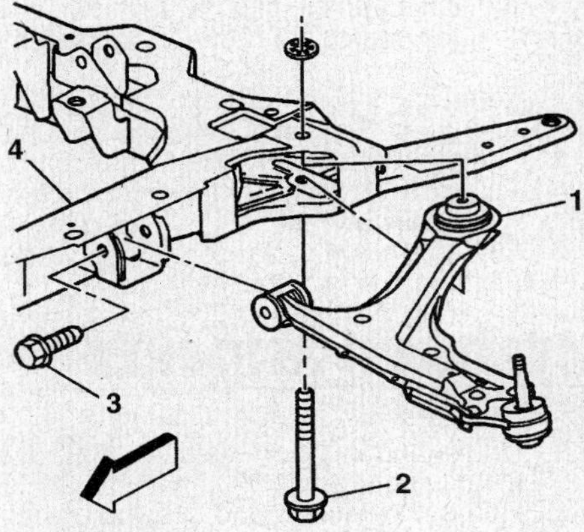

1 ARM
2 REAR MOUNTING BOLT
3 FRONT MOUNTING BOLT
4 CROSSMEMBER

GC2029700276000X

Fig. 10 Lower control arm replacement

   a. Remove transaxle mount-to-crossmember bolt.
   b. Remove rear crossmember to body bolts to provide pipe and hose removal clearance.
   c. Loosen front crossmember bolts.
10. **On all models,** remove steering gear mounting bolts.
11. Place a suitable drain pan below steering gear, then disconnect power steering fluid hoses from gear.
12. Remove steering gear through left-hand wheel opening.
13. Reverse procedure to install. Tighten all fasteners to specifications.

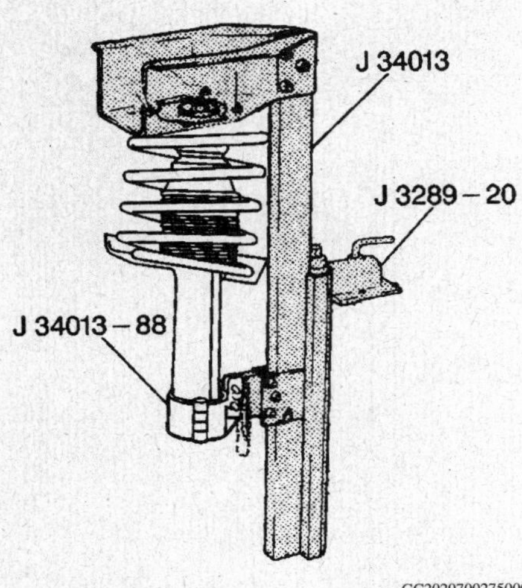

Fig. 9 Strut unit assembly

POWER STEERING PUMP

REPLACE

2.4L ENGINE

1. Siphon as much power steering fluid as possible from reservoir.
2. **On models equipped with variable effort steering,** disconnect variable effort steering electrical connector.
3. **On all models,** place a suitable drain pan in position, then disconnect power steering pump lines at pump, **Fig. 13.**
4. Remove power steering pump mounting bolts, then the pump.
5. Reverse procedure to install, noting the following:
   a. Tighten pump mounting bolts and hose connections to specifications.
   b. Fill pump with proper fluid and bleed air as required.
   c. Inspect for fluid leaks.

3.1L & 3.4L ENGINES

1. Siphon as much power steering fluid as possible from reservoir.
2. Remove engine mount as outlined under "Engine Mount, Replace."
3. Remove serpentine belt as outlined under "Serpentine Drive Belt."
4. Remove alternator bracket retaining hose nut.
5. Remove power steering pump bolts to ease power steering line removal.
6. Place a suitable drain pan in position, then disconnect power steering pump lines at pump and remove pump.
7. Remove transfer pulley if required.
8. Reverse procedure to install. Tighten all fasteners to specifications.

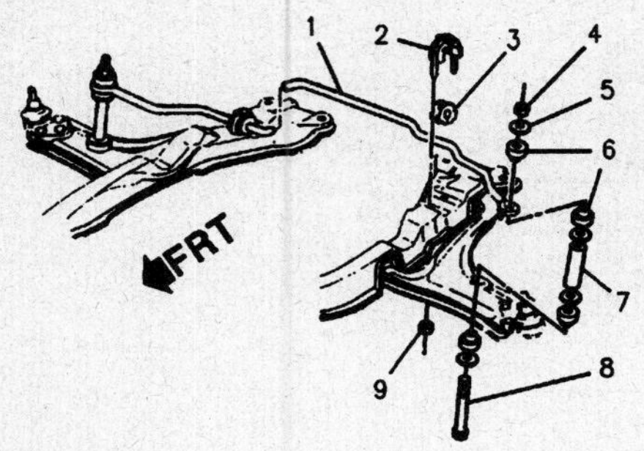

1 SHAFT, STABILIZER
2 CLAMP
3 INSULATOR, STABILIZER SHAFT
4 NUT
5 WASHER
6 INSULATOR, STABILIZER LINK
7 SPACER
8 BOLT
9 NUT

GC2029700277000X

Fig. 11 Typical stabilizer bar replacement

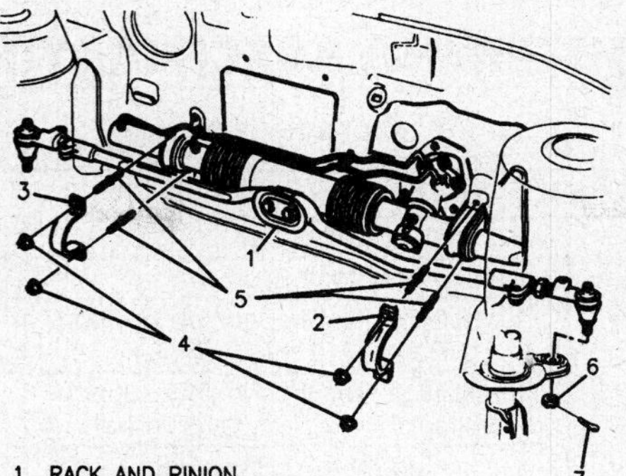

1 RACK AND PINION
2 L.H. CLAMP – HORIZONTAL SLOT AT TOP
3 R.H. CLAMP – HORIZONTAL SLOT AT TOP
4 NUT– HAND START ALL NUTS. TIGHTEN LEFT HAND SIDE CLAMP NUTS FIRST, THEN TIGHTEN RIGHT SIDE NUTS.
5 STUD – AFTER SECOND REUSE OF STUD, THREAD LOCKING KIT NO. 1052624 MUST BE USED.
6 NUT
7 COTTER PIN

GC2029700278000X

Fig. 12 Power rack & pinion steering gear mounting. Achieva, Skylark & 1998 Grand Am

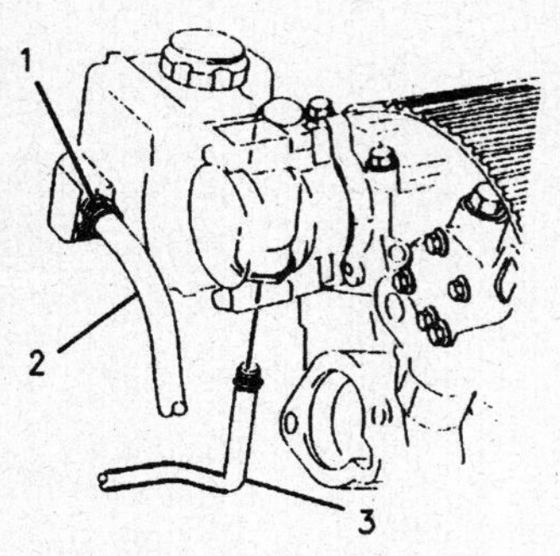

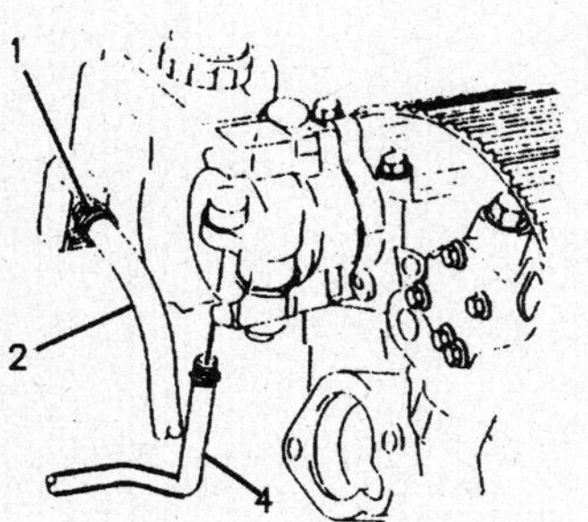

1 CLAMP, HOSE
2 HOSE, OUTLET
3 HOSE, INLET (NON EVO)
4 HOSE, INLET (EVO)

GC6039700056000A

Fig. 13 Power steering pump removal. 2.4L engine

TIGHTENING SPECIFICATIONS

Year	Component	Torque/Ft. Lbs.
ACHIEVA, SKYLARK		
1998	Axle Nut	185
	Ball Joint Stud Nut	41–48
	Control Arm To Suspension Support Bolts At Front Bushing	55②
	Control Arm To Suspension Support Bolts At Rear Vertical Bushing	125
	Control Arm Pivot Bolt	61
	Disc Brake Caliper Bolts	38
	Driveshaft Nut	74③
	Hub & Bearing Assembly To Knuckle Bolts	70
	Hub Nut	185
	Power Steering Line Fittings	20
	Power Steering Pump (2.4L)	19
	Power Steering Pump (3.1L)	25
	Stabilizer Shaft To Control Arm	15
	Stabilizer Shaft Link to Support Nuts	22
	Steering Coupling To Steering Column	30
	Steering Coupling To Stub Shaft	30
	Stabilizer To Support Assembly	16
	Steering Knuckle To Strut Assembly	133
	Strut Assembly To Body	18
	Strut Cartridge Retaining Nut	65
	Suspension Support Assembly	89
	Tie Rod End To Steering Knuckle	37
	Tie Rod End To Strut Nut	42
	Tie Rod Inner Bolts	65
	Tie Rod Pinch Bolts	41
	Wheel Lug Nuts	100
ALERO, CUTLASS, MALIBU		
1999–2002	Axle Nut	284
	Ball Joint To Knuckle (Alero)	41
	Ball Joint To Knuckle For Cotter Pin Installation (1998 Cutlass & Malibu)	7④
	Control Arm Pivot Bolt At Front Bushing (1998 Cutlass & Malibu)	44①
	Control Arm Pivot Bolt At Rear Vertical Bushing (1998 Cutlass & Malibu)	74④
	Control Arm To Frame Bolts At Front Bushing (Alero)	79
	Control Arm To Frame Bolts At Rear Bushing (Alero)	81
	Disc Brake Caliper Bolts	85
	Disc Brake Caliper To Bracket Bolt	23
	Driveshaft Nut	284
	Hub & Bearing Assembly To Knuckle Bolts	70
	Hub Nut	284
	Power Steering Line Fittings	20
	Power Steering Pump (2.4L Engine)	19
	Power Steering Pump (3.1L & 3.4L Engines)	25
	Stabilizer Shaft To Control Arm	13
	Stabilizer Shaft Bushing Clamp To Crossmember Support Nuts	49
	Stabilizer Shaft Link to Control Arm Nuts	13

Continued

TIGHTENING SPECIFICATIONS—Continued

Year	Component	Torque/Ft. Lbs.
ALERO, CUTLASS, MALIBU		
1999–2002	Steering Gear Bolts	89
	Steering Gear Mounting Clamp	22
	Steering Column Upper & Lower Pinch Bolts	16
	Steering Knuckle To Strut Assembly	133
	Strut Assembly To Body	18
	Suspension Support Assembly Bushing (1998 Cutlass & Malibu)	74④
	Strut Nut To Strut Rod	52
	Tie Rod End To Steering Knuckle Nut (1998 Cutlass & Malibu)	15④
	Tie Rod End To Steering Knuckle Nut (1999 Alero)	33
	Tie Rod End To Steering Knuckle Nut (2000–02)	15
	Tie Rod End To Strut Nut (1998 Cutlass & Malibu)	15④
	Tie Rod Jam Nuts	50
	Transaxle Front Mount Bolt (1998 Cutlass & Malibu)	89
	Transaxle Mount Bolt (Alero)	89
	Wheel Lug Nuts	100
GRAND AM		
1998	Axle Nut	185
	Ball Joint Stud Nut	41–48
	Control Arm To Suspension Support Bolts At Front Bushing	55②
	Control Arm To Suspension Support Bolts At Rear Vertical Bushing	125
	Control Arm Pivot Bolt	61
	Disc Brake Caliper Bolts	38
	Driveshaft Nut	74③
	Hub & Bearing Assembly To Knuckle Bolts	70
	Hub Nut	185
	Power Steering Line Fittings	20
	Power Steering Pump (2.4L)	19
	Power Steering Pump (3.1L)	25
	Stabilizer Shaft To Control Arm	15
	Stabilizer Shaft Link to Support Nuts	22
	Steering Coupling To Steering Column	30
	Steering Coupling To Stub Shaft	30
	Stabilizer To Support Assembly	16
	Steering Knuckle To Strut Assembly	133
	Strut Assembly To Body	18
	Strut Cartridge Retaining Nut	65
	Suspension Support Assembly	89
	Tie Rod End To Steering Knuckle	37
	Tie Rod End To Strut Nut	42
	Tie Rod Inner Bolts	65
	Tie Rod Pinch Bolts	41
	Wheel Lug Nuts	100

Continued

TIGHTENING SPECIFICATIONS—Continued

Year	Component	Torque/Ft. Lbs.
GRAND AM		
1999–2002	Axle Nut	284
	Ball Joint To Knuckle	41
	Control Arm To Frame Bolts At Front Bushing	79
	Control Arm To Frame Bolts At Rear Bushing	81
	Disc Brake Caliper Bolts	85
	Disc Brake Caliper To Bracket Bolt	23
	Driveshaft Nut	284
	Hub & Bearing Assembly To Knuckle Bolts	70
	Hub Nut	284
	Power Steering Line Fittings	20
	Power Steering Pump (2.4L Engine)	19
	Power Steering Pump (3.1L & 3.4L Engines)	25
	Stabilizer Shaft To Control Arm	13
	Stabilizer Shaft Bushing Clamp To Crossmember Support Nuts	49
	Stabilizer Shaft Link to Control Arm Nuts	13
	Steering Gear Bolts	89
	Steering Gear Mounting Clamp	22
	Steering Column Upper & Lower Pinch Bolts	16
	Steering Knuckle To Strut Assembly	133
	Strut Assembly To Body	18
	Suspension Crossmember	81
	Strut Nut To Strut Rod	52
	Tie Rod End To Steering Knuckle Nut (1999)	33
	Tie Rod End To Steering Knuckle Nut (2000–02)	15
	Tie Rod Jam Nuts	50
	Transaxle Mount Bolt	89
	Wheel Lug Nuts	100

① — Tighten an additional 120°.
② — Tighten an additional 90°.
③ — Tighten an additional 40°.
④ — Tighten an additional 180°.

Wheel Alignment

INDEX

PRELIMINARY INSPECTION

Ensure all tires are properly inflated.

Before measuring and setting front wheel alignment, rest front wheels on turn plates.

Before setting rear toe, rest rear wheels on slider plates or turn plates.

Before setting any alignment angle, jounce the vehicle three times at each end to establish trim height.

Special adapters are available for using a magnetic hub gauge at rear wheels. Depending on type of equipment used, these may not be required. After removing hub cap and bearing cap, hub gauge will snap into place on brake drum. Magnetic mounting toe gauges may also be installed in the same manner.

Always perform wheel alignment on a level alignment rack. Before doing alignment, proceed as follows:

1. Inspect for worn suspension components.
2. Inspect standing curb height.
3. Remove heavy weights from trunk.
4. Inspect wheel bearings for excessive freeplay.
5. Ensure gas tank is full.
6. Place front seats in full rear position.
7. Inspect rear toe adjustment.
8. Always road test vehicle after adjusting alignment. If vehicle still pulls, switch front tires. If vehicle still pulls in same direction, inspect alignment and rear tracking. If vehicle pulls in opposite direction, rotate tires and road test.

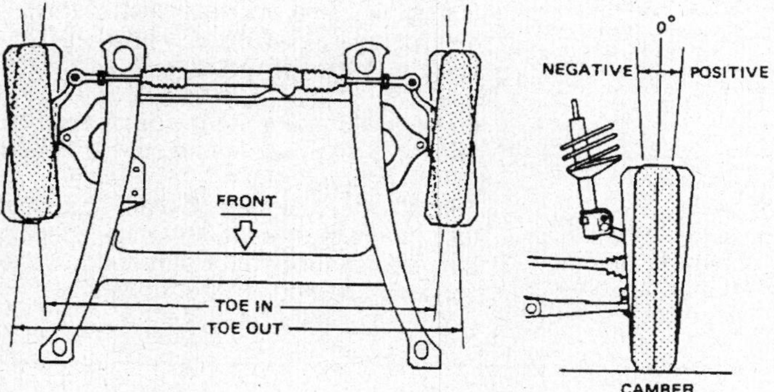

Fig. 1 Caster, camber & toe angles

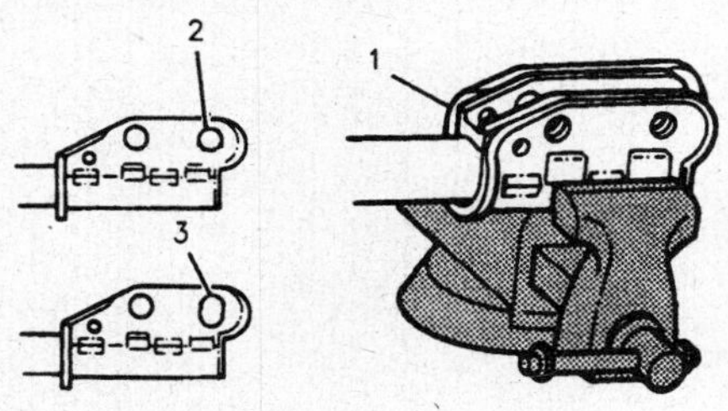

Fig. 2 Strut bracket modification for camber adjustment

FRONT WHEEL ALIGNMENT

CASTER

Caster angle is not adjustable. If caster angle, **Fig. 1,** is not within specifications, inspect suspension support for improper alignment and suspension components for damage. Replace damaged components as required.

CAMBER

Toe setting is the only adjustment normally required. However, in special circumstances, such as damage due to road hazard or collision, camber angle, **Fig. 1,** may be adjusted by modifying strut assembly.

1. If strut is on vehicle, disconnect strut from steering knuckle. If strut is off vehicle, secure bottom of strut assembly in a suitable vise.
2. Enlarge bottom holes in outer flanges with a round file, until holes in outer flanges match slots in inner flanges, **Fig. 2.**
3. Install or connect strut to steering knuckle and install bolts finger tight.
4. Grasp top of tire firmly and move tire inboard or outboard until proper camber reading is obtained. Tighten retaining bolts enough to secure camber setting.
5. Remove wheel and tire assembly if required and tighten strut to steering knuckle retaining bolts to specifications.

TOE

The toe, **Fig. 1,** is controlled by tie rod position.

Achieva, Skylark & 1998 Grand Am

1. Loosen clamp bolts at steering knuckle end of tie rods.
2. Rotating rods to obtain proper toe setting, **Fig. 3.**
3. **Torque** clamp bolts to 31 ft. lbs.

Alero, Cutlass, Malibu & 1999–2002 Grand Am

1. Ensure front wheels are in straight-ahead position.
2. Loosen jam nut, **Fig. 4.**
3. Turn adjuster to obtain proper toe setting.
4. **On 1998 Cutlass and Malibu models, torque** jam nut to 89 inch lbs., then rotate an additional 210° using torque angle meter tool No. J-36660, or equivalent.
5. **On Alero and 1999–2002 Grand Am**

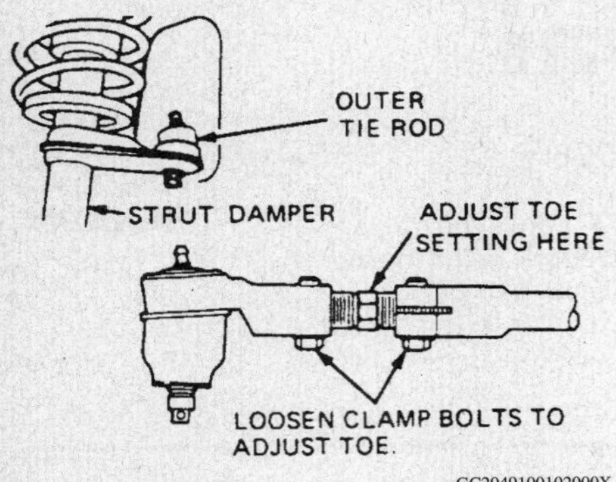

Fig. 3 Toe adjustment. Achieva, Skylark & 1998 Grand Am

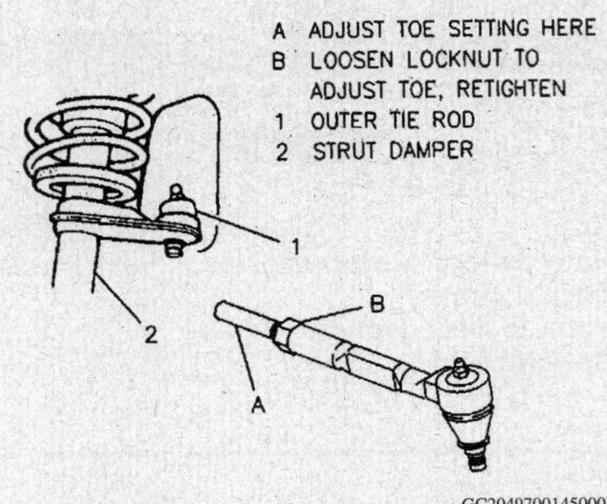

Fig. 4 Toe adjustment. Alero, Cutlass, Malibu & 1999–2002 Grand Am

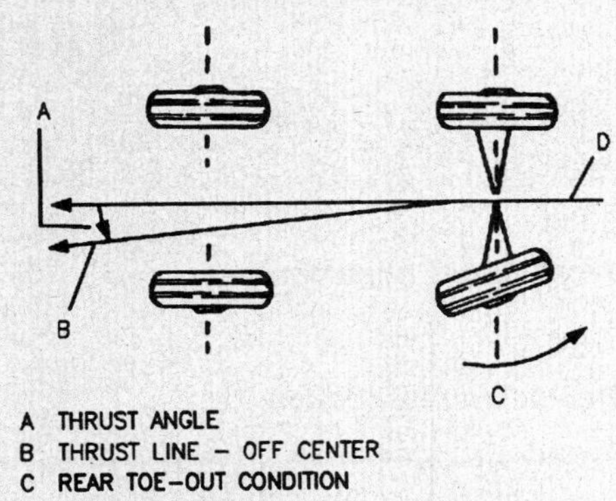

Fig. 5 Thrust angle

models, torque jam nut to 50 ft. lbs.

REAR WHEEL ALIGNMENT

After front wheel alignment has been inspected or adjusted, rear wheel alignment angles should be inspected if vehicle still does not track properly or if excessive rear tire wear is present. Rear wheels should be parallel to and the same distance from the vehicle centerline.

Rear wheel alignment is not adjustable. If alignment angles are not within specification, inspect for bent or damaged suspension arms, components or underbody.

THRUST ANGLE

The vehicle is steered by the front wheels. The path the rear wheels follow is the thrust angle, **Fig. 5.** In an ideal setting, the thrust angle would be aligned with that of the vehicle centerline.

AURORA & RIVIERA

NOTE: Refer To The Rear Of This Manual For Manufacturer's Special Service Tool Supplies.

INDEX OF SERVICE OPERATIONS

Specifications

GENERAL ENGINE SPECIFICATIONS

Engine Liter/VIN Code①	Fuel System	Bore & Stroke	Compression Ratio	Net H.P. @ RPM②	Maximum Torque Ft. Lbs. @ RPM	Normal Oil Pressure, psi
1998						
3800/K	SFI	3.80 X 3.40	9.4	205 @ 5200	230 @ 4000	⑤
3800/1③	SFI	3.80 X 3.40	8.5	240 @ 5200	280 @ 3600	⑤
4.0L/C	SFI	3.43 X 3.31	10.3	250 @ 5600	260 @ 4000	④
1999						
3800/1③	SFI	3.80 X 3.40	8.5	240 @ 5200	280 @ 3600	⑤
4.0L/C	SFI	3.43 X 3.31	10.3	250 @ 5600	260 @ 4000	④
2001–02						
3.5L/H	SFI	3.52 X 3.62	9.3	215 @ 5600	230 @ 4400	⑥
4.0L/C	SFI	3.43 X 3.31	10.3	250 @ 5600	260 @ 4000	④

① — Eighth digit of VIN denotes engine code.
② — Ratings are net-as installed in vehicle.
③ — Supercharged.
④ — 5 psi @ idle speed, 35 psi @ 2000 RPM.
⑤ — 60 psi @ 1850 RPM, using 10W-30 engine oil, w/engine @ operating temperature.
⑥ — 35 psi @ 600 RPM, 80 psi @ 3600 RPM.

TUNE UP SPECIFICATIONS

Engine Liter/VIN Code①	Spark Plug Gap	Ignition Timing		Idle Speed	Fuel Pump Pressure, psi⑤	Valve Clearance, Inch
		Firing Order	Wire Connections Fig.			
1998						
3800/K	.060	②	A	③	48–55	⑦
3800/1	.060	②	A	③	48–55	⑦
4.0L/C	.050	④	B	⑥	⑧	⑦
1999						
3800/1	.060	②	A	③	48–55	⑦
4.0L/C	.050	④	B	⑥	⑧	⑦
2001–02						
3.5L/H	.050	⑨	—	⑥	48–55	⑦
4.0L/C	.050	④	B	⑥	⑧	⑦

① — Eighth digit of VIN denotes engine code.

② — Cylinder numbering from left to right as viewed front of vehicle, front bank 1, 3, 5; rear bank 2, 4, 6. Firing order, 1-6-5-4-3-2

③ — Idle speed is controlled by Idle Air Control Valve.

④ — Cylinder numbering from left to right as viewed from front of vehicle, front bank 2, 4, 6, 8; rear bank 1, 3, 5, 7. Firing order, 1-2-7-3-4-5-6-8.

⑤ — With shop towel wrapped around fuel pressure gauge & fuel pressure test port to prevent spillage, connect fuel pressure gauge to fuel pressure test port. Check fuel pressure w/ignition key in On position and engine not running.

⑥ — Idle speed is controlled by Idle Speed Control Actuator.

⑦ — Equipped w/hydraulic valve lifters; no adjustment required.

⑧ — 1998 models 41–47 psi; 1999 & 2001–02 models, 48–55 psi.

⑨ — Cylinder numbering from left to right as viewed front of vehicle, front bank 2, 4, 6; rear bank 1, 3, 5. Firing order, 1-2-3-4-5-6.

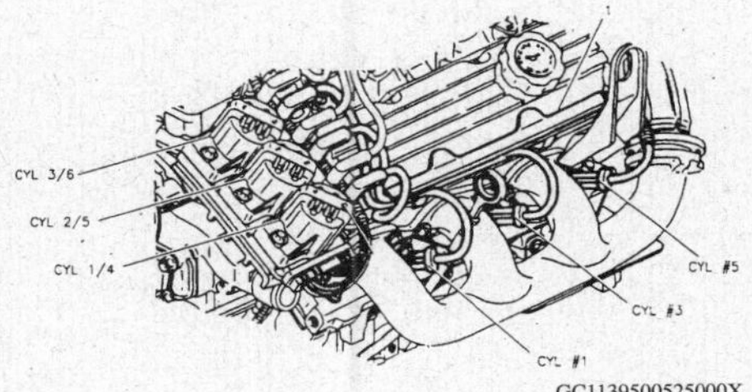

Fig. A

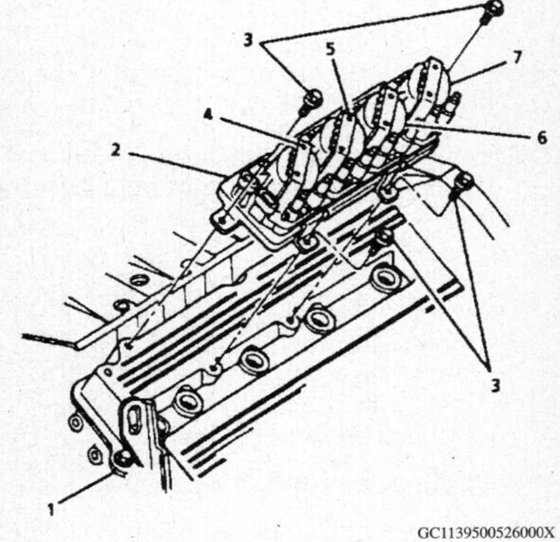

Fig. B

FRONT WHEEL ALIGNMENT SPECIFICATIONS

Year	Model	Caster Angle, Degrees		Camber Angle, Degrees		Total Toe, Degree	Steering Angle, Degrees	Ball Joint Wear
		Limits	Desired	Limits	Desired			
1998–99	All	+5.5 to +6.5	+6	-0.3 to +0.7	+0.2	-0.2 to +0.2	-3 to +3	①
2001	②	+5.5 to +6.5	+6	-0.7 to +0.3	-0.2	0 to +0.4	-3 to +3	①
	③	+4.5 to +5.5	+5	-0.7 to +0.3	-0.2	0 to +0.4	-3 to +3	①
2002	All	+4.5 to +5.5	+5	-0.7 to +0.3	-0.2	0 to +0.4	-3 to +3	①

① — Refer to "Ball Joint Inspection" in "Front Suspension & Steering" section.

② — VIN 14103349 or less.

③ — VIN 14103350 or greater.

REAR WHEEL ALIGNMENT SPECIFICATIONS

Year	Model	Camber Angle, Degrees		Total Toe, Degrees	Thrust Angle, Degrees
		Limits	Desired		
1998–99 & 2001–02	All	-.8 to +0.2	-0.3	0 to +0.4	-0.1 to +0.1

VEHICLE RIDE HEIGHT SPECIFICATIONS

Model	Year	Body Style	Manufacturer's Original Tire Size	Measurement Points & Specifications①③					
				Front			Rear		
				Dim.	Specification		Dim.	Specification	
					Inches	mm		Inches	mm
Riviera	1998–99	All	②	A	23.50	597	B	23.13	588
				C	6.43–7.25	163–184	D	8.37–9.18	213–233
Aurora	1998–99	All	②	A	23.62	600	B	23.25	590
				C	7.06	180	D	9.00	229
	2001–02	All	②	Z	1.20–2.00	30–50	D	3.00–3.80	76–96

Dim. — Dimension.
A Dim. — Measurement from front wheel center to check point on rocker panel.
B Dim. — Measurement from rear wheel center to check point on rocker panel.
C Dim. — Ground to rocker panel, front.
D Dim. — 1998–99, Ground to rocker panel, rear.
D Dim. — 2001–02, Rear suspension measurement from front outboard control arm bolt center line to bottom of control arm wheel bearing and hub face.
Z Dim. — Front suspension measurement from front pivot bolt center line to lower corner of lower ball joint.
① — ±0.0.39 inch (10 mm) front to rear & side to side.
② — See door sticker or inside of glove compartment for manufacturer's original tire size specifications.
③ — Measurement is with fuel, radiator coolant and engine oil full, spare tire, jack, hand tools and mats in designated positions and tires properly inflated.

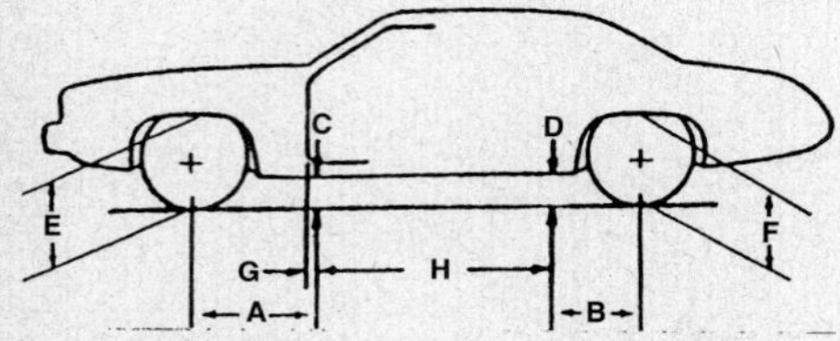

Riviera & 1998–99 Aurora

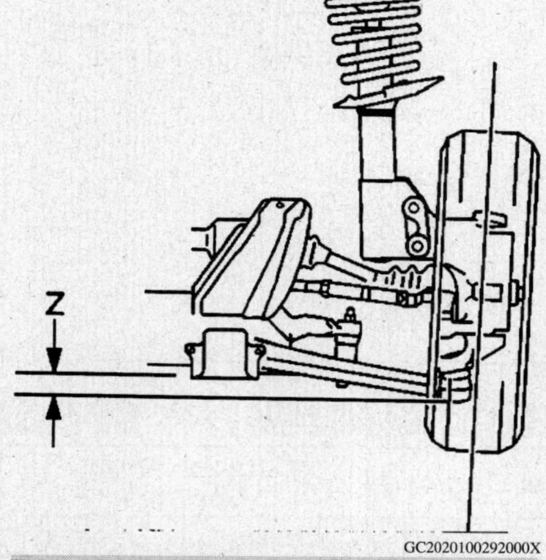

Front suspension. 2001–02 Aurora

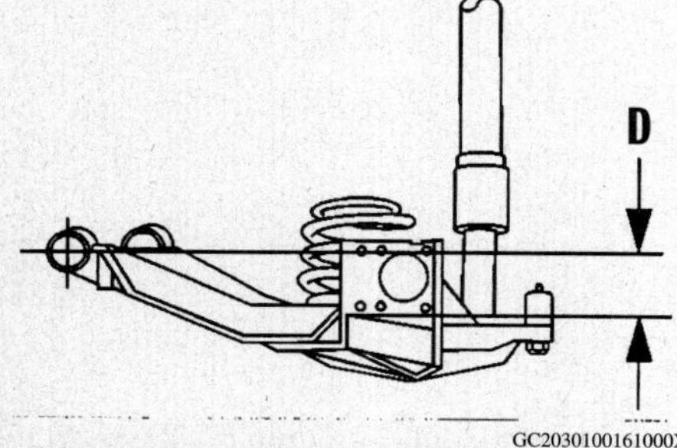

Rear suspension. 2001–02 Aurora

FLUID CAPACITIES & COOLING SYSTEM DATA

Model	Engine Liter/VIN Code①	Coolant Capacity, Qts.	Coolant Type	Radiator Cap Relief Pressure, Lbs.	Thermo Opening Temp.	Fuel Tank, Gallons	Engine Oil Refill, Qts. ④	Auto Transaxle, Qts.
1998–99								
Aurora	4.0L/C	13⑤	DEX-COOL②	15	185	19.4	7.5	③
Riviera	3800/K & 1	13	DEX-COOL②	16	195	19.4	4.5	⑥
2001–02								
Aurora	3.5L/H	10.0	DEX-COOL②	15	195	18.5	6.0	⑥
	4.0L/C	13.0	DEX-COOL②	15	185	17.5	7.0	③

① — Eighth digit of VIN denotes engine code.

② — DEX-COOL, or equivalent, silicant-free antifreeze conforming to GM specification No. 6277M.

③ — Drain & refill, 8 qts.; overhaul, 12.6 qts.; total dry, 15 qts.

④ — With filter change.

⑤ — Add three pellets of GM coolant supplement sealant part No. 3634621, or equivalent.

⑥ — Drain & refill, 7.4 qts.; overhaul, 10 qts.; total dry 13.4 qts.

LUBRICANT DATA

Year	Model	Lubricant Type			
		Automatic Transaxle	Power Steering System	Supercharger	Brake System
1998–99 & 2001–02	All	Dexron III	GM Part No. 1052884	Synthetic Oil GM Part No. 12345982	DOT 3

Electrical

NOTE: On Air Bag Equipped Models, Refer To "Air Bag System Precautions" Located In The Front Of This Manual For System Disarming & Arming Procedures.

NOTE: Refer To "Computer Relearn Procedures" Located In The Front Of This Manual When Battery Power To The Computer Has Been Interrupted.

NOTE: Prior To Performing Any Service Operations Listed In This Section, Consult The "Technical Service Bulletins" Section For Related Information.

INDEX

PRECAUTIONS

AIR BAG SYSTEMS

Refer to "Air Bag System Precautions" in the front of this manual for system disarming and arming procedures.

BATTERY GROUND CABLE

Prior to service, disconnect battery ground cable and isolate as required.

FUSE PANEL & FLASHER LOCATION

1998–99

The instrument panel fuse block is located behind the lefthand side of the instrument panel, behind the trim panel. The rear fuse block is located under the rear seat.

The hazard flasher is located behind the lefthand side of the instrument panel, right of the steering column support. The turn signal flasher is located behind the lefthand side of the instrument panel, attached to the lefthand sound insulator.

2001–02

The rear fuse block is located behind the righthand side of the rear seat. The underhood fuse block is located on the front righthand side of the engine compartment.

The turn signal/hazard lamp control module is located behind the lefthand side of the instrument panel, above the Data Link Connector (DLC).

FUEL PUMP RELAY LOCATION

1998–99

The fuel pump relay is in the passenger compartment relay center, located below the rear seat.

2001–02

The fuel pump relay is located behind the righthand side of the rear seat, in the rear fuse block.

RELAY CENTER LOCATION

1998–99

The passenger compartment relay center is located under the rear seat. The engine compartment relay center is located on the front righthand side of the engine compartment.

2001–02

Relays are located in the rear and underhood fuse blocks, refer to "Fuse Panel & Flasher Location."

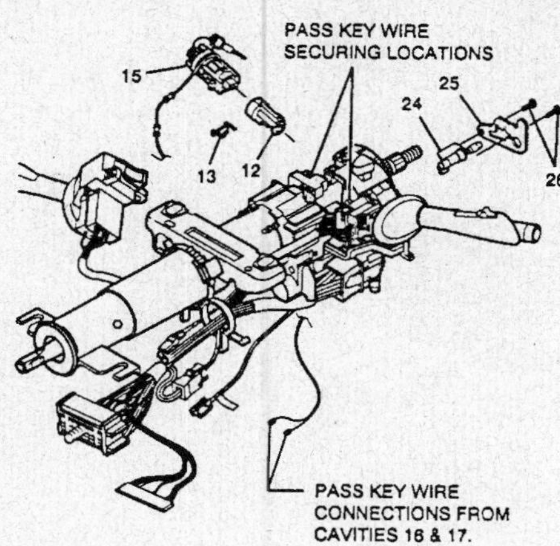

Fig. 1 Lock cylinder & lock bolt replacement. 1998–99

STARTER

REPLACE

3.5L ENGINE

1. Raise and support vehicle.
2. Remove lower air deflector.
3. Remove mounting bolts and torque converter cover.
4. Disconnect battery cable and starter solenoid S terminal wires.
5. Remove starter mounting bolts and starter.
6. Reverse procedure to install, noting the following:
   a. **Torque** starter motor mounting bolts to 37 ft. lbs.
   b. **Torque** nut on solenoid battery terminal to 89 inch lbs.
   c. **Torque** nut on solenoid S terminal to 22 inch lbs.

3800 ENGINE

1. Raise and support vehicle.
2. Remove splash shield
3. Remove mounting bolts and flywheel inspection cover.
4. Disconnect starter wiring.
5. Remove mounting bolts and starter.
6. Reverse procedure to install, noting the following:
   a. **Torque** starter to engine bolts to 32 ft. lbs.
   b. **Torque** nut on solenoid battery terminal to 12 ft. lbs.
   c. **Torque** nut on solenoid S terminal to 22 inch lbs.
   d. **Torque** flywheel inspection cover bolts to 22 inch lbs.

4.0L ENGINE

1. Remove intake manifold as outlined under "Intake Manifold, Replace" in "4.0L Engine" section.
2. Disconnect starter solenoid S and battery terminals electrical connectors.
3. Remove mounting bolts and starter.

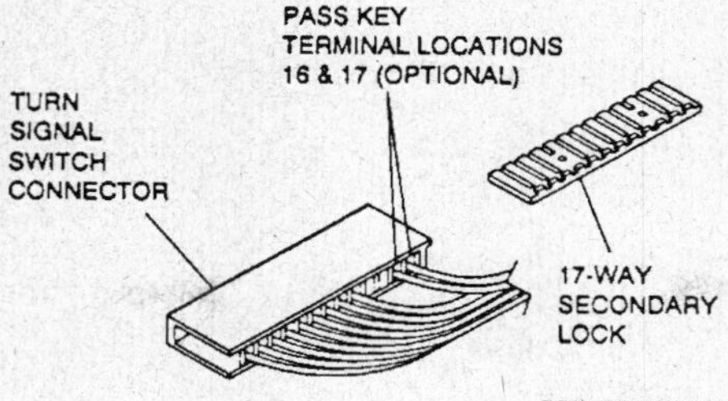

Fig. 2 Pass Key wire connector replacement. 1998–99

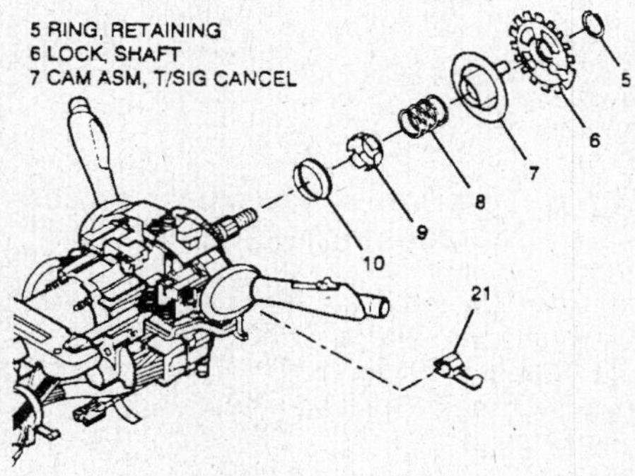

Fig. 4 Upper steering shaft components. 1998–99

4. Reverse procedure to install, noting the following:
   a. **Torque** inner nuts on solenoid terminals to 72 inch lbs.
   b. **Torque** S terminal nut to 26 inch lbs.
   c. **Torque** battery terminal nut to 72 inch lbs.
   d. **Torque** starter mounting bolts to 22 ft. lbs.

ALTERNATOR

REPLACE

3.5L ENGINE

1. Remove accessory drive belt.
2. Remove headlamp/fascia panel support brackets.
3. Remove radiator support brackets and air cleaner.
4. Position PCM aside.
5. Remove upper tie bar mounting bolts and upper tie bar.
6. Disconnect cooling fan motor electrical connectors.
7. Remove clips attaching wiring harness to fan shroud.
8. Raise and support vehicle, then remove lower air deflector.
9. Remove transaxle oil cooler line mounting bolt and clip from fan shroud.
10. Lower vehicle and slide plastic cap off of upper quick connect joint, then disconnect upper transaxle oil cooler line from radiator.
11. Remove shroud mounting bolts and cooling fan.

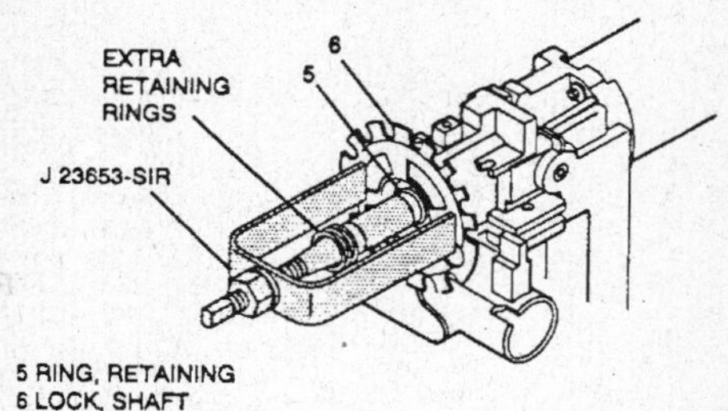

Fig. 3 Shaft lock retaining ring replacement. 1998–99

12. Disconnect alternator electrical connectors.
13. Remove mounting bolt and drive belt idler pulley.
14. Remove alternator upper mounting bolts, then position alternator to access two upper air conditioning compressor mounting bolts.
15. Raise and support vehicle.
16. Remove air conditioning compressor upper mounting bolts and loosen rear compressor mounting nut.
17. Remove front air conditioning compressor mounting nut.
18. Position air conditioning compressor away from engine block.
19. Lower vehicle and remove alternator.
20. Reverse procedure to install, noting the following:
    a. **Torque** air conditioning compressor mounting bolts and front nut to 37 ft. lbs., then the rear nut to 18 ft. lbs.
    b. **Torque** idler pulley bolt to 37 ft. lbs.
    c. **Torque** alternator mounting bolts to 37 ft. lbs.
    d. **Torque** alternator battery output terminal nut to 111 inch lbs.

3800 ENGINE

1. Install engine support fixture tool No. J-28467-360, or equivalent.
2. Remove two bottom engine mount mounting bolts.
3. Remove through bolt and engine mount from bracket.
4. Remove accessory drive belt.
5. **On supercharged engines,** proceed as follows:
   a. Remove ignition module and position aside.
   b. Remove supercharger drive belt.
   c. Remove drive belt tensioner.
6. **On all models,** remove power steering pump and position aside. **Do not disconnect power steering pressure hoses,**
7. Remove mounting nuts and engine mount bracket .
8. Mount holding tool No. J-37096, or equivalent, on flywheel.
9. Remove crankshaft balancer mounting bolt.
10. Remove crankshaft balancer using puller tool No. J-38197, or equivalent.
11. Remove crankshaft sensor shield.
12. Remove mounting bolt and crankshaft sensor.
13. Remove mounting bolts and front cover.

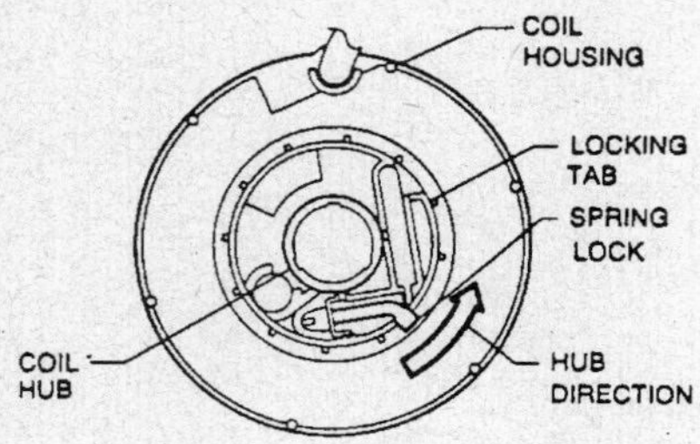

PERFORM THE FOLLOWING STEPS TO CENTER COIL ASSEMBLY

A. WHEELS STRAIGHT AHEAD.
B. REMOVE COIL ASSEMBLY.
C. HOLD COIL ASSEMBLY WITH BOTTOM UP.
D. WHILE HOLDING COIL ASSEMBLY, DEPRESS SPRING LOCK TO ROTATE HUB IN DIRECTION OF ARROW UNTIL IT STOPS.
E. THE COIL RIBBON SHOULD BE WOUND UP SNUG AGAINST CENTER HUB.
F. ROTATE COIL HUB IN OPPOSITE DIRECTION APPROXIMATELY TWO AND A HALF (2-1/2) TURNS. RELEASE SPRING LOCK BETWEEN LOCKING TABS.

GC8019501343000X

Fig. 5 SIR coil installation

14. Remove mounting bolts and alternator rear brace.
15. Remove alternator mounting bolts.
16. Disconnect electrical connector and alternator.
17. Reverse procedure to install, noting the following:
    a. **Torque** alternator mounting bolts to 37 ft. lbs.
    b. **Torque** alternator rear brace bolt to 22 ft. lbs.
    c. **Torque** crankshaft balancer bolt to 111 ft. lbs.
    d. **On supercharged engines, torque** drive belt tensioner bolt to 37 ft. lbs.
    e. **On all models, torque** engine mounting bolts to 52 ft. lbs.

4.0L ENGINE

1. Release accessory drive belt tensioner.
2. Remove power steering pump and alternator drive belt.
3. Raise and support vehicle.
4. Drain cooling system into suitable container and lower vehicle.
5. Remove radiator as outlined under "Radiator, Replace" in "4.0L Engine" section.
6. Disconnect alternator electrical connectors.
7. Loosen lower and remove upper alternator mounting bolts.
8. Remove lower bolt and alternator.
9. Reverse procedure to install. **Torque** alternator mounting bolts to 37 ft. lbs.

COIL PACK

REPLACE

3.5L ENGINE

Left

1. Remove two fuel injector sight shield front mounting nuts.
2. Lift front of sight shield up and slide from engine bracket.
3. Remove oil level indicator tube, then the PCV valve and feed tube from left-hand camshaft cover.
4. Remove ignition coil.
5. Reverse procedure to install.

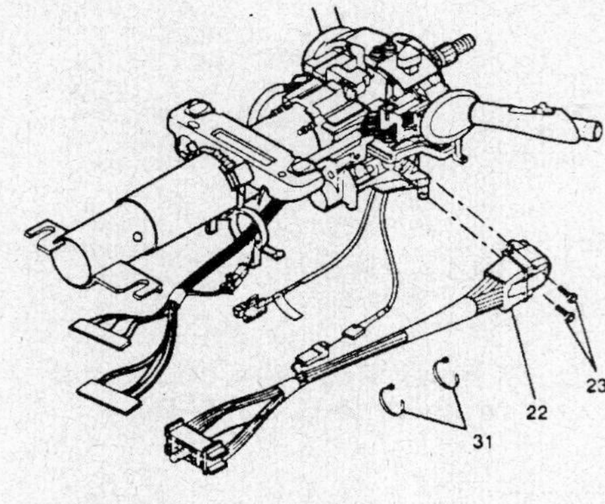

22 SWITCH ASM, IGN & KEY ALARM
23 SCREW, TAPPING
31 STRAP, WIRE

GC6049500156000X

Fig. 6 Ignition & key alarm switch replacement. 1998–99

Right

1. Remove automatic transaxle filler tube.
2. Remove fuel injector sight shield front mounting nuts.
3. Lift front of sight shield up and slide from engine bracket.
4. Remove mounting bolts and fuel injector sight shield bracket .
5. Disconnect PCV feed tube and engine wiring harness clips from front of camshaft cover. Position wiring harness aside.
6. Disconnect oxygen sensor electrical connector and remove connector end from camshaft cover.
7. Remove ignition coil.
8. Reverse procedure to install.

3800 ENGINE

1. Disconnect coil pack (ignition control module) 14-way electrical connector.
2. Mark and disconnect spark plug wires at coils.
3. Remove ignition coil to ignition control module mounting screws.
4. Remove coil.
5. Remove ignition control module mounting screws.
6. Reverse procedure to install.

4.0L ENGINE

1. Disconnect ignition control module four electrical connectors.
2. Mark and disconnect spark plug wires at coils.
3. Remove mounting bolts and ignition coils.
4. Reverse procedure to install. **Torque** mounting bolts to 106 inch lbs.

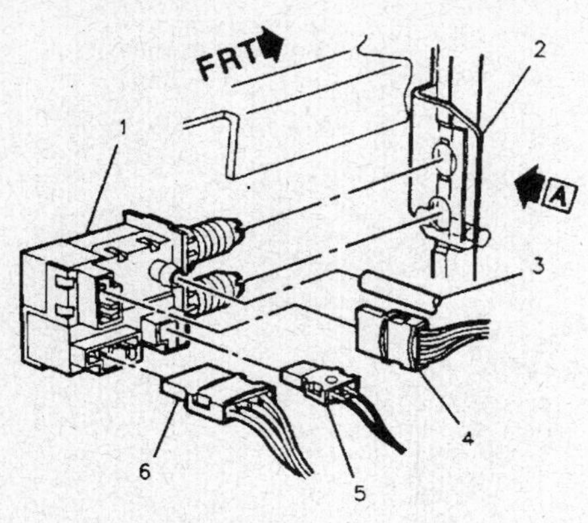

VIEW A CHECKING ADJUSTMENT

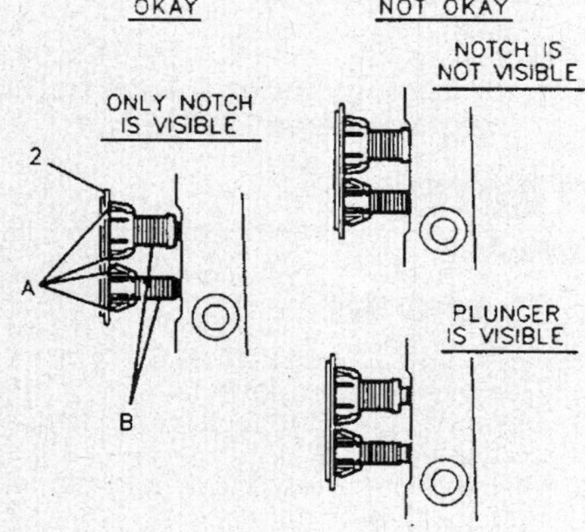

A RETAINING TABS
B SWITCH BARRELS
1 SWITCH
2 MOUNTING BRACKET
3 CRUISE VACUUM LINE
4 CONNECTOR, TCC/ABS (BLACK)
5 CONNECTOR, STOPLAMP SW (GRAY)
6 CONNECTOR, SHIFT-INTERLOCK/CRUISE (BLUE)

GC9049500138000X

Fig. 7 Stop lamp switch replacement & adjustment. 1998–99

IGNITION LOCK

REPLACE

1998-99

Removal

1. Tilt column to center position.
2. Remove mounting screws and upper steering column cover.
3. Remove pivot and pulse switch as outlined under "Pivot & Pulse Switch, Replace," allow switch to hang freely from column.
4. Turn lock cylinder to Run position.

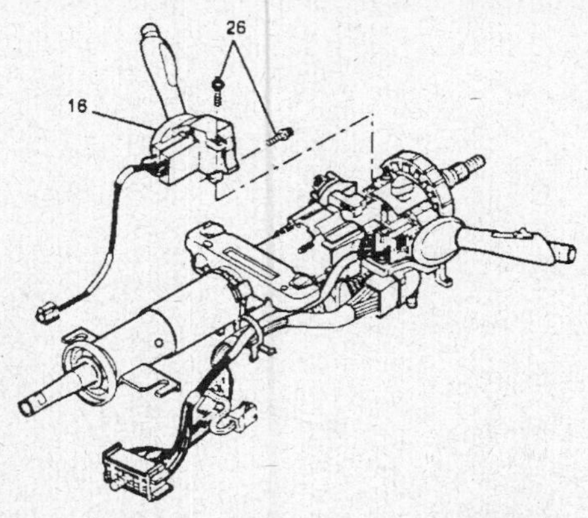

Fig. 8 Pivot & pulse switch replacement. 1998–99

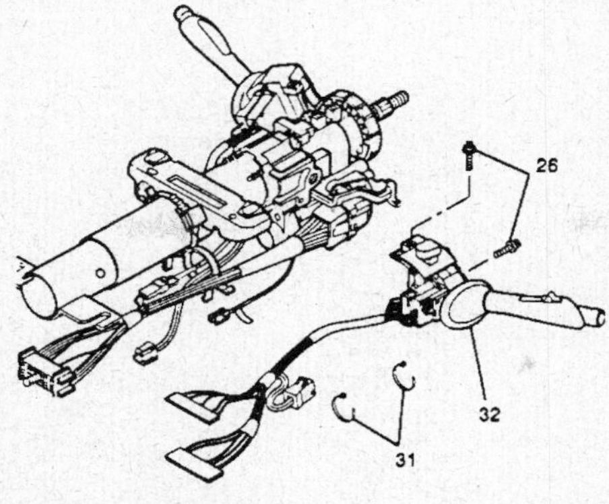

Fig. 9 Turn signal & multi-function switch replacement. 1998

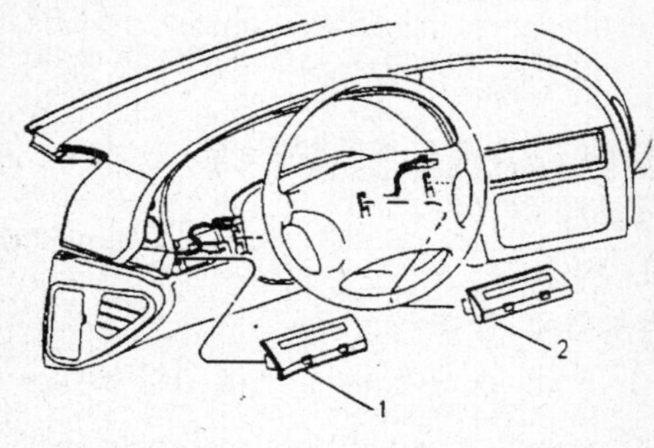

Fig. 10 Instrument panel trim plate replacement. 1998–99 Aurora

5. Push against locking button located on back side of bearing and housing assembly, then remove lock cylinder.
6. Remove lock preload spring, **Fig. 1.**
7. Disconnect vehicle wire harness bulkhead connector.
8. Disconnect bulkhead connector gray turn signal switch connector, **Fig. 2.**
9. Remove turn signal switch connector 17-way secondary lock.
10. Disconnect two Pass Key terminals from gray turn signal switch connector cavities 16 and 17.
11. Disconnect Pass Key wire harness from wire harness strap, multi-function switch and upper head housing.
12. Remove ignition lock actuator from upper head housing using suitable needle nose pliers.
13. Remove mounting screw and tilt lever knob.
14. Pry tabs and remove close out knob.
15. Remove mounting screws and steering column lower cover.
16. Remove steering wheel as outlined under "Steering Wheel, Replace."
17. Remove retaining ring and SIR coil. Allow coil assembly to hang freely from steering column.
18. Push down shaft lock, remove shaft lock retaining ring using lock plate compressor tool No. J-23653-SIR, or equivalent, **Fig. 3.**
19. Remove shaft lock from steering column.
20. Remove turn signal cancel cam, upper bearing spring, upper bearing inner race seat, inner race and tilt lever bracket, **Fig. 4.**
21. Remove mounting bolts and lock bolt support bracket.
22. Remove housing lock bolt.

Installation

1. Install lock bolt and support bracket into housing. **Torque** support bracket mounting screws to 46 inch lbs.
2. Ensure end of lock bolt is flush with support bracket, **Fig. 1,** and install ignition lock actuator into housing,
3. Rotate actuator counterclockwise until it pushes out lock bolt and actuator seats into housing.
4. Rotate actuator clockwise to Run position.
5. Align inner block tooth of lock plate to block tooth of upper shaft.
6. Install tilt lever bracket, inner race, upper bearing inner race seat, upper bearing spring and turn signal cam.
7. Lubricate shaft lock with suitable synthetic grease and install shaft lock into housing.
8. Push down shaft lock and install shaft lock retaining ring using lock plate compressor tool No. J-23653-SIR, or equivalent, **Fig. 3. Ensure ring is seated firmly in shaft groove.**
9. Insert key into lock cylinder and with lock cylinder in Run position, align locking tab with slot in housing and push into position.
10. Insert Pass Key wire harness into column and route wire harness through wiring protector.
11. Secure wiring harness to housing and multi-function switch, then route through wiring harness strap.
12. Connect terminals of wiring harness to cavities 16 and 17 in gray turn signal switch connector.
13. Install 17-way secondary lock onto turn signal switch connector.
14. Connect gray turn signal switch connector to bulkhead connector.
15. Connect bulkhead connector to vehicle wiring harness.
16. Install pivot and pulse switch as outlined under "Pivot & Pulse Switch, Replace."
17. Install upper steering column cover, **torque** cover mounting screws to 46 inch lbs.
18. Install multi-function switch as outlined under "Multi-Function Switch, Replace."
19. Install and center SIR coil, **Fig. 5.**
20. Install steering wheel as outlined under "Steering Wheel, Replace."

2001–02

1. Apply parking brake and remove radio as outlined under "Radio, Replace."
2. Insert ignition key and turn ignition switch to RUN position.
3. Locate ignition lock cylinder release button through radio opening in instrument panel.
4. Depress and hold ignition lock cylinder retaining tab (righthand lower side of ignition switch) using suitable flat-bladed screwdriver.
5. Pull lock cylinder from of instrument panel.
6. Remove lock cylinder reader/exciter ring.
7. Reverse procedure to install.

IGNITION SWITCH

REPLACE

1998–99

1. Tilt column to center position.
2. Remove mounting screws and upper steering column cover.
3. Remove mounting screw and tilt lever knob.
4. Pry locking tabs and remove close out knob.
5. Remove mounting screws and lower steering column cover.
6. Remove two steering column wiring harness wire, **Fig. 6.**
7. Disconnect steering column bulkhead connector from vehicle wiring harness.
8. Disconnect ignition key and alarm switch from wire harness strap.
9. Disconnect turn signal and multi-function switch gray and black connectors from column bulkhead connector.
10. Remove mounting screws, ignition and key alarm switch from column.
11. Reverse procedure to install.

2001–02

1. Remove ignition lock cylinder as outlined under "Ignition Lock, Replace."
2. Remove ignition switch mounting screws.
3. Push and release retaining tab at rear of ignition switch.
4. Disconnect ignition switch electrical connectors, then remove bulb from side of switch.
5. Remove ignition switch through radio opening.

6. Reverse procedure to install. **Torque** ignition switch mounting screws to 80 inch lbs.

NEUTRAL SAFETY SWITCH

REPLACE

1998–99

1. Set parking brake and set gear selector to N position.
2. Remove linkage cable bracket to transaxle shaft mounting nut.
3. Remove linkage cable bracket from transaxle shaft.
4. Remove park/neutral position switch mounting bolts.
5. Disconnect park/neutral position switch electrical connector.
6. Remove terminal nut on starter solenoid and disconnect starter cable.
7. Remove park/neutral position switch.
8. Reverse procedure to install.

2001–02

On these models, the transaxle range function is controlled by an internal transaxle mode switch. Refer to **Motor's "Domestic Transmission Manual"** for automatic transmission mode switch replacement.

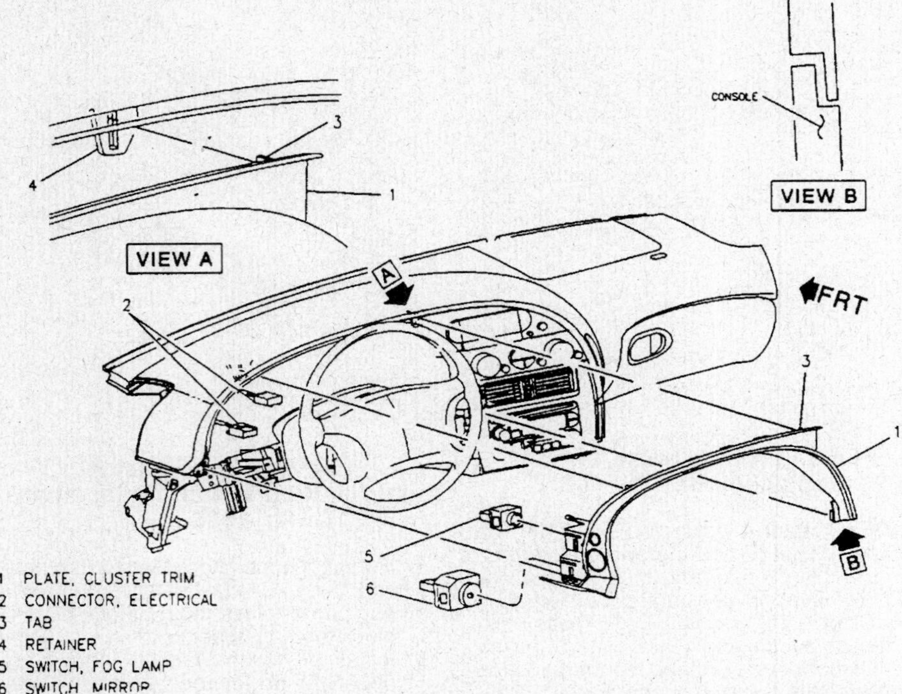

Fig. 11 Instrument cluster trim plate replacement. 1998–99 Aurora

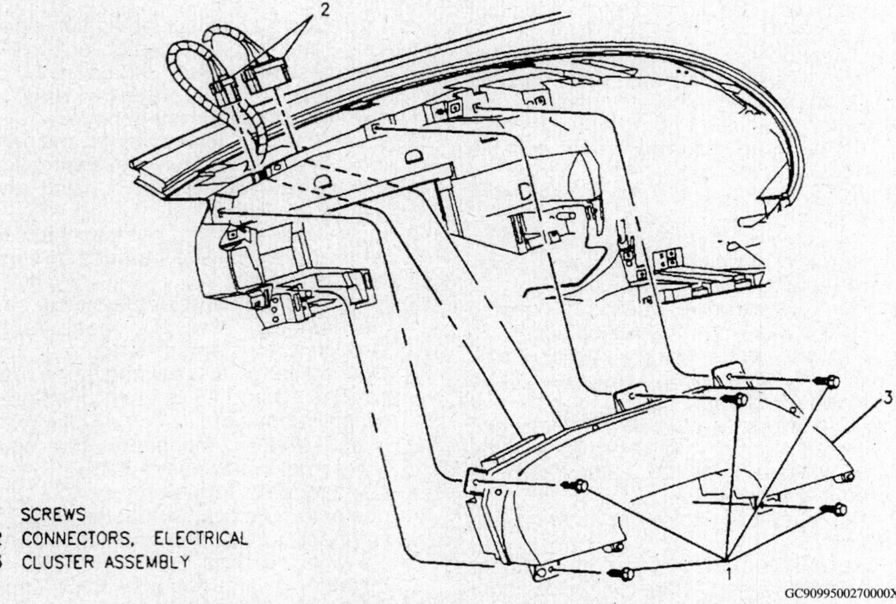

Fig. 12 Instrument cluster replacement. 1998–99 Aurora

STOP LIGHT SWITCH

REPLACE

1998–99

1. Remove lefthand instrument panel sound insulator.
2. Disconnect switch electrical connectors, **Fig. 7.**
3. Disconnect vacuum hose from switch.
4. Remove switch from brake pedal support.
5. Reverse procedure to install, adjust switch as follows:
   a. After installing switch, press brake pedal rearward until no audible clicks remain and release pedal.
   b. Press brake pedal again to ensure no clicks are heard.
   c. Compare switch adjustment, **Fig. 7.**
   d. Only notch should be visible. If plunger is visible or notch is not, repeat adjustment.

2001–02

1. Remove closeout panel from under lefthand side of instrument panel.
2. Turn switch counterclockwise and remove from brake pedal support.
3. Disconnect brake switch electrical connector and remove.
4. Reverse procedure to install.

PIVOT & PULSE SWITCH

REPLACE

1998–99

1. Tilt column to center position.
2. Remove mounting screws and upper steering column cover.
3. Remove two steering column wire harness straps.
4. Disconnect pivot and pulse switch connector from turn signal and multi-function switch wire harness connector.
5. Disconnect pivot and pulse switch harness from wire harness strap.
6. Remove mounting screws, then pivot and pulse switch from column, **Fig. 8.**
7. Reverse procedure to install.

MULTI-FUNCTION SWITCH

REPLACE

1998

1. Tilt column to center position.
2. Remove mounting screws and upper steering column cover.
3. Remove two steering column wire harness wire straps.
4. Disconnect steering column bulkhead

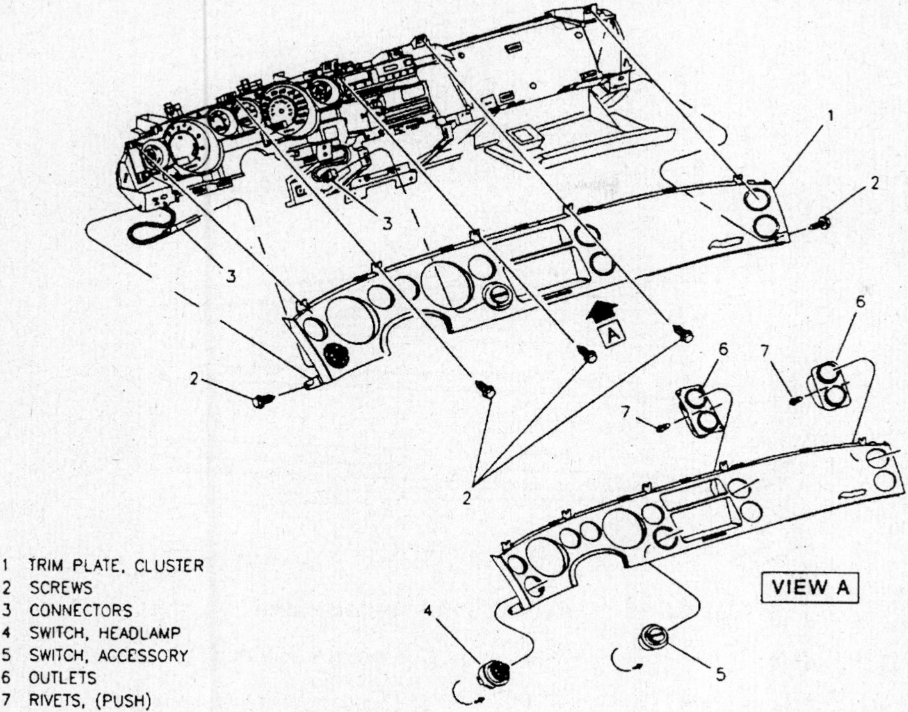

Fig. 13 Instrument panel cluster trim plate replacement. Riviera

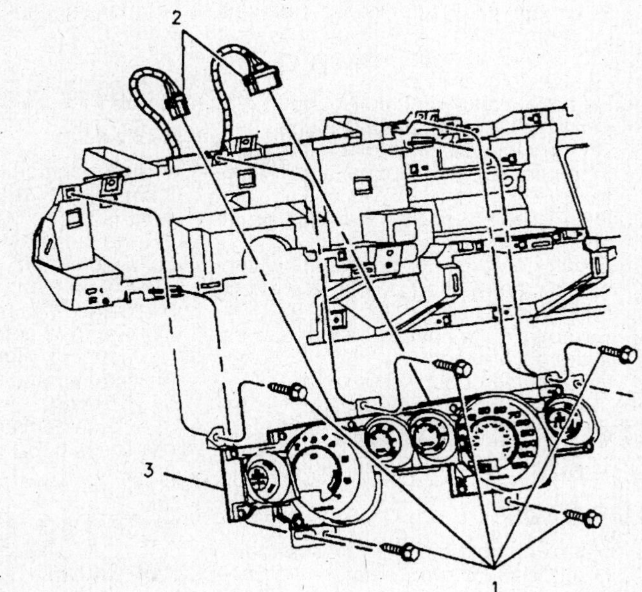

Fig. 14 Instrument cluster replacement. Riviera

connector from vehicle wiring harness.

5. Disconnect turn signal and multi-function switch wiring harness from wiring harness strap.
6. Disconnect pivot and pulse switch connector from multi-function switch wire harness connector.
7. Disconnect gray and black multi-function switch connectors from column bulkhead connector.
8. Remove turn signal switch connector 17-way secondary lock.
9. Disconnect two Pass Key terminals from gray turn signal switch connector cavities 16 and 17.
10. Remove mounting screws and multi-function switch from column, **Fig. 9.**
11. Reverse procedure to install.

1999 & 2001-02

1. Remove steering wheel as outlined under "Steering Wheel Replace."
2. Remove tilt lever by pulling straight out.
3. Remove mounting screws and lower column shroud.
4. Remove mounting screws and upper column shroud.
5. Remove instrument panel trim panel.
6. Remove multi-function switch torx bolts and disconnect switch electrical connector.
7. Remove multi-function switch.
8. Reverse procedure to install.

STEERING WHEEL

REPLACE

1. Remove air bag as outlined in "Passive Restraints Systems" chapter.
2. Remove steering wheel mounting nut, place match marks on shaft and steering wheel.
3. Align mark on steering shaft with steering wheel.
4. Remove steering wheel using pulling tools Nos. J-1859-03 and J-38720, or equivalents.
5. Reverse procedure to install. **Torque** steering wheel mounting nut to 30 ft. lbs.

INSTRUMENT CLUSTER

REPLACE

AURORA

1998-99

1. Remove knee bolster from under steering column.
2. Remove upper steering column bracket nuts and lower steering column.
3. Remove trunk/fuel door release and interior lamp trim plates by pulling rearward, then disconnecting electrical connectors, **Fig. 10.**
4. Remove center air conditioning outlet trim panel.
5. Pull instrument panel cluster trim plate rearward, **Fig. 11.**
6. Remove instrument cluster mounting screws.
7. Pull cluster rearward and disconnect two electrical connectors.
8. Remove cluster, **Fig. 12.**
9. Reverse procedure to install

2001-02

1. Lower tilt steering column to lowest position.
2. Remove ignition lock cylinder bezel.
3. Remove lefthand instrument panel endcap.
4. Remove instrument panel center trim plate.
5. Remove righthand instrument panel endcap.
6. Open glove compartment door and remove righthand accessory trim plate to instrument panel mounting screws.
7. Remove instrument panel righthand accessory trim plate.
8. Remove mounting screws and instrument cluster upper trim cover.
9. Remove lefthand instrument panel air deflector.
10. Remove instrument cluster trim plate mounting screws.
11. Disconnect trim plate electrical connectors and remove instrument panel trim plate.

12. Remove instrument cluster mounting screws.
13. Disconnect cluster electrical connectors and remove cluster.
14. Reverse procedure to install.

RIVIERA

1. Remove cluster trim plate switches and air deflectors, **Fig. 13.**
2. Remove mounting screws and cluster trim plate.
3. Remove instrument cluster mounting screws.
4. Disconnect cluster electrical connectors, **Fig. 14.**
5. Remove instrument cluster.
6. Reverse procedure to install.

RADIO

REPLACE

AURORA

1. Remove instrument panel center trim plate by pulling rearward to disengage retainers.
2. **On 1998–99 models,** remove two radio mounting screws.
3. **On 2001–02 models,** depress spring clip retainers on sides of radio.
4. **On all models,** pull radio outward and disconnect antenna lead and electrical connectors.
5. Remove radio.
6. Reverse procedure to install.

RIVIERA

1. Remove instrument cluster trim plate as outlined under "Instrument Cluster, Replace."
2. Remove two radio mounting screws.
3. Pull radio outward and disconnect antenna lead and electrical connectors.
4. Remove radio.
5. Reverse procedure to install.

WIPER MOTOR

REPLACE

1998–99

1. Turn ignition switch to Accessory position and set wiper switch to Pulse position.
2. Turn ignition switch off when wiper arms are at bottom and not moving.
3. Lift wiper blade up.
4. Pull out retaining latch using suitable screwdriver.
5. Pull wiper arm off transmission driveshaft.
6. Disconnect washer hose.
7. Remove five air inlet panel retainers.
8. Push washer hose into firewall.
9. Remove air inlet panel.
10. Remove wiper motor crank arm transmission drive link socket using wiper transmission separator tool No. J-39232, or equivalent.
11. Pull two harness connector retainers out of wiper motor connector.
12. Disconnect two wiper motor harness connectors.
13. Remove bolts, stud and wiper motor.
14. Reverse procedure to install.

2001–02

1. Ensure wiper arms are in PARK position.
2. Remove mounting nuts and wiper arms.
3. Push air inlet grill panel retainers though grill panel.
4. Disconnect washer hose and remove air inlet grill panel.
5. Remove mounting bolts, nuts and windshield frame reinforcement.
6. Rotate wiper transmission linkage until motor crank arm is opposite PARK position.
7. Remove plenum hole harness grommet.
8. Disconnect wiper motor electrical connector, then push harness and grommet through hole.
9. Remove mounting screws and wiper system drive module .
10. Reverse procedure to install.

BLOWER MOTOR

REPLACE

1998–99

1. Remove righthand sound insulator.
2. Disconnect blower motor electrical connector.
3. Disconnect blower motor cooling tube.
4. Remove blower motor to heater and air conditioning control module mounting screws.
5. Remove blower motor and fan.
6. Reverse procedure to install.

2001–02

1. Remove righthand instrument panel sound insulator panel.
2. Remove glove compartment door to glove compartment mounting screws.
3. Remove mounting screws and glove compartment.
4. Remove Dash Integration Module (DIM) from bracket.
5. Remove mounting screws and DIM bracket .
6. Disconnect blower motor electrical connector.
7. Remove mounting screws and blower motor.
8. Reverse procedure to install.

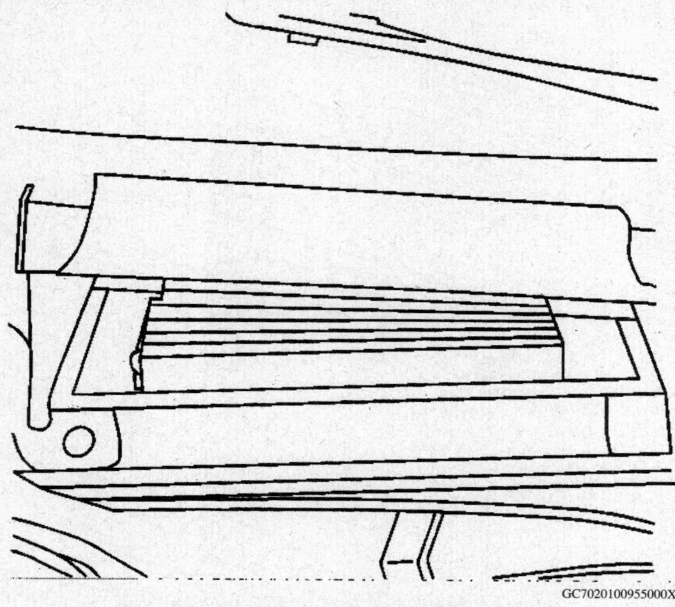

Fig. 15 Cabin air filter replacement

CABIN AIR FILTER

REPLACE

Under normal operating conditions the cabin air filter should be replaced every 12 months or 15,000 miles. In dusty areas change the cabin air filter more often.

1. Open hood.
2. Lift up cabin air filter access cover located on air inlet panel.
3. Remove cabin air filter element from housing, **Fig. 15.**
4. Install new cabin air filter into filter housing.
5. Close cabin air filter access cover.
6. Close hood.

HEATER CORE

REPLACE

1998–99

1. Drain cooling system.
2. Disconnect heater core hoses.
3. Remove left and righthand sound insulators.
4. Remove heater core cover from heater and air conditioning module.
5. Remove heater core retaining straps and heater core.
6. Reverse procedure to install, noting the following:
   a. To aid installation sound insulator seal may be cut in half.
   b. Each half should be placed into respective sides of heater and air conditioning module.

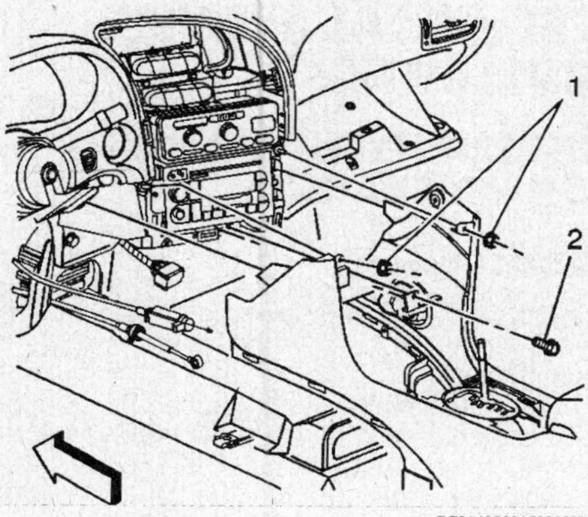

Fig. 16 Center console replacement (Part 1 of 2). 2001–02 Aurora

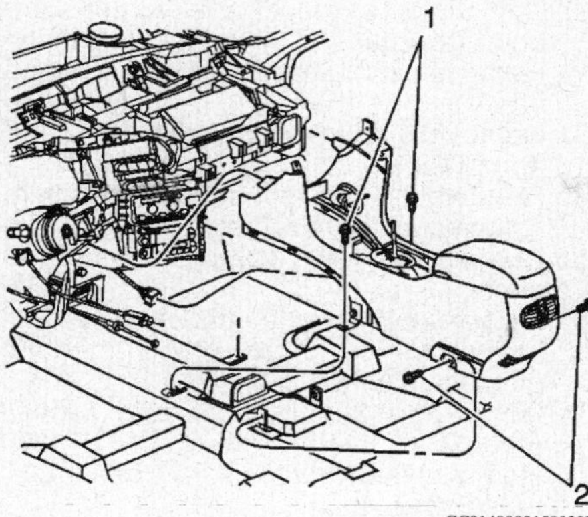

Fig. 16 Center console replacement (Part 2 of 2). 2001–02 Aurora

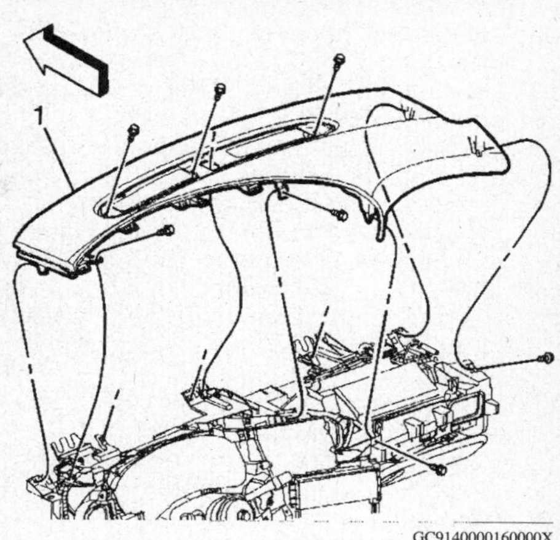

Fig. 17 Upper trim pad replacement. 2001–02 Aurora

2001–02

1. Recover air conditioning refrigerant as outlined in "Air Conditioning" chapter
2. Drain cooling system.
3. Remove heater core hoses.
4. Remove instrument panel left and righthand sound insulators.
5. Remove tray insert, then the center console left and righthand trim plates.
6. Disconnect shifter and park lock cables.
7. Disconnect console main wiring harness connector.
8. Open glove compartment door and remove instrument panel to console mounting screw.
9. Remove console to instrument panel and console to floor mounting screws.
10. Slide console rearward and remove it.
11. Remove auxiliary air distribution duct adapter.
12. Remove mounting screws and air distributor duct.
13. Remove mounting screws and heater core heat shield.
14. Remove mounting screws and heater core cover.
15. Remove mounting screw, strap and heater core.
16. Reverse procedure to install.

EVAPORATOR CORE

REPLACE

1998–99

1. Remove center console storage compartment bin.
2. Remove retainer and shifter handle.
3. Disconnect shift handle electrical connector and remove handle.
4. **On Aurora models,** remove shifter trim plate as follows:
   a. Pull shifter trim plate up to disengage retaining tabs.
   b. Disconnect trim plate electrical connectors and remove center console shifter trim plate.
5. **On Riviera models,** remove shifter trim plate as follows:
   a. Remove upper console trim plate by pulling outward.
   b. Remove shifter trim plate mounting screws.
   c. Pull shifter trim plate upward and disconnect electrical connectors.
   d. Remove center console trim plate.
6. **On all models,** remove center console mounting nuts and bolts.
7. Disconnect console electrical connectors and remove console.
8. Remove cluster trim plate as outlined under "Instrument Cluster, Replace."
9. **On Aurora models,** remove mounting screws and upper trim pad mounting screws.
10. **On Riviera models,** remove instrument panel upper trim pad as follows:
    a. Pry windshield defroster grill upward.
    b. Disconnect sunload temperature and twilight sentinel sensors from defroster grill.
    c. Remove defroster grill.
    d. Remove upper trim pad to instrument panel mounting screws.
    e. Remove instrument panel upper trim pad.
11. **On all models,** remove A pillar trim pads.
12. Remove left and righthand sound insulators.
13. **On Aurora models,** remove mounting screws and knee bolster.
14. **On Riviera models,** remove knee bolster mounting screws. Disconnect electrical connectors, traction control switch and air temperature sensor and remove knee bolster.
15. **On all models,** remove glove compartment.
16. Remove radio as outlined under "Radio, Replace."
17. Remove HVAC control head mounting screws.
18. Disconnect connector and remove HVAC control head.
19. Remove instrument panel to dash panel mounting screws.
20. Pull instrument panel carrier away from dash, then disconnect electrical connectors and antenna cable.
21. Remove instrument panel.
22. Recover refrigerant as outlined under "Air Conditioning" chapter.
23. Remove engine compartment vacuum tank.
24. Remove multi-use bracket to gain access to air conditioning lines.
25. Remove evaporator air conditioning lines and drain cooling system into suitable container.
26. Disconnect heater core hoses.
27. Remove PCM/Programmer bracket.
28. Remove mounting screws and passenger air bag module.
29. Remove defroster duct and disconnect electrical connector near blower housing.
30. Remove connector duct from case and floor.
31. Remove side window ducts.
32. Remove righthand center instrument panel mounting bracket.
33. Remove heater and air conditioning module mounting nuts.
34. Remove heater and air conditioning module.
35. Remove heater and air conditioning module evaporator access panel.
36. Remove mounting straps and evaporator from heater and air conditioning module.
37. Reverse procedure to install.

2001–02

1. Recover air conditioning refrigerant as outlined in "Air Conditioning" chapter.
2. Remove evaporator hose nut and disconnect evaporator hose
3. Drain cooling system into suitable container and remove heater core hoses . Plug heater core and evaporator openings.
4. Remove left and righthand lower dash panel sound insulators.
5. Remove center instrument panel trim plate.
6. Remove center console trim plate screw and pull up on rear of console trim plate to disengage clips.
7. Disconnect center console trim plate electrical connectors and remove trim plate.
8. Remove console compartment.
9. Remove left and righthand console side trim panels.
10. Disconnect shift cable and park lock cable.

11. Disconnect console main wiring harness connector.
12. Open glove compartment and remove mounting screw.
13. Remove remaining mounting screws and console, **Fig. 16.**
14. Remove instrument panel endcaps.
15. Remove left and righthand windshield garnish moldings, then the defroster grille.
16. Remove righthand instrument panel trim panel and instrument cluster trim plate.
17. Remove carrier bolts and instrument panel upper trim pad, **Fig. 17.**
18. Remove steering column as outlined in "Steering Columns" chapter.
19. Remove steering column support.
20. Disconnect instrument panel electrical harnesses.
21. Remove instrument panel center support brackets.
22. Remove brackets and instrument panel.
23. Remove instrument panel lower support bracket.
24. Remove defroster duct mounting screws, nut and defroster duct.
25. Remove screws and air distributor duct.
26. Disconnect blower control module and instrument panel to HVAC module electrical connectors.
27. Remove mounting nuts and HVAC module.
28. Remove heater core and evaporator tubes' seal.
29. Remove upper HVAC evaporator case and evaporator core.
30. Reverse procedure to install.

TECHNICAL SERVICE BULLETINS

INTERMITTENT NO START OR NO CRANK

2001 Aurora

On some of these models there may be an intermittent no start or no crank condition.

This condition may be caused by plastic particles interfering with the ignition switch electrical contacts.

To correct this condition, install improved ignition switch (part No. 25721650).

3.5L Engine

NOTE: On Air Bag Equipped Models, Refer To "Air Bag System Precautions" Located In The Front Of This Manual For System Disarming & Arming Procedures.

NOTE: Refer To "Computer Relearn Procedures" Located In The Front Of This Manual When Battery Power To The Computer Has Been Interrupted.

NOTE: Refer To "3.5L Engine" Section In The "Century, Grand Prix, Impala, Intrigue, Lumina, Monte Carlo & Regal" Chapter For Procedures Not Covered In This Section.

NOTE: Prior To Performing Any Service Operations Listed In This Section, Consult The "Technical Service Bulletins" Section For Related Information.

INDEX

PRECAUTIONS

AIR BAG SYSTEMS

Refer to "Air Bag System Precautions" in the front of this manual for system disarming and arming procedures.

BATTERY GROUND CABLE

Prior to service, disconnect battery ground cable and isolate as required.

FUEL PRESSURE RELIEF

1. Turn ignition off and remove fuel pump relay.
2. Loosen fuel filler cap.
3. Remove mounting nuts and intake manifold top cover.
4. Connect suitable fuel pressure gauge and wrap connection with suitable shop towel to prevent fuel leakage.
5. Install suitable bleed hose into suitable container and open pressure valve to bleed system pressure.

COMPRESSION PRESSURE

ENGINE MOUNT

REPLACE

1. Support engine using engine support fixture tool No. J-28467, or equivalent.
2. Remove mounting bolts and front engine mount support bracket.
3. Raise and support vehicle.
4. Remove engine mount to frame mounting nut.
5. Lower vehicle and remove engine mount.
6. Reverse procedure to install.

ENGINE

REPLACE

1. Relieve fuel system pressure as outlined under "Precautions."
2. Remove accessory drive belt.
3. Remove fuel injector sight shield.
4. Remove power steering pump and position aside. **Do not disconnect power steering pressure lines.**
5. Remove throttle body air intake duct.
6. Disconnect fuel rail lines and position aside.
7. Disconnect fuel vapor line.
8. Disconnect throttle and cruise cables with mounting bracket.
9. Disconnect brake vacuum booster hose from engine.
10. Disconnect air conditioning vacuum hose from engine.
11. Disconnect wiring harness connectors from engine and transaxle.
12. Drain cooling system into suitable container and remove radiator inlet hose from engine.
13. Disconnect transaxle fluid lines from radiator.
14. Remove thermostat housing and disconnect surge tank inlet hose.
15. Disconnect heater hoses from engine.
16. Raise and support vehicle.
17. Drain engine oil into suitable container and disconnect AIR pump outlet pipe from AIR crossover pipe.
18. Remove alternator as outlined in "Electrical" section.
19. Remove air conditioning compressor mounting bolts and nuts. Position compressor aside. **Do not discharge air conditioning system.**
20. Remove torque converter cover and starter motor.
21. Scribe alignment marks on flywheel and torque converter.
22. Remove torque converter to flywheel mounting bolts.
23. Remove lower transaxle to engine mounting bolts.
24. Remove front tire and wheel assemblies.
25. Remove inner fender splash shields.
26. Remove wheel speed sensor harness conduits from lower control arm retainers.
27. Remove tie rod ends from steering knuckle as outlined in "Front Suspension & Steering" section.
28. Remove lower ball joints from steering knuckles as outlined in "Front Suspension & Steering" section.
29. Remove intermediate steering shaft pinch bolt and disconnect intermediate shaft from steering gear.
30. Support engine/transaxle frame using frame table tool No. J-39580, or equivalent.
31. Lower vehicle slightly so frame table is supporting engine/transaxle assembly.
32. Secure vehicle to hoist and remove frame to body mounting bolts.

33. Raise and support vehicle.
34. Remove frame table with engine/transaxle frame.
35. Remove transaxle to engine bracket.
36. Remove upper engine to transaxle mounting bolts and separate engine from transaxle.
37. Reverse procedure to install.

INTAKE MANIFOLD

REPLACE

Refer to "3.5L Engine" section in the "Century, Grand Prix, Impala, Intrigue, Lumina, Monte Carlo & Regal" chapter.

RADIATOR

REPLACE

1. Remove headlamp/fascia panel support brackets.
2. Remove radiator support brackets and air cleaner.
3. Position PCM aside.
4. Remove mounting bolts and upper tie bar.
5. Disconnect cooling fan motor electrical connectors.
6. Remove clips attaching wiring harness to fan shroud.
7. Raise and support vehicle, then remove lower air deflector.
8. Remove transaxle oil cooler line mounting bolt and clip from fan shroud.
9. Lower vehicle and slide plastic cap off of upper quick connect joint, then disconnect upper transaxle oil cooler line from radiator.
10. Remove cooling fan shroud mounting bolts and cooling fan.
11. Disconnect upper and lower radiator hoses.
12. Remove upper radiator seal and headlamps.
13. Remove two condenser mounting bolts and lift condenser out of its lower mounting.
14. Remove radiator.
15. Reverse procedure to install.

FUEL PUMP

REPLACE

1. Relieve fuel system pressure as outlined under "Precautions."
2. Drain fuel tank to at least ¾ of full tank.
3. Remove spare tire cover, jack and spare tire.
4. Remove luggage compartment floor trim.
5. Remove mounting screws and fuel sender access panel.
6. Cover fuel pipe fittings with suitable shop towel to prevent spillage.
7. Remove quick-connect fittings air fuel sender.
8. Disconnect fuel sender and fuel pressure sensor electrical connectors.
9. Remove fuel sender retaining ring using fuel sender locknut wrench tool No. J-39765, or equivalent.
10. Remove fuel tank sender.
11. Reverse procedure to install.

FUEL FILTER

REPLACE

1. Relieve fuel system pressure as outlined under "Precautions."
2. Raise and support vehicle.
3. Disconnect quick-connect fitting at inlet end of in-line fuel filter.
4. Remove outlet end threaded fitting and of filter. Drain remaining fuel into suitable container.
5. Reverse procedure to install.

TECHNICAL SERVICE BULLETINS

HIGH TEMPERATURE GAUGE READING OR OVERHEATING IN COLD WEATHER

2001

On some of these models the temperature gauge may have higher than normal readings or the engine may overheat in cold weather. This condition may occur while idling or driving slowly in traffic when temperature is less than 32°F, with the heater control set to maximum heat and fan.

This condition may be caused by the thermostat not providing adequate coolant flow.

To correct this condition, install enhanced thermostat (part No. 12570247).

ENGINE RUNS HOT, OVERHEATS OR LOSSES COOLANT

1999–2000

On some of these models the engine may run hot, overheat or loss coolant.

This condition may be caused by imperfections in the radiator filler neck sealing surface.

To correct this condition, proceed as follows:

1. **Do not replace radiator.**
2. Polish filler neck sealing surface with 400 grit wet/dry sandpaper backed using suitable flat piece of wood and circular motion.
3. Replace radiator cap.

TIGHTENING SPECIFICATIONS

Year	Component	Torque, Ft. Lbs.
2001–02	Accelerator Cable Bracket	84①
	Air Conditioning Compressor, Front Nut	37
	Air Conditioning Compressor, Hose Fittings	15
	Air Conditioning Compressor, Mounting Bolt	37
	Air Conditioning Compressor, Rear Nut	18
	Air Conditioning Condenser	115①
	Alternator	37
	Ball Joint	41
	Camshaft Bearing Caps	44③
	Camshaft Position Sensor	84①
	Camshaft Sprocket	18②
	Connecting Rod	⑥
	Coolant Temperature Sensor	15
	Cylinder Head	⑤
	EGR to Crossover Pipe	44
	Engine Frame Insulator	12
	Engine Front Cradle	141
	Engine To Transaxle	55
	Exhaust Manifold	18
	Exhaust Manifold, Crossover Stud	18
	Exhaust Manifold, Stud	53①
	EVAP Canister Purge Solenoid	72①
	Flywheel To Torque Converter	47
	Front Cover	11
	Front Cover Coolant Drain Plug	96①
	Front Engine Mount	52
	Front Lift Bracket, Hex Bolt	37
	Front Lift Bracket, Internal Drive Bolt	18
	Fuel Injector Sight Shield	27①
	Idler Pulley	37
	Intake Manifold	60①
	Intermediate Shaft Pinch Bolt	35
	Lower Control Arm	117
	Lower Crankcase	④
	Oil Gallery Plug	41
	Oil Level Sensor	84①
	Oil Pan	18
	Oxygen Sensor	30
	Power Steering Pump	25
	Stabilizer Shaft Link	13
	Steering Rack	48
	Thermostat Housing	80①
	Throttle Body	108①
	Tie Rod	55
	Timing Chain Tensioner	18
	Timing Chain Tensioner Shoe	22
	Transaxle Mount Bracket	37
	Transaxle Mount	48
	Transaxle To Engine	55
	Valve Cover	84①
	Water Pump	11
	Water Pump Pulley	108①
	Water Outlet Housing	84①

① — Inch lbs.
② — Tighten an additional 45°.
③ — Tighten an additional 30°.
④ — Refer to "Main & Rod Bearings" for tightening procedure.
⑤ — Refer to "Cylinder Head, Replace" for tightening procedure.
⑥ — Torque 22 ft. lbs.; loosen completely; torque to 18 ft. lbs.. Final tighten an additional 110°.

3800 Engine

NOTE: On Air Bag Equipped Models, Refer To "Air Bag System Precautions" Located In The Front Of This Manual For System Disarming & Arming Procedures.

NOTE: Refer To "Computer Relearn Procedures" Located In The Front Of This Manual When Battery Power To The Computer Has Been Interrupted.

NOTE: Refer To "3800 Engine" Section In The "Bonneville, Eighty Eight, LeSabre, LSS, Park Avenue & Regency" Chapter For Procedures Not Covered In This Section.

NOTE: Prior To Performing Any Service Operations Listed In This Section, Consult The "Technical Service Bulletins" Section For Related Information.

INDEX

PRECAUTIONS

AIR BAG SYSTEMS

Refer to "Air Bag System Precautions" in the front of this manual for system disarming and arming procedures.

BATTERY GROUND CABLE

Prior to service, disconnect battery ground cable and isolate as required.

FUEL SYSTEM PRESSURE RELIEF

After relieving fuel system pressure, a small amount of fuel may be released when servicing fuel pipes or connections. In order to reduce the risk of personal injury, cover fuel pipe fittings with shop towel before disconnecting to catch any fuel that may leak.

1. Loosen fuel filler cap to relieve tank pressure.
2. Connect suitable fuel pressure gauge to fuel pressure test connector. **Wrap suitable shop towel around connection to avoid fuel spillage.**
3. Insert bleed hose into suitable container and open valve to bleed system.
4. Drain any fuel remaining in fuel gauge into suitable container.

COMPRESSION PRESSURE

Refer to "3800 Engine" section in the "Bonneville, Eighty Eight, LeSabre, LSS, Park Avenue & Regency" chapter

ENGINE MOUNT

REPLACE

1. Raise engine slightly using engine support fixture tool No. J-28467-360, or equivalent.
2. Remove bottom bolts on mount.
3. Remove front and rear engine mount through bolts.
4. Remove engine mount from bracket.
5. Reverse procedure to install.

ENGINE

REPLACE

1. Remove engine hood. Mark hood for installation reference.
2. Relieve fuel system pressure as outlined under "Precautions."
3. Drain coolant and engine oil into suitable containers.
4. Remove radiator and heater hoses.
5. Disconnect battery ground cable from engine.
6. Disconnect engine harness at bulkhead connector.
7. Remove serpentine drive belt.
8. Remove power steering pump engine and position aside.
9. Remove air flow duct.
10. Disconnect throttle cable from throttle linkage mounting bracket and other applicable cables.
11. Disconnect the following wiring harness connectors:
    a. MAT sensor.
    b. Throttle position sensor.
    c. Idle air control valve.
    d. Oxygen sensor.
    e. Air conditioning compressor.
    f. Oil pressure switch.
    g. Power steering cutout switch.
    h. Vehicle speed sensor.
    i. Low oil level sensor.
12. Disconnect ignition coil ground strap from fender inner panel mounting screws.
13. Disconnect fuel feed and return lines from fuel rail and fuel pressure regulator.
14. Disconnect emission control canister hoses from throttle body connections.
15. Disconnect brake booster and heater control hoses from engine vacuum connections.
16. Disconnect vacuum hoses from cruise control and servo.
17. Raise and support vehicle.
18. Remove righthand exhaust manifold exhaust pipe.
19. Remove air conditioning compressor and position aside.
20. Remove righthand front engine to transaxle bracket.
21. Remove flywheel cover and starter motor as outlined under "Starter, Replace" in "Electrical" section.
22. Remove flywheel to torque converter bolts. Scribe marks on flywheel and torque converter for assembly reference.

23. Lower vehicle.
24. Attach suitable lifting device to engine lifting brackets
25. Raise engine slightly and remove torque axis engine mount.
26. Support transaxle and remove engine to transaxle bolts.
27. Separate engine from transaxle. Remove engine.
28. Reverse procedure to install.

INTAKE MANIFOLD

REPLACE

Refer to "3800 Engine" section in the "Bonneville, Eighty Eight, LeSabre, LSS, Park Avenue & Regency" chapter

RADIATOR

REPLACE

1. Raise and support vehicle.
2. Remove lower air dam and drain cooling system into suitable container.
3. Install lower air dam and lower vehicle.
4. Remove upper tie bar.
5. Disconnect cooling fan electrical connectors.
6. Remove left and righthand cooling fans.
7. Disconnect coolant level sensor electrical connector.
8. Disconnect coolant recovery hose from radiator filler neck.
9. Remove upper and lower radiator hoses from radiator.
10. Remove condenser to radiator mounting bolts.
11. Remove transaxle cooler lines from radiator.
12. **On models equipped with engine cooler lines,** disconnect cooler lines from radiator.
13. **On all models,** remove radiator.
14. Reverse procedure to install.

FUEL PUMP

REPLACE

1. Drain fuel tank to at least ¾ of tank.
2. Relieve fuel system pressure as outlined under "Precautions."
3. Remove spare tire cover, jack and tire.
4. Pull back trunk liner and remove fuel sender access panel.
5. Disconnect fuel pump quick-connect fittings, **Fig. 1.**
6. Disconnect fuel pump electrical connectors.
7. Remove fuel pump retaining ring using retaining ring removal tool No. J-39765, or equivalent.
8. Pull fuel pump straight up and hold while pumping fuel from reservoir, noting the following:
   a. When removing fuel pump, reservoir bucket on fuel pump is full of fuel.
   b. **It must be tipped slightly during to avoid damage to float.**
   c. Place remaining fuel into suitable container once fuel pump is removed.
   d. Discard fuel pump gasket.
9. Reverse procedure to install.

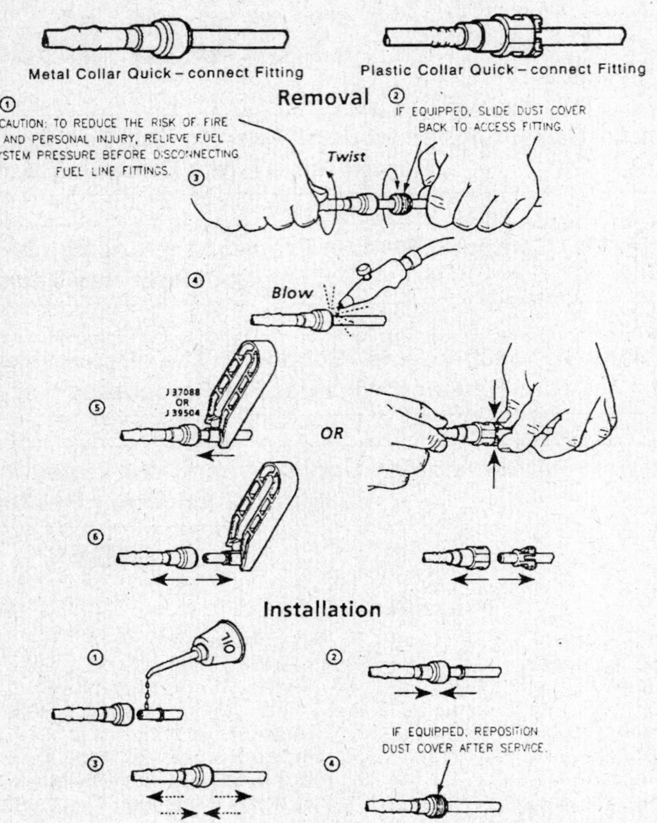

Fig. 1 Servicing fuel line quick-connect fittings

FUEL FILTER

REPLACE

1. Relieve fuel system pressure as outlined under "Precautions."
2. Raise and support vehicle.
3. Disconnect fuel filter quick-connect fittings, **Fig. 1.**
4. Disconnect fuel filter fuel feed pipe and drain remaining fuel into suitable container.
5. Remove fuel filter.
6. Reverse procedure to install.

SUPERCHARGER

REPLACE

Refer to "3800 Engine" section in the "Bonneville, Eighty Eight, LeSabre, LSS, Park Avenue & Regency" chapter

TECHNICAL SERVICE BULLETINS

OIL PAN LEAK

1998-99 Riviera

On some of these models equipped with stamped steel oil pan there may be a leak.

This condition may be caused by uneven, rippled oil pan sealing surface.

To correct this condition, install new gasket and windage tray as follows:

1. Remove oil pan.
2. Remove old RTV from engine block and oil pan sealing surfaces using suitable plastic or metal scraper.
3. Inspect oil pan sealing surface for bends or distortions. Ripples will not affect sealability. **Do not replace oil pan because of ripples.**
4. Clean mating surfaces using solvent part No. 12346139, or equivalent.
5. Apply continuous ¼-inch bead of 5900 RTV sealant, part No. 12346386, or equivalent, to bottom of new gasket. Apply RTV directly over gasket's raised sealing bead.
6. Install gasket to oil pan and align oil pan bolt holes with gasket.
7. Apply continuous ¼-inch bead of RTV sealant to top of new gasket. Apply RTV directly over gasket's raised sealing bead.
8. Install oil pan and **torque** mounting bolts to 124 inch lbs.
9. Allow RTV to set at least 30 minutes before adding engine oil.

ENGINE RUNS HOT, OVERHEATS OR LOSSES COOLANT

1999-2000

On some of these models the engine may run hot, overheat or loss coolant.

This condition may be caused by imperfections in the radiator filler neck sealing surface.

To correct this condition, proceed as follows:

1. **Do not replace radiator.**

2. Polish filler neck sealing surface with 400 grit wet/dry sandpaper backed using suitable flat piece of wood and using circular motion.
3. Replace radiator cap.

POPPING NOISE

1998–99

On some of these models there may be a popping noise after driving at highway speeds and coming to a stop.

This condition may be caused by catalytic converter heat shield expanding.

To correct this condition, proceed as follows:

1. Raise and support vehicle.
2. Remove mounting screws and oxygen sensor wiring rear shield, as required.
3. Remove catalytic converter to exhaust downpipe nuts.
4. Separate catalytic converter from exhaust downpipe.
5. Remove and discard gasket/seal.
6. Drill out rivet above separating flange at center of converter head shield using 3⁄16-inch or larger drill bit.
7. Install new gasket/seal.
8. **Torque** catalytic converter to exhaust downpipe nuts to 18 ft. lbs.
9. Install oxygen sensor wiring rear shield and screws.
10. Lower vehicle.

OIL LEAK

1998 Riviera

On some of these models there may be an oil leak that appear to originate near the oil pan rail.

This condition may be caused by uneven bolt head flanges at the main bearing side bolts.

To correct this condition, proceed as follows:

1. Install oil dye, part No. 1235795, or equivalent, into crankcase.
2. Warm engine to operating temperature by driving vehicle a few miles.
3. Raise and support vehicle with engine running.
4. Thoroughly inspect for oil leaks using suitable black light, noting the following:
   a. Oil leaks originating above oil pan sealing surface may be caused by crankshaft rear oil seal housing gasket, intake end seal, main bearing side bolt or other sources.
   b. **Repair leaks originating above oil pan before replacing oil pan.**
5. Turn engine off and remove flywheel inspection cover.
6. Inspect for flywheel area oil leaks using suitable black light.
7. If leak appears to originate at oil pan flange, proceed as follows:
   a. Install revised oil pan (less oil level sensor part No. 24507900 or w/oil level sensor part No. 24507901) and gasket (part No. 24502397).
   b. **Do use adhesive on gasket.**
   c. Clean mounting bolts thoroughly.
   d. Apply two drops of Loctite No. 242 blue thread locker, or equivalent, to bolts' threaded ends.
   e. **Torque** mounting bolts to 125 inch lbs.
8. If leak appears to originate in flywheel area, proceed as follows:
   a. Remove crankshaft rear oil seal housing.
   b. Install new gasket and rear oil seal.
   c. **Do not use adhesive on housing gasket.**
   d. **Housing plastic inserts are manufacturing assembly and not required for service.**
9. If leak appears to originate above pan rail, but not from rear housing or lower intake manifold end seals, install six new main bearing side bolts (part No. 24505576).

NOISE, VIBRATION OR GROWL FROM FRONT

1998

On some of these models there may be noise, vibration or growl from the front of the vehicle on righthand turns or hard acceleration.

This condition may be caused by the rear transaxle mount grounding out because of a bound or twisted condition within the mount.

To correct this condition, proceed as follows:

1. Raise and support vehicle.
2. Support transaxle using suitable screwjack.
3. Loosen rear transaxle mounting nuts. **Do not remove nuts.**
4. Unload mount by lowering transaxle using screwjack.
5. Eliminate binding or twisting by adjusting mount.
6. Raise transaxle using screwjack until bracket contacts mount.
7. Adjust mount alignment, as required. **Studs will not always be centered in bracket because of cross-car-build variations.**
8. Fully load mount by raising transaxle using screwjack.
9. **Torque** mounting nuts to 33 ft. lbs.
10. Remove screwjack and ensure mount is properly aligned.

TIGHTENING SPECIFICATIONS

Year	Component	Torque/Ft. Lbs.
1998–99	Accessory Drive Belt Tensioner	37
	Alternator Support Through Alternator	36
	Alternator Support To Cylinder Head	11
	Balance Shaft Gear	16⑧
	Balance Shaft Retainer	22
	Belt Tensioner	37
	Boost Control Solenoid To Bypass Actuator	22
	Bypass Actuator To Supercharger	22
	Camshaft Sensor To Front Cover	72①
	Camshaft Sprocket	74⑤
	Connecting Rod	20②
	Coolant Plug	32
	Coolant Temperature Sensor	15
	Crankshaft Balancer	110⑦
	Crankshaft Pulley	110⑦
	Crankshaft Sensor Clamp	40①
	Crankshaft Sensor To Front Cover	22
	Cylinder Block Drain Plug	25
	Cylinder Head To Block	③
	Drive Belt Tensioner To Cylinder Block Bracket	37
	EGR Pipe To EGR Valve	22
	EGR Pipe To Exhaust Manifold	15
	EGR Valve Adapter	37
	EGR Valve To Intake Manifold Adapter	22
	Engine Mount, Front Through Bolt	64
	Engine Mount, Rear Through Bolt	52
	Engine Mount, Rear To Cylinder Block	65
	ESC Knock Sensor	13
	Exhaust Manifold To Cylinder Head	38
	Exhaust Pipe To Manifold	18
	Flywheel Cover	22①
	Flywheel To Crankshaft	11②
	Front Cover To Block	22
	Fuel Feed & Return Pipes	22
	Fuel Filter Outlet Nut	22
	Fuel Rail To Intake Manifold	11
	Heater Hose Fitting To Intake	11
	Ignition Module To Alternator	18
	Intake Manifold To Cylinder Head	84①
	Intake Manifold, Upper To Lower	22
	Main Bearing Cap	26④
	Oil Cooler Adapter Connector	37
	Oil Filter Adapter To Front Cover	22
	Oil Galley Plugs	25
	Oil Level Indicator Tube	11
	Oil Level Sensor To Oil Pan	16
	Oil Pan Drain Plug	22
	Oil Pan To Block	10
	Oil Pan To Front Cover	10
	Oil Pressure Switch	24
	Oil Pump Cover To Front Cover	96①
	Oil Screen Housing To Cylinder Block	11
	Oxygen Sensor	31
	Power Steering Hoses	20

Continued

TIGHTENING SPECIFICATIONS—Continued

Year	Component	Torque/Ft. Lbs.
1998–99	Power Steering Mounts	20
	Righthand Exhaust Manifold To Lefthand Exhaust Manifold	15
	Rocker Arm Cover	88①
	Rocker Arm Pedestal	19⑤
	Spark Plug	12
	Starter Motor	32
	Supercharger To Lower Intake Manifold	17
	Supercharger Bypass Valve Nut	72①
	Thermostat Housing	15
	Throttle Body Adapter To Intake	20
	Throttle Body To Throttle Body Adapter	20
	Throttle Cable Bracket	35①
	Timing Chain Damper	16
	Torque Converter To Flywheel	46
	Transaxle Oil Cooler	20
	Transaxle To Cylinder Block	55
	Upper Tie Bar	89
	Valve Lifter Guide Bolts	22
	Water Pump Pulley	108①
	Water Pump To Front Cover	⑥

①— Inch lbs.
②— Tighten an additional 50°.
③— Refer to "Cylinder Head, Replace."
④— Tighten an additional 50°.
⑤— Tighten an additional 90°.
⑥— Refer to "Water Pump, Replace."
⑦— Tighten an additional 76°.
⑧— Tighten an additional 70°.

4.0L Engine

NOTE: On Air Bag Equipped Models, Refer To "Air Bag System Precautions" Located In The Front Of This Manual For System Disarming & Arming Procedures.

NOTE: Refer To "Computer Relearn Procedures" Located In The Front Of This Manual When Battery Power To The Computer Has Been Interrupted.

NOTE: Prior To Performing Any Service Operations Listed In This Section, Consult The "Technical Service Bulletins" Section For Related Information.

INDEX

PRECAUTIONS

AIR BAG SYSTEMS

Refer to "Air Bag System Precautions" in the front of this manual for system disarming and arming procedures.

BATTERY GROUND CABLE

Prior to service, disconnect battery ground cable and isolate as required.

CAMSHAFT TIMING & TIMING CHAIN

With the timing chain removed or loosened, avoid turning the camshaft or crankshaft. If movement is required, exercise extreme caution to avoid valve damage caused by piston contact.

FUEL SYSTEM PRESSURE RELIEF

After relieving fuel system pressure, a small amount of fuel may be released when servicing fuel pipes or connections. In order to reduce the risk of personal injury, cover fuel pipe fittings with shop towel before disconnecting to catch any fuel that may leak.

1. Loosen fuel filler cap to relieve tank pressure.
2. Connect suitable fuel pressure gauge to fuel pressure test connector. **Wrap suitable shop towel around connection to avoid fuel spillage.**
3. Insert bleed hose into suitable container and open valve to bleed system.
4. Drain any fuel remaining in fuel gauge into suitable container.

COMPRESSION PRESSURE

When checking compression, the lowest cylinder must be within 70 percent of the highest cylinder with a minimum pressure of 100 psi. Perform compression test with engine at normal operating temperature, spark plugs removed and throttle wide open.

ENGINE MOUNT

REPLACE

1. Support engine using support fixture tool No. J-28467-A, or equivalent.
2. Remove windshield washer reservoir.
3. Remove engine mount to body through bolt.
4. Remove torque axis engine mount, **Fig. 1.**
5. Raise and support vehicle.
6. Remove righthand front tire and wheel assembly.
7. Remove wheelwell splash shield.
8. Remove lower center air deflector.
9. Remove lefthand transaxle mount to cradle through bolt.
10. Remove engine mount bracket lower mounting bolt/nut.
11. Remove power steering pump and set aside.
12. Raise engine using support fixture.
13. Remove engine mount bracket.
14. Remove torque axis mount.
15. Reverse procedure to install.

ENGINE

REPLACE

1. Remove air cleaner and intake manifold sight shield.
2. Drain cooling system and engine oil into suitable container.

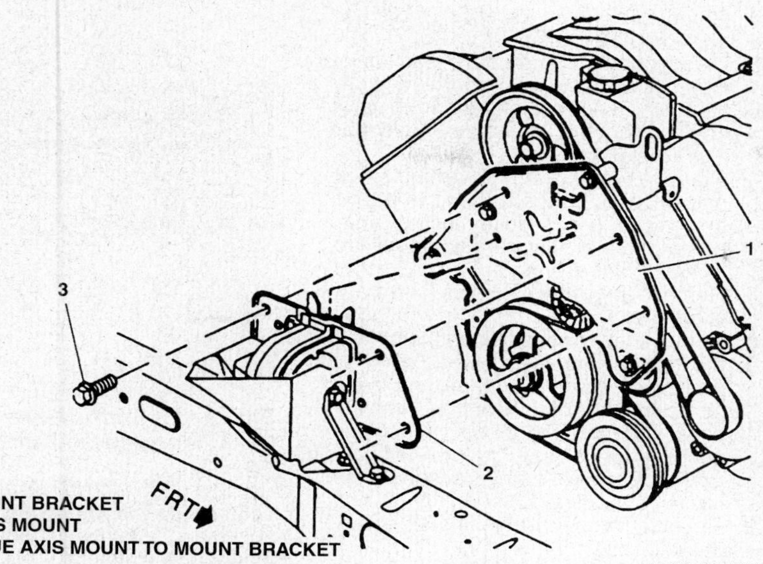

Fig. 1 Front engine mount replacement

3. Relieve fuel system pressure as outlined under "Precautions."
4. Recover refrigerant as outlined in "Air Conditioning" chapter.
5. Disconnect fuel feed and return lines.
6. Disconnect vacuum harness from rear of intake manifold.
7. Disconnect engine wire harness at bulkhead.
8. Disconnect overflow reservoir coolant hoses.
9. Remove coolant crossover upper radiator hose.
10. Remove lower radiator hose at thermostat housing.
11. Disconnect upper transaxle cooler hose at radiator.
12. Disconnect lower transaxle cooler hose at transaxle.
13. Remove heater hoses from coolant pipes at rear of engine.
14. Disconnect brake booster vacuum hose.
15. Remove shift control cable retaining bracket from transaxle.
16. Remove shift control cable from lever on transaxle.
17. Remove vacuum reservoir.
18. Disconnect vacuum and electrical connectors at cruise control servo.
19. Install engine support fixture.
20. Disconnect positive battery cable at junction block.
21. Remove front engine mount through bolt.
22. Remove front plate front engine mounting bolts.
23. Disconnect battery ground cable from engine block.
24. Raise and support vehicle.
25. Remove both front wheels.
26. Remove left and righthand splash shields.
27. Disconnect steering gear electrical connector.
28. Remove left and righthand ball joints cotter pins, then separate ball joints from steering knuckle.
29. Remove left and righthand axle shafts' hubs.
30. Remove exhaust pipe to exhaust manifold mounting bolts and nuts, then separate exhaust system from exhaust manifold.
31. Remove engine oil cooler hoses at adapter.
32. Remove engine to transaxle braces at oil pan, then at front and rear of engine.
33. Remove flywheel cover.
34. Remove flywheel to converter and transaxle to engine bolts.
35. Remove oil filter and adapter.
36. Disconnect air conditioning hose and muffler from rear of air conditioning compressor.
37. Position cradle support table under engine and lower vehicle.
38. Remove lefthand transaxle mount.
39. Support front of lower engine using suitable block of wood.
40. Release engine support.
41. Remove engine cradle bolts.
42. Raise vehicle, then remove engine and transaxle assembly.
43. Reverse procedure to install. **Refer to "Cooling System Bleed."**

INTAKE MANIFOLD

REPLACE

1. Remove intake manifold cover.
2. Relieve fuel system pressure as outlined under "Precautions."
3. Remove air intake duct from throttle body, transaxle vent hose and shift cable.
4. Disconnect throttle position sensor and IAC valve connectors.
5. Disconnect accelerator and cruise control cables. Position cables out of way.
6. Remove lefthand spark plug wires and position out of way.
7. Drain cooling system into suitable container.
8. Disconnect throttle body coolant hoses and surge tank pipe, then the EGR pipe and crankcase ventilation pipe at throttle body spacer.
9. Disconnect intake manifold brake booster vacuum hose.
10. Disconnect righthand cylinder head fuel rail ground wire.
11. Disconnect fuel rail quick connect fittings and fuel rail EGR valve bracket.
12. Disconnect intake manifold PCV hose and injector harness main connector.
13. Remove mounting bolts, studs and intake manifold.
14. Reverse procedure to install. When tightening bolts and studs, start at center and work outward in circular pattern.

EXHAUST MANIFOLD

REPLACE

LEFTHAND

1. Remove drive belt as outlined under "Serpentine Drive Belt."
2. Remove alternator upper mounting bolt.
3. Raise and support vehicle.
4. Remove righthand wheelwell splash shield and lower center air deflector.
5. Remove alternator rear bracket and lower mounting bolt and position alternator aside.
6. Remove exhaust manifold to crossover exhaust pipe bolts.
7. Disconnect oxygen sensor electrical connector.
8. Remove exhaust manifold to cylinder head mounting bolts.
9. Remove exhaust manifold and gasket.
10. Remove oxygen sensor.
11. Reverse procedure to install, coat oxygen sensor threads with suitable high temperature anti-seize lubricant prior to installation.

RIGHTHAND

1. Raise and support vehicle. Support catalytic converter.
2. Remove mounting bolts and exhaust manifold Y pipe from front of catalytic converter and crossover exhaust pipe.
3. Remove crossover pipe.
4. Disconnect oxygen sensor electrical connector.
5. Remove mounting nuts, exhaust manifold, gasket and oxygen sensor.
6. Reverse procedure to install. Coat oxygen sensor threads with suitable high temperature anti-seize lubricant prior to installation.

CYLINDER HEAD

REPLACE

This procedure has been revised by a Technical Service Bulletin.

Align timing marks before removing cylinder heads and timing chains. Especially if only removing one cylinder head.

Do not turn engine with timing chains loose or removed. Valve damage may occur.

1. Remove engine as outlined under "Engine, Replace."

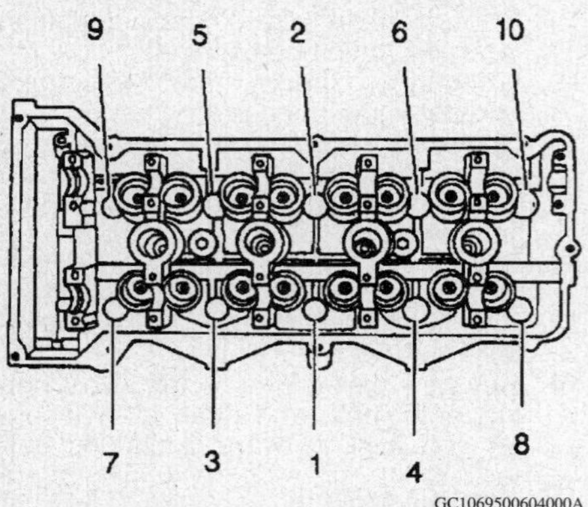

Fig. 2 Cylinder head tightening sequence. Righthand

2. Remove intake manifold as outlined under "Intake Manifold, Replace."
3. Remove valve covers as outlined under "Valve Cover, Replace."
4. Remove crankshaft damper as outlined under "Crankshaft Damper, Replace."
5. Remove front cover as outlined under "Front Cover, Replace."
6. Remove oil pump as outlined under "Oil Pump, Replace."
7. Remove chain tensioner from timing chain and cam sprocket. Timing chain should remain in crankcase.
8. Remove timing chain guides and lever. Access for mounting bolts is through plugs at front of cylinder head.
9. Remove water crossover.
10. Remove exhaust manifold.
11. Remove bolts, cylinder head and gasket.
12. Reverse procedure to install, noting the following:
    a. Clean remaining gasket material from cylinder head and cylinder head mating surface.
    b. **Extreme care must be taken when cleaning aluminum gasket surfaces to prevent damage to sealing surfaces.**
    c. **Use only suitable plastic, wood or dull gasket scrapers. Chemical agents can be used to dissolve gasket materials following manufacturers recommendations.**
    d. Coat washers and underside of cylinder head bolts with suitable anti-seize lubricant, prior to installation.
    e. **Torque** cylinder head bolts to 30 ft. lbs. in sequence, **Figs. 2 and 3.**
    f. Tighten head bolts an additional 70° in sequence.
    g. Tighten bolts an additional 60°.
    h. Final tighten bolts an additional 60°.
    i. **Torque** M6 bolts to 106 inch lbs.

VALVE COVER

REPLACE

LEFTHAND

1. Remove intake manifold cover and partially drain cooling system into suitable container.
2. Remove oil level dipstick, tube and upper radiator hose.
3. Disconnect lefthand spark plug wires.
4. Remove upper core support brace.
5. Remove PCV fresh air tube from valve cover, then the air intake hose and EGR outlet pipe.
6. Remove water pump drive belt shield and drive belt, then the belt tensioner and water pump pulley using water pump drive pulley remover tool No. J-38825, or equivalent.
7. Remove mounting screws and camshaft seal.
8. Remove valve cover mounting bolts.
9. Move cam drive end of valve cover up and pivot entire cover around water pump drive shaft. Continue moving cover upward and pivoting such that cover edge closely follows lefthand edge of intake manifold cover. Remove cover, **Fig. 4.**
10. Reverse procedure to install, noting the following:
    a. Guide valve cover up over cylinder head edge using fingers. **Prevent valve cover seal exposed section from being damaged by cylinder head casting edge.**
    b. Work cover into position by allowing cover top edge to follow intake manifold lefthand edge.
    c. Refer to "Cooling System Bleed."

RIGHTHAND

1. Remove intake manifold cover.
2. Remove vacuum reservoir.
3. Remove cruise control servo and position aside.
4. Disconnect DIS ignition module wiring connectors and remove DIS module mounting bolts.
5. Remove DIS ignition module and spark plug wires from valve cover.
6. Remove PCV valve and fuel vapor canister purge solenoid from valve cover.
7. Raise and support vehicle.
8. Disconnect knock sensor, vehicle speed sensor and power steering pressure switch electrical connectors.
9. Lower vehicle and remove wiring harness retainers from cover.
10. Remove mounting bolts and valve cover.
11. Reverse procedure to install.

VALVE CLEARANCE SPECIFICATIONS

These engines are equipped with hydraulic valve lifters. Valve clearance should be zero.

VALVE ADJUSTMENT

These engines are equipped with hydraulic valve lifters. No adjustment is required.

VALVE GUIDES

Check valve stem to valve guide clearance. Clearance should be 0.005 inch or less. Service valves are available in standard size (.235 inch). If clearance is excessive and new standard size valve stem will not bring clearance within specifications, cylinder head must be replaced.

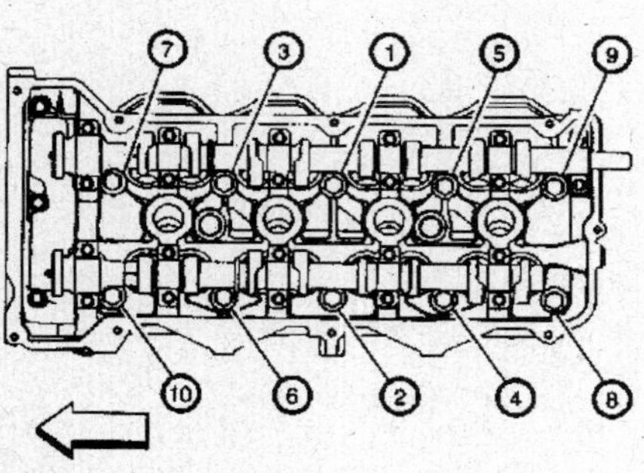

Fig. 3 Cylinder head tightening sequence. Lefthand

HYDRAULIC LIFTERS

REPLACE

If camshafts remain in cylinder head, some valves will always be held open and cylinder head cannot be set on workbench with cylinder head face down. Damage to valves and/or gasket surface will result.

Do not mix cam bearing caps between positions or heads. Each cap must be assembled in the position from which it was removed and in the original orientation (arrow points toward front of engine).

1. Remove cylinder head as outlined under "Cylinder Head, Replace."
2. Place matchmarks on bearing caps.
3. Remove intake and exhaust camshafts by alternately loosening each cam bearing cap bolt two turns at a time until valve spring pressure is completely released.
4. Remove valve lifters and arrange them so they may be installed in original position.
5. Reverse procedure to install, noting the following:
    a. Lubricate camshaft bearing journals with engine oil prior to installation.
    b. Alternately tighten camshaft bearing cap bolts one turn at a time to specifications.

CRANKSHAFT DAMPER

REPLACE

1. Release accessory drive belt tension.
2. Remove torque axis engine mount as outlined under "Engine Mount, Replace."
3. Remove brace between engine oil pan and transaxle case, then install flywheel holder tool No. J-39411, or equivalent.
4. Remove crankshaft damper mounting bolt.

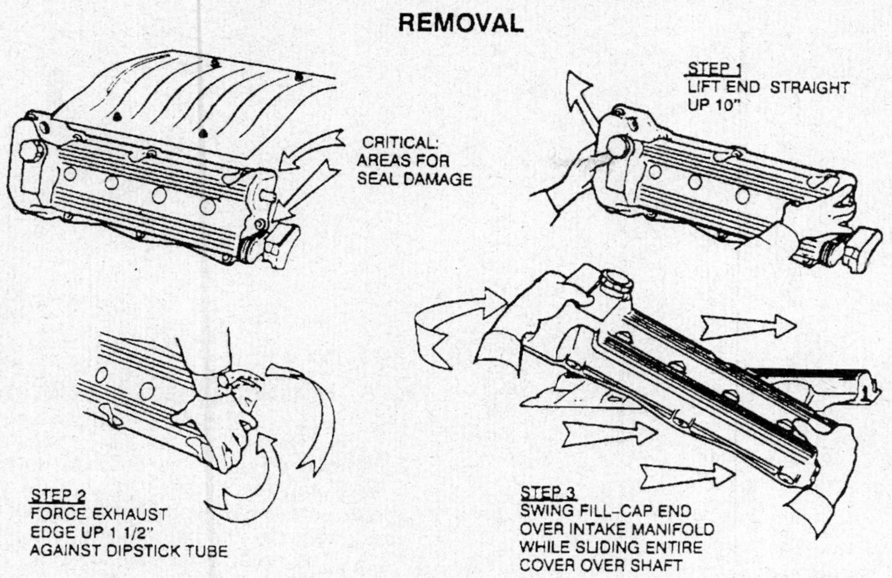
REMOVAL
STEP 1
LIFT END STRAIGHT
UP 10"
CRITICAL:
AREAS FOR
SEAL DAMAGE
STEP 2
FORCE EXHAUST
EDGE UP 1 1/2"
AGAINST DIPSTICK TUBE
STEP 3
SWING FILL-CAP END
OVER INTAKE MANIFOLD
WHILE SLIDING ENTIRE
COVER OVER SHAFT

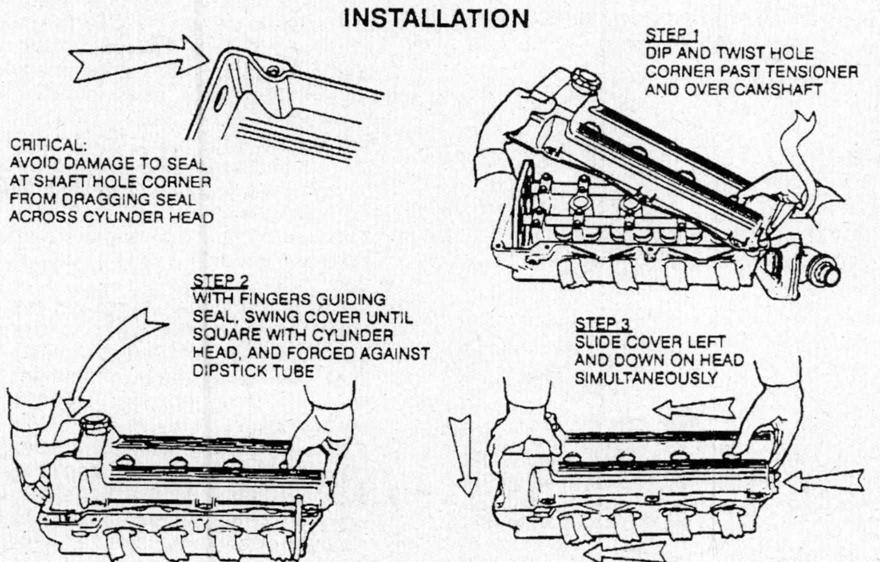
INSTALLATION
STEP 1
DIP AND TWIST HOLE
CORNER PAST TENSIONER
AND OVER CAMSHAFT
CRITICAL:
AVOID DAMAGE TO SEAL
AT SHAFT HOLE CORNER
FROM DRAGGING SEAL
ACROSS CYLINDER HEAD
STEP 2
WITH FINGERS GUIDING
SEAL, SWING COVER UNTIL
SQUARE WITH CYLINDER
HEAD, AND FORCED AGAINST
DIPSTICK TUBE
STEP 3
SLIDE COVER LEFT
AND DOWN ON HEAD
SIMULTANEOUSLY
GC1069500605000X

Fig. 4 Lefthand valve cover replacement

5. Lower engine at support fixture to obtain clearance for pulling tool below body rail.
6. Install pilot tool No. J-39344-2, or equivalent, into end of crankshaft.
7. Remove crankshaft balancer using pulling tool No. J-38416-A, or equivalent.
8. Reverse procedure to install, noting the following:
   a. Thoroughly clean balancer bolt threads.
   b. Apply clean engine oil to balancer bolt threads prior to installation.
   c. Tighten bolt to specification.

FRONT COVER

REPLACE

1. Remove accessory drive belt as outlined under "Serpentine Drive Belt."
2. Remove crankshaft damper as outlined under "Crankshaft Damper, Replace."
3. Remove drive belt tensioner and idler pulley.
4. Remove mounting bolts, front cover and gasket.
5. Reverse procedure to install. Front cover seal is reusable, do not discard unless seal is damaged.

FRONT COVER SEAL

REPLACE

1. Remove crankshaft damper as outlined under "Crankshaft Damper, Replace."
2. Pry seal out of front cover using suitable flat-bladed screwdriver, **Fig. 5.**
3. Reverse procedure to install, noting the following:

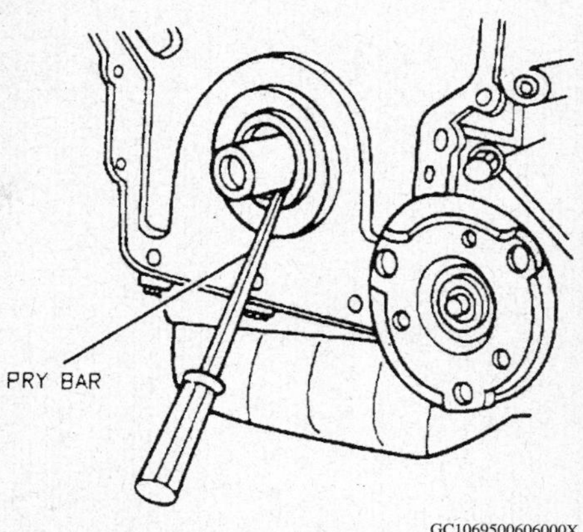
PRY BAR
GC1069500606000X

Fig. 5 Front cover seal replacement

   a. Lubricate seal lips with clean engine oil prior to installation.
   b. Push seal into front cover using seal installer tool No. J-38818, or equivalent, until tool bottoms on cover.

TIMING CHAIN

REPLACE

CAMSHAFT PRIMARY DRIVE CHAIN

1. Remove front cover as outlined under "Front Cover, Replace."
2. Remove oil pump as outlined under "Oil Pump, Replace."
3. Remove valve covers as outlined under "Valve Cover, Replace."
4. Remove timing chain tensioners and camshaft sprockets.
5. Remove secondary drive chains as outlined under "Camshaft Secondary Drive Chain."
6. Remove intermediate shaft sprocket bolt, then slide gears and primary drive chain off crankshaft and intermediate shaft, **Fig. 6.**
7. Reverse procedure to install. Set camshaft timing as outlined under "Setting Camshaft Timing."

CAMSHAFT SECONDARY DRIVE CHAIN

1. Remove front cover as outlined under "Front Cover, Replace."
2. Remove valve covers as outlined under "Valve Cover, Replace."
3. Remove bolts and tensioners.
4. Remove chain guide access plugs noting O-ring seal.
5. Remove camshaft position sensor.
6. Remove mounting bolts and chain guides
7. Remove mounting bolts and slide sprockets off camshafts.
8. Remove sprockets and secondary drive chain together. Leave intermediate sprocket in place.
9. Reverse procedure to install, set camshaft timing as outlined under "Setting Camshaft Timing."

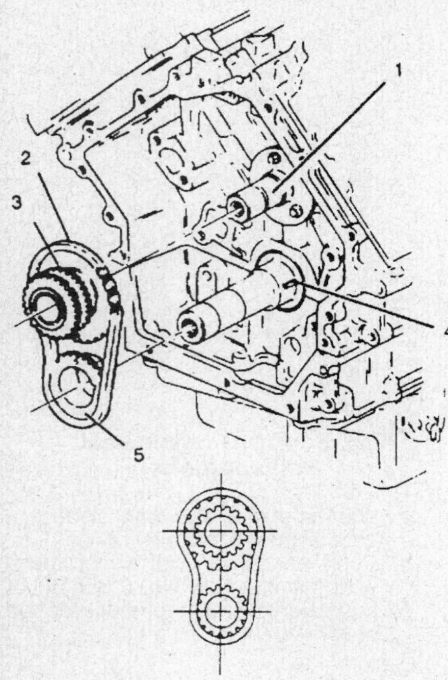

1 INTERMEDIATE SHAFT
2 PRIMARY CHAIN
3 INTERMEDIATE SHAFT SPROCKET
4 CRANKSHAFT SPROCKET KEY
5 SPROCKET

GC1069500607000X

Fig. 6 Primary drive chain replacement

TIMING CHAIN TENSIONER

REPLACE

REMOVAL

1. Remove front cover as outlined under "Front Cover, Replace."
2. Remove transaxle to oil pan brace.
3. Lock flywheel using flywheel holder tool No. J-39411, or equivalent,
4. Remove mounting bolts and tensioner, **Fig. 7.**

INSTALLATION

1. Rotate ratchet release lever counterclockwise and hold, **Fig. 8.**
2. Collapse tensioner retainer shoe and hold.
3. Release ratchet lever and slowly release shoe pressure.
4. Hold tensioner shoe at first click hold, insert suitable pin through hole and release lever, **Fig. 9.**
5. Ensure release lever is facing you, install tensioner and bolts. Tighten to specifications.
6. Remove retaining pin allowing tensioner shoe to extend.
7. Remove flywheel holding tool and install pan brace.
8. Install front cover.

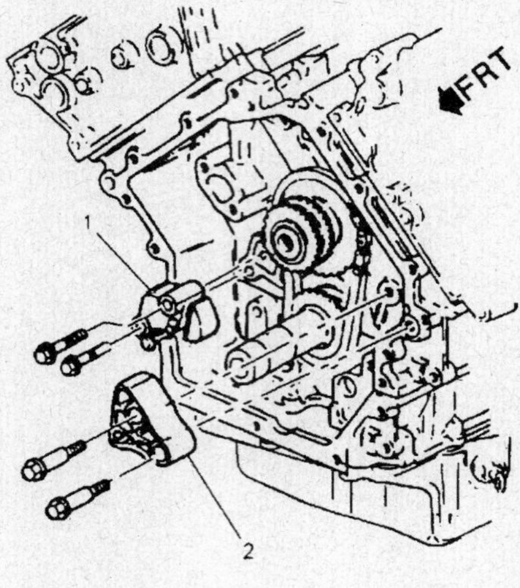

1 PRIMARY CHAIN TENSIONER
2 PRIMARY CHAIN GUIDE

GC1069500608000X

Fig. 7 Primary chain tensioner replacement

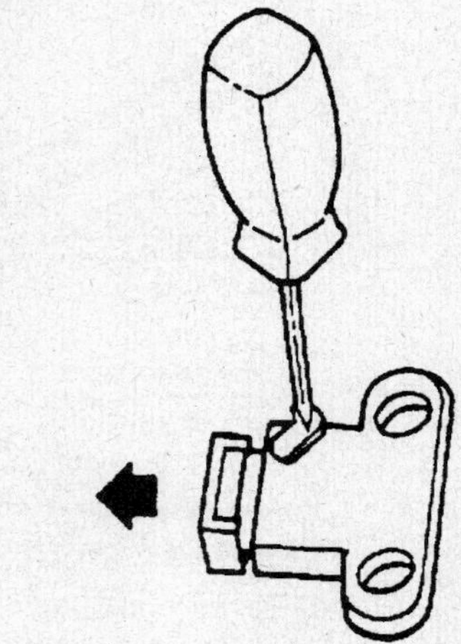

1 RELEASE TO FIRST CLICK
2 INSTALL LOCK PIN

GC1069500610000X

Fig. 9 Locking tensioner

SETTING CAMSHAFT TIMING

This engine is an interference fit engine. The engine is not free spinning and pistons will strike valves if crankshaft is rotated with camshaft drive disconnected or if camshafts are not properly timed.

1. Remove valve covers as outlined under "Valve Cover, Replace."
2. Remove front engine mount as outlined under "Engine Mount, Replace."
3. Support front of engine and remove front cover as outlined under "Front Cover, Replace."
4. Remove three chain tensioners. Chain tensioners may remain in installed position, but must be fully retracted.

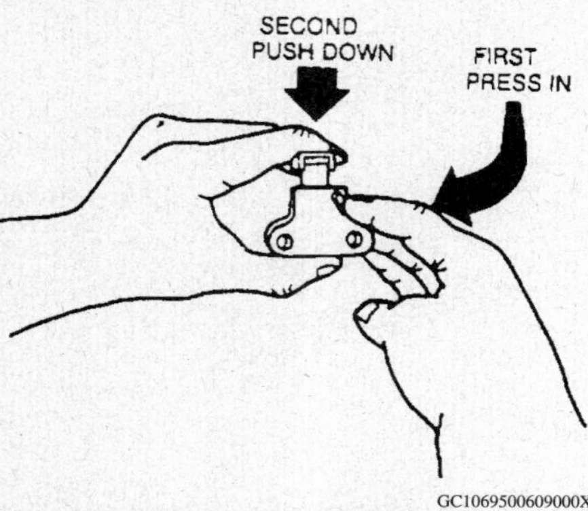

GC1069500609000X

Fig. 8 Rotating tensioner release lever

5. Remove oil pump as outlined under "Oil Pump, Replace."
6. Install crankshaft sprocket drive key. If required, tap into place using suitable small hammer until key bottoms in shaft.
7. Rotate crankshaft until piston No. 1 is at Top Dead Center (TDC) and sprocket drive key is at approximately one o'clock position using suitable socket.
8. Align crankshaft and intermediate shaft sprockets and install with primary drive chain, **Fig. 10.** Rotate crankshaft as required to engage crankshaft key in sprocket without changing timing marks relationship.
9. Install bolt and tighten intermediate sprocket mounting bolt to specification.
10. Install primary chain tensioner and release tensioner shoe as outlined under "Timing Chain Tensioner, Replace."
11. Lock crankshaft into position using flywheel holding tool No. J-39411, or equivalent.
12. If required, install secondary camshaft drive chain guides and access plugs.
13. Route lefthand cylinder head secondary drive chain over inner row of intermediate shaft teeth and chain guide.
14. Install lefthand exhaust cam sprocket to chain so camshaft drive pin engages sprocket notch marked LE. There should be no slack in lower chain section and cam drive pin must be perpendicular to cylinder head face. Camshaft drive pin must be perpendicular to cylinder head face.
15. Install intake cam sprocket into chain so sprocket notch marked LI engages cam drive pin. Pin must be perpendicular to cylinder head face. A hex is cast into camshaft behind lobes for cylinder No. 2 so open end wrench may be used to provide minor camshaft positioning.
16. Loosely install intake and exhaust cam sprocket mounting bolts.
17. Install chain tensioner and release tension on shoe as outlined under "Timing Chain Tensioner, Replace."
18. Route secondary drive chain for righthand cylinder head over outer row of intermediate shaft teeth.
19. Install righthand exhaust cam sprocket

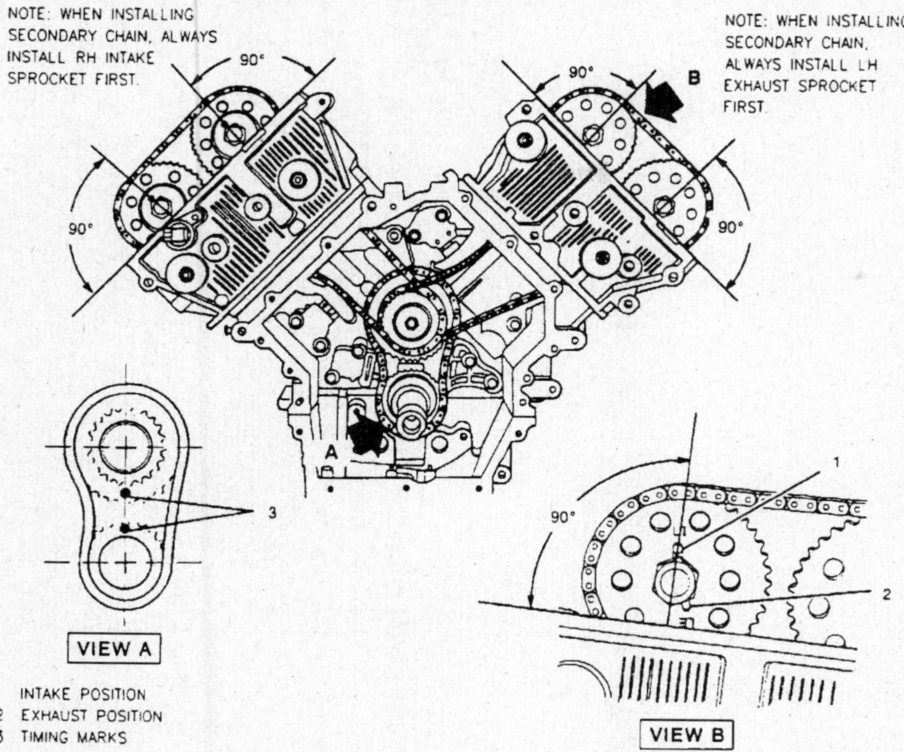
NOTE: WHEN INSTALLING SECONDARY CHAIN, ALWAYS INSTALL RH INTAKE SPROCKET FIRST.
NOTE: WHEN INSTALLING SECONDARY CHAIN, ALWAYS INSTALL LH EXHAUST SPROCKET FIRST.
90°
B
A
3
VIEW A
1 INTAKE POSITION
2 EXHAUST POSITION
3 TIMING MARKS
1
2
VIEW B
GC1069500611000X

Fig. 10 Setting camshaft timing

to chain so camshaft drive pin engages sprocket notch marked RI. There should be no slack in lower chain section and cam drive pin must be perpendicular to cylinder head face. Camshaft drive pin must be perpendicular to cylinder head face.

20. Install intake cam sprocket into chain so sprocket notch marked RE engages cam drive pin. Pin must be perpendicular to cylinder head face. A hex is cast into camshaft behind lobes for cylinder No. 1 so open end wrench may be used to provide minor camshaft positioning.
21. Ensure RE sprocket contains camshaft position sensor pickup and install camshaft position sensor.
22. Loosely install intake and exhaust cam sprocket mounting bolts.
23. Install chain tensioner and release tension on shoe as outlined under "Timing Chain Tensioner, Replace."
24. Install oil pump as outlined under "Oil Pump, Replace."
25. Install front cover as outlined under "Front Cover, Replace."
26. Install valve covers as outlined under "Valve Cover, Replace."
27. Install front engine mount as outlined under "Engine Mount, Replace."

CAMSHAFT

REPLACE

1. Remove valve cover as outlined under "Valve Cover, Replace."
2. Set engine at piston No. 1 TDC and align timing marks to correct position.
3. Secure cam sprocket to timing chain using tie-raps through cam sprocket holes. Use two tie-raps per sprocket. **Sprocket to chain relationship must be maintained throughout this procedure or camshaft timing will be lost and require further engine disassembly for timing.**
4. Working behind sprockets, install cam chain holder J-38822, or equivalent, so it is positioned between chain tensioner and chain guide, **Fig. 11**.
5. Apply tension to tool by tightening tension adjusting screw. **When using cam chain holder tool on righthand cylinder bank, remove wiper motor to gain clearance.**
6. Remove camshaft sprocket bolts. Record relative location of cam drive pins in ends of camshafts.
7. Work sprockets off camshaft using chain play.
8. Alternately loosening each cam bearing cap bolt two turns at a time until valve spring pressure is completely released. **Do not mix cam bearing caps between positions or heads. Each cap must be assembled in position from which it was removed and in original orientation (arrow points toward front of engine).**
9. Remove camshafts.
10. Reverse procedure to install.

PISTON & ROD ASSEMBLY

Refer to **Fig. 12** for piston and rod assembly. Refer to **Fig. 13** for piston installation.

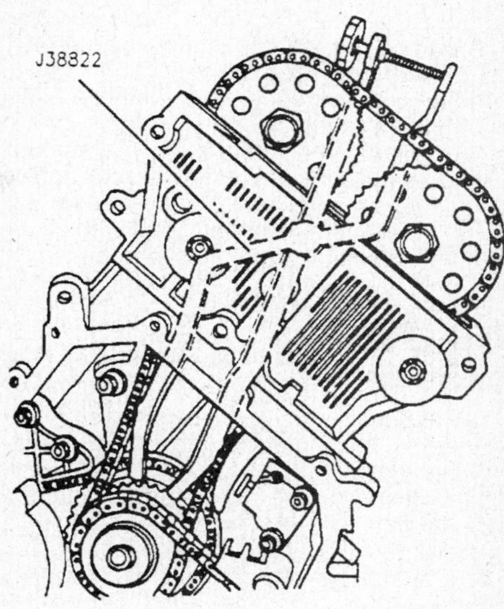
J38822
GC1069500612000X

Fig. 11 Holding drive chain tension

MAIN & ROD BEARINGS

Shell type main bearings of steel backed aluminum are used at all positions. The upper and lower bearing halves are interchangeable except for the upper bearing in the No. 3 position as this is the thrust bearing. Maximum crankshaft endplay is 0.019 inch.

With the crankcase disassembled the main bearing clearance can be measured using suitable plastic gauging material as follows:

1. Wipe oil from crankshaft journals and bearing inserts.
2. Place plastic gauging material across journals to be measured.
3. Install lower crankcase and oil manifold.
4. Install main bearing bolts and tighten bolts to specifications in sequence, **Fig. 14.**
5. Determine clearance by comparing width of flattened plastic gauging material with measurement increments on plastic gauging package.
6. If bearing clearance is more than 0.0025 inch and new bearings do not reduce clearance to 0.0006–0.0020 inch, new crankshaft is required. Undersized bearings are not available and no crankshaft grinding is allowed.

CRANKSHAFT REAR OIL SEAL

REPLACE

1. Remove engine as outlined under "Engine, Replace."
2. Remove mounting bolts, transaxle and flywheel.
3. Drill ⅛ inch hole in seal metal body of seal and use suitable slide hammer to remove seal. **Seal removal can also be done using suitable flat-bladed screwdriver between seal lip and**

crankshaft. Extreme care is required when to avoid crankshaft sealing surface damage.

4. Reverse procedure to install, noting the following:
   a. Place small amount of RTV sealant at crankcase split line across end of upper and lower crankcase seal.
   b. Lubricate rear main seal with clean engine oil prior to installation.

OIL PAN

REPLACE

1. Remove transaxle as outlined in "Automatic Transmission/Transaxle" chapter.
2. Drain engine oil into suitable container.
3. Remove exhaust crossover pipe.
4. Remove mounting bolts and oil pan.
5. Reverse procedure to install. Gasket is reusable unless damaged. **Do not remove gasket from oil pan groove unless replacement is required.** If replacing gasket do not expose new gasket to oil before inserting gasket into pan groove, gasket will expand when exposed to oil and will not stay in pan groove.

OIL PUMP

REPLACE

1. Remove front cover as outlined under "Front Cover, Replace."
2. Remove oil pump mounting bolts.
3. Remove oil pump and drive spacer, **Fig. 15.**
4. Reverse procedure to install.

OIL PUMP SERVICE

DISASSEMBLE

1. Remove drive spacer and screws holding pump housing halves together.
2. Remove inner (drive) and outer (driven) rotors out of housing and mark mating surfaces for assembly.
3. Remove pressure relief valve cap retaining pin and plug without damaging O-ring seal.
4. Slide pressure relief valve spring and piston out of bore.

ASSEMBLE

1. Install inner and outer rotors to pump cover in same position as they were removed (dimples out). Chamfered edge of outer rotor must be face down (closest to engine rear).
2. Install pressure relief valve piston, spring and retaining cap in pump housing.
3. Pack housing with suitable white petroleum jelly.
4. Assemble housing and cover over locating dowel.
5. Insert 3/8 inch drill in pump mounting hole on opposite side to aid in alignment of housing and cover.
6. Install screws and tighten to specifications.

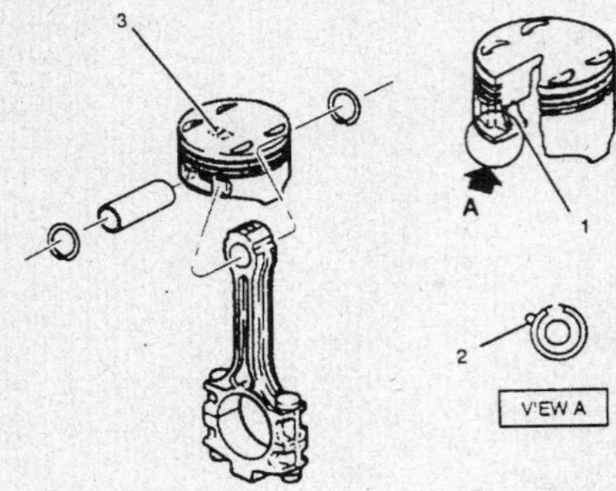

Fig. 12 Piston & rod assembly

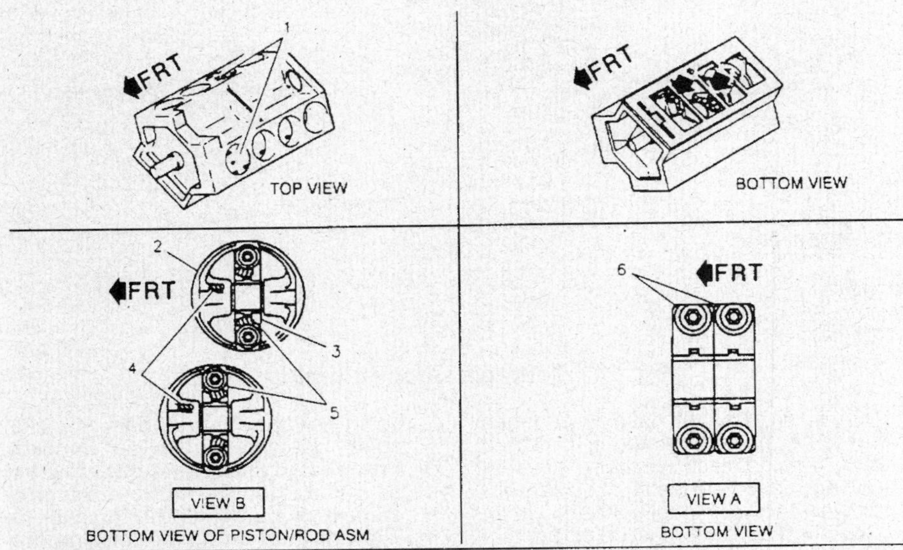

1 PISTON ARROW TOWARD CHAIN CASE ON BOTH SIDES
2 PISTON
3 ROD CAP
4 LOCATER LUGS INDICATE PISTON FRONT TOWARDS ENGINE FRONT
5 BEARING CAP NOTCHES POINT TOWARD EACH OTHER ON PAIRED RODS
6 ROD CAPS

GC1069500614000X

Fig. 13 Piston installation

SERPENTINE DRIVE BELT

BELT, REPLACE

1. Release belt tension, then remove belt from power steering and alternator pulleys.
2. Twist belt to get between tensioner and front cover, then between power steering pulley and engine mount bracket.
3. Raise and support vehicle.
4. Turn wheel to extreme right and remove righthand splash shield.
5. Remove belt from crankshaft and air conditioning compressor pulleys. Twist belt to get between idler pulley and engine mount bracket.
6. Lower vehicle.
7. Twisting new belt to get past front cover, install belt around power steering pump pulley, **Fig. 16.** Allow belt to hang free.
8. Twist belt to get between tensioner and front cover, wrap belt around alternator.
9. Remove belt from power steering pulley and set aside.
10. Raise and support vehicle.
11. Twist belt to get between tensioner and front cover, wrap belt around crankshaft and air conditioning compressor pulleys.
12. Install righthand side splash shield and lower vehicle.
13. Position belt around power steering pulley and release tensioner.

COOLING SYSTEM BLEED

This engine does not require a cooling system bleed procedure. However, the cooling system on aluminum engines a special coolant solution along with GM coolant supplement (sealant) part No.

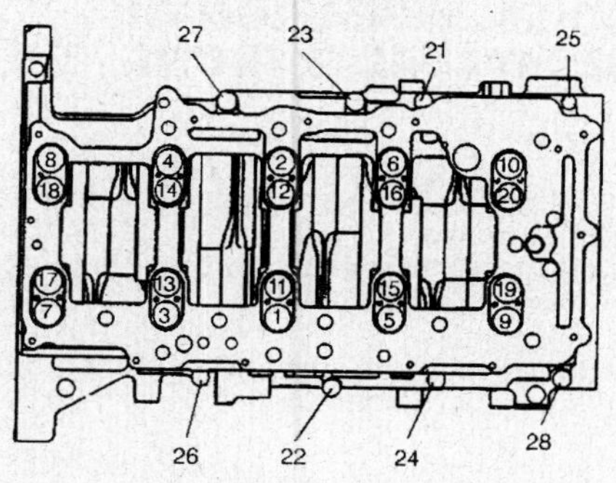

Fig. 14 Main bearing bolt tightening sequence

3634621, or equivalent, must be used. **Failure to add the sealant or the suitable coolant solution could result in major engine damage.** When refilling cooling system add three pellets of engine coolant supplement (sealant) to lower radiator hose.

THERMOSTAT

REPLACE

1. Drain cooling system.
2. Remove air intake duct.
3. Disconnect thermostat housing radiator hose.
4. Remove mounting bolts and thermostat housing, **Fig. 17.**
5. Remove thermostat.
6. Reverse procedure install. Refer to "Cooling System Bleed."

WATER PUMP

REPLACE

1. Drain engine coolant.
2. Remove air intake duct.
3. Remove coolant pump drive belt cover and belt.
4. Remove lower radiator and bypass hoses, then the water pump cover.
5. Remove water pump, seal and gasket by turning coolant remover/installer tool No. J-38816, or equivalent, clockwise, **Fig. 18.**
6. Reverse procedure to install. Refer to "Cooling System Bleed."

RADIATOR

REPLACE

1. Raise and support vehicle.
2. Remove lower air dam and drain cooling system into suitable container.
3. Install lower air dam and lower vehicle.
4. Remove upper tie bar.
5. Disconnect cooling fan electrical connectors.
6. Remove left and righthand cooling fans.
7. Disconnect coolant level sensor electrical connector.
8. Disconnect coolant recovery hose from radiator filler neck.
9. Remove upper and lower radiator hoses from radiator.

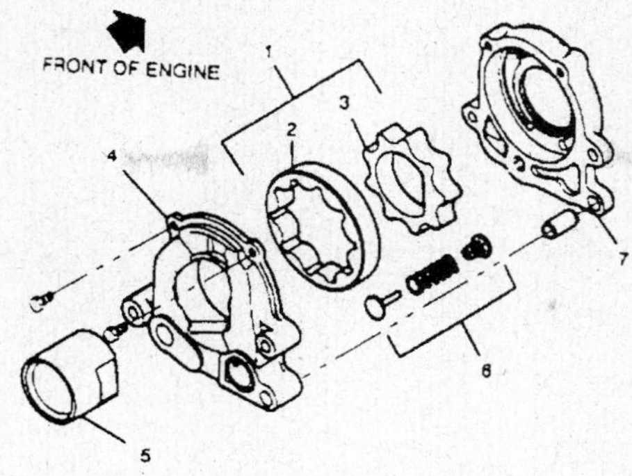

Fig. 15 Exploded view of oil pump

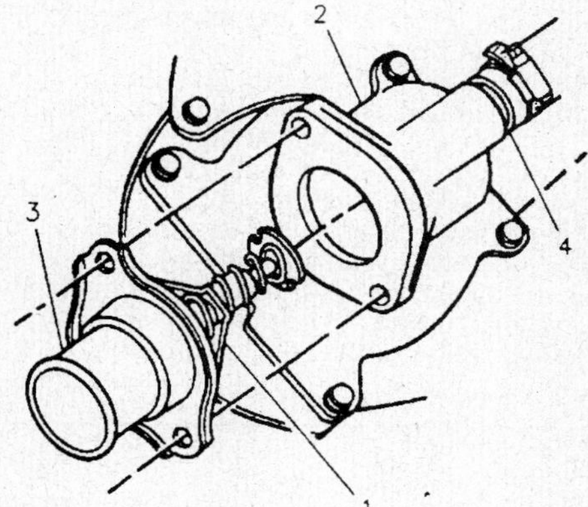

Fig. 17 Thermostat replacement

10. Remove condenser to radiator mounting bolts.
11. Remove transaxle cooler lines from radiator.
12. Remove radiator from vehicle.
13. Reverse procedure to install. Refer to "Cooling System Bleed."

FUEL PUMP

REPLACE

1998–99

Refer to "Fuel Pump, Replace" in "3800 Engine" section for fuel pump replacement procedure.

2001–02

Refer to "Fuel Pump, Replace" in "3.5L Engine" section for fuel pump replacement procedure.

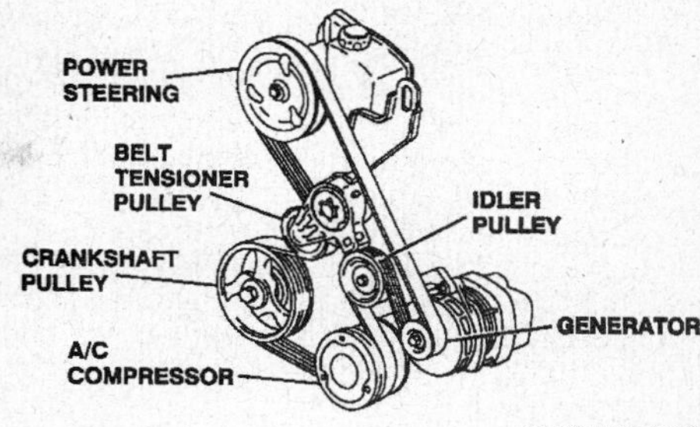

Fig. 16 Serpentine drive belt routing

FUEL FILTER

REPLACE

1998–99

Refer to "Fuel Filter, Replace" in "3800 Engine" section for fuel filter replacement procedure.

2001–02

Refer to "Fuel Filter, Replace" in "3.5L Engine" section for fuel filter replacement procedure.

TECHNICAL SERVICE BULLETINS

ENGINE RUNS HOT, OVERHEATS OR LOSSES COOLANT

1999–2000

On some of these models the engine may run hot, overheat or lose coolant.

This condition may be caused by imperfections in the radiator filler neck sealing surface.

To correct this condition, proceed as follows:

1. **Do not replace radiator.**
2. Polish filler neck sealing surface with 400 grit wet/dry sandpaper backed using suitable flat piece of wood and using circular motion.
3. Replace radiator cap.

COLD ENGINE KNOCK OR TICK

2001–02

On some of these models there may be a tick/knock noise. This may be an upper engine ticking or a deep low knock similar to main bearing knock. These noises are more often heard during engine start up after a long, cold soak. The noise may or may not diminish as engine reaches normal operating temperature. The knock may appear to be loudest at exhaust manifolds. These noises do not change when disconnecting spark plugs or disabling individual fuel injectors.

This condition may be caused by combustion chamber carbon deposits.

To correct this condition, proceed as follows:

1. Start engine and bring coolant temperature to more than 200°F on instrument panel gauge (220°F on scan tool).
2. **Do not raise engine above normal idle speed.**
3. Disconnect PCV hose from valve and slowly spray Top Engine Cleaner, part No. 1052626, or equivalent, into hose.
4. Raise engine speed to approximately 2000 RPM until white smoke comes from exhaust pipe.
5. Shut engine off.
6. Allow vehicle to set at least 20 minutes, preferably overnight.
7. Start engine and remove remaining top cleaner by increasing engine speed to 2000 RPM until white smoke diminishes.

PASSENGER COMPARTMENT POPPING NOISE

1998-99

On some of these models there may be a popping noise after driving at highway speeds and coming to a stop.

This condition may be caused by catalytic converter heat shield expanding.

To correct this condition, proceed as follows:

1. Raise and support vehicle.
2. Remove mounting screws and oxygen sensor wiring rear shield, as required.
3. Remove catalytic converter to exhaust downpipe nuts.

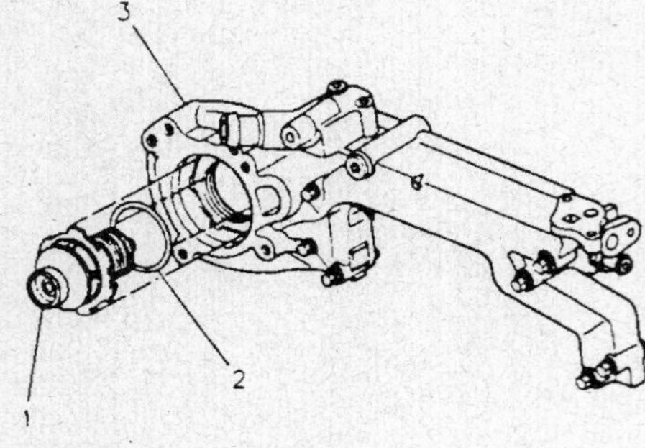

Fig. 18 Coolant pump replacement

4. Separate catalytic converter from exhaust downpipe.
5. Remove and discard gasket/seal.
6. Drill out rivet above separating flange at center of converter head shield using 3/16-inch or larger drill bit.
7. Install new gasket/seal.
8. **Torque** catalytic converter to exhaust downpipe nuts to 18 ft. lbs.
9. Install oxygen sensor wiring rear shield and screws.
10. Lower vehicle.

NOISE, VIBRATION OR GROWL FROM FRONT

1998

On some of these models there may be noise, vibration or growl from the front of the vehicle on righthand turns or hard acceleration.

This condition may be caused by the rear transaxle mount grounding out because of a bound or twisted condition within the mount.

To correct this condition, proceed as follows:

1. Raise and support vehicle.
2. Support transaxle using suitable screwjack.
3. Loosen rear transaxle mounting nuts. **Do not remove nuts.**
4. Unload mount by lowering transaxle using screwjack.
5. Eliminate binding or twisting by adjusting mount.
6. Raise transaxle using screwjack until bracket contacts mount.
7. Adjust mount alignment, as required. **Studs will not always be centered in bracket because of cross-car-build variations.**
8. Fully load mount by raising transaxle using screwjack.
9. **Torque** mounting nuts to 33 ft. lbs.
10. Remove screwjack and ensure mount is properly aligned.

TIGHTENING SPECIFICATIONS

Year	Component	Torque/Ft. lbs.
1998–99 & 2001–02	Belt Idler Pulley	37
	Belt Tensioner	37
	Camshaft Bearing Cap	108⑦
	Camshaft Drive Chain Tensioner	18
	Camshaft Sprocket	89
	Connecting Rod Bearing Cap	⑥
	Crankshaft Damper	37②
	Cylinder Head	④
	Exhaust Manifold To Cylinder Head	18
	Flywheel To Converter	③
	Front Cover	84⑦
	Intake Manifold	84⑦
	Intermediate Sprocket	44
	Main Bearing Cap	15①
	Oil Filter Adapter	12
	Oil Manifold	84⑦
	Oil Pan	84⑦
	Oil Pump	7⑤
	Oxygen Sensor	30
	Primary Chain Tensioner	18
	Upper Crankcase To Lower Crankcase	22
	Valve Cover	84⑦

①— Refer to "Main & Rod Bearings" for tightening sequence.
②— Tighten an additional 150°.
③— Tighten an additional 50°.
④— Refer to "Cylinder Head, Replace" for tightening specifications and sequence.
⑤— Tighten an additional 35°.
⑥— Torque 22 ft. lbs., then back to zero, then 18 ft. lbs. plus an additional 110°.
⑦— Inch lbs.

Rear Suspension

NOTE: On Air Bag Equipped Models, Refer To "Air Bag System Precautions" Located In The Front Of This Manual For System Disarming & Arming Procedures.

NOTE: Refer To "Computer Relearn Procedures" Located In The Front Of This Manual When Battery Power To The Computer Has Been Interrupted.

INDEX

DESCRIPTION

These models utilize an independent rear suspension that is secured to the vehicle body at four points, **Fig. 1.** Control arms, a stabilizer bar and adjustment links are connected to the rear suspension support assembly to provide side to side stability and to allow for rear toe adjustment.

The Electronic Level Control (ELC) system employs rear air adjustable shocks which are anchored at the control arms and allow the system to maintain proper vehicle ride height under various load conditions. The shocks are not manually adjustable and must be replaced if they lose resistance or begin leaking fluid.

The rear wheel bearings have been integrated into the hubs to eliminate the necessity of adjustments and periodic maintenance. This integral hub and bearing also incorporates a wheel speed sensor ring for anti-lock brake operation.

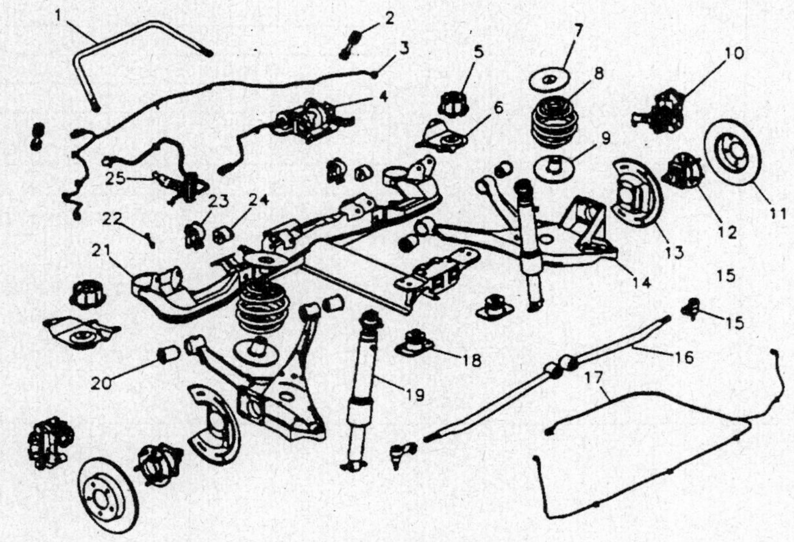

Fig. 1 Exploded view of rear suspension

HUB & BEARING

REPLACE

1. Raise and support vehicle.
2. Remove wheel and disc brake caliper. **It is not required to disconnect hydraulic line from caliper. Support caliper from frame to prevent hydraulic line damage.**
3. Remove brake rotor and ABS sensor wire connector.
4. Remove bolts, then lift hub and bearing.
5. Life brake shield from control arm, **Fig. 2.**
6. Reverse procedure to install. Tighten bolts and wheel lug nuts to specifications.

WHEEL BEARING

ADJUST

Because the hub and bearing are integral parts, the bearing is not adjustable. If the bearing requires service, the entire hub assembly must be replaced.

REAR SUSPENSION

REPLACE

1. Raise and support vehicle. Remove rear wheels and disconnect exhaust system components as required to provide clearance.
2. Remove rear springs as outlined under "Coil Spring, Replace."
3. Remove brake calipers from control arms. **It is not required to disconnect hydraulic line at caliper; support caliper from frame to prevent hydraulic line damage.**
4. Disconnect parking brake cables at calipers and at rear suspension support.
5. Disconnect rear suspension support electrical connectors from electrical harness, then the Electronic Level Control (ELC) electrical connector and vent hose.
6. Disconnect ELC air tube from ELC compressor and support rear suspension using suitable jack, **Fig. 3.**
7. Remove support bracket to body bolts from each side of vehicle.
8. Remove front and rear anchor bolts and lower rear suspension support.

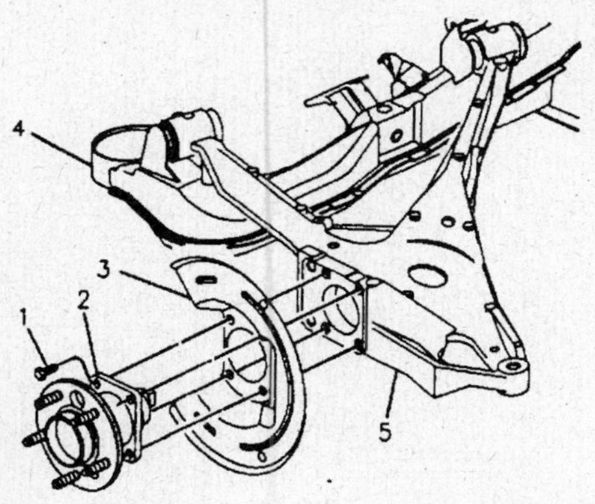

1 BOLT
2 HUB & BEARING
3 BRAKE SHIELD
4 REAR SUSPENSION SUPPORT ASSEMBLY
5 CONTROL ARM

GC2039500108000X

Fig. 2 Hub & bearing replacement

9. Reverse procedure to install. Tighten mounting bolts and nuts to specifications.

SHOCK ABSORBER

REPLACE

1. Raise and support vehicle.
2. Remove wheel and support control arm using suitable jack stand.
3. Disconnect Electronic Level Control (ELC) air tube from shock absorber and remove shock to control arm bolts, **Fig. 4.**
4. Remove luggage compartment trim as required to gain access to shock absorber upper mounting nuts and shock upper cover.
5. Remove upper mounting nuts, reinforcement and shock absorber.
6. Reverse procedure to install. Tighten mounting bolts and nuts to specifications.

COIL SPRING

REPLACE

1. Raise and support vehicle so control arm hangs freely, then remove wheel.
2. Support control arm using suitable jack and disconnect Electronic Level Control (ELC) air tube from shock absorber.
3. Disconnect shock absorber at control arm, then remove adjustment link to knuckle cotter pin and slotted nut,
4. Separate adjustment link from knuckle using universal steering linkage puller tool No. J-24319-B, or equivalent, and slowly lower control arm until it bottoms on rear suspension support.
5. Pry under lower coil spring insulator and remove spring with insulator, **Fig. 5;** then, if required, remove jounce bumper by pulling downward.

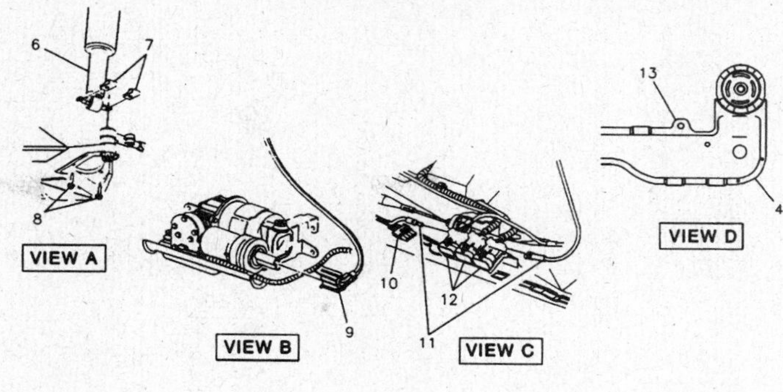

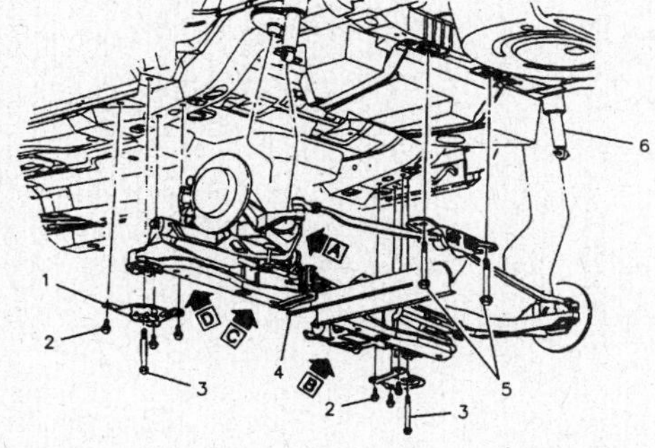

1 SUPPORT BRACKET
2 BOLT 86 N•m (63 LB. FT.)
3 BOLT 191 N•m (141 LB. FT.)
4 REAR SUSPENSION SUPPORT ASSEMBLY
5 BOLT 165 N•m (122 LB. FT.)
6 SHOCK
7 U-NUT
8 BOLT 24 N•m (18 LB. FT.)
9 ELC AIR LINE
10 ELC COMPRESSOR ELECTRICAL CONNECTOR
11 ELC COMPRESSOR VENT TUBE
12 ELECTRICAL CONNECTORS, (ELC HEIGHT SENSOR, FUEL PUMP, ABS HARNESS)
13 GAUGE HOLE

GC2039500109000X

Fig. 3 Rear suspension replacement

6. Reverse procedure to install. Tighten mounting bolts and nuts to specifications.

CONTROL ARM

REPLACE

1. Remove rear suspension support as outlined under "Rear Suspension, Replace."
2. If lefthand control arm is being replaced, remove Electronic Level Control (ELC) height sensor link.
3. Remove stabilizer link bolt and nut and disconnect ABS electrical connector.
4. Remove hub and bearing as outlined under "Hub & Bearing, Replace."
5. Remove control arm to rear suspension support mounting bolt and nut.
6. Reverse procedure to install, noting the following:
   a. Tighten control arm nuts with vehicle weight resting on rear wheels.
   b. Tighten mounting bolts and nuts to specifications.

CONTROL ARM BUSHING

REPLACE

REMOVAL

1. Remove control arm as outlined under "Control Arm, Replace," and assemble bushing replacement tools, **Fig. 6.**
2. Tighten nut until bushing is driven from control arm and remove bushing replacement tools.

INSTALLATION

1. Start new bushing into control arm with flat on bushing positioned vertically and rearward.
2. Assemble bushing tools, **Fig. 6,** and tighten bolt until bushing is seated fully in control arm.
3. Remove bushing tools and install control arm as outlined under "Control Arm, Replace."

STABILIZER SHAFT

REPLACE

1. Raise and support vehicle. Remove wheels and disconnect Electronic Level Control (ELC) height sensor link at control arm.
2. Remove bolts and position ELC height sensor aside.
3. Remove stabilizer shaft link bolt, nut, retainer and insulators from control arm, **Fig. 7.**
4. Remove clamp bolt and bend open end of clamp upward and remove stabilizer shaft and insulators.
5. Reverse procedure to install, noting the following:

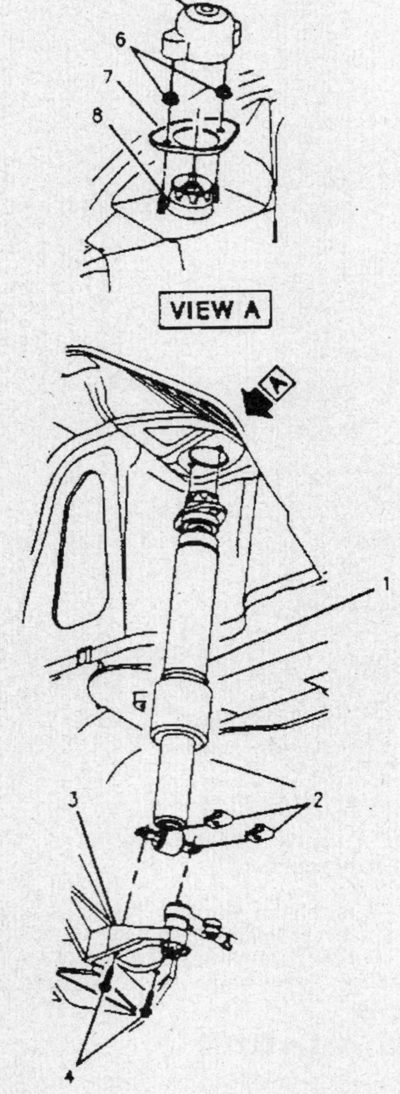

1 SHOCK
2 U-NUTS
3 CONTROL ARM
4 BOLTS 24 N•m (18 LB. FT.)
5 COVER
6 NUTS 20 N•m (15 LB. FT.)
7 REINFORCEMENT
8 MOUNT, UPPER

GC2039500110000X

Fig. 4 Shock absorber replacement

a. Ensure stabilizer shaft is centered before tightening clamp bolt.
b. Tighten mounting bolts and nuts to specifications.

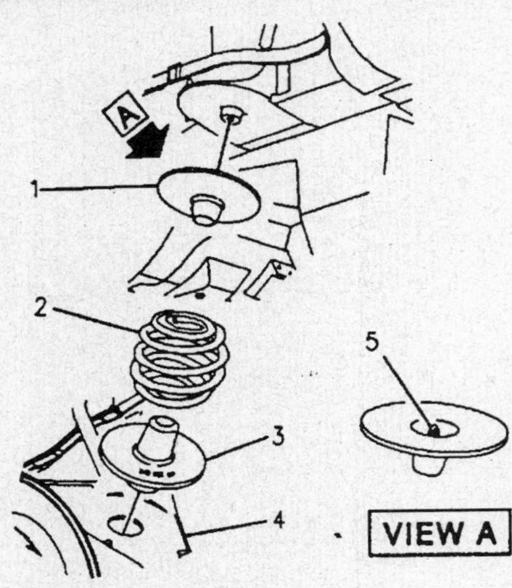

1 JOUNCE BUMPER
2 SPRING
3 LOWER SPRING INSULATOR
4 CONTROL ARM
5 RETAINER

GC2039500111000X

Fig. 5 Coil spring replacement

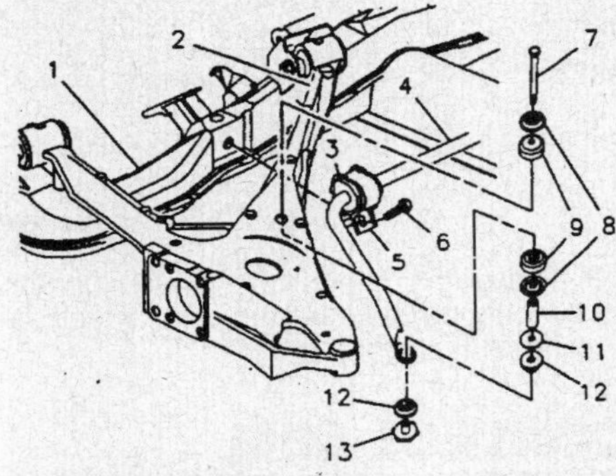

1 REAR SUSPENSION SUPPORT ASSEMBLY
2 CONTROL ARM
3 INSULATOR, STABILIZER SHAFT
4 SHAFT, STABILIZER
5 CLAMP, STABILIZER SHAFT
6 BOLT, 33 N•m (24 LB. IN.)
7 BOLT, 13 N•m (115 LB. IN.)
8 RETAINER, UPPER
9 INSULATOR, UPPER
10 SLEEVE
11 RETAINER, LOWER
12 INSULATOR, LOWER
13 NUT

GC2039500113000X

Fig. 7 Stabilizer shaft replacement

ADJUSTMENT LINK

REPLACE

INNER

1. Raise and support vehicle.

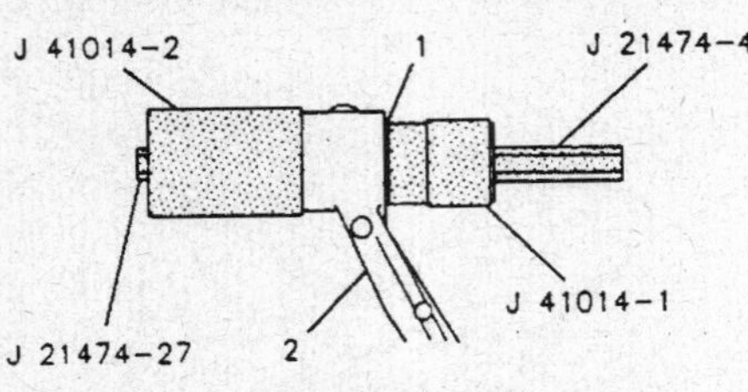

REMOVAL

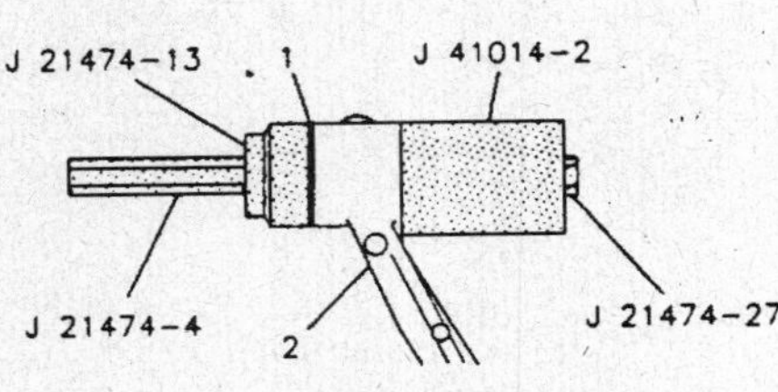

INSTALLATION

1 BUSHING
2 CONTROL ARM

GC2039500112000X

Fig. 6 Control arm bushing replacement tool installation

2. Remove wheel and loosen pinch bolt.
3. Support exhaust and rear suspension support using suitable wood block at least seven inches long.
4. Remove exhaust hangers and rear suspension support mounting bolts.
5. Lower support and exhaust together.
6. Remove cam bolt, nut and adjustment link.
7. Remove inner link from outer link. Record number of turns for installation reference.
8. Reverse procedure to install. Inspect and adjust rear toe as outlined under "Wheel Alignment."

OUTER

1. Raise and support vehicle. Remove wheel.
2. Loosen pinch bolt.
3. Remove cotter pin and clotted hex nut.
4. Separate adjustment link from knuckle using universal steering linkage puller tool No. J-24319-B, or equivalent. **Do not drive wedge between joint and attached part.**
5. Remove outer from inner link. Record number of turns for assembly.
6. Reverse procedure to install. Inspect and adjust rear toe as outlined under "Wheel Alignment."

TIGHTENING SPECIFICATIONS

Year	Component	Torque/Ft. Lbs.
1998–99 & 2001–02	Adjustment Link Pinch Bolt	36
	Adjustment Link To Control Arm	84–96①②
	Adjustment Link To Rear Suspension Support	55
	Control Arm	78
	ELC Height Sensor	60①
	Hub & Bearing	52
	Rear Body	38
	Rear Suspension Support Bracket	63
	Rear Suspension Support To Body Rear	141
	Shock Absorber To Control Arm	18
	Shock Tower	15
	Stabilizer Link	10
	Stabilizer Shaft Clamp	24
	Stabilizer Shaft Link	108–120①
	Wheel Lug Nuts	100

① — Inch lbs.
② — Plus an additional 1/2 turn.

Front Suspension & Steering

NOTE: On Air Bag Equipped Models, Refer To "Air Bag System Precautions" Located In The Front Of This Manual For System Disarming & Arming Procedures.

NOTE: Refer To "Computer Relearn Procedures" Located In The Front Of This Manual When Battery Power To The Computer Has Been Interrupted.

NOTE: Prior To Performing Any Service Operations Listed In This Section, Consult The "Technical Service Bulletins" Section For Related Information.

INDEX

HUB & BEARING

REPLACE

1. Raise and support vehicle, then remove tire and wheel assembly.
2. Insert suitable drift punch or screwdriver into caliper and rotor to prevent rotor from turning.
3. Remove drive axle nut, **Fig. 1.**
4. Remove caliper to steering knuckle bolts and support caliper using mechanics wire.
5. Remove brake rotor.
6. Disconnect ABS front wheel speed sensor connector and unclip from dust shield.
7. Remove hub and bearing mounting bolts and dust shield.
8. Place transmission in P position.
9. Separate hub and bearing from axle using front hub spindle remover tool No. J-28733-B, or equivalent.
10. Reverse procedure to install. Apply thin layer of grease to knuckle bore.

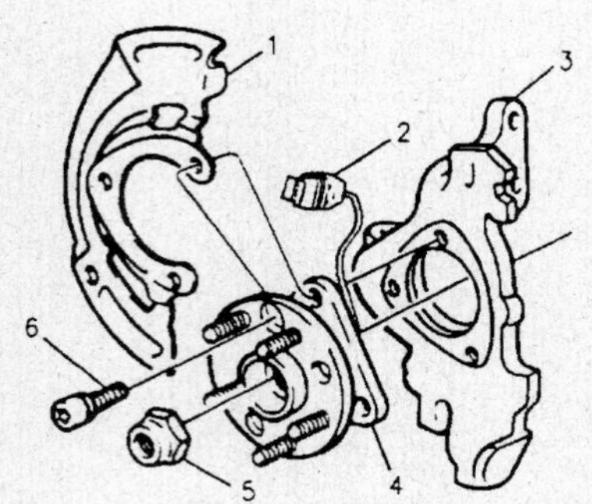

Fig. 1 Hub & bearing replacement

BALL JOINT INSPECTION

1. Raise front of vehicle.
2. Allow suspension to hang free.
3. Grasp tire at top and bottom and move it in and out.
4. Replace ball joint if any horizontal movement in knuckle relative to control arm is detected.
5. Replace ball joint if ball stud is disconnected from knuckle and looseness is detected or ball stud twists in its socket while using hand pressure.
6. Check for ball stud tightness in knuckle boss by shaking wheel and feeling for movement in stud end or nut. If any movement is detected, replace worn or damaged ball joints and knuckles.

BALL JOINT

REPLACE

The ball joint is part of the lower control arm and cannot be serviced separately. Refer to "Lower Control Arm, Replace" for replacement procedure.

STRUT

REPLACE

Care should be taken to avoid chipping or cracking the spring coating. Failure to observe may result in spring breakage.

1. Remove strut to body mounting bolts.
2. Raise and support vehicle with control arms hanging free.
3. Remove tire and wheel assembly.
4. Disconnect ABS front wheel speed sensor connector.
5. Remove speed sensor bracket from strut.
6. Remove brake line bracket from left-hand strut.
7. Chisel position mark across strut to knuckle interface, **Fig. 2.**
8. Scribe strut flange on inboard side along curve of knuckle, **Fig. 2.**
9. Scribe knuckle along lower outboard strut radius, **Fig. 2.**
10. Remove strut-to-knuckle bolts. **Knuckle must be retained after strut-to-knuckle bolts have been removed. Failure to observe this may cause ball joint and/or drive axle damage.**
11. Remove strut.
12. Reverse procedure to install. Adjust wheel alignment as outlined in "Wheel Alignment" section.

STRUT SERVICE

1. Place strut in strut compressor tool No. J-34013-B, or equivalent.
2. Compress spring slightly and remove strut shaft nut while holding strut shaft using suitable open-end wrench.
3. Loosen compressor screw while guiding strut shaft out of assembly.
4. Disassemble strut assembly as required, **Fig. 3.**
5. Reverse procedure to assemble.

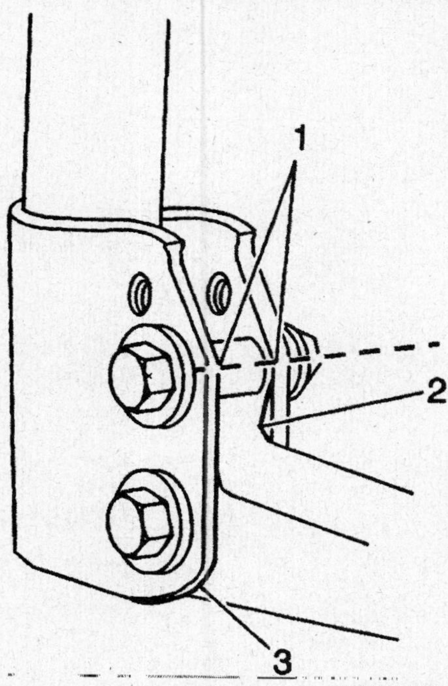

GC2029900274000X

Fig. 2 Strut to knuckle position

CONTROL ARM

REPLACE

1. Raise and support vehicle with control arms hanging free.
2. Remove wheel and tire assembly.
3. Remove stabilizer link to control arm bolt.
4. Remove cotter pin and loosen nut from ball stud.
5. Separate ball joint from knuckle using ball joint separator tool No. J-43828, or equivalent.
6. Remove mounting bolts and control arm.
7. Reverse procedure to install.

STEERING KNUCKLE

REPLACE

1. Raise and support vehicle.
2. Remove wheel and tire assembly.
3. Remove wheel bearing and hub as outlined under "Hub & Wheel Bearing, Replace."
4. Mark relationship of strut to knuckle as outlined under "Strut, Replace."
5. Separate ball joint from steering knuckle as outlined under "Lower Control Arm, Replace."
6. Remove strut to knuckle bolts and steering knuckle.
7. Reverse procedure to install. Adjust wheel alignment as outlined in "Wheel Alignment" section.

STABILIZER BAR

REPLACE

1. Raise and support vehicle with control arms hanging free.
2. Remove front wheels and tires.
3. Remove left and righthand stabilizer link bolts.
4. Remove left and righthand stabilizer bar brackets.
5. Separate lefthand tie rod end from knuckle using universal steering linkage puller tool No. J-24319-B, or equivalent.
6. Remove exhaust pipe from manifold and immediate exhaust hangers and lower exhaust pipe.
7. Turn lefthand strut completely to right and slide stabilizer shaft outboard over lefthand steering knuckle until righthand end comes free.
8. Remove stabilizer shaft out of center of vehicle.
9. Reverse procedures to install.

TIE ROD

REPLACE

INNER

1. Remove steering gear as outlined under "Power Steering Gear, Replace."
2. Remove outer tie rod.
3. Remove inner tie rod jam nut and end clamp.
4. Remove boot clamp using side cutters and discard.
5. Mark breather tube location on steering gear for assembly.
6. Remove rack and pinion boot and breather tube.
7. Loosen inner tie rod shock dampener and slide back on rack.
8. Hold rack in suitable vice.
9. Turn inner tie rod housing counterclockwise using one wrench on rack assembly flats and another on inner tire rod housing flats, then remove it.
10. Reverse procedure to install. Gap between rack and housing stakes should be 0.01 inch.

OUTER

1. Remove cotter pin and hex slotted nut.
2. Loosen jam nut.
3. Remove outer tie rod from steering knuckle using universal steering linkage puller tool No. N-24319-01, or equivalent.
4. Remove outer from inner tie rod.
5. Reverse procedure to install.

POWER STEERING GEAR

REPLACE

1. Raise and support vehicle. Remove front tires and wheels.
2. Disconnect exhaust system from exhaust manifold.
3. Remove fasteners and fold back wheelhouse splash shield enough to allow removal of steering gear.
4. Disconnect tie rod ends from steering knuckles using puller tool No. J-24319-B, or equivalent.
5. Disconnect intermediate shaft lower connection, noting the following:
   a. Vehicle wheels must be straight ahead and steering column in lock position before disconnecting steering column or intermediate shaft from steering gear.
   b. **Failure to disconnect intermediate shaft from rack and pinion stub shaft can result in damage to steering gear and/or intermediate shaft which can cause loss of steering control.**
6. Unsnap and remove power steering heat shield.
7. Disconnect Magnasteer electrical connector.
8. Disconnect steering gear outlet and inlet hoses.
9. Remove steering gear mounting bolts, **Fig. 4.**
10. **On 1998 models,** support rear of frame, remove rear bolts and lower rear of frame to allow steering gear removal. **Do not lower rear of frame too far or engine components may be damaged by cowl,**
11. Remove steering gear through righthand wheel opening.
12. **On 1999 and 2001–02 models,** remove steering gear through lefthand wheel opening.
13. **On all models,** reverse procedure to install. Tighten bolts to specification.

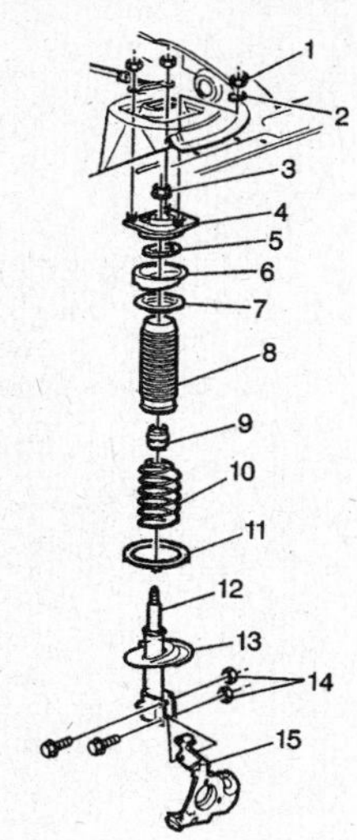

(1) Nut (3)
(2) Washer
(3) Torque Prevailing Nut
(4) Strut Mount
(5) Bearing
(6) Upper Spring Seat
(7) Upper Insulator
(8) Strut Shield
(9) Strut Bumper
(10) Spring
(11) Lower Insulator
(12) Strut
(13) Lower Spring Seat
(14) Torque Prevailing Nut (2)
(15) Steering Knuckle

GC2029900275000X

Fig. 3 Exploded view of strut

POWER STEERING PUMP

REPLACE

AURORA

1. Remove drive belt as outlined under "Serpentine Drive Belt" in "3.5L and 4.0 Engine" section.
2. Remove power steering gear outlet and inlet hoses from pump.
3. Remove mounting bolts.

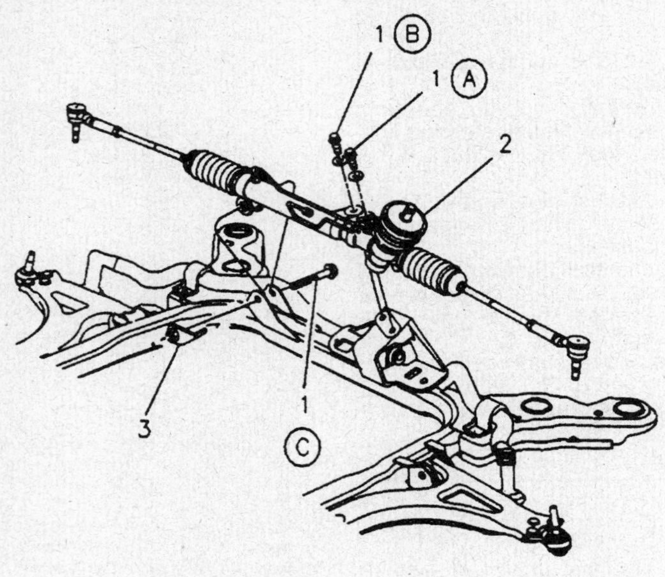

1 BOLT, 65 N•m (48 LB. FT.)
TIGHTEN BOLTS IN
SEQUENCE A THRU C
2 STEERING GEAR
3 TAB NUT

GC2029800224000X

Fig. 4 Steering gear replacement

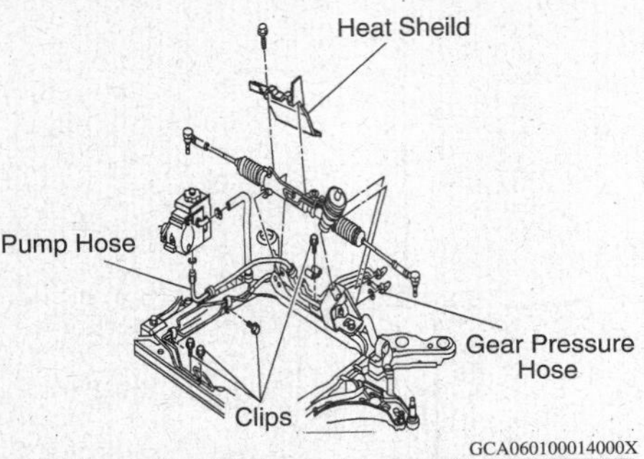

Fig. 5 Power steering gear hose replacement. 1998 Riviera

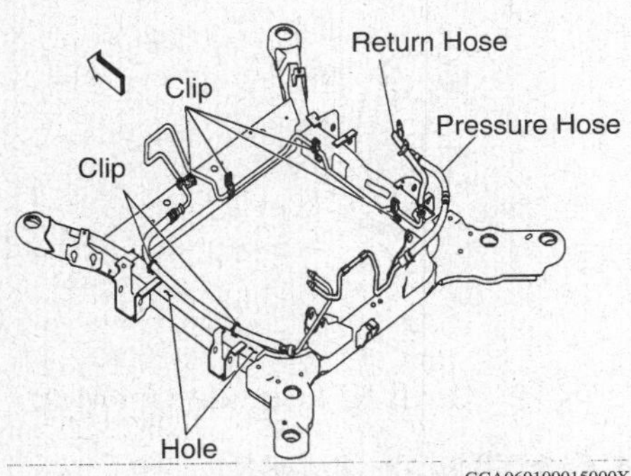

Fig. 6 Power steering gear hose replacements. 1999 Riviera

4. Remove pump and bracket from engine.
5. Reverse procedures to install.

RIVIERA

1. Remove drive belt as outlined under "Serpentine Drive Belt" in "3800 Engine" section.
2. Remove power steering gear outlet and inlet hoses from pump.
3. Remove mounting bolts.
4. Raise and support vehicle.
5. Remove pump from under engine and transfer pulley as required.
6. Reverse procedure to install.

TECHNICAL SERVICE BULLETINS

VIBRATION OR SHUDDER DURING PARKING

1998–99 Riviera

On some of these models there may be a vibration, shudder or moan when steering during parking on dry pavement.

This condition may be caused by the power steering gear hoses.

To correct this condition, proceed as follows:

1. Raise and support vehicle.
2. Drain power steering fluid into suitable container.
3. **On 1999 models,** proceed as follows:
   a. Remove lefthand front tire and wheel assembly.
   b. Remove lefthand lower splash shield.
   c. Remove lower radiator air deflector.
   d. Remove engine splash shield, as required.
4. **On all models,** remove power steering gear heat shield, **Fig. 5.**
5. Disconnect pressure hose from power steering pump.
6. **On 1999 models,** remove return hose from power steering pump.
7. **On all models,** remove retaining clips' mounting bolts/screws.
8. Disconnect pressure hose from power steering gear.
9. **On 1999 models,** disconnect return hose from power steering gear.
10. **On all models,** remove hoses.
11. **On 1999 models,** proceed as follows:
    a. Drill two ¼-inch holes into top surface of lefthand engine frame crossmember approximately 1½ inches rearward from front and rear control arm brackets horizontal flange edge, **Fig. 6.**
    b. Remove two rosebud clips from new hose and install into drilled holes.
    c. Install new lefthand routed power steering return/outlet hose.
    d. From forward side of front engine mount, route pump end to righthand side along righthand engine frame crossmember and up to steering pump.
    e. Route steering gear end to lefthand side of vehicle along lefthand engine frame crossmember and up to steering gear.
12. **On all models,** install pressure hose.
13. Connect hose(s) to pump and gear.
14. **Torque** hoses to 20 ft. lbs.
15. Install retaining clips and **torque** bolts/screws to 53 inch lbs.
16. Install power steering gear heat shield.
17. **On 1999 models,** proceed as follows:
    a. Install engine splash shield, as required.
    b. Install lower radiator air deflector.
    c. Install lefthand lower splash shield.
    d. Install lefthand front tire and wheel assembly.
18. Lower vehicle.
19. Fill and bleed power steering system.

SQUEAK, SQUAWK OR CREAK FROM FRONT STRUT

1999

On some of these models there may be squeak, squawk or creak from the front suspension as the vehicle travels over bumps or road swells.

This condition may be caused by the lower spring isolator/insulator curling or rolling up and contacting lower coil/spring.

To correct this condition, proceed as follows:

1. Raise and support vehicle by frame. Allow control arms to hang free.
2. Remove tire and wheel assembly.
3. **On models built before mid-January 1999 with thick 0.35–0.47 inch lower**

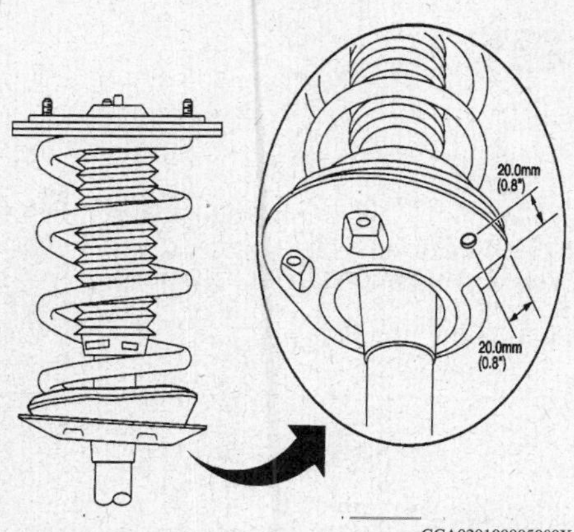

Fig. 7 Lower spring isolator/ insulator

spring isolator/insulator, proceed as follows:

a. Remove front strut .
b. Replace thick isolator/insulator with thin 0.47 inch tapering outward to 0.12 inch isolator/insulator (part No. 22181835).
c. Install front strut.
d. **Do not install tire and wheel assembly now.**

4. **On all models,** mark location for ⅜-inch hole on bottom side of corner of lower spring seat on front strut approximately ¾ of distance from lower end coil, **Fig. 7.**
5. Center punch mark.
6. Hold isolator/insulator to lower spring seat using suitable clamping tool on each side.
7. Drill ⅜-inch pilot hole through lower spring seat and isolator/insulator.
8. Remove clamping tools.
9. Deburr and dress hole edges. Clean area.
10. Apply black touch-up paint to bare metal areas, as required.
11. Install retainer (part No. 22189414) through drilled hole. Ensure point and at least two ribs push through spring seal hole.
12. Install tire and wheel assembly.

CLUNK, RATTLE FROM FRONT OF VEHICLE

1998–99

On some of these models there may be a clunk, rattle or metal-to-metal noise from the left or righthand front of the vehicle. This noise is more noticeable in cold weather.

This condition may be caused by the stabilizer bar rubber insulator walking out of engine frame and stabilizer mounting bracket/clamp during suspension movements.

To correct this condition, proceed as follows:

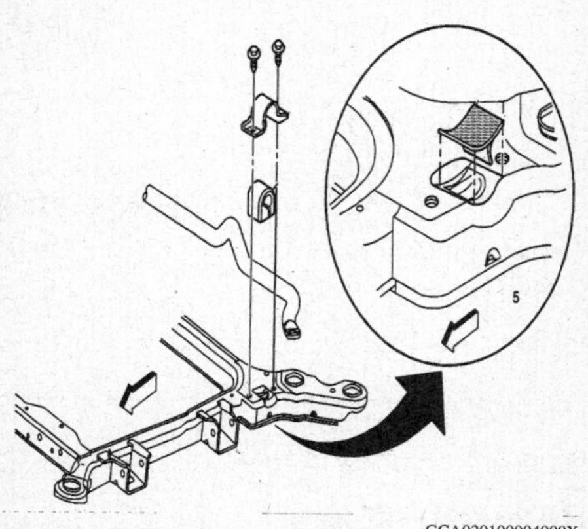

Fig. 8 Stabilizer shaft insulator

1. Raise and support vehicle.
2. Remove stabilizer shaft bolts, bracket/clamp and insulator.
3. Clean engine frame surface.
4. Install 2X1.5-inch strip of anti-slip/friction material such as 3M Safety-Walk General Purpose Treat Tape, or equivalent, to frame rail with adhesive side forward frame and two-inch side fore/aft, **Fig. 8.**
5. Install insulator, clamp and bolts.

TIGHTENING SPECIFICATIONS

Year	Component	Torque Ft. Lbs.
1998–99 & 2001–02	Ball Joint	50
	Brake Caliper Bracket To Knuckle	136
	Brake Line & Speed Sensor Bracket	13
	Caliper	38
	Control Arm, Bolt	117
	Control Arm, Nut	93
	Drive Axle	118
	Frame To Underbody	141
	Hub & Bearing	70
	Hub Nut	118
	Intermediate Steering Shaft Pinch Bolt	35
	Power Steering Gear Hose Connections	20
	Power Steering Gear	48
	Power Steering Pump	20
	Stabilizer Bracket	28
	Stabilizer Shaft Link	13
	Strut To Body	35
	Strut To Knuckle	136
	Tie Rod End To Knuckle	35–52①
	Wheel Lug Nuts	100

① — Do not counter-rotate nut for cotter pin insertion.

Wheel Alignment

INDEX

PRELIMINARY INSPECTION

Inspect tires for proper inflation.

Inspect tie rods for lateral end motion relative to the steering knuckle and tie rod end seals for any visible signs of damage. Replace tie rod end if either of these conditions exist.

Inspect runout of wheels and tires.

Inspect trim height. If out of specifications, correct before alignment. Inspect shocks, rack and pinion and control arms for looseness and proper operation. Replace any damaged steering/suspension components.

If any excess weight is normally carried in the trunk of vehicle, alignment is recommended with load in place.

Ensure vehicle is level.

FRONT WHEEL ALIGNMENT

CASTER

1. Remove top strut nuts and washers.
2. Raise and support front of vehicle to separate strut from inner wheel housing.
3. Drill two 12⁄32 inch holes at front and rear of oval strut mounting hole on left and righthand strut towers, **Fig. 1,** and file excess metal to create slotted holes. **Paint exposed metal with rust resistant paint or primer.**
4. Lower front of vehicle.
5. Install strut mounting nuts, but do not tighten at this time.
6. Adjust caster by moving top of strut towards front or rear. A 0.040 inch position change at tower will change caster approximately .1°.
7. When caster is within specifications, **torque** strut mounting nuts to 35 ft. lbs.

CAMBER

1. Loosen both strut to steering knuckle nuts and install camber adjusting tool No. J-39601, J-29862 or equivalents, and set camber to specifications, **Fig. 2.**
2. **Torque** strut to steering knuckle bolts to 136 ft. lbs.

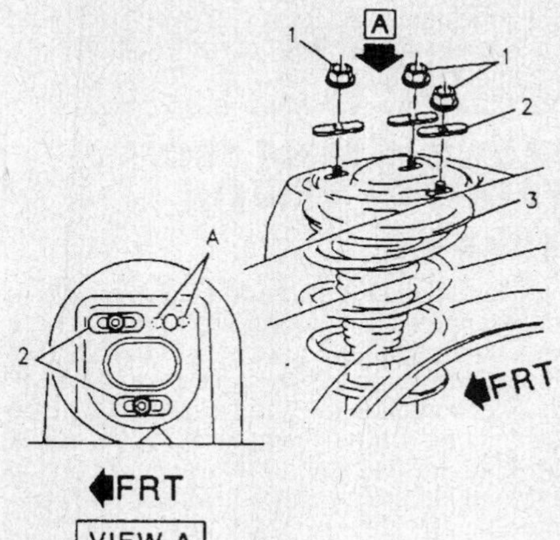

A DRILL 13/32 IN. HOLES
1 NUT, 47 N•m (35 LB. FT.)
2 WASHERS
3 STRUT

GC2049500108000X

Fig. 1 Front caster adjustment

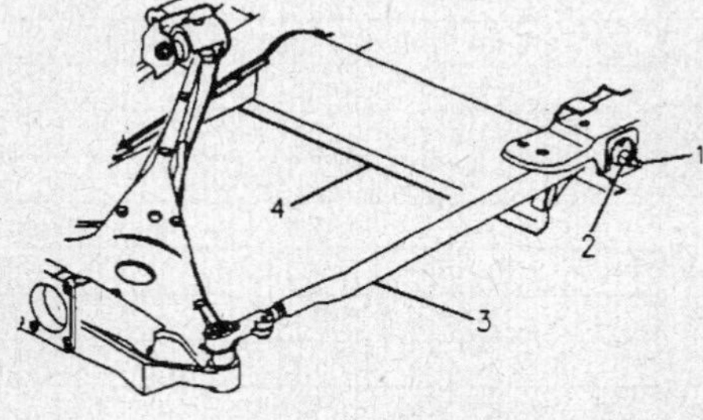

1 CAM BOLT
2 NUT, 75 N•m (55 LB. FT.)
3 INNER ADJUSTMENT LINK
4 REAR SUSPENSION SUPPORT ASSEMBLY

GC2049500110000X

Fig. 3 Rear toe adjustment

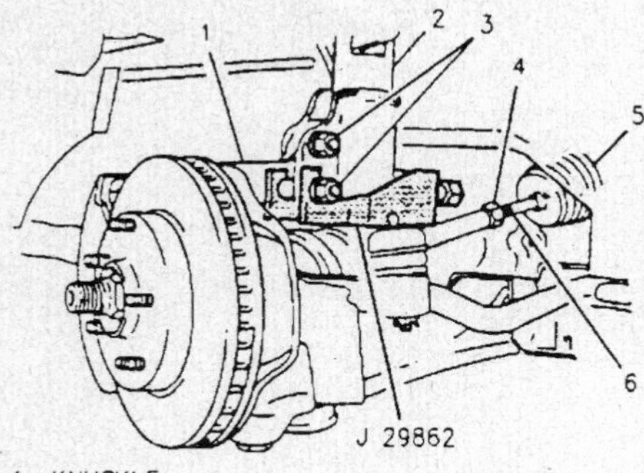

1 KNUCKLE
2 STRUT
3 NUT, 185 N•m (136 LB. FT.)
4 LOCK NUT, 64 N•m (47 LB. FT.)
5 BOOT
6 INNER TIE ROD

GC2049500109000X

Fig. 2 Camber & toe adjustment

TOE

1. Loosen lock nuts on tie rod ends. **Ensure boots are not twisted or damaged during adjustment.**
2. Rotate inner tie rod to adjust toe to specifications, **Fig. 2.**
3. **Torque** lock nuts to 47 ft. lbs.

REAR WHEEL ALIGNMENT

Make left and righthand toe adjustments separately, per wheel.

1. Loosen inner adjustment link cam nut, **Fig. 3.**
2. Rotate cam bolt using suitable wrench or socket, then adjust toe to specifications.
3. **Torque** cam nut to 55 ft. lbs.

VEHICLE RIDE HEIGHT

Refer to "Specifications" section while inspecting vehicle ride height. Ensure vehicle is on level ground and fuel tank is full. Ensure no extra weight is in passenger compartment or trunk.

On vehicle equipped with electronic level control (ELC), ensure ELC is functioning properly.

1. Place front seat to rear position.
2. Bounce vehicle three times at front and rear to normalize suspension.
3. Make measurement D, C, S and Z.
4. Refer to "Specifications" section for specifications.

BONNEVILLE, EIGHTY EIGHT, LESABRE, LSS, PARK AVENUE & REGENCY

NOTE: Refer To The Rear Of This Manual For Vehicle Manufacturer's Special Service Tool Suppliers.

INDEX OF SERVICE OPERATIONS

Specifications

GENERAL ENGINE SPECIFICATIONS

Year/ Engine	VIN Code①	Fuel System	Bore & Stroke	Compression Ratio	Net H.P. @ RPM②	Maximum Torque Ft. Lbs. @ RPM	Normal Oil Pressure psi
1998–2002							
3800	K	SFI	3.80 × 3.40	9.4	205 @ 5200	230 @ 4000	60③
	1	SFI	3.80 × 3.40	8.5	240 @ 5200	280 @ 3200	60③

MFI — Multi-Point Fuel Injection
SFI — Sequential Port Fuel Injection
① — The eighth digit denotes engine code.
② — Ratings are net as installed in vehicle.
③ — At 1850 RPM using SAE 10W-30 motor oil.

TUNE UP SPECIFICATIONS

Engine/VIN Code①	Spark Plug Gap	Ignition Timing: Firing Order Fig.②	Ignition Timing: °BTDC	Ignition Timing: Mark Fig.	Curb Idle Speed	Fast Idle Speed	Fuel Pump Pressure	Valve Clearance, Inch
1998–2000								
3800/K & 1	.060	⑥	⑦	⑧	③	③	48–55⑤	④
2001–02								
3800/K & 1	.060	⑥	⑦	⑧	③	③	53–59⑤	④

BTDC — Before Top Dead Center
① — The eighth digit of the Vehicle Identification Number (VIN) denotes engine code.
② — Before removing wires from distributor cap, determine location of No. 1 wire in cap, as distributor position may have been altered from that illustrated at end of this chart.
③ — Idle speed is controlled by an idle speed control (ISC) motor or an idle air control (IAC) valve.
④ — Equipped w/hydraulic valve lifters. There is no provision for adjustment.
⑤ — With shop towel wrapped around fuel pressure valve to prevent fuel spillage, connect a suitable fuel pressure gauge to fuel pressure valve. Measure fuel pressure w/ignition On, but engine not running.
⑥ — Cylinder numbering left to right as viewed in Figs. A & B from front of vehicle, front bank, 1, 3, 5; rear bank, 2, 4, 6. Firing order 1–6–5–4–3–2. Two different types computer controlled coil ignition systems are used. Refer to **Figs. A and B** for spark plug wire connections at coil unit.
⑦ — Computer controlled. No adjustment.
⑧ — Equipped w/Crankshaft Position Sensor.

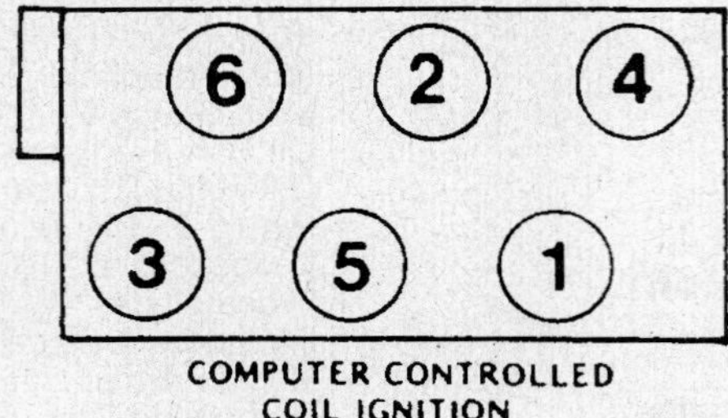

Fig. A

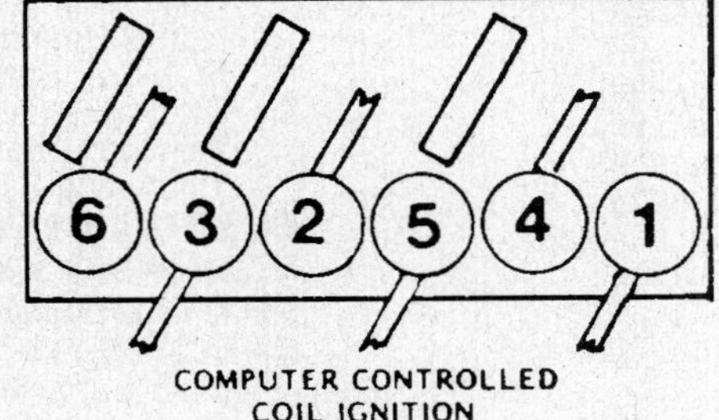

Fig. B

FRONT WHEEL ALIGNMENT SPECIFICATIONS

Year	Model	Caster Angle, Degrees		Camber Angle, Degrees				Total Toe, Degrees	Ball Joint Wear
		Limits	Desired	Limits		Desired			
				Left	Right	Left	Right		
1998–99	Bonneville, Eighty Eight, LeSabre, LSS & Regency	+2.5 to +3.5	+3	–.3 to +.7②	–.3 to +.7②	+.2	+.2	0	①
	Park Avenue	+5.5 to +6.5	+6	–.3 to +.7②	–.3 to +.7②	0	0	+.2	①
2000	Bonneville, LeSabre & Park Avenue	+5.5 to +6.5	+6	–.7 to +.3	–.7 to +.3	–.2	–.2	+.2	①
2001–02	Bonneville, LeSabre & Park Avenue	+4.5 to +5.5	+5	–.7 to +.3	–.7 to +.3	–.2	–.2	+.2	①

① — Refer to "Ball Joint Inspection" in "Front Suspension & Steering" section.

② — Cross caster or camber (LH–RH), 0° (+/- .75°).

REAR WHEEL ALIGNMENT SPECIFICATIONS

Year	Model	Camber Angle, Degrees		Total Toe, Degrees	Thrust Angle, Degrees	Ball Joint Wear
		Limits	Desired			
1998–99	Bonneville, Eighty Eight, LeSabre, LSS & Regency	–.8 to +.2	–.3	+.1	–.1 to +.1	①
1998–2000	Park Avenue	–.8 to +.2	–.3	+.2	–.1 to +.1	①
2000	Bonneville & LeSabre	–.8 to +.2	–.3	+.2	–.1 to +.1	①
2001–02	Bonneville, LeSabre & Park Avenue	–.8 to +.2	–.3	+.2	–.1 to +.1	①

① — Refer to "Ball Joint Inspection" in "Rear Suspension" section.

VEHICLE RIDE HEIGHT SPECIFICATIONS

Model	Year	Body Style	Manufacturer's Original Tire Size	Measurement Points & Specifications①③					
				Front			Rear		
				Dim.	Specification		Dim.	Specification	
					Inches	mm		Inches	mm
LeSabre	1998–99	All	②	A	23.5	600	B	23.5	600
				C	9.47	239	D	9.63	246
	2000	All	②	A	23.5	600	B	23.13	590
				C	6.44–7.25	164–184	D	8.37–9.19	213–233
	2001–02	All	②	Z	3.00–3.80	76.20–96.52	D	1.20–2.00	30.48–50.80
Park Ave	1998–2000	All	②	A	23.5	600	B	23.5	600
				C	6.44–7.25	164–184	D	8.37–9.19	213–233
	2001–02	All	②	Z	3.00–3.80	76.20–96.52	D	1.20–2.00	30.48–50.80
Eighty-Eight, LSS & Regency	1998–99	All	②	A	23.62	600	B	23.62	600
				C	9.37	238	D	9.68	246
Bonneville	1998–99	All	②	A	23.62	600	B	23.62	600
				C	9.37	239	D	9.75	246
				C	9.00–10.50	228.6–266	D	8.62–10.12	219–257
	2000	All	②	A	23.5	600	B	23.12	590
				E	6.43–7.25	164–184	F	8.37–9.18	213–233
	2001–02	All	②	Z	3.00–3.80	76.20–96.52	D	1.20–2.00	30.48–50.80

A Dim. — Measurement From Front Wheel Center to Inspection Point On Rocker Panel
B Dim. — Measurement From Rear Wheel Center to Inspection Point On Rocker Panel
C Dim. — Ground to Rocker Panel, Front
D Dim. — 1998–2000 models, Ground to Rocker Panel, Rear
D Dim. — 2001–02 Models, Lowest Point On Ball Joint Housing Minus Grease Fitting To Centerline Of Rear Bushing.
E Dim. — Ground to Front Underbody Points
F Dim. — Ground to Rear Underbody Points
Z Dim. — Refer to Fig. B for Measurement Locations
Dim. — Dimension
① — ±.0.39 in (10 mm) front to rear & side to side.
② — See door sticker or inside of glove box for manufacturer's original tire size specifications. If tires on vehicle do not match manufacturer's original tire size & measurement is not within limits, it will be necessary to refer to the Non-Standard Tire & Wheel Size Adjustment To Ride Height Specification & Tire Size Adjustment Charts.
③ — Measurement is with fuel, radiator coolant and engine oil full, spare tire, jack, hand tools and mats in designated positions and tires properly inflated.

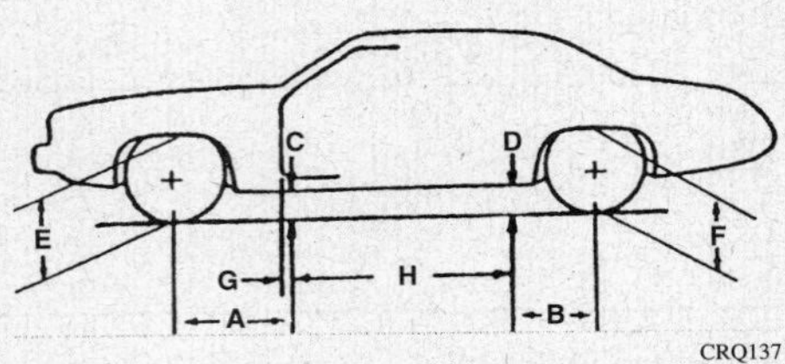

Fig. A Ride height measurement locations. 1998–2000

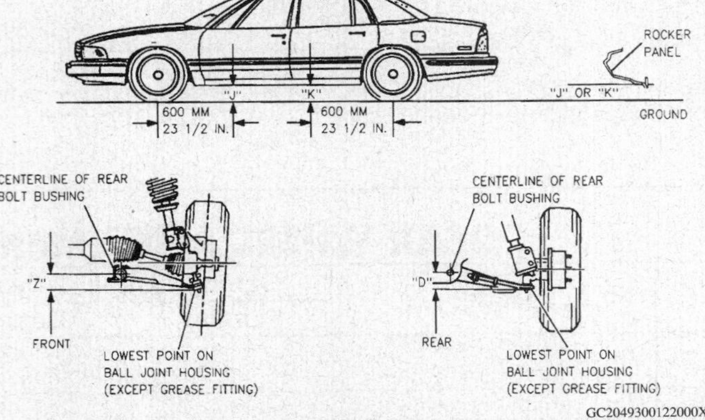

Fig. B Ride height measurement locations. 2001–02

FLUID CAPACITIES & COOLING SYSTEM DATA

Year	Model	Engine	Coolant Capacity, Qts.	Coolant Type	Radiator Cap Relief Pressure, Lbs.	Thermo. Opening Temp.	Fuel Tank Gals.	Engine Oil Refill Qts.	Auto. Transaxle Qts.①
1998–99	Bonneville, Eighty Eight, LeSabre, LSS & Regency	3800	13	Dex-Cool	15	195	19.4	4.5⑤	③
	Park Avenue	3800	13	Dex-Cool	15	195	④	4.5⑤	②
2000	Bonneville, LeSabre & Park Avenue	3800	13	Dex-Cool	⑦	188	18.5	4.0⑤	⑥
2001–02	Bonneville, LeSabre & Park Avenue	3800	10	Dex-Cool	⑦	188	18.5	4.5⑧	⑥

① — Approximate. Make final inspection w/dipstick.
② — Oil pan capacity 6.0 qts.; total capacity 11.0 qts.
③ — Oil pan capacity 7.4 qts.; total capacity 10 qts.
④ — VIN 1 engine 19 gallons; VIN K engine 18 gallons.
⑤ — Add .5 qt. w/filter change.
⑥ — Drain and refill 7.4 qts.; overhaul 10 qts.; dry 13.4 qts.
⑦ — Relief pressure specification is stamped on cap.
⑧ — With filter.

LUBRICANT DATA

Year	Model	Lubricant Type		
		Automatic Transaxle	Power Steering	Brake System
1998–2002	All	Dexron III	Power Steering Fluid①	DOT 3

① — GM part No. 1052884, or equivalent.

Electrical

NOTE: On Air Bag Equipped Models, Refer To "Air Bag System Precautions" Located In The Front Of This Manual For System Disarming & Arming Procedures.

NOTE: Refer To "Computer Relearn Procedures" Located In The Front Of This Manual When Battery Power To The Computer Has Been Interrupted.

INDEX

PRECAUTIONS

AIR BAG SYSTEMS

Refer to "Air Bag System Precautions" in the front of this manual for system disarming and arming procedures.

BATTERY GROUND CABLE

Prior to service, disconnect battery ground cable and isolate as required.

FUSE PANEL & FLASHER LOCATION

The instrument panel fuse panel is located behind the lefthand side of the instrument panel, behind the trim panel. The engine compartment fuse panel is located at the rear center of the engine compartment.

The combined turn signal and hazard flasher module is attached to the lighting control module (LCM) bracket under the instrument panel.

RELAY CENTER LOCATION

The passenger compartment relay center is located behind the righthand side of the instrument panel, on the multi-use bracket. The engine compartment relay center is located at the rear center of the engine compartment.

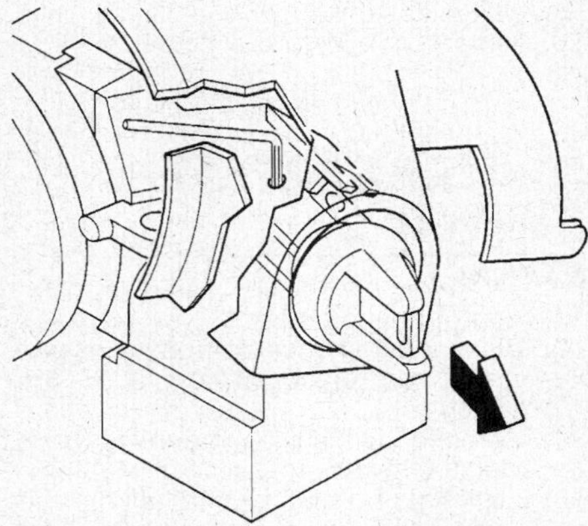

Fig. 1 Lock cylinder removal. Eighty Eight, LeSabre, LSS, Park Avenue & Regency

FUEL PUMP RELAY LOCATION

The fuel pump relay is located in the underhood relay center.

STARTER

REPLACE

When removing starter, note if any shims are used between the starter and mounting surface. If shims are used, install in their original locations.

If starter is noisy during cranking, remove one .015 inch double shim or add one .015 inch single shim to the outer bolt. If starter makes a high pitched whine after engine starts, add .015 inch double shims until noise ceases.

1. Raise and support vehicle.
2. Remove starter braces, shields or other components as required.
3. Support starter, then remove mounting bolts.
4. Lower starter, then disconnect solenoid wires and battery cable.
5. Remove starter from vehicle.
6. Reverse procedure to install.

COIL PACK

REPLACE

1. Tag electrical connectors and spark plug wires to ensure proper installation, then disconnect them from ignition control module.
2. Remove screws securing ignition coils to ignition module, then the coils.
3. Reverse procedure to install.

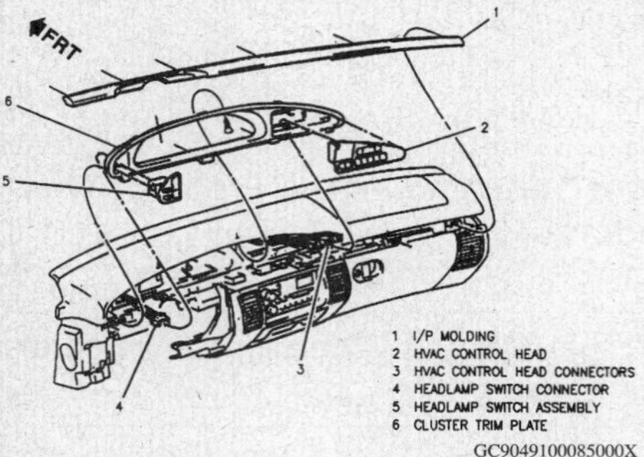

Fig. 2 Headlamp switch removal. 1998 Eighty Eight, LeSabre, LSS, Park Avenue & Regency

IGNITION LOCK

REPLACE

EIGHTY EIGHT, LESABRE, LSS, PARK AVENUE & REGENCY

Removal

1. Remove steering wheel as outlined under "Steering Wheel, Replace."
2. Disconnect SIR wiring harness from wiring protector and wire harness strap.
3. Lower or remove steering column from vehicle.
4. **On models equipped with tilt column,** remove tilt lever.
5. **On all models,** remove column lower and upper shrouds.
6. Remove lock cylinder as follows:
   a. Insert ignition key and hold in Start position.
   b. Push on lock cylinder retaining tab using a 1/16 inch hex wrench, **Fig. 1.**
   c. Release key to Run position and pull lock cylinder from lock module assembly.

Installation

1. Install upper shroud. **Torque** mounting screws to 12 inch lbs.
2. Install lower shroud, ensuring slots on lower shroud engage with tabs on upper shroud.
3. Install lower shroud mounting screws. **Torque** both screws to 53 inch lbs.
4. Install shift and multi-function lever seals to column shrouds.
5. Install tilt lever.
6. Raise or install steering column into vehicle.
7. Install lock cylinder as follows:
   a. Insert key into lock cylinder.
   b. Ensure sector in lock module assembly is in Run position.
   c. Align locking tabs, position tab with slots in lock module assembly and push cylinder into position.
   d. Install lock cylinder through upper shroud and into lock module assembly.

BONNEVILLE

1998-99

Refer to procedure outlined under "Eighty Eight, LeSabre, LSS, Park Avenue & Regency."

2000-02

1. Apply parking brake.
2. Remove instrument panel cluster trim bezel.
3. Remove radio.
4. Remove fasteners from ignition switch.
5. Rotate switch in instrument panel, then disconnect electrical connectors.
6. Remove ignition switch bulb from side of switch.
7. Remove switch through radio opening.
8. Remove ignition switch from bracket.
9. Reverse procedure to install.

IGNITION SWITCH

REPLACE

1. Remove lock cylinder assembly as outlined under "Ignition Lock, Replace."
2. Remove wiring harnesses from steering column as required.
3. Disconnect control coded key connector from wire harness.
4. Pry retaining clip on key alarm switch using a suitable screwdriver, then rotate alarm switch 1/4 turn and remove.
5. Remove ignition switch mounting screws, then the ignition and key alarm switch assembly.
6. Reverse procedure to install.

NEUTRAL SAFETY SWITCH

REPLACE

1. Apply parking brake.
2. Disconnect shift cable from transaxle.
3. Disconnect electrical connector from switch.
4. Remove two switch mounting bolts, then the switch.
5. Align flats on switch with flats on transaxle shaft using alignment tool No. J41545, or equivalent, then push switch over shaft and fully seat on transaxle.
6. Install switch mounting bolts. **Torque** to 18 ft. lbs. **If switch was rotated and pin is broken, reset switch to Neutral position as follows:**
   a. Place transaxle shaft in Neutral position.
   b. Align shift shaft flats to PNP switch flats using alignment tool No. J41545, or equivalent.
   c. Install switch on transaxle as outlined and loosely install mounting bolts.
   d. **Torque** mounting bolts to 18 ft. lbs.

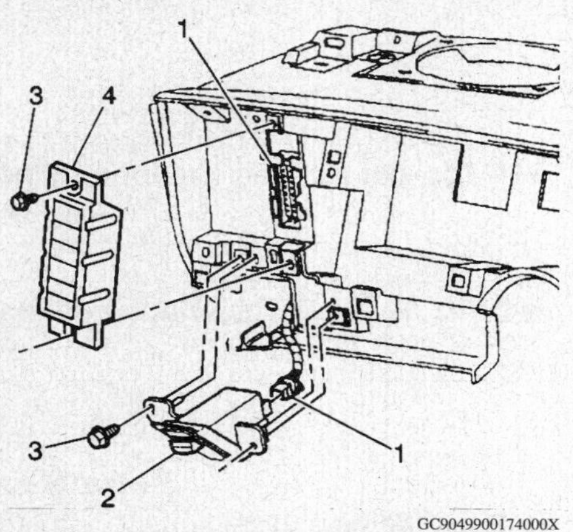

Fig. 3 Headlamp switch replacement. 1999 Eighty Eight, LSS & Regency & 1998–99 Bonneville

BACK-UP LAMP SWITCH

REPLACE

Refer to "Neutral Safety Switch, Replace" for procedure.

HEADLAMP SWITCH

REPLACE

EIGHTY EIGHT, LSS & REGENCY

1998

1. Remove instrument panel molding fasteners in instrument panel compartment, **Fig. 2.**
2. Remove instrument panel molding by carefully pulling rearward.
3. Remove cluster trim plate by removing screws and tilting top of trim plate rearward then pulling bottom of trim plate rearward.
4. Remove HVAC control head and headlamp/park lamp switch from connectors.
5. Disconnect HVAC control head vacuum harness connector, then remove control head by carefully pushing one side outward.
6. Remove headlamp/park lamp switch by carefully pushing one side outward.
7. Reverse procedure to install.

1999

1. Remove instrument panel cluster trim panel.
2. Remove fuel door/trunk release switch screws (3) and electrical connector (1), then the switch (2), **Fig. 3.**
3. Remove headlamp switch screws, then pull rearward to remove switch (4).
4. Reverse procedure to install.

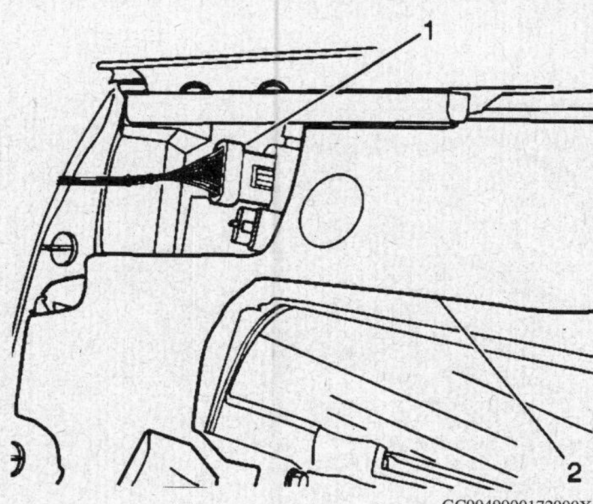

Fig. 4 Headlamp switch electrical connector. 1999 LeSabre & Park Avenue

LESABRE & PARK AVENUE

1998

Refer to "Eighty Eight, LSS & Regency" under "Headlamp Switch, Replace."

1999

1. Remove door trim panel.
2. Disconnect electrical connector, **Fig. 4,** then remove fasteners (2), **Fig. 5,** that retain cover to inner side of trim panel.
3. Remove switch attaching screws, then the switch.
4. Reverse procedure to install.

2000-02

1. Remove lefthand instrument panel accessory trim plate.
2. Remove headlamp switch fasteners, then the switch.
3. Reverse procedure to install.

BONNEVILLE

1998-99

Refer to "1999 Eighty Eight, LSS & Regency."

2000-02

1. Remove lefthand instrument panel accessory trim plate.
2. Remove headlamp switch fasteners, then the switch.
3. Reverse procedure to install.

TURN SIGNAL SWITCH

REPLACE

EIGHTY EIGHT, LSS & REGENCY

1. Remove steering column upper and lower shrouds.
2. Remove retaining ring, SIR coil, wave washer and retaining ring.
3. Remove shaft lock shield assembly.
4. Remove turn signal cancel cam.
5. Remove turn signal switch connector from shifter.
6. Remove turn signal switch mounting screws, then the switch.
7. Reverse procedure to install, noting the following:
   a. Turn signal electrical contact must rest on canceling assembly.
   b. **Torque** turn signal switch mounting screws to 53 inch lbs.

BONNEVILLE, LESABRE & PARK AVENUE

1998-99

Refer to "Eighty Eight, LSS & Regency" for procedure.

2000-02

1. Remove steering wheel and tilt lever.
2. Remove two Torx screws from lower shroud, then tilt shroud down and slide back to disengage locking tabs.
3. Remove shroud protector.
4. Remove two Torx screws from upper shroud, then the shroud.
5. Remove instrument panel trim panel.
6. Remove two Torx screws from multi-function switch.
7. Disconnect multi-function switch electrical connectors, then remove switch.
8. Reverse procedure to install.

DIMMER SWITCH

REPLACE

Refer to "Turn Signal Switch, Replace" for procedure.

STEERING WHEEL

REPLACE

1. Remove air bag module retaining screws from back of steering wheel.
2. Remove module from steering wheel, then disconnect horn contact by pushing slightly and twisting counterclockwise.
3. Remove connector position assurance, then disconnect coil assembly electrical connector, **Fig. 6.**
4. Remove steering wheel retaining nut.
5. Remove wheel using puller tool No. J1859-03 and bolts No. J38720, or equivalents.
6. Reverse procedure to install, noting the following:
   a. **Torque** steering wheel nut to 30 ft. lbs.
   b. Ensure all wiring and electrical connectors are properly routed to avoid pinching.
   c. **Torque** air bag module mounting screws to 27 inch lbs.

INSTRUMENT CLUSTER

REPLACE

LESABRE & PARK AVENUE

1998-99

1. Remove instrument panel trim plates.
2. Remove PRNDL cable.
3. **On 1998 models,** remove instrument panel dimmer switch.
4. **On 1999 models,** remove panel lights twilight sentinel/traction control switch.

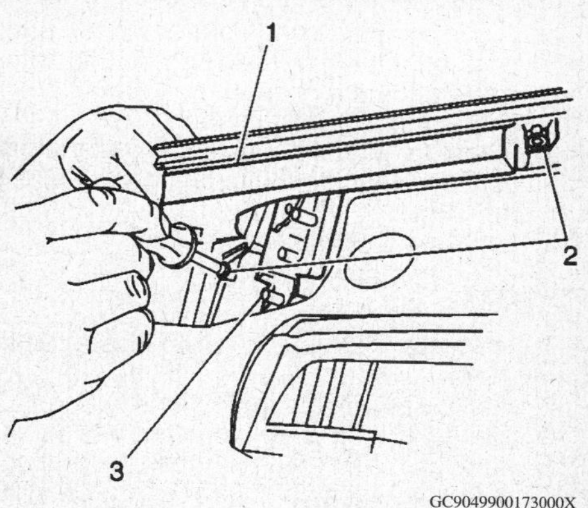

Fig. 5 Headlamp switch attaching hardware. 1999 LeSabre & Park Avenue

5. **On all models,** remove instrument cluster.
6. Reverse procedure to install.

2000-02

1. Carefully pry defroster grill away from instrument panel.
2. Disconnect sunload sensor from grill, then remove grill from instrument panel.
3. Remove righthand and lefthand windshield garnish moldings.
4. Remove instrument panel upper trim pad attaching screws, then the upper trim pad from instrument panel.
5. Lower steering column to its lowest position.
6. Remove instrument cluster trim plate bezel to instrument panel attaching screws.
7. Disengage four upper cluster trim plate bezel retaining clips, then the bottom clips.
8. Disconnect trim bezel driver information center switch electrical connector, then remove trim plate bezel from instrument panel.
9. Remove four instrument cluster pins, then pull cluster rearward to remove.
10. Reverse procedure to install.

EIGHTY EIGHT, LSS & REGENCY

1998

1. Remove instrument panel molding attaching screws, then pull instrument panel molding rearward.
2. Pry defroster grill upward and remove sunload and twilight sentinel sensors.
3. Remove defroster grill from upper trim panel.
4. Tilt top of instrument cluster trim plate rearward, then pull bottom of trim plate rearward.
5. Disconnect HVAC control head and headlamp switch electrical connectors.
6. Disconnect HVAC control head vacuum harness connector.
7. Remove HVAC control head and headlamp switch from instrument cluster trim plate.
8. Remove instrument cluster trim plate.

9. Remove instrument panel upper trim pad attaching screws, then the trim pad from instrument panel, **Fig. 7.**
10. Disconnect PRNDL cable.
11. Remove instrument cluster attaching screws, then the cluster from instrument panel.
12. Reverse procedure to install.

1999

1. Remove instrument panel cluster trim plate.
2. Remove PRNDL cable, if equipped.
3. Remove instrument cluster attaching screws, then the cluster by pulling rearward and disconnecting cluster electrical connector.
4. Reverse procedure to instal.

BONNEVILLE

1998

1. Remove steering column lower filler attaching screws, then the filler panel.
2. Remove steering column support attaching bolts, then lower the steering column and cover to prevent damage.
3. Remove instrument panel trim plate attaching screws.
4. Pull headlamp dimmer and twilight sentinel control knob rearward.
5. Pull panel cluster plate rearward to remove.
6. Remove headlamp switch attaching screws and pull rearward, then remove dimmer and twilight sentinel control knob from switch.
7. Remove instrument panel cluster trim plate.
8. Remove instrument cluster attaching screws, then pull righthand side of cluster rearward, **Fig. 8.**
9. Depress cluster electrical connector locking tab through top righthand side of assembly.
10. Pull bottom of cluster rearward, rotate cluster to face upward, then pull rearward to remove.
11. Reverse procedure to install.

1999

1. Remove steering column filler panel.
2. Lower steering column. Remove steering column lower mounting bolts prior to removing upper steering column mounting bolts or damage to steering column bearing may occur.
3. Remove instrument panel cluster trim plate.
4. Remove instrument cluster attaching screws, then pull righthand end of cluster rearward and rotate cluster assembly to face upward.
5. Reach around top or bottom righthand side of cluster assembly to disconnect cluster connector.
6. Remove instrument cluster by sliding toward center of vehicle.
7. Reverse procedure to install.

2000-02

1. Lower steering column to its lowest position.
2. Remove ignition lock cylinder bezel.

1 CAM TOWER
2 CONNECTOR, SWITCH
3 HORN CONTACT LEAD
4 INFLATOR MODULE
5 SWITCH ASM
6 NUT
7 BOLT/SCREW
8 CONNECTOR, SIR INFLATOR MODULE
9 RETAINER, CPA
10 BOLT/SCREW

VIEW A

GC6049100144000X

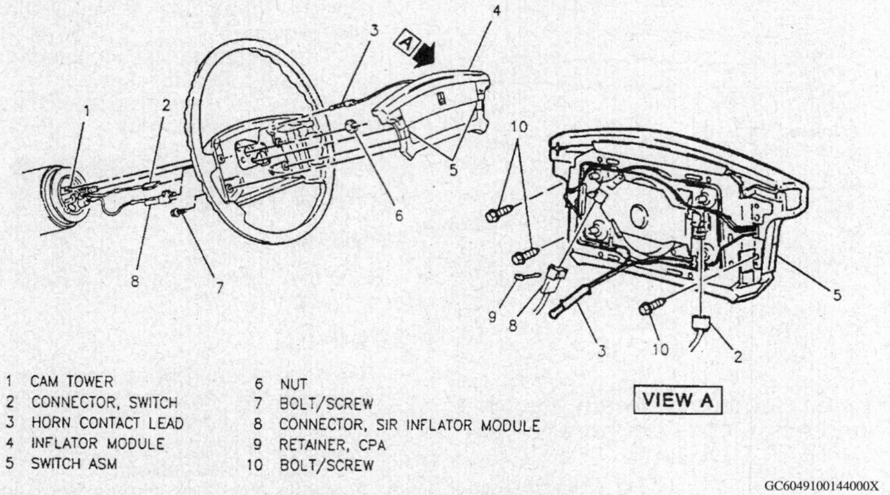

Fig. 6 Inflator module assembly

3. Remove Driver Information Center (DIC) switch.
4. Remove instrument cluster trim plate push-in fasteners.
5. Remove cluster trim plate by carefully pulling rearward and releasing clips.
6. Disconnect DIC switch electrical connector.
7. Release instrument cluster pins, then pull cluster rearward and to right.
8. Disconnect all cluster electrical connectors.
9. Reverse procedure to install, noting the following:
   a. Ensure trim plate is fully seated to instrument panel. This is critical to proper functioning of automatic A/C control in-car sensor.
   b. Ensure all electrical connectors are securely connected.
   c. Push instrument cluster pins into their corresponding locations. An audible snap will be heard when cluster is fully seated.

RADIO

REPLACE

LESABRE & PARK AVENUE

1998

1. Remove instrument panel lower trim plates and four air vent deflectors by prying with suitable tool.
2. Remove bolts and screws that attach glove box to instrument panel, **Fig. 9.**
3. Remove instrument panel trim plate attaching screws.
4. Remove radio to instrument panel attaching bolts and nuts, **Fig. 9.**
5. Pull radio straight back and disconnect electrical connectors and antenna.
6. Reverse procedure to install.

1999-2002

1. Remove instrument panel cluster trim plate.
2. Remove radio mounting screws.
3. Pull radio rearward, then disconnect electrical connectors and antenna lead-in cable.
4. Reverse procedure to install.

EIGHTY EIGHT, LSS & REGENCY

1998

1. Open glove compartment door and remove two center trim plate attaching screws.
2. Pull center trim plate off instrument panel.
3. Remove radio to instrument panel attaching screws.
4. Pull radio rearward, then disconnect electrical connectors and antenna lead-in cable.
5. Remove radio from instrument panel.
6. Reverse procedure to install.

1999

Refer to "LeSabre & Park Avenue" for radio replacement.

BONNEVILLE

1998

1. Pry instrument panel trim panel, pull panel upward, then rearward to remove.
2. Remove radio attaching screws, then pull rearward.
3. Disconnect electrical connectors and antenna lead-in cable.
4. Remove radio assembly, **Fig. 10.**
5. Reverse procedure to install.

1999-2002

Refer to "LeSabre & Park Avenue" for procedure.

WIPER MOTOR

REPLACE

1. Disconnect wiper motor electrical connector.
2. Remove wiper motor mounting screws.
3. Move wiper arms 6–8 inches up windshield from park position.
4. Pull wiper motor away from vehicle.
5. Disconnect transmission drive link

from motor crank arm using separator tool No. J39232, or equivalent.
6. Remove wiper motor from vehicle.
7. Reverse procedure to install, noting the following:
   a. Connect transmission drive link to motor crank arm using installer tool No. J39529, or equivalent.
   b. Install motor onto vehicle. **Torque** mounting screws to 70 inch lbs.
   c. Connect motor electrical connector.

WIPER SWITCH

REPLACE

1. **Make note of lefthand closeout and sound insulator panel fastener positions before removal. Improper installation may lead to possible accelerator or brake pedal binding.**
2. Remove instrument panel lefthand insulator.
3. Remove knee bolster and bracket.
4. Remove steering column bracket bolts. Disconnect electrical connectors from bracket.
5. Remove steering column bracket.
6. Remove steering column trim covers.
7. Remove wire harness assembly from wire restraint clips.
8. Disconnect wiper switch electrical connectors.
9. Depress switch locking tabs.
10. Pull switch assembly out of mounting bracket.
11. Reverse procedure to install, noting the following:
    a. Ensure all electrical connectors and wiring are properly routed to avoid pinching.
    b. Install new wire harness straps.
    c. Install steering column bracket and bolts. **Torque** bolts to 18 inch lbs.
    d. Install bolts and screws to knee bolster bracket at steering column support. **Torque** to 89 inch lbs.
    e. Install bolts and screws to knee bolster bracket at instrument panel. **Torque** to 18 inch lbs.
    f. Ensure lefthand closeout and insulator panel is properly positioned and fasteners are in original locations. **Torque** to 17 inch lbs.

WIPER TRANSMISSION

REPLACE

1. Bring wipers to park position, then turn ignition Off.
2. Disconnect washer hose from air inlet grille panel.
3. Remove wiper arm nut covers.
4. Remove wiper arm nuts.
5. Remove wiper arms from pivot shafts using removal tool No. J39822, or equivalent.
6. Push washer hose into fitting into plenum area using suitable needle-nose pliers.
7. Remove air inlet grille panel retainers, then the panel.
8. Remove windshield frame reinforcement bolts and nuts, then the reinforcement.

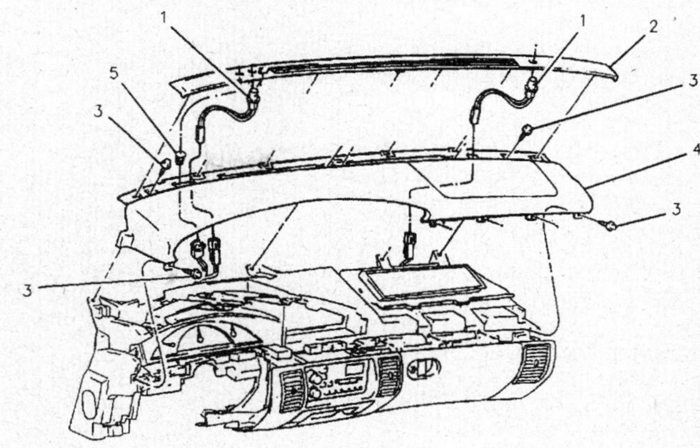

Fig. 7 I/P upper trim pad removal. 1998 Eighty Eight, LSS & Regency

9. Pull or push on wiper transmission linkage to rotate wiper motor crank arm from park position to area opposite park position.
10. Remove harness grommet from hole in plenum.
11. Disconnect wiper motor electrical connector.
12. Push harness and grommet through hole in plenum.
13. Remove wiper system drive module mounting screws, then the module from vehicle.
14. Remove drive links from wiper motor crank arm and wiper transmission driveshafts using separator tool No. J39232, or equivalent.
15. Remove wiper motor mounting screws from drive system module.
16. Reverse procedure to install, noting the following:
    a. Install wiper motor onto drive system module. **Torque** screws to 71 inch lbs.
    b. Install drive links onto wiper motor crank arm and transmission driveshafts using installer tool No. J39529, or equivalent.
    c. Lower the wiper module into upper plenum with motor's nose pointing downward.
    d. Rotate module so motor nose points toward rear of vehicle.
    e. Install wiper drive system module. **Torque** screws to 71 inch lbs.
    f. Install windshield frame reinforcement with three bolts and two nuts. **Torque** to 80 inch lbs.
    g. Install wiper arms in park position. **Torque** arm mounting nuts to 24 ft. lbs.

BLOWER MOTOR

REPLACE

1. Remove righthand side closeout/insulator panel as follows:
   a. Remove fasteners at rear edge of insulator to disengage from lower instrument panel.
   b. Pry out retainers to release panel.
   c. Turn heater temperature sensor ¼ turn to release and allow to remain connected to its wire.
   d. Disconnect electrical connectors, then slide insulator panel rearward to disengage.
2. Pull back carpet near blower motor.
3. Remove glove compartment.
4. Remove Dash Integration Module (DIM) from bracket, then the bracket.
5. Disconnect blower motor electrical connector.
6. Remove blower motor retaining screws, then lower the motor and rotate counterclockwise to remove from vehicle.
7. Reverse procedure to install.

CABIN AIR FILTER

REPLACE

2000–01

1. Open hood.
2. Lift up cabin air filter access cover located on air inlet panel.
3. Remove cabin air filter element from filter housing, **Fig. 11.**
4. Install new cabin air filter into filter housing.
5. Close cabin air filter access cover.

2002

1. **Make note of lefthand closeout and sound insulator panel fastener positions before removal. Improper installation may lead to possible accelerator or brake pedal binding.**
2. Disconnect courtesy lamp, DSIR and heater temperature sensor electrical connectors at closeout panel.
3. Remove lefthand closeout and sound insulator panel.
4. Remove filter access cover by pushing down, then pulling out.
5. Remove tape on first filter.
6. Remove first filter by pulling filter tab.
7. Remove tape on second filter.

8. Remove second filter by pulling filter tab.
9. Remove third filter by pulling filter tab.
10. Reverse procedure to install, noting the following:
    a. Lubricate new filter guides with suitable spray silicon for ease in installation. Keep filters as straight as possible.
    b. Install first filter into HVAC assembly. Use tab or a long screwdriver to raise filter so leading edge catches on holding rib inside filter case.
    c. Install second filter in first filter tab.
    d. Slide second filter into remaining channels of first filter.
    e. Slide third filter into remaining channels of second filter.
    f. Fold second filter tab down and third filter tab up over second.
    g. Install filter access cover.
    h. Ensure lefthand closeout and insulator panel is properly positioned and fasteners are in original locations. **Torque** to 17 inch lbs.

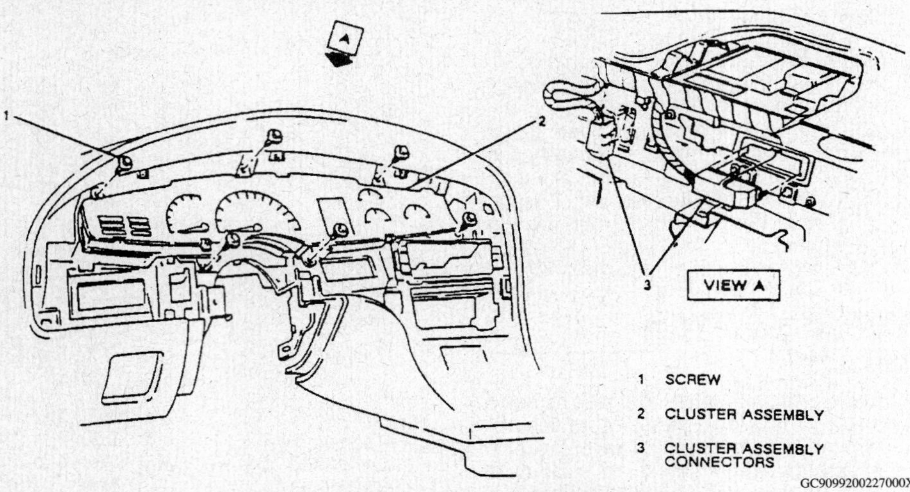

Fig. 8 Cluster removal. 1998 Bonneville

HEATER CORE

REPLACE

EIGHTY EIGHT, LSS & REGENCY

1. Drain cooling system into suitable container.
2. Remove righthand sound insulator.
3. Remove center and lower instrument panel trim plates.
4. **On models equipped with automatic climate control,** proceed as follows:
    a. Remove speaker grille and speaker for access to programmer attaching bolt.
    b. Disconnect wiring and hoses from programmer.
    c. Remove programmer linkage cover and disconnect linkage.
    d. Remove programmer attaching bolt, then the programmer.
5. **On all models,** remove heater core cover, then the splash cover for access to heater hoses.
6. Disconnect heater hoses from heater core.
7. Remove heater core cover, then the heater core.
8. Reverse procedure to install.

BONNEVILLE, LESABRE & PARK AVENUE

1998-99

Refer to "Eighty Eight, LSS & Regency" for procedure.

2000-02

1. Drain cooling system into suitable container.
2. Remove fuel injector sight shield.
3. **Make note of lefthand closeout and sound insulator panel fastener positions before removal. Improper installation may lead to possible accelerator or brake pedal binding.**
4. From inside of vehicle, remove righthand and lefthand side sound insulators.
5. **On models equipped with rear A/C,** remove front console assembly and auxiliary air distribution duct adapter.
6. **On all models,** remove instrument panel lower trim plate.
7. Remove air distributor duct screws (righthand side screw is difficult to remove and may be left out during reassembly), then the air duct.
8. Remove heater core shield and cover.
9. Remove retaining screw and strap from heater core.
10. Remove heater core.
11. Reverse procedure to install. Ensure lefthand closeout and insulator panel is properly positioned and fasteners are in original locations. **Torque** to 17 inch lbs.

EVAPORATOR CORE

REPLACE

EIGHTY EIGHT, LSS & REGENCY

1998

Brazed fittings are used on the condenser and evaporator. These fittings cannot be turned. The brazed fitting that should not be turned is always the same color as the pipe it is brazed to.

1. Recover A/C refrigerant as outlined in "Air Conditioning" chapter.
2. Remove engine rear sight shield.
3. Disconnect electrical connector from pressure cycling switch.
4. Disconnect accumulator inlet and outlet connections, then remove accumulator from vehicle.
5. Remove blower motor resistor, then the vacuum tank.
6. Remove engine coolant reservoir, then the evaporator tube from condenser outlet.
7. Disconnect A/C lines from clamp near shock tower.
8. Remove evaporator tube from vehicle.
9. Remove blower motor, then the brackets and heat shield from blower module assembly, **Fig. 12.**
10. Cut blower module assembly along indicated line, then remove bolts attaching blower module assembly to front of dash (driver's side only).
11. Remove large piece of blower module assembly insulation.
12. Remove screws from evaporator cover, then the evaporator.
13. Reverse procedure to install.

1999

1. Recover A/C refrigerant as outlined under "Air Conditioning."
2. Remove cross vehicle support brace.
3. Remove fuse box cover.
4. Remove accumulator as follows:
    a. Remove sight shield of rear engine.
    b. Loosen retaining clamp screw.
    c. Disconnect accumulator inlet and outlet connections using dual O-ring joint separator tool No. J38042, or equivalent.
    d. Remove retaining clamp screw, then the accumulator.
5. Remove positive booster cable from multi-use relay center.
6. Position under hood fuse block out of way.
7. Remove evaporator tube from evaporator.
8. Remove wire harness clip from HVAC module.
9. Remove accumulator bracket.
10. Remove heat shield of HVAC module.
11. Following cut line, cut top side of HVAC module cover.
12. Raise and support vehicle.
13. Following cut line, cut bottom side of HVAC module cover.
14. Lower vehicle.
15. Remove fuel line clip from HVAC module, then remove insulator from module.
16. Remove bolt that attaches heater and A/C module assembly to inside of vehicle.
17. Remove blower module from HVAC module assembly.
18. Remove evaporator core.
19. Reverse procedure to install.

BONNEVILLE & LESABRE

1998-99

Refer to "Eighty Eight, LSS & Regency" for procedure.

2000-02

1. Remove blower control module assembly as follows:
   a. Recover A/C refrigerant as outlined in "Air Conditioning" chapter.
   b. Remove evaporator hose nut, then disconnect evaporator hose connection at evaporator.
   c. Remove heater hoses from heater core, then pinch off hoses to minimize leakage of coolant.
   d. Raise and support vehicle.
   e. Remove drain tube from A/C module.
   f. Lower vehicle.
   g. **Make note of lefthand closeout and sound insulator panel fastener positions before removal. Improper installation may lead to possible accelerator or brake pedal binding.**
   h. Remove instrument panel assembly.
   i. Remove defroster duct and air distributor duct.
   j. Disconnect blower control module connection and instrument panel to HVAC module connection.
   k. Remove HVAC module retaining nuts, then the module assembly.
2. Remove seal from around heater core and evaporator tubes.
3. Remove upper A/C evaporator case, then the evaporator core.
4. Reverse procedure to install. Ensure lefthand closeout and insulator panel is properly positioned and fasteners are in original locations. **Torque** to 17 inch lbs.

PARK AVENUE

1998

Brazed fittings are used on condenser and evaporator. These fittings cannot be turned. The brazed fitting that should not be turned is always the same color as the pipe it is brazed to.

1. Recover A/C refrigerant as outlined in "Air Conditioning" chapter.
2. Remove vacuum tank.
3. Remove rear sight shield, then disconnect positive battery booster cable from underhood fuse block.
4. Remove underhood fuse block from relay bracket and position aside.
5. Remove relay bracket from dash panel, then the blower resistor from top of evaporator/heater module casing.
6. Disconnect A/C module to accumulator tube from accumulator.
7. Disconnect A/C compressor and condenser hose from accumulator.
8. Remove clamp from accumulator, then disconnect electrical connector from pressure cycling switch.

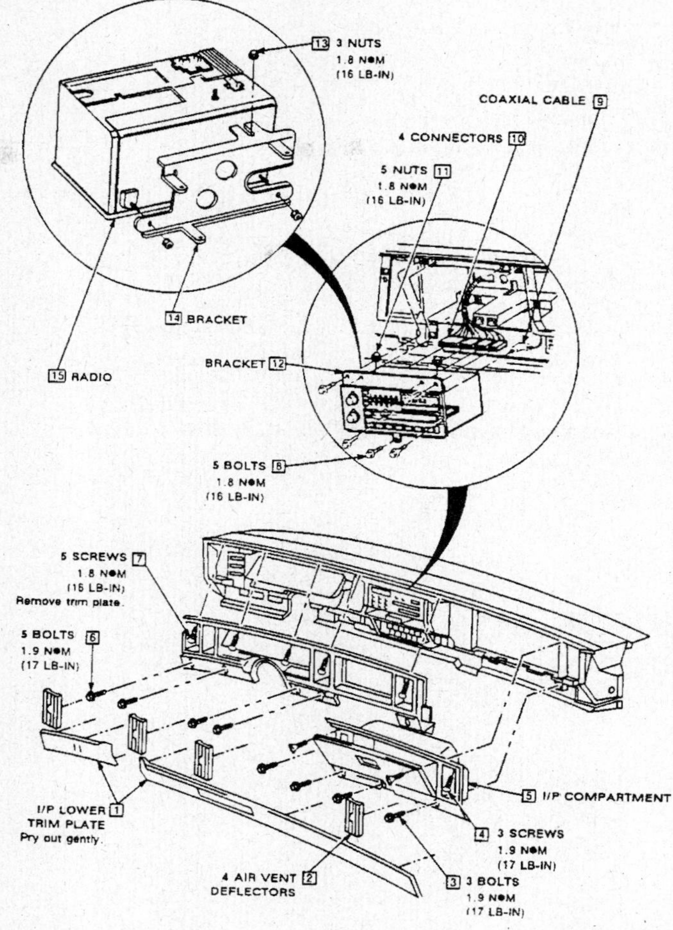

Fig. 9 Radio replacement. 1998 LeSabre & Park Avenue

9. Disconnect evaporator to condenser tube from evaporator case and condenser.
10. Disengage tube from clips holding evaporator tube to fender, then remove tube from vehicle.
11. Remove blower motor and all brackets from evaporator/heater module.
12. Remove heat shield from bottom of evaporator/heater module, then the three screws attaching bottom of module to dash panel.
13. Remove five screws attaching top and side of module to dash panel.
14. Cut insulator on module along line indicated, **Fig. 13.**
15. Remove four module to insulator attaching screws, located behind insulator.
16. Remove Electronic Brake Control Module (EBCM) as follows:
    a. Remove two screws attaching Assembly Line Diagnostic Link (ALDL) connector to righthand side sound insulator.
    b. Remove push-on nuts and attaching bolts from lefthand and righthand sound insulators, **Fig. 13.**
    c. Remove righthand footwell courtesy lamp and oil life module from righthand side sound insulator, then the insulator from vehicle.
    d. Remove lefthand footwell courtesy lamp from lefthand side sound insulator, then the insulator.
    e. Remove two floor outlet assembly to instrument panel attaching screws.
    f. Remove four EBCM bracket to instrument panel attaching screws.
    g. Pull bracket away from instrument panel and remove EBCM to bracket attaching bolt, then slide EBCM out of bracket.
17. Pull down rug and padding, then remove dash panel to evaporator/heater module case attaching screw.
18. Pull module case away from dash panel and remove evaporator.
19. Reverse procedure to install.

1999-2002

Refer to "Bonneville & LeSabre" for procedure.

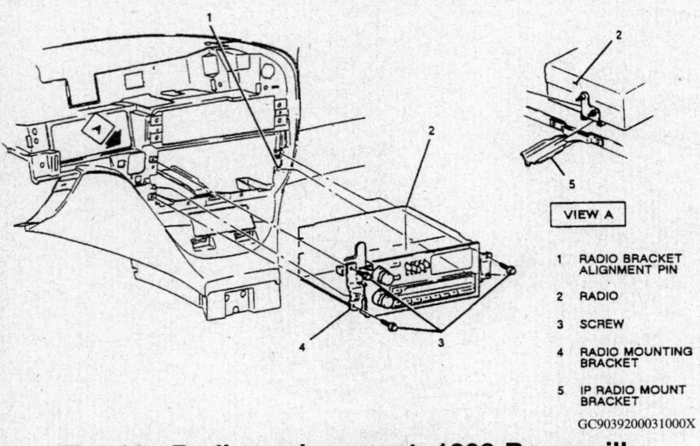

Fig. 10 Radio replacement. 1998 Bonneville

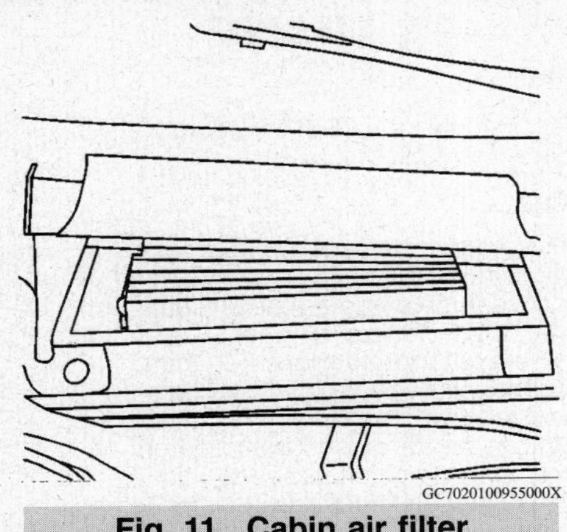

Fig. 11 Cabin air filter replacement. 2000–01

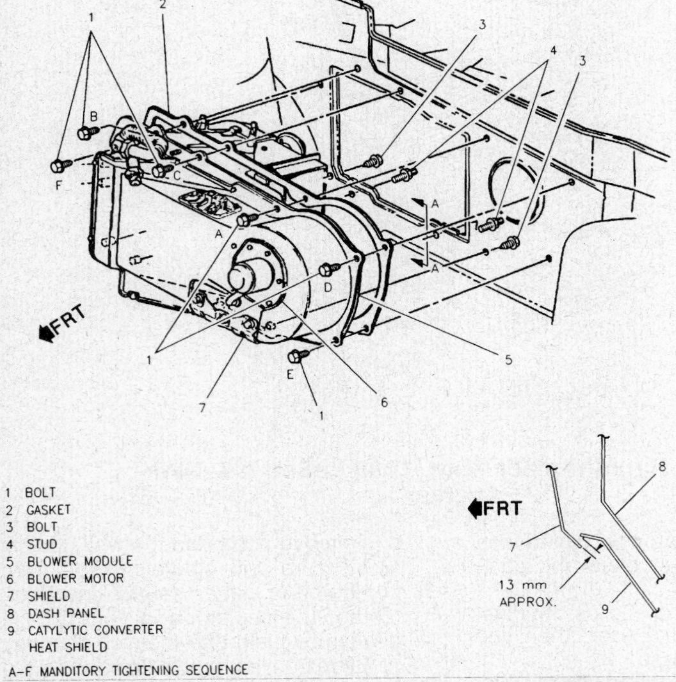

Fig. 12 Evaporator/heater module assembly. 1998 Eighty Eight, LSS, Park Avenue & Regency

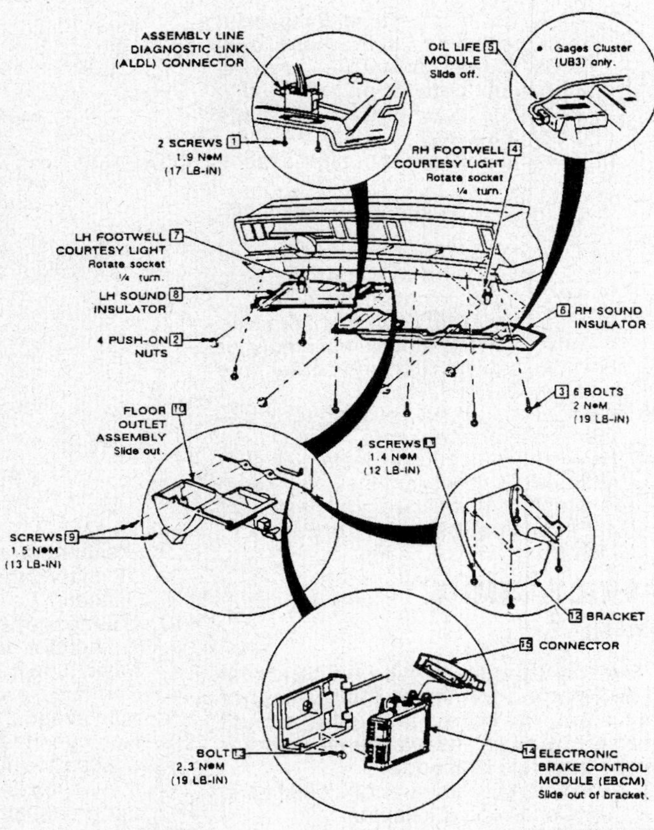

Fig. 13 Electronic Brake Control Module (EBCM) assembly removal. Park Avenue

3800 Engine

NOTE: On Air Bag Equipped Models, Refer To "Air Bag System Precautions" Located In The Front Of This Manual For System Disarming & Arming Procedures.

NOTE: Refer To "Computer Relearn Procedures" Located In The Front Of This Manual When Battery Power To The Computer Has Been Interrupted.

INDEX

PRECAUTIONS

AIR BAG SYSTEMS

Refer to "Air Bag System Precautions" in the front of this manual for system disarming and arming procedures.

FUEL SYSTEM PRESSURE RELIEF

After relieving fuel system pressure, a small amount of fuel may be released when servicing fuel pipes or connections. In order to reduce the risk of personal injury, cover fuel pipe fittings with a suitable shop towel before disconnecting to catch any fuel that may leak.

1. Loosen fuel filler cap to relieve tank pressure.
2. Connect fuel pressure gauge tool No. J34370-1, or equivalent, to fuel pressure connection. Wrap fitting in suitable shop towel.
3. Install bleed hose to suitable container, then open valve and bleed off pressure.
4. Disconnect fuel pressure gauge, then drain gauge in suitable container.

BATTERY GROUND CABLE

Prior to service, disconnect battery ground cable and isolate as required.

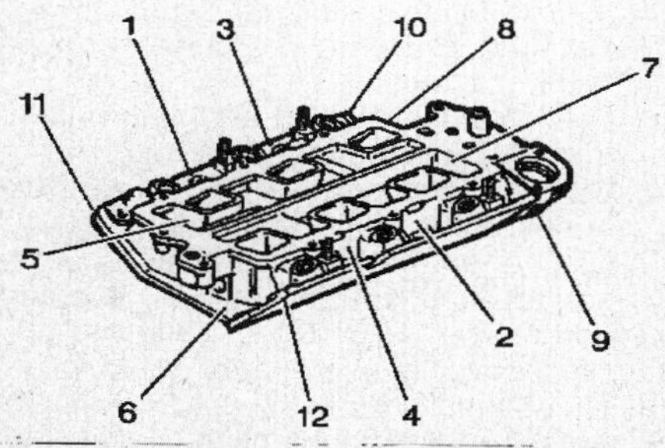

Fig. 1 Intake manifold tightening sequence. VIN K

COMPRESSION PRESSURE

When measuring compression, lowest cylinder must be within 70 percent of the highest cylinder with a minimum pressure of 100 psi. Perform compression test with engine at normal operating temperature, spark plugs removed and throttle wide open.

ENGINE MOUNT

REPLACE

1998–99

Mount

1. Install engine support fixture tool No. J28467-360, or equivalent.
2. Remove mount to bracket bolt.
3. Remove mount to frame bolts, then the engine mount.
4. Reverse procedure to install. Tighten all bolts and nuts to specifications.

Bracket

1. Remove fuel injector sight shield.
2. Using suitable lifting equipment, raise engine slightly to relieve stress on mount.
3. Remove engine mount to bracket nuts, then engine mount to bracket studs.
4. Remove engine mount brackets, then engine mount bracket studs and spacers.
5. Mark running direction with suitable felt pen or chalk, then remove drive belt and supercharger drive belt tensioner if required.

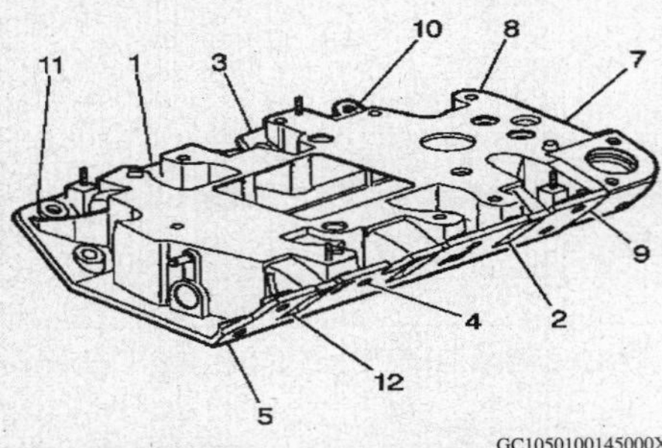

Fig. 2 Intake manifold tightening sequence. VIN 1

6. Without disconnecting lines, remove power steering pump and position aside.
7. Disconnect coil pack assembly, then position aside.
8. Remove coolant pump pulley, then the engine mount bracket.
9. Remove engine mount nuts and bolts, then the engine mount.
10. Reverse procedure to install, noting the following:
    a. **Torque** engine mount bolt nuts to 59 ft. lbs.
    b. **Torque** engine mount bracket stud nuts closest to A/C compressor to 33 ft. lbs.
    c. **Torque** engine mount bracket nuts to 59 ft. lbs.
    d. **Torque** engine mount to engine mount bracket nuts to 59 ft. lbs.

2000-02

Bonneville & LeSabre

1. Remove fuel injector sight shield.
2. Install suitable engine support fixture.
3. Raise and support vehicle.
4. Remove lower engine mount nut from stud.
5. Remove upper horizontal mount bolt in frame rail.
6. Remove nuts from vertical bolts.
7. Lower vehicle.
8. Remove two bolts from vertical bolt flanges on top of frame rail.
9. Raise and support vehicle.
10. Push two vertical bolts upward to clear mount.
11. Remove engine mount through wheelwell.
12. Reverse procedure to install. Tighten all bolts and nuts to specifications.

Park Avenue

1. Remove fuel injector sight shield.
2. Install suitable engine support fixture.
3. Remove engine mount to engine mount bracket nuts, studs and spacers.
4. **On models equipped with VIN 1 engine,** remove supercharger drive belt tensioner.
5. **On all models,** remove power steering pump and position aside.
6. Disconnect coil pack assembly and position aside.
7. Remove water pump pulley.
8. Remove engine mount bracket, engine mount nuts and bolts, then the engine mount.
9. Reverse procedure to install. Tighten all bolts and nuts to specifications.

ENGINE

REPLACE

1. Relieve fuel pressure as outlined under "Precautions."
2. Scribe alignment marks on hood for installation reference, then remove hood.
3. Drain engine coolant into suitable container.
4. Disconnect windshield washer, radiator and heater supply hoses.
5. Disconnect starter electrical connector and wiring.
6. Disconnect main engine harness and battery harness electrical connectors at relay center.
7. Mark running direction with suitable felt pen or chalk, then remove accessory drive belt.
8. Remove power steering pump and position aside.
9. Remove air intake duct and air cleaner assembly.
10. Remove throttle cable from linkage bracket, then other applicable cables.
11. Disconnect electrical connectors from the following:
    a. MAP sensor.
    b. Throttle position switch.
    c. Idle air control valve.
    d. Oxygen sensor.
    e. A/C compressor.
    f. Oil pressure switch.
    g. Power steering cutout switch.
    h. Vehicle speed sensor.
    i. Low oil level sensor.
12. Remove ignition coil ground strap attaching screws.
13. Disconnect fuel feed and return lines from fuel rail and pressure regulator.
14. Disconnect throttle body canister hoses.
15. Disconnect brake booster and heater control hoses from engine vacuum connection.
16. Disconnect cruise control servo vacuum hoses.
17. Raise and support vehicle.
18. Remove exhaust pipe from righthand manifold.
19. Install suitable engine lifting equipment, then raise engine slightly.
20. Remove A/C compressor and position aside.
21. Disconnect engine oil cooler lines, if equipped.
22. Remove front engine mount.
23. Remove righthand front engine to transaxle bracket.
24. Using suitable jack stands, support transaxle.
25. Remove engine to transaxle attaching bolts.
26. Remove flexplate cover.
27. Scribe flexplate installation alignment mark, then remove torque converter to flexplate attaching bolts.
28. Lower vehicle and remove torque axis engine mount.
29. Separate engine from transaxle.

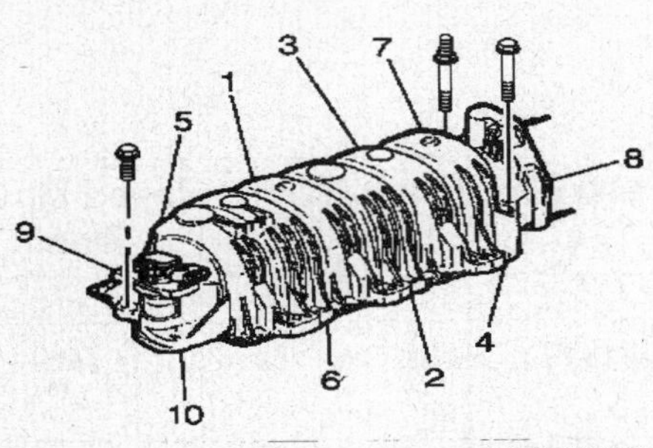

Fig. 3 Upper intake manifold. VIN K

30. Remove engine assembly.
31. Reverse procedure to install. Tighten all bolts and nuts to specifications.

INTAKE MANIFOLD

REPLACE

VIN K

The two bolts which mount the lower intake manifold to the cylinder head are accessible only after removing the upper intake manifold. The bolts are located in the righthand front and the lefthand rear corners of the lower intake manifold.

1. Remove upper intake manifold as described under "Upper Intake Manifold, Replace."
2. Drain cooling system into suitable container, then remove upper radiator hose from coolant outlet.
3. Remove alternator and set aside.
4. Remove drive belt tensioner.
5. Remove EGR valve outlet pipe.
6. Remove intake manifold bolts, then the manifold.
7. Reverse procedure to install, noting the following:
    a. Clean cylinder block, heads and intake manifold sealing surface of all oil using a suitable solvent.
    b. Remove adhesive compound from intake manifold bolts and bolt holes.
    c. Apply thread lock compound part No. 12345493, or equivalent, to intake manifold bolt threads prior to installation.
    d. Tighten intake manifold bolts in sequence, **Fig. 1.**

VIN 1

The two bolts which fasten the lower intake manifold to the cylinder head are accessible only after removing the upper intake manifold. The bolts are located in the righthand front and the lefthand rear corners of the lower intake manifold.

1. Relieve fuel pressure as outlined under "Precautions."
2. Remove fuel injector sight shield.
3. Remove plastic engine cover and air intake duct.
4. Disconnect manifold vacuum source, then drain cooling system into suitable container.

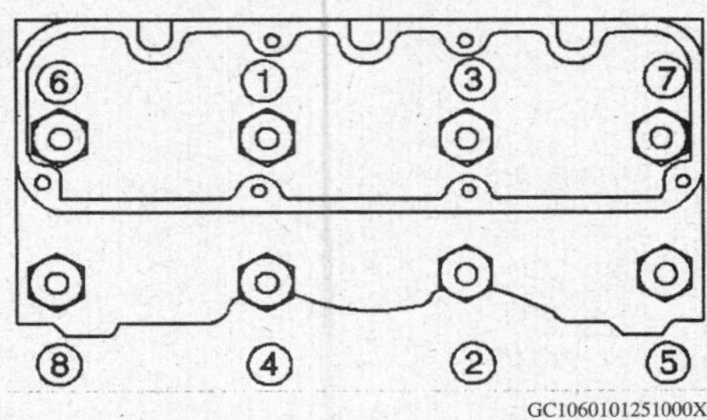

Fig. 4 Cylinder head tightening sequence

5. Disconnect righthand spark plug wires and position aside.
6. Remove fuel rail, then exhaust manifold heat shield.
7. Disconnect upper radiator and bypass hoses from coolant outlet.
8. Disconnect electrical connectors from the following:
   a. Throttle position sensor.
   b. Idle air control valve.
   c. Fuel injectors.
   d. MAP sensor.
9. Remove EGR outlet pipe.
10. Remove throttle and cruise control cables.
11. Remove throttle bracket with power steering reservoir and set aside.
12. Mark running direction with suitable felt pen or chalk, then remove inner accessory drive belt.
13. Disconnect heater hose from intake manifold.
14. Using standard double nut procedure, remove tensioner bracket to supercharger retaining stud.
15. Remove intake manifold attaching bolts, then the manifold.
16. Reverse procedure to install, noting the following:
    a. Clean cylinder block, heads and intake manifold sealing surface of all oil using a suitable solvent.
    b. Remove adhesive compound from intake manifold bolts and bolt holes.
    c. Apply thread lock compound part No. 12345493, or equivalent, to intake manifold bolt threads prior to installation.
    d. Tighten intake manifold bolts in sequence, **Fig. 2.**

UPPER INTAKE MANIFOLD

REPLACE

VIN K

1. Relieve fuel pressure as outlined under "Precautions."
2. Remove fuel injector sight shield and air intake duct.
3. Remove spark plug wires on righthand (rear) side of engine and position aside.
4. Remove fuel rail, then exhaust manifold heat shield.
5. Remove throttle cable bracket to cylinder head mounting bolt.
6. Remove throttle body support bracket.
7. Remove upper intake manifold attaching bolts, then the manifold, **Fig. 3.**
8. Reverse procedure to install. Tighten all bolts and nuts in sequence to specifications.

EXHAUST MANIFOLD

REPLACE

LEFTHAND SIDE (FRONT)

1. Relieve fuel pressure as outlined under "Precautions."
2. Remove two crossover pipe to manifold attaching bolts (VIN K) or two lefthand exhaust manifold to righthand exhaust manifold attaching bolts (VIN 1).
3. Disconnect spark plug wires at spark plugs.
4. Remove oil dipstick tube and dipstick.
5. Remove manifold attaching bolts, then the manifold.
6. Reverse procedure to install. Tighten all bolts and nuts to specifications.

RIGHTHAND SIDE (REAR)

Inspect the EGR outlet pipe for leaks whenever the pipe is removed from the righthand hand exhaust manifold. If a leak exists, replace the EGR adapter.

1. Disconnect spark plug wires from the spark plugs.
2. Remove transaxle oil level dipstick and tube.
3. Disconnect oxygen sensor electrical connector.
4. Remove bolts attaching righthand exhaust manifold to crossover pipe.
5. Raise and support vehicle.
6. Remove front exhaust pipe to exhaust manifold attaching nuts, then remove exhaust pipe from manifold.
7. Lower vehicle.
8. Remove engine lift bracket.
9. Remove exhaust manifold studs, then the exhaust manifold.
10. Reverse procedure to install. Tighten all bolts and nuts to specifications.

CYLINDER HEAD

REPLACE

1. Relieve fuel pressure as outlined under "Precautions."

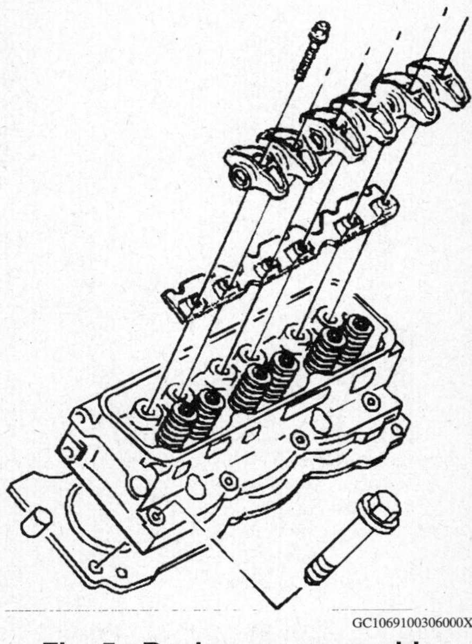

Fig. 5 Rocker arm assembly

2. Remove intake manifolds as outlined under "Intake Manifold, Replace."
3. Remove exhaust manifold as outlined under "Exhaust Manifold, Replace."
4. Remove appropriate valve cover.
5. Remove all wiring or brackets as required.
6. Remove rocker arm assemblies, guide plate and pushrods.
7. Remove and discard cylinder head attaching bolts, then the cylinder head.
8. Reverse procedure to install, noting the following:
   a. Clean all gasket mating surfaces and cylinder head bolt holes in block.
   b. Clean threads in block with appropriate tap.
   c. Apply suitable sealant to new bolt threads.
   d. Install new head gasket with arrow pointing towards front of engine.
   e. **Torque** cylinder head bolts to 37 ft. lbs. in sequence, **Fig. 4.**
   f. Rotate each bolt an additional 120° in sequence using torque angle meter No. J36660, or equivalent.

CAMSHAFT LOBE LIFT SPECIFICATIONS

Engine	Year	Int.	Exh.
3800	1998–2002	.258	.255

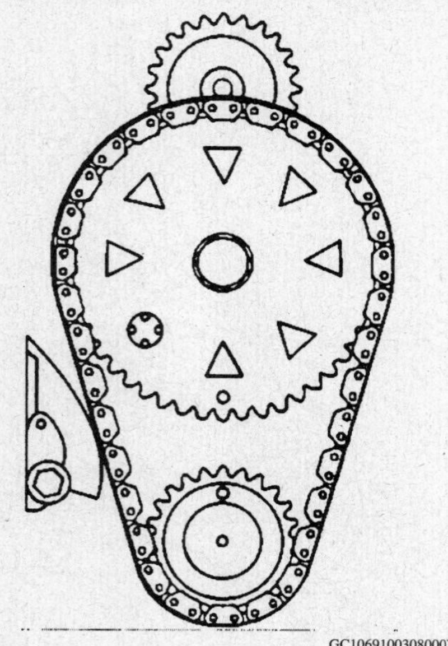

Fig. 6 Timing gear alignment marks

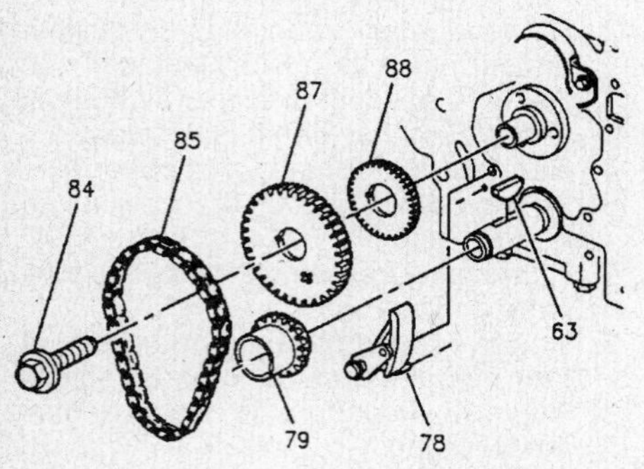

Fig. 7 Timing chain & sprockets

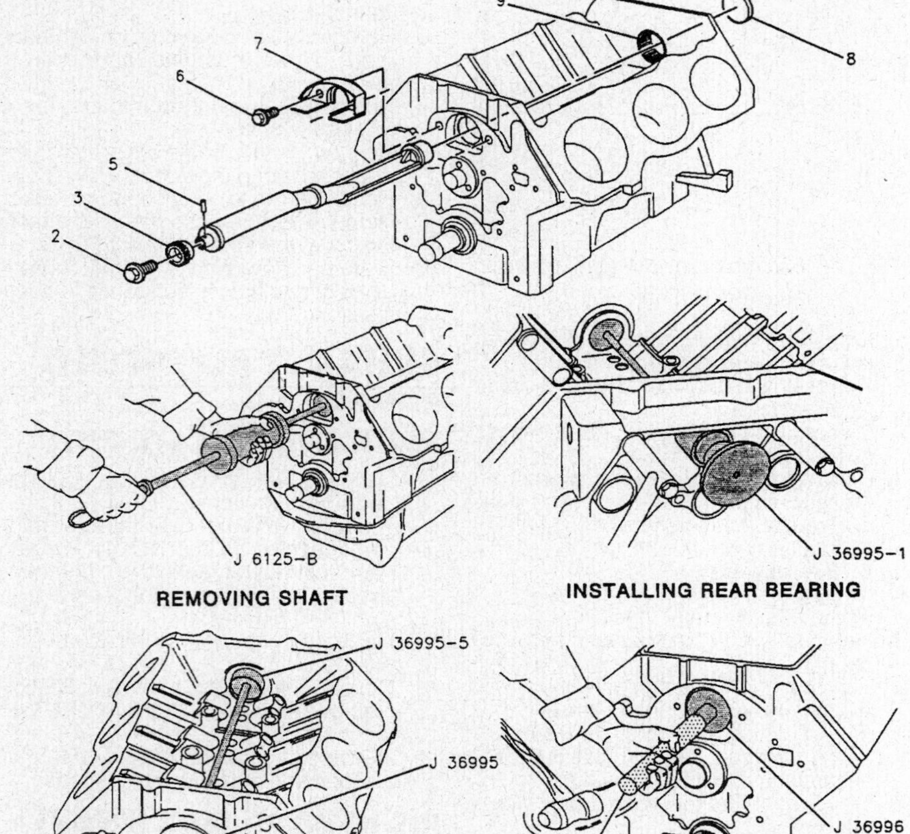

Fig. 8 Balance shaft service

VALVE CLEARANCE SPECIFICATIONS

These engines are equipped with hydraulic valve lifters. Valve clearance should be zero.

VALVE ADJUSTMENT

These engines are equipped with hydraulic valve lifters. There is no provision for adjustment.

ROCKER ARMS

Rocker arms are pedestal mounted over support plates, **Fig. 5.** To replace rocker arms, remove valve cover, pedestal retaining bolt(s), pedestal and the rocker arm. Replace rocker arms and pedestals as an assembly if they are damaged or excessively worn. If rocker arms are to be used again, they must be installed in original position.

VALVE GUIDES

The valve guides are an integral part of the cylinder head and cannot be replaced. If excessive valve stem clearance is noted, the valve guide must be reamed and an oversize valve guide installed. Valves are available in an oversize of .010 inch.

FRONT COVER

REPLACE

1. Remove torque axis mount and bracket.
2. Mark running direction with suitable felt pen or chalk, then remove drive belt.
3. Remove drive belt idler pulley/tensioner assembly.
4. Remove crankshaft balancer, sensor shield and crankshaft sensor.
5. Remove oil pan to front cover bolts.
6. Remove engine front cover attaching bolts, then the front cover.
7. Inspect timing chain for overall in-and-out movement, which should not exceed one inch.
8. Inspect sprockets for visible signs of wear or damage.
9. Clean gasket mating surfaces at timing chain cover and cylinder block.

Fig. 9 Balance shaft endplay measurement

10. If oil pan gasket is excessively swollen, oil pan must be removed and gasket replaced.
11. Reverse procedure to install, noting the following:
    a. Apply sealer No. 12346004, or equivalent, to bolt threads.
    b. Install engine front cover bolts.
    c. **On 1998 models, torque** front cover bolts to 11 ft. lbs.
    d. **On 1999–2002 models, torque** front cover bolts to 15 ft. lbs.
    e. **On all models,** rotate front cover bolts an additional 40° using torque angle meter tool No. J36660, or equivalent.
    f. Install oil pan to front engine cover bolts. **Torque** to 124 inch lbs.
    g. Install crankshaft sensor and shield. **Do not adjust crankshaft sensor.**
    h. Crankshaft sensor bolt is designed to permanently stretch when installed. **Do not install a standard bolt. Components will not be tightened properly if improper bolt is used.**

TIMING CHAIN

REPLACE

1. Remove front cover as outlined under "Front Cover, Replace."
2. Align timing marks on sprockets, **Fig. 6,** so they are as close together as possible.
3. Remove timing chain dampener.
4. Remove camshaft sprocket bolts, **Fig. 7.**
5. Remove camshaft sprocket and chain, then crankshaft sprocket.
6. Reverse procedure to install, noting the following:
    a. Ensure No. 1 piston is at TDC.
    b. Assemble timing chain on sprockets with their timing marks aligned, **Fig. 6.**
    c. Tighten camshaft sprocket bolts to specifications.

CAMSHAFT

REPLACE

1. Relieve fuel pressure as outlined under "Precautions."

Fig. 10 Balance shaft front radial play measurement

2. Remove intake manifold as outlined under "Intake Manifold, Replace."
3. Remove valve cover, rocker arms, pushrods and valve lifters.
4. Remove crankshaft pulley and crankshaft sensor cover.
5. Remove front cover, timing chain and sprockets.
6. Remove camshaft thrust plate and camshaft. **Avoid marring bearing surface when removing or installing camshaft.**
7. Reverse procedure to install. Coat camshaft and valve lifters with prelube part No. 1052365, or equivalent, prior to installation.

BALANCE SHAFT

REPLACE

REMOVAL

1. Remove engine as outlined under "Engine, Replace."
2. Remove flexplate, then the intake manifold as outlined under "Intake Manifold, Replace."
3. Remove lifter guide retainer, then the front cover.
4. Remove balance shaft drive gear bolt, **Fig. 8,** then the camshaft sprocket and timing chain.
5. Remove balance shaft retainer bolts, retainer and gear.
6. Remove balance shaft using slide hammer tool No. J6125-1B, or equivalent. **The balance shaft and both bearings are serviced as a complete package. Use only proper tools for bearing and shaft removal and installation. Inspect balance shaft drive gear and camshaft drive gear for nicks and burrs.**
7. Remove balance shaft rear plug.
8. Remove balance shaft rear bearing using replacement tool No. J36995-5, or equivalent.

INSTALLATION

1. Dip balance shaft rear bearing in clean engine oil.
2. Install bearing with rolled edge facing into engine and manufacturer's markings facing flexplate side using balance shaft bearing replacement tool No. J36995-1, or equivalent.
3. Dip balance shaft front bearing into clean engine oil.
4. Install balance shaft into block using installer tool Nos. J21465-13 and J36996, or equivalent.
5. Temporarily install balance shaft bearing retainer and bolts.
6. Install balance shaft drive gear.
7. Apply suitable sealant to bolt, then install and tighten to specifications.
8. Install balance shaft rear plug.
9. Measure balance shaft endplay, **Fig. 9,** which should not exceed .0067 inch.
10. Measure balance shaft radial play at both front and rear, **Figs. 10 and 11.** Front radial play should be 0–.0011 inch. Rear radial play should be .0005–.0047 inch.
11. With camshaft sprocket temporarily installed, turn camshaft so timing mark is straight down.
12. With camshaft sprocket and camshaft gear removed, turn balance shaft so timing mark on gear points straight down.
13. Install camshaft gear, aligning marks on balance shaft gear and camshaft gear by turning balance shaft, **Fig. 6.**
14. Turn crankshaft so No. 1 piston is at TDC.
15. Install timing chain and camshaft sprocket.
16. Measure gear lash, **Fig. 12,** at four places, every 1/4 turn. Lash should be .002–.005 inch.
17. Install balance shaft front bearing retainer and bolts. Tighten to specifications.
18. Install front cover, then the lifter guide retainer.
19. Install intake manifold, then the flexplate. Tighten flexplate bolts to specifications.
20. Install engine in vehicle.

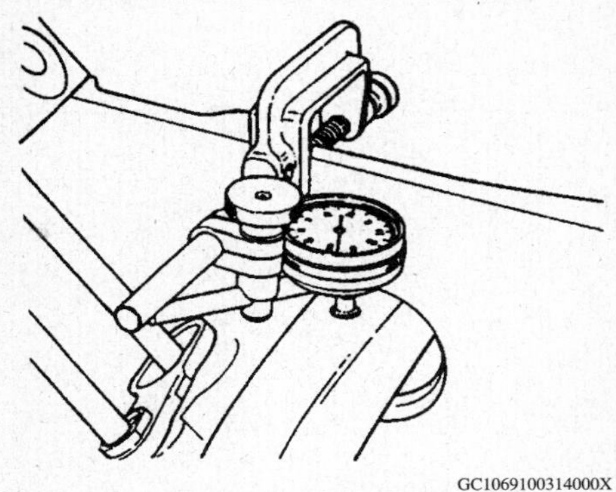

Fig. 11 Balance shaft rear radial play measurement

PISTON & ROD ASSEMBLY

1. Coat piston pin with oil.
2. Install one piston pin retainer into retainer groove.
3. Install connecting rod and piston pin, rod can be installed in either direction.

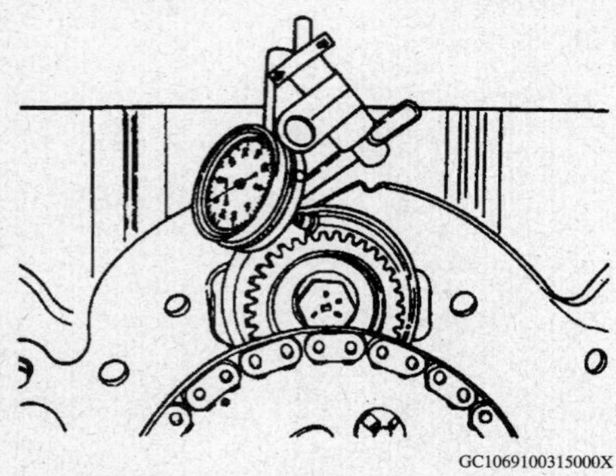

Fig. 12 Balance shaft gear lash inspection

4. Push piston pin in until it bottoms against installed piston pin retainer.
5. Ensure piston moves freely.

PISTONS, PINS & RINGS

Pistons and ring are available in standard sizes and oversizes of .010. Piston pins are supplied with piston and are available in standard size only.

To inspect piston fit in bore, measure bore diameter using suitable telescoping gauges and record reading. Measure piston across skirt at a point 3/4 inch below piston pin center line and record reading. Subtract piston diameter from bore diameter and compare to specified clearance.

MAIN & ROD BEARINGS

Main and rod bearings are available in standard sizes and a variety of undersizes.

CRANKSHAFT SEAL

REPLACE

REMOVAL

1. Remove transaxle assembly and flexplate.
2. Pry out seal using a suitable screwdriver or other flat bladed tool.
3. Clean surfaces and inspect for visual damage or excessive wear. Repair or replace components as required.

INSTALLATION

1. Apply clean engine oil to both sides of new seal.
2. Slide seal over mandrel of rear main oil seal installer tool No. J38196, or equivalent, until back of seal bottoms squarely against collar of tool.
3. Attach main seal oil installer tool to crankshaft by hand or **torque** attaching screws to 54 inch lbs.
4. Turn tool T-handle so that collar pushes seal into bore.
5. Turn handle until collar is tight against case.
6. Loosen T-handle until it comes to a stop, then remove attaching screws.

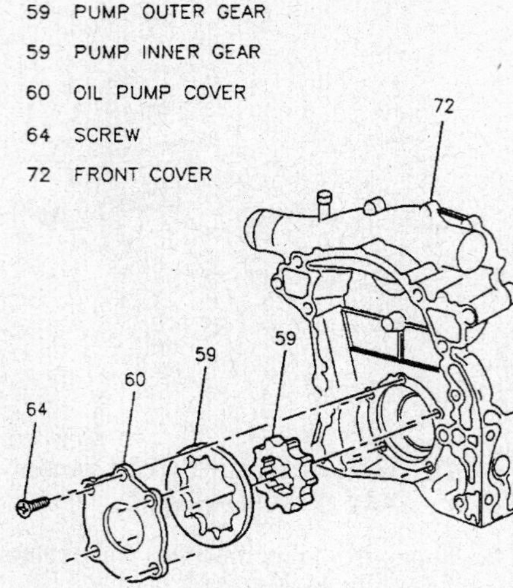

Fig. 13 Oil pump assembly

OIL PAN

REPLACE

1. Raise vehicle and drain engine oil into suitable container.
2. Remove flexplate inspection cover.
3. Remove oil level sensor located in oil pan before oil pan is removed. Damage to sensor will occur if pan is removed with sensor installed.
4. Remove oil filter.
5. Remove oil pan, then the pickup screen.
6. Remove old oil pan gasket.
7. Clean oil pan and cylinder block mating surfaces.
8. Reverse procedure to install. Tighten all bolts and nuts to specifications.

OIL PUMP SERVICE

REMOVAL & INSPECTION

1. Remove front cover as outlined under "Front Cover, Replace."
2. Remove oil filter adapter, pressure regulator valve and spring.
3. Remove oil pump cover and gears, **Fig. 13.**
4. Inspect pump cover and housing for cracks, scoring, porous or damaged casting, damaged threads or excessive wear or galling. Replace as required.
5. Inspect pressure regulator valve for scoring, burrs or sticking in valve bore. Replace as required.
6. Inspect pressure regulator valve spring for tension loss or bending. Replace spring as required.
7. Inspect gears for chipping galling or excessive wear. Replace as required.

ASSEMBLY & INSTALLATION

1. Measure oil pump inner gear tip clearance, **Fig. 14.** Maximum clearance should be .006 inch.
2. Measure oil pump outer gear diameter

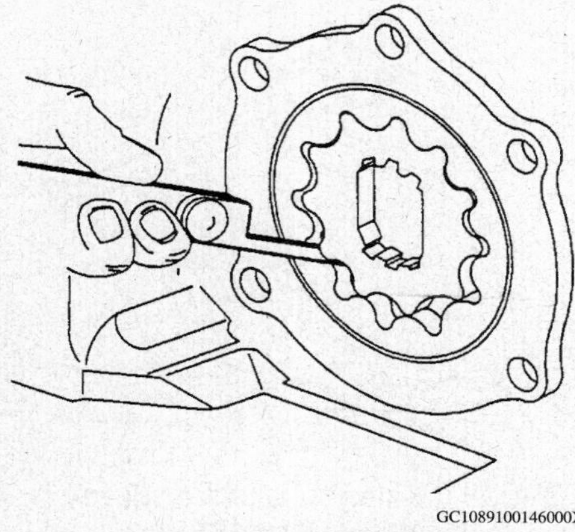

Fig. 14 Oil pump inner gear tip clearance inspection

clearance, **Fig. 15,** which should be .008–.015 inch.
3. Measure oil pump gear end clearance with gear dropped in housing, **Fig. 16,** which should be .0001–.0035 inch.
4. Measure pressure regulator valve for valve to bore clearance of .0015–.0030 inch.
5. Lubricate all gears with clean engine oil, then install gears in housing.
6. Pack pump cavity with suitable petroleum jelly.
7. Install pump cover. Tighten cover attaching screws to specifications.
8. Install pressure regulator valve and spring.
9. Install oil filter adapter using a new gasket. Tighten oil filter adapter attaching bolts to specifications.
10. Install front cover on engine. **Ensure inner pump gear is properly engaged on crankshaft sprocket during front cover installation.**

CRANKSHAFT

REPLACE

REMOVAL

1. Remove engine as outlined under "Engine, Replace" in this section.
2. Mount engine in a suitable stand.
3. Remove oil pan.
4. Remove front cover.
5. Remove timing chain and gears.
6. Remove flexplate.
7. Remove connecting rod caps and lower bearing halves.
8. Remove main bearing caps and lower bearing halves.
9. Remove crankshaft and upper bearing halves.

INSTALLATION

1. Install main bearing upper halves.
2. Lubricate crankshaft to main bearing contact areas with clean engine oil or engine assembly lubricant.
3. Carefully lower crankshaft into position.
4. Crankshaft bearing caps must be tapped into cylinder block cavity using a suitable brass, lead, or leather mallet before installing attaching bolts in

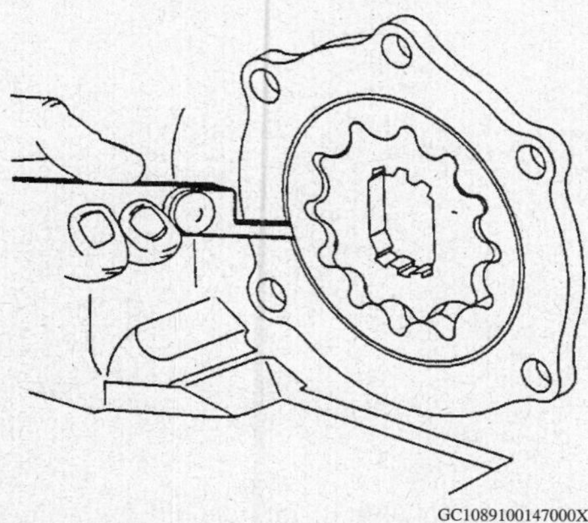

Fig. 15 Oil pump outer gear diameter clearance inspection

order to prevent possibility of cylinder block or crankshaft bearing cap damage. **Do not use attaching bolts to pull crankshaft bearing caps into seats. Failure to heed this precaution may result in cylinder block or bearing cap damage.**

5. Install main bearing lower halves.
6. Install main bearing cap bolts, starting them by hand. Ensure bottom of bearing cap is parallel to bottom of channel.
7. **Torque** all bolts to 52 ft. lbs. in equal increments.
8. Loosen all bolts 360°.
9. **Torque** all bolts to 15 ft. lbs.
10. **Torque** all bolts to 30 ft. lbs.
11. Rotate all bolts an additional 35° using torque angle meter tool No. J36660-A, or equivalent.
12. Rotate all bolts an additional 35°.
13. Rotate all bolts an additional 40°.
14. Apply thread lock compound part No. 12345493, or equivalent, to side main bolts.
15. Install side main bolts. **Torque** to 11 ft. lbs., then rotate an additional 45°.
16. Install connecting rod bearings and bearing caps. **Torque** cap bolts to 20 ft. lbs., then rotate an additional 50°.
17. Pry connecting rod back and forth and inspect for binding. If required, loosen and tighten cap bolts again.
18. Reverse remaining removal steps to complete installation process. Tighten all bolts and nuts to specifications.

BELT TENSION DATA

This engine is equipped with an automatic belt tensioner.

SERPENTINE DRIVE BELT

BELT ROUTING

Refer to **Figs. 17 and 18** for serpentine drive belt routing.

BELT TENSIONER, REPLACE

VIN 1

1. Remove supercharger belt.

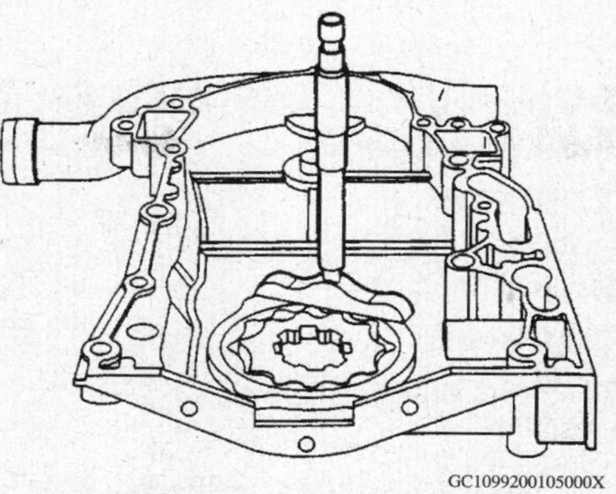

Fig. 16 Oil pump gear end clearance inspection

2. Remove ignition module.
3. Remove tensioner bolts, then the tensioner.
4. Reverse procedure to install.

VIN K

1. Raise and support vehicle.
2. Remove lower splash shield, then drain coolant into suitable container.
3. Install front splash shield, lower vehicle.
4. Mark running direction with suitable felt pen or chalk, then remove drive belt.
5. Remove alternator and heater hoses.
6. Remove drive belt tensioner.
7. Reverse procedure to install. Tighten tensioner bolts to specifications.

COOLING SYSTEM BLEED

1. Fill cooling system and leave radiator cap off.
2. Turn HVAC control to any A/C mode and set temperature to highest setting.
3. Start engine and allow engine to idle until bottom radiator hose is hot.
4. Cycle engine speed up to 3000 RPM and back to idle five times.
5. Slowly open bleed valve on rear of thermostat housing for approximately 15 seconds to expel any trapped air in cooling system.
6. Refill radiator and install pressure cap.
7. Allow engine to return to outside temperature, then fill coolant reservoir to FULL COLD mark.

THERMOSTAT

REPLACE

1. Remove engine cover.
2. With engine cool, drain engine coolant below thermostat level.
3. Disconnect radiator hose from thermostat housing.
4. Remove thermostat housing, gasket and thermostat.
5. Reverse procedure to install, noting the following:
   a. Ensure thermostat gasket sealing surfaces are thoroughly clean prior to installation.

Fig. 17 Serpentine belt routing & replacement. VIN 1

   b. Install thermostat with new gasket.
   c. Tighten thermostat housing retaining bolt(s) to specifications.
   d. Fill and bleed cooling system as outlined under "Cooling System Bleed."

WATER PUMP

REPLACE

VIN K

Removal

1. Drain cooling system into suitable container.
2. Mark running direction with suitable felt pen or chalk, then remove drive belt.
3. Remove water pump pulley.
4. Note their locations, **Fig. 19,** then remove water pump mounting bolts.
5. Remove water pump.

Installation

1. Clean gasket mating surfaces.
2. Install new gasket, then mount water pump in place on engine.
3. Install bolts. **Torque** short bolts (1) to 11 ft. lbs., and long bolts (2) to 22 ft. lbs., **Fig. 19.**
4. Install drive belt.
5. Fill cooling system, then start engine and inspect for leaks.

VIN 1

Removal

1. Remove A/C compressor splash shield.
2. Drain coolant into suitable container.
3. Mark running direction with suitable felt pen or chalk, then remove supercharger and accessory drive belt.

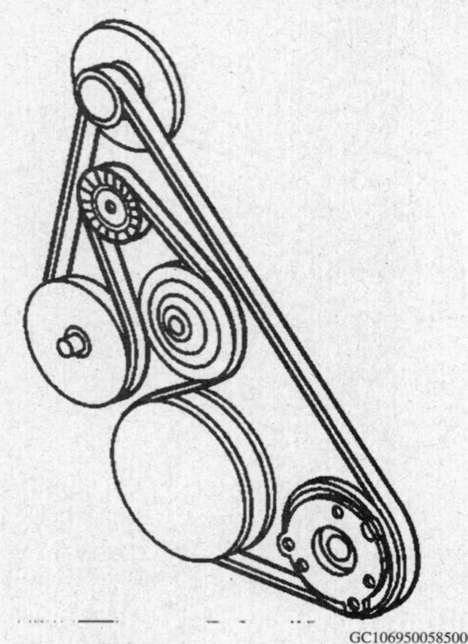

Fig. 18 Serpentine belt routing & replacement. VIN K

4. Remove coil pack mounting hardware and position coil pack out of way.
5. Remove supercharger belt tensioner.
6. Remove engine mount, power steering pump and engine mount bracket.
7. Remove idler pulley and water pump pulley.
8. Remove water pump.
9. Clean gasket mating surfaces.

Installation

1. Install new gasket, then position water pump on engine.
2. Install bolts. **Torque** short bolts (1) to 11 ft. lbs., and long bolts (2) to 22 ft. lbs., **Fig. 19.**
3. Install water pump pulley. Tighten bolts to specifications.
4. Install idler pulley. Tighten bolt to specifications.
5. Install engine mount bracket, power steering pump and engine mount.
6. Install supercharger belt tensioner.
7. Install accessory drive belt, then the supercharger belt.
8. Fill cooling system.
9. Install A/C compressor splash shield.
10. Bleed cooling system as outlined under "Cooling System Bleed."
11. Start engine and inspect for leaks.

RADIATOR

REPLACE

EIGHTY EIGHT, LSS & REGENCY

1. Drain engine coolant into suitable container.
2. Remove upper fan mounting bolts.
3. Remove upper radiator panel.
4. Remove coolant hoses from radiator and coolant recovery tank hose from radiator neck.
5. Disconnect coolant fan electrical connector.
6. Disconnect transaxle oil cooler lines from radiator side tank.
7. Remove radiator from vehicle.
8. Reverse procedure to install.

BONNEVILLE, LESABRE & PARK AVENUE

1998-99

Refer to "Eighty Eight, LSS & Regency" for procedure.

2000-02

1. Drain engine coolant into suitable container.
2. Remove upper radiator seal.
3. **On Park Avenue models,** remove upper two bolts from hood latch support.
4. **On all models,** remove upper radiator support bar.
5. Disconnect and plug coolant overflow hose from radiator.
6. Disconnect upper and lower radiator hoses from radiator and position out of way.
7. Remove bolt from transmission oil cooler pipe clip at lower radiator tie bar.
8. Remove cooling fans.
9. Disconnect transmission fluid cooler lines from radiator using coupling tool No. J41623-B, or equivalent. Position lines aside.
10. Disconnect overflow hose from radiator.
11. **The bolt retaining the condenser to radiator end tank is of a special length and must be used upon installation. Use of other bolts may damage radiator end tank.**
12. Remove condenser mounting bolts, then separate condenser from radiator and remove radiator from vehicle.
13. Reverse procedure to install, noting the following:
    a. **The bolt retaining the condenser to radiator end tank is of a special length and must be used upon installation. Use of other bolts may damage radiator end tank.**
    b. Tighten all bolts and nuts to specifications.
    c. Fill radiator with proper coolant.
    d. Bleed cooling system as outlined under "Cooling System Bleed."
    e. Start engine, then inspect for and correct any leakage.

FUEL PUMP

REPLACE

EIGHTY EIGHT, LSS & REGENCY

1. Relieve fuel pressure as outlined under "Precautions."
2. **Do not handle fuel sender assembly by fuel pipes or damage to fuel pipe joints could occur.**
3. Clean all fuel pipe and hose connections and surrounding areas before disconnecting connections to prevent fuel system contamination.

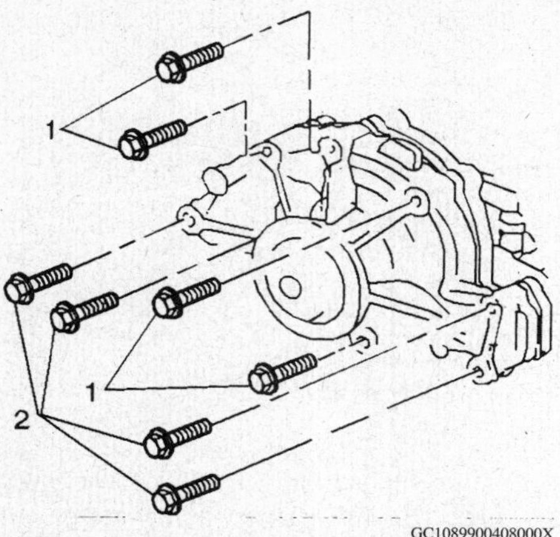

Fig. 19 Water pump bolt locations

4. Drain fuel from tank into a suitable storage unit.
5. Support fuel tank, then remove tank straps and slowly lower tank until fuel line quick-connect fittings are accessible.
6. Disconnect fuel line fittings, then remove fuel tank from vehicle.
7. Remove fuel sender assembly retaining cam using fuel sender wrench tool No. J39765, or equivalent.
8. Remove and discard fuel sender assembly O-ring.
9. Reverse procedure to install, noting the following:
    a. Clean and inspect O-ring sealing surfaces.
    b. Replace fuel sender O-rings when installing sender.
    c. Use care not to fold over or twist fuel pump strainer when installing sender assembly.
    d. Use new O-ring when installing fuel sender/pump assembly.
    e. Attach fuel lines with original type fasteners and hardware.
    f. **Do not repair sections of fuel pipe.**
    g. Upon completion of repairs, turn ignition On for two seconds, then Off for 10 seconds.
    h. Turn ignition back On and inspect for leaks.

BONNEVILLE, LESABRE & PARK AVENUE

1998-99

Refer to "Eighty Eight, LSS & Regency" for procedure.

2000-02

1. Clean fuel pipe connections, hose connections and surrounding areas to prevent fuel system contamination.
2. Do not handle fuel sender/pump assembly by fuel pipes or damage to pipe joints could occur.
3. Relieve fuel system pressure as outlined in "Precautions."

4. Drain fuel from tank into a suitable storage unit.
5. Remove spare tire cover, jack and spare tire.
6. Remove rear compartment floor trim.
7. Remove fuel sender/pump access panel.
8. Remove quick connect fittings and electrical connector at fuel sender/pump assembly.
9. Remove electrical connector at fuel tank pressure sensor.
10. Remove fuel sender/pump retaining ring and assembly retaining cam with fuel sender locknut wrench tool No. J39765, or equivalent.
11. Remove fuel sender/pump from vehicle.
12. Reverse procedure to install, noting the following:
    a. Replace fuel sender O-rings during installation to avoid damaging sender assembly.
    b. Attach fuel lines with original type fasteners and hardware.
    c. **Do not repair sections of fuel pipe.**
    d. Upon completion of repairs, turn ignition On for two seconds, then Off for 10 seconds.
    e. Turn ignition back On and inspect for leaks.

FUEL FILTER

REPLACE

1. Relieve fuel pressure as outlined under "Precautions."

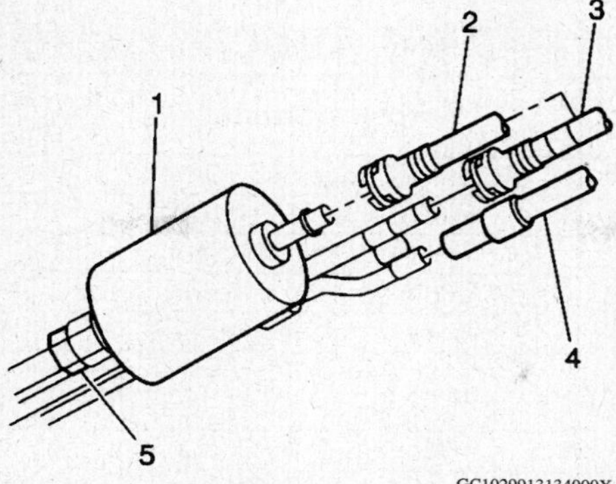

Fig. 20 Fuel filter replacement

2. Raise and support vehicle.
3. Remove quick-connect fitting at fuel feed line (2), **Fig. 20.**
4. Remove threaded connection (5) at inline fuel filter.
5. Inspect fuel lines and O-rings for cuts, swelling, cracks and distortion.
6. Inspect fuel return line and fuel vent pipe.
7. Drain any remaining fuel into suitable container.
8. Reverse procedure to install. Tighten fuel filter outlet nut to specifications.

SUPERCHARGER

REPLACE

1. Relieve fuel pressure as outlined under "Precautions."
2. Remove engine cover.
3. Remove injector sight shield.
4. Remove supercharger belt.
5. Disconnect vacuum brake booster hose from vacuum connections and position aside.
6. Remove evaporative emission canister purge valve, then secure hose to air inlet grille.
7. Remove alternator brace.
8. Disconnect righthand side spark plug wires from ignition module and position aside.
9. Disconnect electrical connectors from fuel injectors.
10. Remove MAP sensor bracket.
11. Remove fuel rail mounting bolts and the fuel rail with injectors.
12. Remove boost control solenoid.
13. Remove throttle body nuts.
14. Remove supercharger.
15. Reverse procedure to install, noting the following:
    a. Clean intake manifold and supercharger mating surfaces.
    b. **Do not use any sealer on supercharger gasket.**
    c. Install supercharger mounting bolts, then tighten to specifications.

TIGHTENING SPECIFICATIONS

Year	Component	Torque/Ft. Lbs.
1998–2002	Accessory Drive Belt Tensioner	37
	Balance Shaft Gear Bolt	16①
	Balance Shaft Retainer	22
	Boost Control Solenoid Retaining Nut	71②
	Bypass Valve Actuator Bolts	18
	Camshaft Sensor To Front Cover	89②
	Camshaft Sprocket Bolts	74⑤
	Connecting Rod Bolts	20④
	Coolant Plug	13
	Coolant Temperature Sensor To Intake	15
	Crankshaft Balancer	110⑥
	Crankshaft Sensor Clamp Bolt	40②
	Crankshaft Sensor To Front Cover	22
	Cylinder Block Drain Plug	13
	Cylinder Head To Block	③
	EGR Pipe To EGR Valve	22
	EGR Pipe To Exhaust Manifold	21
	EGR Valve Adapter	37
	EGR Valve To Intake Manifold Adapter	22
	Engine Mount To Cylinder Block	70
	Engine Mount To Frame Rail	52
	Engine Mount To Mount Bracket	59
	ESC Knock Sensor	14
	Exhaust Manifold To Cylinder Head	22
	Exhaust Pipe To Exhaust Manifold	18
	Flexplate Cover To Transaxle	10
	Flexplate To Crankshaft	11④
	Front Cover To Block	22
	Fuel Rail Hold-Down Bolts & Nuts	89②
	Fuel Filter Outlet Nut	22
	Fuel Injector Rail Stud	18
	Generator Support Through Generator	36
	Generator Support To Cylinder Head	36
	Heater Hose Fitting To Intake	11
	Ignition Module To Generator Support	18
	Intake Manifold To Cylinder Head	11
	Intake Manifold (Upper) To Lower Manifold	89②
	Main Bearing Cap Bolts	⑦
	Oil Filter Adapter To Front Cover (1998–99)	22
	Oil Filter Adapter To Front Cover (2000–02)	11④
	Oil Galley Plugs	22
	Oil Level Indicator Tube	14
	Oil Level Sensor To Oil Pan	15
	Oil Pan Drain Plug	22
	Oil Pan To Block	10
	Oil Pan To Front Cover	10
	Oil Pressure Switch	12
	Oil Pump Cover To Front Cover	98②
	Oil Screen Housing To Cylinder Block	11
	O_2 Sensor	31

Continued

TIGHTENING SPECIFICATIONS—Continued

Year	Component	Torque/Ft. Lbs.
1998–2002	Pulley Assembly To Crankshaft	111⑥
	RH Exhaust Manifold To LH Exhaust Manifold	15
	Rocker Arm Cover	89②
	Rocker Arm Pedestal	11⑤
	Spark Plug	11
	Starter Motor	32
	Supercharger To Lower Intake Manifold	17
	Thermostat Housing	15
	Throttle Cable Bracket	35②
	Timing Chain Damper	16
	Torque Converter To Flexplate	46
	Transaxle To Engine Block	55
	Valve Lifter Guide Bolts	22
	Water Pump Pulley	116②

① — Rotate an additional 70°.
② — Inch lbs.
③ — Refer to "Cylinder Head, Replace."
④ — Rotate an additional 50°.
⑤ — Rotate an additional 90°.
⑥ — Rotate an additional 76°.
⑦ — Refer to "Crankshaft, Replace."

Rear Suspension

NOTE: On Air Bag Equipped Models, Refer To "Air Bag System Precautions" Located In The Front Of This Manual For System Disarming & Arming Procedures.

NOTE: Refer To "Computer Relearn Procedures" Located In The Front Of This Manual When Battery Power To The Computer Has Been Interrupted.

INDEX

DESCRIPTION

The rear suspension components include independent control arms, springs, and struts for each rear wheel. This allows vertical movement of one rear wheel without any effect on the other. A suspension adjustment link on each arm provides for toe adjustment and minimal alignment variation during suspension movement. A stabilizer shaft minimizes body roll.

The bottom of each shock absorber mounts to the suspension knuckle. The top of each shock attaches to a reinforced body area. These shocks are non-adjustable and cannot be refilled. Replace any shock absorber if it suffers from loss of resistance, physical damage or fluid leakage.

Some models are equipped with Electronic Level Control (ELC) which utilizes air adjustable shocks and maintains the rear trim height under a variety of load conditions.

A single unit sealed hub and bearing is bolted to the rear knuckle and does not require wheel bearing adjustments or periodic maintenance. There is an integral speed sensor ring on the inboard side of the bearing for anti-lock brake functions. The wheel speed sensor is incorporated within the knuckle.

HUB & BEARING

REPLACE

DRUM BRAKES

1. Raise and support rear of vehicle.
2. Remove wheel assembly and brake drum. **Do not hammer on drum as bearing damage may occur.**
3. Disconnect ABS sensor wire.
4. Remove four hub and bearing assembly mounting bolts. **These four bolts also support brake assembly. When removing these bolts, support brake assembly with suitable wire. Do not let brake line or ABS electrical wire support weight.**
5. Remove hub and bearing assembly from axle, **Fig. 1.**
6. Reverse procedure to install. Tighten mounting bolts and wheel lug nuts to specifications.

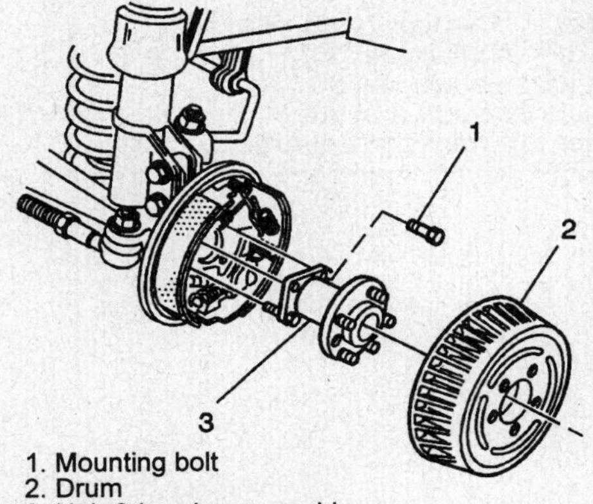

Fig. 1 Hub & bearing assembly

DISC BRAKES

1. Raise and support rear of vehicle.
2. Remove wheel and tire assembly.
3. Remove caliper and position aside.
4. Remove rotor, then disconnect wheel speed sensor electrical connector.
5. Remove four hub and bearing assembly mounting bolts.
6. Remove hub and bearing assembly, then the brake shield.
7. Clean control arm face and bore to remove any debris.
8. Reverse procedure to install. Tighten mounting bolts and wheel lug nuts to specifications.

STRUT

REPLACE

1. Raise and support vehicle, then remove tire and wheel.
2. Support lower control arm with suitable jack stand.
3. Disconnect air line from strut.
4. Remove strut lower mounting bolts, **Fig. 2.**
5. Remove luggage compartment trim to access strut tower mounting nuts, **Fig. 3.**
6. Remove strut tower mounting nuts and upper reinforcement, then the strut from vehicle.
7. Reverse procedure to install. Tighten mounting nuts and wheel lug nuts to specifications.

COIL SPRING

REPLACE

1. Raise and support vehicle.
2. Remove rear wheels and tires.
3. Support control arm with suitable jack stand.
4. Disconnect air line from shock.
5. Remove strut to control arm mounting bolts.
6. Remove cotter pin and slotted hex nut from tie rod.
7. Separate tie rod from lower control arm using linkage puller tool No. J24319-B, or equivalent.
8. Slowly lower control arm until it bottoms on support assembly.
9. Pry under lower spring insulator and remove spring with insulator.
10. Remove upper insulator by pulling downward.
11. Reverse procedure to install. Tighten all bolts and nuts to specifications.

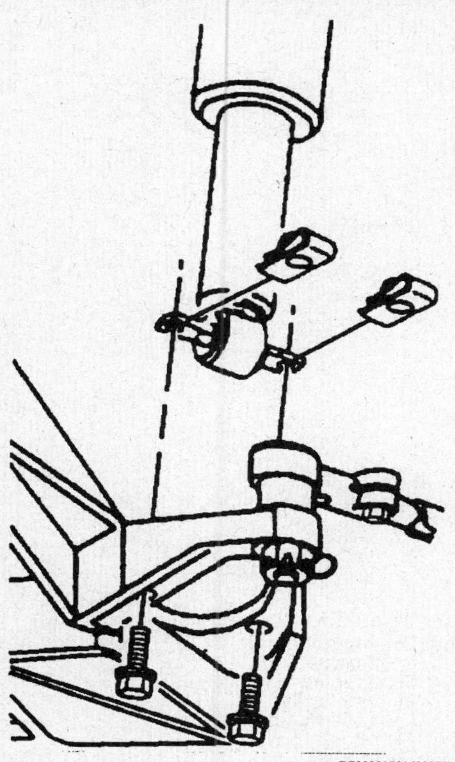
GC2030100163000X

Fig. 2 Rear strut lower mounting

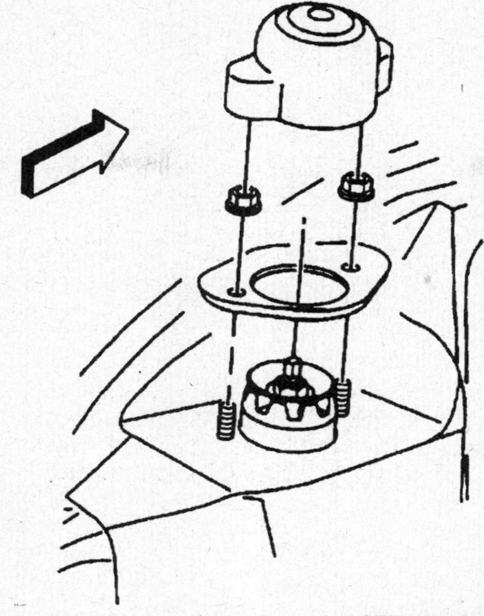
GC2030100164000X

Fig. 3 Strut tower mounting nuts

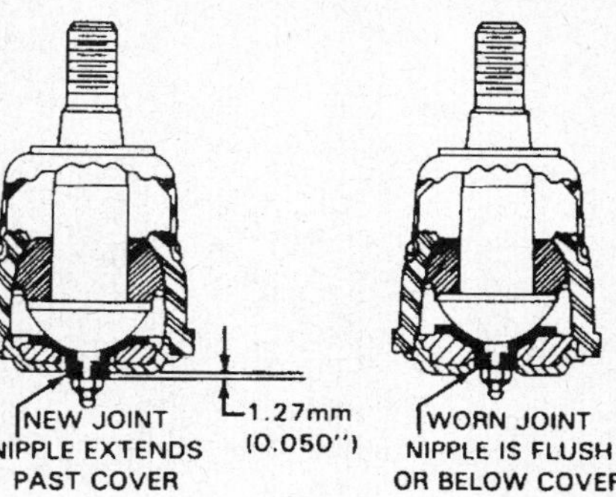

Fig. 4 Ball joint inspection

BALL JOINT INSPECTION

The ball joint has a visual wear indicator. Inspecting the condition of the ball joint is a simple procedure but must be followed accurately to prevent unnecessary ball joint replacement.

The vehicle must be supported by the wheels during inspection to ensure vehicle weight is properly loading the ball joints.

The ball joint is inspected for wear by visual observation alone. Wear is indicated by retraction of the ½ inch diameter nipple into the ball joint cover (the ball joint grease fitting is threaded into this nipple).

The nipple protrudes .050 inch beyond the surface of the ball joint cover on a new unworn joint. Normal wear will result in the surface of this nipple retracting very slowly inward. The ball joint should be replaced if the nipple is flush or below the cover surface, **Fig. 4.**

Ball stud tightness in the knuckle boss should also be inspected when inspecting the ball joint. This may be done by shaking the wheel and feeling for movement of the stud end or castellated nut at the knuckle boss.

Inspecting the fastener tightness at the castellated nut is an alternative method of inspecting (a loose nut can indicate a bent stud or an "opened up" hole in the knuckle boss). If worn, the ball joint and knuckle must be replaced.

If the ball joint is separated from the knuckle for suspension service, the ball joint seal should be inspected for damage. A damaged seal will cause joint failure. If seal damage is found the ball joint should be replaced.

BALL JOINT

REPLACE

BONNEVILLE, EIGHTY EIGHT, LESABRE, LSS & REGENCY

1998-99

1. Raise and support vehicle.
2. Remove wheel and tire.
3. **On models equipped with electronic level control,** remove height sensor link from righthand control arm.
4. **On all models,** remove parking brake cable retaining clip at lefthand control arm.
5. Separate adjustment link from knuckle using universal steering linkage puller No. J24319-01, or equivalent, **Fig. 5.**
6. Support control arm with a suitable jack to prevent spring from forcing it downward.
7. Remove cotter pin and slotted hex nut from ball joint.
8. Separate knuckle from ball joint stud using separator tool No. J43828, or equivalent.
9. Install suitable ball joint removal tools and press ball joint out of control arm, **Fig. 5.**
10. Reverse procedure to install. Tighten all bolts and nuts to specifications.

2000-02

On these models the ball joint is not serviced separately. The complete lower control arm assembly must be replaced. Refer to "Control Arm, Replace" for procedure.

PARK AVENUE

On these models the ball joint is not serviced separately. The complete lower control arm assembly must be replaced. Refer to "Control Arm, Replace" for procedure.

CONTROL ARM

REPLACE

EIGHTY EIGHT, LSS, REGENCY & 1998-1999 BONNEVILLE

1. Remove adjustment link from lower control arm.
2. Remove spring.
3. Using ball joint separator tool No. J34505, or equivalent, separate ball joint stud from knuckle.
4. Remove control arm.
5. Reverse procedure to install.

LESABRE, PARK AVENUE & 2000-02 BONNEVILLE

1. Raise and support vehicle, then remove rear tires and wheels.
2. Remove exhaust system as required.
3. Remove coil springs as outlined under "Coil Spring, Replace."
4. Remove rear brake calipers from control arms, then parking brake cables from calipers.
5. Disconnect electrical connectors from wiring harness.
6. Disconnect Electronic Level Control (ELC) electrical connector and vent hose.
7. Remove ELC air tube from compressor.
8. Support rear suspension support assembly with suitable jack.
9. Remove three bolts per side securing support assembly brackets to vehicle body, **Fig. 6.**
10. Remove front and rear suspension support assembly bolts, then support assembly.
11. On lefthand control arm, remove Electronic Level Control height sensor.
12. Remove stabilizer link bolts and nuts.
13. Remove ABS electrical connectors.
14. Remove hub and bearing as outlined under "Hub & Bearing, Replace."
15. Remove bolt and nut securing control arm to rear suspension support assembly, then the control arm.
16. Reverse procedure to install. Tighten all bolts and nuts to specifications.

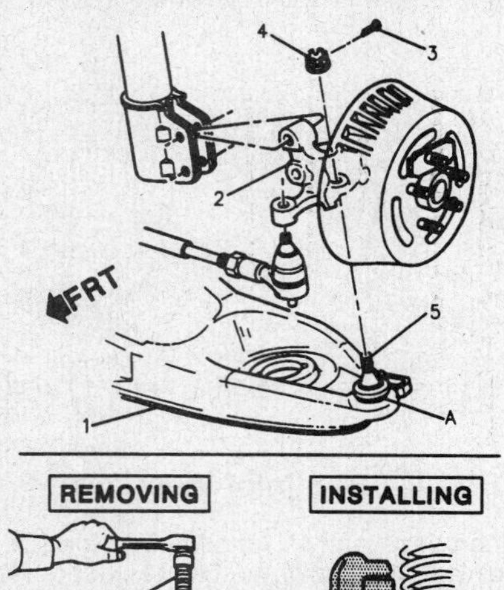

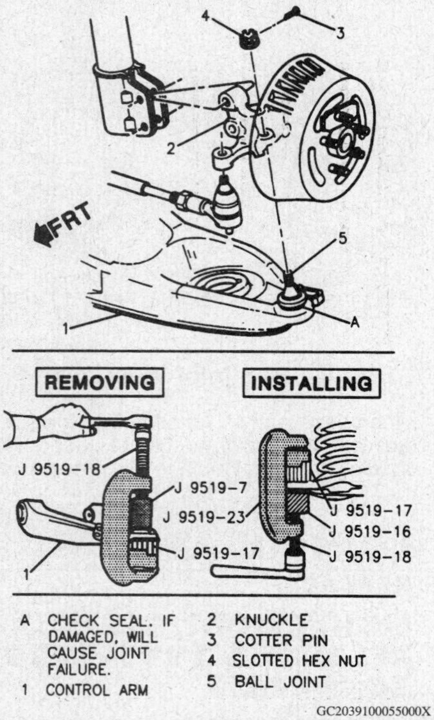

Fig. 5 Rear ball joint replacement

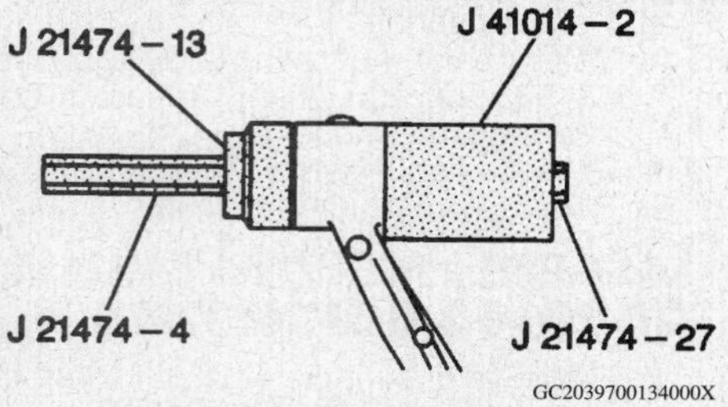

J 21474 – 13
J 41014 – 2
J 21474 – 4
J 21474 – 27
GC2039700134000X

Fig. 8 Control arm bushing installation

CONTROL ARM BUSHING

REPLACE

BONNEVILLE, EIGHTY EIGHT, LESABRE, LSS & REGENCY

1998–99

1. Remove control arm as outlined under "Control Arm, Replace."
2. Refer to **Figs. 7 and 8** when servicing control arm bushings.

2000–02

On these models the ball joint is not serviced separately. The complete lower control arm assembly must be replaced.

PARK AVENUE

On these models the ball joint is not serviced separately. The complete lower control arm assembly must be replaced.

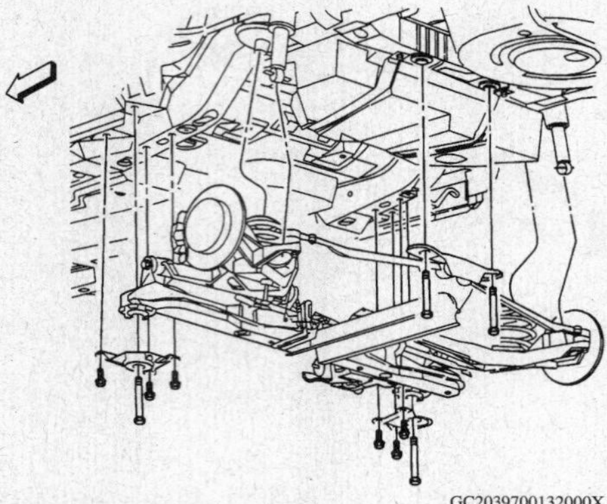

Fig. 6 Rear suspension support assembly removal. LeSabre, Park Avenue & 2000–02 Bonneville

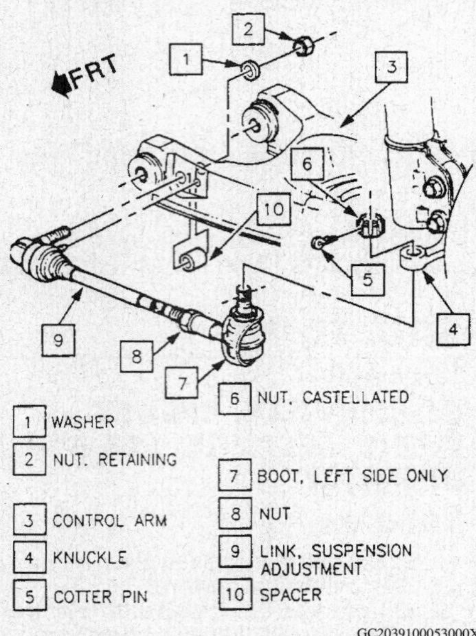

Fig. 9 Tie rod/adjustment link installation

TIE ROD

REPLACE

1. Raise and support vehicle.
2. Remove wheel assembly, cotter key and castle nut, **Fig. 9.**
3. Disconnect outer tie rod/adjustment from lower control arm or knuckle using steering linkage puller tool No. J24319-01, or equivalent. **Do not use a wedge when disconnecting tie rod/adjustment from lower control arm or knuckle since seal damage will occur.**
4. Remove rod/link assembly from lower control arm.
5. Reverse procedure to install, noting the following:
   a. Tighten link retaining nut to specifications.
   b. Tighten ball stud castellated nut to specifications.
   c. Install cotter pin retaining castellated nut, tightening nut as required to insert pin through hole in stud. **Do not loosen nut to align slots with hole.**

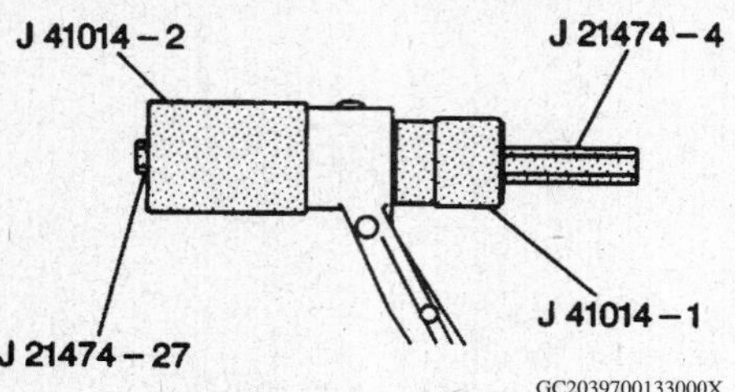

Fig. 7 Control arm bushing removal

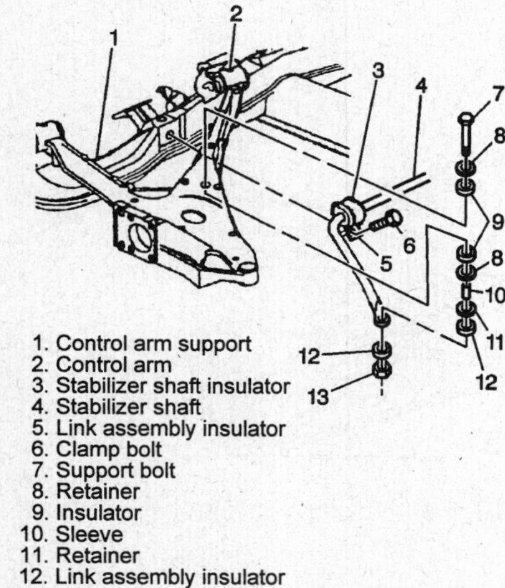

Fig. 10 Stabilizer bar & bushing assembly

STABILIZER BAR

REPLACE

1. Raise and support vehicle.
2. Remove rear wheels and tires.
3. Disconnect ELC height sensor link from control arm.
4. Remove stabilizer shaft support bolt, nut, retainer, sleeve and insulators from lower control arm or knuckle bracket, **Fig. 10.**
5. Remove bushing clip bolt.
6. Bend open end of support assembly downward.
7. Remove stabilizer shaft and bushings.
8. Reverse procedure to install. Tighten all bolts and nuts to specifications.

TIGHTENING SPECIFICATIONS

Year	Component	Torque/Ft. Lbs.
BONNEVILLE, EIGHTY EIGHT, LESABRE, LSS & REGENCY		
1998–99	Adjustment Link Locknut	48
	Adjustment Link To Control Arm	63
	Adjustment Link To Knuckle	33
	Ball Joint	40
	Control Arm Bolts (Optional Torque)	134
	Control Arm Nuts	85
	Hub & Bearing Bolts	52
	Stabilizer Shaft Insulator Link Bolt	17
	Stabilizer Shaft Link Assembly	35
	Stabilizer Shaft Link Nut At Bracket	13
	Stabilizer Shaft Mounting Bracket To Body	14
	Strut To Knuckle	140
	Strut Tower Mounting Nut	35
	Tie Rod Retaining Nut	63
	Tie Rod Slotted Hex Nut	33
	Wheel Lug Nuts	100
2000–02	Adjustment Link Pinch Bolt	38
	Adjustment Link To Suspension Support	67
	Control Arm Nuts	78
	Hub & Bearing Bolts	52
	Rear Body Mount Bolts	38
	Rear Suspension Support To Body Front Bolts	141
	Rear Suspension Support To Body Rear Bolts	191
	Stabilizer Shaft Clamp Bolt	24
	Stabilizer Shaft Link Nut	11
	Strut To Control Arm Bolts	18
	Strut Tower Mounting Nut	15
	Wheel Lug Nuts	100
PARK AVENUE		
1998–2002	Adjustment Link Pinch Bolt	36
	Adjustment Link Retaining Bolt (1998–2001)	55
	Adjustment Link Retaining Bolt (2002)	67
	Body Mount Bolt	38
	Control Arm Nut	78
	Hub Mounting Bolts	52
	Shock To Control Arm Bolts	18
	Shock Tower Mounting Nut	15
	Stabilizer Shaft Clamp Bolt	24
	Stabilizer Shaft Link Bolt	10
	Suspension Support Assembly To Body Front Bolts	141
	Suspension Support Assembly To Body Rear Bolts (1998)	122
	Suspension Support Assembly To Body Rear Bolts (1999–2002)	141
	Suspension Support Assembly To Bracket Bolts	63
	Tie Rod Pinch Bolt	36
	Wheel Lug Nuts	100

Front Suspension & Steering

NOTE: On Air Bag Equipped Models, Refer To "Air Bag System Precautions" Located In The Front Of This Manual For System Disarming & Arming Procedures.

NOTE: Refer To "Computer Relearn Procedures" Located In The Front Of This Manual When Battery Power To The Computer Has Been Interrupted.

INDEX

PRECAUTIONS

AIR BAG SYSTEMS

Refer to "Air Bag System Precautions" in the front of this manual for system disarming and arming procedures.

BATTERY GROUND CABLE

Prior to service, disconnect battery ground cable and isolate as required.

DESCRIPTION

The front suspension is of the McPherson design, **Fig. 1.** The control arm pivots from the cradle and is mounted in rubber bushings. The upper end of the strut is isolated by a rubber mount and contains a bearing to allow for rotation. The lower end of the steering knuckle pivots on a ball joint riveted to the control arm. The ball joint is mounted to the steering knuckle with a castle nut and cotter pin. **Do not use a hammer to remove components from the steering knuckle.**

HUB & BEARING

REPLACE

1. Place transaxle selector lever in Park.
2. Raise and support vehicle, then remove tire and wheel assembly.
3. Clean and lubricate drive axle threads.
4. Insert a suitable drift into caliper and rotor to prevent assembly from rotating, then remove hub nut and washer. Discard hub nut.
5. Remove caliper bracket mounting bolts, caliper and bracket assembly and rotor. Secure assembly aside taking care not to stretch or damage brake hose.
6. Disconnect ABS front wheel speed sensor connector and unclip connector from dust shield.
7. Remove hub and bearing retaining bolts and dust shield, **Fig. 2.**
8. Separate hub and bearing from drive axle using front hub spindle removal tool No. J28733-B, or equivalent, **Fig. 3.**
9. Clean face and bore of knuckle to remove any debris before assembly.
10. Reverse procedure to install, noting the following:
    a. Fill area between seal and bearing assembly with GM lubricant part No. 12377985, or equivalent.
    b. **Do not use old hub nut. Always install a new one.**
    c. Tighten hub attaching bolts, caliper bolts and hub nut to specifications.

BALL JOINT INSPECTION

Ball joints must be replaced if any looseness is detected or ball joint seal is cut or damaged.

To inspect ball joints, raise the front of the vehicle, allowing suspension to hang freely. Grasp the tire at the top and bottom, then move the top of the tire in an in-and-out motion. Inspect for any horizontal movement of the knuckle relative to the control arm. If the ball stud is disconnected from the knuckle and looseness is detected or if the ball stud can be twisted using finger pressure, replace the ball joint.

Ball stud tightness in the knuckle boss should also be inspected. This may be done by shaking the wheel and feeling for movement of the stud end or nut at the knuckle boss. Worn or damaged ball joints and knuckles must be replaced.

BALL JOINT

REPLACE

EIGHTY EIGHT, LSS & REGENCY

1. Raise and support vehicle and place jack stands under cradle. **Vehicle weight should not be placed on control arms.**
2. Remove wheel assembly.
3. Install drive axle boot protectors.
4. Remove cotter key from ball joint nut.
5. Separate ball joint from steering knuckle using ball joint separator tool No. J34505, or equivalent, **Fig. 4.**
6. Drill out ball joint retaining rivets.
7. Remove stabilizer bar bushing to control arm bolt.
8. Pull control arm downward and remove ball joint from steering knuckle and control arm.
9. Reverse procedure to install. Tighten new ball joint attaching nuts to specifications, **Fig. 5.**

LESABRE

1998-99

Refer to "Eighty Eight, LSS & Regency" for procedure.

2000-02

The ball joint is serviced only with the control arm and cannot be serviced separately. Refer to "Control Arm, Replace" for replacement procedure.

PARK AVENUE

The ball joint is serviced only with the control arm and cannot be serviced separately. Refer to "Control Arm, Replace" for replacement procedure.

BONNEVILLE

1998-99

Refer to "Eighty Eight, LSS & Regency," for procedure.

2000-02

The ball joint is serviced only with the control arm and cannot be serviced separately. Refer to "Control Arm, Replace" for replacement procedure.

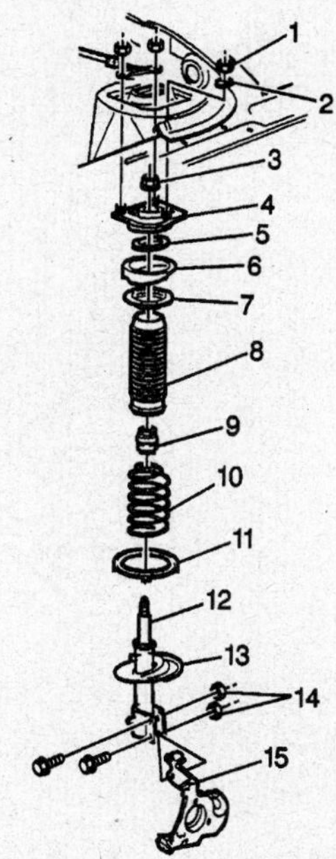

1. Control arm support
2. Control arm
3. Stabilizer shaft insulator
4. Stabilizer shaft
5. Link assembly insulator
6. Clamp bolt
7. Support bolt
8. Retainer
9. Insulator
10. Sleeve
11. Retainer
12. Link assembly insulator
13. Nut

GC2020100301000X

Fig. 1 Exploded view of front suspension

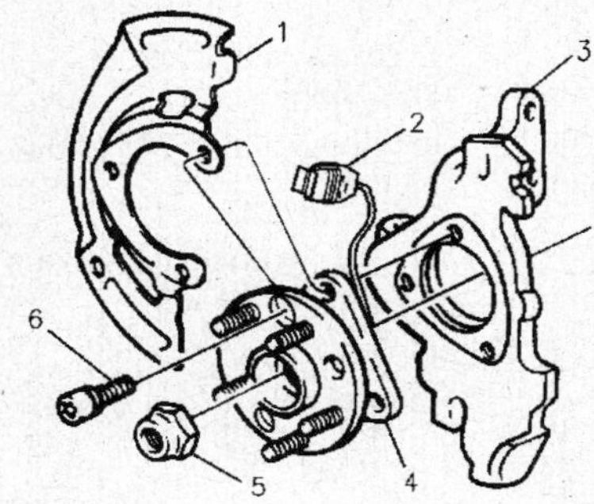

1 DUST SHIELD
2 WHEEL SPEED SENSOR CONNECTOR
3 STEERING KNUCKLE
4 HUB AND BEARING
5 NUT, DRIVE AXLE
6 RETAINING BOLT

GC2029300228000X

Fig. 2 Hub & bearing assembly

STRUT

REPLACE

1. **On 1998–99 Bonneville, Eighty Eight, LeSabre, LSS and Regency models,** loosen strut housing tie bar through-bolts on both ends of tie bar, **Fig. 6.**
2. **On models equipped with CCR,** disconnect CCR connector.
3. **On all models,** remove three strut mount to body bolts or nuts.
4. Raise and support vehicle.
5. Remove wheel and tire.
6. Remove ABS front wheel speed sensor connector.
7. Remove speed sensor bracket from strut.
8. Remove brake line bracket from strut.
9. Retain knuckle in position to prevent damage to ball joint and/or drive axle.
10. Remove strut to knuckle bolts.
11. Remove strut from vehicle.
12. Reverse procedure to install. Avoid cracking or chipping spring coating when handling front suspension coil spring.

STRUT SERVICE

Refer to **Figs. 7 through 10** when performing the following procedure.

1. Remove strut as outlined under "Strut, Replace."
2. Mount strut in compressor tool No. J34013-B and holding fixture tool No. J3289-20, or equivalents.
3. Rotate compressor forcing screw until spring compresses slightly.
4. Hold damper shaft from rotating and remove nut from top of strut assembly.
5. Guide damper shaft from assembly using alignment rod tool No. J34013-38, or equivalent.
6. Loosen compressor forcing screw while guiding damper shaft from assembly. Continue to loosen nut until strut damper and spring can be removed.
7. Reverse procedure to assemble, noting the following:
   a. When assembling spring, flat on upper spring seat must face outward 90° from centerline of vehicle or when mounted in strut compressor.
   b. Seat faces in same direction as steering knuckle mounting flange.
   c. Tighten all bolts and nuts to specifications.

CONTROL ARM

REPLACE

1. Raise and support vehicle.
2. Remove wheel and tire.
3. Disconnect stabilizer link to control arm bolt, **Figs. 11 and 12.**
4. Remove cotter pin and loosen nut from ball joint stud.
5. Remove ball joint from steering knuckle using a suitable ball joint separator tool.
6. Remove control arm mounting bolts, then the control arm from the frame, **Figs. 13 and 14.**
7. Reverse procedure to install, noting the following:
   a. Install control arm to frame and loosely install mounting bolts, washers and nuts. **Do not tighten control arm nuts at this time.** Weight of vehicle must be supported by control arms so that vehicle design trim heights are obtained before tightening control arm mounting bolts.
   b. Install all remaining control arm hardware, then lower vehicle to ground.
   c. Inspect trim height.
   d. Tighten control arm nuts to specifications.

STABILIZER BAR

REPLACE

1. Raise and support vehicle and place jack stands under cradle. **Vehicle weight should not be placed on control arms.**
2. Remove wheel and tire assembly.
3. Install drive axle boot protectors.
4. Remove nuts, washers, bushings and bolt securing stabilizer shaft to each control arm, **Fig. 15.**
5. Remove stabilizer bar mounting bolts, two bolts from each side.
6. Disconnect tie rods from steering knuckles.
7. Remove exhaust pipe between exhaust manifold and catalytic converter.
8. Rotate righthand side strut assembly completely to right.
9. Slide stabilizer bar to right over steering knuckle and pull downward on lefthand side until stabilizer bar clears cradle, **Fig. 16.**
10. Reverse procedure to install. Tighten all bolts and nuts to specifications.

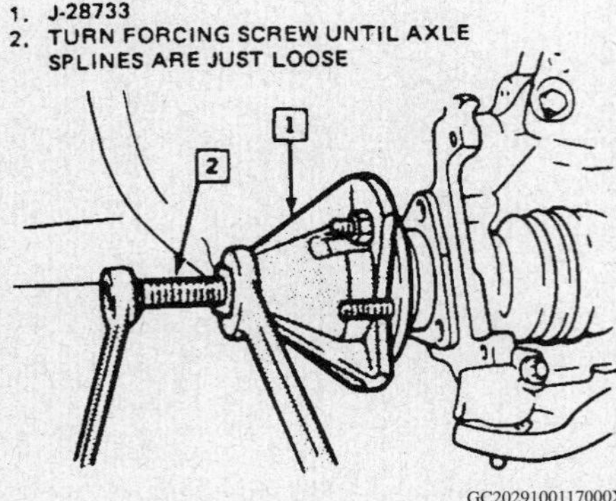

Fig. 3 Separating drive axle from hub

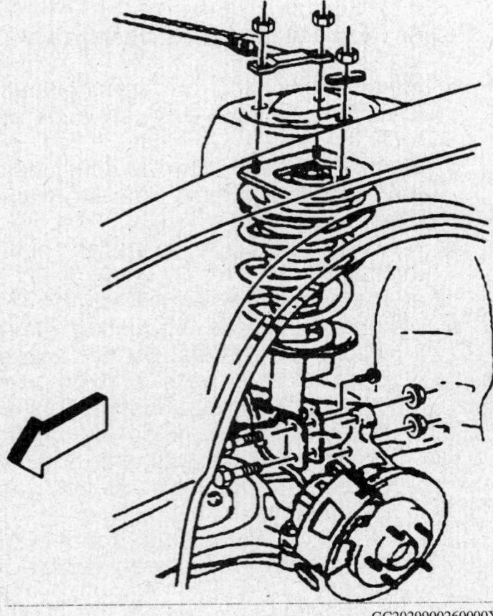

Fig. 6 Strut housing tie bar through-bolts. 1998–99 Bonneville, Eighty Eight, LeSabre, LSS & Regency

POWER STEERING GEAR

REPLACE

1. Ensure front wheels are in straight-ahead position.
2. Lock steering column using lock pin tool No. J42640, or equivalent, **Fig. 17.**
3. Raise and support vehicle with weight resting on suspension.
4. Remove front tire and wheel assemblies.
5. Remove steering gear heat shield.
6. Disconnect intermediate shaft from steering gear stub shaft.
7. Disconnect both tie rod ends from steering knuckles using separator tool No. J24319-B, or equivalent.

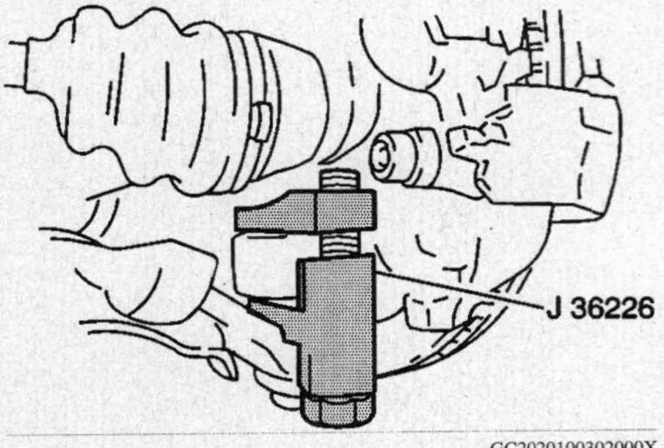

Fig. 4 Ball joint separation from steering knuckle. Eighty Eight, LSS & Regency

8. Remove line retainers and disconnect hydraulic lines from steering gear.
9. Disconnect speed sensitive steering electrical connectors from steering gear.
10. Remove steering gear attaching bolts, **Fig. 18.**
11. Remove steering gear from vehicle by sliding out of side.
12. Reverse procedure to install. Tighten all bolts, nuts and clamps to specifications.

POWER STEERING PUMP

REPLACE

1. Remove air cleaner if required.
2. **On 1998–99 Bonneville, Eighty Eight, LeSabre, LSS and Regency models,** remove strut housing upper tie bar mounting nuts, then the tie bar.
3. **On all models,** mark running direction with suitable felt pen or chalk, then remove accessory drive belt.
4. Raise and support vehicle.
5. Position a suitable drain pan under power steering fluid lines at pump.
6. Disconnect fluid lines and electrical connectors from pump.
7. If required, disconnect righthand outer tie rod end from steering knuckle using tie rod removal tool No. J24319-B, or equivalent.
8. **On Park Avenue models,** remove pump mounting bolts, then the pump from underneath vehicle.
9. **On all models,** lower vehicle.
10. **On Bonneville, Eighty Eight, LeSabre, LSS and Regency models,** remove pump mounting bolts, then the power steering pump.
11. **On all models,** reverse procedure to install, noting the following:
    a. If new pump does not include pulley, remove pulley from old pump using removal tool No. J25034-C, or equivalent, then install onto new pump using installer tool No. J25033-C, or equivalent. Ensure axial tolerance on pump shaft meets specifications, **Fig. 19.**
    b. Tighten all bolts, nuts and clamps to specifications.
    c. Ensure all electrical connectors and wiring are properly routed to avoid pinching.
    d. Fill and bleed power steering system.

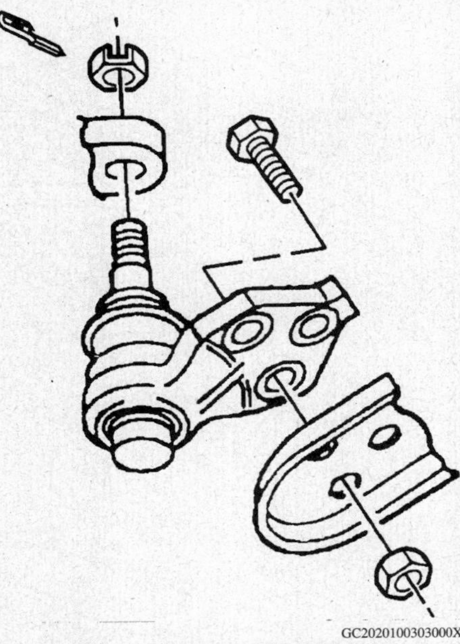

Fig. 5 Service ball joint attachment. Eighty Eight, LeSabre, LSS & Regency

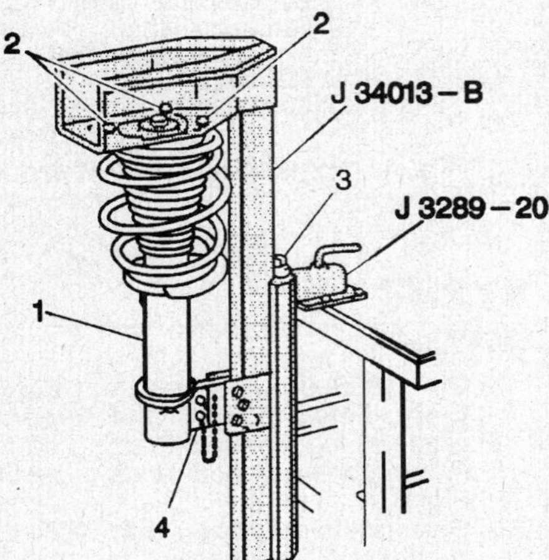

Fig. 7 Strut disassembly

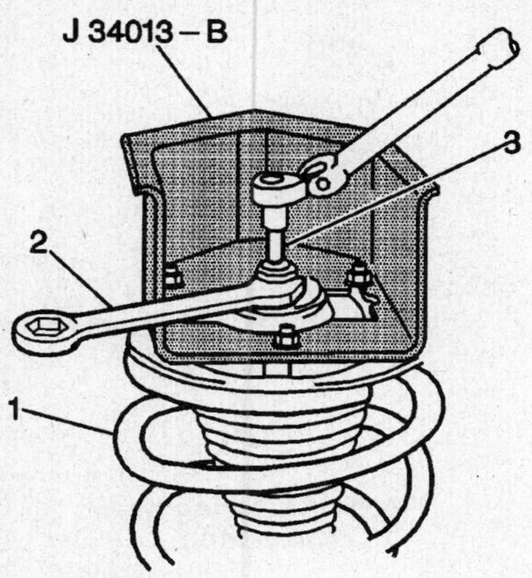

1. Coil spring
2. 24 MM wrench
3. Driver tool

GC2020100305000X

Fig. 8 Coil spring compression

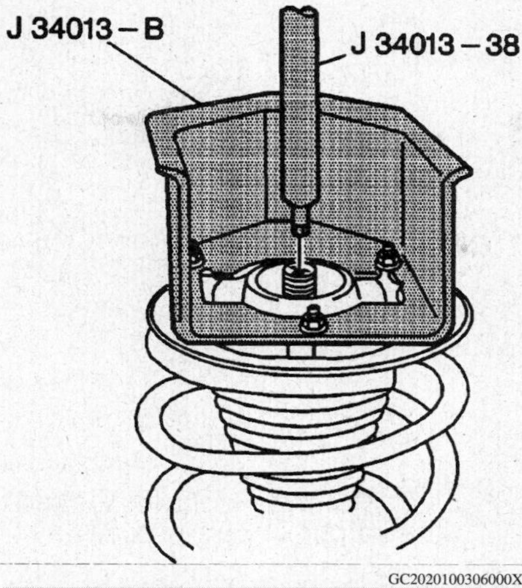

GC2020100306000X

Fig. 9 Strut shaft nut removal

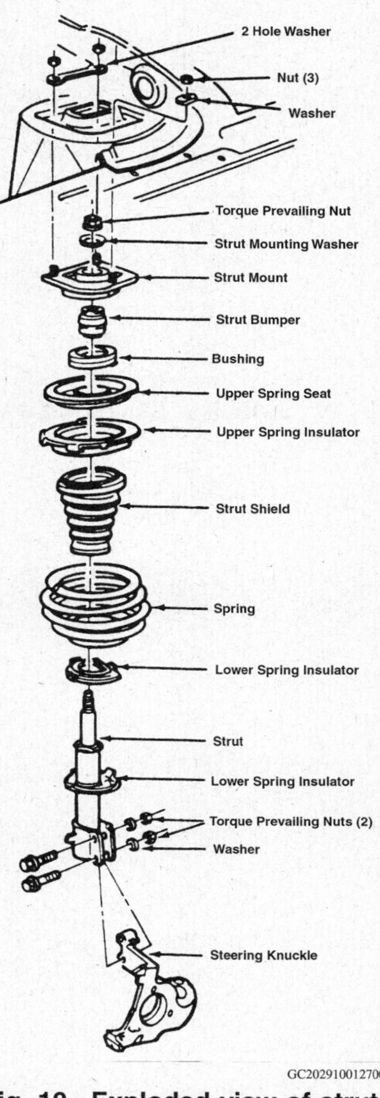

GC2029100127000X

Fig. 10 Exploded view of strut assembly

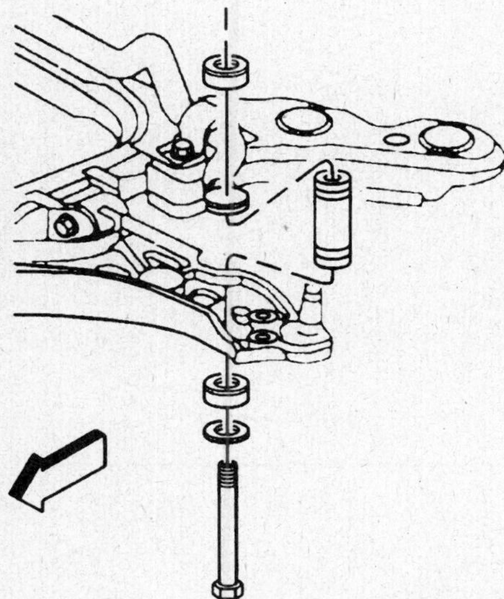

GC2029900261000X

Fig. 11 Stabilizer link to control arm bolt. Park Avenue

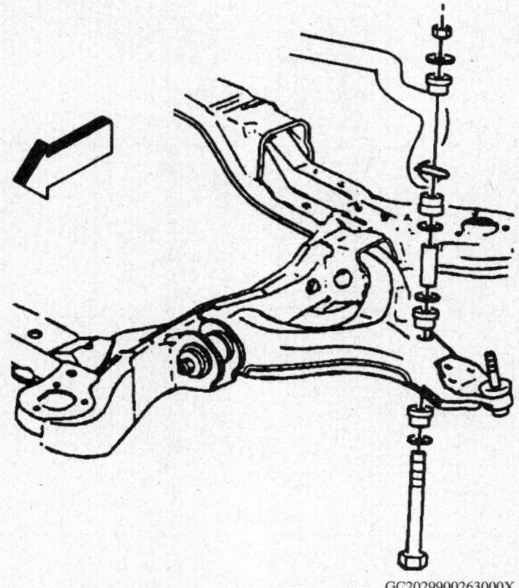

GC2029900263000X

Fig. 12 Stabilizer shaft to control arm bolt. Bonneville, Eighty Eight, LeSabre, LSS & Regency

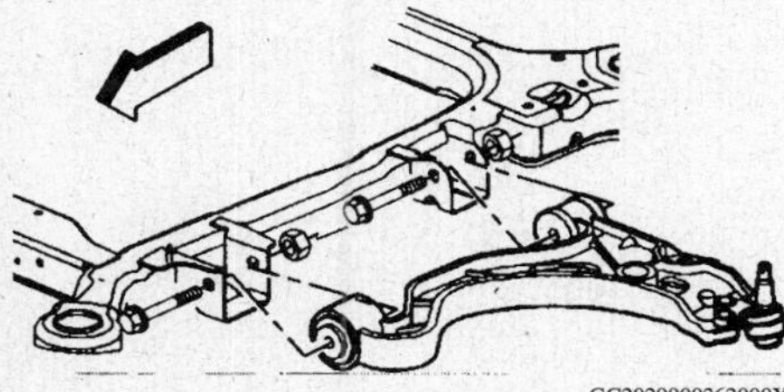

GC2029900262000X

Fig. 13 Lower control arm replacement. Park Avenue

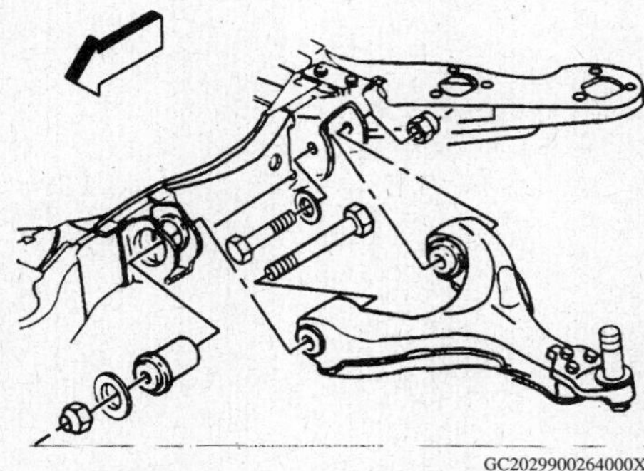

GC2029900264000X

Fig. 14 Lower control arm replacement. Bonneville, Eighty Eight, LeSabre, LSS & Regency

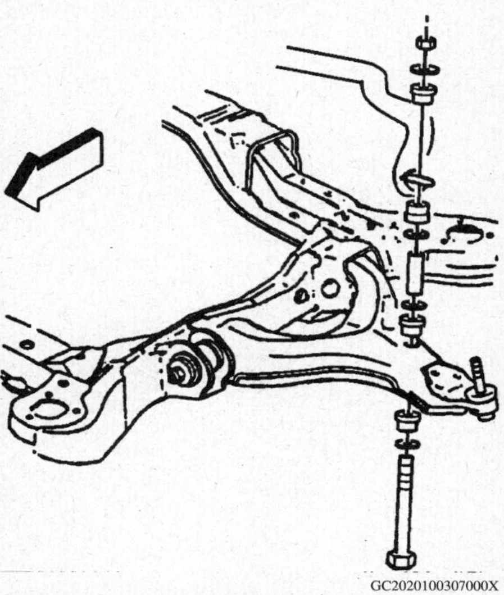

GC2020100307000X

Fig. 15 Stabilizer bar bushing assembly

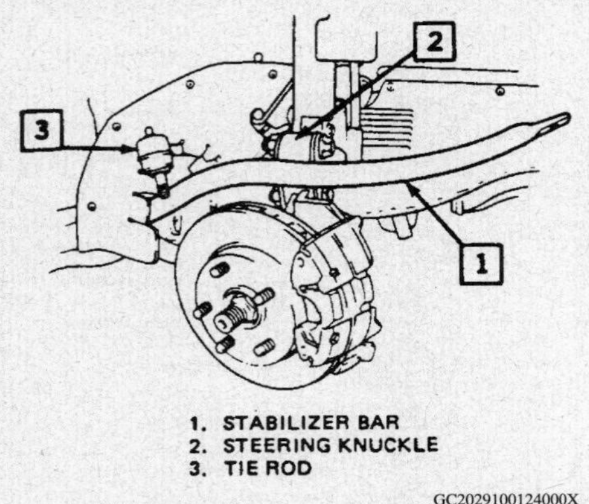

Fig. 16 Stabilizer bar replacement

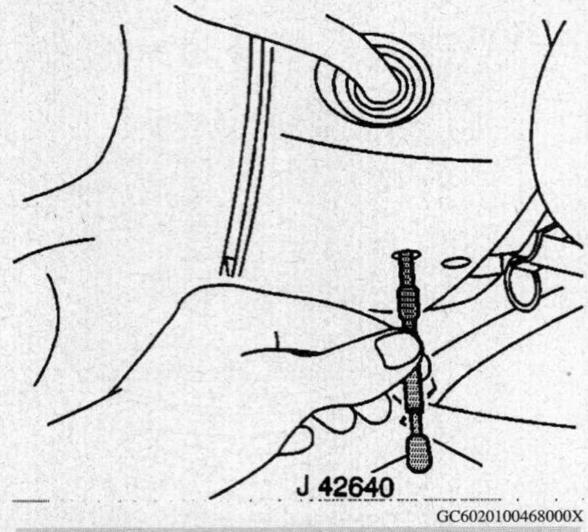

Fig. 17 Steering column locked in straight-ahead position

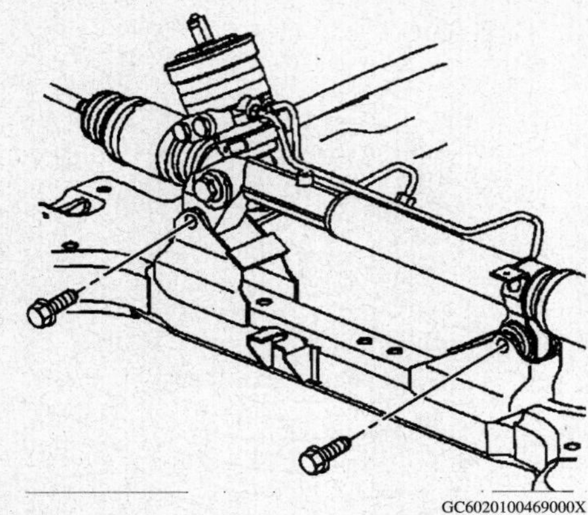

Fig. 18 Steering gear replacement

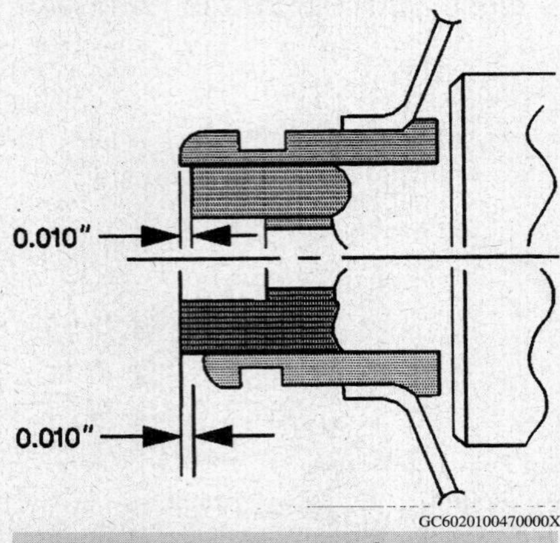

Fig. 19 Power steering pump pulley axial installation

TIGHTENING SPECIFICATIONS

Year	Component	Torque/Ft. Lbs.
BONNEVILLE, EIGHTY EIGHT, LESABRE, LSS & REGENCY		
1998–99	Ball Joint To Knuckle	50
	Brake Bracket To Strut	13
	Brake Caliper To Knuckle	38
	Control Arm Bolts	117
	Control Arm Front Nut	140
	Control Arm Rear Nut	91
	Cross Brace Assembly Through-Bolts	27
	Drive Axle Nut	107
	Hub And Bearing To Knuckle	70
	Inner Tie Rod	74
	Intermediate Shaft Pinch Bolt	34
	Power Steering Gear Hose Fittings To Pump & Steering Gear	20
	Power Steering Gear Mounting Bolts	48
	Power Steering Inlet/Outlet Hose Retainer Bolts	53①
	Power Steering Outer Hose Retaining Clamp Nuts	15
	Power Steering Pump Mounting Bolts	20
	Rack And Pinion Adjuster Plug Nut	50
	Rack And Pinion Cylinder End Fittings	20
	Rack And Pinion Preload	16
	Stabilizer Shaft Bracket Bolt	35
	Stabilizer Shaft Link Nut	13
	Strut Housing Tie Bar Through-Bolts	27
	Strut Mount Nut	55
	Strut Mount To Body Nuts	18
	Strut To Knuckle Nuts	140
	Tie Rod Locknut	50
	Tie Rod End Slotted Hexagon Nut	35
	Tie Rod To Knuckle	35②
	Wheel Speed Sensor Bracket To Strut	13
	Wheel Lug Nut	100
2000–02	Ball Joint To Knuckle	50
	Brake Bracket To Strut	13
	Brake Caliper To Knuckle	38
	Brake Caliper Bracket To Knuckle (2002)	136
	Control Arm Bolts	117
	Control Arm Front Nut	93
	Cross Brace Assembly Through-Bolts	27
	Drive Axle Nut	118
	Hub And Bearing To Knuckle	70
	Inner Tie Rod	74
	Intermediate Shaft Pinch Bolt	33
	Power Steering Gear Hose Fittings To Pump And Steering Gear	20
	Power Steering Gear Mounting Bolts	48
	Power Steering Inlet/Outlet Hose Retainer Bolts	53①
	Power Steering Outer Hose Retaining Clamp Nuts	15
	Power Steering Pump Mounting Bolts	20
	Rack And Pinion Adjuster Plug Nut	50

Continued

TIGHTENING SPECIFICATIONS—Continued

Year	Component	Torque/Ft. Lbs.
BONNEVILLE, EIGHTY EIGHT, LESABRE, LSS & REGENCY		
2000–02	Rack And Pinion Cylinder End Fittings	20
	Stabilizer Shaft Bracket Bolt	35
	Stabilizer Shaft Link Nut	13
	Strut Mount Nut	55
	Strut Mount To Body Nuts	35
	Strut To Knuckle Nuts	136
	Tie Rod Locknut	50
	Tie Rod To Knuckle Castle Nut	35–52
	Wheel Speed Sensor Bracket To Strut	13
	Wheel Lug Nut	100
PARK AVENUE		
1998–2002	Ball Joint Mounting Nuts	50
	Ball Joint To Knuckle	50
	Brake Bracket To Strut	13
	Brake Caliper To Knuckle	38
	Control Arm Front Nut	93
	Control Arm Rear Bolt	117
	Cross Brace Assembly Through-Bolts	27
	Drive Axle Nut	107
	Hub & Bearing To Knuckle	70
	Intermediate Steering Shaft Pinch Bolt	35
	Outer Tie Rod Retaining Nut (1998–2000)	35②
	Outer Tie Rod Retaining Nut (2001–02)	55
	Power Steering Gear Hose Fittings To Pump & Steering Gear	20
	Power Steering Inlet/Outlet Hose Retainer Bolts	53①
	Power Steering Outer Hose Retaining Clamp Nuts	15
	Power Steering Pump Mounting Bolts	20
	Stabilizer Shaft Bracket Bolt (1998–2000)	30
	Stabilizer Shaft Bracket Bolt (2001–02)	35
	Stabilizer Shaft Link Bolt (2001–02)	11
	Stabilizer Shaft Link Nut (1998–2000)	13
	Steering Gear Mounting Bolts	48
	Strut Mount Nut	55
	Strut Mount To Body Nuts	35
	Strut To Knuckle Nuts	136
	Tie Rod End To Knuckle Nut	35
	Wheel Lug Nuts	100
	Wheel Speed Sensor Bracket To Strut	13

① — Inch lbs.

② — Torque nut for cotter pin alignment to 52 ft. lbs. maximum.

Wheel Alignment

INDEX

PRECAUTIONS

AIR BAG SYSTEMS

Refer to "Air Bag System Precautions" in the front of this manual for system disarming and arming procedures.

PRELIMINARY INSPECTION

1. Inspect tires for proper inflation and similar tread wear.
2. Inspect hub and bearing for excessive wear. Repair as required.
3. Inspect ball joints and tie rod ends for excessive looseness.
4. Measure wheel and tire runout.
5. Inspect vehicle ride height.
6. Inspect rack and pinion for looseness at frame.
7. Ensure proper strut operation.
8. Inspect control arm bushings.
9. Inspect stabilizer shaft for loose or missing components.
10. Inspect suspension and steering components for damage. Replace as required.

FRONT WHEEL ALIGNMENT

CASTER

1. Loosen cross brace assembly through-bolts, **Fig. 1.**
2. Remove inboard strut nuts, then the brace assembly.
3. Remove remaining nut over oval strut mounting hole.
4. Lift front of vehicle by body to separate strut from inner wheelhouse.
5. **On Eighty Eight, LSS, Regency and 1998–99 Bonneville and LeSabre models,** drill two 11⁄32 inch holes at front and rear of oval strut mounting hole.
6. **On 1998 Park Avenue models,** drill two 13⁄32 inch holes at front and rear of oval strut mounting hole.
7. **On 1999–2002 Park Avenue and Bonneville and 2000–02 LeSabre models,** remove two guide pins and file to make slotted holes.
8. **On all models,** file excess metal to elongate original holes, then paint exposed metal with primer.
9. Lower front of vehicle.
10. Place cross brace assembly on inboard strut studs and install strut attaching nuts.
11. Set caster to specifications by moving top of strut forward or backward. A .040 inch position change at the tower is approximately equal to a 0.1° caster change.
12. Tighten strut attaching nuts and cross brace bar through-bolts to specifications.

CAMBER

1. Loosen both strut to knuckle attaching nuts.
2. Install camber adjusting tool No. J39601, or equivalent, **Fig. 2.**
3. Inspect camber, and if it does not meet specifications, proceed as follows:
   a. Raise and support vehicle, then remove tire and wheel.
   b. Drive upper and lower bolt and nut out of strut and knuckle. **Do not turn bolts. This will damage serrated shoulders.**
   c. Separate strut from knuckle.
   d. File inner metal plate to outside plate diameter using a suitable round file or die grinder.
   e. File excess metal to create slotted holes.
   f. Paint exposed metal with suitable rust preventive paint or primer.
   g. Connect strut to knuckle. **Do not tighten bolts just yet.**
   h. Install camber adjusting tool No. J39601, or equivalent, to bottom strut bolt.
   i. Tighten upper strut to knuckle nut to specifications.
   j. Remove adjusting tool, then tighten lower strut to knuckle attaching nuts to specifications.
   k. Inspect camber once again. Adjust as required.

TOE

1. Loosen locknuts on both inner tie rods, **Fig. 3.**
2. Adjust toe to specifications by rotating inner tie rod.
3. Tighten locknuts to specifications.
4. Inspect toe setting once again. Adjust as required.

REAR WHEEL ALIGNMENT

When inspecting rear wheel alignment, the electronic leveling system must have the superlift struts inflated with residual pressure only.

Place a weight in luggage compartment. Turn ignition On and move transmission selector from Park to Reverse position and back. This will activate the compressor. Turn ignition Off and remove weight from luggage compartment. Wait 30 seconds for the system to exhaust. Roll vehicle forward one complete wheel rotation. Jounce vehicle before inspecting alignment.

CAMBER

1998-99 Bonneville, Eighty Eight, LeSabre, LSS & Regency

1. Loosen strut to knuckle attaching nuts.
2. Install camber adjusting tool No. J29862, or equivalent, **Fig. 4.**
3. Move strut to set camber to specifications.
4. Remove camber adjusting tool. **Torque** strut to knuckle nuts to 144 ft. lbs.
5. Inspect camber setting once again.

Park Avenue & 2000-02 Bonneville & LeSabre

On these models the rear camber is not adjustable. If rear camber does not meet specifications inspect for worn or damaged suspension components and replace as required.

TOE

Toe adjustment is made by loosening the locknut at tie rod end and turning inner tie

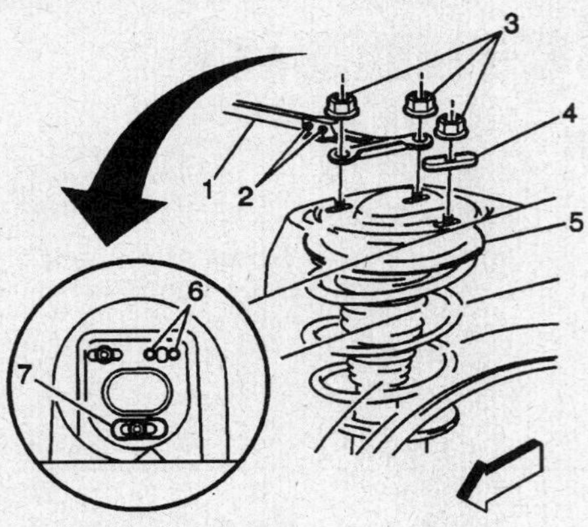

Fig. 1 Cross brace removal

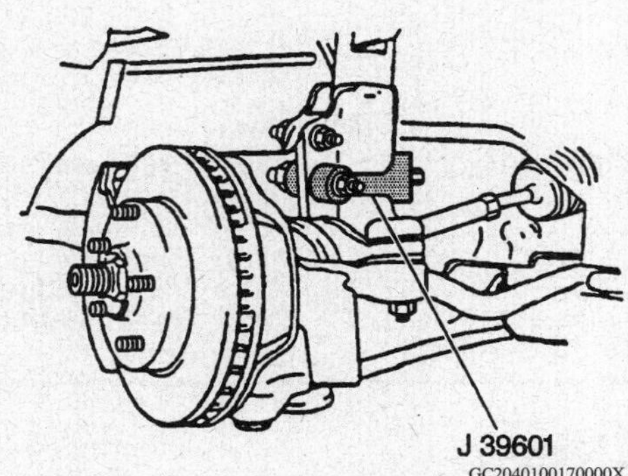

Fig. 2 Camber adjustment tool installation

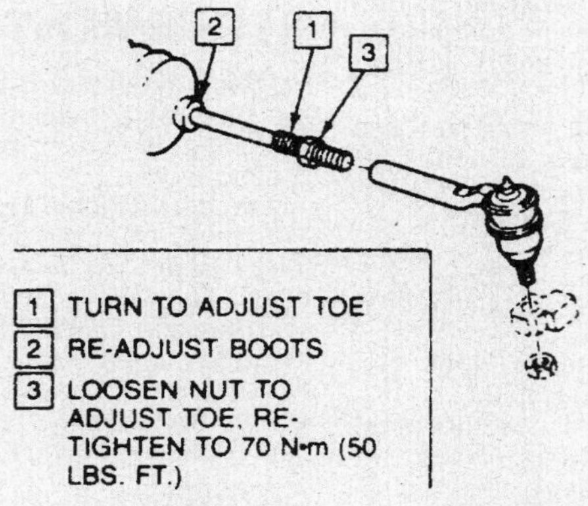

Fig. 3 Toe adjustment

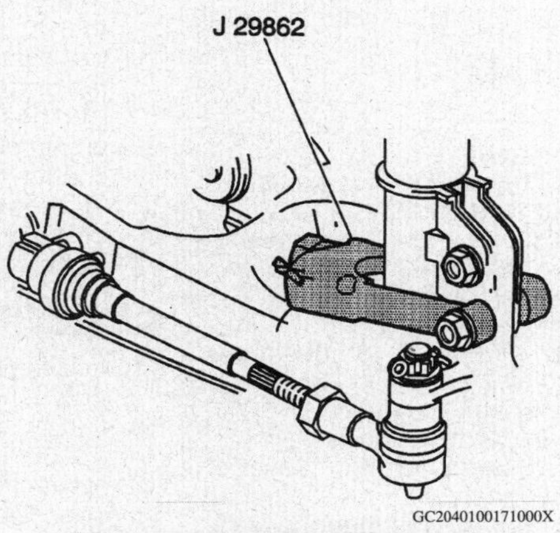

Fig. 4 Rear camber & toe adjustments

rod to set toe to specifications, **Fig. 4.**

CAMARO & FIREBIRD

NOTE: Refer To The Rear Of This Manual For Vehicle Manufacturer's Special Tool Suppliers.

INDEX OF SERVICE OPERATIONS

Specifications

GENERAL ENGINE SPECIFICATIONS

Year	Engine		Fuel System	Bore & Stroke	Compression Ratio	Net Brake H.P. @ RPM②	Maximum Torque	Normal Oil Pressure, psi
	Liter	VIN Code①						
1998–2000	3800	K	SFI	3.80 x 3.40	9.4	200 @ 5200	225 @ 4000	⑤
	5.7L⑥	G	SFI	3.89 x 3.62	10.1	305 @ 5200	335 @ 4000	③
	5.7L④	G	SFI	3.89 x 3.62	10.1	320 @ 5200	345 @ 4400	③
2001–02	3800	K	SFI	3.80 x 3.40	9.4	200 @ 5200	225 @ 4000	⑤
	5.7L⑥	G	SFI	3.90 x 3.62	10.1	310 @ 5200	340 @ 4000	③
	5.7L④	G	SFI	3.90 x 3.62	10.1	325 @ 5200	350 @ 4000	③

SFI — Sequential Fuel Injection
① — The eighth digit of the VIN denotes engine code.
② — Ratings are net-as installed in vehicle.
③ — Minimum, 6 psi @ 1000 RPM; 18 psi @ 2000 RPM; 24 psi @ 4000 RPM.
④ — Models w/ram air.
⑤ — Minimum of 60 psi @ 1850 RPM w/10W-30 motor oil.
⑥ — Models less ram air.

TUNE UP SPECIFICATIONS

Engine Liter (VIN Code)①	Spark Plug Gap	Ignition Timing BTDC				Curb Idle Speed②		Fast Idle Speed		Fuel Pump Pressure, psi	Valve Clearance, Inch
		Firing Order Fig.③	Man. Trans.	Auto. Trans.	Mark	Man. Trans.	Auto. Trans.	Man. Trans.	Auto. Trans.		
3800 (K)	.060	⑥	④	④	⑧	⑤	⑤	⑤	⑤	48-55	⑦
5.7L (G)	.060	⑨	④	④	⑧	⑤	⑤	⑤	⑤	55-60	⑦

BTDC — Before Top Dead Center

D — Drive

N — Neutral

① — The eighth digit of Vehicle Identification Number (VIN) denotes engine code.

② — When adjusting idle speed, set parking brake & block drive wheels.

③ — Before disconnecting wires from distributor cap, determine location of No. 1 wire in cap, as distributor position may have been altered from that outlined at the end of this chart.

④ — Computer controlled, no adjustment.

⑤ — Idle speed is controlled by an Idle Speed Control (ISC) motor, Idle Air Control (IAC) valve or Idle Load Compensator (ILC).

⑥ — Cylinder numbering left to right as viewed from front of vehicle: Front bank, 1, 3, 5; rear bank, 2, 4, 6. Firing order: 1–6–5–4–3–2. Refer to **Fig.A,** for spark plug wire connections at coil unit.

⑦ — Equipped w/hydraulic lifters.

⑧ — Equipped w/crankshaft sensor.

⑨ — Refer to **Fig. B,** for cylinder numbering. Firing order: 1–8–7–2–6–5–4–3.

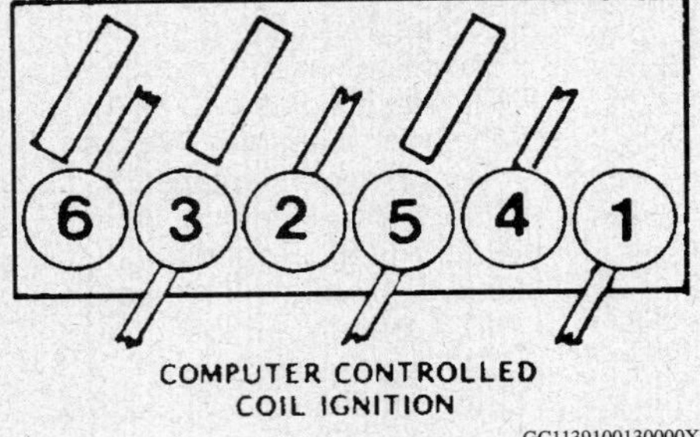

Fig. A

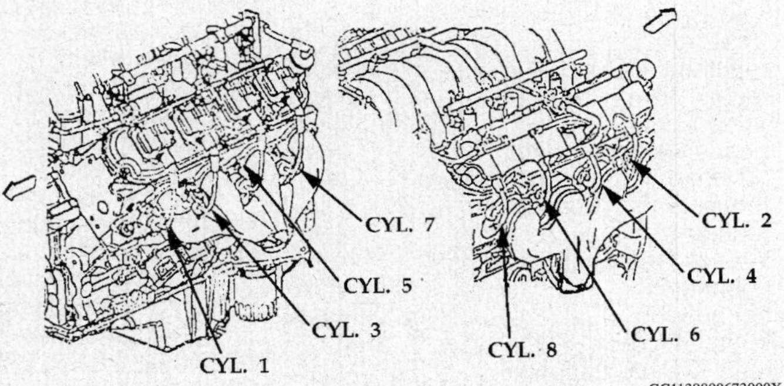

Fig. B

FRONT WHEEL ALIGNMENT SPECIFICATIONS

Year	Caster Angle, Degrees		Camber Angle, Degrees		Total Toe, Degrees	Ball Joint Wear	
	Limits	Desired	Limits	Desired		Lower	Upper
All	+4.5 to +5.5	+5	-.1 to +.9	+.4	-.2 to +.2	②	①

① — Deflection on dial indicator, when positioned against wheel rim, should not exceed .125 inch while moving top of wheel in & out.

② — While reading dial indicator, pry between lower control arm & steering knuckle. Vertical movement should not exceed .046875 inches.

REAR WHEEL ALIGNMENT SPECIFICATIONS

Year	Camber Angle, Degrees		Total Toe, Degrees		Thrust Angle
	Limits	Desired	Limits	Desired	
All	-.6 to +.6	0	-.3 to +.3	0	-.15 to +.15

VEHICLE RIDE HEIGHT SPECIFICATIONS

Model	Year	Body Style	Manufacturer's Original Tire Size	Measurement Points & Specifications①③					
				Front			Rear		
				Dim.	Specification Inches	Specification mm	Dim.	Specification Inches	Specification mm
Camaro	1998–2002	All	②	A	32.62	828	B	17.25	438
				C	8	204	D	8.19	208
Firebird	1998–2002	All	②	A	32.62	828.5	B	17.25	438
				C	8	204	D	8.19	208

A Dim. — Measurement From Front Wheel Center to Check Point On Rocker Panel.
B Dim. — Measurement From Rear Wheel Center to Check Point On Rocker Panel.
C Dim. — Ground to Rocker Panel, Front.
D Dim. — Ground to Rocker Panel, Rear.
Dim. — Dimension.
① — ±0.39 in (10 mm) front to rear & side to side.
② — See door sticker or inside of glove box for manufacturer's original tire size specifications.
③ — Measurement is with fuel, radiator coolant and engine oil full, spare tire, jack, hand tools and mats in designated positions and tires properly inflated.

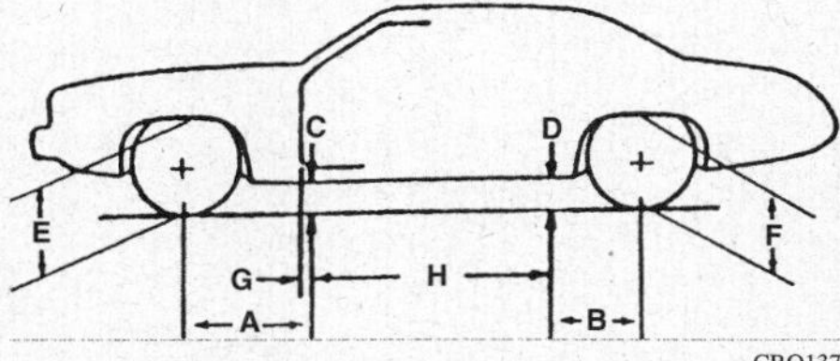

Dimensions A through D

FLUID CAPACITIES & COOLING SYSTEM DATA

Year	Engine Liter (VIN)①	Coolant Capacity, Qts.	Coolant Type	Radiator Cap Relief Pressure, psi	Thermo. Opening Temp. °F	Fuel Tank, Gals.	Engine Oil Refill Qts.	Transmission Oil Man Trans., Pts.	Transmission Oil Auto. Trans., Qts.②	Rear Axle, Pts.⑥
1998–2000	3800 (K)	④	Dex-Cool	18	195	15.5	4.5⑦	8.2	③	3.5
	5.7 (G)	⑤	Dex-Cool	18	180	15.5	5.5⑦	8.2	③	3.5
2001–02	3800 (K)	④	Dex-Cool	18	195	16.8	4⑦	6.8	12.2	3.5
	5.7L (G)	⑤	Dex-Cool	18	180	16.8	5.8⑦	8.0	15.1	3.5

① — The eighth digit of Vehicle Identification Number (VIN) denotes engine code.

② — Approximate, make final inspection w/dipstick.

③ — Total capacity, 11.2 qts.; pan only, 5 qts.

④ — Auto. trans., 12.3 qts.; Man. trans., 12.5 qts.

⑤ — Auto. trans., 15.1 qts.: Man. trans., 15.3 qts.

⑥ — All models require 4 oz. of limited differential additive lubricant P/N 1052358, or equivalent.

⑦ — With filter change.

LUBRICANT DATA

Year	Lubricant Type				
	Transmission		Rear Axle	Power Steering System	Brake System
	Manual	Automatic			
1998–2002	Dexron III	Dexron III	75W-90 GL-5①	Power Steering Fluid②	DOT 3

① — Limited slip differentials also require 4 oz. of lubricant additive (GM P/N 1052358, or equivalent).

② — Meeting GM specification 9985010.

Electrical

NOTE: On Air Bag Equipped Models, Refer To "Air Bag System Precautions" Located In The Front Of This Manual For System Disarming & Arming Procedures.

NOTE: Refer To "Computer Relearn Procedures" Located In The Front Of This Manual When Battery Power To The Computer Has Been Interrupted.

INDEX

PRECAUTIONS

AIR BAG SYSTEMS

Refer to "Air Bag System Precautions" in the front of this manual for system disarming and arming procedures.

BATTERY GROUND CABLE

Prior to service, disconnect battery ground cable and isolate as required.

FUSE PANEL & FLASHER LOCATION

The instrument panel fuse block is attached to a bracket on the left front hinge pillar and is accessed through a removable panel on the instrument panel carrier. The vehicle speed sensor (VSS) and hazard lamp flasher are attached to the relay center (convenience center), located on the lefthand side of the steering column. The turn signal flasher is mounted behind the instrument panel to the right of the steering column on the driver knee bolster bracket.

FUEL PUMP RELAY LOCATION

The fuel pump relay is located on the lefthand side of the engine compartment, in the No. 2 engine compartment relay center, **Fig. 1**.

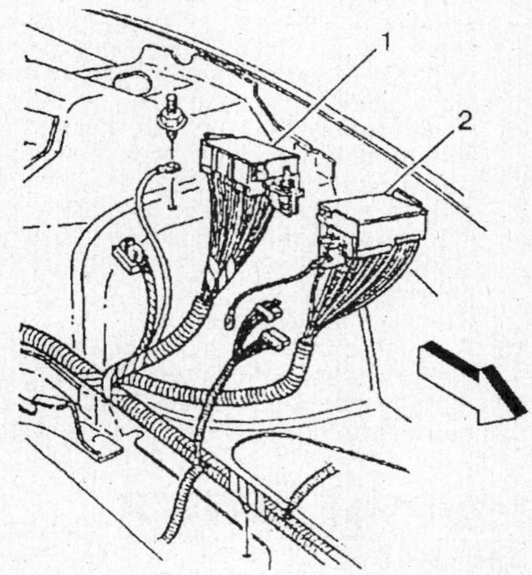

Fig. 1 Fuel pump relay location

RELAY CENTER LOCATION

The No. 1 and 2 relay centers are located in the engine compartment, on the lefthand fenderwell.

STARTER

REPLACE

This vehicle was designed for starter mounting without shims. If single or double shims have been added to correct a noise or engagement problem, they should be reinstalled in their original positions to ensure proper pinion to flywheel assembly engagement.

REMOVAL

1. Raise and support vehicle.
2. **On models equipped with 5.7L engine,** remove left catalytic converter.
3. **On models equipped with 3800 engine,** remove starter shield.
4. **On all models,** remove starter motor attaching bolts and lower starter motor assembly, **Figs. 2 and 3.**
5. Disconnect electrical connectors from starter motor assembly, then remove starter motor assembly.

INSTALLATION

Before connecting electrical connectors, tighten inner nuts on the solenoid terminals. If the nuts are not tight, the solenoid cap may be damaged during installation of connectors.

1. Connect electrical connectors to starter motor assembly, then **torque** BAT terminal nut to 84 inch lbs., and S terminal nut to 18 inch lbs.
2. Install starter motor assembly.
3. **On models equipped with 3800 engine, torque** starter bolt to 35 ft. lbs., and stud to 33 ft. lbs.
4. **On models equipped with 5.7L engine, torque** starter bolts to 37 ft. lbs.
5. **On all models,** measure pinion to flywheel clearance, **Fig. 4,** adding shims

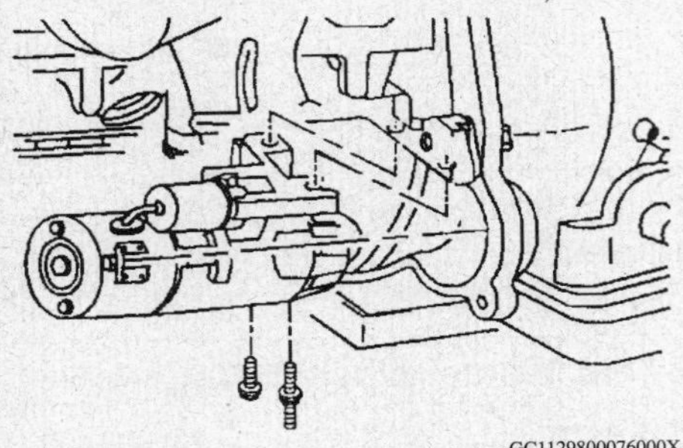

Fig. 2 Starter motor replacement. 3800 engine

if required. Clearance should be .010–.160 inch.

6. **On models equipped with 3800 engine,** install starter shield.
7. **On all models,** connect exhaust to manifolds, then lower vehicle.

ALTERNATOR

REPLACE

3800 ENGINE

1. Remove serpentine drive belt as outlined under "Serpentine Drive Belt" in "3800 Engine" section.
2. Disconnect electrical connector from alternator and battery positive terminal from "BAT" terminal.
3. Remove charcoal canister solenoid from alternator brace.
4. Remove bolt attaching alternator to rear brace, **Fig. 5.**
5. Remove bolts attaching alternator to drive belt tensioner.
6. Reverse procedure to install, noting the following:
   a. **Torque** mounting bolt (8) to 20 ft. lbs. and mounting bolt (11) to 38 ft. lbs.
   b. **Torque** rear brace bolt to 22 ft. lbs.

5.7L ENGINE

1. Remove accessory drive belt as outlined under "Serpentine Drive Belt" in "5.7L Engine" section.
2. Raise and support vehicle.
3. Remove alternator rear bracket bolt, **Fig. 6.**
4. Remove alternator mounting bolts.
5. Disconnect alternator electrical connectors, then remove from vehicle.
6. Reverse procedure to install. **Torque** mounting bolts to 37 ft. lbs. and bracket to 18 ft. lbs.

COIL PACK

REPLACE

1. Remove spark plug wire harness from coil pack/ignition control module.
2. Disconnect electrical harness from coil pack/ignition control module.
3. Remove coil pack/ignition control module attaching bolts, then the coil pack/control module.
4. Reverse procedure to install.

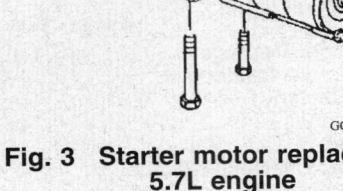

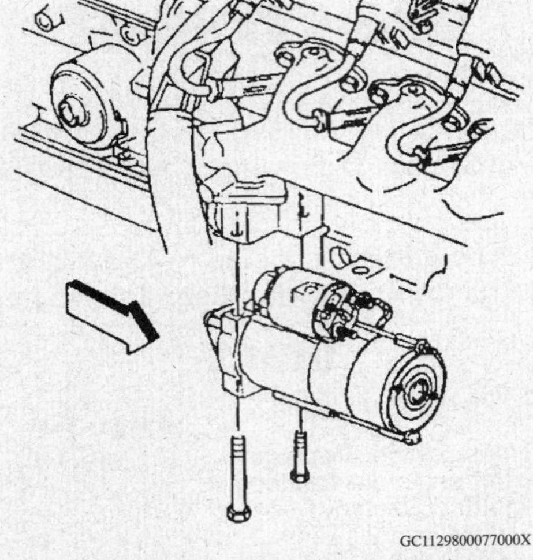

Fig. 3 Starter motor replacement. 5.7L engine

IGNITION LOCK

REPLACE

1. Remove steering wheel as outlined under "Steering Wheel, Replace."
2. Remove turn signal switch as outlined under "Turn Signal Switch, Replace."
3. Remove buzzer switch retaining clip, then the buzzer switch.
4. Place ignition switch in Lock position.
5. Remove lock cylinder retaining screw, **Fig. 7.**
6. Disconnect terminal electrical connector at bulkhead connection to provide slack.
7. Remove wiring connector from steering column.
8. Attach a suitable length of mechanic wire to ignition lock electrical connector for use during installation. Detach wire retaining clip, then carefully pull ignition lock wiring through housing shroud, steering column and lock housing cover.
9. Remove lock cylinder.
10. Reverse procedure to install. Ensure lock cylinder wiring is properly routed through steering column. **Torque** lock cylinder retaining screw to 22 inch lbs.

IGNITION SWITCH

REPLACE

REMOVAL

1. Remove lefthand instrument panel sound insulator assembly, then the instrument panel driver knee bolster assembly and deflector.
2. Ensure steering column lock and ignition switch are in Lock position, then remove steering column upper support nuts and lower column assembly.
3. Disconnect electrical connectors from dimmer switch assembly and ignition switch, then remove dimmer switch actuator rod.
4. Remove dimmer switch assembly, then the ignition switch actuator rod.
5. Remove ignition switch, then disconnect automatic transmission park lock cable assembly, if equipped.

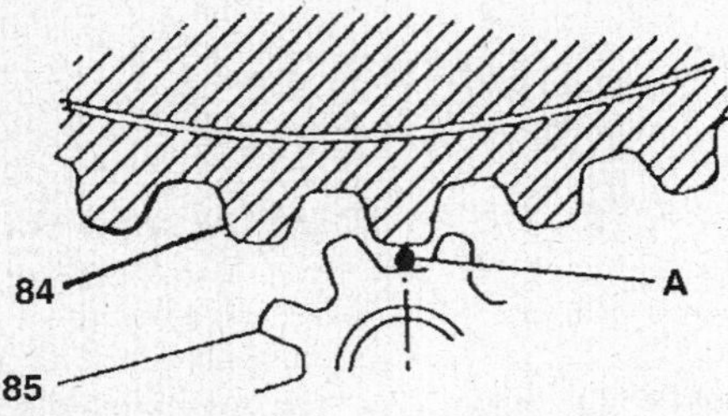

A INSERT WIRE GAGE HERE TO CHECK
84 FLYWHEEL ASSEMBLY
85 PINION, STARTER DRIVE

Fig. 4 Flywheel assembly to pinion clearance inspection

INSTALLATION

1. Connect automatic transmission park lock cable assembly, if equipped, then ensure ignition switch, steering column lock and ignition cylinder assembly are in Lock position.
2. Install ignition switch to jacket, then connect ignition switch actuator rod to ignition switch.
3. **Torque** ignition switch mounting screws to 22 inch lbs.
4. Install dimmer switch assembly, then adjust by pressing switch mechanism slightly to insert a 3/32 inch drill bit and moving dimmer switch assembly to remove tool.
5. **Torque** dimmer switch mounting screws to 35 inch lbs.
6. Install dimmer switch actuator rod, then connect electrical connectors to dimmer switch assembly and ignition switch.
7. Raise column assembly and install upper support nuts.
8. Install instrument panel driver knee bolster assembly and deflector, then the lefthand instrument panel sound insulator assembly.

CLUTCH START SWITCH

REPLACE

1. Remove instrument panel driver knee bolster.
2. Disconnect clutch pedal position switch electrical connector.
3. Remove clutch pedal position switch from pedal bracket.
4. Reverse procedure to install.

NEUTRAL SAFETY SWITCH

REPLACE

REMOVAL

1. Remove floor console, then disconnect electrical connectors from switch.
2. Place shift lever in Neutral position of detent plate, then remove switch attaching screws and switch, **Fig. 8.**

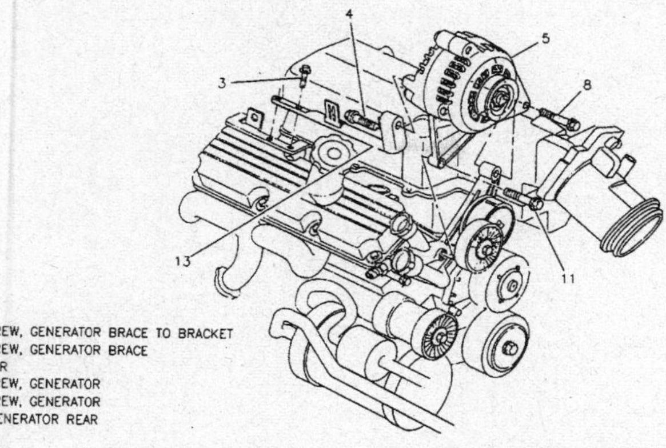

GC1129600065000X

Fig. 5 Alternator replacement. 3800 engine

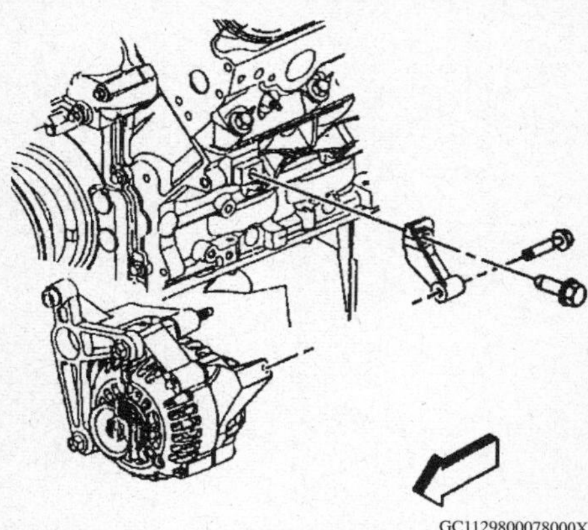

GC1129800078000X

Fig. 6 Alternator replacement. 5.7L engine

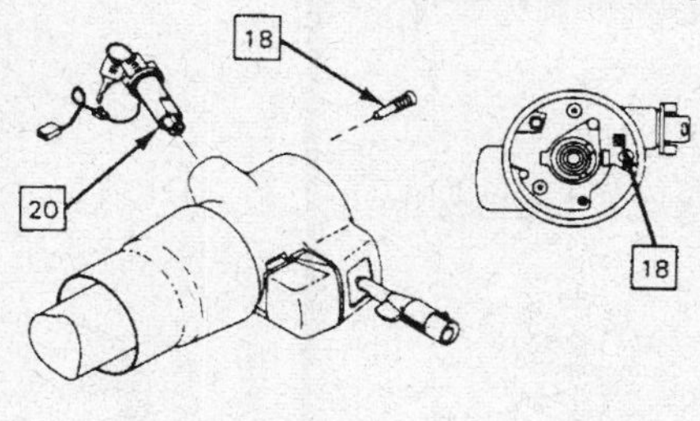

18 LOCK RETAINING SCREW
20 VATS LOCK CYLINDER SET

GC9129100016000X

Fig. 7 Ignition lock cylinder replacement

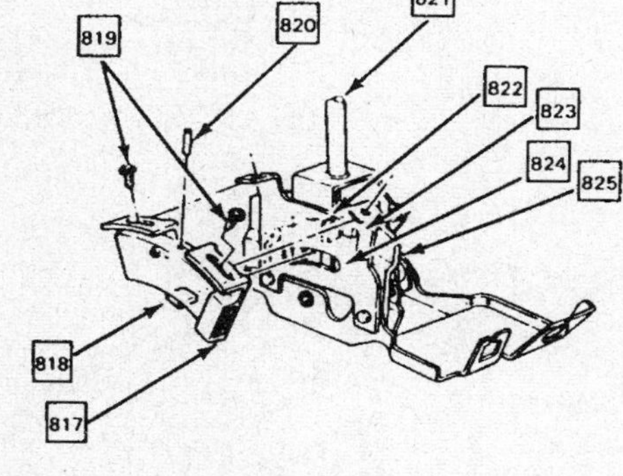

817	SWITCH	822	NEUTRAL NOTCH
818	CARRIER TANG	823	PARK NOTCH
819	BOLTS	824	TANG SLOT
820	GAGE PIN	825	DETENT PLATE
821	SHIFT CONTROL LEVER		

GC9049100061000X

Fig. 8 Neutral safety switch replacement

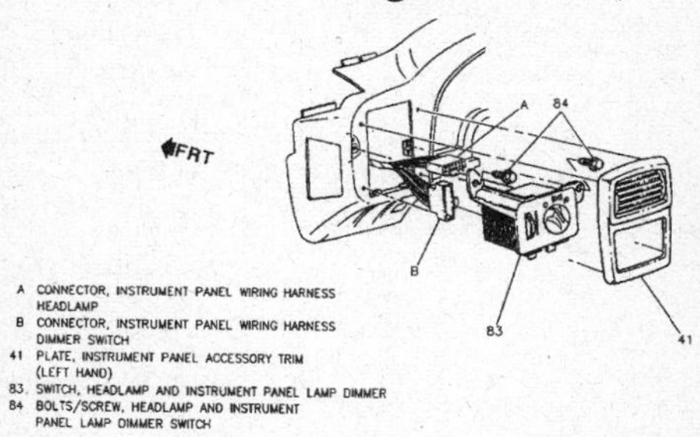

GC9049800163000X

Fig. 9 Headlamp switch replacement. Camaro

INSTALLATION

1. Ensure the shift lever is in Neutral, then position switch on shift lever making sure pin on shaft is in slot of switch.
2. If reinstalling existing switch, rotate switch to align service adjustment hole with carrier tang hole. Insert a $3/32$ inch gauge pin and rotate switch until pin drops in to a depth of $19/32$ inch. **Torque** switch attaching nut to 18 inch lbs., then remove gauge pin.
3. If installing a new switch, **torque** attaching nuts to 18 inch lbs., then move shift lever out of Neutral to shear pin which is a component of new switch.
4. Reconnect electrical connectors to switch, then apply parking brake and start engine. Inspect back-up lights and seat belt warning system for proper operation and ensure engine will start only in Park or Neutral.
5. Turn ignition off and install floor console.

HEADLAMP SWITCH

REPLACE

1. **On Camaro models,** remove switch assembly from bezel assembly, **Fig. 9.**
2. **On Firebird models,** remove switch assembly from carrier, **Fig. 10.**
3. **On all models,** disconnect electrical connector from switch assembly.
4. Reverse procedure to install.

STOP LIGHT SWITCH

REPLACE

1. Remove lefthand instrument panel sound insulator assembly, then disconnect electrical connectors, **Fig. 11.**
2. Remove release switch assembly, stop lamp and TCC switch assembly and clutch switch assembly, or clutch anticipate switch assembly, if equipped, from pedal assembly with bracket.
3. Install release switch assembly, stop lamp and TCC switch assembly and clutch switch assembly, or clutch anticipate switch assembly, if equipped, to pedal assembly with bracket.
4. Connect electrical connectors, then adjust switches as follows:
   a. Depress brake pedal assembly or clutch pedal assembly and insert release switch assembly, stop lamp and TCC switch assembly and clutch switch assembly, or clutch anticipate switch assembly into pedal assembly with bracket until retainer is fully seated.
   b. Slowly pull brake or clutch pedal assembly rearward with a force of 50 lbs. until click sounds can no longer be heard.
   c. Measure release switch assembly and stop lamp and TCC switch assembly contacts, should be open 1 inch or less of pedal assembly travel, and should occur at the same time or before onset of braking.
5. Install lefthand instrument panel sound insulator assembly.

TURN SIGNAL SWITCH

REPLACE

1. Remove steering wheel as outlined under "Steering Wheel, Replace."
2. Place ignition switch in Lock position to retain coil assembly in the centered position.
3. Remove coil assembly retaining ring, **Fig. 12.**
4. Lift coil assembly from steering shaft and allow to hang from wire, then remove wave washer.
5. Install a suitable tool, compress lock plate and remove snap ring (C-ring on tilt models), **Fig. 13.**
6. Remove lock plate, turn signal canceling cam and upper bearing spring, inner race seat and inner race.
7. Place turn signal lever in right hand turn position, then remove multifunction lever and hazard warning flasher knob.
8. Remove turn signal switch lever attaching screw, then remove lever.

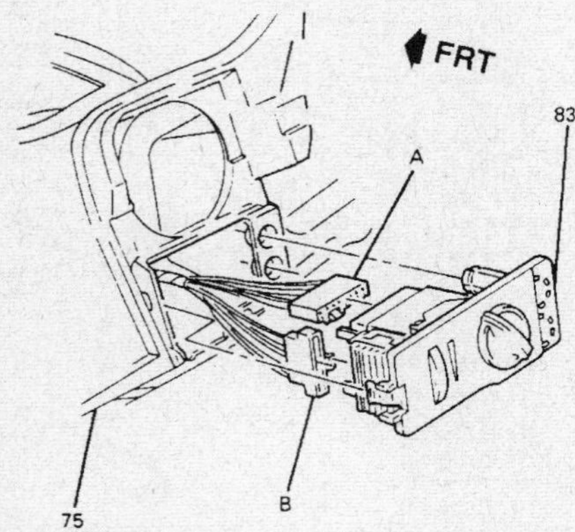

A CONNECTOR, INSTRUMENT PANEL WIRING HARNESS ELECTRICAL
B CONNECTOR, INSTRUMENT PANEL WIRING HARNESS ELECTRICAL
75 CARRIER, INSTRUMENT PANEL
83 SWITCH ASSEMBLY, HEADLAMP AND INSTRUMENT PANEL LAMP DIMMER

GC9049300058000X

Fig. 10 Headlamp switch replacement. Firebird

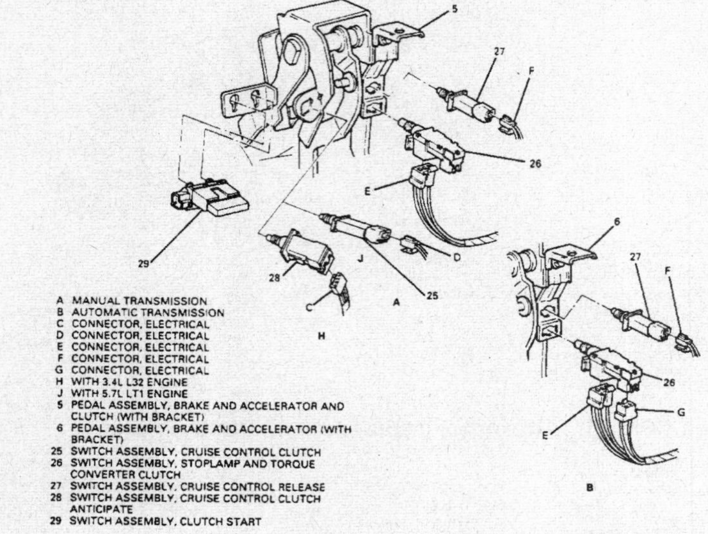

GC9049300060000X

Fig. 11 Stop lamp switch replacement

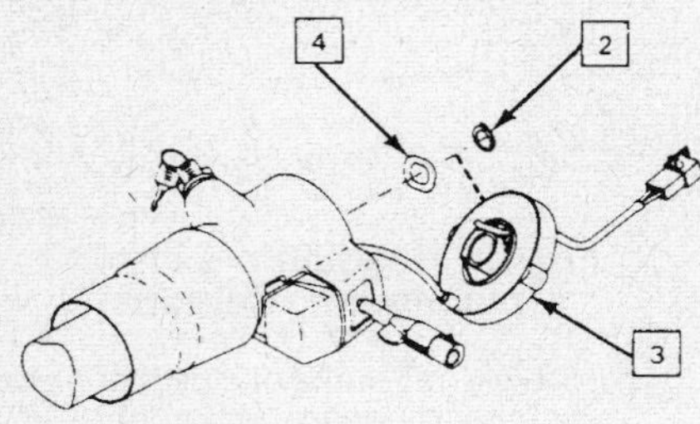

2 RETAINING RING
3 COIL ASSEMBLY
4 WAVE WASHER

GC9049100062000X

Fig. 12 Coil assembly removal

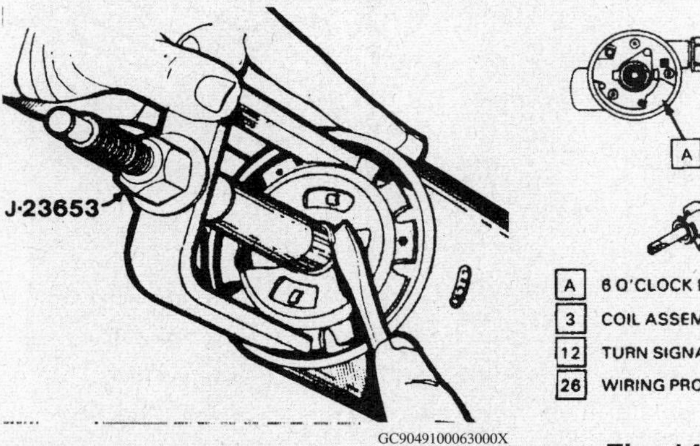

GC9049100063000X

Fig. 13 Lock plate retaining ring removal

A 6 O'CLOCK POSITION: HARNESS THROUGH HERE
3 COIL ASSEMBLY
12 TURN SIGNAL AND HAZARD WARNING SWITCH
26 WIRING PROTECTOR

GC9049100064000X

Fig. 14 Turn signal switch removal

9. Remove turn signal switch attaching screws.
10. Disconnect turn signal switch electrical connector at lower portion of steering column.
11. Remove turn signal switch wiring protector cover from steering column, **Fig. 14.**
12. Carefully pull turn signal switch wiring up and out of steering column.
13. Reverse procedure to install. If coil assembly has become uncentered, refer to **Fig. 15,** for centering procedure.

DIMMER SWITCH

REPLACE

Refer to "Ignition Switch, Replace" for Dimmer Switch replacement.

STEERING WHEEL

REPLACE

REMOVAL

When removing steering wheel, use only specified puller. Do not hammer on end of steering column shaft. Hammering on shaft may damage plastic injections, affecting column assembly rigidity.

When attaching specified puller to steering wheel, use caution to prevent threading bolts through steering wheel hub into Supplemental Inflatable Restraint (SIR) coil assembly, damaging coil assembly.

1. Remove screws from back of steering wheel assembly using a No. 30 Torx driver, then the inflatable restraint steering wheel module assembly from steering wheel assembly.
2. Disconnect SIR coil assembly electrical connector and retainer from inflatable restraint steering wheel module assembly.
3. **On Firebird models,** disconnect radio control switch electrical connector from inflatable restraint steering wheel module assembly, if equipped.
4. **On all models,** disconnect horn lead from column assembly.
5. Remove steering wheel using steering wheel puller tool No. J1859-A and steering wheel puller bolts tool No. J38720, or equivalents.

INSTALLATION

1. Route SIR coil assembly electrical connector to steering wheel, then install steering wheel, aligning block tooth on steering wheel with block tooth on steering column shaft within one female serration.
2. Install nut and **torque** to 32 ft. lbs.
3. Connect horn lead to column assembly.
4. **On Firebird models,** connect radio control switch electrical connector from inflatable restraint steering wheel module assembly, if equipped.
5. **On all models,** connect SIR coil assembly electrical connector and retainer to inflatable restraint steering wheel module assembly.
6. Secure SIR coil assembly electrical connector to steering wheel by inserting thick section of wire into existing retainers.
7. Position inflatable restraint steering wheel module assembly to steering wheel, ensure wiring is not exposed or trapped between module assembly and steering wheel.
8. Install inflatable restraint steering wheel module assembly screws and

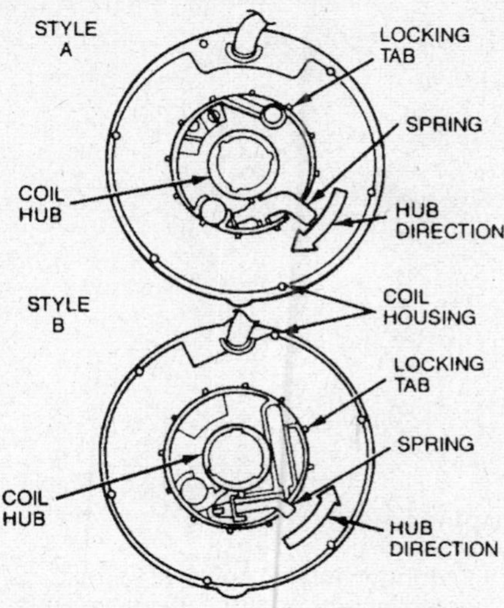

Perform the following steps to center coil assembly:

A. Remove coil assembly.
B. Hold coil assembly with clear bottom up to see coil ribbon.
C. NOTE: There are two different styles of coils. One rotates clockwise and the other rotates counterclockwise.
D. While holding coil assembly, depress spring lock to rotate hub in direction of arrow until it stops.
E. The coil ribbon should be wound up snug against center hub.
F. Rotate coil hub in opposite direction approximately two and a half (2-1/2) turns. Release spring lock between locking tabs in front of arrow.

GC9049100065000X

Fig. 15 Coil assembly centered position

torque to 25 inch lbs.

INSTRUMENT CLUSTER

REPLACE

1. Disconnect instrument panel upper trim panel assembly from lower windshield support, then remove from carrier.
2. Remove instrument cluster assembly from carrier, **Fig. 16.**
3. Reverse procedure to install.

RADIO

REPLACE

1. Remove accessory trim plate, **Fig. 17.**
2. Remove radio bracket bolts, **Fig. 18.**
3. Remove radio from instrument panel, then disconnect antenna cable and electrical connectors.
4. Reverse procedure to install noting the following:
   a. **On Firebird models,** install radio bracket bolts in following order; lower left, upper right, upper left.
   b. **On all models, torque** radio bracket bolts to 16 inch lbs.

WIPER MOTOR

REPLACE

REMOVAL

1. Remove wiper arm and blade assemblies as follows:
   a. Operate wipers at lowest delay setting, then shut Off wipers at inner wipe (end of sweep) position.
   b. Mark windshield at tip of blade assembly to aid installation, then lift wiper arm nut cover and remove nut.
   c. Remove wiper arm from linkage drive shaft using wiper arm puller J39637.
2. Remove lefthand cowl panel and hood seal.
3. Disconnect washer hose assembly from lefthand cowl panel, then the electrical connector from wiper motor assembly.
4. Remove screw and nut from lefthand linkage assembly, **Fig. 19,** then disconnect socket of righthand linkage assembly from ball of lefthand linkage assembly using wiper linkage separator tool No. J39232, or equivalent.
5. Remove lefthand linkage assembly, then the screw from wiper motor assembly.
6. Pull wiper motor assembly free from slots of bracket, then disconnect socket of righthand linkage assembly from crank arm ball of wiper motor assembly using wiper linkage separator.

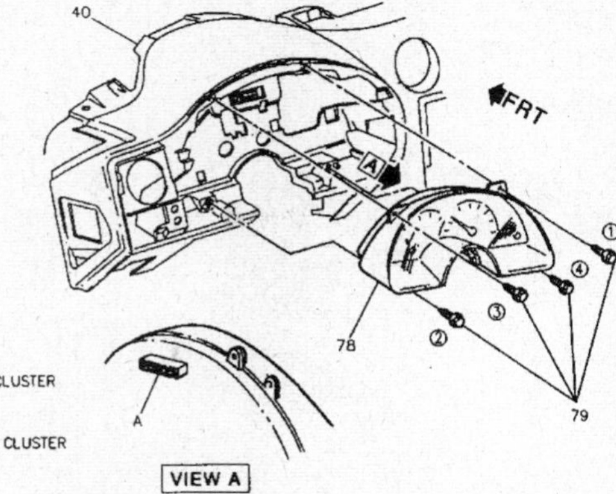

GC9099800671000X

Fig. 16 Instrument cluster

INSTALLATION

When installing wiper motor assembly, ensure crank arm is in inner wipe position. Crank arm drive pin must be engaged in cam pocket.

1. Press socket of righthand linkage assembly into engagement with crank arm ball of wiper motor assembly using wiper linkage installer tool No. J39529, or equivalent.
2. Install wiper motor assembly with two locator pads pressed fully into slots of bracket, then the mounting screw and **torque** to 96 inch lbs.
3. Install lefthand linkage assembly without attaching components, then press socket of righthand linkage assembly into engagement with ball of lefthand linkage assembly using wiper linkage installer.
4. Attach lefthand linkage assembly with screw and nut and **torque** to 90 inch lbs.
5. Connect electrical connector to wiper motor assembly, then the washer hose assembly to lefthand cowl panel and washer nozzle.
6. Install lefthand cowl panel and hood seal.
7. Install wiper arm and blade assemblies as follows:
   a. Install wiper arm and blade assembly onto linkage drive shaft, with tip of blade assembly aligned with mark made at removal.
   b. Install nut on linkage drive shaft and **torque** to 24 ft. lbs. while holding wiper arm.
   c. Close nut cover, then run wipers and inspect for proper wipe pattern. Turn wipers Off and inspect for correct park position.

WIPER SWITCH

REPLACE

1. **On models equipped with cruise control,** remove tilt wheel release lever and access cover, then disconnect electrical connectors.
2. **On all models,** remove wiper switch by grasping firmly and pulling straight out.
3. Reverse procedure to install, noting the following:
   a. Ensure wiper switch is in Off position before installing.
   b. Position tilt lever ± 5° from centerline of column assembly.

WIPER TRANSMISSION

REPLACE

REMOVAL

1. Remove wiper arm and blade assemblies as follows:
   a. Operate wipers at lowest delay setting, then turn wipers Off at inner wipe (end of sweep) position.
   b. Mark windshield at tip of blade assembly to aid installation, then lift wiper arm nut cover and remove nut.
   c. Remove wiper arm from linkage drive shaft using wiper arm puller tool No. J39637, or equivalent.
2. Remove lefthand cowl panel and hood seal, then disconnect washer hose assembly from lefthand cowl panel.

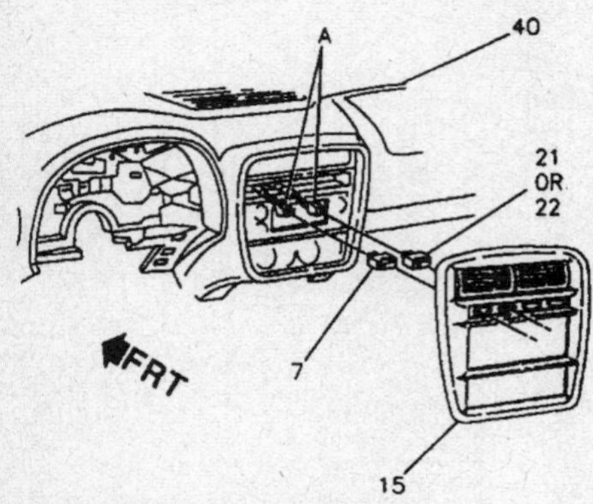

A CONNECTORS, INSTRUMENT PANEL WIRING HARNESS
7 SWITCH, FOG LAMP
15 PLATE, INSTRUMENT PANEL ACCESSORY TRIM
21 SWITCH, TRACTION CONTROL
22 SWITCH, SECOND GEAR START
40 PANEL, INSTRUMENT

GC9099800672000X

Fig. 17 Accessory trim plate removal

3. Remove screw and nut from lefthand linkage assembly, **Fig. 19,** then disconnect socket of righthand linkage assembly from ball of lefthand linkage assembly using wiper linkage separator tool No. J39232, or equivalent.
4. Remove lefthand linkage assembly, then the screws securing righthand linkage assembly.
5. Disconnect socket of righthand linkage assembly from crank arm ball of wiper motor assembly using wiper linkage separator, then remove righthand linkage assembly from slotted plenum access hole.

INSTALLATION

1. Install righthand linkage assembly from slotted plenum access hole, then the screws securing righthand linkage assembly finger tight.
2. Align righthand linkage assembly, then press socket of righthand linkage assembly into engagement with crank arm ball of wiper motor assembly using wiper linkage installer tool No. J39529, or equivalent.
3. Install lefthand linkage assembly without attaching components, then press socket of righthand linkage assembly into engagement with ball of lefthand linkage assembly using wiper linkage installer.
4. Attach lefthand linkage assembly with screw and nut and **torque** to 90 inch lbs.
5. Connect washer hose assembly to lefthand cowl panel and washer nozzle.
6. Install lefthand cowl panel and hood seal.
7. Install wiper arm and blade assemblies as follows:

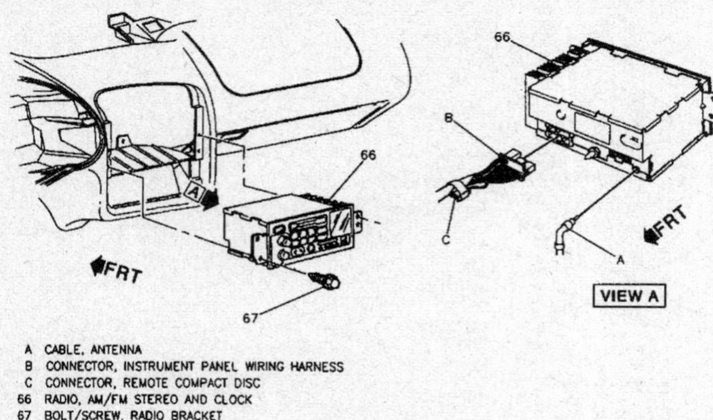

A CABLE, ANTENNA
B CONNECTOR, INSTRUMENT PANEL WIRING HARNESS
C CONNECTOR, REMOTE COMPACT DISC
66 RADIO, AM/FM STEREO AND CLOCK
67 BOLT/SCREW, RADIO BRACKET

GC9099800673000X

Fig. 18 Radio replacement

a. Install wiper arm and blade assembly onto linkage drive shaft, with tip of blade assembly aligned with mark made at removal.
b. Install nut on linkage drive shaft and **torque** to 24 ft. lbs. while holding wiper arm.
c. Close nut cover, then run wipers and inspect for proper wipe pattern. Shut off wipers and inspect for correct park position.

BLOWER MOTOR

REPLACE

1. Ensure ignition switch is in Off position, then remove righthand instrument panel sound insulator assembly and side trim panel.
2. Remove blower motor mounting bolts, then the blower motor.
3. Reverse procedure to install. **Torque** mounting bolts to 20 inch lbs.

HEATER CORE

REPLACE

1. Drain engine coolant into suitable container.
2. Remove heater hoses and pipes.
3. Remove heater core tube clamp and shroud seal.
4. Slide heater rear case downward in order to disengage upper case clip, then remove heater rear case.
5. Remove glove compartment door.
6. Remove heater core clamp, then the heater core.
7. Reverse procedure to install.

EVAPORATOR CORE

REPLACE

1. Evacuate A/C as outlined under "Air Conditioning."
2. Drain engine coolant into suitable container.
3. Remove righthand instrument panel sound insulator panel assembly, then disconnect heater hoses at heater core assembly.
4. Remove instrument panel compartment, then the heater core as outlined under "Heater Core, Replace."
5. Remove evaporator temperature sensor assembly, **Fig. 20,** then disconnect temperature control cable assembly at temperature valve case assembly.
6. Remove bolts (located in engine compartment) from temperature valve case assembly, then the temperature valve case assembly by sliding downward to disengage upper case clip.
7. Remove thermostatic expansion valve assembly.
8. Install a small hand saw, remove perforated section of evaporator module assembly as one piece and retain for reuse.
9. Remove bolts retaining evaporator, then the evaporator from module assembly by sliding evaporator to left and pulling out through opening cut in module.
10. Reverse procedure to install, noting the following:
    a. If replacing evaporator, transfer condensate screen to new evaporator and add 3 fluid ounces of polyalkalene glycol (PAG) synthetic refrigerant oil to new evaporator.
    b. Apply sealer No. 3012078, or equivalent, between evaporator upper and lower case just behind thermostatic expansion valve assembly to prevent air entry from engine compartment.
    c. Use epoxy glue to adhere perforated section of module assembly to module assembly.
    d. Fill radiator and bleed cooling system.
    e. Partially charge system and perform a leak test, then recover refrigerant and evacuate and charge system.

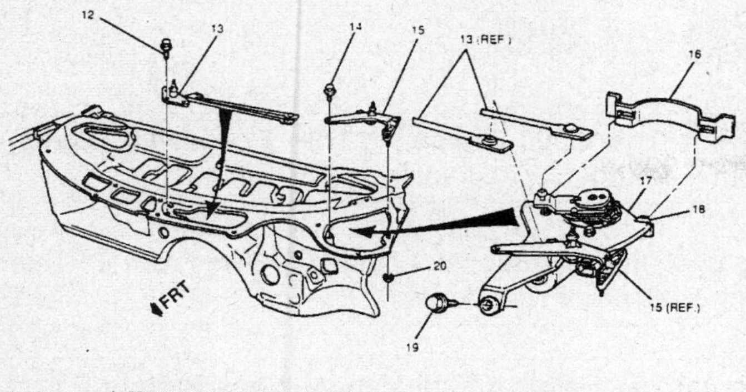

A CRANK ARM DRIVE PIN IN CAM POCKET
12 SCREW (3), 10 N•m (7.5 LB. FT.)
13 LINKAGE ASSEMBLY, RH
14 SCREW, 10 N•m (7.5 LB. FT.)
15 LINKAGE ASSEMBLY, LH
16 BRACKET, WIPER MOTOR
17 MOTOR ASSEMBLY, WIPER
18 PAD, LOCATOR (2)
19 SCREW, 10 N•m (7.5 LB. FT.)
20 NUT, 10 N•m (7.5 LB. FT.)

GC9099300207000X

Fig. 19 Windshield wiper motor/transmission assembly

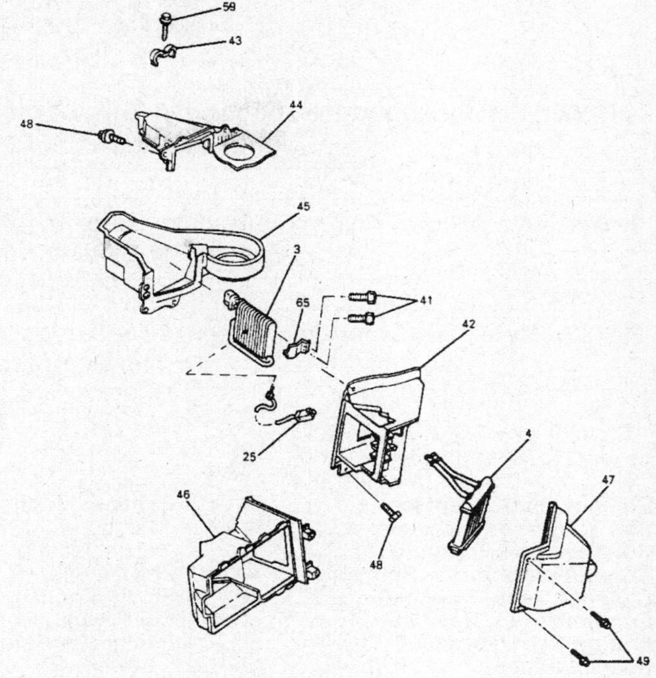

3 EVAPORATOR, AIR CONDITIONING
4 CORE ASSEMBLY, HEATER
25 SENSOR ASSEMBLY, AIR CONDITIONING EVAPORATOR TEMPERATURE
41 BOLT/SCREW, AIR CONDITIONING EVAPORATOR
42 CASE ASSEMBLY, TEMPERATURE VALVE
43 CLAMP, HEATER CORE TUBE
44 CASE, AIR CONDITIONING EVAPORATOR UPPER
45 CASE, AIR CONDITIONING EVAPORATOR LOWER
46 CASE, AIR DISTRIBUTOR UPPER
47 COVER, HEATER AND AIR CONDITIONING EVAPORATOR CASE
48 BOLT/SCREW, TEMPERATURE VALVE CASE ASSEMBLY
49 BOLT/SCREW, HEATER AND AIR CONDITIONING EVAPORATOR CASE COVER
59 BOLT/SCREW, HEATER CORE TUBE CLAMP
65 CLAMP, AIR CONDITIONING EVAPORATOR

GC7029300056000X

Fig. 20 Evaporator core replacement

3800 Engine

NOTE: For Procedures Not Found In This Section, Refer To The "3800 Engine" In The "Bonneville, Eighty Eight, LeSabre, LSS, Park Avenue & Regency" Chapter.

NOTE: On Air Bag Equipped Models, Refer To "Air Bag System Precautions" Located In The Front Of This Manual For System Disarming & Arming Procedures.

NOTE: Refer To "Computer Relearn Procedures" Located In The Front Of This Manual When Battery Power To The Computer Has Been Interrupted.

INDEX

PRECAUTIONS

AIR BAG SYSTEMS

Refer to "Air Bag System Precautions" in the front of this manual for system disarming and arming procedures.

BATTERY GROUND CABLE

Prior to service, disconnect battery ground cable and isolate as required.

FUEL SYSTEM PRESSURE RELIEF

Refer to the "3800 Engine" in the "Bonneville, Eighty Eight, LeSabre, LSS & Park Avenue" chapter for fuel system pressure relief procedure.

ENGINE SUPPORT

When raising the engine for any reason, do not use a jack under the oil pan, crankshaft balancer or any sheet metal, this may result in damage to engine. Always use universal support fixture tool No. J28467-A and engine support adapter tool No. J41044, or equivalents.

COMPRESSION PRESSURE

When inspecting compression, lowest cylinder must be within 70 percent of the highest cylinder with a minimum pressure of 100 psi. Perform compression test with engine at normal operating temperature, spark plugs removed and throttle wide open.

ENGINE MOUNT

REPLACE

1. Remove alternator as outlined under "Alternator, Replace" in "Electrical" section, then ignition control module.
2. Raise and support vehicle.
3. Disconnect exhaust catalytic converter system.
4. Remove engine mount nuts.
5. Disconnect transmission oil cooler lines, if required.
6. Loosen air conditioning compressor and slide forward, if required.
7. Install universal support fixture tool No. J28467-A along with engine support adapter tool No. J41044, or equivalents, and support engine to allow for engine mount bolts/bracket removal and raise engine.
8. Remove engine mount bolts and screws, then remove mounts from engine cradle.
9. Remove engine bracket bolts and screws, then studs and brackets.
10. Reverse procedure to install, noting following:
    a. **Torque** bolts and screws (13) and studs (11), **Fig. 1,** to 74 ft. lbs.
    b. **Torque** bolts and screws (14) to 37 ft. lbs. and engine mount bolts (18) to 43 ft. lbs.

ENGINE

REPLACE

1. Recover refrigerant as outlined under "Air Conditioning" section is this manual.
2. Relieve fuel pressure as outlined under "Precautions."
3. Disconnect A/C compressor and condenser hose from accumulator.
4. Raise and support vehicle and remove front wheels.
5. Drain coolant and engine oil into suitable containers.
6. Disconnect 3-way catalytic converter.
7. Disconnect transmission converter and front fascia lower deflectors.
8. Disconnect stabilizer bar bushing bolts and transmission fluid cooler lines from radiator.
9. Remove radiator inlet hose, shift linkage from transmission and propeller shaft.
10. Disconnect rear axle torque arm from transmission and steering gear coupling shaft from rack and pinion assembly.
11. Disconnect power steering gear inlet and outlet hoses from power steering gear.
12. Disconnect starter motor and electrical ground strap from engine block.
13. Disconnect A/C compressor and condenser hoses.
14. Remove battery ground cable from rear of A/C compressor and engine coolant heater cord from block.
15. Lower vehicle, remove serpentine belt as outlined in "Serpentine Drive Belt," then any remaining hoses/brackets from tensioner.
16. Remove air cleaner outlet rear duct and resonator duct.
17. Remove fuel lines at fuel rail and cruise/accelerator cables from throttle body.
18. Disconnect radiator outlet hose from thermostat housing and brake booster vacuum hose.
19. Disconnect ABS combination valve

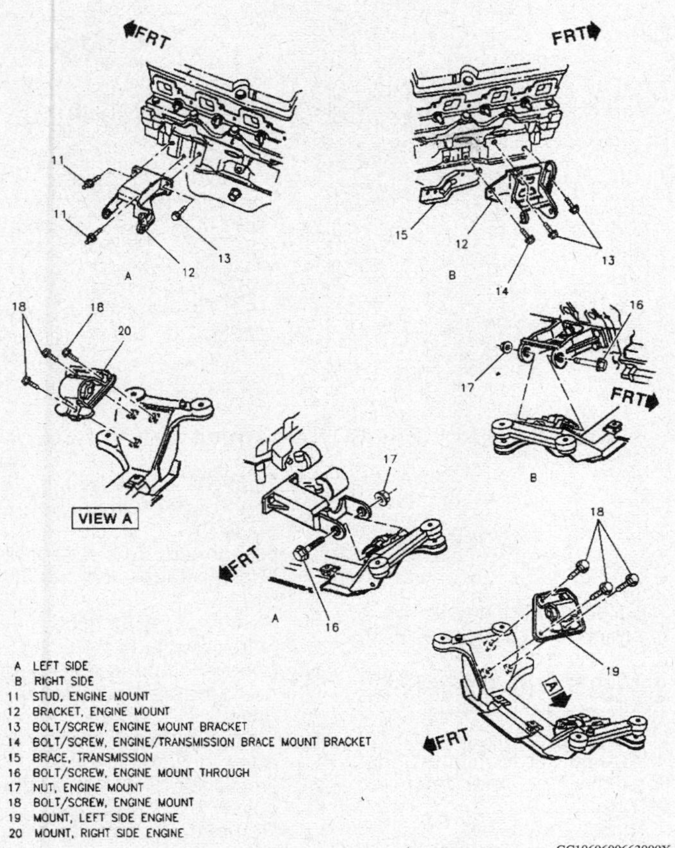

Fig. 1 Engine mount fasteners

from brake lines, clips and hydraulic modulator.

20. Remove righthand body hinge pillar trim panel and the three (blue, black and white) wiring harness connectors.
21. Disconnect the forward lamp wiring harness connectors and PCM and place on top of engine.
22. Disconnect engine wiring harness in passenger compartment and place on top of engine.
23. Disconnect positive lead at alternator.
24. Remove lower shock bolt from lower control arm.
25. Remove upper control arm ball stud from steering knuckle and secure struts.
26. Disconnect electrical connectors to wheel speed sensor at engine frame.
27. Install tool No. J39580, or equivalent, position lift table under engine and frame.
28. Remove engine frame to transmission support bolts.
29. Raise vehicle from engine, transmission and engine frame.
30. Remove transmission.
31. **On models equipped with manual transmission,** remove clutch.
32. **On all models,** remove engine mount through-bolt and separate engine from engine frame.
33. Reverse procedure to install, noting the following:
    a. When installing wiring harness back through front of dash, the rubber grommet must be installed correctly. If grommet is torn or damaged, it must be replaced.
    b. Tighten fasteners to specifications.
    c. Align wheels.

INTAKE MANIFOLD

REPLACE

UPPER

1. Remove right side spark plug wires, then manifold vacuum source.
2. Remove rear alternator mounting bracket bolts.
3. Remove EGR outlet pipe bolt and nut, then separate from intake manifold.
4. Remove throttle body and gasket.
5. Remove fuel rail with injectors attached.
6. Remove upper intake manifold and gasket.
7. Reverse procedure to install, noting the following:
    a. **Torque** vertical bolts in sequence, **Fig. 2,** to 11 ft. lbs.
    b. **Torque** water outlet bolts in sequence, **Fig. 2,** to 20 ft. lbs.
    c. **Torque** side bolts in sequence, **Fig. 2,** to 22 ft. lbs.

LOWER

To remove the lower intake manifold, the upper manifold must be removed first.

1. Remove upper intake manifold as outlined in the "Upper" section of this manual to access two hidden bolts.
2. Remove lower intake manifold bolts, then manifold.
3. Reverse procedure to install, noting the following:
    a. Use a suitable thread locking compound on intake manifold bolts prior to assembly.
    b. Tighten bolts in sequence, **Fig. 3,** to 11 ft. lbs.

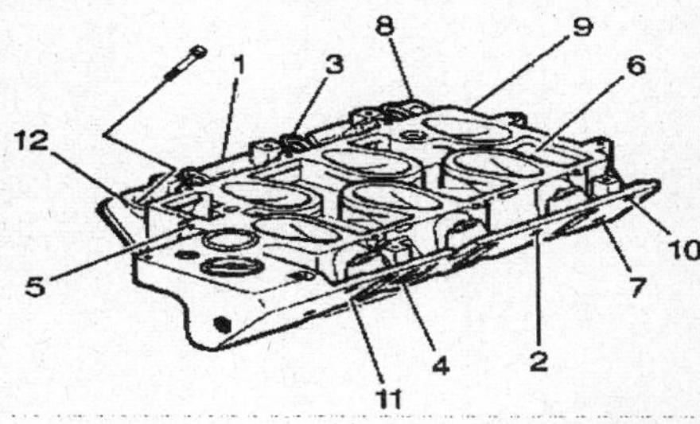

Fig. 2 Upper intake manifold tightening sequence

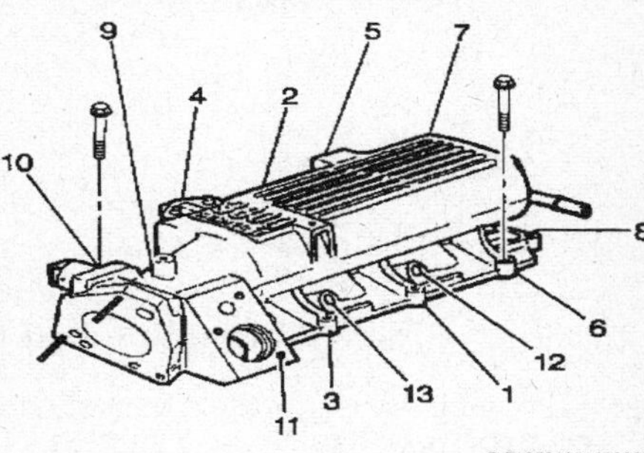

Fig. 3 Lower intake manifold tightening sequence

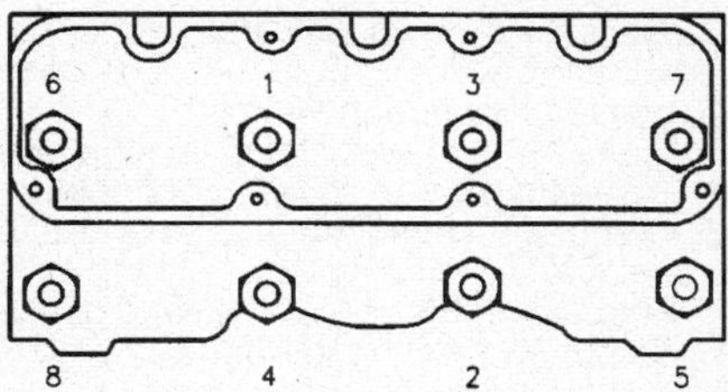

Fig. 4 Cylinder head bolt tightening sequence

EXHAUST MANIFOLD

REPLACE

RIGHTHAND

1. Remove exhaust manifold heat shield nuts, then the shield.
2. Raise and support vehicle.
3. Remove exhaust catalytic converter pipe.
4. Remove heated oxygen sensor electrical connector from bracket.
5. Lower vehicle and remove exhaust manifold studs and bolts, then the manifold.

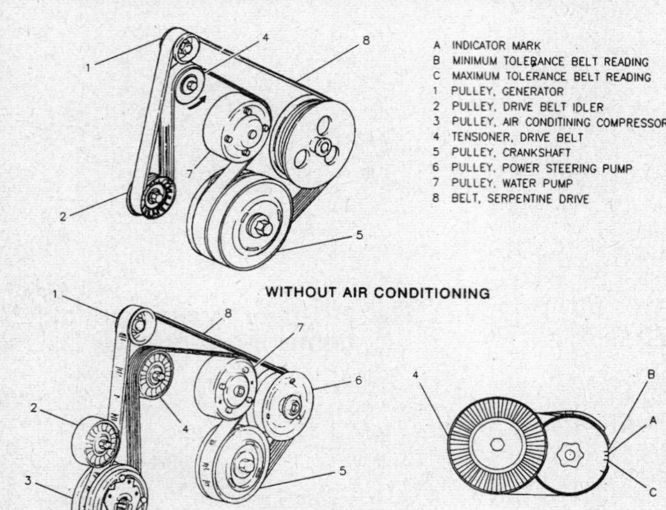

Fig. 5 Serpentine belt routing

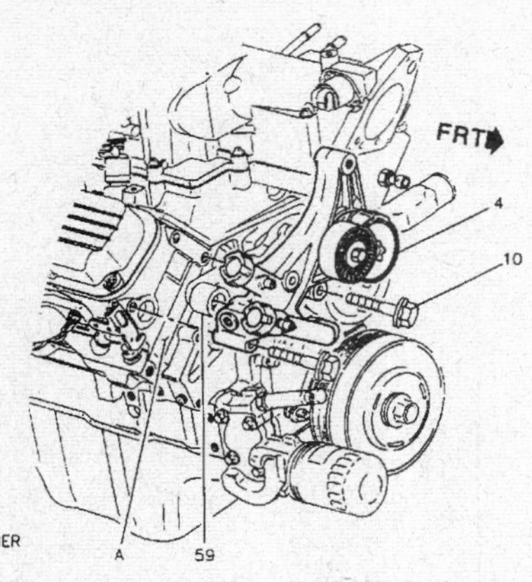

Fig. 6 Serpentine belt tensioner

6. Remove exhaust manifold gasket and clean cylinder head mating surface.
7. Reverse procedure to install.

LEFTHAND

1. Remove EGR valve adapter from exhaust manifold.
2. Remove oil level indicator and tube.
3. Remove exhaust manifold heat shield.
4. Raise and support vehicle.
5. Remove exhaust catalytic converter pipe and oxygen sensor connector.
6. Disconnect spark plug wires and lower vehicle.
7. Remove exhaust manifold and gasket, then clean mating surfaces.
8. Reverse procedure to install, noting the following:
   a. Install new exhaust manifold gasket.
   b. Inspect EGR outlet tube for leaks.

CYLINDER HEAD

REPLACE

1. Remove upper and lower intake manifolds as outlined under "Intake Manifold, Replace."
2. Remove exhaust manifold as outlined under "Exhaust Manifold, Replace."
3. Remove rocker arm covers, rocker arms and push rods.
4. Remove and discard cylinder head bolts.
5. Remove cylinder head.
6. Reverse procedure to install, noting the following:
   a. Clean threads in block with proper size tap.
   b. Install new head gasket with the lefthand gasket, marked "L" and an arrow, pointing forward. The righthand gasket has just the arrow marking. These head gaskets are not interchangeable.
   c. Install new cylinder head bolts, then using sequence, **Fig. 4, torque** cylinder head bolts to 37 ft. lbs.
   d. Install torque angle meter tool No. J36660, or equivalent, tighten each bolt in sequence an additional 120°.

CRANKSHAFT DAMPER

REPLACE

1. Remove drive belt as outlined under "Serpentine Drive Belt," then raise and support vehicle.
2. Remove starter motor as outlined under "Starter, Replace" in "Electrical" section, then transmission braces.
3. Remove transmission access cover.
4. Hold flywheel using tool No. J37096, or equivalent.
5. Remove crankshaft balancer/damper bolt and washer. **Note the relationship of the balancer/damper and crankshaft key as the balancer is removed.**
6. Remove crankshaft balancer using puller tool No. J38197, or equivalent. **The crankshaft damper is serviced as an assembly, do not separate pulley from balancer hub.**
7. Reverse procedure to install, noting the following:
   a. Lubricate balancer and crankshaft mating surface with clean motor oil.
   b. Tighten balancer bolt to specifications.

FRONT COVER

REPLACE

1. Drain engine oil and coolant into suitable containers.
2. Disconnect IAT sensor electrical connector.
3. Remove air intake duct.
4. Loosen water pump pulley bolts.
5. Remove drivebelt tensioner.
6. Install puller No. J25034–B, or equivalent, remove power steering pulley.
7. Place suitable container under power steering pump, then disconnect inlet and return hoses from pump.
8. Remove power steering pump, then raise and support vehicle.
9. Remove crankshaft damper as outlined under "Crankshaft Damper, Replace."
10. Disconnect CKP sensor electrical connector, then remove CKP sensor shield.
11. Remove CKP sensor, then the oil pan to front cover bolts.
12. Loosen oil pans bolts slightly to lower oil pan as an installation aid for front cover.
13. Lower vehicle, then remove water pump pulley.
14. Remove radiator outlet hose from front cover.
15. Remove front cover mounting studs and bolts.
16. Remove front cover and gasket.
17. Remove components from front cover as required if replacing cover.
18. Reverse procedure to install, noting the following:
    a. Apply sealant No. 12346004, or equivalent, to threads of front cover bolts and studs.
    b. **Torque** front cover bolts to 15 ft. lbs., then using torque angle meter No. J36660, or equivalent, tighten bolts and studs an additional 40°.

BALANCE SHAFT

REPLACE

1. Remove drive belt as outlined under "Serpentine Drive Belt."
2. Raise and support vehicle.
3. Remove starter motor as outlined under "Starter Motor, Replace" in "Electrical" section.
4. **On models equipped with manual transmissions,** remove transmission as outlined under "Clutch & Manual Transmission," then the clutch and flywheel.
5. **On models equipped with automatic transmissions,** remove transmission as outlined under "Automatic Transaxles/Transmissions," then the flywheel.
6. **On all models,** remove crankshaft balancer bolt from balancer.
7. Remove crankshaft balancer using crankshaft balancer puller tool No. J38197A, or equivalent.
8. Remove key from crankshaft.

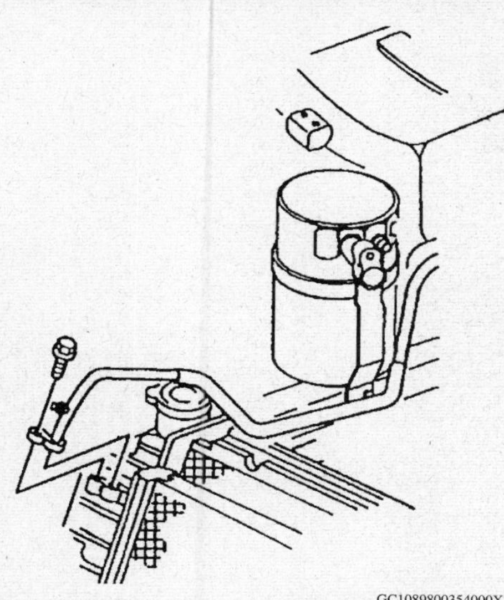

Fig. 7 Evaporator line removal

9. Reverse procedure to install, noting the following:
   a. Lubricate seal surface of crankshaft balancer with suitable engine oil.
   b. Perform crankshaft position system variation learn procedure as outlined under "Computer Relearn Procedures" in the front of this manual.
   c. Tighten to specifications.

OIL PAN

REPLACE

1. Remove ignition coils.
2. Install engine support fixture tool No. J28467-A, or equivalent.
3. Raise and support vehicle.
4. Drain engine oil into suitable container, then remove torque converter cover.
5. Remove exhaust crossover pipe.
6. Remove engine mount through bolts.
7. Raise engine using support fixture.
8. Remove oil level sensor, then the oil pan bolts.
9. Lower rear of oil pan, then rotate outward and remove pan.
10. Reverse procedure to install. Tighten all bolts and nuts to specifications.

SERPENTINE DRIVE BELT

Cracks appearing perpendicular to the belt ribs indicate normal wear. If sections of rib are missing or if the belt is slipping, the belt must be replaced. The belt tensioner has a wear indicator, and if it is out of limits, either the belt or tensioner must be replaced.

1. Install suitable ratchet and socket, push tensioner clockwise and remove serpentine belt, **Fig. 5.**
2. Reverse procedure to install.

BELT TENSIONER

REPLACE

1. Drain engine coolant into suitable container.
2. Remove drive belt as outlined under "Serpentine Drive Belt."
3. Remove transmission oil dipstick and oil filler neck from rocker arm cover.
4. Remove manifold absolute pressure (MAP) sensor from alternator bracket and remove alternator.
5. Remove heater hoses from belt drive tensioner.
6. Remove belt drive tensioner, **Fig. 6.**
7. Reverse procedure to install.

RADIATOR

REPLACE

1. Recover refrigerant as outlined under "Air Conditioning" section.
2. Drain cooling system into suitable container, then remove radiator hoses.
3. Remove upper evaporator tube bracket bolt, **Fig. 7.**
4. Remove evaporator tube from condenser.
5. Remove upper and lower oil cooler lines from radiator.
6. Remove condenser tube from condenser, **Fig. 8.**
7. Remove overflow hose from radiator.
8. Remove air intake duct and air cleaner assembly, then disconnect cooling fan electrical connectors.
9. Remove electric cooling fans, then the coolant level indicator module.
10. Remove radiator and condenser.
11. Reverse procedure to install.

FUEL PUMP

REPLACE

1. Relieve fuel system pressure as outlined under "Precautions."
2. Raise and support vehicle.
3. Drain fuel tank and remove.
4. Remove fuel sender retaining nuts, retaining ring, sender seal (discard seal) and sender assembly.

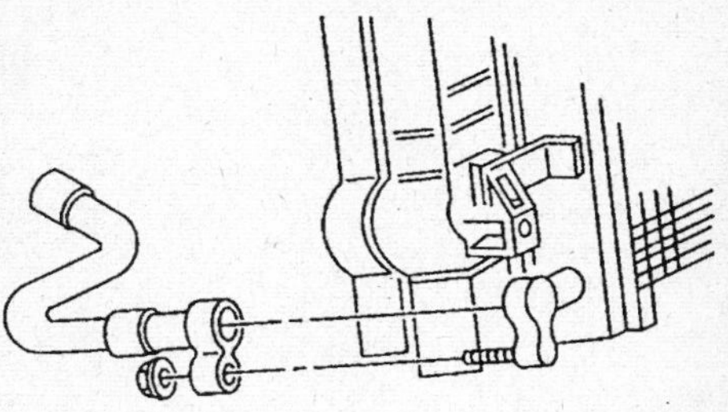

Fig. 8 Condenser tube removal

5. Reverse procedure to install, noting the following:
   a. **Always replace fuel sender seal when servicing sending unit. Do not handle fuel sender assembly by the sender pipes, as this may damage the solder joints.**
   b. Clean fuel sender assembly sealing surfaces.
   c. Fuel pump strainer must be in horizontal position. Ensure fuel pump strainer does not block full travel of float arm.
   d. Gently fold strainer over itself and insert into fuel tank making sure strainer is not damaged or trapped by sump walls.
   e. Inspect for leaks.

FUEL FILTER

REPLACE

1. Relieve fuel system pressure as outlined under "Precautions" then raise and support vehicle.
2. Clean all inline fuel filter connections to avoid contaminating fuel system.
3. Remove quick-connect fitting at filter inlet using quick disconnect tool No. J37088-A, or equivalent, then the threaded fitting from filter outlet. Slide fuel filter from bracket.
4. Reverse procedure to install, noting the following:
   a. Inspect fuel pipe O-ring for cuts, nicks, swelling or distortion and replace, if required.
   b. Inspect for leaks.

TIGHTENING SPECIFICATIONS

Year	Component	Torque/Ft. Lbs.
1998–2002	Balance Shaft Gear	16③
	Balance Shaft Retainer	22
	Camshaft Position Sensor	84⑧
	Camshaft Sprocket	74⑤
	Connecting Rod Bearing Cap	20⑦
	Coolant Outlet	20
	Crankshaft Balancer	111⑨
	Crankshaft Main Bearing Bolt	⑩
	Crankshaft Main Bearing Side Bolt	11④
	Crankshaft Position Sensor Stud	22
	Cylinder Head	①
	Drive Belt Tensioner	37
	EGR Valve Nut	21
	Engine Coolant Temperature Sensor	10
	Engine Front Cover	11⑥
	Engine Mount Bolts	43
	Engine Mount Through Bolt	70
	Engine Mount Through Bolt Nut	59
	Engine Oil Pressure Sensor	10
	ESC Knock Sensor	13
	Exhaust Manifold	22
	Flywheel Bolts (New)	11⑦
	Lower Intake Manifold	11
	Oil Pan	10
	Oil Pump Cover	96⑧
	Oxygen Sensor	31
	Throttle Body	84⑧
	Timing Chain Dampener	16
	Upper Intake Manifold (Two Side Bolts)	22
	Upper Intake Manifold (Two Water Outlet Bolts)	20
	Upper Intake Manifold (10 Vertical Bolts)	11
	Valve Lifter Guide Retainer	22
	Valve Rocker Arm	11⑤
	Water Pump	11②

① — Refer to "Cylinder Head, Replace."
② — Tighten an additional 80.°
③ — Tighten an additional 70.°
④ — Tighten an additional 45.°
⑤ — Tighten an additional 90.°
⑥ — Tighten an additional 40°
⑦ — Tighten an additional 50.°
⑧ — Inch lbs.
⑨ — Models equipped w/manual transmission, plus an additional 114.°
⑩ — Cap bolts to 51 ft. lbs. to seat bearings, then loosen each bolt 1 turn. **To ensure cap seats properly, do not tighten each bolt completely at one time. Make several passes until specified torque is achieved.** Then torque to 30 ft. lbs. Using a suitable torque angle meter, tighten in following steps; 35°, an additional 35°, then an additional 40.°

5.7L Engine

NOTE: For Procedures Not Found In This Section, Refer To The "5.7L Engine" Section In The "Corvette" Chapter.

NOTE: On Air Bag Equipped Models, Refer To "Air Bag System Precautions" Located In The Front Of This Manual For System Disarming & Arming Procedures.

NOTE: Refer To "Computer Relearn Procedures" Located In The Front Of This Manual When Battery Power To The Computer Has Been Interrupted.

INDEX

PRECAUTIONS

AIR BAG SYSTEMS

Refer to "Air Bag System Precautions" in the front of this manual for system disarming and arming procedures.

BATTERY GROUND CABLE

Prior to service, disconnect battery ground cable and isolate as required.

FUEL SYSTEM PRESSURE RELIEF

Before servicing any electrical component, the ignition key must be in the Off or Lock position and all electrical loads must be Off.

1. Turn ignition to Off position.
2. Loosen fuel filler cap in order to relieve fuel tank vapor pressure.
3. Connect J34730-1A fuel pressure gauge to fuel pressure valve.
4. Wrap a shop towel around fitting while connecting gauge in order to avoid spillage.
5. Install bleed hose of the gauge into an approved container.
6. Open valve on gauge to bleed system pressure.
7. The fuel connections are now safe for servicing.
8. Drain any fuel remaining in gauge into an approved container.

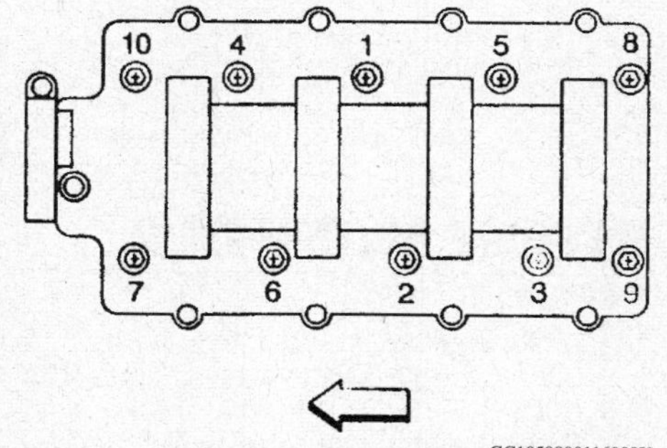

Fig. 1 Intake manifold tightening sequence

COMPRESSION PRESSURE

When inspecting compression, lowest cylinder must be within 70 percent of the highest cylinder with a minimum pressure of 100 psi. Perform compression test with engine at normal operating temperature, spark plugs removed and throttle wide open.

ENGINE MOUNT

REPLACE

LEFTHAND

1. Disconnect MAF and IAT sensor electrical connectors.
2. Remove air duct from throttle body and air cleaner box.
3. Support engine using engine fixture tool Nos. 42451, 28467, 36462 and 41044, or equivalents.
4. Raise and support vehicle, then remove left catalytic converter.
5. Remove engine mount bracket to crossmember bolts.
6. Lower vehicle.
7. Raise left side of engine using fixture tools.
8. Raise and support vehicle, then remove engine mount heat shield.
9. Remove engine mount bracket to block studs.
10. Remove engine mount from vehicle, then separate upper and lower mounts.
11. Reverse procedure to install.

RIGHTHAND

1. Support engine using support tool Nos. J42451, J41044 and J36462, or equivalent.
2. Raise and support vehicle.
3. Remove starter as outlined in "Electrical" section.
4. Remove negative battery cable from engine block.
5. Remove engine mount bracket to crossmember attaching bolts, then lower vehicle.
6. Raise right side of engine using support tool.
7. Raise and support vehicle.
8. Remove engine mount to bracket

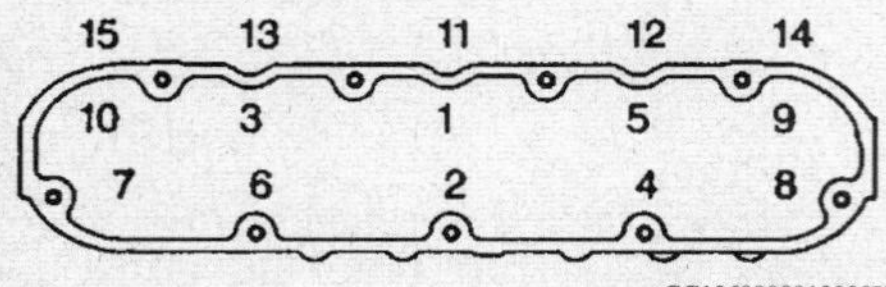

Fig. 2 Cylinder head bolt tightening sequence

bolts, then the mount from vehicle.
9. Reverse procedure to install. Tighten all bolts and nuts to specifications.

ENGINE

REPLACE

The engine and transmission are removed as an assembly.

The accelerator control cable must be replaced whenever the engine is removed.

1. Disconnect IAT and MAF sensor electrical connectors.
2. Remove air intake duct resonator.
3. Recover refrigerant as outlined under "Air Conditioning."
4. Relieve fuel system pressure as outlined under "Precautions" then raise and support vehicle.
5. Drain engine oil into suitable container, then remove front wheel and tire assemblies.
6. Drain engine coolant into suitable container, then remove right catalytic converter.
7. **On models equipped with manual transmission,** drain transmission fluid.
8. **On all models,** remove driveshaft and torque arm.
9. Remove starter motor.
10. **On models equipped with automatic transmission,** remove transmission range select cable.
11. **On models equipped with manual transmission,** remove clutch actuator line using special tool No. 36221, or equivalent.
12. **On all models,** remove left side front air deflector.
13. Remove stabilizer bar brackets.
14. Remove intermediate steering shaft bolt and shaft from rack.
15. Remove ground bolt and straps from front rail.
16. Disconnect front wheel speed sensors.
17. Remove condenser hose bolt from A/C compressor.
18. Remove fuel line heat shield, then remove brake lines from retainer clip.
19. Lower vehicle, then remove A/C compressor hose from accumulator.
20. Remove inlet and outlet heater hoses from water pump.
21. Disconnect fuel line from fuel rail and vapor line from purge valve.
22. Remove accelerator and cruise control cables from throttle lever.
23. Remove accelerator and cruise control cables from servo adjuster as required.
24. Remove inlet hose from water pump.
25. Remove outlet hose from engine.
26. Remove brake booster vacuum hose, then disconnect two front brake lines from brake pressure modulator valve.
27. Disconnect forward lamp wiring harness from engine wiring harness.
28. Disconnect engine harness vacuum tube from bottom of vacuum check valve.
29. Disconnect PCM electrical connectors, then remove PCM.
30. Remove right side insulator panel, then hinge pillar trim panel.
31. Disconnect engine wiring harness from instrument panel harness.
32. Remove engine harness through front of dash.
33. **On models equipped with automatic transmission,** remove floor shift control.
34. **On models equipped with manual transmission,** remove shift control.
35. **On all models,** raise and support vehicle.
36. Remove right and left lower shock bolts.
37. Remove cotter pins and nuts from right and left upper ball joints.
38. Separate upper control arms from knuckles using separator tool No. 39549, or equivalent.
39. Remove both steering knuckles, then place engine support tool No. 39580, or equivalent, under vehicle.
40. Lower vehicle until crossmember is resting on support fixture.
41. Place engine wiring harness on top of engine.
42. Remove front crossmember bolts.
43. Remove transmission support bolts.
44. Raise vehicle to remove engine and transmission from vehicle.
45. Secure crossmember to support fixture.
46. Separate engine and transmission.
47. Reverse procedure to install.

INTAKE MANIFOLD

REPLACE

1. Drain cooling system into suitable container, then disconnect fuel lines from rail.
2. Disconnect IAT and MAF sensor electrical connectors.
3. Remove air intake duct.
4. Disconnect throttle body electrical connectors.
5. Remove accessory drive belt, then disconnect EGR valve connector.
6. Remove EGR valve tube.
7. Remove accelerator and cruise control cables from throttle lever.
8. Remove accelerator and cruise control cable bracket.
9. Disconnect fuel injector electrical connectors.
10. Disconnect MAP sensor electrical connector and vacuum hose.
11. Disconnect knock sensor and all remaining intake manifold electrical connectors.
12. Remove PCV tube, then the fresh air hose from throttle body.
13. Remove throttle body coolant hoses, then the EVAP purge tube.
14. Remove canister purge valve and bracket.

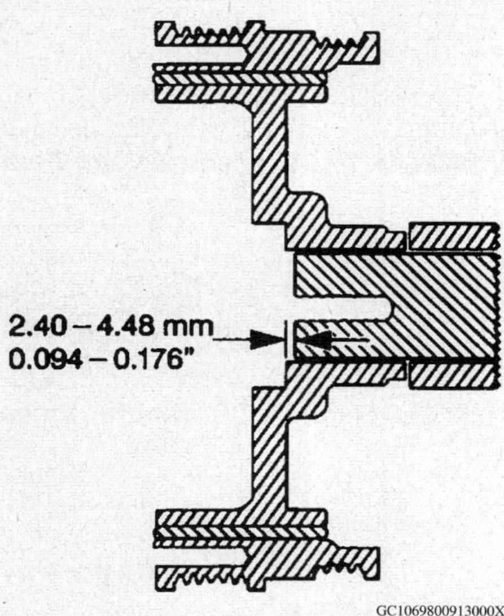

Fig. 3 Crankshaft damper installation

15. Remove intake manifold bolts, then the fuel rail stop bracket.
16. Remove intake manifold and gaskets.
17. Reverse procedure to install noting the following:
    a. Install new intake manifold gaskets.
    b. Apply GM threadlock P/N 12345383, or equivalent to intake manifold bolts.
    c. **Torque** intake manifold bolts to 44 inch lbs., in sequence, **Fig. 1.**
    d. **Torque** intake manifold bolts to 90 inch lbs., in sequence, **Fig. 1.**

EXHAUST MANIFOLD

REPLACE

LEFTHAND

1998-99

1. Relieve fuel pressure as outlined under "Precautions."
2. Disconnect fuel line from fuel rail.
3. Disconnect vapor line from fuel vapor purge valve.
4. Remove fuel rail.
5. Disconnect PCV hose from valve cover.
6. Remove spark plug wires, then the spark plugs.
7. Remove AIR hose and pipe.
8. **On 1998 models,** remove coolant sensor from cylinder head.
9. **On all models,** remove exhaust manifold bolts, then raise and support vehicle.
10. Remove oxygen sensor from manifold, then the exhaust manifold to exhaust pipe attaching nuts.
11. Remove catalytic converter to exhaust pipe attaching nuts.
12. Remove exhaust manifold from vehicle.
13. Reverse procedure to install noting the following:
    a. Install new gasket, then the manifold.
    b. Apply GM threadlock P/N 1234493,

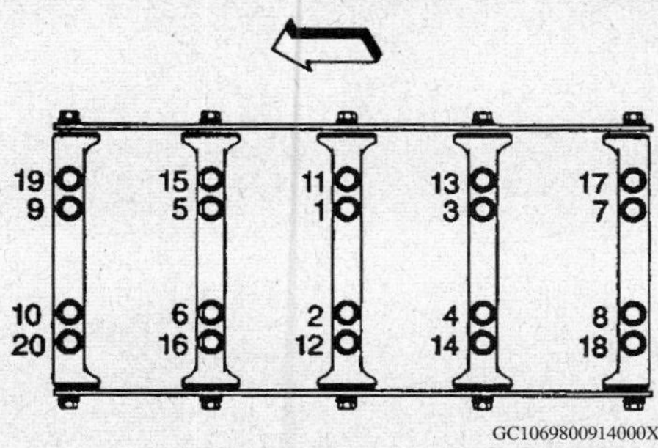

Fig. 4 Main bearing tightening sequence

or equivalent to exhaust manifold bolt threads. Ensure threadlock does not contact first three threads of bolts.

c. Tighten all fasteners to specifications.

2000–02

1. Loosen AIR hose clamps and remove hose assembly.
2. Do not remove check valve from AIR pipe unless service is needed.
3. Remove air pipe with check valve, bolts and gasket from left exhaust manifold.
4. Remove spark plug wires from spark plugs. Do not remove from ignition coils unless required.
5. Do not remove oxygen sensor from exhaust manifold unless required.
6. Remove exhaust manifold bolts and gasket. Discard gasket.
7. Remove heat shield and bolts from manifold.
8. Reverse procedure to install.

RIGHTHAND

1998–99

1. Remove dipstick and tube.
2. Raise and support vehicle.
3. Remove exhaust manifold to exhaust pipe attaching nuts, then lower vehicle.
4. Remove AIR pipe and hose, then disconnect coil harness main connector.
5. Remove spark plug wires and spark plugs.
6. Remove valve cover as outlined under "Valve Cover, Replace."
7. Disconnect EGR valve connector, then remove EGR valve and pipe.
8. Remove exhaust manifold bolts, then the manifold and gasket.
9. Reverse procedure to install noting the following:
   a. Install new gasket, then the manifold.
   b. Apply GM threadlock P/N 1234493, or equivalent to exhaust manifold bolt threads. Ensure threadlock does not contact first three threads of bolts.
   c. Tighten all fasteners to specifications.

2000–02

1. Do not remove EGR valve from pipe assembly unless service is required.
2. Remove EGR pipe and gasket from exhaust manifold.
3. With mild force, pull EGR pipe from intake manifold.
4. Remove O-ring seal from EGR valve pipe and discard.
5. Do not remove check valve from AIR pipe unless service is required.
6. Remove AIR pipe with check valve, from right exhaust manifold.
7. Remove spark plug wires from spark plugs. Do not remove wires from ignition coils unless required.
8. Do not remove oxygen sensor from exhaust manifold unless service is required.
9. Remove manifold and gasket, discard gasket.
10. Remove heat shield from manifold.
11. Reverse procedure to install.

CYLINDER HEAD

REPLACE

LEFTHAND

1. Remove intake manifold as outlined under "Intake Manifold, Replace."
2. Remove vapor vent tube from engine.
3. Remove power steering pump pulley using a suitable puller.
4. Remove power steering pump and bracket.
5. Remove rocker arms, pedestals and pushrods.
6. Remove exhaust manifold as outlined under "Exhaust Manifold, Replace."
7. Remove ground straps from rear of cylinder head.
8. Remove spark plugs.
9. Remove cylinder head bolts, then the cylinder head. Discard M11 head bolts.
10. Reverse procedure to install noting the following:
    a. Clean cylinder head bolt holes, then ensure locating pins are in proper position.
    b. Ensure new gasket is installed facing proper direction.
    c. Install new M11 cylinder head bolts, then apply GM threadlock P/N 12345382, or equivalent to M8 cylinder head bolts and install. M11 cylinder head bolts are identified as 1–10 and M8 bolts are 11–15, **Fig. 2.**
    d. **Torque** M11 head bolts in sequence, **Fig. 2,** to 22 ft. lbs.
    e. Tighten M11 cylinder head bolts in sequence an additional 90° using torque angle meter tool No. J36660, or equivalent.
    f. Tighten M11 head bolts 1–8 an additional 90° and bolts 9 and 10 50° using torque angle meter tool No. J36660, or equivalent.
    g. **Torque** M8 head bolts in sequence to 22 ft. lbs.

RIGHTHAND

1. Remove intake manifold as outlined under "Intake Manifold, Replace."
2. Remove vapor vent tube from engine.
3. Remove exhaust manifold as outlined under "Exhaust Manifold, Replace."

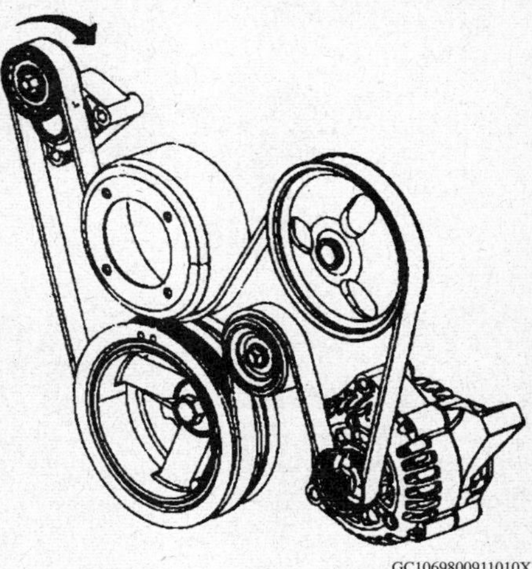

Fig. 5 Accessory drive belt routing (Part 1 of 2)

4. Remove rocker arms, pedestals and pushrods.
5. Remove spark plugs.
6. Remove cylinder head bolts, then the cylinder head. Discard M11 head bolts.
7. Reverse procedure to install noting the following:
   a. Clean cylinder head bolt holes, then ensure locating pins are in proper position.
   b. Ensure new gasket is installed facing proper direction.
   c. Install new M11 cylinder head bolts, then apply GM threadlock P/N 12345382, or equivalent to M8 cylinder head bolts and install. M11 cylinder head bolts are identified as 1–10 and M8 bolts are 11–15, **Fig. 2.**
   d. **Torque** M11 head bolts in sequence, **Fig. 2** to 22 ft. lbs.
   e. Tighten M11 cylinder head bolts in sequence an additional 90° using torque angle meter tool No. J36660, or equivalent.
   f. Tighten M11 head bolts 1–8 an additional 90° and bolts 9 and 10 50° using torque angle meter tool No. J36660, or equivalent.
   g. **Torque** M8 head bolts in sequence to 22 ft. lbs.

VALVE COVER

REPLACE

LEFTHAND

1. Remove fuel lines from vehicle.
2. Remove PCV hose, then disconnect ignition coil main harness connector.
3. Remove spark plug wires, then the AIR hose and pipe.
4. Remove connector position assurance clip.
5. Remove valve cover bolts, then the valve cover.
6. Reverse procedure to install. Tighten to specification.

RIGHTHAND

1. Remove AIR hose and pipe.
2. Disconnect ignition coil main harness.

GC1069800911020X

Fig. 5 Accessory drive belt routing (Part 2 of 2)

3. Remove spark plug wires, then the valve cover bolts and valve cover.
4. Reverse procedure to install. Tighten to specifications.

CAMSHAFT LOBE LIFT SPECIFICATIONS

Year	Engine	Int., Inch	Exh., Inch
1998–2002	5.7L	.292	.292

VALVE ADJUSTMENT

This engine is equipped with hydraulic lifters, no adjustment is required.

CRANKSHAFT DAMPER

REPLACE

1. Remove accessory drive belts.
2. Raise and support vehicle, then remove starter.
3. Remove right torque converter cover, then the transmission oil cooler lines from radiator.
4. Remove power steering cooler if equipped.
5. Install flywheel holder tool No. J42386.
6. Remove crankshaft balancer bolt.
7. Install puller tool Nos. J41816 and J41816-2, or equivalent, then remove damper.
8. Reverse procedure to install noting the following:
   a. Install crankshaft damper using pulley installation tool No. J41665, or equivalent.
   b. Transfer pulley weights if applicable.
   c. **Torque** crankshaft damper to 240 ft. lbs., using old damper bolt.
   d. Remove and discard damper bolt, then ensure nose of crankshaft extends .094–.176 inch into balancer bore, **Fig. 3.**
   e. If measurement is not as specified, repeat installation procedure.
   f. **Torque** new crankshaft damper bolt to 37 ft. lbs., then an additional 240 ft. lbs., then a final 140° using torque angle meter tool No. J36660, or equivalent.

FRONT COVER

REPLACE

1. Raise and support vehicle.
2. Remove cooling fan electrical connectors.
3. Drain engine coolant and engine oil into suitable containers.
4. Lower vehicle, then disconnect IAT and MAF sensors.
5. Remove air intake duct, then the accessory drive belts.
6. Remove coolant hoses from water pump and thermostat housing.
7. Remove upper radiator support, then the cooling fans and belt tensioner.
8. Disconnect overflow hose from radiator.
9. Remove throttle body coolant hoses and idler pulley.
10. Remove water pump as outlined under "Water Pump, Replace."
11. Remove crankshaft damper as outlined under "Crankshaft Damper, Replace."
12. Raise and support vehicle, then remove starter.
13. Remove right torque converter cover, then loosen oil pan attaching bolts.
14. Remove front cover bolts, then the front cover and gasket.
15. Remove front oil seal.
16. Reverse procedure to install noting the following:
    a. Install front cover and gasket to engine, then finger tighten bolts.
    b. Install front cover alignment tool No. J41480, or equivalent and **torque** to 18 ft. lbs.
    c. Install seal alignment tool No. J41476, or equivalent and finger tighten.
    d. **Torque** front cover bolts to 18 ft. lbs.
    e. Place a suitable straightedge across engine block and front cover oil pan sealing surfaces. Avoid contact with portion of gasket that extends into oil pan surface. Insert a suitable feeler gauge between front cover and straightedge. Ensure cover is flush with oil pan surface or .020 inch maximum below flush. If measurements are not as specified, repeat alignment procedure.
    f. Install new crankshaft oil seal using installer tool No. J41478, or equivalent.

MAIN BEARINGS

When replacing crankshaft bearings, it is essential that correct tolerances are achieved. If bearing clearance is not within specification, crankshaft position sensor signals may be affected. When replacing main bearings, the M8 bearing cap side bolts must be replaced. Refer to "Engine Rebuilding Specifications" for correct bearing clearance and to **Fig. 4,** for main bearing cap tightening sequence.

When replacing main bearings, proceed as follows:

1. Finger tighten M10 main bearing cap bolts, then tap caps into place using a suitable plastic hammer.
2. Install new M8 bearing cap side bolts.
3. **Torque** inner main bearing cap M10 bolts to 15 ft. lbs., using sequence, **Fig. 4.**
4. Tap crankshaft backward and then forward to align thrust bearings using a suitable plastic hammer.
5. Tighten M10 inner main bearing cap bolts an additional 80° in sequence using a suitable torque angle meter.
6. **Torque** outer main bearing cap M10 bolts to 15 ft. lbs., using sequence, **Fig. 4.**
7. Tighten M10 outer main bearing cap bolts an additional 53° in sequence using a suitable torque angle meter.
8. **Torque** M8 bearing cap side bolts to 18 ft. lbs. Tighten cap side bolt, then proceed to opposite side.

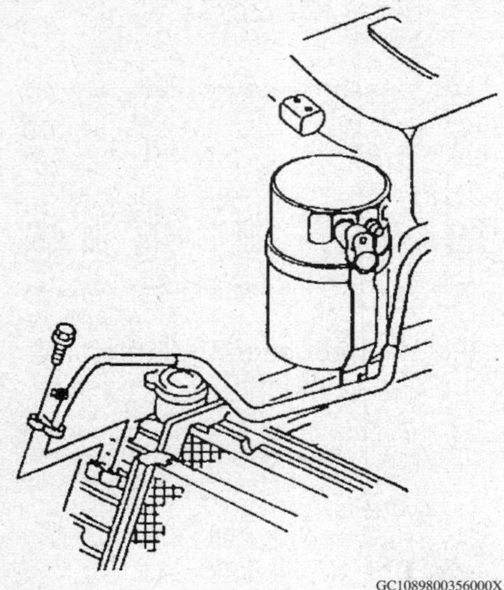

GC1089800356000X

Fig. 6 Evaporator tube removal

REAR COVER

REPLACE

1. Place alignment marks on flywheel and crankshaft for installation reference.
2. Remove flywheel.
3. Remove rear cover attaching bolts, then the cover and gasket.
4. Remove oil seal from cover.
5. Reverse procedure to install noting the following:
   a. Install cover and gasket to engine, then finger tighten bolts.
   b. Install cover alignment tool No. J41480, or equivalent and **torque** to 18 ft. lbs.
   c. Rotate crankshaft until two opposing flywheel bolt holes are parallel to oil pan surface.
   d. Install seal alignment tool No. J41476, or equivalent and finger tighten.
   e. **Torque** rear cover bolts to 18 ft. lbs.
   f. Place a suitable straightedge across engine block and rear cover

oil pan sealing surfaces. Avoid contact with portion of gasket that extends into oil pan surface. Insert a suitable feeler gauge between cover and straightedge. Ensure cover is flush with oil pan surface or .010 inch maximum below flush. If measurements are not as specified, repeat alignment procedure.

g. Install new crankshaft oil seal using installer tool No. J41479, or equivalent.

CRANKSHAFT SEAL

REPLACE

Refer to "Front Cover, Replace" for front crankshaft seal replacement.

CRANKSHAFT REAR OIL SEAL

REPLACE

Refer to "Rear Cover, Replace" for rear crankshaft seal replacement.

OIL PAN

REPLACE

1. Support engine using engine support tool Nos. J41044, J36462-A, J42451 and J28467-B, or equivalent.
2. Raise and support vehicle.
3. Remove oil filter, then drain engine oil into suitable container.
4. Remove right and left engine mount to cradle bolts, then the lower shock bolts.
5. Remove intermediate steering shaft bolt, then support engine cradle.
6. Disconnect and remove oil level sensor.
7. Remove starter, then the right and left torque converter covers.
8. Loosen six cradle bolts. Lower cradle and raise engine as required.
9. Remove oil pan attaching bolts, then the oil pan.
10. Reverse procedure to install noting the following:
    a. Apply a .200 inch bead of GM sealant P/N 12378190, or equivalent where front and rear covers meet engine block.
    b. Install gasket to oil pan. Ensure gasket is properly aligned.
    c. Install oil pan bolts through gasket, then oil pan to engine block. Tighten bolts finger tight.
    d. Ensure oil pan is flush with rear of engine block using a suitable straight edge. Using a suitable feeler gauge, ensure gap between straight edge and oil pan does not exceed .020 inch. If measurement is not within specification, remove oil pan and repeat alignment procedure.
    e. **Torque** oil pan bolts as follows; oil pan to front cover and block, 18 ft. lbs.; oil pan to rear cover, 108 inch lbs.

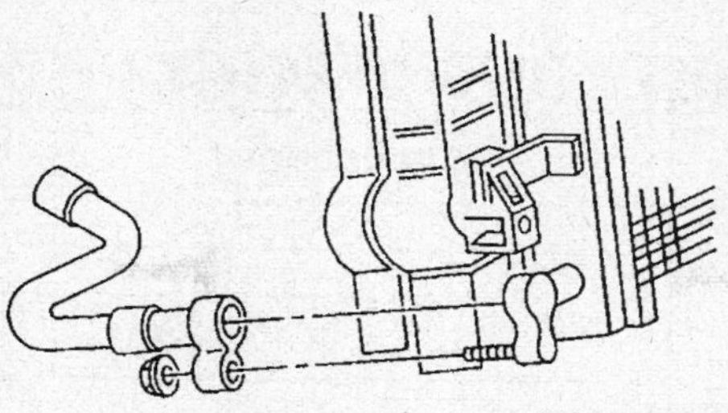

Fig. 7 Condenser tube removal

SERPENTINE DRIVE BELT

1. Rotate drive belt tensioner in clockwise direction.
2. Remove belt, then clean drive belt surfaces.
3. Reverse procedure to install. Refer to **Fig. 5,** for drive belt routing.

COOLING SYSTEM BLEED

1. Fill radiator to below fill neck.
2. Fill coolant recovery bottle to FULL HOT mark.
3. Install coolant recovery reservoir cap.
4. Operate engine with radiator cap off until operating temperature is reached.
5. While engine is at idle, add coolant to radiator until coolant level reaches bottom of fill neck.
6. Install radiator cap and inspect system for leaks.

WATER PUMP

REPLACE

1. Raise and support vehicle.
2. Disconnect cooling fan electrical connectors, then drain coolant into suitable container.
3. Lower vehicle.
4. Disconnect IAT and MAF sensor electrical connectors.
5. Remove air intake duct, then the radiator hose from thermostat housing.
6. Remove water pump inlet hose, then the air cleaner assembly.
7. Remove radiator inlet hose, then the electric cooling fans.
8. Remove accessory drive belts.
9. Remove tensioner from water pump, then the overflow hose from radiator.
10. Remove water pump pulley.
11. Remove water pump attaching bolts, then the water pump.
12. Reverse procedure to install.

RADIATOR

REPLACE

1. Recover refrigerant as outlined under "Air Conditioning" section is this manual.
2. Drain cooling system into suitable container, then remove radiator hoses.
3. Remove upper evaporator tube bracket bolt, **Fig. 6.**
4. Remove evaporator tube from condenser.
5. Remove upper and lower oil cooler lines from radiator, if equipped.
6. Remove condenser tube from condenser, **Fig. 7.**
7. Remove overflow hose from radiator.
8. Remove air intake duct and air cleaner assembly, then disconnect cooling fan electrical connectors.
9. Remove electric cooling fans, then the coolant level indicator module if equipped.
10. Remove radiator and condenser.
11. Reverse procedure to install.

FUEL PUMP

REPLACE

1. Drain fuel tank into suitable container, then remove fuel tank filler pocket.
2. Raise and support vehicle, then remove filler pipe shield.
3. Remove exhaust system and shields from converter to muffler.
4. Remove rear axle as outlined under "Rear Axle, Replace" in the "Rear Axle & Suspension" section.
5. Clean all fuel and EVAP lines, then disconnect and cap ends.
6. Disconnect fuel tank vent hose from rear brake hose bracket, then remove rear line clip.
7. Disconnect fuel electrical harness from fuel tank flange, then the sender and pressure sensor electrical connectors.
8. Support fuel tank, then remove left fuel tank strap bolt from under body bracket.
9. Remove EVAP canister vent solenoid and bracket.
10. Remove right fuel tank strap, then the fuel tank.
11. Remove fuel sender retaining nuts, then the retaining ring, sender assembly and seal.
12. Reverse procedure to install noting the following:
    a. Clean all sealing surfaces and install new seal.
    b. Tighten bolts and nuts to specifications.
    c. Inspect fuel system for leaks.

FUEL FILTER

REPLACE

1. Raise and support vehicle.
2. Clean fuel filter connections.
3. Disconnect fuel filter quick connect fitting using quick disconnect tool No. J37088-A, or equivalent.
4. Disconnect threaded fuel filter line.
5. Cap fuel lines to prevent fuel system contamination.
6. Remove fuel filter from bracket.
7. Reverse procedure to install. Inspect and replace fuel filter O-ring if required.

TIGHTENING SPECIFICATIONS

Year	Component	Torque/Ft. Lbs.
1998–2002	A/C Compressor Bolts	37
	A/C Compressor Bracket Bolts	37
	Air Injection Tube To Exhaust Manifold Bolts	15①
	Alternator Bracket	37
	Belt Tensioner Bolts	37
	Camshaft Retainer Bolts	18
	Camshaft Sensor Bolt	18
	Camshaft Sprocket Bolt	18
	Catalytic Converter Nut	18
	Connecting Rod Bolts	15①
	Coolant Temperature Gauge Sensor	15
	Crankshaft Balancer Bolt	②
	Crankshaft Bearing Cap Bolt	③
	Crankshaft Position Sensor	18
	Cylinder Head Bolts	④
	EGR Pipe To Cylinder Head	37
	EGR Valve	18
	Engine Mount Stud To Engine Block	37
	Engine Mount Through Bolts	70
	Engine Mount Through Bolt Nuts	59
	Engine Mount To Engine Block Bolts	37
	Exhaust Manifold	18
	Flywheel Bolts	⑤
	Front Cover	18
	Fuel Sender	58⑥
	Fuel Tank Straps	24
	Ignition Coil	106⑥
	Intake Manifold	⑦
	Lifter Guide Bolts	106⑥
	Oil Filter	22
	Oil Level Sensor	26
	Oil Pan	⑧
	Oil Pan Drain Plug	18
	Oil Pressure Sensor	13
	Oil Pump To Engine Block	18
	Oil Pump Screen To Pump	106⑥
	Oxygen Sensor	31
	Power Steering Pump	18
	Rear Cover Bolts	18
	Rocker Arms	22
	Spark Plugs	12
	Starter Motor	37
	Thermostat Housing	11
	Throttle Body	106⑥
	Valve Cover	106⑥
	Water Pump	18
	Water Pump Pulley	89⑥

① — Tighten additional 60.°
② — Refer to "Crankshaft Damper, Replace."
③ — Refer to "Main Bearings."
④ — Refer to "Cylinder Head, Replace."
⑤ — Tighten in three steps; 1st step, 15 ft. lbs., 2nd step, 37 ft. lbs., 3rd step 74 ft. lbs.
⑥ — Inch lbs.
⑦ — Refer to "Intake Manifold, Replace."
⑧ — Refer to "Oil Pan, Replace."

Clutch & Manual Transmission

NOTE: On Air Bag Equipped Models, Refer To "Air Bag System Precautions" Located In The Front Of This Manual For System Disarming & Arming Procedures.

NOTE: Refer To "Computer Relearn Procedures" Located In The Front Of This Manual When Battery Power To The Computer Has Been Interrupted.

INDEX

PRECAUTIONS

AIR BAG SYSTEMS

Refer to "Air Bag System Precautions" in the front of this manual for system disarming and arming procedures.

BATTERY GROUND CABLE

Prior to service, disconnect battery ground cable and isolate as required.

ADJUSTMENTS

The hydraulic clutch system sets the clutch pedal height and provides automatic clutch adjustment. No adjustment of clutch or clutch pedal assembly is required.

HYDRAULIC SYSTEM SERVICE

CLUTCH SYSTEM BLEED

1. Fill clutch master cylinder with GM clutch fluid P/N 12345347, or equivalent.
2. Raise and support vehicle.
3. Attach a suitable hose to clutch bleeder screw, then submerge opposite end in approved container of GM clutch fluid.
4. Slowly depress clutch pedal and hold, then loosen bleeder screw, **Figs. 1 and 2.**
5. Allow air to escape, then tighten bleeder screw.
6. Repeat steps 1–4 until no air is present from bleeder hose. Ensure clutch master cylinder is kept full during bleed procedure.

CLUTCH MASTER CYLINDER

REPLACE

1. Remove driver's side instrument panel insulator, then the knee bolster.
2. Remove clutch pedal pin retainer, **Fig. 3.**
3. Remove clutch master cylinder push rod from clutch pedal pin, master cylinder nuts, U-bolt then the clutch master cylinder, **Fig. 3.**
4. Raise and support vehicle.
5. Install hydraulic clutch line separator tool No. J36221, or equivalent, then depress white circular release ring to actuator hose and pull on master cylinder hose to disconnect.
6. Cover both hose coupling ends.
7. Lower vehicle.
8. Remove clutch master cylinder reservoir push pin retainer.
9. Remove clutch master cylinder reservoir and master cylinder.
10. Reverse procedure to install, tighten to specifications.

CLUTCH ACTUATOR CYLINDER

REPLACE

1. Remove manual transmission as outlined under "Transmission, Replace."
2. Remove clutch bleeder from actuator cylinder.
3. Remove rollpin retaining hydraulic fitting to actuator cylinder.
4. Remove clutch actuator cylinder bleed fitting and bolts, **Fig. 4.**
5. Remove clutch actuator cylinder, **Fig. 4.**
6. Reverse procedure to install, tighten to specifications.

CLUTCH

REPLACE

1. Remove manual transmission as outlined under "Transmission, Replace."
2. Remove clutch pressure plate bolts.
3. Remove clutch pressure plate and driven disc.
4. Reverse procedure to install, noting the following:
   a. When clutch driven plate requires replacement, engine flywheel must be replaced along with clutch pressure plate as an assembly.
   b. Install clutch pressure plate bolts, then finger tighten.
   c. Install bushing installer and clutch arbor tool Nos. J38836 and J36660-A, or equivalents, to align clutch driven plate to clutch pilot bearing.
   d. **On models equipped with 6 speed manual transmission, torque** clutch pressure plate bolts to 52 ft. lbs., in sequence, **Fig. 5.**
   e. **On models equipped with 5 speed manual transmission, torque** clutch pressure plate to 15 ft. lbs., plus an additional 45 degrees.

TRANSMISSION

REPLACE

5-SPEED TRANSMISSION

1. Remove front floor console trim plate assembly.
2. Raise and support vehicle, then drain fluid from transmission into suitable container.
3. Disconnect propeller shaft assembly, then support rear axle assembly with a jack stand.
4. Remove rear axle torque arm assembly, then the catalytic converter hanger assembly.
5. Disconnect electrical connectors from back-up lamp switch and speed sensor, then support engine assembly with a jack stand.
6. Remove starter motor as outlined under "Starter, Replace" in "Electrical" section.
7. Remove transmission support and mount assembly, then lower transmission enough to reach control bolts.
8. Remove transmission control bolts, then lower transmission and remove control assembly. **Control must be held while lowering transmission as**

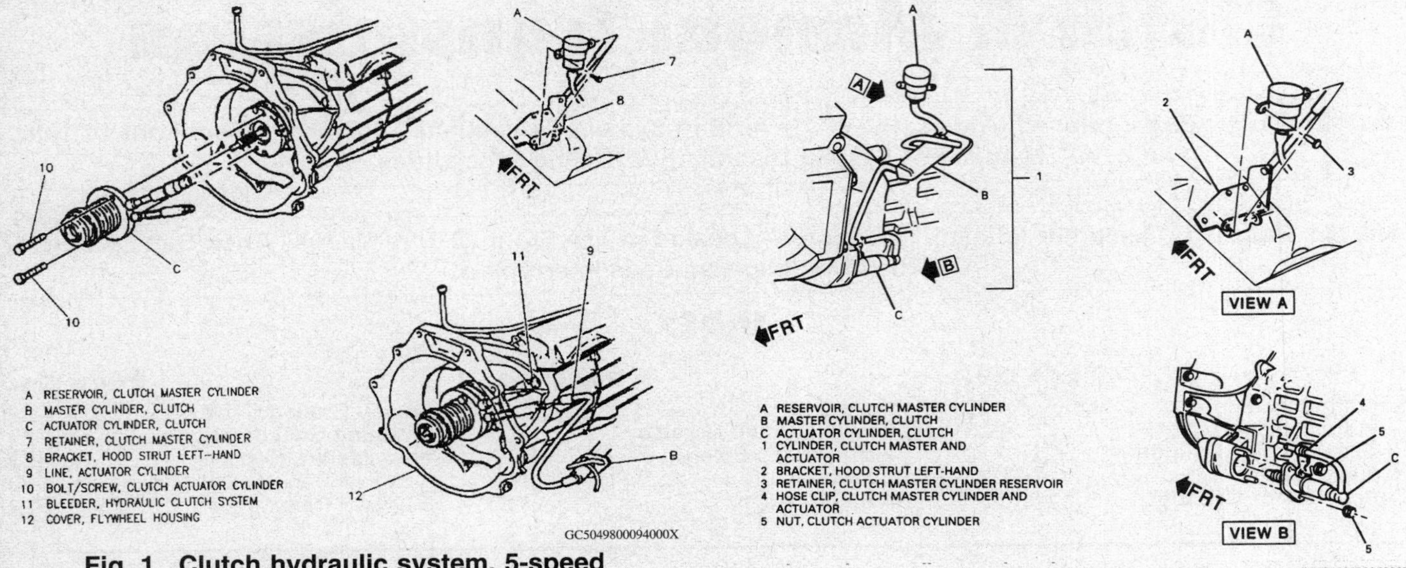

Fig. 1 Clutch hydraulic system. 5-speed transmission

Fig. 2 Clutch hydraulic system. 6-speed transmission

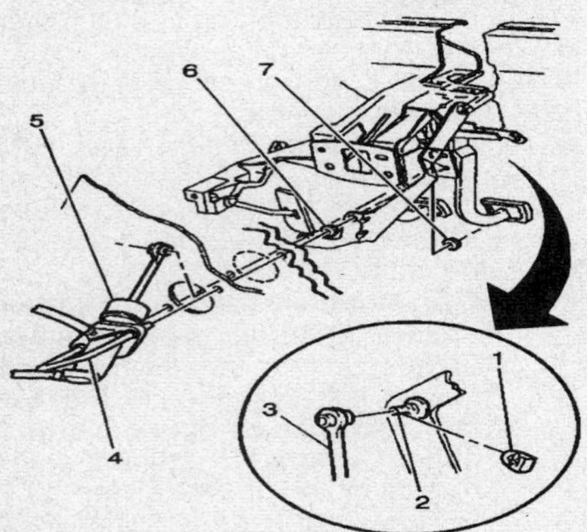

1. Clutch Pedal Pin Retainer
2. Clutch Pedal Pin
3. Clutch Master Cylinder Push Rod
4. U-bolt
5. Clutch Master Cylinder
6. Push-On-Nuts
7. Clutch Master Cylinder Nuts

GC5030100152000X

Fig. 3 Clutch master cylinder & component removal

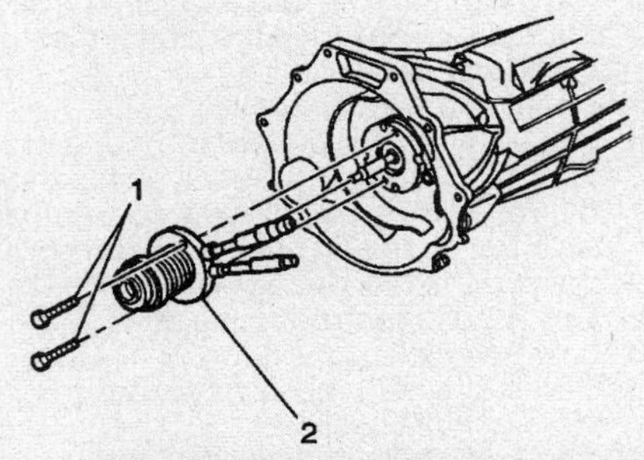

1. Clutch Actuator Cylinder Bolts
2. Clutch Actuator Cylinder

GC5030100153000X

Fig. 4 Clutch actuator cylinder & component removal

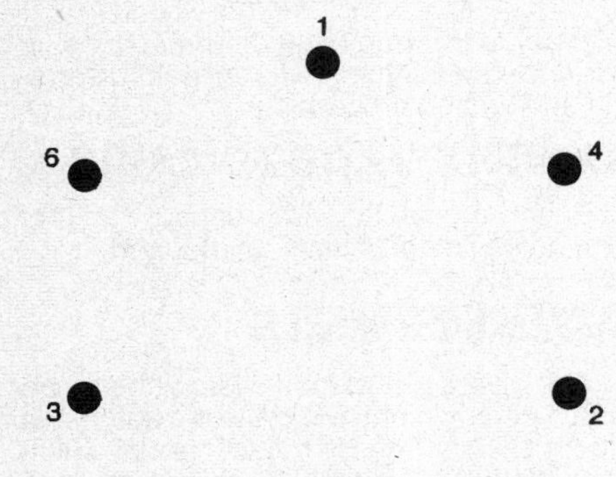

Fig. 5 Clutch pressure plate tightening sequence. 6 speed manual transmission

control is not retained in vehicle and could drop damaging component.

9. Remove transmission assembly.
10. Reverse procedure to install, noting the following:
    a. Tighten fasteners to specifications.
    b. Apply a continuous ⅛ inch bead of RTV sealant P/N 12345739 to extension housing to control assembly sealing surface.

6-SPEED TRANSMISSION

1. Remove front floor console trim plate assembly.
2. Remove control lever handle, then raise and support vehicle.
3. Drain fluid from transmission, then support rear axle assembly with a jack stand.
4. Remove starter motor as outlined under "Starter, Replace" in "Electrical" section.
5. Disconnect propeller shaft assembly, then remove rear axle torque arm.
6. Remove catalytic converter hanger assembly, then disconnect electrical connectors from back-up lamp switch and reverse lockout solenoid.
7. Disconnect clutch master cylinder pushrod from clutch pedal assembly, then remove clutch actuator cylinder and retain with mechanics wire.
8. Remove actuator spacer, then pull clutch fork assembly down to disengage release bearing.
9. Disconnect electrical connector from electronic speed sensor, then support engine assembly with a jack stand.
10. Support transmission assembly with a jack stand, then remove transmission support and mount assembly.
11. Remove transmission assembly.
12. Reverse procedure to install. Tighten fasteners to specifications.

TIGHTENING SPECIFICATIONS

Year	Component	Torque/Ft. Lbs.
CLUTCH		
1998–2002	Brake Pedal Pivot Nut	40
	Clutch Actuator Cylinder Bolt	71①
	Clutch Pressure Plate Bolt (5-Speed)	②
	Clutch Pressure Plate Bolt (6-Speed)	②
	Clutch Master Cylinder Nut	15
	Transmission Bolt (5-Speed)	55①
	Transmission Bolt (6-Speed)	37
5-SPEED		
1998–2002	Back-Up Lamp Switch	28
	Clutch Actuator Cylinder Bolts	71①
	Flywheel Housing Bolts/Nuts	70
	Flywheel Housing Cover Bolts	80①
	Shift Control Closeout Boot Bolts	18①
	Shift Control Knob	27①
	Speed Sensor Bolt	89①
	Transmission Bolts	55
	Transmission To Brace Bolts Left Side Of Engine	21
	Transmission Brace Bolts Left Side To Transmission	37
	Transmission Brace Bolts Right Side	37
	Transmission Case Drain/Fill Plug	20
	Transmission Control Lever Bolts	13
	Transmission Mount Bolt	35
	Transmission Mount Nut	42
	Transmission Support Bolts	42
	Wiring Harness Clip Bolts	97①
6-SPEED		
1998–2002	Back-Up Lamp Switch	20
	Clutch Actuator Cylinder Bolt	71①
	Clutch Housing Bolt	37
	Control Lever Handle Bolt	18
	Gear Select/Skip Shift Solenoid	30
	Reverse Lockout Assembly Bolt	13
	Reverse Lockout Solenoid	30
	Shift Control Bolt	13
	Shift Control Closeout Boot Bolt	18①
	Shift Control Knob	27
	Transmission Bolt	37
	Transmission Drain/Fill Plug	20
	Transmission Mount Bolt	38
	Transmission Mount Nut	77
	Transmission Support Bolt	66
	Vehicle Speed Sensor Bolt	89①

① — Inch lbs.

② — Refer to “Clutch, Replace” for specifications.

Rear Axle & Suspension

NOTE: On Air Bag Equipped Models, Refer To "Air Bag System Precautions" Located In The Front Of This Manual For System Disarming & Arming Procedures.

NOTE: Refer To "Computer Relearn Procedures" Located In The Front Of This Manual When Battery Power To The Computer Has Been Interrupted.

INDEX

REAR AXLE

REPLACE

1. Raise and support vehicle, then remove rear wheels.
2. Remove driveshaft, then the stabilizer shaft.
3. Support axle using a suitable jack.
4. Remove rear shock absorbers, then the track bar.
5. Disconnect brake hose from rear brake hose junction block.
6. Remove coil springs as outlined under "Coil Spring, Replace."
7. Remove parking brake cables from axle housing.
8. Disconnect wheel speed sensors if equipped.
9. Remove torque arm, then the lower control arms.
10. Lower axle from vehicle.
11. Reverse procedure to install noting the following:
    a. Tighten to specifications.
    b. Bleed brake system as outlined under "Hydraulic Brake Systems."

REAR AXLE SHAFT

REPLACE

If the vehicle is equipped with acceleration slip regulation (ASR) traction control, care must be taken not to damage rear wheel speed sensor reluctor wheel. The sensing wheel is located on the axle shaft and must be replaced if damage occurs.

1. Raise and support vehicle.
2. Clean axle housing cover and disconnect parking brake guide.
3. Remove cover bolts and pry cover loose.
4. Drain lubricant, clean old gasket from both sealing surfaces.
5. Remove rear wheels and brake assembly.
6. **On models less traction control,** install exciter ring protector kit tool No. J39446, or equivalent, to speed sensor reluctor wheel and remove.
7. **On all models,** remove differential pinion gear shaft lock bolt (29) from case (33) and then the pinion gear shaft (35), **Fig. 1.**

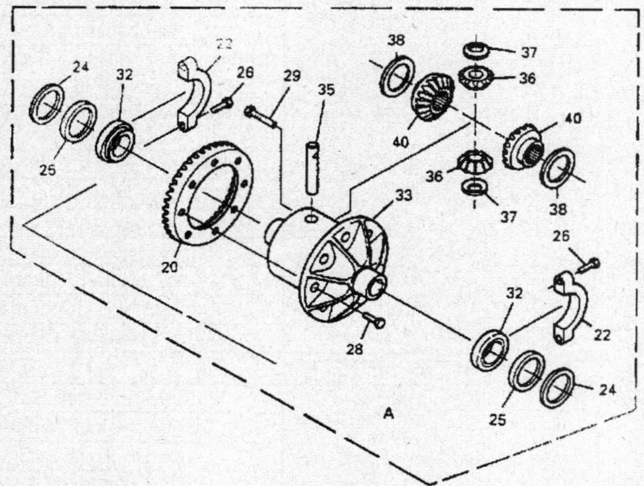

Fig. 1 Pinion gear shaft & lock bolt removal

8. Remove axle shaft lock by pushing flanged end of axle shaft into housing.
9. Slide axle shaft from housing. Take care in removal as splines on end of shaft may damage seal.
10. Reverse procedure to install, noting the following:
    a. Ensure axle shaft splines mesh with splines on side gears.
    b. When installing axle shaft lock, ensure it seats inside counterbore of side gear.
    c. Install Loctite 242, or equivalent, when installing pinion gear shaft bolt and **torque** to 27 ft. lbs.

PROPELLER SHAFT

REPLACE

1. Raise and support vehicle, then mark relationship of propeller shaft assembly to pinion gear yoke.
2. Remove center support bearing and washers from torque arm assembly.
3. **On two-piece propeller shafts,** remove bolts from center support bearing.
4. **On all propeller shafts,** remove bolts and retainers, then the propeller shaft.
5. Reverse procedure to install, noting the following:
    a. Tighten fasteners to specifications.
    b. Lubricate slip yoke with .6 ounces of propeller shaft slip yoke lubricant 1050169, or equivalent.
    c. Align marks on pinion gear yoke and propeller shaft.

SHOCK ABSORBER

REPLACE

1. Fold down seat back frame, then remove quarter trim panel.
2. Pull folding carpet back, then raise and support vehicle.
3. Support rear axle, then remove shock absorber.

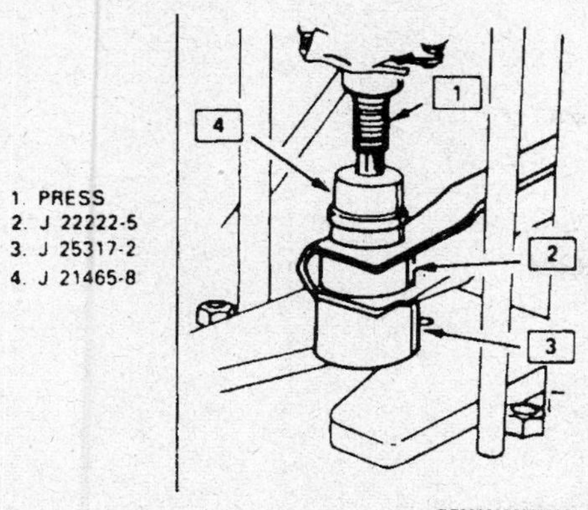

Fig. 2 Control arm bushing removal

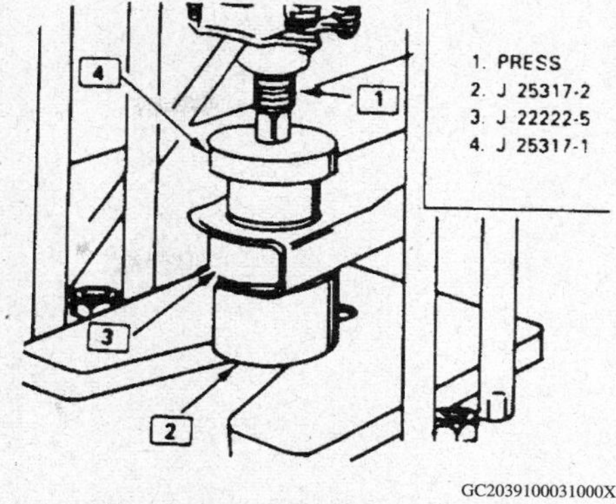

Fig. 3 Control arm bushing installation

4. Reverse procedure to install. Tighten fasteners to specifications.

COIL SPRING

REPLACE

1. Raise and support vehicle, then support rear axle with an adjustable lifting device. **Do not use twin post type hoist.**
2. Remove shock absorber nuts from rear axle, then lower rear axle.
3. Remove upper insulator assembly, then the rear spring.
4. Reverse procedure to install. Tighten fasteners to specifications.

CONTROL ARM

REPLACE

LOWER

If both control arms are to be removed, remove one control arm at a time to prevent axle from slipping or rolling.

1. Raise vehicle and support at frame pads. Support nose of axle housing to prevent assembly from twisting when control arm is removed.
2. Remove bolts securing control arm to chassis and rear axle, and the control arm.
3. Reverse procedure to install.

BUSHINGS

1. Raise and support vehicle and remove control arm as outlined previously.
2. Press bushings out of control arm using suitable tools, **Fig. 2.**
3. Reverse procedure to install, ensure bushing is properly seated in control arm, **Fig. 3. If replacement bushing fits loosely in control arm, or if mounting areas are damaged or deformed, control arm must be replaced.**

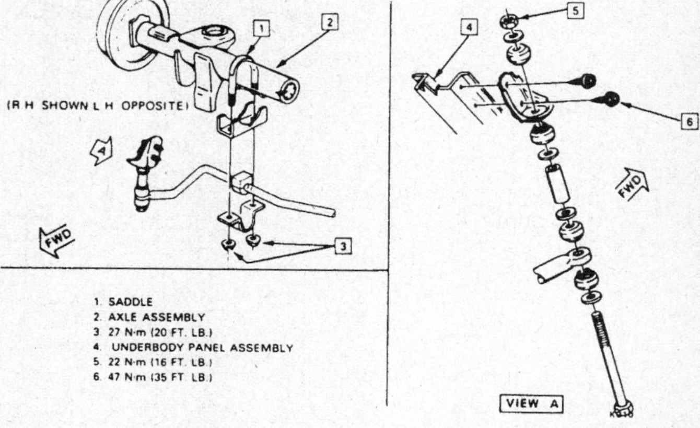

Fig. 4 Stabilizer bar installation

STABILIZER BAR

REPLACE

1. Raise and support vehicle.
2. Remove link bolt nuts, washers, bushings, spacers and link bolts securing stabilizer to chassis, **Fig. 4.**
3. Remove clamps securing stabilizer shaft to rear axle and stabilizer shaft.
4. Reverse procedure to install. Tighten link bolts and U-bolt nuts to specifications.

TRACK ROD

REPLACE

1. Raise vehicle and support rear axle at curb height.
2. Remove track bar mounting bolt and nut from rear axle and from body bracket, then remove track rod, **Fig. 5.**
3. Remove heat shield attaching screws from track bar brace.
4. Remove three track bar to body brace screws.
5. Remove nut and bolt from body bracket, then remove track bar brace.
6. Reverse procedure to install.

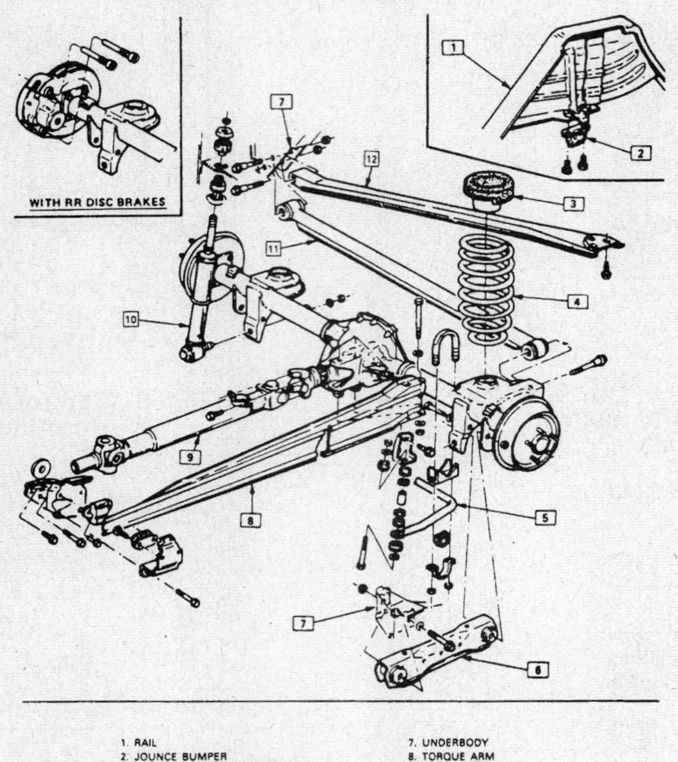

Fig. 5 Track rod replacement

TIGHTENING SPECIFICATIONS

Year	Component	Torque/Ft. lbs.
1998–2002	Control Arm Bolts	80
	Control Arm Nuts	60
	Differential Pinion Gear Shaft Lock Bolt	27
	Shock Absorber Lower Nut	66
	Shock Absorber Upper Nut	13
	Stabilizer Link	16
	Stabilizer Shaft Bracket Bolts	17
	Stabilizer Shaft Nuts	18
	Torque Arm To Rear Axle Bolts	96
	Torque Arm To Transmission Center Bolt	20
	Torque Arm To Transmission Lower & Upper Bolts	37
	Torque Arm To Transmission Nuts	30
	Wheel Lug Nuts	100
	Yoke Nut	①

① — Tighten until endplay is near 0, then measure preload. If using new bearings, preload should be 15–30 inch lbs. If reinstalling old bearings, ensure preload is 10–15 inch lbs.

Front Suspension & Steering

NOTE: On Air Bag Equipped Models, Refer To "Air Bag System Precautions" Located In The Front Of This Manual For System Disarming & Arming Procedures.

NOTE: Refer To "Computer Relearn Procedures" Located In The Front Of This Manual When Battery Power To The Computer Has Been Interrupted.

INDEX

PRECAUTIONS

AIR BAG SYSTEMS

Refer to "Air Bag System Precautions" in the front of this manual for system disarming and arming procedures.

BATTERY GROUND CABLE

Prior to service, disconnect battery ground cable and isolate as required.

DESCRIPTION

The short/long arm (SLA) front suspension assembly, **Fig. 1,** is designed to allow each wheel to compensate for changes in road surface level without significantly affecting the opposite wheel. Each wheel is independently connected to the frame by a steering knuckle, wheel hub, shock absorber and spring, upper and lower ball studs and upper and lower control arms.

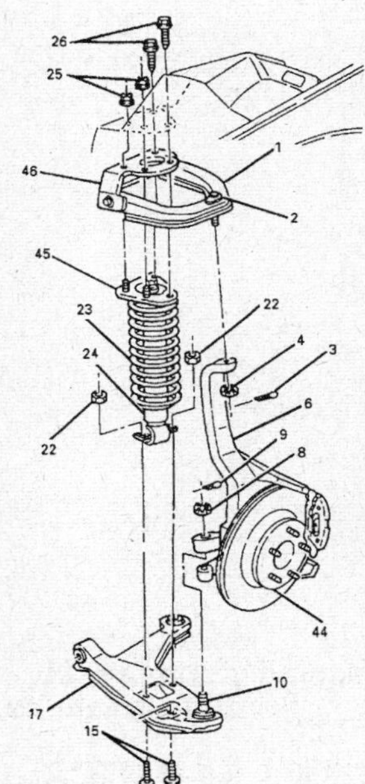

1 ARM ASSEMBLY, FRONT UPPER CONTROL
2 STUD ASSEMBLY, FRONT UPPER CONTROL ARM BALL
3 PIN, FRONT UPPER CONTROL ARM COTTER
4 NUT, FRONT UPPER CONTROL ARM
6 KNUCKLE ASSEMBLY, STEERING
8 NUT, FRONT LOWER CONTROL ARM
9 PIN, FRONT LOWER CONTROL ARM COTTER
10 STUD ASSEMBLY, FRONT LOWER CONTROL ARM BALL
15 BOLT/SCREW, FRONT SHOCK ABSORBER
17 ARM ASSEMBLY, FRONT LOWER CONTROL
22 NUT, FRONT SHOCK ABSORBER LOWER BRACKET
23 SPRING ASSEMBLY, FRONT
24 ABSORBER ASSEMBLY. FRONT SHOCK
25 NUT, FRONT SHOCK ABSORBER UPPER MOUNT
26 BOLT/SCREW. FRONT SHOCK ABSORBER UPPER MOUNT
44 HUB ASSEMBLY, FRONT WHEEL
45 MOUNT ASSEMBLY, FRONT UPPER SHOCK ABSORBER
46 SUPPORT, FRONT UPPER CONTROL ARM

GC2029300074000X

Fig. 1 Exploded view of front suspension

HUB & BEARING

REPLACE

1. Raise and support vehicle, then remove tire and wheel assembly on side to be serviced.
2. Remove brake caliper assembly and brake disc.
3. Disconnect wheel speed sensor electrical connector and secure aside.
4. Remove bolts and screws from hub assembly, then the hub assembly.
5. Reverse procedure to install, **torque** retaining bolts to 63 ft. lbs.

BALL JOINT INSPECTION

LOWER

1. Raise and support vehicle by positioning floor stands under both lower control arms, then wipe grease fitting free of dirt and grease.
2. Position dial indicator against wheel rim.
3. While reading dial indicator, pry between lower control arm and steering knuckle. Vertical movement should not exceed .047 inch, if so, replace ball joint.

UPPER

1. Raise front end of vehicle and position floor stands under both lower control arms as near to ball joints as possible.
2. Position a dial indicator against wheel rim, **Fig. 2.** Push in on bottom of tire while pulling out at top, then reverse procedure.
3. Deflection on dial indicator should not exceed .125 inch. If deflection exceeds specification, replace ball joint.
4. If ball joint is disconnected from steering knuckle, inspect for looseness or see if ball joint can be twisted in its socket using your fingers.
5. If either of the above conditions exist, replace ball joint.

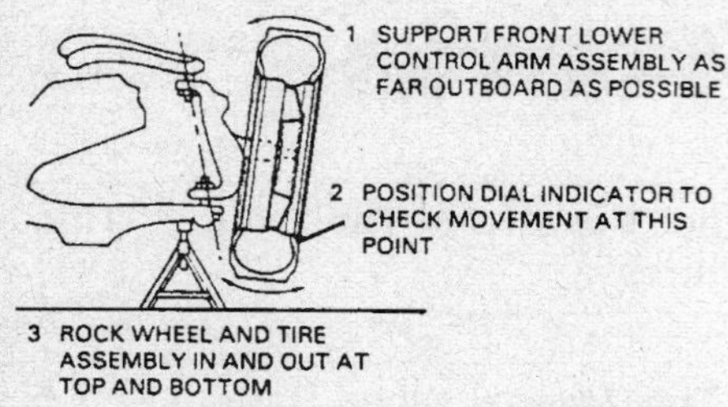

Fig. 2 Upper ball joint inspection

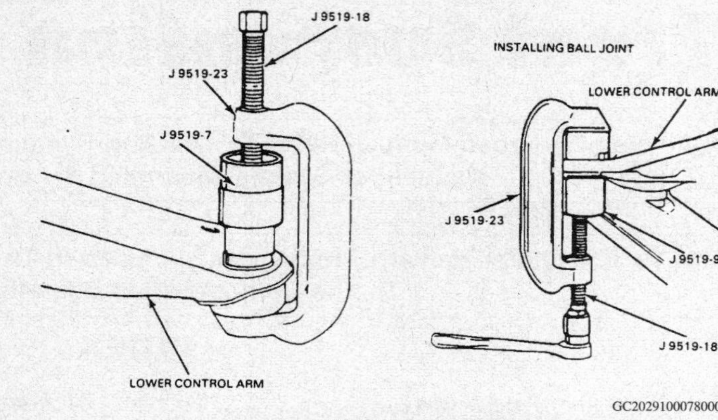

Fig. 3 Lower ball joint replacement

BALL JOINT

REPLACE

LOWER

1. Raise vehicle and support at frame, and remove wheel and tire.
2. Position a suitable jack under lower control arm spring seat, and raise jack to compress coil spring. **Jack must remain in place during ball joint replacement to hold spring and lower control arm in position.**
3. Remove cotter pin and nut securing ball joint stud to steering knuckle, then disconnect joint from knuckle using a suitable tool.
4. Lift knuckle assembly from ball stud, guiding control arm out of splash shield, then support knuckle aside to allow clearance for joint removal.
5. Remove grease fitting, then press ball joint assembly out of lower control arm using a suitable tool, **Fig. 3.**
6. Press replacement joint into arm by reversing removal tools, fit spindle over ball stud, install washer, if equipped, and retaining nut.
7. Tighten retaining nut to specifications.
8. Tighten nut up to an additional 1/16 turn, if required, to align hole in ball stud with nut, then install cotter pin.

UPPER

1. Raise and support vehicle, then remove wheel.
2. Place a floor jack under shock absorber mounting location on lower control. **Jack must remain in place during ball joint replacement to hold spring and lower control arm in position.**
3. Loosen ball joint from steering knuckle, then remove cotter pin and nut.
4. Support steering knuckle with floor stands, then disconnect ball joint from upper control arm using ball joint/tie rod separator tool No. J39549, or equivalent.
5. With upper control arm in raised position, drill out four rivets approximately 1/4 inch deep using a 1/8 inch drill bit.
6. Drill off rivet heads using a 1/2 inch drill bit, then punch out rivets using a small punch and remove ball joint.
7. Position new ball joint and install bolts and nuts supplied with new ball joint.
8. Remove support from steering knuckle, then connect ball joint to steering knuckle.
9. Tighten nut enough to align slot with stud hole, then tighten nut to specifications and install cotter pin.

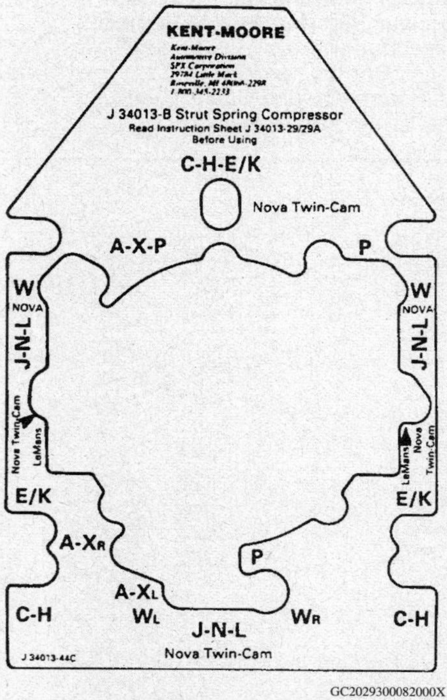

Fig. 4 Modular shock absorber assembly compressor mounting hole locations

STRUT SERVICE

1. If servicing driver's side strut, remove brake master cylinder nuts, then move master cylinder aside.
2. Remove upper shock absorber mounting nuts and bolts, then raise and support vehicle.
3. Remove tire and wheel assembly, then disconnect stabilizer shaft link.
4. Remove lower shock absorber mounting nuts and bolts, then separate lower ball joint from steering knuckle.
5. Mark lower mount location relative to upper mount location, then remove shock absorber and spring assembly.
6. Proceed as follows to disassemble shock absorber assembly:
   a. Install modular shock assembly compressor adapter tool No. J34013-114, or equivalent, onto strut spring compressor tool No. J34013-B, or equivalent, using wing nuts to secure tool to mounting holes C-H in lower left corner and P in upper right corner for driver side shock absorber assembly, **Figs. 4 and 5,** or to holes A-X-P in upper left corner and C-H in lower right corner for passenger side shock absorber assembly, **Fig. 6.**
   b. Install strut compressor adapter tool No. J34013-88, or equivalent, and modular shock support tool No. J34013-218, or equivalent, onto strut spring compressor, **Fig. 7. Ensure strut compressor adapter and modular shock support are aligned so that they can open and close together. If tools are not properly aligned, they will not open.**
   c. Install shock absorber assembly to top of modular shock assembly compressor adapter, **Figs. 8 and 9. Ensure top of shock absorber assembly is flat against modular shock assembly compressor adapter. Shock absorber assembly will not be aligned properly if it does not lay flat against tool.**
   d. Install shock absorber assembly into strut compressor adapter and modular shock support, **Fig. 10,** then close strut compressor adapter and modular shock support and install locking pin. **Ensure mounting ears of shock absorber assembly are facing downward toward rear of strut spring compressor or shock absorber assembly will not align properly.**
   e. Turn screw on strut spring compressor counterclockwise to raise shock absorber assembly up to modular shock assembly compressor adapter. Ensure studs go through guide holes in modular shock assembly compressor adapter and top of shock absorber assembly is flat against tool.
   f. Compress front spring assembly approximately 1/2 inch or three or four complete turns of screw on modular shock assembly compressor adapter. **Do not over compress front spring assembly. Severe overloading may cause tool failure, possibly resulting in**

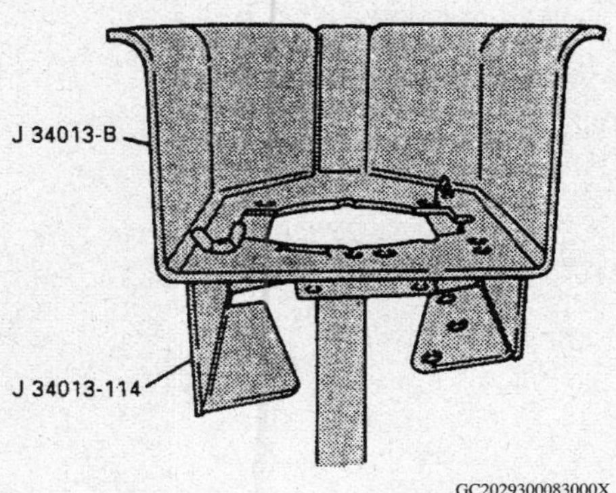

Fig. 5 Modular shock absorber assembly compressor adapter, driver side

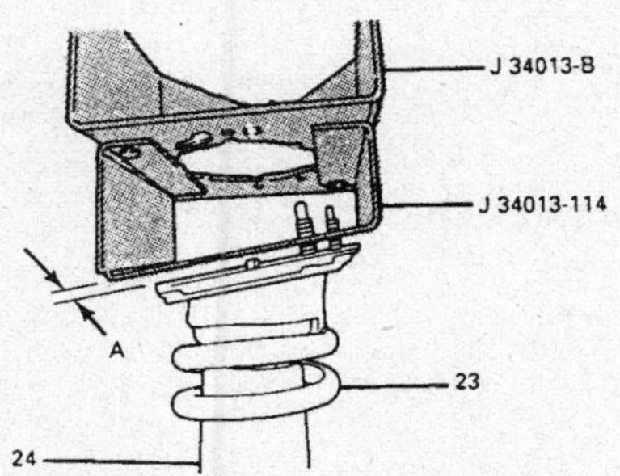

A MATCHING ANGLE BETWEEN SHOCK ABSORBER ASSEMBLY AND J 34013-114
23 SPRING ASSEMBLY, FRONT
24 ABSORBER ASSEMBLY, FRONT SHOCK

GC2029300086000X

Fig. 8 Upper driver side shock absorber assembly to strut spring compressor installation

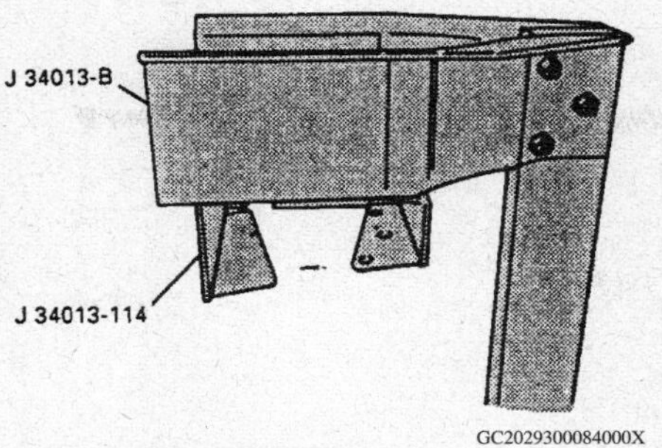

Fig. 6 Modular shock absorber assembly compressor adapter, passenger side

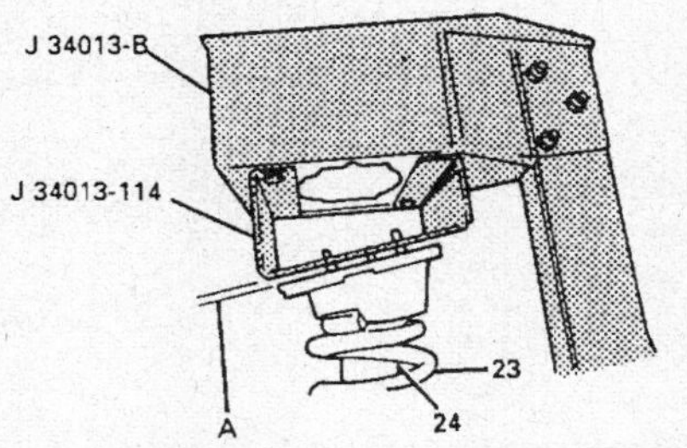

A MATCHING ANGLE BETWEEN SHOCK ABSORBER ASSEMBLY AND J 34013-114
23 SPRING ASSEMBLY, FRONT
24 ABSORBER ASSEMBLY, FRONT SHOCK

GC2029300087000X

Fig. 9 Upper passenger side shock absorber assembly to strut spring compressor installation

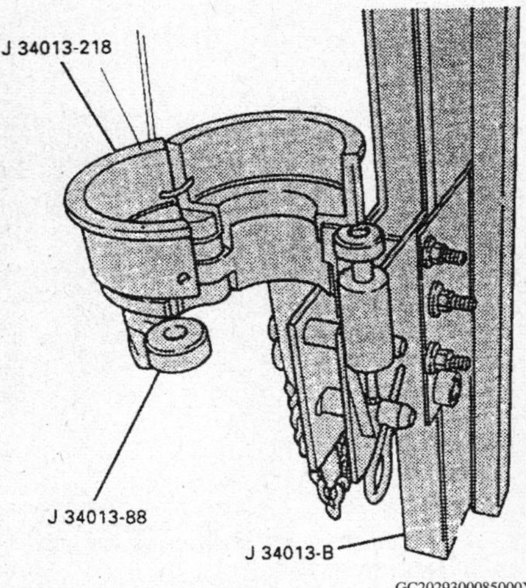

Fig. 7 Strut compressor adapter & modular shock support to strut spring compressor mounting

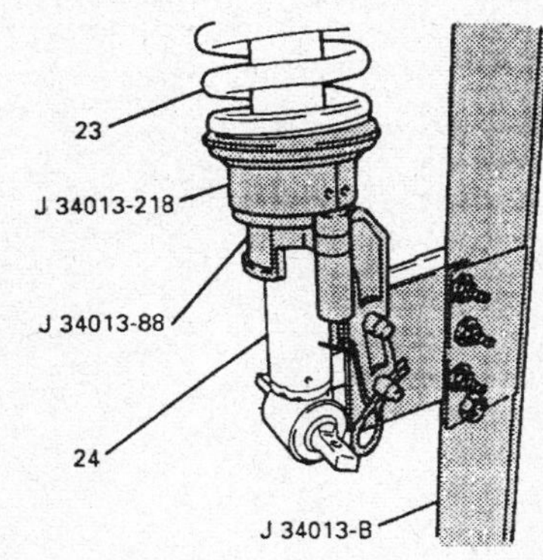

23 SPRING ASSEMBLY, FRONT
24 ABSORBER ASSEMBLY, FRONT SHOCK

GC2029300088000X

Fig. 10 Shock absorber assembly to strut spring compressor installation

personal injury.

g. Insert J39642-1 from modular shock nut removal set tool No. J39642, or equivalent, on shock absorber nut, then insert tool No. J39642-2, or equivalent, from modular shock nut removal set tool Nos. J39642 through J39642-1, or equivalents, to hold shock absorber rod in place.
h. Remove shock absorber nut and discard, then turn strut spring compressor clockwise to relieve spring pressure.

7. Proceed as follows to assemble shock absorber assembly:
   a. Install shock absorber to strut compressor adapter and modular shock support. **Ensure mounting ears of shock absorber assembly are facing downward toward rear of strut spring compressor or shock absorber assembly will not align properly.**
   b. Close strut compressor adapter and modular shock support and install locking pin, then ensure upper and lower spring seats are positioned correctly.
   c. Assemble shock absorber assembly to top of modular shock assembly compressor adapter. **Ensure top of shock absorber assembly is flat against modular shock assembly compressor adapter. Shock absorber assembly will not be aligned properly if it does not lay flat against tool.**
   d. Turn screw on strut spring compressor counterclockwise to raise shock absorber assembly up to modular shock assembly compressor adapter without compressing spring assembly. Ensure studs on shock absorber assembly go through guide holes in modular shock assembly compressor adapter. **Only turn screw until shock absorber assembly is held in strut spring compressor by itself. Do not load spring assembly.**
   e. Place modular shock assembly alignment rod J34013-115 down through top of strut spring compressor, through top of shock absorber assembly and onto shock absorber rod, **Fig. 11. Ensure shock assembly alignment rod is straight with shock absorber assembly. If shock assembly alignment rod is angled, repeat preceding steps until tool is straight.**
   f. Turn operating screw clockwise to compress spring assembly until threaded portion of shock absorber rod is through top of shock absorber assembly. **Do not over compress front spring assembly. Severe overloading may cause tool failure, possibly resulting in personal injury.**
   g. Remove modular shock assembly alignment rod, then insert a new shock absorber nut on shock absorber rod. **Always replace shock absorber nut. Do not turn shock absorber rod when tightening nut or shock absorber assembly could be damaged. Retain shock absorber rod in a stationary position when tightening nut.**
   h. Place tool No. J39642-1, or equivalent, from modular shock nut removal set tool No. J39642, or equivalent, on shock absorber nut, then insert J39642-2 from modular shock nut removal set J–39642 through J39642-1 to hold shock absorber rod in place and tighten nut to specifications.
   i. Remove shock absorber assembly from strut spring compressor.
8. Reverse steps 1 through 5 to install. Tighten fasteners to specifications

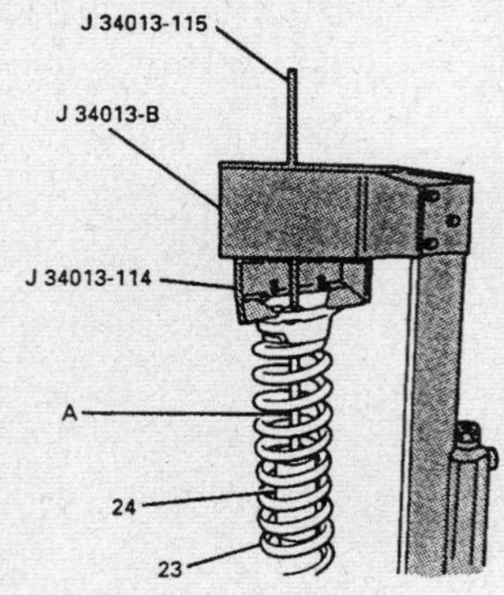

A ROD, FRONT SHOCK ABSORBER
23 SPRING ASSEMBLY, FRONT
24 ABSORBER ASSEMBLY, FRONT SHOCK

GC2029300089000X

Fig. 11 Modular shock assembly alignment rod installation

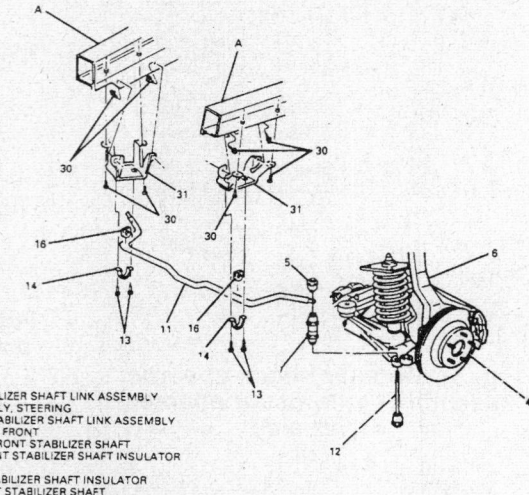

A SIDE RAIL
5 NUT, FRONT STABILIZER SHAFT LINK ASSEMBLY
6 KNUCKLE ASSEMBLY, STEERING
7 SLEEVE, FRONT STABILIZER SHAFT LINK ASSEMBLY
11 STABILIZER SHAFT, FRONT
12 LINK ASSEMBLY, FRONT STABILIZER SHAFT
13 BOLT/SCREW, FRONT STABILIZER SHAFT INSULATOR CLAMP
14 CLAMP, FRONT STABILIZER SHAFT INSULATOR
16 INSULATOR, FRONT STABILIZER SHAFT
30 BOLT/SCREW, FRONT STABILIZER SHAFT BRACKET
31 BRACKET ASSEMBLY, FRONT STABILIZER SHAFT
44 HUB ASSEMBLY, FRONT WHEEL

GC2029500206000X

Fig. 12 Stabilizer shaft replacement

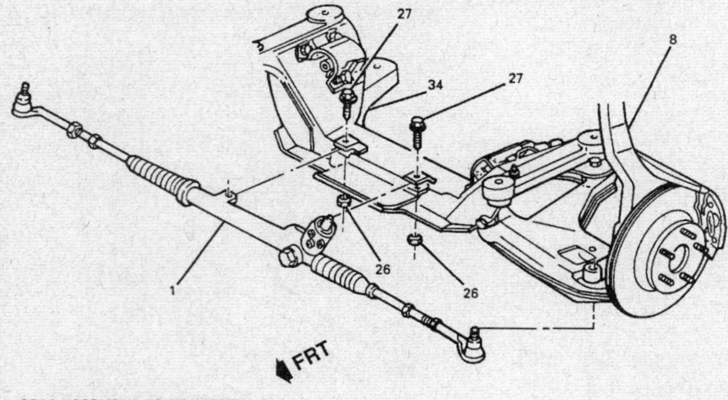

1 GEAR ASSEMBLY, POWER STEERING
8 KNUCKLE ASSEMBLY, STEERING
26 NUT, STEERING GEAR
27 BOLT/SCREW, STEERING GEAR, 85 N•m (63 LB. FT.)
34 CROSSMEMBER ASSEMBLY, FRONT

GC6049300136000X

Fig. 13 Power steering gear installation

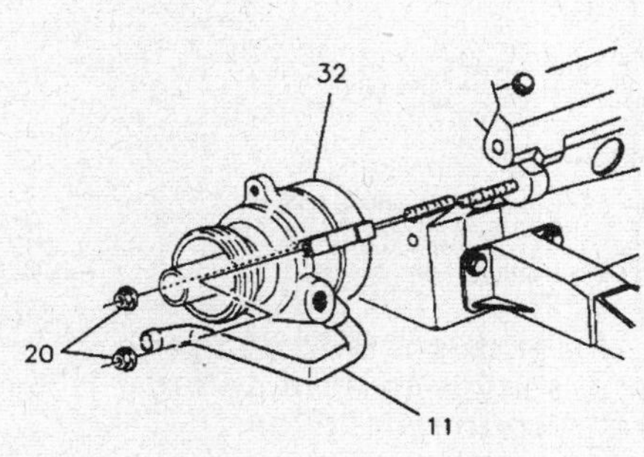

11 HOSE, POWER STEERING FLUID RESERVOIR
20 NUT, POWER STEERING PUMP
32 PUMP, POWER STEERING

GC6049600174000X

Fig. 14 Power steering pump replacement. 3800 engine

STABILIZER BAR

REPLACE

1. Raise and support vehicle.
2. Remove nut from link bolt located at each side, then remove bolt, grommets and bushings, **Fig. 12.**
3. Remove stabilizer shaft to body bolts, then remove stabilizer bar.
4. Reverse procedure to install.

POWER STEERING GEAR

REPLACE

1. Raise and support vehicle, then remove wheels.
2. Disconnect inlet and outlet hoses from steering gear, then the steering linkage outer tie rods from steering knuckles, **Fig. 13.**
3. Disconnect steering gear coupling shaft from steering gear, then remove steering gear.
4. Reverse procedure to install, noting the following:
   a. Tighten fasteners to specifications.
   b. Adjust steering gear so that it aligns as straight as possible with steering gear coupling shaft.
   c. Refill and bleed power steering system.

POWER STEERING PUMP

REPLACE

1. **On models equipped with 5.7L engine,** raise and support vehicle, then drain engine coolant into suitable container.
2. **On all models,** remove serpentine belt, then lower vehicle and remove front air intake duct.
3. **On models equipped with 5.7L engine,** remove alternator, radiator outlet hose and heater inlet/outlet hoses from water pump. Also, remove throttle body heater return from heater outlet hose and pump bolts.
4. **On models equipped with 3800 engine,** remove pulley from pump and mounting nuts.
5. **On all models,** remove pump mounting bolts, **Figs. 14 and 15,** then disconnect inlet and reservoir hoses from pump and remove pump.
6. Reverse procedure to install, noting the following:
   a. Tighten fasteners to specifications.
   b. Refill and bleed power steering system.

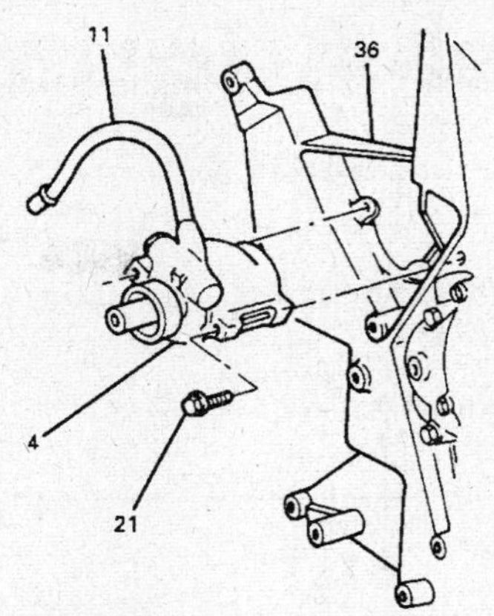

4 PUMP ASSEMBLY, POWER STEERING
11 HOSE ASSEMBLY, POWER STEERING FLUID RESERVOIR
21 BOLT/SCREW, POWER STEERING PUMP, 25 N•m (18 LB. FT.)
36 BRACKET ASSEMBLY, GENERATOR AND AIR CONDITIONER COMPRESSOR AND POWER STEERING PUMP AND DRIVE BELT TENSIONER

GC6049300140000X

Fig. 15 Power steering pump replacement. 5.7L engine

TIGHTENING SPECIFICATIONS

Year	Component	Torque/Ft. Lbs.
1998–2002	Lower Ball Joint Nut	81
	Lower Shock Absorber Nuts	48
	Power Steering Gear Mounting Bolts	63
	Power Steering Pump Bolts (V6 Engine)	23
	Power Steering Pump Bolts (V8 Engine)	18
	Power Steering Pump Support To Pump Nuts & Bolts	37
	Stabilizer Bracket To Frame Bolts	41
	Stabilizer Clamp To Stabilizer Bracket Bolts	41
	Stabilizer Link Nut	17
	Upper Ball Joint Nut	39
	Upper Shock Absorber Mount To Strut Tower Bolts	37
	Upper Shock Absorber Mount To Strut Tower Nuts	32
	Wheel Lug Nuts	100

Wheel Alignment

INDEX

PRELIMINARY INSPECTION

Prior to inspecting or adjusting front suspension alignment, inspect suspension components for damage or excessive wear, and replace as needed. Ensure tire pressures and wheel bearings are properly adjusted, then raise and release front bumper several times to allow vehicle to assume normal ride height.

FRONT WHEEL ALIGNMENT

CASTER

1. Jounce front bumper three times to allow vehicle to return to normal ride height, then raise and support vehicle.
2. Loosen front lower control arm nuts, then install camber/caster adjuster tool No. J38658, or equivalent, to slot holes in lower control arm and front crossmember, **Fig. 1.**
3. Adjust caster to specifications by rotating turnbuckle on camber/caster adjuster. Clockwise increases caster, counterclockwise decreases caster.
4. Remove camber/caster adjuster, then **torque** front lower control arm nuts to 96 ft. lbs.

CAMBER

1. Jounce front bumper three times to allow vehicle to return to normal ride height, then raise and support vehicle.
2. Loosen front lower control arm nuts, then install camber/caster adjuster tool No. J38658, or equivalent, to slot holes in lower control arm and front crossmember, **Fig. 2.**
3. Adjust camber to specifications by rotating turnbuckle on camber/caster adjuster. Clockwise increases caster, counterclockwise decreases caster.
4. Remove camber/caster adjuster, then **torque** front lower control arm nuts to 96 ft. lbs.

TOE-IN

Toe adjustments are made separately at each individual wheel.

1. Ensure steering wheel is set in a straight ahead position within ± 3.5.°
2. Loosen nut on inner tie rod, then adjust toe to specifications. Left and right toe adjustment should be equal within ± .2.°

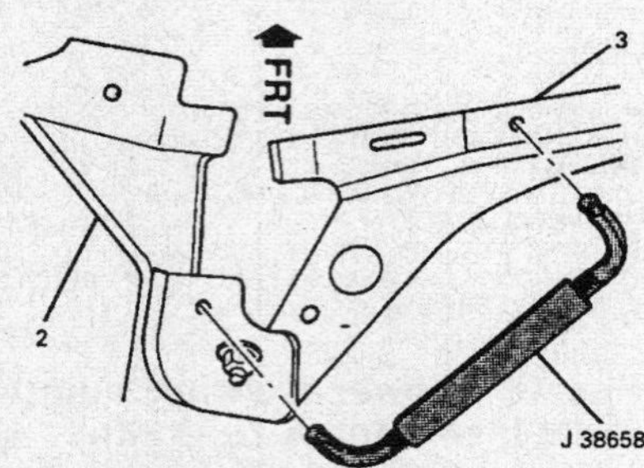

Fig. 1 Front caster adjustment tool installation

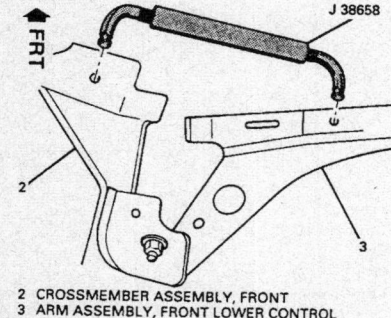

Fig. 2 Front camber adjustment tool installation

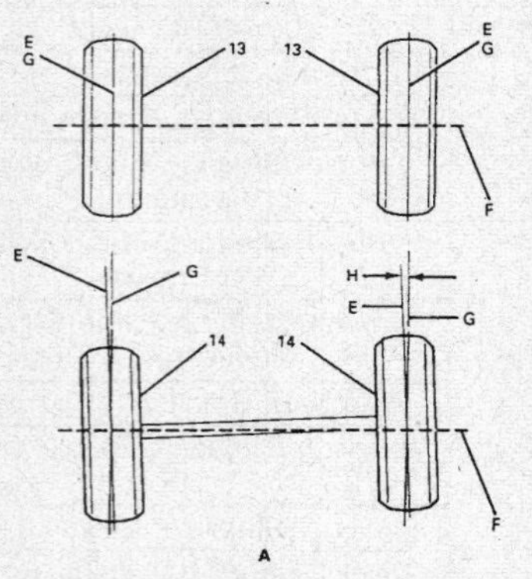
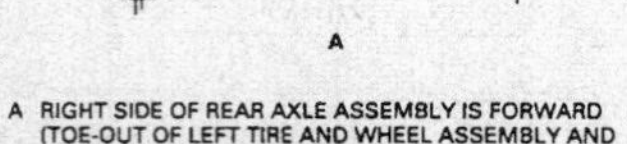

Fig. 3 Rear wheel alignment inspection

3. Ensure steering gear boot is not twisted, then **torque** inner tie rod nut to 35 ft. lbs.

REAR WHEEL ALIGNMENT

After front wheel alignment has been inspected or adjusted, rear wheel alignment angles should be inspected if vehicle still does not track properly or if excessive rear tire wear is present. Rear wheels should be parallel to and the same distance from the vehicle centerline, **Fig. 3.**

Rear wheel alignment is not adjustable. If alignment angles are not within specification, inspect for bent or damaged suspension arms, axle housing or frame.

THRUST ANGLE

If the thrust angle is not within specifications, inspect upper and lower control arms for damage. If control arms are not damaged, inspect frame dimensions.

CATERA

NOTE: Refer To The Rear Of This Manual For Manufacturer's Special Service Tool Suppliers.

INDEX OF SERVICE OPERATIONS

Specifications

GENERAL ENGINE SPECIFICATIONS

Engine	Fuel System	Bore × Stroke, Inches	Comp. Ratio	Net HP @ RPM	Maximum Torque, Ft. Lbs. @ RPM	Minimum Oil Pressure, psi①
3.0L	SMPI	3.4 × 3.4	10.0	200 @ 6000	192 @ 3600	22

SMPI — Sequential Multi-Port Fuel Injection

① — At idle.

TUNE UP SPECIFICATIONS

Engine	Spark Plug Gap, Inch	Ignition Timing		Idle Speed, RPM	Fuel Pressure, psi	Valve Clearance, Inch
		Firing Order	°BTDC			
3.0L	.035–.043	1-2-3-4-5-6	①	③	④	②

BTDC — Before Top Dead Center

① — Not adjustable. Refer to **Fig. A** for spark plug wire harness routing.

② — Zero lash valve train. Not adjustable.

③ — Refer to Vehicle Emission Control Information (VECI) label in engine compartment.

④ — 1998 models, 46–59 psi., 1999–2001 models 40–48 psi.

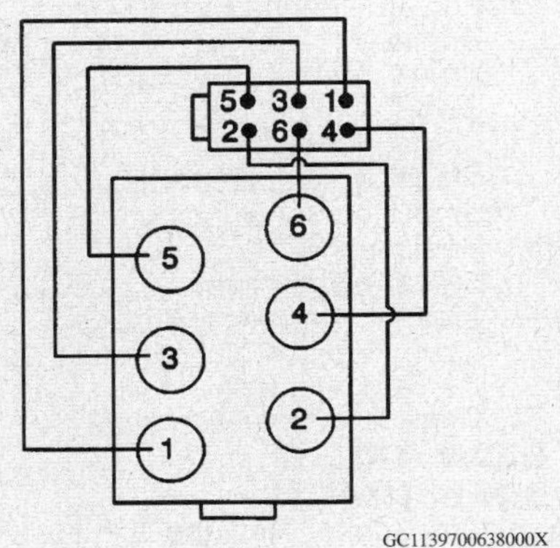

Fig. A

FRONT WHEEL ALIGNMENT SPECIFICATIONS

Year	Caster, Degrees①	Camber, Degrees		Toe, Degrees		Ball Joint Inspection
		Left & Right	Max. Cross Camber	Individual	Total	
1998–2000	+4.0 to +6.0	−1.15 to +1.35	—	+.04 to +.20	+.09 to +.41	②
2001	+4.5 to +5.5	+1.1 to −.10	—	—	+.26 to −.06	②

① — Not adjustable.

② — Refer to “Front Suspension & Steering” section for inspection procedure.

REAR WHEEL ALIGNMENT SPECIFICATIONS

Year	Camber, Degrees	Toe, Degrees	
		Individual	Total
1998–2000	−1.08 to −2.42	−.05 to +.11	−.10 to +.22
2001	−1.35 to −2.15	+.15 to −.15	+.26 to −.06

VEHICLE RIDE HEIGHT SPECIFICATIONS

Model	Year	Body Style	Manufacturer's Original Tire Size	Measurement Points & Specifications①③					
				Front			Rear		
				Dim.	Specification		Dim.	Specification	
					Inches	mm		Inches	mm
Catera	1998–2001	All	②	C	6.87	174	D	6.5	165

C Dim. — Ground to Rocker Panel, Front
D Dim. — Ground to Rocker Panel, Rear
Dim. — Dimension
① — ±.0.39 in (10 mm) front to rear & side to side.
② — See door sticker or inside of glove box for manufacturer's original tire size specifications. If tires on vehicle do not match manufacturer's original tire size & measurement is not within limits, it will be necessary to refer to the "Non-Standard Tire & Wheel Size Adjustment To Ride Height Specification & Tire Size Adjustment Charts" in the front of this manual for approximate changes in ride height specifications.
③ — Measurement is with fuel, radiator coolant and engine oil full, spare tire, jack, hand tools and mats in designated positions and tires properly inflated.

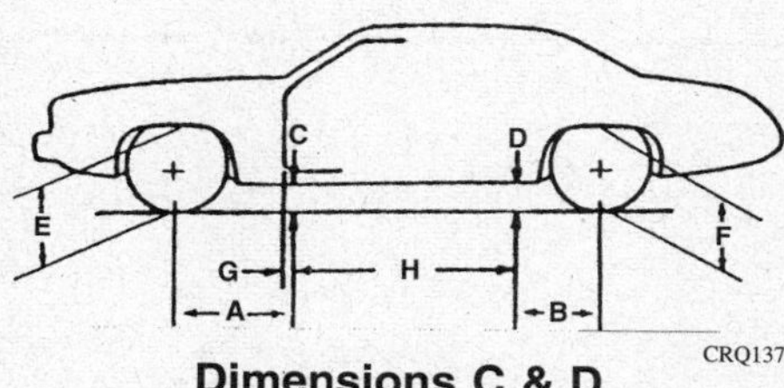

Dimensions C & D

FLUID CAPACITIES & COOLING SYSTEM DATA

Year	Coolant Capacity, Qts.	Coolant Type	Coolant Recovery Reservoir Cap Pressure, Lbs.	Thermo. Opening Temp., °F	Fuel Tank Capacity, Gals.	Engine Oil Refill, Qts.①	Trans. Oil Refill, Qts.	Rear Axle Oil, Qts.
1998–2001	10	Dex-Cool	14	194	18	5.3	7	1.74

① — With oil filter change.

LUBRICANT DATA

Year	Engine	Transmission	Rear Axle	Power Steering	Brake System
All	API 10W-30	Dexron III ATF	SAE 80W-90 GL-5	Dexron III ATF	DOT 3

Electrical

NOTE: On Air Bag Equipped Models, Refer To "Air Bag System Precautions" Located In The Front Of This Manual For System Disarming & Arming Procedures.

NOTE: Refer To "Computer Relearn Procedures" Located In The Front Of This Manual When Battery Power To The Computer Has Been Interrupted.

INDEX

PRECAUTIONS

AIR BAG SYSTEMS

Refer to "Air Bag System Precautions" in the front of this manual for system disarming and arming procedures.

BATTERY GROUND CABLE

Prior to service, disconnect battery ground cable and isolate as required.

FUSE PANEL & FLASHER LOCATION

The fuse panel is located below the lefthand side of the instrument panel, near the lower lefthand portion of the steering column. The turn signal flasher is mounted on the relay box, which is below the instrument panel and to the right of the steering column.

FUEL PUMP RELAY LOCATION

The fuel pump relay is located at the lefthand front of the engine compartment, in the Engine Control Module (ECM) housing.

RELAY CENTER LOCATION

The relay centers are located behind the lefthand side of the instrument panel, **Fig. 1.**

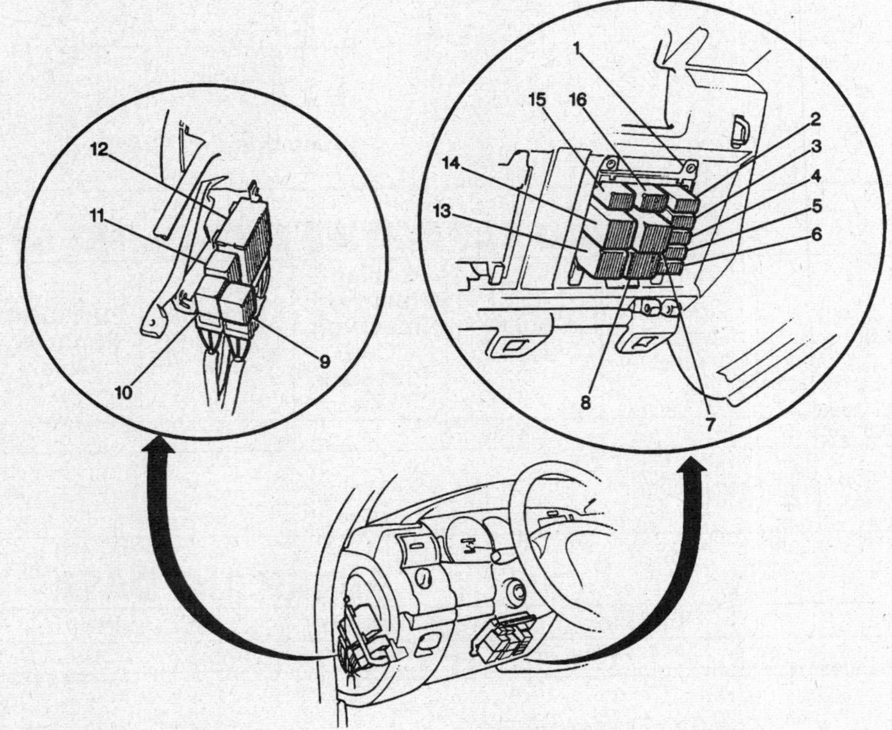

(1) Relay Center
(2) Park Lamp Relay
(3) Low Beam Relay
(4) Not Used
(5) Not Used
(6) LH Headlamp (High Beam) Relay
(7) Turn Signal Lamp Flasher
(8) Horn Relay
(9) Passenger Seat Heater Relay
(10) Driver Seat Heater Relay
(11) Power Steering Control Relay
(12) Multifunction Relay Module
(13) RH Headlamp, (High Beam) Relay
(14) Heated Outside Rear View Mirror and Rear Window Defogger Relay
(15) Daytime Running Lamp Relay
(16) Rear Suspension Leveling Air Compressor Relay

GC9049700156000X

Fig. 1 Relay center location

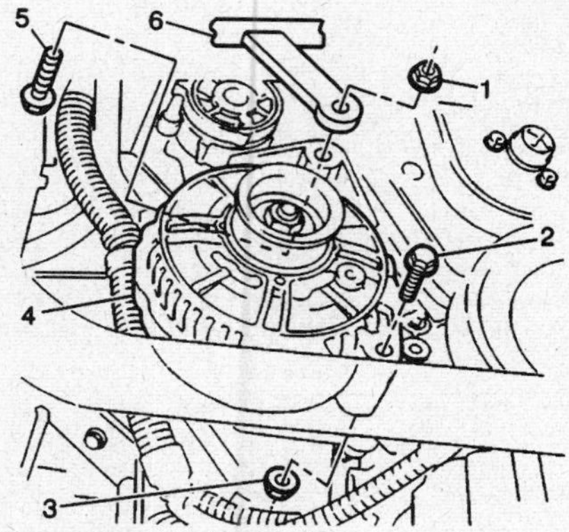

(1) Generator Upper Nut
(2) Generator Lower Bolt
(3) Generator Lower Nut
(4) Generator
(5) Generator Upper Bolt
(6) AIR Injection Crossover Pipe

GC1129700068000X

Fig. 2 Alternator & mounting hardware

STARTER

REPLACE

1. Raise and support vehicle.
2. Remove terminal nuts and disconnect electrical leads at starter.
3. Remove righthand catalytic converter.
4. Remove engine mount and nuts as outlined under "Engine Mount, Replace" in "3.0L Engine" section.
5. Lower vehicle.
6. Remove resonance chamber to throttle body ducts.
7. Install engine support fixture tool No. J28467-A and adapter tool No. J28467-450, or equivalents.
8. Raise righthand side of engine approximately 1½ inches.
9. Raise and support vehicle.
10. Remove engine mount from bracket and cradle.
11. Remove bracket mounting bolts and position bracket aside to gain working clearance.
12. Remove starter.
13. Reverse procedure to install, noting the following:
    a. **Torque** starter mounting bolts to 44 ft. lbs.
    b. When lowering engine, guide mount into position and ensure locator tab engages cradle slot.

ALTERNATOR

REPLACE

1. Remove pre-volume chamber.
2. Remove serpentine drive belt from alternator pulley as outlined under "Serpentine Drive Belt" in "3.0L Engine" section.
3. Raise and support vehicle.
4. Remove terminal nuts and disconnect leads at alternator. **Identify leads for installation reference.**
5. Remove alternator air cooling duct and upper nut, **Fig. 2.**
6. Remove lower mounting bolt and nut.

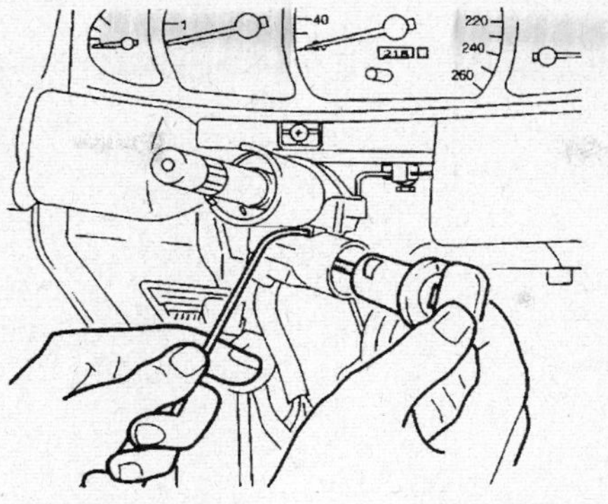

GC9129700044000X

Fig. 3 Ignition lock cylinder removal

7. Separate alternator from engine and slide upper bolt out through bracket.
8. Lower vehicle and remove alternator.
9. Reverse procedure to install. **Torque** alternator mounting bolts to 30 ft. lbs.

COIL PACK

REPLACE

1. Remove wiper arms, then the left and righthand air inlet grilles.
2. Remove wiper motor as outlined under "Wiper Motor, Replace."
3. Disconnect power brake booster vacuum line at intake plenum and spark plug wiring harness at ignition coil.
4. Disconnect coil electrical connector and remove mounting bolts.
5. Remove coil.
6. Reverse procedure to install. **Torque** coil mounting bolts to 72 inch lbs.

IGNITION LOCK

REPLACE

1. Remove Supplemental Inflatable Restraint (SIR) coil.
2. Insert suitable pointed tool into lock cylinder release pin hole and remove cylinder, **Fig. 3.**
3. Reverse procedure to install. Prior to installation, reset wheel locking device as follows:
    a. Locate locking lever in lock cylinder bore.
    b. Carefully push lever down until click is heard, **Fig. 4.**

IGNITION SWITCH

REPLACE

1. Remove Supplemental Inflatable Restraint (SIR) coil and ignition switch setscrew.
2. Turn ignition to On position and depress connector locking tab using suitable flat-bladed screwdriver.
3. Disconnect electrical connector and remove switch.
4. Reverse procedure to install.

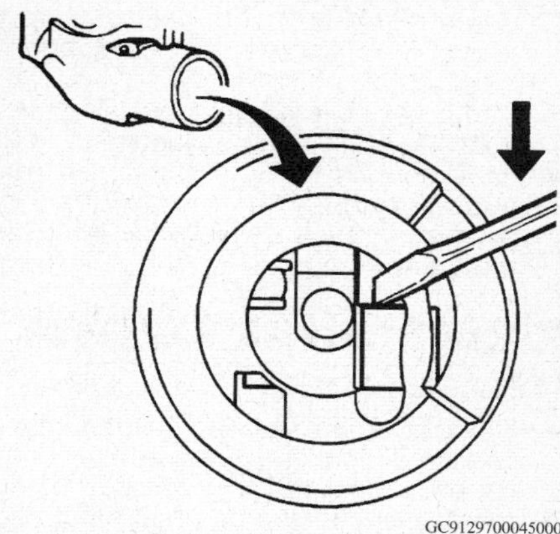

GC9129700045000X

Fig. 4 Steering wheel lock reset

NEUTRAL SAFETY SWITCH

REPLACE

The **Transmission Control Selector Switch** incorporates the functions of a neutral safety and back-up lamp switch.

1. Apply parking brake and place selector lever in Neutral position.
2. Raise and support vehicle, then separate muffler from catalytic converter.
3. Support transmission with suitable jack and remove transmission crossmember to body bolts.
4. Lower transmission enough to access switch and remove switch cover.
5. Disconnect switch wire harness at bracket using suitable pry tool.
6. Remove control selector shaft nut and remove lever from shaft.
7. Remove mounting bolts and switch.
8. Reverse procedure to install, noting the following:
    a. Install bolts loosely.
    b. Place transmission in Neutral position.
    c. Align switch shaft and housing slots.
    d. Ensure alignment is proper during installation by inserting 3/32 inch drill bit.
    e. **Torque** switch bolts to 96–108 inch lbs.
    f. **Torque** crossmember to body bolts to 33 ft. lbs.
    g. **Torque** muffler to catalytic converter bolts to 30 ft. lbs.

HEADLAMP SWITCH

REPLACE

1. Disengage switch from instrument panel by carefully prying on lefthand side using suitable cloth to protect trim.
2. Remove switch from instrument panel.
3. Reverse procedure to install.

STOP LIGHT SWITCH

REPLACE

1. Remove lefthand instrument panel sound insulator.

2. Remove lefthand front floor air outlet duct and disconnect electrical connector at switch.
3. Compress both locking tabs using suitable angled pliers and remove switch.
4. Reverse procedure to install. **Do not push actuating pin into switch. Pin will adjust itself when brake pedal is released.**

TURN SIGNAL SWITCH

REPLACE

1. Remove upper steering column cover caps and mounting screws .
2. Carefully thread tilt lever out of tilt mechanism. It may be required to use suitable non-marring tool.
3. Remove lock cylinder protective cover and mounting screws from lower steering column cover.
4. Remove lower steering column cover, depress tabs and disconnect turn signal switch electrical connector.
5. Remove switch.
6. Reverse procedure to install. Coat tilt lever threads with GM locking compound P/N 12345382, or equivalent, prior to installation.

STEERING WHEEL

REPLACE

1. Remove air bag module mounting screws from steering wheel rear.
2. Disconnect air bag module electrical connector and carefully remove module.
3. Mark relationship between steering wheel and column for alignment during installation.
4. Disengage steering wheel nut locking tab, then remove nut and tab.
5. Remove steering wheel using puller tool No. J1859-A and puller legs tool No. J36541-A, or equivalents. **Do not use hammer on steering shaft.**
6. Reverse procedure to install, noting the following:
   a. **Torque** steering wheel nut to 21 ft. lbs.
   b. **Torque** air bag module screws to 72 inch lbs.

INSTRUMENT CLUSTER

REPLACE

1. Remove center air deflector.
2. Remove righthand instrument cluster screw and turn steering wheel as required to access upper steering column cover screws.
3. Remove upper column cover plugs and mounting, then lift cover away from column.
4. Remove mounting screw and upper column cover collar.
5. Disengage righthand side of cluster and disconnect cluster electrical connector.
6. Slide cluster toward righthand side until lefthand side clears vent housing and gently move cluster out of instrument panel.
7. Reverse procedure to install.

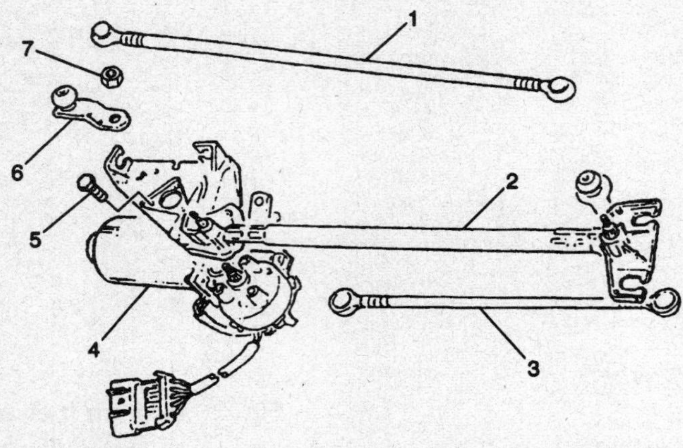

(1) Windshield Wiper Transmission Link (Upper)
(2) Windshield Wiper Transmission
(3) Windshield Wiper Transmission Link (Lower)
(4) Windshield Wiper Motor
(5) Windshield Wiper Motor Bracket Bolt
(6) Windshield Wiper Motor Crank Arm
(7) Windshield Wiper Transmission Nut

GC9029700443000X

Fig. 5 Wiper motor & transmission replacement

RADIO

REPLACE

1. Apply parking brake.
2. Move gear selector lever to full rearward position and remove instrument panel center bezel.
3. Remove radio mounting screws and separate radio from HVAC control head bracket.
4. Disconnect antenna lead and electrical harness at radio, then remove radio.
5. Reverse procedure to install.

WIPER MOTOR

REPLACE

1. Remove wiper transmission as outlined under "Wiper Transmission, Replace."
2. Disconnect wiper transmission upper link at wiper motor crank arm and remove wiper transmission nut from motor.
3. Disconnect wiper motor crank arm at wiper motor, then remove motor bracket bolts, **Fig. 5.**
4. Remove wiper motor from transmission.
5. Reverse procedure to install.

WIPER TRANSMISSION

REPLACE

1. Remove air inlet grilles and disconnect brake booster hose.
2. Disconnect wiper motor harness connector.
3. Remove mounting screws, wiper motor and transmission as an assembly.
4. Remove wiper transmission upper link and wiper motor bracket bolts, **Fig. 5.**
5. Separate wiper motor from transmission.
6. Reverse procedure to install.

BLOWER MOTOR

REPLACE

1. Remove righthand side passenger compartment sound insulator.
2. Disengage clip and remove righthand front floor air outlet.
3. Remove glove compartment.
4. Disconnect supply duct at side air vent and remove blower motor housing screws.
5. Remove blower motor housing.
6. Remove blower motor to housing mounting screws and separate motor from housing.
7. Reverse procedure to install.

HEATER CORE

REPLACE

1. Drain engine coolant into suitable container.
2. Disconnect heater hoses at heater core pipes. **Exercise caution when pulling on quick connect fittings.**
3. Remove steering column as outlined under "Steering Columns."
4. Remove front assist handles, windshield pillar moldings and righthand access panel.
5. Remove righthand air deflector and glove compartment.
6. Remove righthand air ducts, inflatable restraint module trim cover and fasteners.
7. Disconnect inflatable restraint module orange harness connector and remove module.
8. Remove center console and center air duct.
9. Remove radio as outlined under "Radio, Replace."
10. Disconnect and remove climate control head.
11. Remove center air deflector, lefthand access panel and lefthand air deflector.
12. Remove headlamp switch as outlined under "Headlamp Switch, Replace."

13. Remove lefthand vent bracket and remove instrument cluster as outlined under "Instrument Cluster, Replace."
14. Remove mounting screws, fuse and relay panel.
15. Remove steering column support bracket nuts and instrument panel carrier bolts.
16. Remove headlamp automatic control ambient light sensor, disconnect carrier wiring harness and disengage clips.
17. Pull carrier rearward to access heater core. **It is not required to completely remove carrier or to remove instrument panel wiring harness when servicing heater core.**
18. Remove blower motor and housing as an assembly, then the heater core pipe bracket.
19. Remove inlet and outlet pipes and instrument panel support brace bolts.
20. Remove instrument panel support brace, support bracket and heater core mounting screw.
21. Remove heater core and plug ports.

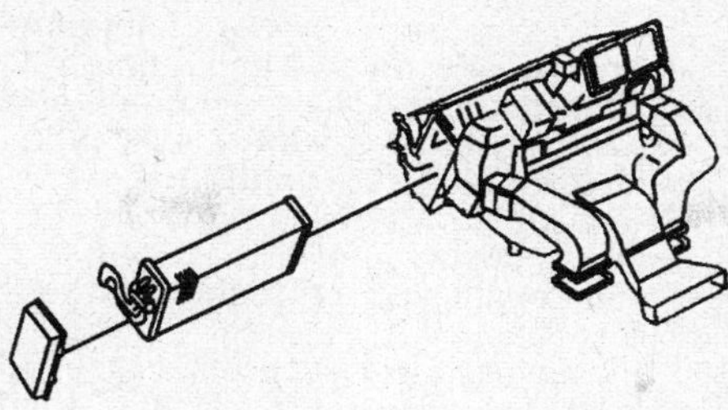

Fig. 6 Evaporator core replacement

22. Remove cavity rubber seal.
23. Reverse procedure to install, noting the following:
    a. **Torque** passenger air bag module mounting bolts to 84–96 inch lbs.
    b. When installing steering column using new shear bolt.
    c. **Torque** rear support bracket bolt, forward support strap nut and coupler to shaft clamp bolt to 16 ft. lbs. Shear bolt head should snap off at approximately 15 ft. lbs.
    d. When connecting heater hoses, ensure quick disconnects are fully seated and retaining sleeves are in locked position.

EVAPORATOR CORE

REPLACE

1. Discharge and recover air conditioning system as outlined under "Air Conditioning."
2. Remove mounting screws and Thermal Expansion Valve (TXV).
3. Remove steering column as outlined under "Steering Columns."
4. Remove brake pedal and bracket as an assembly.
5. Plug evaporator fittings and remove evaporator core, **Fig. 6.**
6. Reverse procedure to install. Install new O-rings lubricated with 525 viscosity mineral oil.

3.0L Engine

NOTE: On Air Bag Equipped Models, Refer To "Air Bag System Precautions" Located In The Front Of This Manual For System Disarming & Arming Procedures.

NOTE: Refer To "Computer Relearn Procedures" Located In The Front Of This Manual When Battery Power To The Computer Has Been Interrupted.

INDEX

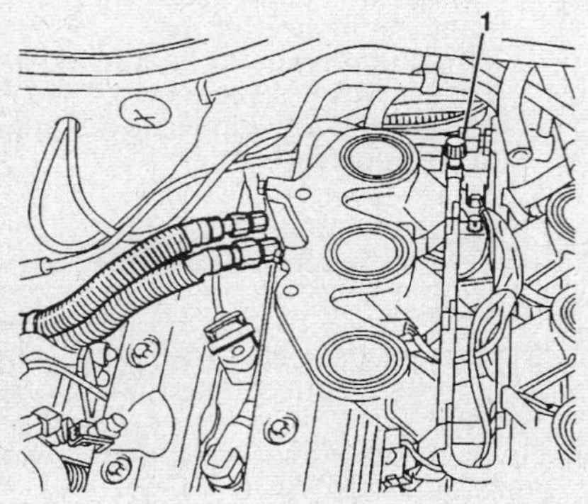

Fig. 1 Fuel pressure service port

PRECAUTIONS

AIR BAG SYSTEMS

Refer to "Air Bag System Precautions" in the front of this manual for system disarming and arming procedures.

BATTERY GROUND CABLE

Prior to service, disconnect battery ground cable and isolate as required.

FUEL SYSTEM PRESSURE RELIEF

In order to avoid personal injury and possible vehicle damage, fuel system pressure must be relieved prior to servicing any component of the fuel system.

1. Loosen fuel filler cap to release tank pressure.
2. Connect fuel pressure gauge tool No. J34730-1A with adapter hose tool No. J42242, or equivalents, to fuel pressure service port on fuel crossover pipe, **Fig. 1.** Wrap shop towel around fitting to prevent spillage during connection.
3. Place end of bleed hose into suitable gasoline container and open valve to bleed system pressure.
4. Drain residual fuel from gauge tool into suitable container.

COMPRESSION PRESSURE

INSPECTION

1. Run engine until normal operating temperature is reached.
2. Shut engine off, disable fuel and ignition systems.
3. Remove spark plugs.
4. Disconnect air ducts at throttle body and block throttle plates open.
5. Install compression tester tool No. J38722, or equivalent, in spark plug hole.
6. Crank engine through at least four compression strokes for test cylinder, noting gauge readings at each stroke.
7. Remove gauge and repeat test for each remaining cylinder. **Minimum pressure for any one cylinder is 100 psi. Compression is acceptable if lowest cylinder reading for all cylinders is within 70% of highest.**
8. Remove throttle plates block and connect air ducts.
9. Install spark plugs and tighten to specifications.
10. Enable fuel and ignition systems.

ENGINE MOUNT

REPLACE

REMOVAL

1. Raise and support vehicle, then remove engine mount lower nut.
2. Lower vehicle and install engine support fixture tool No. J28467-A, or equivalent.
3. Raise and support vehicle, then remove engine mount upper nut.
4. Remove engine mount.

INSTALLATION

1. Raise and support vehicle.
2. Install engine mount. Tighten upper mounting to specifications.
3. Lower vehicle.
4. Lower engine and remove support fixture tool. **Ensure engine mount guide pin engages in crossmember guide hole (1), Fig. 2.**
5. Raise and support vehicle.
6. Tighten engine mount lower nut to specifications.

ENGINE

REPLACE

1. Drain engine coolant and oil into suitable containers. Remove wiper arms.
2. Remove left and righthand air inlet grilles, then the hood. Mark hood position for installation.
3. Remove battery and recover air conditioning system as outlined under "Air Conditioning."
4. Disconnect black wiring harness connector and body ground wire at battery ground cable end. Identify harnesses and wires for installation reference.
5. Disconnect four power supply wires at battery positive cable end and identify for installation reference.
6. Siphon power steering fluid from reservoir, disconnect power steering suction hose and remove clamp.
7. Disconnect power steering discharge hose at pump and remove threaded brake booster fitting from intake manifold plenum.
8. Disconnect vacuum lines at power brake booster hose. Identify lines for installation reference.
9. Disconnect intake plenum switchover valve vacuum and electrical connections, then remove switchover valve mounting bolts.
10. Identify relays and connections for installation.
11. Remove switchover valve and Engine Control Module (ECM) and remove relays.

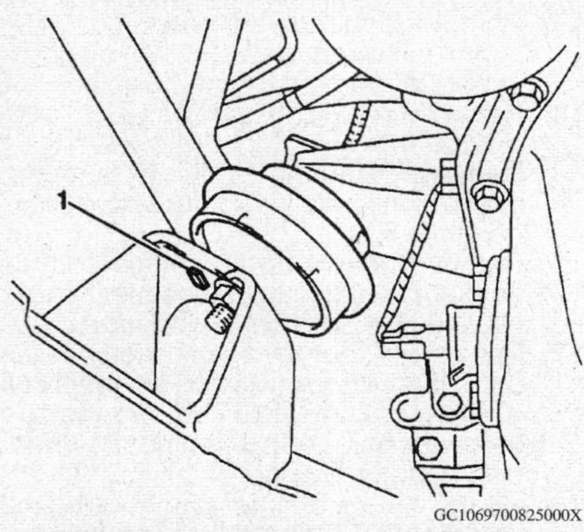

Fig. 2 Engine mount guide pin

12. Disconnect wiring harness at electrical center.
13. Disconnect blue and white wiring harness connectors, then disengage accelerator and cruise control cable retaining clips.
14. Disconnect accelerator and cruise control cables at throttle body.
15. Relieve fuel system pressure as outlined under "Precautions."
16. Disconnect and remove fuel supply and return hoses using suitable back-up tool to prevent fuel rail damage.
17. Disconnect coolant return hose at throttle body and vacuum hose at ventilation chamber purge valve.
18. Disconnect vacuum hose at hot water control valve and coolant reservoir hose at coolant intake pipe.
19. Disconnect heater hoses at heater core pipes.
20. Disconnect Mass Air Flow (MAF) and Intake Air Temperature (IAT) sensor electrical connectors.
21. Disconnect resonance chamber air intake hose at air cleaner housing and MAF sensor, then the Idle Air Control (IAC) inlet hose.
22. Disconnect intake plenum air inlet hoses.
23. Disconnect switchover valve electrical connector and all remaining vacuum connections. Identify connections for installation reference.
24. Remove mounting nuts and resonance chamber.
25. Remove radiator as outlined under "Radiator, Replace."
26. Disconnect air conditioning compressor/condenser hose bracket at body and position aside.
27. Disconnect air conditioning compressor hose quick connect fittings at compressor/condenser hose and at evaporator line extension.
28. Install engine support fixture tool No. J28467-A, or equivalent.
29. Raise and support vehicle.
30. Remove splash shield and disconnect air conditioning compressor electrical connector.
31. Drain transmission fluid into suitable container.
32. Disconnect transmission shift lever rod and remove propeller shaft coupling bolts.

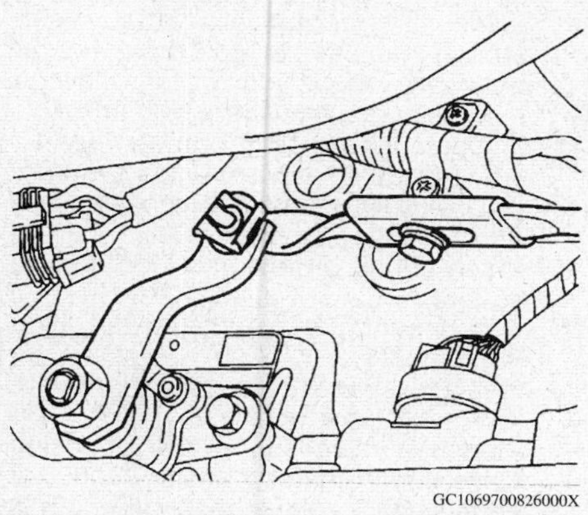
GC1069700826000X

Fig. 3 Shift lever rod adjustment bolt

33. Separate propeller shaft coupling from drive flange using suitable prying tool.
34. Remove transmission oil pan and bellhousing access plugs.
35. Remove flexplate to torque converter bolts. Mark relationship between flexplate and converter for installation reference.
36. Disconnect oil cooler inlet and outlet pipes at center pipes.
37. Disconnect oxygen sensor electrical connectors and remove catalytic converters.
38. Remove transmission housing to engine oil pan bolts and install transmission support.
39. Remove mounting nuts, bolts and crossmember.
40. Lower transmission to access transmission housing to engine block bolts and disconnect ventilation hose at transmission.
41. Disconnect transmission control selector switch, adapter case, main case and speed sensor electrical connectors.
42. With front of engine supported, remove transmission housing to engine block bolts.
43. Remove transmission.
44. Lower vehicle and connect engine lift chains to three support lift shackles.
45. When weight of engine is supported by engine lift, remove support fixture tool.
46. Remove mount nuts and engine.
47. Reverse procedure to install, noting the following:
    a. Tighten mounting bolts and nuts to specifications.
    b. Tighten fuel line connections to specifications using suitable backup tool to prevent fuel rail damage.
    c. Adjust shift lever rod by placing selector lever in Park position and loosening adjustment bolt to allow adjuster to slide freely, **Fig. 3.**
    d. Hold transmission selector lever at rear stop and **torque** adjustment bolt to 72 inch lbs.

INTAKE MANIFOLD

REPLACE

1. Remove clamps and intake plenum air inlet hose from throttle body.
2. Remove brake booster vacuum fitting from intake plenum.
3. Remove mounting bolts and position wiring harness channel out of way.
4. Disconnect switchover valve electrical connections and vacuum hose.
5. Disconnect throttle body control electrical connection.
6. Remove mounting bolts and throttle body from plenum.
7. Remove crankcase vent tube adaptor cover by gently prying up on side.
8. Unclip clamp from righthand side plenum bracket and position heater hoses out of way.
9. Remove caps, mounting bolts then the intake plenum.
10. Relieve fuel system pressure as outlined under "Precautions."
11. Remove fuel supply and return hoses from fuel rail.
12. Disconnect fuel injector electrical harness and fuel pressure regulator vacuum connections.
13. Remove mounting bolts and intake manifold, noting the following:
    a. Mask intake manifold spacer ports.
    b. Clean intake manifold sealing surfaces using suitable nonabrasive tool or solvent.
    c. Ensure machined aluminum surfaces are not damaged.
14. Reverse procedure to install. Tighten intake manifold and plenum bolts to specifications.

EXHAUST MANIFOLD

REPLACE

LEFTHAND

1. Remove engine as outlined under "Engine, Replace."
2. Remove manifold lower and upper heat shields.
3. Remove Secondary Air Injection (AIR) pipe bolts and separate pipe from exhaust manifold to access manifold mounting nuts.
4. Remove coolant pipe/engine lift bracket bolt from cylinder head and dipstick tube by pulling firmly upward.
5. Remove mounting nuts and exhaust manifold.
6. Reverse procedure to install, noting the following:
    a. Tighten mounting bolts and nuts to specifications.
    b. Coat AIR pipe and heat shield bolts with GM high temperature antiseize compound P/N 5613695, or equivalent.

RIGHTHAND

1. Remove transmission as outlined under "Engine, Replace."
2. Remove coolant intake pipe.
3. Raise and support vehicle.
4. Remove exhaust manifold lower heat shield.
5. Remove catalytic converter hanger bolt and two lower rear manifold mounting nuts.
6. Lower vehicle and remove lower front manifold mounting nuts.

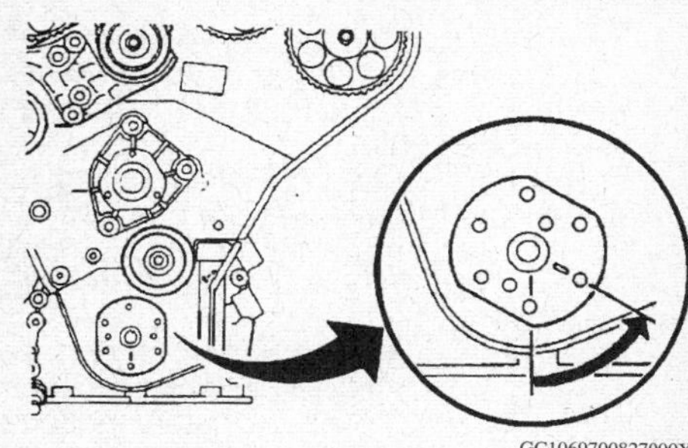
GC1069700827000X

Fig. 4 Crankshaft alignment to 60° BTDC

7. Remove exhaust manifold upper heat shield bolts to access Secondary Air Injection (AIR) pipe. Allow shield to remain in place.
8. Remove AIR pipe bolts and separate pipe from exhaust manifold.
9. Remove mounting nuts and upper manifold.
10. Reverse procedure to install, noting the following:
    a. Tighten mounting bolts and nuts to specifications.
    b. Coat AIR pipe and heat shield bolts with GM high temperature antiseize compound P/N 5613695, or equivalent.

CYLINDER HEAD

REPLACE

LEFT

1. Remove intake plenum as outlined under "Intake Manifold, Replace."
2. Remove resonance chamber as outlined under "Engine, Replace" and intake manifold as outlined under "Intake Manifold, Replace."
3. Remove intake manifold spacer, coolant bridge and lefthand valve cover.
4. Remove front timing belt cover and timing belt as outlined under "Timing Belt, Replace."
5. **Position crankshaft at 60° Before Top Dead Center (BTDC) to prevent valve and piston interference when cylinder head is installed, Fig. 4.**
6. Remove timing belt tensioner bracket.
7. Remove gears from intake and exhaust camshaft Nos. 3 and 4, then from Nos. 1 and 2 as outlined under "Camshaft, Replace."
8. Remove water pump as outlined under "Water Pump, Replace."
9. Remove timing belt rear cover.
10. Disconnect camshaft sensor electrical connector and remove exhaust camshaft No. 4 as outlined under "Camshaft, Replace."
11. Remove coolant pipe/engine lift bracket from cylinder head, grasp dipstick tube firmly and pull upward to remove.
12. Disconnect upper radiator hose from coolant intake pipe and twist pipe to remove.
13. Separate lefthand exhaust manifold from engine block as outlined under "Exhaust Manifold, Replace." **Because this procedure is performed with engine in vehicle, exhaust**

manifold cannot be completely removed. It is not required to remove engine to service manifold during this procedure.

14. Disconnect ignition coil electrical connector and remove cylinder head bolts in reverse order of tightening sequence, **Fig. 5. Discard old cylinder head bolts.**
15. Lift cylinder head off engine, then remove gasket, ignition coil and bracket.
16. Reverse procedure to install, noting the following:
    a. **Ensure crankshaft is still at 60° BTDC to prevent valve and piston interference when cylinder head is installed, Fig. 4.**
    b. Install new cylinder head gasket.
    c. Ensure gasket OBEN/TOP imprint faces front of engine.
    d. **Torque** new cylinder head bolts to 18 ft. lbs. in sequence, **Fig. 5.**
    e. Tighten bolts an additional 90° in sequence.
    f. Tighten bolts an additional 90° in sequence.
    g. Tighten bolts an additional 90° in sequence.
    h. Tighten bolts an additional 15° in sequence.
    i. Install new sealing rings on coolant pipe and lubricate with coolant.
    j. Install new valve cover seals and O-rings as outlined under "Valve Cover, Replace."

RIGHTHAND

1. Remove resonance chamber as outlined under "Engine, Replace."
2. Remove intake plenum and manifold as outlined under "Intake Manifold, Replace," then the manifold spacer.
3. Remove coolant bridge and righthand valve cover.
4. Remove front timing belt cover and timing belt as outlined under "Timing Belt, Replace."
5. Remove timing belt tensioner bracket.
6. **Position crankshaft at 60° Before Top Dead Center (BTDC) to prevent valve and piston interference when cylinder head is installed, Fig. .**
7. Remove camshaft gears for shaft Nos. 3 and 4, and shaft Nos. 1 and 2 as outlined under "Camshaft, Replace."
8. Remove water pump as outlined under "Water Pump, Replace."
9. Remove rear timing belt cover.
10. Remove exhaust camshaft No. 1 as outlined under "Camshaft, Replace."
11. Remove coolant intake pipe.
12. Separate exhaust manifold from cylinder head as outlined under "Exhaust Manifold, Replace."
13. Remove cylinder head bolts in reverse order of tightening sequence, **Fig. 5. Discard old cylinder head bolts.**
14. Remove cylinder head and gasket from engine block.
15. Reverse procedure to install, noting the following:
    a. **Ensure crankshaft is still at 60° BTDC to prevent valve and piston interference when cylinder head is installed, Fig. 4,**
    b. Install new cylinder head gasket.

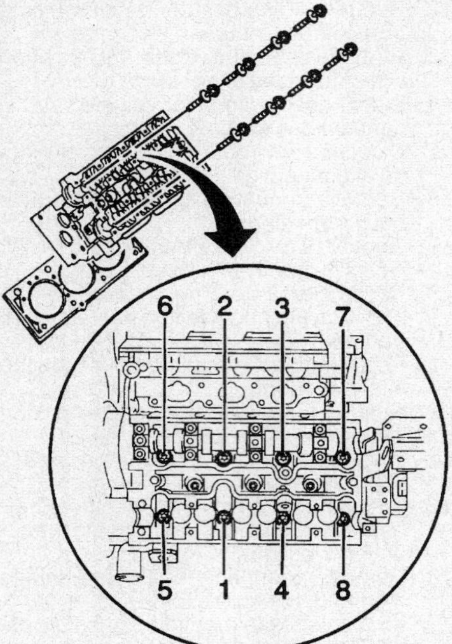

Fig. 5 Cylinder head bolt tightening sequence

c. Ensure gasket OBEN/TOP imprint faces rear of engine.
d. **Torque** new cylinder head bolts to 18 ft. lbs. in sequence, **Fig. 5.**
e. Tighten bolts an additional 90° in sequence.
f. Tighten bolts an additional 90° in sequence.
g. Tighten bolts an additional 90° in sequence.
h. Tighten bolts an additional 15° in sequence.
i. Install new valve cover seals and O-rings as outlined under "Valve Cover, Replace."

COMPONENT SERVICE

CYLINDER HEAD

Disassemble

1. Remove lifters and store in suitable rack. Identify for installation reference.
2. Compress valve springs using valve spring compressor tool No. J8062 and adapter tool No. J41774, or equivalents, and carefully remove stem keys.
3. Remove valve stem caps, springs and seals.
4. Remove valve spring seats and valves from cylinder head. Store valves in suitable rack and identify for installation reference.
5. Clean carbon from combustion chambers and valve train components using suitable brush. **Do not scratch combustion chamber surface.**
6. Clean valve guides.
7. Clean valve stems and heads using suitable buffing wheel.
8. Clean cylinder head bolt holes.

Inspection

1. Inspect cylinder head exhaust ports, combustion chambers and water chamber for cracks. Most cracks occur between exhaust valves or between exhaust valve and spark plug orifice.
2. Inspect valves for burned heads, cracked facing and damaged stems.
3. Ensure valve seats are tight and are not cracked.
4. Place spring on level surface next to square.
5. Rotate spring and measure deviation from square.
6. Replace spring if squareness deviation is .062 inch or less.
7. Measure valve spring tension using valve spring tester tool No. J9666, or equivalent. Replace spring if length is less than 1.338 inches with 56.6 lbs. force.
8. Clamp dial indicator tool No. J8001, or equivalent, on exhaust port side of cylinder head.
9. Position indicator plunger where side to side valve stem movement will be indicated.
10. With valve protruding .39 inch above seat, move valve stem from side to side using light pressure. Record clearance reading.
11. Intake valve clearance should be .0011–.0022 inch and exhaust valve clearance should be .0015–.0026 inch. If not, valve and/or valve guide must be serviced.
12. If valve stem to guide clearance is not as indicated, measure valve stem diameter in three locations.
13. Replace intake valve if stem diameter is less than .2344 inch at narrowest point.
14. Replace exhaust valve if stem diameter is less than .2340 inch at narrowest point, replace valve.
15. Valve guides should be serviced if valve stem diameters are more than minimum specifications.
16. If valve stem to guide clearance is not as indicated and valve stem diameter is satisfactory, use oversize valves and ream valve guides as follows:
    a. Clean guide thoroughly.
    b. Insert reamer tool No. J42096, or equivalent, from top of cylinder head.
    c. Rotate reamer using light hand pressure until it is completely through valve guide.
    d. Remove reamer.
    e. Clean valve guide and combustion chamber to ensure all metal shavings are removed.
17. If clearances are satisfactory and original valves are to be used, valves and seats can be ground to ensure valve seating is optimal, noting the following:
    a. Valves should be ground at 90⅔° angle, **Fig. 6.**
    b. Seats should be ground at 90° angle.
    c. Intake valve seat width should be .039–.055 inch and exhaust valve seat width should be .055–.070 inch.
    d. Control valve seat widths with 30° and 60° stones, **Fig. 7.**

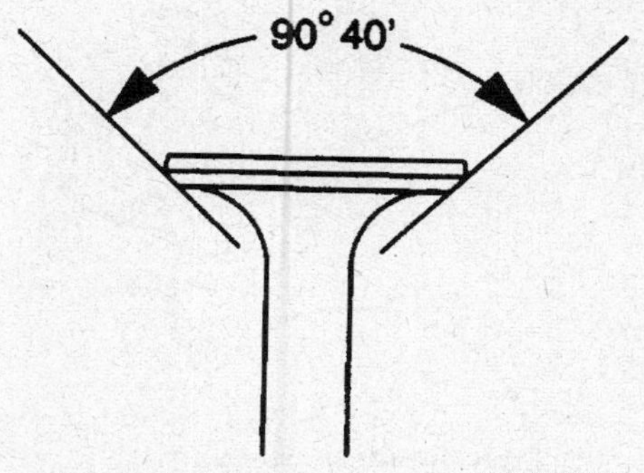

Fig. 6 Valve grinding angle

Assemble

1. Lubricate valve stems with clean engine oil and install valves.
2. Install valve spring seat.
3. Install new valve seal into cylinder head, using seal installer tool No. J41775, or equivalent.
4. Install valve springs and caps.
5. Compress springs using spring compressor tool No. J8062 and adapter tool No. J41774, or equivalents.
6. Install valve stem keys and hold them in place using suitable grease while removing spring compressor and adapter.
7. Ensure keys seat properly in upper groove.
8. Install lifters.

VALVE COVER

REPLACE

1. Remove mounting bolts, throttle body and gasket.
2. Remove crankcase vent tube adapter.
3. Remove mounting bolts and intake plenum.
4. Remove intake manifold as outlined under "Intake Manifold, Replace."
5. **On lefthand side valve cover,** remove oil filler spout by unlocking tab and twisting counter clockwise.
6. **On lefthand side valve cover,** disconnect camshaft position sensor electrical connection and plastic ties.
7. **On both valve covers,** remove spark plug boots from spark plugs and wires from routing retainers.
8. Remove knock sensor wire harness bracket nut and valve cover mounting bolts.
9. Remove valve cover. **Ensure all eight sealing O-rings are accounted for.**

VALVE GUIDES

Refer to "Component Service" for valve guide service information.

VALVE SEATS

Refer to "Component Service" for valve seat service information.

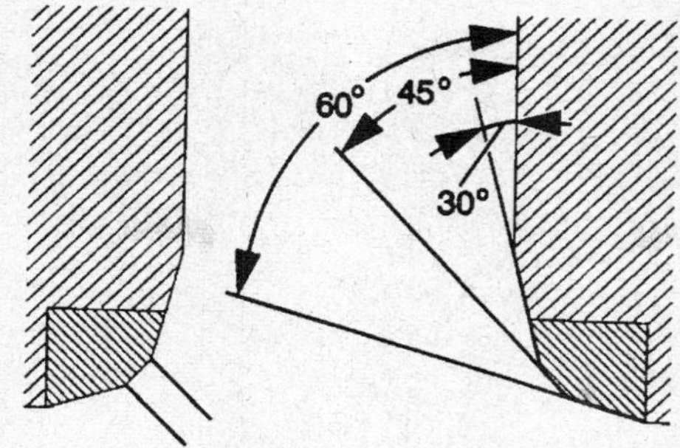

Fig. 7 Valve seat angle

FRONT COVER

REPLACE

Refer to "Timing Belt, Replace" for timing belt front cover replacement procedures.

TIMING BELT

REPLACE

With the timing belt removed, avoid turning the camshaft or crankshaft. If movement is required, exercise extreme caution to avoid valve damage caused by piston contact.

The steps outlined in this procedure are critical in preventing serious engine damage. Adherence to this sequence is imperative.

REMOVAL

1. Disconnect Mass Air Flow (MAF) and Intake Air Temperature (IAT) sensors' electrical connectors.
2. Remove resonance chamber air intake hose from air cleaner housing and MAF sensor.
3. Remove clamp and Idle Air Control (IAC) inlet hose.
4. Remove intake plenum air inlet hoses, switchover valve electrical connector and remaining vacuum connections.
5. Remove mounting nuts and resonance chamber.
6. Remove intake air plenum as outlined under "Intake Manifold, Replace."
7. Raise and support vehicle, then remove mounting bolts and splash shield.
8. Counterhold mounting bolt from alternator back side and remove AIR injection crossover pipe bracket nut.
9. Remove AIR crossover pipe bushing nut from lefthand side of engine bracket.
10. Remove clamps and AIR crossover pipe from rubber hose connections.
11. Lower vehicle.
12. Remove diverter hose clamp and connection, then the AIR crossover pipe.
13. Loosen water and power steering pump pulley mounting bolts, then the harmonic balancer bolts. **Do not remove mounting bolts now.**
14. Remove air conditioning compressor hose support strap bolt from AIR injection crossover bracket.
15. Rotate serpentine belt tensioner pulley clockwise using suitable wrench while sliding belt from water pump pulley.
16. Remove serpentine belt from tensioner and engine.
17. Carefully release retaining tabs and remove wiring harness channel cover.
18. Remove wiring harness from channel. Record routing for installation.
19. Remove mounting bolts and water pump pulley, then the power steering pump pulley and serpentine drive belt tensioner.
20. Remove mounting bolts and harmonic balancer.
21. Remove mounting bolts and front timing belt cover. Replace sealing strip if cracked or torn.
22. Rotate crankshaft clockwise to 60° Before Top Dead Center (BTDC), **Fig. 4.**
23. Install timing belt alignment kit tool No. J42069-10, or equivalent, to crankshaft drive gear, **Fig. 8.**
24. Carefully turn crankshaft clockwise using crank hub Torx socket tool No. J42098, or equivalent, until locking tool lever firmly contacts water pump pulley flange.
25. Secure locking tool's moveable lever to water pump pulley flange.
26. **Ensure crankshaft alignment is not 180° off.**
27. **Camshaft gears alignment marks must align with corresponding notches on timing belt rear cover.**
28. Lock camshaft gears using timing belt alignment kit tool No. J42069-1 and J42069-2, or equivalents, **Fig. 9.** If tools do not fit into camshaft gear teeth, proceed as follows:
    a. Loosen appropriate timing belt idler pulley.
    b. Turn eccentric until tool can be inserted.
    c. Tighten idler pulley to specifications.
29. Loosen timing belt tensioner and remove timing belt. **Do not remove locking tools while belt is removed.**

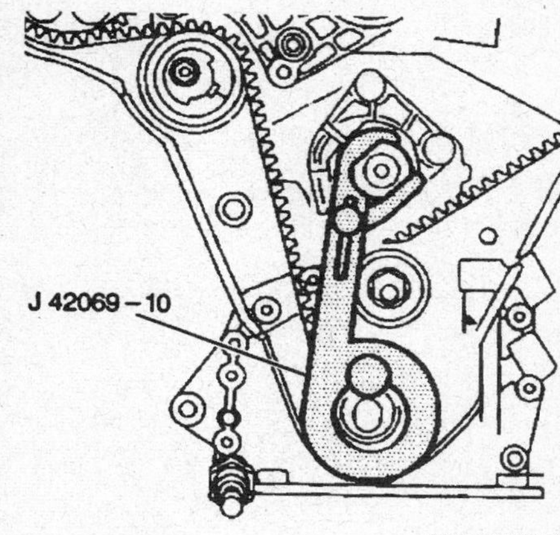

Fig. 8 Crankshaft installation

INSTALLATION

Wait until the engine has cooled off before installing a new timing belt.

1. Start installing timing belt at crankshaft drive gear (1), **Fig. 10.**
2. Install timing belt with double dash

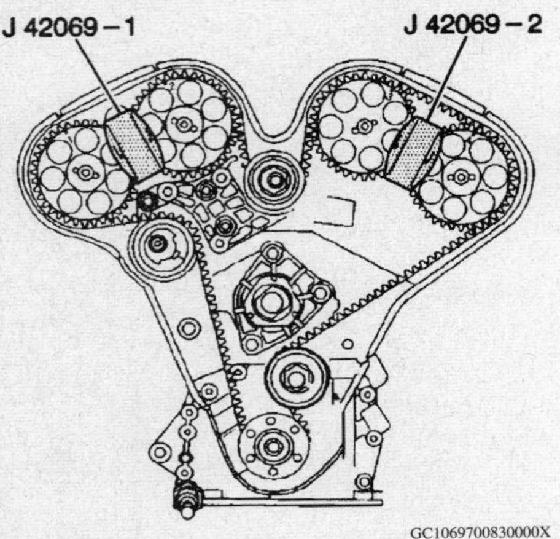

Fig. 9 Locking camshaft gears

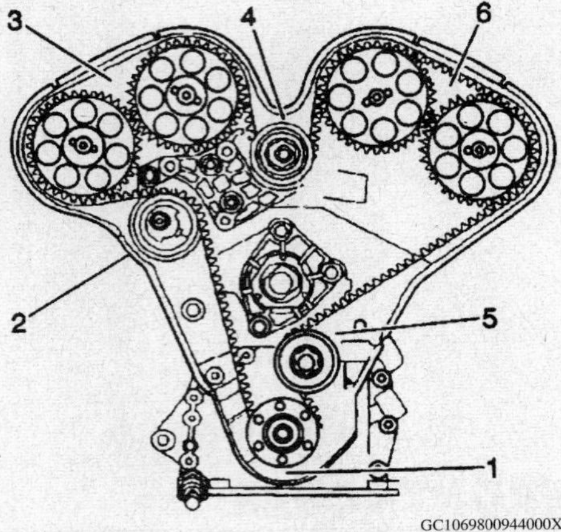

Fig. 10 Timing belt installation sequence

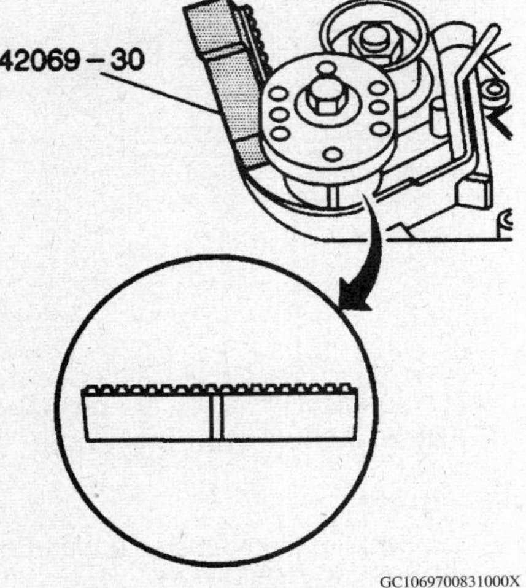

Fig. 11 Timing belt to gear alignment

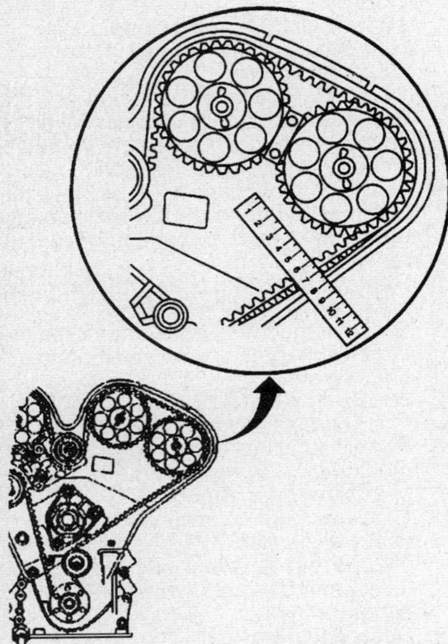

Fig. 12 Measuring timing belt deflection

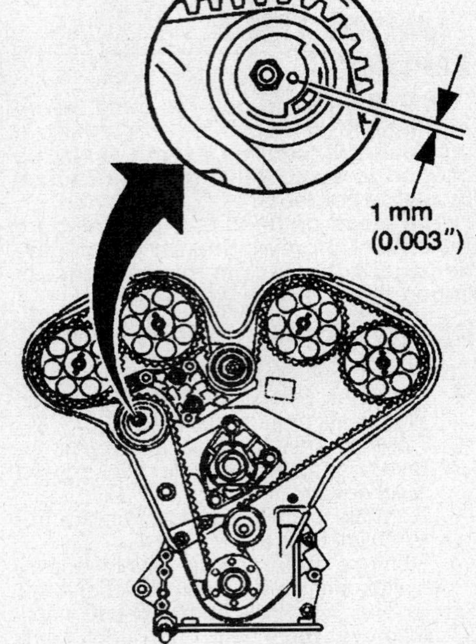

Fig. 13 Initial timing belt tensioner alignment

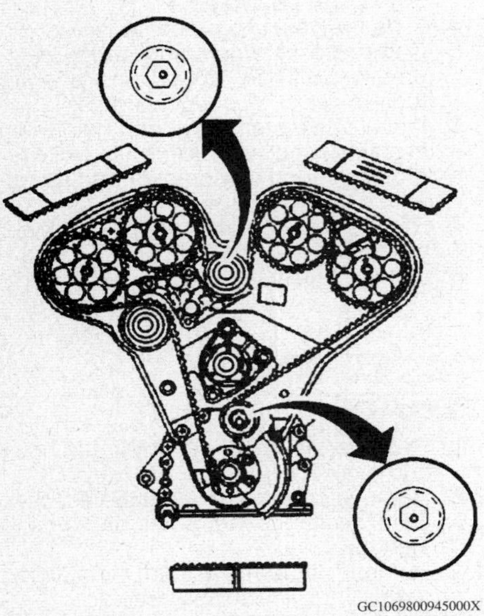

Fig. 14 Timing belt & sprocket alignment marks

(TDC) mark aligned with oil pump and belt drive gear marks, **Fig. 11.**

3. Pinch timing belt to prevent splines from jumping using timing belt alignment kit tool No. J42069-30, or equivalent.
4. Route timing belt through timing belt tensioner (2).
5. Slip timing belt through camshaft sprockets one and two simultaneously (3). Ensure any timing belt dash marks align with camshaft gears' marks and rear cover notches.
6. Route timing belt through camshafts 1 and 2 idler pulley (4).
7. Route timing belt through camshafts 3 and 4 idler pulley (5).
8. Slip timing belt through camshaft sprockets 3 and 4 simultaneously (6). Ensure any timing belt dash marks align with camshaft gears' marks and rear cover notches.
9. Measure timing belt deflection between camshaft gear 4, and camshaft gears 3 and 4 idler pulley, **Fig. 12.**
10. Timing belt deflection should not be more than .4 inch. If timing belt deflection is not is not within specifications, proceed as follows:
    a. Rotate camshafts 3 and 4 timing belt idler pulley eccentric counterclockwise until high point of eccentric is at approximately 12 o'clock position using timing belt alignment kit tool No. No. J42069-40, or equivalent.
    b. Tighten pulley lock bolt until snug while holding eccentric using suitable tool.
11. Apply tension to timing belt at camshafts 1 and 2 idler pulley by turning eccentric high point to approximately nine o'clock position.
12. Apply initial tension to timing belt by turning tensioner eccentric counterclockwise to full stop using suitable hex wrench.
13. Turn eccentric back until reference mark is .04 inch over flange, **Fig. 13.**
14. Tighten tensioner locknut until snug. **Do not fully tighten now.**
15. Inspect timing belt alignment marks to ensure they align with sprockets' reference marks, timing belt rear cover and oil pump housing, **Fig. 14.**
16. Remove tools.
17. Rotate engine two revolutions in clockwise direction stopping at 60° BTDC using crank hub Torx socket tool No. J42098, or equivalent.
18. Install crankshaft locking tool No. J42069-10, or equivalent, to crankshaft drive sprocket.
19. Turn crankshaft until crankshaft locking tool lever firmly contacts water pump pulley flange. Secure tool lever

to water pump pulley flange.

20. Inspect camshaft sprockets reference marks' alignment with rear timing belt cover notches and reference marks' alignment of crankshaft drive gear and oil pump housing. **Timing belt alignment marks will no longer be aligned with camshaft sprockets marks.**
21. Inspect camshaft sprockets 3 and 4, camshaft sprockets 1 and 2 alignment using checking gauge tool No. J420969-20, or equivalent. Reference marks on camshaft sprockets must match exactly with checking gauge marks.
22. If sprocket timing marks are aligned with checking gauge marks, proceed to next step. If sprocket timing marks are not aligned with checking gauge marks, refer to "Timing" procedure.
23. Loosen timing belt tensioner eccentric locknut.
24. Turn eccentric counterclockwise to full stop. Back off eccentric until reference mark is .078–.157 inch above flange reference mark, **Fig. 15.**
25. Tighten timing belt tensioner eccentric locknut to specifications.
26. Hold camshaft 1 and 2, and 3 and 4 tensioner eccentrics in place using adjusting wrench tool No. J42069-40, or equivalent. Tighten idler pulley bolts to specifications.
27. Ensure camshafts 3 and 4 idler pulley eccentric high point is at approximately 12 o'clock position.
28. Ensure camshafts 1 and 2 idler pulley eccentric high point is at approximately nine o'clock position.
29. Remove checking gauge and crankshaft locking tools.
30. Rotate engine in clockwise two revolutions to 60° BTDC.
31. Lock crankshaft drive sprocket using crankshaft locking tool No. J42069-10, or equivalent.
32. Turn crankshaft until crankshaft locking tool lever firmly contacts water pump pulley flange. Secure tool lever to water pump pulley flange.
33. Inspect camshaft sprockets reference marks' alignment with rear timing belt cover notches and reference marks' alignment of crankshaft drive gear and oil pump housing. **Timing belt alignment marks will no longer be aligned with camshaft sprockets marks.**
34. Inspect camshaft sprockets 3 and 4, camshaft sprockets 1 and 2 alignment using checking gauge tool No. J420969-20, or equivalent. Reference marks on camshaft sprockets must match exactly with checking gauge marks.
35. If sprocket timing marks are aligned with checking gauge marks, proceed to next step. If sprocket timing marks are not aligned with checking gauge marks, refer to "Timing" procedure.
36. Remove tools.
37. Install harmonic balancer and tighten mounting bolts to specifications.
38. Install timing belt front cover and tighten mounting bolts to specifications.

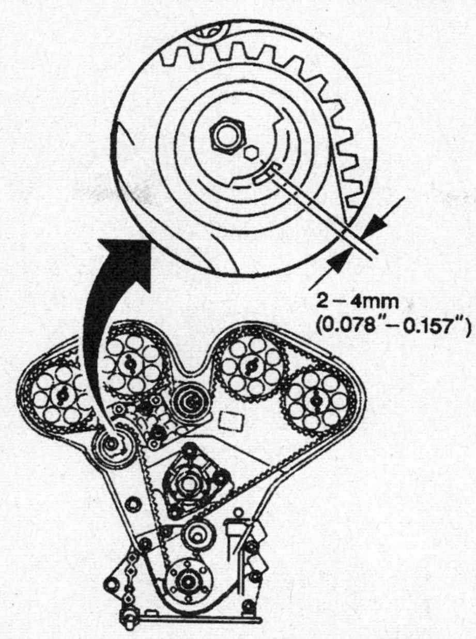

Fig. 15 Timing belt tensioner alignment

39. Install serpentine drive belt tensioner and tighten mounting bolts to specifications.
40. Install power steering pump pulley and tighten mounting bolts snugly.
41. Install water pump pulley and tighten mounting bolts snugly.
42. Route wiring harness into channel and cover.
43. Rotate tensioner clockwise using suitable wrench and install serpentine drive belt. Install over water pump pulley last.
44. Ensure serpentine drive belt is aligned in proper drive pulley grooves.
45. Install air conditioner hose strap bolt and tighten to specifications.
46. Tighten water and power steering pump's pulleys' mounting bolts to specifications.
47. Install AIR diverter hose connections and clamps.
48. Raise and support vehicle.
49. Install AIR crossover pipe into rubber hose connections with clamps.
50. Install AIR crossover pipe bushing nut and tighten to specifications.
51. Install AIR crossover pipe support bracket nut to alternator bolt while counterholding alternator bolt. Tighten mounting nut to specifications.
52. Install splash shield and mounting bolts. Ensure bolts are fully seated and not stripped.
53. Lower vehicle.
54. Install intake plenum, as required.
55. Install pin into rubber mount and resonance chamber. Tighten mounting nuts to specifications.
56. Install switchover valve electrical connector and vacuum hoses.
57. Install intake plenum air inlet hoses, then the IAC inlet hose and clamp.
58. Install resonance chamber air intake hose to air cleaner housing and MAF sensor.
59. Install IAT and MAF sensors' electrical connectors.

TIMING

The following procedure is a continuation of the "Timing Belt, Replace" procedure. **Always start adjustment with camshafts 3 and 4. Be ready to make several repeated adjustments and engine revolutions to arrive at the proper timing belt alignment set points.**

Inspection

1. Inspect alignment of camshaft sprockets 3 and 4, then camshaft sprockets 1 and 2 using checking gauge tool No. J420969-20, or equivalent.
2. Camshaft sprockets' reference marks must match exactly with checking gauge marks.
3. If sprocket timing marks are not aligned with checking gauge marks, refer to the following applicable procedures.

3 & 4 Camshaft Sprocket Marks Align To Left Of Checking Gauge

1. Loosen camshaft sprockets 3 and 4 timing belt idler pulley lock bolt.
2. Turn idler pulley eccentric counterclockwise using adjustment wrench tool No. J42060-40, or equivalent, until camshaft sprocket and checking gauge marks align, **Fig. 16.**
3. Idler pulley eccentric high point will be at approximately 12 o'clock position.
4. Tighten idler pulley bolt to specifications using adjusting wrench tool No. J42069-40, or equivalent, to hold eccentric in place.
5. Remove tools.
6. Rotate engine two clockwise revolutions stopping at 60° BTDC using crank hub Torx socket tool No. J42098, or equivalent.
7. Lock crankshaft drive sprocket using locking tool No. J42069-10, or equivalent.
8. Turn crankshaft until crankshaft locking tool lever firmly contacts water pump pulley flange. Secure tool lever to water pump pulley flange.
9. Inspect camshaft sprockets 3 and 4 alignment using checking gauge tool No. J420969-20, or equivalent.
10. Camshaft sprocket reference marks must match exactly with checking gauge marks.
11. If sprocket timing marks are aligned with checking gauge marks, inspect adjustment of camshaft sprockets 1 and 2. If sprocket timing marks are not aligned with checking gauge marks, repeat procedure.
12. After all timing belt timing adjustments have been completed, proceed to "Tensioner Adjustment" procedure.

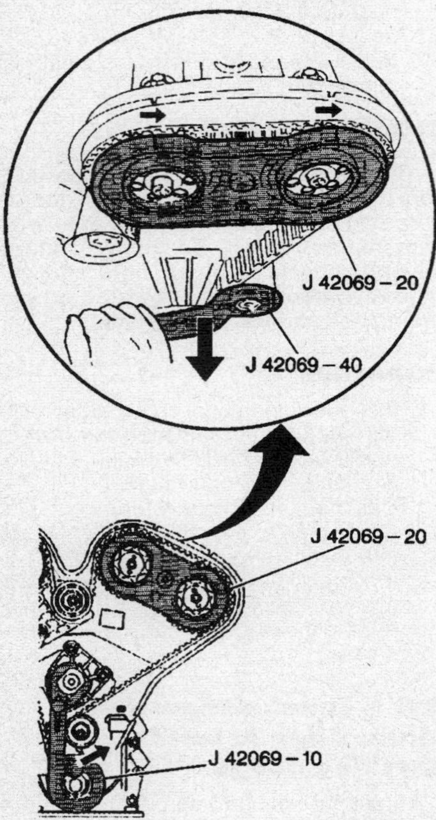

Fig. 16 Camshaft sprockets 3 & 4 mark aligns to left adjustment

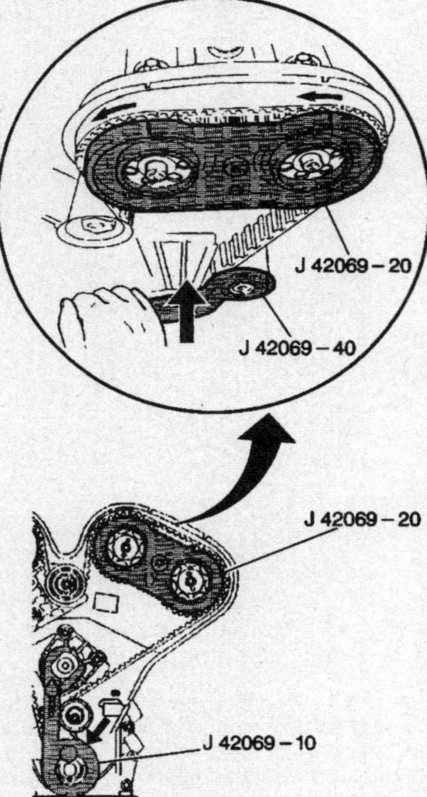

Fig. 17 Camshaft sprockets 3 & 4 aligns to right adjustment

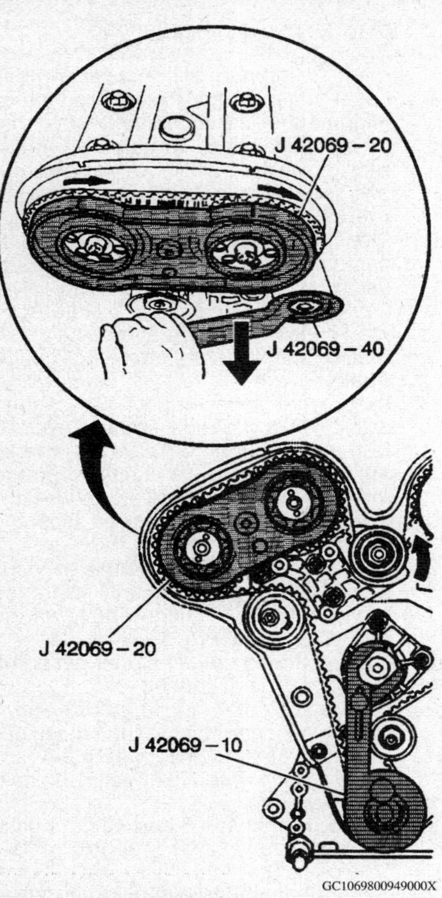

Fig. 18 Camshaft sprockets 1 & 2 aligns to left adjustment

3 & 4 Camshaft Sprocket Marks Align To Right Of Checking Gauge

1. Loosen camshaft sprockets 3 and 4 timing belt idler pulley lock bolt.
2. Turn idler pulley eccentric clockwise using adjustment wrench tool No. J42060-40, or equivalent, until camshaft sprocket and checking gauge tool marks align, **Fig. 17.**
3. Idler pulley eccentric high point will be at approximately 12 o'clock position.
4. Tighten idler pulley bolt to specifications using adjusting wrench tool No. J42069-40, or equivalent, to hold eccentric in place.
5. Remove tools.
6. Rotate engine two clockwise revolutions stopping at 60° BTDC using crank hub Torx socket tool No. J42098, or equivalent.
7. Lock crankshaft drive sprocket using locking tool No. J42069-10, or equivalent.
8. Turn crankshaft until crankshaft locking tool lever firmly contacts water pump pulley flange. Secure tool lever to water pump pulley flange.
9. Inspect camshaft sprockets 3 and 4 alignment using checking gauge tool No. J420969-20, or equivalent.
10. Camshaft sprocket reference marks must match exactly with checking gauge marks.
11. If sprocket timing marks are aligned with checking gauge marks, inspect adjustment of camshaft sprockets 1 and 2. If sprocket timing marks are not aligned with checking gauge marks, repeat procedure.
12. After all timing belt timing adjustments have been completed, proceed to "Tensioner Adjustment" procedure.

1 & 2 Camshaft Sprocket Marks Align To Left Of Checking Gauge

1. Loosen camshaft sprockets 1 and 2 timing belt idler pulley lock bolt.
2. Turn idler pulley eccentric counterclockwise using adjustment wrench tool No. J42060-40, or equivalent, until camshaft sprocket and checking gauge marks align, **Fig. 18.**
3. Idler pulley eccentric high point will be at approximately nine o'clock position.
4. Tighten idler pulley bolt to specifications using adjusting wrench tool No. J42069-40, or equivalent, to hold eccentric in place.
5. Remove tools.
6. Rotate engine two clockwise revolutions stopping at 60° BTDC using crank hub Torx socket tool No. J42098, or equivalent.
7. Lock crankshaft drive sprocket using locking tool No. J42069-10, or equivalent.
8. Turn crankshaft until crankshaft locking tool lever firmly contacts water pump pulley flange. Secure tool lever to water pump pulley flange.
9. Inspect camshaft sprockets 3 and 4 alignment using checking gauge tool No. J420969-20, or equivalent.
10. Camshaft sprocket reference marks must match exactly with checking gauge marks.
11. If sprocket timing marks are aligned with checking gauge marks, inspect adjustment of camshaft sprockets 1 and 2. If sprocket timing marks are not aligned with checking gauge marks, repeat procedure.
12. After all timing belt timing adjustments have been completed, proceed to "Tensioner Adjustment" procedure.

1 & 2 Camshaft Sprocket Marks Align To Right Of Checking Gauge

1. Loosen camshaft sprockets 3 and 4 timing belt idler pulley lock bolt.
2. Turn idler pulley eccentric clockwise using adjustment wrench tool No. J42060-40, or equivalent, until camshaft sprocket and checking gauge tool marks align, **Fig. 19.**
3. Idler pulley eccentric high point will be at approximately nine o'clock position.
4. Tighten idler pulley bolt to specifications using adjusting wrench tool No. J42069-40, or equivalent, to hold eccentric in place.
5. Remove tools.

6. Rotate engine two clockwise revolutions stopping at 60° BTDC using crank hub Torx socket tool No. J42098, or equivalent.
7. Lock crankshaft drive sprocket using locking tool No. J42069-10, or equivalent.
8. Turn crankshaft until crankshaft locking tool lever firmly contacts water pump pulley flange. Secure tool lever to water pump pulley flange.
9. Inspect camshaft sprockets 3 and 4 alignment using checking gauge tool No. J420969-20, or equivalent.
10. Camshaft sprocket reference marks must match exactly with checking gauge marks.
11. If sprocket timing marks are aligned with checking gauge marks, inspect adjustment of camshaft sprockets 1 and 2. If sprocket timing marks are not aligned with checking gauge marks, repeat procedure.
12. After all timing belt timing adjustments have been completed, proceed to "Tensioner Adjustment" procedure.

Tensioner Adjustment

This procedure is the completion of installing and/or adjusting the timing belt. **Do not perform these steps as a stand-alone operation.**

1. Lock crankshaft at TDC using locking tool No. J42069-10, or equivalent, and loosen timing belt tensioner eccentric locknut.
2. Turn eccentric counterclockwise to full stop. Back off eccentric until reference mark is .078–.157 inch above flange reference mark, **Fig. 15.**
3. Tighten timing belt tensioner eccentric locknut to specifications.
4. If not done previously, hold camshaft 3 and 4, and 1 and 2 tensioner eccentrics in place using adjusting wrench tool No. J42069-40, or equivalent and tighten idler pulley bolts to specifications.
5. Ensure camshafts 3 and 4 idler pulley eccentric high point is at approximately 12 o'clock position.
6. Ensure camshafts 1 and 2 idler pulley eccentric high point is at approximately nine o'clock position.
7. Remove checking gauge and crankshaft locking tool.
8. Rotate engine clockwise two revolutions to 60° BTDC.
9. Turn crankshaft until crankshaft locking tool lever firmly contacts water pump pulley flange. Secure tool lever to water pump pulley flange.
10. Inspect camshaft sprockets reference marks' alignment with rear timing belt cover notches and reference marks' alignment of crankshaft drive gear and oil pump housing. **Timing belt alignment marks will no longer be aligned with camshaft sprockets marks.**
11. Inspect camshaft sprockets 3 and 4, camshaft sprockets 1 and 2 alignment using checking gauge tool No. J420969-20, or equivalent. Reference marks on camshaft sprockets must match exactly with checking gauge marks.
12. If sprocket timing marks are aligned with checking gauge marks, no further adjustment is required. If sprocket timing marks are not aligned with checking gauge marks, repeat procedures.

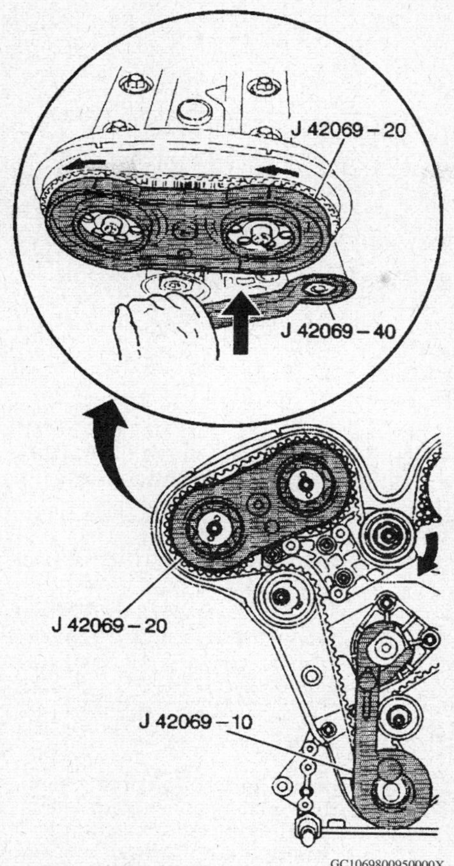

Fig. 19 Camshaft sprockets 1 & 2 aligns to right adjustment

CAMSHAFT

REPLACE

REMOVAL

1. Remove intake plenum as outlined under "Intake Manifold, Replace."
2. Remove resonance chamber as outlined under "Engine, Replace" and appropriate valve cover as outlined under "Valve Cover, Replace."
3. Remove timing belt and front cover as outlined under "Timing Belt, Replace."
4. Turn crankshaft counterclockwise to 60° BTDC, **Fig. 4.**
5. Remove gear bolt using camshaft gear locking tool Nos. J42069-1 and J42069-2, or equivalents, to lock gears in place.
6. Remove camshaft gear, noting the following:
   a. If righthand intake (No. 2) camshaft is being serviced, ensure camshaft pin points toward 11 o'clock position.
   b. If lefthand intake (No. 3) camshaft is being serviced, ensure camshaft pin points toward seven o'clock position.
   c. If lefthand exhaust (No. 4) camshaft is being serviced, ensure camshaft pin points toward 12 o'clock position and disconnect camshaft sensor electrical connector.
   d. Ensure camshaft is under no pressure from lifters.
7. Starting from center and moving outward in spiral pattern, remove camshaft bearing cap bolts and caps.
8. Remove camshaft with seal and separate seal from shaft.

INSTALLATION

1. Lubricate camshaft lobes and lifter contact points with lubricant P/N 12345501, or equivalent.
2. Lubricate bearing surfaces with assembly fluid P/N 1052367, or equivalent.
3. If installing righthand exhaust (No. 1) camshaft, ensure camshaft pin points toward one o'clock position before installing bearing caps.
4. If installing righthand intake (No. 2) camshaft, ensure camshaft pin points toward 11 o'clock position before installing bearing caps.
5. If installing lefthand intake (No. 3) camshaft, ensure camshaft pin points toward seven o'clock position before installing bearing caps.
6. If installing lefthand exhaust (No. 4) camshaft, ensure camshaft pin points toward 12 o'clock position before installing bearing caps.
7. Apply Loctite sealant P/N 573, or equivalent, to bearing cap forward edges prior to installation. **Prevent sealant from entering oil journal.**
8. Position bearing caps over camshafts with reference marks in proper locations, **Figs. 20 and 21. Ensure L coded caps are installed on passenger's side and R coded caps are installed on driver's side.**
9. Tighten camshaft bearing cap bolts to specifications in spiral pattern, starting from center bolts and moving outward.
10. If installing lefthand exhaust (No. 4) camshaft, connect camshaft sensor electrical connector.
11. Coat lip of camshaft seal with suitable chassis grease and tap into place using camshaft seal installer tool No. J35268-A, or equivalent. Ensure seal is seated completely and evenly.
12. Ensure camshaft pins are properly positioned, **Fig. 22,** then install camshaft gear using new bolt.
13. Install camshaft gear locking tool Nos. J42069-1 and J42069-2, or equivalents, to prevent gear rotation while tightening bolt.
14. Tighten camshaft gear bolt as follows:
    a. **Torque** camshaft gear bolt to 37 ft. lbs.
    b. Tighten bolt an additional 60°.
    c. Finally, tighten bolt an additional 15°.
15. Turn crankshaft clockwise to Top Dead Center (TDC) position using crank hub socket tool No. J42098, or equivalent.

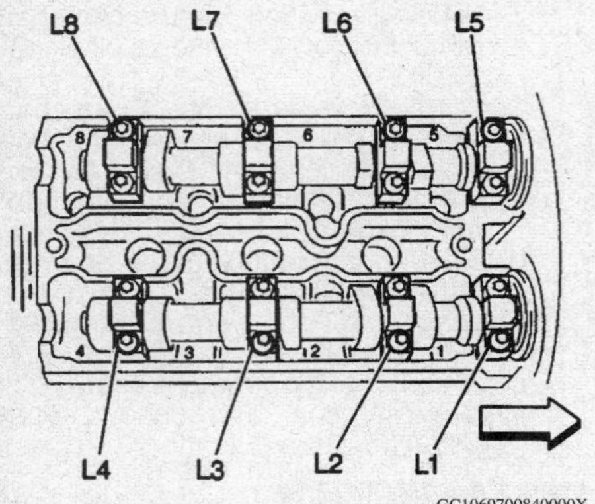

Fig. 20 Righthand bank camshaft bearing cap reference marks

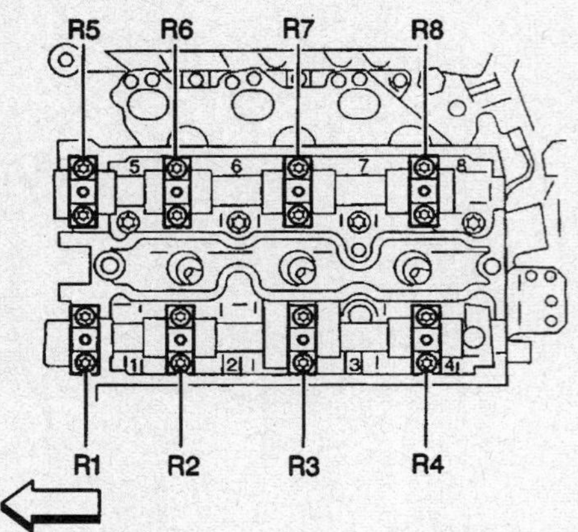

Fig. 21 Lefthand bank camshaft bearing cap reference marks

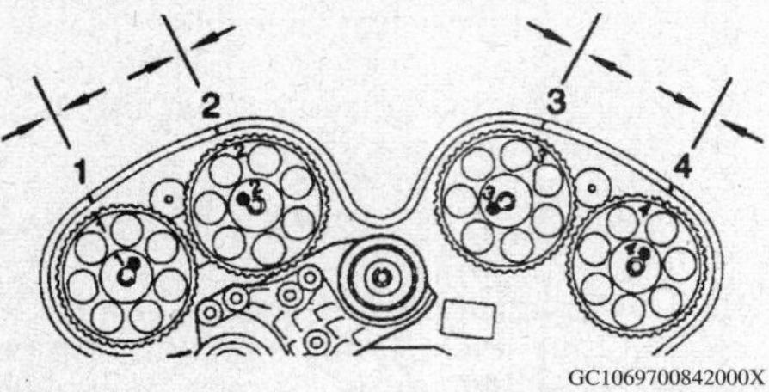

Fig. 22 Camshaft pin orientation

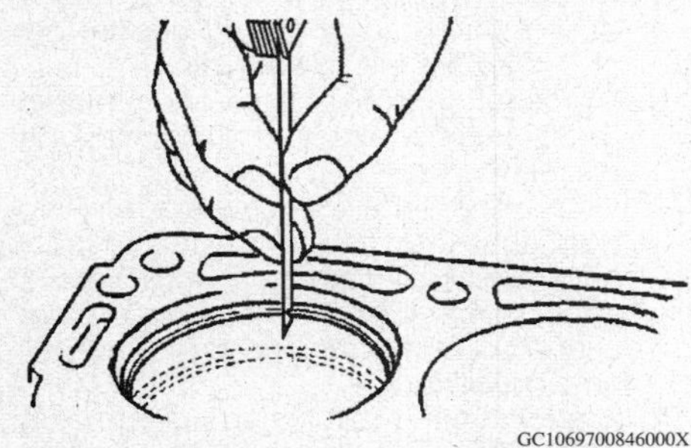

Fig. 24 Piston ring end gap measurement

CYLINDER BORE	PISTON SIZE
(8) 85.976 - 85.985 mm (3.3848 - 3.3852 inch)	(8) 85.940 - 85.950 mm (3.3834 - 3.3838 inch)
(99) 85.985 - 85.995 mm (3.3852 - 3.3856 inch)	(99) 85.950 - 85.960 mm (3.3838 - 3.3842 inch)
(00) 85.995 - 86.005 mm (3.3856 - 3.3860 inch)	(00) 85.960 - 85.970 mm (3.3842 - 3.3846 inch)
(01) 86.005 - 86.015 mm (3.3860 - 3.3864 inch)	(01) 85.970 - 85.980 mm (3.3846 - 3.3850 inch)
(02) 86.015 - 86.025 mm (3.3864 - 3.3868 inch)	(02) 85.980 - 85.990 mm (3.3850 - 3.3854 inch)
† (7 + 0.5) 86.465 - 86.475 mm (3.4041 - 3.4045 inch)	† (7 + 0.5) 86.430 - 86.440 mm (3.4027 - 3.4031 inch)

GC1069700845000X

Fig. 23 Piston selection chart

16. Install and adjust timing belt as outlined under "Timing Belt, Replace."
17. Install timing belt front cover as outlined under "Timing Belt, Replace."
18. Install valve cover as outlined under "Valve Cover, Replace."
19. Install resonance chamber as outlined under "Engine, Replace" and intake plenum as outlined under "Intake Manifold, Replace."
20. Connect battery ground cable.

PISTON & ROD ASSEMBLY

REMOVAL

1. With engine removed and only crankshaft, pistons and rods remaining in block, turn crankshaft until rod bearing cap bolts are accessible.
2. Remove rod bearing cap bolts, cap and insert.
3. Drive piston and rod assembly from block using suitable wooden block.
4. If piston and connecting rod are to be separated, refer to "Pistons, Pins & Rings."

INSTALLATION

1. With piston rings installed and oriented as outlined under "Pistons, Pins & Rings," install guide pin tool No. J41742, or equivalent, in connecting rod end.
2. Install upper rod bearing on rod.
3. Coat piston, rings, cylinder bore and bearing surfaces with Engine Oil Supplement (EOS) P/N 1052368, or equivalent.
4. Compress piston rings using ring compressor tool No. J8037, or equivalent, then gently tap piston into cylinder bore while guiding connecting rod onto crankshaft. **Ensure arrow mark on top of piston faces front of engine.**
5. Remove rod guide pin tool and install connecting rod cap with bearing. **Ensure bumps on connecting rod and cap face rear of engine.**
6. Install new connecting rod cap bolts and tighten bolts alternately as follows:
   a. **Torque** bolts to 26 ft. lbs.
   b. Tighten bolts an additional 45°.
   c. Finally, tighten bolts an additional 15°.

PISTONS, PINS & RINGS

1. If cylinders have been honed, proper size piston must be selected for each bore. Measure cylinder bore after honing and select corresponding piston size, **Fig. 23.**
2. If piston must be separated from connecting rod, note the following:
   a. Heat end of connecting rod to facilitate piston pin replacement.
   b. Press piston pin out of and into piston and connecting rod using press tool No. J24086-C, or equivalent.
   c. When assembling piston and rod, ensure arrow mark on top of piston and bumps on connecting rod face in opposite directions.
   d. Piston arrow mark will face front of engine, while connecting rod bumps will face rear.
3. Measure piston pin bore to piston pin clearance. Maximum clearance is .0003 inch. Replace piston and pin if clearance is more than specifications.
4. After cylinders have been honed, inspect piston ring end gap clearances as follows:
   a. Install compression rings in cylinder bore and measure gap, **Fig. 24.**
   b. Gap should be .0118–.0196 inch.
   c. Install oil control ring in cylinder bore and measure gap.
   d. Gap should be .0157–.0551 inch.
   e. Rings should be replaced if end gap is not as indicated.
5. Inspect piston ring groove clearance, **Fig. 25,** noting the following:
   a. Compression ring groove clearances should be .0008–.0015 inch.
   b. Oil control ring groove clearance should be .0004–.0012 inch.
   c. Replace piston if groove clearance is not as specified.
6. When rings are installed on piston, they must be properly positioned, **Fig. 26.**

MAIN & ROD BEARINGS

MAIN BEARING CLEARANCE INSPECTION

1. Select piece of gauging plastic that is full width of crankshaft bearing and place on journal, **Fig. 27.**
2. Measure all five bearing clearances simultaneously. **Do not turn crankshaft with gauging plastic installed between journal and crankshaft bearing.**
3. Install bearing caps and torsional bearing bridge in original positions.
4. Tighten main bearing cap bolts as follows:
   a. **Torque** main bearing cap bolts to 37 ft. lbs.
   b. Tighten bolts an additional 60°.
   c. Finally, tighten bolts an additional 15°.
5. Tighten torsional bearing bridge bolts

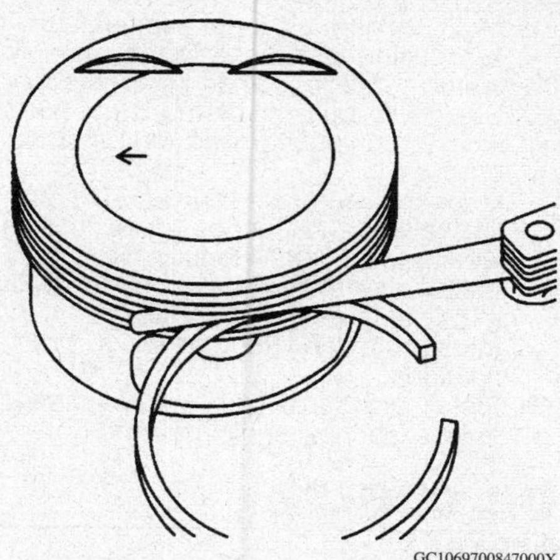

GC1069700847000X

Fig. 25 Piston ring groove clearance measurement

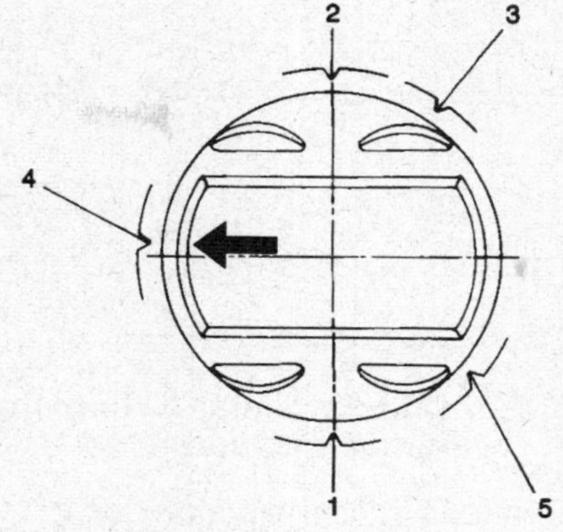

(1) 1st Compression Ring End Gap Location
(2) 2nd Compression Ring End Gap Location
(3) Oil Control Ring Upper Ring End Gap Location
(4) Oil Control Ring Spacer End Gap Location
(5) Oil Control Ring Lower Ring End Gap Location

GC1069700848000X

Fig. 26 Piston ring orientation

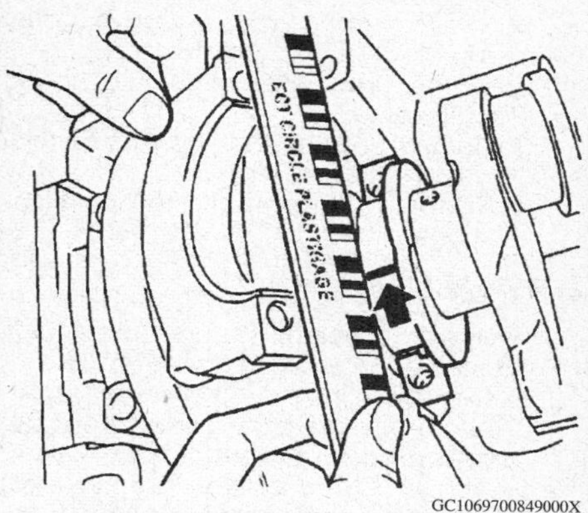

GC1069700849000X

Fig. 27 Main journal gauging plastic installation

to specifications, then remove bearing bridge and bearing caps for gauging plastic inspection.

6. Measure gauging plastic at widest point with scale provided in plastic gauge kit.
7. Bearing clearance should be .0006–.0017 inch.
8. Crankshaft main journal diameter should be 2.6763–2.6766 inches (green) or 2.6766–2.6770 inches (brown).
9. If gauging plastic indicates excessive clearance or clearance irregularity exceeding .0010 inch and crankshaft main journal diameter is as indicated, use standard size bearings. **Always replace upper and lower crankshaft bearings as set.**
10. If specified clearance cannot be achieved with standard bearing, grind crankshaft again and use undersize bearing, available in .010 and .020 inch undersizes.

ROD BEARING CLEARANCE INSPECTION

If the lower half of the connecting rod bearing is worn or damaged, both halves should be replaced. Clearance must be measured at each connecting rod bearing to determine proper sizes, as factory installed bearing sizes may vary between journals.

Using Gauging Plastic

Perform this procedure with pistons and connecting rods installed in engine block. Refer to "Piston & Rod Assembly" for installation procedure.

1. Select piece of gauging plastic that is full width of crankshaft rod bearing and place on journal, **Fig. 28.**
2. Install rod bearing cap in original position. **Do not turn crankshaft while gauging plastic is between journal and bearing.**
3. Tighten bearing cap bolts as outlined under "Piston & Rod Assembly," then remove bearing caps.
4. Measure gauging plastic at widest point using scale provided in plastic gauge kit.

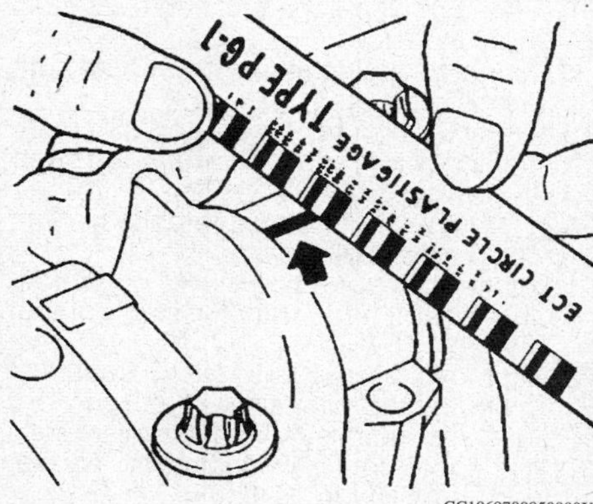

GC1069700850000X

Fig. 28 Rod bearing gauging plastic installation

5. Connecting rod bearing clearance should be .0005–.0024 inch.
6. Connecting rod journal diameter should be 1.927–1.928 inches.
7. If gauging plastic indicates excessive clearance or clearance irregularity exceeding .0010 inch and connecting rod journal diameter is satisfactory, use standard size bearing. **Always replace upper and lower bearings as set.**
8. If proper clearance cannot be achieved using standard size bearings, grind crankshaft again and use undersize bearings, available in .010 and .020 inch undersizes.

Using Micrometer

1. Install connecting rod bearings into rod and cap.
2. Install cap and tighten bolts as outlined under "Piston & Rod Assembly."
3. Measure inside diameter of connecting rod bearings in at least two places 90° apart.
4. Remove bearings and measure connecting rod inside diameter if diameter varies more than .0012 inch.
5. Replace rod if variance is still more than .0012 inch.
6. If diameter does not vary more than .0012 inch, connecting rod is satisfactory.
7. Subtract rod bearing journal diameter from rod bearing inside diameter to obtain bearing clearance.
8. If bearing clearance is not as indicated, replace bearings with new, standard size bearings and measure clearance once again.
9. If clearance is still not as indicated, grind crankshaft again and use undersize bearings.

CRANKSHAFT REAR OIL SEAL

REPLACE

1. Remove transmission as outlined under "Engine, Replace."
2. Hold crankshaft in position and remove flexplate bolts using crank hub socket tool No. J42098, or equivalent.
3. Remove flexplate and center punch rear oil seal steel ring.
4. Carefully drill small, shallow pilot hole into steel ring and thread in self-tapping screw.
5. Pull on screw using suitable pliers and extract oil seal from block.
6. Reverse procedure to install, noting the following:
   a. Coat lip of seal with suitable chassis grease prior to installation.
   b. Install seal using rear main oil seal installer tool No. J42067, or equivalent.

OIL PAN

REPLACE

LOWER

1. Raise and support vehicle, then remove mounting bolts and splash shield.
2. Drain engine oil into suitable container.
3. Disconnect oil level sensor and remove electrical connector C-clip from upper oil pan.
4. Remove mounting bolts and lower oil pan from upper.
5. Pull oil level sensor electrical connector from upper oil pan.

6. Remove mounting bolts and oil level sensor.
7. Reverse procedure to install, noting the following:
   a. Install new oil pan gasket and oil level sensor O-ring.
   b. Tighten oil pan bolts to specifications.

UPPER

1. Remove lower oil pan as previously described.
2. Remove engine mount lower nuts from frame bracket. **Record alignment tab orientation for installation.**
3. Remove air condition compressor hose strap bolt from upper oil pan front.
4. Remove four transmission mounting bolts from upper oil pan.
5. Remove all but four corner upper oil pan mounting bolts.
6. Mark propeller shaft for installation alignment, then remove mounting bolts and slide shaft rearward. Secure propeller shaft in place.
7. Remove catalytic converter mounting bolts from hanger bracket and nuts from exhaust manifold.
8. Lower catalytic converter and secure using suitable mechanic wire.
9. Remove two idler arm mounting bolts from frame and lower relay rod out of way.
10. Lower vehicle.
11. Support and raise engine using support fixture tool No. J28467-A, engine support fixture adapter tool No. J28467-450 and lift bracket tools No. J36857, or equivalents. **Do not damage surrounding components.**
12. Raise and support vehicle.
13. Remove remaining upper oil pan mounting bolts.
14. Remove mounting bolts and oil intake pipe.
15. Remove upper oil pan toward vehicle front. **Do not damage aluminum mating surfaces.**
16. Remove rubber seal and RTV sealant.
17. Thoroughly clean oil pan housing and engine block.
18. Reverse procedure to install, noting the following:
    a. Apply bead of silicone sealing compound No. 12346286, or equivalent, in upper oil pan groove bottom.
    b. **Keep bead at least .4 inch from bolt holes.**
    c. **Oil pan must be installed within 10 minutes of applying sealant.**
    d. Install new seal.
    e. Tighten mounting bolts to specifications.

OIL PUMP

REPLACE

1. Drain engine coolant into suitable container.
2. Remove resonance chamber as outlined under "Engine, Replace" and timing belt as outlined under "Timing Belt, Replace."
3. Remove rear timing belt cover, install crank hub holding tool No. J42065, or equivalent.

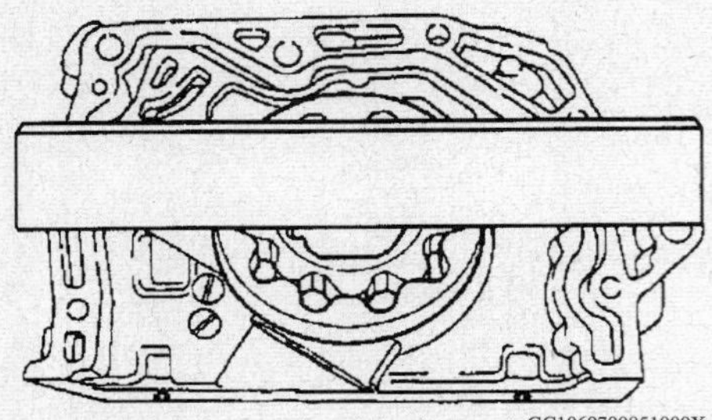

Fig. 29 Oil pump gear to housing clearance measurement

4. Remove crankshaft drive gear bolt using crank hub socket tool No. J42098, or equivalent.
5. Remove crankshaft drive gear and lower alternator bolt.
6. Raise and support vehicle, then remove splash shield and drain engine oil into suitable container.
7. Remove oil pan as outlined under "Oil Pan, Replace."
8. Remove engine mount lower nuts from frame bracket.
9. Remove oil intake pipe and air conditioning compressor hose support strap bolt.
10. Remove oil pan housing bolts leaving four corner bolts in place.
11. Make corresponding marks on propeller shaft and transmission output flange.
12. Remove propeller shaft to transmission flange bolts, slide shaft rearward and secure away from transmission.
13. Remove catalytic converter hanger bolts and lower vehicle.
14. Raise engine slightly and support using support fixture tool No. J28467-A, or equivalent.
15. Raise and support vehicle.
16. Remove remaining mounting bolts, oil pan housing and gasket.
17. Remove mounting bolts and pump.
18. Remove oil pump front main oil seal.
19. Reverse procedure to install, noting the following:
    a. Tighten mounting bolts to specifications.
    b. Install front main oil seal using oil seal installer tool No. J35268-A, or equivalent.
    c. Apply sealant P/N 12345997, or equivalent, to engine block and oil pump joints.
    d. Install crank hub holding tool No. J42065, or equivalent.
    e. Install new crankshaft drive gear bolt and **torque** to 184 ft. lbs.
    f. Finally, tighten gear bolt an additional 15°.
    g. Adjust timing belt as outlined under "Timing Belt, Replace."

OIL PUMP SERVICE

1. Remove oil pump pressure regulating valve plug, seal, valve and spring.
2. Remove oil pump pressure relief valve plug, seal, spring and valve.
3. Remove mounting bolts and oil pump cover, then inner and outer gears.
4. Measure oil pump inner and outer gear to housing clearance using suitable feeler gauge and straightedge, **Fig. 29.** Maximum clearance is .003 inch for inner gear and .004 inch for outer gear.
5. Inspect oil pressure regulating and relief valves and springs for excessive wear and damage. Replace if required.
6. Install inner and outer gears with marks facing cover, **Fig. 30.**
7. Install cover and tighten bolts to specifications.
8. Install pressure relief and regulating valves, springs, seals and plugs.

OIL COOLER

REPLACE

1. Remove intake plenum and manifold as outlined under "Intake Manifold, Replace."
2. Drain engine coolant and oil into suitable containers.
3. Disconnect coolant temperature sensor and sender electrical connectors.
4. Disconnect throttle body and heater inlet hoses at coolant bridge.
5. Remove mounting bolts and upper seals.
6. Remove engine coolant bridge and lower seals.
7. Loosen lefthand exhaust manifold upper heat shield bolts.
8. Disconnect oil feed and return lines at oil cooler.
9. Raise and support vehicle.
10. Remove lefthand catalytic converter and exhaust pipe.
11. Remove oil filter, crank sensor and engine oil cooler line clamp.
12. Disconnect and remove oil feed and return lines at engine block
13. Lower vehicle.
14. Remove oil cooler inlet and outlet nuts, cover and cooler.
15. Reverse procedure to install, noting the following:
    a. Apply .08 inch bead of silicone sealer P/N 12345997, or equivalent, to oil cooler cover groove in place of original seal.
    b. Install new seals on oil cooler oil feed and return line fittings.
    c. Tighten fittings, mounting bolts and nuts to specifications.

BELT TENSION DATA

The serpentine drive belt tensioner features wear indicator marks, **Fig. 31.** These should be used to determine if belt tension is sufficient.

SERPENTINE DRIVE BELT

BELT REPLACEMENT

1. Raise and support vehicle.
2. Remove splash shield, air conditioning compressor hose strap bolt and Secondary Air Injection (AIR) crossover pipe bracket nut. Use suitable back-up wrench on alternator bolt.

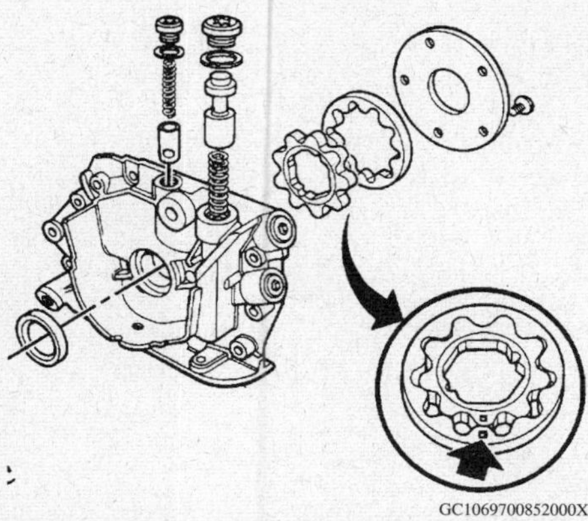

Fig. 30 Oil pump gear orientation

3. Remove AIR crossover pipe bushing nut from bracket and crossover pipe from rubber hose connections. Move pipe aside to gain working clearance.
4. Turn tensioner pulley clockwise, to release serpentine belt tension, then slide belt off pulleys.
5. Reverse procedure to install, noting the following:
   a. Route belt properly, **Fig. 32.**
   b. Turn tensioner clockwise to easy installation..
   c. Install belt over water pump pulley last.

TENSIONER REPLACEMENT

1. Remove serpentine drive belt as outlined under "Belt Replacement" and remove tensioner bolts.
2. Remove tensioner.
3. Reverse procedure to install. Tighten tensioner bolts to specifications.

COOLING SYSTEM BLEED

The cooling system will bleed automatically during engine warm-up. If reservoir is not full, it may be required to add coolant after the engine has cooled.

THERMOSTAT

REPLACE

1. Drain engine coolant into suitable container.
2. Remove intake plenum as outlined under "Intake Manifold, Replace."
3. Remove intake manifold bolts as outlined under "Intake Manifold, Replace."
4. Lift and support manifold while removing seals.
5. Disconnect radiator inlet hose at thermostat outlet pipe and remove pipe.
6. Remove mounting bolts, housing and thermostat.
7. Remove seal ring.
8. Reverse procedure to install, noting the following:
   a. Install new thermostat seal ring.
   b. Tighten mounting bolts to specifications.
   c. Install new intake manifold seal.

WATER PUMP

REPLACE

1. Drain engine coolant into suitable container.
2. Remove resonance chamber as outlined under "Engine, Replace."
3. Remove timing belt front cover as outlined under "Timing Belt, Replace."
4. Remove mounting bolts and water pump.
5. Reverse procedure to install. Tighten water pump bolts to specifications.

RADIATOR

REPLACE

1. Remove battery.
2. Remove upper radiator covers and drain engine coolant into suitable container.
3. Remove resonance chamber as outlined under "Engine, Replace."
4. Disconnect primary cooling fan and cooling fan control switch electrical connectors.
5. Disconnect air bleed hose and transmission oil cooler pipes at radiator. Remove pipe seals.
6. Disconnect coolant hose at secondary auxiliary coolant pump and remove Secondary Air Injection (AIR) cutoff valve bracket bolts from fan housing.
7. Remove condenser to radiator bracket bolts, then disconnect radiator inlet and outlet hoses.
8. Disconnect secondary auxiliary coolant pump electrical connector.
9. Lift radiator and primary fan assembly away from radiator support using rocking motion.
10. Remove upper retainers, primary fan and cooling fan control switches from radiator.
11. Reverse procedure to install. Tighten cooling fan control switches, primary fan bolts and oil cooler pipe fittings to specifications.

FUEL PUMP

REPLACE

The fuel pump is located inside the modular fuel sender. Refer to "Electrical" section for fuel pump relay location.

1. Relieve fuel system pressure as outlined under "Precautions."
2. Drain fuel tank into suitable container using suitable hand operated pump.
3. Raise and support vehicle.
4. Remove rear bumper fascia and rear frame support.
5. Disconnect fuel feed line at fuel filter and fuel return line near filter.
6. Disconnect fuel tank breather and vent hoses, and fuel sender electrical connector.
7. Support fuel tank supported.
8. Remove tank mounting strap front bolts and both straps.
9. Lower fuel tank and disconnect Evaporative Emission (EVAP) tank pressure sensor connector.

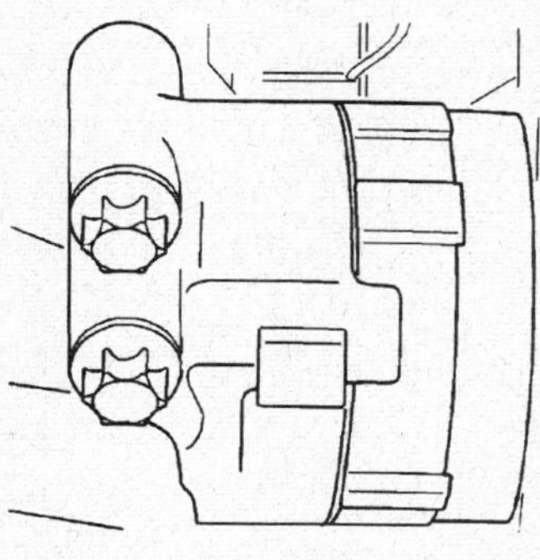

Serpentine Drive Belt Tension Sufficient

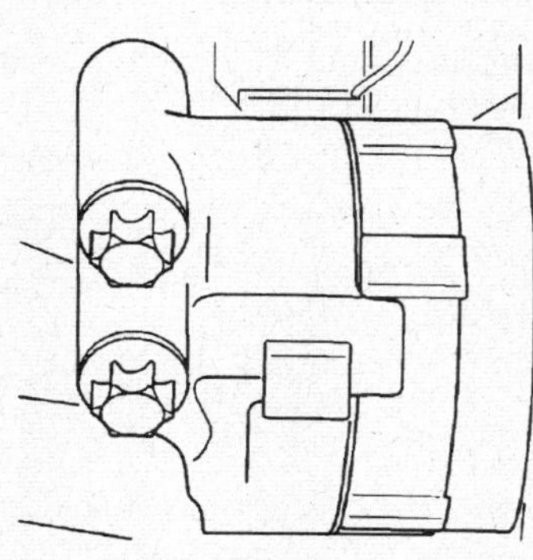

Serpentine Drive Belt Tension Insufficient (Replace Belt)

GC1069700854000X

Fig. 31 Serpentine drive belt tensioner wear indicator

10. Remove spring loaded clamp at fuel tank boot, sending unit and wiring harness from tank using fuel tank sender wrench tool No. J42219, or equivalent.
11. Remove seal from sending unit cover and drain fuel from sender reservoir into suitable container.
12. Remove fuel level sensor from sender and disconnect fuel feed hose at fuel pump.
13. Disconnect fuel pump electrical connectors.
14. Remove damper ring and fuel pump.
15. Remove fuel pump bracket and strainer.
16. Reverse procedure to install, noting the following:
   a. Install new fuel pump strainer and sending unit lip seal.
   b. Apply thin film of oil to inner diameter of lip seal prior to installation.
   c. Tighten fuel tank sender nut and fuel tank straps to specifications.

FUEL FILTER

REPLACE

1. Relieve fuel system pressure as outlined under "Precautions."
2. Grasp filter firmly and remove fuel line fitting bolts.
3. Loosen fuel filter mounting strap and remove filter.
4. Reverse procedure to install.

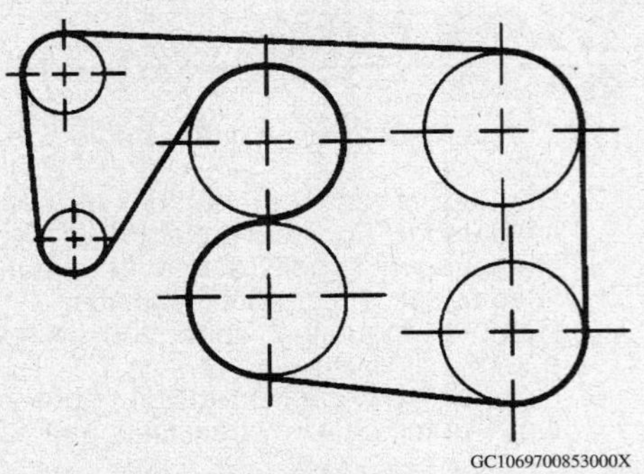

Fig. 32 Serpentine drive belt routing

TIGHTENING SPECIFICATIONS

Year	Component	Torque/Ft. Lbs.
1998–2001	Accelerator & Cruise Control Cable Bracket	72②
	Accessory Bracket	30
	Air Conditioning Compressor Bracket	30
	Air Conditioning Compressor Hose Support Strap	72②
	AIR Injection Crossover Pipe Bushing	108②
	AIR Injection Crossover Pipe Support Bracket	30
	AIR Injection Pipe	15
	Alternator	30
	Camshaft Bearing Cap	72②
	Camshaft Gear	③
	Catalytic Converter	15
	Connecting Rod Caps	⑤
	Coolant Bridge	22
	Cooling Fan Control Switches	16
	Crank Sensor	72②
	Crankshaft Drive Gear	⑥
	Cylinder Head	①
	Cylinder Head Cover	72②
	Engine Mount Lower Nut	41
	Engine Mount Upper Nut	30
	Exhaust Manifold	15
	Exhaust Manifold Heat Shield	72②
	Flexplate To Torque Converter	22
	Fuel Tank Sender	37
	Fuel Tank Straps	26
	Harmonic Balancer	15
	Intake Manifold	15
	Intake Manifold Spacer	15
	Intake Plenum	72②
	Intake Plenum Switchover Valve	72②
	Main Bearing Caps	④
	Oil Cooler Cover	22
	Oil Cooler Inlet & Outlet	15
	Oil Feed & Return Lines	22
	Oil Filter	11
	Oil Intake Pipe	72②
	Oil Pan	72②

Continued

TIGHTENING SPECIFICATIONS—Continued

Year	Component	Torque/Ft. Lbs.
1998–2001	Oil Pan Baffle	72②
	Oil Pan Drain Plug	41
	Oil Pan Housing	11
	Oil Pump Cover	72②
	Oil Pump Housing	53②
	Power Steering Pump Pulley	15
	Primary Cooling Fan To Radiator	35②
	Propeller Shaft Coupling	70
	Resonance Chamber	27②
	Serpentine Drive Belt Tensioner	30
	Spark Plug	19
	Thermostat Housing	15
	Thermostat Outlet Pipe	15
	Timing Belt Cover	72②
	Timing Belt Idler Pulley	30
	Timing Belt Tensioner	15
	Timing Belt Tensioner Bracket	30
	Torsional Bearing Bridge	15
	Transmission Crossmember To Body	33
	Transmission Crossmember To Mount	15
	Transmission Housing To Engine Block	44
	Transmission Housing To Engine Oil Pan	15
	Transmission Oil Cooler Pipes To Radiator	18
	Valve Cover	72②
	Water Pump	18
	Water Pump Pulley	72②

AIR — Secondary Air Injection
① — Refer to "Cylinder Head, Replace" for tightening procedure & specifications.
② — Inch lbs.
③ — Refer to "Camshaft, Replace" for tightening procedure & specifications.
④ — Refer to "Main & Rod Bearings" for tightening procedure & specifications.
⑤ — Refer to "Piston & Rod Assembly" for tightening procedure & specifications.
⑥ — Refer to "Oil Pump, Replace" for tightening procedure & specifications.

Rear Axle & Suspension

NOTE: On Air Bag Equipped Models, Refer To "Air Bag System Precautions" Located In The Front Of This Manual For System Disarming & Arming Procedures.

NOTE: Refer To "Computer Relearn Procedures" Located In The Front Of This Manual When Battery Power To The Computer Has Been Interrupted.

INDEX

DESCRIPTION

The rear axle and suspension assembly is fully independent and is isolated from the vehicle body by rubber bushings at all mounting points, **Fig. 1.** The differential is supported by cradle, which is also the mounting point for stabilizer shaft. Sealed tie rod ends and wheel bearings eliminate the need for periodic lubrication.

The two drive axle assemblies are essentially inner and outer Constant Velocity (CV) joints joined by shaft. The CV joints do not require periodic lubrication and, although the outer joint can be serviced independently of the axle, the inner joint and axle shaft are non-serviceable items.

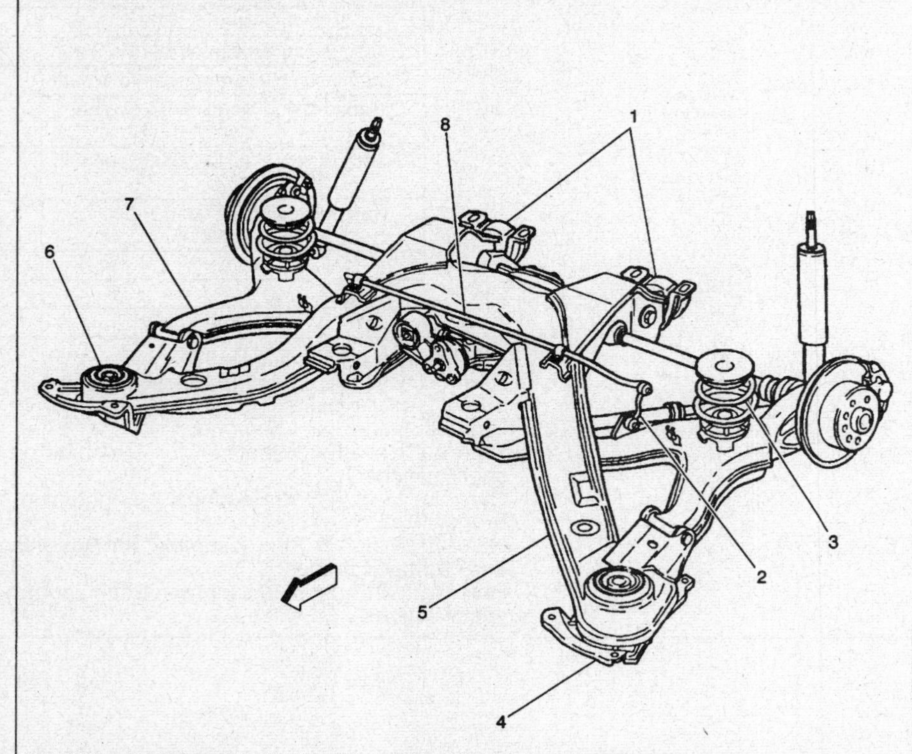

(1) Rear Axle Cradle Mount
(2) Stabilizer Shaft Link
(3) Spring
(4) Rear Axle Support Bushing Flange
(5) Rear Axle Cradle
(6) Rear Axle Support Bushing
(7) Rear Lower Control Arm
(8) Stabilizer Shaft

GC2039700121000X

Fig. 1 Rear axle & suspension assembly

REAR AXLE SHAFT

REPLACE

1. Place gear selector lever in Neutral position, then raise and support vehicle.
2. Remove wheel and install hub flange holding adapter tool No. J42066, or equivalent, on flange using wheel bolts.
3. Hold flange holding adapter tool using suitable ratchet and remove flange bolts.
4. Separate drive axle outer end from wheel bearing hub inner flange.
5. Separate drive axle from differential using drive axle separator tool No. J42071, or equivalent, and suitable hammer. **Ensure beveled side of tool is against differential and not against drive axle.**
6. Reverse procedure to install, noting the following:
   a. Lubricate drive axle spline and seal surfaces with suitable differential lubricant.
   b. Drive axle into differential bore using suitable rubber mallet. **Do not use more force than required to seat axle fully in bore.**
   c. Tighten mounting bolts to specifications.

DIFFERENTIAL CARRIER

REPLACE

1. Raise and support vehicle.
2. Support differential using suitable transmission jack.
3. Disconnect anti-lock brake system electrical connectors and remove drive axles as outlined under "Rear Axle Shaft, Replace."
4. Remove propeller shaft as outlined under "Propeller Shaft, Replace" and coupling.
5. Remove differential support bracket bolts from bracket and bushing bolts

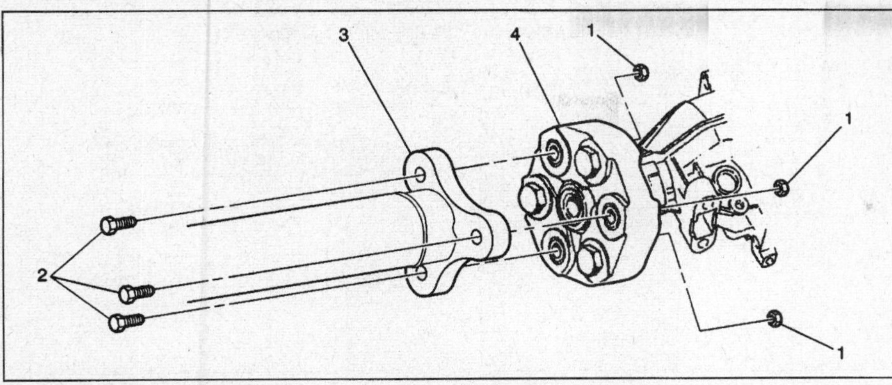

(1) Propeller Shaft Coupling Nut
(2) Propeller Shaft Coupling Bolt
(3) Propeller Shaft
(4) Propeller Shaft Coupling

GC2039700122000X

Fig. 2 Propeller shaft coupling

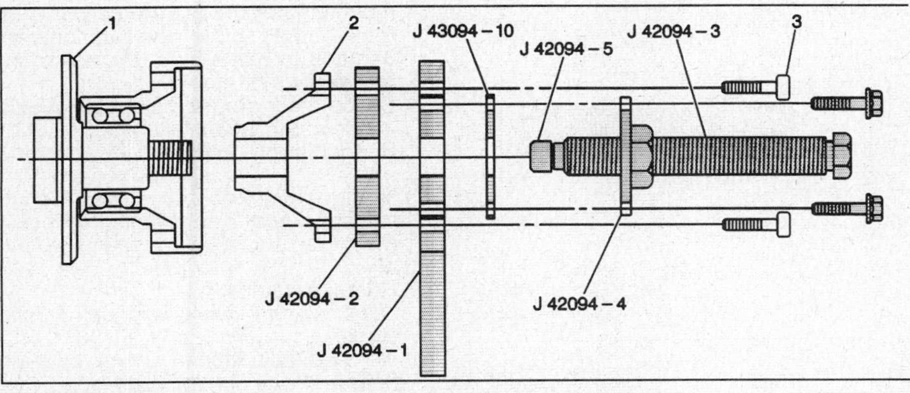

(1) Rear Wheel Hub
(2) Rear Wheel Hub Flange
(3) Driveshaft Bolt

GC2039700123000X

Fig. 3 Hub flange removal tools

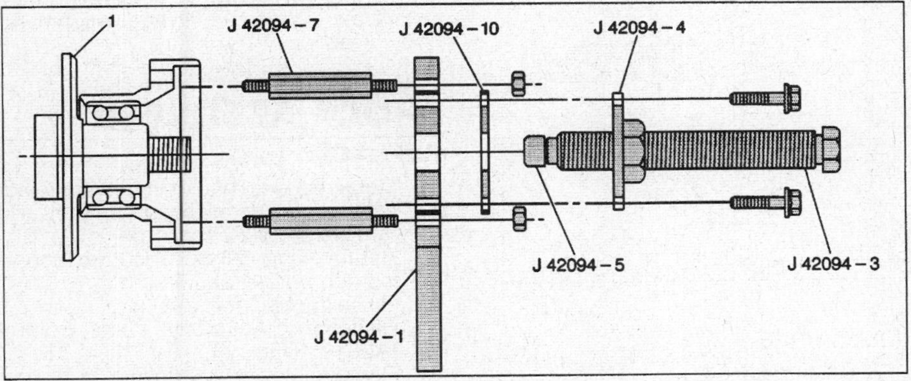

(1) Rear Wheel Hub

GC2039700124000X

Fig. 4 Hub removal tools

from differential.

6. Remove differential carrier.
7. Reverse procedure to install. Tighten differential bushing and support bracket bolts to specifications

PROPELLER SHAFT

REPLACE

1. Place gear selector lever in Neutral position, then raise and support vehicle.
2. Remove heat shields and bolts securing propeller shaft bearing bracket to underbody.
3. Remove front propeller shaft coupling nuts and bolts, **Fig. 2.**
4. Pry front half of shaft rearward until it clears coupling.
5. Remove rear propeller shaft coupling nuts and bolts, then move rear half of shaft forward slightly.
6. Remove shaft by sliding it between exhaust system components and underbody surface.
7. Reverse procedure to install. Tighten front and rear coupling bolts to specifications.

HUB & BEARING

REPLACE

REMOVAL

1. Raise and support vehicle, then remove wheel.
2. Remove driveshaft bolts using holding tool No. J42066, or equivalent, and suitable breaker bar.
3. Separate driveshaft from rear wheel hub flange and suspend in upward direction. **Do not allow shaft to hang freely.**
4. Disengage clip and separate brake pipe from lower control arm.
5. Remove disc brake pads and caliper. Suspend caliper aside. **Do not open hydraulic system.**
6. Loosen setscrew and slide rotor off hub.
7. Back out three of four brake backing plate bolts approximately .47 inch using socket tool No. J42072, or equivalent.
8. Install spacer tool No. J42094-2 and holding fixture tool No. J42094-1, or equivalents, on rear wheel hub flange and remove hub nut.
9. Remove flange from hub using flange removal tools, **Fig. 3.**
10. Press out hub using hub removal tools, **Fig. 4.**
11. If original bearing is to be used again, inspect seal carefully. **Damage may have occur during hub removal.**
12. Remove wheel bearing retaining ring, **Fig. 5.**
13. Remove wheel bearing using wheel bearing removal tools, **Fig. 6.**

INSTALLATION

1. Fully seat bearing using bearing installation tools, **Fig.7.**
2. Install wheel bearing retaining ring, **Fig. 5,** then assemble hub installation tools, **Fig. 8.**
3. Ensure installer tool is on wheel bearing inner ring.
4. Ensure threaded driver tool is properly centered inside wheel bearing to prevent hub from binding as it is drawn into bearing.
5. Adjust threaded spacer pins as required.
6. Draw hub into bearing by holding threaded driver and turning arbor clockwise.
7. Remove tool assembly.
8. Install flange on hub using flange installation tools, **Fig. 9. Ensure splines are properly aligned.**
9. Remove arbor, driver and thrust bearing tools, leaving holding fixture and spacer in place.
10. Install rear wheel hub nut and tighten to specifications. Remove holding fixture and spacer tools.
11. Install retaining washer and stake to hub.

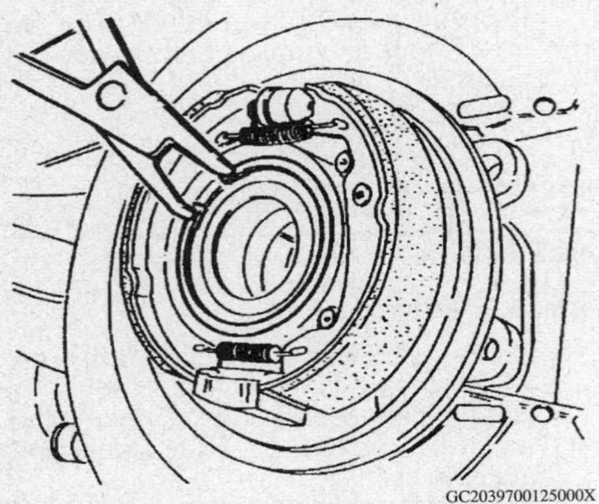

Fig. 5 Wheel bearing retaining ring replacement

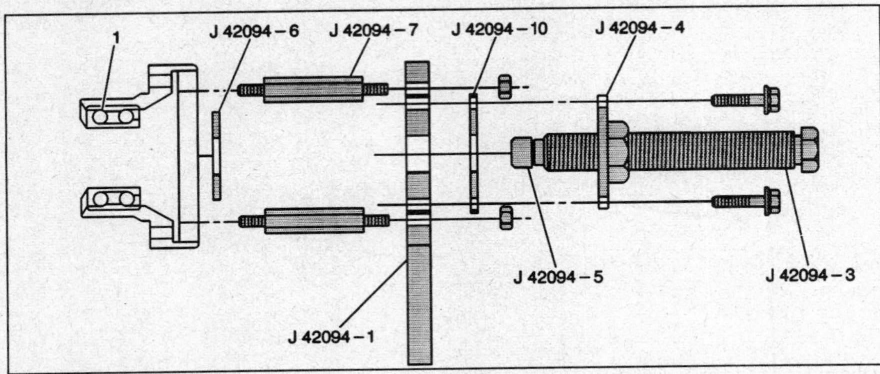

Fig. 6 Wheel bearing removal tools

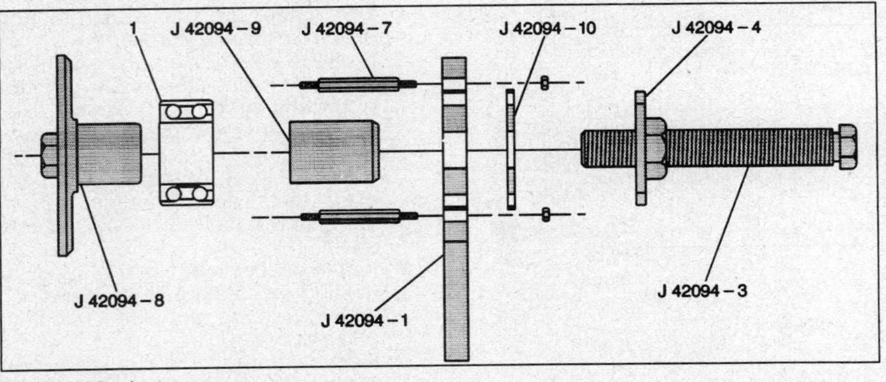

Fig. 7 Wheel bearing installation tools

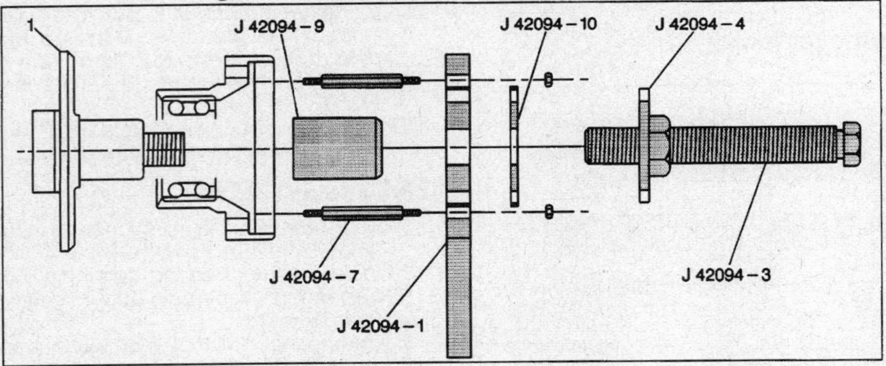

Fig. 8 Hub installation tools

12. Tighten brake backing plate bolts to specifications.
13. Install brake rotor and tighten setscrew to specifications.
14. Install caliper and secure brake pipe to lower control arm with clip.
15. Connect driveshaft to rear wheel hub flange and install bolts.
16. Tighten driveshaft bolts to specifications.
17. Install wheel and lower vehicle.

REAR SUSPENSION

REPLACE

The following procedure is for removal of the differential and axle cradle as a unit. If required, the differential can be replaced independently as outlined under "Differential Carrier, Replace."

1. Raise and support vehicle, allowing working clearance around rear axle support flange bolts.
2. Remove rear wheels and disconnect wheel speed sensor electrical connectors.
3. Remove propeller shaft disc joint bolts from rear differential flange and disconnect exhaust system at rubber body mounts.
4. Disengage clips and separate brake pipes from lower control arms.
5. Release parking brake cables from actuator brackets.
6. Remove disc brake pads and caliper mounting bolts, separate caliper from rotor and suspend aside to prevent damage to brake pipe. **Do not open hydraulic system.**
7. Scribe mark around perimeter of axle cradle mount for installation.
8. Support cradle and each lower control arm.
9. Remove shock absorber lower mounting bolts and cradle mounting bolts. Pivot cradle to allow for spring removal.
10. Remove springs.
11. Lower vehicle while supporting axle cradle.
12. Remove axle support flange, bushing bolts and axle cradle.
13. Reverse procedure to install, noting the following:
    a. Tighten mounting bolts to specifications.
    b. Inspect and adjust wheel alignment as outlined in "Wheel Alignment" section.

SHOCK ABSORBER

REPLACE

1. Move rear seat backrest forward to access upper shock absorber mount and remove protective cap from tower.
2. Remove upper shock absorber mounting nut, washer and grommet.
3. Raise and support vehicle.
4. Disconnect Automatic Level Control (ALC) air line.
5. Remove lower mounting bolt and shock absorber.
6. Reverse procedure to install. Tighten mounting nut and bolt to specifications.

COIL SPRING

REPLACE

1. Raise and support vehicle, then disengage clips and separate brake pipes from lower control arms. **Do not open hydraulic system.**
2. Remove stabilizer shaft link bolts and disconnect link at lower control arms.
3. Disengage exhaust system rubber insulators from hangers to gain working

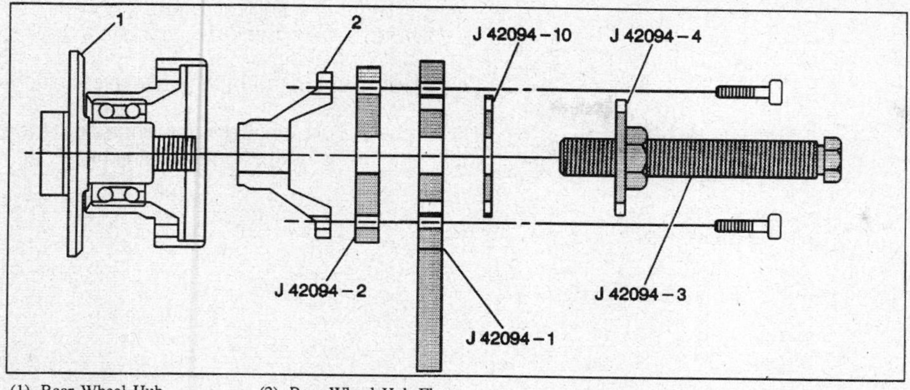

(1) Rear Wheel Hub (2) Rear Wheel Hub Flange

GC2039700129000X

Fig. 9 Hub flange installation tools

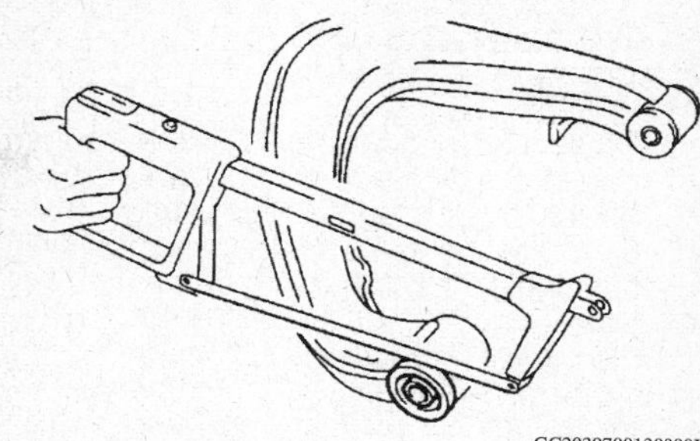
GC2039700130000X

Fig. 10 Control arm bushing collar removal

clearance. **Support exhaust system to prevent damage.**

4. Disconnect rear wheel speed sensor electrical connectors.
5. Support lower control arms.
6. Remove shock absorber lower mount bolt and control arm supports.
7. Support differential.
8. Remove rear axle cradle to vehicle body mounting bolts and lower differential until springs can be removed.
9. Remove spring and seat, then separate seat from spring.
10. Reverse procedure to install.

CONTROL ARM

REPLACE

LOWER

1. Raise and support vehicle, allowing rear axle support flange bolts to remain accessible.
2. Remove wheel and driveshaft bolts while holding rear wheel hub using holding tool No. J42066, or equivalent.
3. Separate driveshaft from rear wheel hub flange and support in upward position. **Do not suspend from spring.**
4. Disengage clip and separate brake pipe from lower control arm.
5. Remove brake pads and caliper.
6. Suspend caliper to prevent brake pipe damage. **Do not open brake hydraulic system.**
7. Loosen setscrew and slide rotor off hub.
8. Release parking brake cable from actuator bracket.
9. Remove hub, flange and bearing as outlined under "Hub & Bearing, Replace."
10. Remove parking brake shoes and related hardware.
11. Remove rear backing plate bolts using socket tool No. J42072, or equivalent, and separate parking brake anchor from rear brake backing plate.
12. Remove backing plate from control arm and disengage exhaust system hangers from rubber body mounts. **Support exhaust system components to prevent damage.**
13. Remove rear outer tie rod nut and outer tie rod from control arm using tie rod puller tool No. J6627-A, or equivalent.
14. Disconnect stabilizer shaft link at control arm and support cradle at differential.
15. Scribe marks around perimeter of cradle mounts for installation and remove cradle to vehicle body mounting bolts.
16. Support lower control arm .
17. Remove lower shock absorber mounting bolt and lower rear cradle to allow for spring removal.
18. Remove rear spring with differential and control arms supported.
19. Lower control arm to access outboard control arm bolt, then remove inboard and outboard control arm bolts.
20. Remove control arm.
21. Reverse procedure to install, noting following:
   a. Tighten mounting bolts and nuts to specifications.
   b. **Torque** steering linkage installer tool No. J42089, or equivalent, to 22 ft. lbs. to seat outer tie rod ball stud taper.
   c. **Install new self-locking tie rod nut.**
   d. Tighten brake backing plate and driveshaft bolts as outlined under "Hub & Bearing, Replace."
   e. Adjust parking brake, as required.
   f. Adjust wheel alignment as outlined in "Wheel Alignment" section.

CONTROL ARM BUSHING

REPLACE

REMOVAL

1. Remove lower control arm as outlined under "Control Arm, Replace."
2. Cut off inboard bushing collar, **Fig. 10.**
3. Cut off outboard control arm rubber collar.
4. Press out bushing using bushing receiver tool No. J21474-5 and lower control arm bushing replacement tool No. J42200, or equivalents.

INSTALLATION

1. Coat new bushings with suitable lubricant and position inboard bushing with collar toward rear differential.
2. Press in new bushing using special tools, **Fig. 11.**
3. Lubricate outboard bushing with silicone spray and press into place, **Fig. 11.**
4. Install lower control arm as outlined under "Control Arm, Replace."

TIE ROD

REPLACE

INNER

1. Raise and support vehicle.
2. Remove inner tie rod bolt from axle cradle.
3. Separate inner tie rod from cradle.
4. Loosen adjuster nut and remove tie rod from adjuster. **Record number of turns required to remove tie rod.**
5. Reverse procedure to install, noting the following:
   a. Thread inner tie rod into adjuster using same number of turns recorded during removal.
   b. Tighten adjuster nut and inner tie rod bolt to specifications.
   c. Adjust wheel alignment as outlined in "Wheel Alignment" section.

OUTER

1. Raise and support vehicle.
2. Remove outer tie rod nut from rear lower control arm.
3. Separate outer tie rod from lower control arm using tie rod puller tool No. J6627-A, or equivalent.
4. Loosen adjuster nut and remove tie rod from adjuster. **Record number of turns required to remove tie rod.**
5. Reverse procedure to install, noting the following:
   a. Thread inner tie rod into adjuster using same number of turns recorded during removal.
   b. Tighten adjuster nut and outer tie rod nut to specifications.
   c. **Torque** steering linkage installer tool No. J42089, or equivalent, to 22 ft. lbs. to seat ball stud taper. **Install new self-locking tie rod nut.**
   d. Adjust wheel alignment as outlined in "Wheel Alignment" section.

STABILIZER SHAFT

REPLACE

1. Raise and support vehicle, then support rear axle cradle at differential.
2. Scribe mark around perimeter of cradle for installation and remove cradle to vehicle body mounting bolts.
3. Lower cradle slightly and remove cradle mount protective shields.
4. Remove stabilizer shaft link bolts from lower control arm and separate link from control arm.
5. Lower cradle and remove bolts from stabilizer shaft mounting brackets.

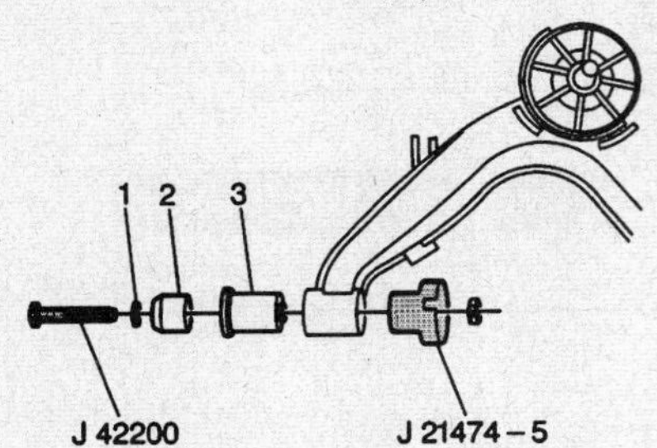

(1) Washer
(2) 30 mm Socket
(3) Bushing

GC2039700131000X

Fig. 11 Control arm bushing installation

6. Remove stabilizer shaft.
7. Reverse procedure to install, noting the following:
   a. Tighten mounting bolts to specifications.
   b. Adjust wheel alignment as outlined in "Wheel Alignment" section.

TIGHTENING SPECIFICATIONS

Year	Component	Torque/Ft. Lbs.
1998–2001	Axle Nut	221
	Brake Backing Plate	37③
	Brake Caliper	59
	Brake Rotor Setscrew	35④
	Differential Bushing To Differential	74
	Differential Support Bracket, Lower	66①
	Differential Support Bracket, Upper	74
	Drive Axle	37②
	Driveshaft Bolts	37⑤
	Driveshaft Nut	221
	Hub Nut	221
	Inner Tie Rod	66
	Lower Control Arm	74
	Outer Tie Rod	44
	Propeller Shaft Bearing Insulator	16
	Propeller Shaft Center Bearing Bracket	15
	Propeller Shaft Couplings	70
	Propeller Shaft Disc Joint To Differential	70
	Rear Axle Cradle Mount To Body	48
	Rear Axle Cradle Mount To Cradle	74
	Rear Axle Filler Plug	15
	Rear Axle Support Bushing	92
	Rear Axle Support Flange	48
	Shock Absorber Lower Mount	81
	Shock Absorber Upper Mount	15
	Stabilizer Shaft Link	15
	Stabilizer Shaft Mounting Bracket	16
	Tie Rod Adjuster	11
	Wheel To Hub	81

①— Tighten an additional 38.°
②— Tighten an additional 67°.
③— Tighten an additional 40.°
④— Inch lbs.
⑤— Tighten an additional 70.°

Front Suspension & Steering

NOTE: On Air Bag Equipped Models, Refer To "Air Bag System Precautions" Located In The Front Of This Manual For System Disarming & Arming Procedures.

NOTE: Refer To "Computer Relearn Procedures" Located In The Front Of This Manual When Battery Power To The Computer Has Been Interrupted.

INDEX

PRECAUTIONS

AIR BAG SYSTEMS

Refer to "Air Bag System Precautions" in the front of this manual for system disarming and arming procedures.

BATTERY GROUND CABLE

Prior to service, disconnect battery ground cable and isolate as required.

DESCRIPTION

The front suspension features McPherson struts with hydraulic bushings in the lower control arms and gas preloaded dampers. The speed sensitive steering system utilizes recirculating ball type steering gear.

HUB, BEARING & SEAL

REPLACE

1. Raise and support vehicle, then remove front wheel.
2. Remove brake pad wear indicator wire and brake hose from strut bracket.
3. Remove caliper bracket from steering knuckle. Suspend caliper aside to prevent brake pipe damage. **Do not open brake hydraulic system.**
4. Loosen set screw and remove brake rotor, dust cap and wheel hub nut.
5. Remove wheel hub, bearing and seal assembly.
6. Reverse procedure to install, noting the following:
   a. Press outer bearing ring into wheel hub using suitable socket, as required.
   b. Remove old locking compound by threading M12 × 1.5 tap through caliper bolt holes.
   c. Install new caliper bolts coated in Threadlocker 272, or equivalent.
   d. Tighten mounting bolts, nuts and setscrews to specifications.

BALL JOINT INSPECTION

The following procedure applies only to the lower control arm ball stud. Before inspecting the ball stud, ensure the corresponding wheel bearing is in satisfactory condition.

1. Raise and support vehicle.
2. Grasp wheel at top and bottom.
3. Move wheel in and out while observing steering knuckle and lower control arm.
4. If steering knuckle moves up and down independently of control arm, proceed as follows:
   a. Inspect steering knuckle pinch bolt area for ball stud slot movement or distortion. Repair as required.
   b. If pinch bolt area is satisfactory but ball stud movement is observed, replace ball stud.
5. If no vertical movement is observed between steering knuckle and control arm while moving wheel, ball stud and slot are satisfactory.

BALL STUD

REPLACE

1. Raise and support vehicle, then remove front wheel.
2. Remove control arm as outlined under "Control Arm, Replace."
3. Drill out ball stud to lower control arm rivet heads and remove stud.
4. Reverse procedure to install, noting the following:
   a. Install ball stud to control arm bolts from upper side of lower control arm.
   b. Tighten bolts to specifications.

COIL SPRING

REPLACE

The coil spring is a component of the strut assembly. Refer to "Strut, Replace" if the entire assembly is to be replaced, or to "Coil Spring & Strut Service" if the spring must be replaced independently.

STRUT

REPLACE

1. Raise and support vehicle, then remove front wheel.
2. Disconnect wheel speed sensor and brake wear indicator electrical connectors, then disengage brake flex hose from clip at strut.
3. Remove caliper bolts and separate caliper from knuckle. Support caliper aside to prevent brake hose damage. **Do not open brake hydraulic system.**
4. Remove stabilizer shaft link nut and separate link from strut.
5. Remove strut lower mounting bolts, lower vehicle and remove upper support plate cap and nut.
6. Remove upper support plate and strut.
7. Reverse procedure to install, noting the following:
   a. Tighten upper support and stabilizer shaft link nuts to specifications.
   b. Install new strut to steering knuckle mounting bolts from front of vehicle toward rear.
   c. Tighten bolts only until snug. Final tightening after wheel alignment procedures have been performed.
   d. Install and tighten caliper as outlined under "Hub, Bearing & Seal, Replace."
   e. Adjust wheel alignment as outlined in "Wheel Alignment" section.
   f. Tighten strut to steering knuckle bolts to specifications.

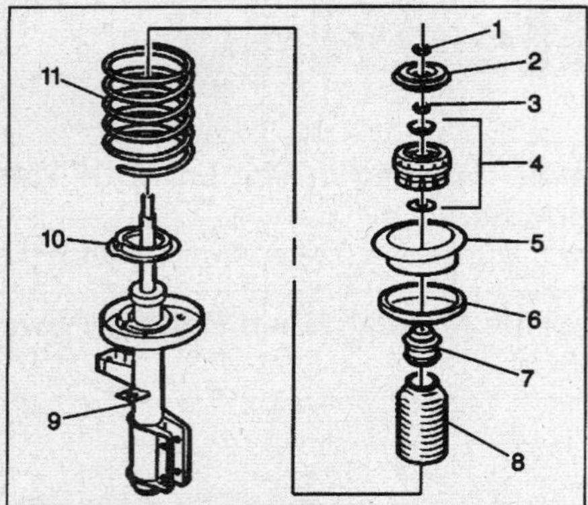

(1) Upper Support Plate Nut
(2) Upper Support Plate
(3) Upper Bearing Support Nut
(4) Bearing and Bearing Plate Assembly
(5) Upper Spring Support Plate
(6) Upper Insulator
(7) Strut Bumper
(8) Strut Cover
(9) Strut
(10) Lower Insulator
(11) Spring

GC2029700219000X

Fig. 1 Coil spring & strut components

COIL SPRING & STRUT SERVICE

1. Place strut in strut spring compressor tool No. J34013-A, or equivalent, with adapter tool No. J34013-88, or equivalent.
2. Prevent strut piston from rotating and remove upper bearing support nut.
3. Compress strut spring, then remove bearing and plate.
4. Release spring and remove upper support plate, insulator, strut bumper and cover, **Fig. 1.**
5. Separate spring from strut and remove lower insulator.
6. Reverse procedure to assemble, noting the following:
   a. **Do not allow coil spring protective coating to be chipped or scratched. Premature spring failure may result.**
   b. Tighten bearing nut to specifications.

CONTROL ARM

REPLACE

LOWER

Removal

1. Raise and support vehicle, then remove front tire and wheel assembly.
2. Separate brake pad wear indicator sleeve from strut and remove wheel speed sensor.
3. Separate brake hose from strut bracket and remove caliper from steering knuckle. Suspend caliper to prevent brake hose damage. **Do not open brake hydraulic system.**
4. Remove outer tie rod ball stud nut, then separate tie rod from knuckle

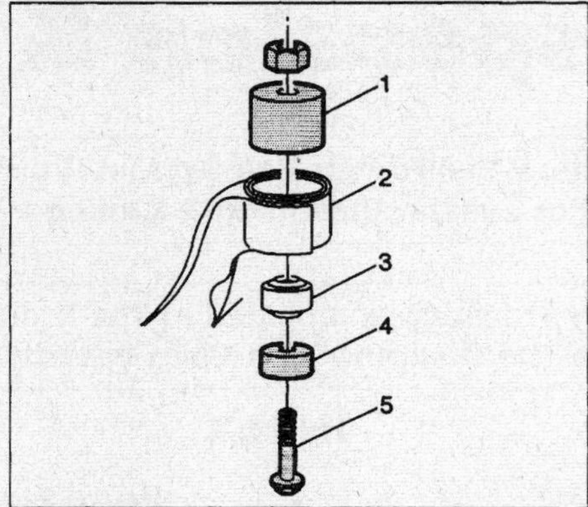

(1) J 42092-1, Receiver
(2) Lower Control Arm
(3) Bushing
(4) J 42092-2, Bushing Remover/Installer Tool
(5) J 42200, Rear Lower Control Arm Bushing Remover/Installer Bolt

GC2029700220000X

Fig. 2 Control arm horizontal bushing replacement

using tie rod separator tool No. J6627-A, or equivalent.
5. Remove stabilizer shaft link nut from shaft and steering knuckle bolts from strut.
6. Remove lower control arm ball stud pinch bolt and separate steering knuckle from ball stud. Allow hub and brake rotor to remain in place.
7. Loosen control arm horizontal and vertical bolts, remove horizontal bolt and turn arm away from support bracket.
8. Remove vertical bolt and control arm.

Installation

1. Install lower control arm and new vertical bolt.
2. Tighten bolt only until snug. Final tightening will occur after horizontal bolt installation.
3. Position front of control arm in support bracket and install new horizontal bolt from rearward side of vehicle.
4. Ensure control arm is in horizontal position and tighten bolts to specifications.
5. Connect steering knuckle to lower control arm ball stud, using new pinch bolt inserted from rear side of vehicle. Tighten pinch bolt to specifications.
6. Connect steering knuckle to strut using new bolts installed from front of vehicle toward rear. Tighten bolts only until snug.
7. Connect stabilizer shaft link to shaft and tighten mounting nut to specifications.
8. Connect outer tie rod to steering knuckle and position linkage installer tool No. J42089, or equivalent, over tie rod ball stud.
9. **Torque** installer tool to 22 ft. lbs. to seat ball stud taper. Remove tool.
10. Install new self-locking tie rod nut and tighten to specifications.
11. Install caliper on steering knuckle as outlined under "Hub, Bearing & Seal, Replace."

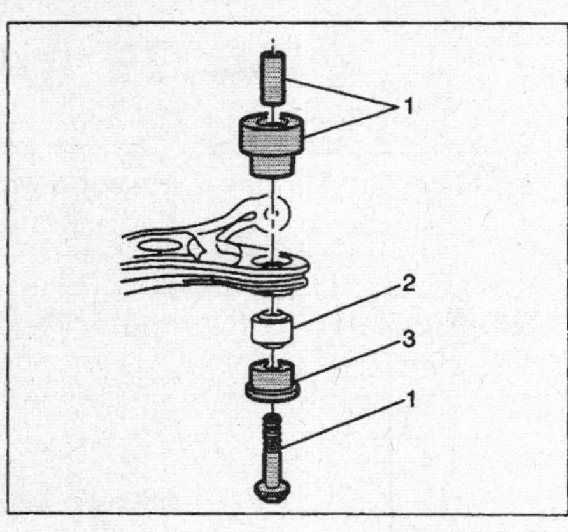

(1) J 21474, Universal Bushing Remover/Installer Kit
(2) Bushing
(3) J 42112-4, Rear Differential Bushing Remover/Installer Tool

GC2029700221000X

Fig. 3 Control arm vertical bushing replacement

12. Attach brake hose to strut bracket, install wheel speed sensor and tighten to specifications.
13. Attach brake pad wear indicator sleeve to strut.
14. Install front wheel and lower vehicle.
15. Adjust wheel alignment as outlined in "Wheel Alignment" section.

CONTROL ARM BUSHING

REPLACE

1. Remove control arm as outlined under "Control Arm, Replace."
2. Press bushing out of control arm using bushing replacement tools turn, **Figs. 2 and 3.**
3. Reverse procedure to install. Ensure bushing is installed flush with control arm.

STEERING KNUCKLE

REPLACE

1. Raise and support vehicle, then remove front wheel.
2. Remove hub as outlined under "Hub, Bearing & Seal, Replace" and brake rotor splash shield.
3. Remove ball stud nut from outer tie rod and separate tie rod from knuckle using tie rod separator tool No. J6627-A, or equivalent.
4. Remove steering knuckle to strut bolts and separate knuckle from strut.
5. Remove lower control arm ball stud pinch bolt and separate knuckle from control arm ball stud.
6. Reverse procedure to install, noting the following:
   a. Install new control arm ball stud pinch bolt and strut to steering knuckle bolts.
   b. Tighten control arm ball stud pinch bolt to specifications.
   c. **Do not tighten strut to steering**

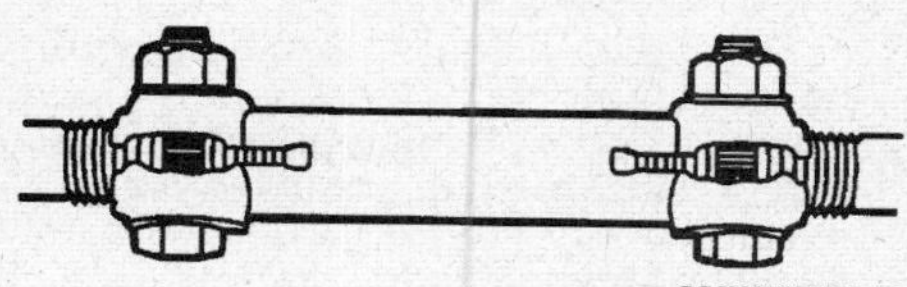

GC6029700117000X

Fig. 4 Tie rod adjuster & clamp orientation

knuckle bolts until wheel alignment is complete.

d. Attach tie rod to knuckle, position linkage using installer tool No. J42089, or equivalent, over tie rod ball stud and **torque** to 22 ft. lbs. to seat taper.
e. Install new self-locking tie rod nut and tighten to specifications.
f. Adjust wheel alignment as outlined in "Wheel Alignment."
g. Tighten strut to steering knuckle bolts as outlined under "Strut, Replace."

STABILIZER BAR

REPLACE

1. Raise and support vehicle.
2. Attach engine support fixture tool No. J28467-A, or equivalent, at engine lift points.
3. Raise and support vehicle, then remove front wheel and tire assemblies.
4. Remove wheel speed sensor and brake wear indicator wires.
5. Remove brake flex hose clips and hose, then the wheel speed sensors.
6. Remove brake caliper and outer tie rods using tie rod/wheel stud puller tool No. J6627-A, or equivalent.
7. Remove lower control arm ball stud pinch bolts and steering knuckles from lower control arm ball studs.
8. Remove stabilizer shaft links from stabilizer shaft and engine mount nuts.
9. Support crossmember frame.
10. Remove mounting bolts and front crossmember frame.
11. Remove insulator bolts and stabilizer shaft.
12. Reverse procedures to install. Tighten bolts to specifications.

STABILIZER BAR BUSHING

REPLACE

Refer to "Stabilizer Bar, Replace" for bar and bushing replacement procedures.

TIE ROD

REPLACE

Never attempt to separate a steering linkage joint by driving a wedge between components.

INNER

1. Raise and support vehicle.
2. Loosen tie rod clamp bolt at end of tie rod adjuster.
3. Remove tie rod ball stud nut and separate ball stud from relay rod using tie rod separator tool No. J6627-A, or equivalent.
4. Remove tie rod from adjuster, counting number of turns for installation reference.
5. Reverse procedure to install, noting the following:
   a. Lubricate tie rod adjuster threads with suitable Extra Pressure (EP) chassis lubricant.
   b. To connect tie rod ball stud to relay rod, position linkage tool No. J42089, or equivalent, over ball stud and **torque** tool to 22 ft. lbs. This will seat taper.
   c. Install new self-locking tie rod ball stud nut and tighten to specifications.
   d. With adjuster and clamps positioned, **Fig. 4,** tighten adjuster clamp bolt to specifications.
   e. Adjust toe as outlined in "Wheel Alignment."

OUTER

1. Raise and support vehicle.
2. Loosen tie rod clamp bolt near tie rod end.
3. Remove tie rod ball stud nut and separate tie rod from knuckle using tie rod puller tool No. J6627-A, or equivalent.
4. Remove tie rod from adjuster, noting the following:
   a. Outer tie rod has lefthand threads.
   b. Count number of turns required to remove tie rod for installation reference.
5. Reverse procedure to install, noting the following:
   a. Lubricate tie rod adjuster threads with Extra Pressure (EP) chassis lubricant.
   b. Connect tie rod ball stud to steering knuckle, position linkage tool No. J42089, or equivalent, over ball stud and **torque** tool to 22 ft. lbs. to seat taper.
   c. Install new self-locking ball stud nut and tighten to specifications.
   d. With adjuster and clamps properly positioned, **Fig. 4,** tighten clamp bolts to specifications.
   e. Adjust toe as outlined under "Wheel Alignment."

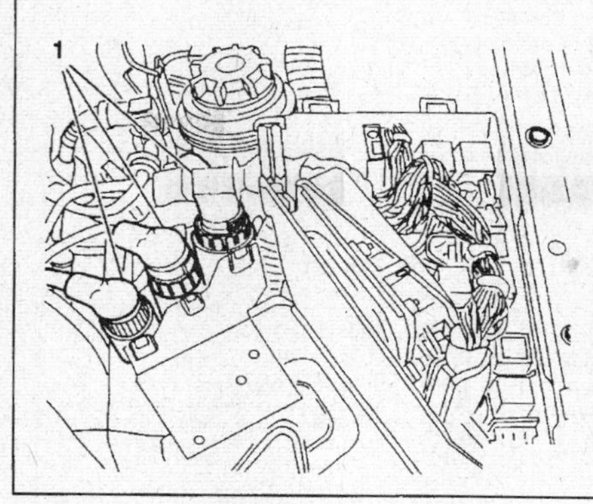

(1) Body Harness Electrical Connector

GC6029700118000X

Fig. 5 Body harness electrical connectors

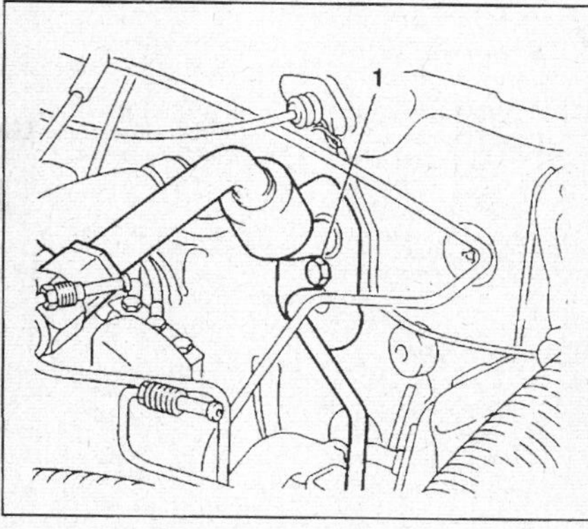

(1) Evaporator Line Extension to Cowl Bolt

GC6029700119000X

Fig. 6 Evaporator line extension bolt

POWER STEERING GEAR

REPLACE

1. Remove windshield wiper assembly.
2. Disconnect three body harness electrical connectors, **Fig. 5,** and remove Engine Control Module (ECM) from electrical box.
3. Drain engine coolant into suitable container and remove upper radiator hose.
4. Discharge and recover air conditioning system as outlined under "Air Conditioning." Remove air conditioning evaporator line extension bolt, **Fig. 6.**
5. Siphon power steering fluid from reservoir, remove reservoir bracket bolt and position reservoir aside.
6. Siphon brake fluid from reservoir and disconnect brake booster vacuum line at intake plenum.
7. Disconnect brake pipes and electrical connector at master cylinder.
8. Make mating marks on steering gear splines and lower steering coupler, then disengage tabs and remove sound insulator.
9. Remove steering coupler mounting bolts. **Do not allow steering wheel to turn when coupler is disconnected.**
10. Place steering wheel in straight ahead position and lock in place. Remove ignition key. **Because substantial steering wheel movement can occur before ignition locking mechanism sets, it is required to lock steering wheel using suitable external locking device.**
11. Carefully spread coupler clamp ears apart until steering shaft can be moved upward and away from steering gear.
12. Remove retaining clip and pin, then disconnect brake pedal from booster link rod.
13. Remove lefthand instrument panel knee bolster, fuse and relay panel screws.
14. Position panels away from upper vacuum booster nuts.

Before bleeding: Inspect steering system. Check, and correct as needed:

Hoses must not touch any other part of vehicle.

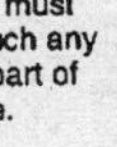
All hose connections must be tight.

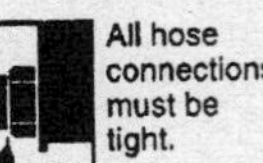

- Steering system noise could be caused by hose touching frame, body, or engine.
- Loose connections might not leak but could allow air into system.

When to bleed:
After any component replacement
After disconnecting fluid line
In case of steering system noise

Why bleed?
To prevent pump damage
To ensure proper system operation
To stop steering system noise

How to bleed:

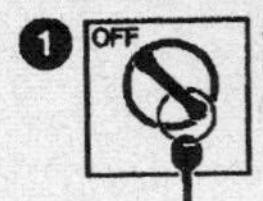
1. Switch ignition off.

2. Raise front wheels off ground.

3. Turn steering wheel full left.

4. Fill fluid reservoir to "FULL COLD" level. Leave cap off.

5. With assistant checking fluid level and condition, turn steering wheel lock-to-lock at least 20 times. Engine remains off.

- On systems with long return lines or fluid coolers, turn steering wheel lock-to-lock at least 40 times.
- Trapped air may cause fluid to overflow. Thoroughly clean any spilled fluid to allow for leak check.
- Keep fluid level at "FULL COLD."

6. While turning wheel, check fluid constantly.

- No bubbles are allowed.
- For any sign of bubbles, recheck connections. Repeat step 5.

7. Start engine. With engine idling, maintain fluid level. Reinstall cap.
8. Return wheels to center. Lower front wheels to ground.
9. Keep engine running for two minutes.
10. Turn steering wheel in both directions.

Verify:
☑ Smooth power assist
☑ Noiseless operation
☑ Proper fluid level
☑ No system leaks
☑ Proper fluid condition
- No bubbles, no foam, no discoloration

11. If all proper conditions apply, procedure is complete.
12. If any problem remains, see "Special Conditions."

Special Conditions:

Fluid

- Foam or bubbles in fluid
  Fluid must be completely free of bubbles. In step 5, be alert to periodic bubbles that could indicate a loose connection or leaky O-ring seal in either the return hose or pressure hose.
- Discolored fluid
  (milky, opaque, or light tan color)

Switch ignition off. Wait two minutes. Recheck hose connections. Repeat steps 7-10. If condition still exists, replace and check a possible cause:
☑ Return hose clamps
☑ Return hose O-ring
☑ Pressure hose O-rings
☑ Gear cylinder line O-rings

Fill system and repeat bleed procedure for each possible cause. Repeat steps 7-10 to verify whether noise has been eliminated.

Noise

- Pump whine or groan

With engine running, recheck hoses for possible contact with frame body or engine. If no contact is found, follow either method below to cool down fluid and repressurize system.

Method 1: Normal Cool Down	Method 2: Partial Fluid Replacement
Switch engine off. Wait for system to cool. Install reservoir cap.	Switch engine off. Use a suction device to remove fluid from reservoir. Refill with cool, clean fluid. Install reservoir cap.

After either method of cooling, start engine and allow engine to come up to operating temperature. If noise persists, remove and replace power steering pump. Repeat bleed procedure following pump replacement.

GC6029700120000X

Fig. 7 Power steering system bleed

15. Remove vacuum booster and master cylinder as an assembly, then disconnect air conditioning evaporator line extension quick connect fitting.
16. Disconnect power steering hoses at steering gear and position away from Electronic Brake/Traction Control Module (EBTCM)/Brake Pressure Modulator Valve (BPMV). Remove EBTCM/BPMV.
17. Remove upper heat shield bolt.
18. Raise and support vehicle.
19. Make mating marks on pitman arm and steering gear splines, then remove pitman arm nut and washer.
20. Remove arm from steering gear using suitable pitman arm puller.
21. Remove lower heat shield nuts and lower steering gear bolts, nuts and washers.
22. Lower vehicle, remove heat shield and disconnect power steering fluid flow control valve actuator electrical connector.
23. Remove upper steering gear bolt and shims. Record shim positions for installation.
24. Remove steering gear.
25. Reverse procedure to install, noting the following:
    a. Prior to installation, turn stub shaft from stop to stop and count number of turns, then turn shaft back ½ that number of turns.
    b. Align stub shaft mark with steering gear case V mark to center gear.
    c. Upper steering gear bolt should be installed and tightened until snug. **Final tightening should not occur until remaining bolts are installed.**
    d. Tighten mounting bolts to specifications.
    e. When connecting air conditioning evaporator line extension fittings, install new O-rings lubricated in 525 viscosity mineral oil.

POWER STEERING PUMP

REPLACE

1. Siphon power steering fluid from reservoir.
2. Loosen power steering pump pulley bolts and remove serpentine drive belt as outlined in "3.0L Engine" section.
3. Remove mounting bolts and pulley, then disconnect gear inlet hose at pump.
4. Remove fluid reservoir inlet hose clamp and hose from power steering pump.
5. Raise and support vehicle.
6. Remove Secondary Air Injection (AIR) crossover pipe support bracket.
7. Remove mounting bolts and power steering pump.
8. Reverse procedure to install. Tighten mounting bolts and hose connections to specifications.

POWER STEERING SYSTEM BLEED

Refer to **Fig. 7,** for power steering system bleed procedures. If the power steering system has been serviced, the system must be bled to obtain an accurate fluid level reading and to ensure proper system operation.

TIGHTENING SPECIFICATIONS

Year	Component	Torque/Ft. Lbs.
1998–2001	Air Conditioning Evaporator Line Extension	15
	Ball Stud To Lower Control Arm	26
	Brake Caliper	70②
	Brake Pipes To Master Cylinder	12
	Brake Rotor Setscrew	35①
	Brake Rotor Splash Shield	35①
	Brake Vacuum Booster	15
	Heat Shield, Lower Nuts	11
	Heat Shield, Upper Bolt	72①
	Hub (Wheel Bearing)	236
	Lower Control Arm	103
	Lower Control Arm Ball Stud Pinch Bolt	74
	Pitman Arm	118
	Power Steering Fluid Reservoir Clamp	60①
	Power Steering Gear Hoses	21
	Power Steering Pump	15
	Power Steering Pump Pulley	15
	Stabilizer Shaft Insulator	15②
	Stabilizer Shaft Link To Shaft	48
	Steering Gear	30
	Strut Bearing	52
	Strut To Steering Knuckle	66③
	Strut Upper Support	41
	Tie Rod Adjuster Clamp	11
	Tie Rod Ball Studs	44
	Wheel Speed Sensor	72①
	Wheel Lug Nut	80

① — Inch lbs.
② — Tighten an additional 37.°
③ — Tighten an additional 52.°

Wheel Alignment

INDEX

PRELIMINARY INSPECTION

1. Ensure all tires are of recommended size and are inflated to proper pressure.
2. Inspect all tires for damage and uneven tread wear.
3. Ensure wheel bearings, control arm ball studs and bushings, relay rods and tie rod ends are in satisfactory condition. Looseness must be corrected before wheels can be aligned.
4. Inspect wheel and tire radial and lateral runout, as follows:
   a. With wheel and tire assembly off vehicle, runout should be approximately .050 inch.
   b. When on vehicle, runout should be approximately .060 inch.
5. If wheel and tire assembly runout specifications cannot be met, separate tire from wheel and measure wheel runout. Wheel runout should be approximately .030 inch.
6. Inspect vehicle ride height as outlined under "Vehicle Ride Height" in "Specifications" section. If corrections are required, complete them prior to setting wheel alignment.
7. Ensure steering gear is not loose at frame mounting.
8. Inspect stabilizer shafts for loose or missing components.
9. Ensure struts and shocks are not leaking or excessively worn and strut upper mounts are in satisfactory condition.
10. Inspect all remaining suspension and steering components for damage and repair or replace prior to setting wheel alignment.
11. Ensure fuel tank is full or compensating ballast is added for proper weight distribution.
12. Ensure vehicle is on level surface and all loads that are normally carried inside vehicle are present.
13. Jounce front and rear of vehicle three times before beginning wheel alignment procedures.

FRONT WHEEL ALIGNMENT

Caster must be satisfactory prior to adjusting camber. Likewise, camber settings must be satisfactory prior to adjusting toe. **Adjust rear toe before adjusting front camber or toe.**

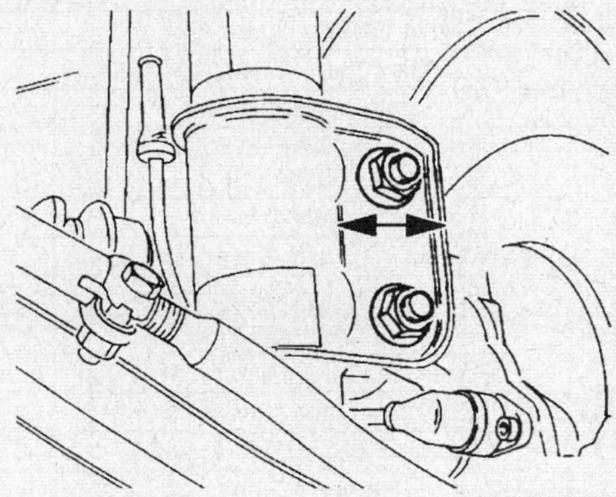

Fig. 1 Front camber adjustment

CASTER

Caster angles can be measured but cannot be adjusted. If angles are improper, service suspension components as required.

CAMBER

1. Raise and support vehicle, then remove front wheel.
2. Separate brake caliper from knuckle. Suspend caliper aside to prevent brake hose damage. **Do not open brake hydraulic system.**
3. Remove strut lower mounting bolts, insert new bolts from front toward rear of vehicle and **torque** to 15 ft. lbs.
4. Inspect brake caliper mounting hole threads in steering knuckle and remove any residual locking compound.
5. Install caliper using new mounting bolts. Coat bolts with suitable thread locking compound.
6. **Torque** mounting bolts to 70 ft. lbs., then tighten an additional 37°.
7. Install wheel and **torque** bolts to 80 ft. lbs.
8. Set camber turn, **Fig. 1.**
9. **Torque** strut lower mounting bolts to 66 ft. lbs., then tighten an additional 52°.

TOE

Toe adjustments are made separately for each wheel.

Fig. 2 Front tie rod adjuster & clamp orientation

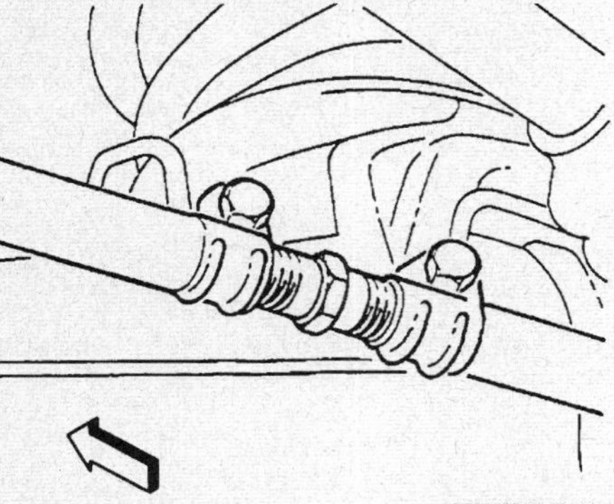

Fig. 3 Rear tie rod adjuster & clamps

1. Set steering wheel in straight ahead position.
2. Turn inner and outer tie rod sockets to limit of control arm ball stud travel.
3. Loosen clamp bolts at each end of tie rod adjuster and turn adjuster until proper toe setting is achieved.
4. Position tie rod adjuster and clamps, **Fig. 2.**
5. **Torque** clamp bolts to 11 ft. lbs.
6. Ensure same number of threads are exposed on either side of adjuster and outer tie rod ends are at right angles to steering knuckles.

REAR WHEEL ALIGNMENT

Adjust rear toe before performing procedures outlined under "Front Wheel Alignment."

TOE

1. Loosen both tie rod adjuster clamps, **Fig. 3.**
2. Turn threaded sleeve until proper toe is achieved.
3. **Torque** tie rod adjuster clamp bolts to 11 ft. lbs.

CAVALIER & SUNFIRE

NOTE: Refer To The Rear Of This Manual For Manufacturer's Special Service Tool Suppliers.

INDEX OF SERVICE OPERATIONS

Specifications

GENERAL ENGINE SPECIFICATIONS

Year	Engine		Fuel System	Bore/ Stroke	Compression Ratio	Net H.P. @ RPM③	Maximum Torque Ft. Lbs. @ RPM	Normal Oil Pressure psi
	Liter	VIN Code②						
1998	2.2L	4	SFI	3.50 × 3.46	9.00	115 @ 5000	135 @ 3600	56④
	2.4L	T	SFI	3.54 × 3.70	9.50	150 @ 5600	155 @ 4400	①
1999–2001	2.2L	4	SFI	3.50 × 3.46	8.85	115 @ 5000	135 @ 3600	56④
	2.4L	T	SFI	3.54 × 3.70	9.50	150 @ 5600	155 @ 4400	①
2002	2.2L/LN2	4	SFI	3.50 × 3.46	8.85	115 @ 5000	135 @ 3600	56④
	2.2L/L61	4	SFI	3.38 x 3.72	10.00	140 @ 5600	150 @ 4000	50–80⑤
	2.4L	T	SFI	3.54 × 3.70	9.50	150 @ 5600	155 @ 4400	①

SFI — Sequential fuel injection
① — 10 @ 900 RPM; 30 @ 3000 RPM.
② — The eighth digit denotes engine code.
③ — Ratings are net as installed in vehicle.
④ — At 3000 RPM.
⑤ — Oil pressure @ 1000 RPM.

TUNE UP SPECIFICATIONS

Year & Engine	Spark Plug Gap	Firing Order Fig.	Ignition Timing BTDC	Timing Mark Fig.	Curb Idle Speed	Fast Idle Speed	Fuel Pump Pressure	Valve Lash
1998								
2.2L	.040	②	⑦	⑥	④	④	41–47③	①
2.4L	.050	⑤	⑦	⑥	④	④	41–47③	①
1999–2001								
2.2L	.040	②	⑦	⑥	④	④	41–47③	①
2.4L	.050	⑤	⑦	⑥	④	④	52–58③	①
2002								
2.2L/LN2	.040	②	⑦	⑥	④	④	41–47③	①
2.2L/L61	.042	②	⑦	⑥	④	④	50–60	①
2.4L	.050	⑤	⑦	⑥	④	④	52–58③	①

BTDC — Before Top Dead Center
① — Equipped w/hydraulic valve lifters. No adjustment is required.
② — Cylinder numbering from front of engine to rear of engine, 1,2,3,4. Firing order 1-3-4-2. Coil connections are stamped on coil assemblies.
③ — Relieve fuel system pressure as outlined under "Fuel System Pressure Relief" under "Precautions" in appropriate engine section. Then, connect suitable fuel pressure gauge between fuel line and fuel rail. Connect battery ground cable. Turn ignition On and record fuel pressure reading.
④ — Idle speeds are controlled by Idle Air Control (IAC) valve.

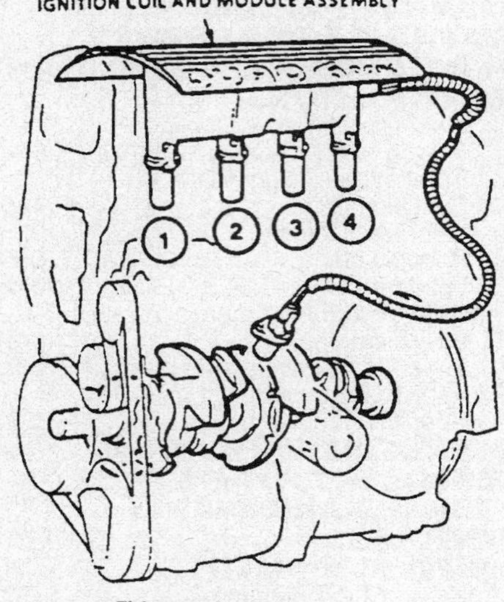

Fig. A

⑤ — Cylinder numbering from front of engine to rear of engine, 1, 2, 3, 4. Firing order 1-3-4-2. Refer to **Fig. 6-2,** for spark plug wire connection at coil unit.
⑥ — Equipped w/crankshaft sensor.
⑦ — No adjustment.

FRONT WHEEL ALIGNMENT SPECIFICATIONS

Year	Caster Angle, Degrees		Camber Angle, Degrees		Total Toe, Degrees	Ball Joint Wear
	Limits	Desired	Limits	Desired		
1998–2002	+3.3 to +5.3①	4.3①	−1 to +1	0	0	②

① — Non-adjustable. For inspection purposes only.

② — Refer to "Front Suspension & Steering" section for ball joint specifications and inspection procedure.

REAR WHEEL ALIGNMENT SPECIFICATIONS

Year	Camber Angle, Degrees①		Thrust Angle, Degrees①		Total Toe, Degrees①	
	Limits	Desired	Limits	Desired	Limits	Desired
1998–2002	−1.15 to +.35	−.4	−.25 to +.25	0	−.1 to +.5	+.2

① — Non-adjustable. For inspection purposes only.

VEHICLE RIDE HEIGHT SPECIFICATIONS

Model	Year	Body Style	Manufacturer's Original Tire Size	Measurement Points & Specifications①③					
				Front			Rear		
				Dim.	Specification		Dim.	Specification	
					Inches	mm		Inches	mm
Cavalier	1998–2002	All	②	A	32.15	816	B	22	558
				C	9.17	233	D	9.45	240
Sunfire	1998–2002	All	②	A	32.15	816.6	B	22	558
				C	9.19	233	D	9.44	240

A Dim. — Measurement From Front Wheel Center to Check Point On Rocker Panel.
B Dim. — Measurement From Rear Wheel Center to Check Point On Rocker Panel.
C Dim. — Ground to Rocker Panel, Front
D Dim. — Ground to Rocker Panel, Rear
Dim. — Dimension

① — ±.0.39 in (10 mm) front to rear & side to side.

② — See door sticker or inside of glove box for manufacturer's original tire size specifications. If tires on vehicle do not match manufacturer's original tire size & measurement is not within limits, it will be necessary to refer to the "Non-Standard Tire & Wheel Size Adjustment To Ride Height Specification & Tire Size Adjustment Charts" in the front of this manual for approximate changes in ride height specifications.

③ — Measurement is with fuel, radiator coolant and engine oil full, spare tire, jack, hand tools and mats in designated positions and tires properly inflated.

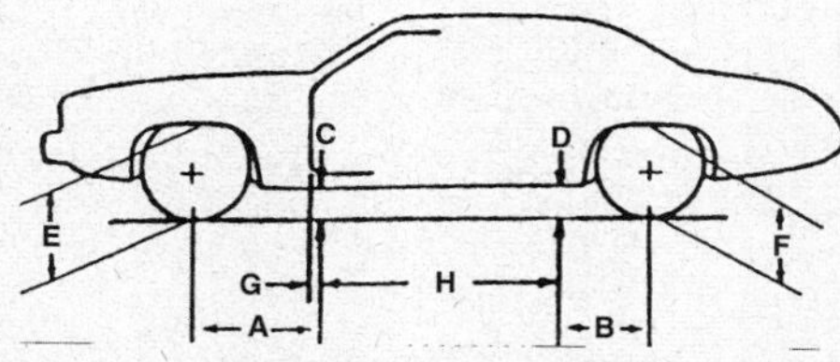

Dimensions A through D

FLUID CAPACITIES & COOLING SYSTEM DATA

Year	Engine	Coolant Capacity, Qts.	Coolant Type	Radiator Cap Relief Pressure, Lbs.	Thermo. Opening Temp.	Fuel Tank Gals.	Engine Oil Refill Qts.②	Transaxle Oil	
								Manual Pts.	Automatic Qts.①
1998	2.2L	10.5	Dex-Cool	15	180	15.2	4	4.0	③
	2.4L	10.5	Dex-Cool	15	180	15.2	4	4.0	③
1999–2001	2.2L	10.3	Dex-Cool	15	180	15.0	4	4.0	④
	2.4L	10.7	Dex-Cool	15	180	15.0	4	4.0	④
2002	2.2L/LN2	10.3	Dex-Cool	15	180	15.0	4	4.0	④
	2.2L/L61	10.0	Dex-Cool	15	195	14.1	4	1.8	⑤
	2.4L	10.7	Dex-Cool	15	180	15.0	4	4.0	④

① — Approximate. Make final inspection w/dipstick.
② — When changing engine oil filter additional oil may be required.
③ — 3T40 auto. trans.: oil pan only, 4 qts. after overhaul, 7 qts. 4T40E auto. trans.: oil pan only, 7.4 qts. after overhaul, 10.6 qts.
④ — 3T40 auto. trans.: oil pan only, 4 qts., after overhaul 7 qts. 4T40E auto. trans.: oil pan only, 6.9 qts., after overhaul 9.5 qts.
⑤ — Oil pan removal, 6.9 qts.; overhaul, 9.5 qts., dry 12.9 qts.

LUBRICANT DATA

Year	Lubricant Type			
	Transaxle		Power Steering	Brake System
	Manual	Automatic		
1998–2002	①	DEXRON III	②	DOT-3

① — Manual transmission fluid GM P/N 12345349, or equivalent.
② — Power steering fluid GM P/N 1052884, or equivalent.

Electrical

NOTE: On Air Bag Equipped Models, Refer To "Air Bag System Precautions" Located In The Front Of This Manual For System Disarming & Arming Procedures.

NOTE: Refer To "Computer Relearn Procedures" Located In The Front Of This Manual When Battery Power To The Computer Has Been Interrupted.

NOTE: On Models Equipped With 2.2L/L61 Engine, Refer To "Achieva, Alero, Cutlass, Grand Am, Malibu & Skylark" Chapter For Procedures.

INDEX

PRECAUTIONS

AIR BAG SYSTEMS

Refer to "Air Bag System Precautions" in the front of this manual for system disarming and arming procedures.

BATTERY GROUND CABLE

Prior to service, disconnect battery ground cable and isolate as required.

FUSE PANEL & FLASHER LOCATION

The fuse panel is located on the lefthand side of the instrument panel. To access the panel, pivot the access door downward.

The turn signal and hazard flasher is located under the instrument panel on the lefthand side of steering column.

FUEL PUMP RELAY LOCATION

The fuel pump relay is located in the front lefthand corner of the engine compartment, in the engine compartment relay center.

RELAY CENTER LOCATION

The relay center is located in the front lefthand corner of the engine compartment, by the strut tower.

STARTER

REPLACE

2.4L & 1998-99 2.2L ENGINES

1. Remove air inlet duct to throttle body.
2. Remove top starter bolt.
3. Raise and support vehicle.
4. Remove lower starter bolt and position starter aside.
5. Disconnect electrical wiring and remove starter.
6. Reverse procedure to install.

2000-02 2.2L ENGINE

1. Remove wiring harness bracket nut from starter bolt.
2. Raise and support vehicle.
3. Remove flywheel inspection shield.
4. Remove electrical connectors.
5. Remove starter bolts, then the starter.
6. Reverse procedure to install, **torque** starter bolts to 37 ft. lbs.

ALTERNATOR

REPLACE

1. Disconnect alternator electrical connectors.
2. Remove drive belt as outlined under "Serpentine Drive Belt" in appropriate engine section.
3. Remove alternator through bolts, then the alternator.
4. Reverse procedure to install, noting the following:
   a. **On models equipped with 2.2L engine, torque** upper alternator mounting bolt to 22 ft. lbs.
   b. **On models equipped with 2.2L engine, torque** lower alternator mounting bolt to 37 ft. lbs.
   c. **On models equipped with 2.4L engine, torque** alternator mounting bolts to 37 ft. lbs.

COIL PACK

REPLACE

1998-99

1. Raise and support vehicle.
2. Remove spark plug and ICM electrical wires.
3. Remove ICM assembly plate attaching bolts, then the ICM.
4. Remove ignition coils from module.
5. Remove module from assembly plate.
6. Reverse procedure to install, **torque** ICM bolts to 18 inch lbs.

2000-02

1. Remove air cleaner outlet from air cleaner.

2. Remove ICM electrical connectors, then the spark plug wires.
3. Remove ignition coil attaching bolts.
4. Remove ignition coils and ICM assembly.
5. Reverse procedure to install, **torque** ignition coil bolts to 35 inch lbs.

IGNITION LOCK

REPLACE

LESS IGNITION KEY

1. Disconnect wiring harness from ignition switch.
2. Disconnect steering column from body as outlined under "Steering Columns."
3. Drill 3/32 hole on back of steering column housing.
4. Remove retainer spring by inserting and turn lock tool No. J-41253, or equivalent, into retain lock retainer spring hole, **Fig. 1.**
5. Hold column vertical and tap on housing to dislodge retainer.
6. Remove lock retainer and lock cylinder from housing.
7. Reverse procedure to install.

WITH IGNITION KEY

1. **On models equipped with tilt column,** remove tilt lever.
2. **On all models,** remove steering column upper and lower trim covers.
3. Turn lock cylinder to Run.
4. Push against locking button on rear side of bearing and housing, then remove lock cylinder by pulling it out of column.
5. Disconnect lock cylinder electrical connector.
6. Reverse procedure to install, noting the following:
   a. Turn lock cylinder to Run position and depress locking button.
   b. Gently push cylinder into place while rotating key approximately 5° counterclockwise.
   c. Inspect for proper operation.

IGNITION SWITCH

REPLACE

1. Remove steering column trim covers.
2. Remove ignition lock cylinder as outlined under "Ignition Lock, Replace."
3. Remove Torx head screws, then the ignition switch from steering column.
4. Reverse procedure to install, noting the following:
   a. **On 1998–99 models, torque** screws to 13 inch lbs.
   b. **On 2000–02 models, torque** screws to 36 inch lbs.

CLUTCH START SWITCH

REPLACE

1. Remove driver's instrument panel knee bolster.
2. Disconnect clutch start switch electrical connector.
3. Remove clutch start switch from pedal bracket.
4. Reverse procedure to install. Ensure starter cranks only when clutch pedal is fully depressed.

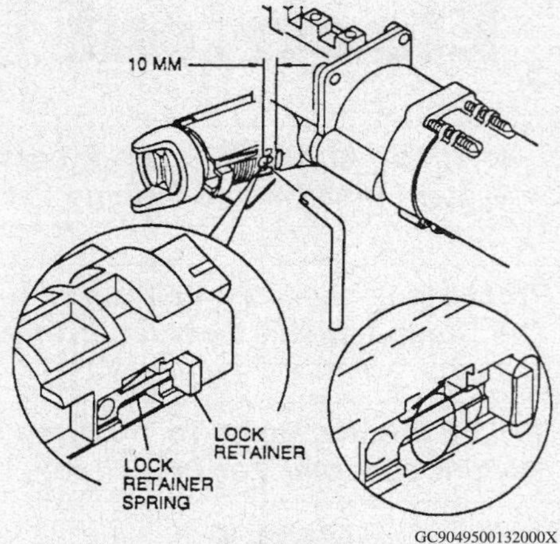

Fig. 1 Lock cylinder removal

NEUTRAL SAFETY SWITCH

REPLACE

On models equipped with automatic transmission, the neutral start and back-up lamp switches are combined into one unit and must be replaced as an assembly.

1. Disconnect shift linkage.
2. Disconnect electrical connector from switch.
3. Remove mounting bolts and switch.
4. If same switch is to be installed again, proceed as follows:
   a. Place shift shaft in Neutral position.
   b. Align flats of shift shaft with switch and install switch.
   c. Loosely install mounting bolts.
   d. Insert gauge pin or 3/32 inch drill bit in service adjustment hole and rotate switch until pin drops to depth of 9/64 inch.
   e. **Torque** mounting bolts to 18 ft. lbs.
5. If new switch is to be installed, proceed as follows:
   a. Place shift shaft in Neutral position.
   b. Align flats of shift shaft with switch and install switch.
   c. If bolt holes do not align with mounting boss on transaxle, ensure shift shaft is in Neutral position and do not rotate switch. Switch is pinned in Neutral position. If switch has been rotated and pin has broken, replace as required.
   d. **Torque** mounting bolts to 18 ft. lbs.
6. Ensure engine will start only in Park or Neutral positions.

HEADLAMP SWITCH

REPLACE

Refer to "Multi-Function Switch, Replace" for replacement procedure.

STOP LIGHT SWITCH

REPLACE

1. Remove driver's side sound insulator.
2. Disconnect and remove electrical connectors.
3. Disconnect brake switch by grasping switch and turning it one quarter turn counterclockwise while pulling toward rear of vehicle.
4. Reverse procedure to install, noting the following for adjustment:
   a. Ensure brake pedal is fully released.
   b. Ensure that stoplamp plunger is fully depressed against brake pedal shanks.
   c. Hold brake pedal forward and ensure stoplamp switch and cruise control switch are fully seated into brake pedal bracket.
   d. Pull brake pedal to rear, against internal stop.
   e. The stoplamp switch and cruise control switch will be adjusted.
   f. Inspect stoplamps for proper operation.

MULTI-FUNCTION SWITCH

REPLACE

1. Remove steering wheel as outlined under "Steering Wheel, Replace."
2. Remove steering column shrouds.
3. Remove two Torx head screws from multi-function switch.
4. Disconnect electrical connectors.
5. Remove multi-function switch from steering column.
6. Reverse procedure to install, noting the following:
   a. **On 1998–99 models, torque** screws to 53 inch lbs.
   b. **On 2000–02 models, torque** screws to 36 inch lbs.

TURN SIGNAL SWITCH

REPLACE

Refer to "Multi-Function Switch, Replace" for turn signal switch replacement procedure.

DIMMER SWITCH

REPLACE

1998–99

1. Remove lefthand sound insulator panel.
2. Disconnect electrical connector.
3. Remove attaching screws to dimmer module.
4. Reverse procedure to install, **torque** screws to 18 inch lbs.

2000–02

Cavalier

1. Remove instrument panel accessory trim plate to access fog lamp switch.
2. Release retainers on fog lamp/dimmer switch housing using suitable flat bladed tool.
3. Remove fog lamp/dimmer switch housing from instrument panel.
4. Release retainers on dimmer switch using a flat bladed tool.

5. Remove dimmer lamp switch from fog lamp/dimmer switch housing.
6. Reverse procedure to install.

Sunfire

1. Remove fog lamp/dimmer switch trim plate from instrument panel using suitable flat bladed tool.
2. Disconnect electrical connectors from fog lamp/dimmer switch.
3. Release retainer tabs on dimmer lamp switch using suitable flat bladed tool on reverse side.
4. Remove dimmer lamp switch from trim plate.
5. Reverse procedure to install.

STEERING WHEEL

REPLACE

1. Remove steering wheel center pad and mounting screws as required.
2. Disable driver's air bag module as outlined under "Air Bag System Precautions" in front of this manual.
3. Remove driver's air bag module as outlined under "Passive Restraint Systems."
4. Disconnect horn electrical connector.
5. Remove steering wheel nut.
6. Remove steering wheel using steering wheel puller No. J1859A, or equivalent.
7. Disconnect electrical connectors from steering wheel.
8. Remove steering wheel from column.
9. Reverse procedure to install, **torque** steering wheel nut to 29 ft. lbs.

INSTRUMENT CLUSTER

REPLACE

1. Remove instrument panel trim plate.
2. Remove screws from top of cluster.
3. Pull cluster rearward.
4. Remove cluster assembly.
5. Reverse procedure to install.

WIPER MOTOR

REPLACE

1. Remove wiper arm assemblies.
2. Disconnect the washer tubing from air inlet screen.
3. Remove air inlet grille panel push-in retainers from panel using door trim pad and garnish clip remover tool No. J38778, or equivalent.
4. Remove air inlet grille panel from vehicle.
5. Remove electrical connector from wiper motor.
6. Remove screws and wiper drive system module from vehicle.
7. Remove wiper transmission from wiper motor crank arm using wiper transmission separator tool No. J39232, or equivalent.
8. Remove screws, then the wiper motor from frame.
9. Reverse procedure to install, **torque** mounting screws to 88 inch lbs.

WIPER SWITCH

REPLACE

1. Remove steering column trim covers.
2. Remove multi-function switch as outlined under "Multi-Function Switch, Replace."
3. Remove retaining screws, then the wiper switch from column.
4. Disconnect electrical connector.
5. Reverse procedure to install, **torque** attaching screws to 36 inch lbs.

WIPER TRANSMISSION

REPLACE

1. Remove wiper arm assemblies.
2. Disconnect the washer tubing from the air inlet screen.
3. Remove air inlet grille panel push-in retainers from panel using door trim pad and garnish clip remover tool No. J38778, or equivalent.
4. Remove air inlet grille panel from vehicle.
5. Remove wiper drive module.
6. Disconnect electrical connector from wiper motor.
7. Remove wiper transmission from wiper motor crank arm using wiper transmission separator tool No. J39232, or equivalent.
8. Remove cap from wiper transmission.
9. Remove screws and wiper transmission from tube frame.
10. Reverse procedure to install, noting the following:
    a. **Torque** wiper transmission screws to 79 inch lbs.
    b. **Torque** wiper drive system module screws to 88 inch lbs.

BLOWER MOTOR

REPLACE

1. Disconnect blower motor electrical connectors.
2. Remove sound insulator panels as required.
3. Remove mounting screws, then the blower motor assembly.
4. Reverse procedure to install, **torque** attaching screws to 44 inch lbs.

HEATER CORE

REPLACE

1. Drain cooling system into suitable container.
2. Recover refrigerant as outlined under "Air Conditioning."
3. Remove evaporator lines to evaporator.
4. Raise and support vehicle.
5. Disconnect heater hoses from heater core.
6. Lower vehicle.
7. Remove evaporator case drain tube.
8. Remove IP carrier as outlined under "Dash Panel Service."
9. Disconnect wiring harness from cross beam.
10. Remove attaching bolts to righthand and lefthand HVAC module.
11. Remove two cross vehicle beam bolts.
12. Remove cross beam.
13. Remove floor console.
14. Reposition floor carpet aside in order to access floor outlet duct connections.
15. Remove floor outlet ducts from heater outlet cover, then the floor outlet ducts.
16. Disconnect wiring harness from HVAC module.
17. Disconnect electrical connections to blower motor and resistor.
18. Remove HVAC module assembly.
19. Remove heater core case cover attaching screws and cover.
20. Remove heater core bracket screws and brackets.
21. Remove heater core from HVAC module assembly.
22. Reverse procedure to install, noting the following:
    a. **Torque** bracket and cover screws to 9 inch lbs.
    b. **Torque** HVAC module mounting bracket bolts and screws to 18 inch lbs.
    c. **Torque** cross vehicle beam bolts and studs to 89 inch lbs.
    d. **Torque** righthand and lefthand side HVAC module support bolts to 18 inch lbs.
    e. **Torque** evaporator tube to evaporator fittings to 18 ft. lbs.

EVAPORATOR CORE

REPLACE

1. Remove HVAC module as outlined under "Heater Core, Replace."
2. Remove heater core as outlined under "Heater Core, Replace."
3. Remove attaching screws and evaporator core brackets.
4. Remove evaporator core assembly.
5. Reverse procedure to install, **torque** evaporator core bracket screws to 9 inch lbs.

2.2L (L61) Engine

NOTE: Refer To "2.2L (L61) Engine" In "Achieva, Alero, Cutlass, Grand Am, Malibu & Skylark" Chapter For Procedures Not Covered In This Section.

NOTE: On Air Bag Equipped Models, Refer To "Air Bag System Precautions" Located In The Front Of This Manual For System Disarming & Arming Procedures.

NOTE: Refer To "Computer Relearn Procedures" Located In The Front Of This Manual When Battery Power To The Computer Has Been Interrupted.

INDEX

PRECAUTIONS

AIR BAG SYSTEMS

Refer to "Air Bag System Precautions" in the front of this manual for system disarming and arming procedures.

BATTERY GROUND CABLE

Prior to service, disconnect battery ground cable and isolate as required.

FUEL SYSTEM PRESSURE RELIEF

1. Disconnect battery ground cable, isolate as required.
2. Install fuel pressure gauge tool No. J34730-1A, or equivalent.
3. Install bleed hose into suitable container, then open valve to bleed system pressure.
4. Disconnect fuel pressure gauge from fuel pressure connection.

COMPRESSION PRESSURE

Refer to "2.2L (L61) Engine" in "Achieva, Alero, Cutlass, Grand Am, Malibu & Skylark" chapter for procedure.

ENGINE MOUNT

REPLACE

RIGHT

1. Remove coolant recovery tank and position aside.
2. Install engine support tool No. J 28467–360, or equivalent, and raise engine off of mount.
3. Remove nuts holding mount to body.
4. Remove bolts holding engine mount to bracket.
5. Remove engine mount assembly.
6. Reverse procedure to install.

ENGINE

REPLACE

AUTOMATIC TRANSMISSION

Always replace accelerator cable with a new cable whenever the engine is removed from vehicle. To avoid cruise control cable damage, position cable out of way when removing or installing engine. Do not pry or lean against cruise control cable, do not kink cruise control cable. Damaged cruise control cables must be replaced.

1. Open hood and mark hinge locations for installation reference, then remove hood.
2. Relieve fuel system pressure as outlined under "Precautions."
3. Drain engine coolant into suitable container.
4. Recover A/C refrigerant with suitable A/C recovery station.
5. Remove air inlet duct and resonator assembly.
6. Disconnect brake booster line at intake manifold.
7. Remove resonator bracket/fuel rail cover.
8. Remove accelerator and cruise control cables from cable bracket.
9. Disconnect engine wiring harness from underhood engine components.
10. Remove cruise control module.
11. Disconnect A/C line from accumulator.
12. Remove drive belt.
13. Remove surge tank.
14. Remove power steering pump from accessory bracket.
15. Remove upper and lower radiator hoses.
16. Remove heater hoses from engine.
17. Remove fuel feed lines at engine.
18. Raise and support vehicle.
19. Remove right side tire and wheel assembly and right engine splash shield.
20. Remove engine mount strut.
21. Remove flywheel inspection cover and starter.
22. Remove exhaust pipe and hanger from exhaust manifold.
23. Remove and support A/C compressor.
24. Remove A/C compressor bracket.
25. Drain engine oil into suitable container.
26. Remove torque converter bolts.
27. Remove transmission to engine support brace.
28. Remove lower transmission to engine bolts, then lower vehicle.
29. Support transmission with suitable jack and install engine lifting device to engine lifting eyes.
30. Remove engine mount as outlined under "Engine Mount, Replace."
31. Remove remaining transmission to engine bolts.
32. Separate engine from transmission and lift engine from vehicle.
33. Reverse procedure to install.

MANUAL TRANSMISSION

1. Relieve fuel system pressure as outlined under "Precautions."
2. Drain cooling system into suitable container.
3. Remove air cleaner outlet duct.
4. Remove upper and lower radiator hoses.
5. Disconnect brake booster vacuum hose, IAC electrical connector and alternator electrical connectors.
6. Disconnect TPS, MAP and EVAP emission solenoid electrical connectors.
7. Disconnect injector harness electrical connectors.
8. Remove accelerator and cruise control

cables from accelerator control bracket.
9. Disconnect ECT, 02S and ignition module electrical connectors.
10. Disconnect engine ground electrical connector.
11. Remove drive belt.
12. Disconnect transmission shift control cable from lever and bracket.
13. Disconnect hydraulic clutch line.
14. Remove coolant surge tank.
15. Disconnect vacuum line near master cylinder.
16. Raise and support vehicle.
17. Remove suspension support frame.
18. Disconnect A/C compressor electrical connector, then remove A/C compressor and position to one side with lines attached.
19. Disconnect vehicle speed sensor electrical connector.
20. Remove starter.
21. Disconnect oil pressure sensor electrical connector and all additional ground wires.
22. Remove both drive axles from transmission and position aside.
23. Lower vehicle until engine/ transmission assembly is on support table.
24. Disconnect heater hoses at front of dash.
25. Disconnect fuel lines.
26. Remove transmission mount through bolts.
27. Remove engine mount assembly.
28. Raise and support vehicle.
29. Separate engine from transmission.
30. Reverse procedure to install.

INTAKE MANIFOLD

REPLACE

Refer to "2.2L (L61) Engine" in "Achieva, Alero, Cutlass, Grand Am, Malibu & Skylark" chapter for procedure.

TIGHTENING SPECIFICATIONS

Year	Component	Torque, Ft. Lbs.
1998–2002	Accelerator & Cruise Control Cable	89②
	Air Cleaner Clamps	44②
	Air Cleaner Outlet Resonator Mounting Bolt	89②
	Alternator	15
	Engine Mount Strut	74①
	Engine To Transmission Bolts	55
	Power Steering Pump	19
	Radiator Drain Cock	18②
	Right Engine Mount Bolts	44①
	Right Engine Mount To Body Nuts	55
	Torque Converter Bolts	46
	Upper Air Cleaner Cover Screws	27②

① — Plus 90.°
② — Inch Lbs.

2.2L (LN2) Engine

NOTE: On Air Bag Equipped Models, Refer To "Air Bag System Precautions" Located In The Front Of This Manual For System Disarming & Arming Procedures.

NOTE: Refer To "Computer Relearn Procedures" Located In The Front Of This Manual When Battery Power To The Computer Has Been Interrupted.

INDEX

PRECAUTIONS

AIR BAG SYSTEMS

Refer to "Air Bag System Precautions" in the front of this manual for system disarming and arming procedures.

BATTERY GROUND CABLE

Prior to service, disconnect battery ground cable and isolate as required.

FUEL SYSTEM PRESSURE RELIEF

1. Raise and support vehicle.
2. Disconnect fuel pump electrical connector.
3. Start engine and run until remaining fuel is consumed.
4. Engage starter for approximately three seconds to ensure relief of any remaining pressure.
5. Disconnect and isolate battery ground cable to avoid possible fuel discharge if any attempt is made to start engine.

COMPRESSION PRESSURE

When inspecting cylinder compression, the throttle should be open, all spark plugs removed and the battery at or near full charge. The lowest reading cylinder should not be less than 70% of the highest and no cylinder reading should be less than 100 psi. Turn ignition key until engine cranks through four compression cycles. Normal compression builds up quickly and evenly to specifications on each cylinder.

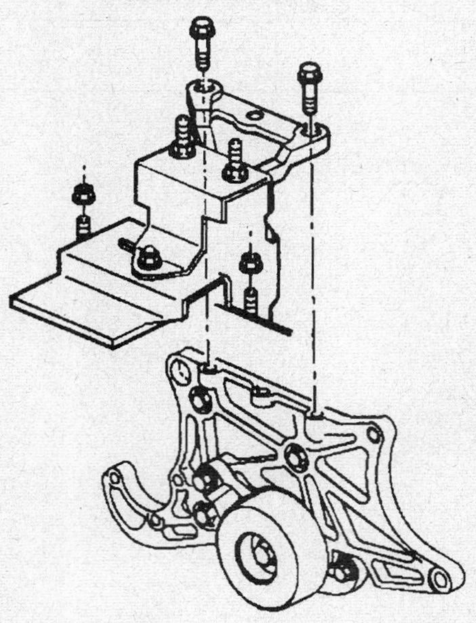

Fig. 1 Engine mount removal

ENGINE MOUNT

REPLACE

1. Install engine support fixture tool No. J-28467-360, or equivalent.
2. Raise engine at front lift hook in order to remove weight from engine mount.
3. Remove coolant recovery tank mounting bolt.
4. Position coolant recovery tank aside with hoses attached.
5. Remove engine mount to drive belt tensioner bracket.
6. Remove two nuts on top of engine mount, **Fig. 1.**
7. Remove engine mount to body nuts.
8. Remove engine mount bracket and engine mount.
9. Reverse procedure to install.

ENGINE MOUNT STRUT & STRUT BRACKET

REPLACE

1. Raise and support vehicle.
2. Remove righthand splash shield.
3. Remove engine mount strut bolts and engine mount strut, **Fig. 2.**
4. Remove air conditioning compressor with lines attached and position aside.
5. Remove transmission brace from engine.
6. Remove engine mount strut bracket bolts and strut bracket.
7. Reverse procedure to install.

ENGINE

REPLACE

AUTOMATIC TRANSAXLE

1. Recover air conditioning refrigerant as outlined under "Air Conditioning."
2. Drain and recover coolant in suitable container.

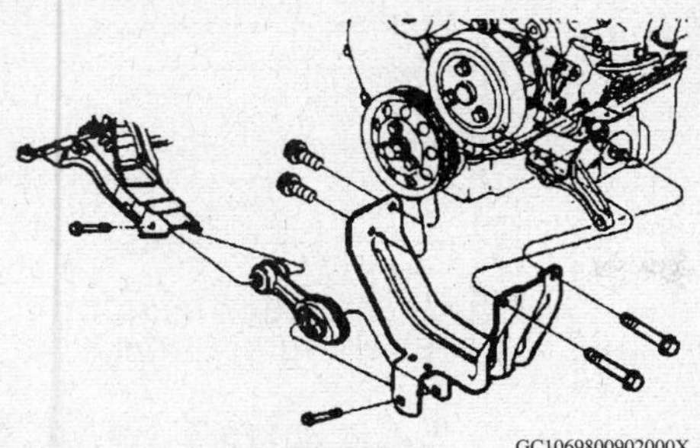

Fig. 2 Engine mount strut & strut bracket removal

3. Mark positions of hinge to hood locations to ease installation and remove hood.
4. Remove air cleaner.
5. Disconnect brake booster vacuum line at intake manifold.
6. Disconnect accelerator control cable.
7. Disconnect speed control cable and position it aside.
8. Remove fuel injector rail cover.
9. Remove accelerator and speed control cables from cable bracket. **Discard accelerator cable.**
10. Disconnect all required electrical connectors from engine components.
11. Remove cruise control module.
12. Disconnect refrigerant lines from accumulator. Discard O-rings.
13. Mark running direction and remove engine accessory drive belt.
14. Remove coolant surge tank.
15. Remove upper and lower radiator hoses.
16. Remove fuel feed lines from engine.
17. Raise and support vehicle.
18. Remove coolant pipe.
19. Remove righthand front wheel and tire.
20. Remove righthand front splash shield.
21. Remove engine mount strut as outlined under "Engine Mount Strut & Strut Bracket, Replace."
22. Remove flexplate inspection cover.
23. Remove exhaust pipe and hanger from exhaust manifold.
24. Remove starter as outlined under "Starter, Replace" in "Electrical" section.
25. Remove and support air conditioning compressor with hoses intact.
26. Remove air conditioning compressor bracket.
27. Drain engine oil into suitable container.
28. Remove torque convertor to flexplate bolts.
29. Remove transaxle to engine support brace.
30. Remove transaxle to engine lower bolts.
31. Lower vehicle.
32. Support transaxle using suitable jack.
33. Install suitable engine lifting device to engine lifting eyes.
34. Remove engine front upper mount as outlined under "Engine Mount, Replace."
35. Remove remaining transaxle to engine bolts.
36. Separate engine from transaxle, carefully lift engine up and out.

(1) Throttle Cable Bracket
(2) Bolt, Intake Manifold Fuel Rail Bracket
(3) Bolt, EGR Pipe
(4) Fuel Line
(5) Retainer, EGR Pipe
(6) EGR Pipe
(7) Nut, EGR Valve
(8) EGR Valve
(9) Gasket, EGR Valve
(10) Bolt, EGR Pipe
(11) Stud, EGR Valve
(12) Bolt, EGR Adapter
(13) EGR Port Cover (EXPORT ONLY)
(14) Gasket, EGR Adapter
(15) EGR Adapter
(16) Bolt, EGR Adapter
(17) Engine Block
(18) Stud, Exhaust Manifold
(19) Gasket, Exhaust Manifold
(20) Nut Exhaust Manifold
(21) Oxygen Sensor
(22) Exhaust Manifold
(23) Stud, Intake Manifold
(24) Intake Manifold
(25) Bolt, Intake Manifold
(26) Nut, Intake Manifold
(27) MAP Sensor
(28) Fuel Rail And Fuel Injectors
(29) Bolt, Fuel Rail
(30) Vacuum Harness
(31) Throttle Body
(32) Bolts, Throttle Body

GC1069800904000X

Fig. 3 Exploded view of intake and exhaust manifold components

37. Reverse procedure to install, noting the following:
    a. Install new accelerator cable.
    b. Install new evaporator O-rings lubricated in clean 525 viscosity refrigerant oil.
    c. Ensure oil pan drain plug is intact with its gasket in place and fill crankcase.
    d. Close radiator petcock and fill cooling system.
    e. Start engine and inspect for any fluid leaks.

MANUAL TRANSAXLE

1. Drain and recover coolant into suitable container.
2. Remove air cleaner outlet duct.
3. Remove upper radiator hose at coolant outlet.
4. Disconnect brake booster vacuum hose.
5. Disconnect IAC electrical connection.
6. Disconnect alternator electrical connector.
7. Disconnect TPS, MAP, EVAP, EGR, ECT, TCC and O2 sensor electrical connectors.
8. Disconnect injector harness electrical connectors.
9. Disconnect engine ground electrical connections.
10. Remove drive belt as outlined under "Serpentine Drive Belt."
11. Remove transmission shift control cable from range select lever and bracket.
12. Remove coolant surge tank and hose.
13. Disconnect vacuum line near master cylinder.
14. Install engine support fixture tool No. J-28467-360, or equivalent.
15. Disconnect lower radiator hose from coolant pump.
16. Raise and support vehicle, then remove front wheels.
17. Remove splash shields.
18. Remove exhaust pipe at exhaust manifold and catalytic converter.
19. Remove engine mount strut as outlined under "Engine Mount Strut & Strut Bracket, Replace."
20. Remove wheel speed sensor wire harness from control arms.
21. Separate ball joints from steering knuckles as outlined under "Ball Joint, Replace" in "Front Suspension &

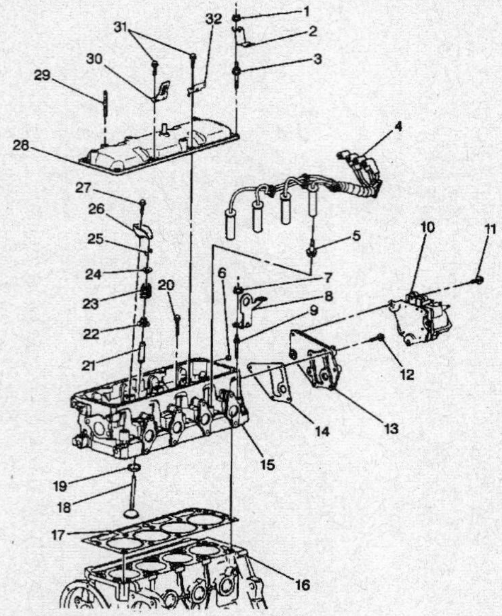

(1) Nut, Secondary Ignition Harness Bracket
(2) Secondary Ignition Harness Bracket
(3) Bolt, Valve Rocker Arm Cover
(4) Secondary Ignition Harness
(5) Spark Plug
(6) Oil Passage Plug
(7) Nut, Engine Lift Hook
(8) Engine Lift Hook
(9) Bolt, Cylinder Head
(10) Ignition Module And Coil Assembly
(11) Bolt, Ignition Coil Bracket
(12) Bolt, Rear Cylinder Head Cover
(13) Rear Cylinder Head Cover
(14) Gasket, Rear Cylinder Head Cover
(15) Cylinder Head
(16) Cylinder Block
(17) Gasket, Cylinder Head
(18) Valve
(19) Valve Seat
(20) Bolt, Cylinder Head
(21) Valve Guide
(22) Valve Guide Seal
(23) Valve Spring
(24) Valve Spring Retainer
(25) Valve Spring Keepers
(26) Valve Rocker Arm
(27) Bolt, Rocker Arm
(28) Valve Rocker Arm Cover
(29) Stud, Fuel Rail Bracket
(30) Bracket, Secondary Ignition Harness
(31) Bolts, Secondary Ignition and Fuel Injector Harness Brackets
(32) Bracket, Fuel Injector Harness

GC1069800905000X

Fig. 4 Exploded view of cylinder head components

Steering" section.

22. Separate tie rod ends from struts.
23. Remove brake lines from suspension support below rack and pinion unit.
24. Remove air conditioning compressor and position aside with lines attached.
25. Disconnect electronic ignition module, VSS, cooling fan, starter, air conditioning compressor, oil pressure sensor, oil level sensor and ground wire electrical connections.
26. Disconnect power steering lines from rack and pinion.
27. Remove flexible coupling joint from rack and pinion.
28. Remove accelerator and cruise control cables from accelerator control bracket.
29. Remove suspension support.
30. Disconnect heater hoses from firewall.
31. Remove drive axles from transaxle and position aside.
32. Disconnect fuel lines and transaxle cooler lines. Cap lines.
33. Remove transmission mount.
34. Remove engine mount as outlined under "Engine Mount, Replace."
35. Lower vehicle until engine rests lightly on suitable support.
36. Remove engine support fixture.
37. Raise and support vehicle.
38. Remove engine and transmission.
39. Place on bench and remove transmission.
40. Reverse procedure to install, noting the following:
    a. Close radiator petcock and fill cooling system.
    b. Ensure all fluids are up to proper levels.
    c. Start engine and inspect for any fluid leaks.

INTAKE MANIFOLD

REPLACE

1. Remove air cleaner inlet duct.
2. Remove resonator and resonator bracket.
3. Remove accelerator and cruise control cables from accelerator control bracket.
4. Disconnect vacuum hoses at throttle body.
5. Disconnect MAP, TPS and IAC electrical connectors.
6. Remove throttle bracket mounting bolts and bracket, **Fig. 3.**
7. Remove throttle body mounting bolts and throttle body.
8. Remove fuel feed.
9. Remove fuel inlet pipe mounting bolts.
10. Remove mounting nuts, bolts and intake manifold.
11. Reverse procedure to install, noting the following:
    a. Clean mating surface of intake manifold and cylinder head.
    b. Inspect manifold for damage and replace as required.

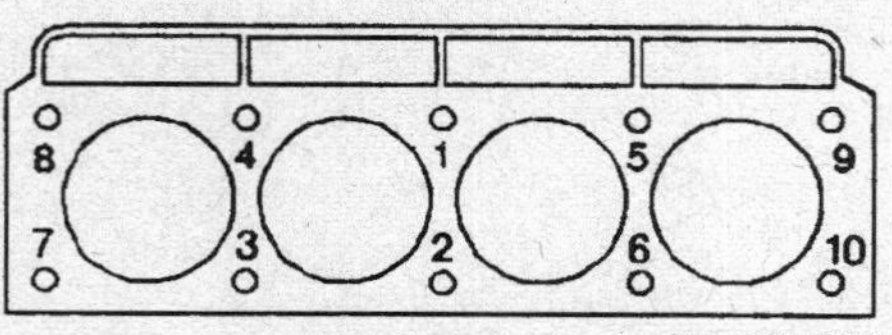

GC1069800903000X

Fig. 5 Cylinder head bolt tightening sequence

EXHAUST MANIFOLD

REPLACE

1. Disconnect lead and remove oxygen sensor.
2. Remove serpentine belt as outlined under "Serpentine Drive Belt."
3. Remove alternator mounting bolts and position it aside.
4. Remove alternator rear brace.
5. Drain coolant into suitable container and remove radiator inlet pipe.
6. Raise and support vehicle.
7. Disconnect exhaust pipe from exhaust manifold and lower vehicle.
8. Remove oil fill tube, exhaust manifold mounting bolts and exhaust manifold.
9. Reverse procedure to install. Tighten manifold mounting bolts to specifications.

CYLINDER HEAD

REPLACE

1. Drain engine coolant into suitable container.
2. Remove accessory drive belt as outlined under "Serpentine Drive Belt."
3. Remove air cleaner outlet duct.
4. Remove engine mount as outlined under "Engine Mount, Replace."
5. Remove intake manifold as outlined under "Intake Manifold, Replace."
6. Remove exhaust manifold as outlined under "Exhaust Manifold, Replace."
7. Disconnect ECT sensor electrical connector.
8. Raise and support vehicle.
9. Lower vehicle and remove valve cover, **Fig. 4.**
10. Remove rocker arms and pushrods. Keep in order for proper installation.
11. Remove alternator rear brace and alternator.
12. Remove power steering pump and position aside with lines intact.
13. Remove radiator inlet pipe.
14. Remove ignition coil.
15. Remove accessory bracket.
16. Reference mark each spark plug wire and remove from spark plugs.
17. Install engine support fixture tool No. J-28467-360, or equivalent.
18. Remove cylinder head bolts and cylinder head using reverse tightening sequence, **Fig. 5.**
19. Reverse procedure to install, noting the following:
    a. Clean cylinder head to engine block and valve cover mating surfaces.
    b. Tighten cylinder head bolts in sequence, **Fig. 5.**
    c. **Torque** long cylinder head bolts Nos. 1, 4, 5, 8 and 9 to 46 ft. lbs.

d. **Torque** short bolts Nos. 2, 3, 6, 7 and 10 to 43 ft. lbs.
e. Finally, tighten cylinder head bolts an additional 90° in sequence.

VALVE CLEARANCE SPECIFICATIONS

This engine is equipped with hydraulic lifters. Clearance is zero.

VALVE ADJUSTMENT

Valve lash is obtained through the use of hydraulic valve lifters. No adjustment is required.

VALVE GUIDES

Valve guides are an integral component of the cylinder head and are not removable. If valve stem clearance becomes excessive, the valve guide should be reamed to the next oversize and the appropriate oversize valves installed. Valves are available in several different oversizes.

HYDRAULIC LIFTERS

REPLACE

1. Remove cylinder head as outlined under "Cylinder Head, Replace."
2. Remove anti-rotation brackets and valve lifters. Keep lifters in order.
3. Inspect lifters for any signs of damage or wear, replacing as required.
4. Reverse procedure to install.

CRANKSHAFT DAMPER

REPLACE

REMOVAL

1. Remove serpentine belt, then raise and support vehicle.
2. Remove righthand front wheel and tire assembly, then inner fender splash shield.
3. Remove three crankshaft pulley mounting bolts, **Fig. 6.**
4. Remove hub bolt and crankshaft pulley.
5. Install crankshaft pulley puller tool No. J-24420-B, or equivalent on hub.
6. Turn puller screw and remove hub.

INSTALLATION

1. Coat front cover seal contact area with engine oil.
2. Apply RTV sealer No. 1052917, or equivalent, to keyway in pulley hub.
3. Place crankshaft pulley hub into position over key on crankshaft.
4. Install crankshaft pulley installer tool No. J-29113, or equivalent, into crankshaft so minimum of ¼ inch of thread is engaged.
5. Pull pulley hub into position and remove tool from crankshaft.
6. Install crankshaft pulley and mounting bolts.
7. Install inner slash shield, then wheel and tire assembly.
8. Lower vehicle and install serpentine belt.

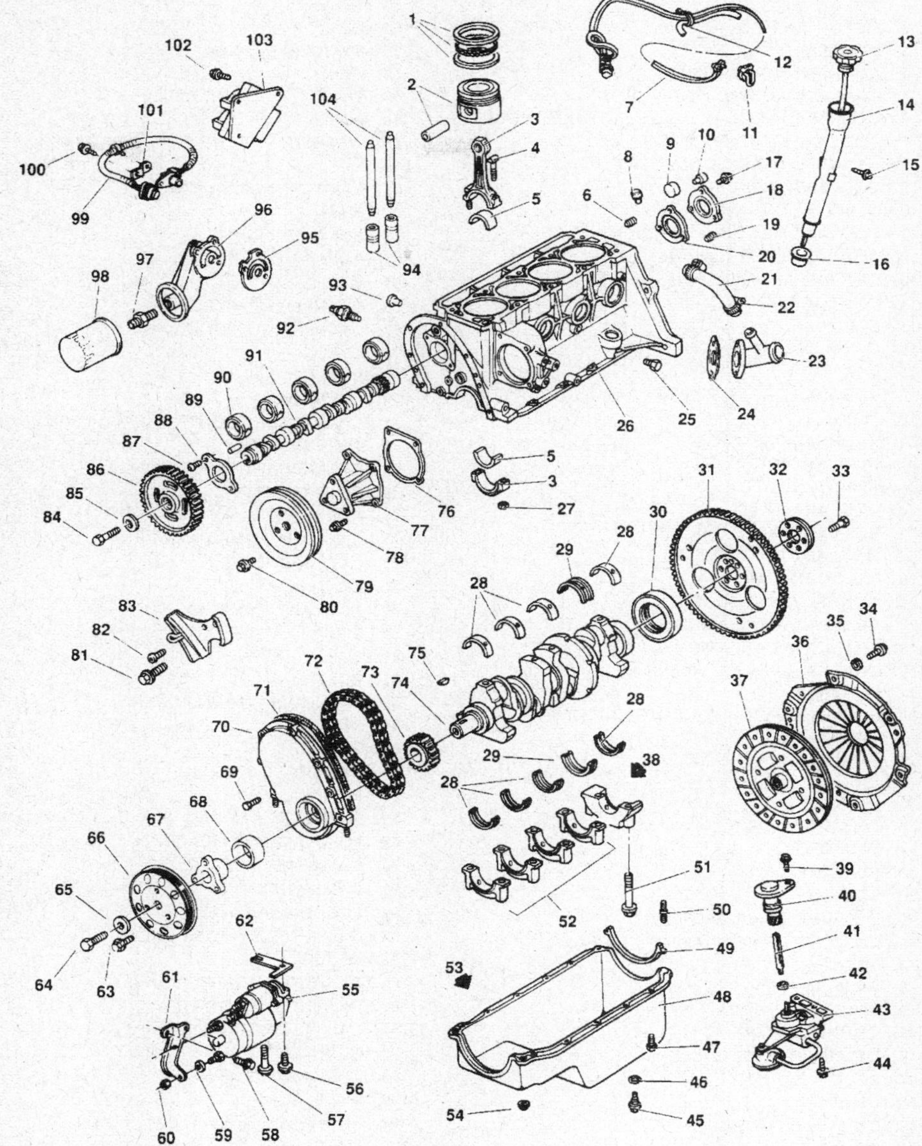

Fig. 6 Exploded view of cylinder block (Part 1 of 2)

FRONT COVER

REPLACE

1. Remove serpentine belt and belt tensioner.
2. Install engine support fixture tool No. J-28467-360, or equivalent.
3. Remove engine mount as outlined under "Engine Mount, Replace."
4. Remove alternator rear brace.
5. Remove alternator as outlined under "Alternator, Replace" in "Electrical" section, then position it aside.
6. Remove power steering pump as outlined under "Front Suspension & Steering," then position it aside with lines attached.
7. Raise and support vehicle.
8. Remove oil pan as outlined under "Oil Pan, Replace."
9. Remove crankshaft pulley and hub.
10. Remove mounting bolts and front cover.
11. Reverse procedure to install.

TIMING CHAIN

REPLACE

1. Remove crankcase front cover as outlined under "Front Cover, Replace."
2. Align marks on crankshaft sprocket and camshaft sprocket, **Fig. 7.**
3. **Before removing chain and sprockets,** measure distance between hole in bracket and unworn tensioner shoe surface. If this distance is more than 0.314 inch, replace both sprockets, tensioner and timing chain.
4. Remove timing chain tensioner bolts.
5. Remove camshaft sprocket and timing chain.
6. Remove mounting bolt and tensioner.

1. PISTON RINGS
2. PISTON AND PIN
3. CONNECTING ROD
4. CONNECTING ROD BOLT
5. CONNECTING ROD BEARING
6. CYLINDER BLOCK OIL GALLERY HOLE PLUG
7. COOLANT HEATER CORD
8. CYLINDER HEAD DOWEL PIN
9. COOLANT JACKET PLUG
10. CLUTCH HOUSING PIN
11. COOLANT HEATER
12. ADJUSTABLE RETAINER
13. OIL LEVEL RETAINER
14. OIL FILL TUBE
15. BOLT
16. OIL FILL TUBE SEAL
17. BOLT
18. CAMSHAFT REAR COVER
19. PLUG
20. CAMSHAFT REAR COVER GASKET
21. COOLANT INLET HOSE
22. CLAMP
23. COOLANT INLET
24. COOLANT INLET GASKET
25. COOLANT DRAIN PLUG
26. CYLINDER BLOCK
27. CONNECTING ROD NUT
28. CRANKSHAFT BEARING
29. CRANKSHAFT BEARING
30. CRANKSHAFT REAR OIL SEAL
31. FLYWHEEL
32. FLYWHEEL RETAINER (AUTOMATIC TRANSAXLE)
33. BOLT
34. BOLT
35. WASHER
36. PRESSURE PLATE
37. CLUTCH DISC
38. SEALANT
39. BOLT
40. OIL PUMP DRIVE ASSEMBLY
41. OIL PUMP DRIVE SHAFT
42. RETAINER
43. OIL PUMP
44. BOLT
45. OIL DRAIN PLUG
46. OIL DRAIN PLUG GASKET
47. BOLT
48. OIL PAN
49. OIL PAN REAR SEAL
50. STUD
51. BOLT
52. MAIN BEARING CAP
53. SEALER
54. NUT
55. STARTER MOTOR
56. BOLT
57. BOLT
58. BOLT
59. WASHER
60. NUT
61. STARTER MOTOR BRACKET
62. SHIM
63. BOLT
64. BOLT
65. WASHER
66. CRANKSHAFT PULLEY
67. CRANKSHAFT PULLEY HUB
68. SEAL
69. BOLT
70. CRANKCASE
71. CRANKCASE FRONT COVER OIL SEAL
72. TIMING CHAIN
73. CRANKSHAFT SPROCKET
74. CRANKSHAFT
75. KEY
76. COOLANT PUMP GASKET
77. COOLANT PUMP
78. BOLT
79. COOLANT PUMP PULLEY
80. BOLT
81. BOLT
82. BOLT
83. TIMING CHAIN TENSIONER
84. BOLT
85. WASHER
86. CAMSHAFT SPROCKET
87. SCREW
88. THRUST PLATE
89. PIN CAMSHAFT BEARING
90. CAMSHAFT BEARING
91. CAMSHAFT
92. FUEL PUMP SWITCH
93. OIL FILTER BY-PASS VALVE
94. LIFTER
95. OIL FILTER ADAPTER GASKET
96. OIL FILTER ADAPTER
97. OIL FILTER CONNECTOR
98. OIL FILTER
99. CRANKSHAFT SENSOR
100. BOLT
101. RETAINER
102. BOLT
103. COIL
104. PUSHROD

GC106910036800BX

Fig. 6 Exploded view of cylinder block (Part 2 of 2)

7. Remove crankshaft sprocket using puller tool No. J-22888-20, or equivalent.
8. Reverse procedure to install, noting the following:
   a. Install crankshaft sprocket fully seated against crankshaft using sprocket installer tool No. J-5590, or equivalent.
   b. Compress tensioner spring and install cotter pin or nail into hole A, **Fig. 8.**
   c. Align marks on camshaft and crankshaft sprockets with tabs on tensioner.
   d. Align dowel in camshaft with dowel hole camshaft sprocket.
   e. Draw camshaft sprocket onto camshaft using mounting bolt.
   f. Tighten mounting bolts to specifications.

CAMSHAFT

REPLACE

1. Remove timing chain as outlined under "Timing Chain, Replace."
2. Drain engine oil into suitable container and remove oil filter.
3. Remove serpentine belt as outlined under "Serpentine Drive Belt."
4. Remove alternator and related brackets as outlined under "Alternator, Replace."
5. Remove power steering pump as outlined under "Front Suspension & Steering."

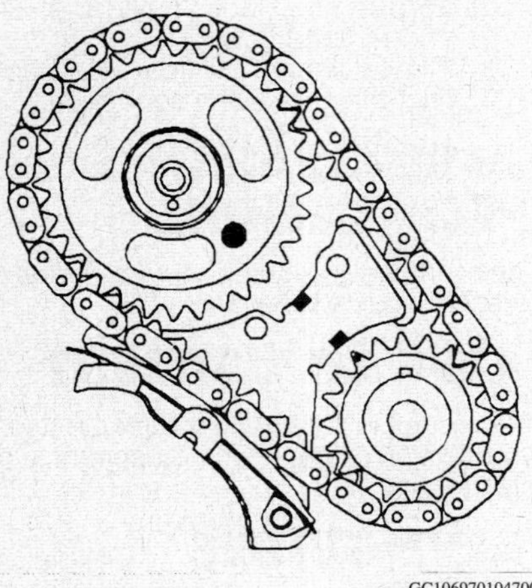

Fig. 7 Timing chain & sprockets

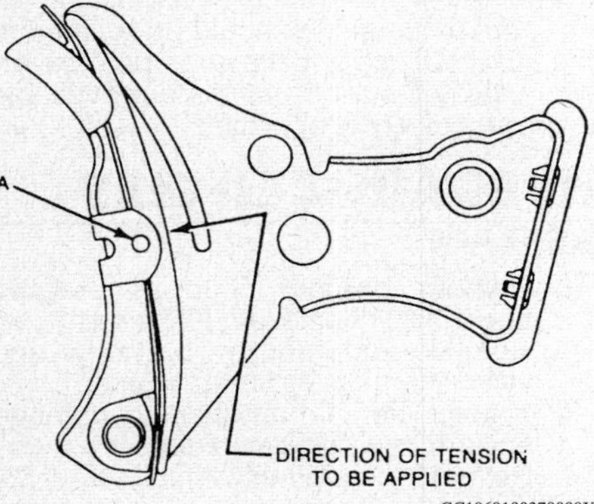

Fig. 8 Timing chain tensioner

6. Remove drive belt tensioner.
7. Remove water pump pulley.
8. Remove crankshaft pulley and hub.
9. Remove cylinder head as outlined under "Cylinder Head, Replace."
10. Remove valve lifters.
11. Remove camshaft sprocket, timing chain and tensioner.
12. Remove oil pump drive.
13. Remove thrust plate.
14. Remove CMP sensor.
15. Carefully remove camshaft. **Avoid damaging camshaft bearings.**
16. Inspect camshaft for galling, gouges, overheating and wear. If any of these conditions exist, replace camshaft.
17. Reverse procedure to install, noting the following:
    a. **Coat camshaft lobes and bearings with camshaft lube No. 1051396, or equivalent.**
    b. **Install camshaft with extreme care to avoid personal injury and gouging of camshaft bearings.**
    c. Tighten thrust plate to specifications.
    d. Lifters must be installed in original bores.
    e. **If new camshaft is installed, replace all valve lifters. Some lifters may be oversized. Ensure marking near lifter bore.**
    f. Valve mechanism components

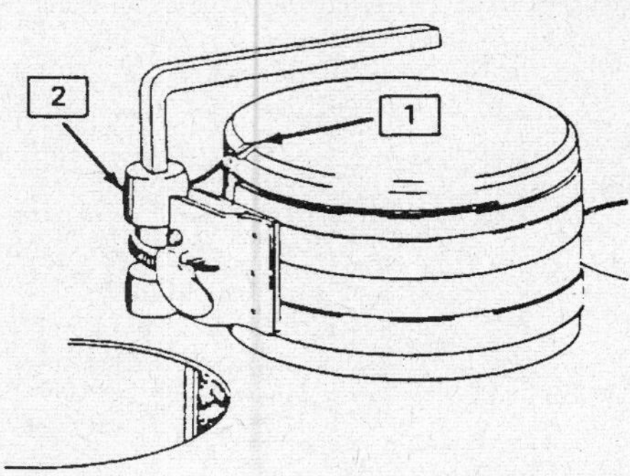

GC1069100371000X

Fig. 9 Piston installation

must be installed in original positions and with same mating surfaces as removed.

g. Replace oil filter.
h. Ensure oil pan drain plug and gasket are intact.

PISTON & ROD ASSEMBLY

Assemble piston to rod with arrow on piston facing toward front of engine, **Fig. 9.**

Measure connecting rod side clearance, Clearance should be .0039–.0149 inch.

PISTONS, PINS & RINGS

Pistons are available in standard size and oversizes of .0015 inch, .002 inch and .004 inch. Piston pins are available in standard size only.

CRANKSHAFT REAR OIL SEAL

REPLACE

1. **On models equipped with automatic transaxle,** remove transaxle as outlined in "Automatic Transaxles/ Transmission" section.
2. **On models equipped with manual transaxle,** remove transaxle, pressure plate and clutch disc as outlined in "Clutch & Manual Transaxle" section.
3. **On all models,** remove flywheel mounting bolts and flywheel.
4. Pry seal out by insert suitable screwdriver through dust lip, **Fig. 10.**
5. Reverse procedure to install, noting the following:
   a. Lubricate seal bore to seal surface with suitable clean engine oil.
   b. Align seal installation tool No. J-34686, or equivalent, dowel pin with crankshaft dowel pin hole and attach tool to crankshaft.
   c. Tighten tool T-handle to push seal into bore. Continue to tighten until tool is flush against block.

OIL PAN

REPLACE

1. Raise and support vehicle.
2. Drain engine oil into suitable container.

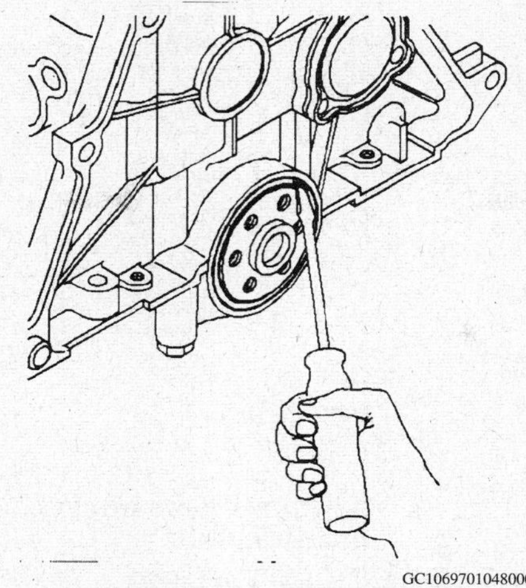

GC1069701048000X

Fig. 10 Crankshaft rear seal removal

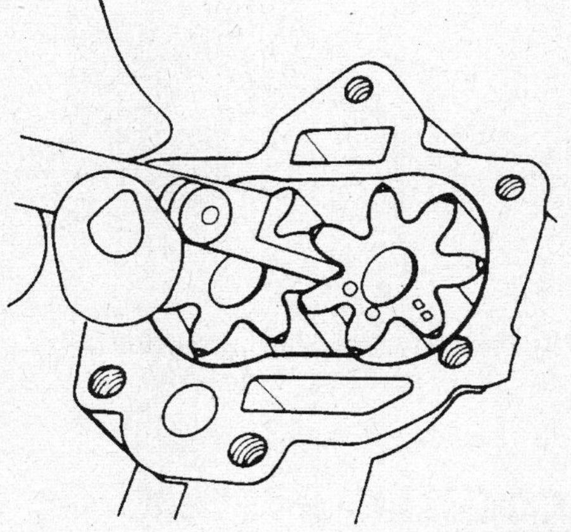

GC1099100052000X

Fig. 12 Oil pump gear lash measurement

3. Remove righthand front tire and wheel.
4. Remove righthand front splash shield.
5. Remove starter bracket at block.
6. Remove starter as outlined under "Starter, Replace" in "Electrical" section.
7. Remove flywheel inspection cover.
8. Remove engine mount strut bracket as outlined under "Engine Mount Strut & Strut Bracket, Replace."
9. Remove oil level sensor.
10. Remove mounting bolts, nuts and oil pan.
11. Reverse procedure to install, noting the following:
    a. Clean all crankcase, front cover and pan sealing surfaces. Ensure all old RTV has been removed from blind mounting holes.
    b. Apply 1/16 inch diameter bead of Loctite 5900 RTV sealer, or equivalent, on oil pan to block sealing flanges. **Do not apply sealer to rear seal mounting surface.**
    c. Install new oil pan rear seal and apply Loctite 5900 RTV sealer, or equivalent, to ends down to ears.

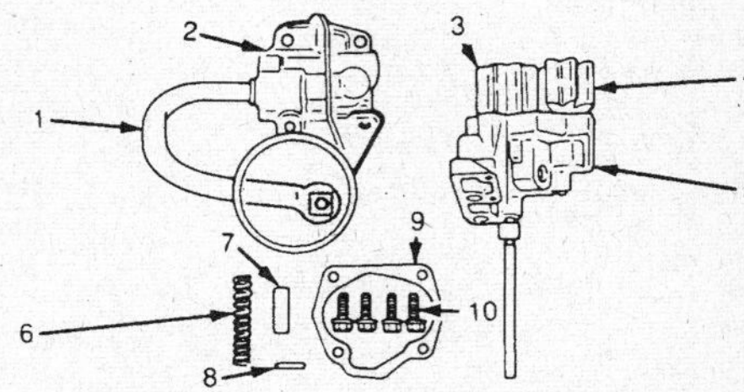

1. PICK UP TUBE AND SCREEN.
2. PUMP COVER.
3. DRIVE GEAR AND SHAFT.
4. IDLER GEAR.
5. PUMP BODY.
6. PRESSURE REGULATOR SPRING
7. PRESSURE REGULATOR VALVE.
8. RETAINING PIN.
9. GASKET.
10. ATTACHING BOLTS.

GC1099100051000X

Fig. 11 Exploded view of oil pump

OIL PUMP SERVICE

REMOVAL

1. Remove oil pan as outlined under "Oil Pan, Replace."
2. Remove pump to rear main bearing cap bolt, pump, extension shaft and retainer.

DISASSEMBLE

1. Drain oil from pump and remove driveshaft, **Fig. 11.**
2. Remove pump cover, **Do not remove pickup tube from cover unless loose or broken.**
3. Remove pump gears and pressure regulator valve. **Pressure regulator valve spring is under pressure.**
4. Remove plug, spring and valve. If valve is stuck, soak pump housing in carburetor cleaning solvent.

INSPECTION

Thoroughly clean all oil pump components and inspect them for excessive wear or damage.

1. Inspect oil pump clearances using straightedge and feeler gauge, **Figs. 12 through 15.**
2. Install gears and measure lash in several places, within .004–.008 inch.
3. Measure depth and diameter of oil pump gear pocket. Depth should be 1.195–1.198 inches. Diameter, 1.503–1.506 inches.
4. Measure gear side clearance to .001–.004.
5. Measure gear end clearance to .002–.006. When determining pump serviceability based on end clearance, consider depth of wear pattern in pump cover and/or cover plate.

ASSEMBLE

1. Lubricate all internal components with engine oil during assembly.
2. Install pump gears. **To avoid engine damage, all pump cavities must be packed with petroleum jelly before installing gears to ensure priming.**
3. Install oil pump cover and gasket.
4. Install pressure regulator valve, spring and retaining pin.

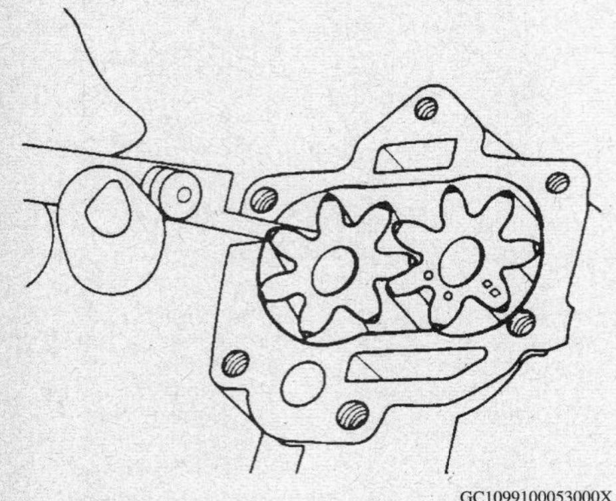

Fig. 13 Gear side clearance measurement

5. Tighten pump cover bolts to specifications. When oil pump is overhauled, clear oil pan of oil and sludge, replace oil filter and fill crankcase with clean oil.

INSTALLATION

1. Heat retainer in hot water, but not so hot it would crack during installation.
2. Install retainer to extension shaft.
3. Install extension to oil pump.
4. Tighten main bearing cap bolt to specifications.
5. Install oil pan.
6. Start engine and ensure oil pressure is as specified.

BELT TENSION DATA

The serpentine belt is automatically adjusted by a spring tensioner. No adjustment is required.

SERPENTINE DRIVE BELT

BELT, REPLACE

1. Rotate tensioner clockwise with suitable wrench and slide belt from alternator pulley.
2. Release tensioner and remove belt.
3. Reverse procedure to install, **Figs. 16 and 17.**

TENSIONER, REPLACE

1998

1. Remove drive belt as outlined under "Serpentine Drive Belt."
2. Remove tensioner bolts.
3. Remove tensioner.
4. Reverse procedure to install.

1999-2002

1. Remove serpentine belt as outlined under "Serpentine Drive Belt."
2. Remove alternator and position it aside.
3. Raise and support vehicle.
4. Remove oil filter.
5. Remove idler pulley.
6. Remove mounting bolt and position air conditioning compressor aside with lines attached.
7. Remove mounting bolts and tensioner.

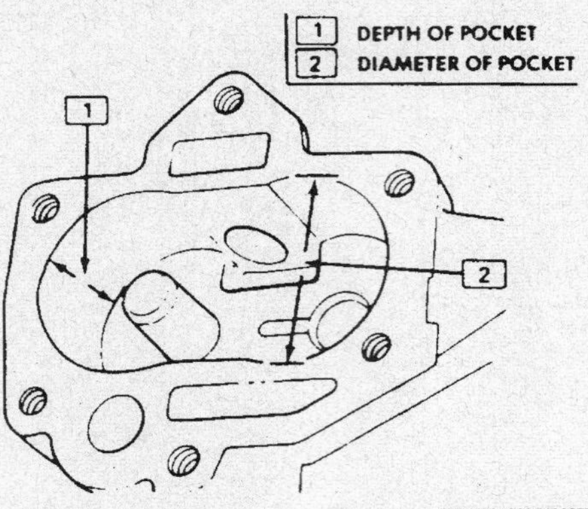

Fig. 14 Oil pump gear pocket measurement

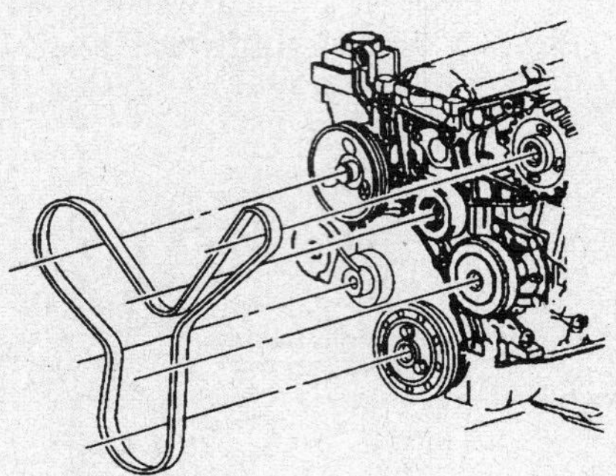

Fig. 16 Serpentine drive belt routing. Less A/C

8. Reverse procedure to install.

COOLING SYSTEM BLEED

1. **On models equipped with bleeder valve,** open valve.
2. **On all models,** fill surge tank or radiator to 1 inch below filler neck.
3. Close bleeder valve.
4. Block drive wheels and apply parking brake.
5. **On models equipped with automatic transaxle,** place shifter in Park position.
6. **On models equipped with manual transaxle,** place shifter in Neutral position.
7. **On all models,** start engine and turn HVAC controls to HEATER and FULL HOT.
8. Allow engine to run until upper radiator hose is hot.
9. Turn engine off and inspect level of coolant in surge tank or radiator.
10. Allow engine to cool and add coolant, as required.

THERMOSTAT

REPLACE

1. Remove air intake duct.
2. With engine cool, drain engine coolant into suitable container below thermostat level. **Never open cooling system with engine hot.**

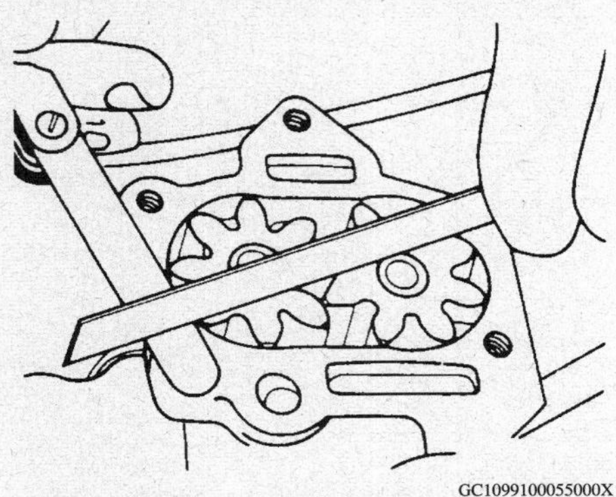

Fig. 15 Oil pump end clearance measurement

3. Disconnect radiator hose or outlet pipe from thermostat housing.
4. Remove mounting nuts, housing, gasket and thermostat.
5. Reverse procedure to install, noting the following:
   a. Ensure thermostat gasket area is thoroughly clean.
   b. Install thermostat with new gasket.
   c. Fill and bleed cooling system as required.

WATER PUMP

REPLACE

1. Drain cooling system into suitable container.
2. Loosen water pump pulley mounting bolts.
3. Remove serpentine drive belt as outlined under "Serpentine Drive Belt."
4. Remove alternator and mounting bracket as outlined under "Alternator, Replace" in "Electrical" section.
5. Remove mounting bolts and water pump pulley, **Fig. 18.**
6. Remove mounting bolts and water pump.
7. Reverse procedure to install.

RADIATOR

REPLACE

1. Drain and recover engine coolant into suitable container.
2. Remove hood latch support from mounting plate.
3. Remove both headlamp assemblies.
4. Remove radiator upper mounts.
5. Raise and support vehicle.
6. Disconnect forward discriminating sensor electrical connector.
7. Remove cooling fan.
8. Remove lower radiator hose from radiator.
9. Remove lower transaxle oil cooler line from radiator and lower vehicle.
10. Remove hood latch support bracket and forward discriminating sensor with electrical harness.
11. Disconnect upper transaxle oil cooler line from radiator.
12. Remove upper radiator hose and overflow hose from radiator.
13. Remove condenser from radiator, if equipped.

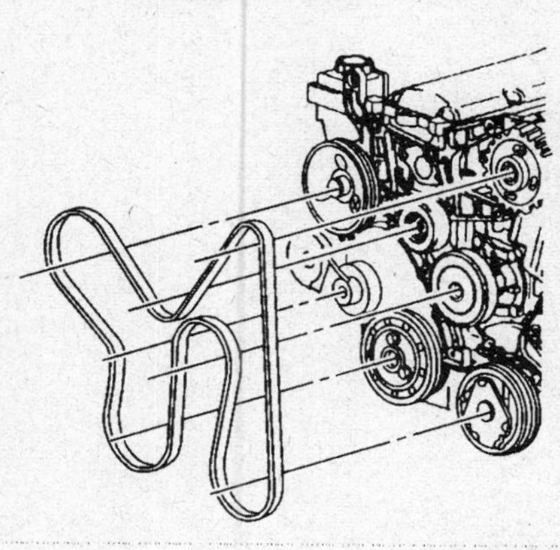

GC1069800907000A

Fig. 17 Serpentine drive belt routing. With A/C

14. Remove radiator.
15. Reverse procedure to install.

FUEL PUMP

REPLACE

1. Drain fuel tank into suitable container.
2. Raise and support vehicle.
3. Disconnect tank meter harness from body harness connector.
4. Remove ground wire mounting screw from underbody and disconnect hoses from fuel meter.
5. Disconnect hoses at tank from filler and vent pipes.
6. Support fuel tank with jack and disconnect fuel tank mounting straps.

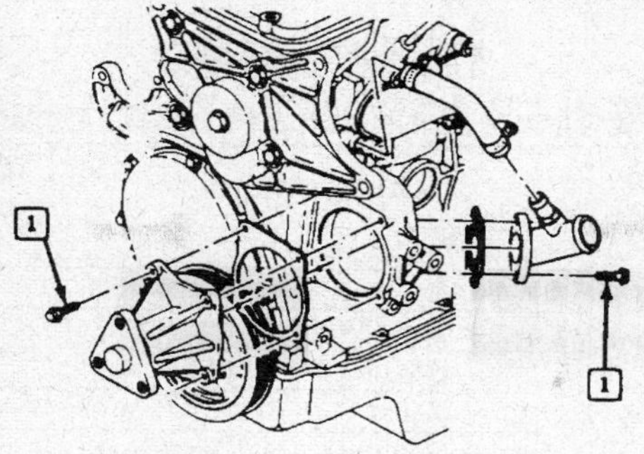

GC1089100159000X

Fig. 18 Water pump installation

7. Remove tank.
8. Remove fuel tank sending unit and pump by turning cam lock ring counterclockwise. **Sending unit might pop up from its position. Reservoir bucket may be full of fuel.** Tip sending unit slightly to avoid float damage.
9. Lift assembly from fuel tank.
10. Reverse procedure to install.

FUEL FILTER

REPLACE

1. Raise and support vehicle.
2. Remove filter fitting using suitable back-up wrench. If nylon fuel lines become kinked and cannot be straightened, they must be replaced.

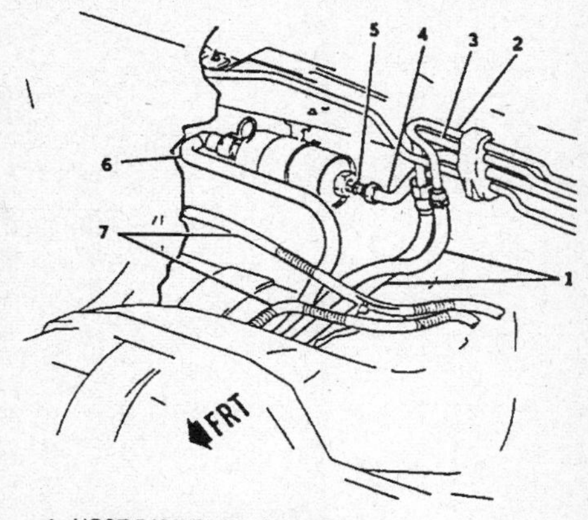

1. HOSE-PART OF FUEL SENDER
2. FUEL VAPOR PIPE
3. FUEL RETURN PIPE
4. FUEL FEED PIPE
5. FUEL FEED PIPE NUT
6. HOSE-PART OF FUEL SENDER
7. ABS AND FUEL SENDER HARNESS

GC1029202728000X

Fig. 19 Fuel filter replacement

3. Twist quick-connect fitting ¼ turn in each direction to loosen dirt within fitting.
4. Clean quick-connect fitting at ends of filter using compressed air.
5. Disconnect quick-connect fittings by squeezing plastic tabs of male end connector and pulling apart.
6. Remove fuel filter, **Fig. 19.**
7. Reverse procedure to install.

TIGHTENING SPECIFICATIONS

Year	Component	Torque/Ft. Lbs.
1998–2002	Accelerator Cable Mounting Bracket	90①
	Accessory Bracket	37
	Accessory Drive Belt Idler Pulley	37
	Camshaft Position Sensor To Block	90①
	Camshaft Rear Cove	108①
	Camshaft Sprocket	96
	Camshaft Thrust Plate	108①
	Clutch Cover & Pressure Plate	15④
	Connecting Rod Cap	38
	Crankcase Front Cover	96①
	Crankshaft Main Bearing Cap	70
	Crankshaft Pulley Hub To Crankshaft	77
	Crankshaft Pulley To Hub	37
	Crankshaft Sensor	72①
	Cylinder Head Bolts	③
	Direct Ignition System Coil	18
	EGR Pipe To Adapter	18
	EGR Pipe To Manifold	90①
	EGR Valve Adapter	96①
	EGR Valve Adapter To Cylinder Head Bolts	90①
	EGR Valve To Adapter	19
	Engine Lift Bracket	37

Continued

TIGHTENING SPECIFICATIONS—Continued

Year	Component	Torque/Ft. Lbs.
1998–2002	Engine Mount Cage	33
	Engine Mount To Accessory Bracket	44②
	Engine Mount To Body	⑤
	Engine Mount Strut	74②
	Engine Mount Strut Bracket (Front)	49
	Engine Mount Strut Bracket (Rear)	44
	Exhaust Manifold	10
	Flexplate Or Flywheel Bolt	55
	Fuel Filter Fitting	20
	Intake Manifold Bolts	17
	Intake Manifold Nuts	17
	Intake Manifold Studs	108①
	Knock Sensor	26
	Large Oil Gallery Plug (Rear Of Engine Block)	24
	Lifter Guide	96①
	Oil Fill Tube	37
	Oil Filter	13
	Oil Filter Adapter	26
	Oil Gallery Plugs (Side Of Block Above Oil Filter)	15
	Oil Pan	90①
	Oil Pump Cover	90①
	Oil Pump Drive	18
	Oil Pump Mounting	32
	Oil Pressure Sensor Switch	108①
	Oxygen Sensor	31
	Rocker Arm	19
	Rocker Arm Cover	90①
	Serpentine Drive Belt Tensioner	37
	Small Oil Gallery Plug (Rear Of Engine Block)	11
	Spark Plugs	13
	Thermostat Housing	10
	Throttle Body To Intake Manifold	90①
	Timing Chain Tensioner	18
	Water Jacket Drain Plug	11
	Water Outlet Pipe	19
	Water Pump	18
	Water Pump Inlet	18
	Water Pump Pulley Bolts	22

① — Inch lbs.

② — Tighten an additional 90.°

③ — Refer to "Cylinder Head, Replace" for tightening sequence and procedure.

④ — Tighten an additional 45.°

⑤ — 1998, 49 ft. lbs.; 1999–2002, 55 ft. lbs.

2.4L Engine

NOTE: On Air Bag Equipped Models, Refer To "Air Bag System Precautions" Located In The Front Of This Manual For System Disarming & Arming Procedures.

NOTE: Refer To "Computer Relearn Procedures" Located In The Front Of This Manual When Battery Power To The Computer Has Been Interrupted.

NOTE: Refer To "2.4L Engine" in "Achieva, Alero, Cutlass, Grand Am, Malibu & Skylark" Chapter For Procedures Not Covered In This Section.

INDEX

PRECAUTIONS

AIR BAG SYSTEMS

Refer to "Air Bag System Precautions" in the front of this manual for system disarming and arming procedures.

BATTERY GROUND CABLE

Prior to service, disconnect battery ground cable and isolate as required.

FUEL SYSTEM PRESSURE RELIEF

1. Raise and support vehicle.
2. Disconnect fuel pump electrical connector.
3. Start engine and run until remaining fuel is consumed.
4. Engage starter for approximately three seconds to ensure relief of any remaining pressure.
5. Disconnect and isolate battery ground cable to avoid possible fuel discharge if any attempt is made to start engine.

COMPRESSION PRESSURE

When inspecting cylinder compression, the throttle should be open, all spark plugs removed and the battery at or near full charge. The lowest reading cylinder should not be less than 70% of the highest and no cylinder reading should be less than 100 psi. Turn ignition key until engine cranks through four compression cycles. Normal compression builds up quickly and evenly to specifications on each cylinder.

ENGINE MOUNT

REPLACE

1. Remove coolant recovery tank mounting bolt and position tank aside.
2. Install engine support tool No. J-28467-360, or equivalent, and raise engine off mount.
3. Remove body to mount mounting nuts, engine bracket to mount bolts and mount.
4. Reverse procedure to install. Tighten mounting nuts and bolts to specifications.

ENGINE MOUNT STRUT

REPLACE

1. Raise and support vehicle.
2. Remove righthand front splash shield.
3. Remove engine mount strut bolts and engine mount strut.
4. Reverse procedure to install. Tighten mounting bolts to specifications.

ENGINE

REPLACE

1. Drain engine coolant into suitable container.
2. **On models equipped with air conditioning,** recover refrigerant and disconnect compressor/condenser hose assembly at compressor.
3. **On all models,** remove lefthand sound insulator and disconnect clutch pushrod from pedal.
4. Disconnect heater hose at thermostat housing and upper radiator hose.
5. Remove air cleaner and coolant fan.
6. Disconnect all vacuum hoses and electrical connectors.
7. Disconnect throttle cable and bracket.
8. Remove power steering rear bracket and power brake vacuum tube as an assembly.
9. Disconnect and position aside power steering pump.
10. Disconnect fuel lines.
11. **On models equipped with automatic transaxle,** disconnect shift cables.
12. **On models equipped with manual transaxle,** disconnect clutch actuator line.
13. **On all models,** remove exhaust manifold and heat shields.
14. Disconnect lower radiator hose, install engine support tool No. J-28467-360, or equivalent, and remove engine mount.
15. Raise and support vehicle, then remove both front tire and wheel assemblies.
16. Remove righthand side splash shield and radiator air deflector.
17. Remove engine and transaxle mount.
18. Separate ball joints from steering knuckles as outlined under "Front Suspension & Steering" section.
19. Remove suspension supports, crossmember and stabilizer shaft as an assembly.
20. Disconnect air conditioning lines from oil pan.
21. Remove air flywheel housing cover.
22. Position suitable support beneath engine and carefully lower vehicle.
23. Mark threads on support fixture hooks so setting can be duplicated when installing engine.
24. Remove engine support J hooks, then slowly raise vehicle away from engine and transaxle.
25. Reverse procedure to install.

RADIATOR

REPLACE

Refer to "Radiator, Replace" in the "2.2L Engine" section of "Cavalier & Sunfire" chapter.

TIGHTENING SPECIFICATIONS

Year	Component	Torque/Ft. Lbs.
1998–2002	Engine Mount Bracket To Block	44①
	Engine Mount, Front Bolts	49
	Engine Mount, Lower Bolts	96
	Engine Mount To Body, Nuts	55
	Engine Mount Strut, Bolts	74②

① — Tighten an additional 90°.
② — 1999–2002, tighten an additional 90°.

Clutch & Manual Transaxle

NOTE: On Air Bag Equipped Models, Refer To "Air Bag System Precautions" Located In The Front Of This Manual For System Disarming & Arming Procedures.

NOTE: Refer To "Computer Relearn Procedures" Located In The Front Of This Manual When Battery Power To The Computer Has Been Interrupted.

INDEX

PRECAUTIONS

AIR BAG SYSTEMS

Refer to "Air Bag System Precautions" in the front of this manual for system disarming and arming procedures.

BATTERY GROUND CABLE

Prior to service, disconnect battery ground cable and isolate as required.

ADJUSTMENTS

CLUTCH PEDAL

These models use a hydraulic clutch system consisting of a dash mounted master cylinder with integral reservoir, a transmission mounted slave cylinder and high pressure tubing to connect the two components.

The hydraulic clutch system provides automatic clutch adjustment. There is no provision for adjustment.

HYDRAULIC SYSTEM SERVICE

HYDRAULIC SYSTEM BLEED

1. Clean dirt and foreign substances from reservoir cap.
2. Fill reservoir with hydraulic clutch fluid No. 12345347, or suitable DOT 3 type brake fluid.
3. Attach hose to clutch actuator bleeder screw and submerge other end in container of clutch fluid.
4. Have assistant depress and hold clutch pedal.
5. Fully loosen bleeder screw located on slave cylinder near inlet connection.
6. While maintaining reservoir fluid level, allow fluid to flow from bleeder valve until steady stream of fluid with no air bubbles is present.
7. **Torque** bleeder screw to 18 inch lbs.
8. Fill reservoir to proper level and start engine.
9. Depress clutch for approximately nine seconds and select reverse gear. If no gear clash is present, system is satisfactory. If gear clash is present, repeat bleeding procedure.

CLUTCH MASTER CYLINDER, REPLACE

Removal

1. Remove sound insulator from inside of vehicle.
2. Disconnect clutch master cylinder pushrod from clutch pedal.
3. Remove clutch master cylinder mounting nuts at front of dash and disconnect remote reservoir.
4. Disconnect fluid master line from actuator line by pushing release slide in, holding and disconnecting halves.
5. Remove clutch master cylinder.

Installation

1. Install clutch master cylinder to front of dash.
2. Connect fluid master line to actuator line by pushing release slide in, holding and connecting halves.
3. Connect remote reservoir.
4. Remove pedal restrictor from pushrod and lubricate pushrod bushing on clutch pedal.
5. Connect pushrod with clutch pedal and install retaining clip.
6. Install sound insulator.
7. Bleed clutch fluid line as outlined under "Hydraulic System Bleed."

CLUTCH ACTUATOR CYLINDER, REPLACE

Removal

1. Disconnect fluid master line from actuator line by pushing release slide in, holding and disconnecting halves.
2. Remove transaxle as outlined under "Transaxle, Replace."
3. Remove cylinder to bellhousing mounting bolts and clutch actuator.

Installation

1. Lubricate inner diameter of release bearing with clutch bearing lubricant No. 12345777, or equivalent.
2. Install clutch actuator cylinder to bellhousing.
3. Install transaxle.
4. Connect fluid master line from actuator line by pushing release slide in, holding and connecting halves.
5. Bleed clutch fluid line as outlined under "Hydraulic System Bleed."

CLUTCH

REPLACE

1. Remove clutch actuator cylinder line.
2. Remove clutch master cylinder assembly from clutch actuator cylinder.
3. Remove transaxle as outlined under "Transaxle, Replace."
4. Remove clutch cover bolts, one turn at a time, until spring pressure is relieved.
5. Remove clutch cover, then the clutch disc.
6. Reverse procedure to install, noting the following:
   a. Align flywheel assembly stamped with an X with clutch cover light side, marked with paint.
   b. Tighten to specifications.
   c. Bleed hydraulic system as required.

TRANSAXLE

REPLACE

1998–99

1. Install engine support fixture tool No. J28467-360, or equivalent.
2. Remove lefthand sound insulator.
3. Remove clutch master cylinder pushrod from clutch pedal.
4. Remove air cleaner and duct assembly from throttle body.

5. Remove wire harness from upper transaxle mount.
6. Remove upper transaxle mount to transaxle bolts, then the upper transaxle mount.
7. Remove master cylinder retaining nuts at front of dash.
8. Remove remote reservoir.
9. Disconnect clutch actuator cylinder line, then remove clutch master cylinder assembly from clutch actuator cylinder.
10. Remove ground cables from transaxle mounting studs.
11. Disconnect back-up light switch.
12. Remove transaxle vent tube.
13. Remove rear transaxle mount bolts, then the mount.
14. Lower safety stand for removal and installation of transaxle.
15. Raise and support vehicle using suitable hoist, support vehicle with safety stand.
16. Drain transaxle into suitable container.
17. Remove front tires and wheels.
18. Remove lefthand front inner splash shield.
19. Remove ABS/WSS connectors.
20. Route lefthand side harness out of way.
21. Remove flywheel housing cover.
22. Disconnect vehicle speed sensor lead from transaxle.
23. Remove vehicle speed sensor bolt, then the vehicle speed sensor retainer.
24. Remove vehicle speed sensor assembly, then the O-ring.
25. Remove lefthand and righthand ball joint nuts as outlined under "Front Suspension & Steering."
26. Remove lefthand stabilizer link pin as outlined under "Front Suspension & Steering."
27. Remove U-bolt from stabilizer bar.
28. Remove lefthand suspension support attaching bolts as follows:
    a. Remove bolt from front suspension support brace and suspension support crossmember.
    b. Remove bolt from front suspension support brace and lower tie bar.
    c. Remove front suspension support brace from vehicle.
29. Disconnect stabilizer link from lower control arm.
30. Disengage axle from hub and bearing using front hub spindle remover tool No. J28733, or equivalent, then separate hub and bearing assembly from drive axle.
31. Move strut and knuckle assembly rearward.
32. Remove inner joint from transaxle using J 33008 attached to J 29794 and J 2619-01, or equivalents, for intermediate shaft, if equipped.
33. Remove front lower transaxle mount bolts, then the mount.
34. Install transaxle case to support stand.
35. Remove transaxle to engine mount bolts.
36. Remove transaxle.
37. Reverse procedure to install, noting the following:
    a. Tighten stabilizer link nut until nut meets end of bolt threads for torque value.
    b. Bleed hydraulic system.

2000-02

1. Remove retaining bolt and battery.
2. Remove washer solvent container.
3. Install engine support fixture tool No. J28467-360, or equivalent.
4. Raise engine to eliminate pressure from transaxle mounts.
5. Remove air cleaner and duct assembly.
6. Drain engine coolant into suitable container.
7. Remove upper radiator hose.
8. Remove wire harness from upper transaxle mount bracket.
9. Remove upper transaxle mount bolts.
10. Remove battery ground cable from transaxle housing.
11. Remove starter as outlined under "Starter, Replace" in "Electrical" section.
12. Disconnect pressure line from clutch actuator cylinder.
13. Disconnect back-up light switch connector.
14. Remove rear transaxle mount bolts.
15. Disconnect vehicle speed sensor.
16. Remove upper transaxle mounting bolts.
17. Disconnect shift cables at transaxle shift control and bracket.
18. Remove cable bracket bolt, then the bracket.
19. Remove rack and pinion mounting bolts.
20. Raise and support vehicle.
21. Remove tire and wheel assemblies
22. Remove front fender liners.
23. Remove power steering gear mounting bolts, secure power steering gear out of way.
24. Remove front suspension support brace.
25. Lower vehicle until front suspension crossmember rests on jack stands.
26. Remove front suspension crossmember mounting bolts, then the front suspension crossmember.
27. Remove flywheel support arm bracket from flywheel cover to engine lower mount.
28. Remove flywheel housing cover bolts, then the flywheel housing cover.
29. Remove drive axles from transaxle.
30. Remove engine strut from bracket.
31. Remove front lower transaxle mount through bolt.
32. Install transaxle case to support stand.
33. Support engine using suitable axle jack.
34. Remove transaxle to engine mount bolts, then the transaxle.
35. Reverse procedure to install, noting the following:
    a. Bleed hydraulic system.
    b. Bleed power steering system.

TIGHTENING SPECIFICATIONS

Year	Component	Torque/Ft. Lbs.
1998–2002	Drain Fill Plug	28
	Front Transmission Mount (1998–99)	55
	Front Transaxle Mount Through Bolt (2000–02)	44
	Intermediate Shaft Bolts	74
	Lower Transaxle Mount Bolts	44
	Rack & Pinion Mounting Bolts	89
	Rear Cover Bolts	18
	Rear Transaxle Mount	55
	Reverse Switch	13
	Ring Gear	66
	Shaft Bolts	74
	Shift Cable Clamp Nut	89①
	Shifter Guide Bolts	18
	Shifter Mounting Bolts	18
	Speed Sensor Bolt	96①
	Transaxle Housing Bolts	18
	Upper Transaxle Mounting Bolts	71

① — Inch lbs.

Rear Axle & Suspension

NOTE: On Air Bag Equipped Models, Refer To "Air Bag System Precautions" Located In The Front Of This Manual For System Disarming & Arming Procedures.

NOTE: Refer To "Computer Relearn Procedures" Located In The Front Of This Manual When Battery Power To The Computer Has Been Interrupted.

INDEX

PRECAUTIONS

AIR BAG SYSTEMS

Refer to "Air Bag System Precautions" in the front of this manual for system disarming and arming procedures.

BATTERY GROUND CABLE

Prior to service, disconnect battery ground cable and isolate as required.

DESCRIPTION

The rear suspension is a semi-independent type consisting of an axle assembly with trailing arms and twisting cross beam, coil springs and coil-over shock absorbers. A stabilizer bar is available and is attached to the inside of the axle beam and to the lower end of the control arms. A single unit hub and bearing assembly is bolted to each end of the axle assembly. The hub and bearing assembly is a sealed, non-serviceable unit and must be replaced as an assembly.

REAR AXLE

REPLACE

1. Raise and support vehicle.
2. Remove rear wheels and tires.
3. Remove brake drums. **Do not hammer on drums.**
4. Remove brake fluid pipe retainer bolts from axle.
5. Disconnect brake pipe at brake hose.
6. Disconnect wheel speed sensor harnesses at sensors.
7. Remove wheel speed sensor harness from retainers on axle.
8. Disconnect parking brake cables from equalizers.
9. Remove parking brake cables from axle.
10. Support rear suspension with suitable jack.
11. Remove shock absorber lower mounting bolts.
12. Remove mounting bolts, washers and nuts from axle.
13. Carefully lower rear axle.
14. Remove control arm to underbody bracket bolts, lower rear axle and remove.
15. Remove hub to rear axle mounting bolts, hubs, bearings and backing plates from rear axle.
16. Reverse procedure to install. Bleed brake system.

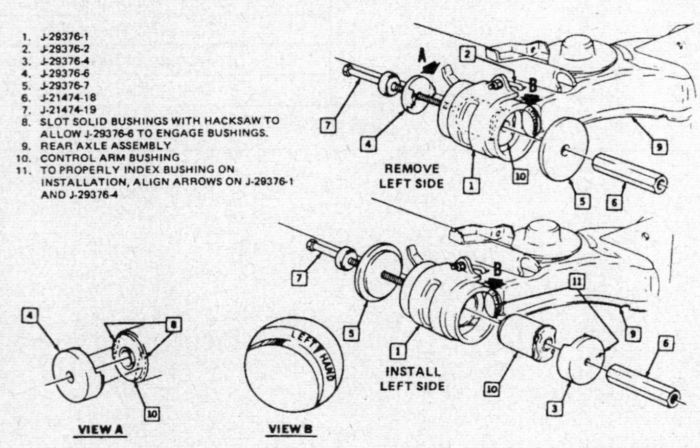

Fig. 1 Control arm bushing replacement

HUB & BEARING

REPLACE

1. Raise and support vehicle, then remove wheel and tire assembly.
2. Remove brake drum. **Do not hammer brake drum.**
3. Disconnect wheel speed sensor electrical connector.
4. Remove mounting bolts and hub/bearing. **Upper rear hub mounting bolt may not clear brake shoe when removing hub and bearing. Partially remove hub and bearing prior to removing this bolt.**
5. Reverse procedure to install. Tighten hub mounting bolts to specifications. **Do not drop hub/bearing assembly.**

SHOCK ABSORBER

REPLACE

1. Raise rear of vehicle and support rear axle using suitable jack.
2. Remove lower mounting bolt, disconnect shock absorber from mounting bracket and remove it.
3. Reverse procedure to install. Tighten mounting bolts to specifications.

CONTROL ARM BUSHING

REPLACE

Remove and install one control arm bushing at a time by proceeding as follows:

1. Raise and support vehicle.
2. Support rear axle with suitable jack.
3. Remove wheels and tires.
4. If replacing righthand bushings, disconnect brake fluid lines at body.
5. If replacing lefthand bushings, disconnect brake fluid line bracket from body and parking brake cable from guide hook on body.
6. Remove control arm to body nut, bolt and washer, then rotate control arm

downward. **Do not allow axle to hang by brake hose.**

7. Reverse procedure to complete installation, noting the following:
   a. Arrow on installer must align with arrow on receiver, **Fig. 1.**
   b. Use high pressure lubricant No. J-23444-A, or equivalent, as required.
   c. When bushing reaches its proper position end flange will sit flush against control arm face.
   d. Ensure bushing washer and nut are installed on outboard side.
   e. Tighten mounting bolt to specifications. **Control arm mounting bolt must be tightened after vehicle is lowered to floor and is in its standing height position.**

TIGHTENING SPECIFICATIONS

Year	Component	Torque/Ft. Lbs.
1998–2002	Brake Pipe Retainer Bolts To Rear Axle	50
	Brake Pipe To Bracket Hose	20
	Control Arm Nuts	59①
	Hub & Bearing Axle Bolts	44
	Rear Axle Mounting Bolts	88
	Shock Absorber Lower Mounting Bolt	110
	Shock Absorber Lower Mounting Bolt	52
	Shock Absorber Lower Nut	18

① — Plus additional 120 degrees rotation.

Front Suspension & Steering

NOTE: On Air Bag Equipped Models, Refer To "Air Bag System Precautions" Located In The Front Of This Manual For System Disarming & Arming Procedures.

NOTE: Refer To "Computer Relearn Procedures" Located In The Front Of This Manual When Battery Power To The Computer Has Been Interrupted.

NOTE: Prior To Performing Any Service Operations Listed In This Section, Consult The "Technical Service Bulletins" Section For Related Information.

INDEX

PRECAUTIONS

AIR BAG SYSTEMS

Refer to "Air Bag System Precautions" in the front of this manual for system disarming and arming procedures.

BATTERY GROUND CABLE

Prior to service, disconnect battery ground cable and isolate as required.

DESCRIPTION

The front suspension on these models is a combination strut and spring design. The control arms pivot from the crossmember, **Fig. 1.** The upper end of the strut is isolated by a rubber mount incorporating a non-serviceable bearing for wheel turning. On base models the lower control arm pivots have conventional rubber bushings. Upgraded models have a cross axis bearing rather than bushings. The tie rods connect to the steering arm on the strut, below the spring seat. The lower end of the steering knuckle pivots on a ball stud which is retained to the lower control arm by rivets and is secured to the steering knuckle with a nut and cotter pin. The sealed wheel bearings are integral with the hub and are serviced as an assembly.

WHEEL BEARING

REPLACE

REMOVAL

1. Raise and support vehicle, then remove tire and wheel assembly.
2. Remove axle shaft nut and washer by inserting suitable drift punch through rotor, **Fig. 2.**
3. Separate ball joint from knuckle using ball joint separator tool No. J-43828, or equivalent.
4. Disengage axle from hub and bearing using front hub spindle remover tool No. J-28733-A, or equivalent.
5. Move axle shaft inward, remove mounting bolts and support caliper.
6. Remove brake rotor, then hub and bearing mounting bolts.
7. Remove hub and bearing.

INSTALLATION

1. Install hub and bearing. Tighten mounting bolts to specifications.
2. Install hub and bearing seal, then the brake rotor.
3. Install caliper, tighten mounting bolts to specifications.
4. Move axle shaft outward and insert suitable drift punch through rotor, **Fig. 2.**
5. Install washer and new shaft nut, tighten shaft nut to specifications.
6. Install ball joint, then remove drift punch and seal protector.
7. Install tire and wheel assembly, then lower vehicle.

BALL JOINT INSPECTION

1. Raise and support vehicle so suspension is allowed to hang free.
2. Grasp wheel and tire assembly at top and bottom, then rock top of wheel and tire assembly inward and outward.
3. While rocking wheel and tire assembly, observe movement between steering knuckle and control arm. If any horizontal movement is present, replace ball joint.
4. If ball joint is disconnected from steering knuckle, use hand to try to twist ball joint in its socket. If ball joint can be twisted in its socket, replace ball joint.

BALL JOINT

REPLACE

REMOVAL

1. Raise and support vehicle, then remove wheel and tire.
2. Remove stabilizer link nut from stabilizer link bolt.
3. Remove wiring harness from lower control arm.
4. Remove ball joint cotter pin.
5. Remove ball joint stud mounting nut.
6. Remove ball joint from steering knuckle using ball joint separator tool No. J43828, or equivalent.
7. Remove lower control arm front and rear mounting bolts, **Fig. 3.**
8. Remove lower control arm from vehicle and place in a suitable vice, **Fig. 3.**
9. Drill out three rivets retaining ball joint to lower control arm. Install a ⅛ inch bit in order to make a pilot hole through rivets. Complete drilling rivets using suitable ½ drill bit, **Fig. 3.**
10. Remove ball joint from control arm, **Fig. 3.**

INSTALLATION

1. Install ball joint into control arm, **Fig. 4.**
2. Install three ball joint bolts and nuts,

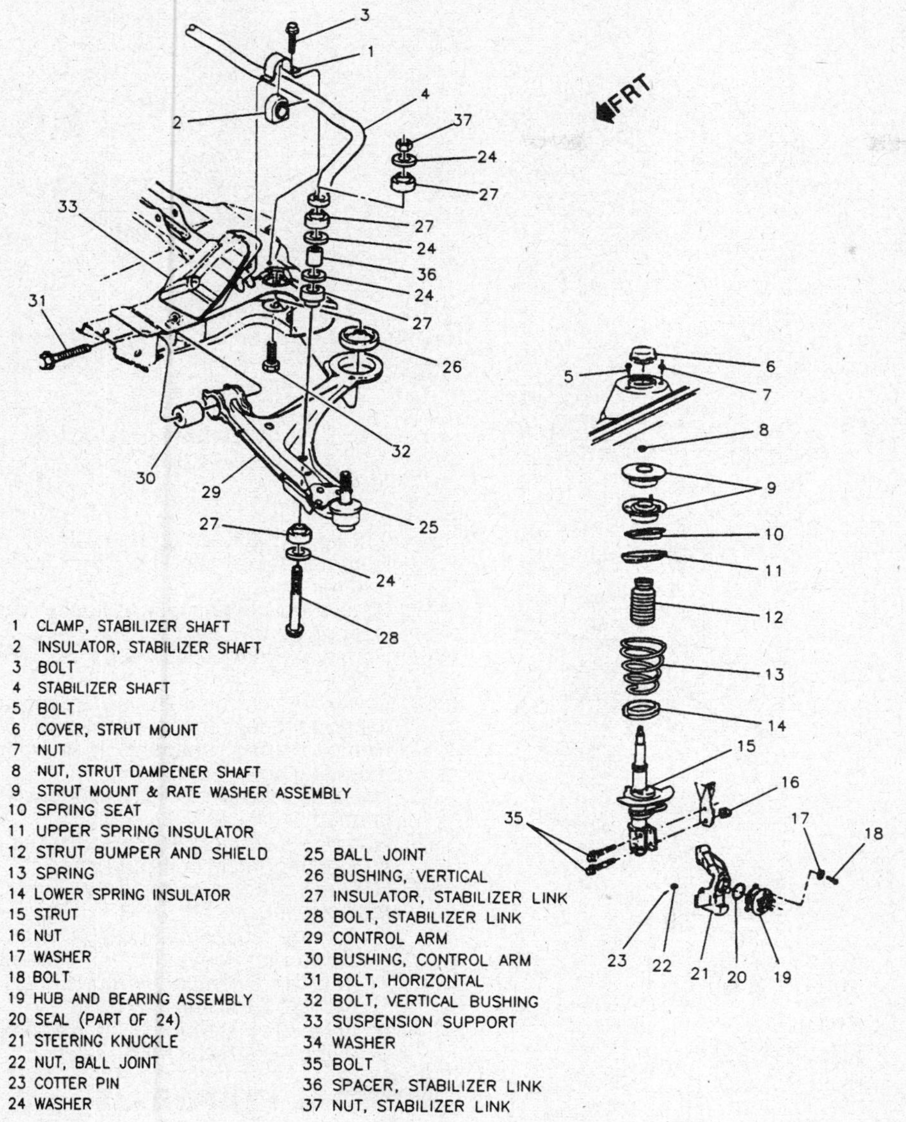

Fig. 1 Exploded view of front suspension

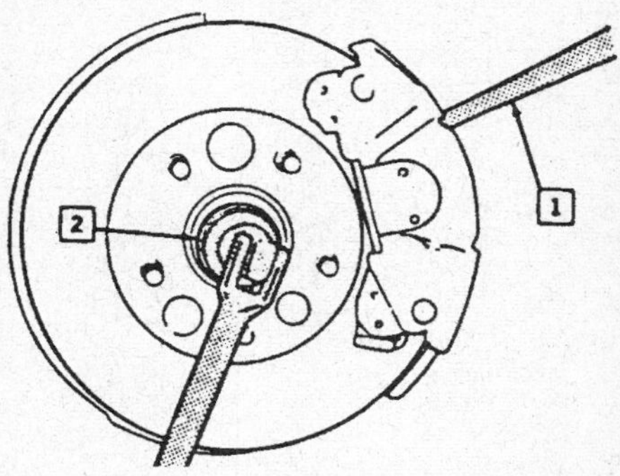

Fig. 2 Shaft nut replacement

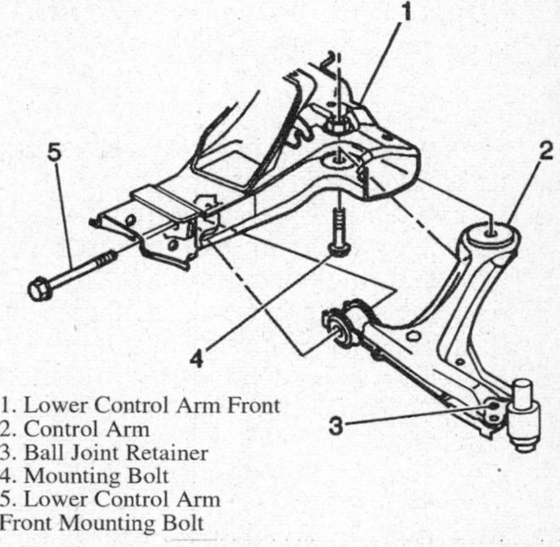

Fig. 3 Lower control arm mounting bolt removal

tighten ball joint bolts according to specifications, **Fig. 4.**
3. Install lower control arm to front suspension support, **Fig. 5.**
4. Install lower control arm front and rear mounting bolts, **Fig. 5.**
5. Install lower ball joint stud to steering knuckle, **Fig. 6.**
6. Install ball joint stud through steering knuckle.
7. Install ball joint nut, tighten to specifications.
8. Install wiring harness to lower control arm and install cotter pin.
9. Install stabilizer link to lower control arm.
10. Install tire and wheel assemblies.
11. Inspect front wheel alignment.

STRUT

REPLACE

1. Remove strut assembly attaching nuts and bolts to body, **Fig. 7.**
2. Raise and support vehicle, install suitable jackstand under crossmember, then lower vehicle for weight to rest slightly on jackstand.
3. Remove tire and wheel assembly.
4. Remove brake line bracket.
5. Scribe strut flange using suitable sharp tool.
6. Remove steering knuckle attaching nuts and bolts to strut assembly, **Fig. 8.**
7. Remove strut assembly.
8. Reverse procedure to install, tighten to specifications and inspect alignment.

CONTROL ARM

REPLACE

1. Raise and support vehicle, then remove wheel and tire.
2. Disconnect stabilizer bar at lower control arm and control arm support.
3. Install modified seal protector tool No. J-34754, or equivalent.
4. Separate ball joint from knuckle using ball joint separator tool No. J-43828, or equivalent.
5. Remove control arm to chassis mounting bolts and control arm.
6. Remove wiring harness from lower control arm.
7. Attach new lower control arm to control arm support.
8. Install control arm support to chassis. Tighten mounting bolts to specifications.
9. Reverse procedure to complete installation. Inspect toe setting and adjust as required.

STEERING KNUCKLE

REPLACE

1. Raise and support vehicle, then remove wheel and tire.
2. Remove front hub and bearing as outlined under "Wheel Bearing, Replace" in this section.
3. Separate ball joint from knuckle using ball joint separator tool No. J-43828, or equivalent.
4. Disconnect tie rod from strut using universal steering linkage puller tool No. J-24319-01, or equivalent.

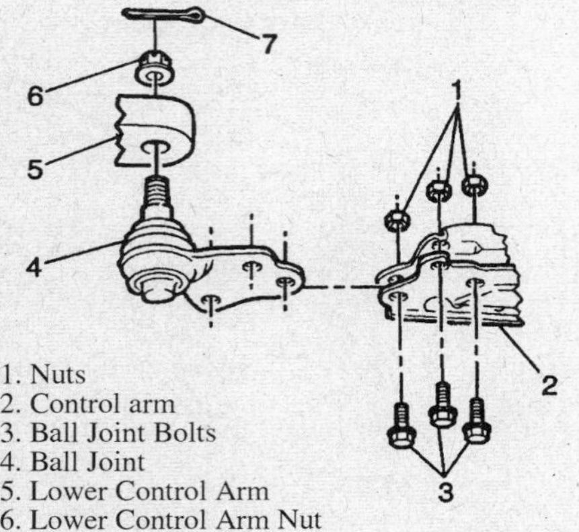

Fig. 4 Ball joint control arm installation

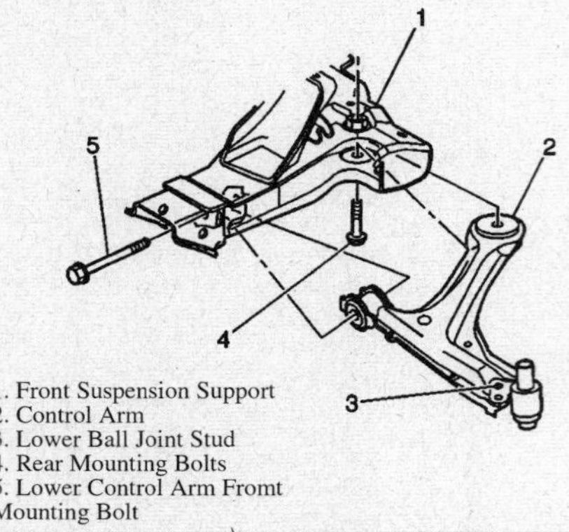

Fig. 5 Lower control arm to front suspension installation

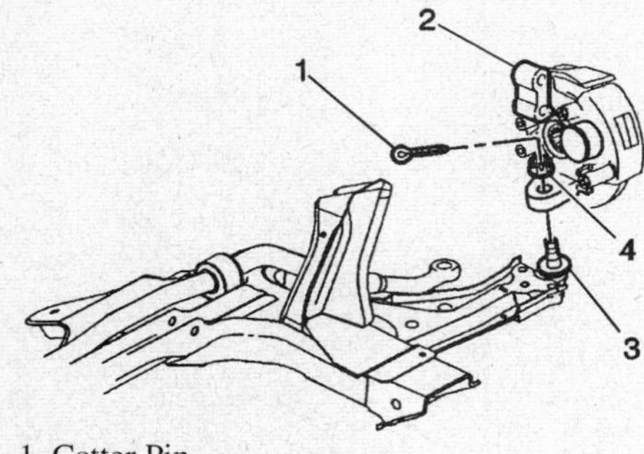

Fig. 6 Lower ball joint stud installation

5. Scribe outlines of strut to knuckle relationship to ease installation.
6. Remove strut to steering knuckle mounting bolts and disconnect strut from steering knuckle.
7. Assemble strut to new steering knuckle and install mounting bolts hand tight.
8. Insert ball joint stud into steering knuckle and tighten stud nut to specifications.
9. Tighten strut to steering knuckle bolts to specifications.
10. Reverse removal procedure to complete installation.

STABILIZER BAR

REPLACE

1. Raise and support vehicle, allowing control arms to hang freely.
2. Remove front wheels and tires.
3. Remove stabilizer shaft links.
4. Support front suspension support with suitable jack.
5. Remove suspension support rear, center and front mounting bolts in order.
6. Lower front suspension support to ease shaft removal.
7. Disconnect stabilizer bar at control arms and control arm supports, **Fig. 9.**
8. Remove stabilizer bar with insulators.
9. Reverse procedure to install, noting the following:
   a. Install stabilizer shaft to vehicle.
   b. Install and hand tighten shaft to suspension support clamp bolts.
   c. Install and hand tighten suspension support front, center and rear mounting bolts in order.
   d. Suspension support lefthand rear, righthand rear, lefthand front and righthand front bolts in order to 71 ft. lbs.
   e. **Torque** stabilizer shaft clamp bolts to 49 ft. lbs.
   f. **Torque** links to 13 ft. lbs.

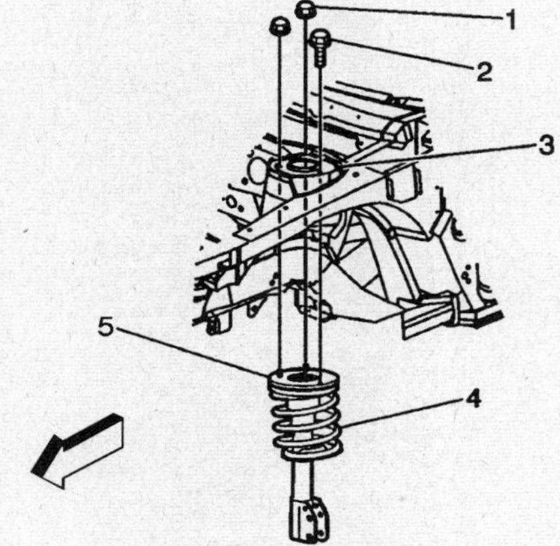

Fig. 7 Strut assembly removal

POWER STEERING GEAR

REPLACE

AUTOMATIC TRANSAXLE

1. Raise and support vehicle.
2. Remove front tires and wheels.
3. Remove righthand and lefthand splash shields.
4. Remove engine strut from lower engine mount and frame.
5. Remove front exhaust pipe.
6. Disconnect ABS wiring harness from wheel speed sensor and body.
7. Remove steering column lower pinch bolt at steering gear.
8. Separate ball joint from knuckle using ball joint separator tool No. J-43828, or equivalent.
9. Disconnect tie rods from knuckles using universal steering linkage puller tool No. J-24319-01, or equivalent.
10. Remove brake fluid lines from frame retainers.
11. Disconnect power steering hoses from steering gear.
12. Remove front suspension support brace.
13. Lower vehicle until front suspension support brace rests on jack stands.
14. Remove front suspension support mounting bolts.
15. Raise vehicle up from front suspension support.
16. Remove steering gear to suspension support mounting bolts and gear.
17. Reverse procedure to install, noting the following:
    a. **Torque** suspension support lefthand rear, righthand rear, lefthand front and righthand front bolts in order to 71 ft. lbs.
    b. Fill power steering fluid reservoir and bleed any air from system.

MANUAL TRANSAXLE

1. Raise and support vehicle.
2. Remove front tires and wheels.
3. Remove power steering hoses from steering gear.
4. Disconnect tie rods from knuckles using universal steering linkage puller tool No. J-24319-01, or equivalent.
5. Remove brake fluid lines from frame retainers.
6. Remove steering column lower pinch bolt at steering gear.
7. Support front suspension support with suitable jack stand.
8. Remove front suspension crossmember mounting bolts.
9. Lower suspension enough to access steering gear mounting bolts.
10. Remove mounting bolts and steering gear.
11. Reverse procedure to install, noting the following:
    a. **Torque** suspension support lefthand rear, righthand rear, lefthand front and righthand front bolts in order to 71 ft. lbs.
    b. Fill power steering fluid reservoir and bleed any air from system.

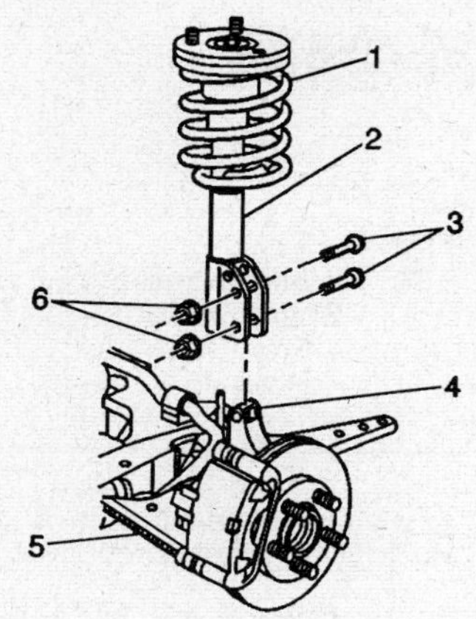

1. Strut Assebly
2. Strut Shaft
3. Strut Attaching Bolts
4. Steering Knuckle
5. Brake Line
6. Strut Attaching Nuts

GC2020100298000X

Fig. 8 Strut to steering knuckle removal

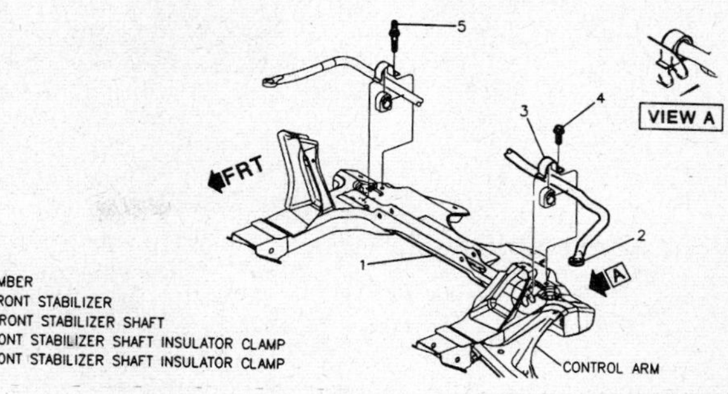

Fig. 9 Stabilizer bar installation

POWER STEERING PUMP

REPLACE

1. **On models equipped with 2.2L engine,** mark running direction and remove serpentine belt.
2. **On all models,** remove power steering fluid lines.
3. Remove power steering pump mounting bolts.
4. Remove pump and transfer pulley, if required.
5. Reverse procedure to install. Tighten mounting bolts to specifications.

TECHNICAL SERVICE BULLETINS

STABILIZER SHAFT SQUAWK/SQUEAK

1998–99

On some of these models there may be a squawk/squeak type noise coming from the front and/or rear suspension. This noise is more apparent when the vehicle is operated over irregular road surfaces and can be heard inside the vehicle passenger compartment.

This condition may be caused by a slip/stick condition between the bushings of the stabilizer shaft and the stabilizer shaft bushings.

To correct this condition, replace the existing stabilizer shaft bushings with newly designed oil-impregnated bushings No. 22619846.

TIGHTENING SPECIFICATIONS

Year	Component	Torque/Ft. Lbs.
1998–2002	Ball Joint To Knuckle	41–50
	Caliper	38
	Control Arm To Crossmember, Front	79
	Control Arm To Crossmember, Rear	125
	Hub & Bearing	70
	Hub Nut	185
	Steering Column Pinch Bolt	16
	Stabilizer Shaft To Control Arm	13
	Stabilizer To Support	49
	Steering Knuckle To Strut	133
	Strut To Body	18
	Strut Piston	34
	Tie Rod Jam Nuts	50
	Tie Rod Stud Nuts	33
	Wheel Lugnuts	100

Wheel Alignment

INDEX

PRELIMINARY INSPECTION

1. Ensure all tires are of recommended size and are inflated to proper pressure.
2. Inspect all tires for damage and uneven tread wear.
3. Ensure wheel bearings, control arm ball studs and bushings, relay rods and tie rod ends are in satisfactory condition. Looseness must be corrected before wheels can be aligned.
4. Inspect wheel and tire radial and lateral runout, as follows:
   a. With wheel and tire assembly off vehicle, runout should be approximately .050 inch.
   b. When on vehicle, runout should be approximately .060 inch.
5. If wheel and tire assembly runout specifications cannot be met, separate tire from wheel and measure wheel runout. Wheel runout should be approximately .030 inch.
6. Inspect vehicle ride height as outlined under "Vehicle Ride Height." If corrections are required, complete them prior to setting wheel alignment.
7. Ensure steering gear is not loose at frame mounting.
8. Inspect stabilizer shafts for loose or missing components.
9. Ensure struts and shocks are not leaking or excessively worn and strut upper mounts are in satisfactory condition.
10. Inspect all remaining suspension and steering components for damage and repair or replace prior to setting wheel alignment.
11. Ensure fuel tank is full or compensating ballast is added for proper weight distribution.
12. Ensure vehicle is on level surface and all loads that are normally carried inside vehicle are present.
13. Jounce front and rear of vehicle three times before beginning wheel alignment procedures.

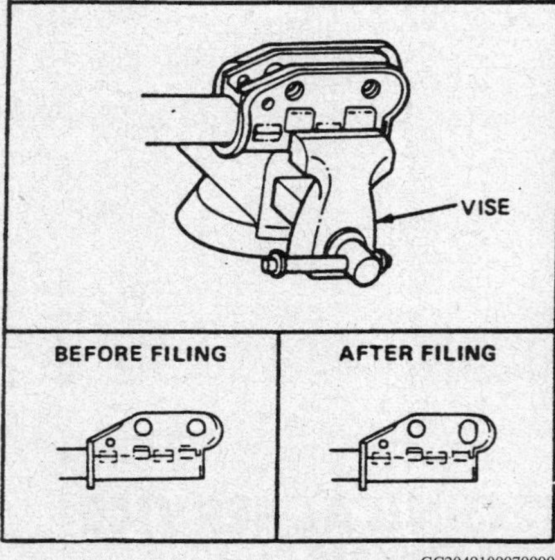

Fig. 1 Strut bracket modification for camber adjustment

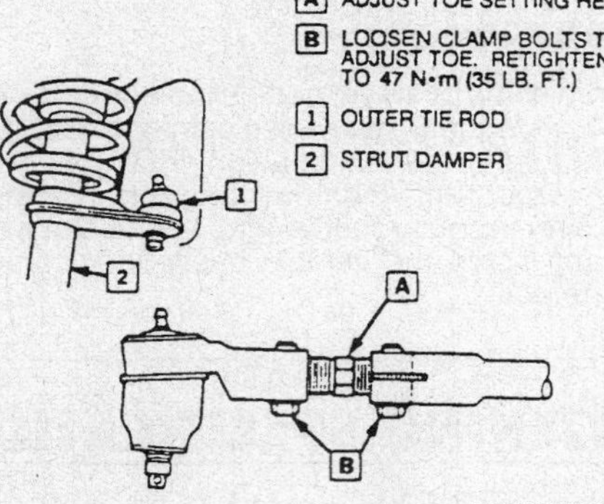

Fig. 2 Typical toe adjustment

FRONT WHEEL ALIGNMENT

CASTER

Caster is not adjustable. If caster angle is not within specifications, inspect for suspension support misalignment or front suspension damage.

CAMBER

Toe setting is the only adjustment normally required. However, in special circumstances, such as damage because of road hazard or collision, camber may be adjusted by modifying the strut. Proceed as follows:

1. Mount strut bottom in suitable vise.
2. Enlarge bottom holes in outer flanges with round file until holes in outer flanges match slots in inner flanges, **Fig. 1.**
3. Connect strut to steering knuckle and install bolts hand tight.
4. Grasp top of tire firmly and move tire inboard or outboard until proper camber reading is obtained. Tighten mounting bolts enough to secure camber setting.
5. Remove wheel and tire and tighten strut to steering knuckle mounting bolts. **Torque** strut to steering knuckle mounting bolt to 133 ft. lbs.

TOE

Toe-out is controlled by tie rod position. Adjustment is made by loosening the clamp bolts or jam nuts at the steering knuckle end of the tie rods and rotating the rods to obtain proper toe setting, **Fig. 2.** After proper toe setting is obtained, tighten mounting nuts and bolts to specifications.

CENTURY, GRAND PRIX, IMPALA, INTRIGUE, LUMINA, MONTE CARLO & REGAL

NOTE: Refer To Rear Of This Manual For Vehicle Manufacturer's Special Service Tool Suppliers.

INDEX OF SERVICE OPERATIONS

Specifications

GENERAL ENGINE SPECIFICATIONS

Year	Engine Displacement	Engine VIN Code②	Fuel System	Bore & Stroke	Compression Ratio	Net H.P. @ RPM③	Maximum Torque Ft. Lbs. @ RPM	Normal Oil Pressure, psi
1998	3.1L	M	SFI	3.50 x 3.31	9.6	160 @ 5200	185 @ 4000	15⑤
	3800 ①	1	SFI	3.80 x 3.40	8.5	240 @ 5200	280 @ 3200	60④
	3800	K	SFI	3.80 x 3.40	9.4	195 @ 5200	220 @ 4000	60④
1999	3.1L	M	SFI	3.50 x 3.31	9.5	160 @ 5200	185 @ 4000	15⑤
	3.5L	H	SFI	3.52 x 3.62	9.3	215 @ 5600	234 @ 4400	⑥
	3800①	1	SFI	3.80 x 3.40	8.5	240 @ 5200	280 @ 3200	60④
	3800	K	SFI	3.80 x 3.40	9.4	200 @ 5200	220 @ 4000	60④
2000	3.1L	M	SFI	3.50 x 3.31	9.5	160 @ 5200	185 @ 4000	15⑤
	3.4L	E	SFI	3.62 x 3.31	9.5	180 @ 5200	205 @ 4000	15⑤
	3.5L	H	SFI	3.52 x 3.62	9.3	215 @ 5600	234 @ 4400	⑥
	3800①	1	SFI	3.80 x 3.40	8.5	240 @ 5200	280 @ 3200	60④
	3800	K	SFI	3.80 x 3.40	9.4	200 @ 5200	220 @ 4000	60④
2001	3.1L	M	SFI	3.50 x 3.31	9.5	160 @ 5200	185 @ 4000	15⑤
	3.4L	E	SFI	3.62 x 3.31	9.5	180 @ 5200	205 @ 4000	15⑤
	3.5L	H	SFI	3.52 x 3.62	9.3	215 @ 5600	234 @ 4400	⑥
	3800①	1	SFI	3.80 x 3.40	8.5	240 @ 5200	280 @ 3200	60④
	3800	K	SFI	3.80 x 3.40	9.4	200 @ 5200	220 @ 4000	60④
2002	3.1L	J	SFI	3.50 x 3.31	9.6	175 @ 5200	195 @ 4000	15⑤
	3.4L	E	SFI	3.62 x 3.31	9.5	180 @ 5200	205 @ 4000	15⑤
	3.5L	H	SFI	3.52 x 3.62	9.3	215 @ 5600	234 @ 4400	⑥
	3800①	1	SFI	3.80 x 3.40	8.5	240 @ 5200	280 @ 3200	60④
	3800	K	SFI	3.80 x 3.40	9.4	200 @ 5200	220 @ 4000	60④

MFI — Multi-Port Fuel Injection
SFI — Sequential-Port Fuel Injection
① — Supercharged engine.
② — The eighth digit of the VIN denotes engine code.
③ — Ratings are net as installed in vehicle.
④ — At 1850 RPM. Engine at operating temperature using 10W-30 engine oil.
⑤ — Minimum @ 1100 RPM. Engine at operating temperature.
⑥ — 35 @ 600 RPM, 80 @ 3600 RPM

TUNE UP SPECIFICATIONS

Year, Engine & VIN Code①	Spark Plug Gap, Inch	Ignition Timing			Curb Idle Speed②	Fast Idle Speed	Fuel Pump Pressure, Psi	Valve Clearance, Inch
		Firing Order Fig.③	°BTDC	Mark Fig.				
1998–99								
3.1L	.060	⑩	④	⑤	⑥	⑥	41–47⑦	⑪
3.5 L	.050	⑨	④	⑤	⑥	⑥	48–55⑦	⑪
3800 (K)	.060	⑧	④	⑤	⑥	⑥	48–55⑦	⑪
3800 (1)	.060	⑧	④	⑤	⑥	⑥	48–55⑦	⑪
2000–01								
3.1L	.060	⑩	④	⑤	⑥	⑥	41–47⑦	⑪
3.4L	.060	⑩	④	⑤	⑥	⑤	41–47⑦	⑪
3.5	.050	⑨	④	⑤	⑥	⑥	48–55⑦	⑪
3800 (K)	.060	⑧	④	⑤	⑥	⑥	48–55⑦	⑪
3800 (1)	.060	⑧	④	⑤	⑥	⑥	48–55⑦	⑪
2002								
3.1L	.060	⑩	④	⑤	⑥	⑥	52–59⑦	⑪
3.4L	.060	⑩	④	⑤	⑥	⑤	41–47⑦	⑪
3.5L	.050	⑨	④	⑤	⑥	⑥	48–55⑦	⑪
3800 (K)	.060	⑧	④	⑤	⑥	⑥	48–55⑦	⑪
3800 (1)	.060	⑧	④	⑤	⑥	⑥	48–55⑦	⑪

BTDC — Before Top Dead Center

① — The eighth digit of Vehicle Identification Number (VIN) denotes engine code.

② — Idle speed is adjusted in Drive. When adjusting idle speed, set parking brake & block drive wheels. Where two idle speeds are listed, the higher speed is w/the idle or A/C solenoid energized.

③ — Before removing wires from distributor cap, determine location of No. 1 wire in cap, as distributor position may have been altered from that shown at the end of this chart.

④ — Computer controlled, no adjustment.

⑤ — Equipped w/crankshaft position sensor.

⑥ — Idle speed is controlled by an idle air control (IAC) valve or idle speed control (ISC) motor.

⑦ — Loosen fuel tank filler cap to relieve fuel vapor pressure. With shop towel wrapped around fuel pressure valve to prevent fuel spillage, connect a suitable fuel pressure gauge to fuel pressure valve. Check fuel pressure w/ignition switch On, engine not running.

⑧ — Cylinder numbering as viewed from front of vehicle, front bank, 1, 3, 5; rear bank, 2, 4, 6. Firing order 1-6-5-4-3-2. Two different types of computer controlled coil ignition systems are used. Refer to **Figs. B & C** for spark plug wire connections at coil unit.

⑨ — Cylinder numbering left to right as viewed from front of vehicle: front bank, 2, 4, 6; rear bank, 1, 3, 5. Firing order: 1-2-3-4-5-6.

⑩ — Cylinder numbering left to right as viewed from front of vehicle: front bank, 2, 4, 6; rear bank, 1, 3, 5. Firing order: 1-2-3-4-5-6. Refer to **Fig. A** for spark plug wire connections at coil unit.

⑪ — Equipped w/hydraulic valve lash adjusters. There is no provision for valve lash adjustment. If valve lash exists, inspect pushrod & rocker arm for excessive wear & check for an inoperative lifter.

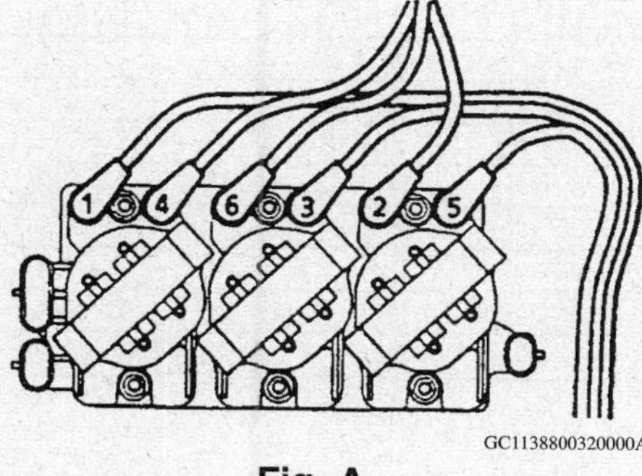

Fig. A

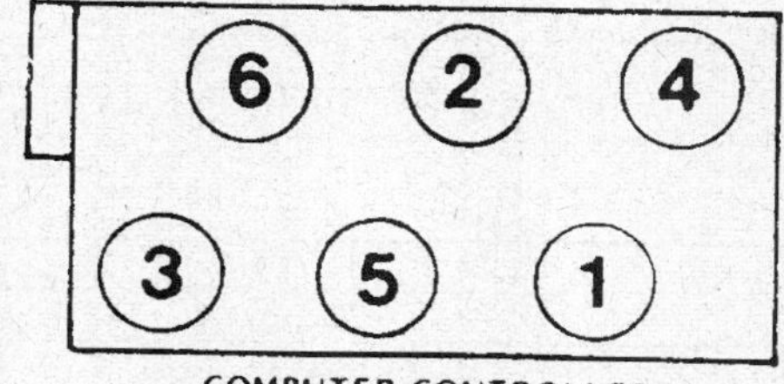

Fig. B

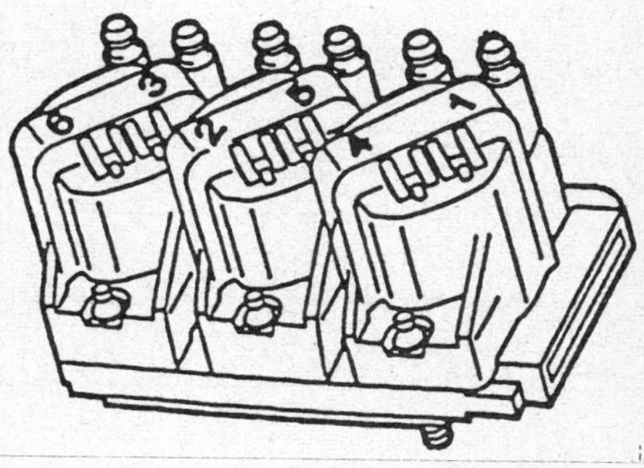

Fig. C

FRONT WHEEL ALIGNMENT SPECIFICATIONS

Year	Model	Caster Angle, Degrees②		Camber Angle, Degrees		Toe-In, Degrees	Steering Angle, Degrees		Ball Joint Wear
		Limits	Desired	Limits	Desired		Limits	Desired	
1998–99	Century, Lumina, Monte Carlo & Regal	+1.3 to +2.3	+1.8	+.20 to +1.20	+.70	-.20 to +.20	-3.5 to +3.5	0	①
	Grand Prix & Intrigue	+2.5 to + 3.5	+3.0	-1.40 to -.40	-.90	-.10 to +.30	-3.5 to +3.5	0	①
2000–02	Century, Grand Prix, Intrigue, Lumina & Regal	+2.5 to +3.5	+3.0	-1.40 to -.40	-.90	-.10 to +.30	-3.5 to +3.5	0	①
	Impala	+2.7 to +3.7	+3.2	-1.35 to -.35	-.85	-.10 to +.30	-3.5 to +3.5	0	①
	Monte Carlo	+2.7 to +3.7	+3.2	-.50 to -.90	-.70	-.10 to +.30	-3.5 to +3.5	0	①

① — With vehicle raised & supported to allow front suspension to hang freely, grasp wheel at top & bottom, attempt to move bottom of wheel inward & outward. Ball joints must be replaced if looseness is observed between knuckle & control arm.

② — Not Adjustable.

REAR WHEEL ALIGNMENT SPECIFICATIONS

Year	Model	Camber Angle, Degrees		Total Toe, Degrees	Thrust Angle, Degrees	
		Limits	Desired		Limits	Desired
1998–99	Century, Lumina, Monte Carlo & Regal	-.65 to +.35	-.15	+.1	-.15 to +.15	0
	Grand Prix & Intrigue	-1.40 to -.40	-.90	0	-.15 to +.15	0
2000–02	Century, Grand Prix, Intrigue, Lumina & Regal	-1.10 to -.10	-.60	-.1 to +.3	-.15 to +.15	0
	Impala	-1.00 to .00	-.50	-.1 to +.3	-.15 to +.15	0
	Monte Carlo	-1.20 to +.20	-.70	-.1 to +.3	-.15 to +.15	0

VEHICLE RIDE HEIGHT SPECIFICATIONS

Model	Year	Body Style	Manufacturer's Original Tire Size	Measurement Points & Specifications②					
				Front			Rear		
				Dim.	Specification Inches	Specification mm	Dim.	Specification Inches	Specification mm
Century & Regal	1998–2002	All	①	A	23.8	606	B	20.7	525
				C	8.4	213	D	8.4	213
Impala	2000–02	All	①	A	23.8	606	B	20.7	525
				C	8.4	213	D	8.4	213
Lumina	1998–2002	All	①	A	23.4	593	B	20.7	525
				C	10.0	254	D	10.2	259
Monte Carlo	1998–99	All	①	A	23.4	593	B	20.7	525
				C	10.0	254	D	10.2	259
	2000–02	All	①	A	23.8	606	B	20.7	525
				C	8.4	213	D	8.4	213
Intrigue	1998–2002	All	①	A	23.8	606	B	20.7	525
				C	8.4	213	D	8.4	213

Continued

VEHICLE RIDE HEIGHT SPECIFICATIONS—Continued

Model	Year	Body Style	Manufacturer's Original Tire Size	Measurement Points & Specifications②					
				Front			Rear		
				Dim.	Specification		Dim.	Specification	
					Inches	mm		Inches	mm
Grand Prix	1998–2002	All	①	A	23.8	606	B	20.7	525
				C	8.4	213	D	8.4	213

A Dim. — Measurement From Front Wheel Center to Check Point On Rocker Panel
B Dim. — Measurement From Rear Wheel Center to Check Point On Rocker Panel
C Dim. — Ground to Rocker Panel, Front
D Dim. — Ground to Rocker Panel, Rear
Dim. — Dimension

① — See door sticker or inside of glove box for manufacturers original tire size specifications. If tires on vehicle do not match manufacturers original tire size & measurement is not within limits, it will be necessary to refer to the "Non-Standard Tire & Wheel Size Adjustment To Ride Height Specification & Tire Size Adjustment Charts" in the front of this manual for approximate changes in ride height specifications.

② — Measurement is with fuel, radiator coolant and engine oil full, spare tire, jack, hand tools and mats in designated positions and tires properly inflated.

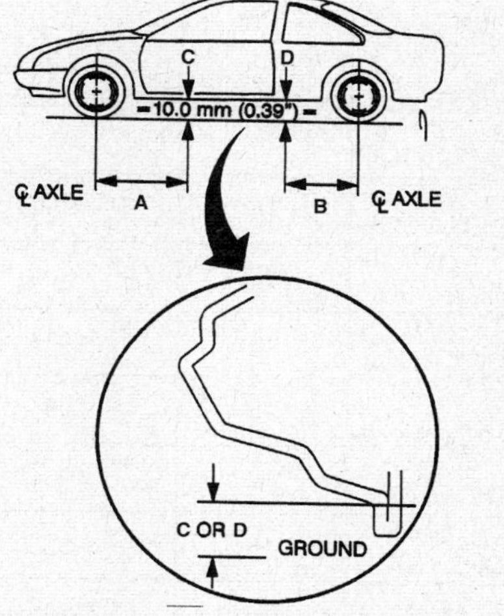

Dimensions A through D

FLUID CAPACITIES & COOLING SYSTEM DATA

Year	Model	Engine	Coolant Capa-city, Qts.	Coolant Type	Radiator Cap Relief Pressure, psi	Thermostat Opening Temp. °F	Fuel Tank Gals.	Engine Oil Refill Qts.①	Transaxle Qts.②	
									Drain & Refill	Total Capacity
1998–99	Century	3.1L	11.6	GM DEX-COOL	15	195	17.5	4.5	7.0	9.6
	Grand Prix	3.1L	11.0	GM DEX-COOL	15	195	17.7	4.5	8.0	10.0
		3800	12.3	GM DEX-COOL	15	195	17.7	4.5	8.0	10.0
	Intrigue	3.5L	9.6	GM DEX-COOL	15	195	17.7	6.0	7.4	10.0
		3800	10.2	GM DEX-COOL	15	195	17.7	4.5	8.0	10.0
	Lumina & Monte Carlo	3.1L	11.6	GM DEX-COOL	15	195	16.6	4.5	7.0	9.6
		3800	11.7	GM DEX-COOL	15	195	16.6	4.5	7.4	10.0
	Regal	3800	12.3	GM DEX-COOL	15	195	17.0	4.5	7.4	10.0
2000	Century	3.1L	11.6	GM DEX-COOL	15	195	17.0	4.5	7.4	10
	Grand Prix	3.1L	11.0	GM DEX-COOL	15	195	17.5	4.5	7.4	10.0
		3800	10.2	GM DEX-COOL	15	195	17.0	4.5	7.4	10.0
	Impala & Monte Carlo	3.4L	11.3	GM DEX-COOL	15	195	17.0	4.5	7.4	10.0
		3800	11.7	GM DEX-COOL	15	195	17.0	4.5	7.4	10.0
	Intrigue	3.5L	9.8	GM DEX-COOL	15	195	17.0	6.0	7.4	10.0
	Regal	3800	12.3	GM DEX-COOL	15	195	17.0	4.5	7.4	10.0
2001–02	Century	3.1L	11.6	GM DEX-COOL	15	195	17.0	4.5	7.4	10
	Grand Prix	3.1L	11.0	GM DEX-COOL	15	195	17.5	4.3	7.4	10.0
		3800	11.2	GM DEX-COOL	15	195	17.5	4.3	7.4	10.0
	Impala & Monte Carlo	3.4L	11.3	GM DEX-COOL	15	195	17.0	4.3	7.4	10.0
		3800	11.7	GM DEX-COOL	15	195	17.0	4.3	7.4	10.0
	Intrigue	3.5L	10.0	GM DEX-COOL	15	195	18.0	6.5	7.4	10.0
	Regal	3800	12.3	GM DEX-COOL	15	195	17.0	4.5	7.4	10.0

① — Additional oil may be required to bring oil level to full mark when changing oil filter.

② — Capacity approximate. Make final check w/dipstick & add fluid as necessary.

LUBRICANT DATA

Year	Lubricant Type		
	Transaxle	Power Steering	Brake System
1998–2002	Dexron III	Power Steering Fluid①	DOT 3

① — Use power steering fluid meeting GM specification 9985010. For cold climates, use GM power steering fluid part No. 12345866 or 12345867, or equivalent. System should be drained, flushed, refilled & bled when changing to cold climate type fluid.

Electrical

NOTE: On Air Bag Equipped Models, Refer To "Air Bag System Precautions" Located In The Front Of This Manual For System Disarming & Arming Procedures.

NOTE: Refer To "Computer Relearn Procedures" Located In The Front Of This Manual When Battery Power To The Computer Has Been Interrupted.

INDEX

PRECAUTIONS

AIR BAG SYSTEMS

Refer to "Air Bag System Precautions" in the front of this manual for system disarming and arming procedures.

RADIO THEFT DETERRENT SYSTEM

Anti-theft radios have a coded theft deterrent circuit. **The security code number must be obtained before disconnecting battery, removing radio fuse or removing radio.**

After service procedure has been performed, reconnect radio power supply, and turn it to its ON position. When "LOC" is displayed, enter security code to reactivate radio.

BATTERY GROUND CABLE

Prior to service, disconnect battery ground cable and isolate as required.

FUSE PANEL & FLASHER LOCATION

CENTURY

The fuse panel is located behind the instrument panel, under the glove compartment. The underhood accessory wiring junction block is located on the righthand side of the engine compartment, mounted on the strut tower. The hazard and turn signal flasher is located behind the lefthand side of the instrument panel, mounted on the multi-purpose bracket, near the Body Control Module (BCM).

GRAND PRIX

Refer to "Century" for fuse panel and flasher locations on these models.

IMPALA

The lefthand instrument panel fuse block is located behind the lefthand side instrument panel cluster trim plate, left of the steering column. The righthand instrument panel fuse block is located behind the fuse block access opening cover, right of the glove compartment. The underhood wiring junction block is located on the righthand side of the engine compartment, mounted on the strut tower. The hazard and turn signal flasher is part of the hazard switch assembly, The hazard switch assembly is located behind the righthand side of the instrument panel, in the instrument panel fuse block.

INTRIGUE

The fuse panel is located behind the instrument panel, under the glove compartment. The underhood accessory wiring junction block is located on the righthand side of the engine compartment, mounted on the strut tower. The hazard and turn signal function is controlled by the hazard switch assembly. The hazard switch assembly is located at the top of the steering column.

LUMINA

The instrument panel fuse block is located behind the righthand side of the instrument panel, right of the glove compartment. The No. 1 engine compartment junction block is located on the righthand side of the engine compartment. The No. 2 engine compartment junction block is located on the front lefthand side of the engine compartment. The hazard and turn signal flasher is located behind the lefthand side of the instrument panel, mounted on the bulkhead.

MONTE CARLO

1998–99

Refer to "Lumina" for fuse panel and flasher locations on these models.

2000–02

Refer to "Impala" for fuse panel and flasher locations on these models.

REGAL

Refer to "Century" for fuse panel and flasher locations on these models.

FUEL PUMP RELAY LOCATION

The fuel pump relay is located in the underhood junction block, on the righthand side of the engine compartment.

STARTER

REPLACE

3.1L ENGINE

1. Remove air cleaner assembly.
2. Raise and support vehicle.
3. Remove torque converter cover attaching bolts, then the cover.
4. Remove starter motor attaching bolts, lower starter and disconnect starter wiring.
5. Remove starter motor and shims (if used).
6. Reverse procedure to install, noting the following:
   a. Install any shims removed in their original location.
   b. **Torque** starter motor attaching bolts to 32 ft. lbs.

3.4L ENGINE

1. Raise and support vehicle.
2. Remove front lower air deflector panel.
3. Remove torque converter covers from transaxle.

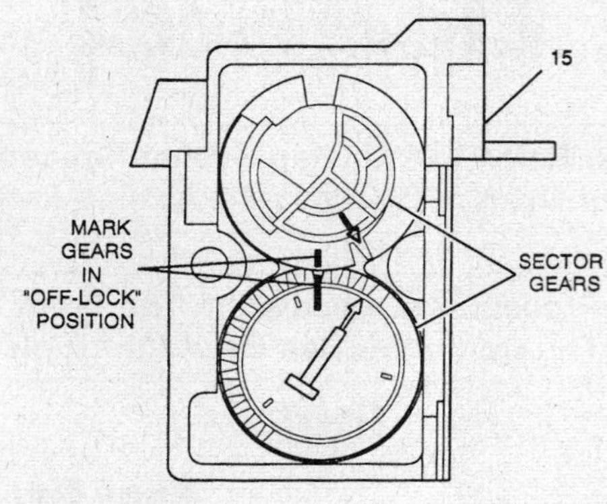

Fig. 1 Lock module sector gear alignment. Century, Grand Prix & Regal

4. Remove retaining nuts, then disconnect starter motor electrical connectors from solenoid.
5. Remove starter motor attaching bolts, then the starter motor.
6. Reverse procedure to install. **Torque** starter motor attaching bolts to 32 ft. lbs.

3.5L ENGINE

1. Raise and support vehicle.
2. Disconnect starter motor electrical connectors.
3. Remove torque converter cover.
4. Remove starter motor bolts and shims, then the starter motor.
5. Reverse procedure to install. **Torque** starter motor attaching bolts to 32 ft. lbs.

3800 ENGINE

1. Raise and support vehicle.
2. Remove torque converter cover attaching bolts, then the cover.
3. Remove starter motor attaching bolts.
4. Disconnect starter motor wiring.
5. Remove starter motor.
6. Reverse procedure to install. **Torque** starter motor attaching bolts to 32 ft. lbs.

ALTERNATOR

REPLACE

3.1L ENGINE

1. Remove serpentine belt at alternator assembly.
2. Remove cross car brace attaching bolts, then the brace.
3. Remove coolant overflow hose from radiator filler neck.
4. Remove coolant reservoir to strut tower attaching bolts, then position reservoir aside.
5. Remove bolts from alternator assembly.
6. Remove power steering gear clip and nut.
7. Remove alternator stud, then disconnect alternator wiring.
8. Loosen alternator front and rear braces from upper intake manifold.
9. Remove alternator assembly.
10. Reverse procedure to install.

3.4L ENGINE

1. Remove engine compartment cross vehicle brace.
2. Remove serpentine belt.
3. Remove coolant recovery reservoir attaching bolts, then position reservoir aside.
4. Remove alternator attaching bolts, then disconnect alternator electrical connector.
5. Remove retaining nut, then disconnect battery lead.
6. Remove alternator.
7. Reverse procedure to install.

3.5L ENGINE

1. Drain coolant into suitable container, then remove right diagonal brace.
2. Position washer solvent reservoir aside, then remove accessory drive belt as outlined under "Serpentine Drive Belt" in the "3.5L Engine" section.
3. Remove thermostat and radiator outlet hose.
4. Remove battery hold down retainer, battery and battery tray.
5. Remove engine mount strut attaching bolts from radiator and engine mounted brackets, then the strut mount.
6. Disconnect cooling fan wiring harness connectors from engine wiring harness.
7. Remove cooling fan shroud attaching bolts, then the cooling fan shroud and cooling fan assembly.
8. Remove outboard alternator bolt, then loosen inboard alternator bolt.
9. Remove idler pulley bolt and idler pulley.
10. Disconnect alternator electrical terminals and connectors.
11. Remove inboard alternator bolt, then the alternator.
12. Reverse procedure to install. **Torque** idler pulley and alternator bolts to 37 ft. lbs.

3800 ENGINE

1. Remove serpentine drive belt as outlined under "Serpentine Drive Belt" in the "3800 Engine" section.
2. Disconnect alternator electrical connectors.
3. Remove alternator retaining bolts, then the alternator.
4. Reverse procedure to install.

COIL PACK

REPLACE

1. Disconnect ignition control module electrical connectors.
2. Remove spark plug wires from ignition coils.
3. Remove screws securing ignition coils to ignition module, then the coils.
4. Reverse procedure to install.

IGNITION LOCK

REPLACE

CENTURY, GRAND PRIX & REGAL

LESS IGNITION KEY

1. Remove steering wheel as outlined under "Steering Wheel, Replace."
2. Remove insulator panel from under lefthand side of instrument panel.
3. Remove trim panel from under steering column.
4. Push top of intermediate shaft seal downward, then remove upper intermediate shaft bolt.
5. **On models equipped with column shift,** remove transaxle shift cable from ball stud on steering column, then the transaxle shift cable casing from steering column bracket.
6. **On models equipped with floor shift,** remove park lock cable.
7. **On all models,** remove lower and upper steering column bolts.
8. Disconnect steering column electrical connector, then the steering column from vehicle.
9. Remove and discard shaft lock retaining ring from top of column using lock plate compressor tool No. J 23653-SIR, or equivalent.
10. Remove shaft lock shield assembly and turn signal cancel cam assembly.
11. Separate key alarm switch from lock module assembly by prying gently with small bladed screwdriver.
12. Remove ignition key and alarm switch assembly attaching screws, allow switch to hang free.
13. Remove lock module assembly attaching screws, then the lock module assembly from column.
14. Mark lock module sector gears at "OFF-LOCK" position for installation reference, **Fig. 1.**
15. Remove sector gears from lock module assembly.
16. Remove positioning tab on end of lock cylinder with a ⅛ inch burring tool, **Fig. 2.**
17. Push on locking tab and remove lock cylinder from module assembly, **Fig. 3.**
18. Reverse procedure to install, noting the following:
    a. Record key code from old lock cylinder, then discard.
    b. Align marks on sector gears.
    c. Ensure lock module assembly is in "OFF-LOCK" position.
    d. Insert new key in lock cylinder and ensure key is in "OFF-LOCK" position.
    e. Align locking tab and positioning tab with lock module slots, then push lock cylinder into lock module.
    f. Rotate lock cylinder to "ACC" position and check alignment arrows on sector gears. Arrows should be pointing towards each other.
    g. Rotate lock cylinder to the "LOCK" position.

WITH IGNITION KEY

1. Remove steering wheel as outlined under "Steering Wheel, Replace."

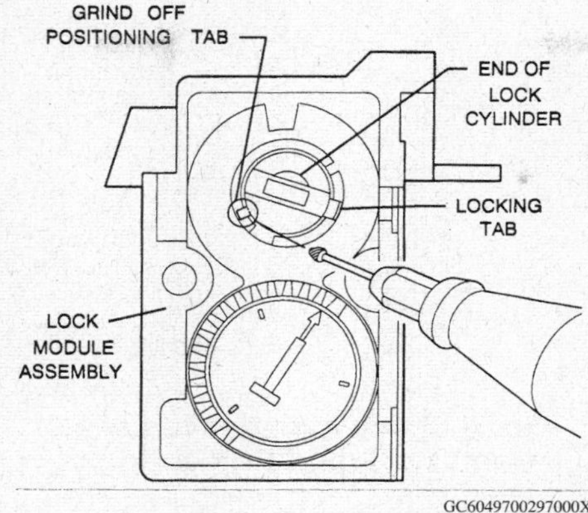

Fig. 2 Lock module positioning tab removal. Century, Grand Prix & Regal

2. Remove insulator panel from under lefthand side of instrument panel.
3. Remove trim panel from under steering column.
4. Push top of intermediate shaft seal downward, then remove upper intermediate shaft bolt.
5. **On models equipped with column shift,** remove transaxle shift cable from ball stud on steering column, then the transaxle shift cable casing from steering column bracket.
6. **On models equipped with floor shift,** remove park lock cable from lock module assembly.
7. **On all models,** remove lower and upper steering column bolts.
8. Disconnect steering column electrical connector, then the steering column from vehicle.
9. Mount steering column in a suitable vise, then remove upper and lower steering column shrouds.
10. Hold ignition key in START position.
11. Push lock cylinder retaining pin with a 1⁄16 inch Allen wrench.
12. Release key to RUN position, then pull lock cylinder set from lock module.
13. Reverse procedure to install.

IMPALA

1. Remove steering column filler panel.
2. Remove knee bolster and bracket from under steering column.
3. Apply parking brake.
4. **On models equipped with column shift,** position shift lever in the "1" position.
5. **On all models,** remove ignition switch cylinder bezel.
6. Remove left and right fuse/relay panel access covers.
7. Remove instrument cluster trim plate bezel attaching screws, then pull cluster trim plate bezel away from instrument panel trim pad.
8. Remove ignition switch retaining bolts, then lower switch away from instrument panel.
9. Insert ignition key and turn switch to the RUN position.
10. Depress detent on bottom of ignition switch housing to release ignition lock cylinder from housing.
11. Disconnect electrical connector from switch housing and remove switch.
12. Reverse procedure to install.

INTRIGUE

1. Remove radio as outlined under "Radio, Replace."
2. Insert ignition key and turn to the ON position.
3. Depress and hold lock cylinder retaining tab with a small flat-bladed tool.
4. Pull lock cylinder from ignition switch.
5. Reverse procedure to install.

LUMINA

1. Remove steering column from vehicle as outlined in "Steering Columns."
2. Remove and discard two lower spring retainers.
3. Remove lower bearing spring and lower bearing seat.
4. Remove nut retainer and jam nut, then the steering wheel.
5. Remove cancel cam assembly, then the hazard knob screw and hazard warning knob.
6. Position turn signal switch so turn signal switch screws and housing screw can be removed through opening in switch.
7. Remove housing screw and column housing cover, then the turn signal switch screws.
8. Remove wiring protector from opening in instrument panel bracket on jacket assembly and separate from wires.
9. Disconnect pivot/pulse switch connector then remove pivot screw and pivot/pulse switch assembly.
10. Disconnect turn signal switch connector from ignition and dimmer switch assembly connector.
11. Disconnect 17-way secondary lock from turn signal connector.
12. Disconnect wires on buzzer switch from turn signal connector using terminal remover tool No. J-35689-A, or equivalent, wrap wire ends with tape.
13. Remove turn signal switch assembly from column.
14. Remove and discard two lower spring retainers.
15. Remove lower bearing spring and seat.
16. Remove adapter screws then the adapter and bearing assembly.
17. **On models equipped with tilt column,** proceed as follows:
    a. Insert Phillips head screwdriver into square opening in spring retainer, push down and turn left to release retainer and wheel tilt spring.
    b. Remove spring retainer, tilt spring and tilt spring guide.
    c. Remove two pivot pins using pivot pin remover tool No. J-21854-01, or equivalent.
18. **On all models,** place lock cylinder in Run position.
19. **On models equipped with tilt column,** pull tilt lever to release steering column housing, then remove steering shaft assembly and steering column housing as a complete unit.

20. **On models less tilt column,** proceed as follows:
    a. Place opening in retaining ring over flat on steering shaft.
    b. Remove retaining ring using a suitable screwdriver.
    c. Remove thrust washer, upper bearing spring and washer.
    d. Remove steering shaft from lower end of jacket and bowl assembly.
    e. Remove housing screws and steering column housing.
    f. Remove housing spacer bearing using a suitable drift. Discard bearing.
21. **On all models,** place lock cylinder in Off-Lock position and remove key.
22. Remove buzzer switch by lifting switch tab with screwdriver and pulling gently on wires.
23. Remove lock retaining screw and lock cylinder.
24. Reverse procedure to install, noting the following:
    a. **Torque** lock retaining screw to 22 inch lbs.
    b. **Torque** steering column housing screws to 88 inch lbs.
    c. **Torque** turn signal switch and column housing cover screws to 35 inch lbs.
    d. **Torque** jam nut to 30 ft. lbs.
    e. Install new lower spring retainers, compressing spring until retainers are positioned 1.14 inches from lower end of steering shaft.

MONTE CARLO

1998-99

Refer to "Lumina" for ignition lock replacement procedure on these models.

2000-02

Refer to "Impala" for ignition lock replacement procedure on these models.

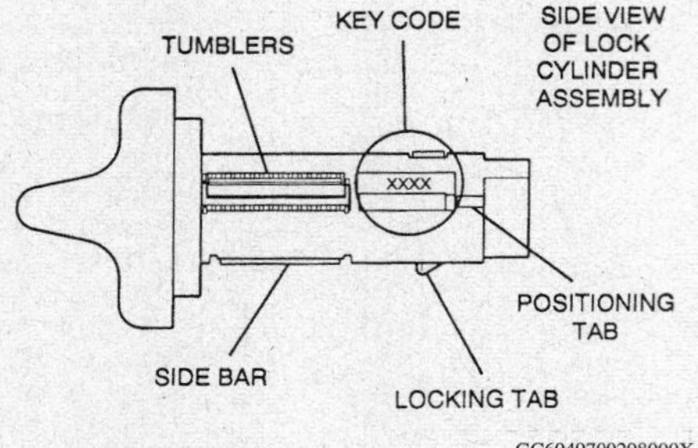

Fig. 3 Lock cylinder removal. Century, Grand Prix & Regal

IMPALA

Refer to "Ignition Lock, Replace" for ignition switch replacement.

INTRIGUE

1. Remove instrument panel center trim plate.
2. Remove radio as outlined under "Radio, Replace."
3. Remove heater and A/C control assembly retaining screws, then pull assembly away from instrument panel and disconnect electrical connectors.
4. Remove heater and A/C control assembly from instrument panel.
5. Remove push-in retainers from instrument panel insulators, then the insulators from under instrument panel, **Fig. 6.**
6. Remove steering column filler panel from under steering column.
7. Remove knee bolster bracket.
8. Turn ignition switch lock cylinder to the ACC position and pull park lock cable from ignition switch.
9. Turn ignition switch lock cylinder to the ON position.
10. Insert a small flat-bladed tool through access hole on right side of ignition switch.
11. Depress locking tab and pull ignition lock cylinder from ignition switch.
12. Disconnect ignition switch electrical connector.
13. Pull ignition switch away from instrument panel.
14. Remove ignition switch to bracket attaching screws, then the bracket from ignition switch.
15. Reverse procedure to install.

LUMINA

REMOVAL

1. Place shift lever in P position and lock cylinder in Off-Lock position.
2. Remove steering column from vehicle as outlined in "Steering Columns" chapter.
3. Disconnect turn signal switch connector from ignition and dimmer switch assembly connector.
4. Disconnect pivot and pulse switch connector from ignition and dimmer switch connector.
5. Remove bowl shield screw, bowl shield nut and bowl shield.
6. Remove dimmer switch nut, then the upper mounting stud.
7. Remove dimmer switch, then the dimmer switch actuator rod.
8. Remove lower mounting stud, then the ignition switch from ignition switch actuator rod.

INSTALLATION

Lock cylinder set must be in the Off-Lock position when installing ignition switch to ensure proper switch slider positioning.

1. Place ignition switch slider in far left position and move back one detent to right, then insert a 3⁄32 inch drill bit in adjustment hole on ignition switch to hold switch slider in proper position during installation.
2. Install ignition switch to switch rod.
3. Install ignition switch to steering column jacket assembly with lower mounting stud. **Torque** to 35 inch lbs.
4. Remove adjustment tool from ignition switch.
5. Install dimmer switch actuator rod through hole in instrument panel bracket and into hole in dimmer switch rod cap.
6. Install dimmer switch assembly on lower mounting stud with dimmer switch nut and upper mounting stud but do not tighten.
7. To adjust dimmer switch, insert a 3⁄32 inch drill bit and push switch against actuator rod to remove all lash.
8. **Torque** dimmer switch nut and upper mounting stud to 35 inch lbs., then remove adjustment tool from dimmer switch.
9. Install bowl shield to column bowl and upper mounting stud, then install shield screw. **Torque** to 35 inch lbs.
10. Install bowl shield nut. **Torque** to 35 inch lbs.
11. Connect turn signal switch connector to ignition and dimmer switch assembly connector and snap in place.
12. Connect pivot and pulse switch connector to ignition and dimmer switch connector.
13. Install steering column and connect battery ground cable.

MONTE CARLO

1998-99

Refer to "Lumina" for ignition switch replacement procedure on these models.

2000-02

Refer to "Impala" for ignition switch replacement procedure on these models.

IGNITION SWITCH

REPLACE

CENTURY, GRAND PRIX & REGAL

1. Remove steering wheel as outlined under "Steering Wheel, Replace."
2. Remove upper and lower steering column shrouds.
3. Remove turn signal and multi-function wire harness retaining straps from steering column and wire harness assembly.
4. Slide turn signal and multi-function switch assembly connectors out of bulkhead connector.
5. Rotate key alarm connector 90°, then pull key alarm connector out of lock module assembly, **Fig. 4.**
6. Remove two ignition and key alarm switch assembly retaining screws, then the ignition and key alarm switch assembly from steering column, **Fig. 5.**
7. Reverse procedure to install.

PARK/NEUTRAL POSITION (PNP) SWITCH

REPLACE

CENTURY, GRAND PRIX, INTRIGUE, LUMINA & REGAL

1. Apply parking brake and block drive wheels.

2. Place selector lever in the NEUTRAL position.
3. Remove throttle body air inlet duct.
4. Remove automatic transaxle range selector cable from switch assembly.
5. Disconnect switch electrical connectors.
6. Remove range selector lever from switch assembly.
7. Remove switch assembly retaining screws, then the switch from transaxle.
8. Reverse procedure to install, noting the following:
   a. **Do not rotate a new switch assembly. The new switch is pinned to the NEUTRAL position. If bolts do not align with mounting boss on transaxle, ensure transaxle shaft is in the NEUTRAL position.**
   b. Align flats of shift shaft to flats of switch.
   c. **Torque** switch mounting bolts to 18 ft. lbs.

IMPALA

The transmission Internal Mode Switch (IMS) sends gear position information to the PCM. The PCM sends this information to the instrument cluster. The transaxle must be removed to replace the IMS switch. Refer to "Automatic Transmissions/ Transaxles" for IMS replacement

MONTE CARLO

1998–99

Refer to "Century, Grand Prix, Intrigue, Lumina & Regal" for Park/Neutral Position switch replacement.

2000–02

Refer to "Impala" for Park/Neutral Position switch replacement.

HEADLAMP SWITCH

REPLACE

CENTURY, GRAND PRIX & REGAL

1. Remove push-in retainers from lefthand side instrument panel sound insulator, then the insulator from under instrument panel.
2. Remove steering column opening filler panel from under steering column.
3. Remove knee bolster bracket from under lefthand side of instrument panel.
4. Remove steering column support to instrument panel retaining bolts, then lower steering column.
5. Pull bottom edge of instrument cluster trim plate away from instrument panel to release retainer clips.
6. Disconnect fog lamp switch electrical connector, then remove instrument cluster trim plate from instrument panel.
7. Pull headlamp switch away from instrument panel and disconnect electrical connector.
8. Reverse procedure to install.

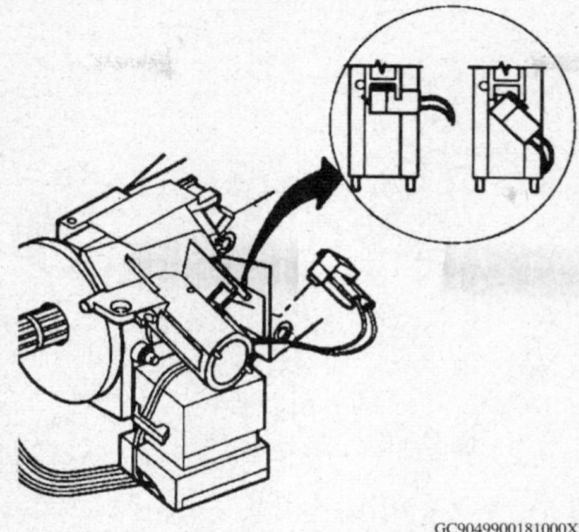

Fig. 4 Key alarm connector. Century, Grand Prix & Regal

IMPALA

1. Remove instrument cluster trim plate as outlined in "Ignition Switch, Replace."
2. Remove headlamp switch housing retaining screws, then the switch housing from instrument panel.
3. Disconnect electrical connector from headlamp switch housing and fog lamp switch.
4. Remove headlamp switch from instrument panel using a suitable flat-bladed tool.
5. Reverse procedure to install.

INTRIGUE

1. Remove push-in retainers from lefthand instrument panel sound insulator.
2. Remove sound insulator from instrument panel.
3. Remove steering column filler panel from under steering column.
4. Remove switch bank retaining screws, then the switch bank from instrument panel.
5. Reverse procedure to install.

LUMINA

1. Move shift lever to the L1 position.
2. Tilt steering column to its lowest position.
3. Unsnap instrument panel cluster trim plate by pulling panel towards the rear.
4. Remove instrument cluster trim plate from instrument panel.
5. Depress headlamp switch locking tabs, then pull switch away from instrument panel and disconnect electrical connector.
6. Reverse procedure to install.

MONTE CARLO

1998–99

Refer to "Lumina" for headlamp switch replacement procedures on these models.

2000–02

Refer to "Impala" for headlamp switch replacement procedures on these models.

STOP LIGHT SWITCH

REPLACE

1. Remove push-in retainers from lefthand instrument panel sound insulator.
2. Remove sound insulator from under lefthand side of instrument panel.
3. Remove brake lamp switch to brake pedal bracket retaining screws.
4. Remove brake lamp switch.
5. Reverse procedure to install, adjust brake and cruise control switches as follows:
   a. Push brake pedal as far forward as possible to set brake push rod into booster.
   b. Pull brake pedal to the rear, against the internal stop. Stop light and cruise control switches are now adjusted.
   c. Ensure brake lamps operate properly.

MULTI-FUNCTION SWITCH

REPLACE

1. Remove steering wheel as outlined under "Steering Wheel, Replace."
2. Remove upper and lower steering column trim covers.
3. Remove wire harness straps from wiring harness and upper tilt head assembly.
4. Remove multi-function switch assembly retaining screws, then the switch assembly from steering column.
5. Reverse procedure to install. **Torque** retaining screws to 62 inch lbs.

TURN SIGNAL SWITCH

REPLACE

Refer to "Multi-Function Switch, Replace" for turn signal switch replacement procedure.

STEERING WHEEL

REPLACE

1. Turn ignition switch to the OFF position.
2. Remove air bag module as outlined in "Air Bag Systems" chapter.
3. Scribe an alignment mark on steering wheel hub inline with slash mark on steering shaft.
4. Loosen steering wheel nut, positioning it flush with end of shaft.
5. Using a suitable puller, loosen steering wheel. **When removing a steering wheel with accessory controls in the hub, use caution to avoid damaging electronic circuits. Steering wheel puller bolts should be turned in no more than four to six threads to avoid contact with electronic circuits.**
6. Remove steering shaft nut and steering wheel.
7. Reverse procedure to install, noting the following:
   a. Align scribe mark.

b. **Torque** steering shaft nut to 30 ft. lbs.

INSTRUMENT CLUSTER

REPLACE

CENTURY, GRAND PRIX & REGAL

1. Remove push-in retainers from left-hand side instrument panel sound insulator, then the insulator from under instrument panel.
2. Remove steering column opening filler panel from under steering column.
3. Remove knee bolster bracket from under lefthand side of instrument panel.
4. Remove steering column support to instrument panel retaining bolts, then lower steering column.
5. Pull bottom edge of instrument cluster trim plate away from instrument panel to release retainer clips.
6. Disconnect fog lamp switch electrical connector, then remove instrument cluster trim plate from instrument panel.
7. Remove instrument cluster retaining screws.
8. Pull instrument cluster towards the rear and upwards to disengage retaining clips.
9. Disconnect cluster electrical connectors and remove cluster from instrument panel.
10. Reverse procedure to install.

IMPALA

1. Remove instrument cluster trim plate bezel as outlined in "Ignition Switch, Replace."
2. Remove instrument cluster attaching bolts.
3. Gently pull cluster away from instrument panel and disconnect electrical connector.
4. Remove cluster from instrument panel.
5. Reverse procedure to install.

INTRIGUE

1. Remove push-in retainers from left-hand instrument panel sound insulator.
2. Remove sound insulator from instrument panel.
3. Remove steering column filler panel from under steering column.
4. Remove trip odometer and reset switch from instrument cluster trim plate.
5. Remove instrument cluster trim plate attaching screws, then the instrument cluster trim plate.
6. Remove instrument cluster retaining screws.
7. Pull cluster towards the rear and disconnect electrical connectors.
8. Remove cluster from instrument panel.
9. Reverse procedure to install.

LUMINA

1. Move shift lever to the L1 position.

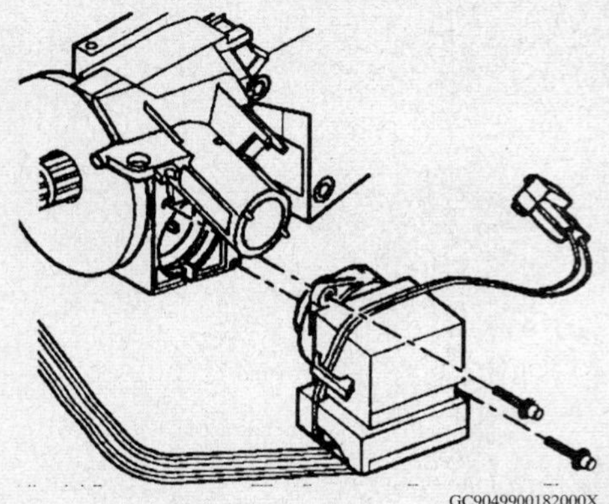

Fig. 5 Ignition & key alarm switch removal. Century, Grand Prix & Regal

2. Tilt steering column to lowest position.
3. Unsnap instrument panel cluster trim plate by pulling panel towards the rear.
4. Remove instrument cluster trim plate from instrument panel.
5. Remove instrument cluster retaining screws.
6. Pull cluster away from instrument panel and disconnect electrical connectors.
7. Reverse procedure to install.

MONTE CARLO

1998–99

Refer to "Lumina" for instrument cluster replacement procedures on these models.

2000–02

Refer to "Impala" for instrument cluster replacement procedures on these models.

RADIO

REPLACE

CENTURY & REGAL

1. Remove push-in retainers from left-hand side instrument panel sound insulator, then the insulator from under instrument panel.
2. Remove steering column opening filler panel from under steering column.
3. Remove instrument panel accessory trim panel attaching screws.
4. Pull accessory trim plate rearward and release two retaining tabs.
5. Remove accessory trim plate from instrument panel.
6. Remove radio retaining screws.
7. Pull radio away from instrument panel, then disconnect electrical connectors and antenna.
8. Reverse procedure to install.

GRAND PRIX

1. Remove push-in retainers from left-hand side instrument panel sound insulator, then the insulator from under instrument panel.
2. Remove steering column opening filler panel from under steering column.
3. Remove knee bolster bracket from under lefthand side of instrument panel.
4. Remove steering column support to instrument panel retaining bolts, then lower steering column.
5. Pull bottom edge of instrument cluster trim plate away from instrument panel to release retainer clips.
6. Disconnect fog lamp switch electrical connector, then remove instrument cluster trim plate from instrument panel.
7. Remove radio retaining screws.
8. Pull radio away from instrument panel and disconnect electrical connectors and antenna.
9. Remove radio from instrument panel.
10. Reverse procedure to install.

IMPALA

1. Remove instrument cluster trim plate bezel as outlined in "Ignition Switch, Replace."
2. Remove radio retaining screws.
3. Pull radio away from instrument panel, then disconnect electrical connectors and antenna.
4. Reverse procedure to install.

INTRIGUE

1. Remove traction control switch from center console trim plate.
2. Open front floor console compartment and remove console trim plate attaching screws.
3. Pull up on trim plate to release retaining clips, then remove console trim plate from console.
4. Remove instrument panel accessory trim plate, then the radio attaching screws.
5. Disconnect electrical connectors, then remove radio.
6. Reverse procedure to install.

LUMINA

1. Move shift lever to the L1 position.
2. Tilt steering column to lowest position.
3. Unsnap instrument panel cluster trim plate by pulling panel towards the rear.
4. Remove instrument cluster trim plate from instrument panel.
5. Remove radio retaining screws.
6. Pull radio away from instrument panel and disconnect electrical connectors and antenna.
7. Remove radio from instrument panel.
8. Reverse procedure to install.

MONTE CARLO

1998–99

Refer to "Lumina" for radio replacement procedures on these models.

2000–02

Refer to "Impala" for radio replacement procedures on these models.

WIPER MOTOR

REPLACE

1. Remove wiper module as outlined in "Wiper Module, Replace."
2. Remove wiper motor crank arm from

wiper transmission using wiper transmission separator tool No. J 39232, or equivalent.
3. Remove wiper motor crank arm to wiper motor retaining nut.
4. Remove wiper motor bracket attaching screws, then the wiper motor assembly from tube frame.
5. Reverse procedure to install.

WIPER SWITCH

REPLACE

Refer to procedure outlined under "Multi-Function Switch, Replace."

WIPER TRANSMISSION

REPLACE

1. Remove wiper module as outlined under "Wiper Motor, Replace."
2. Remove two transmission socket screws, then remove socket from link ball.
3. Remove right, left and bellcrank mounting screws, then the transmission from module.
4. Connect new transmission to module.
5. Ensure wiper motor is in innerwipe position.
6. Align holes in module and bellcrank, then install transmission socket screws.
7. Ensure body seal is in proper place on righthand side of module and install wiper module.
8. Install passenger side wiper arm and blade. Measure from tip of blade to bottom edge of glass. Ensure distance is approximately 9⅛ inches (231 mm), then tighten nut install protective cap and reconnect washer hose.
9. Install driver side wiper arm and blade. Measure from tip of blade to bottom edge of glass. Ensure distance is approximately 2 inches (53 mm), then tighten nut, install protective cap and reconnect washer hose.
10. Run wiper at high and low speeds with wet and tacky windshield. Ensure wiper parks properly and there is no interference between blades.

WIPER MODULE

REPLACE

The windshield wiper module consists of both the wiper motor and the wiper transmission.

1. Turn ignition switch to the ACCY position, then set wiper switch to the PULSE/DELAY position.
2. With wiper arms are in innerwipe position and not moving, turn ignition switch off.
3. Remove hose from nozzle on wiper arm driveshaft.
4. Remove covers from wiper arm retaining nuts.
5. Remove wiper arm retaining nuts, then the wiper arms from wiper transmission driveshaft.
6. Remove inlet shroud attaching bolts, then the inlet shroud from vehicle.

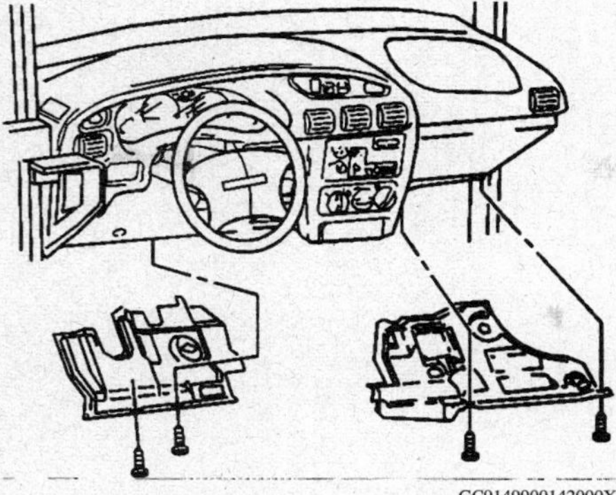

Fig. 6 I/P insulator panel removal. Intrigue

7. Disconnect wiper motor electrical connectors.
8. Remove wiper module assembly attaching bolts, then the wiper module assembly from vehicle.
9. Reverse procedure to install.

BLOWER MOTOR

REPLACE

1. Remove right sound insulator panel from under instrument panel.
2. **On models equipped with convenience center,** remove rear retaining screws from electrical convenience center, then loosen front screw and slide convenience center out.
3. **On all models,** disconnect electrical connector at motor and remove harness from clip.
4. Disconnect blower motor cooling hose.
5. Remove blower motor mounting screws and blower motor.
6. Reverse procedure to install.

CABIN AIR FILTER

REPLACE

1. Place windshield wipers in up position by turning ignition switch Off when wipers reach desired position.
2. Open hood.
3. Lift right side of rear hood seal from flange in area of right air inlet grille.
4. Using a suitable door trim panel pad clip remover, disengage right air inlet grille retaining clips, then remove right inlet grille.
5. Remove cabin air filter element, **Fig. 7.**
6. Reverse procedure to install.

HEATER CORE

REPLACE

1. **On models equipped with 3.1L and 3.4L engines,** remove air cleaner and duct assembly.
2. **On models equipped with 3.5L and 3800 engines,** remove fuel injector sight shield as follows:
   a. Remove oil fill cap.
   b. Remove fuel injector sight shield to fuel injector rail brace stud retaining nut.
   c. Lift fuel injector sight shield up at front and slide tab out of engine bracket.
   d. Install oil fill cap.
3. **On all models,** drain cooling system, then disconnect heater hoses from heater core.
4. **On models equipped with center console,** proceed as follows:
   a. Position transaxle shift lever in the LOW position.
   b. Remove floor console storage compartment rubber mat, then the floor console front attaching bolts.
   c. Remove floor console rear mounting bracket bolts located behind transaxle shift lever.
   d. Remove floor console left and right attaching bolts.
   e. Disconnect console electrical connectors.
   f. Pull console towards the rear and remove from vehicle.
5. **On all models,** remove push-in retainers from instrument panel insulators, then the insulators from under instrument panel.
6. Position heater core outlet cover downward and rearward.
7. Remove heater core outlet cover retaining screws, then disconnect outlet cover from floor duct assembly.
8. Remove heater core cover attaching screws, then the cover.
9. Remove and discard seals from heater core cover and heater core.
10. Remove heater core line clamp retaining screw, heater core retaining clamp and heater core pipe retainer clamp screw.
11. Remove heater core from HVAC lower case.
12. Remove and discard heater core lower, center, upper and side seals from HVAC case.
13. Reverse procedure to install, noting the following:
    a. Install all new seals.
    b. **Torque** heater core line clamp screw to 13 inch lbs.
    c. **Torque** heater core mounting clip screw to 13 inch lbs.
    d. **Torque** heater core cover screws to 13 inch lbs.

EVAPORATOR CORE

REPLACE

CENTURY, INTRIGUE, LUMINA & REGAL

1. Recover A/C refrigerant as outlined in "Air Conditioning" section.
2. Remove air cleaner and duct assembly.
3. Drain engine coolant.
4. Remove instrument panel as outlined in "Dash Panel Service."
5. Remove passenger side air bag module as outlined in "Air Bag Systems."
6. Unclip fuse block and position aside.
7. Remove brake pedal bracket and reinforcement.
8. Remove BCM bracket attaching bolts, then position bracket aside.

9. Release instrument panel wiring harness retaining clips, then position harness aside.
10. Remove HVAC module center support bracket attaching bolts, then the support bracket.
11. Remove HVAC module upper support bracket attaching bolts, then the HVAC module from cross vehicle beam support.
12. Remove support braces from top of engine compartment.
13. Disconnect refrigerant lines from evaporator block fitting.
14. Disconnect heater hoses at heater core.
15. Remove HVAC module to dash panel retaining nuts.
16. Disconnect HVAC module electrical connectors and vacuum hoses. **Note location for installation reference.**
17. Remove HVAC module to cross vehicle support beam attaching bolts and nuts, then the module.
18. Remove all HVAC module outer seals, then the air inlet housing.
19. Unclip and remove heater/defrost valve vacuum actuator from HVAC module.
20. Remove HVAC module case upper screws, then separate module case.
21. Remove module seal and evaporator core from lower case.
22. Remove and discard all evaporator core seals and water core filter.
23. Reverse procedure to install, noting the following:
    a. Replace all seals.
    b. **Torque** HVAC case screws to 13 inch lbs.
    c. Recharge A/C system refrigerant.

IMPALA

1. Remove lefthand fender diagonal brace.

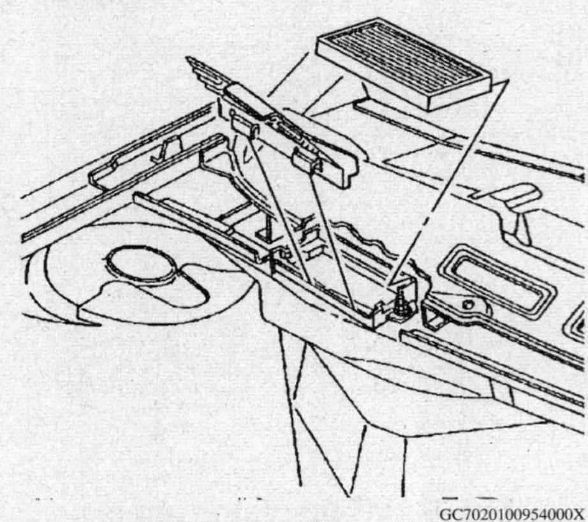

Fig. 7 Cabin air filter replacement

2. Remove cross vehicle brace.
3. Recover A/C refrigerant as outlined in "Air Conditioning" section.
4. Drain cooling system.
5. Disconnect A/C lines from evaporator block fitting, then the heater hoses from heater core.
6. Remove instrument panel as outlined in "Dash Panel Service."
7. Remove cross vehicle beam.
8. Disconnect vacuum hoses and electrical connectors from HVAC module.
9. Disconnect instrument panel wiring harness from HVAC module retainers.
10. Remove evaporator drain elbow.
11. Remove HVAC module to dash panel retaining nuts.
12. Pull HVAC module rearward and disengage from mounting studs.
13. Position dash insulator pad away from HVAC module air inlet opening.
14. Roll HVAC module downward and rearward, then remove heater outlet cover from rear floor air outlet duct.
15. Remove outer HVAC module seals.
16. Remove air inlet housing and heater/defroster valve vacuum actuator from HVAC module.
17. Remove HVAC module case upper screws.
18. Separate module upper case from and lower case.
19. Remove seal from module lower case.
20. Remove evaporator core from case.
21. Reverse procedure to install.

MONTE CARLO

1998–99

Refer to "Century, Intrigue, Lumina & Regal" for evaporator core replacement on these models.

2000–02

Refer to "Impala" for evaporator core replacement on these models.

TECHNICAL SERVICE BULLETINS

IGNITION KEY DIFFICULT TO REMOVE/HARD TO MOVE SHIFT LEVER OUT OF PARK

2000 IMPALA

On some of these vehicles equipped with a column mounted shifter, it may be difficult to remove the ignition key or move the shifter out of the Park position. This condition may be caused by a shift control cable that is too long or routed incorrectly.

To correct this condition, replace shift control cable with part No. 26064241. Refer to "Automatic Transmissions/Transaxles" chapter for replacement procedure.

3.1L Engine

NOTE: On Air Bag Equipped Models, Refer To "Air Bag System Precautions" Located In The Front Of This Manual For System Disarming & Arming Procedures.

NOTE: Refer To "Computer Relearn Procedures" Located In The Front Of This Manual When Battery Power To The Computer Has Been Interrupted.

NOTE: Prior To Performing Any Service Operations Listed In This Section, Consult The "Technical Service Bulletins" Section For Related Information.

INDEX

PRECAUTIONS

AIR BAG SYSTEMS

Refer to "Air Bag System Precautions" in the front of this manual for system disarming and arming procedures.

BATTERY GROUND CABLE

Prior to service, disconnect battery ground cable and isolate as required.

FUEL SYSTEM PRESSURE RELIEF

To reduce the risk of fire and personal injury, it is necessary to relieve the fuel system pressure before servicing fuel system components.

1. Loosen fuel tank filler cap to relieve tank pressure.
2. Connect fuel pressure gauge tool No. J-34730-1, or equivalent, to fuel pressure valve. Wrap a shop towel around fitting while connection gauge to avoid spillage.
3. Install bleed hose into an approved container and open valve to bleed system pressure.

COMPRESSION PRESSURE

When checking compression, lowest cylinder must be within 70 percent of the highest cylinder with a minimum pressure of 100 psi. Perform compression test with engine at normal operating temperature, spark plugs removed and throttle wide open.

ENGINE MOUNT

REPLACE

ENGINE MOUNT

1. Remove throttle body air inlet duct, then the engine mount struts.
2. Raise and support vehicle, then remove right front wheel and tire assembly.
3. Remove catalytic converter pipe from rear exhaust manifold.
4. Remove right engine splash shield, then the engine mount lower nuts.
5. Place a block of wood under the oil pan, then raise engine with suitable floor jack stand.
6. Remove engine mount bracket to oil pan bolts, then the engine mount and engine mount bracket.
7. Remove engine upper mount nuts, then the engine mount from engine mount bracket.
8. Reverse procedure to install.

ENGINE STRUT

1. Remove bolt from engine mount strut bracket, then bolt from bracket.
2. Remove strut assembly.
3. Reverse procedure to install.

TRANSAXLE MOUNT

1. Support transaxle with suitable jack.
2. Remove crossmember to mount attaching nuts, **Fig. 1.**
3. Remove bracket to transaxle attaching bolts.
4. Remove mount and bracket assembly.
5. Separate mount from bracket.
6. Reverse procedure to install.

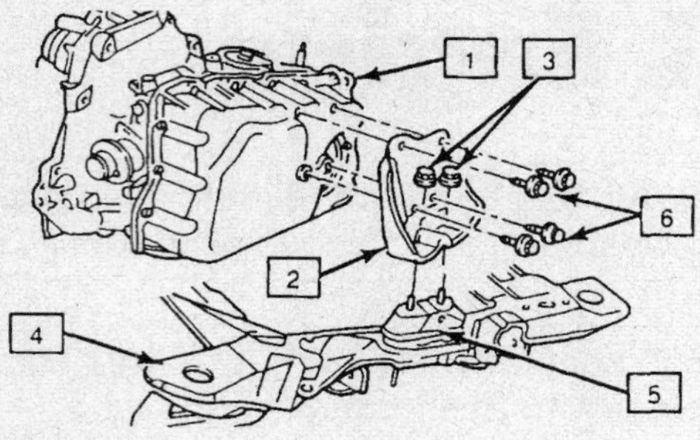

1 COVER ASSEMBLY, TRANSAXLE SIDE
2 BRACKET, TRANSAXLE MOUNT TRANSAXLE SIDE
3 NUT, TRANSAXLE MOUNT TRANSAXLE SIDE BRACKET
4 FRAME ASSEMBLY, DRIVETRAIN AND FRONT SUSPENSION
5 MOUNT ASSEMBLY, TRANSAXLE
6 BOLT/SCREW, TRANSAXLE MOUNT TRANSAXLE SIDE BRACKET

GC1069400816000X

Fig. 1 Transaxle mount

ENGINE

REPLACE

1. Drain engine coolant into a suitable container, then the engine oil.
2. Relieve fuel pressure as outlined under "Precautions."
3. Scribe alignment marks, then remove hood.
4. Remove air flow tube from air cleaner and throttle valve, then the air cleaner assembly.
5. Remove transaxle filler tube assembly.
6. Disconnect necessary electrical wiring, then the throttle and TV cables.
7. Remove engine mount strut bracket.
8. Disconnect fuel lines.
9. Remove AIR pump belt, then the serpentine drive belt cover and belt.
10. Disconnect radiator hoses at engine.
11. Remove A/C compressor bolts from front bracket.
12. Remove power steering pump and position aside.
13. Disconnect heater hoses from engine.
14. Disconnect brake booster vacuum supply line.
15. Disconnect EGR from exhaust.
16. Raise and support vehicle.
17. Remove starter motor assembly.
18. Remove A/C compressor bolts at rear bracket, then position compressor aside.
19. Remove flywheel cover, then disconnect starter and position aside.
20. Remove torque converter bolts, then the transaxle mount bracket.
21. Remove engine front mount retaining nuts.
22. Disconnect exhaust pipe at crossover, then lower vehicle.
23. Remove coolant recovery bottle.
24. Disconnect accelerator control cable bracket and move assemblies aside.
25. Disconnect crossover pipe at left manifold.
26. Remove serpentine belt, then the alternator.
27. Remove power steering pump assembly.
28. Remove plastic cover from front shock tower, then remove automatic transaxle modulator pipe assembly.
29. **On Century and Grand Prix models,** pull engine assembly forward and support in this position.
30. **On all models,** disconnect crossover pipe at right manifold.
31. Disconnect bulkhead connector.
32. **On Century and Grand Prix models,** remove engine support and allow engine to roll to normal position.
33. **On all models,** remove engine to transaxle attaching bolts, attach lifting device to engine and support transaxle.
34. Remove engine assembly.
35. Reverse procedure to install.

INTAKE MANIFOLD

REPLACE

UPPER

1. Disconnect vacuum hose from throttle body air inlet duct, then the wiring harness from intake air temperature sensor.
2. Remove throttle body air inlet duct, then drain engine coolant into a suitable container.
3. Remove accelerator control and cruise control cables with bracket from throttle body.
4. Disconnect wiring harness connectors from throttle body, then the front spark plug wires.
5. Disconnect wiring harness attachment clips from camshaft position sensor, front spark plug wire harness and engine wiring harness.
6. Disconnect thermostat bypass pipe coolant hoses from throttle body.
7. Remove ignition coil bracket with coils, purge solenoid and vacuum canister solenoid.
8. Disconnect vacuum hose at MAP sensor and upper intake manifold, then remove MAP sensor and bracket.
9. Disconnect emission control vacuum harness, then the upper intake manifold to vacuum booster vacuum hose.

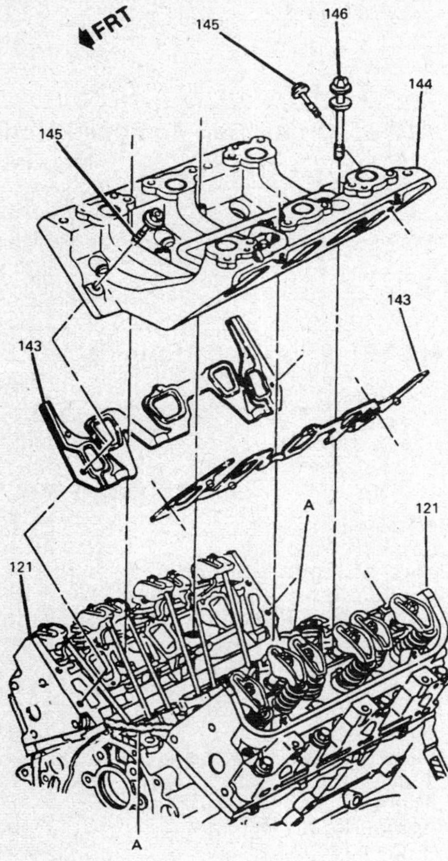

A APPLY SEALANT
121 HEAD ASSEMBLY, CYLINDER
143 GASKET, LOWER INTAKE MANIFOLD
144 BOLT, LOWER INTAKE
145 BOLT, LOWER INTAKE MANIFOLD
146 BOLT, LOWER INTAKE MANIFOLD

GC1059400113000X

Fig. 2 Intake manifold replacement

10. Disconnect automatic transaxle vacuum modulator hose.
11. Disconnect heater/air conditioning vacuum source hose and fuel pressure regulator vacuum hose.
12. Remove front and rear alternator braces, then the alternator bracket.
13. Remove EGR valve, then the upper intake manifold bolts and studs.
14. Remove upper intake manifold and gaskets.
15. Reverse procedure to install.

LOWER

1. Relieve fuel system pressure as outlined under "Precautions."
2. Remove upper intake manifold as outlined under "Upper Intake Manifold, Replace."
3. Remove both valve covers, then disconnect ECT wiring harness.
4. Remove fuel pipe clip bolt, then the fuel pipe clip.
5. Disconnect fuel feed and fuel return pipes from fuel injector rail.

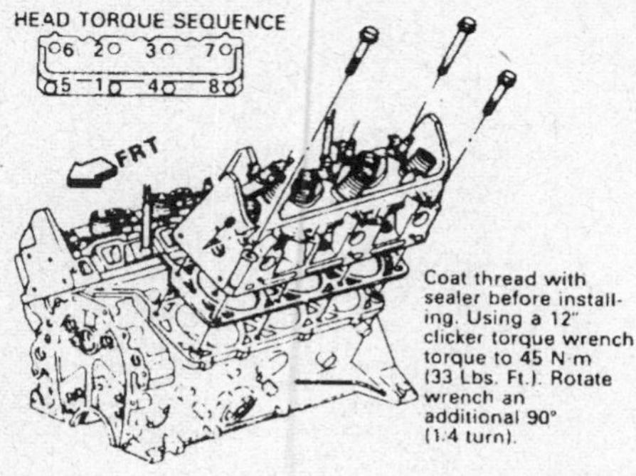

Fig. 3 Cylinder head installation

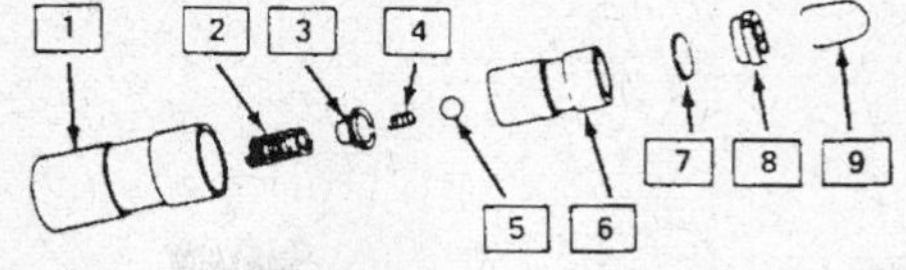

Fig. 4 Exploded view of valve lifter

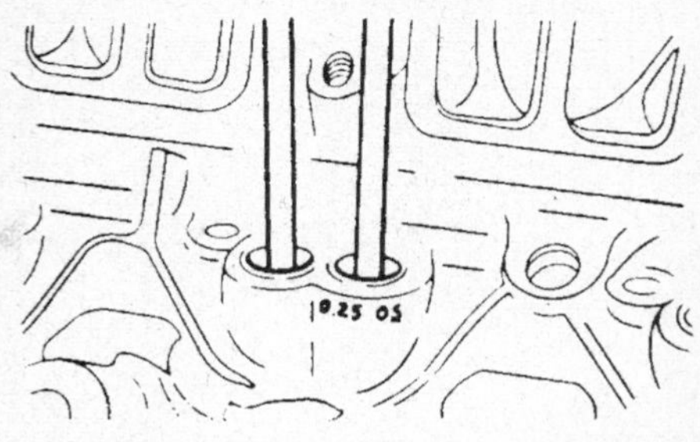

Fig. 5 Oversize lifter marking

6. Remove fuel injector rail, then the power steering pump from front engine cover and set aside.
7. Disconnect heater inlet pipe with heater hose from lower intake manifold and position aside.
8. Disconnect radiator inlet hose from engine, then the thermostat bypass hose from thermostat bypass pipe and lower intake manifold pipe.
9. Remove lower intake manifold bolts, then the lower intake manifold.
10. Remove pushrods, then the lower intake manifold gaskets and seals.
11. Reverse procedure to install, noting the following:
    a. Apply sealant as shown in **Fig. 2.**
    b. **Torque** vertical bolts to 62 inch lbs.
    c. **Torque** diagonal bolts to 62 inch lbs.
    d. **Torque** vertical bolts to 115 inch lbs.
    e. **Torque** diagonal bolts to 115 inch lbs.
    f. **Vertical bolts must be tightened before diagonal bolts or an oil leak could occur.**

EXHAUST MANIFOLD

REPLACE

LEFT

1. Remove throttle body air inlet duct, then drain engine coolant into a suitable container.
2. Remove right engine mount strut bracket, then disconnect radiator inlet hose from engine.
3. Remove automatic transaxle vacuum modulator pipe, then the thermostat bypass pipe.
4. Remove exhaust crossover pipe heat shield, then the exhaust crossover bolts to exhaust manifold.
5. Remove exhaust manifold heat shied bolts, then the heat shield.
6. Remove exhaust manifold nuts, then the exhaust manifold and gasket.
7. Reverse procedure to install.

RIGHT

1. Remove throttle body air inlet duct, then drain engine coolant into a suitable container.
2. Remove right engine mount strut bracket, then disconnect radiator inlet hose from engine.
3. Remove automatic transaxle vacuum modulator pipe, then the thermostat bypass pipe.
4. Remove exhaust crossover pipe heat shield, then the exhaust crossover bolts to exhaust manifold.
5. Remove exhaust manifold heat shied bolts, then the heat shield.
6. Disconnect heated oxygen sensor wiring harness connector, then raise and support vehicle.
7. Remove EGR tube from exhaust manifold, then the exhaust manifold upper heat shield bolts and upper heat shield.
8. Remove exhaust lower heat shield bolts and lower heat shield, then the exhaust manifold nuts and exhaust manifold.
9. Reverse procedure to install.

CYLINDER HEAD

REPLACE

LEFT

1. Drain engine coolant into a suitable container, then the engine oil.
2. Remove upper and lower intake manifolds as outlined under "Intake Manifold, Replace."
3. Remove valve cover as outlined under "Valve Cover, Replace."
4. Remove exhaust crossover, then the oil lever indicator bracket.
5. Remove left exhaust manifold as outlined under "Exhaust Manifold, Replace."
6. Disconnect plug wires at left head, then remove pushrods. Intake and exhaust pushrods are different lengths (exhaust pushrods are longer). Intake pushrods are marked orange and are 5.68 inches long, exhaust pushrods are marked blue and are 6 inches long.
7. remove cylinder head attaching bolts, then the cylinder head.
8. Reverse procedure to install, noting the following:
    a. Clean gasket surfaces on head, cylinder block and intake manifold, cylinder block bolt threads and cylinder head bolts.
    b. Place gasket in position over dowel pins with "This Side Up" marking facing upward.
    c. Coat cylinder head bolt threads with suitable sealant.
    d. Using sequence shown in **Fig. 3,** tighten cylinder head bolts in two steps: First step, **torque** bolts to 37 ft. lbs.; second step, tighten an additional 90.°

RIGHT

1. Raise and support vehicle, then drain engine coolant into a suitable container.
2. Drain engine oil, then lower vehicle.
3. Remove upper and lower intake manifolds as outlined under "Intake Manifold, Replace."
4. Disconnect plug wires at left head, then remove pushrods. Intake and exhaust pushrods are different lengths (exhaust pushrods are longer). Intake pushrods are marked orange and are 5.68 inches long, exhaust pushrods are marked blue and are 6 inches long.
5. Remove exhaust crossover pipe, then the right head spark plug wires and plugs.
6. Remove cylinder head attaching bolts, then the cylinder head.
7. Reverse procedure to install, noting the following:
    a. Clean gasket surfaces on head, cylinder block and intake manifold, cylinder block bolt threads and cylinder head bolts.
    b. Place gasket in position over dowel pins with "This Side Up" marking facing upward.
    c. Coat cylinder head bolt threads with suitable sealant.
    d. Using sequence shown in **Fig. 3,** tighten cylinder head bolts in two steps: First step, **torque** bolts to 37 ft. lbs.; second step, tighten bolts an additional 90.°

VALVE COVER

REPLACE

LEFT

1. Remove lefthand side spark plug wires, then the automatic transaxle vacuum modulator pipe.
2. Remove PCV valve, then the left valve cover bolts.
3. Remove left valve cover and gasket.
4. Reverse procedure to install, noting the following:
    a. Clean sealing surfaces on cylinder head and cover.
    b. Install new gasket and ensure gasket is seated properly in rocker cover groove.

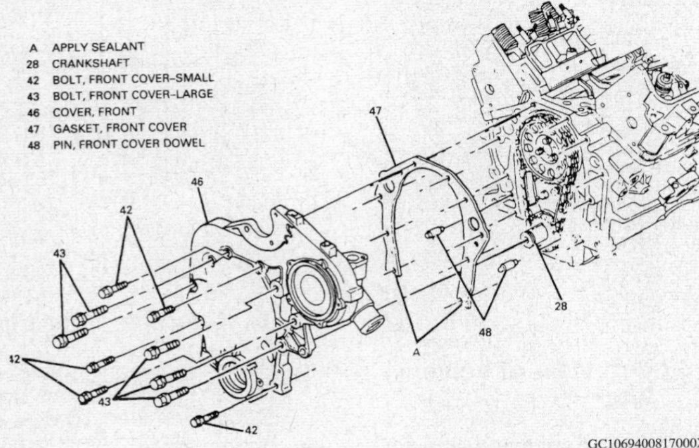

Fig. 6 Front cover installation

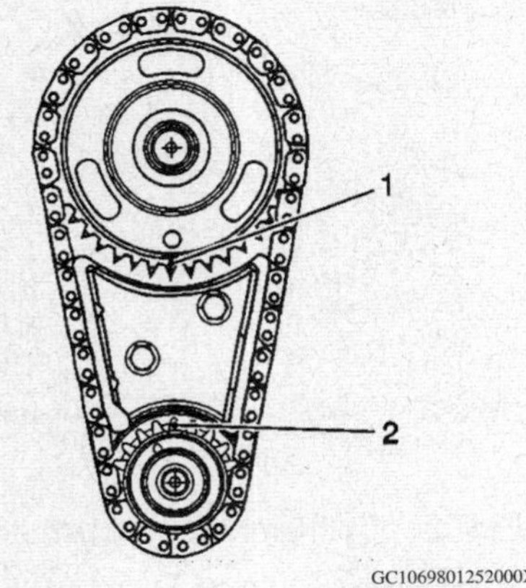

Fig. 7 Timing marks alignment

c. Apply suitable sealer into cylinder head notch.

RIGHT

1. Remove serpentine drive belt, then the alternator braces.
2. Remove alternator, then the right head spark plug wires.
3. Remove ignition coil bracket with coils, then the purge solenoid and vacuum canister solenoid.
4. Remove vacuum hose from grommet in valve cover, then the valve cover bolts.
5. Remove valve cover and gasket.
6. Reverse procedure to install, noting the following:
   a. Clean sealing surfaces on cylinder head and cover.
   b. Install new gasket and ensure gasket is seated properly in rocker cover groove.
   c. Apply suitable sealer into cylinder head notch.

VALVE ARRANGEMENT

FRONT TO REAR

Cowl side ....E-I-E-I-I-E
Radiator side ....E-I-I-E-I-E

VALVE LIFTERS

Roller type valve lifters, **Fig. 4,** are used in this engine. Valve lifters must be replaced whenever camshaft is replaced.

Valve lifters should be kept in order so they will be reinstalled in their original positions. Some engines will have both standard and .010 inch oversize valve lifters.

Where oversize lifters are used, the cylinder case will be marked ".25 OS" with white paint on the lifter boss, **Fig. 5.**

If lifters are removed, they must be installed in their original location. If replacement is necessary, use lifters with a narrow flat ground along the lower ¾ of the lifter. These flats provide additional oil to the cam lobe and lifter surfaces.

CAMSHAFT LOBE LIFT SPECIFICATIONS

Intake.................................... .2500
Exhaust .... .2550

VALVE CLEARANCE SPECIFICATIONS

This engine is equipped with hydraulic lifters; valve lash should always be zero. If valve lash exists, inspect pushrod and rocker arm for excessive wear and check for inoperative lifters.

VALVE ADJUSTMENT

There is no valve adjustment for these engines.

1. Remove valve covers as outlined under "Valve Cover, Replace."
2. Remove rocker arms, identifying components so they can be installed in same location.
3. Remove rocker arm pivot balls and rocker arms, then the pushrods. Intake and exhaust pushrods are different lengths (exhaust pushrods are longer). Intake pushrods are marked orange, exhaust pushrods are marked blue.
4. Reverse procedure to install, noting the following:
   a. Ensure pushrods seat in lifter.
   b. Coat bearing surfaces of rocker arms and pivot balls with Molykote, or equivalent, lubricant.

PUSH RODS

1. Remove valve covers as outlined under "Valve Cover, Replace."
2. Remove rocker arms, identifying components so they can be installed in same location.
3. Remove rocker arm pivot balls and rocker arms, then the pushrods. Intake and exhaust pushrods are different lengths (exhaust pushrods are longer). Intake pushrods are marked orange, exhaust pushrods are marked blue.
4. Reverse procedure to install, noting the following:
   a. Ensure pushrods seat in lifter.
   b. Coat bearing surfaces of rocker arms and pivot balls with Molykote, or equivalent, lubricant.

HYDRAULIC LIFTERS

REPLACE

1. Remove upper and lower intake manifolds as outlined under "Intake Manifold, Replace."
2. Remove valve rocker arms and pushrods as outlined under "Pushrods."
3. Remove intake manifold oil splash shield.
4. Remove lifter guide bolts, lifter guides, then the lifters. **Keep lifters in order for installation reference.**
5. Reverse procedure to install, noting the following:
   a. Clean all gasket surfaces and valve train parts.
   b. Coat lifters with prelube part No. 1052365, or equivalent.
   c. Install lifters in their original position.

FRONT COVER

REPLACE

1. Drain engine coolant into a suitable container.
2. Remove serpentine drive belt cover, then the drive belt.
3. Remove serpentine drive belt tensioner, then the alternator.
4. Detach power steering pump and position aside.
5. Remove cross vehicle brace attaching bolts, then the brace.

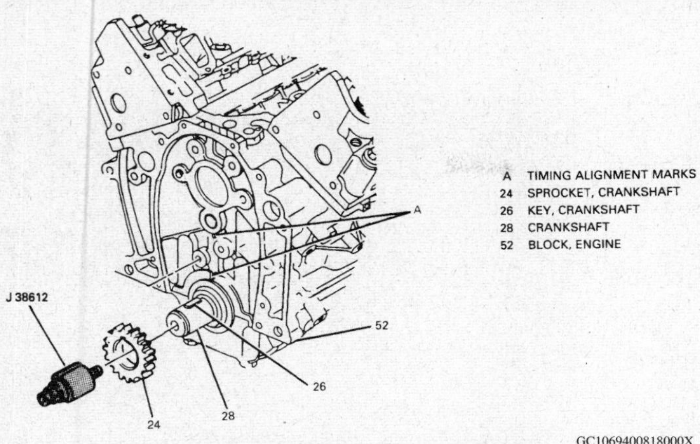

Fig. 8 Timing chain installation

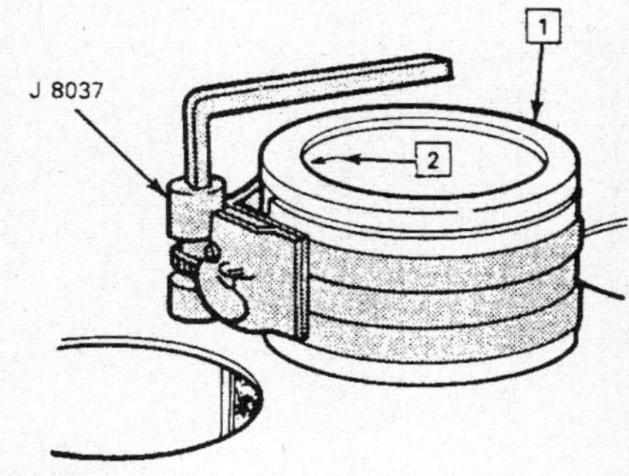

Fig. 9 Piston marking

6. Remove coolant overflow hose from radiator neck.
7. Remove coolant reservoir retaining nuts, then the reservoir from the strut tower.
8. Raise and support vehicle, then drain engine oil into a suitable container.
9. Remove inner splash shield, then the flywheel cover.
10. Remove starter; then the crankshaft balancer, using torsional dampener remover tool No. J-24420, or equivalent.
11. Remove serpentine drive belt idler pulley.
12. Remove lower timing cover attaching bolts, then lower vehicle.
13. Remove throttle body air inlet duct, then the lefthand engine mount strut.
14. Remove spark plug wires from left bank
15. Disconnect radiator hose at water pump and heater coolant hose from cooling system fill pipe.
16. Disconnect bypass, overflow and canister purge hoses.
17. Remove thermostat bypass pipe from front cover.
18. Remove water pump pulley attaching bolts, then the pulley.
19. Remove lower crankshaft position sensor wiring harness bracket from engine front cover.
20. Remove upper timing cover attaching bolts, then the cover.
21. Reverse procedure to install, noting the following:
    a. Clean sealing surfaces on front cover and cylinder block.
    b. Install new gasket.
    c. Apply sealant as shown in **Fig. 6.**

FRONT COVER SEAL

REPLACE

1. Remove inner splash shield.
2. Remove crankshaft balancer, using torsional dampener remover tool No. J-24420, or equivalent.
3. Pry out seal, using a suitable flat-bladed tool. **Do not damage crankshaft.**
4. Reverse procedure to install, noting the following:
    a. Lubricate new seal with clean engine oil and insert in front cover with lip facing engine.
    b. Drive seal into place with front cover alignment and oil seal installer tool No. J-35468, or equivalent.

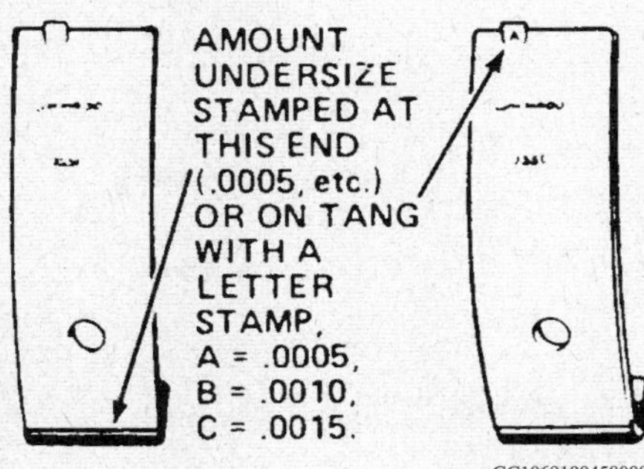

Fig. 10 Main bearing insert markings

TIMING CHAIN

REPLACE

REMOVAL

1. Remove front cover as outlined under "Front Cover, Replace."
2. Rotate crankshaft until timing marks are aligned, **Fig. 7.**
3. Remove camshaft sprocket retaining bolt, then the sprocket and timing chain.
4. Remove timing chain dampener bolts, then the dampener.
5. Remove crankshaft sprocket, using sprocket removal tool No. J-5825-A, or equivalent.

INSTALLATION

1. Install new crankshaft sprocket until sprocket is fully seated on flange of crankshaft, using sprocket installer tool No. J-38612, or equivalent.
2. Coat camshaft and crankshaft sprockets with engine oil.
3. Hold camshaft sprocket with chain hanging down and align marks on camshaft and crankshaft sprockets with cast timing marks on engine block, **Fig. 8.**
4. Install front cover as outlined under "Front Cover, Replace."

CAMSHAFT

REPLACE

1. Remove engine as outlined under "Engine, Replace."
2. Remove valve lifters as outlined under "Hydraulic Lifters, Replace," then the timing chain and sprocket as outlined under "Timing Chain, Replace."
3. Remove camshaft thrust plate attaching bolts, then the thrust plate.
4. Install a suitable large screwdriver into camshaft bolt hole. **Do not damage threads.**
5. Carefully rotate, then pull camshaft from engine.
6. Reverse procedure to install, noting the following:
    a. If installing new camshaft, coat camshaft lobes with GM E.O.S. part No. 1052367, or equivalent.
    b. Lubricate camshaft journals with engine oil.

PISTON & ROD ASSEMBLY

When installing piston and rod assemblies into cylinder block, ensure arrow on top of piston faces toward front of engine, **Fig. 9.**

MAIN & ROD BEARINGS

Engine bearings are of the precision insert type. They are available for service use in standard and various undersizes, **Fig. 10.**

To determine correct replacement insert size, bearing clearance must be measured as follows:

1. Measure crankshaft journal diameter in several places, approximately 90° apart and average the measurements.
2. Measure taper and runout, which should be .0002 inch (maximum).
3. Install bearing inserts and tighten rod and main bearing cap bolts to specifications, then measure I.D. with an inside micrometer. Measure connecting rod I.D. in same direction as length of rod.

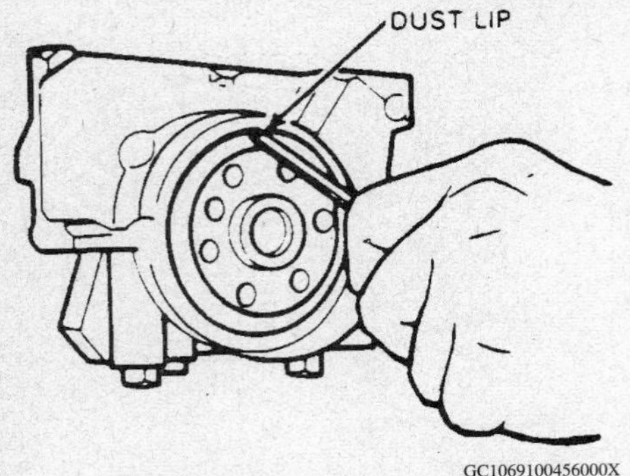

Fig. 11 Rear main seal removal

4. Select a suitable set of inserts to provide specified clearance limits. **Do not mix inserts of different nominal size in same bearing bore.** If clearance limits cannot be met, crankshaft journal must be reconditioned and undersized bearing inserts installed.

CRANKSHAFT REAR OIL SEAL

REPLACE

REMOVAL

1. Support engine with engine support fixture tool No. J-28467, or equivalent, and an extra support leg.
2. Remove transaxle as outlined in "Automatic Transmissions/Transaxles" chapter.
3. Remove flywheel.
4. Remove seal by inserting a suitable tool through the dust lip at an angle, **Fig. 11,** then pry seal out by moving handle of tool toward end of crankshaft pilot, repeating around circumference of seal as necessary. **Be careful not to damage crankshaft outer surface.**

INSTALLATION

1. Check seal bore for nicks or burrs and repair as required.
2. Inspect crankshaft for burrs or nicks on surface which contacts seal, repairing or replacing crankshaft as necessary.
3. Apply engine oil to inner and outer diameters of new seal, then slide seal over mandrel until back of seal bottoms squarely against collar of rear main bearing seal installer tool No. J-34686, or equivalent, **Fig. 12.**
4. Align dowel pin of tool with dowel pin in crankshaft by hand, then **torque** attaching screws to 45 inch lbs., **Fig. 12.**
5. Turn "T" handle of tool so collar pushes seal into bore, turning handle until collar is tight against case.
6. Loosen "T" handle of tool until it comes to a stop, then remove attaching screws.
7. Ensure seal is seated squarely in bore.
8. Install flywheel, then the transaxle.

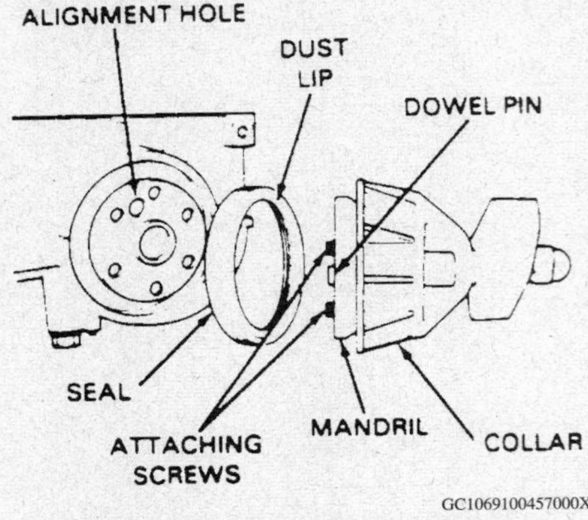

Fig. 12 Rear main seal installation

1 PUMP BODY
2 IDLER GEAR AND DRIVE GEAR
3 PUMP COVER
4 PRESSURE REGULATOR VALVE
5 PRESSURE REGULATOR SPRING
6 RETAINING PIN
7 BOLTS

GC1099100075000X

Fig. 14 Exploded view of oil pump

OIL PAN

REPLACE

1. Remove engine mount struts from engine.
2. Remove A/C compressor mounting bolts and set compressor aside.
3. Install engine support fixture tool No. J 28467–A, engine support fixture adapter tool No. J28467–90 and engine support adapter leg tool No. J 36462, or equivalents.
4. Raise and support vehicle, then disconnect three way catalytic converter pipe from rear exhaust manifold.
5. Drain engine oil, then remove oil level sensor harness connector.
6. Remove starter as outlined under "Starter, Replace" in the "Electrical" section.
7. Remove transaxle brace from oil pan.
8. Remove transaxle mount lower nuts, then the engine mount lower nuts.
9. Raise engine to gain access to oil pan.
10. Remove engine mount bracket with engine mount from oil pan.
11. Remove rear oil pan side bolts, then the front oil pan side bolts.
12. Remove oil pan retaining bolts, then the oil pan and gasket.
13. Reverse procedure to install, noting the following:
    a. Clean oil pan flanges, oil pan rail, front cover, rear main bearing cap and the threaded holes.
    b. Install a new gasket.

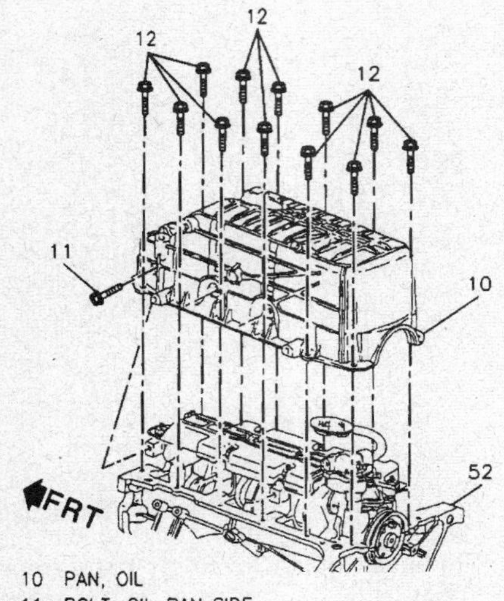

10 PAN, OIL
11 BOLT, OIL PAN SIDE
12 BOLT, OIL PAN RETAINING
52 BLOCK, ENGINE

GC1069600676000X

Fig. 13 Oil pan installation

    c. Install oil pan as shown in **Fig. 13.**

OIL PUMP

REPLACE

1. Remove oil pan as described under "Oil Pan, Replace."
2. Remove crankshaft oil deflector retaining nuts, then the deflector.
3. Remove oil pump mounting bolt, then the oil pump and drive rod.
4. Reverse procedure to install.

OIL PUMP SERVICE

DISASSEMBLE

1. Drain oil from pump.
2. Remove pump cover and pump gears, **Fig. 14.**
3. Remove pressure regulator valve. If valve is stuck, soak pump housing in carburetor cleaning solvent.
4. Carefully remove pressure regulator valve spring retaining pin. **Pressure regulator valve spring may be under pressure.**
5. Clean sludge, oil and/or varnish from all parts.

INSPECTION

1. Inspect pump housing and cover for cracks or damaged threads, replacing as necessary. **Do not attempt to repair pump housing.** Replace spring as necessary.
2. Inspect idler gear shaft. If loose in housing, replace pump.
3. Inspect pressure regulator valve for scoring or sticking. Burrs may be removed with a fine oil stone.
4. Inspect pressure regulator valve spring for loss of tension or bending.
5. Inspect suction pipe and screen assembly for looseness, if permanently pressed into pump body. If pipe is loose or has been removed, pump

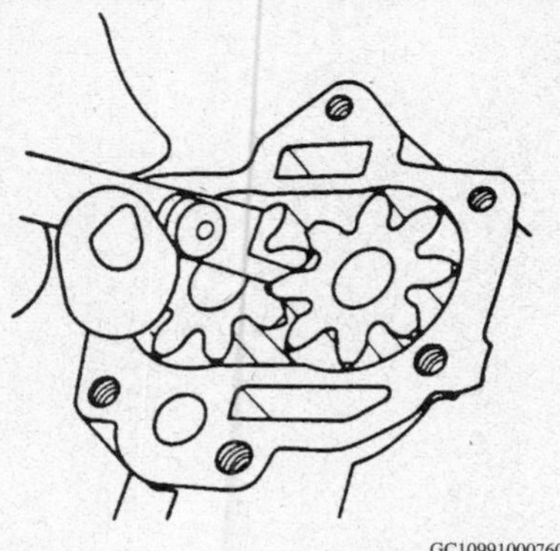

Fig. 15 Oil pump gear lash measurement

body cover must be replaced. Check for broken wire mesh or screen.

6. Inspect gears for chipping, galling or wear.
7. Measure gear lash in several positions, **Fig. 15.** Gear lash should be .0037–.0077 inch.
8. Measure pump housing gear pocket depth, **Fig. 16.** Depth should be as follows:
   a. **On models equipped with an aluminum pump body,** pump depth should be 1.195–1.198 inches.
   b. **On models equipped with a cast pump body,** pump depth should be 1.202–1.204 inches.
9. **On all models,** measure pump housing gear pocket diameter, **Fig. 16.** Pump housing diameter should be 1.503–1.505 inches.
10. Measure pump gear diameters, **Fig. 17.** Gear diameter should be 1.498–1.500 inches.
11. Measure pump gear side clearance, **Fig. 18.** Gear side clearance should be .001–.003 inch.
12. Measure oil pump end clearance, **Fig. 19,** as follows:
   a. **On models equipped with an aluminum pump body,** end clearance should be .0016–.0067 inch.
   b. **On models equipped with a cast pump body,** end clearance should be .0020–.0050 inch.

ASSEMBLE

1. Lubricate all internal parts with engine oil.
2. Install pump gears.
3. Prime engine oil galleries by removing engine oil pump drive unit and rotating oil pump, using drill motor, appropriate socket and extension.
4. Install cover and gasket. **Use only original equipment gaskets as gasket thickness is critical to proper pump operation.**
5. Install pin. Ensure pin is properly secured.
6. Install cover bolts.

BELT TENSION DATA

Belt tension is maintained automatically by a spring tensioned idler pulley. Adjustment of serpentine belt is not necessary.

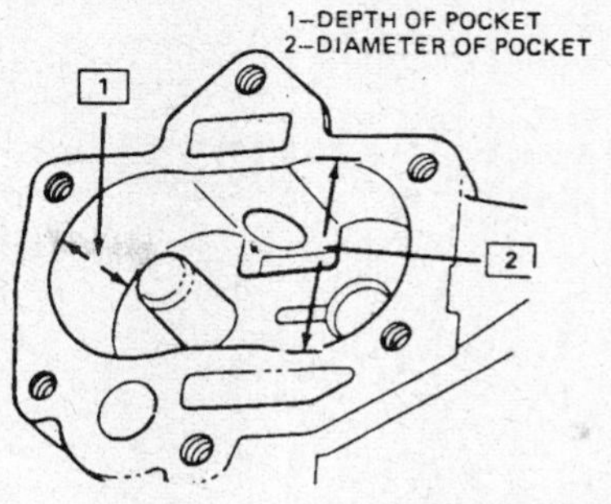

Fig. 16 Oil pump gear pocket measurement

1 CHECK CLEARANCE BETWEEN GEAR TEETH AND SIDE WALL

GC1099100079000X

Fig. 18 Gear side clearance measurement

If belt slippage is indicated and belt tensioner indicator is within normal operating range, measure belt tension as follows:

1. Run engine for ten minutes, then shut off and measure belt tension between any two pulleys using V-belt tension gauge tool No. J 23600-B, or equivalent.
2. Run engine for 30 seconds and repeat measurement.
3. Repeat preceding step, then average all three belt tension measurements. Average tension should be 30–50 lbs.
4. If belt tension is not as specified, replace serpentine drive belt.

SERPENTINE DRIVE BELT

REPLACEMENT

1. Lift or rotate tensioner using a ½ inch breaker bar.
2. Remove serpentine belt.
3. Reverse procedure to install, routing drive belt as shown in **Fig. 20.**

ADJUSTMENT

There is no provision for serpentine belt adjustment. Refer to "Belt Tension Data" for belt tension measurement procedures and to determine whether belt requires replacement.

COOLING SYSTEM BLEED

1. Open vent valves located on thermostat housing and throttle body return

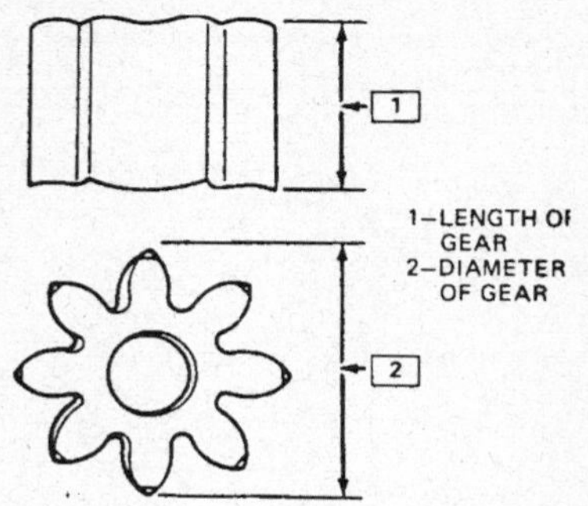

Fig. 17 Oil pump gear measurement

pipe above water pump, **Fig. 21.** Turn both vents screws two to three turns.

2. Fill cooling system to base of radiator neck.
3. Close both vent valves. **Do not over tighten vent valves.**
4. Install radiator cap.
5. Add sufficient coolant to recovery tank.
6. Start engine and observe low coolant warning lamp.
7. If lamp remains illuminated, repeat bleed procedure.

THERMOSTAT

REPLACE

1. Drain engine coolant into a suitable container.
2. Disconnect radiator hose from thermostat housing.
3. Remove thermostat housing bolts, thermostat housing and thermostat.
4. Reverse procedure to install.

WATER PUMP

REPLACE

1. Drain engine coolant into a suitable container.
2. Remove serpentine drive belt, then disconnect radiator and heater hose.
3. Remove water pump attaching bolts, then the water pump, **Fig. 22.**
4. Reverse procedure to install.

RADIATOR

REPLACE

1. Remove battery, then drain cooling system into a suitable container.
2. Remove air cleaner assembly, then drain engine coolant into a suitable container.
3. Remove engine strut upper brace bolts from upper tie bar and rotate strut and brace rearward.
4. Disconnect upper radiator mounting panel bolts and clamps.
5. Disconnect cooling fan electrical connector.
6. Remove cooling fan mounting bolts and fan, then upper radiator bracket.
7. Remove upper and lower radiator hoses at radiator.
8. Disconnect low coolant sensor wiring.
9. Disconnect oil cooler lines, then remove radiator.

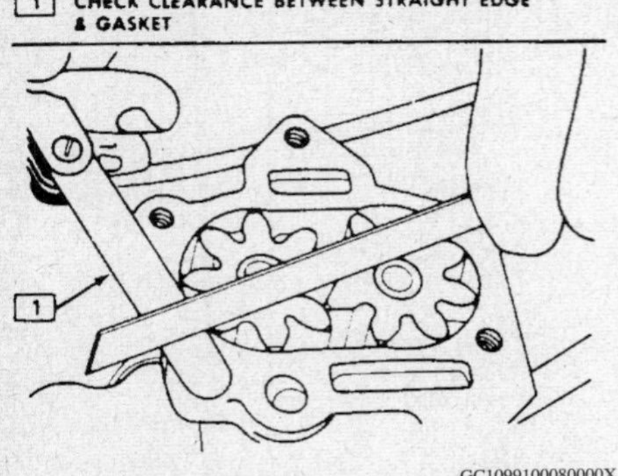

Fig. 19 Oil pump end clearance measurement

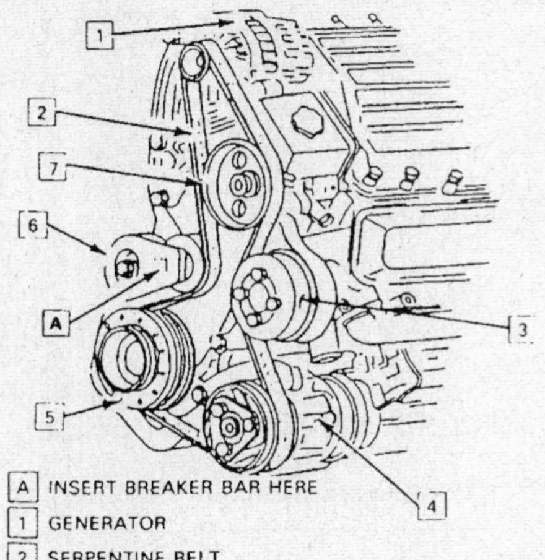

Fig. 20 Serpentine drive belt routing

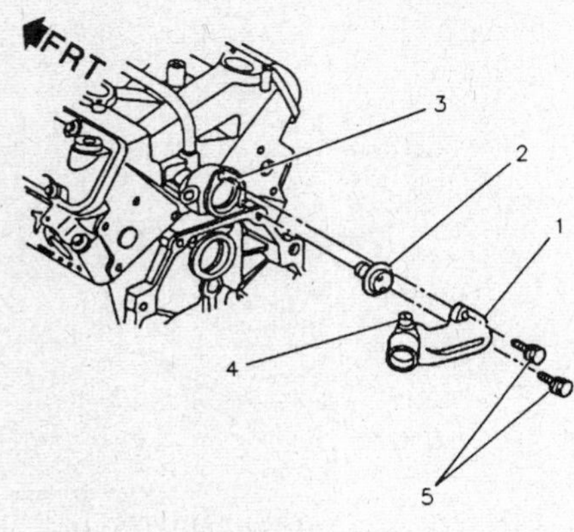

Fig. 21 Cooling system bleed vent

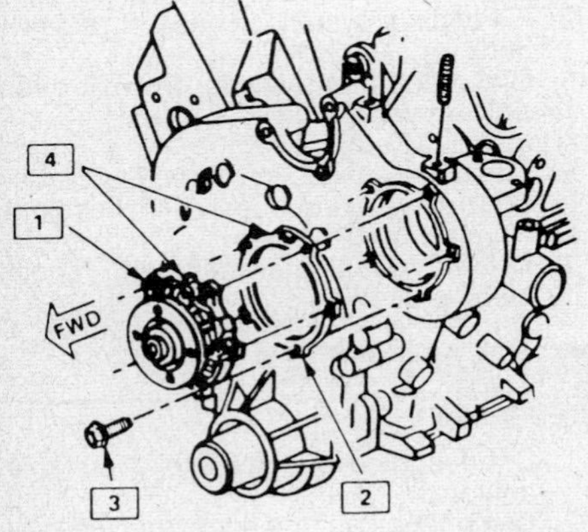

Fig. 22 Water pump mounting

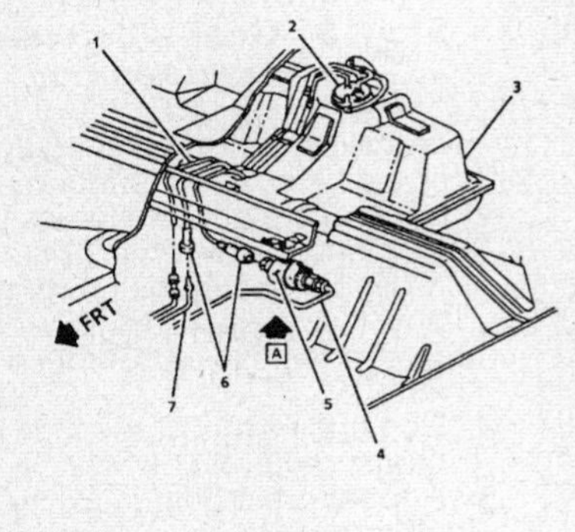
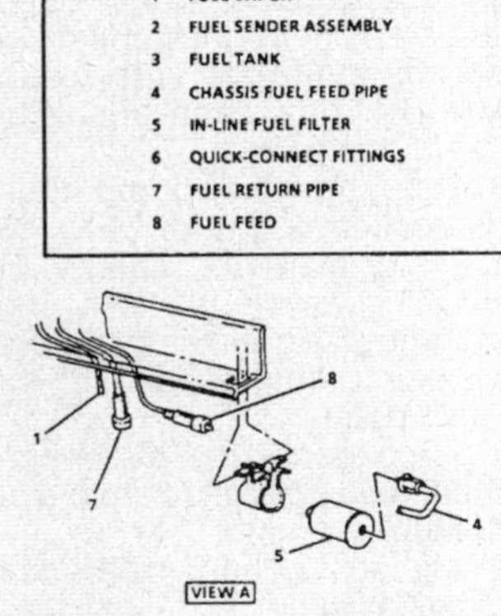

Fig. 23 Fuel filter replacement

10. Reverse procedure to install.

FUEL PUMP

REPLACE

1. Relieve fuel system pressure as outlined under "Precautions."
2. Remove spare tire cover, jack and spare tire, then the trunk liner.
3. Remove seven fuel pump access panel retaining nuts, then the fuel pump access panel.
4. Disconnect fuel tank pressure sensor electrical connector, then clean fuel pipes and fuel pump assembly to prevent fuel contamination.
5. Disconnect quick connect fittings at fuel pump assembly, then remove fuel pump retaining snap ring.
6. Remove modular fuel pump assembly.
7. Reverse procedure to install.

FUEL FILTER

REPLACE

1. Relieve fuel system pressure as outlined under "Precautions."
2. Raise and support vehicle.
3. Remove bracket attaching screw and filter bracket, **Fig. 23.**
4. Grasp filter and fuel line fitting. Twist quick-connect fitting ¼ turn in each direction to loosen any dirt within fitting.
5. Using compressed air, blow out dirt from quick-connect fitting.
6. Remove feed pipe nut from fuel filter, then drain any remaining fuel into a suitable container.
7. Remove fuel filter.
8. Reverse procedure to install.

TECHNICAL SERVICE BULLETINS

COMPOSITE ROCKER COVER ENGINE OIL LEAKS

On some of these models, there may be a rocker cover oil leak. This condition may be caused by the rocker cover material composition.

To correct this condition, install replacement aluminum rocker covers (lefthand, part No. 24504669; righthand, part No. 24504670).

TICKING NOISE DURING COLD ENGINE OPERATION

Some of these engines may exhibit a ticking noise during the first one or two minutes of engine operation or until the engine reaches operating temperature. This condition may be caused by excessive piston to bore clearance in the No. 1 and No. 4 cylinders.

To correct this condition replace pistons with part No. 12564009. This condition is a customer satisfaction issue only. If pistons are not replaced, it will not affect the durability or life of the engine.

TIGHTENING SPECIFICATIONS

Year	Component	Torque/ Ft. Lbs.
1998–2002	Camshaft Position Sensor	89
	Camshaft Sprocket	103
	Camshaft Thrust Plate	89③
	Connecting Rod Bearing Bolt	18⑤
	Coolant Drain Plug	14
	Coolant Temperature Sensor	17
	Crankshaft Balancer	76
	Cylinder Head Bolts	②
	Drive Belt Idler Pulley	37
	Drive Belt Shield Bolt	89③
	Drive Belt Tensioner Bolt	37
	Engine Mount Bracket Bolts	43
	Engine Mount Nuts	35
	Engine Mount Strut Bracket To Engine	35
	Engine Mount Strut Bracket To Radiator	21
	Exhaust Manifold Heat Shield	96③
	Exhaust Manifold Nut	12
	Exhaust Manifold Stud	12
	Flywheel Bolts	52
	Front Cover (Large)	41
	Front Cover (Small)	20
	Intake Manifold Bolts (Lower)	⑥
	Intake Manifold Bolts (Upper)	18
	Intake Manifold Stud (Upper)	18
	Main Bearing Cap Bolts	37④
	Oil Cooler Connector	50
	Oil Filter	10
	Oil Filter Adapter	29
	Oil Level Indicator Retainer Nut	18
	Oil Level Sensor Screw	96③
	Oil Pan (Lower)	18
	Oil Pan (Side)	35
	Oil Pan Drain Plug	18
	Oil Pump	30
	Oil Pump Cover	96③
	Oil Pump Drive Assembly Bolt	27
	Rocker Arm Bolt	14①
	Serpentine Drive Belt Tensioner Bolt	40
	Spark Plugs	15
	Timing Chain Dampener	15
	Valve Cover	89③
	Valve Lifter Guide Bolt	89③
	Water Pump	96③
	Water Pump Pulley	18

① — Tighten an additional 30.°
② — Refer to "Cylinder Head, Replace" for tightening procedure.
③ — Inch lbs.
④ — Tighten an additional 77.°
⑤ — Tighten an additional 100.°
⑥ — Refer to "Intake Manifold, Replace" for tightening procedure.

3.4L Engine

NOTE: On Air Bag Equipped Models, Refer To "Air Bag System Precautions" Located In The Front Of This Manual For System Disarming & Arming Procedures.

NOTE: Refer To "Computer Relearn Procedures" Located In The Front Of This Manual When Battery Power To The Computer Has Been Interrupted.

INDEX

PRECAUTIONS

AIR BAG SYSTEMS

Refer to "Air Bag System Precautions" in the front of this manual for system disarming and arming procedures.

BATTERY GROUND CABLE

Prior to service, disconnect battery ground cable and isolate as required.

FUEL SYSTEM PRESSURE RELIEF

To reduce the risk of fire and personal injury, it is necessary to relieve the fuel system pressure before servicing fuel system components.

1. Loosen fuel tank filler cap to relieve tank pressure.
2. Remove fuel injection sight shield.
3. Connect fuel pressure gauge tool No. J-34730-1, or equivalent, to the fuel pressure valve. Wrap a shop towel around fitting while connection gauge to avoid spillage.
4. Install bleed hose into an approved container and open valve to bleed system pressure.

COMPRESSION PRESSURE

When checking compression, lowest cylinder must be within 70 percent of the highest cylinder with a minimum pressure of 100 psi. Perform compression test with engine at normal operating temperature, spark plugs removed and throttle wide open.

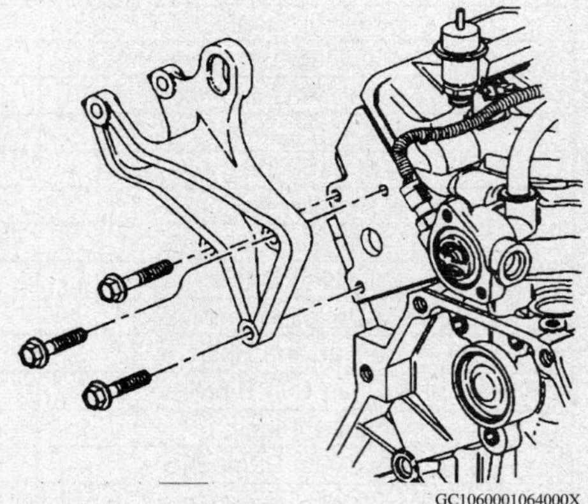

Fig. 1 Left engine mount removal

ENGINE MOUNT

REPLACE

LEFT

1. Remove engine mount strut from engine mount strut bracket.
2. Remove engine exhaust crossover pipe.
3. Remove thermostat housing as outlined in "Thermostat, Replace."
4. Remove engine mount strut bracket attaching bolts, **Fig. 1.**
5. Remove engine mount strut bracket.
6. Reverse procedure to install.

RIGHT LOWER

1. Remove right lower engine mount strut bracket attaching bolts, **Fig. 2.**
2. Remove engine mount retaining nut, then the engine mount.
3. Reverse procedure to install.

RIGHT UPPER

1. Remove right engine mount strut from upper engine strut mount bracket,
2. Remove fuel injector sight shield.
3. Remove EVAP emissions canister purge valve.
4. Remove right upper engine mount strut bracket bolts, then the bracket, **Fig. 3.**
5. **On models equipped with oil cooler,** remove oil cooler pipe bracket bolt from right engine mount strut bracket.
6. **On all models,** remove A/C compressor mounting bolts and position aside.
7. Remove vertical bolt from right engine mount strut bracket, **Fig. 4.**
8. Remove right engine mount bracket.
9. Reverse procedure to install.

FRONT LOWER

1. Disconnect air inlet duct from throttle body.
2. Remove left and right engine mount struts.
3. Raise and support vehicle.

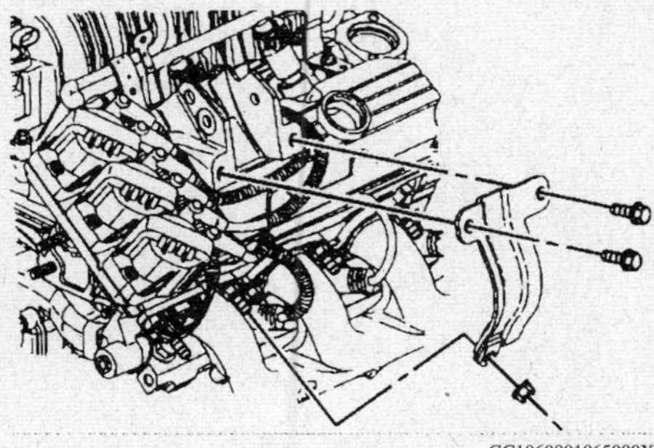

Fig. 2 Right lower engine mount removal

4. Disconnect catalytic converter pipe from right exhaust manifold.
5. Remove right front wheel and tire assembly.
6. Remove right side engine splash shield.
7. Remove engine mount to subframe nuts.
8. Lower vehicle, then install engine lifting tool No. J 28467-B, or equivalent.
9. Raise engine until mount is clear of subframe.
10. Raise and support vehicle.
11. Remove engine mount attaching bolts, **Fig. 5.**
12. Reverse procedure to install.

ENGINE

REPLACE

1. Relieve fuel system pressure as outlined under "Precautions."
2. Remove hood assembly, then the cross vehicle brace from engine compartment.
3. Remove throttle body air inlet duct and mass air flow sensor from air cleaner assembly.
4. Remove engine mount struts, then the accessory drive belt.
5. Disconnect brake booster hose from upper intake manifold.
6. Disconnect and mark the following electrical connectors:
   a. Heated oxygen sensor.
   b. AIR check valve solenoid.
   c. EGR valve.
   d. EVAP valve.
   e. TP sensor.
   f. IAC valve.
   g. Alternator.
   h. Ignition coil.
   i. Wiring harness grounds.
   j. Body wiring harness to engine wiring harness connector.
7. Raise and support vehicle.
8. Remove lower radiator air baffle, then the righthand side engine splash shield.
9. Drain engine cooling system and oil.
10. Remove oil filter, then disconnect the following electrical connectors:
    a. Vehicle speed sensor.
    b. Oil level sensor.
    c. Oil pressure switch.
    d. Engine block heater.
    e. Knock sensor.
    f. Heated oxygen sensor.
    g. Crankshaft position sensor.

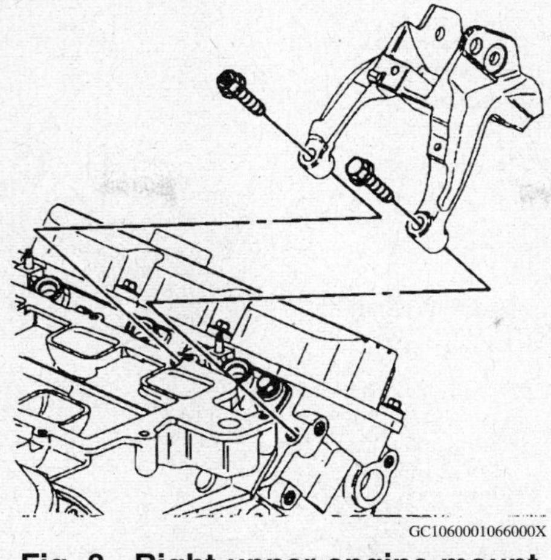

Fig. 3 Right upper engine mount bracket removal

    h. A/C compressor.
    i. Wiring harness grounds.
11. Remove catalytic converter from right exhaust manifold.
12. Remove engine mount lower retaining nuts.
13. Remove torque converter cover, then the starter motor.
14. Remove A/C compressor attaching bolts, then position and secure compressor aside.
15. Remove torque converter attaching bolts.
16. Remove transaxle brace, then the lower transaxle to engine bolt and stud.
17. Disconnect lower radiator outlet hose from engine.
18. Lower vehicle, then disconnect accelerator and cruise control cables from throttle body and cable bracket.
19. Disconnect upper intake manifold and EVAP vacuum hoses.
20. Disconnect fuel feed and return hoses.
21. Disconnect AIR check valve hose.
22. Remove power steering pump and position aside.
23. Disconnect heater inlet and outlet hoses from engine.
24. Disconnect upper radiator hose from engine.
25. Support transaxle assembly with suitable floor stands.
26. Attach a suitable lifting device to engine.
27. Remove upper engine to transaxle bolts.
28. Remove engine assembly from vehicle.
29. Reverse procedure to install.

INTAKE MANIFOLD

REPLACE

UPPER

1. Disconnect vacuum hose from throttle body air inlet duct.
2. Disconnect IAT sensor electrical connector, then the air inlet duct from throttle body.
3. Drain engine coolant.

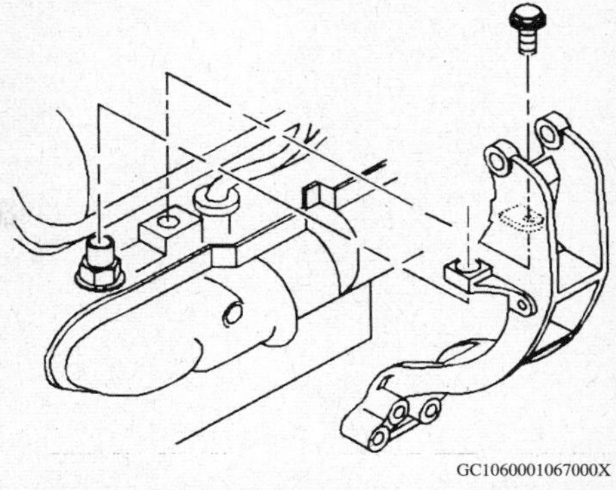

Fig. 4 Right engine mount strut bracket

4. Disconnect accelerator and cruise control cables from throttle body.
5. Disconnect TP sensor and IAC valve electrical connectors.
6. Disconnect wiring harness attachment clips for CMP sensor and lefthand side spark plug wires.
7. Disconnect thermostat bypass hose from throttle body, then remove rear alternator brace.
8. Disconnect vacuum lines from upper intake manifold.
9. Remove MAP sensor, EGR valve, spark plug wires and the ignition control module.
10. Remove upper intake manifold attaching bolts, then the manifold.
11. Reverse procedure to install.

LOWER

1. Relieve fuel system pressure, refer to "Fuel System Pressure Relief."
2. Remove upper intake manifold.
3. Remove valve covers as outlined under "Valve Cover, Replace."
4. Disconnect ECT sensor electrical connector.
5. Disconnect fuel injector and MAP sensor electrical connectors.
6. Remove fuel pipe clip bolt, then the fuel pipe clip.
7. Disconnect fuel feed and return pipes from fuel rail.
8. Remove fuel injector rail.
9. Remove power steering pump from front engine cover and position aside.
10. Disconnect heater inlet pipe with heater hose from lower intake manifold and position aside.
11. Disconnect upper radiator hose from engine, then the thermostat bypass hose from bypass pipe and lower intake manifold pipe.
12. Remove lower intake manifold attaching bolts, then the lower manifold and gaskets.
13. Reverse procedure to install.

EXHAUST MANIFOLD

REPLACE

FRONT

1. Disconnect throttle body air inlet duct.
2. Remove right engine mount strut bracket, then the AIR pipe.

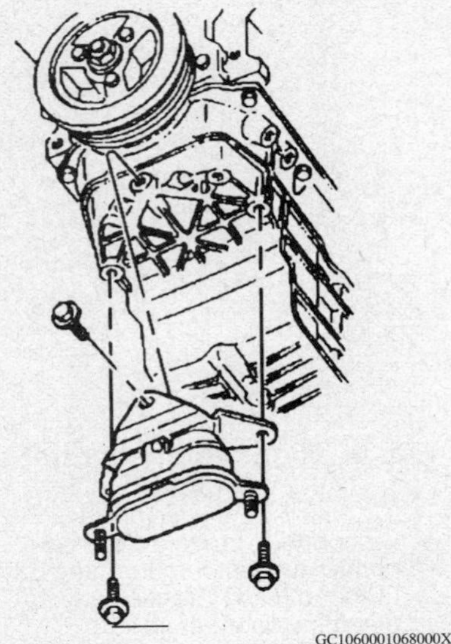

Fig. 5 Front lower engine mount

3. Remove thermostat bypass pipe.
4. Remove exhaust crossover pipe heat shield, then the crossover pipe.
5. Remove exhaust manifold heat shield attaching bolts, then the heat shield.
6. Remove exhaust manifold retaining nuts and the exhaust manifold.
7. Reverse procedure to install.

REAR

1. Disconnect throttle body air inlet duct.
2. Remove AIR check valve.
3. Remove exhaust crossover pipe heat shield, then the crossover pipe.
4. Disconnect oxygen sensor electrical connector.
5. Raise and support vehicle, then remove catalytic converter from exhaust manifold.
6. Remove EGR valve from lower intake manifold.
7. Remove exhaust manifold head shield attaching bolts, then the heat shield.
8. Remove exhaust manifold retaining nuts, then the exhaust manifold and gasket.
9. Reverse procedure to install.

CYLINDER HEAD

REPLACE

FRONT

1. Raise and support vehicle, then drain engine coolant and oil.
2. Lower vehicle, then remove lower intake manifold as outlined under "Intake Manifold, Replace."
3. Remove valve cover as outlined under "Valve Cover, Replace."
4. Remove exhaust crossover pipe, then the right engine mount strut bracket.
5. Remove oil level indicator tube.
6. Remove spark plugs, then the exhaust manifold as outlined under "Exhaust Manifold, Replace."
7. Remove cylinder head attaching bolts, then the cylinder head and gasket.
8. Reverse procedure to install, noting the following:

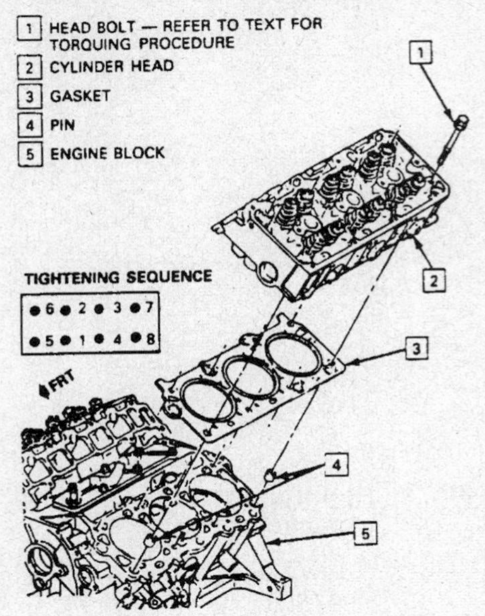

Fig. 6 Cylinder head bolt tightening sequence

   a. Clean all sealing surfaces and install a new gasket.
   b. Using sequence shown in **Fig. 6**, tighten bolts in two steps: First step, **torque** bolts to 37 ft. lbs.; second step, tighten bolts an additional 90° using torque/angle meter tool No. J-36660, or equivalent.

REAR

1. Raise and support vehicle, then drain engine coolant and oil.
2. Lower vehicle, then remove lower intake manifold as outlined under "Intake Manifold, Replace."
3. Remove valve cover as outlined under "Valve Cover, Replace."
4. Remove exhaust crossover pipe.
5. Remove fuel line bracket.
6. Disconnect spark plug wires, then remove spark plugs.
7. Remove exhaust manifold as outlined under "Exhaust Manifold, Replace."
8. Remove cylinder head attaching bolts, then the cylinder head.
9. Reverse procedure to install, noting the following:
   a. Clean all sealing surfaces and install a new gasket.
   b. Using sequence shown in **Fig. 6**, tighten bolts in two steps: First step, **torque** bolts to 37 ft. lbs.; second step, tighten bolts an additional 90° using torque/angle meter tool No. J-36660, or equivalent.

VALVE COVER

REPLACE

FRONT

1. Drain engine coolant.
2. Disconnect spark plug wires, then remove engine mount strut from engine.
3. Remove AIR check valve.

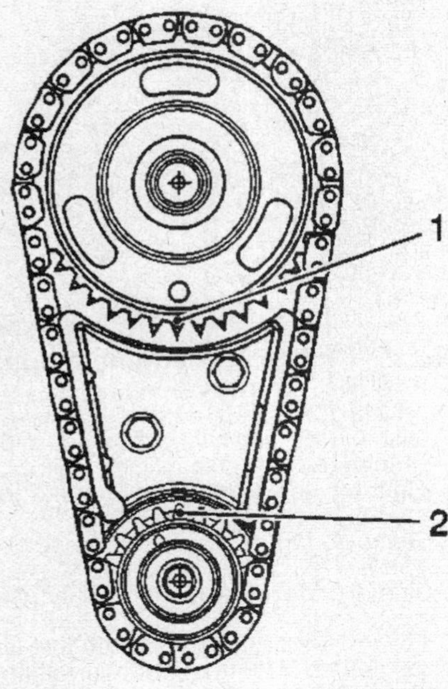

Fig. 7 Timing chain alignment marks

4. Remove thermostat bypass hose and pipe.
5. Remove PCV valve.
6. Remove valve cover attaching bolts, then the valve cover.
7. Reverse procedure to install.

REAR

1. Remove serpentine drive belt as outlined under "Serpentine Drive Belt."
2. Remove alternator as outlined under "Alternator, Replace" in "Electrical" section.
3. Remove alternator bracket.
4. Disconnect righthand spark plug wires, then the EVAP vacuum hoses from EVAP valve.
5. Remove EVAP and AIR check valves.
6. Remove ignition coils and bracket.
7. Remove vacuum hose from valve cover grommet.
8. Remove valve cover attaching bolts, then the valve cover.
9. Reverse procedure to install.

VALVE LIFTERS

REPLACE

1. Remove valve covers as outlined under "Valve Cover, Replace."
2. Remove lower intake manifold as outlined in "Intake Manifold, Replace."
3. Remove rocker arms and pushrods as outlined under "Rocker Arm, Replace."
4. Remove lifter guide bolts, lifter guides and valve lifters.
5. Reverse procedure to install.

CAMSHAFT LOBE LIFT SPECIFICATIONS

Intake ....**2727 inch**
Exhaust...........................**2727 inch**

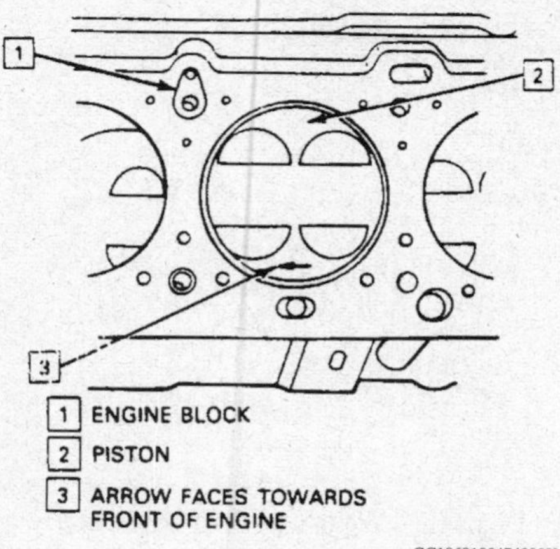

Fig. 8 Piston marking

ROCKER ARMS

REPLACE

1. Remove valve cover as outlined under "Valve Cover, Replace."
2. Remove rocker arm retaining bolts.
3. Remove rocker arms and push rods. Keep valve train components in order.
4. Reverse procedure to install. Ensure valve train components are installed in their original position.

CRANKSHAFT DAMPER

REPLACE

1. Remove serpentine drive belt as outlined under "Serpentine Drive Belt."
2. Raise and support vehicle.
3. Remove right tire and wheel assembly then the engine splash shield.
4. Support frame with a suitable jack, then remove righthand side frame bolts and lower frame to access crankshaft balancer bolt.
5. Remove starter as outlined under "Starter, Replace" in the "Electrical" section.
6. Attach flywheel holding tool No. J-37096, or equivalent, to flywheel.
7. Remove crankshaft pulley bolt and pulley.
8. Remove crankshaft damper/balancer using crankshaft damper removal tool No. J-24430, or equivalent.
9. Reverse procedure to install, noting the following:
   a. Coat front cover oil seal with engine oil.
   b. Install suitable sealant to keyway of damper before installation.
   c. Install damper using crankshaft damper installer tool No. J-29113, or equivalent.

FRONT COVER

REPLACE

1. Raise and support vehicle, then drain engine coolant and oil.
2. Remove crankshaft balancer as outlined under "Crankshaft Damper, Replace."
3. Remove drive belt tensioner attaching bolt, then the drive belt tensioner.

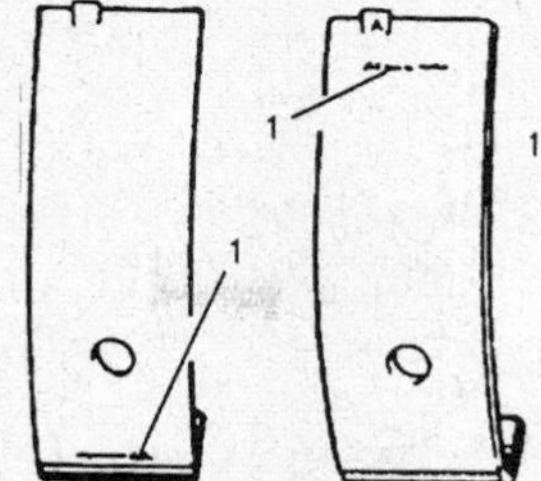

Fig. 9 Bearing marking

4. Remove power steering pump with lines and position aside.
5. Disconnect thermostat bypass pipe from front cover, then the radiator outlet hose from water pump,
6. Remove water pump pulley attaching bolts, then the water pump pulley.
7. Disconnect crankshaft position sensor wiring harness bracket from front cover.
8. Remove front cover attaching bolts, then the front cover and gasket.
9. Remove drive belt shield, crankshaft position sensor and water pump from front cover.
10. Reverse procedure to install.

FRONT COVER SEAL

REPLACE

1. Remove crankshaft pulley and damper as outlined under "Crankshaft Damper, Replace."
2. Pry out seal using a suitable pry tool.
3. Reverse procedure to install, noting the following:
   a. Lubricate seal with oil.
   b. Install seal using seal installer tool No. J-34995, or equivalent.

TIMING CHAIN

REPLACE

1. Remove engine front cover as outlined under "Front Cover, Replace."
2. Rotate crankshaft until timing marks are aligned, **Fig. 7.**
3. Remove camshaft sprocket bolt.
4. Remove camshaft sprocket with timing chain.
5. Reverse procedure to install. Coat crankshaft and camshaft sprockets with oil before installing front cover.

CAMSHAFT

REPLACE

1. Remove timing chain as outlined under "Timing Chain, Replace."
2. Remove camshaft thrust plate attaching bolts, then the thrust plate.
3. Insert a large screwdriver into camshaft bolt hole.
4. Carefully rotate and pull camshaft out of camshaft bearings.
5. Reverse procedure to install, noting the following:
   a. Coat camshaft journals with clean engine oil.
   b. Coat camshaft lobes with prelube part No. 1052365, or equivalent.

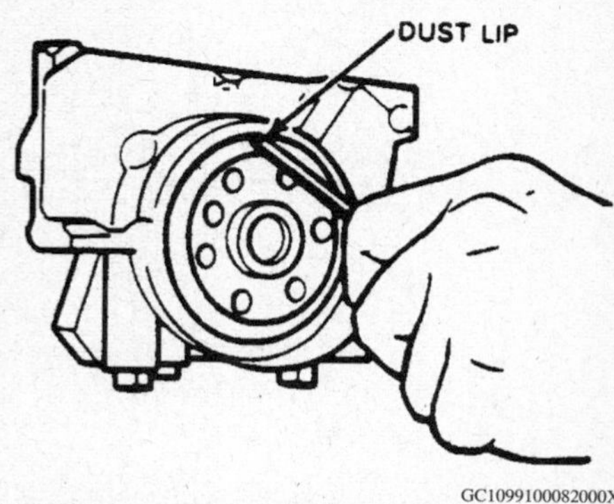

Fig. 10 Rear main seal removal

PISTON & ROD ASSEMBLY

When installing piston and rod assemblies into cylinder block, ensure arrow on top of piston faces toward the front of the engine, **Fig. 8.**

MAIN & ROD BEARINGS

Connecting rod and main bearing are of the precision insert type. They are available for service use in standard and two undersizes of .016 and .032 inch. Bearing undersize amount is stamped at either end of the bearing, **Fig. 9.**

CRANKSHAFT REAR OIL SEAL

REPLACE

1. Remove transaxle assembly as outlined under "Automatic Transmissions/ Transaxles" section.
2. Remove flywheel assembly.
3. Remove oil seal using a suitable pry tool as shown in **Fig. 10.**
4. Reverse procedure to install using seal installer tool No. J-34686, or equivalent.

OIL PAN

REPLACE

1. Remove engine mount struts from engine.
2. Remove A/C compressor mounting bolts, then position compressor aside.
3. Install engine support fixture tool No. J 28467-360, or equivalent.
4. Raise and support vehicle.
5. Remove catalytic converter from exhaust manifold.
6. Drain engine oil, then disconnect oil level sensor electrical connector.
7. Remove starter motor, then the transaxle brace from oil pane.
8. Remove transaxle lower mount retaining nuts.
9. Remove engine mount lower retaining nuts.
10. Raise engine slightly, then remove engine mount bracket and engine mount from oil pan.

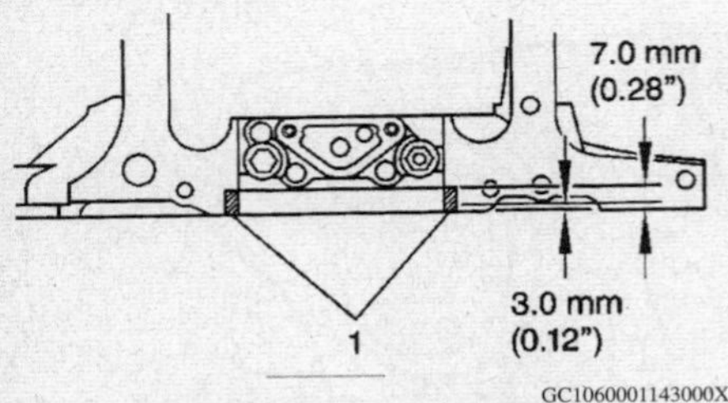

Fig. 11 Oil pan sealant application

11. Remove right and left side oil pan attaching bolts.
12. Remove oil pan to engine block attaching bolts, then the oil pan.
13. Reverse procedure to install. Apply suitable sealant to main bearing cap and engine block as shown in **Fig. 11.**

OIL PUMP

REPLACE

1. Remove oil pan as outlined under "Oil Pan, Replace."
2. Remove oil pump to crankshaft rear bearing cap attaching bolt, then the oil pump.
3. Reverse procedure to install.

BELT TENSION DATA

Belt tension is maintained automatically by a spring tensioned idler pulley. No adjustment of serpentine belt is necessary.

If belt slippage is indicated and belt tensioner indicator is within normal operating range, measure belt tension as follows:

1. Run engine for ten minutes, then shut off and measure belt tension between any two pulleys using V-belt tension gauge tool No. J 23600-B, or equivalent.
2. Run engine for 30 seconds and repeat measurement.
3. Repeat preceding step, then average all three belt tension measurements. Average tension should be 35–55 lbs.
4. If belt tension is not as specified, replace serpentine drive belt.

SERPENTINE DRIVE BELT

BELT REPLACEMENT

1. Rotate tensioner clockwise using a box end wrench.
2. Remove serpentine belt.
3. Reverse procedure to install, routing belt as shown in **Fig. 12.**

TENSIONER REPLACEMENT

1. Remove serpentine drive belt as outlined in this section.
2. Remove tensioner bolt, then the tensioner.
3. Reverse procedure to install.

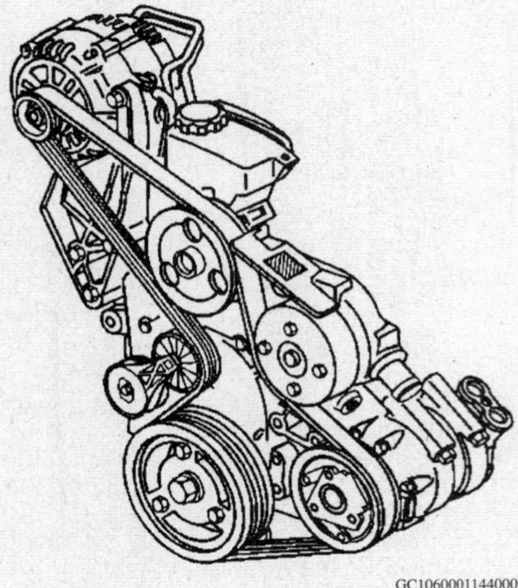

Fig. 12 Serpentine drive belt routing

COOLING SYSTEM BLEED

1. Open air bleed vents on thermostat housing and heater water inlet pipe.
2. Fill system with water and coolant until level of coolant has reached base of radiator neck.
3. Close bleed vents and add clean water if necessary to bring coolant level to base of radiator neck.

THERMOSTAT

REPLACE

1. Remove throttle body air inlet duct.
2. Partially drain cooling system.
3. Remove radiator hose from thermostat housing.
4. Remove exhaust crossover pipe.
5. Remove thermostat housing bolts, then the thermostat housing.
6. Remove thermostat.
7. Reverse procedure to install.

WATER PUMP

REPLACE

1. Remove air cleaner assembly.
2. Drain engine coolant into a suitable container.
3. Remove serpentine drive belt as outlined under "Serpentine Drive Belt."
4. Remove water pump pulley.
5. Remove water pump bolts then the water pump and gasket, **Fig. 13.**
6. Reverse procedure to install.

RADIATOR

REPLACE

1. Remove air cleaner assembly, then drain engine coolant into a suitable container.

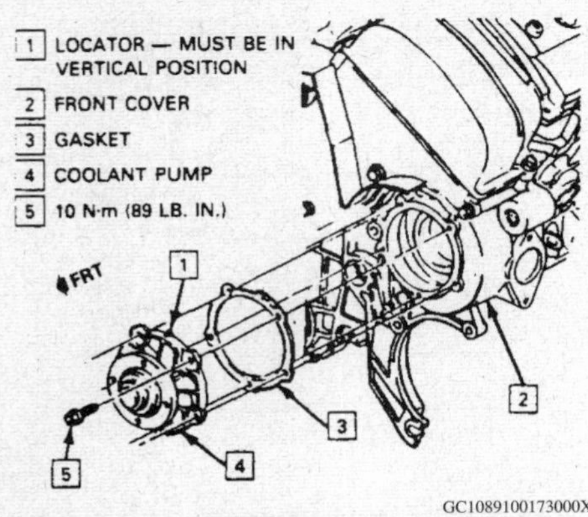

Fig. 13 Water pump assembly

2. Remove engine strut upper brace bolts from upper tie bar and rotate strut and brace rearward.
3. Disconnect upper radiator mounting panel bolts and clamps.
4. Disconnect cooling fan electrical connector.
5. Remove cooling fan mounting bolts and fan, then upper radiator bracket.
6. Remove upper and lower radiator hoses at radiator.
7. Disconnect low coolant sensor wiring.
8. Disconnect oil cooler lines, then remove radiator.
9. Reverse procedure to install.

FUEL PUMP

REPLACE

1. Remove fuel pump/sender assembly access cover from luggage compartment.
2. Remove fuel pump/sender assembly attaching bolts.
3. Pull assembly upward and disconnect electrical connector.
4. Remove pump/sender assembly from fuel tank.
5. Reverse procedure to install.

FUEL FILTER

REPLACE

1. Relieve fuel system pressure as outlined under "Precautions."
2. Raise and support vehicle.
3. Remove bracket attaching screw and filter bracket, **Fig. 14.**
4. Grasp filter and fuel line fitting. Twist quick-connect fitting ¼ turn in each direction to loosen any dirt within fitting.
5. Using compressed air, blow out dirt from quick-connect fitting.
6. Remove feed pipe nut from fuel filter, then drain any remaining fuel into a suitable container.
7. Remove fuel filter.
8. Reverse procedure to install.

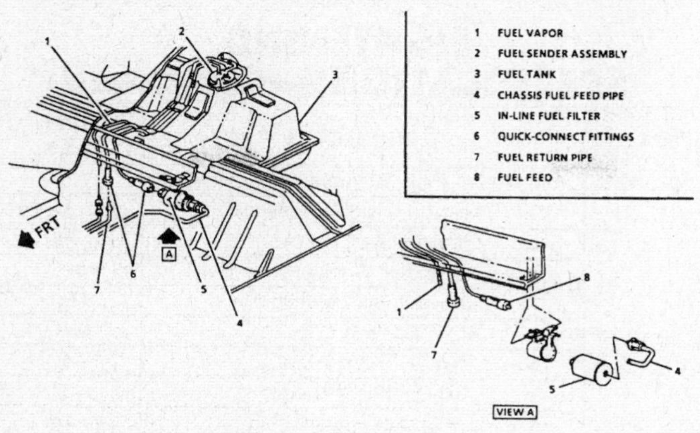

Fig. 14 Fuel filter replacement

TIGHTENING SPECIFICATIONS

Year	Component	Torque/Ft. Lbs.
2000–02	Accelerator Control Cable Bracket	89
	Alternator Brace Bracket	37
	Camshaft Position Sensor Bolt	89①
	Camshaft Sprocket Bolt	103
	Camshaft Thrust Plate Bolt	89①
	Connecting Rod Cap Bolt	15②
	Coolant Drain Plug	14
	Crankshaft Balancer Bolt	76
	Crankshaft Main Bearing Cap Bolt	37④
	Crankshaft Oil Deflector Nut	18
	Crankshaft Position Sensor Bolt	98①
	Crankshaft Position Sensor Stud	98①
	Crankshaft Position Sensor Wiring Bracket	37
	Cylinder Head Bolts	③
	Drive Belt Tensioner Bolt	37
	EGR Valve To EGR Valve Pipe	18
	EGR Valve Adapter Pipe Nut	18
	Engine Flywheel Bolt	52
	Engine Mount Bracket	43
	Engine Mount Lower Nut	32
	Engine Mount Strut & Lift Bracket Bolt	52
	Engine Mount Strut Bolt/Nut	35
	Engine Mount Strut Bracket Bolt (Upper Radiator Support)	21
	Engine Mount Strut Bracket Bolt (Vehicle Righthand Side)	37
	Engine Mont Upper Nut	35
	Engine Oil Pressure Indicator Switch	115①
	Exhaust Crossover Heat Shield	89①
	Exhaust Crossover	18
	Exhaust Manifold Heat Shield	89①
	Exhaust Manifold Nut	12
	Exhaust Manifold Pipe Stud	13
	Front Cover (Large Bolts)	41
	Front Cover (Medium Bolts)	35
	Front Cover (Small Bolts)	15
	Fuel Injector Rail Nut	89①
	Fuel Pipe Clip Bolt	71①

Continued

TIGHTENING SPECIFICATIONS—Continued

Year	Component	Torque/Ft. Lbs.
2000–02	Fuel Return Pipe To Fuel Injector Rail Nut	13
	Heated Oxygen Sensor	31
	Ignition Coil Bracket	18
	Intake Manifold Coolant Pipe Bolt	89①
	Lower Intake Manifold	115①
	Main Bearing Cap Bolt	37④
	MAP Sensor Bolt	44①
	Oil Cooler Connector	37
	Oil Cooler Hose Fitting	14
	Oil Filter	115
	Oil Filter Bypass Hose Plug	14
	Oil Gallery Plug (¼ inch)	14
	Oil Gallery Plug (⅜ inch)	24
	Oil Level Indicator Tube	18
	Oil Level Sensor	89①
	Oil Pan	18
	Oil Pan Drain Plug	18
	Oil Pump Cover	89①
	Oil Pump Drive Clamp Bolt	27
	Oil Pump Mounting Bolt	30
	Spark Plug	20
	Thermostat Bypass Pipe To Cylinder Head Nut	18
	Thermostat Bypass Pipe To Front Cover	106①
	Thermostat Bypass Pipe To Throttle Body	18
	Throttle Body Bolt/Nut	18
	Timing Chain Dampener Bolt	15
	Transaxle To Engine	55
	Upper Intake Manifold	18
	Valve Lifter Guide Bolt	89①
	Valve Rocker Arm Bolt	14⑤
	Valve Rocker Arm Cover	89①
	Water Outlet Bolt	18
	Water Pump	89①
	Water Pump Pulley	18

① — Inch lbs.

② — Tighten an additional 75.°

③ — Refer to "Cylinder Head, Replace."

④ — Tighten an additional 77.°

⑤ — Tighten an additional 30.°

3.5L Engine

NOTE: On Air Bag Equipped Models, Refer To "Air Bag System Precautions" Located In The Front Of This Manual For System Disarming & Arming Procedures.

NOTE: Refer To "Computer Relearn Procedures" Located In The Front Of This Manual When Battery Power To The Computer Has Been Interrupted.

INDEX

PRECAUTIONS

AIR BAG SYSTEMS

Refer to "Air Bag System Precautions" in the front of this manual for system disarming and arming procedures.

BATTERY GROUND CABLE

Prior to service, disconnect battery ground cable and isolate as required.

FUEL SYSTEM PRESSURE RELIEF

To reduce the risk of fire and personal injury, it is necessary to relieve the fuel system pressure before servicing fuel system components.

1. Loosen fuel tank filler cap to relieve tank pressure.
2. Connect fuel pressure gauge tool No. J-34730-1, or equivalent, to fuel pressure valve. Wrap a shop towel around fitting while connection gauge to avoid spillage.
3. Install bleed hose into an approved container and open valve to bleed system pressure.

COMPRESSION PRESSURE

When checking compression, lowest cylinder must be within 70 percent of the highest cylinder with a minimum pressure of 140 psi. Perform compression test with engine at normal operating temperature, spark plugs removed and throttle wide open.

ENGINE MOUNT

REPLACE

ENGINE MOUNT

1. Remove engine mount strut as outlined under "Engine Mount, Replace."
2. Install engine support fixture No. J28467-B using adapter set Nos. J36462-A and J28467-90A, or equivalents.
3. Raise and support vehicle, then remove lower engine mount nuts.
4. Lower vehicle, then raise engine to gain access to engine mount.
5. Raise and support vehicle, then remove upper engine mount nuts.
6. Remove engine mount from bracket.
7. Reverse procedure to install.

ENGINE MOUNT STRUT & BRACKETS

1. Remove bolt and nut from engine mount strut at engine bracket.
2. Remove bolt and nut from engine mount strut at radiator support bracket.
3. Remove engine mount strut, then the bracket from radiator support.
4. Reverse procedure to install.

ENGINE

REPLACE

The throttle cable must be replaced when removing or replacing the engine.

1. Remove fuel injector sight shield and throttle body air inlet duct.
2. Remove engine mount strut as outlined under "Engine Mount, Replace."
3. Relieve fuel pressure as outlined under "Precautions," then disconnect fuel lines from fuel rail and position aside.
4. Disconnect fuel vapor line, then remove throttle and cruise control cables with mounting brackets from throttle body.
5. Disconnect automatic range selector from park/neutral position switch and vacuum booster hose from engine.
6. Disconnect A/C vacuum hose from engine, then the wiring harness connectors from engine and transmissions.
7. Drain coolant into suitable container, then disconnect radiator inlet hose from engine.
8. Disconnect transaxle cooler lines from radiator, surge tank inlet hose and heater hoses from engine.
9. Raise and support vehicle, then drain engine oil.
10. Remove lower radiator air deflector, then disconnect AIR pipe from AIR inlet valve.
11. Remove battery cables from retainers, then disconnect radiator outlet hose from engine.
12. Remove A/C compressor from engine

and secure to frame of vehicle.

13. Remove torque converter cover, then disconnect starter motor electrical connectors and remove starter motor.
14. Reference mark flywheel to torque converter location, then remove flywheel to torque converter attaching bolts.
15. Remove catalytic converter pipe from rear exhaust manifold, then the lower engine to transaxle bolts.
16. Remove front wheel and tire assemblies and the inner fender splash shield.
17. Disconnect fog lamp electrical connectors, then remove wheel speed sensor harness conduits from retainers in lower control arms.
18. Remove tie rod ends and lower ball joints from steering knuckles.
19. Disconnect drive axles from transaxle and secure to vehicle.
20. Remove pinch bolt at intermediate shaft, then disconnect intermediate shaft from steering gear. **This step must be performed to avoid possible damage to the steering gear and intermediate shaft.**
21. Place universal engine support table No. J39580, or equivalent, under engine/transaxle/frame, then lower vehicle to universal engine support table to support engine/transaxle/frame.
22. Suitably secure vehicle to hoist, then remove frame to body bolts.
23. Raise and support vehicle, then remove universal engine support table with engine/transaxle/frame from under vehicle.
24. Remove engine mount bracket to engine bolts, then the transaxle brace.
25. Remove serpentine drive belt and power steering pump from engine and position aside.
26. Remove alternator and upper engine to transaxle bolts.
27. Remove engine from transaxle/frame.
28. Reverse procedure to install. **Ensure intermediate shaft is fully seated prior to installing pinch bolt.**

INTAKE MANIFOLD

REPLACE

1. Disconnect throttle body air inlet duct, then partially drain coolant into suitable container.
2. Remove fuel injector sight shield, then disconnect throttle and cruise control cables from throttle body.
3. Relieve fuel pressure as outlined under Precautions, then disconnect fuel lines and coolant hoses from throttle body.
4. Disconnect fuel vapor line from EVAP canister purge solenoid.
5. Disconnect vacuum hose from brake booster and A/C vacuum hose from intake manifold.
6. Disconnect surge tank inlet pipe retainer from fuel rail.
7. Disconnect electrical connectors from the following:
   a. Fuel injectors.
   b. Throttle position sensor.
   c. IAC valve.
   d. EVAP canister purge solenoid.
   e. MAP sensor.
8. Remove engine wiring harness and channel from valve cover and position aside.
9. Disconnect fuel pressure regulator vacuum line from regulator and throttle body.
10. Remove PCV valve and feed tubes from valve cover and intake manifold.
11. Remove EGR valve outlet pipe and water crossover from intake manifold.
12. Disconnect fuel rail snap lock retainers by pushing toward valve cover and lifting.
13. Remove fuel rail and injectors as an assembly.
14. Remove intake manifold bolts, then the intake manifold.
15. Reverse procedure to install. Remove all sensors, brackets and throttle body from intake manifold and transfer to new one.

GC1059900126000X

Fig. 1 Cylinder head bolt removal

EXHAUST MANIFOLD

REPLACE

LEFT

1. Remove engine as outlined under "Engine, Replace."
2. Remove left exhaust manifold crossover pipe from right exhaust manifold.
3. Disconnect EGR valve pipe from exhaust crossover pipe.
4. Remove left exhaust manifold retaining bolts, then the manifold.
5. Remove O2 sensor and replace as required.
6. Replace exhaust manifold studs as required.
7. reverse procedure to install.

RIGHT

1. Remove fuel injector sight shield, then the engine mount strut and bracket.
2. Drain coolant into suitable container, then remove engine cooling fans.
3. Remove radiator inlet and outlet hoses.
4. Remove transaxle cooler lines from radiator.
5. Remove radiator from vehicle.
6. Remove alternator as outlined under "Alternator, Replace."
7. Remove exhaust manifold heat shield and oil level indicator tube.
8. Disconnect vacuum tube from AIR control valve.
9. Disconnect feed pipe nut from exhaust manifold.
10. Remove AIR control from engine mount strut bracket.
11. Loosen exhaust manifold retaining bolts.
12. Remove exhaust manifold crossover pipe flange retaining studs.
13. Remove exhaust manifold bolts, then the manifold.
14. Reverse procedure to install.

CYLINDER HEAD

REPLACE

1. Remove intake manifold as outlined under "Intake Manifold, Replace."
2. Remove water outlet housing and engine mount strut bracket from right cylinder head.
3. Remove water crossover pipe.
4. Remove exhaust manifold as outlined under "Exhaust Manifold, Replace."
5. Remove camshaft covers, then install camshaft holding fixture No. J42038, or equivalent.
6. Remove primary camshaft drive chain, then the camshafts.
7. Remove rocker arms and lifters.
8. Remove coolant temperature sensor from left cylinder head.
9. Remove and discard M6 and M11 bolts, **Fig. 1. Do not reuse the cylinder head bolts.**
10. Remove cylinder head and ensure no dowel pins are stuck in cylinder head.
11. Reverse procedure to install, noting the following:
    a. Ensure cylinder head locating pins are secured in cylinder block.
    b. Install new M6 and M11 bolts as shown, **Fig. 1.**
    c. Using sequence shown in **Fig. 2,** tighten M11 bolts in three steps: First step, **torque** bolts to 30 ft. lbs.; second step, tighten an additional 100°; third step, tighten an additional 100.°
    d. **Torque** M6 bolts to 106 inch lbs.

VALVE COVER

REPLACE

LEFT

1. Remove fuel injector sight shield and bracket.
2. Disconnect PCV feed tube from left valve cover.
3. Disconnect Inlet hose from coolant over flow tank.
4. Remove coolant over flow tank retaining nuts, then position tank aside.
5. Release clips from power steering lines, then position lines aside.
6. Remove engine wiring harness channel bolt from left valve cover, then position harness aside.
7. Remove engine wiring harness from retainers at left rear camshaft cover.

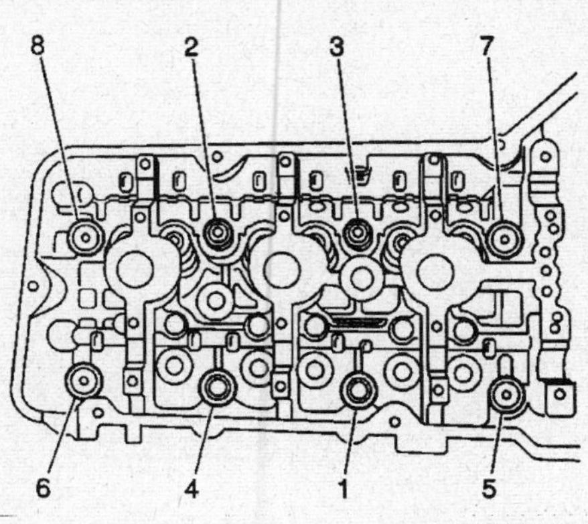

Fig. 2 Cylinder head tightening sequence

8. Disconnect O2 sensor, then remove left coil assembly from valve cover.
9. Remove left valve cover retaining bolts, then lift evenly off of cylinder head.
10. Reverse procedure to install.

RIGHT

1. Remove fuel injector sight shield.
2. Remove oil tube bolt, then adjust tube for access.
3. Disconnect PCV valve and feed tube from right valve cover.
4. Remove coil assembly from left valve cover.
5. Remove engine harness channel bolt from left valve cover, then position harness aside.
6. Remove engine harness from retainers on left valve cover and position aside.
7. Remove left valve cover retaining bolts, then lift cover off evenly.
8. Reverse procedure to install.

VALVE ARRANGEMENT

On lefthand side of engine, exhaust valves are on the left, intake valves on the right. On righthand side of engine, intake valves are on the left, exhaust valves on the right.

CAMSHAFT LOBE LIFT SPECIFICATIONS

Exhaust............................394 inch
Intake...............................413 inch

VALVE ADJUSTMENT

There is no valve adjustment for these engines.

FRONT COVER

REPLACE

1. Drain coolant into suitable container, then remove right diagonal brace.
2. Remove battery and battery tray.
3. Remove engine coolant and washer solvent reservoirs.
4. Reposition underhood accessory wiring junction block for access, then remove serpentine drive belt.
5. Remove power steering pump pulley and serpentine drive belt idler pulley.
6. Remove water pump pulley retaining bolts, then the pulley.
7. Remove water pump and housing as an assembly.
8. Support engine cradle, then remove right side cradle bolts.
9. Lower engine cradle, then remove crankshaft balancer.
10. Remove coolant drain plug from front cover and drain coolant from engine block into suitable container.
11. Remove ten perimeter bolts from front cover.
12. Remove front cover and gasket from engine. **Use plastic scraper when removing remaining gasket material to avoid damage to sealing surfaces.**
13. Reverse procedure to install. Apply short beads of RTV to engine block in locations shown, **Fig. 3.**

FRONT COVER SEAL

REPLACE

1. Remove crankshaft balancer.
2. Carefully pry out seal using small pry bar or flat screwdriver.
3. Install new seal using installer No. J42041, or equivalent.
4. The seal should not be flush with front cover, rather it should protrude .039–.078 inch.
5. Install crankshaft balancer.

TIMING CHAIN

REPLACE

PRIMARY

REMOVAL

1. Remove valve covers as outlined under "Valve Cover, Replace."
2. Install camshaft holding fixture No. J42038, or equivalent.
3. Remove front cover as outlined under "Front Cover, Replace."
4. Remove front engine lift bracket and camshaft position sensor.
5. Remove left cylinder exhaust camshaft sprocket bolt.
6. Remove four chain guide access plugs in cylinder heads.
7. Loosen both primary tensioner bolts, then remove lower tensioner bolt and allow tensioner to swing downward and expand.
8. Remove upper tensioner bolt, then the tensioner.
9. Remove primary timing chain tensioner shoe bolt, then the tensioner shoe by pushing the guide downward slightly and pulling up through cylinder head.
10. Remove primary timing chain from left camshaft sprocket and allow chain to fall into oil pump area of cylinder block.
11. Remove primary timing chain.

INSTALLATION

1. Install primary timing chain.

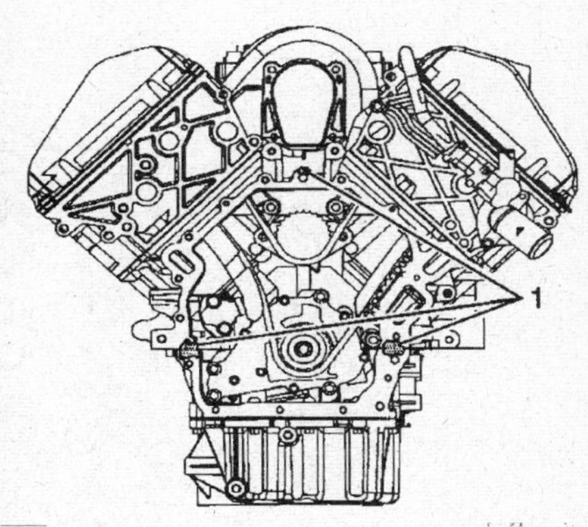

Fig. 3 RTV application points

2. Set base engine timing by rotating crankshaft until cylinder No. 1 is at top dead center as indicated by crankshaft sprocket timing mark (6) in the position shown, **Fig. 4.**
3. Rotate balance shaft until timing mark (7) is in the position shown, **Fig. 4.**
4. Ensure painted marks on timing chain face toward front of engine.
5. Center timing mark on right camshaft sprocket between pair of painted marks on primary timing chain, then wrap chain around sprocket.
6. Fabricate hook tool out of wire, then pull primary timing chain up through left cylinder head to camshaft sprocket.
7. While pulling primary timing chain up, align painted marks with timing marks on balance shaft sprocket and crankshaft sprocket, **Fig. 4.**
8. Wrap primary timing chain around left camshaft sprocket and align painted link with timing mark on sprocket, **Fig. 4.**
9. Install primary timing chain tensioner shoe and retaining bolt through access hole in cylinder head. Ensure all timing marks on sprockets are aligned with painted marks on timing chain.
10. Collapse primary timing chain tensioner as follows:
    a. Rotate ratchet release lever counterclockwise and hold.
    b. Collapse tensioner shoe and hold.
    c. Release ratchet lever and slowly release pressure on shoe.
    d. As ratchet lever moves to first click, hold shoe inward and insert pin through hole in release lever.
    e. The locked ratchet mechanism should hold shoe in collapsed position.
11. Install primary timing chain tensioner.
12. Ensure all timing marks are aligned, then release pin holding tensioner to tighten any slack in primary timing chain.
13. Install four chain guide plugs and front engine lift bracket.
14. Install camshaft position sensor, then

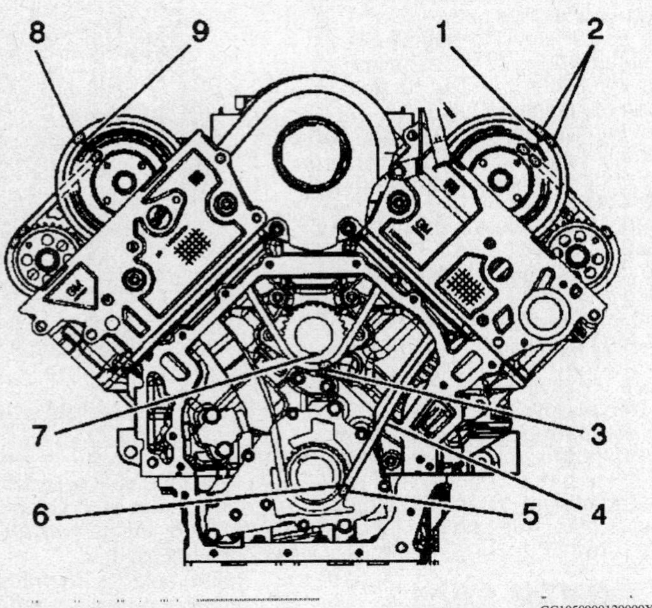

Fig. 4 Primary timing chain alignment

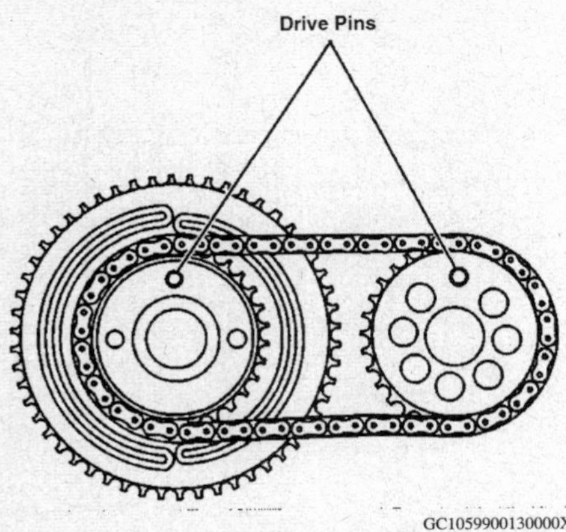

Fig. 5 Secondary sprocket drive pin alignment

remove camshaft holding fixture tool No. J42038.

15. Install valve covers and front cover.

SECONDARY

LEFT

Removal

1. Remove left valve cover as outlined under "Valve Cover, Replace."
2. Install camshaft holding fixture No. J42038, or equivalent.
3. Remove camshaft position sensor.
4. Remove camshaft sprocket bolts, then install sprocket holding fixture No. J42042, or equivalent.
5. Evenly slide secondary drive chain and camshaft sprockets off camshafts on to sprocket holding fixture.

Installation

1. Install secondary timing chain, aligning drive pins as shown, **Fig. 5.**
2. Slide camshaft sprockets off sprocket holding fixture and onto camshafts, then align drive pins in camshafts.
3. Remove sprocket holding fixture, then install intake camshaft sprocket retaining bolts.
4. Remove camshaft holding fixture, then install camshaft position sensor.
5. Install valve cover.

RIGHT

Removal

1. Partially drain coolant into suitable container, then remove thermostat housing.
2. Remove right valve cover as outlined under "Valve Cover, Replace."
3. Install camshaft holding fixture tool No. J42038, or equivalent onto right camshafts.
4. Remove camshaft sprocket bolts, then install sprocket holding fixture No. J42042, or equivalent.
5. Evenly slide secondary drive chain and sprockets onto sprocket holding fixture.

Installation

1. Install secondary timing chain, aligning drive pins as shown, **Fig. 5.**
2. Slide camshaft sprockets off sprocket holding fixture and onto camshafts, then align drive pins in camshafts.
3. Remove sprocket holding fixture, then install intake camshaft sprocket retaining bolts.
4. Remove camshaft holding fixture, then install valve cover.
5. Install thermostat housing. Refill coolant system.

CAMSHAFT

REPLACE

REMOVAL

1. Remove valve cover as outlined under "Valve Cover, Replace."
2. **On right cylinder head,** partially drain coolant into suitable container, then remove thermostat housing.
3. **On left cylinder head,** remove camshaft position sensor.
4. **On all models,** remove camshaft sprockets as outlined under "Timing Chain, Replace."
5. Remove camshaft bearing caps. Identification markings and positions are as follows:
   a. I indicates intake camshaft. E indicates exhaust camshaft.
   b. Number indicates journal position from front of engine.
   c. Raised feature goes toward outboard side of engine.
   d. The cap closest to front of engine is the thrust cap and cannot be installed in any other position.
6. Remove camshafts.

INSTALLATION

1. Apply liberal amount of clean engine oil to rocker arms, then position on lifter and valve tip.
2. Camshafts for right and left cylinder heads are different lengths and identified as follows:
   a. Right cylinder head camshafts are longer than left cylinder head camshafts.
   b. Intake camshaft identification rings are between the first and second sets of lobes.
   c. Exhaust camshaft identification rings are between the second and third sets of lobes.
3. Apply liberal amount of clean engine oil to camshaft journals and camshaft carriers, then install camshafts.
4. Place camshafts in position with notch for camshaft sprocket drive pins at top of rotation.
5. Install camshaft bearing thrust caps in first journal of each camshaft. Thrust caps are wider and have machined undercuts not present on other caps.
6. Tighten bearing caps to specifications.
7. Using hex cast into camshaft, rotate camshaft so rear flat on camshaft is facing cylinder head.
8. Install camshaft holding fixture tool No. J42038, or equivalent.
9. Compress secondary timing chain tensioner and lock into position by inserting wire pin into access hole on side of tensioner.
10. Slowly release pressure on tensioner shoes.
11. Install camshaft sprockets as outlined under "Timing chain, Replace."
12. Remove wire pin from tensioner and allow tensioner shoes to expand.
13. **On left cylinder head,** install camshaft position sensor.

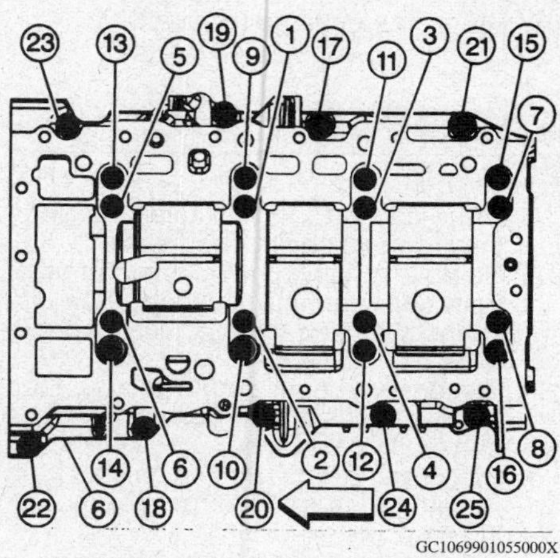

Fig. 6 Lower crankcase bolt identification

14. **On right cylinder head,** install thermostat housing, then fill coolant system.
15. **On all models,** install valve covers.

PISTON & ROD ASSEMBLY

When installing piston and rod assemblies into cylinder block, ensure arrow on top of piston faces toward front of engine.

Tighten connecting rod bolts in four steps: First step, **torque** bolts to 22 ft. lbs.; second step, loosen bolts completely; third step, **torque** bolts to 18 ft. lbs.; fourth step, tighten an additional 110.°

MAIN & ROD BEARINGS

Engine bearings are of the precision insert type. Undersized bearings are not available. Crankshaft or connecting rod replacement is required if bearing clearances exceed specifications.

Using sequence shown in **Fig. 6, torque** lower crankcase bolts numbered 1–16 to 15 ft. lbs., then an additional 70°. **Torque** bolts numbered 17–25 to 22 ft. lbs.

CRANKSHAFT SEAL

REPLACE

FRONT

Refer to "Front Cover Seal, Replace" in this section.

REAR

REMOVAL

1. Remove transaxle as outlined under "Automatic Transmission/Transaxle."
2. Install crankshaft rear oil seal remover tool No. J42841, or equivalent.
3. Using variable speed drill with socket adapter, install eight 1 inch self tapping screws into seal using guide holes in remover tool.
4. Tighten center screw on removal tool to pull seal off end of crankshaft.

INSTALLATION

1. Place small amount of gasket maker part No. 1052942, or equivalent, at crankcase split line across end of upper/lower crankcase seal.
2. Coat outer diameter of cylinder block rear crankshaft seal area with clean engine oil.
3. Coat outer rubber surface of rear crankshaft seal with clean engine oil. **Do not put any oil on green coating of seal. This coating is a sealant that cannot be contaminated.**
4. Loosen center bolt of seal installer No. J42842, or equivalent.
5. Thread three mounting bolts of seal installer into crankshaft flange and tighten until seal installer is firmly mounted on crankshaft.
6. Install seal by tightening center bolt of seal installer until installer bottoms against crankcase.
7. Loosen center bolt, then remove installer tool.
8. Inspect seal to ensure installation depth is equal around the seal circumference.
9. Install transaxle as outlined in "Automatic Transmission/Transaxle" section.

OIL PAN

REPLACE

1. Raise and support vehicle, then drain engine oil.
2. Remove oil filter cap, then discard oil filter element.
3. Disconnect oil level sensor electrical connector. then remove transaxle brace.
4. Remove oil pan retaining bolts, then the oil pan.
5. Transfer oil level switch to new oil pan as required.
6. Reverse procedure to install, noting the following:
   a. Ensure rear edge of oil pan is flush with rear of cylinder block face.
   b. Press forward part of oil pan against transaxle brace when tightening.
   c. Tighten oil pan retaining bolts to specifications using sequence shown, **Fig. 7.**

OIL PUMP

REPLACE

1. Remove front cover as outlined under "Front Cover, Replace."
2. Remove valve covers as outlined under "Valve Cover, Replace."
3. Install camshaft holding fixture tool No. J42038, or equivalent.
4. Remove camshaft drive chain tensioner.
5. Remove primary timing chain from drive sprocket.
6. Remove four large oil pump housing bolts, then slide pump housing with drive sprocket off of crankshaft.
7. Reverse procedure to install, noting the following:
   a. Align crankshaft sprocket splines with oil pump gerotor when installing drive sprocket into oil pump.
   b. Ensure crankshaft sprocket is aligned with drive pin in crankshaft.
   c. Crankshaft sprocket should protrude from oil pump and face of sprocket should be behind machined step in crankshaft.

GC1059900131000X

Fig. 7 Oil pan bolt tightening sequence

OIL PUMP SERVICE

The internal components of the oil pump are not serviceable. The oil pump is replaced as an assembly only.

BELT TENSION DATA

Belt tension is maintained automatically by a spring tensioned idler pulley. Adjustment of serpentine belt is not necessary.

If belt slippage is indicated and belt tensioner indicator is within normal operating range, measure belt tension as follows:

1. Run engine for ten minutes, then shut off and measure belt tension between any two pulleys using V-belt tension gauge tool No. J 23600-B, or equivalent.
2. Run engine for 30 seconds and repeat measurement.
3. Repeat preceding step, then average all three belt tension measurements. Average tension should be 30–50 lbs.
4. If belt tension is not as specified, replace serpentine drive belt.

SERPENTINE DRIVE BELT

REPLACEMENT

1. Lift or rotate tensioner using a ½ inch breaker bar.
2. Remove serpentine belt.
3. Reverse procedure to install, routing drive belt as shown in **Fig. 8.**

ADJUSTMENT

There is no provision for serpentine belt adjustment. Refer to "Belt Tension Data" for belt tension measurement procedures and to determine whether belt requires replacement.

COOLING SYSTEM BLEED

1. Open radiator bleed valve.
2. Fill cooling system until coolant starts to come out of bleed valve.
3. Close bleed valve, then slowly add coolant until level reaches FULL COLD mark.
4. Run engine to operating temperature while adding coolant to FULL mark. Shut engine off and wait 2 minutes.
5. Recheck level and add coolant as required to restore level to FULL COLD mark.
6. Inspect coolant level after engine completes three thermal cycles and add coolant as required.

THERMOSTAT

REPLACE

1. Partially drain coolant into suitable container, then remove hoses from water outlet housing.
2. Remove water housing outlet bolts, then the housing.
3. Replace thermostat and housing as an assembly.
4. Reverse procedure to install.

WATER PUMP

REPLACE

1. Partially drain coolant into suitable container, then loosen water pump pulley bolts.
2. Remove drive belt, idler pulley bolt and idler pulley.
3. Remove water pump pulley bolts and pulley.
4. Remove water pump bolts, then the pump.
5. Reverse procedure to install.

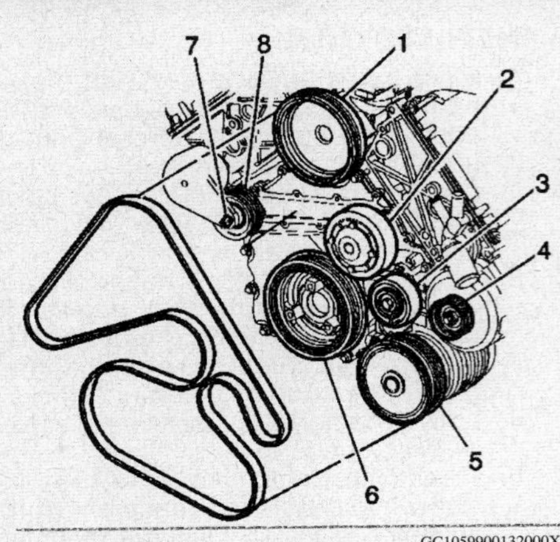

Fig. 8 Serpentine belt routing

RADIATOR

REPLACE

1. Drain coolant into suitable container, then remove engine mount strut.
2. Remove engine mount strut bracket from upper radiator support, then disconnect cooling fan electrical connector.
3. Disconnect hoses from radiator, then remove cooling fan shroud, motors and fans from radiator.
4. Disconnect transaxle cooler lines from radiator, then remove radiator mounting brackets.
5. Remove radiator and mounts.
6. Reverse procedure to install.

FUEL PUMP

REPLACE

Refer to "Fuel Pump Replace" in the "3.1L Engine" section.

FUEL FILTER

REPLACE

Refer to "Fuel Filter Replace" in the "3.1L Engine" section.

TIGHTENING SPECIFICATIONS

Year	Component	Torque/ Ft. Lbs.
1999–2002	Accelerator Cable Bracket	84③
	Camshaft Bearing Caps	71①
	Camshaft Position Sensor	84③
	Camshaft Sprocket Bolt	18②
	Connecting Rod Bolt	⑥
	Coolant Drain Plug (Engine Block)	10
	Coolant Drain Plug (Front Cover)	89③
	Coolant Temperature Sensor	15
	Cylinder Head	⑤
	Cylinder Head Water Jacket Hole Plug	59
	Drive Belt Idler Pulley	37
	Drive Belt Tensioner	37
	EGR to Crossover Pipe	44
	Engine Mount Nuts	35
	Engine Mount Strut Bolt	35
	Engine Mount Strut Bracket Bolt	21
	Engine to Transaxle Bolts	55
	Exhaust Manifold Bolt	18
	Exhaust Manifold Crossover Stud	18
	Exhaust Manifold Stud	53③
	EVAP Canister Purge Solenoid	72⑦
	Flywheel	11⑦
	Front Cover Bolt	11
	Front Cover Coolant Drain Plug	96③
	Front Lift Bracket Hex Bolt	37
	Front Lift Bracket Internal Drive Bolt	18
	Idler Pulley Bolt	37
	Intake Manifold Bolt	60③
	Main Bearing Cap	④
	Lower Crankcase	④
	Oil Gallery Plug (Cylinder Head)	41
	Oil Gallery Plug (Lower Crankcase)	48
	Oil Level Sensor	84③
	Oil Pan	18
	Oil Pan Drain Plug	15
	Oil Pump Cover	97③
	Oil Pump To Cylinder Block	18
	Oxygen Sensor	30
	Power Steering Pump To Cylinder Block	18
	Radiator Bracket Bolt	18
	Throttle Body Bolt	108③
	Timing Chain Guide Access Plug	44③
	Timing Chain Guide Bolt	22
	Timing Chain Tensioner Bolt (Primary)	18
	Timing Chain Tensioner Bolt (Secondary)	106③
	Timing Chain Tensioner Shoe Bolt	22
	Torque Converter Cover	80③
	Transaxle Brace	18
	Valve Cover	80③
	Water Crossover To Cylinder Head	18
	Water Pump Bolt	11
	Water Pump Pulley Bolt	108③
	Water Outlet Housing	84③

① — Tighten an additional 22.°
② — Tighten an additional 45.°
③ — Inch lbs.
④ — Refer to "Main & Rod Bearings" for tightening procedure.
⑤ — Refer to "Cylinder Head, Replace" for tightening procedure.
⑥ — Refer to "Piston & Rod Assembly" for tightening procedure.
⑦ — Tighten an additional 50.°

3800 Engine

NOTE: For Procedures Not Found In This Section, Refer To The "3800 Engine" Section In the "Bonneville, LeSabre, LSS, Park Ave., 88 & Regency" Chapter.

NOTE: On Air Bag Equipped Models, Refer To "Air Bag System Precautions" Located In The Front Of This Manual For System Disarming & Arming Procedures.

NOTE: Refer To "Computer Relearn Procedures" Located In The Front Of This Manual When Battery Power To The Computer Has Been Interrupted.

NOTE: Prior To Performing Any Service Operations Listed In This Section, Consult The "Technical Service Bulletins" Section For Related Information.

INDEX

PRECAUTIONS

AIR BAG SYSTEMS

Refer to "Air Bag System Precautions" in the front of this manual for system disarming and arming procedures.

BATTERY GROUND CABLE

Prior to service, disconnect battery ground cable and isolate as required.

FUEL SYSTEM PRESSURE RELIEF

To reduce the risk of fire and personal injury, it is necessary to relieve the fuel system pressure before servicing fuel system components.

1. Loosen fuel tank filler cap to relieve tank pressure.
2. Connect fuel pressure gauge tool No. J-34730-1, or equivalent, to fuel pressure valve. Wrap a shop towel around fitting while connection gauge to avoid spillage.
3. Install bleed hose into an approved container and open valve to bleed system pressure.

COMPRESSION PRESSURE

When checking compression, lowest cylinder must be within 70 percent of the highest cylinder with a minimum pressure of 100 psi. Perform compression test with engine at normal operating temperature, spark plugs removed and throttle wide open.

ENGINE MOUNT

REPLACE

ENGINE BLOCK MOUNTS

1. Remove engine mount struts, then install engine support fixture tool No. J 28467–A, engine support fixture adapter tool No. J28467–90 and engine support adapter leg tool No. J 36462, or equivalents.
2. Raise and support vehicle, then remove right front wheel and tire assembly.
3. Remove right engine splash shield, then the engine mount lower retaining nuts from frame.
4. Raise and support engine, then remove A/C compressor and position aside.
5. Remove front engine mount bracket bolts, then the rear engine mount bracket from engine.
6. Remove engine mount with engine mount bracket from engine, then the engine mount upper retaining nuts.
7. Remove engine mount from engine mount bracket.
8. Reverse procedure to install.

TRANSAXLE MOUNT

1. Remove engine torque strut from engine.
2. Raise and support vehicle.
3. Remove left tire and wheel assembly and lower splash shield.
4. Support transaxle using a suitable jack.
5. Remove mount nuts then the mount.
6. Reverse procedure to install.

ENGINE

REPLACE

1. Mark and remove hood assembly.
2. Remove air cleaner assembly.
3. Relieve fuel system pressure as described under "Precautions."
4. Remove fuel lines from rail and mounting bracket.
5. Remove coolant bottle and inner fender electrical cover.
6. Remove fuel injector sight cover.
7. Remove throttle cables, bracket and vacuum line from throttle body.
8. Remove heat shield from exhaust crossover pipe then crossover pipe.
9. Remove engine torque strut from engine.
10. Remove engine cooling fan.
11. Remove vacuum line from transaxle module.
12. Remove serpentine drive belt.
13. Remove power steering pump and alternator from engine.
14. Disconnect all necessary electrical connectors.
15. Remove upper and lower radiator and heater hoses from engine.
16. Remove transaxle to engine bolts and ground wire harness with bolt.
17. Raise and support vehicle.
18. Remove right tire and wheel assembly and inner splash shield.
19. Remove flywheel cover and scribe torque converter to flywheel for installation.
20. Remove flywheel to converter bolts.
21. Disconnect wire harness clamps from frame near radiator.

22. Remove A/C compressor and position aside.
23. Remove starter motor.
24. Remove transaxle to engine bolt through wheelwell using suitable extension.
25. Disconnect engine mount to frame nuts.
26. Remove oil filter.
27. Disconnect front exhaust pipe from manifold.
28. Disconnect oil cooler piper from hose connections.
29. Lower vehicle.
30. Install lifting device and remove engine assembly.
31. Reverse procedure to install, noting the following:
    a. Align engine with transaxle dowel pins.
    b. **Torque** torque strut bolts to 41 ft. lbs.
    c. **Torque** flywheel to converter bolts to 46 ft. lbs.

FUEL PUMP

REPLACE

Refer to "Fuel Pump, Replace" in the "3.1L Engine" section.

FUEL FILTER

REPLACE

1. Relieve fuel system pressure as outlined under "Precautions."
2. Raise and support vehicle.
3. Remove bracket attaching screw and filter bracket, **Fig. 1.**
4. Grasp filter and fuel line fitting. Twist quick-connect fitting 1/4 turn in each direction to loosen any dirt within fitting.
5. Using compressed air, blow out dirt from quick-connect fitting.
6. Remove feed pipe nut from fuel filter, then drain any remaining fuel into a suitable container.
7. Remove fuel filter.
8. Reverse procedure to install.

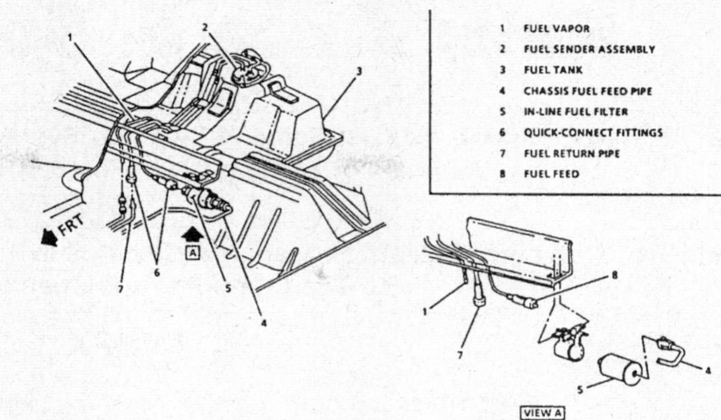

Fig. 1 Fuel filter replacement

TECHNICAL SERVICE BULLETINS

OIL PAN LEAK

1998-99

On some of these models equipped with stamped steel oil pan there may be an oil leak. This condition may be caused by uneven, rippled oil pan sealing surface.

To correct this condition, install new gasket and windage tray as follows:

1. Remove oil pan.
2. Remove old RTV from engine block and oil pan sealing surfaces using suitable plastic or metal scraper.
3. Inspect oil pan sealing surface for bends or distortions. Ripples will not affect sealability. **Do not replace oil pan because of ripples.**
4. Clean mating surfaces using solvent part No. 12346139, or equivalent.
5. Apply a continuous 1/4 inch bead of 5900 RTV sealant, part No. 12346386, or equivalent, to bottom of new gasket. Apply RTV directly over gasket's raised sealing bead.
6. Install gasket to oil pan .
7. Apply a continuous 1/4 inch bead of RTV sealant to top of new gasket. Apply RTV directly over gasket's raised sealing bead.
8. Install oil pan.
9. Allow RTV to set at least 30 minutes before adding engine oil.

ENGINE RUNS HOT, OVERHEATS OR LOSSES COOLANT

1999-2000

On some of these models the engine may run hot, overheat or lose coolant. This condition may be caused by imperfections in the radiator filler neck sealing surface.

To correct this condition, proceed as follows:

1. Polish filler neck sealing surface with 400 grit wet/dry sandpaper and a suitable flat piece of wood.
2. Replace radiator cap. **Do not replace radiator.**

OIL LEAK

1998

On some of these models there may be an oil leak that appears to originate near the oil pan rail. This condition may be caused by uneven bolt head flanges on the main bearing side bolts.

To correct this condition, proceed as follows:

1. Install oil dye, part No. 1235795, or equivalent, into crankcase.
2. Warm engine to operating temperature by driving vehicle a few miles.
3. Raise and support vehicle with engine running.
4. Thoroughly inspect for oil leaks using suitable black light, noting the following:
    a. Oil leaks originating above oil pan sealing surface may be caused by crankshaft rear oil seal housing gasket, intake end seal, main bearing side bolt or other sources.
    b. **Repair leaks originating above oil pan before replacing oil pan.**
5. Turn engine off and remove flywheel inspection cover.
6. Inspect for flywheel area oil leaks using suitable black light.
7. If leak appears to originate at oil pan flange, proceed as follows:
    a. **On models less oil level sensor,** install revised oil pan part No. 24507900 and gasket part No. 24502397.
    b. **On models equipped with oil level sensor,** install revised oil pan part No. 24507901 and gasket part No. 24502397.
    c. **On all models,** clean mounting bolts thoroughly.
    d. Apply two drops of Loctite No. 242 blue thread locker, or equivalent, to bolt threads.
    e. **Torque** bolts to 10 ft. lbs.
8. If leak appears to originate in flywheel area, proceed as follows:
    a. Remove crankshaft rear oil seal housing.
    b. Install new gasket and rear oil seal.
9. If leak appears to originate above pan rail, but not from rear housing or lower intake manifold end seals, install six new main bearing side bolts part No. 24505576.

Rear Axle & Suspension

NOTE: On Air Bag Equipped Models, Refer To "Air Bag System Precautions" Located In The Front Of This Manual For System Disarming & Arming Procedures.

NOTE: Refer To "Computer Relearn Procedures" Located In The Front Of This Manual When Battery Power To The Computer Has Been Interrupted.

INDEX

DESCRIPTION

These vehicles use a tri-link independent rear suspension system with a transverse leaf spring and tubular struts with large lateral links attached to the body crossmember. The three mounting points are the crossmember, strut tower and trailing arm. The crossmember is stamped steel and the composite fiberglass mono leaf spring is transversely mounted to the under side of the crossmember, with its padded ends free riding on the cast knuckle assembly.

HUB & BEARING

REPLACE

The rear hub and bearing assembly is not serviceable. If the hub and/or bearing is damaged, the complete assembly must be replaced.

1. Raise and support vehicle, then remove tire and wheel assembly.
2. Remove brake caliper with hose attached, suspend out of way.
3. Remove brake rotor.
4. Disconnect anti-lock brake system electrical harness connector.
5. Remove hub and bearing to knuckle bolts.
6. Remove parking brake lever bracket, then the parking brake actuator.
7. Remove hub and bearing assembly.
8. Reverse procedure to install.

STRUT

REPLACE

CENTURY, GRAND PRIX, IMPALA, INTRIGUE & REGAL

1. Remove three strut to body mount retaining nuts.

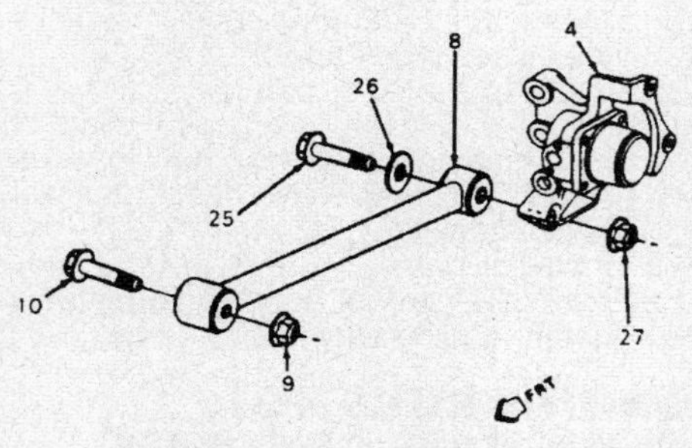

Fig. 1 Trailing arm removal

2. Raise and support vehicle, then remove rear wheel and tire assembly.
3. Disconnect stabilizer shaft link from strut.
4. Scribe matching marks on strut and knuckle.
5. Remove strut to knuckle bolts, then the strut from vehicle.
6. Reverse procedure to install. Check rear wheel alignment as outlined in "Wheel Alignment" section.

LUMINA

1. Raise and support vehicle, then remove wheel and tire assemblies.
2. Place scribe marks on strut and knuckle for installation reference.
3. Remove brake hose bracket at strut, then the strut mount to body nuts.
4. Remove strut/stabilizer shaft bracket from knuckle, then the strut from body.
5. Reverse procedure to install.

MONTE CARLO

1998–99

Refer to "Lumina" for strut replacement procedures on these models.

2000–02

Refer to "Century, Grand Prix, Impala, Intrigue & Regal" for strut replacement procedures on these models.

STRUT SERVICE

1. Position strut assembly into strut spring compressor tool No. J 34013–B, or equivalent.
2. Compress spring assembly approximately ½ inch.
3. Holding shaft with T-45 Torx bit, remove and discard shaft nut.
4. Release spring tension and remove upper mount plate, spring, baffle and lower mount plate.
5. Reverse procedure to assemble.

COIL SPRING

REPLACE

Refer to "Strut Service" for coil spring replacement.

KNUCKLE

REPLACE

CENTURY, GRAND PRIX, IMPALA, INTRIGUE & REGAL

1. Raise and support vehicle.
2. Remove wheel and tire assembly.
3. Scribe matching marks on strut and knuckle assembly, for installation reference.
4. Disconnect rear spindle rods from knuckle.

5. Remove brake caliper and bracket, then the brake rotor.
6. Disconnect ABS electrical connector.
7. Remove wheel hub and bearing.
8. Disconnect trailing arm from knuckle.
9. Remove rear suspension strut to knuckle bolts.
10. Remove knuckle assembly.
11. Reverse procedure to install.

LUMINA

1. Raise and support vehicle, then remove wheel and tire assemblies.
2. Place scribe marks on strut and knuckle to ensure installation in same position.
3. Remove rear wheel spindle rods from knuckle, then the caliper and rotor (brake hose bracket and drum if so equipped).
4. Disconnect ABS connector, then remove rear wheel hub.
5. Disconnect trailing arm from knuckle.
6. Remove strut to knuckle nuts, then the knuckle.
7. Reverse procedure to install.

MONTE CARLO

1998–99

Refer to "Lumina" for strut replacement procedures on these models.

2000–02

Refer to "Century, Grand Prix, Impala, Intrigue & Regal" for strut replacement procedures on these models.

TRAILING ARM

REPLACE

1. Raise and support vehicle.
2. Disconnect ABS electrical harness connector.
3. Remove trailing arm to knuckle attaching nut and bolt, then the trailing rod (link) to body attaching nut and bolt, **Fig. 1.**
4. Remove trailing arm.
5. Reverse procedure to install.

STABILIZER BAR

REPLACE

1. Raise and support vehicle, then remove rear wheel and tire assemblies.
2. Remove right and lefthand stabilizer shaft link bolts, then open brackets to remove insulator.
3. Remove right and lefthand strut to knuckle to stabilizer shaft nuts, **Fig. 2. Do not remove strut to knuckle bolts.**
4. Remove insulator brackets from bolts and from stabilizer shaft, then the stabilizer shaft.
5. Reverse procedure to install, noting the following:
   a. It may be necessary to pry stabilizer shaft to one side for installation clearance at strut. Use caution when prying.

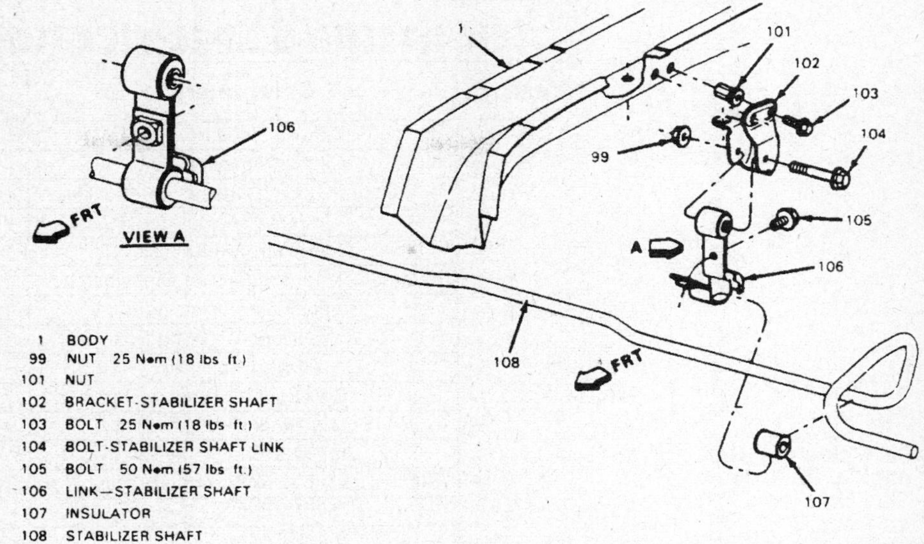

Fig. 2 Stabilizer shaft assembly replacement

LATERAL LINK

REPLACE

FRONT

1. Raise and support vehicle, then remove tire and wheel assembly.
2. Remove rod to knuckle bolt, then the exhaust pipe heat shield.
3. Lower fuel tank to gain access.
4. Remove lateral link to knuckle attaching bolt.
5. Remove lateral link to suspension crossmember attaching nut and bolt, then the lateral link.
6. Reverse procedure to install.

REAR

1. Raise and support vehicle, then remove tire and wheel assembly.
2. Remove transverse spring as outlined under "Leaf Spring Service."
3. Remove lower auxiliary spring bracket from rod.
4. Remove rear lateral link attaching nut from crossmember.
5. Push bolt forward enough to provide clearance for link removal, then remove rear lateral link.
6. Reverse procedure to install.

TECHNICAL SERVICE BULLETINS

REAR STRUT THUMPING OR SQUEAKING

On some of these models, the rear struts may have a muted thumping noise, oil canning or squeak, especially at low speed over irregular road surfaces.

This condition may be caused by the strut jounce bumper system. To correct this condition, replace both rear strut jounce bumper assemblies with revised units, service kit (part No. 22063945).

TIGHTENING SPECIFICATIONS

Year	Component	Torque/ Ft. Lbs.
1998–2002	Caliper Bleeder Valve	60③
	Caliper Mounting Bolt	79
	Caliper Mounting Bracket To Knuckle	148
	Jack Pad Bolt	18
	Lateral Link To Knuckle	157
	Lateral Link To Suspension Crossmember	140
	Proportioning Valve Caps	20
	Rear Caliper Mounting Bolt	92
	Rod To Knuckle	66②
	Rod To Support Crossmember	81①
	Spring Retention Plate Bolt	15
	Stabilizer Shaft Link Bolt	26
	Stabilizer Shaft Link To Body Bracket Nut	35
	Strut Mount To Body	37
	Strut To Knuckle Nut	82
	Suspension Crossmember To Body Bolt	85
	Trailing Arm To Knuckle④	192
	Trailing Arm To Knuckle ⑤	66⑥
	Trailing Link To Body Nut	48
	Upper Strut Bolt	34
	Wheel/Hub/Bearing To Knuckle Bolt	52
	Wheel Lug Nuts	100

① — Tighten an additional 60.°
② — Tighten an additional 90.°
③ — Inch lbs.
④ — Except Lumina & 1998–99 Monte Carlo.
⑤ — Lumina & 1998–99 Monte Carlo.
⑥ — Tighten an additional 75.°

Front Suspension & Steering

NOTE: On Air Bag Equipped Models, Refer To "Air Bag System Precautions" Located In The Front Of This Manual For System Disarming & Arming Procedures.

NOTE: Refer To "Computer Relearn Procedures" Located In The Front Of This Manual When Battery Power To The Computer Has Been Interrupted.

NOTE: Prior To Performing Any Service Operations Listed In This Section, Consult The "Technical Service Bulletins" Section For Related Information.

INDEX

PRECAUTIONS

AIR BAG SYSTEMS

Refer to "Air Bag System Precautions" in the front of this manual for system disarming and arming procedures.

DESCRIPTION

The front suspension system on these vehicles is of the McPherson strut design. This design incorporates McPherson struts with coil springs and a one piece configuration with lower control arms. The use of tapered top coil springs on top of the struts provides a well controlled ride and allows a lower hood profile.

HUB & BEARING

REPLACE

IMPALA & INTRIGUE

1. Raise and support vehicle, then remove tire and wheel assembly.
2. Disconnect wheel speed sensor electrical connector.
3. Remove wheel speed sensor electrical connector from bracket.
4. Remove brake caliper and position aside.
5. Remove caliper bracket and brake rotor.
6. Remove driveshaft nut and discard.
7. Attach front hub spindle remover tool No. J 28733-B, or equivalent, to wheel hub and bearing assembly.
8. Push driveshaft out of wheel hub and bearing assembly.
9. Remove hub and bearing assembly attaching bolts, then the hub and bearing assembly from steering knuckle. Discard attaching bolts.
10. Reverse procedure to install.

MONTE CARLO

2000-02

Refer to "Impala & Intrigue" for hub and bearing replacement procedures on these models.

FRONT WHEEL DRIVESHAFT BEARING

REPLACE

CENTURY, GRAND PRIX & REGAL

1. Raise and support vehicle, then remove tire and wheel assembly.
2. Loosen driveshaft axle nut one turn. **Do not remove axle nut at this time, removing axle nut at this time may cause bearing damage.**
3. Remove brake caliper retaining pins, then the brake caliper assembly. Position aside.
4. Remove caliper bracket attaching bolts, bracket and brake rotor.
5. Remove drive axle shaft nut.
6. Push axle splines back out of front wheel drive shaft bearing, using front hub spindle remover tool No. J 28733, or equivalent.

7. Remove front wheel drive shaft bearing to knuckle attaching bolts.
8. Remove front wheel drive shaft bearing.
9. Reverse procedure to install.

LUMINA

1. Raise and support vehicle, then remove wheel and tire assembly.
2. Loosen drive axle shaft nut one turn.
3. Remove brake caliper and position aside, **Fig. 1.**
4. Remove brake caliper mounting bracket bolts, then the caliper mounting bracket.
5. Remove brake rotor, then the drive axle shaft nut. Discard nut.
6. Loosen front wheel driveshaft bearing to knuckle attaching bolts.
7. Push axle splines back out of bearing assembly, using front hub spindle removal tool No. J 28733-A, or equivalent.
8. Remove driveshaft bearing to knuckle attaching bolts.
9. Remove ABS sensor mounting bolts, then the sensor. Position sensor aside.
10. Remove driveshaft bearing assembly from knuckle.
11. Reverse procedure to install.

MONTE CARLO

1998-99

Refer to "Lumina" for bearing replacement procedures on these models.

BALL JOINT INSPECTION

With vehicle raised and supported to allow front suspension to hang freely, grasp wheel at top and bottom and attempt to move bottom of wheel inward and outward. **Ball joints must be replaced if looseness is observed between knuckle and control arm.**

BALL JOINT

REPLACE

CENTURY, GRAND PRIX, IMPALA, INTRIGUE & REGAL

1. Raise and support vehicle.
2. Remove control arm as outlined under "Control Arm, Replace."
3. Drill out three retaining rivets holding ball joint to control arm, then remove ball joint from control arm.
4. Reverse procedure to install.

LUMINA

1. Raise and support vehicle, then remove wheel and tire assembly.
2. Remove ball joint heat shield attaching bolts, then the heat shield.
3. Remove lower ball joint cotter pin and retaining nut.
4. Loosen stabilizer shaft bushing bolts. **Do not remove bolts.**
5. Separate ball joint from lower control arm using tie rod puller/ball joint remover tool No. J 35917, or equivalent.
6. Drill out four rivets retaining ball joint to steering knuckle. Use a ⅛ inch drill bit to make a pilot hole, then use a ½ inch drill bit to finish drilling rivets.
7. Reverse procedure to install.

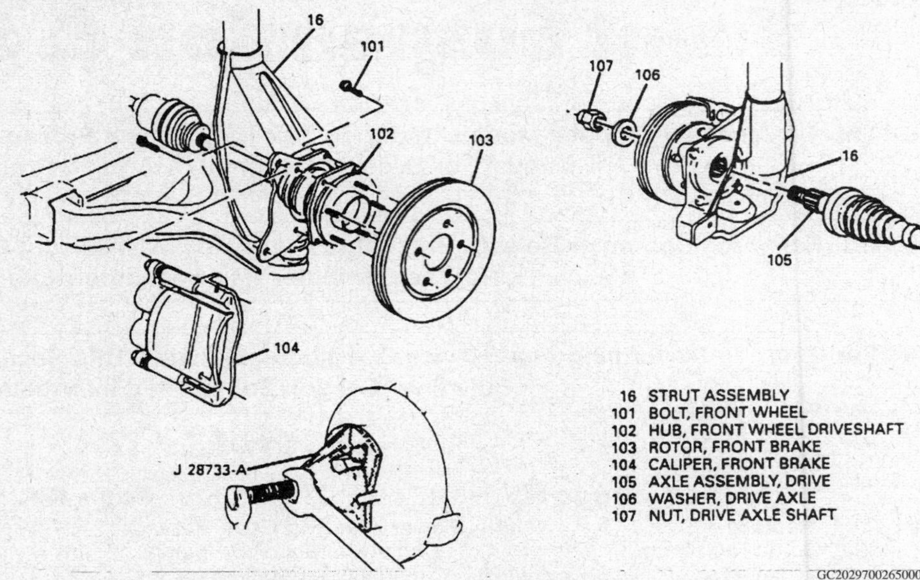

Fig. 1 Front wheel driveshaft bearing replacement. Lumina & 1998–99 Monte Carlo

MONTE CARLO

1998-99

Refer to "Lumina" for ball joint replacement on these models.

2000-02

Refer to "Century, Grand Prix, Impala, Intrigue & Regal" for ball joint replacement on these models.

STRUT

REPLACE

CENTURY, GRAND PRIX, IMPALA, INTRIGUE & REGAL

1. Remove three strut to body nuts, **Fig. 2.**
2. Raise and support vehicle, then remove tire and wheel assembly.
3. Remove strut to knuckle attaching bolts. **After removing bolts, retain knuckle in its original position. Failure to retain knuckle could cause ball joint or drive axle damage.**
4. Remove strut assembly from vehicle.
5. Reverse procedure to install.

LUMINA

1. Scribe alignment marks on cover plate, then loosen cover plate retaining nuts, **Fig. 3.**
2. Raise and support vehicle.
3. Remove tire and wheel assembly.
4. Remove brake caliper and position aside. **Do not disconnect brake hose.**
5. Remove brake rotor, then the hub and bearing as outlined under"Hub & Bearing, Replace."
6. Separate axle from transaxle, then remove tie rod to knuckle attaching nut.
7. Separate tie rod from steering knuckle, using tie rod puller/ball joint removal tool No. J-35917, or equivalent.
8. Remove lower ball joint to knuckle attaching nut.
9. Separate lower ball joint from lower control arm, using tie rod puller/ball joint removal tool No. J-35917, or equivalent.
10. Remove cover plate retaining nuts, then the strut/knuckle assembly.
11. Reverse procedure to install.

MONTE CARLO

1998-99

Refer to "Lumina" for strut replacement on these models.

2000-02

Refer to "Century, Grand Prix, Impala, Intrigue & Regal" for strut replacement on these models.

STRUT CARTRIDGE

REPLACE

LUMINA

Do not service strut unless weight of vehicle is on suspension.

REMOVAL

1. Scribe alignment marks on cover plate, remove cover plate retaining nuts, then the cover plate.
2. Using No. 50 Torx bit and strut rod remover/installer tool No. J-35669, or equivalents, remove strut shaft.
3. Remove strut mount bushing by prying with suitable tool.
4. Remove jounce bumper retainer using

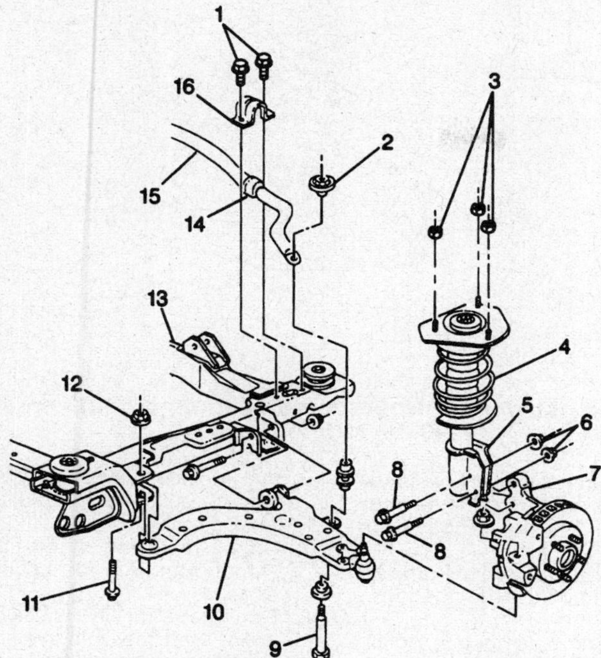

(1) Front Stabilizer Shaft Insulator Clamp Bolt/screw
(2) Front Stabilizer Shaft Link Nut
(3) Front Suspension Strut Mount Nut
(4) Front Suspension Spring
(5) Front Suspension Strut
(6) Strut To Knuckle Nut
(7) Front Steering Knuckle
(8) Strut To Knuckle Bolt/screw
(9) Front Stabilizer Shaft Link]
(10) Front Lower Control Arm
(11) Front Lower Control Arm Bolt/screw
(12) Front Lower Cotrol Arm Nut
(13) Frame
(14) Front Stabilizer Shaft Insulator
(15) Front Stabilizer Shaft
(16) Front Stabilizer Shaft Clamp

GC2029700266000X

Fig. 2 Front suspension. Century, Grand Prix, Impala, Intrigue, Regal & 2000–02 Monte Carlo

strut mount plate wrench tool No. J-35670, or equivalent.

5. Attach strut extension rod tool No. J-35668, or equivalent, to strut shaft and compress shaft down into cartridge, then remove tool and pull out jounce bumper.
6. Attach strut extension rod tool No. J-35668, or equivalent, to strut shaft and extend shaft, then remove tool and, using strut cap nut wrench tool No. J-35671, or equivalent, unscrew closure nut.
7. Remove strut cartridge.
8. Remove oil from strut tube using suction device.

INSTALLATION

1. Using strut cap nut wrench tool No. J-35671, or equivalent, install self contained replacement cartridge.
2. Install jounce bumper, then using strut mount plate wrench tool No. J-35670, or equivalent, the jounce bumper retainer.
3. Install strut mount bushing. If necessary, use strut extension rod tool No. J-35668, or equivalent after bushing is partially installed and position strut shaft as required. Lubricate bushing with a soap solution to ease installation.
4. Using No. 50 Torx bit and strut rod remover/installer tool No. J-35669, or equivalents, install strut shaft nut.
5. Install strut mount cover, aligning scribe marks.

MONTE CARLO

1998–99

Refer to "Lumina" for strut cartridge replacement on these models.

STRUT SERVICE

CENTURY, GRAND PRIX, IMPALA, INTRIGUE & REGAL

DISASSEMBLE

Springs are under high tension. Do not remove strut shaft nut without using a suitable spring compressing tool.

1. Mount strut and knuckle assembly into strut spring compressor tool No. J-34013-A and strut compressor adapter tool No. J-34013-88, or equivalents, then compress spring with compressor forcing screw just enough to release tension from upper spring insulator.
2. Remove strut shaft nut using Torx bit and strut rod nut remover/installer tool No. J-35669, or equivalents.
3. Relieve all spring tension, then remove spring and strut components.

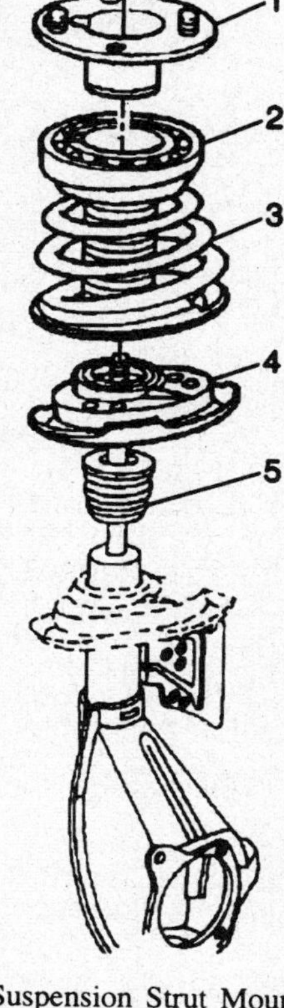

(1) Front Suspension Strut Mount Retainer
(2) Front Spring Upper Insulator
(3) Front Spring
(4) Front Spring Seat
(5) Front Suspension Strut Bumper

GC2029700267000X

Fig. 3 Exploded view of strut assembly. Lumina & 1998–99 Monte Carlo

ASSEMBLE

1. Install spring seat and bearing.
2. Install lower spring insulator. Lower spring coil end must be visible between step and first retention tab of insulator.
3. Install front suspension spring.
4. Install dust shield to lower spring seat.
5. Install jounce bumper.
6. Install upper spring insulator. Upper spring coil end must be between step and location mark on insulator.
7. Using strut mount plate wrench tool No. J-35670, or equivalent, install jounce bumper retainer to strut mount.
8. Install strut mount and upper strut mount bushing.
9. Compress strut assembly using strut spring compressor and strut compressor adapter tools Nos. J-34013-A and J-34013-38, or equivalents.
10. Align strut cartridge shaft with strut extension rod tool No. J-35668, or equivalent.

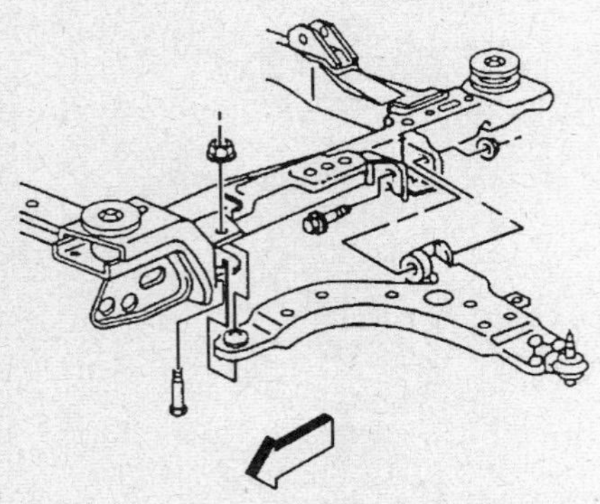
GC2029800225000X

Fig. 4 Lower control arm installation. Century, Grand Prix, Impala, Intrigue, Regal & 2000–02 Monte Carlo

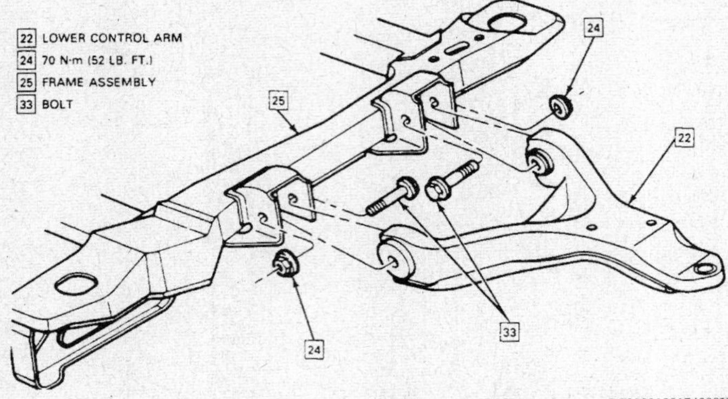

GC2029100174000X

Fig. 5 Lower control arm installation. Lumina & 1998–99 Monte Carlo

11. Install strut shaft nut using strut rod nut remover/installer tool No. J-35669, or equivalent, and a Torx bit.

MONTE CARLO

2000-02

Refer to "Century, Grand Prix, Impala, Intrigue & Regal" for strut service on these models.

CONTROL ARM

REPLACE

CENTURY, GRAND PRIX, IMPALA, INTRIGUE & REGAL

1. Raise and support vehicle, then remove wheel and tire assembly.
2. Remove steering gear outer tie rod from steering knuckle, then the stabilizer shaft to lower control arm insulator bracket bolts.
3. Disconnect ABS speed sensor, then remove control arm mounting bolts.
4. Remove cotter pin, then loosen nut from ball joint, **Fig. 2.**
5. Separate front lower control arm ball joint from steering knuckle, using ball joint separator tool No. J 41820, or equivalent.
6. Remove control arm from frame.
7. Reverse procedure to install, noting the following:
   a. Lower control arm to frame bolts must be installed as shown, **Fig. 4.**
   b. **Torque** lower ball joint nut 40 ft. lbs., then further tighten to align next slot in nut with cotter pin hole in stud. **Do not tighten more than 60° to align with hole and do not loosen nut at any time during installation.**

LUMINA

1. Raise and support vehicle, then remove wheel and tire assembly.
2. Remove engine splash shields.
3. Remove stabilizer shaft to lower control arm insulator bracket bolts.
4. Remove lower ball joint cotter pin and nut, then separate ball joint from lower control arm using tie rod puller/ball joint remover tool No. J-35917, or equivalent.
5. Remove lower control arm to frame attaching nuts and bolts, then the lower control arms.
6. Reverse procedure to install, noting the following:
   a. Lower control arm to frame bolts must be installed as shown, **Fig. 5.**
   b. **Torque** lower ball joint nut 15 ft. lbs. and tighten an additional 90°, then further tighten to align next slot in nut with cotter pin hole in stud. **Do not tighten more than 60° to align with hole and do not loosen nut at any time during installation.**

MONTE CARLO

1998-99

Refer to "Lumina" for control arm replacement procedures on these models.

2000-02

Refer to "Century, Grand Prix, Impala, Intrigue & Regal" for control arm replacement procedures on these models.

STEERING KNUCKLE

REPLACE

CENTURY, GRAND PRIX, IMPALA, INTRIGUE & REGAL

1. Raise and support vehicle, then remove wheel and tire assembly.
2. **On Century, Grand Prix and Regal models,** remove front wheel driveshaft bearing as outlined under "Front Wheel Driveshaft Bearing, Replace."
3. **On Impala, Intrigue and 2000–02 Monte Carlo models,** remove hub and bearing assembly as outlined under "Hub & Bearing, Replace."
4. **On all models,** remove lower control arm ball joint cotter pin and retaining nut.
5. Separate ball joint from control arm, using ball joint stud separator tool No. J 41820, or equivalent.
6. Separate outer tie rod end from steering knuckle, using universal steering linkage puller tool No. J 24319-B, or equivalent.
7. Scribe matching marks on strut and steering knuckle for installation reference.
8. Remove strut to knuckle attaching bolts, then the steering knuckle from vehicle.
9. Reverse procedure to install.

LUMINA

Refer to "Strut, Replace" for strut/knuckle assembly replacement.

MONTE CARLO

1998-99

Refer to "Lumina" for steering knuckle replacement procedures on these models.

2000-02

Refer to "Century, Grand Prix, Impala, Intrigue & Regal" for steering knuckle replacement procedures on these models.

STABILIZER BAR

REPLACE

CENTURY, GRAND PRIX, IMPALA, INTRIGUE & REGAL

REMOVAL

1. Raise and support vehicle, then remove tire and wheel assembly.
2. Move steering shaft dust seal to access lower intermediate shaft pinch bolt, then remove pinch bolt.
3. Loosen all insulator clamp attaching nuts and bolts, **Fig. 6.**
4. Place a jackstand under center of rear frame crossmember.
5. Loosen two front frame to body attaching bolts four turns.
6. Remove two rear frame to body attaching bolts, then lower rear of frame enough to remove stabilizer shaft. Discard frame to body bolts.
7. Remove insulators and clamps from frame.
8. Remove stabilizer bar links from control arms.
9. Pull stabilizer shaft rearward, the

swing shaft downward and remove from left side of vehicle.

INSTALLATION

1. Install stabilizer shaft from left side of vehicle.
2. Loosely install stabilizer shaft link to control arm. **Do not tighten stabilizer link retaining nut at this time. Weight of vehicle must be supported by control arms so that trim height is obtained before tightening link nut.**
3. Install insulator clamps onto frame, then raise frame into position while guiding steering shaft onto steering gear.
4. Install new frame to body attaching bolts and remove jackstand.
5. Install intermediate shaft pinch bolt.
6. Install dust seal onto steering gear.
7. Support vehicle weight with control arms and tighten stabilizer link nut to specification.
8. Install tire and wheel assembly.

LUMINA

1. Raise and support vehicle, then remove wheel and tire assembly.
2. Move steering shaft dust shield to gain access to pinch bolt.
3. Remove pinch bolt from lower intermediate steering shaft.
4. Loosen all insulator clamp attaching nuts and bolts, **Fig. 7.**
5. Place suitable jack under center of rear frame crossmember.
6. Loosen two front frame to body bolts four turns.
7. Remove two rear frame to body bolts.
8. Lower rear of frame just enough to gain access for stabilizer shaft removal.
9. Remove insulators and clamps from frame and control arms.
10. Pull stabilizer shaft rearward, swing down and remove from left side of vehicle.
11. Reverse procedure to install.

MONTE CARLO

1998–99

Refer to "Lumina" for stabilizer bar replacement procedures on these models.

2000–02

Refer to "Century, Grand Prix, Impala, Intrigue & Regal" for stabilizer bar replacement procedures on these models.

TIE ROD END

REPLACE

INNER

Refer to the "Power Steering Gears" chapter for inner tie rod end replacement.

OUTER

1. Raise and support vehicle, then remove tire and wheel assembly.
2. Remove hex torque prevailing nut, then loosen jam nut, **Fig. 8.** Discard hex torque prevailing nut.
3. Separate tie rod end from steering knuckle, using universal steering linkage puller tool No. J 24319-01, or equivalent.
4. Remove outer tie rod from inner tie rod end.
5. Reverse procedure to install.

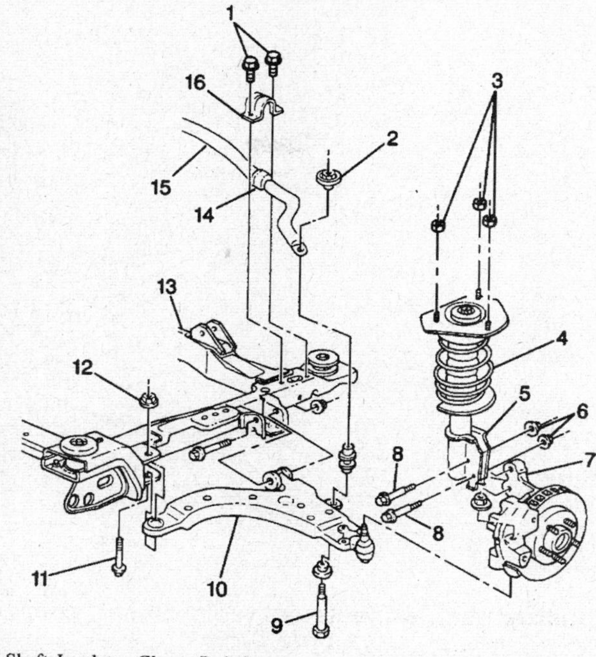

(1) Front Stabilizer Shaft Insulator Clamp Bolt/Screw
(2) Front Stabilizer Shaft Link Nut
(3) Front Suspension Strut Mount Nut
(4) Front Suspension Spring
(5) Front Suspension Strut
(6) Strut-to-Knuckle Nut
(7) Front Steering Knuckle
(8) Strut-to-Knuckle Bolt/Screw
(9) Front Stabilizer Shaft Link
(10) Front Lower Control Arm
(11) Front Lower Control Arm Bolt/Screw
(12) Front Lower Control Arm Nut
(13) Frame
(14) Front Stabilizer Shaft Insulator
(15) Front Stabilizer Shaft
(16) Front Stabilizer Shaft Clamp

GC2029800226000X

Fig. 6 Stabilizer shaft & insulators replacement. Century, Grand Prix, Impala, Intrigue, Regal & 2000–02 Monte Carlo

POWER STEERING GEAR

REPLACE

CENTURY, GRAND PRIX, IMPALA, INTRIGUE & REGAL

1. Set steering wheel to the 12 o'clock position with wheels straight ahead, then turn ignition switch to the LOCK position.
2. Raise and support vehicle, then remove left wheel and tire assembly.
3. Remove steering shaft lower bolt at steering gear.
4. Separate steering shaft from power steering gear. **Failure to disconnect intermediate shaft from rack and pinion shaft stub may result in damage to steering gear and/or intermediate shaft. This damage can cause loss of steering control.**
5. Remove hex torque prevailing nuts, then separate both outer tie rod ends from steering knuckle, using tie rod end puller/ball joint remover tool No. J 35917, or equivalent.
6. Support frame with suitable jackstands.
7. Remove frame bolts, then lower rear of frame. **Do not lower frame too far as damage to engine components nearest to the cowl may result.**
8. Remove pipe retaining clip from steering gear.
9. Remove inlet pipes and outlet line from steering gear.
10. Remove steering gear attaching bolts and nuts.
11. Remove power steering gear through wheel opening.
12. Reverse procedure to install. After completing installation, bleed power steering system as outlined under "Power Steering System Bleed."

LUMINA

1. Raise and support vehicle. **Provide additional support at rear of vehicle.**
2. Remove front wheel and tire assemblies.
3. Remove intermediate shaft lower pinch bolt at steering gear, **Fig. 9.**
4. Remove intermediate shaft from stub shaft. **Failure to disconnect intermediate shaft from rack and pinion shaft stub may result in damage to steering gear and/or intermediate shaft. This damage can cause loss of steering control.**

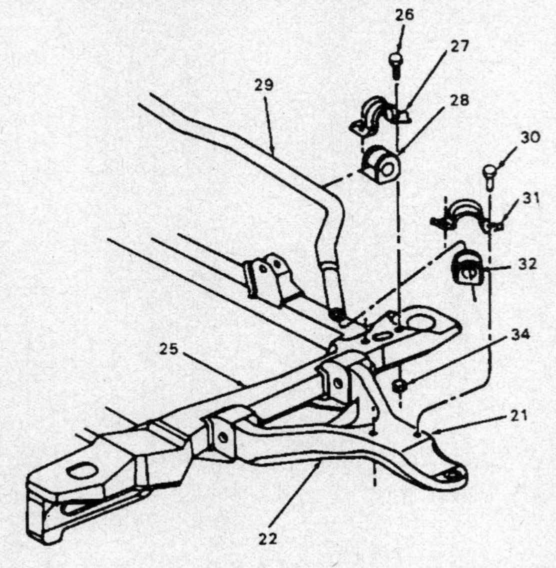

Fig. 7 Stabilizer shaft & insulators replacement. Lumina & 1998–99 Monte Carlo

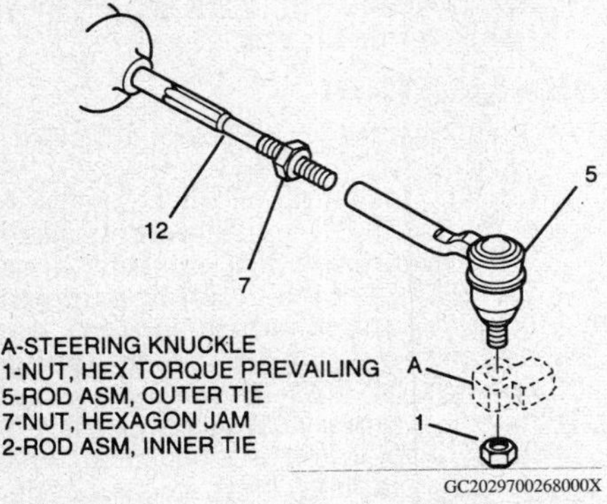

Fig. 8 Tie rod end replacement

5. Disconnect tie rod ends from knuckle and strut assembly, using tie rod puller/ball joint remover tool No. J-35917, or equivalent.
6. Support body with suitable stands, then remove rear frame mounting bolts and lower rear frame no more than 5 inches. **Do not lower rear of frame too far. Damage to engine components nearest to cowl may result.**
7. Remove heat shield, then the pipe retaining clip from steering gear.
8. Disconnect inlet pipes and outlet line from power steering gear.
9. Remove remaining brackets and clips.
10. Remove rack and pinion mounting nuts and bolts, then the rack and pinion assembly through the left wheel opening.
11. Reverse procedure to install. After completing installation, bleed power steering system as outlined under "Power Steering System Bleed."

MONTE CARLO

1998–99

Refer to "Lumina" for power steering gear replacement procedures on these models.

2000–02

Refer to "Century, Grand Prix, Impala, Intrigue & Regal" for power steering gear replacement procedures on these models.

POWER STEERING PUMP

REPLACE

CENTURY, GRAND PRIX & REGAL

1. **On models equipped with 3.1L engine,** remove coolant recovery reservoir and position aside.
2. **On all models,** remove accessory drive belt from pump.
3. **On models equipped with 3.1L engine,** disconnect ignition control wiring harness near pump and position aside.
4. **On all models,** disconnect inlet and outlet hoses from pump.
5. Remove pump assembly attaching bolts, then the pump.
6. Transfer pulley to new pump, if necessary.
7. Reverse procedure to install. Bleed power steering system as outlined under "Power Steering System, Replace."

IMPALA

3.4L ENGINE

1. Place a drain pan under vehicle, then remove coolant recovery reservoir.
2. Remove accessory drive belt from power steering pump pulley.
3. Remove ignition wiring harness from retainer near power steering pump.
4. Disconnect power steering pressure and return hoses.
5. Remove power steering pump mounting bolts, then the pump from engine mounting.
6. Reverse procedure to install.

3800 ENGINE

Refer to "3800 Engine" under "Lumina" for replacement procedure.

INTRIGUE

3.5L ENGINE

1. Place a drain under vehicle, then remove coolant surge tank.
2. Remove fuel injector sight shield.
3. Remove accessory drive belt, then the accessory wiring junction block, position junction block aside.
4. Remove power steering pump pulley, using power steering pump pulley remover tool No. J 25034–C, or equivalent.
5. Remove pressure and return lines from pump.
6. Remove pump mounting bolts, then the pump and reservoir.
7. Remove reservoir from pump.
8. Reverse procedure to install. Bleed power steering system as outlined under "Power Steering System, Replace."

3800 ENGINE

Refer to "3800 Engine" under "Lumina" for replacement procedure.

LUMINA

3.1L ENGINE

Refer to "Century, Grand Prix & Regal" for replacement procedure.

3800 ENGINE

1. Remove accessory drive belt.
2. Raise and support vehicle, then remove tire and wheel assembly.
3. Place a drain pan under vehicle, then disconnect pressure and return lines from power steering pump.
4. Remove power steering pump mounting bolts, then the pump assembly.
5. Remove fluid reservoir from pump, then the pulley.
6. Transfer pulley and reservoir to new pump, if necessary.
7. Reverse procedure to install. Bleed power steering system as outlined under "Power Steering System, Replace."

MONTE CARLO

1998–99

Refer to "Lumina" for power steering pump replacement procedures on these models.

2000–02

Refer to "Impala" for power steering pump replacement procedures on these models.

POWER STEERING SYSTEM BLEED

1. Turn wheels all the way to left.

2. Add power steering to Cold mark on fluid level indicator.
3. Start engine and run at fast idle, then add fluid, if necessary, to bring level to Cold mark.
4. Bleed system by turning wheels from side to side without hitting stops. Keep fluid level at Cold mark.
5. Return wheels to center position and continue running engine for 2–3 minutes.
6. Road test vehicle to ensure steering functions normally and is free of noise.
7. Check fluid level and ensure level is at Hot mark after system has stabilized at its normal operating temperature.

TECHNICAL SERVICE BULLETINS

SCRUNCH OR POPPING NOISE

1998 LUMINA & REGAL

Some of these vehicles may exhibit a scrunch or popping noise during low speed turns. This condition could be caused by a sticking condition between the front suspension strut bumper and the front strut closure nut.

To correct this condition install a front suspension jounce washer part No. 10403367, on each front strut assembly. Refer to "Strut Service" to install jounce washer.

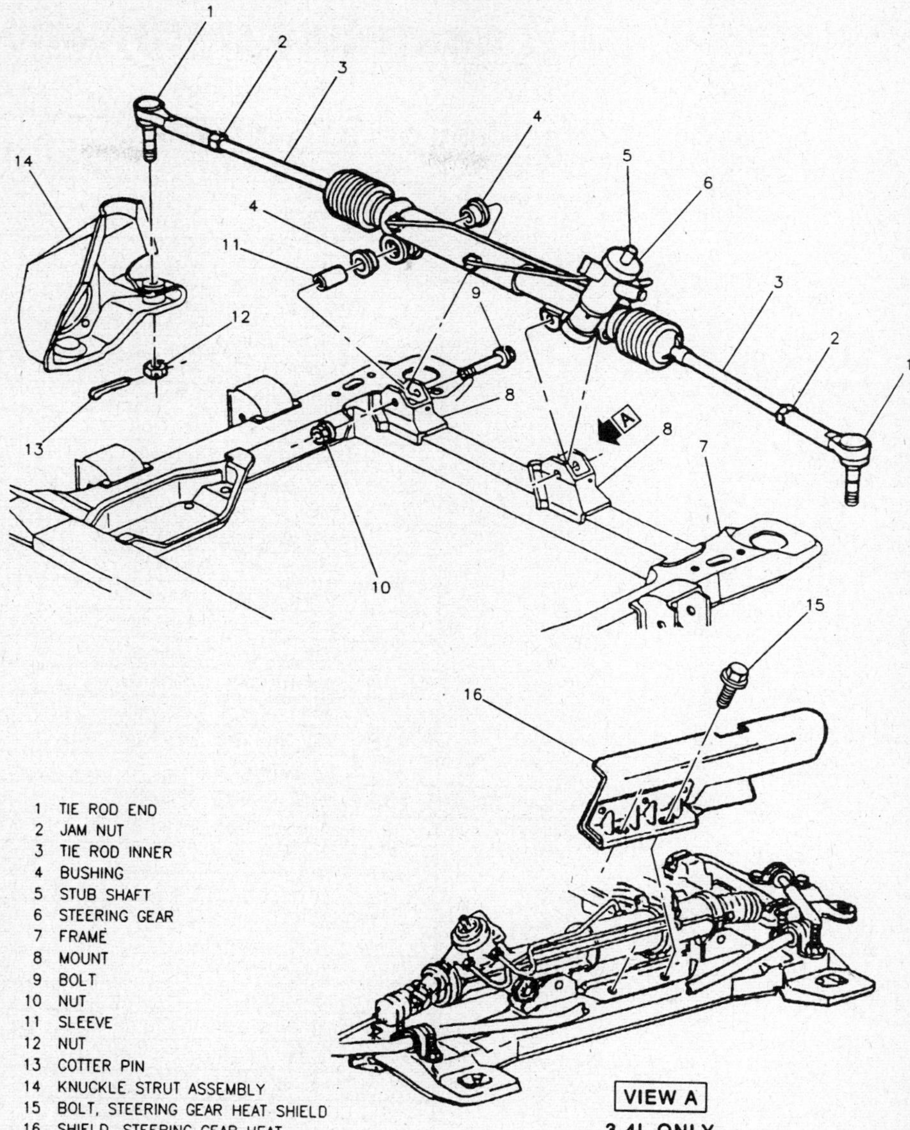

Fig. 9 Power steering gear replacement. Lumina & 1998–99 Monte Carlo

TIGHTENING SPECIFICATIONS

Year	Component	Torque/ Ft. Lbs.
CENTURY, GRAND PRIX & REGAL		
1998–2002	Ball Joint Heat Shield Retaining Nuts	54①
	Ball Joint To Lower Control Arm	50
	Ball Joint To Steering Knuckle	40
	Drive Axle Nut	151
	Frame To Body Bolt	100
	Front Wheel Driveshaft Bearing Bolts	96
	Heat Shield Screws	54①
	Inner Tie Rod To Rack	74
	Intermediate Shaft Pinch Bolt	35
	Lower Ball Joint Nut	40
	Lower Control Arm To Frame Bolts	②
	Outer Tie Rod End To Steering Knuckle Nut	18③
	Power Steering Pipe Fittings	20
	Pump Mounting Bolt	25
	Stabilizer Shaft Bracket Bolts	35
	Stabilizer Shaft Link Nut	17
	Steering Gear Mounting Bolt	59
	Strut To Body Mount Nuts	30
	Strut To Knuckle Bolts	90
	Tie Rod End Jam Nut	50
	Wheel Lug Nuts	100
LUMINA & 1998–99 MONTE CARLO		
1998–2002	Ball Joint Heat Shield Bolts	62①
	Ball Joint Nut	63
	Drive Axle Nut	151
	Front Wheel Driveshaft Bearing To Knuckle	52
	Inner Tie Rod End Nut	74
	Intermediate Shaft Pinch Bolt	35
	Lower Control Arm To Frame Bolts	52
	Outer Tie Rod End Nut	84①⑤
	Power Steering Line Fittings	20
	Stabilizer Shaft Bushing Clamp Bolt	35
	Stabilizer Shaft To Insulator Bracket To Frame	27
	Stabilizer Shaft To Insulator Clamp To Frame	35
	Stabilizer Shaft To Insulator Clamp To Lower Control Arm	35
	Steering Gear Heat Shield	54①
	Steering Gear Mounting Bolts	59
	Strut Closure Nut	82
	Strut Cover Plate Nuts	24
	Strut Piston Shaft Nut	59
	Strut To Knuckle Nuts	90
	Tie Rod End Jam Nut	46
	Wheel Lug Nuts	100

Continued

TIGHTENING SPECIFICATIONS—Continued

Year	Component	Torque/ Ft. Lbs.
IMPALA & 2000–02 MONTE CARLO		
2000–02	Front Wheel Driveshaft Bearing Nut	96
	Intermediate Shaft Lower Pinch Bolt	35
	Intermediate Shaft Upper Pinch Bolt	35
	Lower Control Arm Ball Stud To Control Arm	50
	Lower Control Arm Ball Stud To Knuckle	15④
	Lower Control Arm Mounting Nuts	77
	Power Steering Gear Mounting Bolts	59
	Power Steering Pressure Line To Pump	20
	Power Steering Pressure Line To Steering Gear	20
	Power Steering Pump Mounting Bolts	18
	Power Steering Return Line To Gear	20
	Power Steering Return Line To Pump	20
	Stabilizer Shaft Bracket Bolt	35
	Stabilizer Shaft Link Nut	17
	Strut Mount Nut	52
	Strut To Body Mount Nuts	24
	Strut To Steering Knuckle	90
	Tie Rod End Nut	22④
	Wheel Lug Nuts	100
INTRIGUE		
1998–2002	Ball Joint Stud To Steering Knuckle	15④
	Ball Joint To Lower Control Arm Nut	50
	Front Wheel Driveshaft Bearing Nut	96
	Intermediate Shaft Lower Pinch Bolt	35
	Intermediate Shaft Upper Pinch Bolt	35
	Lower Control Arm Mounting Nuts	77
	Power Steering Cooler Pipe Retainer Bolt	53①
	Power Steering Gear Mounting Bolts	59
	Power Steering Pressure Line To Steering Gear	20
	Power Steering Pressure Line To Pump	20
	Power Steering Pump Mounting Bolts	18
	Power Steering Return Line To Gear	20
	Power Steering Return Line To Pump	20
	Stabilizer Shaft Bracket Bolt	35
	Stabilizer Shaft Link Nut	17
	Strut To Body Mount Nuts	24
	Strut Mount Nut	52
	Strut To Steering Knuckle Bolts	90
	Tie Rod End Nut	22④
	Wheel Lug Nuts	100

① — Inch lbs.

② — Refer to "Control Arm, Replace."

③ — Tighten an additional 180.°

④ — Tighten an additional 120.°

⑤ — Tighten an additional 210.°

Wheel Alignment

INDEX

PRECAUTIONS

When adjusting wheel alignment, always adjust both front and rear alignment. Begin with rear wheel camber, then proceed to rear wheel toe and tracking and, finally, adjustment of front wheel camber and toe.

PRELIMINARY INSPECTION

1. Ensure tires are inflated to correct pressure, and check for uneven wear.
2. Check front wheel bearings and related suspension components for damage and replace as necessary, to eliminate improper alignment due to faulty components.
3. Check ball joints and tie rods.
4. Check vehicle trim heights.
5. Check steering gear for looseness at frame.
6. Check struts for improper operation.
7. Check for loose control arms.
8. Check for loose or missing stabilizer shaft attachments.

FRONT WHEEL ALIGNMENT

CAMBER

CENTURY, GRAND PRIX, IMPALA, INTRIGUE & REGAL

1. Remove strut assembly as outlined in "Front Suspension & Steering" section.
2. Place strut assembly in a suitable vise.
3. File lower strut to knuckle attaching hole oblong, **Fig. 1.**
4. Install strut assembly and adjust camber as necessary.
5. **Torque** strut to knuckle bolts to 88 ft. lbs.

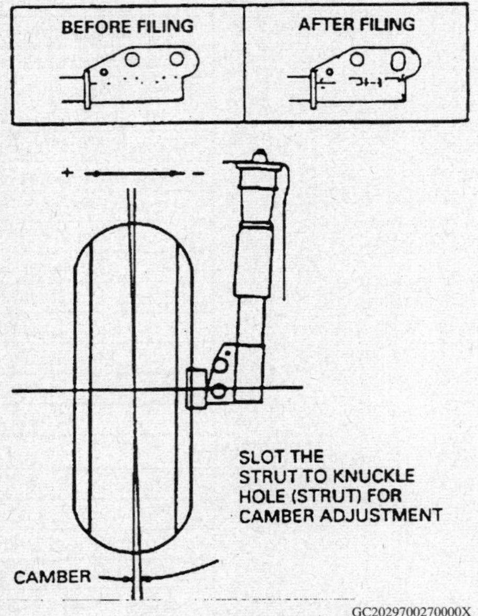

Fig. 1 Front camber adjustment. Century, Grand Prix, Impala, Intrigue, Regal & 2000–02 Monte Carlo

LUMINA

1. Open hood and remove three strut cover plate nuts and cover plate.
2. Lift front of vehicle just to the point that strut stud clears strut tower and cover top of strut. **Do not over extend drive axle. Do not lift by suspension.**
3. Use strut alignment template tool No. J-36892, or equivalent, to mark holes, then file three holes. File inboard or outboard of existing hole depending or camber requirement. Do not file more than .2 inch in either direction. **Paint exposed metal with red oxide primer and, after primer has dried, paint area with paint matching body color.**
4. Lower front of vehicle and guide strut studs into slotted holes.
5. Install three strut cover plate nuts.
6. Set camber to specifications by moving strut, then **torque** strut cover plate nuts to 24 ft. lbs.

MONTE CARLO

1998-99

Refer to "Lumina" for camber adjustment procedures on these models.

2000-02

Refer to "Century, Grand Prix, Impala, Intrigue & Regal" for camber adjustment procedures on these models.

TOE

1. Remove power steering gear seal clamps.
2. With steering wheel in straight ahead position, loosen jam nuts on tie rods.
3. Rotate inner tie rod to obtain proper toe angle, then ensure number of threads showing on each tie rod is approximately equal.
4. Ensure tie rod ends are square, then **torque** jam nuts to 46 ft. lbs.
5. Ensure seals are not twisted and install seal clamps.

REAR WHEEL ALIGNMENT

CAMBER

CENTURY, GRAND PRIX, IMPALA, INTRIGUE & REGAL

1. Remove strut assembly as outlined in "Rear Suspension" section.
2. Place strut assembly in a suitable vise.
3. File upper strut to knuckle attaching hole oblong, **Fig. 2.**
4. Install strut assembly and adjust camber as necessary.
5. **Torque** strut to knuckle bolts to 88 ft. lbs.

LUMINA

1. Raise and support vehicle.
2. Remove tire and wheel assembly.

3. Remove strut assembly as outlined in "Rear Suspension" section.
4. Remove strut/upper auxiliary spring bracket/stabilizer shaft bracket.
5. Place strut in vise.
6. File lower strut to knuckle attaching hole oblong, **Fig. 3**.
7. Place auxiliary spring assembly in vise.
8. File lower strut attaching hole oblong.
9. Place stabilizer bracket in vise.
10. File lower stabilizer bracket to strut attaching hole oblong.
11. Attach strut assembly/stabilizer shaft bracket/upper auxiliary spring bracket to knuckle.
12. Install strut to body bolts and break hose bracket.
13. Install auxiliary spring and install tire and wheel assembly.
14. Adjust camber, then **torque** strut to knuckle nuts to 136 ft. lbs.
15. Check and adjust toe if necessary.

MONTE CARLO

1998-99

Refer to "Lumina" for camber adjustment procedures on these models.

2000-02

Refer to "Century, Grand Prix, Impala, Intrigue & Regal" for camber adjustment procedures on these models.

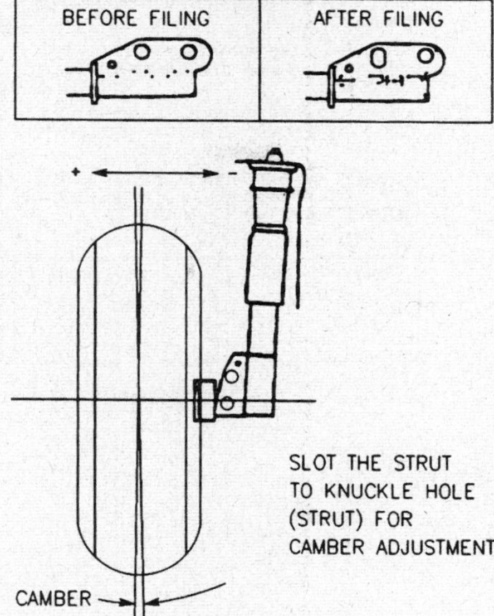

Fig. 2 Rear camber adjustment. Century, Grand Prix, Impala, Intrigue, Regal & 2000–02 Monte Carlo

TOE

CENTURY, GRAND PRIX, IMPALA, INTRIGUE & REGAL

1. Loosen hex nuts at rear wheel spindle rod.
2. Adjust toe to specifications.
3. **Torque** hex nuts to 37 ft. lbs.

LUMINA

1. Install rear toe adjusting tool No. J-38118, or equivalent, after lubricating threads.
2. Hand tighten turnbuckle portion of tool in direction of adjustment. Equal amounts of threads should be showing on both sides of turnbuckle.
3. Loosen rear rod nut at crossmember a minimum of four turns.
4. Rotate turnbuckle portion of tool to reach correct toe specification.
5. **Torque** rear rod to crossmember nut to 81 ft. lbs. plus an additional 60° turn.
6. Remove tool.

MONTE CARLO

1998-99

Refer to "Lumina" for toe adjustment procedures on these models.

2000-02

Refer to "Century, Grand Prix, Impala, Intrigue & Regal" for toe adjustment procedures on these models.

VEHICLE RIDE HEIGHT

Refer to "Vehicle Ride Height Specifications" in the "Specifications" section for vehicle ride height measurement points and specifications.

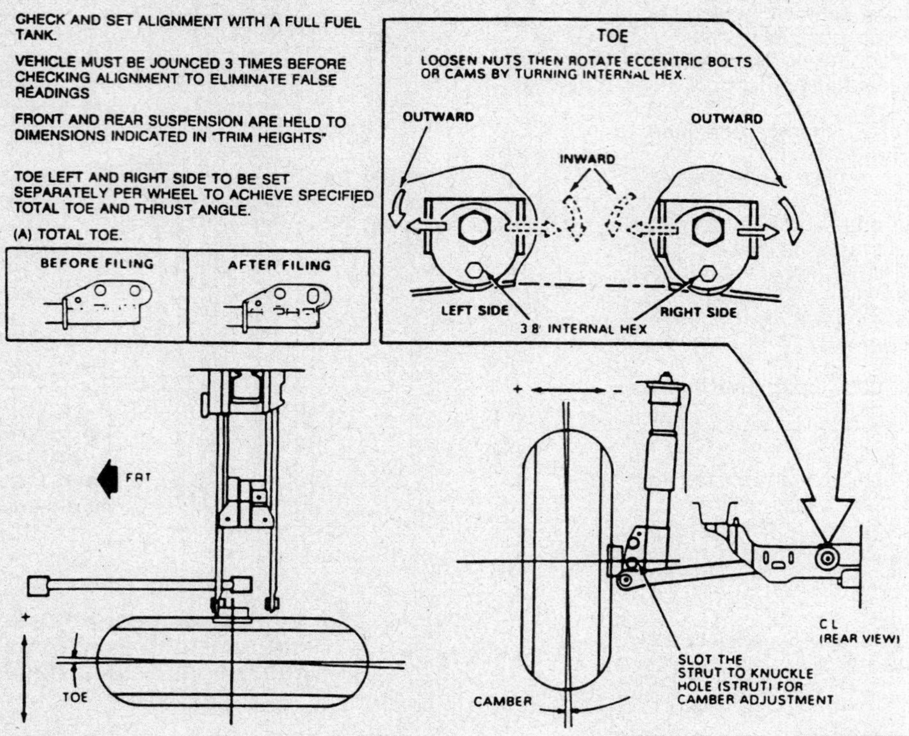
CHECK AND SET ALIGNMENT WITH A FULL FUEL TANK.
VEHICLE MUST BE JOUNCED 3 TIMES BEFORE CHECKING ALIGNMENT TO ELIMINATE FALSE READINGS
FRONT AND REAR SUSPENSION ARE HELD TO DIMENSIONS INDICATED IN "TRIM HEIGHTS"
TOE LEFT AND RIGHT SIDE TO BE SET SEPARATELY PER WHEEL TO ACHIEVE SPECIFIED TOTAL TOE AND THRUST ANGLE.
(A) TOTAL TOE.
BEFORE FILING
AFTER FILING
TOE
LOOSEN NUTS THEN ROTATE ECCENTRIC BOLTS OR CAMS BY TURNING INTERNAL HEX.
OUTWARD
INWARD
OUTWARD
LEFT SIDE
RIGHT SIDE
3/8" INTERNAL HEX
FRT
TOE
CAMBER
C L (REAR VIEW)
SLOT THE STRUT TO KNUCKLE HOLE (STRUT) FOR CAMBER ADJUSTMENT
GC2049100075000X

Fig. 3 Rear alignment inspection & adjustment. Lumina & 1998–99 Monte Carlo

CORVETTE

NOTE: Refer To The Rear Of This Manual For Vehicle Manufacturer's Special Tool Suppliers.

INDEX OF SERVICE OPERATIONS

Specifications

GENERAL ENGINE SPECIFICATIONS

Year	Engine		Fuel System	Bore & Stroke	Compres-sion Ratio	Net Brake H.P. @ RPM②	Maximum Torque	Normal Oil Pressure psi
	Liter	VIN Code①						
1998–2000	5.7L	G	SFI	3.90 x 3.62	10.1	345 @ 5600	350 @ 4400	③
2001–02	5.7L	G	SFI	3.90 x 3.62	10.1	345 @ 5200	④	③
	5.7L	S	SFI	3.90 x 3.62	10.5	405 @ 6000	400 @ 4800	③

SFI — Sequential Fuel Injection.
VIN — Vehicle Identification Number.
① — The eighth digit of the VIN denotes engine code.
② — Ratings are net, as installed in vehicle.
③ — Engine hot, minimum oil pressure @ 1000 RPM, 6 psi.; @ 2000 RPM, 18 psi.; @ 4000 RPM, 24 psi.
④ — Manual transmission, 375 ft. lbs., @ 4400 RPM; automatic transmission, 360 ft. lbs., @ 4000 RPM.

TUNE UP SPECIFICATIONS

Year	Engine	Spark Plug Gap	Ignition Timing BTDC				Curb Idle Speed③		Fast Idle Speed		Fuel Pump Pres-sure psi	Valve Clear-ance Inch
			Firing Order	Man. Trans.	Auto. Trans.	Mark Fig.	Man. Trans.	Auto. Trans.	Man. Trans.	Auto. Trans.		
1998–2002	5.7L	.060	1-8-7-2-6-5-4-3	①	①	—	④	④	④	④	55–61⑤	②

BTDC — Before Top Dead Center
VIN — Vehicle Identification Number
① — Computer controlled. No adjustment.
② — Equipped w/hydraulic lifters. No adjustment is required.
③ — When inspecting idle speed, set parking brake & block drive wheels.
④ — Idle speed is controlled by an idle speed control motor.
⑤ — With shop towel wrapped around fuel pressure fitting to prevent fuel spillage, connect a suitable fuel pressure gauge. Inspect fuel pressure with ignition On, but engine not running.

FRONT WHEEL ALIGNMENT SPECIFICATIONS

Year	Caster Angle, Degrees		Camber Angle, Degrees		Toe Per Wheel, Degrees		Steering Wheel Angle, Degrees	Ball Joint Wear	
	Limits	Desired	Limits	Desired	Limits	Desired		Upper	Lower
1998–2002	+7.4 to +6.4	6.9	0.3 to -0.7	-0.2	0.14 to -0.06	0.04	1.0 to -1.0	①	①

① — Refer to "Front Suspension & Steering."

REAR WHEEL ALIGNMENT SPECIFICATIONS

Year	Camber Angle, Degrees		Toe Per Wheel, Degrees		Thrust Angle, Degrees	
	Limits	Desired	Limits	Desired	Limits	Desired
1998–2002	–.68 to .32	–.18	–.11 to +.09	–.01	–.1 to +.1	0

VEHICLE RIDE HEIGHT SPECIFICATIONS

Model	Year	Body Style	Manufacturer's Original Tire Size	Measurement Points & Specifications①③					
				Front			Rear		
				Dim.	Specification		Dim.	Specification	
					Inches	mm		Inches	mm
Corvette	1998–2002	All	②	C	5.9	150	D	5.31	135

C Dim. — Ground to Rocker Panel, Front
D Dim. — Ground to Rocker Panel, Rear
Dim. — Dimension
① — ±.0.39 in (10 mm) front to rear & side to side.
② — See door sticker or inside of glove box for manufacturer's original tire size specifications. If tires on vehicle do not match manufacturer's original tire size & measurement is not within limits, it will be necessary to refer to the "Non-Standard Tire & Wheel Size Adjustment To Ride Height Specification & Tire Size Adjustment Charts" in the front of this manual for approximate changes in ride height specifications.
③ — Measurement is with fuel, radiator coolant and engine oil full, spare tire, jack, hand tools and mats in designated positions and tires properly inflated.

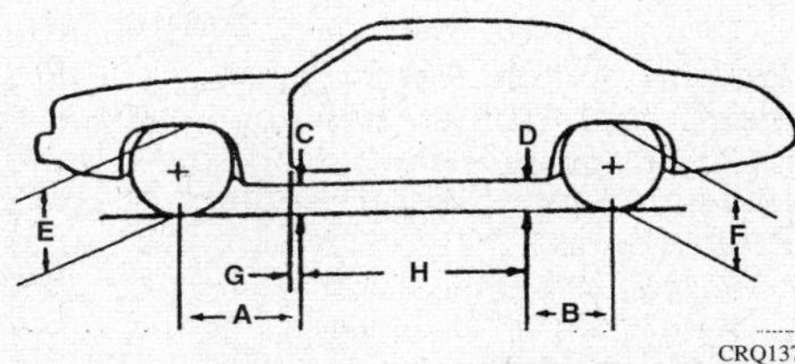

Dimensions C & D

FLUID CAPACITIES & COOLING SYSTEM DATA

Year	Model Or Engine (VIN)①	Coolant Capacity, Qts.	Coolant Type	Radiator Cap Relief Pressure, psi	Thermo. Opening Temp. °F	Fuel Tank, Gals.	Engine Oil, Qts.②		Transmission Oil			Rear Axle Pts.
							Less Filter Change	With Filter Change	Man Trans. Pts.	Auto. Trans. Qts.③		
										Drain & Refill	Total Capacity	
1998–2000	5.7L (G)	⑥	Dex-Cool	15	187	19.1	6④	6.5④	8.2	5	10.8	3.4
2001–02	5.7L (G)	⑤	Dex-Cool	15	187	18.5	6④	6.5④	8.2	5	10.8	3.4
	5.7L (S)	⑤	Dex-Cool	15	187	18.5	6④	6.5④	3.9	—	—	3.4

VIN — Vehicle Identification Number
① — The eighth digit of the VIN denotes engine code.
② — After refilling, inspect oil level again.
③ — Approximate. Make final inspection w/dipstick.
④ — Recommended engine oil SG SAE 5W-30 synthetic engine oil meeting GM specification GM4718M.
⑤ — On models w/A/T, 11.5 qts.; w/M/T, 11.8 qts.
⑥ — On models w/A/T, 12.3 qts.; w/M/T, 12.6 qts.

LUBRICANT DATA

Year	Lubricant Type				
	Transmission		Rear Axle	Power Steering System	Brake System
	Automatic	Manual			
1998	Dexron III	Dexron III	③	②	DOT 3 Brake Fluid
1999–2002	Dexron III	Dexron III	①	②	DOT 3 Brake Fluid

① — 75W-90 synthetic axle lubricant P/N 12378261, or an equivalent meeting GM specification 9986115. When completely draining & filling add 4 ounces of lubricant additive P/N 1052358, or equivalent.
② — Power steering fluid P/N 1052884, 1050017, or equivalents.
③ — Axle lubricant P/N 12345977 & lubricant additive P/N 1052358, or equivalents.

Electrical

NOTE: On Air Bag Equipped Models, Refer To "Air Bag System Precautions" Located In The Front Of This Manual For System Disarming & Arming Procedures.

NOTE: Refer To "Computer Relearn Procedures" Located In The Front Of This Manual When Battery Power To The Computer Has Been Interrupted.

NOTE: Prior To Performing Any Service Operations Listed In This Section, Consult The "Technical Service Bulletins" Section For Related Information.

INDEX

PRECAUTIONS

AIR BAG SYSTEMS

Refer to "Air Bag System Precautions" in the front of this manual for system disarming and arming procedures.

BATTERY GROUND CABLE

Prior to service, disconnect battery ground cable and isolate as required.

FUSE PANEL & FLASHER LOCATION

The fuse panel is located behind the far righthand corner of the instrument panel. The turn signal and hazard flasher is incorporated into the hazard warning switch, which is located behind the center air vent.

FUEL PUMP RELAY LOCATION

The fuel pump relay is located in the underhood electrical center.

RELAY CENTER LOCATION

The relay center, or underhood electrical center, is located on the righthand side of the engine compartment, in front of the battery.

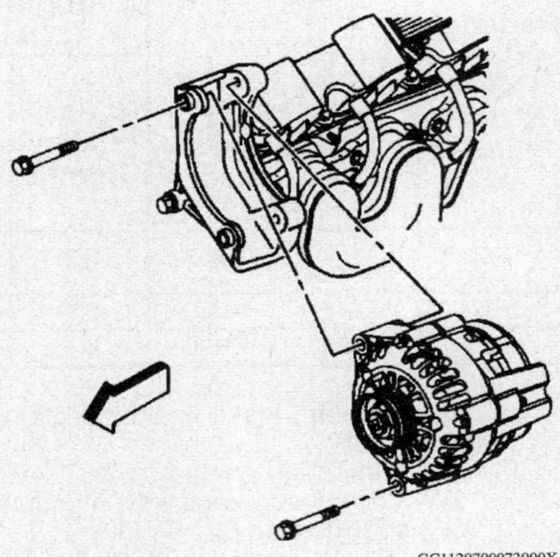

Fig. 1 Alternator removal

STARTER

REPLACE

1. Raise and support vehicle.
2. Disconnect HO2S electrical connectors.
3. Remove takedown pipe flange nuts.
4. Remove intermediate pipe to rear pipe mounting bolts.
5. Remove takedown pipe bracket front exhaust hanger bolts.
6. Remove rear intermediate exhaust pipes rear exhaust hanger bolts.
7. Remove intermediate pipe.
8. Remove intermediate pipe rear HO2S.
9. Record starter motor wiring orientation, then remove nuts and disconnect electrical connections.
10. Remove starter motor mounting bolts while supporting starter motor.
11. Remove starter motor.
12. Reverse procedure to install, noting the following:
    a. **Torque** starter motor mounting bolts to 37 ft. lbs.
    b. **Torque** S-terminal mounting nut to 35 inch lbs.
    c. **Torque** battery cable mounting nuts to 11 ft. lbs.

ALTERNATOR

REPLACE

1. Disconnect regulator electrical connector and battery to alternator terminal.
2. Release accessory drive belt tensioner.
3. Remove accessory drive belt from alternator pulley.
4. Remove alternator mounting bolts, **Fig. 1.**
5. Remove alternator.
6. Reverse procedure to install, noting the following:

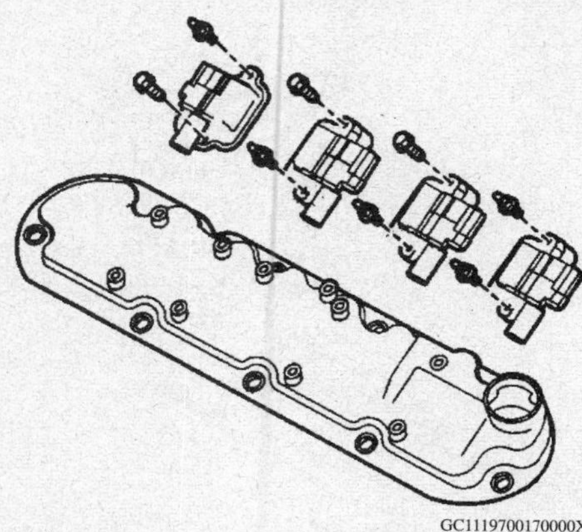

Fig. 2 Coil pack removal. 1998

a. **Torque** alternator mounting bolts to 37 ft. lbs.
b. **Torque** battery terminal nut to 10 ft. lbs.
c. **Torque** battery cable bolt to 11 ft. lbs.

COIL PACK

REPLACE

1. Remove fuel rail cover.
2. Disconnect ignition coil harness electrical connector.
3. Disconnect spark plug wires at ignition coils.
4. Remove ignition coil mounting bolts, **Figs. 2 and 3.**
5. Remove ignition coils.
6. Reverse procedure to install. **Torque** coil mounting bolts to 106 inch lbs.

IGNITION LOCK

REPLACE

1. Apply parking brake and remove console.
2. Remove instrument panel accessory trim plate.
3. Remove driver's knee bolster trim panel.
4. Record routing of ignition switch lock cylinder wire wraps around switch bezel.
5. Remove ignition switch lock cylinder electrical connector from mounting tab.
6. Disconnect lock cylinder electrical connector.
7. Insert key and turn to run position.
8. Depress and hold ignition lock cylinder mounting tab located on righthand lower side of switch, using suitable flat-bladed screwdriver, **Fig. 4.**
9. Pull to remove ignition lock cylinder.
10. Remove ignition switch bezel. Carefully pull to unsnap it.
11. Reverse procedure to install, noting the following:
    a. Wrap ignition switch wire around base of switch bezel as in original fashion.
    b. Align bezel slots to cylinder pins and push to secure in place.
    c. Press cylinder into place and listen for retaining tab to produce definite click.

IGNITION SWITCH

REPLACE

1. Remove ignition lock cylinder as outlined under "Ignition Lock, Replace."
2. Remove hazard warning switch wiring harness from ignition switch retainer.
3. Disconnect ignition switch electrical connectors.
4. **On models equipped with automatic transmission,** disconnect park lock cable from ignition switch using suitable screwdriver to depress retaining tab, **Fig. 5.**
5. **On all models,** remove ignition switch mounting bolts.
6. Remove ignition switch.
7. Reverse procedure to install. **Torque** ignition switch mounting bolts to 49 inch lbs.

CLUTCH START SWITCH

REPLACE

1. Disconnect clutch start switch electrical connector.
2. Insert feeler gauge between switch and clutch pedal bracket to release switch tab.
3. Remove clutch start switch by lifting slightly then pulling.
4. Reverse procedure to install.

NEUTRAL SAFETY SWITCH

REPLACE

1. Raise and support vehicle.
2. Disconnect HO2S connectors.
3. Remove exhaust takedown pipe flange nuts.
4. Remove intermediate pipe to rear pipe mounting bolts.
5. Remove takedown pipe bracket front exhaust hanger bolts.
6. Remove rear intermediate exhaust pipe rear exhaust hanger bolts.
7. Remove intermediate pipe.
8. Remove intermediate pipe rear HO2S.
9. Shift transmission to Neutral position.
10. Remove transmission shift control cable bracket to transmission nuts.
11. Disconnect transmission shift control cable from transmission range selector lever. **Rod end guide tubes cannot endure much abuse.**
12. Position transmission shift cable and bracket aside.
13. Disconnect neutral safety switch electrical connectors.
14. Remove mounting nut and range selector shift lever using suitable wrench on manual shaft flats to prevent rotation.
15. Ensure transmission is still in neutral.
16. Remove neutral safety switch mounting bolts.
17. Slide switch off manual shaft.
18. Reverse procedure to install, noting the following:
    a. Install switch alignment tool No. J41364-A, or equivalent, to neutral safety switch.

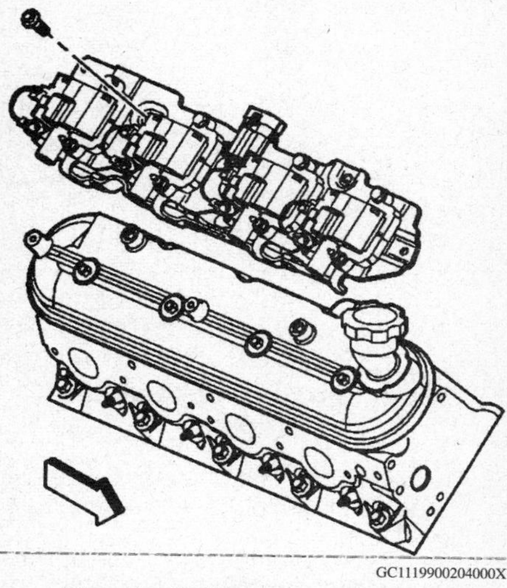

Fig. 3 Coil pack removal. 1999–2002

    b. Align two lower slots on switch with two lower tabs on tool.
    c. Turn tool until its upper pin aligns with slot on top of switch.
    d. Ensure transmission is still in neutral.
    e. Ensure switch hub flats align with those on shaft, then install switch and tool onto manual shaft until switch mounting bracket meets transmission case mounting bosses.
    f. **Torque** switch mounting bolts to 20 ft. lbs.
    g. Remove alignment tool.
    h. **Torque** range selector lever nut to 15 ft. lbs.

HEADLAMP SWITCH

REPLACE

Refer to "Multi-Function Switch, Replace" for headlamp switch replacement procedure.

STOP LIGHT SWITCH

REPLACE

1. Remove instrument panel lower trim panel.
2. Disconnect stop lamp switch electrical connectors.
3. Remove stop lamp switch.
4. Reverse procedure to install, noting the following:
    a. While keeping brake pedal depressed, insert switch into retainer until switch body has seated.
    b. Listen for clicks as threaded portion of switch travels through retainer.
    c. Slowly pull brake pedal fully rearward until clicks have stopped. Switch will move in retainer and self-adjust.

MULTI-FUNCTION SWITCH

REPLACE

1. Release tilt wheel lever locking tab

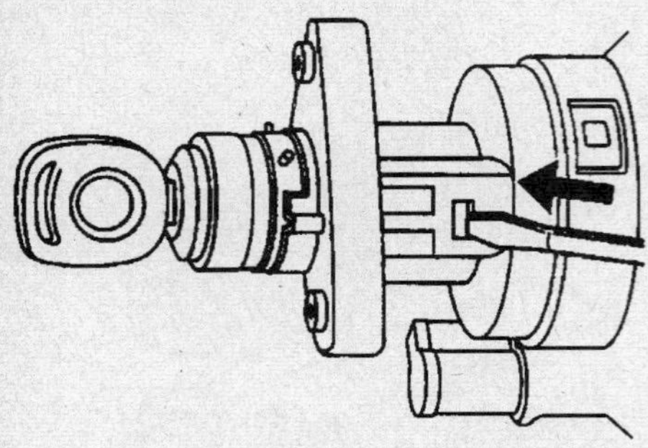

Fig. 4 Ignition lock cylinder removal

using suitable small screwdriver and slide lever straight out of steering column.
2. Remove steering wheel as outlined under "Steering Wheel, Replace."
3. Remove driver's side knee bolster trim panel.
4. Remove upper and lower steering column covers.
5. Disconnect multi-function turn signal switch electrical connectors.
6. Release upper and lower retaining clips.
7. Slide multi-function turn signal switch away from steering column lock module.
8. Reverse procedure to install.

TURN SIGNAL SWITCH

REPLACE

Refer to "Multi-Function Switch, Replace" for procedure.

DIMMER SWITCH

REPLACE

1. Remove instrument panel cluster.
2. Disconnect electrical connectors at instrument panel dimmer switch and driver information center switch.
3. Remove mounting screws and instrument panel cluster bezel.
4. Remove mounting screws and instrument panel dimmer switch.
5. Reverse procedure to install.

STEERING WHEEL

REPLACE

REMOVAL

1. Remove driver's air bag module as outlined under "Passive Restraint Systems."
2. Disconnect steering column horn wiring harness.
3. Disconnect steering column ground wire.
4. Remove and discard steering wheel set nut.
5. Install steering wheel puller and legs tool Nos. J1859-A and J42120, or equivalents, **Fig. 6.**
6. Tighten puller center screw against steering column shaft until wheel slides off shaft.

INSTALLATION

1. Install steering wheel onto column.
2. Install new steering wheel set nut.
3. **Torque** steering wheel set nut to 30 ft. lbs.
4. Connect horn electrical connector.
5. Install air bag as outlined under "Passive Restraint Systems."

INSTRUMENT CLUSTER

REPLACE

1. Remove instrument panel upper trim pad.
2. **On models equipped with Head Up Display (HUD),** carefully lift HUD electrical harness from between cluster and display, then disconnect electrical connector.
3. **On all models,** remove Instrument Panel Cluster (IPC) to steering column bracket mounting screws.
4. Lift rear of IPC slightly to release locator tab, then lift IPC to access and disconnect electrical connectors.
5. Remove IPC.
6. Reverse procedure to install, ensuring cluster retaining tab is properly positioned to steering column bracket.

RADIO

REPLACE

1. Remove front floor kick-up panel.
2. Remove instrument panel electrical center cover.
3. Remove instrument panel electrical center RDO/CD Mini-Fuse No. 5 fuse.
4. Remove console.
5. Remove instrument panel accessory trim plate.
6. Remove screws mounting radio control to instrument panel center support bracket.
7. Remove radio control from center support bracket enough to access rear electrical connectors.
8. Disconnect electrical, audio and coaxial connectors.
9. Remove radio control.
10. Reverse procedure to install.

WIPER MOTOR

REPLACE

1. Remove wiper arm assemblies.
2. Remove air inlet screen.
3. Remove wiper motor module.
4. Disconnect wiper transmission linkage from crank arm using linkage separator tool No. J39232, or equivalent.
5. Remove three wiper motor to wiper motor module mounting screws.
6. Remove wiper motor.
7. Reverse procedure to install, noting the following:
   a. Install motor into module.
   b. Connect linkage to crank arm using linkage installer tool No. J39529, or equivalent.

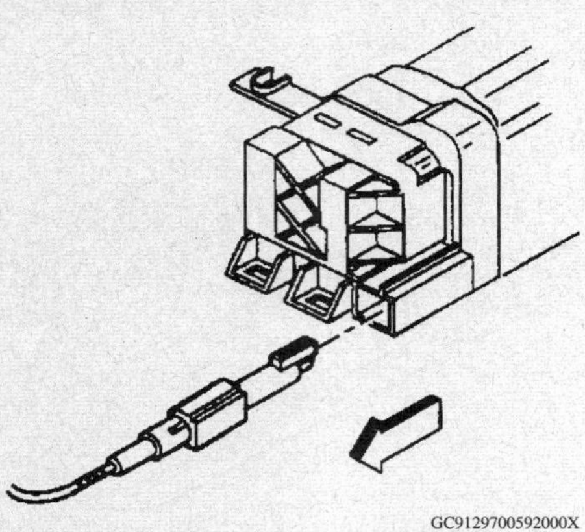

Fig. 5 Park lock cable removal

WIPER SWITCH

REPLACE

1. Remove tilt wheel lever as outlined under "Steering Columns."
2. Remove driver's side knee bolster trim panel.
3. Remove upper and lower steering column covers.
4. Disconnect wiring harness electrical connector.
5. Release upper and lower mounting clips, then slide wiper washer switch from steering column lock module.
6. Reverse procedure to install.

WIPER TRANSMISSION

REPLACE

1. Remove wiper arm assemblies.
2. Remove air inlet screen.
3. Remove wiper motor module.
4. Remove mounting bolts and righthand wiper transmission from linkage.
5. Disconnect wiper transmission linkage from module using linkage separator tool No. J39232, or equivalent.
6. Remove mounting bolts and lefthand wiper transmission from linkage.
7. Reverse procedure to install. Connect linkage to crank arm using linkage installer tool No. J39529, or equivalent.

BLOWER MOTOR

REPLACE

1. Remove front floor kick-up panel.
2. Remove passenger floor hush panel.
3. Disconnect blower motor electrical connectors.
4. Remove cooling tube.
5. Remove blower motor to evaporator and heater core module mounting screws.
6. Remove blower motor and fan.
7. Reverse procedure to install.

HEATER CORE

REPLACE

1. Evacuate air conditioning system refrigerant as outlined under "Air Conditioning."
2. Drain coolant into suitable container.
3. Remove battery and heat shield.

4. Remove intake manifold.
5. Remove heater pipe to dash panel bracket nut.
6. Position heater pipe bracket aside.
7. Remove heater pipe to core mounting bolt.
8. Cap or plug heater pipe and core to prevent contamination and spillage.
9. Remove accumulator hose to evaporator mounting bolt.
10. Disconnect evaporator accumulator hose and tube-rear. Cap or plug air conditioning lines.
11. Remove evaporator and HVAC module drain tube from module.
12. Remove floor console.
13. Remove instrument panel accessory trim plate.
14. Remove glove compartment.
15. Remove righthand hush panel.
16. Remove driver's side knee bolster trim panel.
17. Remove lefthand hush panel.
18. Remove instrument panel upper trim pad.
19. Remove instrument cluster to steering column bracket mounting screws.
20. Position cluster to allow room for HVAC module removal.
21. Remove lefthand side window defroster lower outlet duct.
22. **On models equipped with Automatic Temperature Control (ATC),** remove inside air temperature sensor aspirator duct and muffler.
23. **On all models,** disconnect Daytime Running Lamp (DRL) sensor electrical connector from lefthand side of windshield defroster duct.
24. Disconnect temperature valve actuator electrical connector.
25. Remove instrument panel center support bracket.
26. Remove ignition switch housing bracket.
27. Remove mounting screws and lefthand floor air outlet duct.
28. Remove lefthand rear floor air outlet duct by rotating it 90° clockwise.
29. Remove righthand side window defroster lower outlet.
30. Remove passenger's air bag module bracket and knee bolster bracket.
31. **On models equipped with ATC,** disconnect sunload sensor electrical connector from righthand side of windshield defroster duct.
32. **On all models,** remove mounting screws and righthand floor air outlet duct.
33. Pull front floor carpet away from righthand side of floor tunnel.
34. Remove righthand rear floor air outlet duct by rotating 90° counterclockwise.
35. Remove blower motor.
36. Disconnect instrument panel vacuum harness from HVAC module harness.
37. Disconnect vacuum electric solenoid electrical connector.

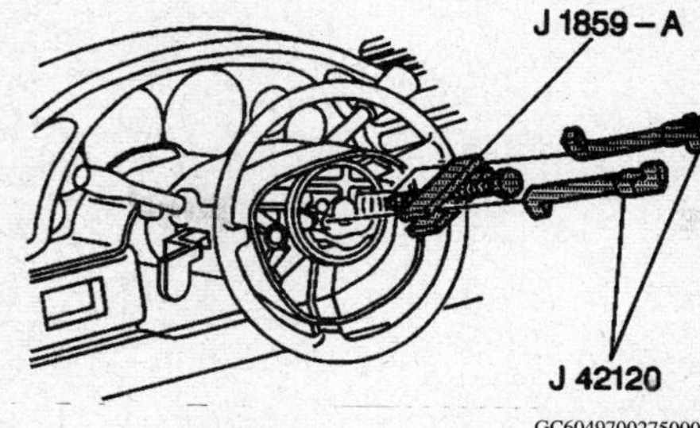

Fig. 6 Steering wheel removal

38. Remove mounting screws and windshield defroster duct.
39. Position air conditioning refrigerant lines to ease removal of HVAC module retaining and sealing nuts from dash panel, as required.
40. Remove instrument panel upper support beam HVAC module mounting screws.
41. Carefully remove HVAC module.
42. Remove and discard seals at module air inlet, drain and plumbing seals.
43. Remove mounting screws and heater core outlet cover.
44. Remove mounting screws and heater core cover.
45. Remove and discard heater core cover cavity, whistle and permagum seals.
46. Remove and discard heater core outer seal.
47. Remove heater core retaining clamp screw, clamp and pipe retainer clamp screw.
48. Remove heater core.
49. Remove and discard heater core lower, center, upper and side seals at HVAC module lower case.
50. Release retaining tab using suitable flat-bladed screwdriver and open up heater core pipe retainer clamp, then remove pipes clamp.
51. Reverse procedure to install, noting the following:
    a. Install new gaskets, O-rings and seals.
    b. **Torque** heater core cover and outlet mounting screws to 14 inch lbs.
    c. Ensure cutouts on dash mat are properly aligned so air inlet, drain and plumbing seals are seated directly against dash panel, not dash mat.
    d. Ensure dash panel drain opening aligns with HVAC module drain.
    e. Coat new refrigerant line O-rings with suitable 525 viscosity refrigerant oil.

EVAPORATOR CORE

REPLACE

1. Remove HVAC module as outlined under "Heater Core, Replace."
2. Release vacuum harness retainers on HVAC case below air inlet housing.
3. Remove upper heater evaporator module screws.
4. Separate upper and lower heater evaporator module halves.
5. Remove and discard seal.
6. Remove evaporator core.
7. Remove and discard lower, side and upper evaporator core seals.
8. Remove and discard water core filter.
9. Reverse procedure to install.

TECHNICAL SERVICE BULLETINS

CHIME SOUNDS WHEN KEY IS REMOVED FROM IGNITION

1998–99 Models

On some of these models, the key warning chime continues to sound after the ignition key has been removed from the ignition lock cylinder. The automatic power door locks will not lock the doors when the key is removed from the ignition lock cylinder and the warning chime is sounding. In addition, there may be an intermittent operation of the passive keyless entry system, the steering column lock or the retracting feature of the memory power seat option when exiting the vehicle.

This condition may be caused by the actuator located in the ignition lock cylinder sticking after the key is removed.

To correct this condition, proceed as follows:

1. Remove ignition lock cylinder for instrument panel as outlined under "Ignition Lock, Replace."
2. With key installed, hold lock cylinder to determine what type of actuator is being used, **Fig. 7.**
3. Hold lock cylinder vertically and remove key, **Fig. 8.**
4. When key is removed, actuator should drop approximately 3/16 inch.
5. Repeat previous step several times.
6. If actuator does not drop down, replace complete lock assembly.
7. **On models equipped with early design actuator,** if actuator does drop down, replace actuator with new design actuator (P/N 12450483).
8. **On all models,** replace actuator as follows:
    a. Install key in lock and grasp actuator end with suitable pair of small long needle nose pliers and pull firmly.
    b. With key still in lock, install new actuator by aligning actuator shaft with lock cylinder opening and pushing actuator into place.
    c. Ensure correct actuator operation by performing test as previously described.

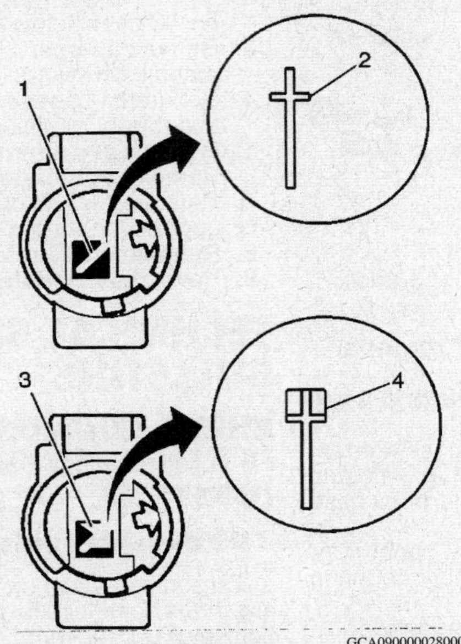

Fig. 7 Ignition lock cylinder actuator identification. 1998-99

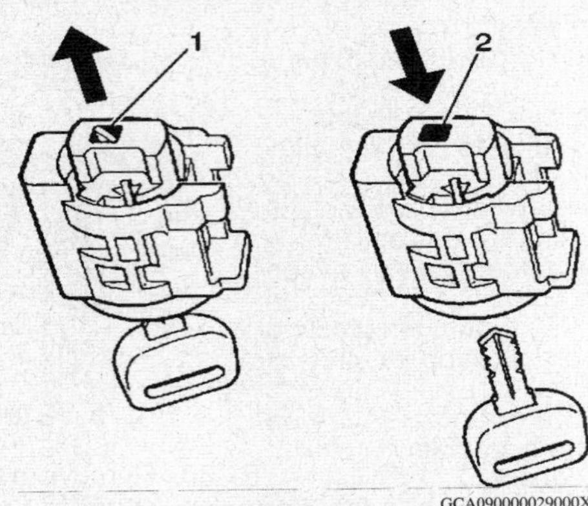

Fig. 8 Lock cylinder testing. 1998-99

5.7L Engine

NOTE: On Air Bag Equipped Models, Refer To "Air Bag System Precautions" Located In The Front Of This Manual For System Disarming & Arming Procedures.

NOTE: Refer To "Computer Relearn Procedures" Located In The Front Of This Manual When Battery Power To The Computer Has Been Interrupted.

NOTE: Prior To Performing Any Service Operations Listed In This Section, Consult The "Technical Service Bulletins" Section For Related Information.

INDEX

PRECAUTIONS

FUEL SYSTEM PRESSURE RELIEF

Failure to relieve system pressure prior to disconnecting fuel system components may cause fire or personal injury.

1. Disconnect and isolate battery ground cable.
2. Remove fuel tank filler cap to release fuel tank pressure.
3. Remove lefthand fuel rail cover.
4. Prior to disconnecting fuel line, position shop towel over fitting.
5. Connect pressure gauge tool No. J34730-1A, or equivalent, to pressure tap on fuel rail.
6. Position bleed hose into suitable container.
7. Slowly relieve fuel system pressure.

BATTERY GROUND CABLE

Prior to service, disconnect battery ground cable and isolate as required.

COMPRESSION PRESSURE

When measuring compression, lowest cylinder must be within 70% of the highest cylinder with a minimum pressure of 100 psi. Compression test results will fall into one of the following categories:

1. Normally, compression builds up quickly and evenly to specifications on each cylinder.
2. If piston rings are faulty, compression will be low on first stroke, then build up on following strokes but will not reach specifications. Improvement is considerable with addition of approximately three squirts oil.
3. If valves are faulty, compression will be low on first stroke and will not tend to build up on following strokes. It will not improve much with addition of oil.
4. Ensure battery is fully charged.
5. Bring engine to operating temperature.
6. Disconnect electrical connector at crankshaft ignition timing sensor.
7. Disable fuel injection system.
8. Remove spark plugs.
9. Ensure throttle is wide open.
10. Install compression gauge tool No. J38722, or equivalent.
11. Crank engine through four complete compression strokes, then record results for each cylinder.

ENGINE MOUNT

REPLACE

1. Remove alternator from accessory mount bracket.
2. Remove windshield washer reservoir.
3. Disconnect coolant switch electrical connector and position wiring aside.
4. Disconnect headlamp electrical connector and position wiring aside.
5. Support engine using engine support tool Nos. J41803 and J28467-B, or equivalent.
6. Raise and support vehicle.

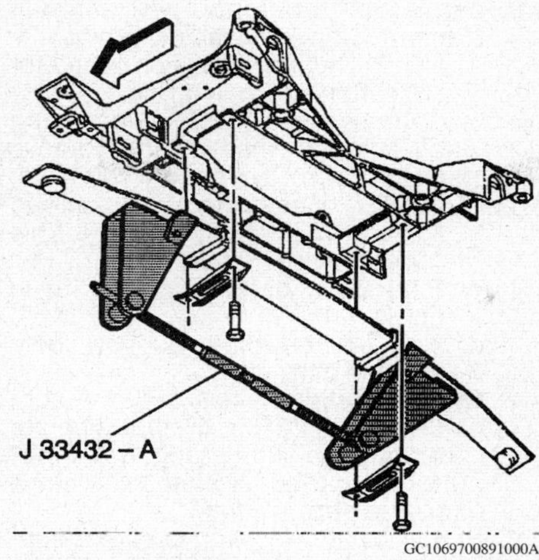

Fig. 1 Transverse leaf spring compression

7. Remove front wheels.
8. Remove tie rod end nuts.
9. Remove tie rod ends from steering knuckles using separator tool No. J42188, or equivalent.
10. Remove stabilizer bar bolts and straps.
11. Disconnect stabilizer from cradle.
12. Remove power steering cooler bolts.
13. Disconnect power steering cooler from cradle and position it upward.
14. Remove power steering gear from cradle and position it upward.
15. Compress spring using transverse leaf spring compressor tool No. J33432-A, or equivalent, **Fig. 1.**
16. Remove shock absorber lower mounting bolts.
17. Loosen, but do not remove, lower ball joint nuts.
18. Separate lower ball joints using separator tool No. J42188, or equivalent.
19. Remove tool and ball joint nuts.
20. Disconnect crossmember electrical connectors.
21. Disconnect cradle electrical harnesses.
22. Remove brake pressure valve modulator valve bracket bolts, then position valve and bracket away from crossmember.
23. Remove motor mount to cradle nuts, **Fig. 2.**
24. Support cradle using suitable transmission jack, or equivalent.
25. Remove mounting nuts and cradle.
26. Remove upper engine mount nut, **Fig. 3.**
27. Remove engine mount.
28. Remove engine block bolts and motor mount bracket.
29. Reverse procedure to install. Tighten mounting bolts, nuts and screws to specifications.

ENGINE

REPLACE

1. Raise and support vehicle.
2. Drain coolant into suitable container.
3. Lower vehicle.
4. Recover air conditioning refrigerant charge.
5. Disconnect electrical connectors at IAT and MAF sensors.
6. Disconnect air intake duct fuel pressure regulator purge tube.
7. Position air intake duct and air cleaner forward.
8. Remove radiator as outlined under "Radiator, Replace."
9. **On 1998 models equipped with front-mounted Electronic Brake Control Module and Brake Pressure Modulator Valve (EBTCM/BPMV) and all 1999–2002 models,** proceed as follows:
    a. Remove EBTCM/BPMV and bracket.
    b. Position brake pipes aside, as required.
    c. Cap and plug lines.
10. **On all models,** remove serpentine belt as outlined under "Serpentine Drive Belt."
11. Remove lefthand fuel line from connector at front of firewall. Cap and plug fittings and openings.
12. Remove engine appearance covers.
13. Disconnect fuel lines at fuel rail. Cap and plug fittings and openings.
14. Disconnect radiator hoses and heater hoses at water pump.
15. Disconnect the following electrical connectors:
    a. Fuel injectors.
    b. Ignition coil main connectors.
    c. EVAP solenoid.
    d. Electric throttle motor.
    e. Throttle position sensor.
    f. ECT sensor.
    g. Air conditioning compressor.
    h. Alternator.
16. Remove alternator rear bracket bolts and bracket.
17. Remove alternator mounting bolts then the alternator as outlined under "Alternator, Replace" in "Electrical" section.
18. Disconnect brake booster vacuum hose.
19. Remove steering intermediate shaft to steering gear bolt.
20. Disconnect steering intermediate shaft from steering gear and position it to lefthand onto frame rail.
21. Disconnect lefthand exhaust manifold AIR hose.
22. Raise and support vehicle, then remove front tires and wheels.
23. Disconnect and unclip intermediate exhaust pipes' HO2S electrical connectors.
24. Remove intermediate exhaust pipes.
25. Remove mounting bolts and closeout panel.
26. Disconnect starter electrical connectors and wiring.
27. Remove starter mounting bolts, then the starter as outlined under "Starter, Replace" in "Electrical" section.
28. Disconnect righthand and rear engine block wiring harness clips.
29. Disconnect oil level, CKP and righthand HO2S sensors electrical connectors.

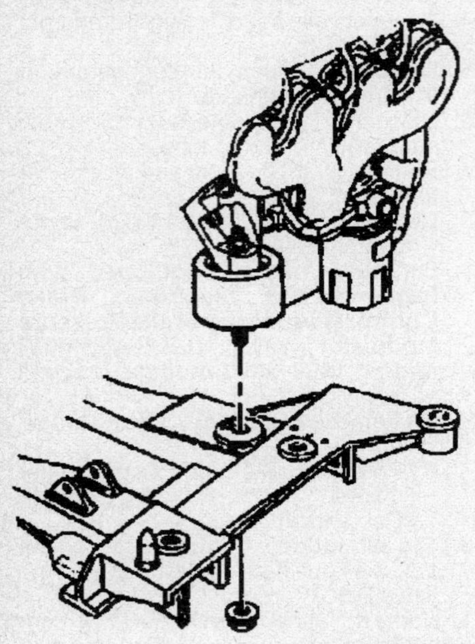

Fig. 2 Engine mount to cradle removal

30. Remove mounting bolt and air conditioning compressor hose.
31. Disconnect engine oil temperature and lefthand HO2S sensors electrical connectors.
32. Remove mounting bolts and straps, then disconnect front stabilizer bar from cradle.
33. Disconnect electric cooling fans' electrical connectors and harness.
34. Slide up and remove electric cooling fans.
35. Loosen nuts and remove tie rod ends from steering knuckles using ball joint separator tool No. J42188, or equivalent.
36. Disconnect ABS electrical, EVO and RTD connectors clips from cradle.
37. Remove lower shock absorber mounting bolts.
38. Compress and remove front transverse spring using transverse spring compressor tool No. J33432-A, or equivalent, **Fig. 1.**
39. **On models equipped with automatic transmission,** proceed as follows:
    a. Disconnect fluid cooler lines at bellhousing junction.
    b. Disconnect cooler pipe clamps from front and rear of engine oil pan.
    c. Disconnect cooler pipes from radiator.
    d. Remove two plugs in driveline support.
    e. Install M10 1.5 × 2.166 inches, or longer bolt, in each plug location, **Fig. 4,** and **torque** to 26 ft. lbs.
    f. Remove bellhousing lower inspection cover.
    g. Position transmission flexplate hub collar downward to access and loosen mounting bolt.
    h. Unclip wiring harness from engine and position it to driveline.
40. **On models equipped with manual transmission,** proceed as follows:
    a. Unclip hydraulic clutch actuator hose from bellhousing clip.
    b. Depress white circular release ring on actuator hose using hydraulic clutch line separator tool No. J36221, or equivalent, while pulling lightly on master cylinder hose. This will separate two portions.
    c. Plug both open hydraulic hose ends.
    d. Remove driveline support bellhousing bolts.
41. **On all models,** install driveline support tool No. J42203, or equivalent, to closeout panel flange, **Fig. 5. Do not support engine weight with driveline line support tool.**
42. Slowly lower vehicle on to engine support table tools Nos. J39580 and No. J39580-500, or equivalents.
43. Remove front and rear cradle nuts by hand.
44. Partially raise vehicle.
45. Remove and position AIR tube bracket bolt to access and remove lefthand rear ground strap at cylinder head.
46. Disconnect following electrical connectors:
    a. Engine oil pressure sensor.
    b. Camshaft position sensor.
    c. MAP sensor.
    d. Knock sensor.
    e. Ground on rear of lefthand head.
    f. All remaining electrical connections.
47. Remove front driveline support bolts.
48. Pry engine loose from driveline using suitable flat-bladed screwdriver, between edge of driveline support and bellhousing.
49. Slowly and carefully pull engine away from driveshaft.
50. Slowly raise vehicle as soon as input shaft clears bellhousing.
51. Slide engine and cradle forward to clear driveshaft spline.
52. **Ensure wiring harnesses are free and clear,** then carefully raise vehicle completely off engine and cradle.
53. Remove power steering pump using pulley removal tool No. J25034-B, or equivalent.
54. Remove mounting bolts, then position power steering pump and reservoir aside.
55. Remove air conditioning belt, mounting bolts, nut, stud and air conditioning compressor.
56. Remove exhaust manifolds' mounting bolts and AIR tube.
57. Install engine lifting brackets tool No. J41798, or equivalent.
58. Install suitable lifting device to lifting brackets.
59. Mark locations, disconnect wires and remove spark plugs.
60. Remove cradle mount nuts and engine.
61. Reverse procedure to install, noting the following:
    a. **Only use hand tools to install new engine cradle nuts.**
    b. **On models equipped with automatic transmission,** tighten flexplate hub collar bolt by hand after bellhousing to driveline support bolts have been tightened.
    c. After running engine to operating temperature and allowing to cool to room temperature, tighten hub collar bolt to specifications.
    d. **On all models,** tighten mounting bolts and nuts to specifications.

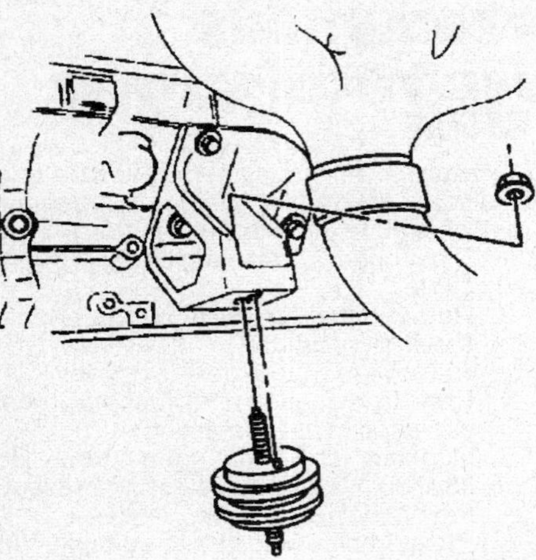

Fig. 3 Upper engine mount removal

INTAKE MANIFOLD

REPLACE

1. Raise and support vehicle.
2. Drain cooling system into suitable container and lower vehicle.
3. Disconnect IAT and MAF sensors electrical connectors.
4. Disconnect air intake duct fuel regulator purge line.
5. Remove air intake duct and air cleaner.
6. Remove fuel rail covers.
7. Disconnect fuel rail lines. Cap and plug open fittings.
8. Remove vacuum and PCV hoses.
9. Remove throttle body coolant outlet hose.
10. Disconnect fuel injector and knock sensor electrical connectors.
11. Disconnect remaining intake manifold electrical connectors.
12. Remove intake manifold bolts and fuel rail stop bracket.
13. Remove lefthand and righthand valve covers' PCV valve pipe.
14. Remove throttle body coolant air bleed hose.
15. Remove throttle body heater outlet hose.
16. Remove intake manifold and gaskets.
17. Remove manifold to cylinder head gaskets from intake manifold.
18. Reverse procedure to install, noting the following:
    a. Install new intake manifold to cylinder head gaskets.
    b. Apply threadlocker P/N 12345383, or equivalent, to intake manifold bolt threads.
    c. **Torque** intake manifold bolts to 44 inch lbs., in sequence, **Fig. 6.**

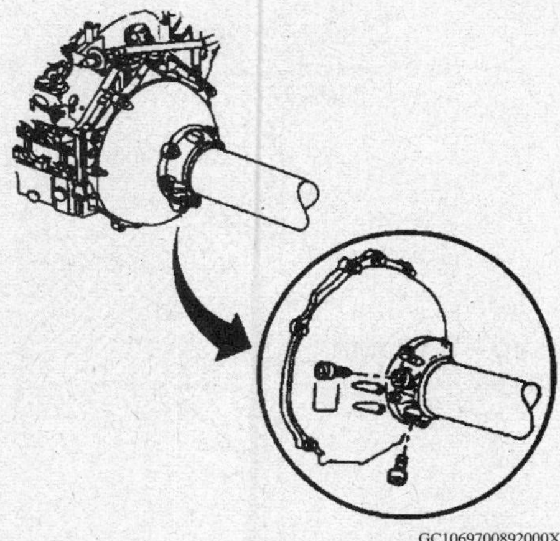

Fig. 4 Propeller shaft support bolt installation

d. Final **torque** bolts to 89 inch lbs., in sequence.
e. Lubricate MAP sensor grommet with suitable clean engine oil before installing.
f. Install new fuel injector O-rings lubricated with suitable clean engine oil.

EXHAUST MANIFOLD

REPLACE

LEFTHAND SIDE

1. Raise and support vehicle.
2. Remove lefthand intermediate exhaust pipe flange nuts from exhaust manifold studs.
3. Disconnect HO2S electrical connector and remove HO2S.
4. Lower vehicle and remove lefthand fuel rail cover.
5. Remove accessory drive belt as outlined under "Serpentine Drive Belt."
6. Remove alternator as outlined under "Alternator, Replace" in "Electrical" section.
7. Remove Secondary Air Injection (SAI) hoses.
8. Remove SAI pipe, bolts and gasket, then position aside.
9. Remove spark plug wires.
10. Remove spark plugs.
11. Remove No. 5 coil bolts and position aside.
12. Remove exhaust manifold and mounting bolts.
13. Reverse procedure to install, noting the following:
    a. Install new exhaust manifold gasket.
    b. Apply threadlocker P/N 12345493, or equivalent, to exhaust manifold bolt threads.
    c. **Torque** exhaust manifold bolts to 11 ft. lbs., beginning with center two bolts, then alternate from side to side and work toward outside bolts.
    d. Final **Torque** to 18 ft. lbs., in sequence.
    e. Bend over exposed edge of exhaust manifold gasket at rear of lefthand cylinder head using suitable flat punch.

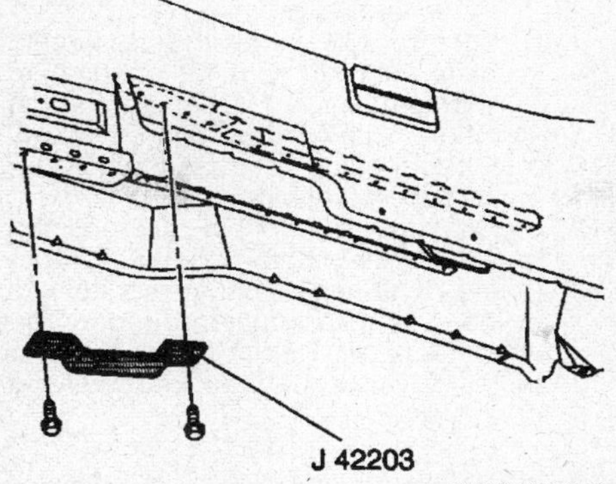

Fig. 5 Driveline support tool installation

f. Install AIR pipe and gasket and **torque** to 15 ft. lbs.

RIGHTHAND SIDE

1. Raise and support vehicle.
2. Remove intermediate exhaust pipe nuts from exhaust manifold studs.
3. Remove HO2S.
4. Lower vehicle.
5. Remove righthand exhaust manifold AIR pipe, bolts and gasket.
6. Remove spark plug wires from spark plugs.
7. Remove engine oil dipstick.
8. Remove mounting bolt and dipstick tube.
9. Remove exhaust manifold and mounting bolts.
10. Reverse procedure to install, noting the following:
    a. Install new exhaust manifold gasket.
    b. Apply threadlocker P/N 12345493, or equivalent, to exhaust manifold bolt threads.
    c. **Torque** exhaust manifold bolts to 11 ft. lbs., beginning with center two bolts, then alternate from side to side and work toward outside bolts.
    d. Final **torque** to 18 ft. lbs., in sequence.
    e. Bend over exposed edge of exhaust manifold gasket at front of righthand cylinder head using suitable flat punch.
    f. Install AIR pipe and gasket and **torque** to 15 ft. lbs.

CYLINDER HEAD

REPLACE

This procedure has been revised by a Technical Service Bulletin.

LEFTHAND SIDE

Removal

1. Remove valve cover, rocker arms, pedestal and pushrods.
2. Remove lefthand exhaust manifold as outlined under "Exhaust Manifold, Replace."
3. Remove intake manifold as outlined under "Intake Manifold, Replace."
4. Remove vapor vent pipe.

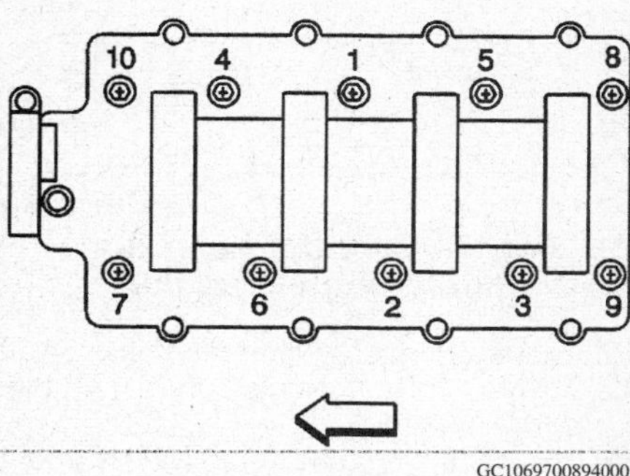

Fig. 6 Intake manifold bolt tightening sequence

5. Remove power steering pump pulley using pulley puller tool No. J25034-B, or equivalent.
6. Remove power steering pump mounting bolts.
7. Remove power steering reservoir bracket bolts, then position pump and reservoir aside.
8. Remove mounting bolts and lower accessory mounting bracket.
9. Remove cylinder head rear ground wire bolt.
10. Remove spark plugs.
11. Remove and discard cylinder head bolts.
12. Remove cylinder head.

Installation

1. Clean cylinder head bolt holes using compressed air.
2. Inspect cylinder head locating pins for proper installation.
3. Install new lefthand cylinder head gasket onto locating pins. When properly installed, tab on lefthand cylinder head gasket will be located left of center or closer to front of engine.
4. **On 1999–2002 models,** ensure THIS SIDE UP and engine displacement are visible.
5. **On all models,** install cylinder head onto locating pins and gasket.
6. Install M11 cylinder head bolts.
7. Apply threadlocker P/N 12345382, or equivalent, to threads of M8 cylinder head bolts.
8. Install M8 cylinder head bolts.
9. Tighten cylinder head bolts as follows:
    a. **Torque** M11 cylinder head bolts 1–10 to 22 ft. lbs., in sequence, **Fig. 7.**
    b. Tighten M11 cylinder head bolts 1–10 an additional 90° in sequence.
    c. Final tighten M11 cylinder head bolts 1–8 an additional 90° in sequence.
    d. Final tighten M11 medium length cylinder head bolts 9 and 10 at front and rear of each head an additional 50° in sequence.
    e. **Torque** M8 inner cylinder head bolts 11–15 to 22 ft. lbs. beginning with center bolt 11, then alternating side to side while working outward.
10. Install spark plugs into cylinder head.
11. Install ground wire bolt into rear of cylinder head.

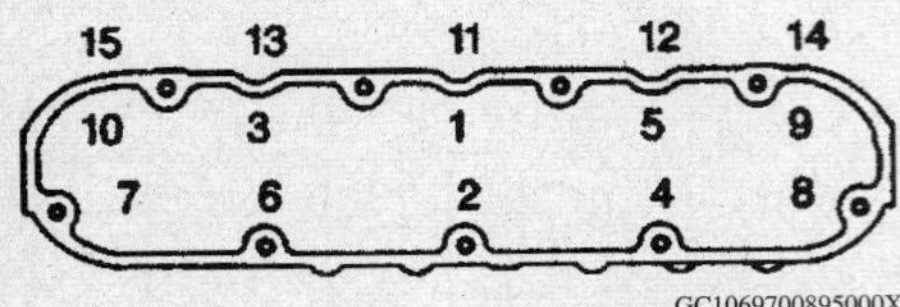

Fig. 7 Cylinder head bolt tightening sequence

12. Install accessory mounting bracket.
13. Install lower accessory mounting bracket bolts.
14. Install power steering reservoir bracket bolts.
15. Install power steering pump mounting bolts.
16. Install power steering pump pulley.
17. Install vapor vent pipe.
18. Install intake manifold as outlined under "Intake Manifold, Replace."
19. Install lefthand exhaust manifold to cylinder head as outlined under "Exhaust Manifold, Replace."
20. Install valve rocker arms, pedestal and pushrods.

RIGHTHAND SIDE

Removal

1. Remove valve rocker arms, pedestal and pushrods.
2. Remove righthand exhaust manifold as outlined under "Exhaust Manifold, Replace."
3. Remove intake manifold as outlined under "Intake Manifold, Replace."
4. Remove vapor vent pipe.
5. Remove spark plugs.
6. Remove and discard cylinder head bolts.
7. Remove cylinder head.

Installation

1. Clean cylinder head bolt holes using compressed air.
2. Inspect cylinder head locating pins for proper installation.
3. Install new righthand cylinder head gasket onto locating pins. When properly installed, tab on righthand cylinder head gasket will be located left of center or closer to front of engine.
4. **On 1999–2002 models,** ensure THIS SIDE UP and engine displacement are visible.
5. **On all models,** install cylinder head onto locating pins and gasket.
6. Install M11 cylinder head bolts.
7. Apply threadlocker P/N 12345382, or equivalent, to threads of M8 cylinder head bolts.
8. Install M8 cylinder head bolts.
9. Tighten cylinder head bolts as follows:
   a. **Torque** M11 cylinder head bolts 1–10 to 22 ft. lbs., in sequence, **Fig. 7.**
   b. Tighten M11 cylinder head bolts 1–10 an additional 90° in sequence.
   c. Final tighten M11 cylinder head bolts 1–8 an additional 90° in sequence.
   d. Final tighten M11 medium length cylinder head bolts 9 and 10 at front and rear of each head an additional 50° in sequence.
   e. **Torque** M8 inner cylinder head bolts 11–15 to 22 ft. lbs., beginning with center bolt 11, then alternating side to side while working outward.
10. Install spark plugs into cylinder head.
11. Install vapor vent pipe.
12. Install intake manifold as outlined under "Intake Manifold, Replace."
13. Install righthand exhaust manifold to cylinder head as outlined under "Exhaust Manifold, Replace."
14. Install valve rocker arms, pedestal and pushrods.

VALVE COVER

REPLACE

LEFTHAND SIDE

1. Remove lefthand fuel rail cover.
2. Disconnect fuel rail lines.
3. Disconnect electrical connectors at alternator and coolant temperature sensors.
4. Disconnect check valve secondary AIR hose.
5. Remove lefthand valve cover PCV valve pipe.
6. Disconnect ignition coils' spark plug wires.
7. Disconnect ignition coil main harness electrical connector.
8. Disconnect EVAP purge solenoid valve hoses.
9. Remove intake manifold EVAP purge solenoid.
10. Remove crankcase vent vacuum tube.
11. Remove valve rocker arm cover bolts and cover.
12. Remove and discard lefthand cover crankcase vent valve grommet.
13. Remove ignition coil wire harness.
14. Remove ignition coils and bolts.
15. Remove cover gasket and bolt grommets.
16. Discard gasket. Bolt grommets may be used again if not damaged.
17. Reverse procedure to install, noting the following:
   a. Install new cover gasket and PCV valve grommet.
   b. **Torque** valve cover mounting bolts to 108 inch lbs.
   c. **Torque** ignition coil mounting bolts to 108 inch lbs.

RIGHTHAND SIDE

1. Remove righthand fuel rail cover.
2. Remove exhaust manifold secondary AIR hose.
3. Disconnect check valve AIR hose.
4. Remove valve cover breather pipes PCV hoses.
5. Remove ignition coils' spark plug wires.
6. Disconnect ignition coil main harness electrical connector.
7. Remove ignition coil, bracket and bolts.
8. Remove valve rocker arm cover bolts and cover.
9. Remove oil fill cap and tube, if required. Discard tube.
10. Remove gasket and bolt grommets.

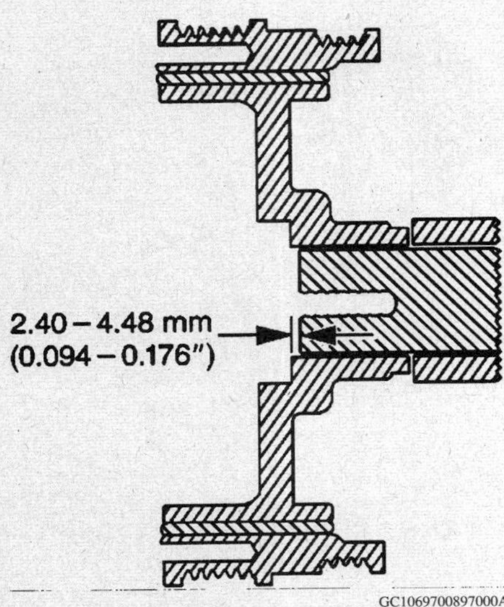

Fig. 8 Damper installed measurement

11. Discard gasket. Bolt grommets may be used again if not damaged.
12. Remove ignition coil bolts, wire harness and coils.
13. Reverse procedure to install, noting the following:
   a. Install new cover gasket.
   b. Install new oil fill tube, as required.
   c. **Torque** valve cover mounting bolts to 108 inch lbs.
   d. **Torque** ignition coil mounting bolts to 108 inch lbs.

VALVE ARRANGEMENT

FRONT TO REAR

All..............................I-E-I-E-I-E-I-E

VALVE CLEARANCE SPECIFICATIONS

This engine is equipped with hydraulic valve lash adjusters. No adjustment is required.

VALVE ADJUSTMENT

This engine is equipped with hydraulic valve lash adjusters. No adjustment is required.

ROCKER ARMS

REMOVAL

It is required to keep components in original order if they will be installed again.

1. Remove valve rocker arm bolts and arms.
2. Remove valve rocker arm pedestals.

INSTALLATION

When using valve train components over again, always install them into original location and position. Valve lash is net build. No valve adjustment is required.

1. Lubricate valve rocker arms with suitable clean engine oil.
2. Lubricate flange of valve rocker arm bolts with suitable clean engine oil.
3. Lubricate flange or washer surface of bolt that will contact valve rocker arm.
4. Install valve rocker arm pedestals.
5. Install rocker arms and bolts. Ensure pushrods seat properly to valve lifter sockets and in ends of rocker arms.
6. Turn crankshaft until number one piston is at top dead center of compression stroke. Cylinders 1, 3, 5 and 7 are lefthand in bank. Cylinders 2, 4, 6 and 8 are in righthand bank. In this position sprocket marks on crankshaft and camshaft will be aligned.
7. With engine in number one firing position, proceed as follows:
   a. **Torque** exhaust valve rocker arm bolts 1, 2, 7 and 8 to 22 ft. lbs.
   b. **Torque** intake valve rocker arm bolts 1, 3, 4 and 5 to 22 ft. lbs.
8. Rotate crankshaft 360° and proceed as follows:
   a. **Torque** exhaust valve rocker arm bolts 3, 4, 5 and 6 to 22 ft. lbs.
   b. **Torque** intake valve rocker arm bolts 2, 6, 7 and 8 to 22 ft. lbs.

PUSH RODS

REMOVAL

It is required to keep components in original order if they will be installed again.

1. Remove valve rocker arm bolts, arms and pedestals as outlined under "Rocker Arms."
2. Remove pushrods.

INSTALLATION

When using valve train components over again, always install them into original location and position. Valve lash is net build. No valve adjustment is required.

1. Lubricate valve rocker arms and pushrods with suitable clean engine oil.
2. Lubricate flange of valve rocker arm bolts with suitable clean engine oil.
3. Lubricate flange or washer surface of bolt that will contact valve rocker arm.
4. Install valve rocker arm pedestal.
5. Install rocker arms and bolts.
6. Install pushrods. Ensure pushrods seat properly to valve lifter sockets and in ends of rocker arms.
7. Turn crankshaft until number one piston is at top dead center of compression stroke. Cylinders 1, 3, 5 and 7 are lefthand in bank. Cylinders 2, 4, 6 and 8 are in righthand bank. In this position sprocket marks on crankshaft and camshaft will be aligned.
8. With engine in number one firing position, proceed as follows:
   a. **Torque** exhaust valve rocker arm bolts 1, 2, 7 and 8 to 22 ft. lbs.
   b. **Torque** intake valve rocker arm bolts 1, 3, 4 and 5 to 22 ft. lbs.
9. Rotate crankshaft 360° and proceed as follows:
   a. **Torque** exhaust valve rocker arm bolts 3, 4, 5 and 6 to 22 ft. lbs.

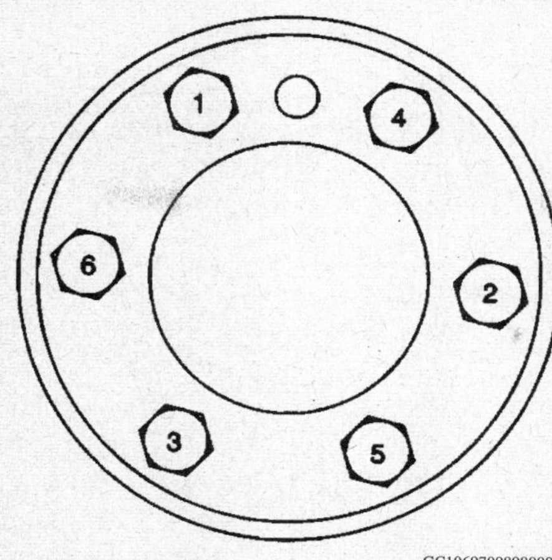

Fig. 9 Flywheel tightening sequence

   b. **Torque** intake valve rocker arm bolts 2, 6, 7 and 8 to 22 ft. lbs.

HYDRAULIC LIFTERS

REPLACE

1. Remove cylinder head as outlined under "Cylinder Head, Replace."
2. Remove valve lifter guide bolts.
3. Remove valve lifters and guide. If lifters stick in bores use valve lifter removal tool No. J3049-A, or equivalent, to remove them.
4. Remove guide valve lifters.
5. Organize or mark components so that they can be installed in original positions,
6. Reverse procedure to install, noting the following:
   a. Lubricate valve lifters and bores with suitable clean engine oil.
   b. Align lifters' and bores' flat sides.

CRANKSHAFT DAMPER

REPLACE

1. Release accessory drive belt tensioner and remove drive belt as outlined under "Serpentine Drive Belt."
2. Remove electronic brake control module from its bracket and position aside. Cap and plug open lines.
3. Remove power steering gear as outlined under "Power Steering Gear, Replace" in "Front Suspension & Steering."
4. Remove starter motor as outlined under "Starter, Replace" in "Electrical" section.
5. Remove power steering cooler mounting bolts and cooler from front crossmember, then position aside.
6. Release tensioner and remove air conditioning drive belt.
7. Install flywheel holding tool No. J42386, or equivalent, and flywheel mounting bolts. **Torque** mounting bolts to 37 ft. lbs.
8. Remove crankshaft damper bolt.
9. Mark crankshaft damper and end of crankshaft. Record damper installed position on crankshaft for installation. Also record location of any weights, which must return to original positions.
10. Remove crankshaft damper using crankshaft end protector and damper removal tool Nos. J41816 and J41816-2, or equivalents.
11. Reverse procedure to install, noting the following:
   a. Install damper using crankshaft balancer and sprocket installer tool No. J41665, or equivalent.
   b. **Torque** used crankshaft damper bolt to 240 ft. lbs.
   c. Remove bolt and measure for properly installed damper, **Fig. 8.**
   d. **Torque** new crankshaft damper bolt to 37 ft. lbs.
   e. Tighten bolt an additional 140°.

FRONT COVER

REPLACE

REMOVAL

1. Drain coolant into suitable container.
2. Disconnect air intake duct fuel regulator purge line.
3. Remove air intake duct and air cleaner.
4. Remove crankshaft damper as outlined under "Crankshaft Damper, Replace."
5. Remove water pump radiator and heater hoses.
6. Remove water pump mounting bolts, pump and gaskets.
7. Remove front cover bolts.
8. Remove front cover and gasket. **Avoid sliding front cover or gasket across oil pan gasket.**
9. Remove and discard crankshaft oil seal.

INSTALLATION

1. Apply .20 inch bead of GM silicone gasket P/N 12378190, or equivalent, to corner where oil pan meets engine block.
2. Install new gasket, front cover and mounting bolts to engine block. Tighten bolts hand tight.
3. Align cover alignment tool No. J41476, or equivalent, on front of crankshaft.
4. Install crankshaft damper bolt and hand tighten.
5. Hand tighten oil pan to cover bolts so cover properly positions itself at pan rail.
6. **Torque** front cover bolts to 18 ft. lbs.
7. Remove alignment tool.
8. Install crankshaft oil seal using oil seal installer tool No. J41478, or equivalent. **Do not lubricate oil seal sealing surface.**
9. Install water pump, gaskets and mounting bolts.
10. Install radiator and heater hoses to water pump.
11. Fill cooling system.
12. Install crankshaft damper as outlined under "Crankshaft Damper, Replace."
13. Install air intake duct and air cleaner.
14. Connect fuel regulator purge line to air intake duct.

REAR COVER

REPLACE

REMOVAL

1. Mark crankshaft end and flywheel for installation, then remove flywheel.
2. Remove engine rear cover mounting bolts and cover. Discard gasket.
3. Remove and discard crankshaft rear cover oil seal.

INSTALLATION

1. Apply .20 inch bead of GM silicone gasket P/N 12378190, or equivalent, to corner were oil pan meets engine block.
2. Install rear cover, gasket and bolts onto engine, hand tighten bolts.
3. Rotate crankshaft until two opposing flywheel bolt holes are parallel to oil pan surface.
4. Install cover alignment tool No. J41476, or equivalent, and bolts onto rear of crankshaft. Hand tighten tool mounting bolts.
5. Hand tighten oil pan to cover bolts so cover properly positions itself at pan rail.
6. **Torque** oil pan to cover bolts to 108 inch lbs.
7. **Torque** rear cover mounting bolts to 18 ft. lbs.
8. Remove alignment tool.
9. Install crankshaft rear oil seal using rear oil seal installer tool No. J41479, or equivalent.
10. Install flywheel as follows:
    a. Align alignment mark made during removal and install mounting bolts hand tight.
    b. **Torque** flywheel mounting bolts to 15 ft. lbs., in sequence, **Fig. 9.**
    c. **Torque** flywheel mounting bolts to 37 ft. lbs., in sequence.
    d. **Torque** flywheel mounting bolts to 74 ft. lbs., in sequence.

TIMING CHAIN

REPLACE

REMOVAL

1. Remove oil pump as outlined under "Oil Pump, Replace."
2. Rotate crankshaft until crankshaft and camshaft sprocket timing marks are aligned.
3. Remove camshaft sprocket bolts.
4. Remove camshaft sprocket and timing chain.
5. Remove crankshaft sprocket using puller tool Nos. J8433, J21427-01, J41816-2 and J41558, or equivalents.
6. Remove crankshaft sprocket key, if required.

INSTALLATION

1. Install key into crankshaft keyway.
2. Install crankshaft sprocket onto front of crankshaft, aligning key with keyway.
3. Install crankshaft sprocket using sprocket installation tool No. J41665, or equivalent. Ensure sprocket fully seats against crankshaft flange.

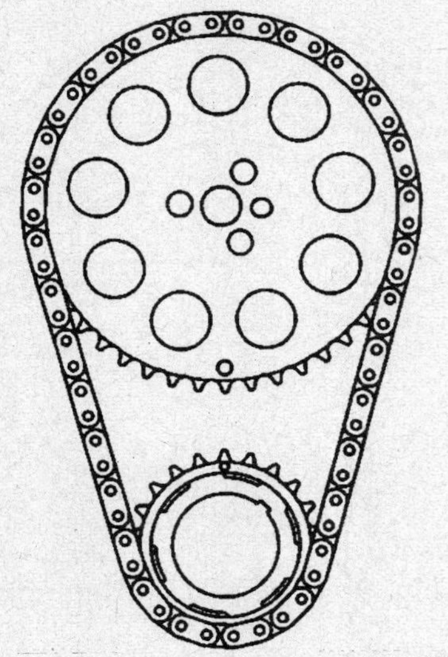

Fig. 10 Camshaft & crankshaft sprocket alignment

4. Rotate crankshaft sprocket until alignment mark is in 12 o'clock position.
5. Install camshaft sprocket and timing chain.
6. Properly locate camshaft sprocket locating pin with camshaft sprocket alignment hole.
7. Sprocket teeth and timing chain must mesh properly.
8. Camshaft and crankshaft sprocket alignment marks must be aligned properly, **Fig. 10.** Locate camshaft sprocket alignment mark in 6 o'clock position.
9. Install camshaft sprocket bolts.
10. Install oil pump as outlined under "Oil Pump, Replace."

CAMSHAFT

REPLACE

1. Remove valve lifters as outlined under "Hydraulic Lifters, Replace."
2. Remove radiator as outlined under "Radiator, Replace."
3. Remove timing chain and sprockets as outlined under "Timing Chain, Replace."
4. Remove camshaft sensor bolt and sensor.
5. Remove camshaft retainer plate bolts and retainer.
6. Install three M8 1.25 × 3.937 inches bolts in camshaft front bolt holes.
7. Carefully rotate and pull camshaft out of engine block using bolts as handle.
8. Remove camshaft bolts.
9. Reverse procedure to install, noting the following:
    a. Ensure camshaft journals are lubricated with suitable clean engine oil before installation.
    b. Install camshaft retainer plate with sealing gasket facing engine block.
    c. Lubricate camshaft sensor O-ring with suitable clean engine oil.

PISTON & ROD ASSEMBLY

1. Insert piston onto piston pin press tool No. J24086-C, or equivalent. Record location of alignment mark on top of piston.
2. Apply mild heat to pin end of connecting rod using torch. This will ease piston and pin assembly.
3. Position connecting rod so bolt flange flat area faces engine block front.
4. Press pin into connecting rod using piston pin press tool.
5. Measure piston, pin and connecting rod for proper assembly as follows:
    a. Place piston and connecting rod with flat top of piston on flat surface.
    b. Slide connecting rod and pin to one side and hold firmly against inside of piston.
    c. Measure pin for proper installation. Properly installed piston pin should protrude .05 inch from piston side.
6. Install piston ring assembly onto piston as follows:
    a. Install oil control ring spacer in groove. Ends of oil control ring spacer should not overlap.
    b. Install upper and lower control rings. Oil control rings do not have dimple or orientation mark and may be installed in either direction.
    c. Stagger three oil control ring end gaps minimum of 90°.
    d. Install upper and lower compression rings. Upper compression ring does not have dimple or orientation mark and may be installed in either direction.
    e. Stagger compression ring end gaps minimum of 1 inch.

PISTONS, PINS & RINGS

Pistons are available in standard and .010 inch oversize.

Piston rings are available in standard and .010 inch oversize.

MAIN & ROD BEARINGS

Connecting rod bearings are available in standard size only.

Main bearings are available in standard size only.

CRANKSHAFT SEAL

REPLACE

Refer to "Front Cover, Replace" for crankshaft front seal replacement.

CRANKSHAFT REAR OIL SEAL

REPLACE

Refer to "Rear Cover, Replace" for crankshaft rear seal replacement.

OIL PAN

REPLACE

1. Drain engine oil into suitable container and remove oil filter.
2. Remove engine cradle as outlined under "Engine Mount, Replace.".
3. **On models equipped with automatic transmission,** remove fluid cooler line front and rear mounting clamp bolts.
4. **On all models,** remove engine flywheel housing to oil pan bolts.
5. Remove engine flywheel housing cover bolts.
6. Remove lefthand and righthand close-out cover bolts and covers.
7. Disconnect electrical connector and remove engine oil level sensor.
8. Disconnect engine oil temperature sensor electrical connector.
9. Remove oil pan mounting bolts and oil pan.
10. Remove and discard oil pan gasket and pan rivets.
11. Remove oil pan baffle bolt and baffle.
12. Reverse procedure to install, noting the following:
    a. Ensure block and oil pan rears are flush or even. **Rear of pan must never protrude beyond block and bellhousing plane.**
    b. Apply .20 inch wide by .80 inch long beads of GM silicone gasket sealer P/N 12378190, or equivalent, to front and rear cover gasket surfaces where covers attach to oil pan mating surface.
    c. Install mounting bolts through oil pan and gasket before installation.

OIL PUMP

REPLACE

1. Remove engine front cover as outlined under "Front Cover, Replace."
2. Remove oil pan as outlined under "Oil Pan, Replace."
3. Remove oil pump screen bolt and nuts.
4. Remove oil pump screen.
5. Remove and discard O-ring seal.
6. Remove remaining crankshaft oil deflector nuts.
7. Remove crankshaft oil deflector.
8. Remove oil pump bolts.
9. Reverse procedure to install, noting the following:
    a. Ensure pump and oil gallery passages are clean and free of obstructions.
    b. Align crankshaft sprocket's and oil pump's splined surfaces.
    c. Install oil pump onto crankshaft sprocket until pump housing contacts engine block face.

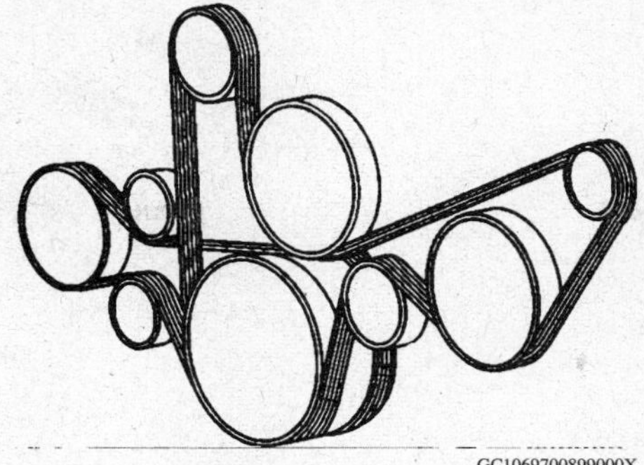

Fig. 11 Serpentine drive belt routing

SERPENTINE DRIVE BELT

BELT ROUTING

Refer to **Fig. 11,** for serpentine drive belt routing.

BELT REPLACEMENT

1. Reduce tension by rotating tensioner away from belts using suitable hex-head socket.
2. Remove accessory drive belts.
3. Clean accessory drive belt surfaces.
4. Install accessory drive belts. Record running direction or arrow markings.
5. Tighten accessory drive belt tensioners to increase tension on accessory drive belts.
6. Ensure accessory drive belts are aligned in proper pulley grooves.

COOLING SYSTEM BLEED

1. Park vehicle on level surface.
2. Fill cooling system.
3. Start engine and let idle for one minute.
4. Install radiator surge tank cap.
5. Cycle RPM from idle to 3000 RPM in 30 second intervals until engine coolant reaches 210°F.
6. Shut off engine and carefully remove radiator surge tank cap.
7. Start engine and idle for one minute.
8. Fill surge tank to ½ inch above COLD FULL mark.
9. Install radiator surge tank cap and cycle RPM as stated.
10. Shut off engine and remove radiator surge tank cap.
11. Fill surge tank to ½ inch above cold full line.
12. Rinse any excess coolant piston from engine and compartment.

THERMOSTAT

REPLACE

1. Drain cooling system into suitable container.
2. Remove radiator outlet hose clamp at thermostat housing using clamp pliers tool No. J38185, or equivalent.
3. Disconnect thermostat housing radiator outlet hose.
4. Record position of thermostat before removing.
5. Remove mounting bolts and thermostat housing.
6. Remove and discard gasket.
7. Reverse procedure to install.

WATER PUMP

REPLACE

1. Drain cooling system into suitable container.
2. Disconnect IAT and MAF sensor electrical connectors.
3. Remove air intake duct fuel regulator purge line.
4. Remove air intake duct cleaner.
5. Remove drive belts as outlined under "Serpentine Drive Belt."
6. Remove radiator inlet and outlet hose clamps, then the water pump hoses using clamp pliers tool No. J38185, or equivalent.
7. Remove heater hose clamps and water pump hoses.
8. Remove water pump pulley bolts and pulley.
9. Remove mounting bolts and water pump.
10. Reverse procedure to install, noting the following:
    a. **On 1998 models, torque** water pump mounting bolts to 30 ft. lbs.
    b. **On 1999–2002 models, torque** water pump mounting bolts to 11 ft. lbs., then to 22 ft. lbs.
    c. **On all models, torque** water pump pulley bolts to 90 inch lbs., then to 18 ft. lbs.

RADIATOR

REPLACE

1. Disconnect Intake Air Temperature (IAT) and Mass Air Flow (MAF) sensor connectors.
2. Remove air intake duct/cleaner.
3. Remove mounting bolts and radiator upper support. Record upper radiator support position in relation to fan shroud for installation.
4. Raise and support vehicle, then drain coolant into suitable container.
5. Remove fan shroud electrical connectors and harness.
6. Remove fan shroud.
7. Remove radiator hoses.
8. **On models equipped with automatic transmission,** remove radiator cooler lines.
9. **On all models,** remove condenser and position forward. **Disconnecting condenser air conditioning lines is not required.**
10. Lower and remove radiator.
11. Reverse procedure to install. Tighten mounting bolts to specifications.

FUEL PUMP

REPLACE

1. Raise and support vehicle.
2. Remove lefthand rear wheel and tire.
3. Clean fuel line connections before disconnecting.

4. Drain lefthand fuel tank into suitable container, then mark and disconnect fuel lines.
5. Cap fuel lines.
6. Disconnect fuel sender electrical connector.
7. Remove fuel tank strap and shield.
8. Support fuel tank.
9. Remove mounting bolts and fuel sender.
10. Record positioning of fuel pump strainer before discarding.
11. Reverse procedure to install, noting the following:
    a. Install new fuel pump strainer, ensuring it is properly positioned as noted during removal.
    b. Align sender cover and tank marks.
    c. Look through tank opening to ensure long side of strainer is visible. It should be approximately one inch from tank opening. Rotate sender counterclockwise approximately 90°, as required.
    d. **On 1998 models, torque** sender mounting bolts to 27 inch lbs., using fuel sender torque tool No. J42940, or equivalent, in sequence, **Fig. 12.**
    e. **On 1999–2002 models,** hand tighten new breakaway head sender mounting bolts, then tighten using suitable wrench until upper heads break off in sequence, **Fig. 12.**

FUEL FILTER

REPLACE

1. Raise and support vehicle.
2. Clean fuel filter connections before disconnecting.
3. **On models equipped with automatic transmission,** proceed as follows:
    a. Disconnect stabilizer bar from rear cradle.
    b. Remove exhaust intermediate pipe to muffler bolts.
    c. Lower lefthand muffler.
4. **On all models,** remove fuel filter bracket nut from mounting stud.
5. Disconnect fuel filter quick-connect fittings and cap fuel lines.
6. **On 1999–2002 models,** disconnect filter mounting stud ground strap.
7. **On all models,** remove fuel filter and bracket, then filter from bracket.
8. Reverse procedure to install. Ensure mounting bracket anti-rotation tab is securely seated into tunnel reinforcement hole.

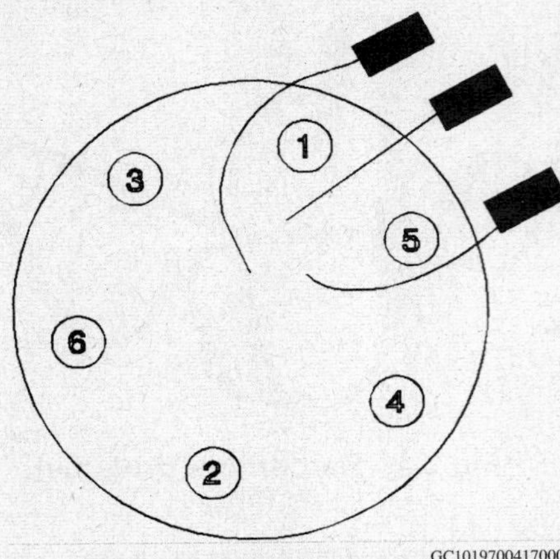

Fig. 12 Fuel sender bolt tightening sequence

TECHNICAL SERVICE BULLETINS

ACCESSORY DRIVE SQUEAK

1998–1999 Models

On some of these models there may be a squeak noise coming from the engine or accessory drive while the engine is running. This squeak may vary in volume and may be heard inside the vehicle with the windows up and the radio on.

This condition may be caused by idler pulley dust shield being distort, then contacting the bearing race and the pulley.

To correct this condition, install new idler pulley with a thicker dust shield (P/N 12564401). Note the following:

1. **Do not over-torque mounting bolt or condition may reoccur.**
2. **Do not use pneumatic or electric tools for installation of idler pulley.**
3. **Torque** idler pulley mounting 37 ft. lbs.

FUEL PUMP NOISE COMING FROM PUMP/TANK

1998 Models

On some of these models there may be a noise coming from the fuel pump or fuel tank area.

This condition may be caused by the fuel pump assembly.

To correct this condition replace the fuel pump assembly with the new kit (P/N 12455734).

TIGHTENING SPECIFICATIONS

Year	Component	Torque/Ft. Lbs.
1998–2002	Air Conditioning Compressor Bracket	37
	Air Conditioning Idler Pulley	37
	Air Conditioning Tensioner	18
	AIR Pipe To Exhaust Manifold	15
	AIR Righthand Side Pipe Bracket To Cylinder Head	15
	Alternator & Power Steering Pump Bracket	37
	Alternator Rear Bracket	37
	Camshaft Retainer	18
	Camshaft Sensor	18
	Camshaft Sprocket	26
	Connecting Rod Bolts	15⑪
	Coolant Temperature Gauge Sensor	15
	Crankshaft Bearing Cap Bolts	15③
	Crankshaft Bearing Cap Side Bolts	18
	Crankshaft Bearing Cap Studs	④
	Crankshaft Damper	②
	Crankshaft Oil Deflector	18
	Crankshaft Position Sensor	18
	Cylinder Head Bolts	⑤
	Cylinder Head Coolant Plug	15
	Cylinder Head Core Hole Plug	15
	Drive Belt Idler Pulley	37
	Drive Belt Tensioner	37
	Engine Block Coolant Drain Plugs	44
	Engine Block Heater	30
	Engine Block Oil Gallery Plugs	44
	Engine Flywheel Hub Collar Bolt (Automatic Transmission)	96
	Engine Front Cover	18
	Engine Mount Bracket To Engine Block	37
	Engine Rear Cover	18
	Engine Service Lift Bracket (M8 Bolts)	18
	Engine Service Lift Bracket (M10 Bolts)	37
	Engine Valley Cover	18
	Exhaust Manifold	⑦
	Flywheel	⑥
	Fuel Injection Fuel Rail	90①
	Ignition Coil	106①
	Ignition Coil Wire Harness Connector	106①
	Intake Manifold Bolts	⑧
	Knock Sensors	15
	Power Steering Pump & Alternator Bracket	37
	Oil Filter	22
	Oil Filter Fitting	40
	Oil Level Indicator Tube	12
	Oil Level Sensor	⑩
	Oil Pan Baffle	106①
	Oil Pan Cover	106①
	Oil Pan Drain Plug	18
	Oil Pan M8 Bolts (Oil Pan To Engine Block & Oil Pan To Front Cover)	18
	Oil Pan M6 Bolts (Oil Pan To Rear Cover)	106①
	Oil Pressure Sensor	15

Continued

TIGHTENING SPECIFICATIONS—Continued

1998–2002	Oil Pump Cover	106①
	Oil Pump Relief Valve Plug	106①
	Oil Pump Screen	18
	Oil Pump Screen To Oil Pump	106①
	Oil Pump To Engine Block	18
	Oil Temperature Sensor	15
	Oil Transfer Cover Bolts	106①
	Oxygen Sensor	30
	Power Steering Pump	18
	Power Steering Reservoir Bracket	37
	Spark Plugs	⑫
	Starter Motor	37
	Throttle Body	106①
	Valve Lifter Guide	106①
	Valve Rocker Arm	22
	Valve Rocker Arm Cover	106①
	Vapor Vent Pipe	106①
	Water Inlet Housing	11
	Water Pump	⑨
	Water Pump Cover	11
	Water Pump Pulley	⑨

①— Inch lbs.
②— Refer to "Crankshaft Damper, Replace."
③— Then tighten an additional 80°.
④— Then tighten an additional 53°.
⑤— Refer to "Cylinder Head, Replace."
⑥— Refer to "Rear Cover, Replace."
⑦— Refer to "Exhaust Manifold, Replace."
⑧— Refer to "Intake Manifold, Replace."
⑨— Refer to "Water Pump, Replace."
⑩— 1998, 26 ft. lbs.; 1999–2002, 115 inch lbs.
⑪— First design (single dimple/mark on bolt head), then tighten an additional 60°; Second design (two dimples/marks on bolt head), then tighten an additional 75°.
⑫— New cylinder head, 15 ft. lbs.; Used cylinder head, 11 ft. lbs.

Clutch & Manual Transmission

NOTE: On Air Bag Equipped Models, Refer To "Air Bag System Precautions" Located In The Front Of This Manual For System Disarming & Arming Procedures.

NOTE: Refer To "Computer Relearn Procedures" Located In The Front Of This Manual When Battery Power To The Computer Has Been Interrupted.

INDEX

ADJUSTMENTS

CLUTCH PEDAL

The clutch release mechanism on these models is hydraulically operated and is not adjustable.

CLUTCH PRESSURE PLATE

Off Vehicle

1. Place clutch pressure plate, with flat surface down, on suitable press.
2. Compress pressure plate diaphragm spring fingers until stepped adjusting ring tension is released.
3. Place two suitable screwdrivers against two of three stepped adjusting ring tension spring stops, just ahead of adjusting ring tension springs.
4. Rotate stepped adjusting ring counterclockwise until adjusting ring steps are fully adjusted out and hold in position.
5. Release pressure plate diaphragm spring fingers pressure.
6. Release adjusting ring tension spring stops.
7. Remove pressure plate.

On Vehicle

1. Raise and support vehicle.
2. Remove engine flywheel inspection cover.
3. With assistance, press clutch pedal until clutch pressure plate stepped adjusting ring tension is released. Continue to hold pedal.
4. Place two suitable screwdrivers against two of three stepped adjusting ring tension spring stops, just ahead of adjusting ring tension springs.
5. Rotate stepped adjusting ring counterclockwise until adjusting ring steps are fully adjusted out and hold in position.
6. Release clutch pedal.
7. Release adjusting ring tension spring stops.
8. Install flywheel inspection cover and lower vehicle.

HYDRAULIC SYSTEM SERVICE

HYDRAULIC SYSTEM BLEED

1. Remove clutch master cylinder reservoir cap with diaphragm.
2. Fill clutch master cylinder reservoir with suitable clutch hydraulic fluid, as required.
3. Raise and support vehicle.
4. Remove intermediate exhaust pipe.
5. Remove driveline tunnel closeout panel.
6. Have assistant depress clutch pedal fully and hold.
7. Loosen bleeder screw on clutch actuator cylinder to purge air and tighten bleeder screw.
8. Release clutch pedal.
9. Repeat previous steps until air is completely evacuated.
10. Fill clutch master cylinder reservoir, if required.
11. Install driveline tunnel closeout panel in propeller shaft.
12. Install exhaust intermediate pipe and lower vehicle.

CLUTCH ACTUATING CYLINDER, REPLACE

1. Remove lefthand instrument panel lower insulator panel.
2. Remove retainer and clutch master cylinder rod.
3. Raise and support vehicle.
4. Remove clutch actuator cylinder hose from retaining clip at engine rear.
5. Disconnect actuator to master cylinder hose connector using hydraulic clutch line separator tool No. J36221, or equivalent. Cover hose ends.
6. Remove driveline support and transaxle.
7. Remove clutch actuator cylinder from driveline support.
8. Reverse procedure to install, noting the following:
   a. Ensure hydraulic hoses are routed away from any interference with other components.
   b. Push actuator hose to master cylinder hose.
   c. Pull outward hoses to ensure secure connection. **Do not rely on audible click or visual appearance alone.**
   d. Bleed clutch hydraulic system.

CLUTCH MASTER CYLINDER, REPLACE

1. Remove lefthand instrument panel lower insulator panel.
2. Remove retainer and clutch master cylinder rod.
3. Remove windshield washer solvent reservoir.
4. Raise and support vehicle.
5. Remove clutch actuator cylinder hose from hose retaining clip at engine rear.
6. Disconnect actuator to master cylinder hose connector using hydraulic clutch line separator tool No. J36221, or equivalent. Cover hose ends.
7. Lower vehicle.
8. Remove clutch master cylinder reservoir push-in fasteners.
9. Rotate counterclockwise 45°, then remove clutch master cylinder and reservoir.
10. Reverse procedure to install, noting the following:
    a. Ensure hydraulic hoses are routed away from any interference with other components.
    b. Push actuator hose to master cylinder hose.
    c. Pull outward on hoses to ensure secure connection **Do not rely on audible click or visual appearance alone.**
    d. Bleed clutch hydraulic system.

CLUTCH

REPLACE

1. Raise and support vehicle.
2. Remove exhaust system.
3. Remove driveline support with transaxle.
4. Remove engine flywheel inspection cover.

5. Loosen visible clutch pressure plate bolts.
6. Rotate engine flywheel and loosen remaining clutch pressure plate bolts.
7. Remove visible clutch pressure plate bolts.
8. Rotate engine flywheel and remove remaining clutch pressure plate bolts.
9. Remove clutch pressure plate and clutch driven plate.
10. Reverse procedure to install, noting the following:
    a. Adjust clutch pressure plate as outlined under "Adjustments," as required.
    b. Align clutch driven plate to pilot bearing using pilot bushing installer tool No. J38836, or equivalent.
    c. **Torque** clutch pressure plate bolts evenly in four increments to 52 ft. lbs., in crisscross pattern.

TRANSMISSION

REPLACE

Observe clearance between rear of engine and composite dash panel. Do not let engine rest unsupported against dash panel.

1. Remove console.
2. Pry off shift control knob button and retainer.
3. Unscrew shift control knob.
4. Grasp sides and release shift boot retaining tabs by applying light pressure toward shift control lever.
5. Continue to release remaining boot retaining tabs using light pressure.
6. Lift and remove boot.
7. Remove instrument panel accessory trim plate.
8. Remove shift control closeout boot mounting nuts.
9. Remove shift control closeout boot.
10. Remove shift control.
11. Remove instrument panel lower insulator panel.
12. Remove retainer and clutch master cylinder pushrod.
13. Raise and support vehicle.
14. Remove clutch actuator cylinder hose from hose retaining clip at engine rear.
15. Disconnect clutch hose connector using clutch line separator tool No. J36221, or equivalent. Cover hose coupling ends.
16. Remove rear tires and wheels.
17. Remove intermediate exhaust pipe.
18. Tie mufflers to underbody to keep them positioned aside.
19. Remove driveline tunnel closeout panel.
20. **On models equipped with rear mounted Electronic Brake and Traction Control Module (EBTCM),** proceed as follows:
    a. Remove EBTCM lefthand mounting bracket bolts.
    b. Remove EBTCM lefthand mounting bracket with EBTCM rubber insulators.
    c. Release EBTCM from righthand mounting bracket insulator by pulling lightly.
    d. Tie EBTCM to underbody support.
21. **On all models,** remove rear suspension crossmember as outlined under "Rear Axle & Suspension."
22. Install transmission support fixture tool No. J42055, or equivalent, to transmission and transmission jack to support fixture.
23. Remove differential to transmission lower nut.
24. Remove transaxle mount bracket to differential bolts.
25. Remove transaxle mount with bracket.
26. Carefully release axle shafts from differential using suitable pry bar.
27. Support axle shafts from underbody.
28. Compress and release retainers securing wiring harness along driveline support using suitable pliers and position harness aside.
29. Slowly lower driveline approximately two inches while simultaneously adjusting angle of tilt.
30. Disconnect Vehicle Speed Sensor (VSS) electrical connector.
31. Disconnect wiring harness retainer from differential rear cover stud.
32. Disconnect wiring harness retainer clip from differential top.
33. Disconnect electrical connectors at back-up lamp switch, reverse lockout solenoid, gear select (skip shift) solenoid and transmission lubricant temperature sensor.
34. Insert suitable putty knife between edge of shifter bracket on side of driveline support and brake pipe retainer on wall of driveline tunnel.
35. Slowly lower driveline, while simultaneously adjusting angle of tilt and observing relationship between top and rear of differential and lowest area of rear compartment panel floor. Differential should not be lowered more than approximately even with specified body point of reference. Avoid engine to dash panel interference.
36. Release wiring harness from harness retainer along transmission top.
37. Ensure wiring harness is free from driveline being removed.
38. Support engine under rear of engine oil pan using suitable jack and block of wood to prevent stressing composite dash panel.
39. Remove driveline support to engine flywheel housing mounting bolts.
40. Bend wiring harness bracket away from driveline toward driveline tunnel wall to make clear path for removal.
41. With assistance, insert suitable flat-bladed screwdriver between edge of driveline support and engine flywheel housing, then pry driveline loose from engine.
42. With assistance, lower driveline until propeller input shaft at driveline support front just clears engine flywheel housing, then lower completely.
43. Lift driveline off jack using suitable chain lift. Position chain so as not to damage exhaust hangers located on driveline support.
44. Disconnect transmission support fixture tool No. J42055, or equivalent, from transmission jack to provide stability while working on bench.
45. Position driveline on workbench with lift still attached.
46. Support driveline and remove lift.
47. Remove transmission to driveline support bolts and studs.
48. Pry driveline support loose from transmission by inserting suitable flat-bladed screwdriver between edge of driveline support and transmission.
49. Slide differential away from transmission.
50. Remove transmission support fixture tool No. J42055, or equivalent, if required.
51. Reverse procedure to install, noting the following:
    a. Avoid engine to dash panel interference.
    b. Install new rear suspension crossmember mounting nuts using hand tools.
    c. Ensure clutch hydraulic hoses are routed away from any interference with other components.
    d. Push clutch actuator hose to master cylinder hose.
    e. Pull outward on hoses to ensure secure connection. **Do not rely on audible click or visual appearance alone.**
    f. Bleed clutch hydraulic system.

TIGHTENING SPECIFICATIONS

Year	Component	Torque/Ft. Lbs.
1998–2002	Back-Up Lamp Switch	15
	Differential To Transmission	37
	Driveline Support To Engine Flywheel Housing	37
	EBTCM Lefthand Mounting Bracket	37
	Gear Select Skip Shift Solenoid	30
	Intermediate Exhaust Pipe To Muffler	37
	Rear Shock Absorber Lower Mounting	162
	Rear Suspension Crossmember	81②
	Reverse Lockout Solenoid	30
	Shift Control	22
	Shift Control Closeout Boot Retaining	106①
	Transaxle Mount Bracket To Differential	37
	Transaxle Mount To Rear Suspension Crossmember	37
	Transmission Fluid Drain & Fill Plugs	20
	Transmission Lubricant Temperature Sensor	20
	Transmission Shift Rod Clamp	22
	Transmission To Driveline Support	37
	Transmission Vent Tube	15

① — Inch lbs.
② — Install new nuts. Tighten using hand tools only.

Rear Axle & Suspension

NOTE: On Air Bag Equipped Models, Refer To "Air Bag System Precautions" Located In The Front Of This Manual For System Disarming & Arming Procedures.

NOTE: Refer To "Computer Relearn Procedures" Located In The Front Of This Manual When Battery Power To The Computer Has Been Interrupted.

INDEX

REAR AXLE

REPLACE

Refer to "Clutch & Manual Transmission" or "Automatic Transaxles/Transmissions" for rear axle replacement.

REAR WHEEL SHAFT

REPLACE

1. Apply parking brake and shift transmission into park or neutral.
2. Raise and support vehicle and remove rear wheel and tire.
3. Prevent wheel hub and bearing turning by insert suitable drift or punch into brake rotor cooling fins and against brake caliper.
4. Remove spindle nut mounting rear wheel driveshaft to hub.
5. Remove drift or punch.
6. Release parking brake.
7. Remove rear transverse spring as outlined under "Transverse Leaf Spring, Replace."
8. Separate outer tie rod end from knuckle and position tie rod toward rear of vehicle. **Do not loosen outer tie rod jam nut.**
9. Disconnect wheel speed sensor electrical connector.
10. Disconnect parking brake cable from parking brake lever at rear hub.
11. Remove parking brake cable from bracket and position toward vehicle rear.
12. Install rear hub spindle remover tool No. J42129, or equivalent, onto wheel hub and secure with lugnuts.
13. Begin to disengage driveshaft from wheel hub and bearing. This will give additional clearance to lower ball joint nut.
14. Separate lower ball joint from suspension knuckle.
15. Disengage driveshaft completely from wheel hub and bearing.
16. Support driveshaft, suspension knuckle and upper control arm, then position knuckle toward front.
17. Remove driveshaft using axle shaft remover, extension and slide hammer tool Nos. J42128, J29794 & J2619-01, or equivalents.
18. Remove rear hub spindle remover tool.
19. Reverse procedure to install.

PROPELLER SHAFT

REPLACE

Refer to "Clutch & Manual Transmission" or "Automatic Transaxles/Transmissions" for propeller shaft replacement.

HUB & BEARING

REPLACE

1. Raise and support vehicle, then remove tire and wheel.
2. Disconnect wheel speed sensor electrical connector.
3. **On models equipped with Real Time Damping (RTD) suspension,** disconnect RTD position sensor link.
4. **On all models,** remove brake caliper and disc rotor.
5. Remove shock absorber solenoid electrical connector.
6. Separate outer tie rod end from suspension knuckle.
7. Remove spindle nut retainer, nut and washer.
8. Separate suspension knuckle from upper control arm.
9. Separate suspension knuckle from lower control arm ball joint stud.
10. Remove suspension knuckle.
11. Remove wheel hub mounting bolts.
12. Remove hub and bearing from suspension knuckle.
13. Reverse procedure to install, noting the following:
    a. **Front and rear hub and bearing are not interchangeable. Ensure proper replacement component is being installed.**
    b. Tighten mounting bolts, nuts and screws to specifications.

SPINDLE KNUCKLE

REPLACE

1. Raise and support vehicle, then remove tire and wheel assembly.
2. Disconnect wheel speed sensor electrical connector.
3. **On models equipped with Real Time Damping (RTD) suspension,** disconnect RTD position sensor link.
4. **On all models,** disconnect shock absorber electrical connector.
5. Remove brake caliper and disc rotor.
6. Separate outer tie rod end from suspension knuckle.
7. Remove spindle nut retainer, nut and washer.
8. Separate suspension knuckle from upper control arm.
9. Separate suspension knuckle from lower control arm ball joint stud.
10. Remove suspension knuckle.
11. Reverse procedure to install.

REAR WHEEL SPINDLE

REPLACE

Refer to "Hub & Bearing, Replace" for rear wheel spindle replacement.

SHOCK ABSORBER

REPLACE

1. Raise and support vehicle, then remove tire and wheel.
2. Disconnect shock absorber solenoid electrical connector.
3. Remove lower shock absorber to lower control arm mounting bolt.
4. Remove upper mounting bolts.
5. Remove shock absorber from lower control arm and shock tower.
6. Remove upper insulator retainer and insulator.
7. Reverse procedure to install.

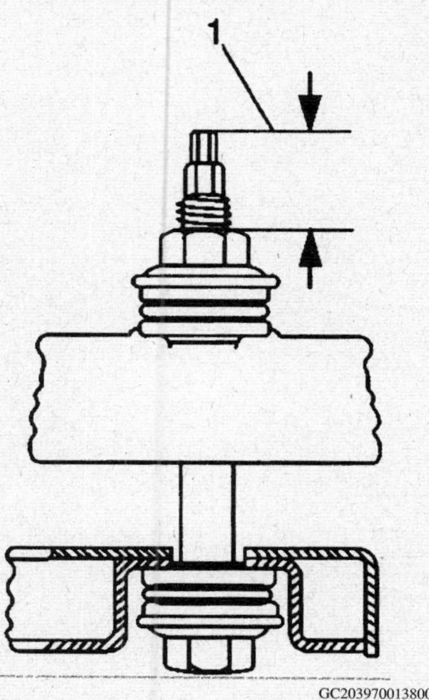

Fig. 1 Spring stud height measurement

TRANSVERSE LEAF SPRING

REPLACE

1. Raise and support vehicle, then remove both rear tires and wheels.
2. Measure transverse spring stud height, **Fig. 1.**
3. Install transverse leaf spring compressor and adapters, tool Nos. J33432-A and J33432-97, or equivalents, **Fig. 2.**
4. Compress spring.
5. Remove spring to control arm mounting nuts, bolts and insulators.
6. Remove spring to crossmember retainer bolts, retainer, spring spacers and insulators.
7. Remove transverse leaf spring.
8. Reverse procedure to install, noting the following:
   a. Set spring stud height to that noted during removal.
   b. Ensure spring stud bolt has minimum of two threads showing above nut.
   c. Tighten mounting bolts, nuts and screws to specifications.

CONTROL ARM

REPLACE

LOWER

1. Raise and support vehicle, then remove tire and wheel.
2. Remove transverse leaf spring as previously described.
3. Support lower control arm using suitable jack stand and remove shock absorber to lower control arm mounting bolt.
4. Loosen lower ball joint stud nut.
5. Separate lower ball joint stud from suspension knuckle using separator tool No. J42188, or equivalent.
6. Remove separator tool and lower ball joint stud nut from suspension knuckle.
7. Remove stabilizer bar link from lower control arm.
8. Mark position of control arm to crossmember cam bolts, washers and nuts, then remove.
9. Remove jack stand and control arm.
10. Reverse procedure to install, noting the following:
    a. Use hex-head wrench to hold ball joint stud in place when installing stud nut, as required.
    b. **Torque** stud nut to 15 ft. lbs., to seat stud.
    c. Turn nut an additional 3½ flats.
    d. Inspect stud nut for minimum final **torque** of 41 ft. lbs.

UPPER

1. Raise and support vehicle, then remove tire and wheel.
2. Support lower control arm using suitable jack stand.
3. **On models equipped with Real Time Damping (RTD) suspension,** disconnect RTD position sensor link at upper control arm.
4. **On all models,** loosen upper ball joint stud nut, but do not remove it.
5. Separate upper ball joint stud from upper control arm using separator tool No. J42188, or equivalent.
6. Remove separator tool and stud nut.
7. Remove mounting bolts and upper control arm.
8. Reverse procedure to install, noting the following:
   a. Use hex-head wrench to hold ball joint stud in place when installing stud nut, as required.
   b. **Torque** stud nut to 15 ft. lbs., to seat stud.
   c. **On 1998 models,** tighten nut an additional four flats and inspect stud nut for minimum final **torque** of 33 ft. lbs.
   d. **On 1999–2002 models,** tighten nut an additional 250° and inspect stud nut for minimum final **torque** of 41 ft. lbs.

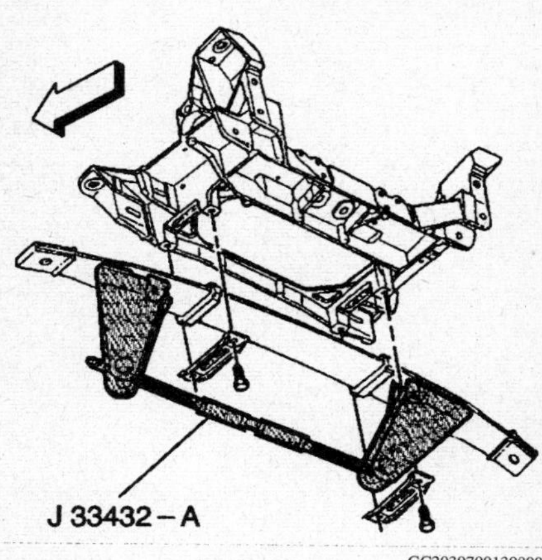

Fig. 2 Transverse leaf spring compressor

TIE ROD

REPLACE

1. Raise and support vehicle, then remove tire and wheel.
2. Loosen outer tie rod end stud nut, but do not remove it.
3. Separate tie rod end from suspension knuckle using ball joint separator tool No. J42188, or equivalent.
4. Remove rear suspension adjustment link to crossmember mounting nut.
5. Remove rear suspension adjustment link.
6. Reverse procedure to install. Tighten outer tie rod end stud nut as follows:
   a. **Torque** to 15 ft. lbs.
   b. Tighten an additional 160°.
   c. **Torque** to 33 ft. lbs.

STABILIZER SHAFT

REPLACE

1. Raise and support vehicle, then remove tires and wheels.
2. Remove stabilizer bar link mounting nuts from lower control arms.
3. Remove stabilizer bar to crossmember bracket mounting bolts and bracket.
4. Remove stabilizer bar.
5. Remove stabilizer bar link mounting nuts and shaft links.
6. Reverse procedure to install.

TIGHTENING SPECIFICATIONS

Year	Component	Torque/Ft. Lbs.
1998–2002	Clutch Actuator Cylinder	106①
	Driveline Support To Engine Flywheel Housing	37
	Driveline Tunnel Closeout Panel	80①
	EBTCM Lefthand Mounting Bracket	37
	Flexplate To Propeller Shaft Rear Bearing	37
	Input Shaft To Front Propeller Shaft Coupler	41
	Lower Control Arm Ball Joint	②
	Lower Control Arm Cam, Front	107
	Lower Control Arm Cam, Rear	70
	Outer Tie Rod	⑤
	Outer Tie Rod End Jam	44
	Propeller Input Shaft Front Bearing	26
	Propeller Shaft Hub Clamp	96
	Rear Axle Driveline	④
	Rear Bearing To Driveline Support Tube	48
	Rear Bearing To Rear Propeller Shaft Coupler	⑥
	Rear Crossmember	81③
	Rear Drive Axle Spindle	118
	Rear Exhaust Hanger	37
	Rear Shock Absorber, Lower	162
	Rear Shock Absorber, Upper	22
	Rear Spring Anchor Plate (1998)	49
	Rear Spring Anchor Plate (1999–2002)	46
	Shift Control	22
	Shift Control Closeout Boot	106①
	Stabilizer Bar Insulator, Lower	70
	Stabilizer Bar Insulator, Upper	49
	Stabilizer Bar Link	53
	Tie Rod	50
	Upper Control Arm	81
	Upper Control Arm Ball Joint	②
	Wheel Hub	96

①— Inch Lbs.
②— Refer to "Control Arm, Replace" for tightening specifications and procedure.
③— Always install new nuts and tighten them using hand tools only.
④— Refer to "Clutch & Manual Transmission" or "Automatic Transaxles/Transmissions" for specifications.
⑤— Refer to "Tie Rod, Replace" for tightening specifications and procedures.
⑥— 1998, 48 ft. lbs.; 1999–2002, 52 ft. lbs.

Front Suspension & Steering

NOTE: On Air Bag Equipped Models, Refer To "Air Bag System Precautions" Located In The Front Of This Manual For System Disarming & Arming Procedures.

NOTE: Refer To "Computer Relearn Procedures" Located In The Front Of This Manual When Battery Power To The Computer Has Been Interrupted.

INDEX

WHEEL BEARING

REPLACE

Refer to "Wheel Hub, Replace" for wheel bearing replacement.

WHEEL HUB

REPLACE

1. Raise and support vehicle, then remove tire and wheel.
2. Remove brake caliper and rotor.
3. Remove stabilizer shaft link from lower control arm.
4. Disconnect wheel speed sensor electrical connector.
5. Support lower control arm using suitable jack stand.
6. Disconnect steering linkage outer tie rod from steering knuckle using separator tool No. J42188, or equivalent.
7. Loosen upper and lower ball joint stud nuts.
8. Separate steering knuckle from upper and lower control arm using ball joint separator tool No. J42188, or equivalent.
9. Remove upper and lower ball joint stud nuts.
10. Remove steering knuckle from upper and lower control arms.
11. Remove wheel hub mounting bolts.
12. Remove hub and bearing from steering knuckle.
13. Reverse procedure to install, noting the following:
    a. **Front and rear hub and bearing are not interchangeable. Ensure proper replacement component is being installed.**
    b. Tighten mounting bolts, nuts and screws to specifications.

BALL JOINT INSPECTION

1. Raise and support front of vehicle, then position jack stands under lower control arms.
2. Shake tire and wheel assembly while inspecting for stud end movement at knuckle bosses.
3. Shake tire and wheel assembly while inspecting for loose prevailing torque nuts at knuckle bosses.
4. Visually inspect for damaged or worn ball studs and knuckles.
5. Replace ball joint if looseness is indicated.

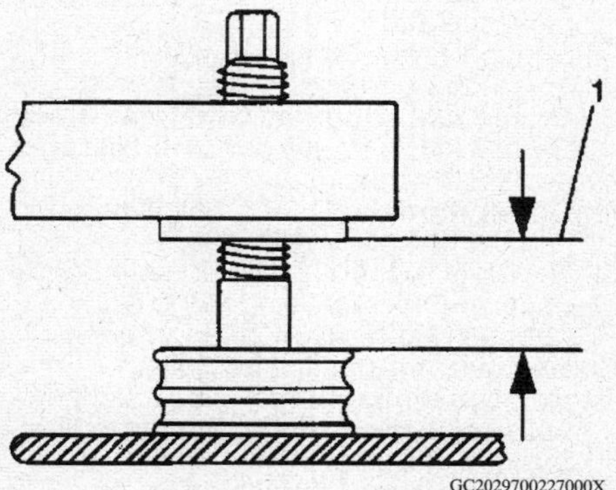

Fig. 1 Transverse spring adjuster gap

BALL JOINT

REPLACE

UPPER BALL JOINT

1. Remove steering knuckle as outlined under "Steering Knuckle, Replace."
2. Remove ball joint from knuckle using ball joint remover kit tool Nos. J9519-E and J21474-5, or equivalents.
3. Install new ball joint into knuckle using ball joint removal tool kit No. J9519-E and installer tool No. J28685, or equivalents.
4. **On 1998 models, torque** ball stud nut to 15 ft. lbs., tighten an additional four flats and inspect nut for final **torque** of 33 ft. lbs.
5. **On 1999–2002 models, torque** ball stud nut to 15 ft. lbs., tighten an additional 250° and inspect nut for final **torque** of 41 ft. lbs.
6. **On all models,** install knuckle onto vehicle.

LOWER BALL JOINT

1. Remove lower control arm as outlined under "Transverse Leaf Spring, Replace."
2. Remove ball joint from control arm using ball joint tool Nos. J9519-98 and J9519-E, or equivalents.
3. Install new ball joint into control arm using ball joint tool Nos. J9519-99 and J9519-E, or equivalents.
4. **On 1998 models, torque** ball stud nut to 15 ft. lbs., tighten an additional 3½ flats and inspect nut for final **torque** of 41 ft. lbs.
5. **On 1999–2002 models, torque** ball stud nut to 15 ft. lbs., tighten an additional 210° and inspect nut for final **torque** of 52 ft. lbs.
6. **On all models,** install lower control arm onto vehicle.

SHOCK ABSORBER

REPLACE

REMOVAL

1. Raise and support vehicle, then remove tire and wheel.
2. Remove shock absorber upper mounting nut, insulator retainer and insulator.
3. Remove shock absorber lower mounting nuts.
4. **On models equipped with heavy duty shock option (FE3),** proceed as follows:
    a. Compress shock absorber from bottom upward using suitable pry bar.

b. Install shock support tool No. J43822, or equivalent, onto shock to keep it compressed.
5. **On all models,** remove shock absorber from lower control arm and shock tower.
6. Remove shock support tool.
7. Remove insulator and retainer.

INSTALLATION

1. **On models less heavy duty shock option (FE3),** proceed as follows:
   a. Install retainer and insulator to new shock absorber.
   b. Install absorber to upper tower.
   c. Install upper insulator, retainer and nut. Tighten to specifications.
   d. Install absorber lower mounting bolts and nuts. Tighten to specifications.
2. **On models equipped with heavy duty shock option (FE3),** proceed as follows:
   a. Install shock support tool No. J43822, or equivalent, onto new shock absorber.
   b. Install absorber onto vehicle.
   c. Install upper insulator, retainer and nut. Tighten to specifications.
   d. Remove shock support tool.
   e. Compress transverse spring using spring compressor tool No. J33432-A, or equivalent.
   f. Raise lower control arm, then install absorber lower mounting bolts and nuts.
   g. Tighten mounting bolts and nuts to specifications.
   h. Remove spring compressor tool.
3. **On all models,** install tire and wheel, then lower vehicle.

TRANSVERSE LEAF SPRING

REPLACE

1. Raise and support vehicle, then remove tires and wheels.
2. Measure and record front spring adjuster bolt gap, **Fig. 1.**
3. Install transverse spring compressor tool No. J33432-A and adapters, or equivalents.
4. Compress transverse spring.
5. Remove lower shock absorber mounting bolts from one lower control arm.
6. Disconnect stabilizer bar link from lower control arm.
7. Loosen lower ball joint nut on control arm, but do not remove it.
8. Separate lower ball joint from steering knuckle using ball joint separator tool No. J42188, or equivalent.
9. Remove separator tool, ball joint nut and ball joint from steering knuckle. Discard ball joint stud nut.
10. Support lower control arms using suitable jack stands.
11. Mark position of cam bolts for reference.
12. Remove cam bolts from lower control arm.
13. Remove lower control arm.
14. Remove transverse spring retainers.
15. Remove and discard transverse spring bolts.
16. Remove transverse leaf spring.
17. Remove compressor tool.
18. Reverse procedure to install, noting the following:
    a. Install spring adjuster bolts to height measured.
    b. Install cam bolts to position marked.
    c. Align front wheels.

CONTROL ARM

REPLACE

UPPER CONTROL ARM

1. Raise and support vehicle, then remove tire and wheel.
2. Support lower control arm using suitable jack stand.
3. **On models equipped with Real Time Damping (RTD) suspension,** disconnect RTD sensor link.
4. **On all models,** loosen ball joint stud nut, but do not remove it.
5. Separate upper ball joint stud from upper control arm using ball joint separator tool No. J42188, or equivalent.
6. Remove tool, nut and ball joint.
7. Remove upper control arm mounting bolts and shims. Record number and position of shims.
8. Remove upper control arm.
9. Reverse procedure to install, noting the following:
   a. **On 1998 models, torque** ball stud nut to 15 ft. lbs., tighten an additional four flats and inspect nut for final **torque** of 33 ft. lbs.
   b. **On 1999–2002 models, torque** ball stud nut to 15 ft. lbs., tighten an additional 250° and inspect nut for final **torque** of 41 ft. lbs.

LOWER CONTROL ARM

Refer to "Transverse Leaf Spring, Replace" for lower control arm replacement procedure.

STEERING KNUCKLE

REPLACE

1. Raise and support vehicle, then remove tire and wheel.
2. Remove brake caliper and rotor.
3. Disconnect stabilizer shaft link from lower control arm.
4. Disconnect wheel speed sensor electrical connector.
5. Support lower control arm using suitable jack stand.
6. Separate outer tie rod ball stud from steering knuckle using ball joint separator tool No. J42188, or equivalent.
7. Separate upper ball joint stud from upper control arm using separator tool.
8. Separate lower ball joint stud from steering knuckle using separator tool.
9. Remove steering knuckle.
10. Reverse procedure to install.

STABILIZER BAR

REPLACE

1. Raise and support vehicle, then remove tire and wheel.
2. Remove stabilizer bar link nuts and link from stabilizer bar and lower control arm.
3. Remove stabilizer bar insulator clamps from front crossmember.
4. Remove stabilizer bar.
5. Reverse procedure to install.

POWER STEERING GEAR

REPLACE

Refer to "Engine Mount, Replace" in "5.7L Engine" section for power steering gear replacement procedure.

POWER STEERING PUMP

REPLACE

1. **On 1998 models equipped with front-mounted Electronic Brake Control Module and Brake Pressure Modulator Valve (EBTCM/BPMV) and all 1999–2002 models,** remove EBTCM/BPMV and bracket. Position brake pipes aside as required. Cap and plug open lines.
2. **On all models,** drain power steering fluid into suitable container.
3. Remove power steering fluid reservoir.
4. Remove accessory drive belt.
5. Remove power steering pump pulley using pulley removal tool No. J25034-B, or equivalent.
6. Disconnect power steering gear inlet hose.
7. Remove power steering pump mounting bolts.
8. Remove power steering pump and bracket.
9. Reverse procedure to install.

TIGHTENING SPECIFICATIONS

Year	Component	Torque/Ft. Lbs.
1998	Crossmember	81①
	Lower Control Arm	125
	Lower Control Arm Ball Stud	②
	Power Steering Pump	18
	Power Steering Reservoir Bracket	37
	Power Steering Line End Fittings	20
	Shock Absorber, Lower	21
	Shock Absorber, Upper	19
	Steering Link Outer Tie Rod End Stud	③
	Stabilizer Bar Insulator Clamp	40
	Stabilizer Bar Link	55
	Transverse Leaf Spring	46①
	Upper Control Arm	42
	Upper Control Arm Ball Stud	②
	Wheel Hub Bearing	70
1999–2002	Crossmember	81①
	Lower Control Arm	125
	Lower Control Arm Ball Stud	②
	Power Steering Pump	18
	Power Steering Reservoir Bracket	37
	Power Steering Line End Fittings	20
	Shock Absorber, Lower	21
	Shock Absorber, Upper	19
	Steering Link Outer Tie Rod End Stud	③
	Stabilizer Bar Insulator Clamp	43
	Stabilizer Bar Link	53
	Transverse Leaf Spring	46①
	Upper Control Arm	48
	Upper Control Arm Ball Stud	②
	Wheel Hub Bearing	96

① — Always install new bolts and nuts. Do not use old bolts and nuts.
② — Refer "Ball Joint, Replace" for tightening specifications and procedure.
③ — **Torque** outer tie rod end nut to 15 ft. lbs., to seat outer tie rod stud. Turn the nut an additional 160 degrees. Inspect outer tie rod end nut for a minimum **torque** of 33 ft. lbs.

Wheel Alignment

INDEX

PRELIMINARY INSPECTION

Prior to inspecting or adjusting front suspension alignment, inspect suspension components and wheel bearings for damage or excessive wear and replace as required. Ensure tire pressure is properly adjusted, then raise and release front bumper several times to allow vehicle to assume normal ride height. The following items should be inspected prior to performing wheel alignment procedures:

1. Inspect tires for proper inflation pressure.
2. Inspect hubs and bearings for excessive wear.
3. Inspect ball joints and tie rod ends for looseness and wear.
4. Inspect for bent wheel rims, wheel runout and faulty tires (belt shifts).
5. Inspect suspension and steering components for looseness and wear.
6. Inspect for excessive cargo loads.
7. Measure vehicle trim height.

FRONT WHEEL ALIGNMENT

CASTER

1. Loosen lower control arm cam bolt nuts.
2. Rotate cam bolts to caster specification setting.
3. Maintain caster setting while **torquing** cam bolt nuts to 125 ft. lbs.

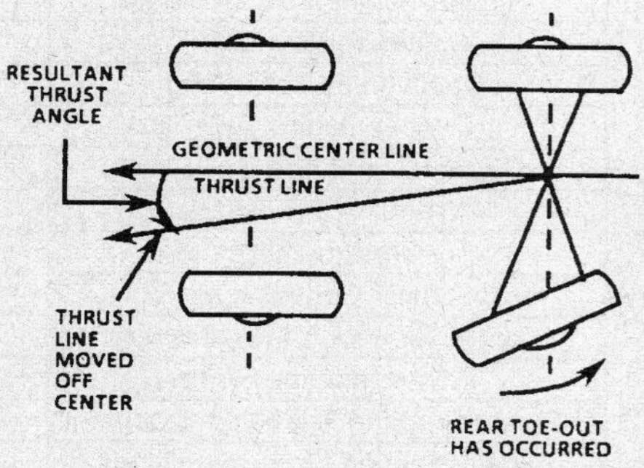

Fig. 1 Vehicle thrust angle

4. Inspect caster and camber settings after tightening. Adjust as required.

CAMBER

1. Loosen lower control arm cam bolt nuts.
2. Rotate cam bolts to required camber specification setting.
3. Maintain camber setting while **torquing** cam bolt nuts to 125 ft. lbs.
4. Inspect caster and camber settings after tightening. Adjust as required.
5. To obtain additional negative camber beyond cam adjustment capability, remove shims from upper control arms.

TOE-IN

1. Loosen jam nut on tie rod.
2. Rotate inner tie rod to toe specification setting.
3. **Torque** jam nut on tie rod end to 50 ft. lbs.
4. Inspect toe setting after tightening. Adjust as required.

REAR WHEEL ALIGNMENT

CAMBER

1. Loosen lower control arm cam bolt nuts.
2. Rotate cam bolts to required camber specification setting.
3. Maintain camber setting while **torquing** front cam bolt nut to 107 ft. lbs., and rear cam bolt nut to 71 ft. lbs.
4. Inspect caster and camber settings after tightening. Adjust as required.

TOE-IN

1. Loosen rear suspension adjustment link locknut.
2. Rotate inner tie rod to toe specification setting.
3. **Torque** rear suspension adjustment link lock nut to 44 ft. lbs.
4. Inspect toe setting after tightening. Adjust as required.

THRUST ANGLE

The vehicle is steered by the front wheels. The path the rear wheels follow is the thrust angle, **Fig. 1.** Thrust angle should be aligned with the vehicle centerline.

ELDORADO, DEVILLE & SEVILLE

NOTE: Refer To Rear Of This Manual For Vehicle Manufacturer's Special Service Tool Suppliers.

INDEX OF SERVICE OPERATIONS

Specifications

GENERAL ENGINE SPECIFICATIONS

Year	Engine		Fuel Injection System	Bore & Stroke	Compr-ession Ratio	Net H.P. @ RPM③	Maximum Torque Ft. Lbs. @ RPM	Normal Oil Pressure Pounds①
	Liter	VIN Code②						
1998–99	4.6L	Y	TPFI	3.66 × 3.31	10.3	275 @ 5600	300 @ 4400	35
	4.6L	9	TPFI	3.66 × 3.31	10.3	300 @ 6000	295 @ 4400	35
2000–01	4.6L	Y	TPFI	3.66 × 3.31	10.0	275 @ 5600	300 @ 4400	35
	4.6L	9	TPFI	3.66 × 3.31	10.0	300 @ 6000	295 @ 4400	35
2002	4.6L	Y	TPFI	3.66 × 3.31	10.0	275 @ 5600	300 @ 4000	35
	4.6L	9	TPFI	3.66 × 3.31	10.0	300 @ 6000	295 @ 4400	35

TPFI — Tuned Port Fuel Injection
① — At 2000 RPM.
② — The eighth digit denotes engine code.
③ — Ratings are net as installed in vehicle.

TUNE UP SPECIFICATIONS

Year & Engine, VIN①	Spark Plug Gap	Ignition Timing			Curb Idle Speed③	Fast Idle Speed	Fuel Pump Pressure, psi	Valve Lash
		Firing Order Fig.④	Degrees BTDC	Mark Fig.				
1998–99								
4.6L/Y	.050	②	10⑤	⑨	⑥	⑥	41–47⑦	⑧
4.6L/9	.050	②	10⑤	⑨	⑥	⑥	41–47⑦	⑧
2000–02								
4.6L/Y	.050	②	⑤	⑨	⑥	⑥	41–47⑦	⑧
4.6L/9	.050	②	⑤	⑨	⑥	⑥	41–47⑦	⑧

BTDC — Before top dead center
① — The eighth digit denotes engine code.
② — Cylinder numbering from left to right as viewed from front of vehicle, front bank, 2, 4, 6, 8; rear bank, 1, 3, 5, 7. Firing order 1–2–7–3–4–5–6–8. Refer to **Fig. A** for spark plug wire connections at coil unit.
③ — On auto. trans. models, idle speed is adjusted in Drive. When adjusting idle speed, set parking brake & block drive wheels.
④ — Before disconnecting wires from distributor cap or coil pack , determine location of No. 1 wire, as position may have been altered from that illustrated at end of this chart.
⑤ — Computer controlled. No adjustment.
⑥ — Idle speed is controlled by an idle speed control (ISC) motor or an idle air control (IAC) valve.
⑦ — With shop towel wrapped around fuel pressure valve to prevent fuel spillage, connect a suitable fuel pressure gauge to fuel pressure valve. Measure fuel pressure w/ignition switch in the On position, engine not running.
⑧ — Equipped w/non adjustable hydraulic valve lifters.
⑨ — Equipped w/crankshaft position sensor.

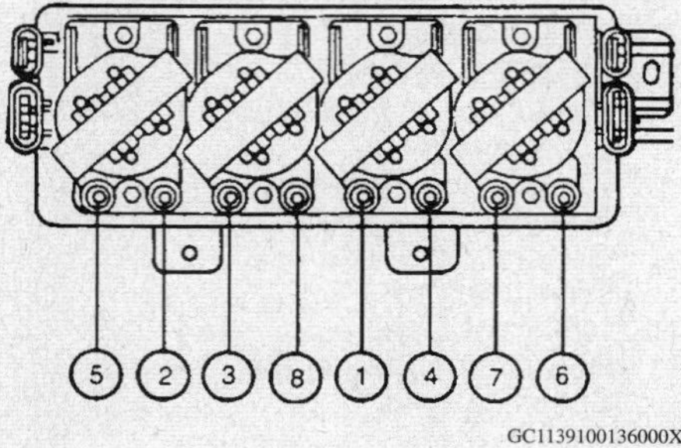

Fig. A

FRONT WHEEL ALIGNMENT SPECIFICATIONS

Year	Model	Caster Angle, Degrees		Camber Angle, Degrees		Total Toe, Degrees①		Ball Joint Inspection
		Limits	Desired	Limits	Desired	Limits	Desired	
1998–99	DeVille	+1.3 to +3.3④	+2.3④	–.5 to +.5③	0③	0 to +.4	+.2	②
	Eldorado	+1.3 to +3.3④	+2.3④	–.5 to +.5③	0③	0 to +.4	+.2	②
	Seville	+5.5 to +6.5⑤	+6.0⑤	–.7 to +.3⑤	–.2⑤	0 to +.4	+.2	②
2000	DeVille	+5.5 to +6.5⑤	+6.0⑤	–.7 to +.3⑤	–.2⑤	0 to +.4	+.2	②
	Seville	+5.5 to +6.5⑤	+6.0⑤	–.7 to +.3⑤	–.2⑤	0 to +.4	+.2	②
2000–02	Eldorado	+1.3 to +3.3④	+2.3④	–.5 to +.5③	0③	0 to +.4	+.2	②
2001–02	DeVille	+4.5 to +5.5⑤	+5.0⑤	–.7 to +.3⑤	–.2⑤	0 to +.4	+.2	②
	Seville	+4.5 to +5.5⑤	+5.0⑤	–.7 to +.3⑤	–.2⑤	0 to +.4	+.2	②

① — Toe-In (+). Toe-Out (–).
② — Refer to "Ball Joint Inspection" in "Front Suspension & Steering."
③ — Cross caster or camber (left to right), 0° (+/-.75°).
④ — Cross caster or camber (left to right), 0° (+/-1°).
⑤ — Cross caster or camber within .5°.

REAR WHEEL ALIGNMENT SPECIFICATIONS

Year	Model	Camber Angle, Degrees		Total Toe, Degrees①		Thrust Angle, Degrees	
		Limits	Desired	Limits	Desired	Limits	Desired
1998	DeVille	–.5 to +.5②	0②	0 to +.4	+.2	–.1 to +.1	0
	Eldorado	–.5 to +.5②	0②	0 to +.4	+.2	–.1 to +.1	0
	Seville	③	④	0 to +.4	+.2	–.1 to +.1	0
1999	DeVille	–.5 to +.5②	0②	0 to +.4	+.2	—	—
	Eldorado	–.5 to +.5②	0②	0 to +.4	+.2	—	—
	Seville	③	④	0 to +.4	+.2	–.1 to +.1	0
2000–02	DeVille	–.8 to +.2	–.3	0 to +.4	+.2	–.1 to +.1	0
	Eldorado	–.5 to +.5②	0②	0 to +.4	+.2	—	—
	Seville	–.8 to +.2	–.3	0 to +.4	+.2	–.1 to +.1	0

① — Toe-In (+). Toe-Out (–).
② — Cross camber (left to right) 0° (+/-.75°).
③ — On Seville models –.8 to +.2; On Seville Touring models –1.1 to –.1. Cross camber (left to right) 0° (+/-.5°).
④ — Kansas –.3; Kentucky –.6.

VEHICLE RIDE HEIGHT SPECIFICATIONS

Model	Year	Body Style	Manufacturer's Original Tire Size	Measurement Points & Specifications①②					
				Front			Rear		
				Dim.	Specification		Dim.	Specification	
					Inches	mm		Inches	mm
Concours	1998–99	All	③	H	1.65	42.00	H	1.12	28.00
DeVille	1998–99	All	③	H	2.00	51.00	H	1.46	37.00
	2000–02	All	③	H	1.57	40.00	H	3.39	86.00
Eldorado	1998–2002	All	③	H	1.96	49.00	I	1.15	29.00
Seville	1998–99	SLS	③	C	7.06	179.00	D	9.00	228.60
		STS	③	C	6.62	168.00	D	8.56	217
	2000–02	SLS④	③	Z	1.20–2.00	30.48–50.80	D	3.00–3.80	76.20–96.52
		SLS⑤	③	Z	.78–1.60	19.81–40.64	D	2.60–3.40	66.04–86.36
		STS	③	Z	.78–1.60	19.81–40.64	D	2.60–3.40	66.04–86.36

C Dim. — Ground to Rocker Panel, Front
D Dim. — 1998–99 models, Ground to Rocker Panel, Rear
D Dim. — 2000–02 Models, Lowest Point On Ball Joint Housing Minus Grease Fitting To Centerline Of Rear Bushing
H Dim. — Distance Between Lower Ball Joint Cover to Center of Lower Arm Bushing Bolt
I Dim. — Distance Between Center of Lower Arm Inner & Outer Bushing Bolts
Z Dim. — Distance Between Pivot Bolt Center Line Down To Lower Corner Of Lower Ball Joint.
Dim. — Dimension

ELDORADO, DEVILLE & SEVILLE

① — ±.39 in (10 MM) front to rear & side to side.
② — Measurement is with fuel, radiator coolant and engine oil full, spare tire, jack, hand tools & mats in designated positions and tires properly inflated.
③ — See door sticker or inside of glove box for manufacturer's original tire size specifications. If tires on vehicle do not match manufacturer's original tire size & measurement is not within limits, refer to the "Non-Standard Tire & Wheel Size Adjustment To Ride Height Specification & Tire Size Adjustment Charts" in the front of this manual for approximate changes in ride height specifications.
④ — FE1 & F45 suspension.
⑤ — FE3 suspension.

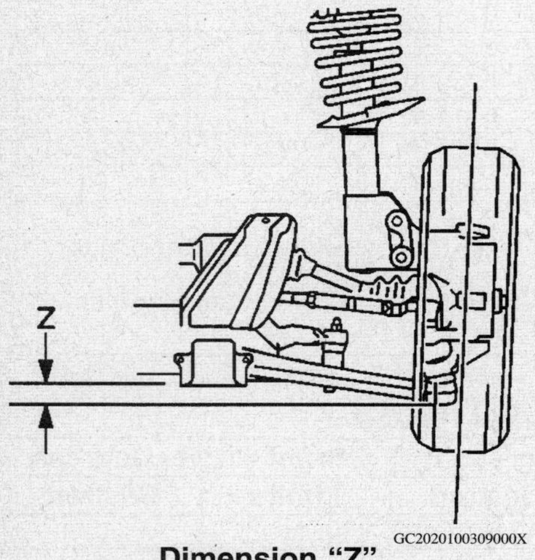

Dimension "Z"

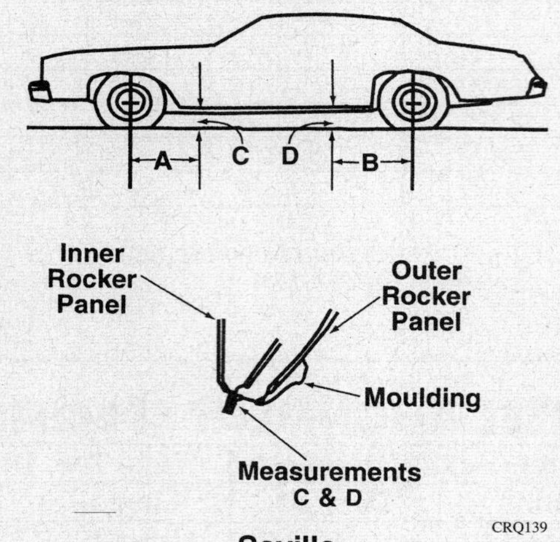

Seville

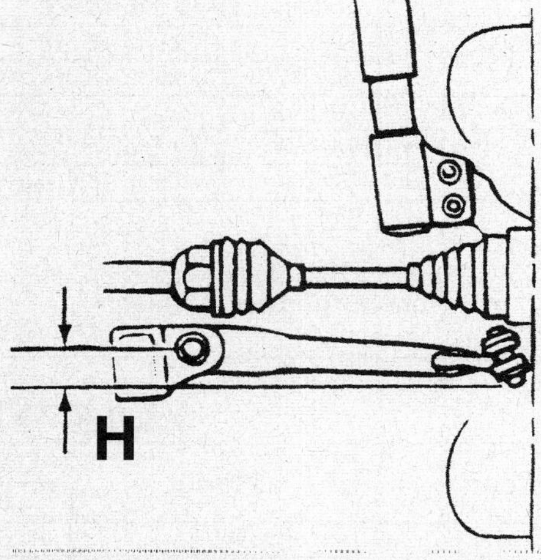

Concours, DeVille & Eldorado

FLUID CAPACITIES & COOLING SYSTEM DATA

Year	Engine/ Liter	Coolant Capacity, Qts.	Coolant Type	Radiator Cap Relief Pressure, Lbs.	Thermostat Opening Temp., °F	Fuel Tank Gals	Engine Oil Refill Qts. ①	ATF Qts.②
DEVILLE								
1998–99	4.6L	10.7	Dex-Cool	15	197	20	7.5	③
2000	4.6L	12.5	Dex-Cool	15	197	19	7.5	④
2001–02	4.6L	12.5	Dex-Cool	18	197	19	7.5	④
ELDORADO								
1998	4.6L	10.7	Dex-Cool	18	197	20	7.5	④
1999–2000	4.6L	10.7	Dex-Cool	15	197	20	7.5	④
2001–02	4.6L	12.5	Dex-Cool	18	197	19	7.5	④
SEVILLE								
1998	4.6L	12.5	Dex-Cool	18	197	19	7.5	④
1999–2000	4.6L	12.5	Dex-Cool	15	197	19	7.5	④
2001–02	4.6L	12.5	Dex-Cool	18	197	19	7.5	④

① — Includes filter.
② — Approximate. Make final inspection w/dipstick.
③ — Oil pan capacity 8 qts.; total capacity 12.6 qts.
④ — Drain & refill 11 qts.; after overhaul 12.6 qts.; dry refill 15 qts.

LUBRICANT DATA

Year	Model	Lubricant Type		
		Automatic Transaxle	Power Steering	Brake System
1998–2001	All	Dexron III	GM Power Steering Fluid①	DOT 3

① — GM part No. 1052884, or equivalent.

Electrical

NOTE: On Air Bag Equipped Models, Refer To "Air Bag System Precautions" Located In The Front Of This Manual For System Disarming & Arming Procedures.

NOTE: Refer To "Computer Relearn Procedures" Located In The Front Of This Manual When Battery Power To The Computer Has Been Interrupted.

INDEX

PRECAUTIONS

AIR BAG SYSTEMS

Refer to "Air Bag System Precautions" in the front of this manual for system disarming and arming procedures.

BATTERY GROUND CABLE

Prior to service, disconnect battery ground cable and isolate as required.

FUSE PANEL & FLASHER LOCATION

ELDORADO & 1998-99 DEVILLE

The engine compartment fuse/relay center is located on the lefthand front side of the engine compartment, near the strut tower. The lefthand and righthand Maxifuse blocks are located on the front lefthand side of the engine compartment, near the fuse/relay center.

The rear compartment fuse block is located in the front lefthand side of the luggage compartment.

The hazard flasher is located under the lefthand side of the instrument panel near the kick panel. The turn flasher module is located under the lefthand side of the instrument panel near the knee bolster.

SEVILLE & 2000-02 DEVILLE

The engine compartment fuse/relay center is located at the righthand rear of the engine compartment near the power steering pump.

The rear fuse block is located in the lefthand rear of passenger compartment under the rear seat.

The hazard/turn flasher is located at the lefthand side of the instrument panel behind the knee bolster.

FUEL PUMP RELAY LOCATION

DEVILLE

1998-99

The fuel pump relay is located on the front lefthand side of the engine compartment, in the engine compartment fuse/relay center.

2000-02

The fuel pump relay is located in the rear fuse block, in the lefthand rear of passenger compartment under the rear seat.

ELDORADO

The fuel pump relay is located on the front lefthand side of the engine compartment, in the engine compartment fuse/relay center.

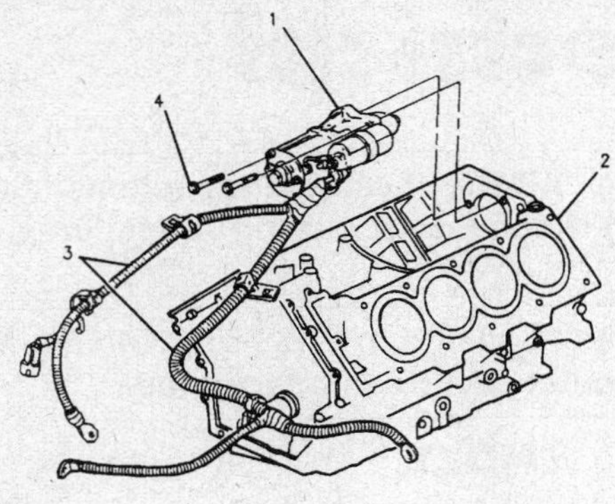

Fig. 1 Starter motor replacement

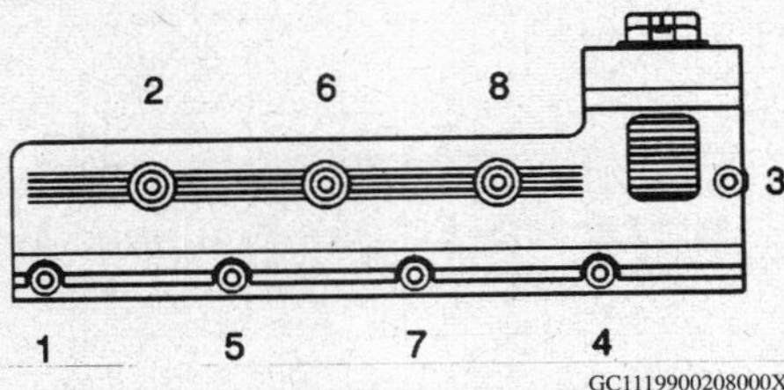

Fig. 2 Ignition control module assembly bolt removal sequence. 2000–02

SEVILLE

The fuel pump relay is located in the rear fuse block, in the lefthand rear of passenger compartment under the rear seat.

RELAY CENTER LOCATION

DEVILLE

1998–99

The engine compartment relay center is located on the front lefthand side of the engine compartment, near the strut tower.

The rear compartment replay center Nos. 1–4 are located on the lefthand rear of the passenger compartment, behind the rear seat.

2000–02

The rear compartment relay center is located in the lefthand rear of passenger compartment under the lefthand side of the rear seat.

ELDORADO

The engine compartment relay center is located on the front lefthand side of the engine compartment, near the strut tower.

The rear compartment replay center Nos. 1–4 are located on the lefthand rear of the passenger compartment, behind the rear seat.

SEVILLE

The rear compartment relay center is located in the lefthand rear of passenger compartment under the lefthand side of the rear seat.

STARTER

REPLACE

1. Remove intake manifold as outlined under "Intake Manifold, Replace" in "4.6L Engine" section.
2. Disconnect starter "S" terminal wire and battery cable, **Fig. 1.**
3. Remove mounting bolts and starter.
4. Remove solenoid and battery cable terminal nuts.
5. Reverse procedure to install, noting the following:
   a. **Torque** starter mounting bolts to 22 ft. lbs.
   b. **Torque** battery cable lead to 89 inch lbs.
   c. **Torque** S terminal nuts to 35 inch lbs.

COIL PACK

REPLACE

1998–99

1. Tag their locations, then disconnect spark plug wires.
2. Disconnect ignition module electrical connectors.
3. Remove mounting bolts and ignition control module.
4. Remove ignition coils from module and module from bracket.
5. Reverse procedure to install, noting the following
   a. **Torque** ignition coils to 30 inch lbs.
   b. **Torque** ignition control module mounting bolts to 108 inch lbs.

2000–02

Lefthand

1. Remove mounting bolts and engine sight shield.
2. Disconnect ignition control module electrical connector.
3. Remove engine oil level indicator as required.
4. Remove ignition assembly mounting bolts in sequence, **Fig. 2.**
5. Remove ignition assembly.
6. Remove mounting screws and ignition control module.
7. Reverse procedure to install, noting the following:
   a. **Torque** ignition control module mounting screws to seven inch lbs.
   b. **Torque** ignition assembly mounting bolts to 80 inch lbs. in reverse of removal sequence, **Fig. 2.**
   c. **Torque** engine sight shield mounting bolts to 70 inch lbs.

Righthand

1. Remove mounting bolts and engine sight shield, then disconnect ignition control module electrical connector.
2. **On models equipped with Secondary Air Injection (AIR),** proceed as follows:
   a. Disconnect AIR vent solenoid.
   b. Remove AIR pipe to exhaust manifold mounting bolts.
   c. Tag their positions, then disconnect AIR vacuum hoses.
   d. Remove AIR assembly.
3. **On all models,** remove ignition assembly bolts in sequence, **Fig. 2.**
4. Remove ignition assembly.
5. Remove mounting screws and ignition control module.
6. Reverse procedure to install, noting the following:
   a. **Torque** ignition control module mounting screws to seven inch lbs.
   b. **Torque** ignition assembly mounting bolts to 80 inch lbs. in reverse of removal sequence, **Fig. 2.**
   c. **Torque** engine sight shield mounting bolts to 70 inch lbs.

IGNITION LOCK

REPLACE

DEVILLE

1998–99

1. Remove lefthand closeout insulator panel as required.
2. Remove steering wheel as outlined under "Steering Wheel, Replace."
3. Remove turn signal switch as outlined under "Turn Signal Switch, Replace."
4. Remove key from lock, then the buzzer switch.
5. Place key in Lock position and remove lock mounting screw, **Fig. 3.**
6. Disconnect electrical connector and retaining clip from housing cover.
7. Remove lock cylinder.
8. Reverse procedure to install, noting the following:
   a. **Torque** lock mounting screw to 25 inch lbs.
   b. **Ensure forward edge of insulator is properly installed onto retainer studs at front of dash. Improper installation may result in brake or accelerator pedal binding.**

2000–02

1. Remove lefthand knee bolster.
2. Remove steering wheel as outlined under "Steering Wheel, Replace."

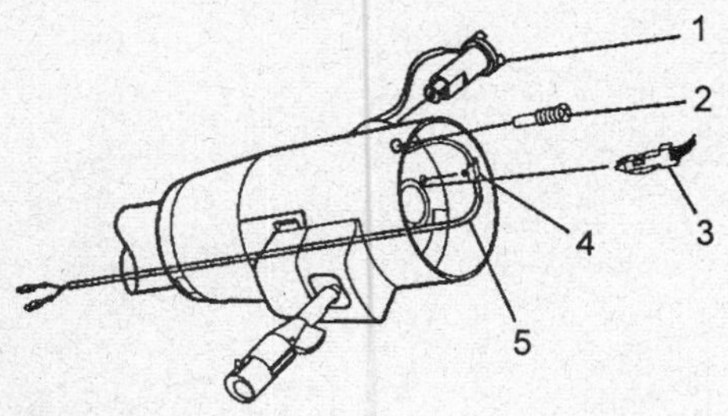

1. Lock cylinder
2. Cylinder retaining screw
3. Warning buzzer switch
4. Retaining clip
5. Wires

GC9120101371000X

Fig. 3 Lock cylinder set replacement. Eldorado & 1998–99 DeVille

3. Remove steering column upper shroud.
4. Remove one screw from upper shroud to access lock cylinder access hole.
5. Turn ignition to Start, then push down on ignition lock cylinder retaining pin through access hole using suitable bent tip awl.
6. Release lock cylinder to Run position and remove it by pulling away from steering column.
7. Reverse procedure to install.

ELDORADO

Refer to "1998–99 DeVille" for ignition lock replacement procedure.

SEVILLE

1. Apply parking brake.
2. Remove radio as outlined under "Radio, Replace."
3. Remove HVAC control head.
4. Turn ignition to Run position.
5. Looking through radio opening, depress lock cylinder retaining tab located on righthand lower side of ignition switch using suitable flat-headed tool.
6. Remove ignition cylinder.
7. Reverse procedure to install, noting the following:
   a. Insert ignition key into lock cylinder, then turn to Run.
   b. Install lock cylinder into instrument panel opening.
   c. Cylinder release button will produce an audible click when fully engaged.
   d. Pull lightly on lock cylinder to ensure secure engagement.

IGNITION SWITCH

REPLACE

DEVILLE

1998-99

1. **On models equipped with floor shift,** place transaxle selector in Park and turn ignition to Run.
2. **On all models,** remove lefthand hush panel, steering column lower cover, toe plate insulator and steering column lower mounting screws.

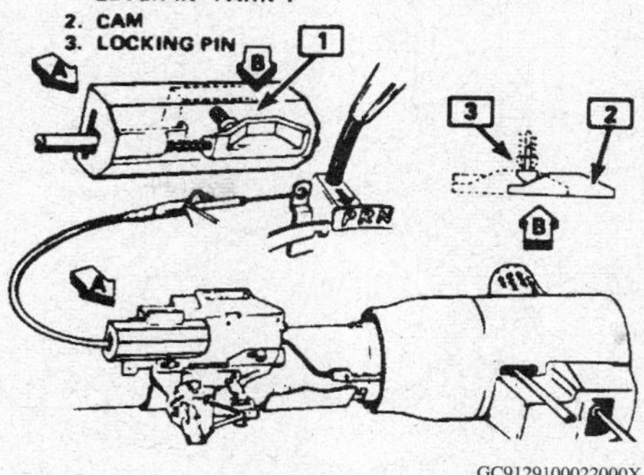

GC9129100022000X

Fig. 4 Park lock cable (Floor shift). 1998–99 DeVille & 1998–2000 Eldorado

3. Remove upper steering column bracket to instrument panel mounting nuts and lower column. Prior to lowering column disconnect shift indicator cable and electrical connectors, as required. **Do not force column down.**
4. Remove mounting nut, screw and dimmer switch. Tape actuator rod to steering column.
5. **On models equipped with floor shift,** proceed as follows:
   a. Ensure ignition is in Run position. **Do not attempt to disconnect park lock cable with switch in any other position.**
   b. Depress park lock cable latch using screwdriver in ignition switch inhibitor.
   c. Disconnect cable from inhibitor, **Fig. 4.**
   d. Turn ignition to Lock position.
6. **On all models,** remove ignition switch stud bolt.
7. Disconnect electrical connector and remove switch.
8. Reverse procedure to install, noting the following:
   a. Move ignition switch slider to extreme right, then one detent to left to place switch in Lock position.
   b. Connect ignition switch electrical connector.
   c. Ensure actuator is properly engaged
   d. **Torque** stud bolt to 35 inch lbs.
   e. Install dimmer switch, depress switch against actuator and insert 3⁄32 inch drill into adjustment slot, **Fig. 5.**
   f. **Torque** mounting nut and screw to 35 inch lbs.
   g. **On models equipped with floor shift,** rotate ignition lock to Run position and install shift lock cable on inhibitor.
   h. **On all models, torque** upper column bracket bolts to 20 ft. lbs. and lower column bolts to 25 ft. lbs.

2000-02

1. Remove lefthand knee bolster.
2. Remove steering column as outlined in "Steering Columns" chapter.
3. Remove ignition lock cylinder.
4. Remove upper and lower trim covers.

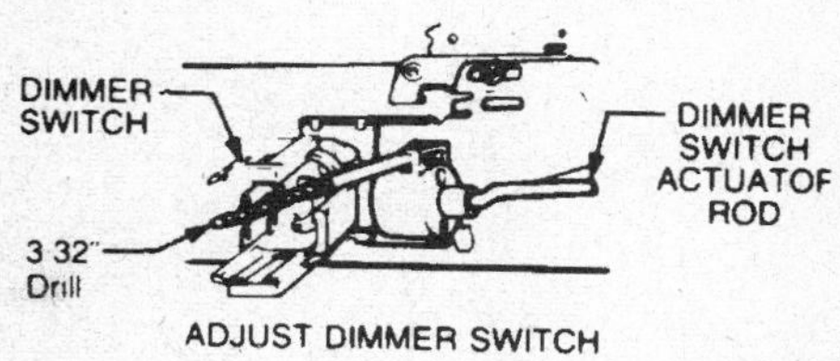

GC9129100023000X

Fig. 5 Dimmer switch installation. 1998–99 DeVille & 1998–2000 Eldorado

5. Disconnect coded key controller electrical connector.
6. Slide coded key controller from the lock module assembly.
7. Disconnect electrical connector from bottom of ignition and key alarm switch assembly.
8. Remove lead inside clip on side of ignition and key alarm switch assembly.
9. Remove ignition and key alarm switch assembly mounting screws, then the switch assembly.
10. Reverse procedure to install. **Torque** ignition and key alarm switch assembly mounting screws to 13 inch lbs.

ELDORADO

1998-2000

Refer to "1998–99" DeVille for ignition switch replacement procedure.

2001-02

1. Remove steering column as outlined in "Steering Columns" chapter.
2. Disconnect headlamp dimmer switch electrical connector.
3. Remove dimmer switch retaining nut and bolt.
4. Disconnect rod from dimmer switch.
5. Remove dimmer switch.
6. Remove ignition switch mounting stud.
7. Remove ignition switch, then disconnect electrical connector.
8. Reverse procedure to install, noting the following:
   a. Ensure all wiring and electrical connectors are properly routed to avoid pinching.
   b. **Torque** headlamp dimmer and ignition switch mounting stud to 35 inch lbs.
   c. **Torque** dimmer switch retaining nut and bolt to 35 inch lbs.

SEVILLE

1. Apply parking brake and ensure ignition switch is in Off or Lock position.
2. Remove radio as outlined under "Radio, Replace."
3. Remove HVAC control head and knee bolster.
4. Lock steering column using lockpin tool No. J42640, or equivalent, in underside of column.
5. Disconnect electrical connectors as required.
6. Remove lamp socket from ignition switch.
7. Disconnect park lock cable from ignition switch.
8. Turn ignition to Run.

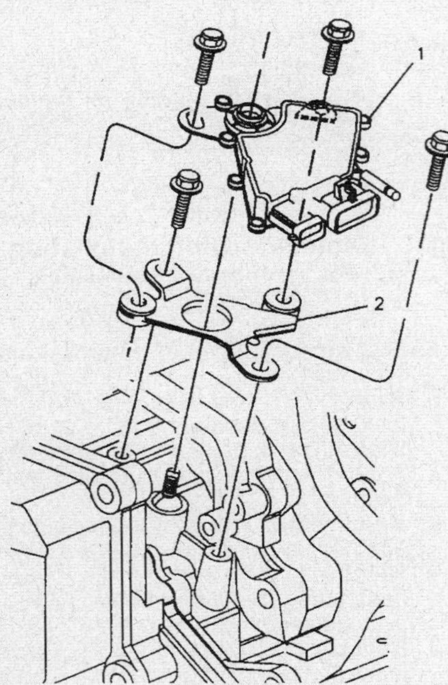

Fig. 6 Neutral safety switch

9. Depress park lock cable release button located on bottom of ignition switch at 6 o'clock position, then pull cable in order to disconnect from ignition switch.
10. Remove ignition lock cylinder as outlined under "Ignition Lock, Replace."
11. Remove ignition switch mounting screws located at access hole in steering column opening and through radio opening, then the switch.
12. Reverse procedure to install. **Torque** ignition switch mounting screws to 18 inch lbs.

NEUTRAL SAFETY SWITCH

REPLACE

1. Apply parking brake.
2. Shift gear selector to Neutral.
3. Disconnect electrical connectors, then remove linkage mounting nut.
4. Disconnect cable and lever.
5. Remove neutral safety switch, **Fig. 6.**
6. Reverse procedure to install, noting the following:
   a. Ensure transaxle is in Neutral.
   b. New switches are pre-aligned to neutral position.
   c. To adjust existing switch refer to "Neutral Safety Switch, Adjust."
   d. **Torque** switch bolts to 18 ft. lbs.
   e. **Torque** linkage mounting nut to 15 ft. lbs.

NEUTRAL SAFETY SWITCH

ADJUST

1. Insert switch alignment tool No.

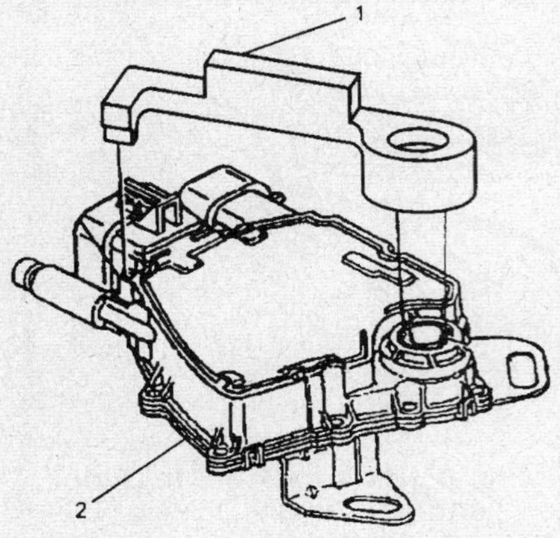

Fig. 7 Neutral safety switch adjustment

J41545, or equivalent, into two slots on switch, **Fig. 7.**
2. Rotate tool until tool rear leg falls into switch slot near hose.
3. Ensure tool is seated in all three slots.
4. Remove tool.

HEADLAMP SWITCH

REPLACE

DEVILLE

1998–99

1. Insert a suitable flat-bladed tool between instrument panel and top of headlamp switch assembly, **Fig. 8,** and depress two tabs securing top of switch to instrument panel.
2. Depress two lower tabs to remove switch.
3. Disconnect electrical connector.
4. Reverse procedure to install, noting the following:
   a. Ensure electrical connector is securely connected.
   b. Push in on switch with even pressure at all four corners and ensure all tabs engage instrument panel.

2000–02

1. Remove lefthand instrument panel end cap.
2. Remove switch by pushing on rear.
3. Disconnect electrical connector.
4. Reverse procedure to install.

ELDORADO

Refer to "1998–99 DeVille" for headlamp switch replacement procedure.

SEVILLE

Refer to "2000–02 DeVille" for headlamp switch replacement procedure.

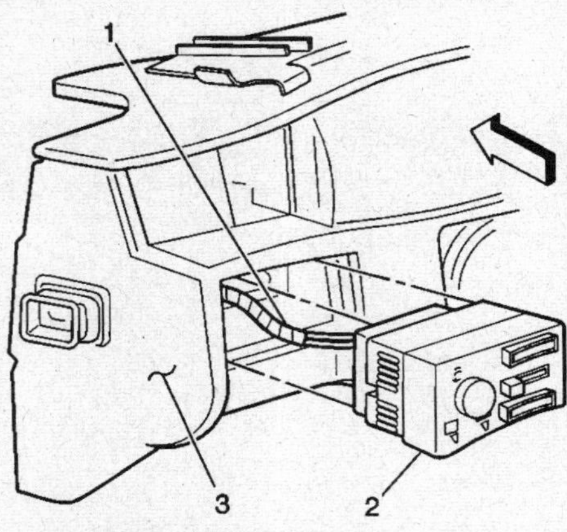

Fig. 8 Headlamp switch replacement. Eldorado & 1998–99 DeVille

TURN SIGNAL SWITCH

REPLACE

DEVILLE

1998–99

1. Remove steering wheel as outlined under "Steering Wheel, Replace."
2. Remove steering column lower trim cover.
3. Remove wave washer.
4. Mount spring compressor tool No. J23653-SIR, or equivalent, on steering shaft, **Fig. 9.**
5. Remove lock plate retaining ring and telescoping wheel components.
6. Remove spring compressor tool.
7. Remove lock plate, canceling cam, upper bearing spring, inner race and seat.
8. Remove multi-function lever.
9. Remove mounting screws and turn signal switch.
10. Reverse procedure to install.

2000–02

1. Remove steering wheel as outlined under "Steering Wheel, Replace."
2. Remove steering column shrouds, trim covers and wiring tie straps as required.
3. Note orientation of steering column wiring harness routing in lower harness shield for proper installation.
4. Remove multi-function switch mounting screws.
5. Disconnect electrical connectors, then remove multi-function switch.
6. Reverse procedure to install. **Torque** multi-function switch mounting screws to 62 inch lbs.

ELDORADO

Refer to "1998–99 DeVille" for turn signal switch replacement procedure.

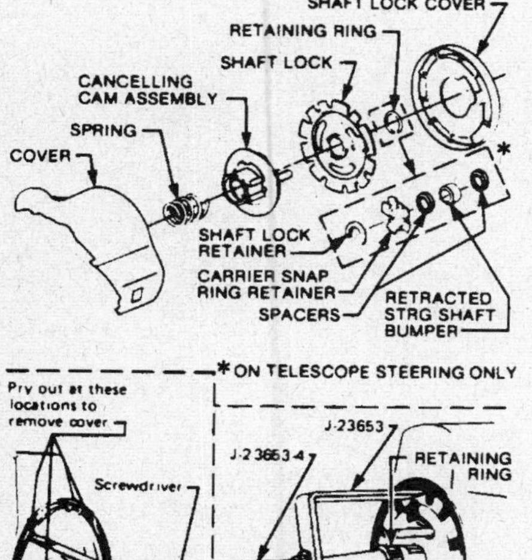

Fig. 9 Lock plate & cancelling cam removal. Eldorado & 1998–99 DeVille

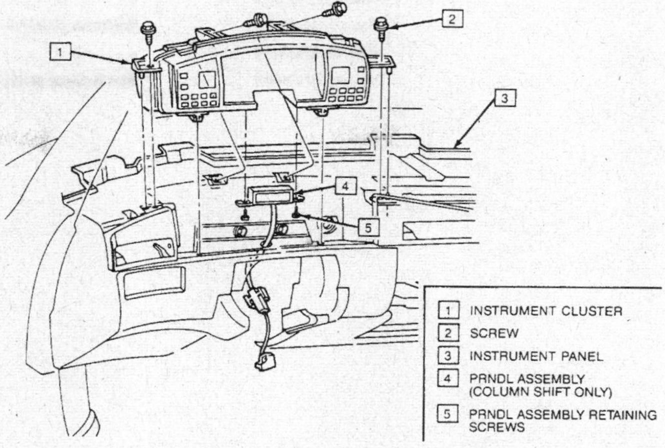

Fig. 10 Instrument cluster replacement. 1998–99 DeVille & Eldorado

SEVILLE

Refer to "2000–02 DeVille" for turn signal switch replacement procedure.

DIMMER SWITCH

REPLACE

Refer to "Ignition Switch, Replace" for dimmer switch replacement procedure.

STEERING WHEEL

REPLACE

1. Turn ignition Off.
2. Remove air bag module as outlined in "Air Bag Systems" chapter.
3. Remove horn contact by pushing slightly and twisting counterclockwise.
4. Disconnect Connector Position Assurance (CPA) and coil assembly electrical connector from air bag module.
5. Remove steering column shaft nut.
6. Remove steering wheel using puller tool No. J1859-A and legs tool No. J42578, or equivalents. **Do not thread puller bolts too far into steering wheel.**
7. Reverse procedure to install.

INSTRUMENT CLUSTER

REPLACE

DEVILLE

1998–99

1. Remove fuses A5 and B5 from rear compartment fuse panel and fuse A3-IGN 1 from engine compartment fuse panel.
2. Remove defroster grille using suitable small flat-bladed tool.
3. Remove sunload and headlamp auto control sensors from defroster grille.
4. Remove three upper trim panel mounting screws through defroster grille opening.
5. Remove heater and air conditioning vents from instrument panel.
6. Remove four upper trim panel mounting screws through vent openings.
7. Remove upper trim panel.
8. Disconnect two electrical connectors from top of instrument panel.
9. Remove instrument cluster mounting screws, **Fig. 10.**
10. Raise cluster and remove PRNDL mechanism mounting screws.
11. Remove instrument cluster.
12. Reverse procedure to install.

2000–02

1. Remove instrument panel upper trim pad.
2. Remove instrument cluster trim panel.
3. Remove cluster to instrument panel retainer mounting screws.
4. Disconnect cluster electrical connectors.
5. Remove cluster assembly from retainer.
6. Reverse procedure to install. **Torque** cluster mounting screws to 14 inch lbs.

ELDORADO

1998–99

Refer to "1998–99 DeVille" for instrument cluster replacement procedure.

2000–02

1. Remove RLY IGN 1, IGN O-BODY and CLUSTER fuses from rear compartment fuse block.
2. Remove HAZARD and MIRROR fuses from front fuse block.
3. Remove instrument panel upper trim pad.
4. Disconnect electrical connectors from top of instrument cluster.
5. Remove cluster to instrument panel mounting screws.
6. Slide cluster upward and remove from vehicle. **Do not allow cluster to sit on its face any more than 15 minutes or damage to the fluid-filled air core gauges may result.**
7. Reverse procedure to install, noting the following:
   a. Ensure all electrical connectors and wiring are properly routed to avoid pinching.
   b. Position cluster locating pins into instrument panel guide holes.
   c. **Torque** cluster mounting screws to 18 inch lbs.

SEVILLE

Refer to "2000–02 DeVille" for instrument cluster replacement procedure.

RADIO

REPLACE

CONSOLE SHIFT

DEVILLE

1998–99

1. Remove shifter trim plate and ashtray.
2. Disconnect Driver Information System switch.
3. Disconnect electrical connectors.
4. Remove screws from radio and HVAC control assembly.
5. Disconnect electrical harness, **Fig. 11.**
6. Remove brackets, **Fig. 12.**
7. Remove plastic loading pin and clip stud from rear of radio.
8. Remove radio.
9. Reverse procedure to install.

2000–02

1. Remove instrument panel center trim plate, then the HVAC control head.
2. Push and hold release tabs on lefthand and righthand sides of radio.
3. Remove radio.
4. Disconnect antenna lead and electrical connectors.
5. Remove mounting brackets and studs. They will need to be transferred if a new radio will be installed.
6. Reverse procedure to install.

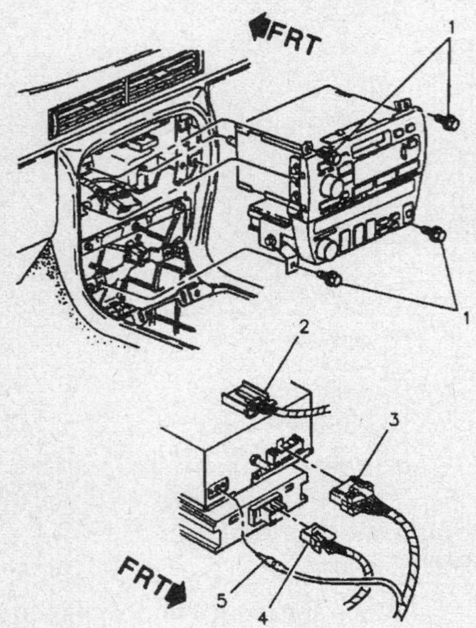

1 SCREW (4)
2 DIC HARNESS
3 RADIO HARNESS
4 HVAC HARNESS
5 ANTENNA COAX

GC9039600042000X

Fig. 11 Radio replacement (console shift). Eldorado & 1998–99 DeVille

2001 w/UY4 Navigation System

1. Remove rear shelf trim panel.
2. Remove rear shelf carrier panel.
3. Remove radio to radio/navigation processor bracket nuts.
4. Disconnect electrical connectors and antenna lead-in from radio.
5. Remove radio from mounting bracket.
6. Reverse procedure to install. **Torque** radio mounting nuts to 44 inch lbs.

ELDORADO

Refer to "1998–99 DeVille" for radio replacement procedure.

COLUMN SHIFT

1. Remove radio trim plate.
2. Push in on locking tabs on side of radio and pull out, **Fig. 13.**
3. Remove electrical harness.
4. Remove both brackets, **Fig. 14.**
5. Remove plastic loading pin and clip stud from rear of radio. They will need to be transferred if a new radio will be installed.
6. Remove radio.
7. Reverse procedure to install.

WIPER MOTOR

REPLACE

DEVILLE

1998–99

1. Remove wiper arm nut caps, then the nuts.

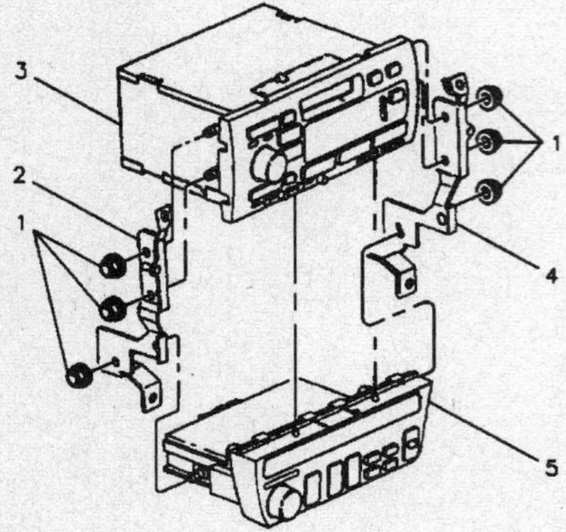

1 NUT (6)
2 LEFT RADIO BRACKET
3 RADIO
4 RIGHT RADIO BRACKET
5 HVAC CONTROLLER

GC9039600044000X

Fig. 12 Radio bracket replacement (console shift). Eldorado & 1998–99 DeVille

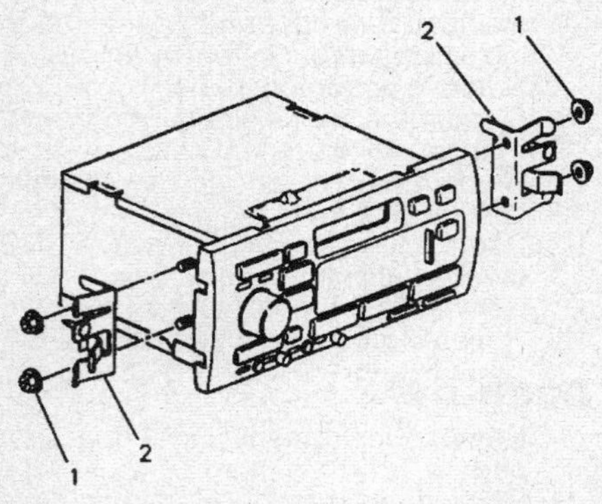

1 NUT (4)
2 LEFT AND RIGHT BRACKET

GC9039600045000X

Fig. 14 Radio bracket replacement. Column shift

2. Remove wiper arms using puller tool No. J39822, or equivalent.
3. Remove air conditioning pipe shroud as required.
4. Remove shroud air inlet grille panel.
5. Disconnect wiper motor electrical connectors.
6. Note position of crank arm on old motor.
7. Disconnect wiper transmission drive link socket from motor crank arm using separator tool No. J39232, or equivalent.
8. Remove air conditioning shroud pipe from wheelhouse as required.
9. Remove motor mounting screws, then the motor.
10. Reverse procedure to install, noting the following:

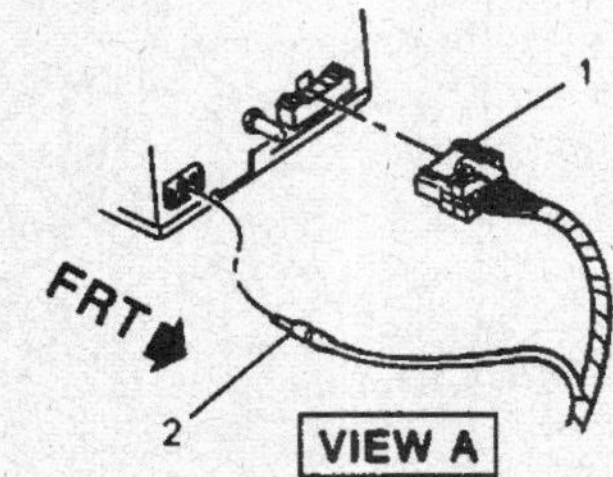

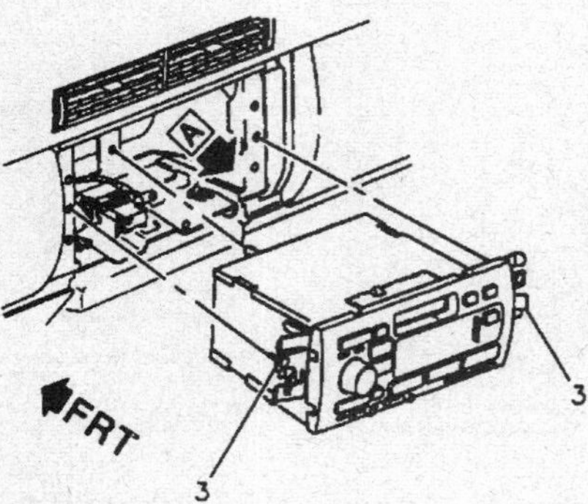

1 HARNESS
2 ANTENNA COAX
3 ALIGNMENT BULLETS AND LOCKING TABS

GC9039600043000X

Fig. 13 Radio replacement. Column shift

a. **Torque** motor mounting screws to 80 inch lbs.
b. Connect transmission drive link socket to motor crank arm ball using installer tool No. J39529, or equivalent.
c. **Torque** wiper arm mounting nuts to 24 ft. lbs.

2000–02

1. Remove wipers arms and air inlet grille panel.
2. Remove windshield frame reinforcement bolts and nuts, then the reinforcement.
3. Rotate wiper motor crank arm to opposite of park position by pushing or pulling on transmission linkage.
4. Disconnect wiper motor electrical connector, then push harness and grommet through hole in plenum.
5. Remove wiper transmission mounting bolts, then the transmission.
6. Remove drive link from wiper motor crank arm using separator tool No. J39232, or equivalent.
7. Remove wiper motor mounting screws, then the motor.
8. Reverse procedure to install, noting the following:
   a. **Torque** motor mounting screws to 71 inch lbs.
   b. Install drive link onto motor crank arm using installer tool No. J39529, or equivalent.
   c. **Torque** wiper transmission mounting screws to 71 inch lbs.

d. **Torque** windshield frame reinforcement bolts and nuts to 80 inch lbs.
e. **Torque** wiper arm nuts to 24 ft. lbs.

ELDORADO

Refer to "1998–99 DeVille" for wiper motor replacement procedure.

SEVILLE

1. Disconnect wiper motor electrical connector.
2. Remove motor mounting screws.
3. Move wiper arms six to eight inches up windshield from park position.
4. Pull wiper motor away from firewall.
5. Disconnect transmission drive link from motor crank arm using removal tool No. J39232, or equivalent.
6. Reverse procedure to install, noting the following:
   a. Ensure wiper arms are still six to eight inches up windshield from park position.
   b. Connect transmission drive link to motor crank arm using installer tool No. J39529, or equivalent.
   c. Mount wiper motor onto firewall. **Torque** screws to 80 inch lbs.

WIPER SWITCH

REPLACE

DEVILLE

1998–99

1. Remove steering wheel as outlined under "Steering Wheel, Replace."
2. Slide connector cover toward front of vehicle, then unplug electrical connector.
3. Push lever in and rotate clockwise ¼ turn, then pull out switch.
4. Reverse procedure to install.

2000–02

1. Remove steering wheel as outlined under "Steering Wheel, Replace."
2. Remove knee bolster and steering column nuts.
3. Lower steering column, then remove tilt lever, steering column shrouds and wire harness assembly.
4. **On models equipped with power tilt and telescope,** disconnect and remove interface module and harness. Record harness placement for installation.
5. **On all models,** depress tabs, then disconnect and remove switch.
6. Reverse procedure to install, noting the following:
   a. **Torque** steering column upper trim cover retaining screw to 13 inch lbs.
   b. **Torque** steering column lower trim cover retaining screws to 31 inch lbs.

ELDORADO

Refer to "1998–99 DeVille" for wiper switch replacement procedure.

SEVILLE

Refer to "2000–02 DeVille" for wiper switch replacement procedure.

WIPER TRANSMISSION

REPLACE

DEVILLE

1998–99

1. Remove wiper arm nut caps, then the nuts.
2. Remove wiper arms using puller tool No. J39822, or equivalent.
3. Remove shroud air inlet grille panel.
4. Remove drive link from wiper motor crank arm using separator tool No. J39232, or equivalent.
5. Remove mounting screws and wiper transmission.
6. Reverse procedure to install, noting the following:
   a. Connect transmission drive link socket to motor crank arm ball using installer tool No. J39529, or equivalent.
   b. **Torque** wiper arm mounting nuts to 24 ft. lbs.

2000–02

Refer to "Wiper Motor, Replace" for wiper transmission replacement procedure.

ELDORADO & SEVILLE

Refer to "1998–99 DeVille" for wiper transmission replacement procedure.

BLOWER MOTOR

REPLACE

DEVILLE

1998–99

1. Remove strut tower cross brace.
2. Remove cowl relay center bracket, then disconnect electrical connector and cooling hose from blower motor.
3. Remove MAP sensor mounting bracket.
4. Remove mounting screws and tilt blower motor in case to allow fan removal. **Fan must be removed prior to blower motor.**
5. Remove retainer and fan from blower motor.
6. Remove blower motor and fan from case.
7. Reverse procedure to install, noting the following:
   a. **Torque** motor mounting screws to 35 inch lbs.
   b. **Torque** inertial plate screws to 35 inch lbs.

2000–02

1. Remove righthand side sound insulator panel.
2. Remove glove compartment as required.
3. Pull back carpet, then remove Dash Integration Module and position aside.
4. Remove mounting screws, then disconnect blower motor electrical connector.
5. Remove blower motor.
6. Reverse procedure to install.

ELDORADO

1998–99

Refer to "1998–99 DeVille" for blower motor replacement procedure.

2000–02

1. Remove righthand cam cover as outlined under "Valve Cover, Replace" in "4.6L Engine" section.
2. Remove inertial plate screws, then the inertial plate from blower motor.
3. Disconnect blower motor electrical connector.
4. Remove blower motor mounting screws, then the motor.
5. Reverse procedure to install, noting the following:
   a. **Torque** motor mounting screws to 35 inch lbs.
   b. **Torque** inertial plate screws to 35 inch lbs.

SEVILLE

Refer to "2000–02 DeVille" for blower motor replacement procedure.

CABIN AIR FILTER

REPLACE

DEVILLE

1. Open hood.
2. Remove cabin air filter access cover from righthand side of cowl panel, **Fig. 15.**
3. Remove cabin air filter element from filter housing. Flex righthand side of filter housing to aid in filter removal, **Fig. 16.**
4. Install new cabin air filter into filter housing. Flex righthand side of filter housing to aid in filter installation, **Fig. 16.**
5. Install cabin air filter access cover.

SEVILLE

1. Remove two retaining screws from rear edge of lefthand sound insulator.
2. Push in on snap tabs to release insulator.
3. Disconnect lefthand sound insulator electrical connectors, then remove insulator.
4. Twist shift cable grommet and position away from cabin air filter access door. Cutting tie strap and peeling back foam insulation may be required to position grommet away from filter door.
5. Remove cabin air filter access cover from HVAC module, **Fig. 17.**
6. Remove tape, then pull out first filter element using filter tab, **Fig. 18.**
7. Remove tape, then pull out second element.
8. Remove tape, then pull out third element.
9. Lubricate new filter guides with suitable silicone spray to ease installation.
10. Install first new filter into case. Raise filter using a long thin-blade screwdriver and filter tab until it is parallel with HVAC module. Ensure leading edge of filter engages filter case holding rib.
11. Engage new second filter in tab of first

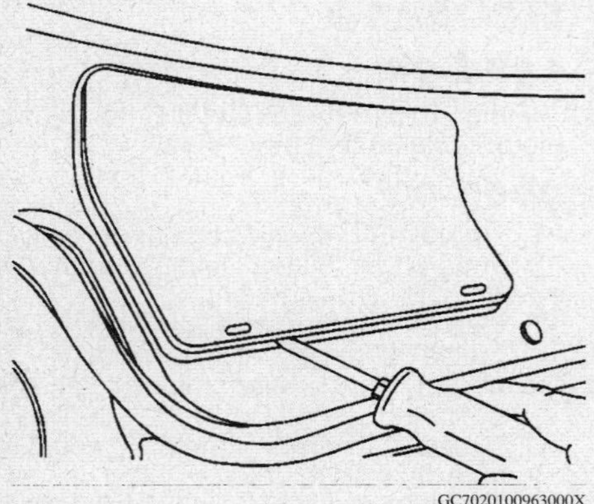

Fig. 15 Cabin air filter access door removal. DeVille

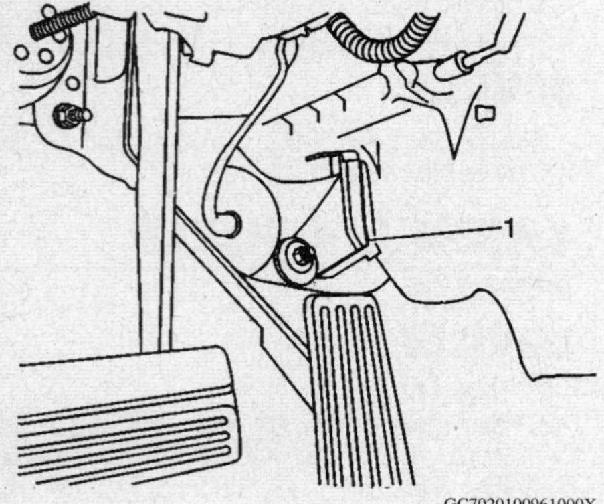

Fig. 18 Cabin air filter replacement. Seville

filter. Slide second filter into remaining channels of first filter. Using filter tab, raise filter until it is parallel with HVAC module. Ensure leading edge of filter engages filter case holding rib.

12. Engage third new cabin air filter in tab of second filter. Slide third filter into remaining channels of second filter.
13. Fold tab of second filter down.
14. Fold tab of third filter up and over second filter.
15. Install A/C and heater module filter cover. Ensure cover is properly seated.
16. Position shift cable grommet, **Fig. 19.**
17. Position lefthand sound insulator to instrument panel, then connect electrical connectors.
18. Install lefthand sound insulator fasteners in proper locations. **Torque** fasteners to 18 inch lbs.

HEATER CORE

REPLACE

DEVILLE

1998–99

1. Drain coolant into a suitable container.
2. Remove mounting screws, glove compartment and righthand lower sound insulator.
3. Remove bracket mounting screws and position Engine Control Module (ECM) aside to access rear programmer mounting screw.
4. Disconnect electrical and vacuum connectors, then remove mounting screws and processor, **Fig. 20.**
5. Disconnect electrical connectors, then remove ECM and mounting bracket.
6. Disconnect lefthand and righthand air mix actuators.
7. Remove heater core cover, then disconnect heater core hoses using clamp tool No. J37097-A, or equivalent.
8. Remove heater core mounting screws, then the core.
9. Reverse procedure to install. Prior to installing glove compartment, adjust air mix door link rods as follows:
   a. Set temperature control for 90°F.
   b. If ambient temperature is above 90°F, disconnect inside air temperature sensor.
   c. Allow 45 seconds for processor arm to travel to maximum heat position.
   d. Move temperature door to full hot position.
   e. Pull driver's temperature door link toward processor until door hits its stop.
   f. Push threaded portion of link into driver's temperature door crank slot.
   g. Pull passenger's door link from temperature door retainer, then snap door link into the retainer.

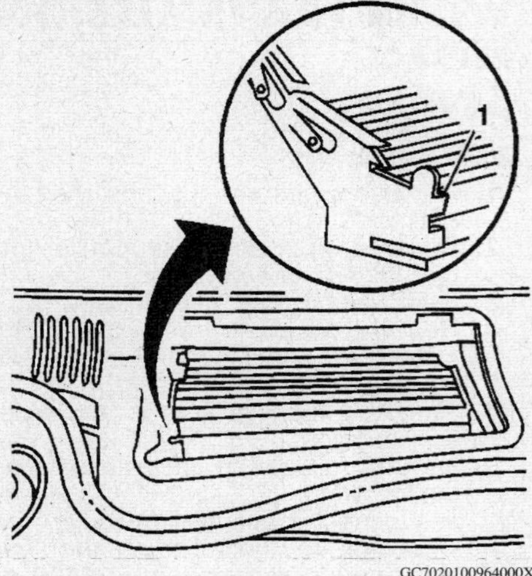

Fig. 16 Cabin air filter replacement. DeVille

2000–02

1. Drain coolant into a suitable container.
2. Disconnect heater hoses from heater core using clamp tool No. J37097-A, or equivalent.
3. Remove instrument panel as outlined in "Dash Panel Service" chapter.
4. Remove heat shield.
5. Remove heater core cover retainers and straps, then the cover.
6. Remove heater core. Discard case side seals.
7. Reverse procedure to install, noting the following:
   a. Install heater core with new case side seals.
   b. Ensure all electrical connectors and wiring are properly routed to avoid pinching.
   c. Fill coolant to proper level and inspect for leakage.

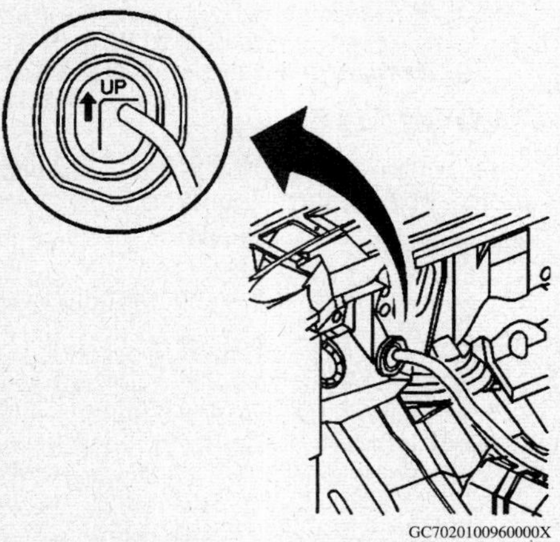

Fig. 17 Cabin air filter access cover location. Seville

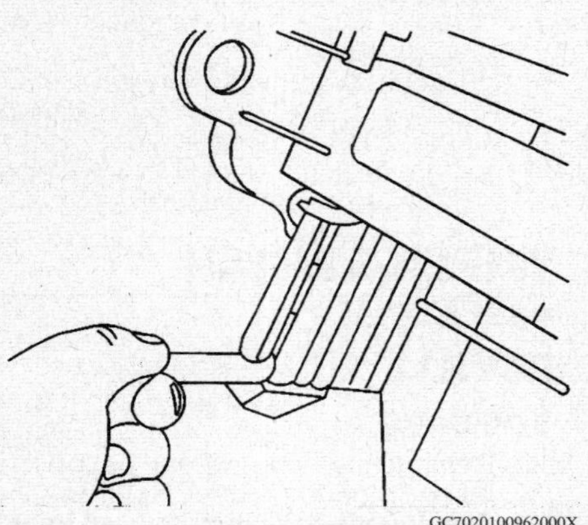

Fig. 19 Positioning shift cable grommet. Seville

ELDORADO

Refer to "1998–99 DeVille" for heater core replacement procedure.

SEVILLE

Refer to "2000–02 DeVille" for hetaer core replacement procedure.

EVAPORATOR CORE

REPLACE

DEVILLE

1998–99

1. Recover refrigerant as outlined in "Air Conditioning" chapter.
2. Drain radiator and coolant into a suitable container.
3. Remove cross-tower support bracket mounting bolts.
4. Remove mounting bolts and position cowl relay center bracket aside.
5. Disconnect power module, blower

motor and blower motor resistor electrical connectors.
6. Disconnect heater core hoses using clamp tool No. J37097-A, or equivalent.
7. Remove evaporator line mounting bracket.
8. Remove evaporator core refrigerant lines. **Cap open fittings.**
9. Remove heater hose T-connector.
10. Remove two engine compartment heat shield mounting screws.
11. Raise and support vehicle.
12. Remove remaining heat shield mounting screws from under vehicle.
13. Remove heat shield.
14. Remove air conditioning module mounting screws.
15. Lower vehicle and remove MAP sensor bracket.
16. Remove diverter valve from righthand side valve cover.
17. Remove valve cover harness hold-down brackets.
18. Remove power module, blower motor and sound insulator.
19. Remove mounting screws, air conditioning module cover, sound insulator and seal.
20. Remove evaporator retaining clamp, and evaporator core.
21. Reverse procedure to install, noting the following:
    a. **Torque** module cover mounting screws to 27 inch lbs.
    b. **Torque** line fitting bolt to 18 ft. lbs.

2000–02

1. Recover refrigerant as outlined in "Air Conditioning" chapter.
2. Disconnect evaporator lines.
3. Disconnect heater hoses using clamp tool No. J37097-A, or equivalent.
4. Remove center console assembly.
5. Remove instrument panel as outlined in "Dash Panel Service" chapter.

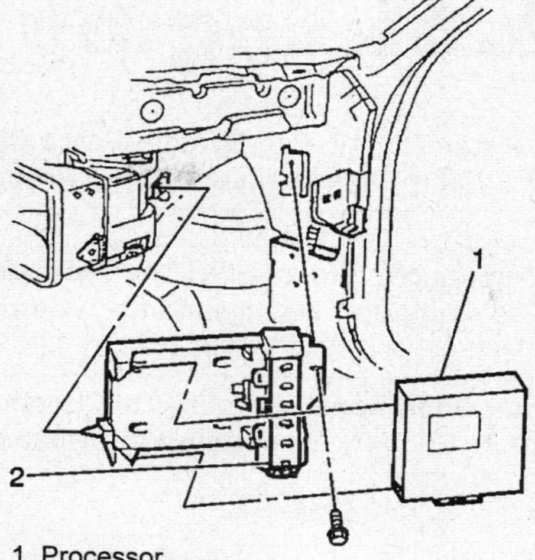

1. Processor
2. Mounting bracket

GC7020100965000X

Fig. 20 Processor removal. Eldorado & 1998–99 DeVille

6. Remove evaporator drain, defroster and heater duct assembly.
7. Remove heater and evaporator module.
8. Remove heater and evaporator tube seal, then the upper evaporator case.
9. Remove evaporator core and case seals.
10. Reverse procedure to install, noting the following:
    a. **Torque** HVAC module retaining nuts to 80 inch lbs.
    b. **Torque** evaporator nut to 18 ft. lbs.

ELDORADO

1. Recover refrigerant as outlined in "Air Conditioning" chapter.
2. Lower engine and transaxle assembly as required. Refer to "Engine, Replace" in "4.6L Engine" section.
3. Disconnect accumulator tube and evaporator tube from evaporator core.
4. Remove blower motor.
5. Remove evaporator core rubber barrier cover and evaporator core cover.
6. Remove evaporator core.
7. Reverse procedure to install, noting the following:
    a. **Torque** evaporator core cover screws to 44 inch lbs.
    b. **Torque** evaporator core rubber barrier cover screws to 44 inch lbs.
    c. Ensure all electrical connectors and wiring are properly routed to avoid pinching.
    d. Charge A/C system, then inspect fittings for leakage using halogen leak detector tool No. J39400-A, or equivalent.

SEVILLE

Refer to "2000–02 DeVille" for evaporator core replacement procedure.

TECHNICAL SERVICE BULLETINS

ANALOG INSTRUMENT CLUSTER ERRATIC OR INOPERATIVE OPERATION

2001 DEVILLE & SEVILLE w/UY9

On these models, DeVille through VIN 1U219979 and Seville through VIN 1U219978, there may be occurrences of fuel gauges sticking on empty, temperature gauges remaining on cold or erratic Driver Information Center (DIC) operation. This may be caused by the cluster software.

To correct this condition, install a replacement cluster assembly part No. 25696232 (88890684 REMAN).

4.6L Engine

NOTE: On Air Bag Equipped Models, Refer To "Air Bag System Precautions" Located In The Front Of This Manual For System Disarming & Arming Procedures.

NOTE: Refer To "Computer Relearn Procedures" Located In The Front Of This Manual When Battery Power To The Computer Has Been Interrupted.

NOTE: Prior To Performing Any Service Operations Listed In This Section, Consult The "Technical Service Bulletins" Section For Related Information.

INDEX

PRECAUTIONS

AIR BAG SYSTEMS

Refer to "Air Bag System Precautions" in the front of this manual for system disarming and arming procedures.

BATTERY GROUND CABLE

Prior to service, disconnect battery ground cable and isolate as required.

FUEL SYSTEM PRESSURE RELIEF

A small amount of fuel may be released when servicing fuel connections even after pressure is released. Cover all fuel connections with shop towel before servicing.

1. Disconnect and isolate battery ground cable.
2. Remove intake manifold top cover.
3. Loosen fuel tank filler cap.
4. Install fuel pressure gauge tool No. J34730-1A, or equivalent, to fuel pressure connection. Wrap shop towel around fitting while connecting gauge.
5. Install bleed hose into approved container, then open valve on gauge to relieve system pressure.

RELEARN PROCEDURES

COMPUTER

Refer to "Computer Relearn Procedure" located in the front of this manual for computer relearn procedures.

THROTTLE POSITION (TP) SENSOR

The TP Sensor Learn Procedure should be performed whenever the TP sensor, throttle body or ECM/PCM is replaced.

1. Ensure nothing is touching or obstructing accelerator or brake pedals.
2. Turn ignition On.
3. Wait 60 seconds.
4. Turn ignition Off.
5. Wait 15 seconds.

IDLE AIR CONTROL (IAC)

If the IAC disconnected or interrupted, proceed as follows:

1. Start and idle engine for 15 seconds.
2. Turn ignition Off.
3. Wait 15 seconds.
4. Start engine and inspect for proper idling function.

COMPRESSION PRESSURE

Perform compression test with engine at normal operating temperature, spark plugs

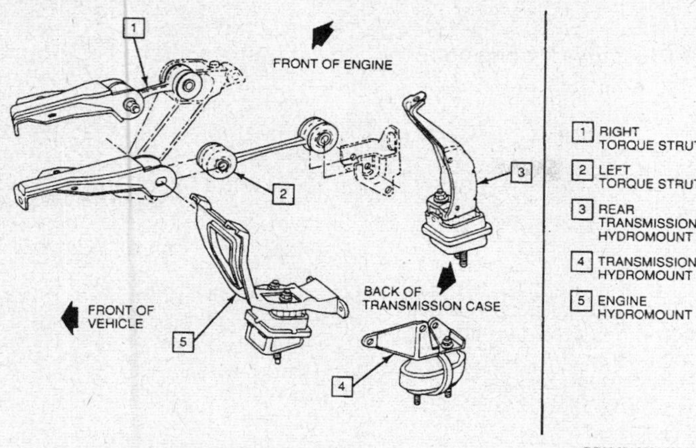

Fig. 1 Engine/transaxle mount replacement. 1998–99 DeVille & Eldorado

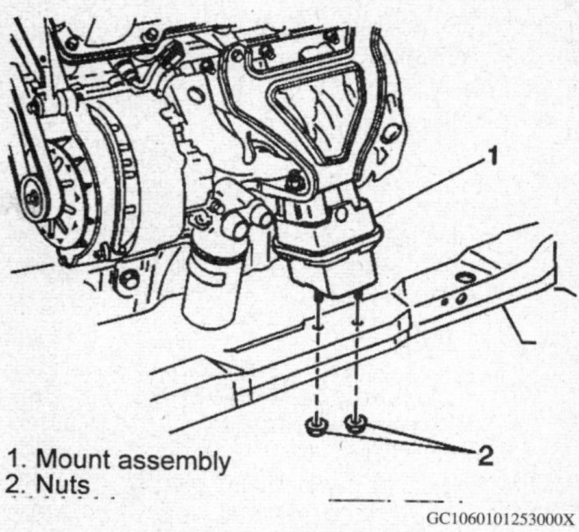

Fig. 2 Front engine mount replacement. 1998–99 DeVille & Eldorado

removed and throttle wide open. Disable the ignition and fuel systems. Lowest cylinder must be within 70% of highest cylinder with a minimum pressure of 140 psi.

ENGINE MOUNT

REPLACE

DeVille

1998–99

1. Remove righthand and lefthand engine cooling fans in sequence.
2. Remove lefthand and righthand torque struts, **Fig. 1.**
3. Install engine support fixture tool No. J28467-A, or equivalent. Use only one support at lefthand rear engine bracket.
4. Raise and support vehicle.
5. Remove mount to engine cradle mounting nuts, **Fig. 2.**
6. Remove motor mount bracket to crankcase mounting bolts.
7. Lower vehicle.
8. Remove mount to cylinder head and bracket mounting bolts.
9. Raise engine, then separate and remove mount and bracket.
10. Reverse procedure to install. Tighten bolts and nuts in following sequence:
    a. **Torque** mount bracket to crankcase bolts to 22 ft. lbs.
    b. **Torque** mount to cradle bolts to 22 ft. lbs.
    c. **Torque** mount bracket to cylinder head bolts to 22 ft. lbs.
    d. **Torque** mount to bracket bolts to 22 ft. lbs.
    e. **Torque** the torque strut fasteners to 37 ft. lbs., then again to 44 ft. lbs. Adjust in order to provide zero preload.
    f. **Torque** lower engine mount bracket nuts to 30 ft. lbs.
    g. **Torque** mount to cradle nuts to 22 ft. lbs.
    h. **Torque** transaxle support brace bolt to 37 ft. lbs.
    i. **Torque** upper engine mount brace bolts to 37 ft. lbs.
    j. Install engine frame. **Torque** front engine mount nuts to 37 ft. lbs.

2000–02

FRONT

1. **On Seville models,** remove radiator cooling fans.
2. **On all models,** install engine lift bracket tool No. J42504 and engine support fixture tool No. J28467-A, or equivalents.
3. Raise and support vehicle.
4. Remove mount bracket to engine block mounting nuts.
5. Remove mount to frame mounting nut.
6. Lower vehicle.
7. Remove bracket to engine upper mounting bolts.
8. Raise engine, then remove mount and bracket.
9. Reverse procedure to install, noting the following:
    a. **Torque** front engine mount to bracket nut to 84 ft. lbs.
    b. **Torque** front engine mount nut to 52 ft. lbs.

RIGHTHAND

1. Raise and support vehicle, then support engine with suitable jack.
2. Remove mount to bracket mounting nut.
3. Lower engine slightly.
4. Remove mounting nut, bolts and mount.
5. Reverse procedure to install.

Eldorado

1998–99

Refer to "1998–99 DeVille" for engine mount replacement procedure.

2000

FRONT

Removal

1. Remove engine cooling fans.
2. Install engine lift bracket tool No. J42504, or equivalent.
3. Install engine support fixture adapters tool No. J42478, or equivalent.
4. Install engine support fixture tool No. J28467-A, or equivalent.
5. Remove two mount to frame nuts.
6. Remove two mount bracket to engine block nuts.
7. Remove two engine mount bracket to engine upper bolts.
8. Remove mount and bracket.

Installation

1. Install mount and bracket.
2. Raise and support vehicle.
3. Install engine support brace.
4. Loosely install two support brace nuts and bolt to support brace.
5. Install two mount to frame nuts.
6. **Torque** mount bracket lefthand nut to 30 ft. lbs.
7. **Torque** mount bracket righthand nut to 30 ft. lbs.
8. **Torque** engine brace bolt to 37 ft. lbs.
9. **On Eldorado models, torque** mount nuts to 37 ft. lbs.
10. **On Seville models, torque** mount nuts to 52 ft. lbs.
11. **On all models, torque** two upper mount brace bolts to 37 ft. lbs.
12. Lower vehicle, then remove engine support fixture tools.
13. Install cooling fans.

MOUNT STRUT

1. Remove bolt through strut at core support.
2. Remove bracket at core support if required.
3. Remove mount strut.
4. Reverse procedure to install, noting the following:
    a. Adjustment is provided where strut connects to core support bracket. Ensure this bolt is loose during assembly.
    b. **Torque** bolt to 58 ft. lbs.

2001–02

FRONT

Removal

1. Raise and support vehicle.
2. Remove front mount to frame nuts.
3. Install powertrain dolly tool No.

J39580, or equivalent.
4. Remove engine frame if required.
5. Remove mount bracket to cylinder head upper bolts.
6. Remove mount bracket to engine block bolts.
7. Remove brace to transaxle bolts.
8. Remove transaxle support brace.
9. Remove engine front mount and bracket.

Installation

1. Position mount bracket to engine.
2. Loosely install upper mount bracket to cylinder head bolts.
3. Install transaxle support brace.
4. Loosely install transaxle support brace and two lower front mount bracket nuts.
5. Tighten nuts and bolts in the following sequence:
   a. **Torque** lower engine mount bracket nuts to 30 ft. lbs.
   b. **Torque** transaxle support brace bolt to 37 ft. lbs.
   c. **Torque** upper engine mount brace bolts to 37 ft. lbs.
   d. **Torque** front engine mount nuts to 37 ft. lbs.

MOUNT STRUT

1. Remove core support sight shield.
2. Remove mount strut to engine bolts, then the mount strut.
3. Reverse procedure to install. Tighten bolts and nuts in following sequence:
   a. Install mount strut to radiator tie bar bolts. **Torque** to 18 ft. lbs.
   b. **Torque** engine mount strut bolts to 58 ft. lbs.

LEFTHAND STRUT BRACKET

1. Partially drain coolant into a suitable container.
2. Remove engine mount strut.
3. Remove secondary AIR pipe retaining bolt from mount strut bracket
4. Disconnect surge tank inlet hose from coolant outlet fitting.
5. Remove coolant outlet fitting.
6. Remove mount strut bracket to water crossover bolts.
7. Reverse procedure to install.

RIGHTHAND STRUT BRACKET

1. Remove engine mount strut.
2. Mark running direction with suitable felt pen or chalk, then remove serpentine belt.
3. Remove power steering return hose to righthand mount strut bracket bolt, then position hose aside.
4. Remove battery ground cable to engine mounting bolt.
5. Remove alternator to mount strut bracket upper mounting bolt.
6. Remove mount strut bracket to cylinder head bolts, then the bracket.
7. Reverse procedure to install.

Seville

1998–99

Refer to "2000–02 DeVille" for engine replacement procedure.

2000–02

Refer to "2000 Eldorado" for engine replacement procedure.

ENGINE

REPLACE

DEVILLE

1998–99

1. Drain coolant into a suitable container.
2. Recover A/C refrigerant as outlined in "Air Conditioning" chapter.
3. Remove tower-to-tower brace.
4. Remove air intake duct and air cleaner assembly.
5. Remove radiator hose at coolant crossover.
6. Remove engine cover.
7. Remove radiator upper cover.
8. Remove upper radiator hoses from engine.
9. Remove forward discriminating sensor from radiator support, then position aside.
10. Remove cooling fans.
11. Disconnect transaxle cooler lines from radiator.
12. Disconnect cruise control servo electrical connectors.
13. Disconnect throttle and cruise control cables from TBI unit.
14. Disconnect shift cable from manual shift lever and bracket.
15. Disconnect vacuum hose from brake booster.
16. Disconnect fuel inlet and return lines using quick-connect tool No. J37088-A, or equivalent.
17. Remove coolant reservoir.
18. Disconnect coolant hoses from pipes at front of engine.
19. Remove battery ground cable from left cylinder head.
20. Disconnect battery positive cable from battery and body retainer.
21. Remove PCM case and PCM.
22. Remove righthand sound insulator.
23. Disconnect engine wiring harness electrical connector and vacuum line under instrument panel.
24. Disconnect wiring harness from pass-through at cowl, then pull harness through cowl.
25. Disconnect three electrical connectors from A/C line near engine cowl.
26. Disconnect vacuum hose from T-fitting near engine harness pass-through.
27. Disconnect front wheel speed sensor electrical connectors.
28. Remove MAP sensor and control motor near master cylinder.
29. Remove engine harness retainer from brake booster.
30. Remove two hoses from power steering cooler.
31. Disconnect engine wiring harness from hood fuse panel.
32. Remove three relays from lower radiator and electrical connector from ABS modulator.
33. Remove front tires and wheels.
34. Separate drive axles from steering knuckles.
35. Remove downstream HO_2S heat shield, then disconnect sensor electrical connector from body harness.
36. Remove hangers from intermediate exhaust pipe.
37. Remove catalytic converter from pipe.
38. Disconnect coupling from steering gear.
39. Remove fuel line bundle from transaxle.
40. Disconnect battery wire from alternator.
41. Remove A/C manifold from A/C compressor. Cap open lines and fittings to prevent system contamination.
42. Remove ABS modulator from subframe, then support using suitable wire or rope.
43. Position powertrain support dolly tool No. J39580, or equivalent under subframe, then lower vehicle onto table.
44. Remove subframe to body bolts.
45. Slowly raise vehicle. **Ensure powertrain and subframe assembly clear all wiring, hoses and fluid lines.**
46. Remove coolant crossover pipe from engine.
47. Remove neutral safety switch from transaxle.
48. Remove engine wiring harness.
49. Remove exhaust Y-pipe.
50. Mark running direction using suitable felt pen or chalk, then remove serpentine belt.
51. Remove power steering pump and hoses. Cap open lines and fittings to prevent entry of dirt and debris.
52. Remove alternator and mounting bracket.
53. Remove A/C compressor and bracket.
54. Remove idler pulley.
55. Remove righthand, lower and lefthand engine to transaxle braces.
56. Attach a suitable lifting crane to engine.
57. Remove engine lefthand mount and bracket.
58. Remove lefthand exhaust manifold.
59. Remove flexplate inspection cover.
60. Remove torque converter to flexplate mounting bolts, then separate torque converter from flexplate.
61. Remove righthand engine mount bracket from engine.
62. Remove transaxle to engine mounting bolts.
63. Lift engine from transaxle and frame assembly.
64. Remove EGR crossunder pipe.
65. Remove righthand exhaust manifold.
66. Reverse procedure to install.

2000–02

1. Drain coolant into a suitable container.
2. Disconnect both battery cables.
3. Recover A/C refrigerant as outlined in "Air Conditioning" chapter.
4. Remove upper filler panel.
5. Disconnect electrical connectors from PCM.
6. Remove air cleaner assembly.
7. Drain engine oil into a suitable container.
8. Remove intake manifold sight shield.
9. Remove lower radiator hose using

clamp tool No. J37097-A, or equivalent.
10. Remove upper radiator hose from thermostat housing using clamp tool No. J38185, or equivalent.
11. Disconnect upper and lower transaxle fluid cooler lines from radiator.
12. Disconnect surge tank inlet hose from engine.
13. Disconnect surge tank outlet hose from heater pipe.
14. **Always replace accelerator cable with a new one whenever engine is removed from vehicle. Position cruise control cable aside during engine removal or installation. Do not pry on, lean against or kink cruise control cable.**
15. Disconnect accelerator and cruise control cables from TBI unit.
16. Disconnect heater hoses from engine.
17. Disconnect two brake fluid lines from master cylinder. Cap open lines and ports to prevent entry of dirt and debris.
18. Remove bracket and shift cable from manual shift lever, then position aside.
19. Disconnect vacuum hose from brake booster.
20. Disconnect hose from EVAP purge valve.
21. Disconnect secondary AIR relay from relay bracket and secure to top of engine.
22. Disconnect fuel inlet and return fittings at fuel rail.
23. Disconnect engine ground wire from body frame rail.
24. Disconnect main engine harness.
25. Disconnect wiring harness from underhood fuse block.
26. Remove strut tower bolts.
27. Raise and support vehicle.
28. Remove front tires and wheels.
29. Disconnect dampening sensor links from lower control arms.
30. Disconnect wheel speed and road sensing suspension sensor electrical connectors.
31. Disconnect two brake lines from both front subframe brackets and at rear of engine subframe. Cap open lines to prevent system contamnation.
32. Remove air deflector.
33. **On 2001–02 models,** remove front fascia extensions.
34. **On all models,** remove and discard engine oil cooler quick-connect fittings from oil filter adapter with oil lines still attached, then position lines aside. **Quick-connect fittings must be replaced whenever they are removed from adapter.**
35. Remove dust cover from quick connect joint.
36. Remove internal spring clip from engine oil cooler fittings.
37. Remove engine oil cooler lines from cooler fittings.
38. **On 2001–02 models,** disconnect the secondary AIR inlet hose from the secondary AIR pump.
39. **On all models,** disconnect A/C suction and discharge hoses from compressor. Cap open lines and fittings to prevent system contamination.
40. Ensure front wheels are in straight-ahead position.
41. Lock steering column using lockpin tool No. J42640, or equivalent, in underside of column.
42. Remove steering intermediate shaft pinch bolt.
43. Disconnect steering gear from intermediate shaft.
44. Disconnect wheel speed and brake wear sensors at strut towers.
45. Disconnect downstream HO_2S electrical connector.
46. Remove front exhaust pipe.
47. Remove engine oil pan to transaxle case brace.
48. Remove flexplate inspection cover.
49. Mark flexplate to torque converter orientation, then remove mounting bolts.
50. Lower vehicle.
51. Position powertrain support dolly tool No. J39580, or equivalent, under engine assembly. Four suitable jack stands may be substituted if a dolly is not available.
52. Remove engine mount to engine mount bracket nuts.
53. Secure front hoist pads to vehicle.
54. Remove subframe mount bolts.
55. Slowly raise vehicle. **Ensure powertrain and subframe assembly clear all wiring, hoses and fluid lines.**
56. Attach a suitable lifting crane to engine.
57. Remove heater pipes.
58. Disconnect coil pack ground wire from cylinder head.
59. Remove crossover pipe from cylinder head.
60. Remove power steering pump.
61. Remove front and rear transaxle brace bolt and nuts, then braces.
62. Remove front engine mount to engine subframe nut.
63. Remove transaxle to engine mounting bolts.
64. Raise engine from subframe and transaxle assembly.
65. Reverse procedure to install.

ELDORADO

1998–2000

Refer to "1998–99 DeVille" for engine replacement procedure.

2001–02

Refer to "2001–02 DeVille" for engine replacement procedure.

SEVILLE

1998–99

1. Drain coolant into a suitable container.
2. Disconnect both battery cables.
3. Recover A/C refrigerant as outlined in "Air Conditioning" chapter.
4. Remove air intake duct.
5. Remove engine cover.
6. Disconnect radiator hose at crossover.
7. Remove upper radiator hose using clamp tool No. J37097-A, or equivalent.
8. Remove radiator upper cover.
9. Remove cooling fans.
10. Disconnect transaxle cooler lines from radiator.
11. Disconnect coolant overflow hose.
12. Remove radiator and A/C condenser assembly.
13. Disconnect cruise control servo electrical connectors.
14. Disconnect throttle and cruise control cables from throttle body.
15. Remove brake pressure switch and bracket.
16. Disconnect brake master cylinder. Cap all open lines and fittings to prevent system contamination.
17. Disconnect shift cable from manual shift lever and bracket.
18. Remove vacuum hose from brake booster.
19. Disconnect fuel inlet and return lines using quick-connect separator tool No. J37088-A, or equivalent.
20. Disconnect battery ground cable at lefthand cylinder head.
21. Disconnect A/C suction and discharge hoses from compressor. Cap open lines and fittings to prevent system contamination.
22. Disconnect electrical harness from underhood relay center.
23. Disconnect electrical pass-through by brake booster.
24. Disconnect road sensing suspension electrical connectors.
25. Raise and support vehicle.
26. Remove lower engine splash shield.
27. Remove front tires and wheels.
28. Disconnect steering gear intermediate shaft.
29. Disconnect wheel speed and brake wear sensor electrical connectors.
30. Disconnect exhaust pipe from exhaust manifold.
31. Disconnect brake line at proportioning valves. Cap open lines and fittings.
32. Disconnect oxygen sensors electrical connectors.
33. Lower vehicle.
34. Remove road sensing suspension wheel speed harness brackets.
35. Remove front and rear engine mount nuts.
36. Remove strut to tower bolts at each strut tower.
37. Position powertrain support dolly tool No. J39580, or equivalent, under engine assembly. Four suitable jack stands may be substituted if a dolly is not available.
38. Remove subframe mount bolts.
39. Slowly raise vehicle. **Ensure powertrain and subframe assembly clear all wiring, hoses and fluid lines.**
40. Remove flexplate inspection cover.
41. Remove torque converter to flexplate bolts.
42. Attach a suitable lifting crane to engine.
43. Disconnect lefthand engine mount from subframe.
44. Remove engine to transaxle bracket.
45. Remove power steering gear heat shield.
46. Remove power steering gear.
47. Disconnect right engine mount to subframe.
48. Remove transaxle to engine bolts.
49. Raise engine from subframe and transaxle assembly.

50. Reverse procedure to install.

2000–02

Refer to "2000–02 DeVille" for engine replacement procedure.

INTAKE MANIFOLD

REPLACE

1. Drain coolant into a suitable container.
2. Remove intake manifold sight shield.
3. Relieve fuel system pressure as outlined under "Precautions."
4. Remove air intake duct from TBI unit.
5. Remove transaxle vent hose and transaxle shift cable at bracket.
6. Disconnect TP sensor and IAC valve electrical connectors.
7. Disconnect accelerator cable and cruise control cable at TBI unit.
8. Tag their locations, then disconnect front bank spark plug wires or coil units and position aside.
9. Disconnect TBI unit coolant hoses at TBI unit and surge tank pipe.
10. Disconnect EGR pipe and crankcase ventilation pipe at TBI unit spacer.
11. Disconnect vacuum lines, PCV hoses and electrical connectors as required.
12. Disconnect brake booster vacuum hose at intake manifold vacuum fitting.
13. Remove fuel rail ground wire at rear cylinder head.
14. Twist fuel rail fuel line female quick-connector fittings ¼ turn in each direction to loosen any dirt within fitting. Blow dirt out of fitting using compressed air.
15. Disconnect fuel line quick-connect fittings using separator tool No. J37088-A, or equivalent.
16. Disconnect fuel rail bracket at EGR valve.
17. Disconnect PCV hose at intake manifold.
18. Disconnect injector harness main electrical connector.
19. Remove intake manifold mounting bolts and studs, then manifold. Carrier gaskets are attached to manifold through a snap-lock feature and will remain attached when removing manifold.
20. If a new manifold will be installed, proceed as follows:
    a. Remove fuel rail.
    b. Remove carrier gaskets from manifold.
    c. Remove TBI unit.
    d. Remove MAP sensor.
21. Reverse procedure to install, noting the following:
    a. Clean all gasket and O-ring sealing surfaces.
    b. After engine has cooled, tighten manifold mounting bolts and nuts to specifications in sequence, **Fig. 3.**
    c. Ensure all electrical connectors and wiring are properly routed to avoid pinching.
    d. Turn ignition On for two seconds, then Off for ten seconds.
    e. Turn ignition On and inspect for fuel leakage.
    f. Install intake manifold sight shield.

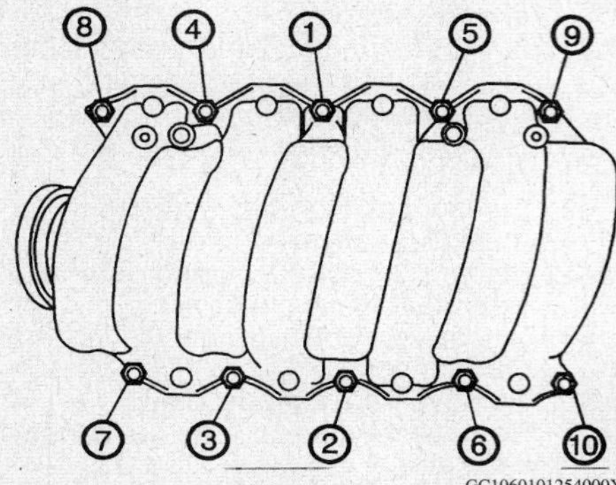

Fig. 3 Intake manifold bolt & nut tightening sequence

EXHAUST MANIFOLD

REPLACE

LEFTHAND

1. Disconnect AIR pipe from manifold as required.
2. Remove engine mount as outlined under "Engine Mount, Replace."
3. **On 1998–99 models,** remove alternator rear bracket.
4. **On all models,** remove manifold outlet flange mounting bolts.
5. Disconnect O_2 sensor electrical connector.
6. Remove manifold mounting bolts.
7. Remove exhaust manifold and oxygen sensor.
8. Reverse procedure to install. Coat oxygen sensor threads with high temperature anti-seize compound.

RIGHTHAND

1. Disconnect both battery cables, then rear O_2 sensor electrical connector and harness clip.
2. **On 2000–02 models,** lock steering column in straight-ahead position using lockpin tool No. J42640, or equivalent in underside of column.
3. **On all models,** raise and support vehicle.
4. Disconnect exhaust pipe from catalytic converter.
5. Disconnect AIR pipe from manifold as required.
6. Disconnect suspension position sensor at both lower control arms.
7. **On 2000–02 models,** proceed as follows:
    a. Remove heat shields from power steering gear, VSS and transaxle.
    b. Remove steering intermediate shaft pinch bolt.
    c. Disconnect intermediate shaft from steering gear.
    d. Remove righthand engine mount to mount bracket nut.
    e. Remove lefthand transaxle mount to mount bracket nut.
8. **On all models,** support engine cradle rear crossmember with suitable screw jack and remove cradle to body mounting bolts.
9. Lower rear of engine cradle.
10. Remove pipe to exhaust manifold and crossover exhaust pipe mounting bolts.
11. Remove righthand side cylinder head to transaxle brace.
12. Remove mounting nuts and exhaust manifold.
13. Reverse procedure to install. Coat oxygen sensor threads with high temperature anti-seize compound.

CYLINDER HEAD

REPLACE

1. **On 1998–99 models,** remove complete powertrain and engine cradle as an assembly.
2. **On all models,** remove exhaust manifolds as outlined under "Exhaust Manifold, Replace."
3. Remove intake manifold as outlined under "Intake Manifold, Replace."
4. Remove valve covers as outlined under "Valve Cover, Replace."
5. Remove crankshaft dampner as outlined under "Crankshaft Dampner, Replace."
6. Remove front cover as outlined under "Front Cover, Replace."
7. Remove timing chain tensioner from cylinder head.
8. Remove camshaft sprockets. **Timing chains should remain in chain case.**
9. Remove timing chain guide mounting screws through access plugs at cylinder head front, **Fig. 4.**
10. Remove water crossover and exhaust manifold as outlined under "Exhaust Manifold, Replace."
11. Remove cylinder head mounting bolts. Discard M11 bolts. M6 bolts can be used again.
12. Remove cylinder head and gasket-**.When camshafts remain in cylinder head some valves will be open at all times. Do not rest cylinder head on a flat surface with head face down.**
13. Reverse procedure to install, noting the following:
    a. Install new M11 bolts. M6 bolts can be used again.
    b. **Torque** M11 bolts to 30 ft. lbs. in sequence, **Figs. 5 and 6.**
    c. Rotate M11 cylinder head bolts an additional 70° in sequence using torque angle meter tool No. J36660-A, or equivalent.
    d. Rotate M11 bolts an additional 60° in sequence.
    e. Finally, rotate M11 bolts an additional 60° in sequence.
    f. **Torque** M6 bolts to 106 inch lbs.

VALVE COVER

REPLACE

DEVILLE

1998–99

Lefthand

1. Disconnect and isolate both battery cables.
2. Partially drain coolant into a suitable container.

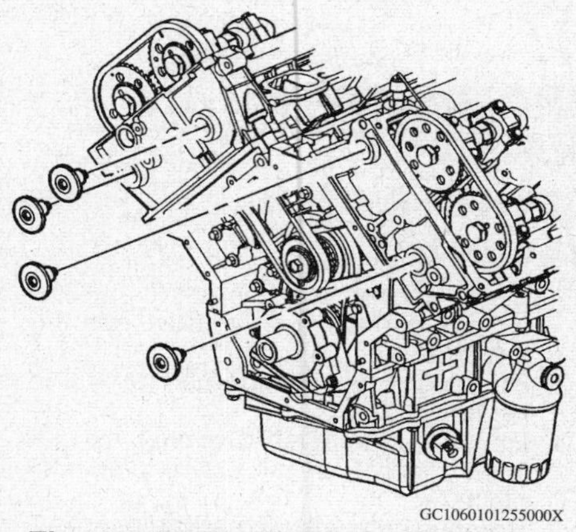

Fig. 4 Chain guide access plug replacement

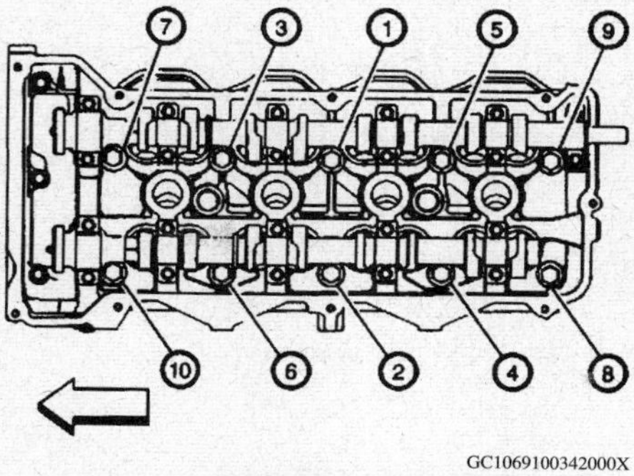

GC1069100342000X

Fig. 5 Cylinder head bolt tightening sequence. Lefthand

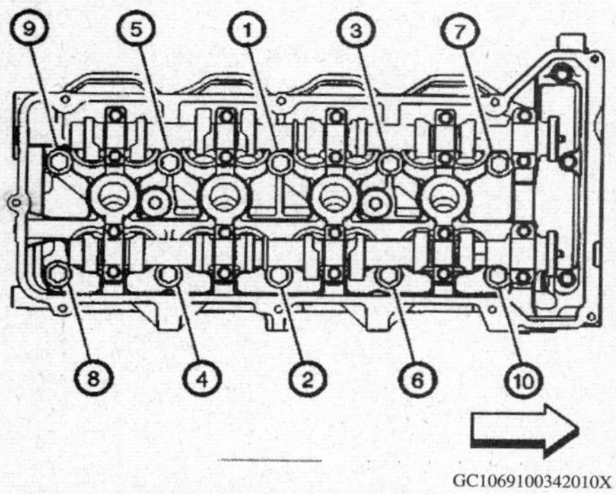

GC1069100342010X

Fig. 6 Cylinder head bolt tightening sequence. Righthand

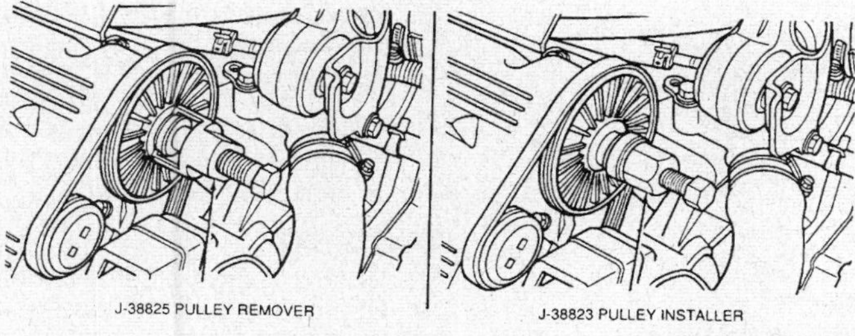

Fig. 7 Water pump pulley replacement. Eldorado & 1998–99 DeVille

3. Disconnect upper radiator hose at water crossover using clamp tool No. J38185, or equivalent.
4. Tag their locations, then disconnect spark plug wires and ignition coil units.
5. Remove righthand cooling fan as required.
6. Disconnect PCV fresh air tube from valve cover.
7. Remove lefthand and righthand torque struts.
8. Remove water pump drive belt shield.
9. Disconnect water pump drive belt.
10. Remove plastic dust cap from end of intake camshaft.
11. Remove water pump pulley, **Fig. 7.**
12. Remove camshaft seal mounting bolts.
13. Remove and discard camshaft seal.
14. Disconnect battery cable retainer at front of valve cover and remove valve cover mounting screws.
15. Remove valve cover mounting bolts, then the cover, **Fig. 8.**
16. Reverse procedure to install, noting the following:
    a. Install a new camshaft seal. Apply sealer part No. 1052080, or equivalent, to retainer bolt threads.
    b. Install water pump pulley using pulley installer tool No. J38823, or equivalent.

Righthand

1. Disconnect and isolate both battery cables.
2. **On 1998–99 models,** proceed as follows:
    a. Remove tower-to-tower brace.
    b. Raise and support vehicle.
    c. Disconnect rear exhaust manifold at converter, then position converter aside.
    d. Lower vehicle.
3. **On all models,** disconnect ignition coil electrical connectors.
4. Tag their locations, then remove mounting bolts, ignition coils and righthand bank spark plug wires.
5. Disconnect PCV valve and remove purge canister solenoid from rear of cover.
6. Remove wiring harness and valve cover mounting screws.
7. Support front of engine cradle and remove front cradle mounting screws.
8. Remove lefthand and righthand torque struts.
9. Lower engine cradle to provide clearance at rear of engine compartment.
10. Remove valve cover mounting bolts, then the cover.
11. Reverse procedure to install.

2000–02

Lefthand

1. Remove intake manifold sight shield and upper filler panel.
2. Partially drain coolant into a suitable container.
3. Remove radiator hose from water crossover and position aside.
4. Disconnect PCV fresh air tube.
5. Tag their locations, then remove ignition coils and spark plug boots.
6. Remove engine coolant heater wire and position aside.
7. Disconnect alternator cooler outlet hose from pipe and position pipe aside.
8. Remove shield and water pump drive belt.
9. Remove water pump belt tensioner and dust cap from end of camshaft.
10. Remove water pump drive pulley using pulley removal tool No. J38825, or equivalent.
11. Remove camshaft seal and discard.
12. Remove valve cover mounting bolts.
13. Lift valve cover drive end and remove reward to clear water pump driveshaft.
14. Reverse procedure install, noting the following:
    a. Install a new camshaft seal. Apply sealer part No. 1052080, or equivalent, to retainer bolt threads.
    b. Install water pump pulley using pulley installer tool No. J38823, or equivalent.

Righthand

1. Remove intake manifold sight shield.
2. Disconnect PCV valve and oxygen sensor wire.
3. Disconnect AIR vent solenoid vacuum tubes and electrical connector, then remove AIR bracket and tube.
4. Tag their locations, then disconnect and remove ignition coils and spark plug boots.
5. Remove valve cover mounting bolts, then the cover.
6. Reverse procedure to install.

ELDORADO

Refer to "1998–99" under "DeVille" for valve cover replacement procedures.

SEVILLE

Refer to "2000–02" under "DeVille" for vlave cover replacement procedures.

VALVE CLEARANCE SPECIFICATIONS

This engine is equipped with hydraulic lifters. Valve adjustment is not required.

VALVE ADJUSTMENT

This engine is equipped with hydraulic lifters. Valve adjustment is not required.

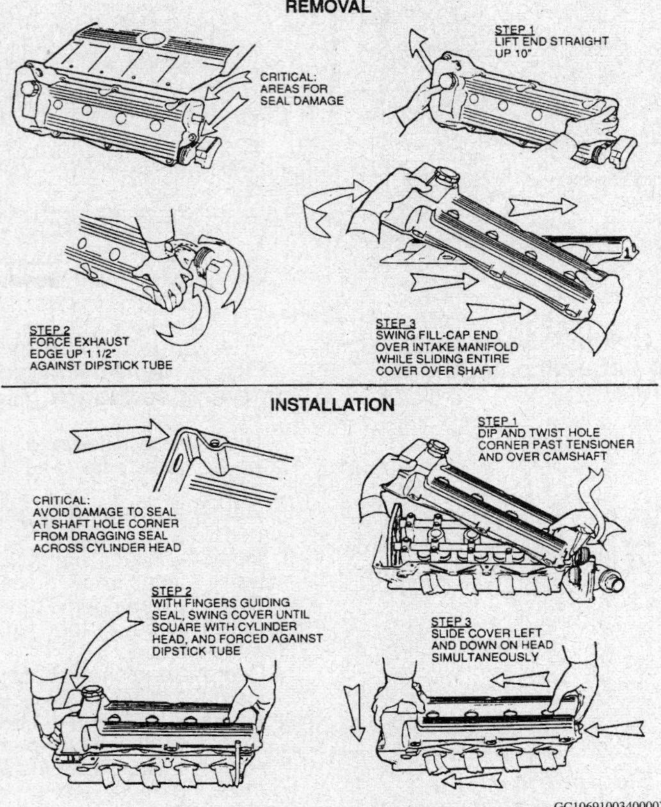
REMOVAL
STEP 1
LIFT END STRAIGHT
UP 10°
CRITICAL:
AREAS FOR
SEAL DAMAGE
STEP 2
FORCE EXHAUST
EDGE UP 1 1/2"
AGAINST DIPSTICK TUBE
STEP 3
SWING FILL-CAP END
OVER INTAKE MANIFOLD
WHILE SLIDING ENTIRE
COVER OVER SHAFT
INSTALLATION
STEP 1
DIP AND TWIST HOLE
CORNER PAST TENSIONER
AND OVER CAMSHAFT
CRITICAL:
AVOID DAMAGE TO SEAL
AT SHAFT HOLE CORNER
FROM DRAGGING SEAL
ACROSS CYLINDER HEAD
STEP 2
WITH FINGERS GUIDING
SEAL, SWING COVER UNTIL
SQUARE WITH CYLINDER
HEAD, AND FORCED AGAINST
DIPSTICK TUBE
STEP 3
SLIDE COVER LEFT
AND DOWN ON HEAD
SIMULTANEOUSLY
GC1069100340000X

Fig. 8 Valve cover replacement. Eldorado & 1998–99 DeVille

CRANKSHAFT DAMPER

REPLACE

1998-99

1. Mark running direction using suitable felt pen or chalk, then remove serpentine belt.
2. Raise and support vehicle.
3. Remove righthand front wheel and splash shields.
4. Remove brace between engine oil pan and transaxle case.
5. Remove flexplate inspection cover.
6. Install flexplate holder tool No. J39411, or equivalent.
7. Remove balancer mounting bolt.
8. Support engine cradle with suitable screw jack.
9. Disconnect RSS sensor from righthand lower control arm.
10. Remove three righthand cradle bolts to allow lowering of cradle to obtain clearance below body rail for balancer puller.
11. Install pilot tool No. J39344-2, or equivalent, into end of crankshaft.
12. Remove crankshaft dampner using puller tool No. J38416, or equivalent.
13. Reverse procedure to install, noting the following:
    a. Install balancer using installer tool No. J39344, or equivalent.
    b. Clean all dirt and debris from balancer bolt threads, then apply clean engine oil.
    c. **Torque** balancer bolt to 37 ft. lbs., then rotate an additional 120° using torque angle meter tool No. J36660-A, or equivalent.

2000-02

1. Mark running direction using suitable felt pen or chalk, then remove serpentine belt.
2. Raise and support vehicle.
3. Remove righthand front wheel and splash shields.
4. Remove brace between engine oil pan and transaxle case.
5. Remove flexplate inspection cover.
6. Install flexplate holder tool No. J44214, or equivalent.
7. Remove balancer mounting bolt.
8. Support engine cradle with suitable screw jack.
9. Remove engine mount to mount bracket nut.
10. Lower the engine assembly to allow clearance for puller tool below body rail.
11. Install pilot into end of crankshaft.
12. Remove crankshaft dampner using puller tool No. J41816, or equivalent.
13. Reverse procedure to install, noting the following:
    a. Install crankshaft balancer using installer tool No. J41998-B, or equivalent.
    b. Clean all dirt and debris from balancer bolt threads, then apply clean engine oil.
    c. **Torque** balancer bolt to 37 ft. lbs., then rotate an additional 120° using torque angle meter tool No. J36660-A, or equivalent.

FRONT COVER

REPLACE

DEVILLE & SEVILLE

1998-99

1. Mark running direction using suitable felt pen or chalk, then remove serpentine belt.
2. Remove power steering hose mounting bolt.
3. Remove crankshaft dampner as outlined under “Crankshaft Dampner, Replace.”
4. Remove belt tensioner and idler pulley.
5. Remove front cover mounting bolts, then the cover. **Do not discard gasket unless it is damaged.**
6. Reverse procedure to install, noting the following:
    a. Apply a small amount of sealant 12345739, or equivalent, at split line of upper and lower crankcases.
    b. Place gasket evenly over dowel pins.

2000-02

1. Remove serpentine drive belt.
2. Remove crankshaft dampner as outlined under “Crankshaft Dampner, Replace.”
3. **On DeVille and Seville models,** remove belt tensioner.
4. **On all models,** remove belt idler pulley.
5. **On DeVille and Seville models,** raise and support vehicle, then support engine assembly using suitable jack.
6. **On all models,** remove engine mount to mount bracket and bracket to engine mounting nuts.
7. Remove front cover mounting bolts, then the cover. **Do not discard gasket unless it is damaged.**
8. Reverse procedure to install, noting the following:
    a. Apply a small amount of sealant part No. 12345739, or equivalent, at split line of upper and lower crankcases.
    b. Place gasket evenly over dowel pins.
    c. Tighten front cover bolts to specifications in sequence, **Fig. 9.**

ELDORADO

1998-2000

Refer to “1998–99” under “DeVille & Seville”for front cover replacement procedure.

2001-02

Refer to “2000–02” under “DeVille & Seville” for front cover replacement procedure.

FRONT COVER SEAL

REPLACE

1. Remove crankshaft dampner as outlined under “Crankshaft Dampner, Replace.”

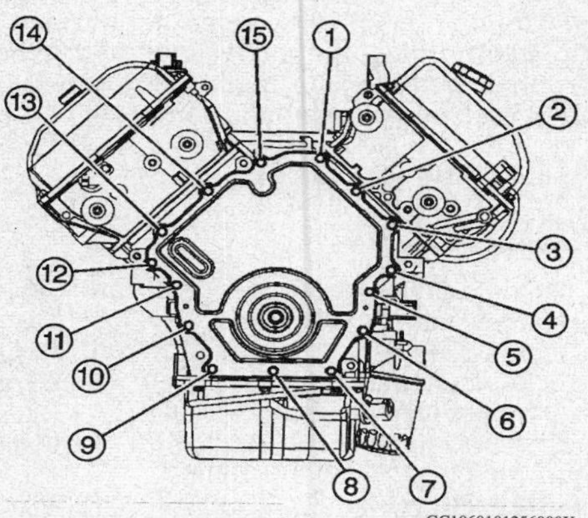

Fig. 9 Front cover bolt tightening sequence. 2000–02 DeVille & Seville & 2001–02 Eldorado

2. Pry out seal using a suitable screwdriver. **Do not score seal or crankshaft cover bore.**
3. Reverse procedure to install, noting the following:
   a. Lubricate seal lips with suitable engine oil.
   b. Position seal to front cover with garter spring side toward engine.
   c. Push seal into front cover using front cover seal installer tool No. J38818 and balancer installer tool No. J39344, or equivalent, until tool bottoms on cover.

TIMING CHAIN

REPLACE

PRIMARY

1. **On 1998–99 models,** remove engine as outlined under "Engine, Replace," then mount on suitable stand.
2. **On all models,** mark running direction using suitable felt pen or chalk, then remove serpentine belt.
3. Remove idler pulley and belt tensioner.
4. Remove front cover as outlined under "Front Cover, Replace."
5. Remove oil pump assembly as outlined under "Oil Pump, Replace."
6. Remove valve covers as outlined under "Valve Cover, Replace."
7. Remove timing chain tensioners and camshaft sprockets.
8. Remove secondary drive chains from intermediate shaft sprocket.
9. Remove one intermediate shaft sprocket bolt, then slide gears and primary drive chain off crankshaft and intermediate shaft.
10. Reverse procedure to install. Time camshafts as outlined under "Camshaft, Replace."

SECONDARY

1. Remove front cover as outlined under "Front Cover, Replace."
2. Remove lefthand valve cover as outlined under "Valve Cover, Replace."
3. Align timing marks.
4. Remove lefthand secondary chain tensioner.
5. Remove lefthand chain guide as outlined under "Cylinder Head, Replace."
6. Remove lefthand cam sprocket bolts and sprockets.
7. Remove lefthand secondary drive chain, **Fig. 10.**
8. Remove righthand secondary drive chain as outlined for lefthand removal in previous steps. Substitute righthand for lefthand.
9. Reverse procedure to install. Time camshafts as outlined under "Camshaft, Replace."

TENSIONER, REPLACE

Removal

1. Remove front cover as outlined under "Front Cover, Replace."
2. Remove mounting bolts and tensioner.

Installation

1. Rotate ratchet release lever counter clockwise and hold, **Fig. 11.**
2. Collapse tensioner shoe and hold.
3. Release ratchet lever and slowly release pressure on shoe.
4. As ratchet lever moves to first click hold tensioner shoe inward and insert pin through release lever hole, **Fig. 12.**
5. Install tensioner and bolts. Tighten to specifications.
6. Remove retaining pin allowing tensioner shoe to extend.
7. Install front cover.

CAMSHAFT

REPLACE

REMOVAL

1. Remove valve cover as outlined under "Valve Cover, Replace."
2. Secure cam sprocket to timing chain by installing four tie wraps per sprocket through sprocket holes.
3. Install cam chain holder tool No. J38822, or equivalent, behind camshaft sprockets, positioned between chain tensioner and chain guide, **Fig. 10.**
4. Apply tension to tool by tightening tension adjusting screw.
5. Remove camshaft sprocket bolts. **Record cam drive pins location in camshafts' end for installation.**
6. Work sprockets off cams using play in chain.
7. Loosen cam bearing cap bolts a few turns at a time until all valve spring pressure has been released.
8. Remove bolts, bearing caps and camshaft.

INSTALLATION

1. Apply camshaft prelube part No. 1052365, or equivalent, to face of each cam lobe.
2. Install camshaft and position cam bearing caps to cylinder head noting the following:
   a. Arrow on top of bearing cap points towards front of engine.

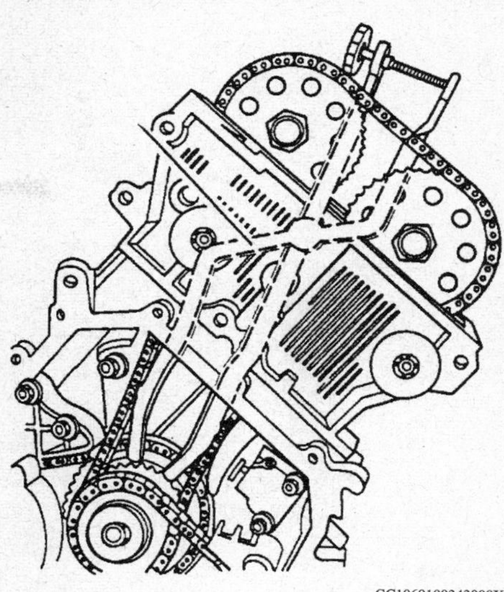

Fig. 10 Drive chain tensioning

   b. "E" mark on top of bearing cap indicates cap for exhaust cam.
   c. "I" mark on top of bearing cap indicates cap for intake cam.
   d. "No. 1" mark on top of bearing cap should be towards front of engine.
3. Loosely install cam bearing cap bolts.
4. Alternately tighten each bearing cap bolt a few turns at a time against valve spring pressure until all bolts are snug.
5. Tighten bearing cap bolts to specifications.
6. Rotate camshaft until drive pins are in position to engage cam sprockets over cams and install retaining bolts. Tighten sprocket bolts to specifications.
7. Remove chain holder tool and tie wraps.
8. Install cam cover.

CAMSHAFT TIMING

Setting camshaft timing is required whenever the camshaft drive system has been disturbed, such that the relationship between any chain and sprocket has been lost. Even when only one sprocket is involved, the following procedure should be observed since one crankshaft rotation will not provide conditions where proper timing can be confirmed.

1. Remove valve covers as outlined under "Valve Cover, Replace."
2. Remove front cover as outlined under "Front Cover, Replace."
3. Remove or retract three chain tensioners. **Tensioners may be in installed positions but must be fully retracted as outlined under "Timing Chain, Replace."**
4. Remove oil pump assembly as outlined under "Oil Pump, Replace."
5. Primary and secondary chain guides should be installed if previously removed.
6. Rotate crankshaft until sprocket drive key is at approximately 1 o'clock position using crankshaft rotation socket tool No. J39946, or equivalent.
7. Install crankshaft and intermediate shaft sprockets to primary drive chain with timing marks aligned, **Fig. 13.**

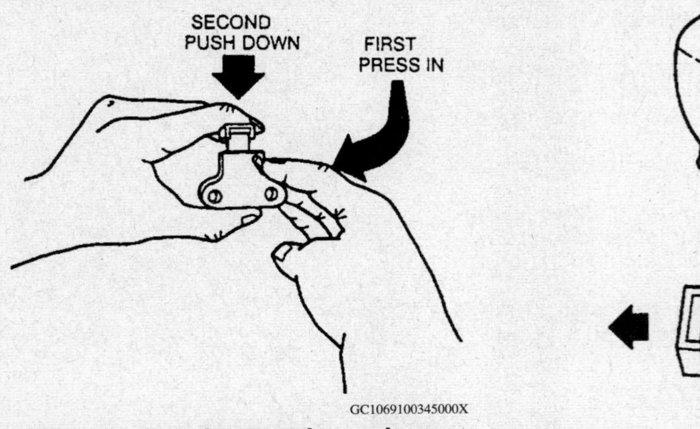

Fig. 11 Tensioner release lever rotation

1 RELEASE TO FIRST CLICK
2 INSTALL LOCK PIN

GC1069100346000X

Fig. 12 Tensioner in collapsed position

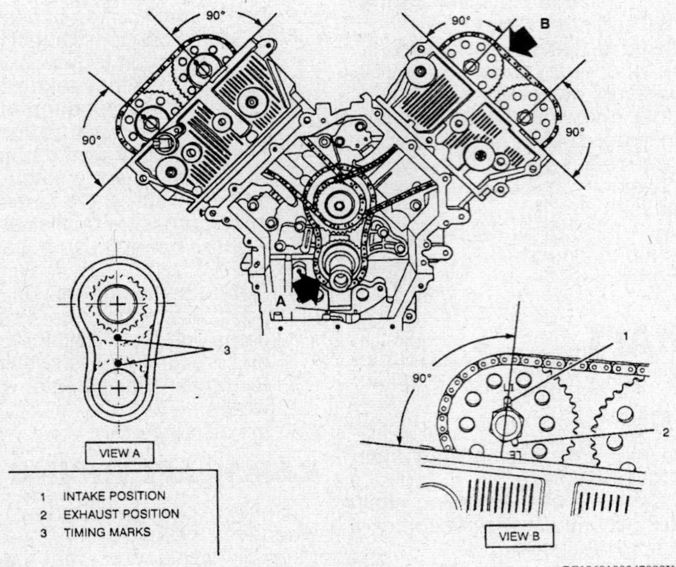

Fig. 13 Camshaft timing procedure

8. Install crank and intermediate shaft sprockets over their respective shafts.
9. Rotate crankshaft so crankshaft key engages sprocket without changing timing mark position using crankshaft rotation socket tool.
10. Tighten intermediate sprocket mounting bolt to specifications.
11. Install primary chain tensioner and release tensioner shoe. Tighten tensioner mounting bolts to specifications.
12. Lock crankshaft in position using flexplate holder tool No. J39411, or equivalent.
13. Route lefthand cylinder head secondary drive chain over intermediate shaft inner row teeth.
14. **Righthand exhaust camshaft sprocket (marked RE) must contain camshaft position sensor pickup.**
15. Route secondary drive chain over chain guide and install exhaust camshaft sprocket to chain so that camshaft drive pin engages lefthand head exhaust sprocket notch (marked LE). There should be no slack in lower section of chain and camshaft drive pin must be perpendicular to cylinder head face, **Fig. 13.**
16. Install intake camshaft sprocket into chain so notch on lefthand head intake sprocket (marked LI) engages cam drive pin while pin remains perpendicular to cylinder head face.
17. A hex is cast into camshafts behind cylinders Nos. 1 and 2 so an open end wrench can be used to provide minor positioning of camshafts.
18. Loosely install exhaust and intake cam sprocket bolts.
19. Install chain tensioner and release tension on shoe. Tighten tensioner mounting bolts to specifications.
20. Tighten camshaft sprocket bolts to specifications.
21. **Righthand exhaust camshaft sprocket (marked RE) must contain camshaft position sensor pickup.**
22. Route righthand cylinder head secondary drive chain over intermediate shaft outer row of teeth, then repeat procedure for righthand cams.

PISTON & ROD ASSEMBLY

Refer to **Fig. 14** for proper piston and rod assembly installation.

Coat piston and rod assemblies with prelube lubricant part No. 1052367, or equivalent, before installation.

The arrow marks on the piston crowns must face the front of the engine.

The locating mark cast into the underside of the piston should point toward the front of the engine. The connecting rod cap locating notch should point toward the rear of the engine on odd-numbered cylinders and toward the front of the engine on even-numbered cylinders.

PISTONS, PINS & RINGS

This procedure has been revised by a Technical Service Bulletin.

When removing and installing piston rings install oil ring expander with ends facing toward piston top. Installing expander with ends facing away from piston top could prevent oil rings from rotating during engine operation.

MAIN & ROD BEARINGS

Shell type main bearings of steel backed aluminum are used at all positions. The upper halves are interchangeable, as are the lower halves except for the No. 3 thrust bearings.

If bearing clearance is more than .003 inch and new bearings do not reduce clearance to .0005–.002 inch, a new crankshaft will be required. Undersized bearing are not available and crankshaft grinding is not allowed.

1. **Torque** lower crankcase bolt Nos. 1–20 in sequence to 15 ft. lbs., **Fig. 15.**
2. Rotate bolt Nos. 1–20 an additional 65° using torque angle meter tool No. J36660-A, or equivalent.
3. **Torque** upper-to-lower crankcase perimeter bolts to 22 ft. lbs. in sequence, **Fig. 16.**
4. Maximum crankshaft endplay is .0197 inch.
5. Coat bearings with prelube lubricant part No. 1052367, or equivalent.
6. Ensure crankshaft journals are covered completely with lubricant.

CRANKSHAFT REAR OIL SEAL

REPLACE

LIP TYPE SEAL

Removal

1. Remove transaxle assembly. Refer to

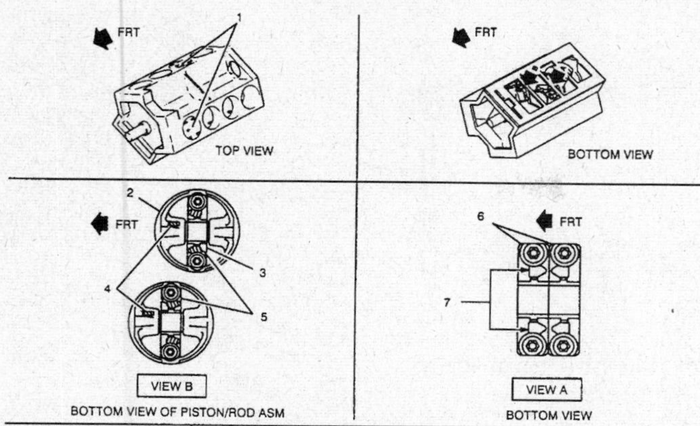

1 PISTON ARROW TOWARD CHAIN CASE ON BOTH SIDES
2 PISTON
3 ROD CAP
4 LOCATER LUGS INDICATE PISTON FRONT TOWARDS ENGINE FRONT
5 BEARING CAP ARROWS POINT TOWARD EACH OTHER ON PAIRED RODS
6 ROD CAPS
7 BEARING CAP ARROWS POINT TOWARD EACH OTHER ON PAIRED RODS

GC1069100349000X

Fig. 14 Piston & rod assembly

"Automatic Transmissions/ Transaxles" chapter.
2. Remove mounting bolts and flexplate.
3. Drill a 1/8 inch hole into rear main seal metal body.
4. Remove seal using suitable slide hammer.

Installation

1. Place small amount of suitable RTV sealant at crankcase split line across end of upper/lower crankcase seal.
2. Lubricate new oil seal with suitable engine oil, then slide seal over arbor of seal installer tool No. J38817, or equivalent.
3. Thread seal installer tool into crankshaft flange, then install seal by turning handle until tool bottoms against crankcase, **Fig. 17.**
4. Install flexplate. Tighten bolts to specifications.

CARTRIDGE TYPE SEAL

Removal

1. Remove transaxle assembly. Refer to "Automatic Transmissions/ Transaxles" chapter.
2. Remove mounting bolts and flexplate.
3. Install eight one inch self-tapping screws using guide holes in crankshaft rear oil seal removal tool No. J42841, or equivalent, and variable speed drill motor with socket adapter.
4. Remove tool mounting bolts, then install tool center screw.
5. Remove seal by tightening tool.

Installation

1. Clean any debris from crankshaft rear oil seal drain.
2. Coat outer diameter of cylinder block with suitable clean engine oil.
3. Oil seal has a pre-applied green sealant coating. **Do not allow engine oil on area where oil seal is to be pressed on crankshaft or on inner diameter of oil seal.**
4. Loosen crankshaft rear oil seal installer tool No. J42842, or equivalent's center bolt until center hub protrudes approximately one inch, then install on to crankshaft by threading mounting bolts to crankshaft flange.
5. Install rear oil seal by tightening rear oil seal installer tool until it bottoms against crankcase. Remove tool.
6. Ensure installation depth of crankshaft rear oil seal is equal around circumference.
7. Install flexplate. Tighten bolts to specifications.

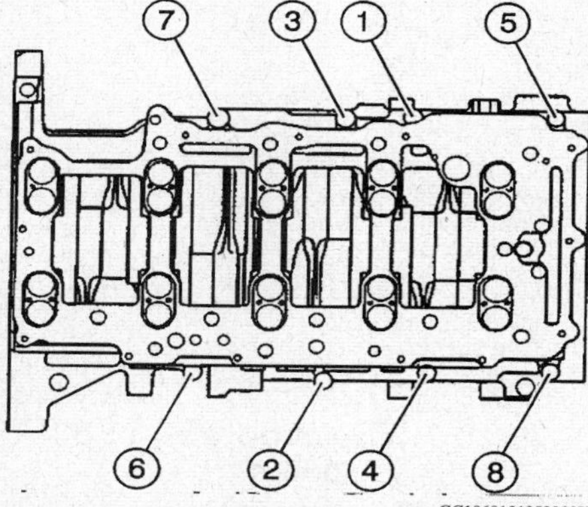

Fig. 16 Crankcase perimeter bolt tightening sequence

OIL PAN

REPLACE

1. Drain engine oil into a suitable container.
2. **On 1998–2000 models,** remove transaxle. Refer to "Automatic Transmissions/Transaxles" chapter.
3. **On all models,** remove exhaust crossover pipe if required. Discard flange gaskets.
4. Remove oil pan mounting bolts, then the pan. **Do not remove gasket from pan groove unless replacement is required. It can be used again if it is not damaged.**
5. Reverse procedure to install. Tighten oil pan bolts to specifications in sequence, **Fig. 18.**

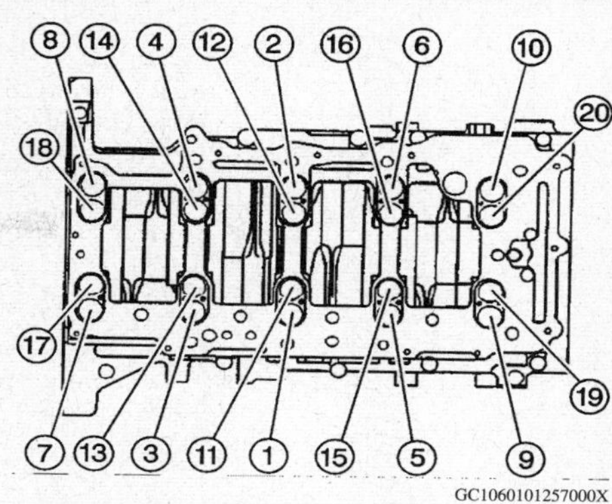

Fig. 15 Lower crankcase bolt tightening sequence

OIL PUMP

REPLACE

REMOVAL

1. Remove front cover as outlined under "Front Cover, Replace."
2. Remove mounting bolts, pump and drive spacer, **Fig. 19.**

INSTALLATION

1. Ensure all gasket and sealing surfaces are clean and free of damage.
2. Install oil pump drive spacer into oil pump from rear so that drive flat engages pump rotor.
3. Position pump over crankshaft and loosely install bolts.
4. Apply upward pressure while tightening mounting bolts.
5. **Torque** pump mounting bolts to 89 inch lbs. in sequence, **Fig. 19.**
6. Rotate bolts an additional 35° using torque angle meter tool No. J36660-A, or equivalent.
7. Install front cover assembly as outlined under "Front Cover, Replace."

OIL PUMP SERVICE

DISASSEMBLY

1. Remove pump housing drive spacer, **Fig. 20.**
2. Remove screws holding pump housing sections together.
3. Mark mating surfaces for installation, then remove inner and outer rotors.
4. Remove pressure relief valve cap retainer pin.
5. Remove retainer cap. **Avoid damaging O-ring.**
6. Slide valve spring and piston from bore.

INSPECTION

Internal components of oil pump are not serviceable. Replace entire pump assembly if wear or damage is noted.

1. Inspect pump housing sections for

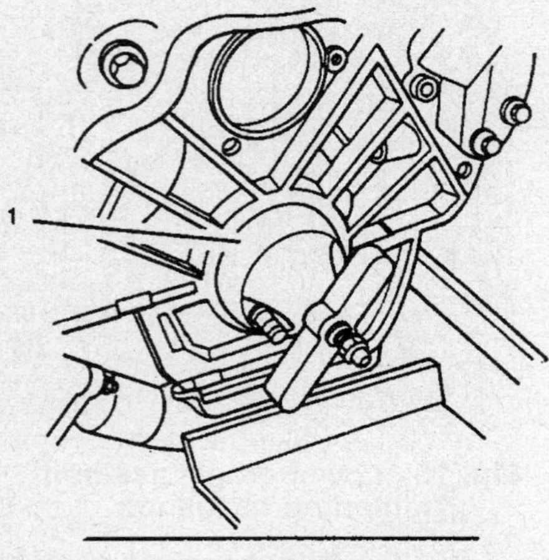

Fig. 17 Rear main seal installation. Lip type seal

nicks, burrs, chips or debris that may cause a leak or binding condition in rotor pocket.
2. Inspect drive or driven rotors for nicks or burrs.
3. Inspect pump cover and interior surface for excessive wear or score marks.

ASSEMBLY

1. Install inner and outer rotors to pump cover. **Align marks made during pump disassembly.**
2. Install pressure relief valve seat, spring and pilot.
3. Assemble housing and cover over locating dowel.
4. Align housing and cover using a suitable drill bit in pump mounting hole on opposite side.

SERPENTINE DRIVE BELT

1. Mark running direction using suitable felt pen or chalk.
2. Rotate drive belt tensioner mechanism upward and away from drive belt using suitable ½ inch breaker bar.
3. Remove serpentine drive belt.
4. Reverse procedure to install. Refer to **Fig. 21** for serpentine drive belt routing.

COOLING SYSTEM BLEED

1. Fill radiator with proper antifreeze solution.
2. Install radiator cap.
3. Start and idle engine.
4. Place HVAC controls in any A/C mode except Max and temperature at highest setting.
5. Idle engine until lower radiator to water pump hose is hot.
6. Turn ignition Off.
7. Allow engine to cool to ambient temperature.

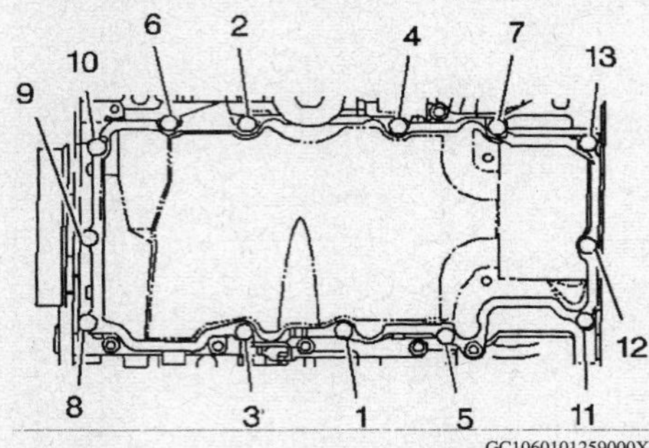

Fig. 18 Oil pan bolt tightening sequence

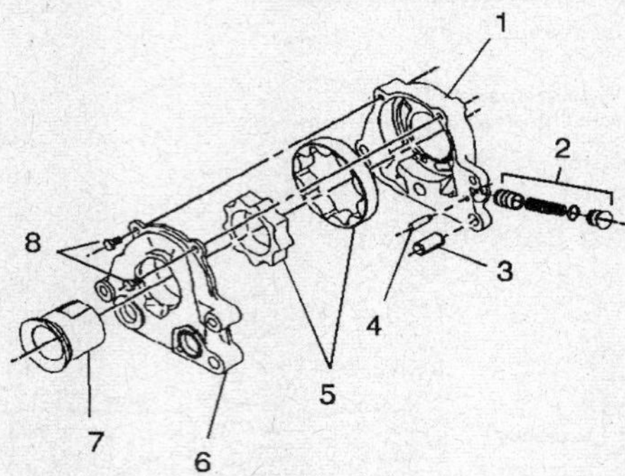

Fig. 20 Exploded view of oil pump

8. Ensure coolant in surge tank is at proper level.

THERMOSTAT

REPLACE

1. Drain coolant into a suitable container.
2. Remove engine cover and air cleaner as required.
3. Disconnect radiator hose at thermostat housing using clamp tool No. J38185, or equivalent.
4. Remove mounting bolts and thermostat housing, **Fig. 22.**
5. Remove thermostat and O-ring.
6. Reverse procedure to install, noting the following:
   a. Ensure all sealing surfaces are free of dirt and debris.
   b. Tighten mounting bolts to specifications.
   c. Fill and bleed cooling system as outlined under "Cooling System Bleed."

WATER PUMP

REPLACE

1. Drain coolant into a suitable container.
2. Remove air cleaner.
3. Remove engine cover and front end filler panel as required.

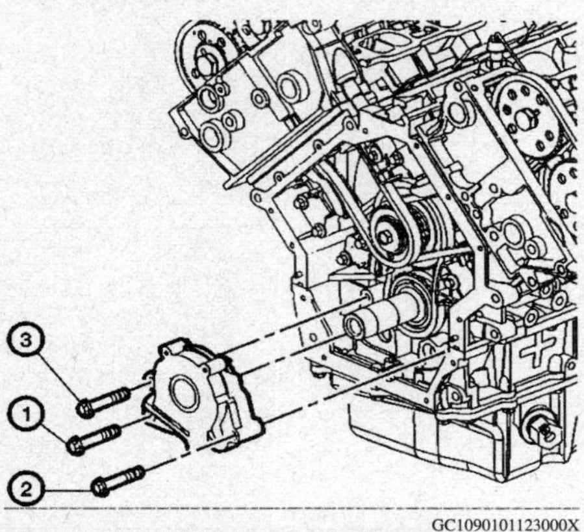

Fig. 19 Oil pump replacement

4. **On models equipped with AIR,** remove check valve.
5. **On all models,** remove water pump belt shield.
6. Mark running direction using suitable felt pen or chalk, then remove water pump drive belt.
7. Disconnect radiator outlet hose from thermostat housing using clamp tool No. J38185, or equivalent.
8. Remove water pump cover bolts, then the cover.
9. Disconnect heater return hose.
10. Rotate pump clockwise to remove from housing using coolant pump remover/installer tool No. J38816-1A, or equivalent.
11. Remove support plate from water housing crossover.
12. Remove water pump assembly.
13. Remove seal from water crossover.
14. Reverse procedure to install, noting the following:
    a. Install new seal into recessed portion of water crossover. **Ensure notched locking ear is in 7 o'clock position.**
    b. Index water pump locking ears with water crossover tangs.
    c. **Torque** remover/installer tool No. J38816-A, or equivalent, counterclockwise to 74 ft. lbs.
    d. Fill and bleed cooling system as outlined under "Cooling System Bleed."

RADIATOR

REPLACE

DEVILLE

1998–99

1. Drain coolant into a suitable container.
2. Remove SRS forward discriminating sensor mounting bolts, then position aside as required.
3. Remove air cleaner.
4. Remove cooling fans as outlined in "Engine Cooling Fans" chapter.
5. Disconnect radiator inlet and outlet hoses using clamp tool No. J38185, or equivalent.
6. Disconnect engine oil cooler lines.
7. Disconnect transaxle fluid cooler lines.

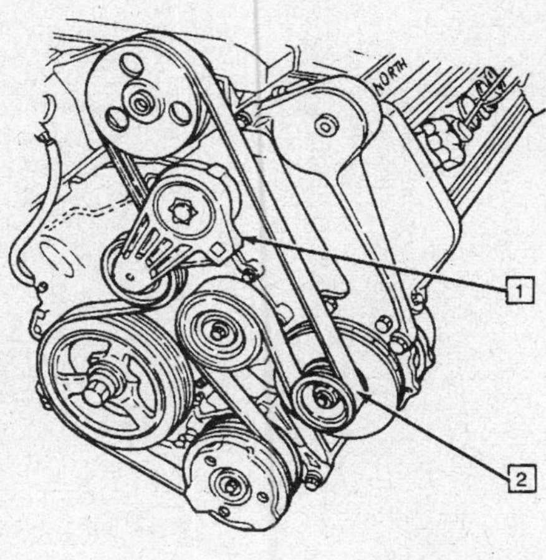

Fig. 21 Serpentine drive belt routing

8. Remove upper radiator support mounting screws.
9. Remove radiator by lifting up and out.
10. Reverse procedure to install. Fill and bleed cooling system as outlined under "Cooling System Bleed."

2000–02

1. Drain coolant into a suitable container.
2. Remove radiator outlet hose using clamp tool No. J38185, or equivalent.
3. Remove cooling fans as outlined in "Engine Cooling Fans" chapter.
4. Disconnect lower transaxle fluid cooler line.
5. Disconnect lower engine oil cooler line.
6. Remove alternator cooler inlet hose.
7. Remove mounting bolts and lift condenser up slightly to release radiator lower mounting feet.
8. Lift up on A/C condenser to release lower mounting feet. **Do not damage radiator and condenser lower attachment points.**
9. Remove radiator by lifting up and out.
10. Reverse procedure to install, noting the following:
    a. Position radiator alignment dowels to align with insulators.
    b. Tighten mounting bolts to specifications.
    c. Fill and bleed cooling system as outlined under "Cooling System Bleed."

ELDORADO

Refer to "1998–99" under "DeVille" for radiator replacment procedures.

SEVILLE

Refer to "2000–02" under "DeVille" for radiator replacment procedures.

FUEL PUMP

REPLACE

The fuel pump is combined with the tank level sending unit and is not serviced separately.

DEVILLE

1998–99

1. Drain fuel from tank into a suitable container.
2. Raise and support vehicle, then remove fuel tank.
3. Remove locking nut using fuel sender locknut wrench tool No. J39765, or equivalent, **Fig. 23.**
4. Remove modular fuel tank sending unit/fuel pump.
5. Remove fuel pump from modular fuel sending unit, **Fig. 24.**
6. Reverse procedure to install.

2000–02

1. Adjust tank fuel level to ¾ full by draining fuel into a suitable container.
2. Remove spare tire cover, jack, spare tire and rear compartment floor trim.
3. Remove fuel sender access panel.
4. Disconnect quick-connect fittings at fuel sender.
5. Disconnect electrical connections at modular fuel sender and fuel tank pressure sensor.
6. Remove fuel sender mounting ring using fuel sender locknut wrench tool No. J39765, or equivalent.
7. Remove fuel sending unit by pulling straight up while pumping fuel from reservoir.
8. Reverse procedure to install. Install new fuel sender O-ring.

ELDORADO

Refer to "1998–99" under "DeVille" fpor fuel pump replacement procedure.

SEVILLE

Refer to "2000–02" under "DeVille" fpor fuel pump replacement procedure.

FUEL FILTER

REPLACE

1. Disconnect fuel filter bracket release tabs.
2. Twist quick-connect fitting ¼ turn in each direction to loosen dirt within fitting.
3. Clean quick-connect fitting at ends of filter.
4. Disconnect quick-connect fittings by squeezing plastic tabs of male end connector and pulling apart.
5. Disconnect threaded fitting at fuel filter outlet.
6. Remove fuel filter.
7. Reverse procedure to install, noting the following:
    a. **Torque** threaded fitting to 22 ft. lbs.
    b. Turn ignition On for two seconds, then Off for ten seconds.
    c. Turn ignition On and inspect for fuel leakage.

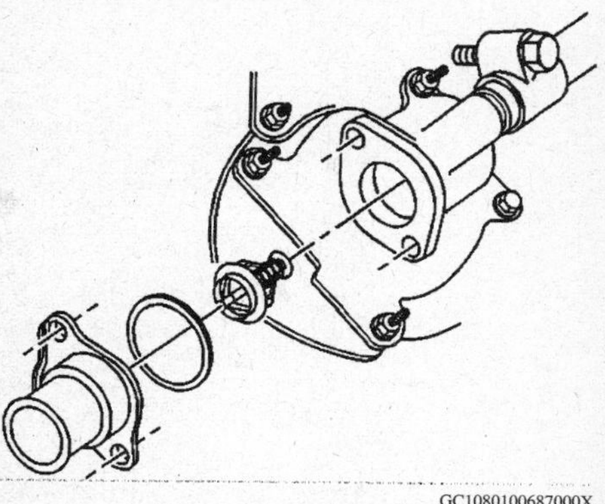

Fig. 22 Thermostat replacement

TECHNICAL SERVICE BULLETINS

POPPING TYPE NOISE IN PASSENGER COMPARTMENT

1998–99 Seville

On some of these models there may be a popping type noise heard in the passenger compartment. This occurs after driving at highway speeds and coming to a stop.

This condition may be caused by the catalytic converter heat shield. When air flow stops, the heat from the converter may cause the shield to expand.

To correct this condition, proceed as follows:

1. Raise and support vehicle.
2. Remove screws and oxygen sensor wiring rear shield.
3. Remove catalytic converter to exhaust inlet pipe mounting nuts.
4. Separate catalytic converter from exhaust inlet pipe.
5. Remove gasket/seal and discard.
6. Drill out rivet above separated flange at converter heat shield center using a $3/16$ inch or larger drill bit.
7. Install new gasket part No. 12554724.
8. Install catalytic converter to exhaust inlet pipe and tighten mounting nuts to specifications.
9. Install oxygen sensor wiring rear shield and screws.

ENGINE OIL COOLER LINE OIL LEAK

1998 DeVille, Eldorado & Seville

On these models the engine oil cooler lines appear to be leaking at the attachment point to the engine.

This condition may be caused by the nut on the engine oil cooler inlet and outlet line assemblies at the engine oil filter adapter becoming loose.

To correct this condition, proceed as follows:

1. **Do not just tighten connection.**
2. Disconnect oil cooler inlet and outlet line assemblies at engine oil filter adapter.

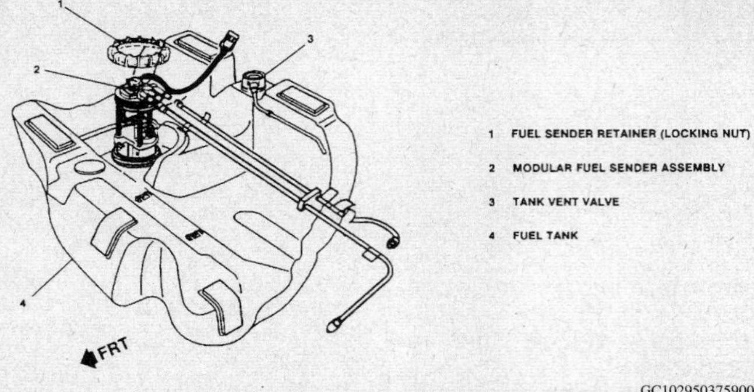

Fig. 23 Modular fuel sending unit/fuel pump removal. Eldorado & 1998–99 DeVille

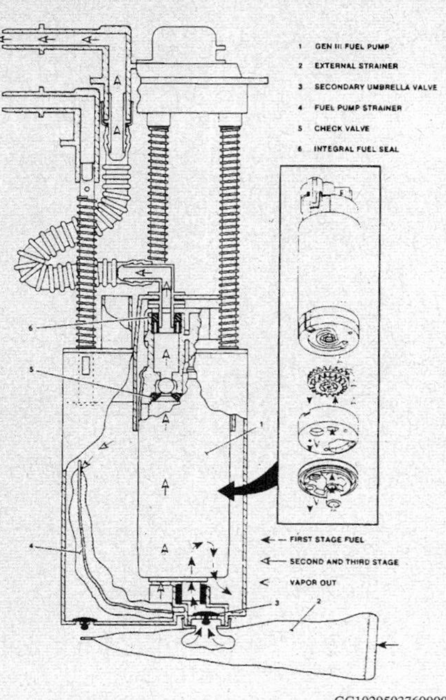

Fig. 24 Fuel pump removal. Eldorado & 1998–99 DeVille

3. Clean oil cooler line nut threads.
4. Apply GM Goodwrench/Loctite 272 threadlocker adhesive, or an equivalent meeting GM specification 9985399.
5. **Torque** oil cooler line nut to 33 ft. lbs.
6. **On models built after 6/20/1998,** note the following:
   a. These models have an adhesive coating applied to threads of connections between oil cooler line and engine assembly.
   b. Tightening oil cooler line nut will break bond of adhesive and negate benefits.
   c. Some residual oil may exist on connection. This is normal.
   d. If there is any question as to connection leaking, an ultraviolet light source and dye should be used to assure connection's condition.

ACCESSORY DRIVE NOISE

1998 DeVille, Eldorado & Seville

On some of these models built before Feb. 1, 1998, there may be chirping, ticking, knocking or trashy noises from the front of the engine. The noise may sound like an under hood squeak, a metallic trashy noise, or an inside vehicle thump.

This condition may be caused by accessory drive system pulley misalignment.

1. Inspect power steering fluid level. Adjust as required.
2. Start vehicle and run for three minutes, idling in park with hood open.
3. Determine type and location of noise while engine is running.
4. Increase engine speed to approximately 2500 RPM and closely listen for noise.
5. Mark running direction with suitable felt pen or chalk, then remove accessory drive belt.
6. Inspect belt grooves for pilling and other damage. Pilling appears as shiny areas in grooves.
7. Start vehicle and listen for noise, noting the following:
   a. If noise is still present, source is not belt or accessory drive components, perform engine mechanical noise diagnosis.
   b. If noise is no longer present, proceed to next step.
8. Inspect accessory drive pulleys for damage such as chips, dings, dents or uncommon wear patterns.
9. Inspect pulleys for trueness or unusual wear. Determine trueness as follows:
   a. Rotate pulley and compare vertical surface to fixed point using suitable measuring device.
   b. If measured distance between two points remains constant, pulley is running true.
   c. If distance varies, pulley is not running true.
10. Replace drive pulleys which are not true, damaged or worn.
11. Remove power steering pump and bracket. Place in suitable vise.
12. Inspect power steering pulley for cracks, chips and excessive runout.
13. Replace damaged pulleys.
14. Remove any flash from mold parting lines in belt contact area of power steering pump pulley, noting the following:
   a. Flash can be detected by running finger nail perpendicular to grooves in pulley.
   b. Remove all flash from entire belt contact area of power steering pump pulley using 400 grit sandpaper folded into V or small smooth file.
   c. Continue to sand pulley until flash can no longer be detected in entire belt contact area by running finger nail perpendicular to grooves.
   d. Thoroughly clean pulley with air and clean shop towel after removing flash.
15. Remove dust cap and inspect power steering pump pulley to shaft flushness with suitable straightedge.
16. Adjust pulley so it is flush with power steering pump shaft using pulley installer tool No. J25033-C and remover tool to. J38825, or equivalents, as required.
17. File chamfer on front face of engine block where power steering pump mounting bracket locating pad is located so sharp corner has been eliminated. **Do not file power steering pump mounting bracket.**
18. Inspect idler pulley assembly for cross threading. Repair as required.
19. **Torque** idler pulley bolt to 37 ft. lbs.
20. Install power steering pump and bracket.
21. Push and hold pump toward engine rear while tightening mounting bolt.
22. **Torque** mounting bolt to 37 ft. lbs.
23. Ensure there is no gap between power steering pump bracket locating ear and engine block.
24. Adjust power steering fluid level as required.
25. Install accessory drive belt.
26. Start engine and ensure all removed components have been properly assembled.
27. Allow vehicle to soak outside overnight.
28. Inspect power steering fluid level. Adjust as required.
29. Start vehicle and run for three minutes, idling in park with hood open.
30. Evaluate for noise.
31. Increase engine speed up to approximately 2500 RPM and listen closely to compressor/alternator area for squeaking noise.
32. If noise is still present, proceed to next step. If noise has been eliminated, replace accessory drive belt.
33. Loosen two rear alternator bracket to block mounting bolts.
34. Remove lower front alternator mounting bolt.
35. Install one shim washer (part No. 00187372, 20 MM outside diameter, 10 MM hole diameter, 1.8 MM thick) between lower front alternator mounting boss and lower front alternator mounting bracket.
36. Install and **torque** lower front alternator mounting bolt to 35 ft. lbs.
37. **Torque** two rear alternator bracket to block mounting bolts to 35 ft. lbs.
38. Install new accessory drive belt.

TIGHTENING SPECIFICATIONS

Year	Component	Torque/Ft. Lbs.
1998–2002	Alternator Upper Mounting Bolt	37
	Belt Tensioner	37
	Camshaft Cover	89①
	Camshaft Bearing Cap (1998–2000)	106①
	Camshaft Bearing Cap (2001–02)	44⑨
	Camshaft Drive Chain Tensioner	18
	Camshaft Seal Retainer To Cover	27①
	Camshaft Sprocket	89
	Catalytic Converter To Exhaust Inlet Pipe	18
	Cooling Fan	53①
	Crankshaft Balancer	37④
	Cylinder Head Bolts	③
	Engine Frame To Body Bolts (DeVille & Seville)	141
	Engine Frame To Body Bolts (Eldorado)	72
	Engine Mount Bracket	⑧
	Engine Mount To Frame	⑧
	Engine Mount Front	⑧
	Engine Mount Righthand	⑧
	Engine To Transaxle	55
	Exhaust Manifold To Cylinder Head Bolt	18
	Exhaust Manifold To Cylinder Head Locknut	18
	Flexplate	11⑤
	Flexplate Inspection Cover	80①
	Front Cover	89①
	Fuel Filter	22
	Ignition Module	80①
	Intake Manifold	⑦
	Intake Manifold Cover	27①
	Lefthand Strut Bracket To Water Crossover	17
	Main Bearing Cap Bolts	⑥
	Oil Filter Adapter	12
	Oil Pan	89①
	Oil Pan Drain Plug	15
	Oil Pump	②
	Oil Pump To Suction Pipe	89①
	O_2 Sensor	30
	Power Steering Return Hose	115①
	Righthand Strur Bracket Bolts	37
	Secondary AIR Pipe Retaining Bolts	80①
	TBI Unit	106①
	Thermostat Housing	89①
	Torque Strut Bracket To Cylinder Head	⑧
	Torque Strut Bracket To Water Manifold	18
	Transaxle Brace	35
	Water Pump Assembly	74
	Water Pump Cover Bolts	89①

①— Inch pounds.
②— Refer to "Oil Pump, Replace" for tightening specifications & sequence.
③— Refer to "Cylinder Head, Replace" for tightening specifications & sequence.

④ — Rotate an additional 120.°
⑤ — Rotate an additional 50.°
⑥ — Refer to "Main & Rod Bearings" for tightening specifications & sequence.
⑦ — Refer to "Intake Manifold, Replace" for tightening specifications & sequence.
⑧ — Refer to "Engine Mount, Replace" for tightening specifications & sequence.
⑨ — Rotate an additional 30.°

Rear Suspension

NOTE: On Air Bag Equipped Models, Refer To "Air Bag System Precautions" Located In The Front Of This Manual For System Disarming & Arming Procedures.

NOTE: Refer To "Computer Relearn Procedures" Located In The Front Of This Manual When Battery Power To The Computer Has Been Interrupted.

NOTE: Prior To Performing Any Service Operations Listed In This Section, Consult The "Technical Service Bulletins" Section For Related Information.

INDEX

PRECAUTIONS

AIR BAG SYSTEMS

Refer to "Air Bag System Precautions" in the front of this manual for system disarming and arming procedures.

BATTERY GROUND CABLE

Prior to service, disconnect battery ground cable and isolate as required.

HUB & BEARING

REPLACE

1998–99

1. Raise and support vehicle, then remove tire and wheel assembly.
2. Remove brake caliper mounting bolts, then position caliper aside using suitable wire or rope. **Do not suspend caliper by brake line.**
3. Remove and discard rotor retainers, if equipped.
4. Remove rotor.
5. Remove hub and bearing mounting bolts, then the hub and bearing.
6. Reverse procedure to install.

2000–02

FE1 & FE3 SUSPENSION

1. Raise and support vehicle.
2. Remove tire and wheel.
3. Remove brake caliper mounting bolts, then position caliper aside using suitable wire or rope. **Disconnecting fluid line from caliper is not required.**
4. Remove brake rotor and ABS sensor wire connector.
5. Remove hub and bearing mounting bolts, then the hub and bearing, **Fig. 1.**
6. Remove brake shield from control arm.
7. Reverse procedure to install.

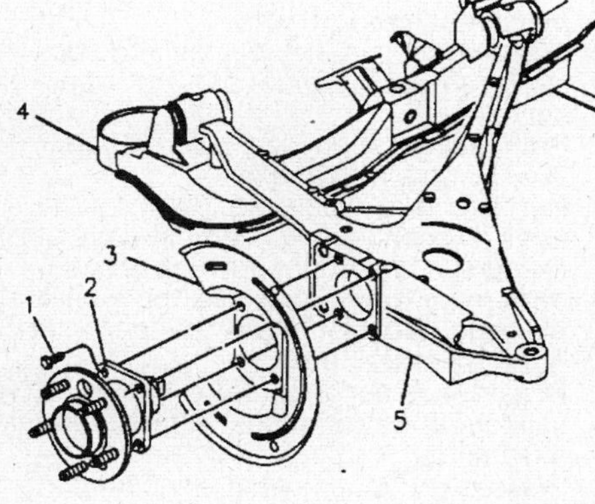

Fig. 1 Hub & bearing replacement. Seville & 2000–02 DeVille w/FE1 & FE3 suspension

FE7 SUSPENSION

1. Raise and support vehicle, then remove tire and wheel assembly.
2. Remove brake caliper mounting bolts, then position caliper aside using suitable wire or rope. **Do not suspend caliper by brake line.**
3. Remove brake rotor.
4. Disconnect ABS sensor electrical connector.
5. Disconnect parking brake cable from lower control arm.
6. Remove wheel speed sensor.
7. Remove hub and bearing retaining bolts, **Fig. 2.**
8. Remove and discard wheel speed sensor reluctor ring. **Do not use reluctor ring again after it has been removed.**
9. Remove bearing nut and washer from hub.
10. Remove brake shield.
11. Remove bearing from hub.
12. Reverse procedure to install, noting the following:
    a. Install a new ABS wheel speed sensor reluctor ring using reluctor installer tool No. J44253, or equivalent. Turn installer to thread the reluctor until it just touches the ring.

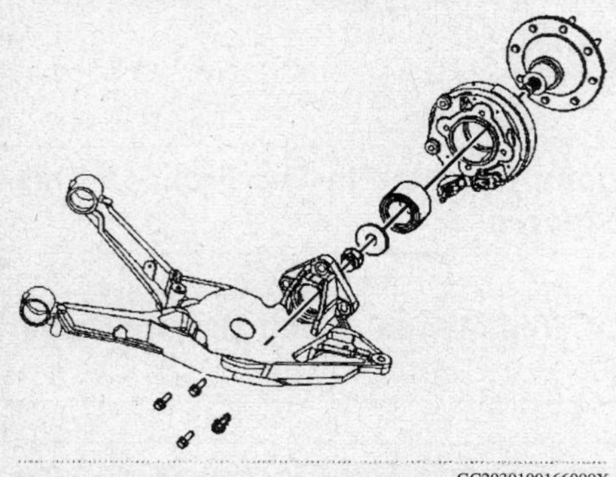

Fig. 2 Hub & bearing replacement. 2000–02 DeVille w/FE7 suspension

b. Install a new ABS sensor using installer tool No. J44252, or equivalent.
c. Measure wheel speed sensor signal AC voltage using a suitable multi-meter. Voltage should be greater than 100 mV while wheel is revolving.

REAR SUSPENSION

REPLACE

DEVILLE

1998–99

1. Raise and support vehicle, then remove rear tires and wheels.
2. Remove lefthand caliper assembly mounting bolts, then position aside using suitable wire or rope. **Do not allow caliper to hang by brake line.**
3. Remove suspension components attached to suspension assembly as required.
4. Remove intermediate parking brake cable from equalizer, then position cable clear of suspension support.
5. Remove rear brake crossover pipe and lefthand rear brake hose from bracket. Plug open fittings to prevent entry of dirt and debris.
6. Disconnect rear chassis wiring harness from main body harness.
7. Support rear suspension using suitable jack stands.
8. Remove suspension support forward arm bolts, upper mounting bolts and lower insulators.
9. Lower jack stands while observing position of brake calipers, brake hoses and fluid lines.
10. Reverse procedure to install, noting the following:
    a. Slowly raise suspension support into vehicle. Align the support with vehicle body as it is raised.
    b. Install both forward arm bolts in proper direction with nuts installed on righthand side of arm. Cup-shaped washer is used on lefthand forward arm bolt installation only.
    c. Tighten righthand side support forward arm nut to specifications.
    d. Tighten lefthand side support forward arm nut to specifications.
    e. Tighten upper mounting bolts to specifications.
    f. Bleed brakes as outlined under "Brake System Bleed" in "Hydraulic Brake Systems" chapter.

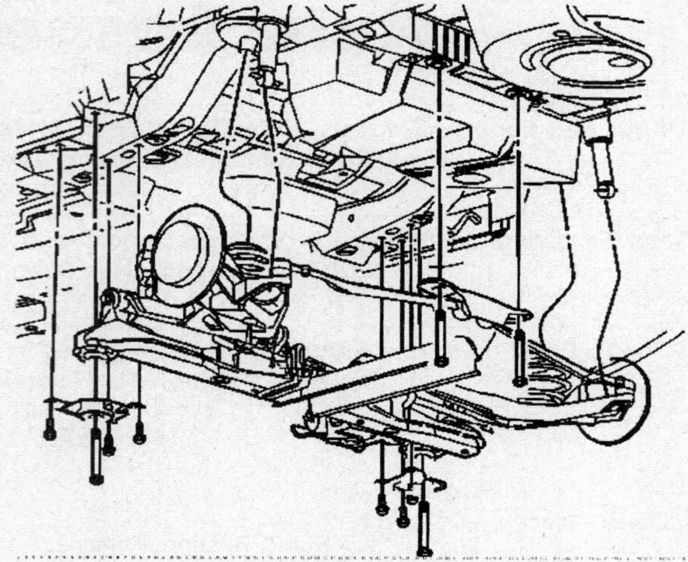

Fig. 3 Rear suspension assembly replacement. Seville & 2000–02 DeVille

2000–02

1. Raise and support vehicle, then remove rear tires and wheels.
2. Disconnect exhaust system components as required to provide clearance.
3. Remove rear springs as outlined under "Coil Spring, Replace."
4. Remove brake calipers from control arms. Disconnecting hydraulic lines at calipers is not required. **Support calipers from frame using suitable wire or rope. Do not allow calipers to hang by brake lines.**
5. Disconnect parking brake cables at calipers and rear suspension support assembly.
6. Disconnect rear suspension support assembly electrical connectors from electrical harness, then the Electronic Level Control (ELC) electrical connector and vent hose.
7. Disconnect ELC air tube from compressor.
8. **On DeVille models equipped with FE7 suspension,** remove center support brackets.
9. **On all models,** support rear suspension using a suitable jack, **Fig. 3.**
10. Remove support bracket to body bolts from each side.
11. Remove front and rear anchor bolts and lower rear suspension support assembly.
12. Reverse procedure to install.

ELDORADO

Refer to "1998–99" under "DeVille" for rear suspension replacement procedure.

SEVILLE

Refer to "2000–02" under "DeVille" for rear suspension replacement procedure.

SHOCK ABSORBER

REPLACE

1. Raise and support vehicle, then remove tire and wheel assembly.
2. Disconnect shock absorber electrical connector from rear suspension support.
3. Relieve spring load by supporting lower control arm using suitable screw type jack.
4. Remove lower shock absorber bolt(s), **Figs. 4 and 5.**
5. Disconnect electrical connector from top of shock absorber.
6. **On Eldorado and 1998–99 DeVille models,** remove upper mounting nut, retainer and insulator using tool No. J35669, or equivalent.
7. **On Seville and 2000–02 DeVille models,** remove upper mounting dust cap, nuts and reinforcement, **Fig. 6.**
8. **On all models,** reverse procedure to install.

COIL SPRING

REPLACE

DEVILLE

1998–99

Refer to "Lower Control Arm, Replace" for coil spring replacement procedures.

2000–02

Removal

1. Raise and support vehicle, then remove tire and wheel assembly.
2. Support control arm using suitable jack.

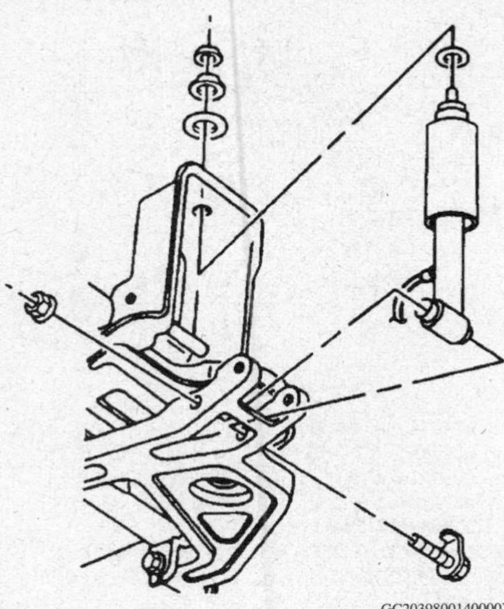

Fig. 4 Shock absorber replacement. Eldorado & 1998–99 DeVille

3. Disconnect electronic level control air tube from shock.
4. Remove shock to control arm mounting bolts.
5. Remove cotter pin and hex nut.
6. Separate adjustment link from knuckle using universal steering linkage puller tool No. J24319-B, or equivalent.
7. **On DeVille models equipped with FE7 suspension,** install coil spring compressor tool No. J4425, or equivalent.
8. **On all models,** lower the control arm until it bottoms on support assembly.
9. Pry under lower spring insulator using suitable pry bar and remove spring with insulator, **Fig. 7.**
10. Remove upper insulator by pulling downward.

Installation

1. **On DeVille models equipped with FE7 suspension,** install coil spring into compressor tool No. J4425, or equivalent.
2. **On all models,** install upper spring insulator in body.
3. Install lower spring insulator in control arm.
4. Install spring, ensuring insulator is seated in control arm.
5. Raise lower control arm and install shock to control arm mounting bolts.
6. Install adjustment link to control arm.
7. **On DeVille models equipped with FE1 and FE3 suspension, torque** adjustment link nut to 22 ft. lbs., then rotate an additional 180.°
8. **On DeVille models equipped with FE7 suspension, torque** adjustment link nut to 22 ft. lbs., then rotate an additional 200.°
9. **On 1998 Seville models, torque** adjustment link nut to 88 inch lbs., then rotate castle nut an additional 270.° **Do not rotate nut more than one flat to install cotter pin.**
10. **On 1999 Seville models, torque** adjustment nut to 36 ft. lbs.
11. **On 2000–02 Seville models, torque** adjustment link nut to 55 ft. lbs.
12. **On all models,** connect electronic level control air tube to shock absorber.
13. Install tire and wheel, then tighten lug nuts to specifications.

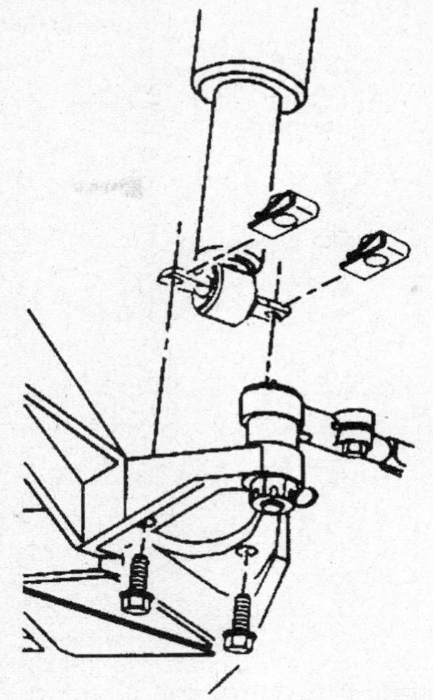

Fig. 5 Shock absorber lower mount replacement. Seville & 2000–02 DeVille

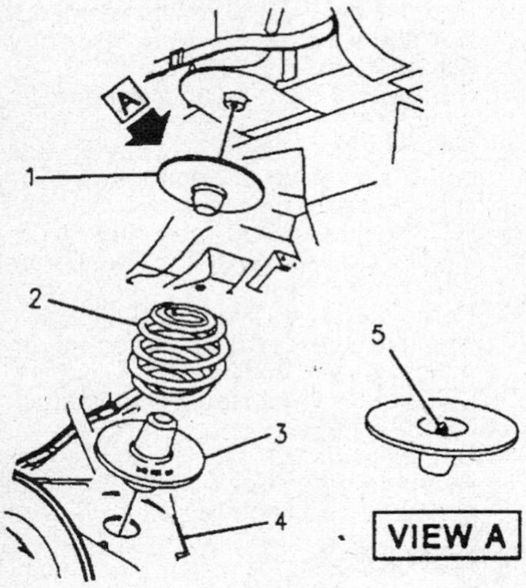

Fig. 7 Coil spring replacement. Seville & 2000–02 DeVille

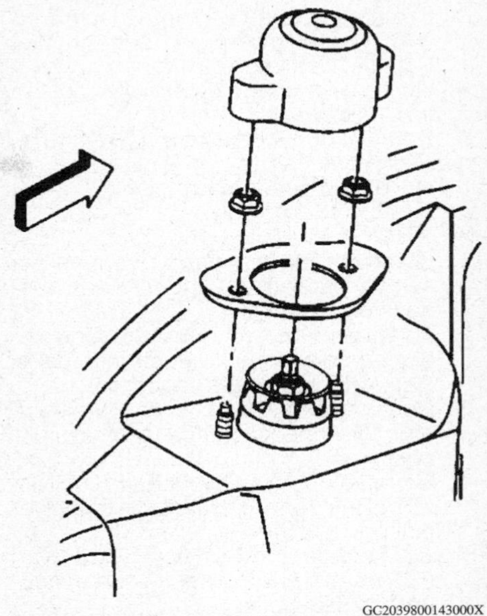

Fig. 6 Shock absorber upper mount replacement. Seville & 2000–02 DeVille

ELDORADO

Refer to “Lower Control Arm, Replace” for coil spring replacement procedures.

SEVILLE

Refer to “Lower Control Arm, Replace” for coil spring replacement procedures.

CONTROL ARM

REPLACE

DEVILLE

1998-99

Lower

1. Raise and support vehicle, then remove tire and wheel assembly.
2. Support inboard end of lower control arm using suitable transmission jack. Position brackets on jack to securely hold control arm.
3. Remove stabilizer link lower attachment.
4. Remove shock absorber lower attachment.
5. Remove inboard lower control arm nuts and bolts.
6. Relieve coil spring pressure by slowly lowering transmission jack.
7. Remove coil spring by pulling lower control arm down.
8. Remove outboard mounting bolt and lower control arm.
9. Reverse procedure to install.

Upper

1. Raise and support vehicle, then remove tire and wheel assembly.
2. Disconnect electronic level control height sensor connector.

3. Disconnect Road Sensing Suspension (RSS) position sensor and bracket from shock tower.
4. Remove inner and outer upper control arm bolts.
5. Remove upper control arm by lifting up and over shock tower.
6. Reverse procedure to install.

2000-02

1. Remove rear suspension support assembly as outlined under "Rear Suspension, Replace."
2. If lefthand control arm is being replaced, disconnect Electronic Level Control (ELC) height sensor link.
3. Remove stabilizer link bolt and nut, then disconnect ABS electrical connector.
4. Remove hub and bearing, if required, as outlined under "Hub & Bearing, Replace."
5. **On DeVille models equipped with FE7 suspension,** remove center support bracket bolts.
6. **On all models,** remove control arm to rear suspension support mounting bolt and nut.
7. Reverse procedure to install, noting the following:
   a. Tighten control arm nuts with vehicle weight resting on rear wheels.
   b. Tighten all bolts and nuts to specifications.
   c. Install tires and wheels. Tighten lug nuts to specifications.

ELDORADO

Refer to "1998–99" under "DeVille" for control arm replacement procedure.

SEVILLE

Refer to "2000–02" under "DeVille" for control arm replacement procedure.

CONTROL ARM BUSHING

REPLACE

DEVILLE

2000-02

1. Remove control arm as outlined under "Control Arm, Replace."
2. Drive bushing from control arm using bushing replacement tools, **Fig. 8.**
3. Remove bushing replacement tools.
4. Reverse procedure to install. Start new bushing into control arm with flat on bushing positioned vertically and rearward.

SEVILLE

Refer to "2000–02" under "DeVille" for control arm bushing replacement procedure.

KNUCKLE

REPLACE

DEVILLE

1998-99

1. Raise and support vehicle, then remove tire and wheel assembly.
2. Remove caliper and position aside. **Do not allow caliper to hang from hydraulic hose.**
3. Remove rotor, hub and bearing assembly.
4. Relieve spring load by support outboard end of lower control arm using suitable screw type jack.
5. Remove lower shock absorber mounting bolt and stabilizer link from control arm.
6. Remove rear toe link outer bolt.
7. Remove upper and lower control arm outer nuts and bolts.
8. Disconnect speed sensor cable bracket from knuckle.
9. Remove knuckle.
10. Reverse procedure to install. Install new rear toe link outer bolt.

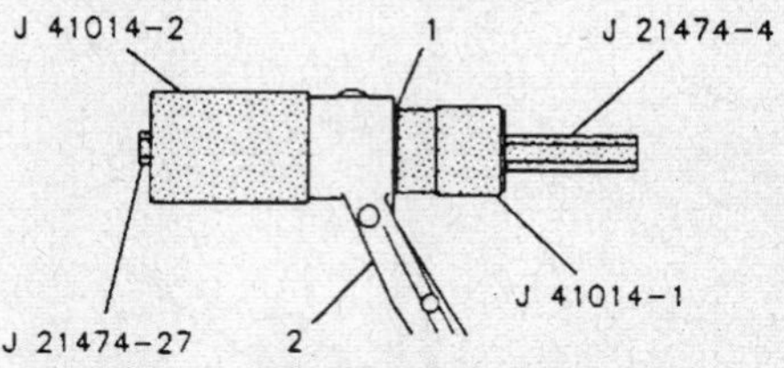

REMOVAL

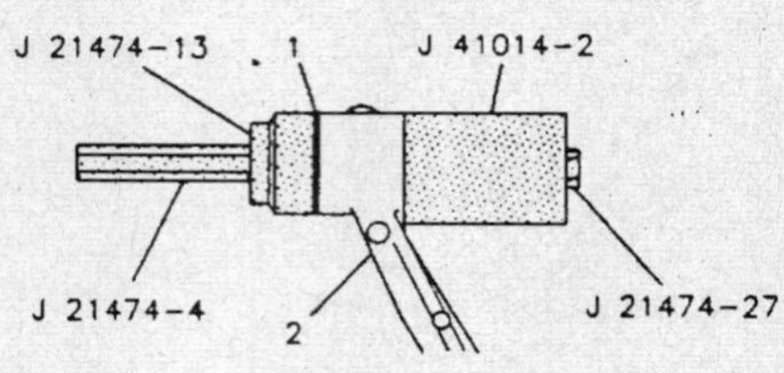

INSTALLATION

1 BUSHING
2 CONTROL ARM

GC2039500112000X

Fig. 8 Control arm bushing replacement tool installation. Seville & 2000–02 DeVille

ELDORADO

Refer to "1998–99" under "DeVille" for knuckle replacement procedure.

REAR CROSSMEMBER

REPLACE

DEVILLE

1998-99

The rear crossmember (suspension support) can be removed without removing or disconnecting the coil spring, shock absorbers, control arms, knuckles, hub and bearing assemblies or rotors.

1. Raise and support vehicle, then remove tire and wheel assemblies.
2. Remove lefthand caliper and position aside. **Do not allow caliper to hang from hydraulic hose.**
3. Remove intermediate parking brake cable from equalizer and move intermediate cable clear of suspension support.
4. Remove rear brake crossover line and rear brake hose from bracket.
5. Disconnect rear chassis wiring harness from main body wiring harness.
6. Support rear crossmember using suitable jack stand.
7. Remove rear crossmember forward arm bolts, upper mounting bolts and lower insulators.
8. Lower rear crossmember slowly. **Avoid damage to brake lines.**
9. Lower jack stands.
10. Reverse procedure to install, noting the following:
    a. Install both forward bolts in proper direction with nuts installed on righthand side of arm.
    b. Cup shaped washer is used on lefthand forward arm bolt only.

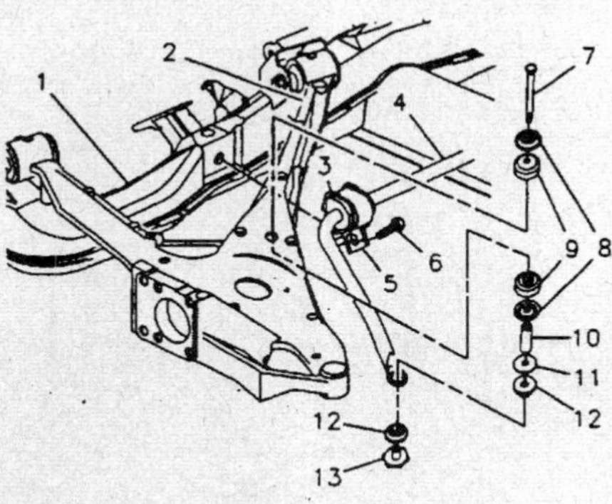

1 REAR SUSPENSION SUPPORT ASSEMBLY
2 CONTROL ARM
3 INSULATOR, STABILIZER SHAFT
4 SHAFT, STABILIZER
5 CLAMP, STABILIZER SHAFT
6 BOLT, 33 N•m (24 LB. IN.)
7 BOLT, 13 N•m (115 LB. IN.)
8 RETAINER, UPPER
9 INSULATOR, UPPER
10 SLEEVE
11 RETAINER, LOWER
12 INSULATOR, LOWER
13 NUT

GC2039500113000X

Fig. 9 Stabilizer shaft replacement. Seville & 2000–02 DeVille

ELDORADO

Refer to "1998–99" under "DeVille" for rear crossmember replacement procedure.

STABILIZER SHAFT

REPLACE

DEVILLE

2000-02

1. Raise and support vehicle, then remove tires and wheels.
2. Remove stabilizer shaft link assembly bolt, nut, retainer and insulators from control arm, **Fig. 9.**
3. Remove clamp bolt, then bend open end of clamp upward.
4. Remove stabilizer shaft and insulators.
5. Reverse procedure to install, noting the following:

a. Install stabilizer shaft insulator to shaft with slit facing forward.
b. Ensure stabilizer shaft is centered before tightening clamp bolt.

SEVILLE

Refer to "2000–02" under "DeVille" for stabilizer shaft replacement procedure.

ADJUSTMENT LINK

REPLACE

DEVILLE

2000–02

1. Raise and support vehicle.
2. Remove adjustment link nut.
3. Separate adjustment link from control arm using universal steering linkage puller tool No. J24319-B, or equivalent.
4. Support exhaust and rear support assembly using suitable block of wood.
5. Remove exhaust hangers and rear support mounting bolts.
6. Lower support assembly and exhaust together.
7. Remove cam nut and bolt, then the adjustment link from rear support.
8. Reverse procedure to install. Inspect and adjust rear toe as outlined in "Wheel Alignment" section.

SEVILLE

Inner

1. Raise and support vehicle, then remove tire and wheel assembly.
2. Loosen pinch bolt.
3. Support exhaust and rear suspension support with suitable wood block at least seven inches long.
4. Remove exhaust hangers and rear suspension support mounting bolts.
5. Lower support and exhaust together.
6. Remove cam bolt and nut, then the adjustment link.
7. Remove inner link from outer link. **Note number of turns for installation.**
8. Reverse procedure to install. Inspect and adjust rear toe as outlined in "Wheel Alignment" section.

Outer

1. Raise and support vehicle, then remove tire and wheel assembly.
2. Loosen pinch bolt.
3. Remove cotter pin and clotted hex nut.
4. Separate adjustment link from knuckle using universal steering linkage puller tool No. J24319-B, or equivalent. **Do not drive wedge between joint and attached part.**
5. Remove outer link from inner link. **Note number of turns for installation.**
6. Reverse procedure to install. Inspect and adjust rear toe as outlined in "Wheel Alignment" section.

TECHNICAL SERVICE BULLETINS

REAR SUSPENSION CLUNK OVER BUMPS

1998 Seville

On these models there may a clunk or thump type noise coming from the rear of the vehicle when going over bumps at low vehicle speeds. such as at railroad tracks or a twist ditch.

This condition may be caused by insufficient staking of tabs on the rear suspension forward body mounts allowing the rear suspension support to move sufficiently to come in contact with the forward body mount brackets.

To correct this condition bend the tabs completely outboard with a suitable large pair of pliers.

TIGHTENING SPECIFICATIONS

Year	Component	Torque/Ft. Lbs.
DEVILLE		
1998–99	Caliper	83
	Crossmember Forward Arm, Nut (Righthand Side)	46
	Crossmember Forward Arm, Nut (Lefthand Side)	75
	Crossmember Upper	75
	Hub	53
	Lower Control Arm	75
	Parking Brake Cable Bracket	32
	Shock Absorber, Lower	75
	Shock Absorber, Upper	55
	Stabilizer Bracket	44
	Stabilizer Link	44
	Toe Link, Inner	42
	Toe Link, Outer	55
	Upper Control Arm	42
	Wheel Lug Nuts	100
DEVILLE w/FE1 & FE3 SUSPENSION		
2000–02	Adjustment Link Cam Nut	59
	Adjustment Link To Control Arm	①
	Control Arm Nuts	78
	ELC Height Sensor	60②
	Hub & Bearing Bolts	50
	Rear Insulator To Body Bolts	57
	Rear Suspension Support Assembly To Body Rear Bolts	141
	Shock Absorber To Control Arm Bolts	18

Continued

TIGHTENING SPECIFICATIONS—Continued

Year	Component	Torque/Ft. Lbs.
DEVILLE w/FE1 & FE3 SUSPENSION		
2000–02	Shock Absorber Upper Bolts	18
	Stabilizer Link	11
	Stabilizer Shaft Clamp	24
	Stabilizer Shaft Link	11
	Wheel Lug Nuts	80
DEVILLE w/FE7 SUSPENSION		
2000–02	Adjustment Link Cam Nut	77
	Adjustment Link To Control Arm	①
	Control Arm Nuts	110
	Front Insulator To Body Bolts	63
	Front Support Assembly To Body Bolts	138
	Hub & Bearing Bolts	87
	Rear Insulator To Body Bolts	57
	Rear Support Assembly To Body Bolts	153
	Shock Absorber To Control Arm Bolts	27
	Shock Absorber Upper Bolts	21
	Stabilizer Link Bolt & Nut	11
	Stabilizer Shaft Bracket Bolt	38
	Suspension Support Insulator Bracket	94
	Wheel Bearing Nut	147
	Wheel Lug Nuts	80
ELDORADO		
1998–2002	Caliper	83
	Crossmember Forward Arm, Nut (Righthand Side)	46
	Crossmember Forward Arm, Nut (Lefthand Side)	75
	Crossmember Upper	75
	Hub	53
	Lower Control Arm Inner Nut	75
	Lower Control Arm Outer Nut (1998–2000)	75
	Lower Control Arm Outer Nut (2001–02)	80
	Parking Brake Cable Bracket	32
	Shock Absorber, Lower	75
	Shock Absorber, Upper	55
	Stabilizer Bracket	44
	Stabilizer Link Lower Bolt	38
	Stabilizer Link Lower Nut	44
	Stabilizer Link Upper Nut	44
	Toe Link, Inner	42
	Toe Link, Outer	55
	Upper Control Arm Inner Nut	42
	Upper Control Arm Outer Nut (1998–2000)	42
	Upper Control Arm Outer Nut (2001–02)	44
	Wheel Lug Nuts	100

Continued

TIGHTENING SPECIFICATIONS—Continued

Year	Component	Torque/Ft. Lbs.
SEVILLE		
1998–2002	Adjustment Link Cam Nut (1998–99)	59
	Adjustment Link Cam Nut (2000–02)	55
	Adjustment Link To Control Arm	①
	Body Bracket Front Bolts	63
	Control Arm Nuts	78
	ELC Height Sensor	60②
	Hub & Bearing	50
	Rear Body Mount Bolts	38
	Rear Suspension Support Assembly To Body Rear	141
	Shock Absorber To Control Arm	18
	Shock Absorber Upper Nuts	18
	Stabilizer Link Bolt & Nut (1998–99)	11
	Stabilizer Link Bolt & Nut (2000–02)	108②
	Stabilizer Shaft Clamp	24
	Wheel Lug Nuts	100

①— Refer to "Coil Spring, Replace" for tightening specifications.
②— Inch lbs.

Front Suspension & Steering

NOTE: On Air Bag Equipped Models, Refer To "Air Bag System Precautions" Located In The Front Of This Manual For System Disarming & Arming Procedures.

NOTE: Refer To "Computer Relearn Procedures" Located In The Front Of This Manual When Battery Power To The Computer Has Been Interrupted.

NOTE: Prior To Performing Any Service Operations Listed In This Section, Consult The "Technical Service Bulletins" Section For Related Information.

INDEX

PRECAUTIONS

AIR BAG SYSTEMS

Refer to "Air Bag System Precautions" in the front of this manual for system disarming and arming procedures.

BATTERY GROUND CABLE

Prior to service, disconnect battery ground cable and isolate as required.

HUB & BEARING

REPLACE

1. Raise and support vehicle, then remove tire and wheel assembly.
2. Remove hub nut and washer using suitable punch to keep rotor stationary. Discard hub nut.
3. Remove caliper, support and rotor.
4. Separate drive axle from hub using drive axle separator tool No. J28733-B, or equivalent, **Fig. 1.**
5. Remove hub and bearing mounting bolts.
6. Disconnect speed sensor connector.
7. Remove hub and bearing assembly.
8. Reverse procedure to install, noting the following:
   a. Clean rust and dirt from knuckle bore, chamber and mounting face allow proper seating of bearing and knuckle.
   b. Apply a light coating of grease to steering knuckle bore.

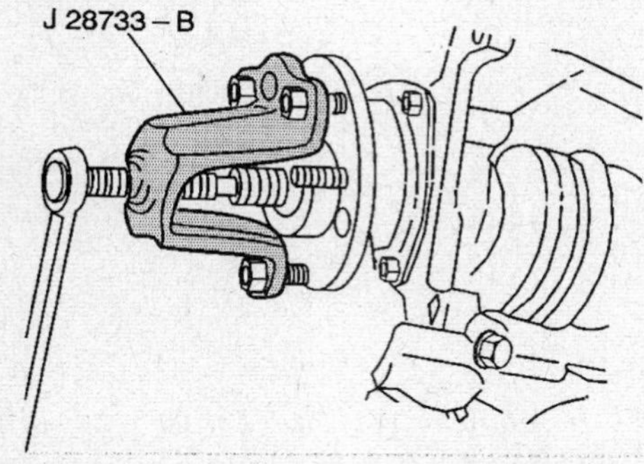

Fig. 1 Drive axle separation

   c. **Do not use old hub nut. Always install a new one.**
   d. Draw hub and bearing onto axle with hub nut.

BALL JOINT INSPECTION

1998–2000

Replace ball joints if any looseness is detected in the joint or ball joint seal is cut. Complete the following steps in order to inspect ball joint.

1. Raise and support front of vehicle, allowing suspension to hang free.
2. Wipe ball joint clean. Inspect seals for tears or cuts.
3. Grasp tire at top and bottom and rock it in and out.
4. Inspect for any horizontal movement in knuckle relative to control arm.
5. Replace ball joint if ball stud is disconnected from knuckle and looseness is detected or ball stud twists in its socket while using hand pressure.
6. Inspect for ball stud tightness in knuckle boss. Shake wheel and feel for movement of stud end or nut at knuckle boss.
7. Replace all worn or damaged ball joints and knuckles.

2001–02

Replace ball joints if any looseness is detected in the joint or ball joint seal is cut. Complete the following steps in order to inspect ball joint.

1. Raise and support front of vehicle.
2. Support lower control arm with a suitable jack stand as far outboard as possible near lower ball joint.
3. Wipe ball joint clean. Inspect seals for tears or cuts.
4. Mount dial indicator kit tool No. J8001, or equivalent, against lowest outboard point on wheel rim.
5. Grasp tire at top and bottom and rock it in and out.
6. Dial indicator reading should not exceed .125 inch. If reading is too high, inspect lower ball joint for vertical looseness as follows:
   a. Wear in ball joints is indicated by a

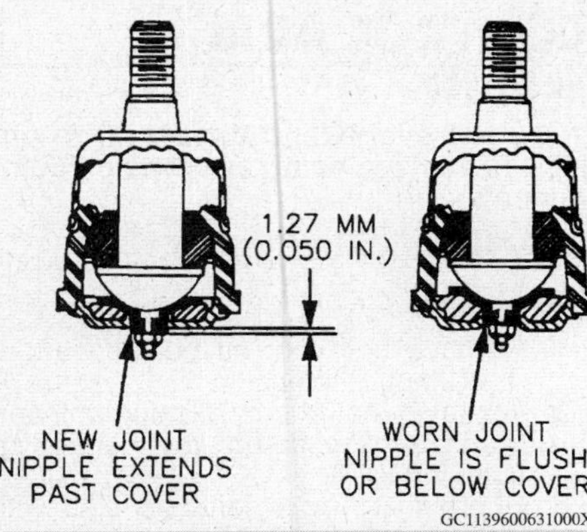

Fig. 2 Ball joint vertical wear inspection

.50 inch diameter nipple which retracts into joint cover as joint wears.

b. Replace ball joint if nipple is flush with or below joint cover, **Fig. 2.**

7. Replace ball joint if ball stud is disconnected from knuckle and looseness is detected or ball stud twists in its socket while using hand pressure.
8. Inspect for ball stud tightness in knuckle boss. Shake wheel and feel for movement of stud end or nut at knuckle boss.
9. Replace all worn or damaged ball joints and knuckles.

BALL JOINT

REPLACE

DEVILLE

1998

1. Raise and support vehicle.
2. Remove tire and wheel assembly.
3. **On models equipped with road sensing suspension,** disconnect position sensor from lower control arm.
4. **On all models,** separate ball joint from knuckle using separator tool No. J35315, or equivalent.
5. Drill out ball joint rivets. Start with a 1/4 inch drill bit, then progress and end with a 1/2 inch bit.
6. Remove ball joint.
7. Reverse procedure to install, noting the following:
   a. **Torque** ball joint castle nut to 84 inch lbs.
   b. Rotate nut an additional 90.°
   c. Rotate nut an additional 120° while noting torque reading.
   d. Rotate nut up to an additional 60° to align holes and install cotter pin.

1999–2002

On these models the ball joint is not serviced separately from the control arm. Refer to "Control Arm, Replace."

ELDORADO

1998

Refer to "1998" under "DeVille" for ball joint replacement procedure.

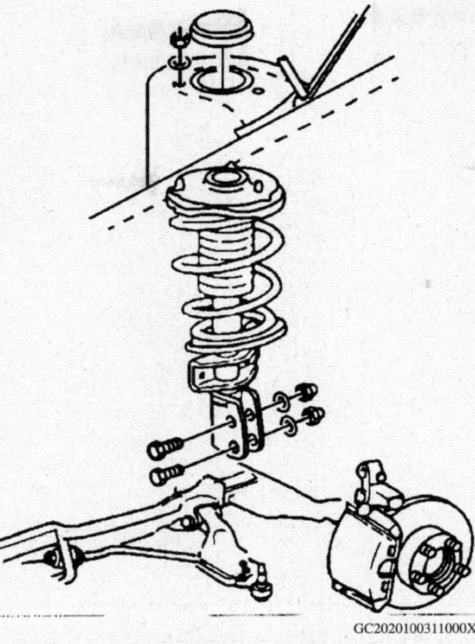

Fig. 3 Steering knuckle & strut replacement. Eldorado & 1998–99 DeVille

1999–2002

On these models the ball joint is not serviced separately from the control arm. Refer to "Control Arm, Replace."

SEVILLE

On these models the ball joint is not serviced separately from the control arm. Refer to "Control Arm, Replace."

STRUT

REPLACE

DEVILLE

1998–99

Do not overextend driveshaft tri-pot joints when replacing suspension components.

1. Remove nuts securing top of strut assembly to body, **Fig. 3.**
2. Raise and support vehicle, then remove tire and wheel.
3. Scribe inboard surface of strut along upper knuckle radius, **Fig. 4.**
4. Scribe knuckle along lower curve of strut.
5. Scribe mark along strut/knuckle interface.
6. Disconnect brake line bracket from strut.
7. Remove strut to stabilizer link mounting bolt and stabilizer link.
8. Remove strut to steering knuckle mounting, then support knuckle using suitable wire or rope.
9. Remove strut.
10. Reverse procedure to install, noting the following:
    a. Align scribe marks made during removal.
    b. Tighten mounting bolts and nuts to specifications.

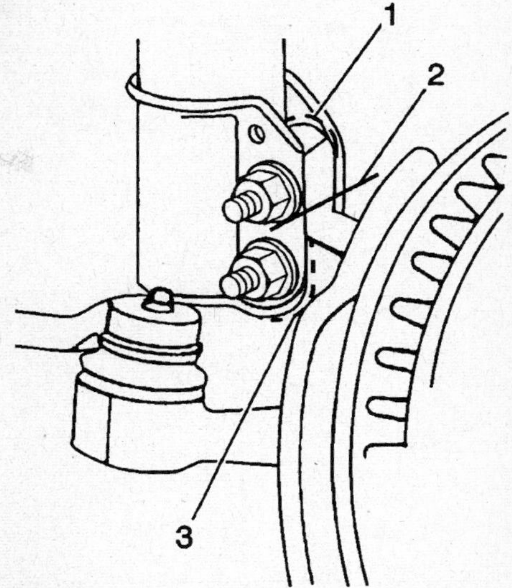

1. Upper knuckle radius
2. Strut/knuckle interface
3. Lower curve of strut

GC2020100312000X

Fig. 4 Steering knuckle & strut alignment marking. Eldorado & 1998–99 DeVille

c. Inspect and adjust alignment as required.

2000–02

1. Remove strut to body mounting bolts.
2. Raise and support vehicle with suspension hanging free.
3. Remove tire and wheel assembly.
4. Disconnect ABS front wheel speed sensor electrical connector.
5. Remove speed sensor bracket from strut.
6. Remove brake line bracket from left-hand strut.
7. Remove strut to knuckle bolts. **Knuckle must be retained after strut to knuckle bolts have been removed.**
8. Remove strut.
9. Reverse procedure to install.

ELDORADO

Refer to "1998–99" under "DeVille" for strut replacement procedure.

SEVILLE

Refer to "2000–02" under "DeVille" for stryt replacement procedure.

STRUT SERVICE

DISASSEMBLY

1. Compress spring slightly using strut compressor tool No. J34013, **Fig. 5.**
2. Remove dampner shaft top nut. Prevent shaft from turning by using a T-50 Torx bit.
3. Guide dampner shaft out of assembly using rod tool No. J34013-38, or equivalent.
4. Loosen compressor screw while guiding dampner shaft out of assembly.
5. Continually loosening compressor

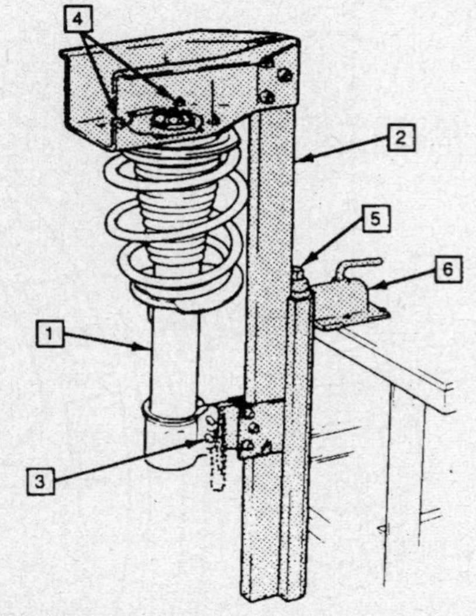

Fig. 5 Strut spring compression

1 ROD J-34013-38 INSTALLED
2 CLAMP J-34013-20 INSTALLED
3 FLAT ON SPRING SEAT MUST FACE SAME DIRECTION AS STEERING KNUCKLE FLANGE
4 BOTH LOCKING PINS INSTALLED
5 COMPRESSOR FORCING SCREW
GC2029100136000X

Fig. 6 Strut assembly

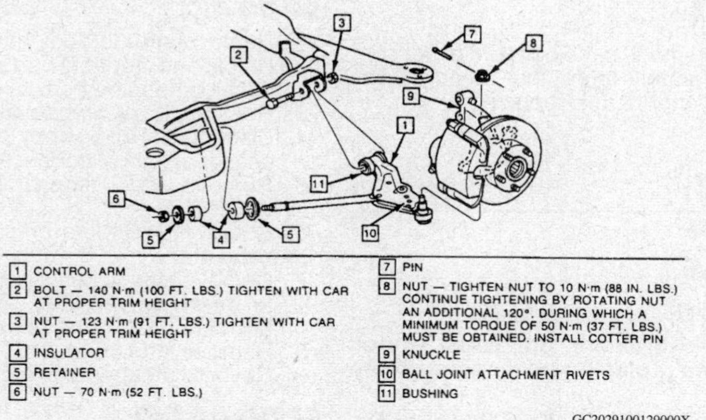

Fig. 7 Lower control arm replacement. Eldorado & 1998–99 DeVille

screw till strut dampner and spring can be removed. **Do not chip or crack spring coating.**

ASSEMBLY

1. Install strut dampner in strut compressor tool No. J34013 with clamp tool No. J34013-20, or equivalents, **Fig. 6.**
2. Install spring over strut in proper position.
3. Move assembly upright in strut compressor and install upper lockpin. **Flat on upper spring seat must face out from centerline of vehicle. If mounted in strut compressor, spring seat faces same direction as steering knuckle mounting flange.**
4. Guide dampner shaft onto strut using installer rod tool No. J34013-38, or equivalent.
5. Center dampner shaft by turning compressor tool screw clockwise while guiding rod.
6. Continue turning compressor screw until dampner shaft threads are visible through top of strut assembly.
7. Install washer and nut. Remove clamp tool.
8. Hold dampner shaft with socket, then tighten dampner shaft nut to specifications.

CONTROL ARM

REPLACE

Do not overextend driveshaft tri-pot joints when replacing suspension components.

DEVILLE

1998–99

1. Remove ball joint as outlined under "Ball Joint, Replace."
2. Remove control arm bushing bolt and brake reaction rod nut, retainer and insulator, **Fig. 7.**
3. Support transaxle lefthand side with suitable screw jack and wood block.
4. Remove two transaxle mount nuts, then raise transaxle to access control arm mounting bolt.
5. Remove mounting bolts and control arm.
6. Reverse procedure to install noting the following:
   a. Install control arm bushing bolt and nut, retainer and insulator. Do not tighten bolt.
   b. **On DeVille models,** tighten bolts to specifications, **Figs. 7 and 8.**
7. **On Eldorado models, torque** ball joint retaining nut to 88 inch lbs., then rotate an additional 150.°
8. **On all models, continue rotating for cotter pin installation if required, but do not exceed 60° additional rotation. Do not back off ball joint nut for cotter pin alignment.**

2000–02

1. Raise and support vehicle with control arms hanging free. Remove tire and wheel.
2. Disconnect stabilizer link to control arm bolt.
3. Remove cotter pin and loosen nut from ball stud.
4. Separate ball joint from knuckle using separator tool No. J35315, or equivalent.
5. Remove mounting bolts and control arm.
6. Reverse procedure to install, noting the following:
   a. **On DeVille models equipped with FE1 and FE3 suspension, torque** ball joint retaining nut to 88 inch lbs., then rotate an additional 150.°
   b. **On DeVille models equipped with FE7 suspension, torque** ball joint nut to 22 ft. lbs., then rotate an additional 190.°
   c. **On 1998–99 Seville models, torque** ball joint nut to 88 inch lbs., then rotate nut 2 ½ flats to a minimum of 41 ft. lbs. for cotter pin installation.
   d. **On 2001–02 Seville models, torque** ball joint retaining nut to 88 inch lbs., then rotate an additional 180–300°, or three to five flats.

e. **On all models, continue rotating for cotter pin installation if required, but do not exceed 60° additional rotation. Do not back off ball joint nut for cotter pin alignment.**

ELDORADO

Refer to "1998–99" under "DeVille" for control arm replacement procedure.

SEVILLE

Refer to "2000–02" under "DeVille" for control arm replacement procedure.

CONTROL ARM BUSHING

REPLACE

On these models the control arm bushings are incorporated into the lower control arm and are not serviced separately.

STEERING KNUCKLE

REPLACE

1. Remove hub and bearing as outlined under "Hub & Bearing, Replace."
2. Disconnect wheel speed sensor electrical connector.
3. Remove tie rod mounting nut.
4. Separate tie rod from knuckle using tie rod separator tool No. J24319-B, or equivalent.
5. Remove cotter pin and lower ball joint mounting nut.
6. Separate ball joint from steering knuckle using ball joint separator tool No. J43828, or equivalent.
7. Remove strut to steering knuckle mounting bolts, then the steering knuckle.
8. Reverse procedure to install, noting the following:
   a. Refer to "Control Arm, Replace" for ball joint nut tightening specifications.
   b. Tighten outer tie rod to knuckle retaining nut to specifications.

STABILIZER BAR

REPLACE

DEVILLE

1998–99

1. Raise and support vehicle. **Ensure vehicle weight rests on frame, not on lower control arms.**
2. Remove righthand front tire and wheel.
3. **On models equipped with road sensing suspension,** disconnect position sensor from lower control arm.
4. **On all models,** remove lefthand and righthand mounting bolts, brackets and insulators, **Fig. 8.**
5. Remove lefthand and righthand stabilizer links.
6. Disconnect exhaust pipe from rear manifold, raise pipe to gain clearance, then remove stabilizer shaft.
7. Reverse procedure to install.

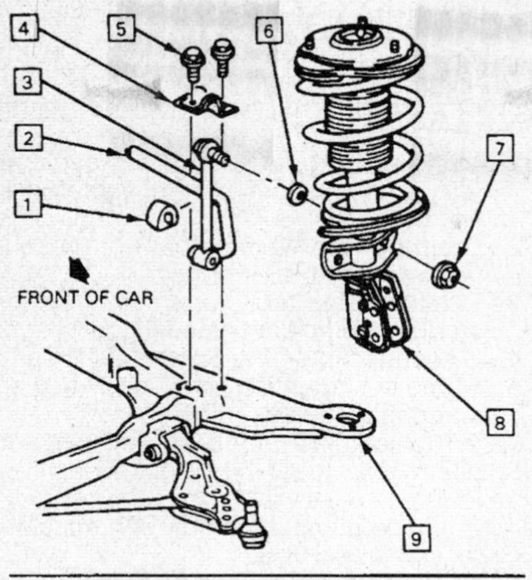

1 INSULATOR – INSTALL WITH SLIT TO REAR OF CAR
2 STABILIZER SHAFT
3 STABILIZER LINK
4 BRACKET
5 BOLT – 47 N·m (35 lbs. ft.)
6 WASHER
7 NUT – 65 N·m (48 lbs. ft.)
8 SPRING & STRUT ASSEMBLY
9 FRAME

GC2029100128000X

Fig. 8 Stabilizer shaft replacement. Eldorado & 1998–99 DeVille

2000–02

1. Raise and support vehicle with control arms hanging free. Remove front tires and wheels.
2. Remove lefthand and righthand stabilizer link bolts.
3. Remove lefthand and righthand stabilizer bar brackets.
4. Remove lefthand tie rod end from knuckle using linkage puller tool No. J24319-B, or equivalent.
5. Separate ball joint from steering knuckle using ball joint separator tool No. J36226, or equivalent.
6. Turn righthand steering knuckle to lefthand, then guide stabilizer shaft out righthand side in an upward direction.
7. Remove stabilizer shaft out of bottom center.
8. Reverse procedure to install.

ELDORADO

Refer to "1998–99" under "DeVille" for stabilizer bar replacement procedure.

SEVILLE

Refer to "2000–02" under "DeVille" for stabilizer bar replacement procedure.

TIE ROD

REPLACE

INNER

1. Remove steering gear as outlined under "Power Steering Gear, Replace."
2. Remove outer tie rod jam nut.
3. Remove inner tie rod assembly jam nut and end clamp.
4. Remove boot clamp using suitable side cutters.
5. Mark breather tube location on steering gear for installation.
6. Remove rack and pinion boot, then the breather tube.
7. Loosen inner tie rod assembly shock dampner and slide back on rack.
8. Hold rack in suitable vise.
9. Turn inner tie rod housing counterclockwise and remove using one wrench on rack assembly flats and another on inner tire rod housing flats.
10. Reverse procedure to install. Gap between rack and housing stakes should be .01 inch.

OUTER

1. Remove cotter pin and hex slotted nut.
2. Loosen jam nut.
3. Remove outer tie rod from steering knuckle using universal steering linkage puller tool No. J24319-01, or equivalent.
4. Remove outer from inner tie rod.
5. Reverse procedure to install.

POWER STEERING GEAR

REPLACE

DEVILLE

1998–99

1. Ensure front wheels are in straight-ahead position, then lock steering wheel.
2. Disconnect intermediate shaft lower coupling.
3. Raise and support vehicle, then remove lefthand front tire and wheel assembly.
4. Disconnect RSS position sensor and links.
5. Disconnect both tie rod ends from knuckles.
6. Disconnect exhaust pipe at converter.
7. Support frame with suitable jack stands.
8. Loosen body mount bolts No. 2 and No. 3, then slightly lower rear of frame. **Do not lower any more than required to access steering gear.**
9. Remove heat shield and plastic line retainer.
10. Disconnect steering gear pressure and return lines.
11. Disconnect Magnasteer electrical connector.
12. Remove mounting bolts and steering gear by sliding out to side.
13. Reverse procedure to install.

2000–02

Removal

1. Ensure front wheels are in straight-ahead position.
2. Lock steering column using lockpin tool No. J42640, or equivalent, in underside of steering column.

3. Disconnect intermediate shaft lower coupling.
4. Disconnect Magnasteer electrical connector and remove heat shield.
5. Separate outer tie rod ends from steering knuckles using separator tool No. J24319-B, or equivalent.
6. Remove righthand transaxle mount. **Frame must be properly supported before partially lowering and should not be lowered any further than required to access steering gear.**
7. Position a suitable drain pan below steering gear fluid pipe fittings.
8. Disconnect steering gear pressure and return pipes.
9. Remove steering gear mounting bolts.
10. Position a suitable floor jack below rear side of frame.
11. Remove rear mounting bolts from frame.
12. Lower the rear portion of frame.
13. Remove steering gear assembly from vehicle.

Installation

1. Install steering gear onto frame.
2. Raise rear portion of frame and install mounting bolts.
3. Install transaxle mount nuts.
4. Install steering gear mounting bolts.
5. Install power steering pressure and return hoses.
6. Connect Magnasteer electrical connector and install heat shield.
7. Connect outer tie rod ends to knuckles.
8. Connect intermediate shaft to steering gear.
9. Install tires and wheels. Tighten lug nuts to specifications.
10. Fill and bleed power steering fluid system as outlined under "Power Steering System Bleed" in "Power Steering" chapter.

ELDORADO

Refer to "1998–99" under "DeVille" for power steering gear replacement procedure.

SEVILLE

Refer to "2000–02" under "DeVille" for power steering gear replacement procedure.

POWER STEERING PUMP

REPLACE

1. Mark running direction using suitable felt pen or chalk, then remove serpentine belt.
2. Drain power steering fluid from reservoir into a suitable container.
3. Position a suitable drain pan below steering pump fluid pipe fittings.
4. Disconnect steering pump fluid lines.
5. Remove mounting bolt and power steering pump assembly.
6. If replacement pump arrived without pulley and reservoir, proceed as follows:
   a. Place pump assembly in a suitable soft jawed vise.
   b. Remove power steering pump and reservoir from bracket.
   c. Remove pump pulley using pulley removal tool No. J25034-C, or equivalent.
   d. Remove pump mounting bracket bolts, then the bracket.
   e. Remove retaining clips from reservoir using clip removal tool No. J42649, or equivalent.
   f. Remove reservoir from pump. Discard O-rings.
7. Reverse procedure to install, noting the following:
   a. Lubricate new O-ring seals with fresh power steering fluid, then install O-rings onto reservoir.
   b. Ensure retaining clip is fully seated on reservoir assembly so reservoir assembly and pump housing are securely installed.
   c. Install power steering pump pulley using pulley installation tool No. J25033-C, or equivalent.

TECHNICAL SERVICE BULLETINS

CLUNK, RATTLE NOISE FROM FRONT OF VEHICLE

1998–99 DeVille, Eldorado & Seville

On some of these models built before April 1, 1999, there may be a clunk, rattle or metal to metal noise from the lefthand or righthand front of the vehicle that can be heard in the passenger compartment. This may be more noticeable in cold weather conditions and may be caused by the stabilizer bar rubber insulator walking out of its seated position between the engine frame and the stabilizer mounting bracket/clamp during large suspension movements.

To correct this condition, proceed as follows:

1. Raise and support vehicle.
2. Remove stabilizer shaft bracket/clamp.
3. Remove stabilizer shaft insulator.
4. Clean engine frame surface of debris or grease.
5. Install a 2 × 1½ inch strip of anti-slip/friction material such as 3M Safety-Walk General Purpose Tread Tape, or equivalent, on engine frame with two-inch side positioned fore/aft.
6. Install stabilizer shaft insulator, bracket/clamp and mounting bolts.

SQUAWK TYPE NOISE FROM FRONT SUSPENSION

1998 Seville

On these models there may a squawk type noise from front suspension when driving on rough or bumpy roads. The condition may be more noticeable in cold weather.

This condition may be caused by either the stabilizer bar insulators rubbing on the bar or the strut lower spring insulator rubbing on the spring.

To correct this condition, proceed as follows:

1. Replace stabilizer bar insulators with revised components (Seville STS part No. 25689665 or Seville SLS part No. 25689666).
2. If noise is still present, determine whether it is from lefthand or righthand front.
3. Remove and disassemble appropriate strut module.
4. Turn spring end-for-end, being careful to properly seat it into insulator.
5. Assemble and install strut module. **Do not lubricate any strut module components.**

TIGHTENING SPECIFICATIONS

Year	Component	Torque/Ft. Lbs.
DEVILLE		
1998–99	Adjuster Plug	50
	Ball Joint To Control Arm	50
	Ball Joint To Knuckle	37
	Brake Reaction Rod To Frame	58
	Caliper	63
	Caliper Mounting Bracket	83
	Control Arm Bushing	100
	Cylinder Line Fittings	20
	Dampner Shaft	55
	Hub & Bearing To Knuckle	70
	Hub To Drive Axle	110
	Inner Tie Rod Housing To Rack	74
	Intermediate Shaft Pinch Bolts	35
	Outer Tie Rod Jam Nut	50
	Pinion Locknut	26
	Pinion Preload	17①
	Power Steering Line Fittings	20
	Stabilizer Bracket To Frame	33
	Stabilizer Link	41
	Strut Mount To Body	18
	Strut To Knuckle	75
	Strut To Strut Top Mount	④
	Tie Rod End To Knuckle	35–52
	Tie Rod Pinch Bolts	41
	Wheel Lug Nuts	100
DEVILLE w/FE1 & FE3 SUSPENSION		
2000–02	Ball Joint To Control Arm Nut	⑦
	Brake Line & Speed Sensor Bracket	13
	Caliper Pin Bolts	②
	Control Arm Bolt	116
	Drive Axle Nut	118
	Hub & Bearing Bolts	96
	Power Steering Gear	70
	Power Steering Gear Hose	22
	Power Steering Pump	37
	Stabilizer Shaft Bracket Bolts	24
	Stabilizer Shaft Link Nuts	13
	Strut Mount Nuts	55
	Strut To Body	30
	Strut To Knuckle	108
	Tie Rod End To Knuckle	22③⑤
	Wheel Lug Nuts	100
DEVILLE w/FE7 SUSPENSION		
2000–02	Ball Joint To Control Arm Nut	⑦
	Brake Line & Speed Sensor Bracket	13
	Caliper Pin Bolts	②
	Control Arm Bolt	108
	Drive Axle Nut	159
	Hub & Bearing Bolts	112
	Power Steering Gear	70
	Power Steering Gear Hose	22
	Power Steering Pump	37
	Stabilizer Shaft Bracket Bolts	49

Continued

TIGHTENING SPECIFICATIONS—Continued

Year	Component	Torque/Ft. Lbs.
DEVILLE w/FE7 SUSPENSION		
2000–02	Stabilizer Shaft Link Nuts	17
	Strut Mount Nuts	55
	Strut To Body	49
	Strut To Knuckle	131
	Tie Rod End To Knuckle	22③⑥
	Wheel Lug Nuts	100
ELDORADO		
1998–2002	Adjuster Plug	50
	Ball Joint To Control Arm	50
	Ball Joint To Knuckle	37
	Brake Reaction Rod To Frame	58
	Caliper Pin Bolts	63
	Caliper Mounting Bracket Bolts	137
	Control Arm Bushing	100
	Cylinder Line Fittings	20
	Hub & Bearing To Knuckle	70
	Hub To Drive Axle	110
	Inner Tie Rod Housing To Rack (1998)	50
	Inner Tie Rod Housing To Rack (1999–2002)	74
	Intermediate Shaft Pinch Bolts	35
	Outer Tie Rod Jam Nut	50
	Power Steering Line Fittings	20
	Stabilizer Bracket To Frame	33
	Stabilizer Link	41
	Strut Mount To Body	18
	Strut To Knuckle	108
	Strut To Strut Top Mount	④
	Tie Rod End To Knuckle (1998–99)	35–52
	Tie Rod End To Knuckle (2000–02)	55
	Tie Rod Pinch Bolts	41
	Wheel Lug Nuts	100
SEVILLE		
1998–2002	Adjuster Plug Nut	55
	Ball Joint	⑦
	Brake Line & Speed Sensor Bracket	13
	Caliper Bracket Bolts	137
	Caliper Pin Bolts	63
	Control Arm Bolt	117
	Drive Axle Nut (1998)	107
	Drive Axle Nut (1999–2002)	118
	Hub & Bearing	96
	Inner Tie Rod	74
	Power Steering Gear	89
	Power Steering Gear Hose	20
	Power Steering Pump	37
	Stabilizer Bracket	24
	Stabilizer Shaft Link	13
	Strut Mount Nut	55
	Strut Tower Bolts (1998)	35

Continued

TIGHTENING SPECIFICATIONS—Continued

Year	Component	Torque/Ft. Lbs.
SEVILLE		
1998–2002	Strut Tower Bolts (1999–2002)	33
	Strut To Knuckle (1998)	125
	Strut To Knuckle (1999–2002)	108
	Tie Rod End To Knuckle (1998)	52③
	Tie Rod End To Knuckle (1999)	55③
	Tie Rod End To Knuckle (2000–02)	35
	Wheel Lug Nuts	100

① — Inch lbs.
② — With standard brakes, 63 ft. lbs.; w/J55 heavy duty brakes, 83 ft. lbs.
③ — Do not counter-rotate nut for cotter pin insertion.
④ — Torque old design (flanged) nut to 75 ft. lbs. & new design (non-flanged) nut to 55 ft. lbs.
⑤ — Rotate an additional 180.°
⑥ — Rotate an additional 200.° If required, rotate another 60° to allow cotter pin installation.
⑦ — Refer to "Control Arm, Replace" for tightening specifications & procedure.

Wheel Alignment

INDEX

PRELIMINARY INSPECTION

1. Inspect all tires for proper inflation pressures and approximately equal tread wear.
2. Inspect hub and bearing assemblies for excessive wear, correcting as required.
3. Inspect ball joints and tie rod ends. If they are excessively loose, correct before making adjustment.
4. Measure runout of wheels and tires.
5. Inspect vehicle trim height, correcting as required before adjusting alignment.
6. Inspect for proper operation of Electronic Level Control system.
7. Inspect strut dampners for proper operation.
8. Inspect control arms for loose bushings.
9. Inspect stabilizer bar for loose or missing components.

FRONT WHEEL ALIGNMENT

1. Install alignment equipment following equipment manufacturers instructions.
2. Jounce front and rear bumpers three times to normalize suspension prior to measuring angles.
3. Measure alignment angles and record the readings.
4. If adjustments are required, they must be made in order:
   a. Caster.
   b. Camber.
   c. Toe.

DEVILLE

1998–99

Caster

1. Support vehicle by wheels, then loosen top strut mounting nuts and washers.
2. Set caster to specification by moving strut forward or rearward, as required. Adjustment sensitivity is approximately .1° per millimeter moved.
3. Tighten top strut mounting nuts and washers to specifications.

Camber

1. Loosen both strut to knuckle bolts just enough to allow movement.
2. Adjust camber by rotating adjustment bolt with adjustment tool No. J39601, or equivalent, **Fig. 1.**
3. Tighten strut to knuckle nuts to specifications.
4. **Torque** camber adjustment bolt to 84 inch lbs.

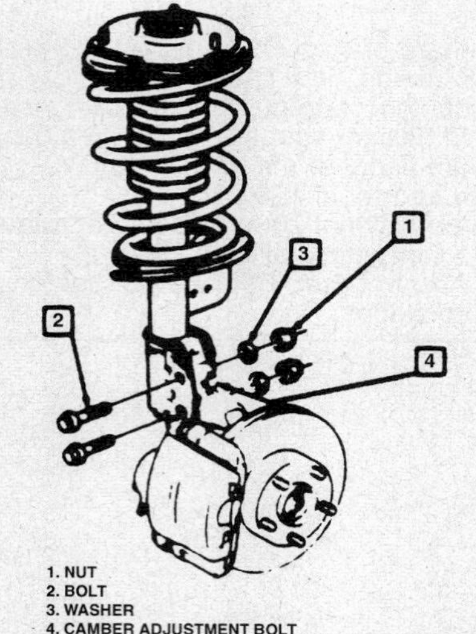

Fig. 1 Front wheel camber adjustment. Eldorado & 1998–99 DeVille

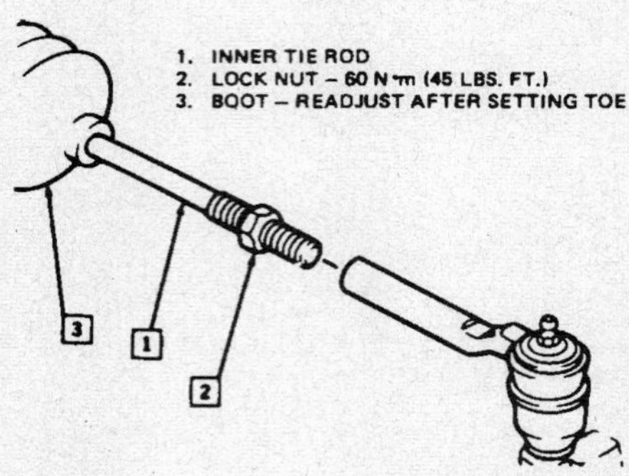

Fig. 2 Front wheel toe adjustment. Eldorado & 1998–99 DeVille

Toe

1. Loosen inner tie rod locknuts, **Fig. 2.**
2. Adjust toe by turning inner tie rods.
3. Adjust boots so they are not twisted.
4. **Torque** locknuts to 46 ft. lbs.

2000–02

Caster

1. Remove top strut nuts and washers.
2. Raise and support front of vehicle to separate strut from inner wheel housing.
3. Drill two 3⁄8 inch holes at front and rear of oval strut mounting hole on lefthand and righthand strut towers, **Fig. 3.**
4. File excess metal to create slotted holes. **Paint exposed metal with rust resistant paint or primer.**
5. Lower front of vehicle.
6. Install strut mounting nuts. **Do not tighten just yet.**
7. Adjust caster by moving top of strut forward or rearward. A .040 inch position change at tower is approximately .1° change in caster.
8. When caster is within specifications, **torque** strut mounting nuts to 35 ft. lbs.

Camber

1. Raise and support vehicle, then remove both front tires and wheels.
2. Tap out upper and lower strut to knuckle bolts, then separate strut from knuckle.
3. Grind lower bolt hole on struts inner metal plate to match outside plates diameter.
4. File excess metal to make slotted holes, then paint exposed metal with rust resistant paint or primer.
5. Replace strut to knuckle and install bolts. **Do not tighten just yet.**
6. Set camber to specifications using camber adjustment tool No. J39601, or equivalent,
7. **On DeVille models equipped with soft or sports suspension, torque** strut to knuckle mounting nuts to 108 ft. lbs.
8. **On Seville models and DeVille equipped with heavy duty suspension, torque** strut to knuckle mounting nuts to 131 ft. lbs.

Toe

1. Loosen locknuts on tie rod ends. **Ensure boots are not twisted or damaged during adjustment.**
2. Rotate inner tie rod to adjust toe to specifications.

3. **Torque** locknuts to 47 ft. lbs.

ELDORADO

Refer to "1998–99" under "DeVille" for front wheel alignment procedure.

SEVILLE

Refer to "2000–02" under "DeVille" for front wheel alignment procedure.

REAR WHEEL ALIGNMENT

DEVILLE

1998–99

Before inspecting rear trim height or measuring rear alignment angles, the following procedure should be performed to ensure the rear air adjustable struts are filled with residual pressure only.

1. Place weight of at least 300 lbs. in vehicle trunk.
2. Turn ignition On, then wait for vehicle leveling lamp to light.
3. Turn ignition Off and remove weight from trunk.
4. Wait at least 30 seconds for ELC system to exhaust.
5. Roll vehicle forward or backward several complete tire rotations to eliminate effects of tire camber change.
6. Jounce front and rear bumpers three times to normalize suspension prior to measuring angles.

Camber

1. Loosen front and rear inside control arm mounting bolts.
2. Move control arm to change camber and adjust to specifications.
3. **Torque** control arm mounting bolts to 66 ft. lbs.

Toe

1. Loosen inner toe link bolts.
2. Insert suitable screwdriver or pry bar between inside rear toe link mounting bolt and rear crossmember assembly.
3. Move toe link to adjust toe and adjust to specifications.
4. **Torque** toe link mounting bolts to 66 ft. lbs.

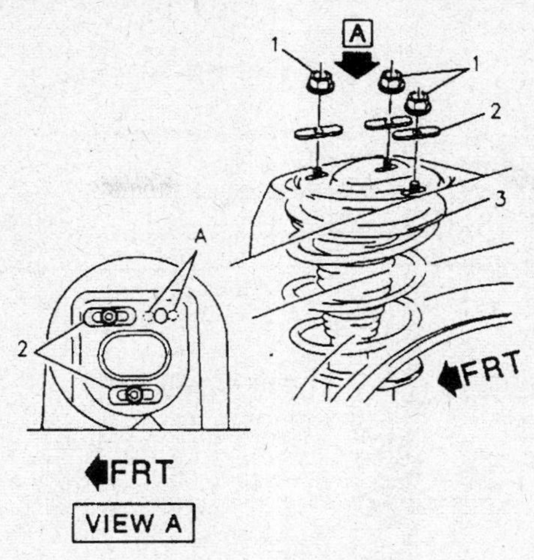

A DRILL 13/32 IN. HOLES
1 NUT, 47 N•m (35 LB. FT.)
2 WASHERS
3 STRUT

GC2049500108000X

Fig. 3 Front caster adjustment. Seville & 2000–02 DeVille

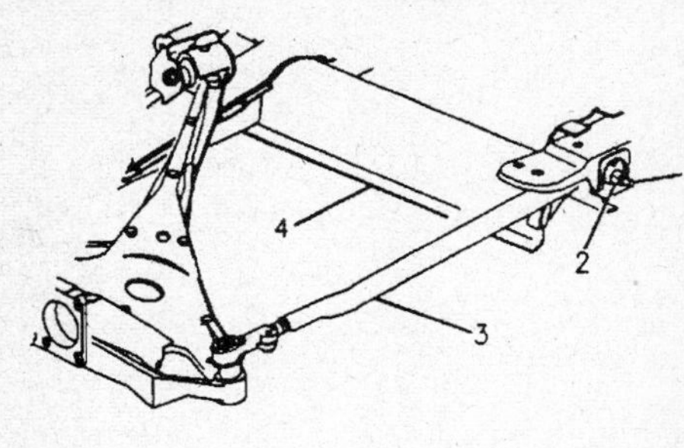

1 CAM BOLT
2 NUT, 75 N•m (55 LB. FT.)
3 INNER ADJUSTMENT LINK
4 REAR SUSPENSION SUPPORT ASSEMBLY

GC2049500110000X

Fig. 4 Rear toe adjustment. Seville & 2000–02 DeVille

2000–02

Make lefthand and righthand toe adjustments separately.

1. Loosen inner adjustment link cam nut, **Fig. 4.**
2. Rotate cam bolt using a suitable 18 MM wrench or socket and adjust toe to specifications.
3. **Torque** cam nut to 74 ft. lbs.

ELDORADO

Refer to "1998–99" under "DeVille" for rear wheel alignment procedure.

SEVILLE

Refer to "2000–02" under "DeVille" for rear wheel alignment procedure.

VEHICLE RIDE HEIGHT

Refer to **Fig. 5** for ride height measurements and to "Vehicle Ride Height Specifications" in "Specifications" section. When inspecting ride height measurements, note the following:

1. Fuel tank should be full.
2. Tires should be at proper pressure.
3. Front seat should be in rearmost position.
4. Luggage compartment should be empty except for spare tire and jack.
5. Vehicle should be on level ground.
6. If fuel tank is not full, add weight to trunk to compensate for amount fuel vehicle is below the full level.
7. Prior to inspecting ride height, lift front bumper upward approximately 1 ½ inches and release three times.
8. Inspect front ride height.
9. Push front bumper downward approximately 1 ½ inches and release three times.
10. Inspect front ride height.
11. Average out both readings to determine vehicle ride height.
12. Inspect rear ride height in same manner, lifting and pushing rear bumper.

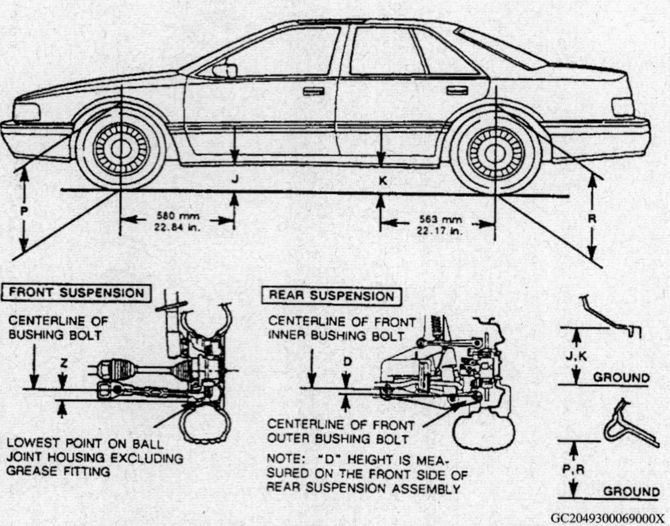

Fig. 5 Ride height measurement locations

METRO

NOTE: Refer To The Rear Of This Manual For Vehicle Manufacturer's Special Tool Suppliers.

INDEX OF SERVICE OPERATIONS

Specifications

GENERAL ENGINE SPECIFICATIONS

Year	Engine Liter	Fuel System	Bore & Stroke Inches	Comp. Ratio	Net. H.P. @ RPM	Maximum Torque, Ft. Lbs. @ RPM	Normal Oil Pressure, psi
1998–2001	1.0L	TBI	2.91 x 3.03	9.5	55 @ 5700	58 @ 3300	47–61
	1.3L	SFI	2.91 x 2.97	9.5	79 @ 6000	75 @ 3000	47–61

TBI — Throttle Body Injection

SFI — Sequential Multi-Port Fuel Injection

TUNE UP SPECIFICATIONS

Engine	Spark Plug Gap	Ignition Timing, BTDC				Curb Idle Speed, RPM		Fast Idle Speed, RPM		Fuel Pump Pressure, psi	Valve Lash
		Firing Order Fig.	Man. Trans.	Auto. Trans.	Mark Fig.	Man. Trans.	Auto. Trans.	Man. Trans.	Auto. Trans.		
1.0L	.041	A	5①	5①	C	850	850	②	②	23–31	③
1.3L	.041	B	5①	5①	C	750–875	750–875	②	②	28–35	③

BTDC: Before Top Dead Center

① — When inspecting ignition timing connect jumper wire between diagnostic connector terminals 4 & 5.

Diagnostic connector is located next to lefthand strut tower.

② — Controlled by an idle speed control motor.

③ — Equipped w/hydraulic valve lash adjusters.

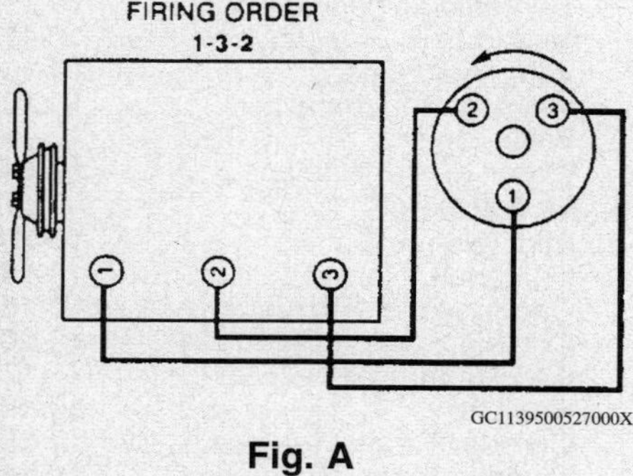

Fig. A

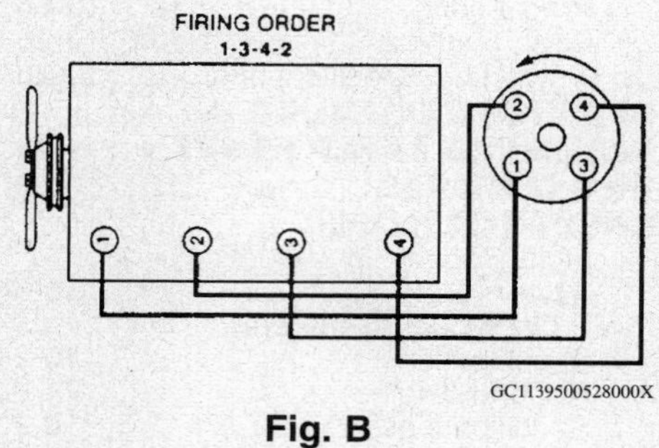

Fig. B

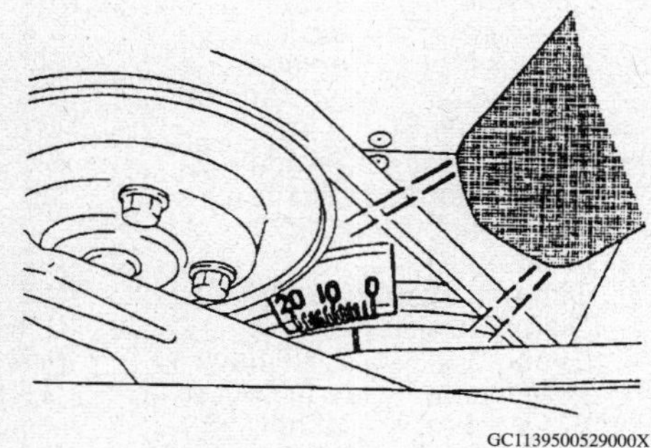

Fig. C

FRONT WHEEL ALIGNMENT SPECIFICATIONS

Year	Caster Angle, Degrees		Camber Angles, Degrees		Total Toe, Degrees	Turning Angle, Degrees		Ball Joint Wear
	Limits	Desired	Limits	Desired		Inner Wheel	Outer Wheel	
1998–2001	+1 to +5	+3	–.5 to +1.5	+.5	0 to +.32	38	32	①

① — Refer to “Ball Joint Inspection,” in the “Front Suspension & Steering” section, for proper inspection of ball joints.

REAR WHEEL ALIGNMENT SPECIFICATIONS

Year	Camber Angles, Degrees				Total Toe, Degree
	Limits		Desired		
	Left	Right	Left	Right	
1998–2001	–.01 to +1	–.01 to +1	0	0	+.3 to +.6

VEHICLE RIDE HEIGHT SPECIFICATIONS

Year	Manufacturer's Original Tire Size	Measurement Points & Specifications①③					
		Front			Rear		
		Dim.	Specification		Dim.	Specification	
			Inches	mm		Inches	mm
1998–2001	②	A	17.75	450	B	17.75	450
		C	8.25	210	D	8.81	225

A Dim. — Measurement From Front Wheel Center to Check Point On Rocker Panel
B Dim. — Measurement From Rear Wheel Center to Check Point On Rocker Panel
C Dim. — Ground to Rocker Panel, Front
D Dim. — Ground to Rocker Panel, Rear

Dim. — Dimension

① — ±.0.39 in (10 mm) front to rear & side to side.

② — See door sticker or inside of glove box for manufacturer's original tire size specifications. If tires on vehicle do not match manufacturer's original tire size & measurement is not within limits, refer to the Non-standard Tire & Wheel Size Adjustment To Ride Height Specification & Tire Size Adjustment Charts.

③ — Measurement is with fuel, radiator coolant and engine oil full, spare tire, jack, hand tools and mats in designated positions and tires properly inflated.

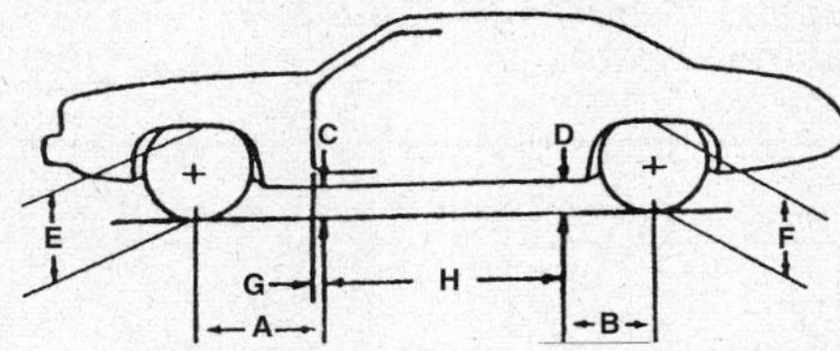

Dimensions A through D

FLUID CAPACITIES & COOLING SYSTEM DATA

Year	Engine	Coolant Capacity, Qts.	Coolant Type	Radiator Cap Relief Pressure, psi	Thermo-stat Open Temp. °F	Fuel Tank Gals.	Engine Oil Qts.	Transaxle	
								Man. Pts.	Auto. Qts.①
1998–2001	1.0L	4.13	Ethylene Glycol	12.8	190	10.6	3.5②	5	③
	1.3L	5.00	Ethylene Glycol	12.8	190	10.6	3.5②	5	③

① — Make final inspection w/dipstick.
② — Additional oil may be required to bring oil level to full mark when changing oil filter.
③ — Oil pan only, 1.6 qts.; after overhaul less torque converter, 3.7 qts.; after overhaul with new torque converter, 5.2 qts.

LUBRICANT DATA

Year	Lubricant Type			
	Transaxle		Power Steering	Brake System
	Manual	Automatic		
1998–2001	75W-90 GL-4①	Dexron III	Dexron III	DOT 3

① — Synthetic type gear lubricant.

Electrical

NOTE: On Air Bag Equipped Models, Refer To "Air Bag System Precautions" Located In The Front Of This Manual For System Disarming & Arming Procedures.

NOTE: Refer To "Computer Relearn Procedures" Located In The Front Of This Manual When Battery Power To The Computer Has Been Interrupted.

INDEX

PRECAUTIONS

AIR BAG SYSTEMS

Refer to "Air Bag System Precautions" in the front of this manual for system disarming and arming procedures.

BATTERY GROUND CABLE

Prior to service, disconnect battery ground cable and isolate as required.

FUSE PANEL & FLASHER LOCATION

The main fuse panel (alternator and ignition switch fuses and main fuse for junction fuse panel) is located in the engine compartment on the lefthand fender apron. The junction fuse panel (fuses for other components) is located under the lefthand side of the instrument panel. The air bag fuse panel, if equipped, is located behind the lefthand side of the instrument panel on the junction block support bracket.

The turn signal and hazard flasher is located under the lefthand side of the instrument panel near the fuel panel.

FUEL PUMP RELAY LOCATION

The fuel pump relay is located in the engine compartment relay center at the front lefthand side of the engine compartment next to battery, **Figs. 1 and 2.**

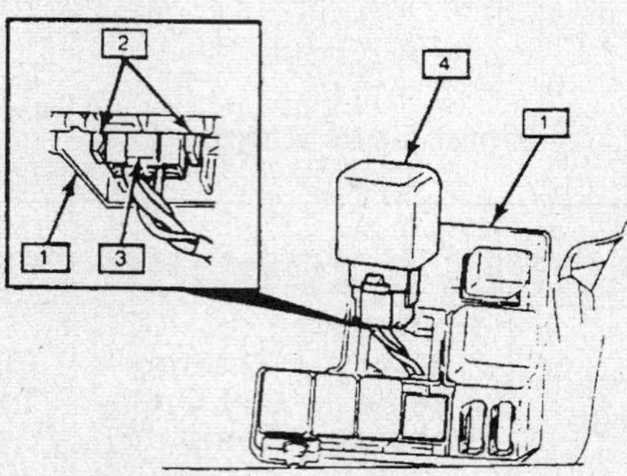

Fig. 1 Fuel pump relay location. 1.0L engine

RELAY CENTER LOCATION

The relay center is located at the lefthand side of the engine compartment, near the battery.

STARTER

REPLACE

1. Disconnect solenoid lead and battery cable.
2. Remove mounting bolts and starter.
3. Reverse procedure to install. **Torque** starter mounting bolts to 17 ft. lbs.

ALTERNATOR

REPLACE

1. Remove air cleaner assembly.
2. Remove rubber insulator and retaining nut, then the battery terminal wire from alternator.
3. Remove alternator upper mounting bolt, then the drive belt.
4. Remove lower alternator mounting bolts, then the alternator.
5. Reverse procedure to install, noting the following:
   a. Adjust drive belt tension so that with 22 lbs., of pressure exerted at the center of the belt, there is .24–.31 inch of deflection.
   b. **Torque** alternator mounting bolts to 17 ft. lbs.
   c. **Torque** battery terminal nut to 71 inch lbs.

DISTRIBUTOR

REPLACE

1. Disconnect electrical connectors and vacuum lines.
2. Remove distributor cap and mark rotor position on housing.
3. Mark distributor position on engine.
4. Remove flange bolts and distributor.
5. Reverse procedure to install. Ensure alignment marks match.

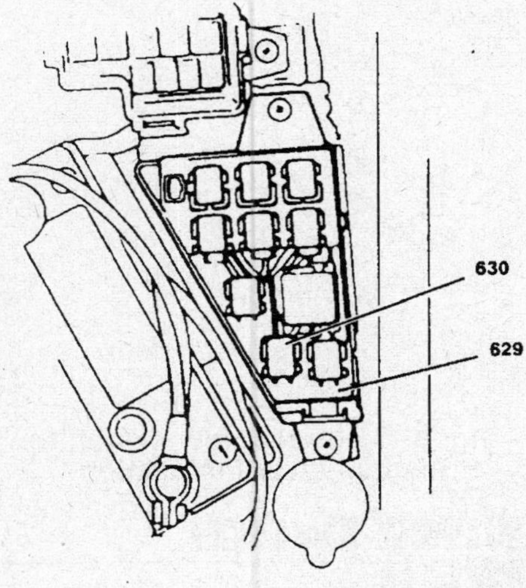

629 RELAY BOX
630 FUEL PUMP RELAY

GC1029503761000X

Fig. 2 Fuel pump relay location. 1.3L engine

IGNITION COIL

REPLACE

1. Disconnect ignition coil spark plug wires and electrical connector.
2. Remove mounting bolts and ignition coil.
3. Reverse procedure to install, **torque** ignition coil mounting bolts to 96 inch lbs.

IGNITION SWITCH

REPLACE

REMOVAL

1. Remove turn signal/dimmer switch as outlined under "Turn Signal Switch, Replace."
2. Disconnect ignition switch and key warning electrical connectors.
3. Lift up floor mat at steering shaft and remove steering column coupling cover.
4. Remove upper steering shaft coupling bolt, then connect ignition switch and key warning electrical connectors.
5. Remove mounting nuts and steering column.
6. Loosen and remove steering lock mounting bolts using suitable center punch, **Fig. 3.**
7. Place ignition switch in ACC or ON position and remove from steering column.

INSTALLATION

1. Position oblong hole on steering shaft at center of hole in steering column, **Fig. 4.**
2. Place ignition switch in ACC or ON position.
3. Position ignition switch to steering column and place switch in LOCK position.

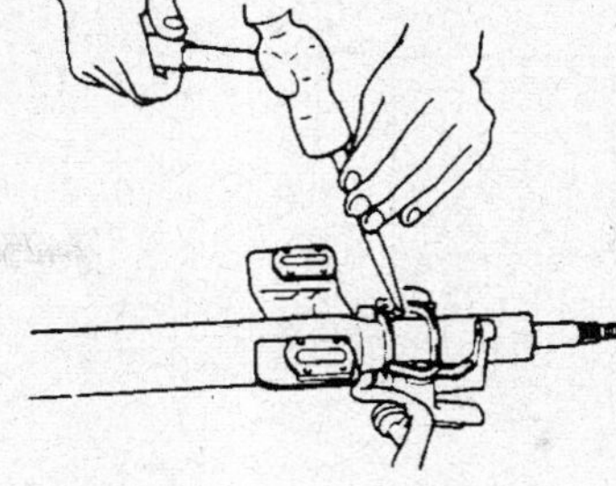

1 CENTER PUNCH (WITH SHARP POINT)
2 IGNITION SWITCH MOUNTING BOLTS

GC9129100029000X

Fig. 3 Ignition switch removal

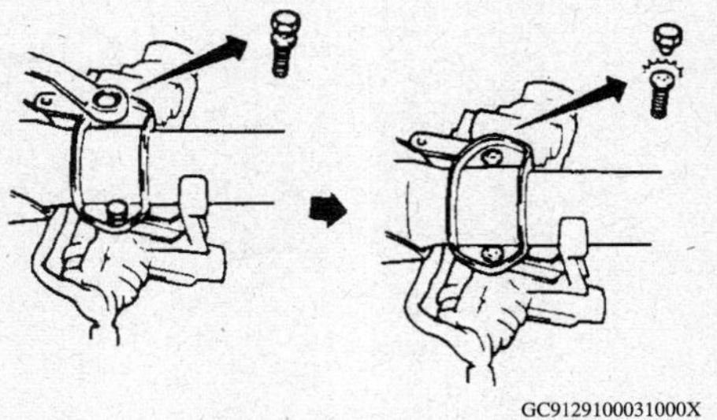

GC9129100031000X

Fig. 5 Ignition switch mounting bolt installation

4. Align ignition switch hub with oblong hole on steering shaft and rotate steering shaft to ensure it locks.
5. Install replacement ignition switch mounting bolts. Tighten bolts until bolt head breaks off, **Fig. 5.**
6. Place ignition switch in ON or ACC and inspect for smooth steering shaft rotation. Also inspect steering shaft lock for proper operation.
7. Align ignition switch hub to steering shaft oblong hole, rotate shaft to ensure steering shaft is locked, **Fig. 6.**
8. Position steering column mounting brackets to mounting studs. **Torque** mounting nuts to 10 ft. lbs.
9. Install steering shaft coupling bolt and **torque** to 18 ft. lbs.
10. Install steering shaft coupling cover.
11. Install turn signal/dimmer switch as outlined under "Turn Signal Switch, Replace."

CLUTCH START SWITCH

ADJUST

1. Disconnect electrical connector at clutch start switch.
2. Loosen switch locknut and back off switch adjustment.
3. Connect suitable ohmmeter between switch terminals.
4. Position clutch pedal at approximately .6–1.2 inches from floor and hold.
5. Rotate switch into bracket until ohmmeter just indicates continuity and tighten locknut. **Torque** locknut to 10 ft. lbs.
6. Connect switch electrical connector.

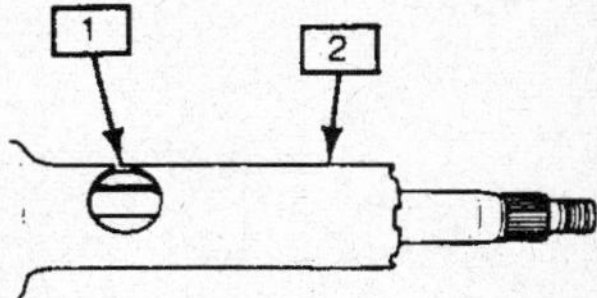

1 STEERING SHAFT
2 STEERING COLUMN

GC9129100030000X

Fig. 4 Steering shaft & column alignment

NEUTRAL SAFETY SWITCH

REPLACE

1. Remove mounting bolt and neutral safety switch.
2. Place shift lever in Neutral position.
3. Position neutral safety switch using suitable screwdriver, **Fig. 7.** Switch should click at this position.
4. Install neutral safety switch to manual shift shaft and loosely install mounting bolt.
5. Rotate switch slightly until click is heard and **torque** mounting bolt to 10–16 ft. lbs., **Fig. 8.**
6. Connect electrical connector to switch and inspect switch for proper operation.

HEADLAMP SWITCH

REPLACE

1. Remove steering column trim panel.
2. Lower steering column.
3. Remove instrument cluster bezel screws and pull bezel out.
4. Remove headlamp switch from bezel.
5. Remove cluster to instrument panel mounting screws.
6. Pull cluster rearward to reach and disconnect headlamp switch connector.
7. Remove headlamp switch.
8. Reverse procedure to install.

STOP LIGHT SWITCH

REPLACE

Pull up brake pedal and adjust switch position so that clearance between end of thread and brake pedal contact plate A is .02–.04 inch, **Fig. 9.** Tighten locknut.

TURN SIGNAL SWITCH

REPLACE

1. Remove steering wheel, refer to "Steering Wheel, Replace."
2. Remove steering column covers, **Fig. 10.**
3. Disconnect turn signal/dimmer switch electrical connector.
4. Remove turn signal/dimmer switch mounting screws and switch, **Fig. 10.**
5. Reverse procedure to install.

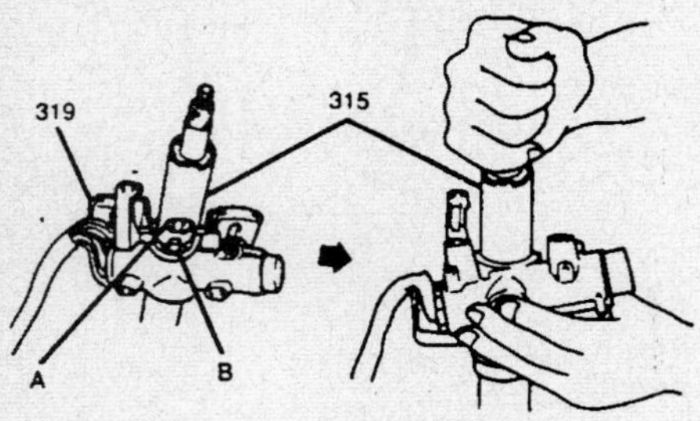

A COLUMN AND SHAFT HOLES
B IGNITION SWITCH HUB
315 STEERING COLUMN
319 IGNITION SWITCH

GC9129500035000X

Fig. 6 Ignition switch hub to steering shaft alignment

DIMMER SWITCH

REPLACE

Replace dimmer switch as an assembly with turn signal switch as outlined under "Turn Signal Switch, Replace."

STEERING WHEEL

REPLACE

1. Remove air bag inflator module as outlined under "Passive Restraint Systems" section.
2. Remove steering wheel nut, then place alignment marks on steering shaft and wheel for use during installation.
3. Remove steering wheel using suitable puller tool.
4. Reverse procedure to install. When installing steering wheel, align marks made during removal. **Torque** steering wheel nut to 24 ft. lbs.

INSTRUMENT CLUSTER

REPLACE

1. Remove cluster lower cover mounting screws and covers.
2. Remove mounting screws and gauge cluster bezel.
3. Depress speedometer plastic tabs to disconnect cable.
4. Remove cluster mounting screw.
5. Disconnect cluster electrical connectors and remove cluster.
6. Reverse procedure to install.

RADIO

REPLACE

1. Through glove compartment, disconnect radio and antenna electrical connector.
2. Pull ashtray outward, push downward and pull ashtray rearward to remove.
3. Remove mounting screws and instrument panel center trim bezel.
4. Through instrument panel ashtray cutout, remove cross recess screw below rear of radio.

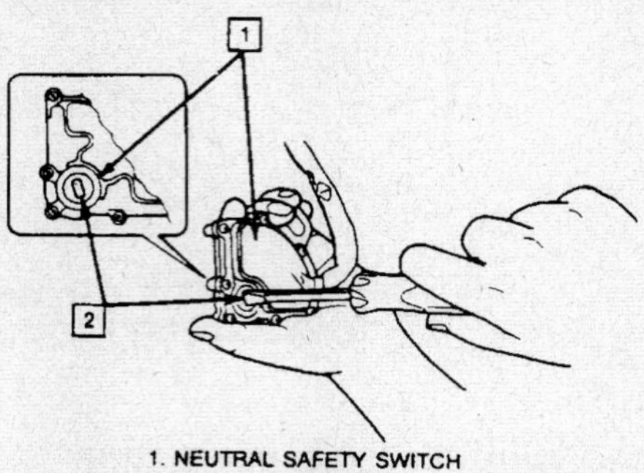

1. NEUTRAL SAFETY SWITCH
2. NEUTRAL SAFETY SWITCH JOINT

GC9049100116000X

Fig. 7 Neutral safety switch position

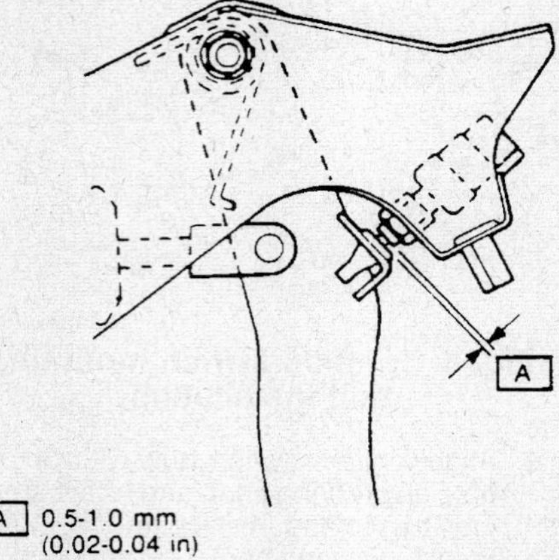

GC9049100118000X

Fig. 9 Stop lamp switch adjustment

5. Remove mounting screws, then pull radio and mounting brackets rearward.
6. Remove mounting bracket to radio mounting screws, if required, and radio.
7. Reverse procedure to install.

WIPER MOTOR

REPLACE

FRONT

1. Disconnect wiper motor electrical connector.
2. Remove wiper motor mounting screws, then wiper linkage to motor mounting nut and washer, **Fig. 11.**
3. Remove wiper motor.
4. Reverse procedure to install.

REAR

1. Disconnect hatchback inner door trim panel clips and remove panel.
2. Disconnect wiper motor electrical connector.
3. Remove wiper motor ground screw, **Fig. 12.**
4. Remove wiper motor mounting nuts.
5. Disconnect wiper linkage and remove wiper motor.
6. Reverse procedure to install. **Torque** wiper motor mounting bolts 15 ft. lbs.

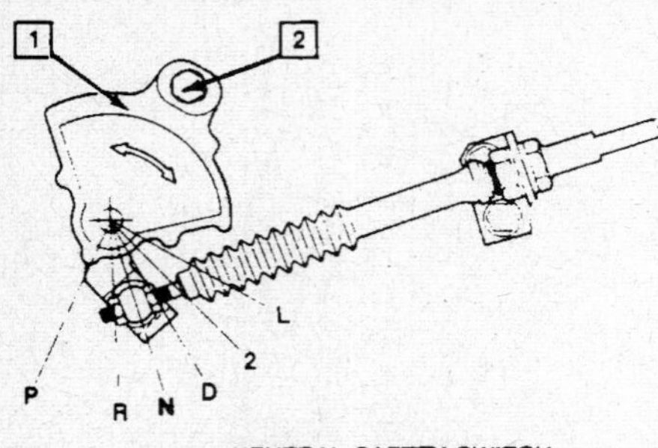

1. NEUTRAL SAFETY SWITCH
2. BOLT

GC9049100117000X

Fig. 8 Neutral safety switch to manual lever installation

WIPER SWITCH

REPLACE

FRONT

1. Remove steering column trim panel.
2. Lower steering column.
3. Remove instrument cluster bezel screws and pull bezel out.
4. Remove wiper switch from bezel.
5. Remove cluster to instrument panel mounting screws.
6. Pull cluster rearward to reach and disconnect wiper switch connector.
7. Remove wiper switch.
8. Reverse procedure to install.

REAR

1. Remove lower steering column trim cover.
2. Remove both steering column mounting nuts and lower steering column.
3. Remove instrument panel cluster trim bezel.
4. Remove rear wiper switch from bezel.
5. Reverse procedure to install.

WIPER TRANSMISSION

REPLACE

FRONT

1. Inspect wiper arms, for proper installation location.
2. Remove wiper arm cover and mounting nut.
3. Disconnect plastic mounting clips and remove cowl vent grill.
4. Remove wiper transmission to cowl mounting nuts.
5. Disconnect wiper motor electrical connector, remove motor mounting bolts and pull motor rearward from bulkhead.
6. Pry wiper transmission from motor crank arm. **Do not disconnect crank arm from motor.**
7. Remove wiper motor and transmission.
8. Reverse procedure to install. **Torque** transmission mounting nuts to 11 ft. lbs.

REAR

1. Inspect wiper arms, for proper installation location.

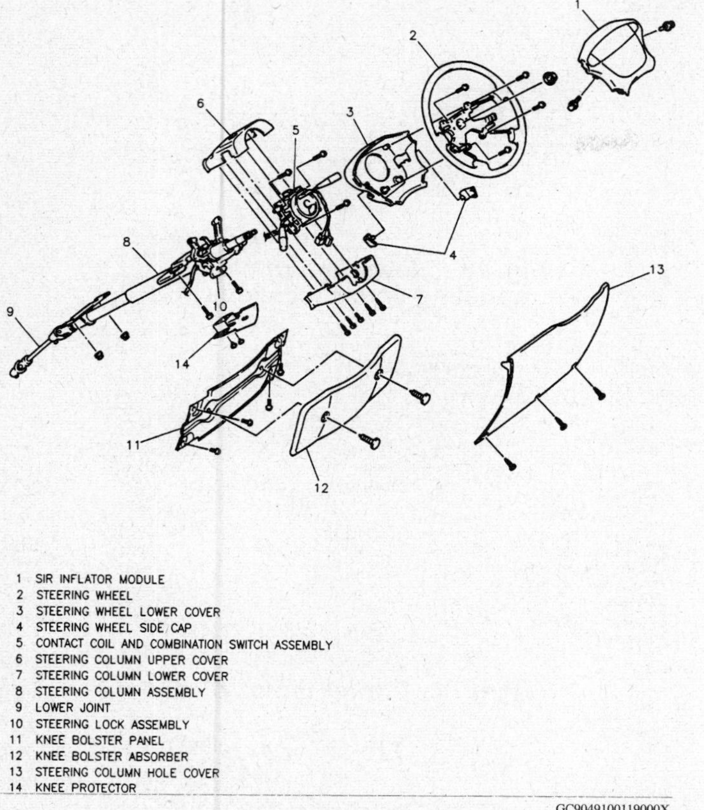

Fig. 10 Turn signal/dimmer switch removal

1 WIPER BLADE
2 WIPER ARM
3 WIPER MOTOR
4 WASHER PUMP
5 WASHER FLUID RESERVOIR
6 WASHER HOSE
7 WASHER NOZZLE AND SEAL

GC9029100237000X

Fig. 11 Front windshield wiper/washer motor & linkage assembly

2. Lift wiper arm nut plastic cover and remove arm mounting nut.
3. Remove wiper arm from transmission.
4. Remove hatchback door inner trim panel.
5. Disconnect wiper motor electrical connector.
6. Remove motor ground lead mounting screw.
7. Remove mounting nuts and separate motor from door.
8. Pry transmission from motor crank arm and wiper arm base, then slide transmission rearward to remove.
9. Remove wiper arm base from door. **Do not disconnect crank arm from motor.**
10. Reverse procedure to install. **Torque** wiper arm nut to 15 ft. lbs.

BLOWER MOTOR

REPLACE

1. Depress glove compartment stopper and pull rearward.
2. Remove glove compartment to instrument panel mounting screws, remove glove compartment.
3. Disconnect electrical connectors, then remove mounting screws and ECM.
4. Disconnect blower motor and blower resistor electrical connectors.
5. Disconnect fresh air control cable from blower motor.
6. Remove mounting bolts and blower motor housing, **Fig. 13.**
7. Remove air hose and mounting screws, then separate blower motor from housing, **Fig. 14.**
8. Reverse procedure to install.

HEATER CORE

REPLACE

1. Remove instrument panel as outlined under "Dash Panel Service."
2. Drain coolant into suitable container.
3. Remove heater core clamps and hoses, through engine compartment.
4. Remove blower case to heater case air duct.
5. Remove heater case mounting nuts and bolts, **Fig. 15,** then heater case.
6. Remove heater case clip and mounting screws, then separate case halves, **Fig. 16.**
7. Remove heater core from case.
8. Reverse procedure to install. **Torque** heater case mounting nuts and bolts to 90 inch lbs.

EVAPORATOR CORE

REPLACE

1. Evacuate and recover refrigerant as outlined under "Air Conditioning."
2. Remove blower motor case as outlined under "Blower Motor, Replace."
3. Disconnect air conditioning amplifier and evaporator thermistor electrical connectors.
4. Disconnect and cap evaporator case refrigerant inlet and outlet pipes.
5. Remove evaporator case drain hose.
6. Remove mounting bolts, nut and evaporator case.
7. Depress lower locking tabs and slide air conditioning amplifier upward to remove.
8. Disengage evaporator case clips, to separate case halves.
9. Remove evaporator core from case.
10. Reverse procedure to install, noting the following:
    a. **Torque** evaporator case bolts to 90 inch lbs.
    b. **Torque** inlet pipe nut to 26 ft. lbs.
    c. **Torque** outlet pipe nut to 33 ft. lbs.

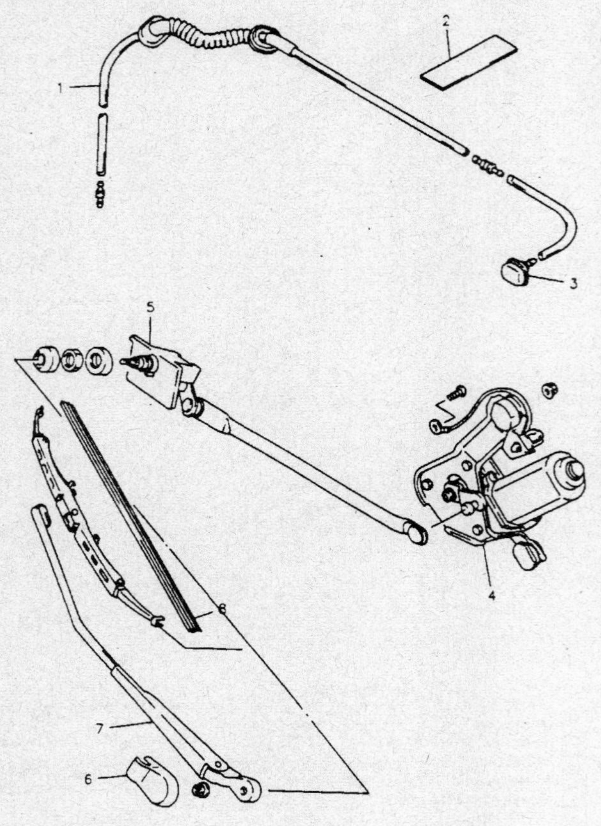

1 REAR WASHER HOSE
2 REAR WASHER HOSE COVER
3 REAR WASHER NOZZLE
4 REAR WIPER MOTOR
5 REAR WIPER LINKAGE
6 REAR WIPER NUT COVER
7 REAR WIPER ARM
8 REAR WIPER BLADE

GC9029500248000X

Fig. 12 Rear windshield wiper motor & linkage assembly

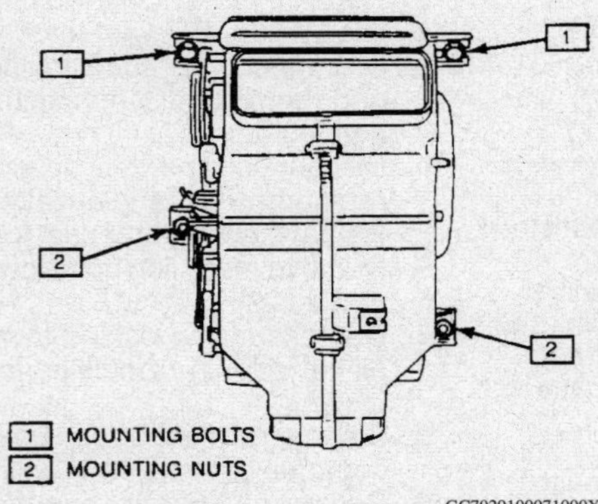

GC7029100071000X

Fig. 15 Heater case mounting bolt & nut locations

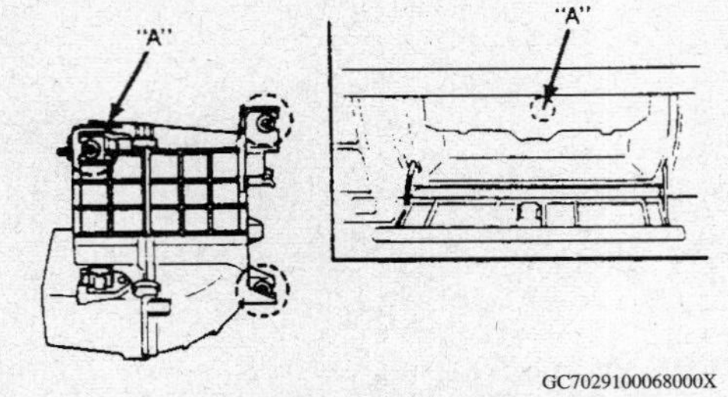

GC7029100068000X

Fig. 13 Blower motor case mounting screw locations

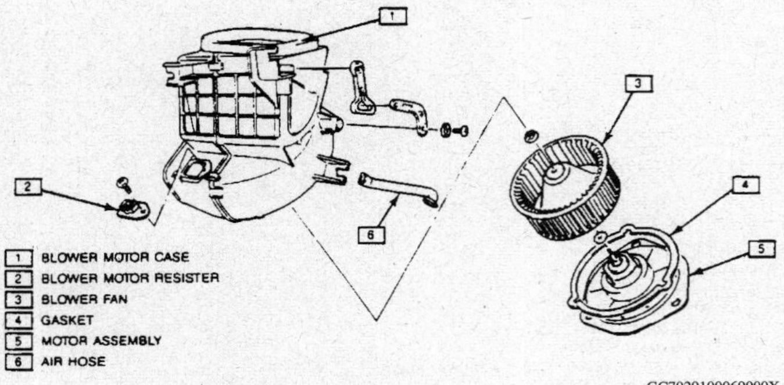

GC7029100069000X

Fig. 14 Blower motor & case

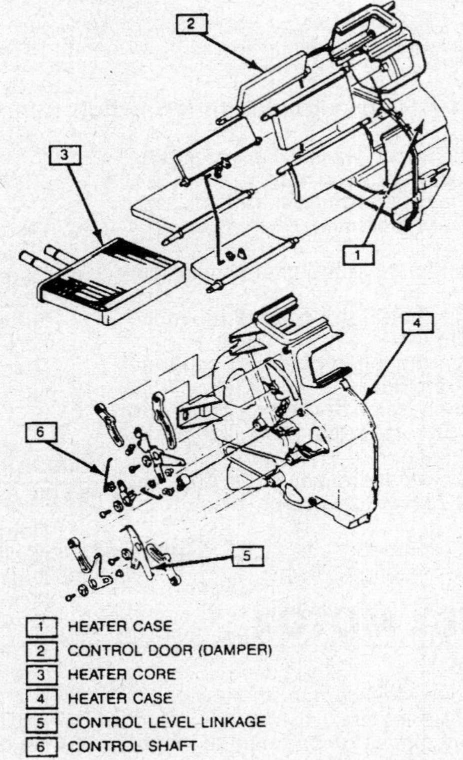

1 HEATER CASE
2 CONTROL DOOR (DAMPER)
3 HEATER CORE
4 HEATER CASE
5 CONTROL LEVEL LINKAGE
6 CONTROL SHAFT

GC7029100072000X

Fig. 16 Exploded view of heater case

1.0L Engine

NOTE: On Air Bag Equipped Models, Refer To "Air Bag System Precautions" Located In The Front Of This Manual For System Disarming & Arming Procedures.

NOTE: Refer To "Computer Relearn Procedures" Located In The Front Of This Manual When Battery Power To The Computer Has Been Interrupted.

INDEX

PRECAUTIONS

AIR BAG SYSTEMS

Refer to "Air Bag System Precautions" in the front of this manual for system disarming and arming procedures.

BATTERY GROUND CABLE

Prior to service, disconnect battery ground cable and isolate as required.

FUEL SYSTEM PRESSURE RELIEF

1. Loosen fuel filler cap to relieve fuel tank pressure
2. Remove fuel pump relay from relay box located at lefthand front of engine compartment, next to battery.
3. Crank engine and allow to stall. Crank engine for several seconds more to ensure relief of any remaining fuel.
4. Remove battery ground cable.

COMPRESSION PRESSURE

1. Turn ignition switch to Lock position.
2. Remove spark plugs.
3. Disconnect distributor electrical connector and remove FI fuse from fuse and relay box.
4. Install spark plug port adapter tool No. J22794, or equivalent and suitable compression gauge into spark plug hole.
5. **On models equipped with manual transaxle,** depress clutch and accelerator to floor.

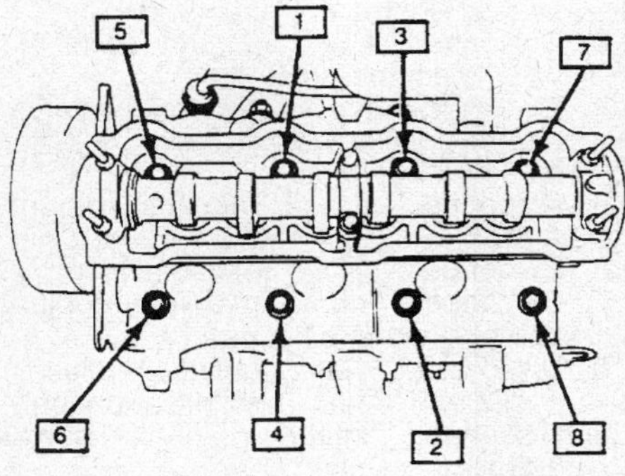

Fig. 1 Cylinder head bolt tightening sequence

6. **On all models,** crank engine and take four pressure readings, recording highest reading obtained.
7. Compression should increase quickly and evenly. Compression pressure at 250 RPM is 199 psi standard and 156 psi minimum. Maximum allowable pressure difference between any two cylinders at 250 RPM is 14 psi.
8. Repeat compression test procedure for remaining cylinders.
9. After completion, install FI fuse, spark plugs and distributor electrical connector.

ENGINE MOUNT

REPLACE

FRONT

1. Remove engine mount nut, then raise and support vehicle.
2. Support engine using suitable engine support fixture.
3. Remove engine mount and frame bracket, then mount from bracket.
4. Reverse procedure to install.

REAR

1. Remove engine mount nut, then raise and support vehicle.
2. Remove nut mounting mount to body bracket.
3. Support engine using suitable engine support fixture.
4. Remove frame bracket and mount.
5. Reverse procedure to install.

ENGINE

REPLACE

1. Remove both battery cables, battery and battery tray.
2. Drain cooling system into suitable container.
3. Remove hood.
4. Remove air cleaner.
5. Remove radiator with cooling fan.
6. Disconnect coolant temperature gauge sensor, throttle position sensor and EGR solenoid electrical connectors.
7. Disconnect EGR bypass valve.
8. Disconnect idle speed control solenoid valve, oxygen sensor, fuel injector, MAP sensor and power steering pressure switch electrical connectors.
9. Disconnect intake manifold ground wires.
10. Disconnect oil pressure switch, alternator and air conditioning compressor electrical connectors.

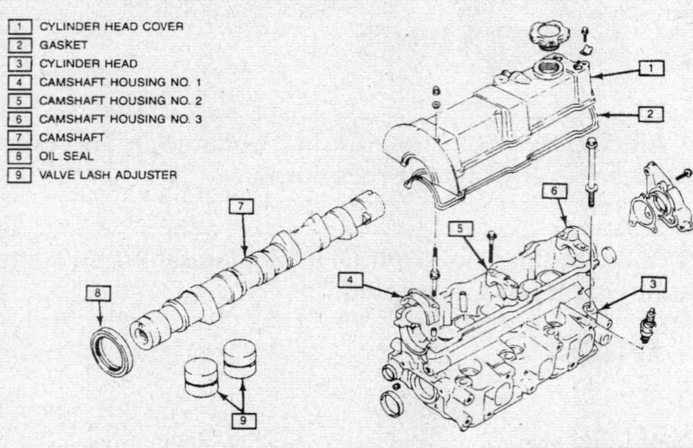

Fig. 2 Camshaft & hydraulic valve lash adjusters

11. Disconnect starter solenoid electrical connector.
12. Disconnect back-up lamp switch.
13. Disconnect direct clutch and second brake solenoids.
14. Release main engine harness from clamps.
15. Disconnect the following vacuum hoses:
    a. Intake manifold front and rear canister purge.
    b. Canister pipe.
    c. Intake manifold pressure sensor.
    d. Intake manifold brake booster.
    e. Throttle body idle speed control.
16. Disconnect the following cables:
    a. Throttle body accelerator.
    b. Transaxle clutch.
    c. Transaxle shift select and throttle valve.
    d. Transaxle speedometer.
17. Remove inlet and outlet hoses.
18. Remove throttle body fuel return and feed hoses.
19. Install universal support fixture tool No. J28467-A with engine support adapters tool No. J28467-89, or equivalents.
20. Raise and support vehicle.
21. Disconnect exhaust system from exhaust manifold.
22. Remove front pipe/catalytic converter.
23. **On models equipped with manual transaxle** remove gearshift control shaft and extension rod.
24. **On all models** drain engine oil and transaxle fluid into suitable container.
25. Remove left and righthand drive axles from transaxle as outlined under "Front Wheel Drive Axle." **It is not required to remove driveshafts from steering knuckles.**
26. Remove air conditioning compressor from bracket and position aside. **Do not disconnect air conditioning hoses from compressor.**
27. Disconnect power steering pump hoses.
28. **On models equipped with automatic transaxle** remove torque rod.
29. **On all models** lower vehicle.
30. Remove tool Nos. J28467-A and J28467-89, or equivalents and install suitable engine lifting device.
31. Remove lefthand transaxle mount, righthand side engine mount and rear engine mount.
32. Remove engine with transaxle.
33. Reverse procedure to install. Tighten mounting bolts and nuts to specifications.

INTAKE MANIFOLD

REPLACE

1. Drain cooling system into suitable container remove air cleaner.
2. Disconnect coolant temperature sender, engine and coolant temperature sensor electrical connectors.
3. Disconnect EGR vacuum switching valve electrical connector.
4. Disconnect idle speed control valve, throttle position switch and fuel injector electrical connectors.
5. Disconnect intake manifold ground wires,
6. Disconnect throttle body fuel hoses.
7. Disconnect intake manifold coolant and MAP sensor hoses.
8. Disconnect evaporative emission hoses from intake manifold and tube.
9. Disconnect intake manifold power brake unit vacuum hose.
10. Disconnect PCV valve hose from cylinder head cover.
11. Disconnect throttle body accelerator cable.
12. Disconnect all other electrical connectors and hoses to permit intake manifold and throttle body removal.
13. Remove intake manifold to cylinder head mounting nuts and bolts, then the intake manifold and throttle body as an assembly.
14. Reverse procedure to Install.

EXHAUST MANIFOLD

REPLACE

1. Disconnect oxygen sensor electrical connector and release wiring harness from clamps.
2. Disconnect exhaust pipe from exhaust manifold.
3. Remove mounting bolts, nuts and exhaust manifold.
4. Reverse procedure to install.

1 CYLINDER HEAD
2 OIL HOLE

GC1069100516000X

Fig. 3 Applying engine oil to camshaft oil holes

CYLINDER HEAD

REPLACE

1. Drain cooling system into suitable container and remove air cleaner.
2. Disconnect distributor cap coil wire.
3. Disconnect distributor electrical connector.
4. Disconnect coolant temperature sender, engine coolant temperature sensor and engine cooling fan switch electrical connectors.
5. Disconnect EGR vacuum switching valve electrical connector.
6. Disconnect idle speed control valve, throttle position switch and fuel injector electrical connectors.
7. Disconnect oxygen sensor electrical connector and wiring harness from clamps.
8. Disconnect intake manifold ground wires.
9. Disconnect intake manifold heater and thermostat housing radiator hoses.
10. Disconnect throttle body fuel hoses.
11. Disconnect intake manifold MAP sensor hose.
12. Disconnect evaporative emission hoses from intake manifold and tube.
13. Disconnect intake manifold power brake unit vacuum hose.
14. Disconnect throttle body accelerator cable.
15. Raise and support vehicle, then disconnect exhaust pipe from exhaust manifold.
16. Lower vehicle and remove cylinder head cover.
17. Remove mounting bolts and cylinder head.
18. Reverse procedure to install. Tighten cylinder head bolts to specifications in several passes in sequence, **Fig. 1.**

VALVE ARRANGEMENT

FRONT TO REAR

1.0L................................I-E-I-E-I-E

VALVE ADJUSTMENT

These engines are equipped with hydraulic valve lash adjusters and no adjustment is required.

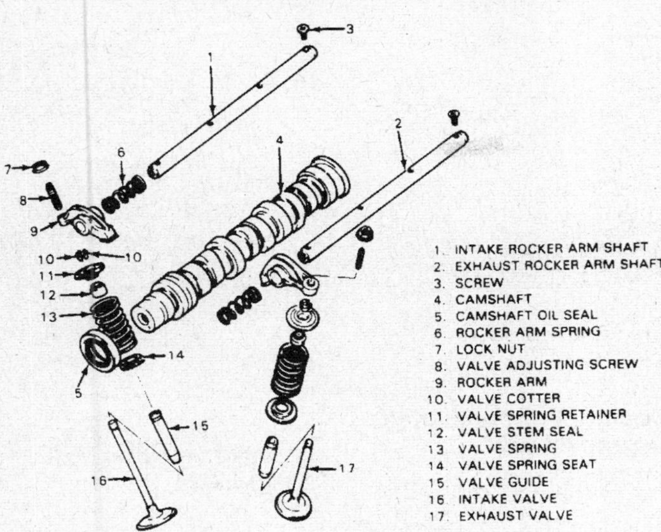

Fig. 4 Timing belt & cover

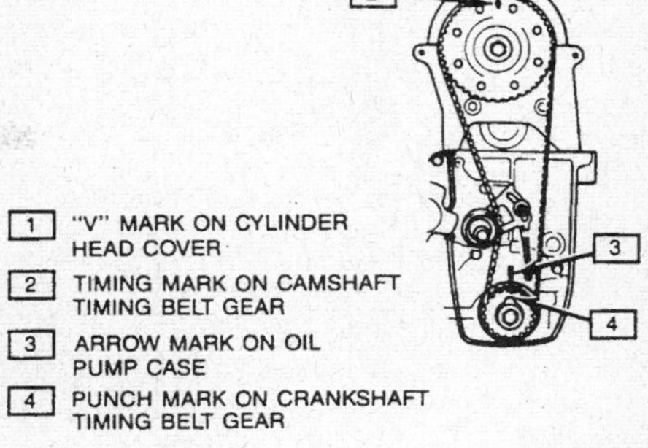

Fig. 5 Camshaft & crankshaft sprocket timing mark alignment

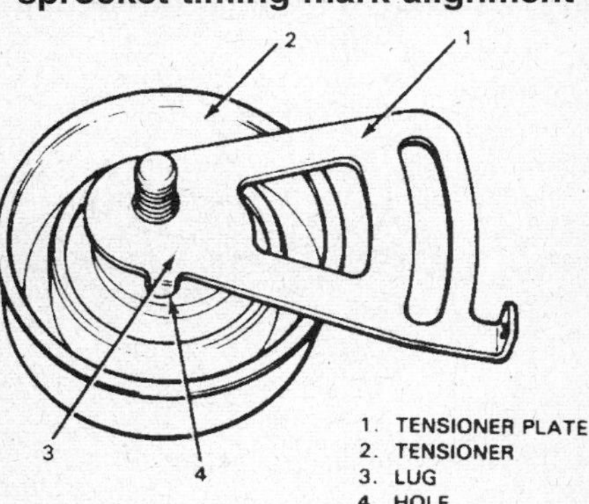

Fig. 6 Tensioner

VALVE GUIDES

Valves and valve guides are available in standard size only. The valve guide can be driven from cylinder bore using valve guide replacement tool No. J37968-1, or equivalent. The valve guide should be driven from the combustion chamber side of the cylinder head out through the valve spring side.

The cylinder head valve guide bore should be reamed with an .433 inch reamer prior to valve guide installation. Heat cylinder head to 176–212°F, then drive valve guide into cylinder head bore using valve guide replacement tool No. J37968-1 and valve guide installer tool No. J37968-2, or equivalents. Valve guide should be driven in until tool contacts cylinder head. Valve guide protrusion should be .45 inch from cylinder head surface. After installation, ream valve guide with .217 inch reamer.

HYDRAULIC VALVE LASH ADJUSTER SERVICE

Hydraulic valve lash adjusters should not be disassembled.

1. Remove camshaft as outlined under "Camshaft, Replace."
2. Remove hydraulic valve lash adjusters, **Fig. 2.**
3. Inspect hydraulic valve lash adjusters for wear and damage and replace as required.
4. Measure outside diameter of hydraulic valve lash adjuster. Outside diameter should be 1.2188–1.2194 inches.
5. Measure hydraulic valve lash adjuster bore in cylinder head. Bore diameter should be 1.2205–1.2214 inches.
6. To determine hydraulic valve lash adjuster to cylinder head bore clearance, subtract adjuster outside diameter from cylinder head adjuster bore diameter. Adjuster to bore clearance should be .0010–.0025 inch. If clearance is more than .0059 inch, replace adjuster or cylinder head, as required.
7. Place valve lash adjuster in clean engine oil prior to installation. Also pour engine oil through camshaft journal oil holes, until oil is emitted from hydraulic valve lash adjuster oil holes, **Fig. 3.**
8. Apply engine oil to valve lash adjuster, position adjuster in cylinder head bore and install camshaft.

TIMING BELT

REPLACE

REMOVAL

1. Raise and support vehicle.
2. Remove fender apron extension from righthand side.
3. Remove drive belt and water pump pulley.
4. Remove mounting bolts and crankshaft pulley.
5. Remove outer timing belt cover, **Fig. 4.**
6. Align camshaft and crankshaft timing marks, **Fig. 5.**
7. Remove timing belt tensioner, tensioner plate, spring and damper.
8. Remove timing belt.

INSPECTION

Inspect timing belt for wear and cracks and replace as required. Inspect timing belt tensioner for smoothness of rotation and replace as required.

INSTALLATION

1. Position lug on tensioner plate to hole in tensioner, **Fig. 6.**
2. Position tensioner and tensioner plate to engine, then install and hand tighten mounting bolt. Ensure tensioner and tensioner plate move in same direction, **Fig. 7.** If movement is not as indicated, remove tensioner and insert tensioner plate lug into tensioner.
3. Ensure camshaft and crankshaft timing marks are aligned, **Fig. 5.**
4. With tensioner plate pushed upward, install timing belt over camshaft and crankshaft pulleys. **Arrow on timing belt should face toward direction of crankshaft rotation. When installing timing belt, keep drive side of belt free of slack.**
5. Install tensioner spring and damper, then hand tighten tensioner stud.
6. Rotate crankshaft two revolutions clockwise direction to remove slack from belt. **Ensure slack is removed from drive belt, and camshaft and crankshaft timing marks are aligned.**
7. Tighten tensioner stud and bolt to specifications.
8. Install timing belt outer cover and crankshaft pulley. **Ensure seal is between oil pump housing and water pump.**
9. Install water pump pulley and drive belt.
10. Install righthand side fender apron extension and lower vehicle.

CAMSHAFT

REPLACE

This procedure has been revised by a Technical Service Bulletin.

REMOVAL

1. Remove air cleaner and cylinder head cover.
2. Remove distributor.
3. Remove timing belt as outlined under "Timing Belt, Replace."

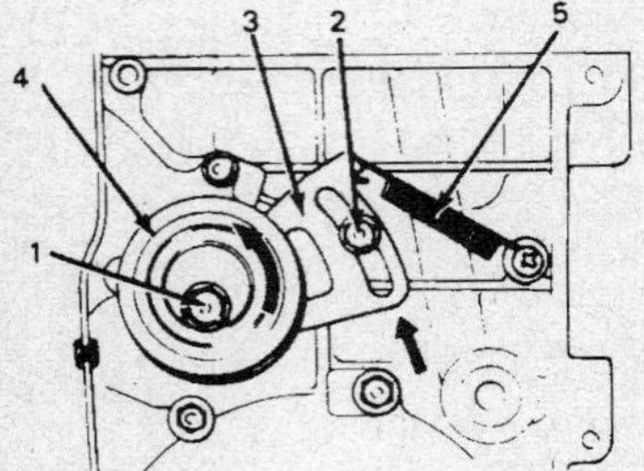

Fig. 7 Tensioner plate movement inspect

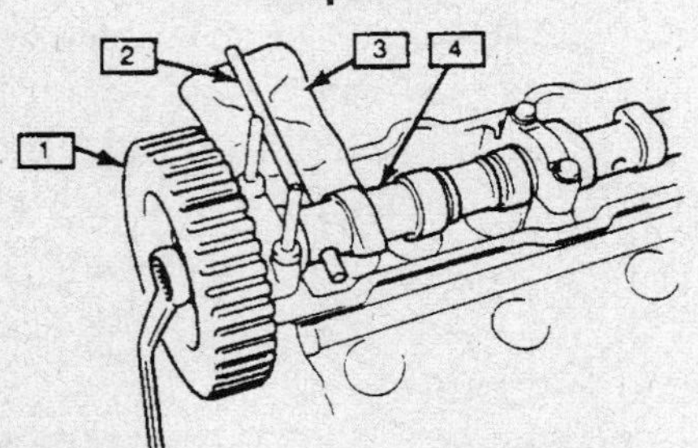

Fig. 10 Camshaft sprocket bolt removal & installation

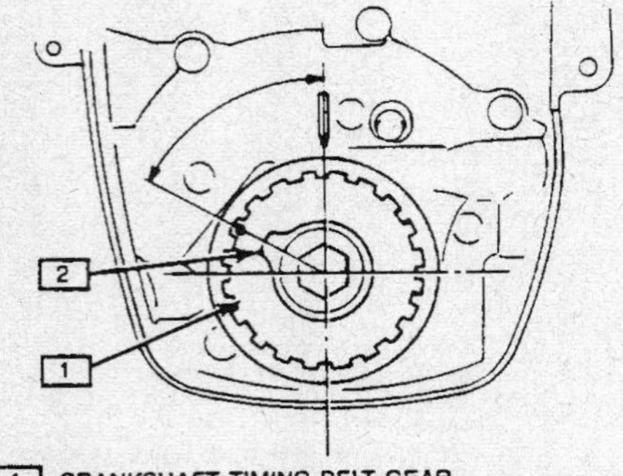

Fig. 8 Positioning crankshaft sprocket key

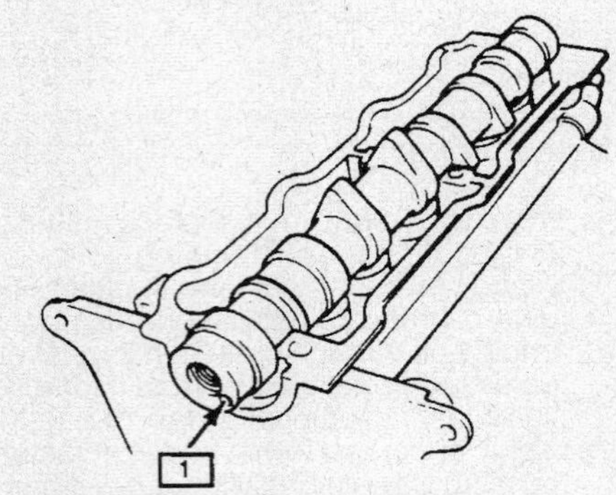

Fig. 11 Position camshaft sprocket pin hole

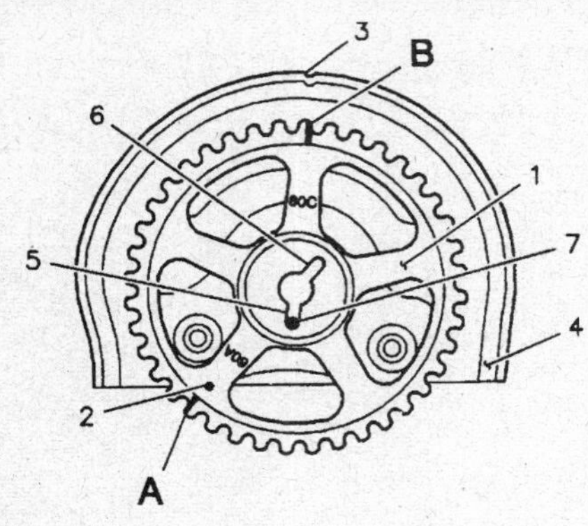

Fig. 9 Camshaft timing gear (spoked type)

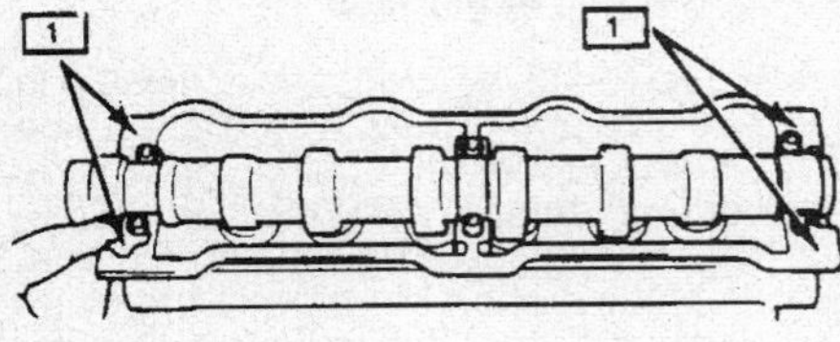

Fig. 12 Camshaft housing to cylinder head surface sealant application

4. Position crankshaft sprocket key, **Fig. 8.**
5. **On models equipped with spoked camshaft timing gear,** position gear so camshaft timing gear pulley pin engages with slot No. 1 on camshaft timing gear, **Fig. 9.**
6. **On all models,** hold camshaft in position by inserting rod into .39 inch hole in camshaft and remove camshaft sprocket mounting bolt, **Fig. 10.** Place shop cloth under rod to prevent damage to cylinder head surface.
7. Remove camshaft housings to cylinder head mounting bolts and studs, **Fig. 2.**
8. Remove camshaft. **Hydraulic valve lash adjusters should also be removed and placed in engine oil until installation.**

INSTALLATION

1. Pour engine oil into camshaft journal oil holes until oil is emitted from hydraulic valve lash adjuster holes, **Fig. 3.**
2. Lubricate valve lash adjusters with engine oil and install on cylinder head.
3. Lubricate camshaft with engine oil and position on cylinder head with sprocket pin hole positioned, **Fig. 11.**
4. **On models equipped with spoked (as opposed to solid) camshaft timing gears,** install gear so pulley pin engages with slot No. 1 on camshaft timing gear.
5. **On all models,** lubricate camshaft journal bores in camshaft housing with engine oil.
6. Apply sealant to cylinder head mating surface of camshaft housings No. 1 and No. 3, **Fig. 12.**
7. Position camshaft housings over camshaft and onto cylinder head mating surface. **Arrow on camshaft housing should face camshaft sprocket side of cylinder head.** Camshaft housings are numbered from one to three. Housings are positioned on cylinder head in numerical order, starting with No. 1 at camshaft sprocket side of cylinder head, **Fig. 13.**
8. Apply engine oil to camshaft housing mounting bolts and studs, then loosely install bolts and studs. Tighten bolts and studs to specifications in sequence, **Fig. 14.**
9. Apply engine oil to camshaft oil seal lip and install seal. Seal surface should be flush with housing surface.
10. Hold camshaft in position by inserting rod into .39 inch hole in camshaft, then install and tighten camshaft sprocket mounting bolt, **Fig. 10.** Place shop cloth under rod.
11. Install cylinder head cover.
12. Install timing belt as outlined under "Timing Belt, Replace."
13. Install ignition distributor and air cleaner.
14. Adjust ignition timing.

PISTON & ROD ASSEMBLY

Refer to **Fig. 15,** when assembling piston and connecting rod. When installing piston and connecting rod, arrow on piston head should face front of engine and oil hole in connecting rod should face intake manifold. When installing connecting rod cap, arrow on cap should face front of engine.

Measure rod bearing side clearance using suitable feeler gauge. Connecting rod bearing side clearance should be .0039 to .0078 inch.

PISTONS, PINS & RINGS

Pistons and rings are available in standard size and oversizes of .010 and .020 inch. Piston pins are supplied with pistons in matched sets.

MAIN & ROD BEARINGS

Main and rod bearings are available in

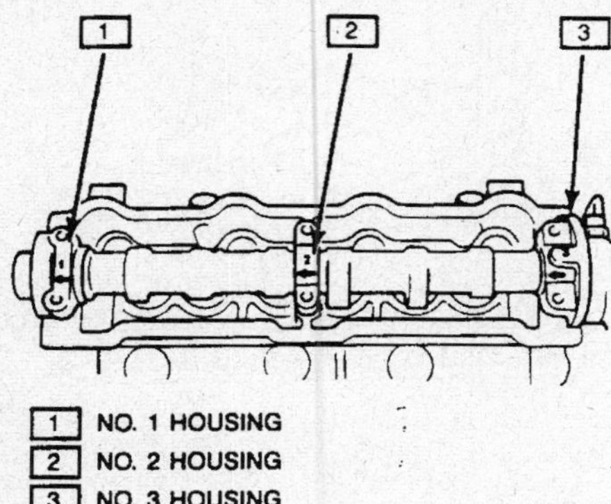

Fig. 13 Camshaft housing locations

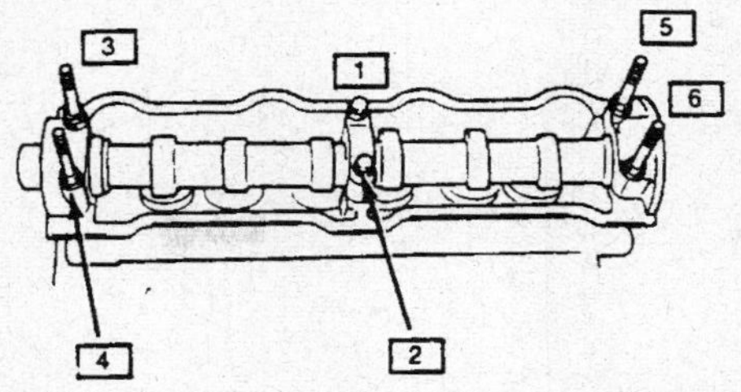

Fig. 14 Camshaft housing bolt tightening sequence

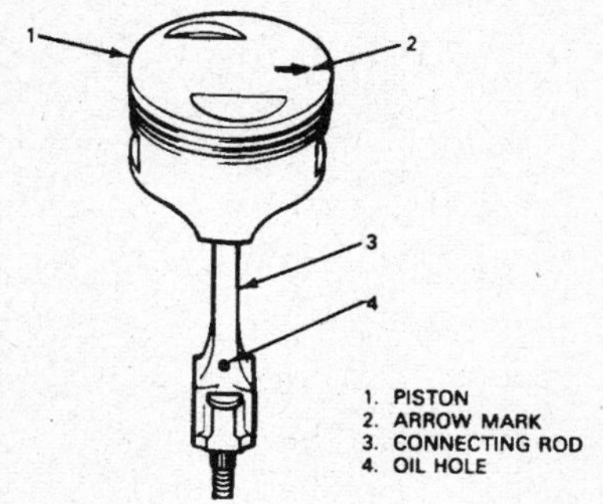

Fig. 15 Piston & connecting rod assembly

standard size and under size of .010 inch. Crankshaft thrust bearings are available in standard size and under size of .005 inch.

CRANKSHAFT REAR OIL SEAL

REPLACE

1. Remove transaxle as outlined under "Transaxle, Replace" in "Automatic Transaxles/Transmissions" or "Clutch & Manual Transaxle" sections.
2. **On models with equipped manual transaxle,** remove pressure plate and clutch disc.
3. **On all models,** remove flywheel.
4. Remove seal retainer and seal from retainer.
5. Reverse procedure to install.

OIL PAN

REPLACE

1. Raise and support vehicle.
2. Drain oil pan into suitable container.
3. Remove flywheel dust cover.
4. Disconnect exhaust pipe at manifold.
5. Remove oil pan bolts and pan, **Fig. 16.**
6. Remove oil pump screen.
7. Reverse procedure to install. Apply continuous bead of silicon type sealer to oil pan flange inside bolt holes. When tightening oil pan mounting bolts, start at center and working outward. Tighten bolts to specifications.

OIL PUMP

REPLACE

REMOVAL

1. Remove timing belt as outlined under "Timing Belt, Replace."
2. Remove oil pan as outlined under "Oil Pan, Replace."
3. Remove crankshaft timing belt sprocket.
4. Remove alternator mounting bracket, if required.
5. **On models equipped with air conditioning,** remove compressor mounting bracket.

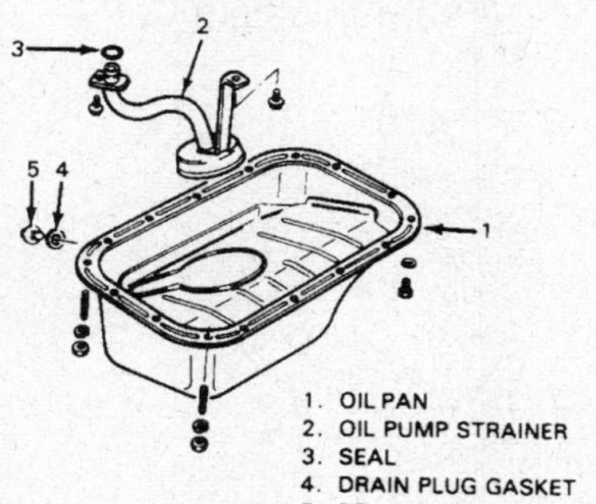

Fig. 16 Oil pan & pick-up tube

6. **On all models,** remove alternator adjusting bolt and upper cover bolt, if required.
7. Remove oil pump bolts and pump, **Fig. 17.**

INSTALLATION

1. Install oil pump pins and gasket on engine block.
2. Install oil seal guide tool No. J34853, or equivalent, onto crankshaft to prevent damage to oil seal lip, **Fig. 18.** Apply engine oil to special tool.
3. Install oil pump onto crankshaft and engine block. Install mounting bolts and tighten to specifications, **Fig. 19.** No. 1 bolts are shorter then No. 2 bolts.
4. After installing oil pump, ensure oil seal lip is not twisted and remove tool.
5. Install rubber seal between oil pump and water pump, **Fig. 20.**
6. Trim oil pump seal edges flush with oil pan mating surface, as required.
7. Install timing belt guide, key and crankshaft timing sprocket. Timing belt guide must be installed so curved side faces oil pump.
8. Install timing belt and tensioner components.
9. Adjust water pump belt tension.
10. Fill crankcase.
11. Run engine to ensure oil pressure is correct.

OIL PUMP SERVICE

1. Remove dipstick tube from oil pump.
2. Remove gear/rotor plate screws and gear plate.
3. Remove outer and inner gears/rotors.
4. Inspect oil seal lip for damage and replace, as required.
5. Inspect outer and inner gears/rotors, gear/rotor plate and oil pump case for excessive wear or damage.
6. Inspect radial clearance between outer gear/rotor and crescent, **Fig. 21.** If clearance is more than .0122 inch, replace outer gear/rotor.
7. Using straightedge and feeler gauge, measure side clearance which should not exceed .0059 inch, **Fig. 22.**
8. Wash, clean and dry all oil pump components.
9. Apply light coat of engine oil to inner and outer gears/rotors, oil seal lip portion and inside surfaces of oil pump case and plate.
10. Install outer and inner gears/rotors in pump case.
11. Install gear/rotor plate and tighten screws. Ensure gears turn smoothly by hand.
12. Install O-ring in pump case and dipstick tube.

BELT TENSION DATA

Belt	Belt Deflection Inch①
AIR CONDITIONING COMPRESSOR	
All	.28–.35
ALTERNATOR & WATER PUMP	
New	.20–.27
Used	.24–.31

① — With thumb pressure applied.

COOLING SYSTEM BLEED

These engines do not require a specific bleed procedure. After filling cooling system, run engine to operating temperature with radiator/pressure cap off. Air will then be automatically bled through cap opening.

THERMOSTAT

REPLACE

1. Drain cooling system into suitable container.
2. Remove radiator inlet hose at thermostat housing.
3. Remove thermostat housing and thermostat.

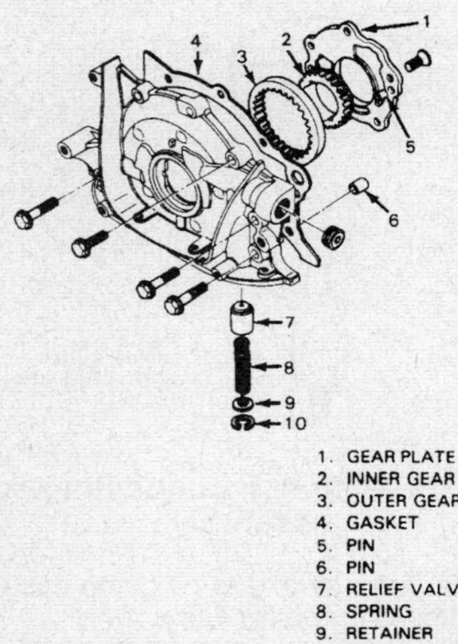

Fig. 17 Rotor type (Trochoid) oil pump

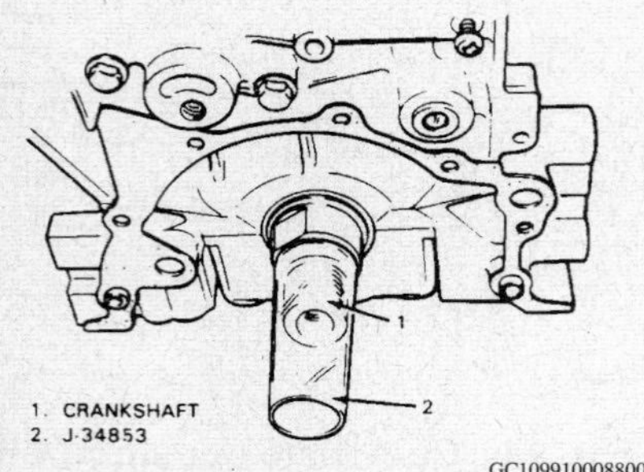

Fig. 18 Crankshaft oil seal guide tool installation

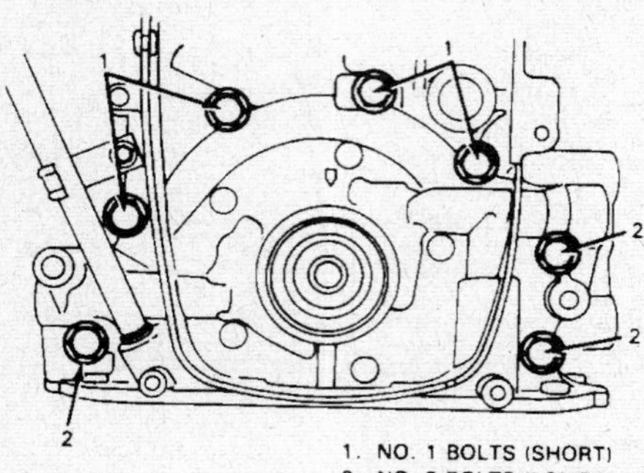

Fig. 19 Oil pump bolt location

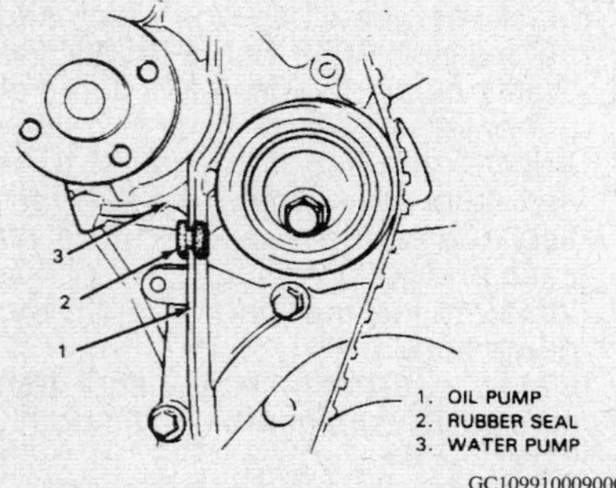

Fig. 20 Rubber seal installation

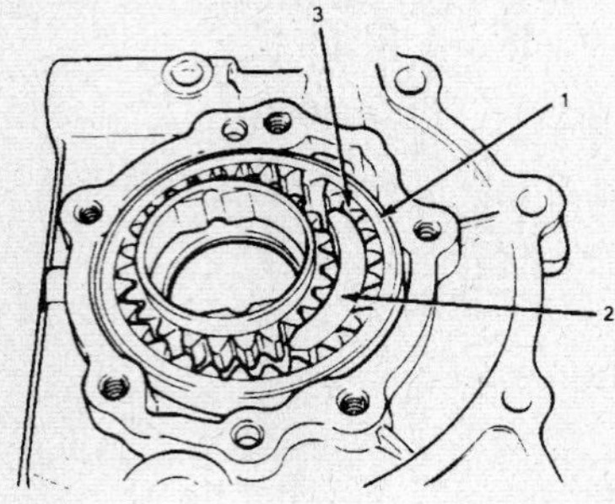

Fig. 21 Oil pump gear radial clearance inspect. Rotor type similar

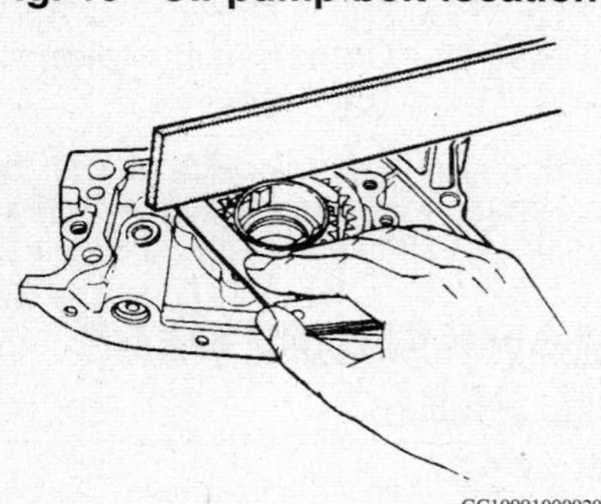

Fig. 22 Oil pump gear side clearance inspect. Rotor type similar

4. Clean both gasket surfaces thoroughly.
5. Reverse procedure to install.

WATER PUMP

REPLACE

1. Drain cooling system into suitable container.
2. Remove drive belt, water pump pulley, crankshaft pulley, timing belt outside cover, timing belt and timing belt tensioner.
3. Remove water pump mounting bolts and nuts and water pump.
4. Install water pump on engine block.
5. Install rubber seals between water pump and oil pump and between water pump and cylinder head, **Fig. 23.**
6. Install timing belt tensioner, timing belt, timing belt outside cover, crankshaft pulley, water pump pulley and drive belt.
7. Tighten drive belt so it deflects .25–.35 inch on span between water pump pulley and crankshaft pulley.
8. Install valve cover and air cleaner.
9. Fill cooling system.

RADIATOR

REPLACE

1. Drain cooling system into suitable container.
2. Remove radiator upper, lower and overflow hoses.
3. Disconnect cooling fan electrical connector.
4. **On models equipped with automatic transaxle,** disconnect transaxle cooling lines from bottom of radiator.
5. **On all models,** remove mounting bolts and radiator/fan assembly.
6. Reverse procedure to install.

FUEL PUMP

REPLACE

1. Remove rear seat cushion, disconnect fuel pump and sending unit electrical connections, then push harness through floor pan grommet.
2. Drain fuel tank into suitable container.
3. Raise and support vehicle.
4. Remove muffler and exhaust pipe.
5. Remove fuel filler neck hose, fuel breather hose and EVAP canister air inlet hose.
6. Remove parking brake cable and position aside.
7. Remove EVAP canister vapor hose, fuel feed and return hoses at fuel tank and pump.

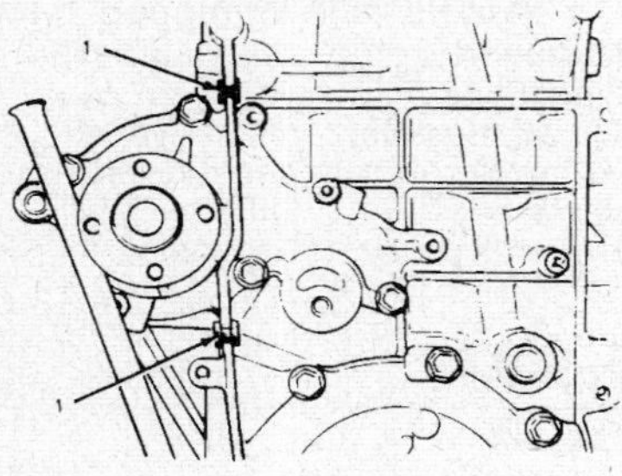

Fig. 23 Rubber seal installation

8. Remove mounting bolts and lower fuel tank.
9. Disconnect fuel sender electrical connections and vapor hoses, then fuel feed and return lines.
10. Remove fuel sender.
11. Separate fuel pump from fuel sender, as required.
12. Reverse procedure to install.

FUEL FILTER

REPLACE

The fuel filter is a component of the fuel sender located in the fuel tank. The fuel sender must be removed in order to replace fuel sender subassembly that contains fuel filter as outlined under "Fuel Pump, Replace."

TIGHTENING SPECIFICATIONS

Tightening specifications are for clean and lightly lubricated threads only.Dry or dirty threads produce increased friction which prevents accurate measurement of tightness.

Year	Component	Torque/Ft. Lbs.
1998–2001	Alternator Mounting	17
	Camshaft Housing To Cylinder Head	97①
	Camshaft Sprocket	44
	Connecting Rod Cap Bolts	26
	Crankshaft Pulley	12
	Crankshaft Sprocket	94
	Cylinder Head	54
	Cylinder Head Cover	97①
	Exhaust Manifold To Cylinder Head	17
	Flywheel To Crankshaft	55
	Ignition Distributor To Cylinder Head	120①
	Intake Manifold To Cylinder Head	17
	Main Bearing Cap Bolts	40
	Oil Pan Drain Plug	26
	Oil Pan To Engine	97①
	Oil Pressure Switch	120①
	Oil Pump Pickup Tube	97①
	Oil Pump Rotor Plate	97①
	Oil Pump To Engine	97①
	Spark Plug	21
	Starter	17
	Timing Belt Cover	97①
	Timing Belt Tensioner Bolt	20
	Timing Belt Tensioner Stud	97①
	Water Pump To Engine	120①

① — Inch lbs.

1.3L Engine

NOTE: On Air Bag Equipped Models, Refer To "Air Bag System Precautions" Located In The Front Of This Manual For System Disarming & Arming Procedures.

NOTE: Refer To "Computer Relearn Procedures" Located In The Front Of This Manual When Battery Power To The Computer Has Been Interrupted.

INDEX

PRECAUTIONS

AIR BAG SYSTEMS

Refer to "Air Bag System Precautions" in the front of this manual for system disarming and arming procedures.

BATTERY GROUND CABLE

Prior to service, disconnect battery ground cable and isolate as required.

FUEL SYSTEM PRESSURE RELIEF

1. Loosen fuel filler cap to relieve fuel tank pressure.
2. Remove fuel pump relay from relay box located at lefthand front of engine compartment, next to battery.
3. Crank engine and allow to stall. Crank engine for several seconds more to ensure relief of any remaining fuel.
4. Remove battery ground cable.

COMPRESSION PRESSURE

1. Turn ignition switch to Lock position.
2. Clean debris from spark plug holes, as required, and remove spark plugs.
3. Disconnect ignition coils electrical connectors.
4. Install spark plug port adapter tool No. J22794, or equivalent and suitable compression gauge into spark plug hole.
5. **On models equipped with manual transaxle,** depress clutch and accelerator to floor.
6. **On all models,** crank engine and take four pressure readings, recording highest reading obtained.
7. Compression should increase quickly and evenly. Compression pressure at 250 RPM is 199 psi standard and 156 psi minimum. Maximum allowable pressure difference between any two cylinders at 250 RPM is 14 psi.
8. Repeat compression test procedure for remaining cylinders.
9. After completion, install FI fuse, spark plugs and distributor electrical connector.

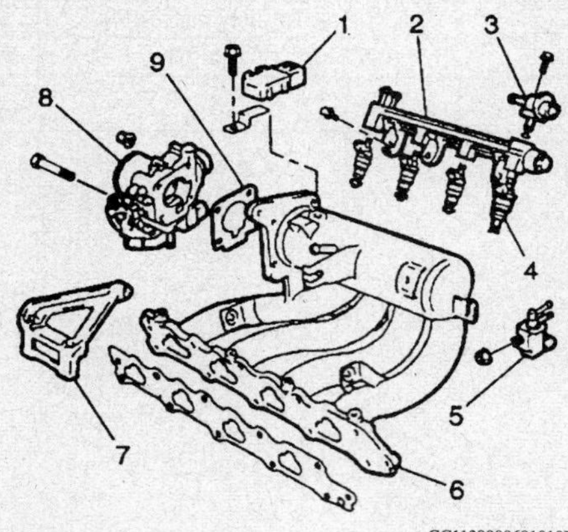

Fig. 1 Intake manifold replacement (Part 1 of 2)

1. MAP SENSOR
2. FUEL RAIL
3. FUEL PRESSURE REGULATOR
4. FUEL INJECTOR
5. EVAP CANISTER PURGE VALVE
6. INTAKE MANIFOLD
7. BRACKET
8. THROTTLE BODY
9. THROTTLE BODY GASKET

GC1139800681020X

Fig. 1 Intake manifold replacement (Part 2 of 2)

ENGINE MOUNT

REPLACE

LEFTHAND

1. Remove engine mount nut, then raise and support vehicle.
2. Support engine using suitable engine support fixture.
3. Remove engine mount and frame bracket, then mount from bracket.
4. Reverse procedure to install.

RIGHTHAND

1. Remove engine mount nut, then raise and support vehicle.
2. Support engine using suitable engine support fixture.
3. Remove engine mount and frame bracket, then mount from bracket.
4. Reverse procedure to install.

REAR

1. Remove engine mount nut, then raise and support vehicle.
2. Remove nut mounting mount to body bracket.
3. Support engine using suitable engine support fixture.
4. Remove frame bracket and mount.

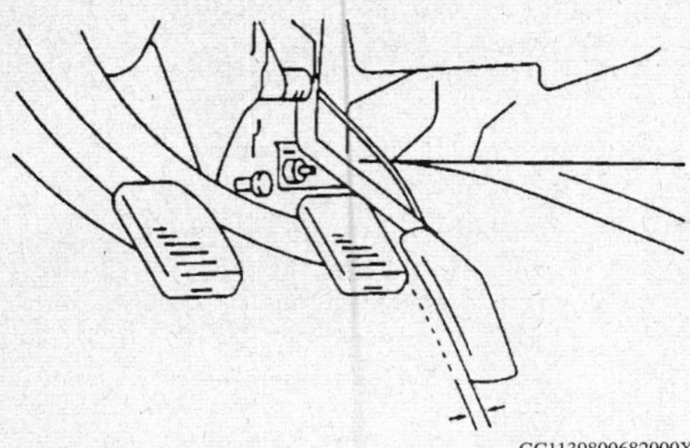

Fig. 2 Accelerator pedal freeplay

5. Reverse procedure to install.

TORQUE ROD

1. Remove engine mount nut, then raise and support vehicle.
2. Remove nut mounting mount to body bracket.
3. Support engine using suitable engine support fixture.
4. Remove frame bracket and mount.
5. Reverse procedure to install.

ENGINE

REPLACE

1. Remove both battery cables, battery and battery tray.
2. Drain cooling system into suitable container.
3. Remove hood.
4. Remove air cleaner.
5. Remove radiator with cooling fan.
6. Disconnect coolant temperature gauge sensor, throttle position sensor and EGR solenoid electrical connectors.
7. Disconnect EGR bypass valve.
8. Disconnect idle speed control solenoid valve, oxygen sensor, fuel injector, MAP sensor and power steering pressure switch electrical connectors.
9. Disconnect intake manifold ground wires.
10. Disconnect oil pressure switch, alternator and air conditioning compressor connectors.
11. Disconnect starter solenoid connectors.
12. Disconnect backup lamp switch.
13. Disconnect direct clutch and second brake solenoids.
14. Release main engine harness from clamps.
15. Disconnect following vacuum hoses:
    a. Intake manifold front and rear canister purge.
    b. Canister pipe.
    c. Intake manifold pressure sensor.
    d. Intake manifold brake booster.
    e. Throttle body idle speed control.
16. Disconnect the following cables:
    a. Throttle body accelerator.
    b. Transaxle clutch.
    c. Transaxle shift select and throttle valve.
    d. Transaxle speedometer.
17. Remove inlet and outlet hoses.
18. Remove throttle body fuel return and feed hoses.
19. Install universal support fixture tool No.

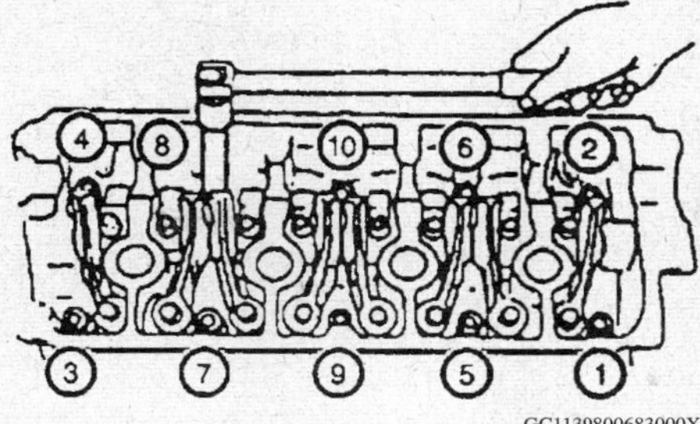

Fig. 3 Cylinder head loosening sequence

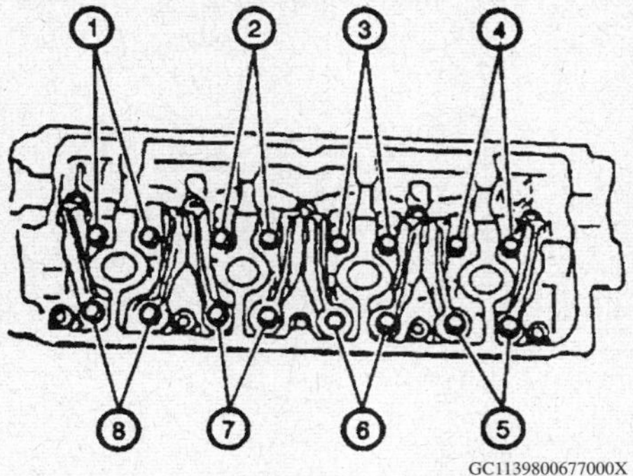

Fig. 5 Valve lash adjustment

J28467-A with engine support adapters tool No. J28467-89, or equivalents.

20. Raise and support vehicle.
21. Disconnect exhaust system from exhaust manifold.
22. Remove front pipe/catalytic converter.
23. **On models equipped with manual transaxle** remove gearshift control shaft and extension rod.
24. **On all models** drain engine oil and transaxle fluid into suitable container.
25. Remove left and righthand drive axles from transaxle as outlined in "Front Wheel Drive Axle" section. **It is not required to remove driveshafts from steering knuckles.**
26. Remove air conditioning compressor from compressor bracket. **Do not disconnect air conditioning hoses from compressor.**
27. Disconnect power steering pump hoses.
28. **On models equipped with automatic transaxle,** remove torque rod.
29. **On all models** lower vehicle.
30. Remove tool Nos. J28467-A and J28467-89, or equivalents, and install suitable engine lifting device.
31. Remove lefthand transaxle mount, righthand side engine mount and rear engine mount.
32. Remove engine with transaxle.
33. Reverse procedure to install. Tightening mounting bolts and nuts to specifications.

INTAKE MANIFOLD

REPLACE

1. Drain cooling system into suitable container.
2. Remove air cleaner.

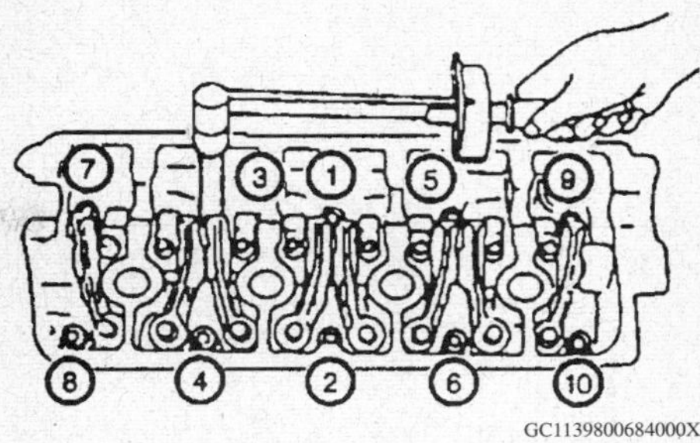

Fig. 4 Cylinder head tightening sequence

3. Disconnect intake manifold ground wires.
4. Disconnect fuel injector, MAP sensor, TP sensor, IAC valve and EVAP canister purge valve electrical connectors, **Fig. 1.**
5. Disconnect wiring harness from retaining clamps.
6. Remove throttle body coolant hoses.
7. Remove intake manifold canister purge and brake booster hoses.
8. Remove throttle body accelerator cable.
9. Remove intake manifold mounting nuts and bolts.
10. Remove intake manifold with throttle body and wire clamps from cylinder head still attached.
11. Reverse procedure to install. Adjust accelerator cable freeplay as follows:
    a. Measure accelerator pedal free play with throttle closed, **Fig. 2.**
    b. If freeplay is not .08–.27 inch, loosen accelerator control cable locknut and turn accelerator control cable adjusting nut.
    c. Depress accelerator pedal to floor.
    d. Measure distance between throttle lever and throttle stop.
    e. If measure is not .02–.07 inch, adjust height of pedal stopper bolt.
    f. Operate accelerator control cable from inside of vehicle to ensure throttle movement is smooth and not binding.

EXHAUST MANIFOLD

REPLACE

1. Raise and support vehicle.
2. Disconnect catalytic converter from manifold and lower vehicle.
3. Disconnect oxygen sensor electrical connector and release wiring harness from clamps.
4. Remove heat shield and engine hanger.
5. Disconnect exhaust pipe from exhaust manifold.
6. Remove mounting bolts and nuts, then the exhaust manifold.
7. Reverse procedure to install, noting the following:
    a. Install new gasket.
    b. Tighten mounting bolts and nuts to specifications.

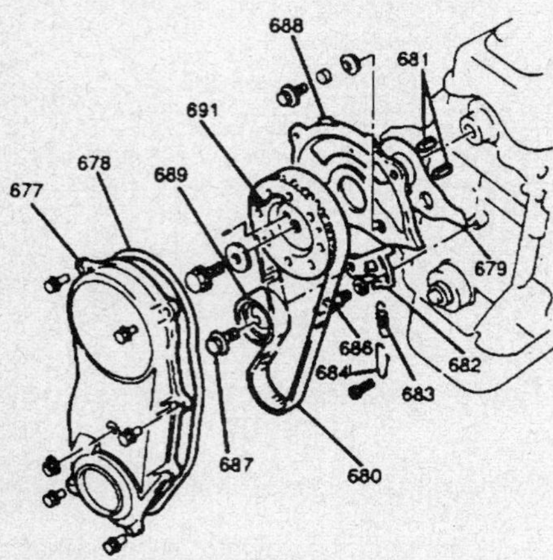

677 TIMING BELT COVER
678 OUTER TIMING BELT COVER GASKET
679 TIMING BELT INNER SEAL
680 TIMING BELT
681 SEAL
682 TENSIONER PLATE
683 TENSIONER SPRING
684 SPRING DAMPER
686 TENSIONER STUD
687 TENSIONER BOLT
688 TIMING BELT INNER COVER
689 TIMING BELT TENSIONER
691 CAMSHAFT TIMING GEAR SPROCKET

GC1069500587000X

Fig. 6 Timing belt assembly

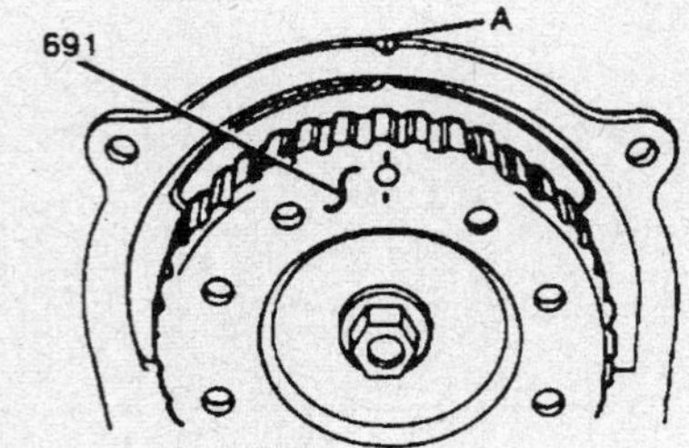

A "V" MARK
691 CAMSHAFT TIMING GEAR SPROCKET

GC1069500588000X

Fig. 7 Camshaft timing mark

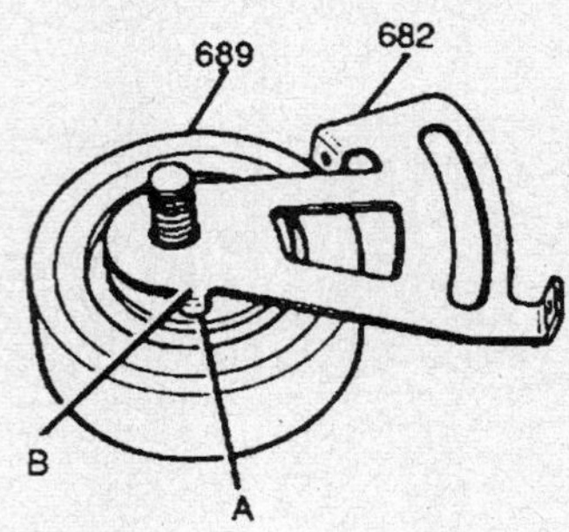

A TIMING BELT TENSIONER HOLE
B TENSIONER PLATE LUG
682 TENSIONER PLATE
689 TIMING BELT TENSIONER

GC1069500590000X

Fig. 9 Timing belt tensioner

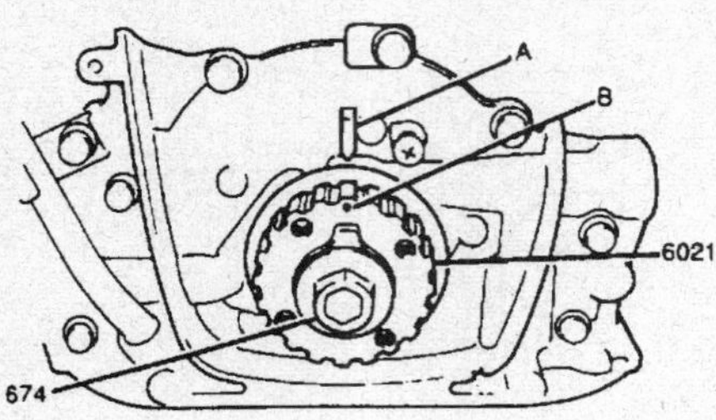

A ARROW MARK ON OIL PUMP CASE
B PUNCH MARK ON CRANKSHAFT TIMING GEAR
674 CRANKSHAFT PULLEY TIMING GEAR BOLT
6021 CRANKSHAFT TIMING GEAR

GC1069500601000X

Fig. 8 Crankshaft timing mark

CYLINDER HEAD

REPLACE

1. Remove intake manifold as outlined under "Intake Manifold, Replace."
2. Remove exhaust manifold as outlined under "Exhaust Manifold, Replace."
3. Remove timing belt and belt tensioner as outlined under "Timing Belt, Replace."
4. Remove valve cover.
5. Loosen all valve lash adjusting screw locknuts.
6. Turn back valve lash adjusting screw until all valve are closed.
7. Remove head bolts in sequence, **Fig. 3.**
8. Remove cylinder head and discard gasket.
9. Reverse procedure to install, noting the following:
   a. Install cylinder head bolts loosely to secure cylinder head.
   b. **Torque** cylinder head bolts evenly and in small increments to 49 ft. lbs., in sequence, **Fig. 4.**
   c. Refill cooling system to specification.

VALVE ARRANGEMENT

FRONT TO REAR

1.3L............................I-E-I-E-I-E-I-E

VALVE ADJUSTMENT

1. Intake valve lash is .005–.007 inch, cold and .007–.009 hot; Exhaust valve lash is .009–.011 cold and .011–.013 hot.
2. Set No. 1 cylinder to top dead center on compression stroke.
3. Ensure camshaft is in proper phase.
4. Adjust valves 1, 2, 8 and 6 **Fig. 5.**
5. Rotate crankshaft 360.°
6. Adjust valves 3, 4, 7 and 5 **Fig. 5.**

VALVE GUIDES

Valves and valve guides are available in standard size only. The valve guide can be driven from cylinder bore using valve guide replacement tool No. J34834, or equivalent. The valve guide should be driven from the combustion chamber side of the cylinder head out through the valve spring side.

The cylinder head valve guide bore should be reamed with .472 inch reamer tool No. 34831, or equivalent, prior to valve guide installation. Drive valve guide into heated cylinder head bore using valve guide replacement tool No. J34834, or equivalent. Valve guide should be driven in until tool contacts cylinder head. Valve guide protrusion should be .55 inch from cylinder head surface. After installation, ream valve guide with .277 inch reamer tool No. J34832, or equivalent.

TIMING BELT

REPLACE

REMOVAL

1. Raise and support vehicle.
2. Remove crankshaft timing pulley.
3. Remove timing belt cover, **Fig. 6.**
4. Align upper and lower timing marks, **Figs. 7 and 8,** by turning crankshaft.
5. Remove tensioner and timing belt.

INSPECTION

1. Inspect radial clearance between outer gear/rotor and crescent, timing belt for wear and cracks and replace.
2. Inspect radial clearance between outer gear/rotor and crescent, timing belt tensioner for smoothness of rotation.
3. Replace as required.

INSTALLATION

1. Position lug on tensioner plate to hole in tensioner, **Fig. 9.**
2. Position tensioner and tensioner plate to engine, then install and hand tighten mounting bolt. Ensure tensioner and tensioner plate move in same direction, **Fig. 10.** If movement is not as indicated, remove tensioner and reinsert tensioner plate lug into tensioner.
3. Ensure camshaft and crankshaft timing marks are aligned.
4. Remove cylinder head cover and completely loosen all valve adjusting screws on intake and exhaust rocker arms. This will permit free rotation of camshaft and prevent damage to valves during timing belt adjustment.
5. With tensioner plate pushed upward, install timing belt over camshaft and crankshaft pulleys. **Arrow on timing belt should face toward direction of crankshaft rotation. When installing timing belt, keep drive side of belt free of slack.**
6. Install tensioner spring and damper, then hand tighten tensioner stud.
7. Rotate crankshaft two revolutions clockwise direction to remove slack from belt. **Ensure slack is removed from drive belt, and camshaft and crankshaft timing marks are aligned.**
8. Tighten tensioner stud and bolt to specifications.
9. Install timing belt outer cover and crankshaft pulley. **Ensure seal is between oil pump housing and water pump.**
10. Adjust valve lash, install cylinder head

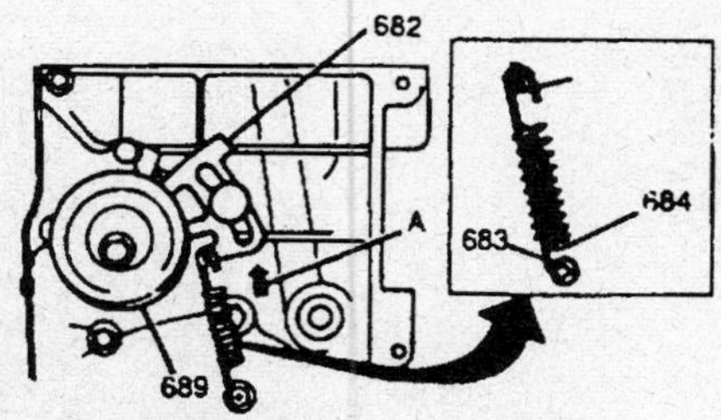

A DIRECTION OF TENSIONER MOVEMENT
682 TENSIONER PLATE
683 TENSIONER SPRING
684 SPRING DAMPER
689 TIMING BELT TENSIONER

GC1069500591000X

Fig. 10 Tensioner adjustment

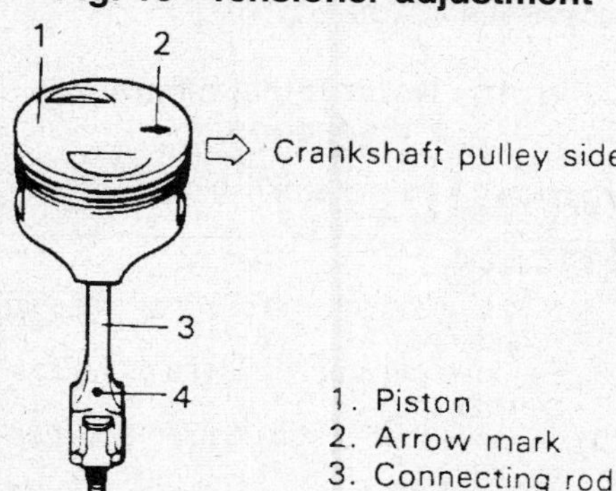

GC1069500595000X

Fig. 13 Piston & connecting rod assembly

cover and lower vehicle.

CAMSHAFT

REPLACE

REMOVAL

1. Remove valve cover as outlined under "Valve Cover, Replace."
2. Remove timing belt and timing belt tensioner as outlined under "Timing Belt, Replace."
3. Remove mounting bolt and camshaft timing sprocket.
4. Disconnect cam sensor electrical connector.
5. Disconnect spark plug wires and ignition coil electrical connectors.
6. Remove ignition coils.
7. Remove cam sensor.
8. Loosen all valve adjusting screw lock nuts, back off adjusting screws to allow rocker arms to move freely.
9. Gradually remove camshaft housing bolts in sequence, **Fig. 11.**

INSTALLATION

1. Apply clean engine oil to camshaft, journals and oil seal.
2. Install camshaft to cylinder head.
3. Apply clean engine oil to housing bolts and **torque** bolts to 96 inch lbs., in sequence, **Fig. 12.**
4. Install camshaft timing sprocket to camshaft.

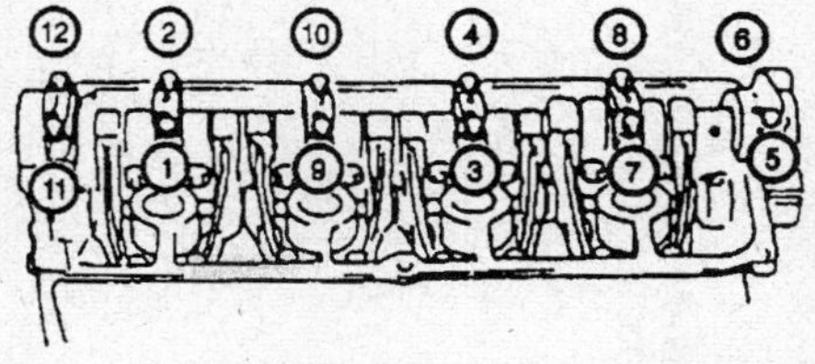

GC1139800686000X

Fig. 11 Camshaft housing bolt removal sequence

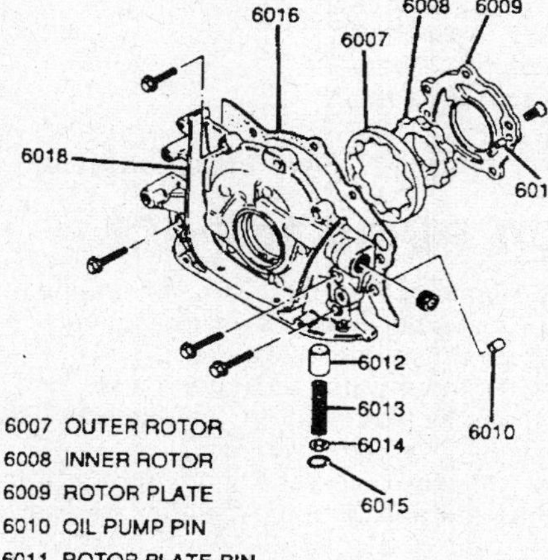

6007 OUTER ROTOR
6008 INNER ROTOR
6009 ROTOR PLATE
6010 OIL PUMP PIN
6011 ROTOR PLATE PIN
6012 RELIEF VALVE
6013 SPRING
6014 RETAINER
6015 RETAINER RING
6016 OIL PUMP GASKET
6018 OIL PUMP BODY

GC1099500107000X

Fig. 14 Rotor type oil pump

5. Ensure pin on camshaft fits slot on sprocket.
6. **Torque** camshaft timing sprocket to 43 ft. lbs.
7. Perform valve lash adjustment as outlined under "Valve Adjustment."
8. Connect cam sensor connector, spark plug wires and ignition coil assemblies.
9. Install timing belt as outlined under "Timing Belt, Replace."
10. Install valve cover.

PISTON & ROD ASSEMBLY

Refer to **Fig. 13,** when assembling piston and connecting rod. When installing piston and connecting rod, arrow on piston head should face front of engine and oil hole in connecting rod should face intake manifold. When installing connecting rod cap, arrow on cap should face front of engine.

Measure rod bearing side clearance using feeler gauge. Connecting rod bearing side clearance should be .0039 to .0078 inch.

PISTONS, PINS & RINGS

Pistons and rings are available in standard size and oversizes of .0098 and .0197

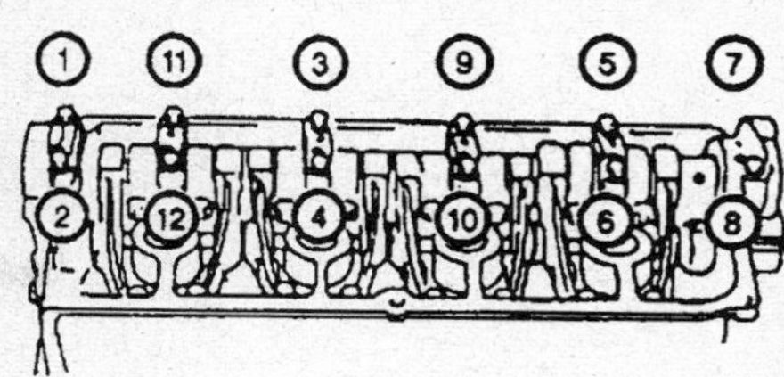

GC1139800687000X

Fig. 12 Camshaft housing bolts tightening sequence

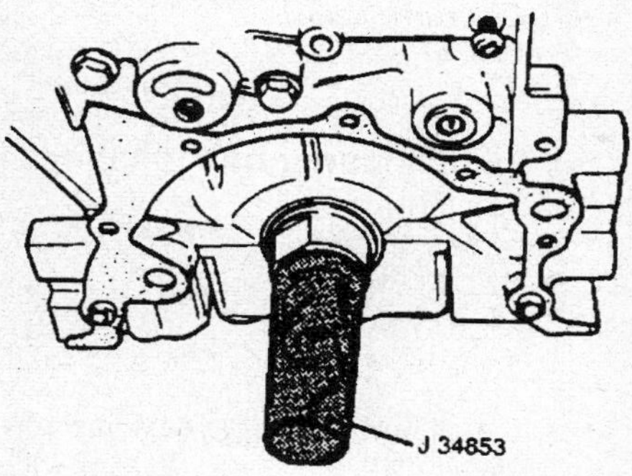

GC1099500108000X

Fig. 15 Crankshaft oil seal guide tool

inch. Piston pins are supplied with pistons in matched sets.

MAIN & ROD BEARINGS

Main and rod bearings are available in standard size and under size of .010 inch.

CRANKSHAFT REAR OIL SEAL

REPLACE

1. Remove transaxle as outlined under "Transaxle, Replace" in "Automatic Transaxles/Transmissions" or "Clutch & Manual Transaxle" sections.
2. **On models equipped with manual transaxle,** remove pressure plate and clutch disc.
3. **On all models,** mark flywheel to engine position and remove flywheel.
4. Remove oil pan as outlined under "Oil Pan, Replace."
5. Remove seal retainer and seal from retainer.
6. Reverse procedure to install, ensuring to install new seal.

OIL PAN

REPLACE

1. Raise and support vehicle.
2. Drain engine oil into suitable container.
3. Remove front pipe/catalytic converter from exhaust manifold and resonator/center pipe.
4. Remove crankshaft position sensor.
5. Remove mounting bolts and nuts and engine oil pan.
6. Reverse procedure to install, noting the following:
   a. Apply continuous bead of silicone

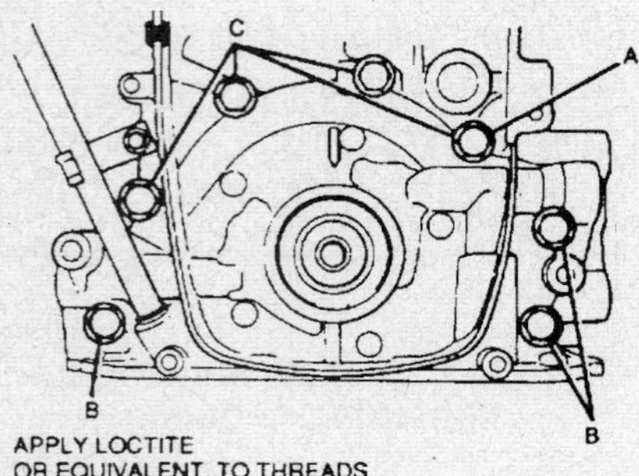

Fig. 16 Oil pump bolt location

P/N 12346240, or equivalent, to engine oil pan mating surface.

b. **Torque** engine oil pan nuts and bolts to 96 inch lbs.
c. **Torque** engine oil drain plug to 26 ft. lbs.
d. Install new front pipe/catalytic converter seal.

OIL PUMP

REPLACE

REMOVAL

1. Remove timing belt as outlined under "Timing Belt, Replace."
2. Remove oil pan as outlined under "Oil Pan, Replace."
3. Remove crankshaft timing belt sprocket.
4. Remove alternator mounting bracket, as required.
5. Remove air conditioning compressor mounting bracket, if equipped.
6. Remove alternator adjusting bolt and upper cover bolt, as required.
7. Remove oil pump bolts and pump, **Fig. 14.**

INSTALLATION

1. Install oil pump pins and gasket on engine block.
2. Install oil seal guide tool No. J34853, or equivalent, onto crankshaft to prevent damage to oil seal lip, **Fig. 15.** Apply engine oil to special tool.
3. Install oil pump onto crankshaft and engine block.
4. Install mounting bolts and tighten to specifications. No. 1 bolts are shorter than No. 2 bolts, **Fig. 16.**
5. Ensure oil seal lip is not twisted and remove tool.
6. Install rubber seal between oil pump and water pump, **Fig. 17.**
7. Trim oil pump seal edges flush with oil pan mating surface, as required.
8. Install timing belt guide, key and crankshaft timing sprocket. Timing belt guide must be installed so curved side faces oil pump.
9. Install timing belt and tensioner components.
10. Adjust water pump belt tension.
11. Fill crankcase.
12. Run engine and ensure oil pressure is correct.

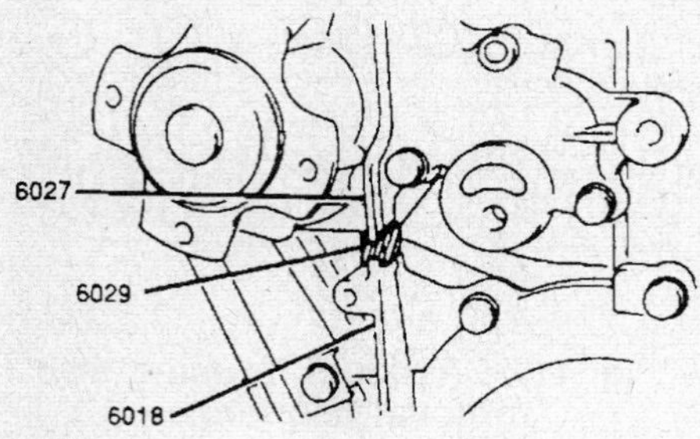

Fig. 17 Seal installation

OIL PUMP SERVICE

1. Drain oil into suitable container and remove dipstick tube from oil pump.
2. Remove rotor plate.
3. Remove outer and inner rotors.
4. Inspect oil seal lip for damage. Replace as required
5. Inspect outer and inner rotors, rotor plate and oil pump case for excessive wear or damage.
6. Inspect radial clearance between outer gear/rotor and crescent, radial clearance between outer rotor and crescent, **Fig. 18.** If clearance is more than .0122 inch, replace outer rotor.
7. Using straightedge and feeler gauge, measure side clearance which should not exceed .0059 inch, **Fig. 19.**
8. Wash, clean and dry all oil pump components.
9. Apply light coat of engine oil to inner and outer rotors, oil seal lip portion and inside surfaces of oil pump case and plate.
10. Install outer and inner rotors in pump case.
11. Install rotor plate and tighten screws. Ensure gears turn smoothly by hand.
12. Install O-ring in pump case and dipstick tube.

BELT TENSION DATA

Belt	Belt Deflection Inch①
Air Conditioning Compressor & Power Steering Pump	.28–.35
Water Pump & Alternator	.25–.32

① — With 22 lbs. pressure applied.

COOLING SYSTEM BLEED

These engines do not require a specific bleed procedure. After filling cooling system, run engine to operating temperature with radiator pressure cap off. Air will then be automatically bled through cap opening.

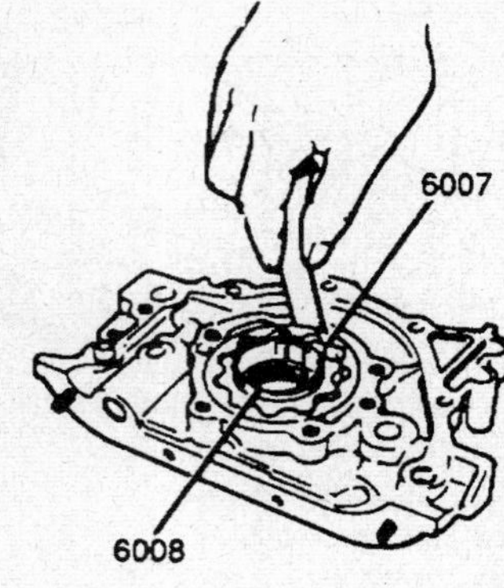

Fig. 18 Rotor radial clearance inspection

THERMOSTAT

REPLACE

1. Drain cooling system into suitable container.
2. Remove radiator inlet hose at thermostat housing.
3. Remove thermostat housing and thermostat.
4. Clean both gasket surfaces thoroughly.
5. Reverse procedure to install, ensuring to use new gasket.

WATER PUMP

REPLACE

REMOVAL

1. Drain cooling system into suitable container.
2. Remove air cleaner.
3. **On models equipped with air conditioning,** remove compressor suction pipe bracket.
4. **On all models,** loosen, but do not remove, water pump bolts.
5. Raise and properly support vehicle.
6. Remove righthand lower splash shield.
7. **On models equipped with air conditioning,** remove compressor drive belt.
8. **On all models,** remove lower alternator cover plate, loosen alternator adjusting bolt and remove water pump/alternator drive belt.
9. Remove crankshaft pulley and water pump pulley.
10. Remove timing belt as outlined under "Timing Belt, Replace."
11. Remove dipstick tube.
12. Remove upper alternator adjusting bracket.
13. Remove rubber seals, **Fig. 20.**
14. Remove water pump mounting bolts, nuts and water pump.

INSTALLATION

1. Install water pump on engine block, ensuring to use new gasket.

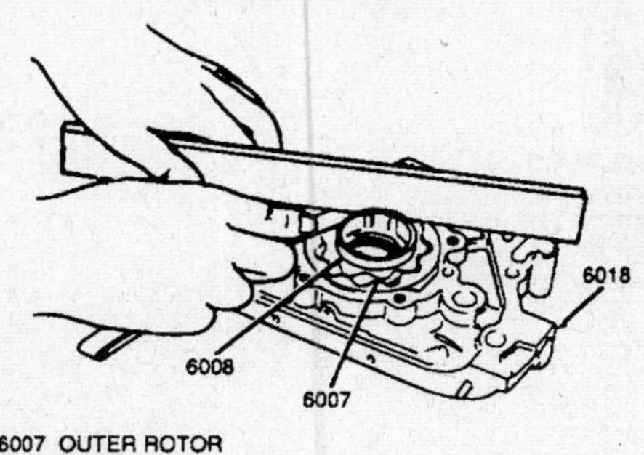

6007 OUTER ROTOR
6008 INNER ROTOR
6018 OIL PUMP BODY

GC1099500112000X

Fig. 19 Rotor side clearance inspection

2. Install rubber seals between water pump and oil pump and between water pump and cylinder head,
3. Install upper alternator adjusting bracket to water pump and tighten to specifications.
4. Install dipstick tube.
5. Install timing belt.
6. Install and hand tighten water pump pulley.
7. Install crankshaft pulley.
8. Install water pump/alternator drive belt and lower alternator cover plate.
9. **On models equipped with air conditioning,** install compressor drive belt.
10. **On all models,** install righthand lower splash shield.
11. Lower vehicle.
12. **On models equipped with air conditioning,** install compressor suction pipe bracket.
13. **On all models,** tighten upper alternator adjustment bolt to specifications.
14. Tighten water pump/alternator drive belt to specifications listed in "Belt Tension Data."
15. Fill cooling system.

RADIATOR

REPLACE

1. Drain cooling system into suitable container.
2. Remove radiator upper, lower and overflow hoses.
3. Disconnect cooling fan electrical connector.
4. **On models equipped with automatic transaxle,** disconnect transaxle cooling lines from bottom of radiator.
5. **On all models,** remove mounting bolts and radiator/fan.
6. Reverse procedure to install.

FUEL PUMP

REPLACE

1. Remove rear seat cushion, disconnect fuel pump and sending unit electrical connections, then push harness through floor pan grommet.
2. Drain fuel tank into suitable container, then raise and support vehicle.
3. Remove muffler and exhaust pipe.
4. Remove fuel filler neck hose, fuel breather hose and EVAP canister air inlet hose.
5. Remove parking brake cable and position aside.
6. Remove EVAP canister vapor hose and fuel feed and return hoses at fuel tank and pump.
7. Remove mounting bolts and lower fuel tank.
8. Disconnect fuel sender electrical connections and vapor hoses, then the fuel feed and return lines.
9. Remove fuel sender.
10. Separate fuel pump from fuel sender, as required.
11. Reverse procedure to install.

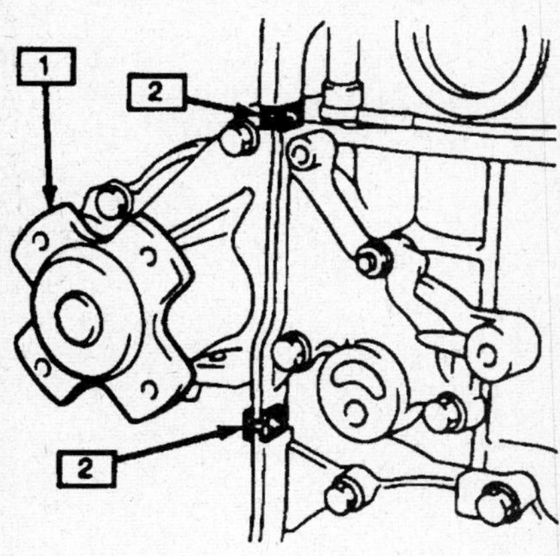

1 COOLANT PUMP
2 RUBBER SEALS

GC1089500243000X

Fig. 20 Water pump rubber seals

FUEL FILTER

REPLACE

The fuel filter is a component of the fuel sender located in the fuel tank. The fuel sender must be removed in order to replace fuel sender subassembly that contains fuel filter as outlined under "Fuel Pump, Replace."

TIGHTENING SPECIFICATIONS

Tightening specifications are for clean and lightly lubricated threads only. Dry or dirty threads produce increased friction which prevents accurate measurement of tightness.

Year	Component	Torque/Ft. Lbs.
1998–2001	Air Cleaner To Cylinder Head	89①
	Camshaft Timing Sprocket	43
	Connecting Bracket To Rear Mount	41
	Connecting Rod Bearing Cap	26
	Coolant Pump Pulley	97①
	Coolant Return Pipe	15
	Crankshaft Timing Pulley	12
	Crankshaft Timing Sprocket	94
	Cylinder Head To Engine Block	49
	Engine Oil Drain Plug	26
	Engine Oil Pan	97①
	Exhaust Manifold	17
	Flywheel (Automatic Transaxle)	69
	Flywheel (Manual Transaxle)	57
	Front Pipe/Catalytic Converter (To Exhaust Manifold)	37
	Front Pipe/Catalytic Converter (To Resonator/Center Pipe)	26
	Main Bearing Cap	40
	Oil Pressure Switch	10
	Oil Pump	97①
	Oil Pump Strainer	97①
	Rear Main Seal Housing	97①
	Rocker Arm Shaft	97①
	Timing Belt Cover	97①
	Timing Belt Tensioner	18
	Timing Belt Tensioner	97①
	Torque Rod Bracket	41

① — Inch lbs.

Clutch & Manual Transaxle

NOTE: On Air Bag Equipped Models, Refer To "Air Bag System Precautions" Located In The Front Of This Manual For System Disarming & Arming Procedures.

NOTE: Refer To "Computer Relearn Procedures" Located In The Front Of This Manual When Battery Power To The Computer Has Been Interrupted.

INDEX

PRECAUTIONS

AIR BAG SYSTEMS

Refer to "Air Bag System Precautions" in the front of this manual for system disarming and arming procedures.

BATTERY GROUND CABLE

Prior to service, disconnect battery ground cable and isolate as required.

ADJUSTMENTS

CLUTCH PEDAL HEIGHT

Clutch pedal height can be adjusted by turning the clutch pedal stop bolt located at the upper end of the clutch pedal lever, at the pedal bracket. Clutch pedal height should be the same as brake pedal height.

CLUTCH RELEASE ARM PLAY

1. Measure clutch pedal freeplay. Clutch pedal freeplay should be .6 to .8 inch.
2. If clutch pedal freeplay is not within specifications, adjust clutch cable joint nut to provide free travel of .08 to .15 inch at release lever, **Fig. 1.**

SHIFT LINKAGE

Inspect radial clearance between outer gear/rotor and crescent, gear shift control lever vertical endplay. Vertical endplay should be 0.0-.007 inch. Inspect radial clearance between outer gear/rotor and crescent, distance between instrument panel and gear shift control lever, with transaxle in neutral, **Fig. 2.** If distance is not approximately 4.8 inches, adjust.

CLUTCH

REPLACE

1. Remove transaxle as outlined under "Transaxle, Replace."
2. Install suitable tool into pilot bearing to support clutch during removal.
3. Inspect radial clearance between outer gear/rotor and crescent, for X mark or white painted letter on pressure plate and corresponding mark stamped on flywheel. If no markings are found, mark flywheel and pressure plate for assembly.
4. Loosen pressure plate to flywheel mounting bolts one turn at a time until spring pressure is released, **Fig. 3.** It may be required to use flywheel holder tool No. J35271, or equivalent, to hold flywheel in position when loosening bolts.
5. Remove bolts, pressure plate and clutch disc.
6. Reverse procedure to install. Lubricate splines of transaxle input shaft and pilot bearing surface and release bearing with suitable lithium grease. **Torque** pressure plate cover bolts to 17 ft. lbs.

SHIFT CABLE

REPLACE

1. Remove clutch cable joint nut and disconnect cable from release arm.
2. Remove clutch cable bracket bolts and bracket.
3. Remove cable mounting bolts at clutch pedal.
4. Remove clutch cable.
5. Reverse procedure to install. Refer to "Adjustments" to adjust cable.

TRANSAXLE

REPLACE

1. Disconnect clutch cable from release lever and bracket.
2. Disconnect electrical connectors from transaxle and remove wiring harness to transaxle mounting brackets.
3. Disconnect speedometer cable from transaxle.
4. Remove upper transaxle mounting bolts.
5. Remove starter motor.
6. Disconnect pressure sensor vacuum hose.
7. Install suitable engine support fixture, then raise and support vehicle.
8. Drain transaxle lubricant into suitable container.
9. Disconnect gear shift control lever from gear shift shaft.
10. Remove mounting nut and extension rod with washers.
11. Remove mounting nuts, bolts and exhaust pipe.
12. Remove clutch housing lower cover.
13. Remove lefthand front wheel.
14. Disconnect lefthand tie rod end and ball joint from steering knuckle.
15. Separate drive axles from transaxle, **Fig. 4.** Support drive axles from chassis using suitable wire.
16. Remove lower transaxle to engine mounting bolts and nuts.
17. Support transaxle using a suitable jack.
18. Remove rear engine mounting nuts, transaxle lefthand mounting bracket mounting nuts and bolts, then the bracket.
19. Lower transaxle and engine to disconnect assembly from stud bolts at rear engine mounting.
20. Pull transaxle outward toward lefthand side to disconnect input shaft from clutch.
21. Lower transaxle and remove.
22. Reverse procedure to install, noting the following:
    a. Lubricate splines of transaxle input shaft and pilot bearing surface and release bearing with suitable lithium grease.
    b. When installing transaxle, guide righthand drive axle into transaxle as it is raised into vehicle. Tighten to specifications.

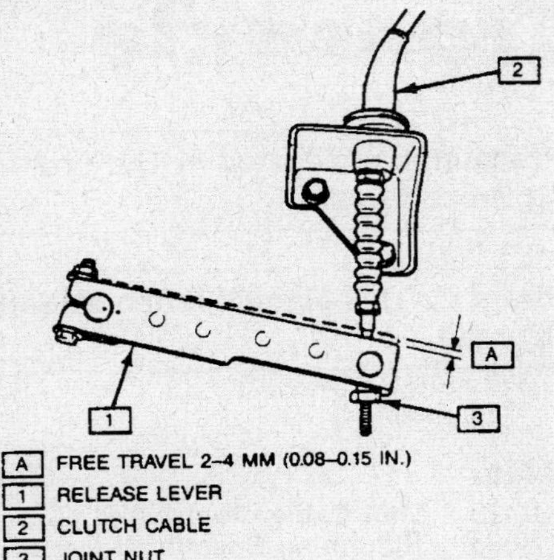

Fig. 1 Clutch cable adjustment

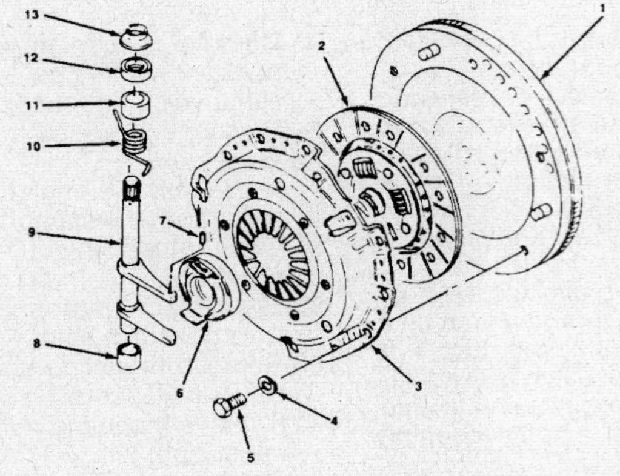

Fig. 3 Clutch assembly

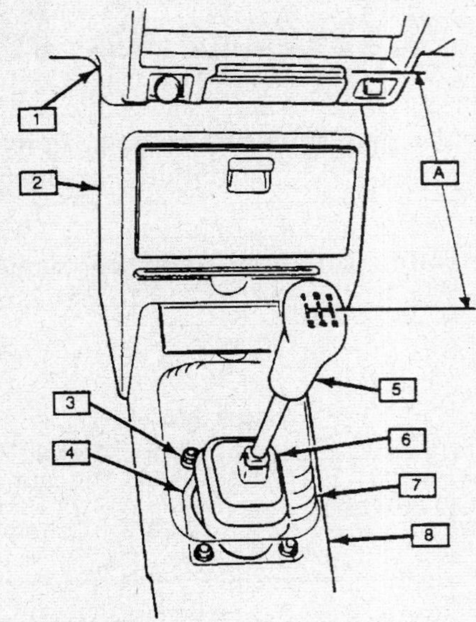

Fig. 2 Gearshift control lever position

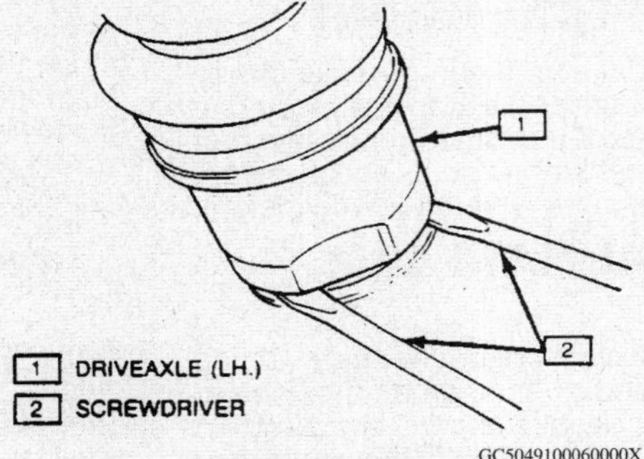

Fig. 4 Front drive axle snap ring removal

TIGHTENING SPECIFICATIONS

Year	Component	Torque/Ft. Lbs.
1998–2001	Back-Up Lamp Switch	17
	Battery Cable To Terminal	89②
	Cable Bracket	21
	Clutch Cover	17
	Clutch Pedal Shaft	15
	Clutch Release Lever	17
	Extension Rod Nut	29
	Flywheel	①
	Gear Shift Control Shaft Bolts & Nuts	15
	Starter	21
	Switch Locknut	10
	Transaxle Hanger	106②
	Transaxle Mounts	44
	Transaxle To Engine Bolts	44
	Transaxle Oil Drain & Filler Plugs	15
	Transaxle Side Cover	106②
	Wheel Lug Nuts	44

① — 1.0L engine, 45 ft. lbs.; 1.3L engine, 57 ft. lbs.
② — Inch lbs.

Rear Axle & Suspension

NOTE: On Air Bag Equipped Models, Refer To "Air Bag System Precautions" Located In The Front Of This Manual For System Disarming & Arming Procedures.

NOTE: Refer To "Computer Relearn Procedures" Located In The Front Of This Manual When Battery Power To The Computer Has Been Interrupted.

INDEX

PRECAUTIONS

AIR BAG SYSTEMS

Refer to "Air Bag System Precautions" in the front of this manual for system disarming and arming procedures.

BATTERY GROUND CABLE

Prior to service, disconnect battery ground cable and isolate as required.

HUB & BEARING

REPLACE

1. Raise and support rear of vehicle, then remove wheel.
2. Remove wheel bearing dust cap from brake drum.
3. Unstake wheel bearing nut using suitable chisel, then remove wheel bearing nut and washer .
4. Loosen parking brake cable adjusting nuts, then remove plug from backing plate and back off drum brake adjustment.
5. Remove brake drum using suitable puller, .
6. Remove wheel bearings from brake drum using suitable brass drift.
7. Reverse procedure to install, noting the following:
   a. Fill Hub cavity (A) with lithium wheel bearing grease, **Fig. 1.**
   b. Install wheel bearings and spacer using bearing and hub installer tool Nos. J7079-2 and J34842, or equivalents, with sealed side facing outward, **Fig. 1.**
   c. Install brake drum on spindle.
   d. Tighten wheel bearing nut to specifications, then stake nut in position.
   e. After completing installation, adjust drum brake and parking brake.
   f. Bleed and inspect brake system for proper operation.

STRUT

REPLACE

1. **On two-door models,** open hatchback for access to upper strut mounting.

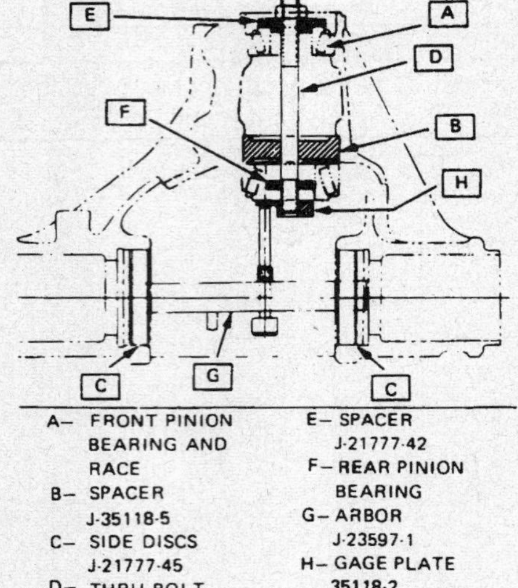

Fig. 1 Wheel bearing installation

2. **On four-door models,** open trunk for access to upper strut mounting.
3. **On all models,** raise and support rear of vehicle, then remove wheel.
4. Support suspension using suitable jack.
5. Remove strut upper support nuts and push downward on strut, **Fig. 2.**
6. Remove strut lower mounting bolt, **Fig. 3.**
7. Separate strut from rear suspension knuckle by compressing strut. **If strut is difficult to remove, open slit on knuckle just enough to allow strut removal.**
8. Reverse procedure to install. When installing strut, align projection on strut with slit on rear suspension knuckle, **Fig. 4.**

COIL SPRING

REPLACE

1. Raise and support rear of vehicle, then remove wheel.
2. Place alignment marks on control rod and control rod washer (A), **Fig. 5,** for setting toe during installation.
3. Remove control rod to body mounting bolt and separate control rod from bracket.
4. Remove nut from rear suspension knuckle stud and disconnect control rod from wheel side of control rod.
5. Loosen, but do not remove suspension arm rear mounting nut.
6. Loosen rear suspension knuckle lower mounting nut.
7. Position suitable jack under suspension arm and remove knuckle lower mounting nut.
8. Raise lower arm slightly to allow removal of rear suspension knuckle lower mounting bolt.
9. Disengage rear suspension knuckle from suspension arm, lower suspension arm and remove coil spring, **Fig. 6.**
10. Remove remaining suspension arm mounting bolts and nuts and remove suspension arm, as required.
11. Reverse procedure to install. When installing spring, position spring end to stepped portion of suspension arm, **Fig. 7.** When installing control rod to body bracket, align marks made on washer and control rod during removal. **Do not tighten control rod or suspension arm mounting nuts and bolts until after vehicle has been lowered.**

CONTROL ARM

REPLACE

1. Raise and support rear of vehicle, then remove wheel.
2. Remove E-ring and detach brake hose from control rod.
3. Place alignment marks on control rod and control rod washer at body bracket for setting toe during installation, **Fig. 5.**
4. Remove control rod to rear suspension knuckle mounting nut, **Fig. 8.**
5. Remove bracket mounting bolt and control rod.

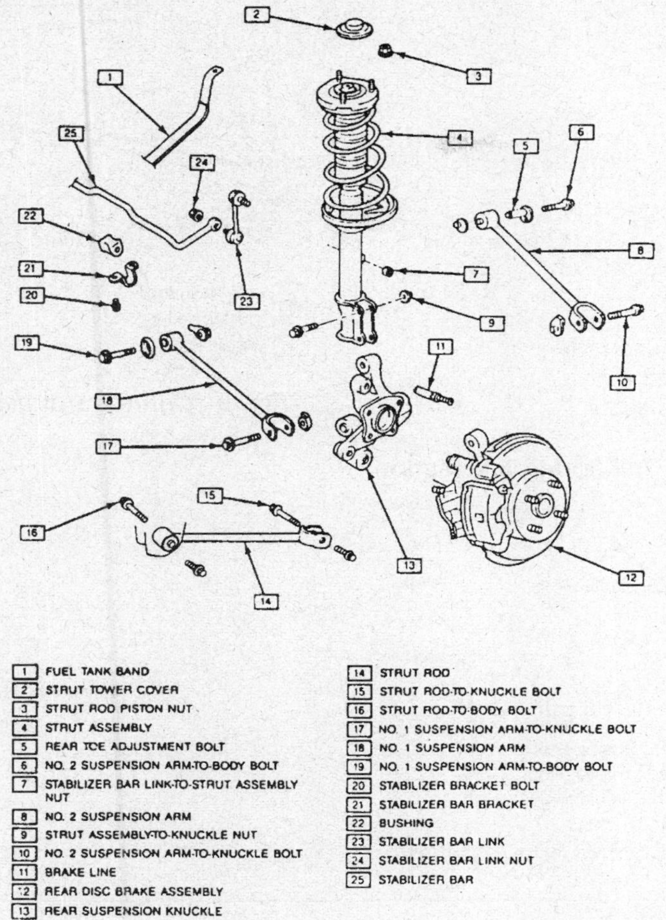

Fig. 2 Strut upper mounting nuts

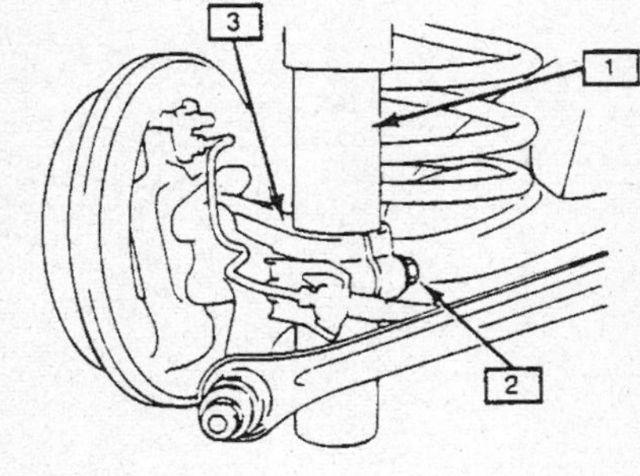

1 STRUT
2 MOUNT BOLT
3 KNUCKLE

GC2039100087000X

Fig. 3 Strut lower mounting bolt

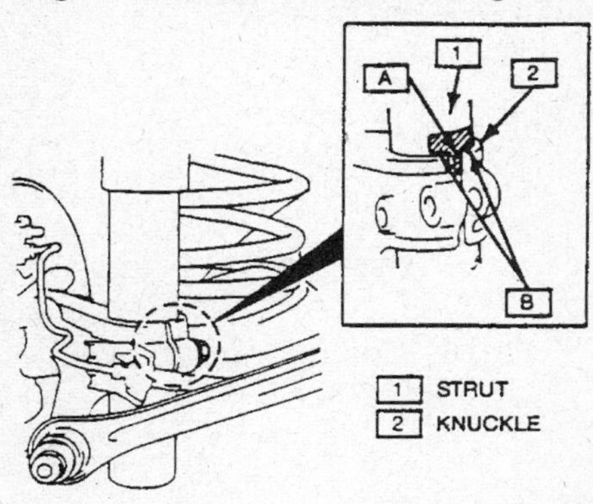

Fig. 4 Strut to rear suspension knuckle position

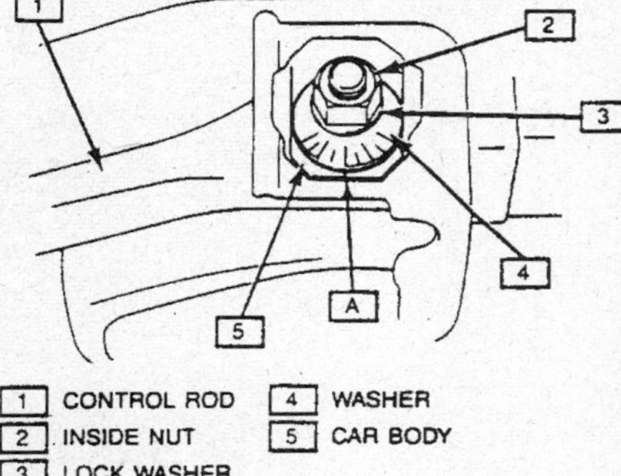

Fig. 5 Control rod inner bolt

6. Reverse procedure to install, noting the following:
   a. Position control rod to vehicle, **Fig. 9.**
   b. When installing control rod to body bracket, align marks made on washer and control rod during removal.
   c. **Do not tighten control rod mounting nuts and bolts until after vehicle has been lowered.**

KNUCKLE

REPLACE

1. Raise and support rear of vehicle, then remove wheel.
2. Remove brake drum and disconnect brake hose from rear suspension knuckle bracket.
3. Disconnect brake line from wheel cylinder. Cap brake line and wheel cylinder fitting bore.
4. Remove mounting bolts and brake backing plate.
5. Position suitable jack under suspension arm.
6. Place alignment marks on control rod and control rod washer at body bracket for setting toe during installation.
7. Remove control rod to body bracket mounting nut and washer.
8. Remove knuckle stud nut and control rod.
9. Remove strut to rear suspension knuckle mounting bolt.
10. Remove strut to suspension arm mounting bolt and separate rear suspension knuckle from suspension arm and strut. **If strut is difficult to remove, open slit on knuckle just enough to allow strut removal.**
11. Reverse procedure to install, noting the following:
    a. When installing control rod to body bracket, align marks made on washer and control rod during removal.
    b. Do not tighten control rod or suspension arm mounting nuts and bolts until after vehicle has been lowered.
    c. Prior to installation, apply sealer to mating surface of brake backing plate and rear suspension knuckle.
    d. When installing brake drum, tighten wheel bearing nut to specification and stake nut in place using suitable chisel.
    e. After completing installation, adjust and bleed brake system, then inspect for proper brake operation before moving vehicle.

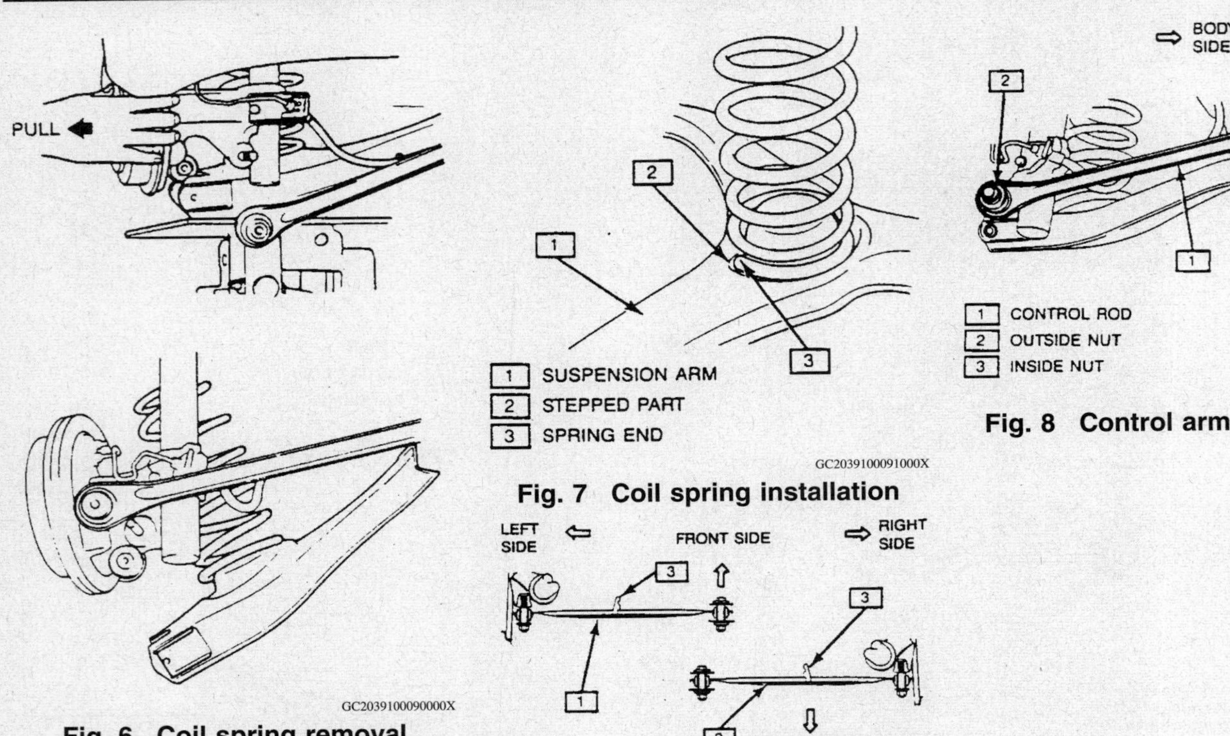

Fig. 6 Coil spring removal

Fig. 7 Coil spring installation

Fig. 8 Control arm installation

Fig. 9 Control arm installation

TIGHTENING SPECIFICATIONS

Year	Component	Torque/Ft. Lbs.
1998–2001	Brake Backing Plate	17
	Brake Line Bracket	17
	Brake Line Fitting To Wheel Cylinder	12
	Control Rod	59
	Rear Suspension Knuckle Arm Lower	27
	Spindle Nut	②
	Stabilizer Bar	19
	Stabilizer Link To Bar	38
	Stabilizer Link To Control Arm	19
	Strut Lower	44
	Strut Support	24
	Strut Upper	37
	Suspension Arm Front Mounting	33
	Suspension Arm To Knuckle	37
	Suspension Arm Rear	27
	Wheel Bearing	74①
	Wheel Lug Nuts	44

① — Tighten nut and stake in position.
② — Revised by Technical Service Bulletin: models less ABS, 74 ft. lbs.; models w/ABS, 120 ft. lbs.

Front Suspension & Steering

NOTE: On Air Bag Equipped Models, Refer To "Air Bag System Precautions" Located In The Front Of This Manual For System Disarming & Arming Procedures.

NOTE: Refer To "Computer Relearn Procedures" Located In The Front Of This Manual When Battery Power To The Computer Has Been Interrupted.

INDEX

PRECAUTIONS

AIR BAG SYSTEMS

Refer to "Air Bag System Precautions" in the front of this manual for system disarming and arming procedures.

BATTERY GROUND CABLE

Prior to service, disconnect battery ground cable and isolate as required.

HUB & BEARING

REPLACE

When inspecting wheel bearings, raise and support front of vehicle, then rotate wheel to inspect bearing for smoothness of rotation and noise. Also inspect wheel bearing endplay with a dial indicator. Wheel bearing endplay should not exceed .016 inch.

REMOVAL

1. Raise and support vehicle, then remove front wheel.
2. Unstake and remove hub mounting nut.
3. Remove mounting bolts and caliper with brake line attached. Suspend caliper from chassis with suitable wire.
4. Measure dimension A for assembly, **Fig. 1.** Pull hub out of knuckle.
5. Disconnect tie rod end from knuckle with tie rod end remover tool No. J21687-02, or equivalent.
6. Remove strut to knuckle bolts and ball joint stud pinch bolt, **Fig. 2.**
7. Remove knuckle.
8. Remove outer and inner bearing from knuckle using suitable drift.

INSTALLATION

1. Apply suitable grease to balls and oil seal lips of wheel bearings. Fill area A, **Fig. 3,** to approximately 40 percent of capacity with suitable grease.
2. Install wheel bearings using bearing installer tool No. J34856, or equivalent. **Install wheel bearings with sealed side facing outward. Ensure spacer is spacer is snug and centered between inner and outer bearings.**
3. Install wheel bearing seal (5) using seal installer tool No. J34881, or equivalent, **Fig. 3.**
4. Install spacer on hub with bevel side first, **Fig. 4.**
5. Ensure wheel bearing spacer bore is aligned with bearing bores. If not, move spacer until aligned.
6. Tap hub lightly into knuckle using suitable plastic hammer. Ensure alignment is maintained.
7. Drive hub until dimension A is obtained using wheel hub installer tool No. J34856 and handle tool No. J7079-2, or equivalents.
8. Install brake caliper.
9. Tighten caliper bolts to specifications.
10. Tighten driveshaft castle nut to specifications
11. Stake nut in position.
12. Install wheel and lower vehicle.

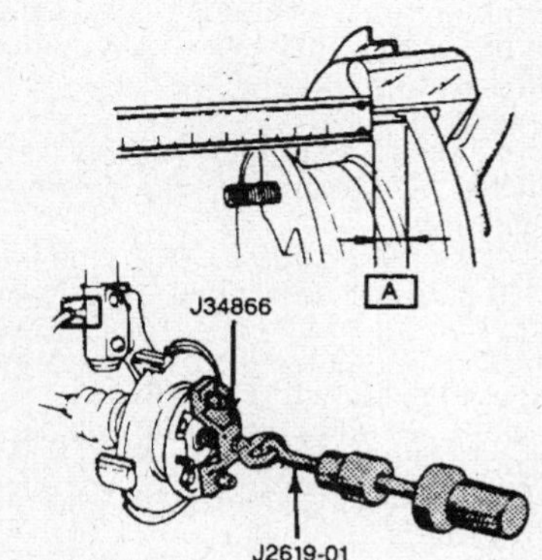

A NOTE DIMENSION "A" AS SHOWN BEFORE HUB REMOVAL AS AN AID IN INSTALLATION.

GC3039100228000X

Fig. 1 Hub installation inspection

STRUT

REPLACE

1. Raise and support vehicle allowing front suspension to hang free.
2. Remove front wheel.
3. Remove E-clip from brake hose and disengage hose from strut bracket, **Fig. 5.**
4. Support lower control arm and knuckle, then remove strut to knuckle bolts.
5. Remove upper strut mount nuts and strut.
6. Reverse procedure to install.

STRUT SERVICE

1. Mount strut in suitable spring compressor.
2. Compress spring approximately ½ inch.
3. Remove nut from strut shaft and remove components, **Fig. 6.**
4. Reverse procedure to assemble. Compress spring so strut shaft protrudes through cap by approximately one inch. Tighten nut to specifications.

CONTROL ARM

REPLACE

1. Raise and support vehicle, then remove wheel.
2. Remove ball joint stud to steering knuckle pinch bolt, **Fig. 7.**
3. Remove control arm bracket nut and bracket bolts.
4. Remove control arm and bracket.
5. If control arm bushing is to be replaced, proceed as follows:
   a. Remove lower control arm as outlined under "Lower Control Arm, Replace."
   b. Press rear bushing from control arm, **Fig. 7.**
   c. Cut flange off front bushing and press front bushing from control arm, **Fig. 8.**

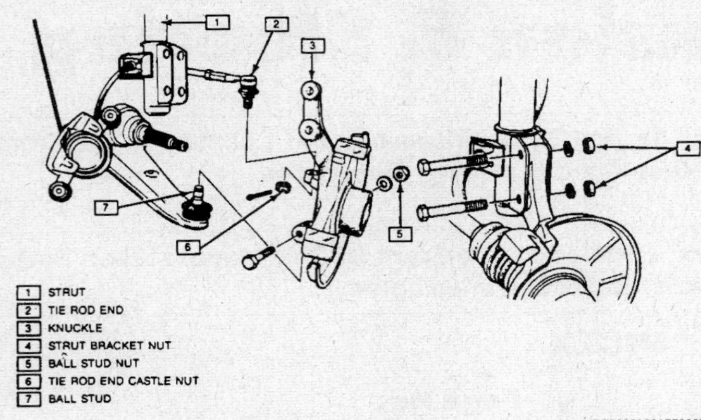

Fig. 2 Steering knuckle removal

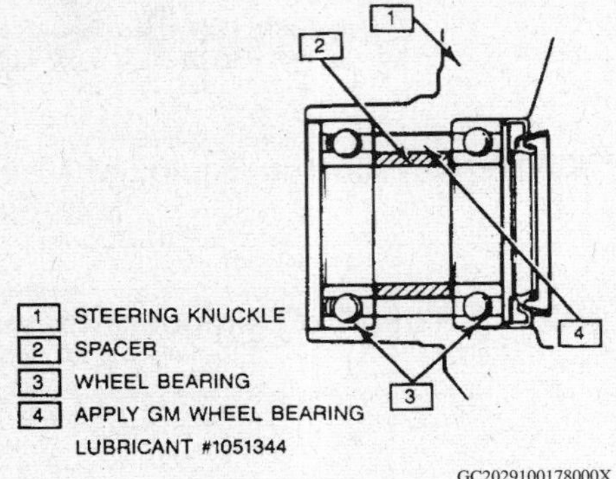

Fig. 3 Steering knuckle hub bearings & seal

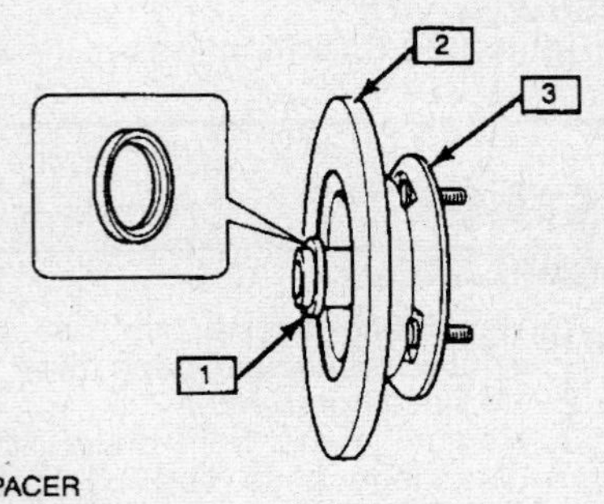

Fig. 4 Wheel hub spacer installation

d. Apply soap and water to outer surface of front bushing, then press front bushing into control arm until centered.
e. Position rear bushing to control arm and drive bushing into control arm, **Figs. 9 and 10.**

6. Reverse procedure to install.

POWER STEERING GEAR

REPLACE

1. Remove forward section of driver's side floor carpeting.
2. Remove steering shaft joint plastic cover, **Fig. 11.**
3. Loosen upper steering shaft joint bolt, **Fig. 12. Do not remove.**
4. Remove lower steering shaft joint bolt to separate shaft from pinion.
5. Raise and support vehicle.
6. Remove both front wheels.
7. Remove cotter pin and castle nut from each tie rod end nut, **Fig. 13.**
8. Separate tie rod ends from right and lefthand steering knuckles using tie rod end remover tool No. J21687-02, or equivalent, **Fig. 14.**
9. Remove front exhaust pipe assembly.
10. Remove shift linkage and extension rod from manual transaxle, if equipped.
11. Remove engine rear torque rod bracket from automatic transaxle, if equipped.
12. Remove steering gear outlet pipe, inlet pipe and cylinder pipe assemblies, **Fig. 15.**
13. Remove four attaching bolts from gear mounting brackets, **Fig. 16.**
14. Remove steering gear from vehicle as follows:
    a. Slide steering gear slightly to driver's side.
    b. Rotate steering gear counterclockwise so that pinion gear is between transaxle case and frame rail.
    c. Slide steering gear to passenger side until lefthand outer tie rod clears through frame opening.
    d. Lower steering gear on a 45 degree angle.
    e. Remove steering gear.
15. Reverse procedure to install, tighten to specifications.

MANUAL STEERING GEAR

REPLACE

1. Slide driver's seat rearward.
2. Pull back front of floor mat on driver's side and remove steering shaft joint cover.
3. Loosen steering shaft upper joint bolt without removing, **Fig. 17.**
4. Remove steering shaft lower joint bolt and disconnect lower joint from pinion.

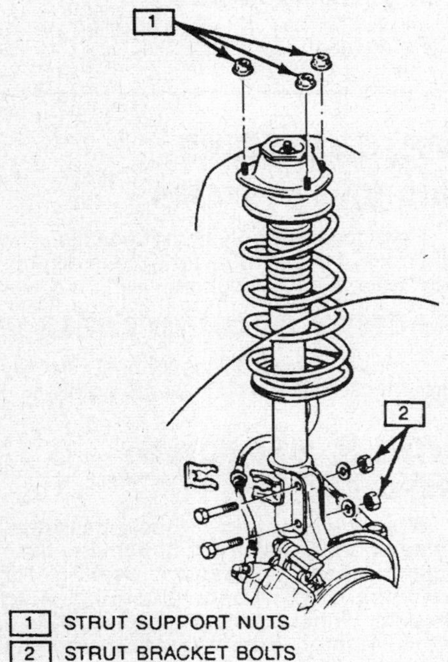

Fig. 5 Strut mounting nut bolt locations

5. Raise and properly support vehicle.
6. Remove front wheel and tire assemblies.
7. Remove cotter pins and castle nuts from tie rod ends.
8. Disconnect tie rods from knuckles using tie rod end remover tool No. J21687-02, or equivalent.
9. Remove steering gear housing mounting bolts, brackets and steering gear, **Fig. 18.**
10. Reverse procedure to install.

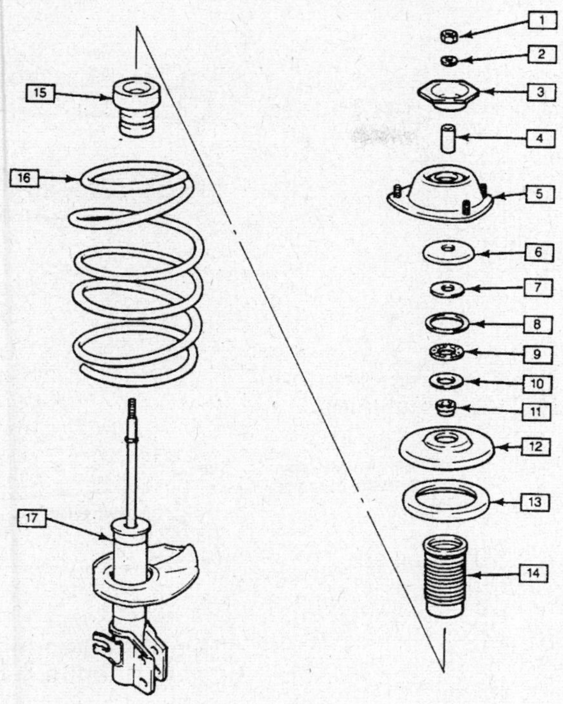

1 NUT
2 WASHER
3 STOPPER
4 INNER SPACER
5 SUPPORT COMP.
6 BEARING SEAT
7 BEARING UPPER WASHER
8 BEARING SEAL
9 BEARING
10 BEARING LOWER WASHER
11 BEARING SPACER
12 COIL SPRING UPPER SEAT
13 COIL SPRING SEAT
14 STRUT COVER
15 BUMP STOPPER
16 COIL SPRING
17 STRUT

GC2029100185000X

Fig. 6 Exploded view of strut

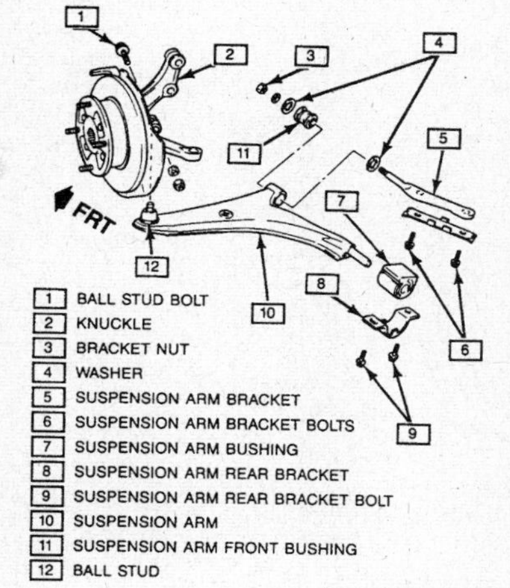

GC2029100180000X

Fig. 7 Lower control arm replacement

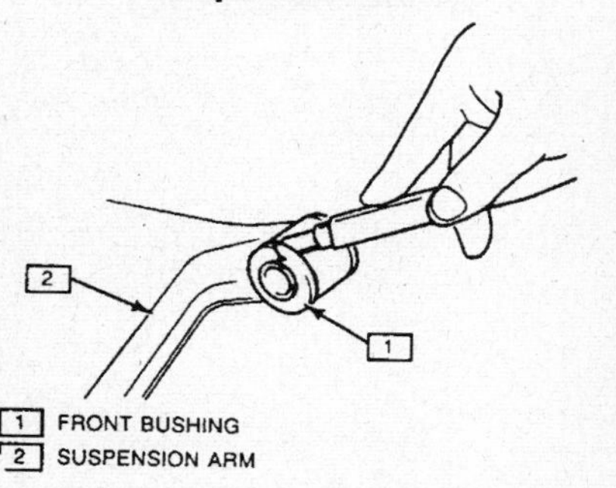

GC2029100181000X

Fig. 8 Cutting flange from control arm front bushing

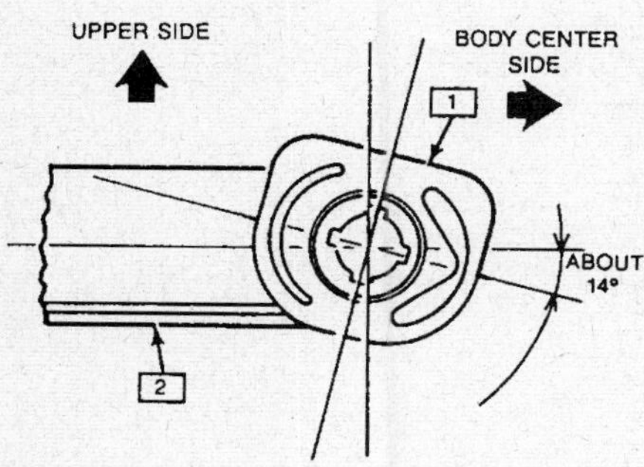

1 REAR BUSHING
2 SUSPENSION ARM

GC2029100182000X

Fig. 9 Rear bushing to control arm installation

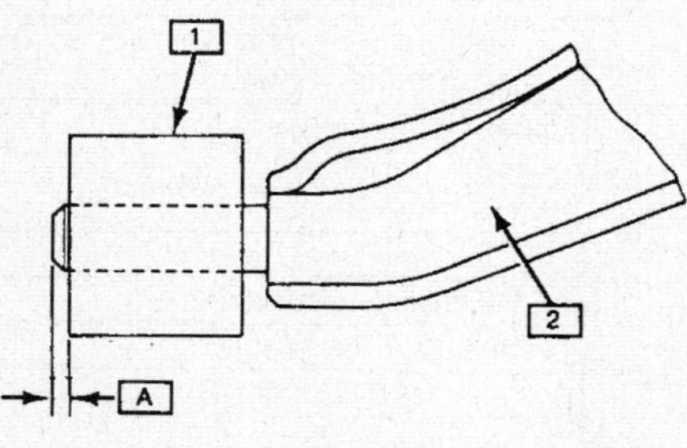

A 5mm ±1
1 REAR BUSHING
2 SUSPENSION ARM

GC2029100183000X

Fig. 10 Rear bushing positioning

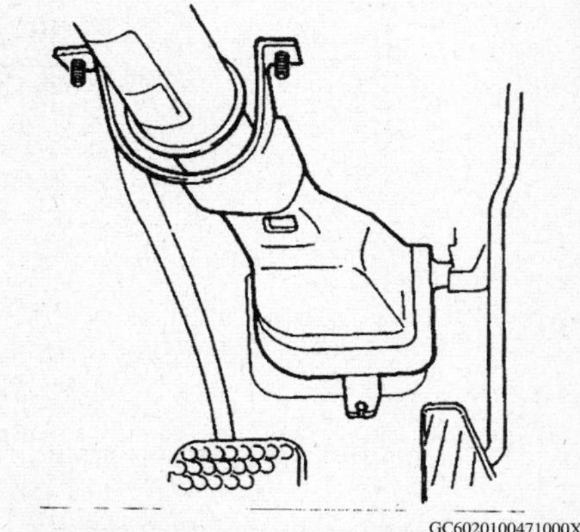

GC6020100471000X

Fig. 11 Steering shaft joint cover removal

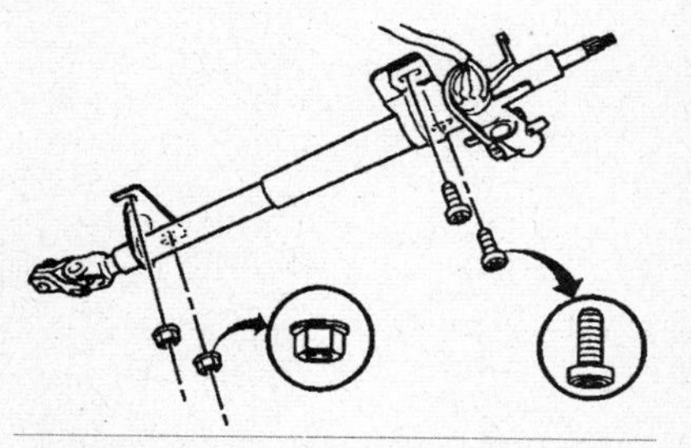

GC6020100472000X

Fig. 12 Upper steering shaft joint bolt

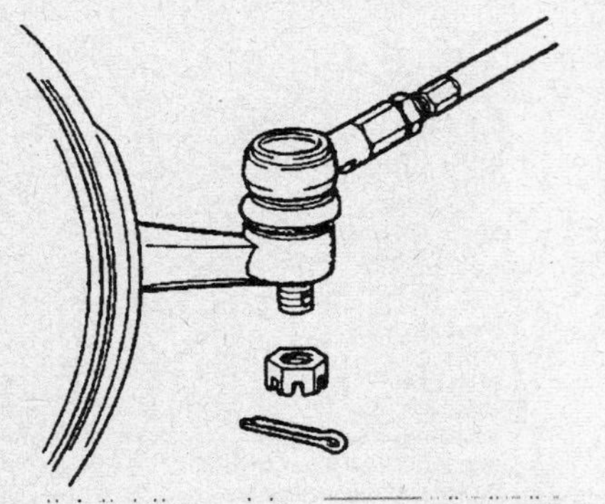

Fig. 13 Cotter pin & castle nut removal

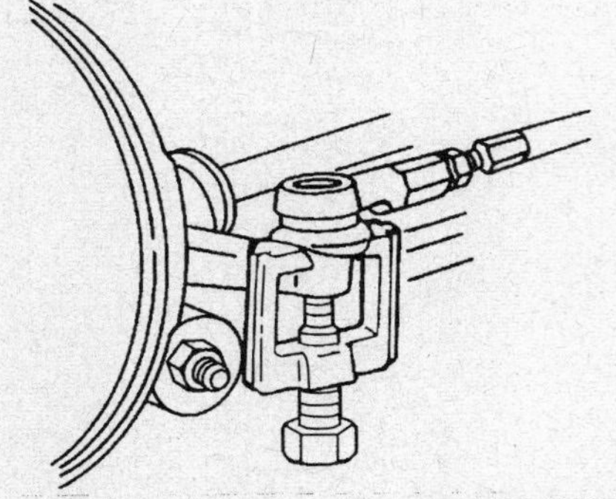

Fig. 14 Tie rod end remover tool No. J21687-02 installation

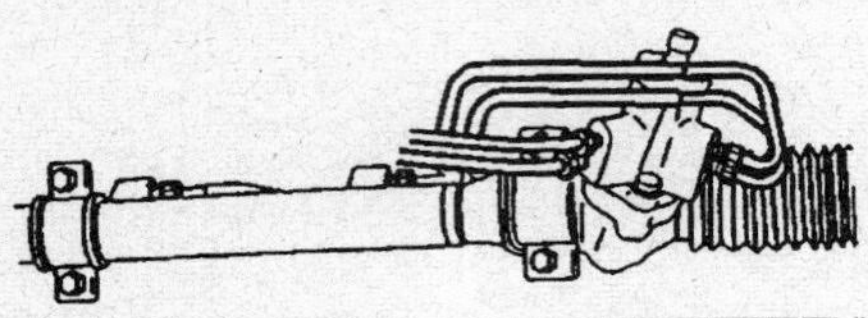

Fig. 15 Steering gear component removal

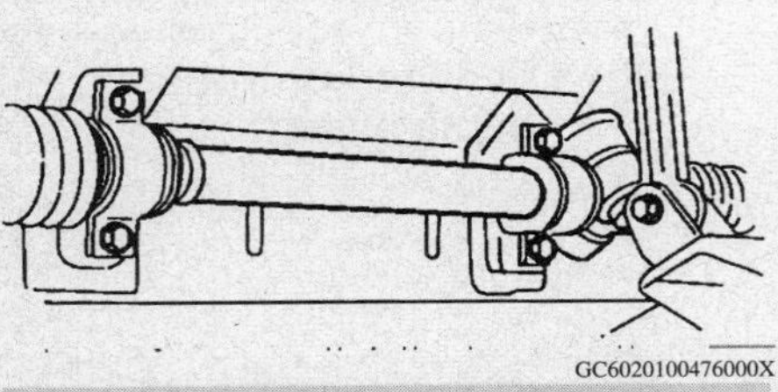

Fig. 16 Gear mounting bracket bolt removal

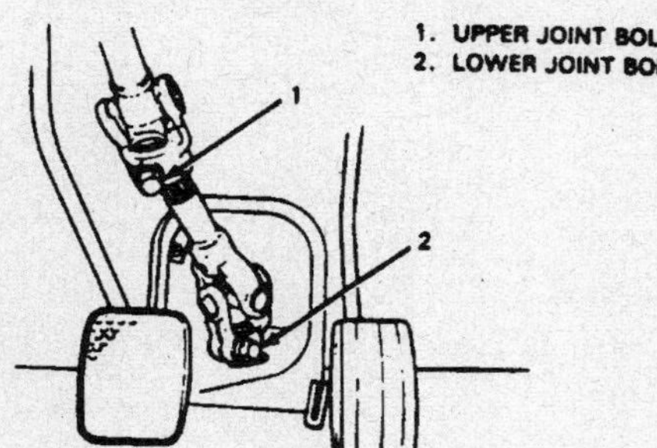

Fig. 17 Steering shaft upper & lower joint bolts

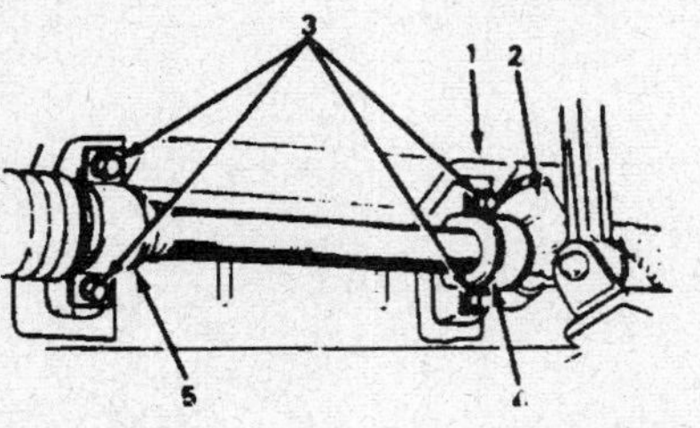

Fig. 18 Steering gear mounting bolts & brackets

TIGHTENING SPECIFICATIONS

Year	Component	Torque/Ft. Lbs.
1998–2001	Ball Joint Stud	44
	Brake Caliper To Knuckle	22
	Control Arm Front Bracket	66
	Control Arm Rear Bracket	32
	Front Control Arm Bracket	92
	Cylinder Pipe Assembly Nuts To Steering Shaft	20
	Cylinder Pipe Assembly Nuts To Pump	13
	Hub Bearing	129①
	Inlet & Outlet Pipes	29
	Stabilizer Bar Link	20
	Stabilizer Bar Mounting	20
	Steering Gear Mounting Bracket	18
	Steering Shaft Coupling	18
	Steering Shaft Joint Bolts	18
	Strut Bracket	59
	Strut Nut	37
	Strut Upper Mounting	21
	Tie Rod Ball	51
	Tie Rod End Castle	32
	Tie Rod End Locknut	32
	Wheel Lug Nuts	44

① — After tightening, stake nut in position.

Wheel Alignment

INDEX

DESCRIPTION

Wheel alignment, is the angular relationship between the wheels, suspension mounting components and ground. The angle of the knuckle away from the vertical, pointing in or out of wheels, tilt of the wheels from vertical (when viewed from front of vehicle) and tilt of suspension members from vertical (when viewed from side of vehicle), all of these are involved in proper alignment, **Fig. 1.**

CAMBER

Camber is the tilting of front and rear wheels from the vertical when viewed from front of vehicle. When wheels tilt outward at top, camber is positive (+). When wheels tilt inward, camber is negative (MI). Amount of tilt is measured in degrees from the vertical and this is camber angle.

CASTER

Caster is tilting of the front steering axis either forward or backward from the vertical (when viewed from side of vehicle). A backward tilt is positive (+) and a forward tilt is negative (–). On short and long arm type suspensions you cannot see a caster angle without using a special instrument, but if you look straight down from the top of the upper control arm to the ground you would find that ball joints do not line up (fore and aft) when a caster angle other than 0° is present.

TOE

Toe is the turning in or out of wheels. The purpose of toe is to ensure parallel rolling of wheels. Excessive toe-in or toe-out may increase tire wear. Toe also serves to offset small deflections of the suspension which occurs when vehicle is moving.

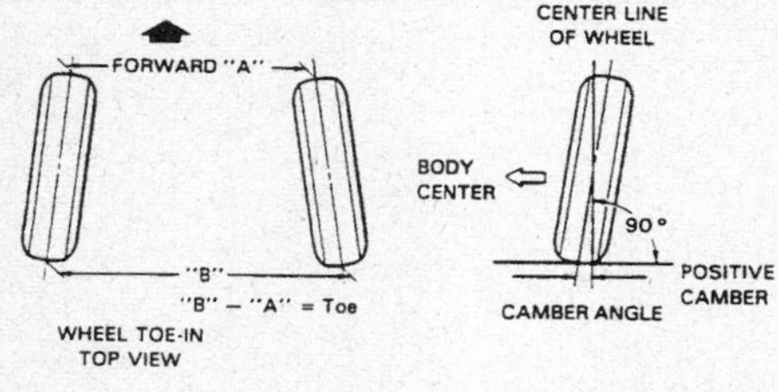

Fig. 1 Suspension geometry

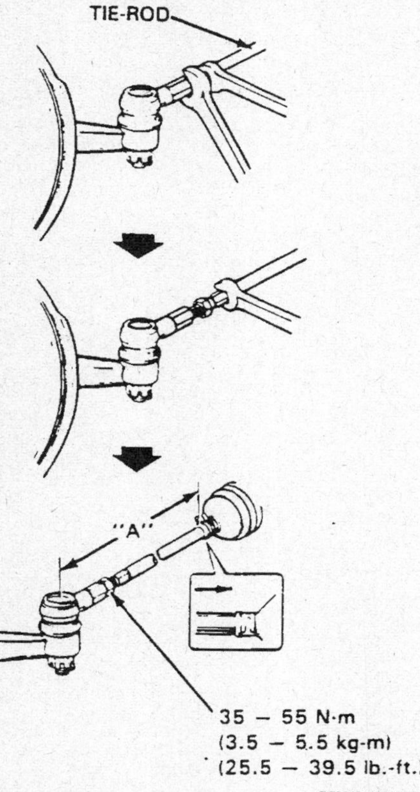

Fig. 2 Front wheel toe adjustment

PRELIMINARY INSPECTION

Steering and vibration problems are not always the result of alignment. An additional problem to be inspected is tire lead because of worn or improperly manufactured tires. "Lead" is the deviation of the vehicle from a straight path on a level road without hand pressure on the steering wheel.

To ensure correct alignment readings and alignment specifications, inspect as follows:

1. Inspect radial clearance between outer gear/rotor and crescent, tire for proper inflation and thread wear.
2. Inspect radial clearance between outer gear/rotor and crescent, for loose ball joints and tie rod ends. If there is excessive looseness, replace faulty components before adjusting toe.
3. Inspect radial clearance between outer gear/rotor and crescent, for wheel runout.
4. Inspect radial clearance between outer gear/rotor and crescent, trim heights. If not within specifications, correct before adjusting toe.
5. Inspect radial clearance between outer gear/rotor and crescent, for loose control arms.
6. Inspect radial clearance between outer gear/rotor and crescent, for loose or missing stabilizer bar components.

FRONT WHEEL ALIGNMENT

CAMBER & CASTER

1. Position vehicle on suitable alignment fixture following manufacturer's instructions and inspect caster and camber angles. Bumper should be bounced three times before inspection, to prevent incorrect reading.
2. Camber and caster cannot be adjusted. Should either be found out of specification, locate the cause first.
3. If improper alignment is caused by damaged, worn or loose suspension components, they should be replaced. If vehicle body or chassis is damaged, it should be repaired.

STEERING ANGLE

When a tie rod or tie rod end is replaced, inspect toe and steering angle with turning radius gauges. If steering angle is not correct, inspect left and righthand tie rods for equal length.

TOE

1. Loosen left and righthand tie rod end locknuts, **Fig. 2.**
2. Apply grease between tie rods and rack boots.
3. Turn left and righthand tie rods by same amount to align toe to specification. Left and righthand tie rods should become equal in length.
4. After adjustment, tighten locknuts and ensure rack boots are not twisted.

REAR WHEEL ALIGNMENT

CAMBER

Camber cannot be adjusted. Should camber be found out of specification, locate the cause. If improper alignment is caused by damaged, worn or loose suspension components, they should be replaced. If vehicle body or chassis is damaged, it should be repaired.

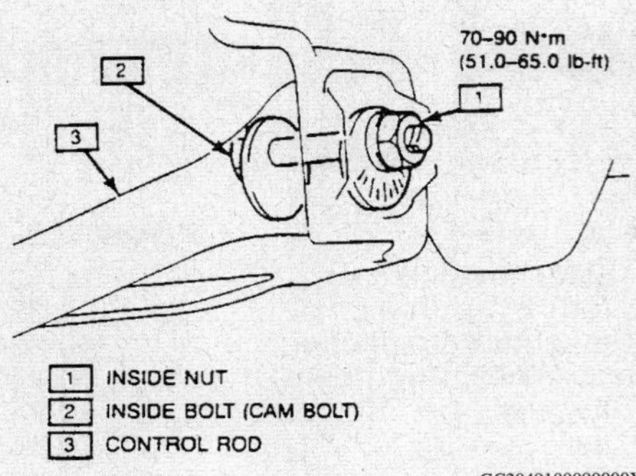

Fig. 3 Rear wheel toe adjustment

TOE

The rear wheel toe is adjusted by the inner control arm cam bolt, **Fig. 3.** If toe is found to out of specification, loosen left and righthand inner control arm cam bolt nuts, then rotate cam bolts by equal amounts to correct toe setting. After completing adjustment, **torque** cam bolt nuts to 51–65 ft. lbs.

PRIZM

NOTE: Refer To Rear Of This Manual For Vehicle Manufacturer's Special Service Tool Suppliers.

INDEX OF SERVICE OPERATIONS

Specifications

GENERAL ENGINE SPECIFICATIONS

Year	Engine Liter	Fuel System	Bore & Stroke, Inch	Compression Ratio	Net H.P. @ RPM	Maximum Torque, Ft. Lbs. @ RPM	Normal Oil Pressure, psi
1998–2000	1.8L	SFI	3.11 × 3.60	10	120 @ 5600	122 @ 4400	—
2001–02	1.8L	SFI	3.11 × 3.60	10	125 @ 5800	125 @ 4000	—

SFI — Sequential Fuel Injection

TUNE UP SPECIFICATIONS

Year & Engine①	Spark Plug Gap, Inch	Ignition Timing BTDC				Curb Idle Speed③		Fast Idle Speed		Fuel Pump Pressure, psi	Valve Clearance, Inch
		Firing Order Fig.②	Man. Trans.	Auto. Trans.	Mark Fig.	Man. Trans.	Auto. Trans.	Man. Trans.	Auto Trans.		
1998											
1.8L	.043	①	10°⑤	10°⑤	A	650–750	650–750N	④	④	44–50	⑥
1999–2002											
1.8L	.043	①	10°⑤	10°⑤	A	650–750	650–750N	④	④	44–50	⑥

BTDC — Before Top Dead Center
N — Neutral
① — Cylinder numbering front of engine to rear 1, 2 , 3, 4. Firing order, 1-3-4-2.
② — Before removing wires from coils or distributor cap, determine location of No. 1 wire, as distributor position may have been altered from that shown.
③ — When adjusting idle speed, set parking brake and block drive wheels.
④ — Electronically controlled.
⑤ — At 700 RPM w/jumper wire connected between terminals of check engine connector. Engine connector is located in the engine compartment on the lefthand inner fender.
⑥ — Intake, 0.006–0.010; exhaust, 0.010–0.014.

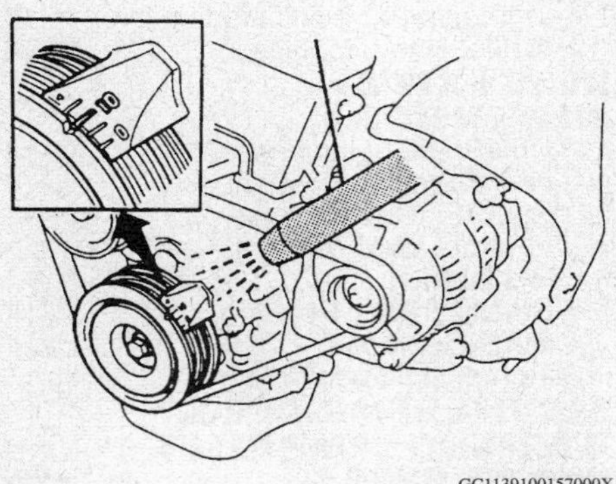

Fig. A

FRONT WHEEL ALIGNMENT SPECIFICATIONS

Year	Model	Caster Angle, Degrees		Camber Angle, Degrees				Toe-In, Inch	Toe Out On Turns, Degrees		Ball Joint Wear
		Limits	Desired	Limits		Desired			Outer Wheel	Inner Wheel	
				Left	Right	Left	Right				
1998–2002	All	+0.57 to +2.07	+1.32	–.93 to +0.57	–.93 to +0.57	–.18	–.18	.04	—	—	①

① — Refer to "Ball Joint Inspection" for proper testing procedure.

REAR WHEEL ALIGNMENT SPECIFICATIONS

Year	Model	Camber Angle, Degrees				Toe-In, Inch	Ball Joint Wear
		Limits		Desired			
		Left	Right	Left	Right		
1998–2002	All	–1.67 to –.17	–1.67 to –.17	–.92	–.92	.16	①

① — Replace ball joint if any looseness is detected or if ball joint seal is cut.

VEHICLE RIDE HEIGHT SPECIFICATIONS

Model	Year	Body Style	Manufacturer's Original Tire Size②	Measurement Points & Specifications①③					
				Front			Rear		
				Dim.	Specification		Dim.	Specification	
					Inches	mm		Inches	mm
Prizm	1998–2002	All	175 Tires	C	7.31	185	D	9.62	244
			185 Tires	C	7.50	190	D	9.81	249

C Dim. — Ground to Rocker Panel, Front
D Dim. — Ground to Rocker Panel, Rear
Dim. — Dimension
① — ±.0.39 in (10 mm) front to rear & side to side.
② — See door sticker or inside of glove box for manufacturer's original tire size specifications. If tires on vehicle do not match manufacturer's original tire size & measurement is not within limits, it will be necessary to refer to the "Non-Standard Tire & Wheel Size Adjustment To Ride Height Specification & Tire Size Adjustment Charts" in the front of this manual for approximate changes in ride height specifications.
③ — Measurement is with fuel, radiator coolant and engine oil full, spare tire, jack, hand tools and mats in designated positions and tires properly inflated.

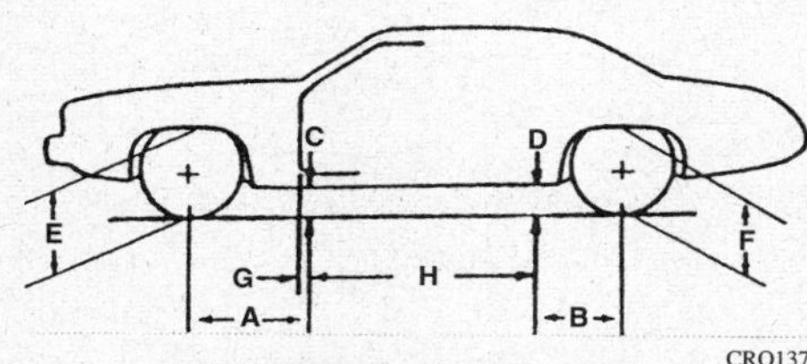

Dimensions C & D

FLUID CAPACITIES & COOLING SYSTEM DATA

Year	Engine	Coolant Capacity, Qts.		Coolant Type	Radiator Cap Relief Pressure, Lbs.	Thermo. Opening Temp., Deg. F	Fuel Tank, Gals.	Engine Oil Refill, Qts.	Transaxle Oil	
		Manual Trans.	Auto. Trans.						Man. Transaxle Qts.	Auto. Transaxle Qts.①
1998–2000	1.8L	6.1	6.0	Dex-Cool	13	180	13.2	3.7②	2	3.3
2001–02	1.8L	5.8	5.7	Dex-Cool	13	180	13.2	3.5	2	3.3

① — Approximate. Make final inspection w/dipstick.
② — Filter change, add 0.2 qt.

LUBRICANT DATA

Year	Model	Lubricant Type			
		Transaxle		Power Steering	Brake System
		Manual	Automatic		
1998–2002	All	①	Dexron III	Dexron III	DOT-3

① — Synthetic manual transmission fluid GM part No. 12346190, or an equivalent 75W-90 GL-4 gear oil.

Electrical

NOTE: On Air Bag Equipped Models, Refer To "Air Bag System Precautions" Located In The Front Of This Manual For System Disarming & Arming Procedures.

NOTE: Refer To "Computer Relearn Procedures" Located In The Front Of This Manual When Battery Power To The Computer Has Been Interrupted.

INDEX

PRECAUTIONS

AIR BAG SYSTEMS

Refer to "Air Bag System Precautions" in the front of this manual for system disarming and arming procedures.

BATTERY GROUND CABLE

Prior to service, disconnect battery ground cable and isolate as required.

FUSE PANEL & FLASHER LOCATION

Fuse and relay block No. 1 is located in the lefthand front of the engine compartment, left of the air cleaner.

Fuse and relay block No. 2 is located in lefthand front engine compartment, left of the battery.

Fuse and relay block No. 3 is located in the righthand front engine compartment.

An additional fuse block is located behind an access cover at the lefthand lower end of the instrument panel.

The hazard and turn signal flasher is located in Junction Block No. 1 under the lefthand body hinge pillar trim panel. The turn/hazard relay is the tallest of the relays in this block.

RELAY CENTER LOCATION

Refer to "Fuse Panel & Flasher Location" for relay center locations.

FUEL PUMP RELAY LOCATION

The circuit opening relay is located at the lower lefthand side of the passenger compartment, above the kick panel, **Fig. 1.**

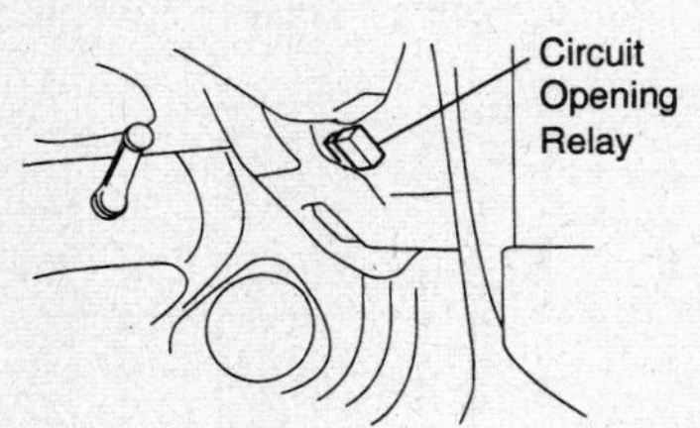

Fig. 1 Circuit opening relay location

STARTER

REPLACE

1. Remove starter motor upper mounting bolt.
2. Raise and support vehicle.
3. Remove righthand splash shield.
4. Disconnect starter electrical connectors and positive battery cable.
5. Remove lower mounting bolt and starter motor.
6. Reverse procedure to install, noting the following:
   a. **Torque** starter mounting bolts to 27 ft. lbs.
   b. **Torque** positive battery cable to starter mounting nut to 78 inch lbs.

IGNITION COIL

REPLACE

1998–99

1. Disconnect ignition coils' spark plug wires.
2. Disconnect electrical connectors.
3. Remove mounting bolts and coils.
4. Reverse procedure to install. **Torque** ignition coil mounting bolts to 77 inch lbs.

2000–02

1. Remove mounting bolts and nuts, retainers and engine cover.
2. Disconnect coils' electrical connectors.
3. Remove coil mounting bolts.
4. Remove mounting bolts and electrical harness
5. Remove ignition coils.
6. Reverse procedure to install. **Torque** ignition coil mounting bolts to 77 inch lbs.

IGNITION LOCK

REPLACE

1. Remove lower and upper steering column covers, **Fig. 2.**
2. Turn ignition switch to ACC position.
3. Push down stop pin and remove cylinder using suitable screwdriver, **Fig. 3.**
4. Reverse procedure to install.

IGNITION SWITCH

REPLACE

1. Remove ignition lock as described under "Ignition Lock, Replace."
2. Remove knee bolster trim panel and knee bolster, as required.
3. Disconnect ignition switch electrical connector.
4. Remove mounting screws and ignition switch.
5. Reverse procedure to install.

COMBINATION SWITCH

REPLACE

1. Remove lower and upper steering column covers.
2. Disconnect electrical connectors and remove combination switch.

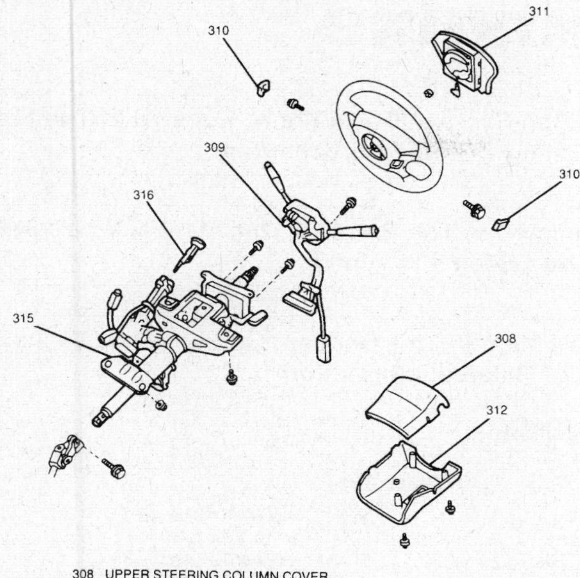

Fig. 2 Steering column exploded view

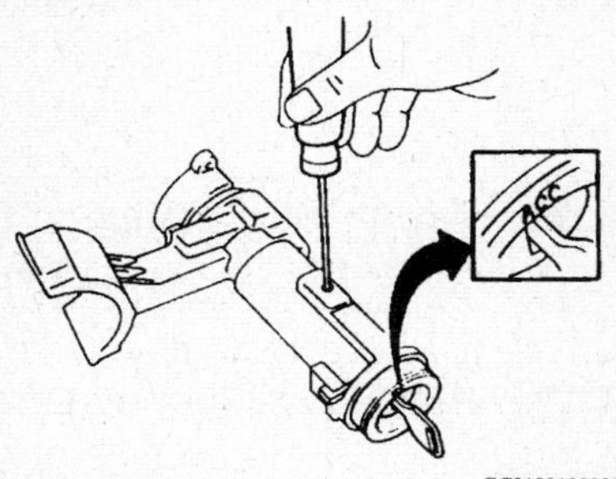

Fig. 3 Ignition lock cylinder removal

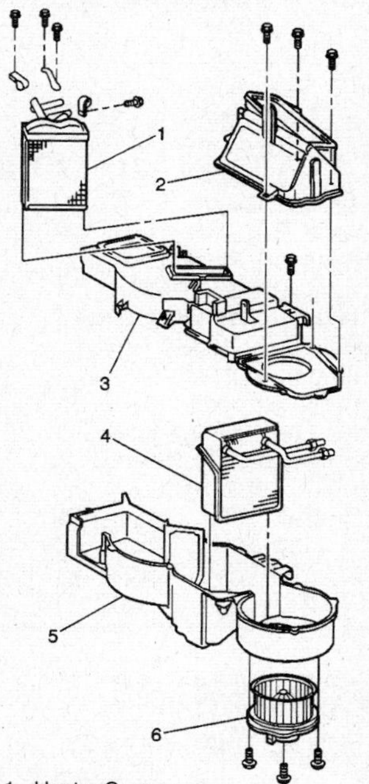

Fig. 4 Evaporator core replacement

3. Reverse procedure to install.

STEERING WHEEL

REPLACE

1. Remove air bag module as outlined in "Passive Restraint Systems" chapter.
2. Disconnect horn electrical connector.
3. Remove steering wheel mounting nut.
4. Mark steering wheel to steering shaft end relationship for installation alignment.
5. Remove steering wheel using steering wheel puller tool No. J-1859-A, or equivalent.
6. Reverse procedure to install. **Torque** steering wheel nut to 25 ft. lbs.

INSTRUMENT CLUSTER

REPLACE

1. Remove instrument cluster bezel screws and bezel by disengaging two lower clips.
2. Remove instrument cluster mounting screws and disconnect electrical connectors.
3. Carefully remove instrument cluster.
4. Reverse procedure to install.

RADIO

REPLACE

1. Remove instrument panel ashtray.
2. Gently pry and release six accessory trim plate to instrument panel mounting clips, using suitable taped flat-bladed tool.
3. Disconnect cigarette lighter and instrument panel ashtray bulb socket electrical connectors.
4. Remove lighter, as required.
5. Remove mounting screws and radio.
6. Disconnect radio electrical connections and antenna lead-in cable.
7. Reverse procedure to install.

WIPER MOTOR

REPLACE

1. Disconnect wiper motor electrical connector.
2. Remove wiper motor mounting bolts.
3. Disconnect wiper linkage from motor crank arm.
4. Remove wiper motor.
5. Reverse procedure to install.

BLOWER MOTOR

REPLACE

1. Remove glove compartment.
2. Disconnect blower motor electrical connector.
3. Remove mounting screws, blower motor and fan.
4. Reverse procedure to install.

HEATER CORE

REPLACE

1. Drain coolant into suitable container.
2. Recover refrigerant charge as outlined in "Air Conditioning" chapter.
3. Remove instrument panel as outlined in "Dash Panel Service" chapter.
4. Remove instrument panel reinforcement.
5. Disconnect blower motor, blower motor resistor and air conditioning compressor control module electrical connectors.
6. Disconnect heater hoses at heater core.
7. Remove speed control servo, as required.
8. Remove evaporator inlet and outlet tubes.
9. Separate rear heater ducts from HVAC module.
10. Remove HVAC module mounting nuts.
11. Carefully pull HVAC module out.
12. Remove brackets and heater core.
13. Reverse procedure to install.

EVAPORATOR CORE

REPLACE

1. Remove heater core as previously under "Heater Core, Replace."
2. Remove blower motor cover, **Fig. 4.**
3. Remove HVAC module case halves' mounting screws.
4. Separate case halves.
5. Remove evaporator core.
6. Reverse procedure to install.

1.8L Engine

NOTE: On Air Bag Equipped Models, Refer To "Air Bag System Precautions" Located In The Front Of This Manual For System Disarming & Arming Procedures.

NOTE: Refer To "Computer Relearn Procedures" Located In The Front Of This Manual When Battery Power To The Computer Has Been Interrupted.

NOTE: Prior To Performing Any Service Operations Listed In This Section, Consult The "Technical Service Bulletins" Section For Related Information.

INDEX

PRECAUTIONS

AIR BAG SYSTEMS

Refer to "Air Bag System Precautions" in the front of this manual for system disarming and arming procedures.

BATTERY GROUND CABLE

Prior to service, disconnect battery ground cable and isolate as required.

FUEL SYSTEM PRESSURE RELEASE

1. Loosen fuel filler cap to release fuel tank pressure.
2. Disconnect circuit opening relay electrical connector.
3. Start engine and allow it to run until it stalls from lack of fuel.
4. Crank engine for an additional three seconds to release remaining fuel pressure.
5. Connect circuit opening relay connector and install radio.
6. Tighten fuel filler cap.

COMPRESSION PRESSURE

Compression readings should be 218 psi, with a minimum of 145 psi. Maximum difference between cylinders should be 15 psi.

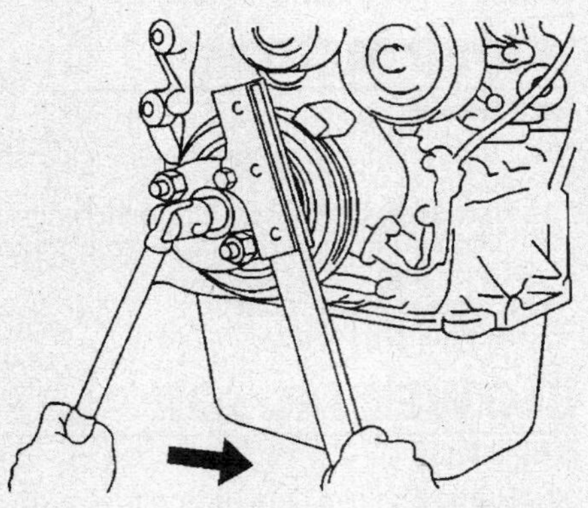

Fig. 1 Crankshaft pulley removal (Part 1 of 2)

ENGINE MOUNT

REPLACE

1. Raise and support engine using engine support tool No. J-28467-360, or equivalent.
2. Remove three righthand side engine mount to frame bracket bolts.
3. Remove righthand side engine mount to engine bracket bolts.
4. Raise engine slightly to provide clearance for engine mount removal.
5. Remove righthand side engine mount.
6. Remove righthand side engine mount to frame bracket.
7. Remove righthand side engine mount to engine bracket.
8. Reverse procedure to install.

ENGINE

REPLACE

1. Relieve fuel system pressure as outlined under "Precautions."
2. **On models equipped with air conditioning,** recover refrigerant charge as outlined in "Air Conditioning" then remove A/C compressor.
3. **On all models,** drain coolant and engine oil into suitable containers.
4. Remove washer hose at hood.
5. Make hood as installation alignment.
6. Remove mounting bolts and hood.
7. Remove spark plug wires from spark plugs and position aside.
8. Remove mounting bolts and ignition coil with plug wires attached.
9. Remove accessory drive belt.
10. **On models equipped with manual transaxle,** proceed as follows:
    a. Remove crankshaft pulley.
    b. Remove alternator.
    c. Remove drive belt tensioner.
11. **On all models,** remove accelerator cable from throttle body.
12. Remove accelerator cable from bracket.
13. **On models equipped with automatic transaxle,** proceed as follows:
    a. Remove transmission Throttle Valve (TV) cable from throttle body.

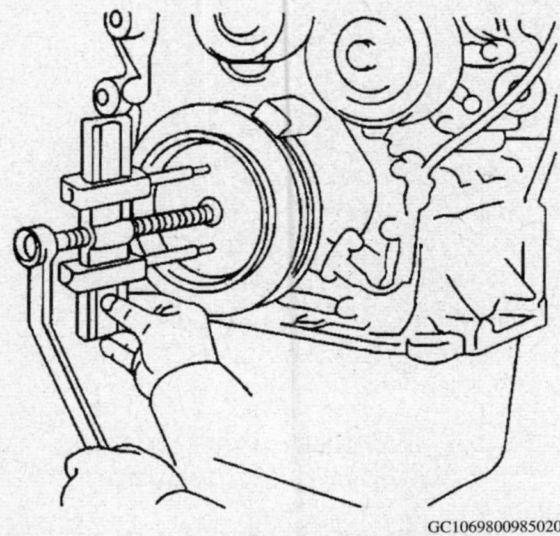

Fig. 1 Crankshaft pulley removal (Part 2 of 2)

b. Remove transmission TV cable from accelerator cable bracket.
14. **On all models,** disconnect Intake Air Temperature (IAT) sensor.
15. Remove air cleaner hose and cap.
16. Remove mounting bolt and Vacuum Switching Valve (VSV) bracket from air cleaner lower case.
17. Remove air filter.
18. Remove mounting bolts and air cleaner lower box.
19. Remove upper radiator hose and washer fluid tank mounting bolt. Position washer fluid tank aside.
20. Disconnect washer pump connector and fluid line. Plug line to prevent fluid leakage.
21. Remove upper alternator mounting bolt.
22. Remove mounting bolt and engine lift hook ground wire.
23. Disconnect hoses and electrical connectors, as required.
24. Disconnect oxygen sensor electrical connector.
25. Remove mounting nuts, oxygen sensor and gasket.
26. Remove bracket bolts and wiring harness brackets.
27. Free engine harness from its routing and position it aside.
28. Remove thermostat housing lower radiator hose.
29. Remove upper starter bolt.
30. Remove mounting bolts, then lower left and righthand side splash shields.
31. Disconnect starter motor electrical connections.
32. Remove lower mounting bolt and starter.
33. **On models equipped with automatic transmission,** remove six torque converter bolts.
34. **On all models,** remove through bolts, nuts and power steering pump.
35. Position power steering pump aside.
36. Remove exhaust pipe to manifold mounting bolts and springs.
37. Remove mounting bolts and axle shaft boot heat shield.
38. Remove lower transmission to engine mounting bolts and lower vehicle.
39. Install suitable engine hoist and remove upper transmission to engine mounting bolts.
40. Remove mounting bolts, nuts and righthand side mounting insulator.
41. Remove righthand side engine mounting bolts and bracket.
42. Ensure wires and hoses are positioned aside.
43. Remove engine and place on heavy duty automotive engine stand tool No. J-36854, or equivalent.
44. Reverse procedure to install. Tighten mounting bolts to specifications.

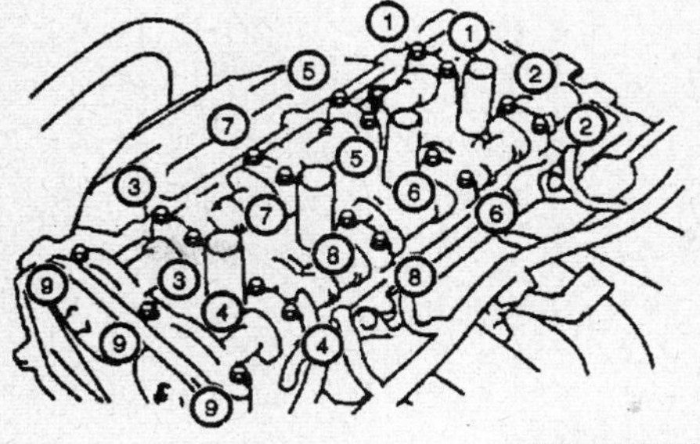

Fig. 2 Camshaft bearing cap loosening sequence

INTAKE MANIFOLD

REPLACE

1. Drain coolant into suitable container.
2. Disconnect accelerator cable from throttle body.
3. **On models equipped with automatic transaxle,** disconnect TV cable.
4. **On all models,** disconnect IAT sensor electrical connector at air cleaner.
5. Disconnect air cleaner hose from throttle body.
6. Remove air cleaner top.
7. Disconnect following components from throttle body:
   a. Throttle Position Sensor (TPS).
   b. Idle Air Control (IAC) valve connector.
   c. Manifold Absolute Pressure (MAP) sensor connector.
   d. Coolant bypass hose clamps and hoses.
8. Disconnect fuel injector electrical connectors.
9. Remove mounting bolts and fuel injector wiring harness from intake manifold.
10. Remove mounting bolts and intake manifold support bracket.
11. Disconnect upper radiator hose at radiator. Position hose aside.
12. Remove upper radiator hose support bracket bolt and nut.
13. Remove intake manifold mounting bolts and nuts.
14. Remove upper radiator hose support bracket.
15. Disconnect vacuum lines at intake manifold.
16. Remove injector harness support brackets and intake manifold with throttle body attached.
17. Reverse procedure to install.

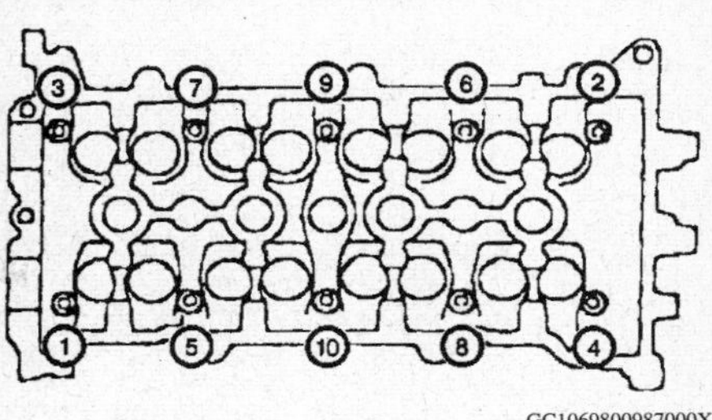

Fig. 3 Cylinder head bolt loosening sequence

EXHAUST MANIFOLD

REPLACE

1. Disconnect Heated Oxygen Sensor (HO2S1) electrical connector.
2. Remove oxygen sensor nuts and gasket from exhaust pipe.
3. Raise and support vehicle.
4. Remove exhaust manifold bolts, springs and gasket.
5. Remove manifold support bracket mounting bolt and lower vehicle.
6. Remove mounting bolts and upper heat insulator.
7. Remove mounting nuts, exhaust manifold and gasket.
8. Remove mounting bolts and lower heat insulator.
9. Reverse procedure to install.

CYLINDER HEAD

REPLACE

1. Drain coolant and engine oil into suitable containers.
2. Remove mounting bolt and position washer fluid tank aside.
3. Disconnect washer pump connector and washer pump fluid line. Plug line.
4. Remove accessory drive belt.
5. Disconnect alternator electrical connector and positive cable at alternator.
6. Remove mounting bolts and alternator.
7. Remove accelerator cable from throttle body.
8. Disconnect IAT sensor, TP sensor and MAP sensor electrical connectors.
9. Remove air cleaner hose and cap.
10. Remove throttle body clamps and coolant bypass hose.
11. Disconnect temperature sensor and fuel injector electrical connectors.
12. Remove upper radiator hose.
13. Remove mounting bolts and fuel injector harness from intake manifold. Position harness above intake manifold.
14. Remove mounting bolts and intake manifold support bracket.
15. Disconnect required vacuum hoses.
16. Remove fuel injector harness brackets.
17. Disconnect oxygen sensor electrical connector.
18. Remove mounting nuts, oxygen sensor and bracket.
19. Raise and support vehicle.
20. Remove mounting bolts and springs from exhaust pipe at manifold.

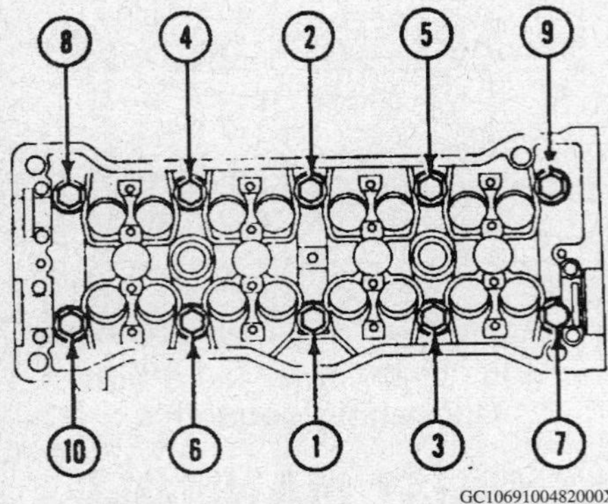

Fig. 4 Cylinder head bolt tightening sequence

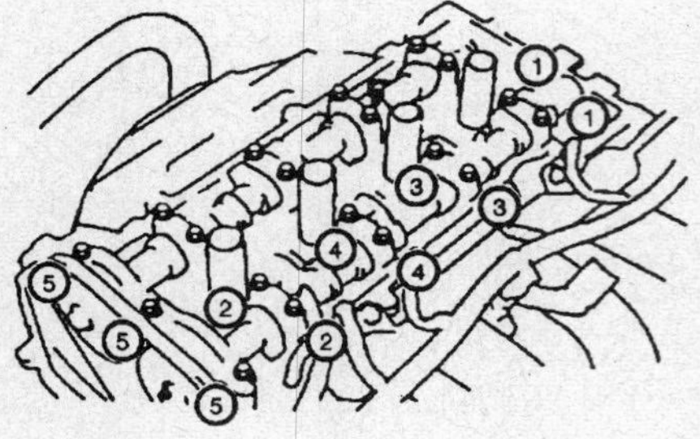

Fig. 5 Intake camshaft cap tightening sequence

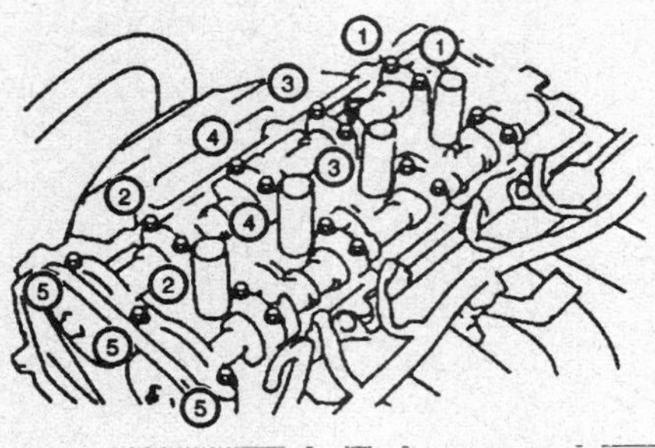

Fig. 6 Exhaust camshaft cap tightening sequence

21. Remove exhaust pipe to manifold seal and one exhaust manifold to support bracket bolt.
22. Lower vehicle.
23. Support engine using engine support fixture tool No. J-28467-A, or equivalent.
24. Remove righthand side mounting insulator mounting bolts and nuts.
25. Loosen air conditioning receiver pinch clamp and lift air conditioning receiver to access righthand side mounting insulator.
26. Remove righthand side mounting insulator.
27. Disconnect ignition coil electrical connectors.
28. Remove injector fuel rail hold-down clamp and spark plug wires from cylinder head cover.
29. Remove mounting bolts and ignition coils with spark plug wires attached.
30. Disconnect fuel line at fuel rail.
31. Remove cylinder head mounting bolts and ground wires.
32. Position injector harness aside and remove heater hose at cylinder head water bypass pipe.
33. Remove mounting bolt and camshaft sensor.
34. Remove engine coolant temperature sensor.
35. Remove cylinder head cover PCV hoses and valve.
36. Remove mounting bolts and cylinder head cover.
37. Place No. 1 piston at Top Dead Center (TDC) and align camshaft timing sprockets.
38. Disconnect power steering pressure switch electrical connector.
39. Raise and support vehicle.
40. Remove righthand side lower engine splash shield.
41. Remove through-bolts and power steering pump. Position pump aside.
42. Remove bolt and crankshaft pulley while holding crankshaft pulley, **Fig. 1.**
43. Remove mounting bolt and crankshaft position sensor.
44. Lower vehicle.
45. Remove mounting nut, bolt and drive belt tensioner.
46. Remove mounting bolts and righthand engine mounting bracket.
47. Remove mounting bolts and timing chain tensioner.
48. Remove mounting bolts, nuts and timing chain cover.
49. Remove crank sensor reluctor, timing chain slipper bolt and slipper.
50. Remove crankshaft sprocket and timing chain.
51. Remove mounting bolts and camshaft sprockets.
52. Remove camshaft bearing cap bolts in sequence, **Fig. 2.**
53. Remove bearing caps and camshafts.
54. Remove valve lifters. Keeping lifters in original order.
55. Raise engine using suitable floor jack. **Protect oil pan with suitable wooden block.**
56. Position holding fixture.
57. Remove cylinder head bolts in sequence, **Fig. 3.**
58. Remove cylinder head.
59. Reverse procedure to install, noting the following:
    a. **Torque** cylinder head bolts to 18 ft. lbs. in sequence, **Fig. 4.**
    b. **Torque** cylinder head bolts to 36 ft. lbs. in sequence.
    c. Tighten bolts an additional 90° in sequence.
    d. Install intake camshaft.
    e. **Torque** camshaft cap bolts No. 1–4 to 10 ft. lbs. in sequence, **Fig. 5.**
    f. **Torque** bolts Nos. 5 to 17 ft. lbs.
    g. Install exhaust camshaft.
    h. **Torque** camshaft cap bolts No. 1–4 to 10 ft. lbs. in sequence, **Fig. 6.**
    i. **Torque** bolts Nos. 5 to 17 ft. lbs.

VALVE CLEARANCE SPECIFICATIONS

Year	Intake	Exhaust
1998–2002	.006–.010	.010–.014

VALVE ADJUSTMENT

Measure and adjust valve clearance while the engine is cold.

1. Remove cylinder head cover.
2. Set No. 1 cylinder at TDC on compression stroke.
3. Turn crankshaft to align groove in crankshaft pulley with 0 mark on No. 1 front cover. **Ensure valve lifters on No. 1 cylinder have freeplay. If not, rotate crankshaft pulley 360° and align 0 mark on front cover.**
4. Measure and record valve lash clearance between intake cam lobes and lifters on cylinder Nos. 1 and 2. Record any clearances which do not meet specifications.
5. Measure and record valve lash clearance between exhaust cam lobes and lifters on cylinder Nos. 1 and 3. Record any clearances which do not meet specifications.
6. Rotate crankshaft pulley 360° and align 0 mark on front cover.
7. Measure and record valve lash clearance between intake cam lobes and lifters on cylinder Nos. 3 and 4. Record any clearances which do not meet specifications.
8. Measure and record valve lash clearance between exhaust cam lobes and lifters on cylinder Nos. 2 and 4. Record any clearances which do not meet specifications.
9. If clearance is not within specifications, refer to "Hydraulic Lifters, Replace."

HYDRAULIC LIFTERS

REPLACE

1. Remove timing chain as described under "Timing Chain, Replace."
2. Remove intake camshaft as described under "Cylinder Head, Replace."
3. Remove valve lifters, as required.
4. Measure removed lifter's thickness using outside micrometer tool No. J-26900-1, or equivalent.
5. Refer to recorded measurement for location.
6. Compare measurements and select valve lifter to provide proper clearance. Lifters are available in 35 different sizes ranging from .1992–.2260 inch in .0008 inch increments.

TIMING CHAIN

REPLACE

1. Drain coolant into suitable container.
2. Remove windshield washer fluid reservoir mounting bolt. Position reservoir to side.
3. Disconnect windshield washer pump connector and fluid line. Plug line.
4. Remove tension from drive belt tensioner by moving tensioner in clockwise direction.
5. Remove accessory drive belt and alternator.

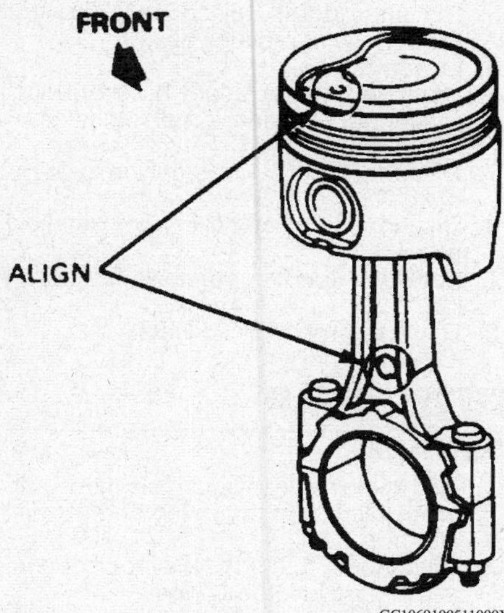

Fig. 7 Piston & rod assembly

6. Support engine using engine support fixture tool No. J-28467-A, or equivalent.
7. Remove righthand side engine mount mounting bolts and nuts.
8. Loosen air conditioning receiver pinch clamp and lift receiver to access righthand side engine mount.
9. Remove righthand side engine mount.
10. Remove cylinder head cover.
11. Rotate No. 1 piston to TDC and align camshaft timing sprockets.
12. Raise and support vehicle.
13. Remove righthand side lower engine splash shield.
14. Disconnect power steering oil pressure switch electrical connector.
15. Remove through-bolts and power steering pump from mount. Position pump aside with hoses attached.
16. Remove mounting bolt and crankshaft pulley while holding crankshaft pulley, **Fig. 1.**
17. Remove mounting bolt and crankshaft position sensor.
18. Lower vehicle and remove drive belt tensioner nut.
19. Remove mounting bolt and drive belt tensioner.
20. Remove three mounting bolts and righthand engine mounting bracket.
21. Remove mounting bolts and timing chain tensioner.
22. Remove mounting bolts, nuts and timing chain cover.
23. Remove crankshaft sensor reluctor, slipper bolts and slipper.
24. Remove timing chain dampener bolt, dampener, shoe bolts and shoe.
25. Remove crankshaft sprocket and timing chain.
26. Reverse procedure to install, noting the following:
    a. Align camshaft timing marks.
    b. Turn crankshaft until crankshaft keyway faces upward.

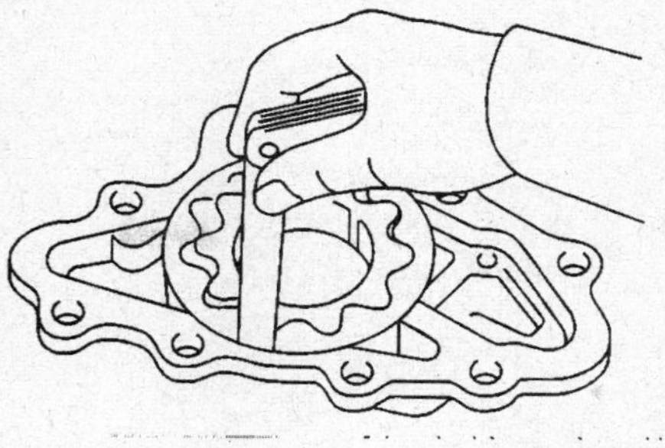

Fig. 8 Oil pump gear to housing clearance inspection

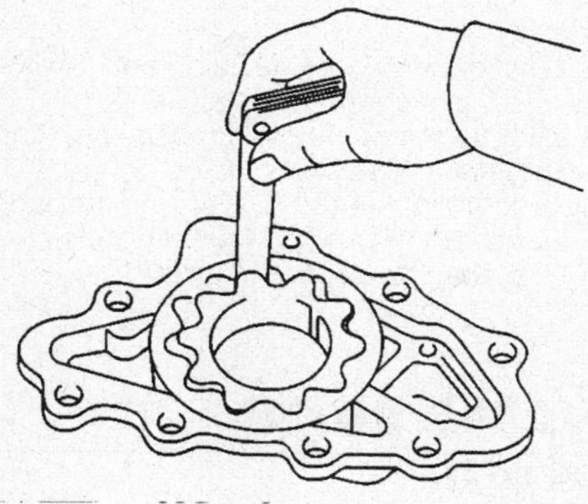

Fig. 10 Oil pump gear tip clearance inspection

CAMSHAFT

REPLACE

Refer to "Cylinder Head, Replace."

PISTON & ROD ASSEMBLY

Refer to **Fig. 7** for piston and rod assembly.

MAIN & ROD BEARINGS

Main bearings are available in four sizes, marked 1–4. If replacing a bearing, replace with one having the same number. If the number of the bearing cannot be determined, select a bearing according to the numbers imprinted on the cylinder block and crankshaft. For example, a 4 block and a 3 crankshaft equals a 7, which calls for bearing No. 3. Totals 0–2 require bearing No. 1. Totals 3–5 require bearing No. 2. Totals 6–8 require bearing No. 3 and totals 9–11 require bearing No. 4.

Rod bearings are available in three sizes, marked 1–3. If replacing a bearing, replace with one having the same number as marked on the connecting rod.

Tighten main bearings as follows:

1. **Torque** main bearing cap to 16 ft. lbs.
2. **Torque** to 32 ft. lbs.
3. **Torque** to 32 ft. lbs.
4. Finally, tighten an additional 90°.

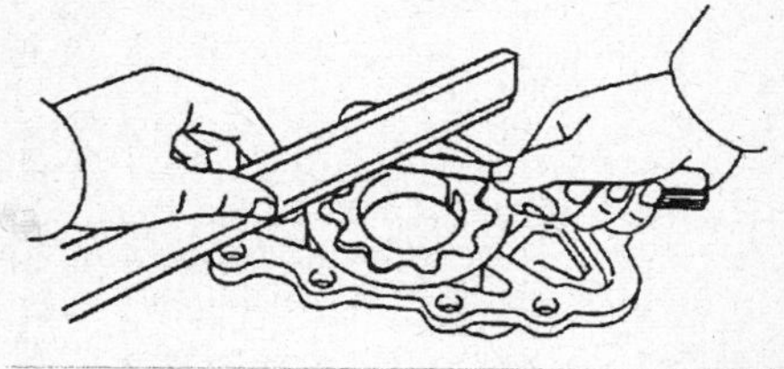

Fig. 9 Oil pump side clearance inspection

CRANKSHAFT REAR OIL SEAL

REPLACE

REMOVAL

1. Remove transaxle as described in "Clutch & Manual Transaxle" section or "Automatic Transmission/Transaxle" chapter.
2. Mark flywheel to crankshaft position and remove flywheel.
3. Remove rear end plate, as required.
4. Pry out old seal using suitable screwdriver with tape-wrapped tip.

INSTALLATION

1. Apply suitable multi-purpose grease to new seal's lip.
2. Carefully tap new seal into place until its surface is flush with retainer edge using suitable hammer.
3. Install flywheel. Ensuring marks are properly aligned.
4. Apply sealant part No. 12345493, or equivalent, to bolt threads.
5. Install transaxle.

OIL PAN

REPLACE

1. Raise and support vehicle.
2. Drain engine oil into suitable container.
3. Remove righthand lower engine splash shield.
4. Remove mounting nuts, bolts and oil pan. **Avoid damaging lower cylinder block oil pan contact surface.**
5. Remove mounting bolts and oil strainer, as required.
6. Reverse procedure to install. Apply continuous bead of silicone sealant part No. 12346240, or equivalent, to engine oil pan mating surface.

OIL PUMP

REPLACE

1. Remove timing chain as described under "Timing Chain, Replace."
2. Remove mounting bolts and pump. Discard gasket.
3. Inspect pump condition as follows:
4. Measure radial clearance between pump outer gear and housing, **Fig. 8.** Replace outer gear or complete pump if clearance is more than 0.0138 inch.

5. Measure side clearance between pump gears and straightedge, **Fig. 9.** Replace gears if clearance is more than 0.0059 inch.
6. Measure tip clearance between gear tips, **Fig. 10.** Replace gears if clearance is more than 0.0138 inch.
7. Reverse procedure to install. Tighten mounting bolts to specifications.

BELT TENSION DATA

This engine is equipped with a serpentine drive belt. Tension is controlled by an automatic tensioner.

SERPENTINE DRIVE BELT

ROUTING

Refer to **Fig. 11** for serpentine drive belt routing.

REMOVAL

1. Remove belt tension using a suitable wrench to rotate tensioner clockwise.
2. Remove belt with pressure applied to wrench and tension relieved from drive belt.

INSTALLATION

1. Raise and support vehicle.
2. Remove righthand side lower engine splash shield.
3. Rotate belt tensioner clockwise using suitable wrench.
4. Route and install drive belt onto drive pulleys with pressure applied to wrench.
5. Release belt tensioner.
6. Install righthand side lower engine splash shield.

COOLING SYSTEM BLEED

This engine does not require a specific bleeding procedure. After filling cooling system, bring engine to operating temperature with radiator/pressure cap off. Air will then be automatically bled through cap opening.

THERMOSTAT

REPLACE

1. Drain engine coolant into suitable container.

Fig. 11 Serpentine drive belt routing

2. Disconnect engine coolant switch electrical connector.
3. Remove mounting nuts, housing, thermostat and gasket or O-ring.
4. Ensure gasket or O-ring contact surfaces are clean and free of debris.
5. Reverse procedure to install.

WATER PUMP

REPLACE

1. Drain coolant into suitable container.
2. Remove engine accessory drive belt.
3. Raise and support vehicle.
4. Remove engine righthand side lower splash shield.
5. Remove mounting bolts, water pump and O-ring.
6. Reverse procedure to install.

RADIATOR

REPLACE

1. Drain coolant into suitable container.
2. Raise and support vehicle.
3. Remove engine left and righthand splash shields.
4. **On models equipped with automatic transaxle,** disconnect transaxle fluid cooler hoses at radiator.
5. **On all models,** disconnect radiator lower hose at radiator.
6. Lower vehicle.
7. Remove radiator upper bracket bolts.
8. Disconnect cooling fan electrical connectors.
9. Disconnect radiator upper hose at radiator.
10. Disconnect radiator filler neck overflow hose.
11. Carefully remove radiator and cooling fan.
12. Reverse procedure to install.

FUEL PUMP

REPLACE

1. Remove rear seat cushion, floor service hole cover mounting screws and cover.
2. Disconnect fuel sender electrical connector and fuel feed hose.
3. Remove fuel return hose.
4. Remove mounting bolts and fuel sender.
5. Remove fuel pump by pulling lower side off bracket.
6. Disconnect fuel pump electrical connector.
7. Remove rubber cushion and strainer.
8. Reverse procedure to install.

FUEL FILTER

REPLACE

1. Remove fuel pump and level sender as previously described.
2. Remove fuel pump.
3. Separate fuel filter from level sender.
4. Reverse procedure to install.

TECHNICAL SERVICE BULLETINS

ENGINE RUNS HOT, OVERHEATS, LOSSES COOLANT

1998–2000 MODELS

On some of these models the engine may run hot, overheat or loss coolant.

This condition may be caused by radiator filler neck sealing surface imperfections.

To correct this condition, polish filler neck using suitable 400 grit wet/dry sandpaper backed with flat piece of wood. **Do not replace radiator.**

TIGHTENING SPECIFICATIONS

Year	Component	Torque/Ft. Lbs.
1998–2002	Alternator (14mm)	18
	Alternator (17mm)	40
	Axle Shaft Heat Shield	13
	Camshaft Bracket	③
	Camshaft Sensor	11
	Camshaft Sprocket	33
	Connecting Rod Cap Bolts	15②
	Coolant Inlet Pipe	11
	Crankshaft Main Bearing Cap Bolts	④
	Crankshaft Position Sensor	106①
	Crankshaft Pulley	105
	Cylinder Head	③
	Drive Belt Tensioner, Bolt	51
	Drive Belt Tensioner, Nut	21
	Engine Mounting Bracket	40
	Exhaust Manifold Bracket	26
	Exhaust Manifold Heat Shield	11
	Exhaust Manifold	36
	Exhaust Pipe	46
	Flywheel, Automatic Transaxle	61⑧
	Flywheel, Manual Transaxle	36⑧
	Front Transaxle Mount	44
	Front Transaxle Mount Through-Bolt	64
	Fuel Injector Wiring Harness	106①
	Ground Wire	78①
	Guide Tube	84①
	Heat Insulator	106①
	Heated Oxygen Sensor	30
	Ignition Coil Bracket	78①
	Intake Manifold	13
	Intake Manifold Support Bracket	37
	Lower Transmission To Engine	47
	Mounting Insulator, Bolt	47
	Mounting Insulator, Nut	38
	Oil Drain Plug	26
	Oil Pan	⑤
	Oil Pump	⑤
	Oil Strainer	⑤
	Oxygen Sensor	14
	Power Steering Pump	29
	Radiator Upper Support Bracket	106①
	Starter	⑥
	Thermostat Housing	80①
	Timing Chain Cover (10mm)	89①
	Timing Chain Cover (12mm)	13
	Timing Chain Cover (13mm)	14
	Timing Chain Slipper, Lefthand	80①
	Timing Chain Slipper, Righthand	20
	Timing Chain Tensioner	89①
	Torque Converter	26
	Washer Fluid Tank	80①
	Water Bypass Pipe To Cylinder Head	80①
	Water Pump	⑦

① — Inch lbs.
② — Tighten an additional 90°.
③ — Refer to "Cylinder Head, Replace" for tightening specifications and sequence.
④ — Refer to "Main & Rod Bearings" for tightening specifications.
⑤ — 1998, 79 inch lbs.; 1999–2002, 97 inch lbs.
⑥ — 1998, 29 ft. lbs.; 1999–2002, 22 ft. lbs.
⑦ — 1998, 10 ft. lbs.; 1999–2002, 106 inch lbs.
⑧ — Tighten an additional 90°.

Clutch & Manual Transaxle

NOTE: On Air Bag Equipped Models, Refer To "Air Bag System Precautions" Located In The Front Of This Manual For System Disarming & Arming Procedures.

NOTE: Refer To "Computer Relearn Procedures" Located In The Front Of This Manual When Battery Power To The Computer Has Been Interrupted.

INDEX

PRECAUTIONS

AIR BAG SYSTEMS

Refer to "Air Bag System Precautions" in the front of this manual for system disarming and arming procedures.

BATTERY GROUND CABLE

Prior to service, disconnect battery ground cable and isolate as required.

ADJUSTMENTS

CLUTCH PEDAL

1. If height, **Fig. 1,** is not 5.45–5.84 inches, adjust as follows:
   a. Remove lower instrument finish panel and air duct.
   b. Loosen locknut.
   c. Turn stopper bolt until clutch pedal height is 5.12–5.51 inches.
   d. Tighten locknut.
2. If freeplay is not .197–.591 inch, adjust as follows:
   a. Depress clutch pedal until resistance is felt.
   b. Loosen locknut.
   c. Turn pushrod until freeplay is .197–.591 inch.
   d. Tighten locknut.
3. Install air duct and lower instrument panel finish panel.

HYDRAULIC SYSTEM SERVICE

HYDRAULIC SYSTEM BLEED

1. Remove cap and fill reservoir with suitable brake fluid.
2. Connect one end of clear vinyl tube to bleeder screw and insert other end of tube into half filled container of brake fluid.
3. Slowly pump clutch pedal several times.

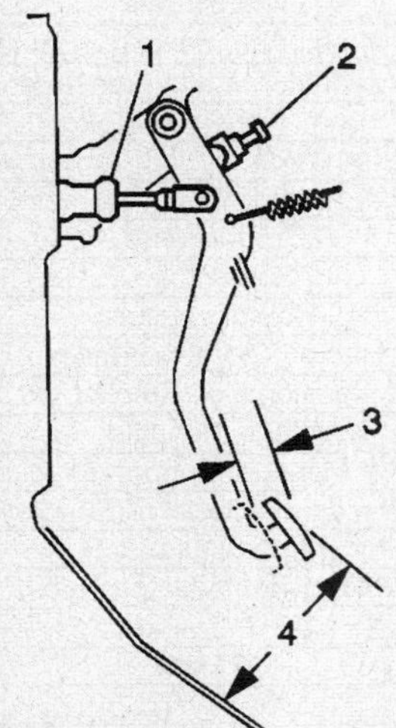

1- Pushrod
2- Locknut
3- Clutch Pedal Freeplay
4- Height

GC5049700099000X

Fig. 1 Clutch pedal adjustment

4. While pumping clutch pedal, loosen bleeder screw until fluid starts to runout.
5. Tighten bleeder screw.
6. Repeat procedure until no air bubbles exist in escaping fluid.

CLUTCH PEDAL POSITION SWITCH

REPLACE

1. Disconnect CPP switch electrical connector.
2. Remove CPP switch from clutch and brake pedal bracket by turning switch counterclockwise.
3. Remove locknut.
4. Reverse procedure to install, noting the following:
   a. Connect digital multimeter tool No. J-39200, or equivalent, to CPP switch electrical connector.
   b. Depress clutch pedal to floor and let it out .6–1.2 inches from floor.
   c. Adjust CPP switch by threading it into pedal bracket until continuity exists.
   d. Tighten CPP switch locknut to specifications.

CLUTCH ACTUATOR

REPLACE

1. Raise and support vehicle.
2. Disconnect clutch hydraulic line at actuator.
3. Remove mounting bolts and actuator.
4. Reverse procedure to install. Bleed system as described under "Hydraulic System Bleed."

CLUTCH PEDAL

REPLACE

1. Remove knee bolster.
2. Remove instrument panel compartment.
3. Remove Daytime Running Lamp (DRL) mounting brackets to instrument panel mounting screws.
4. Disconnect DRL control module electrical connector.
5. Remove DRL control module with mounting brackets attached.
6. Remove one screw and lefthand air duct.
7. Remove clutch pedal return spring, clevis clip and pin.
8. Disconnect Clutch Pedal Position (CPP) switch electrical connector.
9. Remove clutch pedal bracket to clutch master cylinder mounting nuts.
10. Remove bracket to instrument panel bolts and pedal.
11. Reverse procedure to install.

CLUTCH

REPLACE

1. Remove transaxle as described under "Transaxle, Replace."

2. Lock flywheel in place using lock tool No. J-35271, or equivalent.
3. Loosen each set bolt one turn at time until spring tension is released.
4. Remove mounting bolts and clutch.
5. Remove release bearing fork and boot from transaxle.
6. Reverse procedure to install.

TRANSAXLE

REPLACE

1. Remove battery and air cleaner case.
2. Remove three clutch line bracket bolts.
3. Remove mounting bolts, clutch release cylinder and line.
4. Disconnect backup lamp switch and vehicle speed sensor electrical connectors.
5. Disconnect ground cable at transaxle.
6. Disconnect transaxle control cables.
7. Remove starter and transaxle upper side mounting bolts.
8. Support engine using universal support fixture tool No. J-28467-A, or equivalent.
9. Remove lefthand engine mount mounting bolts
10. Lower transaxle side and remove lefthand engine mount.
11. Raise and support vehicle, then remove front wheels.
12. Remove left and righthand engine under covers.
13. Drain transaxle fluid into suitable container.
14. Remove left and righthand driveshafts.
15. Remove mounting bolts and heat insulator.
16. Support suspension crossmember using suitable jack.
17. Remove stabilizer bar bushing bracket mounting bolts, as required.
18. Remove mounting bolts, nuts front sub-frame and lower suspension arm.
19. Disconnect starter electrical connector and wiring.
20. Remove lower side and starter mounting bolt.
21. Slightly raise transaxle and remove transaxle lower side mounting bolts.
22. Lower transaxle lefthand side and separate transaxle from engine.
23. Reverse procedure to install.

TIGHTENING SPECIFICATIONS

Year	Component	Torque/Ft. Lbs.
1998–2002	Actuator & Line Bracket	15
	Actuator Bracket To Instrument Panel	106①
	Back-Up Lamp Switch	17
	Center Crossmember To Main Crossmember	45
	Center Crossmember To Radiator Support	45
	Center Mount To Transaxle	45
	Center & Rear Mounting	45
	Clutch Cover	17
	Clutch Master Cylinder	106①
	Clutch Pedal Bracket To Instrument Panel	11
	Clutch Pedal Position Switch Locknut	115①
	Flywheel, Manual Transaxle	36②
	Front Mount	45
	Front Mount Bracket	45
	Lower A-Frame To Underbody	159
	Main Crossmember To Underbody	167
	Master Cylinder	15
	Mount Bracket	45
	Mount Cover	45
	Mount Through-Bolt	44
	Oil Drain & Fill Plugs	15
	Pedal Bracket To Instrument Panel	11
	Starter	27
	Transaxle To Engine, Lower	34
	Transaxle To Engine, Upper	11
	Vehicle Speed Sensor	53①

① — Inch lbs.

② — Tighten an additional 90°.

Rear Axle & Suspension

NOTE: On Air Bag Equipped Models, Refer To "Air Bag System Precautions" Located In The Front Of This Manual For System Disarming & Arming Procedures.

NOTE: Refer To "Computer Relearn Procedures" Located In The Front Of This Manual When Battery Power To The Computer Has Been Interrupted.

INDEX

HUB & BEARING

REPLACE

1. Raise and support vehicle, then place suitable jack stands under suspension support.
2. Lower vehicle slightly. Ensure weight rests on suspension supports and not arms.
3. Remove tire and wheel assembly.
4. Remove brake drum.
5. Remove mounting bolt and disconnect wheel speed sensor, as required.
6. Remove mounting bolts, and axle hub.
7. Remove and discard backing plate O-ring.
8. Reverse procedure to install. Coat new O-ring with GCLB grease part No. 1051344, or equivalent.

KNUCKLE

REPLACE

1. Remove rear wheel hub as described under "Hub & Bearing, Replace."
2. Remove brake hose brake pipe and backing plate.
3. Disconnect wheel speed sensor, as required.
4. Remove backing plate from rear suspension knuckle.
5. Remove mounting bolt and trailing arm.
6. Remove mounting bolt and lateral link.
7. Remove mounting bolts, nuts and strut.
8. Remove knuckle.
9. Reverse procedure to install, noting the following:
   a. Secure knuckle to strut and tighten mounting bolts.
   b. Install lateral links to knuckle and secure with bolt and nut. **Do not fully tighten now.**
   c. Lower vehicle to ground.
   d. Install trailing arm to knuckle. Tighten lateral link mounting bolts to specifications.

STRUT

REPLACE

1. Remove rear lower seat cushion and rear seatback side cushion.
2. Raise and support vehicle, then place suitable jack stands under suspension support.
3. Lower vehicle slightly. Ensure weight rests on jack stands and not suspension arms.
4. Remove rear wheels.
5. Disconnect ABS speed sensor wiring harness clamp from strut.
6. Remove brake hose brake pipe.
7. Remove bracket clip and brake hose,
8. Prevent master cylinder reservoir from draining by connecting brake pipe to brake hose.
9. Disconnect wheel speed sensor wire harness from strut, as required.
10. Remove stabilizer shaft joint from strut.
11. Remove rear suspension knuckle strut mounting bolts and nuts.
12. Remove suspension support jack stands and lower vehicle.
13. Remove strut support mounting nuts.
14. Remove strut.
15. Reverse procedure to install.

COIL SPRING

REPLACE

1. Remove strut as described under "Strut, Replace."
2. Mount strut compressor tool No. J-34013 into holding fixture tool No. J-3289-20, or equivalents.
3. Mount strut into compressor tool using strut compressor adapter tool No. J-34013-88, or equivalent.
4. Carefully compress coil spring. **Do not compress too far.**
5. Remove strut rod piston nut.
6. Carefully release compressed spring and remove it from strut.
7. Reverse procedure to install.

STABILIZER BAR

REPLACE

1. Raise and support rear of vehicle, then remove rear wheels.
2. Scribe alignment marks between stabilizer shaft bushings, clamps, shaft and body.
3. Remove brake hose from strut.
4. Remove both stabilizer bar links and bushings.
5. Remove left and righthand stabilizer shaft joints.
6. Remove left and righthand stabilizer shaft bushing retainers.
7. Remove stabilizer shaft bushings.
8. Support fuel tank, then remove rear fuel tank bands mounting bolts and allow bands to hang.
9. Support suspension crossmember using suitable jack.
10. Remove six suspension crossmember to body mounting bolts.
11. Lower suspension crossmember.
12. Disconnect EVAP canister hoses.
13. Disconnect fuel filler neck and vapor hoses from fuel tank.
14. Remove stabilizer shaft by aiming it toward lefthand side of vehicle.
15. Reverse procedure to install.

LATERAL LINK & TRAILING ARM

REPLACE

1. Raise and support vehicle.
2. Remove rear tires and wheels.
3. Remove mounting bolts, nuts and trailing arm.
4. Reverse procedure to install. Adjust wheel alignment as required.

TIGHTENING SPECIFICATIONS

Year	Component	Torque/Ft. Lbs.
1998–2002	Axle Hub To Knuckle	59
	Brake Pipe Fittings	11
	Crossmember To Body, Inner	14
	Crossmember To Body, Outer	55
	Fuel Tank Band	29
	Lateral Link	89
	Resonator/Intermediate Pipe To Converter	32
	Resonator/Intermediate Pipe To Muffler	14
	Stabilizer Bar Joint To Shaft	33
	Stabilizer Shaft Bushing	14
	Strut	29
	Stabilizer Bar Joint To Strut	33
	Strut To Knuckle	105
	Trailing Arm	67
	Wheel Speed Sensor	69①

① — Inch lbs.

Front Suspension & Steering

NOTE: On Air Bag Equipped Models, Refer To "Air Bag System Precautions" Located In The Front Of This Manual For System Disarming & Arming Procedures.

NOTE: Refer To "Computer Relearn Procedures" Located In The Front Of This Manual When Battery Power To The Computer Has Been Interrupted.

INDEX

PRECAUTIONS

AIR BAG SYSTEMS

Refer to "Air Bag System Precautions" in the front of this manual for system disarming and arming procedures.

BATTERY GROUND CABLE

Prior to service, disconnect battery ground cable and isolate as required.

DESCRIPTION

The front suspension is a McPherson strut design, **Fig. 1.** The upper end of the strut is anchored to the body by a strut support. The strut and strut support are isolated by a rubber mount. The lower end of the strut is connected to the upper end of the steering knuckle. The lower end of the knuckle is attached to the ball joint, which is attached to the suspension control arm assembly. Movement of the steering wheel is transmitted to the tie rod end and then to the knuckle, turning the wheel and tire assembly.

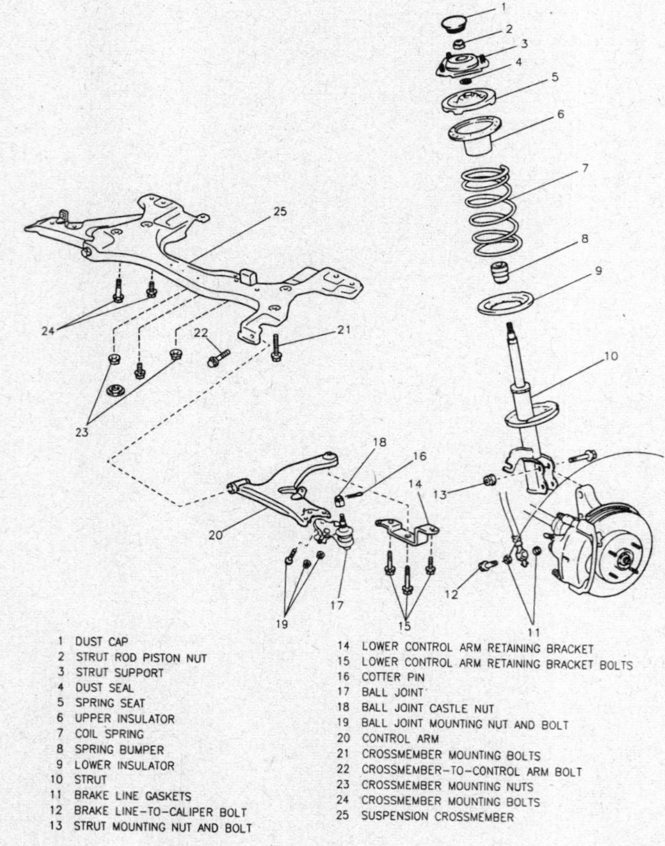

Fig. 1 Disassembled view of front suspension

WHEEL HUB

REPLACE

1. Remove knuckle as outlined in "Steering Knuckle, Replace."
2. Mount knuckle in suitable soft-jawed vise.
3. Record installation direction and remove dust deflector using suitable screwdriver.
4. Remove inner grease seal using seal remover tool No. J-26941 and slide hammer tool No. J-23907, or equivalents, **Fig. 2.**
5. Remove inner bearing snap ring and disc brake dust shield.
6. Push out hub using hub remover tool Nos. J-25287 and J-35378, or equivalents.
7. Remove outer bearing race using hub remover tools.
8. Remove outer grease seal using suitable seal remover tool and slide hammer.
9. Remove bearing using bearing remover tool No. J-22912-01, or equivalent, and suitable press.
10. Remove wheel bearing using driver handle tool No. J-8092 and side bearing installer tool No. J-21784, or equivalents.
11. Remove inner race and receiver cup.

12. Reverse procedure to install, noting the following:
    a. Install hub bearing using bearing installation tool Nos. J-8092 and J-35411, or equivalents.
    b. Apply GCLB grease part No. 1051344, or equivalent, to outer grease seal lip.
    c. Install outer grease seal using seal installation tool No. J-35737-01, or equivalent.
    d. Install hub using installation tool Nos. J-8092 and J-35399, or equivalents.
    e. Install inner grease seal using bearing installer tool No. J-35737-01, or equivalent.
    f. Ensure dust deflector ring faces in its proper direction and install using ring installation tool No. J-35379, or equivalent.

BALL JOINT INSPECTION

1. Remove steering knuckle w/hub, then clamp knuckle into suitable soft-jawed vise.
2. Flip ball stud back & forth five times, then install castle nut onto ball joint stud.
3. Rotate nut continuously for one turn every 2–4 seconds, then note torque reading on fifth turn.
4. Replace ball joint if reading is not 9–26 inch lbs.

BALL JOINT

REPLACE

1. Raise and support vehicle. Place suitable jack stands under suspension crossmember.
2. Lower vehicle slightly so weight of vehicle rests on suspension crossmember and not control arms.
3. Remove steering knuckle with axle hub as described under "Steering Knuckle, Replace."
4. Clamp steering knuckle with axle hub in suitable soft-jawed vise.
5. **On models equipped with ABS,** remove dust deflector.
6. **On all models,** remove cotter pin and nut.
7. Remove ball joint using separator tool No. J-24319-B, or equivalent.
8. Reverse procedure to install, noting the following:
    a. Install new self-locking nut and cotter pin.
    b. . Adjust wheel alignment, as required.

COIL SPRING

REPLACE

Refer to "Strut, Replace" for coil spring replacement procedure.

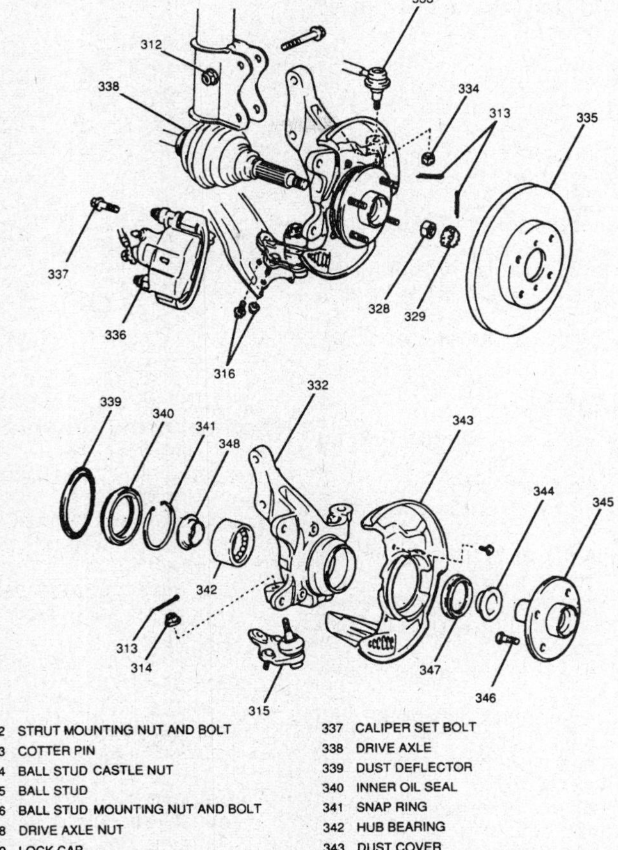

Fig. 2 Disassembled view of hub & bearing

STRUT

REPLACE

1. Raise and support vehicle. Place suitable jack stands under suspension crossmember.
2. Lower vehicle slightly so weight of vehicle rests on suspension crossmember and not control arms.
3. Remove brake hose from disc brake caliper.
4. Remove brake hose clip.
5. Remove brake hose from bracket.
6. Loosen bolts and nuts mounting strut to steering knuckle.
7. Lower vehicle slightly.
8. Remove strut mounting nuts at top of shock tower.
9. Remove strut.
10. Reverse procedure to install, noting the following:
    a. Avoid cracking or scratching spring coating.
    b. Coat threads lower side nuts with suitable clean engine oil.
    c. Install strut lower bolts and nuts. **Do not tighten now.**
    d. Install strut to tower nuts.
    e. Tighten strut lower bolts and nuts.

COIL SPRING & STRUT SERVICE

1. Remove strut as described under "Strut, Replace."
2. Compress spring slightly using strut holding/spring compression tool No. J-34013-B, or equivalent. **Ensure spring seat is secure and will not turn.**
3. Mount compression tool into holding fixture tool No. J-3289-20, or equivalent.
4. Mount strut into holding fixture using adapter tool No. J-34013-88, or equivalent.
5. Remove strut rod dust cap and piston nut.
6. Remove strut support, dust seal, spring seat, upper insulator, coil spring, bumper and lower insulator.
7. Reverse procedure to install.

CONTROL ARM

REPLACE

On models equipped with automatic transaxle, it may be necessary to remove the crossmember, transaxle support, both control arms and stabilizer shaft together as a complete unit.

REMOVAL

1. Install engine support fixture tool No. J-28467-360, or equivalent.
2. Raise and support vehicle.
3. Remove lower control arm mounting nuts and bolts.
4. Disconnect stabilizer bar links, as required.
5. Remove mounting bolts, nuts and suspension crossmember with control arms attached.
6. Remove mounting bolts, nuts and control arm.

INSTALLATION

1. Install control arm. **Do not tighten mounting bolts now.**
2. Install stabilizer shaft and links to control arms. **Do not tighten mounting bolts now.**
3. Install control arm bracket to crossmember. Tighten mounting bolts.
4. Install stabilizer shaft insulator clamps. Tighten mounting nuts. **Do not tighten mounting bolts now.**
5. Tighten control arm to knuckle mounting bolts.
6. Install suspension support brace and tighten mounting bolts.
7. Install tires and wheels, then lower vehicle.
8. Raise vehicle on drive-on lift or suitable alignment rack.
9. Settle suspension by jouncing vehicle up and down few times.
10. Tighten bolt Nos. 9, 1, 3, 11 and 8 in sequence, **Fig. 3.**
11. Tighten stabilizer shaft link stud nut.

CONTROL ARM BUSHING

REPLACE

The control arm bushings are not servicable separately. If the bushing are excessively worn or damaged, replace the control arm assembly.

STEERING KNUCKLE

REPLACE

1. Raise and support vehicle, then remove tire and wheel.
2. **On models equipped with ABS,** remove sensor from knuckle and position aside.
3. **On all models,** remove front brake hose from strut and position aside.
4. Remove control arm to knuckle bolt and nuts.
5. Remove drive axle cotter pin and driveshaft nut retainer.
6. Remove driveshaft nut with assistant holding brake pedal.
7. Remove caliper housing and bracket. Suspend them with suitable wire or rope.
8. Carefully remove brake rotor. Avoid damaging speed sensor rotor, boot and inner oil seal.
9. Loosen nuts on lower side of strut. Do not remove bolts.
10. Remove outer tie rod cotter pin and nut, then separate tie rod end using separator tool No. J-24319-B, or equivalent.
11. Remove strut lower nuts and bolts.
12. Remove knuckle with hub.
13. Remove ball joint cotter pin and nut, then separate ball joint end from knuckle using separator tool No. J-24319-B, or equivalent.
14. Remove hub, bearing and seal as previously described.
15. Reverse procedure to install, noting the following:
    a. Coat strut lower side nut threads with suitable clean engine oil.
    b. Install strut lower bolts and nuts. **Do not tighten now.**
    c. Tighten driveshaft nut while assistant holds brake pedal.
    d. Tighten strut lower bolts and nuts.

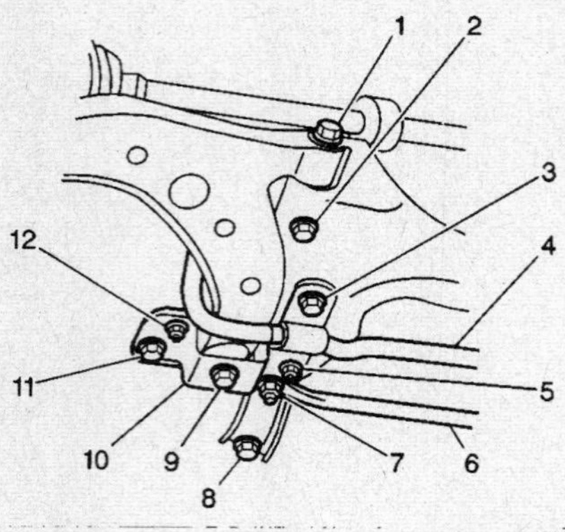

Fig. 3 Front crossmember & control arm tightening sequence

STABILIZER BAR

REPLACE

1. Raise and support vehicle.
2. Remove mounting nuts and stabilizer links.
3. Remove mounting nuts and suspension support brace.
4. Remove stabilizer shaft mounting bolts and stabilizer bar links.
5. Remove clamp bolts, nuts, studs and stabilizer bar.
6. Reverse procedure to install.

TIE ROD END

REPLACE

Refer to "Power Steering Gear, Replace" for tie rod end replacement procedure.

POWER STEERING GEAR

REPLACE

1. Ensure front wheels are in straight-ahead position and remove ignition key.
2. Remove steering column upper column cover from firewall.
3. Remove steering shaft lower coupling bolt.
4. Remove outlet pipe heat shield.
5. Remove lefthand steering gear inlet and outlet pipe clip bolt.
6. Remove righthand steering gear outlet pipe clip bolt.
7. Remove lefthand steering gear inlet and outlet pipe clip.
8. Place suitable drain pan under vehicle to catch power steering fluid.
9. Disconnect steering gear inlet pipe.
10. Disconnect O2S electrical connector, then remove sensor and gasket.
11. Install engine support fixture tool No. J-28467-360, or equivalent.
12. Raise and support vehicle.
13. Remove front tires and wheels.
14. Remove engine left and righthand lower splash shields.
15. Remove driveshaft exhaust heat shield.
16. Remove outer tie rod cotter pin, nut and outer tie rods using separator tool No. J-24319-B, or equivalent.
17. Remove front suspension brace.
18. Remove suspension crossmember, transaxle support, control arms and stabilizer shaft as unit.
19. Remove transaxle rear mount through-bolt and mount.
20. Remove transaxle rear mount bracket.
21. Disconnect exhaust pipe at manifold.
22. Remove steering gear exhaust heat shield.
23. Remove steering gear clamps.
24. Carefully route steering gear to vehicle's righthand side, then lower and remove it through lefthand side.
25. Remove steering gear insulators.
26. Reverse procedure to install, noting the following:
    a. Install new steering gear insulators, as required.
    b. Install new exhaust donut.
    c. Bleed power steering fluid system.
    d. Adjust wheel alignment, as required.

POWER STEERING PUMP

REPLACE

1. Siphon as much power steering fluid from reservoir as possible.
2. Remove pump drive belt.
3. Remove pump gear inlet hose fitting and inlet pipe.
4. Remove fluid reservoir hose.
5. Raise and support vehicle.
6. Remove righthand front tire and wheel.
7. Remove engine righthand lower splash shield.
8. Remove pump mounting bolts.
9. Carefully remove power steering pump.
10. Reverse procedure to install. Bleed power steering fluid system.

TIGHTENING SPECIFICATIONS

Year	Component	Torque/Ft. Lbs.
1998–2002	ABS Hose	22①
	ABS Speed Sensor	71①
	ABS Wire Harness	48①
	Axle Nut	166
	Ball Joint To Control Arm	105
	Ball Joint To Steering Knuckle	91
	Brake Caliper To Steering Knuckle	65
	Control Arm Retainer Bracket, Inner	129
	Control Arm Retainer Bracket, Outer Bolt	109
	Control Arm Retainer Bracket, Outer Nut	14
	Control Arm Retainer Bracket, Rear	91
	Control Arm To Crossmember, Front	158
	Crossmember Front Outer	167
	Drive Axle Nut	166
	Engine Crossmember To Suspension	45
	Front Suspension Crossmember	42
	Front Transaxle Mount	47
	Stabilizer Shaft Link Nut	33
	Stabilizer Shaft Mount Bracket Front Bolt	167
	Stabilizer Shaft Mount Bracket Nut	14
	Stabilizer Shaft Mount Bracket Stud	109
	Strut	29
	Strut Rod Piston	34
	Suspension Support Brace	51
	Tie Rod End	36
	Wheel Lug	76

① — Inch lbs.

Wheel Alignment

INDEX

PRECAUTIONS

AIR BAG SYSTEMS

Refer to "Air Bag System Precautions" in the front of this manual for system disarming and arming procedures.

PRELIMINARY INSPECTION

Steering and vibration problems are not always the result of improper alignment. They may also be caused by wheel and tire imbalance or other factors. To ensure proper alignment readings, the following inspections should be done and corrections made before inspecting caster, camber or toe:

1. Inspect tires for proper inflation pressures and even tread wear.
2. Inspect wheel bearings for looseness.
3. Inspect ball joints and tie rod ends for excessive looseness.
4. Inspect steering gear operation and mounting.
5. Inspect operation of struts.
6. Inspect control arms.
7. Inspect hub and bearing for excessive wear.

FRONT WHEEL ALIGNMENT

CASTER

Caster cannot be adjusted. Should caster be out of specification, locate cause first. If components are damaged, bent, loose, dented or worn, they should be replaced. To prevent an improper caster reading, jounce the bumper three times before inspecting.

CAMBER

1. Estimate amount camber must be adjusted.
2. Select proper combination of bolts, **Fig. 1.**

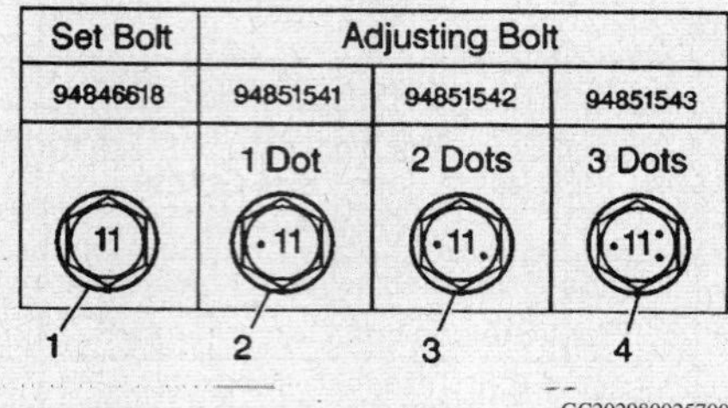

Set Bolt
Adjusting Bolt
94846618
94851541
94851542
94851543
1 Dot
2 Dots
3 Dots
11
1
2
3
4
GC2029800257000X

Fig. 1 Front camber adjustment bolts

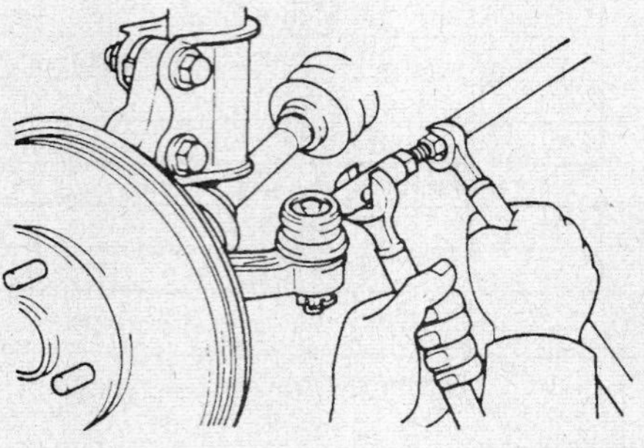

Fig. 2 Front toe adjustment

3. To obtain 0.25° camber, install bolt No. 1 in upper position and bolt No. 2 in lower position.
4. To obtain 0.50° camber, install bolt No. 1 in upper position and bolt No. 3 in lower position.
5. To obtain 0.75° camber, install bolt No. 1 in upper position and bolt No. 4 in lower position.
6. To obtain 1.00° camber, install bolt No. 2 in upper position and bolt No. 4 in lower position.
7. To obtain 1.25° camber, install bolt No. 3 in upper position and bolt No. 4 in lower position.
8. To obtain 1.50° camber, install bolt No. 4 in upper position and bolt No. 4 in lower position.
9. Install bolts, inspect alignment and adjust as required.

TOE-IN

Toe-in is adjusted by changing tie rod length.

1. Loosen boot clamps and slide from boot.
2. Loosen left and righthand tie rod end locknuts.
3. Turn left and righthand tie rods to align toe-in to specifications.
4. Left and righthand tie rods must be equal length, **Fig. 2.**
5. Install boot clamps and tighten nuts.
6. Ensure rack boots are not twisted.
7. Tighten strut to knuckle nut.
8. **Torque** tie rod locking nut to 41 ft. lbs.

REAR WHEEL ALIGNMENT

TOE

1. Loosen left and righthand lateral link or tie rod locknuts.
2. Adjust total rear toe by turning adjusting tubes. One revolution of adjusting tube will adjust rear to approximately 1.2°.
3. **Torque** lateral link or tie rod locknuts to 41 ft. lbs.

CAMBER & CASTER

Rear caster and camber cannot be adjusted. Should camber be out of specification, locate cause first. If components are damaged, bent loose, dented or worn, they should be replaced. To prevent an improper camber reading, jounce the bumper three times before inspecting. If a tie rod or tie rod end is replaced, inspect toe and steering angle with turning radius gauges. If steering angle is not proper, inspect left and righthand tie rods for equal length. If tie rod length is changed to correct steering, inspect toe once again.

SATURN

NOTE: Refer To The Rear Of This Manual For Vehicle Manufacturer's Special Tool Suppliers.

INDEX OF SERVICE OPERATIONS

Specifications

GENERAL ENGINE SPECIFICATIONS

Engine/Liter (VIN)①	Fuel Injection System	Bore & Stoke	Compression Ratio	Net H.P. @ RPM	Maximum Torque, Ft. Lbs. @ RPM	Normal Oil Pressure, psi
1998–99						
1.9L SOHC (8)	MPFI	3.23 X 3.54	9.3	100 @ 5000	114 @ 2400	36.0②
1.9L DOHC (7)	MPFI	3.23 X 3.54	9.5	124 @ 5600	122 @ 4800	36.0②
2000						
1.9L SOHC (8)	MPFI	3.23 X 3.54	9.3	100 @ 5000	114 @ 2400	36.0②
1.9L DOHC (7)	MPFI	3.23 X 3.54	9.5	124 @ 5600	122 @ 4800	36.0②
2.2L DOHC (F)	SPFI	3.38 X 3.72	9.5	137@ 5800	147 @ 4400	65.0③
3.0L DOHC (R)	SPFI	3.38 X 3.34	10.0	182 @ 5600	190 @ 3600	21.7④
2001–02						
1.9L SOHC (8)	SPFI	3.23 X 3.54	9.3	100 @ 5000	114 @ 2400	36.0②
1.9L DOHC (7)	SPFI	3.23 X 3.54	9.5	124 @ 5600	122 @ 4800	36.0②
2.2L DOHC (F)	SPFI	3.39 X 3.72	9.5	135 @ 5200	142 @ 4400	65.0③
3.0L DOHC (R)	SPFI	3.39 X 3.34	10.0	182 @ 5600	190 @ 3600	21.7④

MPFI — Multi-Point Fuel Injection
SPFI — Sequential-Point Fuel Injection
DOHC — Dual Overhead Cam
SOHC — Single Overhead Cam

① — Eighth digit of Vehicle Identification Number (VIN) denotes engine code.

② — At 2000 RPM.

③ — At 1000 RPM.

④ — At Idle.

TUNE UP SPECIFICATIONS

Year & Engine/Liter (VIN) ①	Spark Plug Gap	Ignition Timing BTDC				Curb Idle Speed②		Fast Idle Speed②		Fuel Pump Pressure, psi.	Valve Lash, Inch
		Firing Order	Man. Trans.	Auto. Trans.	Mark Fig.	Man. Trans.	Auto. Trans.	Man. Trans.	Auto. Trans.		
1998–99											
1.9L (8) SOHC MFI	0.040	④	⑤	⑤	⑥	750⑦	650/ 775N⑦	⑦	⑦	40–55⑨	③
1.9L (7) DOHC MFI	0.040	④	⑤	⑤	⑥	850/ 875⑦	750/ 775N⑦	⑦	⑦	65–94⑨	③
2000–02											
1.9L (8) SOHC MFI	0.040	④	⑤	⑤	⑥	700– 800⑦	600– 700D⑦⑪	⑦	⑦	40–55⑨	③
1.9L (7) DOHC MFI	0.040	④	⑤	⑤	⑥	800– 900⑦⑧	700– 800D⑦⑪	⑦	⑦	65–94⑨	③

Continued

TUNE UP SPECIFICATIONS—Continued

Year & Engine/Liter (VIN) ①	Spark Plug Gap	Ignition Timing BTDC				Curb Idle Speed②		Fast Idle Speed②		Fuel Pump Pressure, psi.	Valve Lash, Inch
		Firing Order	Man. Trans.	Auto. Trans.	Mark Fig.	Man. Trans.	Auto. Trans.	Man. Trans.	Auto. Trans.		
2000–02											
2.2L (F) DOHC SPFI	0.045	④	⑤	⑤	⑥	850–875⑦	750–775N⑦	⑦	⑦	50–60⑨	③
3.0L (R) DOHC SPFI	0.039	⑩	—	⑤	⑥	—	750–775N⑦	—	⑦	39–49⑨	③

BTDC — Before Top Dead Center
D — Drive
N — Neutral
① — Eighth digit of Vehicle Identification Number (VIN) denotes engine code.
② — When adjusting idle speed, set parking brake & block drive wheels. Where two idle speeds are listed, higher speed is w/idle or air conditioning solenoid energized.
③ — Equipped w/hydraulic valve lifters.
④ — Cylinder numbering from front of engine to rear 1, 2, 3, 4. Firing order 1-3-4-2. Refer to **Fig. A** for spark plug wire connections at coil unit.
⑤ — Equipped w/Distributorless Ignition System (DIS), no adjustment.
⑥ — Equipped w/crankshaft position sensor.
⑦ — Idle speed is controlled by Idle Air Control (IAC) valve or idle speed control (ISC).
⑧ — With air conditioning on, 825–925 RPM.
⑨ — Wrap shop towel around fuel pressure test port to prevent fuel spillage, connect suitable fuel pressure gauge to fuel pressure test port. Energize fuel pump using a suitably programmed scan tool & check fuel pressure.
⑩ — 1-2-3-4-5-6.
⑪ — With air conditioning on, 725–825 RPM.

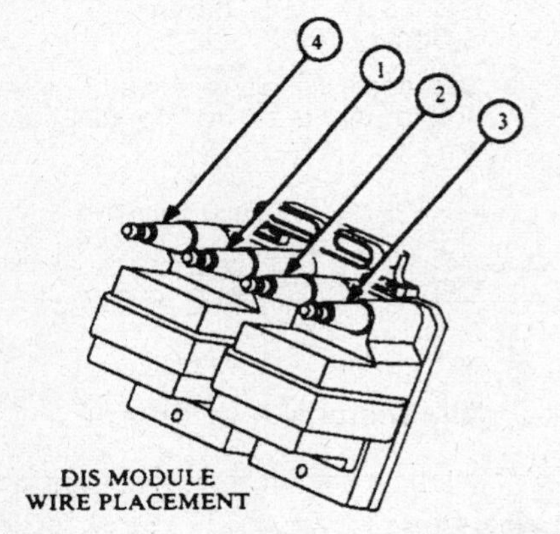

Fig. A

FRONT WHEEL ALIGNMENT SPECIFICATIONS

Model	Caster Angle, Degrees①		Camber Angle, Degrees①		Total Toe, Degrees②		Ball Joint Wear
	Limits	Desired	Limits	Desired	Limits	Desired	
L-Series	+3.2 to +4.2④	+3.7④	-1.75 to -0.50	-1.0	+0.04 to +0.36	+0.20	③
S-Series	+1.1 to +2.3	+1.7	-1.20 to +0.20	-0.5	0 to +0.40	+0.20	③

① — Cross camber, 0° (+/-1°).
② — Toe-In (+). Toe-Out (-).
③ — Refer to "Ball Joint Inspection" in "Front Suspension & Steering" section.
④ — Caster is not adjustable

REAR WHEEL ALIGNMENT SPECIFICATIONS

Model	Year	Camber Angle Degrees		Total Toe, Degrees①	
		Limits	Desired	Limits	Desired
L-Series	2000–02	-1.5 to -0.5	-1.0	+0.13 to +0.47	+0.3
S-Series	1998–99	-1.4 to 0	-0.7	0 to +0.40	+0.2
	2000–02	-1.4 to 0	-0.7	0 to +0.50	+0.2

① — Toe-In (+). Toe-Out (-).

VEHICLE RIDE HEIGHT SPECIFICATIONS

Model	Year	Body Style	Manufacturer's Original Tire Size	Measurement Points & Specifications①②					
				Front			Rear		
				Dim.	Specification		Dim.	Specification	
					Inches	mm		Inches	mm
L-Series	2000–02	All	③	E	15.56	395	F	15.21	386.4
S-Series	1998–2002	Coupe	③	A	5.90	150	B	5.40	138
				C	7.80–9.10	200–232	D	7.90–9.40	201–233
		Sedan	③	A	4.60	117	B	4.10	105
				C	7.80–9.00	200–233	D	8.00–9.30	201–233
		Wagon	③	A	4.60	117	B	4.10	105
				C	7.80–9.10	200–232	D	8.10–9.50	202–234

A Dim. — Measurement From Front Wheel Opening to Check Point On Rocker Panel Flange

B Dim. — Measurement From Rear Wheel Opening to Check Point On Rocker Panel Flange

C Dim. — Distance from Front Rocker Flange Panel to Ground

D Dim. — Distance from Rear Rocker Panel Flange to Ground

E Dim. — Measure from Bottom Center of Front Bumper

F Dim. — Measure from Bottom Center of Rear Bumper

Dim. Dimension

① — Measurement is with fuel, radiator coolant and engine oil full, spare tire, jack, hand tools and mats in designated positions and tires properly inflated.

② — L-Series, ± 0.98″ (25 mm); S-Series, ±0.62 ″ (16 mm).

③ — See door sticker or inside of glove box for manufacturer's original tire size specifications. If tires on vehicle do not match manufacturer's original tire size & measurement is not within limits, it will be necessary to refer to the "Non-Standard Tire & Wheel Size Adjustment To Ride Height Specification & Tire Size Adjustment Charts" in the front of this manual for approximate changes in ride height specifications.

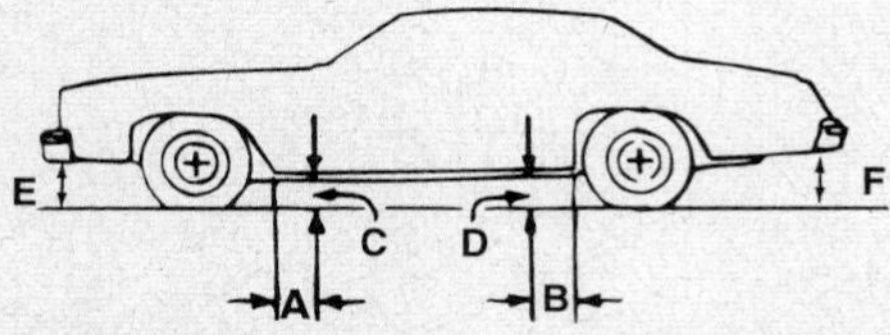

Dimensions A through F

FLUID CAPACITIES & COOLING SYSTEM DATA

Engine/ Liter ①	Cooling Capacity, Qts.	Coolant Type	Radiator Cap Relief Pressure, Lbs.	Thermo. Opening Temp. Deg. F	Fuel Tank Gals.	Engine Oil Refill Qts.③	Transaxle Oil	
							Manual Transaxle Pts.	Auto. Transaxle Qts.②
1998–99								
1.9L	7.2	Dex-Cool	13–17	186	12.1	4.0	5.2	④
2000–01								
1.9L	7.2	Dex-Cool	13–17	186	12.1	4.0	5.2	④
2.2L	7.4	Dex-Cool	13–17	194	12.1	5.0	4.0	⑤
3.0L	7.8	Dex-Cool	20–21	188–196	12.1	5.0	—	⑤
2002								
1.9L	7.2	Dex-Cool	13–17	186	12.1	4.0	5.2	④
2.2L	9.0	Dex-Cool	13–17	194	15.7	5.5	4.0	⑤
3.0L	10.2	Dex-Cool	20–21	188–196	15.7	5.0	—	⑤

① — Eighth digit of Vehicle Identification Number (VIN) denotes engine code.

② — Approximate, make final check w/dipstick.

③ — Additional oil may be necessary to bring oil level to full mark, when changing oil filter.

④ — Drain & refill, 4 qts.; drain & refill w/new filter, 4.2 qts.; total capacity, 7.4 qts.

⑤ — Bottom pan removal, 6.9 qts.; complete overhaul, 9.5 qts.; total capacity, 12.9 qts.

LUBRICANT DATA

Year	Lubricant Type				
	Transaxle		Power Steering	Brake System	Hydraulic Clutch
	Manual	Automatic			
1998–2002	Dexron III	Dexron III	①	DOT 3	DOT 3

① — Must meet GM specification 9985010.

Electrical

NOTE: On Air Bag Equipped Models, Refer To "Air Bag System Precautions" Located In The Front Of This Manual For System Disarming & Arming Procedures.

NOTE: Refer To "Computer Relearn Procedures" Located In The Front Of This Manual When Battery Power To The Computer Has Been Interrupted.

NOTE: Prior To Performing Any Service Operations Listed In This Section, Consult The "Technical Service Bulletins" Section For Related Information.

INDEX

PRECAUTIONS

AIR BAG SYSTEMS

Refer to "Air Bag System Precautions" in the front of this manual for system disarming and arming procedures.

BATTERY GROUND CABLE

Prior to service, disconnect battery ground cable and isolate as required.

FUSE PANEL & FLASHER LOCATION

L-SERIES

The underhood fuse block is located on the rear lefthand side of the engine compartment. The lefthand instrument panel fuse block is located behind the lefthand side kick panel. The righthand instrument panel fuse block is located behind the righthand side kick panel.

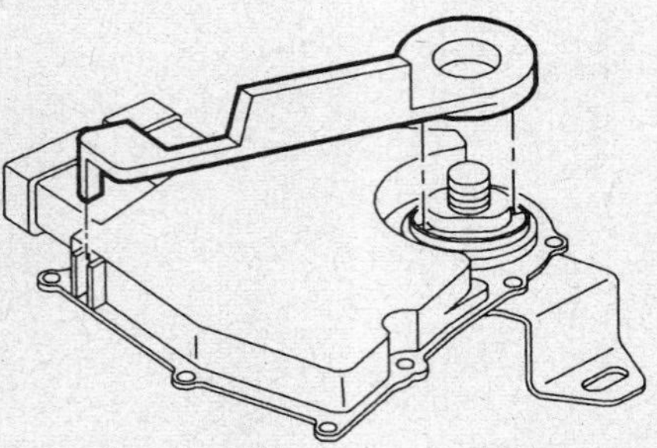

Fig. 1 Transaxle range switch alignment. L-Series

The hazard switch, located in the center of the instrument panel, controls turn signal and hazard lamp flashing.

S-SERIES

The underhood junction block is located at the lefthand front of the engine compartment at the fender apron. The instrument panel junction block and the flasher module are located behind the center instrument panel, in front of the console.

FUEL PUMP RELAY LOCATION

L-SERIES

The fuel pump relay is located behind the lefthand side kick panel, on the lefthand instrument panel fuse block.

S-SERIES

The fuel pump relay is located in the instrument panel fuse block, behind the center of the instrument panel.

RELAY CENTER LOCATION

L-SERIES

Relays are located in three fuse panels.

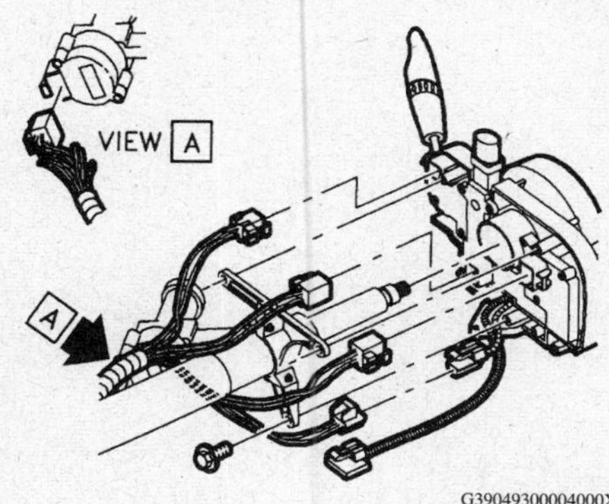

Fig. 2 Multi-function switch replacement. S-Series

Refer to "Fuse Panel & Flasher Location" for fuse block locations.

S-SERIES

Relays are in the located in both the underhood junction block and the instrument panel junction Block. Refer to "Fuse Panel & Flasher Location" for junction block locations.

STARTER

REPLACE

1.9L ENGINE

1. Raise and support vehicle.
2. Disconnect electrical connectors and position aside.
3. Remove starter mounting bolts.
4. Pull starter rearward and toward lefthand side.
5. Remove starter motor.
6. Reverse procedure to install, noting the following:
   a. Starter must be guided into flywheel housing and rotated until starter flange lower bolt hole and engine mounting hole align.
   b. **Torque** starter mounting bolts to 27 ft. lbs.
   c. **Torque** starter solenoid terminal to 44 inch lbs. and positive terminal to 96 inch lbs.

2.2L ENGINE

1. Raise and support vehicle.
2. Disconnect electrical connectors and position aside.
3. Remove mounting bolts and starter.
4. Reverse procedure to install. **Torque** starter mounting bolts to 30 ft. lbs.

3.0L ENGINE

1. Raise and support vehicle.
2. Remove righthand front wheel and disconnect starter electrical connectors.
3. Loosen electrical harness bracket to engine block fastener.
4. Remove lower starter mounting bolt. Lower vehicle.
5. Remove upper starter mounting bolt.
6. Move starter right to clear engine block, then left out of flywheel housing.
7. Reverse procedure to install. **Torque** starter mounting bolts to 30 ft. lbs.

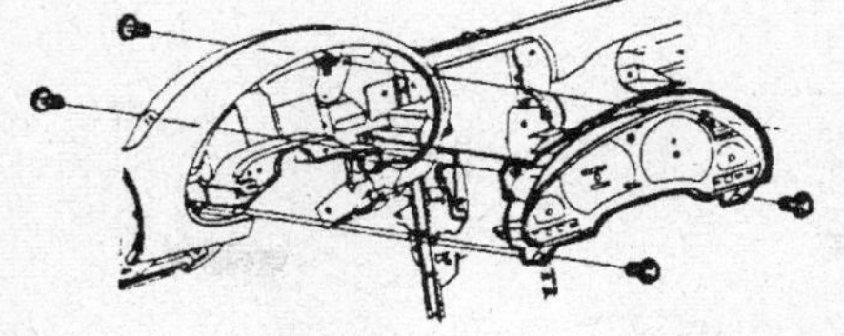

Fig. 3 Instrument cluster replacement. 1998–99 S-Series

ALTERNATOR

REPLACE

1.9L ENGINE

1. Remove drive belt.
2. Raise and support vehicle, then remove righthand wheel.
3. Remove righthand wheelwell and alternator splash shields, then disconnect field wires.
4. Hold B+ output stud from rotating using alternator output stud wrench tool No. SA-9401-C, or equivalent, and disconnect fusible link wire.
5. Remove lower and upper mounting bolts, then the alternator through wheel well opening.
6. Reverse procedure to install, noting the following:
   a. **Torque** mounting bolts to 24 ft. lbs.
   b. Fusible link wire should be between 10 and 11 O'clock position.
   c. **Torque** positive terminal and alternator splash shield to 96 inch lbs.

2.2L ENGINE

1. Remove throttle body air duct and accessory drive belt.
2. Disconnect alternator electrical connectors.
3. Remove mounting bolts and alternator.
4. Reverse procedure to install. **Torque** alternator mounting bolts to 30 ft. lbs.

3.0L ENGINE

1. Remove accessory drive belt and belt tensioner.
2. Remove upper alternator to engine block bolts.
3. Raise and support vehicle.
4. Turn steering wheel towards right to access lower alternator bolt.
5. Remove lower alternator bolt. Lower vehicle.
6. Separate alternator from engine block.
7. Disconnect electrical connectors and remove alternator.
8. Reverse procedure to install. **Torque** alternator mounting bolts to 30 ft. lbs.

COIL PACK

REPLACE

1.9L ENGINE

This procedure has been revised by a Technical Service Bulletin.

1. Turn ignition switch to Off position.
2. Mark spark plug wire positions for installation.

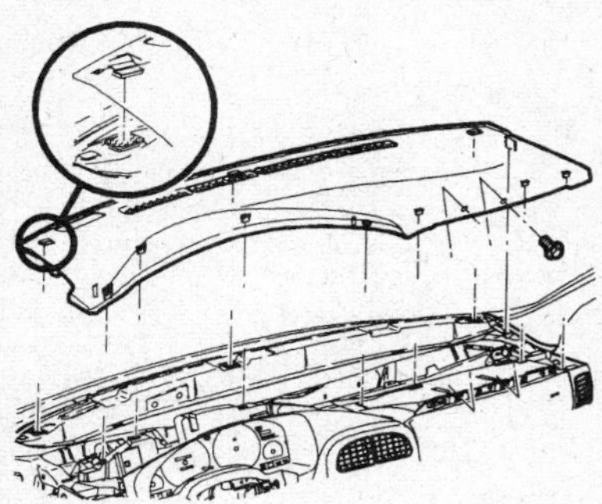

Fig. 4 Upper trim panel replacement. 2000–02 S-Series

3. Remove spark plug wires from coil towers.
4. Remove ignition coil from ignition module by rotating coil upward.
5. Reverse procedure to install, noting the following:
   a. Ensure electrical connectors align before seating.
   b. **Torque** mounting bolts to 71 inch lbs.

2.2L ENGINE

1. Turn ignition switch to Off position.
2. Disconnect ignition module electrical connector.
3. Remove mounting screws and electronic ignition module.
4. Remove mounting bolts and coil pack.
5. Reverse procedure to install, noting the following:
   a. **Torque** coil pack bolts to 84 inch lbs.
   b. **Torque** electronic ignition module mounting screws to 13 inch lbs.

3.0L ENGINE

1. Turn ignition switch to Off position.
2. Remove upper intake manifold runner as outlined under "Intake Manifold, Replace" in "3.0L Engine" section.
3. Disconnect electrical connector, then remove ignition coil and gasket.
4. Reverse procedure to install.

IGNITION LOCK

REPLACE

1. Remove ignition lock bezel.
2. Remove upper steering column shroud panel.
3. Insert ignition key to switch.
4. **On S-Series models,** rotate key to ACC position.
5. **On L-Series models,** rotate key to START position and back to RUN position.
6. **On all models,** depress locking button at top and remove lock cylinder.
7. Reverse procedure to install.

IGNITION SWITCH

REPLACE

L-SERIES

1. Remove ignition lock cylinder bezel from steering column shroud.

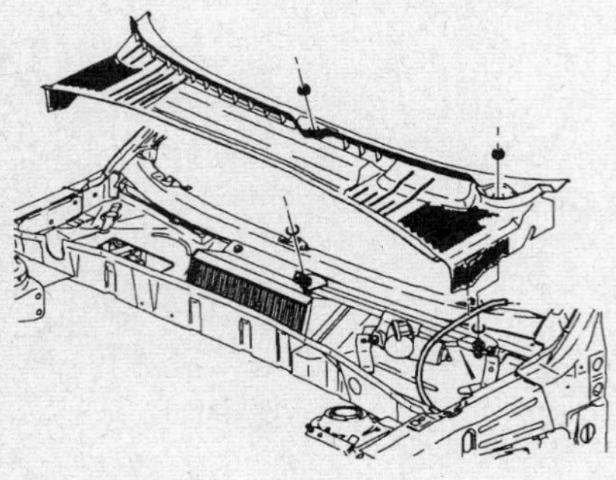

Fig. 5 Windshield cowl screen replacement. L-Series

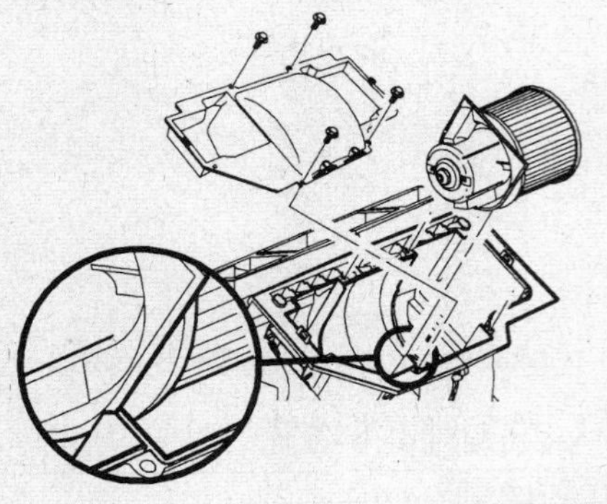

Fig. 6 Blower motor replacement. L-Series

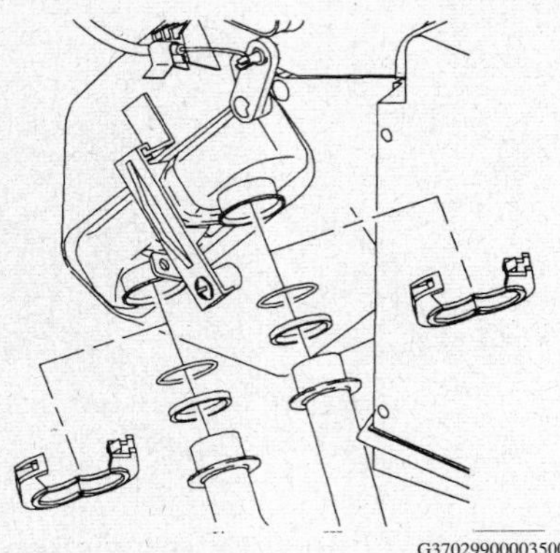

Fig. 7 Heater core pipe replacement. L-Series

2. Remove steering column upper and lower shrouds.
3. Remove ignition switch to steering column mounting screws.
4. Disconnect electrical connector and remove switch.
5. Reverse procedure to install. **Torque** switch mounting screws to 13 inch lbs.

IGNITION MODULE

REPLACE

S-SERIES

1. Remove steering wheel as outlined under "Steering Wheel, Replace."
2. Remove lefthand side lower filler panel mounting screws.
3. Loosen Data Link Connector (DLC) to filler panel mounting screws and lower filler panel.
4. Disconnect hood release cable and remove filler panel.
5. Remove air bag module Connector Position Assurance (CPA) retainer.
6. Disconnect connectors and remove lever control switch.
7. **On models equipped with automatic transaxle,** disconnect park lock cable from ignition module.
8. **On all models,** disconnect pass lock sensor and ignition switch electrical connectors from ignition module.
9. Make small notch in shear bolt head using suitable chisel and hammer.
10. Tap chisel to rotate and loosen bolt.
11. Remove shear bolts.
12. Remove ignition module
13. Reverse procedure to install.

CLUTCH START SWITCH

REPLACE

1. Disconnect clutch switch electrical connector.
2. Remove mounting bolt and switch.
3. Reverse procedure to install. **Torque** clutch switch mounting bolt to 96 inch lbs.

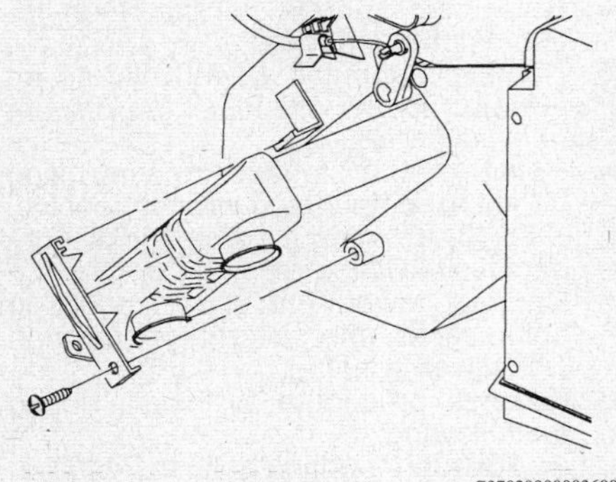

Fig. 8 Heater core replacement. L-Series

TRANSAXLE RANGE SWITCH

REPLACE

L-SERIES

REMOVAL

1. Apply parking brake and place control lever in NEUTRAL position.
2. Remove shift control cable from transaxle range switch lever.
3. Disconnect transaxle range switch electrical connectors.
4. Remove range switch lever nut and lever.
5. Remove mounting bolts and transaxle range.

INSTALLATION

1. Ensure transaxle manual shaft is in NEUTRAL position.
2. Align transaxle shift shaft and transaxle range switch flats, then install switch.
3. Loosely install switch mounting bolts.
4. Insert transaxle range switch alignment tool No. J-41545, or equivalent, over manual shaft, **Fig. 1.**
5. Rotate switch until alignment tool drops into position.
6. **Torque** switch mounting bolts to 15 ft. lbs.
7. **Torque** switch lever mounting nut to 26 ft. lbs.
8. Connect switch electrical connectors.
9. Install control cable and ensure vehicle starts only in PARK or NEUTRAL.

S-SERIES

REMOVAL

1. Turn ignition switch Off position.
2. Remove air cleaner and duct.
3. Disconnect transaxle range switch harness connectors.
4. Disconnect shifter cable from control lever.
5. Place control lever in full clockwise position.
6. Remove control lever to manual shift shaft mounting nut while holding control lever in place.
7. Remove mounting bolts and switch.

INSTALLATION

1. Install switch and mounting bolts. **Do not tighten bolts now.**
2. Install control lever onto manual shaft.
3. **Torque** mounting nut to 108 inch lbs. while holding control lever.
4. Ensure control lever is in PARK position by moving lever to full clockwise position until it clicks and cannot be moved any further.
5. Release control cable adjustment lock tab using suitable screwdriver.
6. Connect control cable to control lever.
7. Move control cable housing back and forth in adjuster. Record endplay.
8. Center control cable in middle of endplay and depress control cable lock tab.
9. Place transaxle in DRIVE position.
10. Connect suitable ohmmeter between transaxle range switch connector terminals.
11. Rotate transaxle range switch toward engine until ohmmeter indicates continuity.
12. **Torque** switch to case mounting bolts to 10 ft. lbs. Ensure continuity still exists between terminals.
13. Connect switch electrical connectors.
14. Install air cleaner and duct.
15. While moving shifter lever to all gear positions, ensure each position reads correctly using suitably programmed scan tool.

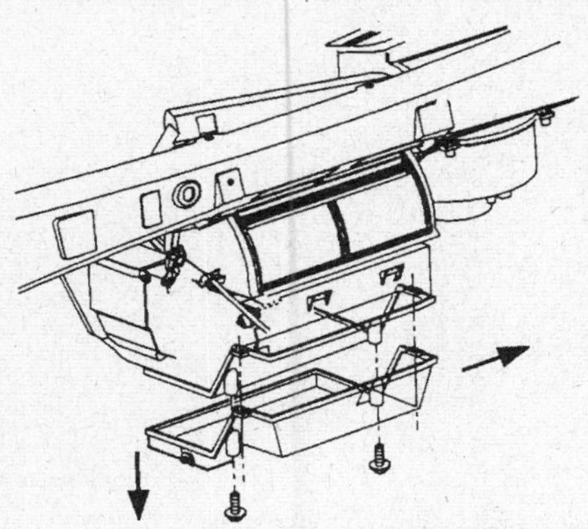

Fig. 9 Lower heater duct replacement. S-Series

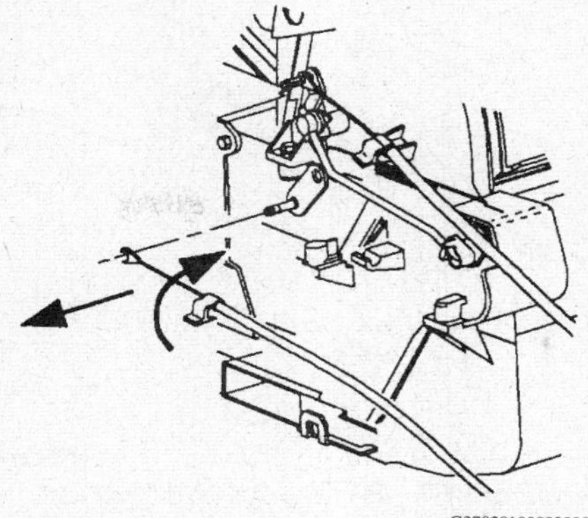

Fig. 10 Temperature cable replacement. S-Series

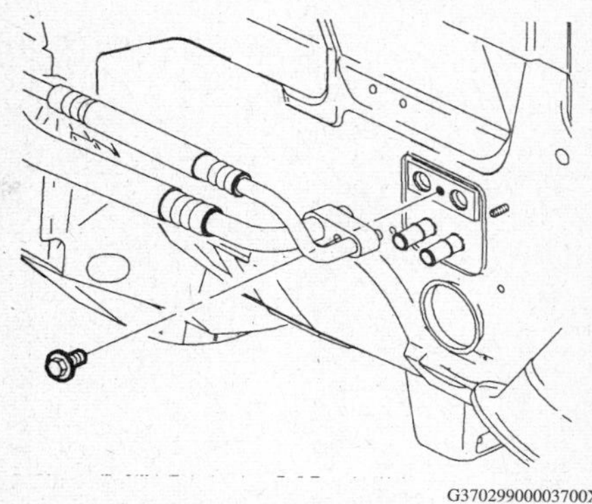

Fig. 11 Suction/liquid line replacement. L-Series

MULTI-FUNCTION SWITCH

REPLACE

S-SERIES

1. Remove steering wheel as described under "Steering Wheel, Replace."
2. Remove Supplemental Inflatable Restraint (SIR) coil assembly as described in "Passive Restraints Systems" chapter.
3. Remove Connector Position Assurance (CPA) device and disconnect electrical connectors from multi-function switch, **Fig. 2.**
4. Remove multi-function switch.
5. Reverse procedure to install.

HEADLAMP/TURN SIGNAL SWITCH

REPLACE

L-SERIES

1. Remove steering wheel as outlined under "Steering Wheel, Replace."
2. Remove ignition switch bezel, then the upper and lower steering column covers.
3. Remove headlamp/turn signal switch.
4. Reverse procedure to install.

S-SERIES

Refer to "Multi-Function Switch, Replace."

STEERING WHEEL

REPLACE

This procedure has been revised by a Technical Service Bulletin.

1. Remove driver's air bag module as outlined in "Passive Restraint Systems" chapter.
2. Disconnect horn switch electrical and cruise control electrical connectors, as required.
3. Remove steering wheel mounting nut.
4. Remove steering wheel using suitable steering wheel puller.
5. Feed electrical wiring through steering wheel and remove steering wheel.

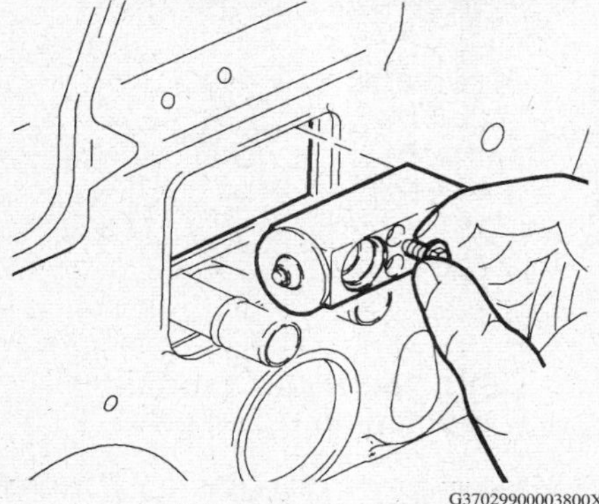

Fig. 12 TXV replacement. L-Series

6. Insert yellow tab into SIR coil or use tape to prevent rotating SIR coil.
7. Reverse procedure to install, noting the following:
   a. **Torque** new steering wheel mounting nut to 26 ft. lbs.
   b. **Torque** inflator module mounting bolts to 96 inch lbs.

INSTRUMENT CLUSTER

REPLACE

L-SERIES

1. Remove steering wheel as outlined under "Steering Wheel, Replace."
2. Remove hush panel from under lefthand side of instrument panel.
3. Remove knee bolster panel from under steering column.
4. Remove upper and lower steering column covers.
5. Lower steering column to its lowest position.
6. Remove mounting screws and instrument cluster trim plate.
7. Remove mounting screws and instrument cluster.
8. Reverse procedure to install.

S-SERIES

1998-99

1. Remove Data Link Connector (DLC) and steering column filler panel screws.
2. Remove hood release cable from lever.
3. Remove steering column filler panel.
4. Disconnect ignition switch electrical connector at righthand steering column bolt.
5. Remove mounting bolts and lower steering column onto front seat.
6. Remove push pin fasteners in top of instrument cluster trim bezel and pull trim bezel rearward at side clip locations.
7. Remove connector locking pins and disconnect electrical connectors from instrument cluster by depressing tabs on each side.
8. Remove front and rear instrument cluster screws, **Fig. 3.**
9. Remove instrument cluster.
10. Reverse procedure to install. **Torque** steering column bolts to 26 ft. lbs.

2000-02

1. Remove instrument panel upper trim pad mounting screws, **Fig. 4.**
2. Disconnect trim panel retaining clips by grasping edges of trim panel and lifting up.
3. Disconnect hook and loop fasteners at rear of upper trim panel by reaching under trim panel and lifting straight up.
4. Raise upper trim panel enough to clear VIN plate.
5. Loosen steering column filler panel mounting bolts. **Do not remove weather strips.**
6. Remove lefthand side endcap to instrument panel mounting screws.
7. Disconnect retaining clips and remove instrument panel endcap.
8. Remove upper and lower steering column covers.
9. Lower steering column to its lowest position.
10. Disconnect retaining clips and pull instrument panel bezel outward.
11. Disconnect dimmer/traction control switch electrical connector.
12. Remove instrument panel bezel.
13. Remove mounting screws and pull cluster away from instrument panel.
14. Disconnect electrical connectors and remove cluster.
15. Reverse procedure to install.

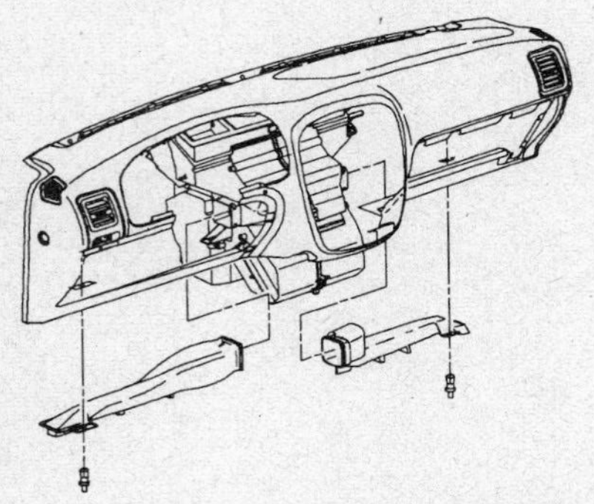
G39149900002500X

Fig. 13 Heater duct replacement. L-Series

RADIO

REPLACE

1. Remove control cover push pin fasteners, then pull radio, and heater and air conditioning control cover rearward.
2. Disconnect single traction control, fog lamp and rear defog electrical connectors.
3. Remove radio mounting screws.
4. Depress both radio side spring clips and pull out slightly.
5. Disconnect antenna and electrical connectors.
6. **On models equipped with base radio,** remove storage tray by pulling out towards front of radio.
7. **On all models,** remove radio.
8. Reverse procedure to install.

WIPER MOTOR

REPLACE

L-SERIES

1. Remove wiper arm finish cap.
2. Scribe wiper arm positions on windshield for installation alignment.
3. Remove mounting nuts and wiper arms.
4. Remove weather strip from rear of hood.
5. Remove mounting nuts and cowl screen, **Fig. 5.**
6. Disconnect wiper motor electrical connector.
7. Remove mounting bolts and wiper motor.
8. Separate wiper motor from transmission.
9. Reverse procedure to install. **Torque** wiper motor mounting bolts to 44 inch lbs. and wiper arm mounting nuts to 21 ft. lbs.

S-SERIES

1. Remove wiper arm finish cap and mounting screw.
2. Lift and remove wiper arm from pivot.
3. Remove cowl trim panel.
4. Remove instrument panel top cover.
5. Remove mounting screws and position defroster duct aside to allow access to wiper module mounting screws.

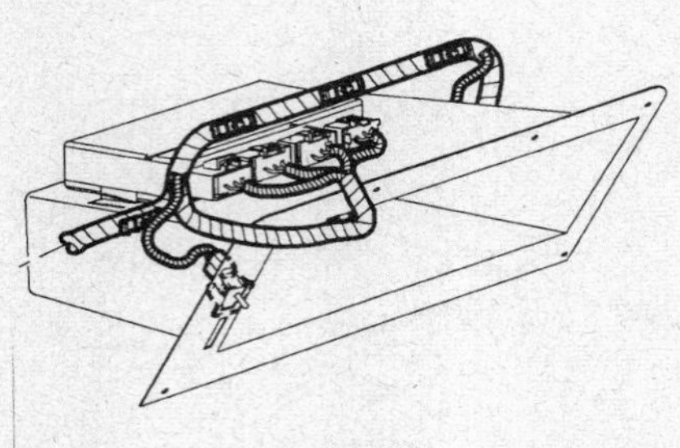
G39149900002600X

Fig. 14 BCM replacement. L-Series

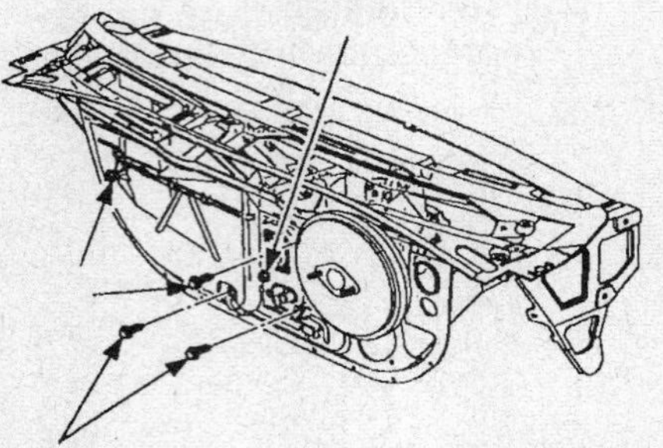
G39149800022000X

Fig. 16 HVAC module replacement. S-Series

6. Place wiper motor arm in 12 o'clock position.
7. Remove wiper module mounting bolts and nuts.
8. Partially remove wiper module and disconnect electrical connectors.
9. Remove wiper module and place in suitable vise.
10. Remove links from motor arm
11. Remove mounting bolts and motor.
12. Reverse procedure to install, noting the following:
    a. **Torque** wiper motor to 96 inch lbs.
    b. Install outboard module bolt first, then inboard bolt.
    c. **Torque** mounting bolts to 13 ft. lbs.
    d. **Torque** mounting nuts to 72 inch lbs.

WIPER SWITCH

REPLACE

L-SERIES

1. Remove steering wheel as outlined under "Steering Wheel, Replace."
2. Remove ignition switch bezel, then the upper and lower steering column covers.
3. Remove wiper/washer switch.
4. Reverse procedure to install.

S-SERIES

Refer to "Multi-Function Switch, Replace."

WIPER TRANSMISSION

REPLACE

Refer to "Wiper Motor, Replace" for wiper motor transmission replacement procedure.

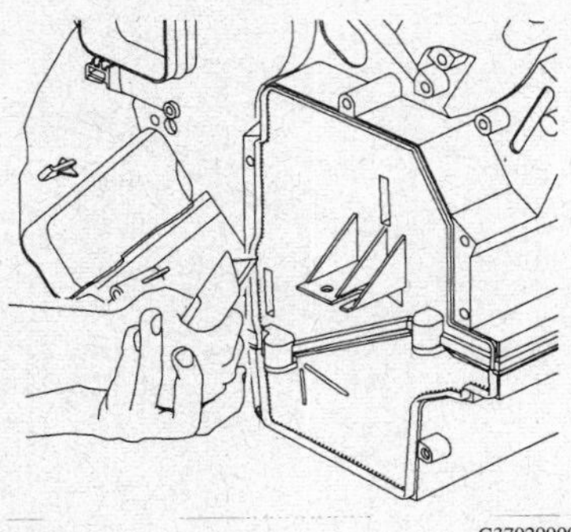
G37029900003900X

Fig. 15 Evaporator core replacement. L-Series

BLOWER MOTOR

REPLACE

L-SERIES

1. Turn ignition switch to ON position, then select outside air on control head.
2. Remove cowl screen as outlined under "Wiper Motor, Replace."
3. Release and remove filter by rotating locking tabs outward.
4. Remove mounting bolts and filter housing.
5. Remove mounting screws and blower motor housing, **Fig. 6.**
6. Disconnect electrical connector and remove blower motor.
7. Reverse procedure to install. **Torque** blower motor housing screws to 9 inch lbs. and filter housing bolts to 31 inch lbs.

S-SERIES

1. Remove righthand instrument panel lower sound insulator.
2. Disconnect blower motor electrical connector.
3. Remove mounting screws and blower motor.
4. Reverse procedure to install.

HEATER CORE

REPLACE

L-SERIES

1. Drain engine coolant into suitable container.
2. Remove heater inlet and return hoses.
3. Place heater return hose end in suitable container, apply low air pressure to inlet hose and blow coolant out of heater core.
4. Remove righthand console extension.
5. Remove heater core pipe to heater core clamps and pipe from core end tank, **Fig. 7.**
6. Remove core mounting screw and strap.
7. Pull center console forward edge outward for access.
8. Pull heater core out of module into passenger foot area, **Fig. 8.**
9. Reverse procedure to install.

S-SERIES

1. Drain coolant into suitable container.

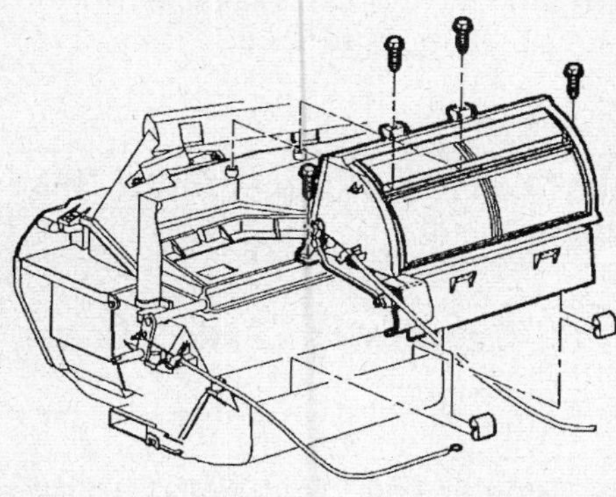

G39149800023000X

Fig. 17 Mode valve replacement. S-Series

2. Raise and support vehicle.
3. Move heater hose clamps upward. Lower vehicle.
4. Remove heater core hoses and blow coolant from heater core using suitable air hose.
5. Disconnect lower instrument panel center trim panels from under instrument panel and rotate trim panels outward to disconnect from front of console.
6. Remove instrument panel lower closeout panel by pulling outward at top edge and rotating downward.
7. Remove mounting screws, drop lower heater duct straight down and slide out sideways, **Fig. 9.**
8. Release temperature cable hold down clip from lower heater core cover by lifting upward on plastic tab while pushing down on top of cable, **Fig. 10.**
9. Slide cable off hook and remove temperature cable.
10. Remove mounting screws and heater core side cover.
11. Remove mounting screws and lower heater core cover.
12. Remove lower heater core retainer mounting screw.
13. Remove heater core.
14. Reverse procedure to install.

EVAPORATOR CORE

REPLACE

L-SERIES

1. Remove blower motor as outlined under "Blower Motor, Replace."
2. Recover refrigerant as outlined in "Air Conditioning" chapter.
3. Remove mounting bolts and suction/liquid line from Thermo Expansion Valve (TXV), **Fig. 11.** Cap suction/liquid line hose.
4. Remove TXV mounting bolts.
5. Install suction/liquid line bolt hand tight.
6. Remove TXV from evaporator by gently pulling forward using bolt as handle, **Fig. 12.**
7. Open glove box door and remove lamp by pulling on plunger.
8. Disconnect glove box lamp electrical connector.
9. Remove righthand side instrument panel lower dash insulator retainers.
10. Pull insulator rearward to disconnect from forward insulator retainers.
11. Remove retainer and righthand side heater duct, **Fig. 13.**
12. Remove glove box door and bin fasteners.
13. Slowly tilt glove box bin downward to expose Body Control Module (BCM), **Fig. 14.**
14. Slide BCM out of mounting slots and remove glove box bin.
15. Remove hush panel support from front of dash.
16. Cut evaporator access door through module wall following inside of raised bead as guide using suitable sharp utility knife, **Fig. 15. Several passes may be required.**
17. Slide evaporator core out through access door opening. Cap pipes.
18. Reverse procedure to install, noting the following:
    a. Add 2.4 ounces of PAG oil to new evaporator.
    b. **Torque** TXV and suction/liquid mounting bolts to 62 inch lbs.
    c. Lubricate O-rings using clean mineral oil.
    d. Apply provided sealant to service door at tongue and groove locations.

S-SERIES

1. Recover refrigerant as outlined in "Air Conditioning" chapter.
2. Remove air cleaner housing cover and air intake tube.
3. Remove suction hose and liquid line from expansion valve.
4. Remove expansion valve from evaporator.
5. Install protective covers over air conditioning lines.
6. Drain cooling system into suitable container and remove heater inlet hose from engine.
7. Blow remaining coolant from heater core using suitable air hose.
8. Raise and support vehicle.
9. Remove heater core hoses. Lower vehicle.
10. Remove instrument panel as outlined in "Dash Panel Service" chapter.
11. Remove wiring harnesses and clips from HVAC module.
12. Disconnect blower and recirc motor electrical connectors.
13. Remove fuel vapor line and clip from HVAC module stud to gain access to nut.
14. Remove HVAC module to cowl mounting nuts and screws, **Fig. 16.**
15. Remove HVAC module.
16. Remove and discard cowl panel seals.
17. Remove mode valve screws and clips, **Fig. 17.**
18. Remove mode valve from HVAC module.
19. Remove upper air inlet case from lower case, **Fig. 18.**
20. Remove evaporator tube clamp and screw.

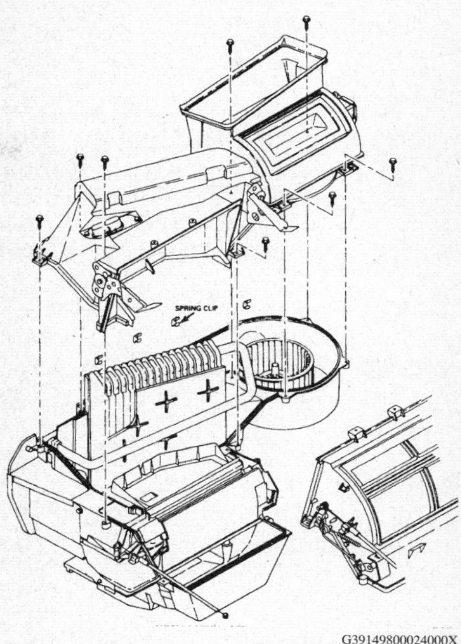

G39149800024000X

Fig. 18 Upper air inlet case replacement. S-Series

21. Lift evaporator from lower case.
22. Reverse procedure to install, noting the following:
    a. Add 2.25 ounces of PAG oil to new evaporator.
    b. **Torque** HVAC module mounting nuts and screws to 44 inch lbs.
    c. **Torque** steering column mounting bolts to 26 ft. lbs.
    d. **Torque** suction hose and liquid line to 19 ft. lbs.

TECHNICAL SERVICE BULLETINS

RATTLE OR BUZZ AT 1500–2500 RPM

1998 MODELS

On some of these models built before VIN WZ252356 there may be a rattle or buzz noise at steady throttle between 1500–2500 RPM.

This condition may be caused by the heater core pipes contact the heater and air conditioning module case or dash panel.

To correct this condition, proceed as follows:

1. Remove front air inlet duct and air cleaner.
2. Run engine at 1500–2500 RPM.
3. Hold heater core pipes. If rattle or buzz goes away, proceed to next step. If noise does not go away, further diagnosis is required.
4. Remove mounting screw and heater core side cover above accelerator pedal.
5. Install heater core pipe clamp (kit part No. 21030351).
6. **Torque** mounting screws to 16 inch lbs.

1.9L Engine

NOTE: On Air Bag Equipped Models, Refer To "Air Bag System Precautions" Located In The Front Of This Manual For System Disarming & Arming Procedures.

NOTE: Refer To "Computer Relearn Procedures" Located In The Front Of This Manual When Battery Power To The Computer Has Been Interrupted.

NOTE: Prior To Performing Any Service Operations Listed In This Section, Consult The "Technical Service Bulletins" Section For Related Information.

INDEX

PRECAUTIONS

AIR BAG SYSTEMS

Refer to "Air Bag System Precautions" in the front of this manual for system disarming and arming procedures.

BATTERY GROUND CABLE

Prior to service, disconnect battery ground cable and isolate as required.

FUEL SYSTEM PRESSURE RELIEF

1. Connect fuel gauge bar kit tool No. SA-9127-E, or equivalent, to fuel pressure test port using adapter tool No. SA-9403-E, or equivalent, **Fig. 1.**
2. Place end of bleed hose into suitable container and open valve to bleed system pressure.
3. Remove gauge and replace cap.

COMPRESSION PRESSURE

1. Start engine and allow to reach normal operating temperature.
2. Turn engine off and disconnect ignition module harness electrical plug.
3. Remove spark plugs.
4. Install compression gauge tool No. SA-9127-E, or equivalent, in spark plug hole.
5. Ensure battery is charged and throttle fully open.
6. Measure compression while cranking engine, noting the following:
   a. Cylinder should puff or compression gauge needle should bounce at least 10 times.
   b. **Do not crank engine for more than 15 seconds.**
7. Repeat preceding steps for each cylinder.
8. Normal compression pressure is 185–205 psi. Minimum pressure is 180 psi.

ENGINE MOUNT

REPLACE

1. Remove engine mount to midrail bracket mounting nuts, **Fig. 2.**
2. Unload mount by raising engine using suitable floor jack under oil pan with suitable wood block between pan and jack.
3. Remove three engine to front cover mounting nuts and engine mount, **Fig. 3.**
4. Reverse procedure to install.

ENGINE

REPLACE

1. Remove coolant bottle cap and drain coolant into suitable container.
2. Remove air cleaner.
3. Disconnect the following engine electrical connectors:
   a. Coolant temperature sensors.
   b. Oxygen sensor and clip, at front transaxle mount bracket.
   c. Idle air control valve.
   d. Ignition coil.
   e. Throttle position sensor.
   f. Manifold absolute pressure sensor.
   g. EGR solenoid.
   h. Cylinder head rear grounds rear at transaxle.
   i. Injectors.
4. Disconnect brake booster hose at booster or intake manifold.
5. Disconnect the following transaxle connectors:
   a. Neutral safety/selector switch.
   b. Valve body actuator.
   c. Turbine speed sensor.

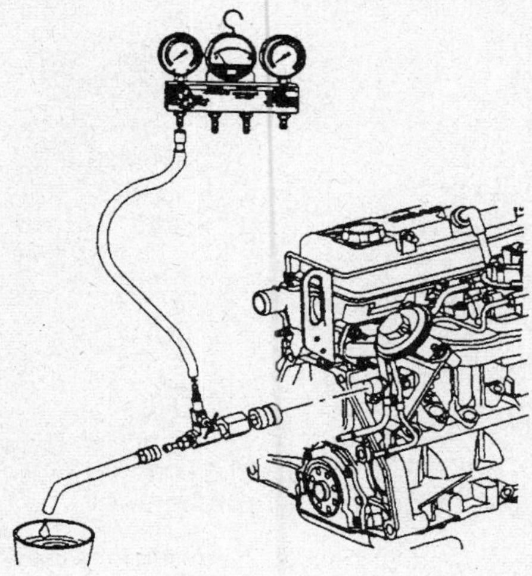

G31029100054000X

Fig. 1 Fuel pressure bleed

d. Temperature sensor.
e. **On models equipped with manual transaxle,** back-up light switch.

6. **On all models,** disconnect accelerator cables.
7. Bleed residual fuel pressure into suitable container using gauge bar tool No. SA-9127-E, or equivalent.
8. **Place cloth around fitting before disconnecting.**
9. Disconnect fuel lines using fuel line tool No. SA-9157-E, or equivalent, **Fig. 4.**
10. **Cap or suspend open fuel lines.**
11. Disconnect upper radiator and deaeration hoses at engine.
12. Disconnect air conditioning compressor and position aside.
13. Pinch tabs to disconnect and plug cooler lines at transaxle. Wrap transaxle cooler line fittings with suitable cloth.
14. **On models equipped with automatic transaxle,** disconnect shifter cable, **Fig. 5.**
15. **On models equipped with manual transaxle,** proceed as follows:
    a. Remove hydraulic damper to clutch housing stud nuts.
    b. Slide damper and bracket from studs.
    c. Disconnect connector and remove by rotating clutch actuator ¼ turn counterclockwise while pushing toward housing.
    d. Position clutch hydraulic system aside.
16. **On all models,** secure radiator, condenser and fan module to front crossbar using suitable wire.
17. Raise and support vehicle.
18. Remove front wheel assemblies, then the front and side shields from cradle.
19. Remove bracket mounting bolts and position caliper aside.
20. Disconnect lower radiator and heater inlet and return hoses at engine.
21. Disconnect steering shaft and power steering pressure switch electrical connector, as required.
22. Remove front exhaust pipe, catalytic converter and powertrain stiffener bracket. **Do not remove torque restrictor bracket to transaxle.**

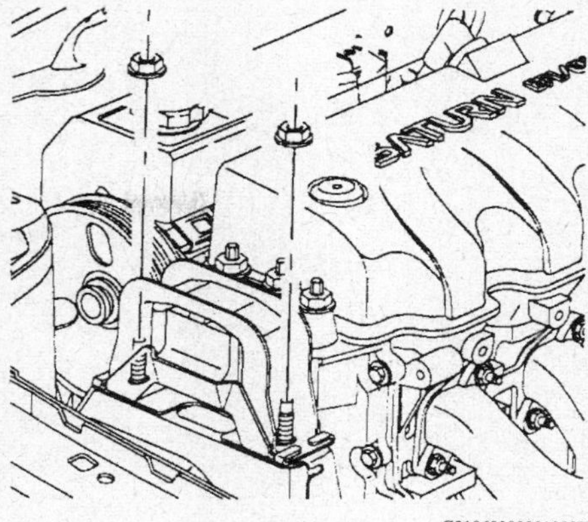

G31069200001000X

Fig. 2 Engine mount to midrail bracket replacement

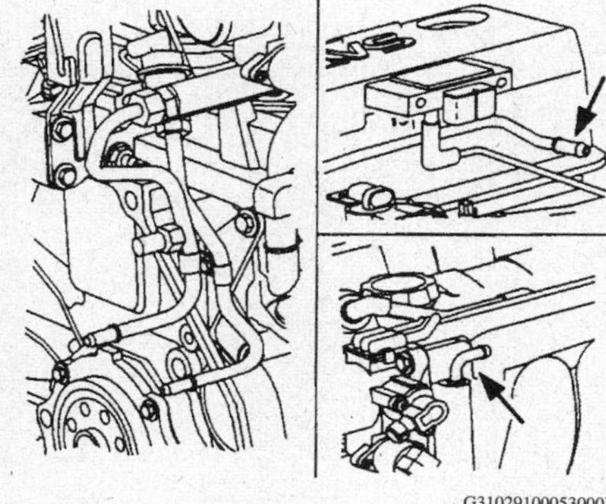

G31029100053000X

Fig. 4 Fuel line removal

23. Remove automatic transaxle flywheel cover and torque converter to flexplate mounting bolts.
24. Remove alternator and starter shields.
25. Disconnect the following electrical connectors:
    a. Starter feed.
    b. Alternator feed.
    c. Oil pressure sensor.
    d. Knock sensor.
    e. Crankshaft position sensor.
    f. EVO solenoid, if equipped.
    g. Vehicle speed sensor.
    h. Canister purge solenoid.
    i. PCM/EC and oxygen sensor.
    j. ABS wheel sensor grounds, if equipped.
26. Disconnect brake lines from rear of cradle and remove electrical harness from engine. Lay electrical harness on underhood junction block and battery cover.
27. Lower vehicle.
28. Place suitable 1 x 1 x 2-inch wood block between torque strut and cradle, **Fig. 6.**
29. Remove upper engine torque axis mount to front cover nuts and mount to midrail bracket nuts.
30. Support cradle using suitable powertrain support dolly and two 4 x 4 x 36-inch wood pieces.
31. Remove cradle to body mounting bolts and lower cradle. Ensure two large rear cradle spacers are attached.

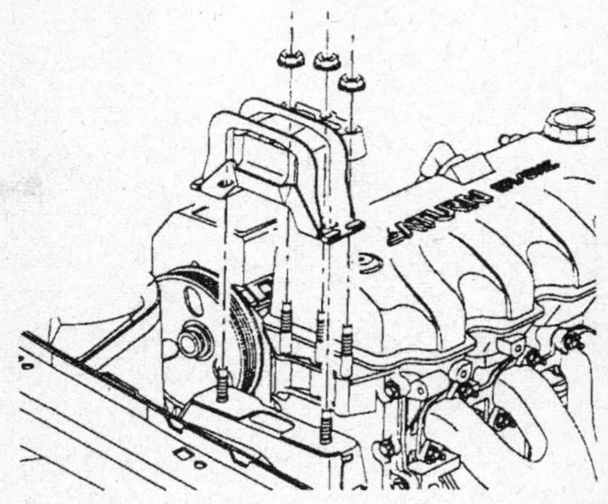

G31069200002000X

Fig. 3 Engine to front cover mount replacement

32. Install suitable engine lifting equipment.
33. Remove spark plug wire ends at ignition module.
34. Remove power steering pump with bracket and attach in upright position to steering gear or cradle using suitable wire.
35. Remove transaxle housing mounting bolts.
36. Remove front engine mount and disconnect motion restrictor, as required.
37. Place ½ x 1 x 3-inch wood block under axle shaft.
38. Remove starter bracket.
39. **On models equipped with DOHC engine,** remove intake manifold bracket.
40. **On all models,** remove three axle shaft bracket bolts and allow bracket to rotate rearward. It may be necessary to lift engine slightly to allow clearance between starter bracket and driveshaft bracket.
41. Place suitable 4 x 4 x 6-inch wood block under transaxle housing.
42. Remove engine strut bracket and torque strut. Engine may have to be lifted slightly to allow engine strut removal, **Fig. 7.**
43. Remove transaxle housing mounting bolts.
44. Lift engine and install on engine stand.
45. Reverse procedure to install.

INTAKE MANIFOLD

REPLACE

SOHC ENGINE

1. Drain engine coolant into suitable container.
2. Remove air cleaner and disconnect fresh air hose at cam cover.
3. Remove PCV hose.
4. Remove fuel line bracket bolt; then disconnect fuel supply and return line by depressing retaining tabs. Discard retainer.
5. Disconnect throttle cable from throttle body and remove bracket mounting nuts.
6. Disconnect the following electrical connectors:
    a. Fuel injectors.

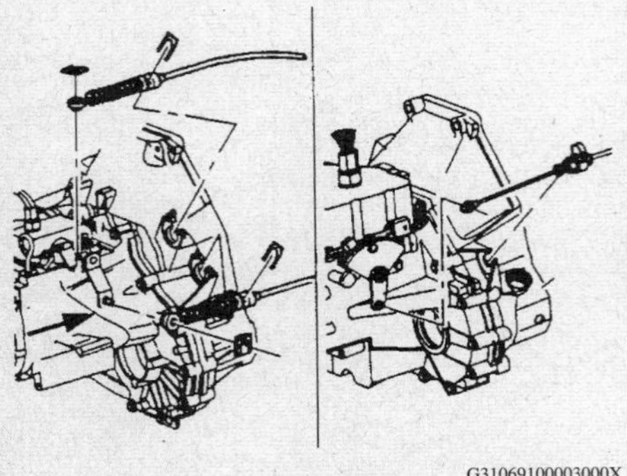

Fig. 5 Transaxle shifter cable replacement

b. Idle air control (IAC).
c. Throttle position sensor (TPS).
d. EGR valve.
e. Manifold absolute pressure sensor.

7. Remove wires with tubes and position harness onto fuel relay.
8. Disconnect and label vacuum hoses.
9. Disconnect heater hose, then remove cylinder head coolant outlet deaeration line fitting and clamps. Position aside.
10. Remove intake manifold support bracket to block mounting bolt and accessory drive belt.
11. Remove mounting bolts and position power steering pump aside.
12. Remove mounting nuts, intake manifold and gasket.
13. Reverse procedure to install. **Torque** intake manifold mounting nuts to 22 ft. lbs. in sequence, **Fig. 8.**

DOHC ENGINE

1. Drain engine coolant into suitable container.
2. Remove air inlet tube/resonator, disconnect fresh air hose at cam cover and lift resonator upward to disconnect from engine.
3. Remove PCV hose.
4. Remove fuel line bracket bolt; then disconnect fuel supply and return lines by depressing plastic retaining tabs of line fitting. Discard retainer.
5. Disconnect throttle cable from throttle body and remove bracket mounting nuts.
6. Disconnect the following electrical connectors:
   a. Fuel injectors.
   b. Idle air control (IAC).
   c. Throttle position sensor (TPS).
   d. Manifold absolute pressure sensor.
   e. EGR valve.
7. Disconnect heater and deaeration hoses at intake manifold outlet.
8. Disconnect EGR solenoid vacuum hose.
9. Position electrical harness over brake master cylinder.
10. Remove intake manifold support bracket to block mounting bolt.
11. Remove accessory drive belt.
12. Remove mounting bolts and position power steering pump aside.
13. Remove upper intake manifold mounting nuts.

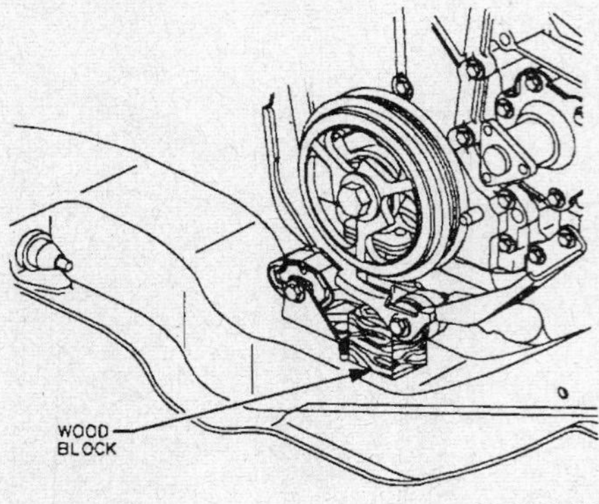

Fig. 6 Torque strut & cradle support

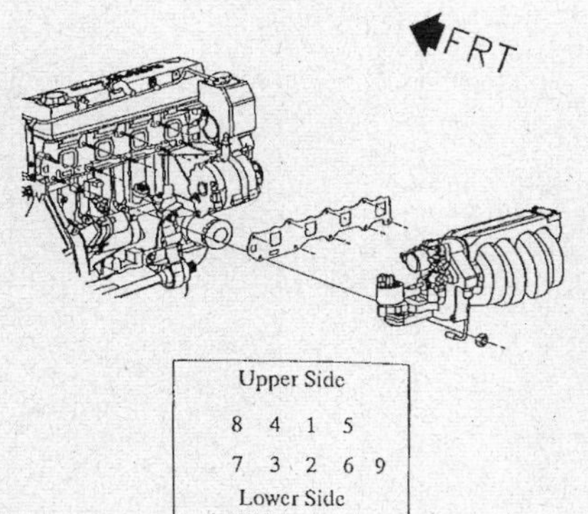

Fig. 8 Intake manifold bolt tightening sequence. SOHC engine

14. Raise and support vehicle.
15. Remove lower power steering bracket.
16. Remove intake manifold bracket mounting bolt.
17. Disconnect canister purge relay and brake booster vacuum hose.
18. Remove lower intake manifold mounting stud.
19. Lower vehicle and remove manifold.
20. Reverse procedure to install. **Torque** intake manifold mounting nuts to 22 ft. lbs. in sequence, **Fig. 9.**

EXHAUST MANIFOLD

REPLACE

1. Raise and support vehicle.
2. Remove exhaust pipe to manifold mounting nuts.
3. Lower exhaust pipe and discard gasket. Lower vehicle.
4. Remove air conditioning compressor and rear compressor bracket.
5. Remove front exhaust pipe to engine stiffening bracket mounting bolts.
6. Disconnect electrical connector and remove oxygen sensor.
7. Remove mounting nuts, exhaust manifold and gasket.
8. Reverse procedure to install, noting the following:
   a. Install new gasket.
   b. **On DOHC models, torque** exhaust manifold mounting nuts to 23 ft. lbs. in sequence, **Fig. 10.**
   c. **On SOHC models, torque** exhaust manifold mounting nuts to 16 ft. lbs. in sequence, **Fig. 10.**

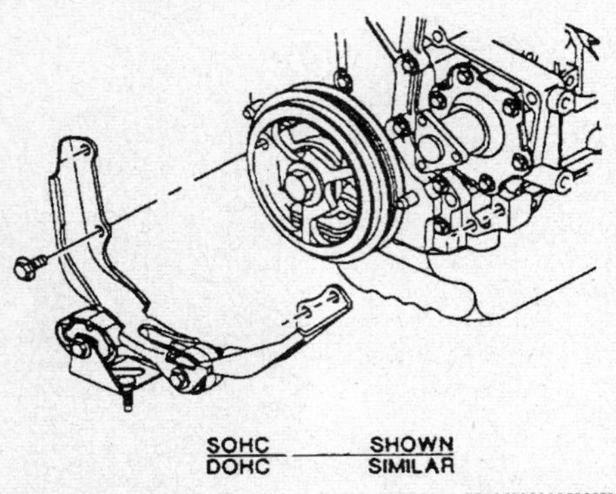

Fig. 7 Engine strut bracket & torque strut replacement

CYLINDER HEAD

REPLACE

SOHC ENGINE

REMOVAL

1. Remove coolant bottle cap.
2. Drain coolant into suitable container.
3. Remove air cleaner and air inlet duct, then disconnect PCV and fresh air hose.
4. Disconnect accelerator cable from throttle lever and bracket from intake manifold.
5. Disconnect the following electrical connectors:
   a. Coolant temperature and PCM.
   b. Injectors.
   c. Idle air control valve.
   d. Manifold air pressure sensor.
   e. Throttle position sensor/switch.
   f. Spark plug wires.
   g. Oxygen sensor.
   h. Air conditioning compressor.
6. Position electrical harness on underhood junction block.
7. Disconnect and label canister purge valve hose and brake booster hose.
8. Disconnect PCV hose at cam cover, fuel regulator vacuum hose and throttle body connector.
9. Disconnect upper radiator hose at cylinder head, heater hose at intake manifold and deaeration hose at throttle body or intake manifold.
10. Remove fuel line clamp to intake manifold base mounting bolt.
11. Disconnect fuel supply and return lines at throttle body.
12. Remove lower intake manifold support bracket stud.
13. Disconnect lower splash shield, then place suitable 1 x 1 x 2-inch wood block between torque strut and cradle.
14. Remove three righthand upper engine torque axis mount to front cover mounting nuts, allowing engine to rest on wood block.
15. Remove accessory drive belt.
16. Disconnect deaeration line at cylinder

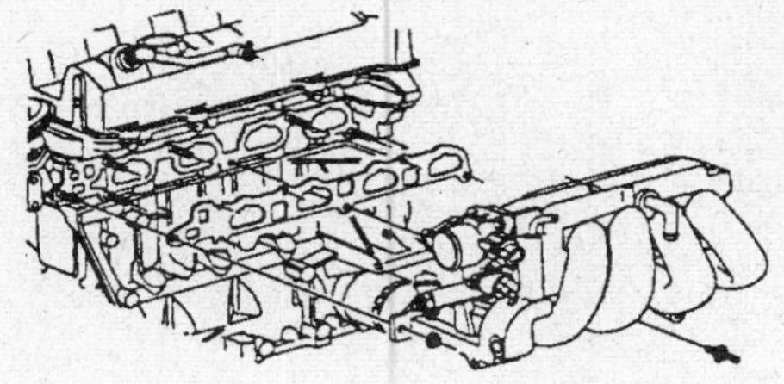

G31059100002000X

Fig. 9 Intake manifold bolt tightening sequence. DOHC engine

head water outlet and support bracket then remove rocker cover, **Fig. 11.**

17. Remove air conditioning compressor front bracket to cylinder head and rear bracket mounting bolts. Position compressor aside. **It is not necessary to recover air conditioning refrigerant.**
18. Remove bracket mounting bolts and position power steering pump aside.
19. Raise and support vehicle, then drain engine oil into suitable container.
20. Remove righthand wheel and splash shield.
21. Remove drive belt tensioner.
22. Remove crankshaft pulley bolt.
23. Remove front crankshaft damper using suitable universal three-jaw puller while holding damper, **Fig. 12. Do not pry against cover.**
24. Hold front crankshaft timing sprocket using crankshaft gear retaining tool No. SA-9104-E, or equivalent, with flat side toward crankshaft sprocket.
25. Remove front oil pan and front cover mounting bolts.
26. Cut RTV seal from front cover using RTV cutter tool No. SA-9123-E, or equivalent.
27. Remove cover using front cover pry tangs.
28. Remove and discard oil gallery transfer seals.
29. **Position crankshaft 90° off Top Dead Center (TDC) to ensure pistons will not contact valves during assembly.**
30. Rotate crankshaft clockwise as viewed from crankshaft accessory belt end. Ensure crankshaft sprocket and keyway timing marks align with main bearing cap split line.
31. Remove timing chain, tensioner, guides, camshaft sprocket and chained, using suitable ⅞ inch wrench to hold camshaft when removing sprocket, **Fig. 13.**
32. Uniformly loosen and remove head bolts in sequence, **Fig. 14.**
33. Remove cylinder head from block dowels.

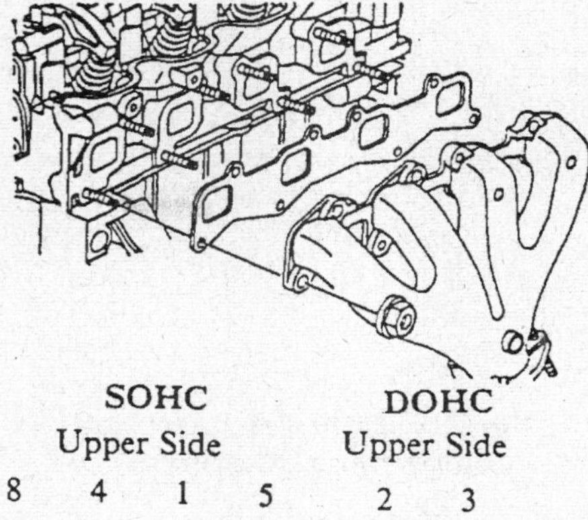

G31079100001000X

Fig. 10 Exhaust manifold bolt tightening sequence

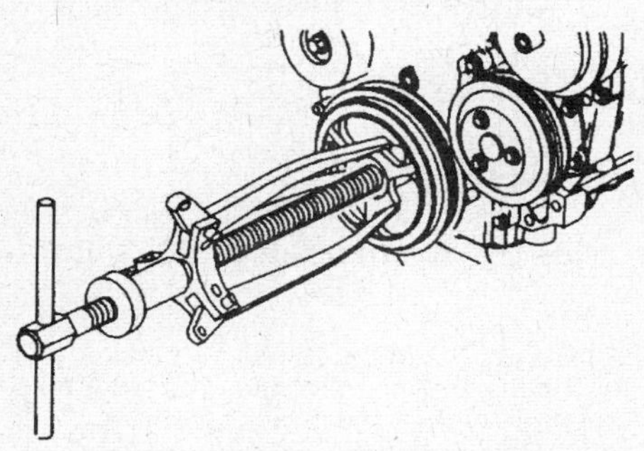

G31069100007000X

Fig. 12 Crankshaft damper removal

INSTALLATION

1. **Torque** cylinder head bolts to 48 ft. lbs. in sequence, **Fig. 15.**
2. Remove bolts and apply light coating of suitable engine oil to threads.
3. **Torque** cylinder head bolts to 22 ft. lbs. in sequence.
4. **Torque** to 33 ft. lbs. in sequence.
5. Finally, tighten cylinder bolts an additional 90° in sequence.
6. Ensure crankshaft is 90° past TDC, **Fig. 16.**
7. Position camshaft to No. 1 TDC by loosely installing sprocket and rotating clockwise until timing pin can be installed, **Fig. 17.**
8. Rotate crankshaft counterclockwise until cylinder No. 1 is at TDC and crankshaft sprocket timing mark will align with cylinder block timing mark, **Fig. 18.**
9. One silver link plate aligns with camshaft sprocket pip marks.
10. Another paired link plates aligns with crankshaft sprocket tooth at 6 o'clock position. Crankshaft sprocket pip mark must be aligned with block timing mark.
11. Place timing chain over camshaft sprocket and under crankshaft sprocket, camshaft sprocket FRT letters must face forward, **Fig. 19.**

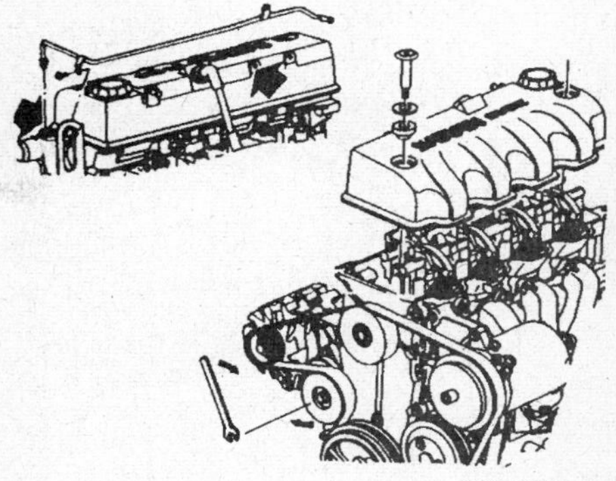

G31069100006000X

Fig. 11 Valve cover replacement. SOHC engine

12. **Keep excess chain slack to chain tensioner side of cylinder block when installing timing chain.**
13. Install camshaft sprocket timing pin, using suitable 3⁄16 inch drill, **Fig. 17.**
14. Install camshaft washer and bolt. Tighten mounting bolt while holding cam.
15. Install fixed chain guide and inspect clearance between block and head.
16. Ensure guide is installed with FRONT facing away from cylinder block and chain is tight against guide.
17. Install pivoting chain guide.
18. Inspect clearance between block and head.
19. Ensure guide pivots freely.
20. Retract tensioner plunger and hold ratchet using suitable ⅛ inch drill. Install tensioner. Remove drill and allow plunger to extend.
21. Ensure timing marks.
22. Remove camshaft timing pins.
23. Install crankshaft timing gear retaining tool No. SA-9104-E, or equivalent.
24. Install front cover and **torque** perimeter mounting bolts to 22 ft. lbs. in sequence, **Fig. 20.**
25. Pump 6–12 drops of oil through front oil seal drain back hole to ensure hole is not plugged.

DOHC ENGINE

REMOVAL

1. Remove coolant bottle cap.
2. Drain coolant into suitable container.
3. Remove air cleaner cover and air inlet duct.
4. Lift resonator upward to disconnect button from engine support bracket.
5. Disconnect cam cover air hose at cam cover.
6. Disconnect accelerator cable from throttle body and intake manifold bracket.
7. Disconnect the following electrical connectors:
   a. Coolant temperature gauge and PCM.
   b. Injectors.
   c. Idle air control valve.
   d. Throttle position sensor/switch.
   e. Manifold air pressure sensor.
   f. Oxygen sensor.
   g. Spark plug wires.
   h. Air conditioning compressor.

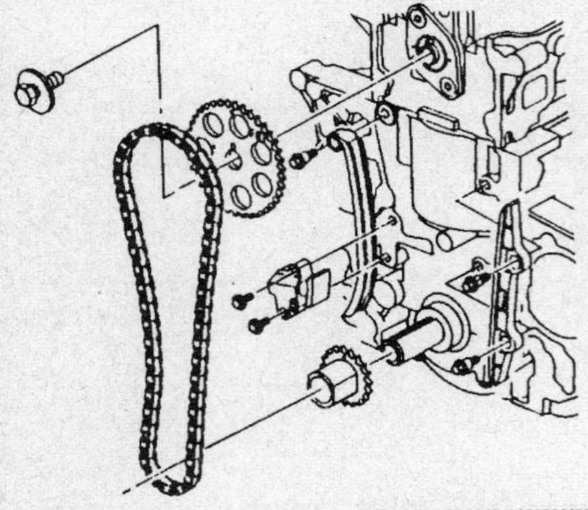

Fig. 13 Timing chain replacement. SOHC engine

i. EGR solenoid.
8. Lay electrical harness onto underhood junction block and battery cover.
9. Disconnect and label the following vacuum hoses:
   a. Canister purge valve.
   b. PCV valve at cam cover.
   c. EGR valve.
   d. Fuel regulator, if equipped.
   e. Throttle body connector.
   f. Brake vacuum booster.
10. Disconnect the following hose clamps using clamp tool No. SA-911-E, or equivalent:
    a. Upper radiator hose at cylinder head outlet.
    b. Deaeration hose at intake manifold.
    c. Heater hose at intake manifold or front of dash.
11. Bleed fuel pressure into suitable container using gauge bar kit tool No. SA-9127-E, or equivalent.
12. Remove fuel line clamp to intake manifold base mounting bolt.
13. Disconnect fuel supply and return line to fuel rail.
14. Disconnect fuel line at regulator.
15. Remove upper intake manifold support bracket mounting bolt.
16. Disconnect lower splash shield and place 1 x 1 x 2-inch wood block between torque strut and cradle.
17. Remove three righthand upper engine torque axis mount to front cover mounting nuts, allowing engine to rest on wood block.
18. Remove accessory drive belt and tensioner. Do not remove water pump pulley.
19. Remove accessory drive belt idler pulley.
20. Remove camshaft cover.
21. Remove bracket mounting bolts and position power steering pump aside.
22. Remove front and rear bracket mounting bolts, then position air conditioning compressor aside. **It is not necessary to recover air conditioning refrigerant.**
23. Raise and support vehicle, then drain engine oil into suitable container.
24. Remove righthand wheel and splash shield.
25. Remove intake manifold bracket to intake manifold mounting bolts.

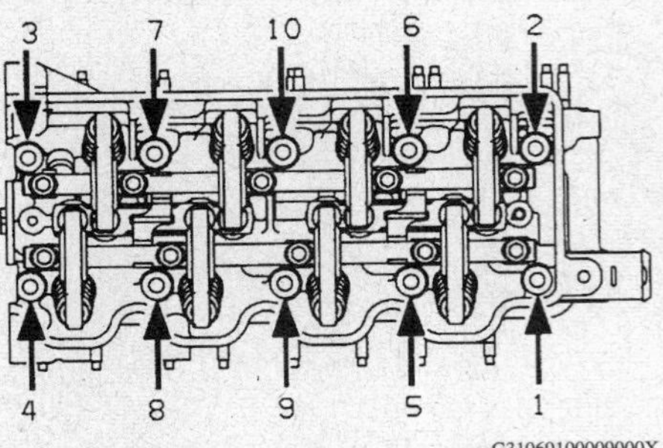

Fig. 14 Cylinder head bolt loosening sequence

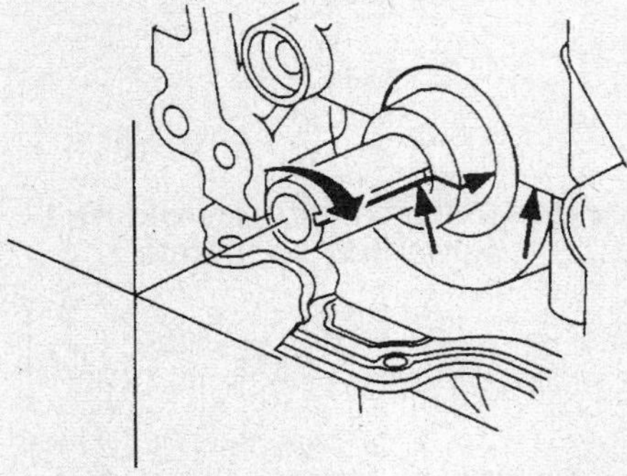

Fig. 16 Crankshaft at 90° past TDC

26. Remove front damper mounting bolt while holding damper with suitable strap wrench or 3/4 inch square x 12-inch long piece of wood wedged between damper spoke and lower rear side of front cover.
27. Remove front crankshaft damper using universal three-jaw puller while holding damper, **Fig. 12. Do not pry against cover.**
28. Disconnect exhaust pipe from exhaust manifold.
29. Hold sprocket using crankshaft gear retaining tool No. SA-9104-E, or equivalent, with flat side toward sprocket.
30. Remove front oil pan bolts and cut seal from front cover using RTV cutter tool No. SA-9123-E, or equivalent.
31. Remove mounting bolts and pry front cover from cylinder block using suitable screwdriver.
32. **Position crankshaft 90° off top dead center to ensure pistons will not contact valves during installation.**
33. Rotate crankshaft clockwise, viewed from crankshaft accessory belt end.
34. Ensure sprocket and keyway timing marks align with main bearing cap split line, **Fig. 21.**
35. Remove timing chain tensioner, guides, camshaft sprockets and chain.
36. Remove sprocket mounting bolts using suitable 7/8 inch wrench to hold camshaft. **Do not place fingers or tools between camshaft sprocket and chain during removal or installation.**
37. Loosen and remove cylinder head bolts in sequence, **Fig. 14.**
38. Remove cylinder head from engine block dowels.

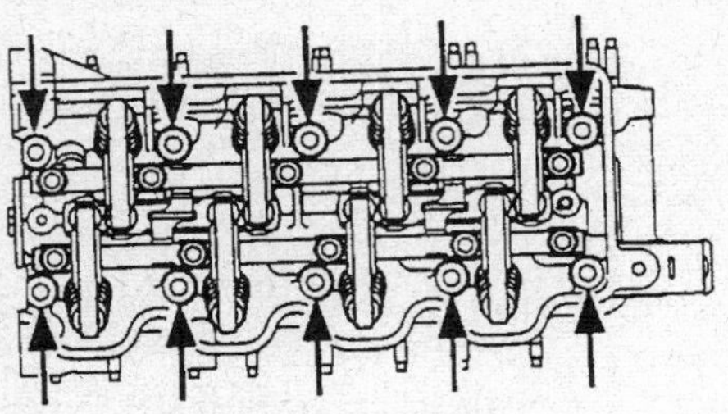

Intake Side

8 4 1 5 9

7 3 2 6 10

Exhaust Side

G31069100010000X

Fig. 15 Cylinder head bolt tightening sequence

INSTALLATION

1. **Torque** cylinder head bolts to 48 ft. lbs. in sequence, **Fig. 15.**
2. Remove bolts and apply light coating of suitable engine oil to threads.
3. **Torque** cylinder head bolts to 22 ft. lbs. in sequence.
4. **Torque** head bolts to 37 ft. lbs. in sequence.
5. Finally, tighten bolts an additional 90° in sequence.
6. Ensure crankshaft is 90° past TDC, **Fig. 16.**
7. Install camshaft timing gears mounting bolts and washer. **Sprocket FRT label must face forward away from cylinder head.**
8. Tighten mounting bolts while holding camshaft.
9. **Do not tighten camshaft mounting bolts against 3/16 inch timing pins.**
10. Position camshaft at cylinder No. 1 TDC by rotating camshaft and sprocket until timing pins can be installed.
11. Rotate crankshaft counterclockwise until cylinder No. 1 is at TDC and crankshaft sprocket and cylinder block timing marks aligns, **Fig. 18.**
12. Align two separated silver link plates with camshaft sprocket pip marks.
13. Align another two paired link plates with crankshaft sprocket tooth at 6 o'clock position. Crankshaft sprocket pip mark must be aligned with block timing mark.
14. Place timing chain over camshaft sprockets and under crankshaft sprocket.
15. **Keep excess chain slack to chain tensioner side (movable guide) of cylinder block.**
16. Position silver colored link plates over pip mark on cam sprocket.
17. Position crankshaft sprocket tooth to pointed downward at 6 o'clock position between two silver colored links. Crankshaft sprocket pip mark should be aligned with block timing mark.
18. Align timing pin holes, crankshaft sprocket pip mark with block mark, colored links with camshaft and crankshaft, **Fig. 22.**

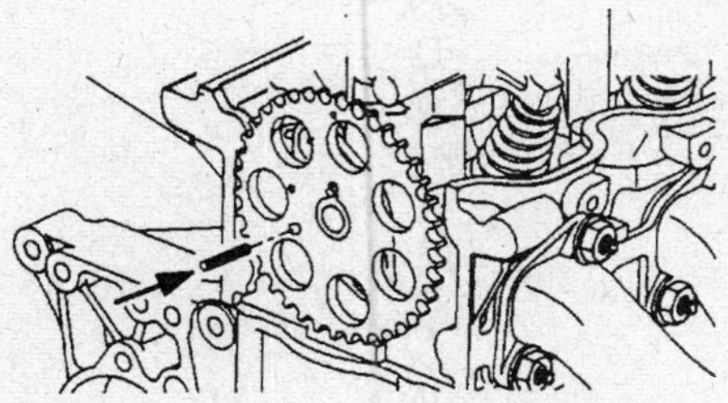

Fig. 17 Camshaft at No. 1 TDC. SOHC engine

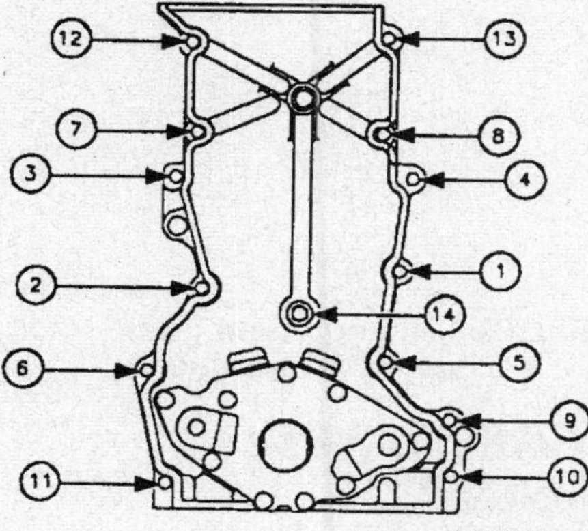

Fig. 20 Front cover tightening sequence. SOHC engine

19. Install fixed guide. Ensure chain is tight against guide.
20. Install pivoting chain guide. Inspect clearance between head and block. Tighten bolt and ensure guide moves freely.
21. Retract tensioner plunger and hold ratchet lever using suitable 1/8 inch drill. Install tensioner.
22. Remove drill and allow plunger to extend.
23. Ensure timing marks align.
24. Remove camshaft timing pins.
25. Install crankshaft retaining tool No. SA-9140-E, or equivalent.
26. Install front cover and **torque** perimeter mounting bolts to 22 ft. lbs. in sequence, **Fig. 23.**
27. Pump 6–12 drops of oil into oil seal drain back hole and ensure hole is not plugged.

VALVE COVER

REPLACE

Refer to procedure in "Cylinder Head, Replace."

CAMSHAFT LOBE LIFT SPECIFICATIONS

Engine	Intake	Exhaust
SOHC	0.2531–0.2556	0.2531–0.2556
DOHC	0.3528–0.3559	0.3409–0.3441

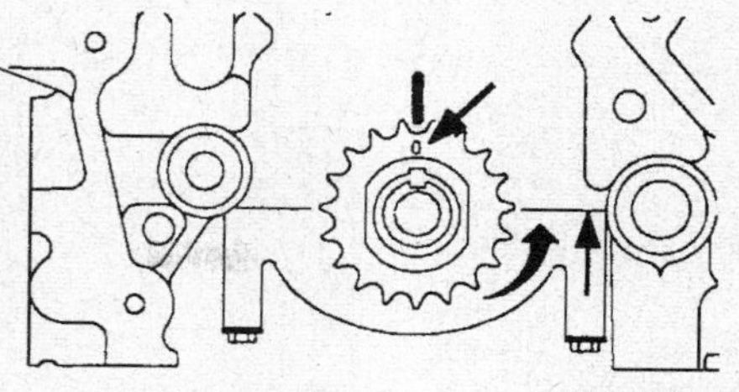

Fig. 18 Crankshaft sprocket & block timing mark alignment

VALVE ADJUSTMENT

This engine is equipped with hydraulic lifters and no adjustment is required.

VALVE GUIDES

Valve guides are an integral part of the cylinder head and are pressed in. If valve stem clearance becomes excessive, the valve guides must be reamed to the oversize and the oversize valves installed. Valves are available in .010 inch oversize.

FRONT COVER

REPLACE

1. Disconnect lower splash shield, then place suitable 1 x 1 x 2-inch long wood block between torque strut and cradle.
2. Remove three righthand upper engine torque axis mount to front cover mounting nuts, allowing engine to rest on wood block.
3. Remove accessory drive belt, idler pulley, tensioner, crankshaft damper and power steering pump.
4. Remove front cover mounting bolts.
5. Remove front cover by prying at upper and lower corners using suitable screwdriver.
6. Reverse procedure to install. Tighten mounting bolts in sequence, **Figs. 20 and 23.**

TIMING CHAIN

REPLACE

Refer to "Cylinder Head, Replace" for timing chain replacement procedure. If required, timing chain may be inspected as follows:

1. Inspect chain for wear and damaged links.
2. Measure chain inner diameter, **Fig. 24.**
3. **On DOHC engine,** standard I.D. is 22.83–22.95 inches. Service limit is 23.15 inches.
4. **On SOHC engine,** standard I.D. is 16.50–16.61 inches. Service limit is 16.77 inches
5. **On all models,** inspect chain guides for wear and cracks.
6. Measure chain track wear, **Fig. 25.** Standard is zero inches. Service limit is 0.0984 inch
7. Inspect timing sprocket teeth on crankshaft, camshaft and key for wear.

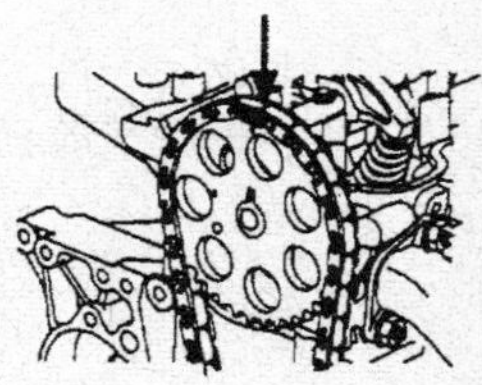

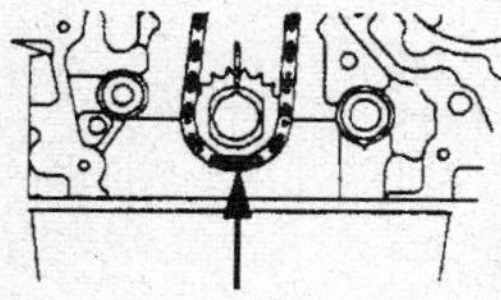

Fig. 19 Timing chain alignment. SOHC engine

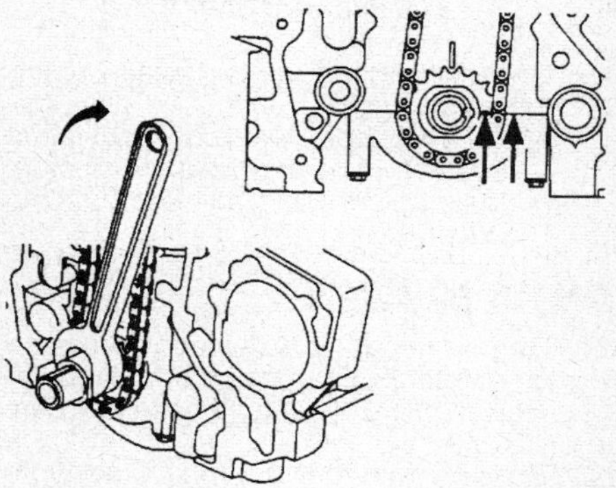

Fig. 21 Crankshaft sprocket & keyway alignment. DOHC engine

8. Inspect camshaft thrust plate and sprocket thrust surface for cracks and wear.
9. Inspect tensioner operation, release plunger lock and ensure piston moves freely.
10. Ensure oil feed hole is open, submerge tensioner in oil or solvent, depress plunger and check flow from tensioner body. Inspect cylinder block port for blockage.
11. Install timing chain and guides installed.
12. Measure plunger travel, **Fig. 26.**
13. **On DOHC engine,** standard is 0.045–0.388 inch. Service limit is 0.8626 inch.
14. **On SOHC engine,** standard is 0.0696–0.4380 inch. Service limit is 0.8626 inch.

CAMSHAFT

REPLACE

SOHC ENGINE

1. Remove battery cover and battery.
2. Remove valve covers, timing chain, gears and guides as outlined under "Cylinder Head, Replace."
3. Remove rocker arms and lifter assemblies.
4. Push camshaft plug inward using suitable driver.
5. Remove camshaft using suitable magnet through rear of cylinder head, **Fig. 27.**

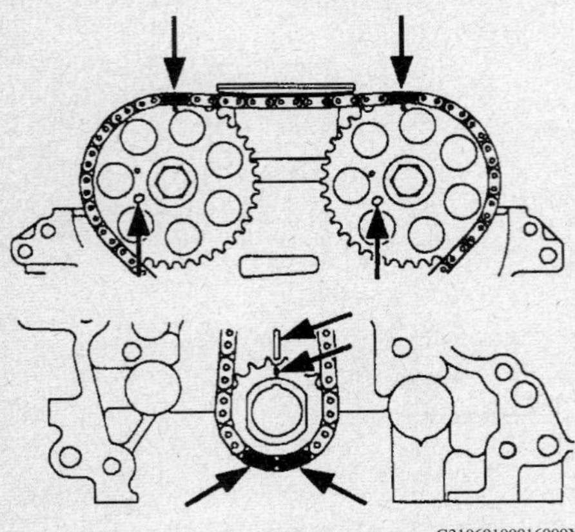

Fig. 22 Crankshaft alignment. DOHC engine

6. Reverse procedure to install, noting the following:
   a. Apply Loctite 242, or equivalent sealant, to new cylinder head plug.
   b. Install plug using suitable bushing driver.

DOHC ENGINE

1. Remove spark plug wires, accessory drive belt, EGR valve solenoid mounting screw, PCV fresh air hose and cam cover.
2. Position cylinder No. 1 to TDC by aligning damper mark with front cover arrow mark, **Fig. 28.**
3. Remove camshaft timing sprocket mounting bolts and washer preventing camshaft from rotating using suitable 7/8 inch open end wrench.
4. Install front support fixture, aligning two holes in each camshaft sprocket, sprocket adapter and front support fixture.
5. Install but do not tighten fixture mounting nuts, **Fig. 29.**
6. Install suitable camshaft sprocket adapter to each camshaft, but do not tighten pilot bolts, **Fig. 30.**
7. Remove upper timing chain guide and front camshaft bearing caps.
8. **Torque** sprocket pilot bolts to 18 ft. lbs. while holding camshaft using suitable 7/8 inch wrench.
9. Move camshaft sprocket off end of each camshaft onto sprocket adapter, **Fig. 31.**
10. Install four 3/8 inch nuts and bolts with blocks through camshaft sprocket, sprocket adapter and front support fixture.
11. Install steel blocks against rearward side of camshaft sprocket.
12. **Torque** nuts and bolts to 18 ft. lbs.
13. Install two 6 mm front support fixture hex bolts to front cover and **torque** bolts to 84 inch lbs.
14. Remove camshaft sprocket pilot bolt while holding camshaft using suitable 7/8 inch wrench.
15. Move cam rearward enough to ensure camshaft end is no longer inside sprocket pilot.
16. Loosen and remove camshaft bearing cap mounting bolts in several passes.

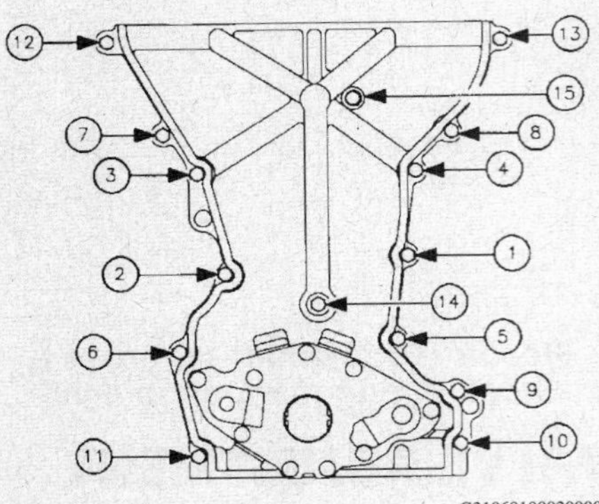

Fig. 23 Front cover tightening sequence. DOHC engine

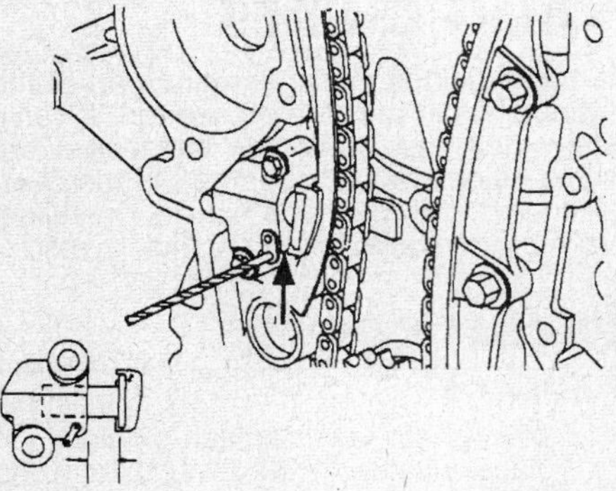

Fig. 26 Timing chain tensioner measurement

If lifters are removed, keep in order for installation. Store with camshaft contact facing downward.

17. Reverse procedure to install.

PISTON & ROD ASSEMBLY

Assemble connecting rod to the piston with the bearing tang slots oriented toward the exhaust manifold, **Fig. 32.**

On DOHC engines, align two eyebrow cuts in piston top toward intake side of engine.

On SOHC engines, align paint dot or pip mark on piston top toward front of engine. If mark is not visible, align piston pin retaining ring pry slots toward intake side of engine.

On all models, if pistons are already install, ensure pin boss with rectangular-shaped casting is pointing toward back of engine, **Fig. 33.**

PISTONS, PINS & RINGS

Pistons are available in 0.005 inch and 0.0157 inch oversizes.

To check piston fit in bore, measure piston diameter at right angle to piston pin hole center line 20 inch from bottom of piston using suitable micrometer. Piston diameter plus piston clearance minus 0.002 inch allowance for finish honing will give piston size to be bored to.

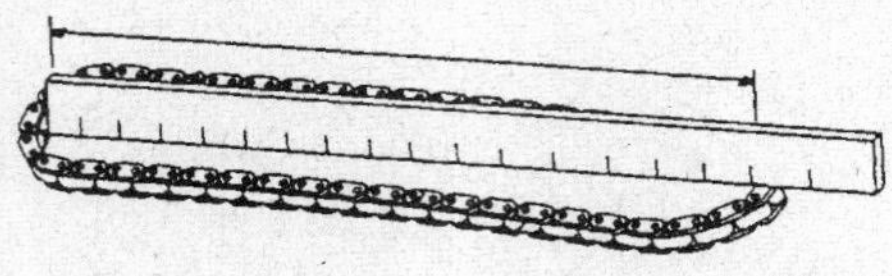

Fig. 24 Timing chain length inspection

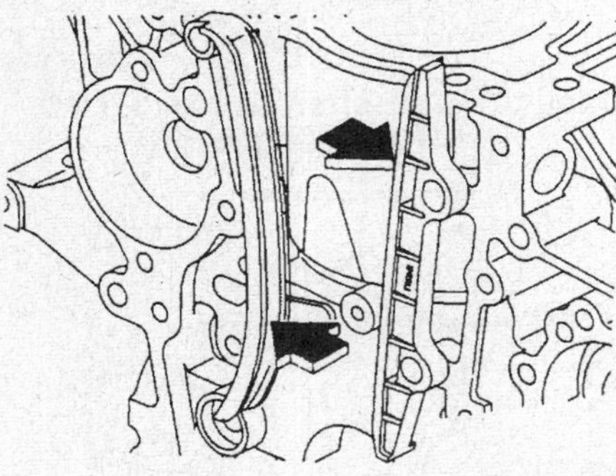

Fig. 25 Timing chain guide track wear measurement

MAIN & ROD BEARINGS

Main and thrust bearings are available in 0.0005 and 0.001 inch undersizes, to adjust for correct main journal clearance.

When installing main bearing caps, ensure arrow points towards the front of the engine.

Torque cap bolts to 37 ft. lbs. in sequence using several steps, **Fig. 34.**

CRANKSHAFT REAR OIL SEAL

REPLACE

This procedure has been revised by a Technical Service Bulletin.

On 2000–01 models equipped with one-piece stamped steel seal, replace one-piece design with two-piece cast aluminum carrier seal (part No. 21006927). Install seal using four new 0.787–inch long bolts (part No. 11513762).

1. Remove transaxle, flywheel and cover.
2. If only oil seal requires replacement, proceed as follows:
   a. Insert suitable screwdriver into pry tangs of seal carrier and remove seal.
   b. Apply engine oil to seal lip and inside diameter of seal carrier.
   c. Install seal using seal installer tool No. SA-9121-E equivalent.
3. If seal and carrier require replacement, proceed as follows:
   a. Remove oil pan as outlined under "Oil Pan, Replace."
   b. Remove seal carrier.
   c. Remove seal from carrier using suitable screwdriver and hammer.
   d. Apply engine oil to seal lip and inside of carrier.
   e. Seal carrier with 0.080 inch diameter bead of suitable RTV.
   f. Install seal carrier.

Fig. 27 Camshaft removal. SOHC engine

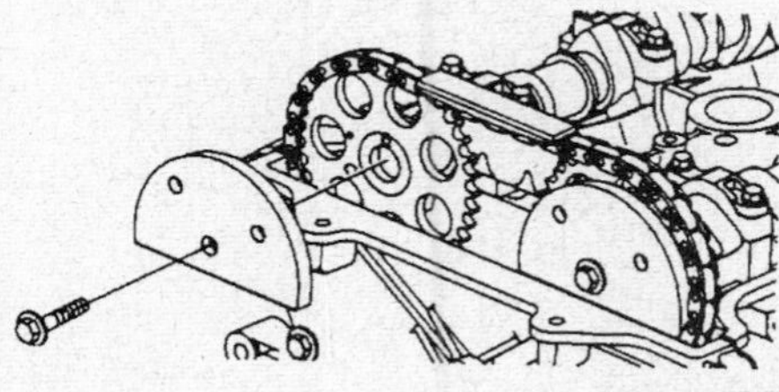

Fig. 30 Camshaft support fixture installation. DOHC engine

g. Install seal using seal installer tool No. SA-9121-E, or equivalent.
4. Install transaxle and flywheel.

OIL PAN

REPLACE

1. Drain engine oil into suitable container.
2. Remove front exhaust pipe.
3. Remove righthand side tire, splash shield and vibration damper.
4. Loosen, but do not remove, four front engine mount mounting bolts approximately ½ inch.
5. Remove oil pan mounting bolts.
6. Pry front engine mount away from cylinder block to allow oil pan removal.
7. Shear seal using RTV removal tool No. SA-9123-E, or equivalent, sharp edge between pan and block.
8. Remove oil pan by tapping sideways using suitable rubber mallet
9. Reverse procedure to install. Apply 0.160 inch bead of RTV sealant to inside edge of oil pan groove.

OIL PUMP

REPLACE

1. Raise and support vehicle.
2. Drain engine oil into suitable container.
3. Remove righthand front wheel assembly and splash shield.
4. Place 1 x 1 x 2-inch wood block between torque strut and cradle.
5. Remove drive belt.
6. Remove crankshaft pulley bolt.
7. Remove front crankshaft damper using universal three-jaw puller while holding damper, **Fig. 12. Do not pry against cover.**
8. Remove idler pulley.

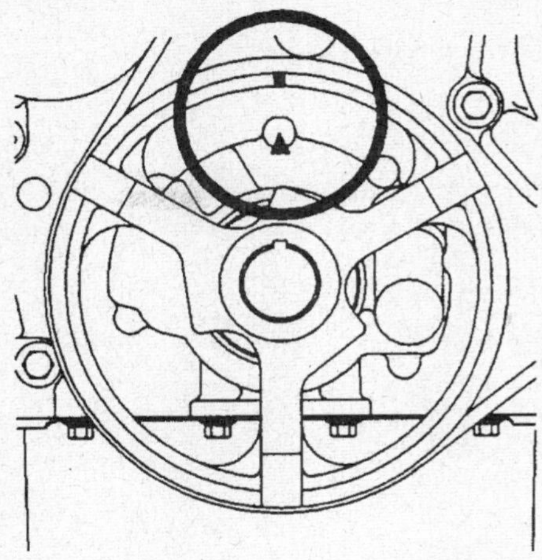

Fig. 28 Cylinder No. 1 at TDC. DOHC engine

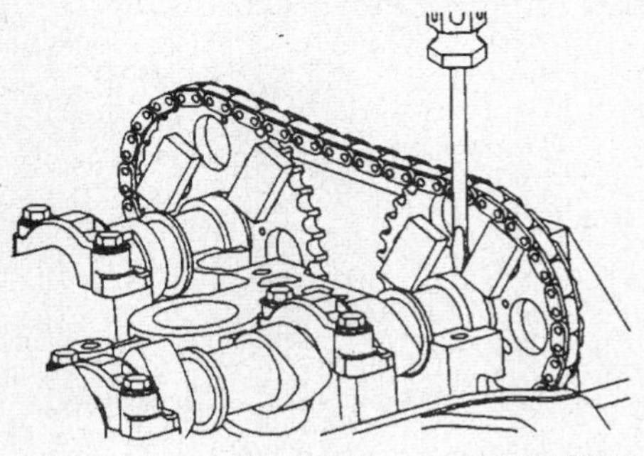

Fig. 31 Camshaft replacement. DOHC engine

9. Remove power steering pump and position aside.
10. Remove belt tensioner.
11. Remove valve cover as outlined under "Valve Cover, Replace."
12. Remove three righthand upper engine torque axis mount to front cover mounting nuts, allowing engine to rest on wood block.
13. Hold front crankshaft timing sprocket using crankshaft timing gear tool No. SA-9104-E, or equivalent, with flat side toward crankshaft sprocket.
14. Remove front oil pan and front cover mounting bolts.
15. Cut RTV seal from front cover using RTV cutter tool No. SA-9123-E, or equivalent.
16. Remove oil gallery transfer seals using front cover pry tangs. Discard seals.
17. Reverse procedure to install.

OIL PUMP SERVICE

DISASSEMBLE

1. Remove cover plate mounting bolts.
2. Remove drive and driven rotors.
3. Remove and discard relief valve using tool No. SA-9103-E, or equivalent.

INSPECTION

1. Measure clearance between driven rotor and pump body, **Fig. 35.** Replace

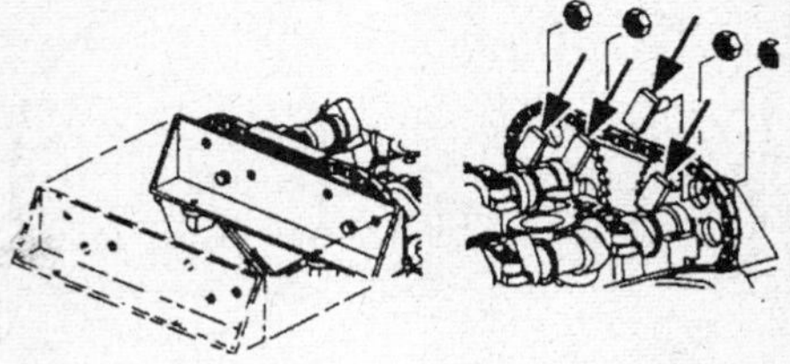

Fig. 29 Camshaft front support fixture. DOHC engine

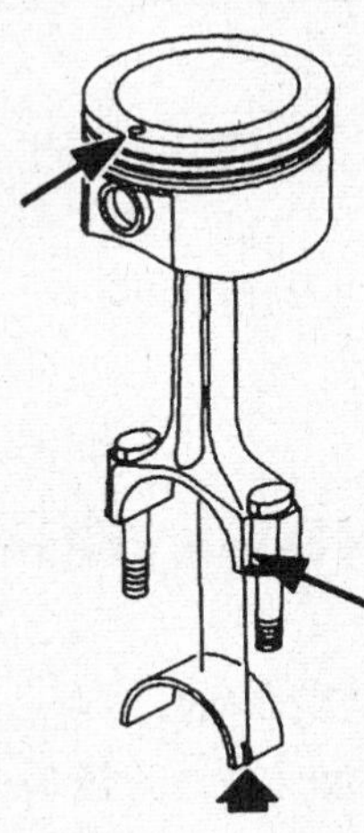

Fig. 32 Piston & rod assembly

pump rotor set is clearance is more than 0.006–0.011 inch.
2. Inspect clearance between both rotor tips, **Fig. 36.** Maximum clearance is 0.006 inch.
3. Measure clearance between side of gear rotor assembly and cover plate, **Fig. 37.** Standard clearance is 0.0016–0.0049 inch and maximum clearance is 0.0050 inch.

ASSEMBLE

1. Remove front cover oil seal using suitable screwdriver or punch.
2. Install new oil seal using seal installer tool No. SA-9140-E, or equivalent, and suitable press.
3. If relief valve was removed, proceed as follows:
   a. Coat new relief valve with suitable engine oil.
   b. Install relief valve using driver tool No. SA-9103-E, or equivalent, and suitable hammer.
4. Pack oil pump with suitable petroleum jelly.
5. Install drive and driven rotors to pump body with chamfer toward front oil seal.
6. Install pump body cover and new bolts.

BELT TENSION DATA

Belt	Tension, Lbs.	
	New	Used
Accessory	50–65	45

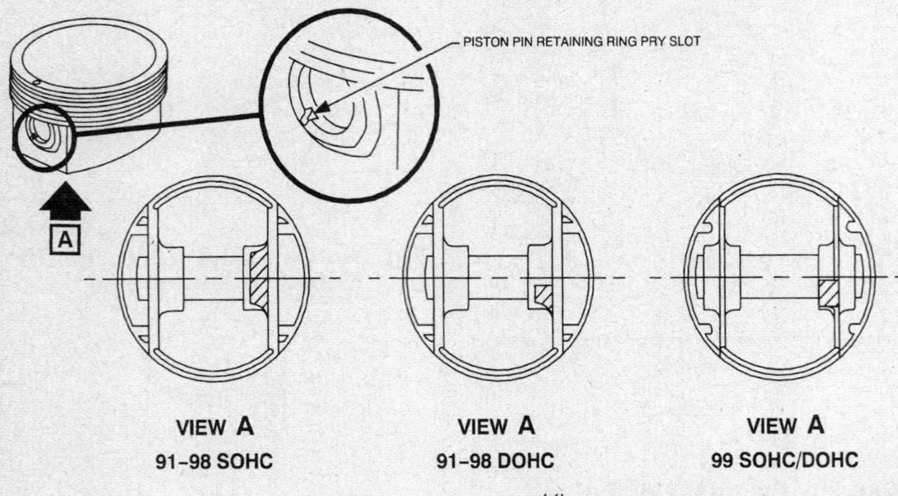

Fig. 33 Piston boss configuration

SERPENTINE DRIVE BELT

BELT ROUTING

Refer to **Figs. 38 and 39** for serpentine belt routing.

TENSIONER, REPLACEMENT

Tensioner internal components are nor serviceable. **Do not disassemble tensioner.**

1. Disconnect lower splash shield and place suitable 1 x 1 x 2-inch wood block between torque strut and cradle.
2. Remove three righthand upper engine torque axis mount to front cover mounting nuts, allowing engine to rest on wood block.
3. Remove belt as outlined under "Belt, Replacement."
4. Remove power steering pump with bracket.
5. Remove tensioner upper and lower mounting bolts, **Fig. 40.**
6. Move engine slightly toward drivers fender using suitable pry bar between steel engine mount and rail, as required.
7. Remove tensioner.
8. Reverse procedure to install.

BELT REPLACEMENT

REMOVAL

1. Depress tensioner arm using suitable wrench, **Fig. 41.**
2. Remove belt from idler and accessory pulleys.

INSTALLATION

1. Route belt over pulleys, except front cover idler or air conditioning compressor.
2. Depress tensioner arm using suitable wrench.
3. Install belt to idler pulley and air conditioning compressor.

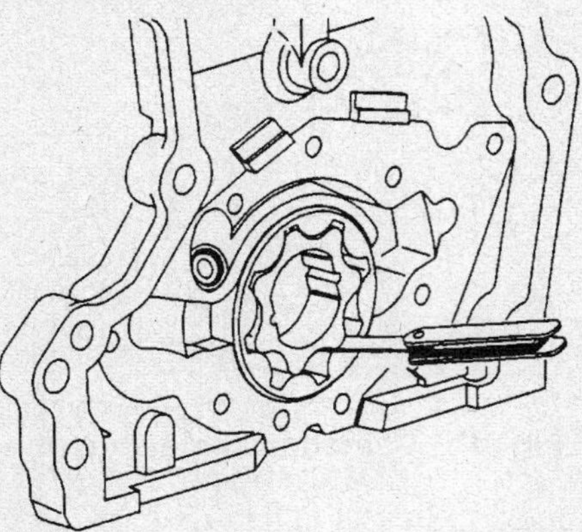

Fig. 36 Oil pump tip clearance measurement

COOLING SYSTEM BLEED

These engines do not require a special bleed procedure. After filling cooling system, run engine and allow to reach normal operating temperature with pressure cap off. Air will then automatically bleed through cap opening.

THERMOSTAT

REPLACE

REMOVAL

Do not remove pressure cap while engine is running or when engine is still warm.

1. Remove engine drain plug at righthand front of engine and open draincock at lower part of radiator to drain coolant into suitable container. Ensure coolant level is below thermostat housing.
2. Disconnect lower radiator hose at thermostat housing using Snap On hose removal tool No. HCP10, or equivalent.
3. Remove water inlet housing mounting bolts.

Intake Side				
8	4	1	5	9
7	3	2	6	10
Exhaust Side				

G31069700076000X

Fig. 34 Main bearing cap bolt tightening sequence

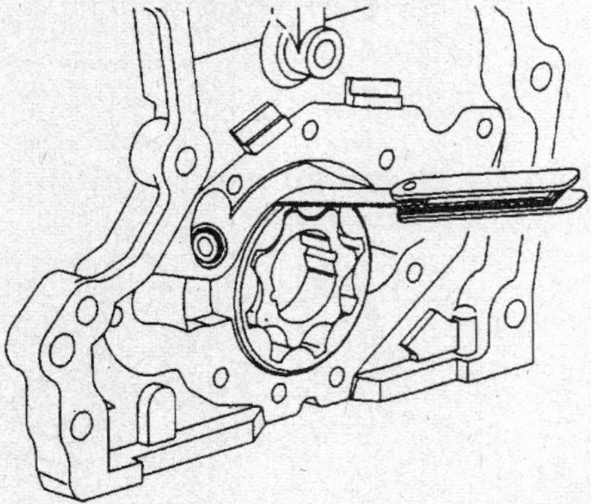

Fig. 35 Oil pump body clearance measurement

4. Remove water inlet and thermostat as an assembly. Discard O-ring.
5. Remove thermostat element using service tool provided with replacement part, noting the following:
   a. New part will not function correctly if oil comes in contact with part.
   b. If oil is found in coolant, flush entire system before replacing thermostat.
6. Ensure no damage or seat deterioration is found within water inlet housing. **Do not damage machined aluminum surfaces.**

INSTALLATION

1. Install new thermostat using service tool provided, ensure tangs are properly seated in legs and piston is correctly positioned in water inlet housing.
2. Install new water inlet housing O-ring.
3. Install water inlet housing and thermostat.
4. Close radiator and engine drain plugs.
5. Install lower radiator hose. Ensure vehicle is on level surface.
6. Fill coolant system.
7. Start engine and run for several minutes.
8. Fill cooling system surge tank to full cold line.
9. Install pressure cap and inspect for leaks.

WATER PUMP

REPLACE

1. Drain coolant into suitable container.
2. Remove accessory drive belt.
3. Raise and support vehicle.
4. Remove righthand wheel assembly, then inner wheelwell splash shield.

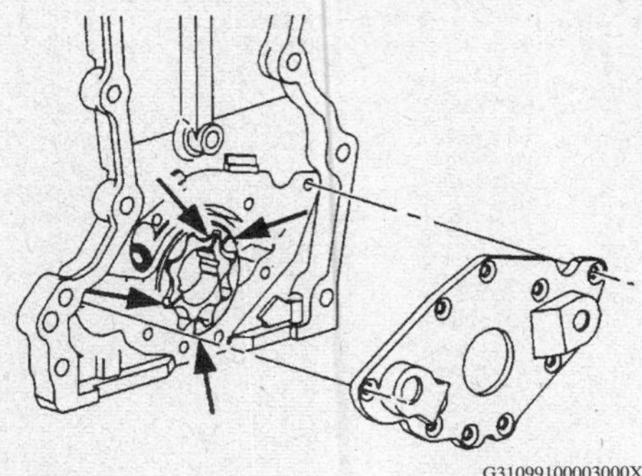

Fig. 37 Oil pump end to end clearance measurement

5. Remove mounting bolts and position air conditioning compressor aside.
6. Place one-inch wood block between crankshaft and water pump pulley.
7. Remove mounting bolts and allow pulley to hang on pump hub.
8. Remove mounting bolts, water pump and gasket.
9. Reverse procedure to install. Install new gasket.

RADIATOR

REPLACE

1. Drain cooling system into suitable container.
2. Remove air intake duct.
3. Remove upper radiator clamp and hose.
4. **On models equipped with automatic transaxle,** remove upper transaxle oil cooler line.
5. **On all models,** remove electric cooling fan.
6. Disconnect lower radiator hose.
7. Raise and support vehicle.
8. Remove lower splash shield.
9. **On models equipped with automatic transaxle,** remove lower transaxle oil cooler line.
10. **On all models,** remove lower condenser bracket to radiator bolts and support condenser with suitable wire.
11. Lower vehicle, then remove upper radiator mounting nuts and brackets.
12. **On models equipped with air conditioning,** remove upper radiator seal.
13. **On all models,** remove radiator.
14. Reverse procedure to install.

FUEL PUMP

REPLACE

When removing fuel system lines and hoses, wrap a suitable shop towel around fitting and have an suitable container available to catch any fuel that may spill.

1. If fuel pump is operational, drain fuel tank into suitable container as follows:
   a. Remove air cleaner inlet hose from throttle body.
   b. Disconnect fuel feed line at fuel rail and install fuel adapter fitting tool No. SA-3097-38, or equivalent.
   c. Connect one end of suitable fuel line to adapter and other end to suitable fuel handling cart.

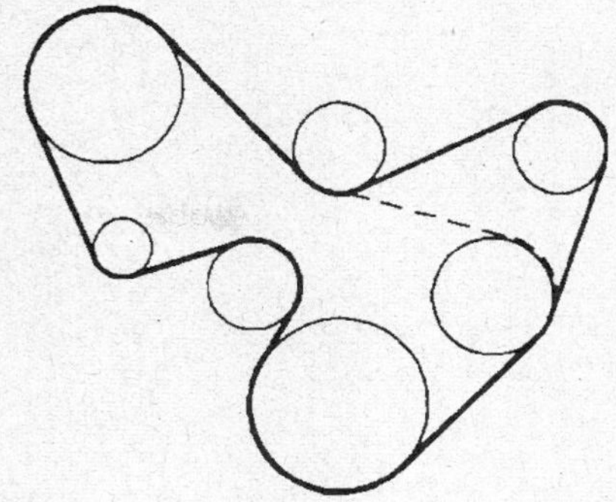

Fig. 38 Serpentine belt routing. DOHC engine

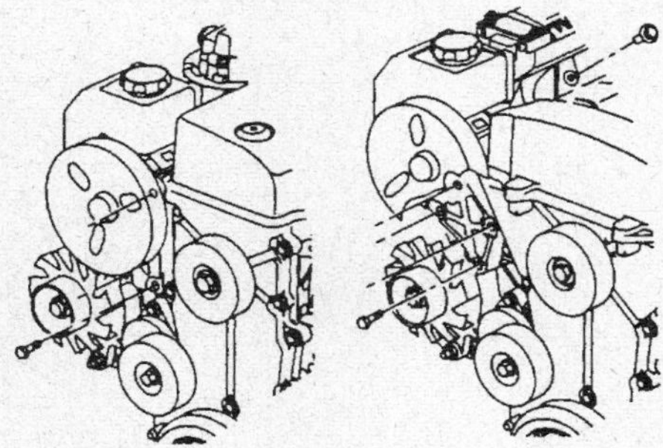

Fig. 40 Belt tensioner replacement

   d. Connect suitably programmed scan tool to Data Link Connector (DLC) and turn ignition switch ON.
   e. Turn fuel pump on using scan tool and pump fuel into suitable container.
2. If fuel pump is inoperative, siphon fuel using siphon hose tool No. SA-980-E, or equivalent, **Fig. 42.**
3. Remove fuel filler cap and rubber close-out grommet.
4. Remove filler pipe mounting screw.
5. Raise and support vehicle.
6. Remove wheelwell inner cover.
7. Disconnect wiring harness from EVAP vent solenoid.
8. Remove filler pipe lower mounting screw.
9. Disconnect EVAP canister vent pipe at ⅝ inch quick connect to canister hose.
10. Remove fuel filler pipe from fuel tank. Ensure fuel fill check valve is not dislodged from filler pipe.
11. Disconnect fuel feed line from fuel pressure regulator.
12. Disconnect fuel vapor line from quick connect fitting.
13. Remove filter bracket from under brake lines.
14. Support fuel tank with suitable lifting device and remove strap mounting bolts.
15. Lower tank enough to access, then disconnect fuel pump and tank pressure sensor electrical connectors.
16. Lower fuel tank.
17. Disconnect fuel feed and return lines from pressure regulator.
18. Disconnect fuel pump vapor line from fuel tank vent pipe.

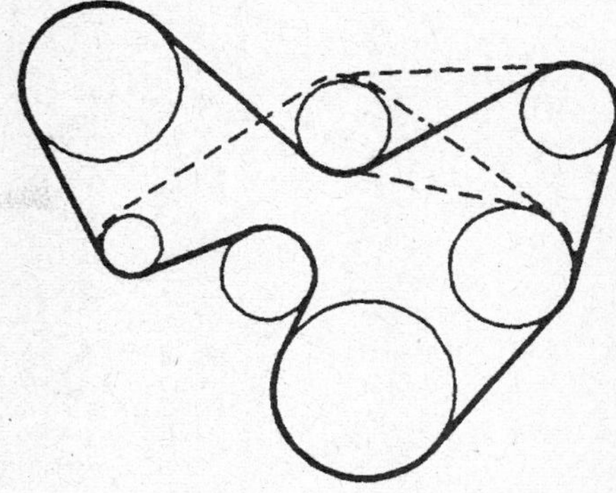

Fig. 39 Serpentine belt routing. SOHC engine

19. Remove fuel pump retaining ring using lock ring removal tool No. SA-9156-E, or equivalent.
20. Lift pump slightly to disconnect tabs and rotate 90° clockwise until lines are facing 1 o'clock position.
21. Lift pump until bottom is close to tank opening.
22. Tilt pump 45° toward righthand side of tank and lift out.
23. Reverse procedure to install, noting the following:
   a. Install new fuel pump green seal. **Do not use black seal.**
   b. White locator button located on lefthand side of fuel tank should be flush with lefthand side rail when installation is complete.
   c. Replace plastic fuel line retainers on lines which were disconnected.

FUEL FILTER

REPLACE

The fuel filter/regulator assembly is located on the underbody near the front lefthand side of the fuel tank.

1. Raise and support vehicle.
2. Remove fuel filter bracket mounting screws.
3. Unlatch fuel line bundle retaining clip at lefthand side of fuel tank.
4. Disconnect EVAP purge line at 90° quick connect.
5. Slide outlet of filter from support on fuel tank bracket and remove fuel feed line at 90° quick connect.
6. Pivot filter down while moving leg of bracket from under brake lines.
7. Disconnect fuel feed and return lines, then remove filter/regulator and bracket.
8. Reverse procedure to install, noting the following:
   a. Install new plastic fuel line retainers.
   b. Ensure fuel feed and purge lines are routed on top of emergency brake cable.
   c. Ensure emergency brake cable is secured firmly to underbody to support lines.
   d. Operate fuel pump and inspect system for leaks.

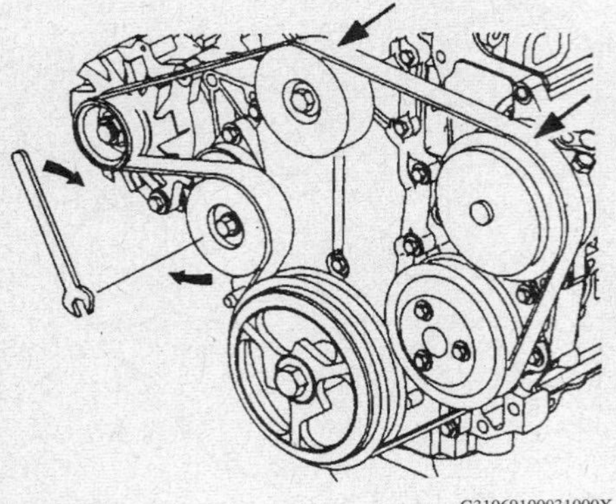
Fig. 41 Belt tensioner arm replacement

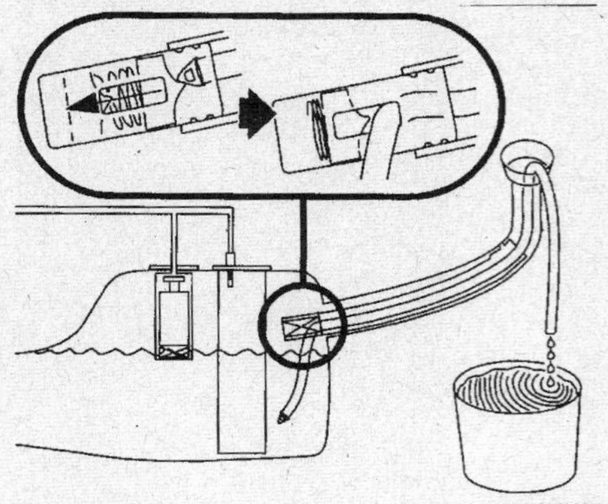
Fig. 42 Fuel tank siphoning

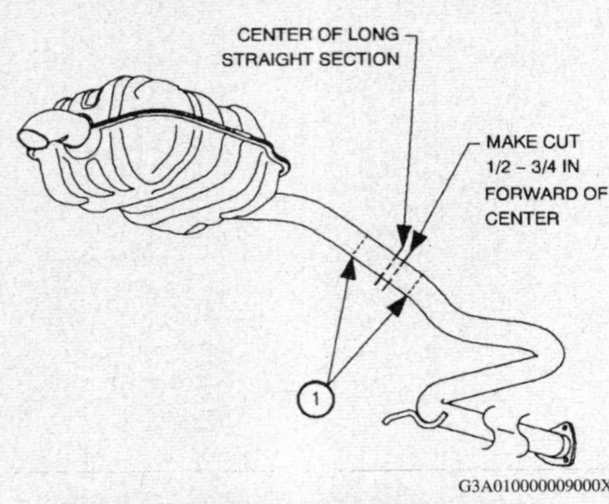

Fig. 43 Intermediate pipe cut location

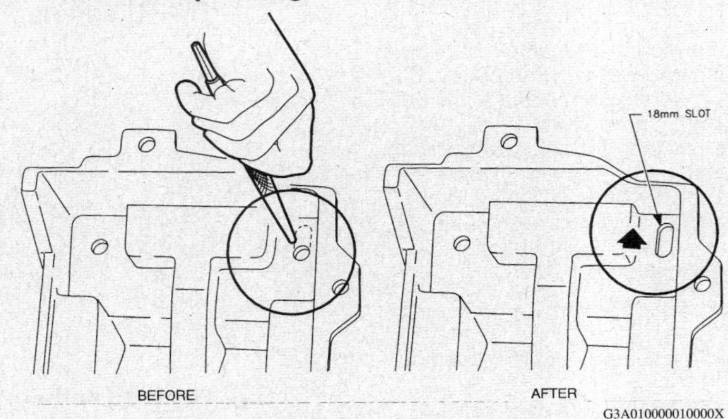

Fig. 44 Battery tray modification

TECHNICAL SERVICE BULLETINS

VALVE TRAIN NOISE

1999–2000 MODELS

On some of these models equipped with DOHC engine built before VIN YZ145977 there may be a light tapping, ticking or knocking noise that increase with engine RPM.

This condition may be caused by misalignment of intake and/or exhausted camshaft bearing caps.

To correct this condition, proceed as follows:

1. Disconnect cam cover air hose at duct.
2. Remove spark plug wires from plugs and cam cover.
3. Disconnect PXV hose at cam cover.
4. Remove mounting bolts and cam cover. Cover camshaft.
5. **Loosen and tighten camshaft bearing caps one at a time.**
6. Starting at front of engine closest to timing chain, loosen camshaft bearing cap bolts until it moves freely.
7. **Torque** camshaft bearing cap bolt to 10 ft. lbs.
8. Repeat previous two steps until all caps have been loosened and tightened.

EXHAUST POP

1998–99 MODELS

On some of these models equipped with base SOHC engine and manual transaxle there may be an exhaust pop during extended deceleration between 3500–3200 RPM in 2nd gear or 2500–2200 RPM in 3rd gear. This includes 1998 models built after VIN WZ216015.

This condition may be caused by fuel delivery during extended deceleration.

To correct this condition, install DOHC intermediate exhaust pipe (part No. 21013306).

SQUEAK OR CHIRP FROM VEHICLE FRONT

1999 MODELS

On some of these models equipped with DOHC engine and California LEV emissions there may be a squeak or chirp from the front of the vehicle at 50–60 mph or 2100–3000 RPM.

This condition may be caused by the secondary air injection (AIR) pump bracket anti-rotation tab wearing against the motor rail slot.

To correct this condition, proceed as follows:

1. Disconnect AIR wiring harness connector.
2. Remove AIR outlet air hose.
3. Remove mounting bolts, air pump and bracket. Place assembly on radiator support.
4. Slide suitable shrink tubing onto anti-rotation tab up to first bracket bend. Position tubing opposite end in middle of tapered section.
5. Shrink tubing using suitable heat gun and allow to cool.
6. Install air pump and bracket. **Torque** mounting bolts to 18 ft. lbs.

RATTLE OR CLUNK FROM REAR

1998–99 MODELS

On some of these models there may be a rattle or clunk from the rear of the vehicle. This condition may exists on 1998 models built after VIN WZ217015, and on 1999 models equipped with DOHC California emissions engines built up to VIN XZ119715, equipped with DOHC Federal emissions engines built up to VIN XZ129456, equipped with SOHC California emissions engines built up to VIN XZ134512, or equipped with SOHC Federal emissions engines built up to VIN XZ129407.

This condition may be caused by the muffler contacting the ramp welded to the spaceframe.

To correct this condition, proceed as follows:

1. Raise and support vehicle.
2. Mark and cut point ½–¾ inch forward of center of long straight (four-inch) section of intermediate pipe using chain cutter tool No. SA-1968-NE, or equivalent, **Fig. 43.**
3. Remove muffler.
4. Loosen replacement muffler inlet clamp.
5. Install muffler and slide inlet pipe over cut section.
6. Tighten clamp with strap in muffler channel.
7. Ensure ¾ inch clearance between muffler and ramp, then **torque** muffler mounting bolt to 16 ft. lbs.
8. Ensure clamp is one inch for inlet pipe end with U-bolt facing away from fuel tank.
9. **Torque** U-bolt clamp to 30 ft. lbs.
10. Ensure exhaust system is properly aligned and clears heat shields. Adjust in isolator block, as required.

POP NOISE FROM UNDERBODY

1998 MODELS

On some of these models there may be a

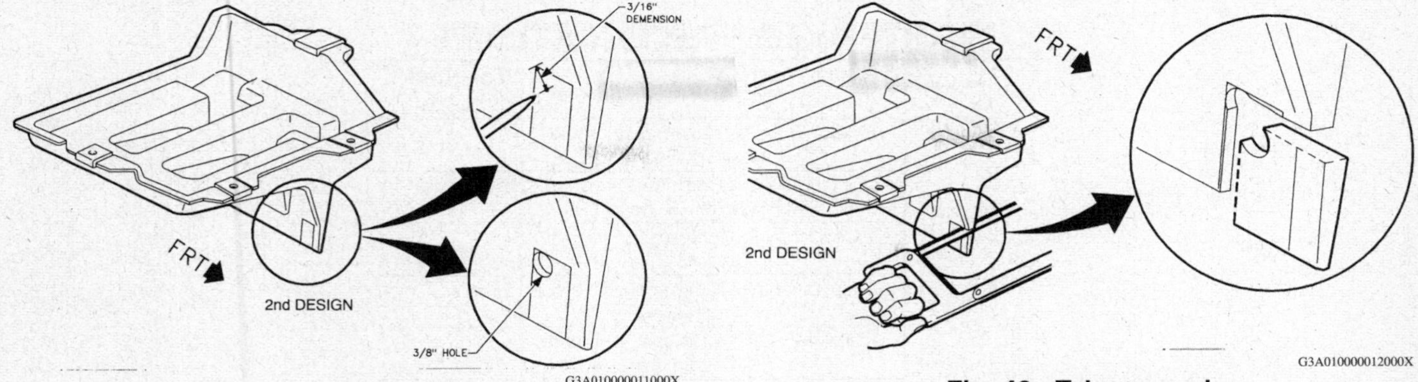

Fig. 45 Pilot hole

Fig. 46 Tab removal

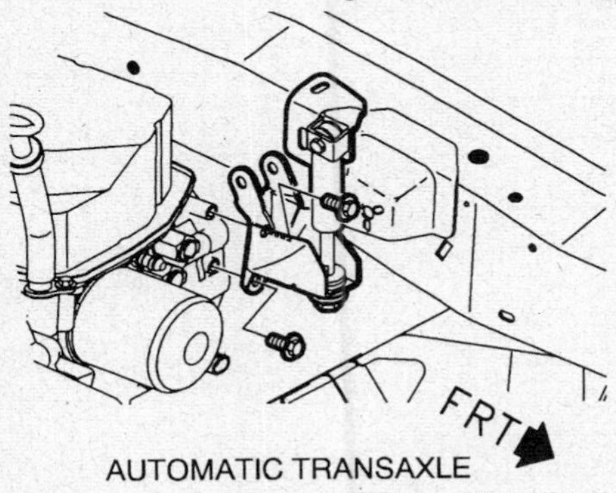

Fig. 47 Damper installation. Automatic transaxle

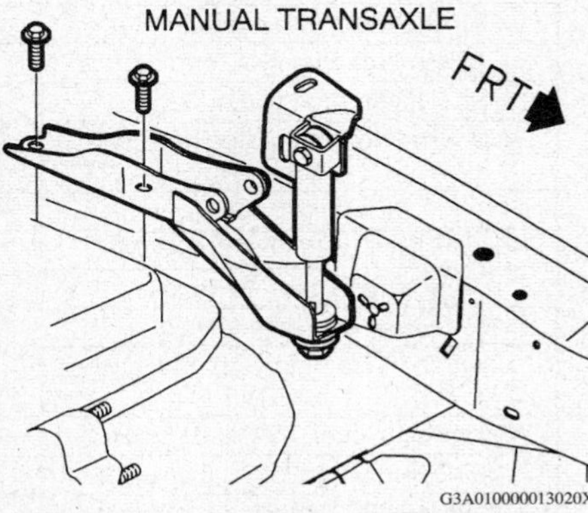

Fig. 48 Damper installation. Manual transaxle

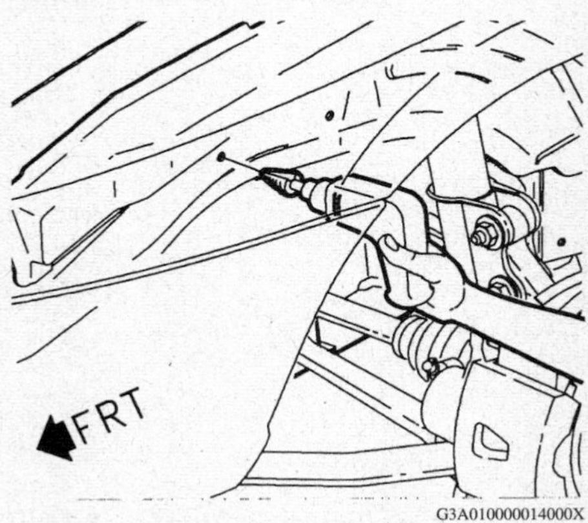

Fig. 49 Midrail hole enlargement

pop noise from underbody when vehicle is parked or idling.

This condition may be caused by loose exhaust heat shield pop rivets.

To correct this condition, replace loose rivets.

VIBRATION AT 48–54 MPH

1998–99 MODELS

On some of these models there may be a vibration at 48–54 mph on smooth roads.

This condition may be caused by insufficient damping between the engine cradle and powertrain.

To correct this condition, install powertrain damper kit (automatic transaxle part No. 21012637 or manual transaxle part No. 21012638) as follows:

1. Remove kit damper shaft first rubber grommet and steel washer.
2. Install damper shaft into appropriate lower bracket, then the rubber grommet and steel washer.
3. **Torque** shaft nut to 89 inch lbs. Hold damper shaft flats using suitable wrench while tightening nut.
4. Remove air induction system and disconnect battery cables.
5. Remove mounting nut, screw and hold-down retainer, then the battery.
6. Remove mounting bolts and battery tray.
7. Place battery tray in suitable vice and elongate forward vertical bolt hole (outboard toward lefthand front tire) by 5/16–23/32 inch using suitable file, **Fig. 44. Do not make slot wider.**
8. Drill 3/8 inch hold 3/16 inch in from upper inside corner of indentation, **Fig. 45.** Maintain rounded corner.
9. Remove tab by cutting in from bottom and side using suitable hacksaw, **Fig. 46.**
10. Remove transaxle strut.
11. Remove mounting bolts and transaxle strut bracket.
12. Install damper in place of transaxle strut bracket, **Figs. 47 and 48.**
13. **Torque** mounting bolts to 40 ft. lbs.
14. Hand start vertical battery tray mounting bolt through damper kit upper bracket.
15. Raise and support vehicle, then remove lefthand front wheel assembly.
16. Ensure upper bracket horizontal hole aligns with midrail hole.
17. Enlarge midrail hole to 11/16 inch using suitable dimension stepped uni-bit, **Fig. 49.**
18. Install M8 x 20 mm bolt using suitable magnetic socket or hold in socket using suitable RTV.
19. Slide bolt, socket and extension through midrail hole and into damper kit upper bracket.
20. **Torque** bolt and nut to 22 ft. lbs.
21. Prime access hole edges with 3M Windo-Weld primer, or equivalent.
22. Install wheel and lower vehicle.
23. Install transaxle strut to modified transaxle strut bracket.
24. **Torque** mounting bolt to 52 ft. lbs.
25. Install battery tray and loosely install mounting bolts.
26. Tighten battery tray mounting bolts and follows:
    a. **Torque** rear horizontal mounting bolt to 89 inch lbs.
    b. **Torque** forward vertical mounting bolt to 15 ft. lbs.
    c. **Torque** rear vertical mounting bolt to 89 inch lbs.
27. Ensure damper-to-upper bracket bolt is **torqued** to 52 ft. lbs.
28. Install transaxle strut-to-midrail and **torque** mounting bolt to 52 ft. lbs.
29. Install battery and hold-down retrain.
30. **Torque** hold-down retrain mounting nut and screw to 80 inch lbs.
31. **Torque** positive and negative battery cables to 13 ft. lbs.
32. Install air induction system.

TIGHTENING SPECIFICATIONS

Year	Component	Torque/Ft. Lbs.
1998–2002	Air Conditioning Compressor Front Bracket To Block	35
	Air Conditioning Compressor Front/ Rear Bracket To Head	23
	Air Conditioning Compressor To Front Bracket	40
	Air Conditioning Compressor To Rear Bracket	22
	Accelerator Cable Bracket To Intake Manifold	19
	Air Cleaner Duct Clamp	15①
	Air Cleaner/Resonator	96①
	Air Cleaner/Resonator Clamp	18①
	Alternator Positive Terminal	84①
	Alternator To Block	24
	Axle Shaft Intermediate Bracket To Block	41
	Battery Cable	13
	Belt Idler Pulley To Front Cover	20
	Belt Tensioner To Block	22
	Block Oil Gallery Plug	22
	Camshaft Bearing Cap To Head (DOHC)	10
	Camshaft Cover To Head (DOHC)	96①
	Camshaft Sprocket To Camshaft	75
	Camshaft Thrust Plate To Head (SOHC)	19
	Canister Band Clamp	31①
	Canister Purge Solenoid To Block	22
	Clutch Pressure Plate To Flywheel	19
	Connecting Rod	19⑥
	Coolant Drain Plug	22
	Coolant Temperature Sensor	72①
	Cradle To Body	151
	Crankshaft Bearing Cap To Block	④
	Crankshaft Damper To Crankshaft	159
	Crankshaft Position Sensor	84①
	Crankshaft Rear Oil Seal Carrier To Block	96①
	Cylinder Head	③
	Deaeration Line Fitting To Head	96①
	Deaeration Line Nut To Head (SOHC)	84①
	EGR Solenoid Bracket (DOHC)	84①
	EGR Solenoid Bracket (SOHC)	19
	EGR Valve	19
	Engine Block Heater To Block	18
	Engine Lift Bracket To Block	22
	Engine Mount To Front Cover	37
	Engine Mount To Midrail Bracket	37
	Engine Support Bracket	23
	ESC Knock Sensor	11
	Exhaust Manifold Studs To Front Pipe	10
	Exhaust Manifold Studs To Head	108①
	Exhaust Manifold To Head	②
	Exhaust Pipe To Converter	35
	Flexplate To Converter	52
	Flexplate To Crankshaft	44

Continued

TIGHTENING SPECIFICATIONS—Continued

Year	Component	Torque/Ft. Lbs.
1998–2002	Flywheel/Flexplate Cover	84①
	Flywheel To Crankshaft	59
	Front Cover To Block (Center)	84①
	Front Cover To Block (Perimeter)	③
	Front Engine Mount To Block	52
	Fuel Canister Bracket To Frame Rail	22
	Fuel Filter Bracket	72①
	Fuel Line Support Bracket	22
	Fuel Line Support Clip	108①
	Fuel Rail To Intake Manifold	84①
	Fuel Tank Fill Hose	35①
	Fuel Tank Fill Pipe Bracket	72①
	Fuel Tank Straps	35
	Fuel/Vapor Line To Body	27①
	Heater Outlet To Intake Manifold	19
	Heater Return Nipple	37
	Idle Air Control Sensor	28
	Idle Air Control Valve	28①
	Ignition Module To Transaxle Case	72①
	Intake Manifold	⑤
	Intake Manifold Bracket To Block (Lefthand)	22
	Intake Manifold Bracket To Block (Righthand) (DOHC)	41
	Intake Manifold Bracket To Manifold (DOHC)	22
	Intake Manifold Bracket To Manifold (SOHC)	21
	Intake Manifold Stud To Fuel Line Clamp (SOHC)	60①
	Intake Manifold Stud To Head	108①
	Intake Manifold Stud To Head (Power Steering Bracket) (DOHC)	22
	Intake Manifold Stud To Head (Power Steering Bracket) (SOHC)	16
	MAP Sensor	44①
	Motion Restrictor Bracket	40
	Motion Restrictor To Side Of Block	22
	Oil Baffle Plate To Block	41
	Oil Drain Plug	26
	Oil Pan To Block	84①
	Oil Pickup Tube (DOHC)	11
	Oil Pipe Bracket To Baffle Plate	11
	Oil Pipe Bracket To Block (DOHC)	11
	Oil Pipe Bracket To Block (SOHC)	41
	Oil Pressure Sensor	26
	Oil Pump Cover	96①
	Oxygen Sensor	33
	Power Steering Hoses	20
	Power Steering Pump Bracket	28
	Power Steering Pump To Bracket	22
	Power Steering Return Hose Clamp	18①
	Radiator Upper Bracket	96①
	Rear Engine Mount To Block	35
	Rocker Arm Cover To Head (SOHC)	22

Continued

TIGHTENING SPECIFICATIONS—Continued

Year	Component	Torque/Ft. Lbs.
1998–2002	Rocker Arm Shaft To Head	19
	Spark Plug	20
	Starter Motor	27
	Starter Motor Bracket To Axle Shaft	22
	Starter Positive Terminal	96①
	Starter Solenoid Terminal	35①
	Steering Joint To Gear	35
	Stiffening Bracket	40
	Strut To Knuckle	148
	Thermostat Housing To Block	22
	Throttle Body To Air Intake Manifold	23
	Throttle Position Sensor	18①
	Timing Chain Guides	19
	Timing Chain Tensioner	14
	Transaxle Case To Block (Lower)	96
	Transaxle Case To Block (Upper)	66
	Transaxle Lower Mount To Cradle	41
	Transaxle Lower Mount To Transaxle	23
	Transaxle Rear Mount	36
	Valve Cover (DOHC)	96①
	Valve Cover (SOHC)	22
	Vapor Canister To Body	22
	Vehicle Speed Sensor	19①
	Water Pump	22
	Water Pump Pulley	18

DOHC — Dual Over Head Cam

SOHC — Single Over Head Cam

① — Inch lbs.

② — Refer to “Exhaust Manifold, Replace” for tightening specifications and sequence.

③ — Refer to “Cylinder Head, Replace” for tightening specifications and sequence.

④ — Refer to “Main & Rod Bearings” for tightening specifications and sequence.

⑤ — Refer to “Intake Manifold, Replace” for tightening specifications and sequence.

⑥ — Tighten an additional 75°.

2.2L Engine

NOTE: On Air Bag Equipped Models, Refer To "Air Bag System Precautions" Located In The Front Of This Manual For System Disarming & Arming Procedures.

NOTE: Refer To "Computer Relearn Procedures" Located In The Front Of This Manual When Battery Power To The Computer Has Been Interrupted.

INDEX

PRECAUTIONS

AIR BAG SYSTEMS

Refer to "Air Bag System Precautions" in the front of this manual for system disarming and arming procedures.

BATTERY GROUND CABLE

Prior to service, disconnect battery ground cable and isolate as required.

FUEL SYSTEM PRESSURE RELIEF

1. Connect gauge bar tool No. 53476, or equivalent, to fuel gauge pressure adapter tool No. 309725, or equivalent, using flexible hose from pressure test kit tool No. SA-9127-E, or equivalent.
2. Ensure needle valve on pressure kit is closed and connect pressure adapter to fuel line test port, **Fig. 1.**
3. Place end of bleed hose in suitable container and open valve to bleed system pressure.
4. Remove gauge and replace cap.

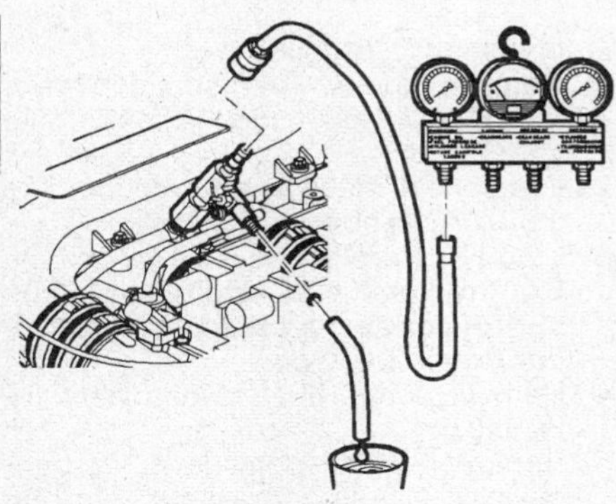

Fig. 1 Fuel pressure bleed

COMPRESSION PRESSURE

1. Start and run engine until it reaches normal operating temperature.
2. Turn engine off, disconnect ignition module wiring and remove spark plugs.
3. Install suitable compression gauge tool in spark plug hole.
4. Ensure battery is charged and throttle is fully open.
5. Crank engine through four compression strokes for each cylinder.
6. Lowest reading cylinder should be within 70% of highest.
7. No cylinder should read less than 100 psi.
8. Place shop towel over spark plug holes and crank engine a few seconds without compression gauge or spark plugs installed.
9. Repeat compression measuring steps on all cylinders.

ENGINE MOUNT

REPLACE

1. Remove air cleaner.
2. Install engine support fixture tool No. SA-9150-E, or equivalent.
3. Remove engine mount to bracket fasteners.
4. Remove engine mount to body mounting bolts, **Fig. 2.**
5. Remove engine mount.
6. Reverse procedure to install.

ENGINE

REPLACE

AUTOMATIC TRANSAXLE

1. Remove battery and disconnect fuse block main wire feed.
2. Disconnect lefthand fenderwell main ground and intake air temperature electrical connector.
3. Remove air cleaner lid and inlet duct.
4. Remove air box and disconnect purge hose from throttle body and position aside.
5. Disconnect EVAP purge solenoid and rear oxygen sensor electrical connectors, then the main master cylinder wiring harness.
6. Remove cowl cover and PCM boot from cowl.
7. Disconnect PCM electrical connector and secure to engine.
8. Remove fuse block lid and disconnect engine harness main connector from bottom of fuse block.
9. Remove battery and fuse block trays.
10. Disconnect cruise control and throttle cables.
11. Disconnect brake assist vacuum line from throttle body and position aside.
12. Remove coolant reservoir cap.
13. Disconnect fuel lines and EVAP purge hose at EVAP purge solenoid.

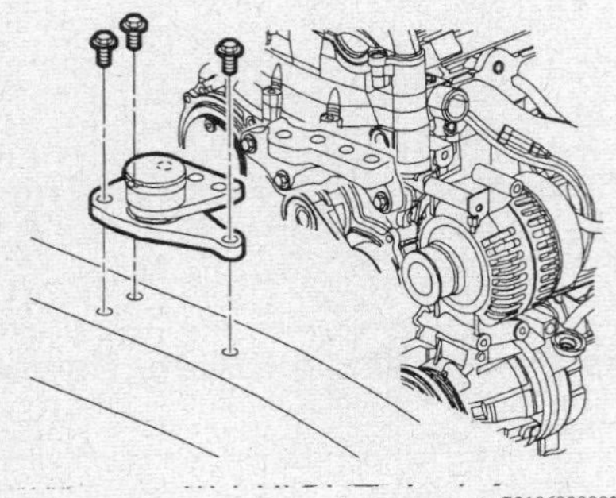

Fig. 2 Engine mount replacement

14. Raise and support vehicle.
15. Drain engine coolant into suitable container.
16. Disconnect heater hoses at lower cowl and remove starter.
17. Remove torque converter bolts.
18. Remove exhaust system from catalytic converter forward.
19. Disconnect transaxle nose bracket, remove mounting bolts and secure air conditioning compressor to frame rail. **Do not disconnect air conditioning lines.**
20. Disconnect lower engine to transaxle bell housing bolts. **Do not remove upper bolts now.**
21. Lower vehicle and remove main hose to coolant reservoir from engine inlet adapter.
22. Remove engine lower and upper radiator hoses.
23. Drain power steering fluid into suitable container by removing smaller hose from under reservoir.
24. Disconnect metal power steering line.
25. Support engine using suitable engine lift hoist to engine lift hooks, **Fig. 3.**
26. Support transaxle weight using suitable floor jack or jack stand.
27. Remove righthand front engine mount from wheel housing and engine mount bracket from engine.
28. Remove upper bell housing bolts and remove engine.
29. Reverse procedure to install.

MANUAL TRANSAXLE

1. Remove steering gear-to-intermediate shaft pinch bolt.
2. Remove battery and disconnect fuse block main wire feed.
3. Disconnect lefthand fenderwell main ground and intake air temperature electrical connector.
4. Remove air cleaner lid and inlet duct.
5. Remove air box, disconnect purge hose from throttle body and position aside.
6. Disconnect EVAP purge solenoid, rear oxygen sensor and transaxle back-up switch electrical connectors, then the master cylinder main harness connector.
7. Remove dash cover front and PCM boot.
8. Disconnect PCM electrical connector and secure to engine.
9. Remove fuse block lid and disconnect engine harness main connector from bottom of fuse block.
10. Remove battery and fuse block trays.
11. Disconnect cruise control and throttle cables.
12. Disconnect brake assist vacuum line from throttle body and lay aside.
13. Loosen control rod to lever pinch bolt. **Control shaft lever retaining pin has spring loaded locking feature securing pin in place.**
14. Remove control shaft lever to shaft retaining pin.
15. Remove control shaft lever to transaxle and frame brackets retaining clips.
16. Remove control shaft lever by pulling straight up from pivot pins.
17. Drain coolant into suitable container.
18. Remove dash front heater hoses, then the radiator upper and lower hoses.
19. Disconnect fuel lines and secure radiator to upper radiator support.
20. Raise and support vehicle, then remove righthand front wheel and tire assembly.
21. Remove righthand front splash shield and lefthand front wheel liner push pin from frame.
22. Install suitable wood blocks between transaxle case and frame, and between crank pulley and frame.
23. Lower vehicle.
24. Disconnect righthand engine and lefthand transaxle mounts by removing mount-to-engine/transaxle bolts. Mount brackets will remain on engine and transaxle.
25. Disconnect rear oxygen sensor harness from frame at two attachment points.
26. Remove exhaust manifold pipe from catalytic converter forward.
27. Remove air conditioning line to frame attachment clip at front of frame. **Do not disconnect air conditioning lines.**
28. Remove air conditioning compressor from engine and secure to cooling module.
29. Remove tie rod-to-steering knuckle bolts and separate tie rod from steering knuckle using tool No. SA-91100-C, or equivalent. Discard tie rod bolts.
30. Remove stabilizer bar links from strut.
31. Remove lower ball stud bolt and separate ball from steering knuckle using suitable tool. **Do not separate ball studs using wedge-type separator tool.**
32. Remove suspension support assemblies and suspension support cage nuts from body. Discard cage nuts.
33. Support powertrain and frame with powertrain lifting table and service tool J-43628, or equivalent, **Fig. 4.**
34. Remove remaining frame-to-body mounting bolts.
35. Carefully lower powertrain and frame.
36. Remove remaining cage nuts and discard.
37. Attach engine lift hoist to engine lift hooks, **Fig. 3.**
38. Place suitable 1¾ x 2 x 4-inch and 1¼ x 2 x 4-inch long wood blocks under transaxle housing support. **Engine must be moved approximately four inches forward in cradle to disconnect input shaft.**
39. Remove transaxle bell housing mounting bolts.
40. Carefully lift engine from cradle and mount on suitable engine stand or transportation pallet.
41. Reverse procedure to install.

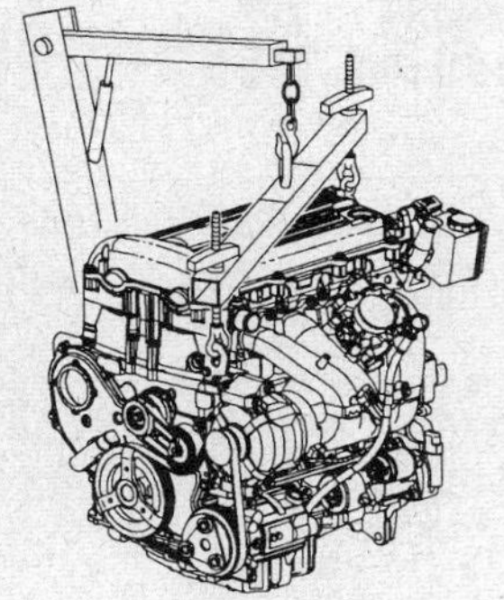

Fig. 3 Engine lift hoist attachment

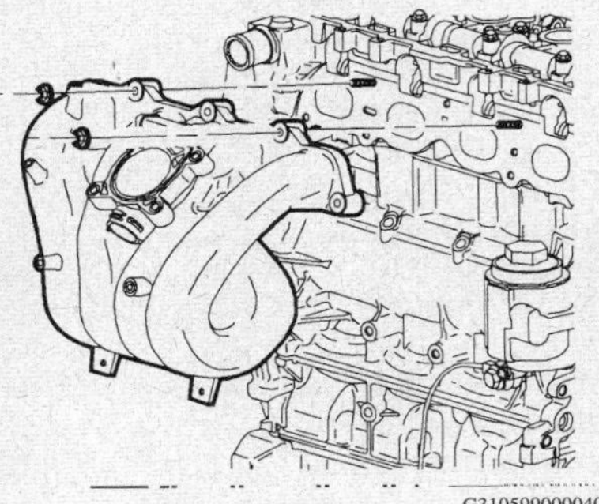

Fig. 5 Intake manifold replacement

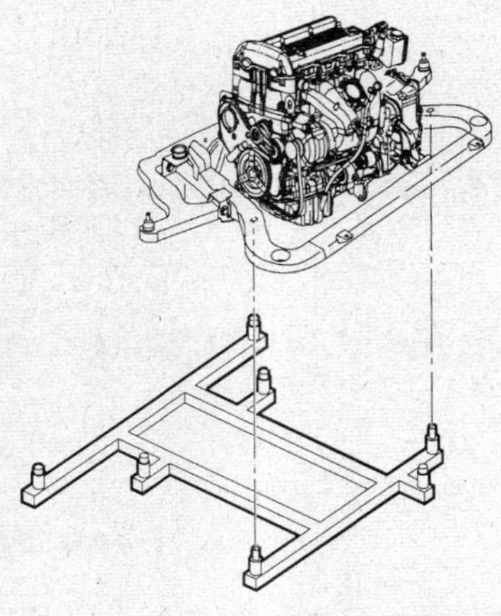

Fig. 4 Frame alignment tool

INTAKE MANIFOLD

REPLACE

Intake manifold is made of a composite plastic and can be damaged if removed when engine is hot. Do not

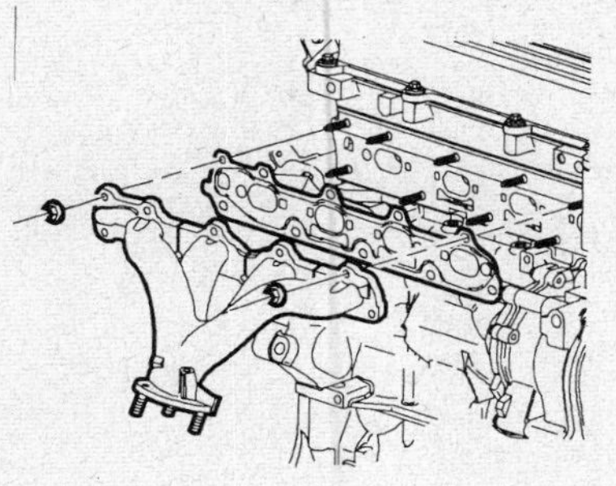
G31079900002000X

Fig. 6 Exhaust manifold replacement

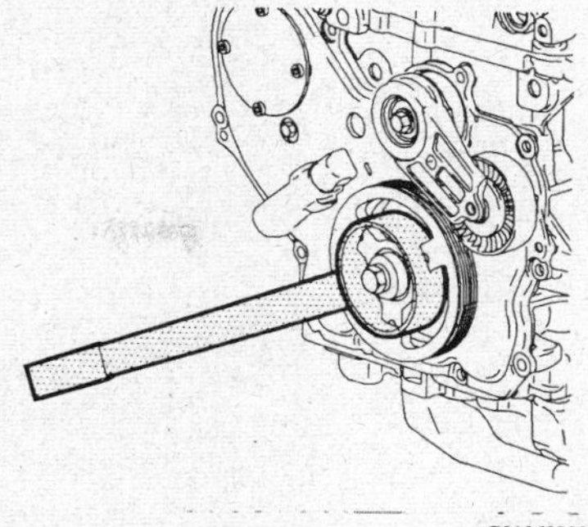
G31069900039000X

Fig. 7 Crankshaft pulley replacement

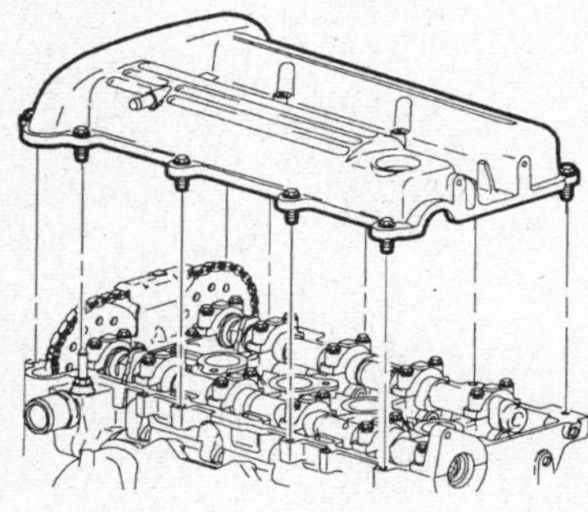
G31069900040000X

Fig. 8 Camshaft cover replacement

remove the intake manifold from a hot engine. Allow engine to cool to ambient temperature.

1. Remove air inlet tube and air cleaner.
2. Disconnect fuel lines using fuel line disconnection tools Nos. J-37088-1A and J-37088-2A, or equivalents.
3. Disconnect throttle position sensor, IAC and MAP sensor electrical connectors.
4. Disconnect throttle and cruise control cables.
5. Disconnect fuel pressure regulator hose from throttle body and fuel rail.
6. Remove mounting bolts and throttle body.
7. Remove fuel rail.
8. Remove mounting bolts, nuts and intake manifold, **Fig. 5.**
9. Remove intake manifold gasket.
10. If intake manifold needs to be replaced, transfer throttle body and gasket.
11. Reverse procedure to install.

EXHAUST MANIFOLD

REPLACE

1. Remove oxygen sensor from exhaust manifold.
2. Remove exhaust manifold heat shield.
3. Remove mounting nuts and exhaust manifold, **Fig. 6.**
4. Reverse procedure to install, noting the following:
   a. Install new exhaust manifold studs.
   b. Coat oxygen sensor threads with anti seize compound, Saturn No. 21485279, or equivalent.

CYLINDER HEAD

REPLACE

REMOVAL

1. Remove exhaust and intake manifolds as described under "Exhaust Manifold, Replace" and "Intake Manifold, Replace."
2. Remove mounting bolt and crankshaft pulley using crankshaft pulley holder tool No. J-38122, or equivalent, **Fig. 7.**
3. Remove camshaft cover grounding strap, ignition module and coil.
4. Remove camshaft cover, **Fig. 8.**
5. Remove accessory drive belt tensioner as outlined under "Tensioner, Replacement."

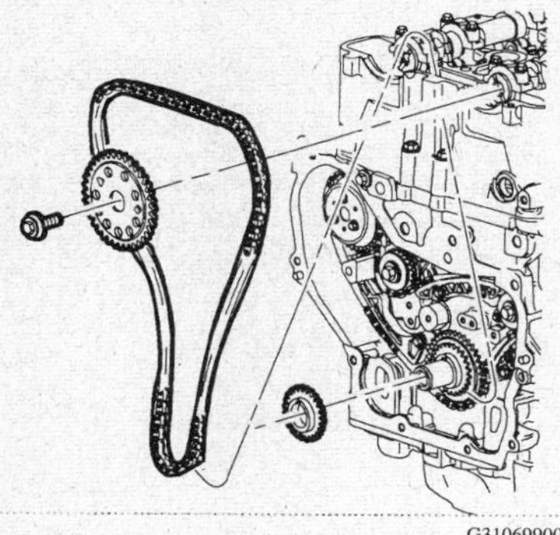
G31069900041000X

Fig. 9 Intake camshaft sprocket timing chain replacement

6. Remove mounting bolts and engine front cover.
7. Remove upper timing chain guide. **Timing chain tensioner must be removed to unload chain tension before timing chain is removed.**
8. Remove timing chain tensioner plunger. **Do not allow any tension on timing chain when loosening camshaft sprocket bolt.**
9. Remove exhaust cam sprocket using suitable ⅞ open end wrench to hold camshaft while loosening camshaft sprocket bolt. Discard bolt.
10. Remove adjustable timing chain guide and fixed timing chain guide bolt access plug.
11. Remove fixed timing guide.
12. Remove intake cam sprocket timing chain through top of cylinder head, **Fig. 9.**
13. Remove crankshaft sprocket and oiling nozzle.
14. Remove each cap one turn at a time until there is no spring tension on camshaft.
15. Mark bearing caps for installation. Keep roller finger followers and hydraulic element adjusters in order so they can be installed in original positions.
16. Remove mounting bolts, intake camshaft bearing caps and camshaft, **Fig. 10.**
17. Remove intake camshaft roller finger followers and hydraulic element adjusters.
18. Remove exhaust camshaft bearing cap bolts, bearing caps and camshaft, **Fig. 11.**
19. Remove balance shaft drive chain tensioner and adjustable balance shaft chain guide.
20. Remove small balance shaft drive chain guide and upper balance shaft chain guide.
21. Remove balance shaft drive chain and crankshaft drive sprocket.
22. Remove bearing carrier bolts and balance shafts, **Fig. 12.**
23. Keep each balance shaft separate. **Do not remove front balance shaft bearing bolts.**
24. Remove thermostat and water feed pipe mounting bolts.
25. Remove thermostat housing and water feed pipe from water pump cover. Ensure bolt through front of engine block is removed.
26. Remove mounting bolts and water pump.
27. Remove cylinder head to block bolts in sequence, **Fig. 13.**
28. Remove cylinder head and gasket.

INSTALLATION

1. Install new gasket and cylinder head. **Do not use any sealing material.**
2. Lightly apply clean engine oil to threads and bottom side of flange of head bolt. Allow oil to drain before installation.
3. **Torque** cylinder head bolts to 22 ft. lbs. in sequence, **Fig. 14.**
4. Tighten cylinder head bolts additional 155° in sequence.
5. **Torque** front cylinder head bolts to 18 ft. lbs., **Fig. 15.**
6. Lubricate and install hydraulic element lash adjusters into cylinder head bores.
7. Lubricate valve tips with suitable engine oil supplement, then position roller followers on tip of valve stem and lash adjuster. Ensure roller followers are lubricated.
8. Set intake and exhaust camshaft on top of roller followers in camshaft bearing journals. Lubricate with engine oil supplement.
9. Install camshaft bearing caps and hand start camshaft cap bolts.
10. Timing chain sprocket alignment notch should be oriented to 11 o'clock position, **Fig. 16.**

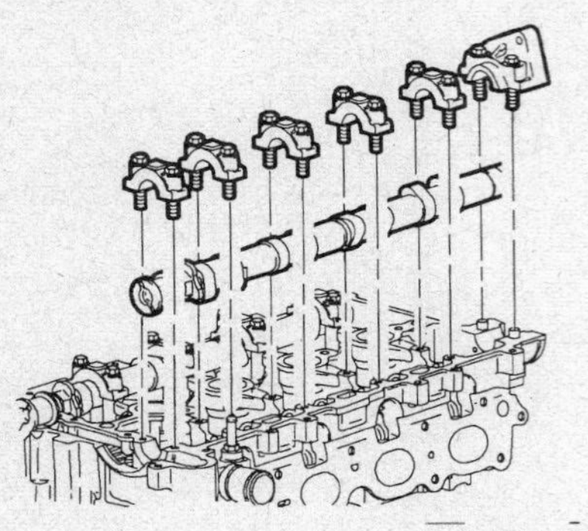

Fig. 10 Intake camshaft & bearing caps replacement

11. Tighten camshaft bearing cap bolts in increments of three turns until seated.
12. Apply 13/64 inch bead of Loctite Anerobic Gasket Maker 578, or equivalent, to rear intake camshaft bearing cap.
13. Place piston No. 1 to top dead center and install balance shaft drive chain sprocket on crankshaft.
14. Install balance shafts in bores.
15. Install water pump, feed tube and thermostat housing.
16. Position chain so copper colored and chrome links are visible, **Fig. 17.**
17. Align copper colored link with intake side balance shaft sprocket timing mark.
18. Working clockwise around chain, align first chrome link with crankshaft drive sprocket timing mark (approximately 5 o'clock position).
19. Align last chrome link with exhaust side balance shaft drive sprocket timing mark and install balance shaft chain guides.
20. Turn tensioner plunger 30° in bore and compress plunger until paper clip can be inserted through holed in plunger body and tensioner plunger.
21. Install timing chain tensioner. Remove paper clip from balance shaft drive chain tensioner.
22. Install timing chain drive sprocket to crankshaft with timing mark in 5 o'clock position.
23. Assemble intake camshaft sprocket to timing chain, align timing mark with copper colored link.
24. Lower timing chain through opening in cylinder head.
25. Route timing chain around crankshaft sprocket and align second link with timing mark on crankshaft sprocket (approximately 5 o'clock position).
26. Install intake camshaft sprocket onto intake camshaft. Hand tighten new sprocket mounting bolt. Sprocket to camshaft offset notch alignment is not required now.
27. Install adjustable timing chain guide through opening in cylinder head.
28. Install exhaust camshaft sprocket onto exhaust camshaft. Hand tighten new sprocket mounting bolt. Align sprocket timing mark with silver link.
29. Ensure colored links and timing marks are aligned.

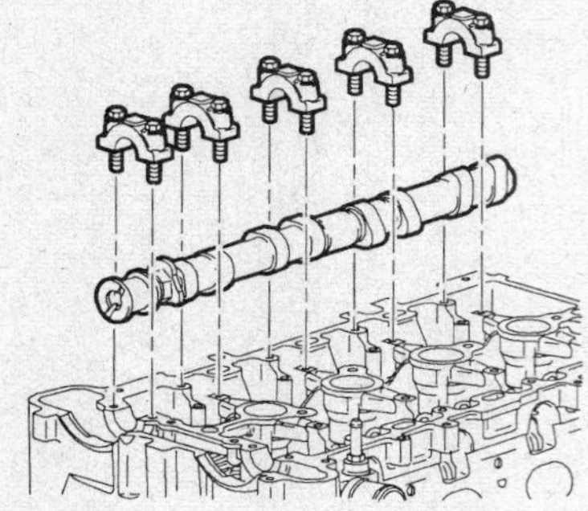

Fig. 11 Exhaust camshaft & bearing caps replacement

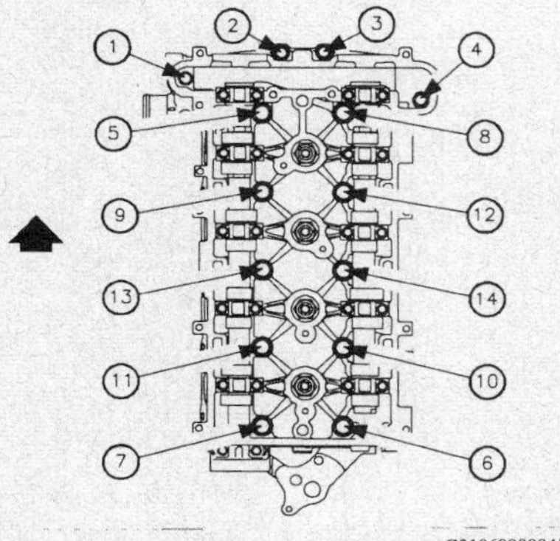

Fig. 13 Cylinder head bolt loosening sequence

30. Install fixed and upper timing chain guides.
31. Tighten intake and exhaust camshafts' hex using suitable 7/8inch wrench, **Fig. 18.**
32. Install new sealing washer and timing chain tensioner.
33. Install timing chain oiling nozzle.
34. Apply Loctite threadlocker 242 compound, or equivalent, and install timing chain guide bolt access hole plug.
35. Install engine front cover and new gasket.
36. Install accessory drive belt tensioner, camshaft cover and gasket.
37. Install crankshaft pulley.
38. Install intake and exhaust manifolds.

VALVE ADJUSTMENT

This engine is equipped with hydraulic lifters and no adjustment is required.

VALVE GUIDES

Valve guides are an integral part of the cylinder head and are pressed in. If valve stem clearance becomes excessive, the valve guides must be hand reamed to the oversize using valve guide reamer tool J-42096, or equivalent. Service valves are available in standard and 0.003 inch oversize.

FRONT COVER

REPLACE

1. Remove air cleaner, then raise and support vehicle.
2. Drain engine oil into suitable container, then remove righthand front wheel and splash shield.
3. Remove engine accessory drive belt as outlined under "Belt Replacement."
4. Install crankshaft holder tool J-38122, or equivalent, onto crankshaft pulley.
5. Remove crankshaft pulley and discard bolt.
6. Remove belt tensioner as outlined under "Tensioner Replacement."
7. Remove righthand engine mount as described under "Engine Mount, Replace.".
8. Remove front cover and gasket.
9. Reverse procedure to install.

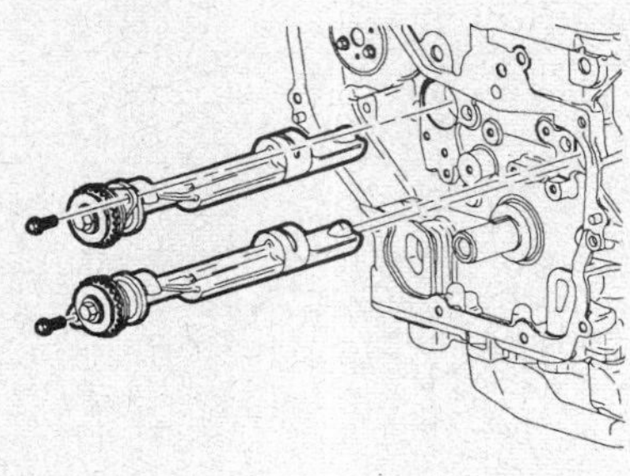

Fig. 12 Balance shaft replacement

TIMING CHAIN

REPLACE

Refer to "Cylinder Head, Replace" for timing chain replacement.

CAMSHAFT

REPLACE

1. Remove ignition coil, accessory drive belt, PCV fresh air hose and cam cover.
2. Position cylinder No. 1 piston at Top Dead Center (TDC) with intake and exhaust valves closed. **Cylinder No. 1 piston must be at TDC when removing or installing camshafts.**
3. Remove upper timing chain guide and timing chain tensioner.
4. Install camshaft sprocket holding tool No. J-43655, or equivalent, onto cylinder head, **Fig. 19, torque** holding tool to 108 inch lbs.
5. Remove camshaft timing sprockets mounting bolts and washers while holding each camshaft in place using suitable 7/8 inch open end wrench.
6. Remove remaining camshaft bearing cap bolts in several passes.
7. Slide camshaft sprockets away from camshafts.
8. Carefully pull camshafts straight up to avoid damaging cylinder head thrust surface, **Fig. 20.**
9. Reverse procedure to install.

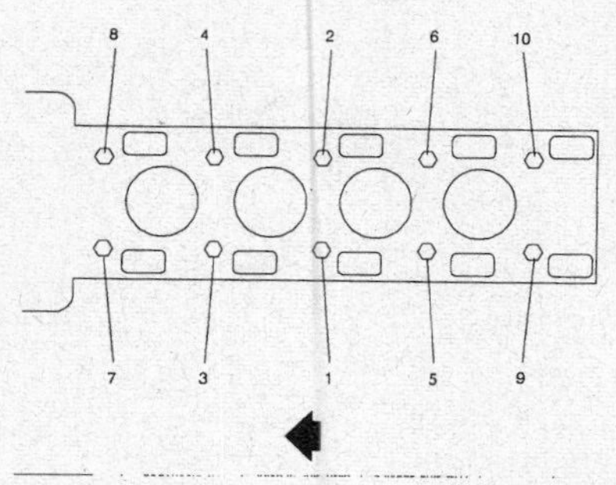

Fig. 14 Cylinder head bolt tightening sequence

PISTON & ROD ASSEMBLY

Install the piston onto the connecting rod with the arrow pointed toward the front of the engine.

PISTONS, PINS & RINGS

Replace any pistons that show signs of damage or excessive wear. Piston pin bores and pins must be free of varnish or scuffing. Use an outside micrometer to measure the piston contact areas and piston pin bore. Subtract the measurement of the piston pin bore from the piston pin.

MAIN & ROD BEARINGS

1. Install crankshaft bearing caps using suitable brass, lead, leather, or equivalent soft-faced mallet. **Do not use lower crankcase bolts to pull bearing caps into seats.**
2. **Torque** lower crankcase inner bolts to 15 ft. lbs. in sequence, **Fig. 21.**
3. **Torque** lower crankcase outer bolt to 15 ft. lbs. in sequence, **Fig. 22.**

CRANKSHAFT REAR OIL SEAL

REPLACE

1. **On models equipped with manual transaxle,** remove transaxle as outlined in "Clutch & Manual Transaxles" section.
2. **On models equipped with automatic transaxle,** remove transaxle as outlined in "Automatic Transaxles" chapter.
3. **On all models,** remove flywheel and cover.
4. Insert suitable screwdriver into pry tangs of seal carrier and remove seal.
5. Apply suitable clean engine oil to seal lip and inside diameter of seal carrier.
6. Install seal using seal installer tool No. J-42067, or equivalent.
7. Install transaxle and flywheel.

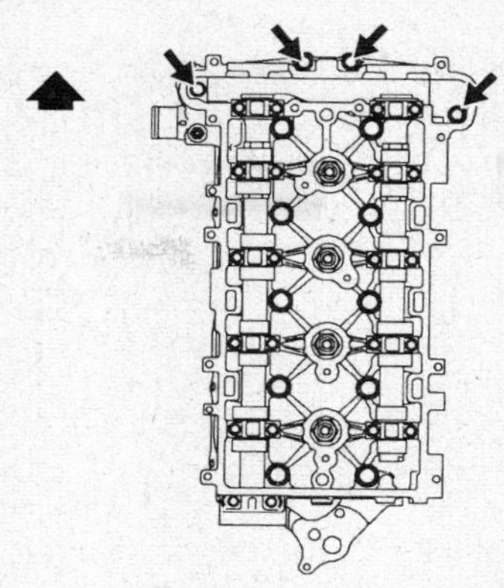

Fig. 15 Front cylinder head bolt locations

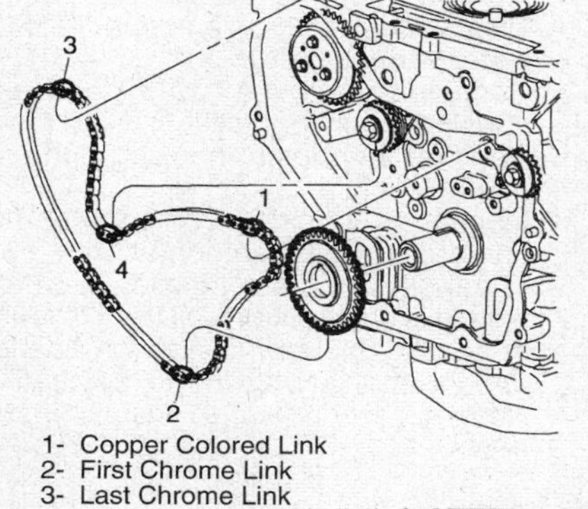

Fig. 17 Balance shaft drive chain installation

OIL PAN

REPLACE

1. Drain engine oil into suitable container and remove front exhaust pipe.
2. Remove righthand front wheel, splash shield and vibration damper.
3. Remove mounting bolts and oil pan.
4. Reverse procedure to install, noting the following:
   a. Apply 0.079 inch bead of RTV Loctite 5900, or equivalent.
   b. Tighten oil pan mounting bolts to 18 ft. lbs. in sequence, **Fig. 23.**

OIL PUMP

REPLACE

1. Remove air cleaner, then raise and support vehicle.
2. Drain engine oil into suitable container, then remove righthand front wheel and splash shield.
3. Remove accessory drive belt.
4. Remove crankshaft pulley using pulley holding tool No. J-38122, or equivalent.
5. Remove belt tensioner as outlined under "Serpentine Drive Belt" "Tensioner Replacement."
6. Install engine support fixture tool No. SA-9150-E, or equivalent.
7. Remove engine mount as described under "Engine Mount, Replace."

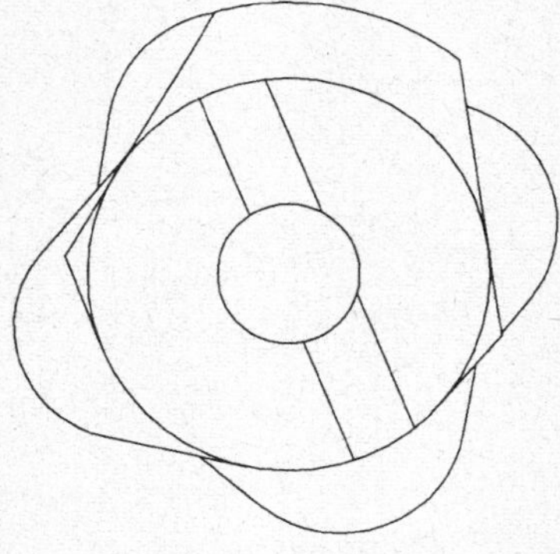

Fig. 16 Timing chain sprocket notch alignment

8. Remove front cover bolts and bolts under water pump cover.
9. Remove front cover and gasket.
10. Reverse procedure to install.

OIL PUMP SERVICE

DISASSEMBLE

1. Remove cover plate mounting bolts.
2. Mark drive and driven rotors for assembly.
3. Remove drive and driven rotors, then the pressure relief valve.

INSPECTION

1. Measure clearance between driven rotor and pump body, **Fig. 24.** Replace oil pump if clearance is more than 0.012 inch.
2. Inspect clearance between both tips, **Fig. 25.** Replace oil pump if clearance is more than 0.006 inch.
3. Measure clearance between side of drive and driven rotors, and oil pump cover plate, **Fig. 26.** Replace oil pump is clearance is more than 0.003 inch.

ASSEMBLE

1. Remove front cover oil seal using suitable screwdriver or punch.
2. Install new oil seal using oil seal installer tool No. J-35268-A, or equivalent, and suitable press.
3. Install pressure relief valve, valve spring and oil pump pressure relief valve plug.
4. Lubricate drive and driven rotors with clean engine oil, then align marks on drive and driven rotors.
5. Install drive and driven rotors into pump body.
6. Fill oil pump with petroleum jelly to prime oil pump.
7. Install oil pump gear cover plate screws.

SERPENTINE DRIVE BELT

BELT ROUTING

Refer to **Fig. 27** for serpentine belt routing.

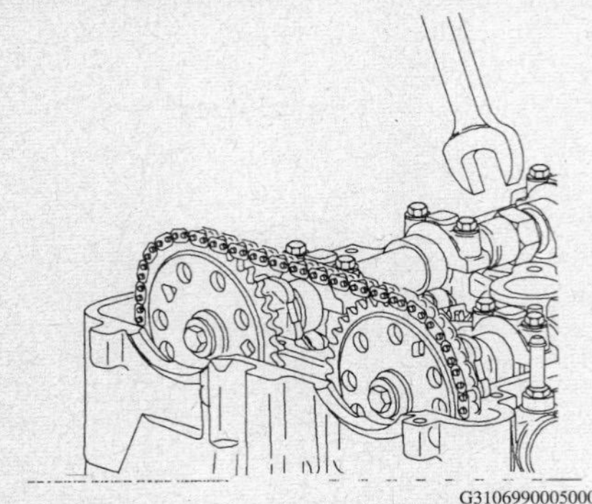

Fig. 18 Camshaft sprocket bolts installation

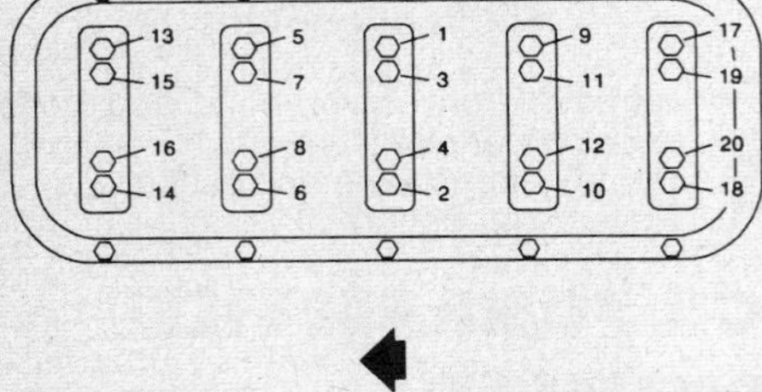

Fig. 21 Lower crankcase inner bolt tightening sequence

TENSIONER REPLACEMENT

The tensioner internal parts are not serviceable. Do not disassemble tensioner.

1. Depress tensioner arm and remove accessory drive belt.
2. Remove mounting bolts and tensioner, **Fig. 28.**
3. Reverse procedure to install.

BELT REPLACEMENT

REMOVAL

1. Depress tensioner arm using suitable 3/8 inch drive breaker bar, **Fig. 27.**
2. Remove belt from idler or air conditioning compressor pulley and accessory pulleys.

INSTALLATION

1. Route belt around pulleys, except for idler pulley.
2. Depress tensioner arm using 3/8 inch drive breaker bar.
3. Ensure belt is properly aligned on pulleys and slip belt over idler pulley.

COOLING SYSTEM BLEED

These engines do not require a special bleed procedure. After filling cooling system, start and run engine until it reaches normal operating temperature with pressure cap off. Air will then automatically bleed through cap opening.

THERMOSTAT

REPLACE

1. Drain engine coolant into suitable container.

Fig. 19 Camshaft sprocket holding tool installation

2. Disconnect lower radiator hose at thermostat housing, using Snap-on hose removal tool HCP10, or equivalent. Twist water feed pipe and remove from water pump.
3. Remove thermostat, water feed and housing mounting bolts
4. Remove thermostat housing and element.
5. Inspect thermostat components for damage and seat deterioration.
6. Thermostat will not function correctly once it is contacted by oil. If oil is found in cooling system, it must be flushed and thermostat's cartridge replaced
7. Reverse procedure to install. Install new O-ring.

WATER PUMP

REPLACE

1. Remove air inlet tube and air cleaner.
2. Drain coolant into suitable container and remove exhaust manifold heat shield.
3. Remove thermostat and water feed mounting bolts.
4. Remove water pump sprocket access plate from front cover and install water pump sprocket holding tool J-43651, or equivalent.
5. Remove mounting bolts accessed from front of engine block.
6. Remove mounting bolts and water pump.
7. Reverse procedure to install.

RADIATOR

REPLACE

1. Remove battery and drain coolant into suitable container.
2. Disconnect cooling fans electrical connectors and slide electrical connectors out of retainers.
3. Remove pusher fan electrical harness from fan shroud retaining tabs.
4. Remove wiring harness from clamp on fan shroud.
5. **On models equipped with automatic transaxle,** remove upper transaxle cooler lines from radiator end tank. Cap line.
6. **On all models,** remove upper radiator hose from radiator.
7. Remove mounting bolts and fan shroud.

Fig. 20 Camshaft replacement

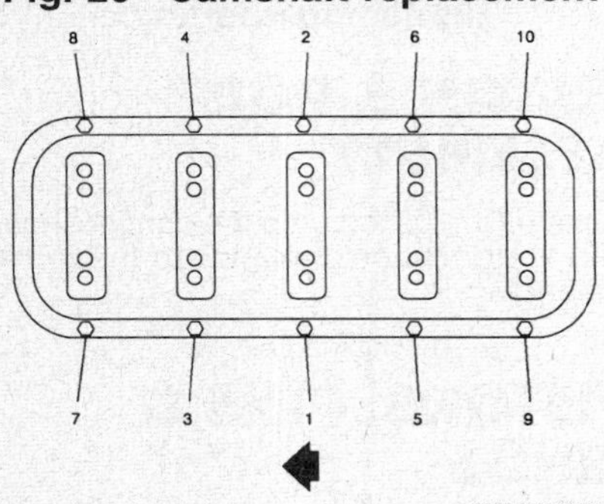

Fig. 22 Lower crankcase outer bolt tightening sequence

8. Remove forward wiring harness from retaining clips and lower radiator hose from radiator.
9. **On models equipped with automatic transaxle,** remove lower transaxle cooler line. Cap line.
10. **On all models,** remove mounting bolts, upper bracket and rubber mounts.
11. Secure condenser away from upper rail using suitable tie strap.
12. Raise and support vehicle.
13. Remove condenser mounting bolts.
14. Pull condenser and pusher fan down slightly to disconnect radiator tabs.
15. Lower vehicle.
16. Remove radiator.
17. Remove upper radiator to condenser gaskets.
18. Reverse procedure to install.

FUEL PUMP

REPLACE

This procedure has been revised by a Technical Service Bulletin.

Whenever fuel line fittings are loosened or removed, wrap a shop cloth around the fitting and have an suitable container available to collect any fuel.

1. Connect suitably programmed scan tool to Diagnostic Link Connector (DLC) and turn ignition to On position.
2. Raise and support vehicle, keeping scan tool outside of vehicle and accessible.
3. Disconnect fuel feed line at outlet to filter.
4. Install 3/8 x 1/4 inch adapter onto flow/pressure adapter tool No. SA-9127E-7, or equivalent, and insert adapter into fuel feed line.

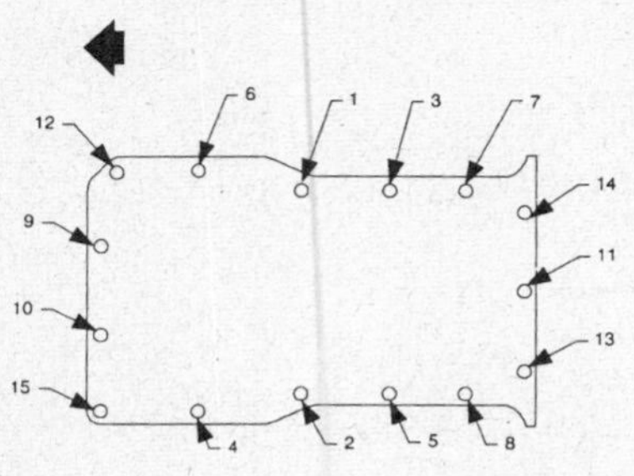

Fig. 23 Oil pan bolt tightening sequence

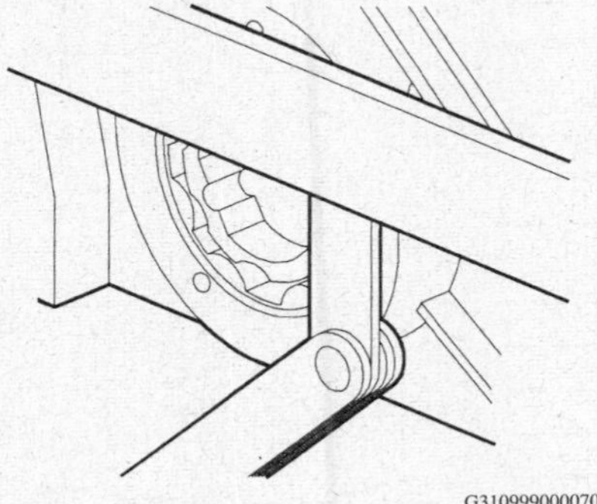

Fig. 26 Oil pump end to end clearance measurement

5. Connect one end of suitable drain hose to other end of adapter and connect other end of drain hose to suitable fuel handling cart.
6. Turn fuel pump on using suitably programmed scan tool and pump fuel into suitable container.
7. If fuel pump is inoperative, proceed as follows:
   a. Insert siphon hose guide/funnel into fuel filler pipe.
   b. Insert siphon hose J-43290, or equivalent, into guide funnel and fuel filler pipe. Some resistance may be encountered when tip of siphon hose reaches inlet check valve. Repeated probing may be required to slide hose tip through check valve.
   c. Begin siphon process and collect fuel inn suitable container.
8. Ensure fuel tank is less than quarter full.
9. Remove exhaust system intermediate pipe and rear heat shield mounting bolts.
10. Remove fuel filler pipe lower bracket mounting screw and disconnect EVAP canister vent hose.
11. Loosen fuel filler pipe hose clamp closest to fuel tank and remove tank ground strap mounting screw near fuel filter.
12. Disconnect fuel feed line after fuel filter.

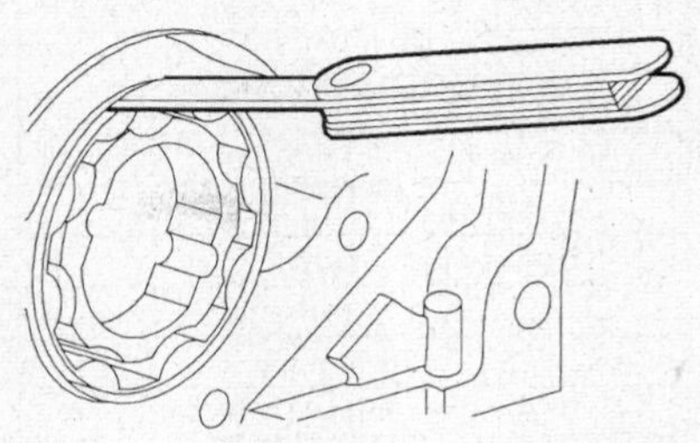

Fig. 24 Oil pump body clearance measurement

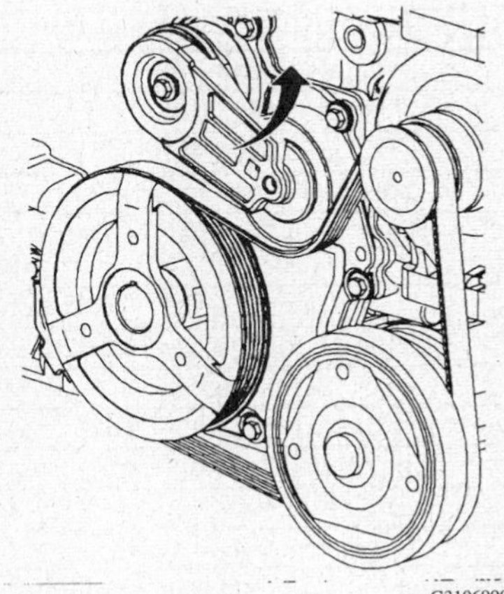

Fig. 27 Serpentine belt routing

13. Disconnect fuel return and EVAP canister purge lines between tank and chassis fuel bundle.
14. Disconnect fuel tank electrical connectors.
15. Loosen front tank strap bolt. **Do not remove.**
16. Remove rear tank mounting strap bolts with assistance.
17. Remove tank by lowering rear, then sliding downward and rearward.
18. Disconnect fuel lines from fuel pump module cover. **Do not attempt to remove retainer using 12-inch, or shorter, ratchet/breaker bar.**
19. Remove fuel pump module retainer ring using lock ring service tool No. J-43827, or equivalent.
20. To prevent bending of sending unit float arm, remove sending unit first by pulling retaining clip toward float arm and lifting upward.
21. Carefully lift fuel pump straight up from fuel tank. To disconnect fuel pump from housing, clips must be disconnected at same time.
22. Discard fuel pump module to tank seal and remove fuel feed line from bottom of fuel pump cover using removal tool No. J-44078, or equivalent.

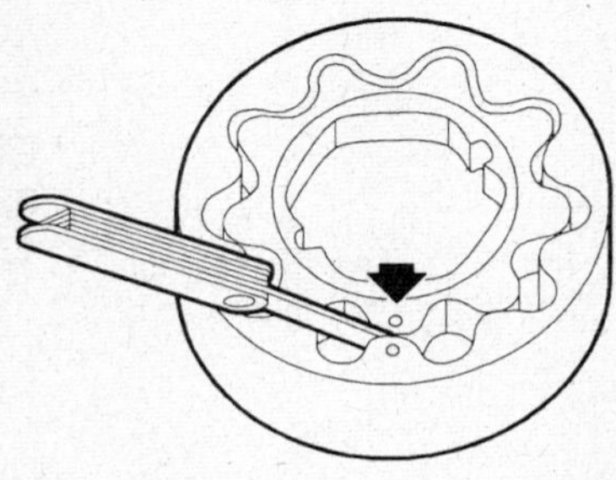

Fig. 25 Oil pump tip clearance measurement

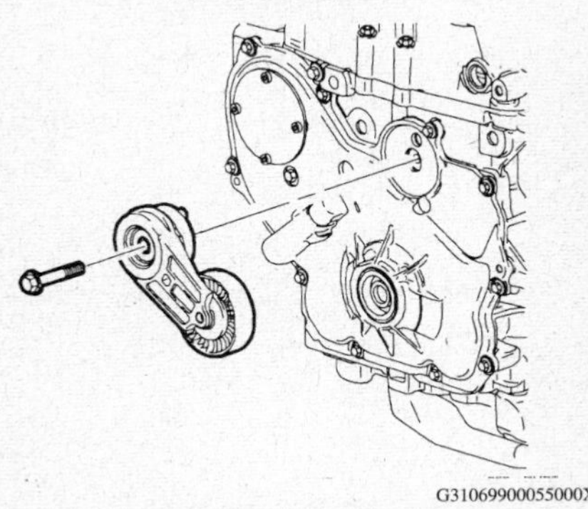

Fig. 28 Belt tensioner replacement

23. Disconnect fuel pump electrical connector from fuel pump cover.
24. Inspect fuel tank for metal chips or debris. Remove contaminants and replace in-line fuel filter before installing new pump.
25. Reverse procedure to install, noting the following:
   a. Replace plastic fuel line retainers.
   b. Install new module to tank seal lubricated with suitable clean engine oil.

FUEL FILTER

REPLACE

1. Raise and support vehicle.
2. Remove fuel filter bracket screw, then disconnect fuel lines from inlet and outlet sides of fuel filter.
3. Slide fuel filter out of bracket
4. Reverse procedure, noting the following:
   a. Cycle ignition On for five seconds and Off for 10 seconds.
   b. Repeat previous step twice.
   c. Crank engine until it starts. **Do not crank starter for more than 20 seconds.**
   d. If engine does not start, repeat previous steps.
   e. Run engine and inspect system for leaks.

TIGHTENING SPECIFICATIONS

Year	Component	Torque/Ft. Lbs.
2000–02	Air Conditioning Compressor To Block	18
	Alternator To Block	18
	Battery Hold-Down Bracket	15
	Battery Terminal	13
	Battery Tray	11
	Belt Tensioner To Block	37
	Block Oil Gallery Plug	26
	Camshaft Bearing Cap	96①
	Cam Cover To Head	96①
	Camshaft Sprocket	39②
	Camshaft Timing Chain Tensioner	44
	Chain Guide Plug	59
	Connecting Rod	18⑨
	Crankshaft Pulley	74⑧
	Crankshaft Position Sensor	96①
	Crankshaft Rear Oil Seal Carrier To Block	96①
	Cylinder Head	③
	EGR Pipe To Cylinder Head	96①
	EGR Valve	18
	Engine Lift Bracket, Front	18
	Engine Lift Bracket, Rear	18
	Engine Mount Bracket	66
	Engine Mount To Body	41
	Exhaust Manifold To Cylinder Head, Stud	18
	Exhaust Manifold To Cylinder Head, Nut	13
	Exhaust Manifold Pipe Flange	12
	Flexplate (Automatic Transaxle)	39 ⑥
	Flywheel (Manual Transaxle)	39 ⑥
	Frame To Body	75④
	Front Cover To Block	18
	Fuel Fill Neck To Fuel Tank Clamp	44①
	Fuel Filter Bracket	35①
	Fuel Line Bracket	96①
	Fuel Line Support Clip	96①
	Fuel Rail Bracket	96①
	Fuel Tank Strap	15
	Fuel Tank Ground Strap	40①
	Fuel Pressure Regulator	44①
	Heater Shield To Exhaust Manifold	96①
	Idle Air Control Motor	27①
	Ignition Coil	96①
	Intake Camshaft Rear Cap	18
	Intake Manifold To Cylinder Head, Bolt	96①
	Intake Manifold To Cylinder Head, Nut	96①
	Intake Manifold To Cylinder Head, Stud	53
	Knock Sensor	18
	Main Bearings	⑤
	Oil Drain Plug	18
	Oil Pan	⑦
	Oil Pump Pressure Relief Valve Plug	30
	Oil Pump Cover	53①
	Oxygen Sensor	22
	Power Steering Pump	18

Continued

TIGHTENING SPECIFICATIONS—Continued

Year	Component	Torque/Ft. Lbs.
2000–02	Radiator Upper Bracket	53①
	Spark Plug	15
	Starter Motor	37
	Thermostat Housing To Block	96①
	Throttle Body	96①
	Throttle Position Sensor	18①
	Timing Chain Guides	96①
	Timing Chain Nozzle	96①
	Transaxle Mount	41
	Transaxle Range Switch	18
	Transaxle Range Switch Lever	26
	Vent Tube To Cylinder Head	11
	Water Pump Access Cover	96①
	Water Pump	18
	Water Pump/Balance Shaft Chain Tensioner	96①
	Water Pump Sprocket	89①

①— Inch lbs.

②— Tighten an additional 30°.

③— Refer to "Cylinder Head, Replace" for tightening specifications and sequence.

④— Tighten an additional 45°.

⑤— Refer to "Main & Rod Bearings" for tightening specifications and sequence.

⑥— Tighten an additional 25°

⑦— Refer to "Oil Pan, Replace" for tightening specifications and sequence.

⑧— Tighten an additional 75°.

⑨— Tighten an additional 70°.

3.0L Engine

NOTE: On Air Bag Equipped Models, Refer To "Air Bag System Precautions" Located In The Front Of This Manual For System Disarming & Arming Procedures.

NOTE: Refer To "Computer Relearn Procedures" Located In The Front Of This Manual When Battery Power To The Computer Has Been Interrupted.

INDEX

PRECAUTIONS

AIR BAG SYSTEMS

Refer to "Air Bag System Precautions" in the front of this manual for system disarming and arming procedures.

BATTERY GROUND CABLE

Prior to service, disconnect battery ground cable and isolate as required.

FUEL SYSTEM PRESSURE RELIEF

WITH SCAN TOOL

Start vehicle and locate SPECIAL TESTS, select ECM, then select fuel delivery. Select FUEL PUMP, then command fuel pump off.

LESS SCAN TOOL

Remove schrader valve cap and install fuel pressure gauge tool No. SA-9127-E, or equivalent. Open valve on pressure gauge and drain fuel into suitable container.

COMPRESSION PRESSURE

1. Start and run engine until it reaches normal operating temperature. Turn engine off.
2. Remove ignition modules and spark plugs.
3. Connect compression gauge tool No. SA-9127-E, or equivalent, into spark plug hole.
4. Open throttle fully.

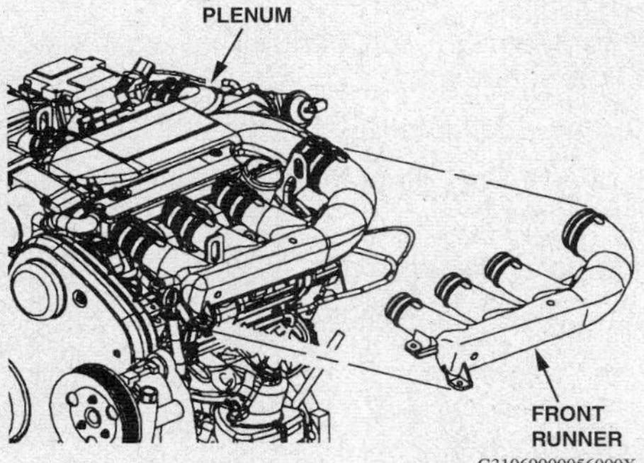

Fig. 1 Upper intake manifold front runner & plenum replacement

5. Crank engine at not less than 250 RPM.
6. Measure compression while cranking engine. Prior to reading compression gauge needle should bounce at least 10 times.
7. Repeat previous steps for each cylinder.
8. Minimum compression on any one cylinder should not be less than 70% of highest cylinder. No cylinder should read less than 100 psi.
9. Place shop towel over spark plug holes and crank engine over a few seconds without compression gauge or spark plugs installed.
10. Repeat compression measuring steps on each cylinder.

ENGINE MOUNT

REPLACE

1. Disconnect MAF sensor and remove air box.
2. Remove EVAP purge assembly and position aside.
3. Install engine support fixture and adapter tools Nos. SA-9150E and J-43405, or equivalents.
4. Remove engine mount and bracket.
5. Reverse procedure to install.

ENGINE

REPLACE

1. Disconnect MAF sensor, then remove air cleaner and battery.
2. Remove positive main feed cable at fuse block.
3. Disconnect main TCM connector under cowl cover and position aside.
4. Disconnect inline TCM connector near brake master cylinder.
5. Disconnect air conditioning pressure connector.
6. Disconnect black engine harness connector from under fuse block and lower weather pack connector inside fuse block.
7. Remove fuse block and position aside.
8. Secure engine harness to top of engine.
9. Remove battery tray.
10. Disconnect EVAP purge connector.
11. Disconnect righthand front speed sensor and secure to engine.

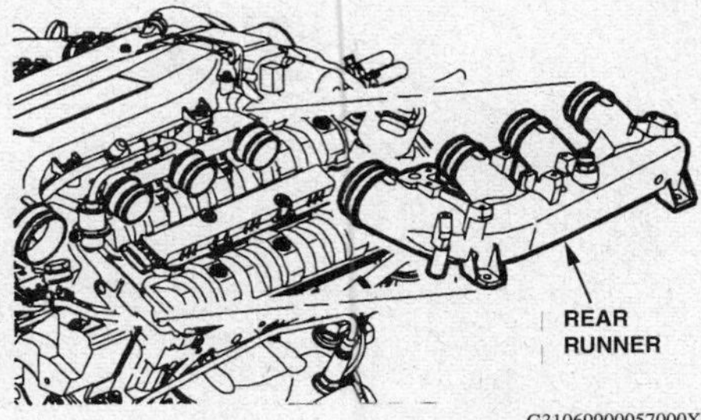

Fig. 2 Upper intake manifold rear runner replacement

12. Disconnect front oxygen sensor.
13. Disconnect transaxle ground, main connector, shift control and rear ECM connectors.
14. Remove brake booster vacuum hose.
15. Disconnect fuel lines and position aside.
16. Disconnect EVAP purge hose at EVAP purge solenoid.
17. Remove starter and torque convertor mounting bolts.
18. Remove exhaust system from catalytic convertor forward.
19. Disconnect transaxle nose bracket.
20. Remove air conditioning compressor and position aside.
21. Drain engine coolant into suitable container and disconnect heater hoses at cowl.
22. Remove lower engine to transaxle bell housing bolts. **Do not remove upper bolts now.**
23. Remove main coolant reservoir hose from engine inlet adapter.
24. Remove upper and lower radiator hoses from engine.
25. Remove small hose under power steering fluid reservoir and drain fluid into suitable container.
26. Disconnect metal power steering line.
27. Remove power steering reservoir and secure to engine.
28. Support engine using suitable engine lift hoist.
29. Remove righthand front engine mount and bracket.
30. Remove upper bell housing bolts.
31. Remove engine.
32. Reverse procedure to install. Ensure engine aligns with dowel pins on transaxle.

INTAKE MANIFOLD

REPLACE

UPPER

1. Remove front runner rubber boot hose clamps using hose clamp pliers tool No. J-43914, or equivalent.
2. Remove front runner, **Fig. 1.**
3. Remove ECM.
4. Remove rear runner rubber boot hose clams using hose clamp pliers tool No. J-43914, or equivalent.
5. Disconnect brake vacuum hose.
6. Disconnect intake plenum switch over valve vacuum hose from switch over valve. Mark hose routing for installation.

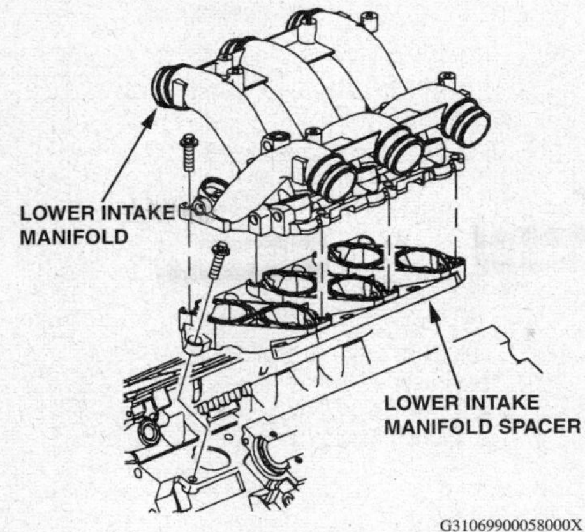

Fig. 3 Lower intake manifold & spacer replacement

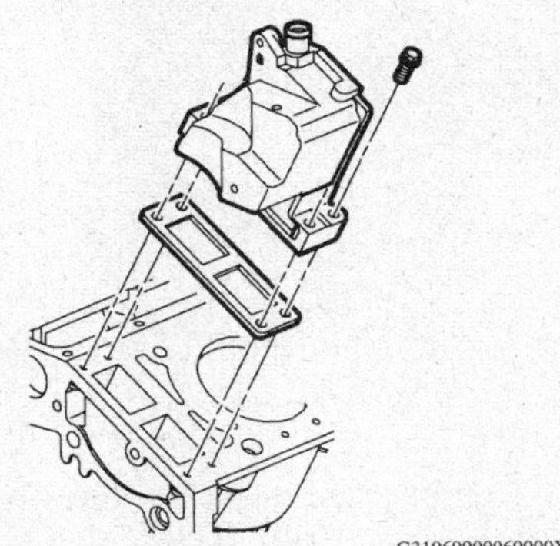

Fig. 5 Engine ventilation chamber replacement

7. Disconnect throttle body vent hose. Mark hose routing for installation.
8. Remove rear runner, **Fig. 2.**
9. Disconnect throttle body electrical connectors.
10. Remove electrical connector and vacuum hoses from plenum switch over valve solenoid.
11. Remove fuel pressure regulator vacuum and throttle body heater hoses.
12. Remove plenum.
13. Mask off ports to lower intake.
14. Remove upper intake manifold.
15. Reverse procedure to install.

LOWER

1. Remove upper intake as described under "Upper."
2. Remove fuel supply and return hoses from fuel rail using fuel line separator tool No. SA-9805-E, or equivalent.
3. Disconnect and remove fuel injector harness.
4. Remove fuel rail.
5. Remove lower intake manifold, **Fig. 3.**
6. Remove lower intake manifold spacer.
7. Mask off ports to lower intake manifold spacer.
8. Remove sealing rings.
9. Clean manifold sealing surfaces with nonabrasive cleaner.
10. Reverse procedure to install. Apply Loctite 242, or equivalent, to lower intake manifold spacer and lower intake manifold mounting bolts.

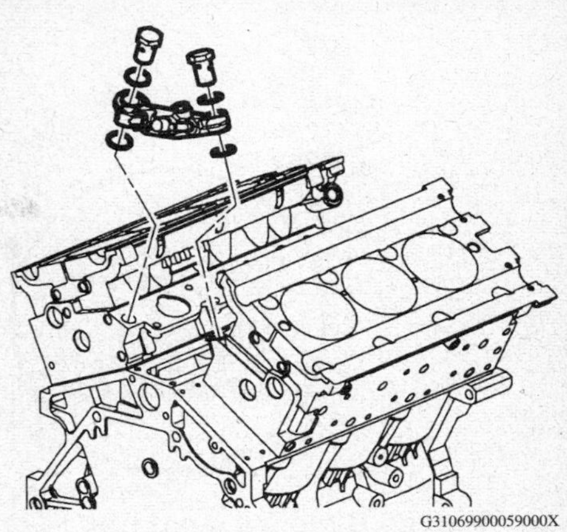

Fig. 4 Coolant bridge replacement

EXHAUST MANIFOLD

REPLACE

1. Remove front oxygen sensor using oxygen sensor socket tool No. J-39194-C, or equivalent.
2. Remove front exhaust manifold and gasket.
3. Remove rear oxygen sensor using oxygen sensor socket tool.
4. Disconnect EGR pipe.
5. Remove rear exhaust manifold and gasket.
6. Reverse procedure to install.

CYLINDER HEAD

REPLACE

1. Remove air cleaner.
2. Remove upper and lower intake manifolds as described under "Intake Manifold, Replace."
3. Remove coolant intake and heater hoses.
4. Remove coolant bridge and seals, **Fig. 4.**
5. Remove engine ventilation chamber, **Fig. 5.**
6. Drain coolant into suitable container.
7. Remove upper radiator hose.
8. Remove exhaust manifold heat shield.
9. Remove exhaust pipe to exhaust manifold mounting nuts.
10. Remove front exhaust pipes from exhaust manifolds.
11. Support powertrain using suitable floor jack under oil pan.
12. Remove front transaxle mount bolt.
13. Raise powertrain using floor jack to gain access to coolant extension housing.
14. Remove oil level indicator tube.
15. Twist and remove coolant extension housing.
16. Remove grounds from front lift bracket.
17. Disconnect oxygen sensor connector.
18. Remove EGR to exhaust manifold pipe.
19. Remove camshaft cover.
20. Remove front timing belt cover as outlined under "Front Cover, Replace."
21. Remove timing belt as outlined under "Timing Belt, Replace."

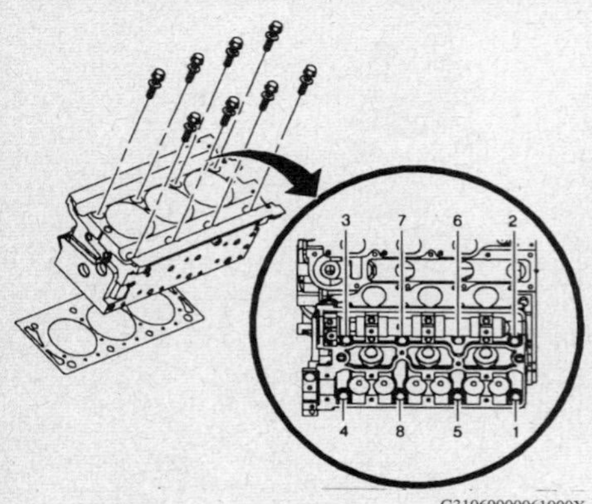

Fig. 6 Cylinder head bolt loosening sequence

22. Remove timing belt tensioner bracket.
23. Remove rear timing belt cover as outlined under "Front Cover, Replace."
24. Disconnect camshaft sensor connector.
25. Remove exhaust camshaft as outlined under "Camshaft, Replace."
26. Loosen and remove cylinder head bolts in several steps in sequence, **Fig. 6.**
27. Remove cylinder head and gasket.
28. Remove exhaust manifold.
29. Clean and inspect cylinder head and sealing surfaces.
30. Reverse procedure to install, noting the following:
    a. Ensure new cylinder head gasket part number imprint is facing towards top of engine.
    b. **Torque** cylinder head bolts to 18 ft. lbs. in sequence, **Fig. 7.**
    c. Tighten cylinder head bolts an additional 90° in sequence.
    d. Tighten head bolts an additional 90° in sequence.
    e. Tighten bolts an additional 90° in sequence.
    f. Finally, tighten cylinder head bolts an additional 15° in sequence.
    g. Replace sealing rings on coolant pipe and lubricate with coolant.

VALVE COVER

REPLACE

1. Remove upper and lower intake manifolds as described under "Intake Manifold, Replace."
2. Remove ignition coils and lift bracket.
3. Remove rear cover knock sensor wire harness and disconnect camshaft position sensor.
4. Remove cover and O-ring seals. Ensure O-rings are accounted for.
5. Clean cover and sealing surfaces.
6. Reverse procedure to install. Apply thin coat of Loctite 5900, or equivalent, to front and rear of cover, **Fig. 8.**

CAMSHAFT LOBE LIFT SPECIFICATIONS

Exhaust cam lobe lift rise 0.3409–0.3441 inch, minimum service limit is 0.339 inch.

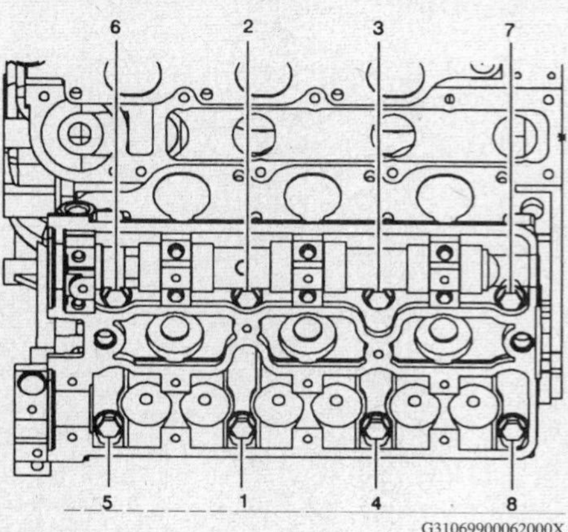

Fig. 7 Cylinder head bolt tightening sequence

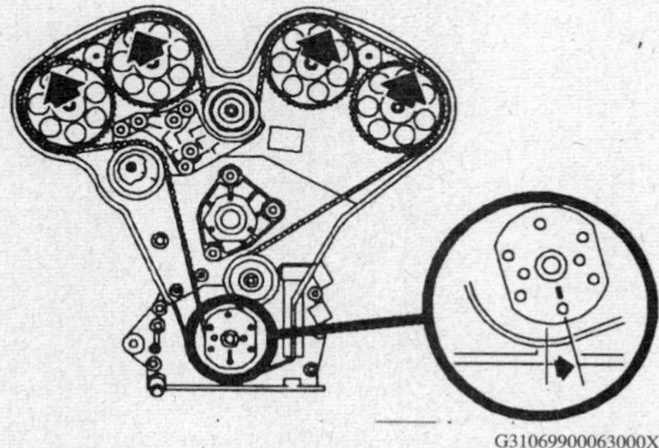

Fig. 9 Crankshaft alignment to 60° BTDC

VALVE ADJUSTMENT

Engine is equipped with hydraulic lifters, no adjustment is required.

FRONT COVER

REPLACE

1. Remove air cleaner.
2. Raise and support vehicle, then remove righthand front wheel and splash shield.
3. Lower vehicle, then loosen but do not remove water pump pulley bolts.
4. Install engine support fixture and adapters tools Nos. SA-9150-E and J-43405, or equivalents.
5. Remove serpentine belt as outlined under "Serpentine Drive Belt."
6. Remove water pump and power steering pulleys.
7. Remove serpentine belt tensioner and crankshaft balancer.
8. Disconnect air conditioning pressure connector to allow additional slack in harness, remove wiring harness channel from front cover and position away from front of engine.
9. Remove timing belt front cover.
10. Inspect outer edge sealing strip on front timing cover for cracks or tears and replace as required.
11. Remove timing belt as outlined under "Timing Belt, Replace."
12. To prevent valve to piston contact, rotate crankshaft counterclockwise to 60° BTDC, **Fig. 9.**
13. Remove camshaft gears using camshaft lock tools Nos. J-42069-1 and J-42069-2, or equivalents, when initially loosening camshaft bolts, **Fig. 10.**

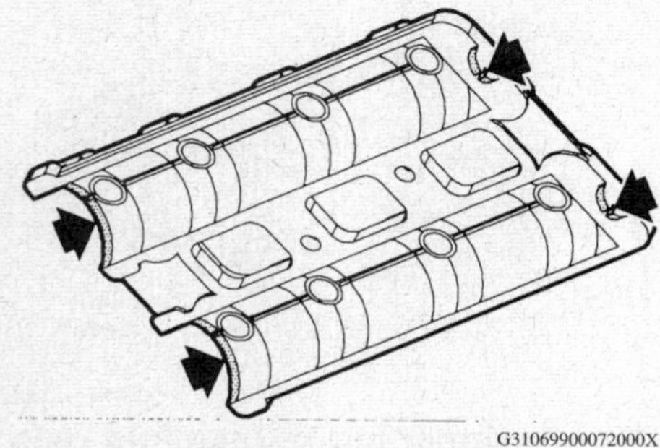

Fig. 8 Valve cover sealant application points

14. Remove timing belt tensioner bracket.
15. Remove timing belt idler pulley for camshaft Nos. 3 and 4, **Fig. 11.**
16. Remove mounting bolts, threaded pin and rear timing belt cover.
17. Reverse procedure to install, noting the following:
    a. Install threaded pin with Loctite 242, or equivalent.
    b. Tighten timing belt idler pulley until snug. After final timing belt adjustments are made, tighten to specifications.
    c. Adjust timing belt as outlined under "Timing Belt, Replace."
    d. Install new camshaft gear bolts.

TIMING BELT

REPLACE

REMOVAL

1. Remove timing belt front cover as described "Front Cover, Replace."
2. Rotate crankshaft using crank hub Torx socket tool No. J-42098, or equivalent, until cylinder No. 1 is at 60° BTDC, **Fig. 9.**
3. Install crankshaft locking tool No. J-42069-10, or equivalent.
4. Rotate crankshaft clockwise using crank hub Torx socket tool No. J-42098, or equivalent, until cylinder No. 1 is at TDC and tighten lever arm to water pump pulley flange.
5. Ensure alignment of crankshaft is not 180° off. Alignment marks must align with corresponding notches on rear timing belt cover.
6. Install camshaft gear locking tools Nos. J-42069-1 and J-42069-2, or equivalents, **Fig. 10.**
7. Remove upper and lower idler pulleys.
8. Remove timing belt tensioner.
9. Remove timing belt.
10. Do not rotate crankshaft if camshaft locking tools are not in place.
11. Do not rotate camshafts unless crankshaft is at 60° BTDC.

INSTALLATION

1. Remove crankshaft locking tool.
2. Mark furthest point from Torx head bolt on upper and lower idler pulleys, **Fig. 12.**

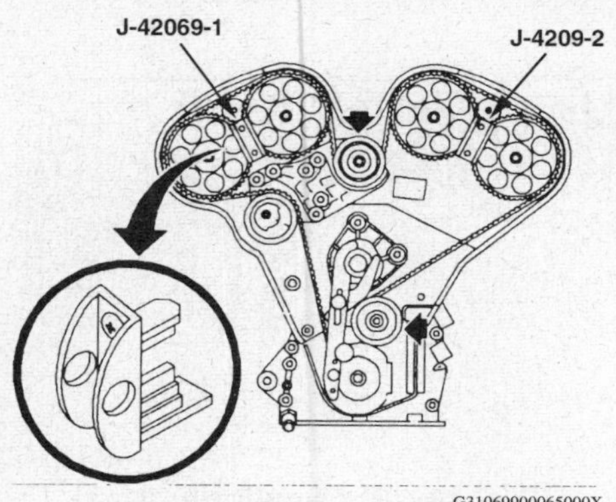

Fig. 10 Camshaft gear locking tool installation

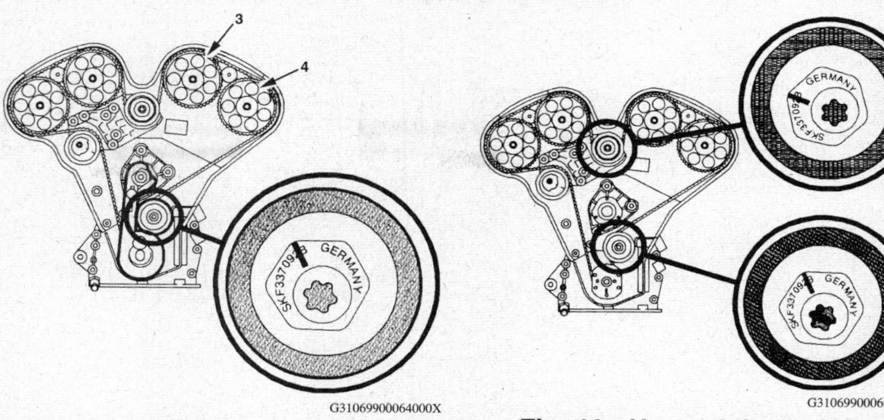

Fig. 11 Camshaft Nos. 3 & 4 idler pulley replacement

Fig. 12 Upper & lower idler pulleys alignment

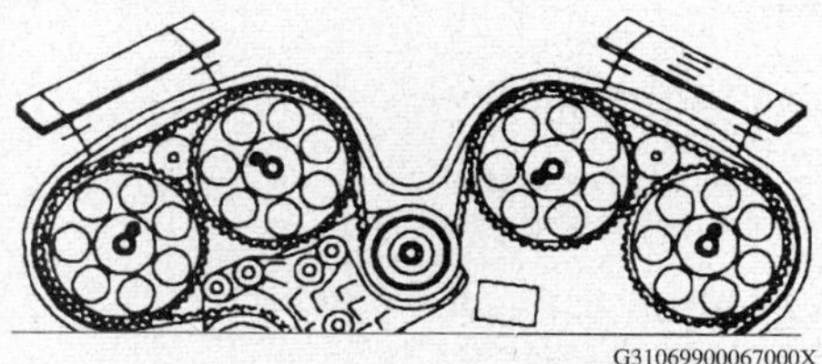

Fig. 13 Timing belt alignment

3. Idler pulleys provide adjustment by rotating eccentric circle around mounting bolt.
4. Install lower idler pulley allowing pulley to rotate with slight resistance using idler pulley wrench tool No. J-42069-40, or equivalent.
5. Align marks on timing belt with marks on camshaft sprockets Nos. 3 and 4, **Fig. 13.**
6. Route timing belt around lower idler pulley and crankshaft sprocket. Ensure timing belt and crankshaft sprocket marks align.
7. Lock timing belt to crankshaft sprocket using plastic wedge tool No. J-42069-30, or equivalent.
8. Route belt around timing belt tensioner, then around Nos. 1 and 2 camshaft sprockets. Ensure timing belt and sprockets' marks align.
9. Install upper idler pulley using idler pulley wrench tool No. J-42069-40, or equivalent. Allow pulley to rotate.
10. Install crankshaft locking tool No. J-42069-10, or equivalent, and tighten lever arm to water pump pulley flange.
11. Adjust timing belt tensioner alignment mark 1/8 inch above mark on spring loaded idler, **Fig. 14.**
12. Adjust mark on upper idler pulley to 10 o'clock position to align Nos. 1 and 2 timing marks close to settings. Snug but do not fully tighten pulley.
13. Adjust mark on lower idler pulley to 11 o'clock position to align Nos. 3 and 4 timing marks close to settings. Snug but do not fully tighten pulley.
14. Remove camshaft locking tools and install checking gauge tool No. J-42069-20, or equivalent.
15. Pull timing belt between tensioner and crankshaft sprocket to remove slack between camshaft Nos. 3 and 4 and lower idler pulley. Ensure timing marks on camshaft Nos. 3 and 4 are 0.0394 inch on retard side, **Fig. 15.** If timing marks are not 0.0394 inch on retard side, turn lower idler clockwise and repeat procedure.
16. Remove crankshaft locking tool.
17. Rotate crankshaft 1¾ turns clockwise and install crankshaft locking tool at TDC.
18. Tighten lever arm to water pump pulley flange.
19. If TDC is passed, do not rotate counterclockwise, rotate crankshaft an additional two turns.
20. Rotate lower idler pulley counterclockwise until timing marks on camshaft sprocket Nos. 3 and 4 align with marks on checking gauge tool.
21. Hold idler pulley using idler pulley wrench tool and tighten.
22. Remove crankshaft locking tool.
23. Rotate crankshaft 1¾ turns clockwise and install crankshaft locking tool. Stop at TDC and tighten lever arm to water pump pulley flange. If TDC is passed, do not rotate counterclockwise, rotate crankshaft an additional two turns.
24. Inspect alignment marks on camshaft Nos. 3 and 4, realign if required.
25. Install checking gauge tool on camshaft Nos. 1 and 2, then install camshaft locking tool on camshaft Nos. 2 and 4.
26. Rotate upper idler pulley counterclockwise until timing marks on camshaft sprocket Nos. 1 and 2 align with marks on checking gauge tool.
27. Hold idler pulley and tighten using idler pulley wrench tool.
28. Remove camshaft and crankshaft locking tools.
29. Rotate crankshaft 1¾ turns clockwise and install crankshaft locking tool. Stop at TDC and tighten lever arm to water pump pulley flange. If TDC is passed, do not rotate counterclockwise, rotate crankshaft an additional two turns.
30. Inspect both pairs of camshaft timing marks using checking gauge tool. Adjust as required.
31. Adjust timing belt tensioner mark 1/8 inch above alignment mark on spring loaded idler, **Fig. 14.**
32. Remove crankshaft locking tool and checking gauge tool.
33. Install timing belt front cover.

CAMSHAFT

REPLACE

REMOVAL

1. Remove upper and lower intake manifold as described under "Intake Manifold, Replace."
2. Remove air cleaner.
3. Remove timing belt cover as outlined under "Front Cover, Replace."
4. Remove timing belt as described "Timing Belt, Replace."
5. Rotate crankshaft counterclockwise to 60° BTDC to prevent valve to piston contact, **Fig. 9.**
6. Remove gear bolt and gear using camshaft locking tools Nos. J-42069-1 and J-42069-2, or equivalents.
7. Ensure camshaft is not under load from lifters.
8. Remove bearing cap bolts, starting in center and moving outward in spiral direction, in stages of ½–1 turn.
9. Code marks on bearing caps are as follows:
   a. Rear cylinder head cylinders Nos. 1, 3 and 5 bearing caps are marked with L followed by a number.
   b. Front cylinder head cylinders Nos. 2, 4 and 6 bearing caps are marked with R followed by a number.
10. Remove camshaft with seal, then clean bearing and sealing surfaces.

INSTALLATION

1. Lubricate camshaft bearing surfaces with oil.
2. Install camshafts as follows:
   a. **When installing rear exhaust**

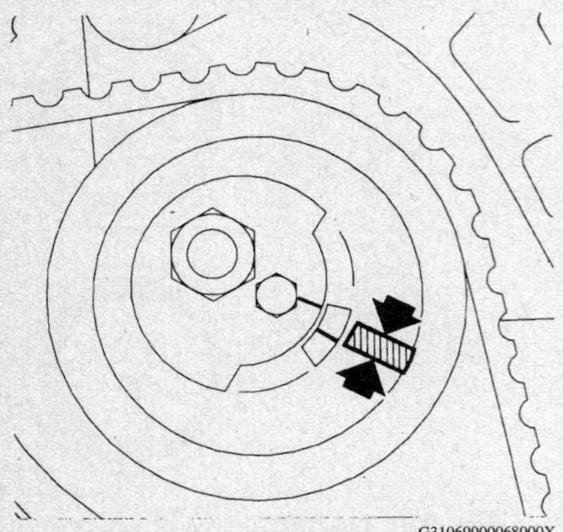

Fig. 14 Timing belt tensioner alignment

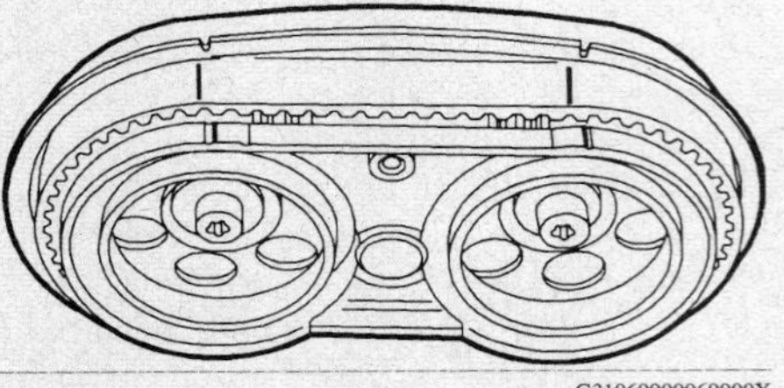

Fig. 15 Timing belt alignment retarded 0.0394 inch

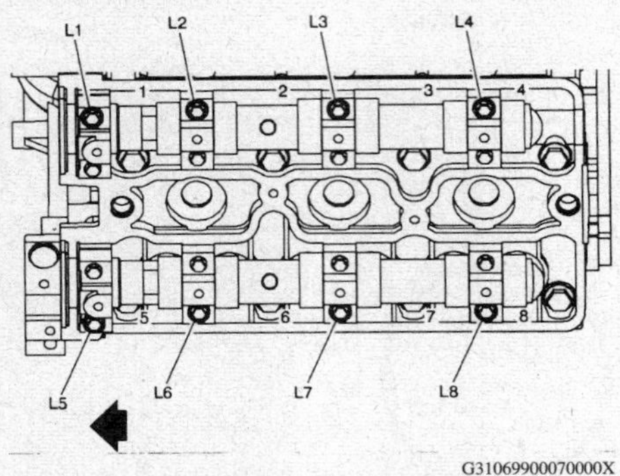

Fig. 16 Rear cylinder head bearing cap locations

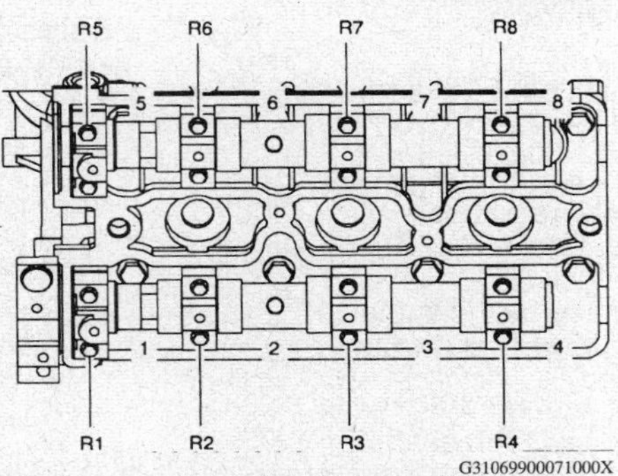

Fig. 17 Front cylinder head bearing cap locations

camshaft, ensure pin points towards 1 o'clock position.

b. **When installing rear intake camshaft,** ensure pin points towards 11 o'clock position.
c. **When installing front exhaust camshaft,** ensure pin points toward 12 o'clock position.
d. **When installing front intake camshaft,** ensure pin points toward 7 o'clock position.

3. Apply sealant Loctite 573, or equivalent, to forward edge of front bearing cap, ensure sealant does not enter oil journal.
4. Install bearing caps in appropriate positions, **Figs. 16 and 17.**
5. Tighten bearing caps, starting in center and moving outward in spiral direction.
6. Coat lip of camshaft seal with engine oil and tap into place using camshaft front seal installer tool No. J-35268-A, or equivalent, ensure seal is fully seated.
7. Install camshaft gear with new bolts and camshaft locking tool.
8. Install new camshaft gear mounting bolts.
9. Install and adjust timing belt.
10. Install valve cover.
11. Install upper and lower intake manifold.
12. Install air cleaner.

PISTON & ROD ASSEMBLY

Ensure arrow on piston head faces towards front of engine and bump on connecting rod face towards rear of engine.

PISTONS, PINS & RINGS

1. If cylinders have been honed, proper size piston must be selected for each bore from chart, **Fig. 18.**
2. If piston must be separated from connecting rod.
3. Remove and install piston pin clips using piston pin clip replacement tool No. J-43654, or equivalent.
4. Remove or install piston from connecting rod using piston pin remover/installer tool No. SA-9101-E, or equivalent.
5. Ensure arrow on top of piston and bump on connecting rod face in opposite directions when assembling piston and rod. Arrow on piston will face front of engine block, bump on connecting rod will face rear of engine block.
6. Measure piston pin bore to piston pin clearance. Replace piston and piston pin if clearance is not 0.0001–0.0003 inch.
7. Hone cylinders.
8. Install 1st and 2nd compression rings in cylinder bore. Gap should be .0118–0.0196 inch.
9. Install oil control ring in cylinder bore. Gap should be 0.0157–0.0551 inch.
10. Replace rings if end gap clearance is more than specified.
11. First and 2nd compression ring groove clearance should be 0.0008–0.0015 inch.
12. Oil control ring groove clearance should be 0.0004–0.0012 inch.
13. Replace piston if ring groove clearance is more than specified.
14. Refer to **Fig. 19** for piston ring orientation.

MAIN & ROD BEARINGS

The crankshaft main bearing caps are numbered 1, 2 and 3 from the front of the engine. The rear bearing cap is not numbered and contains the thrust bearings. The Nos. 2 and 3 bearing shells do not have oil grooves on the cap sides.

There is a 0 or 1 stamped on the cylinder block oil pan mating flange near the end of each main bearing cap. This is the Determining No. The Determining No. corresponds to each crankshaft main bearing size and color to be installed. The main journal diameter for a determining No. 0 is 2.8368–2.8371 inches. The main journal diameter for a determining No. 1 is 2.8371–2.8373 inches.

To select the correct main bearing, measure crankshaft main bearing journal diameter and refer to main bearing selective fits chart, **Fig. 20.**

Tighten connecting rod caps as follows:

1. **Torque** to 26 ft. lbs.
2. Tighten an additional 45°.
3. Finally, tighten an additional 15°.
4. Tighten mounting bolts an additional 60° and final tighten an additional 15°.

Tighten main bearings as follows:

1. **Torque** main bearing cap bolts to 37 ft. lbs.
2. Tighten mounting bolts an additional 60°.
3. Finally, tighten an additional 15°.

CRANKSHAFT REAR OIL SEAL

REPLACE

1. Remove transaxle as outlined in "Automatic Transaxles" chapter.
2. Counterhold crankshaft using crank hub Torx socket tool No. J-42098, or equivalent, and remove flexplate.
3. Center punch steel ring in rear oil seal, then drill small, shallow pilot hole in steel ring.

CYLINDER BORE	PISTON SIZE
(8) 85.976 - 85.985 mm (3.3848 - 3.3852 inch)	(8) 85.940 - 85.950 mm (3.3834 - 3.3838 inch)
(99) 85.985 - 85.995 mm (3.3852 - 3.3856 inch)	(99) 85.950 - 85.960 mm (3.3838 - 3.3842 inch)
(00) 85.995 - 86.005 mm (3.3856 - 3.3860 inch)	(00) 85.960 - 85.970 mm (3.3842 - 3.3846 inch)
(01) 86.005 - 86.015 mm (3.3860 - 3.3864 inch)	(01) 85.970 - 85.980 mm (3.3846 - 3.3850 inch)
(02) 86.015 - 86.025 mm (3.3864 - 3.3868 inch)	(02) 85.980 - 85.990 mm (3.3850 - 3.3854 inch)
† (7 + 0.5) 86.465 - 86.475 mm (3.4041 - 3.4045 inch)	† (7 + 0.5) 86.430 - 86.440 mm (3.4027 - 3.4031 inch)

GC1069700845000X

Fig. 18 Piston selection chart

4. Screw self tapping screw into steel ring and remove rear oil seal using suitable pliers.
5. Reverse procedure to install, noting the following:
   a. Coat lip of rear oil seal with suitable clean engine oil.
   b. Install rear oil seal using rear main oil seal installer tool No. J-42067, or equivalent.

OIL PAN

REPLACE

1. Remove nose cone bracket bolts from oil pan.
2. Remove lower transaxle flange to oil pan bolts.
3. Remove oil pan using RTV cutter tool No. SA-9123-E, or equivalent, to break pan loose from engine block.
4. Reverse procedure to install using Loctite 5900, or equivalent, 0.118 inch from inside edge of oil pan.

OIL PUMP

REPLACE

1. Drain coolant into suitable container.
2. Remove air cleaner.
3. Remove timing belt front and rear covers as outlined under "Front Cover, Replace."
4. Remove timing belt as described under "Timing Belt, Replace."
5. Remove and position air conditioning compressor and power steering pump aside.
6. Pivot alternator aside.
7. Remove oil pan as described under "Oil Pan, Replace."
8. Hold crankshaft drive gear using crank hub holding tool No. J-42065, or equivalent.
9. Remove drive gear using crank hub Torx socket tool No. J-42098, or equivalent.
10. Remove oil pan housing bolts and oil pump.
11. Remove front main oil seal and collar from oil pump.
12. Reverse procedure to install, noting the following:
    a. Coat pump side of new oil pump gasket with anaerobic sealant Loctite 518, or equivalent.
    b. Install oil pump and align using guide pins. Apply thread sealant Loctite 242, or equivalent, to bolts.
    c. Coat lip of front main oil seal with suitable clean engine oil, then install using front main seal installer tool No. J-35268-A, or equivalent. Ensure seal is seated fully and evenly.
    d. Install new crankshaft drive gear bolt.
    e. Tighten oil pump after alternator and drive belt idler pulley for camshafts Nos. 3 and 4 have been tightened.
    f. Fill and bleed cooling system, as required.

BELT TENSION DATA

1. Allow engine to run for approximately 10 minutes with accessories turned on to ensure engine is warmed up.
2. Rotate tensioner arm clockwise until belt becomes loose and slowly apply tension back on belt.
3. Marking on tensioner arm must fall within two marks on tensioner body. Replace drive belt if tensioner marks fall outside operating range.
4. Record belt tension at midspan using calibrated belt tension gauge tool No. SA-9181-NE, or equivalent. This inspection can be performed with engine removed. If engine is in vehicle, upper engine mount must be removed.
5. Repeat previous steps three times. Determine average belt tension.
6. New belt tension should be 50–65 lbs. Used belt should be at least 45 lbs.

SERPENTINE DRIVE BELT

BELT ROUTING

Refer to **Fig. 21** for serpentine belt routing.

BELT REPLACEMENT

1. Remove righthand front engine mount as outlined under "Engine Mount, Replace."
2. Remove belt by rotate tensioner pulley clockwise and sliding drive belt off tensioner or water pump.
3. Reverse procedure to install.

COOLING SYSTEM BLEED

Run engine until thermostat opens, then cycle engine speed from idle to 3000 RPM in 30 second intervals. Add coolant as required to bring level to cold line on reservoir after engine has cooled.

THERMOSTAT

REPLACE

1. Remove thermostat housing extension bolt.
2. Remove extension by pulling it out from thermostat housing.
3. Remove thermostat housing and thermostat.
4. Reverse procedure to install.

WATER PUMP

REPLACE

1. Remove air cleaner inlet duct from throttle body.
2. Remove lefthand front wheel and splash shield.

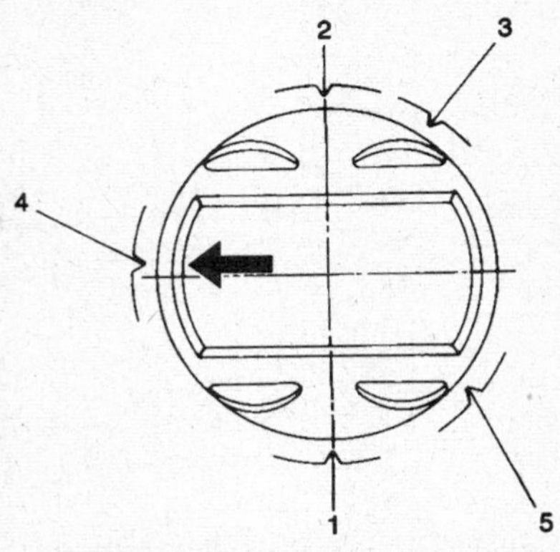

(1) 1st Compression Ring End Gap Location
(2) 2nd Compression Ring End Gap Location
(3) Oil Control Ring Upper Ring End Gap Location
(4) Oil Control Ring Spacer End Gap Location
(5) Oil Control Ring Lower Ring End Gap Location

GC1069700848000X

Fig. 19 Piston ring orientation

3. Loosen but do not remove water pump and power steering pump pulley bolts.
4. Remove accessory drive belt as outlined under "Serpentine Drive Belt."
5. Remove water pump and power steering pump pulleys, then the drive belt tensioner.
6. Remove front timing belt cover as outlined under "Front Cover, Replace."
7. Remove water pump and O-ring.
8. Reverse procedure to install.

RADIATOR

REPLACE

1. Slide fan control module up and off bracket, then position aside.
2. Remove battery.
3. Drain coolant into suitable container.
4. Remove power steering fluid reservoir and position to rear of vehicle.
5. Disconnect both cooling fans and auxiliary water pump, then remove fan shroud harnesses.
6. Remove upper transaxle cooler line and unsnap front end tank retainer.
7. Remove upper radiator hose and auxiliary water pump outlet and inlet hoses.
8. Remove fan shroud and forward wiring harness,
9. Remove lower radiator hose and lower transaxle cooler line from radiator.
10. Remove upper radiator bracket and mounts, then the upper hose.
11. Support condenser from upper rail and remove condenser block bolt from radiator end tank.
12. Remove condenser bolts, then disconnect radiator tabs by pulling condenser and pusher fan down.
13. Remove radiator leaving condenser and pusher fan, then the upper and lower radiator to condenser gaskets.
14. Reverse procedure to install.

FUEL PUMP

REPLACE

1. Drain fuel tank into suitable container using suitable hand operated pump.

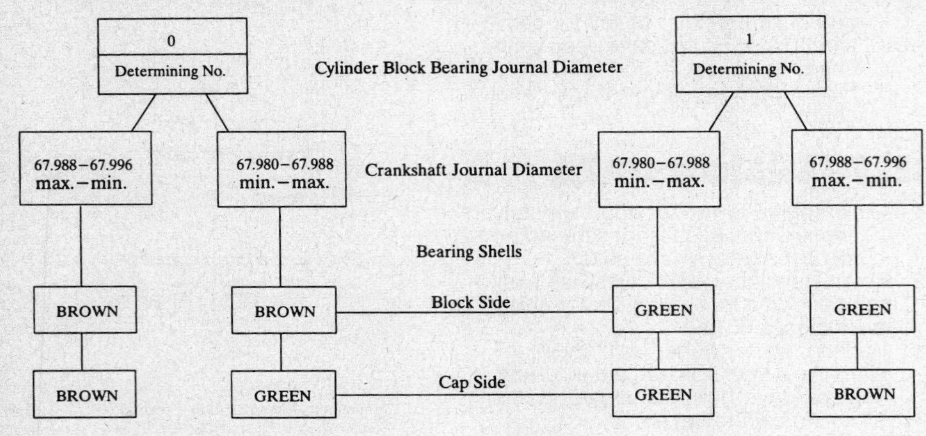

Fig. 20 Main bearing selective fits chart

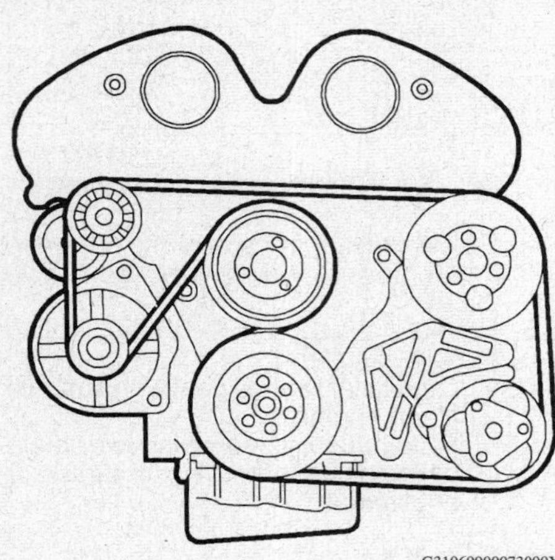

Fig. 21 Serpentine drive belt routing

2. Remove exhaust system intermediate pipe with muffler and heat shield.
3. Remove fuel filler pipe lower bracket and disconnect filler pipe hose from tank.
4. Disconnect EVAP canister vent hose and quick connect at recirc line.
5. Remove fuel tank grounding strap.
6. Disconnect fuel feed line after fuel filter, then the fuel return and EVAP canister purge lines between tank and chassis fuel bundle.
7. Disconnect fuel tank electrical connections.
8. Support fuel tank.
9. Remove rear mounting strap bolts and fuel tank.
10. Remove fuel lines from fuel pump module cover.
11. Remove fuel pump module retaining ring using suitable ½ inch breaker bar and lock ring service tool No. J-43827, or equivalent.
12. Disconnect fuel pump housing clips and remove fuel pump from fuel tank.
13. Remove fuel feed line from bottom of fuel pump using fuel clamp pliers tool No. J-44078, or equivalent.
14. Disconnect fuel pump connector from fuel pump cover.
15. Reverse procedure to install, noting the following:
    a. Install new fuel pump seal.
    b. Install pump cover lock ring with bumps facing away from tank using lock ring service tool.
    c. Install new retainers into female portion of quick connect fitting on fuel and EVAP canister purge lines.

FUEL FILTER

REPLACE

1. Disconnect fuel feed lines.
2. Remove fuel filter.
3. Reverse procedure to install. Install new fuel line retainers into fuel line fittings' female portion.

TIGHTENING SPECIFICATIONS

Year	Component	Torque/Ft. Lbs.
2000–02	Air Conditioning Compressor Bracket	30
	Air Conditioning Compressor Hose Support Strap	71①
	Accelerator Pedal Bracket	89①
	Accelerator Pedal Position Sensor	53①
	Accessory Bracket, Air Conditioning & Power Steering	30
	Accessory Drive Belt Tensioner	30
	Alternator	30
	Battery Hold Down Bracket	15
	Battery Terminal	13
	Battery Tray	11
	Bell Housing	48
	Belt Tensioner	30
	Camshaft Bearing	71①
	Camshaft Cover	71①
	Camshaft Gear	37⑤
	Camshaft Position Sensor	71①
	Catalytic Converter	15
	Catalytic Converter Hanger	15
	Connecting Rod Cap	②
	Coolant Bridge	22
	Crankshaft Balancer	15
	Crankshaft Main Bearing	②
	Crankshaft Torsional Bearing Bridge	15
	Crankshaft Drive Gear	184⑥
	Crankshaft Position Sensor	71①
	Crankshaft Reluctor Ring	11
	Crankshaft Sensor	71①
	Cylinder Head	④
	Drive Belt Tensioner	30
	Engine Control Module	71①
	Engine Coolant Temperature Sensor	13
	Engine Mount	41
	Engine Mount Bracket	41
	Engine Oil Cooler Cover	22
	Engine Oil Cooler Inlet & Outlet	15
	Engine Rear Cover	71①
	Engine Rear Cover Threaded Pin	89①
	Engine Ventilation Chamber	71①
	Exhaust Gas Recirculation Pipe	19
	Exhaust Gas Recirculation Valve	15
	Exhaust Manifold	15
	Flexplate	65
	Front Timing Belt Cover	48③
	Fuel Fill Neck To Fuel Tank Clamp	71①
	Fuel Fill Pipe To Body, Lower	114①
	Fuel Fill Pipe To Body, Upper	35①
	Fuel Filter Bracket	35①
	Fuel Line Stone Chip Guard	106①
	Fuel Rail	71①
	Fuel Tank Mounting Strap	15
	Fuel Tank Pressure Sensor	18①
	Heated Oxygen Sensor	37
	Ignition Coil	71①
	Ignition Module	71①

Continued

TIGHTENING SPECIFICATIONS—Continued

Year	Component	Torque/Ft. Lbs.
2000–02	Intake Manifold	15
	Intake Manifold Spacer	15
	Intake Plenum	71①
	Intake Plenum Switchover Valve	71①
	Intake Runner	71①
	Knock Sensors	15
	Main Bearing	②
	Manifold Absolute Pressure Sensor	44①
	Negative Battery Cable To Chassis	114①
	Oil Cooler Inlet & Outlet	15
	Oil Filter Cap	19
	Oil Filter Cartridge Housing Drain Plug	89①
	Oil Filter Cartridge Housing To Engine Block	33
	Oil Intake Pipe	71①
	Oil Pan Baffle	71①
	Oil Pan	11
	Oil Pan Drain Plug	19
	Oil Pressure Switch	30
	Oil Pump	80①
	Oxygen Sensors, Exhaust Manifold	37
	Oxygen Sensors, Lower Exhaust Pipe	33
	Power Steering Pump Pulley	15
	Rear Timing Belt Cover Threaded Pin	89①
	Rear Timing Cover	71①
	Resonance Chamber	27①
	Spark Plug	19
	Starter	30
	Thermostat Housing	15
	Throttle Boot	71①
	Timing Belt Idler Pulley	30
	Timing Belt Tensioner Bracket	30
	Timing Belt Tensioner	15
	Torque Convertor Bolt	48
	Transaxle Cooler Line, Lower	36①
	Transaxle Cooler Line, Upper	18
	Transaxle Range Switch	18
	Transaxle Range Switch Lever	26
	Water Pump	19
	Water Pump Pulley	71①
	Wheel Bolt	92
	Wiring Channel	71①

①— Inch lbs.
②— Refer to "Main & Rod Bearings" for tighten specifications & sequence.
③— Tighten an additional 30° and final tighten an additional 15°.
④— Refer to "Cylinder Head, Replace" for tighten specifications & sequence.
⑤— Tighten an additional 60° and final tighten an additional 15°.
⑥— Tighten an additional 45° and final tighten an additional 15°.

Clutch & Manual Transaxle

NOTE: On Air Bag Equipped Models, Refer To "Air Bag System Precautions" Located In The Front Of This Manual For System Disarming & Arming Procedures.

NOTE: Refer To "Computer Relearn Procedures" Located In The Front Of This Manual When Battery Power To The Computer Has Been Interrupted.

NOTE: Prior To Performing Any Service Operations Listed In This Section, Consult The "Technical Service Bulletins" Section For Related Information.

INDEX

PRECAUTIONS

AIR BAG SYSTEMS

Refer to "Air Bag System Precautions" in the front of this manual for system disarming and arming procedures.

BATTERY GROUND CABLE

Prior to service, disconnect battery ground cable and isolate as required.

ADJUSTMENTS

CLUTCH PEDAL HEIGHT

The hydraulic clutch system provides automatic clutch adjustment.

If the clutch pedal height, **Fig. 1,** is not 4.6–5.4 inches, check carpet or floor mat under pedal, then inspect for faulty bushing or damaged pedal.

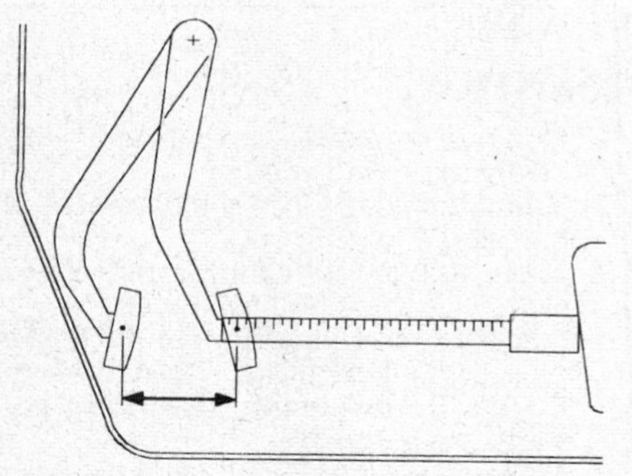

Fig. 1 Clutch pedal height

HYDRAULIC SYSTEM SERVICE

HYDRAULIC CLUTCH SYSTEM BLEED

1.9L ENGINE

The hydraulic system is serviced as a unit; it has been filled with fluid and bled of air. If the system requires any fluid, inspect the hydraulic components for leakage.

1. Remove slave cylinder from clutch housing and inspect for leakage at piston.
2. A slightly wet surface is normal, if excessive, replace system.
3. Clean cap and sides of reservoir before removing cap, then remove diaphragm.
4. Replace diaphragm and cover after filling.

2.2L ENGINE

Manual Bleed

1. Fill brake fluid reservoir with clean brake fluid.
2. Attach transparent hose over clutch bleeder screw nipple. Submerge other end of hose in suitable container of brake fluid.
3. Depress and hold down clutch pedal, then loosen clutch bleeder screw on transaxle hydraulic fitting.
4. Allow brake fluid to drain into suitable container from bleeder screw.
5. Tighten bleeder screw and raise clutch.
6. Repeat steps until no air bubbles are seen.
7. Inspect clutch pedal feel for sponginess. If clutch pedal is spongy, repeat bleeding procedure until condition is corrected.
8. Inspect fluid level in brake fluid reservoir. Add fluid as required.

Pressure Bleed

1. Fill brake fluid reservoir with clean brake fluid.
2. Install bleeder adapter tool No. J-43915, or equivalent, to brake fluid reservoir.
3. Connect pressure bleeder to adapter and charge equipment to 20–25 psi.
4. Attach transparent hose over clutch bleeder screw nipple. Submerge other end of hose in suitable container of brake fluid.
5. Loosen clutch bleeder screw on transaxle hydraulic fitting and bleed system until no bubbles are seen in hose.
6. Tighten clutch bleeder screw, inspect clutch pedal feel for sponginess. If clutch pedal is spongy, repeat bleeding procedure.
7. Remove pressure bleeder equipment.
8. Inspect brake fluid reservoir. Adjust level as required.

SLAVE CYLINDER BLEED

2.2L ENGINE

1. Connect 18-inch long piece of transparent hose to slave cylinder fitting on transaxle.
2. Depress release bearing on slave cylinder towards clutch housing and release it. Even though release bearing will spring back, slave cylinder piston will remain depressed.

3. Connect vacuum pump tool No. SA-9180-NE using pressure adapter J-35555-92, or equivalents, to top of hose.
4. Apply pressure to force brake fluid into slave cylinder, pressure gauge will increase when piston reaches end of travel.
5. Remove vacuum/pressure pump from hose and depress release bearing. Air bubble will appear in hose.
6. Repeat previous steps until no air bubbles appear.
7. Leave slave cylinder piston depressed. Drain into suitable container and remove hose.

CLUTCH HYDRAULIC SYSTEM, REPLACE

1.9L Engine

The clutch hydraulic system must be serviced as a unit. Individual components, with the exception of the slave cylinder actuator pushrod retaining strap, cannot be replaced.

1. Block clutch pedal.
2. Remove air induction tube.
3. Remove battery and battery tray, as required.
4. Rotate actuator ¼ turn counterclockwise while pushing toward housing to disconnect and remove actuator from clutch housing. **Do not remove hydraulic damper before actuator.**
5. Remove hydraulic damper to clutch housing mounting nuts, then slide damper and bracket from studs.
6. Remove clutch pedal pin to slave cylinder pushrod mounting clip and disconnect pushrod from pedal.
7. **On models equipped with ABS,** remove brake master cylinder mounting nuts and move cylinder off studs. Ensure brake lines are not damaged during removal.
8. **On all models,** turn slave cylinder approximately ⅛ turn clockwise and remove.
9. Reverse procedure to install.

CLUTCH MASTER CYLINDER, REPLACE

2.2L ENGINE

1. Remove brake fluid reservoir cap. Ensure there is enough brake fluid to clear passage to clutch cylinder.
2. Disconnect clutch hydraulic line from body retaining clips.
3. Remove clutch hydraulic line from master cylinder and lay aside.
4. Remove lefthand lower instrument panel close out panel and master cylinder push rod from clutch pedal.
5. Remove mounting nuts and master cylinder
6. Reverse procedure to install. Bleed clutch hydraulic system, as required.

CLUTCH SLAVE CYLINDER, REPLACE

2.2L ENGINE

1. Remove transaxle as outlined under "Transaxle Replace."

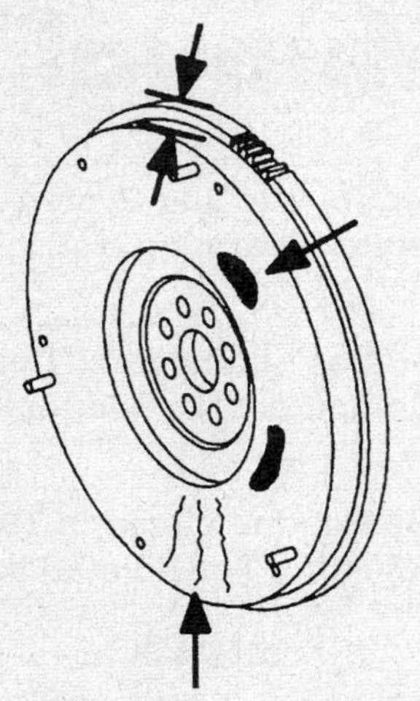

Fig. 2 Pressure plate warpage inspection

2. Remove slave cylinder hydraulic line.
3. Remove mounting bolts and slave cylinder.
4. Reverse procedure to install. Apply Loctite 592, or equivalent sealant, to slave cylinder mounting bolts.

CLUTCH

REPLACE

REMOVAL

1. Remove transaxle as outlined under "Transaxle, Replace."
2. Remove release fork and bearing from ball stud.
3. Slide release bearing from release fork.
4. Inspect release bearing for excessive play or minimal drag. Replace as required. **Do not wash bearing in solvent.**
5. Measure clearance between pressure plate and flywheel. Replace clutch disc if clearance is not 0.205–0.287 inch.
6. Remove pressure plate to flywheel mounting bolts in progressive crisscross pattern.
7. Remove pressure plate and clutch disc.

INSPECTION

1. Inspect pressure plate for excessive wear, chatter marks, cracks or overheating, replace as required. **Random black spotting on friction surface is normal.**
2. Measure pressure plate warpage, **Fig. 2.** Maximum warpage is 0.006 inch.
3. Inspect clutch disc for oil, burn marks and loose damper springs, hub or rivets; replace as required.
4. Inspect flywheel ring gear for wear or damage; replace as required.
5. Measure flywheel thickness, **Fig. 3.** If flywheel is not at least 1.102 inches thick, replace it.
6. Measure flywheel runout while pushing crankshaft forward to take up thrust bearing clearance. Maximum runout is .006 inch. Replace as required.
7. Remove mounting bolts and flywheel.

INSTALLATION

1. Tighten flywheel mounting bolts in sequence, **Fig. 4.**
2. Install clutch disc and pressure plate, with pressure plate yellow dot aligned with flywheel mark.
3. Start pressure plate to flywheel mounting bolts.
4. Insert clutch disc alignment tool No. SA-9145-T, or equivalent, into center hole until it bottoms out in crankshaft.
5. Tighten pressure plate bolts in crisscross pattern.
6. Remove clutch alignment tool and install fork clip.
7. Lubricate fork pivot using high temperature grease No. 21005995, or equivalent, and install release bearing to fork. **Do not lubricate release bearing or quill.**
8. Install release fork and bearing to ball stud.
9. Lubricate input shaft splines and install transaxle as described under "Transaxle, Replace."

TRANSAXLE

REPLACE

1.9L ENGINE

1. Raise and support vehicle, then remove air induction system.
2. Remove battery hold-down, battery and tray.
3. Remove transaxle strut to midrail bracket and cradle bracket mounting bolts.
4. Loosen transaxle strut to transaxle bracket mounting bolt and position strut aside.
5. Disconnect back-up light switch and vehicle speed sensor electrical connectors.
6. Remove and discard vent tube clip.
7. Disconnect upper clutch housing ground terminals and oxygen sensor connector from clutch housing.
8. Remove upper clutch housing engine bolts.
9. Remove mounting screws and DIS coil.
10. Remove shift cables from shift arms and clutch housing, **Fig. 5.**
11. Remove clutch slave cylinder by turning ¼ counterclockwise while pushing into clutch housing.
12. Remove clutch hydraulic dampener mounting bolts.
13. Support hydraulic dampener from upper radiator hose using suitable wire.
14. Secure radiator to upper support with mechanics wire.
15. Install engine lifting equipment.
16. Raise and support vehicle, then drain transaxle fluid into suitable container.
17. Remove front wheels, then lefthand, righthand and front splash shields.
18. Remove engine mount to cradle mounting nuts.

19. Remove engine strut cradle bracket to cradle mounting bolts.
20. Remove transaxle to cradle mount.
21. Remove front exhaust pipe.
22. Remove steering gear to cradle mounting bolts and support steering gear with suitable wire.
23. Remove brake line bracket push pin at rear of cradle.
24. Remove engine to transaxle stiffening bracket.
25. Remove clutch housing dust cover.
26. Remove and discard lower ball joint cotter pins, then loosen nut to top of bolt thread.
27. Separate ball joint from lower control arm using ball joint separator tool No. SA-9132-S, or equivalent. **Outer CV joint has ABS speed sensor ring.**
28. Separate lefthand side axle from transaxle using suitable large screwdriver or pry bar.
29. Pull axle slightly rearward and install axle seal protector tool No. SA-91112-T, or equivalent.
30. Separate righthand axle from intermediate shaft.
31. **On models equipped with DOHC engine,** remove intake support bracket.
32. **On all models,** remove intake to intermediate shaft support bracket.
33. Remove intermediate shaft to engine block bolts.
34. Slide intermediate shaft from transaxle.
35. Support cradle using suitable powertrain support dolly and two 4 x 4 x 36-inch wood pieces .
36. Remove cradle to body mounting bolts and lower cradle. Ensure two large rear cradle spacers are attached.
37. Support transaxle using suitable jack.
38. Remove remaining transaxle to engine bolts and install guide bolt to bottom rear clutch housing bolt hole.
39. Separate lefthand axle from transaxle using suitable screwdriver or pry bar. **Do not allow tool to contact or damage axle seal.**
40. Separate transaxle from engine enough to clear intermediate shaft
41. Lower and remove transaxle.
42. Reverse procedure to install.

2.2L ENGINE

1. Raise and support vehicle, then remove battery.
2. Disconnect battery feed and coolant hose from underhood fuse block.
3. Release tabs and remove underhood fuse block cover.
4. Release tabs on underhood fuse block and roll fuse block back to access electrical connectors.
5. Disconnect connector and lift fuse block off case.
6. Remove harnesses from underhood fuse block case, then the fasteners and case from battery tray.
7. Remove battery tray.
8. Loosen control rod to lever pinch bolt. **Control shaft lever retaining pin has spring loaded locking feature securing pin in place.**
9. Remove control shaft lever to shaft retaining pin.

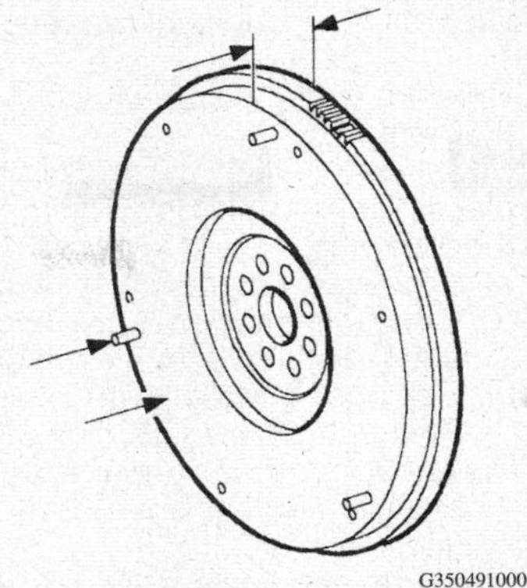

Fig. 3 Flywheel thickness measurement

10. Remove control shaft lever to transaxle and frame bracket retaining clips.
11. Remove control shaft lever by pulling straight up off pivot pins.
12. Disconnect back-up lamp electrical connector and remove wire harness from transaxle.
13. Remove transaxle top hole pin or plug. Discard pin or keep plug.
14. Remove clutch hydraulic fitting from transaxle, then elevate and secure fitting.
15. Remove upper transaxle to engine mounting bolts and install engine support fixture.
16. Mark position and remove lefthand transaxle mount bolts.
17. Remove rear transaxle mount through bolt and transaxle to frame mounting bolt.
18. Secure radiator to upper support using suitable tie straps.
19. Raise and support vehicle.
20. Remove lefthand front wheel and righthand front lower splash shield.
21. Remove lefthand front wheel liner push pin from frame.
22. Disconnect rear oxygen sensor electrical connector and remove harness from frame.
23. Remove front transaxle mount through bolt, remaining rear transaxle mount to frame bolts.
24. Remove clip and air conditioning line from front of frame.
25. Remove mounting bolts and secure steering gear to body.
26. Remove stabilizer bar links from struts.
27. Remove lower ball stud bolt and separate ball stud from steering knuckle.
28. Remove suspension support and cage nuts from body. Discard cage nuts and support bolts.
29. Support frame using powertrain lifting table tool No. J-43628, or equivalent.
30. Remove remaining frame to body mounting bolts.
31. Lower frame. Discard cage nuts and frame bolts.
32. Remove front and rear transaxle mount.
33. **Do not allow CV joint boots to contact other parts during removal. Never pull on shaft assembly.**
34. When removing righthand axle shaft, transaxle stub shaft may come out of transaxle with axle shaft. If this occurs, inspect transaxle axle shaft seal damage. Replace as required.
35. Remove axle shafts from transaxle using suitable pry bar. Leave axle shaft in steering knuckle and secure out of transaxle removal path.
36. Remove retaining clip and drop air conditioning line down from body.
37. Drain transaxle fluid into suitable container and lower vehicle.
38. Lower lefthand side of powertrain with engine support fixture to allow transaxle to clear engine compartment rail.
39. Remove lefthand transaxle mount bracket from transaxle. Raise and support vehicle.
40. Remove control shaft lever pivot pin bracket from transaxle case.
41. Support transaxle using suitable jack and remove remaining engine to transaxle mounting bolts.
42. Separate from engine, then lower and remove transaxle.
43. Reverse procedure to install. Replace spring loaded locking pin with shift lever hole plug.

TECHNICAL SERVICE BULLETINS

ENGINE DOES NOT CRANK

1998 MODELS

On some of these models equipped with manual transmissions the engine will not crank. Additional conditions may include: MIL and ABS lamps are on, park lamps do not operate, fuel gauge is inoperative, and/or radio speakers may be inoperative.

This condition may be caused by the instrument panel wiring harness contacting the clutch pedal pivot bolt/clip.

To correct this condition, proceed as follows:

1. Disarm air bag system as outlined in "Passive Restraint Systems" chapter.
2. Remove connectors and Powertrain Control Module (PCM).
3. Cut wire harness tie strap rose bud clip directly above clutch pedal.
4. Loosen harness clamp approximately three inches from clip.
5. Remove harness tap from starter relay to branch to goes to instrument panel junction box.
6. Separate harness to expose damaged wire and repair as required.
7. Install four inches of suitable conduit to harness and position over clutch pedal pivot clip.

KNOCKING OR RATTLE NOISE FROM FRONT OF VEHICLE DURING DECELERATION

1998

On some of these models built before VIN WZ305220 and equipped manual transaxles, there may be a knocking or rattle noise coming from front of vehicle during deceleration at 4000 RPM and less.

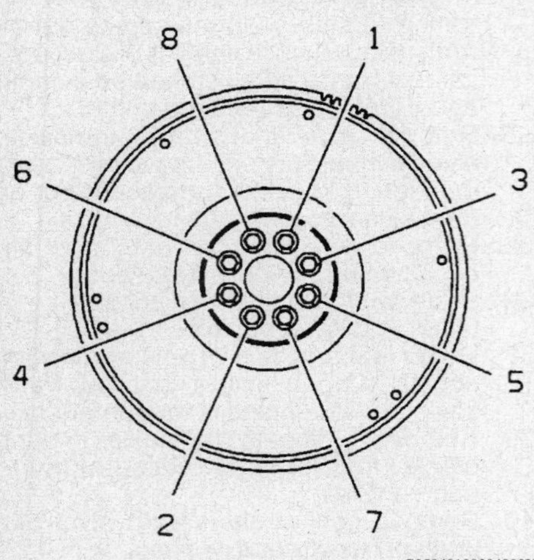

Fig. 4 Flywheel tightening sequence

This condition may be caused by insufficient dampening of engine pulsations by the clutch dampening springs.

To correct this condition, proceed as follows:

1. Remove clutch cover, clutch disc and flywheel.
2. Measure flywheel thickness in three places around circumference, noting the following
   a. All measurements must be made at same distance in from edge and equal distances from each other.
   b. Replace flywheel with chamfered flywheel (part No. 21120535) if flywheel has been resurfaced previously or is less than 1.11 inches thick.
3. Measure and mark flywheel 2.4–2.5 inches starting from outside edge of flat portion of flywheel moving towards inside edge of flywheel.
4. Remove .12–.16 inch from inside edge of flywheel to measured mark with cutting tip at 30° angle to flywheel.
5. Install machined or new flywheel.
6. **Torque** mounting bolts to 59 ft. lbs. in criss-cross pattern.
7. Install new clutch disc with long travel damper (part No. 21120564).
8. Install new clutch cover (part No. 21120582).
9. **Do not tighten cover bolts more than half turn at a time.**

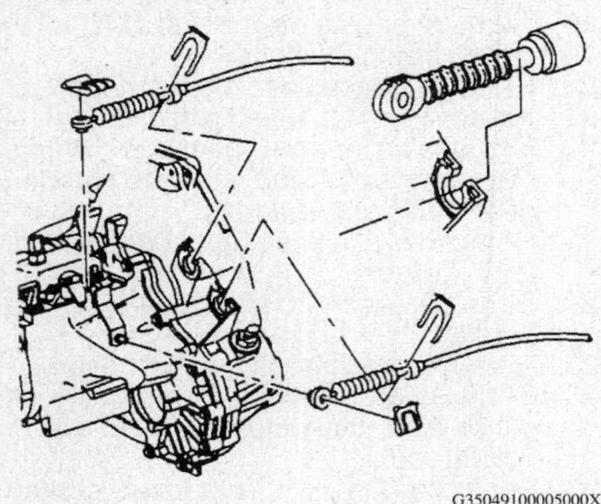

Fig. 5 Shift cable replacement

TIGHTENING SPECIFICATIONS

Year	Component	Torque/Ft. Lbs.
1.9L ENGINE		
1998–2002	Air Box	96①
	Clutch Fork Stabilizer	18
	Clutch Housing Dust Cover	84①
	Clutch Housing To Engine Bolt (Bottom)	103
	Clutch Housing To Engine Stud (Top)	74
	Clutch Hydraulic Damper, Nut	18
	Cradle Bracket To Cradle	52
	Cradle To Body	155
	Down Pipe To Converter	18
	Down Pipe To Exhaust Manifold	23
	Down Pipe To Stiffening Bracket	23
	Engine Strut To Cradle	37
	Flywheel	59
	Ground Terminals To Clutch Housing Studs	18
	Ignition Module	60①
	Intake Support Bracket	22
	Intermediate Shaft Support Bracket	40
	Lower Ball Joint	55
	Lower Transaxle Mount	52
	Pressure Plate	18
	Steering Gear To Cradle	37
	Strut Cradle Bracket To Cradle	52
	Transaxle Bracket To Transaxle	40
	Transaxle Drain Plug	22②
	Transaxle Mount To Case	24
	Transaxle Mount To Cradle	37
	Transaxle Stiffening Bracket	40
	Transaxle Strut To Cradle	52
	Transaxle Strut To Midrail Bracket	37
	Transaxle Strut To Transaxle Bracket	52
	Wheel Lug Nuts	103
2.2L ENGINE		
2000–02	Ball Stud To Steering Knuckle	75
	Back-Up Lamp Switch To Transaxle	18
	Battery Cable Terminals	13
	Battery Hold Down Brackets	15
	Battery Tray	11
	Clutch Master Cylinder	15
	Clutch Pedal To Front Of Dash	15
	Clutch Pedal To Instrument Panel Beam	15
	Clutch Slave Cylinder	96①
	Exhaust Manifold Pipe To Exhaust Manifold	22
	Exhaust Manifold Pipe To Exhaust Pipe	15
	Flywheel To Crankshaft	39③
	Frame To Body	60④
	Pressure Plate To Flywheel	11
	Rear Cover To Transaxle	18

Continued

TIGHTENING SPECIFICATIONS—Continued

Year	Component	Torque/Ft. Lbs.
2.2L ENGINE		
2000–02	Shift Linkage To Transaxle	18
	Stabilizer Bar Link To Strut	50
	Steering Gear To Frame	35⑤
	Tie Rod End To Steering Knuckle	45
	Transaxle Case To Clutch Housing	18
	Transaxle Drain Plug	37
	Transaxle Front Mount Through Bolt	41
	Transaxle Mounts To Transaxle	41
	Transaxle Rear Mount Through Bolt	66
	Transaxle Rear Mount To Frame	44
	Transaxle To Engine	48
	Underhood Fuse Block Case	84①
	Wheel Lug Nut	92

① — Inch lbs.
② — Drain plug seal replacement is not required.
③ — Tighten an additional 25°.
④ — Tighten an additional 45–60°.
⑤ — Tighten an additional 105°.

Rear Axle & Suspension

NOTE: On Air Bag Equipped Models, Refer To "Air Bag System Precautions" Located In The Front Of This Manual For System Disarming & Arming Procedures.

NOTE: Refer To "Computer Relearn Procedures" Located In The Front Of This Manual When Battery Power To The Computer Has Been Interrupted.

NOTE: Prior To Performing Any Service Operations Listed In This Section, Consult The "Technical Service Bulletins" Section For Related Information.

INDEX

PRECAUTIONS

AIR BAG SYSTEMS

Refer to "Air Bag System Precautions" in the front of this manual for system disarming and arming procedures.

BATTERY GROUND CABLE

Prior to service, disconnect battery ground cable and isolate as required.

HUB & BEARING

REPLACE

DISC BRAKES

1. Raise and support vehicle, then remove wheel assembly.
2. Disconnect ABS wheel speed sensor electrical connector.
3. Remove mounting bolts and hang caliper with wire.
4. Remove brake rotor, mounting bolts and hub.
5. Reverse procedure to install.

DRUM BRAKES

1. Raise and support vehicle, then remove wheel assembly.
2. **On models equipped with ABS,** disconnect wheel speed sensor harness.
3. **On all models,** remove brake drum and hub to knuckle mounting bolts.
4. Remove hub.
5. Reverse procedure to install.

STRUT

REPLACE

L-SERIES

1. Raise and support vehicle, then remove wheel assembly.
2. Remove inner wheel liner and shock to knuckle bolt. Discard bolt.
3. Remove upper carrier to body bolts.
4. Loosen lower carrier to body bolts until carrier slides out.
5. Reverse procedure to install.

S-SERIES

This procedure has been revised by a Technical Service Bulletin.

1. Remove rear window trim finish panel.
2. Raise and support vehicle, then remove wheel assembly.
3. Loosen but do not remove knuckle to strut mounting nuts.
4. Support knuckle using suitable floor jack and remove upper strut mounting nuts.
5. Disconnect ABS electrical harness from strut.
6. Remove strut to knuckle nuts and strut.
7. Reverse procedure to install. **On 1998–99 models built before VIN XZ136281,** replace dust boot assembly.

STRUT SERVICE

1. Position strut in strut spring compressor tool No. SA-9155-S, or equivalent, mounted in suitable holding device.
2. Fasten strut to tool using one strut to knuckle bolt and nut in lower strut mounting hole.
3. Compress spring until upper spring supports are completely unladen.
4. Remove strut shaft nut while holding strut shaft in position using suitable Torx wrench.
5. Release spring compressor and tilt strut outward, then remove upper spring support and spring.
6. Remove dust shield and strut from compressor tool.
7. Inspect rubber spring support and dust shield for cracks or deterioration. Replace as required.
8. Inspect spring for signs of damage.
9. Extend and retract strut shaft. Replace strut if movement is not smooth or resistance is not even.
10. Reverse procedure to assemble, noting the following:
    a. Compress spring only enough to install upper washer and shaft nut. **Do not compress spring beyond this point.**
    b. Ensure spring is properly seated in spring supports.

KNUCKLE

REPLACE

DISC BRAKES

1. Raise and support vehicle, then remove wheel assembly.
2. Disconnect ABS wheel speed sensor electrical connector.
3. Remove caliper to knuckle mounting bolts.
4. Suspend caliper with mechanics' wire and remove rotor.
5. Remove mounting bolts, hub and backing plate.
6. Loosen but do not remove lateral link to knuckle mounting bolts.
7. Loosen but do not remove strut to knuckle mounting bolts.
8. Remove trailing arm to knuckle mounting nut and arm to body mounting bolts.

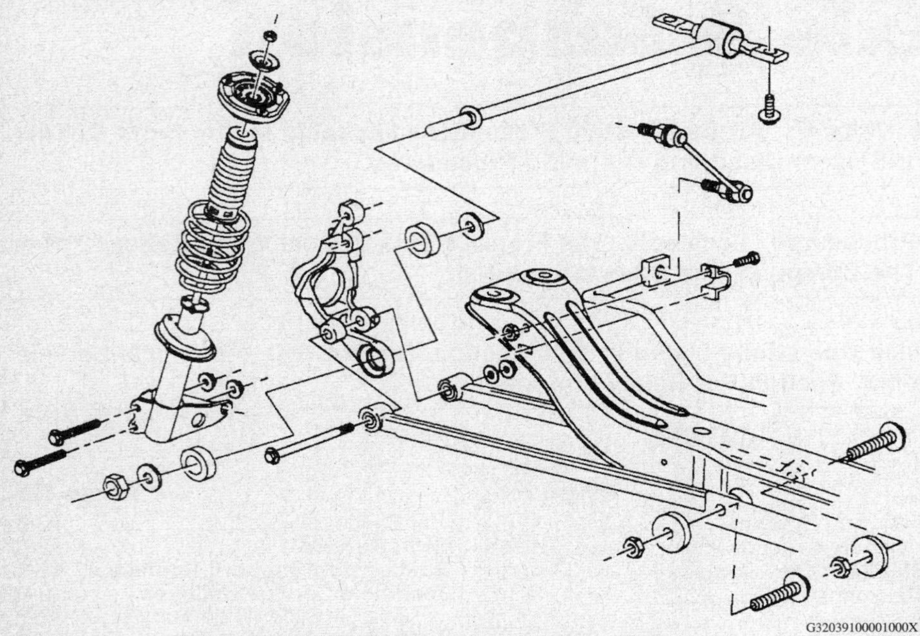

Fig. 1 Exploded view of rear suspension

9. Remove lateral link to knuckle mounting nuts, knuckle to strut bolts and knuckle.
10. Reverse procedure to install.

DRUM BRAKES

1. Raise and support vehicle.
2. Remove wheel assembly and brake drum.
3. Remove mounting bolts and hub.
4. Position brake aside using suitable wire.
5. Loosen but do not remove lateral link and strut to knuckle mounting bolts.
6. Remove trailing arm to knuckle mounting nut and arm to body mounting bolts, then slide arm from knuckle.
7. Remove mounting bolts and link.
8. Reverse procedure to install.

TRAILING ARM

REPLACE

1. Raise and support vehicle, then remove wheel assemblies.
2. Remove trailing arm to knuckle mounting nut, **Fig. 1.**
3. Remove trailing arm to body mounting bolts and slide arm from knuckle.
4. Reverse procedure to install.

SUSPENSION SUPPORT

REPLACE

1. Raise and support vehicle, then remove wheel assemblies.
2. Remove rear exhaust system from resonator back, then heat shield from rear suspension support.
3. Remove upper and lower control arm to rear axle control arm mounting bolts and nuts.
4. Remove both stabilizer bar links from rear axle control arms.
5. Support rear suspension using suitable jack stand.
6. Remove four rear suspension support to body bolts. Discard bolts.
7. Remove rear suspension support.
8. Reverse procedure to install.

STABILIZER BAR

REPLACE

L-SERIES

1. Raise and support vehicle, then remove wheel assemblies.
2. Remove heat shield from rear suspension.
3. Remove left and righthand rear stabilizer bar links to rear axle control arm bolts.
4. Remove mounting bolts and stabilizer bar.
5. Reverse procedure to install.

S-SERIES

1. Raise and support vehicle, then remove wheel assembly.
2. Position suitable drain container at lefthand rear brake line, then disconnect and plug lefthand brake line.
3. Remove left and righthand stabilizer bar link to knuckle mounting nuts, then bar to crossmember nuts.
4. Loosen but do not remove lateral link to knuckle mounting bolts.
5. Remove trailing arm to knuckle and arm to body mounting nuts.
6. Slide trailing arm from knuckle.
7. Remove mounting bolt and swing lateral link downward.

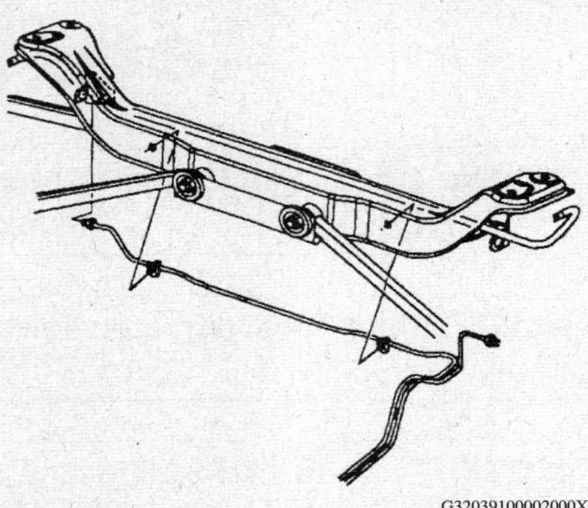

Fig. 2 Brake line replacement

8. Disconnect brake lines from crossmember, **Fig. 2.**
9. Remove stabilizer bar.
10. Reverse procedure to install.

LATERAL LINK

REPLACE

1. Remove fuel tank as described under "Fuel Pump, Replace."
2. Raise and support vehicle, then remove wheel assembly.
3. Remove lateral link to knuckle and lateral link to crossmember mounting bolts, **Fig. 1.**
4. Remove rear lateral link.
5. Remove rear brake line mounting nut.
6. Support crossmember using suitable jackstand.
7. Remove crossmember to body mounting bolts.
8. Lower crossmember and remove inboard lateral link to crossmember mounting bolt.
9. Remove mounting bolt and front lateral link.
10. Reverse procedure to install, noting the following:
    a. Do not tighten lateral link mounting bolts until crossmember is aligned and tightened.
    b. Ensure wheel alignment is within specification.

TECHNICAL SERVICE BULLETINS

RATTLE OR CLICK WHEN TURNING

1999 MODELS

On some of these models there may be a rattle or click noise from vehicle rear when turn at slow speeds and/or when driving over uneven surface.

This condition may be caused by the rear stabilizer shaft link having excessive ball-type joint lash.

To correct this condition, install new rear stabilizer link and **torque** new mounting nuts to 30 ft. lbs.

TIGHTENING SPECIFICATIONS

Year	Component	Torque/Ft. Lbs.
L-SERIES		
2000–02	Heat Shield To Rear Suspension Support	72①
	Rear Axle Control Bracket	65②
	Rear Brake Drum To Hub	35①
	Rear Brake Hose Bracket To Control Arm	72①
	Rear Caliper To Back Plate	59
	Rear Hub To Knuckle	35③
	Stabilizer Bar Clamp	41
	Stabilizer To Control Arm	41
	Strut Carrier To Body	41
	Strut To Knuckle	110③
	Suspension Control Arm To Knuckle	66④
	Suspension Control Arm To Suspension Support	90④
	Suspension Support To Body	66⑤
S-SERIES		
1998–2002	ABS Electrical Harness	53①
	Brake Line	14
	Crossmember To Body	89
	Front Lateral Link To Crossmember	89
	Front Lateral Link To Knuckle	122
	Hub To Knuckle	63
	Lateral Link To Knuckle	122
	Rear Caliper To Knuckle	63
	Rear Lateral Link To Crossmember	89
	Stabilizer Bar Link To Bracket	30
	Stabilizer Bar To Crossmember	41
	Strut Shaft Nut	37
	Strut To Knuckle	126
	Strut Upper Support Nuts	21
	Trailing Arm To Body	89
	Trailing Arm To Knuckle	74
	Wheel Lug Nut	103

① — Inch lbs.

② — Tighten an additional 60°.

③ — Tighten an additional 30°.

④ — Tighten an additional 60–75°.

⑤ — Tighten an additional 90–115°.

Front Suspension & Steering

NOTE: On Air Bag Equipped Models, Refer To "Air Bag System Precautions" Located In The Front Of This Manual For System Disarming & Arming Procedures.

NOTE: Refer To "Computer Relearn Procedures" Located In The Front Of This Manual When Battery Power To The Computer Has Been Interrupted.

NOTE: Prior To Performing Any Service Operations Listed In This Section, Consult The "Technical Service Bulletins" Section For Related Information.

INDEX

PRECAUTIONS

AIR BAG SYSTEMS

Refer to "Air Bag System Precautions" in the front of this manual for system disarming and arming procedures.

BATTERY GROUND CABLE

Prior to service, disconnect battery ground cable and isolate as required.

WHEEL HUB & STEERING KNUCKLE

REPLACE

1. Depress brake pedal and loosen axle to hub nut.
2. Raise and support vehicle, then remove wheel assembly.
3. Remove caliper to knuckle mounting bolts. Suspend caliper with mechanics wire.
4. Loosen but do not remove knuckle to strut mounting bolts.
5. If rotor is difficult to remove, use two M8 X 1.25 self tapping bolts, **Fig. 1.**
6. Remove axle nut and washer, then discard lower control arm ball stud cotter pin.
7. Loosen castle nut until level with top of ball stud.
8. Remove and discard tie rod cotter pin.
9. Remove tie rod and castle nut.
10. Separate lower control arm from knuckle using lower control arm ball stud separator tool No. SA-9132-S, or equivalent. **Do not use wedge type tool to separate.**
11. Remove lower ball joint castle nut, **Fig. 2.**
12. Separate tie rod end from steering knuckle using tie rod separator tool No. SA-91100-C, or equivalent.
13. **On models equipped with Anti-Lock Brake System (ABS),** disconnect wheel speed sensor electrical connector.
14. **On all models,** support or suspend drive axle.
15. Remove strut to knuckle mounting bolts, then knuckle and hub. If it is difficult to separate axle from hub, tap end of drive axle shaft using suitable wood block wood and hammer. **Do not hammer end of axle.**
16. Reverse procedure to install.

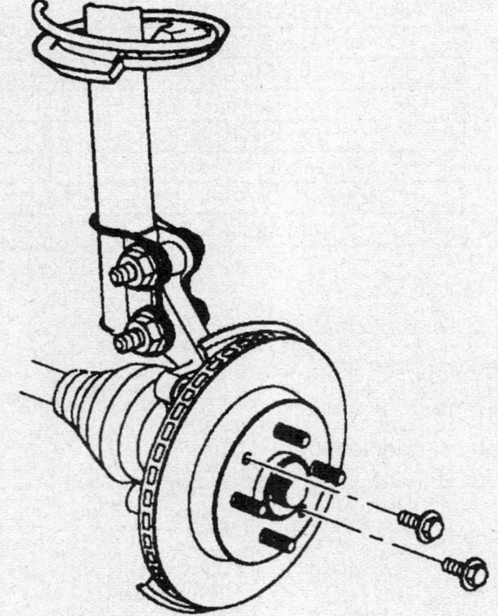

Fig. 1 Brake rotor replacement

HUB & BEARING SERVICE

1. Remove steering knuckle as described under "Wheel Hub & Steering Knuckle, Replace."
2. Remove splash shields and ABS wheel speed sensor.
3. Install wheel bearing/hub removal tool No. SA-9159-S, or equivalent, **Fig. 3.**
4. Place assembly in suitable soft jawed vise.
5. Hold hub drive using suitable wrench. Tighten driver screw to remove hub.
6. Remove inner bearing race using inner race puller, **Fig. 4.**
7. Remove steering knuckle from vise, then the retainer and bridge.
8. Remove bridge snap ring using suitable snap ring pliers.
9. Press out bearing using knuckle support tube and small driver, **Fig. 5.**
10. Reverse procedure to assemble.

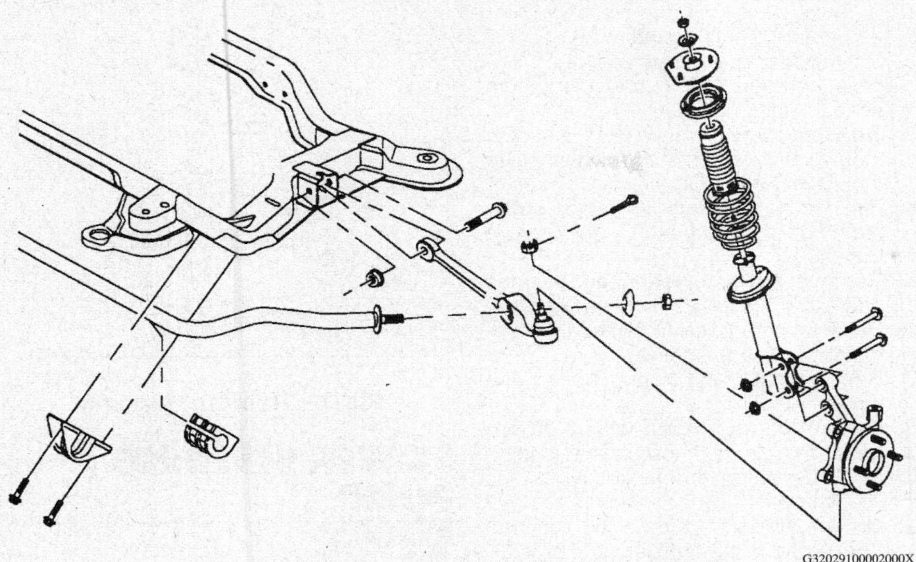

Fig. 2 Exploded view of front suspension

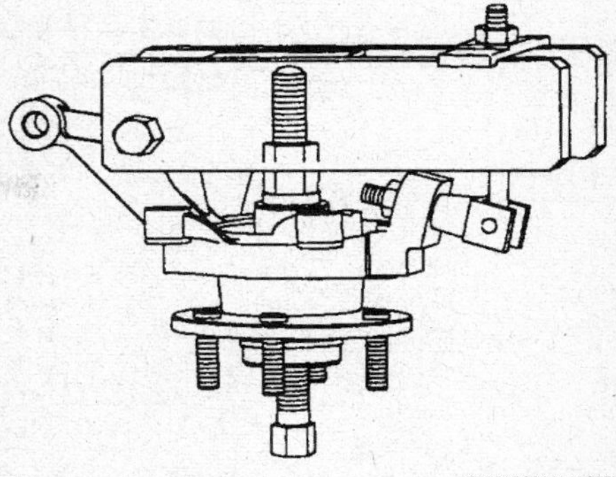

Fig. 3 Wheel bearing/hub removal

BALL JOINT INSPECTION

1. Raise and support front of vehicle.
2. Grasp tire at top and bottom, then move bottom of tire in and out.
3. While moving bottom of tire in and out, observe ball joint for any side to side movement.
4. If any side to side movement is noticed, replace lower control arm.

BALL JOINT

REPLACE

LOWER

The ball joint and the lower control arm are serviced as an assembly. Refer to "Control Arm, Replace" for replacement procedure.

COIL SPRING

REPLACE

Refer to "Strut Service" for coil spring replacement procedure.

STRUT

REPLACE

REMOVAL

1. Raise and support vehicle, then remove wheel assembly.
2. **On models equipped with ABS,** disconnect wheel speed sensor electrical connector bracket.
3. **On all models,** loosen but do not remove steering knuckle to strut housing mounting bolts.
4. Support lower control arm using suitable floor jack.
5. Remove and discard upper strut mounting nuts.
6. Slowly raise vehicle and lower strut.
7. Remove knuckle to housing mounting bolts, **Fig. 2.** Place cloth over CV joint seal.
8. Remove strut.

INSTALLATION

This procedure has been revised by a Technical Service Bulletin.

1. **On 1998–99 models built before VIN XZ136281,** replace dust boot assembly.
2. **On all models,** install new upper strut mounting nuts.
3. Install strut to steering knuckle mounting bolts. **Install new nuts.**
4. **On models equipped with ABS,** install sensor electrical connector bracket.

STRUT SERVICE

DISASSEMBLE

1. Compress spring to unload upper strut mount using spring compressor tool No. SA-9155-C, or equivalent, and suitable holding fixture.
2. While holding strut shaft, remove strut shaft nut.
3. Release spring compressor and tilt strut outward.
4. Remove upper strut assembly, inspect for damage. Replace as required.
5. Remove strut spring and dust shield; inspect for damage and replace as required.
6. Remove strut from holding fixture.

ASSEMBLE

1. Place strut in compressor tool and attach with strut to knuckle bolt through lower mounting hole.
2. Extend strut shaft to travel limit.
3. Install dust shield, spring isolator and mount, ensure spring is properly seated in seat and isolator.
4. Compress spring and install strut shaft mounting nut.

CONTROL ARM

REPLACE

LOWER

1. Raise and support vehicle, then remove wheel assembly.
2. Remove and discard lower control arm ball stud cotter pin.
3. Loosen lower control ball stud castle nut until level with top of ball stud.
4. Separate lower control arm from knuckle using lower control arm ball stud separator tool No. SA-9132-S, or equivalent. **Do not use wedge type tool to separator.**
5. Remove lower control arm ball stud castle nut.
6. Remove inner front fender splash shield.
7. Remove lower control arm to cradle mounting nut and bolt, **Fig. 2.**
8. Remove lower control arm to tension strut mounting nut, then arm.
9. Reverse procedure to install.

TENSION STRUT

REPLACE

1. Raise and support vehicle, then remove wheel assembly.
2. Remove and discard lower control arm ball stud cotter pin.
3. Loosen but do not remove lefthand lower control arm ball stud castle nut.
4. For lefthand side of vehicle, proceed as follows:
   a. Separate lower control arm from steering knuckle using lower control arm ball stud separator tool No. SA-9132-S, or equivalent. **Do not use wedge type tool.**
   b. Remove lower control arm ball joint castle nut.
   c. Remove lefthand front inner fender splash shield.
   d. Remove lower control arm to cradle mounting nut and bolt.
5. For righthand side of vehicle, turn wheel left for access, then remove tension strut to lower control arm mounting nut and washer.
6. For both sides, remove tension strut to cradle bracket mounting bolts.
7. Remove tension strut and lefthand control arm.

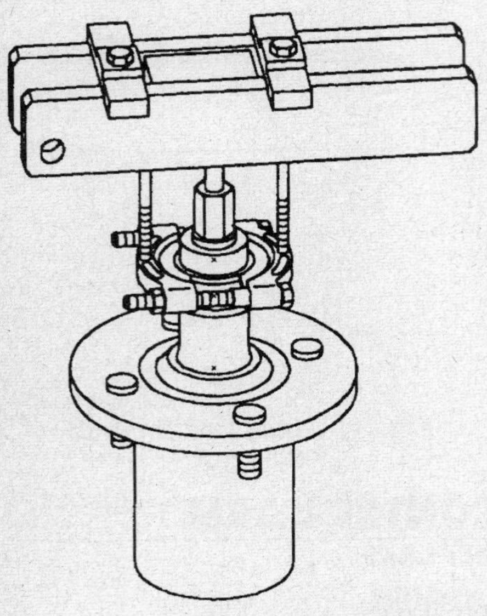

G32049100003000X

Fig. 4 Inner bearing race removal

8. Remove control arm to tension strut mounting nut and washer, then separate.
9. Reverse procedure to install.

TIE ROD

REPLACE

INNER

This procedure has been revised by a Technical Service Bulletin.

1. Raise and support vehicle, then remove wheel assemblies.
2. Remove outer tie road-to-inner tie rod lock nut.
3. Remove steering gear.
4. Unthread outer tie rod from inner tie rod.
5. Remove outer tie rod lock nut.
6. Remove steering gear boot.
7. Remove shock damper from inner tie rod by sliding toward steering gear.
8. Remove inner tie rod, noting the following:
    a. **Hold steering gear rack using suitable wrench on rack teeth.**
    b. **Protect teeth with suitable shop cloth.**
    c. When removing righthand inner tie rod it may be necessary to remove lefthand side boot to access teeth.
9. Reverse procedure to install, noting the following:
    a. Apply Loctite No. 262, or equivalent, evenly to inner tie rod threads.
    b. Install inner tie rod using tool No. SA-9209-C, or equivalent.

POWER STEERING GEAR

REPLACE

L-SERIES

Rotating steering wheel while it is disconnected from the steering gear may damage SIR coil.

1. Remove pinch bolt and disconnect intermediate shaft from steering gear.
2. **On models equipped with 3.0L engine,** remove rear exhaust manifold heat shield.
3. **On all models,** remove rear transaxle mount through bolt and transaxle mount to frame bolt.
4. Place suitable drain container under steering gear pressure and return hoses.
5. Remove power steering gear hoses and allow fluid to drain.
6. Raise and support vehicle, then remove wheel assemblies.
7. Remove righthand front lower splash shield.
8. **On models equipped with 3.0L engine,** remove exhaust manifold pipe and remaining transaxle mount to frame bolts.
9. **On all models,** remove tie rod end torque prevailing nuts, discard nuts.
10. Separate tie rod end from steering knuckle using tie rod end separator tool No. SA-91100-C, or equivalent.
11. Remove steering gear to frame mounting bolts and steering gear heat shield.
12. Remove stabilizer bar links from strut and front suspension supports.
13. Loosen remaining mounting bolts until there is enough clearance to remove gear through lefthand side wheel opening.
14. Remove steering gear.
15. Reverse procedure to install.

S-SERIES

1. Raise and support vehicle.
2. Remove and discard tie rod end cotter pins.
3. Remove tie rod end to knuckle castle nuts.
4. Remove tie rod end from steering knuckle using tie rod separator tool No. SA-91100-C, or equivalent. **Do not separate joint using wedge-type tool.**
5. Remove lefthand inner fender splash shield.
6. Loosen intermediate shaft cover from steering gear.
7. Raise slightly and remove pinch bolt.
8. Disconnect power steering pressure switch, then place suitable drain container under pressure and return hoses.
9. Disconnect pressure and return hoses and allow system to drain.
10. Remove mounting bolts and steering gear through lefthand fenderwell.
11. Reverse procedure to install, noting the following:
    a. Install new steering gear mounting nuts.
    b. Apply Loctite 242, or equivalent, to pinch bolt.

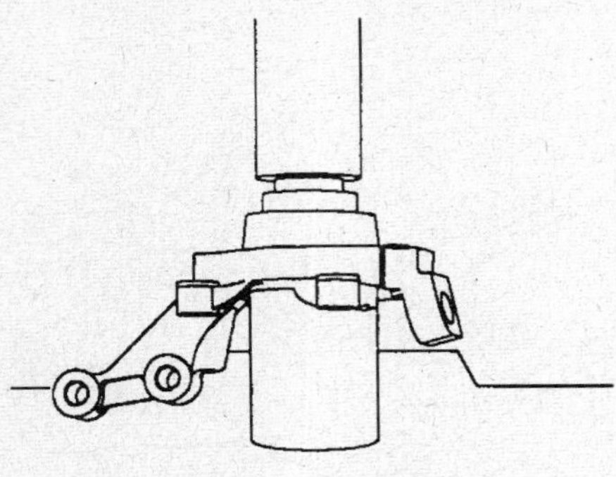

G32049100004000X

Fig. 5 Bearing removal

POWER STEERING PUMP

REPLACE

L-SERIES

2.2L ENGINE

1. Remove power steering pump reservoir fill cap.
2. Place suitable container under power steering hoses at steering gear.
3. Remove steering gear power hoses and allow to drain. **Do not rotate steering wheel.**
4. Remove pressure and return hoses at power steering pump, then pump to cylinder head bolts.
5. Remove pump.
6. Reverse procedure to install.

3.0L ENGINE

1. Remove air cleaner and power steering pulley bolts.
2. Remove accessory drive belt and power steering pump pulley.
3. Place suitable container under power steering pump.
4. Remove power steering pump pressure and return hoses, allow to drain.
5. Remove bracket mounting bolts and power steering pump.
6. Reverse procedure to install.

S-SERIES

1. Remove power steering pump reservoir fill cap.
2. Raise and support vehicle.
3. Place drain container under steering gear hoses.
4. Remove steering gear hoses and allow system to drain. **Do not rotate steering wheel.**
5. Relieve spring tension from accessory drive belt using suitable box end wrench and remove belt, **Fig. 6.**
6. **On models equipped with DOHC engine,** remove pump to intake manifold and pump to engine block brackets.
7. **On all models,** remove pump to engine block mounting bolts.

8. Raise pump and disconnect EVO electrical connector.
9. Remove pump and hose assembly, then the hoses.
10. Reverse procedure to install.

MANUAL STEERING GEAR

REPLACE

1. Raise and support vehicle, then remove front wheel assemblies.
2. Remove and discard tie rod end cotter pins.
3. Remove tie rod end from steering knuckle using tie rod separator tool No. SA-91100-C, or equivalent. **Do not separate joint using wedge type tool.**
4. Remove lefthand inner fender splash shield.
5. Loosen intermediate shaft cover from steering gear.
6. Raise slightly and remove pinch bolt.
7. Remove mounting bolts and steering gear cradle through lefthand fenderwell.
8. Reverse procedure to install, noting the following:
    a. Install new steering gear mounting nuts.
    b. Apply Loctite 242, or equivalent, to pinch bolt.

TECHNICAL SERVICE BULLETINS

STEERING WHEEL SHAKE OR VIBRATION

2000-01 S-SERIES

On some of these models built before VIN YY697119 there may be a steering wheel shake or vibration at highway speeds.

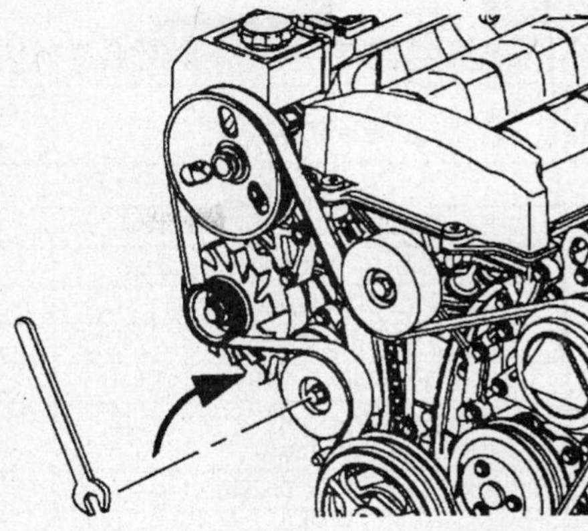

Fig. 6 Belt spring tension release. S-Series

This condition may be caused by vehicle sensitivity to out-of-balance tire and wheel assemblies.

To correct this condition, ensure tire and wheel assemblies are balanced within 0.1 ounce or less, and replace front lower control arm rear bushings as follows:

1. Remove righthand frame lower splash shield.
2. Remove ball stud bolt and nut.
3. Separate ball stud from steering knuckle using suitable pry bar. **Do not damage ABS speed sensor ring.**
4. Remove mounting bolts and lower control arm. Discard bolts.
5. Press out rear control arm bushings using bushing removal tools Nos. KM-907-21, KM-907-22 and KM-671, or equivalents.
6. Install new, updated bushings (part No. 22671497) with notched cut-out areas aligned with front lower control arm weld flanges using bushing installer tools Nos. KM-907-23, KM-907-24 and KM-671, or equivalents.
7. Ensure bushing is fully pressed and seated in control arm.
8. Install control arm using new bolts (part No. 11096192). Hand tighten.
9. Install ball stud to steering knuckle using new bolt (part No. 90496191) and nut (part No. 90538057). **Torque** to 75 ft. lbs.
10. Place suitable under hoist support stand under ball joint area.
11. Load control arm until there is gap between hoist contact pad and vehicle frame.
12. **Torque** front lower control arm bolts to 65 ft. lbs., then tighten an additional 75°.
13. Remove under hoist support stand and install lower splash shield.
14. Vehicle front end wheel alignment is not required.

CREAK, SQUEAK OR POPE FROM FRONT END

1998 MODELS

On some of these models there may be a creak, squeak or pop coming from the front of the vehicle when driving over rough road or when braking at slow speeds.

This condition may be caused by the front strut coil spring being incorrectly positioned.

To correct this condition, proceed as follows:

1. Raise and support vehicle.
2. Rotate lower end of coil spring until end is approximately 1/4 inch from seat ramp using suitable brass drift punch and hammer.

TIGHTENING SPECIFICATIONS

Year	Component	Torque/Ft. Lbs.
L-SERIES		
2000–02	ABS Sensor Bracket To Knuckle	72
	Caliper Bracket To Knuckle	70
	Control Arm To Frame	65
	Frame To Body	66
	Inner Tie Rod To Steering Gear	70
	Intermediate Shaft To Steering Column	20
	Intermediate Shaft To Steering Gear	20
	Power Steering High Pressure Line	20
	Power Steering Pump Pulley	15
	Power Steering Pump To Bracket	15
	Power Steering Pump To Engine	18
	Stabilizer Bar To Link	50
	Steering Wheel Nut	26
	Strut Shaft To Body	40
	Strut Shaft To Mount	40
	Wheel Lug Nut	92
S-SERIES		
1998–2002	ABS Electrical Connector Bracket	72
	Axle To Hub Nut	148
	Ball Joint Stud Castle Nut	55
	Brake Dust Shield	18
	Caliper Bracket To Knuckle	81
	Control Arm To Cradle, Bolt	92
	Control Arm To Cradle, Nut	74
	Control Arm To Tension Strut	106
	Hub To Driveshaft Nut	148
	Inner Tie Rod	70
	Intermediate Shaft To Steering Gear Pinch Bolt	35
	Power Steering Pressure & Return Line Fittings	20
	Power Steering Pump Bracket	28
	Pump To Engine Block	28
	Pump To Intake Manifold Bracket (DOHC)	22
	Steering Gear Cradle	37
	Strut Shaft Nut	37
	Strut To Body	21
	Strut To Steering Knuckle	126
	Tension Strut Bracket To Cradle	103
	Tie Rod End To Steering Knuckle	33
	Upper Strut Mount	21
	Wheel Lug Nuts	103

DOHC — Dual Over Head Cam.

Wheel Alignment

INDEX

PRELIMINARY INSPECTION

1. Road test vehicle.
2. Inspect tires for proper inflation, wear pattern or out of round condition.
3. Inspect suspension and steering components for wear and damage.
4. Inspect strut bushings for wear or damage.
5. Inspect vehicle ride height as described under "Vehicle Ride Height."
6. Wheel alignment should be performed in the following order:
   a. Rear camber.
   b. Rear toe.
   c. Righthand front camber and caster.
   d. Lefthand front camber and caster.
   e. Front toe.

FRONT WHEEL ALIGNMENT

Rear wheel alignment must be set to specifications before front alignment adjustment.

L-SERIES

CASTER

Front wheel caster is non adjustable on these vehicles. These angles can be measured but are set by design of the front suspension.

CAMBER

1. Raise and support vehicle, then remove wheel assemblies.
2. Remove strut to knuckle mounting bolts and discard.
3. Remove material from strut bracket lower hole using suitable file or grinder, **Fig. 1.**
4. To increase negative camber, remove from outside hole, to increase positive camber, remove from inside hole.
5. **Torque** strut to knuckle mounting bolts to 37 ft. lbs., then to 65 ft. lbs. and final tighten an additional 65°.
6. **Torque** wheel lug nuts to 92 ft. lbs. and lower vehicle.
7. Inspect camber angle. Adjust as required.

TOE-IN

This procedure has been revised by a Technical Service Bulletin.

1. Lock steering wheel in straight ahead position.
2. Loosen left and righthand outer tie rod jam nuts.

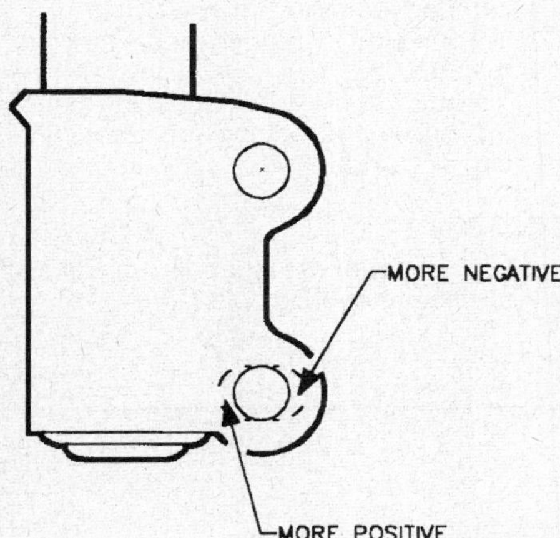

Fig. 1 Front & rear camber adjustment

3. Turn inner tie rod, by flats, to change toe.
4. Tighten outer tie rod end jam nuts, noting the following:
   a. **Torque** outer tie rod end jam nuts 44 ft. lbs.
   b. **On models equipped with torque prevailing nut, torque** new nut to 18 ft. lbs. preventing tie rod stud from turning using suitable wrench.
   c. **On models equipped with torque prevailing nut** final tighten nut an additional 134° preventing tie rod stud from turning using suitable wrench.
5. **Ensure seals do not become twisted.**
6. Inspect toe angle.

S-SERIES

CASTER

1. Lock steering wheel in straight ahead position.
2. Remove and discard upper strut mount mounting nuts.
3. Slide strut forward or rearward to adjust caster. Movement of approximately .157 inch will change caster by approximately ½°.
4. Body attachment holes may need to be filed or ground into oval slots to allow enough front to rear strut movement to adjust caster to specifications. **Do not exceed 0.354 inch in slot width.**
5. **Torque** new upper strut mount mounting nuts to 21 ft. lbs.
6. Inspect caster angle.

CAMBER

1. Lock steering wheel in straight ahead position.
2. Loosen strut to knuckle mounting bolts, then pull or push to adjust.
3. If more than 1.5° of camber is required, inspect for bent suspension components.
4. Raise and support vehicle, then remove wheel assembly.
5. Remove strut to knuckle mounting bolts and separate knuckle from strut bracket.
6. Remove material from strut bracket lower hole using suitable file or grinder, **Fig. 1.**
7. To increase negative camber, remove from outside hole, to increase positive camber, remove from inside hole.
8. **Torque** strut to knuckle mounting bolts to 126 ft. lbs.
9. **Torque** wheel lug nuts to 103 ft. lbs.
10. Inspect camber setting and lower vehicle.

TOE-IN

Refer to the "L-Series."

CRADLE

Inspect cradle to body alignment at two alignment holes using 5⁄16 inch rod, **Fig. 2.** If cradle to body alignment is not correct, loosen cradle mounting bolts and align cradle to body.

REAR WHEEL ALIGNMENT

L-SERIES

Rear wheel alignment involves setting the toe angle. Rear wheel camber is not adjustable.

TOE-IN

1. Remove rear axle control arm bolts and discard.
2. Install new bolts. **Do not tighten now.** Leave inside forward bolt out.
3. Move rear axle control arm in direction of required toe correction using rear toe adjusting tool No. KM-900, or equivalent.
4. Snug rear axle control arm bolts. **Do not tighten now.**
5. Inspect toe. Adjust as required.
6. **Torque** rear axle control arm bolts to 65 ft. lbs., then tighten an additional 30–45°.

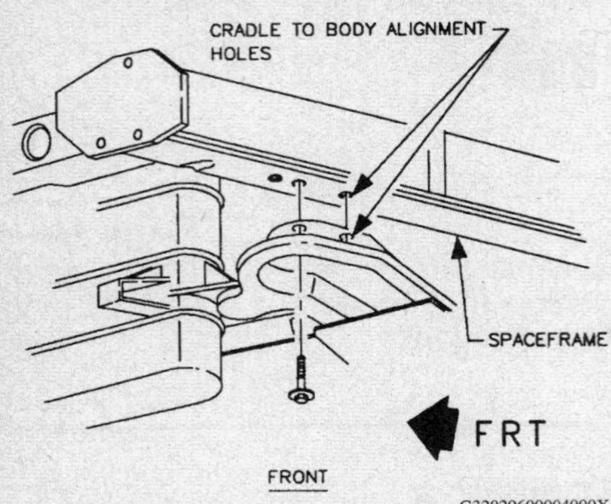

Fig. 2 Cradle alignment. S-Series

7. Repeat procedure for other rear wheel.

S-SERIES

CASTER

Rear wheel caster is not adjustable.

CAMBER

1. Loosen strut to knuckle mounting bolts, then pull or push to adjust.
2. If more than 1.5° of camber is desired, inspect for bent suspension components.
3. Raise and support vehicle, then remove wheel assembly.
4. Remove strut to knuckle mounting bolts and separate knuckle from strut bracket.
5. Remove material from strut bracket lower hole using suitable file or grinder, **Fig. 1.**
6. To increase negative camber, remove from outside hole, to increase positive camber, remove from inside hole.
7. **Torque** strut to knuckle mounting bolts to 126 ft. lbs.
8. **Torque** wheel lug nuts to 103 ft. lbs.
9. Inspect camber setting and lower vehicle.

TOE-IN

1. Loosen rearmost lateral link to crossmember mounting bolts.

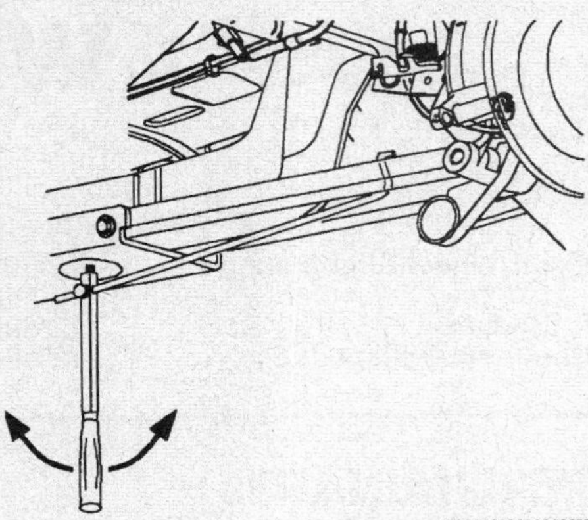

Fig. 3 Rear toe adjustment. S-Series

2. Move lateral link to adjust using rear toe adjusting tool No. SA-9158-C, or equivalent, **Fig. 3.**
3. **Torque** lateral link to 89 ft. lbs.
4. Inspect toe.
5. Repeat procedure for other wheel.

AIR CONDITIONING

TABLE OF CONTENTS

System Testing

NOTE: On Air Bag Equipped Models, Refer To "Air Bag System Precautions" Located In The Front Of This Manual For System Disarming & Arming Procedures.

NOTE: Refer To "Computer Relearn Procedures" Located In The Front Of This Manual When Battery Power To The Computer Has Been Interrupted.

INDEX

PRECAUTIONS

AIR BAG SYSTEMS

Refer to "Air Bag System Precautions" in the front of this manual for system disarming and arming procedures.

BATTERY GROUND CABLE

Prior to service, disconnect battery ground cable and isolate as required.

SYSTEM

R-134a refrigerant is a non toxic, nonflammable, clear and odorless liquefied gas.

R-134a refrigerant is not compatible with R-12 refrigerant. Even small amounts of R-12 in a R-134a system will cause lubricant contamination, compressor failure or improper A/C performance. Never add R-12 to a R-134a system.

Avoid breathing R-134a refrigerant and lubricant vapor or mist. Exposure may irritate eyes, nose and throat. Use only approved service equipment to discharge R-134a systems. Do not heat refrigerant containers with open flame, if container warming is required, place bottom of container in a pail of warm water. R-134a refrigerant will displace oxygen, work only in a well ventilated area to prevent suffocation.

Always wear goggles and wrap clean cloth around fittings, valves and connections when performing work that involves opening the refrigerant system. Keep work area well ventilated and do not steam clean or weld on or near any of the air conditioning lines or components. If liquid coolant does touch the eyes, bathe eyes quickly in cold water, then apply a bland disinfectant oil. See an eye doctor.

Before removing and replacing any of the air conditioning refrigeration lines or components, the refrigerant must be completely removed. The refrigerant system may be evacuated and charged using an air conditioning service charging station or a manifold and gauge set with a 30 lb. drum of R-134a. **Never charge the air conditioning system through the high pressure side of the system.**

For efficient operation of the air conditioning system, be careful not to contaminate the system with foreign materials, such as dirt, air or moisture. Contamination of the air conditioning system will change the chemical stability of the R-134a refrigerant, in turn changing the viscosity of the refrigerant oil. They will also effect pressure, temperature and create corrosion and abnormal wear of moving parts.

TROUBLESHOOTING

EXCEPT SATURN

Refer to **Figs. 1 through 4** for symptom troubleshooting charts.

SATURN

Most A/C system faults can be detected by a thorough inspection of the system and components.

1. Check air intake duct, lower air deflector, condenser to radiator seal and rear hood seal for missing or damaged parts.
2. Check outer surfaces of radiator and condenser cores to ensure air flow is not blocked by dirt, leaves or other matter.
3. Check for kinks in hoses and lines and refrigerant leaks using an electronic leak detector.
4. Check for a worn or loose compressor belt or faulty belt tensioner.
5. Check blower motor operation at all speeds.
6. With blower on High, check for equal distribution of air out of all outlets.
7. Check operation of control mode lever and distribution of air from designated outlets.
8. Press Recirc button with blower on

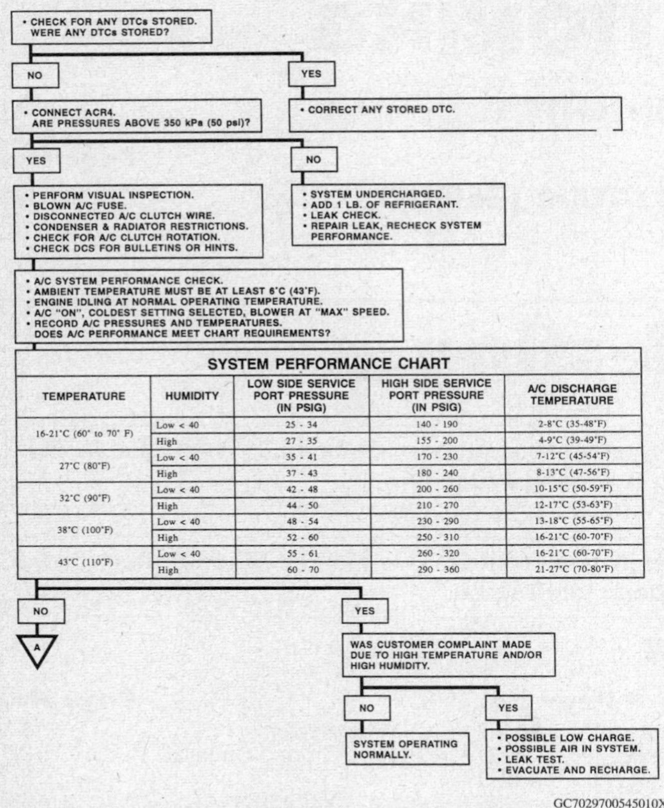

SYSTEM PERFORMANCE CHART

TEMPERATURE	HUMIDITY	LOW SIDE SERVICE PORT PRESSURE (IN PSIG)	HIGH SIDE SERVICE PORT PRESSURE (IN PSIG)	A/C DISCHARGE TEMPERATURE
16-21°C (60° to 70° F)	Low < 40	25 - 34	140 - 190	2-8°C (35-48°F)
	High	27 - 35	155 - 200	4-9°C (39-49°F)
27°C (80°F)	Low < 40	35 - 41	170 - 230	7-12°C (45-54°F)
	High	37 - 43	180 - 240	8-13°C (47-56°F)
32°C (90°F)	Low < 40	42 - 48	200 - 260	10-15°C (50-59°F)
	High	44 - 50	210 - 270	12-17°C (53-63°F)
38°C (100°F)	Low < 40	48 - 54	230 - 290	13-18°C (55-65°F)
	High	52 - 60	250 - 310	16-21°C (60-70°F)
43°C (110°F)	Low < 40	55 - 61	260 - 320	16-21°C (60-70°F)
	High	60 - 70	290 - 360	21-27°C (70-80°F)

Fig. 1 Insufficient A/C cooling troubleshooting (Part 1 of 2). Except Saturn

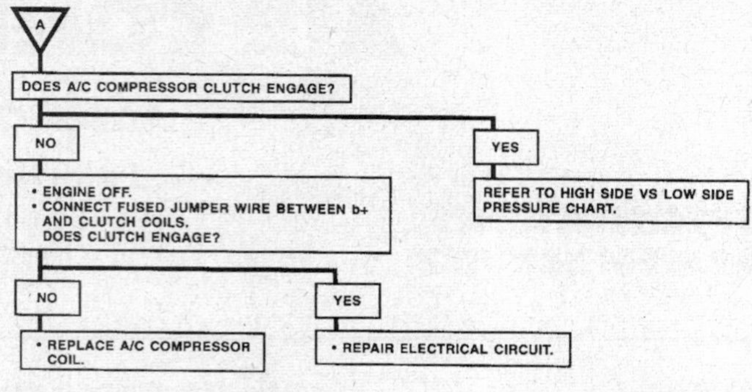

Fig. 1 Insufficient A/C cooling troubleshooting (Part 2 of 2). Except Saturn

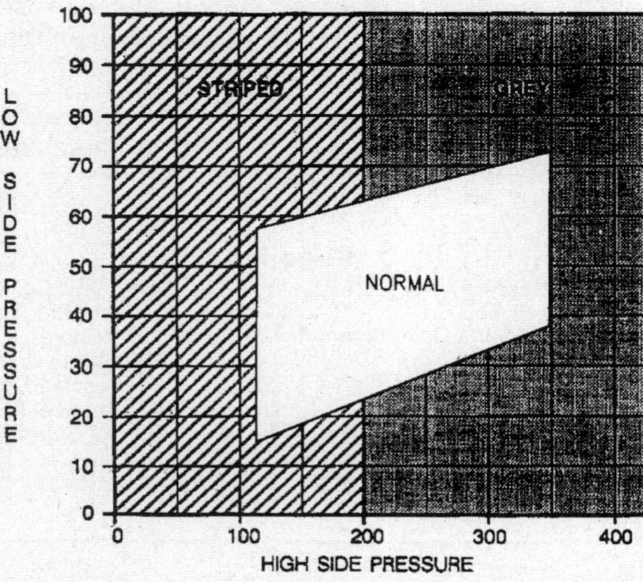

Fig. 2 High side vs. low side pressure chart. Except Saturn

high. A noticeable increase in air flow and sound should occur. Indicator should illuminate.

9. Start engine and run until normal operating temperature is reached.
10. Check operation of temperature control lever and air outlet temperature from hot to cold.
11. Depress A/C button. Indicator should illuminate.
12. Check compressor for clutch engagement, slippage or noise.
13. Check electric cooling fan operation with A/C on.
14. Turn A/C off. Compressor clutch should disengage.

PERFORMANCE TEST

EXCEPT SATURN

Remove leaves and debris from front of the condenser core, mounted at the front of the radiator. All obstructions must be removed, as they will reduce heat transfer and impair the efficiency of the system. Ensure space between the condenser and the radiator is free of foreign matter.

Ensure the evaporator drain is open. The evaporator cools and dehumidifies the air before it enters the passenger compartment. As the core cools the air, moisture condenses on it and is drained through the evaporator water drain tube.

The system should be operated for at least 15 minutes to allow sufficient time for all parts to become completely stabilized. Determine if the system is fully charged by the use of test gauges and sight glass if one is installed on system. Head pressure will read from 180–220 psi or higher, depending upon ambient temperature and the type of unit being tested. The sight glass should be free of bubbles. Low side pressures should read approximately 15–30 psi, depending on the ambient temperature and the unit being tested. The type of control and component installation used on a particular system will directly influence the pressure readings on the high and low sides, **Fig. 5.**

The high side pressure will be affected by the ambient or outside air temperature. Refer to **Fig. 6** for approximate high side pressure readings at various ambient temperatures.

Relative Temperature Of High & Low Sides

The high side of the system should be uniformly hot to the touch throughout. A difference in temperature will indicate a partial blockage of liquid or gas at this point.

The low side of the system should be uniformly cool to the touch with no excessive sweating of the suction line or low side service valve. Excessive sweating or frosting of the low side service valve usually indicates an expansion valve is allowing an excessive amount of refrigerant into the evaporator.

SATURN

Service Stall Test

Record the manifold gauge pressures and outlet temperature with the following preset vehicle conditions:

1. Install thermometer in right center outlet.
2. Open doors and windows to stabilize interior temperature with outside ambient air temperature.
3. Depress Recirc button.
4. Set temperature lever to full cold.
5. Select 3rd blower speed.
6. Depress A/C button.
7. With engine warm, run at 2000 RPM.
8. Continue running until system pressures and outlet temperature stabilize (3–5 minutes).
9. Record pressure and temperature.
10. Compare readings to normal system

Gray Area Diagnosis and Service	
Check the following if pressures intersect in the gray area:	
NOTE V5 clutch cycling can occur when discharge pressure exceeds 400 psi.	
1. Improper condenser operation. This can result from :	• Extremely high ambient humidity. • Insufficient air flow across condenser. • Damaged or dirty condenser fins. • Faulty fan relay.
2. High side refrigerant restriction.	• Feel liquid line before expansion tube (orifice). If line feels cold, it indicates restriction in high side. • Visually check for frost spot to locate restriction and repair as necessary.
3. Refrigerant system overcharged (High discharge and high suction pressures).	• The clutch may cycle on/off and cause the compressor to be noisy.
4. Expansion tube (orifice) blocked (Low suction pressures).	
5. Air in system (High discharge and high suction pressures). Items 4, 5 and 6 in the striped area can be corrected by the same procedure.	• Discharge refrigerant system slowly using the low pressure fitting to prevent oil loss. • Check expansion (orifice) tube for blockage. Clean or replace as required. • Evacuate system to a vacuum. Improper evacuation of system prior to recharge will cause air to remain in system. • Recharge system with proper amount of refrigerant. • Leak check system.

GC7029700547000X

Fig. 3 Gray area diagnosis & service. Except Saturn

performance charts, **Figs. 7 through 9.**

45 mph Test

Recorded manifold gauge pressures and outlet temperature with the vehicle conditions listed under "Service Stall Test," except for the following conditions:

1. Recirc off (outside air).
2. Vehicle running at 45 mph with engine fully warm.
3. Compare readings to normal system performance chart, **Figs. 10 through 12.**

Striped Area Diagnosis and Service	
Check the following if pressures intersect in the striped area:	
1. Compressor may be internally damaged.	• If suction and discharge pressure are equal and do not change when the A/C mode is turned on and off, the compressor may be internally damaged. • Excess heat at the clutch surfaces or a free wheeling clutch driver are signs of internal compressor damage. • When replacing the compressor, follow component replacement procedures to maintain correct oil charge in the system.
2. Missing expansion tube (orifice).	• Feel liquid line after expansion tube. If line is warm, discharge system and inspect for proper installation of expansion tube. If expansion tube or o-ring is missing replace expansion tube. • If expansion tube is present, remove, clean, or replace tube as necessary and install in system. • Evacuate and charge system.
3. Compressor at minimum stroke.	• If compressor discharge pressures remains only 10-30 psi above suction pressure, compressor may be at minimum stroke. • Run engine at approximately 3000 RPM for three minutes until pressures become normal. During this period, cycle mode lever from vent to A/C every 20 seconds. If no change, perform control valve low load test (step 4).
4. Compressor control valve set improperly. Run low load test to verify. Perform low load test as follows. This procedure is designed to create a low cooling load causing the V5 compressor to go toward minimum stroke which is absolutely necessary for evaluation of control valve set point.	• Start engine and run at fast idle speed. • Open hood, close windows and doors. • Set A/C controls to LOW blower and MAX cooling. • Record and evaluate test results: 1. If suction pressure is 25-35 psi, control valve is functioning properly. 2. If suction pressure is outside limits of 25-35 psi, replace control valve.
5. Refrigerant system undercharged.	• This condition may exist when the suction pressure is below 35 psi during the high load test (step 3). • The suction line before the accumulator will be warm if charge is low. • Add 1 lb. of refrigerant and recheck. Pressures should come into white area. If so, find source of refrigerant leak and repair. • Evacuate and charge system with correct amount of refrigerant.
6. Expansion tube (orifice) blocked.	• Refer to step 5 in the gray area for diagnosis.

GC7029700548000X

Fig. 4 Striped area diagnosis & service. Except Saturn

Evaporator Pressure Gauge Reading	Evaporator Temperature F°	High Pressure Gauge Reading	Ambient Temperature
0	-21°	45	20°
0.6	-20°	55	30°
2.4	-15°	72	40°
4.5	-10°	86	50°
6.8	- 5°	105	60°
9.2	0°	126	70°
11.8	5°	140	75°
14.7	10°	160	80°
17.1	15°	185	90°
21.1	20°	195	95°
22.5	22°	220	100°
23.9	24°	240	105°
25.4	26°	260	110°
26.9	28°	275	115°
28.5	30°	290	120°
37.0	40°	305	125°
46.7	50°	325	130°
57.7	60°		
70.1	70°		
84.1	80°		
99.6	90°		
116.9	100°		
136.0	110°		
157.1	120°		
179.0	130°		

GC7029100025000X

Fig. 5 Pressure-temperature relationship, Conditions equivalent to 30 mph or 1750 engine RPM. Except Saturn

LEAK TEST

Before beginning any leak test, attach a manifold gauge set and note pressure. If little or no pressure is indicated, a partial charge must be installed. Inspect all connections, compressor head gasket, oil filler plug and compressor shaft seal for leaks.

ELECTRONIC LEAK DETECTORS

Current versions of electronic leak detectors have three settings, one for R-12, one for R-134a and one for gross. The gross setting is for isolating very large leaks already found in one of the other two settings. Refer to operating instructions for the unit being used and observe these general procedures.

1. Move detector probe one inch per second in areas of suspected leaks.
2. Position probe below test point, as refrigerant gas is heavier than air.
3. Inspect service access gauge port valve fittings, particularly when valve caps are missing, as dirt accumulations can destroy sealing area of valve core when manifold gauge set is attached. Replace missing valve caps after cleaning valve core area. **Valve caps should only be finger tightened. Using pliers to tighten valve caps may distort sealing surface of valve.**
4. Inspect for leaks in manifold gauge set and hoses, as well as rest of system.

FLAME-TYPE (HALIDE) LEAK DETECTORS

1. Adjust detector flame as low as possible to obtain maximum sensitivity. Ensure copper element is cherry red and not burned away, flame will be almost colorless.
2. Slowly move detector along areas of suspected leaks. A slight leak will cause flame to change to a bright yellow-green color. A significant leak will be indicated by a brilliant blue flame. Position flame under areas being tested as refrigerant gas is heavier than air. **Presence of dust in pickup hose may cause a change in color of flame. If not recognized, a false diagnosis could be made. Store leak detector in a clean place and ensure hose is free of dust before leak testing.**
3. Inspect manifold gauge set and hoses for leaks, as well as rest of system.

Ambient Temp., °F	High Side Pressure
80	150–170
90	175–195
95	185–205
100	210–230
105	230–250
110	250–270

Fig. 6 High side pressure specifications. Except Saturn

If the ambient air temperature is . . .	The low side gauge should read . . .	The high side gauge should read . . .	The right center air temperature should be . . .
DEGREES (°F)	SUCTION (psi)	DISCHARGE (psi)	OUTLET (°F)
(70)	(29–31)	(105–133)	(41–46)
(80)	(28–30)	(145–160)	(42–45)
(90)	(27–29)	(185–260)	(45–47)
(100)	(26–28)	(225–310)	(46–48)

G37029900040000X

Fig. 8 Service stall specifications. Saturn w/2.2L engine

If the ambient air temperature is . . .	The low side gauge should read . . .	The high side gauge should read . . .	The right center air temperature should be . . .
DEGREES (°F)	SUCTION (psi)	DISCHARGE (psi)	OUTLET (°F)
(70)	(26–29)	(139–185)	(41–46)
(80)	(25–28)	(190–220)	(42–48)
(90)	(25–27)	(225–340)	(45–48)
(100)	(25–27)	(275–340)	(45–53)

G37029900041000X

Fig. 9 Service stall specifications. Saturn w/3.0L engine

If the ambient air temperature is . . .	The pressure gauge should read–(psi)	The pressure gauge should read–(psi)	The right center air should read–(°F)
DEGREES °F	SUCTION	DISCHARGE	OUTLET °F
70	26~30	115~170	40~48
80	24~28	180~215	42~49
90	22~26	225~270	43~50
100	23~27	275~320	50~56

G37029500025000X

Fig. 7 Service stall test specifications. Saturn w/1.9L engine

NORMAL SYSTEM PERFORMANCE 45 MPH

If the ambient air temperature is . . .	The pressure gauge should read–(psi)	The pressure gauge should read–(psi)	The right center air should read–(°F)
DEGREES °F	SUCTION	DISCHARGE	OUTLET °F
70	29~33	90 ~125	44~48
80	28~32	120~170	44~49
90	26~30	150~200	44~50
100	24~32	180~240	47~53

G37029500026000X

Fig. 10 45 mph test specifications. Saturn w/1.9L engine

4. Use a small fan to ventilate areas where leak detector indicates refrigerant constantly. These areas are contaminated with refrigerant and must be ventilated before leak can be pinpointed.

FLUID LEAK DETECTORS

Apply leak detector solution around joints to be tested. A cluster of bubbles will form immediately if there is a leak. A white foam that forms after a short while will indicate an extremely small leak. In some confined areas such as sections of the evaporator and condenser, use of an electronic leak detector is recommended.

FLUORESCENT LEAK DETECTORS

The high density black light tool No. J-2848-E, tracer dye injector tool No. J-41436 and tracer dye tool No. J-41447, or equivalents, were developed to detect refrigerant leaks on R-134a systems. **Do not use any other tracer dye in these systems. Another type dye may cause premature compressor failure. Use only a ¼ ounce charge of dye, larger amounts may effect system performance.** After adding tracer dye, clean service valves and all affected surfaces of the dye with GM engine degreaser part No. 1050436 or equivalent, to prevent any false leak diagnosis.

DISCHARGING SYSTEM

REFRIGERANT RECOVERY

The refrigerant system must be discharged using an air conditioning refrigerant recovery and recycling system. After completing any necessary repairs the refrigerant system can be evacuated and charged using an air conditioning service charging station. Service fitting caps are color coded for easy reference. Red cap indicates high side port. Blue cap indicates low side port.

Failure to inspect for residual oil from previous recovery can result in adding extra oil to the current vehicle being serviced. This will result in reduced performance and possible compressor damage.

1. Start vehicle and run with A/C On for two minutes, then attach manifold gauge set to A/C system, **Fig. 13.** Attach recovery station inlet hose to center fitting of manifold gauge set.
2. Open both valves of manifold gauge set. Ensure refrigerant tank vapor valve and liquid valve are open.
3. Turn main power switch On.
4. Depress compressor start switch. Amber Compressor On light will come on and compressor will start. Compressor will shutoff automatically when recovery is complete.
5. Wait two minutes and inspect for pressure rise. If pressure rise occurs, depress compressor start switch to repeat recovery procedure.
6. To drain receiver dehydrator of A/C system oil, open receiver dehydrator pressurizing valve for 15 seconds to allow compressor discharge pressure back into receiver dehydrator.
7. Open oil drain valve slowly and drain receiver dehydrator. When oil stops draining, close oil drain valve.
8. **Do not allow receiver dehydrator to completely depressurize.**

REFRIGERANT RECYCLING

1. Turn main power switch On.
2. Open both valves on recovery tank.
3. Turn Recycle Start switch On. Amber Recycle On light will come on and refrigerant pump will start.
4. Refrigerant will be seen going through Moisture Indicator at start up. If there is a sufficient supply of refrigerant, bubbles will clear after a few seconds. When bubbles clear from Moisture Indicator, refrigerant pump is operating at maximum efficiency.
5. Allow station to operate until dot in center of Moisture Indicator turns green. Moisture Indicator Dot should change to a shade indicated on reference decal. Always run recycling system a minimum of 30 minutes. If Moisture Indicator starts out yellow, it could take as long as two hours to turn green, depending on moisture content of refrigerant.
6. Turn Off station when recycling is complete.

REFRIGERANT RECOVERY & RECYCLING OPERATING HINTS

1. When using recovery station in conjunction with a charging station, attach center port hose of manifold gauge set

If the ambient air temperature is . . . DEGREES (°F)	The low side gauge should read . . . SUCTION (psi)	The high side gauge should read . . . DISCHARGE (psi)	The right center air temperature should be . . . OUTLET (°F)
(70)	(30–33)	(86–98)	(42–52)
(80)	(30–31)	(110–120)	(43–57)
(90)	(30–31)	(153–170)	(45–49)
(100)	(28–31)	(175–200)	(45–52)

G37029900042000X

Fig. 11 45 mph test specifications. Saturn w/2.2L engine

If the ambient air temperature is . . . DEGREES (°F)	The low side gauge should read . . . SUCTION (psi)	The high side gauge should read . . . DISCHARGE (psi)	The right center air temperature should be . . . OUTLET (°F)
(70)	(30–32)	(92–120)	(42–48)
(80)	(29–31)	(117–150)	(44–50)
(90)	(28–30)	(145–175)	(43–51)
(100)	(28–30)	(185–200)	(43–55)

G37029900043000X

Fig. 12 45 mph test specifications. Saturn w/3.0L engine

to inlet port of recovery station, then follow normal operating procedures for recovery/recycling station.

2. When using recovery station in conjunction with an automatic charging station, attach exhaust hose to inlet of recovery station.
3. **On automatic A/C service stations,** a hole has been added at rear of cabinet for access to exhaust hose.
4. **On older type stations,** open front doors of cabinet to reach exhaust hose.
5. **On all models,** after attaching exhaust hose to recovery station, depress main power switch on automatic charging station. Depress exhaust switch. Then follow normal operating procedures for recovery station.
6. Air is automatically vented from recovery tank during recycling. This feature eliminates need to purge hoses before recovering refrigerant.
7. Operating engine with A/C Off during recovery may reduce recovery time.
8. To help prevent escape of refrigerant to atmosphere, recovery station can be attached to a Dial A Charge cylinder top vent port when filling cylinder.
9. Always inspect recovery station for residual oil from previous recovery.

SYSTEM EVACUATION

CHARGING STATION

A vacuum pump is built into the charging station. Complete moisture removal from the system is possible only with a vacuum pump constructed for the purpose.

The system must be completely discharged before it can be evacuated. Damage to the vacuum pump may result if pressurized refrigerant is allowed to enter.

1. Connect hose to vacuum pump, if system was discharged through charging station.
2. Open low side gauge hand valve of charging station.
3. Turn vacuum pump on according to instructions for specific station being used.
4. Evacuate system with vacuum pump until low pressure gauge reads at least 28 inches of vacuum. Continue evacuating system for an additional 15 minutes for routine system servicing or 20–30 minutes, if any parts have been replaced.
5. Close low side gauge hand valve, then turn vacuum pump off.
6. Verify ability of system to hold vacuum. Watch low side gauge to see that gauge does not rise at a rate faster than 1 inch vacuum every 4–5 minutes. If low side gauge rises at too rapid a rate, install partial charge and leak test.
7. If system holds vacuum, charge system with refrigerant.

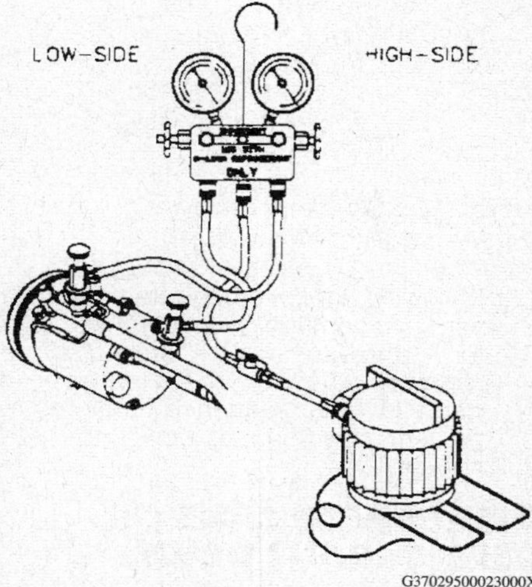

G37029500023000X

Fig. 14 High & low side Schraeder valve location. Saturn

VACUUM PUMP

Except Saturn

The specification for A/C system pump-down is 28–29½ inches vacuum. This reading can be attained at or near sea level only. For each 1000 feet of altitude, the reading will be 1 inch vacuum lower. As an example, at 5000 feet elevation, only 23–24½ inch of vacuum can be obtained. **The system must be completely discharged before it can be evacuated. Damage to vacuum pump may result if pressurized refrigerant is allowed to enter pump.**

1. With manifold gauge set connected to system, remove cap from vacuum hose connector. Install manifold gauge set center hose to vacuum pump connector. Open low side gauge manifold hand valve only.
2. Ensure low side gauge is calibrated correctly. It should be reading zero. If not, adjust calibration.
3. Evacuate system with vacuum pump until low pressure gauge reads at least 28 inches of vacuum.
4. Continue evacuating system for an additional 15 minutes for routine system servicing or 20–30 minutes, if parts have been replaced.
5. When system evacuation is complete, close low side gauge manifold hand valve, then turn vacuum pump off.
6. Verify ability of system to hold vacuum. Watch low side gauge to see that gauge does not rise at a rate faster than 1 inch vacuum every 4–5 minutes. If low side gauge rises at too rapid a rate, install partial charge and leak test.
7. Correct leaks as necessary and evacuate system.
8. If system holds vacuum, charge system with refrigerant.

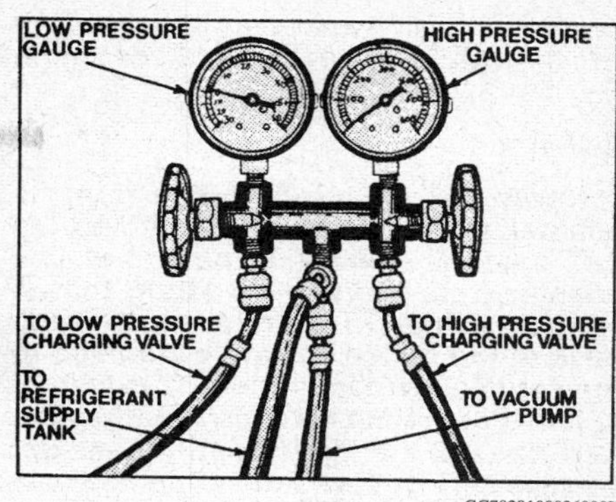

GC7029100026000X

Fig. 13 Manifold gauge set hose connections. Except Saturn

Saturn

1. Connect manifold gauge set and vacuum pump to high and low side Schraeder valves. Refer to **Fig. 14,** for valve locations.
2. Turn vacuum pump on and slowly open high and low side valves to pump. Allow system to evacuate for 20–30 minutes. Note vacuum gauge reading.
3. Close high and low side valves. Shut off vacuum pump.
4. Watch low side gauge for vacuum loss (1–3 minutes).
5. If loss is less than 1 inch Hg., from level recorded in previous step, proceed to "Charging System."
6. If vacuum loss is greater than 1 inch Hg., from level recorded in previous step, charge with ½ lb. of R-134a refrigerant, depending on system type.
7. Leak test, repair leaks and retest. Disconnect high side adapter from service port and check for vacuum loss before leak testing.

CHARGING SYSTEM

CHARGING STATION

EXCEPT SATURN

Use of the following procedures will prevent charging station from being accidentally exposed to high-side vehicle system pressure.

Use instructions provided with charging station noting the following:

1. Do not connect high pressure line to A/C system.
2. Always keep high pressure valve closed on charging station.

3. Perform all evacuation and charging through low-side pressure service fitting.

Saturn

Never remove a gauge line from its adapter when line is connected to the A/C system. Always remove the line adapter from the service fitting to disconnect a line. Do not remove charging hose at the gauge set while attached to the service low-side fitting. This will result in a complete discharge of the system due to the depressed Schraeder valve in service low-side fitting and may cause personal injury due to escaping refrigerant.

Follow charging station manufacturer's instructions with the following exceptions:

1. Open source valve and allow 1 lb. of liquid R-134a to flow into system through low-side service fitting, **Fig. 15.**
2. As soon as 1 lb. has been added to system, start engine, set A/C control to upper outlets, temperature lever to Max cold, blower speed on high and push A/C compressor button to On position (button should illuminate).
3. Slowly draw in remainder of refrigerant charge.
4. Turn off source valve and run engine for 30 seconds to clear lines and gauges.
5. With engine running, remove charging low-side hose adapter from suction pipe service fitting. Remove quickly to avoid excess refrigerant escaping from system.
6. Ensure an O-ring seal is inside of caps before installation, because cap is primary seal for A/C service fittings. Failure to tighten cap will result in refrigerant leakage.
7. Install protective caps on service fittings and hand tighten.
8. Turn engine off, then check system for leaks with electronic leak detector.
9. Do not connect high pressure line to air conditioning system.
10. Keep high pressure valve on charging station closed at all times.
11. Perform entire evacuation and charge procedure through low-side pressure service fitting on suction pipe, **Fig. 15.**

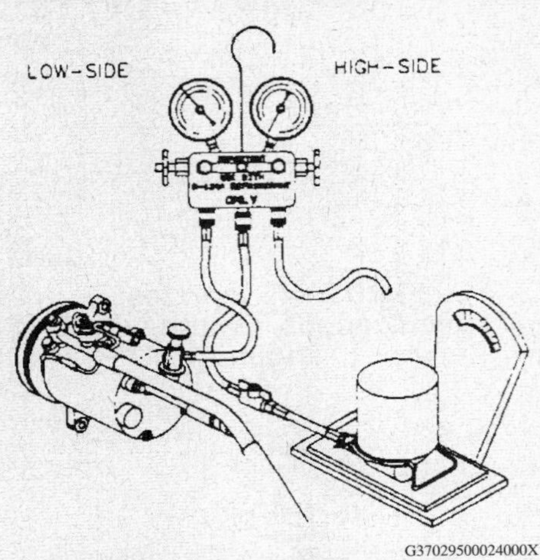

Fig. 15 System charging valve connection. Saturn

12. Following these procedures will prevent accidental high-side vehicle system pressure being subjected to charging station in event an error is made in valve sequence during compressor operation to pull in R-134a charge.

DISPOSABLE CANS OR REFRIGERANT DRUM

EXCEPT SATURN

Never use disposable cans to charge into the high pressure side of the system (compressor discharge port) or into a system that is at high temperature, high system pressures could be transferred into the charging can causing it to explode.

Charging System

1. Start and run engine until normal operating temperature is reached and allow to warm up (choke off, normal idle). Set A/C control lever to OFF.
2. **On all models except Cadillac with display diagnosis,** when 1 lb. of refrigerant has entered system, engage compressor by setting A/C lever to NORM and blower switch to HI to draw in remainder of charge.
3. **On Cadillac models with display diagnosis,** when 1 lb. of refrigerant has entered system, engage compressor by setting climate control panel to AUTO and blower switch to HI to draw in remainder of charge. If system switches to ECON when AUTO is pressed, low refrigerant is indicated, and compressor will not operate. To obtain compressor operation, clear diagnostic trouble codes and select AUTO again.
4. **On all models,** cooling condenser with a large fan will speed up charging procedure by maintaining condenser temperature below charging cylinder temperature.
5. Close refrigerant supply valve and run engine for 30 seconds to clear lines and gauges.
6. With engine running, remove charging low side hose adapter from accumulator service fitting. Unscrew rapidly to avoid excessive refrigerant loss. **Do not remove a gauge line from its adapter when line is connected to A/C system. To disconnect line, always remove line adapter from service fitting. Do not remove charging hose at gauge set while attached to accumulator, as system will be discharged due to depressed Schraeder valve.**
7. Replace protective cap on accumulator fitting and turn engine off.
8. Inspect system for leaks.
9. Start engine and inspect for proper system pressures.

SATURN

Place R-134a drum on scale and note total weight before charging. Watch scale during charging to determine amount of R-134a used.

1. Connect manifold gauge set as follows:
   a. Connect low pressure gauge hose to low pressure service fitting on suction pipe at rear of compressor, **Fig. 15.** Do not connect high pressure line to A/C system.
   b. Connect center hose to R-134a source.
2. Open valve on drum to start flow of refrigerant.

System Service

NOTE: On Air Bag Equipped Models, Refer To "Air Bag System Precautions" Located In The Front Of This Manual For System Disarming & Arming Procedures.

NOTE: Refer To "Computer Relearn Procedures" Located In The Front Of This Manual When Battery Power To The Computer Has Been Interrupted.

NOTE: Prior To Performing Any Service Operations Listed In This Section, Consult The "Technical Service Bulletins" Section For Related Information.

INDEX

OIL CHARGE

EXCEPT SATURN

When replacing certain components of an air conditioning system, an oil charge must be added to the system. Refer to "Oil Charge Data Table" for oil charge specifications.

If the refrigerant charge is abruptly lost due to a large refrigerant leak, approximately three ounces of refrigerant oil will be carried out of the system with the refrigerant. Upon replacement of a component which caused a large refrigerant leak, add three ounces of oil to the system plus the amount required for any component replaced as outlined under "Oil Charge Data Table." If possible, add oil directly to the replacement component.

SATURN

Adding Oil

Adding oil to the A/C system should take place after recovery and before evacuation procedure.

1. Remove refrigeration discharge hose at compressor pipe connection.
2. Pour correct quantity of new Saturn compressor oil or equivalent, into discharge hose pipe.
3. Always lubricate new O-rings with clean compressor oil prior to assembly.
4. Properly connect hose to compressor with new O-ring. Add new oil to components before installation.

Oil Charge Requirements

The A/C system requires the use of Saturn Compressor Oil or equivalent. Refer to the "Oil Charge Data Table" for system capacity.

OIL CHARGE DATA TABLE

EXCEPT SATURN

Model	Year	Compressor Model	Oil Charge (Fl. Oz.) When Replacing Component				
			Compressor	Evaporator	Condenser	Accumulator	Receiver & Dehydrator
BUICK							
Century	1998–2000	V-5	③	3	1	④	—
	2001	V-5	2⑪	3⑪	1⑪	2⑪	—
	2002	V-5	2⑪	3⑪	1⑪	⑩	—
LeSabre	1998–99	V-5	③	3	1	3	—
	2000	V-5	③	2	2	3	—
	2001–02	V-5	2⑪	3⑪	1⑪	2⑩	—
Park Ave.	1998–2000	V-5	③	2	2	3	—
	2001–02	V-5	2⑪	3⑪	1⑪	⑩	—
Regal	1998–2000	V-5	③	3	1	④	—
	2001	V-5	2⑪	3⑪	1⑪	2⑪	—
	2002	V-5	2⑪	3⑪	1⑪	⑩	—
Riviera	1998–99	V-5	③	3	1	3	—
Skylark	1998	V-5	③	3	1	3.5	—
CADILLAC							
Catera	1998–2001	V-5	2⑪	3⑪	1⑪	—	1⑪
DeVille	1998	HD6/HR6-HE	2	2	1	3	—
	1999	HD6	2	2	1	3	—
	2000	HD6	2.8	1	1	4	—
	2001	HD6	2.8⑪	1⑪	1⑪	4⑪	—
	2002	HD6	2.7⑪	1⑪	1⑪	4⑩	—
Eldorado	1998	HD6/HR6-HE	2	2	1	3	—
	1999–2000	HD6	2	2	1	3	—
	2001	HD6	2⑪	3⑪	1⑪	2⑪	—
	2002	HD6	2⑪	3⑪	1⑪	2⑩	—
Seville	1998	HD6/HR6-HE	2.8	2	1	3	—
	1999–2000	HD6	2.8	1	1	4	—
	2001	HD6	2.8⑪	1⑪	1⑪	4⑪	—
	2002	HD6	2.7⑪	1⑪	1⑪	4⑩	—
CHEVROLET/GEO							
Camaro	1998	HD6/HR6-HE	2	3	1	⑩	—
	1999–2000	V-5	2	3	1	⑩	—
	2001–02	V-5 & V-7	2⑪	3⑪	1⑪	2⑩	—
Cavalier	1998–2000	V-5	2.8	2	1	3	—
	2001	V-5	2.8⑪	2⑪	1⑪	3⑪	—
	2002②	V-5	2⑪	2⑪	1⑪	⑩	—
	2002 ⑨	CVC-7	2.5⑪	2⑪	1⑪	⑤	—
Corvette	1998–2000	V-7	③	3	1	④	—
	2001–02	V-7	2⑪	3⑪	1⑪	2⑩	—
Impala	2000	V-5	③	3	1	④	—
	2001	V-5	2	3	1	2	—
	2002	V-5	2	3	1	⑩	—
Lumina	1998–2001	V-5	③	3	1	④	—
Malibu	1998–2000	V-5	2	3	1	3.5	—
	2001	V-5	2⑪	3⑪	1⑪	3.5⑪	—
	2002	V-5	2⑪	3⑪	1⑪	⑩	—
Metro	1998–2001	⑦	3.2	—	0.7–1.0	—	.30
Monte Carlo	1998–2000	V-5	③	3	1	④	—
	2001	V-5	2	3	1	2	—
	2002	V-5	2	3	1	⑩	—
Prizm	1998–2002	V-5	2①	2	2	2	—

Continued

OIL CHARGE DATA TABLE

EXCEPT SATURN—Continued

Model	Year	Compressor Model	Oil Charge (Fl. Oz.) When Replacing Component				
			Com-pressor	Evapor-ator	Con-denser	Accumu-lator	Receiver & Dehydrator
OLDSMOBILE							
Achieva	1998	V-5	③	3	1	3.5	—
Alero	1999–2000	V-5	2	3	1	3.5	—
	2001	V-5	2⑪	3⑪	1⑪	3.5⑪	—
	2002⑨	CVC-7	2.5⑪	2⑪	1⑪	⑥	—
	2002⑧	V-5	2⑪	3⑪	1⑪	⑩	—
Aurora	1998	HD6/HR6-HE	2	3	1	3	—
	1999	V-5	2	2	1	3	—
	2001	HD6	2.7⑪	3⑪	1⑪	2⑪	—
	2002	HD6	2.7⑪	3⑪	1⑪	2⑩	—
Cutlass	1998–99	V-5	2	3	1	3.5	—
Intrigue	1998–99	V-5	③	3	1	1⑤	—
	2000	V-7	2	3	1	1⑤	—
	2001	V-7	2⑪	3⑪	1⑪	2⑪	—
	2002	V-7	2⑪	3⑪	1⑪	2⑩	—
LSS & 88	1998–99	V-5	2	3	1	3	—
PONTIAC							
Bonneville	1998–99	V-5	2	3	1	3	—
	2000	V-5	③	2	2	3	—
	2001–02	V-5	2	3	1	2⑩	—
Firebird	1998	HD6/HR6-HE	2	3	1	⑩	—
	1999–2000	V-5	2	3	1	⑩	—
	2001–02	V-5 & V-7	2⑪	3⑪	1⑪	2⑩	—
Grand Am	1998–2000	V-5	2	3	1	3.5	—
	2001	V-5	2⑪	3⑪	1⑪	3.5⑪	—
	2002⑨	CVC-7	2.5⑪	2⑪	1⑪	⑥	—
	2002⑧	V-5	2⑪	3⑪	1⑪	⑩	—
Grand Prix	1998	V-5	③	3	1	⑤	—
	1999–2000	V-5	2	3	1	⑤	—
	2001	V-5	2⑪	3⑪	1⑪	2⑪	—
	2002	V-5	2⑪	3⑪	1⑪	2⑩	—
Sunfire	1998–2000	V-5	2.8	2	1	3	—
	2001	V-5	2.8⑪	2⑪	1⑪	3⑪	—
	2002②	V-5	2⑪	2⑪	1⑪	⑩	—
	2002 ⑨	CVC-7	2.5⑪	2⑪	1⑪	⑤	—

① — Plus amount drained from old compressor.
② — 2.2L OHV & 2.4L engines.
③ — Drain oil from old compressor and measure, then drain new compressor. If more than 1 ounce is drained from old compressor, add equal amount to new compressor. If less than 1 ounce is drained from compressor, add 2 ounces.
④ — Drain oil from accumulator and measure. Add equal amount of oil to new accumulator, plus 1 ounce. If no oil is drained, add 2 ounces to new accumulator.
⑤ — Drain oil from accumulator and measure. Add equal amount of oil to new accumulator, plus 1 ounce.
⑥ — Drain oil from accumulator and measure. Add equal amount of oil to new accumulator, plus 1.5 ounces. If no oil is drained, add 1.5 ounces to new accumulator.
⑦ — Sanden swash type.
⑧ — 3.4L engine.
⑨ — 2.2L DOHC engine.
⑩ — Drain oil from accumulator and measure. Add equal amount of oil to new accumulator, plus 2 ounces. If no oil is drained, add 2 ounces to new accumulator.
⑪ — If more than specified amount of PAG oil was drained from component, add equal amount of new oil to component.

SATURN

Model	Year	Oil Charge (Fl. Oz.) When Replacing Component			
		Compressor	Evaporator	Condenser	Accumulator
L-Series	2000–02	①	2.40	1.30	0.4
S-Series	1998–2002	①	1.14	0.75	1.0

① — Drain oil from old compressor. Drain oil from replacement compressor. Add equal amount of new compressor oil as drained from removed compressor. New replacement compressors are charged with 2.21 ounces of oil.

OIL LEVEL CHECK

EXCEPT SATURN

Air conditioning oil levels can only be inspected with system discharged and compressor removed from vehicle. Replacement compressor may be shipped with 8–9 ounces of new refrigerant oil. Drain the new oil into a suitable container and retain for later use.

1. Operate system for several minutes to stabilize system. Turn engine Off.
2. Using a suitable refrigerant recovery/recycling station, discharge A/C system.
3. Remove compressor from vehicle.
4. Drain and measure refrigerant oil from old compressor through suction and discharge ports, and drain plug.
5. If no compressor oil leaks were noted and more than one ounce of oil is drained, add drained amount using new refrigerant oil.
6. If less than one ounce of oil is drained from compressor, add two ounces of new refrigerant oil.
7. When replacing other A/C components, add specified amount of new refrigerant oil to component as detailed in "Oil Charge Data Table."
8. Install compressor.
9. Evacuate and recharge system, perform leak test.
10. Ensure A/C system is operating properly.

SATURN

1. To measure compressor oil, compressor must be removed from engine.
2. Install high and low side compressor oil drain adapter tool Nos. SA9149AC-6 and SA9149AC-5, or equivalents, on low and high side ports.
3. Drain oil into suitable clean container from high side port first and move compressor to a different position to remove all oil possible. Turn compressor over to drain oil from low side port and rotate compressor drive plate in both directions to remove oil from compressor chambers.
4. Move compressor to different positions to remove all oil possible. Turn compressor back to high side port to drain and back to low side port to remove maximum amount of oil. Stop oil draining when oil coming from low and high side ports becomes only drops. Measure oil removed and record.
5. Inspect extracted oil for color change from clear to dark brown or black. Also inspect oil for presence of foreign substances, such as metal filings. If oil extracted is found as mentioned, receiver drier must be replaced.
6. Discard extracted oil properly and replace with specified quantity of new Saturn PAG compressor oil or equivalent. Refer to "Specifications" for system capacity.

TECHNICAL SERVICE BULLETINS

LACK OF PERFORMANCE

1998–2000 Grand Prix, Intrigue, Monte Carlo & Regal & 1999–2000 Century & 2000 Impala

On some of these models the air conditioning may lack expected performance in hot humid weather.

This condition may be caused by an undercharged system.

To correct this condition, evacuate and charge system with 2.25 lbs. of R-134a.

Specifications

INDEX

A/C SPECIFICATIONS

EXCEPT SATURN

Model	Year	Refrigerant Capacity, Lbs.	Refrigerant Type	Refrigeration Oil			Compressor Clutch Air Gap, Inch
				Viscosity	Total System Capacity, Ounces	Compressor Oil Level	
BUICK							
Century	1998	1.88	R-134a	②	9.0	①	0.015–0.020
	1999–2000	2.20	R-134a	②	9.0	①	0.015
	2001	2.20	R-134a	⑤	9.0	①	0.015
	2002	2.20	R-134a	②	9.0	①	0.015
LeSabre	1998–99	2.00	R-134a	②	9.0	①	0.015–0.020
	2000	2.20	R-134a	②	9.0	①	0.015
	2001–02	2.20	R-134a	⑤	9.0	①	0.015
Park Avenue	1998–99	2.00	R-134a	②	9.0	①	0.015–0.020
	2000–02	2.20	R-134a	②	9.0	①	0.015
Regal	1998	1.88	R-134a	②	9.0	①	0.015–0.020
	1999–2002	2.20	R-134a	②	9.0	①	0.015
Riviera	1998–99	2.00	R-134a	②	8.0	①	0.020–0.030
Skylark	1998	1.75	R-134a	②	9.0	①	0.015–0.020
CADILLAC							
Catera	1998–2001	2.09	R-134a	⑤	9.0	①	0.015–0.020
	2001	2.09	R-134a	②	9.0	①	0.015–0.020
DeVille	1998–2000	2.00	R-134a	②	9.0	①	0.020–0.030
	2001	2.20	R-134a	⑤	8.8	①	—
	2002	2.20	R-134a	⑤	8.7	①	—
Eldorado	1998–2000	2.00	R-134a	②	9.0	①	0.020–0.030
	2001	2.20	R-134a	⑤	9.0	①	0.020–0.030
	2002	2.20	R-134a	②	9.0	①	0.020–0.030
Seville	1998–2000	2.00	R-134a	③	9.0	①	—
	2001	2.20	R-134a	⑤	8.8	①	—
	2002	2.20	R-134a	⑤	8.7	①	—

Continued

A/C SPECIFICATIONS

EXCEPT SATURN—Continued

Model	Year	Refrigerant Capacity, Lbs.	Refrigerant Type	Refrigeration Oil			Compressor Clutch Air Gap, Inch
				Viscosity	Total System Capacity, Ounces	Compressor Oil Level	
CHEVROLET/GEO							
Camaro	1998–2002	1.50	R-134a	②	9.0	①	④
Cavalier	1998–2000	1.50	R-134a	②	9.0	①	0.015–0.020
	2001	1.50	R-134a	⑤	9.0	①	0.015–0.020
	2002⑨	1.35	R-134a	②	9.0	①	0.015–0.020
	2002⑦	1.35	R-134a	⑧	5.0	①	0.015–0.020
Corvette	1998–99	1.63	R-134a	②	8.0	①	0.015
	2000–02	1.50	R-134a	②	9.0	①	0.015
Impala	2000–02	2.20	R-134a	②	9.0	①	0.015–0.020
Lumina	1998	1.88	R-134a	②	9.0	①	0.015–0.020
	1999–2001	2.20	R-134a	②	9.0	①	0.015–0.020
Malibu	1998–99	1.75	R-134a	②	9.0	①	0.015–0.020
	2000	1.35	R-134a	②	9.5	①	0.016–0.020
	2001	1.35	R-134a	⑤	9.5	①	0.016–0.020
	2002	1.35	R-134a	②	9.0	①	0.015–0.020
Metro	1998–2001	1.10–1.32	R-134a	②	3.4	①	0.014–0.025
Monte Carlo	1998	1.88	R-134a	②	9.0	①	0.015–0.020
	1999–2002	2.20	R-134a	②	9.0	①	0.015–0.020
Prizm	1998–2002	1.65	R-134a	②	8.0	①	0.014–0.025
OLDSMOBILE							
Achieva	1998	1.75	R-134a	②	9.0	①	0.015–0.020
Alero	1999–2000	1.35	R-134a	②	8.0	①	0.016–0.020
	2001	1.35	R-134a	②	9.0	①	0.016–0.020
	2002⑥	1.35	R-134a	②	9.0	①	0.016–0.020
	2002⑦	1.35	R-134a	⑧	5.0	①	0.016–0.020
Aurora	1998–99	2.00	R-134a	②	8.0	①	0.015–0.020
	2001	2.20	R-134a	⑤	9.7	①	—
	2001–02	2.20	R-134a	②	9.0	①	—
Cutlass	1998–99	1.75	R-134a	②	9.0	①	0.015–0.020
Intrigue	1998–2000	2.20	R-134a	②	9.0	①	0.015–0.020
	2001	2.20	R-134a	⑤	9.0	①	0.015
	2002	2.20	R-134a	②	9.0	①	0.015
LSS & 88	1998–99	2.00	R-134a	②	9.0	①	0.015–0.020

Continued

A/C SPECIFICATIONS

EXCEPT SATURN—Continued

Model	Year	Refrigerant Capacity, Lbs.	Refrigerant Type	Refrigeration Oil			Compressor Clutch Air Gap, Inch
				Viscosity	Total System Capacity, Ounces	Compressor Oil Level	
PONTIAC							
Bonneville	1998–99	2.00	R-134a	②	9.0	①	0.015–0.020
	2000	2.20	R-134a	②	9.0	①	0.015–0.020
	2001–02	2.20	R-134a	⑤	9.0	①	0.015–0.020
Firebird	1998–2002	1.50	R-134a	②	9.0	①	④
Grand Am	1998	1.75	R-134a	②	9.0	①	0.015–0.020
	1999–2000	1.35	R-134a	②	8.0	①	0.016–0.020
	2001	1.35	R-134a	②	9.0	①	0.016–0.020
	2002⑥	1.35	R-134a	②	9.0	①	0.016–0.020
	2002⑦	1.35	R-134a	⑧	5.0	①	0.016–0.020
Grand Prix	1998	1.88	R-134a	②	9.0	①	0.015–0.020
	1999–2000	2.20	R-134a	②	9.0	①	0.015
	2001	2.20	R-134a	⑤	9.0	①	0.015
	2002	2.20	R-134a	②	9.0	①	0.015
Sunfire	1998–2000	1.50	R-134a	②	9.0	①	0.015–0.020
	2001	1.50	R-134a	⑤	9.0	①	0.015–0.020
	2002⑨	1.35	R-134a	②	9.0	①	0.015–0.020
	2002⑦	1.35	R-134a	⑧	5.0	①	0.015–0.020

① — Oil Level cannot be checked. Refer to total capacity in ounces.
② — GM PAG refrigerant oil No. 12345923, or equivalent.
③ — SUN PAG oil.
④ — Models w/3.8L engine & V-5 compressor, 0.015–0.020 inch. Models w/5.7L engine & V-7 compressor, 0.015 inch.
⑤ — GM PAG refrigerant oil No. 12356151, or equivalent.
⑥ — 3.4L engine.
⑦ — 2.2L DOHC engine.
⑧ — GM PAG refrigerant oil No. 12378526, or equivalent.
⑨ — 2.2L OHV & 2.4L engines.

SATURN

Engine	Refrigerant Type	Refrigerant Capacity, Lbs.	Refrigerant Oil		Compressor Clutch Air Gap, Inch
			Total System Capacity, Ounces	Compressor Oil Level	
1998–99					
1.9L	R-134a	1.50	5.07	①	0.018–0.030
2000–02					
1.9L	R-134a	1.50	5.07	①	0.018–0.030
2.2L & 3.0L	R-134a	1.88	7.50	①	0.012–0.024

① — Oil level cannot be checked. If compressor replacement is necessary, measure amount removed from old compressor, then add equal amount to new compressor. Saturn service compressors are charged with 5.07 ounces for 1.9L engine & 7.5 ounces for 2.2L & 3.0L engines.

CHARGING VALVE LOCATION

EXCEPT SATURN

The high pressure charging valve is located either on the high pressure line or the muffler, and the low pressure charging valve is located either on the accumulator or low pressure line.

SATURN

Refer to "System Testing" for charging valve locations and illustrations.

BELT TENSION

EXCEPT METRO, PRIZM & SATURN

Belt tension is controlled automatically by the belt tensioner.

METRO & PRIZM

Engine	Belt Deflection, Inch①
METRO	
1.0L	0.28–0.35②
1.3L	0.28–0.35②
PRIZM	
1.6L	0.20–0.32②
1.8L	0.20–0.32②

① — Belt deflection measured in inches, using 22 lbs. of force.

SATURN

Belt	Tension, Lbs.	
	New	Used
Accessory	50–65	45

COOLING FANS

TABLE OF CONTENTS

Variable Speed Fans, General Motors

INDEX

DESCRIPTION

The fan drive clutch, **Fig. 1,** is a fluid coupling containing silicone oil. Fan speed is regulated by the torque carrying capacity of the silicone oil. The more silicone oil in the coupling, the greater the fan speed. The less silicone oil, the slower the fan speed.

Two types of fan drive clutches are in use. On one, **Fig. 2,** a bi-metallic strip and control piston on the front of the fluid coupling regulates the amount of silicone oil entering the coupling. The bi-metallic strip flexes outward with an increase in surrounding temperature and allows a piston to move outward. The piston opens a valve regulating the flow of silicone oil into the coupling from a reserve chamber. The silicone oil is returned to the reserve chamber through a bleed hole when the valve is closed.

On the other type of fan drive clutch, **Fig. 3,** a heat-sensitive, bi-metal spring connected to an opening plate brings about a similar result. Both units cause the fan speed to increase with a rise in temperature and to decrease as the temperature goes down.

In some cases a Flex-Fan is used instead of a Fan Drive Clutch. Flexible blades vary the volume of air being drawn through the radiator, automatically increasing the pitch at low engine speeds.

COMPONENT DIAGNOSIS & TESTING

FAN DRIVE CLUTCH TEST

Do not operate the engine until the fan has been checked for possible cracks and separations.

Run the engine at a fast idle speed (1000 RPM) until normal operating temperature is reached. This process can be expedited by blocking off the front of the radiator with a suitable piece of cardboard. Regardless of temperature, the unit must be operated for at least five minutes before being tested.

Fig. 1 Typical variable speed cooling fan

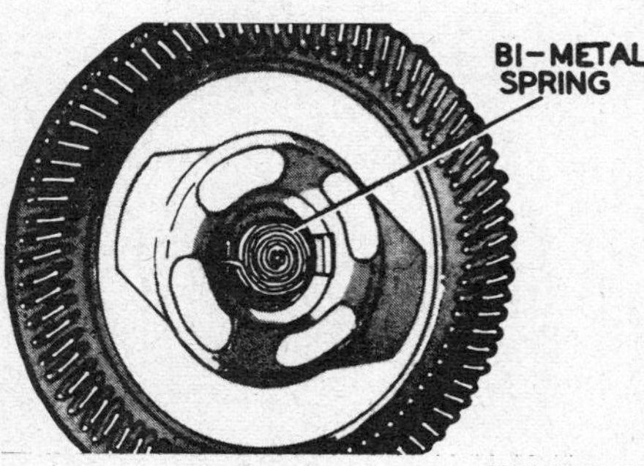

Fig. 3 Variable-speed fan w/coiled bi-metal thermostatic spring

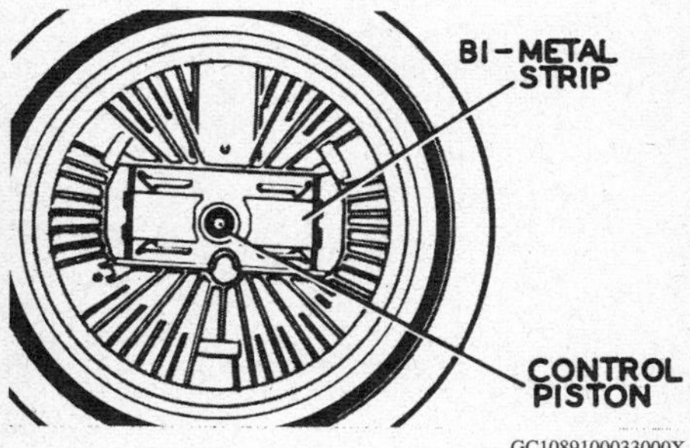

Fig. 2 Variable speed fan w/flat bi-metal thermostatic spring

Stop the engine and, using a glove or a cloth, immediately check the effort required to turn the fan. If considerable effort is required, it can be assumed that the coupling is operating satisfactorily. If very little effort is required to turn the fan, it is an indication that the coupling is not operating properly and should be replaced.

If the clutch fan is the coiled bi-metal spring type, it may be tested while the vehicle is being driven. To check, disconnect the bi-metal spring, **Fig. 4,** and rotate the spring 90° counterclockwise. This disables the temperature controlled free wheeling feature and the clutch performs like a conventional fan. If this cures the overheating condition, replace the fan clutch.

COMPONENT SERVICE

To prevent silicone fluid from draining into fan drive bearing, do not store or place drive unit on bench with rear of shaft pointing downward.

The removal procedure for either type of fan clutch assembly is similar for all vehicles. The unit must be unfastened from the water pump, then it may be lifted from the vehicle.

The type of unit shown in **Fig. 2** may be partially disassembled for inspection and cleaning as follows:

1. Remove bolts holding assembly together and separate fan from drive clutch.
2. Remove metal strip on front of fan clutch by pushing one end toward fan clutch body to clear retaining bracket.
3. Push strip aside until its opposite end springs out of place, then remove small control piston.
4. Inspect piston for free movement in coupling device. If piston sticks, clean it with emery cloth. If bi-metal strip is damaged, replace entire unit. **These strips are not interchangeable.**
5. When reassembling, install control piston so that projection on end will contact metal strip, then install metal strip.
6. After reassembly, clean clutch drive with a solvent soaked cloth. Avoid dipping clutch assembly in any type of liquid.
7. Install assembly in vehicle.

The coil spring type of fan clutch cannot be disassembled, serviced or repaired. If it does not function properly, it must be replaced with a new unit.

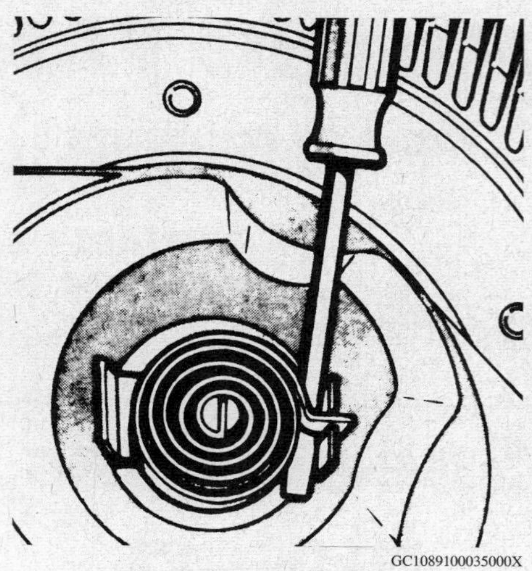

Fig. 4 Bi-metal spring disengagement

Electric Cooling Fans, General Motors

NOTE: On Air Bag Equipped Models, Refer To Air Bag System Precautions Located In The Front Of This Manual For System Disarming & Arming Procedures.

NOTE: "Wire Color Code & Electrical Symbol Identification" Located In The Front Of This Manual Can Be Used As An Aid When Using Wiring Circuits Found In This Section.

NOTE: Refer To "Computer Relearn Procedures" Located In The Front Of This Manual When Battery Power To The Computer Has Been Interrupted.

INDEX

PRECAUTIONS

AIR BAG SYSTEMS

Refer to "Air Bag System Precautions" in the front of this manual for system disarming and arming procedures.

BATTERY GROUND CABLE

Prior to service, disconnect battery ground cable and isolate as required.

DESCRIPTION

ACHIEVA, CAVALIER, SKYLARK & SUNFIRE

Cooling fan operation is controlled by the PCM through the fan relay. The PCM uses signals from the engine coolant temperature sensor, intake air temperature sensor, A/C refrigerant pressure sensor and vehicle speed sensor to determine when and how long the fan should operate. The PCM turns the cooling fan on by providing a ground path for the cooling fan control circuit which activates the coolant fan relay.

The relay will be commanded on anytime engine coolant temperature exceeds 223°F, A/C clutch is requested, vehicle speed is less than 38 mph or any Diagnostic Trouble Code (DTC) that causes the MIL lamp to illuminate.

ALERO

The electric cooling fans are controlled

by the Body Control Module (BCM) which enables the fans through the PCM. The PCM enables the ground path for the three cooling fan relays. The relays are used to control the high current flow to power the cooling fan motors.

When minimum cooling is required, the BCM will command the PCM to energize the No. 1 cooling fan relay and since both fans are connected in series through the Mode Control relay, both fans will run at low speed. When maximum cooling is required, the BCM will command the PCM to energize all three cooling fan relays. Power is supplied to the left fan through the No. 1 cooling fan relay and is grounded through the Mode Control relay. The right fan is powered directly through the No. 2 cooling fan relay, causing both fans to run at high speed.

AURORA

The electric cooling fans are used to cool engine coolant flowing through the radiator. They are also used to cool the refrigerant flowing through the A/C condenser.

The electric cooling fans are controlled by the PCM. The PCM controls the ground path for the three cooling fan relays. The relays are used to control the high current flow to power the cooling fan motors. Both fans operate together. When minimum cooling is required, the PCM energizes the low speed cooling fan relay No. 1, and both fans operate at low speed since the fans are connected in series thorough the series/parallel cooling fan relay No. 2. The series/parallel coolant fan relay is a dual position switch and while de-energized, supplies a ground path for the low speed fan circuit. When maximum cooling is required, the PCM energizes all three cooling fan relays. The left hand coolant fan is still power through the low speed cooling fan relay No. 1, but is now grounded through the series/parallel cooling fan relay No. 2 and operates at high speed. The right hand coolant fan is powered directly through the high speed cooling fan relay No. 3 and also operates at high speed.

The low speed cooling fans are controlled by the PCM based on inputs from the A/C system, Engine Coolant Temperature (ECT) sensor and Vehicle Speed Sensor (VSS). The PCM will command low speed fans to turn On when ECT sensor is above 223°F. The PCM will turn the fans Off when the temperature drops about 5°F. The minimum On time for low speed fans is 50 seconds.

The PCM will command high speed fans to turn On at idle when a certain DTC is set, the ECT is above 230°F or the A/C head pressure is above 248 psi. If the high speed fans were turned On by the ECT, the PCM will switch the fans back to low speed when the temperature drops about 5°F. Minimum On time for high speed fans is 30 seconds.

BONNEVILLE, LESABRE, LSS & REGENCY

1998-99

Power for the fan motors is supplied through the Cooling Fan fuse in the LH Maxi fuse block. The cooling fan relays are energized when current supplied by the Cooling Fan fuse flows through the relay coils to ground through the PCM.

During low speed cooling fan operation the PCM supplies a ground path for the low speed cooling fan relay. This closes the low speed relay contacts, allowing current to flow directly to the righthand cooling fan and through a resistor to the lefthand cooling fan.

During high speed cooling fan operation the PCM enables both relays, supplying current directly to both cooling fan relays.

2000-02

The PCM controls the operation of the cooling fans. This is accomplished by providing a ground path for the cooling fan relay coils within the PCM. The relay contacts will close and complete the circuit between the fusible link at the battery junction block and the fan motors. Whenever the fans are commanded on both fans will be running.

Power for the fan motors is supplied through the Cooling Fan fuse in the righthand Maxi fuse block. The cooling fan relays are energized when current from the Cooling Fan fuse flows through the relay coils to ground through the PCM.

Low speed fan operation will be commanded on anytime engine coolant temperature exceeds 221°F, A/C is requested and ambient temperature is more than 48°F, or A/C pressure is greater than 190 psi.

Before the PCM operates the fans at high speed, it will delay control of the series/parallel and high speed fan relays for six seconds. This six second delay ensures the cooling fan electrical load will not exceed the capacity of the system.

CAMARO & FIREBIRD

Power for the fan motors is supplied through a 40 amp Maxifuse located in the underhood fuse block. The cooling fan relays receive power from a 25 amp fuse located in the underhood fuse block.

During low fan speed operation the PCM supplies a ground path for the No. 1 engine cooling fan relay. This closes the cooling fan relay contacts, allowing current to flow from the 40 amp Maxifuse, through the relays contacts and to left engine cooling fan. The ground path for the left cooling fan is through the No. 3 cooling fan relay and right cooling fan. The result is a series circuit with both fans running at low. The PCM will complete the ground circuit for low speed cooling fan operation anytime engine coolant temperature exceeds 221°F, A/C is requested and ambient temperature is more than 50°F, or A/C pressure is more than 190 psi.

During high speed operation, the PCM supplies a ground path for the No. 1 engine cooling fan relay. After a six second delay, the PCM supplies a ground path for the No. 2 and No. 3 cooling fan relays. The six second delay ensures the cooling fan electrical load will not exceed the capacity of the system. During high speed operation, both coolant fans are supplied current from the 40 amp maxifuse and each cooling fan has its own ground path. The PCM will complete the ground circuit for high speed cooling fan operation anytime engine coolant temperature exceeds 235°F or A/C refrigerant pressure is more than 275 psi.

CATERA

This system consists of one engine coolant fan, two auxiliary coolant fans, two temperature switches, an A/C refrigerant pressure switch, seven fan control relays and a coolant fan resistor.

Battery voltage is supplied to the auxiliary water pump whenever the ignition switch is in the On position. When coolant temperature reaches 212°F (100°C), the primary cooling fan temperature switch stage 1 will close, enabling the Engine Control Module (ECM) relay K48 and the fan control relay K26 to energize. When the ECM relay K48 energizes, battery voltage is applied to the ECM cooling blower. When fan control K26 energizes, battery voltage is applied to the No. 1 and No. 2 auxiliary cooling fans, causing the fans to operate at half speed. The fan control relay K26 will also supply battery voltage to the engine coolant fan through the engine coolant fan resistor. The resistor will cause the engine coolant fan to operate at half speed. The fan control relay K26 will supply battery voltage to the timing control pump through the normally closed contacts of the auxiliary water pump relay K22. This allows the timing control pump to operate. The primary cooling fan temperature switch stage No. 1 contacts will open when the coolant temperature reaches 203°F (95°C). This will turn off all three coolant fans, the ECM blower and the timing control pump, unless the A/C is on.

If the ignition switch is in the OFF position and the coolant temperature is above 212°F (100°C), both auxiliary fans, engine coolant fan and timing control pump will remain on until coolant temperature drops below 203°F (95°C).

CENTURY & REGAL

The engine coolant fan motors receive power from maxifuses located in the underhood electrical center.

During low speed fan operation, the PCM supplies a ground path for the No. 1 Cool Fan relay. This energizes the relay coil, closes the fan relay contacts and supplies current to the primary cooling fan. The ground path for the primary is through the No. 2 Cool Fan relay and secondary fan motor. This results in a series circuit with both fans running at low speed.

To operate the fans at high speed, the PCM first supplies a ground path for the No. 1 Cool Fan relay, then after a three second delay the PCM supplies a ground circuit for the No. 2 and No. 3 Cool Fan relays. This results in a parallel circuit with both fan running at high speed.

CORVETTE

The PCM controls low speed operation by providing a ground path for the Cool Fan 1 relay. This closes the relay switch and allows current to flow from the battery, through the switch to the lefthand cooling fan. The ground circuit for the lefthand fan motor runs through the Cool Fan 3 relay to the righthand cooling fan. This creates a series circuit with both fans running at low speed.

The PCM controls high speed fan operation by providing a ground path for Cool Fan 1, Cool Fan 2 and Cool Fan 3 relays. Providing separate ground paths for the relays creates a parallel circuit, which allows both fans to run at high speed.

CUTLASS & MALIBU

Power for the fan motors is supplied by fuses and relays in the Underhood Electrical Center (U/H BEC). The cooling fan relays are energized when current from the No. 1 and No. 2 Cool Fan fuses flows through the relay coils to ground through the PCM. The No. 1 fan control relay circuit is grounded for low speed fan operation. The No. 1 fan control relay, mode control relay and No. 2 fan control relay are all grounded for high speed fan operation.

During low speed fan operation, the PCM supplies a ground path for the No. 1 fan control relay. This closes the fan control relay contacts, allowing current to flow from the U/H BEC through the relay contacts and to the left cooling fan motor. The ground path for the lefthand cooling fan motor is through the No. 2 fan control relay and righthand cooling fan motor. This results in a series circuit with both fans running at low speed.

During high speed fan operation, the PCM supplies a ground path for the No. 1 fan control relay. The PCM also supplies a ground path for the No. 2 fan control relay and the mode control relay. The No. 1 cooling fan relay is grounded through the Mode Control relay. The right fan is powered directly through the No. 2 cooling fan relay, causing both fans to run at high speed.

DEVILLE, ELDORADO & SEVILLE

The PCM will command low speed fan operation when engine temperature is in excess of 229°F, transaxle fluid temperature is greater than 302°F, when A/C is requested, or after the vehicle is shutoff and coolant temperature is more than 304°F and system voltage is more than 12 volts the fans will stay on for approximately three minutes.

The PCM will command high fan speed operation when engine coolant temperature is in excess of 234°F, transaxle fluid temperature is greater than 304°F, or when certain DTCs are set.

To operate the fans at low speed the PCM provides a ground path for the Cooling Fan No. 1 relay. This allows current to flow through both cooling fans in a series circuit to ground.

To operate the fans at high speed the PCM provides a ground path for all three cooling fan relays. This changes the circuit to parallel and operates both fans at high speed.

GRAND AM

1998

Refer to "Achieva, Cavalier, Skylark & Sunfire" for cooling fan system description.

1999-2002

Refer to "Alero" for cooling fan system description.

GRAND PRIX

The cooling fan motors receive power from maxifuses located in the underhood accessory wiring junction block.

During low speed fan operation, the PCM supplies a ground path for the Cool Fan 1 relay. This energizes the relay coil, closes the relay contacts and supplies current to the lefthand cooling fan motor. The ground path for the lefthand cooling fan motor is through the Cool Fan relay and righthand coolant fan motor. This results in a series circuit with both fans running at low speed.

To operate the fans at high speed, the PCM first supplies a ground path for the Cool Fan 1 relay. After a 3–5 second delay, the PCM supplies a ground path for the Cool Fan and Cool Fan 2 relays. The result is a parallel circuit with both fans running at high speed.

IMPALA & 2000-02 MONTE CARLO

This coolant fan system is equipped with two electric cooling fans and three fan relays which are controlled by the PCM. The relays are wired in a series/parallel arrangement that allows the PCM to operate both fans together at low or high speed.

The PCM controls low fan speed operation by grounding the control circuit for Cool Fan No. 1 relay. The relay supplies current to the No. 1 fan motor. The ground path for the No. 1 fan motor is through the Cool Fan No. 2 relay and the No. 2 fan motor. This results in a series circuit which operates both fans at low speed. The PCM operates the cooling fans at low speed whenever engine coolant temperature exceeds 223°F, A/C operation is requested and ambient temperature is greater than 50°F, A/C refrigerant pressure is greater than 190 psi, or the engine is shutoff and coolant temperature is more than 284.°

To control high speed fan operation, the PCM grounds the control circuit for the Cool Fan No. 1 relay. Then after a three second delay, the PCM grounds the control circuit for Cool Fan No. 2 and No. 3 relays. When the Cool Fan No. 2 relay is energized, both the fans have their own ground path creating a parallel circuit. This parallel circuit causes both fans to operate at high speed. The PCM operates the cooling fans at high speed whenever engine coolant temperature exceeds 230°F, A/C refrigerant pressure exceeds 240 psi.

INTRIGUE

This coolant fan system is equipped with two electric cooling fans and three fan relays which are controlled by the PCM. The relays are wired in a series/parallel arrangement that allows the PCM to operate both fans together at low or high speed.

The PCM controls low fan speed operation by grounding the control circuit for fan relay No. 1. The relay supplies current to the No. 1 fan motor. The ground path for the No. 1 fan motor is through the No. 2 fan relay and the No. 2 fan motor. This results in a series circuit which operates both fans at low speed. The PCM operates the cooling fans at low speed whenever engine coolant temperature exceeds 229°F, A/C operation is requested, or the engine is shutoff and coolant temperature is more than 304°F and system voltage is more than 12 volts. The PCM will shutoff the fans whenever coolant temperature drops below 216°F.

To control high speed fan operation, the PCM grounds the control circuit for the No. 1 fan relay. Then after a three second delay, the PCM grounds the control circuit for the No. 2 and No. 3 fan relays. When the No. 2 fan relay is energized, both the fans have their own ground path creating a parallel circuit. This parallel circuit causes both fans to operate at high speed. The PCM operates the cooling fans at high speed whenever engine coolant temperature exceeds 234°F, A/C refrigerant pressure exceeds 240 psi, or certain Diagnostic Trouble Codes (DTC)s are set.

LUMINA & 1998-99 MONTE CARLO

Power for the cooling fan motors is supplied through a fusible link at the battery junction block. The cooling fans are energized when current flows from the PCM fuse in the No. 1 underhood electrical center and the Fan fuse in the No. 2 underhood electrical center through the relay coils to ground through the PCM.

During low speed fan operation, the PCM supplies a ground path for the No. 1 engine cooling fan relay. This closes the fan relay contacts and allows current to flow to the left engine coolant fan. The ground path for the left cooling fan is the No. 3 cooling fan relay. This results in a series circuit with both cooling fans running at low speed.

During high speed fan operation, the PCM supplies a ground path for the No. 1, No. 2 and No. 3 engine cooling fan relays. With all three relays closed, each fan is supplied current from the battery junction block and has its own ground path.

METRO

Radiator Fan

When ignition switch is in On position, system voltage is applied through ignition fuse to radiator fan switch. Fan switch closes when engine coolant temperature reaches 208°F. With fan switch closed, voltage is applied to radiator fan motor. Since the fan motor is permanently grounded, fan operates as soon as voltage is applied. When temperature falls below 199°F, fan switch opens and voltage to fan motor is interrupted.

A/C Condenser Fan

When ignition switch is in On position, system voltage is applied to dual pressure switch through heater fuse on vehicles equipped with automatic transaxle, or ignition fuse on vehicles equipped with manual transaxle. With dual pressure switch closed, voltage is applied to A/C clutch relay. A/C clutch relay is energized when A/C amplifier grounds coil of relay. With A/C clutch relay energized, voltage is applied through A/C fuse and closed contacts of A/C clutch relay to coil of A/C condenser fan relay. Since A/C condenser fan relay is permanently grounded, relay energizes, contacts close, and voltage is applied to condenser fan. Since condenser fan is permanently grounded, an operates as soon voltage is applied.

PARK AVENUE

Power for the cooling fan motors is supplied by the Cool Fan No. 1 and Cool Fan No. 2 Maxi fuses.

During low speed fan operation, the PCM supplies a ground path for the No. 1 Cool Fan relay through the low speed fan control circuit. This energizes the relay coil, closes the relay contacts and supplies current to the primary cooling fan. The ground path for the primary cooling fan is through the No. 2 Cool Fan (series/parallel) relay and secondary cooling fan motor. This results in a series circuit with both fans running at low speed.

To operate the cooling fans at high speed, the PCM first supplies a ground path for No. 1 Cool Fan relay. After a three second delay the PCM supplies a ground path for the No. 2 and No. 3 Cool Fan relays. During high speed operation, both the primary and secondary cooling fans are supplied current through their respective maxifuse and each fan has its own ground.

PRIZM

When the ignition switch is in either the Run or Start positions, system voltage is applied to the coils of the main engine relay and to fan relay 1. Because the main relay is grounded at G108, the relay is energized, its contacts close, and battery voltage is applied through the relay and the radiator fan fusible link to the contacts of fan relay 1.

When engine coolant temperature is below 194°F, the cooling fan temperature switch provides a ground for relay 1, the relay energizes and its contacts are pulled open.

Whenever engine coolant temperature reaches or exceeds 194°F, the cooling fan temperature switch opens, fan relay 1 is de-energized, its contacts close, and system voltage is applied through the relay to the cooling fan motor. Since the fan motor is grounded at G108, it start to operate as soon as voltage is applied.

When engine coolant temperature drops below 194°F, the cooling fan temperature switch closes to ground, fan relay 1 is energized the relay contacts are pulled open and system voltage is no longer applied to the fan motor.

RIVIERA

The No. 1 coolant fan motor receives power from a 40 amp maxifuse. The No. 2 coolant fan motor receives power from a 30 amp maxifuse. Both maxifuses are located in the underhood electrical center.

To operate the fans at low speed, the PCM supplies a ground path for the No. 1 cooling fan relay through the low speed fan control circuit. This energizes the relay coil and supplies current to the primary cooling fan. The ground path for the primary cooling fan is through the No. 2 cooling fan relay and secondary cooling fan motor. This results in a series circuit with both fans running at low speed.

To run the fans at high speed, the PCM first supplies a ground path for the No. 1 cooling fan relay. After a three second delay, the PCM supplies a ground path for the No. 2 and No. 3 cooling fan relays. During high speed fan operation, both the primary and secondary cooling fans are supplied current through their maxifuses and each has its own ground.

TROUBLESHOOTING

EXCEPT METRO

1. Check for open fuses.
2. Check for open fusible links.
3. Check for corrosion on cooling fan and cooling fan relay connectors.
4. Check for clean and tight grounds.

METRO

Preliminary Check

1. Check A/C fuse for open.
2. Check IG fuse for open.
3. Check fusible link "B"for open.
4. Check radiator fan fuse for open.
5. Check engine coolant level.
6. Check A/C system for proper refrigerant charge.
7. Check grounds G101, G104, and G201 are clean and tight.

System Check

1. Run engine until engine coolant temperature reaches 208°F. Cooling fan should run.
2. Turn A/C switch to On position. A/C compressor clutch should engage and a/c condenser fan motor should run.
3. Turn A/C switch to Off position. A/C compressor clutch should disengage and A/C condenser fan motor should stop.

SYSTEM DIAGNOSIS & TESTING

Wiring Diagrams

ACHIEVA, CAVALIER, SKYLARK, SUNFIRE & 1998 GRAND AM

Refer to **Fig. 1** for wiring diagrams.

CUTLASS & MALIBU

Refer to **Fig. 2** for wiring diagrams.

ALERO & 1999-2002 GRAND AM

Refer to **Fig. 3** for wiring diagrams.

AURORA

Refer to **Figs. 4 and 5** for wiring diagrams.

BONNEVILLE, EIGHTY EIGHT, LESABRE, LSS & REGENCY

Refer to **Figs. 6 and 7** for wiring diagrams.

CAMARO & FIREBIRD

Refer to **Figs. 8 and 9** for wiring diagrams.

CATERA

Refer to **Figs. 10 and 11** for wiring diagrams.

CENTURY & REGAL

Refer to **Fig. 12** for wiring diagrams.

CORVETTE

Refer to **Fig. 13** for wiring diagrams.

DEVILLE, ELDORADO & SEVILLE

Refer to **Figs. 14 and 15** for wiring diagrams.

GRAND PRIX

Refer to **Figs. 16 and 17** for wiring diagrams.

IMPALA & MONTE CARLO

Refer to **Figs. 18 through 20** for wiring diagrams.

INTRIGUE

Refer to **Figs. 21 and 22** for wiring diagrams.

LUMINA

Refer to "Impala & Monte Carlo" for Lumina wiring diagrams.

METRO

Refer to **Fig. 23** for wiring diagrams.

PARK AVENUE

Refer to **Fig. 24** for wiring diagrams.

PRIZM

Refer to **Figs. 25 and 26** for wiring diagrams.

RIVIERA

Refer to **Fig. 27** for wiring diagrams.

Diagnostic Aids

If the temperature light or gauge indicated overheating, but no boil over is detected, the gauge or light should be checked. The gauge accuracy can also be checked using a scan tool to compare the coolant temperature reading with the gauge reading.

If the engine is actually overheating, and the gauge indicates overheating, but the cooling fan is not operating, the Engine Coolant Temperature (ETC) sensor may have shifted out of calibration and should be replaced.

If the engine is overheating and the cooling fan is operating, the cooling system should be checked.

Diagnostic Tests

ACHIEVA, CAVALIER, SKYLARK & SUNFIRE

Refer to **Fig. 28** for diagnostic procedures. Refer to "Diagnostic Aids" as previously outlined when referenced by diagnostic tests.

ALERO, CUTLASS & MALIBU

Refer to **Figs. 29 through 31** for diagnostic procedure. Refer to "Diagnostic Aids" as previously outlined when referenced by diagnostic tests.

AURORA

1998-99

Refer to **Figs. 32 through 37** for diagnostic procedures. Refer to "Diagnostic Aids" as previously outlined when referenced by diagnostic tests.

2001-02

Refer to **Figs. 38 through 40,** for diagnostic procedures. Refer to "Diagnostic Aids" as previously outlined when referenced by diagnostic tests.

BONNEVILLE, EIGHTY EIGHT, LESABRE, LSS, & REGENCY

1998-99

Refer to **Fig. 41** when performing diagnostic procedures. Refer to "Diagnostic Aids" as previously outlined when referenced by diagnostic tests.

2000

Refer to **Figs. 42 through 45** when performing diagnostic procedures. Refer to "Diagnostic Aids" as previously outlined when referenced by diagnostic tests.

2001-02

Refer to **Figs. 46 through 48** when performing diagnostic procedures. Refer to "Diagnostic Aids" as previously outlined when referenced by diagnostic tests.

CAMARO & FIREBIRD

1998-2000

3.8L Engine

Refer to **Figs. 49 through 52,** for diagnostic procedures. Refer to "Diagnostic Aids" as previously outlined when referenced by diagnostic tests.

5.7L Engine

Refer to **Figs. 53 through 56,** for diagnostic procedures. Refer to "Diagnostic Aids" as previously outlined when referenced by diagnostic tests.

2000-01

Refer to **Figs. 57 through 59,** for diagnostic procedures. Refer to "Diagnostic Aids" as previously outlined when referenced by diagnostic tests.

CATERA

1998

Refer to **Figs. 60 through 69,** when performing diagnostic procedures on these systems. Refer to "Diagnostic Aids" as previously outlined when referenced by diagnostic tests.

1999

Refer to **Figs. 70 through 78,** when performing diagnostic procedures on these systems. Refer to "Diagnostic Aids" as previously outlined when referenced by diagnostic tests.

2000-01

Refer to **Figs. 79 through 86,** when performing diagnostic procedures on these systems. Refer to "Diagnostic Aids" as previously outlined when referenced by diagnostic tests.

CENTURY & REGAL

1998-2000

Refer to **Figs. 87 through 90,** when performing diagnostic procedures on these systems. Refer to "Diagnostic Aids" as previously outlined when referenced by diagnostic tests.

2001-02

Refer to **Figs. 91 through 93,** when performing diagnostic procedures on these systems. Refer to "Diagnostic Aids" as previously outlined when referenced by diagnostic tests.

CORVETTE

1998-2000

Refer to **Figs. 94 through 97,** for diagnostic procedures. Refer to "Diagnostic Aids" as previously outlined when referenced by diagnostic tests.

2001-02

Refer to **Figs. 98 through 100** for diagnostic procedures. Refer to "Diagnostic Aids" as previously outlined when referenced by diagnostic tests.

DEVILLE, ELDORADO & SEVILLE

1998-99

Refer to **Figs. 101 through 106,** when performing diagnostic procedures on these systems. Refer to "Diagnostic Aids" as previously outlined when referenced by diagnostic tests.

2000

Refer to **Figs. 107 through 116,** when performing diagnostic procedures. Refer to "Diagnostic Aids" as previously outlined when referenced by diagnostic tests.

2001-02

Refer to **Figs. 117 through 119** when performing diagnostic procedures. Refer to "Diagnostic Aids" as previously outlined when referenced by diagnostic tests.

GRAND AM

1998

Refer to "Achieva, Cavalier, Skylark & Sunfire" for diagnostic procedures.

1999-2002

Refer to "Alero, Cutlass & Malibu" for diagnostic procedures.

GRAND PRIX

1998-99

Refer to **Fig. 120** when performing diagnostic procedures on these systems. Refer to "Diagnostic Aids" as previously outlined when referenced by diagnostic tests.

2000

Refer to **Figs. 121 through 124,** when performing diagnostic procedures on these systems. Refer to "Diagnostic Aids" as previously outlined when referenced by diagnostic tests.

2001-02

Refer to **Figs. 125 through 127** when performing diagnostic procedures on these systems. Refer to "Diagnostic Aids" as previously outlined when referenced by diagnostic tests.

IMPALA, LUMINA & 1998-99 MONTE CARLO

1998-99

Refer to **Fig. 128** when performing diagnostic procedures on these systems. Refer to "Diagnostic Aids" as previously outlined when referenced by diagnostic tests.

2000

Lumina

Refer to **Figs. 129 through 132,** when performing diagnostic procedures on these systems. Refer to "Diagnostic Aids" as previously outlined when referenced by diagnostic tests.

Impala & Monte Carlo

Refer to **Figs. 133 through 136,** when performing diagnostic procedures on these systems. Refer to "Diagnostic Aids" as previously outlined when referenced by diagnostic tests.

2001

Impala & Monte Carlo

Refer to **Figs. 137 through 139** when performing diagnostic procedures on these systems. Refer to "Diagnostic Aids" as previously outlined when referenced by diagnostic tests.

Lumina

Refer to "2000" for 2001 vehicle tests.

2002

Refer to "2001" for 2002 vehicle tests.

INTRIGUE

1998

Refer to **Fig. 140** for diagnostic procedures. Refer to "Diagnostic Aids" as previously outlined when referenced by diagnostic tests.

1999-2000

Refer to **Figs. 141 through 146,** for diagnostic procedures. Refer to "Diagnostic Aids" as previously outlined when referenced by diagnostic tests.

2001-02

Refer to **Figs. 147 through 149** for diagnostic procedures. Refer to "Diagnostic Aids" as previously outlined when referenced by diagnostic tests.

METRO

Refer to **Fig. 150** when performing diagnostic procedures. Refer to "Diagnostic Aids" as previously outlined when referenced by diagnostic tests.

PARK AVENUE

1998-2000

Refer to **Figs. 151 through 154** when performing diagnostic procedures.

2001-02

Refer to **Figs. 155 through 157** when performing diagnostic procedures.

PRIZM

1998-99

Refer to **Figs. 158 through 162** when performing diagnostic procedures. Refer to "Diagnostic Aids" as previously outlined when referenced by diagnostic tests.

2000-02

Refer to **Figs. 163 through 166** when performing diagnostic procedures. Refer to "Diagnostic Aids" as previously outlined when referenced by diagnostic tests.

RIVIERA

Refer to **Fig. 167** for diagnostic procedures.

COMPONENT REPLACEMENT

Cooling Fan

ACHIEVA & SKYLARK

1. Remove fan attaching bolts, then disconnect fan motor electrical connector.
2. Remove fan assembly.
3. Reverse procedure to install.

ALERO

1. Remove A/C line attaching bolt.
2. Remove four upper fan attaching bolts.
3. Raise and support vehicle.
4. Remove four lower fan attaching bolts.
5. Disconnect electrical connector.
6. Remove fan from shroud.
7. Reverse procedure to install.

AURORA & RIVIERA

1. Disconnect wiring harness from fan motor and fan frame.
2. Remove fan guard and hose support as needed.
3. Remove fan assembly from radiator support.
4. Reverse procedure to install.

BONNEVILLE & REGENCY

1. Remove harness from fan motor and fan frame.
2. Remove fan guard and hose support if necessary, then frame to radiator support attaching bolts.
3. Remove fan and frame assembly.
4. Reverse procedure to install.

CAMARO & FIREBIRD

1. Remove air cleaner top.
2. Disconnect wire harness.
3. Remove cooling fan to radiator support bolts.
4. Remove cooling fan assembly.
5. Reverse procedure to install.

CATERA

1. Remove secondary air cutoff bracket bolts, then bracket from cooling fan housing.
2. Remove resonance chamber.
3. Release upper radiator covers self locking tabs.
4. Remove upper radiator covers attaching screws, then covers.
5. Disconnect primary fan motor and primary fan cooling switch electrical connectors.
6. Remove auxiliary water pump from primary fan housing.
7. Remove upper transmission oil cooler fittings.
8. Loosen lower transmission cooler fittings.
9. Remove fan housing bolts, then fan housing from vehicle.
10. Reverse procedure to install.

CAVALIER & SUNFIRE

1. Raise and support vehicle, then remove cooling fan mount bolt.
2. Disconnect wiring harness connector from fan motor.
3. Remove cooling fan assembly by pulling out through bottom of vehicle.
4. Reverse procedure to install.

CENTURY

1. Remove air cleaner and resonator assembly.
2. Disconnect cooling fan electrical connector.
3. Remove cooling fan mounting bolts and the fan.
4. Reverse procedure to install.

CORVETTE

1. Raise and support vehicle, then remove front stabilizer bar bolts.
2. Position front stabilizer bar downward.
3. Disconnect cooling fan motor electrical connectors.
4. Remove wiring harness from fan shrouds.
5. Remove cooling fan assembly mounting bolts.
6. Remove cooling fan assembly from vehicle.
7. Reverse procedure to install.

CUTLASS & MALIBU

1. Remove four fan attaching bolts, then disconnect fan motor electrical connector.
2. Remove fan from shroud.
3. Reverse procedure to install.

DEVILLE

1. Raise and support vehicle.
2. Disconnect fan electrical connectors.
3. Remove fan to lower cradle attaching screws.
4. Lower vehicle.
5. For right fan, remove A/C accumulator from bracket and position out of the way.
6. Remove air cleaner intake duct.
7. Remove fan to upper radiator mounting panel attaching screws.
8. Remove upper radiator mounting panel.
9. Remove cooling fan(s).
10. Reverse procedure to install.

EIGHTY EIGHT & LSS

1. Remove wiring harness from fan motor and fan frame.
2. Remove fan guard and hose support as necessary.
3. Remove fan assembly from radiator support.
4. Reverse procedure to install.

ELDORADO & SEVILLE

1. **On front cooling fan,** proceed as follows:
   a. Remove plastic radiator cover.
   b. Disconnect fan electrical connector.
   c. Remove right headlamp bracket.
   d. Remove three bolts and cooling fan from vehicle.
2. **On rear cooling fan,** proceed as follows:
   a. Remove upper engine to radiator support torque strut.
   b. Disconnect fan electrical connector.
   c. Disconnect oil cooler bracket from fan.
   d. Remove two upper and lower bolts and fan from vehicle.
3. **On both fans,** reverse procedure to install.

GRAND AM

1998

Refer to "Achieva & Skylark" for cooling fan replacement procedure.

1999–2002

Refer to "Alero" for cooling fan replacement procedure.

GRAND PRIX & REGAL

1. Remove air cleaner assembly.
2. Remove wiring harness from fan motor(s) and fan frame(s).
3. Remove fan frame mounting bolts.
4. Remove fan assembly.
5. Reverse procedure to install.

IMPALA, LUMINA & MONTE CARLO

1. Remove air cleaner assembly.
2. Disconnect wiring harness from fan motor(s) and fan frame(s).
3. Remove fan mounting bolts and fan assembly.
4. Reverse procedure to install

METRO

1. Drain cooling system and disconnect upper radiator hose from radiator.
2. Disconnect fan motor electrical connector.
3. Raise and support vehicle, then remove one lower mounting bolt from fan shroud.
4. Lower vehicle and remove two upper cooling fan mounting bolts, then remove fan from vehicle.
5. Reverse procedure to install.

PARK AVENUE & LESABRE

1. Disconnect electrical connector from fan motor and frame.
2. Remove frame to radiator support attaching bolts.
3. Remove fan assembly.
4. Reverse procedure to install.

PRIZM

1. Drain engine coolant from radiator.
2. Disconnect oxygen sensor electrical connector.
3. Remove engine coolant recovery reservoir cap and hoses, then tank.
4. Remove upper radiator hose at radiator.
5. Remove cooling fan mounting bolts, then fan assembly.
6. Reverse procedure to install.

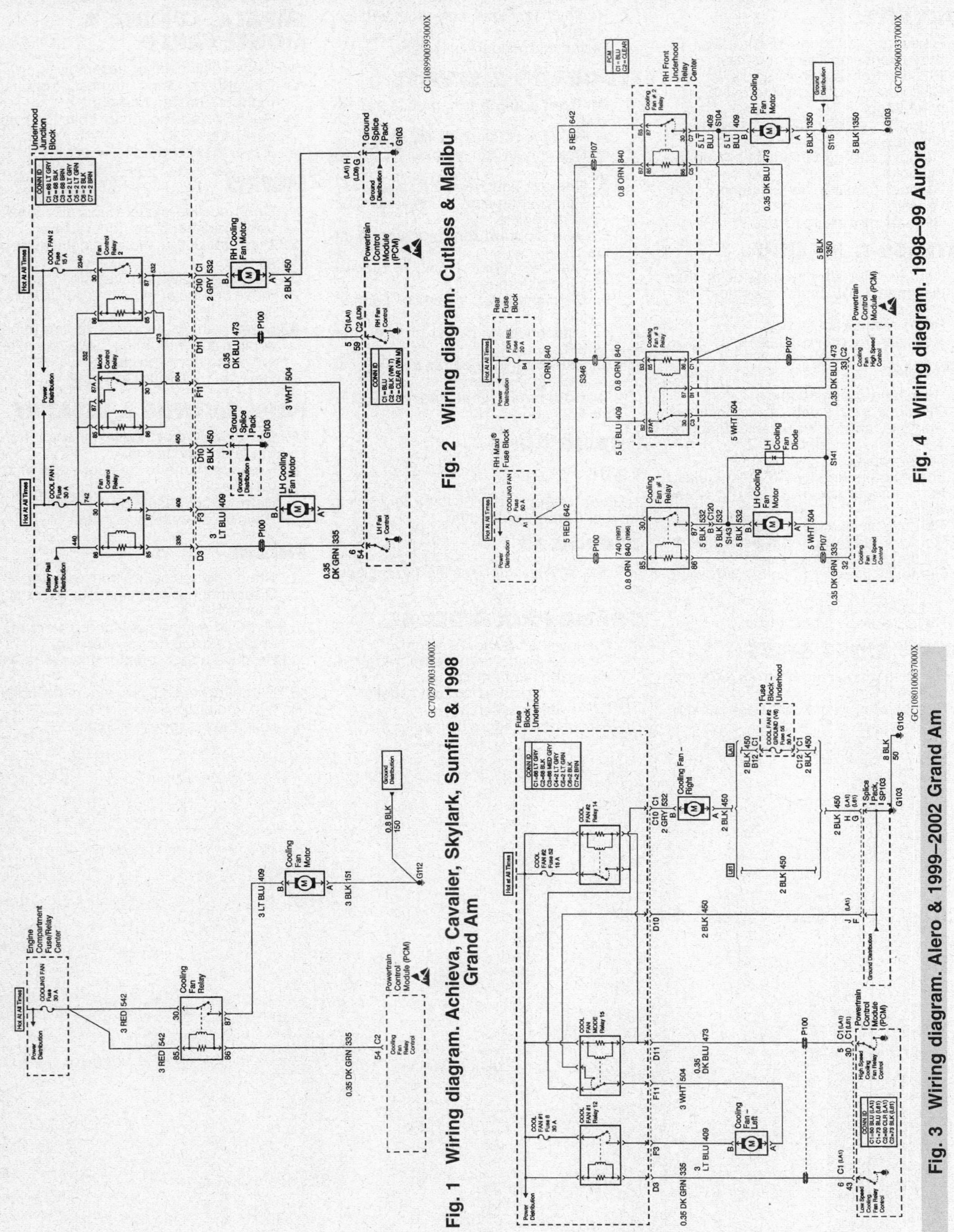

Fig. 1 Wiring diagram. Achieva, Cavalier, Skylark, Sunfire & 1998 Grand Am

Fig. 2 Wiring diagram. Cutlass & Malibu

Fig. 3 Wiring diagram. Alero & 1999–2002 Grand Am

Fig. 4 Wiring diagram. 1998–99 Aurora

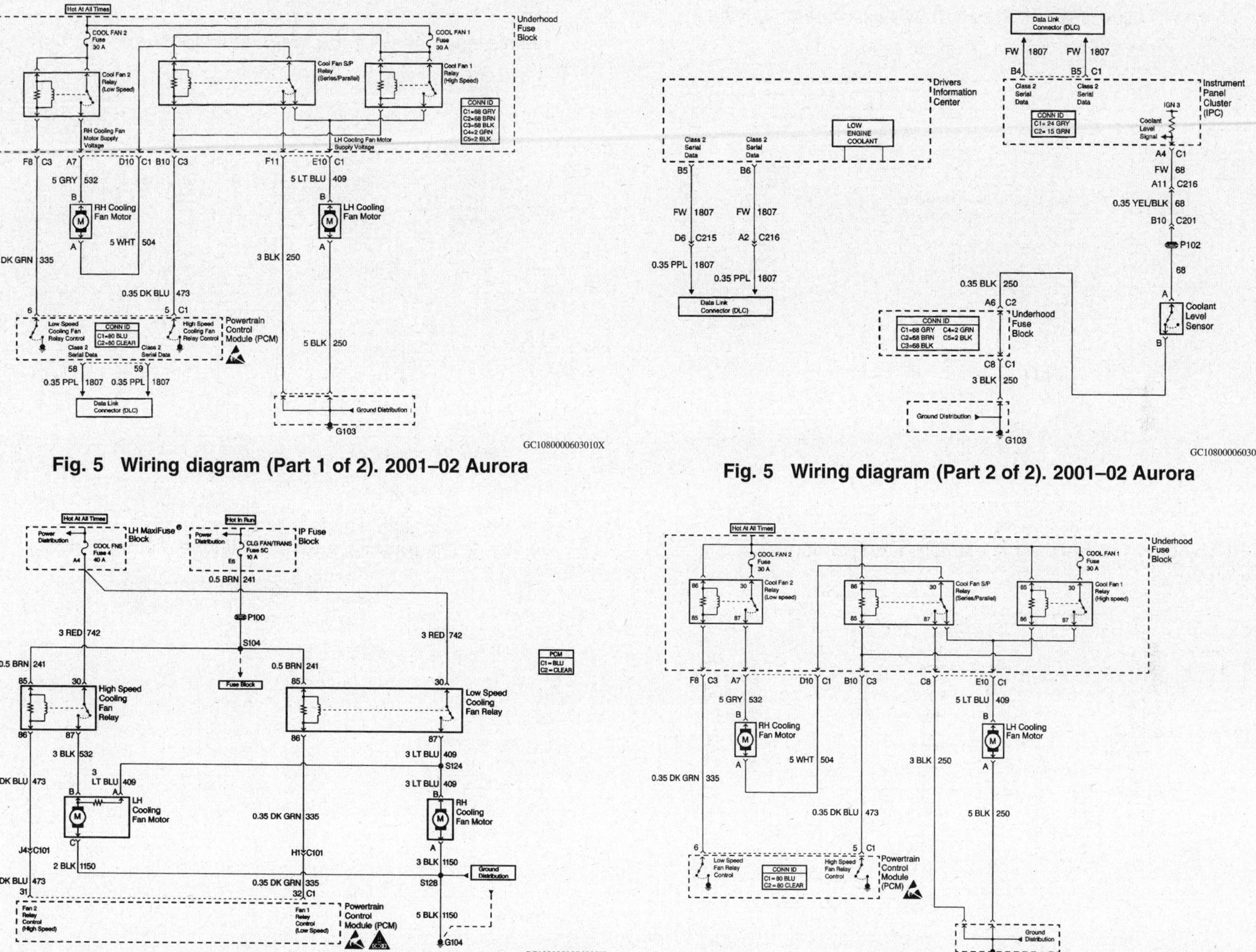

GC1080000603010X

Fig. 5 Wiring diagram (Part 1 of 2). 2001–02 Aurora

GC1080000603020X

Fig. 5 Wiring diagram (Part 2 of 2). 2001–02 Aurora

GC1089800376000X

Fig. 6 Wiring diagram. 1998–99 Bonneville, Eighty Eight, LeSabre, LSS & Regency

GC1080000438000X

Fig. 7 Wiring diagram. 2000–02 Bonneville & LeSabre

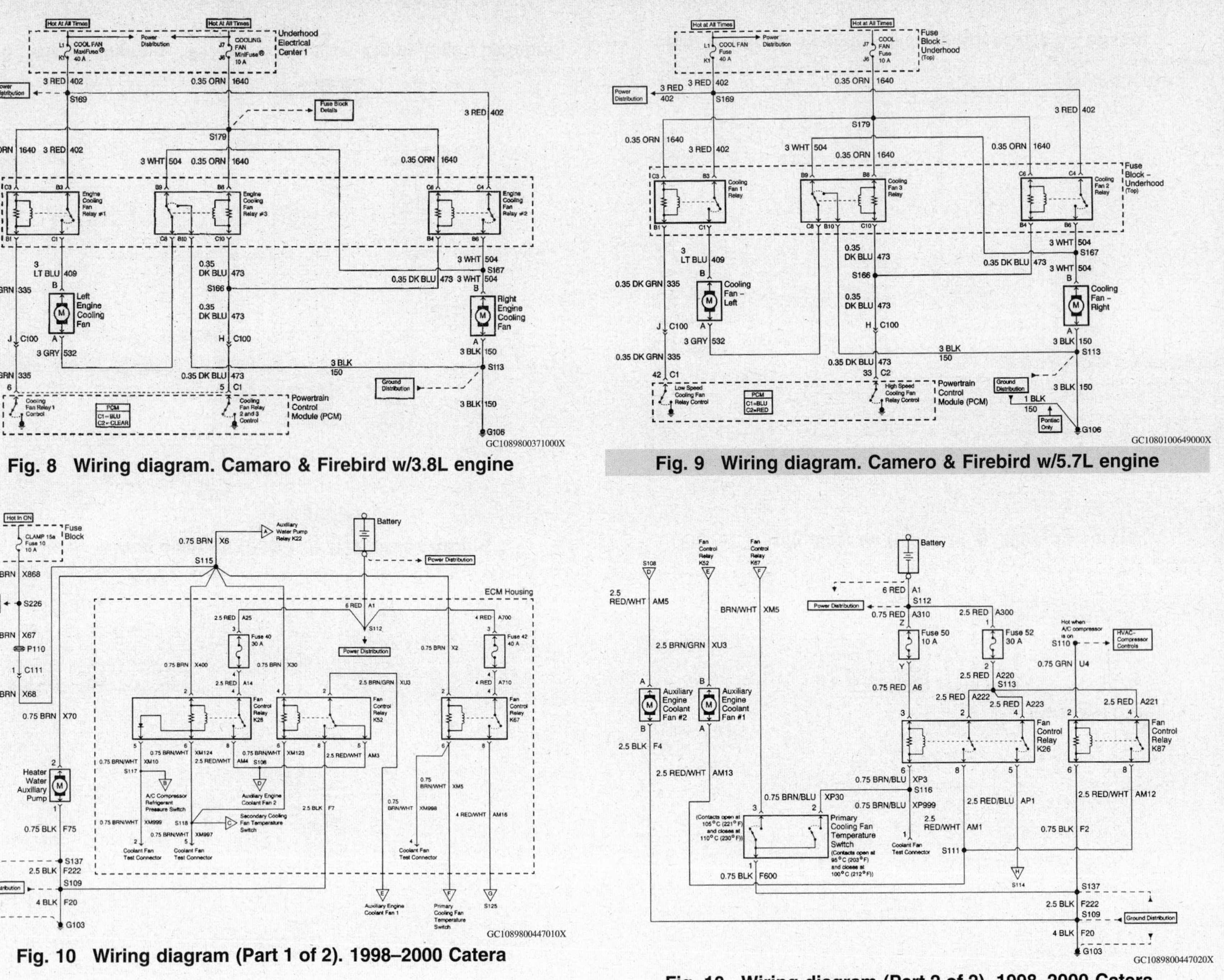

Fig. 8 Wiring diagram. Camaro & Firebird w/3.8L engine

Fig. 9 Wiring diagram. Camero & Firebird w/5.7L engine

Fig. 10 Wiring diagram (Part 1 of 2). 1998–2000 Catera

Fig. 10 Wiring diagram (Part 2 of 2). 1998–2000 Catera

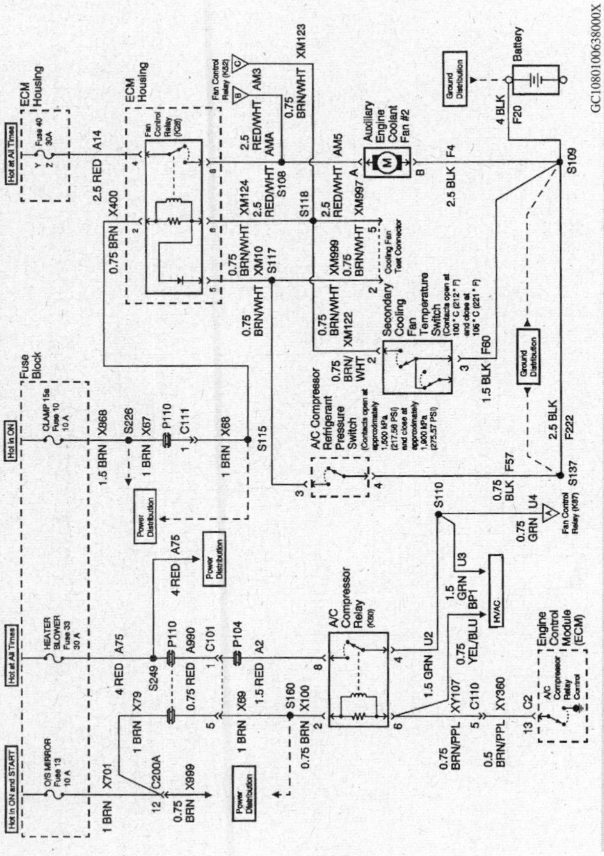

Fig. 11 Wiring diagram. 2001 Catera

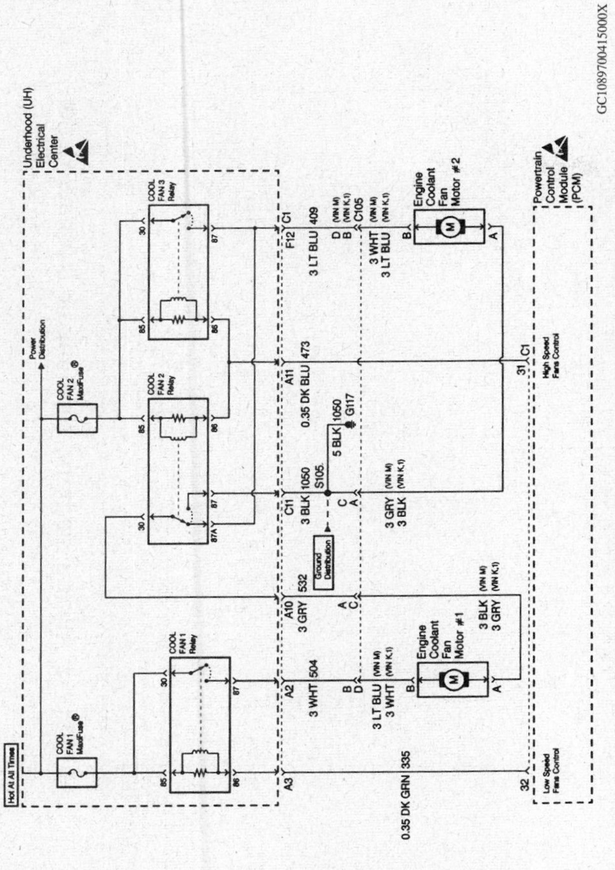

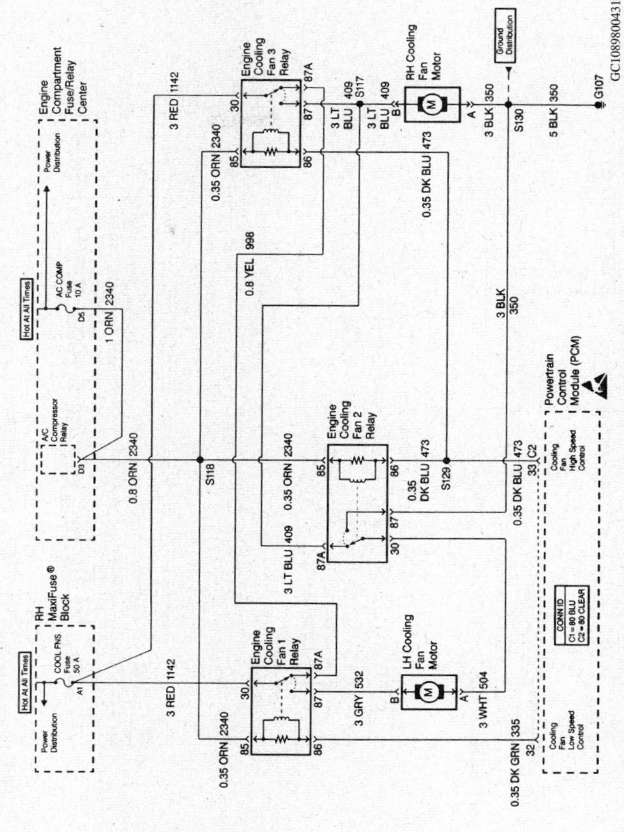

Fig. 12 Wiring diagram. Century & Regal

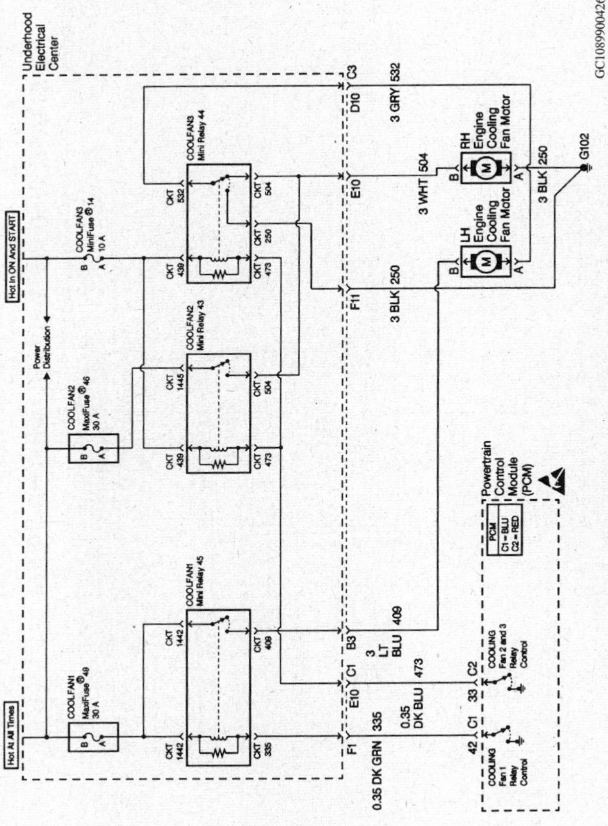

Fig. 13 Wiring diagram. Corvette

Fig. 14 Wiring diagram. 1998–99 DeVille & 1998–2002 Eldorado

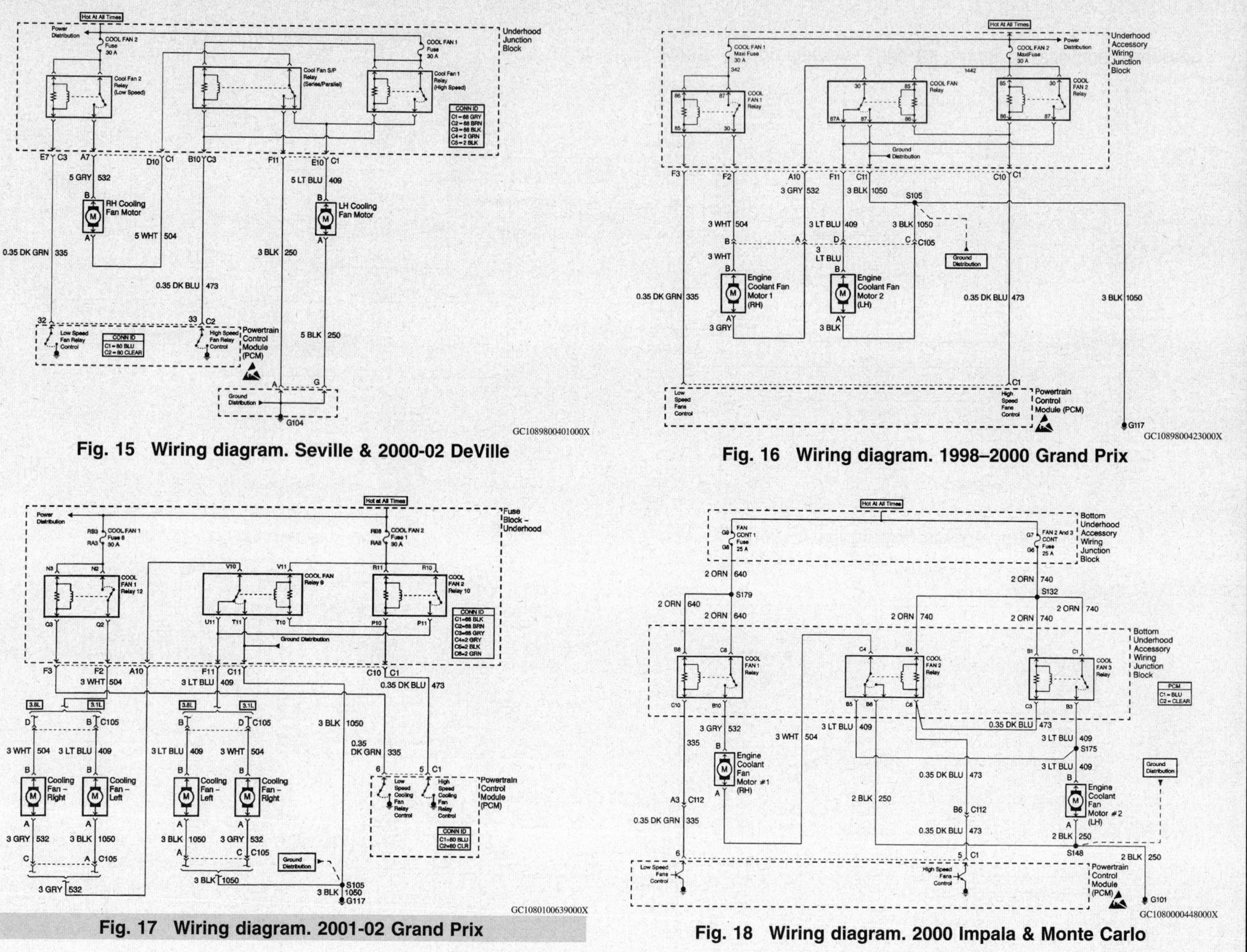

Fig. 15 Wiring diagram. Seville & 2000-02 DeVille

Fig. 16 Wiring diagram. 1998–2000 Grand Prix

Fig. 17 Wiring diagram. 2001-02 Grand Prix

Fig. 18 Wiring diagram. 2000 Impala & Monte Carlo

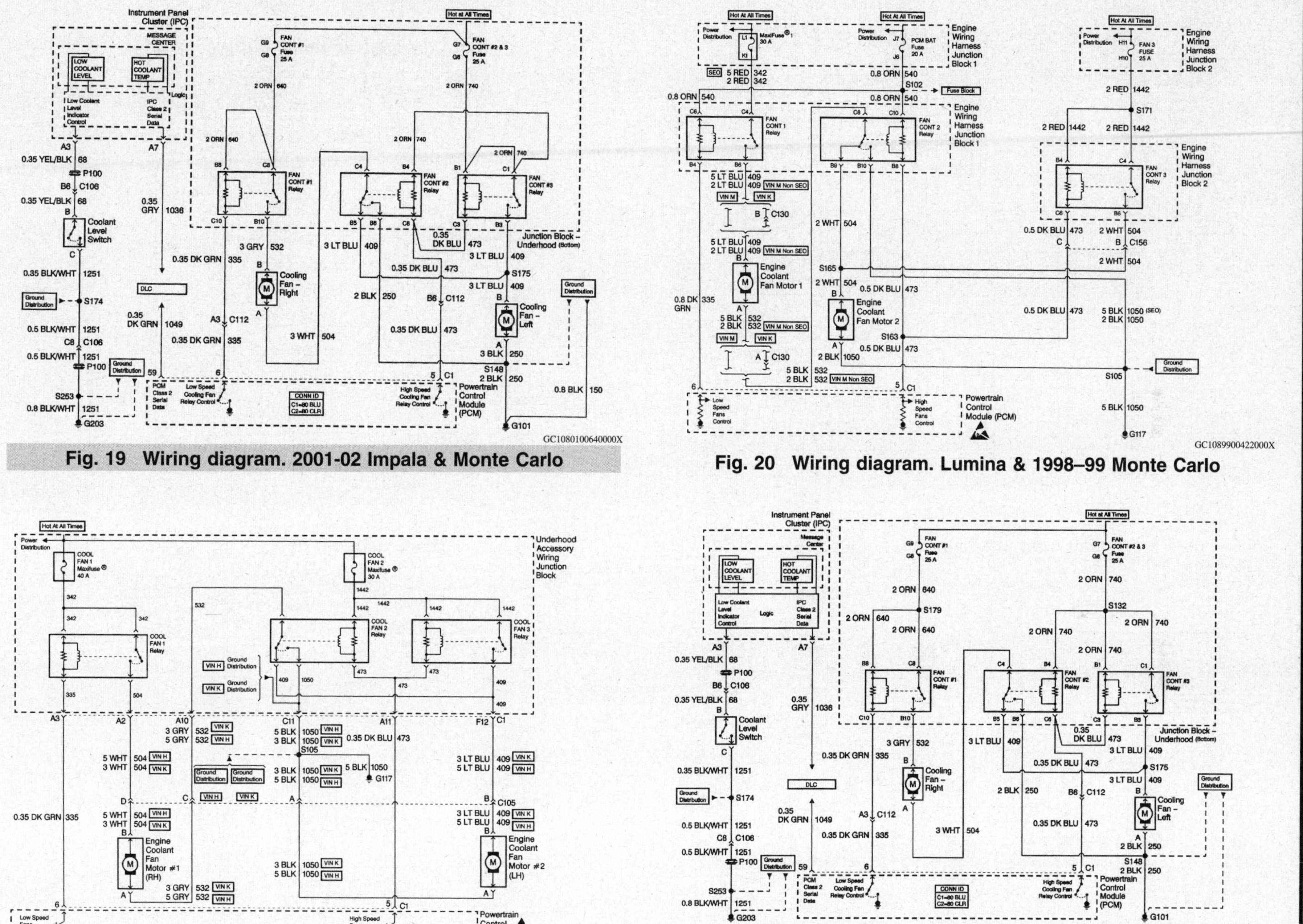

Fig. 19 Wiring diagram. 2001-02 Impala & Monte Carlo

Fig. 20 Wiring diagram. Lumina & 1998–99 Monte Carlo

Fig. 21 Wiring diagram. 1998–2000 Intrigue

Fig. 22 Wiring diagram. 2001-02 Intrigue

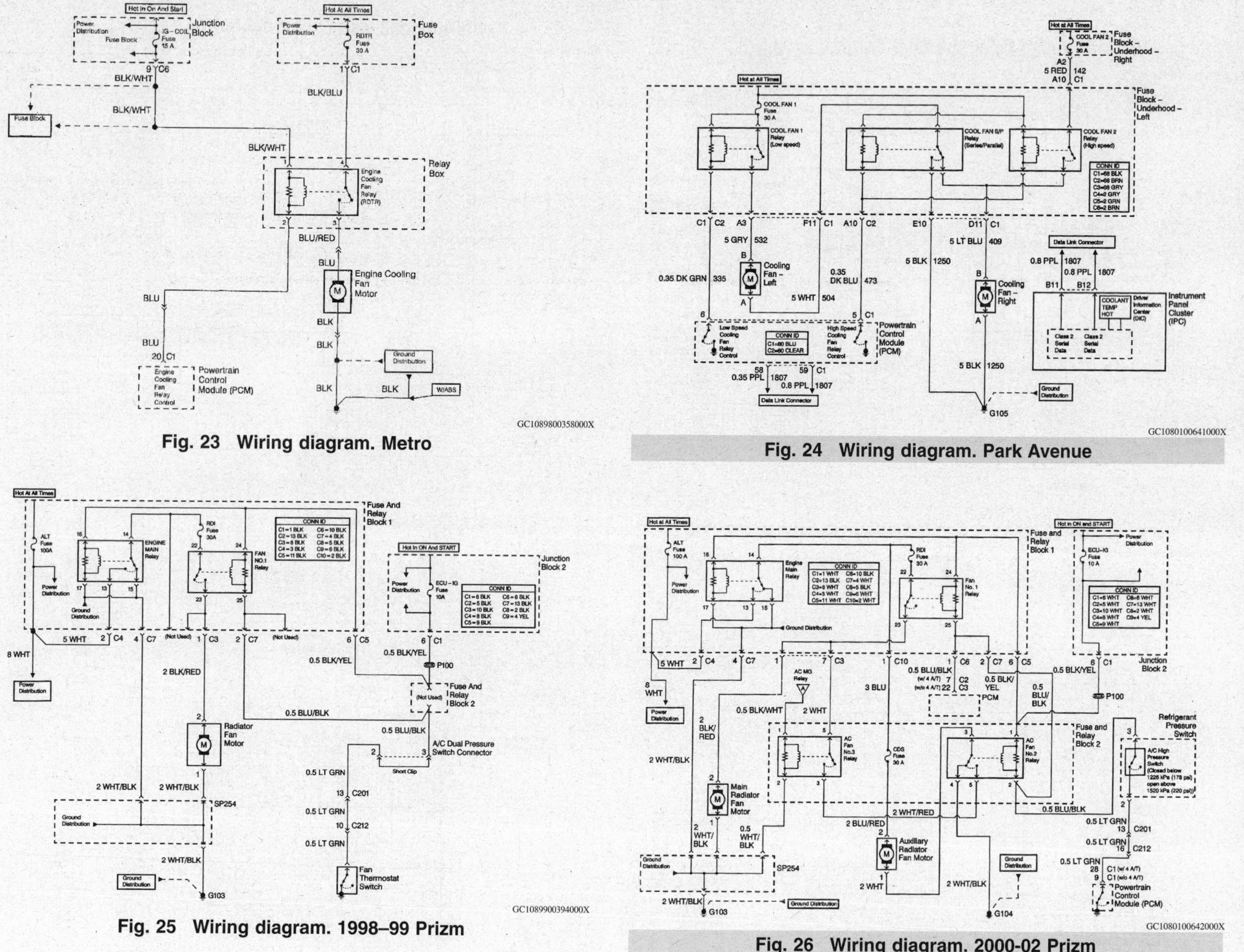

Fig. 23 Wiring diagram. Metro

Fig. 24 Wiring diagram. Park Avenue

Fig. 25 Wiring diagram. 1998–99 Prizm

Fig. 26 Wiring diagram. 2000-02 Prizm

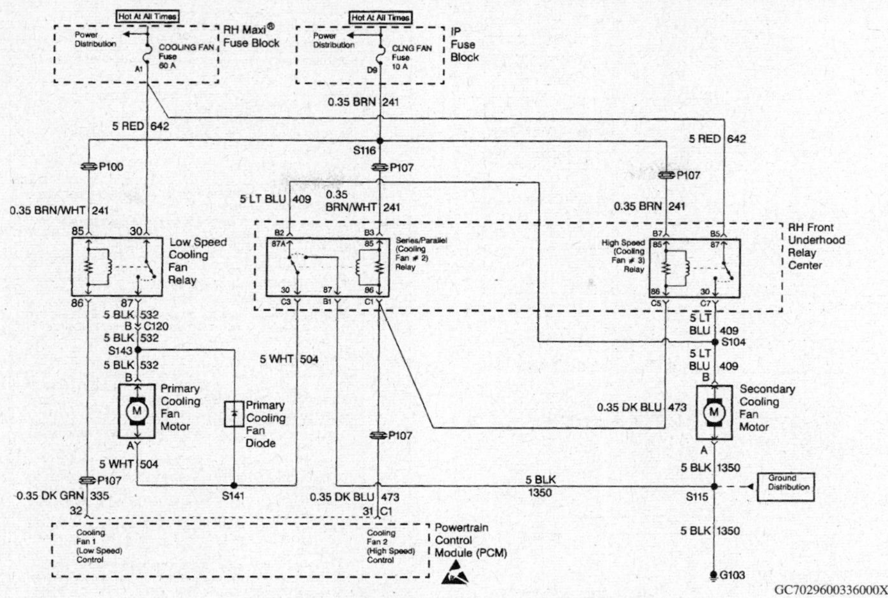

Fig. 27 Wiring diagram. Riviera

Step	Action	Value(s)	Yes	No
1	Was the Powertrain On-Board Diagnostic (OBD) System Check performed? Refer to Motor's "Domestic Engine Performance & Drivability Manual."	—	*Go to Step 2*	Go to *Powertrain OBD System Check*
2	1. Check the cooling system level. 2. Check the water pump belt condition and tension. Were any repairs necessary?	—	*Go to Step 24*	*Go to Step 3*
3	1. Turn the ignition switch ON, with the engine OFF. 2. Install a scan tool. 3. Engine coolant temperature below the specified value. Is the cooling fan OFF?	98°C (209°F)	*Go to Step 4*	*Go to Step 5*
4	Command the cooling fan relay ON. Is the cooling fan ON?	—	*Go to Step 24*	*Go to Step 6*
5	1. Turn the ignition switch OFF. 2. Disconnect the PCM connectors at the PCM. Is the cooling fan OFF?	—	*Go to Step 23*	*Go to Step 7*
6	1. Disconnect the cooling fan relay electrical connector. 2. With a test light to ground, probe the battery feed circuits. Is the test light ON for both terminals?	—	*Go to Step 8*	*Go to Step 9*
7	1. Disconnect the cooling fan relay electrical connector. 2. With a test light connected to ground, probe the cooling fan battery feed circuit. Does the test light illuminate?	—	*Go to Step 10*	*Go to Step 11*
8	Connect a jumper between the cooling fan relay battery feed and cooling fan battery feed circuits. Is the cooling fan ON?	—	*Go to Step 12*	*Go to Step 13*
9	Repair the open battery feed circuit. Is the action complete?	—	*Go to Step 24*	—
10	Repair the short to B+ in the cooling fan battery feed circuit. Is the action complete?	—	*Go to Step 24*	—
11	Connect the test light to B+ and probe the cooling fan control circuit. Does the test light illuminate?	—	*Go to Step 14*	*Go to Step 22*
12	1. With a test light connected to B+, probe the cooling fan control circuit. 2. Command the cooling fan ON. Does the test light illuminate?	—	*Go to Step 15*	*Go to Step 16*
13	1. Jumper still in place. 2. Disconnect the cooling fan electrical connector. 3. With a test light connected to ground, probe the cooling fan battery feed circuit. Does the test light illuminate?	—	*Go to Step 17*	*Go to Step 18*
14	Repair the short to ground in the cooling fan control circuit. Is the action complete?	—	*Go to Step 24*	—

GC1089600288010X

Fig. 28 Cooling fan diagnosis (Part 1 of 2). Achieva, Cavalier, Skylark, Sunfire & 1998 Grand Am

Step	Action	Value(s)	Yes	No
15	Check the terminals to the cooling fan relay and repair as necessary. Was a repair necessary?	—	*Go to Step 24*	*Go to Step 22*
16	Check the cooling fan control circuit for an open or poor connection and repair as necessary. Was a repair necessary?	—	*Go to Step 24*	*Go to Step 23*
17	Connect the test light to B+ and probe the cooling fan ground circuit. Does the test light illuminate?	—	*Go to Step 19*	*Go to Step 20*
18	Repair the open or poor connection in the cooling fan ignition feed circuit. Is the action complete?	—	*Go to Step 24*	—
19	Check for poor connections at the cooling fan electrical connector and repair as necessary. Was a repair necessary.	—	*Go to Step 24*	*Go to Step 21*
20	Repair the open or poor connection in the cooling fan ground circuit. Is the action complete?	—	*Go to Step 24*	—
21	Replace the cooling fan motor. Is the action complete?	—	*Go to Step 24*	—
22	Replace the cooling fan relay. Is the action complete?	—	*Go to Step 24*	—
23	Replace the PCM. Is the action complete?	—	*Go to Step 24*	—
24	1. Turn the ignition switch ON, with the engine OFF. 2. Command the cooling fan ON. Does the cooling turn ON when commanded?	—	System OK	*Go to Step 2*

GC1089600288020X

Fig. 28 Cooling fan diagnosis (Part 2 of 2). Achieva, Cavalier, Skylark, Sunfire & 1998 Grand Am

Step	Action	Yes	No
1	Install a scan tool. Does the scan tool power up?	Go to *Step 2*	Diagnose Data Link Communications
2	1. Turn ON the ignition, with the engine OFF. 2. Attempt to establish communication with the following control modules: • Instrument Cluster • Powertrain Control Module Does the scan tool communicate with the control modules?	Go to *Step 3*	Diagnose Data Link Communications
3	Select the powertrain control module display DTCs function on the scan tool. Does the scan tool display any DTCs?	Go to *Step 4*	Diagnose *Engine Cooling*
4	Does the scan tool display any DTCs which begin with a "U"?	Diagnose Data Link Communications	Diagnose *Trouble Code (DTC)*

GC1080100643000X

Fig. 29 Diagnostic system check. Alero, Cutlass, Malibu & 1999–2002 Grand Am

Step	Action	Yes	No
DEFINITION: One or both engine cooling fan motors run continuously in high or low speed modes.			
1	Did you perform the Engine Cooling Diagnostic System Check?	Go to *Step 2*	Go To *Diagnostic System Check -*
2	Turn ON the ignition, with the engine OFF. Are one or both cooling fans running all the time?	Go to *Step 3*	*Test for Intermittent and Poor Connections*
3	Are both cooling fans running continuously?	Go to *Step 5*	Go to *Step 4*
4	Remove the cooling fan S/P relay. Did the eng cool RH fan turn OFF?	Go to *Step 6*	Go to *Step 7*
5	Repair the short in the eng cool LH fan supply voltage circuit. Did you complete the repair?	Go to *Step 8*	—
6	Repair the short in the eng cool LH fan low circuit. Did you complete the repair?	Go to *Step 8*	—
7	Repair the short in the eng cool RH fan supply voltage circuit. Did you complete the repair?	Go to *Step 8*	—
8	Operate the system in order to verify the repair. Did you correct the condition?	System OK	Go to *Step 2*

GC1080100644000X

Fig. 30 Cooling fan always on. Alero, Cutlass, Malibu & 1999–2002 Grand Am

Step	Action	Yes	No
10	1. Leave the fused jumper wire in place of the cooling fan 1 relay. 2. Connect a 20 Amp fused jumper wire from the cooling fan motor supply voltage circuit of the eng cool RH fan electrical connector to a good ground. Does the eng cool LH fan operate in high speed?	Go to *Step 23*	Go to *Step 24*
11	1. Leave the fused jumper wire in the cooling fan 1 relay. 2. Install the cooling fan S/P relay. 3. Disconnect the eng cool LH fan electrical connector. 4. Connect a 20 Amp fused jumper wire from battery positive voltage circuit of the eng cool LH fan electrical connector to the cooling fan motor ground circuit of the eng cool LH fan electrical connector. Does the eng cool RH fan operate in high speed?	Go to *Step 19*	Go to *Step 12*
12	1. Leave the fused jumper wire in place of the cooling fan 1 relay. 2. Connect a 20 Amp fused jumper wire from battery positive voltage to the eng cool LH fan low circuit of the of the eng cool LH fan electrical connector. Does the eng cool RH fan operate in high speed?	Go to *Step 21*	Go to *Step 25*
13	Is the eng cool RH fan operating properly in high speed?	Go to *Step 14*	Go to *Step 17*
14	1. Remove the cooling fan S/P relay 2. Connect a 20 A fused jumper between the eng cool LH fan low circuit of the cooling fan S/P relay and the ground circuit of the cooling fan S/P relay. Does the eng cool LH fan operate properly in high speed?	Go to *Step 16*	Go to *Step 22*
15	Inspect for poor connections at the cooling fan 1 relay. Did you find and correct the condition?	Go to *Step 31*	Go to *Step 26*
16	Inspect for poor connections at the cooling fan S/P relay. Did you find and correct the condition?	Go to *Step 31*	Go to *Step 27*
17	Inspect for poor connections at the cooling fan 2 relay. Did you find and correct the condition?	Go to *Step 31*	Go to *Step 28*
18	Inspect for poor connections at the harness connector of the eng cool RH fan. Did you find and correct the condition?	Go to *Step 31*	Go to *Step 29*
19	Inspect for poor connections at the harness connector of the eng cool LH fan. Did you find and correct the condition?	Go to *Step 31*	Go to *Step 30*
20	Repair the battery positive voltage circuit of the cooling fan 1 relay switch side. Did you complete the repair?	Go to *Step 31*	—
21	Repair the eng cool LH fan supply voltage circuit. Did you complete the repair?	Go to *Step 31*	—
22	Repair the eng cool LH fan ground circuit. Did you complete the repair?	Go to *Step 31*	—

GC1080100645020X

Fig. 31 Cooling fan inoperative (Part 2 of 3). Alero, Cutlass, Malibu & 1999-2002 Grand Am

Step	Action	Yes	No
DEFINITION: One or both engine cooling fan motors do not operate properly in high or low speed modes.			
1	Did you perform the Engine Cooling Diagnostic System Check?	Go to *Step 2*	Go to *Diagnostic System Check -*
2	1. Install a scan tool. 2. Turn ON the ignition, with the engine OFF. 3. With a scan tool, command the Fans Low Speed ON and OFF. Do the low speed engine cooling fans turn ON and OFF with each command?	Go to *Step 3*	Go to *Step 4*
3	**Important:** Before the PCM changes the speed of the cooling fans, a 3-second delay will occur. With a scan tool, command the Fans High Speed ON and OFF. Do the high speed engine cooling fans turn ON and OFF with each command?	*Test Intermittent and Poor Connections*	Go to *Step 13*
4	1. Turn the ignition OFF. 2. Disconnect the cooling fan 1 relay. 3. Turn the ignition ON, with the engine OFF. 4. Probe the battery positive voltage circuit of the cooling fan 1 relay switch side with a test lamp connected to a good ground. Does the test lamp illuminate?	Go to *Step 5*	Go to *Step 20*
5	Connect a 20 A fused jumper between the battery positive voltage circuit of the cooling fan 1 relay and the cooling fan motor supply voltage circuit of the cooling fan 1 relay. Do both cooling fans operate in low speed?	Go to *Step 15*	Go to *Step 6*
6	1. Leave the fused jumper wire in place of the cooling fan 1 relay. 2. Remove the cooling fan S/P relay 3. Connect a 20 A fused jumper between the eng cool LH fan low circuit of the cooling fan S/P relay and the eng cool RH fan supply voltage circuit of the cooling fan S/P relay. Do both cooling fans operate in low speed?	Go to *Step 16*	Go to *Step 7*
7	1. Leave the fused jumper wire in place of the cooling fan 1 relay. 2. Connect a 20 A fused jumper between the battery positive voltage circuit of the cooling fan S/P relay and the cooling fan motor supply voltage circuit of the cooling fan S/P relay. Does the eng cool RH fan operate in high speed?	Go to *Step 11*	Go to *Step 8*
8	1. Leave the fused jumper wire in place of the cooling fan 1 relay. 2. Install the cooling fan S/P relay. 3. Disconnect the eng cool RH fan electrical connector. Does the eng cool LH fan operate in high speed?	Go to *Step 24*	Go to *Step 9*
9	1. Leave the fused jumper wire in place of the cooling fan 1 relay. 2. Connect a 20 Amp fused jumper wire from the cooling fan motor supply voltage circuit of the eng cool RH fan electrical connector to the cooling fan motor ground circuit of the eng cool RH fan electrical connector. Does the eng cool LH fan operate in high speed?	Go to *Step 18*	Go to *Step 10*

GC1080100645010X

Fig. 31 Cooling fan inoperative (Part 1 of 3). Alero, Cutlass, Malibu & 1999-2002 Grand Am

Step	Action	Yes	No
23	Repair the eng cool RH fan ground circuit. Did you complete the repair?	Go to *Step 31*	—
24	Repair the eng cool RH fan supply voltage circuit. Did you complete the repair?	Go to *Step 31*	—
25	Repair the eng cool LH fan low circuit. Did you complete the repair?	Go to *Step 31*	—
26	Replace the cooling fan 1 relay. Did you complete the repair?	Go to *Step 31*	—
27	Replace the cooling fan S/P relay. Did you complete the repair?	Go to *Step 31*	—
28	Replace the cooling fan 2 relay. Did you complete the repair?	Go to *Step 31*	—
29	Replace the eng cool RH fan. Did you complete the repair?	Go to *Step 31*	—
30	Replace the eng cool LH fan. Did you complete the repair?	Go to *Step 31*	—
31	Operate the system in order to verify the repair. Did you correct the condition?	System OK	Go to *Step 2*

GC1080100645030X

Fig. 31 Cooling fan inoperative (Part 3 of 3). Alero, Cutlass, Malibu & 1999-2002 Grand Am

Circuit Description

To determine if a fault is present perform the Cooling Fan Functional Check. If DTC P1660 is set, or sets during the functional check, it must be diagnosed before proceeding with any of the symptom tables. When the PCM commands low speed fan operation it grounds Cooling Fan Relay 1 which allows current to flow through both cooling fans in a series circuit to ground. If the PCM commands high speed fan operation it grounds all the cooling fan relays, including Fan Relay 1, which changes the circuit to a parallel circuit to ground. If a fault occurs certain symptoms will occur due to the series/parallel circuit design.

The PCM will command fan operation when:

- Low Speed Fan Operation
  - Engine coolant temperature exceeds approximately 106°C (229°F).
  - Transmission fluid temperature exceeds 150°C (302°F).
  - A/C operation is requested.
  - After the vehicle is shut OFF if the coolant temperature at key–off is more than 151°C (304°F) and system voltage was more than 12 volts. The fans will stay ON for approximately 3 minutes.

The fans will switch from low to OFF when the coolant drops below 102°C (216°F).

- High Speed Fan Operation
  - Engine coolant temperature reaches 112°C (234°F).
  - Transmission temperature is more than 151°C (304°F).
  - When certain DTCs set.

The fans will switch from high to low (except DTCs set) when the coolant drops below 106°C (229°F).

- If the cooling fans operate when commanded OFF and DTC P1660 is not set either a cooling fan relay is stuck ON or a cooling fan circuit is shorted to power.
- Whenever a repair is completed repeat the Cooling Fan Functional Check. This will help diagnose possible multiple failures, for example: two water contaminated relays.

Fan Relay Operation Matrix

Operational Mode	OFF	LOW FANS	HIGH FANS
Low Speed Cooling Fan Relay (#1)	De-Energized	Energized	Energized
Series/ Parallel Coling Fan Relay (#2)	De-Energized	De-Energized	Energized
High Speed Cooling Fan (#3)	De-Energized	De-Energized	Energized

*The Series/Parallel Cooling Fan Relay is a dual position switch and while de-energized, supplies a ground path for the low speed fan circuit.

Test Description

Number(s) below refer to the step number(s) on the Functional Table.

1. The Powertrain OBD System Check must be performed first so that mis–diagnosis is avoided, due to the PCM commanding the fans ON due to a DTC set, etc.
2. Checking to see if there is a fault on the cooling fan relay control circuits.
3. Checking to see if any A/C DTCs will set. If A/C DTCs set they must be diagnosed before proceeding with the Cooling Fan Functional Check.
4. Commanding fans ON in sequence to determine the symptom (fault–if any) present.

GC1089600323010X

Fig. 32 Cooling fan function inspection (Part 1 of 3). 1998-99 Aurora

Step	Action	Value(s)	Yes	No
1	Was the Powertrain On–Board Diagnostic (OBD) System Check performed?	—	*Go to Step 2*	Go to *Powertrain OBD System Check*
2	1. Ensure the engine coolant temperature is between the values specified. 2. Turn HVAC controls to OFF. 3. Start and idle the engine. 4. Using the scan tool select Output Tests and while viewing the Quad Driver 1 display, command All Relays OFF for approximately 15 seconds. 5. Using the scan tool select Output Tests and while viewing the Quad Driver 1 display, command All Relays ON for approximately 15 seconds. Did the Quad Driver 1 display indicate a *Fault*?	5°C - 100°C (41°F - 212°F)	Go to *DTC P1660 Cooling Fan Control Circuits*	*Go to Step 3*
3	With the engine idling turn A/C ON to maximum cooling. Have any other DTC(s) failed this ignition?	—	Go to DTC(s) that are set	*Go to Step 4*
4	1. Turn the engine OFF and the key ON. 2. Ensure engine coolant temperature is below the value specified. 3. Observe fan operation while individually commanding Fan Relay 1 ON, then All Relays ON, then All Relays OFF. • With Fan Relay 1 commanded ON both fans should operate at low speed. • With All Relays commanded ON both fans should operate at high speed. • With All Relays commanded OFF both fans should not operate (unless the PCM detects a fault or high temperature condition). Do both cooling fans operate as commanded?	100°C (212°F)	System OK	*Go to Step 5*
5	Does only Cooling Fan #1 (left) operate with Fan Relay 1 commanded ON then both fans operate when All Relays are commanded ON?	—	*Go to Step 6*	*Go to Step 7*
6	Repair CKT 504 shorted to ground. Is the repair complete?	—	*Go to Step 4*	—
7	Does neither cooling fan operate with Fan Relay 1 commanded ON then only Cooling Fan #2 (right) operate with All Relays commanded ON?	—	*Electric Cooling Fan Diagnosis* (Table 1)	*Go to Step 8*
8	Does neither cooling fan operate with Fan Relay 1 commanded ON then only Cooling Fan #1 (left) operate with All Relays commanded ON?	—	*Electric Cooling Fan Diagnosis* (Table 2)	*Go to Step 9*
9	Do both cooling fans operate with Fan Relay 1 commanded ON then only Cooling Fan #2 (right) operate with All Relays commanded ON?	—	*Electric Cooling Fan Diagnosis* (Table 3)	*Go to Step 10*
10	Do both cooling fans operate with Fan Relay 1 commanded ON then only Cooling Fan #1 (left) operate with All Relays commanded ON?	—	*Electric Cooling Fan Diagnosis* (Table 4)	*Go to Step 11*

GC1089600323020X

Fig. 32 Cooling fan function inspection (Part 2 of 3). 1998-99 Aurora

Step	Action	Value(s)	Yes	No
11	Does neither cooling fan operate when Fan Relay 1 is commanded ON and also when All Relays are commanded ON?	—	*Electric Cooling Fan Diagnosis* (Table 5)	*Go to Step 12*
12	Does either cooling fan operate when All Relays is commanded OFF?	—	Go to *Diagnostic Aids*	*Go to Step 4*

GC1089600323030X

Fig. 32 Cooling fan function inspection (Part 3 of 3). 1998-99 Aurora

Step	Action	Value(s)	Yes	No
DEFINITION: No low speed operation of either cooling fan. High speed operation of right cooling fan only. DTC P1660 is not set.				
1	Was the Cooling Fan Functional Check performed?	—	*Go to Step 2*	*Electric Cooling Fan Diagnosis*
2	1. Disconnect Cooling Fan #1 connector. 2. Using the scan tool select Output Tests then Fan Relays. 3. With the key ON command Relay 1 ON. 4. Using DVM J 39200 measure the voltage to ground at Cooling Fan #1 connector terminal B (harness side). Is the voltage the same or more than the value specified?	10.0 volts	*Go to Step 3*	*Go to Step 6*
3	Jumper Cooling Fan #1 connector terminals A and B together. Does Cooling Fan #2 operate while jumpered?	—	*Go to Step 8*	*Go to Step 4*
4	1. With Cooling Fan #1 connector still jumpered, remove Relay #2. 2. Measure the voltage to ground at Relay #2 terminal 30. Is the voltage the same or more than the value specified?	10.0 volts	*Go to Step 5*	*Go to Step 9*
5	Jumper Relay #2 terminals 30 and 87A together. Does Cooling Fan #2 operate while jumpered?	—	*Go to Step 10*	*Go to Step 11*
6	1. Exit Fan Relays. 2. Remove Relay #1. 3. Measure the voltage to ground at Relay #1 terminal 30. Is the voltage the same or more than the value specified?	10.0 volts	*Go to Step 7*	*Go to Step 12*
7	1. Jumper Fan Relay #1 terminals 30 and 87 together. 2. Measure the voltage to ground at Cooling Fan #1 connector terminal B. Is the voltage to ground the same or more than the value specified?	10.0 volts	*Go to Step 13*	*Go to Step 14*
8	Replace Cooling Fan #1 (left). Is the replacement complete?	—	*Electric Cooling Fan Diagnosis*	—
9	Repair the open in CKT 504 between Cooling Fan #1 and Fan Relay #2. Is the repair complete?	—	*Electric Cooling Fan Diagnosis*	—

GC1089600324010X

Fig. 33 Cooling fan symptom table 1 (Part 1 of 2).1998-99 Aurora

Step	Action	Value(s)	Yes	No
DEFINITION: No low speed operation of either cooling fan. High speed operation of right cooling fan only. DTC P1660 is not set.				
10	Replace Fan Relay #2. Is the replacement complete?	—	*Electric Cooling Fan Diagnosis*	—
11	Repair the open in CKT 409 between Fan Relay #2 and the CKT 409 splice. Is the repair complete?	—	*Electric Cooling Fan Diagnosis*	—
12	Repair the open in the circuit between Fan Relay #1 terminal 30 and the Maxi fuse. Is the repair complete?	—	*Electric Cooling Fan Diagnosis*	—
13	Replace Fan Relay #1. Is the replacement complete?	—	*Electric Cooling Fan Diagnosis*	—
14	Repair the open in CKT 532 between Fan Relay #1 and Cooling Fan #1. Is the repair complete?	—	*Electric Cooling Fan Diagnosis*	—

GC1089600324020X

Fig. 33 Cooling fan symptom table 1 (Part 2 of 2). 1998-99 Aurora

Step	Action	Value(s)	Yes	No
DEFINITION: No low speed operation of either cooling fan. High speed operation of left cooling fan only. DTC P1660 is not set.				
1	Was the Cooling Fan Functional Check performed?	—	*Go to Step 2*	*Electric Cooling Fan Diagnosis*
2	1. Disconnect Cooling Fan #2 (right) connector. 2. Using the scan tool select Output Tests than Fan Relays. 3. With the key ON, command Fan Relay 1 ON. 4. Jumper Cooling Fan #2 (right) terminals A and B together. Does Cooling Fan #1 (left) operate while jumpered?	—	*Go to Step 5*	*Go to Step 3*
3	1. With Fan Relay 1 still commanded ON remove Fan Relay #2. 2. Jumper Fan Relay #2 terminals 30 and 87A together. Does left cooling fan operate while jumpered?	—	*Go to Step 6*	*Go to Step 4*
4	With Fan Relay #2 still jumpered use DVM J 39200 and measure the voltage to ground at Cooling Fan #2 connector terminal B (harness side). Is the voltage the same or more than the value specified?	10.0 volts	*Go to Step 7*	*Go to Step 8*
5	Replace Cooling Fan #2 (right). Is the replacement complete?	—	*Electric Cooling Fan Diagnosis*	—
6	Replace Fan Relay #2. Is the replacement complete?	—	*Electric Cooling Fan Diagnosis*	—
7	Repair the open in the BLK circuit between Cooling Fan #2 (right) terminal A and the splice. Is the repair complete?	—	*Electric Cooling Fan Diagnosis*	—
8	Repair the open in CKT 409 between Cooling Fan #2 (right) the CKT 409 splice and Fan Relay #2. Is the repair complete?	—	*Electric Cooling Fan Diagnosis*	—

GC1089600325010X

GC1089600325020X

Fig. 34 Cooling fan symptom table 2 (Part 1 of 2). 1998-99 Aurora

Fig. 34 Cooling fan symptom table 2 (Part 2 of 2). 1998-99 Aurora

Step	Action	Value(s)	Yes	No
DEFINITION: Low speed operation of both fans. High speed operation of right cooling fan only. DTC P1660 not set.				
1	Was the Cooling Fan Functional Check performed?	—	*Go to Step 2*	*Electric Cooling Fan Diagnosis*
2	1. Using the scan tool select Output Tests and then Fan Relays. 2. With the key ON select All Relays ON. 3. Remove Fan Relay #2. 4. Using DVM J 39200 measure the voltage to ground at Fan Relay #2 terminal 85. Is the voltage the same or more than the value specified?	10.0 volts	*Go to Step 3*	*Go to Step 5*
3	1. Remove Fan Relay #3. 2. Measure the resistance between Fan Relay #2 terminal 86 and Fan Relay #3 terminal 86. Is the resistance the same or less than the value specified?	5 ohms	*Go to Step 4*	*Go to Step 6*
4	1. Reconnect Fan Relay #3. 2. With All Relays still commanded ON, jumper Fan Relay #2 terminals 30 and 87 together. Do both cooling fans operate while jumpered?	—	*Go to Step 8*	*Go to Step 7*
5	Repair the open in the ORG circuit between Fan Relay #2 terminal 85 and the splice. Is the repair complete?	—	*Electric Cooling Fan Diagnosis*	—
6	Repair the open in CKT 473 between Fan Relay #2 terminal 86 and the CKT 473 splice. Is the repair complete?	—	*Electric Cooling Fan Diagnosis*	—
7	Repair the open in the BLK circuit between Fan Relay #2 terminal 87 and the splice. Is the repair complete?	—	*Electric Cooling Fan Diagnosis*	—
8	Replace Fan Relay #2. Is the replacement complete?	—	*Electric Cooling Fan Diagnosis*	—

GC1089600326000X

Fig. 35 Cooling fan symptom table 3. 1998-99 Aurora

Step	Action	Value(s)	Yes	No
DEFINITION: Low speed operation of both fans. High speed operation of left cooling fan only. DTC P1660 not set.				
1	Was the Cooling Fan Functional Check performed?	—	*Go to Step 2*	*Electric Cooling Fan Diagnosis*
2	1. Using scan tool select Output Tests then All Relays. 2. With the key ON command All Relays ON. 3. Remove Fan Relay #3. 4. Using DVM J 39200 measure the voltage to ground at Fan Relay #3 terminal 85. Is the voltage the same or more than the value specified?	10.0 volts	*Go to Step 3*	*Go to Step 6*
3	Measure the voltage to ground at Fan Relay #3 terminal 30. Is the voltage the same or more than the value specified?	10.0 volts	*Go to Step 4*	*Go to Step 7*
4	1. Remove Fan Relay #3. 2. Measure the voltage between Fan Relay #3 terminal 86 and Fan Relay #2 terminal 86. Is the resistance the same or less than the value specified?	5 ohms	*Go to Step 5*	*Go to Step 8*
5	1. Reconnect Fan Relay #2. 2. With All Relays still commanded ON, jumper Fan Relay #3 terminals 30 and 87 together. Does Cooling Fan #2 (right) operate while jumpered?	—	*Go to Step 10*	*Go to Step 9*
6	Repair the open in the RED circuit between Fan Relay #3 terminal 30 and the Maxi fuse. Is the repair complete?	—	*Electric Cooling Fan Diagnosis*	—
7	Repair the open in the ORG circuit between Fan Relay #3 terminal 85 and the splice. Is the repair complete?	—	*Electric Cooling Fan Diagnosis*	—
8	Repair the open in CKT 473 between Fan Relay #3 terminal 86 and the CKT 473 splice. Is the repair complete?	—	*Electric Cooling Fan Diagnosis*	—
9	Repair the open in CKT 409 between Fan Relay #3 terminal 87 and the CKT 409 splice. Is the repair complete	—	*Electric Cooling Fan Diagnosis*	—
10	Replace Fan Relay #3. Is the replacement complete?	—	*Electric Cooling Fan Diagnosis*	—

GC1089600327000X

Fig. 36 Cooling fan symptom table 4. 1998-99 Aurora

Step	Action	Value(s)	Yes	No
DEFINITION: No fan operation on either high or low speed. DTC P1660 not set.				
1	Did you perform the Cooling Fan Functional Check?	—	Go to *Step 2*	Go to the Cooling Fan Functional Check
2	Check the condition of the cooling fan Maxi fuse. Is the fuse blown?	—	Go to *Step 4*	Go to *Step 3*
3	1. Remove Fan Relay #1. 2. Using DMM J 39200 measure the voltage to ground at Fan Relay #1 terminal 30. Is the voltage the same or more than the value specified?	10 V	Go to *Step 8*	Go to *Step 9*
4	1. Turn the key to LOCK. 2. Replace the Maxi fuse. Does the fuse immediately blow?	—	Go to *Step 10*	Go to *Step 5*
5	1. Turn the key ON. 2. Using the scan tool select Output Tests and then Fan Relays. 3. Command Fan Relay 1 ON. Does the Maxi fuse blow?	—	Go to *Step 11*	Go to *Step 6*
6	Command All Relays ON. Does the Maxi fuse blow?	—	Go to *Step 7*	Fault not present
7	1. Exit Fan Relays. 2. Replace the Maxi fuse. 3. Select Fan Relays and command Fan Relay 1 ON. Is only Cooling Fan #1 (left) operating?	—	Go to *Step 12*	Go to *Step 13*
8	Repair the open in the BLK circuit between both BLK circuit splices or between the BLK circuit splice and ground or the poor/open ground connection. Is the repair complete?	—	*Powertrain Control Module*	—
9	Repair the open in the RED circuit between the Maxi fuse and both relays. Is the repair complete?	—	*Powertrain Control Module*	—
10	Repair the short to ground in the RED circuit between the Maxi fuse and either Fan Relay 1 or Fan Relay 3. Is the repair complete?	—	*Powertrain Control Module*	—
11	Repair the short to ground in CKT 532 between Fan Relay 1 and Cooling Fan #1 (left). Is the repair complete?	—	*Powertrain Control Module*	—
12	Replace Cooling Fan #2 (right). Is the replacement complete?	—	*Powertrain Control Module*	—
13	Replace Cooling Fan #1 (left). Is the replacement complete?	—	*Powertrain Control Module*	—

GC1089900409000X

Fig. 37 Cooling fan symptom table 5. 1998-99 Aurora

Test Description

The number(s) below refer to the step number(s) on the diagnostic table.

2. Lack of communication may be due to a partial malfunction of the class 2 serial data circuit or due to a total malfunction of the class 2 serial data circuit. The specified procedure will determine the particular condition.

3. The symptom list in Symptoms will determine the correct diagnostic procedure to use.

4. The presence of DTCs which begin with "U" indicate some other module is not communicating. The specified procedure will compile all the available information before tests are performed.

Step	Action	Yes	No
1	1. Install a scan tool. 2. Turn ON the ignition, with the engine OFF. Does the scan tool power up?	Go to Step 2	Go to Scan Tool Does Not Power Up
2	1. Turn ON the ignition, with the engine OFF. 2. Attempt to establish communication with the following: o Instrument Panel Cluster (IPC) o Dash Integration Module (DIM) o Powertrain Control Module (PCM) Does the scan tool communicate with the IPC, DIM and PCM?	Go to Step 3	Go to Scan Tool Does Not Communicate with Class 2 Device
3	Select the IPC, DIM and the PCM display DTC function on the scan tool. Does the scan tool display any DTCs?	Go to Step 4	Go to Symptoms - Engine Cooling
4	Does the scan tool display any DTCs which begin with a U?	Go to Scan Tool Does Not Communicate with Class 2 Device	Go to Step 5
5	Does the scan tool display DTC P1258, P0480, or P0481?	Go to Diagnostic Trouble Code (DTC) List	Go to Step 6
6	Does the scan tool display DTC B1000, B1004, B1007, or B1009?	Go to Diagnostic Trouble Code (DTC) List	Go to Step 7
7	Does the scan tool display DTC B1327, B1513, or B1514?	Go to Diagnostic Trouble Code (DTC)	Go to Control Module References

GC1080000604010X

Fig. 38 Diagnostic system check. 2001–02 Aurora

Step	Action	Yes	No
	DEFINITION: One or both engine cooling fan motors do not operate properly in high or low speed modes. SCHEMATIC REFERENCE: Cooling Fan Motors and Relays		
1	Has the Engine Cooling Diagnostic System Check been performed?	Go to Step 2	Go to A Diagnostic System Check - Engine Cooling
2	1. Install a scan tool. 2. Turn ON the ignition, with the engine OFF. 3. With a scan tool, command the Low Speed Fan Relay ON and OFF. Do the low speed engine cooling fans turn ON and OFF with each command?	Go to Step 3	Go to Step 4
3	**Important:** The cooling fans will remain in low speed operation for 3 seconds before the PCM grounds the high speed fan relay control to turn on the high speed fans. With a scan tool, command the S/P High Speed Fan Relay ON and OFF. Do the high speed engine cooling fans turn ON and OFF with each command?	Go to Testing for Intermittent and Poor Connections	Go to Step 11
4	1. Remove the Cool Fan 2 relay. 2. Connect a 20 A fused jumper between the battery positive voltage circuit of the Cool Fan 2 relay and the cooling fan motor supply voltage circuit of the Cool Fan 2 relay. Do both cooling fans operate in low speed?	Go to Step 13	Go to Step 5
5	1. Leave the fused jumper wire in place of the Cool Fan 2 relay. 2. Remove the Cool Fan S/P relay 3. Connect a 20 A fused jumper between the right cooling fan low circuit of the Cool Fan S/P relay and the left cooling fan motor supply voltage circuit of the Cool Fan S/P relay. Do both cooling fans operate in low speed?	Go to Step 14	Go to Step 6

GC1080000605010X

Fig. 39 Cooling fan inoperative (Part 1 of 6). 2001–02 Aurora

Step	Action	Yes	No
6	1. Leave the fused jumper wire in place of the Cool Fan 2 relay. 2. Connect a 20 A fused jumper between the battery positive voltage circuit of the Cool Fan S/P relay and the cooling fan motor supply voltage circuit of the Cool Fan S/P relay. Does the left cooling fan motor operate in high speed?	Go to Step 9	Go to Step 7
7	1. Leave the fused jumper wire in place of the Cool Fan 2 relay. 2. Install the Cool Fan S/P relay. 3. Disconnect the left cooling fan motor electrical connector. 4. Connect a 20 Amp fused jumper wire from the cooling fan motor supply voltage circuit of the left cooling fan motor electrical connector to the cooling fan motor ground circuit of the left cooling fan motor electrical connector. Does the right cooling fan motor operate in high speed?	Go to Step 16	Go to Step 8
8	1. Leave the fused jumper wire in place of the Cool Fan 2 relay. 2. Connect a 20 Amp fused jumper wire from the cooling fan motor supply voltage circuit of the left cooling fan motor electrical connector to a good ground. Does the right cooling fan motor operate in high speed?	Go to Step 20	Go to Step 21

GC1080000605020X

Fig. 39 Cooling fan inoperative (Part 2 of 6). 2001–02 Aurora

Step	Action	Yes	No
9	1. Leave the fused jumper wire in the Cool Fan 2 relay. 2. Install the Cool Fan S/P relay. 3. Disconnect the right cooling fan motor electrical connector. 4. Connect a 20 Amp fused jumper wire from battery positive voltage circuit of the right cooling fan motor electrical connector to the cooling fan motor ground circuit of the right cooling fan motor electrical connector. Does the left cooling fan motor operate in high speed?	Go to Step 17	Go to Step 10
10	1. Leave the fused jumper wire in place of the Cool Fan 2 relay. 2. Connect a 20 Amp fused jumper wire from battery positive voltage to the right cooling fan motor low circuit of the of the right cooling fan motor electrical connector. Does the left cooling fan motor operate in high speed?	Go to Step 18	Go to Step 22
11	Is the left cooling fan motor operating properly in high speed?	Go to Step 12	Go to Step 15

GC1080000605030X

Fig. 39 Cooling fan inoperative (Part 3 of 6). 2001–02 Aurora

12	1. Remove the Cool Fan S/P relay 2. Connect a 20 A fused jumper between the right cooling fan low circuit of the Cool Fan S/P relay and the ground circuit of the Cool Fan S/P relay. Does the right cooling fan operate properly in high speed?	Go to Step 14	Go to Step 19
13	Inspect for poor connections at the Cool Fan 2 relay. Did you find and correct the condition?	Go to Step 28	Go to Step 23
14	Inspect for poor connections at the Cool Fan S/P relay. Did you find and correct the condition?	Go to Step 28	Go to Step 24
15	Inspect for poor connections at the Cool Fan 1 relay. Did you find and correct the condition?	Go to Step 28 v	Go to Step 25
16	Inspect for poor connections at the harness connector of the left cooling fan motor. Did you find and correct the condition?	Go to Step 28	Go to Step 26

GC1080000605040X

Fig. 39 Cooling fan inoperative (Part 4 of 6). 2001–02 Aurora

17	Inspect for poor connections at the harness connector of the right cooling fan motor. Did you find and correct the condition?	Go to Step 28	Go to Step 27
18	Repair the right cooling fan motor supply voltage circuit. Did you complete the repair?	Go to Step 28	--
19	Repair the right cooling fan motor ground circuit. Did you complete the repair?	Go to Step 28	--
20	Repair the left cooling fan motor ground circuit. Did you complete the repair?	Go to Step 28	--
21	Repair the left cooling fan motor supply voltage circuit. Did you complete the repair?	Go to Step 28	--
22	Repair the right cooling fan motor low circuit. Did you complete the repair?	Go to Step 28	--
23	Replace the Cool Fan 2 relay. Is the repair complete?	Go to Step 28	--
24	Replace the Cool Fan S/P relay. Is the repair complete?	Go to Step 28	--
25	Replace the Cool Fan 1 relay. Is the repair complete?	Go to Step 28	--

GC1080000605050X

Fig. 39 Cooling fan inoperative (Part 5 of 6). 2001–02 Aurora

26	Replace the left cooling fan motor. Is the repair complete?	Go to Step 28	--
27	Replace the right cooling fan motor. Is the repair complete?	Go to Step 28	--
28	Operate the system in order to verify the repair. Did you correct the condition?	System OK	Go to Step 3

GC1080000605060X

Fig. 39 Cooling fan inoperative (Part 6 of 6). 2001–02 Aurora

Step	Action	Yes	No
DEFINITION: One or both engine cooling fan motors run continuously in high or low speed modes. SCHEMATIC REFERENCE: Cooling Fan Motors and Relays			
1	Did you perform the Engine Cooling Diagnostic System Check?	Go to Step 2	Go to A Diagnostic System Check - Engine Cooling
2	Turn ON the ignition, with the engine OFF. Are one or both cooling fans running all the time?	Go to Step 3	Go to Testing for Intermittent and Poor Connections
3	Are both cooling fans running continuously?	Go to Step 5	Go to Step 4
4	Remove the Cool Fan S/P relay. Did the left cooling fan turn OFF?	Go to Step 6	Go to Step 7
5	Repair the short in the right cooling fan motor supply voltage circuit. you complete the repair?	Go to Step 8	--
6	Repair the short in the right cooling fan motor low circuit. Did you complete the repair?	Go to Step 8	--
7	Repair the short in the left cooling fan motor supply voltage circuit. Did you complete the repair?	Go to Step 8	--
8	Operate the system in order to verify the repair. Did you correct the condition?	System OK	Go to Step 2

GC1080000606000X

Fig. 40 Cooling fan always on. 2001–02 Aurora

Step	Action	Value(s)	Yes	No
1	Was the Powertrain On-Board Diagnostic(OBD) System Check performed?	—	*Go to Step 2*	*Go to the Powertrain OBD System Check*
2	Are any PCM DTC(s) stored?	—	Diagnose the DTCs	*Go to Step 3*
3	1. Engine coolant temperature below 100°C (212°F). 2. Ensure that the A/C is OFF. 3. Engine running. Observe the cooling fans. Are the cooling fans running?	—	*Go to Step 30*	*Go to Step 4*
4	Using scan tool output tests command Fan 1 ON. Do both cooling fans run at low speed?	—	*Go to Step 5*	*Go to Step 8*

GC1089600297010X

Fig. 41 Cooling fan diagnosis (Part 1 of 5). 1998–99 Bonneville, Eighty Eight LeSabre, LSS & Regency

Step	Action	Value(s)	Yes	No
5	Using scan tool output tests command Fan 2 ON. Does the left side cooling fan run at high speed?	—	Go to Step 6	Go to Step 18
6	**Important:** Ambient temperature must be above 9°C (48°F). 1. Exit scan tool output tests. 2. Engine running. 3. Turn the A/C ON. Are the cooling fans running?	—	Go to Diagnostic Aids	Go to Step 7
7	View the A/C Request display on the scan tool. Does the scan tool display Yes?	—	Go to Step 44	Air Conditioning Diagnosis
8	1. Turn OFF the ignition switch. 2. Disconnect the low speed cooling fan relay. 3. Turn ON the ignition switch. 4. Probe low speed cooling fan relay harness connector terminal 85 with a test light connected to ground Is the test light ON?	—	Go to Step 9	Go to Step 28
9	Probe low speed cooling fan relay harness connector terminal 30 with a test light to ground. Is the test light ON?	—	Go to Step 10	Go to Step 29
10	1. Connect a fused jumper between low speed cooling fan relay harness connector terminals 87 and 30. 2. Observe the cooling fans. Are both cooling fans running at low speed?	—	Go to Step 11	Go to Step 14
11	1. Using the scan tool output control function, select Fan 1 and command the cooling fans ON. 2. Probe low speed cooling fan harness connector terminal 86 with a test light to B+. Is the test light ON?	—	Go to Step 40	Go to Step 12
12	1. Turn OFF the ignition switch. 2. Disconnect the PCM. 3. Turn ON the ignition switch. 4. Check the low speed cooling fan relay control circuit for an open or short to voltage between the PCM and the low speed cooling fan relay. 5. If a problem is found, repair as necessary. Was a problem found?	—	Go to Step 46	Go to Step 13
13	1. Check the low speed cooling fan relay control circuit for a poor terminal connection at the PCM. 2. If a problem is found, repair as necessary. Was a problem found?	—	Go to Step 46	Go to Step 44
14	1. Disconnect both cooling fan motor 2-way harness connectors (leave low speed cooling fan relay connector terminals 87 and 30 jumpered). 2. Probe terminal B at both cooling fan motor connectors with a test light to ground. Is the test light ON at both cooling fan connectors?	—	Go to Step 15	Go to Step 16
15	Connect the test light between terminals A and B at both cooling fan connectors. Is the test light ON at both cooling fan connectors?	—	Go to Step 45	Go to Step 17

GC1089600297020X

Fig. 41 Cooling fan diagnosis (Part 2 of 5). 1998–99 Bonneville, Eighty Eight LeSabre, LSS & Regency

Step	Action	Value(s)	Yes	No
16	Locate and repair open in CKT 409 to the affected cooling fan motor(s). Is action complete?	—	Go to Step 46	—
17	Locate and repair open in the ground circuit to the affected cooling fan motor(s). Is action complete?	—	Go to Step 46	—
18	1. Disconnect the high speed cooling fan relay 2. Turn ON the ignition switch. 3. Probe high speed cooling fan relay harness connector terminal 30 with a test light to ground. Is the test light ON?	—	Go to Step 19	Go to Step 29
19	Probe high speed cooling fan relay harness connector terminal 86 with a test light to ground. Is the test light ON?	—	Go to Step 20	Go to Step 28
20	1. Connect a fused jumper between high speed cooling fan relay harness connector terminals 30 and 87. 2. Observe the left side cooling fan. Does the left side cooling fan run at high speed?	—	Go to Step 21	Go to Step 24
21	1. Using the scan tool output control function, select Fan 2 and command the fan ON. 2. Wait 6 seconds. 3. Probe high speed cooling fan harness connector terminal 86 with a test light to B+. Is the test light ON?	—	Go to Step 42	Go to Step 22
22	1. Turn OFF the ignition switch. 2. Disconnect the PCM. 3. Turn ON the ignition switch. 4. Check the high speed cooling fan relay control circuit for an open or short to voltage between the PCM and the high speed cooling fan relay. 5. If a problem is found, repair as necessary. Was a problem found?	—	Go to Step 46	Go to Step 23
23	1. Check the high speed cooling fan relay control circuit for a poor terminal connection at the PCM. 2. If a problem is found, repair as necessary. Was a problem found?	—	Go to Step 46	Go to Step 44
24	1. Disconnect the left side cooling fan motor connector (leave high speed cooling fan relay harness connector terminals 30 and 87 jumpered). 2. Probe the left side cooling fan motor harness connector terminal B with a test light to ground. Is the test light ON?	—	Go to Step 25	Go to Step 27
25	Connect the test light between left side cooling fan motor harness connector terminals A and B. Is the test light ON?	—	Go to Step 45	Go to Step 26
26	Locate and repair open in the ground circuit to the left side cooling fan motor. Is action complete?	—	Go to Step 46	—
27	Locate and repair open in CKT 532 to the left side cooling fan. Is action complete?	—	Go to Step 46	—

GC1089600297030X

Fig. 41 Cooling fan diagnosis (Part 3 of 5). 1998–99 Bonneville, Eighty Eight LeSabre, LSS & Regency

Step	Action	Value(s)	Yes	No
28	Locate and repair open in ignition feed (CKT 241) to the affected cooling fan relay. Is action complete?	—	Go to Step 46	—
29	Locate and repair cause of no battery feed to the affected fan relay cavity 30: • Open or short to ground in CKT 742. • Shorted cooling fan motor windings. • CKT 409 shorted to ground. • CKT 532 shorted to ground. Is action complete?	—	Go to Step 46	—
30	Disconnect the high speed cooling fan relay. Is either cooling fan running?	—	Go to Step 35	Go to Step 31
31	Probe the high speed cooling fan relay harness connector terminal 86 with a test light to B+. Is the test light ON?	—	Go to Step 32	Go to Step 43
32	Observe A/C Refrigerant Pressure on the scan tool. Is A/C Refrigerant Pressure greater than the specified value?	260 psi (1800 kPa)	Heater Ventilation and Air Conditioning	Go to Step 33
33	1. Turn OFF the ignition switch. 2. Disconnect the PCM. 3. Turn ON the ignition switch. 4. Probe the high speed cooling fan relay harness connector terminal 86 with a test light to B+. Is the test light ON?	—	Go to Step 34	Go to Step 44
34	Locate and repair the short to ground in the high speed cooling fan relay control circuit. Is action complete?	—	Go to Step 46	—
35	Disconnect the low speed cooling fan relay. Is either cooling fan ON?	—	Go to Step 39	Go to Step 36
36	Probe the low speed cooling fan relay harness connector terminal 86 with a test light to B+. Is the test light ON?	—	Go to Step 37	Go to Step 41
37	1. Turn OFF the ignition switch. 2. Disconnect the PCM. 3. Turn ON the ignition switch. 4. Probe the low speed cooling fan relay harness connector terminal 86 with a test light to B+. Is the test light ON?	—	Go to Step 38	Go to Step 44
38	Locate and repair the short to ground in the low speed cooling fan relay control circuit. Is action complete?	—	Go to Step 46	—
39	Locate and repair short to B+ in affected cooling fan feed CKT 409 or CKT 532. Is action complete?	—	Go to Step 46	—
40	1. Check for poor connections at the low speed cooling fan relay. 2. If a problem is found, repair as necessary. Was a problem found?	—	Go to Step 46	Go to Step 41

GC1089600297040X

Fig. 41 Cooling fan diagnosis (Part 4 of 5). 1998–99 Bonneville, Eighty Eight LeSabre, LSS & Regency

Step	Action	Value(s)	Yes	No
41	Replace the low speed cooling fan relay. Is action complete?	—	Go to Step 46	—
42	1. Check for poor connections at the high speed cooling fan relay. 2. If a problem is found, repair as necessary. Was a problem found?	—	Go to Step 46	Go to Step 43
43	Replace the high speed cooling fan relay. Is action complete?	—	Go to Step 46	—
44	Replace the PCM. **Important:** The replacement PCM must be programmed. Is action complete?	—	Go to Step 46	—
45	Replace the affected cooling fan motor. Is action complete?	—	Go to Step 46	—
46	1. Engine coolant temperature is below 100°C (212°F). 2. Ensure that the A/C is OFF. 3. Engine running. Are the cooling fans running?	—	Go to Step 30	Go to Step 47
47	Using scan tool output tests command Fan 1 ON. Do both cooling fans run at low speed?	—	Go to Step 48	Go to Step 8
48	Using scan tool output tests command Fan 2 ON. Does the left side cooling fan run at high speed?	—	System OK	Go to Step 18

GC1089600297050X

Fig. 41 Cooling fan diagnosis (Part 5 of 5). 1998–99 Bonneville, Eighty Eight LeSabre, LSS & Regency

Step	Action	Value(s)	Yes	No
1	Did you perform the Powertrain On-Board Diagnostic (OBD) System Check?	—	*Go to Step 2*	*Go to A Powertrain On Board Diagnostic (OBD) System Check*
2	Are any DTCs set?	—	Go to applicable DTC Table	*Go to Step 3*
3	1. Install a scan tool. 2. Engine coolant temperature must be below the specified value for all the fan diagnoses. 3. Turn ON the Ignition, with the engine and A/C OFF. Are the cooling fans OFF?	100°C (212°F)	*Go to Step 4*	Go to Cooling Fan table #1
4	With a scan tool, command the low speed cooling fan relay ON. Are both cooling fans ON?	—	*Go to Step 5*	Go to Cooling Fan table #2
5	With a scan tool, command the high speed cooling fan relay ON. Do both cooling fans switch to high speed?	—	*Go to Step 6*	Go to Cooling Fan table #3
6	1. With a scan tool, exit outputs. 2. Idle the engine leaving the A/C OFF. Are the cooling fans ON?	—	*Go to Step 8*	*Go to Step 7*
7	Turn ON the A/C. Are the cooling fans ON?	—	System OK	*Go to Step 9*

GC1080000439010X

Fig. 42 Cooling fan functional check (Part 1 of 2). 2000 Bonneville & LeSabre

Step	Action	Value(s)	Yes	No
1	Did you perform the Cooling Fan Functional Check?	—	*Go to Step 2*	Go to Cooling Fan Functional Check
2	Disconnect the low speed fan relay. Are both fans OFF?	—	*Go to Step 8*	*Go to Step 3*
3	Disconnect the series/parallel fan relay. Are both fans OFF?	—	*Go to Step 4*	*Go to Step 10*
4	1. Disconnect the right fan. 2. Probe the fan feed terminal of the right fan connector using a test lamp that is connected to a good ground. Does the test lamp illuminate?	—	*Go to Step 11*	*Go to Step 5*
5	Probe the series/parallel fan relay switch feed circuit terminal at the right fan connector using a test lamp that is connected to a good ground. Does the test lamp illuminate?	—	*Go to Step 12*	*Go to Step 6*
6	Probe the high speed cooling fan relay control circuit at the series/parallel cooling fan relay connector using a test lamp that is connected to B+. Does the test lamp illuminate?	—	*Go to Step 7*	*Go to Step 13*
7	1. Turn OFF the ignition. 2. Leave the test lamp installed. 3. Disconnect the PCM. 4. Turn ON the ignition, with the engine OFF. Is the test lamp still illuminated?	—	*Go to Step 14*	*Go to Step 16*
8	Probe the low speed cooling fan relay control circuit at the low speed cooling fan relay connector using the test lamp that is connected to B+. Does the test lamp illuminate?	—	*Go to Step 9*	*Go to Step 13*

GC1080000440010X

Fig. 43 Cooling fan table 1 (Part 1 of 2). 2000 Bonneville & LeSabre

Step	Action	Value(s)	Yes	No
1	Did you perform the Cooling Fan Functional Check?	—	*Go to Step 2*	Go to Cooling Fan Functional Check
2	Did either fan turn ON when the low speed cooling fan relay was commanded ON?	—	*Go to Step 3*	*Go to Step 5*
3	1. Install a scan tool. 2. With a scan tool, command the low speed cooling fan relay ON. Did the other fan turn OFF?	—	*Go to Step 19*	*Go to Step 4*
4	Disconnect the high speed fan relay. Did the fan turn OFF?	—	*Go to Step 20*	*Go to Step 21*
5	1. With a scan tool, command the low speed cooling fan relay ON. 2. Disconnect the low speed fan relay. 3. Probe the low speed relay control circuit at the low speed relay connector using a test lamp that is connected to B+. Does the test lamp illuminate?	—	*Go to Step 6*	*Go to Step 13*
6	Probe both feed circuits at the low speed relay connector using a test lamp that is connected to ground. Does test lamp illuminate for both circuits?	—	*Go to Step 7*	*Go to Step 22*

GC1080000441010X

Fig. 44 Cooling fan table 2 (Part 1 of 3). 2000 Bonneville & LeSabre

Step	Action	Value(s)	Yes	No
8	Does the scan tool display A/C request as YES?	—	Diagnose A/C system.	*Go to Step 10*
9	Does the scan tool display A/C request as YES?	—	A/C Refrigerant Pressure Sensor	Diagnose A/C system.
10	**Important:** Program the replacement PCM. Replace the PCM. Is the action complete?	—	System OK	—

GC1080000439020X

Fig. 42 Cooling fan functional check (Part 2 of 2). 2000 Bonneville & LeSabre

Step	Action	Value(s)	Yes	No
9	1. Turn OFF the ignition. 2. Leave the test lamp installed. 3. Disconnect the PCM. 4. Turn ON the ignition, with the engine OFF. Is the test lamp still illuminated?	—	*Go to Step 14*	*Go to Step 16*
10	Repair the LH fan feed circuit for a short to voltage. Did you find and correct the condition?	—	Go to Cooling Fan Functional Check	*Go to Step 15*
11	Repair the RH fan feed circuit for a short to voltage. Is the action complete?	—	Go to Cooling Fan Functional Check	—
12	Repair the short to voltage in the series/parallel relay switch feed circuit. Is the action complete?	—	Go to Cooling Fan Functional Check	—
13	Replace the low speed cooling fan relay. Is the action complete?	—	Go to Cooling Fan Functional Check	—
14	Repair the high speed relay control circuit or the low speed relay control circuit for a short to ground. Is the action complete?	—	Go to Cooling Fan Functional Check	—
15	Replace the high speed cooling fan relay. Is the action complete?	—	Go to Cooling Fan Functional Check	—
16	**Important:** Program the replacement PCM. Replace the PCM. Is the action complete?	—	Go to Cooling Fan Functional Check	—

GC1080000440020X

Fig. 43 Cooling fan table 1 (Part 2 of 2). 2000 Bonneville & LeSabre

Step	Action	Value(s)	Yes	No
7	**Important:** Leave jumper in place for remainder of this table. Connect a fused jumper wire between the switch feed circuit and the RH fan feed circuit at the low speed relay connector. Do both fans turn ON?	—	*Go to Step 23*	*Go to Step 8*
8	1. Disconnect the right fan. 2. Probe the fan feed circuit at the harness connector with a test lamp that is connected to a good ground. Does the test lamp illuminate?	—	*Go to Step 9*	*Go to Step 24*
9	Connect a second fused jumper wire between the fan harness connector terminals. Is the left fan ON?	—	*Go to Step 16*	*Go to Step 10*
10	1. Reconnect the right fan. 2. Disconnect the series/parallel fan relay. 3. Probe the switch feed circuit at the series/parallel fan relay connector using a test lamp that is connected to a good ground. Does the test lamp illuminate?	—	*Go to Step 11*	*Go to Step 25*
11	Using the second jumper wire, jumper the switch ignition feed circuit and the LH fan feed circuit together at the series/parallel relay connector. Do the fans come ON?	—	*Go to Step 26*	*Go to Step 12*
12	1. Reconnect series/parallel fan relay. 2. Disconnect the left fan. 3. Probe fan feed circuit terminal at the harness connector with a test lamp that is connected to a good ground. Is the left fan ON?	—	*Go to Step 16*	*Go to Step 18*
13	1. Test lamp still connected. 2. Turn OFF the ignition. 3. Disconnect the PCM. 4. Probe the low speed cooling fan relay control circuit at the PCM connector, with a fused jumper wire that is connected to a good ground. Is the test lamp ON?	—	*Go to Step 20*	*Go to Step 21*
14	Inspect the PCM connections. Did you find a problem and correct it?	—	Go to Cooling Fan Functional Check	*Go to Step 27*
15	Repair the low speed relay control circuit for an open or short to B+. Is the action complete?	—	Go to Cooling Fan Functional Check	—
16	Inspect the fan motor ground circuit for a open or the fan motor connections and repair as necessary. Did you find and correct the condition?	—	Go to Cooling Fan Functional Check	*Go to Step 17*
17	Replace the fan motor. Is the action complete?	—	Go to Cooling Fan Functional Check	—
18	Repair the LH fan feed circuit for an open. Is the action complete?	—	Go to Cooling Fan Functional Check	—

GC1080000441020X

Fig. 44 Cooling fan table 2 (Part 2 of 3). 2000 Bonneville & LeSabre

Step	Action	Value(s)	Yes	No
19	Replace the fan which was not operating. Is the action complete?	—	Go to Cooling Fan Functional Check	—
20	Replace high speed fan relay. Is the action complete?	—	Go to Cooling Fan Functional Check	—
21	Repair the series/parallel relay switch feed circuit for a short to ground. Did you find and correct the condition?	—	Go to Cooling Fan Functional Check	*Go to Step 26*
22	Repair the open or the grounded circuit for the circuit that did not light. Is the action complete?	—	Go to Cooling Fan Functional Check	—
23	Replace the low speed fan relay. Is the action complete?	—	Go to Cooling Fan Functional Check	—
24	Repair the RH fan feed circuit for an open. Is the action complete?	—	Go to Cooling Fan Functional Check	—
25	Repair the series /parallel relay switch feed circuit for an open. Is the action complete?	—	Go to Cooling Fan Functional Check	—
26	Replace the series/parallel fan relay. Is the action complete?	—	Go to Cooling Fan Functional Check	—
27	**Important:** Program the replacement PCM. Replace the PCM. Is the action complete?	—	Go to Cooling Fan Functional Check	—

GC1080000441030X

Fig. 44 Cooling fan table 2 (Part 3 of 3). 2000 Bonneville & LeSabre

Step	Action	Value(s)	Yes	No
7	Jumper the switch ignition feed circuit and the LH fan feed circuit together at the high speed relay connector. Is the right fan ON?	—	*Go to Step 15*	*Go to Step 16*
8	1. Turn OFF the ignition. 2. Disconnect the PCM. 3. Disconnect the low speed fan relay. 4. Jumper the switch feed circuit and the RH fan feed circuit together at the low speed relay connector locations. 5. Turn the ignition ON. 6. Probe the PCM harness connector for the high speed cooling fan relay control circuit with a fused jumper that is connected to a good ground. Do the fans switch from low to high speed?	—	*Go to Step 22*	*Go to Step 17*
9	1. Disconnect the series/parallel fan relay. 2. Probe the high speed relay control circuit at the series parallel relay connector using a test lamp that is connected to B+. 3. Command the high speed cooling fan relay ON using a scan tool. Does the test lamp illuminate?	—	*Go to Step 10*	*Go to Step 18*
10	Probe the ground circuit at the series /parallel relay connector using a test lamp that is connected to B+. Does the test lamp illuminate?	—	*Go to Step 11*	*Go to Step 19*
11	Probe the coil feed circuit at the series /parallel relay connector using a test lamp that is connected to a good ground. Does the test lamp illuminate?	—	*Go to Step 20*	*Go to Step 21*
12	Repair the high speed relay control circuit for an open between the high speed fan relay and the splice. Is the action complete?	—	Go to Cooling Fan Functional Check	—
13	Repair the open in the high speed relay coil feed circuit. Is the action complete?	—	Go to Cooling Fan Functional Check	—
14	Repair the open in the high speed relay switch feed circuit. Is the action complete?	—	Go to Cooling Fan Functional Check	—
15	Replace the high speed fan relay. Is the action complete?	—	Go to Cooling Fan Functional Check	—
16	Repair the open in the LH fan feed circuit between the high speed fan relay and the splice. Is the action complete?	—	Go to Cooling Fan Functional Check	—
17	Repair the high speed fan relay control circuit for an open or for a short to B+. Is the action complete?	—	Go to Cooling Fan Functional Check	—
18	Repair the open in the high speed fan relay control circuit between the series/parallel fan relay and the splice. Is the action complete?	—	Go to Cooling Fan Functional Check	—
19	Repair the open in the ground circuit. Is the action complete?	—	Go to Cooling Fan Functional Check	—

GC1080000442020X

Fig. 45 Cooling fan table 3 (Part 2 of 2). 2000 Bonneville & LeSabre

Step	Action	Value(s)	Yes	No
1	Did you perform the Cooling Fan Functional Check?	—	*Go to Step 2*	Go to Cooling Fan Functional Check
2	1. With a scan tool, command the low speed cooling fan relay ON. 2. Command high speed cooling fan relay ON while observing the fans. Did both fans operate with no change?	—	*Go to Step 8*	*Go to Step 3*
3	Did the right fan stop operating?	—	*Go to Step 9*	*Go to Step 4*
4	1. Disconnect low speed fan relay. 2. Probe the high speed relay control circuit at the high speed relay connector using a test lamp that is connected to B+. 3. Command the high speed cooling fan relay ON using a scan tool. Does the test lamp illuminate after several seconds?	—	*Go to Step 5*	*Go to Step 12*
5	Probe the coil feed circuit at the high speed relay connector using a test lamp that is connected to a good ground. Does the test lamp illuminate?	—	*Go to Step 6*	*Go to Step 13*
6	Probe the switch feed circuit at the high speed relay connector using a test lamp that is connected to a good ground. Does the test lamp illuminate?	—	*Go to Step 7*	*Go to Step 14*

GC1080000442010X

Fig. 45 Cooling fan table 3 (Part 1 of 2). 2000 Bonneville & LeSabre

Step	Action	Yes	No
1	Install a scan tool. Does the scan tool power up?	Go to *Step 2*	Diagnose Data Link Communications
2	1. Turn ON the ignition, with the engine OFF. 2. Attempt to establish communication with the following control modules: • Instrument Cluster • Powertrain Control Module Does the scan tool communicate with the control modules?	Go to *Step 3*	Diagnose Data Link Communications
3	Select the powertrain control module display DTCs function on the scan tool. Does the scan tool display any DTCs?	Go to *Step 4*	Diagnose *Symptoms - Engine Cooling*
4	Does the scan tool display any DTCs which begin with a "U"?	Diagnose Data Link Communications	Diagnose *Trouble Code*

GC1080100646000X

Fig. 46 Diagnostic system check. 2001-02 Bonneville & LeSabre

Step	Action	Yes	No
DEFINITION: One or both engine cooling fan motors run continuously in high or low speed.			
1	Did you perform the Engine Cooling Diagnostic System Check?	Go to *Step 2*	Go To *Diagnostic System Check -*
2	**Important:** The cooling fan 1 relay and cooling fan 2 relay are improperly identified in the underhood fuse block. Turn ON the ignition, with the engine OFF. Are one or both cooling fans ON?	Go to *Step 3*	*Test Intermittent and Poor Connections*
3	Are both cooling fans running continuously?	Go to *Step 5*	Go to *Step 4*
4	Remove the cooling fan S/P relay. Did the left cooling fan turn OFF?	Go to *Step 6*	Go to *Step 7*
5	Repair the short to voltage in the right cooling fan motor supply voltage circuit. Did you complete the repair?	Go to *Step 8*	—
6	Repair the short to voltage in the cooling fan low reference circuit. Did you complete the repair?	Go to *Step 8*	—
7	Repair the short to voltage in the left cooling fan motor supply voltage circuit. Did you complete the repair?	Go to *Step 8*	—
8	Operate the system in order to verify the repair. Did you correct the condition?	System OK	Go to *Step 2*

GC1080100647000X

Fig. 47 Cooling fan always on. 2001-02 Bonneville & LeSabre

Step	Action	Yes	No
Schematic Reference: *Engine Cooling Schematics*			
1	Did you perform the Engine Cooling Diagnostic System Check?	Go to *Step 2*	Go to *Diagnostic System Check -*
2	**Important:** The cooling fan 1 relay and cooling fan 2 relay are improperly identified in the underhood fuse block. 1. Install a scan tool. 2. Turn ON the ignition, with the engine OFF. 3. With a scan tool, command the Fans Low Speed ON and OFF. Do the low speed engine cooling fans turn ON and OFF with each command?	Go to *Step 3*	Go to *Step 4*
3	**Important:** Before the PCM changes the speed of the cooling fans, a 3-second delay will occur. With a scan tool, command the Fans High Speed ON and OFF. Do the high speed engine cooling fans turn ON and OFF with each command?	*Test Intermittent and Poor Connections*	Go to *Step 11*
4	**Important:** Following this step, do NOT remove the 20-A fused jumper wire that is connected during this step. While performing the following steps, use a second 20-A fused jumper wire. 1. Disconnect the cooling fan 1 relay. 2. Connect a 20-A fused jumper between the battery positive voltage circuit of the cooling fan 1 relay and the cooling fan motor supply voltage circuit of the cooling fan 1 relay. Do both cooling fans operate in low speed?	Go to *Step 13*	Go to *Step 5*

GC1080100648010X

Fig. 48 Cooling fan inoperative (Part 1 of 3). 2001-02 Bonneville & LeSabre

Step	Action	Yes	No
5	1. Disconnect the cooling fan S/P relay. 2. Connect the second 20-A fused jumper between the right cooling fan ground circuit of the cooling fan S/P relay and the left cooling fan motor supply voltage circuit of the cooling fan S/P relay. Do both cooling fans operate in low speed?	Go to *Step 14*	Go to *Step 6*
6	Connect a 20-A fused jumper between the battery positive voltage circuit of the cooling fan S/P relay and the cooling fan motor supply voltage circuit of the cooling fan S/P relay. Does the left cooling fan operate in high speed?	Go to *Step 9*	Go to *Step 7*
7	1. Install the cooling fan S/P relay. 2. Disconnect the left cooling fan electrical connector. 3. Connect the second 20-Amp fused jumper wire from the cooling fan motor supply voltage circuit of the left cooling fan electrical connector to the ground circuit of the left cooling fan electrical connector. Does the right cooling fan operate in high speed?	Go to *Step 16*	Go to *Step 8*
8	Connect a 20-Amp fused jumper wire from the cooling fan motor supply voltage circuit of the left cooling fan electrical connector to a good ground. Does the right cooling fan operate in high speed?	Go to *Step 20*	Go to *Step 21*
9	1. Install the cooling fan S/P relay. 2. Disconnect the right cooling fan electrical connector. 3. Connect the second 20-Amp fused jumper wire from the cooling fan motor supply voltage circuit of the right cooling fan electrical connector to the cooling fan low reference circuit of the right cooling fan electrical connector. Does the left cooling fan operate in high speed?	Go to *Step 17*	Go to *Step 10*
10	Connect the second 20-Amp fused jumper wire from battery positive voltage to the cooling fan low reference circuit of the of the right cooling fan electrical connector. Does the left cooling fan operate in high speed?	Go to *Step 18*	Go to *Step 22*
11	Is the left cooling fan operating properly in high speed?	Go to *Step 12*	Go to *Step 15*
12	1. Disconnect the cooling fan S/P relay. 2. Connect the second 20-A fused jumper between the cooling fan low reference circuit of the cooling fan S/P relay and the ground circuit of the cooling fan S/P relay. Does the right cooling fan operate properly in high speed?	Go to *Step 14*	Go to *Step 19*
13	Inspect for poor connections at the cooling fan 1 relay. Did you find and correct the condition?	Go to *Step 28*	Go to *Step 23*
14	Inspect for poor connections at the cooling fan S/P relay. Did you find and correct the condition?	Go to *Step 28*	Go to *Step 24*
15	Inspect for poor connections at the cooling fan 2 relay. Did you find and correct the condition?	Go to *Step 28*	Go to *Step 25*
16	Inspect for poor connections at the harness connector of the left cooling fan. Did you find and correct the condition?	Go to *Step 28*	Go to *Step 26*

GC1080100648020X

Fig. 48 Cooling fan inoperative (Part 2 of 3). 2001-02 Bonneville & LeSabre

Step	Action	Yes	No
17	Inspect for poor connections at the harness connector of the right cooling fan. Did you find and correct the condition?	Go to *Step 28*	Go to *Step 27*
18	Repair the right cooling fan motor supply voltage circuit. Did you complete the repair?	Go to *Step 28*	—
19	Repair the left cooling fan ground circuit. Did you complete the repair?	Go to *Step 28*	—
20	Repair the right cooling fan ground circuit. Did you complete the repair?	Go to *Step 28*	—
21	Repair the left cooling fan motor supply voltage circuit. Did you complete the repair?	Go to *Step 28*	—
22	Repair the cooling fan low reference circuit. Did you complete the repair?	Go to *Step 28*	—
23	Replace the cooling fan 1 relay. Did you complete the repair?	Go to *Step 28*	—
24	Replace the cooling fan S/P relay. Did you complete the repair?	Go to *Step 28*	—
25	Replace the cooling fan 2 relay. Did you complete the repair?	Go to *Step 28*	—
26	Replace the left cooling fan. Did you complete the repair?	Go to *Step 28*	—
27	Replace the right cooling fan. Did you complete the repair?	Go to *Step 28*	—
28	Operate the system in order to verify the repair. Did you correct the condition?	System OK	Go to *Step 3*

GC1080100648030X

Fig. 48 Cooling fan inoperative (Part 3 of 3). 2001-02 Bonneville & LeSabre

Step	Action	Value(s)	Yes	No
1	Did you perform the Powertrain On-Board Diagnostic (OBD) System Check?	—	*Go to Step 2*	*Go to A Powertrain On Board Diagnostic (OBD) System Check*
2	Are any DTCs set?	—	Go to applicable DTC Table	*Go to Step 3*
3	1. Install a scan tool. 2. Engine coolant temperature must be below the specified value for all the fan diagnoses. 3. Turn ON the Ignition, with the engine and A/C OFF. Are the cooling fans OFF?	100°C (212°F)	*Go to Step 4*	Go to Cooling Fan table #1
4	With a scan tool, command the cooling fan relay #1 ON. Are both cooling fans ON?	—	*Go to Step 5*	Go to Cooling Fan table #2
5	With a scan tool, command cooling fan relays #1, #2, and #3 ON. Do both cooling fans switch to high speed?	—	*Go to Step 6*	Go to Cooling Fan table #3
6	1. Wth a scan tool, exit outputs. 2. Idle the engine leaving the A/C OFF. Are the cooling fans ON?	—	*Go to Step 8*	*Go to Step 7*
7	Turn ON the A/C. Are the cooling fans ON?	—	System OK	*Go to Step 9*
8	Does the scan tool display A/C request as YES?	—	A/C system.	*Go to Step 10*
9	Does the scan tool display A/C request as YES?	—	A/C Refrigerant Pressure Sensor	A/C system.
10	**Important:** Program the replacement PCM. Replace the PCM. Is the action complete?	—	System OK	—

GC1089900411000X

Fig. 49 Cooling fan functional check. 1998–2000 Camaro & Firebird w/3.8L Engine

Step	Action	Value(s)	Yes	No
1	Did you perform the Cooling Fan Functional Check?	—	*Go to Step 2*	Go to Cooling Fan Functional Check
2	Disconnect fan relay #1 Are both fans OFF?	—	*Go to Step 8*	*Go to Step 3*
3	Disconnect fan relay #3 Are both fans OFF?	—	*Go to Step 4*	*Go to Step 10*

GC1089900412010X

Fig. 50 Cooling fan table No. 1 (Part 1 of 2). 1998–2000 Camaro & Firebird w/3.8L Engine

Step	Action	Value(s)	Yes	No
4	1. Disconnect the left fan. 2. Probe terminal B of the left fan connector using a *J 34142-B* test lamp that is connected to a good ground. Does the test light illuminate?	—	*Go to Step 11*	*Go to Step 5*
5	Probe terminal A of the left fan connector using a test lamp that is connected to a good ground. Does the test light illuminate?	—	*Go to Step 12*	*Go to Step 6*
6	Probe the cooling fan relay 2 and 3 control circuit (473) at the cooling fan relay #3 connector location (C10) using a test lamp that is connected to B+. Does the test lamp illuminate?	—	*Go to Step 7*	*Go to Step 13*
7	1. Turn OFF the ignition. 2. Leave the test lamp installed. 3. Disconnect the PCM. 4. Turn ON the ignition, with the engine OFF. Is the test lamp still illuminated?	—	*Go to Step 14*	*Go to Step 16*
8	Probe the cooling fan relay 1 control circuit (335) at the cooling fan relay #1 connector location (B1) using the test lamp that is connected to B+. Does the test lamp illuminate?	—	*Go to Step 9*	*Go to Step 13*
9	1. Turn OFF the ignition. 2. Leave the test lamp installed. 3. Disconnect the PCM. 4. Turn ON the ignition, with the engine OFF. Is the test lamp still illuminated?	—	*Go to Step 14*	*Go to Step 16*
10	Repair the RH fan feed circuit (504) for a short to voltage. Did you find and correct the condition?	—	*Go to Cooling Fan Functional Check*	*Go to Step 15*
11	Repair the LH fan feed circuit (409) for a short to voltage. Is the action complete?	—	*Go to Cooling Fan Functional Check*	—
12	Repair the short to voltage in the relay #3 switch feed circuit (532). Is the action complete?	—	*Go to Cooling Fan Functional Check*	—
13	Replace the cooling fan relay #1. Is the action complete?	—	*Go to Cooling Fan Functional Check*	—
14	Repair the relay 2 and 3 control circuit (473) or the relay 1 control circuit (335) for a short to ground. Is the action complete?	—	*Go to Cooling Fan Functional Check*	—
15	Replace the cooling fan relay #2. Is the action complete?	—	*Go to Cooling Fan Functional Check*	—
16	**Important:** Program the replacement PCM. Replace the PCM. Is the action complete?	—	*Go to Cooling Fan Functional Check*	—

GC1089900412020X

Fig. 50 Cooling fan table No. 1 (Part 2 of 2). 1998–2000 Camaro & Firebird w/3.8L Engine

Step	Action	Value(s)	Yes	No
13	1. Test lamp still connected. 2. Turn OFF the ignition. 3. Disconnect the PCM. 4. Probe the cooling fan #1 relay control circuit at the PCM connector, with a fused jumper wire that is connected to a good ground. Is the test lamp ON?	—	*Go to Step 20*	*Go to Step 21*
14	Inspect the PCM connections. Repair faulty connections as necessary. Did you find a problem and correct it?	—	*Go to Cooling Fan Functional Check*	*Go to Step 27*
15	Repair the relay 1 control circuit (335) for an open or shorted to B+. Is the action complete?	—	*Go to Cooling Fan Functional Check*	—
16	Inspect the fan motor ground circuit for a open or the fan motor connections and repair as necessary. Did you find and correct the condition?	—	*Go to Cooling Fan Functional Check*	*Go to Step 17*
17	Replace the fan motor. Is the action complete?	—	*Go to Cooling Fan Functional Check*	—
18	Repair the RH fan feed circuit (504) for an open. Is the action complete?	—	*Go to Cooling Fan Functional Check*	—
19	Replace the fan which was not operating. Is the action complete?	—	*Go to Cooling Fan Functional Check*	—
20	Replace fan relay #2. Is the action complete?	—	*Go to Cooling Fan Functional Check*	—
21	Repair the relay #3 switch feed circuit (532) for a short to ground. Did you find and correct the condition?	—	*Go to Cooling Fan Functional Check*	*Go to Step 26*
22	Repair the open or the grounded circuit for the circuit that did not light. Is the action complete?	—	*Go to Cooling Fan Functional Check*	—
23	Replace fan relay #1. Is the action complete?	—	*Go to Cooling Fan Functional Check*	—
24	Repair the LH fan feed circuit (409) for a open. Is the action complete?	—	*Go to Cooling Fan Functional Check*	—
25	Repair the relay #3 switch feed circuit (532) for a open. Is the action complete?	—	*Go to Cooling Fan Functional Check*	—
26	Replace fan relay #3. Is the action complete?	—	*Go to Cooling Fan Functional Check*	—
27	**Important:** Program the replacement PCM. Replace the PCM. Is the action complete?	—	*Go to Cooling Fan Functional Check*	—

GC1089900413020X

Fig. 51 Cooling fan table No. 2 (Part 2 of 2). 1998–2000 Camaro & Firebird w/3.8L Engine

Step	Action	Value(s)	Yes	No
1	Did you perform the Cooling Fan Functional Check?	—	*Go to Step 2*	Go to Cooling Fan Functional Check
2	Did either fan turn ON when cooling fan relay #1 was commanded ON?	—	*Go to Step 3*	*Go to Step 5*
3	1. Install a scan tool. 2. With a scan tool, command cooling fan relay #1 ON. Did the other fan turn OFF?	—	*Go to Step 19*	*Go to Step 4*
4	Disconnect fan relay #2. Did the fan turn OFF?	—	*Go to Step 20*	*Go to Step 21*
5	1. With a scan tool, command cooling fan relay #1 ON. 2. Disconnect fan relay #1. 3. Probe the relay 1 control circuit (335) at the relay #1 connector location (B1) using a *J 34142-B* test lamp that is connected to B+. Does the test lamp illuminate?	—	*Go to Step 6*	*Go to Step 13*
6	Probe both feed circuits (1640 and 402) at the relay 1 connector locations (B3 and C3) using a test lamp that is connected to ground. Does test lamp illuminate for both circuits?	—	*Go to Step 7*	*Go to Step 22*
7	**Important:** Leave jumper in place for remainder of this table. Connect a fused jumper wire between the switch feed circuit (402) and the LH fan feed circuit (409) at the relay #1 connector locations (B3 and C1). Do both fans turn ON?	—	*Go to Step 23*	*Go to Step 8*
8	1. Disconnect the left fan. 2. Probe fan harness connector terminal B with a test lamp that is connected to a good ground, Does the test lamp illuminate?	—	*Go to Step 9*	*Go to Step 24*
9	Connect a second fused jumper wire between the fan harness connector terminals. Is the right fan ON?	—	*Go to Step 16*	*Go to Step 10*
10	1. Reconnect the left fan. 2. Disconnect fan relay #3. 3. Probe the switch feed circuit (532) at the fan relay #3 connector location (C8) using a test lamp that is connected to a good ground. Does the test lamp illuminate?	—	*Go to Step 11*	*Go to Step 25*
11	Using the second jumper wire, jumper the switch ignition feed circuit (532) and the RH fan feed circuit (504) together at relay #3 connector locations (B9 and C8). Do the fans come ON?	—	*Go to Step 26*	*Go to Step 12*
12	1. Reconnect fan relay #3. 2. Disconnect the right fan. 3. Probe fan harness connector terminal B with a test lamp that is connected to a good ground. Is the left fan ON?	—	*Go to Step 16*	*Go to Step 18*

GC1089900413010X

Fig. 51 Cooling fan table No. 2 (Part 1 of 2). 1998–2000 Camaro & Firebird w/3.8L Engine

Step	Action	Value(s)	Yes	No
1	Did you perform the Cooling Fan Functional Check?	—	*Go to Step 2*	*Go to Cooling Fan Functional Check*
2	1. With a scan tool, command cooling fan relay #1 ON. 2. Command cooling fan relays #1, #2, and #3 ON while observing the fans. Did both fans operate with no change?	—	*Go to Step 8*	*Go to Step 3*
3	Did the left fan stop operating?	—	*Go to Step 9*	*Go to Step 4*
4	1. Disconnect fan relay #2. 2. Probe the relay 2 and 3 control circuit (473) at relay #2 connector location (B4) using a *J 34142-B* test lamp that is connected to B+. 3. Command cooling fan relay #2 and #3 ON using a scan tool. Does the test lamp illuminate after several seconds?	—	*Go to Step 5*	*Go to Step 12*
5	Probe the coil feed circuit (1640) at relay #2 connector location (C6) using a test lamp that is connected to a good ground. Does the test lamp illuminate?	—	*Go to Step 6*	*Go to Step 13*
6	Probe the switch feed circuit (402) at the relay #2 connector location (C4) using a test lamp that is connected to a good ground. Does the test lamp illuminate?	—	*Go to Step 7*	*Go to Step 14*
7	Jumper the switch ignition feed circuit (402) and the RH fan feed circuit (504) together at the relay #2 connector locations (C4 and B6). Is the right fan ON?	—	*Go to Step 15*	*Go to Step 16*
8	1. Turn OFF the ignition. 2. Disconnect the PCM. 3. Disconnect fan relay #1. 4. Jumper the switch feed circuit (402) and the LH fan feed circuit (409) together at the relay #1 connector locations (B3 and C1). 5. Turn the ignition ON. 6. Probe the PCM harness connector for the cooling fan relay #2 and #3 control with a fused jumper that is connected to a good ground. Do the fans switch from low to high speed?	—	*Go to Step 22*	*Go to Step 17*
9	1. Disconnect fan relay #3. 2. Probe the relay 2 and 3 control circuit (473) at the relay #3 connector location (C10) using a test lamp that is connected to B+. 3. Command cooling fan relay #2 and #3 ON using a scan tool. Does the test lamp illuminate?	—	*Go to Step 10*	*Go to Step 18*
10	Probe the ground circuit (150) at the relay #3 connector location (B10) using a test lamp that is connected to B+. Does the test lamp illuminate?	—	*Go to Step 11*	*Go to Step 19*
11	Probe the coil feed circuit (1640) at the relay #3 connector location (B8) using a test lamp that is connected to a good ground. Does the test lamp illuminate?	—	*Go to Step 20*	*Go to Step 21*

GC1089900414010X

Fig. 52 Cooling fan table No. 3 (Part 1 of 2). 1998–2000 Camaro & Firebird w/3.8L Engine

Step	Action	Value(s)	Yes	No
12	Repair the relay 2 and 3 control circuit (473) for an open between fan relay #2 and the splice. Is the action complete?	—	Go to *Cooling Fan Functional Check*	—
13	Repair the open in the relay #2 coil feed circuit (1640). Is the action complete?	—	Go to *Cooling Fan Functional Check*	—
14	Repair the open in the relay #2 switch feed circuit (402). Is the action complete?	—	Go to *Cooling Fan Functional Check*	—
15	Replace the fan relay #2. Is the action complete?	—	Go to *Cooling Fan Functional Check*	—
16	Repair the open in the RH fan feed circuit (504) between fan relay #2 and the splice. Is the action complete?	—	Go to *Cooling Fan Functional Check*	—
17	Repair the fan 2 and 3 relay control circuit (473) for an open or for a short to B+. Is the action complete?	—	Go to *Cooling Fan Functional Check*	—
18	Repair the open in the fan 2 and 3 relay control circuit (473) between fan relay #3 and the splice. Is the action complete?	—	Go to *Cooling Fan Functional Check*	—
19	Repair the open in the ground circuit (150). Is the action complete?	—	Go to *Cooling Fan Functional Check*	—
20	Replace the fan relay #3. Is the action complete?	—	Go to *Cooling Fan Functional Check*	—
21	Repair the open in relay #3 coil feed circuit (1640). Is the action complete?	—	Go to *Cooling Fan Functional Check*	—
22	1. Inspect the PCM connections. 2. Repair faulty connections as necessary. Did you find and correct the condition?	—	Go to *Cooling Fan Functional Check*	*Go to Step 23*
23	**Important:** Program the replacement PCM. Replace the PCM. Is the action complete?	—	Go to *Cooling Fan Functional Check*	—

GC1089900414020X

Fig. 52 Cooling fan table No. 3 (Part 2 of 2). 1998–2000 Camaro & Firebird w/3.8L Engine

Step	Action	Value(s)	Yes	No
1	Did you perform the Cooling Fan Functional Check?	—	*Go to Step 2*	Go to Cooling Fan Functional Check
2	1. Turn ON the ignition leaving the engine OFF. 2. Disconnect the cooling fan relay #1. Are both of the cooling fans OFF?	—	*Go to Step 6*	*Go to Step 3*
3	Disconnect the cooling fan relay #3. Are both of the cooling fans OFF?	—	*Go to Step 4*	*Go to Step 5*
4	1. Turn OFF the ignition. 2. Raise the vehicle. 3. Disconnect the left cooling fan electrical connector. 4. Probe the cooling fan electrical connector terminal B using the test lamp *J 34142-B* connected to ground. 5. Turn ON the ignition leaving the engine OFF. Does the test lamp illuminate?	—	*Go to Step 7*	*Go to Step 8*
5	Disconnect the cooling fan relay #2. Are both of the cooling fans OFF?	—	*Go to Step 10*	*Go to Step 9*
6	Replace the cooling fan relay #1. Is the action complete	—	Go to Cooling Fan Functional Check	—
7	Repair circuit 409 for a short to B+. Is the action complete	—	Go to Cooling Fan Functional Check	—
8	Repair circuit 532 for a short to B+. Is the action complete	—	Go to Cooling Fan Functional Check	—
9	Repair circuit 504 for a short to B+. Is the action complete?	—	Go to Cooling Fan Functional Check	—
10	Replace the cooling fan relay #2. Is the action complete?	—	Go to Cooling Fan Functional Check	—

GC1080000608000X

Fig. 54 Cooling fan table 1. 1998–2000 Camaro & Firebird w/5.7L Engine

Step	Action	Value(s)	Yes	No
1	Did you perform the Powertrain On-Board Diagnostic (OBD) System Check?	—	*Go to Step 2*	Go to *A Powertrain On Board Diagnostic (OBD) System Check*
2	Are any DTCs set?	—	Go to applicable DTC Table	*Go to Step 3*
3	**Important:** Engine coolant temperature must be below the specified value for all of the cooling fan diagnoses. 1. Idle the engine. 2. Turn the A/C OFF. 3. Monitor the A/C Request parameter using the scan tool. Does the scan tool display the A/C request as YES?	100°C (212°F)	Go to *A/C Request Circuit Diagnosis*	*Go to Step 4*
4	1. Turn OFF the ignition. 2. Turn ON the ignition leaving the engine OFF. Are the cooling fans ON?	—	Go to Cooling Fan table #1	*Go to Step 5*
5	Command the cooling fan relay #1 ON using a scan tool. Are both cooling fans ON?	—	*Go to Step 6*	Go to Cooling Fan table #2
6	Command the cooling fan relays #1, #2 and #3 ON using a scan tool. Do both cooling fans switch to high speed?	—	*Go to Step 7*	Go to Cooling Fan table #3
7	1. Using a scan tool, exit outputs. 2. Idle the engine leaving the A/C OFF. Are the cooling fans ON?	—	Go to Cooling Fan table #1	*Go to Step 8*
8	Turn the A/C ON. Are the cooling fans ON?	—	System OK	*Go to Step 9*
9	Does the scan tool display A/C request as YES?	—	Go to *A Diagnostic Starting Point in* HVAC Systems.	Go to *A/C Request Circuit Diagnosis*

GC1080000607000X

Fig. 53 Cooling fan functional check. 1998–2000 Camaro & Firebird w/5.7L Engine

Step	Action	Value(s)	Yes	No
1	Did you perform the Cooling Fan Functional Check?	—	*Go to Step 2*	Go to Cooling Fan Functional Check
2	1. Turn ON the ignition leaving the engine OFF. 2. Disconnect cooling fan relay #1. 3. Probe the cooling fan relay #1 terminal B3 at the underhood electrical center using the test lamp *J 34142-B* connected to ground. Does the test lamp illuminate?	—	*Go to Step 3*	*Go to Step 11*
3	**Important:** Leave jumper in place for remainder of this table. Connect a fused jumper wire between the cooling fan relay #1 terminals B3 and C1 at the underhood electrical center. Do both cooling fans turn ON?	—	*Go to Step 12*	*Go to Step 4*
4	1. Raise the vehicle. 2. Disconnect the left cooling fan electrical connector. 3. Probe the left cooling fan electrical connector terminal B using the test lamp *J 34142-B* connected to ground. Does the test lamp illuminate?	—	*Go to Step 5*	*Go to Step 13*
5	1. Disconnect the cooling fan relay #3. 2. Probe the cooling fan relay #3 terminal C8 using the test lamp *J 34142-B* connected to B+. Does the test lamp illuminate?	—	*Go to Step 22*	*Go to Step 6*
6	1. Install the cooling fan relay #3. **Important:** Leave jumper in place for remainder of this table. 2. Connect a fused jumper wire between left cooling fan electrical connector terminals A and B. Does the right cooling fan turn ON?	—	*Go to Step 14*	*Go to Step 7*
7	1. Disconnect the cooling fan relay #3. 2. Probe the cooling fan relay #3 terminal C8 at the underhood electrical center using the test lamp *J 34142-B* connected to ground. Does the test lamp illuminate?	—	*Go to Step 8*	*Go to Step 16*
8	**Important:** Leave the jumper in place for remainder of this table. Connect a fused jumper wire between the cooling fan relay #3 terminals C8 and B9 at the underhood electrical center. Does the right cooling fan turn ON?	—	*Go to Step 17*	*Go to Step 9*

GC1080000609010X

Fig. 55 Cooling fan table 2 (Part 1 of 2). 1998–2000 Camaro & Firebird w/5.7L Engine

Step	Action	Value(s)	Yes	No
9	1. Disconnect the right cooling fan electrical connector. 2. Probe the right cooling fan electrical connector terminal B using the test lamp *J 34142-B* connected to ground. Does the test lamp illuminate?	—	*Go to Step 10*	*Go to Step 21*
10	Probe the right cooling fan electrical connector terminal A using the test lamp *J 34142-B* connected to B+. Does the test lamp illuminate?	—	*Go to Step 18*	*Go to Step 20*
11	Repair the cooling fan relay B+ supply circuit. Is the action complete?	—	Go to Cooling Fan Functional Check	—
12	Replace the #1 Cooling fan relay. Is the action complete?	—	Go to Cooling Fan Functional Check	—
13	Repair the open circuit between the cooling fan relay #1 and the left cooling fan motor. Is the action complete?	—	Go to Cooling Fan Functional Check	—
14	1. Inspect for poor connections at the left cooling fan motor. 2. If you find a poor connection, repair the condition as necessary. Did you find and correct the condition?	—	Go to Cooling Fan Functional Check	*Go to Step 15*
15	Replace the LH fan motor. Is the action complete?	—	Go to Cooling Fan Functional Check	—
16	Repair the open circuit between the LH cooling fan electrical connector terminal A and the cooling fan relay #3 terminal C8. Is the action complete?	—	Go to Cooling Fan Functional Check	—
17	Replace the #3 cooling fan relay. Is the action complete?	—	Go to Cooling Fan Functional Check	—
18	1. Inspect for poor connections at the right cooling fan motor. 2. If you find a poor connection, repair the condition as necessary. Did you find and correct the condition?	—	Go to Cooling Fan Functional Check	*Go to Step 19*
19	Replace the RH fan motor. Is the action complete?	—	Go to Cooling Fan Functional Check	—
20	Repair the open ground circuit. Is the action complete?	—	Go to Cooling Fan Functional Check	—
21	Repair the open circuit between the cooling fan relay #3 and the RH cooling fan motor. Is the action complete?	—	Go to Cooling Fan Functional Check	—
22	Repair the short to ground between the left cooling fan motor and relay #3. Is the action complete?	—	Go to Cooling Fan Functional Check	—

GC1080000609020X

Fig. 55 Cooling fan table 2 (Part 2 of 2). 1998–2000 Camaro & Firebird w/5.7L Engine

Step	Action	Value(s)	Yes	No
12	Replace the #2 Cooling fan relay. Is the action complete?	—	Go to Cooling Fan Functional Check	—
13	Repair the cooling fan relay control circuit for an open. Is the action complete?	—	Go to Cooling Fan Functional Check	—
14	Repair circuit 504 for an open. Is the action complete?	—	Go to Cooling Fan Functional Check	—
15	Repair the open ground circuit between cooling fan relay #3 and the splice. Is the action complete?	—	Go to Cooling Fan Functional Check	—
16	Replace the #3 cooling fan relay. Is the action complete?	—	Go to Cooling Fan Functional Check	—
17	1. Inspect for poor relay connections at the underhood electrical. 2. If you find a poor connection, repair the condition as necessary. Is the action complete?	—	Go to Cooling Fan Functional Check	—

GC1080000610020X

Fig. 56 Cooling fan table 3 (Part 2 of 2). 1998–2000 Camaro & Firebird w/5.7L Engine

Step	Action	Value(s)	Yes	No
1	Did you perform the Cooling Fan Functional Check?	—	*Go to Step 2*	Go to Cooling Fan Functional Check
2	1. Turn ON the ignition leaving the engine OFF. 2. Command the cooling fan relays #1, #2 and #3 ON using the scan tool. Is the right cooling fan operating at high speed?	—	*Go to Step 3*	*Go to Step 8*
3	Is the left cooling fan operating at high speed?	—	Go to Cooling Fan Functional Check	*Go to Step 4*
4	1. Remove the cooling fan relay #3. 2. Probe the cooling fan relay #3 terminal B8 at the underhood electrical center using the test lamp *J 34142-B* connected to ground. Does the test lamp illuminate?	—	*Go to Step 5*	*Go to Step 11*
5	1. Probe the cooling fan relay #3 terminal C10 at the underhood electrical center using the test lamp *J 34142-B* connected to B+. 2. Command the cooling fan relays #2 and #3 ON using the scan tool. Does the test lamp illuminate?	—	*Go to step 6*	*Go to Step 13*
6	Connect a fused jumper wire between the cooling fan relay #3 terminals C8 and B10 at the underhood electrical center. Does the left cooling fan turn ON?	—	*Go to Step 16*	*Go to Step 7*
7	Probe the cooling fan relay #3 terminal B10 at the underhood electrical center using the test lamp *J 34142-B* connected to B+. Does the test lamp illuminate?	—	*Go to Step 17*	*Go to Step 15*
8	1. Turn ON the ignition leaving the engine OFF. 2. Disconnect the cooling fan relay #2. 3. Probe the cooling fan relay #2 terminals C4 and C6 at the underhood electrical center using the test lamp *J 34142-B* connected to ground. Does the test lamp illuminate for both terminals?	—	*Go to Step 9*	*Go to Step 11*
9	1. Probe the cooling fan relay #2 terminal B4 at the underhood electrical center using the test lamp *J 34142-B* connected to B+. 2. Command the cooling fan relays #2 and #3 ON using the scan tool. Does the test lamp illuminate?	—	*Go to Step 10*	*Go to Step 13*
10	Jumper the cooling fan relay #2 terminals C4 and B6 at the underhood electrical center using a fused jumper wire. Does the right cooling fan turn ON?	—	*Go to Step 12*	*Go to Step 14*
11	Repair the cooling fan relay B+ circuit for an open. Is the action complete?	—	Go to Cooling Fan Functional Check	—

GC1080000610010X

Fig. 56 Cooling fan table 3 (Part 1 of 2). 1998–2000 Camaro & Firebird w/5.7L Engine

Step	Action	Yes	No
1	Install a scan tool. Does the scan tool power up?	Go to *Step 2*	Diagnose Data Link Communications
2	1. Turn ON the ignition, with the engine OFF. 2. Attempt to establish communication with the following control modules: • Instrument Cluster • Powertrain Control Module Does the scan tool communicate with the control modules?	Go to *Step 3*	Diagnose Data Link Communications
3	Select the powertrain control module display DTCs function on the scan tool. Does the scan tool display any DTCs?	Go to *Step 4*	Diagnose *Engine Cooling*
4	Does the scan tool display any DTCs which begin with a "U"?	Go to *Scan Tool Does Not Communicate with Class 2 Device*	Diagnose *Trouble Code*

GC1080100650000X

Fig. 57 Diagnostic system check. 2001-02 Camaro & Firebird

Step	Action	Yes	No
DEFINITION: One or both engine cooling fan motors run continuously in high or low speed.			
1	Did you perform the Engine Cooling Diagnostic System Check?	Go to *Step 2*	Go To *Diagnostic System Check -*
2	Turn ON the ignition, with the engine OFF. Are one or both cooling fans ON?	Go to *Step 3*	*Test for Intermittent and Poor Connections*
3	Are both cooling fans running continuously?	Go to *Step 5*	Go to *Step 4*
4	Remove the cooling fan 3 relay. Did the right cooling fan turn OFF?	Go to *Step 6*	Go to *Step 7*
5	Repair the short to voltage in the left cooling fan motor supply voltage circuit. Did you complete the repair?	Go to *Step 8*	—
6	Repair the short to voltage in the left cooling fan low reference circuit. Did you complete the repair?	Go to *Step 8*	—
7	Repair the short to voltage in the right cooling fan motor supply voltage circuit. Did you complete the repair?	Go to *Step 8*	—
8	Operate the system in order to verify the repair. Did you correct the condition?	System OK	Go to *Step 2*

GC1080100651000X

Fig. 58 Cooling fan always on. 2001-02 Camaro & Firebird

Step	Action	Yes	No
DEFINITION: One or both engine cooling fan motors do not operate properly in high or low speed modes.			
1	Did you perform the Engine Cooling Diagnostic System Check?	Go to *Step 2*	Go to *Diagnostic System Check -*
2	1. Install a scan tool. 2. Turn ON the ignition, with the engine OFF. 3. With a scan tool, command the Fans Low Speed ON and OFF. Do the low speed engine cooling fans turn ON and OFF with each command?	Go to *Step 3*	Go to *Step 4*
3	**Important:** Before the PCM changes the speed of the cooling fans, a 3-second delay will occur. With a scan tool, command the Fans High Speed ON and OFF. Do the high speed engine cooling fans turn ON and OFF with each command?	*Test for Intermittent and Poor Connections*	Go to *Step 11*
4	**Important:** Following this step, do NOT remove the 20-A fused jumper wire that is connected during this step. While performing the following steps, use a second 20-A fused jumper wire. 1. Remove the cooling fan 1 relay. 2. Connect a 20-A fused jumper between the battery positive voltage circuit of the cooling fan 1 relay and the cooling fan motor supply voltage circuit of the cooling fan 1 relay. Do both cooling fans operate in low speed?	Go to *Step 13*	Go to *Step 5*

GC1080100652010X

Fig. 59 Cooling fan inoperative (Part 1 of 3). 2001-02 Camaro & Firebird

Step	Action	Yes	No
5	1. Disconnect the cooling fan 3 relay 2. Connect the second 20-A fused jumper between the left cooling fan ground circuit of the cooling fan 3 relay and the right cooling fan motor supply voltage circuit of the cooling fan 3 relay. Do both cooling fans operate in low speed?	Go to *Step 14*	Go to *Step 6*
6	Connect the second 20-A fused jumper between the battery positive voltage circuit of the cooling fan 3 relay and the cooling fan motor supply voltage circuit of the cooling fan 3 relay. Does the right cooling fan operate in high speed?	Go to *Step 9*	Go to *Step 7*
7	1. Install the cooling fan 3 relay. 2. Disconnect the right cooling fan electrical connector. 3. Connect the second 20-Amp fused jumper wire from the cooling fan motor supply voltage circuit of the right cooling fan electrical connector to the circuit of the right cooling fan electrical connector. Does the left cooling fan operate in high speed?	Go to *Step 16*	Go to *Step 8*
8	Connect the second 20-Amp fused jumper wire from the cooling fan motor supply voltage circuit of the right cooling fan electrical connector to a good ground. Does the left cooling fan operate in high speed?	Go to *Step 20*	Go to *Step 21*
9	1. Install the cooling fan 3 relay. 2. Disconnect the left cooling fan electrical connector. 3. Connect the second 20-Amp fused jumper wire from the cooling fan motor supply voltage circuit of the left cooling fan electrical connector to the cooling fan low reference circuit of the left cooling fan electrical connector. Does the right cooling fan operate in high speed?	Go to *Step 17*	Go to *Step 10*
10	Connect the second 20-Amp fused jumper wire from battery positive voltage to the low reference circuit of the of the left cooling fan electrical connector. Does the right cooling fan operate in high speed?	Go to *Step 18*	Go to *Step 22*
11	Is the right cooling fan operating properly in high speed?	Go to *Step 12*	Go to *Step 15*
12	1. Disconnect the cooling fan 3 relay 2. Connect the second 20-A fused jumper between the left cooling fan low reference circuit of the cooling fan 3 relay and the ground circuit of the cooling fan 3 relay. Does the left cooling fan operate properly in high speed?	Go to *Step 14*	Go to *Step 19*
13	Inspect for poor connections at the cooling fan 1 relay. Did you find and correct the condition?	Go to *Step 28*	Go to *Step 23*
14	Inspect for poor connections at the cooling fan 3 relay. Did you find and correct the condition?	Go to *Step 28*	Go to *Step 24*
15	Inspect for poor connections at the cooling fan 3 relay. Did you find and correct the condition?	Go to *Step 28*	Go to *Step 25*
16	Inspect for poor connections at the harness connector of the right cooling fan. Did you find and correct the condition?	Go to *Step 28*	Go to *Step 26*

GC1080100652020X

Fig. 59 Cooling fan inoperative (Part 2 of 3). 2001-02 Camaro & Firebird

Step	Action	Yes	No
17	Inspect for poor connections at the harness connector of the left cooling fan. Did you find and correct the condition?	Go to *Step 28*	Go to *Step 27*
18	Repair the left cooling fan motor supply voltage circuit. Did you complete the repair?	Go to *Step 28*	—
19	Repair the left cooling fan low reference circuit. Did you complete the repair?	Go to *Step 28*	—
20	Repair the right cooling fan ground circuit. Did you complete the repair?	Go to *Step 28*	—
21	Repair the right cooling fan motor supply voltage circuit. Did you complete the repair?	Go to *Step 28*	—
22	Repair the left cooling fan low reference circuit. Did you complete the repair?	Go to *Step 28*	—
23	Replace the cooling fan 1 relay. Did you complete the repair?	Go to *Step 28*	—
24	Replace the cooling fan 3 relay. Did you complete the repair?	Go to *Step 28*	—
25	Replace the cooling fan 3 relay. Did you complete the repair?	Go to *Step 28*	—
26	Replace the right cooling fan. Did you complete the repair?	Go to *Step 28*	—
27	Replace the left cooling fan. Did you complete the repair?	Go to *Step 28*	—
28	Operate the system in order to verify the repair. Did you correct the condition?	System OK	Go to *Step 3*

GC1080100652030X

Fig. 59 Cooling fan inoperative (Part 3 of 3). 2001-02 Camaro & Firebird

Step	Action	Normal Result(s)	Abnormal Result(s)*
1	Check in order to ensure that the electric cooling fan operates at normal speed when the primary cooling fan temperature switch reaches the appropriate temperature.	When the primary cooling fan temperature switch reaches 110°C (230°F), terminal 3 of the primary cooling fan temperature switch is grounded, the fan control relay K67 is energized, and the electric cooling fan operates at normal speed.	The electric cooling fan does not operate at normal speed. Refer to *Cooling Fan Inoperative*
2	Check in order to ensure that the electric cooling fan operates at low speed when the primary cooling fan temperature switch reaches the appropriate temperature.	1. When the primary cooling fan temperature switch reaches 100°C (212°F), terminal 2 of the primary cooling fan temperature switch is grounded, the fan control relay K26 is energized, and the electric cooling fan operates at low speed. 2. The electric cooling fan operates at low speed because the engine coolant fan resistor is in series with the electric cooling fan motor.	The electric cooling fan does not operate at low speed. Refer to *Cooling Fan Inoperative at Low Speed*
3	Check in order to ensure that the auxiliary engine coolant fan #1 and auxiliary engine coolant fan #2 operate at low speed when the primary cooling fan temperature switch reaches the appropriate temperature.	When the primary cooling fan temperature switch reaches 100°C (212°F), terminal 2 of the primary cooling fan temperature switch is grounded, the fan control relay K26 is energized, and B+ is supplied to terminal A of the auxiliary engine coolant fan #1. The auxiliary engine coolant fan #1 is wired in series with the auxiliary engine coolant fan #2 through the normally closed contacts of the fan control relay K52. The fans will run at a lower speed until the fan control relay K52 is energized.	The auxiliary engine coolant fan #1 and auxiliary engine coolant fan #2 do not operate at low speed. Refer to *Cooling Fan Inoperative - Auxiliary (Both Aux Eng Cool Fans Inop)*

GC1089800449010X

Fig. 60 Cooling fan system check (Part 1 of 3). 1998 Catera

Step	Action	Normal Result(s)	Abnormal Result(s)*
4	Check in order to ensure that the auxiliary engine coolant fan #1 and auxiliary engine coolant fan #2 operate at normal speed, when the primary cooling fan temperature switch and the secondary cooling fan temperature switch reach their appropriate temperatures.	1. When the secondary cooling fan temperature switch reaches 105°C (221°F), terminal 2 of the secondary cooling fan temperature switch is grounded, the fan control relays K28 and K52 are energized, and ground is supplied to terminal B of the auxiliary engine coolant fan #1 through fan control relay K52. B+ for the auxiliary engine coolant fan #1 is supplied by the previously energized fan control relay K26. 2. When B+ is supplied to terminal A and ground is supplied to terminal B of the auxiliary engine coolant fan #1, the auxiliary engine coolant fan #1 will operate at normal speed. 3. The fan control relay K28 supplies B+ to terminal A of the auxiliary engine coolant fan #2. Terminal B of the auxiliary engine coolant fan #2 is permanently grounded. The auxiliary engine coolant fan runs at normal speed.	1. The auxiliary engine coolant fan #1 does not operate at normal speed. Refer to *Cooling Fan Inoperative - Auxiliary (Aux Engine Coolant Fan #1 Inop).* 2. The auxiliary engine coolant fan #2 does not operate at normal speed. Refer to *Cooling Fan Inoperative - Auxiliary (Aux Engine Coolant Fan #2 Inop).*
5	Check in order to ensure that the auxiliary engine fan #1 and auxiliary engine fan #2 operate at low speed when the A/C compressor clutch coil is energized.	When the A/C compressor clutch coil is engized the fan control relay K87 is energized, and B+ is supplied to terminal A of the auxiliary engine coolant fan #1. The auxiliary engine coolant fan #1 is wired in series with the auxiliary engine coolant fan #2 through the normally closed contacts of the fan control relay K52. The fans will run at low speed until the fan control relay K52 is energized.	The auxiliary engine coolant fan #1 and auxiliary engine coolant fan #2 do not operate at low speed. Refer to *Cooling Fan Inoperative - Auxiliary (A/C Cooling Low Speed).*
6	Check in order to ensure that the auxiliary engine coolant fan #1 and auxiliary engine fan #2 operate at normal speed when the A/C compressor refrigerant pressure switch reaches the appropriate pressure.	When the A/C compressor refrigerant pressure switch reaches 1900 kPa (275 PSI), terminal 3 of the A/C compressor refrigerant pressure switch is grounded, the fan control relay K28 is energized, and the auxiliary engine coolant fan #1 and auxiliary engine coolant fan #2 operate at normal speed.	The auxiliary engine coolant fan #1 and auxiliary engine coolant fan #2 do not operate at normal speed. Refer to *Cooling Fan Inoperative - Auxiliary (A/C Cooling High Speed).*
7	Check in order to ensure that the ECM cooling blower operates at normal speed when the A/C compressor refrigerant pressure switch reaches the appropriate pressure.	When the A/C compressor refrigerant pressure switch reaches 1900 kPa (275 PSI), terminal 3 of the A/C compressor refrigerant pressure switch is grounded, the ECM relay K48 is energized, and the ECM cooling blower operates at normal speed.	The ECM cooling blower does not operate at normal speed. Refer to *ECM Cooling Blower Inoperative.*

GC1089800449020X

Fig. 60 Cooling fan system check (Part 2 of 3). 1998 Catera

Step	Action	Normal Result(s)	Abnormal Result(s)*
8	Check in order to ensure that the water auxiliary pump operates at normal speed when the ignition key is in the ON position.	When the ignition key is turned to the ON position, the auxiliary water pump relay K22 is energized and the water auxiliary pump operates at normal speed.	The water auxiliary pump does not operate at normal speed. Refer to *Water Pump Inoperative - Auxiliary.*
9	Check in order to ensure that the heater water auxiliary pump operates at normal speed when the ignition key is in the ON position.	When the ignition key is in the ON position, B+ is supplied to terminal 2 of the heater water auxiliary pump and the heater water auxiliary pump operates at normal speed.	The heater water auxiliary pump does not operate at normal speed. Refer to *Cooling Fan Circuit Diagnosis (Heater Water Aux Pump Inop).*
* Refer to the appropriate symptom diagnostic table for the applicable abnormal result.			

GC1089800449030X

Fig. 60 Cooling fan system check (Part 3 of 3). 1998 Catera

Step	Action	Value(s)	Yes	No
1	Did you perform the Cooling Fan System Check?	—	*Go to Step 2*	Refer to *Cooling Fan System Check.*
2	1. Turn on the ignition. 2. Locate the coolant fan test connector within the ECM housing. 3. Use a fused jumper to connect terminal 4 of the coolant fan test connector to a known good ground. Does the electric cooling fan turn ON?	—	*Go to Step 3*	*Go to Step 4*
3	1. Locate and repair open or a high resistance in circuits XM5 and/or F600. 2. Replace the primary cooling fan temperature switch if these circuits are OK. Did you complete the repair?	—	*Go to Step 17*	—
4	1. Disconnect the fan control relay K67 connector. 2. Use the DMM in order to measure the resistance between terminal 4 of the coolant fan test connector and terminal 6 of the fan control relay K67. Does the resistance measure near the specified value?	Less than 5 Ω	*Go to Step 6*	*Go to Step 5*
5	1. Locate an open or a high resistance in CKT MX998. 2. Repair the open or the high resistance in CKT MX998. Did you complete the repair?	—	*Go to Step 17*	—
6	Use the DMM in order to measure the voltage between terminal 2 of the fan control relay K67 and a known good ground. Does the voltage measure near the specified value?	B+	*Go to Step 8*	*Go to Step 7*
7	1. Locate an open or a high resistance in CKT X2. 2. Repair the open or the high resistance in CKT X2. Did you complete the repair?	—	*Go to Step 17*	—
8	Use the DMM in order to measure the voltage between terminal 4 of the fan control relay K67 and a known good ground. Does the voltage measure near the specified value?	B+	*Go to Step 10*	*Go to Step. 9*
9	1. Check the integrity of fuse #42. 2. If the fuse is OK, locate an open or a high resistance in circuits A710 and/or A700. 3. Repair the open or the high resistance in circuits A710 and/or A700. Did you complete the repair?	—	*Go to Step 17*	—
10	Connect a fused jumper between terminal 4 and terminal 8 of the fan control relay K67 connector. Does the engine coolant fan turn ON?	—	*Go to Step 11*	*Go to Step 12*
11	Replace the fan control relay K67. Did you complete the repair?	—	*Go to Step 17*	—
12	1. Disconnect the electric cooling fan connector. 2. Use the DMM in order to measure the voltage between terminal A of the electric cooling fan connector and a known good ground. Does the voltage measure near the specified value?	B+	*Go to Step 14*	*Go to Step 13*

GC1089800451010X

Fig. 62 Cooling fan inoperative (Part 1 of 2). 1998 Catera

Step	Action	Value(s)	Yes	No
1	Was the Coolant Fan System Check performed?	B+	*Go to Step 2*	Refer to *Cooling Fan System Check.*
2	1. Disconnect the heater water auxiliary pump connector. 2. Turn the ignition switch to the ON position. 3. Use the DMM to measure the voltage between terminal 2 of the heater water auxiliary pump connector and a known good ground. Is the measured voltage within the specified value?	B+	*Go to Step 4*	*Go to Step 3*
3	1. Locate an open or a high resistance in circuit X70. 2. Repair the open or the high resistance in circuit X70. Is the repair complete?	—	*Go to Step 7*	—
4	Use the DMM to measure the resistance between terminal 1 of the heater water auxiliary pump connector and a known good ground. Is the measured resistance within the specified value?	Less than 5 Ω	*Go to Step 6*	*Go to Step 5*
5	1. Locate an open or a high resistance in circuit F75. 2. Repair the open or the high resistance in circuit F75. Is the repair complete?	—	*Go to Step 7*	—
6	Replace the heater water auxiliary pump. Is the replacement complete?	—	*Go to Step 7*	—
7	1. Connect all connectors and components that were disconnected. 2. Verify the heater water auxiliary pump operates properly? Does the heater water auxiliary pump operate properly?	—	System OK	*Go to Step 1*

GC1089800450000X

Fig. 61 Cooling fan circuit diagnosis (Heater water auxiliary pump inop). 1998 Catera

Step	Action	Value(s)	Yes	No
13	1. Locate an open, high resistance or short to ground in circuits AM16 and/or AM17. 2. Repair an open, high resistance or short to ground in circuits AM16 and/or AM17. Did you complete the repair?	—	*Go to Step 17*	—
14	Use the DMM in order to measure the resistance between terminal B of the electric cooling fan connector and a known good ground. Does the resistance measure near the specified value?	Less than 5 Ω	*Go to Step 16*	*Go to Step 15*
15	1. Locate an open or a high resistance in CKT F100. 2. Repair the open or the high resistance in CKT F100. Did you complete the repair?	—	*Go to Step 17*	—
16	Replace the electric cooling fan. Did you complete the repair?	—	*Go to Step 17*	—
17	1. Connect all connectors and components that were previously disconnected. 2. Verify that the electric cooling fan operates properly. Does the electric cooling fan operate properly?	—	Refer to *Cooling Fan System Check.*	*Go to Step 1*

GC1089800451020X

Fig. 62 Cooling fan inoperative (Part 2 of 2). 1998 Catera

Step	Action	Value(s)	Yes	No
1	Did you perform the Cooling Fan Diagnostic System Check?	—	*Go to Step 2*	Refer to *Cooling Fan System Check.*
2	1. Locate the coolant fan test connector within the ECM housing. 2. Use a fused jumper in order to connect terminal 1 of the coolant fan test connector to a known good ground. Does the electric cooling fan turn ON at low speed?	—	*Go to Step 3*	*Go to Step 4*
3	1. Locate an open or a high resistance in circuits XP30 and/or F600. 2. Repair the open or the high resistance in circuits XP30 and/or F600. 3. Replace the primary cooling fan temperature switch if circuits XP30 and F600 are OK. Did you complete the repair?	—	*Go to Step 19*	—
4	1. Disconnect the fan control relay K26 connector. 2. Use the DMM to measure the resistance between terminal 1 of the coolant fan test connector and terminal 6 of the fan control relay K26. Is the measured resistance within the specified value?	Less than 5 Ω	*Go to Step 6*	*Go to Step 5*
5	1. Locate an open or a high resistance in circuits XP999 and/or XP3. 2. Repair the open or the high resistance in circuits XP999 and/or XP3. Did you complete the repair?	—	*Go to Step 19*	—

GC1089800452010X

Fig. 63 Cooling fan inoperative at low speed (Part 1 of 3). 1998 Catera

Step	Action	Value(s)	Yes	No
6	Use the DMM in order to measure the voltage between terminal 3 of the fan control relay K26 and a known good ground. Does the voltage measure near the specified value?	B+	*Go to Step 8*	*Go to Step 7*
7	1. Inspect fuse #50 for an open. 2. Locate an open or high resistance in circuits A6 and/or A310. 3. Repair the open or the high resistance in circuits A6 and/or A310. Did you complete the repair?	—	*Go to Step 19*	—
8	Use the DMM in order to measure the voltage between terminal 4 of the fan control relay K26 and a known good ground. Does the voltage measure near the specified value?	B+	*Go to Step 10*	*Go to Step 9*
9	1. Inspect fuse #52 for an open. 2. Locate an open or a high resistance in circuits A300, A220 and/or A223 if the fuse in OK. 3. Repair the open or the high resistance in circuits A300, A220 and/or A223. Did you complete the repair?	—	*Go to Step 19*	—
10	Connect a fused jumper between terminal 4 and terminal 5 of the fan control relay K26 connector. Does the engine coolant fan turn ON at half speed?	—	*Go to Step 11*	*Go to Step 12*
11	Replace the fan control relay K26. Did you complete the repair?	—	*Go to Step 19*	—
12	1. Disconnect the engine coolant fan resistor connector. 2. Use the DMM in order to measure the voltage between terminal 1 of the engine coolant fan resistor connector and a known good ground. Does the voltage measure near the specified value?	B+	*Go to Step 14*	*Go to Step 13*
13	1. Locate an open, high resistance or a short to ground in circuits AP2 and/or AP1. 2. Repair an open, high resistance or a short to ground in circuits AP2 and/or AP1. Did you complete the repair?	—	*Go to Step 19*	—
14	1. Disconnect the electric cooling fan connector. 2. Use the DMM in order to measure the resistance between terminal 1 of the engine coolant fan resistor connector and terminal A of the electric cooling fan connector. Does the resistance measure near the specified value?	Less than 5 Ω	*Go to Step 16*	*Go to Step 15*
15	1. Locate an open or a high resistance in circuits AM17 and/or AM6. 2. Repair the open or the high resistance in circuits AM17 and/or AM6. Did you complete the repair?	—	*Go to Step 19*	—
16	Use the DMM in order to measure the resistance between terminal B of the electric cooling fan connector and a known good ground. Does the resistance measure near the specified value?	Less than 5 Ω	*Go to Step 18*	*Go to Step 17*
17	1. Locate an open or a high resistance in CKT F100. 2. Repair the open or the high resistance in CKT F100. Did you complete the repair?	—	*Go to Step 19*	—

GC1089800452020X

Fig. 63 Cooling fan inoperative at low speed (Part 2 of 3). 1998 Catera

Step	Action	Value(s)	Yes	No
1	Did you perform the Cooling Fan Diagnostic System Check?	—	*Go to Step 2*	Go to *Cooling Fan System Check*
2	1. Turn the ignition switch to the OFF positon. 2. Locate the coolant fan test connector within the ECM housing. 3. Use a fused jumper to connect terminal 1 of the coolant fan test connector to a known good ground. Does the auxiliary engine coolant fan #1 and fan #2 operate at low speed?	B+	*Go to Step 3*	Go to *Cooling Fan Inoperative - Auxiliary (Both Aux Eng Cool Fans Inop)*
3	1. Turn the ignition switch to the ON position. 2. Disconnect the fan control relay K52 connector. 3. Use the DMM in order to measure the voltage between terminal 4 of the fan control relay K52 connector and a known good ground. Does the voltage measure near the specified value?	B+	*Go to Step 5*	*Go to Step 4*
4	1. Locate a open or a high resistance in circuit X30. 2. Repair the open or the high resistance in circuit X30. Did you complete the repair?	—	*Go to Step 8*	—

GC1089800454010X

Fig. 64 Cooling fan inoperative (Auxiliary engine coolant fan No. 1, Part 1 of 2). 1998 Catera

Step	Action	Value(s)	Yes	No
18	1. Check the integrity of the engine coolant fan resistor. 2. Replace the engine coolant fan resistor if it is open. 3. Replace the electric cooling fan if the engine coolant fan resistor is OK. Did you complete the repair?	—	*Go to Step 19*	—
19	1. Connect all connectors and components that were previously disconnected. 2. Verify that the electric cooling fan operates properly at low speed. Does the electric cooling fan operate properly at low speed?	—	Refer to *Cooling Fan System Check.*	*Go to Step 1*

GC1089800452030X

Fig. 63 Cooling fan inoperative at low speed (Part 3 of 3). 1998 Catera

Step	Action	Value(s)	Yes	No
5	Use the DMM in order to measure the resistance between terminal 8 of the fan control relay K52 and a known good ground. Does the resistance measure near the specified value?	Less than 5Ω	*Go to Step 7*	*Go to Step 6*
6	1. Locate an open or a high resistance in circuit F7 2. Repair the open or the high resistance in circuits F7. Did you complete the repair?	—	*Go to Step 8*	—
7	1. Locate an open or a high resistance in circuits XM123 or XM997. 2. Repair the open or the high resistance in circuits XM123 or XM997. 3. Replace the fan control relay K52 if these circuits are OK. Did you complete the repair?	—	*Go to Step 8*	—
8	1. Connect all connectors and components that were previously disconnected. 2. Check the auxiliary engine coolant fan #1 for proper operation. Does the auxiliary engine coolant fan #1 operate properly?	—	System OK	*Go to Step 1*

GC1089800454020X

Fig. 64 Cooling fan inoperative (Auxiliary engine coolant fan No. 1, Part 2 of 2). 1998 Catera

Step	Action	Value(s)	Yes	No
1	Did you perform the Cooling Fan Diagnostic System Check?	—	*Go to Step 2*	Go to *Cooling Fan System Check*
2	1. Turn the ignition switch to the OFF position. 2. Locate the coolant fan test connector within the ECM housing. 3. Use a fused jumper to connect terminal 1 of the coolant fan test connector to a known good ground. Does the auxiliary engine coolant fans #1 and auxiliary engine coolant fan #2 operate at low speed?	B+	*Go to Step 3*	Go to *Cooling Fan Inoperative - Auxiliary (Both Aux Eng Cool Fans Inop)*
3	1. Turn the ignition switch to the ON position. 2. Disconnect the fan control relay K28 connector. 3. Use the DMM in order to measure the voltage between terminal 4 of the fan control relay K28 connector and a known good ground. Does the voltage measure near the specified value?	B+	*Go to Step 5*	*Go to Step 4*
4	1. Check the integrity of fuse #40 2. Locate a open or a high resistance in circuit A14 or A25 if fuse #40 is OK. 3. Repair the open or the high resistance in circuit A14 or A25. Did you complete the repair?	—	*Go to Step 10*	—
5	Use the DMM in order to measure the voltage between terminal 2 of the fan control relay K28 and a known good ground. Does the voltage measure near the specified value?	B+	*Go to Step 7*	*Go to Step 6*
6	1. Locate an open or a high resistance in circuit X400 2. Repair the open or the high resistance in circuit X400. Did you complete the repair?	—	*Go to Step 10*	—

GC1089800455010X

Fig. 65 Cooling fan inoperative (Auxiliary engine coolant fan No. 2, Part 1 of 2). 1998 Catera

Step	Action	Value(s)	Yes	No
7	1. Disconnected the auxiliary engine coolant fan #2 connector. 2. Use a DMM in order to measure resistance between terminal 8 of the fan control relay connector and terminal A of the auxiliary engine coolant fan #2 Does the resistance measure near the specified value?	Less than 5Ω	Go to Step 8	Go to Step 9
8	1. Locate an open or a high resistance in circuits XM124 or XM997. 2. Repair the open or the high resistance in circuits XM124 or XM997. 3. Replace the fan control relay K52 if these circuits are OK. Did you complete the repair?	—	Go to Step 10	—
9	1. Locate an open or a high resistance in circuit AM4. 2. Repair the open or the high resistance in circuits AM4. Did you complete the repair?	—	Go to Step 10	—
10	1. Connect all connectors and components that were previously disconnected. 2. Check the auxiliary engine coolant fan #2 for proper operation. Does the auxiliary engine coolant fan #2 operate properly?	—	System OK	Go to Step 1

GC1089800455020X

Fig. 65 Cooling fan inoperative (Auxiliary engine coolant fan No. 2, Part 2 of 2). 1998 Catera

Step	Action	Value(s)	Yes	No
5	1. Inspect fuse #50 for an open. 2. Locate an open or a high resistance in circuits A6 and/or A310 if the fuse is OK. 3. Repair the open or the high resistance in circuits A6 and/or A310. Did you complete the repair?	—	Go to Step 19	—
6	Use the DMM in order to measure the voltage between terminal 2 of the fan control relay K26 connector and a known good ground. Does the voltage measure near the specified value?	B+	Go to Step 8	Go to Step 7
7	1. Inspect fuse #52 for an open. 2. Locate an open or a high resistance in circuits A300, A220, and/or A222 if the fuse is OK. 3. Repair the open or the high resistance in circuits A300, A220, and/or A222. Did you complete the repair?	—	Go to Step 19	—
8	1. Use a fused jumper to connect terminal 1 of the coolant fan test connector to a known good ground. 2. Use the DMM in order to measure the resistance between terminal 6 of the fan control relay K26 connector and a known good ground. Did you measure the resistance near the specified value?	Less than 5Ω	Go to Step 10	Go to Step 9
9	1. Locate an open or a high resistance in circuit XP3 or XP999. 2. Repair the open or the high resistance in circuit XP3 or XP999. Did you complete the repair?	—	Go to Step 19	—
10	1. Place the fan control relay K26 back in the ECM housing. 2. Leave the fused jumper connected between terminal 1 of the coolant fan test connector and a good ground. 3. Disconnect the auxiliary engine coolant fan #1 connector. 4. Use a DMM in order to measure voltage between terminal A of the auxiliary engine coolant fan #1 and a known good ground. Did you measure the voltage near the specified value?	B+	Go to Step 12	Go to Step 11
11	1. Locate an open or a high resistance in circuits AM1 or AM13. 2. Repair the open or the high resistance in circuits AM1 or AM13. 3. Replace the fan control relay K26 if these circuits are OK. Did you complete the repair?	—	Go to Step 19	—
12	1. Remove the fan control relay K52 2. Connect the auxiliary engine fan #1 connector 3. Use a fused jumper to connect from terminal 2 of the fan control relay K52 to a known good ground. Does the auxiliary engine coolant fan #1 operate?	—	Go to Step 14	Go to Step 13

GC1089800456020X

Fig. 66 Cooling fan inoperative (Both auxiliary engine coolant fans, Part 2 of 3). 1998 Catera

Step	Action	Value(s)	Yes	No
1	Did you perform the Cooling Fan Diagnostic System Check?	B+	Go to Step 2	Go to Cooling Fan System Check
2	1. Turn the ignition switch to the ON position. 2. Connect a fused jumper between pin 1 of the coolant fan test connector and a known good ground. 3. Grounding pin 1 of the coolant fan test connector will simulate the closing of the primary cooling fan temperature switch stage 1 contacts, this will energize the fan control relay K26. Does the auxiliary engine coolant fan #1 and auxiliary coolant fan #2 operate at low speed?	—	Go to Step 3	Go to Step 4
3	1. Locate an open or a high resistance in circuit XP30 or F600. 2. Repair the open or the high resistance in circuit XP30 or F600. 3. Replace the primary cooling fan temperature switch if these circuits are OK. Are the engine cooling fans operating properly?	—	Go to Step 19	—
4	1. Disconnect the fused jumper. 2. Disconnect the fan control relay K26 connector. 3. Use the DMM in order to measure the voltage between terminal 3 of the fan control relay K26 connector and a known good ground. Does the voltage measure near the specified value?	B+	Go to Step 6	Go to Step 5

GC1089800456010X

Fig. 66 Cooling fan inoperative (Both auxiliary engine coolant fans, Part 1 of 3). 1998 Catera

Step	Action	Value(s)	Yes	No
13	1. Locate an open or a high resistance in circuit XU3. 2. Repair the open or the high resistance in circuit XU3 3. Replace the auxiliary engine coolant fan #1 if these circuits are OK. Did you complete the repair?	—	Go to Step 19	—
14	Use a DMM in order to measure resistance from terminal B of the auxiliary coolant engine fan #2 connector and a known good ground. Did you measure the resistance near the specified value?	Less than 5Ω	Go to Step 16	Go to Step 15
15	1. Locate an open or a high resistance in circuit F4. 2. Repair the open or the high resistance in circuits F4 Did you complete the repair?	—	Go to Step 19	—
16	1. Remove fan control relay K52 2. With the relay removed determine if the relay contacts are closed. 3. Use a DMM in order to measure resistance between terminal 2 and Terminal 5 of the fan control relay K52. Did you measure the resistance near the specified value?	Less than 5Ω	Go to Step 17	Go to Step 18
17	1. Locate an open or a high resistance in circuit AM3 or AM5. 2. Repair the open or the high resistance in circuit AM3 or AM5. 3. Replace the auxiliary engine coolant fan #2 if these circuits are OK. Did you complete the repair?	—	Go to Step 19	—
18	Replace the fan control relay K52 Did you complete the repair?	—	Go to Step 19	—
19	1. Connect all the connectors and components that were disconnected 2. Verify that the auxiliary engine coolant fans #1 and #2 operate properly. Does the auxiliary engine coolant fans #1 and #2 operate properly?	—	System OK	Go to Step 1

GC1089800456030X

Fig. 66 Cooling fan inoperative (Both auxiliary engine coolant fans, Part 3 of 3). 1998 Catera

Step	Action	Value(s)	Yes	No
1	Did you perform the Cooling Fan Diagnostic System Check?	—	Go to Step 2	Go to Cooling Fan System Check
2	1. Turn the ignition switch to the OFF position. 2. Locate the coolant fan test connector within the ECM housing. 3. Use a fused jumper to connect terminal 1 of the coolant fan test connector to a known good ground. Does the auxiliary engine coolant fan #1 and auxiliary engine coolant fan #2 operate at low speed?	B+	Go to Step 3	Go to Cooling Fan Inoperative - Auxiliary (Both Aux Eng Cool Fans Inop)

GC1089800457010X

Fig. 67 Cooling fan inoperative (A/C cooling low speed, Part 1 of 2). 1998 Catera

Step	Action	Value(s)	Yes	No
3	1. Remove the fused jumper. 2. Turn the ignition switch to the ON position. 3. Disconnect the fan control relay K87 connector. 4. Use the DMM in order to measure the voltage between terminal 4 of the fan control relay K87 connector and a known good ground. Does the voltage measure near the specified value?	B+	Go to Step 5	Go to Step 4
4	1. Locate a open or a high resistance in circuit A221 2. Repair the open or the high resistance in circuit A221. Did you complete the repair?	—	Go to Step 10	—
5	Use the DMM in order to measure the resistance between terminal 6 of the fan control relay K87 and a known good ground. Does the resistance measure near the specified value?	Less than 5Ω	Go to Step 7	Go to Step 6
6	1. Locate an open or a high resistance in circuit F2 2. Repair the open or the high resistance in circuits F2. Did you complete the repair?	—	Go to Step 10	—
7	1. Turn the A/C compressor ON 2. Use the DMM in order to measure the voltage between terminal 2 of the fan control relay K87 and a known good ground. Does the voltage measure near the specified value?	B+	Go to Step 9	Go to Step 8
8	1. Locate an open or a high resistance in circuit U4. 2. Repair the open or the high resistance in circuit U4. 3. Refer to HVAC-Compressor controls for A/C compressor diagnosis if the circuit is OK. Did you complete the repair?	—	Go to Step 10	—
9	1. Locate an open or a high resistance in circuits AM12. 2. Repair the open or the high resistance in circuits AM12. 3. Replace the fan control relay K87 if these circuits are OK. Did you complete the repair?	—	Go to Step 10	—
10	1. Connect all connectors and components that were previously disconnected. 2. Check the auxiliary engine coolant fan #1 for proper operation. Does the auxiliary engine coolant fans operate at low speed?	—	System OK	Go to Step 1

GC1089800457020X

Fig. 67 Cooling fan inoperative (A/C cooling low speed, Part 2 of 2). 1998 Catera

Step	Action	Value(s)	Yes	No
1	Did you perform the Coolant Fan Diagnostic System Check?	—	Go to Step 2	Refer to *Cooling Fan System Check.*
2	1. Turn on the ignition. 2. Locate the coolant fan test connector within the ECM housing. 3. Use a fused jumper to connect terminal 1 of the coolant fan test connector to a known good ground. Does the ECM cooling blower turn ON?	—	Go to Step 3	Go to Step 4
3	1. Locate an open or a high resistance in circuits XP30 and/or F600. 2. Repair the open or the high resistance in circuits XP30 and/or F600. 3. Replace the primary cooling fan temperature switch if these circuits are OK. Did you complete the repair?	—	Go to Step 15	—

GC1089800459010X

Fig. 69 ECM cooling blower inoperative (Part 1 of 2). 1998 Catera

Step	Action	Value(s)	Yes	No
1	Did you perform the Cooling Fan Diagnostic System Check?	—	Go to Step 2	Go to *Cooling Fan System Check*
2	1. Turn the A/C compressor ON. 2. Turn the ignition switch to the ON position. 3. Locate the coolant fan test connector within the ECM housing. 4. Use a fused jumper to connect terminal 2 of the coolant fan test connector to a known good ground. Does the Auxiliary fan #1 and Auxiliary fan #2 operate at high speed?	—	Go to Step 4	Go to Step 3
3	1. Locate an open or a high resistance in circuits XM999 or XM10. 2. Repair the open or the high resistance in circuits XM999 or XM10. 3. Replace the fan control relay K28 if these circuits are OK. Did you complete the repair?	—	Go to Step 5	—
4	1. Locate an open or a high resistance in circuit XM120 or circuit F57. 2. Repair the open or the high resistance in circuit XM120 or circuit F57. 3. Replace the A/C compressor refrigerant pressure switch if these circuit are OK. Did you complete the repair?	—	Go to Step 5	—
5	1. Connect all connectors and components that were previously disconnected. 2. Check the auxiliary engine coolant fan #1 for proper operation. Does the auxiliary engine coolant fans operate at low speed?	—	System OK	Go to Step 1

GC1089800458000X

Fig. 68 Cooling fan inoperative (A/C cooling high speed). 1998 Catera

Step	Action	Value(s)	Yes	No
4	1. Disconnect the ECM relay K48. 2. Use the DMM in order to measure the voltage between terminal 2 of the ECM relay K48 and a known good ground. Does the voltage measure near the specified value?	B+	Go to Step 6	Go to Step 5
5	1. Locate an open or a high resistance in CKT A60. 2. Repair the open or the high resistance in CKT A60. Did you complete the repair?	—	Go to Step 15	—
6	Use the DMM in order to measure the voltage between terminal 4 of the ECM relay K48 and a known good ground. Does the voltage measure near the specified value?	B+	Go to Step 8	Go to Step 7
7	1. Locate an open or a high resistance in CKT X235. 2. Repair the open or the high resistance in CKT X235. Did you complete the repair?	—	Go to Step 15	—
8	Connect a fused jumper between terminal 4 and terminal 8 of the ECM relay K48. Does the ECM cooling blower turn ON?	—	Go to Step 9	Go to Step 10
9	Replace the ECM relay K48. Did you complete the repair?	—	Go to Step 15	—
10	1. Disconnect the ECM cooling blower connector. 2. Use the DMM in order to measure the voltage between terminal 1 of the ECM cooling blower connector and a known good ground. Does the voltage measure near the specified value?	B+	Go to Step 12	Go to Step 11
11	1. Locate an open or a high resistance in CKT FM235. 2. Repair the open or the high resistance in CKT FM235. Did you complete the repair?	—	Go to Step 15	—
12	Use the DMM in order to measure the resistance between terminal 2 of the ECM cooling blower connector and a known good ground. Does the resistance measure near the specified value?	Less than 5 Ω	Go to Step 14	Go to Step 13
13	1. Locate an open or a high resistance in CKT F59. 2. Repair the open or the high resistance in CKT F59. Did you complete the repair?	—	Go to Step 15	—
14	Replace the ECM cooling blower. Did you complete the repair?	—	Go to Step 15	—
15	1. Connect all connectors and components that were previously disconnected. 2. Verify that the ECM cooling blower operates properly. Does the ECM cooling blower operate properly?	—	Refer to *Cooling Fan System Check.*	Go to Step 1

GC1089800459020X

Fig. 69 ECM cooling blower inoperative (Part 2 of 2). 1998 Catera

Step	Action	Yes	No
1	Turn the ignition key to the ON position. Does the heater water auxiliary pump operate?	Go to *Step 2*	Go to *Step 3*
2	Make sure the engine temperature is below 95°C (203°F). Are the auxiliary cooling fans and/or the electric cooling fan inoperative with the engine temperature below 95°C (203°F)?	Go to *Step 4*	Go to *Step 5*
3	The heater water auxiliary pump does not operate. Does the Heater water auxiliary pump operate properly?	Go to *Step 27*	—
4	1. Connect a fused jumper between pin 1 of the coolant fan test connector and a known good ground. 2. Grounding pin 1 of the coolant fan test connector will simulate the closing of the primary cooling fan temperature switch stage 1 contacts, this will energize the fan control relay K26. Does the auxiliary engine coolant fan #1 and auxiliary coolant fan #2 operate at low speed?	Go to *Step 6*	Go to *Step 7*
5	The auxiliary cooling fans run with the engine temperature below 95°C (203°F) Refer to *Cooling Fan Runs Continuously - Auxiliary* Are the engine cooling fans operating properly?	Go to *Step 27*	—
6	Check that the electric cooling fan is operating at low speed. Is the electric cooling fan is operating at low speed?	Go to *Step 9*	Go to *Step 8*
7	The auxiliary engine coolant fan #1 and auxiliary engine coolant fan #2 do not operate. Refer to *Cooling Fan Inoperative - Auxiliary (Both Aux Eng Cool Fans Inop)* Are the engine cooling fans operating properly?	Go to *Step 27*	—
8	The electric cooling fan does not operate at low speed. Refer to *Cooling Fan Inoperative at Low Speed - Electric* Are the engine cooling fans operating properly?	Go to *Step 27*	—
9	Check if the water auxiliary pump is operating. Does the water auxiliary pump operate?	Go to *Step 10*	Go to *Step 11*
10	1. Leave all previously connected jumpers connected. 2. Connect a fused jumper between pin 5 of the coolant fan test connector and a known good ground. 3. Grounding pin 5 of the coolant fan test connector will simulate the closing of the secondary cooling fan temperature switch, this will energize the fan control relay K28 and fan control relay K52. Does the auxiliary engine coolant fan #1 operate at high speed?	Go to *Step 12*	Go to *Step 13*
11	Water auxiliary pump does not operate. Does the water auxiliary pump operate properly?	Go to *Step 27*	—
12	Check if the auxiliary engine coolant fan #2 is operating at high speed. Does the auxiliary engine coolant fan #2 operate at high speed?	Go to *Step 14*	Go to *Step 15*
13	The auxiliary engine coolant fan #1 does not operate at high speed. Refer to *Cooling Fan Inoperative - Auxiliary (Aux Engine Coolant Fan #1 Inop)* Are the engine cooling fans operating properly?	Go to *Step 27*	—

GC1080000563010X

Fig. 70 Cooling fan functional check (Part 1 of 3). 1999 Catera

Step	Action	Yes	No
14	1. Leave all previously connected jumpers connected. 2. Connect a fused jumper between pin 4 of the coolant fan test connector and a known good ground. 3. Grounding pin 4 of the coolant fan test connector will simulate the closing of the primary cooling fan temperature switch stage 2 contacts, this will energize the fan control relay K67. Does the electric cooling fan operate at high speed?	Go to *Step 16*	Go to *Step 17*
15	The auxiliary engine coolant fan #2 does not operate at high speed. Refer to *Cooling Fan Inoperative - Auxiliary (Aux Engine Coolant Fan #2 Inop)* Are the engine cooling fans operating properly?	Go to *Step 27*	—
16	1. Remove all previously connected jumpers. 2. Start the engine and allow it to run. 3. Turn the A/C compressor clutch coil ON. Does the auxiliary engine coolant fan #1 and auxiliary engine coolant fan #2 run at low speed when the compressor clutch coil is turned ON?	Go to *Step 19*	Go to *Step 18*
17	The electrical cooling fan does not operate at high speed. Refer to *Cooling Fan Inoperative* Are the engine cooling fans operating properly?	Go to *Step 27*	—
18	The auxiliary engine coolant fan #1 and auxiliary engine cooling fan #2 do not operate when the compressor is turned ON. Refer to *Cooling Fan Inoperative - Auxiliary (A/C Cooling Low Speed)* Are the engine cooling fans operating properly?	Go to *Step 27*	—
19	1. Install the scan tool. 2. Monitor the engine temperature using the scan tool. 3. Remove any previously connected jumpers. 4. Turn the A/C compressor clutch coil OFF. 5. Allow the engine to run until the primary cooling fan temperature switch reaches 100°C (212°F). The stage 1 contacts should close and energize the fan control relay K26. Does the auxiliary engine coolant fan #1 and auxiliary coolant fan #2 operate at low speed?	Go to *Step 20*	Go to *Step 21*
20	Continue to allow the engine to run until the secondary cooling fan temperature switch reaches 105°C (221°F). The secondary cooling fan temperature switch should close and energize the fan control relay K28 and fan control relay K52. Does the auxiliary engine coolant fan #1 and auxiliary engine coolant fan #2 operate at high speed?	Go to *Step 22*	Go to *Step 23*
21	1. Locate an open or a high resistance in circuit XP30. 2. Repair the open or the high resistance in circuit XP30. 3. Replace the primary cooling fan temperature switch if these circuits are OK. Are the engine cooling fans operating properly?	Go to *Step 27*	—
22	Continue to allow the engine to run until the primary cooling fan temperature switch reaches 110°C (230°F). The stage 2 contacts should close and energize the fan control relay K67. Does the electric cooling fan operate at high speed?	Go to *Step 25*	Go to *Step 24*
23	1. Locate an open or a high resistance in circuit XM122. 2. Repair the open or the high resistance in circuit XM122. 3. Replace the secondary cooling fan temperature switch if these circuits are OK. Are the engine cooling fans operating properly?	Go to *Step 27*	—

GC1080000563020X

Fig. 70 Cooling fan functional check (Part 2 of 3). 1999 Catera

Step	Action	Yes	No
24	1. Locate an open or a high resistance in circuit XM5. 2. Repair the open or the high resistance in circuit XM5. 3. Replace the primary cooling fan temperature switch if these circuits are OK. Are the engine cooling fans operating properly?	Go to *Step 27*	—
25	1. Turn the A/C compressor clutch coil on. 2. Continue to operate the engine until the A/C refrigerant pressure switch reaches 275 psi. Does the auxiliary engine coolant fan #1 and auxiliary engine coolant fan #2 operate at high speed?	Go to *Step 27*	Go to *Step 26*
26	The auxiliary engine coolant fan #1 and fan #2 do not operate at high speed when the A/C refrigerant pressure switch reaches 275 psi. Are the engine cooling fans operating properly?	Go to *Step 27*	—
27	Confirm that the engine cooling fans and auxiliary water pumps operate properly. Do the engine cooling fans and auxiliary water pumps operate properly	System OK	Go to *Step 1*

GC1080000563030X

Fig. 70 Cooling fan functional check (Part 3 of 3). 1999 Catera

Step	Action	Value(s)	Yes	No
1	Did you perform the Cooling Fan System Check?	—	*Go to Step 2*	Go to *Cooling Fan System Check*
2	1. Turn the ignition to the ON position. 2. Disconnect the fan control relay K67 connector. 3. Use the DMM in order to measure the resistance between terminal 4 of the coolant fan test connector and terminal 6 of the fan control relay K67. Does the resistance measure near the specified value?	Less than 2 Ω	*Go to Step 4*	*Go to Step 3*
3	1. Locate an open or a high resistance in CKT MX998. 2. Repair the open or the high resistance in CKT MX998. Did you complete the repair?	—	*Go to Step 15*	—
4	Use the DMM in order to measure the voltage between terminal 2 of the fan control relay K67 and a known good ground. Does the voltage measure near the specified value?	B+	*Go to Step 6*	*Go to Step 5*
5	1. Locate an open or a high resistance in CKT X2. 2. Repair the open or the high resistance in CKT X2. Did you complete the repair?	—	*Go to Step 15*	—
6	Use the DMM in order to measure the voltage between terminal 4 of the fan control relay K67 and a known good ground. Does the voltage measure near the specified value?	B+	*Go to Step 8*	*Go to Step 7*

GC1080000564010X

Fig. 71 Cooling fan inoperative (Part 1 of 2). 1999 Catera

Step	Action	Value(s)	Yes	No
7	1. Check the integrity of fuse #42. If the fuse is open check for a short to ground in the power feed circuit. 2. If the fuse is OK, locate an open or a high resistance in circuits A710 and/or A700. 3. Repair the open or the high resistance in circuits A710 and/or A700. Did you complete the repair?	—	*Go to Step 15*	—
8	Connect a fused jumper between terminal 4 and terminal 8 of the fan control relay K67 connector. Does the engine coolant fan turn ON?	—	*Go to Step 9*	*Go to Step 10*
9	Replace the fan control relay K67. Did you complete the repair?	—	*Go to Step 15*	—
10	1. Leave the fused jumper connected. 2. Disconnect the electric cooling fan connector. 3. Use the DMM in order to measure the voltage between terminal A of the electric cooling fan connector and a known good ground. Does the voltage measure near the specified value?	B+	*Go to Step 12*	*Go to Step 11*
11	1. Locate an open or high resistance in circuits AM16 and/or AM17. 2. Repair an open or high resistance in AM16 and/or AM17. Did you complete the repair?	—	*Go to Step 15*	—
12	Use the DMM in order to measure the resistance between terminal B of the electric cooling fan connector and a known good ground. Does the resistance measure near the specified value?	Less than 2 Ω	*Go to Step 14*	*Go to Step 13*
13	1. Locate an open or a high resistance in CKT F100. 2. Repair the open or the high resistance in CKT F100. Did you complete the repair?	—	*Go to Step 15*	—
14	Replace the electric cooling fan. Did you complete the repair?	—	*Go to Step 15*	—
15	1. Connect all connectors and components that were previously disconnected. 2. Verify that the electric cooling fan operates properly. Does the electric cooling fan operate properly?	—	Go to *Cooling Fan System Check*	*Go to Step 1*

GC1080000564020X

Fig. 71 Cooling fan inoperative (Part 2 of 2). 1999 Catera

Step	Action	Value(s)	Yes	No
1	Did you perform the Cooling Fan Diagnostic System Check?	—	Go to Step 2	Go to Cooling Fan System Check
2	1. Disconnect the fan control relay K26 connector. 2. Use the DMM to measure the resistance between terminal 1 of the coolant fan test connector and terminal 6 of the fan control relay K26. Is the measured resistance within the specified value?	Less than 2 Ω	Go to Step 4	Go to Step 3
3	1. Locate an open or a high resistance in circuits XP999 and/or XP3. 2. Repair the open or the high resistance in circuits XP999 and/or XP3. Did you complete the repair?	—	Go to Step 17	—
4	Use the DMM in order to measure the voltage between terminal 3 of the fan control relay K26 and a known good ground. Does the voltage measure near the specified value?	B+	Go to Step 6	Go to Step 5
5	1. Inspect fuse #50 for an open. If the fuse is open, locate a short to ground in the battery positive voltage circuit. 2. If the fuse is OK, locate an open or high resistance in circuits A6 and/or A310. 3. Repair the open or the high resistance in circuits A6 and/or A310. Did you complete the repair?	—	Go to Step 17	—
6	Use the DMM in order to measure the voltage between terminal 4 of the fan control relay K26 and a known good ground. Does the voltage measure near the specified value?	B+	Go to Step 8	Go to Step 7
7	1. Inspect fuse #52 for an open. If the fuse is open, locate a short to ground in the battery positive voltage circuit. 2. If the fuse is OK, locate an open or a high resistance in circuits A300, A220 and/or A223. 3. Repair the open or the high resistance in circuits A300, A220 and/or A223. Did you complete the repair?	—	Go to Step 17	—
8	Connect a fused jumper between terminal 4 and terminal 5 of the fan control relay K26 connector. Does the engine coolant fan operate at low speed?	—	Go to Step 9	Go to Step 10
9	Replace the fan control relay K26. Did you complete the repair?	—	Go to Step 17	—
10	1. Leave fused jumper connected. 2. Disconnect the engine coolant fan resistor. 3. Use the DMM in order to measure the voltage between terminal 1 circuit AP2 of the engine coolant fan resistor connector and a known good ground. Does the voltage measure near the specified value?	B+	Go to Step 12	Go to Step 11
11	1. Locate an open or high resistance in circuits AP2 and/or AP1. 2. Repair an open or high resistance in circuits AP2 and/or AP1. Did you complete the repair?	—	Go to Step 17	—
12	1. Disconnect the electric cooling fan connector. 2. Use the DMM in order to measure the resistance between terminal 1circuit AM6 of the engine coolant fan resistor connector and terminal A of the electric cooling fan connector. Does the resistance measure near the specified value?	Less than 2 Ω	Go to Step 14	Go to Step 13

GC1080000565010X

Fig. 72 Cooling fan inoperative at low speed (Part 1 of 2). 1999 Catera

Step	Action	Value(s)	Yes	No
13	1. Locate an open or a high resistance in circuits AM17 and/or AM6. 2. Repair the open or the high resistance in circuits AM17 and/or AM6. Did you complete the repair?	—	Go to Step 17	—
14	1. Turn the ignition switch to the OFF position. 2. Use the DMM in order to measure the resistance between terminal B of the electric cooling fan connector and a known good ground. Does the resistance measure near the specified value?	Less than 2 Ω	Go to Step 16	Go to Step 15
15	1. Locate an open or a high resistance in CKT F100. 2. Repair the open or the high resistance in CKT F100. Did you complete the repair?	—	Go to Step 17	—
16	1. Check the integrity of the engine coolant fan resistor. 2. Replace the engine coolant fan resistor if it is open. 3. Replace the electric cooling fan if the engine coolant fan resistor is OK. Did you complete the repair?	—	Go to Step 17	—
17	1. Connect all connectors and components that were previously disconnected. 2. Verify that the electric cooling fan operates properly at low speed. Does the electric cooling fan operate properly at low speed?	—	Go to Cooling Fan System Check	Go to Step 1

GC1080000565020X

Fig. 72 Cooling fan inoperative at low speed (Part 2 of 2). 1999 Catera

Step	Action	Value(s)	Yes	No
1	Did you perform the Cooling Fan Diagnostic System Check?	—	Go to Step 2	Go to Cooling Fan System Check
2	1. Disconnect the fused jumper. 2. Disconnect the fan control relay K26 connector. 3. Use the DMM in order to measure the voltage between terminal 3 of the fan control relay K26 connector and a known good ground. Does the voltage measure near the specified value?	B+	Go to Step 4	Go to Step 3
3	1. Inspect fuse #50 for an open. If fuse #50 is open, locate a short to ground in the batttery voltage circuit. 2. If the fuse #50 is OK, locate an open or a high resistance in circuits A6 and/or A310. 3. Repair the open or the high resistance in circuits A6 and/or A310. Did you complete the repair?	—	Go to Step 17	—
4	Use the DMM in order to measure the voltage between terminal 2 of the fan control relay K26 connector and a known good ground. Does the voltage measure near the specified value?	B+	Go to Step 6	Go to Step 5
5	1. Inspect fuse #52 for an open. If fuse #52 is open, locate a short to ground in the batttery voltage circuit 2. If the fuse is OK, locate an open or a high resistance in circuits A300, A220, or A222. 3. Repair the open or the high resistance in circuits A300, A220, and/or A222. Did you complete the repair?	—	Go to Step 17	—
6	1. Use a fused jumper to connect terminal 1 of the coolant fan test connector to a known good ground. 2. Use the DMM in order to measure the resistance between terminal 6 of the fan control relay K26 connector and a known good ground. Did you measure the resistance near the specified value?	Less than 2Ω	Go to Step 8	Go to Step 7
7	1. Locate an open or a high resistance in circuit XP3 or XP999. 2. Repair the open or the high resistance in circuit XP3 or XP999. Did you complete the repair?	—	Go to Step 17	—

GC1080000566010X

Fig. 73 Cooling fan inoperative-auxiliary (Both fans, Part 1 of 2). 1999 Catera

Step	Action	Value(s)	Yes	No
8	1. Place the fan control relay K26 back in the ECM housing. 2. Leave the fused jumper connected between terminal 1 of the coolant fan test connector and a good ground. 3. Disconnect the auxiliary engine coolant fan #1 connector. 4. Use a DMM in order to measure voltage between terminal A of the auxiliary engine coolant fan #1 and a known good ground. Did you measure the voltage near the specified value?	B+	Go to Step 10	Go to Step 9
9	1. Locate an open or a high resistance in circuits AM1 or AM13. 2. Repair the open or the high resistance in circuits AM1 or AM13. 3. Replace the fan control relay K26 if these circuits are OK. Did you complete the repair?	—	Go to Step 17	—
10	1. Remove the fan control relay K52 2. Connect the auxiliary engine fan #1 connector 3. Use a fused jumper to connect from terminal 2 of the fan control relay K52 to a known good ground. Does the auxiliary engine coolant fan #1 operate?	—	Go to Step 12	Go to Step 11
11	1. Locate an open or a high resistance in circuit XU3. 2. Repair the open or the high resistance in circuit XU3 3. Replace the auxiliary engine coolant fan #1 if these circuits are OK. Did you complete the repair?	—	Go to Step 17	—
12	Use a DMM in order to measure resistance from terminal B of the auxiliary coolant engine fan #2 connector and a known good ground. Did you measure the resistance near the specified value?	Less than 2Ω	Go to Step 14	Go to Step 13
13	1. Locate an open or a high resistance in circuit F4. 2. Repair the open or the high resistance in circuits F4 Did you complete the repair?	—	Go to Step 17	—
14	1. Remove fan control relay K52 2. With the relay removed determine if the contacts are closed. 3. Use a DMM in order to measure resistance between terminal 2 and Terminal 5 of the fan control relay K52. Did you measure the resistance near the specified value?	Less than 2Ω	Go to Step 15	Go to Step 16
15	1. Locate an open or a high resistance in circuit AM3 or AM5. 2. Repair the open or the high resistance in circuit AM3 or AM5. 3. Replace the auxiliary engine coolant fan #2 if these circuits are OK. Did you complete the repair?	—	Go to Step 17	—
16	Replace the fan control relay K52 Did you complete the repair?	—	Go to Step 17	—
17	1. Connect all the connectors and components that were disconnected 2. Verify that the auxiliary engine coolant fans #1 and #2 operate properly. Does the auxiliary engine coolant fans #1 and #2 operate properly?	—	Go to Cooling Fan System Check	Go to Step 1

GC1080000566020X

Fig. 73 Cooling fan inoperative-auxiliary (Both fans, Part 2 of 2). 1999 Catera

Step	Action	Value(s)	Yes	No
1	Did you perform the Cooling Fan Diagnostic System Check?	—	*Go to Step 2*	Go to *Cooling Fan System Check*
2	1. Turn the ignition switch to the OFF positon. 2. Locate the coolant fan test connector within the ECM housing. 3. Use a fused jumper to connect terminal 1 of the coolant fan test connector to a known good ground. Does the auxiliary engine coolant fan #1 and fan #2 operate at low speed?	—	*Go to Step 3*	Go to *Cooling Fan Inoperative - Auxiliary (Both Aux Eng Cool Fans Inop)*
3	1. Turn the ignition switch to the ON position. 2. Disconnect the fan control relay K52 connector. 3. Use the DMM in order to measure the voltage between terminal 4 of the fan control relay K52 connector and a known good ground. Does the voltage measure near the specified value?	B+	*Go to Step 5*	*Go to Step 4*
4	1. Locate a open or a high resistance in circuit X30 2. Repair the open or the high resistance in circuit X30. Did you complete the repair?	—	*Go to Step 8*	—
5	1. Turn the ignition swtich to the OFF position. 2. Use the DMM in order to measure the resistance between terminal 8 of the fan control relay K52 and a known good ground. Does the resistance measure near the specified value?	Less than 2Ω	*Go to Step 7*	*Go to Step 6*
6	1. Locate an open or a high resistance in circuit F7 2. Repair the open or the high resistance in circuits F7. Did you complete the repair?	—	*Go to Step 8*	—
7	1. Locate an open or a high resistance in circuits XM123 or XM997. 2. Repair the open or the high resistance in circuits XM123 or XM997. 3. Replace the fan control relay K52 if these circuits are OK. Did you complete the repair?	—	*Go to Step 8*	—
8	1. Connect all connectors and components that were previously disconnected. 2. Check the auxiliary engine coolant fan #1 for proper operation. Does the auxiliary engine coolant fan #1 operate properly?	—	Go to *Cooling Fan System Check*	*Go to Step 1*

GC1080000567000X

Fig. 74 Cooling fan inoperative-auxiliary (No. 1 fan). 1999 Catera

Step	Action	Value(s)	Yes	No
1	Did you perform the Cooling Fan Diagnostic System Check?	—	*Go to Step 2*	Go to *Cooling Fan System Check*
2	1. Turn the ignition switch to the OFF position. 2. Locate the coolant fan test connector within the ECM housing. 3. Use a fused jumper to connect terminal 1 of the coolant fan test connector to a known good ground. Does the auxiliary engine coolant fans #1 and auxiliary engine coolant fan #2 operate at low speed?	—	*Go to Step 3*	Go to *Cooling Fan Inoperative - Auxiliary (Both Aux Eng Cool Fans Inop)*
3	1. Turn the ignition switch to the ON position. 2. Disconnect the fan control relay K28 connector. 3. Use the DMM in order to measure the voltage between terminal 4 of the fan control relay K28 connector and a known good ground. Does the voltage measure near the specified value?	B+	*Go to Step 5*	*Go to Step 4*
4	1. Check the integrity of fuse #40. If the fuse #40 is open, locate a short to ground in the battery positive voltage circuit. 2. if fuse #40 is OK, locate a open or a high resistance in circuit A14 or A25. 3. Repair the open or the high resistance in circuit A14 or A25. Did you complete the repair?	—	*Go to Step 10*	—
5	Use the DMM in order to measure the voltage between terminal 2 of the fan control relay K28 and a known good ground. Does the voltage measure near the specified value?	B+	*Go to Step 7*	*Go to Step 6*
6	1. Locate an open or a high resistance in circuit X400 2. Repair the open or the high resistance in circuit X400. Did you complete the repair?	—	*Go to Step 10*	—
7	1. Disconnected the auxiliary engine coolant fan #2 connector. 2. Use a DMM in order to measure resistance between terminal 8 of the fan control relay connector and terminal A of the auxiliary engine coolant fan #2 Does the resistance measure near the specified value?	Less than 2Ω	*Go to Step 8*	*Go to Step 9*
8	1. Locate an open or a high resistance in circuits XM124 or XM997. 2. Repair the open or the high resistance in circuits XM124 or XM997. 3. Replace the fan control relay K52 if these circuits are OK. Did you complete the repair?	—	*Go to Step 10*	—
9	1. Locate an open or a high resistance in circuit AM4. 2. Repair the open or the high resistance in circuits AM4. Did you complete the repair?	—	*Go to Step 10*	—
10	1. Connect all connectors and components that were previously disconnected. 2. Check the auxiliary engine coolant fan #2 for proper operation. Does the auxiliary engine coolant fan #2 operate properly?	—	Go to *Cooling Fan System Check*	*Go to Step 1*

GC1080000568000X

Fig. 75 Cooling fan inoperative-auxiliary (No. 2 fan). 1999 Catera

Step	Action	Value(s)	Yes	No
1	Did you perform the Cooling Fan Diagnostic System Check?	—	*Go to Step 2*	Go to *Cooling Fan System Check*
2	1. Turn the ignition switch to the OFF position. 2. Locate the coolant fan test connector within the ECM housing. 3. Use a fused jumper to connect terminal 1 of the coolant fan test connector to a known good ground. Does the auxiliary engine coolant fan #1 and auxiliary engine coolant fan #2 operate at low speed?	—	*Go to Step 3*	Go to *Cooling Fan Inoperative - Auxiliary (Both Aux Eng Cool Fans Inop)*
3	1. Remove the fused jumper. 2. Turn the ignition switch to the ON position. 3. Disconnect the fan control relay K87 connector. 4. Use the DMM in order to measure the voltage between terminal 4 of the fan control relay K87 connector and a known good ground. Does the voltage measure near the specified value?	B+	*Go to Step 5*	*Go to Step 4*
4	1. Locate a open or a high resistance in circuit A221 2. Repair the open or the high resistance in circuit A221. Did you complete the repair?	—	*Go to Step 10*	—
5	Use the DMM in order to measure the resistance between terminal 6 of the fan control relay K87 and a known good ground. Does the resistance measure near the specified value?	Less than 2Ω	*Go to Step 7*	*Go to Step 6*
6	1. Locate an open or a high resistance in circuit F2 2. Repair the open or the high resistance in circuits F2. Did you complete the repair?	—	*Go to Step 10*	—
7	1. Start the engine. 2. Turn the A/C compressor ON 3. With the engine running use the DMM in order to measure the voltage between terminal 2 of the fan control relay K87 and a known good ground. Does the voltage measure near the specified value?	B+	*Go to Step 9*	*Go to Step 8*
8	1. Locate an open or a high resistance in circuit U4. 2. Repair the open or the high resistance in circuit U4. 3. *HVAC Compressor Controls System Check* for A/C compressor diagnosis if the circuit is OK. Did you complete the repair?	—	*Go to Step 10*	—
9	1. Locate an open or a high resistance in circuits AM12. 2. Repair the open or the high resistance in circuits AM12. 3. Replace the fan control relay K87 if these circuits are OK. Did you complete the repair?	—	*Go to Step 10*	—
10	1. Connect all connectors and components that were previously disconnected. 2. Check the auxiliary engine coolant fan #1 for proper operation. Does the auxiliary engine coolant fans operate at low speed?	—	Go to *Cooling Fan System Check*	*Go to Step 1*

GC1080000569000X

Fig. 76 Cooling fan inoperative-auxiliary (A/C cooling low speed). 1999 Catera

Step	Action	Value(s)	Yes	No
1	Did you perform the Cooling Fan Diagnostic System Check?	—	*Go to Step 2*	Go to *Cooling Fan System Check*
2	1. Start the engine. 2. Turn the A/C compressor ON. 3. With the engine running locate the coolant fan test connector within the ECM housing. 4. Use a fused jumper to connect terminal 2 of the coolant fan test connector to a known good ground. Does the Auxiliary fan #1 and Auxiliary fan #2 operate at high speed?	—	*Go to Step 4*	*Go to Step 3*
3	1. Locate an open or a high resistance in circuits XM999 or XM10. 2. Repair the open or the high resistance in circuits XM999 or XM10. 3. Replace the fan control relay K28 if these circuits are OK. Did you complete the repair?	—	*Go to Step 5*	—
4	1. Locate an open or a high resistance in circuit XM120 or circuit F57. 2. Repair the open or the high resistance in circuit XM120 or circuit F57. 3. Replace the A/C compressor refrigerant pressure switch if these circuit are OK. Did you complete the repair?	—	*Go to Step 5*	—
5	1. Connect all connectors and components that were previously disconnected. 2. Check the auxiliary engine coolant fan #1 for proper operation. Does the auxiliary engine coolant fans operate at low speed?	—	Go to *Cooling Fan System Check*	*Go to Step 1*

GC1080000570000X

Fig. 77 Cooling fan inoperative-auxiliary (A/C cooling high speed). 1999 Catera

Step	Action	Value(s)	Yes	No
1	Did you perform the Cooling Fan Diagnostic System Check?	—	*Go to Step 2*	Go to *Cooling Fan System Check*
2	1. Turn the ignition switch to the OFF position. 2. Make sure the engine temperature is below 95°C (203°F). 3. Make sure the A/C compressor refrigerant pressure switch is below 1500kpa (217psi). Does the auxiliary engine coolant fan #1, auxiliary engine coolant fan #2, and electric cooling fan all operate at low speed?	—	*Go to Step 3*	*Go to Step 4*
3	1. Locate an short to ground in circuits XP30, XP3 or XP999. 2. Repair the short to ground in circuits XP30, XP3 or XP999. 3. Replace the primary cooling fan temperature switch if these circuits are OK. Did you complete the repair?	—	*Go to Step 21*	—
4	Does the electric cooling fan operate at low speed?	—	*Go to Step 10*	*Go to Step 5*
5	Does the auxiliary engine coolant fan #1 and auxiliary engine coolant fan #2 operate at low speed?	—	*Go to Step 6*	*Go to Step 11*
6	1. Disconnect the fan control relay K26. 2. Use the DMM in order to measure the voltage between terminal 8 of the fan control relay K26 connector and a known good ground. Did you measure the voltage near the specified value?	B+	*Go to Step 7*	*Go to Step 8*
7	1. Disconnect the fan control relay K87. 2. Use the DMM in order to measure the voltage between terminal 2 of the fan control relay K87 connector and a known good ground. Did you measure the voltage near the specified value?	B+	Go to *HVAC Compressor Controls System Check*	*Go to Step 9*
8	Replace the fan control relay K26. Did you complete the repair?	—	*Go to Step 21*	—
9	1. Locate an short to B+ in circuits AM12, AM1 or AM13. 2. Repair the short to B+ in circuits AM12, AM1 or AM13. 3. Replace the fan control relay K87 if these circuits are OK. Did you complete the repair?	—	*Go to Step 21*	—
10	1. Locate an short to B+ in circuits AP2 or AP1. 2. Repair the short to B+ in circuits AP2 or AP1. 3. Replace the fan control relay K26 if these circuits are OK. Did you complete the repair?	—	*Go to Step 21*	—
11	Turn the ignition switch to the ON position Does the auxiliary engine coolant fan #2 operate at high speed?	—	*Go to Step 12*	*Go to Step 17*
12	1. Disconnect the fan control relay K28. 2. Use the DMM in order to measure the resistance between terminal 6 of the fan control relay K28 connector and a known good ground. Did you measure the resistance near the specified value?	Less than 2Ω	*Go to Step 13*	*Go to Step 14*

GC1080000571010X

Fig. 78 Cooling fan runs continuously-auxiliary (Part 1 of 2). 1999 Catera

Step	Action	Yes	No
1	Turn ON the ignition, with the engine OFF. Does the heater water auxiliary pump operate?	Go to *Step 2*	Go to *Step 3*
2	Make sure the engine temperature is below 95°C (203°F). Are the auxiliary engine coolant fans and/or the electric cooling fan operating with the engine temperature below 95°C (203°F)?	Go to *Step 5*	Go to *Step 4*
3	The heater water auxiliary pump does not operate. Does the heater water auxiliary pump operate properly?	Go to *Step 31*	—
4	1. Connect a 5 A fused jumper between the fan control relay K26 diagnostic enable circuit and a known good ground. 2. Grounding of the fan control relay K26 diagnostic enable circuit will simulate the closing of the primary coolant fan temperature switch stage 1 contacts, this will energize the fan control relay K26. Does the auxiliary engine coolant fan #1 and auxiliary engine coolant fan #2 operate at low speed?	Go to *Step 6*	Go to *Step 7*
5	The auxiliary engine coolant fans and/or the electric cooling fan run with the engine temperature below 95°C (203°F) Refer to *Cooling Fan Always On - Auxiliary.* Are the engine cooling fans operating properly?	Go to *Step 31*	—
6	Observe the electric cooling fan. Is the electric cooling fan operating at low speed?	Go to *Step 9*	Go to *Step 8*
7	The auxiliary engine coolant fan #1 and auxiliary engine coolant fan #2 do not operate. Refer to *Cooling Fan Inoperative - Auxiliary (Both Aux Eng Coolant Fans Inop)* or *Cooling Fan Inoperative - Auxiliary (Aux Engine Coolant Fan #1 Inop)* or *Cooling Fan Inoperative - Auxiliary (Aux Engine Coolant Fan #2 Inop)* or *Cooling Fan Inoperative - Auxiliary (A/C Cooling Low Speed)* or *Cooling Fan Inoperative - Auxiliary (A/C Cooling High Speed).* Are the engine cooling fans operating properly?	Go to *Step 31*	—
8	The electric cooling fan does not operate at low speed. Refer to *Cooling Fan Inoperative at Low Speed - Electric.* Are the engine cooling fans operating properly?	Go to *Step 31*	—
9	1. Turn OFF the ignition. 2. Leave all previously connected jumpers connected. Does the water auxiliary pump operate?	Go to *Step 10*	Go to *Step 11*
10	1. Turn ON the ignition, with the engine OFF. 2. Leave all previously connected jumpers connected. 3. Connect a 5 A fused jumper between the fan control relay K28 and fan control relay K52 diagnostic enable circuit and a known good ground. 4. Grounding of the fan control relay K28 and fan control relay K52 diagnostic enable circuit will simulate the closing of the secondary cooling fan temperature switch, this will energize the fan control relay K28 and fan control relay K52. Does the auxiliary engine coolant fan #1 operate at high speed?	Go to *Step 12*	Go to *Step 13*
11	Water auxiliary pump does not operate. Does the water auxiliary pump operate properly?	Go to *Step 31*	—
12	Observe the auxiliary engine coolant fan #2. Does the auxiliary engine coolant fan #2 operate at high speed?	Go to *Step 14*	Go to *Step 15*

GC1080000576010X

Fig. 79 Cooling fan system check (Part 1 of 3). 2000–01 Catera

Step	Action	Value(s)	Yes	No
13	1. Locate an short to ground in circuits XM124, XM123, XM122, or XM997. 2. Repair the short to ground in circuits XM124, XM123, XM122, or XM997. 3. Replace the secondary cooling fan temperature switch if these circuits are OK. Did you complete the repair?	—	*Go to Step 21*	—
14	Use a DMM in order to measure resistance between terminal 5 of the fan control relay K28 connector and a known good ground. Did you measure the resistance near the specified value?	Less than 2Ω	*Go to Step 15*	*Go to Step 16*
15	1. Locate an short to ground in circuits XM10, XM999, or XM120. 2. Repair the short to ground in circuits XM10, XM999, or XM120. 3. Replace the A/C compressor refrigerant pressure switch if these circuits are OK. Did you complete the repair?	—	*Go to Step 21*	—
16	1. Locate an short to B+ in circuits AM3, AM4, AM5, or XU3. 2. Repair the short to B+ in circuits AM3, AM4, AM5, or XU3. 3. Replace the fan control relay K28 if these circuits are OK. Did you complete the repair?	—	*Go to Step 21*	—
17	Does the electric cooling fan operate at high speed?	—	*Go to Step 18*	*Go to Step 21*
18	1. Disconnect the fan control relay K67. 2. Use a DMM in order to measure resistance between pin 4 of the coolant fan test connector and a known good ground. Did you measure the resistance near the specified value?	Less than Ω	*Go to Step 19*	*Go to Step 20*
19	1. Locate an short to ground in circuits XM5, or XM998. 2. Repair the short to ground in circuits XM5 or, XM998. 3. Replace the primary cooling fan temperature switch if these circuits are OK. Did you complete the repair?	—	*Go to Step 21*	—
20	1. Locate an short to B+ in circuits AM16 or AM6. 2. Repair the short to B+ in circuits AM16 or AM6. 3. Replace the fan control relay K67 if these circuits are OK. Did you complete the repair?	—	*Go to Step 21*	—
21	1. Connect all the connectors and components that were disconnected. 2. Verify that the auxiliary engine coolant fans #1 and #2 operate properly. Does the auxiliary engine coolant fans #1 and #2 operate properly?	—	Go to *Cooling Fan System Check*	*Go to Step 1*

GC1080000571020X

Fig. 78 Cooling fan runs continuously-auxiliary (Part 2 of 2). 1999 Catera

Step	Action	Yes	No
13	The auxiliary engine coolant fan #1 does not operate at high speed. Refer to *Cooling Fan Inoperative* Are the engine cooling fans operating properly?	Go to *Step 31*	—
14	1. Leave all previously connected jumpers connected. 2. Connect a 5 A fused jumper between the fan control relay K67 diagnostic enable circuit and a known good ground. 3. Grounding of the fan control relay K67 diagnostic enable circuit will simulate the closing of the primary cooling fan temperature switch stage 2 contacts, this will energize the fan control relay K67. Does the electric cooling fan operate at high speed?	Go to *Step 16*	Go to *Step 17*
15	The auxiliary engine coolant fan #2 does not operate at high speed. Refer to *Cooling Fan Inoperative* Are the engine cooling fans operating properly?	Go to *Step 31*	—
16	1. Remove all previously connected jumpers. 2. Start the engine and allow it to run. 3. Turn the A/C compressor clutch coil ON. Does the auxiliary engine coolant fan #1 and auxiliary engine coolant fan #2 run at low speed when the compressor clutch coil is turned ON?	Go to *Step 19*	Go to *Step 18*
17	The electrical cooling fan does not operate at high speed. Are the engine cooling fans operating properly?	Go to *Step 31*	—
18	The auxiliary engine coolant fan #1 and auxiliary engine coolant fan #2 do not operate when the compressor is turned ON. Refer to *Cooling Fan Inoperative* Are the engine cooling fans operating properly?	Go to *Step 31*	—
19	1. Install the scan tool. 2. Monitor the engine temperature using the scan tool. 3. Remove any previously connected jumpers. 4. Turn the A/C compressor clutch coil OFF. 5. Allow the engine to run until the primary cooling fan temperature switch reaches 100°C (212°F). The stage 1 contacts should close and energize the fan control relay K26. Does the auxiliary engine coolant fan #1 and auxiliary engine coolant fan #2 operate at low speed?	Go to *Step 20*	Go to *Step 21*
20	Continue to allow the engine to run until the secondary cooling fan temperature switch reaches 105°C (221°F). The secondary cooling fan temperature switch should close and energize the fan control relay K28 and fan control relay K52. Does the auxiliary engine coolant fan #1 and auxiliary engine coolant fan #2 operate at high speed?	Go to *Step 24*	Go to *Step 25*

GC1080000576020X

Fig. 79 Cooling fan system check (Part 2 of 3). 2000–01 Catera

Step	Action	Yes	No
21	Test the control circuit of the fan control relay K26 for an open. Did you find and correct the condition?	Go to *Step 31*	Go to *Step 22*
22	Test the ground circuit of the primary cooling fan temperature switch for an open. Did you find and correct the condition?	Go to *Step 31*	Go to *Step 23*
23	Replace the primary cooling fan temperature switch. Did you complete the repair?	Go to *Step 31*	—
24	Continue to allow the engine to run until the primary cooling fan temperature switch reaches 110°C (230°F). The stage 2 contacts should close and energize the fan control relay K67. Does the electric cooling fan operate at high speed?	Go to *Step 29*	Go to *Step 27*
25	Test the control circuit of the fan control relay K28 and fan control relay K52 for an open. Did you find and correct the condition?	Go to *Step 31*	Go to *Step 26*
26	Replace the secondary cooling fan temperature switch. Did you complete the repair?	Go to *Step 31*	—
27	Test the fan control relay K67 control circuit of the relay coil for an open. Did you find and correct the condition?	Go to *Step 31*	Go to *Step 28*
28	Replace the primary cooling fan temperature switch. Did you complete the repair?	Go to *Step 31*	—
29	1. Install the A/C manifold gauge set to monitor A/C refrigerant pressure. 2. Turn the A/C compressor clutch coil on. 3. Continue to operate the engine until the A/C refrigerant pressure switch reaches 275 psi. Does the auxiliary engine coolant fan #1 and auxiliary engine coolant fan #2 operate at high speed?	Go to *Step 31*	Go to *Step 30*
30	The auxiliary engine coolant fan #1 and auxiliary engine coolant fan #2 do not operate at high speed when the A/C refrigerant pressure switch reaches 275 psi. Refer to *Cooling Fan Inoperative - Auxiliary (Both Aux Eng Coolant Fans Inop)* or *Cooling Fan Inoperative - Auxiliary (Aux Engine Coolant Fan #1 Inop)* or *Cooling Fan Inoperative - Auxiliary (Aux Engine Coolant Fan #2 Inop)* or *Cooling Fan Inoperative - Auxiliary (A/C Cooling Low Speed)* or *Cooling Fan Inoperative - Auxiliary (A/C Cooling High Speed)*. Are the engine cooling fans operating properly?	Go to *Step 31*	—
31	Confirm that the engine cooling fans and auxiliary water pumps operate properly. Do the engine cooling fans and auxiliary water pumps operate properly	System OK	Go to *Step 1*

GC1080000576030X

Fig. 79 Cooling fan system check (Part 3 of 3). 2000–01 Catera

Step	Action	Yes	No
1	Did you perform the Cooling Fan System Check?	Go to *Step 2*	Go to *Cooling Fan System Check*
2	1. Disconnect the fused jumper. 2. Remove fan control relay K26. 3. Test the battery positive voltage circuit of the relay coil of fan control relay K26 connector for a short to ground or an open. Did you find and correct the condition?	Go to *Step 21*	Go to *Step 3*
3	***Notice:*** Refer to *Relay Notice* in Cautions and Notices. Test the battery positive voltage circuit of the auxiliary engine coolant fan #1 and auxiliary engine coolant fan #2 of the fan control relay K26 connector for a short to ground or an open. Did you find and correct the condition?	Go to *Step 21*	Go to *Step 4*
4	Test the supply voltage circuit of the auxiliary engine coolant fan #1 and auxiliary engine coolant fan #2 of the fan control relay K26 connector for a short to ground or an open. Did you find and correct the condition?	Go to *Step 21*	Go to *Step 5*
5	Test the supply voltage circuit of the electric cooling fan of the fan control relay K26 connector for a short to ground. Did you find and correct the condition?	Go to *Step 21*	Go to *Step 6*
6	Test the control circuit of the relay coil of the fan control relay K26 connector for an open. Did you find and correct the condition?	Go to *Step 21*	Go to *Step 7*

GC1080000579010X

Fig. 81 Cooling fan inoperative-auxiliary (Both fans, Part 1 of 3). 2000–01 Catera

Step	Action	Yes	No
1	Did you perform the Cooling Fan System Check?	Go to *Step 2*	Go to *Cooling Fan System Check*
2	1. Turn ON the ignition, with the engine OFF. 2. Remove the fan control relay K67. 3. Test the diagnostic enable circuit of the relay K67 for an open. Did you find and correct the condition?	Go to *Step 13*	Go to *Step 3*
3	Test the ignition voltage supply circuit of the K67 relay for an open. Did you find and correct the condition?	Go to *Step 13*	Go to *Step 4*
4	Test the control circuit of the K67 relay for an open. Did you find and correct the condition?	Go to *Step 13*	Go to *Step 5*
5	Test the battery positive voltage circuit of the relay K67 for a short to ground or an open. Did you find and correct the condition?	Go to *Step 13*	Go to *Step 6*
6	Connect a 20 A fused jumper between the battery positive voltage circuit of the fan control relay K67 and the electric cooling fan motor supply voltage circuit of the fan control relay K67. Does the electric cooling fan operate at high speed?	Go to *Step 7*	Go to *Step 9*
7	Inspect for poor connections at the harness connector of the fan control relay K67. Did you find and correct the condition?	Go to *Step 13*	Go to *Step 8*
8	Replace the fan control relay K67. Did you complete the repair?	Go to *Step 13*	—
9	1. Remove the 20 A fused jumper. 2. Disconnect the electric cooling fan connector. 3. Test the supply voltage circuit of the electric cooling fan motor for a short to ground or an open. Did you find and correct the condition?	Go to *Step 13*	Go to *Step 10*
10	Test the ground circuit of the electric cooling fan motor for an open. Did you find and correct the condition?	Go to *Step 13*	Go to *Step 11*
11	Inspect for poor connections at the harness connector of the electric cooling fan motor. Did you find and correct the condition?	Go to *Step 13*	Go to *Step 12*
12	Replace the electric cooling fan motor. Did you complete the repair?	Go to *Step 13*	—
13	1. Connect all connectors and components that were previously disconnected. 2. Verify that the electric cooling fan operates properly. Does the electric cooling fan operate properly?	Go to *Cooling Fan System Check*	Go to *Step 1*

GC1080000577000X

Fig. 80 Cooling fan inoperative. 2000–01 Catera

Step	Action	Yes	No
7	1. Place the fan control relay K26 back in the ECM housing. 2. Disconnect the auxiliary engine coolant fan #1 connector. 3. Connect a 5 A fused jumper between the fan control relay K26 diagnostic enable circuit and a known good ground. 4. Connect a test lamp between the supply voltage circuit of the auxiliary engine coolant fan #1 connector and a good ground. Does the test lamp illuminate?	Go to *Step 10*	Go to *Step 8*
8	Inspect for poor connections at the harness connector of fan control relay K26. Did you find and correct the condition?	Go to *Step 21*	Go to *Step 9*
9	Replace the fan control relay K26. Did you complete the repair?	Go to *Step 21*	—
10	1. Leave the 20 A fused jumper in place. 2. Remove the fan control relay K52 3. Connect the auxiliary engine fan #1 connector 4. Connect a 20 A fused jumper between the control circuit of the auxiliary engine coolant fan #1 of the fan control relay K52 connector and a good ground. Does the auxiliary engine coolant fan #1 operate?	Go to *Step 14*	Go to *Step 11*
11	Test the control circuit of the auxiliary engine coolant fan #1 for an open. Did you find and correct the condition?	Go to *Step 21*	Go to *Step 12*
12	Inspect for poor connections at the harness connector of the auxiliary engine coolant fan #1. Did you find and correct the condition?	Go to *Step 21*	Go to *Step 13*
13	Replace the auxiliary engine coolant fan #1. Did you complete the repair?	Go to *Step 21*	—
14	Test the ground circuit of the auxiliary engine coolant fan #2 for an open. Did you find and correct the condition?	Go to *Step 21*	Go to *Step 15*
15	1. Leave the 5 A fused jumper wire in place. 2. Connect a 20 A fused jumper wire between the control circuit of the auxiliary engine coolant fan #1 of the fan control relay K52 connector and the supply voltage circuit of the auxiliary engine coolant fan #2 of the fan control relay K52 connector. Does the auxiliary engine coolant fan #1 and the auxiliary engine coolant fan #2 operate at low speed.	Go to *Step 19*	Go to *Step 16*
16	Test the supply voltage circuit of the auxiliary engine coolant fan #2 for an open. Did you find and correct the condition?	Go to *Step 21*	Go to *Step 17*

GC1080000579020X

Fig. 81 Cooling fan inoperative-auxiliary (Both fans, Part 2 of 3). 2000–01 Catera

Step	Action	Yes	No
17	Inspect for poor connections at the harness connector of the auxiliary engine coolant fan #2. Did you find and correct the condition?	Go to *Step 21*	Go to *Step 18*
18	Replace the auxiliary engine coolant fan #2. Did you complete the repair?	Go to *Step 21*	—
19	Inspect for poor connections at the harness connector of the fan control relay K52. Did you find and correct the condition?	Go to *Step 21*	Go to *Step 20*
20	Replace the fan control relay K52 Did you complete the repair?	Go to *Step 21*	—
21	1. Connect all the connectors and components that were disconnected 2. Verify that the auxiliary engine coolant fans #1 and #2 operate properly. Does the auxiliary engine coolant fans #1 and #2 operate properly?	Go to *Cooling Fan System Check*	Go to *Step 1*

GC1080000579030X

Fig. 81 Cooling fan inoperative-auxiliary (Both fans, Part 3 of 3). 2000–01 Catera

Step	Action	Yes	No
5	Test the control circuit of the fan control relay coil of the fan control relay K52 connector for an open. Did you find and correct the condition?	Go to *Step 9*	Go to *Step 6*
6	***Notice:*** Refer to *Relay Notice* in Cautions and Notices. Test the fan control relay K28 and fan control relay K52 diagnostic enable circuit for an open. Did you find and correct the condition?	Go to *Step 9*	Go to *Step 7*
7	Inspect for poor connections at the harness connector of the fan control relay K52. Did you find and correct the condition?	Go to *Step 9*	Go to *Step 8*
8	Replace the fan control relay K52. Did you complete the repair?	Go to *Step 9*	—
9	1. Connect all connectors and components that were previously disconnected. 2. Check the auxiliary engine coolant fan #1 for proper operation. Does the auxiliary engine coolant fan #1 operate properly?	Go to *Cooling Fan System Check*	Go to *Step 1*

GC1080000580020X

Fig. 82 Cooling fan inoperative-auxiliary (Fan No. 1 Part 2 of 2). 2000–01 Catera

Step	Action	Yes	No
5	Test the supply voltage circuit of the auxiliary engine coolant fan #2 for an open. Did you find and correct the condition?	Go to *Step 10*	Go to *Step 6*
6	Test the control circuit of the relay coil of the fan control relay K28 connector for an open. Did you find and correct the condition?	Go to *Step 10*	Go to *Step 7*
7	Test the diagnostic enable circuit of fan control relay K28 for an open. Did you find and correct the condition?	Go to *Step 10*	Go to *Step 8*
8	Inspect for poor connections at the harness connector of the fan control relay K28. Did you find and correct the condition?	Go to *Step 10*	Go to *Step 9*
9	Replace the fan control relay K28. Did you complete the repair?	Go to *Step 10*	—
10	1. Connect all connectors and components that were previously disconnected. 2. Check the auxiliary engine coolant fan #2 for proper operation. Does the auxiliary engine coolant fan #2 operate properly?	Go to *Cooling Fan System Check*	Go to *Step 1*

GC1080000581020X

Fig. 83 Cooling fan inoperative-auxiliary (Fan No. 2 Part 2 of 2). 2000–01 Catera

Step	Action	Yes	No
1	Did you perform the Cooling Fan System Check?	Go to *Step 2*	Go to *Cooling Fan System Check*
2	1. Turn OFF the ignition. 2. Connect a 5 A fused jumper between the fan control relay K26 diagnostic enable circuit and a known good ground. Does the auxiliary engine coolant fan #1 and auxiliary engine coolant fan #2 operate at low speed?	Go to *Step 3*	Go to *Cooling Fan Inoperative - Auxiliary (Both Aux Eng Coolant Fans Inop)* or *Cooling Fan Inoperative - Auxiliary (Aux Engine Coolant Fan #1 Inop)* or *Cooling Fan Inoperative - Auxiliary (Aux Engine Coolant Fan #2 Inop)* or *Cooling Fan Inoperative - Auxiliary (A/C Cooling Low Speed)* or *Cooling Fan Inoperative - Auxiliary (A/C Cooling High Speed)*
3	1. Remove the 5 A jumper. 2. Turn ON the ignition, with the engine OFF. 3. Remove fan control relay K52. 4. Test the ignition voltage supply circuit of the fan control relay K52 connector for an open. Did you find and correct the condition?	Go to *Step 9*	Go to *Step 4*
4	1. Turn OFF the ignition. 2. Test the ground circuit of the auxiliary engine coolant fan #1 of the fan control relay K52 connector for an open. Did you find and correct the condition?	Go to *Step 9*	Go to *Step 5*

GC1080000580010X

Fig. 82 Cooling fan inoperative-auxiliary (Fan No. 1 Part 1 of 2). 2000–01 Catera

Step	Action	Yes	No
1	Did you perform the Cooling Fan System Check?	Go to *Step 2*	Go to *Cooling Fan System Check*
2	1. Turn Off the ignition. 2. Connect a 5 A fused jumper between the fan control relay K26 diagnostic enable circuit and a known good ground. Does the auxiliary engine coolant fan #1 and the auxiliary engine coolant fan #2 operate at low speed?	Go to *Step 3*	Go to *Cooling Fan Inoperative - Auxiliary (Both Aux Eng Coolant Fans Inop)* or *Cooling Fan Inoperative - Auxiliary (Aux Engine Coolant Fan #1 Inop)* or *Cooling Fan Inoperative - Auxiliary (Aux Engine Coolant Fan #2 Inop)* or *Cooling Fan Inoperative - Auxiliary (A/C Cooling Low Speed)* or *Cooling Fan Inoperative - Auxiliary (A/C Cooling High Speed)*
3	1. Turn ON the ignition, with the engine OFF. 2. Remove the fan control relay K28. 3. Test the battery positive voltage circuit of the fan control relay K28 connector for a short to ground or an open. Did you find and correct the condition?	Go to *Step 10*	Go to *Step 4*
4	Test the ignition voltage supply circuit of the fan control relay K28 connector for an open. Did you find and correct the condition?	Go to *Step 10*	Go to *Step 5*

GC1080000581010X

Fig. 83 Cooling fan inoperative-auxiliary (Fan No. 2 Part 1 of 2). 2000–01 Catera

Step	Action	Yes	No
1	Did you perform the Cooling Fan System Check?	Go to *Step 2*	Go to *Cooling Fan System Check*
2	1. Turn OFF the ignition. 2. Connect a 5 A fused jumper between the fan control relay K26 diagnostic enable circuit and a known good ground. Does the auxiliary engine coolant fan #1 and auxiliary engine coolant fan #2 operate at low speed?	Go to *Step 3*	Go to *Cooling Fan Inoperative - Auxiliary (Both Aux Eng Coolant Fans Inop)* or *Cooling Fan Inoperative - Auxiliary (Aux Engine Coolant Fan #1 Inop)* or *Cooling Fan Inoperative - Auxiliary (Aux Engine Coolant Fan #2 Inop)* or *Cooling Fan Inoperative - Auxiliary (A/C Cooling Low Speed)* or *Cooling Fan Inoperative - Auxiliary (A/C Cooling High Speed)*

GC1080000582010X

Fig. 84 Cooling fan inoperative-auxiliary (A/C cooling low speed, Part 1 of 2). 2000–01 Catera

Step	Action	Yes	No
3	1. Remove the fused jumper. 2. Turn ON the ignition, with the engine OFF. 3. Remove fan control relay K87. 4. Test the battery positive voltage circuit of the fan control relay K87 connector for an open. Did you find and correct the condition?	Go to *Step 11*	Go to *Step 4*
4	Test the ground circuit of the relay coil of the fan control relay K87 connector for an open. Did you find and correct the condition?	Go to *Step 11*	Go to *Step 5*
5	1. Start the engine. 2. Turn the A/C compressor ON 3. Connect a test lamp between the supply voltage circuit of the fan control relay coil of the fan control relay K87 connector and a good ground. Does the test lamp illuminate?	Go to *Step 8*	Go to *Step 6*
6	Test the supply voltage circuit for an open. Did you find and correct the condition?	Go to *Step 11*	Go to *Step 7*
7	Refer to HVAC Systems-Automatic. Did you complete the repair?	Go to *Step 11*	—
8	Test the supply voltage circuit of the auxiliary engine coolant fan #1 of the fan control relay K87 connector for an open. Did you find and correct the condition?	Go to *Step 11*	Go to *Step 9*
9	Inspect for poor connections at the harness connector of the fan control relay K87. Did you find and correct the condition?	Go to *Step 11*	Go to *Step 10*
10	Replace the fan control relay K87. Did you complete the repair?	Go to *Step 11*	—
11	1. Connect all connectors and components that were previously disconnected. 2. Check the auxiliary engine coolant fan #1 for proper operation. Does the auxiliary engine coolant fans operate at low speed?	Go to *Cooling Fan System Check*	Go to *Step 1*

GC1080000582020X

Fig. 84 Cooling fan inoperative-auxiliary (A/C cooling low speed, Part 2 of 2). 2000–01 Catera

Step	Action	Yes	No
1	Did you perform the Cooling Fan System Check?	Go to *Step 2*	Go to *Cooling Fan System Check*
2	1. Turn OFF the ignition. 2. Make sure the engine temperature is below 95°C (203°F). 3. Install the A/C manifold gauge set to check A/C compressor refrigerant pressure switch is below 1500kpa (217psi). Are the auxiliary engine coolant fan #1, auxiliary engine coolant fan #2, and electric cooling fan all operating at low speed?	Go to *Step 3*	Go to *Step 6*
3	Test the diagnostic enable circuit of the fan control relay K26 for a short to ground. Did you find and correct the condition?	Go to *Step 29*	Go to *Step 4*
4	Test the control circuit of the relay coil of the fan control relay K26 for a short to ground. Did you find and correct the condition?	Go to *Step 29*	Go to *Step 5*

GC1080000584010X

Fig. 86 Cooling fan always on-auxiliary (Part 1 of 3). 2000–01 Catera

Step	Action	Yes	No
1	Did you perform the Cooling Fan Diagnostic System Check?	Go to *Step 2*	Go to *Cooling Fan System Check*
2	1. Start the engine. 2. Turn the A/C compressor ON. 3. With the engine running locate the coolant fan test connector within the ECM housing. 4. Use a fused jumper to connect the cooling fan relay control circuit of the coolant fan diagnostic enable circuit to a known good ground. Does the Auxiliary fan #1 and Auxiliary fan #2 operate at high speed?	Go to *Step 4*	Go to *Step 3*
3	1. Locate an open or a high resistance in the auxiliary cooling fan relay control circuit or auxiliary cooling fan relay control circuit of the coolant fan diagnostic enable circuit 2. Repair the open or the high resistance in the auxiliary cooling fan relay control circuit or auxiliary cooling fan relay control circuit of the coolant fan diagnostic enable circuit 3. Replace the fan control relay K28 if these circuits are OK. Did you complete the repair?	Go to *Step 5*	—
4	1. Locate an open or a high resistance in the A/C Refrigerant Pressure Cycling Switch Signal circuit or the A/C Refrigerant Pressure Cycling Switch ground circuit 2. Repair the open or the high resistance in the A/C Refrigerant Pressure Cycling Switch Signal circuit or the A/C Refrigerant Pressure Cycling Switch ground circuit. 3. Replace the A/C compressor refrigerant pressure switch if these circuit are OK. Did you complete the repair?	Go to *Step 5*	—
5	1. Connect all connectors and components that were previously disconnected. 2. Check the auxiliary engine coolant fan #1 for proper operation. Do the cooling fans operate properly?	Go to *Cooling Fan System Check*	Go to *Step 1*

GC1080000583000X

Fig. 85 Cooling fan inoperative-auxiliary (A/C cooling high speed). 2000–01 Catera

Step	Action	Yes	No
5	Replace the primary cooling fan temperature switch. Did you complete the repair?	Go to *Step 29*	—
6	Is the electric cooling fan operating at low speed?	Go to *Step 10*	Go to *Step 7*
7	Is the auxiliary engine coolant fan #1 and auxiliary engine coolant fan #2 operating at low speed?	Go to *Step 8*	Go to *Step 15*
8	1. Remove fan control relay K26. 2. Connect a test lamp between the supply voltage circuit of the auxiliary engine coolant fan #1 of the fan control relay K26 connector and a good ground. Does the test lamp illuminate?	Go to *Step 9*	Go to *Step 11*
9	1. Remove fan control relay K87 2. Connect a test lamp between the supply voltage circuit of the relay coil of the fan control relay K87 connector and a good ground. Does the test lamp illuminate?	*Diagnostic Starting Point*	Go to *Step 12*
10	Test the supply voltage circuit of the electric cooling fan of the fan control relay K26 connector for a short to voltage. Did you find and correct the condition?	Go to *Step 29*	Go to *Step 13*
11	Replace the fan control relay K26. Did you complete the repair?	Go to *Step 29*	—
12	Test the supply voltage circuit of the auxiliary engine coolant fan #1 of the fan control relay K26 connector and fan control relay K87 connector for a short to voltage. Did you find and correct the condition?	Go to *Step 29*	Go to *Step 14*
13	Replace the fan control relay K26. Did you complete the repair?	Go to *Step 29*	—
14	Replace the fan control relay K87 Did you complete the repair?	Go to *Step 29*	—
15	Turn ON the ignition, with the engine OFF. Does the auxiliary engine coolant fan #2 operate at high speed?	Go to *Step 16*	Go to *Step 24*
16	1. Remove fan control relay K28. 2. Using the DMM test the control circuit of the relay coil of the fan control relay K28 connector for continuity to a good ground. Is there continuity?	Go to *Step 17*	Go to *Step 19*
17	Test the control circuit of the relay coil of the fan control relay K28 for a short to ground. Did you find and correct the condition?	Go to *Step 29*	Go to *Step 18*
18	Replace the secondary cooling fan temperature switch. Did you complete the repair?	Go to *Step 29*	—
19	Using the DMM test the control circuit of the relay coil of the fan control relay K28 from the A/C compressor refrigerant pressure switch for continuity to a good ground. Is there continuity?	Go to *Step 20*	Go to *Step 22*

GC1080000584020X

Fig. 86 Cooling fan always on-auxiliary (Part 2 of 3). 2000–01 Catera

Step	Action	Yes	No
20	Test the control circuit of the relay coil of the fan control relay K28 from the A/C compressor refrigerant pressure switch for a short to ground. Did you find and correct the condition?	Go to *Step 29*	Go to *Step 21*
21	Replace the A/C compressor refrigerant pressure switch. Did you complete the repair?	Go to *Step 29*	—
22	Test the supply voltage circuit of the auxiliary engine coolant fan #2 for a short to voltage. Did you find and correct the condition?	Go to *Step 29*	Go to *Step 23*
23	Replace the fan control relay K28. Did you complete the repair?	Go to *Step 29*	—
24	Does the electric cooling fan operate at high speed?	Go to *Step 25*	Go to *Step 29*
25	1. Remove fan control relay K67. 2. Test the control circuit of the relay coil of the fan control relay K67 connector for a short to ground. Did you find and correct the condition?	Go to *Step 29*	Go to *Step 26*
26	Replace the primary cooling fan temperature switch. Did you complete the repair?	Go to *Step 29*	—
27	Test the supply voltage circuit of the electric cooling fan of the fan control relay K67 connector for a short to voltage. Did you find and correct the condition?	Go to *Step 29*	Go to *Step 28*
28	Replace the fan control relay K67. Did you complete the repair?	Go to *Step 29*	—
29	1. Connect all the connectors and components that were disconnected. 2. Verify that the auxiliary engine coolant fans #1 and #2 operate properly. Does the auxiliary engine coolant fan #1 and auxiliary engine coolant fan #2 operate properly?	Go to *Cooling Fan System Check*	Go to *Step 1*

GC1080000584030X

Fig. 86 Cooling fan always on-auxiliary (Part 3 of 3). 2000–01 Catera

Step	Action	Value(s)	Yes	No
1	Did you perform the Powertrain On-Board Diagnostic (OBD) System Check?	—	*Go to Step 2*	*Powertrain On Board Diagnostic (OBD) System*
2	Are any DTCs set?	—	Go to applicable DTCs	*Go to Step 3*
3	1. Install a scan tool. 2. Engine coolant temperature must be below the specified value for all the fan diagnoses. 3. Turn on the Ignition, with the engine and A/C off. Are the cooling fans off?	100°C (212°F)	*Go to Step 4*	Go to Cooling Fan table #1
4	With a scan tool, command Low Speed Fans on. Are both cooling fans on?	—	*Go to Step 5*	Go to Cooling Fan table #2
5	**Important:** Allow a 3–5 second delay before determining if the fans have switched from low to high speed. With a scan tool, command High Speed Fans on. Do both cooling fans switch to high speed?	—	*Go to Step 6*	Go to Cooling Fan table #3
6	1. Exit outputs screen on the scan tool. 2. Idle the engine leaving the A/C off. Are the cooling fans on?	—	*Go to Step 8*	*Go to Step 7*
7	Turn on the A/C. Are the cooling fans on?	—	System OK	*Go to Step 9*
8	Does the scan tool display A/C request as YES?	—	Go to *A/C System*	*Go to Step 10*
9	Does the scan tool display A/C request as YES?	—	Go to *A/C System*	Go to *A/C System*
10	**Important:** Program the replacement PCM. Replace the PCM. Is the action complete?	—	System OK	—

GC1089900416000X

Fig. 87 Cooling fan functional check. 1998–2000 Century & Regal

Step	Action	Value(s)	Yes	No
1	Did you perform the Cooling Fan Functional Check?	—	*Go to Step 2*	Go to Cooling Fan Functional Check
2	Disconnect Cool Fan 1 Relay. Are both fans off?	—	*Go to Step 8*	*Go to Step 3*
3	Disconnect Cool Fan 3 Relay. Are both fans off?	—	*Go to Step 4*	*Go to Step 10*
4	1. Disconnect the right fan. 2. Probe terminal B of the right fan connector using a *J 34142-B* test lamp that is connected to a known good ground. Does the *J 34142-B* test lamp illuminate?	—	*Go to Step 11*	*Go to Step 5*

GC1089900417010X

Fig. 88 Cooling fan table No. 1 (Part 1 of 2). 1998–2000 Century & Regal

Step	Action	Value(s)	Yes	No
5	Probe terminal A of the right fan connector using a *J 34142-B* test lamp that is connected to a known good ground. Does the *J 34142-B* test lamp illuminate?	—	*Go to Step 12*	*Go to Step 6*
6	Probe the High Speed Fans control circuit (473) at the Cool Fan 3 Relay connector in the *Underhood Accessory Wiring Junction Block* using a *J 34142-B* test lamp that is connected to battery positive voltage. Does the *J 34142-B* test lamp illuminate?	—	*Go to Step 7*	*Go to Step 13*
7	1. Turn off the ignition. 2. Leave the *J 34142-B* test lamp installed. 3. Disconnect the PCM. 4. Turn on the ignition, with the engine off. Is the *J 34142-B* test lamp still illuminated?	—	*Go to Step 14*	*Go to Step 16*
8	Probe the Low Speed Fans Control circuit (335) at the Cool Fan 1 Relay connector using the *J 34142-B* test lamp that is connected to battery positive voltage. Does the *J 34142-B* test lamp illuminate?	—	*Go to Step 9*	*Go to Step 13*
9	1. Turn off the ignition. 2. Leave the *J 34142-B* test lamp installed. 3. Disconnect the PCM. 4. Turn on the ignition, with the engine off. Is the *J 34142-B* test lamp still illuminated?	—	*Go to Step 14*	*Go to Step 16*
10	Repair the LH fan feed circuit (504) for a short to voltage. Did you find and correct the condition?	—	Go to Cooling Fan Functional Check	*Go to Step 15*
11	Repair the RH fan feed circuit (409) for a short to voltage. Is the action complete?	—	Go to Cooling Fan Functional Check	—
12	Repair the short to voltage in the Cool Fan 2 Relay feed circuit (532). Is the action complete?	—	Go to Cooling Fan Functional Check	—
13	Replace the Cool Fan 1 Relay. Is the action complete?	—	Go to Cooling Fan Functional Check	—
14	Repair the High Speed Fans Control circuit (473) or the Low Speed Fans Control circuit (335) for a short to ground. Is the action complete?	—	Go to Cooling Fan Functional Check	—
15	Replace the Cool Fan 2 Relay. Is the action complete?	—	Go to Cooling Fan Functional Check	—
16	**Important:** Program the replacement PCM. Replace the PCM. Is the action complete?	—	Go to Cooling Fan Functional Check	—

GC1089900417020X

Fig. 88 Cooling fan table No. 1 (Part 2 of 2). 1998–2000 Century & Regal

Step	Action	Value(s)	Yes	No
1	Did you perform the Cooling Fan Functional Check?	—	Go to Step 2	Go to Cooling Fan Functional Check
2	Did either fan turn on when Cool Fan 1 Relay was commanded on?	—	Go to Step 3	Go to Step 5
3	1. Install a scan tool. 2. With a scan tool, command Low Speed Fans on. Did the other fan turn off?	—	Go to Step 19	Go to Step 4
4	Disconnect Cool Fan 2 Relay. Did the fan turn off?	—	Go to Step 20	Go to Step 21
5	1. With a scan tool, command Low Speed Fans on. 2. Disconnect Cool Fan 1 Relay. 3. Probe Low Speed Fans Control circuit (335) at the Cool Fan 1 Relay Connector using a *J 34142-B* test lamp that is connected to battery positive voltage. Does the *J 34142-B* test lamp illuminate?	—	Go to Step 6	Go to Step 13
6	Probe both feed circuits (342) at the Cool Fan 1 Relay Connector locations using a *J 34142-B* test lamp that is connected to ground. Does *J 34142-B* test lamp illuminate for both circuits?	—	Go to Step 7	Go to Step 22
7	**Important:** Leave jumper in place for remainder of this table. Connect a fused jumper wire between the switch feed circuit (342) and the RH fan feed circuit (409) at the Cool Fan 1 Relay Connector locations. Do both fans turn on?	—	Go to Step 23	Go to Step 8
8	1. Disconnect the right fan. 2. Probe fan harness connector terminal B with a *J 34142-B* test lamp that is connected to a known good ground. Does the *J 34142-B* test lamp illuminate?	—	Go to Step 9	Go to Step 24
9	Connect a second fused jumper wire between the right fan harness connector terminals. Is the left fan on?	—	Go to Step 16	Go to Step 10
10	1. Reconnect the right fan. 2. Disconnect Cool Fan 2 Relay. 3. Probe the switch feed circuit (532) at Cool Fan 2 Relay connector using a *J 34142-B* test lamp that is connected to a known good ground. Does the *J 34142-B* test lamp illuminate?	—	Go to Step 11	Go to Step 25
11	Using the second jumper wire, jumper the switch feed circuit (532) and the LH fan feed circuit (504) together at Cool Fan 2 Relay connector. Do the fans come on?	—	Go to Step 26	Go to Step 12
12	1. Reconnect Cool Fan 2 Relay. 2. Disconnect the left fan. 3. Probe left fan harness connector terminal B with a *J 34142-B* test lamp that is connected to a known good ground. Is the right fan on?	—	Go to Step 16	Go to Step 18

GC1089900418010X

Fig. 89 Cooling fan table No. 2 (Part 1 of 2). 1998–2000 Century & Regal

Step	Action	Value(s)	Yes	No
13	1. Keep *J 34142-B* test lamp connected. 2. Turn off the ignition. 3. Disconnect the PCM. 4. Probe the Low Speed Fans Control circuit at the PCM connector, with a fused jumper wire that is connected to a known good ground. Is the *J 34142-B* test lamp on?	—	Go to Step 20	Go to Step 21
14	Inspect the PCM connections. Repair faulty connections as necessary. Did you find a problem and correct the problem?	—	Go to Cooling Fan Functional Check	Go to Step 27
15	Repair the Low Speed Fans Control circuit (335) for an open or shorted to battery positive voltage. Is the action complete?	—	Go to Cooling Fan Functional Check	—
16	Inspect the fan motor ground circuit for a open or the left fan motor connections and repair as necessary. Did you find and correct the condition?	—	Go to Cooling Fan Functional Check	Go to Step 17
17	Replace the left fan motor. Is the action complete?	—	Go to Cooling Fan Functional Check	—
18	Repair the RH fan feed circuit (504) for an open. Is the action complete?	—	Go to Cooling Fan Functional Check	—
19	Replace the fan which was not operating. Is the action complete?	—	Go to Cooling Fan Functional Check	—
20	Replace Cool Fan 3 Relay. Is the action complete?	—	Go to Cooling Fan Functional Check	—
21	Repair the Cool Fan 2 Relay feed circuit (532) for a short to ground. Did you find and correct the condition?	—	Go to Cooling Fan Functional Check	Go to Step 26
22	Repair the open or the grounded circuit for the circuit that did not light. Is the action complete?	—	Go to Cooling Fan Functional Check	—
23	Replace Cool Fan 1 Relay. Is the action complete?	—	Go to Cooling Fan Functional Check	—
24	Repair the LH fan feed circuit (409) for a open. Is the action complete?	—	Go to Cooling Fan Functional Check	—
25	Repair the Cool Fan 2 Relay feed circuit (532) for a open. Is the action complete?	—	Go to Cooling Fan Functional Check	—
26	Replace Cool Fan 2 Relay. Is the action complete?	—	Go to Cooling Fan Functional Check	—
27	**Important:** Program the replacement PCM. Replace the PCM. Is the action complete?	—	Go to Cooling Fan Functional Check	—

GC1089900418020X

Fig. 89 Cooling fan table No. 2 (Part 2 of 2). 1998–2000 Century & Regal

Step	Action	Value(s)	Yes	No
1	Did you perform the Cooling Fan Functional Check?	—	Go to Step 2	Go to Cooling Fan Functional Check
2	1. With a scan tool, command Low Speed Fans on. 2. Command High Speed Fans on. Did both fans operate with no change?	—	Go to Step 8	Go to Step 3
3	Did the left fan stop operating?	—	Go to Step 9	Go to Step 4
4	1. Disconnect Cool Fan 3 Relay. 2. Probe the High Speed Fans Control circuit (473) at Cool Fan 3 Relay connector using a *J 34142-B* test lamp that is connected to battery positive voltage. 3. Command High Speed Fans on using a scan tool. Does the *J 34142-B* test lamp illuminate after several seconds?	—	Go to Step 5	Go to Step 12
5	Probe the coil feed circuit (2140) at Cool Fan Relay connector using a *J 34142-B* test lamp that is connected to a known good ground. Does the *J 34142-B* test lamp illuminate?	—	Go to Step 6	Go to Step 13
6	Probe the switch feed circuit (2140) at the Cool Fan 3 Relay connector using a *J 34142-B* test lamp that is connected to a good ground. Does the *J 34142-B* test lamp illuminate?	—	Go to Step 7	Go to Step 14
7	Jumper the switch feed circuit (2140) and the LH fan feed circuit (504) together at the Cool Fan 3 Relay connector. Is the left fan on?	—	Go to Step 15	Go to Step 16
8	1. Turn off the ignition. 2. Disconnect the PCM. 3. Disconnect Cool Fan 1 Relay. 4. Jumper the switch feed circuit (342) and the RH fan feed circuit (409) together at the Cool Fan 1 Relay connector. 5. Turn the ignition on. 6. Probe the PCM harness connector for the High Speed Fans Control circuit with a fused jumper that is connected to a known good ground. Do the fans switch from low to high speed?	—	Go to Step 22	Go to Step 17
9	1. Disconnect Cool Fan 3 Relay. 2. Probe the High Speed Fans Control Circuit (473) at the Cool Fan 3 Relay connector using a *J 34142-B* test lamp that is connected to battery positive voltage. 3. Command High Speed Fans on using a scan tool. Does the *J 34142-B* test lamp illuminate?	—	Go to Step 10	Go to Step 18
10	Probe the ground circuit (1050) at the Cool Fan 2 Relay connector using a *J 34142-B* test lamp that is connected to battery positive voltage. Does the *J 34142-B* test lamp illuminate?	—	Go to Step 11	Go to Step 19
11	Probe the coil feed circuit (2140) at the Cool Fan 2 Relay connector using a *J 34142-B* test lamp that is connected to a known good ground. Does the *J 34142-B* test lamp illuminate?	—	Go to Step 20	Go to Step 21
12	Repair the High Speed Fans Control circuit (473) for an open between Cool Fan 3 Relay and the splice. Is the action complete?	—	Go to Cooling Fan Functional Check	—

GC1089900419010X

Fig. 90 Cooling fan table No. 3 (Part 1 of 2). 1998–2000 Century & Regal

Step	Action	Value(s)	Yes	No
13	Repair the open in the Cool Fan 3 Relay coil feed circuit (2140). Is the action complete?	—	Go to Cooling Fan Functional Check	—
14	Repair the open in the Cool Fan 3 Relay switch feed circuit (2140). Is the action complete?	—	Go to Cooling Fan Functional Check	—
15	Replace Cool Fan 3 Relay. Is the action complete?	—	Go to Cooling Fan Functional Check	—
16	Repair the open in the LH fan feed circuit (504) between Cool Fan 3 Relay and the splice. Is the action complete?	—	Go to Cooling Fan Functional Check	—
17	Repair the High Speed Fans Control circuit (473) for an open or for a short to battery positive voltage. Is the action complete?	—	Go to Cooling Fan Functional Check	—
18	Repair the open in the High Speed Fans Control circuit (473) between Cool Fan 2 Relay and the splice. Is the action complete?	—	Go to Cooling Fan Functional Check	—
19	Repair the open in the ground circuit (1050). Is the action complete?	—	Go to Cooling Fan Functional Check	—
20	Replace the Cool Fan 2 relay. Is the action complete?	—	Go to Cooling Fan Functional Check	—
21	Repair the open in Cool fan 2 Relay coil feed circuit (2140). Is the action complete?	—	Go to Cooling Fan Functional Check	—
22	1. Inspect the PCM connections. 2. Repair faulty connections as necessary. Did you find and correct the condition?	—	Go to Cooling Fan Functional Check	Go to Step 23
23	**Important:** Program the replacement PCM. Replace the PCM. Is the action complete?	—	Go to Cooling Fan Functional Check	—

GC1089900419020X

Fig. 90 Cooling fan table No. 3 (Part 2 of 2). 1998–2000 Century & Regal

Step	Action	Yes	No
1	Install a scan tool. Does the scan tool power up?	Go to *Step 2*	Diagnose Data Link Communications
2	1. Turn ON the ignition, with the engine OFF. 2. Attempt to establish communication with the following control modules: • Instrument Cluster • Powertrain Control Module Does the scan tool communicate with the control modules?	Go to *Step 3*	Diagnose Data Link Communications
3	Select the powertrain control module display DTCs function on the scan tool. Does the scan tool display any DTCs?	Go to *Step 4*	Diagnose *Engine Cooling*
4	Does the scan tool display any DTCs which begin with a "U"?	Go to *Scan Tool Does Not Communicate with Class 2 Device*	Diagnose *Trouble Code*

GC1080100653000X

Fig. 91 Diagnostic system check. 2001-02 Century & Regal

Step	Action	Yes	No
DEFINITION: One or both engine cooling fan motors do not operate properly in high or low speed modes.			
1	Did you perform the Engine Cooling Diagnostic System Check?	Go to *Step 2*	Go to *Diagnostic System Check*
2	1. Install a scan tool. 2. Turn ON the ignition, with the engine OFF. 3. With a scan tool, command the Fans Low Speed ON and OFF. Do the low speed engine cooling fans turn ON and OFF with each command?	Go to *Step 3*	Go to *Step 4*
3	**Important:** Before the PCM changes the speed of the cooling fans, a 3-second delay will occur. With a scan tool, command the Fans High Speed ON and OFF. Do the high speed engine cooling fans turn ON and OFF with each command?	*Test for Intermittent and Poor Connections*	Go to *Step 11*
4	**Important:** Following this step, do NOT remove the 20-A fused jumper wire that is connected during this step. While performing the following steps, use a second 20-A fused jumper wire. 1. Remove the cooling fan 1 relay. 2. Connect a 20-A fused jumper between the battery positive voltage circuit of the cooling fan 1 relay and the cooling fan motor supply voltage circuit of the cooling fan 1 relay. Do both cooling fans operate in low speed?	Go to *Step 13*	Go to *Step 5*

GC1080100655010X

Fig. 93 Cooling fan inoperative (Part 1 of 3). 2001-02 Century & Regal

Step	Action	Yes	No
5	1. Disconnect the cooling fan 2 relay. 2. Connect a second 20-A fused jumper between the left cooling fan low reference circuit of the cooling fan 2 relay and the right cooling fan supply voltage circuit of the cooling fan 2 relay. Do both cooling fans operate in low speed?	Go to *Step 14*	Go to *Step 6*
6	Connect the second 20-A fused jumper between the battery positive voltage circuit of the cooling fan 2 relay and the cooling fan motor supply voltage circuit of the cooling fan 2 relay. Does the right cooling fan operate in high speed?	Go to *Step 9*	Go to *Step 7*
7	1. Install the cooling fan 2 relay. 2. Disconnect the right cooling fan electrical connector. 3. Connect the second 20-Amp fused jumper wire from the cooling fan motor supply voltage circuit of the right cooling fan electrical connector to the cooling fan ground circuit of the right cooling fan electrical connector. Does the left cooling fan operate in high speed?	Go to *Step 16*	Go to *Step 8*
8	Connect the second 20-Amp fused jumper wire from the cooling fan motor supply voltage circuit of the right cooling fan electrical connector to a good ground. Does the left cooling fan operate in high speed?	Go to *Step 20*	Go to *Step 21*
9	1. Install the cooling fan 2 relay. 2. Disconnect the left cooling fan electrical connector. 3. Connect the second 20-Amp fused jumper wire from the cooling fan motor supply voltage circuit of the left cooling fan electrical connector to the cooling fan ground circuit of the left cooling fan electrical connector. Does the right cooling fan operate in high speed?	Go to *Step 17*	Go to *Step 10*
10	Connect the second 20-Amp fused jumper wire from battery positive voltage to the left cooling fan low circuit of the of the left cooling fan electrical connector. Does the right cooling fan operate in high speed?	Go to *Step 18*	Go to *Step 22*
11	Does the right cooling fan operate in high speed?	Go to *Step 12*	Go to *Step 15*
12	1. Disconnect the cooling fan 2 relay. 2. Connect a 20-A fused jumper between the left cooling fan low reference circuit of the cooling fan 2 relay and the ground circuit of the cooling fan 2 relay. Does the left cooling fan operate properly in high speed?	Go to *Step 14*	Go to *Step 19*
13	Inspect for poor connections at the cooling fan 1 relay. Did you find and correct the condition?	Go to *Step 28*	Go to *Step 23*
14	Inspect for poor connections at the cooling fan 2 relay. Did you find and correct the condition?	Go to *Step 28*	Go to *Step 24*
15	Inspect for poor connections at the cooling fan 3 relay. Did you find and correct the condition?	Go to *Step 28*	Go to *Step 25*
16	Inspect for poor connections at the harness connector of the right cooling fan. Did you find and correct the condition?	Go to *Step 28*	Go to *Step 26*

GC1080100655020X

Fig. 93 Cooling fan inoperative (Part 2 of 3). 2001-02 Century & Regal

Step	Action	Yes	No
DEFINITION: One or both engine cooling fan motors run continuously in high or low speed.			
1	Did you perform the Engine Cooling Diagnostic System Check?	Go to *Step 2*	Go To *Diagnostic System Check*
2	Turn ON the ignition, with the engine OFF. Are one or both cooling fans ON?	Go to *Step 3*	*Test for Intermittent and Poor Connections*
3	Are both cooling fans running continuously?	Go to *Step 5*	Go to *Step 4*
4	Remove the cooling fan 2 relay. Did the right cooling fan turn OFF?	Go to *Step 6*	Go to *Step 7*
5	Repair the short to voltage in the left cooling fan supply voltage circuit. Did you complete the repair?	Go to *Step 8*	—
6	Repair the short to voltage in the left cooling fan low reference circuit. Did you complete the repair?	Go to *Step 8*	—
7	Repair the short to voltage in the right cooling fan supply voltage circuit. Did you complete the repair?	Go to *Step 8*	—
8	Operate the system in order to verify the repair. Did you correct the condition?	System OK	Go to *Step 2*

GC1080100654000X

Fig. 92 Cooling fan always on. 2001-02 Century & Regal

Step	Action	Yes	No
17	Inspect for poor connections at the harness connector of the left cooling fan. Did you find and correct the condition?	Go to *Step 28*	Go to *Step 27*
18	Repair the left cooling fan motor supply voltage circuit. Did you complete the repair?	Go to *Step 28*	—
19	Repair the left cooling fan ground circuit. Did you complete the repair?	Go to *Step 28*	—
20	Repair the right cooling fan ground circuit. Did you complete the repair?	Go to *Step 28*	—
21	Repair the right cooling fan motor supply voltage circuit. Did you complete the repair?	Go to *Step 28*	—
22	Repair the left cooling fan low reference circuit. Did you complete the repair?	Go to *Step 28*	—
23	Replace the cooling fan 1 relay. Did you complete the replacement?	Go to *Step 28*	—
24	Replace the cooling fan 2 relay. Did you complete the replacement?	Go to *Step 28*	—
25	Replace the cooling fan 3 relay. Did you complete the replacement?	Go to *Step 28*	—
26	Replace the right cooling fan. Did you complete the replacement?	Go to *Step 28*	—
27	Replace the left cooling fan. Did you complete the replacement?	Go to *Step 28*	—
28	Operate the system in order to verify the repair. Did you correct the condition?	System OK	Go to *Step 3*

GC1080100655030X

Fig. 93 Cooling fan inoperative (Part 3 of 3). 2001-02 Century & Regal

Step	Action	Value(s)	Yes	No
1	Did you perform the Powertrain On-Board Diagnostic (OBD) System Check?	—	*Go to Step 2*	Go to *Powertrain On Board Diagnostic (OBD) System Check*
2	Are any DTCs set?	—	Go to applicable DTC Table	*Go to Step 3*
3	**Important:** Engine coolant temperature must be below the specified value for all cooling fan diagnoses. 1. Idle the engine. 2. Turn OFF the A/C. 3. Monitor the A/C Request parameter using the scan tool. Does the scan tool display the A/C request as YES?	100° C (212° F)	*A/C Request Circuit*	*Go to Step 4*
4	1. Turn OFF the ignition. 2. Turn ON the ignition leaving the engine OFF. Are the cooling fans ON?	—	Go to Cooling Fan table #1	*Go to Step 5*
5	Command cooling fan relay #1 ON using a scan tool. Are both cooling fans ON?	—	*Go to Step 6*	Go to Cooling Fan table #2
6	Command cooling fan relays #1, #2 and #3 ON using a scan tool. Do both cooling fans swich to high speed?	—	*Go to Step 7*	Go to Cooling Fan table #3
7	1. Using a scan tool, exit outputs. 2. Idle the engine leaving the A/C OFF. Are the cooling fans ON?	—	Go to Cooling Fan table #1	*Go to Step 8*
8	Turn ON the A/C. Are the cooling fans ON?	—	System OK	*Go to Step 9*
9	Does the scan tool display A/C request as YES?	—	*HVAC System*	*A/C Request Circuit*

GC1089900427000X

Fig. 94 Cooling fan functional check. 1998-2000 Corvette

Step	Action	Value(s)	Yes	No
1	Did you perform the Cooling Fan Functional Check?	—	*Go to Step 2*	Go to Cooling Fan Functional Check
2	1. Turn ON the ignition leaving the engine OFF. 2. Disconnect the cooling fan relay #1. Are both of the cooling fans OFF?	—	*Go to Step 6*	*Go to Step 3*
3	Disconnect the cooling fan relay #3. Are both of the cooling fans OFF?	—	*Go to Step 4*	*Go to Step 5*
4	1. Turn OFF the Ignition. 2. Raise the vehicle. 3. Disconnect the left cooling fan electrical connector. 4. Probe the cooling fan electrical connector terminal B using the test lamp *J 34142-B* connected to ground. 5. Turn ON the ignition leaving the engine OFF. Does the test lamp illuminate?	—	*Go to Step 7*	*Go to Step 8*
5	Disconnect the cooling fan relay #2. Are both of the cooling fans OFF?	—	*Go to Step 10*	*Go to Step 9*
6	Replace the cooling fan relay #1. Is the action complete?	—	Go to Cooling Fan Functional Check	—
7	Repair circuit 409 for a short to B+. Is the action complete?	—	Go to Cooling Fan Functional Check	—
8	Repair circuit 532 for a short to B+. Is the action complete?	—	Go to Cooling Fan Functional Check	—
9	Repair circuit 504 for a short to B+. Is the action complete?	—	Go to Cooling Fan Functional Check	—
10	Replace the cooling fan relay #2. Is the action complete?	—	Go to Cooling Fan Functional Check	—

GC1089900428000X

Fig. 95 Cooling fan table 1. 1998-2000 Corvette

Step	Action	Value(s)	Yes	No
1	Did you perform the Cooling Fan Functional Check?	—	*Go to Step 2*	Go to Cooling Fan Functional Check
2	1. Turn ON the ignition leaving the engine OFF. 2. Disconnect cooling fan relay #1. 3. Probe the cooling fan relay B+ terminal (switch side) at the underhood electrical center using the test lamp *J 34142-B* connected to ground. Does the test lamp illuminate?	—	*Go to Step 3*	*Go to Step 11*
3	**Important:** Leave jumper wire in place for remainder of this table. Jumper the cooling fan relay #1 B+ terminal and load terminals together at the underhood electrical center using a fused jumper wire. Do both fans turn ON?	—	*Go to Step 12*	*Go to Step 4*
4	1. Raise the vehicle. 2. Disconnect the left cooling fan electrical connector. 3. Probe the left cooling fan harness connector terminal B using the test lamp *J 34142-B* connected to ground. Does the test lamp illuminate?	—	*Go to Step 5*	*Go to Step 13*
5	1. Disconnect the cooling fan relay #3. 2. Probe the cooling fan relay #3 terminal for circuit 532 at the underhood electrical center using the test lamp *J 34142-B* connected to B+. Does the test lamp illuminate?	—	*Go to Step 22*	*Go to Step 6*
6	1. Install the cooling fan relay #3. **Important:** Leave the jumper wire in place for remainder of this table. 2. Connect a fused jumper wire between the left cooling fan electrical connector terminals A and B. Does the right cooling fan turn ON?	—	*Go to Step 14*	*Go to Step 7*
7	1. Disconnect the cooling fan relay #3. 2. Probe the cooling fan relay #3 terminal for circuit 532 at the underhood electrical center using the test lamp *J 34142-B* connected to ground. Does the test lamp illuminate?	—	*Go to Step 8*	*Go to Step 16*
8	**Important:** Leave the jumper wire in place for remainder of this table. Connect a fused jumper wire between the cooling fan relay #3 terminals for circuits 532 and 504 at the underhood electrical center. Does the right cooling fan turn ON?	—	*Go to Step 17*	*Go to Step 9*

GC1089900429010X

Fig. 96 Cooling fan table 2 (Part 1 of 2). 1998-2000 Corvette

Step	Action	Value(s)	Yes	No
9	1. Disconnect the right cooling fan electrical connector. 2. Probe the right cooling fan electrical connector terminal B using the test lamp *J 34142-B* connected to ground. Does the test lamp illuminate?	—	*Go to Step 10*	*Go to Step 21*
10	Probe the right cooling fan electrical connector terminal A using the test lamp *J 34142-B* connected to B+. Does the test lamp illuminate?	—	*Go to Step 18*	*Go to Step 20*
11	Repair the cooling fan relay B+ supply circuit. Is the action complete?	—	Go to Cooling Fan Functional Check	—
12	Replace the cooling fan relay #1. Is the action complete?	—	Go to Cooling Fan Functional Check	—
13	Repair circuit 409 for an open. Is the action complete?	—	Go to Cooling Fan Functional Check	—
14	1. Inspect for poor connections at the left cooling fan motor. 2. If you find a poor connection, repair the condition as necessary. Did you find and correct the condition?	—	Go to Cooling Fan Functional Check	*Go to Step 15*
15	Replace the LH fan motor. Is the action complete?	—	Go to Cooling Fan Functional Check	—
16	Repair the open in circuit 532 between LH cooling fan connector terminal A and relay #3. Is the action complete?	—	Go to Cooling Fan Functional Check	—
17	Replace the cooling fan relay #3. Is the action complete?	—	Go to Cooling Fan Functional Check	—
18	1. Inspect for poor connections at the right cooling fan motor. 2. If you find a poor connection, repair the condition as necessary. Did you find and correct the condition?	—	Go to Cooling Fan Functional Check	*Go to Step 19*
19	Replace the RH fan motor. Is the action complete?	—	Go to Cooling Fan Functional Check	—
20	Repair the open ground circuit. Is the action complete?	—	Go to Cooling Fan Functional Check	—
21	Repair the open B+ feed circuit to the RH fan motor. Is the action complete?	—	Go to Cooling Fan Functional Check	—
22	Repair the short to ground on the circuit between the left cooling fan motor and relay #3. Is the action complete?	—	Go to Cooling Fan Functional Check	—

GC1089900429020X

Fig. 96 Cooling fan table 2 (Part 2 of 2). 1998-2000 Corvette

Step	Action	Value(s)	Yes	No
1	Did you perform the Cooling Fan Functional Check?	—	Go to Step 2	Go to Cooling Fan Functional Check
2	1. Turn ON the ignition leaving the engine OFF. 2. Command the cooling fan relays #1, #2 and #3 ON using the scan tool. Is the right fan operating at high speed?	—	Go to Step 3	Go to Step 8
3	Is the left fan operating at high speed?	—	Go to Cooling Fan Functional Check	Go to Step 4
4	1. Remove the cooling fan relay #3. 2. Probe the #3 cooling fan relay B+ supply terminal (coil side) at the underhood electrical center, using the test lamp *J 34142-B* connected to ground. Does the test lamp illuminate?	—	Go to Step 5	Go to Step 11
5	1. Probe the cooling fan relay #3 control circuit using the test lamp *J 34142-B* connected to B+. 2. Command the cooling fan relays #2 and #3 ON using the scan tool. Does the test lamp illuminate?	—	Go to Step 6	Go to Step 13
6	Connect a fused jumper wire between the cooling fan relay #3 terminal for circuit 532 and the terminal for circuit 250. Does the left cooling fan turn ON?	—	Go to Step 16	Go to Step 7
7	Probe the cooling fan relay #3 terminal for circuit 250 at the underhood electrical center using the test lamp *J 34142-B* connected to B+. Does the test lamp illuminate?	—	Go to Step 17	Go to Step 15
8	1. Turn ON the ignition leaving the engine OFF. 2. Disconnect the cooling fan relay #2. 3. Probe both of the cooling fan relay #2 B+ supply terminals using the test lamp *J 34142-B* connected to ground. Refer to Diagnostic Aids for terminal identification. Does the test lamp illuminate for both terminals?	—	Go to Step 9	Go to Step 11
9	1. Probe the cooling fan relay #2 control circuit terminal at the underhood electrical center using the test lamp *J 34142-B* connected to B+. 2. Command the cooling fan relays #2 and #3 ON using the scan tool. Does the test lamp illuminate?	—	Go to Step 10	Go to Step 13
10	Connect a fused jumper wire between the cooling fan relay #2 terminals for circuits 1445 and 504 at the underhood electrical center. Does the right cooling fan turn ON?	—	Go to Step 12	Go to Step 14

GC1089900430010X

Fig. 97 Cooling fan table 3 (Part 1 of 2). 1998-2000 Corvette

Test Description

The number(s) below refer to the step number(s) on the diagnostic table.

2. Lack of communication may be due to a partial malfunction of the class 2 serial data circuit or due to a total malfunction of the class 2 serial data circuit. The specified procedure will determine the particular condition.
3. Determine if the Instrument Cluster or Powertrain Control Modules have set DTC's which may affect Engine Cooling operation are present.
4. The presence of DTCs which begin with "U" indicate some other module is not communicating. The specified procedure will compile all the available information before tests are performed.

Step	Action	Yes	No
1	Install a scan tool. Does the scan tool power up?	Go to Step 2	Diagnose Data Link Communications
2	1. Turn ON the ignition, with the engine OFF. 2. Attempt to establish communication with the following control modules: o Instrument Cluster o Powertrain Control Module. Does the scan tool communicate with the control modules?	Go to Step 3	Diagnose Data Link Communications
3	Select the powertrain control module display DTCs function on the scan tool. Does the scan tool display any DTCs?	Go to Step 4	Diagnose Engine Cooling
4	Does the scan tool display any DTCs which begin with a "U"?	Diagnose Data Link Communications	Go to Diagnostic Trouble Code (DTC) List

GC1080100656000X

Fig. 98 Diagnostic system check. 2001-02 Corvette

Step	Action	Value(s)	Yes	No
11	Repair the cooling fan relay B+ circuit for an open. Is the action complete?	—	Go to Cooling Fan Functional Check	—
12	Replace the cooling fan relay #2. Is the action complete?	—	Go to Cooling Fan Functional Check	—
13	Repair the open cooling fan relay control circuit. Is the action complete?	—	Go to Cooling Fan Functional Check	—
14	Repair circuit 504 for an open. Is the action complete?	—	Go to Cooling Fan Functional Check	—
15	Repair the open ground circuit between the cooling fan relay #3 and the splice. Is the action complete?	—	Go to Cooling Fan Functional Check	—
16	Replace the cooling fan relay #3. Is the action complete?	—	Go to Cooling Fan Functional Check	—
17	1. Inspect for poor connections at the underhood electrical center. 2. Repair the condition as necessary. Is the action complete?	—	Go to Cooling Fan Functional Check	—

GC1089900430020X

Fig. 97 Cooling fan table 3 (Part 2 of 2). 1998-2000 Corvette

Step	Action	Yes	No
DEFINITION: One or both engine cooling fan motors run continuously in high or low speed.			
1	Did you perform the Engine Cooling Diagnostic System Check?	Go to Step 2	Go To Diagnostic System Check
2	Turn ON the ignition, with the engine OFF. Are one or both cooling fans ON?	Go to Step 3	Test for Intermittent and Poor Connections
3	Are both cooling fans running continuously?	Go to Step 5	Go to Step 4
4	Remove the cool fan 3 relay. Did the right cooling fan turn OFF?	Go to Step 6	Go to Step 7
5	Repair the short to voltage in the left cooling fan motor supply voltage circuit. Did you complete the repair?	Go to Step 8	--
6	Repair the short to voltage in the left cooling fan low reference circuit. Did you complete the repair?	Go to Step 8	--
7	Repair the short to voltage in the right cooling fan motor supply voltage circuit. Did you complete the repair?	Go to Step 8	--
8	Operate the system in order to verify the repair. Did you correct the condition?	System OK	Go to Step 2

GC1080100657000X

Fig. 99 Cooling fan always on. 2001-02 Corvette

Step	Action	Yes	No
DEFINITION: One or both engine cooling fan motors do not operate properly in high or low speed modes.			
1	Did you perform the Engine Cooling Diagnostic System Check?	Go to Step 2	Go to Diagnostic System Check
2	1. Install a scan tool. 2. Turn ON the ignition, with the engine OFF. 3. With a scan tool, command the Fan Relay 1 ON and OFF. Do the low speed engine cooling fans turn ON and OFF with each command?	Go to Step 3	Go to Step 4
3	With a scan tool, command the Fan Relays 1, 2 & 3 ON and OFF. Do the high speed engine cooling fans turn ON and OFF with each command?	Test Intermittent and Poor Connections	Go to Step 11
4	**Important** Do NOT remove the 20-A fused jumper wire connected during this step. Use a second 20-A fused jumper wire while performing the following steps: 1. Disconnect the cool fan 1 relay. 2. Connect the first 20-A fused jumper between the battery positive voltage circuit of the cool fan 1 relay and the cooling fan motor supply voltage circuit of the cool fan 1 relay. Do both cooling fans operate in low speed?	Go to Step 13	Go to Step 5
5	1. Disconnect the cool fan 3 relay. 2. Connect the second 20-A fused jumper between the left cooling fan circuit of the cool fan 3 relay and the right cooling fan motor supply voltage circuit of the cool fan 3 relay. Do both cooling fans operate in low speed?	Go to Step 14	Go to Step 6

GC1080100658010X

Fig. 100 Cooling fan inoperative (Part 1 of 4). 2001-02 Corvette

Step	Action	Yes	No
6	Connect the second 20-A fused jumper from the battery positive voltage to the cooling fan motor supply voltage circuit of the cool fan 3 relay. Does the right cooling fan operate in high speed?	Go to Step 9	Go to Step 7
7	1. Install the cool fan 3 relay. 2. Disconnect the right cooling fan electrical connector. 3. Connect the second 20-Amp fused jumper wire from the cooling fan motor supply voltage circuit of the right electrical connector to the cooling fan ground circuit of the right electrical connector. Does the left cooling fan operate in high speed?	Go to Step 16	Go to Step 8
8	Connect the second 20-Amp fused jumper wire from the cooling fan supply voltage circuit of the right cooling fan electrical connector to a good ground. Does the left cooling fan motor operate in high speed?	Go to Step 20	Go to Step 21
9	1. Install the cool fan 3 relay. 2. Disconnect the left cooling fan electrical connector. 3. Connect the second 20-Amp fused jumper from the cooling fan motor supply voltage circuit of the left cooling fan electrical connector to the low reference circuit of the left cooling fan electrical connector. Does the right cooling fan motor operate in high speed?	Go to Step 17	Go to Step 10
10	Connect the second 20-Amp fused jumper wire from battery positive voltage to the left cooling fan low reference circuit of the left cooling fan electrical connector. Does the right cooling fan operate in high speed?	Go to Step 18	Go to Step 22
11	Does the right cooling fan operate in high speed?	Go to Step 12	Go to Step 15
12	1. Disconnect the cool fan 3 relay. 2. Connect a 20-A fused jumper between the left cooling fan low reference circuit of the cool fan 3 relay and the ground circuit of the cool fan 3 relay. Does the left cooling fan operate properly in high speed?	Go to Step 14	Go to Step 19
13	Inspect for poor connections at the cool fan 1 relay. Did you find and correct the condition?	Go to Step 28	Go to Step 23
14	Inspect for poor connections at the cool fan 3 relay. Did you find and correct the condition?	Go to Step 28	Go to Step 24
15	Inspect for poor connections at the cool fan 2 relay. Did you find and correct the condition?	Go to Step 28	Go to Step 25

GC1080100658020X

Fig. 100 Cooling fan inoperative (Part 2 of 4). 2001-02 Corvette

Step	Action	Yes	No
16	Inspect for poor connections at the harness connector of the right cooling fan. Did you find and correct the condition?	Go to Step 28	Go to Step 26
17	Inspect for poor connections at the harness connector of the left cooling fan. Did you find and correct the condition?	Go to Step 28	Go to Step 27
18	Repair the left cooling fan motor supply voltage circuit. Did you complete the repair?	Go to Step 28	--
19	Repair the left cooling fan ground circuit. Did you complete the repair?	Go to Step 28	--
20	Repair the right cooling fan ground circuit. Did you complete the repair?	Go to Step 28	--
21	Repair the right cooling fan motor supply voltage circuit. Did you complete the repair?	Go to Step 28	--
22	Repair the left cooling fan low reference circuit. Did you complete the repair?	Go to Step 28	--
23	Replace the cool fan 1 relay. Is the repair complete?	Go to Step 28	--
24	Replace the cool fan 3 relay. Is the repair complete?	Go to Step 28	--

GC1080100658030X

Fig. 100 Cooling fan inoperative (Part 3 of 4). 2001-02 Corvette

Step	Action	Yes	No
25	Replace the cool fan 2 relay. Is the repair complete?	Go to Step 28	--
26	Replace the right cooling fan. Is the repair complete?	Go to Step 28	--
27	Replace the left cooling fan. Is the repair complete?	Go to Step 28	--
28	Operate the system in order to verify the repair. Did you correct the condition?	System OK	Go to Step 3

GC1080100658040X

Fig. 100 Cooling fan inoperative (Part 4 of 4). 2001-02 Corvette

Step	Action	Value(s)	Yes	No
1	Did you perform the Powertrain On-Board Diagnostic (OBD) System Check?	—	*Go to Step 2*	*Go to Powertrain On Board Diagnostic (OBD) System Check*
2	1. Ensure the engine coolant temperature is between the values specified. 2. Turn HVAC controls to OFF. 3. Start and idle the engine. 4. Using the scan tool select Output Tests and while viewing the Driver 1 display, command All Relays OFF for approximately 15 seconds. 5. Using the scan tool select Output Tests and while viewing the Driver 1 display, command All Relays ON for approximately 15 seconds. Did the Driver 1 display ever indicate a FAULT?	5°C - 100°C (41°F - 212°F)	*DTC P1660 Cooling Fan Control Circuits*	*Go to Step 3*
3	With the engine idling turn A/C ON to maximum cooling. Have any other DTC(s) failed this ignition?	—	Go to DTC(s) that are set	*Go to Step 4*
4	1. Turn the key to OFF. 2. Disconnect PCM connector C2. 3. Using a test lamp connected to a known good ground probe PCM connector C2 terminals 32 and 33. Does the test lamp illuminate on both terminals?	—	*Go to Step 5*	*Go to Step 14*
5	1. Reconnect PCM connector C2 (if still disconnected). 2. Turn the key ON while leaving the engine OFF. 3. Ensure engine coolant temperature is below the value specified. 4. Observe fan operation while individually commanding Fan Relay 1 ON, then All Relays ON, then All Relays OFF. • With Fan Relay 1 commanded ON both fans should operate at low speed. • With All Relays commanded ON both fans should operate at high speed. • With All Relays commanded OFF both fans should not operate (unless the PCM detects a fault or high temperature condition). Do both cooling fans operate as commanded?	100°C (212°F)	System OK	*Go to Step 6*
6	Does only Cooling Fan #1 (left) operate with Fan Relay 1 commanded ON then both fans operate when All Relays are commanded ON?	—	*Go to Step 7*	*Go to Step 8*
7	Repair CKT 504 shorted to ground. Is the repair complete?	—	*Go to Step 5*	—
8	Does neither cooling fan operate with Fan Relay 1 commanded ON then only Cooling Fan #2 (right) operate with All Relays commanded ON?	—	Go to Cooling Fan Symptom Table 1	*Go to Step 9*
9	Does neither cooling fan operate with Fan Relay 1 commanded ON then only Cooling Fan #1 (left) operate with All Relays commanded ON?	—	Go to Cooling Fan Symptom Table 2	*Go to Step 9*
10	Do both cooling fans operate with Fan Relay 1 commanded ON then only Cooling Fan #2 (right) operate with All Relays commanded ON?	—	Go to Cooling Fan Symptom Table 3	*Go to Step 11*
11	Do both cooling fans operate with Fan Relay 1 commanded ON then only Cooling Fan #1 (left) operate with All Relays commanded ON?	—	Go to Cooling Fan Symptom Table 4	*Go to Step 12*

GC1089800432010X

Fig. 101 Cooling fan functional check (Part 1 of 2). 1998–99 DeVille, Eldorado & Seville

Step	Action	Value(s)	Yes	No
	DEFINITION: No low speed operation of either cooling fan. High speed operation of right cooling fan only. DTC P1660 is not set.			
1	Was the Cooling Fan Functional Check performed?	—	*Go to Step 2*	Go to Cooling Fan Functional Check
2	1. Disconnect Cooling Fan #1 connector. 2. Using the scan tool select Output Tests then Fan Relays. 3. With the key ON command Relay 1 ON. 4. Using DMM J 39200 measure the voltage to ground at Cooling Fan #1 connector terminal B (harness side). Is the voltage the same or more than the value specified?	10.0 volts	*Go to Step 3*	*Go to Step 6*
3	Jumper Cooling Fan #1 connector terminals A and B together. Does Cooling Fan #2 operate while jumpered?	—	*Go to Step 8*	*Go to Step 4*
4	1. With Cooling Fan #1 connector still jumpered, remove Relay #2. 2. Measure the voltage to ground at Relay #2 terminal 30. Is the voltage the same or more than the value specified?	10.0 volts	*Go to Step 5*	*Go to Step 9*
5	Jumper Relay #2 terminals 30 and 87A together. Does Cooling Fan #2 operate while jumpered?	—	*Go to Step 10*	*Go to Step 11*
6	1. Exit Fan Relays. 2. Remove Relay #1. 3. Measure the voltage to ground at Relay #1 terminal 30. Is the voltage the same or more than the value specified?	10.0 volts	*Go to Step 7*	*Go to Step 12*
7	1. Jumper Fan Relay #1 terminals 30 and 87 together. 2. Measure the voltage to ground at Cooling Fan #1 connector terminal B. Is the voltage to ground the same or more than the value specified?	10.0 volts	*Go to Step 13*	*Go to Step 14*
8	Replace Cooling Fan #1 (left). Is the replacement complete?	—	Go to Cooling Fan Functional Check	—
9	Repair the open in CKT 504 between Cooling Fan #1 and Fan Relay #2. Is the repair complete?	—	Go to Cooling Fan Functional Check	—

GC1089800433010X

Fig. 102 Cooling fan symptom table 1 (Part 1 of 2). 1998–99 DeVille, Eldorado & Seville

Step	Action	Value(s)	Yes	No
12	Does neither cooling fan operate when Fan Relay 1 is commanded ON and also when All Relays are commanded ON?	—	Go to Cooling Fan Symptom Table 5	*Go to Step 13*
13	Does either cooling fan operate when All Relays is commanded OFF?	—	Go to Diagnostic Aids	*Go to Step 5*
14	Repair the cause of no voltage. Possible cause include the following: • A blown relay supply fuse • An open fan relay • An open cooling fan relay control circuit Is the repair complete?	—	*Go to Step 5*	—

GC1089800432020X

Fig. 101 Cooling fan functional check (Part 2 of 2). 1998–99 DeVille, Eldorado & Seville

Step	Action	Value(s)	Yes	No
10	Replace Fan Relay #2. Is the replacement complete?	—	Go to Cooling Fan Functional Check	—
11	Repair the open in CKT 409 between Fan Relay #2 and the CKT 409 splice. Is the repair complete?	—	Go to Cooling Fan Functional Check	—
12	Repair the open in the circuit between Fan Relay #1 terminal 30 and the Maxi fuse. Is the repair complete?	—	Go to Cooling Fan Functional Check	—
13	Replace Fan Relay #1. Is the replacement complete?	—	Go to Cooling Fan Functional Check	—
14	Repair the open in CKT 532 between Fan Relay #1 and Cooling Fan #1. Is the repair complete?	—	Go to Cooling Fan Functional Check	—

GC1089800433020X

Fig. 102 Cooling fan symptom table 1 (Part 2 of 2). 1998–99 DeVille, Eldorado & Seville

Step	Action	Value(s)	Yes	No
	DEFINITION: No low speed operation of either cooling fan. High speed operation of left cooling fan only. DTC P1660 is not set.			
1	Was the Cooling Fan Functional Check performed?	—	*Go to Step 2*	Go to Cooling Fan Functional Check
2	1. Disconnect Cooling Fan #2 (right) connector. 2. Using the scan tool select Output Tests than Fan Relays. 3. With the key ON, command Fan Relay 1 ON. 4. Jumper Cooling Fan #2 (right) terminals A and B together. Does Cooling Fan #1 (left) operate while jumpered?	—	*Go to Step 5*	*Go to Step 3*
3	1. With Fan Relay 1 still commanded ON remove Fan Relay #2. 2. Jumper Fan Relay #2 terminals 30 and 87A together. Does left cooling fan operate while jumpered?	—	*Go to Step 6*	*Go to Step 4*
4	With Fan Relay #2 still jumpered use DMM J 39200 and measure the voltage to ground at Cooling Fan #2 connector terminal B (harness side). Is the voltage the same or more than the value specified?	10.0 volts	*Go to Step 7*	*Go to Step 8*
5	Replace Cooling Fan #2 (right). Is the replacement complete?	—	Go to Cooling Fan Functional Check	—
6	Replace Fan Relay #2. Is the replacement complete?	—	Go to Cooling Fan Functional Check	—
7	Repair the open in the BLK circuit between Cooling Fan #2 (right) terminal A and the splice. Is the repair complete?	—	Go to Cooling Fan Functional Check	—
8	Repair the open in CKT 409 between Cooling Fan #2 (right) the CKT 409 splice and Fan Relay #2. Is the repair complete?	—	Go to Cooling Fan Functional Check	—

GC1089800434000X

Fig. 103 Cooling fan symptom table 2. 1998–99 DeVille, Eldorado & Seville

Step	Action	Value(s)	Yes	No
	DEFINITION: Low speed operation of both fans. High speed operation of right cooling fan only. DTC P1660 not set.			
1	Was the Cooling Fan Functional Check performed?	—	*Go to Step 2*	Go to Cooling Fan Functional Check
2	1. Using the scan tool select Output Tests and then Fan Relays. 2. With the key ON select All Relays ON. 3. Remove Fan Relay #2. 4. Using DMM J 39200 measure the voltage to ground at Fan Relay #2 terminal 85. Is the voltage the same or more than the value specified?	10.0 volts	*Go to Step 3*	*Go to Step 5*
3	1. Remove Fan Relay #3. 2. Measure the resistance between Fan Relay #2 terminal 86 and Fan Relay #3 terminal 86. Is the resistance the same or less than the value specified?	5 ohms	*Go to Step 4*	*Go to Step 6*
4	1. Reconnect Fan Relay #3. 2. With All Relays still commanded ON, jumper Fan Relay #2 terminals 30 and 87 together. Do both cooling fans operate while jumpered?	—	*Go to Step 8*	*Go to Step 7*
5	Repair the open in the ORG circuit between Fan Relay #2 terminal 85 and the splice. Is the repair complete?	—	Go to Cooling Fan Functional Check	—
6	Repair the open in CKT 473 between Fan Relay #2 terminal 86 and the CKT 473 splice. Is the repair complete?	—	Go to Cooling Fan Functional Check	—
7	Repair the open in the BLK circuit between Fan Relay #2 terminal 87 and the splice. Is the repair complete?	—	Go to Cooling Fan Functional Check	—
8	Replace Fan Relay #2. Is the replacement complete?	—	Go to Cooling Fan Functional Check	—

GC1089800435000X

Fig. 104 Cooling fan symptom table 3. 1998–99 DeVille, Eldorado & Seville

Step	Action	Value(s)	Yes	No
DEFINITION: Low speed operation of both fans. High speed operation of left cooling fan only. DTC P1660 not set.				
1	Was the Cooling Fan Functional Check performed?	—	*Go to Step 2*	Go to Cooling Fan Functional Check
2	1. Using scan tool select Output Tests then All Relays. 2. With the key ON command All Relays ON. 3. Remove Fan Relay #3. 4. Using DMM J 39200 measure the voltage to ground at Fan Relay #3 terminal 85. Is the voltage the same or more than the value specified?	10.0 volts	*Go to Step 3*	*Go to Step 7*
3	Measure the voltage to ground at Fan Relay #3 terminal 30. Is the voltage the same or more than the value specified?	10.0 volts	*Go to Step 4*	*Go to Step 6*
4	1. Remove Fan Relay #2. 2. Measure the resistance between Fan Relay #3 terminal 86 and Fan Relay #2 terminal 86. Is the resistance the same or less than the value specified?	5 ohms	*Go to Step 5*	*Go to Step 8*

GC1089800436010X

Fig. 105 Cooling fan symptom table 4 (Part 1 of 2). 1998–99 DeVille, Eldorado & Seville

Step	Action	Value(s)	Yes	No
DEFINITION: No fan operation on either high or low speed. DTC P1660 not set.				
1	Was the Cooling Fan Functional Check performed?	—	*Go to Step 2*	Go to Cooling Fan Functional Check
2	Check the condition of the cooling fan Maxi fuse. Is the fuse blown?	—	*Go to Step 4*	*Go to Step 3*
3	1. Remove Fan Relay #1. 2. Using DMM J 39200 measure the voltage to ground at Fan Relay #1 terminal 30. Is the voltage the same or more than the value specified?	10.0 volts	*Go to Step 8*	*Go to Step 9*
4	1. Turn the key to LOCK. 2. Replace the Maxi fuse. Does the fuse immediately blow?	—	*Go to Step 10*	*Go to Step 5*
5	1. Turn the key ON. 2. Using the scan tool select Output Tests and then Fan Relays. 3. Command Fan Relay 1 ON. Does the Maxi fuse blow?	—	*Go to Step 11*	*Go to Step 6*
6	Command All Relays ON. Does the Maxi fuse blow?	—	*Go to Step 7*	Fault not present
7	1. Exit Fan Relays. 2. Replace the Maxi fuse. 3. Select Fan Relays and command Fan Relay 1 ON. Is only Cooling Fan #1 (left) operating?	—	*Go to Step 12*	*Go to Step 13*
8	Repair the open in the BLK circuit between both BLK circuit splices or between the BLK circuit splice and ground or the poor/open ground connection. Is the repair complete?	—	Go to Cooling Fan Functional Check	—

GC1089800437010X

Fig. 106 Cooling fan symptom table 5 (Part 1 of 2). 1998–99 DeVille, Eldorado & Seville

Step	Action	Values	Yes	No
1	Did you perform the Powertrain On-Board Diagnostic (OBD) System Check?	—	*Go to Step 2*	*Go to A Powertrain On Board Diagnostic (OBD) System Check*
2	**Important:** Ensure that the engine coolant temperature is below the specified value. 1. Ensure that the vehicle battery is fully charged. 2. Turn OFF the ignition. 3. Leave the A/C OFF. Is either or both cooling fans operating?	100°C (212°F)	Go to Cooling Fan Symptom Table 1	*Go to Step 3*
3	**Important:** Ensure that the engine coolant temperature is below the specified value. 1. Turn ON the ignition. 2. Leave the A/C OFF. Is either or both cooling fans operating?	100°C (212°F)	Go to Cooling Fan Symptom Table 1	*Go to Step 4*
4	**Important:** Ensure that the engine coolant temperature is below the specified value. 1. Turn ON the ignition. 2. Leave the A/C OFF. 3. Using the scan tool, check for any DTCs. Are any DTCs set?	100°C (212°F)	Go to the applicable DTC	*Go to Step 5*
5	1. Ensure the ignition is ON. 2. Leave the A/C OFF. 3. Using the scan tool, command low speed cooling fan operation and then command high speed cooling fan operation. 4. Observe the cooling fans during each commanded state. Do both fans operate when low speed and high speed operation is commanded?	—	*Go to Step 6*	*Go to Step 8*
6	**Important:** Ensure that the ambient air temperature is more than 5°C (41°F). 1. Turn ON the ignition. 2. Turn the A/C ON. 3. Observe the cooling fans operation. Are both cooling fans operating?	—	Go to Diagnostic Aids	*Go to Step 7*
7	Observe the A/C Relay display on the scan tool. Does the A/C Relay display on the scan tool indicate ON?	—	*Go to Step 8*	Heating, Ventilation, and Air Conditioning
8	Is one or both cooling fans inoperative with low speed commanded and both fans operate normally with high speed commanded?	—	Go to Cooling Fan Symptom Table 2	*Go to Step 9*
9	Are both cooling fan inoperative with low speed commanded and either cooling fan inoperative with high speed commanded?	—	Go to Cooling Fan Symptom Table 3	*Go to Step 10*
10	Do both cooling fans operate normally with low speed commanded and the left cooling fan inoperative with high speed commanded?	—	Go to Cooling Fan Symptom Table 4	*Go to Step 11*
11	Do both cooling fans operate normally with low speed commanded and the right cooling fan inoperative with high speed commanded?	—	Go to Cooling Fan Symptom Table 5	Go to Diagnostic Aids

GC1080000615000X

Fig. 107 Cooling fan functional check. 2000 DeVille & Seville

Step	Action	Value(s)	Yes	No
5	1. Reconnect Fan Relay #2. 2. With All Relays still commanded ON, jumper Fan Relay #3 terminals 30 and 87 together. Does Cooling Fan #2 (right) operate while jumpered?	—	*Go to Step 10*	*Go to Step 9*
6	Repair the open in the RED circuit between Fan Relay #3 terminal 30 and the Maxi fuse. Is the repair complete?	—	Go to Cooling Fan Functional Check	—
7	Repair the open in the ORG circuit between Fan Relay #3 terminal 85 and the splice. Is the repair complete?	—	Go to Cooling Fan Functional Check	—
8	Repair the open in CKT 473 between Fan Relay #3 terminal 86 and the CKT 473 splice. Is the repair complete?	—	Go to Cooling Fan Functional Check	—
9	Repair the open in CKT 409 between Fan Relay #3 terminal 87 and the CKT 409 splice. Is the repair complete	—	Go to Cooling Fan Functional Check	—
10	Replace Fan Relay #3. Is the replacement complete?	—	Go to Cooling Fan Functional Check	—

GC1089800436020X

Fig. 105 Cooling fan symptom table 4 (Part 2 of 2). 1998–99 DeVille, Eldorado & Seville

Step	Action	Value(s)	Yes	No
9	Repair the open in the RED circuit between the Maxi fuse and both relays. Is the repair complete?	—	Go to Cooling Fan Functional Check	—
10	Repair the short to ground in the RED circuit between the Maxi fuse and either Fan Relay 1 or Fan Relay 3. Is the repair complete?	—	Go to Cooling Fan Functional Check	—
11	Repair the short to ground in CKT 532 between Fan Relay 1 and Cooling Fan #1 (left). Is the repair complete?	—	Go to Cooling Fan Functional Check	—
12	Replace Cooling Fan #2 (right). Is the replacement complete?	—	Go to Cooling Fan Functional Check	—
13	Replace Cooling Fan #1 (left). Is the replacement complete?	—	Go to Cooling Fan Functional Check	—

GC1089800437020X

Fig. 106 Cooling fan symptom table 5 (Part 2 of 2). 1998–99 DeVille, Eldorado & Seville

Step	Action	Values	Yes	No
DEFINITION: One or both cooling fans operate continuously.				
1	Did you perform the Cooling Fan Functional Check?	—	*Go to Step 2*	Go to Cooling Fan Functional Check
2	Are any DTCs set?	—	Go to *Diagnostic Trouble Code (DTC) List/Type*	*Go to Step 3*
3	**Important:** Ensure that the engine coolant temperature is below the specified value? 1. Ensure that the vehicle battery is fully charged. 2. Turn OFF the ignition. 3. Leave the A/C OFF. Are both cooling fans operating?	100°C (212°F)	*Go to Step 7*	*Go to Step 4*
4	Is the left cooling fan operating?	—	*Go to Step 8*	*Go to Step 5*
5	**Important:** Ensure that the engine coolant temperature is below the specified value? 1. Ensure that the vehicle battery is fully charged. 2. Ensure the ignition is ON. 3. Leave the A/C OFF. Are both cooling fans operating?	100°C (212°F)	*Go to Step 9*	*Go to Step 6*
6	Is the left cooling fan operating?	—	*Go to Step 11*	Go to Cooling Fan Functional Check
7	1. Turn OFF the ignition. 2. Leave the A/C OFF. 3. Remove the engine cooling fan relay 2. Are both cooling fans operating?	—	*Go to Step 12*	*Go to Step 13*
8	1. Turn OFF the ignition. 2. Leave the A/C OFF. 3. Remove the engine cooling fan relay 1. Is the left cooling fan operating?	—	*Go to Step 14*	*Go to Step 15*
9	Observe the A/C Relay display on the scan tool. Does the A/C Relay on the scan tool indicate ON?	—	Go to A Diagnostic System Check in HVAC Systems - Automatic	*Go to Step 10*
10	Locate and repair the short between ignition positive voltage and CKT 532. Is the action complete?	—	Go to Cooling Fan Functional Check	—
11	1. Locate and repair the short between ignition positive voltage and the following circuits: • CKT 504 • CKT 409 2. Is the action complete?	—	Go to Cooling Fan Functional Check	—
12	Locate and repair the short between battery positive voltage and CKT 532. Is the action complete?	—	Go to Cooling Fan Functional Check	—
13	Replace the engine cooling fan relay 2. Is the action complete?	—	Go to Cooling Fan Functional Check	—

GC1080000616010X

Fig. 108 Cooling fan symptom table 1 (Part 1 of 2). 2000 DeVille & Seville

Step	Action	Values	Yes	No
14	1. Locate and repair the short between battery positive and the following circuits: • CKT 504 • CKT 409 2. Is the action complete?	—	Go to Cooling Fan Functional Check	—
15	Replace the engine cooling fan relay 1. Is the action complete?	—	Go to Cooling Fan Functional Check	—

GC1080000616020X

Fig. 108 Cooling fan symptom table 1 (Part 2 of 2). 2000 DeVille & Seville

Step	Action	Values	Yes	No
DEFINITION: No low speed operation of both fan. No high speed operation of one cooling fan. No DTCs set.				
1	Did you perform the Cooling Fan Functional Check?	—	*Go to Step 2*	Go to Cooling Fan Functional Check
2	1. Turn ON the ignition. 2. Using the scan tool, command high speed cooling fans operation. Does the left cooling fan operate when high speed operation is commanded?	—	*Go to Step 3*	*Go to Step 7*

GC1080000618010X

Fig. 110 Cooling fan symptom table 3 (Part 1 of 2). 2000 DeVille & Seville

Step	Action	Values	Yes	No
3	1. Remove engine cooling fan S/P relay 2. Connect the appropriate jumper between cavities 30 and 87A in the relay connector. 3. Using the scan tool, command low speed fan operation. Are both fans ON?	—	*Go to Step 8*	*Go to Step 4*
4	1. Leave the jumper connected between cavities 30 and 87A in engine cooling fan S/P relay connector. 2. Remove engine cooling fan relay 2. 3. Connect test lamp between cavity 30 and ground. Is the test lamp ON?	—	*Go to Step 5*	*Go to Step 9*
5	1. Leave the jumper connected between cavities 30 and 87A in engine cooling fan S/P relay connector. 2. Connect the appropriate jumper between cavities 30 and 87 in engine cooling fan relay 2 connector. Are both fans ON?	—	*Go to Step 10*	*Go to Step 6*
6	1. Remove all jumpers. 2. Test for the following conditions: • An open circuit 532 • An open circuit 504 • An open between cavity 87A and splice • Poor connections at the right cooling fan 3. If a condition is found, repair as necessary. Did you find and correct the condition?	—	Go to Electric Cooling Fan Diagnosis	*Go to Step 11*
7	1. Test for the following conditions: • An open circuit 409 • An open circuit 250 • Poor connections at the left cooling fan 2. If the condition is found, repair as necessary. Did you find and correct the condition?	—	Go to Electric Cooling Fan Diagnosis	*Go to Step 12*
8	1. Test for poor connections at the engine cooling fan S/P relay. 2. If the condition is found, repair as necessary. Did you find and correct the condition?	—	Go to Electric Cooling Fan Diagnosis	*Go to Step 13*
9	Locate and repair the open battery positive voltage feed to cavity 30 of engine cooling fan relay 2. Is the action complete??	—	Go to Electric Cooling Fan Diagnosis	—
10	1. Test for poor connections at the engine cooling fan relay 2. 2. If the condition is found, repair as necessary. Did you find and correct the condition?	—	Go to Electric Cooling Fan Diagnosis	*Go to Step 14*
11	Replace the right cooling fan. Is the action complete?	—	Go to Electric Cooling Fan Diagnosis	—
12	Replace the left cooling fan. Is the action complete?	—	Go to Electric Cooling Fan Diagnosis	—
13	Replace engine cooling fan S/P relay. Is the action complete?	—	Go to Electric Cooling Fan Diagnosis	—
14	Replace the engine cooling fan relay 2. Is the action complete?	—	Go to Electric Cooling Fan Diagnosis	—

GC1080000618020X

Fig. 110 Cooling fan symptom table 3 (Part 2 of 2). 2000 DeVille & Seville

Step	Action	Values	Yes	No
DEFINITION: No low speed operation of one or both fans. Normal high speed operation of both fans.				
1	Did you perform the Cooling Fan Functional Check?	—	*Go to Step 2*	Go to Cooling Fan Functional Check
2	1. Remove the engine cooling fan S/P relay. 2. Using the scan tool, command low speed fans operation. Is the right cooling fan operating?	—	*Go to Step 5*	*Go to Step 3*
3	1. Leave the engine cooling fan S/P relay disconnected. 2. Connect the appropriate jumper between cavities 30 and 87A. 3. Using the scan tool, command low speed fans operation. Are both cooling fans operating?	—	*Go to Step 4*	*Go to Step 6*
4	1. Test for poor terminal contact at the engine cooling fan S/P relay connector. 2. If a condition is found, repair as necessary. Did you find and correct the condition?	—	Go to Cooling Fan Functional Check	*Go to Step 7*
5	Locate and repair the short to ground in CKT 504. Is the action complete?	—	Go to Cooling Fan Functional Check	—
6	Locate and repair the open in CKT 409 between cavity 87A and the splice. Is the action complete?	—	Go to Cooling Fan Functional Check	—
7	Replace engine cooling fan S/P relay. Is the action complete?	—	Go to Cooling Fan Functional Check	—

GC1080000617000X

Fig. 109 Cooling fan symptom table 2. 2000 DeVille & Seville

Step	Action	Values	Yes	No
DEFINITION: Normal low speed fans operation. No high speed operation of the left cooling fan. No DTCs set.				
1	Did you perform the Cooling Fan Functional Check?	—	*Go to Step 2*	Go to Cooling Fan Functional Check
2	1. Remove the engine cooling fan relay 1. 2. Connect the appropriate jumper between cavities 30 and 87 in the relay connector. Is the left cooling fan operating?	—	*Go to Step 3*	*Go to Step 6*
3	1. Leave the engine cooling fan relay 1 disconnected. 2. Connect test lamp between cavity 85 and ground. Is the test lamp ON?	—	*Go to Step 4*	*Go to Step 8*
4	1. Test for an open CKT 473 between cavity 86 and the splice connection. 2. If the condition is found, repair as necessary. Did you find and correct the condition?	—	Go to Cooling Fan Functional Check	*Go to Step 5*
5	1. Test for poor terminal contact in the engine cooling fan relay 1 connector. 2. If the condition is found, repair as necessary. Did you find and correct the condition?	—	Go to Cooling Fan Functional Check	*Go to Step 9*
6	1. Test for an open battery positive feed to cavity 30 in the engine cooling fan relay 1 connector. 2. If the condition is found, repair as necessary. Did you find and correct the condition?	—	Go to Cooling Fan Functional Check	*Go to Step 7*
7	Locate and repair the open/faulty splice connection in CKT 409, between cavity 87 and the splice. Is the action complete?	—	Go to Cooling Fan Functional Check	—
8	Locate and repair the open battery positive feed circuit to cavity 85 in the engine cooling fan relay 1 connector. Is the action complete?	—	Go to Cooling Fan Functional Check	—
9	Replace engine cooling fan relay 1. Is the action complete?	—	Go to Cooling Fan Functional Check	—

GC1080000619000X

Fig. 111 Cooling fan symptom table 4. 2000 DeVille & Seville

Step	Action	Values	Yes	No
DEFINITION: Normal low speed fans operation. No high speed operation of the right cooling fan. No DTCs set.				
1	Did you perform the Cooling Fan Functional Check?	—	*Go to Step 2*	Go to Cooling Fan Functional Check
2	1. Remove engine cooling fan S/P relay. 2. Connect the appropriate jumper between cavities 30 and 87 in the relay connector. 3. Using the scan tool, command high speed fans operation. Are both fans operating?	—	*Go to Step 3*	*Go to Step 6*
3	1. Leave engine cooling fan S/P relay disconnected. 2. Connect test lamp between cavity 85 in the relay connector and ground. Is the test lamp ON?	—	*Go to Step 4*	*Go to Step 7*
4	1. Test for an open CKT 473, between cavity 86 and the splice. 2. If the condition is found, repair as necessary. Did you find and correct the condition?	—	Go to Cooling Fan Functional Check	*Go to Step 5*
5	1. Test for poor terminal contact in the engine cooling fan S/P relay connector. 2. If the condition is found, repair as necessary. Did you find and correct the condition?	—	Go to Cooling Fan Functional Check	*Go to Step 8*
6	Locate and repair the open or poor splice connection in CKT 250. Is the action complete?	—	Go to Cooling Fan Functional Check	—
7	Locate and repair the open battery positive feed circuit to cavity 85 in the engine cooling fan S/P relay connector. Is the action complete?	—	Go to Cooling Fan Functional Check	—
8	Replace engine cooling fan S/P relay. Is the action complete?	—	Go to Cooling Fan Functional Check	—

GC1080000620000X

Fig. 112 Cooling fan symptom table 5. 2000 DeVille & Seville

Step	Action	Yes	No
1	Did you perform the Cooling Fan Functional Check?	*Go to Step 2*	Go to Cooling Fan Functional Check
2	1. Raise the vehicle. Refer to *Lifting and Jacking the Vehicle* in General Information. 2. Disconnect the cooling fan relay 1. 3. Turn ON the ignition leaving the engine OFF. Are both of the cooling fans OFF?	*Go to Step 6*	*Go to Step 3*
3	Disconnect the cooling fan relay 2. Are both of the cooling fans OFF?	*Go to Step 4*	*Go to Step 5*
4	1. Turn OFF the ignition. 2. Disconnect the left cooling fan electrical connector. 3. Probe the cooling fan electrical connector terminal B with a test lamp connected to ground. 4. Turn ON the ignition with the engine OFF. Does the test lamp illuminate?	*Go to Step 7*	*Go to Step 8*
5	Disconnect the cooling fan relay 3. Are both of the cooling fans OFF?	*Go to Step 10*	*Go to Step 9*
6	Replace the cooling fan relay 1. Is the action complete	Go to Cooling Fan Functional Check	—
7	Repair circuit 532 for a short to B+. Is the action complete	Go to Cooling Fan Functional Check	—
8	Repair circuit 504 for a short to B+. Is the action complete	Go to Cooling Fan Functional Check	—
9	Repair circuit 409 for a short to B+. Is the action complete?	Go to Cooling Fan Functional Check	—
10	Replace the cooling fan relay 3. Is the action complete?	Go to Cooling Fan Functional Check	—

GC1080000622000X

Fig. 114 Cooling fans on at all times. 2000 Eldorado

Step	Action	Value(s)	Yes	No
1	Did you perform the Powertrain On–Board Diagnostic (OBD) System Check?	—	*Go to Step 2*	Go to *A Powertrain On Board Diagnostic (OBD) System Check*
2	Are any DTCs set?	—	Go to *Diagnostic Trouble Code (DTC) List/Type*	*Go to Step 3*
3	**Important:** Engine coolant temperature must remain below the specified value for all cooling fan diagnoses. 1. Idle the engine. 2. Turn OFF the A/C. 3. Monitor the A/C Request parameter with the scan tool. Does the scan tool display the A/C request as YES?	100°C (212°F)	Go to *PCM Controlled A/C Circuit Diagnosis*	*Go to Step 4*
4	1. Turn OFF the ignition. 2. Turn ON the ignition, with the engine OFF. Are the cooling fans ON?	—	Go to Electric Cooling Fans ON at all times	*Go to Step 5*
5	Command the low speed cooling fans ON with a scan tool. Are both cooling fans ON?	—	*Go to Step 6*	Go to Electric Cooling Fans inoperative low speed commanded
6	Command the high speed cooling fans ON with a scan tool. Do both cooling fans switch to high speed?	—	*Go to Step 7*	Go to Electric Cooling Fans inoperative high speed commanded
7	1. With a scan tool, exit outputs. 2. Idle the engine with the A/C OFF. Are the cooling fans ON?	—	Go to Electric Cooling Fans ON at all times	*Go to Step 8*
8	Turn ON the A/C. Are the cooling fans ON?	—	System OK	*Go to Step 9*
9	Does the scan tool display A/C request as YES?	—	Go to *A Diagnostic System Check*	Go to *PCM Controlled A/C Circuit Diagnosis*

GC1080000621000X

Fig. 113 Cooling fan functional check. 2000 Eldorado

Step	Action	Yes	No
1	Did you perform the Cooling Fan Functional Check?	*Go to Step 2*	Go to Cooling Fan Functional Check
2	Inspect the cooling fan maxi-fuse. Is the fuse open?	*Go to step 14*	*Go to Step 3*
3	Command the low speed cooling fans ON with a scan tool. Does the right cooling fan operate at high speed?	*Go to step 4*	*Go to step 6*
4	1. Raise the vehicle. 2. Remove the cooling fan relay 2. 3. Probe the cooling fan relay 2 harness connector terminal 30 with a test lamp connected to B+. Is the test lamp illuminated?	*Go to step 23*	*Go to step 5*
5	1. Disconnect the right cooling fan harness connector. 2. Probe the right cooling fan harness connector terminal B with a test lamp connected to B+. Is the test lamp illuminated?	*Go to step 24*	*Go to step 28*
6	1. Turn ON the ignition, with the engine OFF. 2. Raise the vehicle. 3. Disconnect cooling fan relay 1. 4. Probe the cooling fan relay 1 B+ supply circuit with a test lamp connected to ground. Is the test lamp illuminated?	*Go to Step 7*	*Go to Step 20*
7	Connect a fused jumper wire between the cooling fan relay 1 switch terminals at the relay harness connector. Do both cooling fans turn ON?	*Go to Step 27*	*Go to Step 8*
8	1. Install the cooling fan relay 1. 2. Disconnect the cooling fan relay 2. 3. Jumper the cooling fan relay 2 harness connector terminal 30 to ground. 4. Command the low speed cooling fans ON with a scan tool. Does the left cooling fan turn ON?	*Go to Step 11*	*Go to step 9*
9	1. Disconnect the left cooling fan harness connector. 2. Probe the left cooling fan harness connector terminal B with a test lamp connected to ground. 3. Command the low speed cooling fans ON with a scan tool. Does the test lamp illuminate?	*Go to step 10*	*Go to step 19*
10	Test the continuity of circuit 504 with a DMM. Does the DMM display continuity?	*Go to step 29*	*Go to step 22*

GC1080000623010X

Fig. 115 Cooling fan inoperative-low speed commanded (Part 1 of 3). 2000 Eldorado

Step	Action	Yes	No
11	1. Install cooling fan relay 2. 2. Disconnect the right cooling fan harness connector. 3. Probe the right cooling fan harness connector terminal B with a test lamp connected to ground. 4. Command the low speed cooling fans ON with a scan tool. Does the test lamp illuminate when the relay is commanded ON?	Go to step 12	Go to step 13
12	Probe the right cooling fan harness connector terminal A with a test lamp connected to B+. Is the test lamp illuminated?	Go to Step 30	Go to Step 25
13	Test the continuity of circuit 409 with a DMM. Does the DMM display continuity?	Go to step 28	Go to step 21
14	1. Raise the vehicle. 2. Disconnect cooling fan relays 1 and 3. 3. Probe the cooling fan relay 1 B+ supply circuit at the harness connector with a test lamp to B+. Is the test lamp illuminated?	Go to step 26	Go to Step 15
15	Probe the cooling fan relay 1 terminal 87A at the harness connector with a test lamp to B+. Is the test lamp illuminated?	Go to step 26	Go to Step 16
16	1. Disconnect the left cooling fan harness connector. 2. Probe the cooling fan relay 1 terminal 87 at the harness connector with a test lamp to B+. Is the test lamp illuminated?	Go to step 26	Go to Step 17
17	1. Install the left cooling fan harness connector. 2. Install cooling fan relay 1. 3. Install a new fuse. 4. Command the high speed cooling fans ON with a scan tool. 5. Inspect the fuse. Is the fuse open?	Go to step 29	Go to step 18
18	1. Install cooling fan relay 3. 2. Remove cooling fan relay 1. 3. Command the high speed cooling fans ON with a scan tool. 4. Inspect the fuse. Is the fuse open?	Go to step 30	Go to *Intermittent Conditions*
19	Repair the open circuit between the cooling fan relay #1 and the left cooling fan motor. Is the action complete?	Go to Cooling Fan Functional Check	—
20	Repair the open cooling fan relay B+ supply circuit. Is the action complete?	Go to Cooling Fan Functional Check	—
21	Repair the open circuit between the cooling fan relay 2 and the right cooling fan motor. Is the action complete?	Go to Cooling Fan Functional Check	—
22	Repair the open circuit between the left cooling fan harness connector terminal A and the cooling fan relay 2. Is the action complete?	Go to Cooling Fan Functional Check	—
23	Repair the short to ground between the left cooling fan motor and relay 2. Is the action complete?	Go to Cooling Fan Functional Check	—

GC1080000623020X

Fig. 115 Cooling fan inoperative-low speed commanded (Part 2 of 3). 2000 Eldorado

Step	Action	Yes	No
24	Repair the short to ground between the right cooling fan motor and relay 2. Is the action complete?	Go to Cooling Fan Functional Check	—
25	Repair the open ground circuit. Is the action complete?	Go to Cooling Fan Functional Check	—
26	Repair the short to ground on the affected circuit. Is the action complete?	Go to Cooling Fan Functional Check	—
27	**Important:** Inspect for poor connections before replacing the relay. Replace the cooling fan relay 1. Is the action complete?	Go to Cooling Fan Functional Check	—
28	**Important:** Inspect for poor connections before replacing the relay. Replace the cooling fan relay 2. Is the action complete?	Go to Cooling Fan Functional Check	—
29	**Important:** Inspect for poor connections before replacing the cooling fan motor. Replace the LH fan motor. Is the action complete?	Go to Cooling Fan Functional Check	—
30	**Important:** Inspect for poor connections before replacing the cooling fan motor. Replace the RH fan motor. Is the action complete?	Go to Cooling Fan Functional Check	—

GC1080000623030X

Fig. 115 Cooling fan inoperative-low speed commanded (Part 3 of 3). 2000 Eldorado

Step	Action	Yes	No
1	Did you perform the Cooling Fan Functional Check?	Go to Step 2	Go to Cooling Fan Functional Check
2	1. Turn ON the ignition with the engine OFF. 2. Command the high speed cooling fans ON with a scan tool. Is the right cooling fan operating at high speed?	Go to Step 3	Go to Step 8
3	Is the left cooling fan operating at high speed?	Go to Cooling Fan Functional Check	Go to Step 4
4	1. Raise the vehicle. Refer to *Lifting and Jacking the Vehicle* in General Information. 2. Remove the cooling fan relay 2. 3. Probe the cooling fan relay 2 terminal 85 with a test lamp connected to ground. Does the test lamp illuminate?	Go to Step 5	Go to Step 11

GC1080000624010X

Fig. 116 Cooling fan inoperative-high speed commanded (Part 1 of 2). 2000 Eldorado

Step	Action	Yes	No
5	1. Probe the cooling fan relay 2 terminal 86 with a test lamp connected to B+. 2. Command the high speed cooling fan relays ON with a scan tool. Does the test lamp illuminate?	Go to step 6	Go to Step 13
6	Connect a fused jumper wire between the cooling fan relay 2 terminals 30 and 87. Does the left cooling fan turn ON?	Go to Step 16	Go to Step 7
7	Probe the cooling fan relay 2 terminal 87 with a test lamp connected to B+. Does the test lamp illuminate?	Go to Step 12	Go to Step 15
8	1. Turn ON the ignition with the engine OFF. 2. Disconnect the cooling fan relay 3. 3. Probe the cooling fan relay 3 terminals 30 and 85 with a test lamp connected to ground. Does the test lamp illuminate for both terminals?	Go to Step 9	Go to Step 11
9	1. Probe the cooling fan relay 3 terminal 86 with a test lamp connected to B+. 2. Command the high speed cooling fans ON with a scan tool. Does the test lamp illuminate?	Go to Step 10	Go to Step 13
10	Jumper the cooling fan relay 3 terminals 30 and 87 with a fused jumper wire. Does the right cooling fan turn ON?	Go to Step 17	Go to Step 14
11	Repair the cooling fan relay B+ circuit for an open. Is the action complete?	Go to Cooling Fan Functional Check	—
12	1. Inspect for poor relay connections. 2. If you find a poor connection, repair the condition as necessary. Is the action complete?	Go to Cooling Fan Functional Check	—
13	Repair the cooling fan relay control circuit for an open. Is the action complete?	Go to Cooling Fan Functional Check	—
14	Repair circuit 409 for an open. System. Is the action complete?	Go to Cooling Fan Functional Check	—
15	Repair the open ground circuit between cooling fan relay 2 and the splice. Is the action complete?	Go to Cooling Fan Functional Check	—
16	Replace the cooling fan relay 2. Is the action complete?	Go to Cooling Fan Functional Check	—
17	Replace the cooling fan relay 3. Is the action complete?	Go to Cooling Fan Functional Check	—

GC1080000624020X

Fig. 116 Cooling fan inoperative-high speed commanded (Part 2 of 2). 2000 Eldorado

Test Description

The number(s) below refer to the step number(s) on the diagnostic table.

2. Lack of communication may be due to a partial malfunction of the class 2 serial data circuit or due to a total malfunction of the class 2 serial data circuit. The specified procedure will determine the particular condition.
3. Determine if the Instrument Cluster or Powertrain Control Modules have set DTC's which may affect Engine Cooling operation are present.
4. The presence of DTCs which begin with "U" indicate some other module is not communicating. The specified procedure will compile all the available information before tests are performed.

Step	Action	Yes	No
1	Install a scan tool. Does the scan tool power up?	Go to Step 2	Diagnose Link Communications
2	1. Turn ON the ignition, with the engine OFF. 2. Attempt to establish communication with the following control modules: • Instrument Cluster • Powertrain Control Module Does the scan tool communicate with the control modules?	Go to Step 3	Diagnose Data Link Communications
3	Select the powertrain control module display DTCs function on the scan tool. Does the scan tool display any DTCs?	Go to Step 4	Diagnose *Engine Cooling*
4	Does the scan tool display any DTCs which begin with a "U"?	Diagnose Data Link Communications	Diagnose *Trouble Code*

GC1080100659000X

Fig. 117 Diagnostic system check. 2001-02 DeVille, Eldorado & Seville

Step	Action	Yes	No
	DEFINITION: One or both engine cooling fan motors run continuously in high or low speed.		
1	Did you perform the Engine Cooling Diagnostic System Check?	Go to Step 2	Engine Cooling
2	Turn ON the ignition, with the engine OFF. Are one or both cooling fans ON?	Go to Step 3	*Test for Intermittent and Poor Connections*
3	Are both cooling fans running continuously?	Go to Step 5	Go to Step 4
4	Remove the cooling fan S/P relay. Did the right cooling fan turn OFF?	Go to Step 6	Go to Step 7
5	Repair the short to voltage in the left cooling fan motor supply voltage circuit. Did you complete the repair?	Go to Step 8	—
6	Repair the short to voltage in the left cooling fan low reference circuit. Did you complete the repair?	Go to Step 8	—
7	Repair the short to voltage in the right cooling fan motor supply voltage circuit. Did you complete the repair?	Go to Step 8	—
8	Operate the system in order to verify the repair. Did you correct the condition?	System OK	Go to Step 2

GC1080100660000X

Fig. 118 Cooling fan always on. 2001-02 DeVille, Eldorado & Seville

Step	Action	Yes	No
DEFINITION: One or both engine cooling fan motors do not operate properly in high or low speed modes.			
1	Did you perform the Engine Cooling Diagnostic System Check?	Go to *Step 2*	*Diagnose Engine Cooling*
2	1. Install a scan tool. 2. Turn ON the ignition, with the engine OFF. 3. With a scan tool, command the Fans Low Speed ON and OFF. Do the low speed engine cooling fans turn ON and OFF with each command?	Go to *Step 3*	Go to *Step 4*
3	**Important:** Before the PCM changes the speed of the cooling fans, a 3-second delay will occur. With a scan tool, command the Fans High Speed ON and OFF. Do the high speed engine cooling fans turn ON and OFF with each command?	*Test for Intermittent and Poor Connections*	Go to *Step 11*
4	**Important:** Following this step, do NOT remove the 20-A fused jumper wire that is connected during this step. While performing the following steps, use a second 20-A fused jumper wire. 1. Remove the cooling fan 1 relay. 2. Connect a 20-A fused jumper between the battery positive voltage circuit of the cooling fan 1 relay and the cooling fan motor supply voltage circuit of the cooling fan 1 relay. Do both cooling fans operate in low speed?	Go to *Step 13*	Go to *Step 5*
5	1. Remove the cooling fan S/P relay 2. Connect the second 20-A fused jumper between the left cooling fan low reference circuit of the cooling fan S/P relay and the right cooling fan supply voltage circuit of the cooling fan S/P relay. Do both cooling fans operate in low speed?	Go to *Step 14*	Go to *Step 6*
6	Connect the second 20-A fused jumper between the battery positive voltage circuit of the cooling fan S/P relay and the cooling fan motor supply voltage circuit of the cooling fan S/P relay. Does the right cooling fan operate in high speed?	Go to *Step 9*	Go to *Step 7*
7	1. Install the cooling fan S/P relay. 2. Disconnect the right cooling fan electrical connector. 3. Connect the second 20-Amp fused jumper wire from the cooling fan motor supply voltage circuit of the right cooling fan electrical connector to the ground circuit of the right cooling fan electrical connector. Does the left cooling fan operate in high speed?	Go to *Step 16*	Go to *Step 8*
8	Connect the second 20-Amp fused jumper wire from the cooling fan motor supply voltage circuit of the right cooling fan electrical connector to a good ground. Does the left cooling fan operate in high speed?	Go to *Step 20*	Go to *Step 21*
9	1. Install the cooling fan S/P relay. 2. Disconnect the left cooling fan electrical connector. 3. Connect the second 20-Amp fused jumper wire from the cooling fan motor supply voltage circuit of the left cooling fan electrical connector to the cooling fan low reference circuit of the left cooling fan electrical connector. Does the right cooling fan operate in high speed?	Go to *Step 17*	Go to *Step 10*
10	1. Leave the fused jumper wire in place of the cooling fan 1 relay. 2. Connect a 20 Amp fused jumper wire from battery positive voltage to the left cooling fan low circuit of the of the left cooling fan electrical connector. Does the right cooling fan operate in high speed?	Go to *Step 18*	Go to *Step 22*
11	Is the right cooling fan operating properly in high speed?	Go to *Step 12*	Go to *Step 15*

GC1080100661010X

Fig. 119 Cooling fan inoperative (Part 1 of 2). 2001-02 DeVille, Eldorado & Seville

Circuit Description:

The engine cooling fan receive power from two separate 30 amp maxifuse located in the Underhood Electrical Center.

During low speed operation, the PCM supplies a ground path for the Cool Fan 1 relay through the Coolant Fan #1 Relay Control circuit. This energizes the relay coil, closes the Fan 1 relay contacts, and supplies current to the primary cooling fan. The ground path for the primary cooling fan is through the series/parallel cooling fan relay (Cool Relay) and the secondary cooling fan motor. The result is a series circuit with both fans running at low speed.

To command high speed cooling fan operation the PCM first supplies a ground path for the low speed cooling fan (Cool Fan #1) relay through the Coolant Fan #1 Relay Control circuit. After a 3 second delay, the PCM supplies a ground path for the series/parallel (Cool Relay) and the high speed cooling fan (Cool Fan #2) relays through the Coolant Fan #2 Relay Control circuit. During high speed operation, both the primary and the secondary cooling fans are supplied current through their respective maxifuse and each fan has its own ground path.

Diagnostic Aids

Check for the following conditions:

- Poor connection at the PCM, cooling fan relays, or cooling fan motors. Inspect harness connectors for backed out terminals, improper mating, broken locks, improperly formed or damaged terminals, and poor terminal to wire connection.
- Damaged harness. Inspect the wiring harness for damage.

GC1089700322010X

Fig. 120 Cooling fan diagnosis (Part 1 of 10). 1998–99 Grand Prix

Step	Action	Yes	No
12	1. Disconnect the cooling fan S/P relay 2. Connect the second 20-A fused jumper between the left cooling fan low reference circuit of the cooling fan S/P relay and the ground circuit of the cooling fan S/P relay. Does the left cooling fan operate properly in high speed?	Go to *Step 14*	Go to *Step 19*
13	Inspect for poor connections at the cooling fan 1 relay. Did you find and correct the condition?	Go to *Step 28*	Go to *Step 23*
14	Inspect for poor connections at the cooling fan S/P relay. Did you find and correct the condition?	Go to *Step 28*	Go to *Step 24*
15	Inspect for poor connections at the cooling fan 2 relay. Did you find and correct the condition?	Go to *Step 28*	Go to *Step 25*
16	Inspect for poor connections at the harness connector of the right cooling fan. Did you find and correct the condition?	Go to *Step 28*	Go to *Step 26*
17	Inspect for poor connections at the harness connector of the left cooling fan. Did you find and correct the condition?	Go to *Step 28*	Go to *Step 27*
18	Repair the left cooling fan motor supply voltage circuit. Did you complete the repair?	Go to *Step 28*	—
19	Repair the left cooling fan ground circuit. Did you complete the repair?	Go to *Step 28*	—
20	Repair the right cooling fan ground circuit. Did you complete the repair?	Go to *Step 28*	—
21	Repair the right cooling fan motor supply voltage circuit. Did you complete the repair?	Go to *Step 28*	—
22	Repair the left cooling fan low reference circuit. Did you complete the repair?	Go to *Step 28*	—
23	Replace the cooling fan 1 relay. Is the repair complete?	Go to *Step 28*	—
24	Replace the cooling fan S/P relay. Is the repair complete?	Go to *Step 28*	—
25	Replace the cooling fan 2 relay. Is the repair complete?	Go to *Step 28*	—
26	Replace the right cooling fan. Is the repair complete?	Go to *Step 28*	—
27	Replace the left cooling fan. Is the repair complete?	Go to *Step 28*	—
28	Operate the system in order to verify the repair. Did you correct the condition?	System OK	Go to *Step 3*

GC1080100661020X

Fig. 119 Cooling fan inoperative (Part 2 of 2). 2001-02 DeVille, Eldorado & Seville

Test Description

Number(s) below refer to the step number(s) on the Diagnostic Table.

2. Stored diagnostic trouble codes may affect engine cooling fans operation. This diagnostic table may lead to improper diagnosis and replacement of good parts if diagnostic trouble codes are present.
6. Ambient temperature must be above 11°C (52°F) before the PCM will enable the cooling fans due to A/C request. The PCM will enable the cooling fans if A/C refrigerant pressure increases regardless of ambient temperature.
77. This vehicle is equipped with a PCM which utilizes an Electrically Erasable Programmable Read Only Memory (EEPROM). When the PCM is being replaced, the new PCM must be programmed.

Step	Action	Value(s)	Yes	No
1	Was the Powertrain On-Board Diagnostic (OBD) System Check performed?	—	Go to *Step 2*	Go to the *Powertrain OBD System Check*
2	Are any PCM DTC(s) stored?	—	Diagnose the PCM DTC(s) first.	Go to *Step 3*
3	1. Ensure that the engine coolant temperature is below 100°C (212°F). 2. Turn OFF the A/C Selector Switch. 3. Engine running. 4. Observe the cooling fans. Are the cooling fans running?	—	Go to *Step 32*	Go to *Step 4*
4	1. Command Fan 1 ON using the scan tool output tests function. 2. Observe the cooling fans. Are both cooling fans running at low speed?	—	Go to *Step 5*	Go to *Step 8*
5	1. Command Fan 2 ON using the scan tool output tests function. 2. Wait 3 seconds. 3. Observe the cooling fans Are both fans running at high speed?	—	Go to *Step 6*	Go to *Step 58*
6	**Important:** Ambient temperature must be above 11°C (52°F). 1. Exit scan tool output tests. 2. Engine running. 3. Turn the A/C ON. Are the cooling fans ON?	—	Go to Diagnostic Aids	Go to *Step 7*
7	View A/C Request on the scan tool. Does A/C Request on the scan tool display Yes?	—	Go to *Step 77*	*PCM Controlled Air Conditioning Diagnosis*
8	Is either cooling fan running?	—	Go to *Step 9*	Go to *Step 16*
9	Is the left cooling fan running?	—	Go to *Step 10*	Go to *Step 14*

GC1089700322020X

Fig. 120 Cooling fan diagnosis (Part 2 of 10). 1998–99 Grand Prix

Step	Action	Value(s)	Yes	No
10	1. Turn OFF the ignition switch. 2. Disconnect the right engine cooling fan. 3. Turn ON the ignition switch. 4. Command Fan 1 ON using the scan tool output tests function. 5. Observe the cooling fans. Is the left engine cooling fan running?		*Go to Step 11*	*Go to Step 80*
11	Remove the engine Cool Fan Relay from the Underhood Electrical Center. Is the left engine cooling fan running?	—	*Go to Step 12*	*Go to Step 13*
12	Locate and repair short to ground in CKT 532. Is action complete?	—	*Go to Step 81*	—
13	1. Check CKT 409 for a short to ground. 2. If a problem is found, repair as necessary and replace Cool Fan 2 maxifuse. Was a problem found?	—	*Go to Step 81*	*Go to Step 76*
14	1. Turn OFF the ignition switch. 2. Disconnect the left engine cooling fan. 3. Turn ON the ignition switch. 4. Command Fan 1 On using the scan tool output tests function. 5. Observe the cooling fans. Is the right engine cooling fan running?	—	*Go to Step 15*	*Go to Step 71*
15	1. Locate and repair the following circuit condition(s): • Short to battery positive in circuit 532 or circuit 504. • Coolant Fan #2 shorted. • Defective engine coolant fan diode. Is action complete?	—	*Go to Step 81*	—
16	1. Ignition On, engine not running. 2. Remove the low speed engine Cool Fan 1 Relay from the Underhood Electrical Center. 3. Probe Cool Fan 1 relay cavity 87 with a test light connected to ground. Is the test light On?	—	*Go to Step 18*	*Go to Step 17*
17	Locate and repair the open in the Cool Fan 1 relay B+ feed to cavity 87. Is action complete?	—	*Go to Step 81*	—
18	Probe Cool Fan 1 relay cavity 86 with a test light connected to ground. Is the test light On?	—	*Go to Step 20*	*Go to Step 19*
19	Locate and repair open in the B+ feed to cavity 86 in the Cool Fan 1 relay connector. Is action complete?	—	*Go to Step 81*	—

GC1089700322030X

Fig. 120 Cooling fan diagnosis (Part 3 of 10). 1998–99 Grand Prix

Step	Action	Value(s)	Yes	No
27	1. Turn OFF the ignition switch. 2. Remove the jumpers from the cooling fan connectors. 3. Reconnect the cooling fans. 4. Install a fused jumper between Cool Fan 1 relay cavities 87 and 30. 5. Remove the Cool Fan Relay from the Underhood Electrical Center. 6. Probe Cool Fan Relay cavity 30 with a test light connected to ground. Is the test light On?	—	*Go to Step 28*	*Go to Step 31*
28	Connect a test light between Cool Fan Relay cavities 30 and 87A in the Underhood Electrical Center. Is the test light ON?	—	*Go to Step 30*	*Go to Step 29*
29	1. Check for an open in CKT 409 between Cool Fan Relay cavity 87A and High Speed Fans terminal B. 2. If a problem is found, repair as necessary. Was a problem found?	—	*Go to Step 81*	*Go to Step 57*
30	1. Check for a poor connection at Cool Fan Relay cavities 30 or 87A in the Underhood Relay Center. 2. If a problem is found, repair as necessary. Was a problem found?	—	*Go to Step 81*	*Go to Step 76*
31	1. Check for an open in CKT 504 between Cool Fan 1 relay cavity 30 and left engine cooling fan harness connector terminal B. 2. If a problem is found, repair as necessary. Was a problem found?	—	*Go to Step 81*	*Go to Step 56*
32	Using scan tool, view A/C Request. Does the scan tool display Yes?	—	*PCM Controlled Air Conditioning Diagnosis*	*Go to Step 33*
33	Are both cooling fans running at low speed?	—	*Go to Step 34*	*Go to Step 40*
34	Remove Cool Fan 1 relay from the Underhood Relay Center. Are the cooling fans running?	—	*Go to Step 35*	*Go to Step 36*
35	Locate and repair short to voltage in CKT 504. Is action complete?	—	*Go to Step 81*	—
36	Using a test light connected to B+, probe Cool Fan 1 relay cavity 85. Is the test light On?	—	*Go to Step 38*	*Go to Step 37*
37	Replace Cool Fan 1 relay. Is action complete?	—	*Go to Step 81*	—
38	1. Turn OFF the ignition switch. 2. Disconnect the blue PCM connector. 3. Probe Cool Fan 1 relay cavity 85 with a test light connected to B+. Is the test light On?	—	*Go to Step 39*	*Go to Step 77*

GC1089700322050X

Fig. 120 Cooling fan diagnosis (Part 5 of 10). 1998–99 Grand Prix

Step	Action	Value(s)	Yes	No
20	1. Turn OFF the ignition switch. 2. Disconnect both cooling fans. 3. Connect terminals A and B together at both cooling fan connectors using fused jumpers. 4. Turn ON the ignition switch. 5. Connect a test light between Cool Fan 1 relay cavities 87 and 30. Is the test light ON?	—	*Go to Step 21*	*Go to Step 27*
21	1. Connect a test light between Cool Fan 1 relay cavities 85 and 86. 2. Turn ON the ignition switch. 3. Command Fan 1 ON using the scan tool output tests function. 4. Observe the test light. Is the test light ON?	—	*Go to Step 22*	*Go to Step 25*
22	1. Turn OFF the ignition switch. 2. Remove the jumpers from the engine cooling fan connectors and reconnect the cooling fans. 3. Install a fused jumper between Cool Fan 1 relay cavities 87 and 30. 4. Turn ON the ignition switch. 5. Observe the cooling fans. Are both cooling fans running?	—	*Go to Step 23*	*Go to Step 24*
23	1. Check for poor Cool Fan 1 relay connections at the Underhood Electrical Center. 2. If a problem is found, repair as necessary. Was a problem found?	—	*Go to Step 81*	*Go to Step 37*
24	1. Check for poor connections at the coolant fan motors. 2. If a problem is found, repair as necessary. Was a problem found?	—	*Go to Step 81*	*Go to Step 63*
25	1. Turn OFF the ignition switch. 2. Disconnect the PCM blue connector C1. 3. Install a fused jumper between Cool Fan 1 relay cavities 30 and 85. 4. Turn ON the ignition switch. 5. Probe Low Speed Fans circuit (CKT 335) at the PCM harness connector with a test light to ground. Is the test light ON?	—	*Go to Step 77*	*Go to Step 26*
26	Locate and repair open in the Low Speed Fans circuit between the PCM and Cooling Fan 1 relay cavity 86. Is action complete?	—	*Go to Step 81*	—

GC1089700322040X

Fig. 120 Cooling fan diagnosis (Part 4 of 10). 1998–99 Grand Prix

Step	Action	Value(s)	Yes	No
39	Locate and repair short to ground in the Low Speed Fans circuit. Is action complete?	—	*Go to Step 81*	—
40	Are both cooling fans running at high speed?	—	*Go to Step 41*	*Go to Step 42*
41	View A/C Pressure on the scan tool. Does the scan tool display voltage less than the specified value?	1.5V	*Go to Step 77*	*Go to Step 44*
42	1. Turn OFF the ignition switch. 2. Disconnect the PCM. 3. Turn ON the ignition switch. 4. Observe the cooling fans. Is the right engine cooling fan running at high speed?	—	*Go to Step 43*	*Go to Step 77*
43	1. Check for a short to ground in the High Speed Fans circuit (CKT 473). 2. If a problem is found, repair as necessary. Was a problem found?	—	*Go to Step 81*	*Go to Step 52*
44	1. Turn off the ignition switch. 2. Disconnect the A/C refrigerant pressure sensor electrical connector. 3. Turn on the ignition switch. 4. View A/C Pressure on the scan tool. Does the scan tool display voltage near the specified value?	0V	*Go to Step 46*	*Go to Step 45*
45	Probe the A/C refrigerant pressure signal circuit with a *J 39200*. Does the digital multimeter display voltage near the specified value?	0V	*Go to Step 77*	*Go to Step 51*
46	Probe the A/C refrigerant pressure sensor ground with a test light to battery positive voltage. Is the test light on?	—	*Go to Step 47*	*Go to Step 49*
47	Probe the A/C refrigerant pressure sensor 5 volt reference B circuit with a *J 39200*. Does the digital multimeter display voltage near the specified value?	5V	*Go to Step 48*	*Go to Step 50*
48	Replace the A/C refrigerant pressure sensor. Is action complete?	—	*Go to Step 81*	—
49	Locate and repair open or short to voltage in the A/C refrigerant pressure sensor ground circuit. Is action complete?	—	*Go to Step 81*	—
50	Locate and repair open or short to ground in the A/C refrigerant pressure sensor 5 volt reference B circuit. Is action complete?	—	*Go to Step 81*	—
51	Locate and repair short to voltage in the A/C refrigerant pressure signal circuit. Is action complete?	—	*Go to Step 81*	—

GC1089700322060X

Fig. 120 Cooling fan diagnosis (Part 6 of 10). 1998–99 Grand Prix

Step	Action	Value(s)	Yes	No
52	1. Remove the Cool Fan 2 relay from the Underhood Electrical Center. 2. Observe the cooling fans. Is the right engine cooling fan running at high speed?	—	Go to Step 53	Go to Step 70
53	Remove the Cool Fan Relay from the Underhood Electrical Center. Is the right engine cooling fan running at high speed?	—	Go to Step 54	Go to Step 55
54	Locate and repair short to battery positive voltage in CKT 409. Is action complete?	—	Go to Step 81	—
55	Locate and repair short to battery positive voltage in CKT 532. Is action complete?	—	Go to Step 81	—
56	1. Check for an open in CKT 532 between Cool Fan Relay cavity 30 and left engine cooling fan terminal A. 2. If a problem is found, repair as necessary. Was a problem found?	—	Go to Step 81	Go to Step 79
57	1. Check for an open in CKT 1050 between right engine cooling fan terminal A and ground. 2. If a problem is found, repair as necessary. Was a problem found?	—	Go to Step 81	Go to Step 80
58	1. Ignition ON, engine not running. 2. Remove the Cool Fan 2 relay from the Underhood Electrical Center. 3. Install a test light between Cool Fan 2 relay cavity 86 and battery positive voltage. 4. Command High speed fans on using the scan tool output controls function. 5. Wait approx. 5-6 seconds. 6. Observe the test light. Is the test light on?	—	Go to Step 61	Go to Step 59
59	1. Remove the Cool Fan Relay from the Underhood Electrical Center. 2. Install a test light between Cool Fan Relay cavity 86 and battery positive voltage. 3. Command high speed fans on using the scan tool output controls function. 4. Wait 6 seconds. 5. Observe the test light. Is the test light ON?	—	Go to Step 78	Go to Step 60

GC1089700322070X

Fig. 120 Cooling fan diagnosis (Part 7 of 10). 1998–99 Grand Prix

Step	Action	Value(s)	Yes	No
60	1. Turn OFF the ignition switch. 2. Disconnect the PCM. 3. Turn ON the ignition switch. 4. Check the High Speed Fans circuit for an open or a short to voltage. 5. If a problem is found, repair as necessary. Was a problem found?	—	Go to Step 81	Go to Step 77
61	1. Turn off the ignition switch. 2. Reinstall the Cool Fan 2 relay. 3. Disconnect both coolant fan electrical connectors. 4. Turn on the ignition switch. 5. Command Fan 2 on using the scan tool output controls function. 6. Wait approx. 5-6 seconds. 7. Probe terminal B at the right engine cooling fan connector with a test light to ground. Is the test light on?	—	Go to Step 62	Go to Step 64
62	Probe terminal A at the left engine cooling fan connector with a test light to B+. Is the test light on?	—	Go to Step 63	Go to Step 71
63	1. Identify cause of inoperative cooling fan: • Open right engine cooling fan motor windings. • Open left engine cooling fan motor windings. • Stalled cooling fans. 2. Replace the affected cooling fan motor. Is action complete?	—	Go to Step 81	—
64	1. Remove the Cool Fan 2 relay from the Underhood Electrical Center. 2. Turn ON the ignition switch. 3. Probe Cool Fan 2 relay cavity 85 with a test light connected to ground. Is the test light on?	—	Go to Step 66	Go to Step 65
65	1. Locate and repair the following circuit condition(s): • Open in the battery positive feed to the Cool Fan and Cool Fan 2 relays. • Short to ground in the battery positive feed to the Cool Fan and Cool Fan 2 relays. Is action complete?	—	Go to Step 81	—
66	Probe Cool Fan 2 relay cavity 30 with a test light connected to ground. Is the test light on?	—	Go to Step 68	Go to Step 67
67	Locate and repair open in battery positive voltage circuit to Cool Fan 2 relay cavity 30. Is action complete?	—	Go to Step 81	—

GC1089700322080X

Fig. 120 Cooling fan diagnosis (Part 8 of 10). 1998–99 Grand Prix

Step	Action	Value(s)	Yes	No
68	1. Check High Speed Fans circuit for an open between right engine cooling fan terminal B and Cool Fan 2 relay cavity 87. 2. If a problem is found, repair as necessary. Was a problem found?	—	Go to Step 81	Go to Step 69
69	1. Check for a poor Cool Fan 2 relay terminal connections at the Underhood Electrical Center. 2. If a problem is found, repair as necessary. Was a problem found?	—	Go to Step 81	Go to Step 70
70	Replace Cool Fan 2 relay. Is action complete?	—	Go to Step 81	—
71	1. Remove the Cool Fan Relay from the Underhood Electrical Center. 2. Turn ON the ignition switch. 3. Probe Cool Fan Relay cavity 85 with a test light connected to ground. Is the test light on?	—	Go to Step 73	Go to Step 72
72	Locate and repair open in battery positive voltage circuit to Cool Fan Relay cavity 85. Is action complete?	—	Go to Step 81	—
73	Probe Cool Fan Relay cavity 87 in the Underhood Electrical Center with a test light to B+. Is the test light on?	—	Go to Step 75	Go to Step 74
74	Locate and repair open in circuit between Cool Fan Relay cavity 87 in the Underhood Electrical Center and ground. Is action complete?	—	Go to Step 81	—
75	1. Check for poor Cool Fan Relay engine terminal connections at the Underhood Electrical Center. 2. If a problem is found, repair as necessary. Was a problem found?	—	Go to Step 81	Go to Step 76
76	Replace the Cool Fan Relay in the Underhood Electrical Center. Is action complete?	—	Go to Step 81	—
77	Replace the PCM. **Important:** The replacement PCM must be programmed. Is action complete?	—	Go to Step 81	—
78	Repair open in the Cool Fan 2 relay control circuit. Is action complete?	—	Go to Step 81	—
79	Replace the left engine cooling fan motor. Is action complete?	—	Go to Step 81	—

GC1089700322090X

Fig. 120 Cooling fan diagnosis (Part 9 of 10). 1998–99 Grand Prix

Step	Action	Value(s)	Yes	No
80	Replace the right engine cooling fan motor. Is action complete?	—	Go to Step 81	—
81	1. Engine coolant below 100°C (212°F). 2. A/C OFF. 3. Engine running. Observe the cooling fans. Are the cooling fans running?	—	Go to Step 32	Go to Step 82
82	1. Command Fan 1 ON using the scan tool output tests function. 2. Observe the cooling fans. Are both cooling fans running at low speed?	—	Go to Step 83	Go to Step 8
83	1. Command High speed fans on using the scan tool output tests function. 2. Wait 6 seconds. 3. Observe the cooling fans. Are both cooling fans running at high speed?	—	System OK	Go to Step 58

GC1089700322100X

Fig. 120 Cooling fan diagnosis (Part 10 of 10). 1998–99 Grand Prix

Step	Action	Value(s)	Yes	No
1	Did you perform the Powertrain On Board Diagnostic (OBD) System Check?	—	*Go to Step 2*	Go to *A Powertrain On Board Diagnostic (OBD) System Check*
2	Are any other DTCs set?	—	Go to *Diagnostic Trouble Code (DTC) List/Type*	*Go to Step 3*
3	1. Install a scan tool. 2. Engine coolant temperature must be below the specified value for all the fan diagnoses. 3. Turn ON the Ignition, with the engine and A/C OFF. Are the cooling fans OFF?	100°C (212°F)	*Go to Step 4*	Go to *Electric Cooling Fan Diagnosis (Cooling Fan Functional Check)* or *Electric Cooling Fan Diagnosis (Cooling Fan Table #1)* or *Electric Cooling Fan Diagnosis (Cooling Fan Table #2)* or *Electric Cooling Fan Diagnosis (Cooling Fan Table #3)* Electric Cooling Fan Table #1
4	With a scan tool, command the low speed cooling fan relay ON. Do both cooling fans turn ON?	—	*Go to Step 5*	Go to *Electric Cooling Fan Diagnosis (Cooling Fan Functional Check)* or *Electric Cooling Fan Diagnosis (Cooling Fan Table #1)* or *Electric Cooling Fan Diagnosis (Cooling Fan Table #2)* or *Electric Cooling Fan Diagnosis (Cooling Fan Table #3)* Electric Cooling Fan Table #2

GC1080000572010X

Fig. 121 Cooling fan functional check (Part 1 of 2). 2000 Grand Prix

Step	Action	Value(s)	Yes	No
5	With a scan tool, command the high speed cooling fan relay ON. Do both cooling fans switch to high speed?	—	*Go to Step 6*	Go to *Electric Cooling Fan Diagnosis (Cooling Fan Functional Check)* or *Electric Cooling Fan Diagnosis (Cooling Fan Table #1)* or *Electric Cooling Fan Diagnosis (Cooling Fan Table #2)* or *Electric Cooling Fan Diagnosis (Cooling Fan Table #3)*
6	1. With a scan tool, exit outputs. 2. Idle the engine leaving the A/C OFF. Are the cooling fans ON?	—	*Go to Step 8*	*Go to Step 7*
7	Turn ON the A/C. Are the cooling fans ON?	—	System OK	*Go to Step 8*
8	Does the scan tool display A/C request as YES?	—	Go to *A Diagnostic System Check* OR *A Diagnostic System Check*	*Go to Step 9*
9	**Important:** Program the replacement PCM. Did you complete the replacement?	—	System OK	—

GC1080000572020X

Fig. 121 Cooling fan functional check (Part 2 of 2). 2000 Grand Prix

Step	Action	Value(s)	Yes	No
1	Did you perform the Electric Cooling Fan Functional Check?	—	*Go to Step 2*	Go to *Electric Cooling Fan Diagnosis (Functional Test)* or *Electric Cooling Fan Diagnosis (Table #1)* or *Electric Cooling Fan Diagnosis (Table #2)* or *Electric Cooling Fan Diagnosis (Table #3)* Electric Cooling Fan Functional Check
2	1. Disconnect the Cool Fan 1 Relay. 2. Turn the ignition ON with the engine OFF. Are both fans OFF?	—	*Go to Step 9*	*Go to Step 3*
3	Disconnect the Cool Fan (Series/Parallel or S/P) Relay. Are both fans OFF?	—	*Go to Step 5*	*Go to Step 4*
4	Remove the Cool Fan 2 Relay. Are both fans OFF?	—	*Go to Step 7*	*Go to Step 11*
5	1. Disconnect the Engine Coolant Fan Motor LH (left Fan). 2. Probe the fan feed terminal of the left fan connector using a test lamp that is connected to ground. Does the test lamp illuminate?	—	*Go to Step 12*	*Go to Step 6*
6	Probe the Cool Fan S/P Relay switch feed terminal at the right fan connector using a test lamp that is connected to ground. Does the test lamp illuminate?	—	*Go to Step 13*	*Go to Step 17*
7	Probe the High Speed Fans control circuit at the Cool Fan S/P Relay connector using a test lamp that is connected to battery positive voltage. Does the test lamp illuminate?	—	*Go to Step 8*	*Go to Step 16*
8	1. Turn OFF the ignition. 2. Leave the test lamp installed. 3. Disconnect the PCM. 4. Turn ON the ignition, with the engine OFF. Is the test lamp still illuminated?	—	*Go to Step 15*	*Go to Step 18*
9	Probe the Low Speed Fans control circuit at the Cool Fan 1 Relay connector using a test lamp that is connected to battery positive voltage. Does the test lamp illuminate?	—	*Go to Step 10*	*Go to Step 14*
10	1. Turn OFF the ignition. 2. Leave the test lamp installed. 3. Disconnect the PCM. 4. Turn ON the ignition, with the engine OFF. Is the test lamp still illuminated?	—	*Go to Step 15*	*Go to Step 18*

GC1080000573010X

Fig. 122 Cooling fan diagnosis table 1 (Part 1 of 4). 2000 Grand Prix

Step	Action	Value(s)	Yes	No
11	Test the right fan feed circuit for a short to voltage and repair as necessary. Did you find and correct a condition?	—	Go to *Electric Cooling Fan Diagnosis (Functional Test)* or *Electric Cooling Fan Diagnosis (Table #1)* or *Electric Cooling Fan Diagnosis (Table #2)* or *Electric Cooling Fan Diagnosis (Table #3)* Electric Cooling Fan Functional Check	*Go to Step 16*
12	Test the left fan feed circuit for a short to voltage and repair as necessary. Did you complete the repair?	—	Go to *Electric Cooling Fan Diagnosis (Functional Test)* or *Electric Cooling Fan Diagnosis (Table #1)* or *Electric Cooling Fan Diagnosis (Table #2)* or *Electric Cooling Fan Diagnosis (Table #3)* Electric Cooling Fan Functional Check	—
13	Repair the short to voltage in the Cool Fan S/P Relay switch feed circuit. The short may be in the *Underhood Accessory Wiring Junction Block.* Did you complete the repair?	—	Go to *Electric Cooling Fan Diagnosis (Functional Test)* or *Electric Cooling Fan Diagnosis (Table #1)* or *Electric Cooling Fan Diagnosis (Table #2)* or *Electric Cooling Fan Diagnosis (Table #3)* Electric Cooling Fan Functional Check	—

GC1080000573020X

Fig. 122 Cooling fan diagnosis table 1 (Part 2 of 4). 2000 Grand Prix

Step	Action	Value(s)	Yes	No
14	Replace the Cool Fan 1 Relay. Did you complete the replacement?	—	Go to *Electric Cooling Fan Diagnosis (Functional Test)* or *Electric Cooling Fan Diagnosis (Table #1)* or *Electric Cooling Fan Diagnosis (Table #2)* or *Electric Cooling Fan Diagnosis (Table #3)* Electric Cooling Fan Functional Check	—
15	Test the High Speed Fans control circuit or the Low Speed Fans control circuit for a short to ground and repair as necessary. short may be in the *Underhood Accessory Wiring Junction Block.* Did you complete the repair?	—	Go to *Electric Cooling Fan Diagnosis (Functional Test)* or *Electric Cooling Fan Diagnosis (Table #1)* or *Electric Cooling Fan Diagnosis (Table #2)* or *Electric Cooling Fan Diagnosis (Table #3)* Electric Cooling Fan Functional Check	—
16	Replace the Cool Fan 2 Relay. Did you complete the replacement?	—	Go to *Electric Cooling Fan Diagnosis (Functional Test)* or *Electric Cooling Fan Diagnosis (Table #1)* or *Electric Cooling Fan Diagnosis (Table #2)* or *Electric Cooling Fan Diagnosis (Table #3)* Electric Cooling Fan Functional Check	—

GC1080000573030X

Fig. 122 Cooling fan diagnosis table 1 (Part 3 of 4). 2000 Grand Prix

Step	Action	Value(s)	Yes	No
17	Replace the Cool Fan S/P Relay. Did you complete the replacement?	—	Go to *Electric Cooling Fan Diagnosis (Functional Test)* or *Electric Cooling Fan Diagnosis (Table #1)* or *Electric Cooling Fan Diagnosis (Table #2)* or *Electric Cooling Fan Diagnosis (Table #3)* Electric Cooling Fan Functional Check	—
18	**Important:** Program the replacement PCM. Replace the PCM. Did you complete the replacement?	—	Go to *Electric Cooling Fan Diagnosis (Functional Test)* or *Electric Cooling Fan Diagnosis (Table #1)* or *Electric Cooling Fan Diagnosis (Table #2)* or *Electric Cooling Fan Diagnosis (Table #3)* Electric Cooling Fan Functional Check	—

GC1080000573040X

Fig. 122 Cooling fan diagnosis table 1 (Part 4 of 4). 2000 Grand Prix

Step	Action	Value(s)	Yes	No
1	Did you perform the Electric Cooling Fan Functional Check?	—	*Go to Step 2*	Go to *Electric Cooling Fan Diagnosis (Functional Test)* or *Electric Cooling Fan Diagnosis (Table #1)* or *Electric Cooling Fan Diagnosis (Table #2)* or *Electric Cooling Fan Diagnosis (Table #3)* Electric Cooling Fan Functional Check
2	Did either fan turn ON when the Low Speed Fans were commanded ON?	—	*Go to Step 3*	*Go to Step 5*
3	With a scan tool, command the High Speed Fans ON. Did the inoperative fan from step 2 turn ON?	—	*Go to Step 4*	*Go to Step 20*
4	Disconnect the Cool Fan 2 Relay. Did the inoperative fan from step 2 turn OFF?	—	*Go to Step 23*	*Go to Step 22*

GC1080000574010X

Fig. 123 Cooling fan diagnosis table 2 (Part 1 of 8). 2000 Grand Prix

Step	Action	Value(s)	Yes	No
5	1. Disconnect the Cool Fan 1 Relay. 2. With a scan tool, command the Low Speed Fans ON. 3. Probe the Low Speed Fans control circuit at the Cool Fan 1 Relay connector using a test lamp that is connected to battery positive voltage. Does the test lamp illuminate?	—	*Go to Step 6*	*Go to Step 13*
6	Probe both feed circuits at the Cool Fan 1 Relay connector using a test lamp that is connected to ground. Does test lamp illuminate for both circuits?	—	*Go to Step 7*	*Go to Step 24*
7	**Important:** Leave the jumper in place for the remainder of this table. Connect a 30 amp fused jumper wire between the switch feed circuit and the left fan feed circuit at the Cool Fan 1 Relay connector. Do both fans turn ON?	—	*Go to Step 25*	*Go to Step 8*
8	1. Disconnect the left fan. 2. Probe the left fan feed circuit at the fan harness connector terminal with a test lamp that is connected to ground. Does the test lamp illuminate?	—	*Go to Step 9*	*Go to Step 27*
9	Connect a second 30 amp fused jumper wire between the right fan harness connector terminals. Does the right fan turn ON?	—	*Go to Step 17*	*Go to Step 10*
10	1. Reconnect the left fan. 2. Disconnect the Cool Fan S/P Relay. 3. Probe the switch feed circuit at the Cool Fan S/P Relay connector using a test lamp that is connected to a good ground. Does the test lamp illuminate?	—	*Go to Step 11*	*Go to Step 28*
11	Using the second jumper wire, jumper the switch feed circuit and the right fan feed circuit together at the Cool Fan S/P Relay connector. Do both fans turn ON?	—	*Go to Step 29*	*Go to Step 12*
12	1. Reconnect the Cool Fan S/P Relay. 2. Disconnect the right fan. 3. Probe the fan feed circuit at the fan harness connector terminal with a test lamp that is connected to ground. Does the test lamp illuminate?	—	*Go to Step 16*	*Go to Step 19*
13	1. Verify that the test lamp is still connected. 2. Turn OFF the ignition. 3. Disconnect the PCM. 4. Probe the Low Speed Fans control circuit at the PCM connector with a 15 amp fused jumper wire that is connected to ground. Does the test lamp illuminate?	—	*Go to Step 14*	*Go to Step 15*

GC1080000574020X

Fig. 123 Cooling fan diagnosis table 2 (Part 2 of 8). 2000 Grand Prix

Step	Action	Value(s)	Yes	No
14	Inspect for faulty connections at the PCM and harness connectors and repair as necessary. Did you find a problem and correct the condition?	—	Go to *Electric Cooling Fan Diagnosis (Functional Test)* or *Electric Cooling Fan Diagnosis (Table #1)* or *Electric Cooling Fan Diagnosis (Table #2)* or *Electric Cooling Fan Diagnosis (Table #3)* Electric Cooling Fan Functional Check	*Go to Step 31*
15	Inspect the Low Speed Fans control circuit for an open or short to battery positive voltage and repair as necessary. The open/short may be in the *Underhood Accessory Wiring Junction Block.* Did you find and correct a condition?	—	Go to *Electric Cooling Fan Diagnosis (Functional Test)* or *Electric Cooling Fan Diagnosis (Table #1)* or *Electric Cooling Fan Diagnosis (Table #2)* or *Electric Cooling Fan Diagnosis (Table #3)* Electric Cooling Fan Functional Check	—
16	Inspect the fan motor ground circuit for an open or poor connections. Did you find and correct the condition?	—	Go to *Electric Cooling Fan Diagnosis (Functional Test)* or *Electric Cooling Fan Diagnosis Table #1)* or *Electric Cooling Fan Diagnosis (Table #2)* or *Electric Cooling Fan Diagnosis (Table #3)* Electric Cooling Fan Functional Check	*Go to Step 17*

GC1080000574030X

Fig. 123 Cooling fan diagnosis table 2 (Part 3 of 8). 2000 Grand Prix

Step	Action	Value(s)	Yes	No
17	Inspect the fan motor and harness connectors for faulty terminals and replace as necessary. Did you find and correct a condition?	—	Go to *Electric Cooling Fan Diagnosis (Functional Test)* or *Electric Cooling Fan Diagnosis (Table #1)* or *Electric Cooling Fan Diagnosis (Table #2)* or *Electric Cooling Fan Diagnosis (Table #3)* Electric Cooling Fan Functional Check	*Go to Step 18*
18	Replace the fan motor. Did you complete the replacement?	—	Go to *Electric Cooling Fan Diagnosis (Functional Test)* or *Electric Cooling Fan Diagnosis (Table #1)* or *Electric Cooling Fan Diagnosis (Table #2)* or *Electric Cooling Fan Diagnosis (Table #3)* Electric Cooling Fan Functional Check	—
19	Test the right fan feed circuit for an open and repair as necessary. The open may be in the *Underhood Accessory Wiring Junction Block.* Did you complete the repair?	—	Go to *Electric Cooling Fan Diagnosis (Functional Test)* or *Electric Cooling Fan Diagnosis (Table #1)* or *Electric Cooling Fan Diagnosis (Table #2)* or *Electric Cooling Fan Diagnosis (Table #3)* Electric Cooling Fan Functional Check	—

GC1080000574040X

Fig. 123 Cooling fan diagnosis table 2 (Part 4 of 8). 2000 Grand Prix

Step	Action	Value(s)	Yes	No
20	Test the supply circuit to the inoperative fan for a short to ground and repair as necessary. The short may be in the *Underhood Accessory Wiring Junction Block.* Did you find and correct a condition?	—	Go to *Electric Cooling Fan Diagnosis (Functional Test)* or *Electric Cooling Fan Diagnosis (Table #1)* or *Electric Cooling Fan Diagnosis (Table #2)* or *Electric Cooling Fan Diagnosis (Table #3)* Electric Cooling Fan Functional Check	*Go to Step 21*
21	Replace the fan which was not operating. Did you complete the replacement?	—	Go to *Electric Cooling Fan Diagnosis (Functional Test)* or *Electric Cooling Fan Diagnosis (Table #1)* or *Electric Cooling Fan Diagnosis (Table #2)* or *Electric Cooling Fan Diagnosis (Table #3)* Electric Cooling Fan Functional Check	—
22	Replace the Cool Fan 2 Relay. Did you complete the replacement?	—	Go to *Electric Cooling Fan Diagnosis (Functional Test)* or *Electric Cooling Fan Diagnosis (Table #1)* or *Electric Cooling Fan Diagnosis (Table #2)* or *Electric Cooling Fan Diagnosis (Table #3)* Electric Cooling Fan Functional Check	—

GC1080000574050X

Fig. 123 Cooling fan diagnosis table 2 (Part 5 of 8). 2000 Grand Prix

Step	Action	Value(s)	Yes	No
23	Test the Cool Fan S/P Relay switch feed circuit for a short to ground and repair as necessary. The short may be in the *Underhood Accessory Wiring Junction Block.* Did you find and correct the condition?	—	Go to *Electric Cooling Fan Diagnosis (Functional Test)* or *Electric Cooling Fan Diagnosis (Table #1)* or *Electric Cooling Fan Diagnosis (Table #2)* or *Electric Cooling Fan Diagnosis (Table #3)* Electric Cooling Fan Functional Check	*Go to Step 29*
24	**Important:** If the fuse is open, locate and repair a short to ground on the load circuit or a shorted component. Repair the open or the grounded circuit for the circuit that did not illuminate the test lamp. The short may be in the *Underhood Accessory Wiring Junction Block.* Did you complete the repair?	—	Go to *Electric Cooling Fan Diagnosis (Functional Test)* or *Electric Cooling Fan Diagnosis (Table #1)* or *Electric Cooling Fan Diagnosis (Table #2)* or *Electric Cooling Fan Diagnosis (Table #3)* Electric Cooling Fan Functional Check	—
25	Inspect the Cool Fan 1 Relay and connector for faulty terminals and replace as necessary. Replace the *Underhood Accessory Wiring Junction Block.* Did you find and correct a condition?	—	Go to *Electric Cooling Fan Diagnosis (Functional Test)* or *Electric Cooling Fan Diagnosis (Table #1)* or *Electric Cooling Fan Diagnosis (Table #2)* or *Electric Cooling Fan Diagnosis (Table #3)* Electric Cooling Fan Functional Check	*Go to Step 26*

GC1080000574060X

Fig. 123 Cooling fan diagnosis table 2 (Part 6 of 8). 2000 Grand Prix

Step	Action	Value(s)	Yes	No
26	Replace the Cool Fan 1 Relay. Did you complete the replacement?	—	Go to *Electric Cooling Fan Diagnosis (Functional Test)* or *Electric Cooling Fan Diagnosis (Table #1)* or *Electric Cooling Fan Diagnosis (Table #2)* or *Electric Cooling Fan Diagnosis (Table #3)* Electric Cooling Fan Functional Check	—
27	Test the left fan feed circuit for an open and repair as necessary. Did you complete the repair?	—	Go to *Electric Cooling Fan Diagnosis (Functional Test)* or *Electric Cooling Fan Diagnosis (Table #1)* or *Electric Cooling Fan Diagnosis (Table #2)* or *Electric Cooling Fan Diagnosis (Table #3)* Electric Cooling Fan Functional Check	—
28	Test the Cool Fan S/P Relay switch feed circuit for an open or poor connections and repair as necessary. The short/poor connection may be in the *Underhood Accessory Wiring Junction Block.* Did you complete the repair?	—	Go to *Electric Cooling Fan Diagnosis (Functional Test)* or *Electric Cooling Fan Diagnosis (Table #1)* or *Electric Cooling Fan Diagnosis (Table #2)* or *Electric Cooling Fan Diagnosis (Table #3)* Electric Cooling Fan Functional Check	—

GC1080000574070X

Fig. 123 Cooling fan diagnosis table 2 (Part 7 of 8). 2000 Grand Prix

Step	Action	Value(s)	Yes	No
29	Inspect the Cool Fan S/P Relay and connector for faulty terminals and replace as necessary. The condition may be in the *Underhood Accessory Wiring Junction Block.* Did you find and correct a condition?	—	Go to *Electric Cooling Fan Diagnosis (Functional Test)* or *Electric Cooling Fan Diagnosis (Table #1)* or *Electric Cooling Fan Diagnosis (Table #2)* or *Electric Cooling Fan Diagnosis (Table #3)* Electric Cooling Fan Functional Check	*Go to Step 30*
30	Replace the Cool Fan S/P Relay. Did you complete the replacement?	—	Go to *Electric Cooling Fan Diagnosis (Functional Test)* or *Electric Cooling Fan Diagnosis (Table #1)* or *Electric Cooling Fan Diagnosis (Table #2)* or *Electric Cooling Fan Diagnosis (Table #3)* Electric Cooling Fan Functional Check	—
31	**Important:** Program the replacement PCM. Did you complete the replacement?	—	Go to *Electric Cooling Fan Diagnosis (Functional Test)* or *Electric Cooling Fan Diagnosis (Table #1)* or *Electric Cooling Fan Diagnosis (Table #2)* or *Electric Cooling Fan Diagnosis (Table #3)* Electric Cooling Fan Functional Check	—

GC1080000574080X

Fig. 123 Cooling fan diagnosis table 2 (Part 8 of 8). 2000 Grand Prix

Step	Action	Value(s)	Yes	No
1	Did you perform the Electric Cooling Fan Functional Check?	—	*Go to Step 2*	Go to *Electric Cooling Fan Diagnosis (Functional Test)* or *Electric Cooling Fan Diagnosis (Table #1)* or *Electric Cooling Fan Diagnosis (Table #2)* or *Electric Cooling Fan Diagnosis (Table #3)* Electric Cooling Fan Functional Check
2	1. With a scan tool, command the Low Speed Fans ON. 2. Command the High Speed Fans ON while observing the fans. Did both fans operate with no change?	—	*Go to Step 8*	*Go to Step 3*
3	Did the left fan stop operating?	—	*Go to Step 9*	*Go to Step 4*
4	1. Disconnect the Cool Fan 2 Relay. 2. Probe the High Speed Fans control circuit at the Cool Fan 2 Relay connector using a test lamp that is connected to battery positive voltage. 3. With a scan tool command the High Speed Fans ON. Does the test lamp illuminate after a few seconds?	—	*Go to Step 5*	*Go to Step 12*
5	Probe the coil feed circuit at the Cool Fan 2 Relay connector using a test lamp that is connected to ground. Does the test lamp illuminate?	—	*Go to Step 6*	*Go to Step 13*
6	Probe the switch feed circuit at the Cool Fan 2 Relay connector using a test lamp that is connected to ground. Does the test lamp illuminate?	—	*Go to Step 7*	*Go to Step 14*
7	Install a 30 amp fused jumper between the Cool Fan 2 Relay switch feed circuit and the right fan feed circuit at the Cool Fan 2 Relay connector. Does the right fan turn ON?	—	*Go to Step 15*	*Go to Step 16*
8	1. Turn OFF the ignition. 2. Disconnect the PCM. 3. Disconnect Cool Fan 1 Relay. 4. Install a 30 amp fused jumper between the switch feed circuit and the left fan feed circuit at the Cool Fan 1 Relay connector. 5. Turn ON the ignition, with the engine OFF. 6. Probe the High Speed Fans Relay control circuit at the PCM harness connector with a fused jumper that is connected to ground. Do the fans switch from low to high speed?	—	*Go to Step 22*	*Go to Step 17*
9	1. Disconnect the Cool Fan S/P Relay. 2. Probe the High Speed Fans control circuit at the Cool Fan S/P Relay connector using a test lamp that is connected to battery positive voltage. 3. With a scan tool command the High Speed fans ON. Does the test lamp illuminate after a few seconds?	—	*Go to Step 10*	*Go to Step 18*

GC1080000575010X

Fig. 124 Cooling fan diagnosis table 3 (Part 1 of 5). 2000 Grand Prix

Step	Action	Value(s)	Yes	No
10	Probe the ground circuit at the Cool Fan S/P Relay connector using a test lamp that is connected to battery positive voltage. Does the test lamp illuminate?	—	*Go to Step 11*	*Go to Step 19*
11	Probe the coil feed circuit at the Cool Fan S/P Relay connector using a test lamp that is connected to ground. Does the test lamp illuminate?	—	*Go to Step 20*	*Go to Step 21*
12	Repair the High Speed Fans control circuit for an open/poor connection between the Cool Fan 2 Relay and the splice. The open/poor connection may be in the *Underhood Accessory Wiring Junction Block.* Did you complete the repair?	—	Go to *Electric Cooling Fan Diagnosis (Functional Test)* or *Electric Cooling Fan Diagnosis (Table #1)* or *Electric Cooling Fan Diagnosis (Table #2)* or *Electric Cooling Fan Diagnosis (Table #3)* Electric Cooling Fan Functional Check	—
13	Repair the open in the Cool Fan 2 Relay coil feed circuit. Replace the *Underhood Accessory Wiring Junction Block.* Did you complete the repair?	—	Go to *Electric Cooling Fan Diagnosis (Functional Test)* or *Electric Cooling Fan Diagnosis (Table #1)* or *Electric Cooling Fan Diagnosis (Table #2)* or *Electric Cooling Fan Diagnosis (Table #3)* Electric Cooling Fan Functional Check	—
14	**Important:** If the fuse is open, locate and repair a short to ground on the load circuit or a shorted component. Repair the open in the Cool Fan 2 Relay switch feed circuit. The short may be in the *Underhood Accessory Wiring Junction Block.* Did you complete the repair?	—	Go to *Electric Cooling Fan Diagnosis (Functional Test)* or *Electric Cooling Fan Diagnosis (Table #1)* or *Electric Cooling Fan Diagnosis (Table #2)* or *Electric Cooling Fan Diagnosis (Table #3)* Electric Cooling Fan Functional Check	—

GC1080000575020X

Fig. 124 Cooling fan diagnosis table 3 (Part 2 of 5). 2000 Grand Prix

Step	Action	Value(s)	Yes	No
15	Replace the Cool Fan 2 relay. Did you complete the replacement?	—	Go to *Electric Cooling Fan Diagnosis (Functional Test)* or *Electric Cooling Fan Diagnosis (Table #1)* or *Electric Cooling Fan Diagnosis (Table #2)* or *Electric Cooling Fan Diagnosis (Table #3)* Electric Cooling Fan Functional Check	—
16	Repair the open in the right fan feed circuit between the Cool Fan 2 Relay and the splice. The open may be in the *Underhood Accessory Wiring Junction Block.* Did you complete the repair?	—	Go to *Electric Cooling Fan Diagnosis (Functional Test)* or *Electric Cooling Fan Diagnosis (Table #1)* or *Electric Cooling Fan Diagnosis (Table #2)* or *Electric Cooling Fan Diagnosis (Table #3)* Electric Cooling Fan Functional Check	—
17	Repair the High Speed Fans control circuit for an open or for a short to battery positive voltage. The open/short may be in the *Underhood Accessory Wiring Junction Block.* Did you complete the repair?	—	Go to *Electric Cooling Fan Diagnosis (Functional Test)* or *Electric Cooling Fan Diagnosis (Table #1)* or *Electric Cooling Fan Diagnosis (Table #2)* or *Electric Cooling Fan Diagnosis (Table #3)* Electric Cooling Fan Functional Check	—

GC1080000575030X

Fig. 124 Cooling fan diagnosis table 3 (Part 3 of 5). 2000 Grand Prix

Step	Action	Value(s)	Yes	No
18	Repair the open in the High Speed Fans control circuit between the Cool Fan S/P Relay and the splice. The open may be in the *Underhood Accessory Wiring Junction Block.* Did you complete the repair?	—	Go to *Electric Cooling Fan Diagnosis (Functional Test)* or *Electric Cooling Fan Diagnosis (Table #1)* or *Electric Cooling Fan Diagnosis (Table #2)* or *Electric Cooling Fan Diagnosis (Table #3)* Electric Cooling Fan Functional Check	—
19	Repair the open in the ground circuit. The short may be in the *Underhood Accessory Wiring Junction Block.* Did you complete the repair?	—	Go to *Electric Cooling Fan Diagnosis (Functional Test)* or *Electric Cooling Fan Diagnosis (Table #1)* or *Electric Cooling Fan Diagnosis (Table #2)* or *Electric Cooling Fan Diagnosis (Table #3)* Electric Cooling Fan Functional Check	—
20	Replace the Cool Fan S/P Relay. Did you complete the replacement?	—	Go to *Electric Cooling Fan Diagnosis (Functional Test)* or *Electric Cooling Fan Diagnosis (Table #1)* or *Electric Cooling Fan Diagnosis (Table #2)* or *Electric Cooling Fan Diagnosis (Table #3)* Electric Cooling Fan Functional Check	—

GC1080000575040X

Fig. 124 Cooling fan diagnosis table 3 (Part 4 of 5). 2000 Grand Prix

Step	Action	Value(s)	Yes	No
21	**Important:** If the fuse is open, locate and repair a short to ground on the load circuit or a shorted component. Repair the open in the Cool Fan S/P Relay coil feed circuit. open/short/poor connection may be in the *Underhood Accessory Wiring Junction Block.* Did you complete the repair?	—	Go to *Electric Cooling Fan Diagnosis (Functional Test)* or *Electric Cooling Fan Diagnosis (Table #1)* or *Electric Cooling Fan Diagnosis (Table #2)* or *Electric Cooling Fan Diagnosis (Table #3)* Electric Cooling Fan Functional Check	—
22	Inspect the PCM connections. Did you find and correct the condition?	—	Go to *Electric Cooling Fan Diagnosis (Functional Test)* or *Electric Cooling Fan Diagnosis (Table #1)* or *Electric Cooling Fan Diagnosis (Table #2)* or *Electric Cooling Fan Diagnosis (Table #3)* Electric Cooling Fan Functional Check	*Go to Step 23*
23	**Important:** Program the replacement PCM. Replace the PCM. Did you complete the replacement?	—	Go to *Electric Cooling Fan Diagnosis (Functional Test)* or *Electric Cooling Fan Diagnosis (Table #1)* or *Electric Cooling Fan Diagnosis (Table #2)* or *Electric Cooling Fan Diagnosis (Table #3)* Electric Cooling Fan Functional Check	—

GC1080000575050X

Fig. 124 Cooling fan diagnosis table 3 (Part 5 of 5). 2000 Grand Prix

Test Description

The number(s) below refer to the step number(s) on the diagnostic table.

2. Lack of communication may be due to a partial malfunction of the class 2 serial data circuit or due to a total malfunction of the class 2 serial data circuit. The specified procedure will determine the particular condition.
3. Determine if the Instrument Cluster or Powertrain Control Modules have set DTCs which may affect Engine Cooling operation are present.
4. The presence of DTCs which begin with "U" indicate some other module is not communicating. The specified procedure will compile all the available information before tests are performed.

Step	Action	Yes	No
1	Install a scan tool. Does the scan tool power up?	Go to *Step 2*	*Diagnose* Data Link Communications
2	1. Turn ON the ignition, with the engine OFF. 2. Attempt to establish communication with the powertrain control module. Does the scan tool communicate with the powertrain control module?	Go to *Step 3*	Data Link Communications
3	Select the powertrain control module display DTCs function on the scan tool. Does the scan tool display any DTCs?	Go to *Step 4*	*Engine Cooling*
4	Does the scan tool display any DTCs which begin with a "U"?	Data Link Communications	*Diagnostic Trouble Code*

GC1080100662000X

Fig. 125 Diagnostic system check. 2001-02 Grand Prix

Step	Action	Yes	No
DEFINITION: One or both engine cooling fan motors run continuously in high or low speed.			
1	Did you perform the Engine Cooling Diagnostic System Check?	Go to *Step 2*	*Diagnose System Check - Engine Cooling*
2	Turn ON the ignition, with the engine OFF. Are one or both cooling fans ON?	Go to *Step 3*	*Test for Intermittent and Poor Connections*
3	Are both cooling fans running continuously?	Go to *Step 5*	Go to *Step 4*
4	Remove the cool fan relay. Did the left cooling fan turn OFF?	Go to *Step 6*	Go to *Step 7*
5	Repair the short to voltage in the right cooling fan supply voltage circuit. Did you complete the repair?	Go to *Step 8*	—
6	Repair the short to voltage in the right cooling fan low reference circuit. Did you complete the repair?	Go to *Step 8*	—
7	Repair the short to voltage in the left cooling fan supply voltage circuit. Did you complete the repair?	Go to *Step 8*	—
8	Operate the system in order to verify the repair. Did you correct the condition?	System OK	Go to *Step 2*

GC1080100663000X

Fig. 126 Cooling fan always on. 2001-02 Grand Prix

Step	Action	Yes	No
12	1. Disconnect the cool fan relay. 2. Connect the second 20-A fused jumper between the right cooling fan low reference circuit of the cool fan relay and the ground circuit of the cool fan relay. Does the right cooling fan operate properly in high speed?	Go to *Step 14*	Go to *Step 19*
13	Inspect for poor connections at the cool fan 1 relay. Did you find and correct the condition?	Go to *Step 28*	Go to *Step 23*
14	Inspect for poor connections at the cool fan relay. Did you find and correct the condition?	Go to *Step 28*	Go to *Step 24*
15	Inspect for poor connections at the cool fan 2 relay. Did you find and correct the condition?	Go to *Step 28*	Go to *Step 25*
16	Inspect for poor connections at the harness connector of the left cooling fan. Did you find and correct the condition?	Go to *Step 28*	Go to *Step 26*
17	Inspect for poor connections at the harness connector of the right cooling fan. Did you find and correct the condition?	Go to *Step 28*	Go to *Step 27*
18	Repair the right cooling fan supply voltage circuit. Did you complete the repair?	Go to *Step 28*	—
19	Repair the right cooling fan ground circuit. Did you complete the repair?	Go to *Step 28*	—
20	Repair the left cooling fan ground circuit. Did you complete the repair?	Go to *Step 28*	—
21	Repair the left cooling fan supply voltage circuit. Did you complete the repair?	Go to *Step 28*	—
22	Repair the right cooling fan low reference circuit. Did you complete the repair?	Go to *Step 28*	—
23	Replace the cool fan 1 relay. Is the repair complete?	Go to *Step 28*	—
24	Replace the cool fan relay. Is the repair complete?	Go to *Step 28*	—
25	Replace the cool fan 2 relay. Is the repair complete?	Go to *Step 28*	—
26	Replace the left cooling fan. Is the repair complete?	Go to *Step 28*	—
27	Replace the right cooling fan. Is the repair complete?	Go to *Step 28*	—
28	Operate the system in order to verify the repair. Did you correct the condition?	System OK	Go to *Step 3*

GC1080100664020X

Fig. 127 Cooling fan inoperative (Part 2 of 2). 2001-02 Grand Prix

Step	Action	Yes	No
DEFINITION: One or both engine cooling fan motors do not operate properly in high or low speed modes.			
1	Did you perform the Engine Cooling Diagnostic System Check?	Go to *Step 2*	*Diagnose Engine Cooling*
2	1. Install a scan tool. 2. Turn ON the ignition, with the engine OFF. 3. With a scan tool, command the Fans Low Speed ON and OFF. Do the low speed engine cooling fans turn ON and OFF with each command?	Go to *Step 3*	Go to *Step 4*
3	**Important:** Before the PCM changes the speed of the cooling fans, a 3-second delay occurs. With a scan tool, command the Fans High Speed ON and OFF. Do the high speed engine cooling fans turn ON and OFF with each command?	*Test for Intermittent and Poor Connections*	Go to *Step 11*
4	**Important:** Following this step, do not remove the 20-A fused jumper wire that is connected during this step. While performing the following steps, use a second 20-A fused jumper wire. 1. Disconnect the cool fan 1 relay. 2. Connect a 20-A fused jumper between the battery positive voltage circuit of the cool fan 1 relay and the cooling fan motor supply voltage circuit of the cool fan 1 relay. Do both cooling fans operate in low speed?	Go to *Step 13*	Go to *Step 5*
5	1. Disconnect the cool fan relay. 2. Connect the second 20-A fused jumper between the right cooling fan low reference circuit of the cool fan relay and the left cooling fan motor supply voltage circuit of the cool fan relay. Do both cooling fans operate in low speed?	Go to *Step 14*	Go to *Step 6*
6	Connect the second 20-A fused jumper between the battery positive voltage circuit of the cool fan relay and the cooling fan motor supply voltage circuit of the cool fan relay. Does the left cooling fan operate in high speed?	Go to *Step 9*	Go to *Step 7*
7	1. Install the cool fan relay. 2. Disconnect the left cooling fan electrical connector. 3. Connect the second 20-Amp fused jumper wire from the cooling fan motor supply voltage circuit of the left cooling fan electrical connector to the cooling fan ground circuit of the left cooling fan electrical connector. Does the right cooling fan operate in high speed?	Go to *Step 16*	Go to *Step 8*
8	Connect the second 20-Amp fused jumper wire from the cooling fan motor supply voltage circuit of the left cooling fan electrical connector to a good ground. Does the right cooling fan operate in high speed?	Go to *Step 20*	Go to *Step 21*
9	1. Install the cool fan relay. 2. Disconnect the right cooling fan electrical connector. 3. Connect the second 20-Amp fused jumper wire from the motor supply voltage circuit of the right cooling fan electrical connector to the low reference circuit of the right cooling fan electrical connector. Does the left cooling fan operate in high speed?	Go to *Step 17*	Go to *Step 10*
10	Connect the second 20-Amp fused jumper wire from battery positive voltage to the right cooling fan low reference circuit of the of the right cooling fan electrical connector. Does the left cooling fan operate in high speed?	Go to *Step 18*	Go to *Step 22*
11	Is the left cooling fan operating properly in high speed?	Go to *Step 12*	Go to *Step 15*

GC1080100664010X

Fig. 127 Cooling fan inoperative (Part 1 of 2). 2001-02 Grand Prix

Step	Action	Value(s)	Yes	No
1	Was the Powertrain On-Board Diagnostic (OBD) System Check performed?	—	*Go to Step 2*	Go to the Powertrain OBD System Check
2	Are any PCM DTC(s) stored?	—	Diagnose the PCM DTC(s) first.	*Go to Step 3*
3	1. Ensure that the engine coolant temperature is below 100°C (212°F). 2. Turn the A/C *off*. 3. Engine running. 4. Observe the cooling fans. Are the cooling fan(s) running?	—	*Go to Step 32*	*Go to Step 4*
4	1. Command Fan 1 *on* using the scan tool output tests function. 2. Observe the cooling fans. Are both cooling fans running at low speed?	—	*Go to Step 5*	*Go to Step 8*

GC1089700320010X

Fig. 128 Cooling fan diagnosis (Part 1 of 9). 1998–99 Lumina & Monte Carlo

Step	Action	Value(s)	Yes	No
5	1. Command Fan 2 *on* using the scan tool output tests function. 2. Wait 6 seconds. 3. Observe the cooling fans Are both fans running at high speed?	—	*Go to Step 6*	*Go to Step 58*
6	**Important:** Ambient temperature must be above 9°C (48°F). 1. Exit scan tool output tests. 2. Engine running. 3. Turn the A/C *on.* Are the cooling fans *on* ?	—	Go to Diagnostic Aids	*Go to Step 7*
7	View A/C Request on the scan tool. Does A/C Request on the scan tool display Yes?	—	*Go to Step 77*	Go to *A/C* Compressor Clutch Control Diagnosis
8	Is either cooling fan running?	—	*Go to Step 9*	*Go to Step 16*
9	Is the left cooling fan running?	—	*Go to Step 10*	*Go to Step 14*
10	1. Turn *off* the ignition switch. 2. Disconnect the right engine cooling fan. 3. Turn *on* the ignition switch. 4. Command Fan 1 *on* using the scan tool output tests function. 5. Observe the cooling fans. Is the left engine cooling fan running?	—	*Go to Step 11*	*Go to Step 80*
11	Remove the engine Fan 2 relay from the Underhood Electrical Center. Is the left engine cooling fan running?	—	*Go to Step 12*	*Go to Step 13*
12	Locate and repair short to ground in CKT 532. Is action complete?	—	*Go to Step 81*	—
13	1. Check CKT 504 for a short to ground. 2. If a problem is found, repair as necessary. Was a problem found?	—	*Go to Step 81*	*Go to Step 70*
14	1. Turn *off* the ignition switch. 2. Disconnect the left engine cooling fan. 3. Turn *on* the ignition switch. 4. Command Fan 1 *on* using the scan tool output tests function. 5. Observe the cooling fans. Is the right engine cooling fan running?	—	*Go to Step 15*	*Go to Step 71*
15	Locate and repair short to battery positive voltage in circuit 532 and 504. If a problem is found repair as necessary. Was a problem found?	—	*Go to Step 81*	*Go to Step 79*

GC1089700320020X

Fig. 128 Cooling fan diagnosis (Part 2 of 9). 1998–99 Lumina & Monte Carlo

Step	Action	Value(s)	Yes	No
16	1. Ignition *on*, engine not running. 2. Remove the low speed engine cooling fan relay #1 from the Underhood Electrical Center. 3. Probe cooling fan relay cavity 30 with a test light connected to ground. Is the test light *on* ?	—	*Go to Step 18*	*Go to Step 17*
17	1. Identify the cause of no battery positive voltage to cooling fan relay #1 cavity 30: • Blown Maxi fuse. If the fuse is blown, locate and correct short circuit. – Stalled right engine or left engine cooling fan. – Shorted right engine or left engine cooling fan motor windings. – Short to ground in CKT 342, CKT 532, or CKT 409. • Open in CKT 342. 2. Repair the cause of no battery positive voltage to Cool Fan 1 relay cavity 30. Is action complete?	—	*Go to Step 81*	—
18	Probe Cool Fan 1 relay cavity 85 with a test light connected to ground. Is the test light *on* ?	—	*Go to Step 20*	*Go to Step 19*
19	1. Identify the cause of no battery positive voltage to Cool Fan 1 relay cavity 85: • Blown fuse. If the fuse is blown, locate short circuit. – CKT 342 open or shorted to ground. – Shorted Cool Fan 1 relay coil. – Shorted Fan 2 relay coil. – Shorted high speed engine Cool Fan 3 relay coil. – Circuit unrelated to cooling fans. 2. Repair cause of no battery positive voltage to Cool Fan 1 relay cavity 85. Is action complete?	—	*Go to Step 81*	—
20	1. Turn *off* the ignition switch. 2. Disconnect both cooling fans. 3. Connect terminals A and B together at both cooling fan connectors using fused jumpers. 4. Turn *off* the ignition switch. 5. Connect a test light between Cool Fan 1 relay cavities 87 and 30. Is the test light ON?	—	*Go to Step 21*	*Go to Step 27*
21	1. Connect a test light between Cool Fan 1 relay cavities 85 and 86. 2. Turn *on* the ignition switch. 3. Command Fan 1 *on* using the scan tool output tests function. 4. Observe the test light. Is the test light *on* ?	—	*Go to Step 22*	*Go to Step 25*

GC1089700320030X

Fig. 128 Cooling fan diagnosis (Part 3 of 9). 1998–99 Lumina & Monte Carlo

Step	Action	Value(s)	Yes	No
22	1. Turn *off* the ignition switch 2. Remove the jumpers from the engine cooling fan connectors and reconnect the cooling fans. 3. Install a fused jumper between Cool Fan 1 relay cavities 87 and 30. 4. Turn *on* the ignition switch. 5. Observe the cooling fans. Are both cooling fans running?	—	*Go to Step 23*	*Go to Step 24*
23	1. Check for poor Cool Fan 1 relay connections at the Underhood Electrical Center. 2. If a problem is found, repair as necessary. Was a problem found?	—	*Go to Step 81*	*Go to Step 37*
24	1. Check for poor connections at the coolant fan motors. 2. If a problem is found, repair as necessary. Was a problem found?	—	*Go to Step 81*	*Go to Step 63*
25	1. Turn *off* the ignition switch. 2. Disconnect the PCM blue connector C1. 3. Install a fused jumper between Cool Fan 1 relay cavities 86 and 85. 4. Turn *on* the ignition switch. 5. Probe Coolant Fan 1 relay control circuit at the PCM harness connector with a test light to ground. Is the test light *on* ?	—	*Go to Step 77*	*Go to Step 26*
26	Locate and repair open in the Coolant Fan 1 relay control circuit between the PCM and Cool Fan 1 relay cavity 86. Is action complete?	—	*Go to Step 81*	—
27	1. Turn *off* the ignition switch. 2. Remove the jumpers from the cooling fan connectors. 3. Reconnect the cooling fans. 4. Install a fused jumper between Cool Fan 1 relay cavities 87 and 30. 5. Remove the Fan 2 relay from the Underhood Electrical Center. 6. Probe Fan 2 relay cavity 30 with a test light connected to ground. Is the test light *on* ?	—	*Go to Step 28*	*Go to Step 31*
28	Connect a test light between Fan 2 relay in Underhood Electrical Center cavities 30 and 87A. Is the test light *on* ?	—	*Go to Step 30*	*Go to Step 29*
29	1. Check for an open in CKT 504 between Fan 2 relay cavity 30 and Engine Coolant Fan Motor #2 terminal B. 2. If a problem is found, repair as necessary. Was a problem found?	—	*Go to Step 81*	*Go to Step 57*
30	1. Check for a poor connection at Fan 2 relay in Underhood Electrical Center cavities 30 or 87A. 2. If a problem is found, repair as necessary. Was a problem found?	—	*Go to Step 81*	*Go to Step 70*

GC1089700320040X

Fig. 128 Cooling fan diagnosis (Part 4 of 9). 1998–99 Lumina & Monte Carlo

Step	Action	Value(s)	Yes	No
31	1. Check for an open in CKT 409 between Cool Fan 1 relay cavity 30 and left engine cooling fan harness connector terminal B. 2. If a problem is found, repair as necessary. Was a problem found?	—	*Go to Step 81*	*Go to Step 56*
32	Using scan tool, view A/C Request. Does the scan tool display Yes?	—	Go to *A/C Compressor Clutch Control Diagnosis A/C* Compressor Clutch Control Diagnosis	*Go to Step 33*
33	Are both cooling fan(s) running at low speed?	—	*Go to Step 34*	*Go to Step 40*
34	Remove Cool Fan 1 relay from the Underhood Electrical Center. Are the cooling fans running?	—	*Go to Step 35*	*Go to Step 36*
35	Locate and repair short to voltage in CKT 409. Is action complete?	—	*Go to Step 81*	—
36	Using a test light connected to battery positive voltage, probe Cool Fan 1 relay cavity 86. Is the test light *on* ?	—	*Go to Step 38*	*Go to Step 37*
37	Replace Cool Fan 1 relay. Is action complete?	—	*Go to Step 81*	—
38	1. Turn *off* the ignition switch 2. Disconnect the blue PCM connector. 3. Probe Cool Fan relay cavity 86 with a test light connected to battery positive voltage. Is the test light *on* ?	—	*Go to Step 39*	*Go to Step 77*
39	Locate and repair short to ground in the Cool Fan 1 relay control circuit. Is action complete?	—	*Go to Step 81*	—
40	Are both cooling fans running at high speed?	—	*Go to Step 41*	*Go to Step 42*
41	View A/C Pressure on the scan tool. Does the scan tool display voltage less than the specified value?	1.2V	*Go to Step 77*	*Go to Step 44*
42	1. Turn *off* the ignition switch. 2. Disconnect the PCM. 3. Turn *off* the ignition switch. 4. Observe the cooling fans. Is the right engine cooling fan running at high speed?	—	*Go to Step 43*	*Go to Step 77*
43	1. Check for a short to ground in the Cool Fan 2 relay and Cool Fan 3 relay control circuit. 2. If a problem is found, repair as necessary. Was a problem found?	—	*Go to Step 81*	*Go to Step 52*

GC1089700320050X

Fig. 128 Cooling fan diagnosis (Part 5 of 9). 1998–99 Lumina & Monte Carlo

Step	Action	Value(s)	Yes	No
44	1. Turn *off* the ignition switch. 2. Disconnect the A/C refrigerant pressure sensor electrical connector. 3. Turn *on* the ignition switch. 4. View A/C Pressure on the scan tool. Does the scan tool display voltage near the specified value?	0V	*Go to Step 46*	*Go to Step 45*
45	Probe the A/C refrigerant pressure signal circuit with a *J 39200* Digital Multimeter connected to the A/C refrigerant pressure sensor ground. Does the digital multimeter display voltage near the specified value?	0V	*Go to Step 77*	*Go to Step 51*
46	Probe the A/C refrigerant pressure sensor ground with a test light to battery positive voltage. Is the test light on?	—	*Go to Step 47*	*Go to Step 49*
47	Probe the A/C refrigerant pressure sensor 5 volt reference circuit with a *J 39200* Digital Multimeter connected to the A/C refrigerant pressure sensor ground. Does the digital multimeter display voltage near the specified value?	5V	*Go to Step 48*	*Go to Step 50*
48	Replace the A/C refrigerant pressure sensor. Is action complete?	—	*Go to Step 81*	—
49	Locate and repair open or short to voltage in the A/C refrigerant pressure sensor ground circuit. Is action complete?	—	*Go to Step 81*	—
50	Locate and repair open or short to ground in the A/C refrigerant pressure sensor 5 volt reference circuit. Is action complete?	—	*Go to Step 81*	—
51	Locate and repair short to voltage in the A/C refrigerant pressure signal circuit. Is action complete?	—	*Go to Step 81*	—
52	1. Remove the Cool Fan 2 relay from the Underhood Electrical Center. 2. Observe the cooling fans. Is the right engine cooling fan running at high speed?	—	*Go to Step 53*	*Go to Step 70*
53	Remove the Fan 3 relay from the Underhood Electrical Center. Is the right engine cooling fan running at high speed?	—	*Go to Step 54*	*Go to Step 55*
54	Locate and repair short to battery positive voltage in CKT 532. Is action complete?	—	*Go to Step 81*	—
55	Locate and repair short to battery positive voltage in CKT 504. If a problem is found repair as necessary. Was a problem found?	—	*Go to Step 81*	*Go to Step 76*
56	1. Check for an open in CKT 532 between Fan 2 relay cavity 30 and left engine cooling fan terminal A. 2. If a problem is found, repair as necessary. Was a problem found?	—	*Go to Step 81*	*Go to Step 79*

GC1089700320060X

Fig. 128 Cooling fan diagnosis (Part 6 of 9). 1998–99 Lumina & Monte Carlo

Step	Action	Value(s)	Yes	No
57	1. Check for an open in CKT 1050 between right engine cooling fan terminal A and ground. 2. If a problem is found, repair as necessary. Was a problem found?	—	*Go to Step 81*	*Go to Step 80*
58	1. Ignition *on*, engine not running. 2. Remove the Cool Fan 2 relay from the Underhood Electrical Center. 3. Install a test light between Cool Fan 2 relay cavity 86 and battery positive voltage. 4. Command High speed fans on using the scan tool output controls function. 5. Wait approx. 5-6 seconds. 6. Observe the test light. Is the test light *on* ?	—	*Go to Step 61*	*Go to Step 59*
59	1. Remove the Fan 3 relay from the Underhood Electrical Center. 2. Install a test light between Fan 3 relay cavity 86 and battery positive voltage. 3. Command high speed fans on using the scan tool output controls function. 4. Wait 6 seconds. 5. Observe the test light. Is the test light *on* ?	—	*Go to Step 78*	*Go to Step 60*
60	1. Turn *off* the ignition switch. 2. Disconnect the PCM. 3. Turn *on* the ignition switch. 4. Check the Cool Fan 2 relay and Cool relay control circuit for an open or a short to voltage. 5. If a problem is found, repair as necessary. Was a problem found?	—	*Go to Step 81*	*Go to Step 77*
61	1. Turn *off* the ignition switch 2. Reinstall the Cool Fan 2 relay. 3. Disconnect both coolant fan electrical connectors. 4. Turn *on* the ignition switch. 5. Command Fan 2 *on* using the scan tool output controls function. 6. Wait approx. 5-6 seconds. 7. Probe terminal B at the right engine cooling fan connector with a test light to ground. Is the test light *on* ?	—	*Go to Step 62*	*Go to Step 64*
62	Probe terminal A at the left engine cooling fan connector with a test light to battery positive voltage. Is the test light *on* ?	—	*Go to Step 63*	*Go to Step 71*
63	1. Identify cause of inoperative cooling fan: • Open right engine cooling fan motor windings. • Open left engine cooling fan motor windings. • Stalled cooling fan(s). 2. Replace the affected cooling fan motor. Is action complete?	—	*Go to Step 81*	—

GC1089700320070X

Fig. 128 Cooling fan diagnosis (Part 7 of 9). 1998–99 Lumina & Monte Carlo

Step	Action	Value(s)	Yes	No
64	1. Remove the high speed engine Cool Fan 2 relay from the Underhood Electrical Center. 2. Turn *on* the ignition switch. 3. Probe Cool Fan 2 relay cavity 85 with a test light connected to ground. Is the test light *on* ?	—	*Go to Step 66*	*Go to Step 65*
65	Locate and repair open in the ignition battery positive voltage circuit to high speed engine Cool Fan 2 relay. Is action complete?	—	*Go to Step 81*	—
66	Probe Cool Fan 2 relay cavity 30 with a test light connected to ground. Is the test light *on* ?	—	*Go to Step 68*	*Go to Step 67*
67	Locate and repair open in battery positive voltage circuit to Cool Fan 2 relay cavity 30. Is action complete?	—	*Go to Step 81*	—
68	1. Check Engine Coolant Fan Motor #1 circuit for an open between right engine cooling fan terminal B and Cool Fan 2 relay cavity 87. 2. If a problem is found, repair as necessary. Was a problem found?	—	*Go to Step 81*	*Go to Step 69*
69	1. Check for a poor Cool Fan 2 relay terminal connections at the Underhood Electrical Center. 2. If a problem is found, repair as necessary. Was a problem found?	—	*Go to Step 81*	*Go to Step 70*
70	Replace Cool Fan 2 relay. Is action complete?	—	*Go to Step 81*	—
71	1. Remove the Fan 3 relay from the Underhood Electrical Center. 2. Turn *on* the ignition switch. 3. Probe Fan 3 relay cavity 85 with a test light connected to ground. Is the test light *on* ?	—	*Go to Step 73*	*Go to Step 72*
72	Locate and repair open in battery positive voltage circuit to Fan 3 relay cavity 85. Is action complete?	—	*Go to Step 81*	—
73	Probe Fan 3 relay cavity 87 in the Underhood Electrical Center with a test light to battery positive voltage. Is the test light *on* ?	—	*Go to Step 75*	*Go to Step 74*
74	Locate and repair open in circuit between Fan 3 cavity 87and Fan 2 relay cavity 87a in the Underhood Electrical Center and ground. Is action complete?	—	*Go to Step 81*	—
75	1. Check for poor Fan 3 relay engine terminal connections at the Underhood Electrical Center. 2. If a problem is found, repair as necessary. Was a problem found?	—	*Go to Step 81*	*Go to Step 76*

GC1089700320080X

Fig. 128 Cooling fan diagnosis (Part 8 of 9). 1998–99 Lumina & Monte Carlo

76	Replace the *Cool Fan 3* relay in the Underhood Electrical Center. Is action complete?	—	*Go to Step 81*	—
77	Replace the PCM. **Important:** The replacement PCM must be programmed. Is action complete?	—	*Go to Step 81*	—
78	Repair open in the *Cool Fan* relay cavity 86 and *Cool Fan 2* relay cavity 86 control circuit to PCM. Is action complete?	—	*Go to Step 81*	—
79	Replace the left engine cooling fan motor. Is action complete?	—	*Go to Step 81*	—
80	Replace the right engine cooling fan motor. Is action complete?	—	*Go to Step 81*	
81	1. Engine coolant below 100 °C (212 °F). 2. A/C *off*. 3. Engine running. 4. Observe the cooling fans. Are the cooling fans running?	—	*Go to Step 32*	*Go to Step 82*
82	1. Command Low Speed Fans *on* using the scan tool output tests function. 2. Observe the cooling fans. Are both cooling fans running at low speed?	—	*Go to Step 83*	*Go to Step 8*
83	1. Command High speed fans *on* using the scan tool output tests function. 2. Wait 6 seconds. 3. Observe the cooling fans. Are both cooling fans running at high speed?	—	System OK	*Go to Step 58*

GC1089700320090X

Fig. 128 Cooling fan diagnosis (Part 9 of 9). 1998–99 Lumina & Monte Carlo

Step	Action	Value(s)	Yes	No
1	Did you perform the Powertrain On-Board Diagnostic (OBD) System Check?	—	*Go to Step 2*	*Go to A Powertrain On Board Diagnostic (OBD) System Check*
2	Are any DTCs set?	—	Go to applicable DTCs	*Go to Step 3*
3	1. Install a scan tool. 2. Engine coolant temperature must be below the specified value for all the fan diagnoses. 3. Turn ON the Ignition, with the engine and A/C OFF. Are the cooling fans OFF?	100°C (212°F)	*Go to Step 4*	Go to Cooling Fan table #1
4	With a scan tool, command Low Speed Fans ON. Are both cooling fans ON?	—	*Go to Step 5*	Go to Cooling Fan table #2
5	**Important:** Allow a 3–5 second delay before determining if the fans have switched from low to high speed. With a scan tool, command High Speed Fans ON. Do both cooling fans switch to high speed?	—	*Go to Step 6*	Go to Cooling Fan table #3
6	1. Exit outputs screen on the scan tool. 2. Idle the engine leaving the A/C OFF. Are the cooling fans ON?	—	*Go to Step 8*	*Go to Step 7*
7	Turn ON the A/C. Are the cooling fans ON?	—	System OK	*Go to Step 9*
8	Does the scan tool display A/C request as YES?	—	Go to *Cooling Insufficient, A/C System*	*Go to Step 10*
9	Does the scan tool display A/C request as YES?	—	Go to *A/C Compressor Control Circuit Diagnosis*	Go to *Cooling Insufficient, A/C System*
10	**Important:** The replacement PCM must be programmed. Replace the PCM. Is the action complete?	—	System OK	—

GC1080000591000X

Fig. 129 Cooling fan functional check. 2000–01 Lumina

Step	Action	Values	Yes	No
1	Did you perform the Cooling Fan Functional Check?	—	*Go to Step 2*	Go to Cooling Fan Functional Check
2	Did either fan turn ON when Cool Fan 1 Relay was commanded ON?	—	*Go to Step 3*	*Go to Step 5*
3	1. Install a scan tool. 2. With a scan tool, command Low Speed Fans ON. Did the other fan turn OFF?	—	*Go to Step 19*	*Go to Step 4*
4	Disconnect Cool Fan 2 Relay. Did the fan turn OFF?	—	*Go to Step 20*	*Go to Step 21*
5	1. With a scan tool, command Low Speed Fans ON. 2. Disconnect Cool Fan 1 Relay. 3. Probe Low Speed Fans Control circuit (335) at the Cool Fan 1 Relay Connector using a test lamp that is connected to battery positive voltage. Does the test lamp illuminate?	—	*Go to Step 6*	*Go to Step 13*
6	Probe both feed circuits (640) at the Cool Fan 1 Relay Connector locations using a test lamp that is connected to ground. Does test lamp illuminate for both circuits?	—	*Go to Step 7*	*Go to Step 22*
7	**Important:** Leave jumper in place for remainder of this table. Connect a fused jumper wire between the switch feed circuit (740) and the RH fan feed circuit (409) at the Cool Fan 1 Relay Connector locations. Do both fans turn ON?	—	*Go to Step 23*	*Go to Step 8*
8	1. Disconnect the right fan. 2. Probe fan harness connector terminal B with a test lamp that is connected to a known good ground. Does the test lamp illuminate?	—	*Go to Step 9*	*Go to Step 24*
9	Connect a second fused jumper wire between the right fan harness connector terminals. Is the left fan ON?	—	*Go to Step 16*	*Go to Step 10*
10	1. Reconnect the right fan. 2. Disconnect Cool Fan 2 Relay. 3. Probe the switch feed circuit (504) at Cool Fan 2 Relay connector using a test lamp that is connected to a known good ground. Does the test lamp illuminate?	—	*Go to Step 11*	*Go to Step 25*
11	Using the second jumper wire, jumper the switch feed circuit (504) and the LH fan feed circuit (409) together at Cool Fan 2 Relay connector. Do the fans come ON?	—	*Go to Step 26*	*Go to Step 12*
12	1. Reconnect Cool Fan 2 Relay. 2. Disconnect the left fan. 3. Probe left fan harness connector terminal B with a test lamp that is connected to a known good ground. Is the right fan ON?	—	*Go to Step 16*	*Go to Step 18*
13	1. Keep test lamp connected. 2. Turn OFF the ignition. 3. Disconnect the PCM. 4. Probe the Low Speed Fans Control circuit at the PCM connector, with a fused jumper wire that is connected to a known good ground. Is the test lamp ON?	—	*Go to Step 20*	*Go to Step 21*

GC1080000593010X

Fig. 131 Cooling fan table 2 (Part 1 of 2). 2000–01 Lumina

Step	Action	Values	Yes	No
1	Did you perform the Cooling Fan Functional Check?	—	*Go to Step 2*	Go to Cooling Fan Functional Check
2	Disconnect Cool Fan 1 Relay. Are both fans OFF?	—	*Go to Step 8*	*Go to Step 3*
3	Disconnect Cool Fan 3 Relay. Are both fans OFF?	—	*Go to Step 4*	*Go to Step 10*
4	1. Disconnect the right fan. 2. Probe terminal B of the right fan connector using a test lamp that is connected to a known good ground. Does the test lamp illuminate?	—	*Go to Step 11*	*Go to Step 5*
5	Probe terminal A of the right fan connector using a test lamp that is connected to a known good ground. Does the test lamp illuminate?	—	*Go to Step 12*	*Go to Step 6*
6	Probe the High Speed Fans control circuit (473) at the Cool Fan 3 Relay connector in the Underhood Accessory Wiring Junction Block using a test lamp that is connected to battery positive voltage. Does the test lamp illuminate?	—	*Go to Step 7*	*Go to Step 13*
7	1. Turn OFF the ignition. 2. Leave the test lamp installed. 3. Disconnect the PCM. 4. Turn ON the ignition, with the engine OFF. Is the test lamp still illuminated?	—	*Go to Step 14*	*Go to Step 16*
8	Probe the Low Speed Fans Control circuit (335) at the Cool Fan 1 Relay connector using the test lamp that is connected to battery positive voltage. Does the test lamp illuminate?	—	*Go to Step 9*	*Go to Step 13*
9	1. Turn OFF the ignition. 2. Leave the test lamp installed. 3. Disconnect the PCM. 4. Turn ON the ignition, with the engine OFF. Is the test lamp still illuminated?	—	*Go to Step 14*	*Go to Step 16*
10	Repair the LH fan feed circuit (409) for a short to voltage. Did you find and correct the condition?	—	Go to Cooling Fan Functional Check	*Go to Step 15*
11	Repair the RH fan feed circuit (532) for a short to voltage. Is the action complete?	—	Go to Cooling Fan Functional Check	—
12	Repair the short to voltage in the Cool Fan 2 Relay feed circuit (740). Is the action complete?	—	Go to Cooling Fan Functional Check	—
13	Replace the Cool Fan 1 Relay. Is the action complete?	—	Go to Cooling Fan Functional Check	—
14	Repair the High Speed Fans Control circuit (473) or the Low Speed Fans Control circuit (335) for a short to ground. Is the action complete?	—	Go to Cooling Fan Functional Check	—
15	Replace the Cool Fan 2 Relay. Is the action complete?	—	Go to Cooling Fan Functional Check	—
16	**Important:** Program the replacement PCM. Replace the PCM. Is the action complete?	—	Go to Cooling Fan Functional Check	—

GC1080000592000X

Fig. 130 Cooling fan table 1. 2000–01 Lumina

Step	Action	Values	Yes	No
14	Inspect the PCM connections. Repair faulty connections as necessary. Did you find a problem and correct the problem?	—	Go to Cooling Fan Functional Check	*Go to Step 27*
15	Repair the Low Speed Fans Control circuit (335) for an open or shorted to battery positive voltage. Is the action complete?	—	Go to Cooling Fan Functional Check	—
16	Inspect the fan motor ground circuit for a open or the left fan motor connections and repair as necessary. Did you find and correct the condition?	—	Go to Cooling Fan Functional Check	*Go to Step 17*
17	Replace the left fan motor. Is the action complete?	—	Go to Cooling Fan Functional Check	—
18	Repair the RH fan feed circuit (504) for an open. Is the action complete?	—	Go to Cooling Fan Functional Check	—
19	Replace the fan which was not operating. Is the action complete?	—	Go to Cooling Fan Functional Check	—
20	Replace Cool Fan 3 Relay. Is the action complete?	—	Go to Cooling Fan Functional Check	—
21	Repair the Cool Fan 2 Relay feed circuit (740) for a short to ground. Did you find and correct the condition?	—	Go to Cooling Fan Functional Check	*Go to Step 26*
22	Repair the open or the grounded circuit for the circuit that did not light. Is the action complete?	—	Go to Cooling Fan Functional Check	—
23	Replace Cool Fan 1 Relay. Is the action complete?	—	Go to Cooling Fan Functional Check	—
24	Repair the LH fan feed circuit (409) for a open. Is the action complete?	—	Go to Cooling Fan Functional Check	—
25	Repair the Cool Fan 2 Relay feed circuit (504) for a open. Is the action complete?	—	Go to Cooling Fan Functional Check	—
26	Replace Cool Fan 2 Relay. Is the action complete?	—	Go to Cooling Fan Functional Check	—
27	**Important:** Program the replacement PCM. Replace the PCM. Is the action complete?	—	Go to Cooling Fan Functional Check	—

GC1080000593020X

Fig. 131 Cooling fan table 2 (Part 2 of 2). 2000–01 Lumina

Step	Action	Values	Yes	No
1	Did you perform the Cooling Fan Functional Check?	—	Go to Step 2	Go to Cooling Fan Functional Check
2	1. With a scan tool, command Low Speed Fans ON. 2. Command High Speed Fans ON. Did both fans operate with no change?	—	Go to Step 8	Go to Step 3
3	Did the left fan stop operating?	—	Go to Step 9	Go to Step 4
4	1. Disconnect Cool Fan 3 Relay. 2. Probe the High Speed Fans Control circuit (473) at Cool Fan 3 Relay connector using a test lamp that is connected to battery positive voltage. 3. Command High Speed Fans ON using a scan tool. Does the test lamp illuminate after several seconds?	—	Go to Step 5	Go to Step 12
5	Probe the coil feed circuit (740) at Cool Fan Relay connector using a test lamp that is connected to a known good ground. Does the test lamp illuminate?	—	Go to Step 6	Go to Step 13
6	Probe the switch feed circuit (740) at the Cool Fan 3 Relay connector using a test lamp that is connected to a good ground. Does the test lamp illuminate?	—	Go to Step 7	Go to Step 14
7	Jumper the switch feed circuit (740) and the LH fan feed circuit (409) together at the Cool Fan 3 Relay connector. Is the left fan ON?	—	Go to Step 15	Go to Step 16
8	1. Turn OFF the ignition. 2. Disconnect the PCM. 3. Disconnect Cool Fan 1 Relay. 4. Jumper the switch feed circuit (640) and the RH fan feed circuit (532) together at the Cool Fan 1 Relay connector. 5. Turn ON the ignition. 6. Probe the PCM harness connector for the High Speed Fans Control circuit with a fused jumper that is connected to a known good ground. Do the fans switch from low to high speed?	—	Go to Step 22	Go to Step 17
9	1. Disconnect Cool Fan 3 Relay. 2. Probe the High Speed Fans Control Ciruict (473) at the Cool Fan 3 Relay connector using a test lamp that is connected to battery positive voltage. 3. Command High Speed Fans ON using a scan tool. Does the test lamp illuminate?	—	Go to Step 10	Go to Step 18
10	Probe the ground circuit (250) at the Cool Fan 2 Relay connector using a test lamp that is connected to battery positive voltage. Does the test lamp illuminate?	—	Go to Step 11	Go to Step 19
11	Probe the coil feed circuit (740) at the Cool Fan 2 Relay connector using a test lamp that is connected to a known good ground. Does the test lamp illuminate?	—	Go to Step 20	Go to Step 21
12	Repair the High Speed Fans Control circuit (473) for an open between Cool Fan 3 Relay and the splice. Is the action complete?	—	Go to Cooling Fan Functional Check	—
13	Repair the open in the Cool Fan 3 Relay coil feed circuit (740). Is the action complete?	—	Go to Cooling Fan Functional Check	—

GC1080000594010X

Fig. 132 Cooling fan table 3 (Part 1 of 2). 2000–01 Lumina

Step	Action	Values	Yes	No
1	Did you perform the Powertrain On-Board Diagnostic (OBD) System Check?	—	Go to Step 2	Go to A Powertrain On Board Diagnostic (OBD) System Check
2	Are any other DTCs set?	—	Go to Diagnostic Trouble Code (DTC) List/Type	Go to Step 3

GC1080000595010X

Fig. 133 Cooling fan functional check (Part 1 of 2). 2000 Impala & Monte Carlo

Step	Action	Values	Yes	No
14	Repair the open in the Cool Fan 3 Relay switch feed circuit (740). Is the action complete?	—	Go to Cooling Fan Functional Check	—
15	Replace Cool Fan 3 Relay. Is the action complete?	—	Go to Cooling Fan Functional Check	—
16	Repair the open in the LH fan feed circuit (409) between Cool Fan 3 Relay and the splice. Is the action complete?	—	Go to Cooling Fan Functional Check	—
17	Repair the High Speed Fans Control circuit (473) for an open or for a short to battery positive voltage. Is the action complete?	—	Go to Cooling Fan Functional Check	—
18	Repair the open in the High Speed Fans Control circuit (473) between Cool Fan 2 Relay and the splice. Is the action complete?	—	Go to Cooling Fan Functional Check	—
19	Repair the open in the ground circuit (250). Is the action complete?	—	Go to Cooling Fan Functional Check	—
20	Replace the Cool Fan 2 relay. Is the action complete?	—	Go to Cooling Fan Functional Check	—
21	Repair the open in Cool fan 2 Relay coil feed circuit (740). Is the action complete?	—	Go to Cooling Fan Functional Check	—
22	1. Inspect the PCM connections. 2. Repair faulty connections as necessary. Did you find and correct the condition?	—	Go to Cooling Fan Functional Check	Go to Step 23
23	**Important:** Program the replacement PCM. Replace the PCM. Is the action complete?	—	Go to Cooling Fan Functional Check	—

GC1080000594020X

Fig. 132 Cooling fan table 3 (Part 2 of 2). 2000–01 Lumina

Step	Action	Values	Yes	No
3	1. Install a scan tool. 2. Engine coolant temperature must be below the specified value for all the fan diagnoses. 3. Turn ON the Ignition, with the engine and A/C OFF. Are the cooling fans OFF?	100°C (212°F)	Go to Step 4	Go to Table #1 in *Electric Cooling Fan Diagnosis (Functional Check)* or *Electric Cooling Fan Diagnosis (Table #1)* or *Electric Cooling Fan Diagnosis (Table #2)* or *Electric Cooling Fan Diagnosis (Table #3)*
4	With a scan tool, command the low speed cooling fan relay ON. Do both cooling fans turn ON?	—	Go to Step 5	Go to Table #2 in *Electric Cooling Fan Diagnosis (Functional Check)* or *Electric Cooling Fan Diagnosis (Table #1)* or *Electric Cooling Fan Diagnosis (Table #2)* or *Electric Cooling Fan Diagnosis (Table #3)*
5	With a scan tool, command the high speed cooling fan relay ON. Do both cooling fans switch to high speed?	—	Go to Step 6	Go to Table #3 in *Electric Cooling Fan Diagnosis (Functional Check)* or *Electric Cooling Fan Diagnosis (Table #1)* or *Electric Cooling Fan Diagnosis (Table #2)* or *Electric Cooling Fan Diagnosis (Table #3)*
6	1. With a scan tool, exit outputs. 2. Idle the engine leaving the A/C OFF. Are the cooling fans ON?	—	Go to Step 8	Go to Step 7
7	Turn ON the A/C. Are the cooling fans ON?	—	System OK	Go to Step 8
8	Does the scan tool display A/C request as YES?	—	Go to A Diagnostic Starting Point	Go to Step 9
9	**Important:** Program the replacement PCM. Replace the PCM. Did you complete the replacement?	—	System OK	—

GC1080000595020X

Fig. 133 Cooling fan functional check (Part 2 of 2). 2000 Impala & Monte Carlo

Step	Action	Values	Yes	No
1	Did you perform the Cooling Fan Functional Check?	—	Go to Step 2	Go to *Electric Cooling Fan Diagnosis (Functional Check)* or *Electric Cooling Fan Diagnosis (Table #2)* or *Electric Cooling Fan Diagnosis (Table #3)*
2	1. Disconnect the low speed cooling fan relay. 2. Turn the ignition ON with the engine OFF. Are both fans OFF?	—	Go to Step 9	Go to Step 3
3	Disconnect the cool fan s/p relay. Are both fans OFF?	—	Go to Step 5	Go to Step 4
4	Remove the high speed cooling fan relay. Are both fans OFF?	—	Go to Step 7	Go to Step 11
5	1. Disconnect the right fan. 2. Probe the fan feed terminal of the right fan connector using a test lamp that is connected to a good ground. Does the test lamp illuminate?	—	Go to Step 12	Go to Step 6
6	Probe the cool fan s/p relay switch feed terminal at the right fan connector using a test lamp that is connected to a good ground. Does the test lamp illuminate?	—	Go to Step 13	Go to Step 17
7	Probe the cool fan s/p relay control circuit at the cool fan s/p relay connector using a test lamp that is connected to B+. Does the test lamp illuminate?	—	Go to Step 8	Go to Step 16
8	1. Turn OFF the ignition. 2. Leave the test lamp installed. 3. Disconnect the PCM. 4. Turn ON the ignition, with the engine OFF. Is the test lamp still illuminated?	—	Go to Step 15	Go to Step 18
9	Probe the low speed cooling fan relay control circuit at the low speed cooling fan relay connector using a test lamp that is connected to B+. Does the test lamp illuminate?	—	Go to Step 10	Go to Step 14
10	1. Turn OFF the ignition. 2. Leave the test lamp installed. 3. Disconnect the PCM. 4. Turn ON the ignition, with the engine OFF. Is the test lamp still illuminated?	—	Go to Step 15	Go to Step 18

GC1080000596010X

Fig. 134 Cooling fan diagnosis table 1 (Part 1 of 3). 2000 Impala & Monte Carlo

Step	Action	Values	Yes	No
11	Test the left fan feed circuit for a short to voltage and repair as necessary. Did you find and correct a condition?	—	Go to the Functional Check in *Electric Cooling Fan Diagnosis (Functional Check)* or *Electric Cooling Fan Diagnosis (Table #2)* or *Electric Cooling Fan Diagnosis (Table #3)*	Go to Step 16
12	Test the right fan feed circuit for a short to voltage and repair as necessary. Did you complete the repair?	—	Go to the Functional Check in *Electric Cooling Fan Diagnosis (Functional Check)* or *Electric Cooling Fan Diagnosis (Table #2)* or *Electric Cooling Fan Diagnosis (Table #3)*	—
13	Repair the short to voltage in the cool fan s/p relay switch feed circuit. Did you complete the repair?	—	Go to the Functional Check in *Electric Cooling Fan Diagnosis (Functional Check)* or *Electric Cooling Fan Diagnosis (Table #2)* or *Electric Cooling Fan Diagnosis (Table #3)*	—
14	Replace the low speed cooling fan relay. Did you complete the replacement?	—	Go to the Functional Check in *Electric Cooling Fan Diagnosis (Functional Check)* or *Electric Cooling Fan Diagnosis (Table #2)* or *Electric Cooling Fan Diagnosis (Table #3)*	—

GC1080000596020X

Fig. 134 Cooling fan diagnosis table 1 (Part 2 of 3). 2000 Impala & Monte Carlo

Step	Action	Values	Yes	No
15	Test the high speed cooling fan relay control circuit or the low speed cooling fan relay control circuit for a short to ground and repair as necessary. Did you complete the repair?	—	Go to the Functional Check in *Electric Cooling Fan Diagnosis (Functional Check)* or *Electric Cooling Fan Diagnosis (Table #2)* or *Electric Cooling Fan Diagnosis (Table #3)*	—
16	Replace the high speed cooling fan relay. Did you complete the replacement?	—	Go to the Functional Check in *Electric Cooling Fan Diagnosis (Functional Check)* or *Electric Cooling Fan Diagnosis (Table #2)* or *Electric Cooling Fan Diagnosis (Table #3)*	—
17	Replace the cool fan s/p relay. Did you complete the replacement?	—	Go to the Functional Check in *Electric Cooling Fan Diagnosis (Functional Check)* or *Electric Cooling Fan Diagnosis (Table #2)* or *Electric Cooling Fan Diagnosis (Table #3)*	—
18	**Important:** Program the replacement PCM. Replace the PCM. Did you complete the replacement?	—	Go to the Functional Check in *Electric Cooling Fan Diagnosis (Functional Check)* or *Electric Cooling Fan Diagnosis (Table #2)* or *Electric Cooling Fan Diagnosis (Table #3)*	—

GC1080000596030X

Fig. 134 Cooling fan diagnosis table 1 (Part 3 of 3). 2000 Impala & Monte Carlo

Step	Action	Values	Yes	No
1	Did you perform the Cooling Fan Functional Check?	—	Go to Step 2	Go to the Functional Check in *Electric Cooling Fan Diagnosis (Functional Check)* or *Electric Cooling Fan Diagnosis (Table #1)* or *Electric Cooling Fan Diagnosis (Table #3)*
2	Did either fan turn ON when the low speed cooling fan relay was commanded ON?	—	Go to Step 3	Go to Step 5
3	With a scan tool, command the high speed cooling fan relay ON. Did the inoperative fan from step 2 turn ON?	—	Go to Step 4	Go to Step 20
4	Disconnect the high speed cooling fan relay. Did the inoperative fan from step 2 turn OFF?	—	Go to Step 23	Go to Step 22
5	1. Disconnect the low speed cooling fan relay. 2. With a scan tool, command the low speed cooling fan relay ON. 3. Probe the low speed cooling fan relay control circuit at the low speed cooling fan relay connector using a test lamp that is connected to B+. Does the test lamp illuminate?	—	Go to Step 6	Go to Step 13
6	Probe both feed circuits at the low speed cooling fan relay connector using a test lamp that is connected to a good ground. Does test lamp illuminate for both circuits?	—	Go to Step 7	Go to Step 24
7	**Important:** Leave the jumper in place for the remainder of this table. Connect a 30 amp fused jumper wire between the switch feed circuit and the right fan feed circuit at the low speed cooling fan relay connector. Do both fans turn ON?	—	Go to Step 25	Go to Step 8
8	1. Disconnect the right fan. 2. Probe the right fan feed circuit at the fan harness connector terminal with a test lamp that is connected to a good ground. Does the test lamp illuminate?	—	Go to Step 9	Go to Step 27
9	Connect a second 30 amp fused jumper wire between the right fan harness connector terminals. Does the left fan turn ON?	—	Go to Step 17	Go to Step 10
10	1. Reconnect the right fan. 2. Disconnect the cool fan s/p relay. 3. Probe the switch feed circuit at the cool fan s/p relay connector using a test lamp that is connected to a good ground. Does the test lamp illuminate?	—	Go to Step 11	Go to Step 28

GC1080000597010X

Fig. 135 Cooling fan diagnosis table 2 (Part 1 of 6). 2000 Impala & Monte Carlo

Step	Action	Values	Yes	No
11	Using the second jumper wire, jumper the switch feed circuit and the left fan feed circuit together at the cool fan s/p relay connector. Do both fans turn ON?	—	*Go to Step 29*	*Go to Step 12*
12	1. Reconnect the cool fan s/p relay. 2. Disconnect the left fan. 3. Probe the fan feed circuit at the fan harness connector terminal with a test lamp that is connected to a good ground. Does the test lamp illuminate?	—	*Go to Step 16*	*Go to Step 19*
13	1. Verify that the test lamp is still connected. 2. Turn OFF the ignition. 3. Disconnect the PCM. 4. Probe the low speed cooling fan relay control circuit at the PCM connector with a test lamp that is connected to a good ground. Does the test lamp illuminate?	—	*Go to Step 14*	*Go to Step 15*
14	Inspect for faulty connections at the PCM and harness connectors and repair as necessary. Did you find a problem and correct the condition?	—	Go to the Functional Check in *Electric Cooling Fan Diagnosis (Functional Check)* or *Electric Cooling Fan Diagnosis (Table #1)* or *Electric Cooling Fan Diagnosis (Table #3)*	*Go to Step 31*
15	Inspect the low speed cooling fan relay control circuit for an open or short to B+ and repair as necessary. Did you find and correct a condition?	—	Go to the Functional Check in *Electric Cooling Fan Diagnosis (Functional Check)* or *Electric Cooling Fan Diagnosis (Table #1)* or *Electric Cooling Fan Diagnosis (Table #3)*	—

GC1080000597020X

Fig. 135 Cooling fan diagnosis table 2 (Part 2 of 6). 2000 Impala & Monte Carlo

Step	Action	Values	Yes	No
20	Test the supply circuit to the inoperative fan for a short to ground and repair as necessary. Did you find and correct a condition?	—	Go to the Functional Check in *Electric Cooling Fan Diagnosis (Functional Check)* or *Electric Cooling Fan Diagnosis (Table #1)* or *Electric Cooling Fan Diagnosis (Table #3)*	*Go to Step 21*
21	Replace the fan which was not operating. Did you complete the replacement?	—	Go to the Functional Check in *Electric Cooling Fan Diagnosis (Functional Check)* or *Electric Cooling Fan Diagnosis (Table #1)* or *Electric Cooling Fan Diagnosis (Table #3)*	—
22	Replace the high speed cooling fan relay. Did you complete the replacement?	—	Go to the Functional Check in *Electric Cooling Fan Diagnosis (Functional Check)* or *Electric Cooling Fan Diagnosis (Table #1)* or *Electric Cooling Fan Diagnosis (Table #3)*	—
23	Test the cool fan s/p relay switch feed circuit for a short to ground and repair as necessary. Did you find and correct the condition?	—	Go to the Functional Check in *Electric Cooling Fan Diagnosis (Functional Check)* or *Electric Cooling Fan Diagnosis (Table #1)* or *Electric Cooling Fan Diagnosis (Table #3)*	*Go to Step 29*

GC1080000597040X

Fig. 135 Cooling fan diagnosis table 2 (Part 4 of 6). 2000 Impala & Monte Carlo

Step	Action	Values	Yes	No
16	1. Inspect the fan motor ground circuit for an open or poor connections. 2. If a problem is found, repair as necessary. Did you find and correct the condition?	—	Go to the Functional Check in *Electric Cooling Fan Diagnosis (Functional Check)* or *Electric Cooling Fan Diagnosis (Table #1)* or *Electric Cooling Fan Diagnosis (Table #3)*	*Go to Step 17*
17	Inspect the fan motor and harness connectors for faulty terminals and replace as necessary. Did you find and correct a condition?	—	Go to the Functional Check in *Electric Cooling Fan Diagnosis (Functional Check)* or *Electric Cooling Fan Diagnosis (Table #1)* or *Electric Cooling Fan Diagnosis (Table #3)*	*Go to Step 18*
18	Replace the fan motor. Did you complete the replacement?	—	Go to the Functional Check in *Electric Cooling Fan Diagnosis (Functional Check)* or *Electric Cooling Fan Diagnosis (Table #1)* or *Electric Cooling Fan Diagnosis (Table #3)*	—
19	Test the left fan feed circuit for an open and repair as necessary. Did you complete the repair?	—	Go to the Functional Check in *Electric Cooling Fan Diagnosis (Functional Check)* or *Electric Cooling Fan Diagnosis (Table #1)* or *Electric Cooling Fan Diagnosis (Table #3)*	—

GC1080000597030X

Fig. 135 Cooling fan diagnosis table 2 (Part 3 of 6). 2000 Impala & Monte Carlo

Step	Action	Values	Yes	No
24	**Important:** If the fuse is blown, locate and repair a short to ground on the load circuit or a shorted component. Repair the open or the grounded circuit for the circuit that did not illuminate the test lamp. Did you complete the repair?	—	Go to the Functional Check in *Electric Cooling Fan Diagnosis (Functional Check)* or *Electric Cooling Fan Diagnosis (Table #1)* or *Electric Cooling Fan Diagnosis (Table #3)*	—
25	Inspect the low speed cooling fan relay and connector for faulty terminals and replace as necessary. Did you find and correct a condition?	—	Go to the Functional Check in *Electric Cooling Fan Diagnosis (Functional Check)* or *Electric Cooling Fan Diagnosis (Table #1)* or *Electric Cooling Fan Diagnosis (Table #3)*	*Go to Step 26*
26	Replace the low speed cooling fan relay. Did you complete the replacement?	—	Go to the Functional Check in *Electric Cooling Fan Diagnosis (Functional Check)* or *Electric Cooling Fan Diagnosis (Table #1)* or *Electric Cooling Fan Diagnosis (Table #3)*	—
27	Test the right fan feed circuit for an open and repair as necessary. Did you complete the repair?	—	Go to the Functional Check in *Electric Cooling Fan Diagnosis (Functional Check)* or *Electric Cooling Fan Diagnosis (Table #1)* or *Electric Cooling Fan Diagnosis (Table #3)*	—
28	Test the cool fan s/p relay switch feed circuit for an open and repair as necessary. Did you complete the repair?	—	Go to the Functional Check in *Electric Cooling Fan Diagnosis (Functional Check)* or *Electric Cooling Fan Diagnosis (Table #1)* or *Electric Cooling Fan Diagnosis (Table #3)*	—

GC1080000597050X

Fig. 135 Cooling fan diagnosis table 2 (Part 5 of 6). 2000 Impala & Monte Carlo

Step	Action	Values	Yes	No
29	Inspect the cool fan s/p relay and connector for faulty terminals and replace as necessary. Did you find and correct a condition?	—	Go to the Functional Check in *Electric Cooling Fan Diagnosis (Functional Check)* or *Electric Cooling Fan Diagnosis (Table #1)* or *Electric Cooling Fan Diagnosis (Table #3)*	*Go to Step 30*
30	Replace the cool fan s/p relay. Did you complete the replacement?	—	Go to the Functional Check in *Electric Cooling Fan Diagnosis (Functional Check)* or *Electric Cooling Fan Diagnosis (Table #1)* or *Electric Cooling Fan Diagnosis (Table #3)*	—
31	**Important:** Program the replacement PCM. Replace the PCM. Did you complete the replacement?	—	Go to the Functional Check in *Electric Cooling Fan Diagnosis (Functional Check)* or *Electric Cooling Fan Diagnosis (Table #1)* or *Electric Cooling Fan Diagnosis (Table #3)*	—

GC1080000597060X

Fig. 135 Cooling fan diagnosis table 2 (Part 6 of 6). 2000 Impala & Monte Carlo

Step	Action	Values	Yes	No
8	1. Turn OFF the ignition. 2. Disconnect the PCM. 3. Disconnect low speed cooling fan relay. 4. Install a 30 amp fused jumper between the switch feed circuit and the right fan feed circuit at the low speed cooling fan relay connector. 5. Turn ON the ignition, with the engine OFF. 6. Probe the high speed cooling fan relay control circuit at the PCM harness connector with a 15 amp fused jumper that is connected to a good ground. Do the fans switch from low to high speed?	—	*Go to Step 22*	*Go to Step 17*
9	1. Disconnect the cool fan s/p relay. 2. Probe the cool fan s/p relay control circuit at the cool fan s/p relay connector using a test lamp that is connected to B+. 3. With a scan tool command the high speed cooling fan relay ON. Does the test lamp illuminate after a few seconds?	—	*Go to Step 10*	*Go to Step 18*
10	Probe the ground circuit at the cool fan s/p relay connector using a test lamp that is connected to B+. Does the test lamp illuminate?	—	*Go to Step 11*	*Go to Step 19*
11	Probe the coil feed circuit at the cseries/parallel connector using a test lamp that is connected to a good ground. Does the test lamp illuminate?	—	*Go to Step 20*	*Go to Step 21*
12	Repair the high speed cooling fan relay control circuit for an open between the high speed fan relay and the splice. Did you complete the repair?	—	Go to the Functional Check in *Electric Cooling Fan Diagnosis (Functional Check)* or *Electric Cooling Fan Diagnosis (Table #1)* or *Electric Cooling Fan Diagnosis (Table #2)*	—
13	Repair the open in the high speed cooling fan relay coil feed circuit. Did you complete the repair?	—	Go to the Functional Check in *Electric Cooling Fan Diagnosis (Functional Check)* or *Electric Cooling Fan Diagnosis (Table #1)* or *Electric Cooling Fan Diagnosis (Table #2)*	—

GC1080000598020X

Fig. 136 Cooling fan diagnosis table 3 (Part 2 of 5). 2000 Impala & Monte Carlo

Step	Action	Values	Yes	No
1	Did you perform the Cooling Fan Functional Check?	—	*Go to Step 2*	Go to the Functional Check in *Electric Cooling Fan Diagnosis (Functional Check)* or *Electric Cooling Fan Diagnosis (Table #1)* or *Electric Cooling Fan Diagnosis (Table #2)*
2	1. With a scan tool, command the low speed cooling fan relay ON. 2. Command the high speed cooling fan relay ON while observing the fans. Did both fans operate with no change?	—	*Go to Step 8*	*Go to Step 3*
3	Did the right fan stop operating?	—	*Go to Step 9*	*Go to Step 4*
4	1. Disconnect the high speed cooling fan relay. 2. Probe the high speed cooling fan relay control circuit at the high speed cooling fan relay connector using a test lamp that is connected to B+. 3. With a scan tool command the high speed cooling fan relay ON. Does the test lamp illuminate after a few seconds?	—	*Go to Step 5*	*Go to Step 12*
5	Probe the coil feed circuit at the high speed cooling fan relay connector using a test lamp that is connected to a good ground. Does the test lamp illuminate?	—	*Go to Step 6*	*Go to Step 13*
6	Probe the switch feed circuit at the high speed cooling fan relay connector using a test lamp that is connected to a good ground. Does the test lamp illuminate?	—	*Go to Step 7*	*Go to Step 14*
7	Install a 30 amp fused jumper between the high speed cooling fan relay switch feed circuit and the left fan feed circuit at the high speed fan relay connector. Does the left fan turn ON?	—	*Go to Step 15*	*Go to Step 16*

GC1080000598010X

Fig. 136 Cooling fan diagnosis table 3 (Part 1 of 5). 2000 Impala & Monte Carlo

Step	Action	Values	Yes	No
14	**Important:** If the fuse is blown, locate and repair a short to ground on the load circuit or a shorted component. Repair the open in the high speed cooling fan relay switch feed circuit. Did you complete the repair?	—	Go to the Functional Check in *Electric Cooling Fan Diagnosis (Functional Check)* or *Electric Cooling Fan Diagnosis (Table #1)* or *Electric Cooling Fan Diagnosis (Table #2)*	—
15	Replace the high speed cooling fan relay. Did you complete the replacement?	—	Go to the Functional Check in *Electric Cooling Fan Diagnosis (Functional Check)* or *Electric Cooling Fan Diagnosis (Table #1)* or *Electric Cooling Fan Diagnosis (Table #2)*	—
16	Repair the open in the left fan feed circuit between the high speed cooling fan relay and the splice. Did you complete the repair?	—	Go to the Functional Check in *Electric Cooling Fan Diagnosis (Functional Check)* or *Electric Cooling Fan Diagnosis (Table #1)* or *Electric Cooling Fan Diagnosis (Table #2)*	—
17	Repair the high speed cooling fan relay control circuit for an open or for a short to B+. Did you complete the repair?	—	Go to the Functional Check in *Electric Cooling Fan Diagnosis (Functional Check)* or *Electric Cooling Fan Diagnosis (Table #1)* or *Electric Cooling Fan Diagnosis (Table #2)*	—

GC1080000598030X

Fig. 136 Cooling fan diagnosis table 3 (Part 3 of 5). 2000 Impala & Monte Carlo

Step	Action	Values	Yes	No
18	Repair the open in the high speed cooling fan relay control circuit between the cool fan s/p relay and the splice. Did you complete the repair?	—	Go to the Functional Check in *Electric Cooling Fan Diagnosis (Functional Check)* or *Electric Cooling Fan Diagnosis (Table #1)* or *Electric Cooling Fan Diagnosis (Table #2)*	—
19	Repair the open in the ground circuit. Did you complete the repair?	—	Go to the Functional Check in *Electric Cooling Fan Diagnosis (Functional Check)* or *Electric Cooling Fan Diagnosis (Table #1)* or *Electric Cooling Fan Diagnosis (Table #2)*	—
20	Replace the cool fan s/p relay. Did you complete the replacement?	—	Go to the Functional Check in *Electric Cooling Fan Diagnosis (Functional Check)* or *Electric Cooling Fan Diagnosis (Table #1)* or *Electric Cooling Fan Diagnosis (Table #2)*	—
21	**Important:** If the fuse is blown, locate and repair a short to ground on the load circuit or a shorted component. Repair the open in the cool fan s/p relay coil feed circuit. Did you complete the repair?	—	Go to the Functional Check in *Electric Cooling Fan Diagnosis (Functional Check)* or *Electric Cooling Fan Diagnosis (Table #1)* or *Electric Cooling Fan Diagnosis (Table #2)*	—

GC1080000598040X

Fig. 136 Cooling fan diagnosis table 3 (Part 4 of 5). 2000 Impala & Monte Carlo

Step	Action	Values	Yes	No
22	1. Inspect the PCM connections. 2. If a problem is found, repair as necessary. Did you find and correct the condition?	—	Go to the Functional Check in *Electric Cooling Fan Diagnosis (Functional Check)* or *Electric Cooling Fan Diagnosis (Table #1)* or *Electric Cooling Fan Diagnosis (Table #2)*	Go to Step 23
23	**Important:** Program the replacement PCM. Replace the PCM. Did you complete the replacement?	—	Go to the Functional Check in *Electric Cooling Fan Diagnosis (Functional Check)* or *Electric Cooling Fan Diagnosis (Table #1)* or *Electric Cooling Fan Diagnosis (Table #2)*	—

GC1080000598050X

Fig. 136 Cooling fan diagnosis table 3 (Part 5 of 5). 2000 Impala & Monte Carlo

Test Description

The number(s) below refer to the step number(s) on the diagnostic table.

2. Lack of communication may be due to a partial malfunction of the class 2 serial data circuit or due to a total malfunction of the class 2 serial data circuit. The specified procedure will determine the particular condition.
3. Determine if the Instrument Cluster or Powertrain Control Modules have set DTCs which may affect Engine Cooling operation are present.
4. The presence of DTCs which begin with "U" indicate some other module is not communicating. The specified procedure will compile all the available information before tests are performed.

Step	Action	Yes	No
1	Install a scan tool. Does the scan tool power up?	Go to Step 2	Diagnose Data Link
2	1. Turn ON the ignition, with the engine OFF. 2. Attempt to establish communication with the following control modules: o Instrument Cluster o Powertrain Control Module Does the scan tool communicate with the control modules?	Go to Step 3	Diagnose Data Link Communications
3	Select the powertrain control module display DTCs function on the scan tool. Does the scan tool display any DTCs?	Go to Step 4	Diagnose Go to Symptoms - Engine Cooling
4	Does the scan tool display any DTCs which begin with a "U"?	Diagnose Device in Data Link Communications	Diagnose Trouble Code (DTC) List

GC1080100665000X

Fig. 137 Diagnostic system check. 2001-02 Impala & Monte Carlo

Step	Action	Yes	No
1	Did you perform the Engine Cooling Diagnostic System Check?	Go to Step 2	Diagnose Engine Cooling
2	Turn ON the ignition, with the engine OFF. Are one or both cooling fans ON?	Go to Step 3	Test for Intermittent and Poor Connections
3	Are both cooling fans running continuously?	Go to Step 5	Go to Step 4
4	Remove the cooling fan 2 relay. Did the left cooling fan turn OFF?	Go to Step 6	Go to Step 7
5	Repair the short to voltage in the right cooling fan motor supply voltage circuit. Did you complete the repair?	Go to Step 8	--
6	Repair the short to voltage in the right cooling fan low reference circuit. Did you complete the repair?	Go to Step 8	--
7	Repair the short to voltage in the left cooling fan motor supply voltage circuit. Did you complete the repair?	Go to Step 8	--
8	Operate the system in order to verify the repair. Did you correct the condition?	System OK	Go to Step 2

GC1080100666000X

Fig. 138 Cooling fan always on. 2001-02 Impala & Monte Carlo

Step	Action	Yes	No
1	Did you perform the Engine Cooling Diagnostic System Check?	Go to Step 2	Diagnose Engine Cooling
2	1. Install a scan tool. 2. Turn ON the ignition, with the engine OFF. 3. With a scan tool, command the Fans Low Speed ON and OFF. Do the low speed engine cooling fans turn ON and OFF with each command?	Go to Step 3	Go to Step 4
3	**Important** Before the PCM changes the speed of the cooling fan, a 3-second delay occurs. With a scan tool, command the Fans High Speed ON and OFF. Do the high speed engine cooling fans turn ON and OFF with each command?	Test for Intermittent and Poor Connections	Go to Step 11
4	**Important** Do NOT remove the 20-A fused jumper wire connected during this step. Use a second 20-A fused jumper wire while performing the following steps. 1. Disconnect the cooling fan 1 relay. 2. Connect a 20-A fused jumper between the battery positive voltage circuit of the cooling fan 1 relay and the cooling fan motor supply voltage circuit of the cooling fan 1 relay. Do both cooling fans operate in low speed?	Go to Step 13	Go to Step 5
5	1. Disconnect the cooling fan 2 relay. 2. Connect the second 20-A fused jumper between the right cooling fan low reference circuit of the cooling fan 2 relay and the left cooling fan motor supply voltage circuit of the cooling fan 2 relay. Do both cooling fans operate in low speed?	Go to Step 14	Go to Step 6

GC1080100667010X

Fig. 139 Cooling fan inoperative (Part 1 of 4). 2001-02 Impala & Monte Carlo

Step	Action	Yes	No
6	Connect the second 20-A fused jumper between the battery positive voltage circuit of the cooling fan 2 relay and the cooling fan motor supply voltage circuit of the cooling fan 2 relay. Does the left cooling fan operate in high speed?	Go to Step 9	Go to Step 7
7	1. Install the cooling fan 2 relay. 2. Disconnect the left cooling fan electrical connector. 3. Connect the second 20-amp fused jumper wire from the cooling fan motor supply voltage circuit of the left cooling fan electrical connector to the cooling fan ground circuit of the left cooling fan electrical connector. Does the right cooling fan operate in high speed?	Go to Step 16	Go to Step 8
8	Connect the second 20-amp fused jumper wire from the cooling fan motor supply voltage circuit of the left cooling fan electrical connector to a good ground. Does the right cooling fan operate in high speed?	Go to Step 20	Go to Step 21
9	1. Install the cooling fan 2 relay. 2. Disconnect the right cooling fan electrical connector. 3. Connect the second 20-amp fused jumper wire from the cooling fan motor supply voltage circuit of the right cooling fan electrical connector to the cooling fan low reference circuit of the right cooling fan electrical connector. Does the left cooling fan operate in high speed?	Go to Step 17	Go to Step 10
10	Connect the second 20-amp fused jumper wire from battery positive voltage to the right cooling fan low reference circuit of the of the right cooling fan electrical connector. Does the left cooling fan operate in high speed?	Go to Step 18	Go to Step 22
11	Does the left cooling fan operate properly in high speed?	Go to Step 12	Go to Step 15
12	1. Disconnect the cooling fan 2 relay. 2. Connect the second 20-A fused jumper between the right cooling fan low reference circuit of the cooling fan 2 relay and the ground circuit of the cooling fan 2 relay. Does the right cooling fan operate properly in high speed?	Go to Step 14	Go to Step 19
13	Inspect for poor connections at the cooling fan 1 relay. Did you find and correct the condition?	Go to Step 28	Go to Step 23
14	Inspect for poor connections at the cooling fan 2 relay. Did you find and correct the condition?	Go to Step 28	Go to Step 24

GC1080100667020X

Fig. 139 Cooling fan inoperative (Part 2 of 4). 2001-02 Impala & Monte Carlo

Step	Action	Yes	No
15	Inspect for poor connections at the cooling fan 3 relay. Did you find and correct the condition?	Go to Step 28	Go to Step 25
16	Inspect for poor connections at the harness connector of the left cooling fan. Did you find and correct the condition?	Go to Step 28	Go to Step 26
17	Inspect for poor connections at the harness connector of the right cooling fan. Did you find and correct the condition?	Go to Step 28	Go to Step 27
18	Repair the right cooling fan motor supply voltage circuit. Did you complete the repair?	Go to Step 28	--
19	Repair the right cooling fan ground circuit. Did you complete the repair?	Go to Step 28	--
20	Repair the left cooling fan ground circuit. Did you complete the repair?	Go to Step 28	--
21	Repair the left cooling fan motor supply voltage circuit. Did you complete the repair?	Go to Step 28	--
22	Repair the right cooling fan low reference circuit. Did you complete the repair?	Go to Step 28	--
23	Replace the cooling fan 1 relay. Did you complete the repair?	Go to Step 28	--
24	Replace the cooling fan 2 relay. Did you complete the repair?	Go to Step 28	--

GC1080100667030X

Fig. 139 Cooling fan inoperative (Part 3 of 4). 2001-02 Impala & Monte Carlo

Step	Action	Yes	No
25	Replace the cooling fan 3 relay. Did you complete the repair?	Go to Step 28	--
26	Replace the left cooling fan. Did you complete the repair?	Go to Step 28	--
27	Replace the right cooling fan. Did you complete the repair?	Go to Step 28	--
28	Operate the system in order to verify the repair. Did you correct the condition?	System OK	Go to Step 3

GC1080100667040X

Fig. 139 Cooling fan inoperative (Part 4 of 4). 2001-02 Impala & Monte Carlo

Step	Action	Value(s)	Yes	No
1	Was the Powertrain On–Board Diagnostic (OBD) System Check performed?	—	Go to Step 2	Powertrain On Board Diagnostic (OBD) System Check
2	Are any PCM DTC(s) stored?	—	Diagnose the PCM DTC(s) first.	Go to Step 3
3	1. Ensure that the engine coolant temperature is below 100°C (212°F). 2. Turn OFF the A/C Selector Switch. 3. Engine running. 4. Observe the cooling fans. Are the cooling fans running?	—	Go to Step 32	Go to Step 4
4	1. Command Fan 1 ON using the scan tool output tests function. 2. Observe the cooling fans. Are both cooling fans running at low speed?	—	Go to Step 5	Go to Step 8
5	1. Command Fan 2 ON using the scan tool output tests function. 2. Wait 3 seconds. 3. Observe the cooling fans Are both fans running at high speed?	—	Go to Step 6	Go to Step 58
6	**Important:** Ambient temperature must be above 9°C (48°F). 1. Exit scan tool output tests. 2. Engine running. 3. Turn the A/C ON. Are the cooling fans ON?	—	Go to Diagnostic Aids	Go to Step 7
7	View A/C Request on the scan tool. Does A/C Request on the scan tool display Yes?	—	Go to Step 77	Go to PCM Controlled A/C Circuit Diagnosis
8	Is either cooling fan running?	—	Go to Step 9	Go to Step 16
9	Is the left cooling fan running?	—	Go to Step 10	Go to Step 14

GC1089900425010X

Fig. 140 Cooling fan diagnosis (Part 1 of 8). 1998 Intrigue

Step	Action	Value(s)	Yes	No
10	1. Turn the ignition switch to the OFF position. 2. Disconnect the right engine cooling fan. 3. Turn the ignition switch to the ON position. 4. Command Fan 1 ON using the scan tool output tests function. 5. Observe the cooling fans. Is the left engine cooling fan running?	—	Go to Step 11	Go to Step 80
11	Remove the engine Cool Fan 2 from the Underhood Electrical Center. Is the left engine cooling fan running?	—	Go to Step 12	Go to Step 13
12	Locate and repair short to ground in CKT 532. Is action complete?	—	Go to Step 81	—
13	1. Check CKT 409 for a short to ground. 2. If a problem is found, repair as necessary and replace Cool Fan 3 maxifuse. Was a problem found?	—	Go to Step 81	Go to Step 76
14	1. Turn the ignition switch to the OFF position. 2. Disconnect the left engine cooling fan. 3. Turn the ignition switch to the ON position. 4. Command Fan 1 On using the scan tool output tests function. 5. Observe the cooling fans. Is the right engine cooling fan running?	—	Go to Step 15	Go to Step 71
15	Locate and repair the following circuit condition(s): 1. Short to battery positive in circuit 532 or circuit 504. 2. Coolant fan #2 shorted. 3. Defective engine coolant fan diode Is action complete?	—	Go to Step 81	—
16	1. Ignition On, engine not running. 2. Remove the Cool Fan 1 Relay from the Underhood Electrical Center. 3. Probe cooling fan relay cavity 30 with a test light connected to ground. Is the test light On?	—	Go to Step 18	Go to Step 17
17	Locate and repair the open in the Cool Fan 1 relay battery positive feed to cavity 30. Is action complete?	—	Go to Step 81	—
18	Probe Cool Fan 1 relay cavity 85 with a test light connected to ground. Is the test light On?	—	Go to Step 20	Go to Step 19
19	Locate and repair open in the battery positive feed to cavity 85 in the Cool Fan 1 relay connector. Is action complete?	—	Go to Step 81	—

GC1089900425020X

Fig. 140 Cooling fan diagnosis (Part 2 of 8). 1998 Intrigue

Step	Action	Value(s)	Yes	No
20	1. Turn the ignition switch to the OFF position. 2. Disconnect both cooling fans. 3. Connect terminals A and B together at both cooling fan connectors using fused jumpers. 4. Turn the ignition switch to the ON position. 5. Connect a test light between Cool Fan 1 relay cavities 87 and 30. Is the test light ON?	—	Go to Step 21	Go to Step 27
21	1. Connect a test light between Cool Fan 1 relay cavities 85 and 86. 2. Turn the ignition switch to the ON position. 3. Command Fan 1 ON using the scan tool output tests function. 4. Observe the test light. Is the test light ON?	—	Go to Step 22	Go to Step 25
22	1. Turn the ignition switch to the OFF position 2. Remove the jumpers from the engine cooling fan connectors and reconnect the cooling fans. 3. Install a fused jumper between Cool Fan 1 relay cavities 87 and 30. 4. Turn the ignition switch to the ON position. 5. Observe the cooling fans. Are both cooling fans running?	—	Go to Step 23	Go to Step 24
23	1. Check for poor Cool Fan 1 relay connections at the Underhood Electrical Center. 2. If a problem is found, repair as necessary. Was a problem found?	—	Go to Step 81	Go to Step 37
24	1. Check for poor connections at the coolant fan motors. 2. If a problem is found, repair as necessary. Was a problem found?	—	Go to Step 81	Go to Step 63
25	1. Turn the ignition switch to the OFF position. 2. Disconnect the PCM blue connector C1. 3. Install a fused jumper between Cool Fan 1 relay cavities 30 and 86. 4. Turn the ignition switch to the ON position. 5. Probe Low Speed Fans control circuit at the PCM harness connector with a test light to ground. Is the test light ON?	—	Go to Step 77	Go to Step 26
26	Locate and repair open in the Low Speed Fans control circuit between the PCM and Cool Fan 1 relay cavity 86. Is action complete?	—	Go to Step 81	—
27	1. Turn the ignition switch to the OFF position. 2. Remove the jumpers from the cooling fan connectors. 3. Reconnect the cooling fans. 4. Install a fused jumper between Cool Fan 1 relay cavities 87 and 30. 5. Remove the Cool Fan 2 from the Underhood Electrical Center. 6. Probe Cool Fan 2 cavity 30 with a test light connected to ground. Is the test light On?	—	Go to Step 28	Go to Step 31

GC1089900425030X

Fig. 140 Cooling fan diagnosis (Part 3 of 8). 1998 Intrigue

Step	Action	Value(s)	Yes	No
28	Connect a test light between Cool Fan 2 cavities 30 and 87A in the Underhood Electrical Center. Is the test light ON?	—	Go to Step 30	Go to Step 29
29	1. Check for an open in CKT 409 between Cool Fan 2 cavity 87A and Engine Coolant Fan Motor #2 terminal B. 2. If a problem is found, repair as necessary. Was a problem found?	—	Go to Step 81	Go to Step 57
30	1. Check for a poor connection at Cool Fan 2 cavities 30 or 87A in the Underhood Relay Center. 2. If a problem is found, repair as necessary. Was a problem found?	—	Go to Step 81	Go to Step 76
31	1. Check for an open in CKT 504 between Cool Fan 1 relay cavity 87 and left engine cooling fan harness connector terminal B. 2. If a problem is found, repair as necessary. Was a problem found?	—	Go to Step 81	Go to Step 56
32	Using scan tool, view A/C Request. Does the scan tool display Yes?	—	PCM Controlled A/C Circuit	Go to Step 33
33	Are both cooling fans running at low speed?	—	Go to Step 34	Go to Step 40
34	Remove Cool Fan 1 relay from the Underhood Relay Center. Are the cooling fans running?	—	Go to Step 35	Go to Step 36
35	Locate and repair short to voltage in CKT 504. Is action complete?	—	Go to Step 81	—
36	Using a test light connected to battery positive voltage, probe Cool Fan 1 relay cavity 86. Is the test light On?	—	Go to Step 38	Go to Step 37
37	Replace Cool Fan 1 relay. Is action complete?	—	Go to Step 81	—
38	1. Turn the ignition switch to the OFF position 2. Disconnect the blue PCM connector. 3. Probe Cool Fan 1 relay cavity 86 with a test light connected to battery positive voltage. Is the test light On?	—	Go to Step 39	Go to Step 77
39	Locate and repair short to ground in the Low Speed Fans control circuit. Is action complete?	—	Go to Step 81	—
40	Are both cooling fans running at high speed?	—	Go to Step 41	Go to Step 42
41	View A/C Pressure on the scan tool. Does the scan tool display voltage less than the specified value?	1.5V	Go to Step 77	Go to Step 44
42	1. Turn the ignition switch to the OFF position. 2. Disconnect the PCM. 3. Turn the ignition switch to the ON position. 4. Observe the cooling fans. Is the right engine cooling fan running at high speed?	—	Go to Step 43	Go to Step 77

GC1089900425040X

Fig. 140 Cooling fan diagnosis (Part 4 of 8). 1998 Intrigue

Step	Action	Value(s)	Yes	No
43	1. Check for a short to ground in the High Speed Fans control circuit. 2. If a problem is found, repair as necessary. Was a problem found?	—	Go to Step 81	Go to Step 52
44	1. Turn the ignition switch to the OFF position. 2. Disconnect the A/C refrigerant pressure sensor electrical connector. 3. Turn the ignition switch to the ON position. 4. View A/C Pressure on the scan tool. Does the scan tool display voltage near the specified value?	0V	Go to Step 46	Go to Step 45
45	Probe the A/C refrigerant pressure signal circuit with a *J 39200* Does the digital multimeter display voltage near the specified value?	0V	Go to Step 77	Go to Step 51
46	Probe the A/C refrigerant pressure sensor ground with a test light to battery positive voltage. Is the test light on?	—	Go to Step 47	Go to Step 49
47	Probe the A/C refrigerant pressure sensor 5 volt reference B circuit with a *J 39200* Does the digital multimeter display voltage near the specified value?	5V	Go to Step 48	Go to Step 50
48	Replace the A/C refrigerant pressure sensor. Is action complete?	—	Go to Step 81	—
49	Locate and repair open or short to voltage in the A/C refrigerant pressure sensor ground circuit. Is action complete?	—	Go to Step 81	—
50	Locate and repair open or short to ground in the A/C refrigerant pressure sensor 5 volt reference B circuit. Is action complete?	—	Go to Step 81	—
51	Locate and repair short to voltage in the A/C refrigerant pressure signal circuit. Is action complete?	—	Go to Step 81	—
52	1. Remove the Cool Fan 3 relay from the Underhood Electrical Center. 2. Observe the cooling fans. Is the right engine cooling fan running at high speed?	—	Go to Step 53	Go to Step 70
53	Remove the Cool Fan 2 from the Underhood Electrical Center. Is the right engine cooling fan running at high speed?	—	Go to Step 54	Go to Step 55
54	Locate and repair short to battery positive voltage in CKT 409. Is action complete?	—	Go to Step 81	—
55	Locate and repair short to battery positive voltage in CKT 532. Is action complete?	—	Go to Step 81	—
56	1. Check for an open in CKT 532 between Cool Fan 2 cavity 30 and left engine cooling fan terminal A. 2. If a problem is found, repair as necessary. Was a problem found?	—	Go to Step 81	Go to Step 79

GC1089900425050X

Fig. 140 Cooling fan diagnosis (Part 5 of 8). 1998 Intrigue

Step	Action	Value(s)	Yes	No
57	1. Check for an open in CKT 1050 between right engine cooling fan terminal A and ground. 2. If a problem is found, repair as necessary. Was a problem found?	—	Go to Step 81	Go to Step 80
58	1. Ignition ON, engine not running. 2. Remove the Cool Fan 3 relay from the Underhood Electrical Center. 3. Install a test light between Cool Fan 3 relay cavity 86 and battery positive voltage. 4. Command High speed fans on using the scan tool output controls function. 5. Wait approx. 5-6 seconds. 6. Observe the test light. Is the test light on?	—	Go to Step 61	Go to Step 59
59	1. Remove the Cool Fan 2 from the Underhood Electrical Center. 2. Install a test light between Cool Fan 2 cavity 86 and battery positive voltage. 3. Command high speed fans on using the scan tool output controls function. 4. Wait 3 seconds. 5. Observe the test light. Is the test light ON?	—	Go to Step 78	Go to Step 60
60	1. Turn the ignition switch to the OFF position. 2. Disconnect the PCM. 3. Turn the ignition switch to the ON position. 4. Check the High Speed Fans control circuit for an open or a short to voltage. 5. If a problem is found, repair as necessary. Was a problem found?	—	Go to Step 81	Go to Step 77
61	1. Turn the ignition switch to the OFF position 2. Reinstall the Cool Fan 3 relay. 3. Disconnect both coolant fan electrical connectors. 4. Turn the ignition switch to the ON position. 5. Command Fan 2 on using the scan tool output controls function. 6. Wait approx. 3 seconds. 7. Probe terminal B at the right engine cooling fan connector with a test light to ground. Is the test light on?	—	Go to Step 62	Go to Step 64
62	Probe terminal A at the left engine cooling fan connector with a test light to battery positive voltage. Is the test light on?	—	Go to Step 63	Go to Step 71
63	1. Identify cause of inoperative cooling fan: • Open right engine cooling fan motor windings. • Open left engine cooling fan motor windings. • Stalled cooling fan(s). 2. Replace the affected cooling fan motor. Is action complete?	—	Go to Step 81	—

GC1089900425060X

Fig. 140 Cooling fan diagnosis (Part 6 of 8). 1998 Intrigue

Step	Action	Value(s)	Yes	No
64	1. Remove the Cool Fan 3 relay from the Underhood Electrical Center. 2. Turn the ignition switch to the ON position. 3. Probe Cool Fan 3 relay cavity 85 with a test light connected to ground. Is the test light on?	—	Go to Step 66	Go to Step 65
65	1. Locate and repair the following circuit condition(s): • Open in the battery positive feed to the Cool and Cool Fan 3 relays. • Short to ground in the battery positive feed to the Cool and Cool Fan 3 relays Is action complete?	—	Go to Step 81	—
66	Probe Cool Fan 3 relay cavity 30 with a test light connected to ground. Is the test light on?	—	Go to Step 68	Go to Step 67
67	Locate and repair open in battery positive voltage circuit to Cool Fan 3 relay cavity 30. Is action complete?	—	Go to Step 81	—
68	1. Check Engine Coolant Fan Motor #2 circuit for an open between right engine cooling fan terminal B and Cool Fan 3 relay cavity 87. 2. If a problem is found, repair as necessary. Was a problem found?	—	Go to Step 81	Go to Step 69
69	1. Check for a poor Cool Fan 3 relay terminal connections at the Underhood Electrical Center. 2. If a problem is found, repair as necessary. Was a problem found?	—	Go to Step 81	Go to Step 70
70	Replace Cool Fan 3 relay. Is action complete?	—	Go to Step 81	—
71	1. Remove the Cool Fan 2 from the Underhood Electrical Center. 2. Turn the ignition switch to the ON position. 3. Probe Cool Fan 2 cavity 85 with a test light connected to ground. Is the test light on?	—	Go to Step 73	Go to Step 72
72	Locate and repair open in battery positive voltage circuit to Cool Fan 2 cavity 85. Is action complete?	—	Go to Step 81	—
73	Probe Cool Fan 2 cavity 87 in the Underhood Electrical Center with a test light to battery positive voltage. Is the test light on?	—	Go to Step 75	Go to Step 74
74	Locate and repair open in circuit between Cool Fan 2 cavity 87 in the Underhood Electrical Center and ground. Is action complete?	—	Go to Step 81	—
75	1. Check for poor Cool Fan 2 engine terminal connections at the Underhood Electrical Center. 2. If a problem is found, repair as necessary. Was a problem found?	—	Go to Step 81	Go to Step 76

GC1089900425070X

Fig. 140 Cooling fan diagnosis (Part 7 of 8). 1998 Intrigue

Step	Action	Value(s)	Yes	No
76	Replace the Cool Fan 2 in the Underhood Electrical Center. Is action complete?	—	Go to Step 81	—
77	Replace the PCM. **Important:** The replacement PCM must be programmed. Is action complete?	—	Go to Step 81	—
78	Repair open in the Cool Fan 3 Relay control circuit. Is action complete?	—	Go to Step 81	—
79	Replace the left engine cooling fan motor. Is action complete?	—	Go to Step 81	—
80	Replace the right engine cooling fan motor. Is action complete?	—	Go to Step 81	—
81	1. Engine coolant below 100°C (212°F). 2. A/C OFF. 3. Engine running. Observe the cooling fans. Are the cooling fans running?	—	Go to Step 32	Go to Step 82
82	1. Command Fan 1 ON using the scan tool output tests function. 2. Observe the cooling fans. Are both cooling fans running at low speed?	—	Go to Step 83	Go to Step 8
83	1. Command High speed fans on using the scan tool output tests function. 2. Wait 6 seconds. 3. Observe the cooling fans. Are both cooling fans running at high speed?	—	System OK	Go to Step 58

GC1089900425080X

Fig. 140 Cooling fan diagnosis (Part 8 of 8). 1998 Intrigue

Step	Action	Value(s)	Yes	No
1	Did you perform the Powertrain On–Board Diagnostic (OBD) System Check?	—	Go to Step 2	Go to A Powertrain On Board Diagnostic (OBD) System Check
2	1. Ensure the engine coolant temperature is between the specified values. 2. Turn the HVAC controls to Off. 3. Start the engine and allow the engine to idle. 4. Using the scan tool command the following in sequence: all fans Off, Fans Low Speed On, Fans High Speed On, all fans Off. Allow approximately 25 seconds in each state. Did either fan relay driver DTC set?	5°C - 100°C (41°F - 212°F)	Go to the appropriate DTC tables	Go to Step 3
3	With the engine idling, turn the A/C on to maximum cooling. Have any other DTCs failed this ignition?	—	Go to the appropriate DTC tables	Go to Step 4
4	1. Turn the A/C off. 2. Turn the engine off. Turn the ignition on. 3. Ensure the engine coolant temperature is less than the specified value. 4. Observe the fan operation while individually commanding Fans Low Speed On, then Fans High Speed On, then all fans Off. • With Fans Low Speed commanded On both fans should operate at low speed. • With Fans High Speed commanded On both fans should operate at high speed. • With all fans commanded Off both fans should not operate, unless the PCM detects a fault or a high temperature condition. Do both cooling fans operate as commanded?	100°C (212°F)	System OK	Go to Step 5
5	Does either cooling fan operate when all fans are commanded Off?	—	Go to Diagnostic Aids	Go to Step 6
6	Does only cooling fan 1 (right) operate with Fans Low Speed commanded On, then both fans operate when Fans High Speed is commanded On?	—	Go to Step 7	Go to Step 8
7	Repair a short to ground in CKT 532. Is the repair complete?	—	Go to Step 4	—
8	Does neither cooling fan operate with Fans Low Speed commanded On, and then only cooling fan 2 (left) operate with Fans High Speed commanded On?	—	Go to Cooling Fan Symptom Table 1	Go to Step 9
9	Does neither cooling fan operate with Fans Low Speed commanded On, and then only cooling fan 1 (right) operate with Fans High Speed commanded On?	—	Go to Cooling Fan Symptom Table 2	Go to Step 10
10	Do both cooling fans operate with Fans Low Speed commanded On, and then only cooling fan 2 (left) operate with Fans High Speed commanded On?	—	Go to Cooling Fan Symptom Table 3	Go to Step 11
11	Do both cooling fans operate with Fans Low Speed commanded On, and then only cooling fan 1 (right) operate with Fans High Speed commanded On?	—	Go to Cooling Fan Symptom Table 4	Go to Step 12

GC1080000585010X

Fig. 141 Cooling fan system check (Part 1 of 2). 1999–2000 Intrigue

Step	Action	Value(s)	Yes	No
DEFINITION: No low speed operation of either cooling fan. High speed operation of cooling fan 2 (left) only. No DTCs are set.				
1	Did you perform the Cooling Fan System Check?	—	Go to Step 2	Go to the Cooling Fan System Check.
2	1. Disconnect cooling fan 1 (right). 2. Command Fans Low Speed On using the scan tool. 3. Using a digital multimeter (DMM), measure the voltage to ground on the harness side of terminal B of the cooling fan 1 connector. Is the voltage near the specified value?	B+	Go to Step 3	Go to Step 5
3	Jumper terminals A and B of the cooling fan 1 connector together. Does cooling fan 2 operate?	—	Go to Step 7	Go to Step 4
4	1. With the cooling fan 1 connector still jumpered, remove relay 2. 2. Measure the voltage to ground at CKT 532 of relay 2. Is the voltage near the specified value?	B+	Go to Step 9	Go to Step 8
5	1. Command all fans Off using the scan tool. 2. Remove relay 1. 3. Measure the voltage to ground at CKT 342 of relay 1. Is the voltage near the specified value?	B+	Go to Step 6	Go to Step 10
6	1. Jumper CKT 342 and CKT 504 of fan relay 1 together. 2. Measure the voltage to ground at terminal B of the cooling fan 1 connector. Is the voltage near the specified value?	B+	Go to Step 11	Go to Step 12
7	Replace cooling fan 1 (right). Is the action complete?	—	Go to the Cooling Fan System Check	—
8	Repair the open in CKT 504 between cooling fan 1 and the fan relay 1. Is the action complete?	—	Go to the Cooling Fan System Check	—
9	Replace fan relay 2. Is the action complete?	—	Go to the Cooling Fan System Check	—
10	Repair the open in CKT 342 between fan relay 1 and the splice. Is the action complete?	—	Go to the Cooling Fan System Check	—
11	Replace fan relay 1. Is the action complete?	—	Go to the Cooling Fan System Check	—
12	Repair the open in CKT 532 between fan relay 2 and cooling fan 1. Is the action complete?	—	Go to the Cooling Fan System Check	—

GC1080000586000X

Fig. 142 Cooling fan symptom table 1. 1999–2000 Intrigue

Step	Action	Value(s)	Yes	No
12	Does neither cooling fan operate with Fans Low Speed commanded On, then both fans operate when Fans High Speed is commanded On?	—	Go to Cooling Fan Symptom Table 5	Go to Step 13
13	Does neither cooling fan operate when Fans Low Speed or Fans High Speed is commanded On?	—	Go to Step 14	Go to Diagnostic Aids
14	Repair the open ground circuit between G117 and the splice. Is the action complete?	—	Go to Step 4	—

GC1080000585020X

Fig. 141 Cooling fan system check (Part 2 of 2). 1999–2000 Intrigue

Step	Action	Value(s)	Yes	No
DEFINITION: No low speed operation of either cooling fan. High speed operation of cooling fan 1 (right) only. No DTCs are set.				
1	Did you perform the Cooling Fan System Check?	—	Go to Step 2	Go to the Cooling Fan System Check.
2	1. Disconnect the cooling fan 2 (left). 2. Jumper terminals A and B of the harness connector for cooling fan 2 (left) together. 3. Command Fans Low Speed On using the scan tool. Does cooling fan 1 (right) operate?	—	Go to Step 4	Go to Step 3
3	1. Using a digital multimeter (DMM), measure the voltage to ground at connector terminal B (harness side) of cooling fan 2. 2. Command Fans Low Speed On using the scan tool. Is the voltage near the specified value?	B+	Go to Step 5	Go to Step 6
4	Replace cooling fan 2 (left). Is the action complete?	—	Go to the Cooling Fan System Check	—
5	Repair the open in the ground circuit of cooling fan 2 (left). Is the action complete?	—	Go to the Cooling Fan System Check	—
6	Repair the open in CKT 409 between cooling fan 2 (left) and fan relay 2. Is the action complete?	—	Go to the Cooling Fan System Check	—

GC1080000587000X

Fig. 143 Cooling fan symptom table 2. 1999–2000 Intrigue

Step	Action	Value(s)	Yes	No
DEFINITION: Low speed operation of both fans. High speed operation of cooling fan 2 (left) only. No DTCs are set.				
1	Did you perform the Cooling Fan System Check?	—	Go to Step 2	Go to the Cooling Fan System Check
2	1. Remove fan relay 2. 2. Command High Speed Fans On using the scan tool. 3. Using a digital multimeter (DMM) measure the voltage to ground in CKT 1442 at fan relay 2. Is the voltage near the specified value?	B+	Go to Step 3	Go to Step 5
3	1. Remove fan relay 3. 2. Measure the resistance of CKT 473 between fan relay 2 and fan relay 3. Is the resistance less than or equal to the specified value?	5 ohms	Go to Step 4	Go to Step 6
4	1. Reconnect fan relay 3. 2. Jumper CKT 532 and CKT 1050 of fan relay 2 together. 3. Command Fans High Speed On using the scan tool. Do both cooling fans operate?	—	Go to Step 8	Go to Step 7
5	Repair the open in CKT 1442 between fan relay 2 and the splice. Is the action complete?	—	Go to the Cooling Fan System Check	—
6	Repair the open in CKT 473 between fan relay 2 and the splice. Is the action complete?	—	Go to the Cooling Fan System Check	—
7	Repair the open in the ground circuit between fan relay 2 and the splice. Is the action complete?	—	Go to the Cooling Fan System Check	—
8	Replace fan relay 2. Is the action complete?	—	Go to the Cooling Fan System Check	—

GC1080000588000X

Fig. 144 Cooling fan symptom table 3. 1999–2000 Intrigue

Step	Action	Value(s)	Yes	No
DEFINITION: Low speed operation of both fans. High speed operation of cooling fan 1 (right) only. No DTCs are set.				
1	Did you perform the Cooling Fan System Check?	—	*Go to Step 2*	*Go to the Cooling Fan System Check*
2	1. Remove fan relay 3. 2. Using a digital multimeter (DMM), measure the voltage to ground at CKT 1442 (2 CKTs) of the fan relay 3. Is the voltage near the specified value on both circuits?	B+	*Go to Step 3*	*Go to Step 5*
3	1. Remove fan relay 2. 2. Measure the resistance of CKT 473 between fan relay 3 and fan relay 2. Is the resistance less than or equal to the specified value?	5 ohms	*Go to Step 4*	*Go to Step 6*
4	Jumper CKT 1442 and CKT 409 of fan relay 3 together. Does cooling fan 2 (left) operate?	—	*Go to Step 8*	*Go to Step 7*
5	Repair the affected leg of CKT 1442 between fan relay 3 and the splice. Is the action complete?	—	*Go to the Cooling Fan System Check*	—
6	Repair the open in CKT 473 between fan relay 3 and the splice. Is the action complete?	—	*Go to the Cooling Fan System Check*	—
7	Repair the open in CKT 409 between fan relay 3 and the splice. Is the action complete?	—	*Go to the Cooling Fan System Check*	—
8	Replace fan relay 3. Is the action complete?	—	*Go to the Cooling Fan System Check*	—

GC1080000589000X

Fig. 145 Cooling fan symptom table 4. 1999–2000 Intrigue

Step	Action	Yes	No
1	Install a scan tool. Does the scan tool power up?	Go to *Step 2*	*Diagnose* Data Link Communications
2	1. Turn ON the ignition, with the engine OFF. 2. Attempt to establish communication with the following control modules: • Instrument Cluster • Powertrain Control Module Does the scan tool communicate with the control modules?	Go to *Step 3*	*Diagnose* Data Link Communications
3	Select the powertrain control module display DTCs function on the scan tool. Does the scan tool display any DTCs?	Go to *Step 4*	*Diagnose Engine Cooling*
4	Does the scan tool display any DTCs which begin with a "U"?	*Diagnose* Data Link Communications	*Diagnose Trouble Code*

GC1080100669000X

Fig. 147 Diagnostic system check. 2001-02 Intrigue

Step	Action	Yes	No
DEFINITION: One or both engine cooling fan motors run continuously in high or low speed.			
1	Did you perform the Engine Cooling Diagnostic System Check?	Go to *Step 2*	*Diagnose Engine Cooling*
2	Turn ON the ignition, with the engine OFF. Are one or both cooling fans ON?	Go to *Step 3*	*Test For Intermittent and Poor Connections*
3	Are both cooling fans running continuously?	Go to *Step 5*	Go to *Step 4*
4	Remove the cooling fan S/P relay. Did the left cooling fan turn OFF?	Go to *Step 6*	Go to *Step 7*
5	Repair the short to voltage in the right cooling fan motor supply voltage circuit. Did you complete the repair?	Go to *Step 8*	—
6	Repair the short to voltage in the right cooling fan low reference circuit. Did you complete the repair?	Go to *Step 8*	—
7	Repair the short to voltage in the left cooling fan motor supply voltage circuit. Did you complete the repair?	Go to *Step 8*	—
8	Operate the system in order to verify the repair. Did you correct the condition?	System OK	Go to *Step 2*

GC1080100670000X

Fig. 148 Cooling fan always on. 2001-02 Intrigue

Step	Action	Value(s)	Yes	No
DEFINITION: No low speed operation of either cooling fan. High speed operation of both fans. No DTCs are set.				
1	Did you perform the Cooling Fan System Check?	—	*Go to Step 2*	*Go to the Cooling Fan System Check*
2	Verify that fan relay 2 is the correct part. Fan relay 2 is a 5 pin relay. Four pin relays like fan relay 1 and relay 3 will plug in to the connector. However, the system will have this symptom. Was a problem found?	—	*Go to Step 4*	*Go to Step 3*
3	1. Remove fan relay 2. 2. Jumper CKT 532 to CKT 409 in the relay connector. 3. Command Fans Low Speed On with the scan tool. Do both fans now operate at low speed?	—	*Go to Step 5*	*Go to Step 6*
4	Replace fan relay 2 with the correct relay. Is the action complete?	—	*Go to the Cooling Fan System Check*	—
5	Replace fan relay 2. Is the action complete?	—	*Go to the Cooling Fan System Check*	—
6	Repair CKT 409 between fan relay 2 and the splice. Is the action complete?	—	*Go to the Cooling Fan System Check*	—

GC1080000590000X

Fig. 146 Cooling fan symptom table 5. 1999–2000 Intrigue

Step	Action	Yes	No
DEFINITION: One or both engine cooling fan motors do not operate properly in high or low speed modes.			
1	Did you perform the Engine Cooling Diagnostic System Check?	Go to *Step 2*	*Diagnose Engine Cooling*
2	1. Install a scan tool. 2. Turn ON the ignition, with the engine OFF. 3. With a scan tool, command the Fans Low Speed ON and OFF. Do the low speed engine cooling fans turn ON and OFF with each command?	Go to *Step 3*	Go to *Step 4*
3	**Important:** A 3-second delay occurs before the PCM changes the colling fan speed. With a scan tool, command the Fans High Speed ON and OFF. Do the high speed engine cooling fans turn ON and OFF with each command?	*Test for Intermittent and Poor Connections*	Go to *Step 11*
4	**Important:** Do NOT remove the 20-A fused jumper wire connected during this step. Use a second 20-A fused jumper wire while performing the following steps. 1. Remove the cooling fan 1 relay. 2. Connect a 20-A fused jumper between the battery positive voltage circuit of the cooling fan 1 relay and the cooling fan motor supply voltage circuit of the cooling fan 1 relay. Do both cooling fans operate in low speed?	Go to *Step 13*	Go to *Step 5*
5	1. Disconnect the cooling fan S/P relay 2. Connect the second 20-A fused jumper between the right cooling fan low reference circuit of the cooling fan S/P relay and the left cooling fan motor supply voltage circuit of the cooling fan S/P relay. Do both cooling fans operate in low speed?	Go to *Step 14*	Go to *Step 6*
6	Connect the second 20-A fused jumper between the battery positive voltage circuit of the cooling fan S/P relay and the cooling fan motor supply voltage circuit of the cooling fan S/P relay. Does the left cooling fan operate in high speed?	Go to *Step 9*	Go to *Step 7*
7	1. Install the cooling fan S/P relay. 2. Disconnect the left cooling fan electrical connector. 3. Connect the second 20-Amp fused jumper wire from the cooling fan motor supply voltage circuit of the left cooling fan electrical connector to the cooling fan ground circuit of the left cooling fan electrical connector. Does the right cooling fan operate in high speed?	Go to *Step 16*	Go to *Step 8*
8	Connect the second 20-Amp fused jumper wire from the cooling fan motor supply voltage circuit of the left cooling fan electrical connector to a good ground. Does the right cooling fan operate in high speed?	Go to *Step 20*	Go to *Step 21*
9	1. Install the cooling fan S/P relay. 2. Disconnect the right cooling fan electrical connector. 3. Connect the second 20-Amp fused jumper wire from the motor supply voltage circuit of the right cooling fan electrical connector to the low reference circuit of the right cooling fan electrical connector. Does the left cooling fan operate in high speed?	Go to *Step 17*	Go to *Step 10*
10	Connect the second 20-Amp fused jumper wire from battery positive voltage to the right cooling fan low reference circuit of the of the right cooling fan electrical connector. Does the left cooling fan operate in high speed?	Go to *Step 18*	Go to *Step 22*
11	Is the left cooling fan operating properly in high speed?	Go to *Step 12*	Go to *Step 15*

GC1080100671010X

Fig. 149 Cooling fan inoperative (Part 1 of 2). 2001-02 Intrigue

Step	Action	Yes	No
12	1. Disconnect the cooling fan S/P relay 2. Connect the second 20-A fused jumper between the right cooling fan low reference circuit of the cooling fan S/P relay and the ground circuit of the cooling fan S/P relay. Does the right cooling fan operate properly in high speed?	Go to *Step 14*	Go to *Step 19*
13	Inspect for poor connections at the cooling fan 1 relay. Did you find and correct the condition?	Go to *Step 28*	Go to *Step 23*
14	Inspect for poor connections at the cooling fan S/P relay. Did you find and correct the condition?	Go to *Step 28*	Go to *Step 24*
15	Inspect for poor connections at the cooling fan 2 relay. Did you find and correct the condition?	Go to *Step 28*	Go to *Step 25*
16	Inspect for poor connections at the harness connector of the left cooling fan. Did you find and correct the condition?	Go to *Step 28*	Go to *Step 26*
17	Inspect for poor connections at the harness connector of the right cooling fan. Did you find and correct the condition?	Go to *Step 28*	Go to *Step 27*
18	Repair the right cooling fan motor supply voltage circuit. Did you complete the repair?	Go to *Step 28*	—
19	Repair the right cooling fan ground circuit. Did you complete the repair?	Go to *Step 28*	—
20	Repair the left cooling fan ground circuit. Did you complete the repair?	Go to *Step 28*	—
21	Repair the left cooling fan motor supply voltage circuit. Did you complete the repair?	Go to *Step 28*	—
22	Repair the right cooling fan low reference circuit. Did you complete the repair?	Go to *Step 28*	—
23	Replace the cooling fan 1 relay. Is the repair complete?	Go to *Step 28*	—
24	Replace the cooling fan S/P relay. Is the repair complete?	Go to *Step 28*	—
25	Replace the cooling fan 2 relay. Is the repair complete?	Go to *Step 28*	—
26	Replace the left cooling fan. Is the repair complete?	Go to *Step 28*	—
27	Replace the right cooling fan. Is the repair complete?	Go to *Step 28*	—
28	Operate the system in order to verify the repair. Did you correct the condition?	System OK	Go to *Step 3*

GC1080100671020X

Fig. 149 Cooling fan inoperative (Part 2 of 2). 2001-02 Intrigue

Step	Action	Value(s)	Yes	No
3	Does the cooling fan turn OFF when the ECT drops below the specified value?	92.5°C (199°F)	***"Inspect ECT and ECT wiring."***	*Go to Step 4*
4	1. Check that the ECT is below the specified value. 2. Disconnect the cooling fan relay. Is the cooling fan OFF?	92.5°C (199°F)	*Go to Step 5*	*Go to Step 6*
5	Probe the cooling fan relay connector cavity 2 with a test lamp connected to B+. Did the test lamp illuminate?	—	*Go to Step 7*	*Go to Step 17*
6	Repair the short to voltage in the power feed circuit between the cooling fan relay and the cooling fan motor Is the action complete?	—	*Go to Step 20*	—
7	1. Check for a short to ground in the cooling fan relay control circuit between the PCM and the cooling fan relay. 2. Repair as necessary. Was a repair necessary?	—	*Go to Step 20*	*Go to Step 18*
8	1. Start the engine. 2. Check that the ECT is above the specified value. 3. Disconnect the cooling fan relay. 4. Probe the cooling fan relay connector cavity 2 with a test lamp connected to B+. Did the test lamp illuminate?	97.5°C (208°F)	*Go to Step 9*	*Go to Step 12*
9	Probe the cooling fan relay connector cavity 1 with a test lamp to ground. Did the test lamp illuminate?	—	*Go to Step 10*	*Go to Step 15*
10	Probe the cooling fan relay connector cavity 4 with a test lamp to ground. Did the test lamp illuminate?	—	*Go to Step 11*	*Go to Step 16*
11	Connect a fused jumper wire between the cooling fan relay connector cavities 3 and 4. Is the cooling fan motor ON?	—	*Go to Step 17*	*Go to Step 13*
12	1. Check for a open in the cooling fan relay control circuit between the PCM and the cooling fan relay. 2. Repair as necessary. Was a repair necessary?	—	*Go to Step 20*	*Go to Step 18*
13	1. Check for a open in the power feed circuit between the cooling fan relay and the cooling fan motor. 2. Repair as necessary. Was a repair necessary?	—	*Go to Step 20*	*Go to Step 14*
14	1. Check for an open or a faulty connection in the ground circuit between the cooling fan motor and **ground.** 2. Repair as necessary. Was a repair necessary?	—	*Go to Step 20*	*Go to Step 19*

GC1089800359020X

Fig. 150 Cooling fan diagnosis (Part 2 of 3). Metro

Step	Action	Value(s)	Yes	No
1	Did you perform the Powertrain On-Board Diagnostic System Check?	—	*Go to Step 2*	Go to *Powertrain OBD System Check*
2	1. Start engine and obtain operating temperature. 2. Turn OFF all the accessories. 3. Install a scan tool. 4. Observe the ECT sensor parameter on the scan tool. Does the cooling fan turn ON when ECT reaches above the specified value?	97.5°C (208°F)	*Go to Step 3*	*Go to Step 8*

GC1089800359010X

Fig. 150 Cooling fan diagnosis (Part 1 of 3). Metro

Step	Action	Value(s)	Yes	No
15	Repair the open in the ignition feed circuit between the cooling fan relay terminal 1 and the junction block. Is the action complete?	—	*Go to Step 20*	—
16	Repair the open in the battery feed circuit between the cooling fan relay terminal 4 and the fuse box. Is the action complete?	—	*Go to Step 20*	—
17	Replace the cooling fan relay. Is the action complete?	—	*Go to Step 20*	—
18	Replace the PCM. Is the action complete?	—	*Go to Step 20*	—
19	Replace the cooling fan motor. Is the action complete?	—	*Go to Step 20*	—
20	1. Clear the scan tool information and road test the vehicle within the Freeze Frame conditions that set the DTC. 2. Review the scan tool data and check for DTCs. The repair is complete if no DTCs are stored. Are any DTCs displayed on the scan tool?	—	Go to the Applicable DTC Table	System OK

GC1089800359030X

Fig. 150 Cooling fan diagnosis (Part 3 of 3). Metro

Step	Action	Value(s)	Yes	No
1	Did you perform the Powertrain On-Board Diagnostic (OBD) System Check?	—	*Go to Step 2*	Go to *A Powertrain On Board Diagnostic (OBD) System Check*
2	Are any DTCs set?	—	Go to applicable DTC Table	*Go to Step 3*
3	1. Install a scan tool. 2. Engine coolant temperature must be below the specified value for all the fan diagnoses. 3. Turn ON the ignition, with the engine and A/C OFF. Are the cooling fans OFF?	100°C (212°F)	*Go to Step 4*	Go to Cooling Fan table #1
4	With a scan tool, command the low speed cooling fan relay ON. Are both cooling fans ON?	—	*Go to Step 5*	Go to Cooling Fan table #2
5	With a scan tool, command the high speed cooling fan relay ON. Do both cooling fans switch to high speed?	—	*Go to Step 6*	Go to Cooling Fan table #3
6	1. With a scan tool, exit outputs. 2. Idle the engine leaving the A/C OFF. Are the cooling fans ON?	—	*Go to Step 8*	*Go to Step 7*
7	Turn ON the A/C. Are the cooling fans ON?	—	System OK	*Go to Step 9*

GC1080000611010X

Fig. 151 Cooling fan functional check (Part 1 of 2). 1998-2000 Park Avenue

Step	Action	Value(s)	Yes	No
8	Does the scan tool display A/C request as YES?	—	Go to *A Diagnostic System Check* for further diagnosis of the A/C system.	*Go to Step 10*
9	Does the scan tool display A/C request as YES?	—	Go to *A Diagnostic System Check* for further diagnosis of the A/C Refrigerant Pressure Sensor	Go to *A Diagnostic System Check* for further diagnosis of the A/C system.
10	**Important:** Program the replacement PCM. Replace the PCM. Is the action complete?	—	System OK	—

GC1080000611020X

Fig. 151 Cooling fan functional check (Part 2 of 2). 1998-2000 Park Avenue

Step	Action	Value(s)	Yes	No
1	Did you perform the Cooling Fan Functional Check?	—	*Go to Step 2*	Go to Cooling Fan Functional Check
2	Disconnect the low speed fan relay. Are both fans OFF?	—	*Go to Step 8*	*Go to Step 3*
3	Disconnect series/parallel fan relay. Are both fans OFF?	—	*Go to Step 4*	*Go to Step 10*
4	1. Disconnect the left fan. 2. Probe the fan feed terminal of the left fan connector using a *J 34142-B* test lamp that is connected to a good ground. Does the test light illuminate?	—	*Go to Step 11*	*Go to Step 5*
5	Probe the series/parallel relay switch feed terminal at the left fan connector using a test lamp that is connected to a good ground. Does the test light illuminate?	—	*Go to Step 12*	*Go to Step 6*
6	Probe the series/parallel cooling fan relay control circuit at the series/parallel cooling fan relay connector using a test lamp that is connected to B+. Does the test lamp illuminate?	—	*Go to Step 7*	*Go to Step 13*
7	1. Turn OFF the ignition. 2. Leave the test lamp installed. 3. Disconnect the PCM. 4. Turn ON the ignition, with the engine OFF. Is the test lamp still illuminated?	—	*Go to Step 14*	*Go to Step 16*
8	Probe the low speed cooling fan relay control circuit at the low speed cooling fan relay connector using the test lamp that is connected to B+. Does the test lamp illuminate?	—	*Go to Step 9*	*Go to Step 13*
9	1. Turn OFF the ignition. 2. Leave the test lamp installed. 3. Disconnect the PCM. 4. Turn ON the ignition, with the engine OFF. Is the test lamp still illuminated?	—	*Go to Step 14*	*Go to Step 16*

GC1080000612010X

Fig. 152 Cooling fan table 1 (Part 1 of 2). 1998-2000 Park Avenue

Step	Action	Value(s)	Yes	No
10	Repair the RH fan feed circuit for a short to voltage. Did you find and correct the condition?	—	Go to Cooling Fan Functional Check	*Go to Step 15*
11	Repair the LH fan feed circuit for a short to voltage. Is the action complete?	—	Go to Cooling Fan Functional Check	—
12	Repair the short to voltage in the series/parallel relay switch feed circuit. Is the action complete?	—	Go to Cooling Fan Functional Check	—
13	Replace the low speed cooling fan relay. Is the action complete?	—	Go to Cooling Fan Functional Check	—
14	Repair the high speed cooling fan relay control circuit or the low speed cooling fan relay control circuit for a short to ground. Is the action complete?	—	Go to Cooling Fan Functional Check	—
15	Replace the high speed cooling fan relay. Is the action complete?	—	Go to Cooling Fan Functional Check	—
16	**Important:** Program the replacement PCM. Replace the PCM. Is the action complete?	—	Go to Cooling Fan Functional Check	—

GC1080000612020X

Fig. 152 Cooling fan table 1 (Part 2 of 2). 1998-2000 Park Avenue

Step	Action	Value(s)	Yes	No
1	Did you perform the Cooling Fan Functional Check?	—	*Go to Step 2*	Go to Cooling Fan Functional Check
2	Did either fan turn ON when the low speed cooling fan relay was commanded ON?	—	*Go to Step 3*	*Go to Step 5*
3	1. Install a scan tool. 2. With a scan tool, command the low speed cooling fan relay ON. Did the other fan turn OFF?	—	*Go to Step 19*	*Go to Step 4*
4	Disconnect the high speed cooling fan relay. Did the fan turn OFF?	—	*Go to Step 20*	*Go to Step 21*
5	1. With a scan tool, command the low speed cooling fan relay ON. 2. Disconnect the low speed cooling fan relay. 3. Probe the low speed cooling relay control circuit at the e low speed cooling fan relay connector using a *J 34142-B* test lamp that is connected to B+. Does the test lamp illuminate?	—	*Go to Step 6*	*Go to Step 13*
6	Probe both feed circuits at the low speed cooling fan relay connector using a test lamp that is connected to ground. Does test lamp illuminate for both circuits?	—	*Go to Step 7*	*Go to Step 22*
7	**Important:** Leave jumper in place for remainder of this table. Connect a fused jumper wire between the switch feed circuit and the LH fan feed circuit at the low speed cooling fan relay connector. Do both fans turn ON?	—	*Go to Step 23*	*Go to Step 8*

GC1080000613010X

Fig. 153 Cooling fan table 2 (Part 1 of 3). 1998-2000 Park Avenue

Step	Action	Value(s)	Yes	No
8	1. Disconnect the left fan. 2. Probe left fan feed circuit at the fan harness connector terminal with a test lamp that is connected to a good ground. Does the test lamp illuminate?	—	*Go to Step 9*	*Go to Step 24*
9	Connect a second fused jumper wire between the left fan harness connector terminals. Is the right fan ON?	—	*Go to Step 16*	*Go to Step 10*
10	1. Reconnect the left fan. 2. Disconnect the Series/Parallel fan relay. 3. Probe the switch feed circuit at the series/parallel fan relay connector using a test lamp that is connected to a good ground. Does the test lamp illuminate?	—	*Go to Step 11*	*Go to Step 25*
11	Using the second jumper wire, jumper the switch ignition feed circuit and the RH fan feed circuit together at the series/parallel relay connector. Do the fans come ON?	—	*Go to Step 26*	*Go to Step 12*
12	1. Reconnect the series/parallel fan relay. 2. Disconnect the right fan. 3. Probe the fan feed circuit at the fan harness connector terminal with a test lamp that is connected to a good ground. Is the left fan ON?	—	*Go to Step 16*	*Go to Step 18*
13	1. Test lamp still connected. 2. Turn OFF the ignition. 3. Disconnect the PCM. 4. Probe the low speed cooling fan relay control circuit at the PCM connector, with a fused jumper wire that is connected to a good ground. Is the test lamp ON?	—	*Go to Step 20*	*Go to Step 21*
14	Inspect the PCM connections. Repair faulty connections as necessary. Did you find a problem and correct it?	—	Go to Cooling Fan Functional Check	*Go to Step 27*
15	Repair the low speed fan relay control circuit for an open or short to B+. Is the action complete?	—	Go to Cooling Fan Functional Check	—
16	Inspect the fan motor ground circuit for an open or the fan motor connections and repair as necessary. Did you find and correct the condition?	—	Go to Cooling Fan Functional Check	*Go to Step 17*
17	Replace the fan motor. Is the action complete?	—	Go to Cooling Fan Functional Check	—
18	Repair the RH fan feed circuit for an open. Is the action complete?	—	Go to Cooling Fan Functional Check	—
19	Replace the fan which was not operating. Is the action complete?	—	Go to Cooling Fan Functional Check	—

GC1080000613020X

Fig. 153 Cooling fan table 2 (Part 2 of 3). 1998-2000 Park Avenue

Step	Action	Value(s)	Yes	No
20	Replace the high speed fan relay. Is the action complete?	—	Go to Cooling Fan Functional Check	—
21	Repair the series/parallel fan relay switch feed circuit for a short to ground. Did you find and correct the condition?	—	Go to Cooling Fan Functional Check	Go to Step 26
22	Repair the open or the grounded circuit for the circuit that did not light. Is the action complete?	—	Go to Cooling Fan Functional Check	—
23	Replace the low speed fan relay. Is the action complete?	—	Go to Cooling Fan Functional Check	—
24	Repair the LH fan feed circuit for an open. Is the action complete?	—	Go to Cooling Fan Functional Check	—
25	Repair the series/parallel relay switch feed circuit for an open. Is the action complete?	—	Go to Cooling Fan Functional Check	—
26	Replace the series/parallel fan relay. Is the action complete?	—	Go to Cooling Fan Functional Check	—
27	**Important:** Program the replacement PCM. Replace the PCM. Is the action complete?	—	Go to Cooling Fan Functional Check	—

GC1080000613030X

Fig. 153 Cooling fan table 2 (Part 3 of 3). 1998-2000 Park Avenue

Step	Action	Value(s)	Yes	No
7	Jumper the switch ignition feed circuit and the RH fan feed circuit together at the high speed fan relay connector. Is the right fan ON?	—	Go to Step 15	Go to Step 16
8	1. Turn OFF the ignition. 2. Disconnect the PCM. 3. Disconnect low speed fan relay. 4. Jumper the switch feed circuit and the LH fan feed circuit together at the low speed fan relay connector. 5. Turn ON the ignition, with the engine OFF. 6. Probe the PCM harness connector for the high speed cooling fan relay control circuit with a fused jumper that is connected to a good ground. Do the fans switch from low to high speed?	—	Go to Step 22	Go to Step 17
9	1. Disconnect the series/parallel fan relay. 2. Probe the high speed fan relay control circuit at the series/parallel fan relay connector using a test lamp that is connected to B+. 3. Command the high speed cooling fan relay ON using a scan tool. Does the test lamp illuminate?	—	Go to Step 10	Go to Step 18
10	Probe the ground circuit at the series/parallel fan relay connector using a test lamp that is connected to B+. Does the test lamp illuminate?	—	Go to Step 11	Go to Step 19
11	Probe the coil feed circuit at the series /parallel relay connector using a test lamp that is connected to a good ground. Does the test lamp illuminate?	—	Go to Step 20	Go to Step 21
12	Repair the high speed fan relay control circuit for an open between the high speed fan relay and the splice. Is the action complete?	—	Go to Cooling Fan Functional Check	—
13	Repair the open in the high speed fan relay coil feed circuit. Is the action complete?	—	Go to Cooling Fan Functional Check	—
14	Repair the open in the high speed fan relay switch feed circuit. Is the action complete?	—	Go to Cooling Fan Functional Check	—
15	Replace the high speed fan relay. Is the action complete?	—	Go to Cooling Fan Functional Check	—
16	Repair the open in the RH fan feed circuit between the high speed fan relay and the splice. Is the action complete?	—	Go to Cooling Fan Functional Check	—
17	Repair the high speed fan relay control circuit for an open or for a short to B+. Is the action complete?	—	Go to Cooling Fan Functional Check	—
18	Repair the open in the high speed fan relay control circuit between the series/parallel fan relay and the splice. Is the action complete?	—	Go to Cooling Fan Functional Check	—
19	Repair the open in the ground circuit. Is the action complete?	—	Go to Cooling Fan Functional Check	—

GC1080000614020X

Fig. 154 Cooling fan table 3 (Part 2 of 3). 1998-2000 Park Avenue

Step	Action	Value(s)	Yes	No
1	Did you perform the Cooling Fan Functional Check?	—	Go to Step 2	Go to Cooling Fan Functional Check
2	1. With a scan tool, command the low speed cooling fan relay ON. 2. Command the high speed cooling fan relay ON while observing the fans. Did both fans operate with no change?	—	Go to Step 8	Go to Step 3
3	Did the left fan stop operating?	—	Go to Step 9	Go to Step 4
4	1. Disconnect the high speed fan relay. 2. Probe the high speed fan relay control circuit at the high speed fan relay connector using a *J 34142-B* test lamp that is connected to B+. 3. Command high speed cooling fan relay ON using a scan tool. Does the test lamp illuminate after several seconds?	—	Go to Step 5	Go to Step 12
5	Probe the coil feed circuit at the high speed fan relay connector location using a test lamp that is connected to a good ground. Does the test lamp illuminate?	—	Go to Step 6	Go to Step 13
6	Probe the switch feed circuit at the high speed fan relay connector using a test lamp that is connected to a good ground. Does the test lamp illuminate?	—	Go to Step 7	Go to Step 14

GC1080000614010X

Fig. 154 Cooling fan table 3 (Part 1 of 3). 1998-2000 Park Avenue

Step	Action	Value(s)	Yes	No
20	Replace the series/parallel fan relay. Is the action complete?	—	Go to Cooling Fan Functional Check	—
21	Repair the open in series/parallel fan relay coil feed circuit. Is the action complete?	—	Go to Cooling Fan Functional Check	—
22	1. Inspect the PCM connections. 2. Repair faulty connections as necessary. Did you find and correct the condition?	—	Go to Cooling Fan Functional Check	Go to Step 23
23	**Important:** Program the replacement PCM. Replace the PCM. Is the action complete?	—	Go to Cooling Fan Functional Check	—

GC1080000614030X

Fig. 154 Cooling fan table 3 (Part 3 of 3). 1998-2000 Park Avenue

Step	Action	Yes	No
1	Install a scan tool. Does the scan tool power up?	Go to *Step 2*	*Diagnose* Data Link Communications
2	1. Turn ON the ignition, with the engine OFF. 2. Attempt to establish communication with the following control modules: • Instrument Cluster • Powertrain Control Module Does the scan tool communicate with the control modules?	Go to *Step 3*	*Diagnose* Data Link Communications
3	Select the powertrain control module display DTCs function on the scan tool. Does the scan tool display any DTCs?	Go to *Step 4*	*Diagnose* Go to *Symptoms - Engine Cooling*
4	Does the scan tool display any DTCs which begin with a "U"?	*Diagnose* Data Link Communications	*Diagnose Trouble Code*

GC1080100672000X

Fig. 155 Diagnostic system check. 2001-02 Park Avenue

Step	Action	Yes	No
DEFINITION: One or both engine cooling fan motors run continuously in high or low speed.			
1	Did you perform the Engine Cooling Diagnostic System Check?	Go to *Step 2*	*Diagnose Engine Cooling*
2	**Important:** The cooling fan 1 relay and cooling fan 2 relay are improperly identified in the underhood fuse block. Turn ON the ignition, with the engine OFF. Are one or both cooling fans ON?	Go to *Step 3*	*Test for Intermittent and Poor Connections*
3	Are both cooling fans running continuously?	Go to *Step 5*	Go to *Step 4*
4	Remove the cooling fan S/P relay. Did the right cooling fan turn OFF?	Go to *Step 6*	Go to *Step 7*
5	Repair the short to voltage in the left cooling fan motor supply voltage circuit. Did you complete the repair?	Go to *Step 8*	—
6	Repair the short to voltage in the left cooling fan low reference circuit. Did you complete the repair?	Go to *Step 8*	—
7	Repair the short to voltage in the right cooling fan motor supply voltage circuit. Did you complete the repair?	Go to *Step 8*	—
8	Operate the system in order to verify the repair. Did you correct the condition?	System OK	Go to *Step 2*

GC1080100673000X

Fig. 156 Cooling fan always on. 2001-02 Park Avenue

Step	Action	Yes	No
DEFINITION: One or both engine cooling fan motors do not operate properly in high or low speed modes.			
1	Did you perform the Engine Cooling Diagnostic System Check?	Go to *Step 2*	*Engine Cooling*
2	**Important:** The cooling fan 1 relay and cooling fan 2 relay are improperly identified in the underhood fuse block. Refer to *Engine Cooling Schematics* for proper identification. 1. Install a scan tool. 2. Turn ON the ignition, with the engine OFF. 3. With a scan tool, command the Fans Low Speed ON and OFF. Do the low speed engine cooling fans turn ON and OFF with each command?	Go to *Step 3*	Go to *Step 4*
3	**Important:** The cooling fans will remain in low speed operation for 3 seconds before the PCM grounds the high speed fan relay control to turn on the high speed fans. With a scan tool, command the Fans High Speed ON and OFF. Do the high speed engine cooling fans turn ON and OFF with each command?	*Test for Intermittent and Poor Connections*	Go to *Step 13*
4	1. Turn the ignition OFF. 2. Disconnect the cooling fan 1 relay. 3. Turn the ignition ON, with the engine OFF. 4. Probe the battery positive voltage circuit of the cool fan 1 relay switch side with a test lamp connected to a good ground. Does the test lamp illuminate?	Go to *Step 5*	Go to *Step 20*
5	**Important:** Following this step, do not remove the 20–A fused jumper wire that is connected during this step. While performing the following steps, use a second 20–A fused jumper wire. Connect a 20-A fused jumper between the battery positive voltage circuit of the cooling fan 1 relay and the cooling fan motor supply voltage circuit of the cooling fan 1 relay. Do both cooling fans operate in low speed?	Go to *Step 15*	Go to *Step 6*
6	1. Disconnect the cooling fan S/P relay. 2. Connect the second 20-A fused jumper between the cooling fan low reference circuit of the cooling fan S/P relay and the right cooling fan motor supply voltage circuit of the cooling fan S/P relay. Do both cooling fans operate in low speed?	Go to *Step 16*	Go to *Step 7*
7	Connect the second 20-A fused jumper between the battery positive voltage circuit of the cooling fan S/P relay and the cooling fan motor supply voltage circuit of the cooling fan S/P relay. Does the right cooling fan operate in high speed?	Go to *Step 11*	Go to *Step 8*
8	1. Turn the ignition OFF. 2. Install the cooling fan S/P relay. 3. Disconnect the right cooling fan electrical connector. 4. Turn the ignition ON, with the engine OFF. Does the left cooling fan operate in high speed?	Go to *Step 24*	Go to *Step 9*
9	Connect the second 20-A fused jumper wire from the cooling fan motor supply voltage circuit of the right cooling fan electrical connector to the ground circuit of the right cooling fan electrical connector. Does the left cooling fan operate in high speed?	Go to *Step 18*	Go to *Step 10*

GC1080100674010X

Fig. 157 Cooling fan inoperative (Part 1 of 3). 2001-02 Park Avenue

Step	Action	Yes	No
10	Connect the second 20-A fused jumper wire from the cooling fan motor supply voltage circuit of the right cooling fan electrical connector to a good ground. Does the left cooling fan operate in high speed?	Go to *Step 23*	Go to *Step 24*
11	1. Install the cooling fan S/P relay. 2. Disconnect the left cooling fan electrical connector. 3. Connect the second 20-A fused jumper wire from the cooling fan motor supply voltage circuit of the left cooling fan electrical connector to the cooling fan low reference circuit of the left cooling fan electrical connector. Does the right cooling fan operate in high speed?	Go to *Step 19*	Go to *Step 12*
12	Connect the second 20-A fused jumper wire from battery positive voltage to the cooling fan low reference circuit of the of the left cooling fan electrical connector. Does the right cooling fan operate in high speed?	Go to *Step 21*	Go to *Step 25*
13	Is the right cooling fan operating properly in high speed?	Go to *Step 14*	Go to *Step 17*
14	1. Disconnect the cooling fan S/P relay 2. Connect the second 20-A fused jumper between the cooling fan low reference circuit of the cooling fan S/P relay and the ground circuit of the cooling fan S/P relay. Does the left cooling fan operate in high speed?	Go to *Step 16*	Go to *Step 22*
15	Inspect for poor connections at the cooling fan 1 relay. Did you find and correct the condition?	Go to *Step 31*	Go to *Step 26*
16	Inspect for poor connections at the cooling fan S/P relay. Did you find and correct the condition?	Go to *Step 31*	Go to *Step 27*
17	Inspect for poor connections at the cooling fan 2 relay. Did you find and correct the condition?	Go to *Step 31*	Go to *Step 28*
18	Inspect for poor connections at the harness connector of the right cooling fan. Did you find and correct the condition?	Go to *Step 31*	Go to *Step 29*
19	Inspect for poor connections at the harness connector of the left cooling fan. Did you find and correct the condition?	Go to *Step 31*	Go to *Step 30*
20	Repair the battery positive voltage circuit of the cool fan 1 relay switch side. Did you complete the repair?	Go to *Step 31*	—
21	Repair the left cooling fan motor supply voltage circuit. Did you complete the repair?	Go to *Step 31*	—
22	Repair the left cooling fan ground circuit. Did you complete the repair?	Go to *Step 31*	—
23	Repair the right cooling fan motor ground circuit. Did you complete the repair?	Go to *Step 31*	—

GC1080100674020X

Fig. 157 Cooling fan inoperative (Part 2 of 3). 2001-02 Park Avenue

Step	Action	Yes	No
24	Repair the right cooling fan motor supply voltage circuit. Did you complete the repair?	Go to *Step 31*	—
25	Repair the left cooling fan low reference circuit. Did you complete the repair?	Go to *Step 31*	—
26	Replace the cooling fan 1 relay. Did you complete the repair?	Go to *Step 31*	—
27	Replace the cooling fan S/P relay. Did you complete the repair?	Go to *Step 31*	—
28	Replace the cooling fan 2 relay. Did you complete the repair?	Go to *Step 31*	—
29	Replace the right cooling fan. Did you complete the repair?	Go to *Step 31*	—
30	Replace the left cooling fan. Did you complete the repair?	Go to *Step 31*	—
31	Operate the system in order to verify the repair. Did you correct the condition?	System OK	Go to *Step 2*

GC1080100674030X

Fig. 157 Cooling fan inoperative (Part 3 of 3). 2001-02 Park Avenue

Step	Action	Normal Result(s)	Abnormal Result(s)*
1	• Start and run the engine until the engine coolant temperature reaches 93°C (199°F) • For vehicles with air conditioning refer to the following in HVAC Systems with A/C-Manual: • HVAC System Check • HVAC Blower Controls Schematic • HVAC Compressor/Condenser Fan Controls Schematics	• The main radiator fan motor and the auxiliary radiator fan motor (with A/C only) run at full speed. • The main radiator fan motor and the auxiliary radiator fan motor stop running when the engine coolant temperature drops below 83° C (181° F)	• Cooling Fan Inoperative - Electric • Cooling Fan Inoperative - Auxiliary
2	1 Run the engine until the engine coolant temperature reaches 93°C (199°F) 2 Turn the blower speed selector switch to any position except OFF. 3 Press the A/C switch to ON	• The main radiator fan motor and the auxiliary radiator fan motor run at half speed. • Once the engine coolant temperature reaches 93°C (199°F), the main radiator fan motor and the auxiliary radiator fan motor run at full speed. • If the A/C system pressure exceeds 1520 kPa (220 psi) at the A/C refrigerant pressure switch, the main radiator fan motor and the auxiliary radiator fan motor will run at full speed.	Cooling Fan Inoperative at Low Speed - Electric
3	Press the A/C switch to OFF	The main radiator fan motor and the auxiliary radiator fan motor stop running once the engine coolant temperature drops below 83°C (181°F).	Cooling Fan Runs Continuously - Auxiliary
* Refer to the appropriate symptom diagnostic table for the applicable abnormal result.			

GC1089900396000X

Fig. 158 Cooling fan system check. 1998–99 Prizm

Step	Action	Value(s)	Yes	No
1	Was the Cooling Fan System Check performed?		Go to Step 2	Go to Cooling Fan System Check
2	1 Run the engine until operating temperature is reached and the thermostat opens. 2 Stop the engine. 3 Disconnect the auxiliary fan motor connector. 4 Connect a test lamp across the auxiliary fan motor connector. 5 Start the engine. Does the test lamp light?		Go to Step 3	Go to Step 4
3	Replace the auxiliary fan motor. Is the repair complete?		Go to Cooling Fan System Check	
4	Test for battery positive at the auxiliary radiator fan motor connector terminal 2. Is battery voltage present?	B+	Go to Step 8	Go to Step 5
5	Inspect the CDS fuse in fuse and relay block 2 for an open. Is the fuse open ?		Go to Step 6	Go to Step 7
6	Repair the short to ground in the BLU/RED wire between the CDS fuse and the auxiliary radiator fan motor connector terminal 2. Is the repair complete?		Go to Cooling Fan System Check	
7	Repair the open in the BLU wire between the CDS fuse and fuse and relay block 1 OR in the BLU/RED wire between the CDS fuse and the auxiliary fan motor connector terminal 2. Is the repair complete?		Go to Cooling Fan System Check	
8	1 Remove the A/C fan no. 2 relay from fuse and relay block 2. 2 Test for an open between the auxiliary fan motor connector terminal 1 and the A/C fan no. 2 relay cavity 3. 3 Test for an open between the A/C fan no. 2 relay cavity 4 and G104. Was an open found?		Go to Step 10	Go to Step 9
9	Replace the fan no. 2 relay. Is the repair complete?		Go to Cooling Fan System Check	
10	Repair the open. Is the repair complete?		Go to Cooling Fan System Check	

GC1089900397000X

Fig. 159 Auxiliary cooling fan inoperative. 1998–99 Prizm

Step	Action	Value(s)	Yes	No
1	Was the Cooling Fan System Check performed?		Go to Step 2	Go to Cooling Fan System Check
2	1 Run the engine until operating temperature is reached and the thermostat opens. 2 Stop the engine. 3 Disconnect the main fan motor connector. 4 Connect a test lamp across the main fan motor connector. 5 Start the engine. Does the test lamp light?		Go to Step 3	Go to Step 4
3	Replace the main fan motor. Is the repair complete?		Go to Cooling Fan System Check	
4	Test for an open in the WHT/BLK wire between the main fan motor terminal 1 and G103. Was an open found?		Go to Step 17	Go to Step 5
5	Test for an open in the BLK/RED wire between the main fan motor terminal 2 and the fan no. 1 relay terminal 23. Was an open found?		Go to Step 6	Go to Step 7
6	1 Test for an open in the BLK/RED wire between the main fan motor terminal 2 and connector 3 terminal 1 of fuse and relay block 1. 2 Test for an open between connector 3 terminal 1 of fuse and relay block 1 and terminal 23 of the fan no. 1 relay. Is the BLK/RED wire open?		Go to Step 17	Go to Step 14
7	Test for battery voltage at the fan no. 1 relay terminal 22 with the engine running. Is battery voltage present?	B+	Go to Step 15	Go to Step 8
8	Test for an open between terminal 22 of the fan no. 1 relay and terminal 14 of the engine main relay in fuse and relay block 1. Was an open found?		Go to Step 14	Go to Step 9
9	Test for battery voltage at the ENGINE MAIN relay terminal 16 with the engine running. Is battery voltage present?	B+	Go to Step 11	Go to Step 10
10	Test for an open in the BLK/YEL wire between fuse and relay block 1 and fuse and relay block 2 OR in the BLK/YEL wire between fuse and relay block 1 and junction block 2. Was an open found?		Go to Step 17	Go to Step 14

GC1089900398010X

Fig. 160 Main cooling fan inoperative (Part 1 of 2). 1998–99 Prizm

Step	Action	Value(s)	Yes	No
11	Test for battery voltage at terminal 13 of the ENGINE MAIN relay with the engine running. Is battery voltage present?	B+	Go to Step 13	Go to Step 12
12	Test for an open in the WHT wire to connector 4 terminal 2 of fuse and relay block 1. Was an open found?		Go to Step 17	Go to Step 14
13	Test for an open in the WHT/BLK wire between fuse and relay block 1 and G103. Was an open found?		Go to Step 17	Go to Step 16
14	Replace fuse and relay block 1. Is the repair complete?		Go to Cooling Fan System Check	
15	Replace the fan no. 1 relay. Is the repair complete?		Go to Cooling Fan System Check	
16	Replace the engine main relay. Is the repair complete?		Go to Cooling Fan System Check	
17	Repair the open. Is the repair complete?		Go to Cooling Fan System Check	

GC1089900398020X

Fig. 160 Main cooling fan inoperative (Part 2 of 2). 1998–99 Prizm

Step	Action	Value(s)	Yes	No
1	Was the Cooling Fan System Check performed?		Go to Step 2	Go to Cooling Fan System Check
2	1 Start the engine. 2 Move the blower speed selector switch to any position except OFF. Does the blower motor run?		Go to Step 3	HVAC System Check
3	Press the A/C switch to the ON position. Does the A/C compressor clutch engage?		Go to Step 4	HVAC Compressor Clutch Does Not Engage

GC1089900399010X

Fig. 161 Main cooling fan inoperative at low speed (Part 1 of 3). 1998–99 Prizm

Step	Action	Value(s)	Yes	No
4	1 Turn the ignition switch to LOCK. 2 Remove the A/C fan no. 3 relay from fuse and relay block 2. 3 Start the engine. 4 Turn the blower speed selector switch to any position except OFF. 5 Measure the voltage between the A/C fan no. 3 relay cavity 1 and ground. Is the value within the specified range?	B+	Go to Step 6	Go to Step 5
5	Repair the open in the BLK/WHT wire between the A/C fan no. 3 relay cavity 1 and the A/C MG relay cavity 3 in fuse and relay block 2. Is the repair complete?		Go to Cooling Fan System Check	
6	Test for an open in the WHT/BLK between the A/C fan no. 3 relay cavity 2 and G103. Was an open found?		Go to Step 9	Go to Step 7
7	Test for an open in the WHT/RED wire between the A/C fan no. 3 relay cavity 3 and the A/C fan no. 2 relay cavity 5. Was an open found?		Go to Step 9	Go to Step 8
8	Test for an open in the WHT wire between the A/C fan no. 3 relay cavity 5 and fuse and relay block 1. Was an open found?		Go to Step 9	Go to Step 10
9	Repair the open. Is the repair complete?		Go to Cooling Fan System Check	

GC1089900399020X

Fig. 161 Main cooling fan inoperative at low speed (Part 2 of 3). 1998–99 Prizm

Step	Action	Value(s)	Yes	No
10	Replace the A/C fan no. 3 relay. Is the repair complete?		Go to Cooling Fan System Check	

GC1089900399030X

Fig. 161 Main cooling fan inoperative at low speed (Part 3 of 3). 1998–99 Prizm

Step	Action	Value(s)	Yes	No
DEFINITION: The main radiator fan motor and/or the auxiliary radiator fan motor runs continuously with the ignition switch in the RUN position.				
1	Was the Cooling Fan System Check performed?		Go to Step 2	Go to the Cooling Fan System Check
2	Are both fans running continuously?		Go to Step 12	Go to Step 3
3	Is only the main radiator fan motor running continuously?		Go to Step 8	Go to Step 4
4	Is only the auxiliary radiator fan motor running continuously?		Go to Step 5	Go to Step 1
5	1 Ensure that the engine coolant temperature is below 93°C (199°F) 2 Remove the A/C fan no. 2 relay from fuse and relay block 2. 3 Start the engine. 4 Turn the A/C off. Does the auxiliary radiator fan motor run?		Go to Step 6	Go to Step 7
6	Repair the short to ground in the WHT wire between the auxiliary radiator fan motor terminal 1 and fuse and relay block 2. Is the repair complete?		Go to the Cooling Fan System Check	
7	Replace the A/C fan no. 2 relay. Is the repair complete?		Go to the Cooling Fan System Check	
8	1 Ensure that the engine coolant temperature is below 93°C (199°F) 2 Remove the fan no. 1 relay from fuse and relay block 1. 3 Start the engine. 4 Turn the A/C off. Does the main radiator fan motor run?		Go to Step 9	Go to Step 10
9	Repair the short to voltage in the BLK/RED wire between the main radiator fan motor terminal 2 and fuse relay block 1. Is the repair complete?		Go to the Cooling Fan System Check	
10	Test for an open in the BLU/BLK wire between the fan no. 1 relay in fuse and relay block 1 and the A/C fan no. 2 relay in fuse and relay block 2. Was an open found?		Go to Step 18	Go to Step 11
11	Replace the fan no. 1 relay. Is the repair complete?		Go to the Cooling Fan System Check	
12	1 Remove the A/C fan no. 3 relay from fuse and relay block 2. 2 Start the engine. 3 Turn the A/C off. Do both fan motors run?		Go to Step 16	Go to Step 13

GC1089900400010X

Fig. 162 Auxiliary cooling fan runs continuously (Part 1 of 2). 1998–99 Prizm

Step	Action	Value(s)	Yes	No
13	1 Test the A/C MG relay for continuity between terminals 3 and 5. 2 Test the A/C fan no. 3 relay for continuity between terminals 3 and 5. Does continuity exist in either relay?		Go to Step 14	Go to Step 15
14	Replace the faulty relay. Is the repair complete?		Go to the Cooling Fan System Check	
15	Repair the short to B+ in the BLK/WHT wire between the A/C fan no. 3 relay terminal 1 in fuse and relay block 2 and the A/C MG relay terminal 3 in fuse and relay block 2. Is the repair complete?		Go to the Cooling Fan System Check	
16	1 Test for an open in the BLU/BLK wire between the A/C fan no. 2 relay and the A/C refrigerant pressure switch connector. 2 Test for an open in the LT GRN wire between the A/C refrigerant pressure switch connector and the fan control switch. Was an open found?		Go to Step 18	Go to Step 17
17	1 Test for an open in the A/C refrigerant pressure switch, if equipped. 2 Test for an open in the A/C refrigerant pressure switch connector shorting clip, if equipped. Was an open found?		Go to Step 19	Go to Step 20
18	Repair the open/short. Is the repair complete?		Go to the Cooling Fan System Check	
19	1 Replace the A/C refrigerant pressure switch, if equipped. 2 Repair or replace the shorting bar, if equipped. Is the repair complete?		Go to the Cooling Fan System Check	
20	Replace the fan control switch. Is the repair complete?		Go to the Cooling Fan System Check	

GC1089900400020X

Fig. 162 Auxiliary cooling fan runs continuously (Part 2 of 2). 1998–99 Prizm

Reference Table

Symptom	Causes
Main fan always ON	• Faulty fan 1 relay • Open in the fan 1 relay coil ground circuit • Short to voltage in the main fan motor supply voltage circuit
Auxiliary fan always ON	• Faulty fan 2 relay • Short to ground in the auxiliary fan motor ground circuit
Both fans always ON	• Faulty fan 3 relay • Faulty A/C MG relay • Open in the fan 2 relay coil ground circuit • Short to voltage in the fan 3 relay coil supply voltage circuit • Engine coolant temperature (ECT) sensor or powertrain control module (PCM) malfunction

Step	Action	Yes	No
The main fan motor is mounted on the left side of the radiator/condenser assembly. The auxiliary fan motor is mounted on the right side of the radiator/condenser assembly. The fans run at low speed in series configuration when the A/C is operating and the engine coolant temperature (ECT) is below 83°C (181°F). The fans run at high speed in parallel configuration when the ECT is above 93°C (199°F). An open in the ground circuit of the A/C fan 1 and 2 relays will cause both fans to operate at high speed when the ECT is below 93°C (199°F). This table assumes that the main fan motor and/or the auxiliary fan motor runs continuously with the ignition switch in the RUN position and the ECT below 93°C (199°F).			
1	Did you review the *Cooling System* and perform the necessary inspections?	Go to *Step 2*	*Engine Cooling*
2	1. Ensure that the ECT is below 93°C (199°F) 2. Depress the A/C switch to the OFF position. 3. Turn the blower switch to the OFF position. 4. Turn the ignition switch to the RUN position. Is only the main fan motor running continuously?	Go to *Step 5*	Go to *Step 3*
3	Is only the auxiliary fan motor running continuously?	Go to *Step 9*	Go to *Step 4*
4	Are both fan motors running continuously?	Go to *Step 12*	Go to *Step 1*
5	Remove the fan 1 relay from fuse and relay block 1. Does the main fan motor run?	Go to *Step 6*	Go to *Step 7*
6	Repair the short to voltage in the main fan motor supply voltage circuit. Did you find and correct the condition?	Go to *Step 18*	—
7	Test the fan 1 relay control circuit for an open. Did you find and correct the condition?	Go to *Step 18*	Go to *Step 8*
8	Replace the fan 1 relay. Did you complete the replacement?	Go to *Step 18*	—
9	Remove the fan 2 relay from fuse and relay block 2. Does the auxiliary fan motor run?	Go to *Step 10*	Go to *Step 11*
10	Repair the short to ground in the circuit between the auxiliary fan motor and fuse and relay block 2. Did you find and correct the condition?	Go to *Step 18*	—
11	Replace the fan 2 relay. Did you complete the replacement?	Go to *Step 18*	—

GC1080100675010X

Fig. 163 Cooling fan always on (Part 1 of 2). 2000-02 Prizm

Problem	Causes
Both fans inoperative	• Open in the supply voltage circuit to the fan 1 and the engine main relays in fuse and relay block 1 • High resistance or poor connection in fuse and relay block 1 • Faulty engine main relay • Short to ground in the fan 1 or the fan 2 coil ground circuit • Engine coolant temperature (ECT) sensor or powertrain control module (PCM) malfunction
Main fan inoperative	• Faulty main fan motor • Faulty fan 1 relay • Open in the main fan circuit
Auxiliary fan inoperative	• Faulty auxiliary fan motor • Faulty fan 2 relay • Open in the auxiliary fan circuit
Both fans inoperative in low speed	• Faulty fan 2 relay • Faulty fan 3 relay • Open in the series portion of fan circuit

GC1080100676010X

Fig. 164 Main cooling fan inoperative (Part 1 of 2). 2001-02 Prizm

Step	Action	Yes	No
12	Remove the fan 3 relay from fuse and relay block 2. Do both fan motors run?	Go to *Step 13*	Go to *Step 15*
13	Test the fan 2 relay control circuit (including the A/C refrigerant pressure switch) for an open. Did you find and correct the condition?	Go to *Step 18*	Go to *Step 14*
14	1. Inspect the ECT sensor for incorrect performance or for an incorrect input to the PCM. 2. If the ECT sensor is operating correctly, replace the PCM. Did you find and correct the condition?	Go to *Step 18*	—
15	1. Test the A/C MG relay for continuity between terminals 3 and 5. 2. Test the fan 3 relay for continuity between terminals 3 and 5. Does continuity exist in either relay?	Go to *Step 16*	Go to *Step 17*
16	Replace the faulty relay. Did you complete the replacement?	Go to *Step 18*	—
17	Repair the short to voltage in the fan 3 relay coil supply voltage circuit. Did you find and correct the condition?	Go to *Step 18*	—
18	Operate the system in order to verify the repair. Did you correct the condition?	System OK	Go to *Step 3*

GC1080100675020X

Fig. 163 Cooling fan always on (Part 2 of 2). 2000-02 Prizm

Step	Action	Yes	No
The main fan motor is mounted on the left side of the radiator/condenser assembly. The fans run at low speed in series configuration when the A/C is operating and the engine coolant temperature (ECT) is below 83°C (181°F). The fans run at high speed in parallel configuration when the ECT is above 93°C (199°F). A short to ground in the coil ground circuit of the fan 1 and 2 relays will cause both fans to be inoperative once the ECT reaches 93°C (199°F). This table assumes that the auxiliary fan motor is functioning normally.			
1	Did you review the *Cooling System* and perform the necessary inspections?	Go to *Step 2*	*Diagnose Engine Cooling*
2	Run the engine until operating temperature is reached and the thermostat opens. Do the cooling fans operate?	*Test for Intermittent and Poor Connections*	Go to *Step 3*
3	Exchange the fan 1 relay with a known good relay (the fan 3 relay, the A/C MG relay, or the horn relay). Did you find and correct the condition?	Go to *Step 14*	Go to *Step 4*
4	1. Stop the engine. 2. Disconnect the main fan motor connector. 3. Connect a test lamp across the main fan motor connector. 4. Start the engine. Does the test lamp illuminate?	Go to *Step 12*	Go to *Step 5*
5	Test the main fan motor ground circuit for an open. Did you find and correct the condition?	Go to *Step 14*	Go to *Step 6*
6	Test the main fan motor supply voltage circuit for an open. Did you find and correct the condition?	Go to *Step 14*	Go to *Step 7*
7	Test the supply voltage circuit to fuse and relay block 1 for an open. This circuit supplies voltage to the coils of the fan 1 relay and the engine main relay. Did you find and correct the condition?	Go to *Step 14*	Go to *Step 8*
8	Test the fan 1 relay switch supply voltage circuit for an open. Did you find and correct the condition?	Go to *Step 14*	Go to *Step 9*
9	Test the engine main relay switch supply voltage circuit for an open. Did you find and correct the condition?	Go to *Step 14*	Go to *Step 10*
10	Test the engine main relay control circuit for an open. Did you find and correct the condition?	Go to *Step 14*	Go to *Step 11*
11	1. Remove fuse and relay block 1 from the inner fender. 2. Inspect the connectors in fuse and relay block 1 for poor connections and high resistance. Did you find and correct the condition?	Go to *Step 14*	—
12	Inspect for a poor connection at the harness connector of the main fan motor. Did you find and correct the condition?	Go to *Step 14*	Go to *Step 13*
13	Replace the main fan motor. Did you complete the replacement?	Go to *Step 14*	—
14	Operate the system in order to verify the repair. Did you correct the condition?	System OK	Go to *Step 3*

GC1080100676020X

Fig. 164 Main cooling fan inoperative (Part 2 of 2). 2001-02 Prizm

Step	Action	Yes	No
	The auxiliary fan motor is mounted on the right side of the radiator/condenser assembly. The fans run at low speed in series configuration when the A/C is operating and the engine coolant temperature (ECT) is below 83°C (181°F). The fans run at high speed in parallel configuration when the ECT is above 93°C (199°F). A short to ground in the ground circuit of the fan 1 and 2 relays will cause both fans to be inoperative once the ECT reaches 93°C (199°F). This table assumes that the main fan motor is functioning normally.		
1	Did you review the *Cooling System* and perform the necessary inspections?	Go to *Step 2*	Diagnose *Engine Cooling*
2	Run the engine until operating temperature is reached and the thermostat opens. Do the cooling fans operate?	*Test for Intermittent and Poor Connections*	Go to *Step 3*
3	1. Stop the engine. 2. Disconnect the auxiliary fan motor connector. 3. Connect a test lamp across the auxiliary fan motor connector. 4. Start the engine. Does the test lamp illuminate?	Go to *Step 7*	Go to *Step 4*
4	Test auxiliary fan motor supply voltage circuit for an open. Did you find and correct the condition?	Go to *Step 9*	Go to *Step 5*
5	1. Remove the fan 2 relay from fuse and relay block 2. 2. Test the circuit between the auxiliary fan motor and the fan 2 relay for an open. 3. Test the fan 2 relay ground circuit for an open. Did you find and correct the condition?	Go to *Step 9*	Go to *Step 6*
6	Replace the fan 2 relay. Did you complete the replacement?	Go to *Step 9*	—
7	Inspect for a poor connection at the harness connector of the auxiliary fan motor. Did you find and correct the condition?	Go to *Step 9*	Go to *Step 8*
8	Replace the auxiliary fan motor. Did you complete the replacement?	Go to *Step 9*	—
9	Operate the system in order to verify the repair. Did you correct the condition?	System OK	Go to *Step 3*

GC1080100677000X

Fig. 165 Auxiliary cooling fan inoperative. 2001-02 Prizm

Step	Action	Yes	No
	The main fan motor is mounted on the left side of the radiator/condenser assembly. The auxiliary fan motor is mounted on the right side of the radiator/condenser assembly. The fans run at low speed in series configuration when the A/C is operating and the engine coolant temperature (ECT) is below 83°C (181°F). The fans run at high speed in parallel configuration when the ECT is above 93°C (199°F). A short to ground in the ground circuit of the fan 1 and 2 relays will cause both fans to be inoperative once the ECT reaches 93°C (199°F). This table assumes that the parallel portion of the circuit and the A/C system are functioning normally. Therefore, the malfunction is in the series portion of the circuit.		
1	Did you review the *Cooling System* and perform the necessary inspections?	Go to *Step 2*	*Engine Cooling*
2	1. Connect a scan tool. The engine must be below operating temperature. 2. Move the blower speed switch to any position except OFF. 3. Depress the A/C switch to the ON position. 4. Use the scan tool to command the A/C compressor clutch (MG) relay ON. When the MG relay is energized the cooling fans will also turn on at low speed. Do the cooling fans operate at low speed?	*Test for Intermittent and Poor Connections*	Go to *Step 3*
3	Exchange the fan 3 relay with a known good relay (the fan 1 relay, the A/C MG relay or the horn relay). Do the cooling fans operate at low speed?	Go to *Step 8*	Go to *Step 4*
4	Test the fan 3 relay coil supply voltage circuit for an open. Did you find and correct the condition?	Go to *Step 9*	Go to *Step 5*
5	Test the fan 3 relay coil ground circuit for an open. Did you find and correct the condition?	Go to *Step 9*	Go to *Step 6*
6	Test the circuit between the fan 3 relay and the fan 2 relay for an open. Did you find and correct the condition?	Go to *Step 9*	Go to *Step 7*
7	Test the fan 3 relay switch supply voltage circuit for an open. Did you find and correct the condition?	Go to *Step 9*	—
8	Replace the fan 3 relay. Did you complete the replacement?	Go to *Step 9*	—
9	Operate the system in order to verify the repair. Did you correct the condition?	System OK	Go to *Step 3*

GC1080100678000X

Fig. 166 Cooling fan inoperative at low speed. 2001-02 Prizm

Circuit Description:

Power for the fan motors is supplied through the Cooling Fan fuse in the RH Maxi fuse block. The cooling fan relays are energized when current flows from the Clng Fan fuse in the IP fuse block through the relay coils to ground through the PCM. The cooling fan 1 control circuit is grounded for low speed fan operation. The cooling fan 1 and cooling fan 2 control circuits are grounded for high speed operation.

During low speed fan operation the PCM supplies a ground path for the low speed cooling fan relay #1. This closes the low speed relay contacts, allowing current to flow from the battery junction block through the relay contacts to the primary cooling fan. During low speed operation, the ground path for the primary cooling fan is through the series/parallel cooling fan relay and secondary cooling fan motor. The result is a series circuit with both fans running at low speed.

To command high speed cooling fan operation the PCM first supplies a ground path for the low speed cooling fan relay through the cooling fan 1 control circuit. After a 6 second delay, the PCM supplies a ground path for the high speed cooling fan relay #3 and the series/parallel cooling fan relay #2 through the cooling fan 2 control circuit. All 3 cooling fan relays are closed for high speed cooling fans operation. During high speed operation, both the primary and the secondary cooling fans are supplied current from the battery junction block and each fan has its own ground path.

Diagnostic Aids

Check for the following conditions:

- Poor connection at the PCM, cooling fan relays, or cooling fan motors. Inspect harness connectors for backed out terminals, improper mating, broken locks, improperly formed or damaged terminals, and poor terminal to wire connection.
- Damaged harness. Inspect the wiring harness for damage.

Test Description

Number(s) below refer to the step number(s) on the Diagnostic Table.

2. Stored diagnostic trouble codes may affect engine cooling fans operation. This diagnostic table may lead to improper diagnosis and replacement of good parts if diagnostic trouble codes are present.
6. Ambient temperature must be greater than 9°C (48°F) before the PCM will enable the cooling fans due to A/C request. The PCM will enable the cooling fans if A/C refrigerant pressure increases regardless of ambient temperature.
77. This vehicle is equipped with a PCM which utilizes an Electrically Erasable Programmable Read Only Memory (EEPROM). When the PCM is being replaced, the new PCM must be programmed.

Step	Action	Value(s)	Yes	No
1	Was the Powertrain On-Board Diagnostic (OBD) System Check performed?	—	*Go to Step 2*	Go to the *Powertrain OBD System Check*
2	Are any powertrain DTC(s) stored?	—	Diagnose the DTC(s) first.	*Go to Step 3*
3	1. Ensure that the engine coolant temperature is less than 100°C (212°F). 2. Turn the A/C OFF. 3. Engine running. 4. Observe the cooling fans. Are the cooling fan(s) running?	—	*Go to Step 32*	*Go to Step 4*
4	1. Command Fan 1 ON using the scan tool output tests function. 2. Observe the cooling fans. Are both cooling fans running at low speed?	—	*Go to Step 5*	*Go to Step 8*

GC1089600329010X

Fig. 167 Cooling fan diagnosis (Part 1 of 10). Riviera

Step	Action	Value(s)	Yes	No
5	1. Command Fan 2 ON using the scan tool output tests function. 2. Wait 6 seconds. 3. Observe the cooling fans. Are both fans running at high speed?	—	*Go to Step 6*	*Go to Step 58*
6	**Important:** Ambient temperature must be greater than 9°C (48°F). 1. Exit scan tool output tests. 2. Engine running. 3. Turn the A/C ON. Are the cooling fans running?	—	Refer to Diagnostic Aids	*Go to Step 7*
7	View A/C Request on the scan tool. Does A/C Request on the scan tool display Yes?	—	*Go to Step 77*	*PCM Controlled Air Conditioning Diagnosis*
8	Is either cooling fan running?	—	*Go to Step 9*	*Go to Step 16*
9	Is the primary cooling fan running?	—	*Go to Step 10*	*Go to Step 14*
10	1. Turn OFF the ignition switch. 2. Disconnect the secondary cooling fan. 3. Turn ON the ignition switch. 4. Command Fan 1 ON using the scan tool output tests function. 5. Observe the cooling fans. Is the primary cooling fan running?	—	*Go to Step 11*	*Go to Step 80*
11	Remove the series/parallel cooling fan #2 relay from the RH Underhood Relay Center. Is the primary cooling fan running?	—	*Go to Step 12*	*Go to Step 13*
12	Locate and repair short to ground in CKT 504. Is action complete?	—	*Go to Step 81*	—
13	1. Check CKT 409 for a short to ground. 2. If a problem is found, repair as necessary. Was a problem found?	—	*Go to Step 81*	*Go to Step 76*
14	1. Turn OFF the ignition switch. 2. Disconnect the primary cooling fan. 3. Turn ON the ignition switch. 4. Command Fan 1 ON using the scan tool output tests function. 5. Observe the cooling fans. Is the secondary cooling fan running?	—	*Go to Step 15*	*Go to Step 79*
15	Replace the primary cooling fan diode. Is action complete?	—	*Go to Step 81*	—
16	1. Ignition ON, engine not running. 2. Disconnect the low speed cooling fan relay. 3. Probe low speed cooling fan relay harness connector cavity 30 with a test light connected to ground. Is the test light ON?	—	*Go to Step 18*	*Go to Step 17*

GC1089600329020X

Fig. 167 Cooling fan diagnosis (Part 2 of 10). Riviera

Step	Action	Value(s)	Yes	No
17	1. Identify the cause of no battery positive voltage to low speed cooling fan relay harness connector cavity 30: • Blown fuse. If the fuse is blown, locate and correct short circuit. – Stalled primary or secondary cooling fan. – Shorted primary or secondary cooling fan motor windings. – Short to ground in CKT 642, CKT 532, or CKT 409. – Shorted primary cooling fan diode. • Open in CKT 642. 2. Repair the cause of no battery positive voltage to low speed cooling fan relay harness connector cavity 30. Is action complete?	—	Go to Step 81	—
18	Probe low speed cooling fan relay harness connector cavity 85 with a test light connected to ground. Is the test light ON?	—	Go to Step 20	Go to Step 19
19	1. Identify the cause of no positive voltage to low speed cooling fan relay harness connector cavity 85: • Blown fuse. If the fuse is blown, locate short circuit. – CKT 241 shorted to ground. – Shorted low speed cooling fan relay coil. – Shorted series/parallel cooling fan #2 relay coil. – Shorted high speed cooling fan #3 relay coil. • CKT 241 open. 2. Repair cause of no positive voltage to low speed cooling fan relay harness connector cavity 85. Is action complete?	—	Go to Step 81	—
20	1. Turn OFF the ignition switch. 2. Disconnect both cooling fans. 3. Connect terminals A and B together at both cooling fan connectors using fused jumpers. 4. Turn ON the ignition switch. 5. Connect a test light between low speed cooling fan relay harness connector cavities 30 and 87. Is the test light ON?	—	Go to Step 21	Go to Step 27
21	1. Connect a test light between low speed cooling fan relay harness connector cavities 85 and 86. 2. Turn ON the ignition switch. 3. Command Fan 1 ON using the scan tool output tests function. 4. Observe the test light. Is the test light ON?	—	Go to Step 22	Go to Step 25

GC1089600329030X

Fig. 167 Cooling fan diagnosis (Part 3 of 10). Riviera

Step	Action	Value(s)	Yes	No
22	1. Turn OFF the ignition switch 2. Remove the jumpers from the engine cooling fan connectors and reconnect the cooling fans. 3. Install a fused jumper between low speed cooling fan relay harness connector cavities 30 and 87. 4. Turn ON the ignition switch. 5. Observe the cooling fans. Are both cooling fans running?	—	Go to Step 23	Go to Step 24
23	1. Check for poor connections at the low speed cooling fan relay. 2. If a problem is found, repair as necessary. Was a problem found?	—	Go to Step 81	Go to Step 37
24	1. Check for poor connections at the cooling fan motors. 2. If a problem is found, repair as necessary. Was a problem found?	—	Go to Step 81	Go to Step 63
25	1. Turn OFF the ignition switch. 2. Disconnect the PCM blue connector C1. 3. Install a fused jumper between low speed cooling fan relay harness connector cavities 30 and 86. 4. Turn ON the ignition switch. 5. Probe PCM harness connector cavity C1-32 with a test light to ground. Is the test light ON?	—	Go to Step 77	Go to Step 26
26	Repair open in the cooling fan 1 control CKT 335 between the PCM and the low speed cooling fan relay. Is action complete?	—	Go to Step 81	—
27	1. Turn OFF the ignition switch. 2. Remove the jumpers from the cooling fan connectors. 3. Reconnect the cooling fans. 4. Install a fused jumper between low speed cooling fan relay harness connector terminals 30 and 87. 5. Remove the series/parallel cooling fan #2 relay from the RH Front Underhood Relay Center. 6. Probe RH Front Underhood Relay Center series/parallel cooling fan #2 relay cavity 30 with a test light connected to ground. Is the test light ON?	—	Go to Step 28	Go to Step 31
28	Connect a test light between RH Front Underhood Relay Center series/parallel cooling fan #2 relay cavities 30 and 87A. Is the test light ON?	—	Go to Step 30	Go to Step 29
29	1. Check for an open in CKT 409 between RH Front Underhood Relay Center series/parallel cooling fan #2 relay cavity 87A and secondary cooling fan terminal B. 2. If a problem is found, repair as necessary. Was a problem found?	—	Go to Step 81	Go to Step 57

GC1089600329040X

Fig. 167 Cooling fan diagnosis (Part 4 of 10). Riviera

Step	Action	Value(s)	Yes	No
30	1. Check for a poor connection at the Underhood Relay Center series/parallel cooling fan #2 relay cavities 87A or 30. 2. If a problem is found, repair as necessary. Was a problem found?	—	Go to Step 81	Go to Step 76
31	1. Check for an open in CKT 532 between the low speed cooling fan relay harness connector cavity 87 and primary cooling fan harness connector terminal B. 2. If a problem is found, repair as necessary. Was a problem found?	—	Go to Step 81	Go to Step 56
32	Using scan tool, view A/C Request. Does the scan tool display Yes?	—	PCM Controlled Air Conditioning	Go to Step 33
33	Are both cooling fan(s) running at low speed?	—	Go to Step 34	Go to Step 40
34	Disconnect the low speed cooling fan relay. Are the cooling fans running?	—	Go to Step 35	Go to Step 36
35	Locate and repair short to voltage in CKT 532. Is action complete?	—	Go to Step 81	—
36	Using a test light connected to B+, probe low speed cooling fan relay harness connector cavity 86. Is the test light ON?	—	Go to Step 38	Go to Step 37
37	Replace the low speed cooling fan relay. Is action complete?	—	Go to Step 81	—
38	1. Turn OFF the ignition switch 2. Disconnect the blue PCM connector C1. 3. Probe low speed cooling fan relay harness connector cavity 86 with a test light connected to B+. Is the test light ON?	—	Go to Step 39	Go to Step 77
39	Locate and repair short to ground in the cooling fan 1 control circuit (CKT 335). Is action complete?	—	Go to Step 81	—
40	Are both cooling fans running at high speed?	—	Go to Step 41	Go to Step 42
41	View A/C High Pressure on the scan tool. Does the scan tool display voltage less than the specified value?	1.2V	Go to Step 77	Go to Step 44
42	1. Turn OFF the ignition switch. 2. Disconnect the PCM. 3. Turn ON the ignition switch. 4. Observe the cooling fans. Is the secondary cooling fan running at high speed?	—	Go to Step 43	Go to Step 77

GC1089600329050X

Fig. 167 Cooling fan diagnosis (Part 5 of 10). Riviera

Step	Action	Value(s)	Yes	No
43	1. Check for a short to ground in the cooling fan 2 control circuit (CKT 473). 2. If a problem is found, repair as necessary. Was a problem found?	—	Go to Step 81	Go to Step 52
44	1. Turn OFF the ignition switch. 2. Disconnect the A/C refrigerant pressure sensor electrical connector. 3. Turn ON the ignition switch. 4. View A/C Pressure on the scan tool. Does the scan tool display voltage near the specified value?	0V	Go to Step 46	Go to Step 45
45	Probe the A/C refrigerant pressure signal circuit with a *J 39200* Digital Multimeter connected to the A/C refrigerant pressure sensor ground. Does the digital multimeter display voltage near the specified value?	0V	Go to Step 77	Go to Step 51
46	Probe the A/C refrigerant pressure sensor ground with a test light to B+. Is the test light ON?	—	Go to Step 47	Go to Step 49
47	Probe the A/C refrigerant pressure sensor 5 volt reference circuit B with a *J 39200* Digital Multimeter connected to the A/C refrigerant pressure sensor ground. Does the digital multimeter display voltage near the specified value?	5V	Go to Step 48	Go to Step 50
48	Replace the A/C refrigerant pressure sensor. Is action complete?	—	Go to Step 81	—
49	Locate and repair open or short to voltage in the A/C refrigerant pressure sensor ground circuit. Is action complete?	—	Go to Step 81	—
50	Locate and repair open or short to ground in the A/C refrigerant pressure sensor 5 volt reference B circuit. Is action complete?	—	Go to Step 81	—
51	Locate and repair short to voltage in the A/C refrigerant pressure signal circuit. Is action complete?	—	Go to Step 81	—
52	1. Remove the high speed cooling fan #3 relay from the RH Front Underhood Relay Center. 2. Observe the cooling fans. Is the secondary cooling fan running at high speed?	—	Go to Step 53	Go to Step 70

GC1089600329060X

Fig. 167 Cooling fan diagnosis (Part 6 of 10). Riviera

Step	Action	Value(s)	Yes	No
53	Remove series/parallel cooling fan #2 relay from the RH Front Underhood Relay Center. Is the secondary cooling fan running at high speed?	—	Go to Step 54	Go to Step 55
54	Locate and repair short to B+ in CKT 409. Is action complete?	—	Go to Step 81	—
55	Locate and repair short to B+ in CKT 504. Is action complete?	—	Go to Step 81	—
56	1. Check for an open between series/parallel #2 relay cavity 30 in the RH Front Underhood Relay Center and primary cooling fan terminal A. 2. If a problem is found, repair as necessary. Was a problem found?	—	Go to Step 81	Go to Step 79
57	1. Check for an open in CKT 1350 between secondary cooling fan terminal A and ground. 2. If a problem is found, repair as necessary. Was a problem found?	—	Go to Step 81	Go to Step 80
58	1. Ignition ON, engine not running. 2. Remove the high speed cooling fan #3 relay from the RH Front Underhood Relay Center. 3. Install a test light between high speed cooling fan #3 relay cavity 86 in the RH Front Underhood Relay Center and B+. 4. Command Fan 2 ON using the scan tool output controls function. 5. Wait 6 seconds. 6. Observe the test light. Is the test light ON?	—	Go to Step 61	Go to Step 59
59	1. Remove the series/parallel cooling fan #2 relay from the RH Front Underhood Relay Center. 2. Install a test light between series/parallel cooling fan #2 relay cavity 86 in the RH Front Underhood Relay Center and B+. 3. Command Fan 2 ON using the scan tool output controls function. 4. Wait 6 seconds. 5. Observe the test light. Is the test light ON?	—	Go to Step 78	Go to Step 60
60	1. Turn OFF the ignition switch. 2. Disconnect the PCM. 3. Turn ON the ignition switch. 4. Check the cooling fan 2 control circuit (CKT 473) for an open or a short to voltage between series/parallel cooling fan #2 relay cavity 86 in the RH Front Underhood Relay Center and the PCM. 5. If a problem is found, repair as necessary. Was a problem found?	—	Go to Step 81	Go to Step 77

GC1089600329070X

Fig. 167 Cooling fan diagnosis (Part 7 of 10). Riviera

Step	Action	Value(s)	Yes	No
61	1. Turn OFF the ignition switch 2. Reinstall high speed cooling fan #3 relay. 3. Disconnect both cooling fan electrical connectors. 4. Turn ON the ignition switch. 5. Command Fan 2 ON using the scan tool output controls function. 6. Wait 6 seconds. 7. Probe terminal B (CKT 409) at the secondary cooling fan connector with a test light to ground. Is the test light ON?	—	Go to Step 62	Go to Step 64
62	Probe terminal A (CKT 504) at the primary cooling fan connector with a test light to B+. Is the test light ON?	—	Go to Step 63	Go to Step 71
63	1. Identify cause of inoperative cooling fan: • Open primary cooling fan motor windings. • Open secondary cooling fan motor windings. • Stalled cooling fan(s). 2. Replace the affected cooling fan motor. Is action complete?	—	Go to Step 81	—
64	1. Remove the high speed cooling fan #3 relay from the RH Front Underhood Relay Center. 2. Turn ON the ignition switch. 3. Probe high speed cooling fan #3 relay cavity 85 in the RH Front Underhood Relay Center with a test light connected to ground. Is the test light ON?	—	Go to Step 66	Go to Step 65
65	Locate and repair open in the ignition positive voltage circuit to high speed cooling fan #3 relay. Is action complete?	—	Go to Step 81	—
66	Probe high speed cooling fan #3 relay cavity 87 in the RH Front Underhood Relay Center with a test light connected to ground. Is the test light ON?	—	Go to Step 68	Go to Step 67
67	Locate and repair open in battery positive voltage circuit to high speed cooling fan #3 relay cavity 87. Is action complete?	—	Go to Step 81	—
68	1. Check CKT 409 for an open between secondary cooling fan terminal B and high speed cooling fan #3 relay cavity 30 in the RH Front Underhood Relay Center. 2. If a problem is found, repair as necessary. Was a problem found?	—	Go to Step 81	Go to Step 69

GC1089600329080X

Fig. 167 Cooling fan diagnosis (Part 8 of 10). Riviera

Step	Action	Value(s)	Yes	No
69	1. Check for poor terminal connections at high speed cooling fan #3 relay. 2. If a problem is found, repair as necessary. Was a problem found?	—	Go to Step 81	Go to Step 70
70	Replace high speed cooling fan #3 relay. Is action complete?	—	Go to Step 81	—
71	1. Remove the series/parallel cooling fan #2 relay. 2. Turn ON the ignition switch. 3. Probe series/parallel cooling fan #2 relay cavity 85 in the RH Front Underhood Relay Center with a test light connected to ground. Is the test light ON?	—	Go to Step 73	Go to Step 72
72	Locate and repair open in battery positive voltage circuit to series/parallel cooling fan #2 relay cavity 85 in the RH Front Underhood Relay Center. Is action complete?	—	Go to Step 81	—
73	Probe series/parallel cooling fan #2 relay cavity 87 in the RH Front Underhood Relay Center with a test light to B+. Is the test light ON?	—	Go to Step 75	Go to Step 74
74	Locate and repair open in CKT 1350 between series/parallel cooling fan #2 relay cavity 87 in the RH Front Underhood Relay Center cavity and ground. Is action complete?	—	Go to Step 81	—
75	1. Check for poor terminal connections at the series/parallel cooling fan #2 relay. 2. If a problem is found, repair as necessary. Was a problem found?	—	Go to Step 81	Go to Step 76
76	Replace the series/parallel cooling fan #2 relay. Is action complete?	—	Go to Step 81	—
77	Replace the PCM. **Important:** The replacement PCM must be programmed. Is action complete?	—	Go to Step 81	—
78	Repair open in the cooling fan 2 control circuit (CKT 473) between the series/parallel cooling fan #2 relay cavity 86 and the high speed cooling fan #3 relay cavity 86. Is action complete?	—	Go to Step 81	—
79	Replace the primary cooling fan motor. Is action complete?	—	Go to Step 81	—
80	Replace the secondary cooling fan motor. Is action complete?	Go to Step 81		

GC1089600329090X

Fig. 167 Cooling fan diagnosis (Part 9 of 10). Riviera

Step	Action	Value(s)	Yes	No
81	1. Engine coolant less than 100°C (212°F). 2. Turn the A/C OFF. 3. Engine running. Observe the cooling fans. Are the cooling fans running?	—	Go to Step 32	Go to Step 82
82	1. Command Fan 1 ON using the scan tool output tests function. 2. Observe the cooling fans. Are both cooling fans running at low speed?	—	Go to Step 83	Go to Step 8
83	1. Command Fan 2 ON using the scan tool output tests function. 2. Wait 6 seconds. 3. Observe the cooling fans. Are both cooling fans running at high speed?	—	System OK	Go to Step 58

GC1089600329100X

Fig. 167 Cooling fan diagnosis (Part 10 of 10). Riviera

Saturn

NOTE: On Air Bag Equipped Models, Refer To "Air Bag System Precautions" Located In The Front Of This Manual For System Disarming & Arming Procedures.

NOTE: "Electrical Symbol & Wire Color Code Identification" Located In The Front Of This Manual Can Be Used As An Aid When Using Wiring Circuits Found In This Section.

NOTE: Refer To "Computer Relearn Procedures" Located In The Front Of This Manual When Battery Power To The Computer Has Been Interrupted.

INDEX

DESCRIPTION

On models equipped with A/C, the cooling fan has five unequally spaced blades to provide air flow through the radiator and condenser. the fan is driven by an electric motor which is attached to the radiator support. The fan motor is activated by a coolant temperature switch.

On models less A/C, the cooling fan has four unequally spaced blades that have curled tips to provide minimum noise. A fan shroud is used to prevent recirculation of air around the fan.

SYSTEM DIAGNOSIS & TESTING

Refer to **Figs. 1 through 3,** for electric cooling fan wiring circuit.

COOLING FAN INOPERATIVE

Refer to **Figs. 4 through 6** for electric cooling fan inoperative diagnosis.

COOLING FAN OPERATES CONSTANTLY

Refer to **Figs. 7 and 8** when diagnosing a cooling fan which operates constantly.

COMPONENT REPLACEMENT

COOLING FAN ASSEMBLY

1.9L Engine

1. Remove intake air ducts and disconnect temperature sensor connector.
2. Disconnect wiring harness from cooling fan motor.

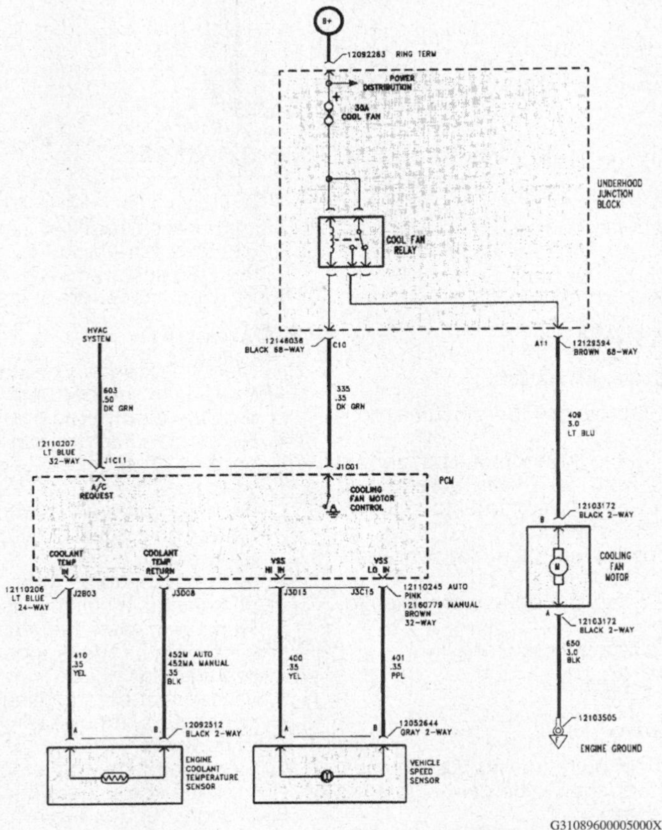

Fig. 1 Cooling fan wiring circuit. 1998–99

3. Loosen and remove top hold-down bolts from cooling fan assembly.
4. **On models equipped with automatic transaxle and A/C,** it may be necessary to loosen top transaxle oil cooler line for clearance.
5. **On all models,** lift cooling fan off of lower mounting brackets. Move assembly to left and rotate counterclockwise while lifting upward past upper

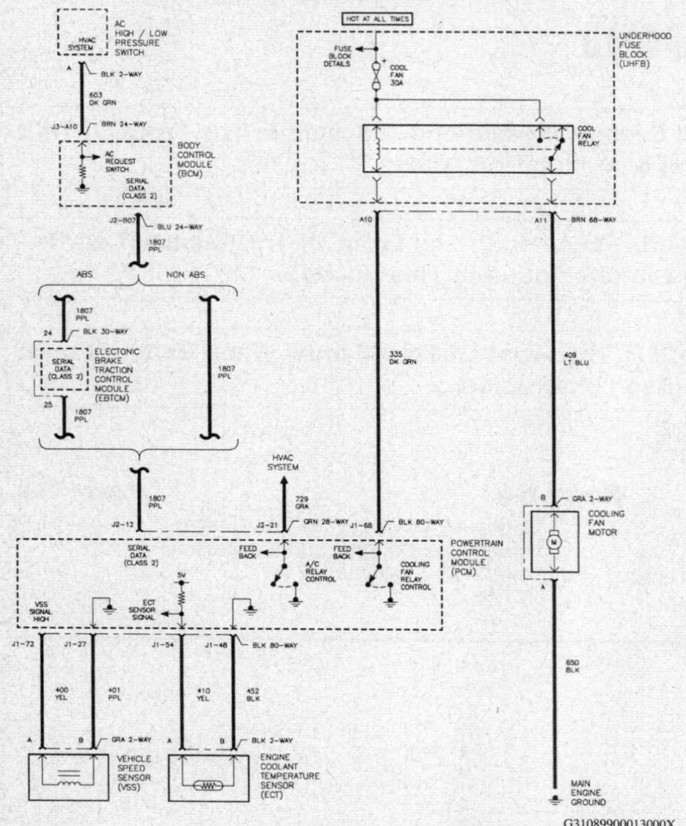

Fig. 2 Cooling fan wiring circuit. 2000–02 w/1.9L engine

G31089900014010X

Fig. 3 Cooling fan wiring circuit (Part 1 of 2). 2.2L & 3.0L engines

radiator hose.

6. Remove cooling fan assembly from vehicle.
7. Reverse procedure to install.

PUSHER FAN

2.2L & 3.0L Engines

1. Disconnect pusher fan electrical connector.
2. Release tabs, then remove pusher fan harness from puller fan shroud and push harness clear of radiator end.
3. Raise and support vehicle, then remove pusher fan to condenser retaining nut.
4. Pull lower fan shroud forward, then remove fan.
5. Reverse procedure to install.

PULLER FAN

2.2L Engine

1. Disconnect both cooling fan electrical connectors, then slide connectors out of retainers.
2. Remove pusher fan electrical harness from fan shroud retainer tabs, then wiring harness from clamp on fan shroud.
3. Remove fan shroud to radiator bolts, then fan and shroud assembly.
4. Reverse procedure to install.

3.0L Engine

1. Disconnect battery ground. **It is not required to disconnect fan control module electrical connector.**
2. Remove fan control module by sliding up and off bracket. Lay module and wiring aside.
3. Remove battery insulator cover, then battery hold down and fan control module bracket.
4. Remove battery, then drain engine coolant into a suitable container.
5. Remove power steering fluid reservoir to fan shroud bolts, position reservoir rearward in vehicle.
6. Disconnect both cooling fan electrical connectors, then slide connectors out of retainers.
7. Remove pusher fan electrical harness from fan shroud retainer tabs.
8. Disconnect auxiliary water pump electrical connector, then remove harness from clip.
9. Remove upper transaxle cooler line from radiator, then unsnap from retainer at radiator end.
10. Remove auxiliary water pump outlet hose from radiator, then remove upper radiator hose.
11. Raise and support vehicle, then remove auxiliary water pump inlet hose from radiator.
12. Lower vehicle, then remove fan shroud to radiator bolts.
13. Remove fan and shroud assembly from vehicle.
14. Reverse procedure to install.

COOLING FAN MOTOR

1.9L Engine

1. Remove cooling fan assembly as described under "Cooling Fan Assembly."
2. While holding fan, remove fan blade to motor nut (lefthand thread). Pull fan blade off of motor shaft.
3. Remove screws securing fan motor to shroud.
4. Remove motor from fan shroud.
5. Reverse procedure to install. **Torque** motor nut to 27–44 inch lbs.

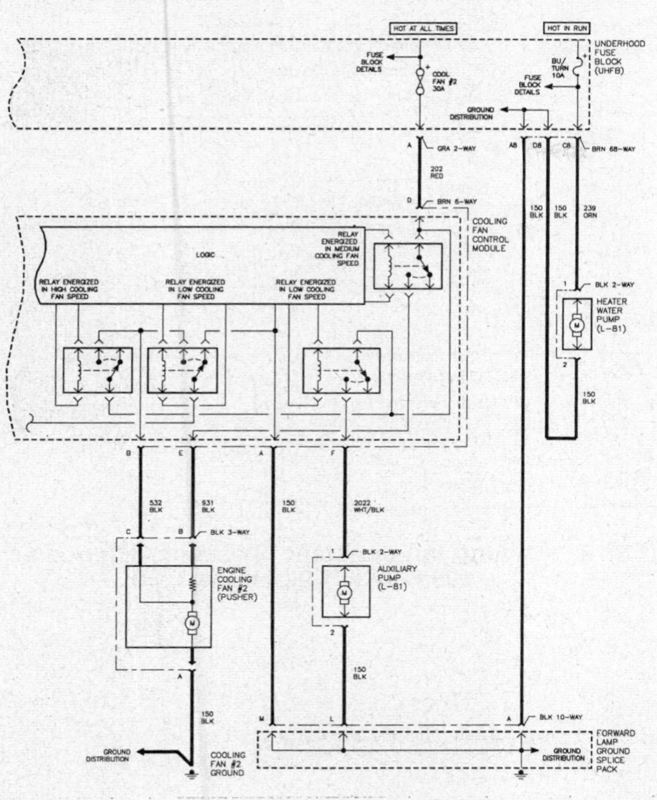

Fig. 3 Cooling fan wiring circuit (Part 2 of 2). 2.2L & 3.0L engines

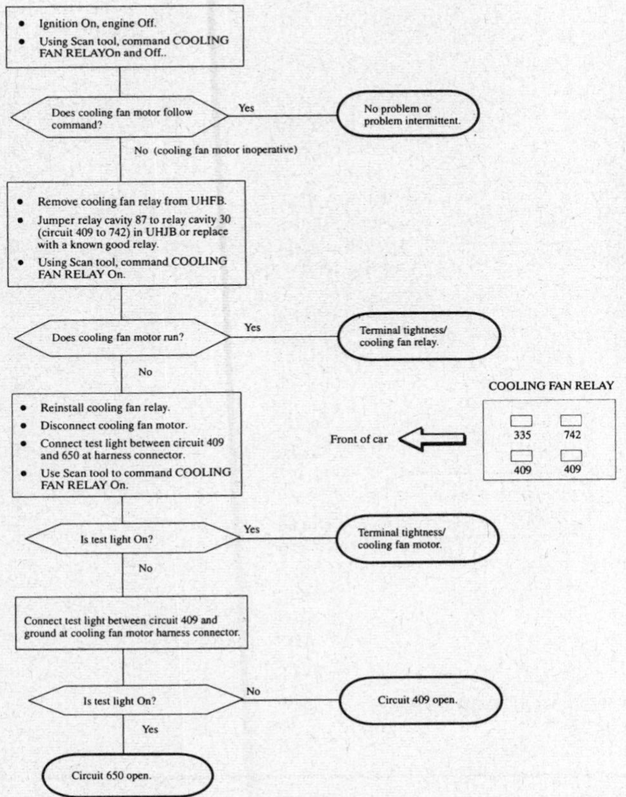

Fig. 5 Cooling fan inoperative. 2000–02 w/1.9L engine

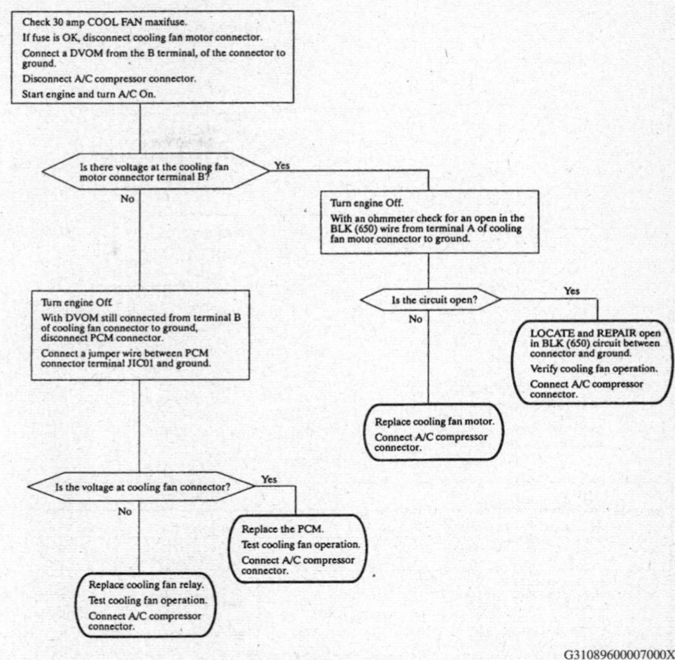

Fig. 4 Cooling fan inoperative. 1998–99 w/1.9L engine

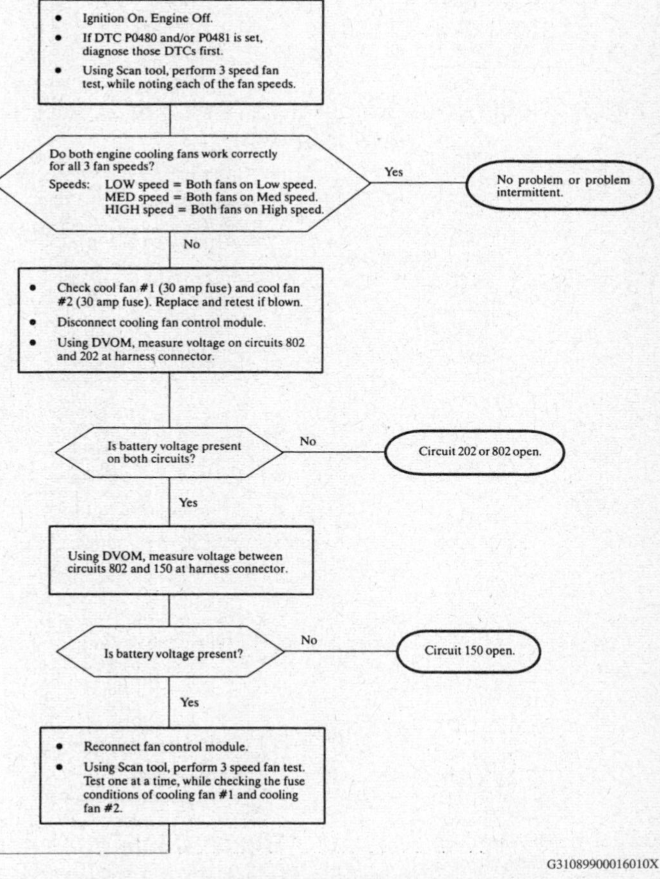

Fig. 6 Cooling fan inoperative (Part 1 of 2). 2.2L & 3.0L engines

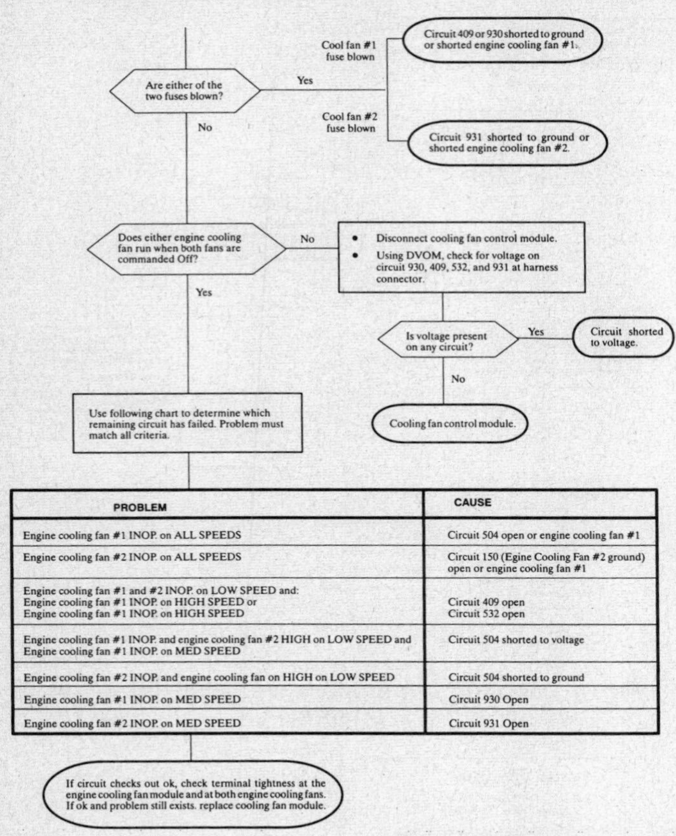

PROBLEM	CAUSE
Engine cooling fan #1 INOP. on ALL SPEEDS	Circuit 504 open or engine cooling fan #1
Engine cooling fan #2 INOP. on ALL SPEEDS	Circuit 150 (Egine Cooling Fan #2 ground) open or engine cooling fan #1
Engine cooling fan #1 and #2 INOP. on LOW SPEED and: Engine cooling fan #1 INOP. on HIGH SPEED or Engine cooling fan #1 INOP. on HIGH SPEED	Circuit 409 open Circuit 532 open
Engine cooling fan #1 INOP. and engine cooling fan #2 HIGH on LOW SPEED and Engine cooling fan #1 INOP. on MED SPEED	Circuit 504 shorted to voltage
Engine cooling fan #2 INOP. and engine cooling fan on HIGH on LOW SPEED	Circuit 504 shorted to ground
Engine cooling fan #1 INOP. on MED SPEED	Circuit 930 Open
Engine cooling fan #2 INOP. on MED SPEED	Circuit 931 Open

Fig. 6 Cooling fan inoperative (Part 2 of 2). 2.2L & 3.0L engines

Disconnect negative battery cable.
Remove cooling fan relay.
Connect negative battery cable.

Does cooling fan still operate?

No

Replace engine cooling fan relay.
If the fan operates with a new relay, check for a short to ground in the DK GRN (335) wire to the PCM.
If a short is found, repair.
If no short, replace PCM.

Yes

Repair short to power in LT/BLU (409) wire from underhood junction block to cooling fan motor.

G31089600006000X

Fig. 7 Cooling fan constant operation diagnosis. 1998–99 w/1.9L engine

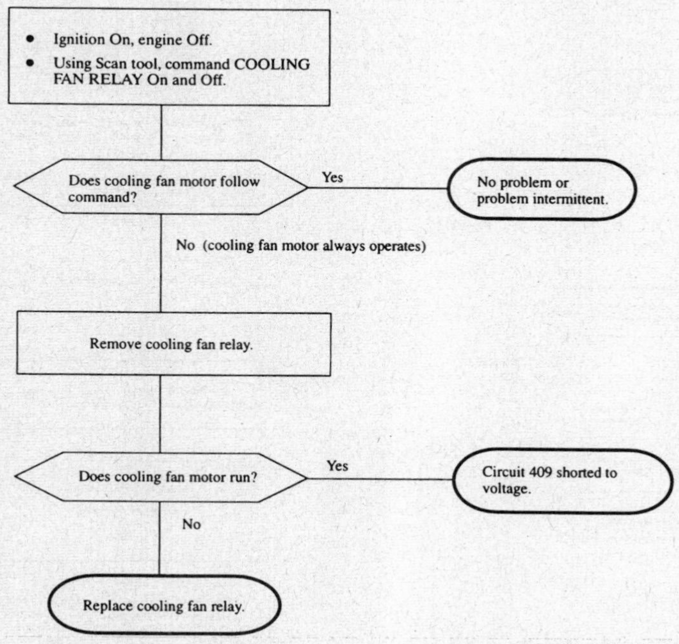

Fig. 8 Cooling fan constant operation diagnosis. 2000–02 w/1.9L engine

STARTER MOTORS

TABLE OF CONTENTS

AC-Delco Starters, General Motors

NOTE: On Air Bag Equipped Models, Refer To "Air Bag System Precautions" Located In The Front Of This Manual For System Disarming & Arming Procedures.

NOTE: Refer To "Computer Relearn Procedures" Located In The Front Of This Manual When Battery Power To The Computer Has Been Interrupted.

INDEX

APPLICATION CHART

Year	Engine	VIN①	Model
ACHIEVA, ALERO, GRAND AM & SKYLARK			
1998	2.4L	T	SD
	3.1L	M	SD
1999–2002	2.4L	T	PG
	3.4L	E	PG
AURORA & RIVIERA			
1998–99	3.8L	1	PG
	3.8L	K	PG
	4.0L	C	PG
AURORA			
2001–02	3.5L	H	PG
	4.0L	C	PG
BONNEVILLE, LESABRE, LSS & 88			
1998	3.8L	K	SD
	3.8L	1	SD
1999–2002	3.8L	K	PG
	3.8L	1	PG
CAMARO & FIREBIRD			
1998–2002	3.8L	K	PG
	5.7L	G	PG
CAVALIER & SUNFIRE			
1998	2.2L	4	SD
	2.4L	T	SD
1999–2002	2.2L	4	PG
	2.4L	T	PG

Continued

APPLICATION CHART—Continued

Year	Engine	VIN①	Model
CENTURY, GRAND PRIX, INTRIGUE, LUMINA, MONTE CARLO & REGAL			
1998	3.1L	M	PG
	3.8L	1	PG
	3.8L	K	PG
1999–2002	3.1L	J	PG
	3.5L	H	PG
	3.8L	1	PG
	3.8L	K	PG
CORVETTE			
1998–2002	5.7L	G	PG
CUTLASS			
1998–99	2.4L	T	PG
	3.1L	M	PG
DEVILLE, ELDORADO & SEVILLE			
1998–2002	4.6L	9	PG
	4.6L	Y	PG
IMPALA			
2000–02	3.4L	E	PG
	3.8L	K	PG
MALIBU			
1998–2002	2.4L	T	PG
	3.1L	M	PG
PARK AVENUE			
1998–2002	3.8L	1	PG
	3.8L	K	PG

① — The eighth digit of VIN denotes engine code.

PRECAUTIONS

AIR BAG SYSTEMS

Refer to "Air Bag System Precautions" in the front of this manual for system disarming and arming procedures.

BATTERY GROUND CABLE

Prior to service, disconnect battery ground cable and isolate as required.

DESCRIPTION

PG SERIES

The PG starter motors are a non-repairable starter motor. They have pole pieces that are arranged around the armature. Both solenoid windings are energized. The pull-in winding circuit is completed to the ground through the starter motor. The windings work together magnetically to pull and hold in the plunger moves the shift lever. This action causes the starter drive assembly to rotate on the armature shaft spline as it engages with the flywheel ring gear on the engine. Moving at the same time, the plunger also closes the solenoid switch contacts in the starter solenoid. Full battery voltage is applied directly to the starter motor and it cranks the engine.

SD SERIES

The SD starter motor has pole pieces that are arranged around the armature. Wound field coils energize the pole pieces. The solenoid windings are energized when the ignition switch is turned to start position. The resulting plunger and shift lever movement causes the pinion to engage the flywheel ring gear and the solenoid main contact switch to close. When the engine starts, pinion overrun protects the armature from excessive speed until the switch is opened. Once the solenoid windings are de-energized, the return springs causes the pinion to disengage.

TROUBLESHOOTING

PG SERIES

Refer to **Figs 1 through 4,** for troubleshooting procedures.

SD SERIES

Refer to **Fig. 5 through 8,** for troubleshooting procedures.

DIAGNOSIS & TESTING

Refer to **MOTORS "Domestic Engine Performance & Driveability Manual"** for diagnosis and testing procedures.

Step	Action	Yes	No
1	Did you perform the Battery Inspection/Test?	Go to *Step 2*	*Battery Inspection/Test*
2	1. Install a scan tool 2. Turn ON the ignition, with the engine OFF. Does the scan tool power up?	Go to *Step 3*	Go to *Scan Tool Does Not Power Up*
3	Attempt to establish communication with the following components: • Body Control Module (BCM) • Instrument Panel Cluster (IPC) • Powertrain Control Module (PCM) • Vehicle Theft Deterrent Module (VTD) Does the scan tool communicate with the BCM, IPC, PCM and VTD?	Go to *Step 4*	*Scan Tool Does Not Communicate with Class 2 Device*
4	Select the BCM, IPC, PCM and VTD display DTC function on the scan tool. Does the scan tool display any DTCs?	Go to *Step 5*	Go to *Symptoms*
5	Does the scan tool display any DTCs which begin with a U?	*Scan Tool Does Not Communicate with Class 2 Device*	Go to *Step 6*
6	Does the scan tool display any DTCs in the PCM which begin with a P?	*Diagnostic Trouble Code (DTC) List/Type*	Go to *Step 7*
7	Does the scan tool display any DTCs in the VTD which begin with B?	*Diagnostic Trouble Code (DTC) List/Type*	Go to *Step 8*
8	Does the scan tool display any DTCs in the BCM which begin with B?	*Diagnostic Trouble Code (DTC) List/Type*	Go to *Step 9*
9	Does the scan tool display any DTCs in the IPC which begin with B?	*Diagnostic Trouble Code (DTC) List/Type*	System OK

GC1120100173000X

Fig. 1 System check. PG Series

Step	Action	Yes	No
6	1. Turn OFF the ignition. 2. Disconnect the CRANK relay. 3. Turn ON the ignition, with the Engine OFF. 4. Connect a test lamp between the battery positive voltage circuit of the CRANK relay coil and a good ground. Does the test lamp illuminate?	Go to *Step 7*	Go to *Step 14*
7	1. Connect a test lamp between the battery positive voltage circuit of the CRANK relay coil and the control circuit of the CRANK relay. 2. Turn the ignition to the START position. Does the test lamp illuminate?	Go to *Step 18*	Go to *Step 15*
8	1. Turn OFF the ignition. 2. Disconnect the CRANK relay. 3. Connect a test lamp between the battery positive voltage circuit of the CRANK relay switch circuit and a good ground. Does the test lamp illuminate?	Go to *Step 9*	Go to *Step 22*
9	Connect a 30 amp fused jumper between the battery positive voltage circuit of the START relay switch circuit and the supply voltage circuit of the starter solenoid. Does the engine crank?	Go to *Step 18*	Go to *Step 10*
10	1. Disconnect the park neutral position (PNP) switch. 2. Connect a 30 amp fused jumper between the starter solenoid supply voltage circuits of the PNP switch harness connector. Does the engine crank?	Go to *Step 17*	Go to *Step 11*
11	Does the fuse in either jumper open?	Go to *Step 23*	Go to *Step 16*
12	Test the crank request signal circuit of the PCM for an open or high resistance. Did you find and correct the condition?	Go to *Step 29*	Go to *Step 19*
13	Test the crank signal circuit of the IPC for an open or high resistance. Did you find and correct the condition?	Go to *Step 29*	Go to *Step 20*
14	Test the battery positive voltage circuit of the CRANK relay coil for an open or high resistance. Did you find and correct the condition?	Go to *Step 29*	Go to *Step 20*
15	Test the control circuit of the CRANK relay for an open, high resistance or short to battery voltage. Did you find and correct the condition?	Go to *Step 29*	Go to *Step 19*
16	Test the supply voltage circuit of the starter solenoid for an open or high resistance. Did you find and correct the condition?	Go to *Step 29*	Go to *Step 21*
17	1. Inspect the PNP switch for proper operation. 2. Inspect for poor connection at the PNP switch harness connector. Did you find and correct the condition?	Go to *Step 29*	Go to *Step 24*
18	Inspect for poor connections at the CRANK relay. Did you find and correct the condition?	Go to *Step 29*	Go to *Step 25*

GC1120100170020X

Fig. 2 Starter solenoid does not click (Part 2 of 3). PG Series

Step	Action	Yes	No
1	Did you perform the Diagnostic System Check for starting and charging?	Go to *Step 2*	*System Check*
2	Turn the ignition to the START position. Does the engine crank?	Go to *Intermittent and Poor Connections*	Go to *Step 3*
3	1. Install a scan tool. 2. With a scan tool, observe the Crank Request parameter in the PCM data list. 3. Turn the ignition switch to the START position. Does the scan tool display Yes?	Go to *Step 5*	Go to *Step 4*
4	1. With a scan tool, observe the Crank parameter in the IPC data list. 2. Turn the ignition switch to the START position. Does the scan tool display Yes?	Go to *Step 12*	Go to *Step 13*
5	Turn the ignition to the START position. Does the CRANK relay click?	Go to *Step 8*	Go to *Step 6*

GC1120100170010X

Fig. 2 Starter solenoid does not click (Part 1 of 3). PG Series

Step	Action	Yes	No
19	Inspect for poor connection at the PCM harness connector. Did you find and correct the condition?	Go to *Step 29*	Go to *Step 26*
20	Inspect for poor connections at the ignition switch harness connector. Did you find and correct the condition?	Go to *Step 29*	Go to *Step 27*
21	Inspect for poor connections at the starter solenoid. Did you find and correct the condition?	Go to *Step 29*	Go to *Step 28*
22	Repair the open or high resistance in the battery positive voltage circuit of the CRANK relay switch. Did you complete the repair?	Go to *Step 29*	—
23	Repair the high resistance or short to ground in the supply voltage circuit of the starter solenoid. Did you complete the repair?	Go to *Step 29*	—
24	Replace the PNP switch. Did you complete the replacement?	Go to *Step 29*	—
25	Replace the crank relay. Did you complete the replacement?	Go to *Step 29*	—
26	**Important:** Perform the set up procedures for the PCM. Replace the PCM. Did you complete the replacement?	Go to *Step 29*	—
27	Replace the Ignition Switch. Did you complete the replacement?	Go to *Step 29*	—
28	Replace the Starter Motor. Did you complete the replacement?	Go to *Step 29*	—
29	Operate the system for which the symptom occurred. Did you correct the condition?	System OK	Go to *Step 2*

GC1120100170030X

Fig. 2 Starter solenoid does not click (Part 3 of 3). PG Series

Step	Action	Yes	No
1	Did you perform the Diagnostic System Check for starting and charging?	Go to *Step 2*	*System Check*
2	Turn the ignition to the START position. Did the starter solenoid click?	Go to *Step 3*	Go to *Starter Solenoid Does Not Click*
3	Inspect the engine and belt drive system for mechanical binding (seized engine, seized generator). Does the engine move freely?	Go to *Step 4*	Go to *Engine Overhaul*
4	Test the battery positive cable between the battery and the starter solenoid for high resistance. Did you find and correct the condition?	Go to *Step 8*	Go to *Step 5*
5	Test the ground circuit between the battery and the starter motor for a high resistance. Did you find and correct the condition?	Go to *Step 8*	Go to *Step 6*
6	Inspect for poor connections at the starter. Did you find and correct the condition?	Go to *Step 8*	Go to *Step 7*
7	Replace the Starter. Did you complete the replacement?	Go to *Step 8*	—
8	Operate the system for which the symptom occurred. Did you correct the condition?	System OK	Go to *Step 2*

GC1120100171000X

Fig. 3 Starter solenoid clicks, engine does not crank. PG Series

Step	Action	Yes	No
1	Did you review the engine electrical operation and perform the necessary inspections?	Go to *Step 2*	Go to *Symptoms*
2	Start the engine. Does the starter operate normally?	*Test Intermittent and Poor Connections*	Go to *Step 3*
3	Start the engine while listening to the starter motor turn. Is there a loud "whoop" (it may sound like a siren if the engine is revved while the starter is engaged) after the engine starts, but while the starter is still held in the engaged position?	Go to *Step 6*	Go to *Step 4*
4	Do you hear a "rumble", a "growl", or, in some cases, a "knock" as the starter is coasting down to a stop after starting the engine?	Go to *Step 7*	Go to *Step 5*
5	When the engine is cranked, do you hear a high-pitched whine after the engine cranks and starts normally? (This is often diagnosed as a starter drive gear hang-in or a weak solenoid.)	Go to *Step 8*	Go to *Step 7*
6	Inspect the flywheel ring gear for the following: • Chipped gear teeth • Missing gear teeth • milled teeth Does the flywheel have damaged teeth or is bent?	Go to *Step 9*	Go to *Step 10*
7	1. Remove the starter motor. 2. Inspect the starter motor bushings and clutch gear. Does the clutch gear have chipped or milled teeth or worn bushings?	Go to *Step 10*	Go to *Step 9*
8	Shim the starter motor away from the flywheel by adding shims one at a time, between the starter motor and the engine block. Flywheel runout may make this noise appear to be intermittent. Did you complete the repair?	Go to *Step 11*	—
9	Replace the flywheel. Did you complete the replacement?	Go to *Step 11*	—
10	Replace the starter motor. Has the noise stopped?	Go to *Step 11*	—
11	Operate the system in order to verify the repair. Did you correct the condition?	System OK	Go to *Step 2*

GC1120100172000X

Fig. 4 Starter motor noise. PG Series

Step	Action	Value(s)	Yes	No
1	1. Turn the ignition switch to the START position. 2. Observe the SECURITY indicator. Does the indicator stay on or flash continuously?	—	*PASS-Key®II Diagnostic System Check*	*Go to Step 2*
2	Perform the battery load test. Did the battery check as OK?	—	*Go to Step 3*	*Go to Step 11*
3	Check the battery cables and connections. Are the battery cables and connections OK?	—	*Go to Step 4*	*Go to Step 12*
4	1. Remove the INJECTOR Fuse 7 from the IP Junction Block to prevent the engine from starting. 2. Turn the ignition switch to the START position. 3. Using a DMM, measure the voltage at the starter solenoid terminal S, CKT 6 (PPL) to ground. Is the measured voltage greater than the specified value?	8 V	*Go to Step 13*	*Go to Step 5*
5	1. Disconnect CKT 6 (PPL) from the starter solenoid. 2. Turn the ignition switch to the START position. 3. Using a DMM, measure the voltage at the starter enable relay terminal A2, CKT 6 (PPL) to ground. Is the measured voltage greater than the specified value?	8 V	*Go to Step 14*	*Go to Step 6*
6	1. Reconnect CKT 6 (PPL) to the starter solenoid. 2. Backprobe with a test lamp between Battery Positive Voltage (B+) and the park/neutral position (PNP) switch connector C1 terminal G, CKT 575 (YEL). 3. Place the gear selector lever in the PARK position. Does the test lamp light?	—	*Go to Step 7*	*Go to Step 15*
7	1. Connect a test lamp between the starter enable relay terminal C2, CKT 806 (PPL) and ground. 2. Place the ignition switch in the START position. Does the test lamp light?	—	*Go to Step 9*	*Go to Step 8*
8	1. Remove the AIRBAG/VATS Fuse 2E from the I/P Fuse Block. 2. Connect a test lamp between the AIRBAG/VATS Fuse 2E terminal B1, CKT 5 (YEL) and ground. 3. Place the ignition switch in the START position. Does the test lamp light?	—	*Go to Step 19*	*Go to Step 22*
9	1. Turn the ignition switch to the START position. 2. Using a DMM, measure the voltage at the starter enable relay terminal C1, CKT 5 (YEL) to ground. Is the measured voltage greater than the specified value?	8 V	*Go to Step 10*	*Go to Step 30*
10	Check for an open in CKT 575 (YEL). Is CKT 575 OK?	—	*Go to Step 31*	*Go to Step 32*
11	Replace the battery. Is the battery replacement complete?	—	*Starting System Check*	—
12	Repair the battery cable connections or replace battery cables as needed. Is the battery cable repair complete?	—	*Starting System Check*	—

GC1120100177010X

Fig. 6 Starter solenoid does not click (Part 1 of 3). SD Series

Step	Action	Normal Result(s)	Abnormal Result(s)*
1	Turn ignition switch to the START position.	Engine cranks.	• *Starter Solenoid Does Not Click* • *Starter Solenoid Clicks, Engine Does Not Crank*
2	Ignition switch in run, engine running.	Charging system operating properly. Volt/charge indicator operating properly	• *Battery Is Undercharged or Overcharged* • *Charge Indicator Always On* • *Charge Indicator Inoperative*
* Refer to the appropriate symptom diagnostic table for the applicable abnormal result.			

GC1120100176000X

Fig. 5 System check. SD Series

Step	Action	Value(s)	Yes	No
13	1. Check for poor connections at starter solenoid terminal S, CKT 6 (PPL). 2. Check for dirty or poor ground between starter and engine block. 3. If OK, replace the starter. Is the starter replacement complete?	—	*Starting System Check*	—
14	Repair the open or short to ground in CKT 6 (PPL). in Wiring Systems. Is the circuit repair complete?	—	*Starting System Check*	—
15	Backprobe with a test lamp between Battery Positive Voltage (B+) and the PNP switch connector C1 terminal E, CKT 625 (YEL/BLK). Does the test lamp light?	—	*Go to Step 16*	*Go to Step 17*
16	Replace the park/neutral position (PNP) switch. Is the park/neutral position (PNP) switch replacement complete?	—	*Starting System Check*	—
17	Check for an open in CKT 625 (YEL/BLK). Is CKT 625 OK?	—	*Go to Step 18*	*Go to Step 32*
18	Replace the Pass-Key®II Decoder Module. Is the Pass-Key®II Decoder Module replacement complete?	—	*Starting System Check*	—
19	Check the AIRBAG/VATS Fuse 2E in the I/P Fuse Block for an open. Is the AIRBAG/VATS Fuse 2E OK?	—	*Go to Step 21*	*Go to Step 20*
20	1. Repair the short to ground in CKT 806 (PPL). 2. Replace the AIRBAG/VATS Fuse 2E in the I/P Fuse Block. Is the circuit repair and fuse replacement complete?	—	*Starting System Check*	—
21	Repair the open in CKT 806 (PPL). Is the circuit repair complete?	—	*Starting System Check*	—
22	1. Turn the ignition switch to the START position. 2. Using a DMM, measure the voltage at the starter enable relay terminal C1, CKT 5 (YEL) to ground. Is the measured voltage greater than the specified value?	8 V	*Go to Step 23*	*Go to Step 24*
23	Repair the open in CKT 5 (YEL) between S217 and the I/P Fuse Block. Is the circuit repair complete?	—	*Starting System Check*	—
24	Backprobe with a test lamp between the ignition switch connector C202 terminal D5, CKT 1342 (RED). Does the test lamp light?	—	*Go to Step 25*	*Go to Step 27*
25	Check for an open in CKT 5 (YEL) between S217 and the ignition switch connector C202. Is the CKT 5 OK?	—	*Go to Step 26*	*Go to Step 32*
26	Replace the ignition switch. Is the ignition switch replacement complete?	—	*Starting System Check*	—

GC1120100177020X

Fig. 6 Starter solenoid does not click (Part 2 of 3). SD Series

Step	Action	Value(s)	Yes	No
27	Check the IGN SW Fuse in the RH MaxiFuse® Block for an open. Is the IGN SW Fuse OK?	—	*Go to Step 29*	*Go to Step 28*
28	Repair the short to ground in CKT 1342 (RED). Is the circuit repair complete?	—	*Starting System Check*	—
29	Repair the open in CKT 1342 (RED). Is the circuit repair complete?	—	*Starting System Check*	—
30	Repair the open in CKT 5 (YEL) between S217 and the starter enable relay. Is the circuit repair complete?	—	*Starting System Check*	—
31	Replace the starter enable relay. Is the starter enable relay replacement complete?	—	*Starting System Check*	—
32	Repair the suspect circuit. Is the circuit repair complete?	—	*Starting System Check*	—

GC1120100177030X

Fig. 6 Starter solenoid does not click (Part 3 of 3). SD Series

Step	Action	Value(s)	Yes	No
1	1. Inspect the battery hydrometer. 2. Remove the INJECTOR Fuse 7 from the IP Junction Block to prevent the engine from starting. 3. Place the ignition switch in CRANK for 15 seconds. 4. Using a DMM, measure the voltage between the battery terminals. Is the measured voltage greater than the specified value?	8 V	*Go to Step 2*	*Go to Step 5*
2	Using a DMM, measure the voltage between the negative battery terminal and the engine block while the ignition switch is placed in CRANK for 15 seconds. Is the measured voltage less than the specified value?	0.5 V	*Go to Step 3*	*Go to Step 7*
3	Using a DMM, measure the voltage between the positive battery terminal and the starter solenoid terminal B while the ignition switch is placed in CRANK for 15 seconds. Is the voltage less than the specified value?	0.5 V	*Go to Step 4*	*Go to Step 8*
4	Replace the starter motor. Is the starter motor replacement complete?	—	*Starting System Check*	—
5	Perform the parasitic load test. Does the battery test OK?	—	*Go to Step 6*	*Go to Step 9*
6	Check the battery and starter motor terminals for corrosion or poor contact. Is the repair completed?	—	*Starting System Check*	—
7	1. Clean the negative battery cable connections and repeat the test. 2. If the measured voltage is still greater than the specified value, replace the negative battery cable. Is the repair complete?	0.5 V	*Starting System Check*	—

GC1120100178010X

Fig. 7 Starter solenoid clicks, engine does not crank (Part 1 of 2). SD Series

Step	Action	Value(s)	Yes	No
8	1. Clean the positive battery cable connections and repeat the test. 2. If the measured voltage is still greater than the specified value, replace the positive battery cable. Is the repair complete?	0.5 V	*Starting System Check*	—
9	Replace the battery. Is the battery replacement complete?	—	*Starting System Check*	—

GC1120100178020X

Fig. 7 Starter solenoid clicks, engine does not crank (Part 2 of 2). SD Series

Step	Action	Value(s)	Yes	No
1	Does the engine emit a high pitched whine during cranking but the engine cranks and starts OK?	—	*Go to Step 2*	*Go to Step 3*
2	Decrease the distance between the starter drive pinion and the flywheel. Has the noise disappeared?	—	System OK	—
3	Does the engine emit a high pitched whine as the ignition key is being released, but the engine cranks and starts OK?	—	*Go to Step 4*	*Go to Step 5*
4	Increase the distance between the starter drive pinion and the flywheel. Has the noise disappeared?	—	System OK	—
5	Does the engine make a loud whoop after the engine starts as the starter drive pinion is still engaged?	—	*Go to Step 7*	*Go to Step 6*
6	Does the engine rumble, growl or knock as the starter motor is coasting down to a stop after the engine is started?	—	*Go to Step 7*	*Go to Step 8*
7	Repair or replace the starter drive Has the noise disappeared?	—	System OK	—
8	Repair or replace the starter armature. Has the noise disappeared?	—	System OK	—

GC1120100179000X

Fig. 8 Starter motor noise. SD Series

STARTER SPECIFICATIONS

Starter Identification No.	Free Speed Test			Solenoid	
	Amps	Volts	RPM	Hold-In Windings, Amps	Pull-In Windings, Amps
PG260	60–120	10.0	2900–3400	—	—
PG260 F1	40–90	12.0	3200–4800	6–12	30–45
PG260 F2	35–85	12.0	2550–4150	6–12	30–45
PG260 M	60–96	11.5	2925–3375	6–12	30–45
SD-255①	45–75	10.0	8600–13,000	10–20	60–85
SD-255②	50–75	10.0	6000–12,000	—	—
SD-205③	50–75	10.0	6000–12,000	—	—

① — 1998 models VIN K and 1.
② — 1998 models VIN T.
③ — 1998 models VIN M.

AC-Delco Starters, Saturn

NOTE: On Air Bag Equipped Models, Refer To "Air Bag System Precautions" Located In The Front Of This Manual For System Disarming & Arming Procedures.

NOTE: Refer To "Computer Relearn Procedures" Located In The Front Of This Manual When Battery Power To The Computer Has Been Interrupted.

INDEX

APPLICATION CHART

Year	Model	Part No.①
1998–99	All	21024210
2000–02	All	21024332

① — Core #21024316.

PRECAUTIONS

AIR BAG SYSTEMS

Refer to "Air Bag System Precautions" in the front of this manual for system disarming and arming procedures.

BATTERY GROUND CABLE

Prior to service, disconnect battery ground cable and isolate as required.

DESCRIPTION

These planetary gear reduction starters consist of an armature, a frame with permanent magnet poles, a planetary drive mechanism, a solenoid and a housing.

The starters use a planetary gear drive between the armature and motor pinion. The gear drive allows the use of permanent magnets eliminating heat that normally would be produced by coil fields and also simplifies motor construction since there are no internal field coils and connections.

TROUBLESHOOTING

Refer to starting/charging system troubleshooting procedures, **Fig. 1.**

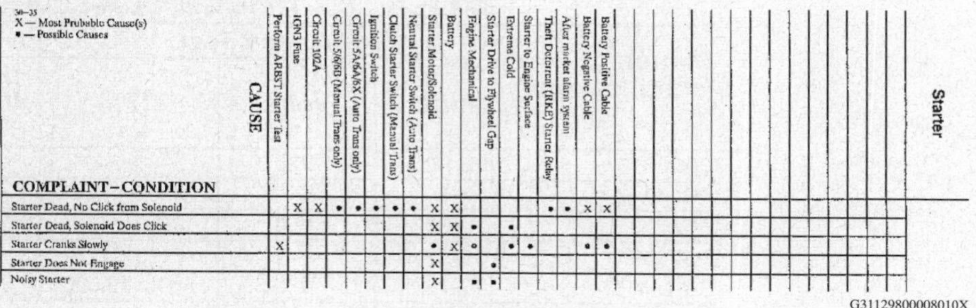

30–35
X — Most Probable Cause(s)
• — Possible Causes

Starter

COMPLAINT–CONDITION / CAUSE	Perform ARBST Starter Test	IGN3 Fuse	Circuit 102A	Circuit 5/6/6B (Manual Trans only)	Circuit 5A/6A/6X (Auto Trans only)	Ignition Switch	Clutch Starter Switch (Manual Trans)	Neutral Starter Switch (Auto Trans)	Starter Motor/Solenoid	Battery	Engine Mechanical	Starter Drive to Flywheel Gap	Extreme Cold	Starter to Engine Surface	Theft Deterrent (RKE) Starter Relay	After market alarm system	Battery Negative Cable	Battery Positive Cable
Starter Dead, No Click from Solenoid		X	X	•	•	•	•	•	X	X					•	•	X	X
Starter Dead, Solenoid Does Click									X	X	•		•					
Starter Cranks Slowly	X								•	X	•		•	•			•	•
Starter Does Not Engage									X			•						
Noisy Starter									X		•	•						

G311298000008010X

Fig. 1 Troubleshooting (Part 1 of 3)

DIAGNOSIS & TESTING

ON-VEHICLE STARTER TEST

Ensure battery is in satisfactory condition before performing test. If battery power is insufficient, the start motor will not function properly.

Electronic system tester tool No. SA9154Z, or equivalent, is required for the following starter system test.

1. Connect red and black tester cables to battery. Place gray inductive current pick-up around positive battery cable.
2. Ensure arrow on gray inductive current pick-up is pointing toward starter motor solenoid.
3. Disable ignition system by disconnecting electrical connection at ignition module.
4. Press "Starter Test" button on system tester.
5. Position tester so display can be seen from driver's seat. When display reads "Crank Engine," turn ignition to Start position.
6. Tester will continue to display "Crank Engine" for 15 seconds.
7. The System Tester will display following information:
   a. **Cranking Amps:** This displays average amperage drawn by starter motor during cranking. Refer to "Starter Specifications" chart for normal operation amperage specifications.
   b. **Cranking Voltage:** This displays average battery voltage during cranking. If voltage is below 9.5 volts, ensure battery is in satisfactory condition and properly charged. Correct cranking voltage and a slow stator indicates loose or corroded cables.
   c. **Good Starter/Bad Starter:** If display reads "Bad Starter," replace starter motor only after determining there is no engine mechanical faults or flywheel binding problems.

CLUTCH START SWITCH

1.9L Engine

1. Inspect resistance through switch.
2. Circuit should be open with clutch is engaged.
3. Less than two ohms should exist when clutch is fully depressed.

2.2L Engine

1. Disconnect electrical connector from clutch start switch.
2. Using a jumper wire connect terminal A to Terminal B.
3. If engine cranks normal, replace switch.

NEUTRAL START SWITCH

1. Inspect resistance through switch from Pin A to Pin B.
2. Circuit should be open when transaxle shifter is in R, 3 or 2.
3. Resistance should be less than 2 ohms when transaxle shifter is in P or N.

TRANSAXLE RANGE SWITCH

1. Disconnect electrical connector transaxle range switch.
2. Using a jumper wire connect terminal E to Terminal G.
3. If engine cranks normal, replace switch.

COMPLAINT/CONDITION	POSSIBLE CAUSE(S)	CORRECTION(S)
No Click, No Crank During Starting.	Faulty or discharged battery.	Check the battery.
	If voltage at the starter solenoid "small" terminal is less than 9 volts, then the control circuit is the probable cause.	Check starter ground: a. paint on mounting surface b. battery negative grounds. c. other loose connections d. Refer to component section
	If voltage at the starter solenoid small terminal is greater than 9 volts, then the motor is the probable cause.	Replace the starter motor.
Click, No Crank During Startup.	If voltage at the starter solenoid small terminal is greater than 6 volts, possible causes could be damaged internal starter ground, excess solenoid temperature, excess voltage drop between the brushes and commutator, or defect at internal solenoid connection.	Check the battery. Replace the starter motor.
	If voltage at the starter solenoid small terminal is greater than 6 volts, a possible cause could be the radial and axial fit between the starter drive gear and flywheel.	Replace starter or flywheel, whichever is found to be damaged.
	Check flywheel runout.	**IMPORTANT:** Saturn starter motors should not be shimmed.
Starter Motor Continues to Run After Starting.	Starter motor internal short (at contact assembly or solenoid coil) or external short between battery and starter solenoid small terminal or faulty ignition key switch.	Check external ring terminals and wires for possible touching between battery and switch terminal lead. If no external short exists, replace starter motor.
	Internal starter motor damage; either electrical (welded contact, short between motor and battery terminal) or mechanical (contact rod).	Replace starter motor.

G31129800008020X

Fig. 1 Troubleshooting (Part 2 of 3)

COMPLAINT/CONDITION	POSSIBLE CAUSE(S)	CORRECTION(S)
High Pitched Whine During Cranking (before the Engine Fires Over), but Engine Cranks and Starts.	The distance between the flywheel and starter drive gear is too great. Check the flywheel for damage such as a bent flywheel or excessive or unusual wear patterns.	Start the engine and carefully touch the outside diameter of the flywheel with chalk or crayon to show high point of tooth runout when the engine is turned off. Turn the engine off and rotate the engine by hand so that the marked teeth are in the area of inspection. If the runout is present, the flywheel may have to be replaced. If no runout exists, check the starter drive gear and starter housing for any unusual conditions that would cause it not to mesh properly. If a problem exists, replace the starter motor. **IMPORTANT:** Saturn starter motors are not shimmed.
High Pitched Whine after Engine Fires Over as Key is being Released (Starter Hang-in, or Solenoid Weak).	The distance between the flywheel and starter drive gear is too small.	Check flywheel runout; if it is acceptable, replace the starter motor. **IMPORTANT:** The starter motor is not shimmed for service.
A Loud Whoop after the Engine Fires Over; but While the Starter is Still Engaged. May Sound like a Siren If Engine is Revved while the Starter is Engaged.	The most probable cause is starter drive assembly.	Replace the starter motor.
A Rumble or Growl, or in Several Cases A Knock as the Starter Motor is Coasting Down to a Stop after Starting the Engine.	The most probable cause is a bent or unbalanced starter armature.	Replace the starter motor.
High Pitched Whine during Starting.	Check the flywheel for damage such as a bent flywheel or unusual wear patterns.	Start the engine and, using chalk, mark the high point of the tooth runout when the engine is turned off. If runout is present, the flywheel may have to be replaced. If no runout exists, the starter drive gear or housing may be preventing the gears from meshing properly. If a condition exists, replace the starter motor.
High Pitched Whine after the Engine Fires over.	Check flywheel runout.	If flywheel runout is acceptable, replace the starter motor.
Rumble or Knock As Starter Motor Coasts Down after Starting.	Starter motor.	Replace the starter motor.

G31129800008030X

Fig. 1 Troubleshooting (Part 3 of 3)

STARTER SPECIFICATIONS

Engine Temperature	Cranking Amperage
–4°F	230–280 amps
40°F	90–130 amps
40–80°F	80–120 amps
120°F	70–110 amps

Mitsubishi & Nippondenso Starters

NOTE: On Air Bag Equipped Models, Refer To "Air Bag System Precautions" Located In The Front Of This Manual For System Disarming & Arming Procedures.

NOTE: Refer To "Computer Relearn Procedures" Located In The Front Of This Manual When Battery Power To The Computer Has Been Interrupted.

INDEX

APPLICATION CHART

Year	Engine	VIN①	Ident. No.
CATERA			
1998–2001	3.0L	R	90542967
METRO			
1998	1.0L②	6	30005925
	1.0L③	6	30005226
	1.3L②	9	30005925
	1.3L③	9	30005226
1999–2001	1.0L②	6	30005925
	1.0L③	6	30005226
	1.3L②	2	30005925
	1.3L③	2	30005563
PRIZM			
1998–2002	1.8L	8	94857220

①— The eighth digit of VIN denotes engine code.
②— Automatic transaxle.
③— Manual transaxle.

PRECAUTIONS

AIR BAG SYSTEMS

Refer to "Air Bag System Precautions" in the front of this manual for system disarming and arming procedures.

BATTERY GROUND CABLE

Prior to service, disconnect battery ground cable and isolate as required.

DESCRIPTION

Nippondenso starters, **Figs. 1 and 2,** are either conventional or reduction gear types. The conventional type used on manual transmissions consists of a frame and field assembly, an armature assembly, an overrunning clutch assembly, a starter solenoid assembly, a commutator end housing, a brush holder and a shift lever. The reduction gear type starters used on automatic transmissions use all of the above components along with a reduction gear and shock absorber assembly.

TROUBLESHOOTING

SLOW OR NOT CRANKING

1. Turn headlamps On.
2. Ensure headlamps are burning with normal intensity.
3. If headlamps are burning dim, inspect battery charge condition, then charge as required.
4. If battery is fully charged, operate starter motor.
5. Note whether headlamps go out, dim considerably, or stay bright without starter activating.
6. Refer to the following diagnostic procedures as applicable.

Lamps Go Out

If the lamps go out as the starter switch is closed, it indicates a poor connection between the battery and starter motor.

1. Inspect battery terminals.
2. If corroded, remove, clean and reinstall.
3. Apply corrosion inhibitor to terminals to retard formation of corrosion.

Lamps Dim

If the lamps dim considerably as the starter switch is closed and the starter operates slowly or not at all, perform the following:

1. Inspect for a discharged battery, recharge or replace as required.
2. If the battery is fully charged, inspect the engine or the starter motor.
3. Inspect the engine for tight bearings, pistons, or other components.
4. Inspect engine timing, adjust as required.
5. Inspect for heavy engine oil. Low temperatures thicken engine oil and add considerable load to starting system.
6. Inspect starter motor for bent armature, loose pole screws, or worn bearings.
7. Inspect for thrown armature windings or commutator bars.

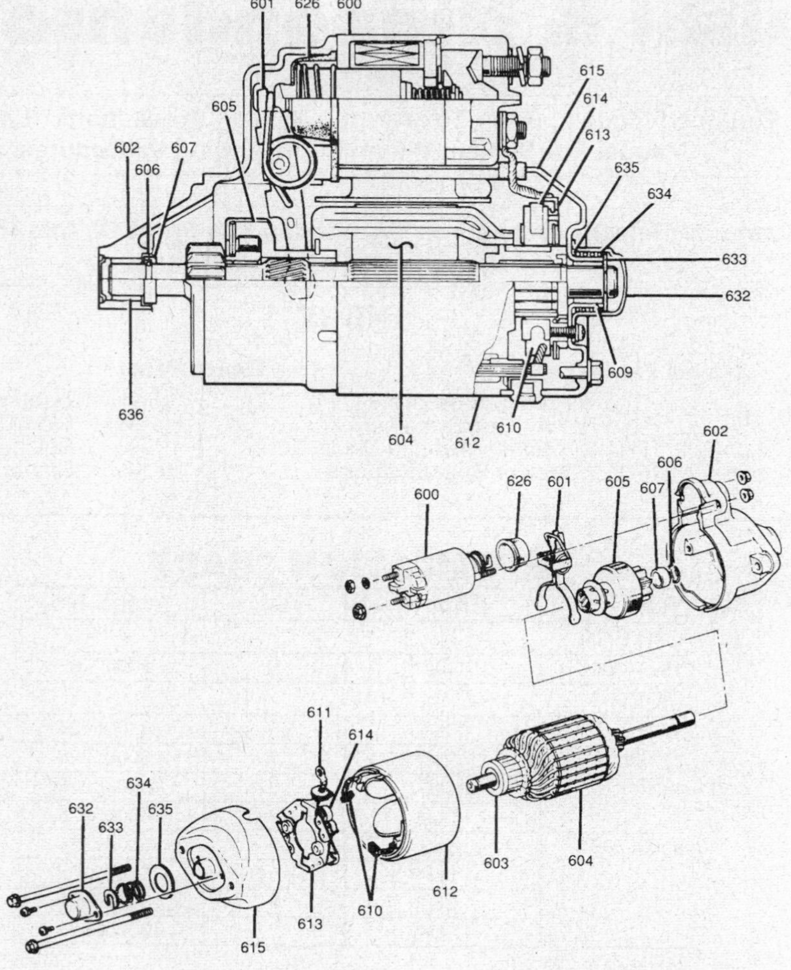

600	SOLENOID	607	ARMATURE STOP RING	615	COMMUTATOR END COVER
601	PINION DRIVE LEVER	609	COMMUTATOR END BUSHING	626	BOOT
602	DRIVE HOUSING	610	BRUSHES	632	COMMUTATOR END CAP
603	COMMUTATOR END	611	FIELD COIL LEAD WIRE	633	ARMATURE PLATE
604	ARMATURE	612	YOKE	634	ARMATURE BRAKE SPRING
605	OVERRUNNING CLUTCH ASSEMBLY	613	BRUSH HOLDER	635	END CAP GASKET
606	ARMATURE RETAINING RING	614	BRUSH SPRINGS	636	DRIVE HOUSING BUSHING

GC1129100033000X

Fig. 1 Exploded view of starter motor. Conventional w/manual transaxle

Lamps Stay Bright, No Cranking Action

Inspect for an open circuit in the starter, the starter switch or control circuit.

1. Place a heavy jumper lead across solenoid main terminals.
2. Starter should engage and operate.
3. If starter fails to perform as indicated, remove and inspect starter.

STARTER DRIVE PROBLEMS

If the starter does not turn over or if it drags, inspect the starter or electrical supply system. If the starter is noisy, if it turns but does not engage the engine, or if the starter will not disengage after the engine is started, inspect for the following:

1. Worn or chipped ring gear or starter pinion.
2. Improper pinion clearance.
3. Bent starter armature shaft. Maximum radial runout is .003 inch.

Drive Clutch Failure

The overrunning clutch is directly activated by a fork and lever. If the overrunning clutch will not turn engine over, inspect for worn out overrunning clutch. Proper meshing of the pinion is controlled by the end clearance between the pinion gear and the starter housing or pinion stop, if used.

1. Inspect and adjust pinion clearance (if applicable).
2. If pinion clearance is not adjustable, remove starter and inspect for excessive wear of solenoid linkage, shift lever mechanism, or improper assembly of components.
3. Inspect overrunning clutch for signs of overheating.
4. If clutch shows signs of overheating (bluish color), inspect for rust or gum buildup between armature shaft and drive or for burred splines.
5. Clean or deburr splines as required.
6. Overrunning clutches are not serviceable. Replace as required.

Drive Failure

If a Bendix type drive does not engage, inspect the following:

1. Inspect for a broken drive spring, or for sheared drive spring bolts.
2. If spring is broken, or spring bolts are sheared off, remove drive and replace damaged components.
3. Inspect for screw shaft.
4. If screw shaft threads are gummed or

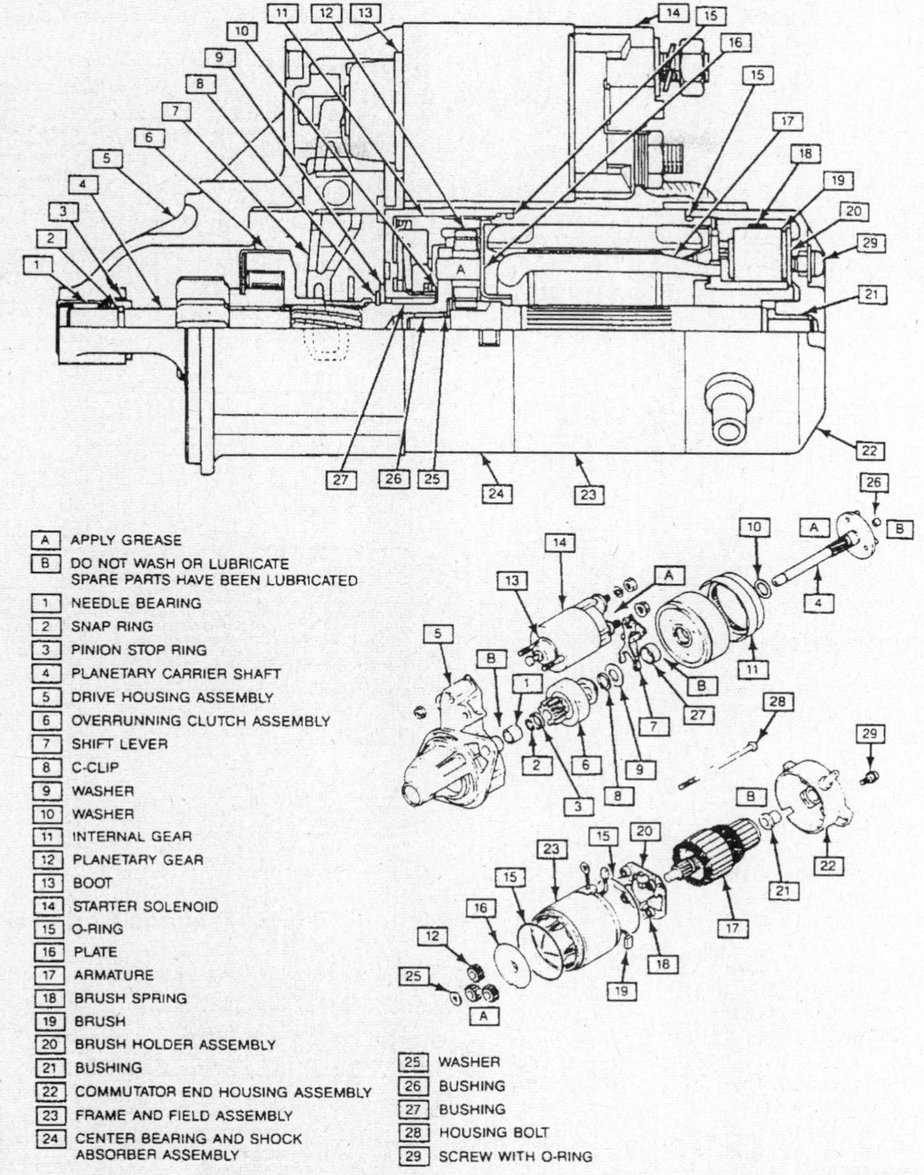

Fig. 2 Exploded view of starter motor. Reduction w/automatic transaxle

rusty, clean with kerosene or steel wool.

5. Ensure flywheel has adequate ventilation. Inspect breather hole in bottom of flywheel housing and clean if required.
6. If screw shaft threads are clean and rust free, look for mechanical failure within the drive itself.

SOLENOID SWITCHES

The solenoid switch on a cranking motor closes the circuit between the battery and the cranking motor and also shifts the drive pinion into mesh with the engine flywheel ring gear. This is done by means of a linkage between the solenoid switch plunger and the shift lever on the cranking motor.

There are two windings in the solenoid: a pull-in and a hold-in. Both windings are energized when the external control switch is closed. They produce a magnetic field which pulls the plunger in so that the drive pinion is shifted into mesh, and the main contacts in the solenoid switch are closed to connect the battery directly to the cranking motor. Closing the main switch contacts shorts out the pull-in winding since this winding is connected across the main contacts. The magnetism produced by the hold-in winding is sufficient to hold the plunger in, and shorting out the pull-in winding reduces battery drain. When the control switch is opened, it disconnects the hold-in winding from the battery. When the hold-in winding is disconnected from the battery, the shift lever spring withdraws the plunger from the solenoid, opening the solenoid switch contacts and at the same time withdrawing the drive pinion from mesh. Proper operation of the switch depends on maintaining a definite balance between the magnetic strength of the pull-in and hold-in windings.

This balance is determined by the size of the wire and the number of turns specified. An open circuit in the hold-in winding or attempts to crank with a discharged battery will cause the switch to chatter.

DIAGNOSIS & TESTING

Refer to **Fig. 3,** when troubleshooting these starter motors.

CIRCUIT INSPECTION w/VOLTMETER

Excessive resistance in the circuit between the battery and starter will reduce cranking performance. The resistance can

CHART #1
ENGINE DOES NOT CRANK AND STARTER SOLENOID DOES NOT CLICK

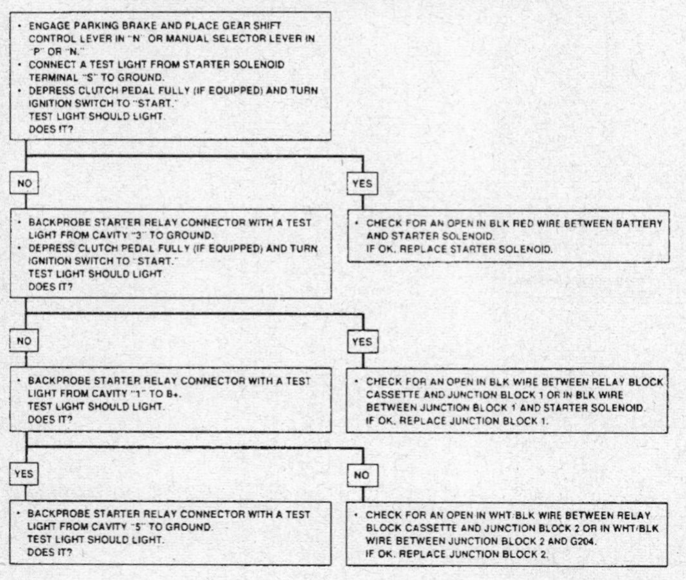

Fig. 3 Diagnosis chart (Part 1 of 4)

be inspected by using a voltmeter to measure voltage drop in the circuits while the starter is operated. Inspect for the following three conditions:

1. Voltage drop between vehicle frame and grounded battery terminal post.
2. Voltage drop between vehicle frame and starter motor field frame.
3. Voltage drop between insulated battery terminal post and starter motor terminal stud, or the battery terminal stud of the solenoid.

Measurements should show no more than one tenth (.1) volt drop when the starter motor is cranking the engine. Do not use the starter for more than 30 seconds at a time to avoid overheating it.

If excessive voltage drop is found, disconnect the cables, clean the connections, then connect the cables again. A coating of petroleum jelly on the battery cables and terminal clamps will retard corrosion.

On some models, extra long battery cables may be required due to the location of the battery and starter. This may result in somewhat higher voltage drop than the above recommended .1 volt. To determine the normal voltage drop, test several comparable vehicles and compare the results. If the voltage drop is well above the normal figure for all vehicles inspected, abnormal resistance will be indicated and corrections can be made as required.

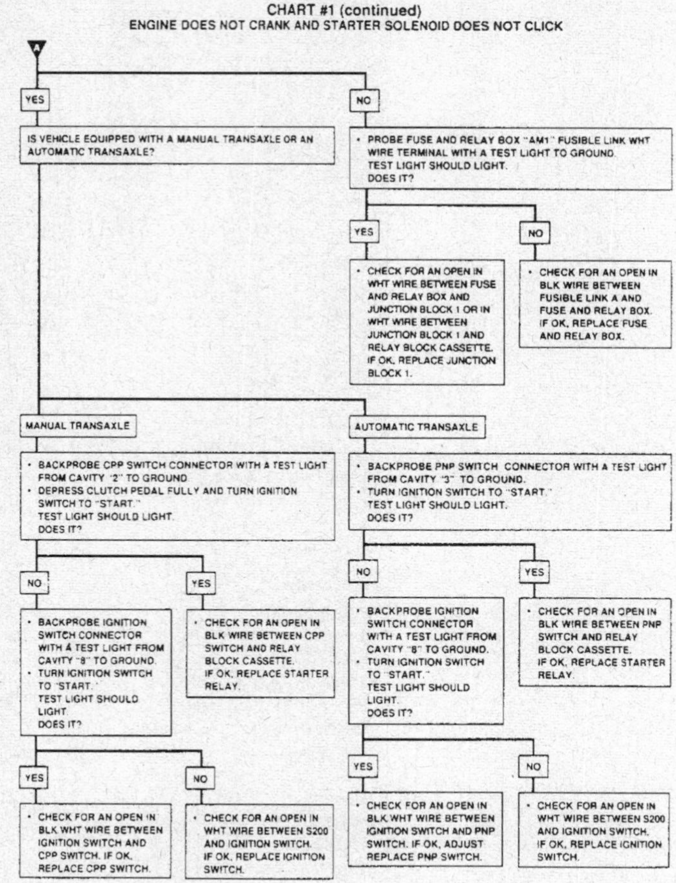

Fig. 3 Diagnosis chart (Part 2 of 4)

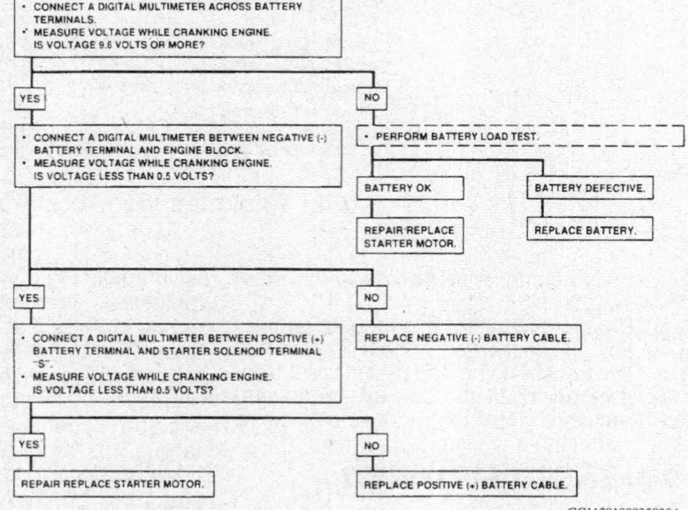

Fig. 3 Diagnosis chart (Part 3 of 4)

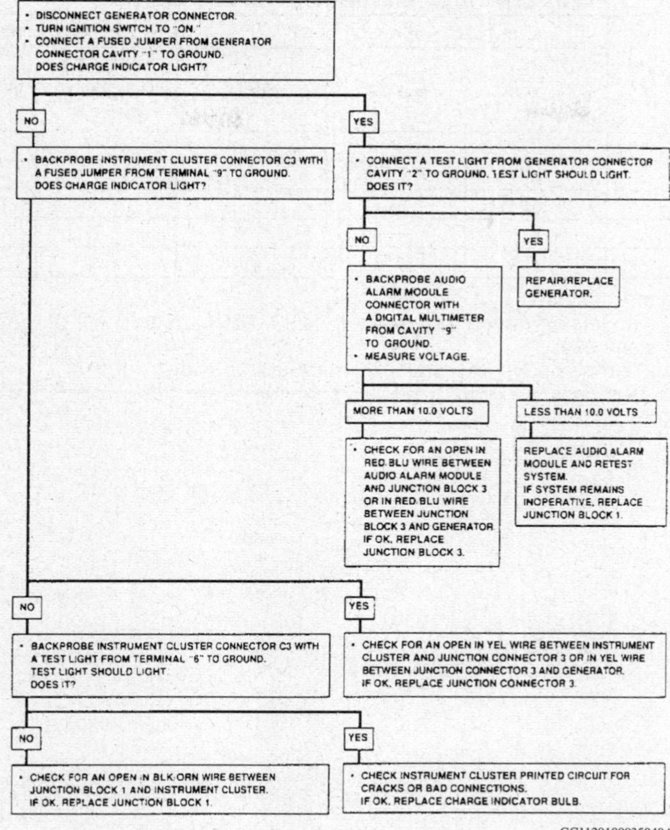

Fig. 3 Diagnosis chart (Part 4 of 4)

STARTER SPECIFICATIONS

Starter Identification No.	Free Speed Test			Solenoid	
	Amps	Volts	RPM	Hold-In Windings, Amps	Pull-In Windings, Amps
30005925①	75	11	—	—	—
30005226②	60	11	—	—	—
30005563③	60	11	—	—	—
90542967	—	—	—	—	—
94857220	90	11.5	3000	—	—

① — Automatic transaxle.
② — All 1998 models w/manual transaxle & 1999–2001 models w/1.0L engine & manual transaxle.
③ — 1999–2002 models w/1.3L engine & manual transaxle.

ALTERNATORS

TABLE OF CONTENTS

Application Chart

Model	Alternator Manufacturer
BUICK	
Century	Delphi
LeSabre	Delphi
Park Avenue	Delphi
Regal	Delphi
Riviera	Delphi
Skylark	Delphi
CADILLAC	
Catera	Bosch
DeVille	②
Eldorado	Delphi
Seville	②
CHEVROLET	
Camaro	Delphi
Cavalier	Delphi
Corvette	Valeo
Impala	Bosch①
	Delphi
Lumina	Delphi
Malibu	Delphi
Metro	Mitsubishi
Monte Carlo	Bosch
	Delphi
Prizm	Denso
OLDSMOBILE	
Achieva	Delphi
Alero	Delphi
	Valeo
Aurora	Delphi
Cutlass	Delphi
Intrigue	Delphi
LSS, Regency & 88	Delphi
PONTIAC	
Bonneville	Delphi
Firebird	Delphi
Grand Am	Delphi
	Valeo
Grand Prix	Delphi
Sunfire	Delphi
SATURN	
1.9L & 2.2L Engines	Delphi
3.0L Engine	Bosch

① — A Bosch NCB1 125 amp alternator is used for police and taxi options.

② — 1998–2001 models, Delphi; 2002 models, Denso.

Delphi Alternators, General Motors

NOTE: On Air Bag Equipped Models, Refer To "Air Bag System Precautions" Located In The Front Of This Manual For System Disarming & Arming Procedures.

NOTE: Refer To "Computer Relearn Procedure" Located In The Front Of This Manual When Battery Power To The Computer Has Been Interrupted.

INDEX

APPLICATION CHART

Model	Year	Alternator Model
BUICK		
Century	1998	CS130D
	1999–2001	CS130DP
	2002	CS130D
LeSabre	1998	CS144
	1999	CS130
	2000–02	AD230
Park Avenue	1998	CS130D
	1999	CS130DP
	2000–02	②
Regal	1998	CS130D
	1999–2001	CS130DP
	2002	CS130D
Riviera	1998–99	CS144
Skylark	1998–99	①
CADILLAC		
DeVille	1998	CS144
	1999	CS144 Gen II
	2000–01	LR 630
Eldorado	1998	CS144
	1999–2002	CS144 Gen II
Seville	1998–2001	LR630 Water Cooled
CHEVROLET		
Camaro	1998–2002	CS130D
Cavalier	1998–2002	CS130D
Impala	2000–02	CS130D
Lumina	1998–2001	③
Malibu	1998–99	CS130
	2000–02	CS130D
Monte Carlo	1998–2000	③
	2001–02	CS130D
OLDSMOBILE		
Achieva	1998	①
Alero	1999–2001	CS130D
Aurora	1998–99	CS144
	2001–02	AD 237

Continued

APPLICATION CHART—Continued

Model	Year	Alternator Model
OLDSMOBILE		
Cutlass	1998–99	CS130
Intrigue	1998–99	CS144
	2000–02	AD 237
LSS, Regency & 88	1998	CS144
	1999	CS130
PONTIAC		
Bonneville	1998	CS144
	1999	CS130
	2000–02	②
Firebird	1998–2002	CS130D
Grand Am	1998	①
	1999–2002	CS130D
Grand Prix	1998	CS130D
	1999–2001	CS130DP
	2002	CS130D
Sunfire	1998–2002	CS130D

① — 2.4L engine CS130D; 3.1L engine CS130.
② — VIN K engine AD230; VIN 1 engine AD237.
③ — Standard application CS130D; optional high output application CS144.

PRECAUTIONS

AIR BAG SYSTEMS

Refer to "Air Bag System Precautions" in the front of this manual for system disarming and arming procedures.

BATTERY GROUND CABLE

Prior to service, disconnect battery ground cable and isolate as required.

CHARGING SYSTEM

1. Ensure battery polarity is proper when servicing units. Reversed battery polarity will damage rectifiers and regulators.
2. If booster battery is used for starting, use proper polarity in hookup.
3. When a fast charger is used to charge a vehicle battery, vehicle battery cables should be disconnected unless fast charger is equipped with a special Alternator Protector, in which case vehicle battery cables need not be disconnected. **Fast chargers should never be used to start a vehicle as rectifier damage will result.**
4. Unless this system includes a load relay or field relay, grounding alternator output terminal will damage alternator and/or circuits. This is true even when system is not in operation since no circuit breaker is used and battery is applied to alternator output terminal at all times. The field or load relay acts as a circuit breaker in that it is controlled by ignition switch.
5. Before making any on vehicle tests of alternator or regulator, battery should be inspected and circuit inspected for faulty wiring or insulation. loose or corroded connections and poor ground circuits.

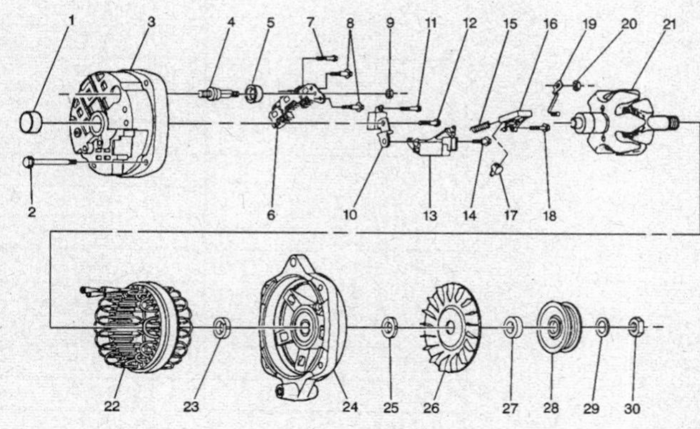

(1) Generator Rotor Slip Ring End Frame Bearing
(2) Generator Through Bolt
(3) Generator Slip Ring End Frame
(4) Generator Battery Terminal Stud
(5) Generator Battery Terminal Sleeve
(6) Generator Rectifier Bridge
(7) Generator Rectifier Bridge Bolt
(8) Generator Rectifier Bridge Bolt (Insulated)
(9) Generator Battery Terminal Nut
(10) Generator Capacitor
(11) Generator Rectifier Bridge Bolt
(12) Generator Capacitor/Rectifier Bolt (Insulated)
(13) Generator Voltage Regulator
(14) Generator Voltage Regulator Attaching Bolt (Insulated)
(15) Generator Brush Spring
(16) Generator Brush Holder
(17) Dust Shield
(18) Generator Brush Holder Bolt
(19) Generator Voltage Regulator Connector Strap
(20) Generator Stator Lead Attaching Nut
(21) Generator Rotor
(22) Generator Stator
(23) Generator Rotor Drive End Bearing Inside Collar
(24) Generator Rotor Drive End Bearing Frame
(25) Generator Rotor Drive End Bearing Outside Collar
(26) Generator Fan
(27) Generator Rotor Drive End Fan Collar
(28) Generator Pulley
(29) Generator Rotor Shaft Drive End Washer
(30) Generator Rotor Shaft Drive End Nut

GC1129700090000X

Fig. 1 Exploded view of CS type alternator

6. Inspect alternator belt tension and condition.
7. Ignition should be Off and battery ground cable disconnected before making any test connections to prevent system damage.
8. Do not reverse connections to alternator.
9. Do not short across or ground any of terminals in charging system.
10. Never disconnect output terminal while alternator is running.

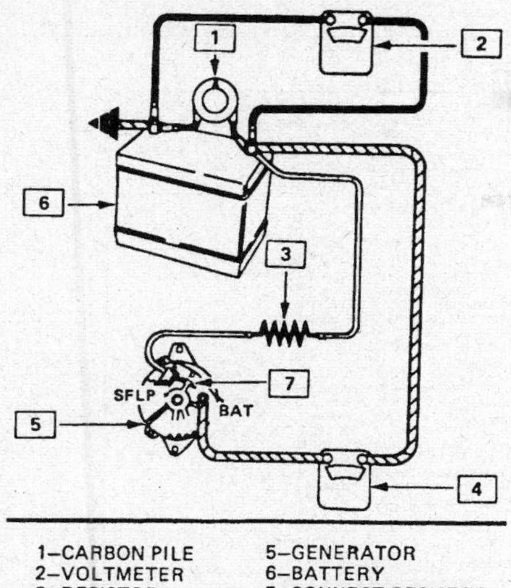

1–CARBON PILE
2–VOLTMETER
3–RESISTOR
4–TESTAMMETER
5–GENERATOR
6–BATTERY
7–CONNECT RESISTOR TO "L" TERMINAL

GC1129100038000X

Fig. 2 Alternator bench inspection

11. The vehicle battery must be fully charged when testing charging system.

Step	Action	Value(s)	Yes	No
DEFINITION: Generator on-vehicle test which will test the generator independently from the vehicle wiring.				
2	1. Connect the red alligator clip of a *J 41450-B* CS Generator Electronic Tester to the generator output terminal. (The output wire is attached to the generator with a ring terminal and nut.) 2. Connect the black alligator clip of the *J 41450-B* to the metal generator housing. The green POWER lamp of the tester should light and remain lighted while the tester is being used. Does the green POWER lamp on the tester light?	—	Go to *Step 9*	Go to *Step 3*
3	1. Recheck the alligator clip connections that were made in Step 2. 2. Correct the connections if they were reversed. Does the green POWER lamp on the tester light after the correct connections are verified?	—	Go to *Step 9*	Go to *Step 4*
4	Connect a *J 39200* digital multimeter (DMM) from the generator output terminal to the generator metal housing. Is the measured voltage within the specified range?	Above 12 V	Go to *Step 18*	Go to *Step 5*
5	Use a DMM to check the voltage between the battery terminals. Is the measured voltage within the specified range?	Above 12 V	Go to *Step 6*	Go to *Step 8*

GC1129800091010X

Fig. 3 Charging system test (Part 1 of 5). LR series alternator

Step	Action	Value(s)	Yes	No
6	1. Inspect the circuit between the generator output terminal and the battery positive terminal for a loose connection or open circuit condition. Be sure to check for an open fusible link and/or any blown in-line fuses that may be used on the vehicle. 2. If a loose connection or open circuit was located, repair it. If an open fusible link or blown fuse was found, be sure to check the system for possible causes of a circuit overload, such as a direct B+ short to ground. Is the circuit okay between the generator output terminal and the battery positive terminal?	—	Go to *Step 7*	—
7	Repair the loose connection or open circuit between the battery negative terminal and the generator housing. Is the repair complete?	—	Go to *Step 26*	—
8	1. Inspect the battery. 2. Charge or replace the battery if necessary. Is the battery OK?	—	Go to *Step 26*	—
9	1. Leave the *J 41450-B* alligator clips attached as in Step 2, and disconnect the vehicle 4-way generator connector. 2. Locate the matching 4-way connector of the *J 41450-B* and connect it to the generator. Does the red DIAGNOSTIC lamp on the tester light?	—	Go to *Step 11*	Go to *Step 10*
10	Perform the following test of the DIAGNOSTIC lamp of the *J 41450-B* : 1. Disconnect the *J 41450-B* 4-way connector from the generator, but leave the J41450-B alligator clips connected as in step 2. 2. Prepare a jumper wire with an in-line 100 ohm resistor. The watt rating of the resistor is not important. (An inexpensive 100Ω resistor can be purchased at an electronics supply store.) 3. At one end of the prepared jumper wire, attach a Metri-Pack 150 male terminal probe adapter from a *J 35616-A* Connector Test Adapter Kit. 4. Connect the prepared jumper wire to the *J 41450-B* L terminal (which is called the B terminal on CS 130D, LR, and AD generators). The tester connector terminals are the same as the generator connector terminals, so terminal identification on the *J 41450-B* can be accomplished by referring to Starting and Charging Connector End Views. 5. Connect the other end of the jumper to the battery negative terminal. Does the red DIAGNOSTIC lamp on the tester light when the jumper is connected?	—	Go to *Step 19*	Go to *Step 18*

GC1129800091020X

Fig. 3 Charging system test (Part 2 of 5). LR series alternator

GENERAL INFORMATION

Alternators are composed of the same functional components as the conventional DC generator but they operate differently. The field is called a rotor and is the turning portion of the unit. The generating part, called a stator, is the stationary member, comparable to the armature in a DC generator. The regulator, similar to those used in a DC system, regulates the alternator-rectifier system output.

The power source of the system is the alternator. Current is transmitted from the field terminal of the regulator through a slip ring to the field coil and back to ground through another slip ring. The strength of the field regulates the output of the alternating current. This alternating current is then transmitted from the alternator to the rectifier where it is converted to direct current.

These alternators employ a three-phase stator winding in which the phase windings are electrically 120° apart. The rotor consists of a field coil encased between interleaved sections producing. When the rotor is energized, a magnetic field with alternate north and south poles is created. By rotating the rotor inside the stator the alternating current is induced in the stator windings. This alternating current is rectified (changed to DC) by silicon diodes and brought out to the output terminal of the alternator.

DIODE RECTIFIERS

Six silicon diode rectifiers are used and act as electrical one-way valves. Three of the diodes have ground polarity and are pressed or screwed into a heat sink which is grounded. The other three diodes (ungrounded) are pressed or screwed into and insulated from the end head; these diodes are connected to the alternator output terminal.

Since the diodes have a high resistance to the flow of current in one direction and a low resistance in the opposite direction, they may be connected in a manner which allows current to flow from the alternator to the battery in the low resistance direction. The high resistance in the opposite direction prevents the flow of current from the battery to the alternator. Because of this feature no circuit breaker is required between the alternator and battery.

DESCRIPTION

CS ALTERNATORS

The CS alternator is available in two sizes: CS130 and CS144, **Fig. 1.** The numerals denote the outer diameter of the stator laminations in millimeters and the letters CS stand for charging system.

These alternators use a conventional fan mounted next to the pulley to pull air through the assembly for cooling. An internal fan mounted on the rotor pulls air through the slip ring end frame to cool the rectifier, bridge and regulator. Air is expelled through openings in the frame. No periodic maintenance is required.

LR ALTERNATORS

The LR series alternator is available in only one size with an output of 140 amps. The LR series alternator has a liquid cooled end frame. Engine coolant is passed through a tube molded into the end frame next to the electronic components of the alternator. This cooling supplements the air cooling action of the internal fans and helps

Step	Action	Value(s)	Yes	No
11	***Caution: Make sure that the load is completely turned off before connecting or disconnecting a carbon pile load tester to the battery. Otherwise, sparking could ignite battery gasses which are extremely flammable and may explode violently.*** 1. Prior to connecting a carbon pile load tester, make sure that the load dial of the carbon pile tester is turned completely to the OFF position. 2. Connect the cable leads of the carbon pile tester to the battery of the vehicle. 3. Connect an inductive ammeter to the output lead(s) of the generator. Make sure that all output leads pass through the ammeter inductive clip. The carbon pile tester may have its own inductive ammeter, or use a *J 35590* Current Clamp. 4. Start the engine and allow it to idle briefly. Does the red DIAGNOSTIC lamp on the *J 41450-B* light?	—	Go to *Step 19*	Go to *Step 12*
12	Increase the engine speed to 2500 RPM. Does the red DIAGNOSTIC lamp on the *J 41450-B* light?	—	Go to *Step 19*	Go to *Step 13*
13	1. Maintain the engine speed at 2500 RPM. 2. Turn on the load of the carbon pile tester, and increase the load until the generator output is equal to the load test value given in Generator Usage. As the load is increased, is the generator capable of producing the amount of load test current specified in Generator Usage?	—	Go to *Step 14*	Go to *Step 19*
14	Maintain the engine speed at 2500 RPM and continue to operate the generator at the load test value. Is the red DIAGNOSTIC lamp on the *J 41450-B* lit?	—	Go to *Step 19*	Go to *Step 15*
15	1. Maintain the engine speed at 2500 RPM and continue to operate the generator at the load test value. 2. Connect a DMM from the generator output terminal to the battery positive (+) terminal. Is the measured voltage within the specified range?	Above 0.5 V	Go to *Step 22*	Go to *Step 16*
16	1. Maintain the engine speed at 2500 RPM and continue to operate the generator at the load test value. 2. Connect a DMM from the generator metal housing to the battery negative (–) terminal. Is the measured voltage within the specified range?	Above 0.5 V	Go to *Step 23*	Go to *Step 17*
17	***Caution: Make sure that the load is completely turned off before connecting or disconnecting a carbon pile load tester to the battery. Otherwise, sparking could ignite battery gasses which are extremely flammable and may explode violently.*** 1. Disconnect the DMM. 2. Turn OFF the load in the carbon pile tester. 3. Turn the ignition switch to LOCK to stop the engine. 4. Disconnect the carbon pile tester cables from the battery. 5. Disconnect the *J 41450-B* 4-way connector from the generator. 6. Inspect the generator 4-way connector on the vehicle. Does the vehicle have a wire in the L terminal cavity (or B terminal for CS 130D, LR, and AD generators) of the generator 4-way connector?	—	Go to *Step 26*	Go to *Step 24*

GC1129800091030X

Fig. 3 Charging system test (Part 3 of 5). LR series alternator

Step	Action	Value(s)	Yes	No
18	There is an internal problem in the *J 41450-B*. Replace the *J 41450-B*. Has the *J 41450-B* been replaced?	—	Go to *Step 26*	—
19	**Important:** Before generator repair or replacement, the L terminal circuit (if applicable) must be tested for resistance in order to avoid a repeat failure. Disconnect and examine the generator 4-way connector. Is there a wire in the L cavity (or B cavity for CS 130D, LR, and AD generators) of the generator connector?	—	Go to *Step 20*	Go to *Step 24*
20	1. Be sure the 4-way generator connector is disconnected. 2. Turn the ignition key to the RUN position. 3. Connect a fused jumper wire *J 36169-A* (with a 5 amp fuse) from ground to the vehicle 4-way generator connector terminal L (or B terminal for CS 130D, LR, and AD generators). To connect the jumper to the generator, use a Metri-Pack 150 connector test adapter from *J 35616-A*. Refer to Starting and Charging Connector End Views. Does the fuse blow?	—	Go to *Step 21*	Go to *Step 25*
21	There is a short to B+ voltage when the ignition key is in the RUN position. The short may be a result of a miswired condition. The L terminal circuit must be a resistance circuit either through a charge indicator or the PCM. If direct battery voltage is applied to the generator at the L terminal, the regulator will eventually be destroyed, causing a repeat failure. Repair the short to B+ voltage in the L terminal circuit (or B terminal circuit for CS 130D, LR, and AD generators). Is the short circuit repaired?	—	Go to *Step 25*	—
22	1. Turn off the engine. 2. Disconnect the battery negative terminal. 3. Inspect the circuit between the battery positive terminal and the generator output terminal for a high-resistance connection. Disassemble and clean all connections in this circuit. 4. Assemble the connections 5. Connect the battery negative terminal. Is the repair complete?	—	Go to *Step 26*	—
23	1. Turn off the engine. 2. Inspect the ground circuit for high resistance from the battery negative terminal to the generator housing. Disassemble and clean all connections. 3. Assemble the connections Is the repair complete?	—	Go to *Step 26*	—

GC1129800091040X

Fig. 3 Charging system test (Part 4 of 5). LR series alternator

prevent overheating of the alternator during periods of high electrical demands.

AD ALTERNATORS

The AD alternators are similar to CS type alternators except for their dual cooling fans. The "AD" stands for Air-Cooled Dual internal fan. The "2" is an electric design designator. The "30" or "37" denotes the outside diameter of the stator laminations in millimeters.

SYSTEM OPERATION

CS ALTERNATORS

CS130 and CS144 alternators may be used with only two connections. The battery positive BAT terminal must be connected to a battery during operation. The second required connection is through the Powertrain Control Module (PCM) to the indicator lamp. Three other regulator terminals are available for optional use in vehicle systems. The P terminal is connected to the stator and may be connected to a tachometer or other device. The F terminal is connected internally to field positive and may be used as a fault indicator. The S terminal may be connected externally to a voltage, such as battery voltage, to sense voltage to be controlled.

The regulator voltage setting varies with temperature, and limits system voltage by controlling rotor field current. Unlike others regulators, this regulator switches field current on and off at a fixed frequency of about 400 cycles per second. By varying on–off time, proper average field current is obtained to provide proper system voltage. At high speeds, the on time may be 10% and off time 90%. At low speeds with high electrical loads, on–off time may be 90% and 10% respectively.

LR ALTERNATORS

The LR series alternator provides the voltage to operate the vehicle's electrical system and to charge the battery through circuit No. 1 (red). When the ignition is turned On, voltage is supplied to the alternator L terminal by the Powertrain Control Module (PCM), turning on the voltage regulator. The voltage regulator controls current to the rotor, which controls alternator output voltage. When the engine starts, the regulator senses alternator rotation by detecting AC voltage at the stator through an internal wire. Once the engine is running, the regulator varies the field current by controlling the pulse width. The alternator F terminal is connected internally to the voltage regulator and externally to the PCM. The PCM monitors the field voltage on the alternator F terminal.

The PCM turns on the CHARGE indicator lamp by sending a message to the instrument cluster whenever a under-voltage, over-voltage or a stopped alternator is detected.

AD ALTERNATORS

Refer to "CS Alternators" for system operation.

DIAGNOSIS & TESTING

CS ALTERNATORS

In-Vehicle Test

When the charging system is operating properly, the indicator lamp will light when the ignition is turned On and will go out when the engine starts. If the lamp operates abnormally, or if a battery undercharge or overcharge condition occurs, use the following procedure to diagnose the charging system.

1. Before beginning test, inspect the following:
   a. An undercharged battery is often caused by accessories being left on for extended periods of time or an accessory lamp staying on. Ensure all lamps and accessories are turned off.
   b. If alternator is noisy inspect for a loose drive pulley, loose mounting bolts, worn or dirty bearings, faulty diodes or a faulty stator.
2. Turn ignition and all electrical accessory loads Off.
3. Connect ammeter in series at alternator output BAT terminal, then connect voltmeter and carbon pile across battery terminal.

Step	Action	Value(s)	Yes	No
24	The tester turns the generator on in a different way than the vehicle does, so an additional test is necessary. This Step is applicable only for vehicles that do not use an L terminal connection (or B terminal for CS 130D, LR, and AD generators). 1. Remove the 4-way connector from the generator. 2. Measure the generator internal resistance between the L and I/F terminals (B and C terminals for CS 130D, LR, and AD generators). Use Metri-Pack 150 terminal adapters from a *J 35616-A* Connector Test Adapter Kit. The L and I/F terminals are the two middle terminals on the generator. Is the measured resistance within the specified range?	Below 500 Ω	Go to *Step 26*	Go to *Step 25*
25	Repair or replace the generator. Is the repair complete?	—	Go to *Step 26*	—
26	1. Make sure any components removed during diagnosis are installed in place and that all connectors are connected. 2. Repeat the system check. Is the system check complete?	—	System OK	—

GC1129800091050X

Fig. 3 Charging system test (Part 5 of 5). LR series alternator

4. Connect positive lead of universal electronic CS generator tester tool No. J41450-CS, or equivalent, to alternator output terminal and negative lead to alternator housing. If tester lamp lights, proceed to next step. If tester lamp does not light, proceed as follows:
   a. Measure voltage between alternator output terminal and battery ground terminal using a suitable voltmeter. If battery voltage is indicated, proceed to next step. If battery voltage is not indicated, locate and repair open in alternator output circuit.
   b. Connect a jumper wire between alternator housing and battery ground terminal. If test lamp lights, proceed to next step. If test lamp does not light, repair open in ground circuit from alternator housing to battery ground terminal.
5. Disconnect alternator connector and connect matching connector of tester to alternator. If red tester lamp lights, proceed to next step. If red tester lamp does not light, proceed as follows:
   a. Disconnect tester lead from alternator.
   b. Turn ignition On and probe connector terminal "L" of vehicle harness connector with a fused jumper wire.
   c. If fuse does not blow, replace alternator. If fuse blows, repair direct short to battery voltage in terminal "L" circuit, then replace alternator.
6. Turn off all accessories and close doors to ensure there is no load on battery.
7. Connect positive lead of universal electronic CS generator tester tool No. J41450-CS, or equivalent, to alternator output terminal and negative lead to alternator housing.
8. Start engine and let idle briefly. If red tester lamp does not light, proceed to next step. If red tester lamp lights, replace alternator.
9. Increase engine speed to 2500 RPM. If red tester lamp does not light, proceed to next step. If red tester lamp lights, replace alternator.
10. With engine speed still at 2500 RPM, turn load on carbon pile load tester to ON and adjust until alternator output is at Load Test value. If red tester lamp does not light, alternator is satisfactory. If red tester lamp lights, replace alternator.

Bench Testing

1. Make connections as illustrated, **Fig. 2,** but leave carbon pile disconnected. The ground polarity of alternator and battery must be same. Battery must be fully charged. Use a 30–500 ohm resistor between battery and L terminal.
2. Slowly increase alternator speed and observe voltage.
3. If voltage is uncontrolled and increases above 16 volts, rotor field is shorted, regulator is faulty or both. A shorted rotor field can cause regulator to become faulty. **Battery must be fully charged when making this test.**
4. If voltage is below 16 volts, increase speed and adjust carbon pile obtain maximum amperage output, maintain voltage above 13 volts.
5. If output is within 15 amps of rated output, alternator is satisfactory.
6. If output is not within 15 amps of rated output, alternator is faulty and requires repair.

LR ALTERNATORS

Refer to **Fig. 3** for alternator and charging system diagnosis. The LR series alternator is serviced by replacement only.

AD ALTERNATORS

Refer to "CS Alternators" for system diagnosis and testing procedure.

ALTERNATOR SPECIFICATIONS

Alternator Model	Rated Hot Output Amps
AD230	105
AD237	105
CS130	105
CS130D	105
CS130 DIF	105
CS130DP	107
CS144①	124
CS144②	150
LR630	150

① — Except service part identification code KG9.
② — Service part identification code KG9.

Delphi Alternators, Saturn

INDEX

APPLICATION CHART

Model	Alternator Model
Saturn	CS130
	CS121

DESCRIPTION

The alternator is constructed of a rotor mounted on bearings in two end frames, a stator assembly, six silicon diodes, an internally mounted voltage regulator and an integral mounted shield. the alternator develops AC voltages which are converted to DC current by a rectifier circuit.

The Powertrain Control Module (PCM) monitors battery voltage and will increase idle speed if battery voltage drops below a calibrated amount.

TROUBLESHOOTING

Refer to **Figs. 1 and 2** for alternator system troubleshooting procedures.

X — Most Probable Cause(s)
• — Possible Causes

COMPLAINT–CONDITION / CAUSE	IGN4 Fuse	IGN3 Fuse	IGN1 Fuse	Circuit 15A (Battery Ground)	Circuit 2B	Circuit 3C	Circuit 39C	Circuit 25/25A	I/P Cluster	Generator	Ignition Switch	Excessive Electrical Load	Constant Running at Low RPM	Loose Belt	Broken Belt	Loose Mounting Bolts	Parasitic Load	Fusible Link Circuit 2C
Charge Warning Telltale Lamp Does Not Light	X		X		X	X	X	X	•	•	•							
Charge Warning Telltale Lamp stays on with Engine on								X	•	•		•	•	•	•			
Battery is Undercharged				X	X					•		•	•	•	•		X	X
Battery is Overcharged										X								
Lights Dim at Idle												X	•	•	X			•
Lights Dim at Over 1000 RPM										•				X	•	•		
Mechanical Noise										•				X		•		
Radio Noise/Hum or Whistle										X								
Output Exceeds 16V																		

G311295000007000X

Fig. 1 Alternator system troubleshooting chart

DIAGNOSIS & TESTING

PRECAUTIONS

Ensure engine is stopped, ignition is Off and drive belt is at proper tension before connecting any test equipment to alternator. Refer to "Belt Tension Data" for tension specifications.

CHARGING SYSTEM LAMP FUNCTION TEST

1. Turn ignition Off. Charge indicator lamp should be off.
2. Turn ignition On. Charge indicator lamp should be on.
3. Crank engine. Charge indicator lamp should turn off and stay off once engine is running.

ALTERNATOR TEST

Electronic system tester tool No. SA9154Z-A, or equivalent, is required for the following starter system test.

1. Clean battery terminals and attach electronic system tester clamps to appropriate terminals. The gray inductive current pickup should be clamped around battery positive cable between positive terminal and starter motor solenoid connection.
2. Clamp current probe to wire leading to battery ground terminal. Arrow on probe should point toward battery.
3. Press "Charging System Test." Display should show proper number of cylinders.
4. Run engine at 2000 RPM until display flashes "Maintain 2000 RPM."
5. Hold at 2000 RPM until counter counts down from ten seconds.
6. When ten seconds are over, run engine at idle until display reads "Maintain Idle." Hold this momentarily until display reads "Test Complete."
7. Press "Continue" to view results. Electronic System Tester will display alternator voltage and current output as follows:
   a. Voltage output should be 13–15.5 volts.
   b. Current output should be a minimum of 60 amps.
8. If alternator does not meet specifications, proceed as follows:
   a. Ensure battery is sufficiently charged and electrical system is not excessively loaded.
   b. If battery has sufficient charge, if electrical loads are not excessive and alternator performance is still not as specified, replace alternator.
   c. Repeat test to ensure alternator is functioning properly.

COMPLAINT/CONDITION	POSSIBLE CAUSE(S)	CORRECTION(S)
High Pitch Whine with High Electrical Loads	– Magnetic noise from generator – Bearing noise	– Verify additional electrical loads from accessories (e.g., cell phone, CB radio, radar detector, etc.). – Disconnect regulator connector if the whine is no longer present; tighten to specification all generator mounting bolts. Reconnect regulator; if whine still exists, replace generator.
Squeal, Click, Chirp, or Squeak Seems To Follow Engine rpm	– Serpentine belt – Generator bearing noise or rotor rub	– Spray belt dressing on serpentine belt. If noise goes away, replace belt. – Check belt tension and ensure all belted accessories are tight. If noise is still present, replace generator.

G31129900009000X

Fig. 2 Alternator system troubleshooting chart

ALTERNATOR SPECIFICATIONS

Type	Model	Max. Rated Output Amps	Temp. Deg. F	Approx. Output Amps @ RPM
Saturn	CS121 & CS130	96	81	91 @ 2000
			221	71 @ 2000

Bosch Alternators

NOTE: On Air Bag Equipped Models, Refer To "Air Bag System Precautions" Located In The Front Of This Manual For System Disarming & Arming Procedures.

NOTE: Refer To "Computer Relearn Procedure" Located In The Front Of This Manual When Battery Power To The Computer Has Been Interrupted.

NOTE: "Electrical Symbol & Wire Color Code Identification" Located In The Front Of This Manual May Be Used As An Aid When Using Wiring Circuits Found In This Section.

INDEX

APPLICATION CHART

Model	Year	Rated Hot Output Amps
Catera	1998–2001	120
Impala	2000–02	125
Monte Carlo	2000–02	125

GENERAL INFORMATION

Refer to "Delphi Alternators" for general information.

PRECAUTIONS

AIR BAG SYSTEMS

Refer to "Air Bag System Precautions" in the front of this manual for system disarming and arming procedures.

BATTERY GROUND CABLE

Prior to service, disconnect battery ground cable and isolate as required.

CHARGING SYSTEM

1. Ensure battery polarity is proper when servicing units. Reversed battery polarity will damage rectifiers and regulators.
2. If booster battery is used for starting, use proper polarity in hookup.
3. When a fast charger is used to charge a vehicle battery, vehicle battery cables should be disconnected unless fast charger is equipped with a special Alternator Protector, in which case vehicle battery cables need not be disconnected. **Fast chargers should never be used to start a vehicle as rectifier damage will result.**
4. Unless system includes a load relay or field relay, grounding alternator output terminal will damage alternator and/or circuits. This is true even when system is not in operation since no circuit breaker is used and battery is applied to alternator output terminal at all times. The field or load relay acts as a circuit breaker in that it is controlled by ignition switch.
5. Before making any on vehicle tests of alternator or regulator, battery should be inspected and circuit inspected for faulty wiring or insulation. loose or corroded connections and poor ground circuits.
6. Inspect alternator belt tension and condition.
7. Ignition should be Off and battery ground cable disconnected before making any test connections to prevent damage to system.
8. Do not reverse connections to alternator.
9. Do not short across or ground any of terminals in charging system.
10. Never disconnect output terminal while alternator is running.
11. The vehicle battery must be fully charged when testing charging system.

DESCRIPTION

CATERA

The Bosch alternator is a 120 amp output alternator. The main components are the rotor, field coil, regulator and rectifier bridge, **Fig. 1.** The alternator is water cooled. The coolant hose runs directly from the radiator to the alternator housing. No periodic maintenance is required.

IMPALA & MONTE CARLO

The Bosch alternator is a 125 amp output alternator. The main components are the rotor, field coil, rectifier bridge and a digital regulator.

SYSTEM OPERATION

A regulator supplies current to the field coil of the rotor. When the field coil is supplied with voltage, a magnetic field is created. As the rotor turns, this magnetic field creates AC voltage and current in the stator windings. The AC voltage and current is converted to DC by a rectifier bridge which is available to the vehicle's electrical system.

DIAGNOSIS & TESTING

CATERA

Refer to wiring diagram, **Fig. 2** and diagnosis charts, **Figs. 3 through 5,** for charging system diagnosis.

IMPALA & MONTE CARLO

Refer to wiring diagrams, **Figs. 6 and 7,** and to diagnosis tests, **Fig. 8 and 9,** for charging system diagnosis.

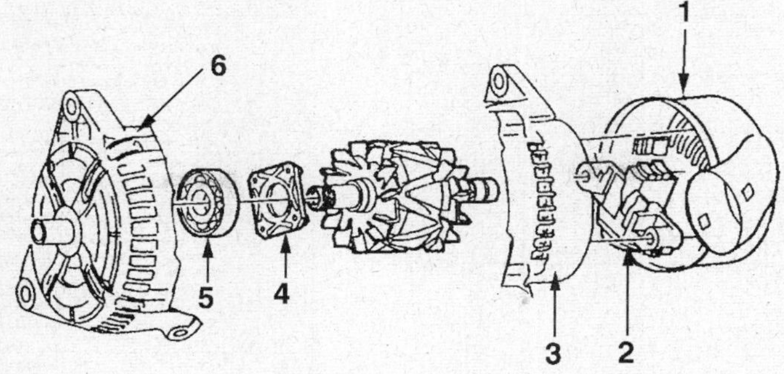

1. REAR CAP
2. REGULATOR
3. REAR COVER
4. FRONT BEARING RETAINER
5. FRONT BEARING
6. FRONT COVER
7. ARMATURE

GC1129800080000X

Fig. 1 Exploded view of Bosch alternator

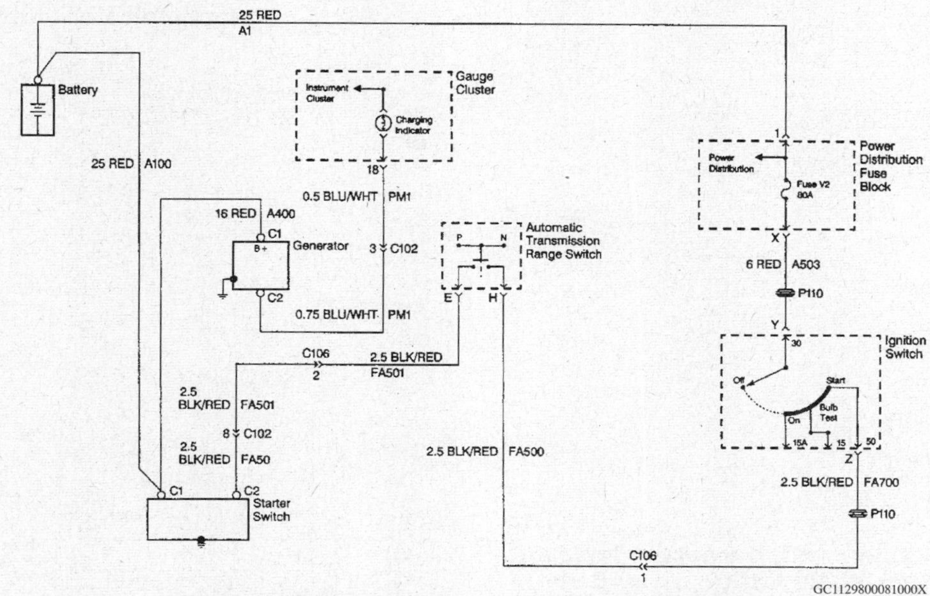

GC1129800081000X

Fig. 2 Charging system wiring diagram. Catera

Step	Action	Value(s)	Yes	No
1.	1. Disconnect the generator connector C2. 2. Turn the ignition switch to the ON position. 3. Use the DMM to measure the voltage between the generator connector C2 and a known good ground. Is the measured voltage within the specified value?	B+	*Go to Step 3*	*Go to Step 2*
2	1. Locate an open or a high resistance in circuit PM1. 2. Repair the open or the high resistance in circuit PM1. Is the repair complete?	—	*Go to Step 8*	—
3	Disconnect generator connector C1. 2. Use the DMM to measure the voltage between the generator connector C1 and a known good ground. Is the measured voltage within the specified value?	B+	*Go to Step 5*	*Go to Step 4*
4	1. Locate an open or a high resistance in circuits A100 and/or A400. 2. Repair the open or the high resistance in circuits A100 and/or A400. Is the repair complete?	—	*Go to Step 5*	—

GC1129800082010X

Fig. 3 Battery is undercharged or overcharged (Part 1 of 2). Catera

Step	Action	Value(s)	Yes	No
5	1. Reconnect the generator connector. 2. Turn OFF all the accessories. 3. Run the engine at fast idle. 4. Use the DMM to measure the voltage between the positive and the negative terminals of the battery. Is the measured voltage within the specified value?	12.5–14.5V	*Go to Step 7*	*Go to Step 6*
6	Repair or replace the generator. Is the repair or replacement complete?	—	*Go to Step 8*	—
7	1. Load test the generator. 2. Replace the battery if the generator passed the load test. Is the replacement complete?	—	*Go to Step 8*	—
8	1. Connect all of the connectors and components that were disconnected. 2. Verify that the generator operates properly. Does the generator operate properly?	—	System OK	*Go to Step 1*

GC1129800082020X

Fig. 3 Battery is undercharged or overcharged (Part 2 of 2). Catera

Step	Action	Value(s)	Yes	No
1	1. Disconnect generator connector C2. 2. Turn the ignition switch to the ON position. Is the charging indicator lamp illuminated?	—	Go to Step 3	Go to Step 2
2	Repair or replace the generator. Is the repair or replacement complete?	—	Go to Step 6	—
3	Disconnect connector C102. Is the charging indicator lamp illuminated?	—	Go to Step 5	Go to Step 4
4	1. Locate the short to ground in circuit PM1 between the generator connector C2 and connector C102 terminal 3. 2. Repair the short to ground in circuit PM1. Is the repair complete?	—	Go to Step 6	—
5	1. Locate a short to ground in circuit PM1 between the gauge cluster connector terminal 18 and connector C102 terminal 3. 2. Repair the short to ground in circuit PM1 between the gauge cluster connector terminal 18 and connector C102 terminal 3. 3. Replace the gauge cluster if circuit PM1 is OK. Is the repair or replacement complete?	—	Go to Step 6	—
6	1. Connect all connectors and components that were disconnected. 2. Verify that the charging indicator lamp operates properly. Does the charging indicator lamp operate properly?	—	System OK	Go to Step 1

GC1129800083000X

Fig. 4 Charge indicator always on. Catera

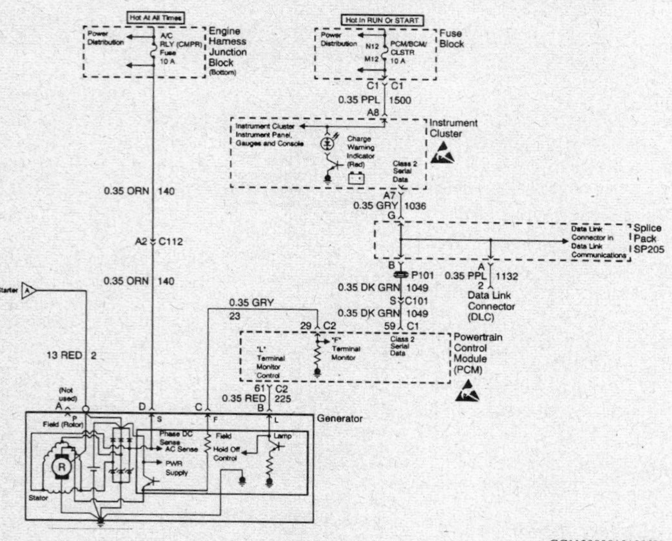

GC1120000101000X

Fig. 6 Charging system wiring diagram. Impala & 2000 Monte Carlo

Step	Action	Value(s)	Yes	No
1	1. Disconnect generator connector C2. 2. Attach a fused jumper from the generator connector C2 to ground. 3. Turn the ignition switch to the ON position. Is the charging indicator lamp illuminated?	—	Go to Step 2	Go to Step 3
2	Repair or replace the generator. Is the repair or replacement complete?	—	Go to Step 6	—
3	1. Disconnect connector C102. 2. Attach a fused jumper between terminal 3 of connector C102 and a known good ground. Is the charging indicator lamp illuminated?	—	Go to Step 4	Go to Step 6
4	1. Locate an open or a high resistance in circuit PM1 between terminal 3 of connector C102 and the generator connector C2. 2. Repair the open or the high resistance in circuit PM1 between terminal 3 of connector C102 and the generator connector C2. Is the repair complete?	—	Go to Step 6	—
5	1. Locate an open or a high resistance in circuit PM1 between terminal 3 of connector C102 and terminal 18 of the gauge cluster connector. 2. Repair the open or the high resistance in circuit PM1 between terminal 3 of connector C102 and terminal 18 of the gauge cluster connector. 3. Replace the gauge cluster if circuit PM1 is OK. Is the repair or replacement complete?	—	Go to Step 6	—
6	1. Connect all of the connectors and components that were disconnected. 2. Verify that the charging indicator operates properly. Does the charging indicator lamp operate properly?	—	System OK	Go to Step 1

GC1129800084000X

Fig. 5 Charge indicator inoperative. Catera

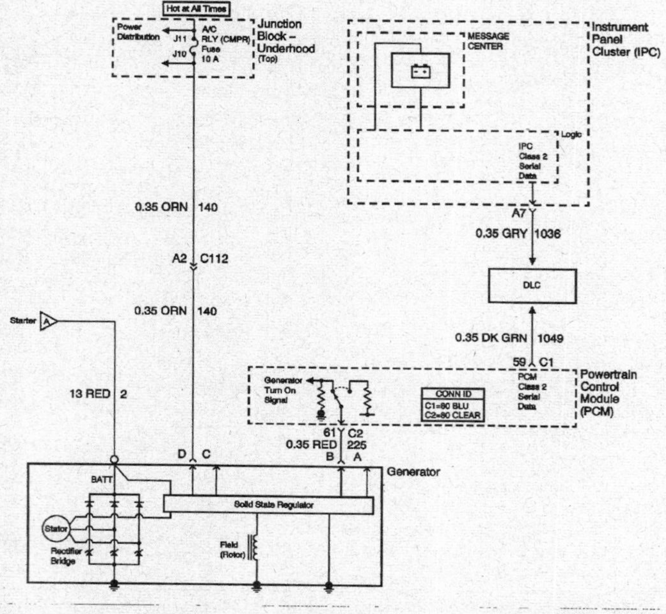

GC1120100184000X

Fig. 7 Charging system wiring diagram. 2001–02 Monte Carlo

Step	Action	Value(s)	Yes	No
1	**Inspect battery & starting system.** **Are systems operating properly?**		Go to Step 2	**Repair or replace components as needed**
2	Connect the J 41450-B to the generator. Does the green POWER lamp on the tester light?		Go to Step 4	Go to Step 3
3	Measure the voltage from the output terminal of the J 41450-B to the metal housing of the generator. Does the voltage measure greater than the specified value?	12 V	Go to Step 12	Go to Step 4
4	1 Disconnect the generator harness connector. 2 Locate the matching harness connector on the J 41450-B and connect it to the generator. Does the red DIAGNOSTIC lamp on the tester light?		Go to Step 6	Go to Step 5
5	**Notice:** The J 41450-B connector terminals are the same as the generator connector terminals. 1 Disconnect the J 41450-B harness connector from the generator. 2 Prepare a jumper wire with an in-line 100Ω resistor. 3 Attach a Metri-Pack 150 male terminal probe adapter from a J 35616-A . 4 Connect the jumper wire between the L terminal of the J 41450-B and a good ground. Does the red DIAGNOSTIC lamp on the tester light?		Go to Step 15	Go to Step 13

GC1120000102010X

Fig. 8 Charging system test (Part 1 of 3). Impala

Step	Action	Value(s)	Yes	No
11	1 Maintain the engine speed at 2500 RPM and continue to operate the generator at the load test value. 2 Measure the voltage from the housing of the generator to a good ground. Does the voltage measure greater than the specified value?	0.5 V	Go to Step 15	Go to Step 13
12	There is an internal problem in the J 41450-B . Replace the J 41450-B . Has the J 41450-B been replaced?		Go to Step 2	
13	Test the output circuit of the generator for a high resistance or an open. Did you find and correct the condition?		Go to Step 17	Go to Step 14
14	Test the ground circuit of the generator for a high resistance or an open. Did you find and correct the condition?		Go to Step 17	Go to Step 15
15	Inspect for poor connections at the harness connector of the generator. Did you find and correct the condition?		Go to Step 17	Go to Step 16
16	Replace the generator. Is the repair complete?		Go to Step 17	
17	Operate the system for which the symptom occurred. Does the symptom reoccur?		Go to Step 2	System OK

GC1120000102030X

Fig. 8 Charging system test (Part 3 of 3). Impala

Step	Action	Value(s)	Yes	No
6	**Caution** **Make sure that the load is completely turned off before connecting or disconnecting a carbon pile load tester to the battery. Otherwise, sparking could ignite battery gasses which are extremely flammable and may explode violently.** 1 Connect a carbon pile tester to the vehicle. 2 Connect an inductive ammeter to the output circuit of the generator. 3 Start the engine and allow it to idle briefly. Does the red DIAGNOSTIC lamp on the tester light?		Go to Step 15	Go to Step 7
7	Increase the engine speed to 2500 RPM. Does the red DIAGNOSTIC lamp on the tester light?		Go to Step 15	Go to Step 8
8	1 Maintain the engine speed at 2500 RPM. 2 Turn on the load of the carbon pile tester and increase the load until the generator output is equal to the load test value. Is the generator output greater than the load test value?		Go to Step 9	Go to Step 15
9	Maintain the engine speed at 2500 RPM and continue to operate the generator at the load test value. Does the red DIAGNOSTIC lamp on the tester light?		Go to Step 15	Go to Step 10
10	1 Maintain the engine speed at 2500 RPM and continue to operate the generator at the load test value. 2 Measure the voltage from the output terminal of the generator to the positive terminal on the front relay block. Does the voltage measure greater than the specified value?	0.5 V	Go to Step 15	Go to Step 11

GC1120000102020X

Fig. 8 Charging system test (Part 2 of 3). Impala

Step	Action	Value(s)	Yes	No
1	Did you perform the Diagnostic System Check for Engine Electrical?	--	Go to Step 2	Perform Diagnostic System Check - Engine Electrical
2	1. Start the engine. 2. Install a scan tool. 3. With a scan tool view the Ignition 0 parameter in the IPC data list. Does the scan tool indicate the voltage is less than the specified value?	12.6 volts	Go to Step 3	Go to Symptoms - Engine Electrical
3	1. Turn OFF the ignition. 2. Connect a charging system tester to the battery (follow the manufactures instructions). 3. Operate the engine at 2500 RPM. 4. Adjust the carbon pile as necessary in order to obtain the maximum current output. Is the generator output within 10 A of the specified value?	87 A	Go to Step 9	Go to Step 4
4	1. Maintain the engine speed at 2500 RPM and continue to operate the generator at the load test value. 2. Measure the voltage drop between the generator output terminal and the battery positive terminal. Is the voltage above the specified value?	0.5 V	Go to Step 6	Go to Step 5
5	1. Maintain the engine speed at 2500 RPM and continue to operate the generator at the load test value. 2. Measure the voltage drop between the battery negative terminal and the generator metal housing. Is the voltage above the specified value?	0.5 V	Go to Step 7	Go to Step 8

GC1120100185010X

Fig. 9 Charging system test (Part 1 of 2). Monte Carlo

6	Test the battery positive circuit between the generator output terminal and the battery positive terminal for a high resistance. Did you find and correct the condition?	-	Go to Step 9	Go to Step 7
7	Repair the high resistance in the ground circuit between the generator housing and the battery negative terminal. Did you complete the repair?	-	Go to Step 9	--
8	Replace the generator. Did you complete the repair?	-	Go to Step 9	--
9	Operate the system in order to verify the repair. Did you correct the condition?	-	System OK	Go to Step 3

GC1120100185020X

Fig. 9 Charging system test (Part 2 of 2). Monte Carlo

ALTERNATOR SPECIFICATIONS

Model	Year	Rated Hot Output Amps	Regulated Voltage	Brush Length Minimum, Inch	Commutator Diameter Minimum, Inch
Catera	1998–2001	120	14.7–15	.315	1.228
Impala	2000–02	125	—	—	—
Monte Carlo	2000–02	125	—	—	—

Denso & Mitsubishi Alternators

NOTE: On Air Bag Equipped Models, Refer To "Air Bag System Precautions" Located In The Front Of This Manual For System Disarming & Arming Procedures.

NOTE: Refer To "Computer Relearn Procedure" Located In The Front Of This Manual When Battery Power To The Computer Has Been Interrupted.

INDEX

APPLICATION CHART

Model	Year	Manufacturer	Rated Hot Output Amps
Metro	1998–2001	Mitsubishi	55
DeVille	2002	Denso	140
Prizm	1998	Denso	70
	1999–2002	Denso	80
Seville	2002	Denso	140

GENERAL INFORMATION

Refer to "Delphi Alternators" for general information.

PRECAUTIONS

AIR BAG SYSTEMS

Refer to "Air Bag System Precautions" in the front of this manual for system disarming and arming procedures.

BATTERY GROUND CABLE

Prior to service, disconnect battery ground cable and isolate as required.

CHARGING SYSTEM

1. Ensure battery polarity is proper when servicing units. Reversed battery polarity will damage rectifiers and regulators.
2. If booster battery is used for starting, use proper polarity in hookup.
3. When a fast charger is used to charge a vehicle battery, vehicle battery cables should be disconnected unless fast charger is equipped with a special Alternator Protector, in which case vehicle battery cables need not be disconnected. **Fast chargers should never be used to start a vehicle as rectifier damage will result.**
4. Unless system includes a load relay or field relay, grounding alternator output terminal will damage alternator and/or circuits. This is true even when system is not in operation since no circuit breaker is used and battery is applied to alternator output terminal at all times. The field or load relay acts as a circuit breaker in that it is controlled by ignition switch.
5. Before making any on vehicle tests of alternator or regulator, battery should be inspected and circuit inspected for faulty wiring or insulation. loose or corroded connections and poor ground circuits.
6. Inspect alternator belt tension and condition.
7. Ignition should be Off and battery ground cable disconnected before making any test connections to prevent system damage.
8. Do not reverse connections to alternator.
9. Do not short across or ground any of terminals in charging system.
10. Never disconnect output terminal while alternator is running.
11. The vehicle battery must be fully charged when testing charging system.

DESCRIPTION

These alternators have IC integral solid state regulators, **Figs. 1 and 2.** All regulator components are enclosed into a solid mold and are attached to the slip ring end frame along with the brush holder assembly. The alternator voltage setting cannot be adjusted.

The alternator rotor bearings contain enough grease to eliminate the need for periodic lubrication. Two brushes carry current through the two slip rings to the field coil mounted on the rotor.

The stator windings are assembled on the inside of a laminated core that form part of the alternator frame. The rectifier bridge contains six diodes which electrically change stator AC voltage into DC voltage. The neutral diodes serve to convert the voltage fluctuation at the neutral point to direct current for increasing generator output.

DIAGNOSIS & TESTING

SYSTEM TEST

1. Connect a voltmeter across battery.
2. Start engine and allow to run at 2,000 RPM, then inspect voltmeter reading, which should be at least 13.5 volts.
3. If voltage reading is not as specified, disconnect battery ground cable.
4. Disconnect alternator B terminal wire.
5. Connect ammeter red lead to alternator B terminal and black lead to disconnected B terminal wire.
6. Connect a voltmeter between alternator B terminal and chassis ground.
7. Connect battery ground cable, then start engine and turn all accessories on.
8. Operate engine at sufficient RPM (approximately 2000 RPM) to obtain maximum alternator current output.
9. Repair or replace alternator if current

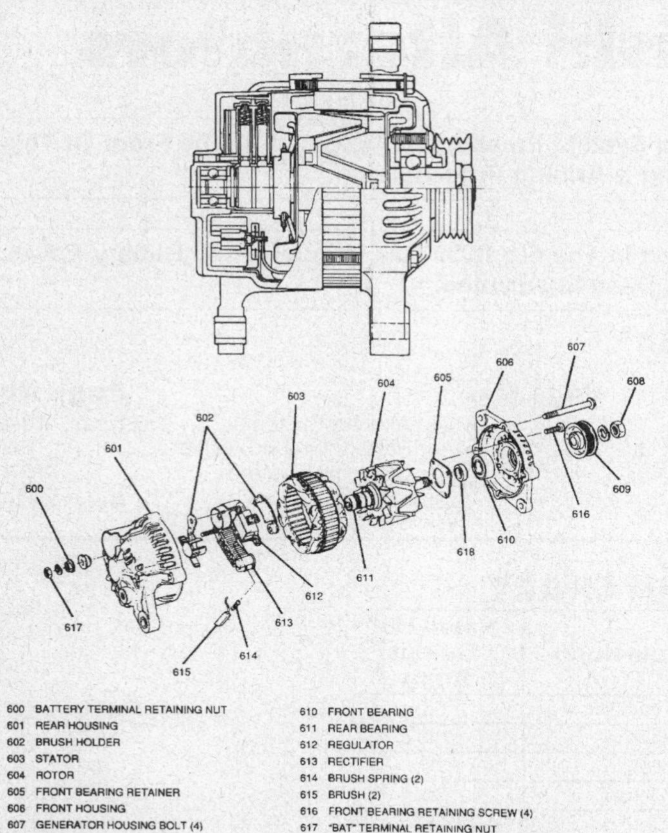

Fig. 1 Exploded view of Mitsubishi alternator

609 ROTOR
614 FRONT BEARING
615 FRONT BEARING RETAINER
616 PULLEY
617 PULLEY NUT
618 BRUSH
619 REAR BEARING
620 BEARING COVER
621 RECTIFIER END FRAME
622 RUBBER INSULATOR
623 IC REGULATOR
634 TERMINAL INSULATOR
635 BRUSH HOLDER
637 BRUSH HOLDER COVER
638 REAR END COVER
639 RECTIFIER HOLDER
640 DRIVE END FRAME

GC1129100036000X

Fig. 2 Exploded view of Denso alternator

reading is not within 10 amps of maximum rated output or voltage reading is not 13.5–16 volts.

REGULATOR TEST

1. Connect a voltmeter and fast charger to battery.
2. Turn ignition On and slowly increase charge rate. Indicator lamp in vehicle will begin to dim when voltage setting is reached.
3. Observe voltmeter. Lamp should dim at 13.5–16.0 volts.
4. If no voltage is present, replace voltage regulator.

ALTERNATOR SPECIFICATIONS

Model	Year	Alternator Manufacturer	Rated Hot Output Amps	Regulated Voltage
DeVille	2002	Denso	140	13.5–15
Metro	1998–2001	Mitsubishi	55	14.7–15
Prizm	1998	Denso	70	13.5–15
	1999–2002	Denso	80	13.5–15
Seville	2002	Denso	140	13.5–15

Valeo Alternators

NOTE: On Air Bag Equipped Models, Refer To "Air Bag System Precautions" Located In The Front Of This Manual For System Disarming & Arming Procedures.

NOTE: Refer To "Computer Relearn Procedure" Located In The Front Of This Manual When Battery Power To The Computer Has Been Interrupted.

NOTE: "Electrical Symbol & Wire Color Code Identification" Located In The Front Of This Manual May Be Used As An Aid When Using Wiring Circuits Found In This Section.

INDEX

APPLICATION CHART

Model	Year	Rated Output Amps
Alero	2002	102
Corvette	1998–2002	110
Grand Am	2002	102

GENERAL INFORMATION

Refer to "Delphi Alternators" for general information.

PRECAUTIONS

AIR BAG SYSTEMS

Refer to "Air Bag System Precautions" in the front of this manual for system disarming and arming procedures.

BATTERY GROUND CABLE

Prior to service, disconnect battery ground cable and isolate as required.

CHARGING SYSTEM

1. Ensure battery polarity is proper when servicing units. Reversed battery polarity will damage rectifiers and regulators.
2. If booster battery is used for starting, use proper polarity in hookup.
3. When a fast charger is used to charge a vehicle battery, vehicle battery cables should be disconnected unless fast charger is equipped with a special Alternator Protector, in which case vehicle battery cables need not be disconnected. **Fast chargers should never be used to start a vehicle as rectifier damage will result.**
4. Unless system includes a load relay or field relay, grounding alternator output terminal will damage alternator and/or circuits. This is true even when system is not in operation since no circuit breaker is used and battery is applied to alternator output terminal at all times. The field or load relay acts as a circuit breaker in that it is controlled by ignition switch.
5. Before making any on vehicle tests of alternator or regulator, battery should be inspected and circuit inspected for faulty wiring or insulation. loose or corroded connections and poor ground circuits.
6. Inspect alternator belt tension and condition.
7. The ignition should be Off and battery ground cable disconnected before making any test connections to prevent damage to system.
8. Do not reverse connections to alternator.
9. Do not short across or ground any terminals in charging system.
10. Never disconnect output terminal while alternator is running.
11. The vehicle battery must be fully charged when testing charging system.

DESCRIPTION

The Valeo alternator is available in one size with a maximum output of 110 amps. The main components are the rotor, regulator and rectifier bridge. No periodic maintenance is required.

DIAGNOSIS & TESTING

Refer to wiring diagrams, **Figs. 1 and 2**, and to diagnosis charts, **Figs. 3 through 14** for charging system diagnosis.

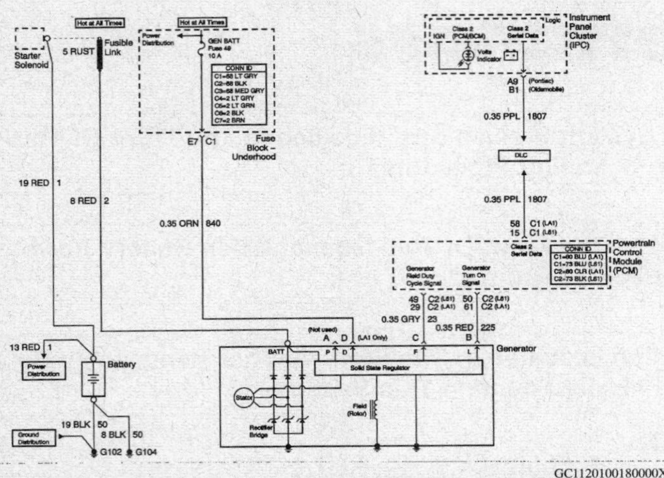

Fig. 1 Charging system wiring diagram. Alero & Grand Am

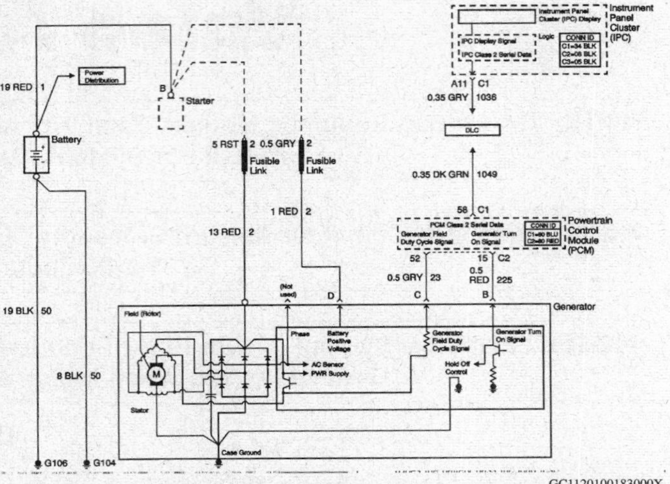

Fig. 2 Charging system wiring diagram. Corvette

Step	Action	Values	Yes	No
1	Did you perform the Diagnostic System Check for Engine Electrical?	--	Go to Step 2	Perform Diagnostic System Check - Engine Electrical
2	Start the engine, observe the charge indicator on the instrument cluster (IPC) or message in the driver information center (DIC). Does the charge indicator illuminate or the DIC display a charging system message?	--	Go to Step 3	Test for Intermittent and Poor Connections in Wiring Systems
3	**Important** The green POWER lamp of the tester should remain illuminated while the tester is being used. 1. Turn OFF the ignition. 2. Connect the red lead of the J 41450-B to the generator output terminal. 3. Connect the black lead of the J 41450-B to the metal generator housing. Does the green POWER lamp on the tester illuminate?	--	Go to Step 6	Go to Step 4
4	Measure the voltage from the output terminal of the generator to the generator metal housing. Does the voltage measure equal to the specified value?	B+	Go to Step 14	Go to Step 5
5	Measure the voltage from the output terminal of the generator to the battery negative terminal. Does the voltage measure equal to the specified value?	B+	Go to Step 12	Go to Step 11

GC1120100186010X

Fig. 3 Charging system inspection (Part 1 of 3). Alero & Grand Am

Step	Action	Values	Yes	No
6	**Caution** **Make sure that the load is completely turned off before connecting or disconnecting a carbon pile load tester to the battery. Otherwise, sparking could ignite battery gasses which are extremely flammable and may explode violently.** 1. Connect a carbon pile tester to the vehicle. **Important** Be sure all of generator output circuit wires pass through the inductive probe. 2. Connect an inductive ammeter to the output circuit of the generator. 3. Disconnect the generator harness connector. 4. Locate the matching harness connector on the J 41450-B and connect it to the generator. Does the red DIAGNOSTIC lamp on the tester light?	--	Go to Step 7	Go to Step 13
7	1. Start the engine and allow it to idle for 30 seconds. 2. Increase the engine speed to 2,500 RPM. Does the red DIAGNOSTIC lamp on the tester illuminate?	--	Go to Step 15	Go to Step 8
8	1. Maintain the engine speed at 2,500 RPM. **Important** If the generator is not capable of producing the Load Test amps, operate the generator at it's maximum possible output. 2. Turn ON the load of the carbon pile tester and increase the load until the generator output is greater than or equal to the load test value Does the red DIAGNOSTIC lamp on the tester illuminate?	--	Go to Step 15	Go to Step 9
9	1. Maintain the engine speed at 2,500 RPM and continue to operate the generator at the load test value. 2. Measure the voltage drop from the output terminal of the generator to the positive terminal on the battery. Does the voltage measure greater than the specified value?	0.5 V	Go to Step 11	Go to Step 10

GC1120100186020X

Fig. 3 Charging system inspection (Part 2 of 3). Alero & Grand Am

Step	Action	Value(s)	Yes	No
10	1. Maintain the engine speed at 2,500 RPM and continue to operate the generator at the load test value. 2. Measure the voltage drop from the battery negative terminal to the metal housing of the generator. Does the voltage measure greater than the specified value?	0.5 V	Go to Step 12	Go to Step 16
11	Repair the high resistance or an open in the output circuit of the generator. Did you complete the repair?	--	Go to Step 16	--
12	Repair the high resistance or open in the ground circuit of the generator. Did you complete the repair?	--	Go to Step 16	--
13	1. Disconnect the J 41450-B tester harness connector from the generator, but leave the alligator clips connected so that the green POWER lamp remains illuminated. 2. Connect a jumper lead, with an in-line 100-ohm resistor between the J 41450-B tester harness connector terminal B and a good ground. Does the red DIAGNOSTIC lamp illuminate?	--	Go to Step 15	Go to Step 14
14	There is a problem with the J 41450-B . Refer to the manufacturers instructions on how to test the J 41450-B for proper operation. Has the J 41450-B tester been replaced?	--	Go to Step 3	--
15	Replace the generator. Did you complete the replacement?	--	Go to Step 16	--
16	Operate the vehicle in order to verify the repair. Did you correct the condition?	--	System OK	Go to Step 2

GC1120100186030X

Fig. 3 Charging system inspection (Part 3 of 3). Alero & Grand Am

Step	Action	Normal Result(s)	Abnormal Result(s)*
3	1. Install the scan tool to the diagnostic link connector. 2. Turn the ignition switch to the ON position. 3. Select display DTC function with the scan tool. 4. Check for any stored PCM, BCM, or communication DTCs related to theft deterrent, starting or charging system operation.	No DTCs are stored in memory or current status.	• DTC is stored in memory or current status (refer to appropriate DTC table). • Scan Tool Does Not Communicate with Component.
4	1. Start the engine and allow it to idle in PARK. 2. Press the HVAC MODE control button until the LOWER floor position is displayed. 3. Depress the fan control button until the fan reaches high speed. 4. Turn the headlamp switch to the ON position (headlights ON). 5. Move the wiper switch to the HI position (maintain some moisture on the windshield while the wipers are in operation). 6. Maintain engine speed between 800 and 1000 RPMs. 7. Connect a DMM between the battery positive terminal and negative terminal. 8. Observe the voltage reading at the DMM.	1. The generator operates without unusual noises. 2. The battery indicator light on the instrument cluster extinguishes after the engine is started. 3. The SERVICE ENGINE SOON malfunction indicator lamp extinguishes when the engine starts. 4. The DMM reads approximately between 12.0 and 16.0 volts while the engine is idling.	• Battery is Undercharged or Overcharged (Low/High Voltage Message). • Indicator-Always ON (Charge System Fault Message). • Voltmeter Displaying High or Low.

GC1129700089020X

Fig. 4 Charging system inspection (Part 2 of 2). Corvette

Step	Action	Normal Result(s)	Abnormal Result(s)*
1	1. Inspect the battery for proper installation. 2. Inspect the battery for cracking or other damage. 3. Inspect the battery terminals for proper connection. 4. Inspect the battery terminals for excessive corrosion. 5. Inspect the battery cables for proper installation. 6. Check that all ground connections are clean and tight. 7. Inspect the battery hydrometer (eye) for a green dot. 8. Connect a DMM between the battery's positive and negative terminals. 9. Ensure that any aftermarket accessory equipment is de-energized. 10. Observe the battery voltage.	1. The battery is properly installed. 2. The battery is free from physical damage. 3. The battery terminals are free from corrosion. 4. The battery cables are properly connected. 5. The battery cables are properly installed. 6. The battery hydrometer displays a green dot. 7. Battery voltage is approximately between 11.5 to 13.0 volts.	• Battery Hydrometer Displays Dark or Yellow Dot. • Common Causes of Battery Failure. • Battery is undercharged (refer to Battery Charging).
2	1. Remove the DMM from the battery terminals. 2. Perform a load test on the battery	Battery maintains a specified voltage level according to the Battery Temperature vs. Voltage Drop table.	Battery does not maintain the specified voltage level during the load test, replace the battery

GC1129700089010X

Fig. 4 Charging system inspection (Part 1 of 2). Corvette

Step	Action	Value(s)	Yes	No
DEFINITION: The vehicle's charging system has begun to either undercharge or overcharge the battery. The regulated voltage has dropped below 13.5 volts or raised above 15.5 volts with the vehicle in normal operation. The Instrument Panel Cluster (IPC) has detected this condition through monitoring the Ignition 1 voltage at the IPC connector terminal A13. If the voltage reading at the IPC terminal A13 falls out of the normal range, the IPC will inform the driver by illuminating across the Driver's Information Center either the LOW VOLTAGE or HIGH VOLTAGE warning message. The voltmeter indicator may or may not indicate abnormal voltage readings. If PCM fault codes P0562 or P0563 exist, diagnose those first before proceeding with this table. Always ensure that a good battery is installed in the vehicle, charging system operation depends heavily on the battery condition.				
1	Were you sent here from the Charging System Check?	—	Go to Step 2	Go to Charging System Check
2	Load test the battery. Does the battery pass the load test?	—	Go to Step 5	Go to Step 3
3	1. Recharge the battery. 2. After charging, load test the battery again. Does the battery pass the load test?	—	Go to Step 5	Go to Step 4
4	Replace the battery. Is the repair complete?	—	Go to Charging System Check	—
5	1. Start the engine and allow it to idle in Park. 2. Load the electrical system by turning on the headlights and the high blower. 3. Connect a DMM between the battery terminals. 4. Measure the available voltage at the battery with the engine running and the electrical system under load. Is the voltage within the specified values?	10.0-14.0V	Go to Step 6	Go to Step 11
6	1. Turn the ignition switch to the OFF position. 2. Disconnect the instrument panel cluster connector. 3. Return the ignition switch to the ON position. 4. Connect a DMM between ground and the instrument panel cluster terminal A13. 5. Measure the available voltage at the instrument panel cluster terminal A13. Is the voltage within the specified values?	10.0-14.0V	Go to Step 7	Go to Step 8
7	Replace the instrument panel cluster (IPC). Is the repair complete?	—	Go to Charging System Check	—
8	Check the IPC MiniFuse #19 fuse for an open circuit. Is this fuse open?	—	Go to Step 9	Go to Step 10
9	Repair a short to ground in CKT 139. Is the repair complete?	—	Go to Charging System Check	—
10	Repair the open in CKT 139. Is the repair complete?	—	Go to Charging System Check	—
11	1. Connect a DMM between the BATTERY terminal (CKT 2-large red wire) in the back of the generator and ground. 2. Measure the available voltage at the BATTERY terminal (CKT 2-large red wire) in the back of the generator. Is the voltage within the specified values?	10.0-14.0V	Go to Step 15	Go to Step 12
12	Check the fusible link at the starter motor between the medium gauge blue wire (CKT 2) and the heavy gauge red wire (CKT 2). See wiring schematic for further detail. Is the fusible link open?	—	Go to Step 13	Go to Step 14

GC1129700086010X

Fig. 5 Battery is undercharged or overcharged (Part 1 of 3). Corvette

Step	Action	Value(s)	Yes	No
13	Repair a short to ground in CKT 2 (13 red wire) between the generator BATTERY terminal and the fusible link. Is the repair complete?	—	Go to Charging System Check	—
14	Repair an open in CKT 1 (19 red wire), CKT 2 (3 blue wire) or CKT 2 (13 red wire) between the generator BATTERY terminal and the positive battery terminal. Is the repair complete?	—	Go to Charging System Check	—
15	1. Disconnect the generator connector. 2. Connect a DMM between the generator connector terminal D (CKT 2-medium red wire) and ground. 3. Measure the available voltage at the generator connector terminal D (CKT 2-medium red wire). Is the voltage within the specified values?	10.0-14.0V	*Go to Step 19*	*Go to Step 16*
16	Check the fusible link at the starter motor between the small gauge grey wire (CKT 2) and the medium gauge red wire (CKT 2). See wiring schematic for further detail. Is the fusible link open?	—	*Go to Step 17*	*Go to Step 18*
17	Repair a short to ground in CKT 2 (1 red wire) between the generator connector terminal D and the fusible link. Is the repair complete?	—	Go to Charging System Check	—
18	Repair an open in CKT 1 (19 red wire), CKT 2 (0.5 grey wire) or CKT 2 (1 red wire) between the generator connector terminal D and the positive battery terminal. Is the repair complete?	—	Go to Charging System Check	—
19	1. Disconnect the powertrain control module connector C2. 2. Connect a DMM between the generator connector terminal C (CKT 23) and the powertrain control module connector C2 terminal 11. 3. Measure CKT 23 for continuity between these two connectors. Is CKT 23 continuous between the generator connector and the powertrain control module connector C2?	—	*Go to Step 20*	*Go to Step 22*
20	1. Powertrain control module connector C2 and generator connector are still disconnected. 2. Connect the DMM between the generator connector terminal C (CKT 23) and ground. 3. Measure CKT 23 for continuity to ground. Is CKT 23 shorted to ground?	—	*Go to Step 23*	*Go to Step 21*
21	1. Powertrain control module connector C2 and generator connector are still disconnected. 2. DMM still connected between the generator connector terminal C (CKT 23) and ground. 3. Turn the ignition switch to the ON position. 4. Measure CKT 23 for available voltage. Is CKT 23 shorted to battery power?	—	*Go to Step 24*	*Go to Step 25*

GC1129700086020X

Fig. 5 Battery is undercharged or overcharged (Part 2 of 3). Corvette

Step	Action	Values	Yes	No
1	Did you perform the Diagnostic System Check for Starting and Charging?	--	Go to Step 2	Perform Diagnostic System Check
2	Start the engine. Does the battery charge indicator remain illuminated after the five second bulb check?	--	Go to Step 3	Test Intermittent and Poor Connections
3	1. Install a scan tool 2. With a scan tool, observe the Ignition 1 Signal parameter in the PCM data list. Does the voltage measure within the normal operating range?	10 V - 15 V	Go to Step 4	Perform Charging System Test
4	Replace the instrument panel cluster. Did you complete the replacement?	--	Go to Step 5	--
5	Operate the system in order to verify the repair. Did you correct the condition?	--	System OK	Go to Step 2

GC1120100181000X

Fig. 6 Charge indicator always on. Alero & Grand Am

Step	Action	Value(s)	Yes	No
22	Repair the open in CKT 23 between the generator connector and the powertrain control module connector C2. Is the repair complete?	—	Go to Charging System Check	—
23	Repair the short to ground in CKT 23 between the generator connector and the powertrain control module connector C2. Is the repair complete?	—	Go to Charging System Check	—
24	Repair the short to battery power in CKT 23 between the generator connector and the powertrain control module connector C2. Is the repair complete?	—	Go to Charging System Check	—
25	1. Connect a DMM between the generator connector terminal B (CKT 225) and the powertrain control module connector C2 terminal 77. 2. Measure CKT 225 for continuity between these two connectors. Is CKT 225 continuous between the generator connector and the powertrain control module connector C2?	—	*Go to Step 26*	*Go to Step 28*
26	1. Powertrain control module connector C2 and generator connector are still disconnected. 2. Connect the DMM between the generator connector terminal B (CKT 225) and ground. 3. Measure CKT 225 for continuity to ground. Is CKT 225 shorted to ground?	—	*Go to Step 29*	*Go to Step 27*
27	1. Powertrain control module connector C2 and generator connector are still disconnected. 2. DMM still connected between the generator connector terminal B (CKT 225) and ground. 3. Turn the ignition switch to the ON position. 4. Measure CKT 225 for available voltage. Is CKT 225 shorted to battery power?	—	*Go to Step 30*	*Go to Step 31*
28	Repair the open in CKT 225 between the generator connector and the powertrain control module connector C2. Is the repair complete?	—	Go to Charging System Check	—
29	Repair the short to ground in CKT 225 between the generator connector and the powertrain control module connector C2. Is the repair complete?	—	Go to Charging System Check	—
30	Repair the short to battery power in CKT 225 between the generator connector and the powertrain control module connector C2. Is the repair complete?	—	Go to Charging System Check	—
31	Replace the generator. Is the repair complete?	—	Go to Charging System Check	—

GC1129700086030X

Fig. 5 Battery is undercharged or overcharged (Part 3 of 3). Corvette

Step	Action	Value(s)	Yes	No
DEFINITION: A charging system fault has been detected by the Powertrain Control Module (PCM). The PCM monitors CKT 225 at connector C2 terminal 77. If the incorrect voltage reading is detected at connector C2 terminal 77, the PCM will send a Class 2 message to the IPC indicating a charging system fault. The CHARGE SYSTEM FAULT warning message will then illuminate across the Driver's Information Center. The voltmeter indicator may or may not indicate abnormal voltage readings. If PCM fault codes P0562 or P0563 exist, diagnose those first before proceeding with this table. Always ensure that a good battery is installed in the vehicle, charging system operation depends heavily on the battery condition.				
1	Were you sent here from the Charging System Check?	—	*Go to Step 2*	Go to Charging System Check
2	Load test the battery. Does the battery pass the load test?	—	*Go to Step 5*	*Go to Step 3*
3	1. Recharge the battery. 2. After charging, load test the battery again. Does the battery pass the load test?	—	*Go to Step 5*	*Go to Step 4*
4	Replace the battery. Is the repair complete?	—	Go to Charging System Check	—
5	1. Start the engine and allow it to idle in Park. 2. Load the electrical system by turning on the headlights and the high blower. 3. Connect a DMM between the battery terminals. 4. Measure the available voltage at the battery with the engine running and the electrical system under load. Is the voltage within the specified values?	10.0-14.0V	*Go to Step 6*	*Go to Step 11*
6	1. Turn the ignition switch to the OFF position. 2. Disconnect the powertrain control module connector C2. 3. Return the ignition switch to the ON position. 4. Connect a DMM between ground and: • the powertrain control module connector C2 terminal 61. • the powertrain control module connector C2 terminal 20. • the powertrain control module connector C2 terminal 19. 5. Measure the available voltage at these powertrain control module terminals. Is the voltage within the specified values?	10.0-14.0V	*Go to Step 7*	*Go to Step 8*
7	Replace the Powertrain Control Module (PCM). Is the repair complete?	—	Go to Charging System Check	—
8	Check the following fuses for an open ciruict. • PCMB MiniFuse #23 • PCM MiniFuse #16 Is either of these fuses open?	—	*Go to Step 9*	*Go to Step 10*
9	Repair a short to ground in the circuit relative to the open fuse. • CKT 340 = PCMB MiniFuse #23 • CKT 239 = PCM MiniFuse #16 Is the repair complete?	—	Go to Charging System Check	—

GC1129700087010X

Fig. 7 Charge indicator always on (Part 1 of 4). 1998 Corvette

Step	Action	Value(s)	Yes	No
10	Repair the open in the circuit relative to the PCM terminal lacking voltage. • CKT 340 = PCM connector C2 terminals 20 and 61 • CKT 239 = PCM connector C2 terminal 19 Is the repair complete?	—	Go to Charging System Check	—
11	1. Connect a DMM between the BATTERY terminal (CKT 2-large red wire) in the back of the generator and ground. 2. Measure the available voltage at the BATTERY terminal (CKT 2-large red wire) in the back of the generator. Is the voltage within the specified values?	10.0-14.0V	*Go to Step 15*	*Go to Step 12*
12	Check the fusible link located down at the starter motor between the medium gauge blue wire (CKT 2) and the heavy gauge red wire (CKT 2). Is the fusible link open?	—	*Go to Step 13*	*Go to Step 14*
13	Repair a short to ground in CKT 2 (13 red wire) between the generator BATTERY terminal and the fusible link. Is the repair complete?	—	Go to Charging System Check	—
14	Repair an open in CKT 1 (19 red wire), CKT 2 (3 blue wire) or CKT 2 (13 red wire) between the generator BATTERY terminal and the positive battery terminal. Is the repair complete?	—	Go to Charging System Check	—
15	1. Disconnect the generator connector. 2. Connect a DMM between the generator connector terminal D (CKT 2-medium red wire) and ground. 3. Measure the available voltage at the generator connector terminal D (CKT 2-medium red wire). Is the voltage within the specified values?	10.0-14.0V	*Go to Step 19*	*Go to Step 16*
16	Check the fusible link located down at the starter motor between the small gauge grey wire (CKT 2) and the medium gauge red wire (CKT 2). Is the fusible link open?	—	*Go to Step 17*	*Go to Step 18*
17	Repair a short to ground in CKT 2 (1 red wire) between the generator connector terminal D and the fusible link. Is the repair complete?	—	Go to Charging System Check	—
18	Repair an open in CKT 1 (19 red wire), CKT 2 (0.5 grey wire) or CKT 2 (1 red wire) between the generator connector terminal D and the positive battery terminal. Is the repair complete?	—	Go to Charging System Check	—
19	1. Disconnect the powertrain control module connector C2. 2. Connect a DMM between the generator connector terminal C (CKT 23) and the powertrain control module connector C2 terminal 11. 3. Measure CKT 23 for continuity between these two connectors. Is CKT 23 continuous between the generator connector and the powertrain control module connector C2?	—	*Go to Step 20*	*Go to Step 22*

GC1129700087020X

Fig. 7 Charge indicator always on (Part 2 of 4). 1998 Corvette

Step	Action	Value(s)	Yes	No
30	Repair the short to battery power in CKT 225 between the generator connector and the powertrain control module connector C2. Is the repair complete?	—	Go to Charging System Check	—
31	Replace the generator. Is the repair complete?	—	Go to Charging System Check	—

GC1129700087040X

Fig. 7 Charge indicator always on (Part 4 of 4). 1998 Corvette

Step	Action	Value(s)	Yes	No
20	1. Powertrain control module connector C2 and generator connector are still disconnected. 2. Connect the DMM between the generator connector terminal C (CKT 23) and ground. 3. Measure CKT 23 for continuity to ground. Is CKT 23 shorted to ground?	—	*Go to Step 23*	*Go to Step 21*
21	1. Powertrain control module connector C2 and generator connector are still disconnected. 2. DMM still connected between the generator connector terminal C (CKT 23) and ground. 3. Turn the ignition switch to the ON position. 4. Measure CKT 23 for available voltage. Is CKT 23 shorted to battery power?	—	*Go to Step 24*	*Go to Step 25*
22	Repair the open in CKT 23 between the generator connector and the powertrain control module connector C2. Is the repair complete?	—	Go to Charging System Check	—
23	Repair the short to ground in CKT 23 between the generator connector and the powertrain control module connector C2. Is the repair complete?	—	Go to Charging System Check	—
24	Repair the short to battery power in CKT 23 between the generator connector and the powertrain control module connector C2. Is the repair complete?	—	Go to Charging System Check	—
25	1. Connect a DMM between the generator connector terminal B (CKT 225) and the powertrain control module connector C2 terminal 77. 2. Measure CKT 225 for continuity between these two connectors. Is CKT 225 continuous between the generator connector and the powertrain control module connector C2?	—	*Go to Step 26*	*Go to Step 28*
26	1. Powertrain control module connector C2 and generator connector are still disconnected. 2. Connect the DMM between the generator connector terminal B (CKT 225) and ground. 3. Measure CKT 225 for continuity to ground. Is CKT 225 shorted to ground?	—	*Go to Step 29*	*Go to Step 27*
27	1. Powertrain control module connector C2 and generator connector are still disconnected. 2. DMM still connected between the generator connector terminal B (CKT 225) and ground. 3. Turn the ignition switch to the ON position. 4. Measure CKT 225 for available voltage. Is CKT 225 shorted to battery power?	—	*Go to Step 30*	*Go to Step 31*
28	Repair the open in CKT 225 between the generator connector and the powertrain control module connector C2. Is the repair complete?	—	Go to Charging System Check	—
29	Repair the short to ground in CKT 225 between the generator connector and the powertrain control module connector C2. Is the repair complete?	—	Go to Charging System Check	—

GC1129700087030X

Fig. 7 Charge indicator always on (Part 3 of 4). 1998 Corvette

Step	Action	Value (s)	Yes	No
DEFINITION: The CHARGE SYSTEM FAULT message is displayed across the Driver Information Center.				
1	Were you sent here from the Charging System Check?	--	Go to Step 2	Go to Charging System Check
2	1. Recharge the battery if necessary. 2. Load test the battery. Does the battery pass the load test?	--	Go to Step 4	Go to Step 3
3	Replace the battery. Is the repair complete?	--	Go to Charging System Check	--
4	1. Start the engine and allow it to idle in park. 2. Load the electrical system by turning on the highbeam headlamps and the heater blower to high. 3. Connect a DMM to the vehicle battery and measure the voltage. Is the voltage within specified values?	13.5-15.0 V	Go to Step 5	Diagnose Battery Undercharge or Overcharge

GC1120100187010X

Fig. 8 Charge indicator always on (Part 1 of 2). 1999 Corvette

Step	Action	Value	Yes	No
5	1. Install a scan tool. 2. Check the PCM DTC's Is DTC P0562 or P0563 stored in the PCM?	-	Go to DTC P0562 System Voltage Low or DTC P0563 System Voltage High	Go to Step 6
6	Does the Instrument Panel Cluster volt gauge indicate abnormal voltage readings?	-	Diagnose Volt Gage Inaccurate or Inoperative	Go to Step 7
7	Replace the Instrument Panel Cluster. Refer to Instrument Panel Cluster (IPC) Replacement . Is the repair complete?	-	Go to Charging System Check	--

GC1120100187020X

Fig. 8 Charge indicator always on (Part 2 of 2). 1999 Corvette

Step	Action	Value	Yes	No
7	Inspect for poor connections at the PCM harness connector. Did you find and correct the condition?	-	Go to Step 9	Go to Step 8
8	**IMPORTANT:** Perform the set up procedures for the PCM. Replace the PCM. Did you complete the replacement?	-	Go to Step 9	--
9	Operate the system for which the symptom occurred. Did you correct the condition?	-	System OK	Go to Step 2

GC1120100188020X

Fig. 9 Charge indicator always on (Part 2 of 2). 2000–02 Corvette

Step	Action	Yes	No
1	Did you perform the Engine Electrical Diagnostic System Check?	Go to Step 2	Perform Diagnostic System Check - Engine Electrical
2	1. Turn OFF the ignition. 2. Turn ON the ignition, with the engine OFF. 3. Observe the battery charge indicator on the instrument cluster (IPC) during the bulb check. Does the battery charge indicator illuminate during the bulb check?	Test for Intermittent and Poor Connections	Go to Step 3
3	Replace the instrument cluster (IPC). Did you complete the repair?	Go to Step 4	--
4	Operate the system in order to verify the repair. Did you correct the condition?	System OK	Go to Step 2

GC1120100182000X

Fig. 10 Charge indicator inoperative. Alero & Grand Am

Step	Action	Value	Yes	No
1	Did you perform the Engine Electrical Diagnostic System Check?	--	Go to Step 2	Perform Diagnostic System Check - Engine Electrical
2	Start the engine. Does the Charge System Fault message remain ON?	--	Go to Step 3	Test for Intermittent and Poor Connections
3	1. Install a scan tool. 2. With a scan tool, observe the Ignition 1 Signal parameter in the PCM data list. Is the voltage within the specified value?	11.0-15.5 Volts	Go to Step 4	Go to Charging System Test
4	1. Turn OFF the ignition. 2. Disconnect the PCM. 3. Turn ON the ignition, with the engine OFF. Is the Charge System Fault message ON?	--	Go to Step 5	Go to Step 7
5	Inspect for poor connections at the harness connector of the IPC. Did you find and correct the condition?	--	Go to Step 9	Go to Step 6
6	Replace the instrument panel cluster. Did you complete the replacement?	--	Go to Step 9	

GC1120100188010X

Fig. 9 Charge indicator always on (Part 1 of 2). 2000–02 Corvette

Step	Action	Value(s)	Yes	No
DEFINITION: The voltmeter is indicating abnormal voltage readings. The Instrument Panel Cluster (IPC) monitors Ignition 1 voltage at the IPC connector terminal A13. If the voltage reading at the IPC terminal A13 falls out of the normal range, the IPC should inform the driver by illuminating across the Driver's Information Center either the LOW VOLTAGE or HIGH VOLTAGE warning message. If PCM fault codes P0562 or P0563 exist, diagnose those first before proceeding with this table. Always ensure that a good battery is installed in the vehicle, charging system operation depends heavily on the battery condition.				
1	Were you sent here from the Charging System Check?	—	*Go to Step 2*	Go to Charging System Check
2	Load test the battery. Does the battery pass the load test?	—	*Go to Step 5*	*Go to Step 3*
3	1. Recharge the battery. 2. After charging, load test the battery again. Does the battery pass the load test?	—	*Go to Step 5*	*Go to Step 4*
4	Replace the battery. Is the repair complete?	—	Go to Charging System Check	—
5	1. Start the engine and allow it to idle in Park. 2. Load the electrical system by turning on the headlights and the high blower. 3. Connect a DMM between the battery terminals. 4. Measure the available voltage at the battery with the engine running and the electrical system under load. Is the voltage within the specified values?	10.0-14.0V	*Go to Step 6*	*Go to Step 11*
6	1. Turn the ignition switch to the OFF position. 2. Disconnect the instrument panel cluster connector. 3. Connect one DMM between the battery terminals. 4. Connect another DMM between ground and the instrument panel cluster terminal A13. 5. Start the engine and allow it to idle in Park. 6. Load the electrical system by turning on the headlights and the high blower. 7. Compare the voltage readings at the instrument panel cluster terminal A13 to the voltage reading at the battery. Are the voltage readings within 0.1 to 1.5 volts of each other?	—	*Go to Step 7*	*Go to Step 8*
7	Replace the instrument panel cluster (IPC). Is the repair complete?	—	Go to Charging System Check	—
8	Check the IPC MiniFuse #19 fuse for an open circuit. Is this fuse open?	—	*Go to Step 9*	*Go to Step 10*

GC1129700088010X

Fig. 11 Voltmeter displaying high or low (Part 1 of 4). Alero, Grand Am & 1998 Corvette

Step	Action	Value(s)	Yes	No
9	Repair a short to ground in CKT 139 between the IPC and the instrument panel electrical center. Is the repair complete?	—	Go to Charging System Check	—
10	Repair the open or high resistance in CKT 139 between the IPC and the instrument panel electrical center. Is the repair complete?	—	Go to Charging System Check	—
11	1. Connect a DMM between the BATTERY terminal (CKT 2-large red wire) in the back of the generator and ground. 2. Measure the available voltage at the BATTERY terminal (CKT 2-large red wire) in the back of the generator. Is the voltage within the specified values?	10.0-14.0V	Go to Step 15	Go to Step 12
12	Check the fusible link located down at the starter motor between the medium gauge blue wire (CKT 2) and the heavy gauge red wire (CKT 2). Is the fusible link open?	—	Go to Step 13	Go to Step 14
13	Repair a short to ground in CKT 2 (13 red wire) between the generator BATTERY terminal and the fusible link. Is the repair complete?	—	Go to Charging System Check	—
14	Repair an open in CKT 1 (19 red wire), CKT 2 (3 blue wire) or CKT 2 (13 red wire) between the generator BATTERY terminal and the positive battery terminal. Is the repair complete?	—	Go to Charging System Check	—
15	1. Disconnect the generator connector. 2. Connect a DMM between the generator connector terminal D (CKT 2-medium red wire) and ground. 3. Measure the available voltage at the generator connector terminal D (CKT 2-medium red wire). Is the voltage within the specified values?	10.0-14.0V	Go to Step 19	Go to Step 16
16	Check the fusible link located down at the starter motor between the small gauge grey wire (CKT 2) and the medium gauge red wire (CKT 2). Is the fusible link open?	—	Go to Step 17	Go to Step 18
17	Repair a short to ground in CKT 2 (1 red wire) between the generator connector terminal D and the fusible link. Is the repair complete?	—	Go to Charging System Check	—
18	Repair an open in CKT 1 (19 red wire), CKT 2 (0.5 grey wire) or CKT 2 (1 red wire) between the generator connector terminal D and the positive battery terminal. Is the repair complete?	—	Go to Charging System Check	—

GC1129700088020X

Fig. 11 Voltmeter displaying high or low (Part 2 of 4). Alero, Grand Am & 1998 Corvette

Step	Action	Value(s)	Yes	No
28	Repair the open in CKT 225 between the generator connector and the powertrain control module connector C2. Is the repair complete?	—	Go to Charging System Check	—
29	Repair the short to ground in CKT 225 between the generator connector and the powertrain control module connector C2. Is the repair complete?	—	Go to Charging System Check	—
30	Repair the short to battery power in CKT 225 between the generator connector and the powertrain control module connector C2. Is the repair complete?	—	Go to Charging System Check	—
31	Replace the generator. Is the repair complete?	—	Go to Charging System Check	—

GC1129700088040X

Fig. 11 Voltmeter displaying high or low (Part 4 of 4). Alero, Grand Am & 1998 Corvette

Step	Action	Value(s)	Yes	No
19	1. Disconnect the powertrain control module connector C2. 2. Connect a DMM between the generator connector terminal C (CKT 23) and the powertrain control module connector C2 terminal 11. 3. Measure CKT 23 for continuity between these two connectors. Is CKT 23 continuous between the generator connector and the powertrain control module connector C2?	—	Go to Step 20	Go to Step 22
20	1. Powertrain control module connector C2 and generator connector are still disconnected. 2. Connect the DMM between the generator connector terminal C (CKT 23) and ground. 3. Measure CKT 23 for continuity to ground. Is CKT 23 shorted to ground?	—	Go to Step 23	Go to Step 21
21	1. Powertrain control module connector C2 and generator connector are still disconnected. 2. DMM still connected between the generator connector terminal C (CKT 23) and ground. 3. Turn the ignition switch to the ON position. 4. Measure CKT 23 for available voltage. Is CKT 23 shorted to battery power?	—	Go to Step 24	Go to Step 25
22	Repair the open in CKT 23 between the generator connector and the powertrain control module connector C2. Is the repair complete?	—	Go to Charging System Check	—
23	Repair the short to ground in CKT 23 between the generator connector and the powertrain control module connector C2. Is the repair complete?	—	Go to Charging System Check	—
24	Repair the short to battery power in CKT 23 between the generator connector and the powertrain control module connector C2. Is the repair complete?	—	Go to Charging System Check	—
25	1. Connect a DMM between the generator connector terminal B (CKT 225) and the powertrain control module connector C2 terminal 77. 2. Measure CKT 225 for continuity between these two connectors. Is CKT 225 continuous between the generator connector and the powertrain control module connector C2?	—	Go to Step 26	Go to Step 28
26	1. Powertrain control module connector C2 and generator connector are still disconnected. 2. Connect the DMM between the generator connector terminal B (CKT 225) and ground. 3. Measure CKT 225 for continuity to ground. Is CKT 225 shorted to ground?	—	Go to Step 29	Go to Step 27
27	1. Powertrain control module connector C2 and generator connector are still disconnected. 2. DMM still connected between the generator connector terminal B (CKT 225) and ground. 3. Turn the ignition switch to the ON position. 4. Measure CKT 225 for available voltage. Is CKT 225 shorted to battery power?	—	Go to Step 30	Go to Step 31

GC1129700088030X

Fig. 11 Voltmeter displaying high or low (Part 3 of 4). Alero, Grand Am & 1998 Corvette

Action	Value(s)	Yes	No	
DEFINITION: The LOW VOLTAGE or HIGH VOLTAGE message is displayed across the driver information center.				
1	Were you sent here from the Charging System Check?	--	Go to Step 2	Go to Charging System Check
2	1. Recharge the battery if necessary. 2. Load test the battery. Does the battery pass the load test?	--	Go to Step 4	Go to Step 3
3	Replace the battery. Is the repair complete?	--	Go to Charging System Check	--
4	1. Start the engine and allow it to idle in park. 2. Load the electrical system by turning on the highbeam headlamps and the heater blower to high. 3. Connect a DMM to the vehicle battery and measure the voltage. Is the voltage within specified values?	13.5-15.0 V	Go to Charging System Check	Go to Step 5
5	1. Connect the red alligator clip of the J 41450-B CS Generator Electronic Tester to the generator output terminal. 2. Connect the black alligator clip to the generator housing. 3. The green POWER lamp of the tester should light and remain lighted while the tester is being used. Does the green POWER lamp of the tester light?	--	Go to Step 6	Go to Step 7
6	1. With the alligator clips connected. 2. Disconnect the generator four way connector. 3. Locate the matching four way connector of the J 41450-B and connect it to the generator. Does the red DIAGNOSTIC lamp of the tester light?	--	Go to Step 8	Go to Step 30

GC1120100189010X

Fig. 12 Voltmeter displaying high or low (Part 1 of 5). 1999 Corvette

7	Repair the open in the generator output circuit or the battery ground circuit. Is the repair complete?	--	Go to Charging System Check	--
8	1. Prior to connecting a carbon pile load tester, make sure that the load dial is completely turned to the off position. 2. Connect the leads of the carbon pile to the vehicle battery. 3. Connect an inductive ammeter to the generator output circuit. 4. Start the engine and allow it to idle. Does the red DIAGNOSTIC lamp of the tester light?	--	Go to Step 30	Go to Step 9
9	Increase the engine speed to 2500 RPM. Does the red DIAGNOSTIC lamp of the tester light?	--	Go to Step 30	Go to Step 10
10	1. Maintain the engine speed at 2500 RPM 2. Turn on the load of the carbon pile tester. 3. Using caution not to load the battery beyond manufacturers load test values, increase the load while monitoring generator output current. As the load is increased, is the generator capable of producing the amount of load test current specified in generator usage?	--	Go to Step 11	Go to Step 12
11	With the engine speed at 2500 RPM and the generator operating at load test value, is the red DIAGNOSTIC lamp of the tester lighted?	--	Go to Step 30	Go to Step 12
12	1. Maintain the engine speed at 2500 RPM and continue to operate the generator at the load test value. 2. Using a DMM measure the voltage from the generator output terminal to the battery positive terminal. Is the voltage under the specified value?	0.5 V	Go to Step 13	Go to Step 14
13	1. Maintain the engine speed at 2500 RPM and continue to operate the generator at the load test value. 2. Using a DMM measure the voltage from the generator housing to the battery negative terminal. Is the voltage under the specified value?	0.5 V	Go to Step 16	Go to Step 15

GC1120100189020X

Fig. 12 Voltmeter displaying high or low (Part 2 of 5). 1999 Corvette

14	1. Turn off the engine. 2. Disconnect the battery negative terminal. 3. Inspect the circuit between the battery positive terminal and the generator output terminal for high resistance. 4. Disassemble and clean or replace the terminals and wire in this circuit as necessary. Is the repair complete?	--	Go to Charging System Check	--
15	1. Turn off the engine. 2. Inspect the circuit between the negative battery terminal and the generator housing for high resistance. 3. Disassemble and clean or replace the terminals and wire in this circuit as necessary. Is the repair complete?	--	Go to Charging System Check	--
16	1. Turn the ignition switch to the off position. 2. Disconnect the negative battery terminal. 3. Disconnect the circuit 2 from the starter terminal. 4. Using a DMM measure the resistance of this circuit from the generator four wire connector terminal D to the starter connector terminal. Is the resistance within specified values?	0-2 ohms	Go to Step 18	Go to Step 17
17	Repair the open in circuit 2 between the starter terminal and the generator connector. Is the repair complete?	--	Go to Charging System Check	--
18	1. Disconnect the powertrain control module connector C2. 2. Connect a DMM between the powertrain control module connector C2 terminal 52 and the generator four wire connector terminal C. 3. Measure the resistance of circuit 23. Is the resistance within specified values?	0-2 ohms	Go to Step 19	Go to Step 24
19	With the powertrain control module connector C2 and the generator four wire connector disconnected, measure the resistance to ground of circuit 23. Is circuit 23 shorted to ground?	--	Go to Step 20	Go to Step 25
20	With the powertrain control module connector C2 and the generator four wire connector disconnected, measure circuit 23 for a short to voltage. Is circuit 23 shorted to voltage?	--	Go to Step 26	Go to Step 21

GC1120100189030X

Fig. 12 Voltmeter displaying high or low (Part 3 of 5). 1999 Corvette

21	1. Disconnect the powertrain control module connector C2. 2. Connect a DMM between the powertrain control module connector C2 terminal 15 and the generator four wire connector terminal B. 3. Measure the resistance of circuit 225. Is the resistance within specified values?	-	Go to Step 22	Go to Step 27
22	With the powertrain control module connector C2 and the generator four wire connector disconnected, measure the resistance to ground of circuit 225. Is circuit 225 shorted to ground?	-	Go to Step 23	Go to Step 28
23	With the powertrain control module connector C2 and the generator four wire connector disconnected, measure circuit 225 for a short to voltage. Is circuit 225 shorted to voltage?	-	Go to Step 29	Go to Charging System Check
24	Repair the open in circuit 23. Is the repair complete?	-	Go to Charging System Check	--
25	Repair the short to ground in circuit 23. Is the repair complete?	-	Go to Charging System Check	--
26	Repair the short to voltage in circuit 23. Is the repair complete?	-	Go to Charging System Check	

GC1120100189040X

Fig. 12 Voltmeter displaying high or low (Part 4 of 5). 1999 Corvette

27	Repair the open in circuit 225. Is the repair complete?	-	Go to Charging System Check	--
28	Repair the short to ground in circuit 225. Is the repair complete?	-	Go to Charging System Check	--
29	Repair the short to voltage in circuit 225. Is the repair complete?	-	Go to Charging System Check	--
30	1. Disconnect the powertrain control module connector C2, and the generator four wire connector. 2. Turn the ignition switch to the on position. 3. Measure circuit 225 for a short to voltage. Is circuit 225 shorted to voltage?	-	Go to Step 31	Go to Step 32
31	Repair the short to voltage in circuit 225. Is the repair complete?	-	Go to Step 32	--
32	Replace or repair the generator. Is the repair complete?	-	Go to Charging System Check	--

GC1120100189050X

Fig. 12 Voltmeter displaying high or low (Part 5 of 5). 1999 Corvette

Step	Action	Value (s)	Yes	No
1	Did you perform the Engine Electrical Diagnostic System Check?	--	Go to Step 2	Perform Diagnostic System Check - Engine Electrical
2	1. Install a scan tool. 2. Turn ON the ignition, with the engine OFF. 3. With a scan tool, observe the Ignition 1 Signal parameter in the PCM data list . Does the scan tool indicate that the Ignition 1 Signal parameter is greater than the specified range?	10.5 V	Go to Step 6	Go to Step 3
3	Measure the voltage at the battery and compare it with the Ignition 1 Signal parameter in the PCM data list Are the battery voltage and PCM Ignition 1 readings different by more than the value specified?	0.5 V	Go to Step 4	Go to Charging System Test
4	Test the battery positive voltage circuit of the PCM for a high resistance. Did you find and correct the condition?	--	Go to Step 7	Go to Step 5
5	Inspect for poor connections at the harness connector of the PCM. Did you find and correct the condition?	--	Go to Step 7	Go to Step 6
6	**Important** The replacement PCM must be programmed. Replace the PCM. Is action complete?	--	Go to Step 7	--
7	1. Review and record the scan tool Fail Records data. 2. Use the scan tool in order to clear the DTC(s). 3. Operate the vehicle within the Conditions for Running the DTC 4. Using the scan tool, observe the Specific DTC Information for DTC P0562 until the test runs. Does the scan tool indicate that DTC P0562 failed this Inspection?	--	Go to Step 2	System Ok

GC1120100190000X

Fig. 13 Voltmeter displaying low. 2000–02 Corvette

Step	Action	Value (s)	Yes	No
1	Did you perform the Engine Electrical Diagnostic System Check?	--	Go to Step 2	Perform Diagnostic System Check - Engine Electrical
2	1. Install a scan tool. 2. Turn ON the ignition, with the engine OFF. 3. With a scan tool, observe the Ignition 1 Signal parameter in the PCM data list . Does the scan tool indicate that the Ignition 1 Signal parameter is less than the specified range?	16.0 V	Go to Step 4	Go to Step 3
3	Measure the voltage at the battery and compare it with the Ignition 1 Signal parameter in the PCM data list Are the battery voltage and PCM Ignition 1 readings different by more than the value specified?	0.5 V	Go to Step 4	Go to Charging System Test
4	**Important** The replacement PCM must be programmed. Replace the PCM. Is action complete?	--	Go to Step 5	--
5	1. Review and record the scan tool Fail Records data. 2. Use the scan tool in order to clear the DTC(s). 3. Operate the vehicle within the Conditions for Running the DTC 4. Using the scan tool, observe the Specific DTC Information for DTC P0563 until the test runs. Does the scan tool indicate that DTC P0563 failed this ignition?	--	Go to Step 2	System OK

GC1120100191000X

Fig. 14 Voltmeter displaying high. 2000–02 Corvette

ALTERNATOR SPECIFICATIONS

Model	Year	Rated Hot Output Amps
Alero & Grand Am	2002	①
Corvette	1998–2002	110

① — Models equipped w/2.2L engine 105 amps; models equipped w/3.4L engine 102 amps.

STEERING COLUMNS

TABLE OF CONTENTS

General Motors

NOTE: On Air Bag Equipped Models, Refer To "Air Bag System Precautions" Located In The Front Of This Manual For System Disarming & Arming Procedures.

NOTE: Refer To "Computer Relearn Procedures" Located In The Front Of This Manual When Battery Power To The Computer Has Been Interrupted.

NOTE: Prior To Performing Any Service Operations Listed In This Section, Consult The "Technical Service Bulletins" Section For Related Information.

INDEX

STEERING COLUMN EXPLODED VIEWS

Model	Year	Type		Shifter Position		Page No.	Fig. No.
		Standard	Tilt	Column	Floor		
Achieva & Skylark	1998	X	—	—	X	17-11	17
		—	X	—	X	17-12	18
Alero	1999–2002	—	X	—	X	17-13	19
Aurora	1998–99	—	X	X	—	17-14	20
		—	X	—	X	17-15	21
	2001–02	—	X	—	X	17-16	22
Bonneville & LeSabre	1998–99	—	X	X	—	17-21	27
		—	X	—	X	17-22	28
	2000–02	—	X	X	—	17-24	31
Camaro & Firebird	1998–2002	—	X	—	X	17-17	23
Catera	1998–2002	—	X	—	X	17-25	32
Cavalier & Sunfire	1998–2002	X	—	—	X	17-26	34
		—	X	—	X	17-26	35
Century	1998–2002	—	X	X	—	17-29	40
Corvette	1998–2002	—	X	—	X	17-18	24①
		—	X	—	X	17-19	25②
		—	X	—	X	17-20	26③
Cutlass	1998–99	—	X	—	X	17-27	36
DeVille, Eldorado & Seville	1998–2002	—	X	X	—	17-30	41
		—	X	—	X	17-30	42
Grand Am	1998	X	—	—	X	17-11	17
		—	X	—	X	17-12	18
	1999–2002	—	X	—	X	17-13	19
Grand Prix, Intrigue & Regal	1998–2002	—	X	—	X	17-29	39
		—	X	X	—	17-29	40
Impala	2000–02	—	X	X	—	17-33	58
		—	X	—	X	17-33	58
Lumina	1998–2001	—	X	X	—	17-31	47
		—	X	—	X	17-32	48
LSS, Regency & 88	1998–99	—	X	X	—	17-21	27
		—	X	—	X	17-22	28
Malibu	1998–2002	—	X	—	X	17-27	36
Metro	1998–2001	X	—	—	X	17-34	62
Monte Carlo	1998–99	—	X	—	X	17-32	48
	2000–02	—	X	—	X	17-33	58
Park Avenue	1998–2002	—	X	X	—	17-34	64
Prizm	1998–2002	—	X	—	X	17-35	65
Riviera	1998–99	—	X	X	—	17-14	20
		—	X	—	X	17-15	21

① — Non telescoping less sensor. ② — Non telescoping w/sensor. ③ — Telescoping.

PRECAUTIONS

AIR BAG SYSTEMS

Refer to "Air Bag System Precautions" in the front of this manual for system disarming and arming procedures.

BATTERY GROUND CABLE

Prior to service, disconnect battery ground cable and isolate as required.

SERVICE

Use only the specified screws, bolts and nuts during the mandatory assembling sequence and tighten to specifications to ensure proper breakaway action of column under impact. Avoid using excessively long bolts as they may prevent a portion of the steering column from collapsing under impact.

When removing or installing, steering wheel, ignition switch or lock, turn signal switch, adjusting transmission linkage, or installing and adjusting neutral-start or back-up light switch, refer to appropriate car chapter.

If a shift tube shows a sheared plastic injection, a new shift tube must be installed. If a steering shaft shows a sheared plastic, but it is not bent, it can be repaired by using a service steering shaft repair kit part No. 7810077. The kit contains instructions and dimensions for all steering columns. On some models, the attaching brackets will shear under impact and must also be replaced.

STEERING COLUMN DAMAGE

When the steering column is removed, it is extremely susceptible to damage. Dropping the steering column on its end could collapse the steering shaft or loosen plastic injections that keep the steering column rigid. Leaning on the steering column could cause the jacket to bend or deform. Any of these conditions could impair the steering

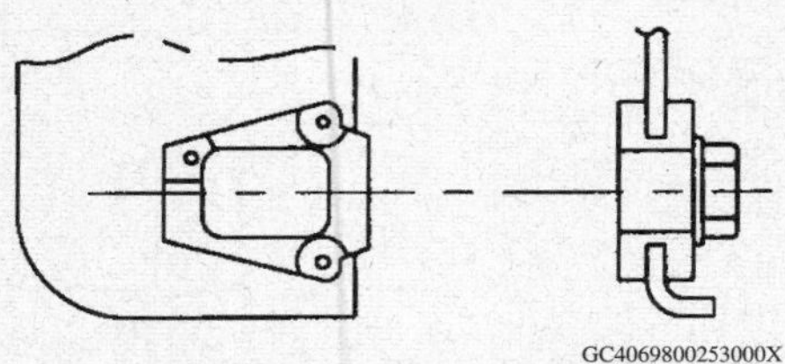

Fig. 1 Inspecting for looseness on steering column bracket assembly

column's collapsible design. If the steering wheel must be removed, use only the specified steering wheel puller and steering wheel puller bolts. Never hammer on the end of the shaft.

SIR COIL DAMAGE

The front wheels of the vehicle must be in a straight ahead position and the steering column must be in the locked position before disconnecting the steering column or intermediate shaft. Failure to follow these procedures will cause improper alignment of some components during installation and result in damage to the SIR coil.

STEERING COLUMN COLLISION DAMAGE

Vehicles involved in accidents resulting in frame damage, major body or sheet metal damage, or where steering column has been impacted, or where supplemental inflatable restraints systems deployed, may also have a damaged or misaligned steering column. When performing service operations on steering columns, inspect the following components:

1. Ensure steering column bracket capsules are securely seated in bracket slots.
2. Inspected for steering column bracket capsules any looseness when pushed or pulled by hand, **Fig. 1.**
3. Replace bracket or jacket, as required.
4. Inspect for jacket assembly collapse by measuring distance from lower edge of upper jacket,**Fig. 2.** If measured dimensions are not as specified, replace jacket assembly.
5. Visually inspect steering column for sheared plastic, **Fig. 3.**
6. If steering shaft shows sheared plastic, replace steering shaft.
7. Remove inflatable restraint coil and allow to hang freely.
8. Rotate steering wheel and measure steering shaft lower end runout using suitable dial indicator.
9. If runout is more than 0.063 inch, replace steering shaft.

TROUBLESHOOTING

Refer to **Fig. 4** for steering column troubleshooting.

STEERING COLUMN

REPLACE

ACHIEVA & SKYLARK & 1998 GRAND AM

1. Remove inflator module as outlined in

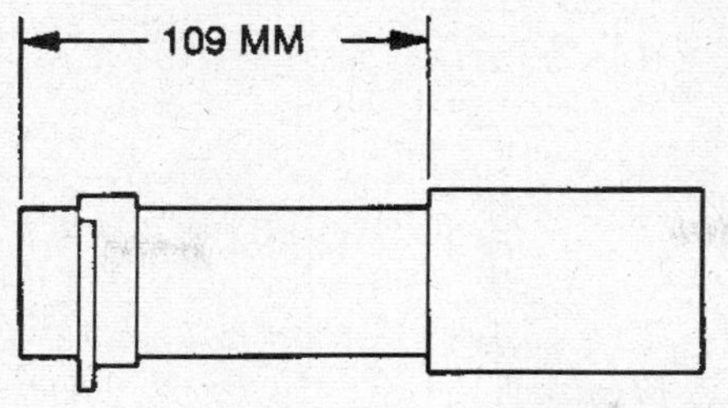

Fig. 2 Jacket assembly collapse measurement

"Passive Restraints Systems" chapter.
2. Remove lefthand lower insulator panel and lower steering column filler panel.
3. Disconnect yellow two-way SIR connectors and remove steering wheel.
4. Remove tilt lever, then the upper and lower steering column covers.
5. Disconnect lock cylinder wire from connector, then the headlamp switch and windshield wiper switch connectors.
6. Disconnect park lock/brake transmission shift interlock cable from ignition switch, then remove upper flexible column bolt.
7. Remove column bracket support bolts and steering column.
8. Reverse procedure to install, noting the following:
   a. Tighten mounting bolts to specifications.
   b. Ensure steering shaft is centered in mast jacket.
   c. Position column as required.

ALERO & 1999-2002 GRAND AM

1. Remove inflator module as outlined in "Passive Restraints Systems" chapter.
2. Remove steering wheel.
3. Remove tilt lever, as required.
4. Remove upper mounting screws and steering column cover.
5. Remove lower mounting screws and steering column cover.
6. Disconnect headlamp switch and windshield wiper switch.
7. Disconnect cruise control electrical connector.
8. Remove instrument panel trim plate and instrument cluster.
9. Cut plastic wire wrap and route SIR coil wiring out of way.
10. Remove lefthand lower sound insulator.
11. Position upper intermediate shaft boot out of way and remove upper shaft pinch bolt.
12. Remove lower steering column bracket support bolts.
13. Loosen upper column bolts.
14. Spread lower steering column intermediate shaft joint apart with suitable screwdriver.
15. Remove upper column bolts.
16. Rotate steering column 45° counterclockwise and remove steering column.
17. Reverse procedure to install. Tighten

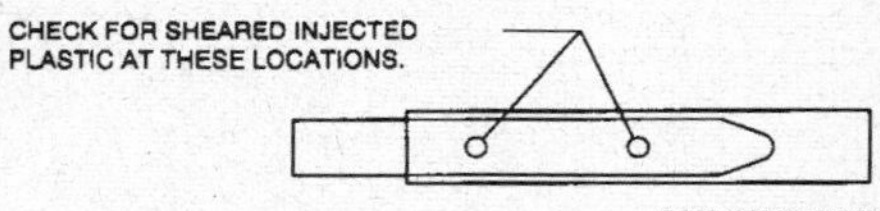

Fig. 3 Inspecting for sheared plastic

mounting bolts and nuts to specifications.

RIVIERA & 1998-99 AURORA

1. Remove inflator module as outlined in "Passive Restraints Systems" chapter.
2. Remove air bag module and steering wheel, **Fig. 5.**
3. Remove knee bolster and reinforcement bracket.
4. **On models equipped with column shift,** remove shift lever cable.
5. **On models equipped with console shift,** unlock ignition, then remove park lock cable and lock ignition.
6. **On all models,** disconnect steering column wiring harness connector from main body wiring harness.
7. Disconnect steering column shaft from intermediate shaft, position seal, as required.
8. Loosen but do not remove lower steering column support mounting nuts.
9. Support column and remove upper steering column support mounting nuts. Discard upper steering column support clips, if present.
10. Remove steering column.
11. Reverse procedure to install, noting the following:
    a. Loosely install nuts on lower support bracket studs, position steering column into vehicle and slide lower support onto nuts.
    b. Tighten mounting bolts and nuts to specifications.

2001-02 AURORA

The steering column should never be supported only by the lower support bracket.

1. Ensure wheels are straight ahead and steering column is in LOCK position.
2. Turn ignition key must to OFF or LOCK position.
3. Lock steering column by inserting steering column lock pin tool No. J-42640, or equivalent, into steering column access hole.
4. If steering column is to be disassemble, remove steering wheel as described in "Electrical" section of "Aurora & Riviera" chassis chapter.
5. Push in hazard button.
6. Remove knee bolster and bracket or reinforcement.
7. Disconnect steering column wiring harness connector from main body wiring harness.
8. Remove steering column shaft from intermediate shaft. Position seal, as required.
9. Remove upper intermediate shaft pinch bolt.
10. Support column.

Condition	Cause
The lock system does not lock.	• A broken lock bolt spring • A worn lock bolt spring • A damaged sector • A damaged lock cylinder • A burr on the lock bolt • A damaged housing • A damaged rack • Interference between the bowl and the rack coupling • A binding ignition switch • A restricted actuator rod • The sector is installed incorrectly. • The shift lever is not in the PARK position. • The park lock cable is incorrectly adjusted. • The park lock components are damaged.

Condition	Cause
The lock system sticks in START.	• A deformed actuator rod • *High Lock Effort Between the Off Lock Positions*

Condition	Cause
The key cannot be removed in the OFF-LOCK position.	• The ignition switch is not set correctly. • A damaged lock cylinder • An improperly adjusted linkage • The shift lever is not in the PARK position.

Condition	Cause
The lock cylinder can be removed without depressing the retainer.	A missing lock cylinder retaining screw

Condition	Cause
The lock cylinder effort between OFF and OFF-LOCK is high.	A distorted rack

Condition	Cause
The lock bolt hits the shift lock in the OFF position and the PARK position.	The ignition switch is set incorrectly.

GC6049900276010X

Fig. 4 Steering column troubleshooting chart (Part 1 of 5)

Condition	Causes
A high lock effort exists.	• The lock cylinder is damaged. • The ignition switch is damaged. • A rack preload spring is broken. • A rack preload spring is broken. • Burrs exist on the following items: – The sector – The rack – The housing – The support – The actuator rod coupling • The sector shaft is bent. • A rack is damaged. • The housing is extreme misaligned to the cover. • A coupling slot in the rack is distorted. • An actuator rod is damaged. • The ignition switch mounting bracket is bent. • An actuator rod is restricted. • The key cut is damaged. • The key cut is incorrect. • The park lock cable is incorrectly adjusted. • The park lock components are damaged.

Condition	Causes
Noise is present in the steering column.	• The pinch bolts are loose in the intermediate shaft coupling. • The column is misaligned • The contact ring is not lubricated. • The bearing lacks lubrication. • The column components are loose. • The steering shaft bearings are worn. • The steering shaft bearings are broken. • The shaft lock snap ring is not seated. • The spherical joint is not lubricated. • The dust seal is rubbing the column shaft coupling. • The contact ring is worn. • The contact ring is damaged. • The brushes are worn. • The brushes are damaged. • The lock bolt is bolt. • The lock bolt is improperly lubricated.

GC6049900276020X

Fig. 4 Steering column troubleshooting chart (Part 2 of 5)

11. Remove upper steering column support mounting nuts. Discard upper steering column support clips, if equipped.
12. Remove steering column.
13. Reverse procedure to install, noting the following:
    a. Use correct bolts and nuts in proper location.
    b. **Do not use paints, lubricants or corrosion inhibitors on bolts and nuts or joint surfaces unless specified.**
    c. Tighten pinch bolt, upper and lower support mounting nuts, and wiring harness mounting bolt to specifications.

BONNEVILLE, LESABRE, LSS, REGENCY & 88

1. Remove inflator module as outlined in "Passive Restraints Systems" chapter, then the steering wheel.
2. Remove trim plate and knee bolster deflector.
3. **On models equipped with column shift,** disconnect shift indicator cable.
4. **On all models,** loosen column support bracket bolts.
5. Remove mounting bolt and steering column support brace, **Fig. 6.**
6. Disconnect steering column wiring harness, then support column and remove support bracket bolts, **Fig. 7.**
7. **On models equipped with column shift,** disconnect shift control cable from actuator and from slot in lower column bracket, as required.
8. **On models equipped with console shift,** disconnect park lock cable from ignition switch inhibitor.
9. **On all models,** position seal, as required, and loosen or remove upper intermediate steering shaft pinch bolt.
10. Disconnect steering column shaft from intermediate steering shaft.
11. Remove steering column.
12. Reverse procedure to install, noting the following:
    a. Hand start one bolt into lower right-hand steering column support bracket.
    b. Tighten mounting bolts to specifications.

CAMARO & FIREBIRD

1. Remove lefthand instrument panel insulator, knee bolster and deflector.
2. Remove inflator module as outlined in "Passive Restraints Systems" chapter, then the steering wheel.
3. Remove intermediate steering shaft bolt from steering gear coupling shaft and column, then the cover from dash panel, **Fig. 8.**
4. Disconnect electrical connectors, then remove steering column support nuts and shims.
5. **On models equipped with automatic transmission,** disconnect park lock cable from ignition switch.
6. **On all models,** remove steering column.
7. Reverse procedure to install. Tighten mounting bolts and nuts to specifications.

CATERA

If service replacement steering column is being installed, do not remove the anti-rotation pin until after the column has been connected to the steering gear. Removing the anti-rotation pin before the column is connected to the steering gear may cause damage to the SIR coil.

1. Remove inflator module as outlined in "Passive Restraints Systems" chapter, then the steering wheel.
2. Remove SIR coil.
3. Remove ignition lock cylinder.
4. Disconnect and remove theft deterrent immobilizer.
5. Remove ignition switch, windshield washer switch and turn signal switch.
6. Remove driver's knee bolster and sound insulator.
7. Remove coupler bolt from steering column shaft connection.
8. Separate coupler enough to allow for shaft removal.
9. Remove forward support strap nut.
10. Rotate forward support strap shear bolt to remove using suitable chisel.
11. Remove rear support bracket bolt.
12. Pull steering column straight back through dash.
13. Reverse procedure to install. Tighten mounting bolts and nuts to specifications

CAVALIER & SUNFIRE

1. Remove inflator module as outlined in "Passive Restraints Systems" chapter and steering wheel.
2. Remove lefthand lower sound insulator and side instrument panel covers.
3. Remove instrument panel pad by removing defroster vent screw, under defroster vent screw, one screw on each side panel, two screws in glove compartment toward lefthand rear and

Condition	Causes
High steering shaft effort exists.	• The column is misaligned. • The dust sel is improperly installed. • The dust seal is deformed. • The upper bearing is damaged. • The lower bearing is damaged. • The intermediate steering shaft universal joint is tight. • The shroud is rubbing on the column cover.

Condition	Causes
Lash exists in the steering column.	• The IP-to-column mounting bolts for the upper bracket are loose. • The IP-to-column mounting bolts for the lower bracket are loose. • The weld nuts on the jacket are broken. • The IP upper bracket capsule is sheared. • The shoes in the housing are loose. • The tilt head pivot pins are loose. • The shoe lock pin in the support is loose. • The support screws are loose. • The upper bracket-to-jacket bolts in the column are loose. • The lower bracket-to-jacket bolts in the column are loose. • The lower bracket-to-adapter screws are loose. • The bearing assembly mounting screws are loose. • The IP-to-jacket mounting bolts are loose.

Condition	Causes
The steering wheel is loose.	• Excessive clearance exists between the pivot pin diameters and the holes in the support or in the housing. • The anti-lash spring in the spheres is damaged. • The anti-lash spring in the spheres is missing. • The upper bearing is not seated in the housing. • The inner race seal is missing from the upper bearing. • The support screws are loose. • The bearing preload spring is missing. • The bearing preload spring is broken.

Condition	Causes
The steering wheel is loose in every other tilt position.	• A loose fit exists between the shoe and the shoe pivot pin. • The shoe is not free in the slot.

GC6049900276030X

Fig. 4 Steering column troubleshooting chart (Part 3 of 5)

Condition	Causes
The steering wheel does not lock in any tilt position.	• The shoe seized on the pivot pin. • Burrs are present in the shoe grooves. • Dirt is present in the shoe grooves. • The shoe lock spring is weak. • The shoe lock spring is broken.

Condition	Causes
The steering wheel does not return to the top tilt position.	• The pivot pins are binding. • The wheel tilt spring is broken. • The wheel tilt spring is weak. • The turn signal switch wires are too tight.

Condition	Causes
Noise is present when tilting the column.	• The upper tilt bumpers are worn. • The tilt spring rubs in the housing.

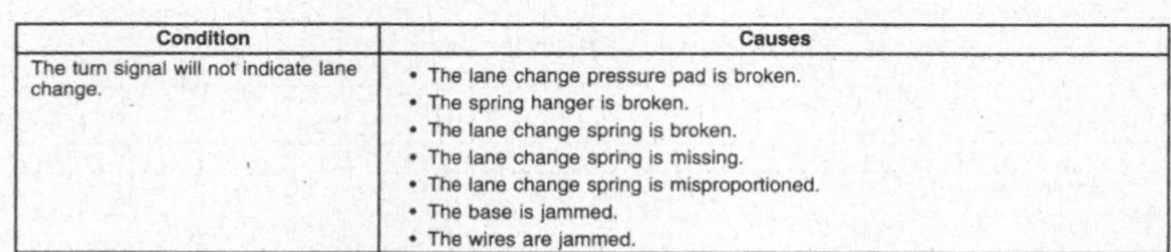

Condition	Causes
The turn signal will not indicate lane change.	• The lane change pressure pad is broken. • The spring hanger is broken. • The lane change spring is broken. • The lane change spring is missing. • The lane change spring is misproportioned. • The base is jammed. • The wires are jammed.

Condition	Causes
The turn signal will not stay in the turn position.	• Foreign material is impeding movement of the yoke. • Loose parts are impeding movement of the yoke. • A detent is broken. • A detent is missing. • A canceling spring is broken. • A canceling spring is missing.

GC6049900276040X

Fig. 4 Steering column troubleshooting chart (Part 4 of 5)

three screws along glove compartment top.

4. Remove tilt lever, then the upper and lower column covers as outlined under "Steering Column Cover."
5. Disconnect cruise control, headlamp switch and windshield wiper switch connectors, then the ignition switch.
6. Disconnect Passlock cylinder connector.
7. **On models equipped with automatic transaxle**, disconnect park lock/brake transmission shift interlock cable from lock cylinder housing.
8. **On all models,** remove upper flexible joint pinch bolt and lefthand side wire harness retainer clip, **Fig. 9.**
9. Loosen lower column bracket support bolts and remove upper column support bolts.
10. Spread lower steering column flexible joint apart using suitable screwdriver and remove steering column.
11. Reverse procedure to install. Tighten mounting bolts to specifications.

CORVETTE

1. Remove inflator module as outlined in "Passive Restraints Systems" chapter.
2. Turn steering wheel to left to access upper intermediate steering shaft pinch bolt and remove pinch bolt.
3. Turn steering wheel until wheels are in straight ahead position and lock steering column.
4. Remove steering wheel and tilt lever.
5. Remove lefthand knee bolster trim panel and knee bolster.
6. Disconnect electrical connectors from column and remove lower steering column support plate nuts, **Fig. 10.**
7. Remove upper steering column bracket nuts and steering column.
8. Reverse procedure to install. Tighten mounting bolts and nuts to specifications.

CUTLASS & MALIBU

1. Remove inflator module as outlined in "Passive Restraints Systems" chapter, then the steering wheel.
2. Remove column covers as outlined under "Steering Column Cover."
3. Remove tilt lever, then disconnect cruise control, headlamp and windshield wiper switch connectors.
4. Remove instrument panel trim plate and instrument cluster.
5. Remove lefthand lower sound insulator, disconnect SIR coil wiring harness and cut plastic zip tie.
6. Position upper intermediate shaft boot aside and remove shaft pinch bolt.
7. Loosen steering column bracket and upper column bolts, **Fig. 11.**
8. Spread lower steering column intermediate shaft joint apart using screwdriver and remove upper column bolts.
9. Rotate column counterclockwise approximately 45° and remove column.
10. Reverse procedure to install. Tighten mounting bolts and nuts to specifications

CENTURY, GRAND PRIX, INTRIGUE, LUMINA, MONTE CARLO & REGAL

1. Remove inflator module as outlined in "Passive Restraints Systems" chapter, then the steering wheel.
2. Remove lefthand instrument panel insulator.
3. **On Century and Regal models,** remove knee bolster bracket.
4. **On all models,** remove trim panel below steering column.
5. Push top of intermediate shaft seal down, then remove upper intermediate steering shaft pinch bolt, **Fig. 12.**
6. **On models equipped with console shift,** disconnect shift indicator cable end and casing from shift cam and automatic transmission control indicator adjuster, or park lock cable.
7. **On models equipped with column shift,** disconnect transaxle shift cable from ball stud on steering column and transaxle shift cable casing from steering column bracket.
8. **On all models,** remove lower and upper steering column bolts.
9. Disconnect electrical connector and remove steering column.
10. Reverse procedure to install. Tighten mounting bolts to specifications.

DEVILLE, ELDORADO & SEVILLE

1. Remove inflator module as outlined in "Passive Restraints Systems" chapter.
2. Remove knee bolster and steering column reinforcement plate.
3. Disconnect electrical connectors from column.
4. Remove pinch bolt from intermediate shaft, **Fig. 13.**
5. Remove lower support bracket.
6. Remove upper support and column.
7. Reverse procedure to install, noting the following:
   a. Install column and support upper bracket with two bolts, **Fig. 14. Do not tighten now.**
   b. Tighten mounting bolts to specifications.

Condition	Causes
The turn signal will not cancel.	• The switch mounting screws are loose. • A switch is broken. • The anchor bosses are broken. • A detent is broken. • A return is broken. • A canceling spring is broken. • A detent is missing. • A return is missing. • A canceling spring is missing. • A detent is out-of-position. • A return is out-of-position. • A canceling spring is out-of-position. • A cancelling cam is worn.

Condition	Causes
The turn signal is difficult to operate.	• A turn signal lever screw is loose. • A yoke is broken. Replace the switch. • A yoke is distorted. Replace the switch. • The springs are loose. • The springs are mispositioned. • Interference caused by foreign material exists. • The turn signal switch mounting screws are loose.

Condition	Causes
The electrical system will not function.	• The ignition switch is damaged. • The ignition switch is improperly adjusted. • A loose connection at the ignition switch exists. • A loose connection at the column connectors exists.

Condition	Causes
The switch cannot be set correctly.	• The switch actuator rod is deformed. • The sector is engaged in the wrong rack tooth.

GC6049900276050X

Fig. 4 Steering column troubleshooting chart (Part 5 of 5)

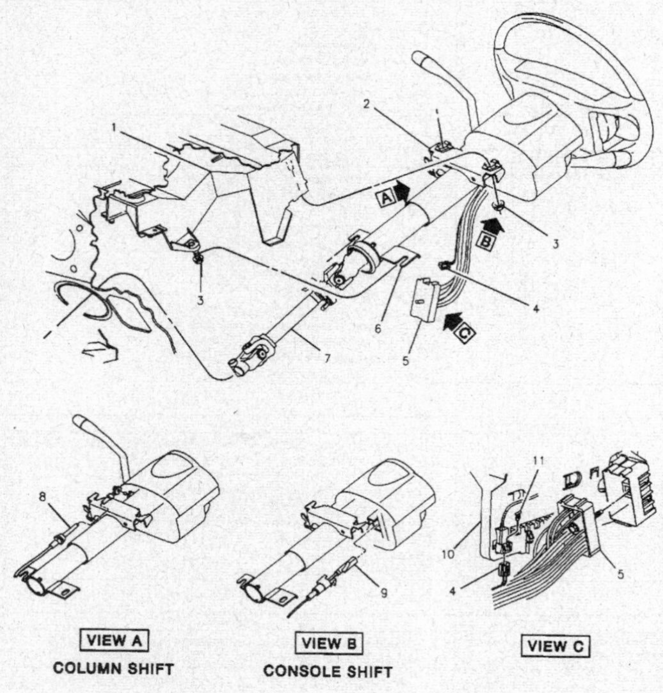

1 BRACKET, STEERING COLUMN SUPPORT
2 SUPPORT, STEERING COLUMN UPPER
3 NUT, 27 N·m (20 LB. FT.)
4 CONNECTOR, SIR
5 CONNECTOR, STEERING COLUMN WIRING HARNESS
6 SUPPORT, STEERING COLUMN LOWER
7 INTERMEDIATE STEERING SHAFT
8 SHIFT LEVER CABLE
9 PARK LOCK CABLE
10 BRACKET, MULTIUSE MODULE
11 CONNECTOR, POSITION ASSURANCE (CPA)

GC6049500173000X

Fig. 5 Steering column replacement. Riviera & 1998–99 Aurora

IMPALA

Do not support steering column by only the lower or upper support bracket. Damage to column lower bearing adapter could result.

1. Remove inflator module as outlined in "Passive Restraints Systems" chapter.
2. Remove steering wheel.
3. Remove lefthand instrument panel insulator.
4. Remove trim panel below steering column.
5. Remove steering column knee bolster.
6. Remove steering column intermediate shaft from steering column.
7. Remove shift indicator cable, casing from shift cam and automatic control indicator adjuster or park lock cable.
8. Disconnect transaxle range selector cable from ball stud on steering column.
9. Remove transaxle shift cable casing from steering column bracket by depressing two tabs.
10. Disconnect steering column electrical connectors.
11. Loosen steering column electrical connector bolt.
12. Separate two steering column electrical connector halves.
13. Remove lower steering column mounting bolts.
14. Remove upper mounting bolts and steering column.
15. Reverse procedure to install, noting the following:
    a. **When installing steering column to intermediate shaft, ensure shaft is seated prior to pinch bolt installation.**
    b. Tighten mounting bolts to specifications.
    c. Tighten righthand lower bolt first, then lefthand lower bolt, lefthand upper nut and righthand upper nut.

METRO

1. Remove inflator module as outlined in "Passive Restraints Systems" chapter, then the steering wheel.
2. Remove knee bolster, then loosen upper steering column support bolts and lower column slightly.
3. Disconnect SIR coil and combination switch connectors, then remove upper and lower steering column covers by removing screws from lower cover, **Fig. 15.**
4. Remove SIR coil and combination switch, then disconnect ignition wiring connectors from junction block.
5. Pull aside steering shaft joint cover and remove steering shaft joint upper pinch bolt.
6. Remove lower and upper steering column mounting nuts and bolts.
7. Lower steering column and disconnect shift interlock cable from ignition switch.
8. Remove steering column, then the ignition switch from steering column.
9. Reverse procedure to install. Tighten mounting bolts and nuts to specifications.

PARK AVENUE

1. Remove inflator module as outlined in "Passive Restraints Systems" chapter, then the steering wheel.
2. Push in hazard button, then remove knee bolster and bracket.
3. **On models equipped with column shift,** remove shift lever cable.
4. **On models equipped with console shift,** unlock ignition and remove park lock cable, then lock ignition.
5. **On all models,** disconnect steering column electrical connectors and remove upper intermediate shaft pinch bolt, **Fig.16.**
6. Remove steering column shaft from intermediate shaft, loosen but do not remove lower steering column support mounting nuts.
7. Support steering column and remove upper steering column support mounting nuts. **Discard upper steering column support clips.**
8. Remove lower support nuts and steering column.
9. Reverse procedure to install. Tighten mounting bolts and nuts to specifications.

PRIZM

1. Remove inflator module as outlined in "Passive Restraints Systems" chapter.
2. Remove steering wheel.
3. Unclip lefthand front carpet retainer, loosen mounting screws and disconnect hood release lever from knee bolster.
4. Remove trim caps and knee bolster to

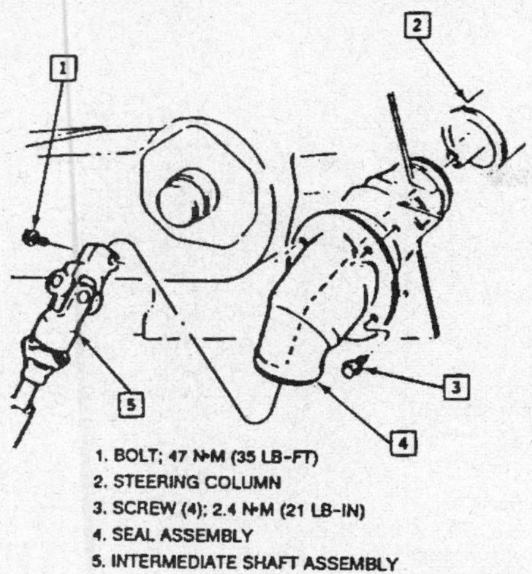

Fig. 6 Intermediate shaft & boot installation. Bonneville, LeSabre, LSS, Regency & 88

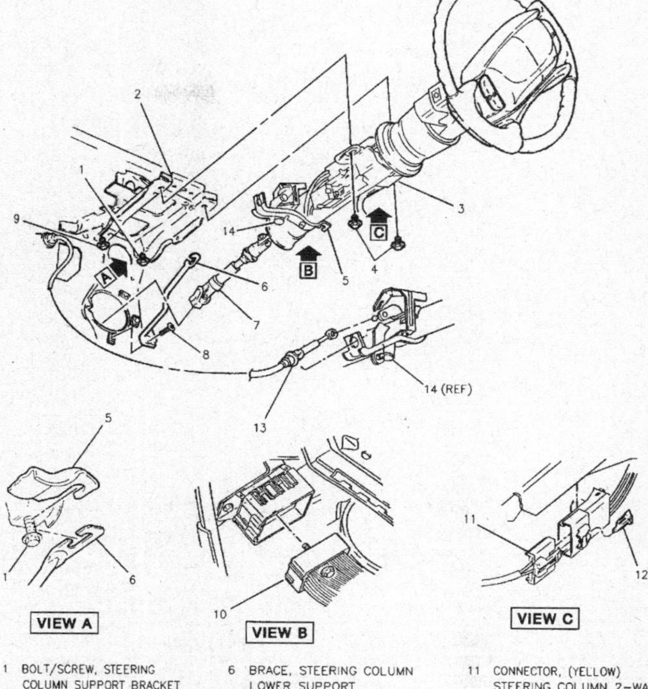

Fig. 7 Steering column replacement. Bonneville, LeSabre, LSS, Regency & 88

instrument panel mounting bolts.
5. Pull out instrument panel lefthand side ventilation duct.
6. Loosen screws, then remove upper and lower steering column trim covers.
7. Disconnect steering column electrical connectors.
8. Remove steering column pinch bolt.
9. Remove mounting bolts, nuts and steering column.
10. Reverse procedure to install. Tighten mounting bolts to specifications.

STEERING COLUMN SERVICE

ACHIEVA & SKYLARK & 1998 GRAND AM

Refer to **Figs. 17 and 18** for exploded views of these steering columns.

STEERING COLUMN COVERS

1. Remove lower mounting screws and separate column covers by snapping apart.
2. Reverse procedure to install.

TURN SIGNAL SWITCH

Refer to the "Electrical" section of the "Achieva, Alero, Cutlass, Grand Am, Malibu & Skylark" chassis chapter for turn signal switch replacement.

WASH/WIPE SWITCH

Refer to the "Electrical" section of the "Achieva, Alero, Cutlass, Grand Am, Malibu & Skylark" chassis chapter for wash/wipe switch replacement.

IGNITION SWITCH

Refer to the "Electrical" section of the "Achieva, Alero, Cutlass, Grand Am, Malibu & Skylark" chassis chapter for ignition switch replacement.

INTERLOCK SOLENOID

1. Remove steering wheel as outlined in "Electrical" section of "Achieva, Alero, Cutlass, Grand Am, Malibu & Skylark" chassis chapter.
2. Place shifter lever in Park position and ignition key in Off-Lock position, then remove key.
3. Disconnect wire connector from interlock solenoid.
4. Remove interlock solenoid mounting screws and interlock solenoid.
5. Reverse procedure to install. Tighten mounting screws to specifications.

LOCK CYLINDER

Refer to the "Electrical" section of the "Achieva, Alero, Cutlass, Grand Am, Malibu & Skylark" chassis chapter, for ignition lock replacement.

PARK LOCK CABLE

1. Remove steering wheel as outlined in "Electrical" section of "Achieva, Alero, Cutlass, Grand Am, Malibu & Skylark" chassis chapter.
2. Place key in RUN position and disconnect park lock cable from lock cylinder housing.
3. **On models equipped with column shift,** disconnect park lock cable from shift gate.
4. **On all models,** reverse procedure to install, noting the following:
   a. Place key in RUN position and shift lever in PARK position.
   b. Snap connector body of cable to lock cylinder, ensure locking tab is fully engaged into lock cylinder housing.
   c. **On models equipped with column shift,** place key in Off-Lock position and pull key half way out of lock cylinder housing.
   d. **On all models,** route cable end fitting through park lock latch, depress adjuster button and snap cable adjuster to shift gate.
   e. Snap cable into cable retainer, depress adjuster button and pull cable sheathing towards lock cylinder to remove lash from system.
   f. Release sheathing and release button.

COLUMN JACKET BUSHING, ORIENTATION PLATE CAM, TURN SIGNAL CANCEL CAM, UPPER BEARING SPRING, BEARING, COLUMN SHAFT, COLUMN HOUSING & JACKET

Standard Column

1. Remove steering wheel as outlined in "Electrical" section of "Achieva, Alero, Cutlass, Grand Am, Malibu & Skylark" chassis chapter.
2. Remove SIR coil and allow to hang freely
3. Remove steering column as previously described.

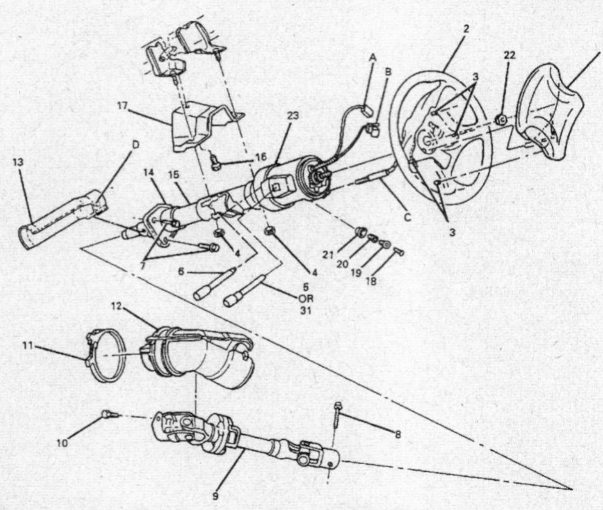

A CONNECTOR, RADIO ASSEMBLY ELECTRICAL (PONTIAC ONLY)
B CONNECTOR, SIR COIL ASSEMBLY ELECTRICAL
C LEAD, HORN
D BUTTON, STEERING GEAR COUPLING HEAT SHIELD
1 MODULE ASSEMBLY, INFLATABLE RESTRAINT STEERING WHEEL
2 WHEEL ASSEMBLY, STEERING
3 BOLT/SCREW, STEERING WHEEL
4 NUT, STEERING COLUMN UPPER SUPPORT
5 LEVER ASSEMBLY, TURN SIGNAL AND HEADLAMP DIMMER SWITCH AND CRUISE CONTROL ACTUATOR AND WINDSHIELD WIPER AND WINDSHIELD WASHER
6 LEVER ASSEMBLY, STEERING COLUMN TILT WHEEL RELEASE
7 BOLT/SCREW, STEERING COLUMN
8 BOLT/SCREW, INTERMEDIATE STEERING SHAFT
9 SHAFT ASSEMBLY, STEERING GEAR COUPLING
10 BOLT/SCREW, INTERMEDIATE STEERING SHAFT
11 CLAMP, STEERING GEAR COUPLING SHIELD
12 BOOT, STEERING GEAR
13 SHIELD, STEERING GEAR COUPLING HEAT
14 COVER ASSEMBLY, STEERING COLUMN DASH PANEL
15 COLUMN ASSEMBLY, STEERING
16 BOLT/SCREW, STEERING COLUMN GUIDE,
17 GUIDE, STEERING COLUMN
18 BOLT/SCREW, HAZARD WARNING SWITCH KNOB
19 BUTTON, HAZARD WARNING SWITCH
20 SPRING, HAZARD WARNING SWITCH KNOB
21 KNOB, HAZARD WARNING SWITCH
22 NUT, STEERING WHEEL
23 SEALER, STEERING COLUMN
31 LEVER ASSEMBLY, TURN SIGNAL AND HEADLAMP DIMMER SWITCH AND WINDSHIELD WIPER AND WINDSHIELD WASHER

GC6049100052000A

Fig. 8 Steering column replacement. Camaro & Firebird

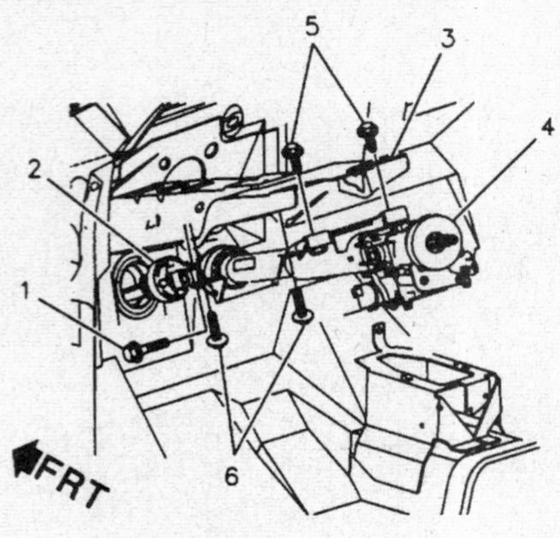

1 UPPER PINCH BOLT
2 FLANGE AND STEERING COUPLING
3 UPPER COLUMN SUPPORT
4 STEERING COLUMN
5 UPPER COLUMN BOLT
6 LOWER COLUMN BOLT

GC6049700227000X

Fig. 9 Steering column replacement. Cavalier & Sunfire

4. Remove shaft lock retaining ring using lock plate compressor No. J-23653-SIR or equivalent.
5. Remove shaft lock and turn signal cancel cam, then the upper bearing spring and spacer.
6. Remove steering column jacket bushing and shaft from lower end of steering column jacket.
7. Remove bushing and retaining ring from steering shaft.
8. Reverse procedure to install.

Tilt Column

1. Remove steering wheel as outlined in "Electrical" section of "Achieva, Alero, Cutlass, Grand Am, Malibu & Skylark" chassis chapter.
2. Remove SIR coil.
3. Remove steering column as previously described.
4. Put key in Run position, push on locking tab on end of lock cable and remove cable.
5. Remove wire restraint clip from bottom of steering column jacket support.
6. Tilt column to Up position.
7. Push tilt wheel spring retainer down and turn counterclockwise to release using suitable Phillips head screwdriver.
8. Remove column jacket bushing, or position sensor and bushing from jacket.
9. Move shift lever to Park position.
10. Remove two pivot pins using pivot pin remover tool No. J-21854-01, or equivalent.
11. Install and pull tilt arm to disengage steering wheel lock shoes from dowel pins in steering column jacket support.
12. Remove bearing and housing with steering shaft.
13. Reverse procedure to install.

ALERO & 1999–2002 GRAND AM

Refer to **Fig. 19** for exploded view of this steering column.

TILT SPRING

1. Move tilt column into up position.
2. Pry spring upward until bulge occurs and most of spring tension is removed.
3. Secure locking spring with locking pliers.
4. Continue prying on spring until tilt spring disengages from post on steering column support and steering column housing and bearing.
5. Remove tilt spring guide from tilt spring.
6. Reverse procedure to install.

STEERING COLUMN TILT HEAD

1. Remove steering column as previously described.
2. Remove SIR coil.
3. Compress cam orientation plate using lock plate compressor No. J-23653-SIR and cam orientation plate adapter No. J-42137, or equivalents.
4. Remove and dispose of bearing retainer.
5. Remove cam orientation plate.
6. Remove turn signal cam.
7. Remove upper bearing spring, inner race seat and inner race.
8. Remove pivot pins using pivot pin remover No. J-21854-1, or equivalent.
9. Pull tilt arm to disengage steering wheel lock shoes from dowel pins in steering column support.
10. Remove bearing and housing.
11. Reverse procedure to assemble, noting the following:
    a. Lubricate pivot pins with grease.
    b. Press pivot pins until seated and stake at three locations.

LOWER STEERING SHAFT, LOWER BEARING & COLUMN JACKET

1. Remove steering column as previously described.
2. Remove steering shaft seal from sensor retainer.
3. Remove sensor retainer from end of steering shaft.
4. Remove lower spring retainer and steering wheel speed sensor, then the lower bearing spring and seat from steering shaft.
5. Remove adapter and bearing from steering column jacket.
6. Remove upper tilt head components as previously described.
7. Remove steering shaft from steering column support.
8. Remove mounting screws from steering column support.
9. Remove steering column support from steering column jacket.
10. Mark race, upper and lower steering shaft to ensure proper assembly.
11. Tilt race and upper shaft 90° toward each other.
12. Disengage, then remove race and upper shaft.
13. Remove centering sphere from race

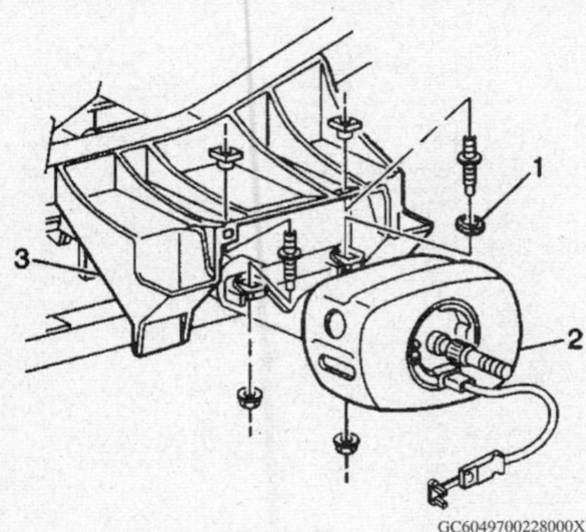

Fig. 10 Steering column replacement. Corvette

and upper shaft by rotating centering sphere 90°.

14. Lift centering sphere out of race and upper shaft.
15. Remove joint preload spring from centering sphere.
16. Inspect centering sphere and joint preload spring. Replace parts, as required.
17. Reverse procedure to install, noting the following:
    a. Grease centering sphere with lithium grease.
    b. Assemble centering sphere and joint preload spring using centering sphere installer tool No. J-41688, or equivalent.
    c. Apply lithium grease to exposed shaft engagement areas.

SIR COIL CENTERING

The SIR coil will become uncentered if the steering column is separated from the steering gear and rotates, or if the centering spring is pushed down and the hub rotates while the coil is removed from the steering column. To center the coil, proceed as follows:

1. Remove coil from steering column.
2. Hold coil with bottom facing upward.
3. Depress spring lock and rotate hub counterclockwise until it stops.
4. Ensure coil ribbon is wound against center hub.
5. Rotate coil hub clockwise approximately 2½ turns.
6. Release spring lock between locking tabs.

RIVIERA & 1998–99 AURORA

Refer to **Figs. 20 and 21** for exploded view of these steering columns.

STEERING COLUMN COVERS

1. Lower or remove steering column as previously described.
2. Disable SIR system.
3. **On 1998 models,** proceed as follows:
    a. Remove upper cover mounting screws.
    b. Remove upper cover and mounting screw.

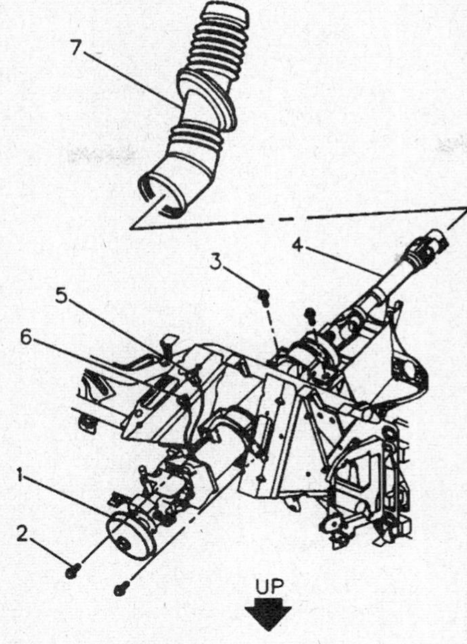

(1) Coil, SIR
(2) Bolt, Steering Column (Lower)
(3) Bolt, Steering Column (Upper)
(4) Intermediate Shaft
(5) Connection, SIR
(6) Connector, Cruise
(7) Intermediate Shaft Boot

GC6049700224000X

Fig. 11 Steering column replacement. Cutlass & Malibu

    c. Remove tilt knob lever and shift lever seal.
    d. Remove close out knob by prying locking tabs from bearing and housing.
    e. Remove mounting screws and cover.
4. **On 1999–2000 models,** proceed as follows:
    a. Steering wheel must be in 12 o'clock position and place column on modular column holding fixture tool No. J-41352, or equivalent.
    b. Remove upper, then lower mounting screws and column cover.
5. **On all models,** reverse procedure to install. Tighten mounting screws to specifications.

TURN SIGNAL SWITCH

Refer to the "Electrical" section of the "Aurora & Riviera" chassis chapter, for turn signal switch replacement.

WASH/WIPER SWITCH

Refer to the "Electrical" section of the "Aurora & Riviera" chassis chapter, for wash and wiper switch replacement.

IGNITION SWITCH

Refer to the "Electrical" section of the "Aurora & Riviera" chassis chapter for ignition switch replacement.

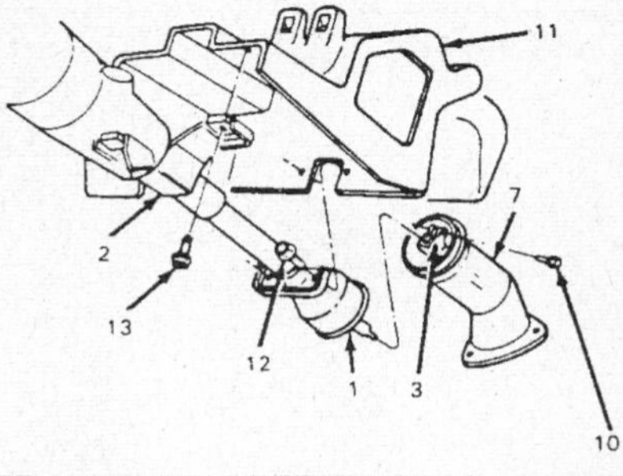

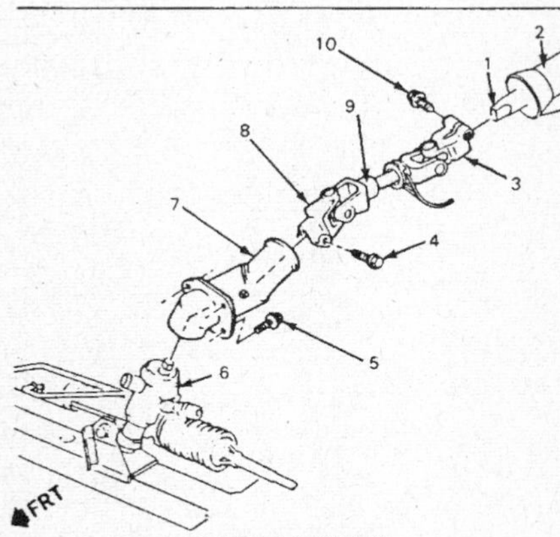

1 STEERING SHAFT-LOWER END
2 STEERING COLUMN ASSEMBLY
3 INTERMEDIATE SHAFT COUPLING-UPPER
4 PINCH BOLT-LOWER COUPLING
5 SCREW
6 STEERING GEAR
7 SEAL-INTERMEDIATE SHAFT
8 INTERMEDIATE SHAFT COUPLING-LOWER
9 INTERMEDIATE SHAFT
10 PINCH BOLT-UPPER COUPLING
11 BRACKET-BRAKE PEDAL
12 BOLT-LOWER STEERING COLUMN
13 BOLT-UPPER STEERING COLUMN

GC6049100057000X

Fig. 12 Steering column replacement. Century, Grand Prix, Intrigue, Lumina, Monte Carlo & Regal

INTERLOCK SOLENOID

Column Shift

1. Remove steering wheel as outlined in "Electrical" section of "Aurora & Riviera" chassis chapter.
2. Remove upper and lower column covers as previously described.
3. Remove mounting screws from bottom of bearing and housing.
4. Disconnect interlock solenoid wire connector from turn signal and multifunction switch wire harness.
5. Remove interlock solenoid.
6. Reverse procedure to install. Tighten mounting screws to specifications.

LOCK CYLINDER

Refer to the "Electrical" section of the "Aurora & Riviera" chassis chapter for ignition lock cylinder replacement.

PARK LOCK CABLE

1. Remove steering wheel as outlined in "Electrical" section of "Aurora & Riviera" chassis chapter.

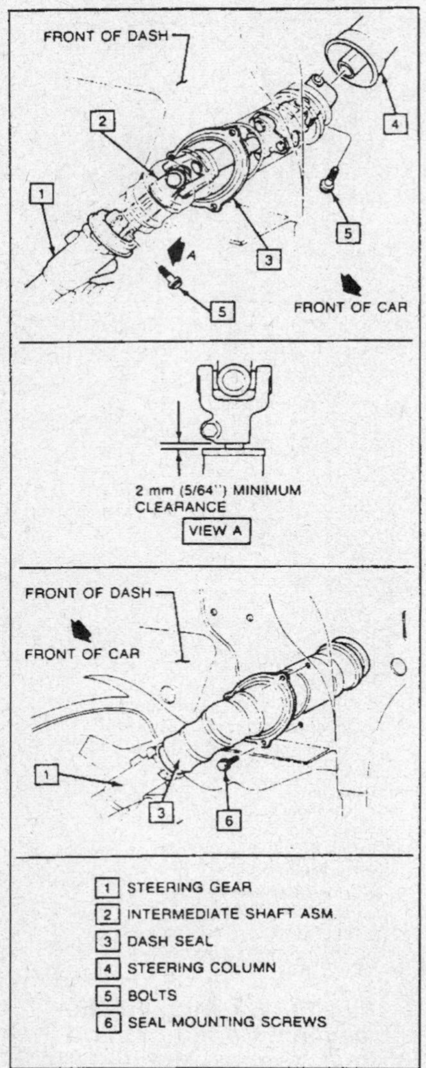

GC6049100048000X

Fig. 13 Intermediate shaft & boot. DeVille, Eldorado & Seville

2. Remove upper and lower column covers as previously described.
3. Turn key to Run position.
4. Press in locking tab on end of cable, then remove cable from bottom of bearing and housing.
5. Pry locking tab on opposite end of cable and remove cable from linear shift base adapter.
6. Remove wire cable from park lock latch.
7. Place shift lever in Neutral position.
8. If required, remove shift lever spring as follows:
   a. Pry off shift lever spring leg.
   b. Remove shift lever clip from shift lever pin.
   c. Remove shift lever pin with drift.
   d. Remove shift lever spring with linear shift lever.
9. Remove mounting screws.
10. Remove linear shift base adapter from column.
11. Remove transaxle cable from ball stud on linear shift base adapter.

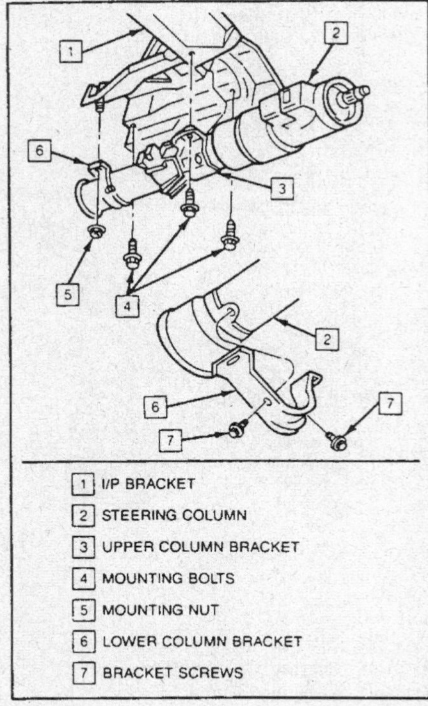

GC6049100049000X

Fig. 14 Steering column installation. DeVille, Eldorado & Seville

12. Reverse procedure to install. Tighten mounting screws to specifications.

UPPER HEAD HOUSING COMPONENTS, SHAFT LOCK, TURN SIGNAL CANCEL CAM, UPPER BEARING SPRING, UPPER BEARING INNER RACE SEAT & INNER RACE

1. Remove steering wheel as outlined in "Electrical" section of "Aurora & Riviera" chassis chapter.
2. Remove SIR coil.
3. Remove shaft lock retaining ring using lock plate compressor tool No. J-23653-SIR, or equivalent, to push down shaft lock.
4. Remove shaft lock and turn signal cancel cam.
5. Remove upper bearing spring, upper bearing inner race seat and inner race.
6. Remove tilt lever bracket.
7. Reverse procedure to install.

2001–02 AURORA

Refer to **Fig. 22** for exploded view of steering column.

INTERMEDIATE STEERING SHAFT

1. Ensure wheels are straight ahead and steering column is in LOCK position.
2. Turn ignition key must to OFF or LOCK position.
3. Lock steering column by inserting steering column lock pin tool No. J-42640, or equivalent, into steering column access hole.

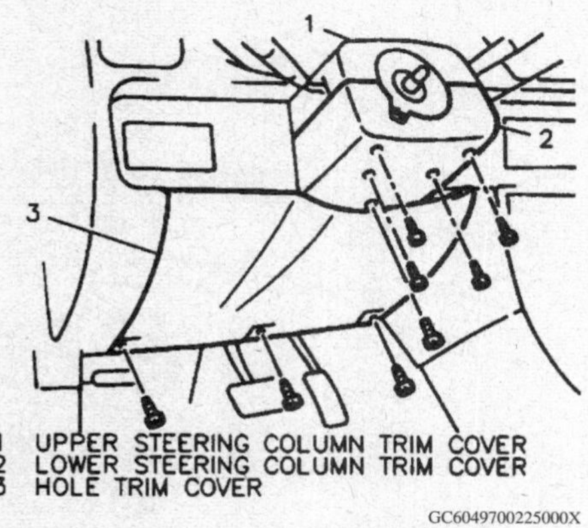

GC6049700225000X

Fig. 15 Steering column cover replacement. Metro

4. Remove steering gear stub shaft pinch bolt.
5. Remove lefthand instrument panel sound insulator.
6. Position shaft dust seal for access, as required.
7. Remove upper intermediate shaft pinch bolt.
8. Disconnect and remove shaft.
9. Reverse procedure to install, noting the following:
   a. Use correct bolts and nuts in proper location.
   b. **Do not use paints, lubricants or corrosion inhibitors on bolts and nuts or joint surfaces unless specified.**
   c. Tighten pinch bolt to specifications.

TURN SIGNAL & MULTI-FUNCTION SWITCH

Refer to the "Electrical" section in the "Aurora & Riviera" chassis chapter.

STEERING WHEEL

Refer to the "Electrical" section in the "Aurora & Riviera" chassis chapter.

STEERING COLUMN COVERS

1. Remove steering column as previously described.
2. Place bottom of modular column holding fixture tool No. J-41352, or equivalent, into suitable vise.
3. Set steering column in bottom of fixture.
4. Place top piece of tool onto column and secure suitable screws.
5. Remove mounting screws and unsnap lower close-out shroud.
6. Remove lower shroud.
7. Remove mounting screw and upper shroud with close-out.
8. Remove close-out shroud, as required.
9. Reverse procedure to install, noting the following:
   a. Use correct bolts and nuts in proper location.
   b. **Do not use paints, lubricants or corrosion inhibitors on bolts and nuts or joint surfaces unless specified.**
   c. Ensure shift lever seal seat correctly in the shrouds.

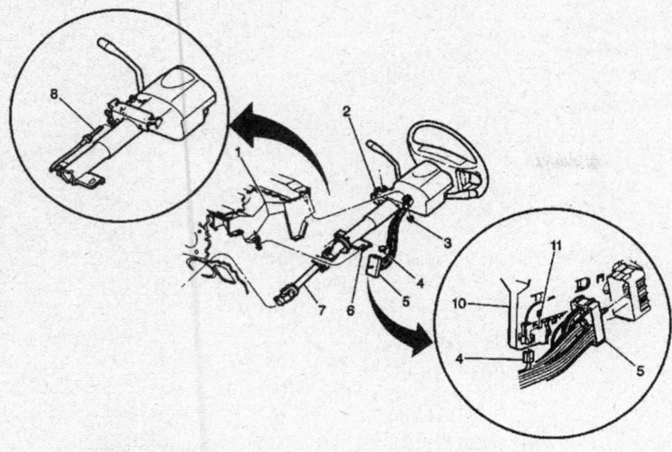

(1) Bracket, Steering Column Support
(2) Support, Steering Column Upper
(3) Nut
(4) Connector, SIR
(5) Connector, Steering Column Wiring Harness
(6) Support, Steering Column Lower
(7) Intermediate Steering Shaft
(8) Shift Lever Cable
(9) Park Lock Cable
(10) Bracket, Multiuse Module
(11) Connector, Position Assurance (CPA)

GC6049700226000X

Fig. 16 Steering column replacement. Park Avenue

d. Tighten mounting screws to specifications.

TILT SPRING

Removal

1. Remove steering column as previously described.
2. Remove upper and lower covers as previously described.
3. Tilt column to up position using tilt lever.
4. Pry tilt spring up until bulge occurs and most of tilt spring tension is removed.
5. Secure tilt spring and continue prying until it disengages from steering column support assembly post and tilt head.
6. Remove spring guide from tilt spring.

Installation

1. Lubricate spring guide with suitable synthetic grease.
2. Install spring guide into tilt spring.
3. Install tilt spring to steering column support assembly post and secure.
4. Install upper and lower covers as previously described.

TURN SIGNAL CANCEL CAM & UPPER BEARING INNER RACE

1. Remove steering column as previously described.
2. Remove upper and lower covers as previously described.
3. Remove wire harness from wire restraint clip, then the straps.
4. Remove black SIR connector from fused jumper assembly connector.
5. Remove retaining ring using suitable snap ring pliers, then the SIR coil
6. Remove wave washer
7. Remove bearing retainer using lock plate compressor tool No. J-23653-SIR, or equivalent. Remove tool.
8. Remove shaft lock shield and turn signal cancel cam.
9. Remove upper bearing spring, inner race seat and inner race.
10. Disconnect pivot and pulse switch connector, as required.
11. Press locking tabs, then pull pivot and pulse switch out of switch mounting bracket.
12. Remove mounting screws and bracket.
13. Reverse procedure to install, noting the following:
    a. Use correct bolts and nuts in proper location.
    b. **Do not use paints, lubricants or corrosion inhibitors on bolts and nuts or joint surfaces unless specified.**
    c. Tighten mounting bolts and screws to specifications.
    d. Lubricate turn signal cancel cam.
    e. Turn signal and multi-function switch electrical contact must rest on turn signal cancel cam.
    f. Center inflatable restraint steering wheel module coil as described under "Inflatable Restraint Steering Wheel Module Coil, Centering."
    g. **Improper routing of wire harness may damage inflatable restraint steering wheel module coil.**

INFLATABLE RESTRAINT STEERING WHEEL MODULE COIL, CENTERING.

New

A new inflatable restraint steering wheel module coil is precentered. **Do not remove the centering tab until the installation is complete.**

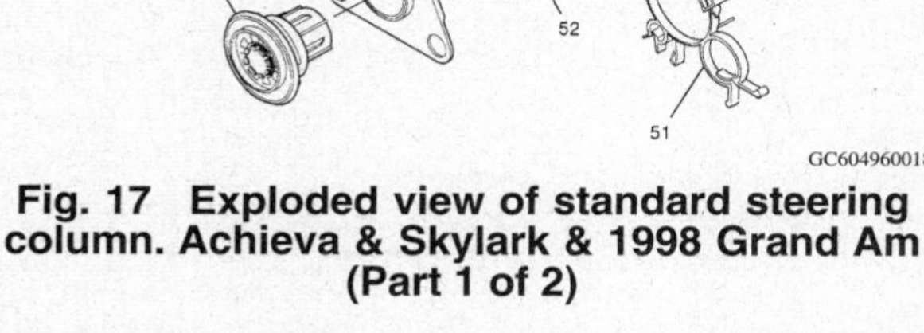

GC604960018400AX

Fig. 17 Exploded view of standard steering column. Achieva & Skylark & 1998 Grand Am (Part 1 of 2)

1. Ensure wheels are straight ahead.
2. Align steering shaft block tooth to 12 O.' clock position.
3. Ensure ignition switch is in LOCK position.
4. Align SIR coil with the horn tower sticking through shaft lock shield.
5. Slide inflatable restraint steering wheel module coil onto steering shaft.
6. Remove and discard new inflatable restraint steering wheel module coil centering tab.

Existing

1. Ensure wheels are straight ahead.
2. Align steering shaft block tooth to 12 O.' clock position.
3. Ensure ignition switch is in LOCK position.
4. If inflatable restraint steering wheel module coil front has centering window and back has spring service lock, proceed as follows:
    a. Hold inflatable restraint steering wheel module coil with face up.
    b. While depressing spring service lock, rotate coil hub clockwise until coil ribbon stops.
    c. Rotate coil hub slowly, counterclockwise, until centering window appears yellow and both arrows line up.
    d. Release spring service lock between locking tab.
    e. Coil is now centered.
    f. Align centered coil with horn tower and slide onto steering column shaft.

1- NUT, HEX LOCKING (M14x1.5)
2- RING, RETAINING
3- COIL ASM, SIR
4- WASHER, WAVE
5- RING, RETAINING
6- LOCK, SHAFT
7- CAM ASM, T/SIG CANCEL
8- SPRING, UPPER BEARING
9- SPACER, UPPER BEARING
10- SCREW, ADAPTER
11- HOUSING ASM, STRG COLUMN
12- ACTUATOR ASM, IGNITION LOCK
13- LOCK CYL SET, STRG COLUMN
14- SPRING, LOCK PRE-LOAD
15- STRAP, GROUND
16- SPRING, LOCK BOLT
17- PLATE, MOUNTING
18- RETAINER, BEARING
19- SWITCH ASM, IGNITION
20- SCREW, TAPPING
21- BOLT ASM, LOCK
22- BRACKET, LOCK BOLT SUPPORT
23- SCREW, TAPPING
25- RING, RETAINING
26- SHAFT ASM, STEERING
43- ELEC PARK LOCK, STRG COL
44- SCREW, TAPPING
45- SCREW, SUPPORT
49- ADAPTER, SUPPORT MOUNTING
51- STRAP, WIRE
52- JACKET ASM, STRG COL
54- BOLT, FLNG HEX HD (M8X1.25)
55- BUSHING ASM, COLUMN JACKET
56- CLIP, WIRE RESTRAINT

GC604960018400BX

Fig. 17 Exploded view of standard steering column. Achieva & Skylark & 1998 Grand Am (Part 2 of 2)

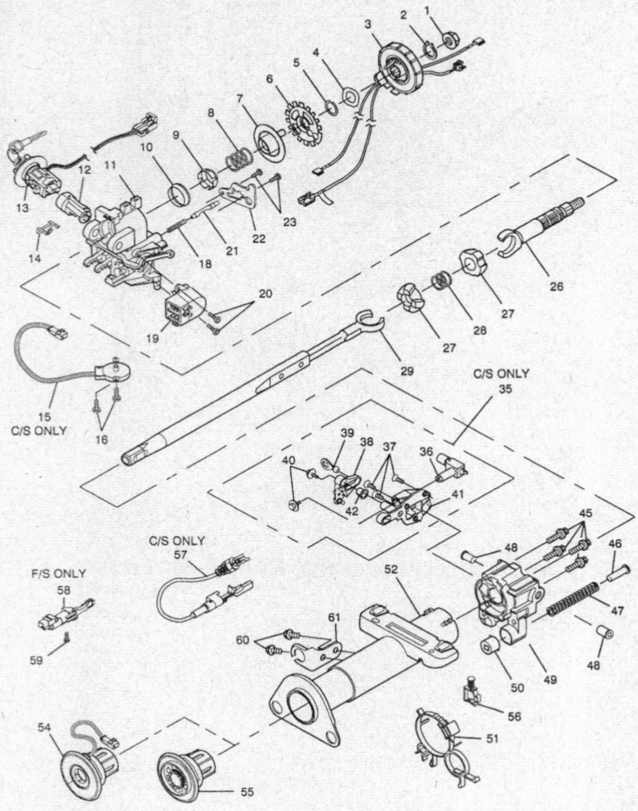

Fig. 18 Exploded view of tilt steering column (Part 1 of 2). Achieva & Skylark & 1998 Grand Am

5. If inflatable restraint steering wheel module coil front has centering window and back has no spring service lock, proceed as follows:
   a. Hold inflatable restraint steering wheel module coil with face up.
   b. Rotate coil hub clockwise until coil ribbon stops.
   c. Rotate coil hub slowly, counterclockwise until centering window appears yellow and both arrows line up.
   d. Coil is now centered.
   e. While holding coil hub in center position, align coil with horn tower and slide onto steering column shaft assembly.
6. If inflatable restraint steering wheel module coil front has no centering window, but back has spring service lock, proceed as follows:
   a. Hold coil with back side up.
   b. While depressing spring service lock, rotate coil hub counterclockwise until coil ribbon stops.
   c. Still pressing spring service lock, rotate coil hub in opposite direction 2½ revolutions.
   d. Release spring service lock between locking tabs.
   e. Coil is now centered.
   f. Align centered coil with horn tower and slide onto steering column shaft.
7. If inflatable restraint steering wheel module coil front has no centering window and back has no spring service lock, proceed as follows:
   a. Hold coil with face up.
   b. Rotate coil hub clockwise until coil ribbon stops.
   c. Rotate coil hub slowly counterclockwise for 2½ revolutions.
   d. Coil is now centered.
   e. While maintaining coil hub in center position, align centered coil with horn tower and slide onto steering column.

STEERING SHAFT, LOWER BEARING & JACKET

1. Remove switch mounting bracket as described under "Turn Signal Cancel Cam & Upper Bearing Inner Race."
2. Remove turn signal and multi-function switch.
3. Remove tilt spring as previously described.
4. Remove steering column support pivot pins using pivot pin remover tool No. J-21854-1, or equivalent.
5. Remove dual triangle sensor.
6. Remove boot seal, steering shaft seal, sensor retainer and steering shaft seal.
7. Remove mounting screws and cable support bracket.
8. Remove tilt head with lower steering shaft attached.
9. Remove tilt head assembly from steering shaft.
10. Mark race and upper shaft, then the lower steering shaft to ensure proper assembly.
11. Tilt upper shaft assembly 90° and disengage.
12. Reverse procedure to install, noting the following:
    a. Apply suitable lithium grease to race and upper shaft.
    b. Lubricate bracket mounting screws with suitable Loctite.
    c. Use correct bolts and nuts in proper location.
    d. **Do not use paints, lubricants or corrosion inhibitors on bolts and nuts or joint surfaces unless specified.**
    e. Tighten mounting bolts and screws to specifications.
    f. **Replace steering column support assembly if it has been staked three times.**
    g. Lubricate pivot pins with suitable synthetic grease.

1- NUT, HEX LOCKING (M14x1.5)
2- RING, RETAINING
3- COIL ASM, SIR
4- WASHER, WAVE
5- RING, RETAINING
6- LOCK, SHAFT
7- CAM ASM, TURN SIG CANCEL
8- SPRING, UPPER BEARING
9- SEAT, UPPER BEARING INNER RACE
10- RACE, INNER
11- HOUSING ASM, BRG &
12- ACTUATOR ASM, IGNITION LOCK
13- LOCK CYL SET, STRG COLUMN
14- SPRING, LOCK PRELOAD
15- SOLENOID ASM, INTERLOCK
16- SCREW, TAPPING
18- SPRING, LOCK BOLT
19- SWITCH ASM, IGNITION
20- SCREW, TAPPING
21-BOLT ASM, LOCK
22-BRACKET, LOCK BOLT SUPPORT
23-SCREW, TAPPING
26-SHAFT ASM, RACE & UPPER
27-SPHERE, CENTERING
28-SPRING, JOINT PRELOAD
29-SHAFT ASM, LOWER
35-SHIFT ASM, LINEAR
36-CLEVIS, SHIFT LEVER
37-SCREW, FLAT HD TAPPING
38-CAM ASM, CABLE SHIFT
39-ACTUATOR ASM, BALL
40-BOLT, HEX FLANGE HEAD
41-BRACKET, GS LEVER ASM SUPPORT
42-BUSHING,CAM
45-SCREW, SUPPORT
46-GUIDE, SPRING
47-SPRING, TILT WHEEL
48-PIN, PIVOT
49-SUPPORT ASM, STRG COL JACKET
50-RETAINER, SPRING
51-STRAP, WIRE
52-JACKET ASM, STRG COL
54-BUSHING ASM, POSITION SENSOR &
55-BUSHING ASM, COLUMN JACKET
56-CLIP, WIRE RESTRAINT
57-CABLE ASM, PARK LOCK
58-ELECTRIC PARK LOCK, STRG COL
59-SCREW, TAPPING
60-BOLT, FLANGED
61-BRACKET, CABLE SUPPORT

GC604960018500BX

Fig. 18 Exploded view of tilt steering column (Part 2 of 2). Achieva & Skylark & 1998 Grand Am

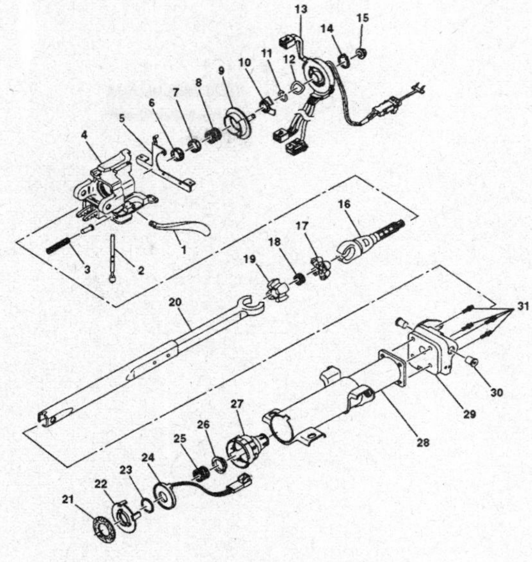

(1) Tilt Lever
(2) Anti-Rotation Pin
(3) Tilt Spring and Guide
(4) Bearing and Housing Assembly
(5) Switch Adapter Plate
(6) Upper Bearing Spring
(7) Upper Bearing Inner Race Seat
(8) Upper Bearing Spring
(9) Turn Signal Cancel Cam Assembly
(10) Cam Orientation Plate
(11) Bearing Retainer
(12) Wave Washer
(13) SIR Coil Assembly
(14) Snap Ring
(15) Flanged Prevailing Torque Nut
(16) Race and Upper Shaft Assembly
(17) Centering Sphere
(18) Joint Preload Spring
(19) Centering Sphere
(20) Lower Shaft Assembly

GC6049900252000X

Fig. 19 Exploded view of tilt steering column. Alero & 1999–2002 Grand Am

CAMARO, CORVETTE, FIREBIRD, LSS, REGENCY & 88 & 1998–99 BONNEVILLE & LESABRE

Refer to **Figs. 23 through 28** for exploded view of steering columns.

COIL, SHAFT LOCK, TURN SIGNAL CANCELING CAM, UPPER BEARING SPRING & SEAT, INNER RACE, TURN SIGNAL SWITCH, BUZZER SWITCH & LOCK CYLINDER SET

1. Remove inflator module as outlined in "Passive Restraints Systems" chapter and coil retaining ring.
2. Remove coil and let hang freely. Remove wave washer.
3. Remove shaft lock retaining ring lock plate using compressor tool No. J-23653-SIR, or equivalent, and shaft lock.
4. Remove turn signal cancel cam and upper bearing spring.
5. Remove upper bearing race seat and inner race.
6. Remove turn signal switch as outlined in "Electrical" section of appropriate chassis chapter.
7. **On Bonneville, LeSabre, LSS, Regency and 88 models,** disconnect RSWC connector from turn signal harness.
8. **On all models,** remove wire protector and wire harness strap.
9. Attach suitable length of mechanics wire to both coil terminal connectors to aid in assembly and gently pull wire through column.
10. Remove key from pass key lock cylinder set, then the buzzer switch.
11. Insert key in pass key lock cylinder and remove lock mounting screw.
12. Disconnect pass key lock cylinder terminal connector from bulkhead connector and remove wire protector.
13. Attach suitable length of mechanics wire to aid in assembly.
14. Remove retaining clip from housing cover and gently pull wire harness through column.
15. Reverse procedure to install. Tighten mounting screws to specifications.

LOCK HOUSING COVER, COVER END CAP, PIVOT & SWITCH, DIMMER SWITCH ROD ACTUATOR & TILT SPRING

1. Disassemble coil, shaft lock, turn signal cancel cam, upper bearing spring and seat, inner race turn signal switch, buzzer switch and lock cylinder set as previously described.
2. Remove lock cover housing end cap.
3. Remove mounting screws, lock housing cover and tilt lever.
4. Remove base plate and dimmer switch rod actuator, then gently pull pivot switch wiring harness through column housing and gear shift lever bowl.
5. **On models equipped with cruise control,** unplug connector from base plate and remove multi-function lever.
6. **On all models,** remove pin, pivot and switch.
7. Remove retainer, spring and guide.
8. Reverse procedure to install, noting the following:
   a. Coat spring guide and spring with lithium grease.
   b. Tighten lock housing cover screw in 12 o'clock position first, screw in 8 o'clock position second and screw in 3 o'clock position third
   c. Tighten mounting screws to specifications in previous step's order.

COLUMN HOUSING, LOCK SHOES, ACTUATOR SECTOR, SWITCH ACTUATOR RACK, BEARINGS & LOCK BOLT

1. Disassemble coil, shaft lock, turn signal cancel cam, upper bearing spring and seat, inner race turn signal switch,

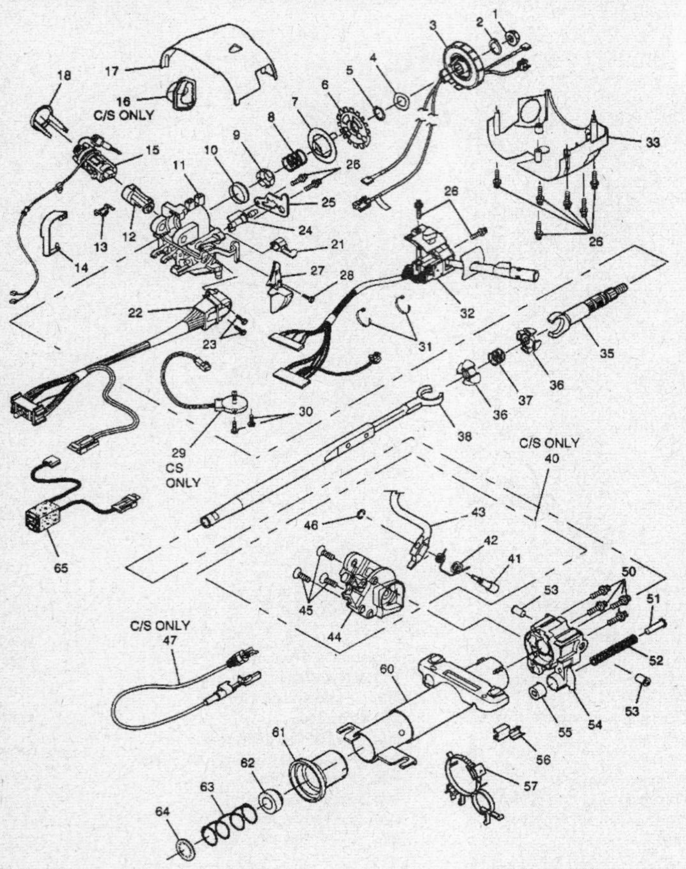

Fig. 20 Exploded view of steering column w/ column shift (Part 1 of 2). Aurora & Riviera

1-NUT, HEXAGON LOCKING (M14x1.5)
2-RING, RETAINING
3-COIL ASM, SIR
4-WASHER, WAVE
5-RING, RETAINING
6-LOCK, SHAFT
7-CAM ASM, T/SIG CANCEL
8-SPRING, UPPER BEARING
9-SEAT, UPPER BEARING INNER RACE
10-RACE, INNER
11-HOUSING ASM, BRG &
12-ACTUATOR ASM, IGNITION LOCK
13-SPRING, LOCK PRE-LOAD
14-PROTECTOR, WIRING
15-LOCK CYL SET, STRG COLUMN
16-SEAL ASM, SHIFT LEVER
17-COVER, UPPER
18-KNOB, CLOSE OUT
21-BRACKET, TILT LEVER
22-SWITCH ASM, IGN & KEY ALARM
23-SCREW, TAPPING
24-BOLT ASM, LOCK
25-BRACKET, LOCK BOLT SUPPORT
26-SCREW, TAPPING
27-KNOB, TILT LEVER
28-SCREW, PAN HEAD
29-SOLENOID ASM, INTERLOCK
30-SCREW, TAPPING
31-STRAP, WIRE HARNESS
32-SWITCH ASM, T/S & MULTIFUNC
33-COVER, LOWER
35-SHAFT ASM, UPPER
36-SPHERE, CENTERING
37-SPRING, JOINT PRELOAD
38-SHAFT ASM, LOWER STRG
40-SHIFT ASM, LINEAR
41-PIN, SHIFT LEVER
42-SPRING, SHIFT LEVER
43-LEVER ASM, LINEAR SHIFT
44-ADAPTER, LINEAR SHIFT BASE (NC)
45-SCREW, FLT HD TAPPING
46-CLIP, SHIFT LEVER
47-CABLE ASM, PARK LOCK
50-SCREW, SUPPORT
51-GUIDE, SPRING
52-SPRING, TILT WHEEL
53-PIN, PIVOT
54-SUPPORT ASM, STRG COL JACKET
55-RETAINER, SPRING
56-CLIP, WIRE RESTRAINT
57-STRAP, WIRE HARNESS
60-JACKET ASM, STRG COL
61-BEARING ASM, ADAPTER &
62-SEAT, LOWER BEARING
63-SPRING, LOWER BEARING
64-RETAINER, LOWER SPRING
65-HARNESS ASM, JUMPER

GC604970022900BX

Fig. 20 Exploded view of steering column w/ column shift (Part 2 of 2). Riviera & 1998–99 Aurora

buzzer switch and lock cylinder set as previously described.

2. Disassemble lock housing cover, cover end cap, pivot and switch, dimmer switch rod actuator and tilt spring as previously described.
3. Remove mounting screws, lock housing cover and tilt lever.
4. Remove cover housing end cap, base plate and dimmer switch rod actuator, then gently pull pivot switch wire harness through column housing and gear shift lever bowl.
5. **On models equipped with cruise control,** unplug connector from base plate and remove multi-function lever.
6. **On all models,** remove retainer, spring and guide.
7. Remove pivot pins using pivot pin removal tool No. J-21854-01, or equivalent, **Fig. 29,** then install tilt lever.
8. Remove column housing by pulling back on tilt lever and pulling housing down and away from column.
9. Remove bearing and mounting screw.
10. Remove lock bolt spring and lock bolt, then the switch actuator rack and rack preload spring.
11. Remove driveshaft and switch actuator sector.
12. Remove release lever pin and shoe release lever.
13. Remove release lever spring and dowel pin.
14. Remove steering wheel lock shoes and lock shoe springs.
15. Reverse procedure to install.

SHAFT, COLUMN HOUSING SUPPORT, SHIFT TUBE, IGNITION SWITCH, DIMMER SWITCH & LOWER BEARING

1. Remove inflator module as outlined in "Passive Restraints Systems" chapter.
2. Remove mounting screw, nut and ground wire with ring terminal from stud, **Fig. 30.**
3. Remove dimmer switch from dimmer switch rod and wiring harness strap.
4. Disconnect positive assurance terminal connector from bulkhead connector and dimmer switch wires from bulkhead connector positions 4B, 5B and 5C.
5. Reverse procedure to install, noting the following:
   a. Connect dimmer switch wires; Tan — 4B; Green — 5B; Yellow — 5 C.
   b. Tighten mounting screws to specifications.

2000–02 BONNEVILLE & LESABRE

Refer to **Fig. 31** for exploded view this steering column.

SIR COIL

1. Remove steering column as previously described.
2. Remove inflator module as outlined in "Passive Restraints Systems" chapter.
3. Remove steering wheel as outlined in "Electrical" section of appropriate chassis chapter.
4. Remove upper and lower steering column shrouds.
5. Remove wire harness straps and wire harness from wire restraint clip.
6. Remove black SIR connector from fused jumper connector.
7. Remove retaining ring using suitable snap ring pliers, then the SIR coil.
8. Remove wave washer.
9. Reverse procedure to assemble.

LINEAR SHIFT

1. Remove steering column as previously described.
2. Remove inflator module as outlined in "Passive Restraints Systems" chapter.
3. Remove steering wheel as outlined in "Electrical" section of appropriate chassis chapter.
4. Remove upper and lower steering column shrouds.
5. Remove wire harness straps and wire harness from wire restraint clip.
6. Disconnect shift lever electrical connector, slide shift lever seal up shift lever and remove lever mounting screw.
7. Remove shift lever and electric BTSI actuator from steering column.
8. Lock cylinder should be in Off-Lock position.

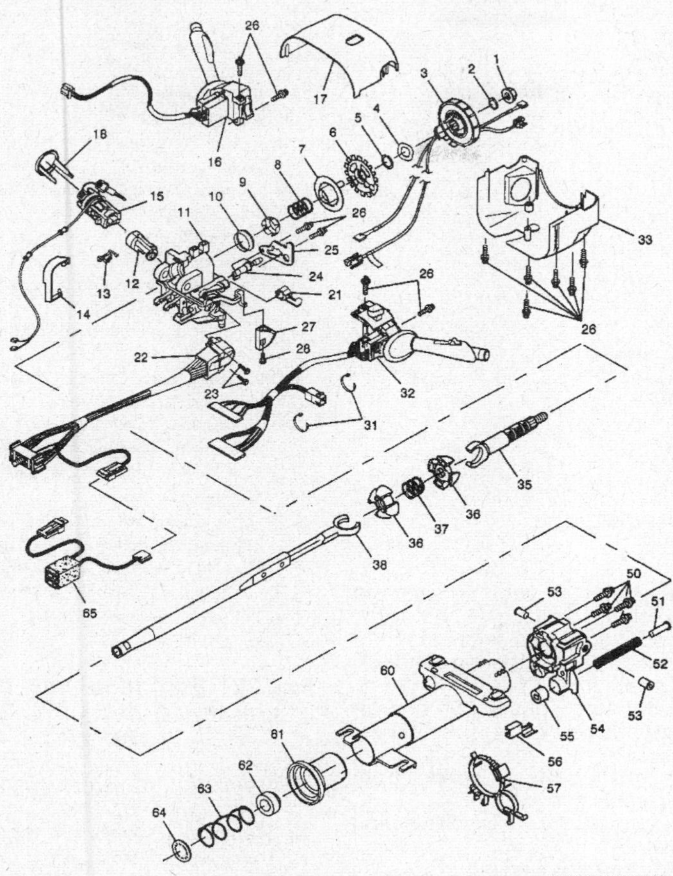

Fig. 21 Exploded view of steering column w/floor shift (Part 1 of 2). Riviera & 1998–99 Aurora

1- NUT, HEXAGON LOCKING (M14x1.5)
2- RING, RETAINING
3- COIL ASM, SIR
4- WASHER, WAVE
5- RING, RETAINING
6- LOCK, SHAFT
7- CAM ASM, T/SIG CANCEL
8- SPRING, UPPER BEARING
9- SEAT, UPPER BEARING INNER RACE
10- RACE, INNER
11- HOUSING ASM, BRG &
12- ACTUATOR ASM, IGNITION LOCK
13- SPRING, LOCK PRE-LOAD
14- PROTECTOR, WIRING
15- LOCK CYL SET, STRG COLUMN
16- SWITCH ASM, PIVOT & (PULSE)
17- COVER, UPPER
18- KNOB, CLOSE OUT
21- BRACKET, TILT LEVER
22- SWITCH ASM, IGN & KEY ALARM
23- SCREW, TAPPING
24- BOLT ASM, LOCK
25- BRACKET, LOCK BOLT SUPPORT
26- SCREW, TAPPING
27- KNOB, TILT LEVER
28- SCREW, PAN HEAD
31- STRAP, WIRE
32- SWITCH ASM, T/S & MULTIFUNC
33- COVER, LOWER
35- SHAFT ASM, UPPER
36- SPHERE, CENTERING
37- SPRING, JOINT PRELOAD
38- SHAFT ASM, LOWER STRG
50- SCREW, SUPPORT
51- GUIDE, SPRING
52- SPRING, WHEEL TILT
53- PIN, PIVOT
54- SUPPORT ASM, STRG COL JACKET
55- RETAINER, SPRING
56- CLIP, WIRE RESTRAINT
57- STRAP, WIRE HARNESS
60- JACKET ASM, STRG COL
61- BEARING ASM, ADAPTER &
62- SEAT, LOWER BEARING
63- SPRING, LOWER BEARING
64- RETAINER, LOWER SPRING
65- HARNESS ASM, JUMPER

GC604970023000BX

Fig. 21 Exploded view of steering column w/floor shift (Part 2 of 2). Riviera & 1998–99 Aurora

9. Remove mounting screws and linear shift from steering column.
10. Reverse procedure to assemble. Tighten to specification.

TILT SPRING

The tilt spring and guide are under pressure and could become projectiles. During disassembly and assembly procedures, secure the tilt spring.

1. Remove upper and lower steering column shrouds.
2. Tilt steering column Up position.
3. Pry tilt spring until bulge occurs and most of tilt spring tension is removed.
4. Secure tilt spring and continue to pry until tilt spring disengages from post on steering wheel column and column tilt head.
5. Remove tilt spring guide from tilt spring.
6. Reverse procedure to assemble.

LOCK MODULE

1. Remove coded key controller, ignition and key alarm switch.
2. Remove upper tilt head components as previously described.
3. Lock cylinder should be in Off-Lock position.
4. Insert suitable small screwdriver into slot on lock module, push against locking tab to remove.
5. Disconnect park lock cable.
6. Remove mounting screws and lock module.
7. Reverse procedure to assemble. Adjust park lock cable as follows:
   a. Put column in park position with gear shift lever.
   b. Put ignition switch in Off-Lock position. Remove key.
   c. Unlock adjuster ring on park lock cable with park lock cable pliers tool No. J-41396, or equivalent.
   d. Pull on cable until park lock latch contacts gear shift lever. Release cable.
   e. Lock adjuster ring securely in place on park lock cable with cable pliers.

STEERING COLUMN TILT HEAD HOUSING

1. Remove SIR as previously described.
2. Remove bearing retainer using bearing remover tool No. J-23653-SIR, or equivalent.
3. Remove shaft lock shield and turn signal cancel cam.
4. Remove upper bearing spring and inner race seat.
5. Remove inner race.
6. Reverse procedure to assemble.

STEERING SHAFT, LOWER BEARING & JACKET

1. Remove upper tilt head components as previously described.
2. Disconnect electrical connector from pivot and pulse switch, as required.
3. Press on locking tabs of pivot and pulse switch, then pull out pivot and pulse switch from mounting bracket.
4. Remove screws and mounting bracket.
5. Remove turn signal and multi-function switch.
6. Remove tilt spring, linear shift, shift lever and BTSI actuator.
7. Remove steering column support pivot pins using pivot pin remover tool No. J-21854-1, or equivalent.
8. Remove dual triangle sensor, if equipped.
9. Remove boot and steering shaft seals.
10. Remove sensor retainer and steering shaft seal.
11. Remove mounting screws and cable support bracket.
12. Remove tilt head with lower steering shaft still attached from steering column support.
13. Remove tilt head from steering shaft.

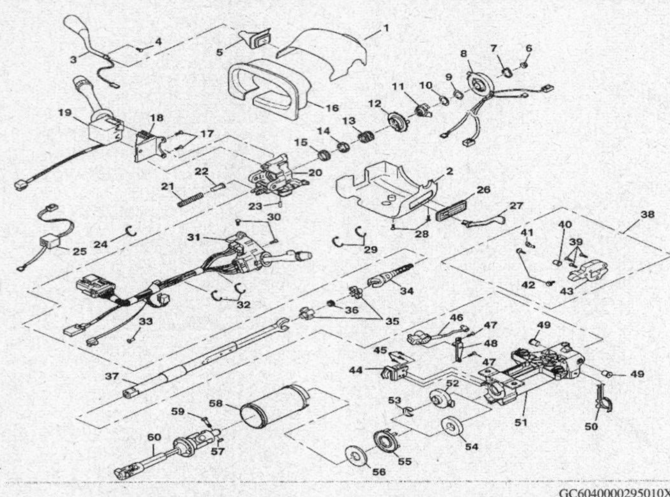

Fig. 22 Exploded view of steering column (Part 1 of 3). 2001–02 Aurora

14. Mark race and upper shaft and lower steering shaft to ensure proper assembly.
15. Reverse procedure to assemble.

CATERA

Refer to **Fig. 32** for exploded view this steering column.

STEERING COLUMN HOUSING

1. Remove mounting screws and signal switch housing.
2. Remove heads from lock housing shear bolts using suitable ¼ inch drill bit.
3. Remove steering column housing lock housing and shear bolts using suitable locking type pliers.
4. Remove retaining ring using lock plate compressor tool No. J-23653-SIR, with compressor plate adapter tool No. J-23653-91, or equivalents.
5. Remove spring retainer, upper bearing spring, inner race seat and inner race.
6. Insert No. 2 Phillips head screwdriver into square opening in tilt spring retainer, **Fig. 33,** then depress tilt spring retainer and turn screwdriver to unlock tilt spring retainer.
7. Remove tilt spring retainer and tilt spring by pushing spring out towards front of column.
8. Remove pivot pins using pivot pin remover tool No. J-21854-01, or equivalent, and pull tilt lever forward to release tilt shoes from column support.
9. Remove steering column.
10. Reverse procedure to install. Install new retaining ring.

LOWER STEERING SHAFT, LOWER BEARING & COLUMN JACKET

1. Remove steering column housing as previously described.
2. Remove steering shaft from steering column housing support and jacket . **Make alignment marks on upper and lower steering shaft prior to disassembly.**
3. Remove bearing, support screws and steering column housing.
4. Disconnect upper and lower steering shaft by tilting upper steering shaft 90° from lower steering shaft.
5. Rotate centering sphere 90° and lift centering sphere away from upper steering shaft.
6. Remove shaft preload spring from centering sphere.
7. Reverse procedure to install, noting the following:
   a. Install new centering sphere.
   b. Preload spring using centering sphere installer tool No. J-41688, or equivalent, and suitable vise.
   c. Tighten mounting screws to specifications.

CAVALIER & SUNFIRE

Refer to **Figs. 34 and 35** for exploded views of these steering columns.

SHAFT LOCK, TURN SIGNAL CANCEL CAM, UPPER BEARING SPRING, UPPER BEARING INNER RACE SEAT, INNER RACE, THRUST WASHER, BUZZER SWITCH & COLUMN LOCK CYLINDER SET

Standard Column

1. Remove inflator module as outlined in "Passive Restraints Systems" chapter.
2. Remove steering wheel as outlined in "Electrical" section of "Cavalier & Sunfire" chassis chapter.
3. Remove shaft lock cover and shaft lock retaining ring using plate compressor tool No. J-23653-SIR, or equivalent, to depress shaft lock.
4. Remove shaft lock, turn signal canceling cam, upper bearing spring and thrust washer.
5. Move turn signal to righthand turn position.
6. Remove multi-function lever and hazard knob.
7. Remove screw and signal switch arm, then the turn signal switch screws.

(1) Upper Trim Cover
(2) Lower Trim Cover
(3) Shift Lever Assembly
(4) Shift Lever Screw
(5) Shift Lever Seal
(6) Flanged Prevailing Torque Nut
(7) Retaining Ring
(8) Inflatable Restraint Steering Wheel Module Coil
(9) Wave Washer
(10) Bearing Retainer
(11) Cam Orientation Plate
(12) Turn Signal Cancel Cam Assembly
(13) Upper Bearing Spring
(14) Upper Bearing Inner Race Seat
(15) Inner Race
(16) Steering Column Closeout Trim Cover
(17) Pan Head Tapping Screw
(18) Turn Signal Switch Housing
(19) Windshield Wiper and Washer Switch Assembly
(20) Steering Column Tilt Head Assembly
(21) Tilt Spring
(22) Spring Guide
(23) Release Lever Pin
(24) Wire Harness Strap
(25) Fused Jumper Assembly
(26) Tilt Lever Closeout
(27) Tilt Knob

GC6040000295020X

Fig. 22 Exploded view of steering column (Part 2 of 3). 2001–02 Aurora

8. Remove turn signal switch and allow switch to hang freely.
9. Remove key from lock cylinder set, then the buzzer switch.
10. Install key in lock cylinder and turn to Lock position.
11. Remove mounting screw and lock cylinder set.
12. Reverse procedure to install. Tighten mounting screws to specifications.

Tilt Column

1. Remove inflator module as outlined in "Passive Restraints Systems" chapter.
2. Remove steering wheel as outlined in "Electrical" section of "Cavalier & Sunfire" chassis chapter.
3. Remove shaft lock cover and retaining ring using plate compressor J-23653-C, or equivalent, to depress shaft lock.
4. Remove shaft lock, turn signal canceling cam, upper bearing spring, upper bearing inner race seat and inner race.
5. Move turn signal to righthand turn position.
6. Remove multi-function lever and hazard knob.
7. Remove screw and signal switch arm, then the turn signal switch screws.
8. Remove turn signal switch and allow switch to hang freely.
9. Remove key from lock cylinder set, then the buzzer switch.
10. Install key in lock cylinder and turn to Lock position.
11. Remove mounting screw and lock cylinder.
12. Reverse procedure to install. Tighten mounting screws to specifications.

(28) Pan Head Tapping Screws
(29) Wire Harness Straps
(30) Pan Head Tapping Screws
(31) Turn Signal and Multifunction Switch Assembly
(32) Wire Harness Straps
(33) Axial Position Assurance Connector
(34) Race and Upper Shaft Assembly
(35) Centering Sphere
(36) Joint Preload Spring
(37) Lower Shaft Assembly
(38) Linear Shift Assembly
(39) Flat Head 6-Lobed Soc Tap Screw
(40) Cam Bushing
(41) Ball and Actuator Assembly
(42) Hexagon Flange Head Bolt
(43) Gearshift Lever Assembly Support Bracket
(44) Cable Support Bracket
(45) Flat Head Screw
(46) Automatic Transmission Shift Lock Control
(47) Pan Head Tapping Screw
(47) Pan Head Tapping Screw
(48) Automatic Transmission Shift Lock Control Mounting Bracket Assembly
(49) Pivot Pin
(49) Pivot Pin
(50) Wire Restraint Clip
(51) Steering Column Support Assembly
(52) Dual Triangle Sensor Assembly
(53) Sensor Locator
(54) Boot Seal
(55) Sensor Retainer
(56) Steering Shaft Seal
(57) Bolt Retainer
(58) Boot
(59) Bolt and Retainer Assembly
(60) Intermediate Steering Shaft Assembly

GC6040000295030X

Fig. 22 Exploded view of steering column (Part 3 of 3). 2001–02 Aurora

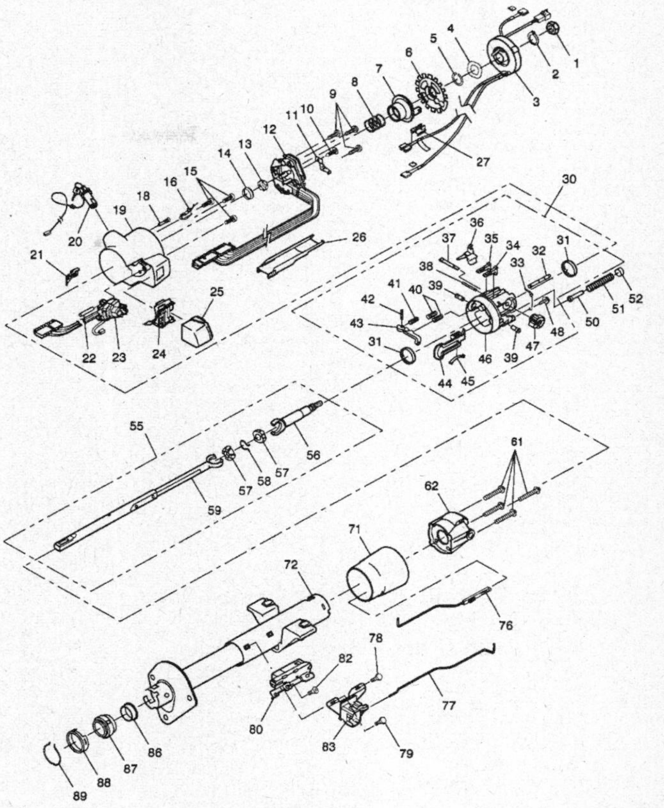

GC604910009700AA

Fig. 23 Exploded view of steering column (Part 1 of 2). Camaro & Firebird

STEERING SHAFT, STEERING WHEEL LOCK SHOE, TURN SIGNAL SWITCH, COLUMN HOUSING, COLUMN HOUSING SUPPORT, SWITCH ACTUATOR PIVOT, SWITCH ACTUATOR RACK, SPRING & BOLT, LOCK BOLT, BEARING, SWITCH ACTUATOR SECTOR & IGNITION SWITCH ACTUATOR

Standard Column

1. Remove inflator module as outlined in "Passive Restraints Systems" chapter
2. Remove steering wheel as outlined in "Electrical" section of "Cavalier & Sunfire" chassis chapter.
3. Remove steering column as previously described.
4. Inspect steering column for damage.
5. Remove steering shaft and retaining ring from shaft.
6. Inspect column shaft for damage.
7. Remove mounting bolts and steering column support bracket.
8. Remove wiring protector, turn signal switch, mounting screw and nut.
9. Remove dimmer switch, dimmer switch rod and switch mounting stud.
10. Remove ignition switch, mounting screws and inhibitor housing.
11. Remove cover screws and lock housing cover with floor shift lever bowl and shift bowl shroud. Pull housing cover from jacket and remove upper bearing retainer.
12. Remove mounting screws, floor shift lever bowl with shift bowl shroud and shroud from bowl.
13. If required, disassemble steering column housing as follows:
    a. Remove switch actuator rack with spring and bolt.
    b. Remove spring and bolt from switch actuator rack.
    c. Remove switch actuator rod from rack.
    d. Remove spring thrust washer from spring and bolt.
    e. Remove switch actuator sector, rack preload spring, switch actuator pivot pin and switch actuator pivot.
    f. Remove bearing retaining bushing using suitable punch.
    g. Remove bearing using suitable punch.
14. Reverse procedure to install, noting the following:
    a. Assemble spring and bolt with switch actuator rack to housing. **First tooth of rack must interact with first and second tooth of sector. With rack fully inserted, block tooth of sector will rest in block tooth of rack.**
    b. Tighten mounting screws to specifications.

Tilt Column

1. Remove inflator module as outlined in "Passive Restraints Systems" chapter.
2. Remove steering wheel as outlined in "Electrical" section of "Cavalier & Sunfire" chassis chapter.
3. Remove steering column as previously described.
4. Inspect steering column for damage.
5. Disassemble lock housing cover, column housing cover end cap, pivot and pulse switch, dimmer switch rod actuator and tilt spring as previously described.
6. Remove turn signal switch with lock housing cover from steering column.
7. Remove mounting bolts and support bracket from steering column.
8. Remove wiring protectors and gently pull wire harness through column.
9. Remove pivot pins using pivot pin removal tool No. J-21854-01, or equivalent, and install tilt lever.
10. Remove steering column housing and pull back on tilt lever, then pull steering column housing down and away from column.
11. If required, disassemble steering column housing as follows:
    a. Remove bearing , mounting screw,

1- NUT, HEX LOCKING (M14x1.5)
2- RING, RETAINING
3- COIL ASM, INFL RESTRAINT
4- WASHER, WAVE
5- RING, RETAINING
6- LOCK, SHAFT
7- CAM ASM, TURN SIG CANCEL
8- SPRING, UPPER BEARING
9- SCREW, BNDG HD CR RECESS
10- SCREW, RD WASH HD (M4.2x1.41)
11- ARM ASM, SIGNAL SWITCH
12- SWITCH ASM, TURN SIGNAL
13- SEAT, UPPER BRG INNER RACE
14- RACE, INNER
15- SCREW, PAN HD SOC TAP
16- SWITCH ASM, BUZZER
18- SCREW, LOCK RETAINING
19- COVER ASM, LOCK HOUSING
20- LOCK CYLINDER SET, STRG COL PASS KEY
21- ACTUATOR, DIMMER SW ROD
22- PIN, SWITCH ACTUATOR PIVOT
23- SWITCH ASM, PIVOT & (PULSE)
24- BASE PLATE, COL HSG CVR END
25- CAP, COL HSG COVER END
26- PROTECTOR, WIRING
27- SHROUD, CONNECTOR
30- HOUSING ASM, STRG COLUMN
31- BEARING ASM
32- BOLT, LOCK
33- SPRING, LOCK BOLT
34- SHOE, STEERING WHEEL LOCK
35- SHOE, STEERING WHEEL LOCK
36- SHIELD, WIRE PROTECTOR
37- SHAFT, DRIVE
38- PIN, DOWEL
39- PIN, PIVOT
40- SPRING, SHOE
41- SPRING, RELEASE LEVER
42- PIN, RELEASE LEVER
43- LEVER, SHOE RELEASE
44- RACK, SWITCH ACTUATOR
45- SPRING, RACK PRELOAD
46- HOUSING, STRG COLUMN
47- SECTOR, SWITCH ACTUATOR
48- SCREW, HEX WASHER HEAD
50- GUIDE, SPRING
51- SPRING, WHEEL TILT
52- RETAINER, SPRING
55- SHAFT ASM, STEERING COLUMN
56- SHAFT ASM, RACE & UPPER
57- SPHERE, CENTERING
58- SPRING, JOINT PRELOAD
59- SHAFT ASM, LOWER STEERING
61- SCREW, SUPPORT
62- SUPPORT ASM, STRG COL HSG
71- SHROUD, STRG COLUMN HOUSING
72- JACKET ASM, STRG COL
76- ACTUATOR ASM, IGNITION SWITCH
77- ROD, DIMMER SWITCH
78- SCREW, WASH HD (#10-24X.25)
79- SCREW, HEX WASH HD TAP
80- SWITCH ASM, IGNITION
82- SCREW, FLT HD (#10-24X.31)
83- SWITCH ASM, DIMMER
86- ADAPTER, LOWER BEARING
87- BEARING ASM
88- RETAINER, BEARING ADAPTER
89- CLIP, LOWER BEARING ADAPTER

Service Kits

201- RACK SERV KIT, COL SECTOR & -INCLUDES: 14,31,33,44,47,48
202- SPRING SERV KIT, TILT COLUMN -INCLUDES: 13,14,39,50,51,52
203- COIL SERV KIT, INFL RESTRAINT -INCLUDES: 3,4,27
204- SPHERE SERV KIT, TILT COLUMN -INCLUDES: 57,58
205- GREASE SERV KIT, (SYNTHETIC)

GC604910009700BA

Fig. 23 Exploded view of steering column (Part 2 of 2). Camaro & Firebird (Part 2 of 2)

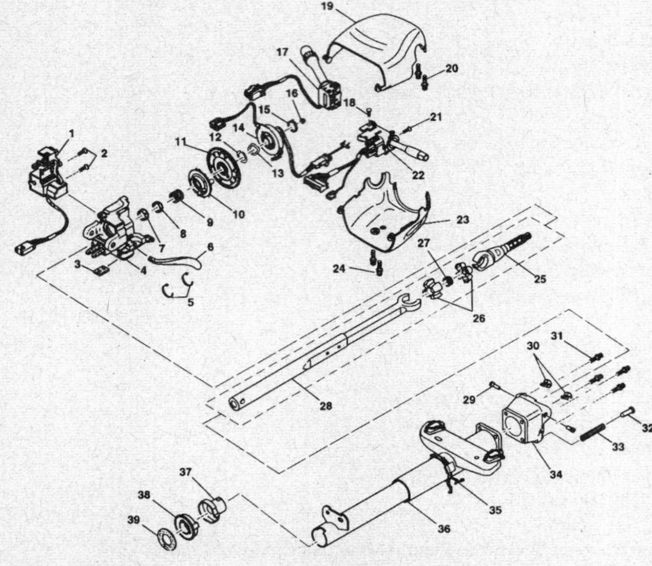

(1) Electric Column Lock
(2) Pan Head Tapping Screws
(3) Wire Harness Spacer
(4) Steering Column Tilt Head Assembly
(5) Wire Harness Straps
(6) Tilt Lever
(7) Inner Race
(8) Upper Bearing Inner Race Seat
(9) Upper Bearing Spring
(10) Turn Signal Cancel Cam Assembly
(11) Shaft Lock Shield Assembly
(12) Bearing Retainer
(13) Wave Washer
(14) SIR Coil Assembly
(15) Retaining Ring
(16) Flanged Prevailing Torque Nut
(17) Pivot and Pulse Switch Assembly
(18) Pan Head Tapping Screws
(19) Upper Shroud
(20) TORX® Head Screw
(21) Pan Head Tapping Screws
(22) Turn Signal and Multifunction Switch Assembly
(23) Lower Shroud
(24) Torx Head Screw
(25) Race and Upper Shaft Assembly

GC6049900278010X

Fig. 24 Exploded view of steering column (Part 1 of 2). Corvette non telescoping less sensor

lock bolt spring, lock bolt, switch actuator rack and rack preload spring.

b. Remove driveshaft and switch actuator sector.
c. Remove release lever pin using lock shoe and release lever pin remover/installer tool No. J-22635, or equivalent.
d. Remove shoe release lever, release lever spring and dowel pin using lock shoe and release lever pin remover/installer tool.
e. Remove lock shoes and shoe springs.

12. If required, assemble steering column housing as follows:
    a. Install shoe springs and lock shoes.
    b. Install dowel pin using lock shoe and release lever pin remover/installer.
    c. Install release lever spring and shoe release lever.
    d. Install release lever pin using lock shoe and release lever pin remover/installer tool.
    e. Install switch actuator sector, driveshaft and rack preload spring.
    f. Install switch actuator rack to actuator sector.
    g. Assemble bearing lubricated with lithium grease to column housing using steering column housing bearing installer tool No. J-38639 and driver handle tool No. J-8092, or equivalents.
    h. Install lock bolt, lock bolt spring and mounting screw. Tighten mounting screw to specifications.
13. Remove steering column jacket bushing and shaft.
14. Inspect steering column shaft for damage.
15. Mark upper and lower steering shaft to ensure proper assembly.
16. If required, disassemble steering column shaft as follows:
    a. Disassemble upper shaft from lower steering shaft. Tilt 90° to each other and disengage.
    b. Disassemble centering sphere from upper shaft. Rotate sphere 90° and slip out.
    c. Remove joint preload spring from centering sphere.
17. If required, assemble steering column shaft as follows:
    a. Install joint preload spring to centering sphere.
    b. Lubricate centering sphere with lithium grease.
    c. Slip into upper shaft and rotate sphere 90°.
    d. Install upper shaft to lower steering shaft.
    e. Align marks and tilt assemblies 90° to each other.
18. Remove mounting screws and column housing support with dimmer switch rod from steering column jacket. Remove rod from support.
19. Remove lock plate from steering column jacket and housing shroud.
20. Remove mounting nut, screw and dimmer switch from rod.
21. Remove mounting stud and ignition switch with switch actuator.
22. Remove switch actuator.
23. Remove mounting screws and ignition switch inhibitor housing.
24. Remove ignition switch inhibitor from ignition switch.
25. Reverse procedure to install, Tighten mounting screws to specifications.

LOCK HOUSING COVER, COLUMN HOUSING COVER END CAP, PIVOT & PULSE SWITCH, DIMMER SWITCH ROD ACTUATOR & TILT SPRING

Tilt Column

1. Remove inflator module as outlined in "Passive Restraints Systems" chapter
2. Remove steering wheel as outlined in "Electrical" section of "Cavalier & Sunfire" chassis chapter.
3. Remove tilt lever, cover screws and lock housing cover. Let cover hang freely.
4. Remove column housing cover end cap with dimmer switch rod actuator and actuator from end cap.
5. Remove pivot, pivot and pulse switch actuator.
6. Remove spring retainer using suitable cross recess head screwdriver to push retainer down and turn clockwise to release.
7. Remove spring and spring guide.
8. Reverse procedure to install, noting the following:
    a. Install lock housing cover and mounting screws.
    b. Tighten screw in 12 o'clock position

(26) Centering Sphere
(27) Joint Preload Spring
(28) Lower Steering Shaft Assembly
(29) Pivot Pin
(30) Tilt Bumper
(31) TORX® Head Screw
(32) Spring Guide
(33) Tilt Spring
(34) Steering Column Support Assembly
(35) Wire Harness Strap
(36) Steering Column Jacket Assembly
(37) Adapter and Bearing Assembly
(38) Sensor Retainer
(39) Steering Shaft Seal

GC6049900278020X

Fig. 24 Exploded view of steering column (Part 2 of 2). Corvette non telescoping less sensor

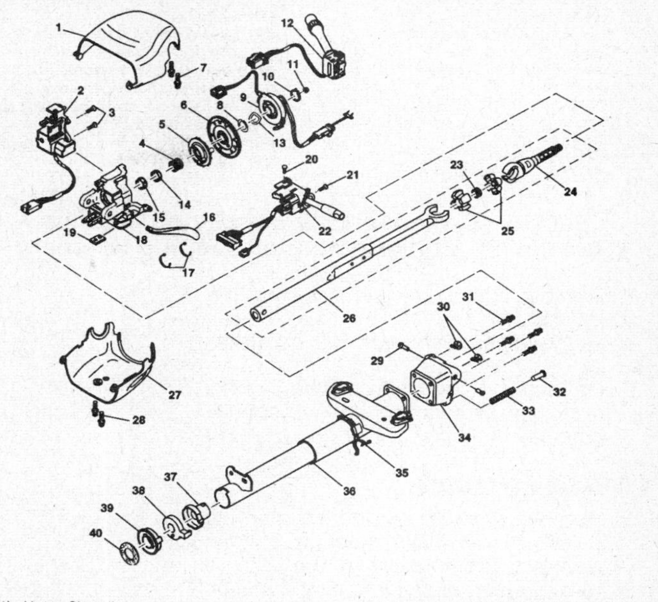

(1) Upper Shroud
(2) Electric Column Lock
(3) Pan Head Tapping Screw
(4) Upper Bearing Spring
(5) Turn Signal Cancel Cam Assembly
(6) Shaft Lock Shield Assembly
(7) Torx Head Screw
(8) Bearing Retainer
(9) SIR Coil Assembly
(10) Retaining Ring
(11) Flanged Prevailing Torque Nut
(12) Pivot and Pulse Switch Assembly
(13) Wave Washer
(14) Upper Bearing Inner Race Seat
(15) Inner Race
(16) Tilt Lever
(17) Wire Harness Straps
(18) Steering Column Tilt Head Assembly
(19) Wire Harness Spacer
(20) Pan Head Tapping Screws
(21) Pan Head Tapping Screws
(22) Turn Signal and Multifunction Switch Assembly

GC6049900277010X

Fig. 25 Exploded view of steering column (Part 1 of 2). Corvette non telescoping w/sensor

first, screw in 8 o'clock position second and screw in 3 o'clock position third.

c. Tighten mounting screws to specification in previous step's order.

CUTLASS & MALIBU

Refer to **Fig. 36** for exploded view of this steering column.

STEERING COLUMN COVERS

1. Remove tilt lever and lower steering column cover mounting screws.
2. Separate column covers by snapping apart.
3. Reverse procedure to install.

SIR COIL

1. Remove steering column as previously described.
2. Remove inflator module as outlined under "Passive Restraints Systems" chapter.
3. Remove steering wheel as outlined under "Electrical" section of "Achieva, Alero, Cutlass, Grand Am, Malibu & Skylark" chassis chapter.
4. Remove nut, retaining ring and coil.
5. Remove wave washer.
6. Reverse procedure to install.

SHAFT LOCK, TURN SIGNAL CANCEL CAM, TILT SPRING, UPPER BEARING SPRING, UPPER BEARING INNER RACE SEAT, INNER RACE, PIVOT PINS & STEERING COLUMN HOUSING

1. Remove coil as previously described.
2. Remove retaining ring using lock plate compressor tool No. J-23653-SIR, or equivalent.
3. Remove turn signal cancel cam orientation plate and turn signal cancel cam.
4. Remove tilt spring, guide and upper bearing spring.
5. Remove upper bearing inner race seat and race.
6. Remove two pivot pins using pivot pin remover tool No. J-21854-01, or equivalent.
7. Pull tilt arm to disengage steering wheel lock shoes from dowel pins in steering column support.
8. Remove steering column housing and bearing.
9. Reverse procedure to install.

STEERING COLUMN SHAFT

1. Remove upper tilt head components as previously described.
2. Remove steering shaft seal and sensor retainer, then the lower bearing seat, spring and retainer, **Fig. 37.**
3. Remove adapter and bearing from jacket, then the steering shaft from steering column jacket.
4. Remove lower and upper steering shaft.
5. Remove centering sphere from upper shaft by rotating sphere 90° and slipping out, **Fig. 38.**
6. Remove shaft preload spring from centering sphere.
7. Reverse procedure to install, noting the following:
   a. Install new centering sphere.
   b. Preload spring, using centering sphere installer tool No. J-41688, or equivalent, and suitable vise.
   c. Install lower bearing seat, lower bearing spring and lower spring retainer.
   d. Compressing lower bearing spring to 0.91–0.94 inches between lower bearing seat and retainer.

CENTURY, GRAND PRIX, INTRIGUE & REGAL

Refer to **Figs. 39 and 40** for exploded view of steering column.

STEERING COLUMN COVERS

1. Remove inflator module as outlined in "Passive Restraints Systems" chapter.
2. Remove intermediate steering shaft pinch bolt and steering column.
3. Remove tilt lever and lower column cover mounting screws.
4. Remove lock cylinder.
5. Remove lower and upper column cover mounting screws.
6. Remove upper column cover.
7. Reverse procedure to install. Tighten mounting bolts and screws to specifications.

UPPER COLUMN

1. Remove steering column cover as previously described, then steering wheel.
2. Remove retaining ring and coil.
3. Remove shaft lock retaining ring using lock plate compressor tool No. J-23653-SIR, or equivalent, and shaft lock plate.
4. Remove turn signal cancel cam, then the upper bearing spring, race seat and inner race.
5. Reverse procedure to install.

MID COLUMN (COLUMN SHIFT)

1. Remove steering column cover as previously described.
2. Remove mounting bolt, ball and actuator.
3. Disconnect park lock cable and remove park lock cable mounting screws.
4. Remove shift lever clevis and park lock cable from support bracket.
5. Disconnect BTSI actuator arm from outer shift cable ball stud and transaxle shift cable from inner ball stud.
6. Remove mounting bolt and cable shift cam.

(23) Joint Preload Spring
(24) Race and Upper Shaft Assembly
(25) Centering Sphere
(26) Lower Steering Shaft Assembly
(27) Lower Shroud
(28) TORX® Head Screw
(29) Pivot Pin
(30) Tilt Bumper
(31) TORX® Head Screw
(32) Spring Guide
(33) Tilt Spring
(34) Steering Column Support Assembly
(35) Wire Harness Strap
(36) Steering Column Jacket Assembly
(37) Adapter and Bearing Assembly
(38) High Resolution Steering Wheel Position Sensor Assembly
(39) Sensor Retainer
(40) Steering Shaft Seal

GC6049900277020X

Fig. 25 Exploded view of steering column (Part 2 of 2). Corvette non telescoping w/sensor

7. Remove cam bushing and cam mounting screws.
8. Remove gearshift lever support bracket.
9. Reverse procedure to install. Tighten mounting screws and bolts to specifications.

LOWER COLUMN

1. Remove steering guide from steering column jacket and steering column covers as previously described.
2. Remove turn signal and multi-function switch.
3. Remove cam mounting bolt, ball and actuator.
4. Disconnect park lock cable and remove park lock cable mounting screws.
5. Remove shift lever clevis.
6. Pry up on tilt spring and spring guide until bulge appears and most spring tension is removed.
7. Secure spring with suitable pair of locking pliers and continue to pry until spring disengages from post. **Tilt spring and spring guide are under pressure. Secured with suitable pair of locking pliers.**
8. Remove spring guide from spring.
9. Remove steering shaft seal and sensor retainer from adapter and bearing.
10. Remove lower spring retainer, bearing spring and seat.
11. Remove adapter and bearing from steering column jacket.
12. Remove pivot pins using pivot pin removal tool No J-21854-01, or equivalent.
13. Remove steering column tilt head with steering shaft by installing and pulling tilt arm to disengage steering wheel lock shoes from dowel pins in steering column support.
14. Disconnect upper and lower steering shaft by tilting upper steering shaft 90° from lower steering shaft.
15. Rotate centering sphere 90° and lift centering sphere away from upper steering shaft.
16. Remove shaft preload spring from centering sphere.
17. Reverse procedure to install, noting the following:
    a. Install new centering sphere.
    b. Preload spring, using centering sphere installer tool No. J-41688, or equivalent, and suitable vise.

(1) Pan Head Tapping Screws
(2) Electric Column Lock
(3) Pan Head Tapping Screws
(4) Steering Column Tilt Head Assembly
(5) Inner Race
(6) Upper Bearing Inner Race Seat
(7) Upper Bearing Spring
(8) Turn Signal Cancel Cam Assembly
(9) Shaft Lock Shield Assembly
(10) Bearing Retainer
(11) Wave Washer
(12) SIR Coil Assembly
(13) Retaining Ring
(14) Flanged Prevailing Torque Nut
(15) Pivot and Pulse Switch Assembly
(16) Upper Shroud
(17) TORX® Head Screw
(18) Pan Head Tapping Screws
(19) Turn Signal and Multifunction Switch Assembly
(20) Pan Head Tapping Screws
(21) Tilt Lever
(22) Wire Harness Strap
(23) Steering Shaft Assembly
(24) Lower Steering Yoke Assembly
(25) Centering Sphere

GC6049900279010X

Fig. 26 Exploded view of steering column (Part 1 of 2). Corvette telescoping

SHAFT LOCK SHIELD, TURN SIGNAL CAM, UPPER BEARING SPRING, UPPER BEARING INNER RACE SEAT & INNER RACE

1. Remove SIR coil and let hang freely.
2. Remove shaft lock by push down using lock plate compressor tool No. J-23653-SIR, or equivalent.
3. Remove shaft lock shield.
4. Remove turn signal cancel cam.
5. Remove upper bearing spring, inner race seat, and inner race.
6. Reverse procedure to install.

LOCK MODULE

1. Remove shaft lock shield, turn signal cam, upper bearing spring, upper bearing inner race seat, and inner race as previously described.
2. Put lock cylinder in Off-Lock position and gear shift into Park position.
3. Insert small blade screwdriver into slot in lock module.
4. Push against locking tab on end of cable and remove.
5. Pry retaining clip on alarm switch with suitable small blade screwdriver.
6. Rotate alarm switch 1/4 turn and remove.
7. Remove from ignition and key alarm switch mounting screws. Let switch hang freely.
8. **Lock bolt is under slight spring pressure from lock bolt spring. Hold lock bolt in place while removing lock module.**
9. Remove mounting screws and lock module.
10. Remove lock bolt with spring.
11. Remove spring from lock bolt.
12. Remove lock cylinder.
13. Reverse procedure to install.

ELECTRIC PARK LOCK

1. Remove transmission fuse No. 24 in instrument panel fuse panel.
2. Remove filler plug on bottom of lower shroud.
3. Insert suitable small screwdriver into hole and push up on manual override of electric park lock.
4. Turn key to Lock position, and remove.
5. Remove upper and lower steering column covers as previously described.
6. Remove mounting screw and black connector.
7. Remove electronic park lock from lock module with suitable small screwdriver.

(26) Joint Preload Spring
(27) Race and Upper Shaft Assembly
(28) Steering Column Close Out Shroud
(29) Telescoping Switch Assembly
(30) Lower Shroud
(31) Pan Head Tapping Screw
(32) Telescope Motor and Bracket Assembly
(33) Connector Clip
(34) Telescope Drive Motor Assembly
(35) Pan Head Tapping Screws
(36) Telescope Drive Bracket
(37) Pan Head Tapping Screws
(38) Flat Head 6–Lobed Soc Tap Screw
(39) Telescope Adapter Assembly
(40) Telescope Drive Ball
(41) Telescope Drive Bolt
(42) TORX® Head Screw
(43) Telescope Actuator Assembly
(44) TORX® Head Screw
(45) Cable Assembly
(46) Steering Shaft Seal
(47) Sensor Retainer
(48) Hi Resolution Steering Wheel Position Sensor Assembly
(49) Lower Spring Retainer
(50) Adapter and Bearing Assembly
(51) Switch Housing Blocking Plug
(52) Telebearing and Jacket Assembly
(53) Shoulder Bolt
(54) Retaining Ring
(55) Compression Spring
(56) Anti Rotation Ball
(57) Pivot Pin
(58) Steering Column Support Assembly
(59) Tilt Bumper
(60) Tilt Spring
(61) Pivot Pin
(62) Spring Guide
(63) Support Screw

GC6049900279020X

Fig. 26 Exploded view of steering column (Part 2 of 2). Corvette telescoping

8. Reverse procedure to install.

TILT SPRING

Tilt spring and spring guide are under pressure. During removal and installation secure spring with locking pliers.

1. Remove lower shroud mounting screws.
2. Tilt shroud down, slide back to disengage locking tabs and remove.
3. Tilt column to up position.
4. Pry spring up until bulge occurs and most of spring tension is removed.
5. Secure spring with locking pliers and continue prying until spring disengages from post on steering column.
6. Remove spring guide from tilt spring.
7. Reverse procedure to install.

LINEAR SHIFT

Linear shift may be removed as an assembly or certain components may be disassembled as required to do repairs. Remove or disassemble only those components required to do repairs.

1. Remove upper and lower covers as previously described.
2. Place lock cylinder in Off-Lock position and gear shift in Park position.
3. Insert suitable small blade screwdriver into slot in lock module.
4. Push against locking tab on end of cable to release and remove park lock cable.
5. Pry actuator arm of electrical actuator from outer shift cable ball stud on cable shift cam and mounting pin on jacket.
6. Remove transaxle cable from inner shift cable ball stud on cable shift cam.
7. Shift column to Neutral position to gain access to lower mounting screw.
8. Remove mounting screws and linear shift.
9. Reverse procedure to install.

DEVILLE, ELDORADO & SEVILLE

Refer to **Figs. 41 and 42** for exploded view of these steering column.

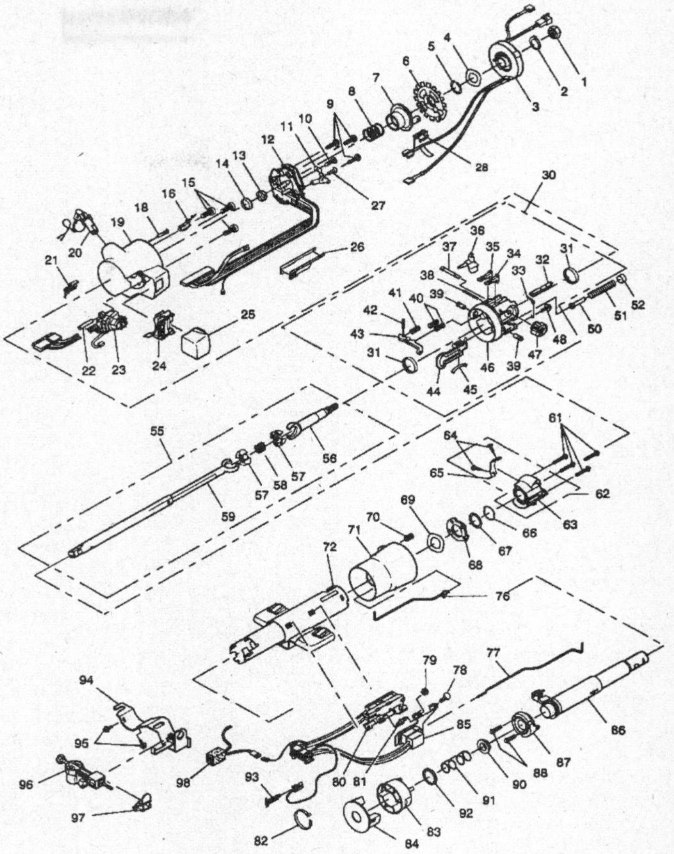

GC604970023200AX

Fig. 27 Exploded view of steering column (Part 1 of 2). LSS, Regency & 88 & 1998–99 Bonneville & LeSabre w/column shift

AIR BAG COIL, SHAFT LOCK, TURN SIGNAL CANCELING CAM, UPPER BEARING SPRING, UPPER BEARING INNER RACE SEAT, INNER RACE, TURN SIGNAL SWITCH, BUZZER SWITCH & STEERING COLUMN PASS KEY LOCK CYLINDER SET

1. Remove inflator module and steering wheel as previously described.
2. Remove retaining ring and coil. Remove wave washer.
3. Remove shaft lock retaining ring using compressor tool No. J-23653-C, or equivalent, to push down shaft lock.
4. Remove shaft lock and turn signal canceling cam.
5. Remove upper bearing spring and upper bearing inner race seat.
6. Remove inner race and move turn signal to righthand turn position (up).
7. Remove multi-function lever and hazard knob.
8. Remove signal switch arm and mounting screws.
9. Disconnect turn signal switch connector from bulkhead connector.
10. Remove wiring protector.
11. Gently pull wire harness through column.
12. **Coil will become uncentered if steering column is separated from steering gear and is allowed to rotate; or if centering spring is pushed down, letting hub rotate while coil is removed from steering column.**
13. Remove coil terminal from vehicle harness.
14. Remove yellow connector shroud from black terminal connector.
15. Remove wiring protector.
16. Attach suitable length of mechanics wire to coil terminal connector to aid in assembling.
17. Gently pull wire through column.
18. Remove key from pass key lock cylinder set, **Fig. 43.**
19. Remove buzzer switch and insert key in pass key in lock cylinder. Ensure key is in Lock position.
20. Remove lock mounting screw.
21. Disconnect pivot switch connector from bulkhead connector and remove 13-way secondary lock.
22. Disconnect terminals of pass key wire harness from switch connector cavities 12 and 13.
23. Remove wiring protector and attach suitable piece of mechanics wire to terminal to aid in assembling.
24. Remove retaining clip from housing cover and gently pull wire harness

1-NUT, HEX LOCKING (M14x1.5)
2-RING, RETAINING
3-COIL ASM, SIR
4-WASHER, WAVE
5-RING, RETAINING
6-LOCK, SHAFT
7-CAM ASM, TURN SIG CANCEL
8-SPRING, UPPER BEARING
9-SCREW, BNDG HD CR RECESS
10-SCREW, C/S TAPPING (#8-18X.75)
11-ARM ASM, SIGNAL SWITCH
12-SWITCH ASM, TURN SIGNAL
13-SEAT, UPPER BRG INNER RACE
14-RACE, INNER
15-SCREW, PAN HD SOC TAP
16-SWITCH ASM, BUZZER
18-SCREW, LOCK RETAINING
19-COVER ASM, LOCK HOUSING
20-LOCK CYLINDER SET, STRG COL (PASS KEY)
21-ACTUATOR, DIMMER SW ROD
22-PIN, SWITCH ACTUATOR PIVOT
23-SWITCH ASM, PIVOT & (PULSE)
24-BASE PLATE, COL HSG CVR END
25-CAP, COL HSG COVER END
26-PROTECTOR, WIRING
27-SCREW, FLT HD TAPPING
28-SHROUD, CONNECTOR
30-HOUSING ASM, STRG COLUMN
31-BEARING ASM
32-BOLT, LOCK
33-SPRING, LOCK BOLT
34-SHOE, STRG WHEEL LOCK
35-SHOE, STRG WHEEL LOCK
36-SHIELD, WIRE PROTECTOR
37-SHAFT, DRIVE
38-PIN, DOWEL
39-PIN, PIVOT
40-SPRING, SHOE
41-SPRING, RELEASE LEVER
42-PIN, RELEASE LEVER
43-LEVER, SHOE RELEASE
44-RACK, SWITCH ACTUATOR
45-SPRING, RACK PRELOAD
46-HOUSING, STRG COLUMN
47-SECTOR, SWITCH ACTUATOR
48-SCREW, HEX WASHER HEAD
50-GUIDE, SPRING
51-SPRING, WHEEL TILT
52-RETAINER, SPRING
55-SHAFT ASM, STEERING
56-SHAFT ASM, RACE & UPPER
57-SPHERE, CENTERING
58-SPRING, JOINT PRELOAD
59-SHAFT ASM, LOWER STEERING
61-SCREW, SUPPORT
62-SUPPORT ASM, STRG COL HSG
63-SUPPORT, STRG COL HSG
64-SCREW, OVL HD CROSS RECESS
65-GATE, SHIFT LEVER
66-RING, SHIFT TUBE RETAINING
67-WASHER, THRUST
68-PLATE, LOCK
69-WASHER, WAVE
70-SPRING, SHIFT LEVER
71-BOWL ASM, GEARSHIFT LEVER
72-JACKET ASM, STRG COL
76-ACTUATOR ASM, IGN SWITCH
77-ROD, DIMMER SWITCH
78-SCREW, WASH HD (#10-24x.25)
79-NUT, HEXAGON (#10-24)
80-SWITCH ASM, IGNITION & DIMR
81-STUD, DIMR & IGN SW MTG
82-STRAP, WIRE HARNESS
83-RETAINER, BEARING & SEAL
84-WASHER ASM, RETAINER
85-SWITCH ASM, DIMMER
86-TUBE ASM, SHIFT
87-BEARING ASM, ADAPTER &
88-SCREW, HEX WASHER HD TAP
90-SEAT, LOWER BEARING
91-SPRING, LOWER BEARING
92-RETAINER, LOWER SPRING
93-CONNECTOR, AXIAL POSN ASSUR
94-SUPPORT, STRG COL LOWER
95-BOLT, HEX FLNG HD (M6x1x14)
96-ACTUATOR, ELECTRICAL (BTSI)
97-CLIP, ADJUSTMENT RETAINING
98-HARNESS ASM, JUMPER

GC604970023200BX

Fig. 27 Exploded view of steering column (Part 2 of 2). LSS, Regency & 88 & 1998–99 Bonneville & LeSabre w/column shift

through column.

25. Reverse procedure to install, noting the following:
    a. Route wire from pass key lock cylinder, **Fig. 44,** and snap retaining clip into hole in housing.
    b. Tighten mounting screws to specifications.
    c. While holding coil, depress spring lock to rotate hub in direction of arrow until it stops, **Fig. 45.**
    d. Rotate coil hub in opposite direction approximately 2½ turns. Release spring lock between locking tabs in front of arrow, **Fig. 45.**
    e. Align opening in coil with horn tower and locating bump between two tabs on housing cover, **Fig. 46.**

LOCK HOUSING COVER, COLUMN HOUSING COVER END CAP, PIVOT & PULSE SWITCH, DIMMER SWITCH ROD ACTUATOR & TILT SPRING

1. Remove upper column as previously described.
2. Remove housing end cap.
3. Remove cruise control and multi-function lever connectors from base plate and disconnect.
4. Remove multi-function lever.
5. Remove cover screws and tilt lever.
6. Remove lock housing cover.
7. Remove base plate and dimmer switch rod actuator.
8. Remove pin, pivot and pulse switch actuator, noting the following:
    a. Allow switch to hang freely if removal is not required.
    b. Disconnect pivot and switch connector from bulkhead connector.
    c. Gently pull wire harness through column.

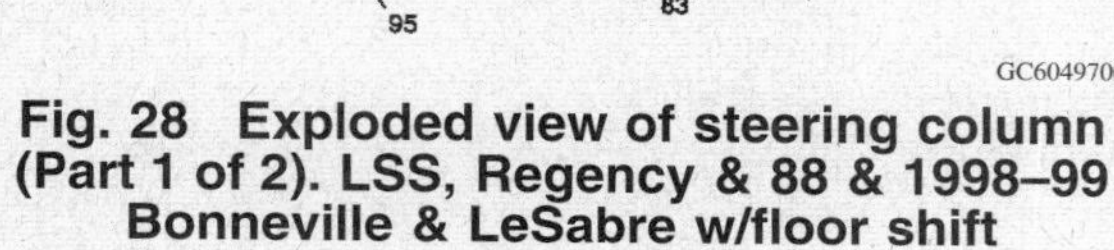

GC604970023400AX

Fig. 28 Exploded view of steering column (Part 1 of 2). LSS, Regency & 88 & 1998–99 Bonneville & LeSabre w/floor shift

9. Remove spring retainer, spring and spring guide.
10. Reverse procedure to install, noting the following:
    a. Tighten lock housing cover screws in 12 o'clock position first, 8 o'clock position second and 3 o'clock position last.
    b. Tighten mounting screws in previous step's order.

STEERING COLUMN HOUSING, STEERING WHEEL LOCK SHOE, SWITCH ACTUATOR SECTOR, SWITCH ACTUATOR RACK, BEARING, LOCK BOLT, STEERING COLUMN HOUSING SUPPORT, STEERING SHAFT & SHIFT TUBE

1. Remove steering column as previously described.
2. Perform all disassembling steps outlined under "Housing Cover."
3. Remove pivot pins using pivot pin removal tool No. J-21854-01, or equivalent. Install tilt lever.
4. Remove steering column housing. Pull back on tilt lever and pull steering column housing down and away from column.
5. Remove the following components to disassemble steering column housing assembly:
    a. Bearing.
    b. Wire abrasion shield.
    c. Mounting screw.
    d. Lock bolt spring.
    e. Lock bolt.
    f. Switch actuator rack and rack preload spring.
    g. Driveshaft.
    h. Switch actuator sector.
    i. Release lever pin using lock shoe and release lever pin tool No. J-22635, or equivalent.
    j. Shoe release lever.
    k. Release lever spring.
    l. Dowel pin using lock show and release lever pin tool.
    m. Lock shoes and shoe springs.
6. Remove lower spring retainer.
7. Remove bearing and seal retainer.
8. Remove lower spring retainer.
9. Remove lower bearing spring and lower bearing seat.
10. Remove mounting bolts, adapter and bearing.
11. Remove steering column shaft.
12. Mark upper shaft and lower steering shaft to ensure proper assembly.
13. Disassemble steering column shaft as follows:
    a. Separate upper shaft from lower steering shaft. Tilt 90° to each other and disengage.
    b. Separate centering sphere from

1-NUT, HEX LOCKING (M14x1.5)
2-RING, RETAINING
3-COIL ASM, INFL RESTRAINT
4-WASHER, WAVE
5-RING, RETAINING
6-LOCK, SHAFT
7-CAM ASM, TURN SIG CANCEL
8-SPRING, UPPER BEARING
9-SCREW, BNDG HD CR RECESS
10-SCREW, C/S TAPPING (8-18X.75)
11-ARM ASM, SIGNAL SWITCH
12-SWITCH ASM, TURN SIGNAL
13-SEAT, UPPER BRG INNER RACE
14-RACE, INNER
15-SCREW, PAN HD SOC TAP
16-SWITCH ASM, BUZZER
18-SCREW, LOCK RETAINING
19-COVER ASM, LOCK HOUSING
20-LOCK CYLINDER SET, STRG COL (PASS KEY)
21-ACTUATOR, DIMMER SW ROD
22-PIN, SWITCH ACTUATOR PIVOT
23-SWITCH ASM, PIVOT & (PULSE)
24-BASE PLATE, COL HSG CVR END
25-CAP, COL HSG COVER END
26-PROTECTOR, WIRING
27-SCREW, FLT HD TAPPING
28-SHROUD, CONNECTOR
30-HOUSING ASM, STRG COLUMN
31-BEARING ASM
32-BOLT, LOCK
33-SPRING, LOCK BOLT
34-SHOE, STRG WHEEL LOCK
35-SHOE, STRG WHEEL LOCK
36-SHIELD, WIRE PROTECTOR
37-SHAFT, DRIVE
38-PIN, DOWEL
39-PIN, PIVOT
40-SPRING, SHOE
41-SPRING, RELEASE LEVER
42-PIN, RELEASE LEVER
43-LEVER, SHOE RELEASE
44-RACK, SWITCH ACTUATOR
45-SPRING, RACK PRELOAD
46-HOUSING, STRG COLUMN
47-SECTOR, SWITCH ACTUATOR
48-SCREW, HEX WASHER HEAD
50-GUIDE, SPRING
51-SPRING, WHEEL TILT
52-RETAINER, SPRING
55-SHAFT ASM, STEERING
56-SHAFT ASM, RACE & UPPER
57-SPHERE, CENTERING
58-SPRING, JOINT PRELOAD
59-SHAFT ASM, LOWER STEERING
61-SCREW, SUPPORT
62-SUPPORT ASM, STRG COL HSG
68-PLATE, LOCK
71-SHROUD, STRG COL HSG
72-JACKET ASM, STRG COL
76-ACTUATOR ASM, IGN SWITCH
77-ROD, DIMMER SWITCH
78-SCREW, WASH HD (#10-24x.25)
79-NUT, HEXAGON (#10-24)
80-SWITCH ASM, IGN & DIMMER
81-STUD, DIMR & IGN SW MTG
82-SWITCH ASM, DIMMER
83-STRAP, WIRE HARNESS
87-BEARING ASM, ADAPTER &
88-SCREW, HEX WASHER HD TAP
90-SEAT, LOWER BEARING
91-SPRING, LOWER BEARING
92-RETAINER, LOWER SPRING
93-RETAINER, BEARING & SEAL
94-WASHER ASM, RETAINER
95-HARNESS ASM, JUMPER

GC604970023400BX

Fig. 28 Exploded view of steering column (Part 2 of 2). LSS, Regency & 88 & 1998–99 Bonneville & LeSabre w/floor shift

upper shaft by rotating sphere 90° and sliding out.

c. Remove joint preload spring from centering sphere.

14. Remove mounting screws and column housing support with dimmer switch rod from steering column jacket.
15. Remove mounting screws and shift lever gate from support.
16. Remove shift tube retaining ring, thrust washers and lock plate.
17. Remove wave washer and thrust washers, then the gearshift lever bowl with gearshift bowl shroud and shift tube.
18. Remove shroud from bowl.
19. Remove shift lever spring and shift tube from bowl. Use suitable press, as required.
20. Remove PRNDL adjuster mounting nut and screw.
21. Remove PRNDL adjuster bracket and dimmer switch.
22. Remove dimmer and ignition switch mounting stud.
23. Remove ignition switch from ignition switch actuator.
24. Remove cam retainer.
25. Remove dimmer and ignition switch mounting screw and stud.
26. Remove cable clip from upper location of steering column jacket.
27. Remove cable mounting clip from solenoid bracket.
28. Remove ball joint socket from solenoid.
29. Remove ball joint spring.
30. Remove interlock solenoid and solenoid bracket to steering column jacket mounting screw.
31. Remove solenoid bracket to steering column jacket mounting screws
32. Reverse procedure to install. Tighten mounting screws to specifications.

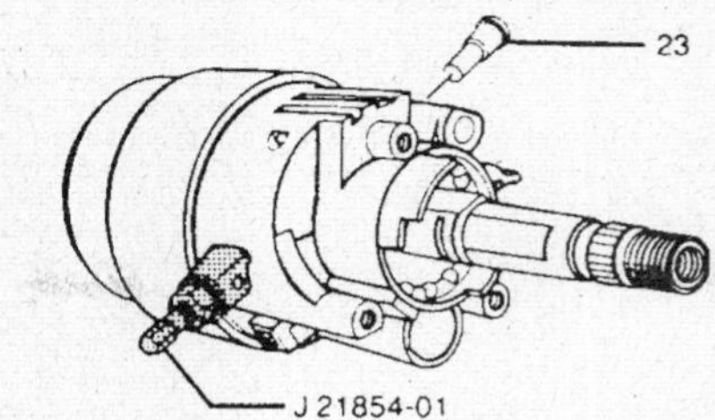

23 PIN, PIVOT

GC6049100092000X

Fig. 29 Pivot pin removal. Bonneville, Camaro, Corvette, DeVille, Firebird, LeSabre, LSS, Park Avenue & 88

LUMINA & 1998-99 MONTE CARLO

Refer to **Figs. 47 and 48** for exploded views of these columns.

UPPER COLUMN

Do not allow steering column to be supported only by the upper or lower support brackets. Damage to the column lower bearing adapter could result.

1. Remove SIR retaining ring.
2. Remove wave washer.
3. Push down on shaft lock using lock plate compressor tool No. J-23653-SIR, or equivalent. Remove bearing retainer.
4. Remove turn signal canceling cam.
5. Remove upper bearing spring, inner race seat, and inner race.
6. Remove multi-function lever.
7. Push top and bottom edges of housing end cover cap out of slots in housing using fingers.
8. Remove mounting screws, then the pivot and pulse dimmer switch connector from bulkhead connector.
9. Pry on upper and lower wings of switch body using suitable screwdriver, **Fig. 49.**
10. Remove wiring protector and wire harness clamp from tab inside housing, pull wire harness from column.
11. Pry knob from hazard warning switch using suitable small screwdriver.
12. Place turn signal switch to righthand turn position.
13. Remove turn signal switch mounting screws. Allow switch to hang freely.
14. Remove wiring protector from SIR coil and attach suitable length of mechanics wire to coil terminal terminals to ease assembly.
15. Remove coil and pull wires through column.
16. Remove key from lock cylinder set.
17. Remove buzzer switch.
18. Insert key and move switch to Lock position.
19. Remove steering lock cylinder set mounting screw.
20. Remove terminal of pass key wiring harness from vehicle wire harness.
21. Remove wiring protector.
22. Attach suitable length of mechanics wire to terminal for ease of assembly.

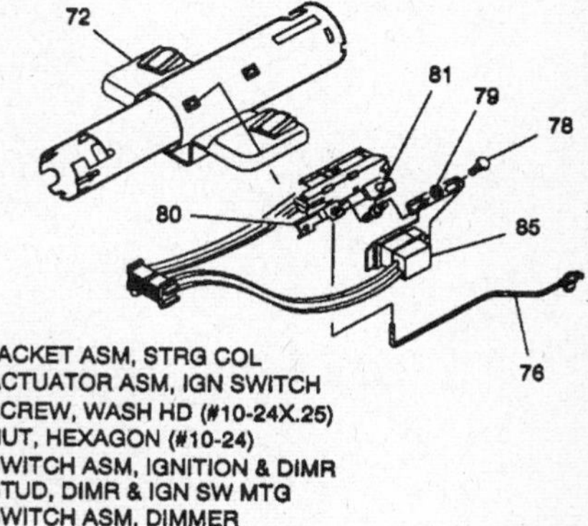

72 JACKET ASM, STRG COL
76 ACTUATOR ASM, IGN SWITCH
78 SCREW, WASH HD (#10-24X.25)
79 NUT, HEXAGON (#10-24)
80 SWITCH ASM, IGNITION & DIMR
81 STUD, DIMR & IGN SW MTG
85 SWITCH ASM, DIMMER

GC6049700231000X

Fig. 30 Ignition & dimmer switch replacement. Bonneville, Camaro, Corvette, Firebird, LeSabre, LSS, Regency & 88

23. Remove steering column lock cylinder set retaining clip, pull lock and wiring harness through steering column.
24. Remove mounting screws, tilt lever, lock housing cover and sleeve, then the wire protector shield.
25. Seat counterbore of tilt spring compressor No. J-39246, or equivalent, over end race and upper shaft.
26. Thread and seat standard flanged previously torqued nut on to race and upper shaft assembly, **Fig. 50.**
27. Align square extension on end of tool bolt with square hole in spring retainer and seat.
28. Rotate tool bolt clockwise with wrench until it contacts surface of tool block.
29. Spring retainer must be compressed approximately ¼ inch into steering column housing.
30. Rotate hexagon section on end of tool bolt counterclockwise approximately ¼ turn.
31. Unscrew tool boot until spring and spring retainer are loose and free of tool.
32. Remove spring retainer, tilt spring and spring guide.
33. Reverse procedure to install, noting the following:
    a. Refer to **Fig. 51** for proper wire routing.
    b. Tighten mounting screws to specifications.
    c. Set steering shaft so block tooth on race and upper shaft is at 12 o'clock position. Wheels should be straight ahead.
    d. Set steering column lock cylinder set to Lock position.
    e. **SIR coil will become uncentered if steering column is allowed to rotate or centering spring is pushed down, letting hub rotate while coil is removed from column. If this occurs, proceed to next step and refer to Fig. 52.**
    f. Position vehicle wheels straight ahead.
    g. Remove coil
    h. Hold coil assembly with bottom up.
    i. While holding coil, depress spring lock to rotate hub in direction of

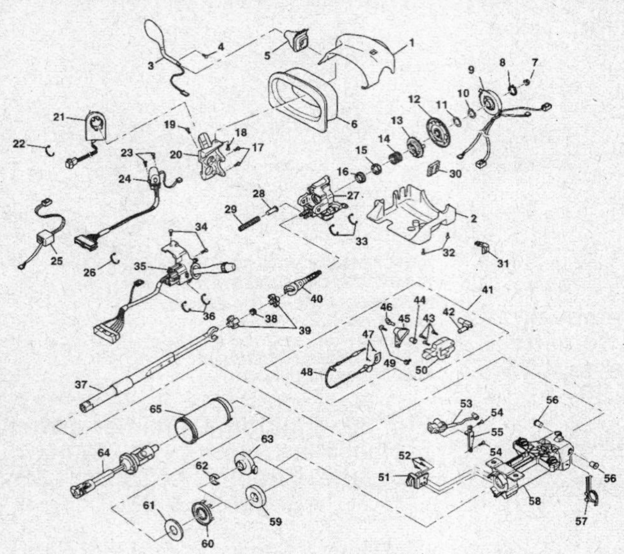

(1) Upper Shroud
(2) Lower Shroud
(3) Automatic Transmission Control Lever Assembly
(4) Shift Lever Screw
(5) Shift Lever Seal
(6) Steering Column Closeout Shroud
(7) Hexagon Locking Nut
(8) Retaining Ring
(9) SIR Coil Assembly
(10) Wave Washer
(11) Bearing Retainer
(12) Shaft Lock Shield Assembly
(13) Turn Signal Cancel Cam Assembly
(14) Upper Bearing Spring
(15) Upper Bearing Inner Race Seat
(16) Inner Race
(17) Pan Head Tapping Screw
(18) TORX® Head Screw
(19) Pan Head Tapping Screw
(20) Lock Module Assembly
(21) Coded Key Controller
(22) Wire Harness Strap
(23) Tapping Screw

GC6049900286010X

Fig. 31 Exploded view of steering column (Part 1 of 2). 2000–02 Bonneville & LeSabre w/ column shift

(24) Ignition & Key Alarm Switch Assembly
(25) Fused Jumper Assembly
(26) Wire Harness Strap
(27) Tilt Spring
(28) Spring Guide
(29) Steering Column Tilt Head Assembly
(30) Shroud Protector
(31) Tilt Lever Assembly
(32) Pan Head Tapping Screw
(33) Wire Harness Strap
(34) Pan Head Tapping Screw
(35) Turn Signal and Multifunction Switch
(36) Wire Harness Strap
(37) Lower Steering Shaft Assembly
(38) Joint Preload Spring
(39) Centering Sphere
(40) Race and Upper Shaft Assembly
(41) Linear Shift Assembly
(42) Shift Lever Clevis
(43) Flat Head 6–Lobed Socket Tapping Screw
(44) Cam Bushing
(45) Cable Shift Cam Assembly
(46) Ball and Actuator Assembly
(47) Oval Head 6–Lobed Socket Tapping Screw
(48) Park Lock Cable Assembly
(49) Hex Flanged Head Bolt
(50) Gear Shift Lever Assembly Support Bracket
(51) Cable Support Bracket
(52) Flat Head Screw
(53) Electrical BTSI Actuator
(54) Pan Head Tapping Screw
(55) BTSI Mounting Bracket Assembly
(56) Pivot Pin
(57) Wire Restraint Clip
(58) Steering Column Support Assembly
(59) Steering Shaft Seal
(60) Sensor Retainer
(61) Steering Shaft Seal
(62) Sensor Locator
(63) Sensor Steer Sensor Assembly
(64) Intermediate Steering Shaft Assembly
(65) Boot Seal

GC6049900286020X

Fig. 31 Exploded view of steering column (Part 2 of 2). 2000–02 Bonneville & LeSabre w/ column shift

arrow until it stops.
j. Coil ribbon should be wound up snug against center hub.
k. Rotate coil hub in opposite direction approximately 2½ turns.
l. Release spring lock between locking tabs.

34. If new SIR coil is being installed, assemble precentered coil to steering column. Remove and dispose of centering tab.
35. SIR coil wires must be kept tight with no slack while installing SIR coil assembly.

MID COLUMN

1. Remove steering column.
2. Remove upper column as previously described.
3. Remove pivot pins using pivot pin remover No. J-21854-01 or equivalent.
4. Install tilt lever.
5. Pull back on tilt lever and pull steering column housing down and away from column.
6. Remove sensor retainer.
7. Remove steering wheel speed sensor from adapter and bearing.
8. Remove and dispose of lower spring retainer.
9. Remove lower spring.
10. Remove lower bearing seat.
11. Remove adapter and bearing.
12. Remove steering shaft.
13. Disassemble lower steering shaft from race and upper shaft.
14. Tilt lower steering shaft assembly 90° to race and upper shaft and disengage.
15. Remove housing support.
16. Remove shift lever gate from steering column housing support.
17. Remove shift tube retaining ring and thrust washers.
18. Turn gearshift lever bowl clockwise to 4 o'clock position.
19. Push lock plate with thumb and rotate counterclockwise until loose.
20. Remove wave washer, two thrust washers, and cam retainer.
21. Remove gearshift lever bowl with shift tube.
22. Remove shift lever spring and shift tube from bowl using suitable press.
23. Remove shift bowl protector from gearshift lever bowl.
24. Remove park position switch from stud and bracket.
25. Remove PRNDL adjuster bracket.
26. Remove ignition switch from ignition switch actuator.
27. Remove BTSI cable assembly from interlock solenoid and ignition switch actuator.
28. Ensure BTSI cable remains straight and does not become kinked during removal and installation.

LOWER COLUMN

1. Remove axial position assurance connector and vehicle wire harness connector from interlock solenoid.
2. Remove BTSI cable from interlock solenoid. Ensure BTSI cable does not become kinked during removal. Remove interlock solenoid.

STEERING COLUMN HOUSING

Remove only those components required to do repairs.

1. To disassemble steering column housing, remove the following:
   a. Switch actuator rack.
   b. Rack preload spring.
   c. Mounting screw.
   d. Lock bolt spring and shaft lock bolt, **Fig. 53.**
   e. Switch actuator sector.
   f. Drive shaft.
   g. Bearing.
   h. Release lever pin, using lock shoe and release lever pin remover and installer No. J-22635, or equivalent.
   i. Shoe release lever, **Fig. 54.**
   j. Release lever spring.
   k. Dowel pin using tool No. J-22635, or equivalent.
   l. Steering wheel lock shoes.
   m. Shoe springs.

STEERING SHAFT

1. Tilt race and upper and lower steering shaft 90° to each other and disengage.
2. Rotate centering sphere 90° and slip out.
3. Remove joint preload spring from centering sphere, **Fig. 55.**

CENTERING SPHERE

1. Remove old centering spring and sphere.
2. Clean and inspect, replace components, as required.
3. Grease sphere with lithium grease. Grease lower half of sphere in upper shaft engagement areas.
4. Grease upper half of sphere in shaft engagement areas opposite to greased areas of lower half of sphere.
5. Place centering sphere installer tool No. J-41688, or equivalent, in suitable vise.
6. Place bottom half of centering sphere, spring, top half of centering sphere and driver in installer tool, **Fig. 56.**

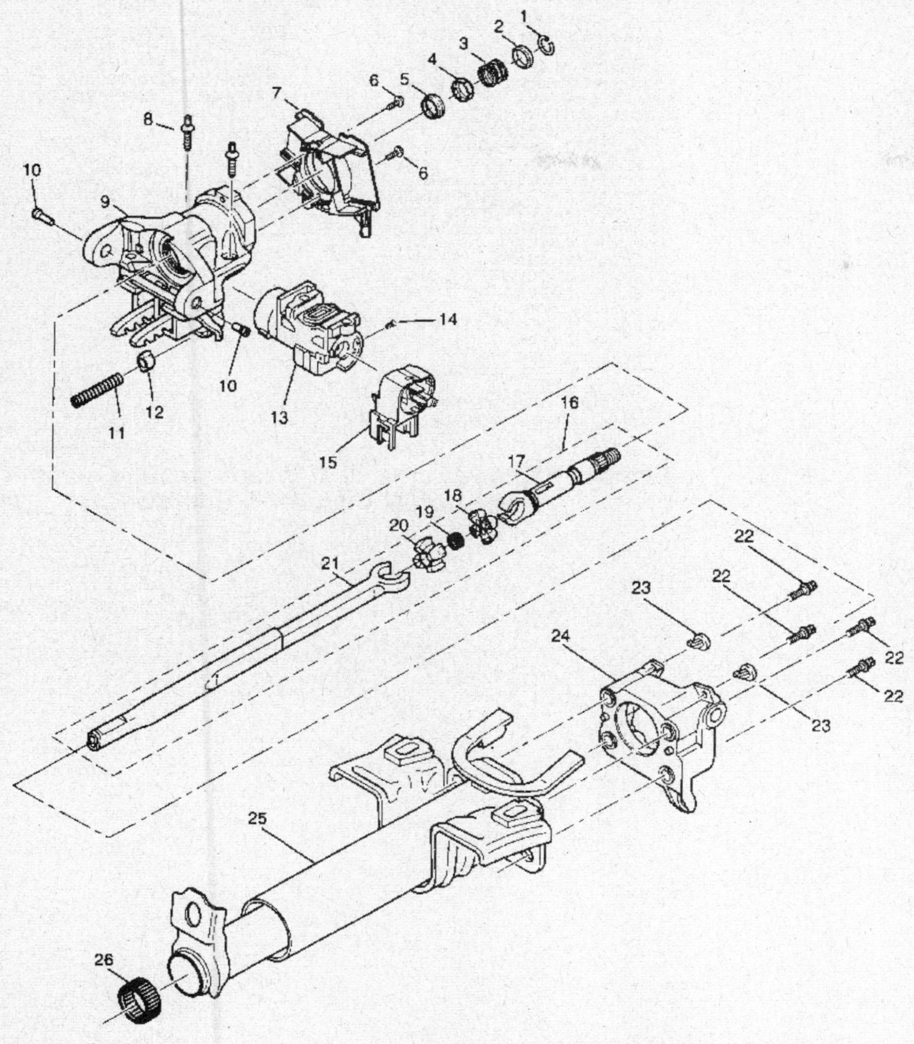

1. Ring, Retaining
2. Retainer, Spring
3. Spring, Upper Bearing
4. Seat, Inner Race
5. Race, Inner
6. Screw, Support
7. Housing, Signal Switch
8. Bolt, Shear
9. Housing, Steering Column
10. Pin, Pivot
11. Spring, Wheel Tilt
12. Retainer, Spring
13. Housing Asm, Lock Ay A/Trns
14. Screw, Set
15. Switch Asm, Ignition
16. Shaft Assembly, Steering
17. Shaft Assembly, Race and Upper
18. Sphere, Centering
19. Spring, Joint Preload
20. Sphere, Centering
21. Shaft Assembly, Lower Steering
22. Screw, Support
23. Bumper
24. Support, Strging Column Housing
25. Jacket Asm, Steering Column
26. Bearing Assembly, Lower Shaft

GC6049700242000X

Fig. 32 Exploded view of steering column. Catera

7. Compress spring and rotate driver 90° in clockwise direction.
8. Ensure feet of driver slide into grooves in base. Rotate driver until arms lock in place.
9. Once sphere is locked in place, attach race and upper shaft.
10. After race and upper shaft is attached to centering sphere, rotate shaft 90° downward to lock centering sphere in place.
11. Remove centering sphere installer, race and upper shaft from vise.
12. Disassemble tool by separating base, then remove shaft and sphere.
13. Apply lithium grease to exposed shaft engagement area and install lower shaft.

IGNITION SWITCH

Removal

1. Remove steering column as previously described.
2. Remove PRNDL adjuster bracket.
3. Remove mounting screws and dimmer switch mounting stud, then the switch from ignition switch actuator.
4. Remove turn signal switch connector from bulkhead connector.
5. Remove pivot and pulse dimmer switch connector from bulkhead connector.

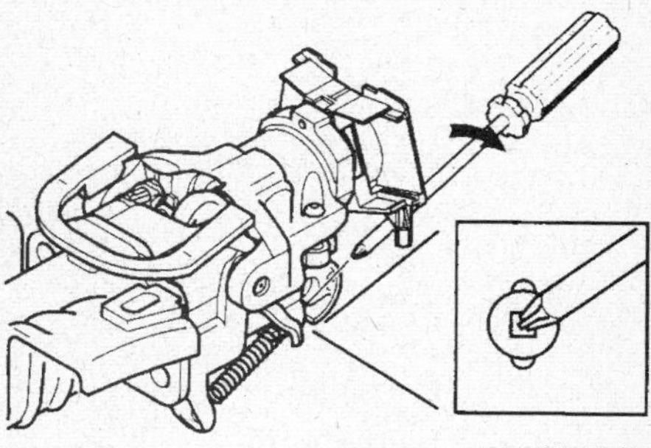

Fig. 33 Tilt spring replacement. Catera

Installation

1. Install ignition switch to steering column jacket with ignition switch in Off-Lock position.
2. New ignition switch will be pinned in Off-Lock position. Remove plastic pin after switch is assembled to column.
3. Move slider switch to extreme right-hand position.
4. Move slider switch one detent to left Off-Lock position.
5. Install 3⁄32 inch drill bit in hole on switch to limit travel.
6. Install ignition switch to ignition switch actuator.
7. Install dimmer switch mounting stud and tighten to specifications.
8. Install mounting screw and tighten to specifications.
9. Remove drill bit from ignition switch.
10. Install remaining components in reverse order of removal.

ADAPTER & BEARING, STEERING WHEEL SPEED SENSOR

1. Remove steering column as previously described.
2. Remove sensor retainer and steering shaft seal from retainer.
3. Remove steering wheel speed sensor from adapter and bearing.
4. Remove and dispose of lower spring retainer.
5. Remove lower bearing spring and seat.
6. Remove adapter and bearing.
7. Lubricate inner surface of lower bearing with suitable lithium grease.
8. Install adapter and bearing, lower bearing seat and lower bearing spring.
9. Install new lower spring retainer and press retainer onto steering shaft until spring retainer is flush with adapter and bearing, **Fig. 57.**

IMPALA & 2000–02 MONTE CARLO

Refer to **Fig. 58** for exploded view of this steering column.

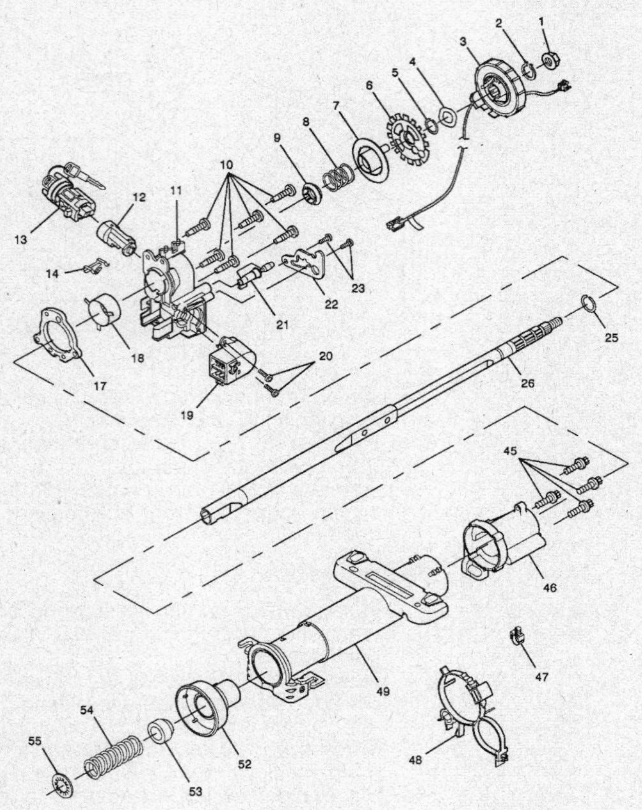

GC604950016600AX

Fig. 34 Exploded view of standard steering column (Part 1 of 2). Cavalier & Sunfire

1-NUT, HEX LOCKING (M14x1.5)
2-RING, RETAINING
3-COIL ASM, SIR
4-WASHER, WAVE
5-RING, RETAINING
6-LOCK, SHAFT
7-CAM ASM, T/SIG CANCEL
8-SPRING, UPPER BEARING
9-SPACER, UPPER BEARING
10-SCREW, ADAPTER
11-HOUSING ASM, STRG COLUMN
12-ACTUATOR ASM, IGNITION LOCK
13-LOCK CYL SET, STRG COLUMN
14-SPRING, LOCK PRE-LOAD
17-PLATE, MOUNTING
18-RETAINER, BEARING
19-SWITCH ASM, IGNITION
20-SCREW, TAPPING
21-BOLT ASM, LOCK
22-BRACKET, LOCK BOLT SUPPORT
23-SCREW, TAPPING
25-RING, RETAINING
26-SHAFT ASM, STEERING
45-SCREW, SUPPORT
46-ADAPTER, SUPPORT MOUNTING
47- CLIP, WIRE RESTRAINT
48-STRAP, WIRE
49-JACKET ASM, STRG COL
52-BEARING ASM, ADAPTER &
53-SEAT, LOWER BEARING
54-SPRING, LOWER BEARING
55-RETAINER, LOWER SPRING

Service Kits

201-GREASE SERV KIT, (SYNTHETIC)

GC604950016600BX

Fig. 34 Exploded view of standard steering column (Part 2 of 2). Cavalier & Sunfire

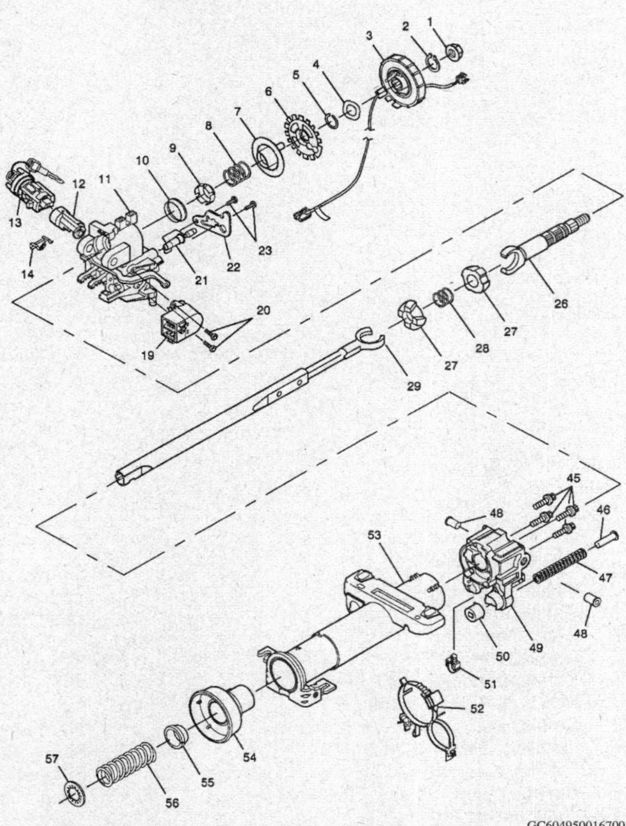

GC604950016700AX

Fig. 35 Exploded view of tilt steering column (Part 1 of 2). Cavalier & Sunfire

INTERMEDIATE STEERING SHAFT

1. Raise and support vehicle.
2. Position intermediate steering shaft seal in order to provide access to lower pinch bolt.
3. Remove intermediate steering shaft lower pinch bolt from power steering gear stub shaft, **Fig. 59. Front wheels must be maintained in straight ahead position and steering column must be in Lock position before disconnecting steering column or intermediate shaft.**
4. Remove intermediate steering shaft from power steering gear stub shaft.
5. Lower vehicle.
6. Remove lefthand instrument panel insulator.
7. Position intermediate steering shaft seal to gain access to upper pinch bolt.
8. Remove intermediate steering shaft from steering column.
9. Disconnect intermediate steering shaft from steering column.
10. Remove intermediate shaft.
11. Reverse procedure to install. Tighten mounting bolts to specifications.

STEERING COLUMN COVER

1. Remove tilt lever.
2. Remove ignition lock cylinder.
3. Remove mounting screws and steering column trim covers, **Figs. 60 and 61.**
4. Reverse procedure to install. Tighten mounting screws to specifications.

STEERING WHEEL CONTROL SWITCH

1. Remove inflator module as outlined in "Passive Restraints Systems" chapter.
2. Remove steering wheel controls, wire harness from retainers in steering wheel aluminum insert and plastic back shroud.
3. Remove cruise control switch bezel to steering wheel insert mounting screw.
4. Disconnect electrical connector from back of cruise control switch.
5. Remove steering wheel controls switch and bezel from steering wheel.
6. Reverse procedure to install.

TILT LEVER

Removal

1. Rock tilt lever back and forth to remove it from steering column.
2. Pull lever away from steering column.

1- NUT, HEX LOCKING (M14x1.5)
2- RING, RETAINING
3- COIL ASM, SIR
4- WASHER, WAVE
5- RING, RETAINING
6- LOCK, SHAFT
7- CAM ASM, T/SIG CANCEL
8- SPRING, UPPER BEARING
9- SEAT, UPPER BEARING INNER RACE
10- RACE, INNER
11- HOUSING ASM, BRG &
12- ACTUATOR ASM, IGNITION LOCK
13- LOCK CYL SET, STRG COLUMN
14- SPRING, LOCK PRE-LOAD
19- SWITCH ASM, IGNITION
20- SCREW, TAPPING
21- BOLT ASM, LOCK
22- BRACKET, LOCK BOLT SUPPORT
23- SCREW, TAPPING
26- SHAFT ASM, RACE & UPPER
27- SPHERE, CENTERING
28- SPRING, JOINT PRELOAD
29- SHAFT ASM, LOWER
45- SCREW, SUPPORT
46- GUIDE, SPRING
47- SPRING, WHEEL TILT
48- PIN, PIVOT
49- SUPPORT ASM, STRG COL
50- RETAINER, SPRING
51- CLIP, WIRE RESTRAINT
52- STRAP, WIRE
53- JACKET ASM, STRG COL
54- BEARING ASM, ADAPTER &
55- SEAT, LOWER BEARING
56- SPRING, LOWER BEARING
57- RETAINER, LOWER SPRING

Service Kits

201- SPRING SERV KIT, TILT COLUMN -INCLUDES: 9,10,47
202- SPHERE SERV KIT, TILT COLUMN -INCLUDES: 27,28
203- GREASE SERV KIT, (SYNTHETIC)

GC604950016700BX

Fig. 35 Exploded view of tilt steering column (Part 2 of 2). Cavalier & Sunfire

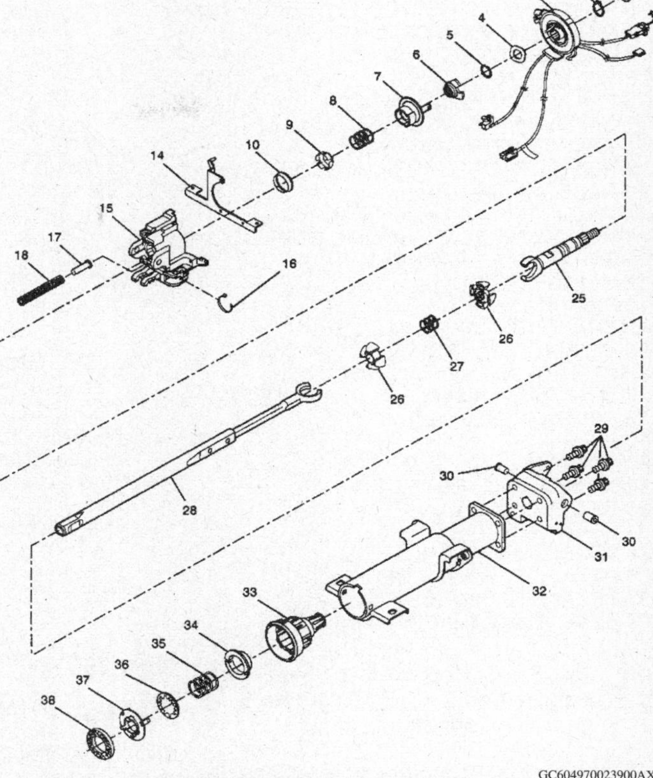

Fig. 36 Exploded view of steering column (Part 1 of 2). Cutlass & Malibu

Installation

1. Press tilt wheel lever into place.
2. Ensure tilt lever operates properly.

METRO

Refer to **Fig. 62** for exploded view of this steering column.

SIR COIL, TURN SIGNAL & DIMMER SWITCH

1. Remove inflator module as outlined in "Passive Restraints Systems" chapter.
2. Remove steering wheel as outlined in "Electrical" section of "Metro" chassis chapter.
3. Remove knee bolster, loosen upper steering column mounting bolts and lower column slightly.
4. Remove upper and lower steering column covers, then disconnect coil and combination switch electrical connectors.
5. Loosen switch electrical harness wire bands on lower steering column, then remove coil and combination switch screws.
6. Remove coil and combination switch.
7. Disconnect all wiring connectors from junction block and pull back forward section of driver's side floor carpet.
8. Move aside steering shaft joint cover by hand, then remove steering shaft joint upper pinch bolt and lower column.
9. Disconnect shift interlock cable from ignition switch and remove steering column.
10. Remove ignition switch from steering column.
11. Reverse procedure to install. Tighten mounting bolts and screws to specifications.

STEERING COLUMN LOCK

1. Remove steering wheel as previously described.
2. Remove mounting screw and ignition switch.
3. Remove mounting screws and ignition key warning switch.
4. Loosen and remove steering column lock mounting bolts using suitable center punch, **Fig. 63. Do not damage aluminum parts.**
5. Turn ignition key to On or ACC position and remove lock from steering column.
6. Reverse procedure to install.

PARK AVENUE

Refer to **Fig. 64** for exploded view of steering column.

STEERING COLUMN COVERS

1. Remove inflator module as outlined in "Passive Restraints Systems" chapter.
2. Remove tilt lever and lower column cover mounting screws.
3. Tilt lower column cover downward, slide back cover to disengage from locking tabs and remove column cover protector.
4. Remove mounting screws and upper column cover.
5. Reverse procedure to install. Tighten mounting screws to specifications.

COIL , SHAFT LOCK, TURN SIGNAL CANCEL CAM, UPPER BEARING SPRING, UPPER BEARING INNER RACE SEAT & INNER RACE

1. Remove column covers Do not damage aluminum parts.
2. Remove inflator module as outlined in "Passive Restraints Systems" chapter
3. Remove steering column wiring harness straps and coil retaining ring.
4. Remove coil and wave washer.
5. Remove retaining ring using lock plate compressor tool No. J-23653-SIR, or equivalent, and shaft lock.
6. Remove turn signal cancel cam and upper bearing spring.
7. Remove upper bearing inner race seat and race.
8. Reverse procedure to install.

LINEAR SHIFT, SHIFT LEVER CLEVIS, PARK LOCK CABLE, SHIFT GATE LEVER, BALL & ACTUATOR

1. Remove steering column as previously described.
2. Tilt column to center position and remove lower column cover mounting screws.
3. Remove lower and upper column cover mounting screws.
4. Remove upper column cover and shift lever.
5. Remove shift lever seal and park lock cable from lock module.
6. Pry actuator arm of electrical actuator from outer shift cable ball stud on cable shift cam and mounting pin on jacket.
7. Remove mounting bolt, ball and actuator.
8. Lifting up on shift gate, rotate shift lever clevis and remove clevis from gearshift lever support bracket.

1-NUT, HEXAGON LOCKING (M14x1.5)
2-RING, RETAINING
3-COIL ASM, SIR (2 CONDUCTOR)
3-COIL ASM, SIR (6 CONDUCTOR)
4-WASHER, WAVE
5-RING, RETAINING
6-PLATE, CAM ORIENTATION
7-CAM ASM, T/SIG CANCEL
8-SPRING, UPPER BEARING
9-SEAT, UPPER BEARING INNER RACE
10-RACE, INNER
14-PLATE, SWITCH ADAPTER
15-HOUSING & BEARING ASM, STRG COL
16-STRAP, WIRE HARNESS
17-GUIDE, SPRING
18-SPRING, TILT
25-SHAFT ASM, RACE & UPPER
26-SPHERE, CENTERING
27-SPRING, JOINT PRELOAD
28-SHAFT ASM, LOWER
29-SCREW, TORX HEAD
30-PIN, PIVOT
31-SUPPORT ASM, STRG COL
32-JACKET ASM, STRG COL
33-BEARING ASM, ADAPTER &
34-SEAT, LOWER BEARING
35-SPRING, LOWER BEARING
36-RETAINER, LOWER SPRING
37-RETAINER, SENSOR
38-SEAL, STRG SHAFT

GC604970023900BX

Fig. 36 Exploded view of steering column (Part 2 of 2). Cutlass & Malibu

9. Pry locking ring off of park lock cable and move park lock latch to gain access to lower mounting screw.
10. Remove shift gate mounting screws and park lock cable.
11. Pry transaxle shift cable from inner ball stud on cable shift cam and remove mounting bolt.
12. Remove cam bushing from cable shift cam and mounting screws.
13. Remove gearshift lever support bracket.
14. Reverse procedure to install. Tighten mounting bolts and screws to specifications.

PRIZM

The steering column cannot be serviced, a faulty column can only be replaced.

Refer to **Fig. 65** for exploded view of steering column.

1. Disconnect combination switch electrical connector.
2. Loosen mounting screws and remove combination switch from steering column.
3. Mark ignition switch housing mounting bolt using suitable center punch.
4. Drill into bolts using suitable 0.12–0.16 inch drill bit.
5. Remove mounting bolts using suitable bolt extractor.
6. Remove ignition switch housing.

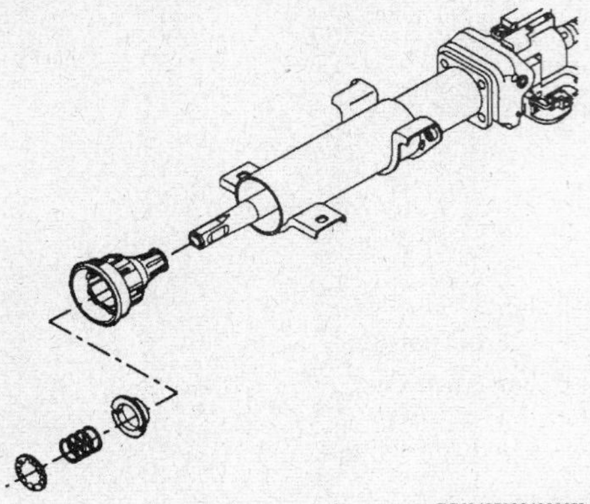

GC6049700240000X

Fig. 37 Steering column shaft. Cutlass & Malibu

7. Remove upper snap ring using suitable snap ring pliers.
8. Remove shaft from steering column tube.
9. Remove snap ring from shaft.
10. Reverse procedure to install. Tighten tapered-head bolts until heads snap off.

TECHNICAL SERVICE BULLETINS

CLUNK FROM FRONT DURING TURNING

1998–2001 Cavalier & Sunfire

On some of these models there may be a clunk from the front of the vehicle during turning. This condition may be felt when turning the vehicle from stop to stop every 180°,

This condition may be caused by inadequate steering intermediate shaft lubrication.

To correct this condition, install revised steering intermediate shaft (part No. 26050292).

STEERING COLUMN SQUEAK

1998–2001 Catera

On some of these models there may be a squeak from the steering column. This condition is most noticeable in cold ambient temperatures.

This condition may be caused by lack of lubricant in the lower bearing cage.

To correct this condition, procedure as follows:

1. Remove steering column.
2. Remove bearing assembly.
3. Clean old lubricant from lower bearing.
4. Restore steering column shaft lower bearing contact surfaced using Scotchbrite pad, or equivalent.
5. Thoroughly lubricate bearing using Dielectric Silicone Grease part No. 12345579, or equivalent.
6. Install lower steering column bearing.
7. Assembly steering column and install it in vehicle.

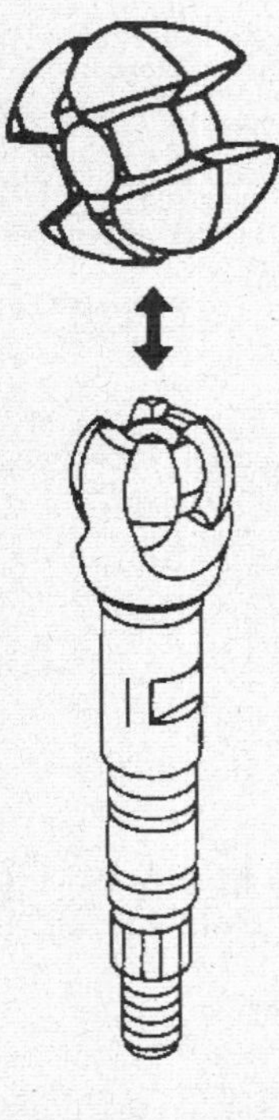

GC6049700241000X

Fig. 38 Lower steering shaft. Cutlass & Malibu

STEERING WHEEL SQUEAKS

1999–2001 Camaro & Firebird

On some of these models built before Feb. 1, 2001, there may be a steering wheel squeak when turning.

This condition may be caused by air bag module mounting tabs contacting the inner steering wheel.

To correct this condition, proceed as follows:

1. Disarm air bag.
2. Remove mounting screws, air bag module and CPA.
3. Disconnect radio controls, as required.
4. Cut two pieces of adhesive flocking tape (part No. 12378189) to 5/8 by 3/4 inch.
5. Clean mounting tabs using suitable dray shop rags.
6. Install tape on each tab, **Fig. 66.**
7. Connect and install air bag module. **Torque** mounting screws to 25 inch lbs.
8. Arm air bag.

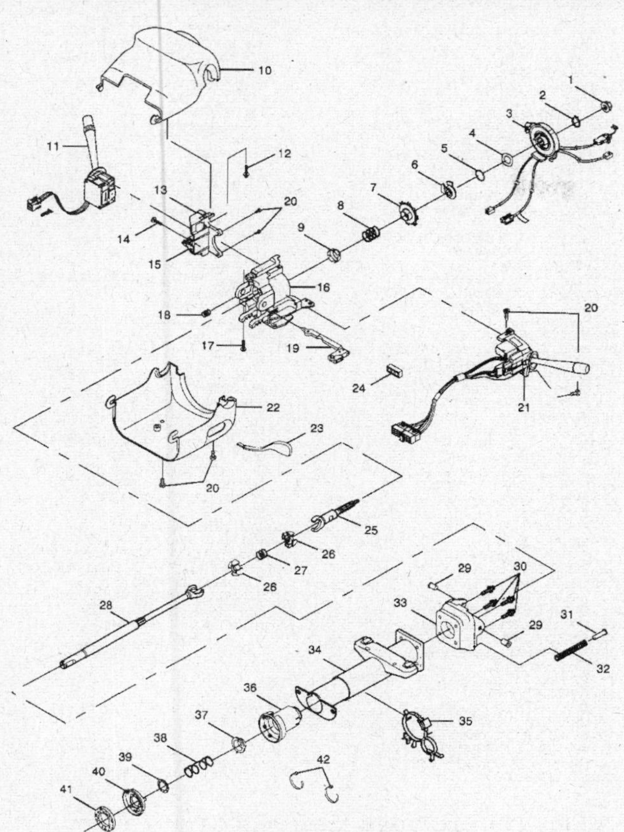

GC604980024600AX

Fig. 39 Exploded view of steering column (Part 1 of 2). Intrigue & Grand Prix w/floor shift

1-NUT, FLANGED PREVAIL TORQUE
2-RING, RETAINING
3-SIR, COIL ASSEMBLY
4-WASHER, WAVE
5-RING, RETAINING
6-SHIELD, SHAFT LOCK
7-CAM, T/S CANCEL
8-SPRING, UPPER BEARING
9-SEAT, UPPER BEARING
10-SHROUD, UPPER
11-SWITCH ASM, PIVOT & PULSE
12-SCREW, TORX HEAD
13-BRACKET, SWITCH MOUNTING
14-SCREW, TORX HEAD
16-TILT HEAD ASM, STRG COLUMN
17-SCREW, TORX HEAD
18-SPRING, TILT LEVER
19-LEVER ASM, SHOE RELEASE
20-SCREW, PAN HEAD TAPPING
21-SWITCH ASM, T/S MULTIFUNCTION
22-SHROUD, LOWER
23-LEVER ASM, TILT
24-SPACER, WIRE HARNESS
25-SHAFT ASM, RACE & UPPER
26-SPHERE, CENTERING
27-SPRING, JOINT PRELOAD
28-SHAFT ASM, LOWER STRG
29-PIN, PIVOT
30-SCREW, TORX HEAD
31-SPRING, GUIDE
32-SPRING, TILT
33-SUPPORT ASM, STRG COLUMN
34-JACKET ASM, STRG COLUMN
35-STRAP, WIRE HARNESS
36-BEARING ASM, ADAPTER &
37-SEAT, LOWER BEARING
38-SPRING, LOWER BEARING
39-RETAINER, LOWER SPRING
40-RETAINER, SENSOR
41-SEAL, STRG SHAFT
42-STRAP, WIRE HARNESS

GC604980024600BX

Fig. 39 Exploded view of steering column (Part 2 of 2). Intrigue & Grand Prix w/floor shift

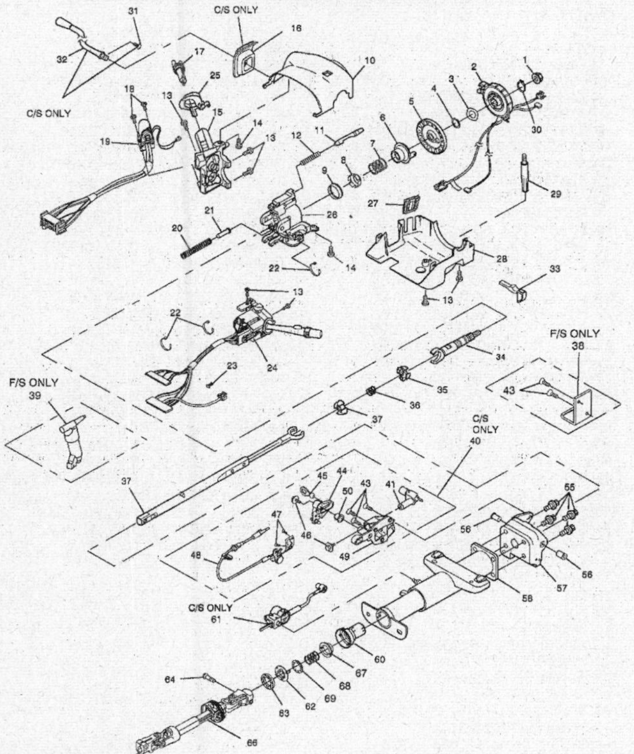

GC604970024500AX

Fig. 40 Exploded view of steering column (Part 1 of 2). Century, Grand Prix & Regal w/column shift

1-NUT, HEXAGON LOCKING (M14x1.5)
2-COIL ASM, SIR
3-WASHER, WAVE
4-RING, RETAINING
5-SHIELD ASM, SHAFT LOCK
6-CAM ASM, T/SIG CANCEL
7-SPRING, UPPER BEARING
8-SEAT, UPPER BEARING INNER RACE
9-RACE, INNER
10-SHROUD, UPPER
11-BOLT ASM, LOCK
12-SPRING, LOCK BOLT
13-SCREW, PAN HD TAPPING
14-SCREW, TORX HEAD
15-ASM, LOCK MODULE
16-SEAL, SHIFT LEVER
17-LOCK CYL SET, STRG COLUMN
18-SCREW, TAPPING
19-SWITCH ASM, IGN & KEY ALARM
20-SPRING, TILT
21-GUIDE, SPRING
22-STRAP, WIRE HARNESS
23-CONNECTOR, AXIAL POSN ASSUR
24-SWITCH ASM, T/S & MULTIFUNCTION
25-RING, TRIM
26- TILT HEAD ASM, STRG COL
27-PROTECTOR, SHROUD
28-SHROUD, LOWER
29-STUD, SHROUD MOUNTING
30-RING, RETAINING
31- SCREW, SHIFT LEVER
32-LEVER ASM, A/TRNS CONTROL
33-LEVER ASM, TILT
34-SHAFT ASM, RACE & UPPER
35-SPHERE, CENTERING
36-SPRING, JOINT PRELOAD
37-SHAFT ASM, LOWER STRG
38-STRAP REINFORCEMENT, STRG
39-ELEC PARK LOCK, STRG COL
40-SHIFT ASM, LINEAR
41-CLEVIS, SHIFT LEVER
43-SCREW, FLAT HD 6-LOBED SOC TAP
44-CAM ASM, CABLE SHIFT
45-ACTUATOR ASM, BALL &
46-BOLT, HEX FLANGE HEAD
47-SCREW, OVAL HD 6-LOBED SOC TAP
48-CABLE ASM, PARK LOCK
49-BRACKET, G/S LEVER ASM SUPPORT
50-BUSHING, CAM
55-SCREW, TORX HEAD
56-PIN, PIVOT
57-SUPPORT ASM, STRG COL
58-JACKET ASM, STRG COL
60-BEARING ASM, ADAPTER &
61-ACTUATOR, ELECTRICAL (BTSI)
62-RETAINER, SENSOR
63-SEAL, STEERING SHAFT
64-BOLT, PINCH
65-SHAFT ASM, INTER STRG
66-SHAFT ASM, INTER STRG
67-SEAT, LOWER BEARING
68-SPRING, LOWER BEARING
69-RETAINER, LOWER SPRING

GC604970024500BX

Fig. 40 Exploded view of steering column (Part 2 of 2). Century, Grand Prix & Regal w/column shift

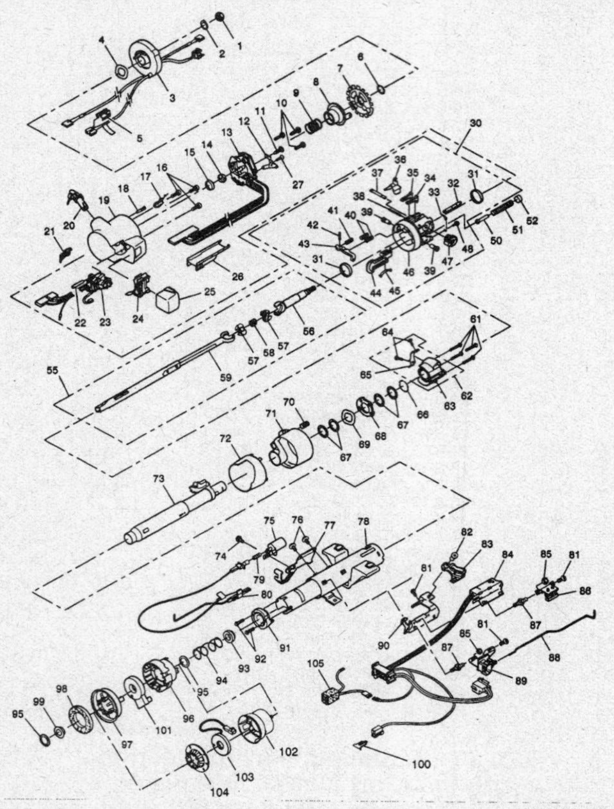

GC604970023500AX

Fig. 41 Exploded view of steering column (Part 1 of 2). DeVille, Eldorado & Seville w/column shift

1 - NUT, HEXAGON LOCKING (M14x1.5)
2 - RING, RETAINING
3 - COIL ASM, SIR
4 - WASHER, WAVE
5 - SHROUD, CONNECTOR
6 - RING, RETAINING
7 - LOCK, SHAFT
8 - CAM ASM, T/SIG CANCEL
9 - SPRING, UPPER BEARING
10 - SCREW, BNDG HD CR RECESS
11 - SCREW, RD WASH HD (M4.2x1.41)
12 - ARM ASM, SIGNAL SWITCH
13 - SWITCH ASM, TURN SIGNAL
14 - SEAT, UPPER BRG INNER RACE
15 - RACE, INNER
16 - SCREW, PAN HD 6 LOBED SOC TAP
17 - SWITCH ASM, BUZZER
18 - SCREW, LOCK RETAINING
19 - COVER ASM, LOCK HOUSING
20 - LOCK CYLINDER SET, STRG COL
21 - ACTUATOR, DIMMER SW ROD
22 - PIN, SWITCH ACTUATOR PIVOT
23 - SWITCH ASM, PIVOT & (PULSE)
24 - BASE PLATE, COL HSG CVR END
25 - CAP, COL HSG COVER END
26 - PROTECTOR, WIRING
27 - SCREW, FLAT HEAD TAPPING
30 - HOUSING ASM, STRG COLUMN
31 - BEARING ASM
32 - BOLT, LOCK
33 - SPRING, LOCK BOLT
34 - SHOE, STEERING WHEEL LOCK
35 - SHOE, STEERING WHEEL LOCK
36 - SHIELD, WIRE PROTECTOR
37 - SHAFT, DRIVE
38 - PIN, DOWEL
39 - PIN, PIVOT
40 - SPRING, SHOE
41 - SPRING, RELEASE LEVER
42 - PIN, RELEASE LEVER
43 - LEVER, SHOE RELEASE
44 - RACK, SWITCH ACTUATOR
45 - SPRING, RACK PRELOAD
46 - HOUSING, STRG COLUMN
47 - SECTOR, SWITCH ACTUATOR
48 - SCREW, HEX WASHER HEAD
50 - GUIDE, SPRING
51 - SPRING, WHEEL TILT
52 - RETAINER, SPRING
55 - SHAFT ASM, STEERING
56 - SHAFT ASM, RACE & UPPER
57 - SPHERE, CENTERING
58 - SPRING, JOINT PRELOAD
59 - SHAFT ASM, LOWER STEERING
61 - SCREW, SUPPORT
62 - SUPPORT ASM, STRG COL HSG
63 - SUPPORT, STRG COL HSG
64 - SCREW, OVL HD CROSS RECESS
65 - GATE, SHIFT LEVER
66 - RING, SHIFT TUBE RETAINING
67 - WASHER, THRUST
68 - PLATE, LOCK
69 - WASHER, WAVE
70 - SPRING, SHIFT LEVER
71 - BOWL ASM, GEARSHIFT LEVER
72 - SHROUD, GEARSHIFT BOWL
73 - TUBE ASM, SHIFT
74 - SCREW, HEX WASH HD (#10-24X.25)
75 - SOLENOID ASM, INTERLOCK
76 - SCREW, WASH HD (#10-24X.25)
77 - BRACKET, SOLENOID
78 - JACKET ASM, STRG COL
79 - SPRING, BALL JOINT
80 - ACTUATOR ASM, IGNITION SWITCH
81 - SCREW, TORX WASHER HEAD
82 - RETAINER, CAM
83 - CAM ASM, CABLE SHIFT
84 - SWITCH ASM, IGNITION
85 - NUT, HEXAGON (#10-24)
86 - ADJUSTER ASM, PRNDL
87 - STUD, DIMR SW MTG
88 - ROD, DIMMER SWITCH
89 - SWITCH ASM, DIMMER
90 - BRACKET ASM, STUD &
91 - BEARING ASM, ADAPTER &
92 - SCREW, HEX WASHER HD TAP
93 - SEAT, LOWER BEARING
94 - SPRING, LOWER BEARING
95 - RETAINER, LOWER SPRING
96 - ADAPTER, STRG SENSOR
97 - RETAINER, SENSOR
98 - SEAL, STEERING SHAFT
99 - BUSHING, SEAL RETAINING
100 - CONNECTOR, AXIAL POSN ASSURANCE
101 - SENSOR ASM, HI RES STRG WHL POSN
102 - RETAINER, BEARING
103 - SENSOR ASM, STRG WHL POSN
104 - DAMPENER ASM, ROTATIONAL
105 - HARNESS ASM, JUMPER

GC604970023500BX

Fig. 41 Exploded view of steering column (Part 2 of 2). DeVille, Eldorado & Seville w/column shift

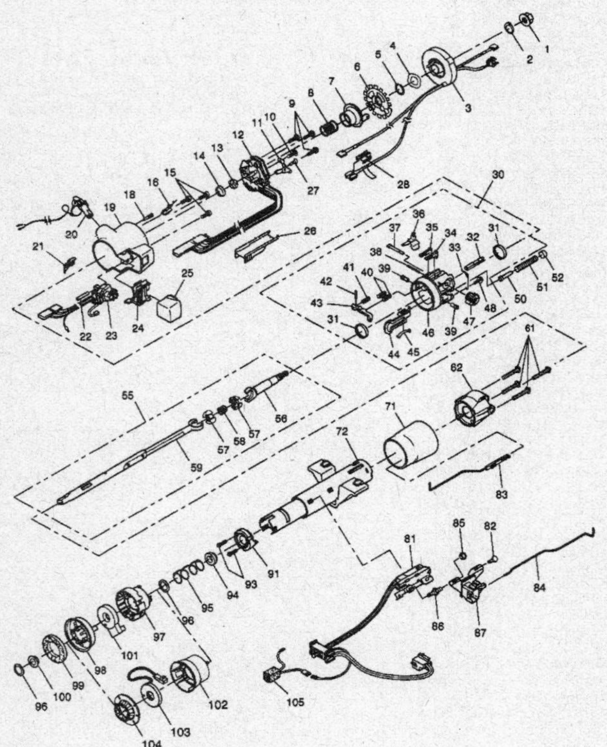

GC604970023600AX

Fig. 42 Exploded view of steering column (Part 1 of 2). DeVille, Eldorado & Seville w/console shift

1- NUT, HEX LOCKING (M14x1.5)
2- RING, RETAINING
3- COIL ASM, SIR
4- WASHER, WAVE
5- RING, RETAINING
6- LOCK, SHAFT
7- CAM ASM, T/SIG CANCEL
8- SPRING, UPPER BEARING
9- SCREW, BNDG HD CR RECESS
10- SCREW, RD WASH HD (M4.2x1.41)
11- ARM ASM, SIGNAL SWITCH
12- SWITCH ASM, TURN SIGNAL
13- SEAT, UPPER BRG INNER RACE
14- RACE, INNER
15- SCREW, PAN HD 6 LOBED SOC TAP
16- SWITCH ASM, BUZZER
18- SCREW, LOCK RETAINING
19- COVER ASM, LOCK HOUSING
20- LOCK CYLINDER SET, STRG COL PASS KEY
21- ACTUATOR, DIMMER SWITCH ROD
22- PIN, SWITCH ACTUATOR PIVOT
23- SWITCH ASM, PIVOT & (PULSE)
24- BASE PLATE, COL HSG CVR END
25- CAP, COL HSG COVER END
26- PROTECTOR, WIRING
27- SCREW, FLT HD TAPPING
28- SHROUD, CONNECTOR
30- HOUSING ASM, STRG COLUMN
31- BEARING ASM
32- BOLT, LOCK
33- SPRING, LOCK BOLT
34- SHOE, STEERING WHEEL LOCK
35- SHOE, STEERING WHEEL LOCK
36- SHIELD, WIRE PROTECTOR
37- SHAFT, DRIVE
38- PIN, DOWEL
39- PIN, PIVOT
40- SPRING, SHOE
41- SPRING, RELEASE LEVER
42- PIN, RELEASE LEVER
43- LEVER, SHOE RELEASE
44- RACK, SWITCH ACTUATOR
45- SPRING, RACK PRELOAD
46- HOUSING, STRG COLUMN
47- SECTOR, SWITCH ACTUATOR
48- SCREW, HEX WASHER HEAD
50- GUIDE, SPRING
51- SPRING, WHEEL TILT
52- RETAINER, SPRING
55- SHAFT ASM, STEERING
56- SHAFT ASM, RACE & UPPER
57- SPHERE, CENTERING
58- SPRING, JOINT PRELOAD
59- SHAFT ASM, LOWER STEERING
61- SCREW, HEX WASHER HD TAPPING
62- SUPPORT ASM, STRG COL HSG
71- SHROUD, STRG COLUMN HSG
72- JACKET ASM, STRG COL
81- SWITCH ASM, COL LOCK & IGN
82- SCREW, WASH HD (#10-24X.25)
83- ACTUATOR ASM, IGNITION SWITCH
84- ROD, DIMMER SWITCH
85- NUT, HEXAGON (#10-24)
86- STUD, DIMR & IGN SW MTG
87- SWITCH ASM, DIMMER
91- BEARING ASM, ADAPTER &
93- SCREW, HEX WASHER HD TAP
94- SEAT, LOWER BEARING
95- SPRING, LOWER BEARING
96- RETAINER, LOWER SPRING
97- ADAPTER, STRG SENSOR
98- RETAINER, SENSOR
99- SEAL, STEERING SHAFT
100- BUSHING, SEAL RETAINING
101- SENSOR ASM, HI RES STRG WHL POSN
102- RETAINER, BEARING
103- SENSOR ASM, STRG WHL POSN
104- DAMPENER ASM, ROTATIONAL
105- HARNESS ASM, JUMPER

GC604970023600BX

Fig. 42 Exploded view of steering column (Part 2 of 2). DeVille, Eldorado & Seville w/console shift

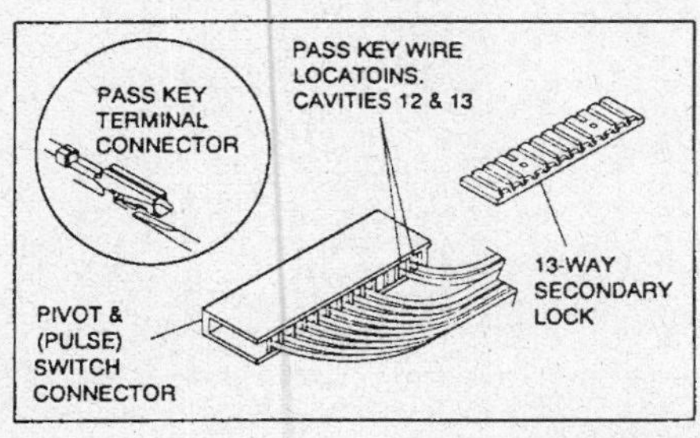

Fig. 43 Pass key wire connection locations. DeVille, Eldorado & Seville

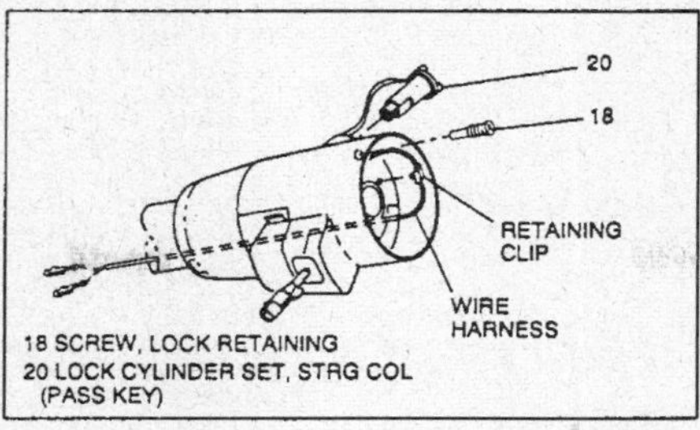

Fig. 44 Pass key wire installation. DeVille, Eldorado & Seville

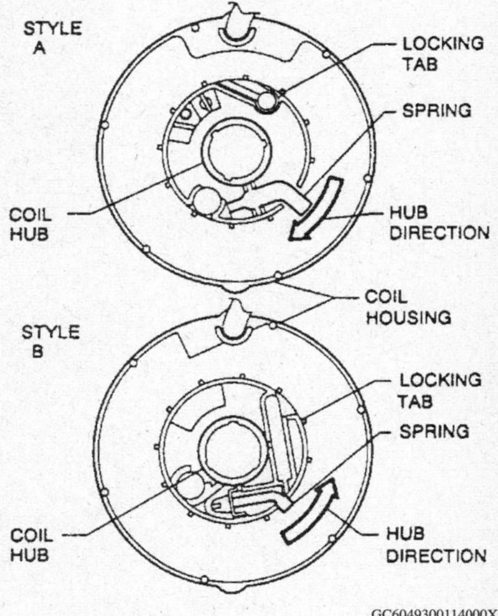

Fig. 45 Coil centering. DeVille, Eldorado & Seville

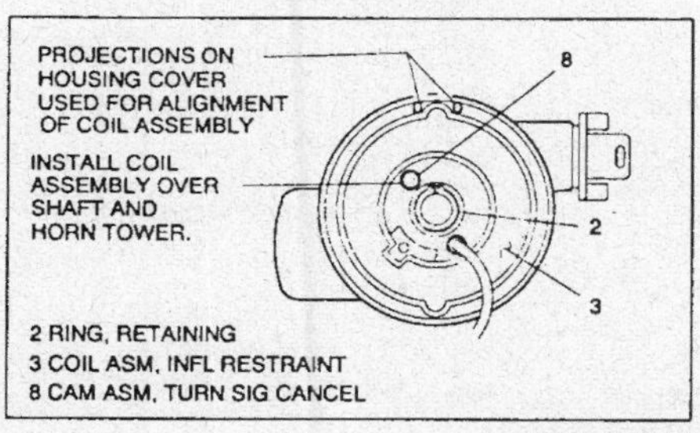

Fig. 46 Coil installation. DeVille, Eldorado & Seville

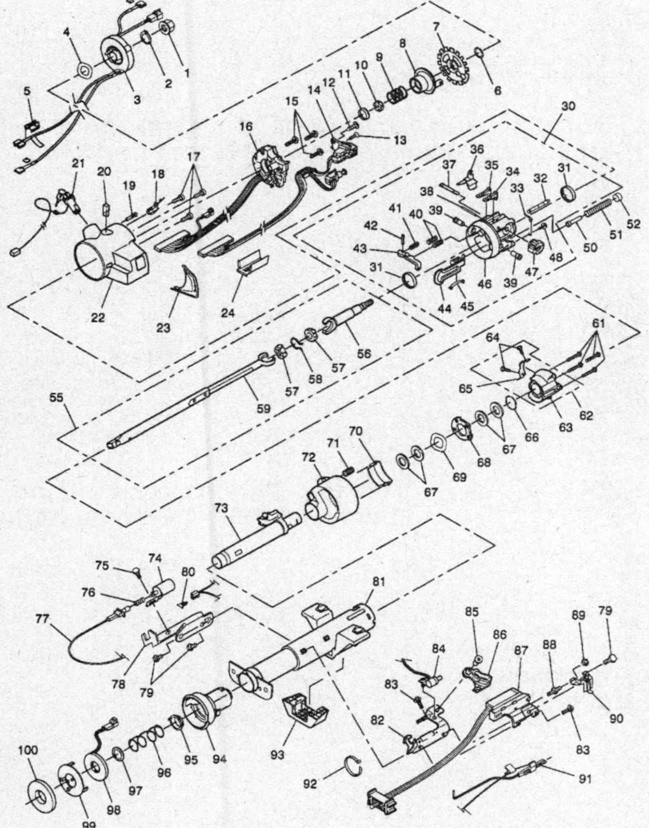

Fig. 47 Exploded view of tilt steering column (Part 1 of 2). Lumina w/column shift

1-NUT, HEXAGON LOCKING (M14x1.5)
2-RING, RETAINING
3-COIL ASM, SIR
4-WASHER, WAVE
5-SHROUD, CONNECTOR
6-RING, RETAINING
7-LOCK, SHAFT
8-CAM ASM, T/SIG CANCEL
9-SPRING, UPPER BEARING
10-SEAT, UPPER BRG INNER RACE
11-RACE, INNER
12-SCREW, RD WASH HD (M4.2X1.41)
13-SCREW, FLAT HEAD
14-SW ASM, PIVOT & (PULSE-DIMMER)
15-SCREW, BNDG HD CR RECESS
16-SWITCH ASM, TURN SIGNAL
17-SCREW, PAN HD 6-LOBED SOC TAP
18-SWITCH ASM, BUZZER
19-SCREW, LOCK RETAINING
20-KNOB, HAZARD WARNING SW
21-LOCK CYLINDER SET, STRG COL
22-COVER & SLEEVE ASM, LOCK HSG
23-CAP, HSG COVER END
24-PROTECTOR, WIRING
30-HOUSING ASM, STRG COLUMN
31-BEARING ASM
32-BOLT ASM, SHAFT LOCK
33-SPRING, LOCK BOLT
34-SHOE, STEERING WHEEL LOCK
35-SHOE, STEERING WHEEL LOCK
36-SHIELD, PROTECTOR WIRE
37-SHAFT, DRIVE
38-PIN, DOWEL
39-PIN, PIVOT
40-SPRING, SHOE
41-SPRING, RELEASE LEVER
42-PIN, RELEASE LEVER
43-LEVER ASM, SHOE RELEASE
44-RACK, SWITCH ACTUATOR
45-SPRING, RACK PRELOAD
46-HOUSING, STRG COLUMN
47-SECTOR, SWITCH ACTUATOR
48-SCREW, HEX WASHER HEAD
50-GUIDE, SPRING
51-SPRING, WHEEL TILT
52-RETAINER, SPRING
55-SHAFT ASM, STEERING
56-SHAFT ASM, RACE & UPPER
57-SPHERE, CENTERING
58-SPRING, JOINT PRELOAD
59-SHAFT ASM, LOWER STEERING
61-SCREW, SUPPORT
62-SUPPORT ASM, STRG COL HSG
63-SUPPORT, STRG COL HSG
64-SCREW, OVL HD CROSS RECESS
65-GATE, SHIFT LEVER
66-RING, SHIFT TUBE RETAINING
67-WASHER, THRUST
68-PLATE, LOCK
69-WASHER, WAVE
70-PROTECTOR, SHIFT BOWL
71-SPRING, SHIFT LEVER
72-BOWL ASM, GEARSHIFT LEVER
73-TUBE ASM, SHIFT
74-SOLENOID ASM, INTERLOCK
75-SCREW, HEX WASHER HEAD
76-SPRING, BALL JOINT
77-CABLE ASM, BTSI
78-BRACKET, SOLENOID ADAPTER
79-SCREW, HEX WASH HD (#10-24X0.25)
80-CONNECTOR, AXIAL POSN ASSUR
81-JACKET ASM, STRG COL
82-BRACKET ASM, STUD &
83-SCREW, TORX WASHER HEAD
84-SWITCH ASM, PARK POSITION
85-RETAINER, CAM
86-CAM ASM, CABLE SHIFT
87-SWITCH ASM, IGNITION
88-STUD, DIMR SW MOUNTING
89-NUT, HEXAGON (#10-24)
90-ADJUSTER ASM, PRNDL
91-ACTUATOR ASM, IGNITION SWITCH
92-STRAP, WIRE HARNESS
93-CAPSULE,STRG COL SUPPORT
94-BEARING ASM, ADAPTER &
95-SEAT, LOWER BEARING
96-SPRING, LOWER BEARING
97-RETAINER, LOWER SPRING
98-SENSOR ASM, STRG WHL SPD
99-RETAINER, SENSOR
100-SEAL, STEERING SHAFT

Service Kits

201-RACK SERV KIT, COL SECTOR &
-INCLUDES: 11,31,33,44,47,48
202-SPRING SERV KIT, TILT COLUMN
-INCLUDES: 10,11,39,50,51,52
203-COIL ASM SERV KIT, SIR
-INCLUDES: 3,4,5
204-SPHERE SERV KIT, TILT COLUMN
-INCLUDES: 57,58
205-GREASE SERV KIT, (SYNTHETIC)

GC604940016900BX

Fig. 47 Exploded view of tilt steering column (Part 2 of 2). Lumina w/column shift

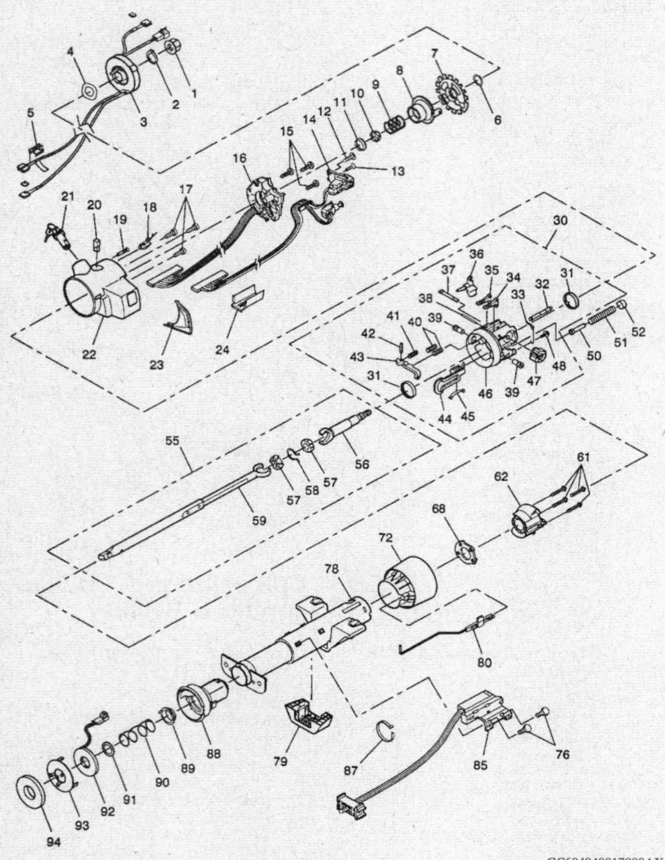

GC604940017000AX

Fig. 48 Exploded view of tilt steering column (Part 1 of 2). Lumina & 1998–99 Monte Carlo w/floor shift

1-NUT, HEXAGON LOCKING (M14x1.5)
2-RING, RETAINING
3-COIL ASM, SIR
4-WASHER, WAVE
5-SHROUD, CONNECTOR
6-RING, RETAINING
7-LOCK, SHAFT
8-CAM ASM, T/SIG CANCEL
9-SPRING, UPPER BEARING
10-SEAT, UPPER BRG INNER RACE
11-RACE, INNER
12-SCREW, RD WASH HD (M4.2X1.41)
13-SCREW, FLAT HEAD
14-SW ASM, PIVOT & (PULSE-DIMMER)
15-SCREW, BNDG HD CR RECESS
16-SWITCH ASM, TURN SIGNAL
17-SCREW, PAN HD 6-LOBED SOC TAP
18-SWITCH ASM, BUZZER
19-SCREW, LOCK RETAINING
20-KNOB, HAZARD WARNING SW
21-LOCK CYLINDER SET, STRG COL
22-COVER & SLEEVE ASM, LOCK HSG
23-CAP, HSG COVER END
24-PROTECTOR, WIRING
30-HOUSING ASM, STRG COLUMN
31-BEARING ASM
32-BOLT ASM, SHAFT LOCK
33-SPRING, LOCK BOLT
34-SHOE, STEERING WHEEL LOCK
35-SHOE, STEERING WHEEL LOCK
36-SHIELD, PROTECTOR WIRE
37-SHAFT, DRIVE
38-PIN, DOWEL
39-PIN, PIVOT
40-SPRING, SHOE
41-SPRING, RELEASE LEVER
42-PIN, RELEASE LEVER
43-LEVER ASM, SHOE RELEASE
44-RACK, SWITCH ACTUATOR
45-SPRING, RACK PRELOAD
46-HOUSING, STRG COLUMN
47-SECTOR, SWITCH ACTUATOR
48-SCREW, HEX WASHER HEAD
50-GUIDE, SPRING
51-SPRING, TILT
52-RETAINER, SPRING
55-SHAFT ASM, STEERING
56-SHAFT ASM, RACE & UPPER
57-SPHERE, CENTERING
58-SPRING, JOINT PRELOAD
59-SHAFT ASM, LOWER STEERING
61-SCREW, SUPPORT
62-SUPPORT ASM, STRG COL HSG
68-PLATE, LOCK
72-SHROUD, STRG COL
76-SCREW, WASH HD (#10-24X0.25)
78-JACKET ASM, STRG COL
79-CAPSULE, STRG COL SUPPORT
80-ACTUATOR ASM, IGNITION SWITCH
85-SWITCH ASM, COLUMN LOCK & IGN
87-STRAP, WIRE HARNESS
88-BEARING ASM, ADAPTER &
89-SEAT, LOWER BEARING
90-SPRING, LOWER BEARING
91-RETAINER, LOWER SPRING
92-SENSOR ASM, STRG WHL SPD
93-RETAINER, SENSOR
94-SEAL,STEERING SHAFT

Service Kits

201-RACK SERV KIT, COL SECTOR &
-INCLUDES: 11,31,33,44,47,48
202-SPRING SERV KIT, TILT COLUMN
-INCLUDES: 10,11,39,50,51,52
203-COIL SERV KIT, INFL RESTRAINT
-INCLUDES: 3,4,5
204-SPHERE SERV KIT, TILT COLUMN
-INCLUDES: 57,58
205-GREASE SERV KIT, (SYNTHETIC)

GC604940017000BX

Fig. 48 Exploded view of tilt steering column (Part 2 of 2). Lumina & 1998–99 Monte Carlo w/floor shift

12
13
14
TOP WING
WIRE HARNESS CLAMP
22
PRY
BOTTOM WING

12 SCREW, RD WASH HD (M4.2X1.41)
13 SCREW, FLAT HEAD
14 SW ASM, PIVOT & (PULSE-DIMMER)
22 COVER & SLEEVE ASM, LOCK HSG

GC6049700239000X

Fig. 49 Pivot & pulse dimmer switch removal. Lumina & 1998–99 Monte Carlo

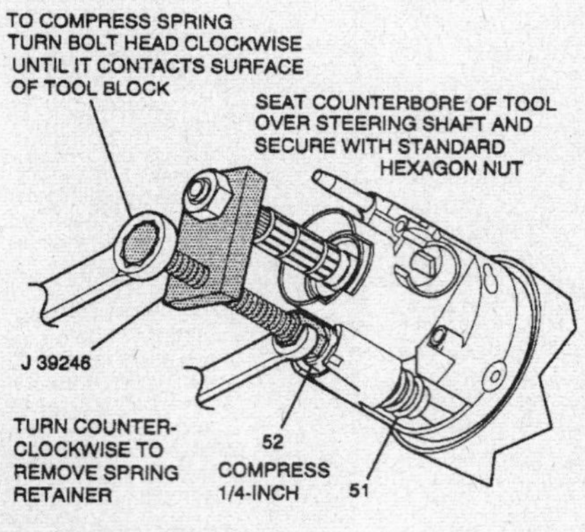

51 SPRING, WHEEL TILT
52 RETAINER, SPRING

GC6049700247000X

Fig. 50 Tilt spring removal. Lumina & 1998–99 Monte Carlo

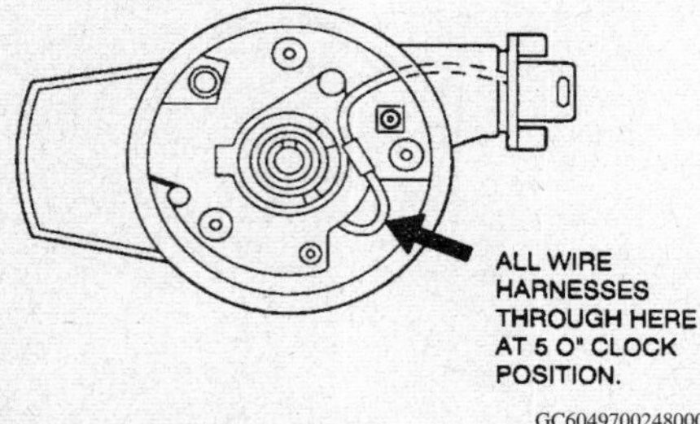

GC6049700248000X

Fig. 51 Wire harness routing. Lumina & 1998–99 Monte Carlo

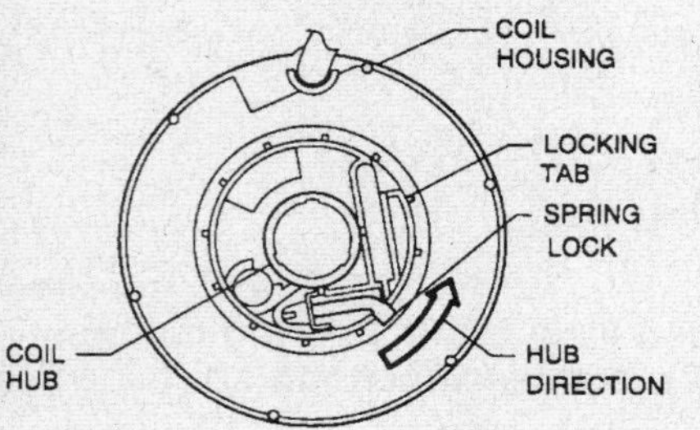

GC6049700249000X

Fig. 52 Centering SIR coil. Lumina & 1998–99 Monte Carlo

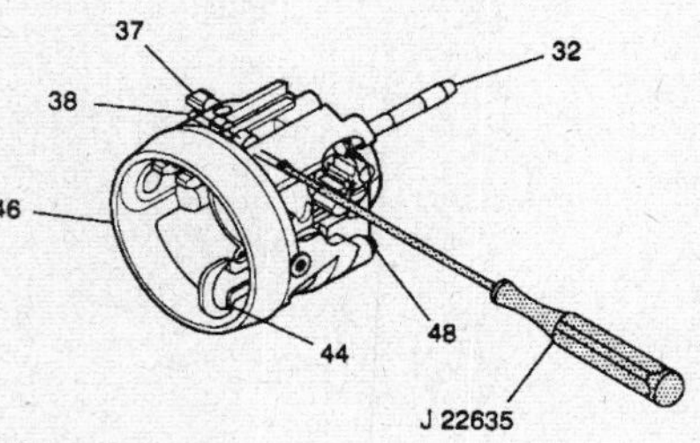

32 BOLT ASM, SHAFT LOCK
37 SHAFT, DRIVE
38 PIN, DOWEL
44 RACK, SWITCH ACTUATOR
46 HOUSING, STRG COLUMN
48 SCREW, HEX WASHER HEAD

GC6049700251000X

Fig. 53 Steering column housing. Lumina & 1998–99 Monte Carlo

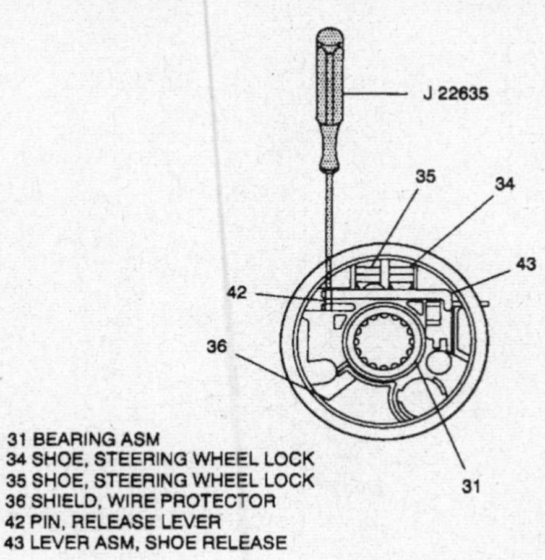

Fig. 54 Lock housing cover components. Lumina & 1998–99 Monte Carlo

59
57
58
57
ALIGNMENT MARK
TILT 90° AND SEPARATE
ALIGNMENT MARK
ROTATE SPHERE 90° AND LIFT
56

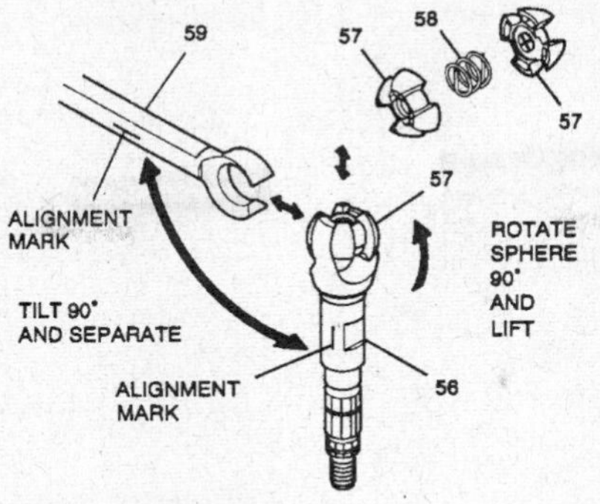

56 SHAFT ASM, RACE & UPPER
57 SPHERE, CENTERING
58 SPRING, JOINT PRELOAD
59 SHAFT ASM, LOWER STEERING

GC6049700245000X

Fig. 55 Steering shaft components. Lumina & 1998–99 Monte Carlo

GREASE APPLICATION AREAS

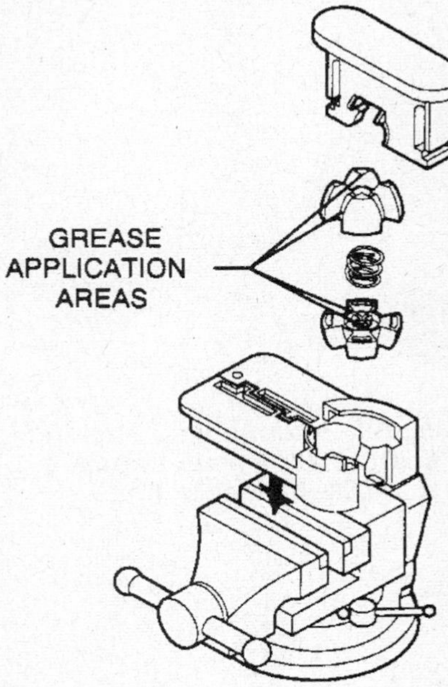

GC6049700246000X

Fig. 56 Centering sphere installation tool. Lumina & 1998–99 Monte Carlo

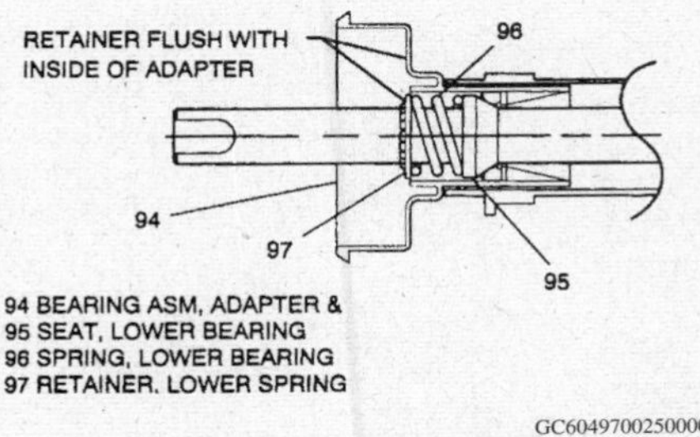

Fig. 57 Spring height measurement. Lumina & 1998–99 Monte Carlo

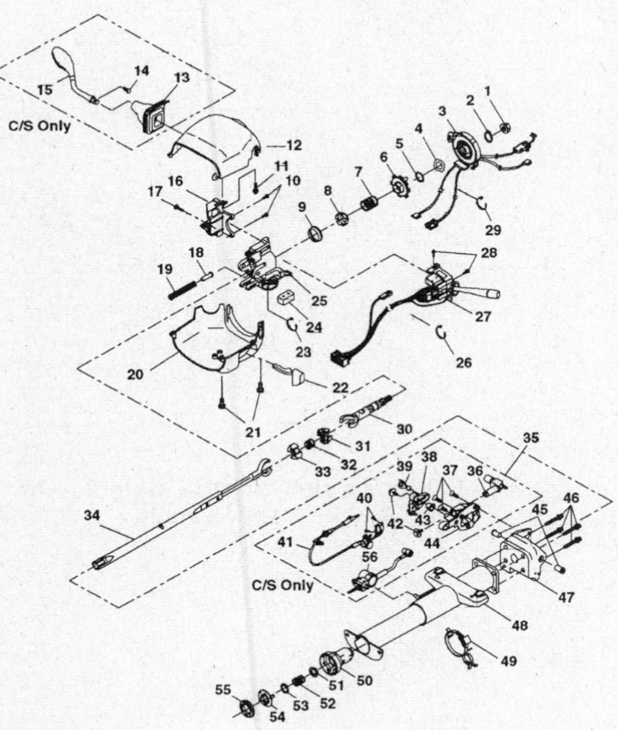

Fig. 58 Exploded view of steering column (Part 1 of 2). Impala & 2000–02 Monte Carlo

1. Hexagon Nut
2. Retaining Ring
3. SIR Coil Assembly
4. Wave Washer
5. Bearing Retainer
6. Turn Signal Cancel Cam Assembly
7. Upper Bearing Spring
8. Upper Bearing Inner Race Seat
9. Inner Race
10. Flat Head Screw
11. Pan Head Tapping Screw
12. Upper Shroud
13. Shift Lever Seal
14. Shift Lever Screw
15. Automatic Transmission Control Lever Assembly
16. Switch Mounting Bracket
17. Flat Head Screw
18. Spring Guide
19. Tilt Spring
20. Lower Shroud
21. TORX® Head Screw
22. Tilt Lever Assembly
23. Wire Harness Strap
24. Spacer
25. Steering Column Tilt Head
26. Wire Harness Strap
27. Turn Signal And Multifunction Switch Assembly
28. Pan Head Tapping Screw
29. Wire Harness Strap
30. Race And Upper Shaft Assembly
31. Centering Sphere
32. Joint Preload Spring
33. Centering Sphere
34. Lower Steering Shaft Assembly
35. Linear Shift Assembly
36. Shift Lever Clevis
37. Flat Head 6-Lobed Socket Tapping Screw
38. Cable Shift Cam Assembly
39. Ball and Actuator
40. Oval Head 6-Lobed Socket Tapping Screw
41. Park Lock Cable Assembly
42. Hex Flange Head Bolt
43. Cam Bushing
44. Gear Shift Lever Assembly Support Bracket
45. Pivot Pin
46. TORX® Head Screw
47. Steering Column Support Assembly
48. Steering Column Jacket Assembly
49. Wire Harness Strap
50. Adapter and Bearing Assembly
51. Lower Bearing Seat
52. Lower Bearing Spring
53. Lower Spring Retainer
54. Sensor Retainer
55. Steering Shaft Seal
56. Electrical (BTSI) Actuator

GC6040000291020X

Fig. 58 Exploded view of steering column (Part 2 of 2). Impala & 2000–02 Monte Carlo

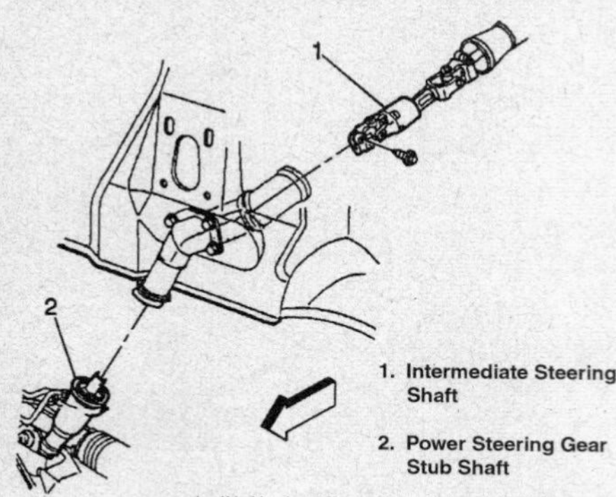

Fig. 59 Intermediate steering shaft replacement. Impala & 2000–02 Monte Carlo

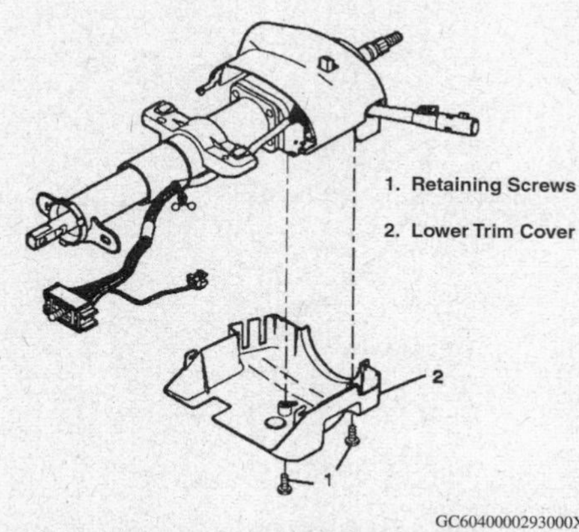

Fig. 60 Steering column trim cover replacement (Lower). Impala & 2000–02 Monte Carlo

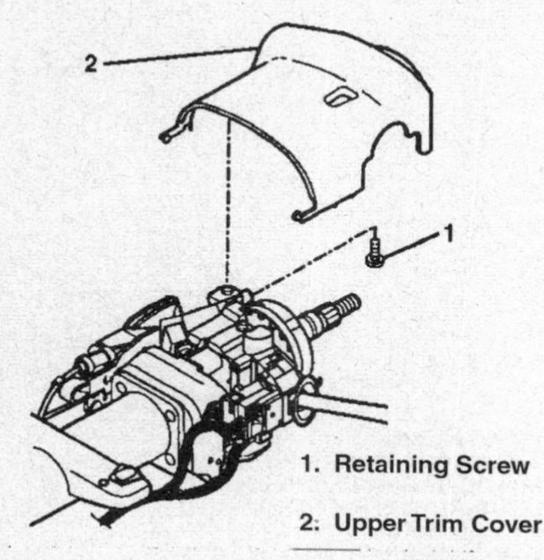

Fig. 61 Steering column trim cover replacement (Upper). Impala & 2000–02 Monte Carlo

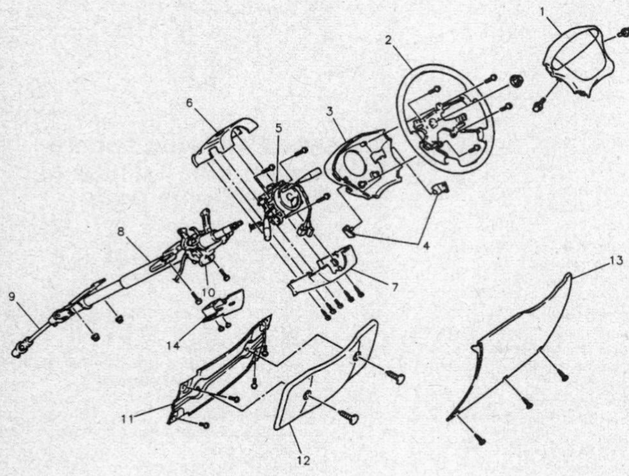

Fig. 62 Exploded view of steering column. Metro

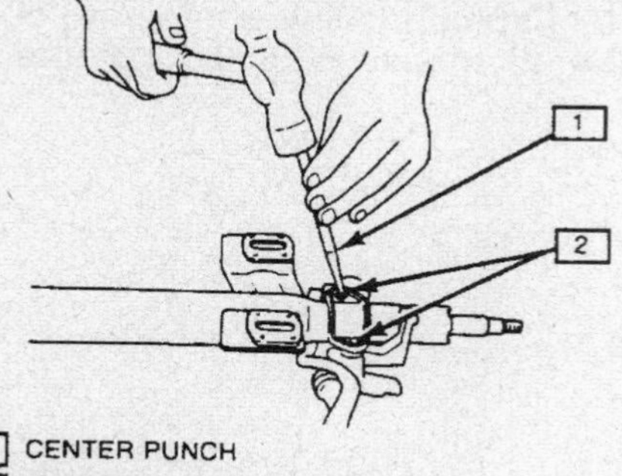

Fig. 63 Steering column lock bolts removal. Metro

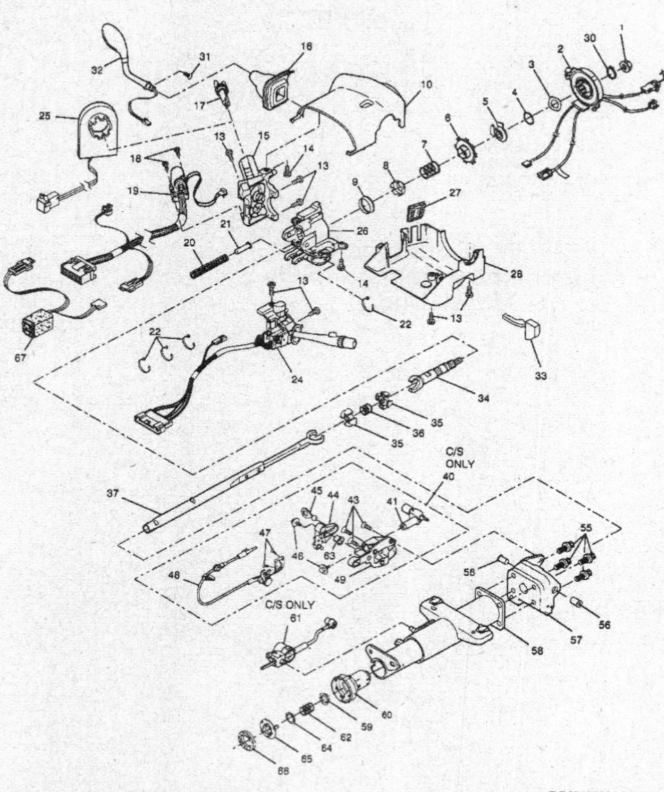

Fig. 64 Exploded view of steering column (Part 1 of 2). Park Avenue

1-NUT,FLANGED PREVAIL TORQUE
2-COIL ASM, SIR
3-WASHER, WAVE
4-RING, RETAINER
5-SHIELD ASM, SHAFT LOCK
6-CAM ASM, T/SIG CANCEL
7-SPRING, UPPER BEARING
8-SEAT, UPPER BEARING INNER RACE
9-RACE, INNER
10-SHROUD, UPPER
11-BOLT ASM, LOCK
12-SPRING, LOCK BOLT
13-SCREW, PAN HD TAPPING
14-SCREW, TORX HEAD
15-ASM, LOCK MODULE
16-SEAL, SHIFT LEVER
17-LOCK CYL SET, STRG COLUMN
18-SCREW, TAPPING
19-SWITCH ASM, IGN & KEY ALARM
20-SPRING, TILT
21-GUIDE, SPRING
22-STRAP, WIRE HARNESS
24-SWITCH ASM, T/S & MULTIFUNCTION
25-CONTROL CODED KEY
26-TILT HEAD ASM, STRG COL
27-PROTECTOR, SHROUD
28-SHROUD, LOWER
29-STUD, SHROUD MOUNTING
30-RING, RETAINING
31-SCREW, SHIFT LEVER
32-LEVER ASM, A/TRNS CONTROL
33-LEVER ASM, TILT
34-SHAFT ASM, RACE & UPPER
35-SPHERE, CENTERING
36-SPRING, JOINT PRELOAD
37-SHAFT ASM, LOWER STRG
40-SHIFT ASM, LINEAR
41-CLEVIS, SHIFT LEVER
43-SCREW, FLAT HD 6-LOBED SOC TAP
44-CAM ASM, CABLE SHIFT
45-ACTUATOR ASM, BALL &
46-BOLT, HEX FLANGE HEAD
47-SCREW, OVAL HD 6-LOBED SOC TAP
48-CABLE ASM, PARK LOCK
49-BRACKET, G/S LEVER ASM SUPPORT
55-SCREW, TORX HEAD
56-PIN, PIVOT
57-SUPPORT ASM, STRG COL
58-JACKET ASM, STRG COL
59-SEAT, LOWER BEARING
60-BEARING ASM, ADAPTER &
61-ACTUATOR, ELECTRICAL (BTSI)
62-SPRING, LOWER BEARING
63-BUSHING, CAM
64-RETAINER, LOWER SPRING
65-RETAINER, SENSOR
66-SEAL, STEERING SHAFT
67-HARNESS ASM, JUMPER

GC604970023800BX

Fig. 64 Exploded view of steering column (Part 2 of 2). Park Avenue

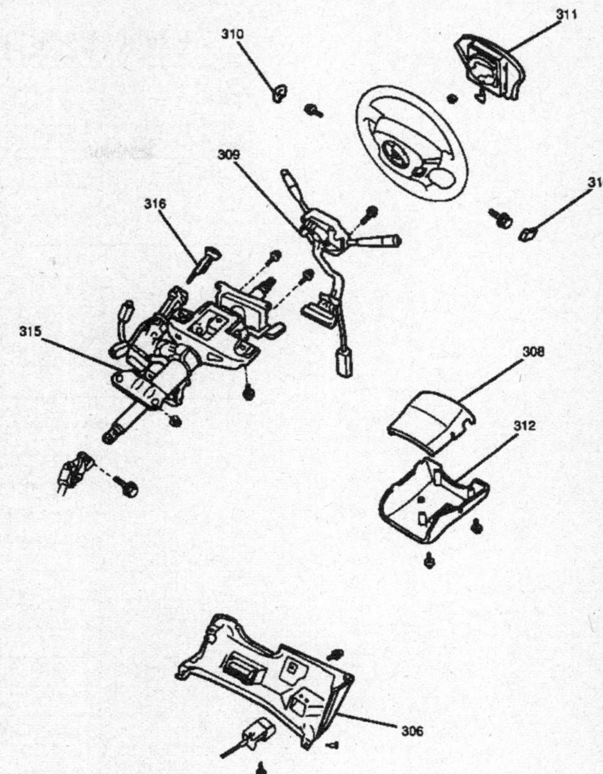

306 KNEE BOLSTER
308 UPPER STEERING COLUMN COVER
309 COMBINATION SWITCH
310 SIDE TRIM COVERS
311 INFLATOR MODULE
312 LOWER STEERING COLUMN COVER
315 STEERING COLUMN ASSEMBLY
316 IGNITION SWITCH

GC6049700237000X

Fig. 65 Exploded view of steering column. Prizm

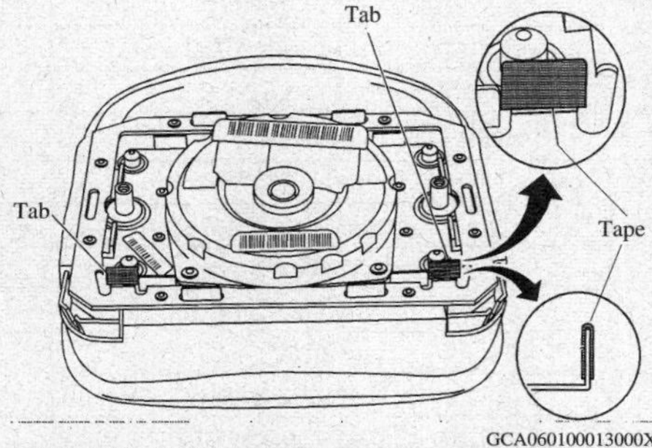

Fig. 66 Flocking tape installation. 1998-2001 Cavalier & Sunfire

TIGHTENING SPECIFICATIONS

Year	Component	Torque/Ft. Lbs.
ACHIEVA & SKYLARK		
1998	Interlock Solenoid	21①
	Pinch Bolt	30
	Mounting	20
ALERO		
1999–2000	Column Bracket Support	19
	Intermediate Shaft Pinch Bolt	16
	Steering Wheel.	30
AURORA		
1998–99	Column Cover, Pan Head	30①
	Column Cover, Tapping	②
	Interlock Solenoid	15①
	Park Lock Cable	84①
	Pinch Bolt	35
	Support	20
	Wiring Harness Connector	72①
2001–02	Cable Support	89①
	Lower Cover	31①
	Upper Cover	13①
	Intermediate Shaft Pinch Bolt	35
	Intermediate Shaft Seal	21①
	Steering Wheel	30
	Support	20
	Switch Bracket	62①
	Wiring Harness Connector	71①
BONNEVILLE & LESABRE		
1998–2000	Dimmer Switch	35①
	Lock Housing Cover	96①
	Lower Support Brace	84①
	Pass Key Lock Cylinder	22①
	Support Bracket	20
	Turn Signal Switch	30①
	Turn Signal Switch Arm	20①
	Wiring Harness Connector	42①
CAMARO & FIREBIRD		
1998–2000	Dimmer Switch	35①
	Electrical Connectors	14
	Lock Housing Cover	96①
	Pass Key Lock Cylinder	22①
	Support	18
	Turn Signal Switch	30①
	Turn Signal Switch Arm	20①
CATERA		
1998–2000	Connector	16
	Pass Key Lock Cylinder	22①
	Signal Switch Housing	35①
	Support Bracket, Rear	16
	Support Shear Bolt, Forward	15
	Support Strap, Forward	16

Continued

TIGHTENING SPECIFICATIONS—Continued

Year	Component	Torque/Ft. Lbs.
CAVALIER & SUNFIRE		
1998–2000	Cover	47①
	Cross Recess Screws	17①
	Dimmer Switch	35①
	Ignition Switch	35①
	Lock Bolt	35①
	Lock Cylinder Set	40①
	Lock Housing	80①
	Pinch Bolt	30
	Support	22
	Switch Actuator Pivot Pin	27①
	Turn Signal Switch	30①
	Signal Switch Arm	20①
CENTURY, GRAND PRIX & REGAL		
1998–2000	Column Cover, Lower	30①
	Column Cover, Upper	12①
	Mounting	18
	Park Lock Cable	58①
	Pinch Bolt	35
	Turn Signal Cam, Screws	84①
	Turn Signal Cam, Bolt	13
CORVETTE		
1998–2000	Bracket	17
	Dimmer Switch	35①
	Lock Housing Cover	96①
	Pass Key Lock Cylinder	22①
	Pinch Bolt	35
	Support Plate	17
	Turn Signal Switch	30①
	Turn Signal Switch Arm	20①
CUTLASS		
1998–99	Intermediate Shaft Pinch Bolt	16
	Steering Wheel	35
	Support Bracket	18
DEVILLE, ELDORADO & SEVILLE		
1998–2000	Cable Shift Cam	35①
	Gate	33①
	Interlock Solenoid Bracket	35①
	Lock	22①
	Lower Bracket	12
	Lock Housing	80①
	Pinch Bolt	35
	Support	20
	Turn Signal Switch	30①
	Turn Signal Switch Arm	20①
GRAND AM		
1998	Interlock Solenoid	21①
	Pinch Bolt	30
	Mounting Bolts	20
1999–2000	Column Bracket Support	19
	Intermediate Shaft Pinch Bolt	16
	Steering Wheel.	30

Continued

TIGHTENING SPECIFICATIONS—Continued

Year	Component	Torque/Ft. Lbs.
IMPALA		
2000–02	Cover, Lower Trim	31①
	Cover, Upper Trim	13①
	Mount	18
	Pinch Bolt	35
INTRIGUE		
1998–2000	Column Cover, Lower	30①
	Column Cover, Upper	12①
	Mounting	18
	Park Lock Cable	58①
	Pinch Bolt	35
	Turn Signal Cam, Screws	84①
	Turn Signal Cam, Bolt	13
LSS, REGENCY & 88		
1998–99	Dimmer Switch	35①
	Lock Housing Cover	96①
	Lower Support Brace	84①
	Pass Key Lock Cylinder	22①
	Support Bracket	20
	Turn Signal Switch	30①
	Turn Signal Switch Arm	20①
	Wiring Harness Connector	42①
LUMINA		
1998–2000	Cylinder Lock	22①
	Dimmer Switch	35①
	Mounting	18
	Pinch Bolt	35
	Turn Signal Switch	31①
MALIBU		
1998–2000	Intermediate Shaft Pinch Bolt	16
	Steering Wheel	35
	Support Bracket	18
METRO		
1998–2000	Mount	10
	Upper Pinch Bolt	18
MONTE CARLO		
1998–99	Cylinder Lock	22①
	Dimmer Switch	35①
	Mounting	18
	Pinch Bolt	35
	Turn Signal Switch	31①
2000–02	Cover, Lower Trim	31①
	Cover, Upper Trim	13①
	Mount	18
	Pinch Bolt	35
PARK AVENUE		
1998–2000	Cover, Lower	60①
	Cover, Upper	13①
	Pinch Bolt	35
	Shift Lever, Bolt	14
	Shift Lever, Flat Head Tap Screw	84①
	Shift Lever, Oval Head Tap Screw	58①
	Support	20
	Wiring Harness Connector	72①

Continued

TIGHTENING SPECIFICATIONS—Continued

Year	Component	Torque/Ft. Lbs.
PRIZM		
1998–2000	Knee Bolster	84①
	Mount	19
	Pinch Bolt	26
RIVIERA		
1998–99	Column Cover, Pan Head	30①
	Column Cover, Tapping	②
	Interlock Solenoid	15①
	Park Lock Cable	84①
	Pinch Bolt	35
	Support	20
	Wiring Harness Connector	72①

① — Inch lbs.
② — 1998, 46 inch lbs.; 1999, 5 inch lbs.

Saturn

NOTE: On Air Bag Equipped Models, Refer To "Air Bag System Precautions" Located In The Front Of This Manual For System Disarming & Arming Procedures.

NOTE: Refer To "Computer Relearn Procedures" Located In The Front Of This Manual When Battery Power To The Computer Has Been Interrupted.

NOTE: Prior To Performing Any Service Operations Listed In This Section, Consult The "Technical Service Bulletins" Section For Related Information.

INDEX

PRECAUTIONS

AIR BAG SYSTEMS

Refer to "Air Bag System Precautions" in the front of this manual for system disarming and arming procedures.

BATTERY GROUND CABLE

Prior to service, disconnect battery ground cable and isolate as required.

STEERING COLUMN

REPLACE

L-SERIES

1. Remove steering wheel as described in "Electrical" section and Supplemental Inflatable Restraint (SIR) coil as described in "Passive Restraints Systems" chapter.
2. Remove HVAC duct and knee bolster.
3. Disconnect the following electrical connectors:
   a. Wiper/washer and headlamp/turn signal switches.
   b. Ignition switch from lefthand side of steering column.
   c. Interlock solenoid to right of steering column.
   d. Ignition switch to right of steering wheel.
4. Remove wiper/washer and headlamp/turn signal switches.
5. Remove signal switch housing and upper intermediate shaft bolt, then disconnect shaft from steering column.
6. Remove lower and upper steering column support bolts and nuts.
7. Remove steering column.
8. If new column is to be installed, ignition module must be removed as follows:
   a. Place steering column in suitable soft-jawed vise.
   b. Mark ignition module shear bolts center using suitable center punch.
   c. Drill ⅛ inch hole in bolts at each center mark.
   d. Remove bolts using suitable screw extractor and separate ignition module from column.
9. Reverse procedure to install, noting the following:
   a. When installing ignition module, use new shear bolts and tighten until bolt heads break off.
   b. Tighten mounting bolts to specifications.

S-SERIES

1. Remove steering wheel as described

in "Electrical" section and Supplemental Inflatable Restraint (SIR) coil as described in "Passive Restraints Systems" chapter.
2. Remove steering column lower filler panel screws and loosen Data Link Connector (DLC) screws, then pull filler panel outward and down.
3. Release hood release cable housing retainer.
4. Pull cable and housing downward until cable can pass through cutout in handle, then slide cable out of handle.
5. Remove steering column lower filler panel and multi-function switch as described in "Electrical" section.
6. Disconnect ignition switch electrical connector from steering column upper support bracket, as required.
7. **On models equipped with automatic transmission,** disconnect park lock cable from ignition module.
8. **On all models,** remove intermediate shaft bolt and disconnect shaft from column.
9. Remove upper and lower column mounting bolts and nuts.
10. Disconnect harness clamps and remove steering column.
11. If new column is to be installed, ignition module must be removed as follows:
    a. Place steering column in suitable soft-jawed vise.
    b. Mark ignition module shear bolts center using suitable center punch.
    c. Drill 1/8 inch hole in bolts from each center mark.
    d. Remove bolts using suitable screw extractor and separate ignition module from column.
12. Reverse procedure to install, noting the following:
    a. When installing ignition module, use new shear bolts and tighten until bolt heads break off.
    b. Tighten intermediate shaft bolt to specification.

STEERING COLUMN SERVICE

The steering column is serviced only as an assembly. If a steering column fault or defect is found, replacement as required.

TECHNICAL SERVICE BULLETINS

BUZZING NOISE FROM STEERING COLUMN

1998

On some of these models up to and including VIN WZ166759, the steering column may emit a buss noise when driving over bumps at 15–25 mph.

This condition may be caused by excessive lash in lower steering column bearing.

To correct this condition, replace steering column.

TIGHTENING SPECIFICATIONS

Year	Component	Torque/Ft. Lbs.
L-SERIES		
2000–02	Intermediate Shaft Pinch Bolt	22
	Signal Switch Housing To Steering Column	14①
	Steering Column To I/P Support Beam	22
S-SERIES		
1998–99	Intermediate Shaft	34
2000–01	Intermediate Shaft Pinch Bolt	22
	Signal Switch Housing To Steering Column	14①
	Steering Column To I/P Support Beam	22

① — Inch lbs.

MANUAL STEERING GEARS

TABLE OF CONTENTS

Suzuki Rack & Pinion, Metro

INDEX

DESCRIPTION

The rack and pinion steering system consists of two main components: the rack and the pinion. The motion of turning the steering wheel is transferred to the pinion. The rotary motion of the pinion is then transferred through the pinion teeth which mesh with the rack teeth and, in turn, gives the rack linear motion. The linear motion is then transmitted through the inner and outer tie rods to the steering knuckles which turn the wheels.

STEERING GEAR SERVICE

Refer to **Fig. 1** when servicing the steering gear.

STEERING RACK

Disassemble

1. Mark position of outer tie rod end locknuts on inner tie rod threads.
2. Remove outer tie rod ends from inner tie rods.
3. Remove boot wires and clips, then slide boots toward tie rod end.
4. Unstake ball nut.
5. Remove inner tie rods from rack.
6. Clean dirt and grease from all steering gear components using a suitable solvent.
7. Remove pinion seal using socket tool No. J34871-A, or equivalent.

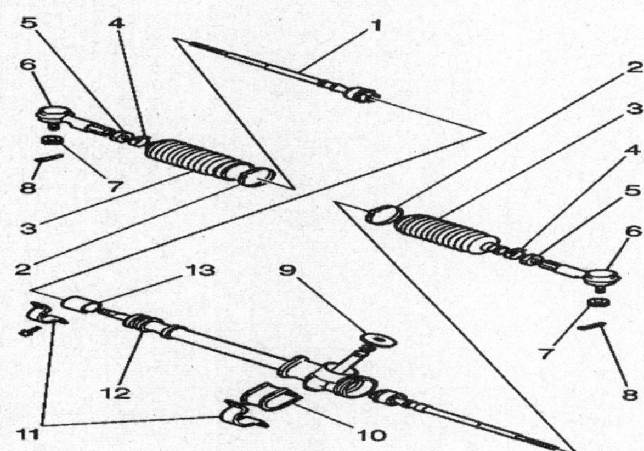

(1) Tie Rod
(2) Steering Gear Boot Clamp
(3) Steering Gear Boot
(4) Outer Boot Clamp
(5) Tie Rod End Locknut
(6) Tie Rod End
(7) Castle Nut
(8) Cotter Pin
(9) Steering Pinion Seal
(10) Steering Pinion Side Mount
(11) Steering Rack Mount Bracket
(12) Steering Rack Housing and Gear Case
(13) Steering Rack Side Mount

GC6030100057000X

Fig. 1 Exploded view of manual rack & pinion steering gear

Inspection

1. Inspect all components for damage and wear. Replace as required.
2. Inspect pinion oil seal and rack boots for damage, tears or wear. Replace as required.
3. Measure pinion's resistance to rotation using a suitable torque wrench and socket tool No. J34871-A, or equivalent. Resistance should be 9–13 inch lbs. Replace steering gear if resistance does not meet specifications.

Assemble

1. Coat inside of ball stud dust seal with chassis grease part No. 12377985, or equivalent.
2. Install seal to ball stud.
3. Install new inner tie rods to rack. Tighten ball nuts to specifications.
4. Stake each ball nut until flat spots, **Fig. 2,** are 0.95 inch apart.
5. Coat inside of outer end of each boot with manual steering gear lubricant

part No. 1052182, or equivalent.
6. Position boots on steering gear housing grooves and inner tie rods.
7. Install outer boot clamps.
8. Install a new inner boot clamp and secure using clamping tool No. J-22610, or equivalent.
9. Inspect all boots and ensure they are not twisted or improperly folded. Ensure boot clamps are secure.
10. Copy marks from old inner tie rods to the new ones.
11. Install outer tie rod ends to inner tie rods and tighten nuts to specifications. Ensure lock washer tabs are properly bent.

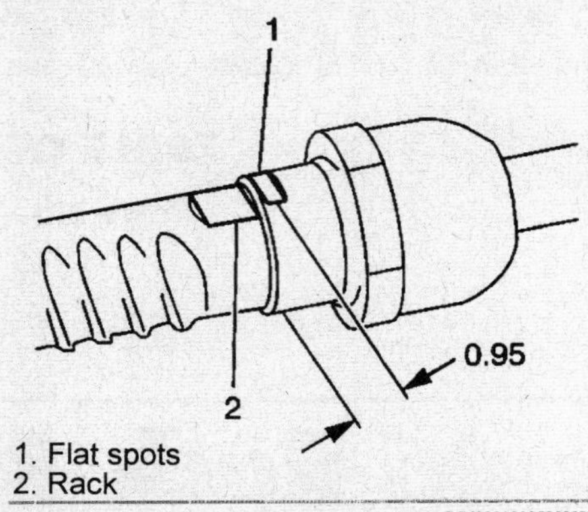

Fig. 2 Ball nut staking

TIGHTENING SPECIFICATIONS

Component	Torque, Ft. Lbs.
Adjuster Plug Locknut	70
Flange & Coupling Pinch Bolt	18
Coupling To Column Pinch Bolt	18
Outer Tie Rod Jam Nuts	32
Pinion Preload	9–13①
Steering Gear Mounting Bracket Bolts	18
Steering Shaft Joint Bolts	18
Tie Rod Ball Nuts	51
Tie Rod End Castle Nuts & Locknuts	32

① — Inch lbs.

Saturn

INDEX

DESCRIPTION

The manual steering system is a rack and pinion design. The major components of the steering system are the steering wheel, steering column and shaft, intermediate shaft, manual steering gear, tie rods and steering knuckles.

When the steering wheel is turned, the steering shaft turns the intermediate shaft which turns the steering gear pinion. The pinion gear teeth mesh with the straight rack mating teeth inside the steering gear. Rotation of the pinion converts to a straight-line motion of the rack across the vehicle that moves the tie rods either left or right. This motion causes the steering knuckle to pivot either clockwise or counterclockwise, steering the front wheels.

TROUBLESHOOTING

Refer to **Fig. 1** for manual steering system troubleshooting.

ADJUSTMENTS

BEARING PRELOAD

The following adjustment should be made with the front wheels raised and the steering wheel centered.

1. Loosen adjuster plug locknut on steering gear housing.
2. Turn adjuster plug clockwise until it bottoms in steering gear housing, **Fig. 2.**
3. **Torque** adjuster plug to 108 inch lbs.
4. Back adjuster plug off 50° (approximately one flat of nut).
5. **Torque** locknut to 52 ft. lbs. while holding adjuster plug.
6. Inspect steering wheel return following adjustment.

STEERING GEAR SERVICE

The steering gear must be serviced as an assembly.

Complaint/Condition	Possible Cause(s)	Correction(s)
Hard Steering	Front tire(s) improperly inflated.	Inflate tire(s) correctly.
	Improperly adjusted, improperly lubricated, or damaged steering gear.	Adjust, lubricate (check for damaged boots), or replace steering gear.
	Worn or binding lower control arm ball stud(s).	Replace lower control arm(s).
	Worn or binding inner or outer tie rod end(s).	Replace inner or outer tie rod end(s).
	Worn or binding upper strut mount(s).	Replace mount(s).
	Worn or binding intermediate steering shaft joint(s).	Replace intermediate steering shaft.
	Binding within steering column or intermediate steering shaft boot.	Correct condition.
Poor return of steering wheel to center.	Front tire(s) improperly inflated.	Inflate tire(s) correctly.
	Improperly adjusted, lubricated, or damaged steering gear.	Adjust, lubricate (check for damaged boots), or replace steering gear.
	Worn or binding lower control arm ball stud(s).	Replace lower control arm(s).
	Worn or binding inner or outer tie rod end(s).	Replace inner or outer tie rod end(s).
	Worn or binding upper strut mount(s).	Replace mount(s).
	Worn or binding intermediate steering shaft joint(s).	Replace intermediate steering shaft.
	Binding within steering column or intermediate steering shaft boot.	Correct condition.
	Incorrect front wheel caster.	Perform alignment.
Excessive free play in steering.	Wheel bearing(s) worn.	Replace wheel bearing(s).
	Steering gear mounting bolt(s) loose.	Tighten bolt(s).
	Steering gear out of adjustment or worn.	Adjust or replace steering gear.
	Intermediate steering shaft joint(s) worn.	Replace intermediate steering shaft.
	Inner or outer steering tie rod(s) worn.	Replace tie rod(s).
	Lower control arm ball stud(s) worn.	Replace lower control arm(s).
	Front stabilizer shaft bushings worn.	Replace bushings.
Rattle and/or clunking noise in steering.	Inner or outer tie rod end(s) worn.	Replace tie rod end(s).
	Steering gear out of adjustment or worn.	Adjust or replace steering gear.
	Worn or loose steering gearright-hand bushing.	Repair or replace steering gear.
	Intermediate steering shaft joint(s) worn.	Replace intermediate steering shaft.
	Steering gear mounting bolt(s) loose.	Tighten bolt(s).
	Worn wheel bearing(s).	Replace wheel bearing(s).

G36030100001000X

Fig. 1 Steering system troubleshooting

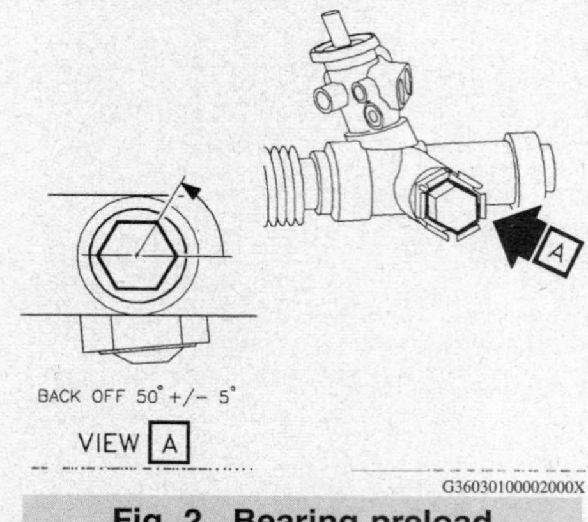

Fig. 2 Bearing preload adjustment

POWER STEERING

TABLE OF CONTENTS

Application Chart

Model	Year	Power Steering Type
BUICK		
Century	1998–2002	Saginaw Rack & Pinion
LeSabre	1998–2002	Saginaw Rack & Pinion
Park Avenue	1998–2002	Saginaw Rack & Pinion
Regal	1998–2002	Saginaw Rack & Pinion
Riviera	1998–99	Saginaw Rack & Pinion
Skylark	1998	Saginaw Rack & Pinion
CADILLAC		
Catera	1998–2001	Saginaw Rotary Valve
DeVille	1998–2002	Saginaw Rack & Pinion
Eldorado	1998–2002	Saginaw Rack & Pinion
Seville	1998–2002	Saginaw Rack & Pinion
CHEVROLET		
Camaro	1998–2002	Saginaw Rack & Pinion
Cavalier	1998–2002	Saginaw Rack & Pinion
Corvette	1998–2001	Saginaw Rack & Pinion
Impala	2000–02	Saginaw Rack & Pinion
Lumina	1998–2001	Saginaw Rack & Pinion
Malibu	1998–2002	Saginaw Rack & Pinion
Metro	1998–2001	Saginaw Rack & Pinion
Monte Carlo	1998–2002	Saginaw Rack & Pinion
Prizm	1998–2002	Toyota
OLDSMOBILE		
Achieva	1998	Saginaw Rack & Pinion
Alero	1999–2002	Saginaw Rack & Pinion
Aurora	1998–2002	Saginaw Rack & Pinion
Cutlass	1998–99	Saginaw Rack & Pinion
Eighty-Eight	1998–99	Saginaw Rack & Pinion
Intrigue	1998–2002	Saginaw Rack & Pinion
LSS	1998–99	Saginaw Rack & Pinion
Regency	1998	Saginaw Rack & Pinion

Continued

Model	Year	Power Steering Type
PONTIAC		
Bonneville	1998–2002	Saginaw Rack & Pinion
Firebird	1998–2002	Saginaw Rack & Pinion
Grand Am	1998–2002	Saginaw Rack & Pinion
Grand Prix	1998–2002	Saginaw Rack & Pinion
Sunfire	1998–2002	Saginaw Rack & Pinion
SATURN		
All	1998–2002	Saturn

Power Steering Pressure Specifications

Model	Engine	Maximum Pressure Reading, Gauge Valve Open	Minimum Pressure Reading, Gauge Valve Closed
Achieva	2.3L, 2.4L, 3.1L & 3.3L	150	1000
Alero	2.2L	230	1200
	2.4L & 3.4L	150	1300
Aurora	4.0L	200	1500
Bonneville	3800	80–125	1500
Camaro	3800 & 5.7L	150	1300
Catera	3.0L	150	1600
Cavalier	2.2L	230	1300
	2.4L	150	1000
Century	3.1L & 3800	80–125	1000
Corvette	5.7L	150	1250
Cutlass	3.1L	150	1000
DeVille	4.6L	150	1700
Eighty Eight	3800	150	1000
Eldorado	4.6L	200	1500
Firebird	3800 & 5.7L	150	1300
Grand Am	2.2L	230	1200
	2.4L, 3.1L & 3.4L	150	1300
Grand Prix	3.1L & 3800	80–125	1000
Impala	3.4L & 3800	150	1250
Intrigue	3.5L & 3800	150	1000
LeSabre	3800	80–125	1500
LSS	3800	80–125	1500
Lumina	3.1L, 3.4L & 3800	80–125	1000
Malibu	2.4L & 3.1L	150	1000
Metro	1.0L & 1.3L	142	924
Monte Carlo	3.1L, 3.4L & 3800	150	1000
Park Avenue	3800	200	1500
Prizm	1.8L	—	924
Regal	3.1L & 3800	80–125	1000
Regency	3800	150	1000
Riviera	3800	200	1500
Seville	4.6L	150	1700
Skylark	2.4L & 3.1L	150	1000
Sunfire	2.2L	230	1300
	2.4L	150	1000

Power Steering Pumps, General Motors

NOTE: On Air Bag Equipped Models, Refer To "Air Bag System Precautions" Located In The Front Of This Manual For System Disarming & Arming Procedures.

NOTE: Refer To "Computer Relearn Procedures" Located In The Front Of This Manual When Battery Power To The Computer Has Been Interrupted.

INDEX

DIAGNOSIS & TESTING

SYSTEM PRESSURE TEST

When performing system test procedures, power steering pressures can easily exceed 1000 psi. Extreme caution must be exercised when performing these tests to prevent personal injury.

Except Catera, Metro & Prizm

1. Disconnect pressure hose at pump. Use a suitable container to catch any fluid leakage.
2. Connect a spare pressure hose to pump.
3. Connect pressure gauge tool kit No. J44721, or equivalent test components, **Fig. 1.**
4. Open valve on gauge.
5. Start engine and allow system to reach normal operating temperature.
6. Inspect fluid level and ensure it is at proper level. Add fluid as required.
7. When engine is at operating temperature, pressure reading on gauge should be as specified under "Power Steering Pressure Specifications." If pressure is more than maximum specification, inspect hoses for restrictions.
8. **Do not leave valve fully closed for more than five seconds or pump could be damaged.**
9. Fully close valve three times, noting the following:
   a. Three readings should be within 50 psi of each other.
   b. If pressure readings are at least minimum as specified under "Power Steering Pressure Specifications" and are within 50 psi of each other, pump is functioning properly.
   c. If pressure readings are at least minimum as specified under "Power Steering Pressure Specifications" but not within 50 psi of each other, flow control valve is sticking and requires removal and cleaning. Burrs can be removed using crocus cloth.
10. If pressure readings are within specifications, leave valve open and turn steering wheel to both stops. If pressure at stops is not same as maximum pressure as specified under "Power Steering Pressure Specifications," steering gear is leaking internally.
11. Turn engine off and remove testing gauge and hoses.
12. Connect pressure hose and inspect fluid level.

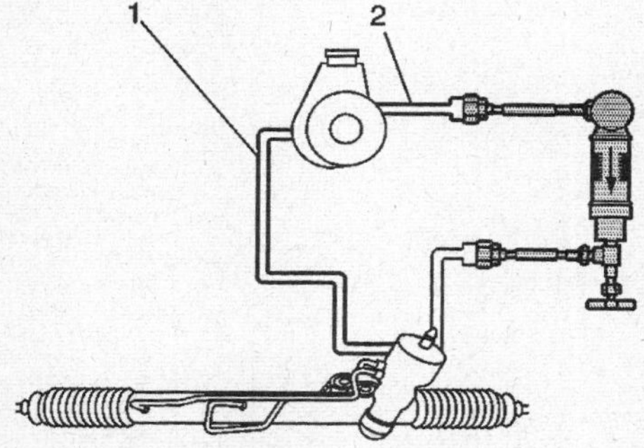

Fig. 1 Power steering pressure gauge connections. Except Catera & Metro

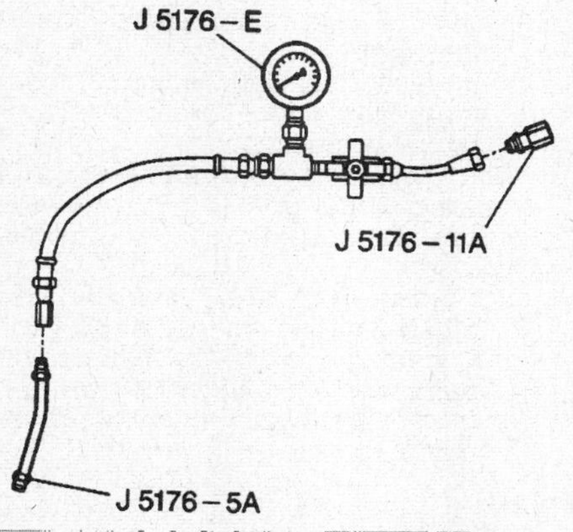

Fig. 2 Power steering pressure gauge connections. Catera

Catera

1. Disconnect power steering pump pressure hose from pump. Use a suitable container to catch any fluid leakage.
2. Connect gauge tool No. J5176-E and pressure tester adapter tool No. J5176-5A, or equivalents, to pump, **Fig. 2.**
3. Connect pressure tester to power steering pressure hose using pressure test adapter tool No. J5176-11A, or equivalent.
4. Open valve on pressure tester.
5. Bleed power steering system as outlined under "Power Steering System Service."
6. Start engine and allow it to reach normal operating temperature.
7. Pressure should be no more than 150 psi with engine at idle and valve open. If pressure is more than specified, inspect for following conditions:
   a. Inspect hoses and pipes for restrictions or kinks.
   b. Inspect valve on steering gear inlet hose fitting for proper operation.
   c. Inspect valve on steering gear inlet hose fitting for restrictions.
8. **Do not leave valve fully closed for more than five seconds or damage to pump could result.**
9. Close valve on gauge three times, noting the following:
   a. Each reading should be at least 1600 psi and be within 50 psi of each other.
   b. If pressure readings are as specified and within 50 psi of each other, pump is operating properly.

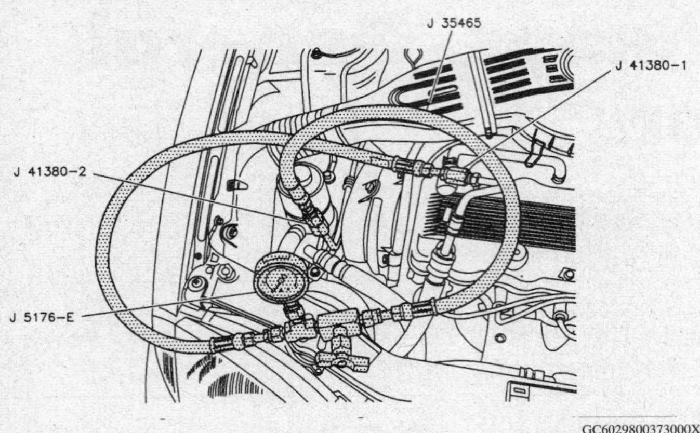

Fig. 3 Power steering pressure gauge connections. Metro

c. If pressure readings are below 1600 psi, replace pump.

10. With valve in open position, turn steering wheel to both stops, noting the following:
    a. Pressure reading should be same as maximum pressure reading as specified under "Power Steering Pressure Specifications."
    b. If pressure is not as specified, steering gear is leaking internally.
11. Turn ignition Off, then remove pressure test tools.
12. Connect pump pressure hose to pump.
13. **Torque** pressure hose fitting to 21 ft. lbs.
14. Bleed power steering system as outlined under "Power Steering System Service."

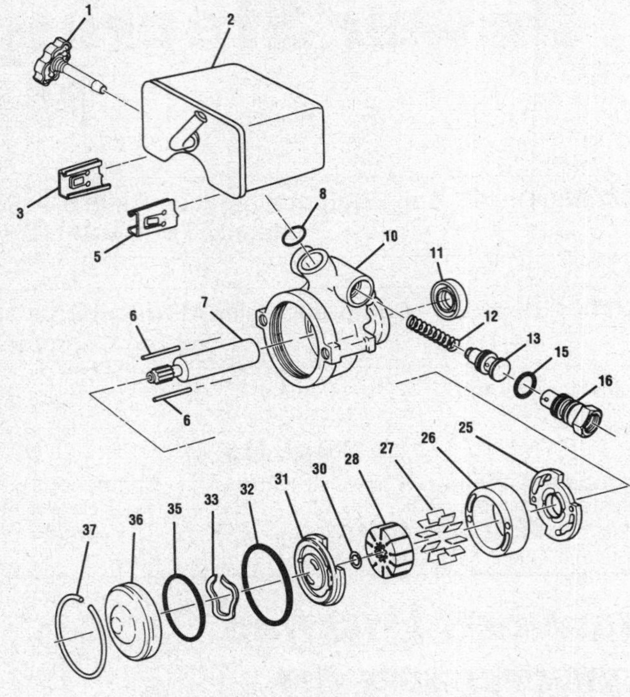

Fig. 4 Exploded view of CB series power steering pump

Metro

1. Remove one 10 MM bolt retaining high pressure hose and pipe to core support, then disconnect hose to high pressure pipe at core support.
2. Install pressure gauge tool No. J5176-E, pressure tester adapter hose tool No. J35465 and pressure tester adapter kit tool No. J41380, or equivalents, as follows:
    a. Connect gauge side of pressure gauge to pressure hose from pump.
    b. Connect valve side of gauge to pressure line to rack, **Fig. 3.**
3. Bleed power steering system as outlined under "Power Steering System Bleed."
4. Start engine, then turn steering wheel from righthand and lefthand stops two or three times.
5. Ensure fluid level is at proper level.
6. Turn off engine and ensure fluid temperature is at least 176°F.
7. Start and run engine at idle.
8. Inspect pressure, noting the following:
    a. With valve open and engine idling, pressure reading should be no more than 142 psi.
    b. If pressure reading is more than 142 psi, inspect hoses for restrictions or control valve for damage.
9. **Do not leave valve closed for more than 10 seconds or pump damage could result.** Inspect fluid pressure reading with valve closed, noting the following:
    a. If pressure reading is below 825 psi, repair or replace power steering pump.
    b. If pressure gauge reading is higher than 924 psi, possible cause is relief valve malfunction.
10. With engine idling and valve open, turn steering wheel to full right or full left and read pressure, noting the following:
    a. Pressure should be no lower than 825 psi and no higher than 924 psi.
    b. If reading is lower than 825 psi, repair or replace rack and pinion.
    c. If reading is higher than 924 psi, repair or replace relief valve.

Prizm

1. Disconnect pressure line from gear housing.
2. Connect pressure gauge tool No. J5176 and gauge adapter tool No. J35465, or equivalents to power steering system, **Fig. 1.**
3. Bleed system, then start engine and turn steering wheel from righthand to lefthand stops two or three times.
4. Shut off engine and ensure fluid temperature is at least 176°F and reservoir is full.
5. Start engine and run at idle speed.
6. Inspect fluid pressure with valve on pressure gauge closed. **Do not keep valve closed for more than five seconds. This could damage power steering system.**
7. If pressure is below 924 psi, power steering pump is faulty. Repair or replace as required.
8. Open valve on power steering gear and record pressure reading at 1000 RPM and at 3000 RPM. If there is more than 71 psi difference between 1000–3000 RPM inspections, repair or replace steering gear valve.

POWER STEERING SYSTEM SERVICE

Component Service

CB SERIES PUMP

Disassembly

1. Remove power steering pump from

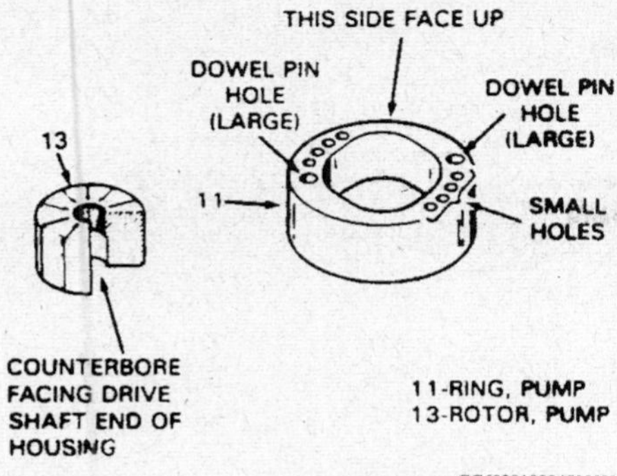

Fig. 5 Rotor and/or pump ring installation. CB series power steering pump

vehicle. Refer to "Front Suspension & Steering" in appropriate chassis chapter.

2. Remove union fitting with O-ring and O-ring seal, **Fig. 4.**
3. Remove control valve assembly and flow control spring.
4. Protect driveshaft with shim stock and remove driveshaft seal by cutting with small chisel. Discard seal.
5. Remove end cover retaining ring by inserting punch in access hole.
6. Gently push on driveshaft to assist in removing end cover, O-ring, pressure plate spring, pump ring, pump vanes and driveshaft subassembly.
7. Remove O-ring from housing.
8. Note orientation of pump ring holes and dowel pins.
9. Remove dowel pins, then driveshaft seal if not previously removed.
10. Remove pressure plate, pressure plate spring and O-ring from end cover.
11. Remove shaft retaining ring from driveshaft, then the pump rotor and thrust plate.

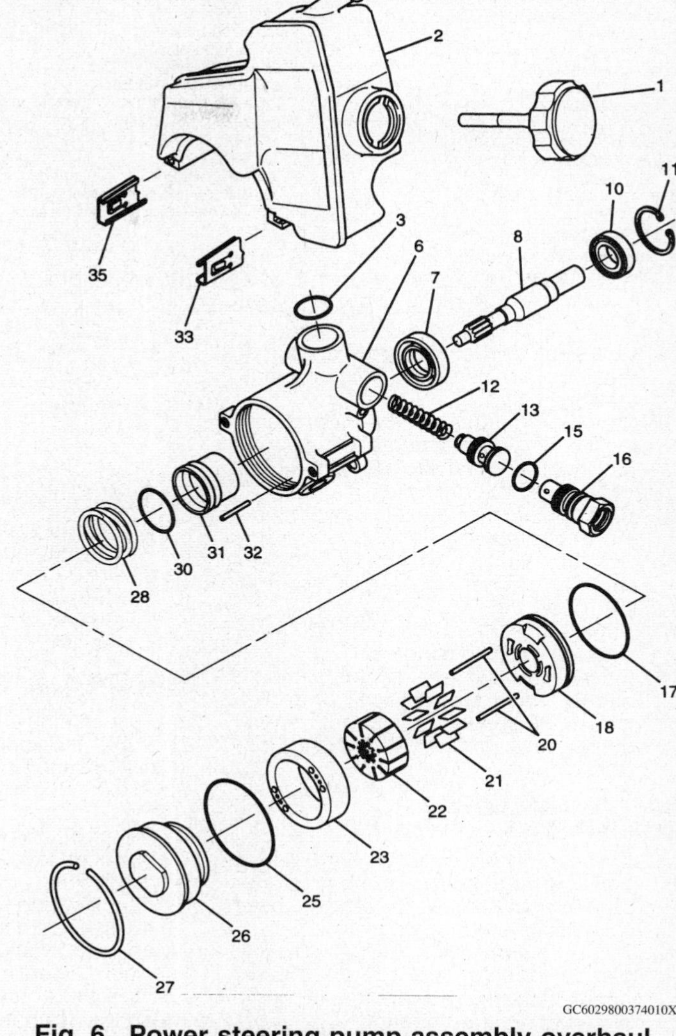

Fig. 6 Power steering pump assembly overhaul (Part 1 of 2). TC Series

Inspection

1. Clean all components in clean power steering fluid, then dry thoroughly.
2. Inspect pump ring, vanes, thrust plate, pressure plate and driveshaft for scoring, pitting or chatter marks, replacing components as required.

Assembly

1. Lubricate new driveshaft seal with power steering fluid, then press driveshaft seal into pump housing using seal installer tool No. J7728, or equivalent.
2. Install pump ring dowel pins into housing.
3. Install thrust plate and pump rotor onto driveshaft, **Fig. 5.**
4. Install new shaft retaining ring onto driveshaft.
5. Install driveshaft subassembly into housing.
6. Install pump ring with holes positioned properly onto dowel pins, **Fig. 5,** in housing.
7. Install vanes into pump rotor.
8. Lubricate new large O-ring with power steering fluid and install O-ring into end cover.
9. Install pressure plate and pressure plate spring.
10. Lubricate new small O-ring and install O-ring into end cover.
11. Lubricate outer edge of end cover with power steering fluid and press end cover into housing.
12. Insert retaining ring into groove in housing with ring opening near access hole opening.

TC SERIES PUMP

Refer to **Fig. 6** for service procedures on this power steering pump.

Power Steering System Bleed

EXCEPT AURORA & RIVIERA

Inspect steering system before bleeding, looking for power steering lines touching frame, body or engine. Also inspect all hose connections for looseness or leaks and tighten as required.

Bleed power steering system after any component replacement, fluid line disconnection or in case of steering system noise. Bleed system to prevent pump damage, stop steering noise and to ensure proper system operation.

1. Remove power steering pump reservoir cap.
2. Fill reservoir with proper fluid to "full cold" level.
3. Connect vacuum pump tool No. J35555 and power steering bleeder adapter tool No. J43485, or equivalents, to reservoir filler neck, **Fig. 7.**
4. Apply a maximum vacuum of 20 inches, then wait five minutes.
5. Inspect vacuum level after five minute break, which typically will drop 2–3 inches. If vacuum does not remain steady, refer to "Special Bleeding Conditions."
6. Install reservoir cap, then start and idle engine.
7. Stop engine, then inspect power steering fluid level.

Key No.	Part Name	Key No.	Part Name
1	CAPSTICK ASM, RESERVOIR	20	PIN, PUMP RING DOWEL (2)
2	RESERVOIR ASM, HYD PUMP	21	VANE (10)
3	SEAL, O-RING	22	ROTOR, PUMP
6	HOUSING ASM, HYD PUMP	23	RING, PUMP
7	SEAL, DRIVE SHAFT	25	SEAL, O-RING
8	SHAFT, DRIVE	26	PLATE ASM, THRUST
10	BEARING ASM, BALL	27	RING, THRUST PLATE RETAINING
11	RING, RETAINING	28	SPRING, PRESSURE PLATE
12	SPRING, FLOW CONTROL	30	SEAL, O-RING
13	VALVE ASM, CONTROL	31	SLEEVE ASM
15	SEAL, O-RING	32	PIN, DOWEL
16	FITTING, O-RING UNION	33	CLIP, RESERVOIR RETAINING (RH)
17	SEAL, O-RING	35	CLIP, RESERVOIR RETAINING (LH)
18	PLATE, PRESSURE		

GC6029800374020X

Fig. 6 Power steering pump assembly overhaul (Part 2 of 2). TC Series

8. Wait another five minutes, then repeat previous two steps until fluid level has stabilized.
9. Start and idle engine, then turn steering wheel 180–360° degrees in both directions five times. **Do not turn wheel all the way to stops.**
10. Stop engine, then inspect power steering fluid level again.
11. Connect vacuum pump and power steering bleeder adapter to reservoir filler neck, **Fig. 7.**
12. Apply a maximum vacuum of 20 inches, then wait five minutes.
13. Inspect vacuum level after five minute break, which typically will drop 2–3 inches. If vacuum does not remain steady, refer to "Special Bleeding Conditions."

SPECIAL BLEEDING CONDITIONS

1. If vacuum continued to drop during bleeding procedure, remove power steering pressure and return hoses from power steering pump.
2. Install plugs from power steering bleeder adapter tool No. J43485, or equivalents, into power steering pump pressure and return ports.
3. Connect vacuum pump and power steering bleeder adapter to reservoir filler neck as illustrated, **Fig. 7.**
4. Apply a maximum vacuum of 20 inches.
5. **If vacuum drops again,** repair or replace power steering pump as required. **If vacuum holds steady,** proceed as follows:
   a. Inspect power steering fluid and ensure it is free of bubbles and is not discolored.
   b. Replace return hose clamps and O-rings.
   c. Replace pressure hose O-rings and reservoir to pump O-ring.
   d. Repeat bleeding procedure from very beginning.
   e. Drive vehicle approximately 10 miles on a smooth, flat surface to ensure power steering system reaches full operating temperature.

AURORA & RIVIERA

1. Turn ignition Off.
2. Raise and support front of vehicle until tires clear ground.
3. Rotate steering wheel to full lefthand turn.
4. Fill power steering fluid reservoir to "full cold" level. Leave reservoir cap off at this time.
5. Turn steering wheel lock to lock at least 40 times with engine stopped while an assistant inspects fluid level and condition. **Ensure fluid level remains at "full cold" level. Trapped air might cause fluid to overflow. Clean up any spills immediately.**
6. If any bubbles appear, inspect for loose fluid line connections and correct as required.
7. Start and idle engine, ensuring fluid is kept at proper level.
8. Install reservoir cap.
9. Turn steering wheel until front tires reach center position.
10. Lower the vehicle and allow engine to idle for two minutes.
11. Turn steering wheel in both directions and ensure it rotates smoothly and noiselessly.

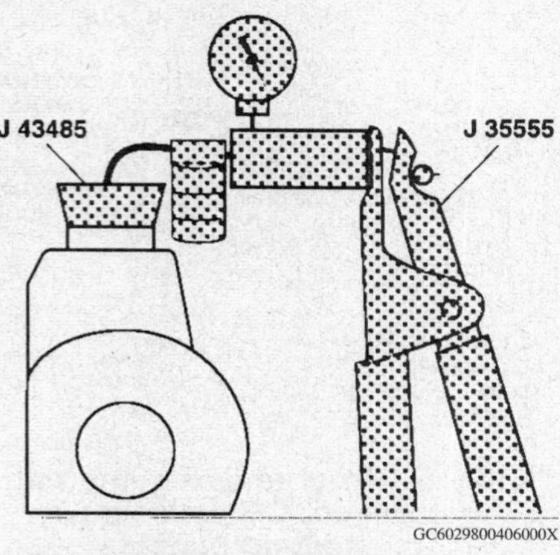

GC6029800406000X

Fig. 7 Power steering bleeder tool installation in reservoir

12. Ensure fluid remains at proper level, has no bubbles, foam or discoloration and does not leak.
13. If bubbles, discoloration or foam appear in fluid, proceed as follows:
    a. Turn ignition Off.
    b. Wait two minutes, then inspect hose connections again.
    c. Start and idle engine while maintaining fluid at proper level.
    d. Install reservoir cap.
    e. Turn steering wheel in both directions and ensure it rotates smoothly and noiselessly.
    f. If a fluid fault condition persists, inspect and replace return hose clamps and O-rings, pressure hose O-rings and gear cylinder line O-rings.
14. If pump groans or whines, idle engine and inspect for hose contact and interference with body, engine and frame. Correct as required.
15. If no hose contact or interference is found, proceed as follows:
    a. Stop engine and allow power steering system to cool off.
    b. Siphon fluid from reservoir using a suitable suction device.
    c. Refill reservoir with cool, clean specified power steering fluid.
    d. Install reservoir cap, then start engine and bring to operating temperature.
16. If noises persist, replace power steering pump assembly, then repeat bleeding procedure.

Saginaw Rack & Pinion Power Steering Gear Less Speed Sensitive Steering, General Motors

NOTE: On Air Bag Equipped Models, Refer To "Air Bag System Precautions" Located In The Front Of This Manual For System Disarming & Arming Procedures.

NOTE: Refer To "Computer Relearn Procedures" Located In The Front Of This Manual When Battery Power To The Computer Has Been Interrupted.

INDEX

DESCRIPTION

POWER STEERING GEAR

This power steering gear assembly incorporates an integral tube and housing containing a pinion shaft and steering rack. The tube and housing are joined by a plastic injection-bonding process. The pinion shaft is supported in the housing by thrust bearings and bushings. A bushing and bulkhead assembly supports the steering in the tube.

A rotary-type valve body is used to control the hydraulic steering assist. Fluid under pressure is directed to the gear housing and into the valve body. The valve body then directs fluid to the power cylinder.

A spool valve, connected to the stub shaft by a locating pin, rotates within the valve body. Fluid directional passages, machined into the spool valve, are aligned with fluid passages in the valve body as the spool valve rotates. Fluid is directed through these passages, into either side of the power cylinder through the externally mounted oil lines.

DIAGNOSIS & TESTING

EXTERNAL LEAK INSPECTION

1. With engine off, wipe entire power steering system clean and dry.
2. Ensure fluid level is at proper level.
3. Start engine, then turn steering wheel from stop to stop a few times. Do not hold at stop for a long period.
4. Find exact area of leak and repair as required, **Fig. 1.**

POWER STEERING SYSTEM SERVICE

Component Service

POWER STEERING GEAR

DISASSEMBLY

Refer to **Figs. 2 through 4** for service procedures.

OUTER TIE ROD

1. Remove prevailing torque nut or cotter pin and hex slotted nut from outer tie rod assembly, **Figs. 5 and 6.**
2. **On Achieva, Skylark and 1998 Grand Am models,** proceed as follows:
   a. Loosen outer tie rod pinch bolts, then separate outer tie rod from steering knuckle using steering linkage puller, tool No. J24319-01, or equivalent.
   b. Remove outer tie rod from tie rod adjuster.
3. **On all models except Achieva, Skylark and 1998 Grand Am,** proceed as follows:
   a. Loosen jam nut, then remove outer tie rod from steering knuckle using steering linkage remover tool No. J24319-01, or equivalent.
   b. Remove outer tie rod from inner tie rod.
4. **On all models,** reverse procedure to install, noting the following:
   a. **On all models except 1998–2001 Century, Grand Prix and Regal, torque** hex slotted nut to 35 ft. lbs. with a maximum of 52 ft. lbs. to install cotter pin. **Do not back off nut when installing cotter pin.**
   b. **On 1998–2001 Century, Grand Prix and Regal models, torque** prevailing nut to tie rod end to 22 ft. lbs., then rotate an additional 120°.
   c. **On all models,** adjust toe by turning inner tie rod.
   d. **Torque** jam nut against outer tie rod to 50 ft. lbs.

INNER TIE ROD

ACHIEVA, SKYLARK & 1998 GRAND AM

1. Remove and dispose of lock plate from inner tie rod bolts, **Fig. 7.**
2. Remove inner tie rod bolt.
3. Slide out and remove inner tie rod between bolt support plate and rack and pinion boot. **If both inner tie rods are to be removed, after removing the first tie rod, install bolt again to keep rack and pinion and other components aligned.**
4. Reverse procedure to install, noting the following:
   a. Ensure center housing cover washers are fitted into rack and pinion boot.
   b. Install new lock plate with notches in proper position over flats of inner tie rod bolts.

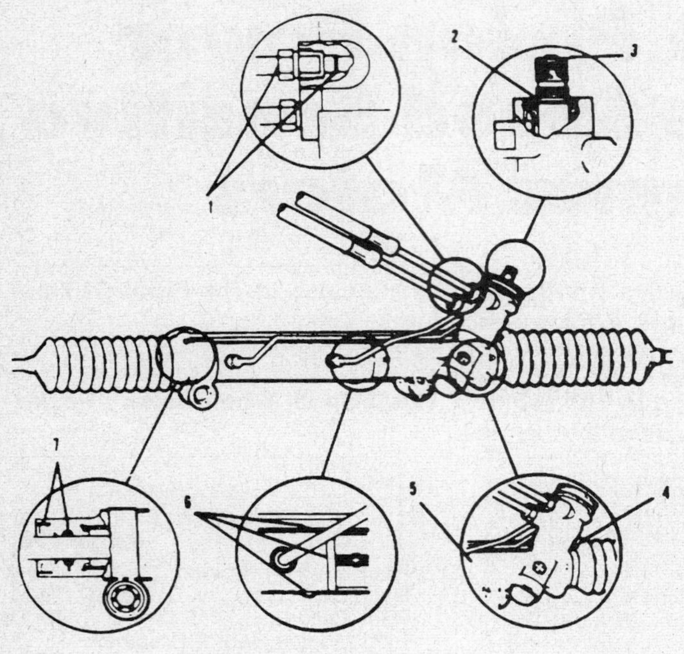

1 TIGHTEN FITTING TO 27 N m (20 LB FT) IF LEAKAGE PERSISTS, REPLACE O-RING SEAL IF LEAKAGE IS DUE TO DAMAGED THREADS, REPAIR FITTING NUT OR REPLACE LINE AS REQUIRED IF HOUSING THREADS ARE BADLY DAMAGED, REPLACE HOUSING
2 REPLACE DUST AND STUB SHAFT SEALS
3 IF LEAKAGE IS OBSERVED BETWEEN TORSION BAR AND STUB SHAFT, PARTIAL GEAR REPLACEMENT WILL BE REQUIRED
4 IF LEAKAGE IS OBSERVED AT DRIVER SIDE AND IS NOT AFFECTED BY THE DIRECTION OF TURN, PARTIAL GEAR REPLACEMENT WILL BE REQUIRED
5 IF LEAKAGE IS OBSERVED AT THE HOUSING END AND SPURTS WHEN BOTTOMED IN LEFT TURN, PARTIAL GEAR REPLACEMENT WILL BE REQUIRED
6 PARTIAL GEAR REPLACEMENT MAY BE REQUIRED
7 IF LEAKAGE IS OBSERVED AT PASSENGER SIDE, IT IS NECESSARY TO REPLACE WITH A PARTIAL GEAR ASSEMBLY.

GC6029700407000X

Fig. 1 Power rack & pinion steering gear leak diagnosis

c. Tighten inner tie rod bolts to specifications.

EXCEPT ACHIEVA, SKYLARK & 1998 GRAND AM

Removal

Rack must be held during inner tie rod removal to prevent internal gear damage.

1. Remove rack and pinion steering assembly from vehicle.
2. Remove outer tie rod from inner tie rod assembly, then rack and pinion boot.
3. Place wrench on flat of rack assembly and place wrench on flats of inner tie rod housing, **Fig. 8.**
4. Rotate housing counterclockwise until inner tie rod separates from rack.

Installation

Rack must be held during inner tie rod installation to prevent internal gear damage.

1. Install inner tie rod on rack and tighten to specifications, **Fig. 9.**
2. Support rack and housing of inner tie rod assembly, then stake both sides of inner tie rod housing to flats on rack, **Fig. 10.**
3. Inspect both stakes by inserting a .010 inch feeler gauge between rack and housing stake. **When properly staked, feeler gauge must not pass between rack and housing stakes.**
4. Slide shock damper over housing until it engages.
5. Install boot and rack outer tie rod, then the rack and pinion assembly to vehicle.

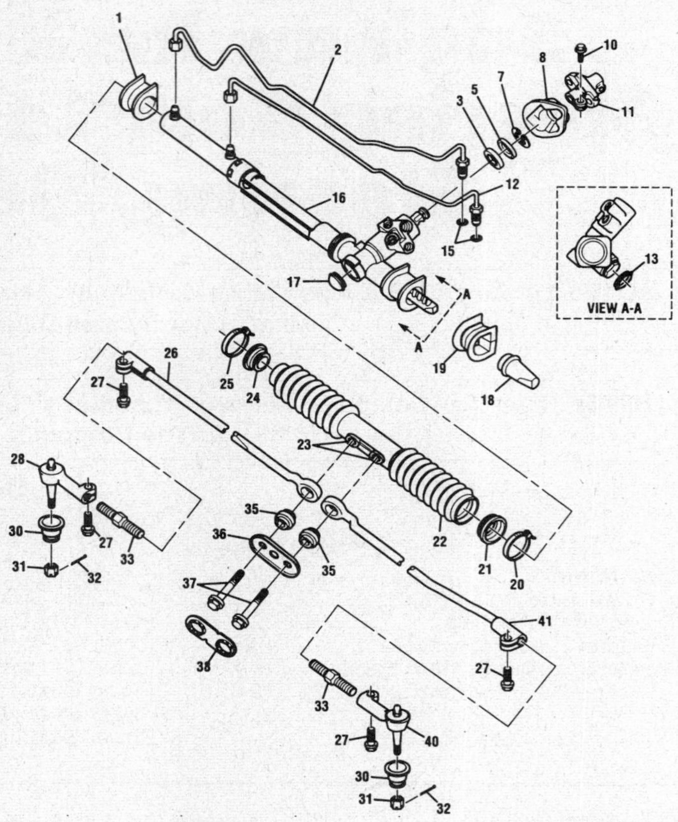

GC6029700408010X

Fig. 2 Exploded view of power rack & pinion assembly (Part 1 of 2). Achieva, Skylark & 1998 Grand Am

1 - GROMMET, MOUNTING
2 - LINE ASM, CYLINDER (LT)
3 - ANNULUS ASM, BEARING
5 - SEAL, STUB SHAFT
7 - RING, RETAINING
8 - SEAL, DASH
10 - BOLT, PINCH
11 - COUPLING, FLANGE & STEERING
12 - LINE ASM, CYLINDER (RT)
13 - NUT, ADJUSTER PLUG LOCK
15 - SEAL, O-RING
16 - HOUSING, RACK & PINION
17 - COVER, DUST
18 - COVER, HOUSING END
19 - GROMMET, MOUNTING
20 - CLAMP, BOOT
21 - BUSHING, BOOT RETAINING
22 - BOOT, RACK & PINION
23 - WASHER, CENTER HOUSING COVER (PART OF 22)
24 - BUSHING, BOOT RETAINING
25 - CLAMP, BOOT
26 - ASSEMBLY, INNER TIE ROD
27 - BOLT, PINCH
28 - ASSEMBLY, OUTER TIE ROD
30 - SEAL, TIE ROD
31 - NUT, HEX SLOTTED
32 - PIN, COTTER
33 - ADJUSTER, TIE ROD
35 - BUSHING, INNER PIVOT
36 - PLATE, BOLT SUPPORT
37 - BOLT, INNER TIE ROD
38 - PLATE, LOCK
40 - ASSEMBLY, OUTER TIE ROD
41 - ASSEMBLY, INNER TIE ROD

GC6029700408020X

Fig. 2 Exploded view of power rack & pinion assembly (Part 2 of 2). Achieva, Skylark & 1998 Grand Am

RACK BEARING PRELOAD

EXCEPT ACHIEVA, SKYLARK & 1998 GRAND AM

On all models except Century, Grand Prix and Regal, make adjustment with front wheels raised and steering wheel centered. Ensure steering wheel returns to center position after adjustment.

On Century, Grand Prix and Regal models, make adjustment with the steering rack assembly removed from the vehicle.

1. Loosen locknut, turn adjuster plug clockwise until it bottoms in housing, then back off 50–70°.
2. Tighten locknut to specifications while holding adjuster plug.

ACHIEVA, SKYLARK & 1998 GRAND AM

On Vehicle Adjustment

Make adjustment with front wheels

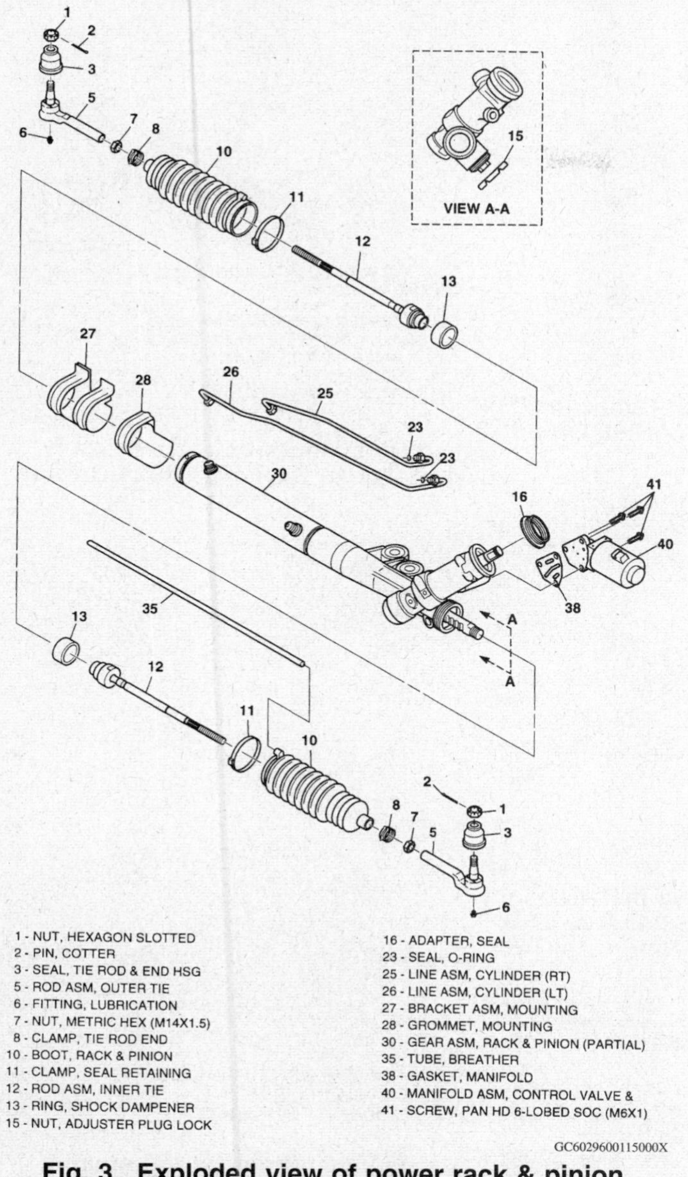

Fig. 3 Exploded view of power rack & pinion assembly. Except Achieva, Camaro, Firebird, Skylark, 1998 Grand Am & Intrigue

GC6029700409010X

Fig. 4 Exploded view of power rack & pinion assembly (Part 1 of 2). Camaro & Firebird

1 - NUT, HEXAGON SLOTTED
2 - PIN, COTTER
3 - SEAL, TIE ROD
5 - ROD ASM, OUTER TIE
6 - FITTING, LUBE (90 DEG ELBOW)
7 - NUT, METRIC HEX (M14 X 1.5)
8 - CLAMP, TIE ROD END
10 - BOOT, RACK & PINION
11 - CLAMP, SEAL RETAINING
12 - ROD ASM, INNER TIE
13 - RING, SHOCK DAMPENER
15 - NUT, ADJUSTER PLUG LOCK
16 - ADAPTER, SEAL
17 - RING, RETAINING
20 - SEAL, STUB SHAFT
21 - BEARING ANNULUS ASM, NEEDLE
23 - SEAL, O-RING (4.50 I.D.)
25 - LINE ASM, CYLINDER (RT)
26 - LINE ASM, CYLINDER (LT)
30 - GEAR ASM, RACK & PINION (PARTIAL)
32 - NUT, HEX LOCK
33 - COVER, DUST
35 - CLIP, PIPE
36 - BUSHING, STEERING GEAR
37 - SLEEVE, STEERING GEAR BUSHING

GC6029700409020X

Fig. 4 Exploded view of power rack & pinion assembly (Part 2 of 2). Camaro & Firebird

raised and steering wheel centered. Ensure the steering wheel returns to the center position after adjustment.

1. Loosen locknut, turn adjuster plug clockwise until it bottoms in housing, then back off 35–45°.
2. Tighten adjuster plug locknut to specifications while holding adjuster plug.

RACK, PINION BOOT & BREATHER TUBE

EXCEPT ACHIEVA, SKYLARK & 1998 GRAND AM

Removal

1. Remove outer tie rod.
2. Remove hex jam nut from inner tie rod assembly.
3. Remove tie rod end clamp, **Fig. 11**, then remove and discard boot clamp using suitable side cutters.
4. Mark location of breather tube on housing before removing tube, then remove boot and breather tube.

Installation

1. Install new boot clamp onto boot.
2. Apply grease to inner tie rod or housing, **Fig. 12.**

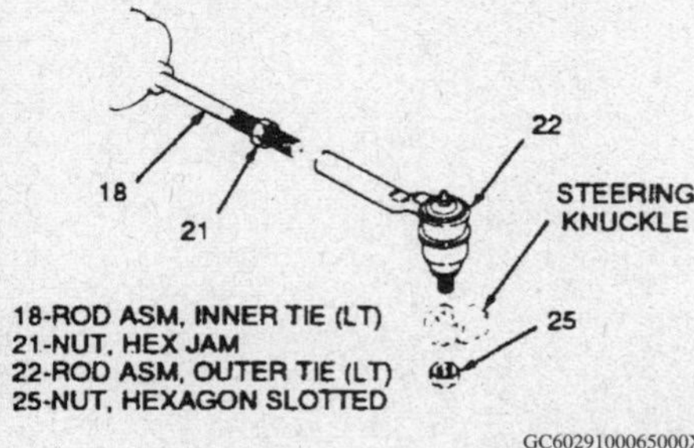

Fig. 5 Outer tie rod replacement. Except Achieva, Skylark & 1998 Grand Am

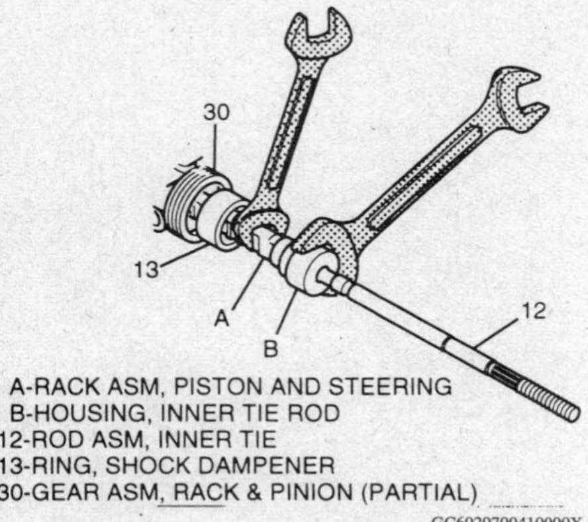

Fig. 8 Inner tie rod removal. Except Achieva, Skylark & 1998 Grand Am

3. Align and install breather tube.
4. Install boot onto housing until seated in housing groove tang.
5. Position boot clamp on boot and crimp.
6. Position tie rod end clamp on boot and secure with pliers.

PINION SEAL, DUST SEAL & BEARING ANNULUS

EXCEPT ACHIEVA, SKYLARK & 1998 GRAND AM

Removal

1. Remove rack and pinion steering assembly from vehicle.
2. Remove adjuster plug locknut from adjuster plug, **Fig. 13.**
3. Remove adjuster plug from housing, then the adjuster spring and rack bearing.
4. Remove retaining ring from valve bore of housing, then the dust cover, **Fig. 14.**
5. Holding stub shaft, remove hex locknut from pinion and valve assembly. **Stub shaft must be held to prevent damage to pinion teeth.**
6. Press on threaded end of pinion using an arbor press, **Fig. 15,** until it is possible to remove stub shaft, dust seal, stub shaft seal and annulus bearing.

Installation

1. While holding valve stub shaft, install hex locknut onto pinion. Tighten locknut to specifications. **Damage to pinion teeth will occur if stub shaft is not held.**
2. Install dust cover to gear assembly.
3. Install stub shaft bearing annulus assembly onto valve stub shaft.
4. Install seal protector tool No. J29810, or equivalent, onto valve stub shaft.
5. Apply a small amount of grease between seals, then install stub shaft seal and dust seal over protector and into gear assembly.
6. Install retaining ring into groove in gear assembly.
7. Lubricate stub shaft and dust seal area with grease.
8. Coat rack bearing, adjuster spring and adjuster plug with lithium base grease and install gear assembly.
9. Adjust assembly as follows:
   a. With rack centered in gear assembly, turn adjuster plug clockwise until it bottoms in gear assembly, then back off 50–70°.
   b. Measure pinion rotational torque. Maximum preload torque should be 16 inch lbs.
10. Install adjuster plug locknut to adjuster plug.
11. Tighten adjuster plug firmly against gear assembly while holding adjuster plug stationary.
12. Install rack and pinion assembly.

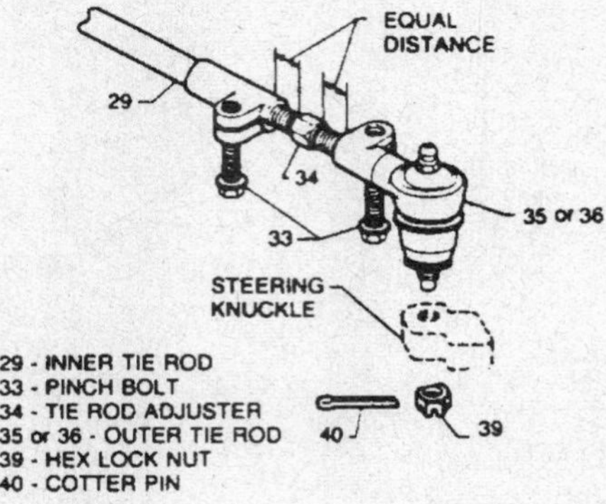

Fig. 6 Outer tie rod replacement. Achieva, Skylark & 1998 Grand Am

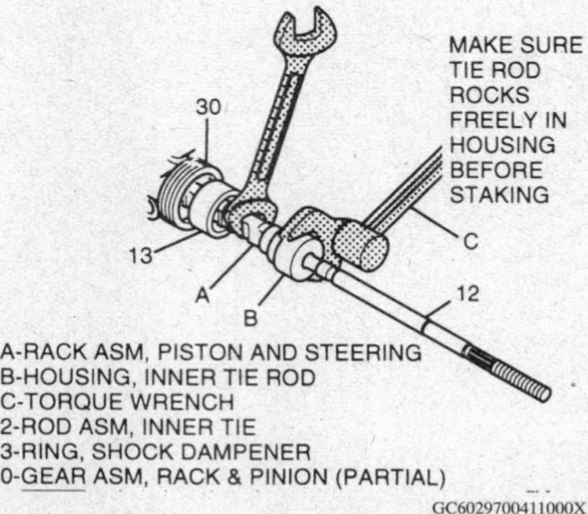

Fig. 9 Inner tie rod installation. Except Achieva, Skylark & 1998 Grand Am

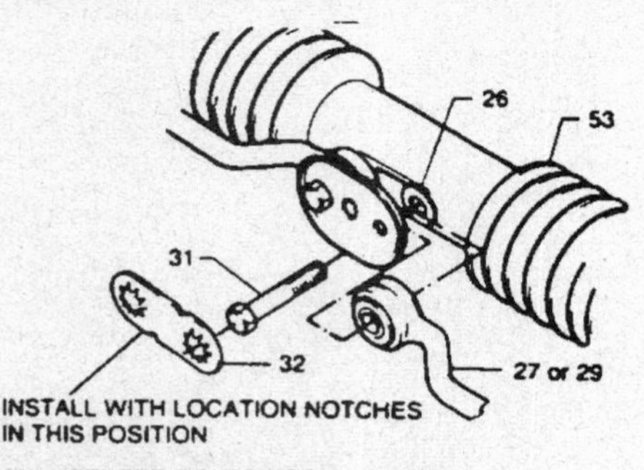

Fig. 7 Inner tie rod assembly. Achieva, Skylark & 1998 Grand Am

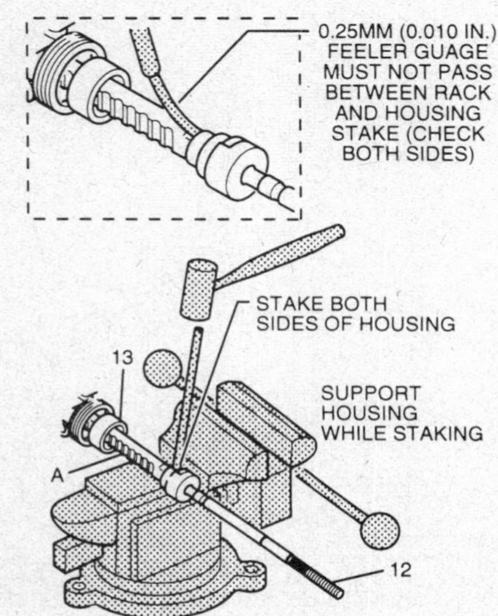

Fig. 10 Inner tie rod staking procedure. Except Achieva, Skylark & 1998 Grand Am

INNER PIVOT BUSHINGS

ACHIEVA, SKYLARK & 1998 GRAND AM

Refer to **Figs. 16 and 17** for removal and installation procedures.

FLANGE & STEERING COUPLING ASSEMBLY

ACHIEVA, SKYLARK & 1998 GRAND AM

1. Remove rack and pinion assembly from vehicle.
2. Remove pinch bolt from flange and steering coupling assembly, then the coupling, **Fig. 18.**

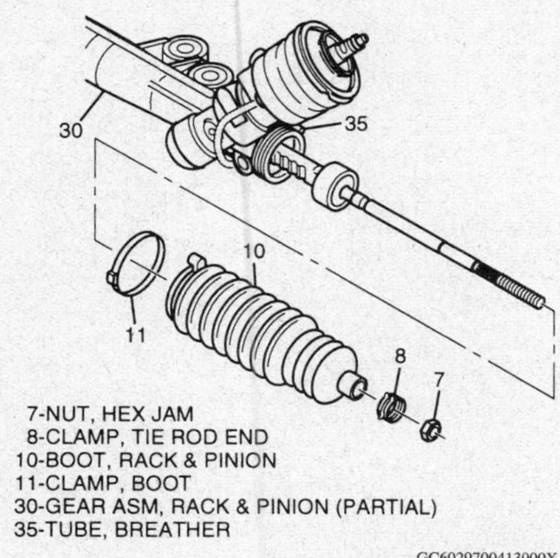

Fig. 11 Boot replacement. Except Achieva, Skylark & 1998 Grand Am

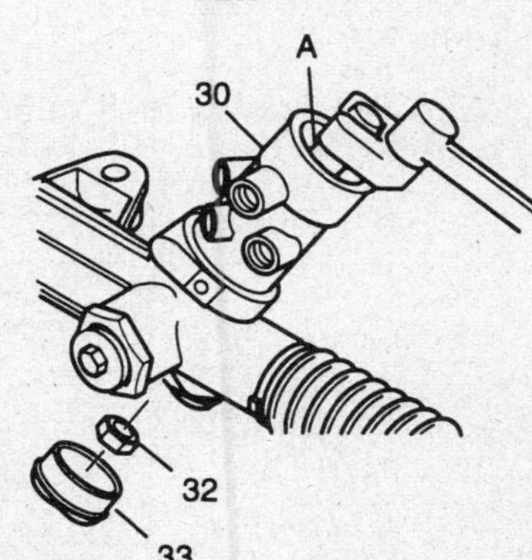

Fig. 14 Retaining ring & locknut removal. Except Achieva, Skylark & 1998 Grand Am

3. Reverse procedure to install. **Torque** pinch bolt to 30 ft. lbs.

HYDRAULIC CYLINDER LINES

ACHIEVA, SKYLARK & 1998 GRAND AM

Refer to **Fig. 2** for replacement procedure. Ensure new O-rings are installed. **Torque** line fittings at valve end to 14 ft. lbs. **Torque** line fittings at cylinder end to 20 ft. lbs.

RACK GUIDE

ACHIEVA, SKYLARK & 1998 GRAND AM

Removal

1. Remove rack and pinion steering assembly from vehicle.
2. Remove lock plate from inner tie rod bolts and discard, **Figs. 2 and 19.**
3. Remove inner tie rod bolts, bolt support plate, cylinder lines and inner tie rod assemblies.
4. Cut and remove mounting grommet

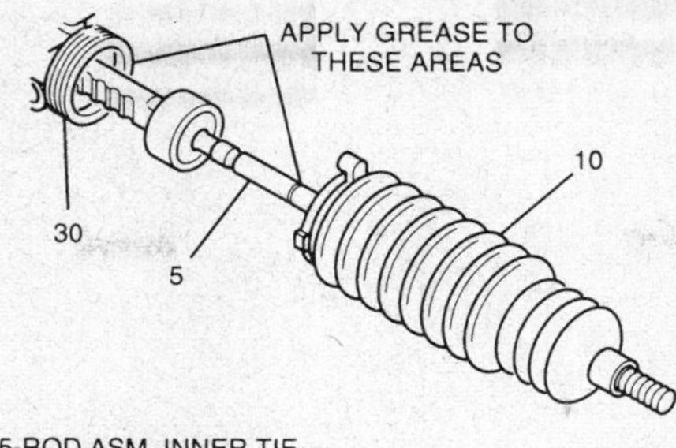

Fig. 12 Boot seal application. Except Achieva, Skylark & 1998 Grand Am

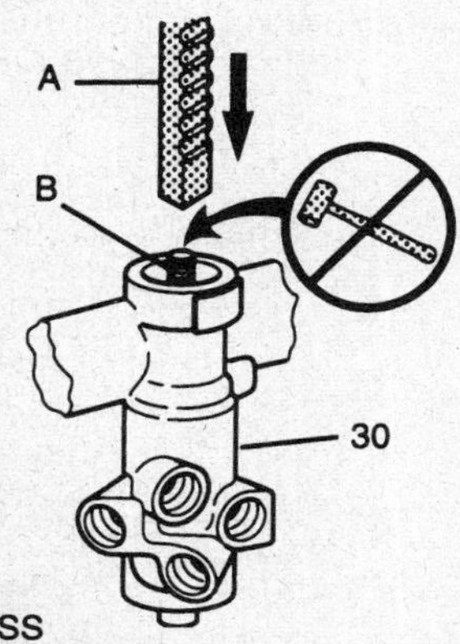

Fig. 15 Stub shaft, dust seal & stub shaft seal removal. Except Achieva, Skylark & 1998 Grand Am

and boot clamp.

5. Slide boot retaining bushing from rack and pinion boot, then boot assembly from rack and pinion housing.
6. Insert rack guide assembly from rod and rack assembly if required.

Installation

1. Slide boot retaining bushing from rack and pinion housing.
2. Slide new boot clamp on rack and pinion boot, then install boot retaining bushing into rack and pinion boot.
3. Install rack guide on rack.
4. Coat inner lip of boot retaining bushing lightly with grease, then install boot on housing. Ensure center housing cover washers are in place on boot.
5. Install inner tie rod bolts through cover washers and rack and pinion boot. Screw into rack lightly.
6. Slide boot and boot retaining bushing until seated in bushing groove in housing. Crimp new boot clamp.
7. Slide other end of boot into boot groove on cylinder end of housing.
8. Slide other end of boot into boot groove on cylinder end of housing and crimp new boot clamp. **Boot clamp bridge must be crimped over split in boot retaining bushing to ensure**

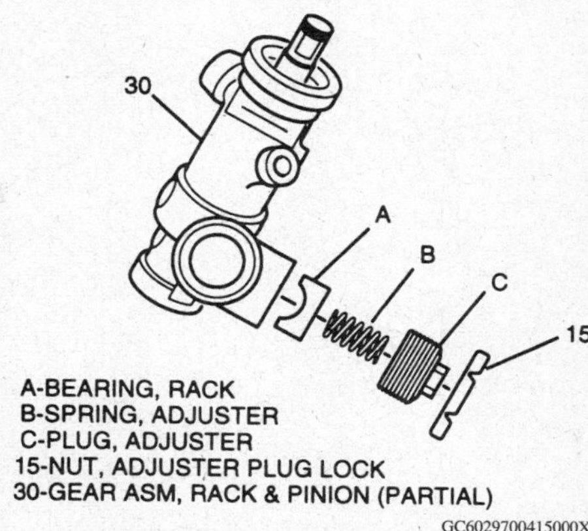

Fig. 13 Rack bearing removal. Except Achieva, Skylark & 1998 Grand Am

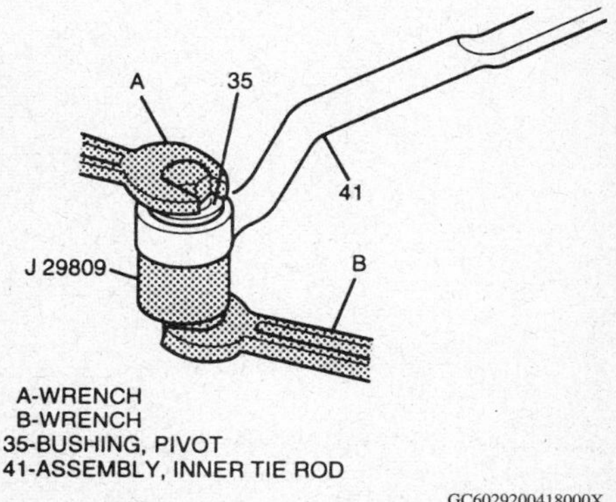

Fig. 16 Inner pivot bushing removal. Achieva, Skylark & 1998 Grand Am

proper sealing, Fig. 20.

9. Install new lock plate with notches in proper position over flats of inner tie rod bolts.

RACK BEARINGS

ACHIEVA, SKYLARK & 1998 GRAND AM

Removal

1. Remove rack and pinion assembly from vehicle.
2. Remove adjuster plug nut from adjuster plug, then adjuster plug from housing, **Fig. 21.**
3. Remove adjuster spring and rack bearing with O-ring seal attached.

Installation

1. Coat components with lithium grease, then install rack bearing with O-ring seal adjuster spring and adjuster plug into housing.
2. With rack centered in housing, turn adjuster plug clockwise until it bottoms in housing, then back off 35–45° and measure pinion torque. Maximum preload torque is 16 inch lbs.
3. Install locknut to adjuster plug and tighten to specifications while holding adjuster plug stationary, **Fig. 22.**

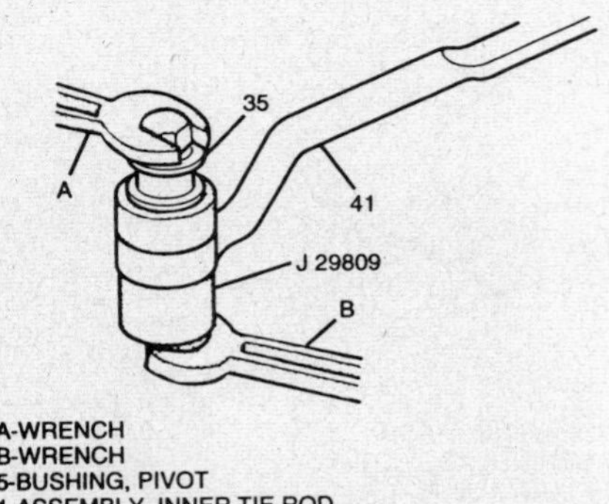

Fig. 17 Inner pivot bushing installation. Achieva, Skylark & 1998 Grand Am

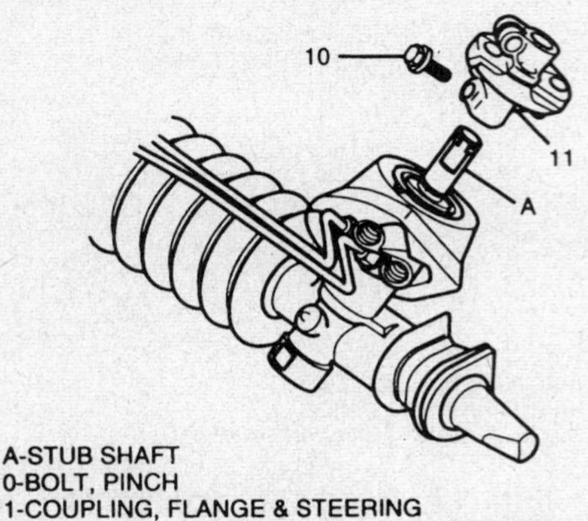

Fig. 18 Flange & steering coupling assembly. Achieva, Skylark & 1998 Grand Am

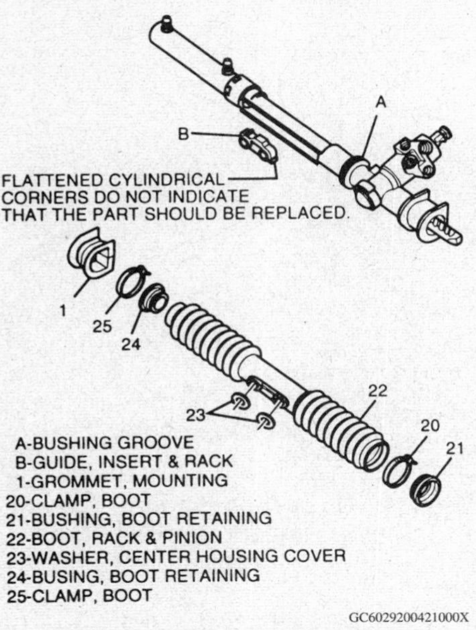

Fig. 19 Boot & rack guide assembly. Achieva, Grand Am & Skylark

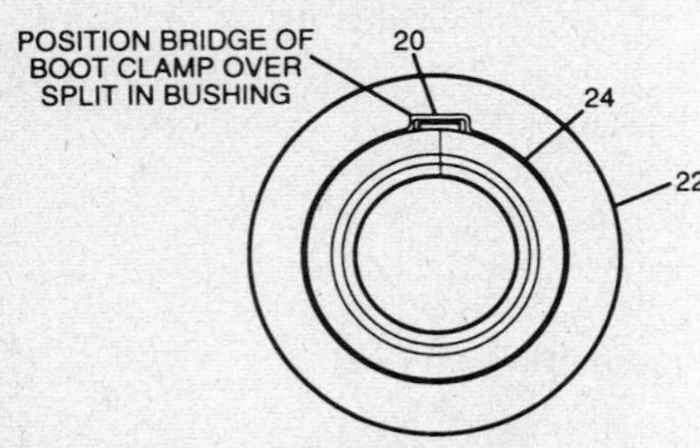

Fig. 20 Boot clamp position. Achieva, Skylark & 1998 Grand Am

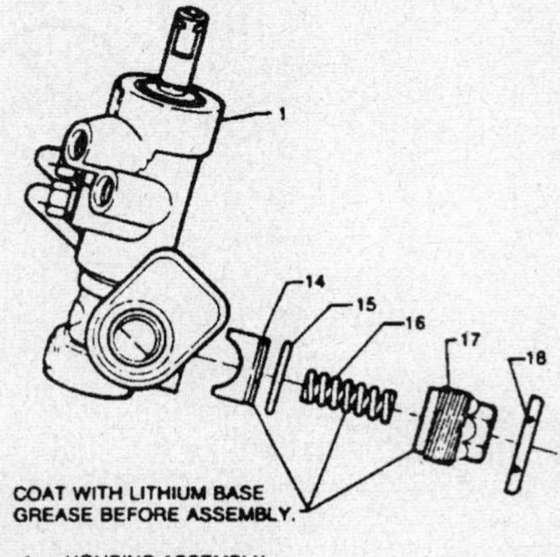

Fig. 21 Rack bearing assembly. Achieva, Skylark & 1998 Grand Am

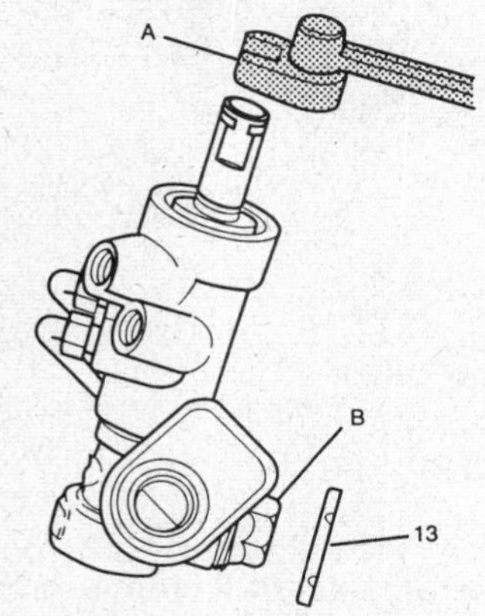

Fig. 22 Rack bearing adjustment. Achieva, Skylark & 1998 Grand Am

STUB SHAFT SEALS & UPPER BEARING

ACHIEVA, SKYLARK & 1998 GRAND AM

Removal

1. Remove rack and pinion assembly from vehicle.
2. Remove retaining ring and dust cover, **Fig. 23.**
3. While holding stub shaft, remove locknut from pinion. **Damage to pinion teeth will occur if stub shaft is not held.**
4. Press on threaded end of pinion until flush with ball bearing assembly using suitable press equipment. Complete removal of valve and pinion assembly is not required.
5. Remove stub shaft dust seal, stub shaft seal and stub shaft bearing annulus assembly from valve end of housing.

Installation

1. Install annulus assembly into gear.
2. Place seal protector tool No. J29810, or equivalent onto stub shaft and install stub shaft seal and stub shaft dust seal over protector and into housing.
3. Seat pinion locknut and tighten to specifications while holding stub shaft firmly.

BOOT OR RACK GUIDE

ACHIEVA, SKYLARK & 1998 GRAND AM

1. Cut off righthand hand mounting grommet and boot clamps, **Fig. 2.**
2. Slide boot retaining bushing from rack and pinion boot.
3. Slide boot assembly from rack and pinion housing.
4. Remove insert and rack guide assembly as required.
5. Slide boot retaining bushing from rack and pinion boot.
6. Slide new boot clamp onto rack and pinion boot.
7. Insert boot retaining bushing into rack and pinion boot.
8. Coat inner lip of boot retaining bushing lightly with suitable grease to facilitate assembly, then slide assembly onto housing assembly.
9. Ensure center housing cover washers are in place on rack and pinion boot.
10. Insert inner tie rod bolt through center housing cover washers, then the insert and rack guide and lightly thread bolt into rod and rack assembly to keep components in proper alignment.
11. Place boot retaining bushing onto cylinder tube of rack and pinion assembly, then slide into end of rack and pinion boot.
12. Slide boot clamp over cylinder end of housing and position on rack and pinion boot.
13. Slide rack and pinion boot and boot retaining bushing until seated in bushing groove in housing.
14. Position boot clamp on rack and pinion boot and crimp clamp.
15. Position boot clamp bridge over split in boot retaining bushing and crimp clamp. **Boot clamp bridge must be crimped over split in boot retaining bushing to ensure proper sealing.**

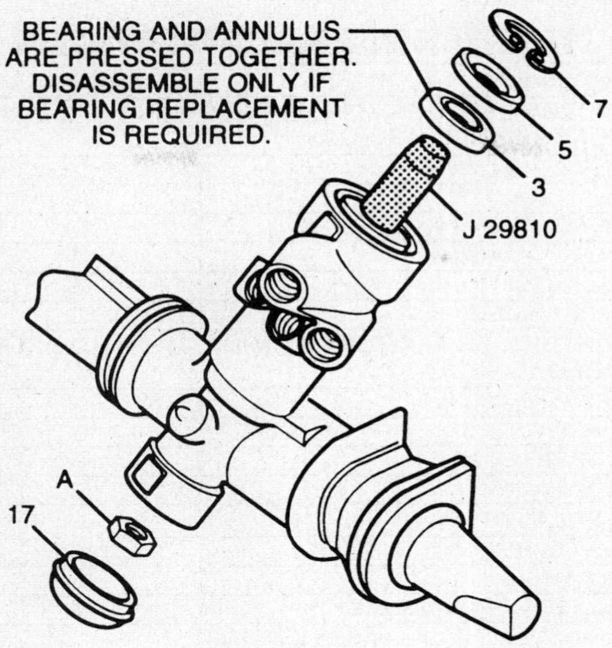
BEARING AND ANNULUS
ARE PRESSED TOGETHER.
DISASSEMBLE ONLY IF
BEARING REPLACEMENT
IS REQUIRED.
7
5
3
J 29810
A
17

A-NUT, HEX LOCK
3-ANNULUS ASM, BEARING
5-SEAL, STUB SHAFT
7-RING, RETAINING
17-COVER, DUST

GC6029200424000X

Fig. 23 Stub shaft seals & upper bearing assembly. Achieva, Skylark & 1998 Grand Am

TIGHTENING SPECIFICATIONS

Component	Torque/Ft. Lbs.
EXCEPT CENTURY, GRAND PRIX, IMPALA, LUMINA, MONTE CARLO & REGAL	
Adjuster Plug Locknut	50
Hex Locknut	22
Hex Nut	50
Hexagon Slotted Nut	35
Inner Tie Rod Housing To Rack	70
Tie Rod Jam Nut	50
CENTURY, GRAND PRIX, LUMINA, MONTE CARLO & REGAL	
Adjuster Plug Locknut	55
Inner Tie Rod Housing To Rack	74
Tie Rod End Nuts	22②
Tie Rod Jam Nut	50
IMPALA	
Fluid Cooler Pipe Bolt	84①
Inner Tie Rod	74
Intermediate Shaft Pinch Bolts	35
Steering Gear Cylinder Line Fittings	13
Steering Gear Mounting Bolts	59
Steering Gear Valve End Fittings	20
Steering Pump Mounting Bolts	25
Tie Rod End Nuts	22②
Tie Rod Jam Nuts	50

① — Inch lbs.
② — Rotate an additional 120°.

Saginaw Rack & Pinion Power Steering Gear w/Speed Sensitive Steering, General Motors

NOTE: On Air Bag Equipped Models, Refer To "Air Bag System Precautions" Located In The Front Of This Manual For System Disarming & Arming Procedures.

NOTE: Refer To "Computer Relearn Procedures" Located In The Front Of This Manual When Battery Power To The Computer Has Been Interrupted.

NOTE: "Electrical Symbol & Wire Color Code Identification" Located In The Front Of This Manual May Be Used As An Aid When Using Wiring Circuits Found In This Section.

INDEX

DESCRIPTION

Speed sensitive steering (Variable Effort or Magnasteer) varies the driver effort required to steer as vehicle speed changes. At low speeds, the system provides maximum power assist. At higher speeds, steering effort is increased to provide firmer steering and directional stability. Variable steering effort is accomplished by reducing power steering fluid flow from the pump as vehicle speed increases. When the vehicle is stationary, the system provides maximum flow. The speed sensitive steering system is made up of an Electronic Brake Control Module (EBCM) or Electronic Brake Traction Control Module (EBCTM), power steering fluid flow actuating device, steering wheel speed sensor, power rack and pinion and power steering pump.

Except for differences in valve machining, the design of the speed sensitive power rack and pinion assembly is the same as for the non-speed sensitive power rack and pinion.

DIAGNOSIS & TESTING

Accessing Diagnostic Trouble Codes

Diagnostic Trouble Codes (DTCs) must be read using a suitably programmed scan tool. There are no provisions for flash code diagnostics.

1. Turn ignition Off.
2. Connect suitably programmed scan tool to Data Link Connector (DLC).
3. Turn ignition On.
4. Select scan tool's Special Functions.
5. Read and record DTCs.

Diagnostic Trouble Code Interpretation

Refer to **Fig. 1** for diagnostic trouble code interpretation.

Wiring Diagrams

Refer to **Figs. 2 through 27** for wiring diagrams.

Diagnostic Tests

Refer to **Figs. 28 through 55** for diagnostic tests.

Clearing Diagnostic Trouble Codes

DTCs cannot be cleared by disconnecting EBTCM or battery cables. Follow the scan tool manufacturer's instructions to clear DTCs.

POWER STEERING SYSTEM SERVICE

Component Service

POWER STEERING GEAR

Disassembly

Refer to **Figs. 56 through 59** for exploded views of power steering gears. For procedures not covered in this section, refer to "Saginaw Rack & Pinion Power Steering Gear Less Speed Sensitive Steering."

EBCM

1. Disconnect EBCM from bracket using pressure tabs.
2. Disconnect EBCM electrical connectors.
3. Remove EBCM.
4. Reverse procedure to install.

VARIABLE EFFORT STEERING PROGRAMMING

Bonneville, Eighty Eight, LeSabre, LSS, Park Avenue, Regency & 2001 Aurora

Refer to **Fig. 60** for variable effort steering programming procedures.

Eldorado & Seville

Refer to **Fig. 61** for variable effort steering programming procedures.

Code	Description
C0450	Steering Assist Control Actuator Circuit Malfunction
C0455	Steering Position Sensor Circuit Malfunction
C1241	Speed Sensitive Steering Circuit Malfunction
C1241	Magnasteer Malfunction
C1243	Steering Wheel Position Sensor Circuit Malfunction
C1273	Actuator Circuit Open Or Shorted To Ground
C1274	Actuator Circuit Shorted Or Solenoid Shorted
C1287	Steering Position Sensor Open Or Shorted Or Yaw Rate Sensor Data Mismatch
C1288	Yaw Rate Sensor Data Mismatch

Fig. 1 Diagnostic trouble code interpretation

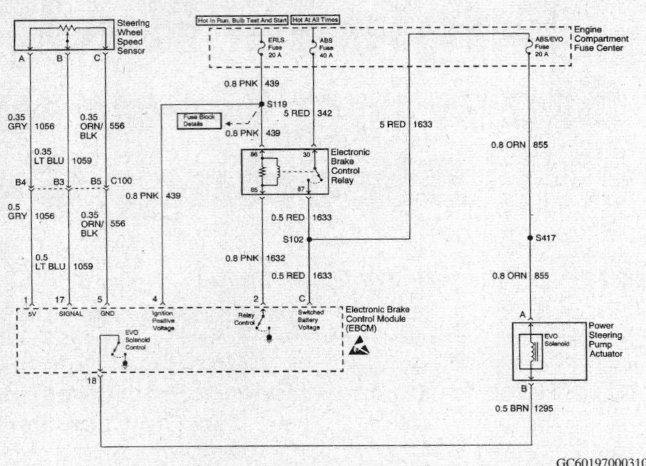

Fig. 2 Wiring diagram. Achieva & 1998 Grand Am

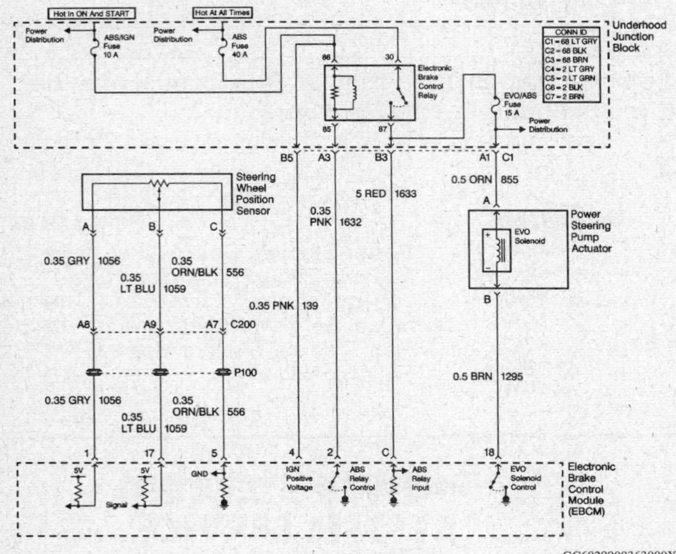

Fig. 3 Wiring diagram. 1999–2000 Alero & Grand Am

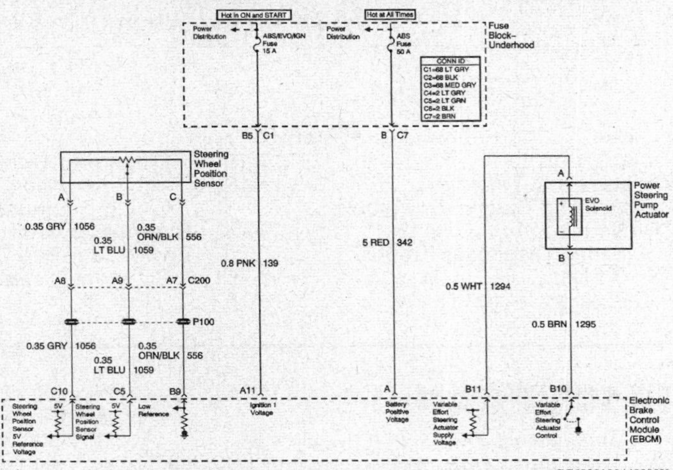

Fig. 4 Wiring diagram. 2001 Alero & Grand Am

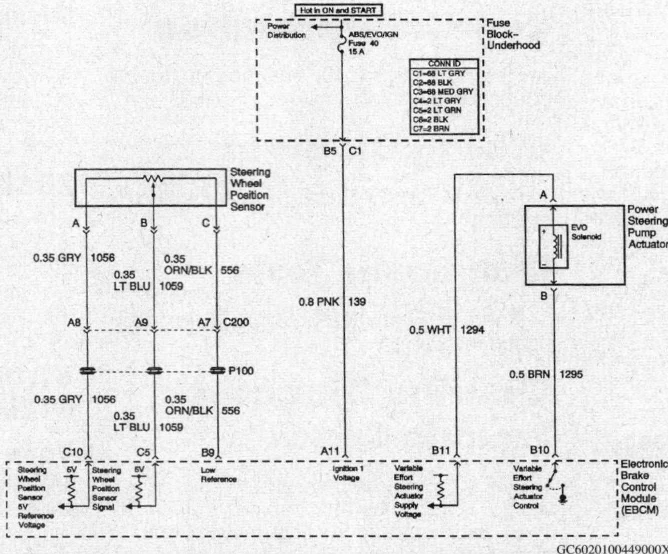

Fig. 5 Wiring diagram. 2002 Alero & Grand Am

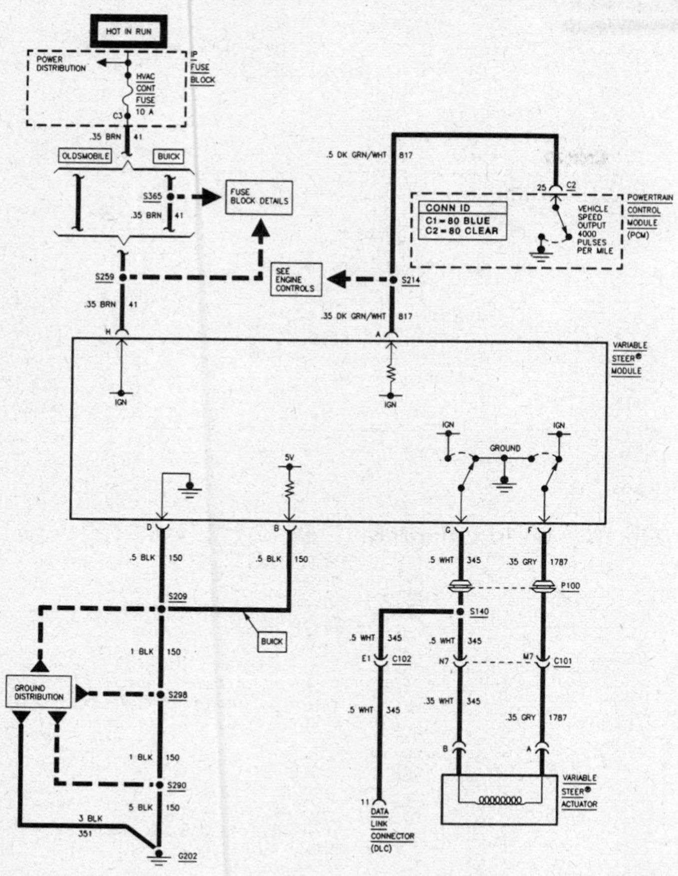

Fig. 6 Wiring diagram. 1998 Aurora & Riviera

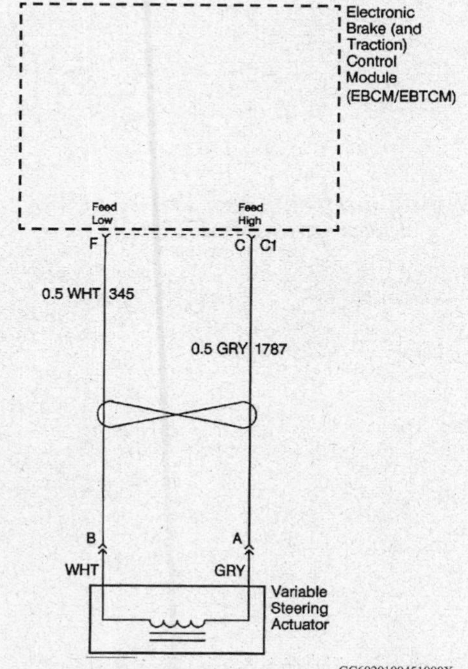

Fig. 9 Wiring diagram. 1998–99 Bonneville, Eighty Eight, LSS, LeSabre & Park Avenue

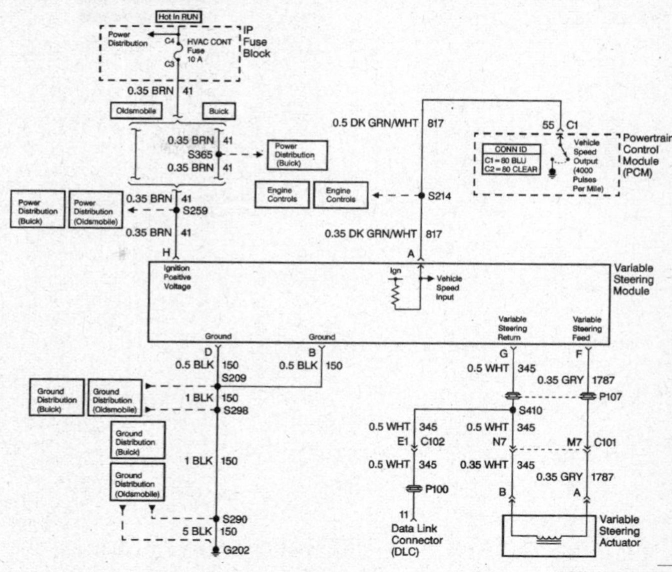

Fig. 7 Wiring diagram. 1999 Aurora & Riviera

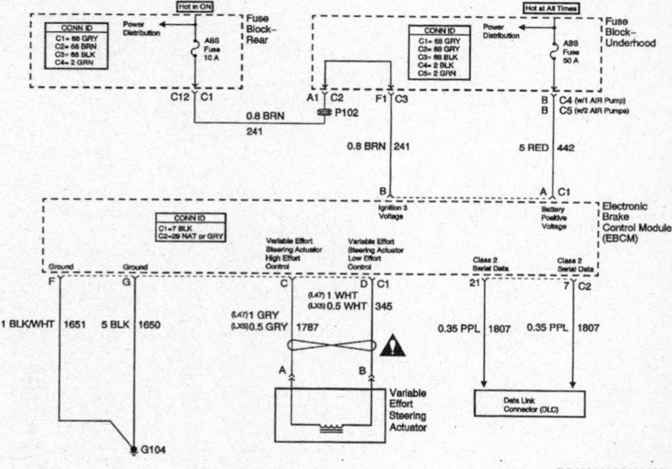

Fig. 8 Wiring diagram. 2001–02 Aurora

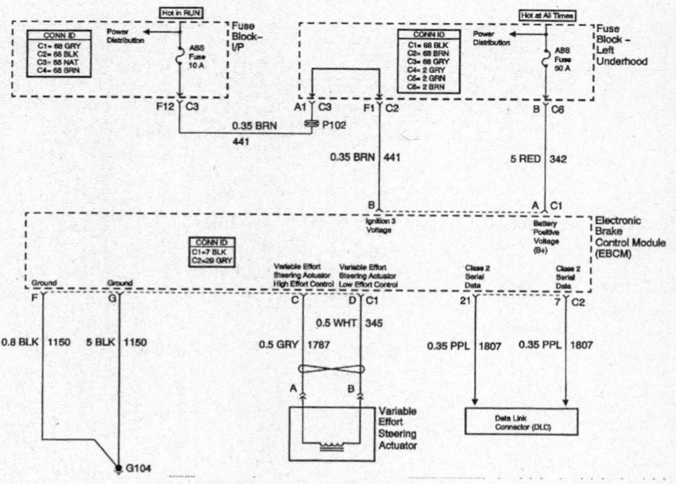

Fig. 10 Wiring diagram. 2000–02 Bonneville, LeSabre & Park Avenue

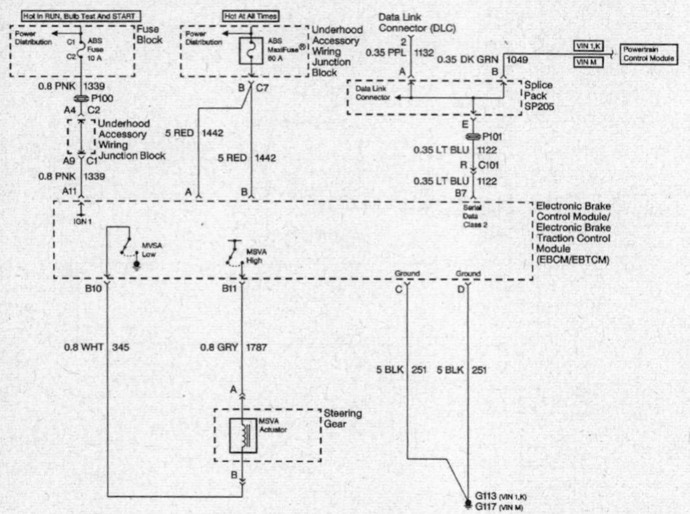

Fig. 11 Wiring diagram. 1999–2002 Century & Regal

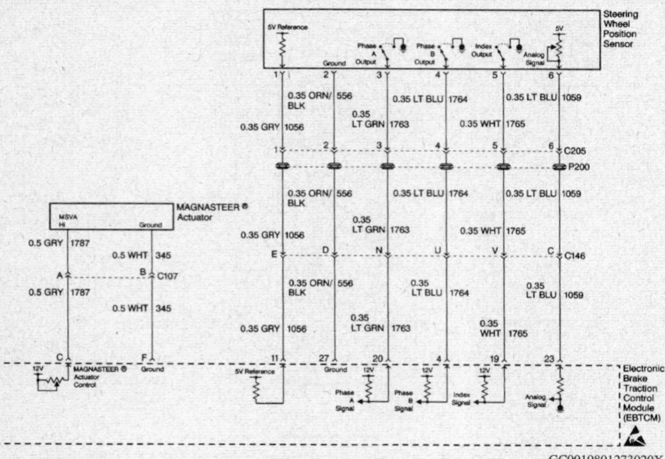

Fig. 12 Wiring diagram (Part 2 of 2). 1998 Corvette w/rear mounted EBTCM

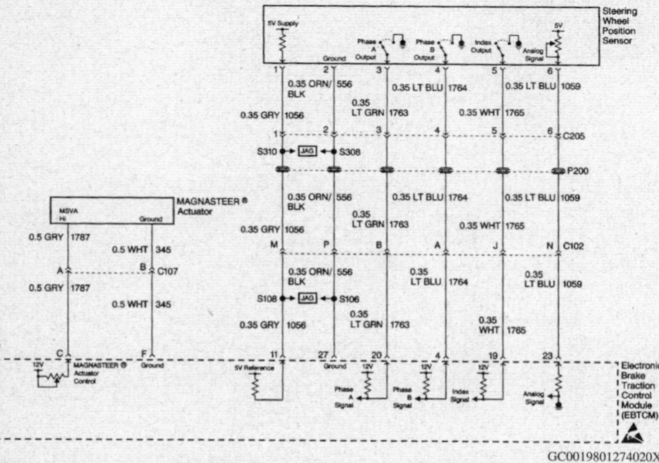

Fig. 13 Wiring diagram (Part 2 of 2). 1998 Corvette w/front mounted EBTCM

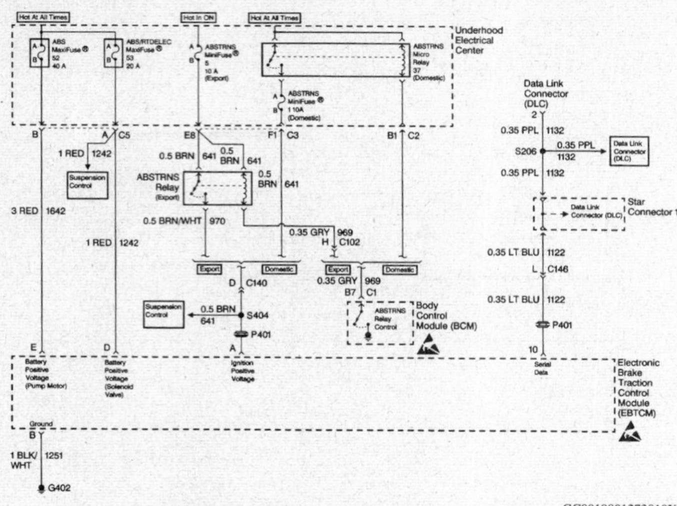

Fig. 12 Wiring diagram (Part 1 of 2). 1998 Corvette w/rear mounted EBTCM

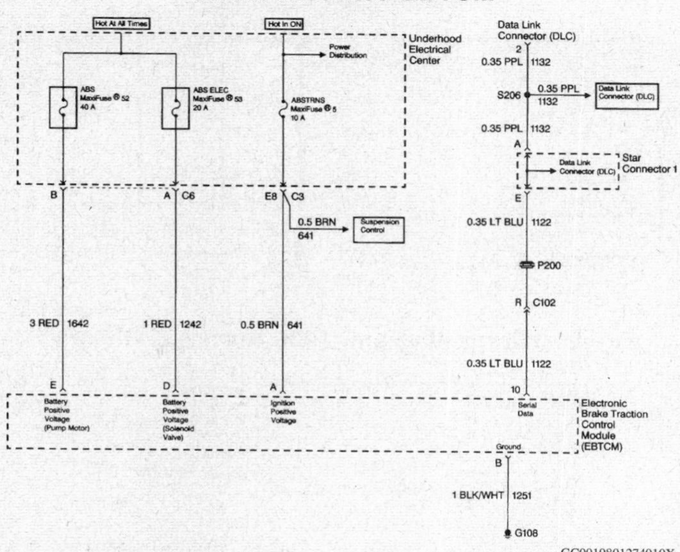

Fig. 13 Wiring diagram (Part 1 of 2). 1998 Corvette w/front mounted EBTCM

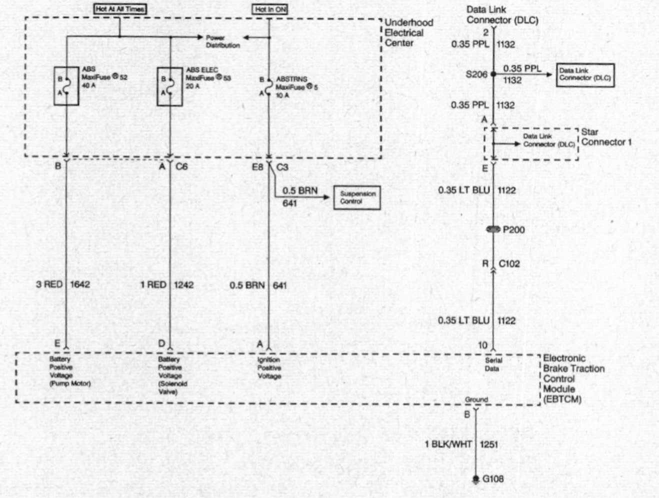

Fig. 14 Wiring diagram (Part 1 of 2). 1999–2000 Corvette

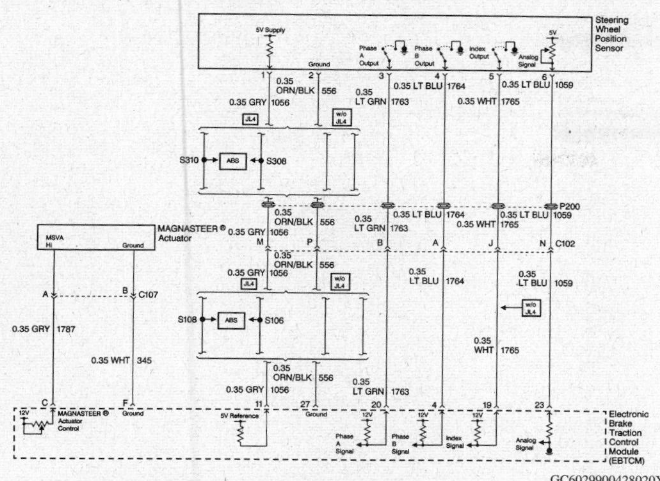

Fig. 14 Wiring diagram (Part 2 of 2). 1999–2000 Corvette

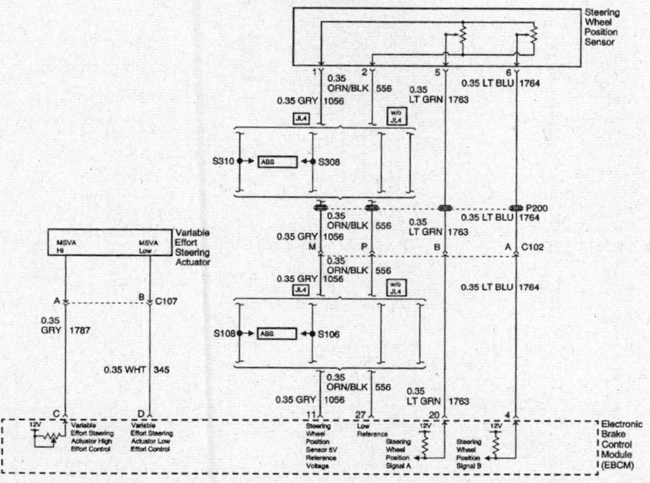

Fig. 15 Wiring diagram (Part 2 of 2). 2001–02 Corvette

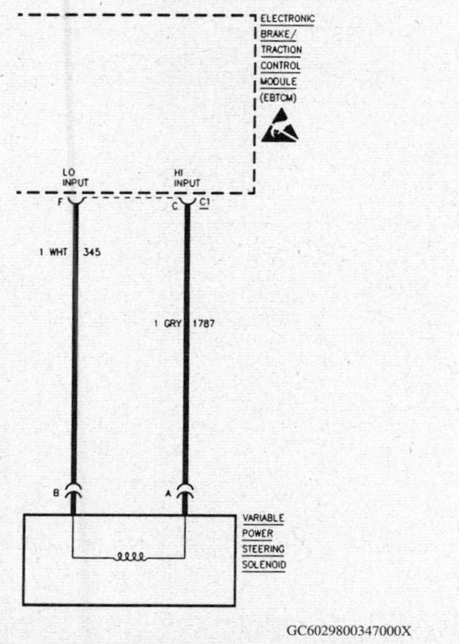

Fig. 16 Wiring diagram. 1998–99 DeVille & Eldorado

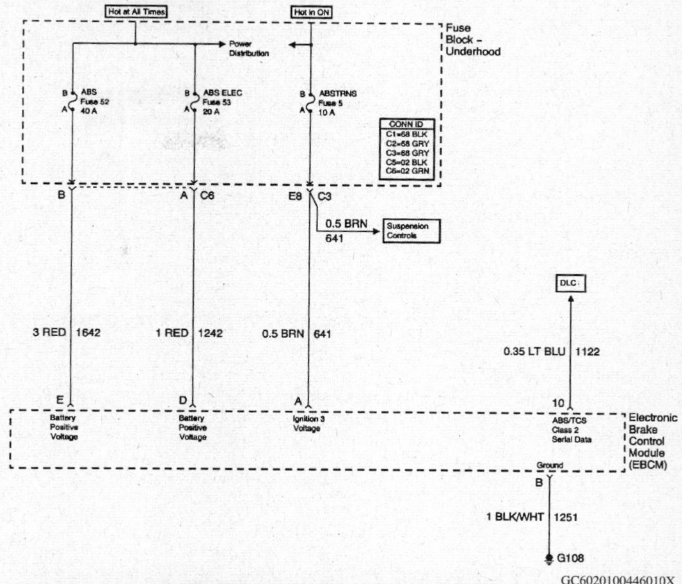

Fig. 15 Wiring diagram (Part 1 of 2). 2001–02 Corvette

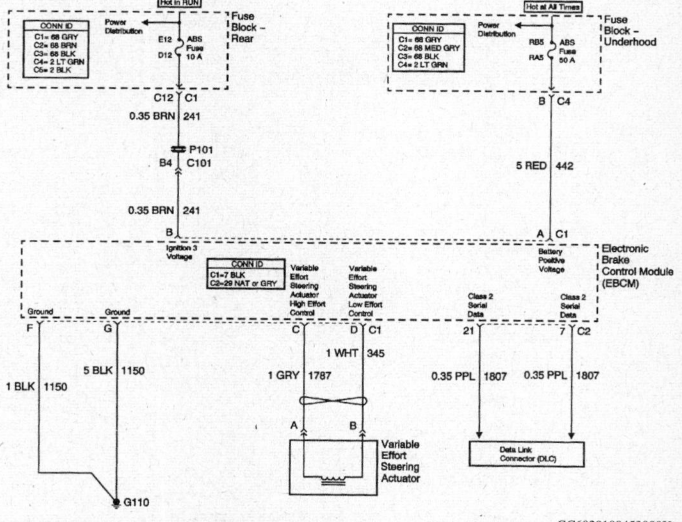

Fig. 17 Wiring diagram. 2000–02 DeVille

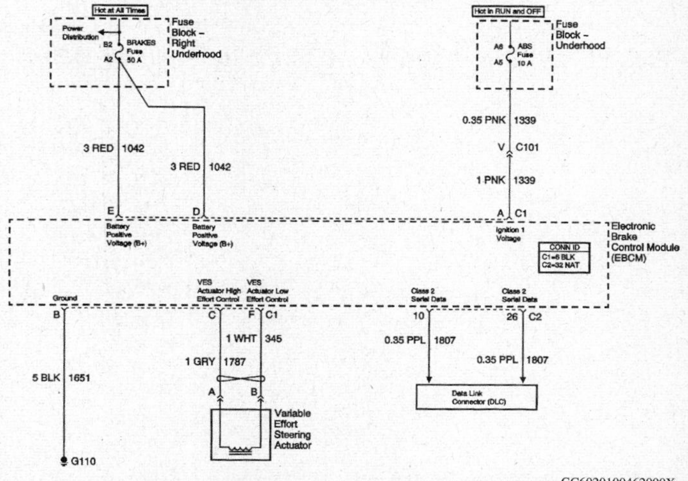

Fig. 18 Wiring diagram. 2000–02 Eldorado

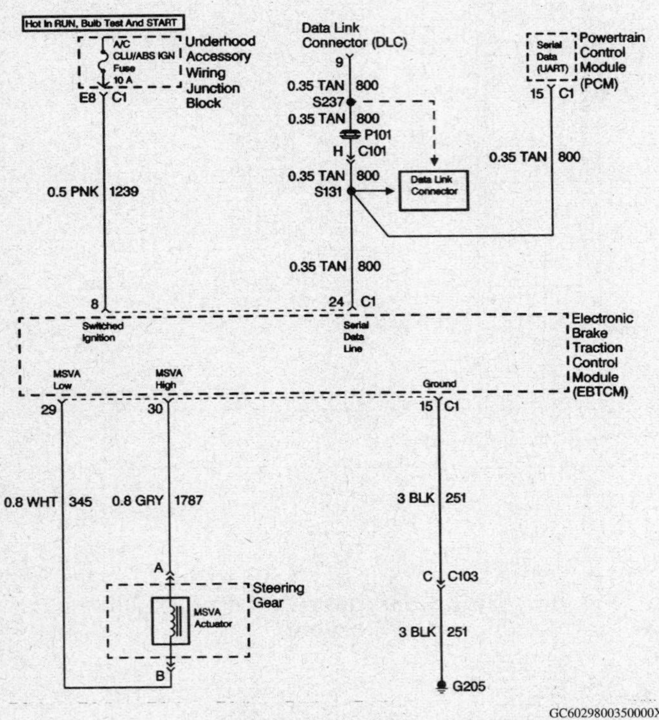

Fig. 19 Wiring diagram. Grand Prix

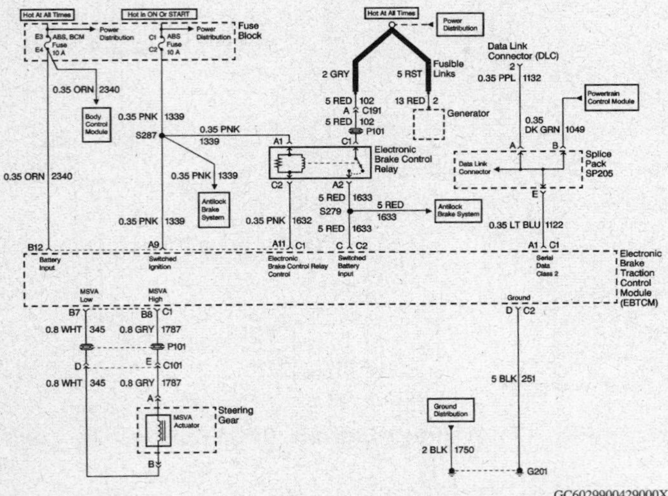

Fig. 21 Wiring diagram. 1999 Intrigue w/L36 Delco VI

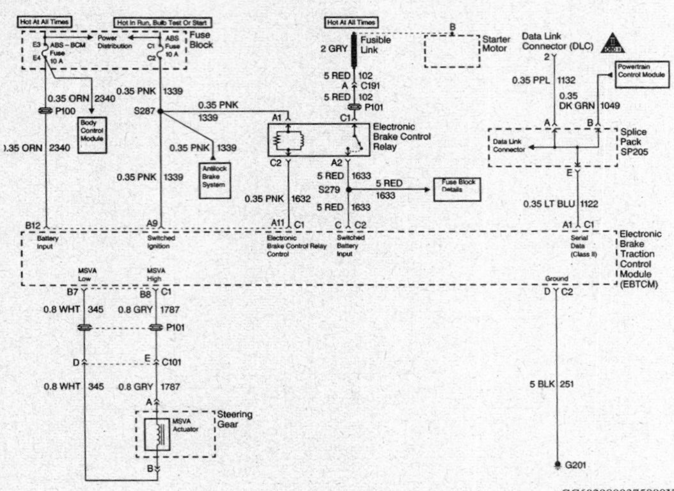

Fig. 20 Wiring diagram. 1998 Intrigue

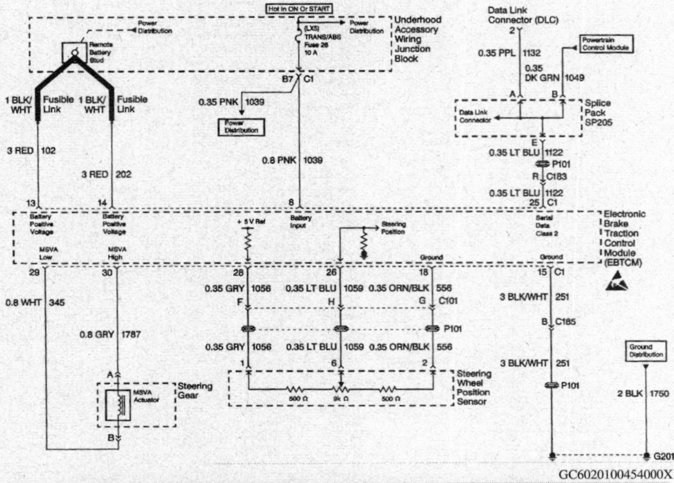

Fig. 22 Wiring diagram. 1999 Intrigue w/LX5 Bosch 5.3

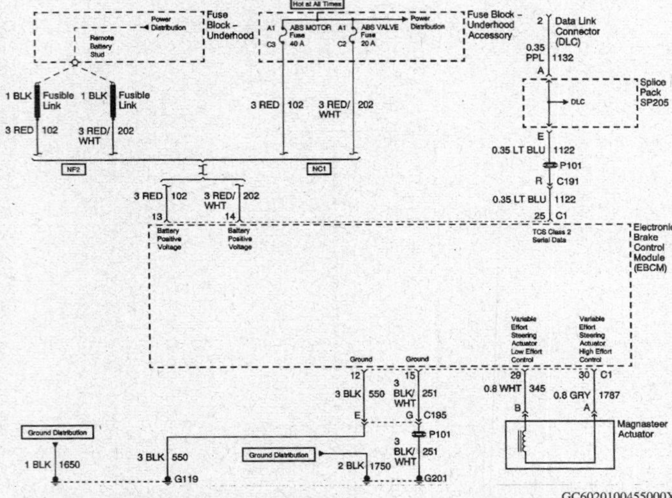

Fig. 23 Wiring diagram (steering actuator). 2000–01 Intrigue

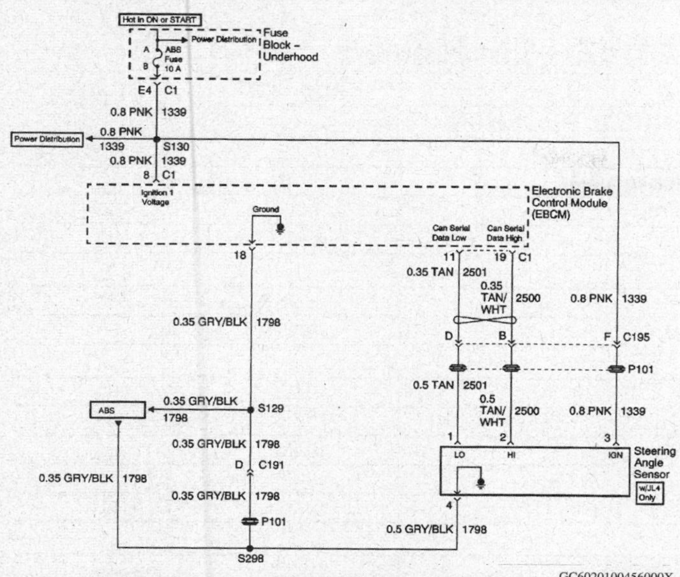

Fig. 24 Wiring diagram (steering position sensor). 2000–01 Intrigue w/JL4

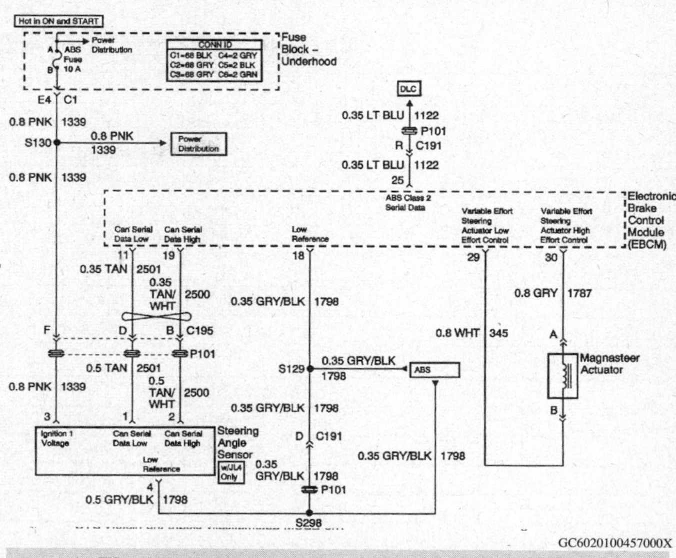

Fig. 25 Wiring diagram. 2002 Intrigue

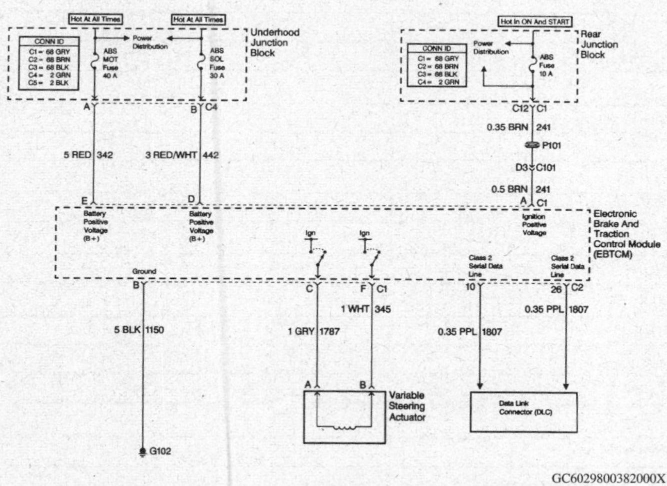

Fig. 26 Wiring diagram. 1998–99 Seville

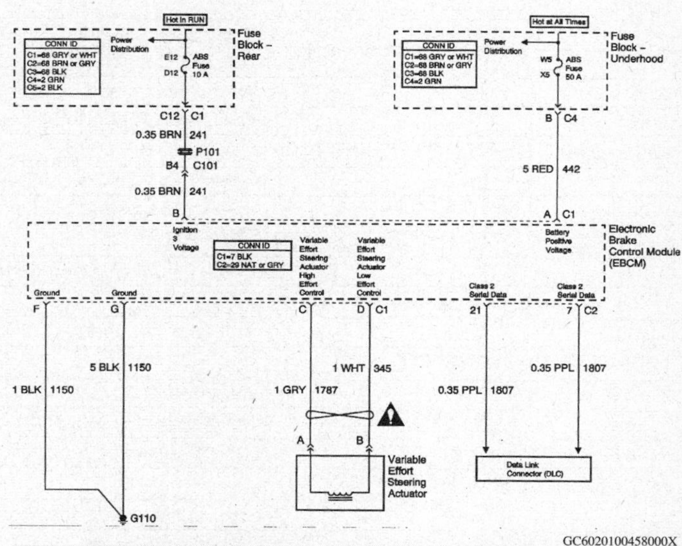

Fig. 27 Wiring diagram. 2000–02 Seville

DIAGNOSTIC CHART INDEX

Code	Description	Page No.	Fig. No.
ACHIEVA, ALERO & GRAND AM			
C1243	Steering Wheel Position Sensor Circuit Malfunction	19-34	49
C1273	Actuator Circuit Open Or Shorted To Ground	19-35	50
C1274	Actuator Circuit Shorted Or Solenoid Shorted	19-37	52
C1287	Yaw Rate Sensor Data Mismatch (2001)	19-37	54
C1287	Steering Position Sensor Shorted Or Open (2002)	19-39	55
C1288	Yaw Rate Sensor Data Mismatch	19-37	54
AURORA			
—	Variable Effort Steering System Inspection (1998–99)	19-23	28
—	Variable Effort Steering Electrical Diagnosis (1998–99)	19-23	29
—	Diagnostic System Inspection (2001–02)	19-23	30
C1241	Speed Sensitive Steering Circuit Malfunction (2001–02)	19-27	37

Continued

DIAGNOSTIC CHART INDEX—Continued

Code	Description	Page No.	Fig. No.
BONNEVILLE, EIGHTY EIGHT, LESABRE, LSS, PARK AVENUE & REGENCY			
—	Diagnostic System Inspection (1999–2002)	19-23	30
C1241	Speed Sensitive Steering Circuit Malfunction (1998)	19-26	35
C1241	Speed Sensitive Steering Circuit Malfunction (1999)	19-27	36
C1241	Speed Sensitive Steering Circuit Malfunction (2000–02)	19-27	37
GRAND PRIX			
—	Variable Effort Steering System Inspection	19-23	31
C0450	Steering Assist Control Actuator Circuit Malfunction	19-25	33
INTRIGUE			
—	Variable Effort Steering System Inspection (1999–2002)	19-23	31
C0450	Steering Assist Control Actuator Circuit Malfunction (2002)	19-25	33
C0455	Steering Position Sensor Circuit Malfunction	19-25	34
C1273	Actuator Circuit Open Or Shorted To Ground (1998–99)	19-36	51
C1274	Actuator Open Or Shorted Or Solenoid Shorted (1998–99)	19-37	53
RIVIERA			
—	Variable Effort Steering System Inspection	19-23	28
—	Variable Effort Steering Electrical Diagnosis	19-23	29
1998 CENTURY & REGAL			
—	Variable Effort Steering System Inspection	19-23	31
C0450	Steering Assist Control Actuator Circuit Malfunction	19-24	32
C1273	Actuator Circuit Open Or Shorted To Ground	19-36	51
C1274	Actuator Open Or Shorted Or Solenoid Shorted	19-37	53
1999–2002 CENTURY & REGAL			
—	Variable Effort Steering System Inspection	19-23	31
C1241	Magnasteer Malfunction	19-31	43
1998 CORVETTE w/REAR MOUNTED EBCM			
C1241	Speed Sensitive Steering Circuit Malfunction	19-28	38
1998 CORVETTE w/FRONT MOUNTED EBCM			
C1241	Speed Sensitive Steering Circuit Malfunction	19-28	39
1999–2002 CORVETTE			
C1241	Magnasteer Malfunction (1999–2000)	19-29	40
C1241	Magnasteer Malfunction (2001)	19-30	41
C1241	Magnasteer Malfunction (2002)	19-30	42
1998 DEVILLE & ELDORADO			
C1241	Speed Sensitive Steering Circuit Malfunction	19-32	44
1998 SEVILLE			
C1241	Speed Sensitive Steering Circuit Malfunction	19-32	45
1999 DEVILLE, ELDORADO & SEVILLE			
—	Diagnostic System Inspection	19-23	30
C1241	Magnasteer Malfunction	19-33	46
2000–02 DEVILLE & SEVILLE			
C1241	Speed Sensitive Steering Circuit Malfunction	19-33	47
2000–02 ELDORADO			
—	Diagnostic System Inspection	19-23	30
C1241	Magnasteer Malfunction	19-34	48

Step	Action	Normal Result(s)	Abnormal Result(s)*
1	1. Turn on the ignition with the engine running. 2. Place the gear selector in PARK. 3. Turn the steering wheel several times in both directions.	The steering wheel turns with minimal effort.	Go to *Variable Effort Steering Electrical Diagnosis*
2	1. Drive the vehicle. 2. Turn the steering wheel several times in both directions.	• As the vehicle speed increases, the level of effort needed to turn the steering wheel increases. • As the vehicle speed decreases, the level of effort needed to turn the steering wheel decreases.	Go to *Variable Effort Steering Electrical Diagnosis*

GC6019900019000X

Fig. 28 Variable Effort Steering System Inspection. Riviera & 1998–99 Aurora

Step	Action	Value(s)	Yes	No
12	Use a *J 39200* DMM in order to measure the voltage between the variable steering module connector terminal G and a good ground. Is the voltage greater than the specified value?	1 V	Go to *Step 23*	Go to *Step 13*
13	1. Raise the vehicle. 2. Place the gear selector in NEUTRAL. 3. Set the *J 39200* DMM to the DC scale. 4. Use a *J 39200* DMM in order to measure the voltage between the variable steering module connector terminal A and terminal D. 5. By hand, turn a drive wheel. Does the voltage vary within the specified range?	0–5 V	Go to *Step 15*	Go to *Step 24*
14	Replace the variable steering actuator. Did you complete the repair?	—	Go to *Variable Effort Steering System Check*	—
15	Replace the variable steering module. Did you complete the repair?	—	Go to *Variable Effort Steering System Check*	—
16	Repair the open in CKT 41 (BRN). Did you complete the repair?	—	Go to *Variable Effort Steering System Check*	—
17	Repair the open in CKT 150 (BLK). Did you complete the repair?	—	Go to *Variable Effort Steering System Check*	—
18	Repair the open in CKT 1787 (GRY). Did you complete the repair?	—	Go to *Variable Effort Steering System Check*	—
19	Repair the open in CKT 345 (WHT). Did you complete the repair?	—	Go to *Variable Effort Steering System Check*	—
20	Repair the short to ground in CKT 1787 (GRY). Did you complete the repair?	—	Go to *Variable Effort Steering System Check*	—
21	Repair the short to ground in CKT 1787 (GRY). Did you complete the repair?	—	Go to *Variable Effort Steering System Check*	—
22	Repair the short to ground in CKT 345 (WHT). Did you complete the repair?	—	Go to *Variable Effort Steering System Check*	—
23	Repair the short to voltage in CKT 345 (WHT). Did you complete the repair?	—	Go to *Variable Effort Steering System Check*	—
24	Repair the open or short in CKT 817 (DK GRN/WHT). Did you complete the repair?	—	Go to *Variable Effort Steering System Check*	—

GC6019900019020X

Fig. 29 Variable Effort Steering Electrical Diagnosis (Part 2 of 2). Riviera & 1998–99 Aurora

Step	Action	Value (s)	Yes	No
1	Install a scan tool. Does the scan tool power up?	--	Go to Step 2	Tool Does Not Power Up in Data Link Communications
2	1. Start the engine. 2. Attempt to establish communications with the EBCM. Does the scan tool communicate with the EBCM?	--	Go to Step 3	Scan Tool Does Not Communicate with Class 2 Device
3	Select the Magna Steer display DTC function on the scan tool. Does the scan tool display any DRP/ABS/TCS/VSES (if equipped) DTCs?	--	Go to A Diagnostic System Check - ABS in Antilock Brake System	Go to Step 4
4	Select the Magna Steer display DTC function on the scan tool. Does the scan tool display DTC C1241?	--	Go to DTC C1241	Go to Power Steering

GC6010100020000X

Fig. 30 Diagnostic System Inspection. 1999–2002 Bonneville, DeVille, Eighty Eight, Eldorado, LeSabre, LSS, Park Avenue, Regency, Seville & 2001–02 Aurora

Step	Action	Value(s)	Yes	No
1	Did you perform the Variable Effort Steering System Check?	—	Go to *Step 2*	Go to *Variable Effort Steering System Check*
2	Inspect the wiring and the connectors for damage. Is physical damage evident?	—	Go to *Step 3*	Go to *Step 4*
3	Repair damage to the wiring and connectors. Did you complete the repair?	—	Go to *Variable Effort Steering System Check*	—
4	1. Turn OFF the ignition. 2. Disconnect the variable steering module connector. 3. Turn ON the ignition leaving the engine OFF. 4. Use a *J 39200* DMM in order to measure the voltage between the variable steering module connector terminal H and a good ground. Is the voltage within the specified range?	Battery Voltage	Go to *Step 5*	Go to *Step 16*
5	1. Use a *J 39200* DMM in order to measure the voltage between the variable steering module connector terminal H and terminal D. 2. Use a *J 39200* DMM in order to measure the voltage between the variable steering module connector terminal H and terminal B. Is the voltage within the specified range for both measurements?	Battery Voltage	Go to *Step 6*	Go to *Step 17*
6	1. Turn OFF the ignition. 2. Use a *J 39200* DMM in order to measure the resistance between the variable steering module connector terminal G and terminal F. Is the resistance within the specified range?	1.6–3.1 Ω	Go to *Step 9*	Go to *Step 7*
7	1. Disconnect the variable steering actuator connector. 2. Use a *J 39200* DMM in order to measure the resistance between the variable steering module connector terminal F and the variable steering actuator connector terminal A. Is the resistance less than the specified value?	5 Ω	Go to *Step 8*	Go to *Step 18*
8	Use a *J 39200* DMM in order to measure the resistance between the variable steering module connector terminal G and the variable steering actuator connector terminal B. Is the resistance less than the specified value?	5 Ω	Go to *Step 14*	Go to *Step 19*
9	Use a *J 39200* DMM in order to measure the resistance between the variable steering module terminal F and a good ground. Is the resistance less than the specified value?	OL (Infinite)	Go to *Step 20*	Go to *Step 10*
10	Use a *J 39200* DMM in order to measure the voltage between the variable steering module connector terminal F and a good ground. Is the voltage greater than the specified value?	1 V	Go to *Step 21*	Go to *Step 11*
11	Use a *J 39200* DMM in order to measure the resistance between the variable steering module terminal G and a good ground. Is the resistance less than the specified value?	OL (Infinite)	Go to *Step 22*	Go to *Step 12*

GC6019900019010X

Fig. 29 Variable Effort Steering Electrical Diagnosis (Part 1 of 2). Riviera & 1998–99 Aurora

Step	Action	Value (s)	Yes	No
1	Connect a scan tool to the Data Link Connector (DLC). Does the scan tool communicate with the electronic brake traction control module (EBCM/EBTCM)?	--	Go to Step 2	Go to Diagnostic System
2	Using the scan tool, inspect for DTC C1241 in the ABS Diagnostic Trouble Codes (DTC). Does the scan tool displays DTC C1241 as current or history DTC?	--	Go to DTC C1241 Magnasteer Malfunction	Go to Step 3
3	Does the scan tool read any other current or history ABS DTC(s)?	--	Go to Diagnostic Trouble Code (DTC) List	Go to Step 4
4	1. Start the engine. 2. Turn the steering wheel to the right. 3. Turn the steering wheel to the left. Does the steering wheel turn with little effort?	--	Go to Step 5	Diagnose Steering Effort Hard in One or Both Directions
5	1. Drive the vehicle. 2. While driving the vehicle perform several turns and listen for any unusual sounds. Are there any unusual noises (hissing, rattle, groaning, whining, or growling) heard from the vehicle when turning?	--	Diagnose Power Steering System Inspection or Power Steering Gear	System OK

GC6020100460000X

Fig. 31 Variable Effort Steering System Inspection. Century, Grand Prix, Regal & 1999–2002 Intrigue

Circuit Description

The Magnetic Steering Variable Assist (MSVA), also known as MAGNASTEER® incorporates its controller into the electronic brake control module (EBCM). The EBCM controls the amount of current supplied to the MAGNASTEER® actuator based on input from the following components:

- The wheel speed sensors
- The steering wheel position sensor

Conditions for Setting the DTC

The MAGNASTEER® actuator or one or both of the MAGNASTEER® actuator circuit wires becomes open or shorted.

Action Taken When the DTC Sets

- A malfunction DTC is stored.
- No antilock brake system (ABS)/traction control system (TRAC OFF) indicators are turned ON.
- The MAGNASTEER® is disabled.

The ABS/TCS remains functional.

Conditions for Clearing the DTC

1. A history DTC will clear after 100 consecutive ignition cycles if the condition for the malfunction is no longer present.
2. You may use a scan tool in order to clear the DTC.

Diagnostic Aids

1. The following conditions may cause an intermittent malfunction to occur:
   - A poor connection
   - A rubbed-through wire insulation
   - A broken wire inside the insulation
2. Inspect the frequency of the malfunction by using the enhanced diagnostic function of the scan tool.
3. Inspect any circuitry that may cause the intermittent complaint for the following conditions:
   - Backed out terminals
   - Improper mating
   - Broken locks
   - Improperly formed terminals
   - Damaged terminals
   - Poor terminal to wiring connections
   - Physical damage to the wiring harness

Test Description

The numbers below refer to step numbers on the diagnostic table.

2. This step checks for an open or high resistance in the MAGNASTEER® circuit.
3. This step determines if the open or high resistance is in the MAGNASTEER® actuator, or the wiring harness.
16. This step checks if the MAGNASTEER® actuator is shorted to the steering gear case.

GC6019900025010X

Fig. 32 Code C0450: Steering Assist Control Actuator Circuit Malfunction (Part 1 of 4). 1998 Century & Regal & 1999–2001 Grand Prix & Intrigue

Step	Action	Value(s)	Yes	No
1	Was the Variable Effort Steering System Check performed?	—	Go to *Step 2*	Go to *Variable Effort Steering System Check*
2	1. Turn the ignition switch to the OFF position. 2. Disconnect the electronic brake control module (EBCM) harness connector. 3. Install the universal pinout box using the J 39700-530 cable adaptor to the EBCM harness connector only. 4. Use the DMM in order to measure the resistance between the following components: • The universal pinout box terminal 29 • Terminal 30 Is the resistance within the specified range?	1.6 - 3.1 Ω	Go to *Step 11*	Go to *Step 3*
3	1. Disconnect the two-way MAGNASTEER® actuator connector. 2. Using the DMM, measure the resistance between the following components: • MAGNASTEER® actuator pin A • MAGNASTEER® actuator pin B Is the resistance within the specified range?	1.6 - 3.1 Ω	Go to *Step 5*	Go to *Step 4*
4	Replace the MAGNASTEER® actuator. Is the repair complete?	—	Go to *Variable Effort Steering System Check*	—
5	Using the DMM, measure the resistance between the following components: • The universal pinout box terminal 29 • The MAGNASTEER® actuator harness connector terminal B Is the resistance within the specified range?	0–2 Ω	Go to *Step 7*	Go to *Step 6*
6	Repair the open or high resistance in CKT 345. Is the repair complete?	—	Go to *Variable Effort Steering System Check*	—
7	Using the DMM, measure the resistance between the following components: • The universal pinout box terminal 30 • The MAGNASTEER® actuator harness connector terminal A Is the resistance within the specified range?	0–2 Ω	Go to *Step 9*	Go to *Step 8*
8	Repair the open or high resistance in CKT 1787. Is the repair complete?	—	Go to *Variable Effort Steering System Check*	—
9	Using the DMM, measure the resistance between the following components: • The universal pinout box terminal 29 • The universal pinout box terminal 30 Is the resistance within the specified range?	OL (Infinite)	Go to *Step 22*	Go to *Step 10*
10	Repair the short between CKT 345 and CKT 1787. Is the repair complete?	—	Go to *Variable Effort Steering System Check*	—
11	Using the DMM, measure the resistance between the following components: • The universal pinout box terminal 15 • The universal pinout box terminal 29 Is the resistance within the specified range?	OL (Infinite)	Go to *Step 17*	Go to *Step 12*

GC6019900025020X

Fig. 32 Code C0450: Steering Assist Control Actuator Circuit Malfunction (Part 2 of 4). 1998 Century & Regal & 1999–2001 Grand Prix & Intrigue

Step	Action	Value(s)	Yes	No
12	1. Disconnect the two-way MAGNASTEER® actuator connector. 2. Using the DMM, measure the resistance between the following components: • The universal pinout box terminal 15 • The universal pinout box terminal 29 Is the resistance within the specified range?	OL (Infinite)	Go to *Step 14*	Go to *Step 13*
13	Repair the short to ground in CKT 345. Is the repair complete?	—	Go to *Variable Effort Steering System Check*	—
14	Using the DMM, measure the resistance between the following components: • The universal pinout box terminal 15 • Terminal 30 Is the resistance within the specified range?	OL (Infinite)	Go to *Step 16*	Go to *Step 15*
15	Repair the short to ground in CKT 1787. Is the repair complete?	—	Go to *Variable Effort Steering System Check*	—
16	Using the DMM, measure the resistance between the following components: • The MAGNASTEER® actuator pin A • The steering gear case Is the resistance within the specified range?	OL (Infinite)	Go to *Step 22*	Go to *Step 4*
17	1. Turn the ignition switch to the ON position with the engine OFF. 2. Using the DMM, measure the voltage between the following components: • The universal pinout box terminal 15 • Terminal 29 Is the voltage within the specified range?	0–1 V	Go to *Step 22*	Go to *Step 18*
18	1. Disconnect the two-way MAGNASTEER® actuator connector. 2. Using the DMM, measure the voltage between the following components: • The universal pinout box terminal 15 • Terminal 29. Is the voltage within the specified range?	0–1 V	Go to *Step 20*	Go to *Step 19*
19	Repair the short to voltage in CKT 345. Is the repair complete?	—	Go to *Variable Effort Steering System Check*	—
20	Using the DMM, measure the voltage between the following components: • The universal pinout box terminal 15 • Terminal 30 Is the voltage within the specified range?	0–1 V	Go to *Step 22*	Go to *Step 21*
21	Repair the short to voltage in CKT 1787. Is the repair complete?	—	Go to *Variable Effort Steering System Check*	—

GC6019900025030X

Fig. 32 Code C0450: Steering Assist Control Actuator Circuit Malfunction (Part 3 of 4). 1998 Century & Regal & 1999–2001 Grand Prix & Intrigue

Step	Action	Value(s)	Yes	No
22	1. Turn the ignition switch to the OFF position. **Important:** Damage or corrosion may result in an open or short with all of the connectors connected. 2. Inspect the EBCM harness connectors for the following conditions: • Damage • Corrosion **Important:** Damage or corrosion may result in an open or short with all of the connectors connected. 3. Inspect the two-way MAGNASTEER® actuator harness connector for the following conditions: • Damage • Corrosion Do the connectors exhibit signs of corrosion or damage?	—	Go to *Step 23*	Go to *Step 24*
23	1. Repair the damaged or corroded harness connectors in the EBCM. 2. Repair the damaged or corroded two-way MAGNASTEER® actuator harness connector. Is the repair complete?	—	Go to *Variable Effort Steering System Check*	—
24	1. Reconnect all of the connectors. 2. Test drive the vehicle to a speed greater than 40 km/h (25 mph). Did the DTC C0450 reset?	—	Go to *Step 25*	Go to *Variable Effort Steering System Check*
25	Replace the EBCM. Is the repair complete?	—	Go to *Variable Effort Steering System Check*	—

GC6019900025040X

Fig. 32 Code C0450: Steering Assist Control Actuator Circuit Malfunction (Part 4 of 4). 1998 Century & Regal & 1999–2001 Grand Prix & Intrigue

Step	Action	Value(s)	Yes	No
1	Did you perform the Variable Effort Steering Diagnostic System Check?	--	Go to Step 2	Perform Diagnostic System Check - Variable Effort Steering
2	1. Install a scan tool. 2. Turn the ignition ON, with the engine OFF. 3. With the scan tool, select the Diagnostic Trouble Codes (DTC) function. Does the scan tool indicate that DTC C0450 is a history DTC ?	--	Test for Intermittent and Poor Connections	Go to Step 3
3	1. Turn OFF the ignition. 2. Disconnect the VES actuator harness connector. 3. Measure the resistance of the VES actuator. Does the resistance measure within the specified range?	1.6-3.1 ohms	Go to Step 4	Go to Step 8
4	Test the High Effort Control circuit of the VES actuator for a short to ground. Did you find and correct the condition?	--	Go to Step 12	Go to Step 5
5	Test the High Effort Control circuit for an open or short to voltage. Did you find and correct the condition?	--	Go to Step 12	Go to Step 6
6	Test the Low Effort Control circuit for a short to ground. Did you find and correct the condition?	--	Go to Step 12	Go to Step 7
7	Test the Low Effort Control circuit for an open or short to voltage. Did you find and correct the condition?	--	Go to Step 12	Go to Step 9

GC6020100461010X

Fig. 33 Code C0450: Steering Assist Control Actuator Circuit Malfunction (Part 1 of 2). 2002 Grand Prix & Intrigue

Step	Action	Value(s)	Yes	No
8	Inspect for poor connections at the harness connector of the VES actuator. Did you find and correct the condition?	--	Go to Step 12	Go to Step 10
9	Inspect for poor connections at the harness connector of the EBCM. Did you find and correct the condition?	--	Go to Step 12	Go to Step 11
10	Replace the VES actuator. Did you complete the repair?	--	Go to Step 12	--
11	Replace the EBCM Did you complete the repair?	--	Go to Step 12	--
12	1. Use the scan tool in order to clear the DTCs. 2. Operate the vehicle within the Conditions for Running the DTC Does the DTC reset?	--	Go to Step 2	System OK

GC6020100461020X

Fig. 33 Code C0450: Steering Assist Control Actuator Circuit Malfunction (Part 2 of 2). 2002 Grand Prix & Intrigue

Circuit Description

The steering wheel position sensor provides the EBCM with an analog voltage reading from 0.15–4.84 V depending on the steering wheel angle. The EBCM uses the analog voltage for the centering routine. The EBCM runs a centering routine when the vehicle speed goes above 30 km/h (18 mph). When the vehicle reaches 30 km/h (18 mph), the EBCM monitors the steering wheel position sensor inputs (Analog voltage) to see if the steering wheel is moving. If the steering wheel is not moving for a set period of time then the EBCM assumes the vehicle is going in a straight line. At this point, the EBCM looks at the analog voltage signal and reads the voltage. This voltage, normally around 2.5 V, is then considered the center position and the digital degrees also become zero at the same time. This centering routine is necessary to compensate for wear in the steering and suspension. Wear in the steering and suspension can result in a change in the relationship between the steering wheel and the front wheels. By running the centering routine, the EBCM can compensate for these changes by changing the digital and analog center position.

Conditions for Setting the DTC

- The center position is +/-21.5° deviation from the previous nominal center point (0°) after the centering routine is complete.
- The steering wheel position sensor analog output voltage falls outside the 0.15–4.84 V range.

Action Taken When the DTC Sets

- Correct function of the steering wheel position sensor is incorrect and the EBCM stops using the sensor's data.
- MAGNASTEER® remains active using wheel speed data only.
- A malfunction DTC is stored.
- No ABS/TCS indicators are turned on and ABS/TCS remains active.

Conditions for Clearing the DTC

- Condition for DTC is no longer present and scan tool clear DTC function is used.
- 100 ignition cycles have passed with no DTCs detected.

GC6019900026010X

Fig. 34 Code C0455: Steering Position Sensor Circuit Malfunction (Part 1 of 4). Intrigue

Diagnostic Aids

The following are possible causes:

- The steering wheel was rotated with the steering gear disconnected.
- A malfunctioning steering wheel position sensor.
- A steering wheel position sensor circuit open.
- A steering wheel position sensor circuit shorted.
- A malfunctioning EBCM.

Perform an inspection of the wiring and of the connectors. Failure to carefully inspect the wiring and the connectors may result in misdiagnosis. Misdiagnosis causes part replacement with reappearance of the malfunction.

Test Description

The numbers below refer to the step numbers on the diagnostic table.

5. Re-centers the steering wheel position sensor.
11. Checks for an open in CKT 556.
12. Checks for a short to voltage in CKT 1059.
14. Checks for a short to ground in CKT 1059.
16. Checks for an open in CKT 1059.
18. Checks for a short to battery in CKT 1056.
20. Checks for an open in CKT 1056.
22. Checks for a short to ground in CKT 1056.

Step	Action	Value(s)	Yes	No
1	Was the Variable Effort Steering System Check performed?	—	*Go to Step 2*	*Go to Variable Effort Steering System Check*
2	1. Point the front wheels straight ahead. 2. Using a scan tool check the steering wheel position sensor analog voltage. Is the voltage within the range specified within the value(s) column?	2–3 V	*Go to Step 4*	*Go to Step 3*
3	Is the voltage in the range specified within the values(s) column?	0.15–4.84 V	*Go to Step 5*	*Go to Step 9*
4	Replace the EBCM. Is the repair complete?	—	*Go to Variable Effort Steering System Check*	—
5	1. Turn the ignition switch to the OFF position. 2. Disable the Supplemental Inflatable Restraint (SIR). 3. Remove the Inflatable Restraint Steering Wheel Module Coil. 4. Remove the Intermediate Steering Shaft. 5. Turn the ignition switch to the ON position, engine off. 6. Using a scan tool monitor the steering wheel position sensor analog voltage as you rotate the steering column shaft. 7. Turn the steering column shaft until the analog voltage is close to 2.5 volts. Does the analog voltage move smoothly to, or close to, 2.5 volts?	—	*Go to Step 7*	*Go to Step 6*
6	Replace the Steering Wheel Position Sensor. Is the replacement complete?	—	*Go to Variable Effort Steering System Check*	—

GC6019900026020X

Fig. 34 Code C0455: Steering Position Sensor Circuit Malfunction (Part 2 of 4). Intrigue

Step	Action	Value(s)	Yes	No
7	1. Leave the steering column shaft centered at 2.5 volts. 2. Turn the ignition switch to the OFF position. 3. Install the Intermediate Steering Shaft. 4. Install the Inflatable Restraint Steering Wheel Module Coil. 5. Enable the SIR. Is the repair complete?	—	*Go to Step 8*	—
8	1. Turn the ignition switch to the ON position, engine off. 2. Using a scan tool, clear DTC C0455. 3. Drive vehicle above 30 km/h (18 mph) for several minutes in a straight line. 4. Using a scan tool check for DTC C0455. Did DTC C0455 set as a current DTC?	—	*Go to Step 4*	Go to *Variable Effort Steering System Check*
9	1. Turn the ignition switch to the OFF position. 2. Disconnect the EBCM. 3. Install the *J 39700* universal pinout box using the J 39700-530 cable adapter to the EBCM harness connector and the EBCM. 4. Turn the ignition switch to the ON position, engine off. 5. Using *J 39200* DMM, measure the voltage between ground and terminal 26 of *J 39700*. Is the voltage within the range specified in the value(s) column?	0.15–4.84 V	*Go to Step 4*	*Go to Step 10*
10	1. Turn the ignition switch to the OFF position. 2. Disconnect the steering wheel position sensor connector. 3. Turn the ignition switch to the ON position, engine off. 4. Using the *J 39200* DMM, measure the voltage between ground and terminal 1 of the steering wheel position sensor harness connector. Is the voltage within the range specified in the value(s) column?	4.75–5.25 V	*Go to Step 11*	*Go to Step 18*
11	Using *J 39200* DMM, measure the resistance between the steering wheel position sensor harness connector terminal 2 and a good ground. Is the resistance within the range specified in the value(s) column?	0–5 Ω	*Go to Step 12*	*Go to Step 24*
12	1. Turn the ignition switch to the ON position, engine off. 2. Using the *J 39200* DMM, measure the voltage at terminal 6 of the steering wheel position sensor harness connector. Is the voltage above the value specified in the value(s) column?	1 V	*Go to Step 13*	*Go to Step 14*
13	Repair CKT 1059 for a short to voltage, being sure to check for a short to CKT 1056. Is the repair complete?	—	Go to *Variable Effort Steering System Check*	—
14	1. Turn the ignition switch to the OFF position. 2. Disconnect the J 39700-530 cable adapter from the EBCM leaving the J 39700-530 cable adapter connected to the EBCM harness connector. 3. Using *J 39200* DMM, measure the resistance between terminals 26 and 15 of *J 39700*. Is the resistance within the range specified within the value(s) column?	OL (infinite)	*Go to Step 16*	*Go to Step 15*

GC6019900026030X

Fig. 34 Code C0455: Steering Position Sensor Circuit Malfunction (Part 3 of 4). Intrigue

Step	Action	Value(s)	Yes	No
15	Repair CKT 1059 for a short to ground, being sure to check for a short to CKT 556. Is the repair complete?	—	Go to *Variable Effort Steering System Check*	—
16	1. Connect a jumper wire between terminals 26 and 18 of *J 39700*. 2. Using *J 39200* DMM, measure the resistance between the steering wheel position sensors harness connector terminals 2 and 6. Is the resistance within the range specified within the value(s) column?	0–5 Ω	*Go to Step 6*	*Go to Step 17*
17	Repair CKT 1059 for an open or high resistance. Is the repair complete?	—	Go to *Variable Effort Steering System Check*	—
18	Using the *J 39200* DMM, measure the voltage at terminal 1 of the steering wheel position sensor harness connector. Is the voltage above the value specified in the value(s) column?	5.25 V	*Go to Step 19*	*Go to Step 20*
19	Repair CKT 1056 for a short to battery. Is the repair complete?	—	Go to *Variable Effort Steering System Check*	—
20	1. Turn the ignition switch to the OFF position. 2. Disconnect the J 39700-530 cable adapter from the EBCM leaving the J 39700-530 cable adapter connected to the EBCM harness connector. 3. Connect a jumper wire between terminals 28 and 15 of *J 39700*. 4. Using *J 39200* DMM, measure the resistance between the steering wheel position sensor harness connector terminal 1 and a good ground. Is the resistance within the range specified within the value(s) column?	0–5 Ω	*Go to Step 22*	*Go to Step 21*
21	Repair CKT 1056 for an open or high resistance. Is the repair complete?	—	Go to *Variable Effort Steering System Check*	—
22	1. Remove the jumper wire from *J 39700*. 2. Using *J 39200* DMM, measure the resistance between the steering wheel position sensor harness connector terminal 1 and a good ground. Is the resistance within the range specified in the values column?	OL (infinite)	*Go to Step 4*	*Go to Step 23*
23	Repair CKT 1056 for a short to ground. Is the repair complete?	—	Go to *Variable Effort Steering System Check*	—
24	1. Turn the ignition switch to the OFF position. 2. Disconnect the J 39700-530 cable adapter from the EBCM leaving the J 39700-530 cable adapter connected to the EBCM harness connector. 3. Using the *J 39200* DMM, measure the resistance between the *J 39700* terminal 18 and terminal 2 of the steering wheel position sensor harness connector. Is the resistance within the range specified in the value(s) column?	0–5 Ω	*Go to Step 4*	*Go to Step 25*
25	Repair CKT 556 for an open or high resistance. Is the repair complete?	—	Go to *Variable Effort Steering System Check*	—

GC6019900026040X

Fig. 34 Code C0455: Steering Position Sensor Circuit Malfunction (Part 4 of 4). Intrigue

Step	Action	Value(s)	Yes	No
1	Was the Steering Controls Diagnostic System Check performed?	-	Go to Step 2	Go to System Check.
2	Inspect wiring and connectors for damage. Is physical damage evident?	-	Go to Step 3	Go to Step 4
3	Repair as necessary. Is repair complete?	-	Go to System Check.	-
4	1. Disconnect Variable Power Steering Solenoid connector. 2. Using J39200, measure the resistance between terminals A and B on the Variable Power Steering Solenoid. Is the resistance within the specified range?	1.6 - 3.1 Ω	Go to Step 5	Go to Step 6
5	1. Using J39200, measure the resistance between terminal A and a good ground. 2. Using J39200, measure the resistance between terminal B and a good ground. Was the resistance of either measurement within the specified range?	-	Go to Step 6	Go to Step 7
6	Replace the Variable Power Steering Solenoid. Is the actuator replacement complete?	-	Go to System Check.	-
7	1. Turn the ignition switch to the OFF position. 2. Disconnect the Electronic Brake/Traction Control Module (EBTCM) connector C1. 3. Install a J39700 universal pinout box using J39700-25 cable adapter to the EBTCM harness only. 4. Using J39200, measure the resistance between terminals C and B of J39700. Is the resistance within the specified range?	Less than OL	Go to Step 8	Go to Step 9
8	Repair CKT 1787 (GRY) for a short to ground. Is the repair complete?	-	Go to System Check.	-
9	Using J39200, measure the resistance between terminals F and B of J39700. Is the resistance within the range specified?	Less than OL	Go to Step 10	Go to Step 11
10	Repair CKT 345 (WHT) for a short to ground. Is the repair complete?	-	Go to System Check.	-

GC6029800355010X

Fig. 35 Code C1241: Speed Sensitive Steering Circuit Malfunction (Part 1 of 2). 1998 Bonneville, Eighty Eight, LeSabre, LSS, Park Avenue & Regency

Step	Action	Value(s)	Yes	No
11	1. Reconnect the Variable Power Steering Solenoid connector. 2. Using J39200, measure the resistance between terminals C and F of J39700. Is the resistance within the specified range?	1.6 - 3.1 Ω	Go to Step 17	Go to Step 12
12	Is the resistance less than the range specified in the value(s) column?	-	Go to Step 13	Go to Step 14
13	Repair CKT 1787 (GRY) and 345 (WHT) for a short together.	-	Go to System Check.	-
14	1. Connect a fused jumper wire between terminals C and B of J39700. 2. Disconnect the Variable Power Steering Solenoid. 3. Using J39200, measure the resistance between the Variable Power Steering Solenoid harness connector terminal A and a good ground. Is the resistance within the specified range?	0 - 5 Ω	Go to Step 15	Go to Step 16
15	Repair CKT 345 (WHT) for an open. Is the wire repair complete?	-	Go to System Check.	-
16	Repair CKT 1787 (GRY) for an open. Is the wire repair complete?	-	Go to System Check.	-
17	1. Turn the ignition switch to the RUN position. 2. Using J39200, measure for voltage at terminal C of J39700. Is the voltage within the specified range?	above 1 volt	Go to Step 18	Go to Step 19
18	Repair CKT 1787 (GRY) for a short to voltage. Is the repair complete?	-	Go to System Check.	-
19	Using J39200, measure for voltage at terminal F of J39700. Is the voltage within the specified range?	above 1 volt	Go to Step 20	Go to Step 21
20	Repair CKT 345 (WHT) for a short to voltage. Is the repair complete?	-	Go to System Check.	-
21	Replace the EBTCM. Is the module replacement complete?	-	Go to System Check.	-

GC6029800355020X

Fig. 35 Code C1241: Speed Sensitive Steering Circuit Malfunction (Part 2 of 2). 1998 Bonneville, Eighty Eight, LeSabre, LSS, Park Avenue & Regency

Step	Action	Value(s)	Yes	No
1	Did you perform the Variable Effort Steering System Inspection?	—	Go to *Step 2*	Refer to System Inspection
2	Inspect the wiring and the connectors for damage. Is physical damage evident?	—	Go to *Step 3*	Go to *Step 4*
3	Repair damage to the wiring and connectors. Did you complete the repair?	—	Refer to System Inspection	—
4	1. Turn OFF the ignition. 2. Disconnect the EBCM/EBTCM connector. 3. Install the *J 39700* universal pinout box using the *J 39700 - 25* cable adapter to the EBCM/EBTCM harness connector only. 4. Use the *J 39200* DMM to measure the resistance between the *J 39700* terminal C and terminal F. Is the resistance within the specified range?	1.6–3.1 Ω	Go to *Step 19*	Go to *Step 5*
5	1. Disconnect the variable steering actuator connector. 2. Use the *J 39200* to measure the resistance between the variable steering actuator terminal A and terminal C. Is the resistance within the specified range?	1.6–3.1 Ω	Go to *Step 6*	Go to *Step 12*
6	Use the *J 39200* to measure the resistance between the *J 39700* terminal C and the variable steering actuator connector terminal A. Is the resistance less than the specified value?	0.5 Ω	Go to *Step 7*	Go to *Step 13*
7	Use the *J 39200* to measure the resistance between the *J 39700* terminal F and the variable steering actuator connector terminal B. Is the resistance less than the specified value?	0.5 Ω	Go to *Step 8*	Go to *Step 14*
8	Use the *J 39200* to measure the resistance between the *J 39700* terminal F and a good ground. Is the resistance less than the specified value?	OL	Go to *Step 15*	Go to *Step 9*
9	Use the *J 39200* to measure the resistance between the *J 39700* terminal F and a good ground. Is the resistance greater than the specified value?	1 V	Go to *Step 16*	Go to *Step 10*
10	Use the *J 39200* to measure the resistance between the *J 39700* terminal C and a good ground. Is the resistance less than the specified value?	OL	Go to *Step 17*	Go to *Step 11*
11	Use the *J 39200* to measure the resistance between the *J 39700* terminal C and a good ground. Is the resistance greater than the specified value?	1 V	Go to *Step 18*	Go to *Step 19*
12	Replace the variable steering actuator. Did you complete the repair?	—	Refer to System Inspection	—
13	Repair the open in CKT 1787. Did you complete the repair?	—	Refer to System Inspection	—
14	Repair the open in CKT 345. Did you complete the repair?	—	Refer to System Inspection	—

GC6029900426010X

Fig. 36 Code C1241: Speed Sensitive Steering Circuit Malfunction (Part 1 of 2). 1999 Bonneville, Eighty Eight, LeSabre, LSS, Park Avenue & Regency

Step	Action	Value(s)	Yes	No
15	Repair the short to ground in CKT 345. Did you complete the repair?	—	Refer to System Inspection	—
16	Repair the short to voltage in CKT 345. Did you complete the repair?	—	Refer to System Inspection	—
17	Repair the short to ground in CKT 1787. Did you complete the repair?	—	Refer to System Inspection	—
18	Repair the short to voltage in CKT 1787. Did you complete the repair?	—	Refer to System Inspection	—
19	Replace the EBCM/EBTCM. Did you complete the repair?	—	Refer to System Inspection	—

GC6029900426020X

Fig. 36 Code C1241: Speed Sensitive Steering Circuit Malfunction (Part 2 of 2). 1999 Bonneville, Eighty Eight, LeSabre, LSS, Park Avenue & Regency

Circuit Description

The EBCM controls a bi-directional magnetic rotary solenoid. The solenoid is in the steering gear. The solenoid adjusts the amount of power steering assist in order to achieve a given level of driver effort in turning the vehicle. The EBCM varies the steering assist by adjusting the current flow through the solenoid. The amount of steering assist adjusted for steering is dependent upon vehicle speed. As the vehicle speed increases, the following actions occur:

- The steering assist decreases
- The driver effort increases.

As the vehicle speed decreases, the following actions occur:

- The steering assist increases
- The driver effort decreases.

Conditions for Running the DTC

The EBCM performs 2 diagnostic tests for the VES circuits when the ignition voltage is between 10.5 volts and 17 volts. The numbers below corresponds to the numbers in Conditions for Setting the DTC.

1. Off State Test (Open Circuit Test) - When the ignition is first turned ON, the EBCM performs an open circuit test independent of vehicle speed or engine running.
2. On State Test (Open or Short Circuit Test) - If the Off State Test is passed, the EBCM runs the On State Test during VES operations.

The VES operations occur during driving. The EBCM detects an open or short in the VES circuit by comparing the feedback current to the commanded current.

Conditions for Setting the DTC

The EBCM performs 2 different tests to detect a DTC condition. The numbers below correspond to the number in Conditions for Running the DTC.

1. The EBCM detects an open in the VES circuit.
2. The EBCM detects an open or short in the VES circuit when the feedback current is less than 155 mA while the absolute value of the commanded current is greater than 826 mA for 2.5 seconds.

Action Taken When the DTC Sets

The EBCM disables the variable effort steering (VES) for the duration of the ignition cycle.

Conditions for Clearing the DTC

- The condition for the DTC is no longer present (the DTC is not current) and you used the scan tool Clear DTC function.
- The EBCM automatically clears the history DTC when a current DTC is not detected in 100 consecutive drive cycles.

GC6010000021010X

Fig. 37 Code C1241: Speed Sensitive Steering Circuit Malfunction (Part 1 of 3). 2000–02 Bonneville, LeSabre & Park Avenue & 2001–02 Aurora

Diagnostic Aids

The vehicle may need to be driven to view non-zero values of the Magna Steer Commanded Current and Magna Steer Feedback Current on the scan tool.

Test Description

The numbers below refer to the step numbers on the diagnostic table.

2. This step uses the scan tool to check the Magna Steer Feedback Current parameter.
6. This step checks for an open in the variable effort steering actuator and circuit.

Step	Action	Value(s)	Yes	No
1	Did you perform the Variable Effort Steering Diagnostic System Check?	—	Go to *Step 2*	Go to *A Diagnostic System Check - Variable Effort Steering*
2	1. Install a scan tool. 2. Start the engine. 3. With a scan tool, observe the Magna Steer Commanded Current and Magna Steer Feedback Current parameters in the Magna Steer data list. 4. Carefully test drive the vehicle so that the Magna Steer Commanded Current is greater than 826 mA. Does the scan tool indicate that the Magna Steer Feedback Current is greater than the specified value?	155 mA	Go to *Intermittent*	Go to *Step 3*
3	1. Turn OFF the ignition. 2. Disconnect the variable effort steering actuator connector. 3. Measure the resistance across the variable effort steering actuator. Does the resistance measure within the specified range?	1.6–3.1 Ω	Go to *Step 5*	Go to *Step 4*
4	Test both variable effort steering control circuits for a high resistance or an open between the variable effort steering actuator pigtail connector and the variable effort steering actuator. Did you find and correct the condition?	—	Go to *Step 13*	Go to *Step 8*
5	Test both variable effort steering control circuits for a short between the variable effort steering actuator pigtail connector and the variable effort steering actuator housing. Did you find and correct the condition?	—	Go to *Step 13*	Go to *Step 6*
6	1. Turn OFF the ignition. 2. Reconnect the variable effort steering actuator connector. **Important:** Removing battery voltage or ground from the EBCM will result in the following conditions. • Loss of the TIM learned tire inflation configuration parameters • Set DTC C1245 Low Tire Pressure Detected When the diagnosis is complete, inspect the tire pressures and perform the TIM reset. 3. Disconnect the EBCM harness connector. 4. Install the *J 39700* universal pinout box using the *J 39700-300* cable adapter to the EBCM harness connector only. 5. Measure the resistance at the *J 39700* universal pinout box between the variable effort steering control circuits. Does the resistance measure within the specified range?	1.6–5 Ω	Go to *Step 7*	Go to *Step 9*

GC6010000021020X

Fig. 37 Code C1241: Speed Sensitive Steering Circuit Malfunction (Part 2 of 3). 2000–02 Bonneville, LeSabre & Park Avenue & 2001–02 Aurora

Step	Action	Value(s)	Yes	No
7	Test both variable effort steering control circuits for a short to ground or short to voltage between the EBCM and the variable effort steering actuator pigtail connector. Did you find and correct the condition?	—	Go to *Step 13*	Go to *Step 12*
8	Inspect for poor connections at the harness connector of the variable effort steering actuator. Did you find and correct the condition?	—	Go to *Step 13*	Go to *Step 11*
9	Inspect for poor connections at the harness connector of the EBCM. Did you find and correct the condition?	—	Go to *Step 13*	Go to *Step 10*
10	Test for and repair one of the following conditions in the suspect variable effort steering control circuit between the EBCM and the variable effort steering actuator pigtail connector. • An open • A high resistance • A short between the control circuits Refer to *Wiring Repairs* in Wiring System. Did you complete the repair?	—	Go to *Step 13*	—
11	Replace the variable effort steering actuator. Did you complete the repair?	—	Go to *Step 13*	—
12	**Important:** Perform the setup procedure for the EBCM. An unprogrammed EBCM will result in the following conditions: • Inoperative or poorly functioning DRP/ABS/TCS/VSES/VES/TIM (if equipped) • Set DTC C1248 EBCM Turned the Red Brake Warning Indicator On • Set DTC C1255m3 EBCM Internal Malfunction Replace the EBCM. Did you complete the repair?	—	Go to *Step 13*	—
13	1. Use the scan tool in order to clear the DTCs. 2. Operate the vehicle within the Conditions for Running the DTC as specified in the supporting text. Does the DTC reset?	—	Go to *Step 2*	System OK

GC6010000021030X

Fig. 37 Code C1241: Speed Sensitive Steering Circuit Malfunction (Part 3 of 3). 2000–02 Bonneville, LeSabre & Park Avenue & 2001–02 Aurora

Step	Action	Value(s)	Yes	No
1	Was the ABS Diagnostic System Check performed?	—	*Go to Step 2*	Refer to ABS
2	1. Inspect the Magnasteer wiring and connectors for damage. 2. Inspect the Magnasteer Actuator for looseness or damage. Is physical damage of Actuator evident?	—	*Go to Step 3*	*Go to Step 4*
3	Repair as necessary. Is the repair complete?	—	Refer to ABS	—
4	1. Turn the ignition switch to the OFF position. 2. Disconnect the EBTCM. 3. Install the *J 39700* Universal Pinout Box using the *J 39700-25* cable adapter to the EBTCM harness connector only. 4. Using *J 39200* DMM, measure the resistance between terminals C and F of *J 39700*. Is the resistance within the range specified in the value(s) column?	2–3Ω	*Go to Step 12*	*Go to Step 5*
5	1. Disconnect the Magnasteer Actuator. 2. Using *J 39200* DMM, measure the resistance between terminals A and B of the Magnasteer Actuator Connector. Is the resistance within the range specified in the value(s) column?	2–3Ω	*Go to Step 6*	*Go to Step 11*
6	1. Connect a jumper between the Magnasteer Actuator harness connector terminal A and ground. 2. Using *J 39200* DMM, measure the resistance between terminals C and B of *J 39700*. Is the resistance within the range specified in the value(s) column?	0–5Ω	*Go to Step 8*	*Go to Step 7*
7	Repair CKT 1787 for an open or high resistance. Is the repair complete?	—	Refer to ABS	—
8	1. Connect a jumper between the Magnasteer Actuator harness connector terminal B and ground. 2. Using *J 39200* DMM, measure the resistance between terminals F and B of *J 39700*. Is the resistance within the range specified in the value(s) column?	0–5Ω	*Go to Step 10*	*Go to Step 9*
9	Repair CKT 345 for an open or high resistance. Is the repair complete?	—	Refer to ABS	—
10	Malfunction is intermittent. Inspect all connectors and harnesses for damage that may result in an open or high resistance when connected. Is the repair complete?	—	Refer to ABS	—
11	Replace the Power Steering Gear. Is the replacement complete?	—	Refer to ABS	—

GC6029800360010X

Fig. 38 Code C1241: Speed Sensitive Steering Circuit Malfunction (Part 1 of 2). 1998 Corvette w/Rear Mounted EBCM

Step	Action	Value(s)	Yes	No
12	Using *J 39200* DMM, measure the resistance between terminals C and B of *J 39700*. Is the resistance within the range specified in the value(s) column?	OL (infinite)	*Go to Step 19*	*Go to Step 13*
13	1. Disconnect the Magnasteer Actuator. 2. Using *J 39200* DMM, measure the resistance between terminal A and ground of the Magnasteer Actuator Connector. Is the resistance within the range specified in the value(s) column?	OL (infinite)	*Go to Step 14*	*Go to Step 11*
14	Using *J 39200* DMM, measure the resistance between terminals F and B of *J 39700*. Is the resistance within the range specified in the value(s) column?	OL (infinite)	*Go to Step 16*	*Go to Step 15*
15	Repair CKT 345 for a short to ground. Is the repair complete?	—	Refer to ABS	—
16	Using *J 39200* DMM, measure the resistance between terminals C and B of *J 39700*. Is the resistance within the range specified in the value(s) column?	OL (infinite)	*Go to Step 17*	*Go to Step 18*
17	Malfunction is intermittent. Inspect all connectors and harnesses for damage that may result in a short to ground when connected. Is the repair complete?	—	Refer to ABS	—
18	Repair CKT 1787 for a short to ground. Is the repair complete?	—	Refer to ABS	—
19	1. Disconnect the Magnasteer Actuator. 2. Turn the ignition switch to the ON position, engine off. 3. Using *J 39200* DMM, measure the voltage at terminal F of *J 39700*. Is the voltage within the range specified in the value(s) column?	Above 1V	*Go to Step 20*	*Go to Step 21*
20	Repair CKT 345 for a short to voltage. Is the repair complete?	—	Refer to ABS	—
21	Using *J 39200* DMM, measure the voltage at terminal C of *J 39700*. Is the voltage within the range specified in the value(s) column?	Above 1V	*Go to Step 22*	*Go to Step 23*
22	Repair CKT 1787 for a short to voltage. Is the repair complete?	—	Refer to ABS	—
23	Replace the EBTCM. Is the replacement complete?	—	Refer to ABS	—

GC6029800360020X

Fig. 38 Code C1241: Speed Sensitive Steering Circuit Malfunction (Part 2 of 2). 1998 Corvette w/Rear Mounted EBCM

Step	Action	Value(s)	Yes	No
1	Was the ABS Diagnostic System Check performed?	—	*Go to Step 2*	Refer to ABS
2	1. Inspect the Magnasteer wiring and connectors for damage. 2. Inspect the Magnasteer Actuator for looseness or damage. Is physical damage of Actuator evident?	—	*Go to Step 3*	*Go to Step 4*
3	Repair as necessary. Is the repair complete?	—	Refer to ABS	—
4	1. Turn the ignition switch to the OFF position. 2. Disconnect the EBTCM. 3. Install the *J 39700* Universal Pinout Box using the *J 39700-25* cable adapter to the EBTCM harness connector only. 4. Using *J 39200* DMM, measure the resistance between terminals C and F of *J 39700*. Is the resistance within the range specified in the value(s) column?	2–3Ω	*Go to Step 12*	*Go to Step 5*
5	1. Disconnect the Magnasteer Actuator. 2. Using *J 39200* DMM, measure the resistance between terminals A and B of the Magnasteer Actuator Connector. Is the resistance within the range specified in the value(s) column?	2–3Ω	*Go to Step 6*	*Go to Step 11*
6	1. Connect a jumper between the Magnasteer Actuator harness connector terminal A and ground. 2. Using *J 39200* DMM, measure the resistance between terminals C and B of *J 39700*. Is the resistance within the range specified in the value(s) column?	0–5Ω	*Go to Step 8*	*Go to Step 7*
7	Repair CKT 1787 for an open or high resistance. Is the repair complete?	—	Refer to ABS	—
8	1. Connect a jumper between the Magnasteer Actuator harness connector terminal B and ground. 2. Using *J 39200* DMM, measure the resistance between terminals F and B of *J 39700*. Is the resistance within the range specified in the value(s) column?	0–5Ω	*Go to Step 10*	*Go to Step 9*
9	Repair CKT 345 for an open or high resistance. Is the repair complete?	—	Refer to ABS	—
10	Malfunction is intermittent. Inspect all connectors and harnesses for damage that may result in an open or high resistance when connected. Is the repair complete?	—	Refer to ABS	—
11	Replace the Power Steering Gear. Is the replacement complete?	—	Refer to ABS	—

GC6029800361010X

Fig. 39 Code C1241: Speed Sensitive Steering Circuit Malfunction (Part 1 of 2). 1998 Corvette w/Front Mounted EBCM

Step	Action	Value(s)	Yes	No
12	Using *J 39200* DMM, measure the resistance between terminals C and B of *J 39700*. Is the resistance within the range specified in the value(s) column?	OL (infinite)	*Go to Step 19*	*Go to Step 13*
13	1. Disconnect the Magnasteer Actuator. 2. Using *J 39200* DMM, measure the resistance between terminal A and ground of the Magnasteer Actuator Connector. Is the resistance within the range specified in the value(s) column?	OL (infinite)	*Go to Step 14*	*Go to Step 11*
14	Using *J 39200* DMM, measure the resistance between terminals F and B of *J 39700*. Is the resistance within the range specified in the value(s) column?	OL (infinite)	*Go to Step 16*	*Go to Step 15*
15	Repair CKT 345 for a short to ground. Is the repair complete?	—	Refer to ABS	—
16	Using *J 39200* DMM, measure the resistance between terminals C and B of *J 39700*. Is the resistance within the range specified in the value(s) column?	OL (infinite)	*Go to Step 17*	*Go to Step 18*
17	Malfunction is intermittent. Inspect all connectors and harnesses for damage that may result in a short to ground when connected. Is the repair complete?	—	Refer to ABS	—
18	Repair CKT 1787 for a short to ground. Is the repair complete?	—	Refer to ABS	—
19	1. Disconnect the Magnasteer Actuator. 2. Turn the ignition switch to the ON position, engine off. 3. Using *J 39200* DMM, measure the voltage at terminal F of *J 39700*. Is the voltage within the range specified in the value(s) column?	Above 1V	*Go to Step 20*	*Go to Step 21*
20	Repair CKT 345 for a short to voltage. Is the repair complete?	—	Refer to ABS	—
21	Using *J 39200* DMM, measure the voltage at terminal C of *J 39700*. Is the voltage within the range specified in the value(s) column?	Above 1V	*Go to Step 22*	*Go to Step 23*
22	Repair CKT 1787 for a short to voltage. Is the repair complete?	—	Refer to ABS	—
23	Replace the EBTCM. Is the replacement complete?	—	Refer to ABS	—

GC6029800361020X

Fig. 39 Code C1241: Speed Sensitive Steering Circuit Malfunction (Part 2 of 2). 1998 Corvette w/Front Mounted EBCM

Circuit Description

The Speed dependent Steering System (Magnasteer®) incorporates its controller into the EBCM. The EBCM controls the amount of current supplied to the Magnasteer® actuator based on input from the wheel speed sensors.

Magnasteer® 2 also uses inputs from the wheel speed sensors along with added input from the Steering Wheel Position Sensor.

Conditions for Setting the DTC

One or both of the Magnasteer® actuator circuit wires become open or shorted.

Action Taken When the DTC Sets

A malfunction DTC is stored. No ABS or Car Icon (TCS indicator) indicators are turned on but Magnasteer® is disabled. ABS/TCS remains functional.

Conditions for Clearing the DTC

- Condition for DTC is no longer present and scan tool clear DTC function is used.
- Fifty ignition cycles have passed with no DTC(s) detected.

Diagnostic Aids

- It is very important that a thorough inspection of the wiring and connectors be performed. Failure to carefully and fully inspect wiring and connectors may result in misdiagnosis, causing part replacement with reappearance of the malfunction.
- An intermittent malfunction can be caused by poor connections, broken insulation, or a wire that is broken inside the insulation.

Test Description

The numbers below refer to step numbers on the diagnostic table.

4. Checks for an open in the Magnasteer® actuator or Magnasteer® CKT.
12. Checks for a short to ground in the Magnasteer® actuator or Magnasteer® CKT.
19. Checks for a short to voltage in the Magnasteer® CKT.
21. Checks for a short to voltage in the Magnasteer® CKT.

GC6020100465010X

Fig. 40 Code C1241: Magnasteer Malfunction (Part 1 of 4). 1999–2000 Corvette

Step	Action	Value (s)	Yes	No
1	Was the ABS Diagnostic System Check performed?	--	Go to Step 2	Perform Diagnostic System Check -
2	1. Inspect the Magnasteer® wiring and connectors for damage. 2. Inspect the Magnasteer® Actuator for looseness or damage. Is physical damage of Actuator evident?	--	Go to Step 3	Go to Step 4
3	Repair as necessary. Is the repair complete?	--	Perform Diagnostic System Check -	--
4	1. Turn the ignition switch to the OFF position. 2. Disconnect the EBCM. 3. Install the J 39700 Universal Pinout Box using the J 39700-25 cable adapter to the EBCM harness connector only. 4. Using J 39200 DMM, measure the resistance between terminals C and F of J 39700 . Is the resistance within the range specified in the value(s) column?	2-3 ohms	Go to Step 12	Go to Step 5
5	1. Disconnect the Magnasteer® Actuator. 2. Using J 39200 DMM, measure the resistance between terminals A and B of the Magnasteer® Actuator Connector. Is the resistance within the range specified in the value(s) column?	2-3 ohms	Go to Step 6	Go to Step 11
6	1. Connect a jumper between the Magnasteer® Actuator harness connector terminal A and ground. 2. Using J 39200 DMM, measure the resistance between terminals C and B of J 39700 . Is the resistance within the range specified in the value(s) column?	0-5 ohms	Go to Step 8	Go to Step 7
7	Repair CKT 1787 for an open or high resistance. Is the repair complete?	--	Perform Diagnostic System Check -	--

GC6020100465020X

Fig. 40 Code C1241: Magnasteer Malfunction (Part 2 of 4). 1999–2000 Corvette

Step	Action	Value (s)	Yes	No
8	1. Connect a jumper between the Magnasteer® Actuator harness connector terminal B and ground. 2. Using J 39200 DMM, measure the resistance between terminals F and B of J 39700 . Is the resistance within the range specified in the value(s) column?	0-5 ohms	Go to Step 10	Go to Step 9
9	Repair CKT 345 for an open or high resistance. Is the repair complete?	--	Perform Diagnostic System Check -	--
10	Malfunction is intermittent. Inspect all connectors and harnesses for damage that may result in an open or high resistance when connected. Is the repair complete?	--	Perform Diagnostic System Check -	--
11	Replace the Power Steering Gear. Is the replacement complete?	--	Perform Diagnostic System Check -	--
12	Using J 39200 DMM, measure the resistance between terminals C and B of J 39700 . Is the resistance within the range specified in the value(s) column?	OL (infinite)	Go to Step 19	Go to Step 13
13	1. Disconnect the Magnasteer® Actuator. 2. Using J 39200 DMM, measure the resistance between terminal A and ground of the Magnasteer® Actuator Connector. Is the resistance within the range specified in the value(s) column?	OL (infinite)	Go to Step 14	Go to Step 11
14	Using J 39200 DMM, measure the resistance between terminals F and B of J 39700 . Is the resistance within the range specified in the value(s) column?	OL (infinite)	Go to Step 16	Go to Step 15
15	Repair CKT 345 for a short to ground. Is the repair complete?	--	Perform Diagnostic System Check -	--

GC6020100465030X

Fig. 40 Code C1241: Magnasteer Malfunction (Part 3 of 4). 1999–2000 Corvette

Step	Action	Value (s)	Yes	No
16	Using J 39200 DMM, measure the resistance between terminals C and B of J 39700 . Is the resistance within the range specified in the value(s) column?	OL (infinite)	Go to Step 17	Go to Step 18
17	Malfunction is intermittent. Inspect all connectors and harnesses for damage that may result in a short to ground when connected. Is the repair complete?	--	Perform Diagnostic System Check -	--
18	Repair CKT 1787 for a short to ground. Is the repair complete?	--	Perform Diagnostic System Check -	--
19	1. Disconnect the Magnasteer® Actuator. 2. Turn the ignition switch to the ON position, engine off. 3. Using J 39200 DMM, measure the voltage at terminal F of J 39700 . Is the voltage within the range specified in the value(s) column?	Above 1V	Go to Step 20	Go to Step 21
20	Repair CKT 345 for a short to voltage. Is the repair complete?	--	Perform Diagnostic System Check -	--
21	Using J 39200 DMM, measure the voltage at terminal C of J 39700 . Is the voltage within the range specified in the value(s) column?	Above 1V	Go to Step 22	Go to Step 23
22	Repair CKT 1787 for a short to voltage Is the repair complete?	--	Perform Diagnostic System Check -	--
23	Replace the EBCM. Is the replacement complete?	--	Perform Diagnostic System Check -	--

GC6020100465040X

Fig. 40 Code C1241: Magnasteer Malfunction (Part 4 of 4). 1999–2000 Corvette

Circuit Description

The Speed dependent Steering System (MAGNASTEER®) incorporates its controller into the EBCM. The EBCM controls the amount of current supplied to the MAGNASTEER® actuator based on input from the wheel speed sensors.

MAGNASTEER® 2 also uses inputs from the wheel speed sensors along with added input from the Steering Wheel Position Sensor.

Conditions for Setting the DTC

One or both of the MAGNASTEER® actuator circuit wires become open or shorted.

Action Taken When the DTC Sets

A malfunction DTC is stored. No ABS or Car Icon (TCS indicator) indicators are turned on but MAGNASTEER® is disabled. ABS/TCS remains functional.

Conditions for Clearing the DTC

- Condition for DTC is no longer present and scan tool clear DTC function is used.
- Fifty ignition cycles have passed with no DTC(s) detected.

Diagnostic Aids

- It is very important that a thorough inspection of the wiring and connectors be performed. Failure to carefully and fully inspect wiring and connectors may result in misdiagnosis, causing part replacement with reappearance of the malfunction.
- An intermittent malfunction can be caused by poor connections, broken insulation, or a wire that is broken inside the insulation.

Test Description

The numbers below refer to the step numbers on the diagnostic table.

2. This step uses the scan tool to check the Magna Steer Feedback Current parameter.

6. This step checks for an open in the variable effort steering actuator and circuit.

GC6020100466010X

Fig. 41 Code C1241: Magnasteer Malfunction (Part 1 of 3). 2001 Corvette

Step	Action	Value(s)	Yes	No
1	Did you perform the Variable Effort Steering Diagnostic System Check?	--	Go to Step 2	Perform System Check
2	1. Install a scan tool. 2. Start the engine. 3. With a scan tool, observe the MAGNASTEER® Commanded Current and MAGNASTEER® Feedback Current parameters in the MAGNASTEER® data list. 4. Carefully test drive the vehicle so that the MAGNASTEER® Commanded Current is greater than 826 mA. Does the scan tool indicate that the MAGNASTEER® Feedback Current is greater than the specified value?	155 mA	Repair Intermittent and Poor Connections	Go to Step 3
3	1. Turn OFF the ignition. 2. Disconnect the variable effort steering actuator connector. 3. Measure the resistance across the variable effort steering actuator. Does the resistance measure within the specified range?	1.6-3.1 ohms	Go to Step 4	Go to Step 5
4	Test both variable effort steering actuator control circuits for a short to ground, short to voltage, an or open between the EBCM and the variable effort steering actuator pigtail connector. Did you find and correct the condition?	--	Go to Step 9	Go to Step 6
5	Inspect for poor connections at the harness connector of the variable effort steering actuator. Did you find and correct the condition?	--	Go to Step 9	Go to Step 7
6	Inspect for poor connections at the harness connector of the EBCM. Did you find and correct the condition?	--	Go to Step 9	Go to Step 8

GC6020100466020X

Fig. 41 Code C1241: Magnasteer Malfunction (Part 2 of 3). 2001 Corvette

7	Replace the variable effort steering actuator. Did you complete the repair?	--	Go to Step 9	--
8	**Important** Perform the setup procedure for the EBCM. An unprogrammed EBCM will result in the following conditions: • Inoperative or poorly functioning DRP/ABS/TCS/VSES/VES (if equipped) • Set DTC C1248 EBCM Turned the Red Brake Warning Indicator On • Set DTC C1255 EBCM Internal Malfunction Replace the EBCM. Did you complete the repair?	--	Go to Step 9	--
9	1. Use the scan tool in order to clear the DTCs. 2. Operate the vehicle within the Conditions for Running the DTC as specified in the supporting text. Does the DTC reset?	--	Go to Step 2	System OK

GC6020100466030X

Fig. 41 Code C1241: Magnasteer Malfunction (Part 3 of 3). 2001 Corvette

Circuit Description

The Variable Effort Steering (VES) system uses the Electronic Brake Control Module (EBCM) to control current to a bi-directional electromagnetic rotary actuator. The EBCM commands current from negative two amps to positive three amps to the actuator. At low speeds, a negative current is commanded, which assists steering. At medium speeds, no current is commanded and steering is assisted by hydraulics only. At high speeds, a positive current is commanded, which creates steering resistance.

Conditions for running the DTC

- Ignition voltage between 10.5 and 17 volts
- Off state test - Initial ignition ON, no engine rpm or vehicle speed present.
- On state test - If off state test passes, engine rpm and vehicle speed present.

Conditions for Setting the DTC

An open, short to ground, or short to voltage in the VES actuator or the circuits to the actuator.

Action Taken When the DTC Sets

- A DTC C1241 is stored in memory
- The DIC may display the SERVICE STEERING SYS warning message.
- The VES system is disabled.

Conditions for Clearing the DTC

- A current DTC will clear when malfunction is no longer present.
- A history DTC will clear after 100 consecutive ignition cycles with no malfunction present.
- Using the scan tool

Diagnostic Aids

The vehicle needs to be driven to view full commanded and feedback current ranges on the scan tool.

GC6020100467010X

Fig. 42 Code C1241: Magnasteer Malfunction (Part 1 of 4). 2002 Corvette

Test Description

The numbers below refer to the step numbers on the diagnostic table.

2. Tests if the Commanded and Feedback current parameters are at the specified value in there active state.
3. Tests if the resistance of the VES actuator is in the specified range.
5. Tests the High Effort Control circuit for an open or short to voltage.
6. Tests the Low Effort Control circuit for a short to ground.
8. Tests for poor connections at the VES actuator harness connector.
11. Perform the setup procedure after EBCM replacement.

GC6020100467020X

Fig. 42 Code C1241: Magnasteer Malfunction (Part 2 of 4). 2002 Corvette

Step	Action	Value(s)	Yes	No
1	Did you perform the Variable Effort Steering Diagnostic System Check?	--	Go to Step 2	Perform Diagnostic System Check - Variable Effort Steering
2	1. Install a scan tool. 2. Start the engine. 3. With the scan tool, observe the Magna Steer Commanded Current and the Magna Steer Feedback Current data parameters in the Magna Steer data list. Does the scan tool indicate that the Magna Steer Commanded and Magna Steer Feedback current parameters are within .05 amps of each other and within specified range?	-1.84 to -1.99 A	Repair Intermittent and Poor Connections	Go to Step 3
3	1. Turn OFF the ignition. 2. Disconnect the VES actuator harness connector. 3. Measure the resistance of the VES actuator. Does the resistance measure within the specified range?	1.6-3.1 ohms	Go to Step 4	Go to Step 8
4	Test the High Effort Control circuit of the VES actuator for a short to ground. Did you find and correct the condition?	--	Go to Step 12	Go to Step 5
5	Test the High Effort Control circuit of the VES actuator for an open or short to voltage. Did you find and correct the condition?	--	Go to Step 12	Go to Step 6
6	Test the Low Effort Control circuit of the VES actuator for a short to ground. Did you find and correct the condition?	--	Go to Step 12	Go to Step 7

GC6020100467030X

Fig. 42 Code C1241: Magnasteer Malfunction (Part 3 of 4). 2002 Corvette

Step	Action	Value(s)	Yes	No
7	Test the Low Effort Control circuit of the VES actuator for an open or short to voltage Did you find and correct the condition?	-	Go to Step 12	Go to Step 9
8	Inspect for poor connections at the harness connector of the VES actuator. Did you find and correct the condition?	-	Go to Step 12	Go to Step 10
9	Inspect for poor connections at the harness connector of the EBCM. Did you find and correct the condition?	-	Go to Step 12	Go to Step 11
10	Replace the VES actuator. Did you complete the repair?	-	Go to Step 12	--
11	**Important** Perform the setup procedure for the EBCM. An unprogrammed EBCM will result in the following conditions: • Inoperative, or poorly functioning DRP/ABS/TCS/VSES/VES/TPM, if equipped, system. • Set DTC C1248 • Set DTC C1255 Replace the EBCM. Did you complete the repair?	-	Go to Step 12	--
12	1. Use the scan tool in order to clear the DTCs. 2. Operate the vehicle within the Conditions for Running the DTC as specified in the supporting text. Does the DTC reset?	-	Go to Step 2	System OK

GC6020100467040X

Fig. 42 Code C1241: Magnasteer Malfunction (Part 4 of 4). 2002 Corvette

Circuit Description

The Magnetic Steering Variable Assist (MSVA) system, also known as Magnasteer®, uses inputs from the ABS wheel speed sensors to determine the desired amount of power steering assist. The speed dependent Steering System is incorporated into the EBTCM. The EBTCM controls the amount of current supplied to the MSVA actuator based on inputs from the wheel speed sensors.

Conditions for Setting the DTC

DTC C1241 is set when the ignition voltage is between 17.0 and 10.5 volts, and either of the MSVA steering system actuator circuits (CKT 1787 or CKT 345) become open or shorted.

Action Taken When the DTC Sets

- A Malfunction DTC C1241 is stored within the EBTCM.
- The Antilock Brake System (ABS), Enhanced Traction Control (ETS), or the Traction Control System (TCS) indicator lamps are NOT illuminated.
- The MSVA system is disabled.
- The ABS/ETS/TCS remains functional.

Conditions for Clearing the DTC

1. A history DTC will clear after 100 consecutive ignition cycles if the condition for the malfunction is no longer present.
2. You may use a scan tool in order to clear the DTC.

Diagnostic Aids

- Possible causes for DTC C1241 to set are:
  - One or both MSVA circuits open.
  - One or both MSVA circuits short to battery.
  - One or both MSVA circuits short to ground.
- It is very important that a thorough inspection of the wiring and connectors be performed. Failure to carefully and fully inspect wiring and connectors may result in misdiagnosis, causing part replacement with reappearance of the malfunction.
- Inspect all of the circuitry that may cause the intermittent complaint for the following conditions:
  - Broken wire inside the insulation
  - Backed out terminals
  - Improper mating
  - Improperly formed terminals
  - Damaged terminals
  - Poor terminal to wiring connections
  - Physical damage to the wiring harness

GC6019900028010X

Fig. 43 Code C1241: Magnasteer Malfunction (Part 1 of 4). 1999–2002 Century & Regal

Step	Action	Value(s)	Yes	No
1	Was the Variable Effort System (VES) Diagnostic System Check performed?	—	Go to *Step 2*	Go to *Variable Effort Steering System Check*
2	1. Turn the ignition switch to the OFF position. 2. Disconnect the EBTCM connector. 3. Install the *J 39700* Universal Pinout Box using the *J 39700-99* Cable Adaptor to the EBTCM harness connector only. 4. Using *J 39200* DMM, measure the resistance between terminals B10 and B11 of *J 39700* Universal Pinout Box. Is the resistance within the specified range?	1.6–3.1 Ω	Go to *Step 11*	Go to *Step 3*
3	1. Disconnect the two-way MSVA actuator connector. 2. Using the DMM, measure the resistance between terminal A and B of MSVA connector. Is the resistance within the specified range?	1.6–3.1 Ω	Go to *Step 5*	Go to *Step 4*
4	Replace the MSVA actuator. Is the repair complete?	—	Go to *Variable Effort Steering System Check*	—
5	1. Use the Universal Pinout box with the Cable Adaptor still connected to EBTCM harness only. 2. Use the DMM to measure the resistance between terminal B10 of the universal pinout box and the MSVA connector terminal B. Is the resistance within the specified range?	0–2 Ω	Go to *Step 7*	Go to *Step 6*
6	Repair open or high resistance in CKT 345. Is the repair complete?	—	Go to *Variable Effort Steering System Check*	—
7	Using the DMM, measure the resistance between terminal B11 of the universal pinout box and the MSVA connector terminal A. Is the resistance within the specified range?	0–2 Ω	Go to *Step 9*	Go to *Step 8*
8	Repair open or high resistance in CKT 1787. Is the repair complete?	—	Go to *Variable Effort Steering System Check*	—
9	1. MSVA connector still disconnected. 2. Use the DMM to measure the resistance between terminals B10 and B11 of the Universal Pinout Box. Is continuity present between the terminals B10 and B11 of the Universal Pinout Box?	—	Go to *Step 10*	Go to *Step 20*
10	Repair the short between CKT 345 and CKT 1787. Is the repair complete?	—	Go to *Variable Effort Steering System Check*	—
11	1. Disconnect the two-way MSVA actuator connector. 2. Using the DMM, measure the resistance between terminals B10 and D of the Universal Pinout Box. Is continuity present between the terminals B10 and D of the Universal Pinout Box?	—	Go to *Step 12*	Go to *Step 13*
12	Repair the short to ground in CKT 345. Is the repair complete?	—	Go to *Variable Effort Steering System Check*	—

GC6019900028020X

Fig. 43 Code C1241: Magnasteer Malfunction (Part 2 of 4). 1999–2002 Century & Regal

Step	Action	Value(s)	Yes	No
13	Using the DMM, measure the resistance between terminals B11 and D of the Universal Pinout Box. Is continuity present between terminals B11 and D of the Universal Pinout Box?	—	Go to *Step 14*	Go to *Step 15*
14	Repair the short to ground in CKT 1787. Is the repair complete?	—	Go to *Variable Effort Steering System Check*	—
15	1. Using the DMM, measure the resistance between the MSVA actuator terminal A and the steering gear case. 2. Check for an internal short to ground inside the MSVA actuator. Is continuity present between the MSVA actuator terminal A and the steering gear case?	—	Go to *Step 4*	Go to *Step 16*
16	1. Disconnect the two-way MAGNASTEER® actuator connector. 2. Turn the ignition switch to the RUN position, engine off. 3. Connect the DMM between terminals B10 and D of the Universal Pinout Box. 4. Check for voltage at terminal B10 of the Universal Pinout Box. Is any voltage present at terminal B10 of the Universal Pinout Box?	—	Go to *Step 17*	Go to *Step 18*
17	1. Repair the short to voltage in CKT 345. 2. Inspect the variable effort steering system. Is the repair complete?	—	Go to *Variable Effort Steering System Check*	—
18	1. Ignition switch still in the RUN position, engine off. 2. Connect the DMM between terminals B11 and D of the Universal Pinout Box. 3. Check for voltage at terminal B11 of the Universal Pinout Box. Is any voltage present at terminal B11 of the Universal Pinout Box?	—	Go to *Step 19*	Go to *Step 20*
19	Repair the short to voltage in CKT 1787. Is the repair complete?	—	Go to *Variable Effort Steering System Check*	—
20	1. Turn the ignition switch to the OFF position. **Important:** Damage or corrosion may result in an open or short with all of the connectors connected. 2. Inspect the EBTCM harness connectors for the following conditions: • Damage • Corrosion **Important:** Damage or corrosion may result in an open or short with all of the connectors connected. 3. Inspect the two-way MSVA actuator harness connector for the following conditions: • Damage • Corrosion Do the connectors exhibit signs of corrosion or damage?	—	Go to *Step 21*	Go to *Step 22*

GC6019900028030X

Fig. 43 Code C1241: Magnasteer Malfunction (Part 3 of 4). 1999–2002 Century & Regal

Step	Action	Value(s)	Yes	No
1	1. Turn the ignition switch to the OFF position. 2. Disconnect the Electronic Brake/Traction Control Module (EBTCM). 3. Disconnect the Variable Power Steering Solenoid. 4. Using a DMM, measure voltage at the Variable Power Steering Solenoid connector terminal B and B+. Is any voltage measured?	—	Go to Step 2	Go to Step 3
2	Repair the short to ground in the wire. Has the repair been made and the system rechecked?	—	System OK	—
3	Using a DMM, measure voltage at the Variable Power Steering Solenoid connector terminal B and ground. Is any voltage measured?	—	Go to Step 4	Go to Step 5
4	Repair the short to B+ in the wire. Has the repair been made and the system rechecked?	—	System OK	—
5	Using a DMM, measure voltage at the Variable Power Steering Solenoid connector terminal A and B+. Is any voltage measured?	—	Go to Step 2	Go to Step 6
6	Using a DMM, measure voltage at the Variable Power Steering Solenoid connector terminal A and ground. Is any voltage measured?	—	Go to Step 4	Go to Step 7
7	1. Reconnect the EBTCM. 2. Using a DMM, measure voltage at the Variable Power Steering Solenoid connector terminal B and B+. Is the voltage level acceptable?	9-14V	Go to Step 8	Go to Step 9
8	Using a DMM, measure voltage at the Variable Power Steering Solenoid connector terminal A and B+. Is the voltage level acceptable?	9-14V	Go to Step 10	Go to Step 11
9	Using a DMM, measure voltage at the EBTCM connector C1 terminal F and B+. Is the voltage level acceptable?	9-14V	Go to Step 12	Go to Step 13
10	Replace the Variable Power Steering Solenoid. Has the repair been made and the system rechecked?	—	System OK	—
11	Using a DMM, measure voltage at the EBTCM connector C1 terminal C and B+. Is the voltage level acceptable?	9-14V	Go to Step 12	Go to Step 13
12	Repair the open in the wire. Has the repair been made and the system rechecked?	—	System OK	—
13	Replace the EBTCM. Has the repair been made and the system rechecked?	—	System OK	—

GC6029800348000X

Fig. 44 Code C1241: Speed Sensitive Steering Circuit Malfunction. 1998 DeVille & Eldorado

Step	Action	Value(s)	Yes	No
21	1. Repair the damaged or corroded harness connectors in the EBTCM. 2. Repair the damaged or corroded two-way MSVA actuator harness connector. 3. Inspect the variable effort steering system. Is the repair complete?	—	Go to *Variable Effort Steering System Check*	—
22	1. Reconnect all of the connectors. 2. Install the scan tool to the data link connector. 3. Select VES Data within the scan tool menus. 4. Start the engine and allow vehicle to idle in Park. 5. Monitor VES Actuator Commanded and VES Actuator Feedback. 6. Test drive vehicle while monitoring VES Actuator Commanded and VES Actuator Feedback signals. 7. Compare the values to those given below. • 0 km/h (0 mph) = 0 to -2 amps • 72 km/h (45 mph) = 0 amps • 72 km/h or higher (45 mph or higher) = 0 to 2 amps Does the VES Actuator Commanded and VES Actuator Feedback signals respond according to the given values?	—	Go to *Step 4*	Go to *Step 23*
23	1. Replace the EBTCM. 2. Inspect the variable effort steering system. Is the repair complete?	—	Go to *Variable Effort Steering System Check*	—

GC6019900028040X

Fig. 43 Code C1241: Magnasteer Malfunction (Part 4 of 4). 1999–2002 Century & Regal

Step	Action	Value(s)	Yes	No
1	Was the Variable Effort Steering System Check performed?	—	*Go to Step 2*	REFER TO SYSTEM CHECK
2	Inspect wiring and connectors for damage. Is physical damage evident?	—	*Go to Step 3*	*Go to Step 4*
3	Repair wiring as necessary. Is repair complete?	—	REFER TO SYSTEM CHECK	—
4	1. Turn ignition OFF. 2. Disconnect the Variable Steering Actuator connector. 3. Using a DMM, measure the resistance between Variable Steering Actuator connector terminals A and B. Is the resistance within the specified value?	1.6–3.1 Ω	*Go to Step 5*	*Go to Step 6*
5	1. Using a DMM, measure the resistance between Variable Steering Actuator connector terminal A and ground. 2. Using a DMM, measure the resistance between Variable Steering Actuator connector terminal B and ground. Was the resistance within the specified value?	Less than OL	*Go to Step 6*	*Go to Step 7*
6	Replace the Variable Steering Actuator Is the repair completed?	—	REFER TO SYSTEM CHECK	—
7	1. Disconnect the EBTCM connector. 2. Install a J39700 universal pinout box using J39700-25 cable adapter to the EBTCM harness only. 3. Using a DMM, measure the resistance between terminals C and B of J39700. Is the resistance within the specified range?	Less than OL	*Go to Step 8*	*Go to Step 9*
8	Repair CKT 1787 (GRY). Is repair completed?	—	REFER TO SYSTEM CHECK	—
9	Using a DMM, measure the resistance between F and B of the J39700 Is the resistance within the specified value?	Less than OL	*Go to Step 10*	*Go to Step 11*
10	Repair CKT 345 (WHT). Is the repair completed?	—	REFER TO SYSTEM CHECK	—
11	1. Reconnect the Variable Steering Actuator. 2. Using a DMM, measure the resistance between terminals C and F of J39700. Is the resistance within the specified value?	1.6–3.1 Ω	*Go to Step 14*	*Go to Step 12*
12	Is the resistance less than the specified value?	1.6–3.1 Ω	*Go to Step 8*	*Go to Step 13*

GC6029800349010X

Fig. 45 Code C1241: Speed Sensitive Steering Circuit Malfunction (Part 1 of 2). 1998 Seville

Step	Action	Value(s)	Yes	No
13	1. Connect a fused jumper between terminals C and B of J39700. 2. Using a DMM, measure the resistance between the Variable Steering Actuator harness connector terminal A and ground. Is the resistance within the specified range?	0–5 Ω	*Go to Step 10*	*Go to Step 8*
14	1. Turn the ignition switch to the ON position. 2. Using a DMM, measure the voltage at terminal C of J39700. Is the voltage within the specified range?	Above 1 volt	*Go to Step 8*	*Go to Step 15*
15	Using a DMM, measure the voltage at terminal F of J39700. Is the voltage within the specified value?	Above 1 volt	*Go to Step 10*	*Go to Step 16*
16	Replace the EBTCM Is the repair completed?	—	REFER TO SYSTEM CHECK	—

GC6029800349020X

Fig. 45 Code C1241: Speed Sensitive Steering Circuit Malfunction (Part 2 of 2). 1998 Seville

Step	Action	Value(s)	Yes	No
1	Did you perform the Variable Effort Steering System Inspection?	—	Go to *Step 2*	Refer to System Inspection
2	Inspect the wiring and the connectors for damage. Is physical damage evident?	—	Go to *Step 3*	Go to *Step 4*
3	Repair damage to the wiring and connectors. Did you complete the repair?	—	Refer to System Inspection	—
4	1. Turn OFF the ignition. 2. Disconnect the EBTCM connector. 3. Install the *J 39700* universal pinout box using the *J 39700-25* cable adapter to the EBTCM harness connector only. 4. Use a *J 39200* DMM in order to measure the resistance between terminal C and terminal F of the *J 39700*. Is the resistance within the specified range?	1.6–3.1 Ω	Go to *Step 19*	Go to *Step 5*
5	1. Disconnect the variable steering actuator connector. 2. Use a *J 39200* DMM in order to measure the resistance between the variable steering actuator terminal A and terminal B. Is the resistance within the specified range?	1.6–3.1 Ω	Go to *Step 6*	Go to *Step 12*
6	Use a *J 39200* DMM in order to measure the resistance between terminal C of the *J 39700* and the variable steering actuator connector terminal A. Is the resistance less than the specified value?	0.5 Ω	Go to *Step 7*	Go to *Step 13*
7	Use a *J 39200* DMM in order to measure the resistance between terminal F of the *J 39700* and the variable steering actuator connector terminal B. Is the resistance less than the specified value?	0.5 Ω	Go to *Step 8*	Go to *Step 14*
8	Use a *J 39200* DMM in order to measure the resistance between terminal F of the *J 39700* and a good ground. Is the resistance less than the specified value?	OL	Go to *Step 15*	Go to *Step 9*
9	Use a *J 39200* DMM in order to measure the voltage between terminal F of the *J 39700* and a good ground. Is the voltage greater than the specified value?	1 V	Go to *Step 16*	Go to *Step 10*
10	Use a *J 39200* DMM in order to measure the resistance between terminal C of the *J 39700* and a good ground. Is the resistance less than the specified value?	OL	Go to *Step 17*	Go to *Step 11*
11	Use a *J 39200* DMM in order to measure the voltage between terminal C of the *J 39700* and a good ground. Is the voltage greater than the specified value?	1 V	Go to *Step 18*	Go to *Step 19*
12	Replace the variable steering actuator. Did you complete the repair?	—	Refer to System Inspection	—
13	Repair the open in CKT 1787 (GRY). Did you complete the repair?	—	Refer to System Inspection	—

GC6029900425010X

Fig. 46 Code C1241: Magnasteer Malfunction (Part 1 of 2). 1999 DeVille, Eldorado & Seville

Conditions for Setting the DTC

The EBCM performs 2 different tests to detect a DTC condition. The numbers below correspond to the number in Conditions for Running the DTC.

1. The EBCM detects an open in the VES circuit.
2. The EBCM detects an open or short in the VES circuit when the feedback current is less than 155 mA while the absolute value of the commanded current is greater than 826 mA for 2.5 seconds.

Action Taken When the DTC Sets

- The EBCM disables the variable effort steering (VES) for the duration of the ignition cycle.
- The DIC displays the SERVICE STEERING SYS message.

Conditions for Clearing the DTC

- The condition for the DTC is no longer present (the DTC is not current) and you used the scan tool Clear DTC function.
- The condition for the DTC is no longer present (the DTC is not current) and you used the On-Board Diagnostics Clear DTC function.
- The EBCM automatically clears the history DTC when a current DTC is not detected in 100 consecutive drive cycles.

Diagnostic Aids

The vehicle may need to be driven to view non-zero values of the Magna Steer Commanded Current and Magna Steer Feedback Current on the scan tool.

Test Description

The numbers below refer to the step numbers on the diagnostic table.

2. This step uses the scan tool to check the Magna Steer Feedback Current parameter.
6. This step checks for an open in the variable effort steering actuator and circuit.

Step	Action	Value(s)	Yes	No
1	Did you perform the Variable Effort Steering Diagnostic System Check?	—	Go to *Step 2*	Go to *A Diagnostic System Check - Variable Effort Steering*
2	1. Install a scan tool. 2. Start the engine. 3. With a scan tool, observe the Magna Steer Commanded Current and Magna Steer Feedback Current parameters in the Magna Steer data list. 4. Carefully test drive the vehicle so that the Magna Steer Commanded Current is greater than 826 mA. Does the scan tool indicate that the Magna Steer Feedback Current is greater than the specified value?	155 mA	Go to *Intermittent*	Go to *Step 3*
3	1. Turn OFF the ignition. 2. Disconnect the variable effort steering actuator connector. 3. Measure the resistance across the variable effort steering actuator. Does the resistance measure within the specified range?	1.6–3.1 Ω	Go to *Step 5*	Go to *Step 4*
4	Test both variable effort steering control circuits for a high resistance or an open between the variable effort steering actuator pigtail connector and the variable effort steering actuator. Did you find and correct the condition?	—	Go to *Step 13*	Go to *Step 8*
5	Test both variable effort steering control circuits for a short between the variable effort steering actuator pigtail connector and the variable effort steering actuator housing. Did you find and correct the condition?	—	Go to *Step 13*	Go to *Step 6*

GC6010000022020X

Fig. 47 Code C1241: Speed Sensitive Steering Circuit Malfunction (Part 2 of 3). 2000–02 DeVille & Seville

Step	Action	Value(s)	Yes	No
14	Repair the open in CKT 345 (WHT). Did you complete the repair?	—	Refer to System Inspection	—
15	Repair the short to ground in CKT 345 (WHT). Did you complete the repair?	—	Refer to System Inspection	—
16	Repair the short to voltage in CKT 345 (WHT). Did you complete the repair?	—	Refer to System Inspection	—
17	Repair the short to ground in CKT 1787 (GRY). Did you complete the repair?	—	Refer to System Inspection	—
18	Repair the short to voltage in CKT 1787 (GRY). Did you complete the repair?	—	Refer to System Inspection	—
19	Replace the EBTCM. Did you complete the repair?	—	Refer to System Inspection	—

GC6029900425020X

Fig. 46 Code C1241: Magnasteer Malfunction (Part 2 of 2). 1999 DeVille, Eldorado & Seville

Circuit Description

The EBCM controls a bi-directional magnetic rotary solenoid. The solenoid is in the steering gear. The solenoid adjusts the amount of power steering assist in order to achieve a given level of driver effort in turning the vehicle. The EBCM varies the steering assist by adjusting the current flow through the solenoid. The amount of steering assist adjusted for steering is dependent upon vehicle speed. As the vehicle speed increases, the following actions occur:

- The steering assist decreases
- The driver effort increases.

As the vehicle speed decreases, the following actions occur:

- The steering assist increases
- The driver effort decreases.

Conditions for Running the DTC

The EBCM performs 2 diagnostic tests for the VES circuits when the ignition voltage is between 10.5 volts and 17 volts. The numbers below corresponds to the numbers in Conditions for Setting the DTC.

1. Off State Test (Open Circuit Test) - When the ignition is first turned ON, the EBCM performs an open circuit test independent of vehicle speed or engine running.
2. On State Test (Open or Short Circuit Test) - If the Off State Test is passed, the EBCM runs the On State Test during VES operations. The VES operations occur during driving. The EBCM detects an open or short in the VES circuit by comparing the feedback current to the commanded current.

GC6010000022010X

Fig. 47 Code C1241: Speed Sensitive Steering Circuit Malfunction (Part 1 of 3). 2000–02 DeVille & Seville

Step	Action	Value(s)	Yes	No
6	1. Turn OFF the ignition. 2. Reconnect the variable effort steering actuator connector. 3. Disconnect the EBCM harness connector. 4. Install the *J 39700* universal pinout box using the *J 39700-300* cable adapter to the EBCM harness connector only. 5. Measure the resistance at the *J 39700* universal pinout box between the variable effort steering control circuits. Does the resistance measure within the specified range?	1.6–5 Ω	Go to *Step 7*	Go to *Step 9*
7	Test both variable effort steering control circuits for a short to ground or short to voltage between the EBCM and the variable effort steering actuator pigtail connector. Did you find and correct the condition?	—	Go to *Step 13*	Go to *Step 12*
8	Inspect for poor connections at the harness connector of the variable effort steering actuator. Did you find and correct the condition?	—	Go to *Step 13*	Go to *Step 11*
9	Inspect for poor connections at the harness connector of the EBCM. Did you find and correct the condition?	—	Go to *Step 13*	Go to *Step 10*
10	Test for and repair one of the following conditions in the suspect variable effort steering control circuit between the EBCM and the variable effort steering actuator pigtail connector. • An open • A high resistance • A short between the control circuits Did you complete the repair?	—	Go to *Step 13*	—
11	Replace the variable effort steering actuator. Did you complete the repair?	—	Go to *Step 13*	—
12	**Important:** Perform the setup procedure for the EBCM. An unprogrammed EBCM will result in the following conditions: • Inoperative or poorly functioning DRP/ABS/TCS/VSES/VES (if equipped) • Set DTC C1248 EBCM Turned the Red Brake Warning Indicator On • Set DTC C1255m3 EBCM Internal Malfunction Replace the EBCM. Did you complete the repair?	—	Go to *Step 13*	—
13	1. Use the scan tool in order to clear the DTCs. 2. Operate the vehicle within the Conditions for Running the DTC as specified in the supporting text. Does the DTC reset?	—	Go to *Step 2*	System OK

GC6010000022030X

Fig. 47 Code C1241: Speed Sensitive Steering Circuit Malfunction (Part 3 of 3). 2000–02 DeVille & Seville

Circuit Description

The EBCM controls a bi-directional magnetic rotary solenoid. The solenoid is in the steering gear.
The solenoid adjusts the amount of power steering assist in order to achieve a given level of driver effort in turning the vehicle. The EBCM varies the steering assist by adjusting the current flow through the solenoid. The amount of steering assist adjusted for steering is dependent upon vehicle speed. As the vehicle speed increases, the following actions occur:

- The steering assist decreases
- The driver effort increases.

As the vehicle speed decreases, the following actions occur:

- The steering assist increases
- The driver effort decreases.

Conditions for Running the DTC

The ignition is ON.

Conditions for Setting the DTC

The EBCM detects an open or short in the VES circuit when the feedback current is less than 360 mA while the absolute value of the commanded current is greater than 826 mA for 2.5 seconds.

Action Taken When the DTC Sets

- The EBCM disables the variable effort steering (VES) for the duration of the ignition cycle.
- The DIC displays the SERVICE STEERING SYS message.

Conditions for Clearing the DTC

- The condition for the DTC is no longer present (the DTC is not current) and you used the scan tool Clear DTC function.
- The condition for the DTC is no longer present (the DTC is not current) and you used the On-Board Diagnostics Clear DTC function.
- The EBCM automatically clears the history DTC when a current DTC is not detected in 50 consecutive drive cycles.

Diagnostic Aids

The vehicle may need to be driven to view non-zero values of the Magna Steer Commanded Current and Magna Steer Feedback Current on the scan tool.

Test Description

The numbers below refer to the step numbers on the diagnostic table.

2. This step uses the scan tool to check the Magna Steer Feedback Current parameter.
6. This step checks for an open in the variable effort steering actuator and circuit.

GC6010000023010X

Fig. 48 Code C1241: Magnasteer Malfunction (Part 1 of 3). 2000–02 Eldorado

Step	Action	Value(s)	Yes	No
1	Did you perform the Variable Effort Steering Diagnostic System Check?	—	Go to *Step 2*	Go to *A Diagnostic System Check - Variable Effort Steering*
2	1. Install a scan tool. 2. Start the engine. 3. With the scan tool, observe the Magna Steer Commanded Current and Magna Steer Feedback Current parameters in the Delco/Bosch ABS/TCS ICCS (if equipped) data list. 4. Carefully test drive the vehicle so that the Magna Steer Commanded Current is greater than 826 mA. Does the scan tool indicate that the Magna Steer Feedback Current is greater than the specified value?	360 mA	Go to *Testing for Intermittent and Poor Connections* in Wiring Systems	Go to *Step 3*
3	1. Turn OFF the ignition. 2. Disconnect the variable effort steering actuator connector. 3. Measure the resistance across the variable effort steering actuator. Does the resistance measure within the specified range?	1.6–3.1 Ω	Go to *Step 5*	Go to *Step 4*
4	Test both variable effort steering control circuits for a high resistance or an open between the variable effort steering actuator pigtail connector and the variable effort steering actuator. Did you find and correct the condition?	—	Go to *Step 13*	Go to *Step 8*
5	Test both variable effort steering control circuits for a short between the variable effort steering actuator pigtail connector and the variable effort steering actuator housing. Refer to *Circuit Testing* and *Wiring Repairs* in Wiring System. Did you find and correct the condition?	—	Go to *Step 13*	Go to *Step 6*
6	1. Turn OFF the ignition. 2. Reconnect the variable effort steering actuator connector. 3. Disconnect the EBCM harness connector. 4. Install the *J 39700* universal pinout box using the *J 39700-25* cable adapter to the EBCM harness connector only. 5. Measure the resistance at the *J 39700* universal pinout box between the variable effort steering control circuits. Does the resistance measure within the specified range?	1.6–5 Ω	Go to *Step 7*	Go to *Step 9*
7	Test both variable effort steering control circuits for a short to ground or short to voltage between the EBCM and the variable effort steering actuator pigtail connector. Did you find and correct the condition?	—	Go to *Step 13*	Go to *Step 12*
8	Inspect for poor connections at the harness connector of the variable effort steering actuator. Did you find and correct the condition?	—	Go to *Step 13*	Go to *Step 11*
9	Inspect for poor connections at the harness connector of the EBCM. Did you find and correct the condition?	—	Go to *Step 13*	Go to *Step 10*

GC6010000023020X

Fig. 48 Code C1241: Magnasteer Malfunction (Part 2 of 3). 2000–02 Eldorado

Step	Action	Value(s)	Yes	No
10	Test for and repair one of the following conditions in the suspect variable effort steering control circuit between the EBCM and the variable effort steering actuator pigtail connector. • An open • A high resistance • A short between the control circuits Did you complete the repair?	—	Go to *Step 13*	—
11	Replace the variable effort steering actuator. Did you complete the repair?	—	Go to *Step 13*	—
12	Replace the EBCM. Did you complete the repair?	—	Go to *Step 13*	—
13	1. Use the scan tool in order to clear the DTCs. 2. Operate the vehicle within the Conditions for Running the DTC as specified in the supporting text. Does the DTC reset?	—	Go to *Step 2*	System OK

GC6010000023030X

Fig. 48 Code C1241: Magnasteer Malfunction (Part 3 of 3). 2000–02 Eldorado

Step	Action	Value(s)	Yes	No
1	Was the ABS Diagnostic System Check performed?	—	Go to Step 2	**Refer to Anti-Lock Brakes**
2	1. Start the engine. 2. Using a scan tool, select DATA LIST and monitor the steering wheel sensor voltage while rotating the steering wheel from stop-to-stop. Is the voltage within the range specified?	0-.5V	Go to Step 5	Go to Step 3
3	Is the voltage from Step 2 within the range specified in the Value(s) column?	4.7-5V	Go to Step 14	Go to Step 4
4	Does the voltage from Step 2 vary?	—	Go to Step 21	Go to Step 1
5	1. Turn the ignition switch to the OFF position. 2. Disconnect the steering wheel position sensor. 3. Disconnect the ECBM harness connector. 4. Using the J 39200, measure the resistance between the ECBM harness connector terminals 17 and 5. Is the resistance within the range specified in the Value(s) column?	Infinite	Go to Step 6	Go to Step 29
6	Using the J 39200, measure the resistance between the ECBM harness connector terminals 1 and 5. Is the resistance within the range specified in the Value(s) column?	Infinite	Go to Step 7	Go to Step 30
7	Using the J 39200, measure the resistance between the ECBM harness connector terminal 17 and ground. Is the resistance within the range specified in the Value(s) column?	Infinite	Go to Step 8	Go to Step 31
8	Using the J 39200, measure the resistance between the ECBM harness connector terminal 1 and ground. Is the resistance within the range specified in the Value(s) column?	Infinite	Go to Step 9	Go to Step 32
9	Using the J 39200, measure the resistance between the ECBM harness connector terminal 1 and the steering wheel position sensor harness connector terminal A. Is the resistance within the range specified in the Value(s) column?	0-2 Ω	Go to Step 10	Go to Step 33
10	Using the J 39200, measure the resistance between the ECBM harness connector terminal 17 and the steering wheel position sensor harness connector terminal B. Is the resistance within the range specified in the Value(s) column?	0-2 Ω	Go to Step 11	Go to Step 34

GC6029800352010X

Fig. 49 Code C1243: Steering Wheel Position Sensor Circuit Malfunction (Part 1 of 5). Achieva, Alero & Grand Am

Step	Action	Value(s)	Yes	No
11	Inspect the ECBM harness connector terminals 1 and 17 and all steering wheel position sensor terminals for poor terminal contact. Is poor terminal contact evident?	—	Go to Step 35	Go to Step 12
12	1. Reconnect the ECBM harness connector. 2. Turn the ignition switch to the RUN position. 3. Using the J 39200, measure the voltage between the steering wheel position sensor harness connector terminals A and C. Is the voltage greater than the value listed in the Value(s) column?	4.0V	Go to Step 41	Go to Step 13
13	1. Turn the ignition switch to the OFF position. 2. Inspect CKTs 1056, 1059, and 556 for damage which may result in shorts between the circuits or shorts to ground. Repair damage if evident. 3. Reconnect all connectors. 4. Turn the ignition switch to the RUN position. Is DTC C1243 set as a current DTC?	—	Go to Step 42	**Refer to Anti-Lock Brakes**
14	1. Turn the ignition switch to the OFF position. 2. Disconnect steering wheel position sensor. 3. Turn the ignition switch to the RUN position. Does the scan tool display the steering wheel position sensor voltage within the range specified in the Value(s) column?	0-1V	Go to Step 15	Go to Step 16
15	Using the J 39200, measure the resistance between the steering wheel sensor harness connector terminal C and ground. Is the resistance within the range specified in the Value(s) column?	0-5 Ω	Go to Step 41	Go to Step 18
16	1. Turn the ignition switch to the OFF position. 2. Disconnect ECBM harness connector. 3. Turn the ignition switch to the RUN position. 4. Using the J 39200, measure the voltage between the ECBM harness connector terminal 17 and ground. Is the voltage within the range specified in the Value(s) column?	0-1V	Go to Step 17	Go to Step 38
17	1. Turn the ignition switch to the OFF position. 2. Inspect CKT 1059 for any damage which may result in a short to voltage with all connectors connected. Repair any damage if evident. 3. Reconnect all connectors. 4. Turn the ignition switch to the RUN position. Is DTC C1243 set as a current DTC?	—	Go to Step 42	**Refer to Anti-Lock Brakes**

GC6029800352020X

Fig. 49 Code C1243: Steering Wheel Position Sensor Circuit Malfunction (Part 2 of 5). Achieva, Alero & Grand Am

Step	Action	Value(s)	Yes	No
18	1. Turn the ignition switch to the OFF position. 2. Disconnect ECBM harness connector. 3. Using the J 39200, measure the resistance between the steering wheel position sensor harness connector terminal C and the ECBM harness connector terminal 5. Is the resistance within the range specified in the Value(s) column?	0-2 Ω	Go to Step 19	Go to Step 36
19	1. Turn the ignition switch to the RUN position. 2. Using the J 39200, measure the voltage between the ECBM harness connector terminal 5 and ground. Is the voltage within the range specified in the Value(s) column?	0-1V	Go to Step 20	Go to Step 37
20	1. Turn the ignition switch to the OFF position. 2. Inspect the ECBM harness connector and the steering wheel position sensor terminals for poor terminal contact. Replace any terminals with poor terminal contact. 3. Inspect all steering wheel position sensor circuits for damage which may result in a short to voltage or an open with all connectors connected. Repair damage if evident. 4. Reconnect all connectors. 5. Turn the ignition switch to the RUN position. Is DTC C1243 set as a current DTC?	—	Go to Step 42	Refer to "Diagnosis & Testing" in "Anti-lock Brakes"
21	1. Turn the ignition switch to the RUN position. 2. Using the J 39200, measure the voltage by backprobing between the steering wheel position sensor harness connector terminals A and C. Is the voltage within the the range listed in the Value(s) column?	4.5-5.5V	Go to Step 22	Go to Step 23
22	1. Turn the ignition switch to the OFF position. 2. Disconnect the steering wheel position sensor. 3. Turn the ignition switch to the RUN position. 4. Using the J39200, measure the voltage by backprobing between the steering wheel position sensor harness connector terminals A and C. Is the voltage within the the range listed in the Value(s) column?	4.5-5.5V	Go to Step 27	Go to Step 41
23	1. Turn the ignition switch to the OFF position. 2. Disconnect the ECBM harness connector. 3. Disconnect the steering wheel position sensor harness connector. 4. Measure the resistance between the ECBM harness connector terminals 1 and 17. Is the resistance within the range specified in the Value(s) column?	Infinite	Go to Step 24	Go to Step 40

GC6029800352030X

Fig. 49 Code C1243: Steering Wheel Position Sensor Circuit Malfunction (Part 3 of 5). Achieva, Alero & Grand Am

Step	Action	Value(s)	Yes	No
24	Using the MIN/MAX function of the J 39200, measure the resistance between the steering wheel position sensor terminals A and B while rotating the steering wheel slowly from stop-to-stop. Is the resistance within the range specified in the Value(s) column?	390-12,000 Ω	Go to Step 25	Go to Step 41
25	1. Inspect CKTs 1056 and 1059 for damage which may result in a short between the two circuits with all connectors connected. Repair damage if evident. 2. Reconnect all connectors. 3. Being very careful not to move the steering wheel, turn the ignition switch to the RUN position. Is DTC C1243 set as a current DTC?	—	Go to Step 42	Go to Step 26
26	Turn the steering wheel slowly from stop-to-stop. Is DTC C1243 set as a current DTC?	—	Go to Step 41	Refer to Anti-Lock Brakes
27	1. Turn the ignition switch to the OFF position. 2. Disconnect the ECBM harness connector. 3. Turn the ignition switch to the RUN position. 4. Using the J 39200, measure the voltage between the ECBM harness connector terminal 1 and ground. Is the voltage within the the range listed in the Value(s) column?	4.5-5.5V	Go to Step 39	Go to Step 28
28	1. Turn the ignition switch to the OFF position. 2. Inspect CKT 1056 for any damage which may result in a short to voltage with all connectors connected. Repair any damage if evident. 3. Reconnect all connectors. 4. Turn the ignition switch to the RUN position. Is DTC C1243 set as a current DTC?	—	Go to Step 42	Refer to Anti-Lock Brakes
29	Repair the short between CKTs 1059 and 556. Is the repair complete?	—	Refer to Anti-Lock Brakes	—
30	Repair the short between CKTs 1056 and 556. Is the repair complete?	—	Refer to Anti-Lock Brakes	—
31	Repair the short to ground in CKT 1059. Is the repair complete?	—	Refer to Anti-Lock Brakes	—
32	Repair the short to ground in CKT 1056. Is the repair complete?	—	Refer to Anti-Lock Brakes	—

GC6029800352040X

Fig. 49 Code C1243: Steering Wheel Position Sensor Circuit Malfunction (Part 4 of 5). Achieva, Alero & Grand Am

Step	Action	Value(s)	Yes	No
33	Repair the open or high resistance in CKT 1056. Is the repair complete?	—	Refer to Anti-Lock Brakes	—
34	Repair the open or high resistance in CKT 1059. Is the repair complete?	—	Refer to Anti-Lock Brakes	—
35	Replace the terminals that exhibit poor contact. Is the repair complete?	—	Refer to Anti-Lock Brakes	—
36	Repair the open or high resistance in CKT 556. Is the repair complete?	—	Refer to Anti-Lock Brakes	—
37	Repair the short to voltage in CKT 556. Is the repair complete?	—	Refer to Anti-Lock Brakes	—
38	Repair the short to voltage in CKT 1059. Is the repair complete?	—	Refer to Anti-Lock Brakes	—
39	Repair the short to voltage in CKT 1056. Is the repair complete?	—	Refer to Anti-Lock Brakes	—
40	Repair the short between CKTs 1056 and 1059. Is the repair complete?	—	Refer to Anti-Lock Brakes	—
41	Replace the steering wheel position sensor. Is the repair complete?	—	Refer to Anti-Lock Brakes	—
42	Replace the ECBM. Is the repair complete?	—	Refer to Anti-Lock Brakes	—

GC6029800352050X

Fig. 49 Code C1243: Steering Wheel Position Sensor Circuit Malfunction (Part 5 of 5). Achieva, Alero & Grand Am

Step	Action	Value(s)	Yes	No
1	Was the ABS Diagnostic System Check performed?	—	Go to Step 2	Refer to ABS
2	1. Turn the ignition switch to the RUN position. 2. Using the scan tool, select MISC. TESTS, select VES MANUAL CONTROL function, and command EVO actuator ON. Is the feedback current greater than the value listed in the Value(s) column?	100 mA	Go to Step 14	Go to Step 3
3	1. Turn the ignition switch to the OFF position. 2. Disconnect the ECBM harness connector. 3. Disconnect the 2-way EVO actuator connector. 4. Using the J 39200, measure the resistance between the 2-way EVO actuator harness connector terminal B and the ECBM harness connector terminal 18. Is the resistance within the range specified in the Value(s) column?	0-2 Ω	Go to Step 4	Go to Step 10
4	Using the J 39200, measure the resistance between the ECBM harness connector terminal 18 and ground. Is the resistance within the range specified in the Value(s) column?	Infinite	Go to Step 5	Go to Step 11
5	Using the J 39200, measure the resistance between the 2-way EVO actuator harness connector terminal A and the ECBM harness connector terminal C. Is the resistance within the range specified in the Value(s) column?	0-2 Ω	Go to Step 6	Go to Step 12
6	Using the J 39200, measure the resistance between the ECBM harness connector terminal C and ground. Is the resistance within the range specified in the Value(s) column?	Infinite	Go to Step 7	Go to Step 13
7	1. Reconnect the EVO actuator connector. 2. Using the J 39200, measure the resistance between the ECBM harness connector terminal 18 and ground. Is the resistance within the range specified in the Value(s) column?	Infinite	Go to Step 8	Go to Step 15
8	Using the J 39200, measure the resistance between the ECBM harness connector terminals 18 and C. Is the resistance within the range specified in the Value(s) column?	7-19 Ω	Go to Step 9	Go to Step 15

GC6029800353010X

Fig. 50 Code C1273: Actuator Circuit Open Or Shorted To Ground (Part 1 of 2). Achieva, Alero & Grand Am

Step	Action	Value(s)	Yes	No
9	1. Inspect the ECBM harness connector and the 2-way EVO actuator harness connector for poor terminal contact or corrosion. Replace any terminals with poor terminal contact or corrosion. 2. Inspect CKT 1295 for damage which may result in a short to ground or an open with all connectors connected. Repair the damage if evident. 3. Reconnect all connectors. 4. Turn the ignition switch to the RUN position. Is DTC C1273 set as a current DTC?	—	Check wiring circuit for damage or loose connections	Check wiring circuit for damage or loose connections
10	Repair the open or high resistance in CKT 1295. Is the repair complete?	—	Refer to ABS	—
11	Repair the short to ground in CKT 1295. Is the repair complete?	—	Refer to ABS	—
12	Repair the open or high resistance in CKT 1294/1633. Is the repair complete?	—	Refer to ABS	—
13	Repair short to ground in CKT 1633/1294 or 855. Is the repair complete?	—	Refer to ABS	—
14	Malfunction is intermittent.	—	Go to Diagnostic Aids	Go to Diagnostic Aids
15	Replace the EVO actuator. Is the repair complete?	—	Refer to ABS	—
16	Replace the ECBM. Is the repair complete?	—	Refer to ABS	—

GC6029800353020X

Fig. 50 Code C1273: Actuator Circuit Open Or Shorted To Ground (Part 2 of 2). Achieva, Alero & Grand Am

Ensure that all the ABS DTCs are diagnosed and corrected prior to cleaning VES DTCs. Cleaning the VES DTCs will automatically clear the ABS DTCs resulting in a loss of DTC history data. Refer to *A Diagnostic System Check* in Antilock Brake System for more information.

Use the enhanced diagnostic function of the scan tool in order to measure the frequency of the malfunction. Refer to *Enhanced Diagnostics* for more information.

Important: Zero the *J 39200* digital multimeter (DMM) test leads prior to making any resistance measurements. Refer to J 39200 user's manual.

Clear the DTCs after completing the diagnosis. Test drive the vehicle for three drive cycles in order to verify that the DTC does not reset. Use the following procedure in order to complete one drive cycle:

1. Start the vehicle.
2. Drive the vehicle over 16 km/h (10 mph).
3. Stop the vehicle.
4. Turn the ignition switch off.

Test Description

The number(s) below refer to the step number(s) on the diagnostic table.

2. This step checks for proper currect feedback values.
3. This step checks for an open in circuit 345.
4. This step checks for a short ground in circuit 345.
5. This step checks for an open in circuit 1787.
6. This step checks for a short ground in circuit 1787.
7. This step checks for a faulty MSVA actuator.
8. This step checks for a faulty MSVA actuator.
9. This step determines whether the EBTCM is faulty or the condition is intermittent.

Step	Action	Value(s)	Yes	No
1	Was the ABS Diagnostic System Check performed?	—	*Go to Step 2*	*Go to A Diagnostic System Check* in Antilock Brake System
2	1. Turn the ignition switch on. 2. Using the *Scan Tool* scan tool, command the Variable Effort Steering (VES) actuator on. 3. Observe the feedback current on the *Scan Tool* scan tool. Is the feedback current greater than the value listed?	100 mA	*Go to Step 16*	*Go to Step 3*
3	1. Turn the ignition switch off. 2. Disconnect the Electronic Brake Traction Control Module (EBTCM) harness connectors. 3. Disconnect the MSVA actuator connector. 4. Using a *J 39200* digital multimeter (DMM), measure the resistance between the MSVA actuator harness connector terminal B and the EBTCM harness connector C1 terminal B7. Is the measured resistance within the specified range?	Less than 2Ω	*Go to Step 4*	*Go to Step 10*
4	Using a *J 39200* DMM, measure the resistance between the EBTCM harness connector C1 terminal B7 and ground. Is the measured resistance within the specified range?	∞	*Go to Step 5*	*Go to Step 11*
5	Using a *J 39200* DMM, measure the resistance between the MSVA actuator harness connector terminal A and the EBTCM harness connector C1 terminal B8. Is the measured resistance within the specified range?	Less than 2Ω	*Go to Step 6*	*Go to Step 12*
6	Using a *J 39200* DMM, measure the resistance between the EBTCM harness connector C1 terminal B8 and ground. Is the measured resistance within the specified range?	∞	*Go to Step 7*	*Go to Step 13*

GC6019800029020X

Fig. 51 Code C1273: Actuator Circuit Open Or Shorted To Ground (Part 2 of 3). 1998 Century & Regal & 1998–99 Intrigue

Circuit Description

When the Electronic Brake Traction Control Module (EBTCM) commands the electronic brake control relay ON, B+ is supplied through the EBTCM connector C1 terminal B8 to the MAGNASTEER actuator connector terminal A. Ground/control for the MAGNASTEER actuator is provided through the EBTCM connector C1 terminal B7 to MAGNASTEER actuator connector terminal B. The EBTCM controls the amount of current supplied to the MAGNASTEER actuator based on the input from the wheel speed sensors.

Conditions for Setting the DTC

The EBTCM sets DTC C1273 when these conditions are met:

- The electronic brake control relay is commanded ON.
- Vehicle speed is above 16 km/h (10 mph) when the MAGNASTEER actuator is commanded ON.
- Commanded current is greater than 0.5A and the sense current is less than half the command current.
- The MAGNASTEER actuator control circuit is below 1.7V (B+ expected).

Action Taken When the DTC Sets

- The EBTCM stores DTC C1273 in memory.
- The Antilock Brake System (ABS) and Variable Effort Steering (VES) are disabled.
- The amber ABS warning indicator lamp turns on.
- The power steering returns to medium assist.

If the malfunction occurs during an ABS event, the ABS disable action is delayed until the ABS event is over.

Conditions for Clearing the DTC

DTC C1273 setting conditions no longer exist when the ignition switch is turned off.

Diagnostic Aids

The following conditions may cause this malfunction to occur:

- An open or short to ground in circuit 345.
- An open or short to ground in circuit 1787.
- A poor connection.
- Rubbed-through wire insulation.
- A broken wire inside the insulation.
- Backed out terminals.
- Improper mating.
- Broken locks.
- Improperly formed or damaged terminals.
- Poor terminal to wiring connections.
- Physical damage to the wiring harness.

GC6019800029010X

Fig. 51 Code C1273: Actuator Circuit Open Or Shorted To Ground (Part 1 of 3). 1998 Century & Regal & 1998–99 Intrigue

Step	Action	Value(s)	Yes	No
7	1. Reconnect the MSVA actuator connector. 2. Using a *J 39200* DMM, measure the resistance between the EBTCM harness connector C1 terminal B7 and ground. Is the measured resistance within the specified range?	∞	*Go to Step 8*	*Go to Step 14*
8	Using a *J 39200* DMM, measure the resistance between the EBTCM harness connector C1 terminal B7 and C1 terminal B8. Is the measured resistance within the specified range?	7–19Ω	*Go to Step 9*	*Go to Step 14*
9	1. Inspect the EBTCM harness connectors and the MSVA actuator harness connector for poor terminal contact or corrosion. 2. Inspect circuit 345 for damage which may result in a short to ground or an open with all connectors connected. Repair the damage if evident. 3. Reconnect all the connectors. 4. Turn the ignition switch on. 5. Clear Diagnostic Trouble Codes (DTCs) 6. Check for DTCs Refer to *Displaying DTCs* for more information. Is DTC C1273 set as a current DTC?	—	*Go to Step 15*	*Go to Step 16*
10	Repair poor connection or open in circuit 345. Is the repair complete?	—	*Go to Step 17*	—
11	Repair short to ground in circuit 345. Is the repair complete?	—	*Go to Step 17*	—
12	Repair poor connection or open in circuit 1787. Is the repair complete?	—	*Go to Step 17*	—
13	Repair short to ground in circuit 1787. Is the repair complete?	—	*Go to Step 17*	—
14	Replace the MSVA actuator. Is the repair complete?	—	*Go to Step 17*	—
15	Replace the EBTCM. Is the repair complete?	—	*Go to Step 17*	—
16	The malfunction is not present at this time. Is the action complete?	—	System OK	—
17	1. Turn the ignition switch off. 2. Reconnect connectors/components removed. Is the action complete?	—	Go to Brake System	—

GC6019800029030X

Fig. 51 Code C1273: Actuator Circuit Open Or Shorted To Ground (Part 3 of 3). 1998 Century & Regal & 1998–99 Intrigue

Step	Action	Value(s)	Yes	No
1	Was the ABS Diagnostic System Check performed?	—	Go to Step 2	Refer to ABS
2	1. Turn the ignition switch to the OFF position. 2. Disconnect the ECBM harness connector. 3. Turn the ignition switch to the RUN position. 4. Using the J 39200, measure the voltage between the ECBM harness connector terminal 18 and ground. Is the voltage within the range specified in the Value(s) column?	0-1V	Go to Step 3	Go to Step 6
3	1. Turn the ignition switch to the OFF position. 2. Using the J 39200, measure the resistance between the ECBM harness connector terminals 18 and C. Is the resistance within the range specified in the Value(s) column?	7-19 Ω	Go to Step 4	Go to Step 5
4	1. Inspect the ECBM harness connector and the 2-way EVO actuator harness connector for damage which may result in a short to voltage or an open with all connectors connected. Repair the damage if evident. 2. Reconnect all connectors. 3. Start the engine. Wait 10 seconds. Does DTC C1274 set as a current DTC?	—	Go to Step 10	Go to Step 8
5	1. Disconnect the 2-way EVO actuator connector. 2. Using the J 39200, measure the resistance between the ECBM harness connector terminals 18 and C. Is the resistance within the range specified in the Value(s) column?	Infinite	Go to Step 9	Go to Step 7
6	Repair the short to voltage in CKT 1295. Is the repair complete?	—	Refer to ABS	—
7	Repair the short between CKTs 1295 and 1294/1633. Is the repair complete?	—	Refer to ABS	—
8	Malfunction is intermittent.	—	—	—
9	Replace the EVO actuator. Is the repair complete?	—	Refer to ABS	—
10	Replace the ECBM. Is the repair complete?	—	Refer to ABS	—

GC6029800354000X

Fig. 52 Code C1274: Actuator Circuit Shorted Or Solenoid Shorted. Achieva, Alero & Grand Am

Step	Action	Value(s)	Yes	No
1	Was the ABS Diagnostic System Check performed?	—	Go to Step 2	Go to Antilock Brake System
2	1. Turn the ignition switch off. 2. Disconnect the Electronic Brake Traction Control Module (EBTCM) harness connectors. 3. Turn the ignition switch on. 4. Using a *J 39200* DMM, measure the voltage between the EBTCM harness connector C1 terminal B7 and ground. Is the measured voltage within the specified range?	Less than 2V	Go to Step 3	Go to Step 6
3	1. Turn the ignition switch off. 2. Using a *J 39200* DMM, measure the resistance between the EBTCM harness connector C1 terminal B7 and C1 terminal B8. Is the measured resistance within the specified range?	7–19Ω	Go to Step 4	Go to Step 5
4	1. Inspect the EBCM harness connectors and the MSVA actuator harness connector for damage which may result in a short to voltage or an open with all the connectors connected. Repair the damage if evident. 2. Reconnect all the connectors. 3. Clear Variable Effort Steering (VES) Diagnostic Trouble Codes (DTCs). 4. Start the engine. Wait 10 seconds. 5. Check for VES DTCs. Does DTC C1274 reset as a current DTC?	—	Go to Step 9	Go to Step 10
5	1. Disconnect the MSVA actuator connector. 2. Using a DMM, measure the resistance between the EBTCM harness connectors C1 terminal B7 and C1 terminal B8. Is the measured resistance within the specified range?	∞	Go to Step 8	Go to Step 7
6	Repair short to voltage in circuit 345. Is the repair complete?	—	Go to Step 11	—
7	Repair short between circuits 345 and 1787. Is the repair complete?	—	Go to Step 11	—
8	Replace the MSVA actuator. Is the repair complete?	—	Go to Step 11	—
9	Replace the EBTCM. Is the repair complete?	—	Go to Step 11	—
10	The malfunction is not present at this time. Is the action complete?	—	System OK	—
11	1. Turn the ignition switch off. 2. Reconnect connectors/components removed. Is the action complete?	—	Go to Antilock Brake System	—

GC6019800030030X

Fig. 53 Code C1274: Actuator Open Or Shorted Or Solenoid Shorted (Part 3 of 3). 1998 Century & Regal & 1998–99 Intrigue

Circuit Description

When the Electronic Brake Traction Control Module (EBTCM) commands the electronic brake control relay ON, B+ is supplied through the EBTCM connector C1 terminal B8 to the MAGNASTEER actuator connector terminal A. Ground/control for the MAGNASTEER actuator is provided through the EBTCM connector C1 terminal B7 to MAGNASTEER actuator connector terminal B. The EBTCM controls the amount of current supplied to the MAGNASTEER actuator based on the input from the wheel speed sensors.

Conditions for Setting the DTC

- DTC C1274 can be set once the electronic brake control relay is commanded ON.
- Voltage drop is greater than 2.5V across the MAGNASTEER actuator driver.

Action Taken When the DTC Sets

- The EBTCM stores DTC C1274 in memory.
- The Antilock Brake System (ABS) is not disabled.
- The amber ABS warning indicator lamp does not turn on.
- The power steering returns to full assist.

Conditions for Clearing the DTC

DTC C1274 setting conditions no longer exist when the ignition switch is turned off.

GC6019800030010X

Fig. 53 Code C1274: Actuator Open Or Shorted Or Solenoid Shorted (Part 1 of 3). 1998 Century & Regal & 1998–99 Intrigue

Diagnostic Aids

The following conditions may cause this malfunction to occur:

- A short to B+ in circuit 345 or 1787.
- Circuit 345 and 1787 shorted together.
- Faulty MSVA actuator.
- Rubbed-through wire insulation.
- Improperly formed or damaged terminals.
- Physical damage to the wiring harness.

Ensure that all the ABS DTCs are diagnosed and corrected prior to cleaning VES DTCs. Cleaning the VES DTCs will automatically clear the ABS DTCs resulting in a loss of DTC history data.

Use the enhanced diagnostic function of the scan tool in order to measure the frequency of the malfunction.

Important: Zero the *J 39200* digital multimeter (DMM) test leads prior to making any resistance measurements. Refer to J 39200 user's manual.
Clear the DTCs after completing the diagnosis. Test drive the vehicle for three drive cycles in order to verify that the DTC does not reset. Use the following procedure in order to complete one drive cycle:

1. Start the vehicle.
2. Drive the vehicle over 16 km/h (10 mph).
3. Stop the vehicle.
4. Turn the ignition switch off.

Test Description

The number(s) below refer to the step number(s) on the diagnostic table.

2. This step checks for a short to B+ in circuit 345.
3. This step checks for proper resistance value of the MSVA actuator.
4. This step determines whether the EBTCM is faulty or the malfunction is intermittent.
5. This step determines whether the MSVA actuator is faulty or circuits 345 and 1787 are shorted together.

GC6019800030020X

Fig. 53 Code C1274: Actuator Open Or Shorted Or Solenoid Shorted (Part 2 of 3). 1998 Century & Regal & 1998–99 Intrigue

Circuit Description

The vehicle stability enhancement system (VSES) is activated by the EBCM calculating the desired yaw rate and comparing it to the actual yaw rate input. The desired yaw rate is calculated from measured steering wheel position, vehicle speed, and lateral acceleration. The difference between the desired yaw rate and actual yaw rate is the yaw rate error, which is a measurement of oversteer or understeer. If the yaw rate error becomes too large, the EBCM will attempt to correct the vehicle's yaw motion by applying differential braking to the left or right front wheel.

The VSES activations generally occur during aggressive driving, in the turns or bumpy roads without much use of the accelerator pedal. When braking during VSES activation, the brake pedal will feel different than the ABS pedal pulsation. The brake pedal pulsates at a higher frequency during VSES activation.

The usable output voltage range for the lateral accelerometer and yaw rate sensors is 0.25-4.75 volts. The scan tool will report zero lateral acceleration or yaw rate as 2.5 volts with no sensor bias present. The sensor bias compensates for sensor mounting alignment errors, electronic signal errors, temperature changes, and manufacturing differences.

The steering wheel position sensor supplies 2 analog inputs, Phase A and Phase B, to the EBCM. The 2 input signals are approximately 90 degrees out of phase. By interpreting the relationship between the 2 inputs, the EBCM can determine the position of the steering wheel and the direction of steering wheel rotation.

Steer angle centering is the process by which the EBCM calibrates the steering sensor output so that the output reads zero when the steering wheel is centered. Using the yaw rate input, lateral accelerometer input, and wheel speed sensor inputs, the initial steering center position is calculated after driving greater than 10 km/h (6 mph) for more than 10 seconds in a straight line on a level surface.

Conditions for Running the DTC

The ignition is ON.

Conditions for Setting the DTC

C1287

One of the following conditions exists:

- The steering wheel position sensor is synchronized and the steer rate (speed that the steering wheel appears to be turning) is greater than 1100 degrees/second.
- The steer rate is less than 80 degrees/second and the difference in the phase angle between Phase A and Phase B is greater than 20 degrees.
- The 2 steering sensor signals (Phase A and Phase B) do not agree for 1 second. Under this condition, this DTC will set along with DTC C1281.

GC6020100464010X

Fig. 54 Codes C1287 & C1288: Yaw Rate Sensor Data Mismatch (Part 1 of 6). 2001 Alero & Grand Am

C1288

One of the following conditions exists:

- Both Phase A and Phase B are greater than 4.9 volts for 1.6 seconds.
- Both Phase A and Phase B are less than 0.2 volts for 1.6 seconds.
- The difference in the changes in Phase A and Phase B is greater than 35.2 degrees for 9.76 milliseconds.

Action Taken When the DTC Sets

- The EBCM disables the VSES for the duration of the ignition cycle.
- The DIC displays the Service Stability System message.
- The ABS/TCS remains functional.

Conditions for Clearing the DTC

- The condition for the DTC is no longer present and you used the scan tool Clear DTC function.
- The EBCM automatically clears the history DTC when a current DTC is not detected in 100 consecutive drive cycles.

Diagnostic Aids

- During diagnosis, park the vehicle on a level surface.
- Check the vehicle for proper alignment. The car should not pull in either direction while driving straight on a level surface.
- Find out from the driver under what conditions the DTC was set (when the DIC displayed the Service Stability System message). This information will help to duplicate the failure.
- The Snapshot function on the scan tool can help find an intermittent DTC.

Test Description

The numbers below refer to the step numbers on the diagnostic table.

2. Perform the Steering Position Sensor Test in order to verify if the steering wheel position sensor (SWPS) is operating properly.
3. Tests for the proper operation of the steering wheel position signal A circuit in the low voltage range.
4. Tests for the proper operation of the steering wheel position signal B circuit in the low voltage range.
5. Tests for the proper operation of the steering wheel position signal A circuit in the high voltage range. If the fuse in the jumper opens when you perform this test, the signal circuit is shorted to ground.
6. Tests for the proper operation of the steering wheel position signal B circuit in the high voltage range. If the fuse in the jumper opens when you perform this test, the signal circuit is shorted to ground.
7. Tests for a short to voltage in the 5 volt reference circuit.
8. Tests for a high resistance or an open in the low reference circuit.

GC6020100464020X

Fig. 54 Code C1287 & C1288: Yaw Rate Sensor Data Mismatch (Part 2 of 6). 2001 Alero & Grand Am

Step	Action	Value (s)	Yes	No
1	Did you perform the ABS Diagnostic System Check?	--	Go to Step 2	Perform Diagnostic System Check -
2	1. Install a scan tool. 2. Turn ON the ignition, with the engine OFF. 3. With the scan tool, perform the Steering Position Sensor Test. Did the SWPS pass the test?	--	Go to Diagnostic Aids	Go to Step 3
3	1. Turn OFF the ignition. 2. Disconnect the steering wheel position sensor (SWPS) connector. 3. Turn ON the ignition, with the engine OFF. 4. With the scan tool, observe the Dual Analog SWPS Input A parameter in the VSES data list. Does the scan tool indicate the Dual Analog SWPS Input A parameter is less than the specified value?	0.2 V	Go to Step 4	Go to Step 13
4	With the scan tool, observe the Dual Analog SWPS Input B parameter. Does the scan tool indicate the Dual Analog SWPS Input B parameter is less than the specified value?	0.2 V	Go to Step 5	Go to Step 14
5	1. Turn OFF the ignition. 2. Connect a 3 amp fused jumper wire between the 5 volt reference circuit of the steering wheel position sensor (SWPS) and the signal A circuit of the steering wheel position sensor (SWPS). 3. Turn ON the ignition, with the engine OFF. 4. With the scan tool, observe the Dual Analog SWPS Input A parameter. Does the scan tool indicate that the Dual Analog SWPS Input A parameter is greater than the specified value?	4.9 V	Go to Step 6	Go to Step 10

GC6020100464030X

Fig. 54 Code C1287 & C1288: Yaw Rate Sensor Data Mismatch (Part 3 of 6). 2001 Alero & Grand Am

Step	Action	Value (s)	Yes	No
6	1. Turn OFF the ignition. 2. Disconnect the fused jumper wire. 3. Connect a 3 amp fused jumper wire between the 5 volt reference circuit of the steering wheel position sensor (SWPS) and the signal B circuit of the steering wheel position sensor (SWPS). 4. Turn ON the ignition, with the engine OFF. 5. With the scan tool, observe the Dual Analog SWPS Input B parameter. Does the scan tool indicate that the Dual Analog SWPS Input B parameter is greater than the specified value?	4.9 V	Go to Step 7	Go to Step 10
7	1. Disconnect the fused jumper wire. 2. Measure the voltage between the 5 volt reference circuit of the steering wheel position sensor (SWPS) and the low reference circuit of the steering wheel position sensor (SWPS). Does the voltage measure less the specified value?	5 V	Go to Step 8	Go to Step 9
8	1. Turn OFF the ignition. 2. Disconnect the negative battery cable. 3. Measure the resistance from the low reference circuit of the steering wheel position sensor (SWPS) to a good ground. Does the resistance measure less than the specified value?	5 ohms	Go to Step 16	Go to Step 15
9	Test the 5 volt reference circuit of the steering wheel position sensor (SWPS) for a short to voltage. Did you find and correct the condition?	--	Go to Step 20	Go to Step 17
10	Test the 5 volt reference circuit of the steering wheel position sensor (SWPS) for the following conditions: • An open • A short to ground • A high resistance Did you find and correct the condition?	--	Go to Step 20	Go to Step 11
11	Test the signal A circuit of the steering wheel position sensor (SWPS) for the following conditions: • An open • A short to ground • A high resistance Did you find and correct the condition?	--	Go to Step 20	Go to Step 12

GC6020100464040X

Fig. 54 Code C1287 & C1288: Yaw Rate Sensor Data Mismatch (Part 4 of 6). 2001 Alero & Grand Am

Step	Action	Value (s)	Yes	No
12	Test the signal B circuit of the steering wheel position sensor (SWPS) for the following conditions: • An open • A short to ground • A high resistance Did you find and correct the condition?	-	Go to Step 20	Go to Step 17
13	Test the signal A circuit of the steering wheel position sensor (SWPS) for a short to voltage. Did you find and correct the condition?	-	Go to Step 20	Go to Step 17
14	Test the signal B circuit of the steering wheel position sensor (SWPS) for a short to voltage. Did you find and correct the condition?	-	Go to Step 20	Go to Step 17
15	**Important** Removing battery voltage or ground from the EBCM will result in the following conditions: o Loss of the TIM learned tire inflation configuration parameters in the EBCM o The EBCM sets DTC C1245 When the diagnosis is complete, inspect the tire pressures and perform the TIM reset when. 1. Disconnect the EBCM harness connector. 2. Install the J 39700 universal pinout box using the J 39700-300 cable adapter to the EBCM harness connector only. 3. Test the low reference circuit of the steering wheel position sensor (SWPS) for a high resistance or an open. Did you find and correct the condition?	-	Go to Step 20	Go to Step 17
16	Inspect for poor connections at the harness connector of the steering wheel position sensor (SWPS). Did you find and correct the condition?	-	Go to Step 20	Go to Step 18

GC6020100464050X

Fig. 54 Code C1287 & C1288: Yaw Rate Sensor Data Mismatch (Part 5 of 6). 2001 Alero & Grand Am

17	Inspect for poor connections at the harness connector of the EBCM. Did you find and correct the condition?	-	Go to Step 20	Go to Step 19
18	Replace the steering wheel position sensor (SWPS). Did you complete the repair?	-	Go to Step 20	--
19	**Important** Perform the setup procedure for the EBCM. An unprogrammed EBCM will result in the following conditions: • Inoperative or poorly functioning system operations • The EBCM sets DTC C1248 and DTC C1255m3 Did you complete the repair?	-	Go to Step 20	--
20	1. Clear the DTCs using the scan tool. 2. Operate the vehicle within the Conditions for Running the DTC as specified in the supporting text. Does the DTC reset?	-	Go to Step 2	System OK

GC6020100464060X

Fig. 54 Code C1287 & C1288: Yaw Rate Sensor Data Mismatch (Part 6 of 6). 2001 Alero & Grand Am

Step	Action	Value(s)	Yes	No
1	Did you perform the Variable Effort Steering Diagnostic System Check?	--	Go to Step 2	Perform Diagnostic System Check - Variable Effort Steering
2	1. Install a scan tool. 2. Turn ON the ignition, with the engine OFF. 3. With the scan tool, observe the Steering Position Sensor data parameter in the VES data list. Does the scan tool indicate that the Steering Position Sensor data parameter is within the specified range?	0.39 V-4.86 V	Test for Intermittent and Poor Connections	Go to Step 3
3	1. Turn OFF the ignition. 2. Disconnect the steering position sensor harness connector. 3. Turn ON the ignition, with the engine OFF. 4. With a scan tool, observe the Steering Position Sensor data parameter. Does the scan tool indicate that the Steering Position Sensor data parameter is less than the specified value?	0.39 V	Go to Step 4	Go to Step 10
4	1. Turn OFF the ignition. 2. Connect a 3 amp fused jumper wire between the 5 volt reference circuit and the signal circuit of the steering position sensor harness connector. 3. Turn ON the ignition, with the engine OFF. 4. With a scan tool, observe the Steering Position Sensor data parameter. Does the scan tool indicate that the Steering Position Sensor data parameter is greater than the specified value?	4.86 V	Go to Step 5	Go to Step 8

GC6020100463020X

Fig. 55 Code C1287: Steering Position Sensor Shorted Or Open (Part 2 of 4). 2002 Alero & Grand Am

Circuit Description

The Steering Position Sensor is a 5 volt sensor that is used by the Variable Effort Steering (VES) system to detect rapid steering wheel movement. The valid voltage range of the sensor is 0.39-4.86 V. The signal circuit voltage will increase and decrease within the valid voltage range as the steering wheel is turned. The Electronic Brake Control Module (EBCM) monitors the signal voltage from the steering position sensor. If the EBCM detects rapid steering wheel movement, during abrupt driving maneuvers, less current is commanded to the VES actuator to provide full steering assists.

Conditions for Running the DTC

The ignition is on, and ignition voltage is between 10.5-17.0 volts.

Conditions for Setting the DTC

- The steering position sensor signal voltage is less than 0.39 V or greater than 4.89 V for more than 2 seconds.
- The steering position sensor signal voltage changes by more than 2.5 V within 0.02 seconds.

Action Taken When the DTC Sets

- A DTC C1287 is stored in memory.
- The VES system is disabled for the remainder of the ignition cycle.

Conditions for Clearing the DTC

- A current DTC will clear when the malfunction is no longer present.
- A history DTC will clear after 100 consecutive malfunction free ignition cycles.
- Using the scan tool

Test Description

The numbers below refer to the step numbers on the diagnostic table.

2. Tests if the sensor is with in the valid voltage range.
3. Tests for the proper operation of the signal circuit in the low voltage range.
4. Tests for the proper operation of the signal circuit in the high voltage range. If the fuse in the jumper opens when you perform this test, the signal circuit is shorted to ground.
5. Tests for a short to voltage in the 5 volt reference circuit.
6. Tests for a high resistance or an open in the low reference circuit.
15. Perform the setup procedure after EBCM replacement.

GC6020100463010X

Fig. 55 Code C1287: Steering Position Sensor Shorted Or Open (Part 1 of 4). 2002 Alero & Grand Am

5	1. Disconnect the fused jumper wire. 2. Measure the voltage between the 5 volt reference circuit and the low reference circuit of the steering position sensor harness connector. Does the voltage measure less than the specified value?	5 V	Go to Step 6	Go to Step 7
6	1. Turn OFF the ignition. 2. Disconnect the negative battery cable. 3. Measure the resistance from the low reference circuit of the steering position sensor to a good ground. Does the resistance measure less than the specified value?	5 ohms	Go to Step 12	Go to Step 11
7	Test the 5 volt reference circuit of the steering position sensor for a short to voltage. Did you find and correct the condition?	--	Go to Step 16	Go to Step 13
8	Test the 5 volt reference circuit of the steering position sensor for a short to ground, a high resistance, or an open. Did you find and correct the condition?	--	Go to Step 16	Go to Step 9
9	Test the signal circuit of the steering position sensor for a short to ground, a high resistance, or an open. Did you find and correct the condition?	--	Go to Step 16	Go to Step 13
10	Test the signal circuit of the steering position sensor for a short to voltage. Did you find and correct the condition?	--	Go to Step 16	Go to Step 13
11	1. Disconnect the EBCM. 2. Test the low reference circuit of the steering position sensor for a high resistance or an open. Did you find and correct the condition?	--	Go to Step 16	Go to Step 13

GC6020100463030X

Fig. 55 Code C1287: Steering Position Sensor Shorted Or Open (Part 3 of 4). 2002 Alero & Grand Am

Step	Action	Value(s)	Yes	No
12	Inspect for poor connections at the harness connector of the steering position sensor. Did you find and correct the condition?	-	Go to Step 16	Go to Step 14
13	Inspect for poor connections at the harness connector of the EBCM. Did you find and correct the condition?	-	Go to Step 16	Go to Step 15
14	Replace the steering position sensor. Did you complete the replacement?	-	Go to Step 16	--
15	**Important** Perform the set up procedure for the EBCM . Replace the EBCM. Did you complete the replacement?	-	Go to Step 16	--
16	1. Use the scan tool in order to clear the DTCs. 2. Operate the vehicle within the Conditions for Running the DTC as specified in the supporting text. Does the DTC reset?	-	Go to Step 2	System OK

GC6020100463040X

Fig. 55 Code C1287: Steering Position Sensor Shorted Or Open (Part 4 of 4). 2002 Alero & Grand Am

1 - NUT, HEXAGON SLOTTED
2 - PIN, COTTER
3 - SEAL, TIE ROD
5 - ROD ASM, OUTER TIE
6 - FITTING, LUBRICATION
7 - NUT, HEX JAM
8 - CLAMP, TIE ROD END
10 - BOOT, RACK & PINION
11 - CLAMP, BOOT
12 - ROD ASM, INNER TIE
13 - RING, SHOCK DAMPENER
15 - NUT, ADJUSTER PLUG LOCK
23 - SEAL, O-RING
25 - LINE ASM, CYLINDER (RH)
26 - LINE ASM, CYLINDER (LH)
30 - GEAR ASM, RACK & PINION (PARTIAL)
33 - COVER, DUST (ADD)
35 - TUBE, BREATHER

GC6029500134020A

Fig. 56 Exploded view of power rack & pinion assembly (Part 2 of 2). Aurora & Riviera

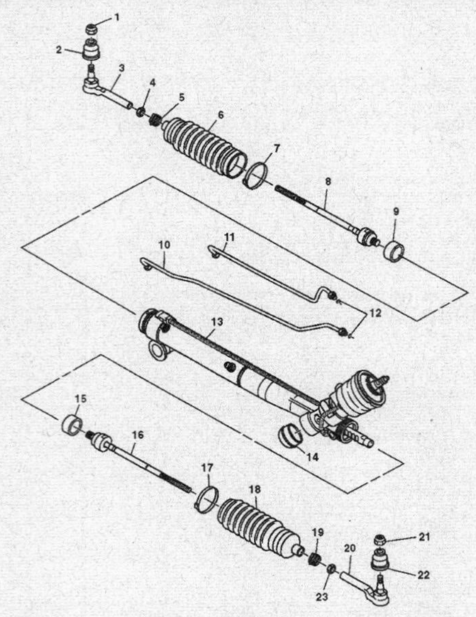

(1) Prevailing Torque Nut
(2) Tie Rod Seal
(3) Outer Tie Rod Assembly
(4) Hex Jam Nut
(5) Tie Rod End Clamp
(6) Rack and Pinion Boot
(7) Boot Clamp
(8) Inner Tie Rod Assembly
(9) Shock Dampener Ring
(10) Cylinder Line Assembly (LH)
(11) Cylinder Line Assembly (RH)
(12) O-ring Seal
(13) Rack and Pinion Gear Assembly (Partial)
(14) Dust Cover
(15) Shock Dampener Ring
(16) Inner Tie Rod Assembly
(17) Boot Clamp
(18) Rack and Pinion Boot
(19) Tie Rod End Clamp
(20) Outer Tie Rod Assembly
(21) Prevailing Torque Nut
(22) Tie Rod Seal
(23) Hex Jam Nut

GC6029800362000X

Fig. 57 Exploded view of power rack & pinion assembly. Corvette & Intrigue

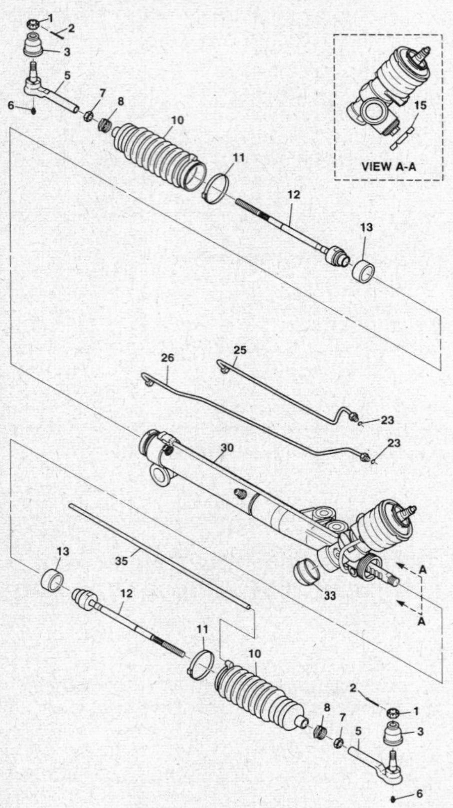

GC6029500134010A

Fig. 56 Exploded view of power rack & pinion assembly (Part 1 of 2). Aurora & Riviera

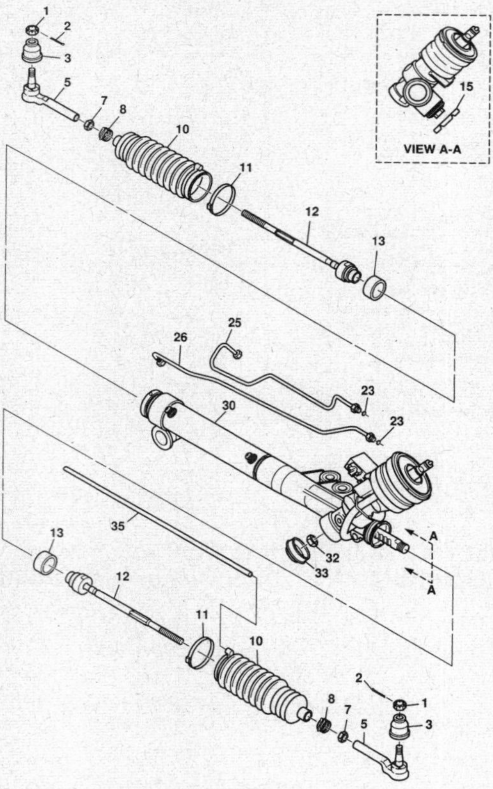

GC6029800386010X

Fig. 58 Exploded view of power rack & pinion assembly (Part 1 of 2). DeVille, Eldorado & Seville

1 - NUT, HEXAGON SLOTTED
2 - PIN, COTTER
3 - SEAL, TIE ROD
5 - ROD ASM, OUTER TIE
7 - NUT, HEX JAM
8 - CLAMP, TIE ROD END
10 - BOOT, RACK & PINION
11 - CLAMP, BOOT
12 - ROD ASM, INNER TIE
13 - RING, SHOCK DAMPENER
15 - NUT, ADJUSTER PLUG LOCK
16 - ADAPTER, SEAL
17 - RING, RETAINING
20 - SEAL, STUB SHAFT
21 - ANNULUS ASM, BEARING
22 - PLUG ASM, O-RING
23 - SEAL, O-RING
25 - LINE ASM, CYLINDER (RH)
26 - LINE ASM, CYLINDER (LH)
27 - BRACKET ASM, MOUNTING
28 - GROMMET, MOUNTING
30 - GEAR ASM, RACK & PINION (PARTIAL)
32 - NUT, HEX LOCK
33 - COVER, DUST
35 - TUBE, BREATHER

GC6029800386020X

Fig. 58 Exploded view of power rack & pinion assembly (Part 2 of 2). DeVille, Eldorado & Seville

1 - NUT, HEX TORQUE PREVAILING
3 - SEAL, TIE ROD
5 - ROD ASM, OUTER TIE
7 - NUT, HEX JAM
8 - CLAMP, TIE ROD END
10 - BOOT, RACK & PINION
11 - CLAMP, BOOT
12 - ROD ASM, INNER TIE
13 - RING, SHOCK DAMPENER
15 - NUT, ADJUSTER PLUG LOCK
16 - ADAPTER, SEAL
17 - RING, RETAINING
20 - SEAL, STUB SHAFT
21 - ANNULUS BEARING ASM
23 - SEAL, O-RING
25 - LINE ASM, CYLINDER (RH)
26 - LINE ASM, CYLINDER (LH)
30 - GEAR ASM, RACK & PINION (PARTIAL)
32 - NUT, HEX LOCK
33 - COVER, DUST
35 - BREATHER TUBE

GC6029800385020X

Fig. 59 Exploded view of power rack & pinion assembly (Part 2 of 2). Alero, Bonneville, Century, Eighty-Eight, Grand Prix, LeSabre, LSS, Park Avenue, Regal, Regency & 1999–2001 Grand Am

Step	Action	Scan Tool Display
1	1. Connect a scan tool to the data link connector (DLC). 2. Input the vehicle information and select Chassis.	• Delco Bosch ABS/TCS • Magna Steer
2	Select Magna Steer.	• Diagnostics • Recalibration
3	Select Recalibration.	• Magna Steer Recalibration Procedure - Ensure that the ignition is ON and the engine is OFF. • Press ENTER to Start.
4	Press ENTER.	Is the VIN correct?
5	Select YES.	Does the vehicle have Magna Steer RPO # <NV8 ?
6	Select YES.	Is the vehicle equipped with the Gran Touring Package RPO # <Y56 ?
7	Select YES.	Recal with the FACTORY STANDARD calibration
8	Select NO.	Select the calibration: • More firm • Factory calibration • Less firm
9	Select the desired response mode.	• Magna Steer Recalibration Procedure is complete. • Press EXIT in order to return to the menu.
10	Exit the scan tool.	Reprogramming is complete.

GC6029900427000X

Fig. 60 Variable effort steering programming. Bonneville, Eighty Eight, LeSabre, LSS, Park Avenue, Regency & 2001–02 Aurora

Action	Result
1. Install a *Scan Tool.* 2. Input the vehicle information and select Chassis.	• ABS/TCS/ICCS • Magna Steer
Select Magna Steer.	• Diagnostics • Recalibration
Select Recalibration.	Magna Steer Recalibration Procedure - Be sure Ignition is ON Engine OFF Press [ENTER] to Start
Press [ENTER].	Is VIN Correct?
Select YES.	Factory Standard Calibration Will Be Used For This VIN. Press [ENTER] to Start
Press [ENTER].	Magna Steer Recalibration Procedure is complete Press [EXIT] to Return to Menu.
Exit the scan tool.	Reprogramming is complete.

GC6019800016000X

Fig. 61 Variable effort steering programming. Eldorado & Seville

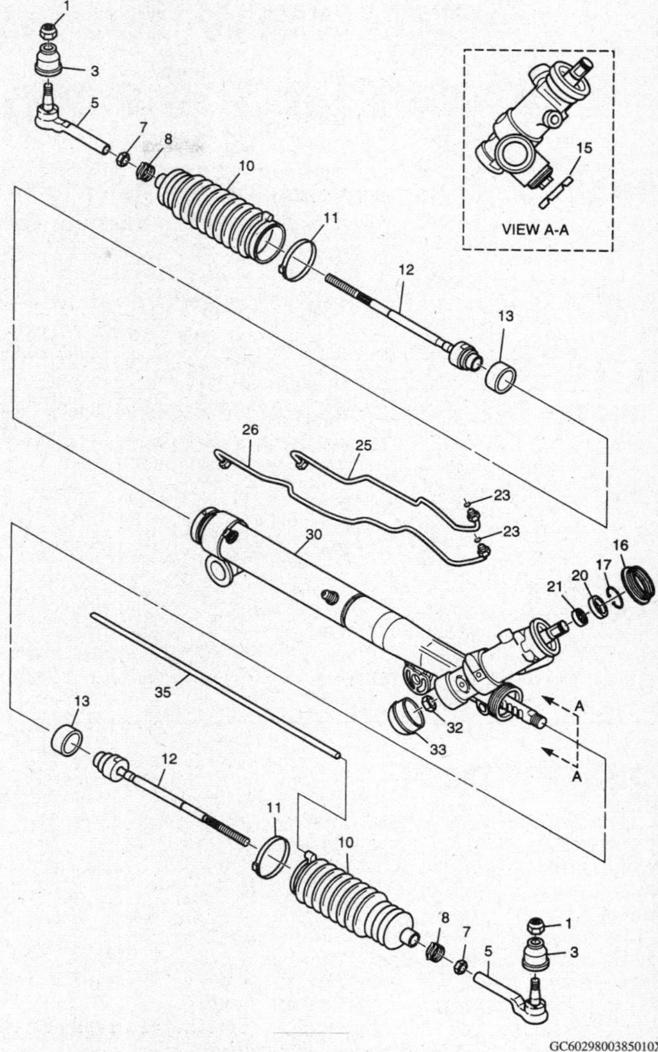

Fig. 59 Exploded view of power rack & pinion assembly (Part 1 of 2). Alero, Bonneville, Century, Eighty-Eight, Grand Prix, LeSabre, LSS, Park Avenue, Regal, Regency & 1999–2000 Grand Am

TECHNICAL SERVICE BULLETINS

POWER STEERING SYSTEM MOAN & SQUAWK NOISE

2001 Park Avenue & Ultra w/Y56 Performance Package

On these models these noises may be heard during low speed turns. They may be caused by a steering gear valve instability which results in a pressure disturbance, creating the noises and transmitting them through the vehicle structure.

To correct this condition, install a replacement steering gear part No. 26098491, pressure hose part No. 25739393 and clip bolt part No. 10082184.

Saginaw Rotary Valve Power Steering Gear, General Motors

NOTE: On Air Bag Equipped Models, Refer To "Air Bag System Precautions" Located In The Front Of This Manual For System Disarming & Arming Procedures.

NOTE: Refer To "Computer Relearn Procedures" Located In The Front Of This Manual When Battery Power To The Computer Has Been Interrupted.

NOTE: "Electrical Symbol & Wire Color Code Identification" Located In The Front Of This Manual May Be Used As An Aid When Using Wiring Circuits Found In This Section.

INDEX

DESCRIPTION

The Saginaw rotary valve steering gear incorporates a recirculating ball system in which steel balls act as a rolling thread between a steering worm shaft and the rack piston.

Variable Effort Steering (VES) or Speed Sensitive Steering (SSS) is a power steering system varies the steering effort required to steer the vehicle at different speeds. At low speeds, the system provides maximum power assist. At higher speeds, increased steering effort will provide firmer steering (road feel) and direction stability. The power steering control module uses speed input from the Electronic Braking Traction Control Module (EBTCM) to control the power steering fluid flow control valve actuator. The power steering fluid flow control valve actuator utilizes a pintle valve to control fluid flow to the steering gear.

DIAGNOSIS & TESTING

Accessing Diagnostic Trouble Codes

Diagnostic Trouble Codes (DTCs) may be read using a suitably programmed scan tool. There are no provisions for flash code diagnostics.

1. Turn ignition Off.
2. Connect suitably programmed scan tool to Data Link Connector (DLC).
3. Turn ignition On.
4. Select scan tool's Special Functions.
5. Read and record DTCs.

Code	Description
21	No Speed Signal
22	Solenoid Short To Ground/Open
23	Power Steering Control Module Malfunction

Fig. 1 Diagnostic trouble code interpretation

Diagnostic Trouble Code Interpretation

Refer to **Fig. 1** for diagnostic trouble code interpretation.

Wiring Diagrams

Refer to **Fig. 2** for wiring diagram.

Diagnostic Tests

Refer to **Fig. 3** for system inspection and **Figs. 4 through 6** for diagnostic trouble code tests.

Clearing Diagnostic Trouble Codes

DTCs cannot be cleared by disconnecting EBTCM or battery cables. Follow the scan tool manufacturer's instructions to clear DTCs.

POWER STEERING SYSTEM SERVICE

POWER STEERING CONTROL MODULE

1. Twist self-locking screws to allow front of sound insulator to drop down, **Fig. 7.**
2. Remove sound insulator.
3. Disconnect control module electrical connectors, **Fig. 8.**
4. Remove power steering control module.
5. Reverse procedure to install.

FLOW CONTROL VALVE ACTUATOR

1. Remove steering gear as outlined under "Front Suspension & Steering" in appropriate chassis section of this manual.
2. Remove flow control valve actuator retaining screws, then the flow control valve actuator.
3. Reverse procedure to install. Tighten flow control valve actuator retaining screws to specifications.

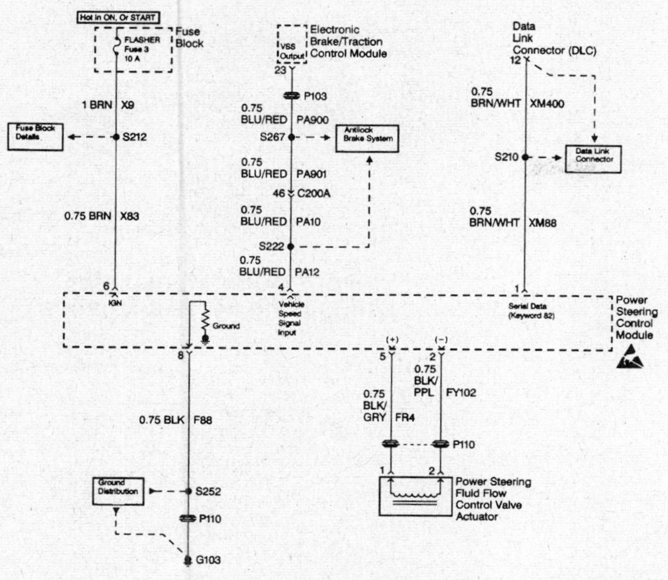

GC6029800364000X

Fig. 2 Wiring diagram

Step	Action	Value(s)	Yes	No
1	Was the Variable Effort Steering System Check performed?	—	Go to Step 2	Check Speedometer
2	Does the speedometer operate properly?	—	Go to Step 3	Check Speedometer
3	1. Disconnect the power steering control module connector. 2. Raise the drive wheels. 3. Turn the ignition switch to the ON position. 4. Use the DMM, on the AC scale, to measure the voltage between terminals 4 and 8 of the power steering control module connector while rotating the LH rear wheel. Is the measured voltage within the specified value?	Greater than 1 VAC	Go to Step 5	Go to Step 4
4	1. Locate an open or a high resistance in circuit PA12. 2. Repair the open or the high resistance in circuit PA12. Is the repair complete?	—	Go to Step 6	—
5	Replace the power steering control module. Is the replacement complete?	—	Go to Step 6	—
6	1. Connect all connectors and components that were disconnected. 2. Road test the vehicle. 3. After road test, install the scan tool again. 4. Check for DTC 21. Is DTC 21 present?	—	Go to Step 1	System OK

GC6029800365000X

Fig. 4 Code 21: No Speed Signal

Step	Action	Value(s)	Yes	No
1	1. Prepare the vehicle for a road test. 2. Check the power steering fluid level. 3. Check the power steering belt tension. 4. Check the tire inflation. 5. Road test the vehicle using various parking maneuvers and a level stretch of highway. Does the steering force lessen when parking and require more force as the vehicle speed increases?	—	Go to Step 3	Go to Step 2
2	Was the problem found and repaired?	—	Go to Step 9	—
3	1. The procedure for reading DTCs is to use the scan tool. 2. When reading DTCs, follow the instructions that are supplied by the scan tool manufacturer. 3. Connect the scan tool to the data link connector (DLC). 4. Establish communication with the power steering control module. Does the scan tool communicate with the power steering control module?	—	Go to Step 5	Go to Step 4
4	ST Does Not Communicate with PS Control Module	—	—	—
5	Are there any current DTCs displayed?	—	Go to Step 6	Go to Step 7
6	1. If DTC 21 is present, refer to DTC 21. 2. If DTC 22 is present, refer to DTC 22. 3. If DTC 23 is present, refer to DTC 23. Go to the appropriate table to diagnose the DTC.	—	—	—
7	Are any history or intermittent codes displayed?	—	Go to Step 8	Go to Step 9
8	Locate and repair the problem. Was the intermittent problem found and repaired?	—	Go to Step 9	—
9	1. Connect all connectors and components that were disconnected. 2. Install the scan tool. 3. Check for any current or history or intermittent DTCs. Are there any current or history or intermittent DTCs present?	—	Go to Step 1	System OK

GC6029800380000X

Fig. 3 System Inspection

Step	Action	Value(s)	Yes	No
1	Was the Variable Effort Steering System Check performed?	—	Go to Step 2	Refer to System Check
2	1. Connect the scan tool to the data link connector (DTC). 2. Check for a current DTC 22. Is a current DTC 22 displayed?	—	Go to Step 3	Go to Step 4
3	1. Remove the power steering control module (PSCM). 2. Use a DMM to measure the resistance across terminals 2 and 5 of the module connector. Is the measured resistance within the specified value?	7–8 Ω	Go to Step 6	Go to Step 7
4	Check for a history or an intermittent DTC 22. Is a history or an intermittent DTC 22 displayed?	—	Go to Step 5	Go to Step 6
5	1. Locate an intermittent in circuits FR4 and/or FY102. 2. Repair the intermittent in circuits FR4 and/or FY102. Is the repair complete?	—	Go to Step 10	—
6	1. Use the DMM to measure the resistance between terminal 2 of the PSCM connector and a known good ground. 2. Use the DMM to measure the resistance between terminal 5 of the PSCM connector and a known good ground. Is the measured resistance for both measurements within the specified value?	OL	Go to Step 8	Go to Step 9
7	1. Locate an open or a high resistance in circuits FR4 and/or FY102. 2. Repair the open or the high resistance in circuits FR4 and/or FY102. 3. Replace the power steering fluid flow control valve actuator if these circuits are OK. Is the repair or replacement complete?	—	Go to Step 10	—
8	1. Check power and ground circuits to the module. 2. Replace the power steering control module if power and ground is OK. Is the replacement complete?	—	Go to Step 10	—

GC6029800366010X

Fig. 5 Code 22: Solenoid Circuit Short To Ground/Open (Part 1 of 2)

Step	Action	Value(s)	Yes	No
9	1. If any continuity readings were observed, locate a short to ground in circuits FR4 and/or FY102. 2. Repair the short to ground in circuits FR4 and/or FY102. Is the repair complete?	—	Go to Step 10	—
10	1. Connect all connectors or components that were disconnected. 2. Road test the vehicle. 3. After the road test, install the scan tool again. 4. Check for DTC 22. Is DTC 22 displayed?	—	Go to Step 1	System OK

GC6029800366020X

Fig. 5 Code 22: Solenoid Circuit Short To Ground/Open (Part 2 of 2)

Step	Action	Value(s)	Yes	No
1	Was the Variable Effort Steering System Check performed?	—	*Go to Step 2*	Refer to System Check
2	1. Remove the power steering control module (PSCM). 2. Turn the ignition switch to the ON position. 3. Use a DMM to measure the voltage between terminal 6 of the PSCM connector and a known good ground. Is the measured voltage within the specified value?	B+	*Go to Step 4*	*Go to Step 3*
3	1. Locate an open or a high resistance in circuit X83. 2. Repair the open or the high resistance in circuit X83. Is the repair complete?	—	*Go to Step 7*	—
4	Use the DMM to measure the resistance between terminal 8 of the PSCM connector and a known good ground. Is the measured resistance within the specified value?	Less than 5 Ω	*Go to Step 6*	*Go to Step 5*
5	1. Locate an open or a high resistance in circuit F88. 2. Repair the open or the high resistance in circuit F88. Is the repair complete?	—	*Go to Step 7*	—
6	Replace the power steering control module. Effort Steering. Is the replacement complete?	—	*Go to Step 7*	—
7	1. Connect all of the connectors and components that were disconnected. 2. Road test the vehicle. 3. Install the scan tool after the road test. 4. Check for DTC 23. Is DTC 23 displayed?	—	*Go to Step 1*	System OK

GC6029800367000X

Fig. 6 Code 23: Power Steering Control Module Malfunction

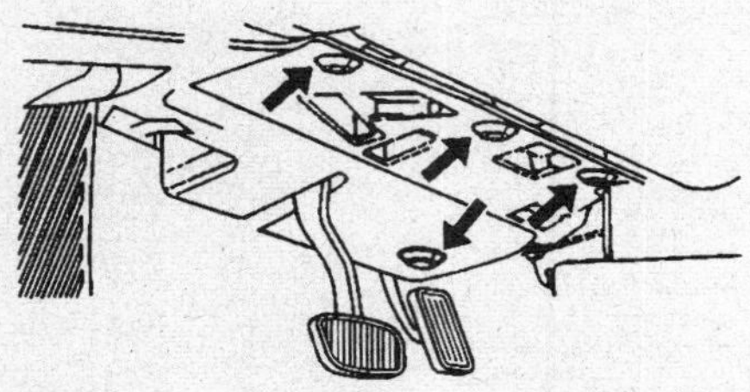

GC6029800368000X

Fig. 7 Sound insulator self-locking screws location

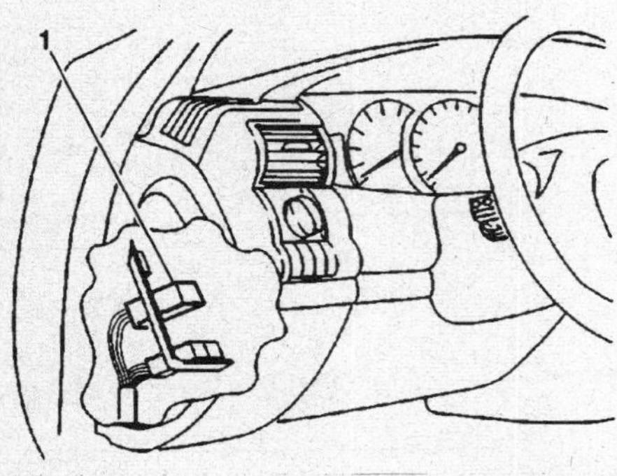

GC6029800369000X

Fig. 8 Power steering control module location

TIGHTENING SPECIFICATIONS

Component	Torque/Ft. Lbs.
Ball Stud Nut (1998)	44
Ball Stud Nut (1999–2001)	44①
Flow Control Valve Actuator	27②
Idler Arm Bolts	44
Tie Rod Adjuster Clamp Bolt	11
Steering Gear Bolts	30
Steering Gear Coupler Bolt	16

① — Rotate an additional 52°.

② — Inch lbs.

Toyota Rack & Pinion Power Steering Gear, Prizm

NOTE: On Air Bag Equipped Models, Refer To "Air Bag System Precautions" Located In The Front Of This Manual For System Disarming & Arming Procedures.

NOTE: Refer To "Computer Relearn Procedures" Located In The Front Of This Manual When Battery Power To The Computer Has Been Interrupted.

INDEX

DESCRIPTION

This steering system converts rotary motion to linear motion as follows: when the steering wheel is turned, rotary motion is transferred to the steering shaft, the shaft joint and rack pinion. The pinion teeth mesh with teeth on the rack and the rotary motion is transferred to the rack and changed to linear motion. The linear force is then transmitted through the tie rods to the steering knuckles which steer the front wheels.

POWER STEERING SYSTEM SERVICE

STEERING GEAR

REMOVAL

1. Ensure front wheels are in straight-ahead position, then turn ignition to Lock.
2. Remove steering column upper cover bolts from firewall.
3. Remove steering column shaft lower coupling pinch bolt.
4. Remove power steering fluid outlet pipe heat shield.
5. Remove lefthand and righthand steering gear inlet and outlet pipe clips and bolts.
6. Locate a suitable drain pan to collect power steering fluid spillage.
7. Disconnect inlet and outlet pipes from steering gear.
8. Remove oxygen sensor as required. Discard gasket.
9. Install engine support tool No. J28467-360, or equivalent.
10. Raise and support vehicle.
11. Remove engine righthand and lefthand lower splash shields.
12. Remove driveshaft exhaust heat shield.
13. Remove front tires and wheels.
14. Remove outer tie rods using puller tool No. J24319-B, or equivalent.
15. Remove front suspension brace nuts, then the brace.
16. Remove front suspension crossmember, transaxle support, control arms and front stabilizer shaft as a complete unit.
17. Remove rear transaxle mount through-bolt, then the mount.
18. Remove rear transaxle mount bracket bolts, then the bracket.
19. Disconnect exhaust pipe from manifold.
20. Remove steering gear boot heat shield.
21. Remove steering gear clamp fasteners, then the clamps.
22. Remove steering gear to righthand side of vehicle, then lower and remove from lefthand side.
23. Remove insulators from steering gear.

DISASSEMBLY

Do not disassemble the steering gear on these models.

INSTALLATION

Reverse removal procedure to install, noting the following:

1. Replace exhaust flange gasket.
2. Install a new gasket when installing oxygen sensor.
3. Tighten all bolts and nuts to specifications.
4. Bleed power steering fluid system.
5. Inspect for and correct any leakage.

TIGHTENING SPECIFICATIONS

Component	Torque/Ft. Lbs.
Driveshaft Heat Shield Bolts & Nuts	48①
Front Suspension Brace Nuts	51
Inner Tie Rod Housing To Rack (1998–99)	32
Inner Tie Rod Housing To Rack (2000–02)	46
Inner Tie Rod Pinch Bolts	46
Outer Tie Rod Jam Nut	41
Outer Tie Rod Castle Nut	②
Power Steering Gear Inlet & Outlet Pipe Nuts	108①
Power Steering Inlet Hose Fitting	40
Return Elbow Flare Nut	32
Steering Gear Mounting Bolts & Nuts	52
Steering Shaft Lower Coupling Bolt	26
Transaxle Rear Mount Bolts	57
Transaxle Rear Mount Through-Bolts	64

① — Inch lbs.
② — Torque to 36 ft. lbs. Rotate an additional 1/6 turn or 52 ft. lbs. to align cotter pin slots. Do not back nut off for cotter pin installation.

Saturn

NOTE: On Air Bag Equipped Models, Refer To "Air Bag System Precautions" Located In The Front Of This Manual For System Disarming & Arming Procedures.

NOTE: Refer To "Computer Relearn Procedures" Located In The Front Of This Manual When Battery Power To The Computer Has Been Interrupted.

NOTE: Prior To Performing Any Service Operations Listed In This Section, Consult The "Technical Service Bulletins" Section For Related Information.

INDEX

DESCRIPTION

STEERING SYSTEM

The power steering system is a rack and pinion design featuring a constant flow or Electronic Variable Orifice (EVO) system. Models equipped with the DOHC engine utilize the EVO system while models equipped with the SOHC engine utilize the constant flow design.

Unlike conventional power steering systems, the EVO feature adjusts the amount of steering assist according to the speed of the vehicle, which is monitored by a vehicle speed sensor (VSS). This information is read electronically by the Powertrain Control Module (PCM), which commands the EVO actuator to control the power steering pump output flow.

At low speeds, where high levels of assist are desired, the EVO actuator is opened more widely, providing more flow to the steering gear and greater assist. At higher speeds, the actuator is closed further, providing less pump flow and less steering assist and improved road feeling. All of the additional flow of the pump that is not needed by the gear is allowed to return to the reservoir through a bypass.

EVO ACTUATOR

The EVO actuator is a 10 ohm linear solenoid. The PCM controls the current to the high and low side of the actuator so current control is retained in the presence of any output fault condition.

The control of the actuator is accomplished by pulse width modulating (PWM) voltage to the actuator ad monitoring the actual current flow. The PCM varies the PWM signal in order to make the actual current equal to the desired current.

TROUBLESHOOTING

Refer to **Fig. 1** for power steering system troubleshooting.

DIAGNOSIS & TESTING

HYDRAULIC SYSTEM TEST

1. Disconnect high pressure line at steering gear and install power steering system tester tool No. SA9134C, or equivalent.
2. Open gate valve on power steering system tester.
3. Run engine until it has reached normal operating temperature. Replace any power steering fluid lost during tester installation, then bleed system if required.
4. With engine idling, record pressure and flow rate. If pressure reading is greater than 150 psi, stop engine and inspect power steering lines for restrictions. **Do not turn steering wheel while performing this test.**
5. Slowly close gate valve until 700 psi is indicated on power steering tester. Record pressure and flow rate.
6. Flow rate should not drop more than one gallon per minute from recorded flow rate.
7. If flow rate drops more than one gallon per minute, replace ring, rotor and vanes in pump. Also inspect pressure plate and thrust plates for wear.
8. Completely close and open gate valve three times. **Do not close gate valve for more than five seconds at a time.** Record fluid pressure each time valve is closed.
9. If all three readings are not within 50 psi, replace flow control valve.
10. With gate valve open, increase engine speed to 1600 RPM and record fluid pressure and flow rate. **Do not turn steering wheel.**
11. Flow rate should not vary more than one gallon per minute from flow rate recorded in step 4.
12. Ensure flow control valve moves freely in pump housing. Inspect valve for burrs.
13. Turn steering wheel completely to left, then completely to right. Record fluid pressure and flow rate at each stop.
14. If flow rate is greater than one gallon per minute, steering gear is leaking internally and must be replaced.

EVO SUBSYSTEM TEST

1. Disconnect high pressure line at power steering pump and install Power Steering System Tester tool No. SA9134C, or equivalent.
2. Connect a Powertrain Diagnostic Tool (PDT) to ALDL diagnostic port. Follow tool manufacturer's instructions.
3. Open gate valve on steering system tester.
4. Run engine until normal operating temperature is reached. Replace any power steering fluid lost during tester installation, then bleed system if required.
5. Select "EVO Subsystem Test" using PDT tool in special test menu.
6. Command EVO actuator to provide "full assist" using PDT. Record power steering fluid flow rate as indicated on power steering system tester. Replace EVO actuator if flow rate is not between 2.35–2.85 gallons per minute.
7. Command EVO actuator to provide "no assist" using PDT. Record fluid flow rate as indicated on steering tester. Replace EVO actuator if flow

COMPLAINT/CONDITION	POSSIBLE CAUSE(S)	CORRECTION(S)
Hard Steering	Front tire(s) improperly inflated.	Inflate tire(s) correctly.
	Improperly adjusted, improperly lubricated or damaged steering gear.	Adjust, lubricate (check for damaged boots), or replace steering gear.
	Worn or binding lower control arm ball stud(s).	Replace lower control arm(s).
	Worn or binding inner or outer tie rod(s).	Replace inner or outer tie rod end(s).
	Worn or binding upper strut mount(s).	Replace mount(s).
	Worn or binding intermediate shaft joint(s).	Replace intermediate shaft.
	Accessory drive belt loose.	Check accessory drive belt tension.
	Power steering fluid level low.	Add power steering fluid.
	Insufficient power steering pump pressure.	Repair or replace power steering pump.
	Faulty EVO actuator.	Replace EVO actuator.
	Restricted or leaking power steering hoses.	Replace hoses or tighten hose connections.
	High internal leakage in steering gear.	Replace steering gear.
	Excessive front wheel caster.	Perform alignment.
	Binding within steering column or intermediate shaft boot.	Correct condition.
Poor return of steering wheel to center.	Front tire(s) improperly inflated.	Inflate tire(s) correctly.
	Improperly adjusted, improperly lubricated, or binding steering gear.	Adjust, lubricate (check for damaged boots), or replace steering gear.
	Incorrect front wheel caster.	Perform alignment.
	Worn or binding inner or outer tie rod end(s).	Replace inner or outer tie rod end(s).
	Worn or binding upper strut mount(s).	Replace mount(s).
	Worn or binding intermediate shaft joint(s).	Replace intermediate shaft.
	Binding within steering column or intermediate shaft boot.	Correct condition.

G36029100001010A

Fig. 1 Power steering system troubleshooting (Part 1 of 3)

rate is not between .4–.9 gallons per minute.

POWER STEERING SYSTEM SERVICE

Component Service

POWER STEERING PUMP OVERHAUL

Disassembly

1. Remove power steering pump from vehicle.
2. Remove reservoir retaining clips from reservoir assembly.
3. Remove reservoir from housing.
4. Remove O-ring seal from pump housing, then the pulley using puller tool No. SA9162C, or equivalent.
5. Remove three power steering pump to bracket fasteners and remove bracket from pump.
6. Remove EVO actuator assembly using removal tool No. SA9116C, or equivalent.
7. Remove flow control valve and spring.
8. Remove retaining ring, **Fig. 2,** as follows:
   a. Use a suitable C-clamp (one side on end cover, other on pump driveshaft) to depress end cover, easing removal of retaining ring.
   b. Insert a piece of wood between C-clamp and pump driveshaft.
   c. Place a punch into pump housing access hole and remove retaining ring.
9. Push on driveshaft to assist in removing end cover.
10. Remove internal pump components in two groups, **Fig. 3,** as follows:
    a. Remove end cover, O-ring, pressure plate spring and pressure plate.
    b. Remove driveshaft with pump rotor, pump vanes, pump ring, thrust plate and shaft retaining ring.
11. Remove O-ring seal (A), two dowel pins (B) and driveshaft seal (C) from pump housing, **Fig. 4.**
12. Remove pressure plate, pressure plate spring and O-ring from end cover.
13. Remove shaft retaining ring from driveshaft.
14. Remove pump rotor, pump vanes, pump ring and thrust plate from driveshaft, **Fig. 5.**
15. Separate pump rotor, pump vanes and pump ring.
16. Clean all components with new power steering fluid.
17. Inspect pump ring, pump vanes, thrust plate and driveshaft for scoring, pitting or chatter marks.
18. Replace any damaged components. Do not attempt to remove damage with abrasive cleaners.

COMPLAINT/CONDITION	POSSIBLE CAUSE(S)	CORRECTION(S)
Excessive free play in steering.	Wheel bearing(s) worn.	Replace wheel bearing(s).
	Steering gear mounting bolt(s) loose.	Tighten bolt(s).
	Steering gear out of adjustment or worn.	Adjust or replace steering gear.
	Worn inner or outer steering tie rod(s).	Replace tie rod(s).
	Lower control arm ball stud(s) worn.	Replace lower control arm(s).
	Front stabilizer bar bushings worn.	Replace bushings.
Rattle and/or clunking noise in steering	Inner or outer tie rod end(s) worn.	Replace inner or outer tie rod end(s).
	Steering gear out of adjustment or worn.	Adjust or replace steering gear.
	Intermediate shaft joint(s) worn.	Replace intermediate shaft.
	Steering gear mounting bolt(s) loose.	Tighten bolt(s).
	Worn wheel bearing(s).	Replace wheel bearing(s).
Momentary increase in steering effort when steering wheel is turned quickly with system at warm operating temperature.	High internal leakage in steering gear.	Replace steering gear.
	Low power steering fluid level.	Correct power steering fluid level.
	Insufficient pump pressure.	Repair or replace power steering pump.
	Damaged EVO actuator.	Replace actuator.
	EVO electrical circuit malfunction.	Correct condition.
Steering wheel surges or jerks when turning at low speeds.	Insufficient power steering pump pressure.	Repair or replace power steering pump.
	High internal leakage in steering gear.	Replace steering gear.
	Loose accessory drive belt.	Check accessory drive belt tension.
Insufficient system pressure – caused by pump.	Flow control valve stuck or inoperative.	Free or replace flow control valve.
	EVO system malfunction.	Refer to EVO system diagnosis.
	Pressure plate not flat against pump ring.	Correct condition.
	Worn pump ring.	Replace pump ring.
	Scored pressure plate, thrust plate, or rotor.	Replace components.
	Vane(s) sticking in rotor slot(s).	Clean rotor/vanes or replace component(s).
	Cracked or broken thrust or pressure plate.	Replace components.

G36029100001020A

Fig. 1 Power steering system troubleshooting (Part 2 of 3)

COMPLAINT/CONDITION	POSSIBLE CAUSE(S)	CORRECTION(S)
Insufficient system pressure – caused by steering gear.	Leaking steering gear piston seals or inner rack seal.	Replace steering gear.
Growling noise in power steering pump.	Excessive back pressure in hoses or steering gear caused by restriction.	Eliminate restriction.
	Scored pressure plate, thrust plate, or rotor.	Replace component(s)
	Worn pump ring.	Replace pump ring.
	Air in power steering fluid.	Add power steering fluid and bleed system.
	Pump mounting loose.	Tighten pump mounting.
Rattling noise in power steering pump.	Vane(s) sticking in rotor slot(s).	Clean rotor/vanes or replace component(s).
Swishing noise in power steering pump.	Damaged flow control valve.	Replace flow control valve.
Whining noise in power steering pump.	Pump shaft being scored.	Replace pump.

G36029100001030A

Fig. 1 Power steering system troubleshooting (Part 3 of 3)

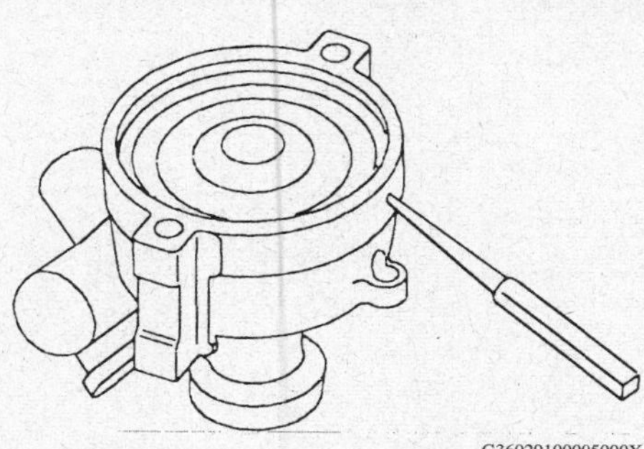

Fig. 2 Pump retaining ring removal

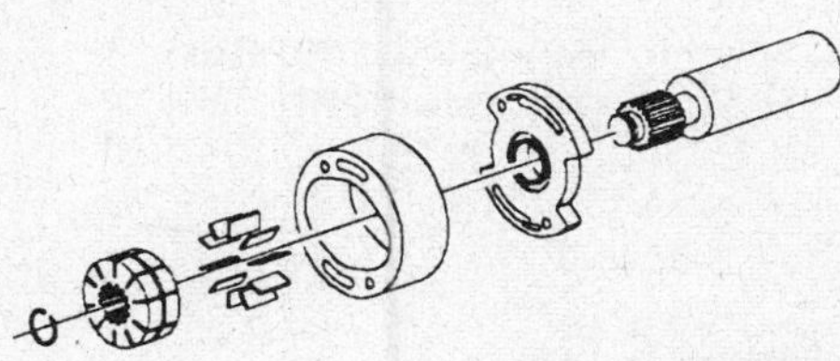

Fig. 5 Removing rotor, vanes, ring & thrust plate from driveshaft

19. A wavy pattern on pump ring face will be present with low mileage and should not be mistaken for premature wear or damage.

Assembly

1. Lubricate driveshaft with new power steering fluid.
2. Install new driveshaft seal into pump housing using a suitably sized socket as a driver.
3. Install thrust plate and pump rotor onto driveshaft.
4. Install driveshaft/rotor/thrust plate assembly into housing, **Fig. 6.**
5. Install pump ring dowel pins into pump housing through thrust plate. Install pump ring (with holes properly positioned onto dowel pins) into housing, **Fig. 7.**
6. Pump ring face has a indentation on one side near dowel hole. The ring must be installed with the indentation facing up. **Pump will not function if ring is installed upside down.**
7. Install vanes into pump rotor. Vanes may be installed in either direction.
8. Lubricate new pump housing O-ring with power steering fluid and install into groove in housing.
9. Align pressure plate dowel holes with dowel pins and install plate into housing.
10. Position pressure plate spring against pressure plate. Lubricate new end cover O-ring with power steering fluid and install onto end cover, **Fig. 8.**
11. Lubricate outer edge of end cover with power steering fluid, then press end cover into pump housing.
12. Install retaining ring into groove in pump housing, with ring opening near access hole in housing. Ensure ring is fully seated in housing groove.
13. Install three O-ring seals onto EVO actuator, if removed during disassembly procedure. **Install three seals (A, B and C) in proper position, Fig. 9.**

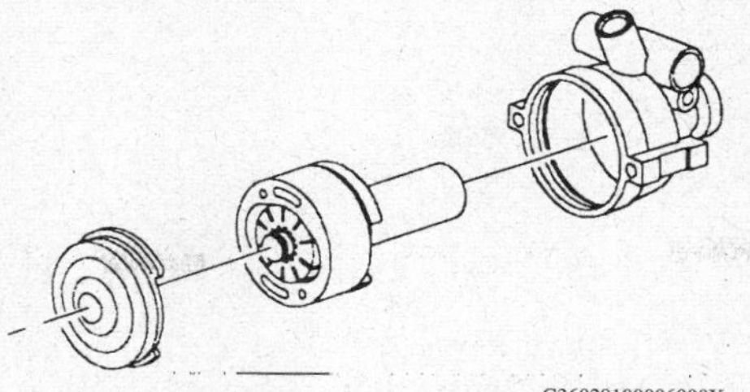

Fig. 3 Pump internal component removal

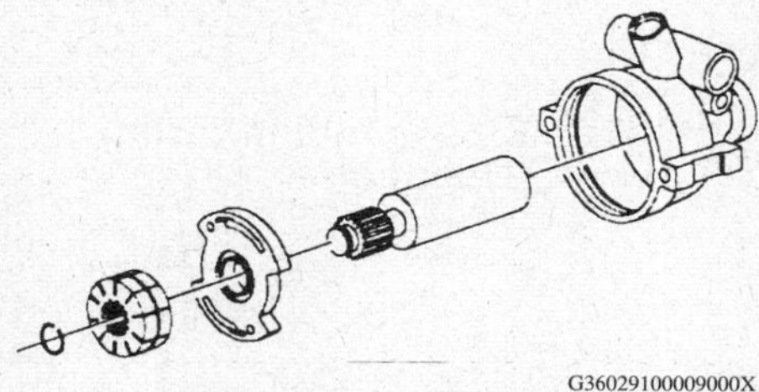

Fig. 6 Driveshaft/rotor/thrust plate assembly

14. Properly position EVO actuator and discharge fitting to pump assembly, **Fig. 10.**
15. **Torque** EVO actuator to 46 ft. lbs. using installation tool No. SA9116C, or equivalent, **Fig. 10.**
16. Install power steering pump bracket onto power steering pump with three fasteners. **Torque** to 28 ft. lbs.
17. Install pump pulley using installation tool No. SA9162C, or equivalent.
18. Lubricate new reservoir O-ring with power steering fluid and install onto reservoir.
19. Install reservoir into pump housing. Push reservoir straight into housing, then install retaining clips.
20. Install pump on engine and bleed power steering system as outlined in this section.

ELECTRONIC VARIABLE ORIFICE (EVO) ACTUATOR, REPLACE

1. Remove pump from vehicle, then disconnect EVO electrical connector locating clip.
2. Remove EVO actuator assembly using socket removal tool No. SA91116C, or equivalent, **Fig. 10. Do not pivot socket tool during removal.**
3. Remove discharge fitting from actuator.
4. Remove three O-ring seals from actuator. Note size and location of O-ring seals.
5. Reverse procedure to install, noting the following:
   a. Refer to **Fig. 9.**
   b. **Torque** EVO actuator to 46 ft. lbs.
   c. Install pump and bleed power steering system as outlined in this section.

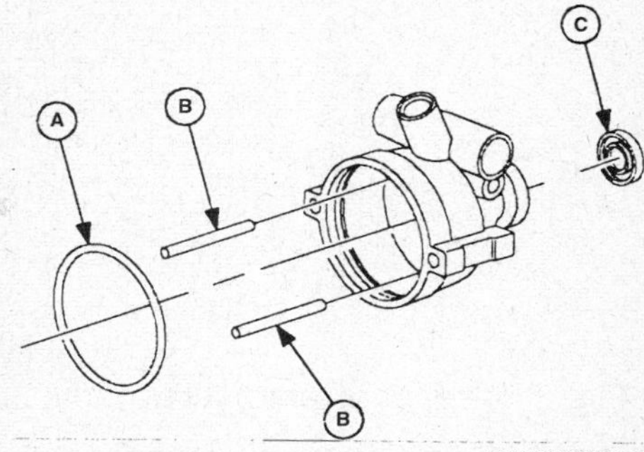

Fig. 4 Pump housing O-ring seal, dowel pins & driveshaft seal removal

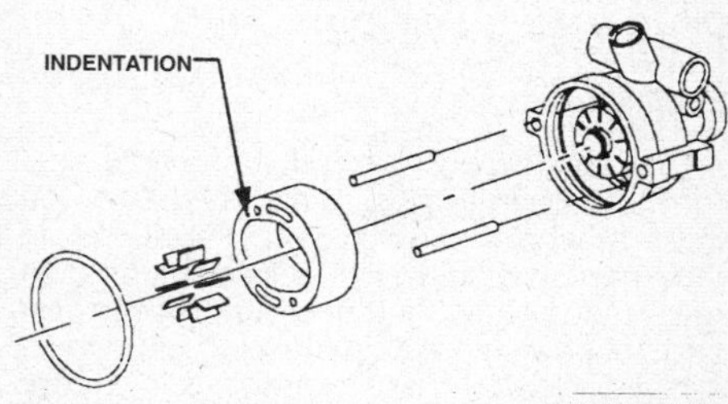

Fig. 7 Pump ring dowel pins & pump ring assembly

Power Steering System Bleed

1. Turn front wheels completely toward lefthand side, then turn ignition Off.
2. Raise and support vehicle until front tires clear ground.
3. Inspect reservoir fluid level. Add fluid if required.
4. Bleed system by turning wheels from side to side several times without contacting stops.
5. Start engine and inspect fluid level. Add fluid if required.
6. Return steering wheel to straight ahead position, lower front wheels and allow engine to idle for two to three minutes.
7. Road test vehicle to ensure steering functions normally and is free of noise.

Adjustments

STEERING GEAR BEARING PRELOAD

The following adjustment should be made with the front wheels raised and the steering wheel centered.

1. Loosen adjuster plug locknut on steering gear housing.
2. Turn adjuster plug clockwise until it bottoms in steering gear housing, **Fig. 11.**
3. **Torque** adjuster plug to 108 inch lbs.
4. Back adjuster plug off 50° (approximately one flat of nut).
5. **Torque** locknut to 52 ft. lbs. while holding adjuster plug.
6. Inspect steering wheel return following adjustment.

Fig. 8 Pressure plate assembly

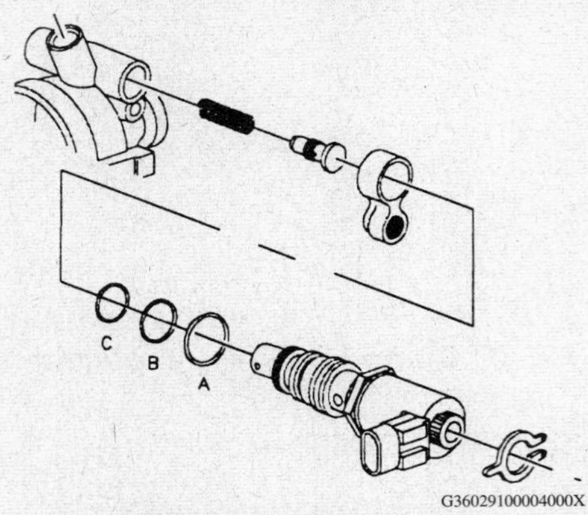

Fig. 9 EVO actuator O-ring locations

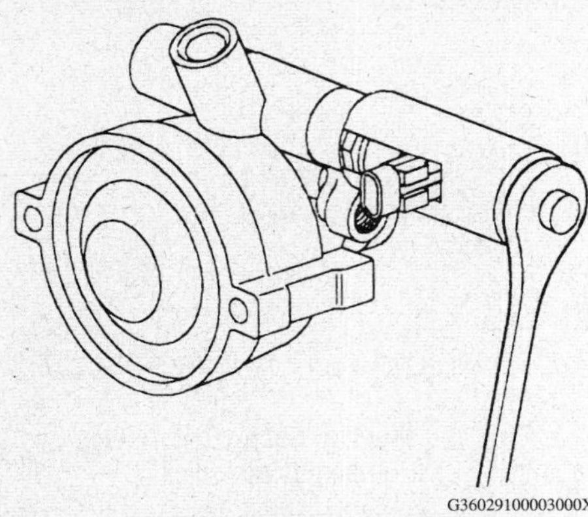

Fig. 10 EVO actuator replacement

TECHNICAL SERVICE BULLETINS

CLUNK NOISE FROM STEERING GEAR

1998

On these models a clunk noise may emit from the steering gear. This noise may be present when driving over variations in pavement at 5–10 mph. This condition may be caused by insufficient steering gear preload. Inspect and adjust steering gear bearing preload as outlined under "Adjustments" in this section.

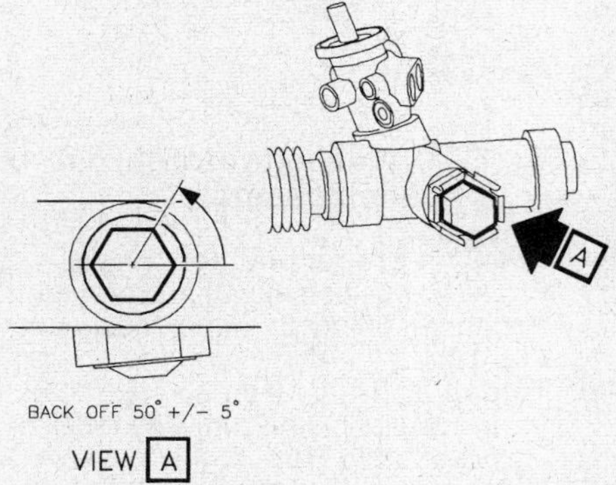

Fig. 11 Bearing preload adjustment

DISC BRAKES

TABLE OF CONTENTS

Application Chart

Model	Year	Front/Rear Brakes	Application
BUICK			
Century	1998–2002	Front	AC Delco Single Piston
	1998–2002	Rear	AC Delco Single Piston Type 1
LeSabre	1998–2002	Front	AC Delco Single Piston
Park Avenue	1998–2002	Front	AC Delco Single Piston
	1998–2002	Rear	AC Delco Single Piston Type 2
Regal	1998–2002	Front	AC Delco Single Piston
	1998–2002	Rear	AC Delco Single Piston Type 1
Riviera	1998–99	Front	AC Delco Single Piston
	1998–99	Rear	AC Delco Single Piston Type 2
Skylark	1998	Front	AC Delco Single Piston
CADILLAC			
Catera	1998–2001	Front	AC Delco Single Piston
	1998–2001	Rear	AC Delco Dual Piston
DeVille	1998–2002	Front	AC Delco Single Piston
	1998–2002	Rear	AC Delco Single Piston Type 2
Eldorado	1998–2002	Front	AC Delco Single Piston
	1998–2002	Rear	AC Delco Single Piston Type 2
Seville	1998–2002	Front	AC Delco Single Piston
	1998–2002	Rear	AC Delco Single Piston Type 2
CHEVROLET			
Camaro	1998–2002	Rear	PBR Single Piston
	1998–2002	Front	AC Delco Dual Piston
Cavalier	1998–2002	Front	AC Delco Single Piston
Corvette	1998–2002	Front	PBR Dual Piston
	1998–2002	Rear	PBR Single Piston
Impala	2000–02	Front	AC Delco Single Piston
		Rear	AC Delco Single Piston Type 2
Lumina	1998–99	Front	AC Delco Dual Piston
	2000–01	Front	AC Delco Single Piston
	1998–2001	Rear	AC Delco Single Piston Type 2

Continued

Model	Year	Front/Rear Brakes	Application
CHEVROLET			
Malibu	1998–2002	Front	AC Delco Single Piston
Monte Carlo	1998–99	Front	AC Delco Dual Piston
	2000–02	Front	AC Delco Single Piston
	1998–2002	Rear	AC Delco Single Piston Type 2
Metro	1998–2001	Front	Aisin Seiki Type 1
Prizm	1998–2002	Front	Toyota/GM
OLDSMOBILE			
Achieva	1998	Front	AC Delco Single Piston
Alero	1999–2002	Front	AC Delco Single Piston
		Rear	AC Delco Single Piston Type 2
Aurora	1998–99	Front	AC Delco Single Piston
	1998–99	Rear	AC Delco Single Piston Type 2
	2001–02	Front	AC Delco Single Piston
		Rear	AC Delco Single Piston Type 2
Cutlass	1998–99	Front	AC Delco Single Piston
Eighty-Eight	1998–99	Front	AC Delco Single Piston
Intrigue	1998–2002	Front	AC Delco Single Piston
	1998–2002	Rear	AC Delco Single Piston Type 1
LSS	1998	Front	AC Delco Single Piston
Regency	1998	Front	AC Delco Single Piston
PONTIAC			
Bonneville	1998–2002	Front	AC Delco Single Piston
Firebird	1998–2002	Rear	PBR Single Piston
	1998–2002	Front	AC Delco Dual Piston
Grand Am	1998–2002	Front	AC Delco Single Piston
	1998–2002	Rear	AC Delco Single Piston Type 2
Grand Prix	1998–2002	Front	AC Delco Single Piston
	1998–2002	Rear	AC Delco Single Piston Type 1
Sunfire	1998–2002	Front	AC Delco Single Piston

Aisin-Seiki Single Piston Front Disc Brake

NOTE: On Air Bag Equipped Models, Refer To "Air Bag System Precautions" Located In The Front Of This Manual For System Disarming & Arming Procedures.

NOTE: Refer To "Computer Relearn Procedures" Located In The Front Of This Manual When Battery Power To The Computer Has Been Interrupted.

INDEX

PRECAUTIONS

1. Grease or any other foreign material must be kept off brake linings, caliper, surfaces of disc and external surfaces of hub during service procedures.
2. Handling brake disc and caliper should be done in a way to avoid deformation of disc and nicking or scratching brake linings.
3. If inspection reveals worn or damaged rubber piston seals, they should be replaced.
4. During removal and installation of a wheel assembly, ensure not to interfere with or damage caliper splash shield or bleeder screw.
5. Front wheel bearing preload should be adjusted to specifications.
6. Ensure vehicle is centered on hoist before servicing any front end components to avoid bending or damaging disc splash shield on full righthand or lefthand wheel turns.
7. Before vehicle is moved after any brake service work, obtain a firm brake pedal.
8. Assembly bolts of two piece caliper housings should not be disturbed unless caliper requires service.

DESCRIPTION

This single piston sliding caliper assembly, **Fig. 1,** is mounted to a support bracket by two slide pins. The caliper assembly slides on the two mounting pins. Upon brake application, fluid pressure against the piston forces the inboard shoe and lining assembly against the inboard side of the disc. This action causes the caliper assembly to slide until the outboard lining comes into contact with the disc.

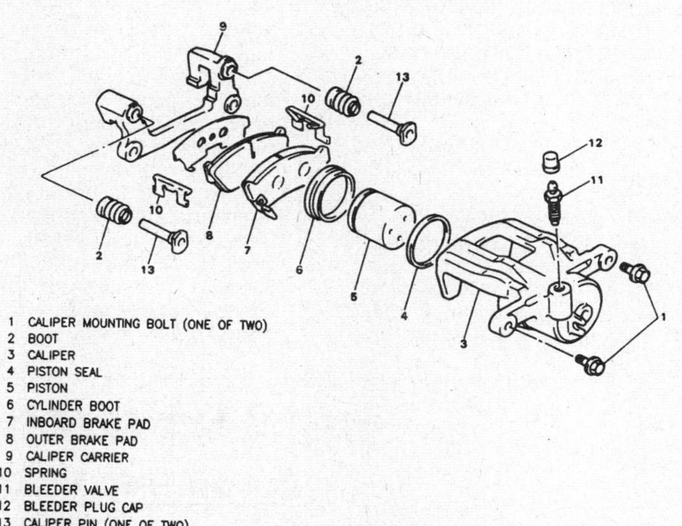

Fig. 1 Exploded view of disc brake caliper assembly

TROUBLESHOOTING

BRAKE ROUGHNESS

The most common cause of brake chatter on disc brakes is a variation in thickness of the disc. If roughness or vibration is encountered during highway operation or if pedal pulsation is experienced at low speeds, the disc may have excessive thickness variation. To inspect for this condition, measure the disc at 12 points with a micrometer at a radius approximately one inch from edge of disc. If thickness measurements vary by more than .0005 inch, the disc should be replaced with a new one.

Excessive lateral runout of braking disc may cause a piston "knocking back," possibly creating increased pedal travel and vibration when brakes are applied.

Before inspecting the runout, the wheel bearings should be adjusted. The adjustment is very important and will be required at the completion of the test to prevent bearing failure. Adjust the wheel bearings as outlined under "Front Suspension & Steering" section.

BRAKE PAD SERVICE

1. Remove approximately ⅔ of brake fluid from master cylinder.
2. Raise and support vehicle.
3. Mark relationship between front wheel and axle, then remove wheel and tire assembly.
4. Remove two caliper slide pins from bracket.
5. Unfasten caliper and support with a length of rope or wire, leaving hydraulic lines connected.

6. Remove brake pads, shims, wear indicators and retainers, **Fig. 1.**
7. Reverse procedure to install.

CALIPER SERVICE

REMOVAL

1. Remove approximately ⅔ of brake fluid from master cylinder.
2. Raise and support vehicle.
3. Mark relationship between front wheel and axle, then remove wheel and tire assembly.
4. If caliper assembly is to be serviced, remove inlet fitting attaching bolt, copper washer, and inlet fitting from caliper housing. Plug opening in inlet fitting to prevent fluid loss and contamination. **Do not crimp brake hose, since this may damage internal structure of hose. If only shoe and lining assemblies are to be replaced, do not disconnect brake line fitting from caliper.**
5. Remove caliper slide pins and caliper. If only shoe and lining assemblies are to be replaced, suspend caliper from chassis using suitable hanger. **Do not allow caliper to hang by brake hose.**
6. Remove shoe and lining assembly.
7. Remove bracket attaching bolts, then the bracket.
8. Remove slide pin boot from bracket.

DISASSEMBLE

1. Drain brake fluid from caliper.
2. Use clean shop towels to pad interior of caliper assembly, then remove piston by directing compressed air into caliper brake hose inlet hole, **Fig. 2. Use just enough air pressure to ease piston out of bore. Do not place fingers in front of piston for any reason when applying compressed air. This could result in serious personal injury.**

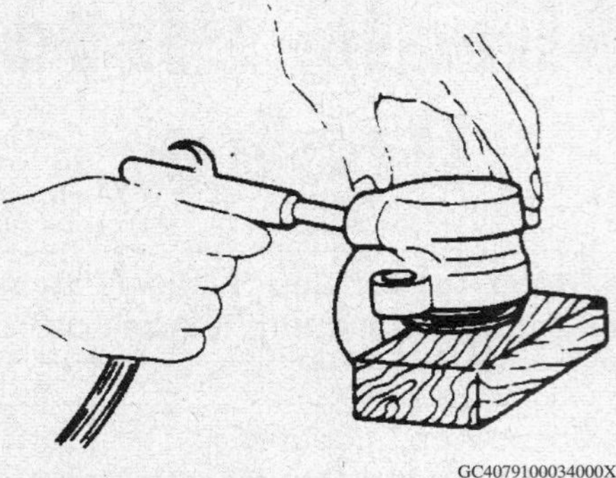

Fig. 2 Caliper piston removal

3. Remove dust boot from piston.
4. Using a small piece of wood or plastic, remove piston seal from bore. **Do not use a metal tool of any kind to remove seal since it may damage bore.**
5. Remove bleeder valve.
6. Inspect piston for scoring, nicks, corrosion, and wear.
7. Inspect caliper housing and seal groove for corrosion, nicks, scoring and excessive wear. Use crocus cloth to polish away corrosion from housing bore. Replace caliper housing if corrosion in and around seal groove will not clean up with crocus cloth.
8. Clean all components with denatured alcohol then dry with compressed air.
9. Blow out all passages in housing and bleeder valve.

ASSEMBLE

1. Apply suitable grease to piston seal and cylinder wall, then install the seal. Ensure piston seal is not twisted.
2. Apply suitable grease to sliding portion of piston and install dust boot.
3. Insert edge of dust boot into boot groove, then slowly force piston fully into cylinder.
4. Install bleeder valve.

INSTALLATION

1. Apply suitable grease to inner face of slide pin boot.
2. Install slide pin boot to bracket.
3. Install bracket and attaching bolts.
4. Install shoe and lining assembly. Ensure wear indicators are located on trailing edge of shoe assemblies during forward wheel rotation.
5. Install caliper assembly to bracket. Tighten attaching bolts to specifications.
6. Attach hose to caliper.
7. Install wheel and tire assembly, then lower the vehicle.
8. Fill master cylinder to proper level and bleed brakes as outlined under "Hydraulic Brake Systems" chapter. **Before moving vehicle, pump brake pedal several times to ensure it is firm. Do not move vehicle until a firm pedal is obtained.**

ROTOR

REPLACE

1. Remove caliper assembly from rotor as outlined under "Brake Pad Service."
2. Remove rotor from wheel hub.
3. Reverse procedure to install.

DISC BRAKE SPECIFICATIONS

ROTOR SPECIFICATIONS

Model	Year	Brake Lining Wear Limit, Inch	Nominal Thickness, Inch	Minimum Refinish Thickness, Inch	Discard Limit, Inch①	Thickness Variation Parallelism, Inch	Lateral Run Out (TIR) Inch
Metro	1998	.040	.670	—	.590	.0039	.004
	1999–2001	.040	.670	—	.590	.0005	.004

① — Discard thickness is stamped on rotor.

TIGHTENING SPECIFICATIONS

Year	Component	Torque/Ft. Lbs.
1998–2001	Bleeder Valve	89①
	Brake Hose Union Bolt	17
	Brake Pipe Fittings	12
	Caliper Mounting Bracket	29–43
	Caliper Mounting Slide Pins	22

① — Inch lbs.

AC-Delco Single Piston Front Disc Brake

NOTE: On Air Bag Equipped Models, Refer To "Air Bag System Precautions" Located In The Front Of This Manual For System Disarming & Arming Procedures.

NOTE: Refer To "Computer Relearn Procedures" Located In The Front Of This Manual When Battery Power To The Computer Has Been Interrupted.

INDEX

PRECAUTIONS

1. Grease or any other foreign material must be kept off brake linings, caliper, surfaces of disc and external surfaces of hub during service procedures.
2. Handling brake disc and caliper should be done in a way to avoid deformation of disc and nicking or scratching brake linings.
3. If inspection reveals worn or damaged rubber piston seals, they should be replaced.
4. During removal and installation of a wheel assembly, ensure not to interfere with or damage caliper splash shield, or bleeder screw.
5. Front wheel bearing preload should be adjusted to specifications.
6. Ensure vehicle is centered on hoist before servicing any front end components to avoid bending or damaging disc splash shield on full righthand or lefthand wheel turns.
7. Before vehicle is moved after any brake service work, ensure to obtain a firm brake pedal.
8. Assembly bolts of two piece caliper housings should not be disturbed unless caliper requires service.

DESCRIPTION

The caliper has a single piston and is mounted to the support bracket by two mounting bolts, **Figs. 1 through 3.** The caliper assembly slides on the two mounting bolts. Upon brake application, fluid pressure against the piston forces the inboard shoe and lining assembly against the inboard side of the disc. This action causes the caliper assembly to slide until the outboard lining comes into contact with the disc. As pressure builds up the linings are pressed against the disc with increased force.

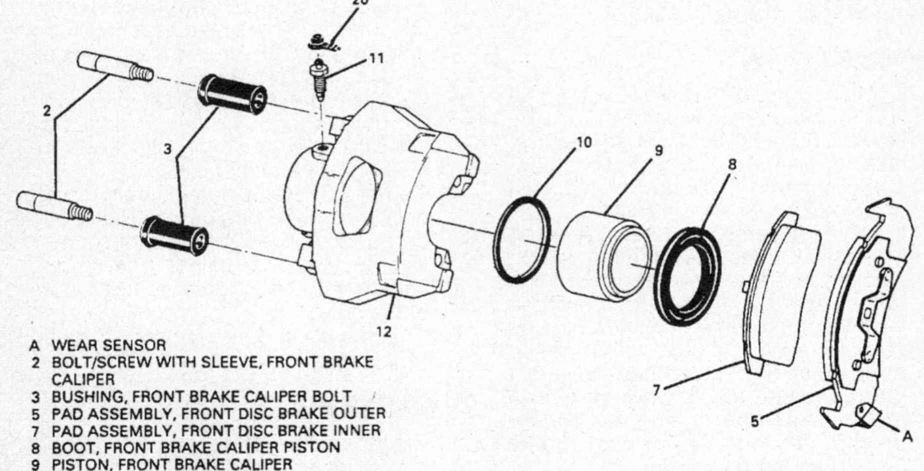

Fig. 1 Exploded view of caliper. Achieva, Alero, Cavalier, Eighty-Eight, Grand Am, LSS, Regency, Skylark, Sunfire & 1998–99 LeSabre

TROUBLESHOOTING

BRAKE ROUGHNESS

The most common cause of brake chatter on disc brakes is a variation in disc thickness. If roughness or vibration is encountered during highway operation or if pedal pulsation is experienced at low speeds, the disc may have excessive thickness variation. To inspect for this condition, measure the disc at 12 points with a micrometer at a radius approximately one inch from edge of disc. If thickness measurements vary by more than .0005 inch, the disc should be replaced with a new one.

Excessive lateral runout of braking disc may cause a piston "knocking back," possibly creating increased pedal travel and vibration when brakes are applied.

Before inspecting the runout, the wheel bearings should be adjusted. The adjustment is very important and will be required at the completion of the test to prevent bearing failure. Adjust the wheel bearings as outlined under "Front Suspension & Steering" section.

BRAKE PAD SERVICE

1. Remove caliper as outlined under "Caliper Service."
2. Remove brake pads and pad retainers from caliper bracket, **Figs. 1 through 3.**
3. Reverse procedure to install.

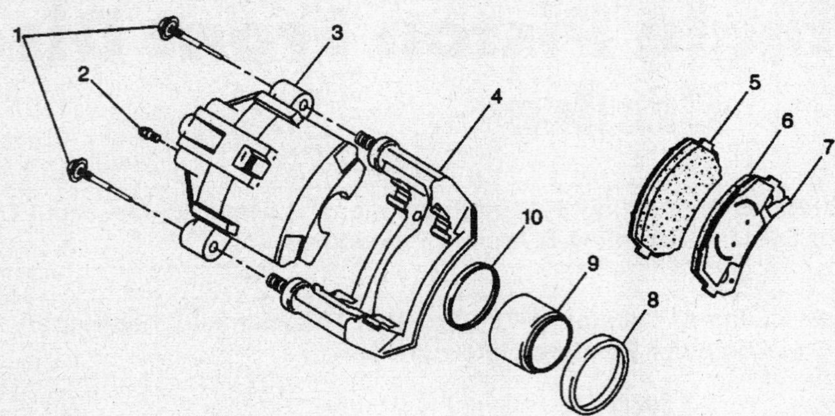

(1) Caliper Bolts
(2) Bleeder Valve
(3) Caliper Housing
(4) Caliper Bracket
(5) Inboard Pad
(6) Outboard Pad
(7) Wear Sensor
(8) Caliper Boot
(9) Piston
(10) Piston Seal

GC4079700137000X

Fig. 2 Exploded view of caliper. Aurora, Century, DeVille, Eldorado, Grand Prix, Intrigue, Regal, Riviera, Seville & 2000–02 LeSabre

CALIPER SERVICE

REPLACEMENT

1. Remove approximately ⅔ of brake fluid from master cylinder.
2. Raise and support front of vehicle, then remove wheel and tire assembly.
3. Using suitable C-clamp, push piston back into caliper bore, **Fig. 4.**
4. If caliper assembly is being removed for service, remove inlet fitting attaching bolt, copper washer, and inlet fitting from caliper housing. Plug opening in inlet fitting to prevent fluid loss and contamination. **Do not crimp brake hose since this may damage hose's internal structure. If only shoe and lining assemblies are to be replaced, do not disconnect brake line fitting from caliper.**
5. **On Catera models,** carefully separate sensor from inner brake pad, **Fig. 5,** by placing a small screwdriver between lower section of sensor and brake pad.
6. **On all models,** remove caliper mounting bolts, **Fig. 6,** if signs of corrosion are indicated, replace bolts when installing caliper assembly.
7. Remove caliper assembly from disc. If only shoe and lining assemblies are to be replaced, use a length of rope or wire to suspend caliper from spring coil. Never allow caliper to hang from brake hose.
8. Reverse procedure to install. Tighten to specifications.

DISASSEMBLE

1. Clean outside of caliper, then drain brake fluid from caliper.
2. Remove piston by directing compressed air into caliper brake hose inlet hole, place clean shop towels to pad interior of caliper assembly, **Fig. 7. Use just enough air pressure to ease piston out of bore. Do not place fingers in front of piston for any reason when applying compressed air. This could result in serious personal injury.**
3. Remove dust boot from caliper bore using a suitable screwdriver, **Fig. 8.**
4. Remove piston seal from bore using a small piece of wood or plastic, **Do not use a metal tool of any kind to remove seal since it may damage bore.**
5. Remove bleeder valve.
6. Inspect piston for scoring, nicks, corrosion, and wear and replace as needed.
7. Inspect caliper housing and seal groove for corrosion, nicks, scoring and excessive wear, then use crocus cloth to polish away corrosion from housing bore.
8. Replace caliper housing if corrosion in and around seal groove will not clean up with crocus cloth.
9. Clean all components with denatured alcohol and dry with compressed air.
10. Blow out all passages in housing and bleeder valve.
11. Reverse procedure to assemble. Ensure to properly seat dust boot using installer tool No. J-36349, or equivalent, **Fig. 9.**

ROTOR

REPLACE

1. Raise and support vehicle, then remove tire and wheel assembly.
2. Remove caliper assembly from rotor as outlined under "Caliper Service."
3. Remove caliper assembly mounting bracket attaching bolts, then the mounting bracket.
4. Remove rotor from hub and bearing assembly.
5. Reverse procedure to install.

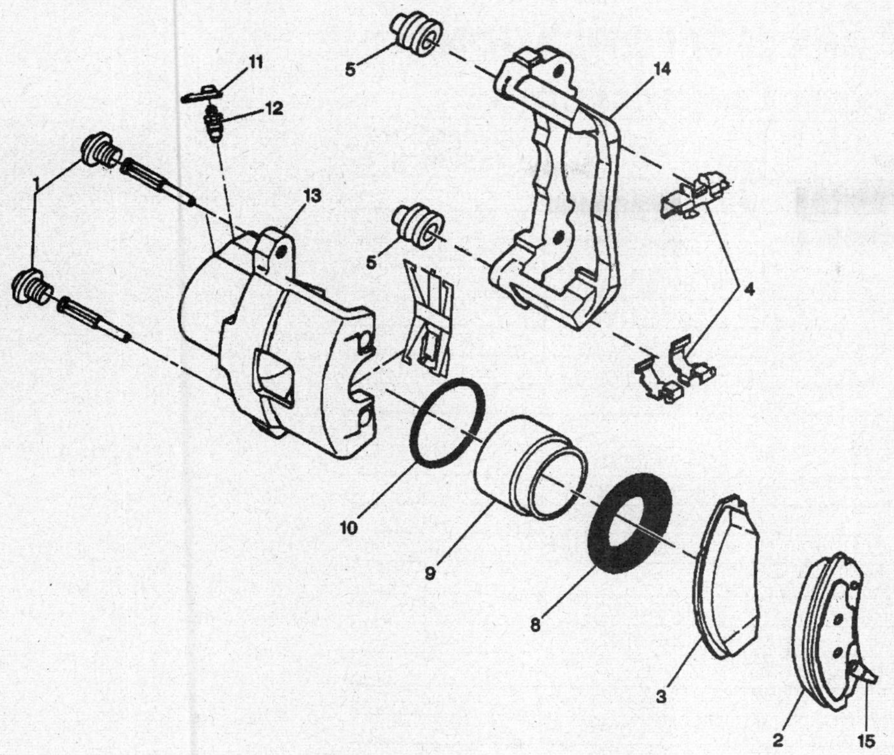

(1) Bolt and Slide Pin Assemblies
(2) Outboard Brake Pad
(3) Inboard Brake Pad
(4) Clips, Brake Pad
(5) Boot, Brake Pin Slide
(8) Seal, Brake Caliper Dust
(9) Piston, Brake Caliper
(10) Seal, Brake Caliper Piston
(11) Cap, Brake Bleeder Screw
(12) Screw, Brake Bleeder
(13) Caliper, Brake
(14) Bracket, Caliper to Knuckle
(15) Wear Sensor

GC4079700138000X

Fig. 3 Exploded view of caliper. Cutlass & Malibu

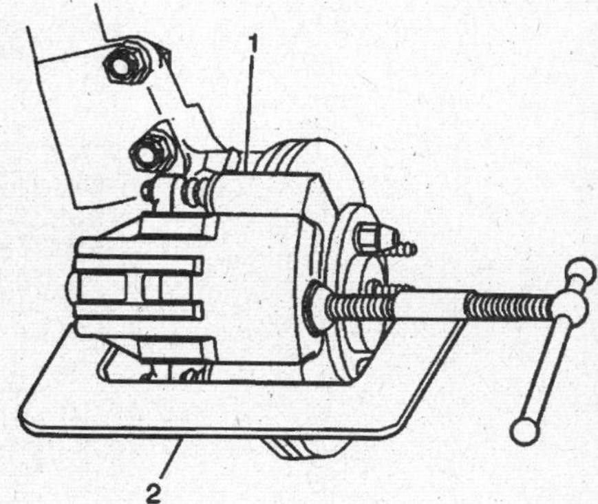

(1) Caliper
(2) C-Clamp

GC4079700136000X

Fig. 4 Piston compression

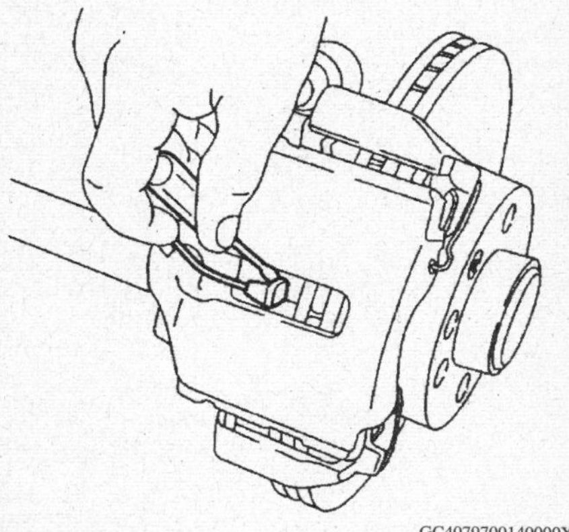

GC4079700140000X

Fig. 5 Brake pad sensor removal. Catera

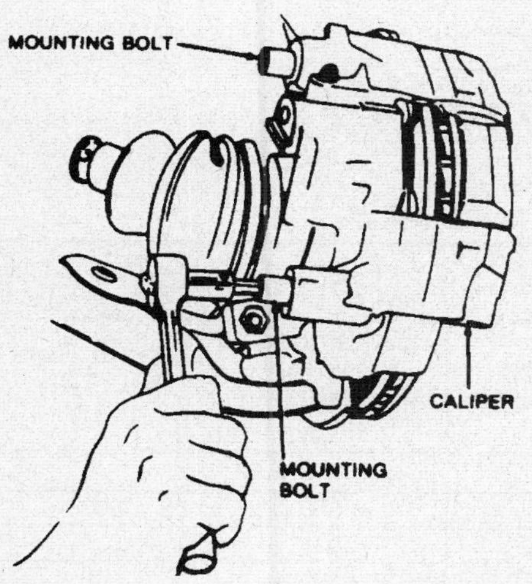

GC4079100059000X

Fig. 6 Caliper mounting bolts replacement

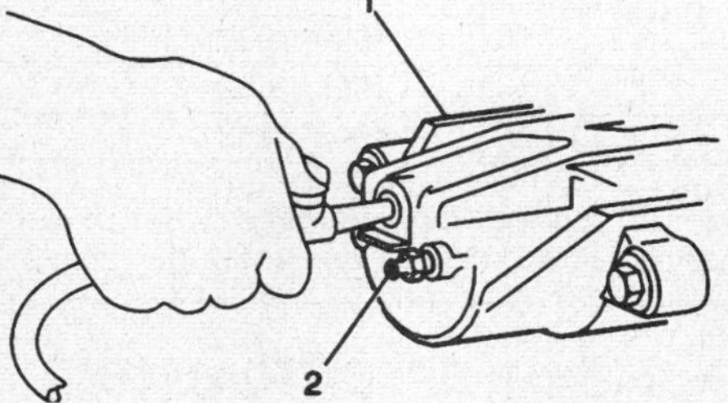

GC4079700147000X

Fig. 7 Caliper piston removal

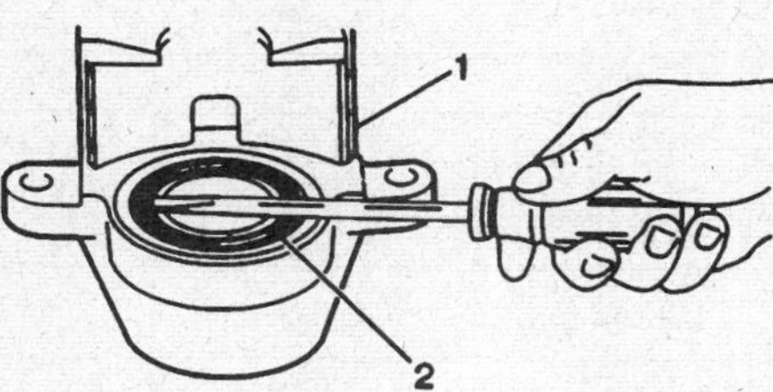

GC4079700148000X

Fig. 8 Dust boot removal

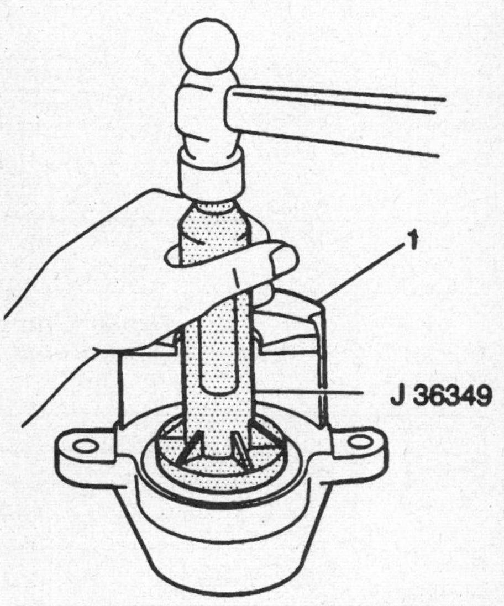

GC4079700149000X

Fig. 9 Dust boot installation in caliper

DISC BRAKE SPECIFICATIONS

CALIPER SPECIFICATIONS

Model	Year	Caliper Bore Dia. Inch
BUICK		
Century	1998–2002	2.50
LeSabre	1998–99	2.50
	2000–02	①
Park Avenue	1998–2002	2.52
Regal	1998–2002	2.50
Riviera	1998–99	2.52
Skylark	1998	2.24
CADILLAC		
Catera	1998–2001	2.24
DeVille	1998–2002	2.52
Eldorado	1998–2002	2.52
Seville	1998–2002	2.52
CHEVROLET		
Cavalier	1998–2002	2.24
Malibu	1998–2002	2.36
OLDSMOBILE		
Achieva	1998	2.24
Alero	1999–2002	2.36
Aurora	1998–99	2.52
	2001–02	2.52
Cutlass	1998–99	—
Eighty-Eight	1998–99	2.52
Intrigue	1998–2002	2.50
LSS	1998	2.52
Regency	1998	2.52
PONTIAC		
Bonneville	1998–2002	2.52
Grand Am	1998	2.24
	1999–2002	2.36
Grand Prix	1998–2002	2.50
Sunfire	1998–2002	2.24

① — Inspect for scoring, nicks, cracks, wear or corrosion. Do not hone caliper, replace as required.

ROTOR SPECIFICATIONS

Model	Year	Brake Lining Wear Limit, Inch	Nominal Thickness, Inch	Minimum Refinish Thickness, Inch	Discard Limit, Inch①	Thickness Variation Parallelism, Inch	Lateral Run Out (TIR) Inch
BUICK							
Century	1998–2002	.030	1.270	1.250	1.210	.0005	.003
LeSabre	1998–99	.030	1.260	1.224	1.209	.0005	.002
	2000–02	.030	1.267	1.224	1.200	.0005	.002
Park Avenue	1998–2002	.030	1.267	1.224	1.200	.0005	.002
Regal	1998–2002	.030	1.270	1.250	1.210	.0005	.003
Riviera	1998–99	.030	1.267	1.224	1.200	.0005	.002
Skylark	1998	.030	.796	.751	.736	.0005	.003
CADILLAC							
Catera	1998–2001	.315②	1.102	1.043	.984	.0005	.004
Deville	1998–99	.030	1.267	1.224	1.200	.0005	.002
	2000–02	.030	1.267	1.224	1.209	.0005	.002

Continued

ROTOR SPECIFICATIONS—Continued

Model	Year	Brake Lining Wear Limit, Inch	Nominal Thickness, Inch	Minimum Refinish Thickness, Inch	Discard Limit, Inch①	Thickness Variation Parallelism, Inch	Lateral Run Out (TIR) Inch
CADILLAC							
Eldorado	1998–2002	.030	1.267	1.224	1.200	.0005	.002
Seville	1998–2002	.030	1.267	1.224	1.209	.0005	.002
CHEVROLET							
Cavalier	1998–2002	.030	.796	.751	.736	.0005	.003
Malibu	1998–99	.030	1.031	.987	.972	.0005	.0025
	2000–02	.030	1.030	.980	.970	.0005	.003
OLDSMOBILE							
Achieva	1998	.030	.796	.751	.736	.0005	.003
Alero	1999–2002	.030	1.030	.980	.970	.0005	.002
Aurora	1998–99 & 2001–02	.030	1.267	1.224	1.200	.0005	.002
Cutlass	1998–99	.030	1.031	.987	.972	.0005	.0025
Eighty-Eight	1998–99	.030	1.260	1.224	1.209	.0005	.002
Intrigue	1998–2002	.030	1.270	1.250	1.210	.0005	.003
LSS	1998	.030	1.260	1.224	1.209	.0005	.002
Regency	1998	.030	1.260	1.224	1.209	.0005	.002
PONTIAC							
Bonneville	1998–99	.030	1.260	1.224	1.209	.0005	.002
	2000–02	.030	1.267	1.224	1.200	.0005	.002
Firebird	1998	.030	1.260	1.223	1.209	.0005	.005
	1999–2002	.030	1.260	1.223	1.209	.0005	.005
Grand Am	1998	.030	.796	.751	.736	.0005	.003
	1999–2002	.030	1.030	.980	.970	.0005	.002
Grand Prix	1998–2002	.030	1.270	1.250	1.210	.0005	.003
Sunfire	1998–2002	.030	.796	.751	.736	.0005	.003

① — Discard thickness is stamped on rotor.

② — Includes backing plate.

TIGHTENING SPECIFICATIONS

Year	Component	Torque/Ft. Lbs.
1998–2002	Brake Hose To Caliper (Achieva, Alero, Cavalier, Grand Am, Skylark & Sunfire)	32
	Brake Hose To Caliper (Catera)	30
	Brake Hose To Caliper (Century, Cutlass, Intrigue, Malibu, Regal)	40
	Brake Hose To Caliper (Aurora, Bonneville, DeVille, Eighty-Eight, Eldorado, LSS, LeSabre, Park Avenue, Regency, Riviera & Seville)	33
	Caliper Bleeder Screw (Except Catera)	115②
	Caliper Bleeder Screw (Catera)	81②
	Caliper Bracket Mounting Bolts (Except Catera)	137
	Caliper Bracket Mounting Bolts (Catera)	70①
	Caliper Mounting Bolts (Except Achieva, Alero, Bonneville, Catera, Cavalier, Eighty-Eight, Grand Am, LeSabre, LSS, Regency, Skylark & Sunfire)	63
	Caliper Mounting Bolts (Achieva, Alero, Bonneville, Cavalier, Eighty-Eight, Grand Am, LeSabre, LSS, Regency, Skylark & Sunfire)	38
	Caliper Mounting Bolts (Catera)	22
	Rotor Setscrew (Catera)	35②
	Wheel Speed Sensor Mounting Bolt	96②
	Wheel Lug Nuts (Except Catera)	100
	Wheel Lug Nuts (Catera)	80

① — Rotate an additional 37°.
② — Inch lbs.

AC-Delco Dual Piston Front Disc Brake

NOTE: On Air Bag Equipped Models, Refer To "Air Bag System Precautions" Located In The Front Of This Manual For System Disarming & Arming Procedures.

NOTE: Refer To "Computer Relearn Procedures" Located In The Front Of This Manual When Battery Power To The Computer Has Been Interrupted.

INDEX

PRECAUTIONS

1. Grease or any other foreign material must be kept off brake linings, caliper, surfaces of disc and external surfaces of hub during service procedures.
2. Handling brake disc and caliper should be done in a way to avoid deformation of disc and nicking or scratching brake linings.
3. If inspection reveals worn or damaged rubber piston seals, they should be replaced.
4. During removal and installation of a wheel assembly, ensure not to interfere with or damage caliper splash shield, or bleeder screw.
5. Front wheel bearings preload should be adjusted to specifications.
6. Ensure vehicle is centered on hoist before servicing any front end components to avoid bending or damaging disc splash shield on full righthand or lefthand wheel turns.
7. Before vehicle is moved after any brake service work, obtain a firm brake pedal.
8. Assembly bolts of two piece caliper housings should not be disturbed unless caliper requires service.

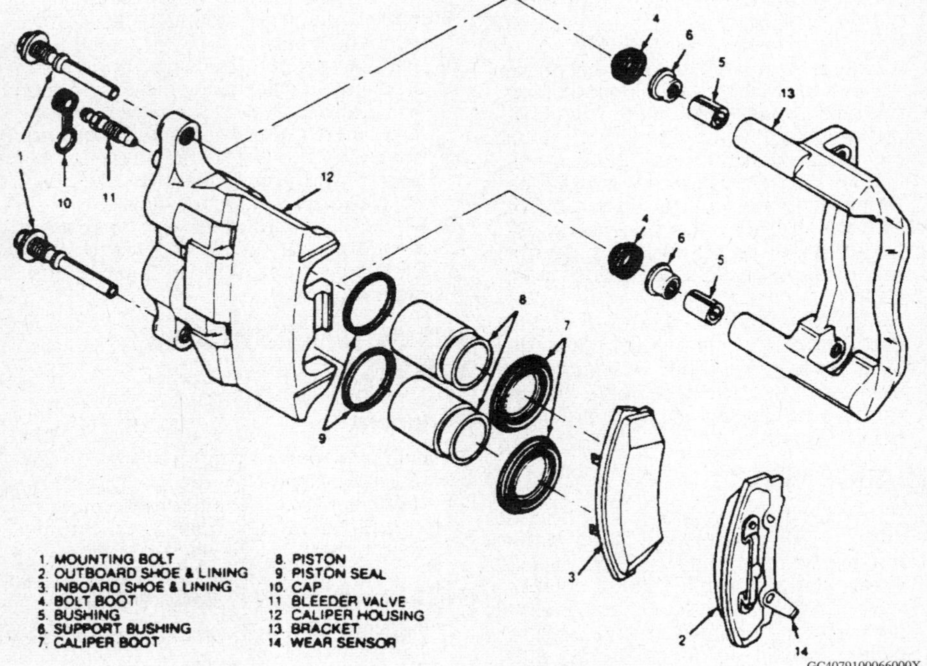

Fig. 1 Exploded view of AC-Delco 3242 series dual piston caliper

DESCRIPTION

This dual piston sliding caliper, **Fig. 1,** is comprised of two interconnected bores and is attached to a mounting bracket with two mounting bolts. Hydraulic pressure acting on the bottom of the caliper bores forces the pistons outward, enabling the caliper to slide inward, thereby clamping the brake shoes against the rotor.

TROUBLESHOOTING

BRAKE ROUGHNESS

The most common cause of brake chatter on disc brakes is a variation in disc thickness. If roughness or vibration is encountered during highway operation or if pedal pulsation is experienced at low speeds, the disc may have excessive thickness variation. To inspect for this condition, measure the disc at 12 points with a micrometer at a radius approximately one inch from edge of disc. If thickness measurements vary by more than .0005 inch, the disc should be replaced with a new one.

Excessive lateral runout of braking disc may cause a piston "knocking back," possibly creating increased pedal travel and vibration when brakes are applied.

Before inspecting the runout, the wheel bearings should be adjusted. The adjustment is very important and will be required at the completion of the test to prevent bearing failure. Adjust the wheel bearings as outlined under "Front Suspension & Steering" section.

BRAKE PAD SERVICE

1. Remove caliper as outlined under "Caliper Service."

2. Lift upward on outward shoe retaining spring of outboard shoe until it clears center lug, then remove shoe from caliper.
3. Pull inboard shoe outward to disengage retainer springs from pistons, then remove inboard shoe from caliper.
4. Reverse procedure to install, noting the following:
   a. Install inboard shoe into caliper. Ensure retainer spring tangs are fully positioned into pistons.
   b. Snap outboard shoe retaining spring over housing center lug, then install outboard shoe into caliper.

CALIPER SERVICE

REMOVAL

1. Siphon enough brake fluid out of master cylinder to bring fluid level to ⅓ full to avoid fluid overflow when caliper pistons are pushed back into bores.
2. Raise and support vehicle, then remove front wheels.
3. Mark relationship between wheel to hub and bearing assembly.
4. Using a suitable C-clamp and, if required, a block of wood, push pistons back together into caliper bores.
5. If caliper assembly is to be serviced, remove inlet fitting attaching bolt, copper washer, and inlet fitting from caliper housing. Plug opening in inlet fitting to prevent fluid loss and contamination. **Do not crimp brake hose, as this may damage internal structure of hose. If only shoe and lining assemblies are to be replaced, do not disconnect brake line fitting from caliper.**
6. Remove two mounting bolts, then the caliper. If only shoe and lining assemblies are to be replaced, suspend caliper from chassis using suitable rope or wire. **Do not allow caliper to hang by brake hose.**

DISASSEMBLE

1. Remove caliper assembly as outlined under "Caliper Service," then drain brake fluid from caliper.
2. Position shop towel in interior component of caliper, then slowly apply compressed air to inlet port and remove pistons. **It is imperative that one piston be partially installed to facilitate removal of second piston from bore. A pad or wooden spacer may be used to prevent complete removal of first piston.**
3. Remove piston boots from caliper bores, then using suitable wooden or plastic tool, pry piston seals from caliper bore grooves. **Do not use a metal tool of any kind to remove seal since it may damage bore.**
4. Remove bleeder valve from caliper.
5. Inspect piston for scoring, nicks, corrosion, and wear.
6. Inspect caliper housing and seal grooves for corrosion, nicks, scoring and excessive wear. Use crocus cloth to polish away corrosion from housing bore. Replace caliper housing if corrosion in and around seal grooves will not clean up with crocus cloth.
7. Clean all components with denatured alcohol and dry with compressed air.
8. Blow out all passages in housing and bleeder valve.

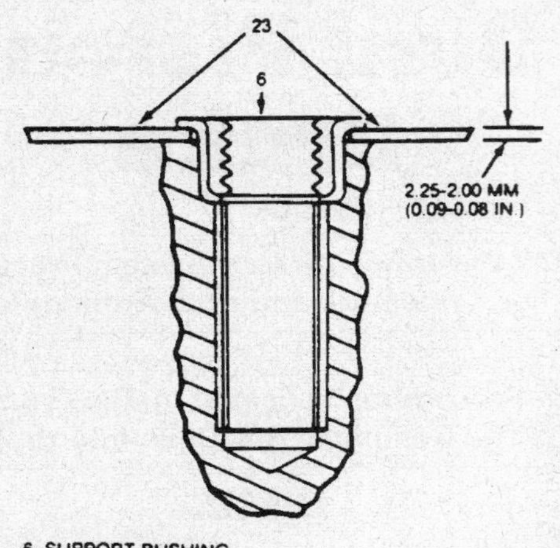

Fig. 2 Support bushing installation

MOUNTING BRACKET SERVICE

Removal

1. Remove caliper as outlined under "Caliper Service."
2. Using suitable Torx bit, remove mounting bracket attaching bolts and mounting bracket.

Bushing & Boot Replacement

1. Remove mounting bracket from vehicle.
2. Remove bolt boots from support bushings, **Fig. 1.**
3. Clamp bracket in a suitable vise, then pry support bushings from inner bushings in bracket ears with small screwdriver.
4. Using a paper clip, pull inner bushings from mounting bracket ears.
5. Lubricate inner bushings with silicone based grease, then install bushings flush with bracket ears.
6. Position an .080–.090 inch thick shim stock on bracket ear face, then drive support bushings into inner bushings, **Fig. 2.** When properly installed, bushing should protrude .080–.090 inch above bracket ear face.
7. Snap new bolt boots over support bushing lip.

Installation

1. Coat mounting bracket attaching bolt threads with Loctite sealant, or equivalent.
2. Align mounting bracket holes, then install mounting bracket and tighten attaching bolts to specifications.

ASSEMBLE

1. Install bleeder valve.
2. Lubricate piston seals with clean brake fluid, then carefully install seals into caliper bore grooves. **Ensure seals are not twisted.**
3. Lubricate boots and install onto pistons, then push pistons fully into caliper bores.
4. Seat boots into caliper bores using boot seal installer tool No. J-36349, or equivalent.

INSTALLATION

1. Position caliper over rotor and onto mounting bracket.
2. Lubricate entire length of mounting bolts with silicone based grease, then install bolts and tighten to specifications.
3. If inlet fitting was removed, install fitting using new copper washer.
4. Install front wheels, fill master cylinder to proper level, then bleed brake as outlined under "Hydraulic Brake Systems" chapter. **Before moving vehicle, pump brake pedal several times to ensure it is firm. Do not move vehicle until a firm pedal is obtained.**

ROTOR

REPLACE

1. Raise and support vehicle, then remove tire and wheel assembly.
2. Remove caliper and caliper mounting bracket as outlined under "Caliper Service."
3. Remove rotor from hub and bearing assembly.
4. Reverse procedure to install.

DISC BRAKE SPECIFICATIONS

CALIPER SPECIFICATIONS

Model	Year	Caliper Bore Dia. Inch
Camaro & Firebird	1998–2002	2.50
Lumina & Monte Carlo	1998–99	1.654

ROTOR SPECIFICATIONS

Model	Year	Brake Lining Wear Limit, Inch	Nominal Thickness, Inch	Minimum Refinish Thickness, Inch	Discard Limit, Inch①	Thickness Variation Parallelism, Inch	Lateral Run Out (TIR) Inch
Camaro	1998–2002	.030	1.260	1.223	1.209	.0005	.005
Firebird	1998–2002	.030	1.260	1.223	1.209	.0005	.005
Lumina	1998–99	.030	1.039	.987	.972	.0005	.003
Monte Carlo	1998–99	.030	1.039	.987	.972	.0005	.003

① — Discard thickness is stamped on rotor.

TIGHTENING SPECIFICATIONS

Year	Component	Torque/Ft. Lbs.
CAMARO & FIREBIRD		
1998–2002	Brake Hose To Caliper Inlet Fitting Bolt	30
	Brake Pipe Connection	11
	Caliper Bleeder Valve (1998)	115①
	Caliper Bleeder Valve (1999–2002)	106①
	Caliper Mounting Bracket Bolt (1998)	162
	Caliper Mounting Bracket Bolt (1999–2002)	74
	Caliper Slide Bolt	23
LUMINA & MONTE CARLO		
1998–99	Brake Hose To Caliper Inlet Fitting Bolt (1998)	33
	Brake Hose To Caliper Inlet Fitting Bolt (1999)	40
	Brake Pipe Connection	11
	Caliper Bleeder Valve (1998)	115①
	Caliper Bleeder Valve (1999)	106①
	Caliper Mounting Bracket Bolt (1998)	148
	Caliper Mounting Bracket Bolt (1999)	137
	Caliper Slide Bolt	80

① — Inch lbs.

PBR Dual Piston Front Disc Brake

NOTE: On Air Bag Equipped Models, Refer To "Air Bag System Precautions" Located In The Front Of This Manual For System Disarming & Arming Procedures.

NOTE: Refer To "Computer Relearn Procedures" Located In The Front Of This Manual When Battery Power To The Computer Has Been Interrupted.

INDEX

PRECAUTIONS

1. Grease or any other foreign material must be kept off brake linings, caliper, surfaces of disc and external surfaces of hub during service procedures.
2. Handling brake disc and caliper should be done in a way to avoid deformation of disc and nicking or scratching brake linings.
3. If inspection reveals worn or damaged rubber piston seals, they should be replaced.
4. During removal and installation of a wheel assembly, ensure not to interfere with or damage caliper splash shield, or bleeder screw.
5. Front wheel bearings preload should be adjusted to specifications.
6. Ensure vehicle is centered on hoist before servicing any front end components to avoid bending or damaging disc splash shield on full righthand or lefthand wheel turns.
7. Before vehicle is moved after any brake service work, obtain a firm brake pedal.
8. Assembly bolts of two piece caliper housings should not be disturbed unless caliper requires service.

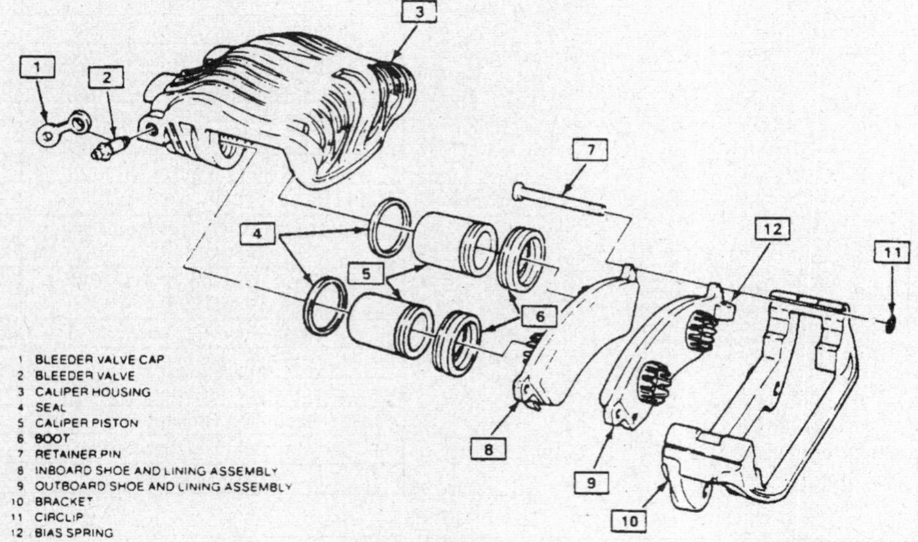

Fig. 1 Exploded view of PBR dual piston front caliper

DESCRIPTION

This front caliper, **Fig. 1,** consists of dual pistons and an aluminum housing which is suspended on the shoe and lining assemblies. Hydraulic pressure, created by applying force to the brake pedal, acts equally against the pistons and the bottom of the caliper bores to move the pistons outward. This action slides the caliper inward, resulting in a clamping action on the brake rotor. This clamping action forces the linings against the rotor, creating the friction required to stop the vehicle.

TROUBLESHOOTING

BRAKE ROUGHNESS

The most common cause of brake chatter on disc brakes is a variation in disc thickness. If roughness or vibration is encountered during highway operation or if pedal pulsation is experienced at low speeds, the disc may have excessive thickness variation. To inspect for this condition, measure the disc at 12 points with a micrometer at a radius approximately one inch from edge of disc. If thickness measurements vary by more than .0005 inch, the disc should be replaced with a new one.

Excessive lateral runout of braking disc may cause a piston "knocking back," possibly creating increased pedal travel and vibration when brakes are applied.

Before inspecting the runout, the wheel bearings should be adjusted. The adjustment is very important and will be required at the completion of the test to prevent bearing failure. Adjust the wheel bearings as outlined under "Front Suspension & Steering" section.

BRAKE PAD SERVICE

REMOVAL

1. Remove brake caliper as outlined under "Caliper Service."
2. Position suitable pliers over caliper and center of inboard shoe and lining, **Fig. 2,** then squeeze pliers to bottom pistons in caliper bores.
3. Remove shoe and lining assemblies.

INSTALLATION

1. Install inboard shoe and lining.
2. Ensure tangs on shoe fully engage pistons. When properly installed, shoe should be flush with piston.
3. Install outboard shoe and lining into caliper housing. Ensure insulators are fully seated into holes in outboard side of housing.
4. Install caliper as outlined under "Caliper Service."

CALIPER SERVICE

REMOVAL

1. Remove ⅔ of total brake fluid capacity from master cylinder reservoir.
2. Raise and support vehicle, then remove tire and wheel assembly.
3. If caliper requires overhaul, remove inlet fitting attaching bolt, then disconnect inlet fitting from caliper housing.
4. Discard both gaskets, then plug openings in inlet fitting and caliper to prevent loss or contamination of fluid. **Do not crimp brake hose since this may damage hose's internal structure.**
5. Remove caliper guide pin bolts, then the caliper from rotor and caliper mounting bracket. If only shoe and linings require replacement, suspend caliper from upper control arm to prevent damage to brake hose.

DISASSEMBLE

1. Remove shoe and lining assemblies.
2. Pad interior of caliper housing with shop towels to prevent damage to pistons during removal.
3. Position shop towel in interior component of caliper, then slowly apply compressed air to inlet port and remove pistons. **It is imperative that one piston be partially installed to facilitate removal of second piston from bore. A pad or wooden spacer may be used to prevent complete removal of first piston.**
4. Remove dust boots from pistons.
5. Using a small piece of wood or plastic, remove piston seal from bore. **Do not use a metal tool of any kind to remove seal since it may damage bore.**
6. Remove bleeder valve cap and bleeder valve.
7. Inspect piston for scoring, nicks, corrosion, and wear.
8. Inspect caliper housing and seal groove for corrosion, nicks, scoring and excessive wear.
9. Use crocus cloth to polish away corrosion from housing bore. Replace caliper housing if corrosion in and around seal groove will not clean up with crocus cloth.
10. Clean all components with denatured alcohol, then dry with compressed air.
11. Blow out all passages in housing and bleeder valve.

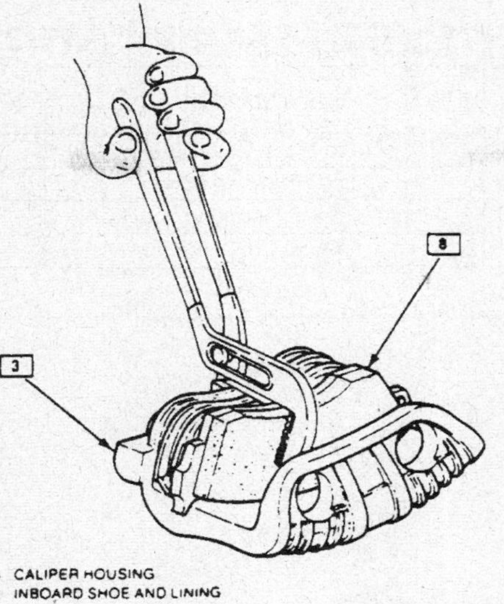

Fig. 2 Piston retraction in caliper bores

ASSEMBLE

1. Install cap onto bleeder valve, then install bleeder valve into caliper.
2. Using clean brake fluid, lubricate piston seals, then install seals into caliper bore grooves. Ensure seals are not twisted during installation.
3. Using clean brake fluid, lubricate caliper bores and piston assemblies.
4. Install boot over end of piston.
5. Place piston into caliper bore, then push downward until fully bottomed in bore. Ensure boot is properly seated into groove around piston and into groove in caliper bore.
6. Repeat Step 3 and 4 for remaining piston.
7. Install shoes and linings as described in this section, then bleed brake system.

INSTALLATION

1. Ensure guiding surfaces on shoe and lining assemblies and mounting bracket are seated properly, then position caliper over rotor and onto mounting bracket.
2. Press caliper housing downward to compress bias springs (12), **Fig. 1,** then install new retainer pin and circlip. **Two sets of retainer pins are available for service. One is for base calipers and one is for heavy duty. Since circlip grooves are cut in different positions, ensure proper retainer pin is used.**
3. If caliper was overhauled, connect inlet fitting using new gaskets, then bleed brake system as required.
4. Install wheel and tire assembly, then lower the vehicle.
5. Fill master cylinder to proper level, then pump brake pedal to bring pads into contact with brake rotor.

ROTOR

REPLACE

1. Remove caliper as outlined under "Caliper Service."
2. Remove caliper mounting bracket attaching bolts, then the mounting bracket.
3. Remove rotor from hub assembly.
4. Reverse procedure to install.

DISC BRAKE SPECIFICATIONS

CALIPER SPECIFICATIONS

Model	Year	Caliper Bore Dia. Inch
Corvette	1998–2002	1.50

ROTOR SPECIFICATIONS

Model	Year	Brake Lining Wear Limit, Inch	Nominal Thickness, Inch	Minimum Refinish Thickness, Inch	Discard Limit, Inch①	Thickness Variation Parallelism, Inch	Lateral Run Out (TIR) Inch
Corvette	1998–2002	.030	1.260	1.205	1.190	.0005	.003

① — Discard thickness is stamped on rotor.

TIGHTENING SPECIFICATIONS

Year	Component	Torque/Ft. Lbs.
1998–2002	Brake Hose To Caliper	30
	Caliper Bleeder Screw	108①
	Front Caliper Mounting Bracket	125
	Wheel Lug Nuts	100

① — Inch lbs.

AC-Delco Dual Piston Rear Disc Brake

NOTE: On Air Bag Equipped Models, Refer To "Air Bag System Precautions" Located In The Front Of This Manual For System Disarming & Arming Procedures.

NOTE: Refer To "Computer Relearn Procedures" Located In The Front Of This Manual When Battery Power To The Computer Has Been Interrupted.

INDEX

PRECAUTIONS

1. Grease or any other foreign material must be kept off brake linings, caliper, surfaces of disc and external surfaces of hub during service procedures.
2. Handling brake disc and caliper should be done in a way to avoid deformation of disc and nicking or scratching brake linings.
3. If inspection reveals rubber piston seals are worn or damaged, they should be replaced.
4. During removal and installation of a wheel assembly, ensure not to interfere with or damage caliper splash shield, or bleeder screw.
5. Front wheel bearings preload should be adjusted to specifications .
6. Ensure vehicle is centered on hoist before servicing any front end components to avoid bending or damaging disc splash shield on full righthand or lefthand wheel turns.
7. Before vehicle is moved after any brake service work, ensure to obtain a firm brake pedal.
8. Assembly bolts of two piece caliper housings should not be disturbed unless caliper requires service.

DESCRIPTION

The rear disc brake caliper contains opposing dual pistons in a two piece cast iron housing which bolts directly to the mounting flange of the rear suspension lower trailing arm. Hydraulic pressure, created by applying force to the brake pedal, acts equally against all surfaces of both pistons and both piston bore cavity surfaces. The parking brake application is completely independent of the hydraulic braking system.

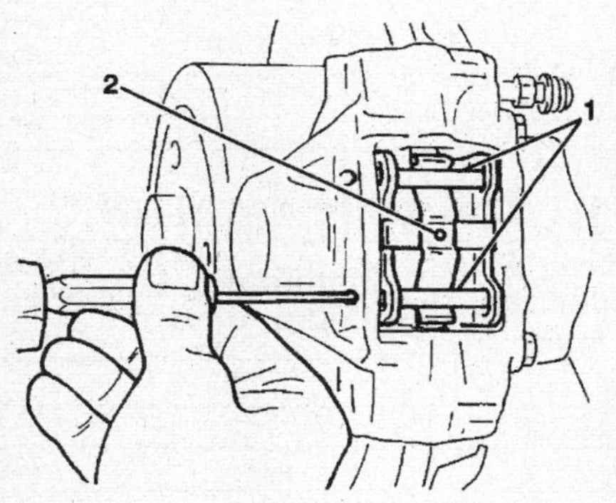

(1) Rear Brake Caliper Retaining Pins
(2) Rear Brake Caliper Spring Retainer

GC4079700141000X

Fig. 1 Rear brake pad removal

TROUBLESHOOTING

BRAKE ROUGHNESS

The most common cause of brake chatter on disc brakes is a variation in thickness of the disc. If roughness or vibration is encountered during highway operation or if pedal pulsation is experienced at low speeds, the disc may have excessive thickness variation. To inspect for this condition, measure the disc at 12 points with a micrometer at a radius approximately one inch from edge of disc. If thickness measurements vary by more than .0005 inch, the disc should be replaced with a new one.

Excessive lateral runout of braking disc may cause a piston "knocking back," possibly creating increased pedal travel and vibration when brakes are applied.

Before inspecting the runout, the wheel bearings should be adjusted. The adjustment is very important and will be required at the completion of the test to prevent bearing failure. Adjust the wheel bearings as outlined under "Front Suspension & Steering" section.

BRAKE PAD SERVICE

1. Remove approximately ⅓ of brake fluid from master cylinder.
2. Raise and support vehicle, then remove wheel and tire assembly.
3. Using a screwdriver, gently pry between rotor and each brake pad to bottom each piston in its bore.
4. Remove brake caliper retaining pins from brake caliper, **Fig. 1,** then the brake pads.
5. Reverse procedure to install.

CALIPER SERVICE

REPLACEMENT

1. Remove brake pads as outlined under "Brake Pad Service" then the rear caliper pipe, **Fig. 2.**
2. Remove rear brake caliper bolts, then the caliper from rotor.
3. Reverse procedure to install. Tighten rear brake caliper bolts and brake pipe fitting to specifications.

DISASSEMBLE

1. Install piston retainer tool No. J-22429, or equivalent on opposite cylinder to be removed.
2. Remove piston by directing dry filtered compressed air into fluid channel port of caliper housing, then cover exposed bore with tool No. J-22429, or equivalent, and remove opposing piston using dry compressed air.
3. Using a small piece of wood or plastic, remove piston seal from bore. **Do not**

use a metal tool of any kind to remove seal since it may damage bore.

4. Remove bleeder valve cap and rear brake caliper bleeder valve.

ASSEMBLE

1. Install new bleeder valve and cap, then the new piston seals lubricated with clean brake fluid.
2. Install dust boots lubricated with clean brake fluid onto pistons, then the pistons into caliper housing bores.
3. With pistons bottomed in bores, ensure outer edge of dust boots are around caliper housing embossments.

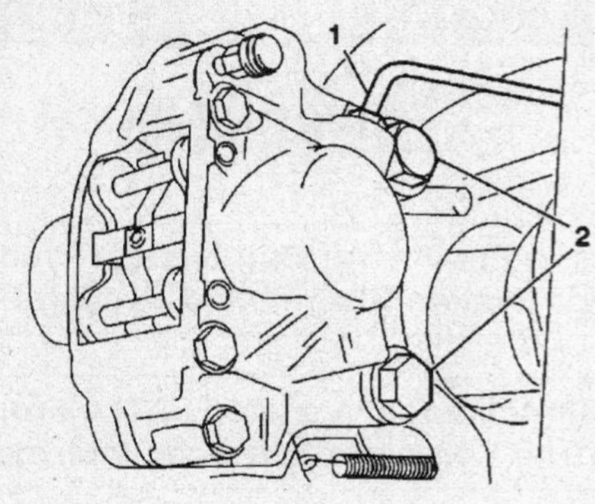

(1) Rear Brake Caliper Pipe
(2) Rear Brake Caliper Bolt

GC4079700142000X

Fig. 2 Rear brake caliper removal

ROTOR

REPLACE

1. Remove caliper as outlined under "Caliper Service" then the rotor setscrew.
2. Remove rotor from vehicle.
3. Reverse procedure to install.

DISC BRAKE SPECIFICATIONS

CALIPER SPECIFICATIONS

Model	Year	Caliper Bore Dia. Inch
Catera	1998–2001	1.57

ROTOR SPECIFICATIONS

Model	Year	Nominal Thickness, Inch	Minimum Refinish, Inch	Discard Thickness, Inch	Variation (Parallelism), Inch	Lateral Runout, Inch
CATERA						
Standard Rotor	1998–2001	.472	.433	.393	.0005	.004
Vented Rotor	2001	.787	.748	.709	.0005	.004

TIGHTENING SPECIFICATIONS

Year	Component	Torque/Ft. Lbs.
1998–2001	Rear Brake Caliper Bolts	59
	Rear Brake Caliper Pipe	12

AC-Delco Single Piston Rear Disc Brake (Type 1)

NOTE: On Air Bag Equipped Models, Refer To "Air Bag System Precautions" Located In The Front Of This Manual For System Disarming & Arming Procedures.

NOTE: Refer To "Computer Relearn Procedures" Located In The Front Of This Manual When Battery Power To The Computer Has Been Interrupted.

INDEX

PRECAUTIONS

1. Grease or any other foreign material must be kept off brake linings, caliper, surfaces of disc and external surfaces of hub during service procedures.
2. Handling brake disc and caliper should be done in a way to avoid deformation of disc and nicking or scratching brake linings.
3. If inspection reveals worn or damaged rubber piston seals, they should be replaced.
4. During removal and installation of a wheel assembly, ensure not to interfere with or damage caliper splash shield, or bleeder screw.
5. Front wheel bearings preload should be adjusted to specifications.
6. Ensure vehicle is centered on hoist before servicing any front end components to avoid bending or damaging disc splash shield on full righthand or lefthand wheel turns.
7. Before vehicle is moved after any brake service work, ensure to obtain a firm brake pedal.
8. Assembly bolts of two piece caliper housings should not be disturbed unless caliper requires service.

DESCRIPTION

The caliper has a single piston, **Fig. 1**, and is mounted to the support bracket by two mounting bolts. The caliper assembly slides on the two mounting bolts. Upon brake application, fluid pressure against the piston forces the inboard shoe and lining assembly against the inboard side of the disc. This action causes the caliper assembly to slide until the outboard lining comes into contact with the disc. As pressure builds up the linings are pressed against the disc with increased force.

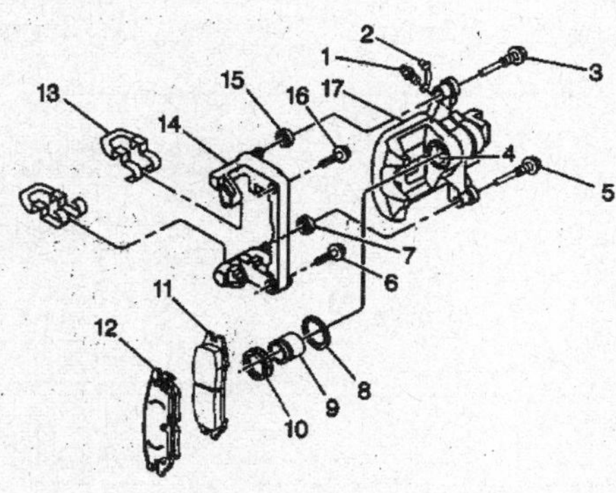

(1) Valve, Caliper Bleeder
(2) Cap, Bleeder Valve
(3) Bolt, Caliper
(4) Caliper Bore
(5) Bolt, Caliper
(6) Bolt, Caliper Bracket
(7) Boot, Caliper
(8) Seal, Caliper Piston
(9) Piston, Caliper
(10) Boot, Caliper Piston
(11) Pad, Inner
(12) Pad, Outer
(13) Clips, Retainer
(14) Bracket, Caliper
(15) Boot, Caliper
(16) Bolt, Caliper Bracket
(17) Housing, Caliper

GC4079700143000X

Fig. 1 Exploded view of rear caliper. Century, Grand Prix, Intrigue & Regal

TROUBLESHOOTING

BRAKE ROUGHNESS

The most common cause of brake chatter on disc brakes is a variation in disc thickness. If roughness or vibration is encountered during highway operation or if pedal pulsation is experienced at low speeds, the disc may have excessive thickness variation. To inspect for this condition, measure the disc at 12 points with a micrometer at a radius approximately one inch from edge of disc. If thickness measurements vary by more than .0005 inch, the disc should be replaced with a new one.

Excessive lateral runout of braking disc may cause a piston "knocking back," possibly creating increased pedal travel and vibration when brakes are applied.

Before inspecting the runout, the wheel bearings should be adjusted. The adjustment is very important and will be required at the completion of the test to prevent bearing failure. Adjust the wheel bearings as outlined under "Front Suspension & Steering" section.

BRAKE PAD SERVICE

1. Remove ⅔ of brake fluid from master cylinder reservoir.
2. Raise and support vehicle.
3. Mark relationship of wheel to axle flange, then remove wheel and tire assembly.
4. Using a suitable C-clamp, compress

caliper piston enough for clearance, then remove upper caliper bolt.
5. Pivot caliper body down in order to access the pads. **Do not remove the caliper body.**
6. Remove brake pads and pad clips from caliper bracket.
7. Reverse procedure to install. Tighten caliper bolt to specifications.

CALIPER SERVICE

REPLACEMENT

1. Remove ⅔ of brake fluid from master cylinder reservoir.
2. Raise and support vehicle.
3. Mark relationship of wheel to axle flange, then remove wheel and tire assembly.
4. Using a suitable C-clamp, compress caliper piston enough for clearance.
5. Remove brake hose from caliper plug openings in caliper and brake hose to prevent fluid loss and contamination.
6. Remove caliper bolts, then the caliper housing from rotor and caliper bracket.
7. Reverse procedure to install. Tighten fasteners to specifications.

DISASSEMBLE

1. Pad interior of caliper assembly with a clean shop towel, then remove piston assembly using low pressure compressed air into caliper inlet hole. **Do not place fingers in front of piston in an attempt to catch or protect piston when applying compressed air. This could result in serious injury.**
2. Using a small screwdriver, pry up one end of boot ring and work boot ring out of caliper groove.
3. Using a small wooden or plastic tool, remove piston seal from caliper bore groove.
4. Remove bleeder valve and bleeder valve cap.
5. Clean all components in clean denatured alcohol, then dry with low pressure compressed air.
6. Blow out all passages in caliper body and bleeder valve.
7. Inspect piston assembly for nicks, cracks, wear or corrosion.
8. Inspect piston bore for scoring, nicks, wear or corrosion. Use crocus cloth to polish out light corrosion. Replace caliper if any heavy corrosion is found. **Do not hone caliper bore.**
9. Inspect seal groove for nicks or burrs.
10. Inspect boots for cuts, tears or deterioration.

ASSEMBLE

1. Install bleeder valve and bleeder valve cap. Tighten to specifications.
2. Install new lubricated piston seal into caliper bore grooves, then the piston boot onto piston.
3. Lubricate piston with clean brake fluid, then install piston and boot into bore of caliper.
4. Install piston ring. Ensure outside edge of piston boot is seated smoothly in counterbore of caliper body.
5. Install caliper.

ROTOR

REPLACE

1. Remove caliper assembly as outlined under "Caliper Service."
2. Remove caliper mounting bracket attaching bolts, then the mounting bracket.
3. Remove rotor from hub and bearing assembly.
4. Reverse procedure to install.

DISC BRAKE SPECIFICATIONS

CALIPER SPECIFICATIONS

Model	Year	Caliper Bore Dia. Inch
All	1998–2002	1.50

ROTOR SPECIFICATIONS

Model	Year	Nominal Thickness, Inch	Minimum Refinish Thickness, Inch	Discard Thickness, Inch	Thickness Variation, Inch	Lateral Runout (T.I.R.), Inch
All	1998–2002	.430	.410	.350	.0001	.003

TIGHTENING SPECIFICATIONS

Year	Component	Torque/Ft. Lbs.
1998–2002	Brake Hose To Caliper	40
	Caliper Bleeder Screw (1998)	96①
	Caliper Bleeder Screw (1999–2002)	62①
	Caliper Bracket Bolts	92
	Caliper Mounting Bolts	32

① — Inch lbs.

AC-Delco Single Piston Rear Disc Brake (Type 2)

NOTE: On Air Bag Equipped Models, Refer To "Air Bag System Precautions" Located In The Front Of This Manual For System Disarming & Arming Procedures.

NOTE: Refer To "Computer Relearn Procedures" Located In The Front Of This Manual When Battery Power To The Computer Has Been Interrupted.

INDEX

PRECAUTIONS

1. Grease or any other foreign material must be kept off brake linings, caliper, surfaces of disc and external surfaces of hub during service procedures.
2. Handling brake disc and caliper should be done in a way to avoid deformation of disc and nicking or scratching brake linings.
3. If inspection reveals rubber piston seals are worn or damaged, they should be replaced.
4. During removal and installation of a wheel assembly, ensure not to interfere with or damage caliper splash shield, or bleeder screw.
5. Front wheel bearings preload should be adjusted to specifications.
6. Ensure vehicle is centered on hoist before servicing any front end components to avoid bending or damaging disc splash shield on full righthand or lefthand wheel turns.
7. Before vehicle is moved after any brake service work, obtain a firm brake pedal.
8. Assembly bolts of two piece caliper housings should not be disturbed unless caliper requires service.

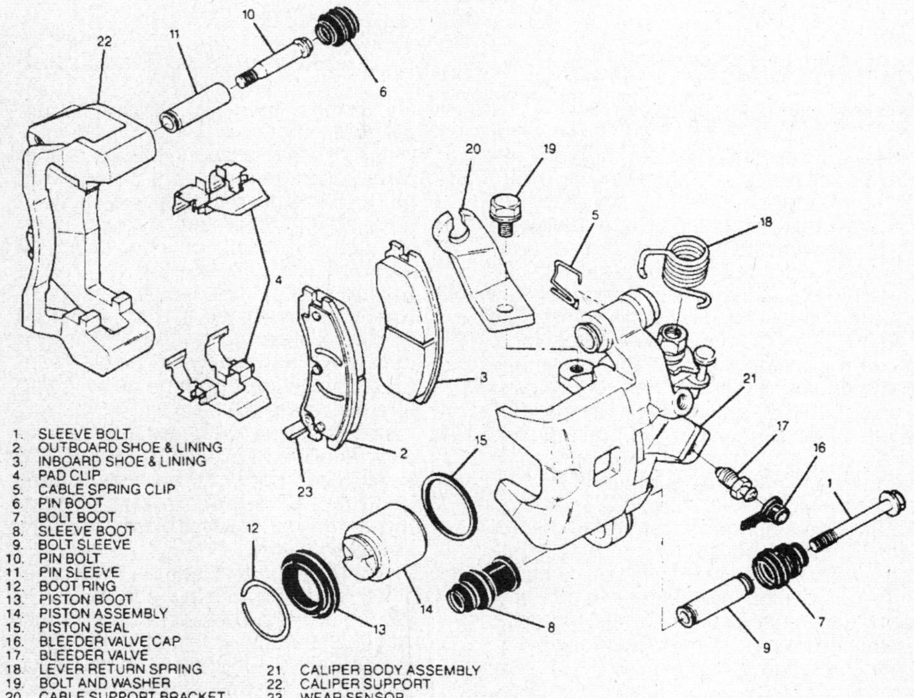

Fig. 1 Exploded view of AC-Delco single piston rear disc brake caliper

DESCRIPTION

The caliper assembly, **Fig. 1,** has a single bore and is mounted to the support bracket with two mounting bolt and sleeve assemblies. Hydraulic pressure created by applying the brake pedal is converted by the caliper to a stopping force. This force acts equally against the piston and the bottom of the piston bore to move the piston outward and to slide the caliper inward resulting in a clamping action. This clamping action presses the linings against the rotor, creating friction to stop the vehicle.

When the parking brake is applied, the external caliper parking brake lever moves and rotates a spindle within the caliper housing. As the spindle rotates, a connecting rod is pushed against an internal adjusting screw which is threaded into a sleeve nut in the piston assembly. This causes the piston assembly to move outward bringing the inboard shoe and lining assembly against the rotor. As the inboard shoe and lining contacts the rotor, a reaction force causes the caliper housing to slide inward pressing the outboard shoe and lining against the rotor.

The piston assembly contains a self adjusting mechanism to keep the parking brake in proper adjustment. As the linings are worn, the piston moves through the seal to maintain proper lining to rotor clearance. The parking brake adjusts to proper

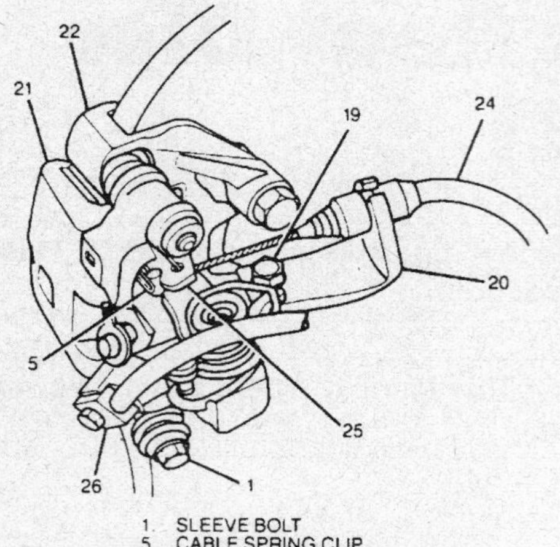

Fig. 2 Caliper assembly

clearances through an internal sleeve nut that rotates and moves as one unit with the piston.

TROUBLESHOOTING

BRAKE ROUGHNESS

The most common cause of brake chatter on disc brakes is a variation in disc thickness. If roughness or vibration is encountered during highway operation or if pedal pulsation is experienced at low speeds, the disc may have excessive thickness variation. To inspect for this condition, measure the disc at 12 points with a micrometer at a radius approximately one inch from edge of disc. If thickness measurements vary by more than .0005 inch, the disc should be replaced with a new one.

Excessive lateral runout of braking disc may cause a piston "knocking back," possibly creating increased pedal travel and vibration when brakes are applied.

Before inspecting the runout, the wheel bearings should be adjusted. The adjustment is very important and will be required at the completion of the test to prevent bearing failure. Adjust the wheel bearings as outlined under "Front Suspension & Steering" section.

BRAKE PAD SERVICE

1. Remove ⅔ of brake fluid from master cylinder reservoir.
2. Raise and support vehicle.
3. Mark relationship of wheel to axle flange, then remove wheel and tire assembly.
4. Remove bolt and washer attaching cable support bracket to caliper body, **Fig. 2.**
5. Remove sleeve bolt and pivot caliper assembly up, **Fig. 3. Do not completely remove caliper assembly body.**
6. Remove outboard and inboard shoe

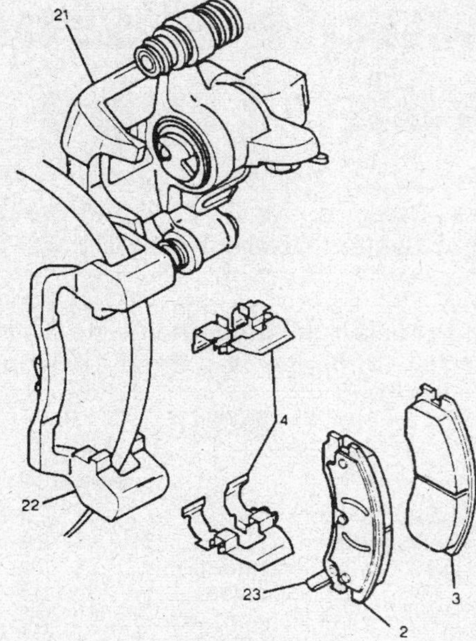

Fig. 3 Shoe & lining installation

and linings, then two pad clips from caliper support.

7. Using a suitable spanner type tool in piston slots, turn piston assembly and thread it into caliper body assembly.
8. After bottoming piston, lift inner edge of boot next to piston assembly and press out any trapped air.
9. Ensure slots in end of piston are positioned as illustrated in **Fig. 4,** before pivoting caliper body assembly down over shoe and linings in caliper support. Use suitable spanner type tool to turn piston as required.
10. Install pad clips, outboard and inboard shoe and linings in caliper support. **Ensure wear sensor is on outboard shoe positioned downward at leading edge of rotor during forward wheel rotation.**
11. Pivot caliper body assembly down over shoe and lining assemblies. Avoid damaging piston boot on inboard shoe.
12. After caliper body is in position, inspect installation of pad clips again. If required, use a small screwdriver to reseat or center the pad clips on support abutments.
13. Install sleeve bolt and **torque** to 20 ft. lbs.
14. Install cable support bracket and **torque** bolt to 32 ft. lbs.
15. Install wheels and tires, aligning previous marks, then lower the vehicle.
16. Apply approximately 175 lbs. of force to brake pedal three times to seat shoe and linings against rotor.

CALIPER SERVICE

REPLACEMENT

1. Raise and support vehicle.

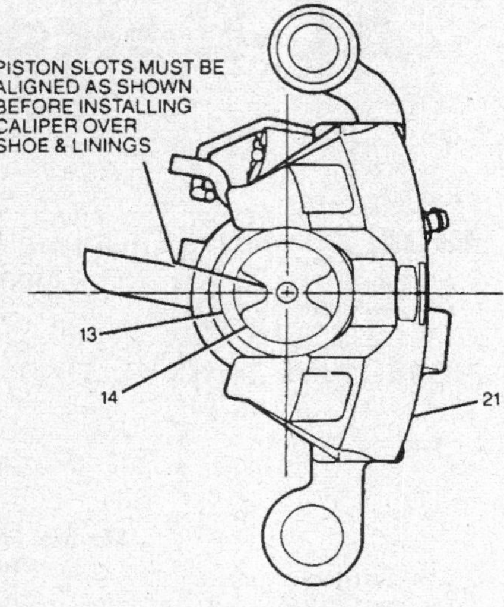

Fig. 4 Positioning piston slots

2. Mark relationship of wheel to axle flange, then remove wheel and tire assembly.
3. Remove brake hose from caliper, **Fig. 2.** Plug openings in caliper and brake hose to prevent fluid loss and contamination.
4. Lift up on end of cable spring to free end of cable from lever, then disconnect parking brake cable from lever.
5. Remove bolt and washer attaching cable support bracket to caliper body assembly.
6. Remove sleeve bolt and caliper body assembly.
7. Reverse procedure to install, noting the following:
   a. **Torque** sleeve bolt to 20 ft. lbs.
   b. **Torque** cable support bracket to 32 ft. lbs.
   c. Bleed brakes.

DISASSEMBLE

1. Remove caliper from vehicle as outlined under "Caliper Service."
2. Pad interior of caliper assembly with a clean shop towel, then remove piston assembly using low pressure compressed air into caliper inlet hole, **Fig. 5. Do not place fingers in front of piston in an attempt to catch or protect piston when applying compressed air. This could result in serious injury.**
3. Using a small screwdriver, pry up one end of boot ring, **Fig. 6.** Work boot ring out of caliper groove.
4. Using a small wooden or plastic tool, remove piston seal from caliper bore groove.
5. Remove bleeder valve and bleeder valve cap.
6. If lever return spring replacement is required, remove by using a screwdriver to disengage return spring from parking brake lever, then unhook spring from stopper pin, **Fig. 7.**
7. Remove pin boot and pin bolt, then the

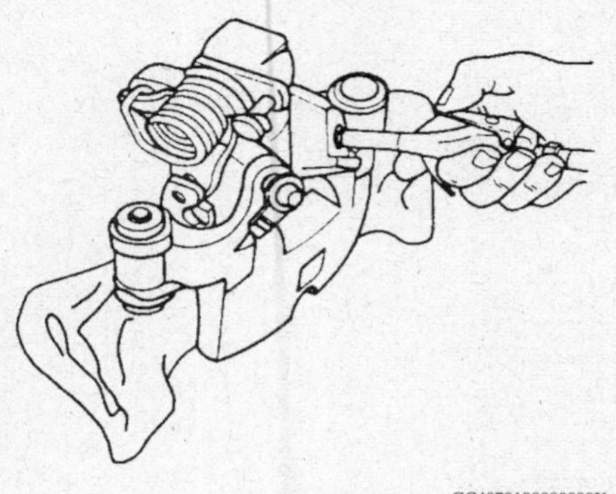

Fig. 5 Removing piston

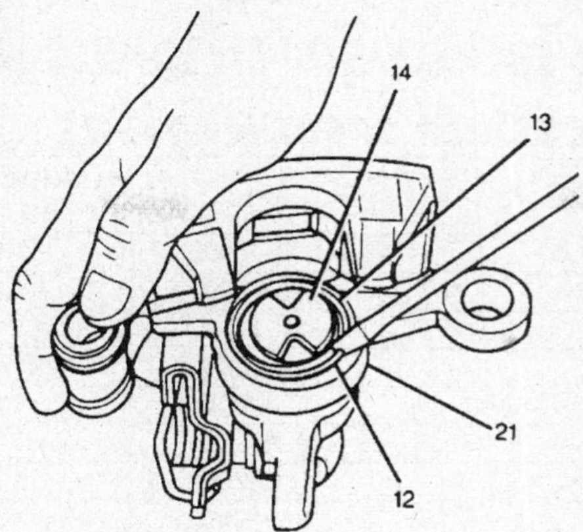

12. BOOT RING
13. PISTON BOOT
14. PISTON ASSEMBLY
21. CALIPER BODY ASSEMBLY

Fig. 6 Removing boot ring

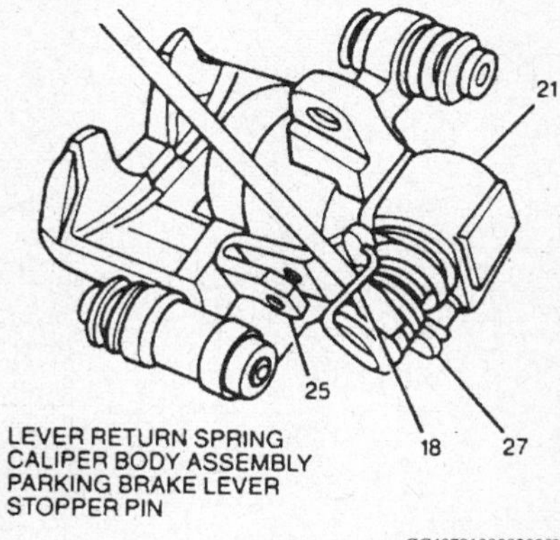

18. LEVER RETURN SPRING
21. CALIPER BODY ASSEMBLY
25. PARKING BRAKE LEVER
27. STOPPER PIN

Fig. 7 Removing lever return spring

bolt sleeve and sleeve bolt from caliper body.

8. Remove pin bolt and pin sleeve from caliper support.
9. Clean all components in clean denatured alcohol, then dry with low pressure compressed air.
10. Blow out all passages in caliper body and bleeder valve.
11. Inspect piston assembly for nicks, cracks, wear or corrosion.
12. Inspect piston bore for scoring, nicks, wear or corrosion. Use crocus cloth to polish out light corrosion. Replace caliper if any heavy corrosion is found. **Do not hone caliper bore.**
13. Inspect seal groove for nicks or burrs.
14. Inspect boots for cuts, tears or deterioration.
15. Inspect bolt sleeve and pin sleeve for corrosion or damage. **Do not attempt to polish away corrosion.**

ASSEMBLE

1. Lubricate pin sleeve with silicone grease, then install pin bolts and pin sleeve to caliper support.
2. Lubricate sleeve boot with silicone grease, then compress lip on sleeve boot and push it through caliper body assembly until lip emerges and seals on inboard face of caliper ear.
3. Lubricate push bolt sleeve with silicone grease, then push it in through lip end of boot until boot seats in sleeve groove at other end.
4. Install bolt boot onto caliper body.
5. Install small end of pin boot over pin sleeve until boot seats in pin groove.
6. If removed, position new lever return spring with hook end around stopper pin, then pry other end of spring over lever.
7. Install bleeder valve and bleeder valve cap.
8. Lubricate new piston seal with clean brake fluid and install in groove in caliper bore. Ensure it is not twisted.
9. Install piston boot onto piston assembly.
10. Lubricate piston assembly with clean brake fluid.
11. Start piston assembly in by hand, then thread into bottom of caliper bore using spanner type tool in slots in end of piston assembly.
12. Ensure outside edge of piston boot is smoothly seated in counterbore of caliper body assembly.
13. Work boot ring into groove near open end of caliper bore using care not to pinch piston boot between boot ring and caliper body.
14. After installing ring, lift inner edge of boot next to piston assembly and press out any trapped air. Boot must lay flat.
15. Install caliper on vehicle as outlined under "Caliper Service."

ROTOR

REPLACE

1. Remove caliper assembly as outlined under "Caliper Service."
2. Remove caliper mounting bracket attaching bolts, then the mounting bracket.
3. Remove rotor from hub and bearing assembly.
4. Reverse procedure to install. Adjust parking brake as outlined under "Adjustments."

ADJUSTMENTS

PARKING BRAKE

1. Cycle brake system as follows:
   a. Apply service brake with a pedal force of 175 lbs., and release.
   b. Fully apply parking brake using approximately 125 lbs., of force on final stroke, then release.
   c. Apply and release parking brake two additional times as described above.
2. Inspect parking brake pedal assembly for full release by turning ignition On and observing brake warning lamp, which should be off.
3. If brake warning lamp is on and parking brake appears to be fully released, operate manual pedal release lever and pull downward on front park brake cable to remove slack from pedal assembly.
4. Raise and support vehicle.
5. Inspect parking brake levers on rear calipers, noting the following:
   a. Levers should be against stops on caliper housing.
   b. If levers are not against stops, inspect for binding in rear brake cables and position levers against stops.
6. Tighten parking brake cable at adjuster until either lefthand or righthand lever begins to move off of stop.
7. Loosen adjuster until lever which previously moved off the stop is again resting on the stop. **Both levers should be resting on caliper stops after completing this step.**
8. Operate parking brake several times to inspect adjustment.
9. A firm pedal feel should be obtained by pumping pedal less than one stroke.
10. Inspect lefthand and righthand caliper levers. Both levers must be resting on stops after adjustment of parking brake.
11. Inspect operation of parking brake. If possible, place vehicle on a grade and inspect parking brake holding ability.

DISC BRAKE SPECIFICATIONS

CALIPER SPECIFICATIONS

Model	Year	Caliper Bore Dia. Inch
Alero & Grand Am	1998–2002	1.50
Aurora & Riviera	1998–99	1.50
Aurora	2001–02	1.50
DeVille	1998–2002	1.50
Eldorado & Seville	1998–2002	1.50
Lumina	1998–99	1.50
Monte Carlo	1998–2002	1.50
Park Avenue	1999–2002	1.50

ROTOR SPECIFICATIONS

Model	Year	Nominal Thickness, Inch	Minimum Refinish Thickness, Inch	Discard Thickness, Inch	Thickness Variation, Inch	Lateral Runout (T.I.R.), Inch
Alero & Grand Am	1998–2002	.430	.410	.350	.0005	—
Aurora & Riviera	1998–99	.433	.423	.374	.0005	.002
	2001–02	.433	.423	.374	.0005	.002
DeVille Standard Brakes)	1998–99	.433	.389	.374	.0005	.002
	2000–01	.433	.390	.374	.0005	.002
DeVille (Heavy Duty Brakes)	2000–01	.787	.728	.724	.0004	.004
Eldorado	1998–2002	.433	.423	.374	.0005	.002
Lumina	1998–2000	.433	.385	.370	.0005	.003
Monte Carlo	1998–99	.433	.385	.370	.0005	.003
	2000–01	.430	.410	.350	.0005	.003
	2002	.430	.410	.350	.0005	.002
Park Avenue	1998–2002	.433	.423	.374	.0005	.002

TIGHTENING SPECIFICATIONS

Year	Component	Torque/Ft. Lbs.
1998–2002	Brake Hose To Caliper	33
	Caliper Bleeder Screw	10
	Caliper Bracket Mounting Bolts (Except 2001-02 Aurora)	83
	Caliper Bracket Mounting Bolt (2001-02 Aurora)	94
	Caliper Mounting Bolts	63
	Caliper Pin Bolts (2001 Aurora)	20
	Master Cylinder To Booster	22
	Wheel Lug Nuts	100
	Wheel Speed Sensor Mounting Bolt	108①

① — Inch lbs.

PBR Single Piston Rear Disc Brake

NOTE: On Air Bag Equipped Models, Refer To "Air Bag System Precautions" Located In The Front Of This Manual For System Disarming & Arming Procedures.

NOTE: Refer To "Computer Relearn Procedures" Located In The Front Of This Manual When Battery Power To The Computer Has Been Interrupted.

INDEX

PRECAUTIONS

1. Grease or any other foreign material must be kept off brake linings, caliper, surfaces of disc and external surfaces of hub during service procedures.
2. Handling brake disc and caliper should be done in a way to avoid deformation of disc and nicking or scratching brake linings.
3. If inspection reveals worn or damaged rubber piston seals, they should be replaced.
4. During removal and installation of a wheel assembly, ensure not to interfere with or damage caliper splash shield, or bleeder screw.
5. Front wheel bearings preload should be adjusted to specifications.
6. Ensure vehicle is centered on hoist before servicing any front end components to avoid bending or damaging disc splash shield on full righthand or lefthand wheel turns.
7. Before vehicle is moved after any brake service work, obtain a firm brake pedal.
8. Assembly bolts of two piece caliper housings should not be disturbed unless caliper requires service.

DESCRIPTION

This rear caliper, **Fig. 1,** consists of a single piston and an aluminum housing which is suspended in a mounting bracket through two slide pins. Hydraulic pressure, created by applying force to the brake pedal, acts equally against the piston and the bottom of the caliper bore to move the piston outward. This action slides the caliper inward, resulting in a clamping action on the brake rotor. This clamping action forces the linings against the rotor, creating the friction required to stop the vehicle.

The parking brake mechanism on this caliper is completely independent of the hydraulic brake system. When the parking brake is applied, the lever on the caliper causes the pushrod, actuating collar and clamp rod assembly to move outward. This causes the caliper to move inward, mechanically forcing the linings against the rotor.

TROUBLESHOOTING

BRAKE ROUGHNESS

The most common cause of brake chatter on disc brakes is a variation in disc thickness. If roughness or vibration is encountered during highway operation or if pedal pulsation is experienced at low speeds, the disc may have excessive thickness variation. To inspect for this condition, measure the disc at 12 points with a micrometer at a radius approximately one inch from edge of disc. If thickness measurements vary by more than .0005 inch, the disc should be replaced with a new one.

Excessive lateral runout of braking disc may cause a piston "knocking back," possibly creating increased pedal travel and vibration when brakes are applied.

Before inspecting the runout, the wheel bearings should be adjusted. The adjustment is very important and will be required at the completion of the test to prevent bearing failure. Adjust the wheel bearings as outlined under "Front Suspension & Steering" section.

BRAKE PAD SERVICE

REMOVAL

1. Remove ⅔ of total brake fluid capacity from master cylinder reservoir.
2. Raise and support vehicle, then remove tire and wheel assembly.
3. Install two wheel lug nuts to retain rotor in position.
4. Position one end of a suitable C-clamp against inlet fitting bolt and other end against outboard shoe and lining.
5. Tighten clamp, **Fig. 2,** until piston fully bottoms in caliper bore.
6. Remove upper guide pin bolt and discard.
7. Loosen lower guide pin bolt, then pivot caliper downward on lower guide pin bolt to expose shoe and lining assemblies.
8. Remove shoes and linings from mounting bracket.

INSTALLATION

1. Install outboard shoe and lining onto mounting bracket. Ensure insulator on shoe is positioned toward caliper housing.
2. Install inboard shoe and lining.
3. Ensure wear sensor is positioned nearest caliper piston. When properly installed, sensor should be in trailing position when wheel is rotated in forward direction.
4. Pivot caliper into position over shoes and linings, noting the following:
   a. Ensure springs on outboard shoe do not protrude through inspection hole in housing.
   b. If protrusion is evident, lift caliper housing and adjust position of outboard shoe and lining.
5. Install and tighten new upper guide pin bolt, then tighten lower bolt.
6. Fill master cylinder to proper level, then pump brake pedal to bring pads into contact with brake rotor.

CALIPER SERVICE

REPLACEMENT

Camaro & Firebird

1. Raise and support vehicle, then disconnect park brake cable at equalizer.
2. Remove tire and wheel assemblies, then install two wheel nuts to retain rotor.
3. If caliper is to be overhauled, remove brake hose fitting bolt/screw, brake hose and brake hose gasket.
4. If return spring coils are open, remove park brake lever return spring.

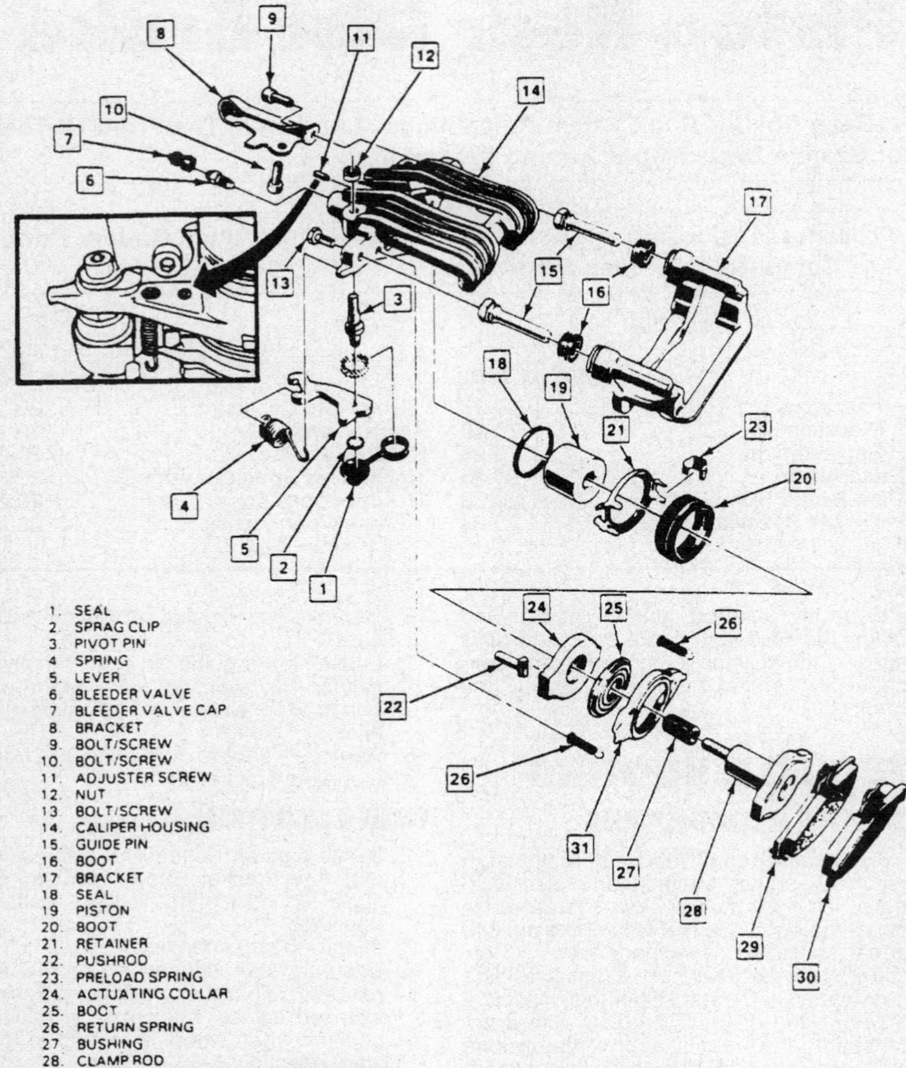

Fig. 1 Typical exploded view of PBR single piston rear caliper

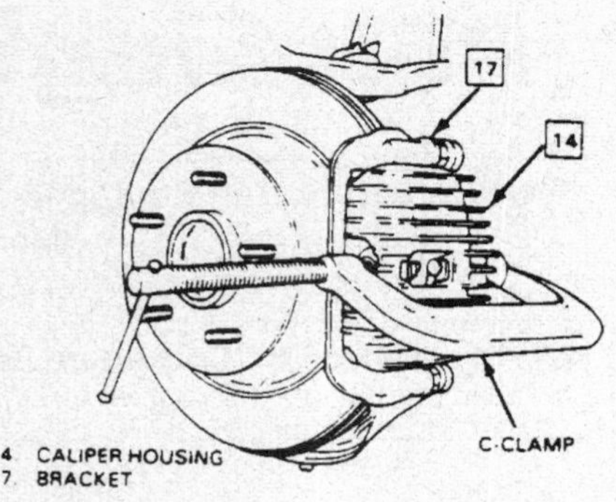

Fig. 2 Piston compression in caliper bore

5. Disconnect park brake cable from park brake actuator lever and park brake cable bracket.
6. If required, remove vibration dampener nut and vibration dampener from park brake cable bracket.
7. Remove brake caliper guide pin bolt and discard, then the rear caliper bolt and discard.
8. Remove rear brake caliper from rotor and caliper mounting plate.
9. Reverse procedure to install, noting the following:
   a. **Torque** brake caliper guide pin bolt to 27 ft. lbs.
   b. **Torque** rear caliper bolt to 22 ft. lbs.
   c. **Torque** brake hose fitting bolt or screw to 22 ft. lbs.
   d. **Torque** vibration dampener nut to 37 ft. lbs.

Corvette

1. Raise and support vehicle, then remove tire and wheel assembly.
2. If caliper requires overhaul, remove inlet fitting attaching bolt, then disconnect inlet fitting from caliper housing.
3. Discard the two gaskets, then plug openings in inlet fitting and caliper to prevent loss or contamination of fluid.
4. Remove brake caliper guide pin bolts, then the caliper from rotor and mounting bracket.
5. Reverse procedure to install, noting the following:
   a. **Torque** brake caliper guide pin bolts to 23 ft. lbs.
   b. **Torque** inlet fitting bolt to 30 ft. lbs.

DISASSEMBLE

1. Remove the two return springs from actuating collar, then pull collar out of caliper housing and remove clamp rod (28) and bushing (27), **Fig. 1.**
2. Discard bushing.
3. Bend back boot retainer tabs, then remove retainers (21, 31), boots (20, 25) and pushrod (22) from actuating collar.
4. Remove preload spring (23) from retainer (31), then discard retainers and boots.
5. Use clean shop towels to pad interior of caliper assembly, then remove piston by directing compressed air into caliper brake hose inlet hole, **Use just enough air pressure to ease piston out of bore. Do not place fingers in front of piston for any reason when applying compressed air. This could result in serious personal injury.**
6. Using a small piece of wood or plastic, remove piston seal from bore. **Do not use a metal tool of any kind to remove seal since it may damage bore.**
7. Remove bleeder valve cap and bleeder valve.
8. Remove seal (1), sprag clip (2) and lever (5) from pivot pin (3), then discard sprag clip.
9. Clean all metal components with suitable solvent, then dry with compressed air.
10. Inspect parking brake lever components, piston, caliper bore and mounting bracket for scoring, excessive wear or corrosion.

ASSEMBLE

1. Using clean brake fluid, lubricate piston seal, then install seal into caliper bore groove. Ensure seal is not twisted during installation.
2. Using clean brake fluid, lubricate caliper bore and piston.
3. Place piston into caliper bore, then push downward until fully bottomed in bore.
4. Apply lubricant provided in repair kit to actuating collar (24), then install pushrod (22), new boots (20, 25) and new retainers (21, 31) onto collar, **Fig. 1.**
5. Clamp retainers firmly against collar, then bend tabs on retainer (21) to hold assembly together.
6. Connect preload spring (23) onto retainer (31).
7. Apply lubricant provided in repair kit to clamp rod (28), then slide rod through holes in boot (25) and actuating collar (24). Ensure boot is firmly positioned against reaction plate on clamp rod.
8. Lubricate new compliance bushing

(27), then install bushing onto clamp rod (28).

9. Lubricate grooved bead of inner boot (20), boot groove in caliper housing and actuating collar with lubricant provided in repair kit.
10. Push clamp rod to bottom of piston mating hole, then pull actuating collar (24) and seat inner boot (20) into boot groove in caliper housing.
11. Ensure pushrod (22) is positioned in hole in caliper housing, then install bleeder cap and valve.
12. If removed, install pivot pin (3) and new nut (12) onto caliper. Tighten nut to specifications, then lubricate parking brake lever (5) and pivot pin.
13. Install pivot pin seal (1), parking brake lever and new sprag clip (2).
14. Ensure teeth of sprag clip face away from lever, then snap seal cap over pivot pin.
15. Install two collar return springs (26) onto retainer (31). Ensure retainer enters springs at end of second coil.
16. Install adjustment screw (11) into caliper housing until actuating collar is parallel to piston bore face of housing.
17. Lubricate guide pins with suitable grease, then slide boots onto pins.
18. Fill boots with grease, then install into mounting bracket. Ensure boots are properly positioned in grooves in pins and mounting bracket.
19. Install caliper and bleed brake system, then adjust parking brake free travel as outlined under "Caliper Service."

ROTOR

REPLACE

1. Remove caliper as outlined under "Caliper Service."
2. Remove caliper mounting bracket attaching bolts, then the mounting bracket.
3. Remove rotor from hub and bearing assembly.
4. Reverse procedure to install. Adjust parking brake as outlined under "Adjustments" if required.

ADJUSTMENTS

PARKING BRAKE

1. Release parking brake lever, then raise and support vehicle.
2. Remove rear wheels, then install lug nuts on two opposite wheel studs to hold brake rotor in position.
3. Back caliper pistons into bores.
4. Loosen parking brake cable adjusting nut until there is no tension on parking brake shoes.
5. Turn each brake rotor until parking brake shoe star adjuster is visible through hole in rotor.
6. Adjusting one side at a time, tighten adjuster until rotor cannot be turned by hand, then back star wheel off 5–7 notches. **Adjust parking brake shoes by inserting a suitable tool through hole in rotor. On driver's side, tighten adjuster by moving tool handle upward. On passenger's side, tighten adjuster by moving tool handle downward.**
7. Install rear wheels and pull parking lever up two notches.
8. Tighten cable adjusting nut at equalizer until there is drag on wheels.
9. Release parking brake lever and inspect adjustment. No drag should be felt when rotating wheels.

DISC BRAKE SPECIFICATIONS

CALIPER SPECIFICATIONS

Model	Year	Caliper Bore Dia. Inch
CHEVROLET		
Camaro	1998–2002	1.595
Corvette	1998–2002	1.600
PONTIAC		
Firebird	1998–2002	1.595

ROTOR SPECIFICATIONS

Model	Year	Nominal Thickness, Inch	Minimum Refinish Thickness, Inch	Discard Thickness, Inch	Thickness Variation (Parallelism), Inch	Lateral Runout (T.I.R.), Inch
Camaro & Firebird	1998	—	.985	.970	.0005	.006
	1999–2002	1.020	.980	.965	.0005	.006
Corvette	1998–2002	1.020	.980	.965	.0005	.003

TIGHTENING SPECIFICATIONS

Year	Component	Torque/Ft. lbs.
1998–2002	Brake Hose To Caliper	①
	Caliper Bleeder Screw	108②
	Front Caliper Mounting Bracket	125
	Rear Caliper Mounting Bracket	125
	Rear Lower Guide Pin Bolt	①
	Rear Pivot Pin Nut	16
	Rear Upper Guide Pin Bolt	①
	Wheel Lug Nuts	100

①— Refer to "Caliper Service" for tightening specifications.
②— Inch lbs.

Toyota/GM Single Piston Caliper

NOTE: On Air Bag Equipped Models, Refer To "Air Bag System Precautions" Located In The Front Of This Manual For System Disarming & Arming Procedures.

NOTE: Refer To "Computer Relearn Procedures" Located In The Front Of This Manual When Battery Power To The Computer Has Been Interrupted.

INDEX

PRECAUTIONS

1. Grease or any other foreign material must be kept off brake linings, caliper, surfaces of disc and external surfaces of hub during service procedures.
2. Handling brake disc and caliper should be done in a way to avoid deformation of disc and nicking or scratching brake linings.
3. If inspection reveals worn or damaged rubber piston seals, they should be replaced.
4. During removal and installation of a wheel assembly, ensure not to interfere with or damage caliper splash shield, or bleeder screw.
5. Front wheel bearing preload should be adjusted to specifications.
6. Ensure vehicle is centered on hoist before servicing any front end components to avoid bending or damaging disc splash shield on full righthand or lefthand wheel turns.
7. Before vehicle is moved after any brake service work, ensure to obtain a firm brake pedal.
8. Assembly bolts of two piece caliper housings should not be disturbed unless caliper requires service.

DESCRIPTION

The caliper is a single bore design and is mounted to a carrier assembly. Hydraulic pressure, created by applying the brake pedal, is converted by the caliper to a stopping force. This force acts equally against the piston and bottom of caliper bore to move the piston outward and to slide the caliper inward, resulting in a clamping action on the rotor. The clamping action forces the linings against the rotor, creating friction required to stop the vehicle.

TROUBLESHOOTING

BRAKE ROUGHNESS

The most common cause of brake chatter on disc brakes is a variation in disc thickness. If roughness or vibration is encountered during highway operation or if pedal pulsation is experienced at low speeds, the disc may have excessive thickness variation. To inspect for this condition, measure the disc at 12 points with a micrometer at a radius approximately one inch from edge of disc. If thickness measurements vary by more than .0005 inch, the disc should be replaced with a new one.

Excessive lateral runout of braking disc may cause a piston "knocking back," possibly creating increased pedal travel and vibration when brakes are applied.

Before inspecting the runout, the wheel bearings should be adjusted. The adjustment is very important and will be required at the completion of the test to prevent bearing failure. Adjust the wheel bearings as outlined under "Front Suspension & Steering" section.

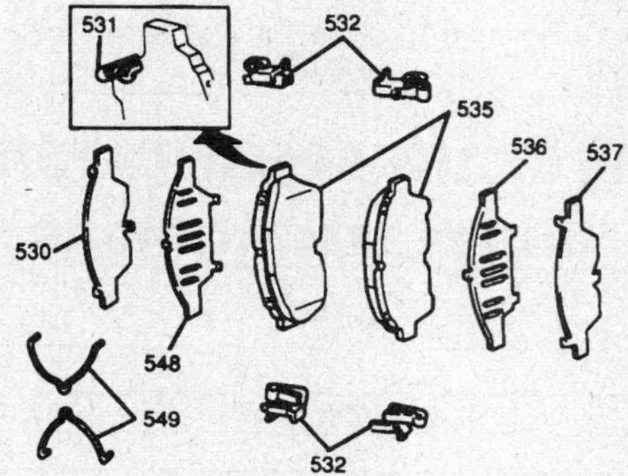

530 ANTI-SQUEAL SHIM (INBOARD)
531 PAD WEAR INDICATOR PLATE
532 ANTI-RATTLE SPRINGS
535 BRAKE PADS
536 ANTI-SQUEAL SHIM (INNER OUTBOARD)
537 ANTI-SQUEAL SHIM (OUTBOARD)
548 ANTI-SQUEAL SHIM (INNER INBOARD)
549 ANTI-SQUEAL SPRINGS

GC4079700150000X

Fig. 1 Brake pad assembly

BRAKE PAD SERVICE

REMOVAL

Replace brake pads on one wheel at a time to prevent opposite side caliper piston from being forced out of bore.

1. Remove caliper as outlined under "Caliper Service," leaving brake hose connected, and secure caliper aside.
2. Remove anti-rattle clips, then the brake pads, **Fig. 1.**
3. Remove pad wear indicator plates and anti-squeal shims.
4. Remove support plates.

INSTALLATION

1. Install new support plates on caliper mounting bracket.
2. Install new wear indicators and anti-squeal shims on each pad, **Fig. 1,** then position pads in caliper mounting bracket. **Ensure arrow on wear indicator is pointing in rotating direction of rotor.**
3. Install anti-rattle springs.
4. Seat piston in caliper bore, then install caliper and mounting bolts. Tighten bolts to specifications.
5. Fill master cylinder, then bleed brakes as outlined under "Hydraulic Brake Systems" chapter.

CALIPER SERVICE

REMOVAL

1. Siphon ⅔ of brake fluid from master cylinder.
2. Raise and support vehicle, then remove wheels.
3. Install two wheel lug nuts to retain rotor, then remove caliper mounting bolts, **Fig. 2.**
4. Remove union nut securing brake hose to caliper and drain fluid into a suitable container. **If caliper is only being removed for brake pad replacement, do not disconnect brake hose.**

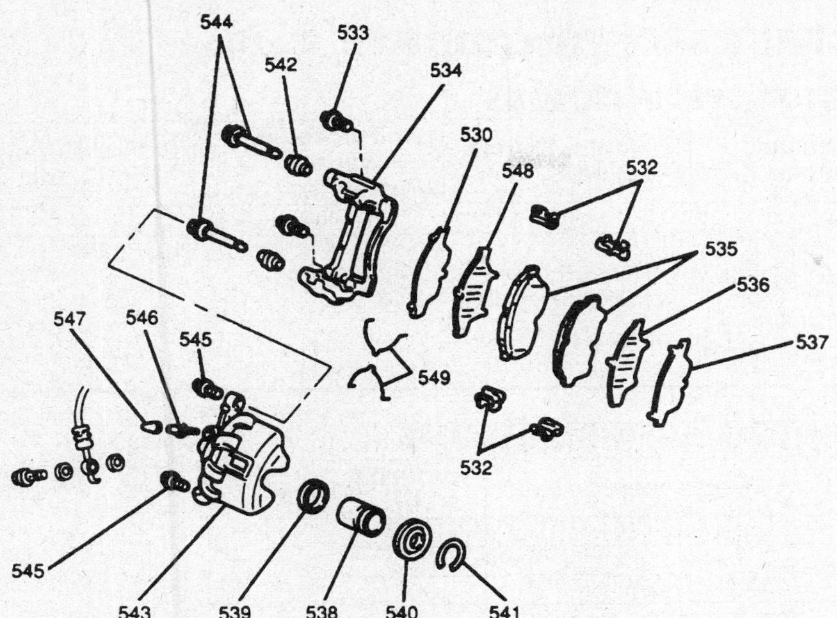

530	ANTI-SQUEAL SHIM (INBOARD)	540	PISTON BOOT
532	ANTI-RATTLE SPRINGS	541	CALIPER SET RING
533	CALIPER CARRIER BOLTS	542	DUST BOOTS
534	CALIPER CARRIER	543	CALIPER HOUSING
535	BRAKE PADS	544	SLIDE PINS
536	ANTI-SQUEAL SHIM (INNER OUTBOARD)	545	CALIPER MOUNTING BOLTS
537	ANTI-SQUEAL SHIM (OUTBOARD)	546	BLEEDER SCREW
538	PISTON	547	CAP
539	PISTON SEAL	548	ANTI-SQUEAL SHIM (INNER INBOARD)
		549	ANTI-SQUEAL SPRINGS

GC4079700151000X

Fig. 2 Exploded view of brake caliper

5. Compress piston as needed, then remove caliper. If brake hose remains connected, secure caliper aside to prevent hose from being stretched.

DISASSEMBLE

1. Remove two caliper slide bushings, four dust boots and spacer collars, **Fig. 2.**
2. Pry out caliper dust boot retaining ring, then remove dust boot.
3. Place clean shop towels in caliper web to protect piston, then apply compressed air to caliper fluid inlet to force piston from bore. **Keep fingers clear of caliper web when removing piston. Use only enough air pressure to ease piston out of bore or piston may be damaged.**
4. Remove piston seal from caliper bore. Ensure not to mar machined surface of caliper.
5. Remove bleeder valve.
6. Clean components with alcohol and wipe dry with clean, lint free shop towels.

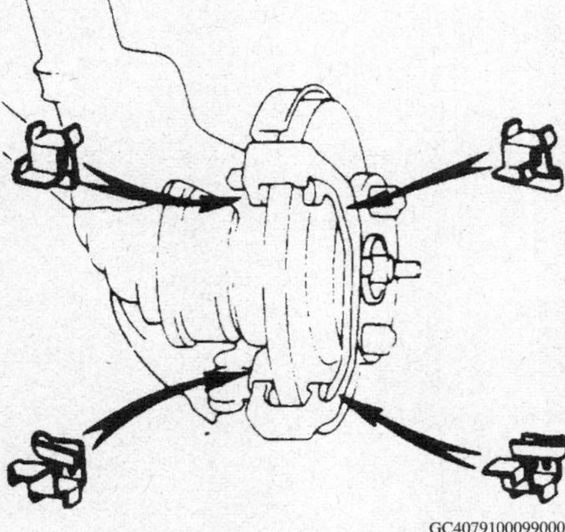

GC4079100099000X

Fig. 4 Caliper support installation

7. Blow out caliper body and fluid passages with clean, filtered compressed air.
8. Inspect caliper and piston for damage, distortion, excessive wear and pitting.

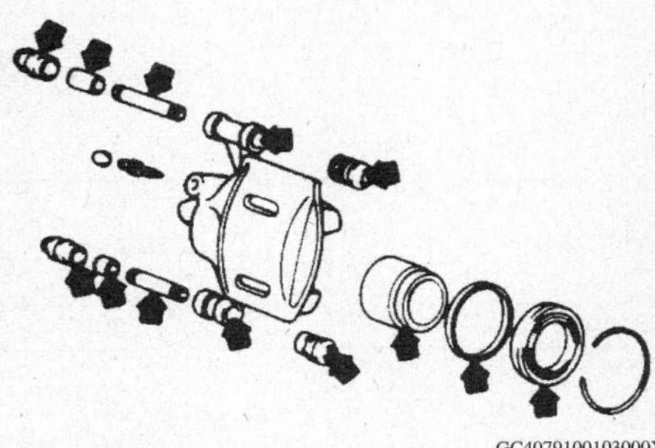

GC4079100103000X

Fig. 3 Caliper piston installation

9. Replace mounting bolts, collars and caliper slides if they are damaged or worn.

ASSEMBLE

1. Apply lithium soap base glycol grease to components, **Fig. 3.**
2. Install piston seal in caliper. Ensure seal is squarely seated in groove.
3. Press piston into bore. Ensure piston enters bore straight.
4. Seat piston dust boot in caliper groove, then install retaining ring.
5. Install two collars and four slide bushing dust boots, **Fig. 2,** rotating boots as they are pressed in to ensure they are fully seated.
6. Install slide bushings through dust boots. Ensure boots remain seated in caliper grooves.

INSTALLATION

1. Seat piston in caliper bore. Ensure not to damage piston.
2. Ensure support plates, **Fig. 4,** and anti-rattle springs are properly positioned, then mount caliper over rotor onto mounting bracket.
3. Install caliper mounting bolts and tighten to specifications.
4. Install brake hose and mounting bolts, using new copper gaskets, then tighten bolts to specifications.
5. Fill master cylinder, then bleed brake system as outlined under "Hydraulic Brake Systems" chapter.

ROTOR

REPLACE

1. Remove caliper as outlined under "Caliper Service."
2. Remove anti-rattle springs from caliper carrier.
3. Remove caliper carrier mounting bolts, then the caliper carrier.
4. Remove brake rotor from wheel hub. If rotor cannot be removed by hand, install two 8 MM bolts into rotor. Tightening bolts will force rotor off wheel hub.
5. Reverse procedure to install.

DISC BRAKE SPECIFICATIONS

ROTOR SPECIFICATIONS

Model	Year	Nominal Thickness, Inch	Minimum Refinish Thickness, Inch①	Thickness Variation (Parallelism), Inch	Lateral Runout (T.I.R.), Inch
Prizm	1998–2002	—	.787	.0005	.002

① — All brake rotors have a discard dimension cast into them. This is a wear dimension, not a refinish dimension. Any rotor that does not meet specifications should be discarded.

TIGHTENING SPECIFICATIONS

Year	Component	Torque/Ft. Lbs.
1998–2002	ABS Wheel Speed Sensor Bolt	72①
	Bleeder Valve	72①
	Brake Hose Union Bolt	22
	Caliper Carrier Mounting Bolts	65
	Caliper Mounting Bolts	25

① — Inch lbs.

Saturn

NOTE: On Air Bag Equipped Models, Refer To "Air Bag System Precautions" Located In The Front Of This Manual For System Disarming & Arming Procedures.

NOTE: Refer To "Computer Relearn Procedures" Located In The Front Of This Manual When Battery Power To The Computer Has Been Interrupted.

NOTE: Prior To Performing Any Service Operations Listed In This Section, Consult The "Technical Service Bulletins" Section For Related Information.

INDEX

BRAKE SYSTEM BLEED

Refer to "Hydraulic Brake Systems" for manual and pressure bleeding procedures.

BRAKE PAD SERVICE

S-Series

FRONT

1. Raise and support vehicle.
2. Remove front wheel assemblies.
3. Remove caliper lockpin.
4. Pivot caliper upward around guide pin.
5. Remove brake pads.
6. Remove two pad clips from caliper support.
7. Reverse procedure to install.

REAR

1. Raise and support vehicle.
2. Remove wheel assemblies.
3. Remove caliper lockpin and guide pin.
4. Remove caliper from support and suspend with mechanics wire.
5. Remove brake pads from caliper support.
6. Remove two pad clips from caliper support.
7. Reverse procedure to install.

L-Series

FRONT

1. Raise and support vehicle.
2. Remove front wheel assemblies.
3. Pry off locking plate, then remove brake pressure hose from strut.
4. Remove pad retainer spring, then caliper-to-bracket guide pins and caliper assembly.
5. Remove inboard, then outboard brake pads from caliper assembly.
6. Reverse procedure to install.

REAR

1. Raise and support vehicle.
2. Remove rear wheel assemblies.
3. Drive out brake pad retaining pins from outside to inside, then remove pins, retaining spring and pads.
4. Reverse procedure to install.

CALIPER SERVICE

S-Series

FRONT

REPLACEMENT

1. Raise and support vehicle.
2. Remove wheel assemblies.
3. Disconnect caliper brake fluid lines and plug opening.
4. Remove caliper lockpin, guide pin and pin boots.
5. Remove caliper from caliper support, ensure not to damage pin boots.
6. Remove brake pads.
7. Remove two pad clips from caliper support.
8. Reverse procedure to install.

DISASSEMBLE

1. Inspect lockpin and guide pin boots for damage. replace as required.
2. Inspect piston boot and lockpin for damage, replace as required.
3. Using a small screwdriver, remove piston boot ring and boot.
4. Pad caliper interior with a suitable cushion, then apply non-lubricated compressed air to caliper inlet hole to remove piston.
5. Remove piston seal, then bleeder valve and cap.
6. Clean all components in clean denatured alcohol, then dry with non-lubricated compressed air, then blow out all caliper body and bleeder valve passages.
7. Inspect piston for damage, replace as required.
8. Inspect caliper bore for damage. Slight corrosion may be removed using suitable crocus cloth, if damage is excessive, replace caliper. **Do not hone caliper bore.**
9. Inspect seal groove for damage, replace as required.

ASSEMBLE

1. Install bleeder valve.
2. Lubricate piston seal using clean brake fluid, then install, ensuring seal is not twisted.
3. Install lubricated piston boot to piston.
4. Install lubricated piston to body, push piston to bottom of bore.
5. Install boot ring, ensure piston boot outer edge is smoothly seated in counterbore, work boot ring into groove near open end of caliper bore. **Do not pinch piston ring between boot ring and body.**
6. Lift piston boot inner edge to release trapped air, then install caliper and bleed brake system.

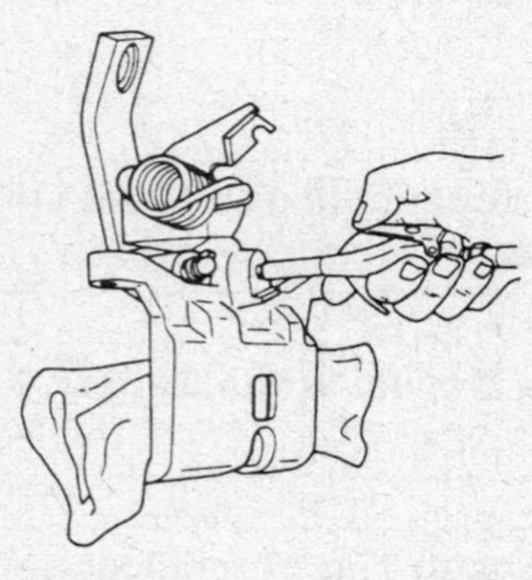

G34079100003000X

Fig. 1 Rear caliper piston removal. S-Series

REAR

REPLACEMENT

1. Raise and support vehicle.
2. Remove wheel assemblies.
3. Disconnect caliper brake fluid lines and plug opening.
4. Slip parking brake cable end from brake lever, then, using cable release tool No. SA9151BR, or equivalent, remove cable outer housing.
5. Remove caliper lockpin and guide pin.
6. Remove caliper from caliper support, ensuring not to damage pin boots.
7. Remove lockpin and guide pins from caliper support.
8. Reverse procedure to install.

DISASSEMBLE

1. Inspect lockpin and guide pin boots for damage, replace as required.
2. Inspect piston boot and lockpin for damage, replace as required.
3. Using a small screwdriver, remove piston boot ring and boot.
4. Pad the caliper interior with suitable cushion, then apply non-lubricated compressed air to caliper inlet hole to remove piston, **Fig. 1.**
5. Remove piston seal, then bleeder valve and cap.
6. Clean all components in clean denatured alcohol, then dry with non-lubricated compressed air.
7. Blow out all caliper body and bleeder valve passages.
8. Inspect piston for damage, replacing as required.
9. Inspect caliper bore for damage. Slight corrosion may be removed using suitable crocus cloth. If damage is excessive, replace caliper. **Do not hone caliper bore.**
10. Inspect seal groove for damage, replacing as required.

ASSEMBLE

1. Install bleeder valve and cap.
2. Lubricate piston seal using clean brake fluid, then install, ensuring seal is not twisted.
3. Install lubricated piston boot to piston.
4. Install lubricated piston to body, push piston by hand, then install piston installation tool No. SA91110NE, or equivalent, to piston slots. Rotate piston clockwise to install, **Fig. 2.**
5. Install boot ring, ensuring piston boot outer edge is smoothly seated in counterbore, then work boot ring into groove near open end of caliper bore. **Do not pinch piston ring between boot ring and body.**
6. Lift piston boot inner edge to release trapped air, then install caliper and bleed brake system.

L-Series

FRONT

REPLACEMENT

1. Raise and support vehicle, then remove wheel assemblies.
2. Remove brake hose from caliper and plug opening.
3. Remove brake pad retaining spring from caliper, then caliper-to-bracket guide pins.
4. Remove caliper from support bracket, then pads from caliper.
5. Reverse procedure to install.

DISASSEMBLE

1. Inspect guide pin sleeves and covers for damage, replacing as required.
2. Inspect boot for deterioration. If damaged overhaul caliper.
3. Using a small screwdriver, remove piston boot ring and boot.
4. Pad caliper interior with a suitable cushion, then apply non-lubricated compressed air to caliper inlet hole to remove piston.
5. Remove piston seal, then bleeder valve and cap.
6. Clean all components in clean denatured alcohol, then dry with non-lubricated compressed air.
7. Blow out all caliper body and bleeder valve passages.
8. Inspect piston for damage, replacing as required.
9. Inspect caliper bore for damage, noting the following:
   a. Slight corrosion may be removed using suitable crocus cloth.
   b. If damage is excessive, replace caliper.
   c. **Do not hone caliper bore.**
10. Inspect seal groove for damage, replace as required.

ASSEMBLE

1. Install bleeder valve.
2. Lubricate piston seal using clean brake fluid, then install. Ensure seal is not twisted.
3. Install lubricated piston boot to piston.
4. Install lubricated piston to body, push piston to bottom of bore.
5. Install boot ring, noting the following:
   a. Ensure piston boot outer edge is smoothly seated in counterbore.
   b. Work boot ring into groove near open end of caliper bore.
   c. **Do not pinch piston ring between boot ring and body.**
6. Lift piston boot inner edge to release trapped air, then install caliper and bleed brake system.

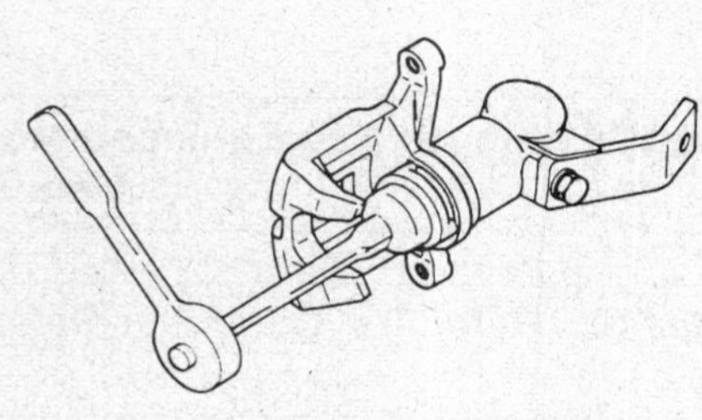

G34079100004000X

Fig. 2 Rear caliper piston installation. S-Series

REAR

REPLACEMENT

1. Raise and support vehicle, then remove wheel assemblies.
2. Drive out brake pad retaining pins from outside-to-inside, then remove pins, retaining spring and pads.
3. Remove brake pipe from caliper and plug opening.
4. Remove caliper to rear axle control arm fasteners, then the caliper assembly.
5. Reverse procedure to install.

DISASSEMBLE

The rear caliper has a dual piston design. The caliper must not be completely disassembled. Just disassemble only one piston at a time.

1. Carefully pry out piston boot clamp using a small screwdriver, then remove piston boot.
2. Pad caliper interior with suitable cushion, then apply non-lubricated compressed air to caliper inlet hole to remove piston.
3. Remove piston seal, then bleeder valve and cap.
4. Clean all components in clean denatured alcohol, then dry with non-lubricated compressed air.
5. Blow out all caliper body and bleeder valve passages.
6. Inspect piston for damage, replace as required.
7. Inspect caliper bore for damage, noting the following:
   a. Slight corrosion may be removed using suitable crocus cloth.
   b. If damage is excessive, replace caliper.
   c. **Do not hone caliper bore.**
8. Inspect seal groove for damage, replace as required.

ASSEMBLE

1. Install bleeder valve and cap.
2. Lubricate piston seal using clean brake fluid, then install. Ensure seal is not twisted.
3. Install lubricated piston boot to piston.
4. Insert lubricated piston into body, then install caliper and bleed brake system.

ROTOR

REPLACE

S-SERIES

1. Raise and support vehicle.
2. Remove tire and wheel assembly.
3. Remove caliper support to knuckle bolts, then separate and suspend caliper from strut spring with wire.
4. Remove rotor.
5. Reverse procedure to install. Tighten caliper bolts to specifications.

L-SERIES

1. Raise and support vehicle, then remove tire and wheel assembly.
2. Pry off locking plate, then remove brake pressure hose from strut.
3. Remove caliper bracket to steering knuckle bolts, then suspend caliper using wire.
4. Remove rotor retaining screw, then the rotor.
5. Reverse procedure to install.

PARKING BRAKE SERVICE

PARKING BRAKE EQUALIZER CABLE, REPLACE

1. Remove center console as outlined under "Dash Panel Service" section.
2. Remove adjuster nut, then cables from equalizer assembly, **Fig. 3.**
3. Place parking brake lever to highest position.
4. Lift equalizer cable over parking brake indicator switch and swing forward. Pull cable down and out of parking brake lever.
5. Reverse procedure to install. Adjust parking brake cable.

PARKING BRAKE CABLE, REPLACE

S-SERIES

1. Remove center console as outlined under "Dash Panel Service" section.
2. Loosen adjuster nut.
3. Remove parking brake cables from equalizer, then from parking brake base.
4. Remove rear seat bottom cushion, then pull carpet back.
5. Raise and support vehicle.
6. Remove parking brake cable grommet from floor pan.
7. Remove parking brake cable attaching brackets and tie strap.
8. Disconnect cable end from caliper. Remove cable from bracket using parking brake release tool No. SA9151BR, or equivalent.
9. Remove cable from vehicle.
10. Reverse procedure to install. Adjust parking brake cable.

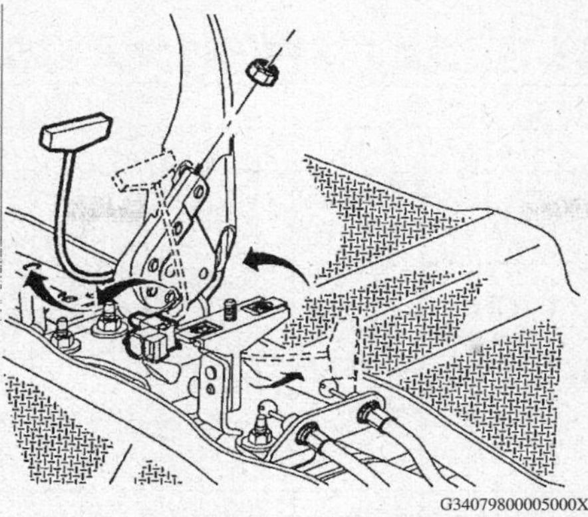

Fig. 3 Parking brake equalizer cable removal

L-SERIES

1. Release parking brake.
2. Remove parking brake boot by squeezing boot in sides while pulling upwards.
3. Loosen parking brake adjuster nut to provide ample slack in brake cable.
4. Raise and support vehicle, then disconnect exhaust resonator from exhaust manifold pipe.
5. Remove exhaust pipe to body insulator, then lower exhaust resonator pipe and muffler assembly from vehicle.
6. Remove exhaust heat shield, then disengage parking brake cable from rear parking brake cable and discard clips.
7. Disengage front parking brake cable from equalizer.
8. Remove cable body attachment points.
9. Reverse procedure to install. Adjust parking brake cable as outlined under "Adjustments."

PARKING BRAKE SHOES, REPLACE

1. Raise and support vehicle, then remove rear wheel assemblies.
2. Remove rear caliper to rear axle control arm bolts, then suspend caliper using wire.
3. Remove rotor retaining screw, then rotor.
4. Remove return springs from parking brake shoes, then brake shoe hold-down retainers.
5. Remove parking brake shoes and adjuster.
6. Reverse procedure to install. Adjust parking brake as outlined under "Adjustments."

ADJUSTMENTS

PARKING BRAKE

S-SERIES

1. Lift parking brake lever, then remove cover attaching screw and cover.
2. Raise and support vehicle.
3. Pull parking brake lever to first click.
4. Tighten adjuster nut until moderate drag is felt at both rear wheels when turned by hand.
5. Pull up on parking brake lever until twelfth or thirteenth click is heard. Repeat 3 to 4 times.
6. Ensure no drag exists when parking brake is in rest position.
7. Pull lever to first click and ensure moderate drag exists at both rear wheels. Repeat procedure until proper adjustment is reached.

L-SERIES

1. Remove parking brake boot by squeezing boot in sides while pulling upwards.
2. Raise and support vehicle, then remove rear wheel assemblies.
3. Access to parking brake adjuster is through a hole in front face of rotor.
4. Turn adjuster at rear rotor until brake disc locks. Turn back adjuster until disc just moves freely.
5. Pull parking brake lever to third click.
6. Tighten adjuster nut until heavy drag is felt at both rear wheels when turned by hand.
7. Apply and release parking brake several times. There should be no drag when lever is in rest position.
8. Pull lever to third click and ensure heavy drag exists at both rear wheels. Repeat procedure until proper adjustment is reached.

TECHNICAL SERVICE BULLETINS

REAR DISC BRAKE NOISE/ PULSATION

1998

Models equipped with rear disc brakes (JL9), built up to and including WZ223951, may exhibit disc brake grind/growl, squeak/ squeal noise and/or pulsation during slow braking.

Brake noise may be caused by vibration of brake components and/or contact between the disc brake pad and rotor during stopping. Some intermittent brake noises are normal. In high corrosion areas of the country, semi-metallic pads, interacting with the rear rotor, may contribute to the corrosion process leaving a rear disc brake pad shaped "footprint" on the rotor. This may cause rear disc brake pulsation. In addition, the pulsation may be caused by thickness variation worn into the rotor by the disc brake pads. The new disc brake pads, installed on 1998 vehicles built after WZ223951, cause less rotor thickness variation as a result of wear.

Replace rear disc brake pads with new non-asbestos organic pads P/N 21013126, or equivalent, according to procedures outlined in this section.

DISC BRAKE SPECIFICATIONS

Model	Year	Front Disc Brake						Rear Disc Brake					
		Brake Lining Wear Limit, Inch②	Rotor					Brake Lining Wear Limit, Inch②	Rotor				
			Thickness, Inch			Thickness Variation Parallelism Inch	Lateral Run Out (T.I.R.) Inch		Thickness, Inch			Thickness Variation Parallelism Inch	Lateral Run-Out (T.I.R.) Inch
			Nominal	Min. Refinish	Discard Limit①				Nominal	Min. Refinish	Discard Limit①		
L-Series	2000–02	.080	.980	.900	.870	.0003	.001	.080	.390	.350	.310	.0004	.001
S-Series	1998–2002	.080	.710	.633	.625	.0005	.0024	.080	.440	.370	.350	.0005	.0024

① — Discard thickness is stamped on rotor.

② — Above rivet head or backing plate. Original equipment type brake lining.

TIGHTENING SPECIFICATIONS

Year	Component	Torque/Ft. Lbs.
L-SERIES		
2000–02	Bleed Valve①	17③
	Bleed Valve②	72③
	Brake Hose To Brake Pipe	13
	Brake Hose To Brake Caliper	30
	Brake Pipe To Caliper	12
	Brake Lever To Floor Nut	84③
	Caliper to Bracket Guide Pins	22
	Caliper To Steering Knuckle	70
	Caliper To Rear Axle Control Arm	59
	Exhaust Heat Shield	35③
	Wheel Lug Nuts	92④
	Wheel Speed Sensor To Knuckle	72③
S-SERIES		
1998–2002	Backing Plate To Knuckle②	63
	Bleed Valve	96③
	Brake Hose To Caliper	36
	Brake Lever To Floor Nut	23
	Brake Line To Brake Hose	18
	Brake Line To Master Cylinder	24
	Caliper Lock & Guide Pins	27
	Caliper Mount Bracket①	81
	Caliper To Caliper Support①	27
	Caliper To Knuckle②	63
	Wheel Lug Nuts	103
	Wheel Speed Sensor To Knuckle	84③

① — Front.
② — Rear.
③ — Inch lbs.
④ — For steel wheel & optional aluminum wheel w/large center cap, install wheel cover or cap. With socket, hand tighten five cap nuts then, with wrench, tighten each cap an additional 90°.

DRUM BRAKES

TABLE OF CONTENTS

Application Chart

Model	Application
BUICK	
Century	Type 5
LeSabre	Type 5
Skylark	Type 1
CHEVROLET	
Cavalier	Type 1
Lumina	Type 5
Malibu	Type 5
Metro	Type 4
Prizm	Type 3
OLDSMOBILE	
Achieva	Type 1
Alero	Type 5
Cutlass	Type 5
Eighty Eight	Type 5
LSS	Type 5
Regency	Type 5
PONTIAC	
Bonneville	Type 5
Grand Am (1998)	Type 1
Grand Am (1999–2002)	Type 5
Sunfire	Type 1
SATURN	
All	Type 2

Type 1

NOTE: On Air Bag Equipped Models, Refer To "Air Bag System Precautions" Located In The Front Of This Manual For System Disarming & Arming Procedures.

NOTE: Refer To "Computer Relearn Procedures" Located In The Front Of This Manual When Battery Power To The Computer Has Been Interrupted.

INDEX

PRECAUTIONS

When working on or around brake assemblies, care must be taken to prevent breathing asbestos dust, as many manufacturers incorporate asbestos fibers in the production of brake linings. During routine service operations the amount of asbestos dust from brake lining wear is at a low level due to a chemical breakdown during use, and a few precautions will minimize exposure.

1. Do not sand or grind brake linings unless suitable local exhaust ventilation equipment is used to prevent excessive asbestos exposure.
2. Wear a suitable respirator approved for asbestos dust use during all repair procedures.
3. When cleaning brake dust from brake components, use a vacuum cleaner with a highly efficient filter system. If a suitable vacuum cleaner is not available, use a water soaked rag. **Do not use compressed air or dry brush to clean brake components.**
4. Keep work area clean using same equipment as for cleaning brake components.
5. Properly dispose of rags and vacuum cleaner bags by placing them in plastic bags.
6. Do not smoke or eat while working on brake systems. **Never use gasoline, kerosene, alcohol, motor oil, transmission fluid, or any fluid containing mineral oil to clean brake system components. These fluids will damage the rubber caps and seals. If system contamination is suspected, inspect brake fluid in the reservoir for dirt, discoloration, or separation (breakdown) of the brake fluid into distinct layers. Drain and flush the hydraulic system with clean brake fluid if contamination is suspected.**

INSPECTION

1. Inspect components for damage or wear. Replace as required.
2. Inspect wheel cylinder boots for tears, cuts or heat damage. Replace as required.
3. Remove wheel cylinder links. If fluid spills from boot center hole, replace wheel cylinder.
4. Light fluid coatings on piston within cylinder is considered normal.
5. Inspect backing plate for evidence of axle seal leakage. If leakage exists, refer to individual vehicle chapters for axle seal replacement procedures.
6. Inspect backing plate attaching bolts and ensure they are tight.
7. Using fine emery cloth or other suitable abrasive, clean rust and dirt from shoe contact surface on backing plate.

BRAKE DRUMS

Any time the brake drums are removed for brake service, the braking surface diameter should be inspected with a suitable brake drum micrometer at several points to determine if they are within the safe oversize limit stamped on the brake drum outer surface. If the braking surface diameter exceeds specifications, the drum must be replaced. If the braking surface diameter is within specifications, drums should be cleaned and inspected for cracks, scores, deep grooves, taper, out-of-round and heat spotting. If drums are cracked or heat spotted, they must be replaced. Minor scores should be removed with sandpaper. Grooves and large scores can only be removed by machining with special equipment, as long as the braking surface is within specifications stamped on brake drum outer surface. Any brake drum sufficiently out-of-round to cause vehicle vibration or noise while braking or showing taper should also be machined, removing only enough stock to true up the brake drum.

After a brake drum is machined, wipe the braking surface diameter with a denatured alcohol soaked cloth. If one brake drum is machined, the other should also be machined to the same diameter to maintain equal braking forces.

BRAKE LININGS & SPRINGS

Inspect brake linings for excessive wear, damage, oil, grease or brake fluid contamination. If any of the above conditions exists, brake linings should be replaced. Do not attempt to replace only one set of brake shoes; they should be replaced as an axle set only to maintain equal braking forces. Examine brake shoe webbing, hold-down and return springs for signs of overheating indicated by a slight blue color. If any component exhibits overheating signs, replace hold-down and return springs with new ones. Overheated springs lose their pull and could cause brake linings to wear out prematurely. Inspect all springs for sags, bends and external damage and replace as required.

Inspect hold-down retainers and pins for bends, rust and corrosion. If any of the above is found, replace as required.

BACKING PLATE

Inspect backing plate shoe contact surface for grooves that may restrict shoe movement and cannot be removed by lightly sanding with emery cloth or other suitable abrasive. If backing plate exhibits above condition, it should be replaced. Also inspect for signs of cracks, warpage and excessive rust, indicating need for replacement.

ADJUSTER MECHANISM

Inspect all components for rust, corrosion, bends and fatigue. Replace as required. **On adjuster mechanism equipped with adjuster cable,** inspect cable for kinks, fraying or elongation of eyelet and replace as required.

PARKING BRAKE CABLE

Inspect parking brake cable end for kinks, fraying and elongation and replace as required. Use a small hose clamp to compress clamp where it enters backing plate to remove it.

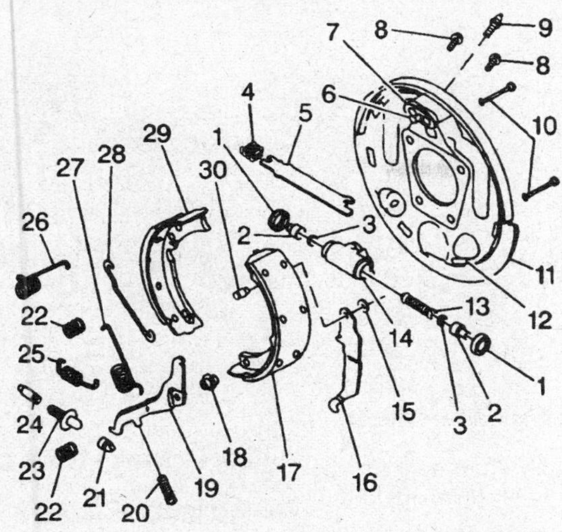

1. Boot
2. Piston
3. Seal
4. Strut Spring
5. Strut
6. Shoe Retainer
7. Anchor Pin
8. Bolt
9. Bleeder Screw
10. Hold down Pins
11. Backing Plate
12. Shoe Contact Points
13. Piston Spring
14. Cylinder
15. Reatainer Ring
16. Parking Brake Lever
17. Secondary Shoe
18. Sleeve
19. Actuator Lever
20. Return Spring
21. Socket
22. Hold Down Spring
23. Star Wheel
24. Pivot Nut
25. Adjuster Spring
26. Return Spring

GC4089700045000X

Fig. 1 Drum brake assembly

BRAKE SERVICE

REMOVAL

1. Raise and support rear of vehicle, then remove tire and wheel assembly.
2. Mark drum and axle hub, then remove brake drum. If brake lining is dragging on brake drum, back off brake adjustment by rotating adjustment screw. Refer to individual vehicle chapter for procedure. **If brake drum is rusted or corroded to axle flange and cannot be removed, lightly tap axle flange to drum mounting surface with a suitable hammer.**
3. Using brake spring removal and installation tool Nos. J-8049 or J-29840, or their equivalents, unhook primary and secondary return springs, **Fig. 1. Observe location of brake components being removed to aid during installation.**
4. Remove brake hold-down springs with suitable tool.
5. Lift actuating lever, then unhook and remove actuating link from anchor pin.
6. Remove actuating lever(s) and return spring.
7. Spread shoes apart and remove parking brake strut and spring.
8. Disconnect parking brake cable from lever, then remove brake shoes from backing plate.
9. Separate brake shoes by removing adjusting screw and spring, then unhook parking brake lever from shoe assembly.
10. Clean dirt from brake drum, backing plate and all other components. **Do not use compressed air or dry brush to clean brake components. Many brake components contain asbestos fibers which, if inhaled, can cause serious injury. Clean brake components with a water soaked rag or a suitable vacuum cleaner to minimize airborne dust.**

INSTALLATION

1. Lubricate parking brake lever fulcrum with suitable brake lubricant, then attach lever to brake shoe. Ensure lever operates smoothly.
2. Connect brake shoes with adjusting screw spring, then position adjusting screw. **Ensure adjusting screw star wheel does not contact adjusting screw spring after installation and also ensure righthand thread adjusting screw is installed on lefthand side of vehicle and lefthand thread adjusting screw is installed on righthand side of vehicle. When brake shoe installation is completed, ensure star wheel lines up with adjusting hole in backing plate.**
3. Lubricate backing plate shoe contact surfaces with suitable brake lubricant, then the area where parking brake cable contacts backing plate.
4. Install brake shoes on backing plate while engaging wheel cylinder links (if equipped) with shoe webbing. Connect parking brake cable to parking brake lever. **The primary shoe (short lining) faces towards front of vehicle. The end without the strut spring should engage parking brake lever and secondary shoe. The end with the strut spring should engage the primary shoe.**
5. Install actuating levers, actuating link and return spring, **Figs. 1.**
6. Install hold-down springs with suitable tool.
7. Install primary and secondary shoe return springs using brake spring pliers or equivalent.
8. Using suitable brake drum to shoe gauge, measure brake drum inside diameter. Adjust brake shoes to dimension obtained on outside portion of gauge.
9. Install brake drum, wheel and tire assembly.
10. If any hydraulic connections have been opened, bleed brake system.
11. Adjust parking brake. Refer to individual vehicle chapters for procedures.
12. Inspect all hydraulic lines and connections for leakage and repair as required.
13. Inspect master cylinder fluid level and replenish as required.
14. Inspect brake pedal for proper feel and return.
15. Lower vehicle and road test. **Do not severely apply brakes immediately after installation of new brake linings or permanent damage may occur to linings, and/or brake drums may become scored. Brakes must be used moderately during first several hundred miles of operation to ensure proper burnishing of linings.**

ADJUSTMENTS

These brakes have self-adjusting shoe mechanisms that ensure proper lining-to-drum clearances at all times. The automatic adjusters operate only when the brakes are applied as the vehicle is moving rearward.

An initial adjustment is required after the brake shoes have been relined or replaced, or when the length of the adjusting screw has been changed during service operations.

Frequent usage of an automatic transmission forward range to halt reverse vehicle motion may prevent the automatic adjusters from functioning, thereby inducing low pedal heights. Should low pedal heights be encountered, it is recommended that numerous forward and reverse stops be made until satisfactory pedal height is obtained. **If a low pedal condition cannot be corrected by making numerous reverse stops (provided the hydraulic system is free of air) it indicates that the self-adjusting mechanism is not functioning. Therefore, it will be necessary to remove the brake drum, clean, free up and lubricate the adjusting mechanism. Then adjust the brakes as follows, ensuring the parking brake is fully released.**

SERVICE BRAKE

Brake adjustment cannot be performed

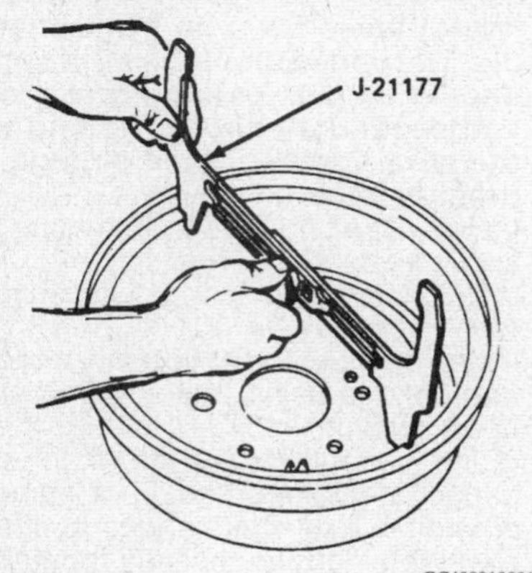
J-21177
GC4089100019000X

Fig. 2 Brake drum measurement

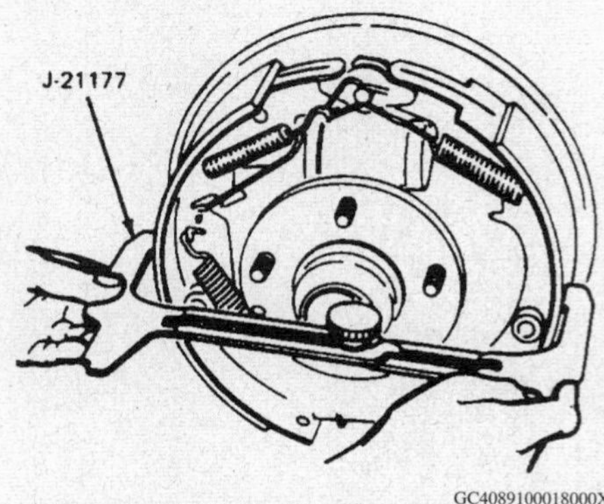
J-21177
GC4089100018000X

Fig. 3 Brake shoe measurement

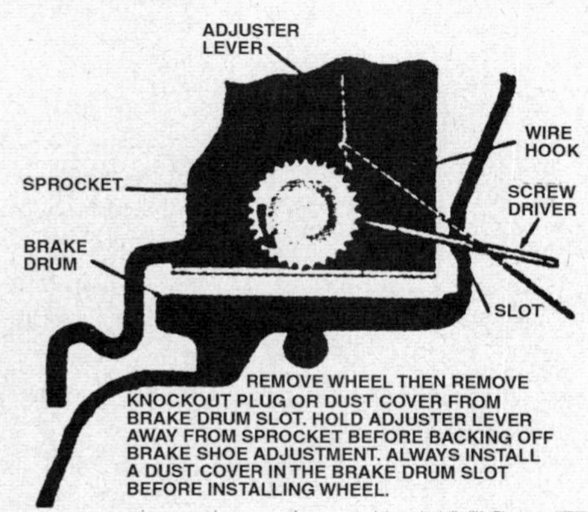
ADJUSTER LEVER
WIRE HOOK
SPROCKET
SCREW DRIVER
BRAKE DRUM
SLOT
REMOVE WHEEL THEN REMOVE KNOCKOUT PLUG OR DUST COVER FROM BRAKE DRUM SLOT. HOLD ADJUSTER LEVER AWAY FROM SPROCKET BEFORE BACKING OFF BRAKE SHOE ADJUSTMENT. ALWAYS INSTALL A DUST COVER IN THE BRAKE DRUM SLOT BEFORE INSTALLING WHEEL.
GC4089100013000X

Fig. 4 Brake shoe adjustment

with the drums installed. The following procedure is mandatory after new linings are installed, or when the length of the brake shoe adjusting screw has been changed.

1. With brake drums removed, position the caliper as illustrated in **Fig. 2,** to the inside diameter of the drum, then tighten the clamp screw.
2. Position brake shoe end of the caliper tool over the brake shoes as illustrated in **Fig. 3.**
3. Rotate gauge slightly around shoes to ensure gauge contacts linings at largest diameter.
4. Adjust brake shoes until their outside diameter is .030 inch less than that of drum's inside diameter. **If it is necessary to back off the brake shoe adjustment, it will be necessary to hold the adjuster lever away from the adjuster screw, Fig. 4.**

PARKING BRAKE

On these brake systems, no adjustment is required. These models have a self-adjusting parking brake system and it should not be adjusted or modified in any way.

On brakes, by fully applying and releasing the parking brake 4–6 times the system will perform its self-adjustment procedure.

DRUM BRAKE SPECIFICATIONS

Model	Year	Brake Lining Wear Limit, Inch②	Brake Drum Inside Diameter, Inches			Drum Runout Limit, Inch	Drum Maximum Out Of Roundness, Inch②
			Nominal	Maximum Refinish	Maximum Inside Diameter (Discard Limit)①		
BUICK							
Skylark	1998	.030	7.874–7.890	7.899	7.929	.006	—
CHEVROLET							
Cavalier	1998–2002	.030	7.874–7.890	7.899	7.929	.006	—
OLDSMOBILE							
Achieva	1998	.030	7.874–7.890	7.899	7.929	.006	—
Grand Am	1998	.030	7.874–7.890	7.899	7.929	.006	—
Sunfire	1998–2002	.030	7.874–7.890	7.899	7.929	.006	—

① — Maximum brake drum inside diameter (discard limit) is stamped on drum.

② — Above rivet head or shoe. Original equipment type brake linings.

TIGHTENING SPECIFICATIONS

Year	Component	Torque/ Ft. Lbs.
1998–2002	Wheel Cylinder Bleeder Screw	60①
	Wheel Cylinder Line Fitting	18
	Wheel Cylinder To Backing Plate	15
	Wheel Lug Nuts	②

① — Inch lbs.

② — Tighten lug nuts in sequence in increments of 20 ft. lbs. until the final torque of 100 ft. lbs., is reached.

Type 2

NOTE: On Air Bag Equipped Models, Refer To "Air Bag System Precautions" Located In The Front Of This Manual For System Disarming & Arming Procedures.

NOTE: Refer To "Computer Relearn Procedures" Located In The Front Of This Manual When Battery Power To The Computer Has Been Interrupted.

INDEX

INSPECTION

1. Release parking brake.
2. Raise and support vehicle.
3. Remove rear wheels and tires.
4. Remove brake drum. **Do not pry against brake backing plate.**
5. Inspect adjuster assembly, ensuring screw threads turn smoothly into nut over full threaded length.
6. Inspect wheel cylinder for damage, leakage or seizure. Replace as required.

BRAKE SERVICE

1. Release parking brake.
2. Raise and support vehicle.
3. Remove rear wheels.
4. Remove brake drum. **Do not pry against brake backing plate.**
5. Remove lower return spring, **Fig. 1.**
6. Remove adjuster spring.
7. Remove leading brake shoe hold-down, spring and pin.
8. Remove adjuster assembly and lever. If difficult, pull leading shoe toward front of vehicle, then or turn star wheel on adjuster to shorten length.
9. Twist shoe from upper return spring engagement to remove.
10. Remove parking brake shoe upper return spring.
11. Remove park brake shoe hold-down cup, spring and pin.
12. Push park brake lever into cable spring to remove park brake cable from lever.
13. Remove park brake lever retainer and wave washer and separate from park brake shoe.
14. Reverse procedure to install noting the following:
    a. Lubricate adjuster assembly, adjuster lever surface, backing plate at shoe contact pads and park brake lever pin and brake shoe web contact surface.
    b. Using brake drum clearance tool No. SA91109NE, or equivalent, measure drum inner diameter, then the brake shoe assembly outer diameter. Adjust brake adjuster to obtain a measurement .050 inch less than drum inner diameter.

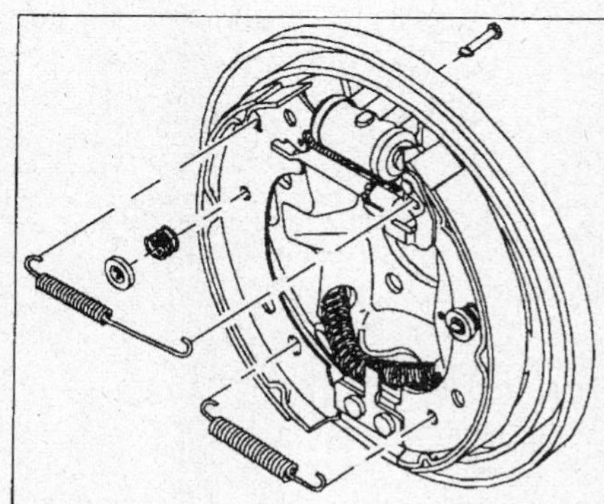

G34089100001000X

Fig. 1 Rear brake assembly

ADJUSTMENTS

PARKING BRAKE

Refer to "Adjustments" under "Disc Brakes" for parking brake adjustment.

DRUM BRAKE SPECIFICATIONS

Model	Year	Brake Lining Wear Limit, Inch②	Brake Drum Inside Diameter, Inches: Nominal	Maximum Refinish	Maximum Inside Diameter (Discard Limit)①	Drum Runout Limit, Inch	Drum Maximum Out Of Roundness, Inch②
SATURN							
L-Series	2000–02	.080	9.050	9.080	9.090	.002	—
S-Series	1998–2002	.040	7.870	7.900	7.930	.006	—

① — Maximum brake drum inside diameter (discard limit) is stamped on drum.

② — Above rivet head or shoe. Original equipment type brake linings.

TIGHTENING SPECIFICATIONS

Year	Component	Torque/ Ft. Lbs.
1998–2002	Backing Plate To Knuckle	63
	Bleed Valve	66①
	Brake Line To Brake Hose	18
	Brake Line To Wheel Cylinder	36
	Brake Pipe To Union	14
	Wheel Cylinder To Backing Plate	84①
	Wheel Lug Nuts (L-Series)	92②
	Wheel Lug Nuts (S-Series)	103

① — Inch lbs.
② — For steel wheel & optional aluminum wheel w/large center cap, install wheel cover or cap. With socket, hand tighten five cap nuts then, with wrench, tighten each cap nut an additional 90°.

Type 3

NOTE: On Air Bag Equipped Models, Refer To "Air Bag System Precautions" Located In The Front Of This Manual For System Disarming & Arming Procedures.

NOTE: Refer To "Computer Relearn Procedures" Located In The Front Of This Manual When Battery Power To The Computer Has Been Interrupted.

INDEX

PRECAUTIONS

When working on or around brake assemblies, care must be taken to prevent breathing asbestos dust, as many manufacturers incorporate asbestos fibers in the production of brake linings. During routine service operations the amount of asbestos dust from brake lining wear is at a low level due to a chemical breakdown during use, and a few precautions will minimize exposure.

1. Do not sand or grind brake linings unless suitable local exhaust ventilation equipment is used to prevent excessive asbestos exposure.
2. Wear a suitable respirator approved for asbestos dust use during all repair procedures.
3. When cleaning brake dust from brake components, use a vacuum cleaner with a highly efficient filter system. If a suitable vacuum cleaner is not available, use a water soaked rag. **Do not use compressed air or dry brush to clean brake components.**
4. Keep work area clean using same equipment as for cleaning brake components.
5. Properly dispose of rags and vacuum cleaner bags by placing them in plastic bags.
6. Do not smoke or eat while working on brake systems. **Never use gasoline, kerosene, alcohol, motor oil, transmission fluid, or any fluid containing mineral oil to clean brake system components. These fluids will damage the rubber caps and seals. If system contamination is suspected, inspect brake fluid in the reservoir for dirt, discoloration, or separation (breakdown) of the brake fluid into distinct layers. Drain and flush the hydraulic system with clean brake fluid if contamination is suspected.**

INSPECTION

1. Inspect brake drum, shoes, strut, auto adjuster lever, springs and backing plate for wear, distortion, cracks or other abnormal conditions.
2. If any components are of doubtful strength or quality due to damage, heat discoloration, stress or wear, replace them.
3. Measure brake drum inside diameter and the brake shoe lining thickness.
4. Inspect lining and drum for proper contact.

BRAKE DRUMS

Any time the brake drums are removed for brake service, the braking surface diameter should be inspected with a suitable brake drum micrometer at several points to determine if they are within the safe oversize limit stamped on the brake drum outer surface. If the braking surface diameter exceeds specifications, the drum must be replaced. If the braking surface diameter is within specifications, drums should be cleaned and inspected for cracks, scores, deep grooves, taper, out-of-round and heat spotting. If drums are cracked or heat spotted, they must be replaced. Minor scores should be removed with sandpaper. Grooves and large scores can only be removed by machining with special equipment, as long as the braking surface is within specifications stamped on brake drum outer surface. Any brake drum sufficiently out-of-round to cause vehicle vibration or noise while braking or showing taper should also be machined, removing only enough stock to true up the brake drum.

After a brake drum is machined, wipe the braking surface diameter with a denatured alcohol soaked cloth. If one brake drum is machined, the other should also be machined to the same diameter to maintain equal braking forces.

BRAKE LININGS & SPRINGS

Inspect brake linings for excessive wear, damage, oil, grease or brake fluid contamination. If any of the above conditions exists, brake linings should be replaced. Do not attempt to replace only one set of brake shoes; they should be replaced as an axle set only to maintain equal braking forces. Examine brake shoe webbing, hold-down and return springs for signs of overheating indicated by a slight blue color. If any component exhibits overheating signs, replace hold-down and return springs with new ones. Overheated springs lose their pull and could cause brake linings to wear out prematurely. Inspect all springs for sags, bends and external damage and replace as required.

Inspect hold-down retainers and pins for bends, rust and corrosion. If any of the above is found, replace as required.

BACKING PLATE

Inspect backing plate shoe contact surface for grooves that may restrict shoe movement and cannot be removed by lightly sanding with emery cloth or other suitable abrasive. If backing plate exhibits above condition, it should be replaced. Also inspect for signs of cracks, warpage and excessive rust, indicating need for replacement.

ADJUSTER MECHANISM

Inspect all components for rust, corrosion, bends and fatigue. Replace as required. On adjuster mechanism equipped with adjuster cable, inspect cable for kinks, fraying or elongation of eyelet and replace as required.

PARKING BRAKE CABLE

Inspect parking brake cable end for kinks, fraying and elongation and replace as required. Use a small hose clamp to compress clamp where it enters backing plate to remove.

BRAKE SERVICE

REMOVAL

1. Raise and support vehicle.

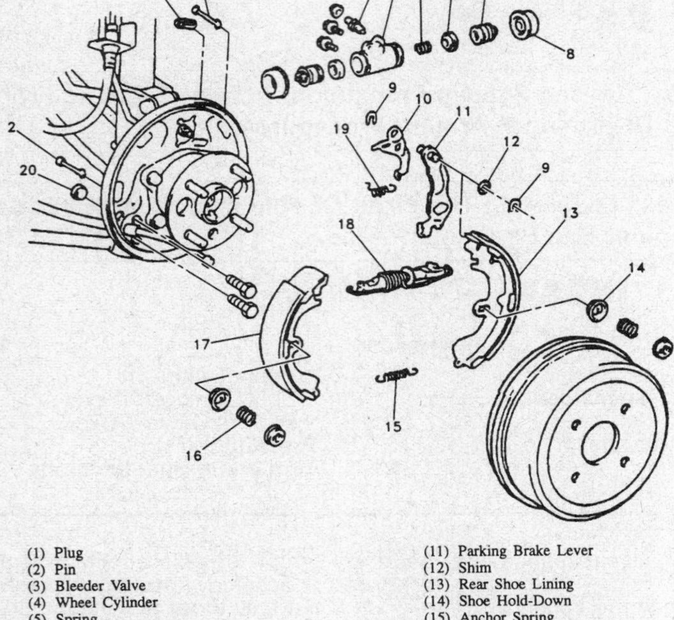

(1) Plug
(2) Pin
(3) Bleeder Valve
(4) Wheel Cylinder
(5) Spring
(6) Cup
(7) Piston
(8) Boot
(9) C-Clip
(10) Automatic Adjuster Lever
(11) Parking Brake Lever
(12) Shim
(13) Rear Shoe Lining
(14) Shoe Hold-Down
(15) Anchor Spring
(16) Shoe Hold-Down Spring
(17) Front Shoe Lining
(18) Adjuster
(19) Automatic Adjuster Lever Spring
(20) Inspection Hole Plug

GC4089700046000X

Fig. 1 Drum brake assembly

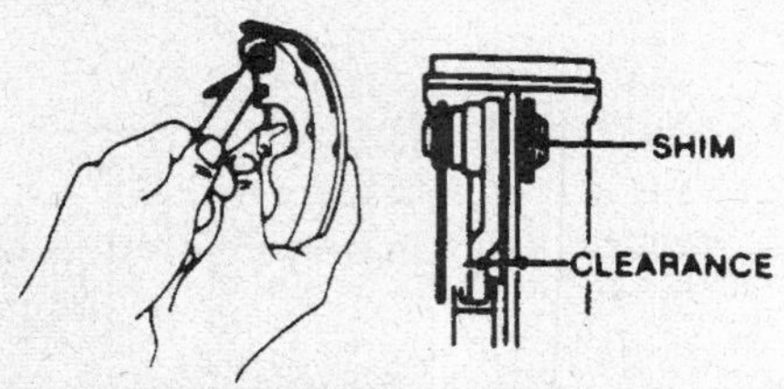

SHIM THICKNESS	
THICKNESS	THICKNESS
0.2 MM (0.008 IN.)	0.5 MM (0.020 IN.)
0.3 MM (0.012 IN.)	0.6 MM (0.024 IN.)
0.4 MM (0.016 IN.)	0.9 MM (0.035 IN.)

GC4089100025000X

Fig. 2 Lever to shoe clearance inspection

2. Mark relationship of wheel to axle, then remove wheel and tire assembly.
3. Remove brake drum. If drum is difficult to remove, insert screwdriver through hole in backing plate and hold automatic adjusting lever away from adjusting bolt, then, using a second screwdriver, reduce brake shoe adjustment.
4. Remove return spring, **Fig. 1.**
5. Remove hold-down spring, retainers and pin retaining front shoe.
6. Disconnect anchor spring from front shoe, then remove front shoe.
7. Remove anchor spring.
8. Remove hold-down spring, retainers and pin retaining rear shoe.
9. Using screwdriver, disconnect parking brake cable from anchor plate.
10. Using pliers, disconnect parking brake cable from lever and remove rear shoe together with strut.
11. Remove adjusting lever spring, then the strut together with return spring.
12. Remove parking brake lever and automatic adjusting lever from rear shoe by prying out "C" washer and removing shims and levers.
13. Clean dirt from brake drum, backing plate and all other components. **Do not use compressed air or dry brush to clean brake components. Many brake components contain asbestos fibers which, if inhaled, can cause serious injury. Clean brake components with a water soaked rag or a suitable vacuum cleaner to minimize airborne dust.**

INSTALLATION

1. Apply white lithium grease part No. 1050109, or a suitable equivalent to backing plate brake shoe contact points, anchor plate brake shoe contact points, strut and adjusting bolt contact points and the strut and brake shoe contact points.
2. Install parking brake lever and automatic adjusting lever to rear shoe as follows:
   a. Temporarily install levers and shim with a new "C" washer.
   b. Using feeler gauge, measure clearance between shoe and lever, **Fig. 2.**
   c. If clearance is not 0–.0138 inch, adjust by installing replacement shim.
   d. Using pliers, stake "C" washer.
3. Set strut and return spring in place on rear shoe and install adjusting lever spring.
4. Install rear shoe as follows:
   a. Using pliers, connect parking brake cable to lever.
   b. Pass parking brake cable through notch in anchor plate.
   c. Set rear shoe in place with end of shoe inserted in wheel cylinder and other end in anchor plate.
   d. Install hold-down spring, retainers and pin.
5. Install front shoe as follows:
   a. Install anchor spring between front and rear shoes.
   b. Set front shoe in place with end of shoe inserted in wheel cylinder and the strut in place.
   c. Install hold-down spring, retainers and pin.
   d. Connect return spring.
6. Inspect operation of automatic adjuster mechanism as follows:
   a. Move parking brake lever of rear shoe back and forth and ensure adjusting bolt turns. If bolt does not turn, inspect brakes for improper installation.
   b. Adjust strut length to shortest possible distance.
   c. Install brake drum.
   d. Pull parking brake lever all the way up until a clicking sound can no longer be heard.
7. Inspect clearance between brake shoes and drum. Remove drum and measure brake drum inside diameter and diameter of brake shoes.
8. If clearance is not .024 inch, inspect parking brake system.
9. Install brake drum and the wheel and tire assembly.
10. Fill master cylinder as required and bleed brake system.
11. Inspect for fluid leakage.

ADJUSTMENTS

SERVICE BRAKE

Adjustment is accomplished automatically by pulling the parking brake lever all the way up until a clicking sound can no longer be heard.

PARKING BRAKE

1. Ensure parking brake lever travel is proper by pulling parking brake lever all the way up and counting the number of clicks.
2. Parking brake lever travel should be 4–7 clicks. If not, remove console, loosen locknut and turn adjusting nut until proper travel is achieved.

DRUM BRAKE SPECIFICATIONS

Model	Year	Brake Lining Wear Limit, Inch②	Brake Drum Inside Diameter, Inches			Drum Runout Limit, Inch	Drum Maximum Out Of Roundness, Inch②
			Nominal	Maximum Refinish	Maximum Inside Diameter (Discard Limit)①		
CHEVROLET							
Prizm	1998–2002	.039	7.874	—	7.913	.0016	.0004

① — Maximum brake drum inside diameter (discard limit) is stamped on drum.

② — Above rivet head or shoe. Original equipment type brake linings.

TIGHTENING SPECIFICATIONS

Year	Component	Torque/ Ft. Lbs.
1998–2002	Brake Line To Wheel Cylinder Fitting	11
	Hub Retaining Bolts	59
	Wheel Cylinder Bleeder Screw	72①
	Wheel Cylinder Retaining Bolts	89①
	Wheel Lug Nuts	76

① — Inch lbs.

Type 4

NOTE: On Air Bag Equipped Models, Refer To "Air Bag System Precautions" Located In The Front Of This Manual For System Disarming & Arming Procedures.

NOTE: Refer To "Computer Relearn Procedures" Located In The Front Of This Manual When Battery Power To The Computer Has Been Interrupted.

INDEX

PRECAUTIONS

When working on or around brake assemblies, care must be taken to prevent breathing asbestos dust, as many manufacturers incorporate asbestos fibers in the production of brake linings. During routine service operations the amount of asbestos dust from brake lining wear is at a low level due to a chemical breakdown during use, and a few precautions will minimize exposure.

1. Do not sand or grind brake linings unless suitable local exhaust ventilation equipment is used to prevent excessive asbestos exposure.
2. Wear a suitable respirator approved for asbestos dust use during all repair procedures.
3. When cleaning brake dust from brake components, use a vacuum cleaner with a highly efficient filter system. If a suitable vacuum cleaner is not available, use a water soaked rag. **Do not use compressed air or dry brush to clean brake components.**
4. Keep work area clean using same equipment as for cleaning brake components.
5. Properly dispose of rags and vacuum cleaner bags by placing them in plastic bags.
6. Do not smoke or eat while working on brake systems. **Never use gasoline, kerosene, alcohol, motor oil, transmission fluid, or any fluid containing mineral oil to clean brake system components. These fluids will damage the rubber caps and seals. If system contamination is suspected, inspect brake fluid in the reservoir for dirt, discoloration, or separation (breakdown) of the brake fluid into distinct layers. Drain and flush the hydraulic system with clean brake fluid if contamination is suspected.**

INSPECTION

1. If any components are of doubtful strength or quality due to heat discoloration, or are worn, replace them.
2. Inspect wheel cylinder dust boots for signs of excessive wear or damage. If any leakage is apparent replace or rebuild wheel cylinder.
3. Clean dirt and/or rust from brake drum, backing plate and all other components. **Do not use compressed air or dry brush to clean brake components. Many brake components contain asbestos fibers which, if inhaled, can cause serious injury. Clean brake components with a water soaked rag or a suitable vacuum cleaner to minimize airborne dust.**

BRAKE DRUMS

Any time the brake drums are removed for brake service, the braking surface diameter should be inspected with a suitable brake drum micrometer at several points to determine if they are within the safe oversize limit stamped on the brake drum outer surface. If the braking surface diameter exceeds specifications, the drum must be replaced. If the braking surface diameter is within specifications, drums should be cleaned and inspected for cracks, scores, deep grooves, taper, out-of-round and heat spotting. If drums are cracked or heat spotted, they must be replaced. Minor scores should be removed with sandpaper. Grooves and large scores can only be removed by machining with special equipment, as long as the braking surface is within specifications stamped on brake drum outer surface. Any brake drum sufficiently out-of-round to cause vehicle vibration or noise while braking or showing taper should also be machined, removing only enough stock to true up the brake drum.

After a brake drum is machined, wipe the braking surface diameter with a denatured alcohol soaked cloth. If one brake drum is machined, the other should also be machined to the same diameter to maintain equal braking forces.

BRAKE LININGS & SPRINGS

Inspect brake linings for excessive wear, damage, oil, grease or brake fluid contamination. If any of the above conditions exists, brake linings should be replaced. Do not attempt to replace only one set of brake shoes. They should be replaced as an axle set only to maintain equal braking forces. Examine brake shoe webbing, hold-down and return springs for signs of overheating indicated by a slight blue color. If any component exhibits overheating signs, replace hold-down and return springs with new ones. Overheated springs lose their pull and could cause brake linings to wear out prematurely. Inspect all springs for sags, bends and external damage and replace as required.

Inspect hold-down retainers and pins for bends, rust and corrosion. If any of the above is found, replace as required.

BACKING PLATE

Inspect backing plate shoe contact surface for grooves that may restrict shoe movement and cannot be removed by lightly sanding with emery cloth or other suitable abrasive. If backing plate exhibits above condition, it should be replaced. Also inspect for signs of cracks, warpage and excessive rust, indicating need for replacement.

ADJUSTER MECHANISM

Inspect all components for rust, corrosion, bends and fatigue. Replace as required. **On adjuster mechanism equipped with adjuster cable,** inspect cable for kinks, fraying or elongation of eyelet and replace as required.

PARKING BRAKE CABLE

Inspect parking brake cable end for kinks, fraying and elongation and replace as required. Use a small hose clamp to compress clamp where it enters backing plate to remove.

BRAKE SERVICE

REMOVAL

1. Raise and support vehicle.
2. Remove spindle cap by hammering lightly at three points around cap.
3. Remove cotter pin or unfasten staked portion of nut, then remove castle nut and washer.
4. Loosen parking brake cable adjusting nuts.
5. Remove backing plate plug, **Fig. 1.**
6. Insert screwdriver into plug hole until it contacts shoe hold-down spring, then push in direction illustrated, **Fig. 1.** This pushes hold-down spring up and releases parking brake shoe lever from hold-down spring, resulting in added clearance between shoe and drum.
7. **On models equipped with ABS,** install two 8 MM bolts into drum, then tighten them to remove drum from hub.
8. **On models less ABS,** using slide hammer tool No. J-2619-01 and brake drum remover tool No. J-34866, or their equivalents, pull off brake drum.
9. **On all models,** remove brake shoe hold-down springs by turning hold-down pins.
10. Disconnect parking brake cable from parking brake shoe lever and remove brake shoes.
11. Remove spring (1) in **Fig. 2,** pull primary shoe in direction of arrow and disengage strut (4) and return spring (2).
12. Disconnect return spring (3) from shoe.
13. Disconnect parking brake shoe lever from shoe.

INSTALLATION

1. Apply white lithium grease part No. 1050109, or a suitable equivalent to backing plate brake shoe contact points and to anchor plate brake shoe contact points.
2. Assemble brake shoes, levers and springs as illustrated in **Fig. 3.**
3. Push shoe hold-down springs down into place. Turn hold-down pins to engage springs.
4. To minimize dimension "A–A," **Fig. 4,** push strut towards backplate while pushing out on shoe as illustrated.
5. Position tab of spring clip behind parking brake lever.
6. Install brake drum and tighten castle nut to specifications.
7. Install cotter pin.
8. Install spindle cap.
9. Install wheel.
10. Depress brake pedal several times to obtain proper drum to shoe clearance and adjust parking brake.
11. Ensure brake drums do not drag.
12. Lower the vehicle and test brake operation.

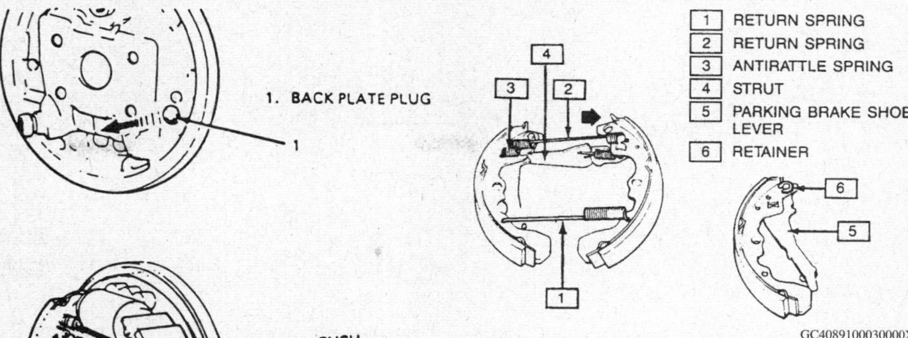

Fig. 2 Brake shoe return spring identification

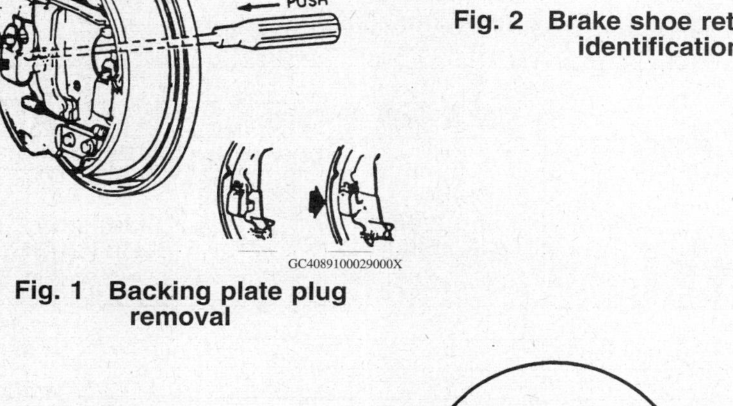

Fig. 1 Backing plate plug removal

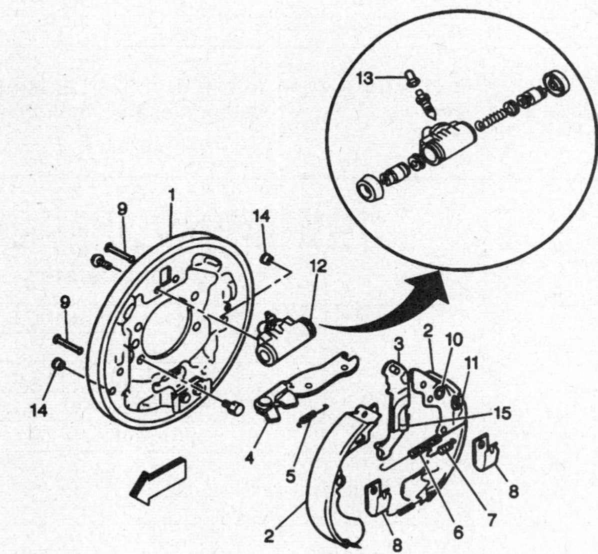

(1) Backing Plate
(2) Shoe
(3) Parking Brake Shoe Lever
(4) Adjuster
(5) Adjuster Spring
(6) Shoe Return Spring
(7) Spring
(8) Shoe Hold Down Spring
(9) Shoe Hold Down Pin
(10) Shim
(11) C-Clip
(12) Wheel Cylinder
(13) Bleeder Cap
(14) Plug

GC4089700047000X

Fig. 3 Rear brake unit assembly

ADJUSTMENTS

SERVICE BRAKE

Adjustment is accomplished automatically by applying brake pedal 3–5 times with 66 lbs. of pressure. Brake pedal should be cycled 3–5 times when replacement components are installed to ensure proper adjustment.

PARKING BRAKE

The parking brake lever should be adjusted so lever comes up 3–6 notches with 44 ft. lbs., of pull applied.

Adjust travel by loosening adjustment nuts, **Fig. 5.**

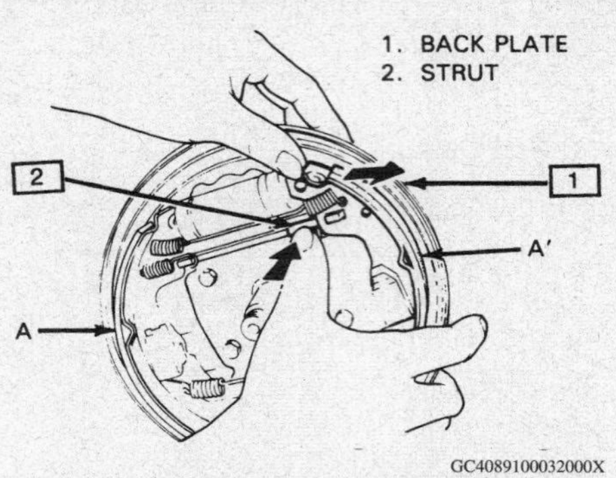

Fig. 4 Brake lining installation

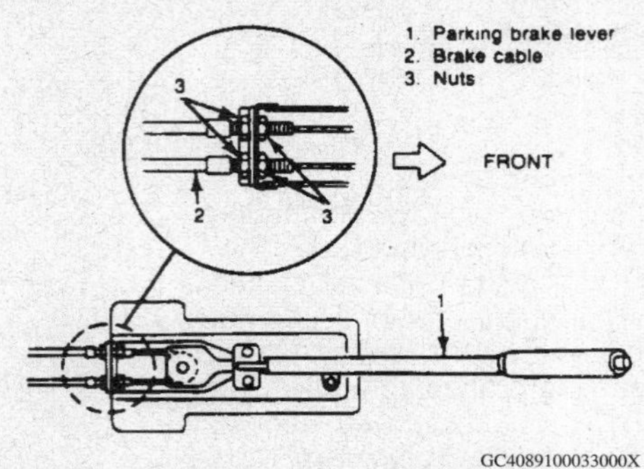

Fig. 5 Parking brake adjustment

DRUM BRAKE SPECIFICATIONS

Model	Year	Brake Lining Wear Limit, Inch②	Brake Drum Inside Diameter, Inches: Nominal	Brake Drum Inside Diameter, Inches: Maximum Refinish	Brake Drum Inside Diameter, Inches: Maximum Inside Diameter (Discard Limit)①	Drum Runout Limit, Inch	Drum Maximum Out Of Roundness, Inch②
CHEVROLET							
Metro 2 Door	1998–2001	.040	—	—	7.160	.0016	.0004
Metro 4 Door	1998–2001	.040	—	—	7.950	.0016	.0004

① — Maximum brake drum inside diameter (discard limit) is stamped on drum.

② — Above rivet head or shoe. Original equipment type brake linings.

TIGHTENING SPECIFICATIONS

Year	Component	Torque/ Ft. Lbs.
1998–2001	Backing Plate Mounting Bolts	17
	Bleeder Valve	89①
	Brake Fluid Pipe Nut	12
	Hub Assembly Spindle Nut	58–87
	Wheel Lug Nuts	44

① — Inch lbs.

Type 5

NOTE: On Air Bag Equipped Models, Refer To "Air Bag System Precautions" Located In The Front Of This Manual For System Disarming & Arming Procedures.

NOTE: Refer To "Computer Relearn Procedures" Located In The Front Of This Manual When Battery Power To The Computer Has Been Interrupted.

INDEX

DESCRIPTION

This brake assembly operates with fewer components, but is equal to other drum brake systems in performance. In this assembly, a single spring holds both shoe and lining to the backing plate and acts as a retractor spring for the shoe and lining assemblies, **Fig. 1.**

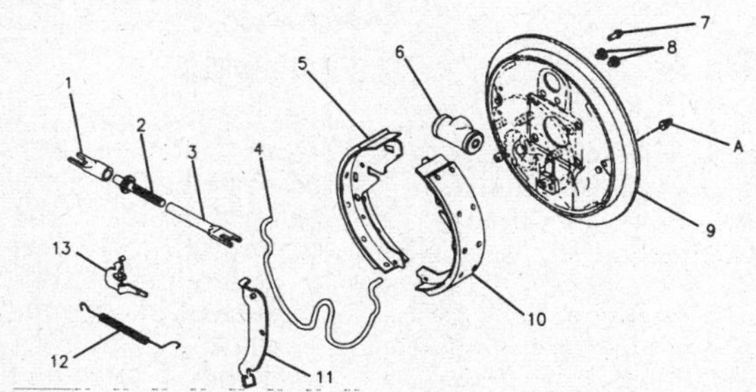

Fig. 1 Brake drum assembly

PRECAUTIONS

When working on or around brake assemblies, care must be taken to prevent breathing asbestos dust, as many manufacturers incorporate asbestos fibers in the production of brake linings. During routine service operations the amount of asbestos dust from brake lining wear is at a low level due to a chemical breakdown during use, and a few precautions will minimize exposure.

1. Do not sand or grind brake linings unless suitable local exhaust ventilation equipment is used to prevent excessive asbestos exposure.
2. Wear a suitable respirator approved for asbestos dust use during all repair procedures.
3. When cleaning brake dust from brake components, use a vacuum cleaner with a highly efficient filter system. If a suitable vacuum cleaner is not available, use a water soaked rag. **Do not use compressed air or dry brush to clean brake components.**
4. Keep work area clean using same equipment as for cleaning brake components.
5. Properly dispose of rags and vacuum cleaner bags by placing them in plastic bags.
6. Do not smoke or eat while working on brake systems. **Never use gasoline, kerosene, alcohol, motor oil, transmission fluid, or any fluid containing mineral oil to clean brake system components. These fluids will damage the rubber caps and seals. If system contamination is suspected, inspect brake fluid in the reservoir for dirt, discoloration, or separation (breakdown) of the brake fluid into distinct layers. Drain and flush the hydraulic system with clean brake fluid if contamination is suspected.**

INSPECTION

1. If any components are of doubtful strength or quality due to heat discoloration, or are worn, replace them.
2. Inspect wheel cylinder dust boots for signs of excessive wear or damage. If any leakage is apparent replace wheel cylinder.
3. Clean dirt and/or rust from brake drum, backing plate and all other components. **Do not use compressed air or dry brush to clean brake components. Many brake components contain asbestos fibers which, if inhaled, can cause serious injury. Clean brake components with a water soaked rag or a suitable vacuum cleaner to minimize airborne dust.**

BRAKE DRUMS

Any time the brake drums are removed for brake service, the braking surface diameter should be inspected with a suitable brake drum micrometer at several points to determine if they are within the safe oversize limit stamped on the brake drum outer surface. If the braking surface diameter exceeds specifications, the drum must be replaced. If the braking surface diameter is within specifications, drums should be cleaned and inspected for cracks, scores, deep grooves, taper, out-of-round and heat spotting. If drums are cracked or heat spotted, they must be replaced. Minor scores should be removed with sandpaper. Grooves and large scores can only be removed by machining with special equipment, as long as the braking surface is within specifications stamped on brake drum outer surface. Any brake drum sufficiently out-of-round to cause vehicle vibration or noise while braking or showing taper should also be machined, removing only enough stock to true up the brake drum.

After a brake drum is machined, wipe the braking surface diameter with a denatured

Fig. 2 Loosening drum through splash shield

alcohol soaked cloth. If one brake drum is machined, the other should also be machined to the same diameter to maintain equal braking forces.

BRAKE LININGS & SPRINGS

Inspect brake linings for excessive wear, damage, oil, grease or brake fluid contamination. If any of the above conditions exists, brake linings should be replaced. Do not attempt to replace only one set of brake shoes. they should be replaced as an axle set only to maintain equal braking forces. Examine brake shoe webbing, hold-down and return springs for signs of overheating indicated by a slight blue color. If any component exhibits overheating signs, replace hold-down and return springs with new ones. Overheated springs lose their pull and could cause brake linings to wear out prematurely. Inspect all springs for sags, bends and external damage and replace as required.

Inspect hold-down retainers and pins for bends, rust and corrosion. If any of the above is found, replace as required.

BACKING PLATE

Inspect backing plate shoe contact surface for grooves that may restrict shoe movement and cannot be removed by lightly sanding with emery cloth or other suitable abrasive. If backing plate exhibits above condition, it should be replaced. Also inspect for signs of cracks, warpage and excessive rust, indicating need for replacement.

ADJUSTER MECHANISM

Inspect all components for rust, corrosion, bends and fatigue. Replace as required. **On adjuster mechanism equipped with adjuster cable,** inspect cable for kinks, fraying or elongation of eyelet and replace as required.

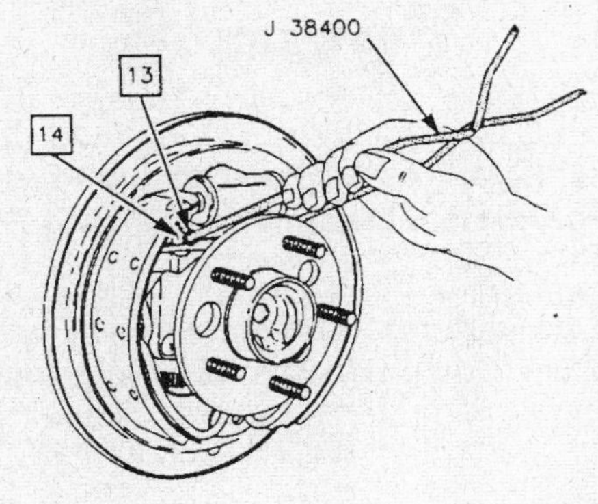

Fig. 3 Actuator spring removal

PARKING BRAKE CABLE

Inspect parking brake cable end for kinks, fraying and elongation and replace as required. Use a small hose clamp to compress clamp where it enters backing plate to remove.

BRAKE SERVICE

REMOVAL

1. Raise and support vehicle.
2. Mark relationship of wheel to axle, then remove wheel and tire assembly.
3. Remove brake drum. If drum is difficult to remove, proceed as follows:
   a. Ensure parking brake is released.
   b. Back off parking brake cable adjustment.
   c. Remove access hole plug from backing plate, insert screwdriver through hole and push parking brake lever off its stop.
   d. Insert punch through hole in splash shield **Fig. 2,** tap on punch to loosen drum, then remove drum.
4. Remove actuator spring using brake tool No. J-38400, or equivalent to pry loop end of spring from adjuster actuator, **Fig. 3. Do not over stretch the spring as this will reduce its effectiveness.**
5. Remove end of retractor spring from adjuster shoe and lining assembly, **Fig. 4. Keep finger away from retractor spring to prevent pinching.**
6. Remove adjuster shoe and lining assembly, adjuster actuator, then the adjusting screw assembly.
7. Remove park brake lever from shoe assembly, do not remove parking brake cable from lever unless parking brake lever is being replaced.
8. Remove retractor spring from park brake shoe and lining.
9. Pry end of retractor spring toward axle using brake tool, until it snaps off shoe web onto backing plate. Remove park brake shoe.

INSTALLATION

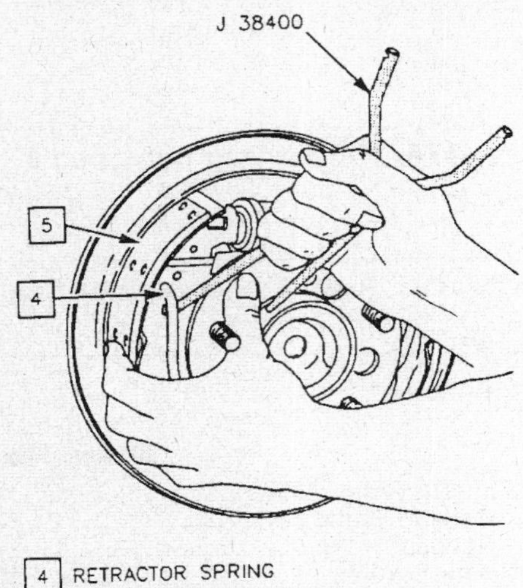

Fig. 4 Retractor spring disengagement

1. Using brake lubricant No. 1052196, or equivalent, lubricate raised shoe pads on backing plate, anchor surfaces on backing plate and adjuster screw threads.
2. Install retractor spring if removed by hooking center spring section under tab on anchor.
3. Install park shoe and lining assembly as follows:
   a. Place shoe on backing plate.
   b. Using brake tool No. J-38400, or equivalent, pull end of retractor spring up to rest on web of brake shoe, **Fig. 5.**
   c. Pull end of retractor spring over until it locks into slot of brake shoe, **Fig. 6.**
4. Install park brake lever.
5. Install adjuster screw and adjuster shoe as follows:
   a. Place shoe on backing plate.
   b. Using brake tool, pull end of retractor spring up to rest on web of brake shoe.
   c. Pull end of retractor spring over until if locks into slot of brake shoe.
6. Install adjuster actuator by spreading shoes using brake tool, **Fig. 7,** then move actuator into place.
7. Install actuator spring.
8. Adjust brakes using suitable adjustment tool. The shoes' outer diameter should be .050 inch less than inside diameter of each drum.
9. Install drums, wheels and tires, aligning marks made during removal.

ADJUSTMENTS

SERVICE BRAKE

1. Raise and support vehicle.
2. Mark relationship of wheel to axle, then remove wheel and tire assembly.
3. Remove brake drum. If drum is difficult to remove, proceed as follows:

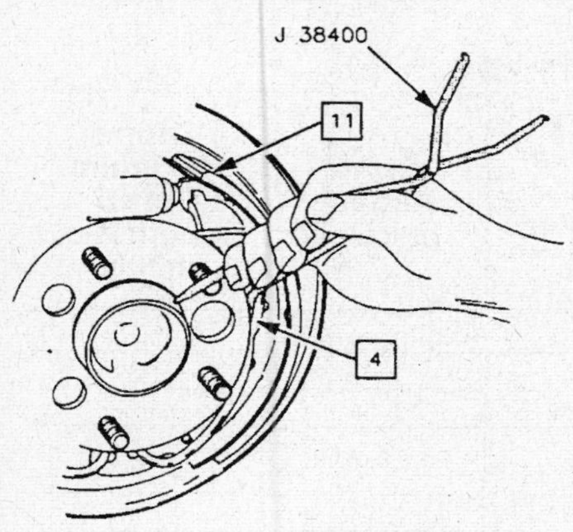

Fig. 5 Spring end installation onto shoe web

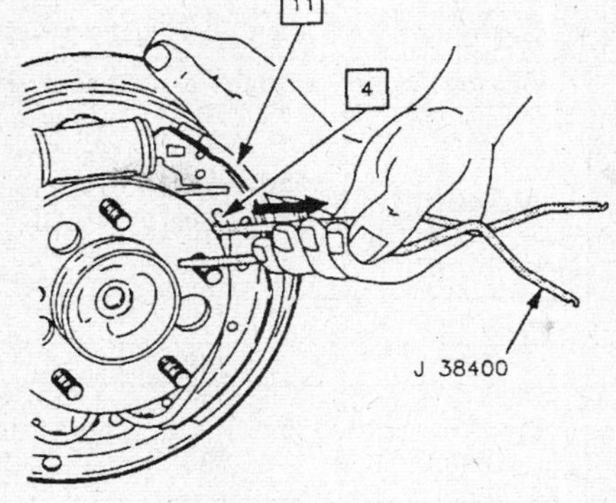

Fig. 6 Spring end installation into shoe slot

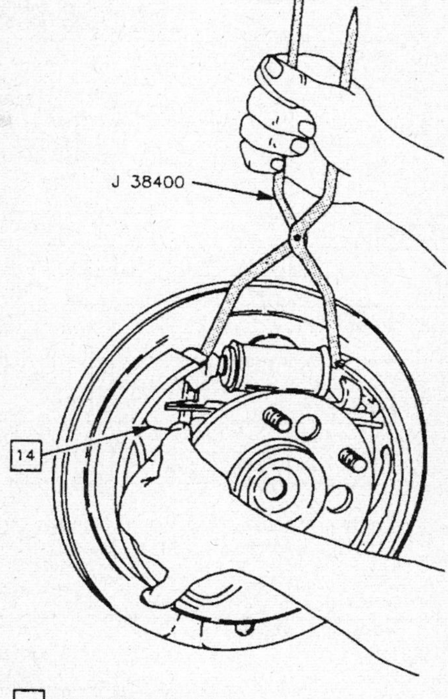

Fig. 7 Shoe spreading to install adjuster actuator

a. Ensure parking brake is released.
b. Back off parking brake cable adjustment.
c. Remove access hole plug from backing plate, insert screwdriver through hole and push parking brake lever off its stop.
d. Insert punch through hole in splash shield, **Fig. 2,** tap on punch to loosen drum, then remove drum.

4. Measure inside diameter of drum using tool Nos. J-21177-A or J-22364-01, or their equivalents.
5. Adjust by turning star wheel adjuster. Lining diameter should be .050 inch less than inside diameter of each drum.
6. Install drums, wheels and tires.
7. Lower the vehicle, then tighten wheel lug nuts to specifications.

PARKING BRAKE

1. Adjust brakes as outlined in "Service Brake."
2. Apply and release parking brake five times to six clicks.

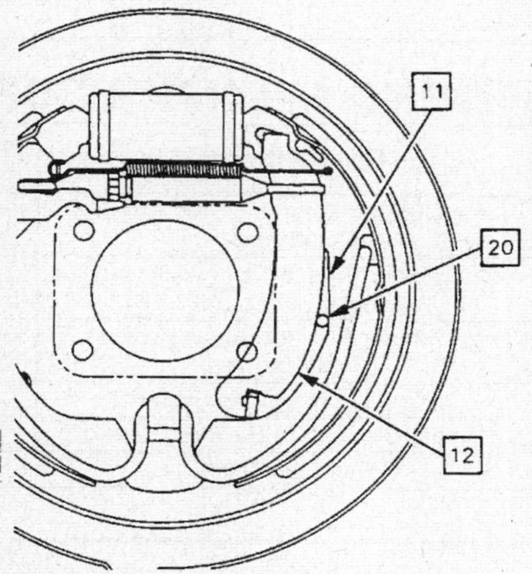

Fig. 8 Parking brake adjustment

3. Ensure pedal is fully released by turning ignition On. The brake warning lamp should be off.
4. If brake warning lamp is lit, operate pedal release lever and pull downward on front parking brake cable.
5. Raise and support vehicle, then remove access hole plug.
6. Adjust cable until a ⅛ inch drill bit can be inserted through access hole into space between shoe web and park lever, **Fig. 8.** Proper adjustment lets a ⅛ inch drill bit fit in the space but not a ¼ inch bit.
7. Release brake, then ensure wheels rotate freely.
8. Replace access hole plug, then lower the vehicle.

DRUM BRAKE SPECIFICATIONS

Model	Year	Brake Lining Wear Limit, Inch②	Brake Drum Inside Diameter, Inches			Drum Runout Limit, Inch	Drum Maximum Out Of Roundness, Inch②
			Nominal	Maximum Refinish	Maximum Inside Diameter (Discard Limit)①		
BUICK							
Century	1998–2002	.030	8.863	8.909	8.920	.006	—
LeSabre	1998–99	.030	8.863	8.880	8.909	.006	—
Regal	1998–2002	.030	8.863	8.909	8.920	.006	—
CHEVROLET							
Lumina	1998–2001	.030	8.863	8.909	8.920	.006	—
Malibu	1998–2002	.030	8.863	8.909	8.920	.006	—

Continued

DRUM BRAKE SPECIFICATIONS—Continued

Model	Year	Brake Lining Wear Limit, Inch②	Brake Drum Inside Diameter, Inches			Drum Runout Limit, Inch	Drum Maximum Out Of Roundness, Inch②
			Nominal	Maximum Refinish	Maximum Inside Diameter (Discard Limit)①		
OLDSMOBILE							
Alero	1999–2002	.030	8.863	8.909	8.920	.006	—
Cutlass	1998–99	.030	—	8.880	8.909	.006	—
Eighty Eight & LSS	1998–99	.030	8.863	8.880	8.909	.006	—
Regency	1998	.030	8.863	8.880	8.909	.006	—
PONTIAC							
Bonneville	1998–99	.030	8.863	8.880	8.909	.006	—
Grand Am	1998–2001	.030	8.863	8.909	8.920	.006	—

①— Maximum brake drum inside diameter (discard limit) is stamped on drum.

②— Above rivet head or shoe. Original equipment type brake linings.

TIGHTENING SPECIFICATIONS

Year	Component	Torque/ Ft. Lbs.
1998–2002	Wheel Cylinder Bleeder Screw (Alero & Grand Am)	115①
	Wheel Cylinder Bleeder Screw (Bonneville, Eighty Eight, LeSabre & LSS)	89①
	Wheel Cylinder Bleeder Screw (Cutlass & Malibu)	62①
	Wheel Cylinder Line Fitting	11
	Wheel Cylinder To Backing Plate	108①
	Wheel Lug Nuts	100

①— Inch lbs.

HYDRAULIC BRAKE SYSTEMS

TABLE OF CONTENTS

General Motors

NOTE: On Air Bag Equipped Models, Refer To "Air Bag System Precautions" Located In The Front Of This Manual For System Disarming & Arming Procedures.

NOTE: Refer To "Computer Relearn Procedures" Located In The Front Of This Manual When Battery Power To The Computer Has Been Interrupted.

INDEX

DESCRIPTION

FRONT & REAR SPLIT SYSTEM

When the brake pedal is depressed, both the primary (front brake) and the secondary (rear brake) master cylinder pistons are moved simultaneously to exert hydraulic fluid pressure on their respective systems, **Fig. 1.**

If the rear (secondary) brake system fails, initial brake pedal movement will cause the unrestricted secondary piston to bottom in the master cylinder bore. Primary piston movement will displace hydraulic fluid in the primary section of the master cylinder to actuate the front brake system.

If the front (primary) brake system fails, initial brake pedal movement will cause the unrestricted primary piston to bottom out against the secondary piston. Continued downward movement of the brake pedal moves the secondary piston to displace hydraulic fluid in the rear brake system to actuate the rear brakes.

DIAGONALLY SPLIT SYSTEM

This system operates on the same principle as conventional front and rear split systems, using primary and secondary master cylinders which move simultaneously to exert hydraulic pressure on their respective systems. The hydraulic brake lines on this system, however, have been diagonally split front to rear (lefthand front to righthand rear and righthand front to lefthand rear) in place of separate lines to the front and rear wheels, **Fig. 2.**

In the event of a system failure, the remaining non-failed system will do all the braking on one front wheel and one rear wheel, maintaining 50% of the total braking force.

COMPONENTS

Warning Lamp

The warning lamp should illuminate when the ignition switch is in the start position and turn off when the switch returns to run. If the brake lamp remains on after the ignition returns to run, check fluid level in master cylinder reservoir and inspect parking brake. If the warning lamp does not turn on during cranking, inspect for defective bulb or blown fuse.

Fluid Level Sensor

This sensor, mounted on the master cylinder, will activate the brake warning lamp if a low brake fluid level is detected. The lamp will turn off once the fluid level is corrected.

Brake Warning Lamp Switches

In **Fig. 3,** as pressure falls in one system, the other system's normal pressure forces the piston to the inoperative side, contacting the switch terminal, causing the warning lamp on the instrument panel to glow.

The switch is mounted directly in the master cylinder assembly, **Fig. 4.** Whenever there is a specified differential pressure, the switch piston will activate the brake failure warning switch and cause the brake warning lamp to glow.

Combination Valve

The combination valve is a metering valve, failure warning switch, and a proportioner in one assembly and is used on disc brake applications, **Fig. 5.** The metering valve delays front disc braking until the rear drum brake shoes contact the drum. The failure warning switch is actuated in event of front or rear brake system failure, in turn activating a dash warning lamp. The proportioner balances front to rear braking action during rapid deceleration.

Metering Valve

When the brakes are not applied, the metering valve permits the brake fluid to flow through the valve allowing the fluid to expand and contract with temperature changes.

When the brakes are initially applied, the metering valve stem moves to the left, preventing fluid to flow through the valve to the front disc brakes. This is accomplished by the smooth end of the metering valve stem contacting the metering valve seal lip at 4–30 psi, **Fig. 6.** The metering valve spring

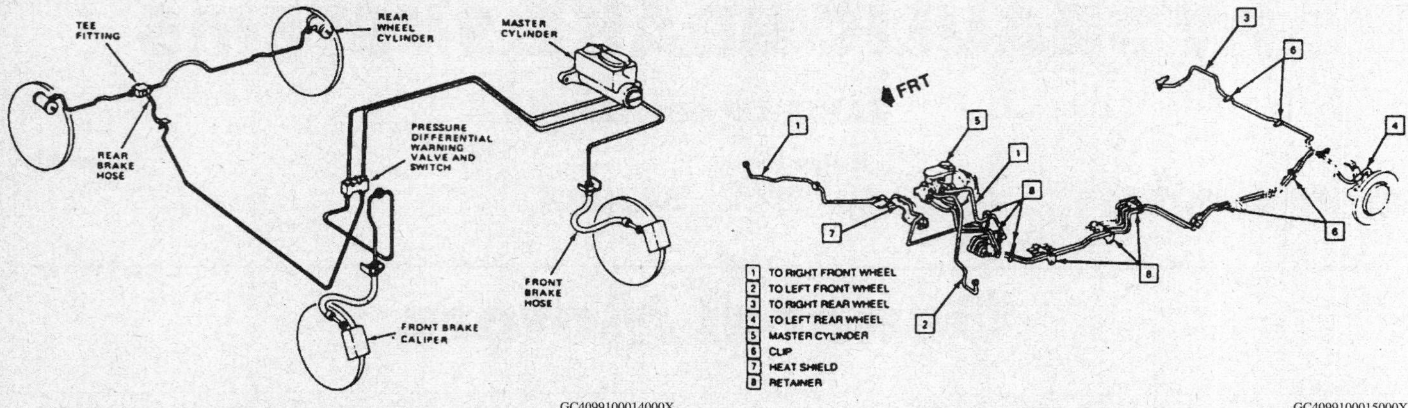

Fig. 1 Front & rear split brake system

Fig. 2 Diagonally split brake system

holds the retainer against the seal until a predetermined pressure is produced at the valve inlet port which overcomes the spring pressure and permits hydraulic pressure to actuate the front disc brakes, **Fig. 7.** The increased pressure into the valve is metered through the valve seal, to the front disc brakes, producing an increased force on the diaphragm. The diaphragm then pulls the pin, in turn pulling the retainer, and reduces the spring pressure on the metering valve seal. Eventually, the pressure reaches a point at which the spring is pulled away by the diaphragm pin and retainer, leaving the metering valve unrestricted, permitting full pressure to pass through the metering valve.

Failure Warning Switch

If the rear brake system fails, the front system pressure forces the switch piston to the right, **Fig. 8.** The switch pin is then forced up into the switch, completing the electrical circuit and activates the dash warning lamp.

When repairs are made and pressure returns to the system, the piston moves to the left, resetting the switch. The detent on the piston requires approximately 100–450 psi to permit full reset of the piston. In event of front brake system failure, the piston moves to the left and the same sequence of events is followed as for rear system failure except the piston resets to the right.

Proportioning Or Pressure Control Valve

During rapid deceleration, a portion of vehicle weight is transferred to the front wheels. This resultant loss of weight at rear wheels must be compensated for to avoid early rear wheel skid. The proportioner or pressure control valve reduces rear brake system pressure, delaying rear wheel skid. When the proportioner or pressure control valve is incorporated in the combination valve assembly, pressure developed within the valve acts against the large end of the piston, overcoming the spring pressure, moving the piston left, **Fig. 9.** The piston then contacts the stem seat and restricts line pressure through the valve.

During normal braking operation, the proportioner or pressure control valve is not functional. Brake fluid flows into the proportioner or pressure control valve between the piston center hole and the valve stem, through the stop plate and to the rear brakes. Spring pressure loads the piston during normal braking, causing it to rest against the stop plate, **Fig. 10.**

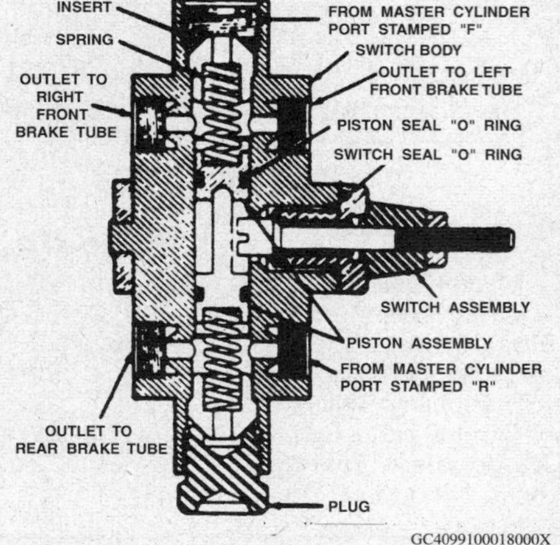

Fig. 3 Pressure differential valve & brake warning lamp switch

On diagonally split brake systems, two proportioners or pressure control valves are used. One controls the lefthand rear brake, the other the righthand rear brake. The proportioners or pressure control valves are installed in the master cylinder rear brake outlet ports, **Fig. 10.**

Brake Distribution Valve & Switch

This switch assembly is used on some diagonally split brake systems and Corvette four-wheel disc brake systems, **Fig. 11.** It is connected to the outlet ports of the master cylinder and to the brake warning lamp and warns the driver if either the primary or secondary brake system has failed.

When hydraulic pressure is equal in both primary and secondary brake systems, the switch remains centered, **Fig. 12.** If pressure fails in one of the systems, the piston moves toward the inoperative side, **Fig. 13.** The shoulder of the piston contacts the switch terminal, providing a ground and lighting the warning lamp.

TROUBLESHOOTING

When troubleshooting the hydraulic brake system, perform the following checks and inspections. If problem still exists within system, refer to **Figs. 14 and 15.**

MASTER CYLINDER INTERNAL FLUID LEAKAGE CHECK

Start engine and depress the brake pedal. If the pedal gradually falls under constant pressure, the hydraulic system may be leaking. Raise the vehicle on a lift and check all tubing lines and backing plates for signs of leakage. It may be necessary to lift or remove the carpeting or floor mats to check for booster or master cylinder leakage.

ROAD TEST

When testing brakes, ensure the road is level and dry. Test brakes at both light and heavy pedal pressure. Do not lock up brakes or slide tires during a brake test.

Check the tires on the vehicle before performing a brake test. Tires should be equally inflated, identical in size and with equal tread pattern. Excessive camber and caster will cause the brakes to pull. An overloaded vehicle will also brake erratically.

DIAGNOSIS & TESTING

Refer to **Fig. 16,** for diagnosis chart.

COMPONENT REPLACEMENT

MASTER CYLINDER

1. Disconnect fluid level sensor retainer and electrical connector.
2. Drain master cylinder reservoir brake fluid into suitable container.
3. Plug hose.
4. Disconnect master cylinder brake pipes. Plug open pipes.
5. Remove mounting nuts and master cylinder.
6. Remove reservoir, as required.
7. Reverse procedure to install, noting the following:

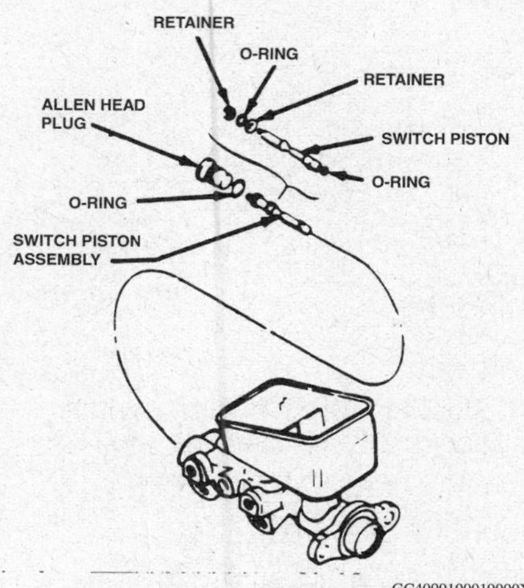

Fig. 4 Dual master cylinder w/built in warning lamp switch

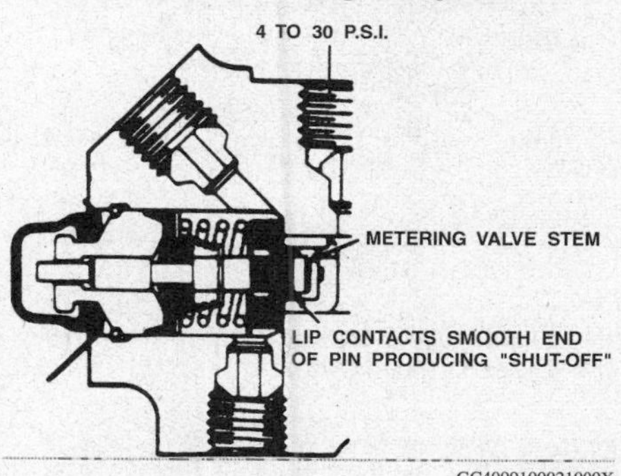

Fig. 6 Metering valve. Initial braking

a. Tighten to specifications.
b. Bleed hydraulic system as outlined under "Brake System Bleed."

COMPONENT SERVICE

MASTER CYLINDER OVERHAUL

EXCEPT AURORA, BONNEVILLE, EIGHTY-EIGHT, LESABRE, LSS, PARK AVENUE, REGENCY & RIVIERA

Disassemble

Refer to **Figs. 17 and 18,** when performing the following procedures.

1. Disconnect and plug hydraulic lines.
2. Remove mounting nuts and master cylinder.
3. Remove reservoir cover and diaphragm. Discard old brake fluid in reservoir.
4. Inspect cover and diaphragm.
5. Remove fluid level switch, if equipped.
6. **On models equipped with compact master cylinder,** remove proportioner valve, **Fig. 18.**
7. **On all models,** depress primary piston and remove lock ring.
8. Plug primary fluid outlet (outlet nearest to cowl when master cylinder is installed), then remove primary and secondary pistons by applying compressed air into secondary fluid outlet.
9. Remove secondary piston spring retainer and seals.
10. Clamp master cylinder in suitable vise and remove reservoir using suitable pry bar, **Fig. 19.**
11. Remove reservoir grommets.
12. Inspect master cylinder bore for corrosion. **Do not use abrasive material on master cylinder bore.**

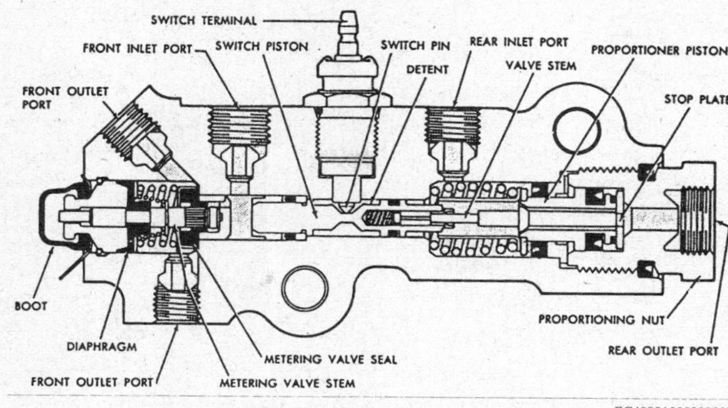

Fig. 5 Combination valve

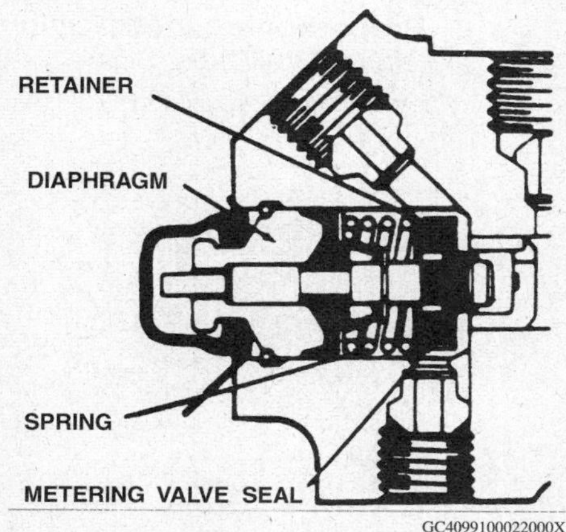

Fig. 7 Metering valve. Continued braking

Assemble

Clean all parts not included in repair kit with suitable brake fluid. **Do not dry with compressed air.** Lubricate all rubber parts with clean brake fluid prior to installation.

1. Lubricate new reservoir grommets with suitable silicone brake lube.
2. Press grommets into master cylinder body. Ensure grommets are properly seated.
3. Lay reservoir upside down on flat, hard surface.
4. Press master cylinder body onto reservoir using rocking motion.
5. Install new seals on secondary piston and spring retainer.
6. Install spring and secondary piston into cylinder.
7. Install primary piston.
8. Depress primary piston into cylinder and install lock ring.
9. Install fluid level switch, if equipped.
10. **On models equipped with compact master cylinder,** install proportioner valve, **Fig. 18.**
11. **On all models,** install diaphragm into reservoir cover and cover onto reservoir.
12. Install master cylinder and bleed brake system.

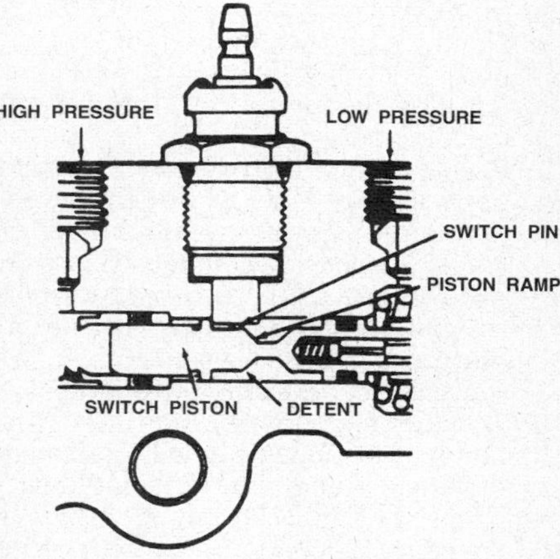

Fig. 8 Failure warning switch. Rear system failure

AURORA, BONNEVILLE, EIGHTY-EIGHT, LESABRE, LSS, PARK AVENUE, REGENCY & RIVIERA

These master cylinders are not serviceable. Master cylinder must be replaced as a complete unit. **Do not attempt to overhaul the master cylinder.**

CORVETTE

1. Remove reservoir cap and diaphragm.
2. Drain fluid into suitable container.
3. Remove master cylinder prime pipe clamp and prime pipe.
4. Remove mounting screw and reservoir, **Fig. 20.**
5. Remove reservoir O-rings.
6. Slightly depress piston and remove retaining ring using suitable retaining ring pliers.
7. Invert cylinder so reservoir wells face downward.
8. Depress primary and secondary pistons until fully bottomed in bore using suitable brass rod or wooden dowel.

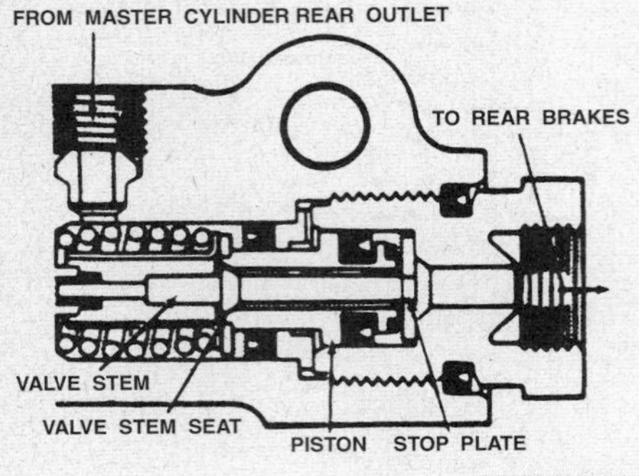

Fig. 9 Proportion

Secondary stop pin should fall freely from cylinder.

9. Gently bump open end of cylinder body against suitable wood piece to dislodge primary piston. Remove primary piston.
10. Gently bump open end of cylinder body against suitable wood piece to dislodge secondary piston and center valve. Remove secondary piston. **Do not remove or disturb screw which retains primary spring to secondary piston.**
11. Remove secondary return spring.
12. Remove secondary piston spring retainer using suitable small screwdriver to lift crimp and allow retainer to slide off piston, **Fig. 21.**
13. Remove secondary piston center valve plunger and spring.
14. Remove primary piston seal retainer using suitable sharp knife or razor blade to cut and remove plastic retaining cup retaining ring, **Fig. 22.**
15. Remove recuperating guide.
16. Remove pistons' rubber seals, **Figs. 23 and 24. Do not damage any piston surfaces, particularly areas where seals seat.**
17. Remove pressure differential switch. **Do not disassemble spring or probe.**
18. Remove end plug and O-ring. **Do not lose small electrical bias spring located just inside end plug.**
19. Remove warning switch. **Keep warning switch and probe together as an assembly.**
20. Remove end plug, O-ring and electrical bias spring.
21. Gently tap cylinder body against suitable wood piece to dislodge proportioning valve spool.
22. Remove proportioning valve spool including O-ring and spacer. **Do not disassemble proportioning valve.**
23. Proportioning valve is lubricated with special grease. **Do not use cleaning solution to clean it or parts included in repair kit.** Clean other parts in suitable denatured alcohol. Dry parts and passages within cylinder using filtered unlubricated compressed air.
24. Reverse procedure to assemble. Ensure seals and parts are lubricated with clean brake fluid.

FAILURE WARNING SWITCH

O-RINGS

PROPORTIONERS

GC4099100026000X

Fig. 10 Proportioners installed in master cylinder

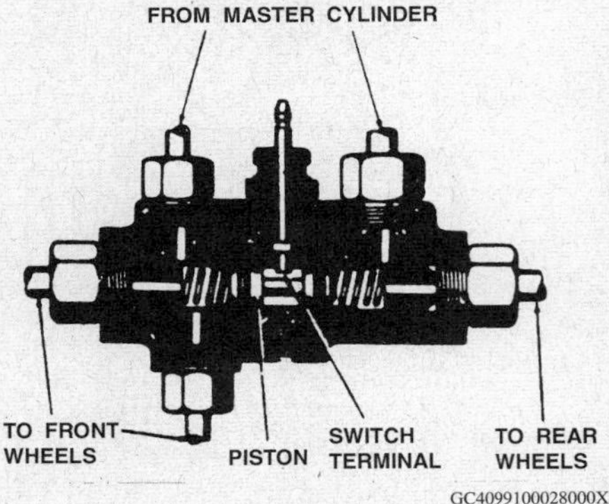

Fig. 12 Brake distribution switch. Normal

WHEEL CYLINDER OVERHAUL

Disassemble

1. Raise and support vehicle.
2. Remove wheel, drum and brake shoes.
3. Disconnect hydraulic line at wheel cylinder. **Do not pull metal line away from cylinder.** Line will separate from cylinder when cylinder is moved away from brake backing plate.
4. Remove mounting screws and wheel cylinder.
5. Remove boots, pistons, springs and cups, **Fig. 25.**

Assemble

1. Clean parts with suitable brake fluid.
2. Inspect cylinder bore. Scored bore may be honed as long as diameter is not increased by more than .005 inch.
3. Ensure hands are clean before proceeding.
4. Lubricate cylinder wall and rubber cups with suitable brake fluid.
5. Install springs, cups, pistons and boots.
6. Wipe end of hydraulic line to remove any foreign matter and place wheel cylinder in position.
7. Enter tubing into cylinder and start threads on fitting.
8. Secure cylinder to backing plate and complete tightening of tubing fitting.

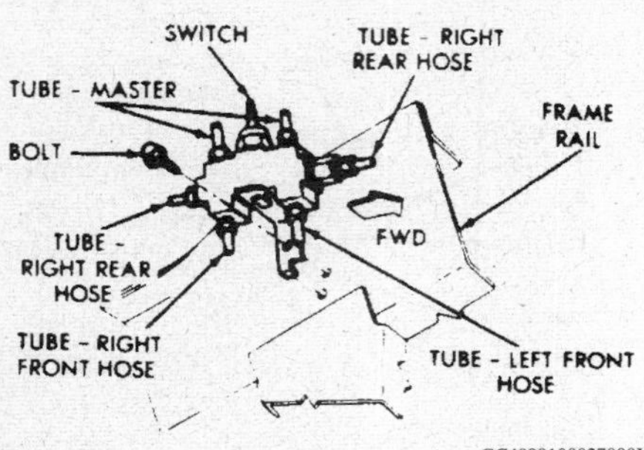

Fig. 11 Distribution switch. Diagonally split brake systems

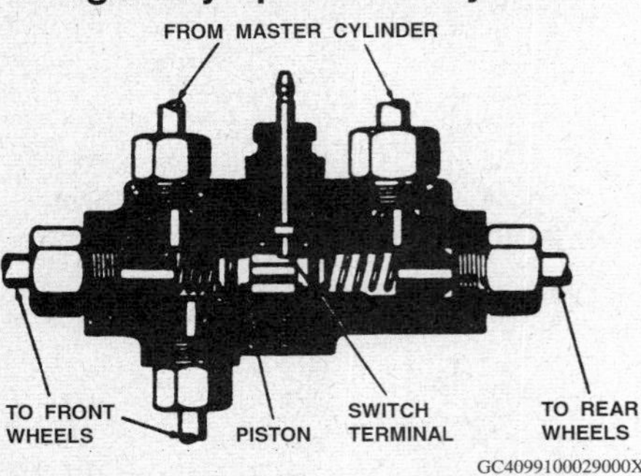

Fig. 13 Brake distribution switch. Failed

9. Install brake shoes, drum and wheel.
10. Bleed brake system and adjust brakes.

BRAKE SYSTEM BLEED

MANUAL

Pressure bleeding is recommended for all hydraulic systems. However, if a pressure bleeder is unavailable, use the following procedure. **Brake fluid damages painted surfaces. Immediately clean any spilled fluid.**

1. Remove vacuum reserve by pumping brakes several times with engine off.
2. Fill master cylinder reservoir with clean brake fluid. **Do not let reservoir fall below half full during bleeding procedure.**
3. If necessary, bleed master cylinder as follows:
   a. Loosen master cylinder forward brake line connection until fluid flows from reservoir, then tighten brake line.
   b. Have assistant to slowly depress brake pedal one time and hold.
   c. Loosen front brake line connection and purge air from cylinder.
   d. Tighten connection and slowly release brake pedal.
   e. Wait 15 seconds, then repeat previous steps until all air is purged.
   f. Bleed rearward brake line connection by repeating previous steps.
4. Loosen and tighten bleeder valves at all four wheels.
5. Bleed calipers or wheel cylinders in sequence outlined under "Bleed Sequence."
6. Place one end of transparent tube over bleeder valve and submerge other end

into transparent container filled with clean brake fluid, **Fig. 26.**

7. Have assistant slowly depress brake pedal one time and hold.
8. Loosen bleeder valve and purge air from wheel cylinder or caliper. Tighten bleeder screw and slowly release pedal.
9. Wait 15 seconds and repeat previous steps until all air is bled from system.

PRESSURE

1. Loosen and tighten bleeder valves at all four wheels.
2. Install suitable bleeder adapter to master cylinder using diaphragm type pressure bleeder, **Fig. 26.**
3. Charge bleeder ball to 20–25 psi.
4. Connect pressure bleeder line to adapter.
5. Open line valve on pressure bleeder and depress bleed-off valve on adapter until small amount of brake fluid is released.
6. Raise and support vehicle.
7. Bleed calipers or wheel cylinders in sequence as outlined under "Bleed Sequence."
8. Place one end of transparent tube over bleeder valve and submerge other end into transparent container filled with clean brake fluid, **Fig. 26.**
9. Open bleeder valve ½–¾ turn and allow fluid to flow into container until all air is purged from line.

BLEED SEQUENCE

Rear wheel drive models: if manual bleeding, righthand rear-lefthand rear-righthand front-lefthand front; if pressure bleeding, bleed front brakes together and rear brakes together.

Front wheel drive models: righthand rear-lefthand front-lefthand rear-righthand front.

HYDRAULIC SYSTEM FLUSH

If brake fluid is old, contaminated, or whenever new hydraulic system parts are installed, the system must be flushed. Bleed brakes, allowing at least one quart of clean brake fluid to pass through system. Any rubber parts in the hydraulic system which were exposed to contaminated fluid must be replaced.

CAUSE \ SYMPTOM	Excessive Brake Pedal Travel	Brake Pedal Travel Gradually Increases	Excessive Brake Pedal Effort	Excessive Braking Action	Brakes Slow To Respond	Brakes Slow To Release	Brakes Drag	Uneven Braking Action (Side To Side)	Uneven Braking Action (Front To Rear)	Scraping Noise From Brakes	Brakes Squeak During Application*	Brakes Squeak During Stop*	Brakes Chatter (Roughness)	Brakes Groan At End Of Stop*	Brake Warning Lamp Glows During Stop
Leaking Brake Line or Connection	X	XX							X						XX
Leaking Wheel Cylinder or Piston Seal	X	XX		X				X							X
Leaking Master Cylinder	X	XX													X
Air in Brake System	XX								X						XX
Contaminated or Improper Brake Fluid					X	X	X								X
Leaking Vacuum System			XX		X										
Restricted Air Passage in Power Head			X		XX	X									
Damaged Power Head			X	X	X	X	X								
Improperly Assembled Power Head Valving			X	X	X	X	XX								
Worn Out Brake Lining-Replace			X	X				X	X	X	X	X		X	
Uneven Brake Lining Wear-Replace and Correct	X			X				X	X	X	X	XX		X	X
Glazed Brake Lining			XX		X			X	X		X	X			
Incorrect Lining Material-Replace			X	X				X	X			X		X	
Contaminated Brake Lining-Replace				XX				XX	XX	X	X	X		X	
Linings Damaged by Abusive Use-Replace			X	XX				X	X	X	X	X		X	
Excessive Brake Lining Dust			X	XX				XX	XX		X	XX		X	
Heat Spotted or Scored Brake Drums or Rotors				X				X	X		X	X	XX	X	
Out-of-Round or Vibrating Brake Drums												X	XX		
Improper Thickness Variation on Brake Rotors													XX		
Excessive Lateral Run-Out													X		
Faulty Automatic Adjusters	X						X	X	X						X
Incorrect Wheel Cylinder Sizes			X	X				X	X						
Weak or Incorrect Brake Shoe Retention Springs				X		X	XX	X	X	XX	X	XX			
Brake Assembly Attachments-Missing or Loose	X						X	X	X	X		X	X	X	
Insufficient Brake Shoe Guide Lubricant						X	X	X	X	XX	XX				
Restricted Brake Fluid Passage or Sticking Wheel Cylinder Piston		X	X		X	X	X	X	X						
Faulty Metering Valve	X		X	X	X	X	X		X						X
Brake Pedal Linkage Interference or Binding			X		X	XX	XX								
Improperly Adjusted Parking Brake							X								
Drums Tapered or Threaded										XX					
Incorrect Front End Alignment								XX							
Incorrect Tire Pressure								X	X						
Incorrect Wheel Bearing Adjustment	X									X			X		
Loose Front Suspension Attachments								X		XX			X	X	
Out-of-Balance Wheel Assemblies													XX		
Operator Riding Brake Pedal	X	X	X				X		X					X	
Improperly Adjusted Booster Pushrod	X					X	XX								X
Sticking Wheel Cylinder or Caliper Pistons			X			X	X	X	X						
Faulty Proportioning Valve			X		X	X	X								

XX — Indicates more probable cause(s) X — Indicates other causes *May be a normal condition.

GC4099100030010X

Fig. 14 Brake diagnosis chart. Front disc/rear drum system

CAUSE / SYMPTOM	Excessive Brake Pedal Travel	Brake Pedal Travel Gradually Increases	Excessive Brake Pedal Effort	Excessive Braking Action	Brakes Slow To Respond	Brakes Slow To Release	Brakes Drag	Uneven Braking Action (Side To Side)	Uneven Braking Action (Front To Rear)	Scraping Noise From Brakes	Brakes Squeak During Application*	Brakes Squeak During Stop*	Brakes Chatter (Roughness)	Brakes Groan At End Of Stop*	Brake Warning Lamp Glows
Leaking Brake Line or Connection	X	XX	X						X						XX
Leaking Piston Seal	X	XX	X	X				X	X						X
Leaking Master Cylinder	X	XX	X						X						X
Air in Brake System	XX		X						X						XX
Contaminated or Improper Brake Fluid	X				X	X	X	X	X						X
Leaking Vacuum System			XX		X										
Restricted Air Passage in Power Head		X	X		XX	X									
Damaged Power Head		X	X	X	X	XX									
Worn Out Brake Lining			X	X				X	X	X	X	X		X	
Uneven Brake Lining Wear-Replace	X			X				X	X	X	X	XX		X	X
Glazed Brake Lining			XX		X			X	X		X	X			
Incorrect Lining Material-Replace			X	X		X		X	X			X		X	
Contaminated Brake Lining-Replace				XX		X		XX	XX	X	X	X		X	
Linings Damaged by Abusive Use-Replace			X	XX				X	X	X	X	X		X	
Heat Spotted or Scored Discs				X				X	X		X	X	XX	X	
Improper Thickness Variation	X												XX		
Excessive Lateral Run-Out	X												X		
Automatic Adjuster Problem	X	X					X	X	X						X
Brake Assembly Attachments-Missing or Loose	X						X	X	X	X		X	X	X	
Restricted Brake Fluid Passage		X	X		X	X	X	X	X						X
Improperly Adjusted Stoplamp Switch Or Cruise Control Vacuum Dump							X								
Metering Valve Problem		X	X	X	X	X	X		X						X
Proportioning Valve Problem		X	X	X	X	X	X		X						X
Brake Pedal Linkage Interference or Binding			X		X	XX	XX								
Improperly Adjusted Parking Brake							X		X						
Improper Length Booster Pushrod	X			X		X	XX		X						
Incorrect Front End Alignment								XX							
Incorrect Tire Pressure								X	X						
Incorrect Wheel Bearing Adjustment	X									X			X		
Loose Front Suspension Attachments							X	X		XX			X	X	
Out-of-Balance Wheel Assemblies													XX		
Operator Riding Brake Pedal			X				X		X					X	
Sticking Caliper or Wheel Cylinder Pistons					X	X	XX	X	X						
Park Brake Switch Circuit Grounded															XX
Park Brake Not Releasing						X		X							XX

XX — Indicates more probable cause(s)

X — Indicates other causes

*May be a normal condition.

GC4099100030020X

Fig. 15 Brake diagnosis chart. Four wheel disc system

The same types of brake trouble are encountered with power brakes as with standard brakes. Before checking power brake system for source of trouble, refer to the brake system diagnosis charts. After these possible causes have been eliminated, check for cause as outlined below:

HARD PEDAL

CAUSE	CORRECTION
Broken or damaged hydraulic brake pipes.	Inspect and replace as necessary.
Vacuum failure.	Check for: Faulty vacuum check valve or grommet. Replace. Collapsed or damaged vacuum hose. Replace. Plugged or loose vacuum fitting. Repair. Faulty air valve seal or support plate seal. Replace. Damaged floating control valve. Replace. Bad stud welds on front or rear housing or power head. Replace unless easily repaired.
Faulty diaphragm.	Replace.
Restricted air filter element.	Replace.
Worn or distorted reaction plate or levers.	Replace plate or levers.
Cracked or broken power pistons or retainer.	Replace power pistons and piston rod retainer.

GRABBY BRAKES
(Apparent Off-On Condition)

CAUSE	CORRECTION
Broken or damaged hydraulic brake pipes.	Inspect and replace as necessary.
Insufficient fluid in master cylinder.	Fill reservoirs with approved brake fluid. Check for leaks.
Faulty master cylinder seals.	Repair or replace as necessary.
Cracked master cylinder casting.	Replace.
Leaks in pipes or connections at disc brake calipers or wheel cylinders.	Inspect and repair as necessary.
Air in hydraulic system.	Bleed system.

BRAKES FAIL TO RELEASE

CAUSE	CORRECTION
Blocked passage in power piston.	Inspect and repair or replace as necessary.
Air valve sticking shut.	Check for proper lubrication of air valve "O" ring.
Broken piston return spring.	Replace.
Broken air valve spring.	Replace.
Tight pedal linkage.	Repair or replace as necessary.

GC4099100031000X

Fig. 16 Power brake diagnosis chart

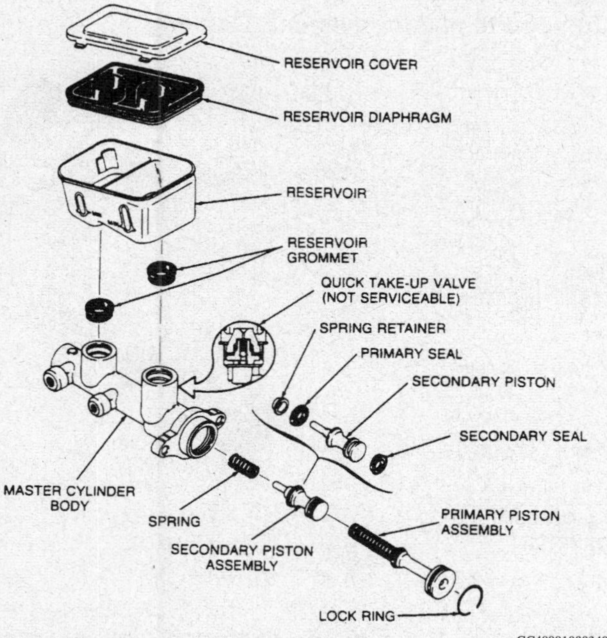

Fig. 17 Dual master cylinder assembly. Composite type

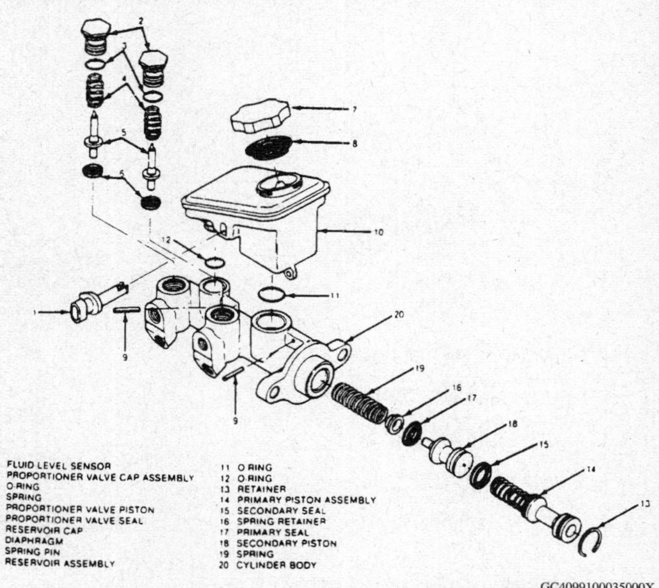

Fig. 18 Compact master cylinder assembly

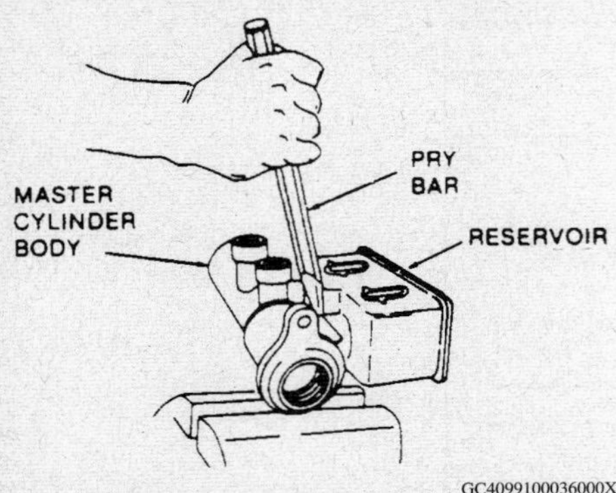

Fig. 19 Master cylinder reservoir removal. Composite type

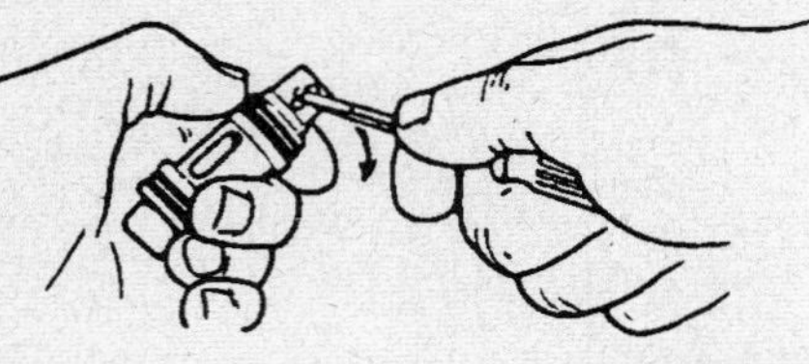

Fig. 21 Lifting crimp on secondary spring retainer. Corvette

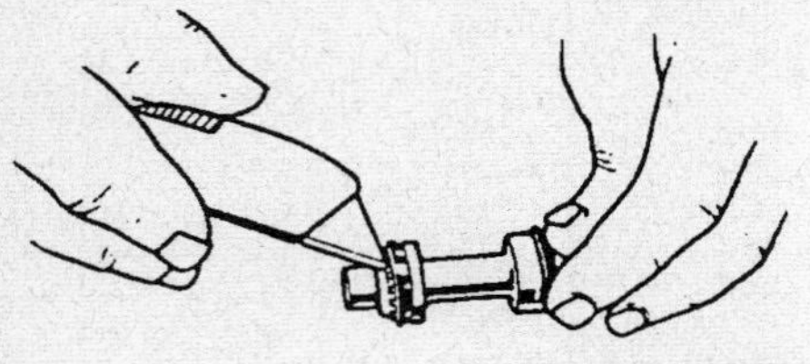

Fig. 22 Seal retainer cutting. Corvette

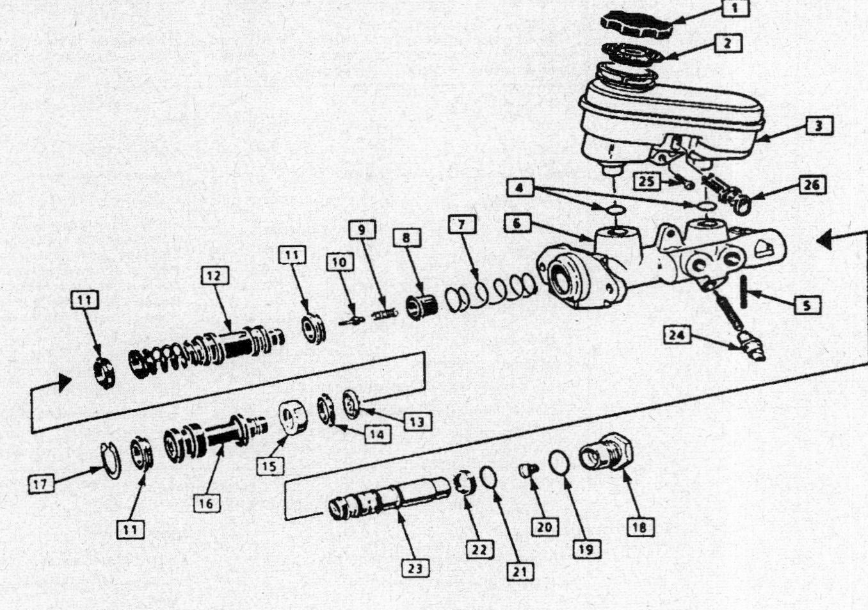

1 RESERVOIR CAP
2 RESERVOIR CAP DIAPHRAGM
3 RESERVOIR BODY
4 RESERVOIR 'O' RING
5 SECONDARY PISTON STOP PIN
6 CYLINDER BODY
7 SECONDARY RETURN SPRING
8 SECONDARY SPRING RETAINER
9 CENTER VALVE SPRING
10 CENTER VALVE PLUNGER
11 'L' TYPE CUP SEAL
12 SECONDARY PISTON ASSEMBLY
13 PRIMARY CUP RETAINING RING
14 RECUPERATING TYPE CUP SEAL
15 RECUPERATING GUIDE
16 PRIMARY PISTON
17 RETAINING RING
18 ENG PLUG
19 END PLUG 'O' RING
20 ELECTRICAL BIAS SPRING
21 PROPORTIONING VALVE O-RING
22 PROPORTIONING VALVE SPACER
23 PROPORTIONING VALVE/PRESSURE DIFFERENTIAL ASSEMBLY
24 PRESSURE DIFFERENTIAL WARNING SWITCH ASSEMBLY
25 RESERVOIR RETAINER SCREW
26 FLUID LEVEL SWITCH ASSEMBLY

GC4099200037000X

Fig. 20 Composite master cylinder. Corvette

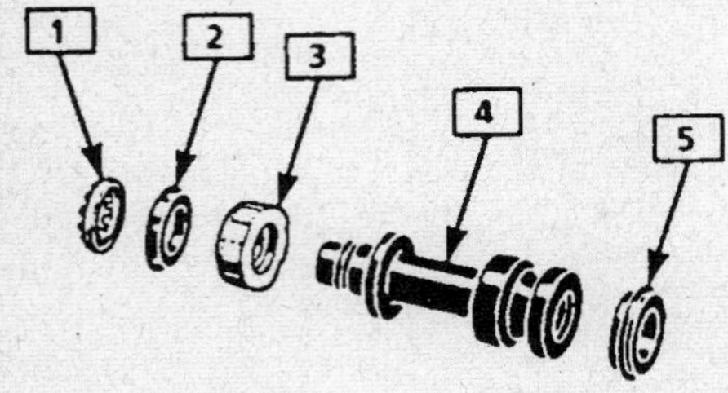

1 PRIMARY CUP RETAINING RING
2 RECUPERATING TYPE CUP SEAL
3 RECUPERATING GUIDE
4 PRIMARY PISTON
5 'L' TYPE CUP SEAL

GC4099200040000X

Fig. 23 Primary piston components. Corvette

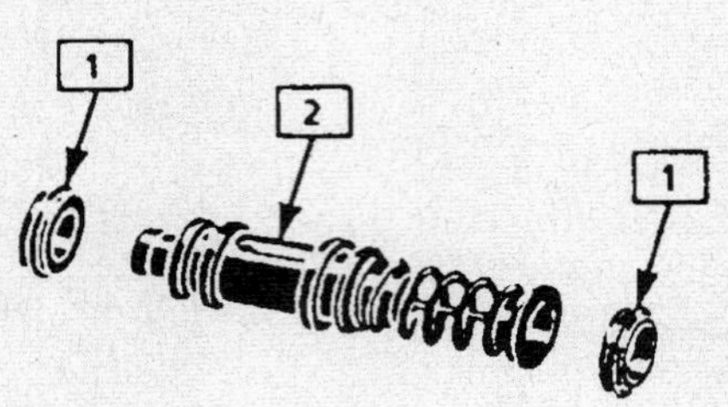

1 'L' TYPE CUP SEAL
2 SECONDARY PISTON ASSEMBLY

GC4099200041000X

Fig. 24 Secondary piston components. Corvette

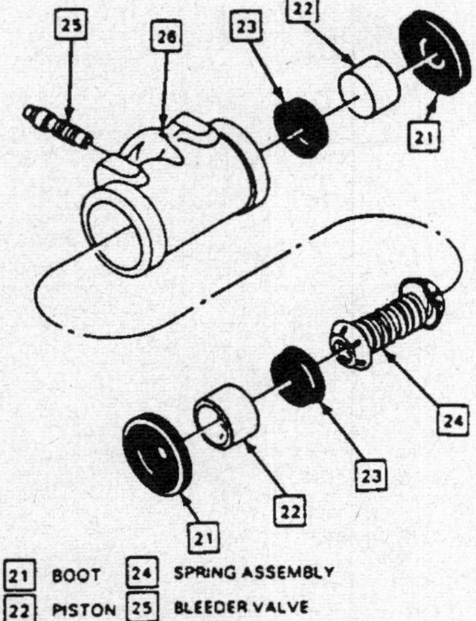

Fig. 25 Exploded view of wheel cylinder

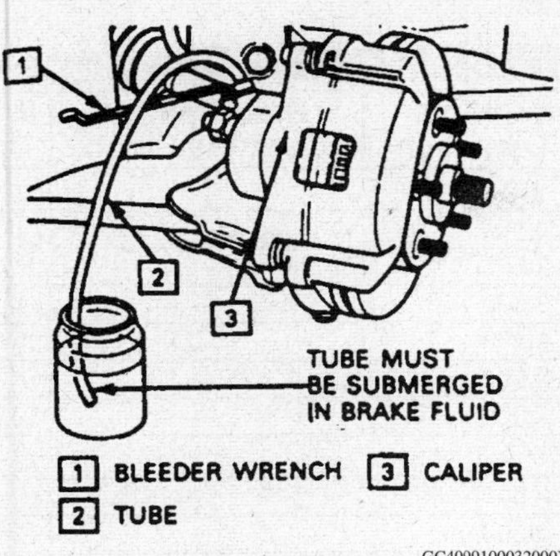

Fig. 26 Brake bleed

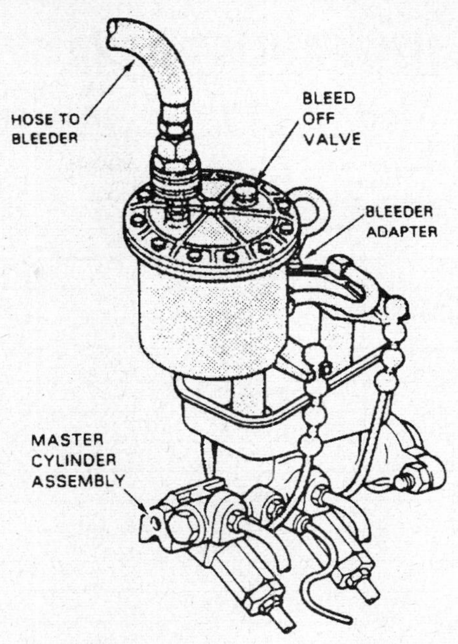

Fig. 27 Pressure bleeder adapter installation

HYDRAULIC BRAKE SYSTEM SPECIFICATIONS

Model	Year	Master Cylinder Bore Dia., Inch	Front Caliper Bore Dia., Inch	Rear Caliper Bore Dia., Inch	Wheel Cylinder Bore Dia., Inch
BUICK					
Century	1998–2002	1.000	2.500	1.500	.874
LeSabre	1998	1.000④	2.520	—	.937
	1999	1.000④	2.500	—	.937
	2000–02	1.000④	2.500	1.500	—
Park Avenue	1998	1.000④	2.520	1.500	—
	1999–2002	1.000④	2.500	1.500	—
Regal	1998–2002	1.000	2.500	1.500	—
Riviera	1998–99	1.000④	2.520	1.500	—
Skylark	1998	.874	2.244	—	.689
CADILLAC					
Catera	1998–2001	①	2.244	1.574	—
DeVille	1998	1.000	2.500	1.500	.937
	1999–2002	1.000	2.500	1.500	—
Eldorado	1998–2002	1.000	2.500	1.500	—
Seville	1998–2002	1.000	2.520	1.500	.937
CHEVROLET/GEO					
Camaro	1998–2002	1.000	2.500	1.595	.810
Cavalier	1998–2002	.874	2.244	—	.689
Corvette	1998–2002	.930	1.500③	1.590	—
Lumina	1998–2002	.945	1.654	—	.874
Malibu	1998–2002	1.000	2.362	—	.874
Metro	1998–2001	.810	1.889	—	.685
Monte Carlo	1998–2002	.945	1.654	—	.874
Prizm	1998–2002	②	2.128	—	.688
OLDSMOBILE					
Achieva	1998	.874	2.244	—	.689
Alero	1999–2002	1.000	2.360	1.500	.874
Aurora	1998–99	1.000④	2.520	1.500	—
	2001–02	1.000④	2.500	1.50	—

Continued

HYDRAULIC BRAKE SYSTEM SPECIFICATIONS—Continued

Model	Year	Master Cylinder Bore Dia., Inch	Front Caliper Bore Dia., Inch	Rear Caliper Bore Dia., Inch	Wheel Cylinder Bore Dia., Inch
OLDSMOBILE					
Cutlass	1998–99	1.000	2.362	—	.874
Eighty-Eight	1998	1.000④	2.500	—	.937
	1999	1.000④	2.500	—	.937
Intrigue	1998–2002	1.000	2.500	1.500	—
LSS	1998	1.000④	2.500	—	.937
Regency	1998	1.000④	2.500	—	.937
PONTIAC					
Bonneville	1998	1.000④	2.500	—	.937
	1999	1.000④	2.500	—	.937
	2000–02	1.000④	2.500	1.500	—
Firebird	1998–2002	1.000	2.500	1.595	.810
Grand Am	1998	.874	2.244	—	.689
	1999–2002	1.000	2.360	1.500	.874
Grand Prix	1998–2002	1.000	2.500	1.500	—
Sunfire	1998–2002	.874	2.244	—	.689

① — Primary piston, .960 inch; secondary piston, .812 inch.
② — Less ABS, .812 inch; w/ABS, .875 inch.
③ — Dual piston caliper.
④ — Master cylinder cannot be overhauled.

TIGHTENING SPECIFICATIONS

Year	Component	Torque Ft. Lbs.
1998–2002	ABS Brake Modulator To Master Cylinder Banjo Nuts	18
	Brake Combination Valve Pipe Fittings	24
	Brake Pipe Fittings At Master Cylinder	②
	Gear Cover To Master Cylinder To Torx Screws	36①
	Master Cylinder Mounting Nuts	18–20③
	Motor Pack To Brake Modulator Torx Screws	44①
	Power Steering Reservoir Bracket Bolt	62①

① — Inch lbs.

② — Acheiva, Alero, Cavalier, Cutlass, Grand Am, Malibu & Sunfire, 17 ft. lbs.; Century, Eighty-Eight, Grand Prix, LSS, Lumina, Regal, Regency & Riviera, 11 ft. lbs.; Corvette & Intrigue, 18 ft. lbs.; 1998–2000 Aurora, Bonneville, Deville, Eldorado, LeSabre, Park Avenue & Seville, 11 ft. lbs., Camaro, Firebird & 2001–02 Aurora, Bonneville, Deville, Eldorado, LeSabre, Park Avenue & Seville, 24 ft. lbs.; Metro & Prizm, 12 ft. lbs.;

③ — All Except Metro & Prizm, 18–20 ft. lbs.; Metro & Prizm models, 115 inch lbs.

Saturn

NOTE: On Air Bag Equipped Models, Refer To "Air Bag System Precautions" Located In The Front Of This Manual For System Disarming & Arming Procedures.

NOTE: Refer To "Computer Relearn Procedures" Located In The Front Of This Manual When Battery Power To The Computer Has Been Interrupted.

INDEX

DESCRIPTION

These vehicles use a diagonally split hydraulic system, **Fig. 1.** This system combines the lefthand front and righthand rear brake on one hydraulic circuit, while the righthand front and lefthand rear are on the other.

Installed in master cylinder are integral brake proportioning valves, which limit the fluid pressure to the rear brakes after a predetermined rear brake pressure has been reached. These valves are used to minimize the occurrence of rear wheel lock-up when the brakes are applied and the vehicle is lightly loaded in the rear.

A brake fluid level sensor, located in the brake fluid reservoir, will activate the brake warning lamp if the brake fluid becomes low. After the brake fluid level is corrected and a moderately high brake pedal force is applied, the brake warning lamp should go off.

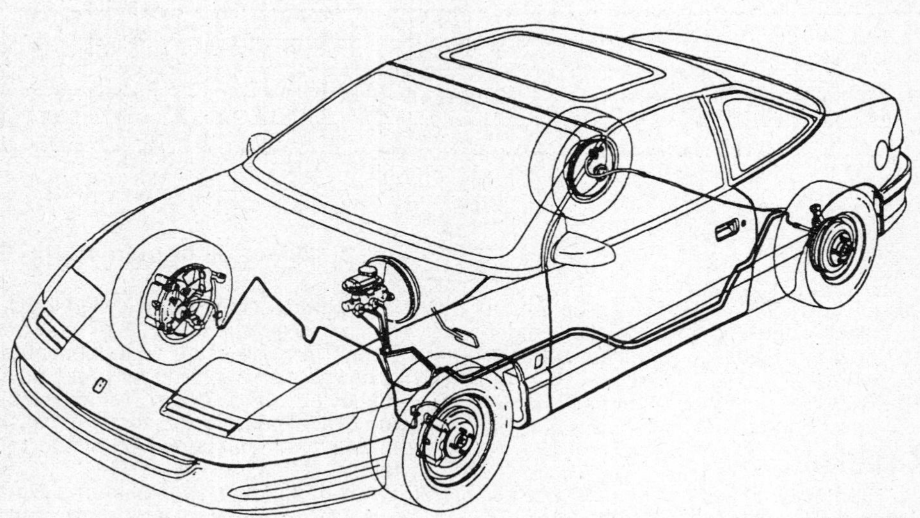

Fig. 1 Diagonally split brake system

TROUBLESHOOTING

When troubleshooting the hydraulic brake system, perform the following checks and inspections. If a fault still exists within the system, refer to the brake system diagnosis chart, **Fig. 2,** and the troubleshooting chart, **Fig. 3.**

ROAD TESTING

When testing brakes, ensure the road is level and dry. Test brakes at both light and heavy pedal pressure. Do not lock up brakes or slide tires during a brake test.

Check the tires on the vehicle before performing a brake test. Tires should be equally inflated, identical in size and of equal tread pattern. Excessive camber and caster will cause the brakes to pull. An overloaded vehicle will also brake erratically.

FLUID LEAKS

Start engine and depress the brake pedal. If the pedal gradually falls under constant pressure, the hydraulic system may be leaking. Raise and support vehicle and check all tubing lines and backing plates for signs of leakage. It may be necessary to lift or remove the carpeting or floor mats to check for booster or master cylinder leakage.

COMPONENT REPLACEMENT

MASTER CYLINDER

1. Remove brake fluid level sensor electrical connector.
2. Remove master cylinder brake line fitting nuts. **Plug open lines and fittings.**
3. Remove mounting nuts and master cylinder.
4. Reverse procedure to install. Tighten to specifications.

FLUID RESERVOIR

S-SERIES

1. Remove master cylinder as outlined under "Component Replacement."
2. Wipe reservoir cap clean, remove cap and inspect reservoir cap and diaphragm for cuts, nicks or deformation. Replace damaged parts, as required.
3. Drain reservoir brake fluid into suitable container.
4. **On models equipped with anti-lock brakes,** remove modulator and motor pack.
5. **On all models,** remove brake fluid level sensor.
6. Place master cylinder in suitable vice. **Do not clamp on master cylinder body.**
7. Drive out spring pins using suitable ⅛ inch punch, **Fig. 4.**
8. Pull reservoir out of cylinder body and remove reservoir bayonets' O-rings, **Fig. 5.**

18

X — Most Probable Cause(s)
● — Possible Causes

COMPLAINT—CONDITION / CAUSE	Low Brake Fluid Level	Leaking Brak Pipe or Connection	Leaking Wheel Cylinder or Piston Seal	Leaking Master Cylinder	Air in Brake System	Contaminated or Improper Brake Fluid	Leaking Vacuum System	Restricted Air Passage in Vacuum Booster	Damaged Vacuum Booster	Worn Out Brake Lining	Glazed Brake Lining	Uneven Brake Lining Wear	Incorrect Lining Material	Contaminated Brake Lining	Excessive Brake Lining Dust	Heat Spotted/Scored Drums/Rotors	Out-of-Round Brake Drums	Excessive Rotor Thickness Variation	Excessive Rotor/Hub Lateral Runout	Faulty Automatic Adjusters	Weak or Incorrect Brake Shoe Springs	Brake Asm. Bolts Missing or Loose	Insufficient Brake Shoe Guide Lubricant	Restricted Fluid Passage	Sticking Wheel Cylinder/Caliper Piston	Incorrect Stoplamp Switch Adjustment	Brake Pedal Linkage Interference/Binding	Improperly Adjusted Park Brake	Park Brake Cable Seized	Drum Tapered or Threaded	Operator Riding Brake Pedal	Improper Booster Pushrod Length	Caliper Not Sliding Freely
Excessive Brake Pedal Travel	●	●	●	●	X							●							●	●		●									●	●	●
Brake Pedal Travel Gradually Increases		X	X	X																											●		
Excessive Brake Pedal Effort	●						X	●	●	●	X		●		●									●	●		●				●		
Excessive Braking Action			●						●	●		●	●	X	X	●					●												
Brakes Slow to Respond						●	●	X	●		●													●	●		●						
Brakes Slow to Release						●		●	●												●		●	●	●		X		●			●	
Brakes Drag						●			●											●	●	●	●	●	●	X	●	X	●		●	X	X
Uneven Braking Action (Side-to-Side)		●	●							●	●	●	●	X	X	●				●	●	●	●	●	●								
Uneven Braking Action (Front-to-Rear)		●			●					●	●	●	●	X	X	●				●	●	●	●	●	●				●		●		
Scraping Noise from Brakes										●		●		●	●						X	●	X							X			●
Brakes Squeak During Application										●	●	●		●	●	●			●		●		X										
Brakes Squeak During Stop										●	●	●	●	●	X	●	●				X	●									●		
Brakes Pulsate (Roughness)																X	X	X	●			●				●							X
Brakes Groan at End of Stop										●			●	●	●	●						●											
Brake Warning Lamp Glows	X	●	●	●																													

G34099100002000A

Fig. 2 Brake diagnosis chart

9. Clean reservoir with clean denatured alcohol and inspect for cracks or deformation. Replace reservoir, as required.
10. Reverse procedure to install. Install new O-rings.

L-SERIES

1. Remove master cylinder as outlined under "Component Replacement."
2. Unclip hold down clamps and remove reservoir by pulling upward.
3. Reverse procedure to install. Tighten to specifications.

COMPONENT SERVICE

MASTER CYLINDER OVERHAUL

Disassemble

1. Remove master cylinder as outlined under "Component Replacement."
2. Wipe reservoir cap clean, remove cap and inspect reservoir cap and diaphragm for cuts, nicks or deformation. Replace damaged parts, as required
3. Drain reservoir brake fluid into suitable container.
4. **On models equipped with anti-lock brakes,** remove modulator and motor pack.
5. **On all models,** remove brake fluid level sensor.
6. Remove reservoir as outlined under "Component Replacement."
7. While depressing master cylinder piston, remove retainer clip, **Fig. 6.**
8. Apply low pressure non-lubricated compressed air into upper brake fluid output port, **Fig. 7.** This will facilitate removal of primary and secondary pistons as well as spring and spring retainer.
9. Clean parts with clean denatured alcohol. Dry with unlubricated, low pressure compressed air. Blow out cylinder body passages.
10. Inspect pistons and seals for nicks, cuts, cracks, wear or corrosion. Replace worn or damaged parts, as required.
11. Inspect master cylinder bore for scoring or corrosion. If cylinder bore is damaged, replace master cylinder. **Do not hone master cylinder bore.**

Assemble

1. Lubricate secondary seal and master cylinder bore with clean brake fluid.
2. Install spring and secondary piston into master cylinder bore, **Fig. 8.**
3. Lubricate primary seal and master cylinder bore with clean brake fluid.
4. Install primary piston into master cylinder bore.
5. While depressing master cylinder piston, install retainer clip.
6. Install reservoir as outlined under "Component Replacement."
7. Install brake fluid level sensor.
8. **On models equipped with anti-lock brakes,** install modulator and motor pack.
9. **On all models,** install master cylinder as outlined under "Component Replacement."

BRAKE SYSTEM BLEED

Brake fluid is corrosive to painted surfaces. Care must be taken not to allow brake fluid to come in contact with painted surfaces on vehicle.

When bleeding the brake system, always bleed righthand rear wheel circuit first, followed by the lefthand front, lefthand rear and, finally, righthand front.

MANUAL BLEED

1. Fill master cylinder reservoir. Keep reservoir at least half full during bleeding procedure.
2. If master cylinder is suspected to have air trapped inside, it must be bled before bleeding brake lines. Bleed master cylinder as follows:
   a. Depress brake pedal slowly one time and hold.
   b. Loosen front brake line at master cylinder and allow brake fluid to flow from front master cylinder port.
   c. Tighten front brake line to master cylinder.
   d. Repeat previous steps until all air is removed from master cylinder bore.
3. Loosen and slightly tighten bleeder valves at all four wheels. Repair any broken, stripped or frozen valves at this time.
4. Proceed to appropriate wheel first and

Complaint/Condition	Possible Cause(s)	Correction(s)
Pedal Feel		
Excessive Pedal Travel	Air in brake system.	Bleed brake system.
	Front or rear brakes not adjusting to lining wear.	Check adjuster mechanism and replace or repair as needed.
	Leaking wheel cylinder or caliper piston seal.	Replace wheel cylinder or overhaul caliper
	Leaking at brake line or hose connections.	Tighten connection. Replace line or hose.
	Internal master cylinder seal leak.	Overhaul or replace master cylinder.
	Uneven lining wear or damaged lining.	Replace lining.
	Rotor or drum out of specifications (i.e. rotor too thin, parallelism, out of round, bell shaped etc.).	Replace rotor, or drum.
	Improper vacuum booster to master cylinder length.	Replace booster and pushrod.
Pedal Creeps Down	Internal master cylinder seal leak or defective master cylinder bore.	Repair or replace master cylinder.
	Leaking wheel cylinder or caliper piston seal.	Replace wheel cylinder or overhaul caliper
	Leaking at brake line or hose connections.	Tighten connection. Replace lines or hose.
	Damaged vacuum booster check valve or grommet.	Replace check valve and grommet.
Pedal Pulses	Rotor or drum out of specifications (i.e. lateral runout, parallelism, out of round, bell shaped etc.).	Replace or turn rotor or drum.
	Worn out linings or linings wearing unevenly.	Replace linings.
	Wheel bearings worn.	Replace wheel bearing.
	Damaged suspension, knuckle or axle.	Replace defective parts.

G34099100003010X

Fig. 3 Brake system troubleshooting chart (Part 1 of 6)

Complaint/Condition	Possible Cause(s)	Correction(s)
Excessive Pedal Effort	Leaking or damaged vacuum booster (i.e. cut diaphragm, restricted vacuum hose, damaged vacuum check valve, cracked power piston, restricted air passages)	Replace booster.
	Worn out brake linings (glazed)	Replace linings.
	Damage to braking surface of rotor or drum.	Replace rotor or drum.
	Crimped brake line or collapsed brake hose.	Replace line or hose.
	Engine out of specifications.	Check engine to specification.
Pedal Goes to the Floor	Low fluid level, large amount of air in system.	Bleed brake system.
	Broken brake line or brake hose.	Replace line or hose.
	Cut, torn or nicked master cylinder secondary seals.	Repair or replace master cylinder.
	Brake pedal not connected to push rod.	Check connection and repair.
	Wheel cylinder or caliper piston falls out.	Check assembly and repair.

G34099100003020X

Fig. 3 Brake system troubleshooting chart (Part 2 of 6)

Complaint/Condition	Possible Cause(s)	Correction(s)
Noise		
Squeal/Scrape While Not Braking	Worn linings, sensor scraping on rotor (normal).	Replace linings.
	Loose drum brake component (spring, lever, adjuster, etc.).	Check drum brake and repair.
	Loose front suspension attachments.	Tighten attachments or replace.
	Caliper interference with rotor.	Check clearance and repair.
	Bent or cracked suspension parts.	Replace components.
	Drum or rotor contacting backing plate or dust shield.	Check clearance and repair.
Squeal/Scrape While Braking	Linings worn out, shoe contacting drum or rotor.	Replace linings.
	Lack of lubrication on backing plate or on adjuster screw.	Lubricate backing plate or adjuster screw.
	Lack of lubrication on caliper sliding surfaces.	Lubricate.
	Lack of lubrication on brake pedal attachments.	Lubricate.
	Damage to insulator between disc brake shoe and caliper piston.	Replace insulator and pads as needed.
	Hot spots or worn surface on drum or rotor.	Replace rotor or drum.
	Weak hold down springs or worn drum brake components.	Replace drum brake springs.
Chatters/Rattles	Hot spots or worn surface on drum or rotor.	Replace drum or rotor.
	Rotor or drum out of specifications (i.e. lateral runout, parallelism, out of round, bell shaped, etc.).	Replace or turn rotor or drum.
	Lining contaminated with foreign substances.	Replace linings.
	Linings wearing unevenly.	Replace linings.
	Bent or loose brake shoes.	Replace show and linings.
	Weak or broken retractor springs.	Replace drum brake springs.
	Loose brake cable, brake line, or ABS wiring.	Check cable or line connection and tighten or replace as needed.
Groans (at/near stop)	Linings worn out.	Replace linings.
	Incorrect or damaged lining material.	Replace linings.
	Hot spots or worn surface on drum or rotor.	Replace drum or rotor.
	Cracked or bent knuckle or suspension parts.	Replace suspension component.
	Loose suspension.	Tighten suspension or replace.

G34099100003030X

Fig. 3 Brake system troubleshooting chart (Part 3 of 6)

follow righthand rear-lefthand front-lefthand rear-righthand front bleeding sequence.

5. Place transparent tube over bleeder valve and allow tube to hang down into transparent container. Ensure end of tube is submerged in clean brake fluid.
6. Have assistant to slowly depress brake pedal one time and hold.
7. Crack open bleeder valve and purging air from cylinder.
8. Tighten bleeder screw and slowly release pedal.
9. Repeat previous steps until all air is bled from system.
10. Check fluid level after bleeding each wheel. Adjust fluid lever, as required.

PRESSURE BLEED

Pressure bleeding equipment must be the diaphragm type. It must have a rubber diaphragm between the air supply and the brake fluid to prevent air, moisture and other contaminants from entering brake system.

1. Clean brake fluid reservoir cap and area around cap, then remove cap.
2. Fill master cylinder reservoir.
3. Install bleeder adapter tool No. SA-9150-BR, or equivalent, on brake fluid reservoir, **Fig. 9.**
4. Connect pressure bleeder to adapter and set pressure to 20–25 psi.
5. Loosen front brake line at master cylinder and allow brake fluid to flow from front master cylinder port until all air is bled.
6. Tighten front brake line.
7. Open each bleeder valve until all air is bled, then tighten bleeder screw.
8. Remove pressure bleeder and ensure fluid level is full.

HYDRAULIC BRAKE SYSTEM FLUSH

If brake fluid is old, rusty or contaminated or whenever new parts are installed in hydraulic system, the system must be flushed. Bleed brakes, allowing at least one quart of clean brake fluid to pass through system. Any rubber parts in hydraulic system which were exposed to contaminated fluid must be replaced.

Complaint/Condition	Possible Cause(s)	Correction(s)
Performance		
Brake Pull Left/Right	Caliper pistons sticking.	Overhaul caliper and replace piston.
	Loose wheel bearings or suspension attachments.	Replace wheel bearings or tighten suspension attachments.
	Worn suspension components.	Replace suspension components.
	Loose steering or steering gear.	Repair or replace steering components.
	Uneven wear on tires, tires not properly inflated or incorrect tires for vehicle.	Check tire and replace if necessary.
	Uneven worn linings.	Replace linings.
	Front suspension out of line.	Align suspension.
	Restricted brake line or hose.	Replace line or hose.
Brakes Grab	Contaminated brake linings.	Replace linings.
	Damage to braking surface of rotors or drums.	Replace rotors or drums.
	Rotor or drum out of specifications (i.e. lateral runout, parallelism, out of round, bell shaped, etc.).	Replace or turn rotor or drum.
	Damaged vacuum booster.	Replace booster.
Brakes Drag	Caliper pistons stuck.	Overhaul caliper and replace piston.
	Corroded caliper bolts. Caliper will not retract.	Replace bolts and bolt boots.
	Compensating port or bypass hole in master cylinder clogged.	Clean master cylinder and rebuild.
	Worn or damaged drum brake return springs.	Replace drum brake springs.
	Contaminated or improper brake fluid, rubber seals are swollen.	Flush brake system and replace all rubber parts including hoses.
	Parking brake not releasing.	Check cable and cable attachments.
	Self-adjusters over adjusting for lining wear.	Overhaul or replace adjusters.
	Improper vacuum booster push rod length.	Gage booster push rod and replace if needed.
Brake Action Uneven (Front – Rear)	Uneven wear on tires, tires improperly inflated or incorrect tires installed.	Check tires and replace if needed.
	Proportioning valve not functioning properly.	Replace master cylinder.
	Linings wearing unevenly front to rear.	Replace linings.
	Fluid leak in system.	Check system for leaks and repair or replace components.
	Hot spots or worn surface on drum or rotor.	Replace drum or rotor.

G34099100003040X

Fig. 3 Brake system troubleshooting chart (Part 4 of 6)

Complaint/Condition	Possible Cause(s)	Correction(s)
Brakes Slow to Release	Caliper piston sticking.	Overhaul caliper and replace piston.
	Corroded caliper bolts. Caliper will not retract.	Replace bolts and bolt boots.
	Contaminated or improper brake fluid, rubber seals are swollen.	Flush brake system and replace all rubber parts including hoses.
	Worn caliper piston seals.	Overhaul calipers.
	Worn or damaged drum brake return springs.	Replace drum brake springs.
	Worn or damaged master cylinder seals.	Overhaul master cylinder.
	Damage to mechanical action of brake pedal.	Check pedal and repair or replace.
Slow Response/Excessive Stopping Distance	Rotor not turned to proper surface finish.	Check rotor surface finish and turn rotor or replace.
	Linings not adjusting properly, damaged self-adjusters or worn piston seal.	Overhaul drum brake or caliper.
	Caliper pistons sticking.	Overhaul caliper and replace piston.
	Worn or glazed linings.	Replace linings.
	Proportioning valve not functioning properly.	Replace master cylinder.
Odor	Linings over heated.	
	Lining contaminated with foreign substances.	Replace lining.
Poor Fuel Economy	Linings over heated.	
	Egg shaped drum or bent rotor/knuckle.	Replace drum, rotor or knuckle.

G34099100003050X

Fig. 3 Brake system troubleshooting chart (Part 5 of 6)

Complaint/Condition	Possible Cause(s)	Correction(s)
Telltale		
Red (Brake) Telltale On	Park brake on.	Release park brake.
	Low brake fluid level in master cylinder (check for leaks).	Fill reservoir. Check for leaks.
	Improperly adjusted park brake switch.	Check park brake switch connection and adjustment.
	Damaged park brake switch or switch circuit.	Replace switch or repair circuit.
	Antilock brake system (ABS) problem	Refer to ABS
Amber (ABS) Telltale On (Solid/Flashing)	Refer to ABS	
Parking Brake		
Does Not Hold	Park brake not adjusted properly.	Adjust park brake.
	Brakes not adjusting properly.	Check brake adjusters and repair or replace as needed.
	Linings worn out.	Replace linings.
	Linings contaminated with foreign material.	Replace linings.
	Cable disconnected from lever.	Connect cable.
	Lever bent or loose.	Replace lever.
	Cable slipping.	Replace cable.
Does Not Release	Park brake cables binding.	Check cable and cable attachments.
	Release lever broken or binding.	Replace park brake lever.
Parking Brake Lever Hard to Apply	Lack of lubrication on apply mechanism.	Lubricate apply mechanism.
	Park brake cables binding.	Check cables and cable attachments.

G34099100003060X

Fig. 3 Brake system troubleshooting chart (Part 6 of 6)

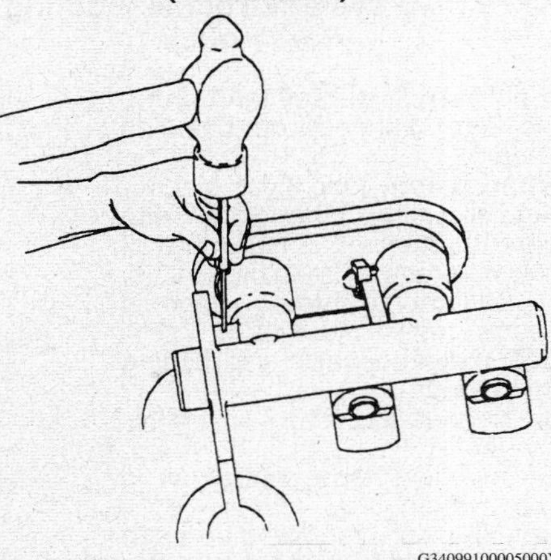

G34099100005000X

Fig. 4 Master cylinder reservoir spring pin removal. S-Series

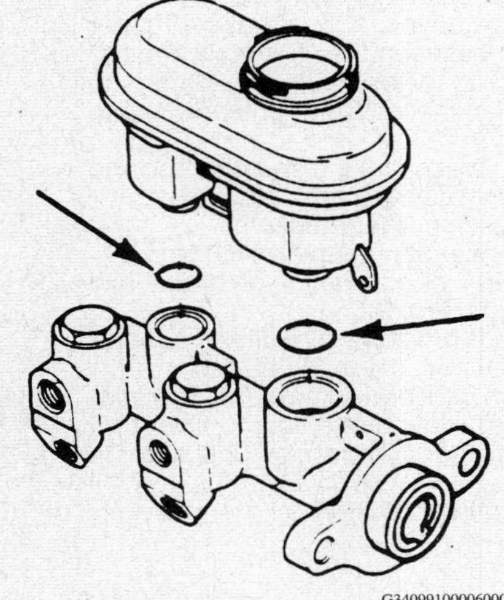

G34099100006000X

Fig. 5 Reservoir & O-ring replacement. S-Series

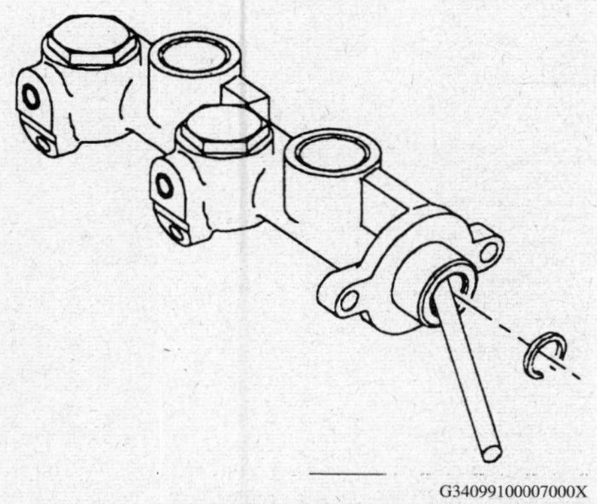

Fig. 6 Master cylinder retainer clip removal

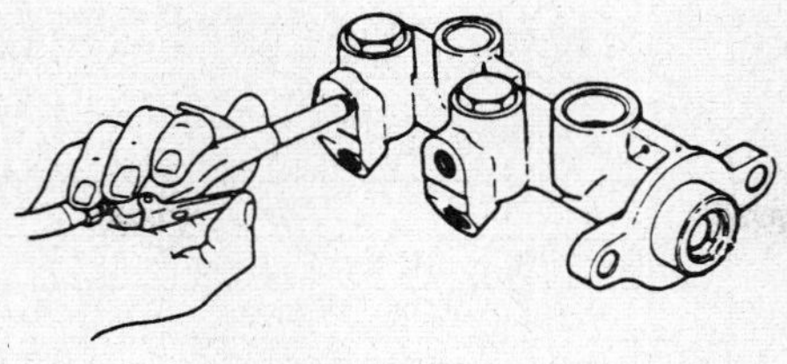

Fig. 7 Master cylinder piston removal

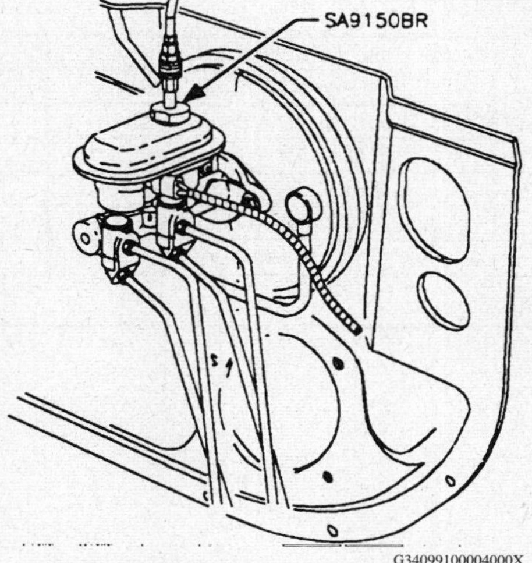

Fig. 9 Brake pressure bleeder adapter installation

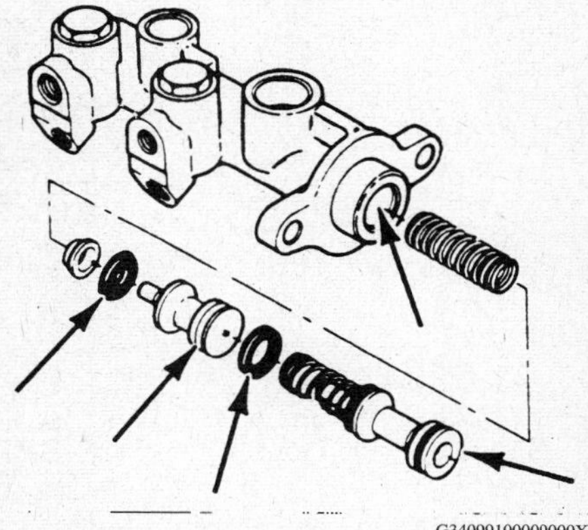

Fig. 8 Exploded view of master cylinder

TIGHTENING SPECIFICATIONS

Year	Component	Torque Ft. Lbs.
L-SERIES		
2000-02	Brake Pipe To Master Cylinder Nuts	12
	Caliper Bleed Valves	71①
	Cylinder To Brake Booster Nuts	25
	Proportioning Valve	12
	Rear Brake Hose	12
	Rear Crossover	12
S-SERIES		
1998-2002	Brake Hose To Caliper/Wheel Cylinder	36
	Brake Pipes To Brake Hoses	18
	Brake Pipes To Master Cylinder	24
	Brake Pipes To Union	14
	Front Bleeder Valve	97①
	Master Cylinder To Brake Booster	20
	Rear Bleeder Valve	66①

① — Inch lbs.

POWER BRAKE UNITS

NOTE: On Air Bag Equipped Models, Refer To "Air Bag System Precautions" Located In The Front Of This Manual For System Disarming & Arming Procedures.

NOTE: Refer To "Computer Relearn Procedures" Located In The Front Of This Manual When Battery Power To The Computer Has Been Interrupted.

INDEX

APPLICATION CHART

Model	Power Brake Type
All Except Metro & Prizm	AC-Delco Tandem Diaphragm
Metro	AC-Delco Single Diaphragm
Prizm	Toyota/GM Single Diaphragm

PRECAUTIONS

1. After disassembling power brake unit, soak metal components in solvent.
2. Use only alcohol on components containing rubber. After components have been thoroughly cleaned and rinsed in solvent, they should be washed again in clean alcohol before assembly.
3. Use compressed air to blow dirt and cleaning fluid from recesses and internal passages.
4. Always use all components furnished in repair kit.
5. **Use extreme caution when disassembling power assist mechanisms. If internal spring tension is suddenly released it could cause damage or personal injury.**

DESCRIPTION

AC-DELCO TANDEM DIAPHRAGM TYPE

This unit utilizes a vacuum power chamber, consisting of a front and rear shell, housing divider, front and rear diaphragm, plate assemblies, hydraulic pushrod and a diaphragm return spring, **Fig. 1.**

In normal operating mode, with service brakes in released position, the booster operates with vacuum on both sides of its diaphragms. When brakes are applied, air at atmospheric pressure is admitted to one side of each diaphragm to provide power assist. When the service brake is released, atmospheric air is shut off from one side of each diaphragm. The air is then drawn from the booster through the vacuum check valve to the vacuum source.

AC-DELCO SINGLE DIAPHRAGM TYPE

The AC-Delco power booster assembly is located along the bulkhead in the left-hand side engine compartment, between the brake pedal and master cylinder, **Fig. 2.** It is designed to take advantage of the vacuum produced by the engine. The applied force created when brake pedal is applied is mechanically increased with assistance of engine vacuum.

TOYOTA/GM SINGLE DIAPHRAGM TYPE

The Toyota/GM single diaphragm type booster assembly is located between the master cylinder and brake pedal, **Fig. 3.** When the brake pedal is depressed, the force is transmitted to the master cylinder piston through the valve operating rod, booster air valve, reaction disc and piston rod. The force of the booster piston is developed because of the pressure difference between the front and rear chambers.

TROUBLESHOOTING

BRAKES GRAB

1. Contaminated, worn or faulty brake linings.
2. Drum or brake rotor out-of-round.
3. Faulty brake booster.

HARD PEDAL/BRAKES INEFFICIENT

1. Contaminated, glazed or faulty brake linings.
2. Frozen caliper piston.
3. Faulty vacuum pump, or leak in booster vacuum supply system.
4. Faulty brake booster.

SLOW OR NO RELEASE

1. Faulty pushrod adjustment.
2. Bind in linkage.

ADJUSTMENTS

BRAKE PEDAL

TOYOTA/GM SINGLE DIAPHRAGM TYPE

1. With engine running and brake pedal in rest position, measure distance between face of pedal and floor mat.
2. Distance should be 5.850–6.244 inches.
3. If distance is not as specified, adjust pedal height as follows:
   a. Remove lefthand lower instrument panel trim section and air duct.
   b. Loosen stop lamp switch sufficiently to access pedal adjustment.
   c. Loosen locknut and rotate pedal pushrod as required to obtain specified pedal height. Tighten locknut.
   d. Adjust brake lamp switch position so plunger lightly contacts pedal stopper and brake lamps are off when pedal is released.
   e. Inspect pedal free travel.
4. With engine stopped, depress brake pedal several times to ensure there is no vacuum pressure in booster.
5. Release pedal and press pedal down until beginning of resistance is felt. Measure pedal travel. **Pedal free travel is amount brake booster air valve is moved by pedal pushrod.**

1 BOOT
2 AIR FILTER
3 VACUUM CHECK VALVE
4 GROMMET
7 FRONT HOUSING SEAL
8 PRIMARY PISTON BEARING
9 REAR HOUSING
10 FRONT HOUSING
11 RETURN SPRING
12 PISTON ROD (GAGED)
13 REACTION RETAINER
14 AIR SILENCER
15 DIAPHRAGM RETAINER
16 PRIMARY DIAPHRAGM
17 PRIMARY SUPPORT PLATE
18 SECONDARY PISTON BEARING
19 HOUSING DIVIDER
20 SECONDARY DIAPHRAGM
21 SECONDARY SUPPORT PLATE
22 REACTION DISC
23 REACTION PISTON
24 REACTION BODY RETAINER
25 REACTION BODY
26 AIR VALVE SPRING
27 REACTION BUMPER
28 RETAINING RING
29 SILENCER
30 RETAINER
31 O-RING
32 AIR VALVE PUSH ROD ASSEMBLY
33 POWER PISTON

GC4099700059000X

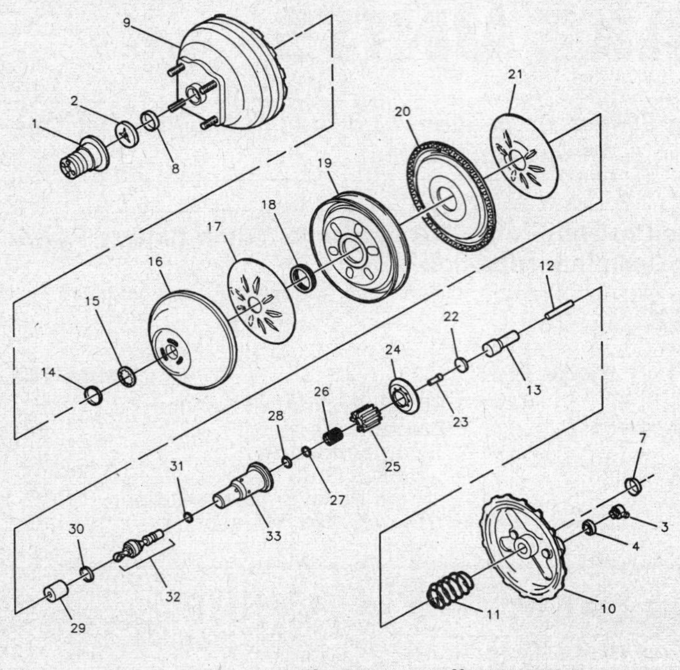

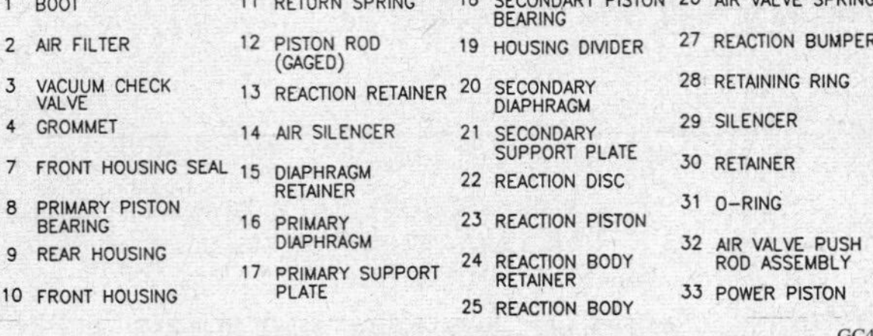

Fig. 1 Exploded view of AC-Delco tandem diaphragm booster

565 PUSHROD ADJUSTMENT NUT
566 COTTER PIN
569 CLEVIS PIN
570 CLEVIS
571 PUSHROD BRACKET
572 BOOSTER FRONT HALF
573 BOOSTER PISTON RETURN SPRING
574 PISTON ROD RETAINER
575 PISTON ROD
576 REACTION DISC
577 BOOSTER PISTON
578 AIR VALVE ASSEMBLY
579 VALVE STOPPER KEY
580 BODY BOOT
581 AIR CLEANER ELEMENTS
582 BOOSTER REAR HALF OIL SEAL
583 BOOSTER REAR HALF
584 DIAPHRAGM

GC4099400052000A

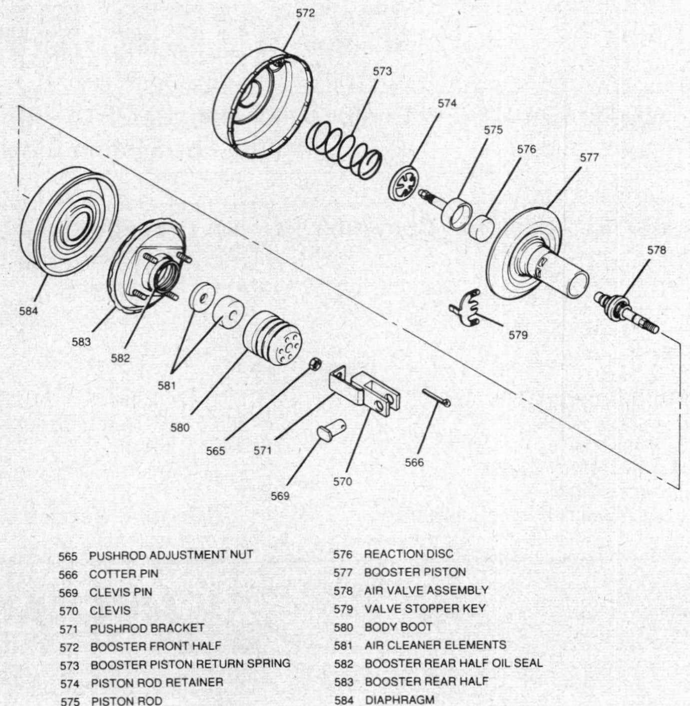

Fig. 2 Exploded view of AC-Delco single diaphragm booster

1 CIRCULAR RING
2 BODY SEAL
3 FRONT BODY
4 DIAPHRAGM SPRING
5 PUSH ROD
6 REACTION DISC
7 STOPPER KEY
8 VALVE BODY
9 OPERATING ROD
10 BOOSTER PISTON
11 DIAPHRAGM
12 REAR BODY
13 BODY SEAL
14 SPONGE ELEMENT
15 FELT ELEMENT
16 BOOT
17 NUT

GC4099100050000A

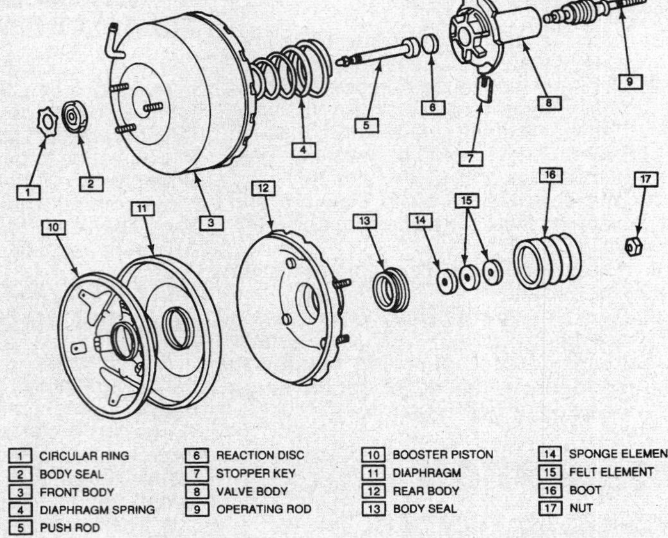

Fig. 3 Exploded view of Toyota/GM brake booster

6. If pedal travel is not .12–.24 inch, adjust pedal freeplay as follows:
   a. Adjust pedal free travel by loosening locknut and rotating pedal pushrod.
   b. Ensure brake lamp switch and pedal height are properly adjusted.
   c. Start engine and confirm free travel still exists.
   d. Inspect pedal reserve distance.
7. Release parking brake and start engine.
8. Depress brake pedal with applied force of 110 lbs. and measure distance from face of pedal to floor mat.
9. Pedal reserve distance should not be more than 3.35 inches.
10. If pedal reserve distance does not meet specifications, inspect and repair brake system as needed.

PUSHROD

Proper adjustment of the master cylinder pushrod is required to ensure proper operation of the power brake system. A pushrod that is too long will cause the master cylinder piston to close off the compensating port, preventing hydraulic pressure from being released and resulting in brake drag. A pushrod that is too short will cause excessive brake pedal travel and cause groaning noises to come from the booster when the brakes are applied. A properly adjusted pushrod that remains assembled to the booster with which it was matched during production should not require service adjustment. However, if the booster, master cylinder or pushrod are serviced, the pushrod may require adjustment.

There are two methods that can be used to inspect for proper pushrod length and installation. These are the gauge method and air method. Usually, if the power unit pushrod requires adjustment, use the power unit repair kit gauge. The gauge measures from the end of the pushrod to the power unit shell.

GAUGE METHOD

AC-Delco Tandem Diaphragm Type

The master cylinder pushrod length is fixed and is usually only inspected after the unit has been overhauled. This procedure can be performed with the unit removed from the vehicle if a suitable vacuum source is available.

1. Assemble booster unit and install pushrod. Ensure pushrod is fully seated.
2. Apply 20 inches or maximum engine

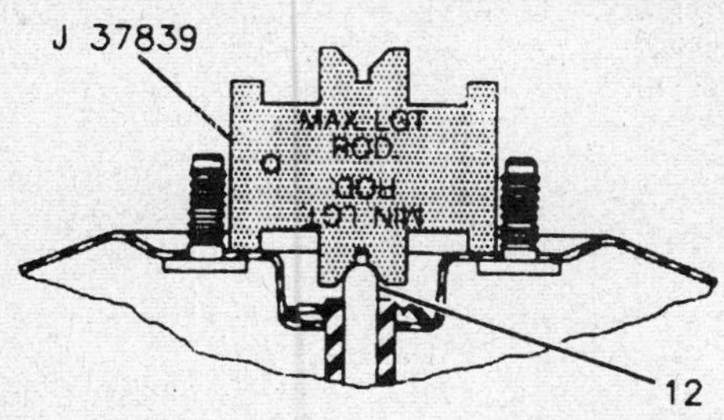

Fig. 4 Master cylinder measurement. AC-Delco tandem diaphragm type

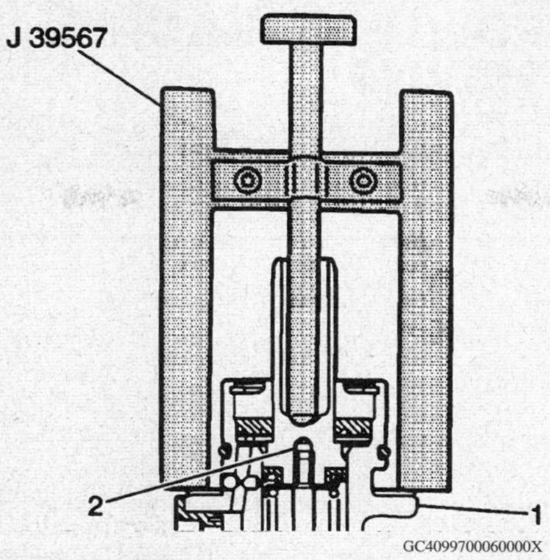

Fig. 5 Master cylinder adjustment tool. AC-Delco & Toyota/GM single diaphragm type

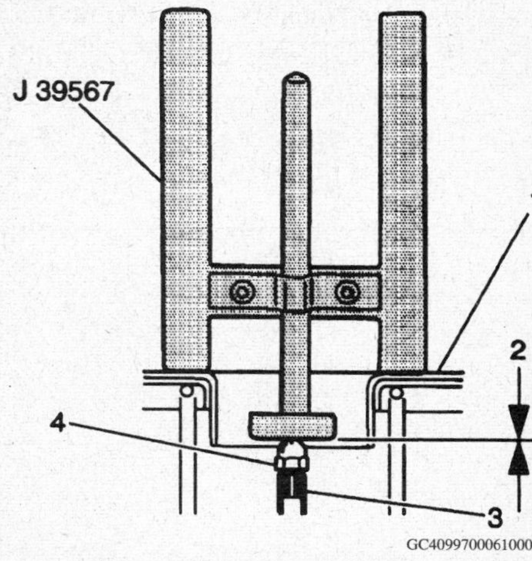

Fig. 6 Booster piston rod adjustment. AC-Delco & Toyota/GM single diaphragm type

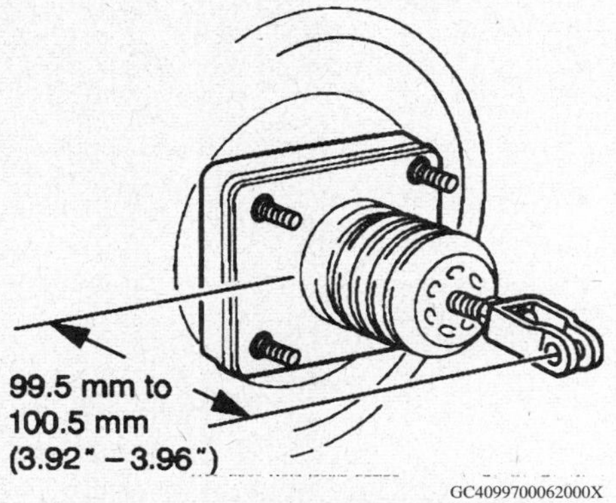

Fig. 7 Pushrod clevis length adjustment. AC-Delco diaphragm type

vacuum to booster.

3. Position gauge tool No. J-37839, or equivalent, over pushrod, **Fig. 4.**
4. Replace booster if output button length is not within gauge limits.
5. Install power unit and inspect adjustment.
6. Ensure master cylinder compensating port is open with engine running and brake pedal released.

AC-Delco Single Diaphragm Type

The length of the booster piston rod is adjusted to provide specified clearance between the piston rod end and master cylinder piston. Before making an adjustment, push piston rod several times to ensure reaction disc is in place. Ensure gasket is installed to master cylinder and keep inside of booster at atmospheric pressure.

1. Place booster pin rod gauge tool No. J-39567, or equivalent, on master cylinder (1) and push pin until it contacts piston (2), **Fig. 5.**
2. Turn tool upside down and place it on booster. Adjust booster piston rod length until rod end contacts pin head.
3. Adjust clearance by turning adjusting bolt (4) of piston rod (3), **Fig. 6.** There should be no clearance between booster piston rod and gauge tool (2).
4. **On Metro models,** adjust pushrod clevis length to 3.92–3.96 inches, **Fig. 7,** then **Torque** locknut to 18 ft. lbs.

Toyota/GM Single Diaphragm Type

Refer to "AC-Delco Single Diaphragm Type" for pushrod adjustment procedures.

AIR METHOD

1. Ensure master cylinder mounting nuts are tight.
2. Remove master cylinder filler cap.
3. With brake released, force compressed air into hydraulic outlet of master cylinder. **Regulate air pressure to value of approximately 5 psi to prevent spraying brake fluid from master cylinder. Care must be taken not to allow brake fluid to contact painted surfaces of vehicle, skin or eyes, as damage or personal injury will result.**
4. If air passes through compensating port, which is smaller of two holes in bottom of master cylinder reservoir, adjustment is satisfactory.
5. If air does not flow through compensating port, adjust pushrod as required, either by means of adjustment screw (if provided) or by adding shims between master cylinder and power unit shell until air flows freely.
6. Connect brake lines and bleed system.

GENERAL SERVICE

Two basic types of power assist mechanisms are used: vacuum assist diaphragm assemblies, which use engine vacuum or, in some cases vacuum pressure developed by an external vacuum pump. The second type is a hydraulic pressure assist mechanism, which use pressure developed by an external pump (usually the power steering pump). Both systems act to increase the force exerted on the master cylinder piston by the operator. This in turn increases the hydraulic pressure delivered to the wheel cylinders while decreasing driver effort required to obtain acceptable stopping performance.

Vacuum assist units are similar in operation and get their energy by opposing engine vacuum to atmospheric pressure. A piston and cylinder, flexible diaphragm (bellows) utilize this energy to provide brake assistance. The fundamental difference between these types of vacuum assist systems lies simply in how the diaphragm within the power unit is suspended when the brakes are not applied.

In order to properly diagnose vacuum assist system malfunctions it is important to know whether the diaphragm within a power unit is air suspended or vacuum suspended. Air-suspended units are under atmospheric pressure until the brakes are applied. Engine vacuum is then admitted, causing the piston or diaphragm to move (or the bellows to collapse). Vacuum-suspended types are balanced with engine vacuum until the brake pedal is depressed, allowing atmospheric pressure to unbalance the unit and apply force to the brake system.

Regardless of whether the brakes are vacuum or hydraulically assisted, certain general service procedures apply. Only specified, clean brake fluid should be used in brake systems. On hydro-boost systems, use of the specified hydraulic fluid in the boost circuit is essential to proper system operation. Care must be taken not to mix the fluids of the two separate operating circuits.

POWER BRAKE UNIT SERVICE

This brake booster is not serviceable and should be replaced as an assembly.

AUTOMATIC TRANSMISSIONS/ TRANSAXLES

TABLE OF CONTENTS

Application Chart

Year	Engine	Type
ACHIEVA & SKYLARK		
1998	All	4T60-E
ALERO		
1999–2002	2.4L	4T40-E
	3.4L	4T45-E
AURORA		
1998–99	All	4T80-E
2001–02	3.5L	4T65-E
	4.0L	4T80-E
BONNEVILLE		
1998–2002	3.8L①	4T65-E
	3.8L②	4T65-E-HD
CAMARO & FIREBIRD		
1998–2002	All	4L60-E
CATERA		
1998–2001	All	4L30-E
CAVALIER & SUNFIRE		
1998–2001	2.2L	3T40
		4T40-E
	2.4L	4T40-E
2002	All	4T40-E
CENTURY		
1998–2002	All	4T60-E
CORVETTE		
1998–2002	All	4L60-E
CUTLASS		
1998	3.1L	4T40-E
1999	3.1L	4T45-E

Continued

AUTOMATIC TRANSMISSIONS/TRANSAXLES

Year	Engine	Type
DEVILLE, ELDORADO & SEVILLE		
1998–2002	All	4T80-E
EIGHTY EIGHT		
1998–99	3.8L①	4T65-E
	3.8L②	4T65-E-HD
GRAND AM		
1998	All	4T60-E
1999–2002	2.4L	4T40-E
	3.4L	4T45-E
GRAND PRIX		
1998	3.4L	4T60-E
	3.8L①	4T65-E
	3.8L②	4T65-E-HD
1999–2002	3.1L	4T60-E
	3.8L①	4T65-E
	3.8L②	4T65-E-HD
IMPALA		
2000–02	All	4T65-E
INTRIGUE		
1998–2002	All	4T65-E
LESABRE		
1998–99	3.8L①	4T65-E
	3.8L②	4T65-E-HD
2000–02	All	4T65-E
LSS & REGENCY		
1998	3.8L①	4T65-E
	3.8L②	4T65-E-HD
LUMINA		
1998	All	4T60-E
1999	3.1L	4T60-E
	3.8L	4T65-E
2000–01	All	4T65-E
MALIBU		
1998	All	4T40-E
1999	2.4L	4T40-E
	3.1L	4T45-E
2000–02	All	4T40-E
		4T45-E
METRO		
1998–2001	All	Aisin Seiki
MONTE CARLO		
1998	3.4L	4T60-E
	3.8L	4T65-E
1999	3.1L	4T60-E
	3.8L	4T65-E
2000–02	All	4T65-E
PARK AVENUE		
1998–2002	3.8L①	4T65-E
	3.8L②	4T65-E-HD
PRIZM		
1998–2002	All	A131L
		A245-E
REGAL		
1998–2002	3.8L①	4T65-E
	3.8L②	4T65-E-HD
RIVIERA		
1998–99	All	4T65-E-HD

Continued

Year	Engine	Type
SATURN L-SERIES		
2000–02	2.2L	4T40-E
	3.0L	4T45-E
SATURN S-SEIRES		
1998–2002	All	Saturn Four-Speed

① — VIN K.
② — VIN 1.

Aisin Seiki Three-Speed Automatic Transaxle

NOTE: On Air Bag Equipped Models, Refer To "Air Bag System Precautions" Located In The Front Of This Manual For System Disarming & Arming Procedures.

NOTE: Refer To "Computer Relearn Procedures" Located In The Front Of This Manual When Battery Power To The Computer Has Been Interrupted.

INDEX

PRECAUTIONS

AIR BAG SYSTEMS

Refer to "Air Bag System Precautions" in the front of this manual for system disarming and arming procedures.

BATTERY GROUND CABLE

Prior to service, disconnect battery ground cable and isolate as required.

IDENTIFICATION

The transaxle identification number is located on the top center of the transaxle, **Fig. 1.**

TROUBLESHOOTING

1. Ensure engine coolant is at normal operating temperature.
2. Ensure engine idle speed is 800–900 RPM.
3. Ensure transaxle fluid level is correct and at normal operating temperature.
4. Ensure accelerator cable, oil pressure control cable and selector cable are properly adjusted.
5. Ensure gear shift control system wiring is in good condition.
6. Ensure vacuum switch hose is properly connected.
7. Refer to **Fig. 2,** for transaxle troubleshooting.

MAINTENANCE

Refer to "Lubricant Data" chart in the appropriate chassis chapter of this manual for transmission fluid specifications.

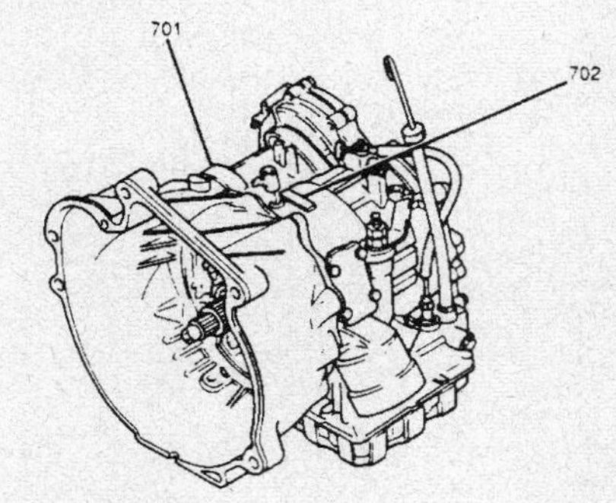

701 TRANSAXLE CASE
702 TRANSAXLE IDENTIFICATION NUMBER LOCATION
GC5029200461000X

Fig. 1 Transaxle identification number location

FLUID CHECK

1. Drive vehicle for approximately 15 minutes to bring fluid to normal operating temperature.
2. With vehicle on level surface, apply parking brake and block drive wheels.
3. With selector lever in Park, start engine and move selector lever through each range and return to Park.
4. Remove dipstick and check fluid level.
5. Fluid level should be between two HOT marks on dipstick.
6. Add fluid as required to bring fluid to specified level.

FLUID CHANGE

Under normal driving conditions, fluid should be changed and oil strainer cleaned every 100,000 miles. Under harsh driving conditions fluid should be changed every 15,000 miles. To service, proceed as follows:

1. Raise and support front of vehicle.
2. Remove plug and drain fluid into suitable container.
3. Remove mounting bolts and oil pan.
4. Remove mounting bolts and oil strainer.
5. Clean strainer and oil pan in solvent. Engine magnet in oil pan is positioned directly below oil strainer.
6. Install oil strainer and mounting bolts.
7. Install oil pan using new gasket. **Two of oil pan mounting bolts have crossed grooves on bolt head. When installing these two bolts, coat threads with suitable sealant, Fig. 3.**
8. Lower vehicle and fill oil pan.
9. Adjust fluid level as required.

ADJUSTMENTS

THROTTLE VALVE (TV) CABLE

1. Inspect accelerator cable for play and adjust as required.
2. Start engine and allow it to run at idle speed until operating temperature is reached.
3. Remove TV cable adjustment cover.
4. Measure TV cable boot to inner stopper clearance. If clearance is more than 0.02 inch, adjust TV cable, **Fig. 4.**
5. Turn TV cable adjustment nuts A until correct clearance is obtained. If correct

CONDITION	INSPECT COMPONENT	FOR CAUSE
HARSH ENGAGEMENT INTO ANY FORWARD RANGE	FLUID LEVEL INDICATOR	– LOW FLUID LEVEL
	TV CABLE	– MISADJUSTED, BINDING OR DAMAGED
	SHIFT SELECT CABLE	– MISADJUSTED, BINDING OR DAMAGED
	VALVE BODY	– MANUAL VALVE BINDING OR STICKING – THROTTLE VALVE BINDING OR STICKING – B2 CONTROL VALVE BINDING OR STICKING
	ACCUMULATORS	– PISTONS DAMAGED OR LEAKING – SEALS CUT OR DAMAGED – BROKEN OR DISTORTED SPRINGS
	FLUID PRESSURE	– INSPECT FOR CAUSES OF HIGH OR LOW FLUID PRESSURE
SLIPS IN 1ST GEAR	FLUID LEVEL INDICATOR	– LOW FLUID LEVEL
	TV CABLE	– MISADJUSTED, BINDING OR DAMAGED
	SHIFT SELECT CABLE	– MISADJUSTED, BINDING OR DAMAGED
	VALVE BODY	– THROTTLE VALVE BINDING OR STICKING – PRIMARY REGULATOR VALVE BINDING OR STICKING
	ACCUMULATORS	– PISTONS DAMAGED OR LEAKING – SEALS CUT OR DAMAGED – BROKEN OR DISTORTED SPRINGS
	FORWARD CLUTCH	– CLUTCH DISCS WORN – FORWARD CLUTCH PISTON OR SEAL LEAKING OR DAMAGED – INPUT SHAFT O-RINGS CUT OR DAMAGED
	ONE-WAY CLUTCH	– NOT HOLDING OR DAMAGED
	FLUID PRESSURE	– INSPECT FOR CAUSES OF HIGH OR LOW FLUID PRESSURE

GC5029300495010X

Fig. 2 Troubleshooting chart (Part 1 of 6)

CONDITION	INSPECT COMPONENT	FOR CAUSE
1ST GEAR ONLY — NO UPSHIFT	TV CABLE	– MISADJUSTED, BINDING OR DAMAGED
	VALVE BODY	– THROTTLE VALVE BINDING OR STICKING – 1–2 SHIFT VALVE BINDING OR STICKING – PRIMARY REGULATOR VALVE BINDING OR STICKING
	INTERMEDIATE SERVO	– SEALS CUT OR DAMAGED – PISTON BINDING OR STICKING – PISTON ROD NOT ENGAGED
	2ND BRAKE BAND	– WORN OR MISALIGNED
	FLUID PRESSURE	– INSPECT FOR CAUSES OF HIGH OR LOW FLUID PRESSURE
SLIPPING OR ROUGH 1–2 UPSHIFT	FLUID LEVEL INDICATOR	– LOW FLUID LEVEL
	TV CABLE	– MISADJUSTED, BINDING OR DAMAGED
	VALVE BODY	– THROTTLE VALVE BINDING OR STICKING – 1–2 SHIFT VALVE BINDING OR STICKING – PRIMARY REGULATOR VALVE BINDING OR STICKING
	INTERMEDIATE SERVO	– SEALS CUT OR DAMAGED – PISTON BINDING OR STICKING – PISTON ROD NOT ENGAGED
	2ND BRAKE BAND	– WORN OR MISALIGNED
	TORQUE CONVERTER	– INTERNAL DAMAGE
	FORWARD CLUTCH	– CLUTCH DISCS WORN – FORWARD CLUTCH PISTON OR SEAL LEAKING OR DAMAGED – INPUT SHAFT O-RINGS CUT OR DAMAGED
	FLUID PRESSURE	– INSPECT FOR CAUSES OF HIGH OR LOW FLUID PRESSURE

GC5029300495020X

Fig. 2 Troubleshooting chart (Part 2 of 6)

clearance cannot be obtained using adjustment nuts A, use adjustment nuts B.

PARK/NEUTRAL POSITION (PNP) SWITCH

1. Remove park/neutral position switch from transaxle as described under "Park/Neutral Position Switch, Replace."
2. Move transaxle lever to Neutral position.
3. Turn park/neutral switch joint clockwise or counterclockwise using flat-bladed screwdriver until distinct click is heard, **Fig. 5.**
4. Install PNP switch to transaxle as described under "Park/Neutral Position Switch, Replace."

IN-VEHICLE REPAIRS

BRAKE TRANSAXLE SHIFT INTERLOCK, REPLACE

1. Remove selector knob to selector lever mounting screws, **Fig. 6.**
2. Remove mounting screws and center console.
3. Remove manual selector bulb socket from manual selector cover.
4. Remove manual selector cover to selector lever mounting screws.
5. Remove retainer clip and clevis pin, then disconnect shift select cable from selector lever.
6. Disconnect interlock cable end from key release plate on manual selector.
7. Remove interlock cable to selector mounting bolt and disconnect cable.
8. Disconnect shift lock solenoid electrical connector located under carpet.
9. Raise and support vehicle.
10. Remove selector lever housing seat mounting nuts.
11. Lower vehicle, then remove selector lever housing and selector lever.
12. Reverse procedure to install, noting the following:
    a. Adjust interlock cable as outlined under "Interlock Cable, Replace."
    b. Adjust shift select cable as outline under "Shift Select Cable, Replace."
    c. Apply lithium grease under solenoid lock plate, **Fig. 7.**

SHIFT SELECT CABLE, REPLACE

1. Remove selector lever knob to selector lever mounting screws.
2. Remove mounting screws and center console.
3. Remove manual selector cover lamp bulb socket from selector cover, **Fig. 8.**
4. Remove selector cover to selector lever mounting screws.
5. Remove retainer clip and clevis pin, then disconnect shift select cable from selector lever.
6. Remove front carpet retainers and pull back carpet.
7. Remove retaining clip and shift select cable from transaxle mounting bracket.
8. Remove nut and disconnect shift select cable from manual shift lever.
9. Remove bolts from bulkhead grommet and pull shift select cable out of bulkhead from engine compartment side of bulkhead.
10. Reverse procedure to install, noting the following:
    a. After connecting shift select cable to transaxle mounting bracket, tighten adjustment nut A by hand until it contacts shift select cable joint, **Fig. 9.**
    b. Tighten adjustment nut B using suitable open end wrench until it is jammed against manual shift select cable joint.
    c. Apply lithium grease to shift select cable clevis pin.

PARK/NEUTRAL POSITION SWITCH, REPLACE

1. Disconnect park/neutral position switch electrical connector.
2. Remove position switch wiring harness from retaining clips.
3. Remove switch to transaxle mounting bolt.
4. Reverse procedure to install. Adjust position switch described under "Adjustments."

INTERLOCK CABLE, REPLACE

REMOVAL

1. Remove selector lever knob to selector lever mounting screws.
2. Remove mounting screws and center console.
3. Remove manual selector cover lamp bulb socket from selector cover.
4. Remove selector cover to selector lever mounting screws.
5. Disconnect interlock cable end from

CONDITION	INSPECT COMPONENT	FOR CAUSE
NO 2–3 SHIFT OR 2–3 SHIFT SLIPPING	FLUID LEVEL INDICATOR	– LOW FLUID LEVEL
	TV CABLE	– MISADJUSTED, BINDING OR DAMAGED
	VALVE BODY	– THROTTLE VALVE BINDING OR STICKING – 2–3 SHIFT VALVE BINDING OR STICKING – PRIMARY REGULATOR VALVE BINDING OR STICKING
	INTERMEDIATE SERVO	– PISTON BINDING OR STICKING – PISTON ROD BINDING
	2ND BRAKE BAND	– NOT RELEASING
	TORQUE CONVERTER	– INTERNAL DAMAGE
	DIRECT CLUTCH	– CLUTCH DISCS WORN – DIRECT CLUTCH PISTON OR SEAL LEAKING OR DAMAGED
	FLUID PRESSURE	– INSPECT FOR CAUSES OF HIGH OR LOW FLUID PRESSURE
HIGH OR LOW SHIFT POINTS	FLUID LEVEL INDICATOR	– LOW FLUID LEVEL
	TV CABLE	– MISADJUSTED, BINDING OR DAMAGED
	VALVE BODY	– SPACER PLATE OR GASKETS MISPOSITIONED OR DAMAGED – THROTTLE VALVE BINDING OR STICKING – CHECK BALLS OMITTED OR MISPOSITIONED
	TORQUE CONVERTER	– INTERNAL DAMAGE
	FORWARD CLUTCH	– FORWARD CLUTCH PISTON OR SEAL LEAKING OR DAMAGED – INPUT SHAFT O-RINGS CUT OR DAMAGED
	DIRECT CLUTCH	– DIRECT CLUTCH PISTON OR SEAL LEAKING OR DAMAGED
	FLUID PRESSURE	– INSPECT FOR CAUSES OF HIGH OR LOW FLUID PRESSURE

GC5029300495030X

Fig. 2 Troubleshooting chart (Part 3 of 6)

CONDITION	INSPECT COMPONENT	FOR CAUSE
NO PART THROTTLE OR DELAYED DOWNSHIFT	TV CABLE	– MISADJUSTED, BINDING OR DAMAGED
	VALVE BODY	– THROTTLE VALVE BINDING OR STICKING – 2–3 SHIFT VALVE BINDING OR STICKING – 1–2 SHIFT VALVE BINDING OR STICKING – PRIMARY REGULATOR VALVE BINDING OR STICKING – BROKEN OR DISTORTED VALVE SPRINGS – DAMAGED OR POROUS VALVE BODY CASTING
	INTERMEDIATE SERVO	– PISTON BINDING OR STICKING – PISTON SEALS CUT OR DAMAGED – PISTON ROD BINDING
	2ND BRAKE BAND	– WORN OR MISPOSITIONED
	1ST-REVERSE BRAKE	– CLUTCH DISCS WORN – 1ST-REVERSE BRAKE PISTON OR SEAL LEAKING OR DAMAGED
	ONE-WAY CLUTCH	– NOT HOLDING OR DAMAGED
NO ENGINE BRAKING OR 3–2–1 MANUAL DOWNSHIFT	SHIFT SELECT CABLE	– MISADJUSTED, BINDING OR DAMAGED
	VALVE BODY	– MANUAL VALVE BINDING OR STICKING – 2–3 SHIFT VALVE BINDING OR STICKING – 1–2 SHIFT VALVE BINDING OR STICKING – PRIMARY REGULATOR VALVE BINDING OR STICKING – BROKEN OR DISTORTED VALVE SPRINGS – DAMAGED OR POROUS VALVE BODY CASTING
	INTERMEDIATE SERVO	– PISTON BINDING OR STICKING – PISTON SEALS CUT OR DAMAGED – PISTON ROD BINDING
	2ND BRAKE BAND	– WORN OR MISPOSITIONED
	1ST-REVERSE BRAKE	– CLUTCH DISCS WORN – 1ST-REVERSE BRAKE PISTON OR SEAL LEAKING OR DAMAGED
	ONE-WAY CLUTCH	– NOT HOLDING OR DAMAGED

GC5029300495040X

Fig. 2 Troubleshooting chart (Part 4 of 6)

key release plate on manual selector, **Fig. 10.**

6. Remove interlock cable mounting bolt.
7. Disconnect interlock cable from selector lever housing bracket.
8. Remove front carpet retainers and pull back front carpet.
9. Remove upper and lower steering column covers.
10. Remove upper and lower mounting nuts, then lower steering column.
11. Remove screw and interlock cable mounting clamp from ignition switch.
12. Push release shaft in at ignition switch lock mechanism.
13. Remove cable end from ignition switch and interlock cable.

INSTALLATION

1. Install cable into vehicle and route it to ignition switch.
2. Push release shaft in at ignition switch and insert cable end.
3. Attach interlock cable mounting clamp to ignition switch and secure with screw.
4. Position steering column and install mounting nuts.
5. Install steering column covers.
6. Refit front carpet and install carpet retainers.
7. Attach interlock cable to selector lever housing bracket.
8. Attach cable end to key release plate.
9. Move selector lever to Park position and hold selector button in.
10. Rotate key release plate and insert small screwdriver through key release plate to hold it in position, **Fig. 11.**
11. Allow retaining spring to position interlock control bracket.
12. Ensure ignition key can be moved from ACC to Lock and removed from ignition switch when selector lever is in Park position.
13. Ensure ignition switch cannot be turned to ACC or Lock position when selector lever is in any position other than Park.
14. Install manual selector cover onto selector lever.
15. Install manual selector cover lamp bulb socket into cover.
16. Install console and selector knob.

SHIFT LOCK SOLENOID, REPLACE

REMOVAL

1. Remove selector lever knob to selector lever mounting screws.
2. Remove center console mounting screws and center console.
3. Remove selector lever upper cover and lower cover.
4. Disconnect shift solenoid electrical connector located under carpet.
5. Remove shift lock solenoid mounting screws and shift lock solenoid from selector lever housing, **Fig. 12.**

INSTALLATION

1. Move selector lever to Park position.
2. Apply lithium grease to upper and lower edges of solenoid lock plate.
3. Attach shift lock solenoid to selector lever housing and hand tighten mounting screws.
4. Connect shift lock solenoid electrical connector.
5. Adjust shift lock solenoid so it operates as follows:
   a. When ignition switch is turned off, solenoid is not actuated.
   b. When ignition switch is turned on and brake pedal is depressed, solenoid is actuated and solenoid lock plate should be positioned, **Fig. 12.**
   c. There should be no clearance between solenoid lock plate and selector lever.
   d. If manual override is enabled with ignition switch in OFF position, selector lever can be moved to any range or position.
6. Tighten shift lock solenoid mounting screws. **Ensure selector lever locks in P position and cannot be shifted to any other position.**
7. Install lower cover onto selector lever.
8. Install upper cover onto selector lever.
9. Install console and selector lever knob.

TV CABLE, REPLACE

1. Remove TV cable adjustment cover, **Fig. 13.**
2. Disconnect TV cable from accelerator cable and bracket.
3. Raise and support vehicle.
4. Remove transaxle drain plug and drain fluid into suitable container.
5. Remove transaxle oil pan guard, oil pan and gasket.
6. Disconnect TV cable from throttle valve cam.

CONDITION	INSPECT COMPONENT	FOR CAUSE
NO REVERSE OR SLIPS IN REVERSE	FLUID LEVEL INDICATOR	– LOW FLUID LEVEL
	SHIFT SELECT CABLE	– MISADJUSTED, BINDING OR DAMAGED
	VALVE BODY	– SPACER PLATE OR GASKETS MISPOSITIONED OR DAMAGED – CHECK BALLS OMITTED OR MISPOSITIONED – MANUAL VALVE BINDING OR STICKING – MANUAL VALVE LINK DISCONNECTED
	DIRECT CLUTCH	– DIRECT CLUTCH PISTON OR SEAL LEAKING OR DAMAGED
	FLUID PRESSURE	– INSPECT FOR CAUSES OF HIGH OR LOW FLUID PRESSURE
FLUID PRESSURE HIGH OR LOW (VERIFY WITH GAGE	FLUID PUMP	– INTERNAL FLUID PUMP LEAK – FLUID PUMP DRIVE AND DRIVEN GEARS WORN OR DAMAGED – FLUID PUMP COVER SEAL RINGS CUT OR DAMAGED – FLUID PUMP BODY OR COVER CASTING POROUS OR DAMAGED
	TV CABLE	– TV CABLE LINK LOOSE OR DISCONNECTED – MISADJUSTED, BINDING OR DAMAGED
	VALVE BODY	– SPACER PLATE OR GASKETS MISPOSITIONED OR DAMAGED – CHECK BALLS OMITTED OR MISPOSITIONED – MANUAL VALVE BINDING OR STICKING – MANUAL VALVE LINK DISCONNECTED – PRIMARY REGULATOR VALVE BINDING OR STICKING
	CASE	– INTERNAL LEAK IN FORWARD CLUTCH FLUID CIRCUIT – INTERNAL LEAK IN DIRECT CLUTCH FLUID CIRCUIT – FLUID PASSAGES BLOCKED OR RESTRICTED

GC5029300495050X

Fig. 2 Troubleshooting chart (Part 5 of 6)

CONDITION	INSPECT COMPONENT	FOR CAUSE
NO PARK OR RATCHETING NOISE IN PARK	SHIFT SELECT CABLE	– MISADJUSTED, BINDING OR DAMAGED
	LOCK PAWL SPRING	– DISCONNECTED OR BROKEN
	PARKING LOCK ROD	– DISCONNECTED OR BROKEN
	PARKING LOCK PAWL	– LOOSE OR DISCONNECTED
	LOCK PAWL SPRING	– WEAK OR DAMAGED
VEHICLE DOES NOT MOVE IN ANY RANGE — FORWARD OR REVERSE	FLUID LEVEL INDICATOR	– LITTLE OR NO FLUID
	SHIFT SELECT CABLE	– MISADJUSTED, BINDING OR DAMAGED
	PARKING LOCK PAWL	– MECHANISM LOCKED OR FROZEN
	TORQUE CONVERTER	– BROKEN TORQUE CONVERTER-TO-FLYWHEEL BOLTS – STATOR ONE-WAY CLUTCH NOT HOLDING – INTERNAL DAMAGE
	VALVE BODY	– SPACER PLATE OR GASKETS MISPOSITIONED OR DAMAGED – CHECK BALLS OMITTED OR MISPOSITIONED – MANUAL VALVE BINDING OR STICKING – MANUAL VALVE LINK DISCONNECTED
	FLUID PRESSURE	– INSPECT FOR CAUSES OF HIGH OR LOW FLUID PRESSURE

GC5029300495060X

Fig. 2 Troubleshooting chart (Part 6 of 6)

7. Reverse procedure to install. Adjust TV cable as described under "Adjustments."

TRANSAXLE CONTROL MODULE, REPLACE

1. Disconnect Transaxle Control Module (TCM) electrical connectors.
2. Remove mounting bolts and TCM from under lefthand side of instrument panel, **Fig. 14.**
3. Reverse procedure to install.

INTERMEDIATE SERVO, REPLACE

1. Raise and support vehicle.
2. Remove three transaxle fluid pan bolts, **Fig. 15.**
3. Install piston cover depressor tool No. J-35534, or equivalent, onto transaxle oil pan, **Fig. 16.**
4. Tighten adjustment bolt on tool until servo cover snap ring can be removed.
5. Remove servo cover snap ring and slowly loosen adjustment bolt.
6. Remove servo cover, servo piston, springs and piston rod, **Fig. 17.**
7. Reverse procedure to install. Apply transmission fluid liberally to all servo components prior to installation.

DRIVE AXLE SHAFT FLUID SEAL, REPLACE

1. Raise and support vehicle.
2. Remove wheel cover or center cap.
3. Unstake drive axle nut, then remove drive axle nut and washer.
4. Remove tire and wheel assembly.
5. Drain transaxle fluid and install two boot protectors tool No. J-28712, or

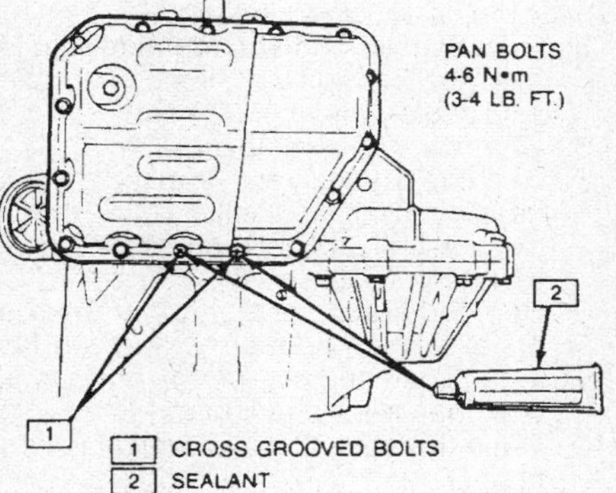

GC5029100465000X

Fig. 3 Oil pan installation

equivalent, onto inner and outer drive axle boots.
6. Pry differential side joint away from transaxle using suitable screwdriver and remove differential side gear snap ring.
7. Remove ball stud and nut, then separate steering knuckle from control arm.
8. Remove drive axle by removing differential side joint from differential side gear.
9. Remove drive axle fluid seal from transaxle.
10. Reverse procedure to install, noting the following:
    a. Install seal using axle shaft seal installer tool No. J-35538, or equivalent.
    b. Coat transaxle oil pan drain plug with Loctite pipe sealant part No. 1052080, or equivalent.

VALVE BODY & ACCUMULATOR, REPLACE

REMOVAL

1. Raise and support vehicle.
2. Drain transaxle fluid into suitable container, then remove oil pan and gasket.
3. Disconnect direct clutch and 2nd brake solenoid electrical connectors.
4. Pry forward clutch accumulator and 2nd brake fluid pipes from lower valve body using suitable screwdriver.
5. Disconnect TV cable from throttle valve cam.
6. Remove mounting bolts and fluid filter screen.
7. Remove valve body mounting bolts, **Fig. 18.**
8. Remove forward clutch and 2nd brake accumulators from transaxle case by covering accumulator bores with cloth and slowly applying low pressure compressed air into fluid pressure passage, **Fig. 19.**

INSTALLATION

Torque sequence and specification is very important to valve body operation. If bolts are tightened at random, valve bores may become distorted and inhibit valve operation. Ensure all parts are clean and free of damage prior to their installation. When installing valve body to case, ensure accumulators and springs are in their correct positions, and all valve body bolts are installed according to length and position. **Do not use air powered tools when installing valve body.**

1. Apply transjel transmission assembly lubricant No. J-36850, or equivalent, to seals.
2. Install forward clutch and 2nd brake accumulators in case bores.
3. Install valve body into transaxle case aligning manual valve with shift lever pin.
4. Install and hand tighten valve body bolts in correct positions, **Fig. 20.**

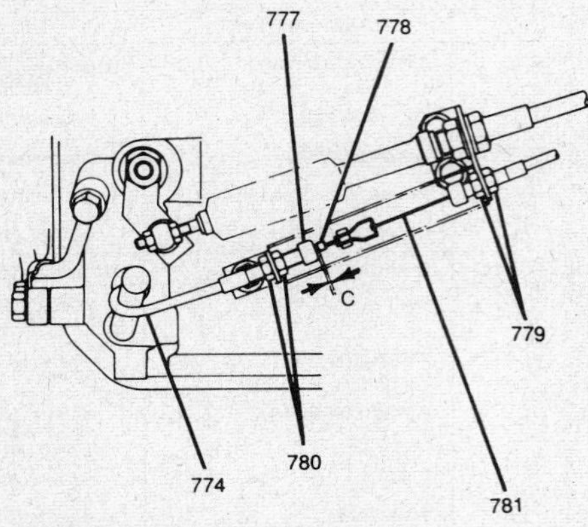

C 0.0–0.5 mm (0.0–0.02")
774 TV CABLE ASSEMBLY
777 TV CABLE BOOT
778 INNER CABLE STOPPER
779 ACCELERATOR CABLE ADJUSTMENT NUTS "B"
780 TV CABLE ADJUSTMENT NUTS "A"
781 ACCELERATOR CABLE

GC5029300477000X

Fig. 4 TV cable adjustment

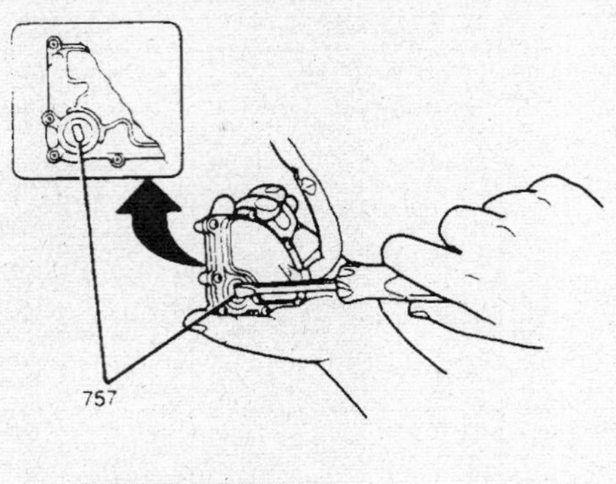

757 PNP SWITCH JOINT

GC5029300482000X

Fig. 5 Park/Neutral position switch adjustment

5. Tighten bolts A and B first, then tighten remaining bolts in diagonal pattern.
6. Install fluid filter screen.
7. Attach TV cable to throttle valve cam.
8. Install forward clutch accumulator and 2nd brake fluid pipes.
9. Connect direct clutch and 2nd brake solenoid connectors.
10. Install oil pan with new oil pan gasket.
11. Coat transaxle oil pan drain plug with Loctite pipe sealant part No. 1052080, or equivalent.
12. Fill transaxle with fluid and check level.

SHIFT SOLENOIDS & WIRING HARNESS, REPLACE

1. Raise and support vehicle.
2. Drain transaxle fluid into suitable container and remove transaxle oil pan.
3. Disconnect direct clutch and 2nd brake solenoid electrical connectors.
4. Remove direct clutch solenoid and 2nd brake solenoid mounting bolts, **Fig. 21.**
5. Remove solenoid wiring harness mounting nut and plate.
6. Pull wiring harness out of transaxle case.
7. Reverse procedure to install. Coat transaxle oil pan drain plug with Loctite pipe sealant part No. 1052080, or equivalent.

TRANSAXLE

REPLACE

1. Remove mounting bolts and hood.
2. Remove hold down bolt, bracket and battery.
3. Remove adjustment cover and TV cable, then the adjustment nut and shift select cable.
4. Remove engine wire harness bracket, then the vehicle speed sensor, shift solenoid harness and transaxle range switch electrical connectors.
5. Remove clip and speedometer cable, then the clamps and inlet and outlet fluid cooler hoses. Plug hoses.
6. Remove starter motor.
7. Remove upper rear transaxle bulkhead mounting bolt, rear mount through bolt and nut, and upper engine mounting bolts.
8. Remove ground cable from transaxle.
9. Install universal support fixture tool No. J-28467-A and adapters, or equivalent, then raise and support vehicle.
10. Drain transaxle fluid into suitable container.
11. Remove front wheel assemblies, then left and righthand splash shields.
12. Remove left and righthand ball stud nuts and bolts, then separate control arms from steering knuckles.
13. Install drive axle boot protector tool No. J-28712, or equivalent, on differential side and wheel side joints of both axles.
14. Remove wheel center cap, cotter pin and driveshaft nut, then the wheel nuts and wheel assembly.
15. Remove snap ring from spline of differential side joint using suitable screwdriver.
16. Remove stabilizer bar bracket bolts and ball stud bolt, then the ball stud from steering knuckle by pulling down on stabilizer bar.
17. Disconnect inboard joint from differential side gear and wheel side joint from steering knuckle.
18. Remove drive axle.
19. Remove mounting bolts and rear engine torque rod, then the mounting bolts and flywheel cover.
20. Remove torque converter mounting bolts using suitable screwdriver in notch provided to hold driveplate, **Fig. 22.**
21. Remove exhaust hanger bracket and lower rear engine mount bulkhead bolt.
22. Remove mounting nuts, bolts and rear engine mount bracket.
23. Lower vehicle and slightly lower engine.
24. Raise and support vehicle, then support transaxle with suitable hydraulic jack.
25. Remove bolts and lefthand transaxle mount and bracket.
26. Remove lower mounting bolt, nut and stud.
27. Move transaxle toward lefthand side of engine compartment and remove transaxle.
28. Reverse procedure to install, noting the following:
    a. Apply suitable grease around torque converter center cup.
    b. Measure distance A, **Fig. 23.**
    c. If distance is less than 0.85 inch, converter is improperly installed.
    d. Guide righthand drive axle into differential side gear as transaxle is being raised.
    e. After installing inboard joints into differential side gear, push inboard joints into side gears until snap rings on drive axles engage side gears.
    f. Adjust oil pressure control cable, as required.
    g. Fill transaxle with fluid.

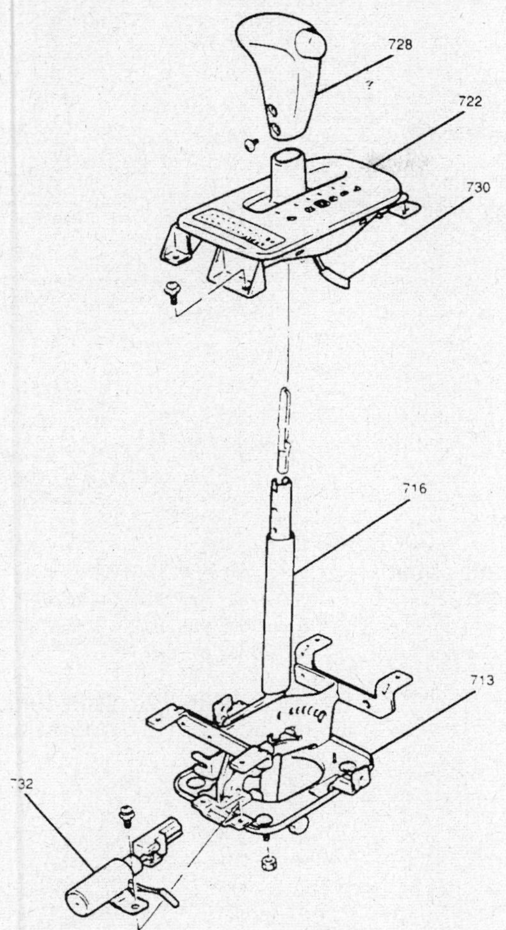

713 SELECTOR LEVER HOUSING
716 SELECTOR LEVER
722 SELECTOR COVER
728 SELECTOR LEVER KNOB
730 INDICATOR LAMP
732 SHIFT LOCK SOLENOID

GC5029300478000X

Fig. 6 Manual selector

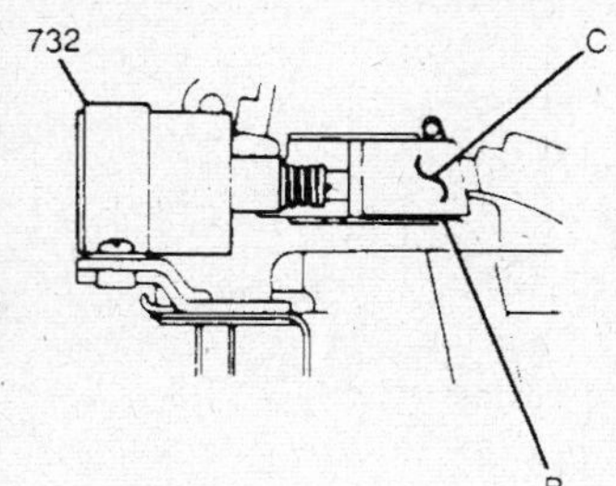

B LITHIUM GREASE
C MANUAL OVERRIDE SOLENOID LOCK PLATE
732 SHIFT LOCK SOLENOID

GC5029300479000X

Fig. 7 Solenoid lock plate

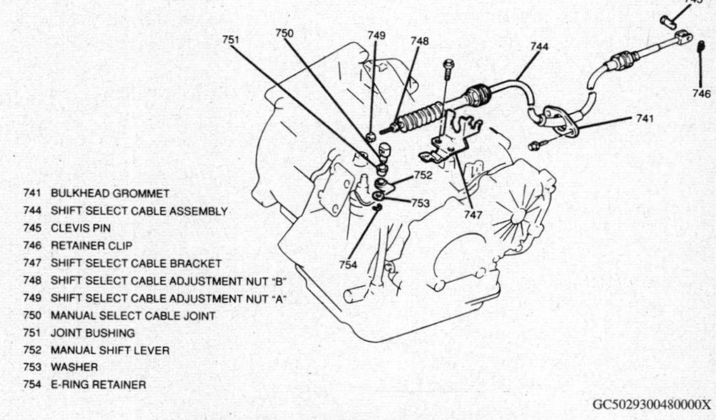

741 BULKHEAD GROMMET
744 SHIFT SELECT CABLE ASSEMBLY
745 CLEVIS PIN
746 RETAINER CLIP
747 SHIFT SELECT CABLE BRACKET
748 SHIFT SELECT CABLE ADJUSTMENT NUT "B"
749 SHIFT SELECT CABLE ADJUSTMENT NUT "A"
750 MANUAL SELECT CABLE JOINT
751 JOINT BUSHING
752 MANUAL SHIFT LEVER
753 WASHER
754 E-RING RETAINER

GC5029300480000X

Fig. 8 Shift select cable

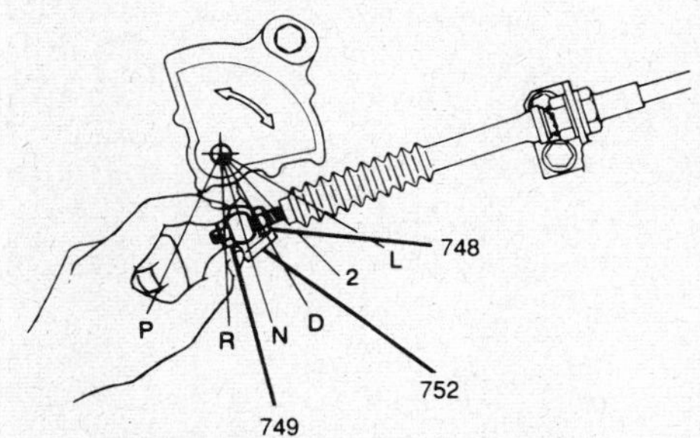

748 SHIFT SELECT CABLE ADJUSTMENT NUT "B"
749 SHIFT SELECT CABLE ADJUSTMENT NUT "A"
752 MANUAL SHIFT LEVER

GC5029300481000X

Fig. 9 Shift select cable installation

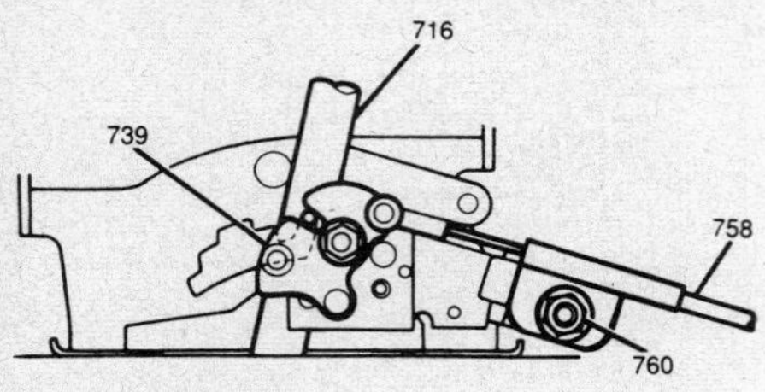

716 SELECTOR LEVER
739 KEY RELEASE PLATE
758 INTERLOCK CABLE ASSEMBLY
760 INTERLOCK CABLE BOLT

GC5029300483000X

Fig. 10 Interlock cable & manual selector

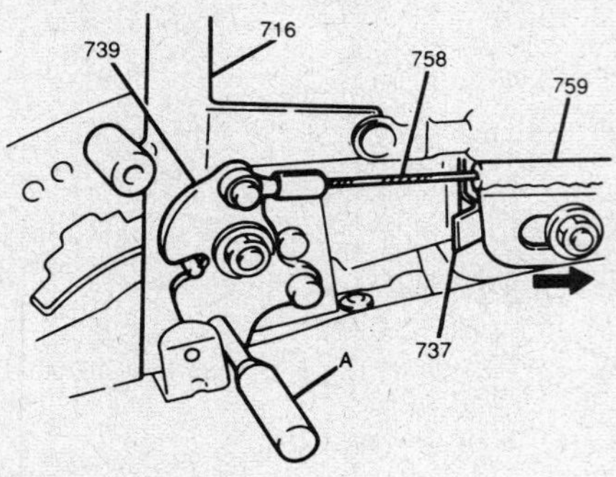

A SMALL SCREWDRIVER
716 SELECTOR LEVER
737 RETAINING SPRING
739 KEY RELEASE PLATE
758 INTERLOCK CABLE
759 INTERLOCK CABLE BRACKET

GC5029300484000X

Fig. 11 Interlock cable adjustment

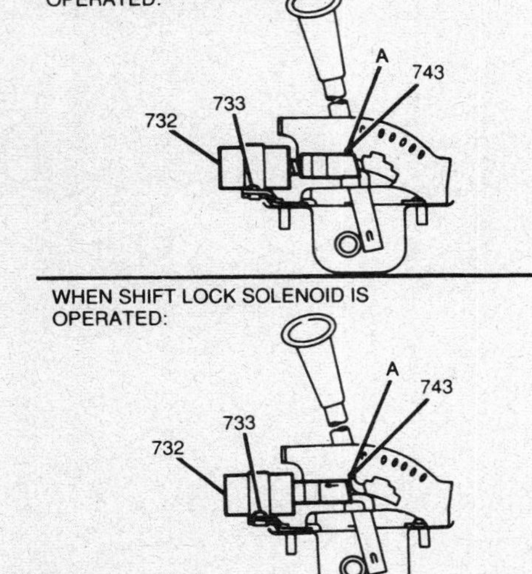

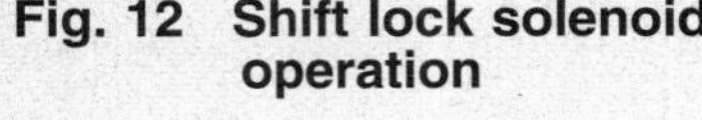

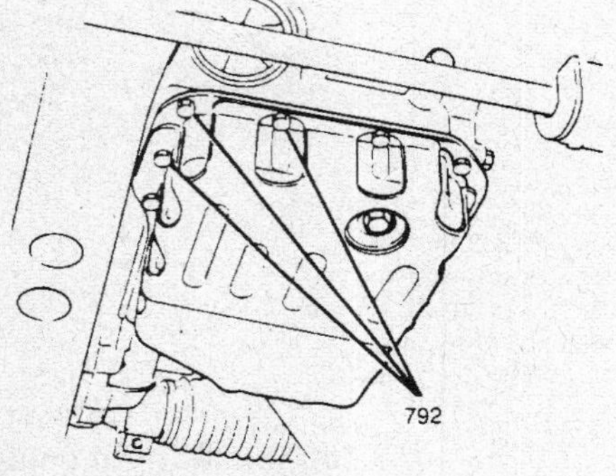

A APPLY LITHIUM GREASE
732 SHIFT LOCK SOLENOID
733 SHIFT LOCK SOLENOID RETAINING SCREW
743 DETENT PIN

GC5029300485000X

Fig. 12 Shift lock solenoid operation

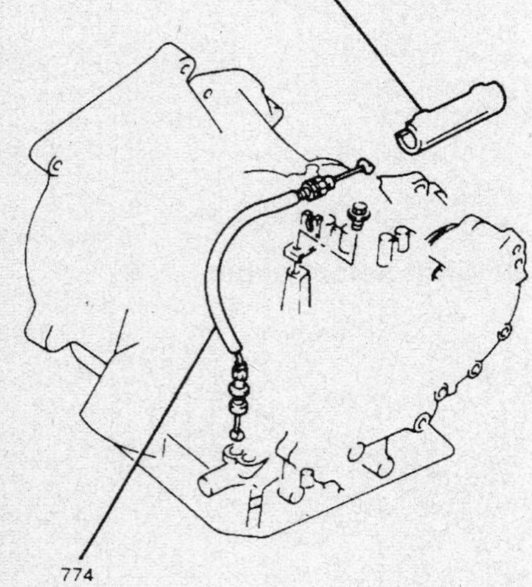

774 TV CABLE ASSEMBLY
775 TV CABLE ADJUSTMENT COVER

GC5029300486000X

Fig. 13 TV cable & adjustment cover

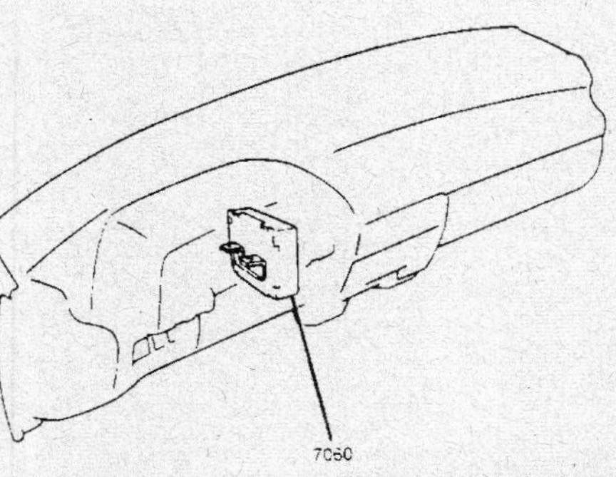

GC5029300487000X

Fig. 14 Transaxle control module location

792 TRANSAXLE FLUID PAN BOLTS

GC5029300488000X

Fig. 15 Transaxle fluid pan bolts

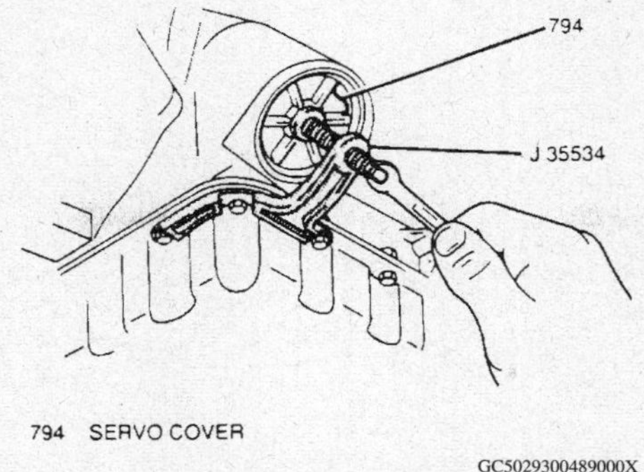

Fig. 16 Piston cover depressor tool installation

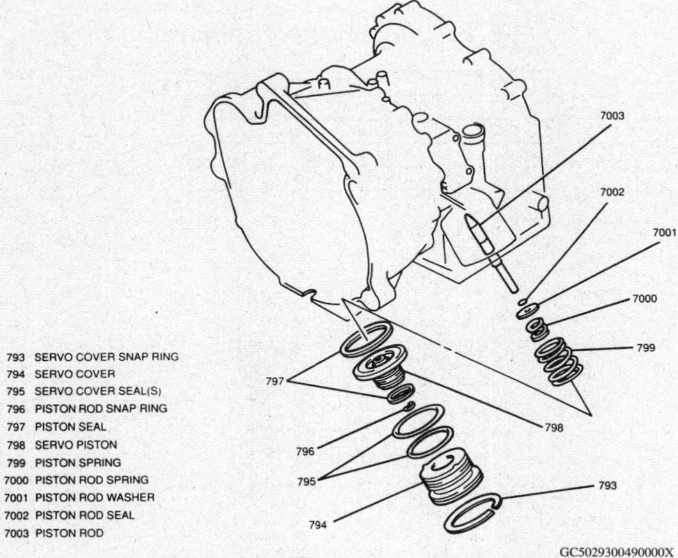

Fig. 17 Intermediate servo components

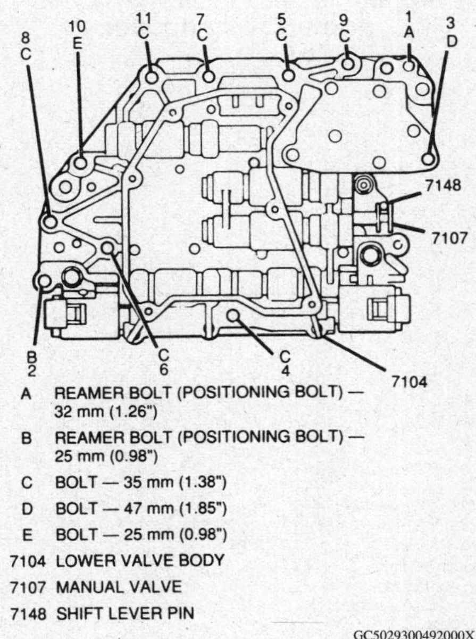

Fig. 18 Valve body bolt locations

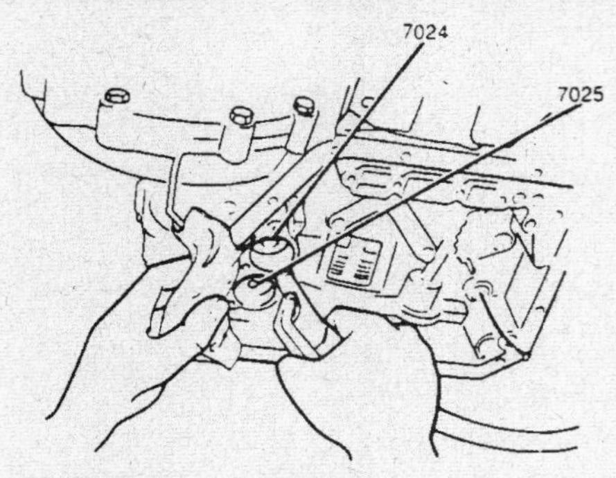

Fig. 19 Accumulator removal

BOLT	LENGTH	PIECES
A	29.5 mm (1.16")	6
B	38 mm (1.49")	6
C	44 mm (1.73")	2
D	REAMER BOLT	2

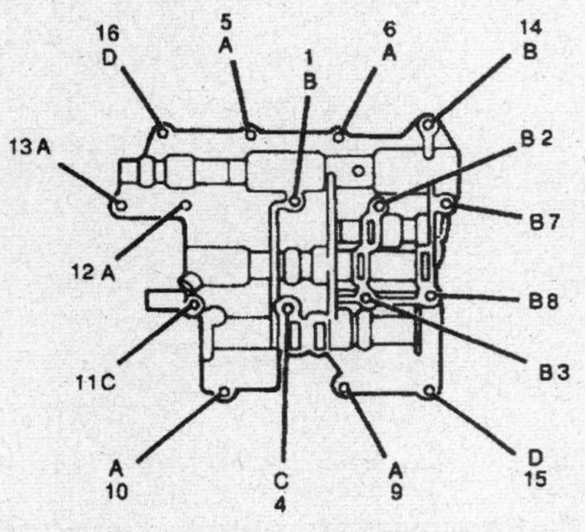

Fig. 20 Upper valve body bolt tightening sequence

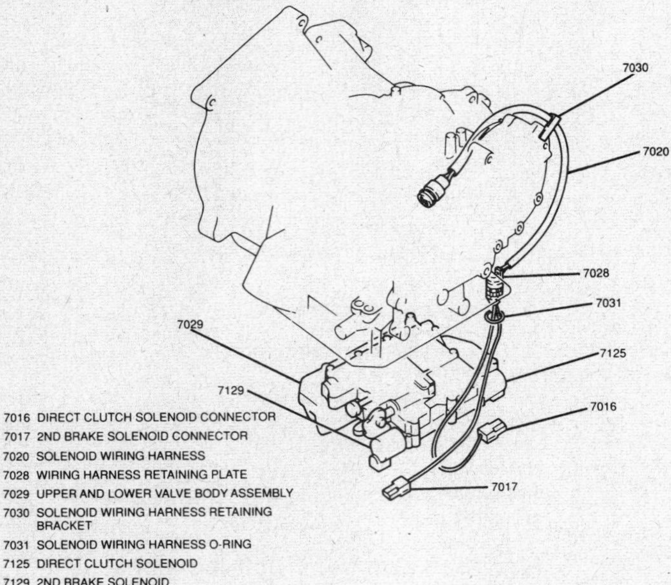

Fig. 21 Shift solenoids & wiring harness

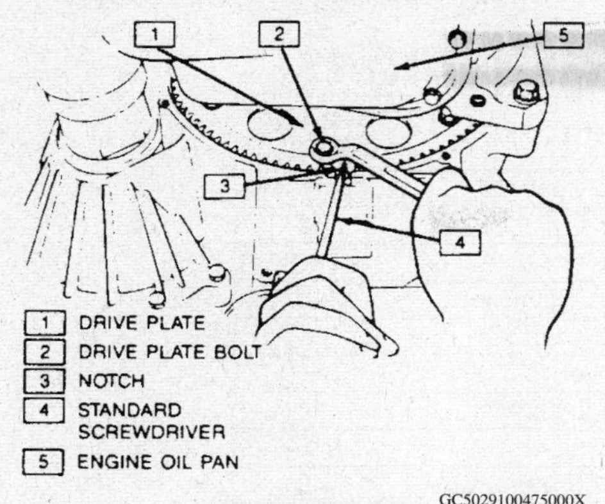

Fig. 22 Driveplate bolt removal

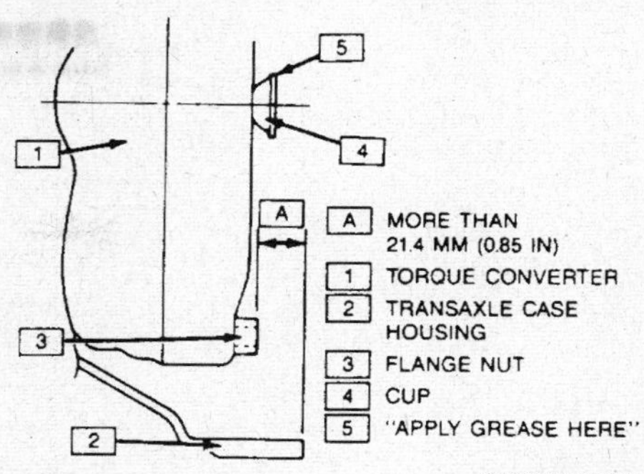

Fig. 23 Torque converter installation

TIGHTENING SPECIFICATIONS

Year	Component	Torque/Ft. Lbs.
1998–2001	Automatic Transaxle Controller	11
	Ball Stud	44
	Direct Clutch Solenoid	35①
	Engine Wiring Harness Bracket	12
	Filler Tube Bracket & Screen	53①
	Flywheel Cover	84①
	Flywheel To Torque Converter	14
	Inlet & Outlet Union	16
	Lefthand Transaxle Mount Bracket	40
	Lower Engine To Transaxle	40
	Lower Rear Engine Mount To Bulkhead	40
	Lower Valve Body	108①
	Lower Valve Body Cover	35①
	Rear Engine Mount Bracket	40
	Rear Engine Torque Rod	40
	Second Brake Solenoid	35①
	Selector Lever Housing Seat	12
	Shift Lever Back-up & Neutral Safety Switch	17
	Shift Select Cable Bulkhead Grommet	15
	Solenoid Wiring Harness Retaining Bracket	15
	Speedometer Driven Gear Case	11
	Starter Motor	17
	Transaxle Cooler Pipe Bracket	20
	Transaxle Drain Plug	17
	Transaxle Fluid Pan	53①
	Upper Rear Transaxle Mount To Bulkhead	40
	Upper Transaxle To Engine	40
	Upper Valve Body	53①
	Vehicle Speed Sensor	17

① — Inch lbs.

Aisin Warner A131L Automatic Transaxle

NOTE: On Air Bag Equipped Models, Refer To "Air Bag System Precautions" Located In The Front Of This Manual For System Disarming & Arming Procedures.

NOTE: Refer To "Computer Relearn Procedures" Located In The Front Of This Manual When Battery Power To The Computer Has Been Interrupted.

INDEX

PRECAUTIONS

AIR BAG SYSTEMS

Refer to "Air Bag System Precautions" in the front of this manual for system disarming and arming procedures.

BATTERY GROUND CABLE

Prior to service, disconnect battery ground cable and isolate as required.

IDENTIFICATION

The transaxle identification number is located on the top of the transaxle case above the lefthand drive axle, **Fig. 1.**

DESCRIPTION

The torque converter is equipped with an integral lock-up clutch. For higher performance, greater fuel economy and quietness, a high efficiency torque converter, wider gear ratio, compact high-precision valve body, high efficiency oil pump and a light weight durable integral transaxle case are used.

TROUBLESHOOTING

Refer to **Figs. 2 through 13** for troubleshooting.

MAINTENANCE

Refer to "Lubricant Data" chart in the appropriate chassis chapter of this manual for transmission fluid specifications.

FLUID CHECK

1. Start engine and allow transaxle fluid to reach 158–176°F.

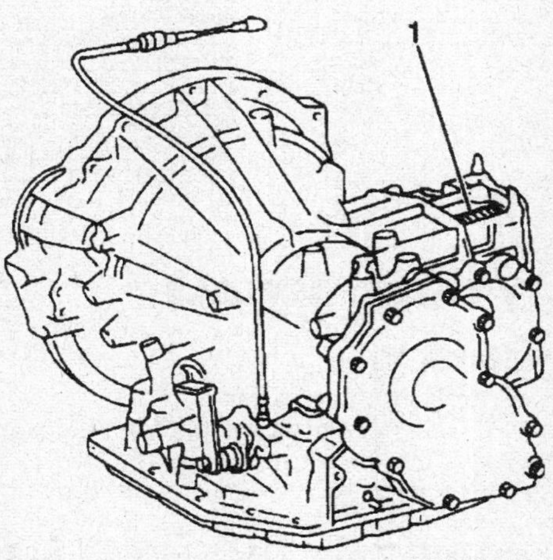

Fig. 1 Transaxle identification number plate location

2. Position vehicle on level surface and set parking brake.
3. With engine idling and brake pedal depressed, move shift lever through all positions.
4. Remove transaxle dipstick, wipe clean and replace.
5. Remove dipstick again. Ensure fluid is at HOT level.

FLUID CHANGE

1. Raise and support vehicle.
2. Remove splash shield.
3. Remove plug and drain fluid into suitable container.
4. Remove bolts, oil pan and gasket.
5. Remove bolts, filter screen and gasket.
6. Clean screen and magnets with suitable solvent and dry thoroughly.
7. Install new gasket, screen and mounting bolts.
8. Install new gasket, oil pan and mounting bolts.
9. Install new drain plug.
10. Install splash shield, then lower vehicle and fill transaxle.
11. Start engine and move selector lever through all ranges, ending in P position.
12. With engine idling, check and adjust fluid level.

ADJUSTMENTS

THROTTLE VALVE (TV) CABLE

1. Inspect TV cable for deflection or looseness.
2. Ensure TV is in fully closed position.
3. Measure TV cable boot to inner cable stopper clearance, **Fig. 14.** If clearance is more than 0.04 inch, proceed to next step.
4. Adjust TV cable boot to inner cable stopper clearance by turning adjustment nuts until clearance is as specified.

IN-VEHICLE REPAIRS

VALVE BODY, REPLACE

REMOVAL

1. Raise and support vehicle.
2. Clean area around oil pan and drain transmission fluid into suitable container.
3. Remove oil pan, gasket and oil strainer.
4. Remove mounting bolts, bracket and oil apply tube.

Problem	Action
Low fluid.	Add fluid.
TV cable out of adjustment, binding or damaged.	Adjust or replace throttle valve cable.
Shift select cable out of adjustment, biding or damaged.	Adjust or replace shift select cable.
Manual valve binding or sticking.	Inspect valve body.
Throttle valve binding or sticking.	Inspect valve body.
B2 control valve binding or sticking.	Inspect valve body.
Accumulator(s) pistons damaged or leaking.	Inspect accumulator pistons.
Accumulator(s) seals cut or damaged.	Inspect accumulator seals.
Accumulator(s) broken or distorted springs.	Inspect accumulator springs.
Incorrect line pressure.	Perform line pressure diagnosis.

GC5029800944000X

Fig. 2 Harsh engagement into any drive range

Problem	Action
Fluid level is low.	Add fluid.
TV cable is out of adjustment, binding or damaged.	Adjust or replace throttle valve cable.
Shift select cable is out of adjustment, biding or damaged.	Adjust or replace shift select cable.
Throttle valve is binding or sticking.	Inspect valve body.
Primary regulator valve is binding or sticking.	Inspect valve body.
Accumulator pistons are damaged or leaking.	Inspect accumulator pistons.
Accumulator seals are cut or damaged.	Inspect accumulator seals.
Accumulator springs are broken or distorted.	Inspect accumulator springs.
Forward clutch discs are worn.	Replace forward clutch discs.
Forward clutch piston or seal is leaking or damaged.	Inspect forward clutch piston seal.
Input shaft O-rings are cut or damaged.	Inspect input shaft O-ring.
One-way clutch is not holding or damaged.	Inspect one-way clutch.
Fluid pressure is incorrect.	Perform line pressure diagnosis.

GC5029800945000X

Fig. 3 Slips in first gear

Problem	Action
Throttle valve cable is out of adjustment, binding or damaged.	Adjust or replace throttle valve cable.
Throttle valve is binding or sticking.	Inspect valve body.
1-2 shift valve is binding or sticking.	Inspect valve body.
Primary regulator valve is binding or sticking.	Inspect valve body.
Intermediate servo seals are cut or damaged.	Inspect intermediate servo seals.
Intermediate servo piston is binding or sticking.	Inspect intermediate servo piston.
2nd brake band is worn or out of alignment.	Inspect 2nd brake band.
Fluid pressure is incorrect	Perform line pressure diagnosis.

GC5029800946000X

Fig. 4 First gear only

Problem	Action
Fluid level is low.	Add fluid.
Throttle valve cable out of adjustment, binding or damaged.	Adjust or replace throttle valve cable.
Throttle valve binding or sticking.	Inspect valve body.
1-2 shift valve binding or sticking.	Inspect valve body.
Primary regulator valve binding or sticking.	Inspect valve body.
Intermediate servo seals are cut or damaged.	Inspect valve body.
Intermediate servo piston is binding or sticking.	Inspect intermediate servo seals.
Intermediate servo piston rod is not engaged.	Inspect intermediate servo piston.
2nd brake band is worn or out of alignment.	Inspect 2nd brake band.
Internal damage to torque converter.	Replace torque converter.
Forward clutch discs are worn.	Replace forward clutch discs.
Forward clutch piston or seal are leaking or damaged.	Inspect forward clutch piston and seal.
Input shaft O-rings are cut or damaged.	Inspect input shaft O-rings.
Fluid pressure is incorrect.	Perform line pressure diagnosis.

GC5029800947000X

Fig. 5 Slipping or rough 1-2 shift

Problem	Action
Fluid level is low.	Add fluid.
Throttle valve cable out of adjustment, binding or damaged.	Adjust or replace throttle valve cable.
Throttle valve binding or sticking.	Inspect valve body.
2-3 shift valve binding or sticking.	Inspect valve body.
Primary regulator valve binding or sticking.	Inspect valve body.
Intermediate servo piston binding or sticking.	Inspect intermediate servo seals.
Intermediate servo piston rod not engaged.	Inspect intermediate servo piston.
2nd brake band not releasing.	Inspect 2nd brake band.
Torque converter internal damage.	Replace torque converter.
Direct clutch discs are worn.	Replace direct clutch discs.
Direct clutch piston or seal is leaking or damaged.	Inspect direct clutch piston and seal.
Fluid pressure is incorrect.	Perform line pressure diagnosis.

GC5029800948000X

Fig. 6 No 2-3 shift or 2-3 shift slipping

Problem	Action
Fluid level is low.	Add fluid.
Throttle valve cable out of adjustment, binding or damaged.	Adjust or replace throttle valve cable.
Valve body spacer plate or gaskets damaged or not positioned correctly.	Inspect valve body.
Throttle valve is binding or sticking.	Inspect valve body.
Check balls omitted or not positioned correctly.	Inspect valve body.
Internal damage to torque converter.	Replace torque converter.
Direct clutch piston or seal leaking or damaged.	Inspect direct clutch piston and seal.
Fluid pressure is incorrect.	Perform the line pressure diagnosis.

GC5029800949000X

Fig. 7 High or low shift points

5. Remove oil tubes using suitable screwdriver, then the manual detent spring.
6. Remove mounting bolts and manual valve.
7. Remove valve body to cable bracket mounting bolt and disconnect throttle cable.
8. Remove mounting bolts, valve body, governor, apply gasket and governor oil gasket.

INSTALLATION

1. Install governor oil gasket, governor and governor apply gasket.
2. Hold valve body in place, manually retain cam in downward position and slip cable end into slot.
3. Position valve body into place and install.
4. Hand tighten mounting bolts, then tighten bolts to specification, **Fig. 15.**
5. Align manual valve with pin on manual valve lever and install manual valve body.
6. Insert and hand tighten mounting bolts. Tighten to specification, **Fig. 16.**
7. Install detent spring, then insert and hand tighten mounting bolts.
8. Ensure manual lever is in contact with center of roller at tip of detent spring and install oil tubes.
9. Install apply tube bracket and oil strainer.
10. Insert magnet into oil pan and pan with new gasket.
11. Insert oil pan mounting bolts.
12. Install drain plug with new gasket.
13. Fill transaxle to specifications.

TV CABLE, REPLACE

REMOVAL

1. Loosen TV cable jam nuts.
2. Disconnect throttle cable from bracket and throttle plate.
3. Remove neutral start and back-up switch.
4. Remove valve body and throttle cable end from throttle pressure valve cam.
5. Pull cable from transaxle case.

INSTALLATION

1. Insert cable into transaxle case, then install retaining plate and bolt.
2. Install valve body.
3. Bend cable to approximately 7.87 inches radius, **Fig. 17.**
4. Lightly pull inner cable from housing until slight resistance is felt and hold in position.
5. Stake stopper onto inner cable so 0.031–0.059 inch clearance exists between stop and cable housing. **Cable stop is not staked in place on replacement cable.**
6. Connect throttle cable to throttle linkage and adjust cable.
7. Install neutral safety switch and manual shift lever.
8. Adjust switch,
9. Adjust fluid level, as required.

GOVERNOR VALVE, REPLACE

1. Raise and support vehicle.
2. Remove transaxle cover and lefthand driveshaft.
3. Remove governor cover and O-ring.
4. Remove governor body with thrust washer.
5. Remove washer and governor body adapter.
6. Reverse procedure to install.

SECOND BRAKE SERVO, REPLACE

REMOVAL

1. Raise and support vehicle.
2. Drain fluid into suitable container.
3. Remove shift cable bracket at transaxle.
4. Compress second brake servo using second brake servo compressor tool No. J-35549-A, or equivalent.
5. Remove second brake servo snap ring and second brake servo compressor.
6. Remove cover.
7. Remove piston and outer spring.

INSTALLATION

1. Insert piston, less outer spring, then install snap ring.
2. Install brake apply rod tool No. J-35679, or equivalent, and observe

Problem	Action
Throttle valve is cable out of adjustment, binding or damaged.	Adjust or replace throttle valve cable.
Throttle valve is binding or sticking.	Inspect valve body.
1-2 shift valve is binding or sticking.	Inspect valve body.
2-3 shift valve is binding or sticking.	Inspect valve body.
Primary regulator is valve binding or sticking.	Inspect valve body.
Valve springs are broken or distorted.	Inspect valve body.
Valve body casting is damaged or porous.	Inspect valve body.
Intermediate servo piston is binding or sticking.	Inspect intermediate servo piston.
Intermediate servo piston seals are cut or damaged.	Inspect intermediate servo piston seals.
Intermediate servo piston rod is binding.	Inspect intermediate sero piston rod.
2nd brake band is worn or out of alignment.	Replace 1st-reverse brake clutch discs.
1st-reverse brake clutch discs worn.	Replace 1st-reverse brake clutch.
1st-reverse brake piston or seal is leaking or damaged.	Inspect 1st-reverse brake piston.
One-way clutch not holding or damaged.	Inspect one-way clutch.

GC5029800950000X

Fig. 8 No part throttle or delayed downshifts

Problem	Action
Shift select cable is out of adjustment, binding or damaged.	Adjust or replace shift select cable.
Manual valve is binding or sticking.	Inspect valve body.
1-2 shift valve is binding or sticking.	Inspect valve body.
2-3 shift valve is binding or sticking.	Inspect valve body.
Valve springs are broken or distorted.	Inspect valve body.
Valve body casting is damaged or porous.	Inspect valve body.
Intermediate servo piston is binding or sticking.	Inspect intermediate servo piston.
Intermediate servo piston seals are cut or damaged.	Inspect intermediate servo piston seals.
Intermediate servo piston rod is binding.	Inspect intermediate servo piston rod.
2nd brake band is worn or out of alignment.	Inspect 2nd brake band.
1st-reverse brake clutch disc worn.	Replace 1st-reverse brake clutch discs.
1st-reverse brake piston or seal leaking or damaged.	Inspect 1st-reverse brake piston.
One-way clutch not holding or damaged.	Inspect one-way clutch.

GC5029800951000X

Fig. 9 No engine braking or 3-2-1 manual downshift

Problem	Action
Fluid level is low.	Add fluid.
Shift select cable is out of adjustment, binding or damaged.	Adjust or replace shift select cable.
Valve body spacer plate or gaskets not positioned correctly or damaged.	Inspect valve body.
Check balls omitted or not positioned correctly.	Inspect valve body.
Manual valve binding or sticking.	Inspect valve body.
Manual valve link disconnected.	Inspect manual valve link.
Direct clutch piston or seals leaking or damaged.	Inspect direct clutch piston and seals.
Incorrect line pressure.	Perform Line Pressure Test diagnosis.

GC5029800952000X

Fig. 10 No reverse or slips in reverse

Problem	Action
Fluid pump is internally leaking.	Inspect fluid pump.
Fluid pump drive and driven gears worn or damaged.	Repair fluid pump drive and driven gears.
Fluid pump cover seal rings cut or damaged.	Inspect fluid pump seal rings.
Fluid pump body or cover casting is porous or damaged.	Repair/replace fluid pump.
Throttle valve cable out of adjustment, binding or damaged.	Adjust or replace throttle valve cable.
Throttle valve cable link is loose or disconnected.	Inspect throttle valve cable link.
Valve body spacer plate or gaskets not positioned correctly or damaged.	Inspect valve body.
Check balls omitted or not positioned correctly or damaged.	Inspect valve body.
Manual valve binding or sticking.	Inspect valve body.
Manual valve link is disconnected.	Inspect manual valve link.
Primary regulator valve binding or sticking.	Inspect valve body.
Case internal leak in forward clutch fluid circuit.	Repair and replace case.
Case internal leak in direct clutch fluid circuit.	Repair and replace case.
Case fluid passages blocked or restricted.	Repair and replace case.

GC5029800953000X

Fig. 11 Fluid pressure high or low

Problem	Action
Shift select cable is out of adjustment, binding or damaged.	Adjust shift select cable.
Parking lock rod, pawl or spring is faulty.	Inspect parking lock assembly.

GC5029800954000X

Fig. 12 No Park or ratcheting noise in Park

Problem	Action
Low or no fluid.	Add fluid.
Shift cable out of adjustment, binding or damaged.	Adjust or replace select cable.
Parking lock pawl mechanism locked or frozen.	Inspect parking lock pawl.
Broken torque converter to flywheel bolts.	Replace bolts.
Torque converter stator one-way clutch no holding.	Replace torque converter.
Torque converter failure.	Replace torque converter.
Valve body spacer plate or gaskets improper position or damaged.	Inspect valve body.
Check balls omitted or improper position.	Inspect valve body.
Manual valve binding or sticking.	Inspect valve body.
Manual valve link disconnected.	Inspect manual valve linkage.
Incorrect line pressure.	Perform line pressure diagnosis.

GC5029800955000X

Fig. 13 Unable to run in all ranges

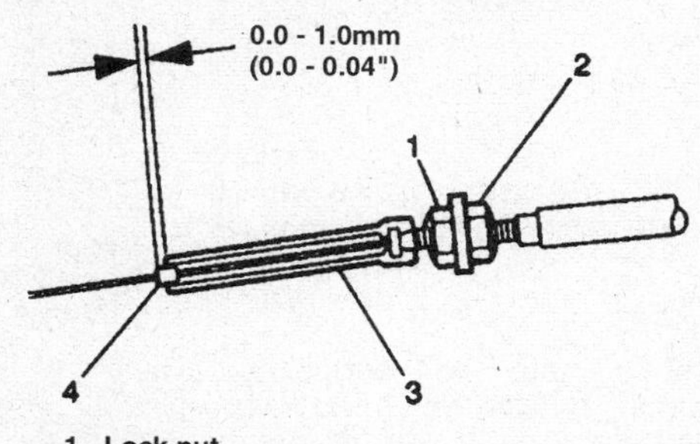

1- Lock nut
2- Lock nut
3- Cable boot
4- Inner cable stopper

GC5029100428000A

Fig. 14 TV cable adjustment

groove on plunger of tool.

3. Push button on tool, **Fig. 18,** and note the following:
   a. This allows tool to push brake apply rod into case.
   b. If groove is visible, piston stroke is correct 0.059–0.118 inch).
   c. If stroke is greater than specified, replace piston rod with 2.870 inch or 2.811 inch rod, as required.
4. Remove snap ring, then install piston and outer spring.
5. Compress spring using spring compressor tool No. J-35549, or equivalent, and insert snap ring.
6. Install cover and shift cable bracket.
7. Lower vehicle.

BRAKE TRANSMISSION SHIFT INTERLOCK, REPLACE

The automatic transmission control lever solenoid is part of the brake transmission shift interlock system.

1. Remove rear console.
2. Disconnect electrical connector from shift interlock solenoid.
3. Remove indicator bulb.
4. Remove two shift indicator cover mounting bolts.
5. Raise and rotate shift indicator cover to access mounting screws on shift interlock solenoid.
6. Remove mounting screws shift interlock solenoid.
7. Reverse procedure to install.

MANUAL SELECTOR, REPLACE

1. Remove center console.
2. Remove one spring clip and shift select cable from manual selector lever, **Fig. 19.**
3. Remove one E-clip and shift select cable from manual selector base, **Fig. 20.**
4. Remove mounting bolts and manual selector.
5. Reverse procedure to install.

TRANSAXLE

REPLACE

1. Disconnect Intake Air Temperature (IAT) sensor electrical connector.
2. Remove air cleaner cover and filter.
3. Loosen air cleaner intake tube clamp.
4. Remove mounting bolts and air cleaner.
5. Disconnect Park/Neutral Position (PNP) switch electrical connector.
6. Disconnect solenoid wire harness electrical connector.
7. Remove transaxle case ground strap and loosen TV cable locknut.
8. Disconnect throttle cable from throttle linkage and TV cable bracket.
9. Disconnect vehicle speed sensor electrical connector.
10. Remove shift select cable from manual lever.
11. Remove E-clip and shift select cable from bracket.
12. Remove TV cable guide bracket from transaxle case.
13. Remove two upper transaxle to engine mounting bolts.
14. Remove starter.
15. Install universal support fixture tool No. J-28467-A, or equivalent.
16. Remove mounting bolts and lefthand

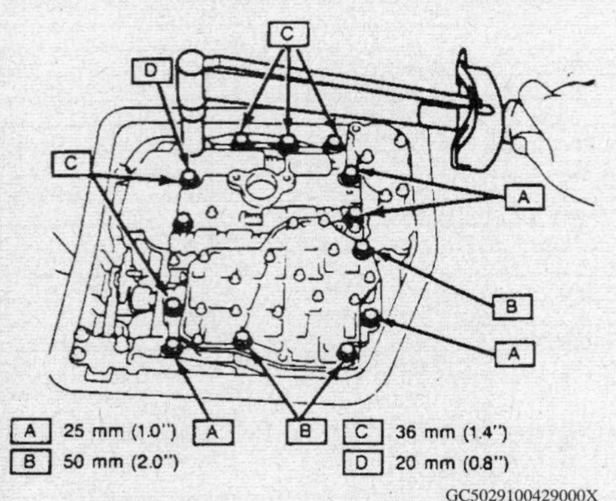

Fig. 15 Valve body bolt identification

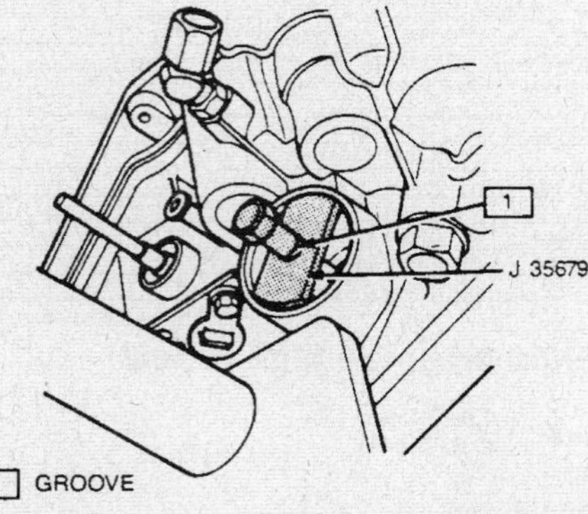

Fig. 18 Second brake servo plunger installation

transaxle mounting bracket reinforcement.

17. Remove one lefthand transaxle mounting bracket mounting bolt.
18. Raise and support vehicle, then place suitable container under transaxle.
19. Remove transaxle drain plug and drain fluid.
20. Remove differential drain plug and drain fluid from differential case.
21. Remove left and righthand splash shields.
22. Remove hose clamps, then the inner and outer fluid cooler hoses from fluid cooler pipes at transaxle. **Plug fluid cooler hoses.**
23. Remove two mounting bolts from lefthand transaxle mounting bracket.

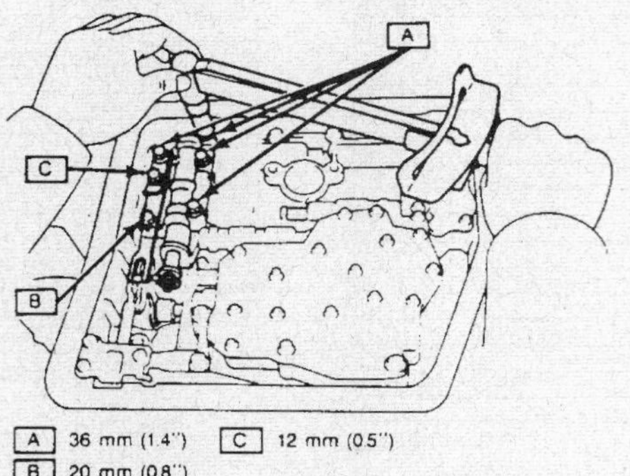

Fig. 16 Manual valve body bolt identification

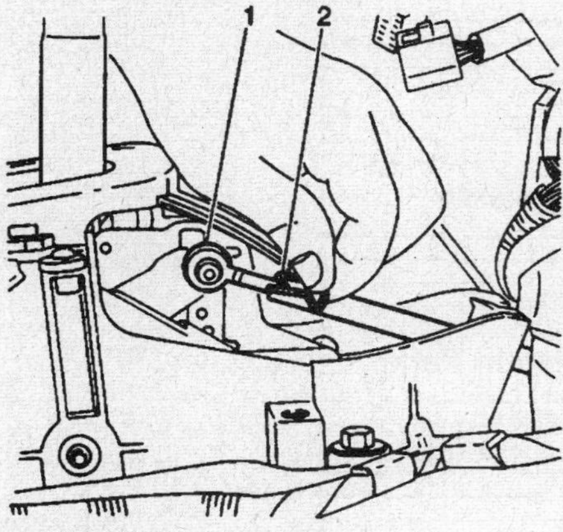

Fig. 19 Shift cable to selector lever removal

24. Remove front wheels.
25. Remove left and righthand drive axles.
26. Remove mounting bolts, nut and exhaust pipe support from center crossmember.
27. Remove mounting bolts from front exhaust pipe to three-way catalytic converter mating flange.
28. Disconnect electrical connector from oxygen sensor at front exhaust pipe.
29. Remove mounting bolts and front exhaust pipe from exhaust manifold.
30. Remove crossmember plastic access cover from center crossmember.
31. Remove front transaxle and rear transaxle mounts' mounting bolts and nuts.
32. Remove mounting bolts and front suspension crossmember.
33. Support transmission using a suitable hydraulic transmission jack.
34. Remove mounting bolts and engine reinforcement brace.
35. Remove access cover and flywheel mounting bolts.
36. Remove lower transaxle to engine mounting bolts and transaxle.
37. Reverse procedure to install.

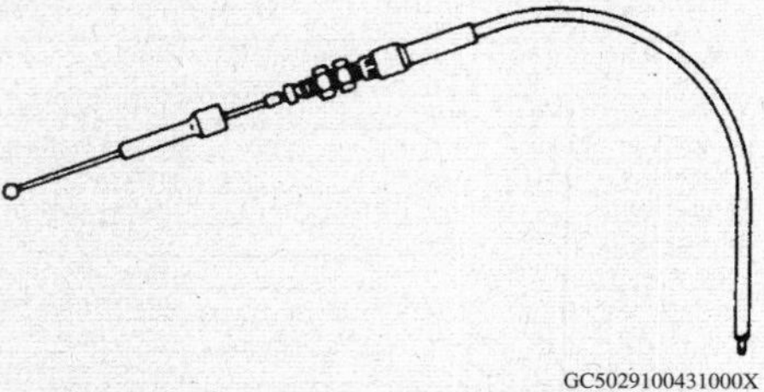

Fig. 17 TV cable positioning for stopper installation

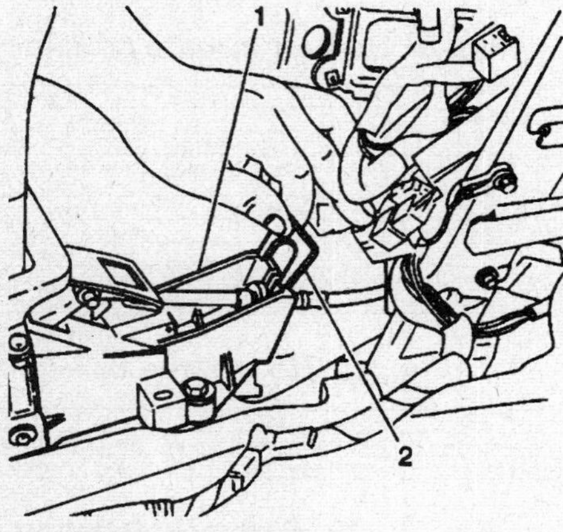

Fig. 20 Shift cable to selector base removal

TIGHTENING SPECIFICATIONS

Year	Component	Torque/Ft. Lbs.
1998–2002	Cable End	15
	Center Crossmember To Main Crossmember	45
	Center Crossmember To Radiator Support	45
	Center Mount	45
	Center Mount To Transaxle	45
	Detent Spring	72①
	Differential Check Fill Plug	29
	Differential Fill & Drain Plug	29
	Drain Plug	29
	Exhaust Hanger Bracket	10
	Fill Tube To Case	96①
	Front, Center & Rear Mount	45
	Front Mount	45
	Front Mount Bracket	13
	Front Mount Through Bolt	64
	Governor Cover	96①
	Lefthand Mount Brace	13
	Lefthand Mount Through Bolt	66
	Lower A-Frame To Underbody	94
	Lower Mount To Bracket	45
	Lower Transaxle Mount	45
	Main Crossmember To Underbody	152
	Manual Lever Cap	84①
	Manual Valve & Manual Detent Spring	84①
	Mount Cover & Brace	13
	Neutral Start Switch	72①
	Oil Apply Tube	44①
	Oil Cooler Line	20
	Oil Cooler Pipe Fittings	15
	Oil Filter	84①
	Oil Pan	44①
	Oil Pan Drain Plug	29
	Oil Pump	16
	Rear Mount Through Bolt	64
	Shift Control	15
	Side Case Cover Bolts	44①
	Starter Motor	29
	Switch	84①
	Throttle Valve Cable Adjusting Nut	72①
	Throttle Valve Cable Housing Locknuts	84①
	Torque Converter	14
	Transaxle Fluid Drain Plug	29
	Transaxle To Engine	47
	Upper Mount To Bracket	45
	Upper Transaxle Mount Bracket	45
	Valve Body	84①
	Wheel Lug Nuts	76

① — Inch lbs.

Aisin Warner A245-E Automatic Transaxle

NOTE: On Air Bag Equipped Models, Refer To "Air Bag System Precautions" Located In The Front Of This Manual For System Disarming & Arming Procedures.

NOTE: Refer To "Computer Relearn Procedures" Located In The Front Of This Manual When Battery Power To The Computer Has Been Interrupted.

NOTE: Prior To Performing Any Service Operations Listed In This Section, Consult The "Technical Service Bulletins" Section For Related Information.

INDEX

PRECAUTIONS

AIR BAG SYSTEMS

Refer to "Air Bag System Precautions" in the front of this manual for system disarming and arming procedures.

BATTERY GROUND CABLE

Prior to service, disconnect battery ground cable and isolate as required.

IDENTIFICATION

The A245E four-speed automatic transaxle identification number is located on top of the transaxle case in front of the vent tube, **Fig. 1.**

DESCRIPTION

The A245E transaxle is equipped with an integral lock-up mechanism, fuel consumption has been reduced and power output increased by more precise shift control and monitoring of the throttle opening angle.

TROUBLESHOOTING

Refer to **Figs. 2 through 10** for troubleshooting.

MAINTENANCE

Refer to "Aisin Warner A131L Automatic Transaxle" section for procedures.

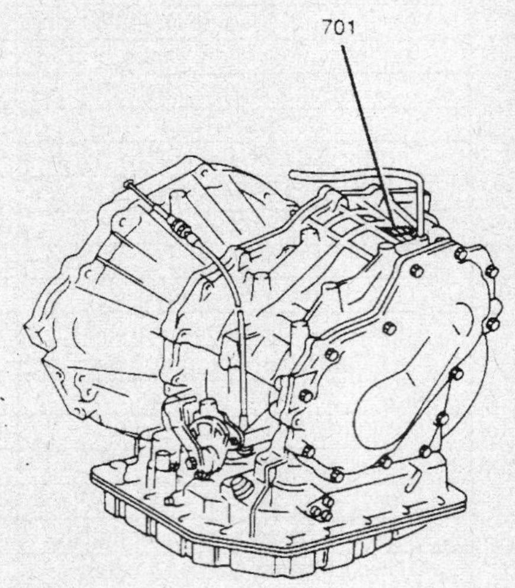

Fig. 1 Transaxle identification number location

ADJUSTMENTS

THROTTLE VALVE (TV) CABLE

Refer to "Adjustments" in the "Aisin Warner A131L Automatic Transaxle" section for procedure.

IN-VEHICLE REPAIRS

BRAKE TRANSMISSION SHIFT INTERLOCK, REPLACE

Refer to "Adjustments" in the "Aisin Warner A131L Automatic Transaxle" section for procedure.

MANUAL SELECTOR, REPLACE

Refer to "Adjustments" in the "Aisin Warner A131L Automatic Transaxle" section for procedure.

VALVE BODY & ACCUMULATOR, REPLACE

1. Raise and support vehicle.
2. Remove six bolts and lefthand splash shield.
3. Place suitable container under transaxle oil pan.
4. Remove drain plug and drain transaxle fluid.
5. Remove transaxle fluid pan. Use suitable rubber mallet and wooden block if pan is frozen to transaxle. **Do not use metal objects (crow bar, screwdriver, etc.) to free pan.**
6. Remove filter and screen from valve body.
7. Disconnect solenoid electrical connectors from shift solenoid Nos. 1 and 2 and TCC solenoid, **Fig. 11.**
8. Remove bolt and solenoid wire harness clip from valve body and detent spring.
9. Remove TV cable from throttle valve cam. **B2 accumulator, checkball and**

Problem	Action
The Fluid is contaminated.	Flush and add fresh fluid.
Torque converter is faulty.	Replace torque converter.
Transaxle is faulty.	Overhaul transaxle.

GC5029800958000X

Fig. 2 Fluid discolored or smells burnt

Problem	Action
Low fluid.	Add fluid.
TV cable out of adjustment, binding or damaged.	Adjust or replace throttle valve cable.
Shift select cable out of adjustment, biding or damaged.	Adjust or replace shift select cable.
Manual valve binding or sticking.	Inspect valve body.
Throttle valve binding or sticking.	Inspect valve body.
B2 control valve binding or sticking.	Inspect valve body.
Accumulator(s) pistons damaged or leaking.	Inspect accumulator pistons.
Accumulator(s) seals cut or damaged.	Inspect accumulator seals.
Accumulator(s) broken or distorted springs.	Inspect accumulator springs.
Incorrect line pressure.	Perform line pressure diagnosis.

GC5029800960000X

Fig. 4 Harsh engagement into any drive range

Problem	Action
Valve body is faulty.	Inspect valve body.
Shift solenoid is faulty.	Inspect shift solenoid.
Fault within electronic control system.	Perform Powertrain On-Board Diagnostic (OBD) system check

GC5029800962000X

Fig. 6 No downshift when coasting

Problem	Action
Shift solenoid is Faulty.	Inspect shift solenoid.
Fault within electronic control system.	Perform Powertrain On-Board Diagnostic (OBD) system check
Faulty valve body.	Inspect valve body.
Throttle valve cable is faulty.	Inspect throttle valve cable.

GC5029800964000X

Fig. 8 No OD-3, 3-2 or 2-1 kickdown

Problem	Action
Low or no fluid.	Add fluid.
Shift cable out of adjustment, binding or damaged.	Adjust or replace select cable.
Parking lock pawl mechanism locked or frozen.	Inspect parking lock pawl.
Broken torque converter to flywheel bolts.	Replace bolts.
Torque converter stator one-way clutch no holding.	Replace torque converter.
Torque converter failure.	Replace torque converter.
Valve body spacer plate or gaskets improper position or damaged.	Inspect valve body.
Check balls omitted or improper position.	Inspect valve body.
Manual valve binding or sticking.	Inspect valve body.
Manual valve link disconnected.	Inspect manual valve linkage.
Incorrect line pressure.	Perform line pressure diagnosis.

GC5029800959000X

Fig. 3 Unable to Run in all ranges

Problem	Action
Throttle valve cable out of adjustment.	Adjust throttle valve cable.
Faulty throttle vavle cable and cam.	Inpsect throttle valve cable and cam.
Faulty accumulator pistons.	Inspect accumulator pistons.
Faulty valve body.	Inspect valve body.
Faulty transaxle.	Overhaul transaxle.

GC5029800961000X

Fig. 5 Harsh downshift

Problem	Action
Throttle valve cable is faulty.	Inspect throttle valve cable.
Valve body is faulty.	Inspect valve body.
Transaxle is faulty.	Overhaul transaxle.
Shift solenoid is faulty.	Inspect shift solenoid.
Fault within electronic control system.	Perform Powertrain On-Board Diagnostic (OBD) system check

GC5029800963000X

Fig. 7 Downshift occurs too quickly or too late

Problem	Action
Shift solenoid is faulty.	Inspect shift solenoid.
Fault within electronic control system.	Perform Powertrain On-Board Diagnostic (OBD) system check
Valve body is faulty.	Inspect valve body.
Transaxle is faulty	Inspect the transaxle.

GC5029800965000X

Fig. 9 No engine braking in 2 or L range

Problem	Action
Shift select cable out of adjustment.	Adjust shift select cable.
Faulty parking lock pawl and spring.	Inspect cam and spring.

GC5029800966000X

Fig. 10 Vehicle does not hold in Park range.

spring may drop from transaxle during valve body removal. B2 accumulator is under intense spring pressure and may push valve body down after valve body bolts are loosened.

10. Remove mounting bolts and valve body while simultaneously disconnecting manual valve link from manual lever, **Fig. 12.**
11. Remove checkball body and spring from transaxle and B2 accumulator piston and spring. **When using compressed air to remove components from transaxle case, air pressure should never exceed 14 psi.**
12. Remove C2, C1 and C3 accumulator pistons and springs from transaxle case by slowly applying low pressure compressed air into accumulator apply passages, **Figs. 13 through 15.**
13. Reverse procedure to install. Inspect transaxle case for nicks or scars, accumulator seals for cuts or damage and accumulator pistons for cracks or porosity.

TV CABLE, REPLACE

1. Loosen TV cable locknut and adjust nut, **Fig. 16.**
2. Disconnect TV cable from TV linkage and TV cable bracket, then from cable guide bracket at top of transaxle.
3. Raise and support vehicle.
4. Remove lefthand splash shield.
5. Disconnect Park/Neutral Position (PNP) switch from transaxle and place suitable container under transaxle fluid pan.
6. Drain transaxle fluid and remove pan.
7. Disconnect TV cable from throttle valve cam at valve body.
8. Remove cable mounting bolt and cable.
9. Inspect TV cable for fraying, kinks, excessive wear or damage.
10. New TV cables do not have staked TV cable stopper. **New stopper must be staked if using new cable.** To stake cable stopper, proceed as follows:
    a. Bend cable to approximately 7.87 inches radius, **Fig. 17.**
    b. Lightly pull inner cable from housing until slight resistance is felt and hold in position.
    c. Stake stopper onto inner cable so 0.031–0.059 inch clearance exists between stop and cable housing.
11. Reverse procedure to install.

TRANSAXLE

REPLACE

1. Remove battery, hold down bracket and tray.
2. Disconnect Intake Air Temperature (IAT) connector.
3. Remove air cleaner cover and air cleaner.
4. Disconnect solenoid wire harness electrical connector from solenoid wire harness.
5. Disconnect PNP switch connector.
6. Remove ground strap from transaxle case and loosen TV cable locknut and adjust nut.
7. Disconnect TV cable from throttle linkage and TV cable bracket.
8. Disconnect Vehicle Speed Sensor (VSS) electrical connector.
9. Remove shift select cable from manual lever and shift select cable bracket.
10. Remove cable guide bracket from transaxle case and upper transaxle to engine bolts.
11. Remove upper starter motor mounting bolt.
12. Remove reinforcement bolts and lefthand transaxle mounting bracket
13. Remove bolt from lefthand transaxle mounting bracket.
14. Raise and support vehicle.
15. Drain transaxle fluid into suitable container.
16. Remove starter positive terminal nut, positive battery cable and electrical connector.
17. Remove mounting bolt and starter.
18. Remove both splash shields and plug

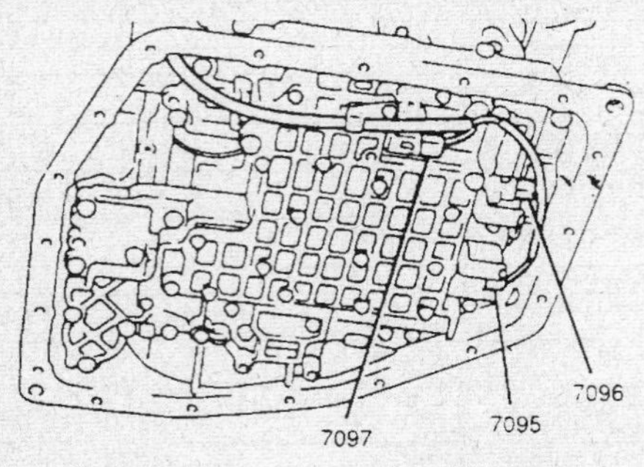

7095 SHIFT SOLENOID NO. 1 ELECTRICAL CONNECTOR
7096 SHIFT SOLENOID NO. 2 ELECTRICAL CONNECTOR
7097 TORQUE CONVERTER CLUTCH (TCC) SOLENOID ELECTRICAL CONNECTOR
GC5029300439000X

Fig. 11 Solenoid electrical connectors

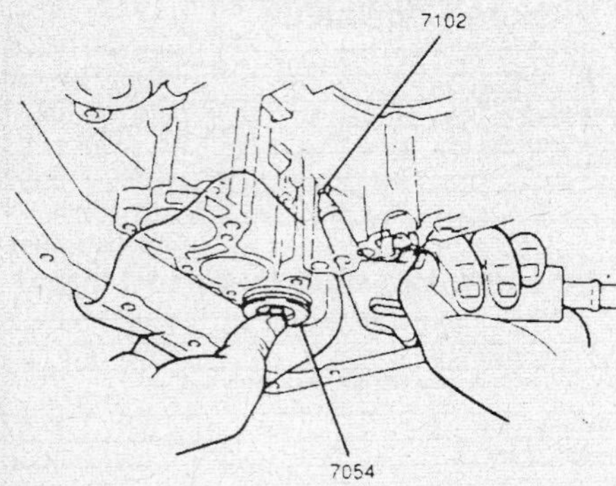

7054 C1 ACCUMULATOR PISTON
7102 C1 ACCUMULATOR APPLY PASSAGE
GC5029300442000X

Fig. 14 C1 accumulator piston & spring removal

fluid cooler pipes to prevent transaxle fluid cooler leakage.

19. Remove inner and outer cooler hoses and pipes at transaxle.
20. Remove bolts from lefthand transaxle mounting bracket.
21. Remove both front wheel assemblies.
22. Remove both drive axles.
23. Remove exhaust pipe support bolts and center crossmember.
24. **On models equipped with Federal emissions,** remove front exhaust pipe to three-way catalytic converter mating flange bolts.
25. **On models equipped with California emissions,** remove mating flange nuts and front exhaust pipe from warm up three-way catalytic converter.
26. **On all models,** remove mating flange nuts and front exhaust pipe from exhaust manifold.
27. Remove center crossmember plastic access cover, then the front transaxle mount mounting bolts and nuts.
28. Remove front suspension and center crossmembers, then support transaxle with suitable jack.
29. Remove engine rear end plate access cover and flywheel mounting bolts.

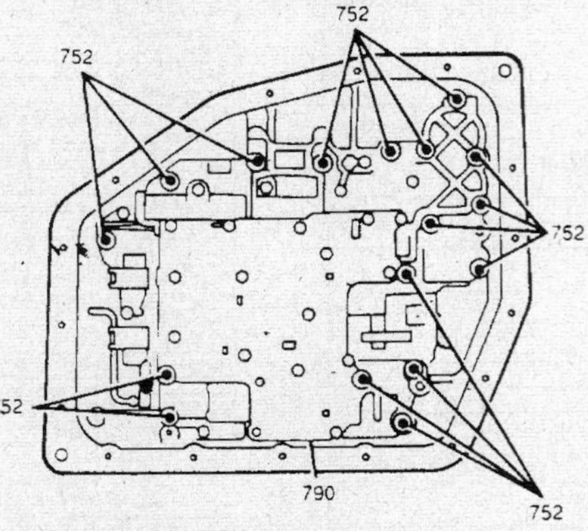

752 VALVE BODY ASSEMBLY BOLTS
790 VALVE BODY ASSEMBLY
GC5029300440000X

Fig. 12 Valve body bolt location

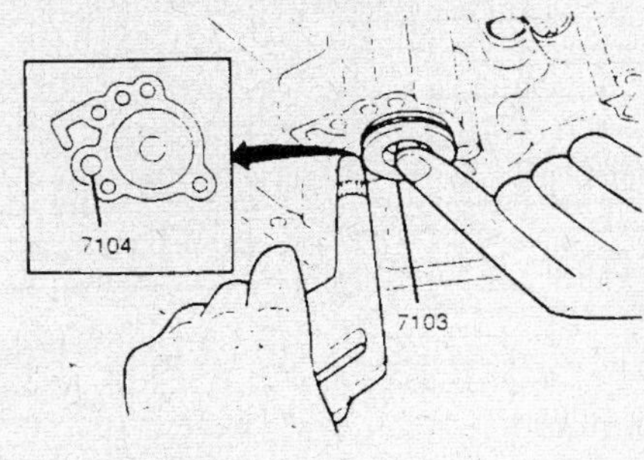

7103 C3 ACCUMULATOR PISTON
7104 C3 ACCUMULATOR APPLY PASSAGE
GC5029300443000X

Fig. 15 C3 accumulator piston & spring removal

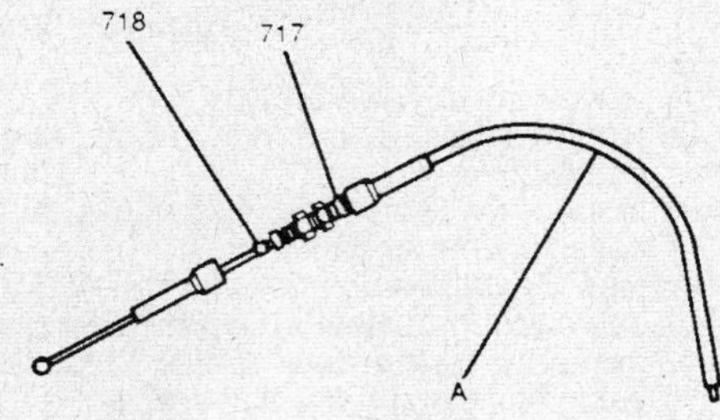

A 200 mm (7.87") RADIUS
717 TV CABLE
718 TV CABLE STOPPER
GC5029300445000X

Fig. 17 TV cable stopper staking

30. Remove drain pan from underneath transaxle.
31. Remove lower transaxle to engine mounting bolts.
32. Disconnect transaxle from engine by carefully moving transaxle away from engine toward lefthand side of engine compartment and very slowly lowering hydraulic jack ensuring no obstructions exist.

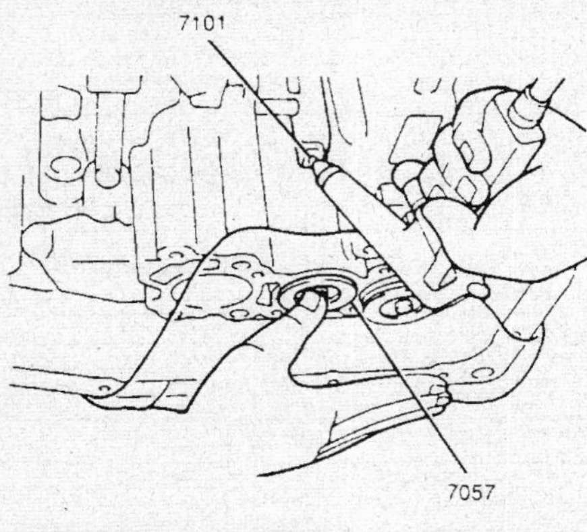

7057 C2 ACCUMULATOR PISTON
7101 C2 ACCUMULATOR APPLY PASSAGE
GC5029300441000X

Fig. 13 C2 accumulator piston & spring removal

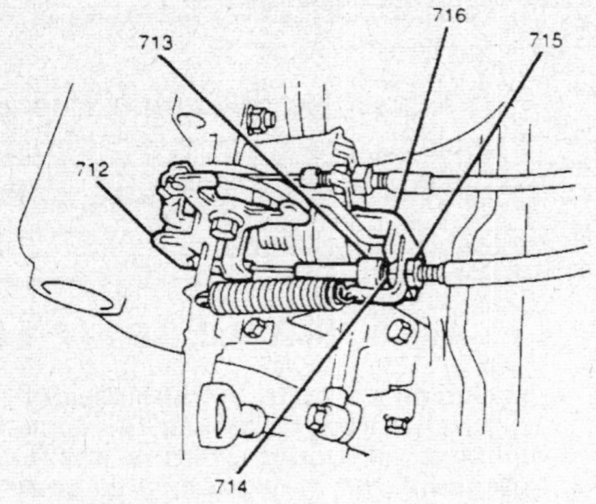

712 THROTTLE VALVE LINKAGE
713 OUTER CABLE BOOT
714 TV CABLE ADJUST NUT
715 TV CABLE LOCKNUT
716 TV CABLE BRACKET
GC5029300444000X

Fig. 16 TV cable locknut & adjust nut location

33. Reverse procedure to install.

TECHNICAL SERVICE BULLETINS

DELAYED UPSHIFT WHEN CRUISE CONTROL IS ENGAGED

1998

On some of these models there may be a delayed upshift when the cruise control is engaged. The transaxle may not upshift immediately when a grade is crested.

This condition may be caused by the cruise control module software.

To correct this condition, install revised cruise control module (part No. 94859069).

TIGHTENING SPECIFICATIONS

Year	Component	Torque/Ft. Lbs.
1998–2002	Air Cleaner	44①
	Axle Nut	129
	Ball Stud	44
	Battery Ground Cable	11
	Battery Hold-Down Bracket, Bolt	44①
	Battery Hold-Down Bracket, Nut	72①
	Bulkhead Grommet	15
	Center Crossmember Rear	45
	Detent Spring	84①
	Direct Clutch Solenoid	35①
	Drain Plug	17
	Driveshaft Nut	129
	Fluid Filter Screen	84①
	Flywheel To Torque Converter	14
	Front Exhaust Pipe Support	14
	Front Exhaust Pipe Support	14
	Front Exhaust Pipe To Exhaust Manifold	46
	Front Exhaust Pipe To Three-Way Catalytic Converter Mating Flange, Bolts	32
	Front Exhaust Pipe To Warm Up Three-Way Catalytic Converter Mating Flange, Nuts	46
	Front Suspension Crossmember	152
	Front Transaxle Mount	35
	Front Transaxle Mount Through Bolt & Nut	64
	Ground Strap	10
	Hub Nut	129
	Interlock Cable	10
	Lefthand Transaxle Mounting Bracket	35
	Lefthand Transaxle Mounting Bracket Reinforcement	15
	Lefthand Transaxle Mount Through Bolt	64
	Lower Engine Reinforcement Brace	47
	Oil Pan	53①
	Oil Strainer	53①
	Park Neutral Position Switch	48①

Continued

TIGHTENING SPECIFICATIONS—Continued

Year	Component	Torque/Ft. Lbs.
1998–2002	Rear Transaxle Mount	42
	Rear Transaxle Mount Through Bolt	64
	Selector Lever Housing	25
	Second Gear Brake Solenoid	35①
	Solenoid Wire Harness	53①
	Solenoid Wire Harness Clip	53①
	Solenoid Wire Harness Retaining Plate & Bracket	15
	Speedometer Driven Gear	11
	Splash Shield	44①
	Starter Motor Positive Terminal	44①
	Starter Motor	29
	Transaxle Fluid Drain Plug	13
	Transaxle Fluid Pan	43①
	Transaxle To Engine	47
	Transmission Control Module	11
	TV Cable	72①
	TV Cable Guide Bracket	72①
	TV Cable Locknut	72①
	Valve Body	84①
	Vehicle Speed Sensor	53①

① — Inch lbs.

Saturn Four-Speed Automatic Transaxle

NOTE: On Air Bag Equipped Models, Refer To "Air Bag System Precautions" Located In The Front Of This Manual For System Disarming & Arming Procedures.

NOTE: Refer To "Computer Relearn Procedures" Located In The Front Of This Manual When Battery Power To The Computer Has Been Interrupted.

NOTE: Prior To Performing Any Service Operations Listed In This Section, Consult The "Technical Service Bulletins" Section For Related Information.

INDEX

PRECAUTIONS

AIR BAG SYSTEMS

Refer to "Air Bag System Precautions" in the front of this manual for system disarming and arming procedures.

BATTERY GROUND CABLE

Prior to service, disconnect battery ground cable and isolate as required.

IDENTIFICATION

The transaxle identification plate is located on the torque converter housing, **Fig. 1**.

DESCRIPTION

This fully automatic four-speed transaxle consists of four multiple disc clutches, a four-element torque converter with a lock up clutch, 1st gear sprag clutch and a servo actuated dog clutch, **Fig. 2**.

The transaxle employs an electronic control system, which utilizes five electro-hydraulic solenoids in conjunction with a Powertrain Control Module (PCM) and its sensors to control shift timing, shift feel and on-board diagnostics.

TROUBLESHOOTING

Refer to **Figs. 3 through 7** for transaxle troubleshooting and **Fig. 8** for Brake/Transaxle Shift Interlock (BTSI) system troubleshooting.

MAINTENANCE

Refer to "Lubricant Data" chart in the appropriate chassis chapter of this manual for transmission fluid specifications.

FLUID CHECK

1. Start engine and operate vehicle for 15 minutes to reach normal operating temperature.
2. With vehicle on level surface, apply parking brake.
3. Move selector through all gear positions.
4. Move gear selector to Park position.
5. Allow engine to idle for three minutes with accessories off.
6. Check fluid level, color and condition, noting the following:
   a. Fluid level must be in cross-hatched area of dipstick.
   b. If fluid level is below ADD mark, add only enough transaxle fluid to bring level to middle of cross-hatched area.

FLUID CHANGE

1. Fluid may be drained when operating temperature of 190–200°F is reached.
2. Turn engine Off, then raise and support vehicle.
3. Remove transaxle drain plug, then allow fluid five minutes to drain into suitable container.
4. Install new drain plug washer and drain plug.
5. Lower vehicle and remove air induction tubing and air filter box.
6. Remove fluid filter using suitable strap wrench.
7. Remove magnet from filter, wipe clean and install on new filter.
8. Lubricate new filter seal with transaxle fluid, then install.
9. Install air filter box, as required.
10. Fill transaxle slowly, or use vented funnel.

ADJUSTMENTS

SELECTOR SWITCH

1. Place transaxle in D4 position.
2. Inspect for continuity across selector switch terminals.
3. If continuity is not indicated, rotate switch until continuity is present.
4. Tighten mounting bolts and inspect for continuity.

SHIFT CABLE

1. Move cable housing back and forth in adjuster.
2. Center cable housing in middle of endplay.
3. Press in lock tab.
4. Ensure correct operation.

IN-VEHICLE REPAIRS

SELECTOR SWITCH, REPLACE

REMOVAL

1. Remove air induction system.
2. Disconnect gear selector switch electrical connector.

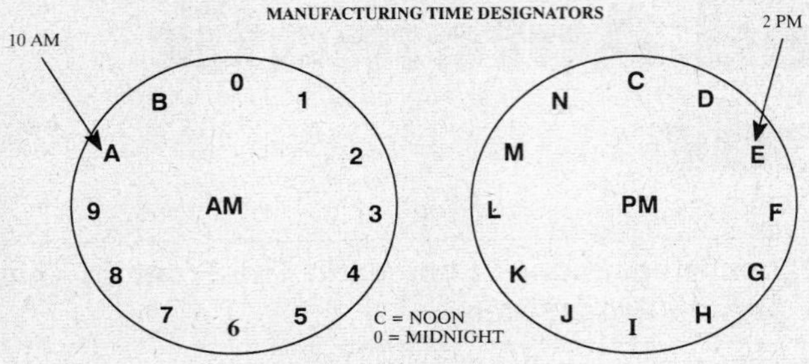

HOUR OF THE DAY CLOCKS

TRANSAXLE BUILD DATE CODES

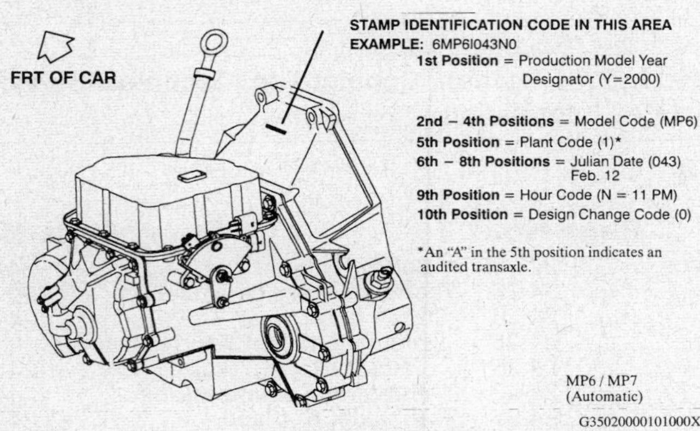

Fig. 1 Transaxle identification

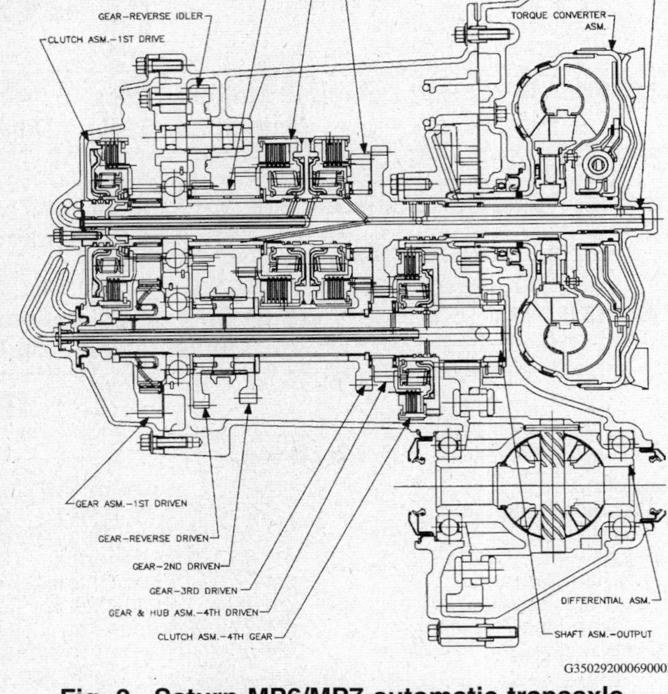

Fig. 2 Saturn MP6/MP7 automatic transaxle

3. Remove mounting nut and manual control lever shaft lever. Record position for installation.
4. Remove mounting bolts and selector switch.

INSTALLATION

1. Install switch and mounting bolt. Hand tighten.
2. Install manual lever to control shaft retainer.
3. Adjust switch.
4. Install cable to control lever.
5. Adjust cable.
6. Connect switch electrical connector.
7. Install air induction tube.

SHIFT CABLE, REPLACE

REMOVAL

1. Tape release button on shifter lever handle.
2. Remove rear storage tray liner from console and screws below liner.
3. Remove front console mounting screws.
4. Apply parking brake and remove trim panel below park brake lever.
5. Remove ashtrays and disconnect front ashtray electrical connector.
6. **On models equipped with power window/mirrors,** lift window/lock/mirror switch rear edge, slide switch rearward and disconnect electrical connectors.
7. **On all models,** remove side trim panels.
8. Lift rear of console, slide console rearward and lift straight up to remove.
9. Position shifter in second gear and disconnect cable end from shifter.
10. Depress cable housing tabs and remove cable from shifter.
11. Remove air induction tube.
12. Disconnect cable from shifter lever.
13. Depress retaining tabs and remove cable from converter housing.
14. Raise and support vehicle.
15. Remove cable grommet from front of dash.
16. Remove mounting nuts and feed grommet plate through dash hole.

INSTALLATION

1. Feed cable and plate through front of dash and install plate.
2. Connect cable to shift lever.
3. Install cable housing to shifter.
4. Install console.
5. Install cable to converter housing.
6. Ensure transaxle and shifter are in Park position.
7. Release cable adjustment lock tab, using suitable screwdriver to pry lock tab up and lift with hand.
8. Connect cable to shift lever and install retainer.
9. Adjust cable.
10. Install air induction tube.

PARK LOCK CABLE, REPLACE

REMOVAL

1. Remove console as outlined under "Shift Cable, Replace."
2. Remove mounting screws, upper cover, ignition cylinder and lower cover.
3. Depress cable retaining tab and remove ignition module cable.
4. Unsnap park lock cable end terminal from shifter plastic lock out lever.
5. Depress cable housing end fitting tabs and remove cable from shifter.
6. Remove cable. Record cable routing for installation.

INSTALLATION

1. Ensure cable is routed through accelerator pedal bracket retainer.
2. Install cable, route cable same as cable was removed.
3. Install ignition module cable cassette end and park lock cable fitting end to shifter. Ensure cable is completely seated.
4. Lift cable end fitting lock tab using suitable screwdriver to allow housing to move freely in end fitting.
5. Attach park lock cable end terminal to plastic lock out lever on shifter.
6. Install lower column cover, top column cover and ignition cylinder.
7. With ignition off, shifter in park, depress cable end fitting lock and remove adjustment clip from new cable end terminal.
8. If connecting cable does not have adjustment clip, adjust clip to provide 0.005 inch gap between cable and end and cable to park lock connector.
9. Ensure interlock operation.
10. Install console.

VALVE BODY, REPLACE

REMOVAL

1. Remove air cleaner and duct.

X — Most Probable Cause(s)
• — Possible Causes

COMPLAINT–CONDITION / CAUSE	MAT	CTS	Dis. Primary	Dis. Secondary	Fuel Delivery System	EGR System	TPS	MAP Sensor	Eng. Vac.	Engine Mech. System	PCM/TC Calibration	Trans. 1st Gear Hyd./Mech.	Trans. Line Act. System	Trans. 2nd Act. System	Trans. 3rd Act. System	Trans. 4th Act. System	Trans. TCC Act. System	Trans. Hydra/Mech.	Trans. Perf/Norm Sw.	Shift to 2 Lt. Circuit	PRNDL Sel. Circuit	Brake Switch Circuit	Trans. Master Enable Circuit	Clutch Clearance	Gear Clearance Incorrect	1st Clutch Defective	2nd Clutch Defective	3rd Clutch Defective	4th Clutch Defective	Park Pawl Mech.	Reverse Fork Mech.	TCC Defective	Input Shaft Nut
Trans Hard Up-Shift:	X	•	•		•	X	•	X			•		X					•	•		•			X			•						
1st–2nd													X	•													•	•					
2nd–3rd													X	•	•													•	•				
3rd–4th													X		•	•																	
Trans Vibration:			•		•												X	X															
While Cruising				•	•												•	X															
Idling			•		•					•								X															
Accelerating			•		•												•	X															
Cold Ambient			•		•												•	X															
Normal Operating Temperature			•		•												•	X															
Cold Engine		X	•		•												•	•															
Decelerating						•											•	X															
Accessory Load			•		•												•	X															
Under Load			•		•												•	X															
Always			•		•												•	X															
Trans Shudder:			•	•	•	•				•				•	•	•	•	•															
Acceleration				X										•	•	•	•																
Normal Operating Temperature				•													•	•															
Deceleration																	•	•															
Braking																						•											
Under Load			•	X	•	•				•				•	•	•	•	•															
2nd Gear				X										•			X	•															
3rd Gear			X			•									•		X	•															
4th Gear				X		X										•	X	•															
Reverse				•										•				X															

G35029100061010X

Fig. 3 Transaxle troubleshooting chart (Part 1 of 2)

2. Remove battery shield, battery and tray.
3. Disconnect PCM black electrical connector.
4. Remove mounting bolts and position PCM aside.
5. Loosen transaxle connector mounting bolt and disconnect electrical connector.
6. Remove master cylinder to booster mounting nuts and lift cylinder slightly to remove valve body cover. Position cylinder back on booster studs.
7. Remove valve body cover mounting bolts.
8. Remove 11 valve body to case bolts, **Fig. 9.**

INSTALLATION

1. Install manual valve to manual link with manual valve flat facing upwards.
2. Lower valve body and install manual link to manual valve.
3. Valve body to case mounting bolts must be installed to valve body prior to installation, **Fig. 10.**
4. Clean and lubricate mounting bolts with transmission fluid.
5. Tighten valve body bolts in sequence, **Fig. 11.**
6. Tighten valve body to case mounting bolts in sequence, **Fig. 12.**
7. Clean valve body cover gasket surface using suitable carburetor cleaner.
8. Install mounting bolts and tighten in sequence, **Fig. 13.**
9. Install master cylinder to booster mounting nuts.
10. Connect transaxle electrical connector.
11. Install PCM and attach black PCM electrical connector.
12. Install battery tray.
13. Install battery and shield mounting bolts.
14. Install air cleaner and duct.

COOLING LINE REPLACE

1. Remove air induction system.
2. Depress cooler line to transaxle plastic tabs and pull connector rearward with retainer on cooler line.
3. Disconnect upper transaxle cooler line from radiator using suitable line wrench.
4. Raise and support vehicle, then remove front splash shield.
5. Disconnect lower transaxle cooler line from radiator using suitable line wrench.
6. Disconnect lower transaxle cooler line from transaxle by depressing plastic tabs at connector and pull line out of connector.
7. Remove plastic retainer from line and pry tabs away from line far enough to slip retainer over rib on lines using suitable small screwdriver, **Fig. 14.**
8. Inspect plastic retainer for cracks or damage, replace as required.
9. Remove transaxle cooler line fitting is leak is indicated.
10. Reverse procedure to install.

TRANSAXLE

REPLACE

1. Remove air induction system.
2. Remove battery and tray.
3. Disconnect electronic ignition module spark plug wires and electrical connectors.
4. Remove electronic ignition module.
5. Remove top two converter housing to engine bolts.
6. Remove transaxle strut to midrail bracket mounting bolt.
7. Loosen transaxle strut to transaxle bracket mounting bolt and position aside.
8. Disconnect the following electrical connectors:
   a. Solenoid connector.
   b. Vehicle and turbine speed sensor.
   c. Transaxle temperature sensor.
   d. Selector switch connector.
   e. Ground terminals from top converter housing bolts.
   f. Ground wire from park/neutral position switch.
9. Secure radiator to upper radiator support with mechanics wire.
10. Install support bar feet on outer edge of shock tower, **Fig. 15.**
11. Connect bar hooks to engine support brackets.
12. Position stabilizer foot on engine block to right of engine oil dipstick.
13. Adjust hooks and stabilize to remove looseness.

X — Most Probable Cause(s)
• — Possible Causes

COMPLAINT–CONDITION / CAUSE	MAT	CTS	Dis. Primary	Dis. Secondary	Fuel Delivery System	EGR System	TPS	MAP Sensor	Eng. Vac.	Engine Mech. System	PCM/TCM Calibration	Trans. 1st Gear Hyd./Mech.	Trans. Line Act. System	Trans. 2nd Act. System	Trans. 3rd Act. System	Trans. 4th Act. System	Trans. TCC Act. System	Trans. Hydra/Mech.	Trans. Perf/Norm Sw.	Shift to 2 Lt. Circuit	PRNDL Sel. Circuit	Brake Switch Circuit	Trans. Master Enable Circuit	Clutch Clearance	Gear Clearance Incorrect	1st Clutch Defective	2nd Clutch Defective	3rd Clutch Defective	4th Clutch Defective	Park Pawl Mech.	Reverse Fork Mech.	TCC Defective	Input Shaft Nut
Trans Hard Downshift			•				•						X						•		•						•	•	•				
Accelerating													X						X								•	•	•				
Decelerating													X				X		X														
Shift to Two (2) Light													X				X																
Trans Slipping:													X	•	•	•	•									•	•	•	•			•	
Accelerating													X	•	•	•	•									•	•	•	•				
Normal Operating Temperature												•	X	•	•	•	•																
Cold Engine													X	•	•	•	•									•	•	•	•				
From Launch												•	X																				
1st Gear													X													X							
2nd Gear														X													X						•
3rd Gear															X													•					
4th Gear																X													•				
Reverse														X				X									X						
TCC																	X														X		
Trans Gear Missing:													X	•	•	•	•				•		•			•	•	•	•			X	
Reverse														•													X				X		•
Drives in Neutral																								X	•	•	•	•	•				
Trans No Park																														X			
Trans Stuck In Park																														X			
Trans Hunting/Gears, TCC:		•					X	X	X		•	•		X	X	X	X		•		•	X											
While Cruising		•					X	X	X		•				•																		
Cold Engine		X					•	•	•					•	•	•	•		•														
Under Load							X	X	X				•	•	•	•	•				•												

G35029100061020X

Fig. 3 Transaxle troubleshooting chart (Part 2 of 2)

14. Raise and support vehicle, then drain transaxle fluid into suitable container.
15. Remove front wheel assemblies and splash shields.
16. Remove engine strut cradle bracket and transaxle mount to cradle mounting bolts.
17. Remove down pipe to manifold, down pipe to powertrain stiffening bracket and down pipe to catalytic converter mounting bolts and nuts, then the down pipe.
18. Discard front exhaust pipe to manifold and converter gaskets.
19. Remove steering gear to cradle mounting bolts, support steering gear with mechanics wire.
20. Remove brake pipe bracket push pin at rear of cradle and engine to transaxle stiffening brace.
21. Remove mounting bolts and converter housing dust cover.
22. Remove torque converter mounting bolts.
23. Remove and discard outer cotter pin from lower ball joints.
24. Loosen mounting nut and back off until top of nut is even with top of threads.
25. Separate ball joint from steering knuckle using ball joint tool No. SA9132S, or equivalent. **Outer CV joint has ABS speed sensor ring. Incorrect tool usage may result in ring damage or loss of ABS.**
26. Separate left and righthand axles from transaxle using suitable large screwdriver or pry bar. **Do not allow pry tool to contact axle seal.**
27. **On models equipped with DOHC engines,** remove intake bracket to intake manifold bolt.
28. **On all models,** remove intake bracket to intermediate shaft support and intermediate shaft to engine block mounting bolts.
29. Slide intermediate shaft out of transaxle.
30. Support cradle on suitable powertrain support dolly using two 4 x 4 x 36 inch pieces of wood.
31. Depress transaxle connector plastic tabs and pull cooler lines from transaxle. Install 3/8 inch rubber hose between cooler lines.
32. Remove cradle to body mounting bolts, then lower cradle.
33. Ensure two large spacing washers between cradle and body are attached.
34. Support transaxle with suitable jack and remove torque converter housing to engine bolts.
35. Separate transaxle from engine and lower enough to reach transaxle shifter cable.
36. Disconnect and remove shifter cable from converter housing.
37. Remove transaxle.
38. Reverse procedure to install.

TECHNICAL SERVICE BULLETINS

CASE LEAK

1998

On some of these models there may be an ATF leak coming from the upper lefthand corner of the case.

This condition may be caused by an thin-walled section weep or leaking ATF.

To correct this condition, proceed as follows:

1. Pour dye from black light kit (part No. SA9175-NE) into transaxle.
2. Bring transaxle to normal operating temperature by driving vehicle.
3. Raise and support vehicle.
4. Remove lefthand side splash shield.
5. Direct black light toward suspected leak area, noting the following:
   a. If leak is coming from upper lefthand corner near case end cover assembly joint, **Fig. 16,** replace transaxle case.
   b. If leak does not appear to coming from upper lefthand corner, further diagnosis is required.

INTERMITTENT NO CLICK, NO CRANK, NO START

1998

On some of these models built between VINs WZ240305–WZ260290 there may be an intermittent no click, no crank or no start condition. Vehicle may start after shifter is moved through pattern and firmly placed in Park position.

This condition may be caused by the Park-Neutral Position (PNP) switch.

To correct this condition, replace PNP switch with Julian build date, **Fig. 17,** between 7O22–7N06 with revised switch (part No. 210223303).

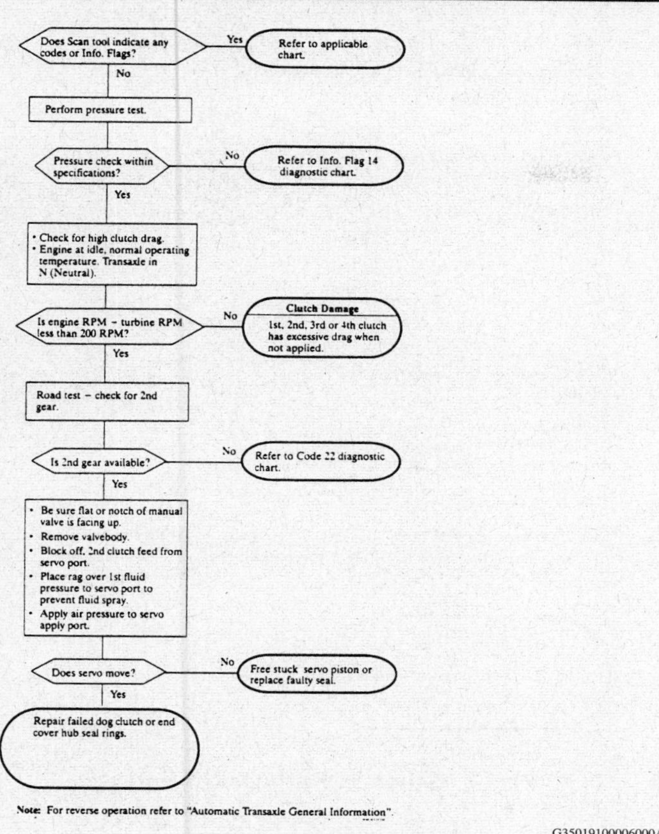

Fig. 4 No Reverse

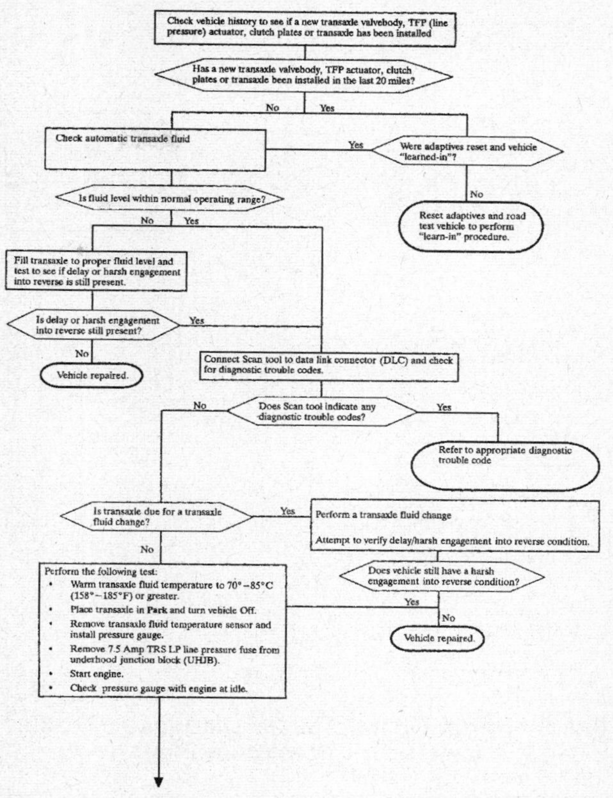

Fig. 5 Delay Or Harsh Engagement Into Reverse (Part 1 of 3)

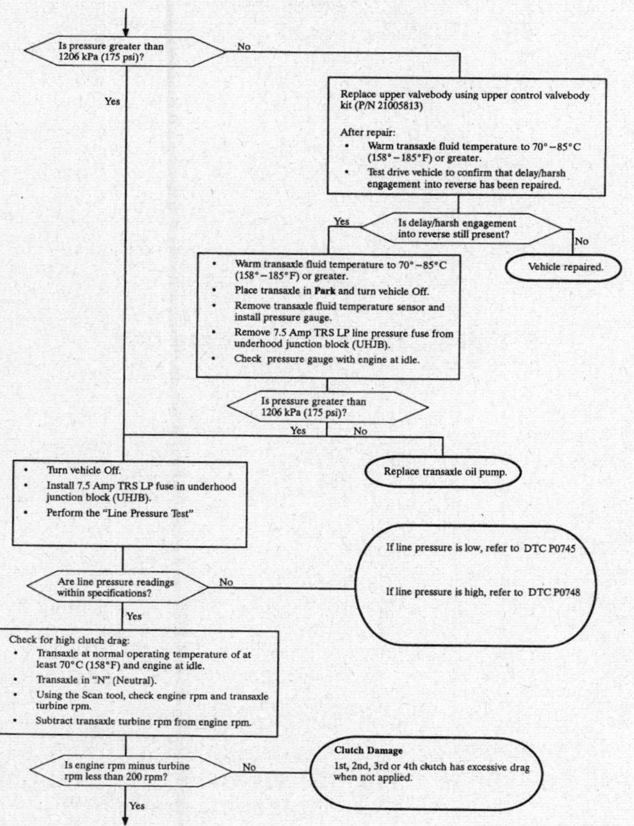

Fig. 5 Delay Or Harsh Engagement Into Reverse (Part 2 of 3)

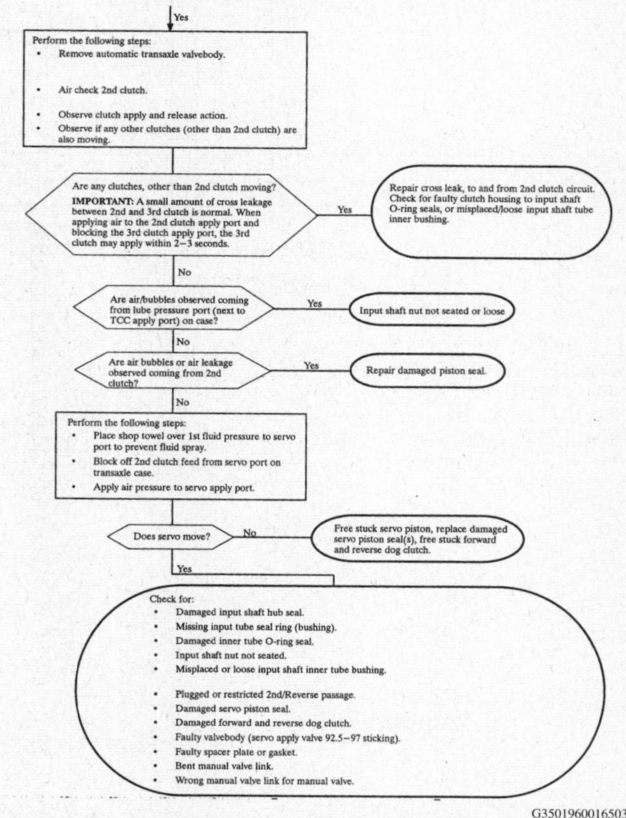

Fig. 5 Delay Or Harsh Engagement Into Reverse (Part 3 of 3)

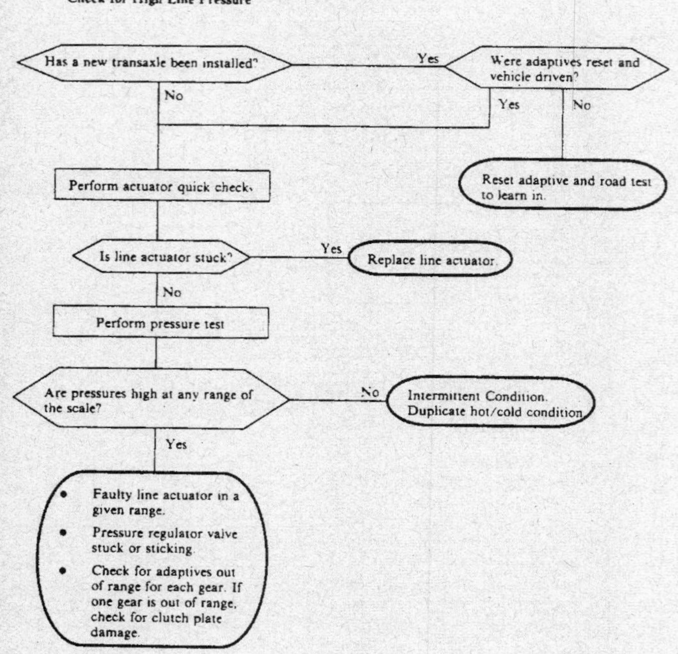

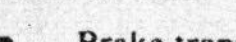

Fig. 6 Harsh Upshifts & No Diagnostic Trouble Codes Or Information Flags

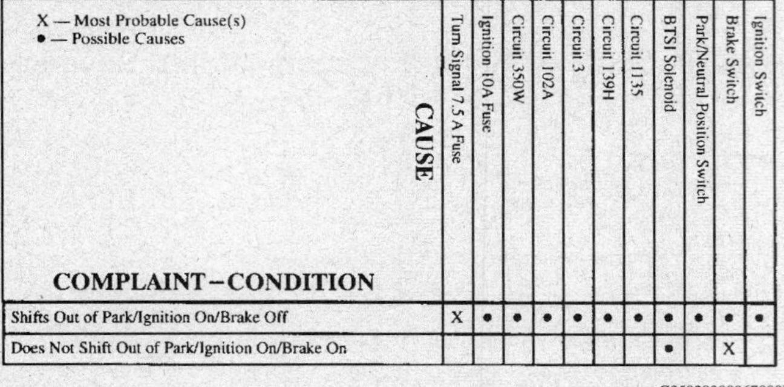

X — Most Probable Cause(s)
• — Possible Causes

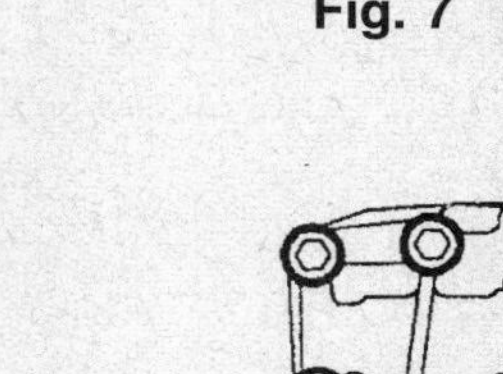

COMPLAINT—CONDITION	Turn Signal 7.5 A Fuse	Ignition 10A Fuse	Circuit 350W	Circuit 102A	Circuit 3	Circuit 139H	Circuit 1135	BTSI Solenoid	Park/Neutral Position Switch	Brake Switch	Ignition Switch
Shifts Out of Park/Ignition On/Brake Off	X	•	•	•	•	•	•	•	•	•	•
Does Not Shift Out of Park/Ignition On/Brake On								•		X	

G35029300067000X

Fig. 8 Brake/Transaxle Shift Interlock (BTSI) troubleshooting chart

Stuck in Park:

- Brake transmission shift interlock (BTSI) system.
- Parked on steep grade.
- Park pawl assembly faulty.
- Park lever actuator rod faulty.

No Park:

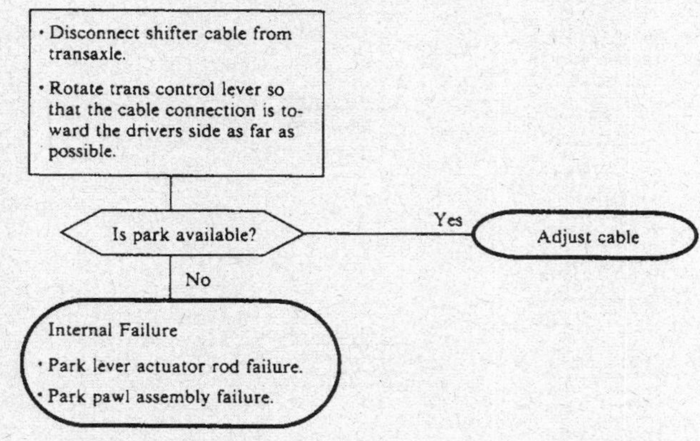

Fig. 7 Stuck In Park Or No Park

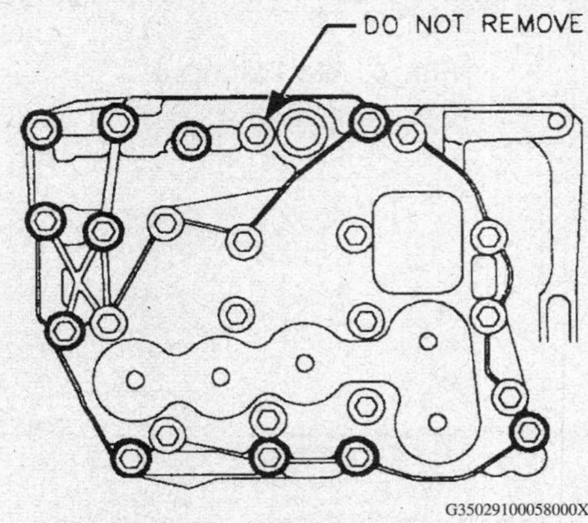

Fig. 9 Valve body to case bolt removal

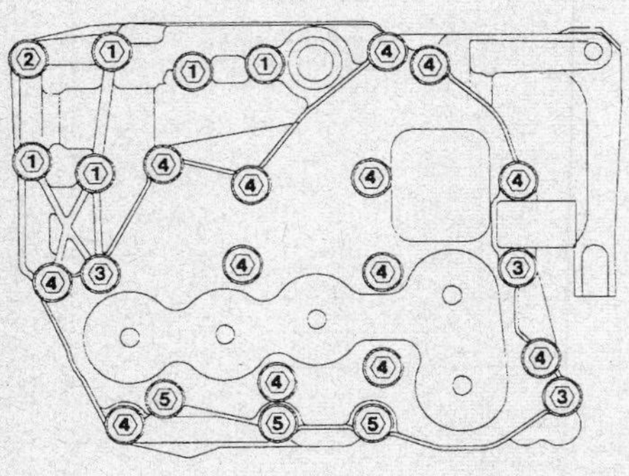

Fig. 10 Valve body to case bolt location

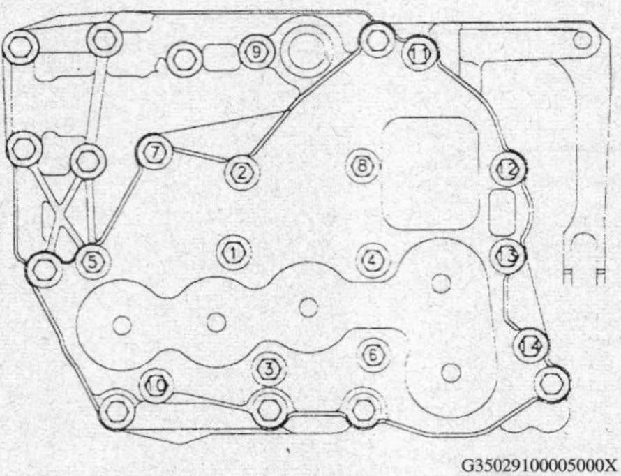

Fig. 11 Valve body bolt tightening sequence

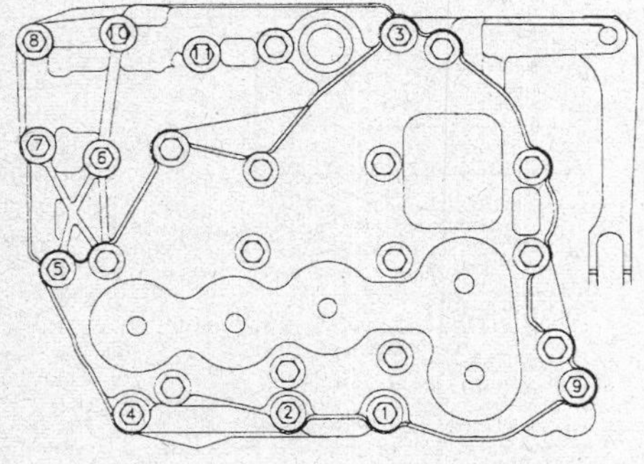

Fig. 12 Valve body to case bolt tightening sequence

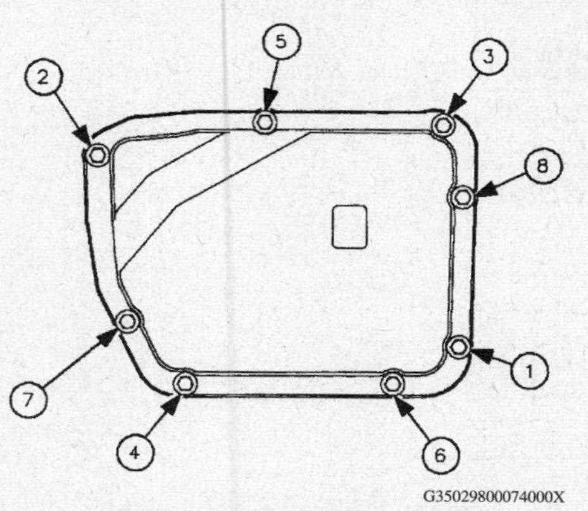

Fig. 13 Valve body cover tightening sequence

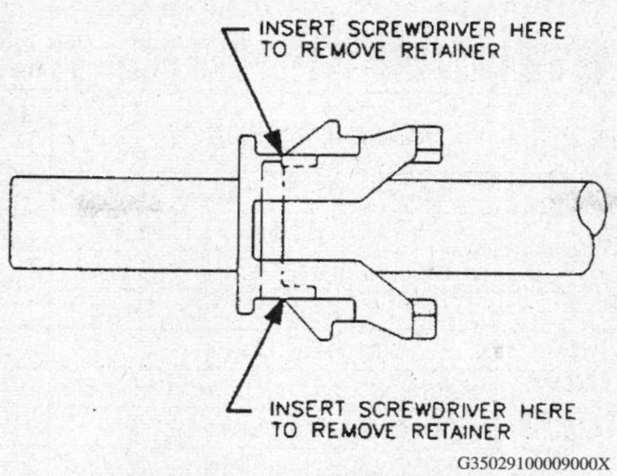

Fig. 14 Transaxle cooler line retainer removal

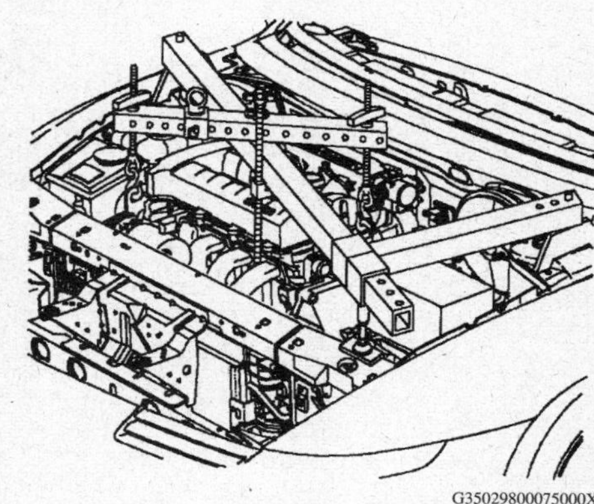

Fig. 15 Engine support bar installation

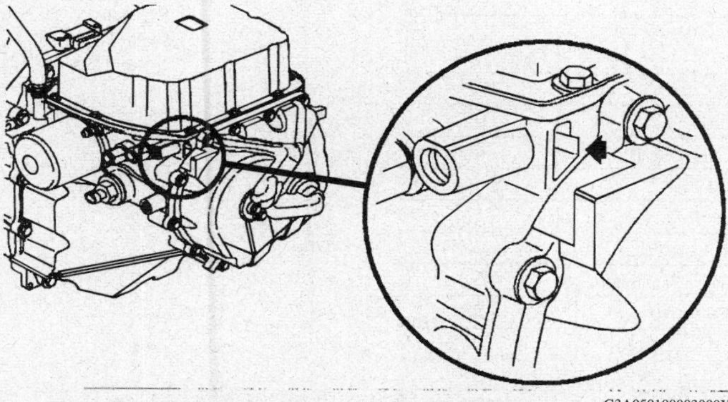

Fig. 16 Thin-walled section leak

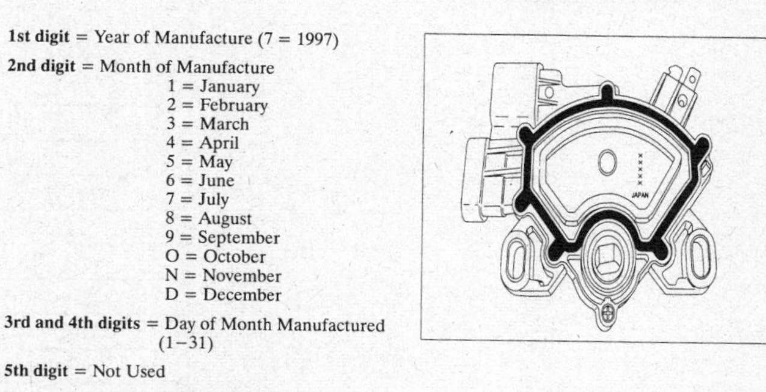

1st digit = Year of Manufacture (7 = 1997)
2nd digit = Month of Manufacture
1 = January
2 = February
3 = March
4 = April
5 = May
6 = June
7 = July
8 = August
9 = September
O = October
N = November
D = December
3rd and 4th digits = Day of Month Manufactured (1–31)
5th digit = Not Used
Example: 7O30E = October 30, 1997
G3A040000001000X

Fig. 17 PNP switch Julian build date

TIGHTENING SPECIFICATIONS

Year	Component	Torque/Ft. Lbs.
1998–2002	Air Cleaner Box To Battery Tray	84①
	Brake Master Cylinder To Booster	20
	Converter Housing To Case, Short	18
	Converter Housing To Case, Long	21
	Cradle To Body	155
	Distributorless Ignition System Module	72①
	Dust Cover To Converter Housing	96①
	Engine Strut Bracket To Cradle	37
	Exhaust Down Pipe To Catalytic Converter	18
	Exhaust Down Pipe To Exhaust Manifold	23
	Flywheel To Crankshaft	44
	Ground Terminal To Converter Housing	18
	Input Shaft Clamp	111
	Intake Bracket	22
	Intermediate Shaft Bracket	40
	Lower Ball Joint Nut	55②
	Shifter To Floor	19
	Steering Rack To Cradle	37
	Torque Converter To Flexplate	52
	Transaxle Drain Plug	22
	Transaxle Electrical Connector	27①
	Transaxle Mount To Cradle	37
	Transaxle Mount To Transaxle	24
	Transaxle Oil Indicator Tube	108①
	Transaxle To Engine, Bolt	103
	Transaxle To Engine, Stud	74
	Valve Body Cover	108①
	Valve Body To Case	96①
	Wheel Lug Nuts	103

① — Inch lbs.
② — Tighten, then align nut slot to cotter pin hole.

Turbo Hydra-Matic 3T40 Automatic Transaxle

NOTE: On Air Bag Equipped Models, Refer To "Air Bag System Precautions" Located In The Front Of This Manual For System Disarming & Arming Procedures.

NOTE: Refer To "Computer Relearn Procedures" Located In The Front Of This Manual When Battery Power To The Computer Has Been Interrupted.

NOTE: Prior To Performing Any Service Operations Listed In This Section, Consult The "Technical Service Bulletins" Section For Related Information.

INDEX

PRECAUTIONS

AIR BAG SYSTEMS

Refer to "Air Bag System Precautions" in the front of this manual for system disarming and arming procedures.

BATTERY GROUND CABLE

Prior to service, disconnect battery ground cable and isolate as required.

IDENTIFICATION

These transaxles may be identified by a model tag attached to the oil pan flange pad to the right if the oil dipstick at the rear of the transaxle, **Fig. 1.**

DESCRIPTION

This automatic transaxle is designed for use with FWD vehicles. It consists primarily of a compound planetary gear set, dual sprocket and drive link assembly, intermediate band and valve body assemblies, one roller clutch, three multiple disc clutches, vane type oil pump and a four-element torque converter. Refer to **Fig. 2** for transaxle cross-sectional view.

TROUBLESHOOTING

Always check for the following conditions when troubleshooting any type of transaxle malfunction:

1. Incorrect oil.
2. Improperly adjusted, disconnected, bound or broken TV cable.
3. Manual linkage improperly adjusted.
4. Incorrect oil pressure.

CHATTERS OR SLIPS IN FIRST GEAR

1. Low oil level.
2. Restricted feed to forward clutch.
3. Burned clutch plates.
4. Drive sprocket support.
5. Incorrect case cover gasket.

NO REVERSE OR SLIPS IN REVERSE

1. Forward clutch:
   a. Burned clutch plates.
   b. Seal ring off piston.
   c. Exhaust checkball sticking.
2. Low/Reverse clutch:
   a. Housing cup plug restricted or not fully seated.
   b. Leaking seals.
3. Low and reverse pipe O-ring seal damaged or missing.
4. Incorrect, damaged or leaking case to cover gasket.
5. Burned direct clutch plates.
6. Burned low and reverse clutch plates.
7. Low line pressure.

NO UPSHIFTS, DELAYED UPSHIFTS OR FULL THROTTLE SHIFTS

1. Governor or speed sensor:
   a. Cover worn.
   b. Thrust washer missing.
   c. Governor seal worn or cut.
   d. Governor spring not seated.
   e. Governor weights binding on pin.
   f. Ball missing.
   g. Governor driven gear stripped.
2. Intermediate servo:

a. Wrong or sticking apply pin.
b. Seals cut, damaged or missing.
c. Porosity in case servo bore.
d. Damaged or sticking piston.

3. Control valve:
   a. Valves sticking.
   b. Spacer plate gaskets leaking or incorrectly installed.
4. Valve body spacer:
   a. Governor feed orifice to 1-2 and 2-3 shift valve plugged.
   b. Drive to governor orifice plugged.
5. Burned or worn intermediate band.
6. Case cover:
   a. Porosity.
   b. Undrilled holes.
   c. Missing cup plugs.
   d. Second oil passage leaking.
7. Leaks in governor passage and/or pipe.

SLIPPING OR ROUGH 1-2 SHIFT

1. Intermediate servo:
   a. Seals cut, damaged or leaking.
   b. Piston damaged.
   c. Servo bore in case damaged.
   d. Apply pin too long or too short.
   e. Servo orifice bleed cup plug missing.
   f. Leak between servo apply pin and case.
2. Binding intermediate servo band apply pin.
3. Incorrect TV link or bent TV link.
4. Control valve:
   a. TV plunger binding.
   b. Shift TV linkage binding.
   c. 1-2 accumulator valve binding.
5. 1-2 accumulator:
   a. Binding piston.
   b. Broken spring.
   c. Piston seal or groove damaged.
   d. Bore damaged.
6. Incorrect spacer plate or gasket, or gasket incorrectly installed.
7. Second oil passage leaking.

2-3 SHIFT ROUGH OR DELAYED

1. Plugged accumulator exhaust port.
2. Direct clutch exhaust No. 1 checkball mispositioned or missing.
3. Control valve:
   a. Binding plunger and throttle valve.
   b. Binding shift TV valve.

2-3 SHIFT SOFT, SLIPS OR EARLY

1. Intermediate servo:
   a. Piston to case oil seal damaged.
   b. Servo piston damaged.
   c. Servo bore in case damaged.
2. Accumulator exhaust check valve not seating in case.
3. Spacer plate:
   a. Plugged or restricted direct clutch feed orifice.
   b. Incorrect case cover gaskets.
   c. Leaking, damaged or incorrectly installed spacer plate or gasket.
   d. Drive sprocket support passages interconnected, leaking or restricted.
   e. Sleeve loose or out of position.

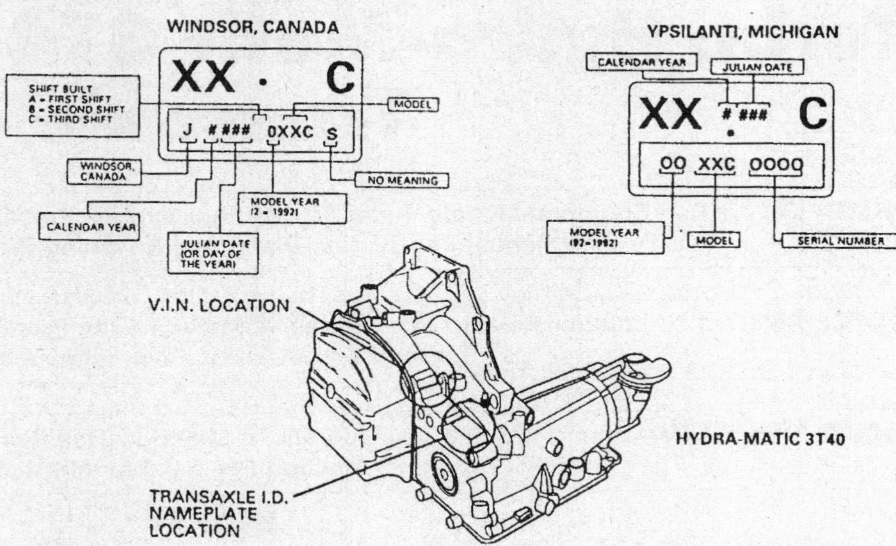

TH5028800099000X

Fig. 1 Transaxle identification

4. Checkball No. 5 not seating or missing.
5. Case Cover:
   a. Porosity in direct clutch case cover passage.
   b. Incorrect gasket.
   c. Interconnected, leaking or restricted driven sprocket support passages.
   d. Damaged or missing driven sprocket support oil seal rings.
6. Direct clutch:
   a. Checkball leaking.
   b. Checkball capsule damaged.
   c. Damaged or missing seals.
   d. Cracked or damaged housing or piston.
   e. Missing or incorrect apply ring.
   f. Wrong number of clutch plates.

NO 2-3 SHIFT OR 2-3 SHIFT DELAYED

1. Governor or speed sensor:
   a. Cover worn.
   b. Thrust washer missing.
   c. Governor seal worn or cut.
   d. Governor weights binding on pin.
   e. Governor spring not seated.
   f. Ball missing.
   g. Governor driven gear stripped.
2. Intermediate servo:
   a. Piston to case oil seal damaged.
   b. Servo piston damaged.
   c. Servo bore damaged.
   d. Servo orifice bleed cup plug missing in case.
3. Accumulator exhaust check valve is not seating in case.
4. Case:
   a. Direct clutch accumulator cup plug (third oil) leaking or missing.
   b. Case to governor shaft sleeve missing or damaged.
   c. Center gasket leaking.
5. Case cover:
   a. Case cover bolts loose.
   b. Drive sprocket support passages interconnected, leaking or restricted.
   c. Drive sprocket support oil seal rings damaged or missing.
   d. Sleeve loose or out of position.
6. Throttle lever and bracket binding.
7. TV link incorrect, disconnected or binding.
8. Control valve:
   a. 2-3 shift valve, 2-3 TV valve sticking.
   b. Shift TV valve sticking.
   c. Governor feed to 2-3 shift valve restricted.
   d. Direct clutch feed orifice restricted.
   e. No. 5 checkball missing or mislocated.
9. Spacer plate or gaskets leaking, damaged or incorrectly installed.
10. Case to governor shaft sleeve damaged or missing.
11. Direct clutch:
    a. Checkball leaking.
    b. Checkball capsule damaged.
    c. Seals damaged or missing.
    d. Cracked or damaged housing or piston.
    e. Backing plate snap ring out of groove.
    f. Clutch plates damaged or missing.

ENGINE STALLS DURING REVERSE OR DRIVE ENGAGEMENT

Missing or clogged TCC auxiliary valve body filter.

DELAY IN DRIVE & REVERSE

1. Converter, drive sprocket and support bushings.
2. Turbine shaft scarf seals damaged or leaking.

NO DRIVE IN DRIVE OR INTERMEDIATE RANGE

Low roller clutch springs missing, rollers galled or missing.

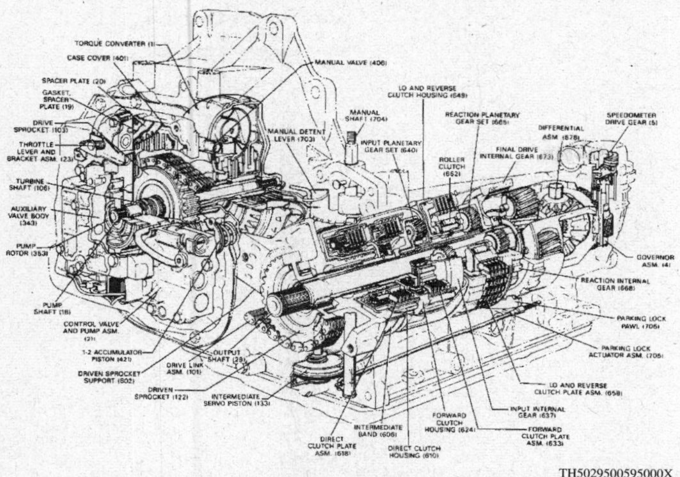

Fig. 2 Cross–sectional view of 3T40 transaxle

Noise In All Ranges

Checks	Cause
Definition: A whine which may be RPM or load sensitive, or ceases when the TCC engages	
Torque Converter (1)	Verify that the noise is internal to the torque converter by placing your left foot on the brake with the gear selector in drive. Then momentarily stall the engine. The torque converter noise increases under load.

Whine Noise Varying w/ RPM or Fluid Pressure

Checks	Cause
Definition: Additionally, a popping noise similar to popcorn popping	
Oil Pump System	• Verify that the noise is internal to the oil pump during a preliminary oil pressure check. An increase in line pressure will vary an oil pump noise • Pump cavitation is indicated by bubbles on the fluid level indicator • Check the transmission fluid strainer for a filter seam leak • Check the transmission fluid strainer seal for proper positioning or for a cut seal

Buzz Noise or High Frequency Rattle Sound

Checks	Cause
• Trace Cooler Pipes • Check for binding or contact at the Radiator other than the Cooler Pipe Connectors	Verify a pressure buzz by watching for a needle vibration on the pressure gage. A road test may be necessary.

Whine/Growl Noise that Changes w/ Vehicle Speed

Checks	Cause
Definition: Additionally, noise is most noticeable under light throttle	
Drive Link Assembly System	Verify a noise from the sprockets or the drive link assembly (chain) by placing your left foot on the brake and by moving the gear selector from Park or Neutral to Drive or Reverse. If the noise stops, check the remaining items in this list.
Drive Link (Chain) Assembly (101)	Stretched
Drive Sprocket and Driven Sprocket (103, 102)	Broken or sheared teeth
Drive and Driven Sprocket Support Bearing Assemblies (108, 121)	Bearing race or roller bearing surfaces are rough or pitted
Drive Sprocket Support and Driven Sprocket Support (109, 602)	Bearing outer race support is rough or nicked

TH5028800101010A

Fig. 3 Noise troubleshooting (Part 1 of 2)

NO DRIVE IN ANY FORWARD RANGE

1. Manual linkage not moving manual valve.
2. Drive sprocket support:
   a. Drive oil passage blocked in driven sprocket support.
   b. Sleeve loose or mislocated.
3. Case cover drive oil passage leak.
4. Forward clutch plates burned or damaged.
5. Control valve body pipe leaking or missing.

NO DRIVE IN ALL RANGES

1. Oil pressure:
   a. Pressure regulator valve sticking in bushing.
   b. Worn pump seals.
   c. Oil pump shaft broken.
2. Differential damaged or broken.
3. Drive link broken or interference between drive link and sprocket.
4. Manual valve retainer clip missing.
5. Input shaft loose or broken away from forward clutch drum.
6. Reaction carrier broken at Low roller clutch cam.

NO DRIVE IN DRIVE RANGE

1. Forward clutch feed in input shaft restricted with cold engine at fast idle.
2. Case cover:
   a. Leak between case cover and driven sprocket passages.
   b. Incorrect gaskets between case cover and driven sprocket support passages.

SECOND SPEED START

1. Governor springs distorted or out of position.
2. Governor weights binding on pin.
3. Control valve:
   a. 1-2 shift valve sticking in upshifted position.
   b. 1-2 throttle valve sticking in upshifted position.

SHIFTS 1-3, MISSES SECOND

1. Intermediate servo:
   a. Wrong or sticking apply pin.
   b. Seals cut, damaged or missing.
   c. Damaged or sticking piston.
   d. Porosity in case servo bore.
2. Accumulator exhaust valve sticking or not seating.
3. Control valve 1-2 shift valve sticking.
4. Spacer plate:
   a. Gaskets incorrectly installed.
   b. Governor feed to 1-2 shift valve blocked.
   c. Intermediate band apply feed orifice blocked.
   d. Wrong spacer plate.
5. Intermediate servo apply passage blocked.
6. Intermediate band improperly installed, burned or broken.

SHIFTS 3-1 AT HIGH SPEEDS FOR PASSING GEAR

1. Governor or speed sensor:
   a. Cover worn.
   b. Thrust washer missing.
   c. Governor seal worn or cut.
   d. Governor spring not seated.
   e. Governor weights binding on pin.
   f. Ball missing.
   g. Governor driven gear stripped.
2. Intermediate servo sticking.
3. Restriction in direct clutch orifice controlled by No. 2 checkball.
4. 1-2 accumulator piston missing or seal leaking.

NO FULL THROTTLE DOWNSHIFT

1. Throttle cable not opening sufficiently.
2. Control valve shift TV valve binding.
3. Spacer plate holes plugged, gasket not positioned correctly or damaged.

NO OVERRUN BRAKING IN LOW

1. Manual linkage improperly adjusted.
2. Low/Reverse clutch pipe leaking.
3. Piston seals are leaking.
4. Control valve low blow off valve damaged.

NO INTERMEDIATE RANGE

1. Intermediate servo oil seal ring missing or damaged.
2. Intermediate band mispositioned, broken or burned.
3. 1-2 accumulator piston or pin missing or damaged.

BINDS IN THIRD GEAR

Direct clutch center seal missing.

NOISE IN ALL RANGES

Refer to **Fig. 3** for noise troubleshooting procedures.

BRAKE TRANSAXLE SHIFT INTERLOCK (BTSI) SYSTEM

Refer to **Fig. 4** for wiring diagram.

Noise In 2nd

Checks	Cause
Reaction Gear Set	—
Reaction Internal Gear (637)	Gears are worn or pitted
Reaction Carrier Assembly (665)	The thrust washer or the thrust bearing mating surfaces are rough or pitted.
Reaction Sun Gear (646)	—
Reaction Sun Gear to Reaction Internal Gear Thrust Bearing (667)	Thrust bearing races or roller bearing surfaces are rough or pitted

Final Drive Noise or Hum Under Light Throttle

Checks	Cause
Definition: Noise may occur in First, Second, or Third	
Final Drive Gear Set	—
Final Drive Internal Gear (673)	—
Differential Carrier (678)	—
Final Drive Sun Gear (675)	—
Differential Pinions (816)	—
Differential Side Gears (687)	• Gears are worn or pitted • The thrust washer or the thrust bearing mating surfaces are rough or pitted
Final Drive Sun Gear to Final Drive Internal Gear Thrust Bearing (676	—
Final Drive Sun Gear to Differential Carrier Thrust Bearing (674)	Thrust bearing races or roller bearing surfaces are rough or pitted
Differential Carrier to Case thrust Bearing (681)	—

Metallic Rattle Noise In Second or Third Gear

Checks	Cause
Definition: Between 25-40 mph under coast or drive operation	
Lo and Reverse Clutch Pack (688, 659)	• Steel plates are not flat • Clutch pack clearance • Parallel grooved fiber plates
Case (15)	Excess plate-to-case clearance due to case machining

TH5028800101020A

Fig. 3 Noise troubleshooting (Part 2 of 2)

TRANSAXLE DOES NOT SHIFT OUT OF PARK w/BRAKE PEDAL DEPRESSED & IGNITION IN RUN

1. Place gear selector in Park and turn ignition switch to Run position.
2. Disconnect stop lamp switch connector.
3. Backprobe BTSI solenoid between terminal A and ground using suitable test lamp.
4. If test lamp lights, repair short to battery voltage in circuit from stop lamp switch to BTSI solenoid. If test lamp does not light, proceed to next step.
5. Connect stop lamp switch.
6. Depress brake pedal, then backprobe circuit between stop lamp switch and BTSI solenoid with suitable test lamp.
7. If test lamp lights, adjust or replace stop lamp switch. If test lamp does not light, inspect shift linkage for binding.
8. If linkage is satisfactory, replace BTSI solenoid.

TRANSAXLE DOES NOT SHIFT OUT OF PARK w/IGNITION SWITCH IN RUN & BRAKE PEDAL NOT DEPRESSED

1. Place gear selector in Park and turn ignition switch to Run.
2. Backprobe BTSI solenoid between terminal A and ground using suitable test lamp.
3. If test lamp lights, inspect BTSI ground circuit. If ground circuit is satisfactory, replace BTSI solenoid. If test lamp does not light, proceed to next step.
4. Backprobe stop lamp switch connector terminal between stop lamp switch and BTSI solenoid using suitable test lamp.
5. If test lamp does not light, inspect for open in circuit between fuse panel and stop lamp switch. If circuit is satisfactory, adjust or replace stop lamp switch.
6. If test lamp lights, find and repair open in circuit between stop lamp switch and BTSI solenoid.

MAINTENANCE

Refer to "Lubricant Data" chart in the appropriate chassis chapter of this manual for transmission fluid specifications.

FLUID CHECK

The transaxle oil level should be approximately ½ inch above the FULL mark at standing temperature (65–85°F), or between the two dimples on the dipstick, **Fig. 5.** The oil level at normal vehicle operating temperature (190–200°F) should be between the ADD and FULL marks. Vehicle must be driven a minimum of 15 minutes to allow transaxle oil to reach normal operating temperature. To bring oil level from ADD mark to FULL mark requires approximately one pint of fluid. Check oil level with vehicle on level surface, parking brake applied, engine idling at operating temperature and transaxle in Park.

When adding fluid, do not over fill, as foaming and loss of fluid through vent may occur as fluid heats up. Also, if fluid level is too low, complete loss of drive may occur especially when cold, which can cause transaxle failure.

FLUID CHANGE

An early change to a darker color from the usual red or green color and/or a strong

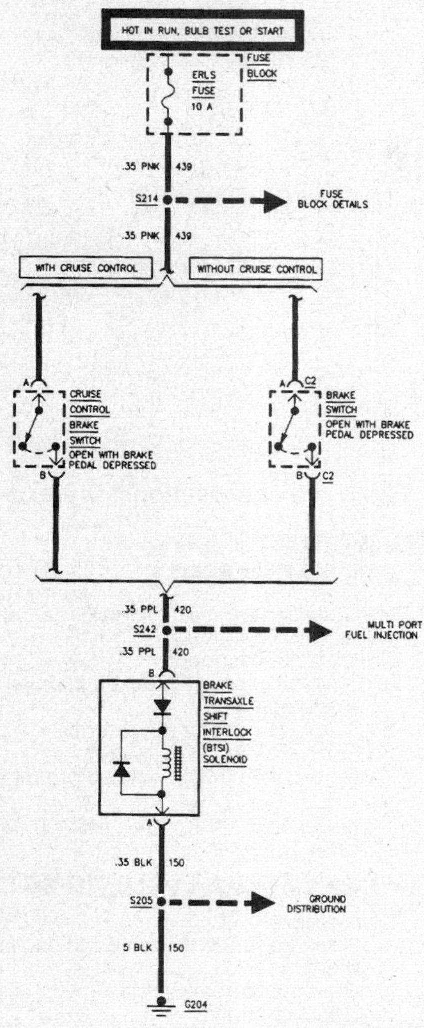

Fig. 4 BTSI wiring diagram

odor that is usually associated with overheated fluid is normal and should not be considered as a positive sign of required maintenance or unit failure.

1. Raise and support vehicle, then position suitable drain pan below transaxle oil pan.
2. Remove front and side oil pan mounting bolts, then loosen rear bolts approximately four turns.
3. Pry pan loose from transaxle case and allow fluid to drain.
4. Remove remaining mounting bolts, oil pan and gasket. Thoroughly clean pan before installing.
5. Remove and discard filter and seal.
6. Lubricate new O-ring seal with assembly lube No. J-36850, or equivalent.
7. Install new filter and O-ring seal with screen located against dipstick stop.
8. Apply GM Threadlocker, or equivalent, to pan mounting bolts.
9. Install gasket on oil pan, pan and mounting bolts.
10. Lower vehicle and add proper amount of transaxle fluid.

11. Place gear selector in Park, start engine and operate at slow idle. **Do not race engine.**
12. Check fluid level and adjust, as required. Ensure pan has no oil leaks.

ADJUSTMENTS

PARK/LOCK CABLE

1. Place floor shift lever in Park position.
2. Place ignition in lock position.
3. Unseat body housing lock from body housing.
4. Ensure there is no gap between metal terminal stop and protruding end of blue plastic collar. If gap exists, adjust position of park/lock cable.
5. Ensure blue plastic collar is flush or recessed 0.04 inch within ignition park/lock housing. If collar position is not as specified, adjust position of park/lock cable.
6. Adjust outer cable conduit to obtain proper location of white plastic housing in ignition switch. Ensure body housing is still attached to shift control mounting bracket.
7. Seat body housing lock in body housing while holding outer cable conduit in position.

THROTTLE VALVE (TV) CABLE

1998

1. Depress and hold adjustment tab.
2. Pull cable conduit out until slider mechanism contacts stopper.
3. Release button and remove floor mat.
4. Firmly depress accelerator pedal to wide open throttle position.
5. Ensure cable moves freely with engine cold and hot.
6. Road test vehicle to ensure proper operation.

1999–2001

1. Depress and hold adjustment tab.
2. Pull cable conduit out until slider mechanism contacts stopper.
3. Release button and position 17mm socket and torque wrench onto throttle body pulley cam.
4. Rotate torque wrench to full wide open throttle position and apply 62–69 inch lbs. of torque.
5. Release applied pressure on torque wrench.
6. Remove torque wrench and socket.
7. Ensure cable moves freely. Check with engine cold and hot.
8. Road test vehicle to ensure proper operation.

IN-VEHICLE REPAIRS

VALVE BODY, REPLACE

The auxiliary valve body, valve body and oil pump are replaced as an assembly.

1. Remove TV cable from transmission.
2. Remove transmission mount bracket.
3. Remove valve body cover.
4. Remove mounting bolt and TCC solenoid.

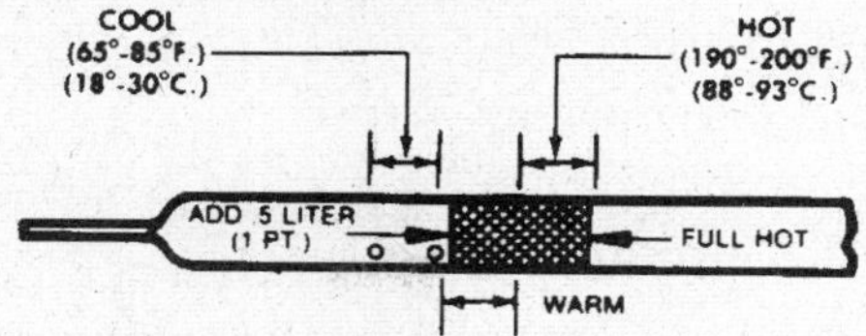

TH5028800100000X

Fig. 5 Transaxle dipstick oil level readings

5. Remove TCC solenoid wiring connector from case connector.
6. Disconnect TCC wires from pressure switches.
7. Remove mounting bolts and TV lever.
8. Remove TV cable link.
9. **Do not lose six checkballs. Do not remove green bolt.** Remove remaining valve body to case cover mounting bolts.
10. Remove valve body from case cover and green bolt.
11. Separate valve body from oil pump.
12. Remove checkball behind control valve.

INTERMEDIATE SERVO & ACCUMULATOR CHECK VALVE, REPLACE

1. Raise and support vehicle.
2. Remove transaxle oil pan and gasket, then the screen and O-ring.
3. Remove reverse oil pipe mounting brackets, intermediate servo cover and gasket.
4. Remove accumulator valve and spring.
5. Remove intermediate servo.
6. Reverse procedure to install

GOVERNOR, REPLACE

1. Raise and support vehicle.
2. Disconnect vehicle speed sensor lead from transaxle.
3. Remove mounting bolts and speed sensor housing, **Fig. 6.**
4. Remove speed sensor housing O-ring.
5. Remove governor, shaft screen and seal.

PARKING PAWL ACTUATOR, REPLACE

1. Raise and support vehicle.
2. Remove transaxle oil pan.
3. Remove oil strainer and filter seal.
4. Remove fluid level indicator stop bracket.
5. Remove spring shaft retainer.
6. Remove parking pawl actuator bracket and clip.
7. Remove manual shift shaft pin.
8. Remove manual valve with retainer rod.
9. Remove manual valve pin.
10. Remove parking pawl spring.
11. Reverse procedure to install.

TRANSAXLE SIDE CASE COVER, REPLACE

1. Remove transmission bracket.
2. Remove valve body cover.
3. Disconnect TCC wire from case connector.
4. Remove mounting bolts and control valve body.
5. Remove mounting bolts and oil pump.
6. Remove oil pump drive shaft.
7. Remove control valve body spacer plate and gaskets.
8. Remove mounting bolts and case cover.
9. Install two 12 x 1.95 x 14 bolts in dowel pin holes and tighten equally in order to pull case cover loose.

TV CABLE, REPLACE

1998

1. Depress and hold adjustment tab.
2. Pull cable conduit out until slider mechanism contacts stopper.
3. Release button and remove floor mat.
4. Firmly depress accelerator pedal to wide open throttle position.
5. Ensure cable moves freely with engine cold and hot.
6. Road test vehicle to ensure proper operation.

1999–2002

1. Depress and hold adjustment tab.
2. Pull cable conduit out until slider mechanism contacts stopper.
3. Release button, then position 17mm socket and torque wrench onto throttle body pulley cam.
4. Rotate torque wrench to full wide open throttle position and apply 62–69 inch lbs. of torque.
5. Release applied pressure on torque wrench.
6. Remove torque wrench and socket.
7. Ensure cable moves freely. Check with engine cold and hot.
8. Road test vehicle to ensure proper operation.

TRANSAXLE

REPLACE

1. Remove intake air duct and TV cable, if equipped.
2. Remove shift cable and bracket.

3. Remove vacuum lines and disconnect electrical connectors.
4. Remove power steering pump and lay off to side.
5. Remove filler tube and install engine support fixture tool No. J-28467-360, or equivalent, to transmission.
6. Remove top transmission to engine mounting bolts.
7. Raise and support vehicle.
8. Remove both front tire and wheel assemblies.
9. Remove lefthand splash shield.
10. Remove both front ABS wheel speed sensors and harness from lefthand suspension support.
11. Remove both lower ball joints and stabilizer shaft links.
12. Remove front air deflector and lefthand suspension support.
13. Remove both drive axles and engine to transmission brace.
14. Remove transmission converter cover and starter.
15. Remove flywheel to torque converter mounting bolts.
16. Remove cooler pipes and ground wires from engine to transmission bolt.
17. Remove cooler pipe and exhaust braces.
18. Remove engine and transmission mount mounting bolts.
19. Support transmission with suitable transmission jack.
20. Remove transmission mount to body mounting bolts.
21. Remove heater core hose pipe brace to transmission nut and bolt.

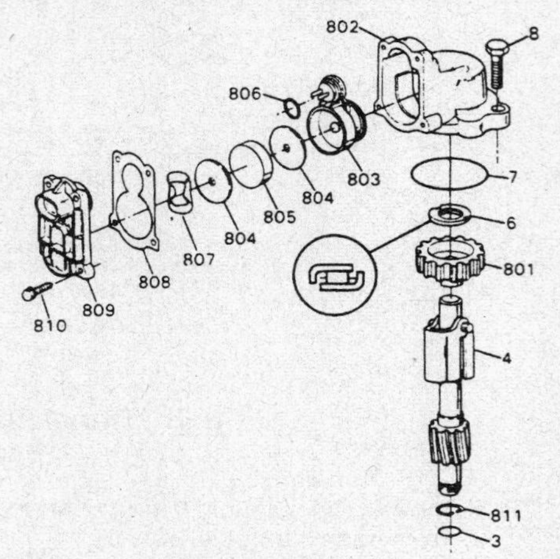

ILL. NO.	DESCRIPTION
3	RING, FLUID SEAL (GOVERNOR SHAFT)
4	GOVERNOR ASSEMBLY
6	BEARING ASSEMBLY, ROTOR THRUST
7	SEAL, "O" RING (GOVERNOR COVER FLUID)
8	SCREW, GOVERNOR COVER — M6 X 1 X 25
801	ROTOR, SPEED SENSOR
802	HOUSING, SPEED SENSOR
803	COIL ASSEMBLY
804	WASHER
805	MAGNET
806	SEAL, "O" RING
807	WASHER, WAVE SPRING
808	GASKET, COVER
809	COVER, SPEED SENSOR HOUSING
810	SCREW, SPEED SENSOR COVER — M4 X 0.7 X 13
811	RING, GOVERNOR COMPRESSION

TH5028800112000X

Fig. 6 Governor replacement

22. Remove remaining transmission to engine bolts and transmission.
23. Reverse procedures to install.

TECHNICAL SERVICE BULLETINS

TRANSMISSION WHINE AT 2800–3200 RPM

1998

On some of these models there may be a whine from the transmission at 2800–3200 RPM.

This condition may be caused by an internal coolant flow restrictor in the heater inlet hose.

To correct this condition replace the heater inlet hose (part No. 22615693) using new stainless steel clamp that comes with hose.

DELAYED, SLOW OR NO SECOND TO THIRD GEAR UPSHIFT

1998

On some of these models there may be a delayed, slow or no second to third gear upshift.

This condition may be caused by a fluid pressure leak between the driven sprocket support and the case cover assembly.

To correct this condition, replace the case cover assembly and gaskets, or replace the transaxle.

TIGHTENING SPECIFICATIONS

Year	Component	Torque/Ft. Lbs.
1998–2001	Auxiliary Oil Cooler	12①
	Axle Nut	184
	Case Cover	18
	Control Assembly	18
	Converter Shield	96①
	Cooler Connector	23
	Engine Mount	34
	Fill Tube	31
	Flywheel To Torque Converter	46
	Frame Insulator	40
	Frame To Crossmember	37
	Governor Cover To Case	96①
	Intermediate Servo Cover	96①
	Intermediate Steering Shaft	40
	Manual Detent Spring To Case	96①
	Neutral Start Switch	22
	Oil Cooler Line To Radiator	23
	Oil Cooler Line To Transaxle	16
	Oil Pan & Valve Body Cover	96①
	Parking Lock Bracket	18
	Pipe Extension	41
	Pipe Retainer	18
	Pressure Switch	96①
	Pump Cover To Case Cover (6mm)	96①
	Pump Cover To Case Cover (8mm)	18
	Reverse Pipe Retainer To Case	18
	Shift Cable Bracket	20
	Solenoid Valve To Valve Body	96①
	Speedometer Driven Gear	72①
	Starter Motor	32
	Throttle Valve Cable	84①
	Transaxle Control Lever	15
	Transaxle Mount Pipe Expansion	41
	Transaxle Mount Support Brace	18
	Transaxle Mount Through Bolt	82
	Transaxle Mount To Support	49
	Transaxle Mount To Transaxle	41
	Transaxle Support	55
	Transaxle To Engine Brace	32
	Transaxle To Engine Mount	71
	Valve Body Cover	11
	Valve Body To Case	18
	Valve Body To Case Cover	96①
	Valve Body To Sprocket Support	18
	Vehicle Speed Sensor	96①

① — Inch lbs.

Turbo Hydra-Matic 4L30-E Automatic Transmission

NOTE: On Air Bag Equipped Models, Refer To "Air Bag System Precautions" Located In The Front Of This Manual For System Disarming & Arming Procedures.

NOTE: Refer To "Computer Relearn Procedures" Located In The Front Of This Manual When Battery Power To The Computer Has Been Interrupted.

INDEX

PRECAUTIONS

AIR BAG SYSTEMS

Refer to "Air Bag System Precautions" in the front of this manual for system disarming and arming procedures.

BATTERY GROUND CABLE

Prior to service, disconnect battery ground cable and isolate as required.

IDENTIFICATION

Refer to **Fig. 1** for transmission identification.

DESCRIPTION

The 4L30-E transmission is a four-speed automatic with a torque converter clutch that provides a direct coupling to the engine when desired, **Fig. 2.** Gear changes, line pressure and torque converter clutch operation are controlled by a separate Transmission Control Module (TCM). There are three driver-selectable, shift programs.

TROUBLESHOOTING

ENGINE WILL NOT START

1. Selector level not in Park or Neutral.
2. Selector level position switch/shift linkage adjustment is incorrect.
3. Fluid pump is blocked.
4. Torque converter is blocked.

SELECTOR POSITION P WILL NOT ENGAGE

1. Selector level position switch/shift linkage is incorrectly adjusted.
2. Shift gate at selector lever position P is damaged.

RATTLING NOISES IN TRANSMISSION

1. Worn parking lock return spring.

REAR WHEELS LOCKED

1. Worn parking lock return spring.

DELAY IN SHIFTING FROM NEUTRAL TO DRIVE

1. Transmission fluid is too low.
2. Fluid pressure is too low.
3. Brake band valve is jammed.

SLIPS OR SHUDDERS IN FIRST GEAR

1. Transmission fluid pressure too low.
2. Torque converter is defective.
3. Loss of fluid in circuit between accumulator and brake band.
4. Brake band incorrectly adjusted.
5. Free wheel (planetary set or 4th gear unit) is defective.
6. Fluid loss in converter clutch fluid circuit.

NO REVERSE GEAR

1. Selector lever position switch/shift linkage is incorrectly adjusted. Only recognizable upon transmission removal and disassembly.
2. Clutch for reverse gear is defective.

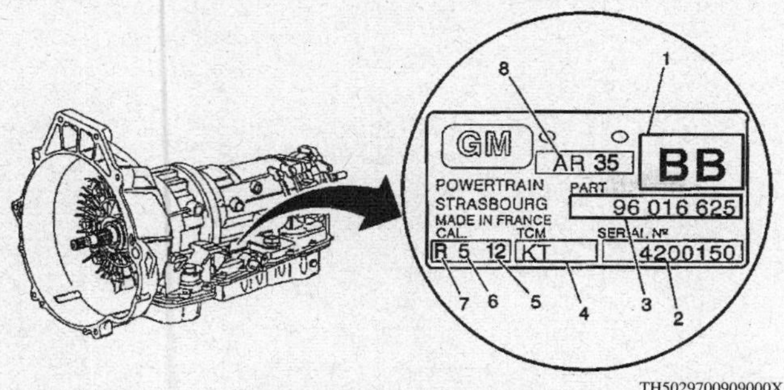

Fig. 1 Transmission identification

(1) Torque Converter Housing
(2) Torque Converter
(3) Turbine Shaft
(4) Oil Pump Assembly
(5) Adapter Case
(6) Overdrive Clutch Roller Assembly
(7) Overrun Clutch Plate Assembly
(8) Overdrive Complete Carrier Assembly
(9) Reverse Clutch Plate Assembly
(10) 2nd Clutch Plate Assembly
(11) Main Case
(12) 3rd Clutch Plate Assembly
(13) Sprag, Cage Assembly
(14) Extension Housing
(15) Output Shaft
(16) Speed Sensor Assembly
(17) Drive Flange
(18) Speedo Wheel
(19) Parking Lock Wheel
(20) Band Assembly
(21) Servo Piston Assembly
(22) Planetary Carrier Assembly
(23) Detent Lever
(24) Center Support
(25) Main Case Valve Body Assembly
(26) 4th Clutch Plate Assembly
(27) Adapter Case Control Valve Assembly
(28) TCC Solenoid Assembly
(29) Converter Pump Assembly
(30) Stator
(31) Turbine Assembly
(32) Pressure Plate

GC5020001066010X

Fig. 2 Cross-sectional view of 4L30-E transmission

COARSE SHIFTING FROM NEUTRAL TO DRIVE

1. Brake band valve is blocked or defective.
2. Cable connection to pressure regulator is defective.
3. Pressure regulator is defective.

POOR ACCELERATION

1. Engine performance is degraded.
2. Winter program is selected.
3. Default mode is active.
4. Torque converter is defective.

NO 1-2 UPSHIFT

1. Selector Lever is in position 1.
2. An incorrectly adjusted selector level position switch/shift linkage.
3. A blocked solenoid valve for 1-2/3-4 shift or on-off valve in valve body.
4. Loss of fluid in clutch C2 or in fluid circuit. Only recognizable upon transmission removal and disassembly.

DIFFICULTY IN SHIFTING BETWEEN 1-2 GEAR

1. Incorrect fluid pressure in clutch C2.
2. Accumulator valve for 1-2 shift is blocked or leaking.
3. Loss of fluid in clutch C2 or in fluid circuit. Only recognizable upon transmission removal and disassembly.
4. Main pressure incorrect.

NO 2-3 UPSHIFT

1. Selector lever in Position 2.
2. Selector lever position switch/shift linkage is incorrectly adjusted.
3. Solenoid valve for 2-3 shift or on-off valve in valve body is defective.

DIFFICULTY IN SHIFTING BETWEEN 2-3 GEAR

1. Brake band is incorrectly adjusted.
2. Loss of fluid in return line between accumulator and brake band.
3. Loss of fluid in clutch C3 or in fluid circuit.
4. Defective or blocked brake band valve.
5. Fluid pressure is incorrect.

NO 3-4 UPSHIFT

1. Selector lever is in position 3.
2. Selector lever position switch/shift linkage is incorrectly adjusted.
3. Solenoid valve for 1-2/3-4 shift or on-off valve in valve body is defective.
4. Loss of hydraulic fluid in clutch C4 or in fluid circuit.

DIFFICULTY IN SHIFTING BETWEEN 3-4 GEAR

1. Loss of fluid in clutch C4 or in fluid circuit.
2. Incorrect fluid pressure.
3. Bridging 4th gear clutch (4th gear lockup clutch) cannot be released.

NO ENGAGEMENT OF TORQUE CONVERTER CLUTCH

1. Solenoid valve for converter clutch is defective.
2. There is interruption in signal circuit.
3. There is fluid loss in fluid circuit of converter clutch.

RATTLING IN TORQUE CONVERTER CLUTCH

1. Torque converter clutch is defective.
2. Fluid pressure is inadequate.

CANNOT RELEASE TORQUE CONVERTER CLUTCH

1. Solenoid valve for converter clutch is defective.
2. Return line is blocked.

VIBRATION IN SECOND GEAR

Solenoid valve of converter clutch is jammed in position active so converter clutch is engaged.

NO SPORT PROGRAM

1. Tip switch is defective.
2. There is electrical circuit interruption.

NO WINTER PROGRAM

1. Tip switch is defective.
2. There is electrical circuit interruption.

NO KICKDOWN PROGRAM

1. WOT switch is defective.
2. There is electrical circuit interruption.

NO DOWNSHIFT POSSIBLE

1. 1-2/3-4 or 2-3 Shift solenoid valves are defective or on-off valve in valve body is locked.

NO ENGINE BRAKING

Bridging clutch for 4th gear (4th gear lockup clutch) is defective or there is loss of fluid in fluid circuit.

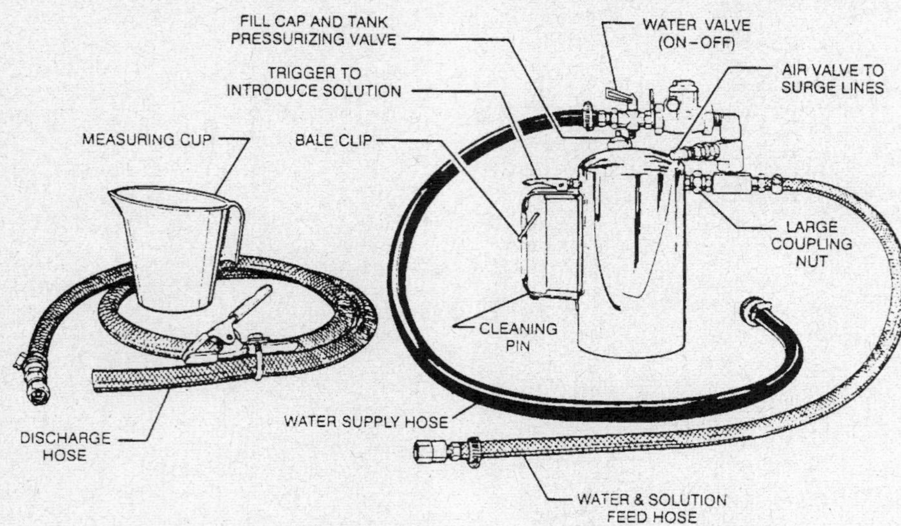

Fig. 3 Oil cooler flushing tool

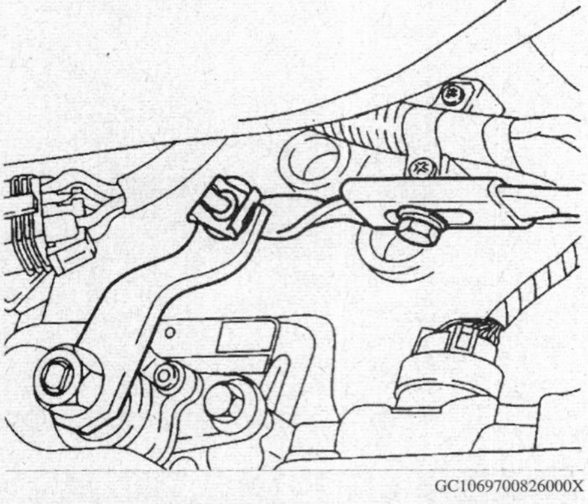

Fig. 4 Shift lever rod adjustment bolt

TRANSMISSION OVERHEATING & FLUID LEAKING FROM VENTILATION

1. Transmission fluid level is too high.
2. Torque converter clutch is not functioning.
3. There is and extreme load in default mode or in winter mode.

MAINTENANCE

Refer to "Lubricant Data" chart in the appropriate chassis chapter of this manual for transmission fluid specifications.

FLUID CHECK

This transmission does not have a dipstick. The fluid level can be checked by removing a plug on the side of the transmission fluid pan.

1. Ensure transmission fluid is at normal operating temperature (113–185°F), which is usually obtained after 15 miles of highway driving.
2. Place transmission range selector in P position and apply parking brake.
3. Wait for engine to cool to ambient temperature.
4. Connect suitably programmed scan tool to vehicle system.
5. Raise and support vehicle.
6. Start engine, move gear select through all gears and return to P position.
7. With engine idling, remove transmission oil pan fill plug.
8. Fluid level should be at plug opening's lower edge. Add fluid, as required.
9. Install oil plug, lower vehicle, disconnect scan tool and test drive vehicle.

FLUID CHANGE

1. Raise and support vehicle, then place suitable container under oil pan.
2. Remove bolts from front and sides of pan, then loosen rear pan bolts.
3. Separate oil pan from transmission case by lightly tapping pan with suitable rubber mallet and flat-bladed screwdriver, then drain fluid.
4. Remove rear bolts, pan and gasket.
5. Remove mounting bolts and filter.
6. Clean case, front adapter case and oil pan gasket surfaces with suitable solvent and air dry.
7. Install gasket, filter and mounting bolts and front oil pan, gasket and mounting bolts.
8. Fill transmission to lower edge of oil pan fill plug opening, install plug and tighten.
9. Lower vehicle and check fluid level.

TRANSMISSION OIL COOLER FLUSH

Use cooler flusher tool No. J-35944, **Fig. 3,** and flushing solution funnel tool No. J-35944-20, or equivalents. Do not substitute the recommended flushing solution. The use of other solutions can result in damage to the tool, components or other improper flushing of the cooler. **Air supply must be equipped with a water/oil filter and must not exceed 120 psi.**

1. Fill flushing tool No. J-35944-A, or equivalent, with 20–21 ounces of flushing solution J-35944-20, or equivalent. **Do not overfill.**
2. Secure cap and pressurize can to 80–120 psi.
3. Connect discharge hose to transmission fitting end of oil cooler pipe that goes to top fitting at radiator and clip discharge hose into suitable drain container.
4. Mount flushing tool to undercarriage using hook provided.
5. Connect hose from flushing tool to remaining oil cooler pipe and with flushing tool water valve in Off position, connect water hose from water supply to flushing tool.
6. Open water supply at faucet and switch flushing tool water valve to On position and allow water to flow through oil cooler for 10 seconds, noting the following:
   a. If water does not flow through cooler, do not continue with flushing procedure.
   b. Cooling system may be plugged.
   c. Excess pressure may cause personal injury.
   d. Replacement of cooler pipe and/or cooler may be required.
7. Switch flushing tool water valve to Off position and clip discharge hose into five-gallon pail with lid, or place shop towel over end of discharge hose to prevent splash. **Discharge will foam when solution and water mix.**
8. Switch flushing tool water valve to On position and depress trigger on handle. **Use bale clip provided on handle to hold trigger.**
9. Flush cooler for two minutes while applying air to air valve for 3–5 seconds. **Apply air at 15–20 seconds intervals to create surging action.**
10. Release trigger and switch flushing tool water valve to Off position and disconnect hoses from cooler pipes.
11. Reverse positions and connect to cooler pipes to back flush system.
12. Repeat previous suitably programmed scan tools and release trigger and allow water to flow to rinse oil cooler for one minute.
13. Switch flushing tool water valve to Off position and turn off water supply at faucet.
14. Dry system with compressed air for at least two minutes or until there is no moisture coming from discharge hose. Use air chuck clip, if available.
15. **Excess residual moisture may corrode cooler, pipes and damage transmission. If following suitably programmed scan tools cannot be completed at this time, use suitable squirt type oil can filled with ATF to rinse cooler and pipes.**
16. Connect cooler feed pipe to transmission (top connector is feed, bottom connector is cooler return).
17. Attach discharge hose to cooler return pipe and place into suitable oil drain container.
18. Fill transmission to appropriate level

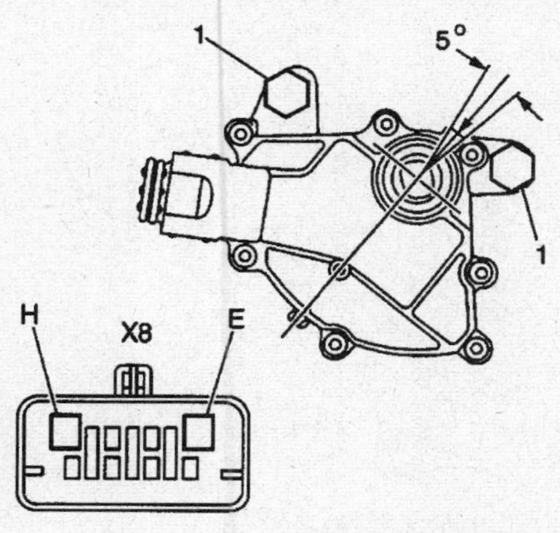

Fig. 5 Mode switch adjustment

with suitable ATF.

19. Start engine and allow to run for 30 seconds. Minimum of two quarts must flow through discharge hose.
20. If fluid flow is not sufficient, disconnect oil feed line at radiator and restart engine and inspect flow rate. If flow rate is not sufficient, inspect oil cooler feed and transmission for cause. If flow rate is sufficient, repeat oil cooler flushing and fluid flow inspection procedures. If flow is not sufficient, replace oil cooler.
21. Remove discharge hose and connect cooler return pipe to transmission, then fill transmission to proper fluid level.
22. Thoroughly clean flushing tool with water. **Do not store tool with flushing solution in tank.**

ADJUSTMENTS

SHIFT LEVER ROD

1. Place shift lever in Park position.
2. Raise and support vehicle.
3. Loosen adjustment bolt to allow adjuster to slide freely, **Fig. 4.**
4. Hold selector against rear stop and tighten adjustment bolt.
5. Lower vehicle and ensure engine starts when selector is in Park or Neutral positions only.

TRANSMISSION CONTROL SELECTOR SWITCH

1. Apply parking brake and position selector in Neutral position.
2. Raise and support vehicle.
3. Remove transmission and selector lever position switch covers.
4. Remove transmission selector lever nut and intermediate lever.
5. Disconnect mode switch electrical connector.
6. Connect suitable multimeter to mode switch electrical connector terminals E and H, **Fig. 5.**
7. Loosen mounting bolts and rotate mode switch in both directions to determine electrical contact range.
8. Position switch in middle of range.
9. Reverse procedure to install.

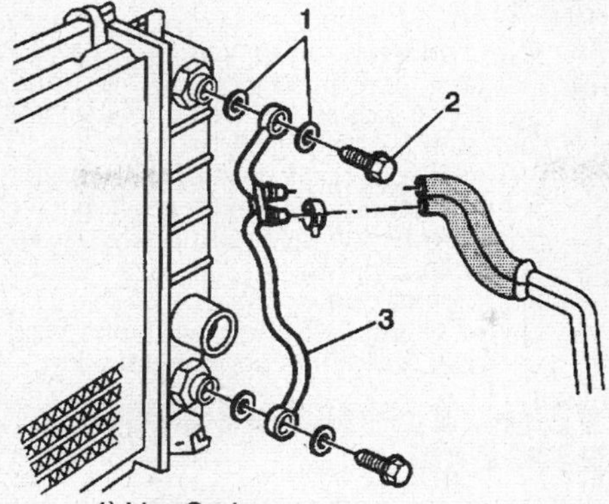

1) Line Seals
2) Line Attaching Bolt
3) Oil Cooling Line

Fig. 6 Front oil cooling line replacement

THIRD CLUTCH SERVO PISTON

1. Hold adjusting sleeve with wrench and loosen lock nut.
2. **Torque** adjusting screw to 40 inch lbs.
3. Loosen adjusting screw five turns.
4. Hold adjusting sleeve and screw, **torque** locknut to 14 ft. lbs.

IN-VEHICLE REPAIRS

BRAKE TRANSMISSION SHIFT INTERLOCK (BTSI) SOLENOID, REPLACE

1. Remove floor console, parking brake and shift selector boots.
2. Remove low and second blockout switch and transmission control indicator and shift plate.
3. Raise and support vehicle.
4. Remove Brake Transmission Shift Interlock (BTSI) solenoid mounting screw.
5. Lower vehicle.
6. Remove electrical connector and BTSI solenoid.
7. Reverse procedure to install.

AUTOMATIC TRANSMISSION CONTROL, REPLACE

1. Remove console and mounting nuts and rear air duct front and console rear supports.
2. Slide rear air duct to rear and disconnect automatic transmission control electrical connector.
3. Raise and support vehicle.
4. Remove clip and slide rod off shift lever.
5. Lower vehicle, drill out rivets and remove automatic transmission control.
6. Reverse procedure to install.

DRIVE FLANGE & CASE EXTENSION SEAL, REPLACE

1. Raise and support vehicle.
2. Remove bolts and pry propeller shaft

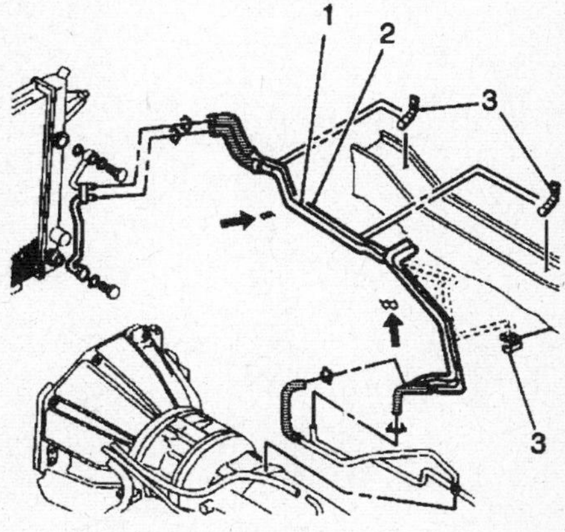

1) Inlet Cooling Line
2) Outlet Cooling LIne
3) Cooling Line Retaining Clip

Fig. 7 Middle oil cooling line replacement

coupling away from drive flange using suitable screwdriver.

3. Hold drive flange with rear hub holding tool No. J-42066, or equivalent, and remove mounting nut.
4. Remove flange and pry out seal with suitable screwdriver.
5. Reverse procedure to install, noting following:
   a. Install new seal using transmission extension housing seal installer tool No. J-42080, or equivalent.
   b. Install new drive flange nut.

CASE EXTENSION, REPLACE

1. Raise and support vehicle. Support transmission with suitable transmission jack.
2. Remove body bolts and crossmember, then the mounting bolts and mount.
3. Remove drive flange.
4. Remove mounting bolts and catalytic converter support bracket.
5. Remove electrical connector, mounting bolt and speed sensor. Do not pry sensor out.
6. Remove oxygen sensor harness clips.
7. Remove mounting bolts, extension and gasket.
8. Remove speed sensor ring and extension seal.
9. Press bearing out of extension case rear using suitable size spacer.
10. Reverse procedure to install.

SOLENOID VALVES, REPLACE

The 2-3 shift, 1-2/3-4 shift and band control solenoid valves are located in the main case. The Torque Convert Clutch (TCC) and force motor solenoid valves are located in the front case.

1. Remove oil pan and filter as outlined under "Oil Pan, Replace."
2. Remove solenoid valve electrical connectors.
3. Remove retaining pin and remove valves using suitable pliers.
4. Reverse procedure to install.

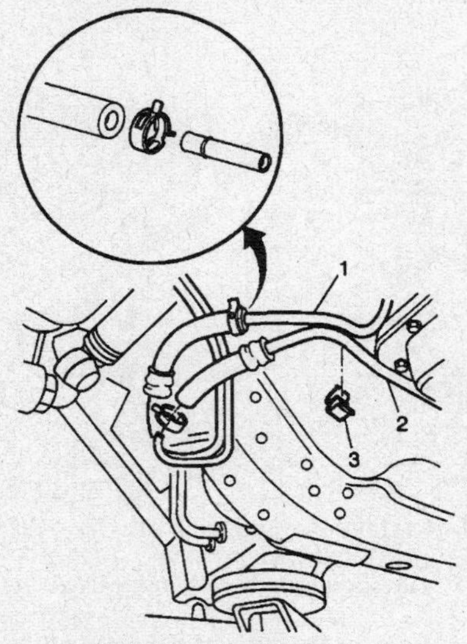

Fig. 8 Rear oil cooling line replacement

TRANSMISSION CONTROL MODULE (TCM), REPLACE

1. Remove righthand side sound insulator panel and retainer.
2. Remove side floor air outlet and glove compartment.
3. Remove mounting nuts, pull Transmission Control Module (TCM) away from studs, slide down and away from upper clip, then remove.
4. Reverse procedure to install.

COOLING LINES, REPLACE

FRONT

1. Remove air filter housing and alternator cooling duct.
2. Remove center inlet and outlet line hoses from oil cooling line, then the upper line fitting seals from radiator, **Fig. 6.**
3. Raise and support vehicle, then remove lower line fitting and seals from radiator.
4. Remove front cooling line.
5. Reverse procedure to install, ensuring to install seals upon installation.

MIDDLE

1. Remove air filter housing and alternator cooling duct.
2. Remove fuel vapor fresh air inlet hose, then the center inlet and outlet line hoses at radiator, **Fig. 7.**
3. Remove center inlet and outlet lines from upper body retaining clips, then raise and support vehicle.
4. Remove center inlet and outlet line hoses from inlet and outlet lines at transmission, then the center inlet and outlet lines from lower body retaining clips.
5. Remove lines.
6. Reverse procedure to install.

REAR

1. Raise and support vehicle.
2. Remove center oil cooling inlet and outlet line hoses from oil cooling inlet and outlet lines, **Fig. 8.**
3. Remove oil cooling inlet and outlet lines retainer, then the oil cooling inlet and outlet lines fittings and seals from transmission, **Fig. 9.**
4. Remove oil cooling lines.
5. Reverse procedure to install, ensuring to install new seals upon installation.

VEHICLE SPEED SENSOR, REPLACE

1. Raise and support vehicle.
2. Disconnect electrical connector.
3. Remove mounting bolt, sensor and seal. Use hand pressure to rotate back and forth while pulling outward. **Do not pry on sensor.**
4. Reverse procedure to install.

TRANSMISSION MOUNT, REPLACE

1. Raise and support vehicle.
2. Support transmission using suitable transmission jack and remove transmission crossmember to mount nuts.
3. Remove mounting bolts and crossmember.
4. Remove mounting bolts and transmission mount.
5. Reverse procedure to install.

MANUAL SHAFT SHIFT POSITION SWITCH, REPLACE

1. Place shift lever in Neutral position, then raise and support vehicle.
2. Remove exhaust muffler to catalytic converter nuts and bolts, then support transmission with suitable transmission jack.
3. Remove crossmember to body bolts, then lower transmission enough to access to switch.
4. Remove switch cover and disconnect switch wire harness connector from bracket.
5. Remove transmission control selector shaft nut and lever from shaft.
6. Remove mounting bolts and switch.
7. Reverse procedure to install. Adjust transmission control selector switch.

BAND CONTROL SOLENOID, REPLACE

1. Raise and support vehicle.
2. Remove pan and filter, then disconnect solenoid valve electrical connector.
3. Remove retaining pin using suitable pliers, then the solenoid.
4. Remove solenoid valve and wave washer.
5. Reverse procedure to install.

CONVERTER CLUTCH SOLENOID, REPLACE

1. Raise and support vehicle.

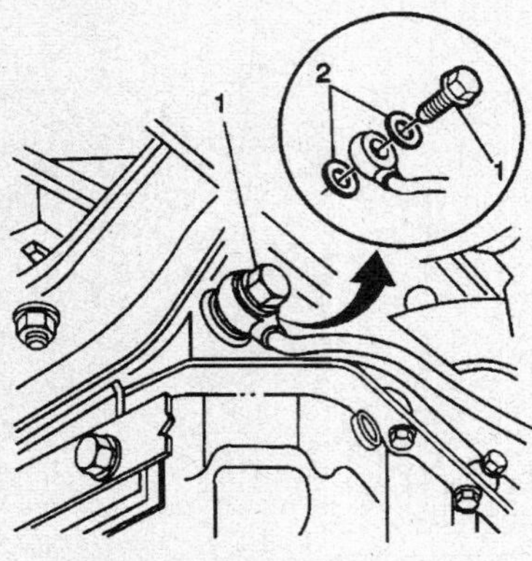

Fig. 9 Rear oil cooling line fittings

2. Remove adapter case oil pan and electrical connectors from solenoid valves.
3. Remove mounting bolts, clip and force motor solenoid valve.
4. Remove torque converter clutch solenoid valve.
5. Reverse procedure to install.

TRANSMISSION

REPLACE

1. Raise and support vehicle.
2. Drain transmission fluid into suitable container.
3. Disconnect transmission shift lever rod and remove propeller shaft coupling bolts.
4. Separate propeller shaft coupling from drive flange using suitable pry tool, then remove transmission oil pan and bellhousing access plugs.
5. Remove flexplate to torque converter bolts. Mark relationship between flexplate and converter for installation reference.
6. Disconnect oil cooler inlet and outlet pipes at center pipes.
7. Disconnect oxygen sensor electrical connectors and remove catalytic converters.
8. Remove transmission housing to engine oil pan mounting bolts and install suitable transmission support.
9. Remove mounting nuts, bolts and transmission crossmember.
10. Lower transmission to access transmission housing to engine block bolts and disconnect ventilation hose at transmission.
11. Disconnect transmission control selector switch, adapter case, main case and speed sensor electrical connectors.
12. With front of engine supported, remove transmission housing to engine block bolts.
13. Remove transmission.
14. Reverse procedure to install. Adjust shift lever rod.

TIGHTENING SPECIFICATIONS

Year	Component	Torque/Ft. Lbs.
1998–2001	Catalytic Converter Support	15
	Catalytic Converter To Muffler	30
	Console Rear Support	35①
	Control Valve	15
	Crossmember to Body	33
	Crossmember to Mount	15
	Drive Flange Nut	74
	Extension Housing To Main Case	24
	Flex Plate	22
	Force Motor Solenoid Valve	84①
	Front Oil Pan	96①
	Manual Shaft	16
	Manual Shaft Shift Position Switch	113①
	Oil Cooler Fittings At Radiator	18
	Oil Cooler Inlet	18
	Oil Cooler Outlet	22
	Oil Pan	96①
	Oil Pan Fill Plug	33
	Oil Pressure Test Hole Plug	108①
	Propeller Shaft Coupling	70
	Rear Air Duct Front Support	87①
	Shift Lever Rod Adjustment	87①
	TCC Solenoid Valve	87①
	Transmission Case Extension, Nut	15
	Transmission Case Extension, Bolt	23
	Transmission Control Selector Switch	10
	Transmission Control Solenoid	96①
	Transmission Crossmember To Body	33
	Transmission Crossmember To Mount	15
	Transmission Housing To Engine Block	44
	Transmission Housing To Engine Oil Pan	15
	Transmission Mount	30
	Transmission Oil Filter	15
	Transmission Speed Sensor	78①

① — Inch Lbs.

Turbo Hydra-Matic 4L60-E Automatic Transmission

NOTE: On Air Bag Equipped Models, Refer To "Air Bag System Precautions" Located In The Front Of This Manual For System Disarming & Arming Procedures.

NOTE: Refer To "Computer Relearn Procedures" Located In The Front Of This Manual When Battery Power To The Computer Has Been Interrupted.

NOTE: Prior To Performing Any Service Operations Listed In This Section, Consult The "Technical Service Bulletins" Section For Related Information.

INDEX

PRECAUTIONS

AIR BAG SYSTEMS

Refer to "Air Bag System Precautions" in the front of this manual for system disarming and arming procedures.

BATTERY GROUND CABLE

Prior to service, disconnect battery ground cable and isolate as required.

IDENTIFICATION

The transmission identification code is located on the rear righthand side of the transmission above the oil pan, **Fig. 1.** For code and model interpretation, refer to **Fig. 2.** The code numbers that indicate the Julian date tell what day of the year the transmission was built. It should be noted that the transmission model year starts in mid year. This means that the first transmission built in any model year will start with a higher Julian date.

DESCRIPTION

The 4L60-E **Fig. 3** is an electronically controlled transmission. A Powertrain Control Module (PCM) manages engine and transmission functions as a single system. The PCM retards engine spark for an instant during each gear shift which reduces engine torque as the gear is engaged. After the shift is completed, spark is advanced and torque is brought to normal operating levels. Shifting is accomplished by sensor-driven servos located within the transmission valve body.

The torque converter couples the engine power to the gearsets and hydraulically provides additional torque multiplication when required. Also, through the converter clutch, the converter drive and driven members operate as one unit when applied, providing mechanical drive from the engine through the transmission.

The gear ratio changes are fully automatic in relation to the vehicle speed and engine torque. Vehicle speed and engine torque are directed to the transmission providing the proper gear ratio for maximum efficiency and performance at all throttle openings.

A hydraulic system pressurized by a variable capacity vane-type pump, provides the operating pressure required for the operation of the friction elements and automatic controls.

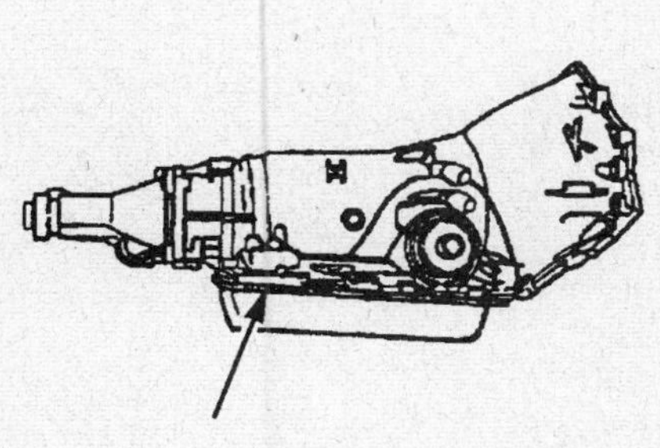

TH5028800357000A

Fig. 1 Transmission identification

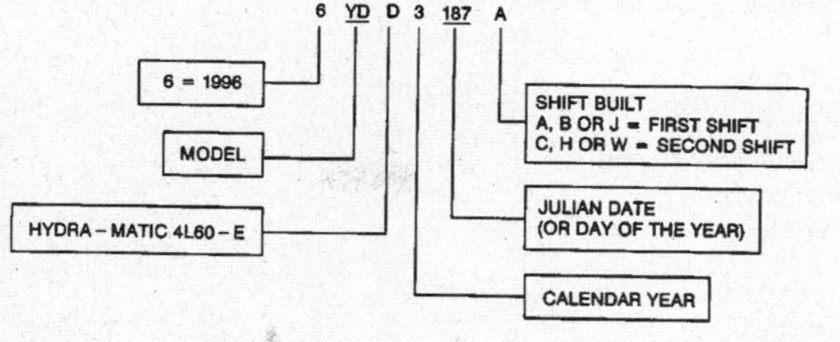

Fig. 2 Transmission code interpretation

TROUBLESHOOTING

OIL PRESSURE HIGH OR LOW

1. Oil pump pressure regulator valve stuck.
2. Oil pump pressure regulator valve spring damaged.
3. Oil pump rotor guide omitted or incorrectly assembled.
4. Oil pump rotor cracked or damaged.
5. TV valve and reverse boost valve or bushing stuck, damaged or incorrectly assembled.
6. Orifice hole in pressure regulator valve plugged.
7. Oil pump slide sticking or excessive rotor clearance.
8. Oil pump pressure relief ball not seated or damaged.
9. Oil pump cover or body porous.
10. Incorrect pump cover or defective pump faces.
11. Oil filter intake pipe and filter body restricted or cracked.
12. Oil filter O-ring seal missing, cut or damaged.
13. TV exhaust ball stuck or damaged.
14. Throttle lever and bracket or throttle link binding, damaged or incorrectly assembled.
15. Valve body manual valve scored or damaged.
16. Valve body spacer plate or gaskets incorrect, damaged or incorrectly assembled.
17. Valve body throttle valve sticking, sleeve rotated in bore or retaining pin not seated.
18. TV limit valve, line bias valve, modulated downshift valve or 2-3 shift valve stuck.
19. Valve body checkballs omitted or incorrectly assembled.

HARSH SHIFTS

1. Throttle position sensor open or shorted circuit.
2. Vehicle speed sensor open or shorted circuit.
3. Pressure switch contaminated or damaged seals.
4. Transmission fluid temperature sensor open or shorted circuit.
5. Engine coolant temperature sensor circuit open or shorted circuit.
6. Pressure control solenoid contaminated or damage to pins.

INACCURATE SHIFT POINTS

1. Oil pump has stuck pressure regulator valve or sticking pump slide.
2. Valve body has incorrect, damaged or incorrectly assembled spacer plate or gaskets.
3. Case has the following conditions:
   a. Porous or damaged valve body pad.
   b. 2-4 servo has damaged servo piston seals, improper length or damaged apply pin, or accumulator porosity.
   c. 2-4 band is burned or anchor pin is not engaged.
4. Throttle position sensor is disconnected or damaged.
5. Vehicle speed sensor is disconnected or damaged.
6. Four wheel drive low switch is disconnected or damaged.

HIGH OR LOW SHIFT POINTS

1. TV cable binding or incorrectly adjusted.
2. TV exhaust ball stuck or damaged.
3. Throttle lever and bracket binding, damaged or incorrectly assembled.
4. Sticking oil pump slide, pressure regulator valve or TV boost valve.
5. Valve body modulated TV up or down valves sticking.
6. TV limit valve, throttle valve or plunger sticking.
7. Valve body spacer plate or gaskets damaged or incorrect.

FIRST SPEED ONLY-NO UPSHIFT

1. Governor valve sticking.
2. Governor driven gear loose or damaged.
3. Governor driven gear retaining pin missing.
4. Nicks or burrs on output shaft, governor sleeve or case bore.
5. Governor support pin in case too long or short.
6. Governor weights or springs missing, binding or damaged.
7. 1-2 shift valve sticking.
8. Valve body spacer plate or gaskets damaged or incorrectly installed.
9. Case to valve body face not flat or damaged.
10. Governor screen restricted or damaged.
11. Restricted or blocked 2-4 servo apply passages.
12. Nicks or burrs on 2-4 servo pin or pin bore in case.
13. Missing or damaged 2-4 servo piston or pin seals.
14. Fourth servo piston installed backwards.
15. 2-4 band worn or damaged.
16. 2-4 band anchor pin not engaged.

SLIPS IN FIRST GEAR

1. Forward clutch plates worn.
2. Porosity or damage in forward clutch piston.
3. Forward clutch piston inner and outer seals missing, cut or damaged.
4. Input housing to forward clutch housing O-ring seal missing, cut or damaged.
5. Forward clutch housing damaged.
6. Forward clutch housing retainer and ball not sealing or damaged.
7. Turbine shaft seals missing, cut or damaged.
8. Valve body accumulator valve stuck.
9. Valve body face not flat, damaged lands or interconnected passages.
10. Valve body spacer plate or gaskets incorrect, damaged or incorrectly assembled.
11. TV cable binding or broken.
12. Damaged ring grooves on 1-2 accumulator piston.
13. 1-2 accumulator piston seal missing, cut or damaged.
14. 1-2 accumulator cover gasket missing or damaged.
15. Leak between 1-2 accumulator piston and pin.
16. Broken 1-2 accumulator spring.
17. Fourth servo piston installed backwards.
18. Incorrect oil pressure. Refer to "Oil Pressure High Or Low."

1-2 SHIFT SPEED-HIGH OR LOW

1. TV cable binding, broken or incorrectly adjusted.
2. Faulty governor. Refer to "First Speed Only-No Upshift."
3. Throttle lever and bracket damaged, binding or incorrectly assembled.
4. TV link missing, binding or damaged.
5. TV exhaust checkball and TV plunger sticking.
6. Valve body or oil pump face not flat.

1-2 SHIFT SLIPPING OR ROUGH

1. Throttle lever and bracket incorrectly installed or damaged.
2. TV cable broken or damaged.
3. Throttle valve sticking.
4. TV bushing turned in its bore.
5. 1-2 shift valve train stuck.
6. Valve body gaskets or spacer plate incorrect, damaged or incorrectly installed.
7. TV limit valve, line bias valve or accumulator valve stuck.
8. Valve body face not flat.
9. 2-4 servo apply pin too long or short.
10. 2-4 servo seals or O-ring seals missing, cut or damaged.
11. 2-4 servo bore damaged.
12. Restricted or missing 2-4 servo oil passages.
13. Porosity in 1-2 accumulator housing or piston.
14. Second accumulator piston seal or groove damaged.
15. Nicks or burrs in 1-2 accumulator housing.
16. 2-4 band worn or incorrectly installed.
17. Oil pump faces not flat.

NO 2-3 SHIFT OR 2-3 SHIFT SLIPPING, ROUGH OR HUNTING

1. Internal converter damage.
2. Governor valve stuck.
3. Governor drive gear retaining pin missing or loose.
4. Governor weights binding.
5. Governor drive gear damaged.
6. Governor support pin in case too long or short.
7. Oil pump stator shaft sleeve scored or improperly installed.
8. Accumulator valve, throttle valve, TV limit valve or 2-3 valve train stuck.
9. Valve body spacer plate or gaskets incorrect, damaged or incorrectly installed.
10. Forward or 3-4 clutch plates worn.
11. Excessive clutch plate travel.
12. Cut or damaged piston seals in input housing.
13. Porosity in 3-4 clutch housing or piston.
14. 3-4 piston checkball stuck, damaged or incorrectly sealing.
15. Restricted input housing apply passages.
16. Forward clutch piston retainer and ball not seating.
17. Input housing sealing balls loose or missing.
18. Third accumulator retainer and ball not seating.
19. Second apply piston seals missing, cut or damaged.
20. 2-4 servo pin seals missing, cut or damaged.

1ST & 4TH OR 2ND & 3RD GEARS ONLY

Shift solenoids have accumulated sediment, damaged seal or bad electrical connection.

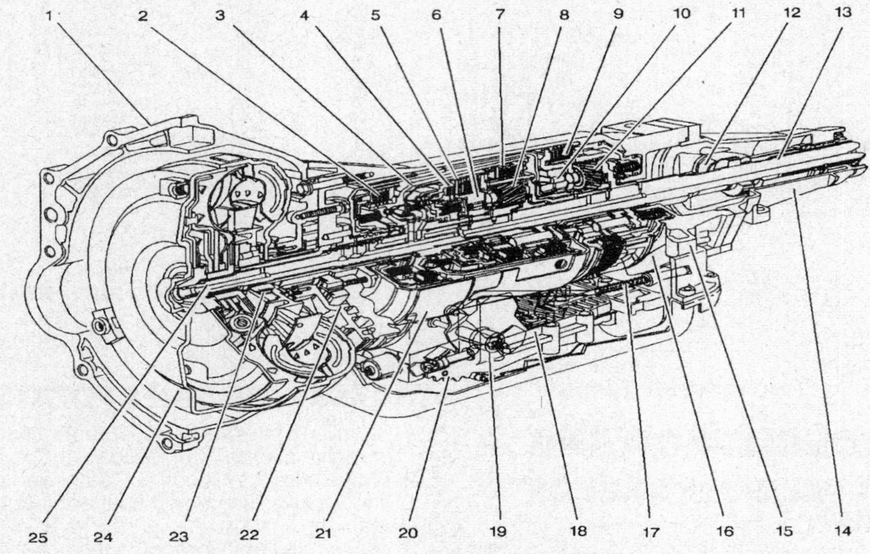

(1) Converter Housing
(2) Reverse Input Clutch
(3) Input Clutch Housing
(4) Overrun Clutch
(5) Forward Clutch
(6) Forward Sprag Clutch Assembly
(7) 3-4 Clutch
(8) Input Planetary Gear Set
(9) Lo and Reverse Clutch
(10) Lo Roller Clutch Assembly
(11) Reaction Planetary Gear Set
(12) Speed Sensor
(13) Output Shaft
(14) Case Extension
(15) Main Section Case
(16) Parking Pawl
(17) Parking Lock Actuator Assembly
(18) Control Valve Assembly
(19) Manual Shaft
(20) Inside Detent Lever
(21) 2-4 Band Assembly
(22) Pump Assembly
(23) Stator Roller Clutch
(24) Torque Converter Assembly
(25) Turbine Shaft

TH502940048I000A

Fig. 3 Cross-sectional view of transmission

3-2 FLARE OR TIE-UP

3-2 control solenoid is contaminated, has damaged seal or is shorted or damaged.

NO 3-4 SHIFT OR ROUGH 3-4 SHIFT

1. Governor weights binding.
2. Governor valve stuck.
3. Governor drive gear retaining pin missing or loose.
4. Governor drive gear damaged.
5. Governor support pin in case too long or short.
6. Oil pump faces not flat.
7. Pump cover retainer and ball omitted or damaged.
8. Accumulator valve, throttle valve, TV limit valve, 3-2 control valve, 1-2 shift valve train or 2-3 shift valve train stuck.
9. Manual valve link bent or damaged.
10. Valve body spacer plates or gaskets incorrect, damaged or incorrectly installed.
11. Incorrect 2-4 servo band apply pin.
12. Missing or damaged 2-4 servo seals.
13. Porosity in 2-4 servo pistons, cover and case.
14. Damaged 2-4 servo piston seal grooves.
15. Plugged or missing orifice cup plug in 2-4 servo.
16. Third accumulator retainer and ball leaking.
17. Porosity in 3-4 accumulator piston or bore.
18. 3-4 accumulator piston seal or seal grooves damaged.
19. Plugged or missing orifice cup plug.
20. Restricted case oil passage.
21. Faulty input housing. Refer to "No 2-3 Shift Or 2-3 Shift Slipping, Rough Or Hunting."
22. 2-4 band worn or incorrectly installed.

NO REVERSE OR SLIPS IN REVERSE

1. 3-4 apply ring stuck in applied position.
2. Forward clutch not releasing.
3. Turbine shaft seals missing, cut or damaged.
4. Manual linkage incorrectly adjusted.
5. Oil pump retainer and ball missing or damaged.

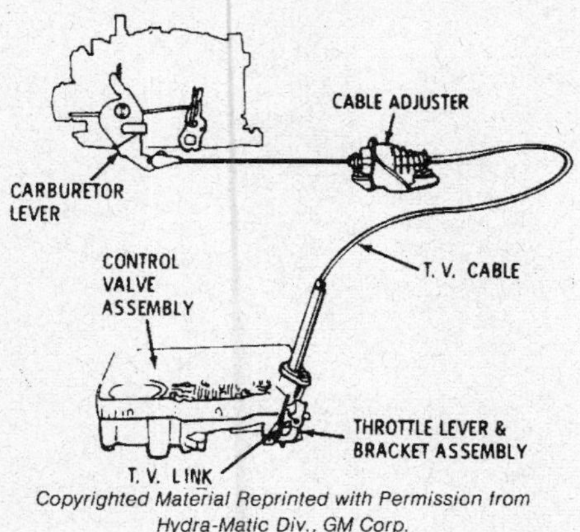

TH5028800368000X

Fig. 4 Throttle cable & linkage

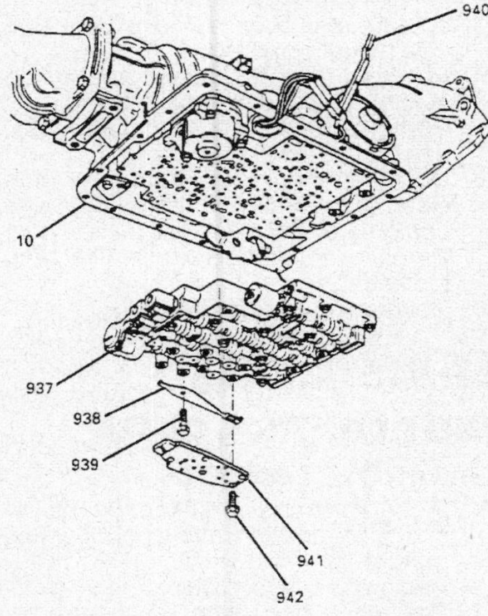

10 CASE, TRANSMISSION
937 VALVE ASSEMBLY, CONTROL BODY
938 SPRING ASSEMBLY, MANUAL DETENT
939 BOLT/SCREW, MANUAL DETENT SPRING
940 SOLENOID ASSEMBLY, WIRING HARNESS AND
941 SWITCH ASSEMBLY, TRANSMISSION PRESSURE
942 BOLT/SCREW, PRESSURE SWITCH ASSEMBLY

GC5029400450000X

Fig. 7 Control valve & pressure switch

6. Oil pump stator shaft sleeve scored or damaged.
7. Reverse boost valve stuck, damaged or incorrectly installed.
8. Oil pump cup plug missing.
9. Oil pump converter clutch apply valve stuck.
10. Oil pump face not flat or restricted oil passage.
11. 2-3 shift valve stuck.
12. Valve body spacer plate and gaskets incorrect, damaged or incorrectly installed.
13. Reverse input clutch plate worn.
14. Reverse input housing and drum cracked at weld.
15. Reverse input clutch plate retaining ring out of groove.
16. Reverse input clutch return spring retaining ring out of groove.

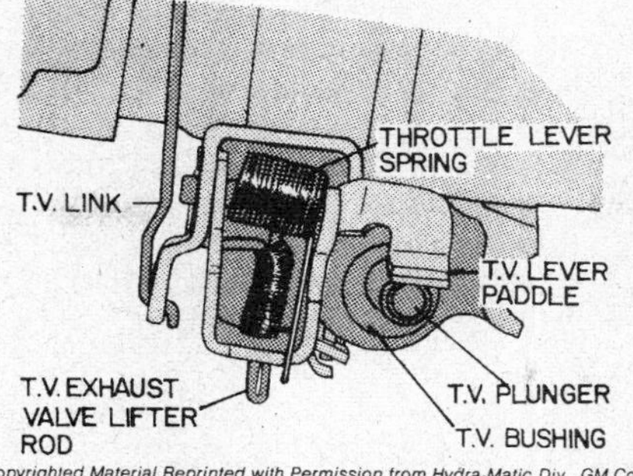

TH5028800369000X

Fig. 5 Throttle lever & bracket

17. Reverse input clutch seals cut or damaged.
18. Reverse input clutch retainer and ball not sealing.
19. Restricted oil apply passage in reverse input clutch.
20. Low/Reverse clutch plates worn.
21. Low/Reverse clutch plate retaining ring incorrectly installed.
22. Porosity in Low/Reverse clutch piston.
23. Low/Reverse clutch seals damaged or oil apply passage restricted.
24. Case cover plate gasket missing, damaged or incorrectly tightened.

NO PART THROTTLE OR DELAYED DOWNSHIFTS

1. Throttle linkage incorrectly adjusted.
2. 2-4 servo apply pin cut or damaged.
3. 2-4 servo cover retaining ring omitted or incorrectly assembled.
4. Fourth apply piston damaged or incorrectly assembled.
5. 2-4 servo inner housing damaged or incorrectly assembled.
6. Governor weights binding.
7. Governor valve stuck.
8. Throttle valve, 3-2 control valve or TV modulated downshift valve stuck.
9. TV sleeve turned in bore.
10. 4-3 sequence valve body channel blocked.
11. No. 5 checkball omitted from valve body.

HARSH GARAGE SHIFT

Valve body orifice cup plug missing or checkball missing.

NO OVERRUN BRAKING-MANUAL 3-2-1

1. Throttle linkage incorrectly adjusted.
2. Throttle valve or 4-3 sequence valve stuck.
3. No. 3 checkball incorrectly installed.
4. Valve body spacer plate and gaskets incorrect, damaged or incorrectly installed.
5. Turbine shaft oil passages plugged or not drilled.
6. Turbine shaft seal rings damaged.
7. Turbine shaft sealing balls loose or missing.
8. Porosity in forward or overrun clutch piston.
9. Overrun piston seals cut or damaged.
10. Overrun piston checkball not sealing.

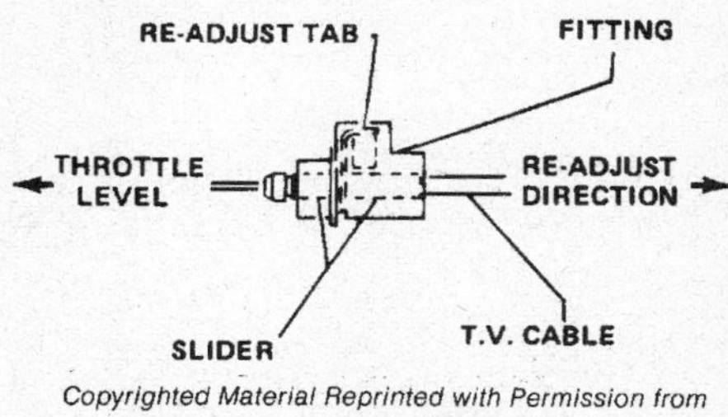

TH5028800370000X

Fig. 6 Throttle cable adjustment

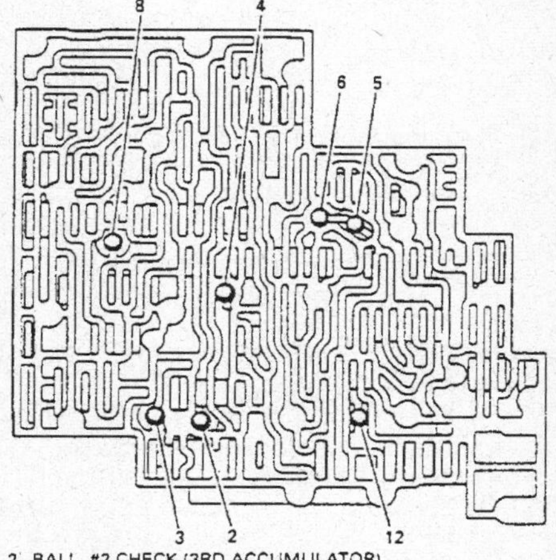

2 BALL, #2 CHECK (3RD ACCUMULATOR)
3 BALL, #3 CHECK (REVERSE INPUT)
4 BALL, #4 CHECK (3-4 CLUTCH EXHAUST)
5 BALL, #5 CHECK (OVERRUN CLUTCH FEED)
6 BALL, #6 CHECK (OVERRUN CLUTCH CONTROL)
8 BALL, #8 CHECK (1-2 UPSHIFT)
12 BALL, #2 CHECK (FORWARD CLUTCH ACCUM.)

GC5029400457000X

Fig. 8 Control valve body checkball locations

NO TORQUE CONVERTER CLUTCH APPLY

1. Battery voltage not being applied to transmission.
2. Defective outside electrical connector.
3. Defective inside electrical connector, wiring harness or solenoid.
4. Solenoid shorted or incorrectly grounded.
5. Incorrect or damaged pressure switches.
6. Internal converter damage.
7. Oil pump converter clutch apply valve stuck or incorrectly assembled.
8. Oil pump converter clutch apply valve retaining ring incorrectly assembled.
9. Oil pump to case gasket incorrectly assembled.
10. Oil pump orifice cup plug clogged.
11. Oil pump solenoid O-ring seal cut or damaged.
12. Oil pump orifice cup plug omitted from cooler in passage.
13. High or uneven oil pump body to cover bolt torque.
14. Converter clutch shift valve or throttle valve stuck.
15. Turbine shaft O-ring seal cut or damaged.
16. Turbine shaft retainer and ball plugged.

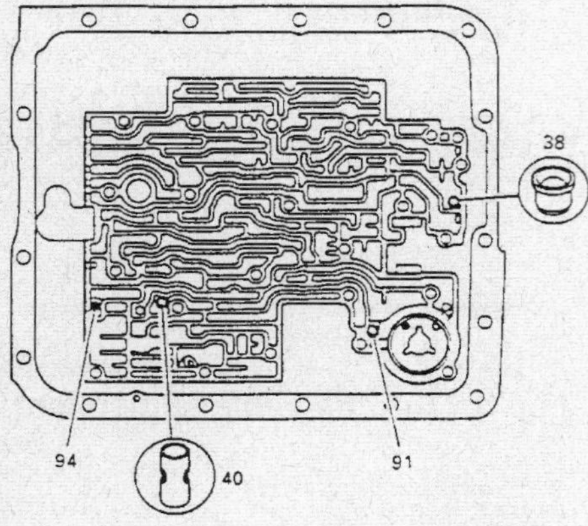

38 PLUG, TRANSMISSION CASE (ACCUM. BLEED)
40 RETAINER AND BALL ASSEMBLY, 3RD ACCUM.
91 NO. 1 CHECKBALL
94 SCREEN, TCC

GC5029400458000X

Fig. 9 Transmission case checkball locations

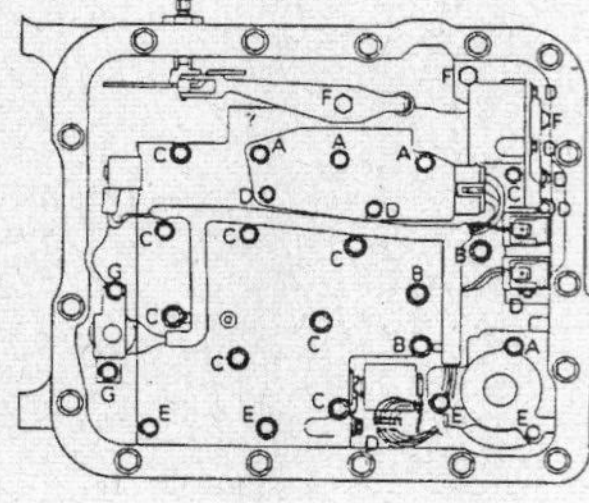

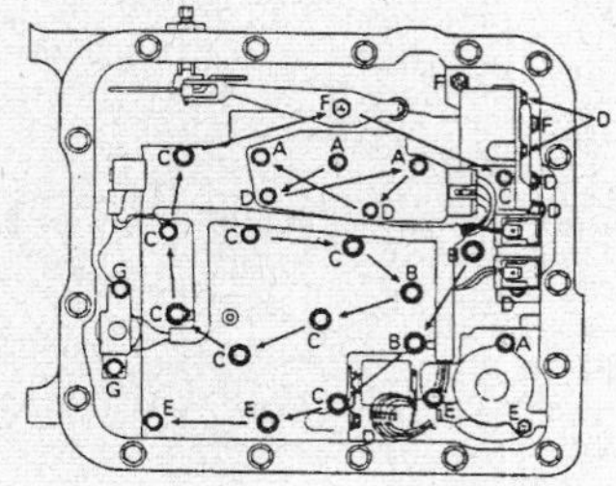

A M6 X 1.0 X 65.0
B M6 X 1.0 X 54.4
C M6 X 1.0 X 47.5
D M6 X 1.0 X 18.0
E M6 X 1.0 X 35.0
F M8 X 1.25 X 20.0
G M6 X 1.0 X 12.0

GC5029400451000X

Fig. 10 Control valve body bolts & tightening pattern

TORQUE CONVERTER CLUTCH SHUDDER

1. Internal torque converter damage.
2. Converter clutch shift valve stuck.
3. Oil pump converter clutch apply valve stuck.
4. Restricted oil pump oil passage.
5. Crack in oil filter body or restriction in filler neck.
6. Oil filter O-ring seal cut or damaged.
7. Low oil pressure or engine not properly tuned.
8. Turbine shaft O-ring cut or damaged.
9. Turbine shaft retainer and ball damaged.

NO TORQUE CONVERTER CLUTCH RELEASE

1. Oil pump converter clutch apply valve stuck.
2. Internal torque converter damage.
3. Solenoid grounded.

DRIVES IN NEUTRAL

1. Forward clutch burned or not releasing.
2. Manual linkage disconnected or incorrectly adjusted.
3. Internal leakage in case or case face not flat.

SECOND GEAR START IN DRIVE RANGE

1. Governor valve stuck.
2. Governor support pin too long or missing.
3. Forward sprag clutch installed backwards.

NO PARK

1. Parking linkage actuator rod bent or damaged.
2. Parking linkage actuator rod spring binding or improperly crimped.
3. Parking linkage actuator rod not attached to inside detent lever.
4. Parking linkage bracket damaged or not tightened properly.
5. Inside detent lever not tightened properly.
6. Detent roller improperly installed.
7. Parking pawl binding or damaged.

RATCHETING NOISE

Parking pawl return spring weak, damaged or incorrectly assembled.

OIL OUT OF VENT

1. Chamfer in oil pump body rotor pocket too large.
2. TV limit valve stuck.

VIBRATION IN REVERSE & WHINING NOISE IN PARK

Broken vane rings in oil pump.

NO DRIVE IN ALL RANGES

Torque converter to flex plate bolts missing.

NO DRIVE IN DRIVE RANGE

1. Stator roller clutch not holding.
2. Torque converter not bolted to flex plate.

DELAY IN DRIVE & REVERSE

Torque converter drain back.

MAINTENANCE

Refer to "Lubricant Data" chart in the appropriate chassis chapter of this manual for transmission fluid specifications.

FLUID CHECK

1. Ensure vehicle is on level surface, then move gear selector to Park position.
2. Apply parking brake and block drive wheels.
3. Allow engine to run at idle speed for three minutes with all accessories off.
4. Check fluid level, color and condition.

FLUID CHANGE

1. Raise and support vehicle.
2. Place suitable drain pan under transmission oil pan.
3. Loosen rear bolts, remove front and side mounting bolts.
4. Pry front of pan to break seal using suitable tool and allow fluid to drain.
5. Remove remaining mounting bolts, pan and gasket.
6. Drain remaining fluid from pan, then clean pan and dry thoroughly with compressed air.
7. Remove mounting bolt, oil filter and gasket.
8. Reverse procedure to install.

ADJUSTMENTS

SHIFT CONTROL CABLE

CAMARO & FIREBIRD

1. Place transmission shift control lever into Park position and apply parking brake.
2. Raise and support vehicle.
3. Position transmission range selector lever to park by rotating range selector lever clockwise until it reaches full mechanical stop position.
4. Snap transmission shift cable into bracket with cable adjustment button up.
5. Snap shift cable onto range selector lever pin and press cable adjustment button down.
6. Insert retainer to fitting of shift cable.
7. Lower vehicle.

CORVETTE

1. Raise and support vehicle.
2. Shift transmission into Neutral position.
3. Release transmission shift control cable adjustment lock by prying with flat bladed screwdriver.
4. Ensure transmission floor shift control and transmission are in neutral detent position.
5. Press to secure transmission shift control cable adjustment lock and lower vehicle.
6. Check cable adjustment by rotating control lever through detents.

THROTTLE CABLE

The throttle cable controls line pressures, shift points, shift feel, part throttle

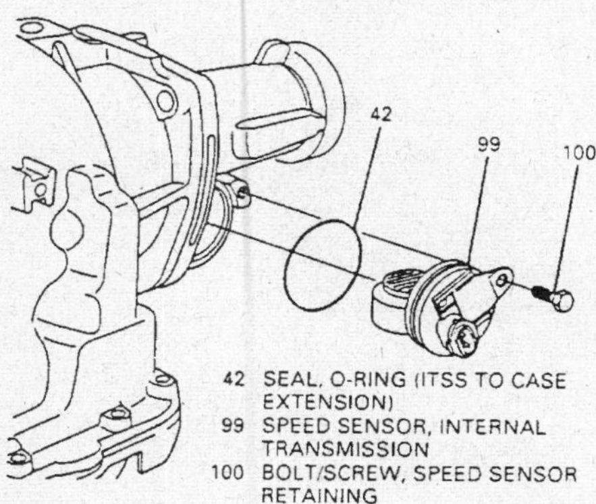

Fig. 11 Vehicle speed sensor replacement. Corvette

downshifts and detent downshifts. The function of the cable is similar to the combined functions of a vacuum modulator and detent downshift cable. The cable operates the throttle lever and bracket, **Figs. 4 and 5.**

1. Stop engine.
2. Depress and hold down adjust tab, **Fig. 6,** move slider through fitting, away from lever, until slider stops against fitting.
3. Release adjust tab and open throttle lever to its full throttle position to automatically adjust cable.
4. Release throttle lever and inspect cable for sticking or binding. **Cable may appear to function properly with engine stopped and cold. Inspect cable with engine at normal operating temperature.**
5. Road test vehicle.

IN-VEHICLE REPAIRS

GOVERNOR, REPLACE

1. Raise and support vehicle
2. Remove governor cover from case using extreme care not to damage cover. If cover is damaged, it should be replaced.
3. Remove governor.
4. Reverse procedure to install and check fluid level.

CONTROL VALVE BODY & PRESSURE SWITCH, REPLACE

1. Raise and support vehicle.
2. Remove oil pan and gasket
3. Remove oil filter and filter seal.
4. Disconnect electrical connectors from control valve body components.
5. Remove TCC solenoid bolts and solenoid with O-ring seal.
6. Remove wiring harness mounting bolts and set harness aside, **Fig. 7.**
7. Remove manual detent spring mounting bolt.
8. Remove remaining control valve body mounting bolts.
9. Remove manual valve link and control valve body.
10. Reverse procedure to install, noting the following:
    a. Before installing valve body, ensure valve body and transmission case checkballs are in correct locations, **Figs. 8 and 9.**
    b. Install all control valve body bolts.
    c. Tighten mounting bolts in spiral sequence, **Fig. 10.**

SPEEDOMETER DRIVEN GEAR, REPLACE

1. Disconnect speedometer cable or pulse generator electrical connector at transmission.
2. Remove retainer bolt, retainer, pulse generator (if equipped), speedometer driven gear and O-ring seal.
3. Reverse procedure to install, using new O-ring and adding fluid, as required.

VEHICLE SPEED SENSOR (VSS) , REPLACE

CAMARO & FIREBIRD

1. Raise and support vehicle.
2. Remove righthand muffler and disconnect VSS electrical connector.
3. Remove mounting bolt and vehicle speed sensor.
4. Reverse procedure to install.

CORVETTE

1. Raise and support vehicle.
2. Disconnect speed sensor electrical connector.
3. Remove speed sensor mounting bolt, **Fig. 11.**
4. Remove speed sensor and O-ring seal.
5. Reverse procedure to install.

AUXILIARY VALVE BODY, REPLACE

1. Raise and support vehicle, then drain transmission fluid into suitable container.
2. Remove transmission oil pan and filter.
3. Remove auxiliary accumulator valve tube to control valve and accumulator valve body mounting bolts.
4. Remove two tube clamps, gently pry tube loose from oil pump and auxiliary accumulator valve body.
5. Remove three auxiliary accumulator valve body to transmission case mounting bolts.
6. Remove auxiliary valve body and checkball.
7. Reverse procedure to install.

ACCUMULATOR, REPLACE

1. Raise and support vehicle.
2. Remove oil pan and gasket.
3. Remove oil filter and filter seal.
4. Remove control valve body as described under "Control Valve Body & Pressure Switch, Replace."
5. Remove accumulator cover bolts, **Fig. 12.**
6. Remove 1-2 accumulator cover, piston and spring.
7. Remove spacer plate support bolts.
8. Remove spacer plate and spacer plate gaskets.

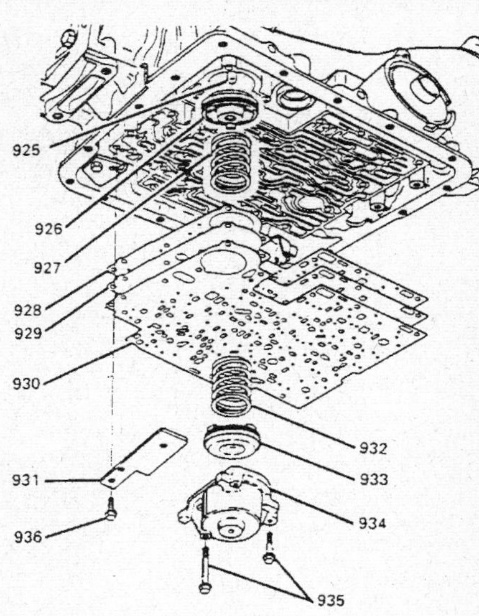

Fig. 12 Accumulator replacement

9. Remove 3-4 accumulator spring, piston and pin.
10. Remove accumulator.
11. Reverse procedure to install, noting the following:
    a. When installing 3-4 accumulator piston onto pin, piston legs must face valve body.
    b. When installing case and valve body gaskets, case gasket will be marked with C and valve body gasket will be marked with V.

CONTROL & SHIFT SOLENOIDS, REPLACE

1. Raise and support vehicle.
2. Remove oil pan, oil filter and filter seal.
3. Remove accumulator cover bolts.
4. Remove 1-2 accumulator cover, piston and spring.
5. Disconnect control and shift solenoid electrical connectors.
6. Remove pressure control solenoid retainer bolt, retainer and solenoid, **Fig. 13.**
7. Remove shift solenoid retainers and shift solenoids.
8. Remove 3-2 control solenoid retainer and control solenoid.
9. Reverse procedure to install.

TCC SOLENOID & WIRING HARNESS, REPLACE

CAMARO & FIREBIRD

1. Raise and support vehicle.
2. Remove exhaust crossover pipe to exhaust manifold mounting nuts.

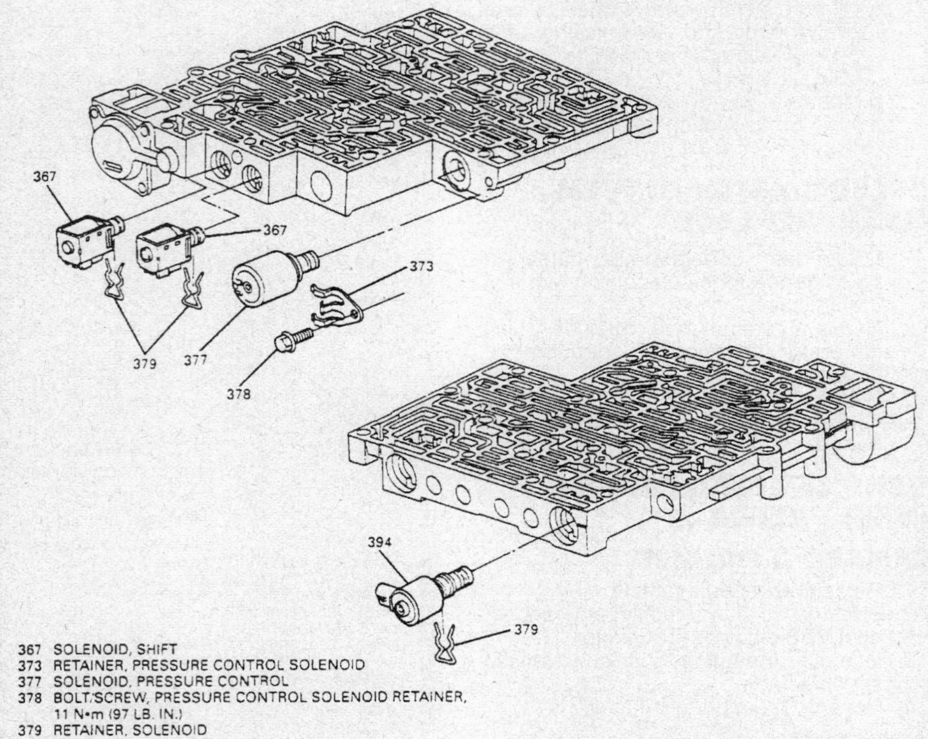

Fig. 13 Electrical component locations

3. Remove exhaust pipe to catalytic converter mounting bolts and nuts.
4. Remove catalytic converter and crossover pipe.
5. Remove transmission oil pan, oil filter and seal.
6. Disconnect external wiring harness connector from transmission pass through connector.
7. Remove accumulator cover bolts, 1-2 accumulator cover, piston and spring.
8. Disconnect component electrical connectors.
9. Remove pressure control solenoid retainer bolt, retainer and solenoid.
10. Remove TCC solenoid mounting bolts.
11. Remove pass-through electrical connector from transmission case by positioning small end of power piston seal protector and diaphragm retainer installer tool No. J-28458, or equivalent, over top of connector. Twist tool to release tabs while, at same time, pulling harness through case.
12. Remove TCC solenoid with wiring harness from transmission case.
13. Reverse procedure to install. When installing 1-2 accumulator piston to accumulator cover, piston legs must face towards case.

CORVETTE

1. Raise and support vehicle.
2. Remove righthand muffler.
3. Remove transmission oil pan, oil filter and seal.
4. Disconnect external wiring harness connector from transmission pass through connector by squeezing fore and aft flats on connector in order to release locking tabs.
5. Remove 1-2 accumulator cover bolts, cover, piston and piston spring.
6. Disconnect electrical connectors and remove TCC PWM solenoid retainer.
7. Remove TCC PWM solenoid from control valve body.
8. Remove pressure control solenoid retainer bolt, retainer and solenoid from control valve body.
9. Remove TCC solenoid bolts and wiring harness bolts.
10. Remove pass-through electrical connector from transmission case by positioning small end of power piston seal protector and diaphragm retainer installer tool No. J-28458, or equivalent, over top of connector. Twist tool to release tabs while, at same time, pulling harness through case.
11. Remove TCC solenoid with wiring harness from transmission case.
12. Reverse procedure to install. When installing 1-2 accumulator piston to accumulator cover, piston legs must face towards case.

SERVO, REPLACE

1. Remove exhaust system as required.
2. Remove transmission oil pan bolt below servo cover, **Fig. 14.**
3. Install servo cover depressor tool No. J-29714-A, or equivalent, on oil pan and install bolt included with tool, **Fig. 14.**
4. Depress servo cover and remove mounting ring.
5. Remove tool.
6. Remove cover and seal ring.

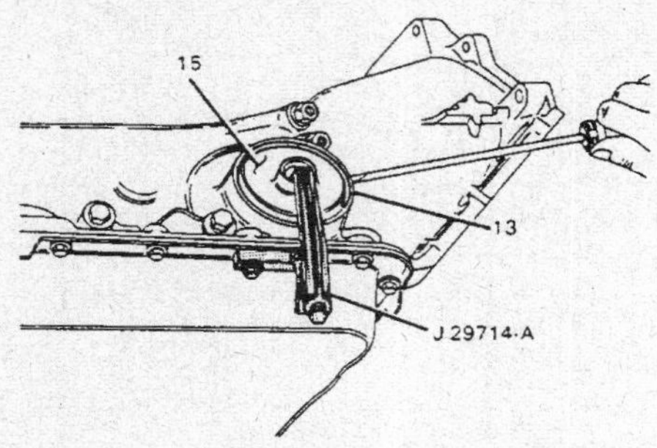

Fig. 14 Servo cover removal

7. Remove servo piston and bore apply pin.
8. Reverse procedure to install.

PUMP PRESSURE REGULATOR VALVE, REPLACE

1. Raise and support vehicle.
2. Remove transmission oil pan and gasket.
3. Compress pressure regulator valve with suitable small screwdriver, **Fig. 15.**
4. Remove retaining ring and slowly release spring tension.
5. Remove pressure regulator bore plug, valve, spring and guide.
6. Reverse procedure to install.

DRIVESHAFT OIL SEAL, REPLACE

1. Remove driveshaft and tunnel strap, if equipped.
2. Pry out lip oil seal using suitable tool.
3. Coat outer casting of new oil seal with suitable sealer and drive into place with seal installer tool No. J-21426, or equivalent.
4. Install tunnel strap, if used, and driveshaft.

TRANSMISSION

REPLACE

CAMARO & FIREBIRD

1. Remove air intake duct and disconnect electrical connector from intake air temperature sensor.
2. Remove transmission fluid level indicator.
3. Raise and support vehicle.
4. Remove catalytic converter and range selector lever cable.
5. Remove center support bearing from torque arm and propeller shaft.
6. Support rear axle with jack and remove rear axle torque arm.
7. Remove starter motor and loosen righthand side rear engine mount bracket bolts.
8. Remove mounting bolts and transmission support braces.
9. Remove transmission converter cover bolts and cover.

10. Remove torque converter mounting bolts.
11. Remove oil cooler pipes at transmission and disconnect electrical connectors.
12. Support transmission and remove transmission bolts.
13. Remove transmission fluid fill tube and separate transmission from engine.
14. Retain torque converter using torque converter holding fixture tool No. J-21366, or equivalent, when moving transmission.
15. Lower transmission.
16. Reverse procedure to install.

CORVETTE

1. Raise and support vehicle.
2. Remove rear tire and wheel assemblies.
3. Shift transmission into Neutral position and remove intermediate exhaust pipe.
4. Tie off lefthand muffler to underbody to support out of way.
5. Remove righthand muffler and driveline tunnel closeout panel.
6. Remove rear bellhousing access plug using suitable flat bladed screwdriver.
7. Match mark transmission flexplate to transmission torque converter through access hole in rear bellhousing.
8. Remove transmission flexplate and plug bolts from front of driveline support.
9. Install two propeller input shaft front bearing positioning bolts, M10-1.5 X 55 mm, or longer, in place of plug bolts.
10. **Torque** propeller input shaft front bearing positioning bolts to 26 ft. lbs.
11. Bolts must remain tightened and in place until instructed otherwise.
12. Remove engine flywheel housing access plug using suitable flat bladed screwdriver.
13. Loosen propeller shaft hub clamp bolt and rotate engine at flywheel for alignment, as required.
14. Shift transmission into Park position and remove transmission shift cable bracket mounting nuts.
15. Disconnect transmission shift control cable from transmission shift lever by unsnapping cable.
16. Position transmission shift cable and bracket.
17. Remove Electronic Brake Traction Control Module (EBTCM) lefthand mounting bracket bolts.
18. Remove EBTCM lefthand mounting bracket with EBTCM rubber insulators.
19. Pull lightly to release EBTCM from insulator attached to EBTCM righthand mounting bracket. Tie off EBTCM to underbody to support out of way.
20. Remove rear transverse spring and support lower control arm with suitable straight jack.
21. Disconnect outer tie rod end from suspension knuckle and shock absorber lower mounting bolt.
22. Disconnect lower ball joint from suspension knuckle.
23. Remove straight jack from control arm. Repeat previous steps to other side suspension components.

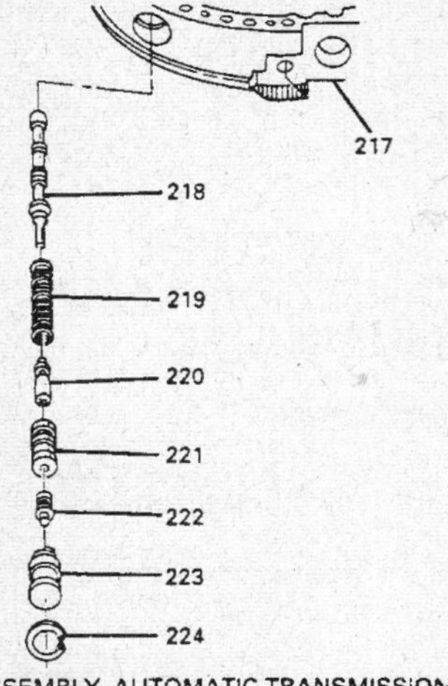

217 PUMP ASSEMBLY, AUTOMATIC TRANSMISSION OI
218 VALVE, PRESSURE REGULATOR
219 SPRING, PRESSURE REGULATOR VALVE
220 VALVE, REVERSE BOOST
221 BUSHING, REVERSE BOOST VALVE
222 VALVE, TV BOOST
223 BUSHING, TV BOOST VALVE
224 RING, TV BOOST VALVE BUSHING RETAINER

GC5029400456000X

Fig. 15 Pump pressure regulator valve

24. Install transmission support fixture tool No. J-42055, or equivalent, with transmission jack to transmission.
25. Disconnect wiring harness and brake pipe clip retainers from rear suspension crossmember.
26. Remove differential to transmission lower nut. Removing nut at this time will aid in separating differential from transmission after driveline has been removed.
27. Remove transmission mount to rear crossmember nuts.
28. Position transmission jack under rear suspension crossmember and firmly secure crossmember to jack.
29. By hand, remove rear suspension crossmember mounting nuts.
30. Slowly lower rear suspension crossmember away from vehicle frame rails with aid of assistant and remove.
31. Remove mounting bolts and transmission mount bracket.
32. Release axle shafts from differential using suitable pry bar.
33. Tie off axle shafts to underbody to support out of way.
34. Compress and release four retainers securing wiring harness along driveline support using suitable and push harness out of way.
35. Slowly lower driveline approximately two inches, while adjusting angle of tilt in order to access electrical connectors.
36. Disconnect vehicle speed sensor and wiring harness retainer from stud at differential rear cover.
37. Disconnect wiring harness retainer clip from top of differential.
38. Have assistant guide front of driveline during removal of driveline.
39. Slowly lower driveline while adjusting angle of tilt and pulling driveline away from engine until propeller input shaft at front of driveline support just clears engine flywheel housing.
40. Slowly lower driveline completely out of vehicle.
41. Position suitable lift device chain fall, to protect transmission oil cooler rear pipes and rear exhaust hangers located on driveline support.
42. Raise driveline to relieve weight from transmission jack using suitable lift device.
43. Disconnect support fixture from transmission jack only. Support fixture will provide stability to driveline components while working on bench.
44. Position driveline on workbench with lift device still attached, then support driveline support and differential for additional balance.
45. Remove lift device from driveline and disconnect transmission oil cooler rear pipes from fittings on transmission.
46. Remove transmission to driveline support bolts, insert suitable flat bladed screwdriver or similar tool between support and transmission, and begin to pry driveline support loose from transmission.
47. Slowly slide driveline support away from transmission while supporting transmission torque converter to transmission.
48. Remove differential to transmission bolts and nuts.
49. Use care when separating differential from transmission to not damage transmission output shaft seal in differential plate. Slowly slide differential from transmission.
50. Remove differential plate from differential.
51. Remove transmission from support fixture.
52. Reverse procedure to install.

TECHNICAL SERVICE BULLETINS

PARK/NEUTRAL POSITION SWITCH CONNECTOR CANNOT BE REMOVED

1998–2001

On some of these models it may be difficult to remove the Park/Neutral Position (PNP) switch connectors. In rare cases there may be related electrical conditions, such as improper or no shift indication, or no back-up light operation.

This condition may be caused by high ambient heat causing the switch sealing compound to melt and flow into the connectors, sealing the connectors to the switch.

Normally the switch can be removed and installed without removing the connectors.

To correct this condition, install new switch using old connector as a pattern to ensure that the new wires are connected to the harness correctly. **It is very important to solder the wires and use heat-shrink tubing to ensure water-tight connections.**

HARSH 1-2 UPSHIFT

1998-2000

On some of these models built before Jan. 15, 1999 (Julian Date 9015), there may be a harsh 1-2 upshift that may also have set the MIL. There may be a show historic Diagnostic Trouble Code (DTC) P1870 set. Typically, these vehicles will have been driven more than 20,000 miles.

This condition may be caused by wear in the control valve body. This wear occurs in the bore that contains the TCC isolator and regulator valves, and results in poor, or no, TCC apply.

To correct this condition install a control valve body with the revised TCC regulator and isolator valves. These valves are used in all transmissions produced after Jan. 15, 1999 (Julian Date 9015) and all General Motors SPO parts.

MALFUNCTION INDICATION LAMP ILLUMINATED

1998-99

On some of these models built before April 8, 1999 (Julian date 098), the Malfunction Indication Lamp (MIL) may be illuminated and Diagnostic Trouble Code (DTC) P1810 set.

This condition may be caused by debris from aluminum shavings, bronze material and certain clutch material causing the pressure switches in the Transmission Fluid Pressure Manual Valve Position (TFP) switch assembly to stick or electrically short out.

To correct this condition, install a new TFP switch assembly with a plastic shield (part No 24215111).

TIGHTENING SPECIFICATIONS

Year	Component	Torque/Ft. Lbs.
CAMARO & FIREBIRD		
1998–99	Accumulator Cover	72–120①
	Case Extension	35–39
	Converter Housing	48–55
	Cooler Pipe Connector	26–30
	Detent Spring	15–20
	Forward Accumulator Cover	72–120①
	Line Pressure Plug	72–120①
	Manual Shaft	20–25
	Oil Cooler Pipe Fitting	26–30
	Oil Pan	84–120①
	Oil Passage Cover	72–120①
	Park Brake Bracket	20–25
	Pressure Control Solenoid Bracket	72–120①
	Pump	19–24
	Pump Cover	15–20
	Solenoid	72–120①
	Speed Sensor	92–120①
	TFP Manual Valve Position Switch	72–120①
	Transmission To Engine	35
	Valve Body	72–120①
2000–02	Accumulator Cover	72–120①
	Case Extension	31–35
	Converter Cover	89①
	Converter Housing	48–55
	Cooler Pipe Connection	26–30
	Detent Spring	15–20
	Floorshift Control	89①
	Forward Accumulaor Cover	72–120①
	Heat Shield	13
	Line Pressure Plug	72–120①
	Manual Shaft	20–25
	Mount	18
	Oil Cooler Pipe Fitting	72–120①
	Oil Level Indicator	35
	Oil Pan	84–120①
	Oil Passage Cover	72–120①
	Park Brake Bracket	20–25
	PNP Switch	27①
	Pressure Control Solenoid Bracket	72–120①
	Pump	19–24
	Pump Cover	15–20
2000–02	Shift Cable Grommet	15①
	Shift Control Cable	15
	Speed Sensor	92–120①
	TCC Solenoid	72–120①
	TFP Manual Valve Position Switch	72–120①
	Transmission To Engine	35
	Valve Body	72–120①

Continued

TIGHTENING SPECIFICATIONS—Continued

Year	Component	Torque/Ft. Lbs.
CORVETTE		
1998–99	Accumulator Cover	97①
	Control Valve Body	97①
	Differential To Transmission	37
	Driveline Support	37
	EBTCM	37
	Flexplate	47
	Floor Shift Control	89①
	Fluid Check/Fill Plug	47
	Oil Cooler Clamp	106①
	Oil Cooler Pipe, Flared Fitting	30
	Oil Cooler Pipe, Sealed Washer	12
	Oil Pan	97
	Pressure Control Solenoid	97①
	Shift Control Bracket	15
	Spacer Plate Support	97①
	TCC Solenoid	97①
2000–02	Accumulator Cover	72–120①
	Case Extension	31–35
	Converter Cover	89①
	Converter Housing	48–55
	Cooler Pipe Connection	26–30
	Detent Spring	15–20
	Extension Stud	13–16
	Floorshift Control	89①
	Forward Accumulaor Cover	72–120①
	Heat Shield	13
	Line Pressure Plug	72–120①
	Manual Shaft	20–25
	Mount	18
	Oil Cooler Pipe Fitting	84–120①
	Oil Level Indicator	35
	Oil Pan	72–120①
	Oil Passage Cover	72–120①
	Park Brake Bracket	20–25
	PNP Switch	27①
	Plug	21–24
	Pressure Control Solenoid Bracket	72–120①
	Pump	19–24
	Pump Cover	15–20
	Shift Cable Grommet	15①
	Shift Control Cable	15
	Speed Sensor	92–120①
	TCC Solenoid	72–120①
	TFP Manual Valve Position Switch	72–120①
	Transmission To Engine	35
	Valve Body	72–120①

① — Inch lbs.

Turbo Hydra-Matic 4T40-E & 4T45-E Automatic Transaxles

NOTE: On Air Bag Equipped Models, Refer To "Air Bag System Precautions" Located In The Front Of This Manual For System Disarming & Arming Procedures.

NOTE: Refer To "Computer Relearn Procedures" Located In The Front Of This Manual When Battery Power To The Computer Has Been Interrupted.

NOTE: Prior To Performing Any Service Operations Listed In This Section, Consult The "Technical Service Bulletins" Section For Related Information.

INDEX

PRECAUTIONS

AIR BAG SYSTEMS

Refer to "Air Bag System Precautions" in the front of this manual for system disarming and arming procedures.

BATTERY GROUND CABLE

Prior to service, disconnect battery ground cable and isolate as required.

IDENTIFICATION

The transaxle identification tag is located on the rear righthand side of the transaxle housing, **Fig. 1.**

DESCRIPTION

The 4T40-E and 4T45-E automatic transaxles are fully automatic electronically controlled front wheel drive transaxles with four forward gear ranges including overdrive and one reverse gear range, **Fig. 2.** Oil pressure is supplied by a variable displacement vane type oil pump. Two shift solenoids, operated by the PCM, control shift points and TCC apply rates, which are influenced by various sensor inputs. The transaxle unit includes a three-element hydraulic torque converter and lockup clutching element, four multiple disc clutch packs, roller clutch, sprag clutch, two bands and a compound reaction planetary gearset. Power is transmitted to the drive wheels from the planetary gear through a final drive gearset and differential assembly.

TROUBLESHOOTING

HIGH OR LOW LINE PRESSURE

1. Oil level high or low.
2. Pressure regulator valve stuck.
3. Pressure regulator valve spring or isolator stuck.
4. Pressure regulator boots valve stuck.
5. Pressure control solenoid contaminated, O-rings damaged or leaking, connector loose or pins damaged, or pipes damaged.

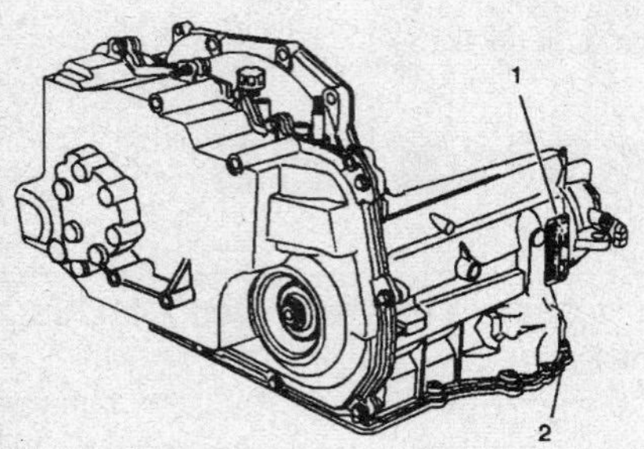

(1) Transmission ID Location
(2) VIN Location
(3) Calendar Year (9 = 1999)
(4) Julian Date
(5) Shift and Line Number
(6) Calendar Year (9 = 1999)
(7) Model
(8) Serial Number in Base Code 31
(9) J = Windsor Plant
(10) Broadcast Code
(11) Transmission (4T40-E)

TH5029600810000A

Fig. 1 Transaxle identification tag location

(1) TFP Manual Valve Position Switch Assembly
(2) Control Valve Body Assembly
(3) Torque Converter Assembly
(4) Manual Shaft and Detent Lever Assembly
(5) 2nd Clutch
(6) Reverse Clutch
(7) Coast Clutch
(8) Direct Clutch
(9) Reaction Planetary Gear Set
(10) Input Planetary Gear Set
(11) Forward Clutch
(12) Lo Roller Clutch
(13) Parking Lock Actuator Assembly
(14) Differential and Final Drive Assembly
(15) Output Stub Shaft
(16) Output Speed Sensor
(17) Lo/Reverse Servo Assembly
(18) Lo/Reverse Band
(19) Oil Feed Tube Assembly
(20) Input Sprag Clutch Assembly
(21) Oil Filter Assembly
(22) 2nd Roller Clutch
(23) Oil Level Control Valve
(24) Drive Link Assembly
(25) Driven Sprocket
(26) Output Shaft
(27) Channel Plate Assembly
(28) Input Speed Sensor
(29) Drive Sprocket
(30) Control Valve Body Assembly
(31) Oil Pump Assembly

TH5029600811000A

Fig. 2 Cross sectional view of 4T40–E & 4T45–E transaxles

6. Pressure control solenoid contaminated, or O-rings damaged or leaking, or pipes damaged.
7. Pressure control solenoid connector loose or pins damaged.
8. Torque signal regulator valve stuck.
9. Transaxle wiring harness connector loose, pins damaged, contaminated or shorted.
10. Pressure switch connector loose, or O-ring damaged or missing.
11. Oil filter clogged, broken or loose.
12. Oil filter seal leaking.
13. Cooler lines clogged or restricted.
14. Cooler line seals leaking.
15. Oil pump damaged, sticking, porous or leaking.
16. Oil pump drive shaft damaged.
17. Pressure relief valve spring damaged or checkball missing.
18. Transaxle case porous, circuits leaking or surfaces finish uneven.
19. Valve body porous, circuits leaking or surfaces finish uneven.
20. Channel plate porous, leaking circuits or surfaces finish uneven.
21. Throttle position sensor damaged, sticking or disconnected.
22. Throttle position sensor intermittent open or short circuit.

INACCURATE/ INCONSISTENT SHIFT POINTS

1. Shift solenoids contaminated.
2. Shift solenoids intermittent open or short circuit.
3. Throttle position sensor damaged or disconnected.
4. Throttle position sensor intermittent open or shorted circuit.
5. Output or input speed sensors intermittent open or short circuit.
6. Output or input speed sensors damaged, disconnected or loose.
7. Line pressure high.
8. Checkballs missing or orifice not applied.
9. Accumulator springs or pistons binding.
10. Accumulator valve stuck.
11. Reverse or direct clutch housing exhaust checkballs plugged.

HARSH SHIFTS

1. Line pressure high.
2. Checkballs missing or orifices not applied.
3. Accumulator missing.
4. Accumulator springs binding.
5. Accumulator piston binding.
6. Accumulator valve stuck.

NO REVERSE OR SLIPS IN REVERSE

1. Fluid level low.
2. Fluid pressure low.
3. Shift linkage disconnected or misaligned.
4. Low/reverse band anchor pin broken.
5. Fluid feed tube broken, bent or plugged
6. Fluid feed tube seals missing or leaking.
7. Low/reverse band servo piston broken or binding.
8. Low/reverse servo piston seals leaking.
9. Servo pin and spring binding.
10. Low/reverse servo cover broken, loose or leaking.
11. Checkball No. 1 missing.
12. Manual valve and link to detent lever disconnected or misaligned.
13. Control valve body, gaskets and channel plate porous, fluid leaking across channels, misalignment, damage or fluid restriction.
14. Driven sprocket support seals leaking.
15. Driven sprocket support porous, cracked or misaligned.
16. Reverse clutch slipping or not applying.
17. Reverse clutch piston binding, cracked or leaking.
18. Reverse clutch center retainer and seal plugged.
19. Reverse clutch plates friction material worn or splines broken.
20. Reverse clutch snap ring out of position.
21. Reverse clutch housing cracked, feed holes plugged or tangs broken.
22. Reverse clutch housing exhaust checkball missing or out of position.
23. Reverse clutch spring and retainer binding.
24. Reverse clutch fluid routing leak or restriction.
25. Low/reverse band binding, broken, worn or out of position.
26. Low/reverse band not applying or slipping.
27. Case porous, fluid leak or restricted.

NO 1ST GEAR, SLIPS IN 1ST GEAR

1. Line pressure low.
2. Oil feed tube bent, broken or plugged.
3. Oil feed tube seals leaking.
4. TFP manual valve position switch O-ring leaking.
5. 1-2 shift solenoid valve failed Off.

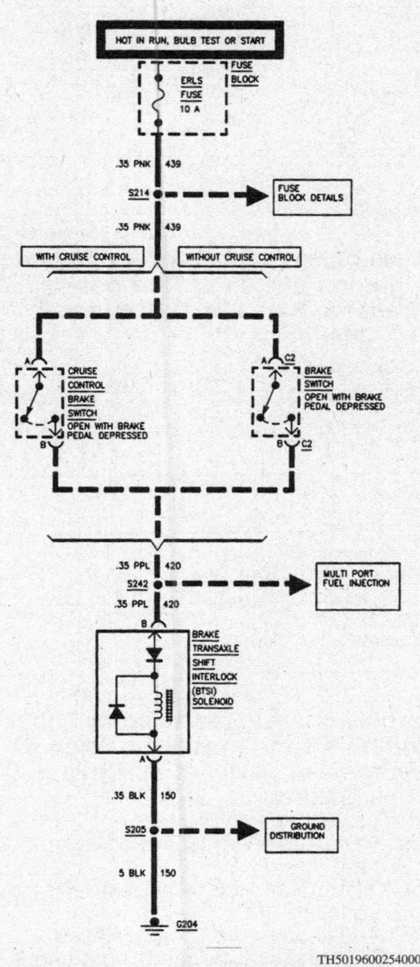

Fig. 3 BTSI wiring diagram. Cavalier & Sunfire

6. 1-2 shift solenoid leaking.
7. 1-2 shift valve stuck in upshift position.
8. 2-3 shift solenoid valve failed On.
9. 2-3 shift solenoid exhaust plugged.
10. Channel plate and gasket porous, misaligned, fluid leaking across channels or restricted.
11. Manual valve or shift linkage misaligned.
12. Shift cable misaligned.
13. Forward clutch not applying or slipping.
14. Forward clutch piston binding, cracked or leaking.
15. Forward clutch inner seal and sleeve plugged.
16. Forward clutch plates friction material worn or splines broken.
17. Forward clutch snap ring out of position.
18. Forward clutch housing cracked or feed holes plugged.
19. Forward clutch housing exhaust checkball missing or out of position.
20. Forward clutch return springs binding.
21. Input sprag damaged or not holding.
22. Low roller clutch damaged or not holding.
23. Forward clutch fluid routing passages leaking or restricted.
24. Forward clutch support porous.
25. Forward clutch support seal rings leaking or damaged.
26. Forward clutch support feed holes plugged.
27. Torque converter stator roller clutch not holding.
28. PSA drive switch O-ring leaking.

NO 2ND GEAR, SLIPS IN 2ND GEAR

1. Line pressure low.
2. Manual valve position switch electrical or hydraulic malfunction.
3. 1-2 shift solenoid stuck On.
4. 1-2 shift solenoid plugged.
5. 2-3 shift valve stuck in upshift position.
6. 1-2 accumulator valve stuck.
7. Control valve body porous, misalignment, loose, restricted or fluid leaking across channels.
8. Control valve body gaskets and spacer plate porous, misalignment, loose, restricted or fluid leaking across channels.
9. Channel plate and gasket porous, misalignment, loose, restricted or fluid leaking across channels.
10. Driven sprocket support porous, misalignment, loose, restricted or fluid leaking across channels.
11. 1-2 accumulator piston seal leak.
12. Channel plate or case porous near 1-2 accumulator.
13. Second clutch piston binding, cracked or leaking.
14. Second clutch plates friction material worn or splines broken.
15. Second clutch sprint mounting ring out of position.
16. Second clutch spring binding.
17. Driven sprocket support damaged, leaking or porous.
18. Second clutch fluid routing leak or restriction.
19. Second roller clutch broken or not holding.
20. Oil level low.
21. Second clutch not applying or slipping.
22. PSA malfunction.

NO 3RD GEAR, SLIPS IN 3RD GEAR

1. Line pressure low.
2. TFP manual valve position switch electrical or hydraulic malfunction.
3. 2-3 shift solenoid stuck Off,
4. 2-3 shift solenoid leaking.
5. 3-4 shift valve stuck in upshift position.
6. 2-3 accumulator valve stuck.
7. 2-3 accumulator piston seal leak
8. Channel plate or case porous near 2-3 accumulator.
9. Control valve body porous, misalignment, loose, restricted or fluid leaking across channels.
10. Gaskets and spacer plate porous, misalignment, loose, restricted or fluid leaking across channels.
11. Channel plate and gasket porous, misalignment, loose, restricted or fluid leaking across channels.
12. Driven sprocket support porous, misalignment, loose, restricted or fluid leaking across channels.

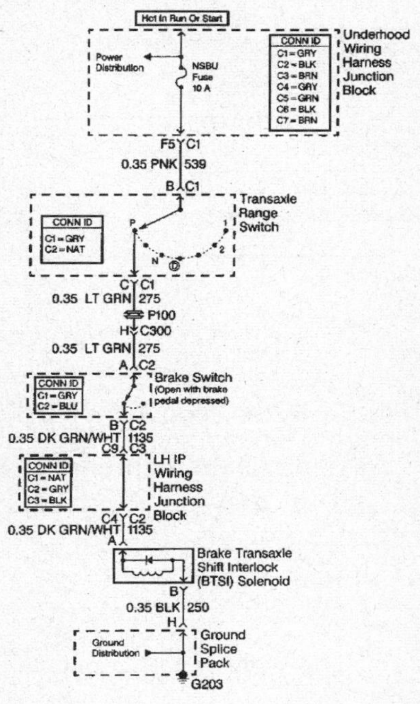

Fig. 4 BTSI wiring diagram. Cutlass & Malibu

13. Input shaft seals leaking.
14. Input shaft sleeve damaged or misaligned.
15. Driven sprocket support seals leaking.
16. Direct clutch piston binding, cracked or leaking.
17. Direct clutch plates friction material worn or splines broken.
18. Direct clutch spring retainer ring out of position.
19. Direct clutch spring and retainer binding.
20. Coast clutch housing damaged or cracked.
21. Input shaft or feed holes restricted.
22. Direct and coast clutch housing feed holes restricted.
23. Direct and coast clutch and input shaft housing direct clutch exhaust checkball missing or out of position.
24. Direct clutch fluid routing leak or restriction.
25. Direct clutch not applying or slipping.
26. PSA malfunction.

2ND GEAR ONLY

1-2 shift valve stuck in downshift position.

NO 4TH GEAR, SLIPS IN 4TH GEAR

1. Line pressure low.
2. TFP manual valve position switch electrical or hydraulic malfunction.
3. 1-2 shift solenoid stuck Off.
4. 1-2 shift solenoid leaking.
5. 3-4 shift valve stuck in downshifted position.
6. 3-4 accumulator valve stuck.
7. Manual valve misaligned in manual 3rd gear.

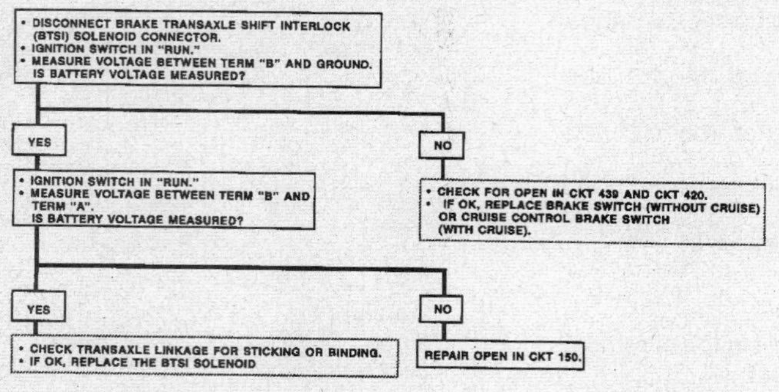

Fig. 5 BTSI diagnosis chart (gear selector shifts out of Park w/ignition switch in Run position & brake pedal not depressed). Cavalier & Sunfire

Step	Action	Value(s)	Yes	No
4	Repair the short to B+ in circuit 1135 between the LH IP Wiring Harness Junction Block and the Brake Switch. Is repair complete?	—	System OK	—
5	Disconnect the LH IP Wiring Harness Junction Block connector C2. Can the Transaxle be shifted out of PARK?	—	Go to Step 6	Go to Step 7
6	Replace the LH IP Wiring Harness Junction Block. Is repair complete?	—	System OK	—
7	Disconnect the Brake Transaxle Shift Interlock (BTSI) Solenoid connector. Can the Transaxle be shifted out of PARK?	—	Go to Step 8	Go to Step 9
8	Repair the short to B+ in circuit 1135 between the LH IP Wiring Harness Junction Block and the Brake Transaxle Shift Interlock (BTSI) Solenoid. Is repair complete?	—	System OK	—
9	Replace the Brake Transaxle Shift Interlock (BTSI) Solenoid. Is repair complete?	—	System OK	—

TH5029800942020X

Fig. 6 BTSI diagnosis chart (gear selector does not shift out of Park w/ignition switch in Run position & brake pedal depressed, Part 2 of 2). Cutlass & Malibu

Step	Action	Value(s)	Yes	No
1	1. Disconnect the Brake Switch connector C2. 2. Turn the Ignition Switch to the RUN position. Can the Transaxle be shifted out of PARK?	—	Go to Step 2	Go to Step 3
2	Check the adjustment of the Brake Switch, if OK replace the Brake Switch. Is repair complete?	—	System OK	—
3	Disconnect the LH IP Wiring Harness Junction Block connector C3. Can the Transaxle be shifted out of PARK?	—	Go to Step 4	Go to Step 5

TH5029800942010X

Fig. 6 BTSI diagnosis chart (gear selector does not shift out of Park w/ignition switch in Run position & brake pedal depressed, Part 1 of 2). Cutlass & Malibu

Step	Action	Value(s)	Yes	No
1	1. Disconnect the Transaxle Range Switch connector C1. 2. Turn the Ignition Switch to the RUN position. 3. Connect a test lamp between terminal B of the Transaxle Range Switch connector C1 and ground. Does the test lamp light?	—	Go to Step 2	Go to Step 3
2	Connect a fused jumper between terminal B and terminal C of the Transaxle Range Switch connector C1. Can the Transaxle be shifted out of PARK?	—	Go to Step 4	Go to Step 5
3	Backprobe the Underhood Wiring Harness Junction Block connector C1 with a test lamp between terminal F5 and ground. Does the test lamp light?	—	Go to Step 6	Go to Step 7
4	1. Reconnect the Transaxle Range Switch connector C1. 2. Backprobe the Brake Switch connector C2 with a test lamp between terminal A and ground. Does the test lamp light?	—	Go to Step 8	Go to Step 9

TH5029800943010X

Fig. 7 BTSI diagnosis chart (gear selector shifts out of Park w/ignition switch in Run position & brake pedal not depressed, Part 1 of 3). Cutlass & Malibu

8. Control valve body porous, misalignment, loose, restricted or fluid leaking across channels.
9. Gaskets and spacer plate porous, misalignment, loose, restricted or fluid leaking across channels.
10. Transaxle case porous, misalignment or fluid leaking across channels.
11. Driven sprocket support porous, misalignment, loose, restricted or fluid leaking across channels.
12. 3-4 accumulator piston seal leak
13. Channel plate or case porous near 3-4 accumulator valve.
14. Intermediate/fourth band and servo slipping or not applying.
15. Intermediate/fourth servo piston broken or binding.
16. Intermediate/fourth servo piston or cover seals leaking.
17. Intermediate/fourth servo apply pin and return springs binding.
18. Intermediate/fourth servo cover broken, loose or leaking.
19. Transaxle case band seat cracked.
20. Band fluid routing leak or restriction.
21. Oil level low.
22. Band broken, worn or out of position.
23. PSA malfunction.

LOSS OF DRIVE

1. Torque converter lugs broken or lug weld failed.
2. Torque converter to flexplate bolts sheared.
3. Turbine shaft splines worn.
4. Torque converter internal failure.
5. Torque converter cover cracked at weld.
6. Fluid level low.
7. Shift linkage disconnected.
8. Oil filter and seal plugged or missing.
9. Oil pump seized or gears broken.
10. Oil pump drive shaft broken or splines stripped.
11. Drive/driven sprockets and chain broken.
12. Control valve body, gaskets and spacer plate damaged, leaking or misaligned.
13. Channel plate and gasket damaged, leaking or misaligned.
14. Turbine shaft splines stripped.
15. Input sprag damaged or not holding.
16. Forward clutch damaged or not holding.
17. Low roller clutch damaged or not holding.
18. Planetary gears failure or lacks lubricant.
19. Different and final drive failure or lacks lubricant.
20. Axle shafts worn, loose or failed.
21. Filter and seal plugged or missing.
22. Hydraulic system tie up or fluid circuit leaks.

LOSS OF POWER

1. Fluid level low.
2. 1-2 shift solenoid stuck Off.
3. 2-3 shift solenoids stuck On.
4. TCC stuck On or dragging.
5. Torque converter contaminated or damaged.

ENGINE STALL

1. TCC stuck On or dragging.
2. TCC control PWM solenoid stuck On.
3. TCC control PWM solenoid exhaust plugged.
4. TCC regulated apply valve stuck in apply position.

1ST & 2ND GEARS ONLY

1. 2-3 shift solenoid stuck Off.
2. 2-3 shift solenoid leaking.
3. 2-3 shift solenoid electrical malfunction.
4. 2-3 shift valve stuck in downshift position.
5. Direct clutch failed.

3RD & 4TH GEARS ONLY

1. 2-3 shift solenoid stuck On.
2. 2-3 shift solenoid plugged.
3. 2-3 shift solenoid electrical malfunction.

Step	Action	Value(s)	Yes	No
5	Check the adjustment of the Transaxle Range Switch. If OK, replace the Transaxle Range Switch. Is repair complete?	—	System OK	—
6	Repair the open in circuit 539 between the Underhood Wiring Harness Junction Block and the Transaxle Range Switch. Is repair complete?	—	System OK	—
7	Replace the Underhood Wiring Harness Junction Block. Is repair complete?	—	System OK	—
8	Backprobe the Brake Switch connector C2 with a test lamp between terminal B and ground. Does the test lamp light?	—	Go to Step 10	Go to Step 11
9	Repair the open in circuit 275 between the Transaxle Range Switch and the Brake Switch. Is repair complete?	—	System OK	—
10	Backprobe the LH IP Wiring Harness Junction Block connector C3 with a test lamp between terminal C9 and ground. Does the test lamp light?	—	Go to Step 12	Go to Step 13
11	Check the adjustment of the Brake Switch, if OK replace the Brake Switch. Is repair complete?	—	System OK	—
12	Backprobe the LH IP Wiring Harness Junction Block connector C2 with a test lamp between terminal C4 and ground. Does the test lamp light?	—	Go to Step 14	Go to Step 15
13	Repair the open in circuit 1135 between the Brake Switch and the LH IP Wiring Harness Junction Block. Is repair complete?	—	System OK	—
14	1. Disconnect the Brake Transaxle Shift Interlock (BTSI) Solenoid connector. 2. Connect a test lamp between terminal A of the Brake Transaxle Shift Interlock (BTSI) Solenoid connector and ground. Does the test lamp light?	—	Go to Step 16	Go to Step 17
15	Replace the LH IP Wiring Harness Junction Block. Is repair complete?	—	System OK	—

TH5029800943020X

Fig. 7 BTSI diagnosis chart (gear selector shifts out of Park w/ignition switch in Run position & brake pedal not depressed, Part 2 of 3). Cutlass & Malibu

4. 1-2 and 2-3 shift valves stuck in upshift position.

1ST & 4TH GEARS ONLY

1. 1-2 shift solenoid stuck On.
2. 1-2 shift solenoid plugged.
3. 1-2 shift solenoid electrical malfunction.

2ND & 3RD GEARS ONLY

1. 1-2 shift solenoid stuck Off.
2. 1-2 shift solenoid leaking.
3. 1-2 shift solenoid electrical malfunction.

NO PARK

1. Parking lock actuator bent or rod damaged.
2. Parking lock actuator spring binding or broken
3. Parking lock actuator rod not attached to manual shaft and detent lever.
4. Manual detent spring and roller loose.
5. Manual detent spring and roller bent or damaged.
6. Manual shaft to case pin missing.
7. Manual valve to detent lever link bent.
8. Parking lock pawl damaged or tooth broken.
9. Park lock gear teeth or splines damaged.
10. Park pawl return spring broken or missing.
11. Shift linkage misadjusted.

NO ENGINE BRAKING: ALL MANUAL RANGES

1. Oil level low.
2. 3-4 shift valve stuck in 4th gear position.
3. Manual valve misaligned.
4. Control valve body porous, misaligned, loose, fluid restriction or leak across channels.
5. Channel plate and gasket porous, misaligned, loose, fluid restriction or leak across channels.
6. Driven sprocket support porous, misaligned, loose, fluid restriction or leak across channels.
7. Driven sprocket support seals leaking.
8. Input shaft seals leaking,
9. Input shaft bushing damaged or misaligned.
10. Coast clutch plates friction material worn or splines broken.
11. Coast clutch release spring binding.
12. Direct and coast clutch housing damaged or cracked.
13. Direct and coast clutch housing feed holes restricted.
14. Direct and coast clutch housing exhaust checkball missing or out of position.
15. Coast clutch fluid routing leak or restriction.

Step	Action	Value(s)	Yes	No
16	Connect a test lamp between terminal A and terminal B of the Brake Transaxle Shift Interlock (BTSI) Solenoid connector. Does the test lamp light?	—	Go to Step 18	Go to Step 19
17	Repair the open in circuit 1135 between the LH IP Wiring Harness Junction Block and the Brake Transaxle Shift Interlock (BTSI) Solenoid. Is repair complete?	—	System OK	—
18	Replace the Brake Transaxle Shift Interlock (BTSI) Solenoid. Is repair complete?	—	System OK	—
19	Repair the open in circuit 250 between the Brake Transaxle Shift Interlock (BTSI) Solenoid and Ground Splice Pack G203. Is repair complete?	—	System OK	—

TH5029800943030X

Fig. 7 BTSI diagnosis chart (gear selector shifts out of Park w/ignition switch in Run position & brake pedal not depressed, Part 3 of 3). Cutlass & Malibu

16. Coast clutch no applying or slipping.
17. Coast clutch piston and seal binding, cracked or leaking.

NO ENGINE BRAKING: MANUAL 2ND GEAR

1. Output speed sensor reads 0 mph.
2. TFP manual valve position switch leaking or inoperative.
3. Coast clutch no applied.
4. Intermediate or fourth band no applied.

NO ENGINE BRAKING: MANUAL 1ST GEAR

1. Low/reverse servo no applied.
2. TFP manual valve position switch leaking or inoperative.
3. Checkball No. 1 missing.
4. Coast clutch no applied.

DRIVES IN NEUTRAL

1. Manual valve and linkage to detent lever misaligned.
2. Forward clutch not releasing.
3. Reverse clutch and low/reverse servo not releasing.

NO GEAR SELECTION

1. Shift linkage disconnected.
2. Manual valve to detent lever link broken or missing.
3. Manual valve to link clip disconnected.
4. Manual valve stuck.
5. Control valve body fluid channels blocked.
6. Channel plate fluid channels blocked.
7. Transaxle case fluid channels blocked.
8. Control valve body, channel plate and case fluid channels broken.

SHIFT INDICATOR INDICATES WRONG GEAR SELECTION

1. Manual detent spring and roller broken or missing.
2. Manual detent spring and roller bolt loose.
3. Manual valve not connected to detent lever link.
4. Indicator linkage misadjusted.

NO TCC RELEASE

1. TCC control PWM solenoid internal

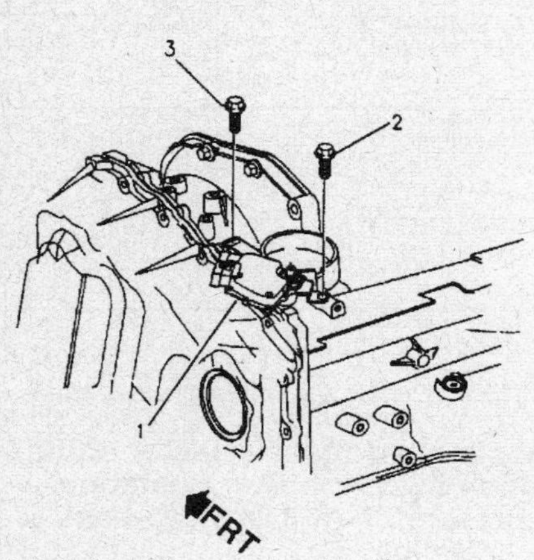

Fig. 8 Park/Neutral position switch adjustment

failure or fluid exhaust plugged.
2. TCC control PWM solenoid external ground.
3. TCC regulated apply and control valves stuck in TCC apply position.
4. Torque converter internal failure.

TCC APPLY w/COLD ENGINE

Engine coolant temperature sensor malfunction.

FLUID FOAMING

1. Fluid degraded, contaminated (coolant) or transaxle overfilled.
2. Cooler lines plugged.
3. Oil filter clogged or cracked.
4. Filter seal leaking.
5. Side over seal damaged.
6. Engine overheated.
7. Vehicle overloaded.
8. Oil level control valve damaged or loose.

VIBRATION

1. Torque converter out of balance.
2. Torque converter bolts/lugs missing or loose.
3. Torque converter internal failure.
4. Output or stub shafts out of balance.
5. Output or stub shafts bushings worn.
6. Turbine shaft out of balance.
7. Turbine shaft bushings worn.
8. Transaxle or engine misaligned.

RPM SENSITIVE WHINE

Ensure noise is internal to torque converter by applying brake with transaxle in Drive position and momentarily stalling engine. Torque converter noise should increase under load.

HIGH PITCH WHINE

Ensure noise is internal to oil pump during preliminary oil pressure check. Increase in line pressure will vary noise.

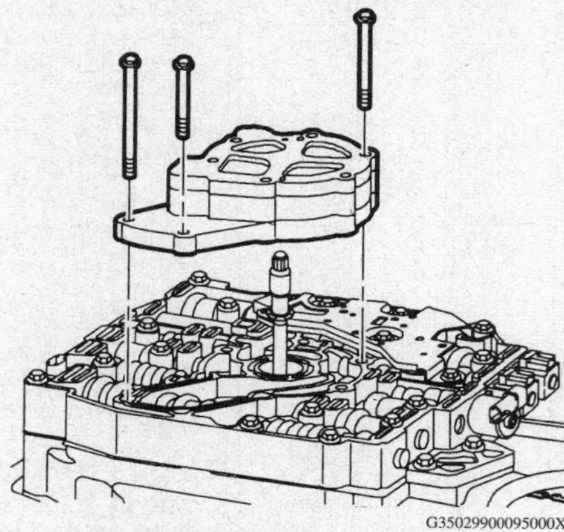

Fig. 9 Oil pump & shaft replacement

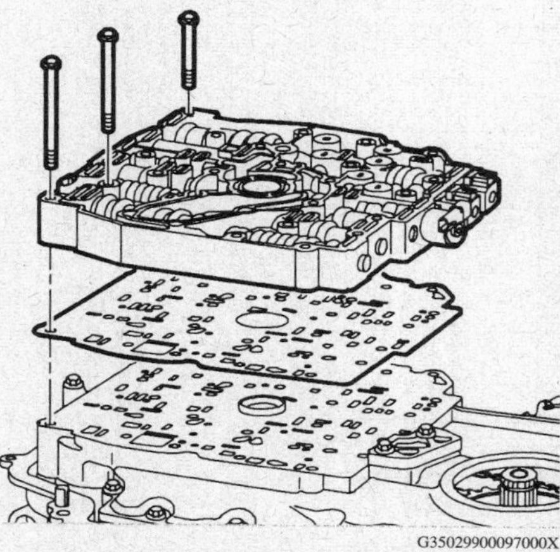

Fig. 11 Valve body replacement

POPPING

1. Inspect transaxle filter for leaking seam.
2. Inspect filter seal for improper positioning or cut.
3. Inspect oil level control valve for proper operation and obstructions.
4. Inspect for oil pump cavitation indications of fluid bubbles.

BUZZ OR HIGH FREQUENCY RATTLE

1. Ensure pressure buzz by watching of gauge needle vibration.
2. Road test as required.
3. Trace cooler pipes and inspect for binding or contact at radiator and other connectors.

WHINE OR GROWL

Ensure noise comes from drive link sprockets or chain by apply brake and moving gear selector from Park or Reverse position. Noise should stop. Inspect as follows:

1. Drive chain stretched.
2. Drive and driven sprockets broken or sheared teeth.
3. Drive and driven sprocket support surfaces nicked or scored.
4. Drive and driven sprocket support inner bearing race or roller surfaces

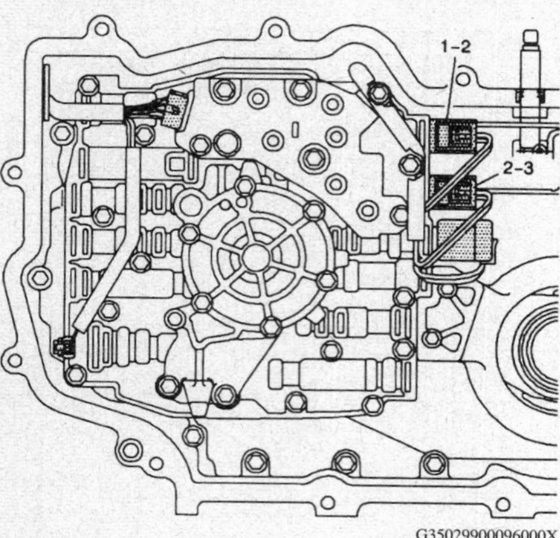

Fig. 10 1-2 & 2-3 shift solenoid harness connectors

rough or pitted, or bearing damaged.
5. Drive and driven sprocket support bearing outer race rough or nicked.

FINAL DRIVE HUM

1. Final drive and differential drive planet pinion gears worn.
2. Final drive and differential pinion thrust washers worn.
3. Final drive sun gear worn or teeth damaged.
4. Final drive internal gear worn or teeth damaged.
5. Final drive and differential pinion gears worn or pitted.
6. Final drive and differential pinion thrust washers damaged.
7. Final drive and differential side gear thrust washers damaged.

FORWARD RANGES NOISES

1. Final drive sun gear worn or damaged.
2. Final drive planet pinion gear worn or damaged.

RATCHETING NOISE

Parking pawl return spring damaged, weak or misassembled.

BRAKE TRANSAXLE SHIFT INTERLOCK (BTSI)

1. Ensure brake light operation.
2. If brake lights do not operate, refer to **Figs. 3 and 4** for wiring diagrams and **Figs. 5 through 7** for diagnostic procedures.
3. Inspect for proper installation of aftermarket equipment or for broken or partially broken wires inside of insulation. This could cause system failures, but not be indicated in continuity or voltage check.

MAINTENANCE

Refer to "Lubricant Data" chart in the appropriate chassis chapter of this manual for transmission fluid specifications.

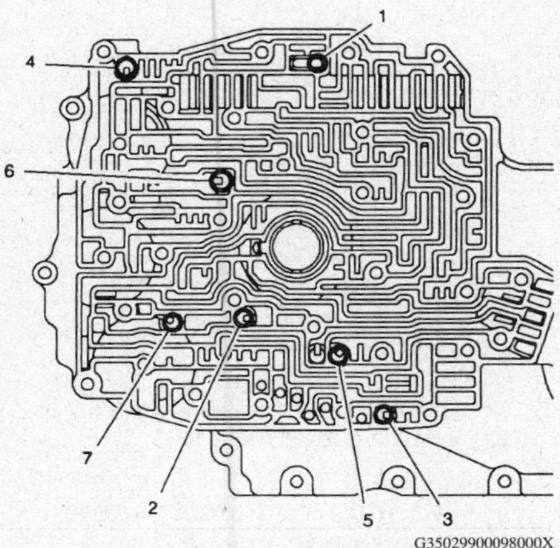

Fig. 12 Channel plate checkball locations

FLUID CHECK

Start engine and drive vehicle approximately 15 miles or until the transaxle reaches operating temperature of 180–200°F.

1. Allow engine to run at idle speed for 3–5 minutes with accessories off.
2. Apply brake and move shift lever through all gear ranges, pausing three seconds in each range.
3. Place shift lever in Park position.
4. Raise and support vehicle. Ensure vehicle is level.
5. Place oil container under check plug.
6. Ensure oil level is at bottom of oil check hole. Because transaxle operates over range of fluid levels, fluid may or may not drain out of screw hole when screw is removed.
7. If fluid drains through screw hole, transaxle may have been overfilled. When fluid stops draining, fluid level is correct.
8. If fluid does not drain through screw hole, transaxle fluid level may have been low. Add fluid at vent cap location in one pint increments until oil level is at bottom of oil check hole.
9. Install oil check plug.
10. Lower vehicle.

FLUID CHANGE

This is a fill for life transaxle and does not require fluid changing. Additionally, there is no dip stick.

ADJUSTMENTS

SHIFT LINKAGE

1. Place shift lever in Neutral position.
2. Place shift control in Neutral position.
3. Pull cable locking clip fully upward.
4. Push cable adjuster to adjust cable in cable mounting bracket.

NEUTRAL SAFETY SWITCH

1. Place transaxle control shifter in detent plate Neutral position notch.
2. Loosen switch mounting bolts, **Fig. 8.**
3. Rotate switch on shifter to align service adjustment hole with carrier tang hole.

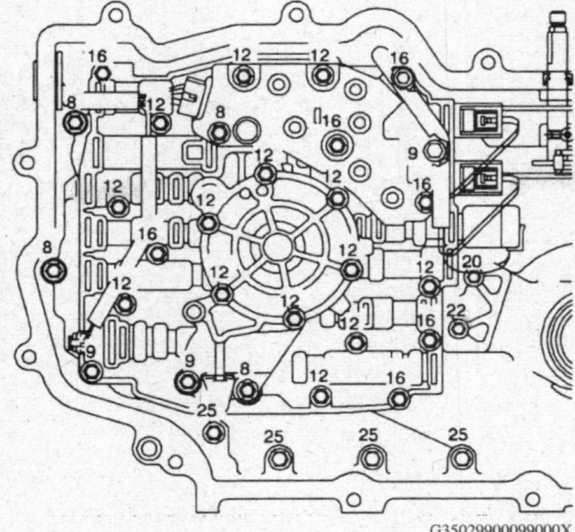

Fig. 13 Valve body bolt locations

BOTTOM VIEW

1 TRANSAXLE BOTTOM PAN
2 TRANSAXLE ASSEMBLY
3 VEHICLE SPEED SENSOR

TH5029600814000X

Fig. 15 Vehicle speed sensor replacement

4. Insert 3/32 inch maximum diameter gauge pin to depth of 9/64 inch.
5. Remove gauge pin.

PARK LOCK CABLE

1. Place floor shift lever in Park position.
2. Place ignition switch in lock position.
3. Unseat body housing lock from body housing.
4. Ensure there is no gap between metal terminal stop and protruding end of white plastic collar. If gap exists, adjust position of park/lock cable.
5. Ensure white plastic collar is flush or recessed approximately 0.04 inch with ignition park/lock housing. If collar is not in proper location, adjust position of park/lock cable.

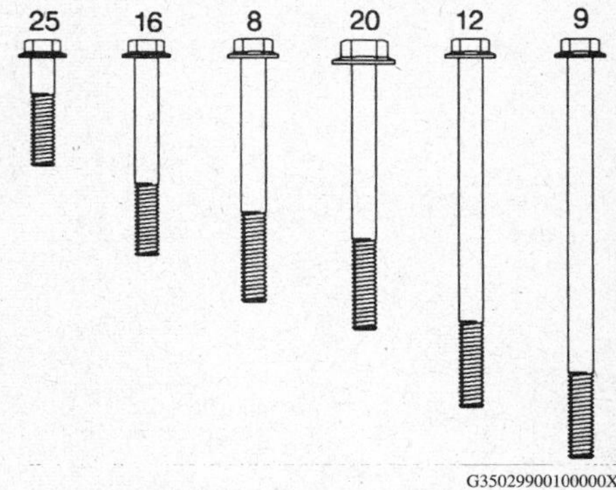

Fig. 14 Valve body bolt identification

6. Adjust outer cable conduit in order to obtain proper location of white plastic housing in ignition switch.
7. Ensure body housing is still attached to shift control mounting bracket.
8. Seat body housing lock in body housing while holding outer cable conduit in position.
9. Inspect park/lock control cable as described under "In-Vehicle Repairs."

IN-VEHICLE REPAIRS

OIL FILTER & SEAL, REPLACE

1. Raise and support vehicle.
2. Place suitable container under transaxle.
3. Remove front and side oil pan mounting bolts, then loosen rear bolts four turns. **Do not damage sealing surfaces.**
4. Lightly tap oil pan with suitable rubber mallet or pry to allow fluid to drain.
5. Remove rear mounting bolts, oil pan and gasket.
6. Remove oil filter using suitable long screwdriver to pry oil filter neck out of seal.
7. Remove seal using slide hammer tool No. J-6125-1B and axle boot remover tool No. J-23129, or equivalents, from transaxle case using suitable small screwdriver, as required.
8. Reverse procedure to install, noting the following:
   a. Install new seal, as required.
   b. Coat new seal with small amount of Transjel part No. J-36850, or equivalent petroleum jelly.
   c. Install new oil filter and seal.
   d. Oil pan gasket may be reused, unless sealing ribs are damaged.

OIL PAN, REPLACE

Refer to "Oil Filter & Seal, Replace."

VALVE BODY, REPLACE

REMOVAL

1. Remove case side cover.
2. Remove mounting bolts and oil pump, **Fig. 9.**
3. Disconnect pressure control solenoid and 1-2, 2-3 shift solenoids connectors, **Fig. 10.**

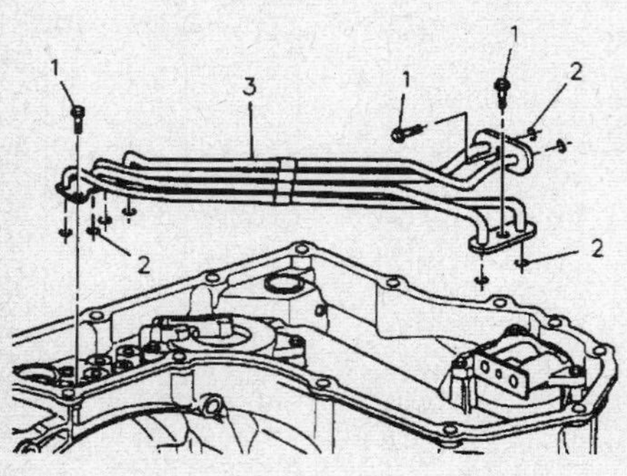

1 BOLT, TUBE ASSEMBLY
2 SEAL, OIL FEED TUBE ASSEMBLY
3 TUBE ASSEMBLY, OIL FEED

TH5029600823000X

Fig. 16 Oil feed pipe

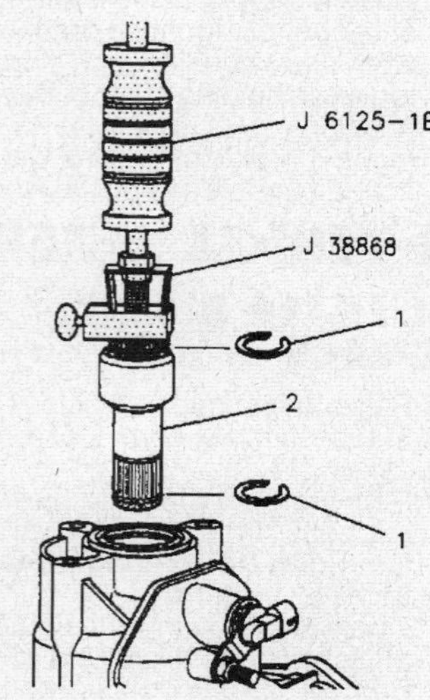

1 RING, OUTPUT/STUB SHAFT SNAP
2 SHAFT, OUTPUT STUB

TH5029600825000X

Fig. 19 Stub shaft removal

4. Disconnect TFP switch and TCC solenoid connectors.
5. Remove TFP switch from valve body. TFP switch O-rings are reusable if not damaged and should remain with switch.
6. Remove remaining mounting bolts and control valve body, **Fig. 11.**
7. Remove and discard valve body to spacer plate gasket.
8. Remove support and spacer plate with filter. Discard spacer plate to channel plate gasket. **Checkballs may fall out of channel plate. Retain balls with suitable petroleum jelly.**

INSTALLATION

1. Ensure checkballs are in proper locations on channel plate, **Fig. 12.**
2. Install new gasket and spacer plate with filter attached.
3. Hand start mounting bolts and install spacer plate support.
4. Install gasket and valve body.
5. Hand start mounting bolts to hold valve body in place.
6. Install TFP switch onto control valve body.
7. Install and hand start remaining control valve body mounting bolts, **Figs. 13 and 14.**
8. Connect transaxle wiring harness connectors to TFP switch, pressure control, 1-2 and 2-3 solenoids.
9. Install oil pump shaft into control valve body, oil pump onto oil pump shaft and valve body.
10. Install transaxle case side gaskets and seals, then the driven sprocket thrust washer and retain with suitable petroleum jelly.

VEHICLE SPEED SENSOR, REPLACE

1. Raise and support vehicle.
2. Disconnect electrical connector.
3. Remove speed sensor mounting bolt, **Fig. 15.**
4. Remove speed sensor from case extension.
5. Remove O-ring from speed sensor.
6. Reverse procedure to install. Replace O-ring.

OIL FEED PIPES & GASKETS, REPLACE

1. Raise and support vehicle.
2. Remove transaxle oil pan and filter.
3. Remove oil feed pipe mounting bolts, **Fig. 16.**
4. Remove oil feed pipe and seals.
5. Reverse procedure to install, noting the following:
   a. Inspect pipes for plugged passages, bends or cracks.
   b. Inspect seal rings. Replace if cut, swelled or damaged.
   c. Replace oil pan gasket if damaged.

PARK LOCK CONTROL CABLE, REPLACE

REMOVAL

1. Remove console.
2. Remove lefthand sound insulator.
3. Remove knee bolster.
4. Loosen bracket mounting bolts and lower steering column.
5. Place transaxle shift lever in Park position.

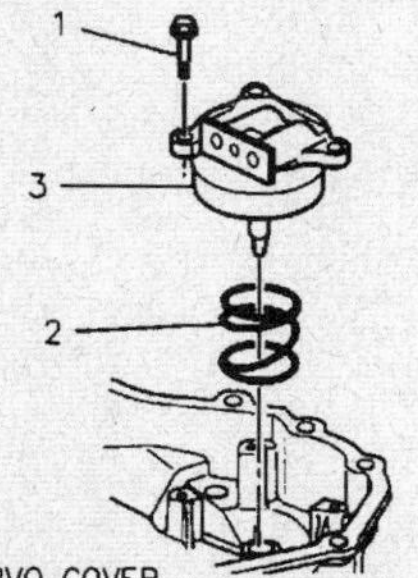

1 BOLT, SERVO COVER
2 SPRING, SERVO RETURN (LO/REVERSE)
3 COVER, SERVO (LO/REVERSE)

TH5029600815000X

Fig. 17 Low/Reverse servo replacement

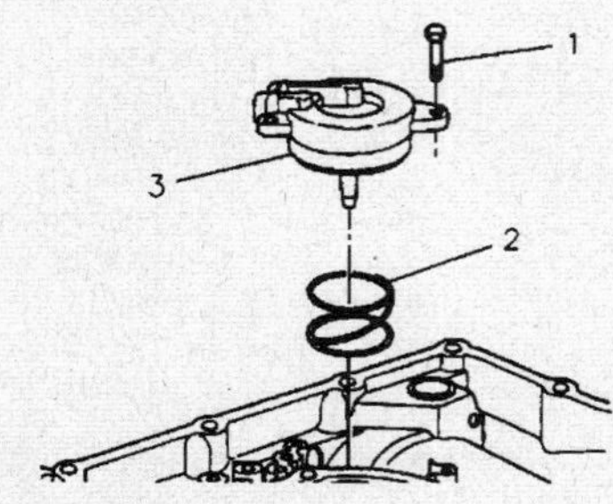

1 BOLT, SERVO COVER
2 SPRING, SERVO RETURN (INTERMEDIATE/4TH)
3 COVER, SERVO (INTERMEDIATE/4TH)

TH5029600816000X

Fig. 18 Intermediate/4th servo replacement

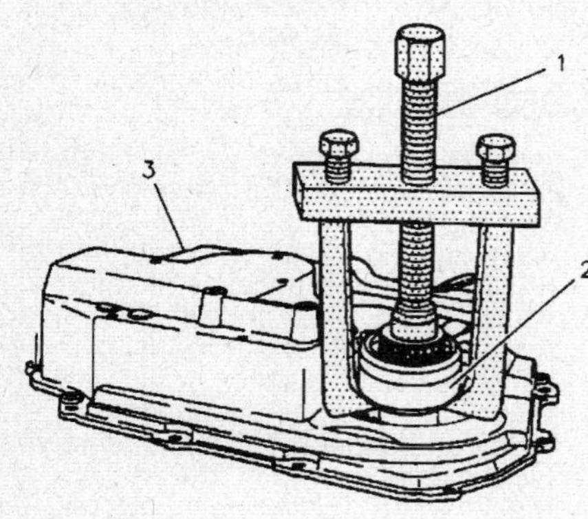

1 J 41227
2 SLEEVE, OUTPUT/STUB SHAFT
3 TRANSAXLE

TH5029600826000X

Fig. 20 Sleeve removal

6. Place ignition in Run position. **Do not proceed to next step with key in any other position.**
7. Insert screwdriver blade into slot provided in ignition switch inhibitor.
8. Depress cable latch and pull control cable from inhibitor.
9. Push cable connector lock button at shifter base to up position.
10. Snap cable from park/lock lever pin.
11. Depress and remove control cable latches from automatic transaxle control.
12. Remove control cable clips.

INSTALLATION

When installing a new park/lock cable, keep the shipping cover gauge attached until instructed to detach it. The shipping cover gauge will aid in the proper positioning of cable.

1. Ensure cable lock button is in Up position and place shift lever in Park position.
2. Snap control cable connector into automatic transaxle control.
3. Place ignition in Run position. **Do not insert cable with key in any other position.**
4. Snap control cable into inhibitor housing until snap lock is seated.
5. Remove shipping cover gauge.

6. Place ignition in Lock position.
7. Snap control cable end onto shift park/lock lever pin.
8. Push cable connector hose forward in order to remove any slack.
9. With no load applied to connector nose, snap cable connector lock button down. Ensure proper operation of park/lock control cable before installing steering column to instrument panel.
10. Raise and connect steering column bracket bolts.
11. Install knee bolster and lefthand sound insulator.
12. Install console.

FUNCTION INSPECTION

1. Ensure there is no gap between metal terminal stop and protruding end of white plastic collar. If gap exists, adjust position of park/lock cable.
2. Ensure white plastic collar is flush or 0.04 inch recessed within park/lock housing. If collar position is not as specified, adjust position of park/lock cable.
3. Ensure terminal stop on column end of park/lock cable is touching white collar that protrudes from ignition switch.
4. Place ignition in Lock position.
5. Place floor shift lever into Park position.
6. Ensure terminal stop is in correct position.
7. Ensure ignition remains in Lock position.
8. Ensure floor shift lever remains in Park position.
9. Gently depress park/lock button on floor shift lever until resistance is felt.
10. Ensure white plastic collar travels no more than 0.06 inch. **Floor shift lever must not come out of Park.**
11. Place ignition switch in On position.
12. Ensure proper movement of floor shift lever through all gear ranges.
13. While moving shift lever through drive gears, ensure ignition cannot be turned to lock position.
14. Ensure key can be removed with ignition in Lock position and floor shift lever in Park position.
15. If one or more inspections have failed, adjust park/lock cable as described under "Adjustments."

SERVO, REPLACE

1. Raise and support vehicle.
2. Remove oil pan.
3. Remove mounting bolts and servo cover, **Figs. 17 and 18.**
4. Remove snap ring, piston, sealing ring and servo spring.
5. Reverse procedure to install.

CASE SIDE COVER, REPLACE

1. Remove park/neutral position switch.
2. Raise and support vehicle.
3. Remove lefthand front wheel.
4. Remove inner splash shield.
5. Remove tie rod end from knuckle.
6. Remove stabilizer shaft link from lower control arm.
7. Remove ball joint from steering knuckle.

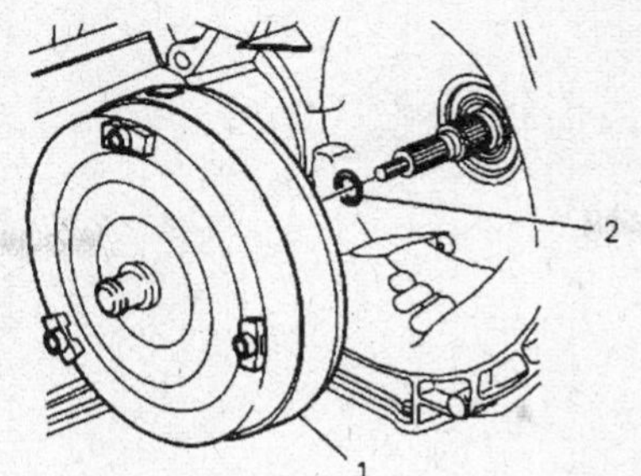

1 SEAL, O-RING (TORQUE CONVERTER)
2 TORQUE CONVERTER ASSEMBLY

TH5029600822000X

Fig. 21 Torque converter & turbine shaft seal replacement

8. Remove drive axle from transaxle.
9. Remove pinch bolt from intermediate shaft. **Failure to disconnect intermediate shaft from rack and pinion steering gear stub shaft can result in damage to steering gear or intermediate shaft.**
10. Remove intermediate shaft from steering gear.
11. Support transaxle oil pan with suitable transaxle jack.
12. Remove three frame to body mounting bolts on lefthand side.
13. Lower transaxle to gain access to case side cover.
14. Remove oil cooler pipes at case.
15. Remove mounting bolts and case side cover.
16. Reverse procedure to install.

STUB AXLE SHAFT, RIGHTHAND OUTPUT AXLE SHAFT OIL SEALS & SLEEVES, REPLACE

1. Raise and support vehicle.
2. Remove tire and wheel assembly.
3. Remove inner splash shield and separate tie rod from steering knuckle.
4. Remove ball joint from steering knuckle.
5. Remove drive axle.
6. Remove snap ring from stub axle shaft. Discard snap ring.
7. Pull lightly on shaft and rotate it until output shaft snap ring at differential seats in taper on differential side gear.
8. Remove stub shaft from transaxle using slide hammer tool No. J-6125 and output shaft removal tool No. J-38868, or equivalents, **Fig. 19.**
9. Remove sleeve from stub shaft using sleeve puller tool No. J-41227, or equivalent, **Fig. 20.**
10. Remove righthand axle seal from transaxle using axle boot remover tool No. J-23129 and slide hammer tool No. J-6125, or equivalents.
11. Remove transaxle side cover.
12. Remove sleeve from output shaft using sleeve puller tool No. J-41227, or equivalent, **Fig. 20.**
13. Reverse procedure to install, noting the following:
    a. Lubricate seal lip with light wipe of transaxle fluid.
    b. Install new seal using axle seal installer tool No. J-41102, or equivalent.
    c. Install shaft sleeves with sleeve installer tool No. J-41228, or equivalent.
    d. Install new snap rings on stub shaft.
    e. Carefully guide axle shaft past lip seal. **Do not allow shaft splines to contact any portion of seal lip surface.**

TORQUE CONVERTER & TURBINE SHAFT SEAL, REPLACE

1. Remove transaxle.
2. Remove torque converter from transaxle, **Fig. 21.**
3. Remove turbine shaft O-ring from end of turbine shaft using suitable screw driver.
4. Reverse procedure to install.

SOLENOID, REPLACE

1. Remove transaxle case side cover.
2. Remove retainer clip from solenoid using suitable small screwdriver, **Fig. 22.**
3. Remove solenoids and O-rings from transaxle. Shift solenoids have one O-ring and pressure control and TCC solenoids have two O-rings.
4. Inspect solenoids and O-rings for damage.
5. Reverse procedure to install. Install new O-rings.

SHIFT LINKAGE, REPLACE

1. Disconnect cable from transaxle selector lever.
2. Disconnect cable from transaxle cable bracket.
3. Remove center console.
4. Disconnect cable at shift control.
5. Remove cable grommet at cowl.
6. Remove cable.
7. Reverse procedure to install, adjust cable as required.

TRANSAXLE

REPLACE

ALERO, CUTLASS, GRAND AM & MALIBU

1. Support engine using engine support fixture tool No. J-28467-360, or equivalent.
2. Support transaxle with suitable safety stand.
3. Raise vehicle. Ensure pressure is off transaxle mounts.
4. Remove splash shield.
5. Remove air cleaner and duct from throttle body.
6. Remove wire harness from upper transaxle mount bracket.
7. Remove upper transaxle mount.
8. Remove shifter cable.
9. Remove ground cables from transaxle mounting studs.
10. Disconnect park/neutral switch connector.

11. Remove transaxle vent tube and rear transaxle mount.
12. Raise and support vehicle.
13. Drain transaxle fluid into suitable container.
14. Remove both front wheels.
15. Remove lefthand front inner splash shield.
16. Remove front ABS wheel speed sensor connectors.
17. Remove lefthand side harness from its routing.
18. Remove mounting bolts and housing cover.
19. Remove vehicle speed sensor.
20. Remove torque converter bolts.
21. Remove left and righthand ball joint nuts.
22. Remove lefthand suspension support mounting bolts.
23. Remove drive axles.
24. Remove mounting bolts and front lower transaxle mount.
25. Attach transaxle case to support stand.
26. Remove transaxle to engine mount bolts.
27. Remove transaxle.
28. Reverse procedure to install.

CAVALIER & SUNFIRE

1. Remove air cleaner.
2. Remove shift linkage from transaxle.
3. Disconnect wiring connections from transaxle.
4. Support engine using engine support fixture tool No. J-28467-360, or equivalent.
5. Remove upper transaxle to engine mounting bolts.
6. Raise and support vehicle.
7. Remove both front wheel assemblies.
8. Remove left and righthand splash shields.
9. Remove front ABS wheel speed sensors and disconnect harness from lefthand side suspension support.
10. Remove outer tie rods from steering knuckle.
11. Remove ball joints from knuckle.
12. Remove mounting bolts and front suspension support brace.
13. Remove engine mount strut from strut mount bracket.
14. Remove mounting bolts and lower suspension support.
15. Disconnect steering coupling and power steering fluid lines, then remove suspension support.
16. Remove drive axles from transaxle.
17. Remove engine to transaxle brace and shift cable bracket.
18. Remove starter and transaxle converter cover.
19. Mark flywheel to torque converter for assembly and remove torque converter to flywheel bolts.
20. Remove transaxle cooler pipes and brake hose bracket to body.
21. Remove transaxle mount to body bolts.
22. Lower vehicle and transaxle with engine support fixture enough to remove transaxle.
23. Raise vehicle and support transaxle.
24. Remove mounting bolts and transaxle.
25. Reverse procedure to install.

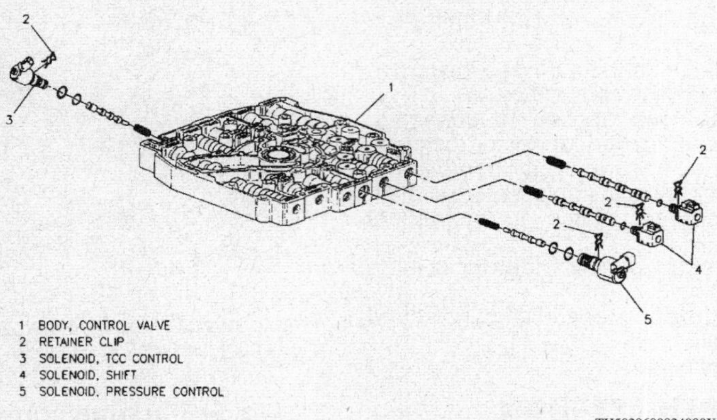

Fig. 22 TCC control, shift & pressure control solenoid replacement

SATURN L-SERIES

1. Remove battery hold down bracket and battery.
2. Remove underhood fuse block and battery tray.
3. Disconnect control cable from transaxle range switch lever using suitable screwdriver.
4. Remove control cable bracket from rear powertrain mount. Tie cable and bracket to dash panel.
5. Remove electrical connector, ground wire and all wiring attachments from transaxle.
6. Disconnect transaxle range switch electrical connectors and remove upper engine to transaxle bolts.
7. **On models equipped with 3.0L engine,** remove accessory drive belt, tensioner and alternator.
8. **On all models,** disconnect output speed sensor electrical connector and remove harness from mounting stud.
9. Install engine support fixture to engine.
10. Remove frame.
11. Pry out axle shafts from transaxle, leaving axle shafts in steering knuckles and secure away from transaxle removal path.
12. **On models equipped with 3.0L engine,** remove wiring harness mounting bracket from rear of engine block for access to starter.
13. **On all models,** remove engine to transaxle bracket and starter electrical connectors.
14. Remove flexplate to torque converter bolts using torque converter tool No. J-44014, or equivalent.
15. Remove oil cooler line from transaxle.
16. Remove lower two engine to transaxle mounting bolts and lower vehicle.
17. Mark position of lefthand transaxle mount and remove mounting bolts.
18. Raise and support vehicle.
19. Slide suitable hydraulic lift table under transaxle.
20. Lower vehicle slowly until transaxle is on hydraulic lift table. Place suitable wood block between barrel of transaxle and surface of table.
21. Remove remaining engine to transaxle mounting bolts.
22. Slide transaxle away from engine and raise vehicle from transaxle.
23. Reverse procedure to install.

TECHNICAL SERVICE BULLETINS

SHIFT LEVER HANDLE DIFFICULT TO OPERATE

1999–2000 ALERO & GRAND AM

On some of these models the shift lever handle may be difficult for some drivers to operate.

To correct this condition install different design handle that does not require the use of the thumb (part No. 12557279).

TIGHTENING SPECIFICATIONS

Year	Component	Torque/Ft. Lbs.
ALERO & GRAND AM		
1999–2002	Case Cover	18
	Case Side Cover	15
	Channel Plate To Case	106①
	Channel Plate To Driven Sprocket Support	10
	Converter Shield	18
	Cooler Pipes At Case	71①
	Cooler Pipes At Radiator	15–30
	Detent Spring	106①
	Drive Sprocket Support	106①
	Driven Sprocket Support	10
	Flywheel To Torque Converter	46
	Input Speed Sensor	106①
	Intermediate/4th Servo Cover	106①
	Low/Reverse Servo Cover	86①
	Park/Neutral Position Switch To Case	18
	Oil Check Plug	10
	Oil Feed Pipe	106①
	Oil Pan	10
	Oil Pump	106①
	Pressure Switch	106①
	Shift Control Cable	17①
	Shift Lever	15
	TFP Switch	106–124①
	Speed Sensor Housing	97①
	Transaxle Mount Through Bolts	89
	Transaxle Mount To Cradle, Front	89
	Transaxle Mount To Cradle, Rear	49
	Transaxle Mount To Engine	99
	Transaxle Mount To Engine Brace	32
	Transaxle Support Fixture	97①
	Transaxle Range Switch	18
	Valve Body	106–124①
	Wiring Harness	106①

Continued

TIGHTENING SPECIFICATIONS—Continued

Year	Component	Torque/Ft. Lbs.
CAVALIER & SUNFIRE		
1998	Case Cover	18
	Case Side Cover	15
	Converter Shield	18
	Cooler Pipes At Case	71①
	Cooler Pipes At Radiator	15–30
	Drive Sprocket Support	106①
	Flywheel To Torque Converter	46
	Low/Reverse Servo Cover	86①
	Park/Neutral Position Switch To Case	18
	Oil Check Plug	10
	Oil Feed Pipe	10
	Oil Pan	10
	Pressure Switch	106①
	Shift Control Cable	17①
	Shift Lever	15
	Speed Sensor Housing	97①
	Transaxle Mount Through Bolts	89
	Transaxle Mount To Cradle, Front	89
	Transaxle Mount To Cradle, Rear	49
	Transaxle Mount To Engine	99
	Transaxle Mount To Engine Brace	32
	Transaxle Range Switch	18
	Transaxle Support Fixture	97①
1999–2002	Bottom Pan	106①
	Case Cover	15–22
	Channel Plate To Case	106①
	Channel Plate To Driven Sprocket Support	10
	Detent To Channel Plate Spring & Roller	106①
	Drive Sprocket Support	106①
	Driven Sprocket Support	10
	Input Speed Sensor	106①
	Intermediate 4th Servo Cover	106①
	Low/Reverse Servo Cover	106①
	Oil Feed Pipe	106①
	Oil Pump	106①
	Pipe Plug	106①
	Side Cover	15
	TFP Switch	106①
	Transaxle To Engine Mount	66
	Transaxle Support Fixture	97①
	Tube Assembly	106①
	Valve Body	106①
	Vehicle Speed Sensor	106①
	Wiring Harness	106①

Continued

TIGHTENING SPECIFICATIONS—Continued

Year	Component	Torque/Ft. Lbs.
CUTLASS		
1998	Case Cover	18
	Case Side Cover	21
	Converter Shield	18
	Cooler Pipes At Case	71①
	Cooler Pipes At Radiator	15–30
	Drive Sprocket Support	106①
	Flywheel To Torque Converter	46
	Low/Reverse Servo Cover	86①
	Oil Check Plug	10
	Oil Feed Tube Bolts	10
	Oil Pan	10
	Park/Neutral Position Switch To Case	18
	Pressure Switch	106①
	Shift Control Cable	17①
	Shift Lever	15
	Speed Sensor Housing	97①
	Transaxle Mount Through Bolts	89
	Transaxle Mount To Cradle, Front	89
	Transaxle Mount To Cradle, Rear	49
	Transaxle Mount To Engine	99
	Transaxle Mount To Engine Brace	32
	Transaxle To Engine Mount	66
	Transaxle Range Switch	18
	Transaxle Support Fixture	97①
	TV Cable	80①
MALIBU		
1998	Case Cover	18
	Case Side Cover	21
	Converter Shield	18
	Cooler Pipes At Case	71①
	Cooler Pipes At Radiator	15–30
	Drive Sprocket Support	106①
	Flywheel To Torque Converter	46
	Low/Reverse Servo Cover	86①
	Oil Check Plug	10
	Oil Feed Tube Bolts	10
	Oil Pan	10
	Park/Neutral Position Switch To Case	18
	Pressure Switch	106①
	Shift Control Cable	17①
	Shift Lever	15
	Speed Sensor Housing	97①
	Transaxle Mount Through Bolts	89
	Transaxle Mount To Cradle, Front	89
	Transaxle Mount To Cradle, Rear	49
	Transaxle Mount To Engine	99
	Transaxle Mount To Engine Brace	32
	Transaxle To Engine Mount	66
	Transaxle Range Switch	18
	Transaxle Support Fixture	97①
	TV Cable	80①

Continued

TIGHTENING SPECIFICATIONS—Continued

Year	Component	Torque/Ft. Lbs.
MALIBU		
1999–2002	Bottom Pan	106①
	Case Cover	15–22
	Channel Plate To Case	106①
	Channel Plate To Driven Sprocket Support	10
	Detent To Channel Plate Spring & Roller	106①
	Drive Sprocket Support	106①
	Driven Sprocket Support	10
	Input Speed Sensor	106①
	Intermediate 4th Servo Cover	106①
	Low/Reverse Servo Cover	106①
	Oil Feed Pipe	106①
	Oil Pump	106①
	Pipe Plug	106①
	Side Cover	15
	TFP Switch	106①
	Transaxle Fixture	97①
	Transaxle Range Switch	18
	Tube Assembly	106①
	Valve Body	106①
	Vehicle Speed Sensor	106①
	Wiring Harness	106①
SATURN L-SERIES		
2000–02	Case Cover	15–22
	Channel Plate To Case	106①
	Channel Plate To Driven Sprocket Support	10
	Control Cable	15
	Cooler Line	71①
	Detent Spring	106①
	Drive Sprocket Support	106①
	Driven Sprocket Support	10
	Engine To Transaxle	48
	Engine To Transaxle Bracket	26
	Flexplate To Torque Converter	33
	Intermediate/4th Servo Cover	106①
	Low/Reverse Servo Cover	106①
	Input Speed Sensor	106①
	Oil Feed Pipe	106①
	Oil Level Plug	106①
	Oil Pan	106①
	Oil Pump	106①

Continued

TIGHTENING SPECIFICATIONS—Continued

Year	Component	Torque/Ft. Lbs.
SATURN L-SERIES		
2000–02	Servo Cover	106①
	Side Cover	15
	TFP Switch	106–124①
	Transaxle Fixture	97①
	Transaxle Mount Bracket	66
	Transaxle Mount Through Bolt, Front	41
	Transaxle Mount Through Bolt, Rear	66
	Transaxle Mount To Bracket	41
	Transaxle Mount To Engine	15
	Transaxle Mount To Frame	44
	Transaxle Range Switch	15
	Transaxle Range Switch Lever	26
	Valve Body	106①
	Vehicle Speed Sensor	96①
	Wiring Harness	15

① — Inch lbs.

Turbo Hydra-Matic 4T60-E, 4T65-E & 4T65-E-HD Automatic Transaxles

NOTE: On Air Bag Equipped Models, Refer To "Air Bag System Precautions" Located In The Front Of This Manual For System Disarming & Arming Procedures.

NOTE: Refer To "Computer Relearn Procedures" Located In The Front Of This Manual When Battery Power To The Computer Has Been Interrupted.

NOTE: Prior To Performing Any Service Operations Listed In This Section, Consult The "Technical Service Bulletins" Section For Related Information.

INDEX

PRECAUTIONS

AIR BAG SYSTEMS

Refer to "Air Bag System Precautions" in the front of this manual for system disarming and arming procedures.

BATTERY GROUND CABLE

Prior to service, disconnect battery ground cable and isolate as required.

IDENTIFICATION

This transaxle may be identified by codes stamped into the horizontal cast rib on the righthand rear side of the transaxle housing, **Fig. 1.**

DESCRIPTION

The 4T60-E & 4T65-E transaxles are

fully automatic units which provide four forward speeds including an overdrive top gear, **Fig. 2.** The transmission units include a three-element hydraulic torque converter and lock-up clutching element, four multiple disc clutch, two bands and a compound reaction planetary gear set. Power is transmitted to the drive wheels from the planetary gear through a final drive gear set and differential assembly.

The converter is designed to provide torque multiplication during acceleration and at slow vehicle speed and lock-up during normal operation for increase operating economy. Operation of the converter lock-up is controlled automatically by the engine fuel system electronic control module. In addition, the converter drives the vane type oil pump by means of a shaft splined to the converter cover.

The torque converter hydraulically couples the engine to the planetary gears through a turbine and shaft assembly which drives the transmission output shaft by means of a drive link chain and sprockets.

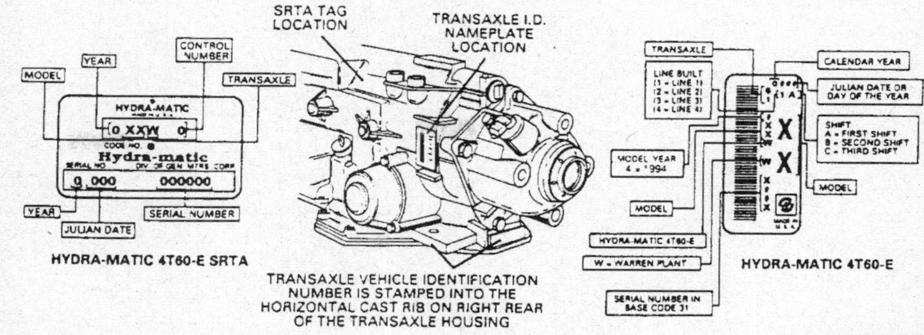

Fig. 1 Transaxle identification plate

TROUBLESHOOTING

OIL LEAK

1. Side cover distorted.
2. Vent.
3. Reverse servo cover seal.
4. Drive shaft oil seal.
5. Forward servo cover.
6. Park pawl actuator guide seal.
7. Electrical connector seal.
8. Torque converter oil seal.
9. Oil pan mounting bolts loose.
10. Oil pan gaskets damaged.
11. Oil fill tube seal.
12. Vehicle speed sensor seal.
13. Manual shaft seal damaged.
14. Governor cover and/or servo covers O-rings damaged.
15. Cooler fittings and/or pressure taps insufficiently tightened, or threads stripped.
16. Axle seals damaged, or garter spring missing.
17. Modulator O-ring damaged.
18. Parking plunger guide O-ring damaged.

OIL FORCED OUT VENT OR FOAMING OIL

1. High fluid level.
2. Overheated or contaminated oil.
3. Damaged filter or filter seal.
4. Leaking accumulator cover pipe or drive socket support lubrication pipes.
5. Thermo element not closing properly.
6. Thermo element improperly installed or incorrect pin height.
7. Defective or improperly installed modulator port gasket.
8. Plugged drive sprocket support drain back holes.

OIL PRESSURE HIGH OR LOW

1. Incorrect fluid level.
2. Contaminated fluid or engine overheating.
3. Thermo element is misadjusted or damaged.
4. Wiring harness is disconnected or damaged.
5. Vacuum line leaking.
6. Modulator leaking or modulator diaphragm damaged.
7. Nicked, scored or stuck modulator valve.
8. Pressure control solenoid valve is damaged or seal is leaking.
9. Pressure regulator valve is damaged valve spring is missing.
10. Actuator feed limit valve is damaged.
11. Line blow off valve is damaged.
12. Oil pump damaged or restricted.
13. Aspirator T blocked or incorrectly installed.

DELAYED ENGAGEMENT

1. Low oil level.
2. Low transmission main line pressure.
3. Reverse band servo piston oil seal ring is damaged.
4. Forward band servo piston oil seal ring is damaged.
5. Control valve body reverse or forward boost valves are damaged.
6. Control valve body spacer plate is damaged or is not functioning properly.
7. Torque converter clutch blowoff ball valve is not seating.
8. Cooler checkball not seating.
9. Input clutch is damaged.
10. Damaged or defective reverse servo seal.
11. Damaged or defective 1-2 servo seal.
12. Leaking 1-2 servo oil pipes.

NO DRIVE IN D RANGE

1. Low fluid level.
2. Low oil pressure.
3. Manual linkage improperly adjusted or disconnected.
4. Oil filter is plugged or damaged.
5. Accumulator and manual 2-1 band servo is loose, damaged or leaking.
6. Forward band servo is damaged or leaking.
7. Checkball is missing in control valve body.
8. Torque converter stator roller clutch sluggish or converter not properly attached to flex plate.
9. Drive axles disengaged.
10. Damaged or broken drive link chain, sprockets or bearings.
11. Input clutch is damaged or misassembled.
12. Damaged 1-2 servo or incorrect apply pin.
13. 1-2 servo oil pipes or pipe seals leaking.
14. Damaged oil pump or pump driveshaft.
15. Input clutch reverse checkball out of position.
16. Burned input clutch plates, damaged clutch seals or damaged piston.
17. Leaking input housing checkball.
18. Damaged input shaft seals or blocked input shaft passages.
19. Defective input sprag or improper sprag and input sun gear. **When servicing transaxle for intermittent or complete loss of drive, input sprag should always be replaced.**
20. Third roller clutch burned because of lack of lubrication.
21. Damaged input carrier and/or reaction carrier.
22. Damaged or improperly installed output shaft.
23. Burned or improperly installed 1-2 band.
24. Damaged final drive and/or final drive sun gear shaft.
25. Broken parking pawl spring.

SLIPS IN DRIVE

1. Incorrect oil level.
2. Cut or damaged vacuum line to modulator or defective modulator.
3. Low oil pressure.
4. Damaged 1-2 servo or servo piston seal.
5. Plugged filter screen.
6. Leaking servo oil pipes or pipe seals.
7. Defective converter stator clutch.
8. Defective input clutch accumulator or damaged input shaft seals.
9. Damaged or defective input clutch or leaks at ball capsule.

NO 1-2 UPSHIFT, 1ST SPEED ONLY

1. Stuck or binding 1-2 shift valve.
2. Debris in control valve body or spacer plate.
3. Control valve body spacer plate or gaskets damaged or improperly positioned.
4. Damaged or improperly assembled second clutch.
5. Damaged splines on reverse reaction drum.

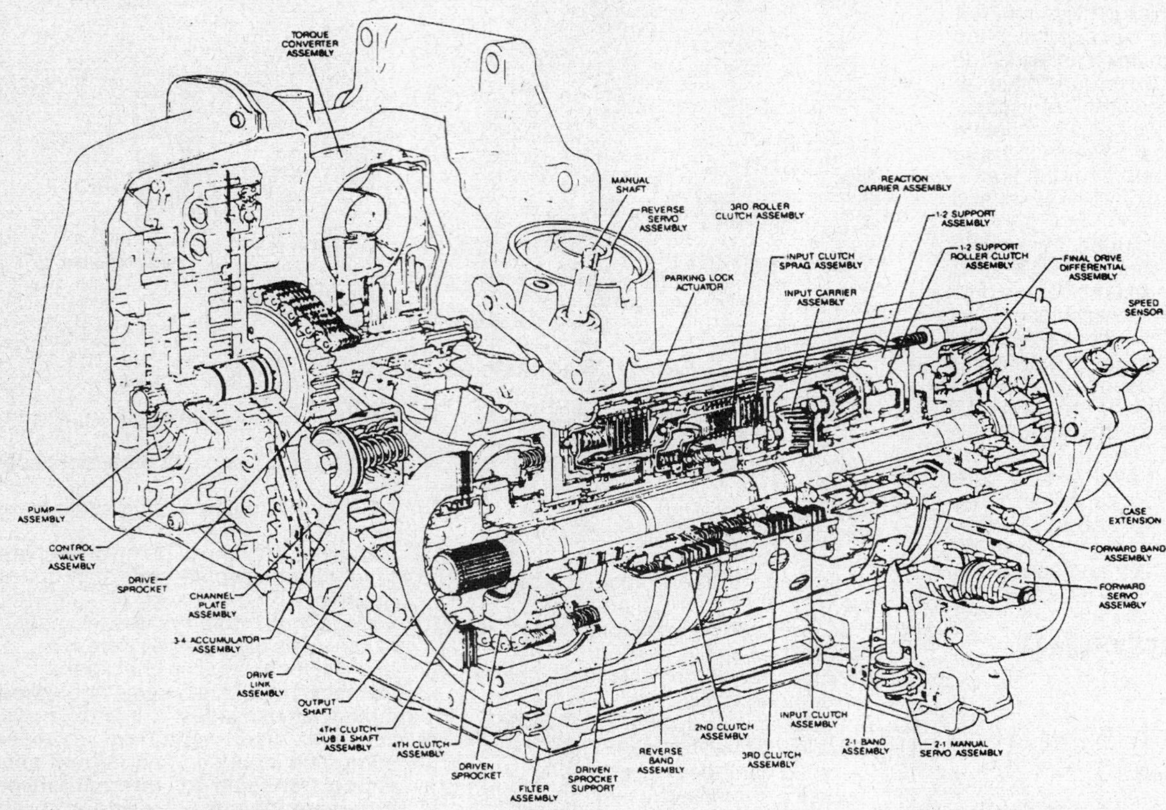

TH5029200003000X

Fig. 2 Cross sectional view of Turbo Hydra-Matic 4T60-E & 4T65-E automatic transaxles

6. Damaged driven sprocket support oil rings.
7. Damaged reverse reaction drum splines or missing drum plate.

HARSH OR SOFT 1-2 SHIFT

1. Low fluid level.
2. Incorrect oil pressure.
3. Oil filter plugged or damaged.
4. 1-2 accumulator cover bolts improperly tightened.
5. Accumulator pistons, seals or springs damaged.
6. Control valve accumulator valve stuck or binding.
7. Checkball missing or improperly installed.
8. Driven sprocket support seal or bushing damaged.
9. Second clutch damaged or improperly installed.

NO 2-3 UPSHIFT, 1ST & 2ND SPEEDS ONLY

4T60-E TRANSAXLE

1. Accumulator cover oil hole blocked.
2. Leaking drive sprocket support oil pipe.
3. 2-3 shift valve binding or sticking.
4. Control valve bolts improperly tightened.
5. Leaking or improperly positioned checkballs.
6. Sticking 2-3 accumulator valve.
7. Leaking 1-2 servo release oil pipe.
8. Improperly installed channel plate gasket.
9. Blocked oil passage to driven sprocket support.
10. Damaged input housing and shaft seals or blocked oil passages.
11. Damaged third clutch.
12. Damaged third clutch piston checkball.
13. Damaged third roller clutch.
14. Third roller clutch improperly assembled on input sun gear shaft.

4T65-E TRANSAXLE

1. Faulty 2-3 shift solenoid valve.
2. Debris in control valve body or spacer plate.

HARSH OR SOFT 2-3 SHIFT

4T60-E TRANSAXLE

1. Low fluid level.
2. Incorrect oil pressure.
3. Oil filter plugged or damaged.
4. No. 4 checkball mislocated causing soft shift.
5. No. 9 checkball mislocated causing harsh shift.
6. Missing or damaged seals or springs on 2-3 accumulator piston.

4T65-E TRANSAXLE

1. Low fluid level.
2. Low fluid pressure.
3. Oil filter is plugged or damaged.
4. Misassembled 2-3 accumulator.
5. Damaged or missing 2-3 accumulator piston oil sealing ring.
6. Damaged or missing 2-3 accumulator piston cushion spring or outer spring.
7. Stuck or binding 2-3 accumulator piston.
8. Debris in control valve body or spacer plate.
9. Missing or mislocated control valve body checkballs.
10. Stuck or binding 2-3 accumulator valve.
11. Plugged third clutch oil passage in driven sprocket support.
12. Input clutch housing oil seal rings are missing or damaged.
13. Third clutch ball check valve is damaged or missing.
14. Third clutch piston or piston inner seal is damaged.
15. Third clutch plates are worn or misassembled.

NO 3-4 UPSHIFT

1. 3-4 shift valve binding or stuck.
2. 4-3 manual shift valve binding or stuck.
3. Spline damage on fourth clutch shaft.
4. Damaged fourth clutch shift spline.
5. Damaged or improperly assembled fourth clutch.

HARSH OR SOFT 3-4 SHIFT

4T60-E TRANSAXLE

1. Incorrect oil pressure.
2. Accumulator cover and pistons seal damaged or springs missing.
3. Checkball No. 10 improperly located.
4. 3-4 accumulator valve stuck.

4T65-E TRANSAXLE

1. Low fluid level.

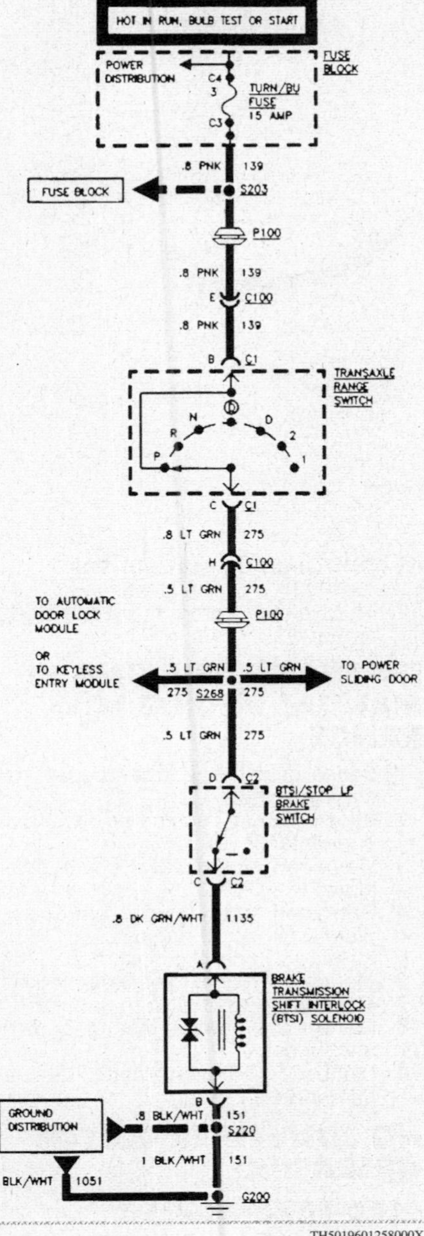

Fig. 3 BTSI wiring diagram

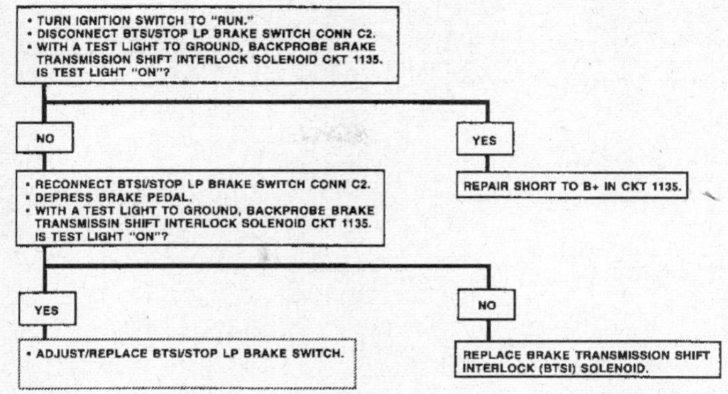

Fig. 4 BTSI diagnosis chart (Part 1 of 2)

2. Low or high main line fluid pressure.
3. Oil filter is plugged or damaged.
4. Misassembled 3-4 accumulator.
5. Missing or damaged 3-4 accumulator piston oil seal ring.
6. Stuck or binding 3-4 accumulator piston.
7. Debris in control valve body or spacer plate.
8. Misassembled, stuck or binding 3-4 accumulator valve.
9. Damaged or misassembled 3-4 accumulator valve spring or retainer.
10. Missing or damaged fourth clutch orifice in driven sprocket support.
11. Damaged driven sprocket support.
12. Worn, damaged or misassembled clutch plates in fourth clutch.
13. Fourth clutch spring not seated or missing.
14. Damaged piston or spring in fourth clutch.
15. Worn or damaged fourth clutch piston seals.

HIGH OR LOW UPSHIFT OR DOWNSHIFT SPEED

1. Incorrect PCM calibration.
2. Misadjusted or faulty TP sensor.

1ST & 2ND GEAR ONLY (2-3 SOLENOID STUCK ON)

1. Faulty 2-3 shift solenoid valve.
2. Debris in control valve body or spacer plate.

1ST & 4TH GEAR ONLY (1-2 SOLENOID STUCK ON)

1. Faulty 1-2, 3-4 shift solenoid valve.
2. Debris in control valve body or spacer plate.

2ND & 3RD GEAR ONLY (1-2 SOLENOID STUCK OFF)

1. Faulty 1-2, 3-4 shift solenoid valve.
2. Missing or damaged shift solenoid valve O-ring seal.
3. Plugged or damaged solenoid valve screen/seal.
4. Debris in control valve body or spacer plate.
5. Stuck, binding or missing actuator feed limit valve.

3RD & 4TH GEAR ONLY (2-3 SOLENOID STUCK OFF)

1. Faulty 2-3 shift solenoid valve.
2. Mislocated 2-3 shift solenoid valve and retainer.
3. Missing or damaged shift solenoid valve O-ring seal.
4. Plugged or damaged solenoid valve screen/seal.
5. Debris in control valve body or spacer plate.

1ST GEAR ONLY

1. Stuck or binding 1-2 shift valve.
2. Debris in control valve body or spacer plate.
3. Misassembled control valve body spacer plate or gaskets.
4. Second clutch backing plate retaining ring not seated or missing.
5. Second clutch backing plate misassembled.
6. Worn or damaged clutch plates in second clutch.
7. Second clutch spring retaining ring not seated or missing.
8. Second clutch housing ball check valve damaged or missing.
9. Damaged splines of reverse reaction drum.

2ND GEAR ONLY

1. Stuck or binding 1-2 shift valve.
2. Debris in control valve body or spacer plate.
3. Misassembled control valve body spacer plate or gaskets.
4. Damaged input sun gear.
5. Damaged input carrier planetary gear.

3RD GEAR ONLY

1. Debris in control valve body or spacer plate.
2. Misassembled control valve body spacer plate or gaskets.

4TH GEAR ONLY

1. Debris in control valve body or spacer plate.
2. Misassembled control valve body spacer plate or gaskets.

SLIPPING OR NO 1ST GEAR

1. Low fluid level.
2. Low fluid pressure.
3. Oil filter is plugged or damaged.
4. Oil filter seal is damaged or missing.
5. Loose or damaged forward band servo oil pipe.
6. Loose manual 2-1 band servo cover.
7. Damaged manual 2-1 servo cover gasket.
8. Damaged accumulator cover spacer plate.
9. Forward band servo piston oil seal ring is damaged.
10. Forward band servo piston is damaged or stuck in servo cover.
11. Forward band servo piston cushion

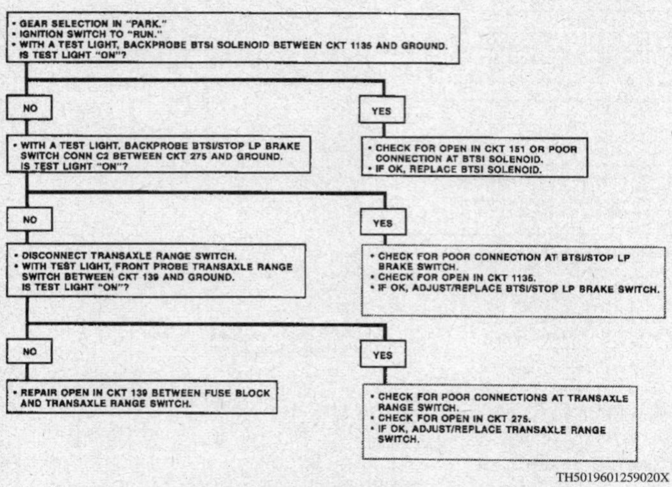

Fig. 4 BTSI diagnosis chart (Part 2 of 2)

1. CABLE, SHIFT
2. STUD, STRUT TOWER
3. LOCK, CABLE
4. NUT, RANGE SELECTOR LEVER
5. LEVER, RANGE SELECTOR
6. BRACKET, RANGE SELECTOR LEVER
7. BOLT/SCREW, RANGE SELECTOR LEVER CABLE BRACKET
8. CLIP, NEUTRAL START

GC5029400448000X

Fig. 5 Shift control cable adjustment

spring or retainer is missing or damaged.

12. Servo piston pin is not engaged to forward band.
13. Forward band is worn or burned.
14. Forward band is disengaged from anchor pin.
15. Band anchor pin is loose or missing.
16. 1-2 shift valve is stuck or binding.
17. Control valve body No. 3 check valve is missing.
18. Input clutch sprag is damaged or misassembled.
19. Input clutch housing oil seal rings are missing or damaged.
20. Input clutch housing ball check valve is damaged or missing.
21. Input clutch piston inner/outer seals are missing or damaged.
22. Input clutch piston is damaged.
23. Input clutch plates are worn.
24. 1-2 clutch roller is damaged.

SLIPPING OR NO 2ND GEAR

1. Low fluid level.
2. Low fluid pressure.
3. Oil filter is plugged or damaged.
4. Oil filter seal is damaged or missing.
5. 1-2 shift valve is stuck or binding.
6. Debris in control valve body or spacer plate.
7. Damaged second clutch housing oil seal rings.
8. Lobe oil seal rings damaged.
9. Second clutch housing bushings worn or damaged.
10. Second clutch backing plate retaining ring missing or not seated.
11. Second clutch backing plate misassembled.
12. Worn or damaged second clutch plates.
13. Second clutch spring retaining ring missing or not seated.
14. Damaged second clutch spring or piston.
15. Damaged second clutch housing ball check valve.
16. Damaged second clutch housing.

SLIPPING OR NO THIRD GEAR

1. Low fluid level.
2. Low fluid pressure.
3. Oil filter is plugged or damaged.
4. Oil filter seal is damaged or missing.
5. 2-3 shift valve or 3-2 manual downshift valve is stuck or binding.
6. Debris in control valve body or spacer plate.
7. No. 4 and No. 9 control valve body checkballs missing or mislocated.
8. Plugged third clutch oil passage in driven sprocket support.
9. Third clutch input clutch housing oil seal rings are missing or damaged.
10. Third clutch ball check valve is missing or damaged.
11. Third clutch piston is damaged.
12. Third clutch piston inner seal is missing or damaged.
13. Third clutch plates are worn or misassembled.
14. Third clutch sprag is damaged or misassembled.

SLIPPING OR NO 4TH GEAR

1. Low fluid level.
2. Low fluid pressure.
3. Oil filter is plugged or damaged.
4. Oil filter seal is damaged or missing.
5. Control valve body 3-4 shift valve or 4-3 manual downshift valve is stuck or binding.
6. Debris in control valve body or spacer plate.
7. Manual valve or case cover distorted or damaged.
8. Plugged third clutch oil passage in driven sprocket support.
9. Fourth clutch plates worn or misassembled.
10. Fourth clutch spring retaining ring missing or not seated.
11. Fourth clutch spring or piston damaged.
12. Third clutch sprag misassembled or damaged.

NO ENGINE BRAKING IN MANUAL 2ND OR LOW RANGE

1. Loose or damaged manual 2-1 band servo oil pipe.
2. Loose manual band servo cover or accumulator cover,
3. Damaged accumulator cover spacer plate.
4. Damaged servo piston seal or servo piston cylinder O-ring seal.
5. Missing servo exhaust screen.
6. Manual 2-1 servo misassembled.
7. Manual 2-1 band is worn or burned.
8. Manual 2-1 band is disengaged from anchor pin.
9. Manual 2-1 band anchor pin is loose or damaged.

NO CONVERTER CLUTCH OPERATION

4T60-E TRANSAXLE

1. Ensure proper PCM operation or wiring.
2. Pinched wires or damaged connectors.
3. Stuck converter clutch valve.
4. Stuck converter clutch regulator valve.
5. TCC solenoid O-ring leaking.
6. Solenoid screen blocked.
7. Damaged torque converter.
8. Damaged turbine shaft seals.
9. Damaged oil pump driveshaft seal.
10. Improperly seated or damaged converter clutch blow-off checkball.
11. No. 1 checkball missing.

4T65-E TRANSAXLE

1. TCC PWM solenoid is stuck off.
2. TCC control valve or TCC regulator apply valve is stuck or binding.
3. No. 10 control valve body check valve is missing or mislocated
4. Control valve body spacer plate and gaskets are misassembled.

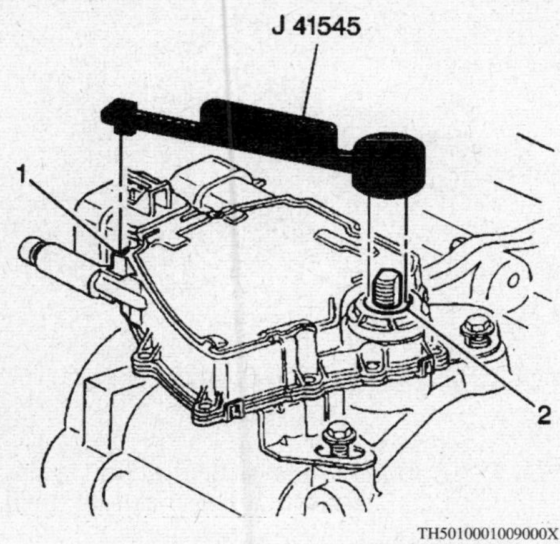

Fig. 6 PNP switch alignment

5. TCC blowoff ball valve or spring is damaged or not seating.
6. Turbine shaft O-ring seal is damaged or missing.
7. Turbine shaft oil seal rings are damaged or missing.
8. Turbine shaft is damaged.
9. Turbine shaft bushing is worn or damaged.
10. Torque converter is faulty.

CONVERTER CLUTCH DOES NOT RELEASE

4T60-E TRANSAXLE

1. No PCM signal to solenoid or defective solenoid, if equipped.
2. Sticking converter clutch apply piston.
3. Missing TCC orifice screen.

4T65-E TRANSAXLE

1. TCC control valve or TCC regulator apply valve is stuck or binding.
2. Control valve body spacer plate and gaskets are misassembled.
3. Faulty torque converter.

ROUGH CONVERTER CLUTCH OPERATION

1. Sticking converter clutch regulator valve.
2. Turbine shaft seals damaged or missing.
3. Converter clutch blow-off valve checkball damaged.
4. Drive sprocket support bushing worn.
5. Worn or glazed fiber material in torque converter.

HARSH CONVERTER CLUTCH APPLY OR RELEASE

1. TCC regulator apply valve stuck or binding.
2. TCC regulator apply valve spring is missing or damaged.
3. TCC control valve spring is missing or damaged.
4. Control valve body spacer plate or gaskets are misassembled.
5. Faulty torque converter.

HARSH 4-3 DOWNSHIFT

1. Control valve checkball No. 10 missing.

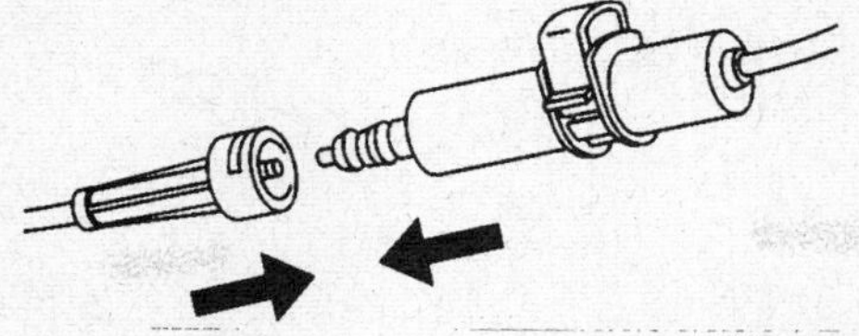

Fig. 7 A/T range selector cable connection

2. 3-4 accumulator seal cut or damaged.
3. 3-4 accumulator valve stuck.

HARSH 3-2 DOWNSHIFT

1. Control valve No. 9 checkball missing.
2. 2-3 accumulator seal cut or damaged.
3. 2-3 accumulator valve stuck.

HARSH 2-1 DOWNSHIFT

1. Wrong spacer plate installed.
2. 1-2 accumulator seal cut or damaged.
3. 1-2 accumulator valve stuck.

NO REVERSE IN R RANGE

1. Incorrect oil pressure.
2. Damaged reverse servo piston or seal.
3. Reverse servo improperly assembled or improper apply pin installed.
4. Damaged or defective oil pump.
5. Damaged input clutch accumulator piston seal.
6. Damaged drive link.
7. Burned, damaged or improperly installed reverse band.
8. Damaged or defective input clutch.
9. Defective input sprag.
10. Reverse reaction drum splines, input carrier and/or reaction carrier damaged.

SLIPS IN REVERSE

1. Incorrect oil pressure.
2. Damaged reverse servo seal.
3. Damaged reverse reaction carrier splines.
4. Refer to "Slips In Drive" comments.

WILL NOT HOLD IN PARK

1. Damaged or disconnect manual linkage.
2. Damaged parking pawl spring, pawl and/or parking gear.
3. Damaged actuator or actuator spring.

HARSH N-D OR D-N SHIFT

1. Improper vacuum signal to modulator or defective modulator.
2. Broken reverse servo cushion spring.
3. No. 5 checkball missing from control valve (harsh into reverse).
4. No. 6 checkball missing from control valve (harsh into drive).
5. Broken forward servo cushion spring.
6. Thermal element does not close when hot.

2ND GEAR STARTS

1-2 shift valve stuck.

HARSH ENGAGEMENT OR SHUDDER IN REVERSE

1. 2nd clutch housing drum surface

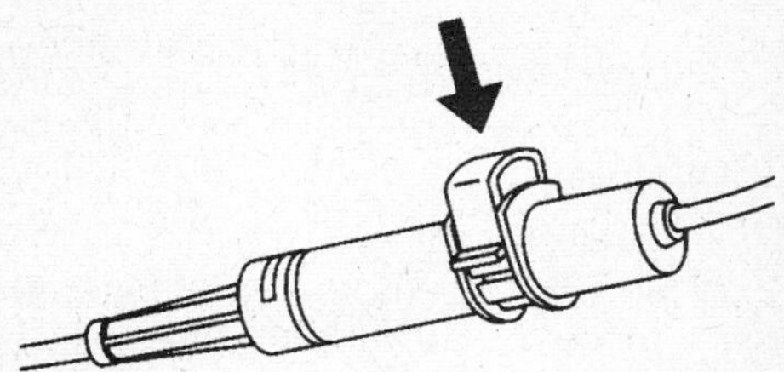

Fig. 8 Adjuster clip position

scored or hot spots caused by band slippage.
2. Burned fiber material on reverse band.
3. No. 5 checkball missing or mislocated.
4. Damaged servo cushion spring.

SHUDDER IN 1-2 SHIFT

1. 2nd clutch worn plates.
2. Leaking 2nd valve checkball.
3. 2nd clutch cut seal.
4. Damaged 2nd clutch plates.
5. Mispositioned 2nd clutch snap ring.

NO PARK RANGE

1. Park pawl spring.
2. Parking pawl.
3. Damaged parking gear.
4. Accumulator spring damage.

NO ENGINE BRAKING IN MANUAL 2ND OR LOW

1. 2-1 manual band burned or glazed material.
2. Cut or damaged seals.
3. Missing filter allowing foreign material to damage seal and bore.
4. Bolts improperly tightened.

BRAKE TRANSAXLE SHIFT INTERLOCK (BTSI)

1. Ensure brake light operation.
2. If brake lights do not operate, refer to **Fig. 3** for wiring diagram and **Fig. 4** for diagnostic procedure.
3. Inspect for proper installation of aftermarket equipment or for broken or partially broken wires inside of insulation. This could cause system failures, but not be indicated in continuity or voltage check.

MAINTENANCE

Refer to "Lubricant Data" chart in the appropriate chassis chapter of this manual for transmission fluid specifications.

FLUID CHECK

To check fluid, drive vehicle for at least 15 minutes to bring fluid to operating temperature (200°F). With vehicle on a level surface and engine idling in Park and parking brake applied, the level on the dipstick should be at the FULL mark. To bring the fluid level from the ADD mark to the FULL mark requires one pint of fluid. If vehicle cannot be driven sufficiently to bring fluid to operating temperature, the level on the dipstick should be between the two dimples on

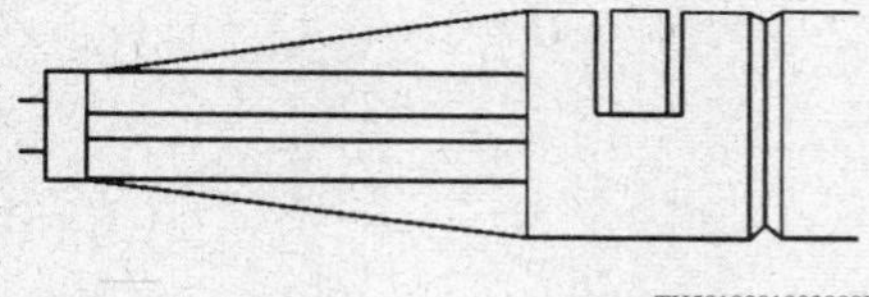

Fig. 9 Horseshoe clip engagement

the dipstick with fluid temperature at 70°F. Note that the two dimples are located above the FULL mark.

An early change to a darker color from the usual red color and/or a strong odor that is usually associated with overheated fluid is normal and should not be considered as a positive sign of required maintenance or unit failure.

When adding fluid, do not overfill, as foaming and loss of fluid through the vent may occur as the fluid heats up. Also, if fluid level is too low, complete loss of drive may occur especially when cold, which can cause transmission failure.

FLUID CHANGE

1. Raise and support vehicle. Position suitable drain pan under oil pan.
2. Remove front and side oil pan mounting bolts, then loosen rear pan mounting bolts.
3. Pry oil pan loose from transaxle case and allow fluid to drain.
4. Remove remaining mounting bolt, oil pan and gasket. Thoroughly clean pan before installing.
5. Remove and discard screen and O-ring seal.
6. Install replacement screen and O-ring seal, locating screen against dipstick stop.
7. Install gasket on oil pan and apply Loctite 242, or equivalent to oil pan bolts to prevent leakage.
8. Lower vehicle and add fluid.
9. With selector in park, parking brake applied and engine at idle speed and operating temperature, check fluid level and adjust fluid, as required. **Do not race engine or move shift lever through ranges.**

ADJUSTMENTS

SHIFT CONTROL CABLE

ACHEIVA, GRAND AM & SKYLARK

1. Apply parking brake and block wheels.
2. Position range selector into Neutral position.
3. Lift up range selector cable locking button.
4. Remove range selector cable end from transaxle range selector level, **Fig. 5.**
5. Position transaxle range selector lever into L position. Obtain L position by rotating transaxle range selector lever toward front of vehicle until it stops.
6. Snap range selector cable end onto transaxle range selector lever.
7. Press range selector cable locking button down into locked position.

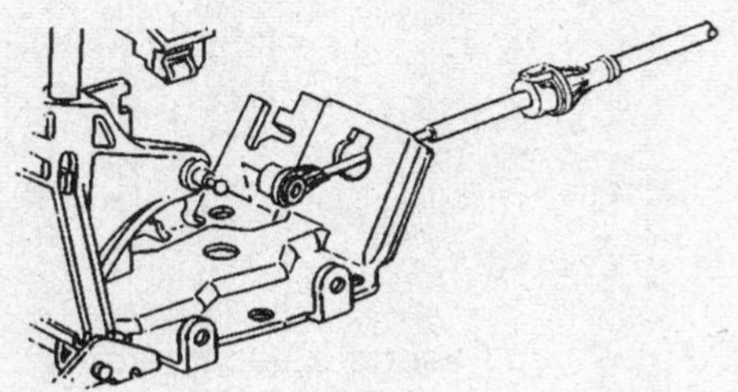

Fig. 10 Console shift control removal

8. Position range selector lever into PARK position.
9. Remove wheel blocks and release parking brake.

BONNEVILLE, EIGHTY EIGHT, LESABRE, LSS, PARK AVENUE, REGENCY & RIVIERA & 2001 AURORA

Adjust shift cable only when transaxle and gear selector are in N position. Failure to do so may result in shift cable misalignment.

1. Apply parking brake and remove shift cable terminal from transaxle manual shaft lever pin.
2. Lift lock button, ensuring adjuster is free to move.
3. Place manual shaft lever in N position by rotating fully counterclockwise to P position and rotating two audible clicks clockwise to desired position.
4. Place gear selector in N position.
5. Grasp shift cable terminal and pull toward pin on manual shaft lever.
6. Shift cable adjuster spring should compress as terminal is moved toward pin.
7. Attach pin to lever by pushing downward until it snaps.
8. Press adjuster lock button down flush with adjuster body.
9. Shift to P position and release parking brake while applying service brakes.
10. Start engine and ensure all indicated gear positions match vehicle response.

CENTURY, GRAND PRIX, IMPALA, INTRIGUE, LUMINA, MONTE CARLO & REGAL

Adjust shift cable only when transaxle and gear selector are in N position. Failure to do so may result in shift cable misalignment.

1. Apply parking brake and disconnect shift cables at both ends.
2. Do not attempt to separate metal couplings. Both cable sections will be damaged if two metal couplings are disconnected.
3. Push up to adjustment position to release adjuster until cable housings separate.
4. Depress adjuster clip once. This mobilizes adjuster housing toward transaxle end fitting.
5. Position end fittings so they slide together until parts can be felt coming together and locking.
6. Depress adjuster clip completely. This locks cable into adjusted position.

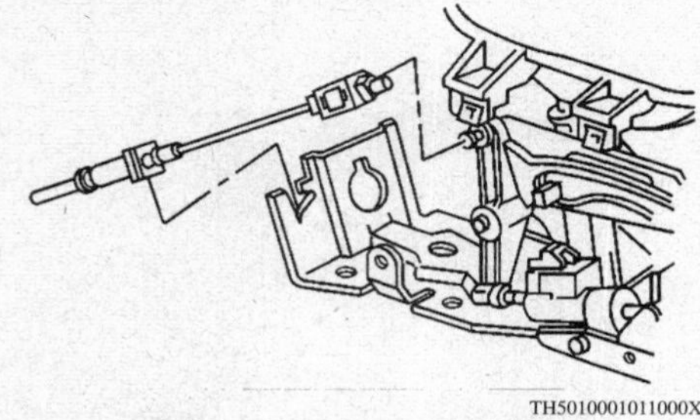

Fig. 11 Control shift cable removal

7. Pull conduit in opposite direction to ensure full system adjustment of shift cable.
8. Ensure conduit is fully engaged.
9. Horseshoe clip with tab is not flush when not fully engaged.
10. Install shift cable retainer and wiring harness clip or strap.
11. Start engine and ensure all indicated gear positions match vehicle response.

SHIFT CONTROL CABLE/AT RANGE SELECTOR CABLE

Adjust shift cable only when transaxle and gear selector are in N position. Failure to do so may result in shift cable misalignment.

BONNEVILLE, EIGHTY EIGHT, LESABRE, LSS, PARK AVENUE, REGENCY & RIVIERA & 2001 AURORA

1. Apply parking brake and remove shift cable terminal from transaxle manual shaft lever pin.
2. Lift lock button, ensuring adjuster is free to move.
3. Place manual shaft lever in N position by rotating fully counterclockwise to P position and rotating two audible clicks clockwise to neutral position.
4. Place gear selector in N position.
5. Grasp shift cable terminal and pull toward pin on manual shaft lever.
6. Shift cable adjuster spring should compress as terminal is moved toward pin.
7. Attach pin to lever by pushing downward until it snaps.
8. Press adjuster lock button down flush with adjuster body.
9. Shift to P position and release parking brake while applying service brakes.
10. Start engine and ensure all indicated gear positions match vehicle response.

CENTURY, GRAND PRIX, IMPALA, INTRIGUE, LUMINA, MONTE CARLO & REGAL

1. Apply parking brake and disconnect shift cables at both ends.
2. Do not attempt to separate metal couplings. Both cable sections will be damaged if two metal couplings are disconnected.
3. Push up to adjustment position to release adjuster until cable housings separate.

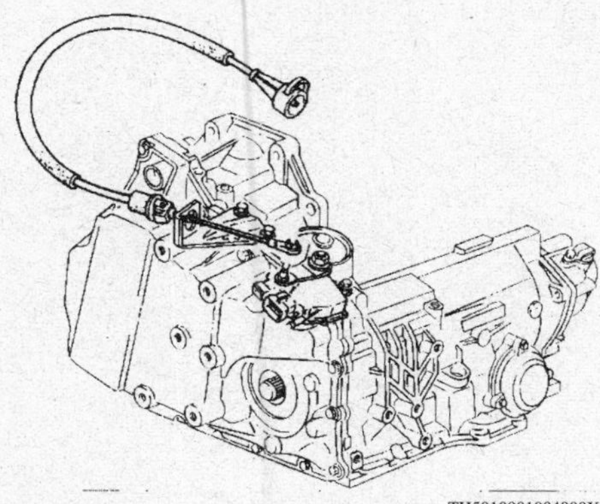

Fig. 12 Automatic transaxle selector cable removal

4. Depress adjuster clip once. This mobilizes adjuster housing toward transaxle end fitting.
5. Position end fittings so they slide together until parts can be felt coming together and locking.
6. Depress adjuster clip completely. This locks cable into adjusted position.
7. Pull conduit in opposite direction to ensure full system adjustment of shift cable.
8. Ensure conduit is fully engaged.
9. Horseshoe clip with tab is not flush when not fully engaged.
10. Install shift cable retainer and wiring harness clip or strap.
11. Start engine and ensure all indicated gear positions match vehicle response.

PNP SWITCH

1. Place shift shaft in Neutral position.
2. Align slots of PNP switch to neutral position using park/neutral switch alignment tool No. J-41545, or equivalent.
3. Align shift shaft and PNP switch flats.
4. Install PNP switch to mounting boss and loosely install mounting bolts.
5. Align PNP switch using alignment tool, **Fig. 6.**
6. Install mounting bolts.

IN-VEHICLE REPAIRS

SHIFT CONTROL CABLE/AT RANGE SELECTOR CABLE, REPLACE

The automatic transaxle range selector cable is made out of two cable sections. After initial connection, never separate the two metal couplings from one another.

1. Set parking brake and block wheels. Ensure shift control is in neutral position.
2. Connect each cable section, **Fig. 7**
3. Install to automatic transaxle range selector lever and shift cable bracket.
4. Install to column or console shift control, retainer and wiring harness clip.
5. Connect metal end fitting of shift control cable into transaxle cable end.
6. Ensure metal post of cables snaps into place.

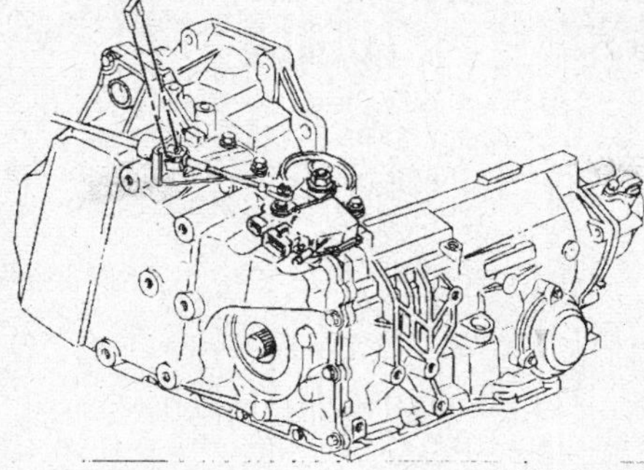

Fig. 13 Automatic transaxle selector cable removal/shift console

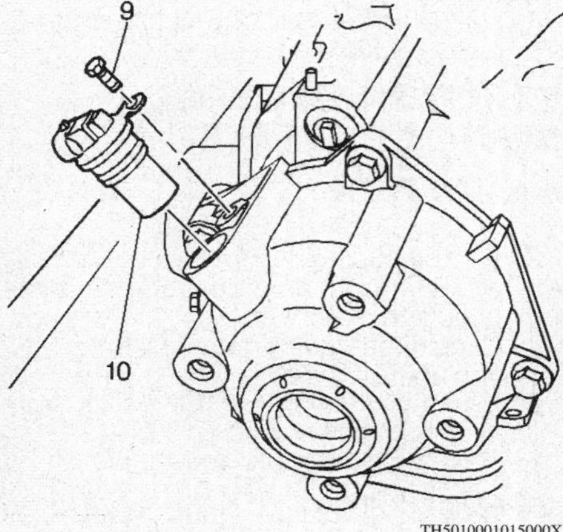

Fig. 15 Vehicle speed sensor removal

7. Depress adjuster clip once, this mobilizes adjuster housing toward transaxle end fitting.
8. Ensure end fittings are aligned so they slide together until parts come together and lock.
9. Depress adjuster clip completely. Pull conduit in opposite direction to ensure full system adjustment, **Fig. 8.**
10. Ensure horseshoe clip is flush, this will ensure conduit is engaged, **Fig. 9.**
11. Install shift cable retainer and wiring harness clip or strap.

FLOOR SHIFT CONTROL, REPLACE

1. Remove shift knob from shifter.
2. Remove console as outlined in "Shift Control Cable/AT Range Selector Cable, Console Switch."
3. Remove park/lock cable from floorshift control, **Fig. 10.**
4. Remove shift control cable from floorshift, **Fig. 11.**
5. Remove mounting bolts and floorshift control.
6. Reverse procedures to install.

SHIFT CONTROL CABLE/AT RANGE SELECTOR CABLE, PNP SWITCH, REPLACE

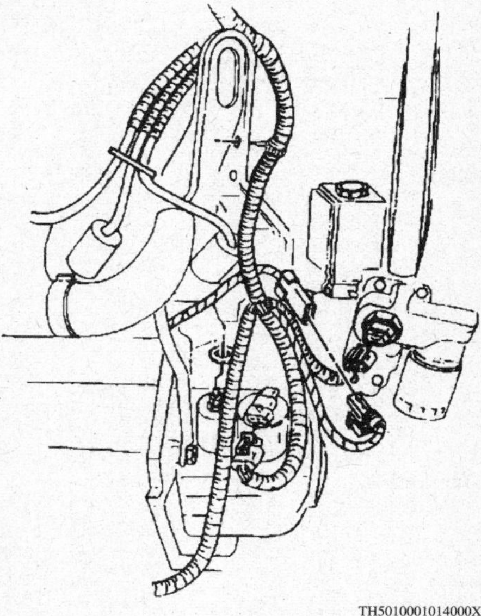

Fig. 14 Vehicle speed sensor electrical connector removal

The automatic transaxle range selector cable is made out of two cable sections. After initial connection, never separate the two metal couplings from one another.

1. Remove throttle body air inlet duct.
2. Remove automatic transaxle range selector cable from lever and bracket, **Fig. 12.**
3. Remove automatic transaxle range selector cable from console/column shift control, **Fig. 13.**
4. Pull automatic transaxle range selector cable through dash from engine compartment side.
5. Reverse procedures to install.

SHIFT CONTROL CABLE/AT RANGE SELECTOR CABLE, CONSOLE SWITCH, REPLACE

The automatic transaxle range selector cable is made out of two cable sections. After initial connection, never separate the two metal couplings from one another.

1. Remove automatic transaxle range selector cable from wiring harness clip or retainer in engine compartment.
2. Remove control lever handle retainer and handle.
3. Remove center trim plate and pry up plate over switches.
4. Disconnect electrical connector.
5. Remove console front and rear fasteners.
6. Remove console.
7. Pull carpet back to expose automatic transaxle range selector cable and remove cable from retaining clips.
8. Disengage, then remove automatic transaxle range selector cable retainer and cable from console shift control.
9. Remove automatic transaxle range selector cable through hole in cowl.
10. Remove automatic transaxle range selector cable from PNP switch.

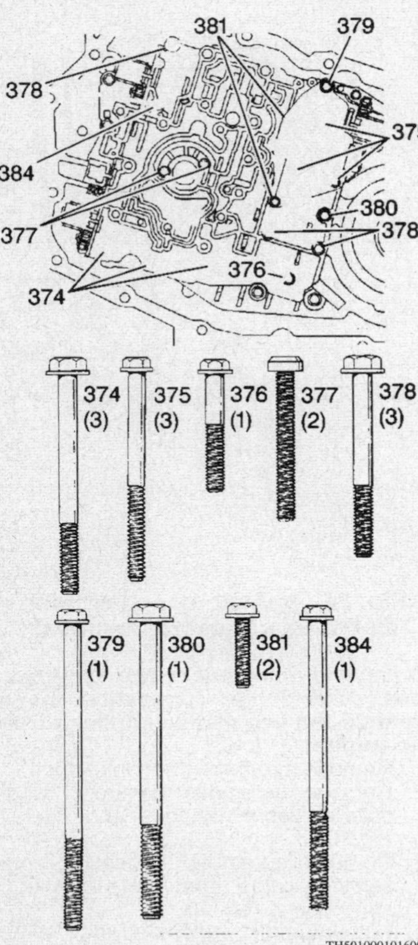

Fig. 16 Valve body removal

11. Reverse procedures to install.

BRAKE TRANSAXLE SHIFT INTERLOCK SOLENOID, REPLACE

CENTURY & REGAL

1. Place transaxle shift lever to Low position.
2. Remove front floor console trim plate by pulling upward on trim plate in order to release tabs from retainers.
3. Disconnect electrical connectors.
4. Remove front floor trim plate.
5. Remove rubber mat from storage compartment.
6. Remove bolts from front floor console mounting bracket.
7. Remove bolts from both sides of front floor console.
8. Disconnect electrical connectors.
9. Remove front floor console.
10. Remove spring clip and shift select cable from manual lever.
11. Remove E-clip and shift select cable from manual selector base.
12. Remove mounting bolts and manual selector.
13. Reverse procedures to install.

BONNEVILLE, EIGHTY EIGHT, LESABRE, LSS, PARK AVENUE, REGENCY & RIVIERA

1. Remove lever handle from shifter.
2. Disassemble and remove center console as outlined in "Shift Control Cable/AT Range Selector Cable, Console Switch."
3. Remove park/lock cable from shift control.
4. Remove shift control cable from shift control.
5. Disconnect electrical connectors.
6. Remove shift control.
7. Remove BTSI solenoid from steering column lower support with trim pad removal tool No. J-38778, or equivalent.
8. Remove BTSI from shift control cable with suitable flat bladed screwdriver.
9. Reverse procedure to install. Inspect shift lever for proper function and adjust shift cable as required.

TRACTION CONTROL SWITCH, REPLACE

GRAND PRIX

1. Open console storage lid.
2. Ensure cup holder is open.
3. Remove front floor console trim plate bolts and plate.
4. Disconnect wiring harness from traction control switch.
5. Remove traction control switch from front floor console trim plate.
6. Reverse procedures to install.

VEHICLE SPEED SENSOR

1. Raise and support vehicle as required.
2. Remove front righthand tire and wheel.
3. Remove righthand engine splash shield.
4. Remove electrical connector at vehicle speed sensor, **Fig. 14.**
5. Remove mounting bolt and sensor, **Fig. 15.**
6. Reverse procedures to install.

VALVE BODY, REPLACE

1. Remove throttle body air inlet duct or air cleaner inlet duct from engine.
2. Install engine support fixture tool No. J-28467-A, or equivalent.
3. Remove engine mount struts.
4. Raise and support vehicle.
5. Remove lefthand front wheel.
6. Remove lefthand engine splash shield.
7. Remove stabilizer shaft bracket from lower control arms
8. Remove stabilizer shaft link bolts and nuts.
9. Remove stabilizer shaft link.
10. Remove front wheel drive shaft bearing.
11. Remove front lower control arm ball stud to knuckle cotter pin and nut.
12. Separate front lower control arm stud from front steering knuckle using ball joint/stud separator tool No. J-41820, or equivalent.
13. Remove outer tie rod to steering knuckle.
14. Scribe strut to knuckle.

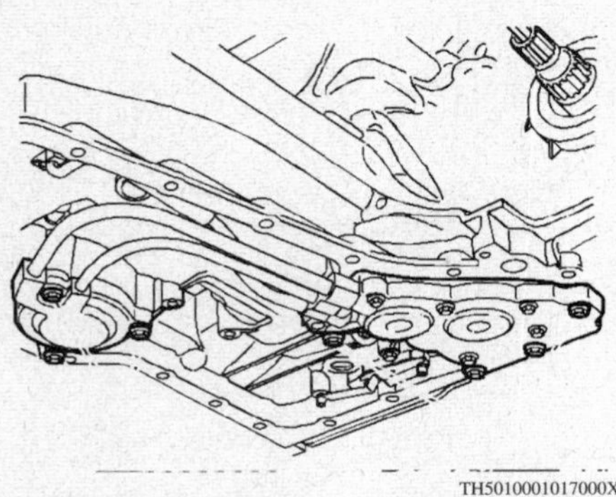

Fig. 17 Accumulator mounting bolt removal

15. Remove mounting bolts and knuckle.
16. Remove wheel speed sensor harness connector.
17. Remove lower control arm.
18. Secure lower control arm in suitable vice.
19. Drill or grind off ball stud rivet heads.
20. Use hammer or drift punch to remove rivets.
21. Remove ball stud from lower control arm.
22. Remove front wheel drive shaft nut. Insert suitable flat bladed tool into caliper and rotor to prevent rotor from turning.
23. Ensure outer tie rod is disconnected.
24. Ensure ball joint and steering knuckle are separated.
25. Separate front wheel drive axle from front wheel drive shaft bearing using front hub spindle tool No. J-28733-B, or equivalent.
26. Remove front wheel drive axle from transaxle.
27. Secure drive axle to steering knuckle or strut.
28. Position intermediate steering shaft seal to access lower pinch bolt.
29. Remove intermediate steering shaft lower pinch bolt from power steering gear stub shaft.
30. Remove intermediate shaft from steering gear.
31. Disconnect catalytic converter pipe to righthand rear exhaust manifold.
32. Support left and righthand side of frame with jackstands.
33. Remove transaxle bracket to transaxle mount upper nuts and bolts.
34. Remove transaxle bracket.
35. Remove lower mounting nuts and transaxle mount.
36. Loosen engine mount lower nuts.
37. Position jackstand under engine for support.
38. Loosen righthand side frame to body bolts.
39. Remove lefthand side frame to body bolts.
40. Adjust jackstand to lower lefthand side of frame.
41. Position suitable drain pan under transaxle.
42. Remove wiring harness connector.
43. Remove case side cover bolts.
44. Remove case side cover and side

cover inner gasket.
45. Remove oil pump to valve body bolts, **Fig. 16.**
46. Remove valve body to channel plate bolts.
47. Remove valve body, leaving spacer plate with transmission.
48. Remove spacer plate and spacer plate gasket as required.
49. Remove solenoid screens.
50. Reverse procedure to install. Apply assembly lube part No. J-36850 Transjel, or equivalent, to components.

ACCUMULATOR, REPLACE

1. Raise and support vehicle.
2. Drain transaxle fluid into suitable container and remove oil pan.
3. Remove oil filter and seal, then the mounting bolts and accumulator cover, **Fig. 17.**
4. Remove accumulator, **Fig. 18.**
5. Remove 2-1 manual servo piston cover bolts.
6. Remove 2-1 manual servo piston and filter, then the seal, **Fig. 19.**
7. Disassemble, then inspect accumulator and 2-1 manual servo.
8. Reverse procedure to install.

REVERSE SERVO, REPLACE

1. Remove air cleaner.
2. Remove righthand exhaust manifold.
3. Raise drivers side of car so it is higher than differential side.
4. Depress servo cover, then remove snap ring, servo cover, servo piston, sealing ring, apply pin and servo spring, **Fig. 20.**
5. Reverse procedure to install.

FORWARD SERVO, REPLACE

1. Install engine support fixture tool No. J-28467-A, engine support fixture adapter tool No. J-28467-90 and engine support adapter leg tool No. J-36462, or equivalents.
2. Raise and support vehicle.
3. Remove power steering rack and pinion heat shield.
4. Remove power steering rack and pinion mounting bolts and hang steering rack from exhaust pipe flange.
5. Disconnect transaxle and engine mounts.
6. Support rear of frame with suitable jackstand, loosen front frame bolts and remove rear frame bolts.
7. Lower frame from jackstand and disconnect power steering lines from righthand side of frame.
8. Remove mounting bolts, servo cover, servo piston, sealing ring, apply pin, servo spring retainer and servo spring, **Fig. 21.**
9. Reverse procedure to install.

TRANSAXLE

REPLACE

ACHIEVA, GRAND AM & SKYLARK

1. Remove air intake duct.

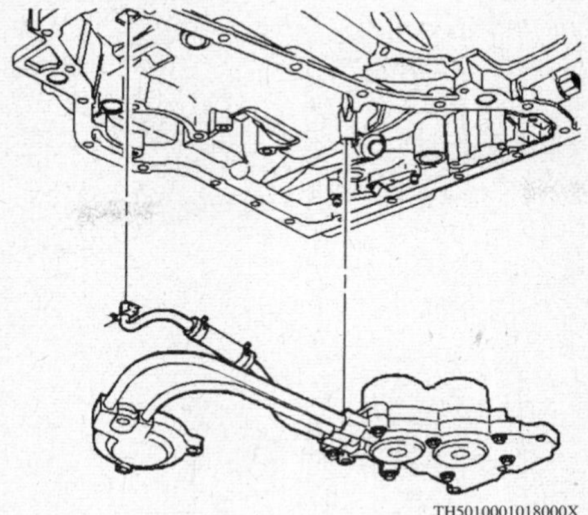

Fig. 18 Accumulator removal

2. Remove shift linkage from transmission.
3. Disconnect vacuum modulator line at modulator.
4. Disconnect electrical connectors from torque converter clutch, park/neutral position switch and shift solenoid.
5. Support engine using engine support fixture tool No. J-28467-360, or equivalent.
6. Remove two top transmission to engine mounting bolts.
7. Remove rubber hose from transmission to vent pipe and remaining upper engine to transmission mounting bolts.
8. Raise and support vehicle, then remove both front wheels.
9. Remove left and righthand splash shield.
10. Remove both front ABS wheel speed sensors and harness from lefthand side suspension support.
11. Remove both ball joints from control arms and lefthand stabilizer shaft link pin bolt.
12. Remove lefthand stabilizer shaft frame bushing clamp nuts.
13. Remove lefthand suspension support and drive axles.
14. Remove engine to transmission brace and starter motor.
15. Remove transmission converter cover, then the heater core hose pipe brace to transmission mounting nut and bolt.
16. Remove torque converter to flywheel mounting bolts. Mark flywheel to torque converter relationship for proper installation.
17. Remove oil level indicator and fill tube, then the transmission oil cooler pipes. Plug pipes.
18. Remove vehicle speed sensor and vacuum reserve tank.
19. Position suitable transmission jack under transmission.
20. Remove transmission mount to body mounting bolts and remaining engine to transmission mounting bolts.
21. Remove transmission.
22. Reverse procedure to install.

AURORA

1. Support engine with engine support adapters tool No. J-28467-90A, engine support adapter leg set tools No. J-36462-A and universal engine support fixture tool No. J-28467-B, or equivalents.
2. Remove air cleaner.
3. Disconnect transaxle electrical connector.
4. Disconnect shift control cable bracket with cable attached.
5. Remove six upper transaxle case to engine bolts.
6. Remove upper bolt from rear transaxle mount.
7. Disconnect oxygen sensor connector.
8. Remove vacuum reservoir.
9. Raise and support vehicle, then remove tire and wheel assemblies. Allow control arms to hang free.
10. Disconnect stabilizer link to control arm bolt.
11. Remove cotter pin and loosen ball stud nut.
12. Install suitable drive axle joint seal protectors.
13. Remove ball joints from steering knuckle using ball joint separator tool No. J-43828, or equivalent.
14. Remove push in retainers and lefthand front wheelhouse extension.
15. Disconnect Secondary Air Injection (AIR) pump and leave on frame.
16. Unbolt ABS module from lefthand front bracket.
17. Remove left and righthand front splash shields.
18. Remove retainers and front air deflector.
19. Remove steering gear heat shield.
20. Remove mounting bolts and power steering lines' brackets from engine frame.
21. Remove front and rear transmission mounts' mounting nuts.
22. Remove steering gear mounting bolts.
23. Support engine frame with suitable jack.
24. Remove frame insulator bolts, lower and remove frame.
25. Loosen or remove stabilizer shaft link mounting bolts, as required.
26. Remove hub nuts. Keep rotor from turn by inserting suitable drift or screwdriver into caliper and rotor.
27. Disconnect axles from hub using front hub spindles remover tool No. J-28733-B, or equivalent. Hubs may be partially installed to protect threads.
28. Move struts and knuckles rearward.
29. **Do not overextend wheel drive shafts.**
30. Disengage drive axles from transaxle using axle shaft remover tool No. J-42128 and slide hammer tool No. J-2619-01 with adapter, or equivalents.
31. Remove drive axles.
32. Remove mounting bolts and torque converter cover.
33. Remove flywheel to torque converter mounting bolts. Mark flywheel to converter relationship to ensure proper assembly.
34. Disconnect input speed sensor electrical connectors.
35. Remove engine to transaxle brace.
36. Remove bracket mounting bolt, fluid filler tube and seal.

37. Remove mounting bolt, nuts and righthand transaxle mount.
38. Remove remaining transaxle to engine bolts.
39. Remove transaxle using suitable transmission jack.
40. Reverse procedure to install, noting the following:
    a. Align transaxle with engine alignment dowels.
    b. **Do not use paints, lubricants, or corrosion inhibitors on mounting bolts, nuts and screws or their mounting surfaces unless specified.**
    c. Apply Dexron III ATF, or equivalent, to fluid filler tube seal.
    d. **Do not place seal on fluid filler tube when installing.**
    e. Inspect transaxle tripot housing seal surface for corrosion.
    f. Remove corrosion using suitable 320 grit emery cloth in rotational motion until smooth.
    g. Lubricate tripot housing surface with suitable clean ATF.
    h. Use care when installing righthand side drive axle into transaxle case.
    i. Splined shaft can easily damage seal.
    j. Ensure drive axle is seated by grasping inner joint housing and pulling.
    k. **Do not pull on drive axle shaft.**
    l. Install new hub nut.
    m. **Torque** ball joint nut to 88 inch lbs.
    n. Then, tighten two flats to minimum **torque** of 41 ft. lbs. to align cotter pin slot.
    o. Ensure transaxle range selector cable functions properly.

BONNEVILLE, EIGHTY EIGHT, LSS, LESABRE & REGENCY

1. Loosen bar through-bolts.
2. Remove inboard strut nuts.
3. Remove cross brace.
4. Install inboard strut nuts.
5. Remove air intake duct.
6. Remove cruise control cable at throttle body, vacuum hoses at servo and servo.
7. Remove shift control linkage mounting bracket at transaxle and lever at manual shaft.
8. Disconnect wiring connectors at: transaxle Park/Neutral Position switch and back up lamp switch, transaxle electrical connector and vehicle speed sensor.
9. Remove fuel pipe retainers and disconnect vacuum modulator hose at modulator.
10. Remove top three transaxle-to-engine bolts and install engine support fixture. **Load support fixture by tightening wing nuts several turns to relieve tension on frame and mounts.**
11. Raise and support vehicle.
12. Remove front wheel and ball joint assemblies.
13. Separate control arms from steering knuckles. **Drive axle seal protector tool No. J-34754, or equivalent,**

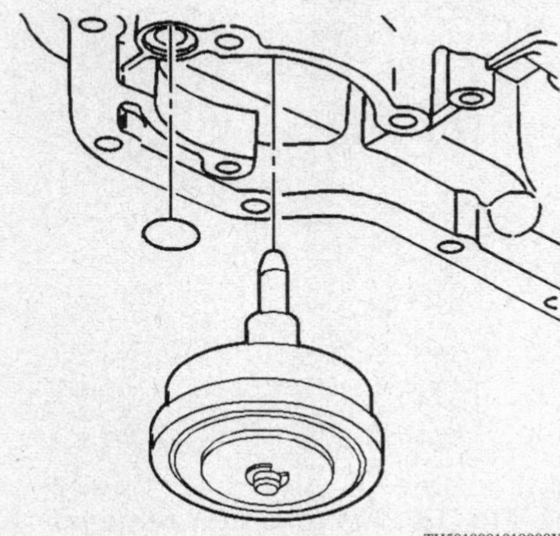

Fig. 19 Manual 2-1 servo removal

should be modified and installed on any drive axle prior to service.

14. Remove righthand drive axle from transaxle only. **Do not remove from hub/knuckle.**
15. Remove lefthand drive axle from transaxle and hub/knuckle.
16. Support transaxle with jackstand and remove lefthand front transaxle mount.
17. Remove torque strut bracket from transaxle and lefthand rear transaxle mount-to-transaxle bolts.
18. Remove transaxle brace from engine bracket and stabilizer shaft link-to-control arm bolt.
19. Remove flywheel cover bolts, flywheel cover and flywheel-to-converter bolts. Mark flywheel to converter relationship to ensure proper installation.
20. Remove bolts mounting rear frame member to front frame dog leg.
21. Remove front lefthand frame-to-body bolts and front lefthand frame dog leg-to-righthand frame member bolts.
22. Remove frame by swinging aside and supporting with suitable stand, then disconnect cooler pipes at transaxle.
23. Remove remaining transaxle-to-engine bolts. **One bolt is located between transaxle case and engine block and is installed in opposite direction.**
24. Lower transaxle.
25. Reverse procedure to install.

CENTURY, GRAND PRIX, IMPALA, INTRIGUE, MONTE CARLO, LUMINA & REGAL

1. Remove throttle body air inlet duct.
2. Install engine support adapter tool No. J-28467-90, or equivalent
3. Install engine support fixture tool No. J-28467-A, or equivalent.
4. Install engine support adapter leg set tool No. J-36462, or equivalent.
5. **On models with 3.1L and 3.5L engine,** remove engine mount struts as follows:
    a. Remove engine mount strut from lefthand engine mount strut bracket.
    b. Remove mounting bolts and engine mount strut bracket from lefthand cylinder head.
    c. Remove air conditioning compressor mounting bolts.
    d. Remove and set aside air conditioning compressor.
    e. Remove vertical bolt and righthand strut bracket.
    f. Remove engine mount struts.
6. **On models equipped with 3.8L engine,** remove engine mount struts as follows:
    a. Remove bolt and nut from left/righthand engine mount strut at left/righthand engine mount bracket on engine and upper radiator support.
    b. Remove engine mount struts.
7. **On all models,** remove wiring harness connectors from transaxle.
8. Remove auto transaxle range selector cable from PNP switch as described in "Shift Control Cable/AT Range Selector Cable, PNP Switch."
9. Remove automatic transaxle range selector from selector lever.
10. Remove automatic transaxle range selector cable from bracket.
11. Remove mounting bolts and cable bracket.
12. Remove mounting bolts and PNP switch.
13. Disconnect HO2S wiring harness connectors and retainers.
14. Support exhaust system.
15. Remove catalytic converter bolts and gasket.
16. Remove exhaust manifold pipe stud nuts.
17. Remove catalytic converter.
18. Remove bracket mounting bolt and fluid filler tube.
19. Remove upper transaxle bolts and wiring harness grounds.
20. Raise and support vehicle.
21. Remove front wheel and tire assemblies.
22. Remove engine splash shields.
23. Remove stabilizer link shaft bolts and nuts.
24. Remove stabilizer link from vehicle.
25. Remove front wheel drive shaft nut, inserting suitable flat bladed tool into caliper/rotor to prevent rotor from turning.
26. Remove prevailing torque nut from outer tie rod.
27. Loosen jam nut on inner tie rod.
28. Remove outer tie rod from steering knuckle using tie rod puller tool No. J-24319-01, or equivalent.
29. Remove power steering gear heat shield.
30. Remove power steering gear mounting bolts and power steering gear from frame.
31. Secure power steering gear with wire and remove power steering cooler line clamps from frame.
32. Remove engine mount lower nuts.
33. Remove lower ball joints from steering knuckles.
34. Remove torque converter cover and starter motor.
35. Remove torque converter bolts and drain transaxle fluid into suitable container.

36. Remove transaxle cooler hoses from transaxle.
37. Disconnect drive axles from transaxle, then secure to steering knuckles and struts.
38. Disconnect wheel speed sensor and vehicle speed sensor wiring harness connectors.
39. Support transaxle and frame, then remove transaxle brace.
40. Remove lower transaxle bolt and stud.
41. Remove frame to body bolts, lower transaxle and frame.
42. Remove transaxle from frame.
43. Reverse procedure to install.

PARK AVENUE

1. Remove air cleaner cover and disconnect transaxle electrical connector.
2. Disconnect shift control cable bracket with cable attached.
3. Remove top transaxle case bolts and top bolt from rear transaxle mount.
4. Remove lefthand steering gear mount bolts.
5. Disconnect O2 sensor connector.
6. Install engine support fixture J-28467-A, or equivalent.
7. Load fixture by tightening wing nuts several turns to relieve tension on frame and mounts.
8. Raise and support vehicle.
9. Remove wheel and tire assemblies.
10. Remove lefthand splash shield.
11. Remove power steering line bracket from engine frame.
12. Remove righthand splash shield and lefthand transaxle mount from engine frame.
13. Remove righthand transaxle mount from frame.
14. Remove righthand steering rack mount bolts from engine frame.
15. Secure steering gear to exhaust with wire.
16. Disconnect transaxle cooler lines from engine frame.
17. Remove sway bar mounts from lower control arms.
18. Separate lower ball joints from steering knuckles and hand tighten ball joint nuts.
19. Remove engine frame bolts.
20. Remove ball joint nuts and lower engine frame.
21. Remove drive axles from transaxle.
22. Remove cover and torque converter bolts.
23. Mark flywheel to torque converter position for proper assembly.
24. Disconnect input speed sensor connectors.
25. Remove engine to transaxle bracket.
26. Remove transaxle fluid filler tube.
27. Remove rear engine mount and remaining transaxle bolts.
28. Remove transaxle.
29. Reverse procedure to install.

RIVIERA

1. Remove air intake duct.
2. Disconnect cruise control cable at throttle body, shift control cables and brackets from transaxle.

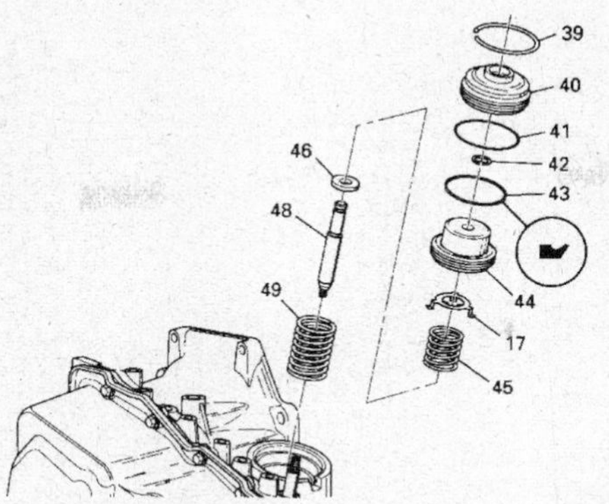

17 RETAINER, SERVO SPRING (1ST AND 2ND)
39 RING, SERVO COVER RETAINING
40 COVER, SERVO
41 SEAL, O-RING (SERVO COVER)
42 RING, INTERNAL RETAINING
43 RING, OIL SEAL PISTON
44 PISTON, SERVO REVERSE
45 SPRING, REVERSE SERVO CUSHION
46 RETAINER, SERVO CUSHION SPRING
48 PIN, REVERSE APPLY
49 SPRING, SERVO RETURN

TH5029500808000X

Fig. 20 Reverse servo

3. Disconnect vacuum line and electrical connectors from transaxle.
4. Remove exhaust crossover pipe and heater hose retainer bracket.
5. Disconnect oxygen sensor connector and remove top transaxle to engine bolts.
6. Install engine support fixture tool No. J-28467-A, or equivalent, and raise powertrain slightly to relieve tension on mounts.
7. Raise and support vehicle.
8. Remove both front wheels.
9. Remove lefthand steering rack mounting bolts and lefthand front splash shield.
10. Remove left and righthand ball joint mounting nuts, then separate both control arms from knuckles.
11. Remove lower front air deflector and power steering line brackets at frame.
12. Remove righthand side steering rack through bolt and support frame with suitable jack.
13. Remove left and righthand transaxle mount through bolts, then frame.
14. Remove flywheel cover and mark torque converter and flywheel for assembly.
15. Remove torque converter to flywheel bolts.
16. Remove starter and disconnect speed sensor connector.
17. Remove drive axles.
18. Support transaxle with suitable jackstand and remove rear transaxle mount.
19. Disconnect righthand side spark plug wires from spark plugs and remove transaxle filler tube.
20. Remove righthand exhaust manifold and lower transaxle to engine bolts.
21. Disconnect transaxle oil cooler lines and remove rear transaxle mount bracket.
22. Remove transaxle.
23. Reverse procedure to install, noting the following:
    a. Ensure torque converter to flywheel match marks are aligned.
    b. Tighten mounting bolts in two steps.
    c. Tighten engine to transaxle brace engine bolts first, then transaxle bolts.
    d. Installing righthand axle using seal protector tool No. J-37292-B, or equivalent.

TECHNICAL SERVICE BULLETINS

NOISE AND/OR VIBRATION DURING LOW SPEED ACCELERATION

1999 PARK AVENUE & RIVIERA

On some of these models built before Park Avenue VIN 4623629 and Riviera VIN 4701065 there may be a noise and/or vibration during low speed acceleration or brake torquing. This sound may be similar to that of the exhaust system contacting the floor pan.

This condition may be caused by the rear transaxle mount grounding out because of a bound or twisted condition within the mount.

To correct this condition, proceed as follows:

1. Raise and suitably support vehicle.
2. Disconnect and position heat shield aside to access rear transaxle mount upper two nuts.
3. Support transaxle rear with suitable floor jack.
4. Remove upper two nuts retaining bracket to transaxle rear mount.
5. Remove lower two bolts and nut retaining mount to engine frame.
6. Raise transaxle using suitable floor jack, then remove rear transaxle mount.
7. Install rear transaxle mount to engine frame.
8. Lower transaxle until bracket contacts rear transaxle mount using suitable floor jack.
9. Position rear transaxle mount to align mounting holes, as required.
10. Install lower two bolts and nut.
11. Lower transaxle completely onto rear transaxle mount.
12. **Torque** mounting bolts and nut to 37 ft. lbs.
13. Install upper two nuts. **Torque** nuts to 30 ft. lbs.
14. Remove floor jack.
15. Install steering gear heat shield.
16. Ensure frame mounts are not bound up and are properly seated. If engine frame mounts are bound up or are not properly seated, proceed as follows:
    a. Loosen engine frame mount.
    b. Unbind and seat engine frame mounts (shake engine down).

HARSH UPSHIFT/GARAGE SHIFT, LAUNCH SHUDDERS

1999–2000 LESABRE, PARK AVENUE, REGAL & RIVIERA & 1999 BONNEVILLE, EIGHTY EIGHT, GRAND PRIX, INTRIGUE, LUMINA & MONTE CARLO

On some of these models there may be harsh upshifts or harsh garage shifts, soft shifts, shudders on hard acceleration, or erratic shifts

This condition may be caused by sediment inside the Pressure Control Solenoid (PCS) or the valve body, or incorrect transaxle oil level.

To correct this condition replace the pressure control solenoid valve.

HARSH 3-4 SHIFT

1998 PARK AVENUE, LESABRE, RIVIERA & REGAL

On some of these models there may be harsh 3-4 shift.

This condition may be caused by a scored 3-4 accumulator valve and/or accumulator valve bore.

To correct this condition replace the valve body.

DELAYED SHIFTS, SLIPS, FLARES OR EXTENDED SHIFTS DURING COLD OPERATION

2001 AURORA, BONNEVILLE, CENTURY, GRAND PRIX, IMPALA, INTRIGUE, LESABRE, LUMINA, MONTE CARLO, PARK AVENUE & REGAL

On some of these models there may be delayed shifts, slips, flares or extended shifts during cold operation. This condition affects 1-2 shift only. The transmission won't shift out of 1st gear until the temperature is high enough to unstick the solenoid. This condition can last up to several shift patterns. These symptoms can return after the vehicle sits, usually six hours or more.

This condition may be caused by the 1-2, 3-4 shift solenoid valve not exhausting.

To correct this condition replace the 1-2, 3-4 shift solenoid valve.

HIGH EFFORT TO OPERATE RANGE SELECTOR LEVER

1998–2000 PARK AVENUE

On some of these models built before VIN Y4129012 there may be a high effort to move the gear shift control lever to a desired position. The high effort can occur in either direction.

This condition may be caused by the range selector lever cable.

To correct this condition remove the transaxle range selector lever cable with an improved unit (part No. 25713062).

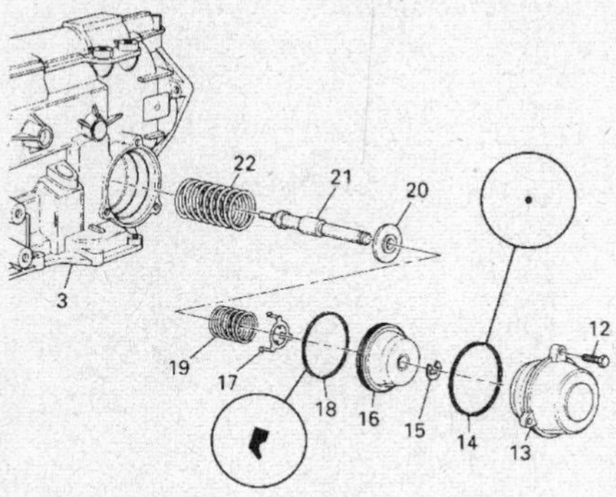

3 CASE, TRANSMISSION
12 BOLT, FWD. SERVO COVER TO CASE M6 X 1.0 X 20.0 (3)
13 COVER, FORWARD SERVO
14 SEAL, O-RING (SERVO COVER)
15 RING, INTERNAL RETAINING
16 PISTON, SERVO FORWARD
17 RETAINER, SERVO SPRING (1ST AND 2ND)
18 RING, OIL SEAL PISTON
19 SPRING, FORWARD SERVO CUSHION
20 RETAINER, SERVO CUSHION SPRING
21 PIN, FORWARD BAND APPLY
22 SPRING, SERVO RETURN

TH5029500807000X

Fig. 21 Forward servo

HIGH EFFORT TO TURN IGNITION KEY/REMOVE SHIFT LEVER FROM PARK

2000 BONNEVILLE & IMPALA

On some of these models equipped with column shift the transaxle shift lever may be difficult to move from the park position. In addition, it may take a high effort to rotate or turn the ignition key.

This condition may be caused by a steering column mounted linear shift control cable that attaches to the ignition switch being too long and routed incorrectly.

To correct this condition install a new shorter cable with adjustment feature (Bonneville part No. 26089928 and Impala part No. 26064241) as follows:

1. Disarm air bag system as outlined in "Passive Restraint Systems" chapter.
2. Remove lefthand side lower instrument panel insulator.
3. **On Bonneville models,** proceed as follows:
   a. Remove cover and driver's side knee bolster.
   b. Remove ignition lock/switch and instrument cluster bezels.
4. **On Impala models,** proceed as follows:
   a. Remove lower steering column filler panel.
   b. Remove aluminum knee bolster bracket.
5. **On all models,** remove tilt lever.
6. Remove lower and upper steering column covers.
7. **On Bonneville models,** remove two nuts, loosen two bolts and lower steering column for access to linear shift control cable assembly.
8. **On Impala models,** remove two support mounting nuts and lower column.
9. **On all models,** cut any plastic tie bands that secure or route cable assembly to ignition switch, noting the following:
   a. **Plastic tie bands have to be replaced when servicing linear shift control cable assembly.**
   b. **Do not remove plastic tie bands from new assembly.**
10. **On Impala models,** depress black tab on end of cable and pull cable out of backside of ignition switch/lock cylinder.
11. **On all models,** disconnect shift cable and brake/transaxle safety interlock rod from linear shift control cable.
12. Remove mounting screw and shift lever. Discard screw.
13. Remove three linear shift control cable mounting screws. Discard screws.
14. **On Bonneville models,** proceed as follows:
   a. Remove radio.
   b. Remove ignition lock/switch from instrument panel.
   c. Depress black tab on end of cable and pull cable out of backside of ignition lock/switch.
15. **On all models,** remove linear shift control cable.
16. Reverse procedure to install, noting the following:
   a. Inspect cable routing for clearance with brake switches.
   b. Ensure shift control works properly.
   c. Adjust cable length by moving white adjustment tab outwards from adjuster body located in middle of cable.
   d. Move shift lever from PARK to REVERSE and back to PARK position.
   e. Turn ignition key to OFF position.
   f. Press white adjustment tab inwards until it locks in place.
   g. Ensure proper operation.

SHIFT LEVER IS DIFFICULT TO MOVE

1998–2001 CENTURY

On some of these models the range selector lever is difficult to move/shift.

This condition may be caused by the original shift lever not imparting enough mechanical advantage on the shift linkage to provide low enough effort when shifting gears.

To correct this condition, install improved revised shift lever, noting the following:

1. Shift levers do not have part numbers on them.
2. Identify lever version by shape, length and style.
3. Original part is an S-shaped lever that is slightly shorter than new design.
4. Base of lever where plastic covering begins, is a single flared plastic stop.
5. Revised lever has double ringed raised lever stop.

SHAKING SENSATION BETWEEN 35–55 MPH

1998–99 CENTURY & REGAL

On some of these models there may be a shaking sensation when between 35–55 mph on a smooth road surface with curves or dips. This condition may be further aggravated by elevated ambient temperatures.

This condition may be caused by engine being vertically displaced or bounced in its' mounts, resulting in the transmitting of a vibration into the body structure.

To correct this replace existing elastromeric transaxle mount with hydraulic transmission mount (part No. 22178939). **Do not install transaxle mount (part No. 22178939) in an attempt to correct any condition other than this vibration.**

GEAR RANGE SELECTOR DIFFICULT TO SHIFT

1998–99 CENTURY

On some of these models the range selector is difficult to move/shift.

This condition may be caused by the original shift cable binding and/or allowing too much friction to build up within the cable sheathing and the internal cable.

To correct this condition on 1998 models replace the shift cable and the brake transmission interlock solenoid (BTSI) with new design units (cable part No. 12454863 and BTSI part No. 26064467).

To correct this condition on 1999 models replace shift cable with new design unit (part No. 12458110).

TIGHTENING SPECIFICATIONS

Year	Component	Torque/Ft. Lbs.
ACHIEVA, GRAND AM & SKYLARK		
1998	Case Cover	18
	Case Side Cover	96①
	Cooler Pipes At Case	16
	Cooler Pipes At Radiator	20
	Flywheel To Torque Converter	46
	Oil Pan	96–108①
	Park/Neutral Position Switch To Case	18
	Shift Lever To Transaxle	15
	Speed Sensor Housing To Case	96①
	Transaxle To Engine	66
	Valve Body To Case	15–20
AURORA		
2001–02	Accumulator Cover	106①
	Ball Joint	③
	Case Cover	106①
	Case Extension	26
	Case Side Cover	18
	Detent Spring	106①
	Fluid Filler Tube	79①
	Forward Band Servo Cover	106①
	Frame Insulator	12
	Manual Shaft	23
	Oil Cooler Quick Connect	28
	Oil Pan	10
	Oil Pressure Test Hole Plug	106①
	Power Steering Line Bracket	53①
	Pump	11
	Pump Cover To Case	106①
	Pump Cover To Body	70①
	Rack & Pinion	48
	Speed Sensor	106①
	Stabilizer Link	13
	TFP Switch To Case	11
	TFP Switch To Case Cover	106①
	TFP Switch To Valve Body	70①
	Torque Converter	47
	Torque Converter Cover	115①
	Transaxle Brace	44
	Transaxle Mount, Bolt	42
	Transaxle Mount, Nut	48
	Transaxle To Engine	55
	Valve Body	106①
	Wheel Hub	107
	2-1 Servo	18

Continued

TIGHTENING SPECIFICATIONS—Continued

Year	Component	Torque/Ft. Lbs.
BONNEVILLE, EIGHTY EIGHT, LESABRE, LSS & PARK AVENUE		
1998–2002	Flywheel Cover	11
	Governor Cover	11
	Lefthand Front & Righthand Rear Mount To Transaxle	40
	Lefthand Rear Mount To Transaxle	30
	Neutral Start & Back-Up Switch	20
	Oil Cooler Lines At Radiator	20
	Oil Cooler Lines At Transaxle	16
	Starter	32
	Throttle Cable To Transaxle	72①
	Torque Converter	46
	Transaxle Mount To Frame	30
	Transaxle To Engine	55
	Wheel Lug Nuts	100
CENTURY		
1998–2002	Bracket To Transaxle	41
	Channel Plate	41
	Console Shift Control	18
	Fill Tube	18
	Flywheel Cover	84①
	Governor Housing	96①
	Modulator	20
	Mount To Bracket	35
	Oil Pan	12
	Park/Neutral Switch	21
	Shift Control Bracket	18
	Shift Control Lever	15
	TCC Solenoid	10
	Torque Converter	46
	Transaxle Case Side Cover	10
	Transaxle Cooler Pipe Clip	35
	Transaxle Cooler Pipe To Radiator	13
	Valve Body	10
	Wheel Lug Nuts	100

Continued

TIGHTENING SPECIFICATIONS—Continued

Year	Component	Torque/Ft. Lbs.
GRAND PRIX, IMPALA, INTRIGUE, LUMINA, MONTE CARLO & REGAL		
1998–2002	Auxiliary Oil Cooler, Bolt	18
	Auxiliary Oil Cooler, Nut	84①
	Bracket To Transaxle, Front	35
	Bracket To Transaxle, Top	61
	Console Shift Control	18
	Engine To Transaxle Brace	35
	Fill Tube	18
	Flywheel Cover	84①
	Governor Housing	96①
	Modulator Retaining	18
	Mount To Support	35
	Neutral Start Switch	18
	Oil Cooler Line Clip	35
	Oil Cooler Line To Radiator	13
	Oil Pan	13
	Oil Scoop	72①
	Shift Control Bracket	18
	Shift Control Lever	15
	Support Frame, Bolt	38
	Support Frame, Nut	32
	TCC Solenoid	10
	Throttle Cable	84①
	Torque Converter	44
	Transaxle Case Side Cover	10
	Transaxle To Engine	55
	Valve Body	10
	Wheel Lug Nuts	100
RIVIERA		
1998–99	Accumulator	20
	Auxiliary Oil Cooler Pipe Fitting	20
	Brace To Engine Bracket	37
	Brace To Transaxle	33
	Bracket To Transaxle Mount	30
	Case Extension	27
	Case Side Cover	84–120①
	Engine Bracket To Engine	70
	Engine To Transaxle	55
	Extension Cover	22–30
	Filler Tube Bracket	15
	Flywheel Cover	10
	Frame	30
	Frame To Body	83
	Front Side Of Bracket To Transaxle	47
	Front Top Of Bracket To Transaxle/ Engine	55
	Modulator	15–20
	Neutral Start Switch	20

Continued

TIGHTENING SPECIFICATIONS—Continued

Year	Component	Torque/Ft. Lbs.
RIVIERA		
1998–99	Neutral Start Switch Shift Lever	15
	Oil Cooler Line Ball Check Fitting At Transaxle	43
	Oil Cooler Line To Radiator	20
	Oil Cooler Line To Transaxle	33
	Oil Pan	12–13
	Oil Scoop	44–97①
	Rear Top Of Bracket To Transaxle	43
	Shift Control Cable Bracket To Transaxle	18
	Shift Lever To Neutral Start Switch	15
	Speed Sensor To Case Extension	96①
	Starter	32
	Torque Converter	46②
	Transaxle Mount To Body Rail	37
	Transaxle To Body Rail Mount, Bracket to Transaxle	55
	Transaxle To Body Rail Mount	29
	Transaxle To Engine	55
	Transaxle To Subframe Mount	75
	Transaxle To Subframe Mount, Bracket to Engine	42
	Transaxle To Subframe Mount, Bracket to Frame	53
	Wheel Lug Nuts	100

① — Inch lbs.
② — Tighten in two steps.
③ — Tighten all torque converter to flywheel bolts twice.

Turbo Hydra-Matic 4T80-E Automatic Transaxle

NOTE: On Air Bag Equipped Models, Refer To "Air Bag System Precautions" Located In The Front Of This Manual For System Disarming & Arming Procedures.

NOTE: Refer To "Computer Relearn Procedures" Located In The Front Of This Manual When Battery Power To The Computer Has Been Interrupted.

NOTE: Prior To Performing Any Service Operations Listed In This Section, Consult The "Technical Service Bulletins" Section For Related Information.

INDEX

PRECAUTIONS

AIR BAG SYSTEMS

Refer to "Air Bag System Precautions" in the front of this manual for system disarming and arming procedures.

BATTERY GROUND CABLE

Prior to service, disconnect battery ground cable and isolate as required.

IDENTIFICATION

Refer to **Fig. 1** for transaxle identification location.

DESCRIPTION

The 4T80-E transaxle is a fully automatic electronically controlled transaxle, **Fig. 2.** It has four forward ranges, including overdrive. Two shift solenoids, operated by the PCM, control shift points. Oil pressure is supplied by three gear type oil pumps and regulated by a transaxle pressure control solenoid (force motor) which is controlled by the PCM. Shift schedule and TCC apply rates, which are influenced by many sensor inputs, are controlled by the PCM. Refer to **Fig. 3** for transaxle electronic component locations.

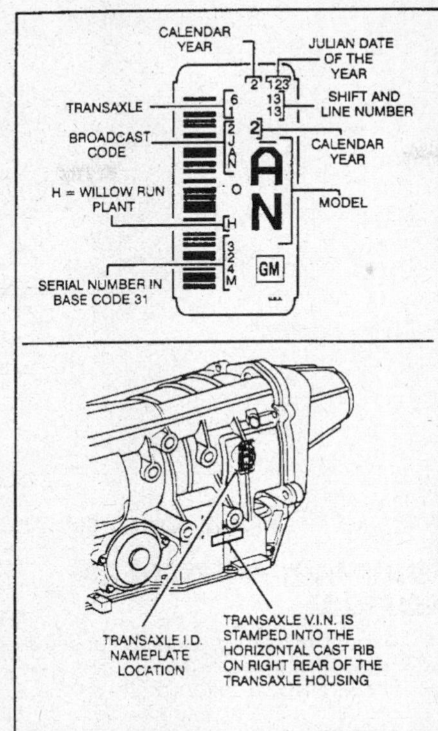

THA059000035000X

Fig. 1 Transaxle identification location

TROUBLESHOOTING

HARSH SHIFTS

1. Pressure regulator valve stuck at high torque signal because of undersized bore, sediment or pressure control solenoid failure.
2. Pressure control solenoid circuit has intermittent short or loose connector.
3. Pressure Control Solenoid (PCS) failed Off or intermittent short.
4. PCS feed valve stuck.
5. Pressure regulator boost valve stuck open.
6. Transaxle fluid pressure valve position switch loose connector.
7. Transaxle wiring harness loose connection connector at vehicle harness.
8. Checkballs missing.
9. Final drive internal gear snap ring missing.
10. Actuator feed limit valve stuck open.

INCORRECT LINE PRESSURE

1. Scavenge pump body or gasket leak.
2. Restricted scavenge pipe.
3. Scavenge pipe seal is damaged, cut or leaking.
4. Oil leakage at primary pump body or gasket.
5. Scavenge screens clogged.
6. Pressure regulator valve stuck because of sediment.
7. Low ATF level.
8. Cooler lines clogged or restricted.

SECOND GEAR STARTS

1. 1-2 shift solenoid stuck off or pinched wire to ground.
2. Pressure control solenoid inoperative, leaking or pinched wire to ground.
3. Driven sprocket support staked checkball missing.

TRANSAXLE SLIPS IN REVERSE

1. ATF level too high or low.
2. Line pressure low.
3. Scavenge pump gears worn or broken.
4. Primary pump gears worn or broken.
5. Scavenge pipe debris.
6. Scavenge pipe seal cut or damaged.
7. Reverse clutch seals cut, damaged or leaking.
8. Reverse clutch plates damaged or burned.
9. Reverse band damaged, burned or slipping.
10. Reverse servo piston damaged or cracked.
11. Reverse servo seals cut, damaged or leaking.
12. Reverse servo pin binding or too short.
13. Reverse band anchor pins loose or missing.

SOFT SHIFTS

1. Line pressure low.
2. Pressure control solenoid stuck On.
3. Pressure control solenoid clamp broken.
4. PCM PROM calibration incorrect.

NO FIRST GEAR D2, D3 & D4

1. Forward and coast clutch checkballs missing.
2. Low/Reverse servo apply pin damaged.
3. 1-2 shift valve stuck in upshift position.
4. Forward and coast clutch support seals damaged.
5. Forward and coast clutch studs damaged or broken.
6. Low roller clutch worn or damaged.
7. 1-2 shift solenoid valve debris, failed Off, or pinched or damaged wires, or inoperative.
8. Forward clutch piston damaged or cracked.
9. Forward clutch piston seals rolled, cut or damaged.
10. Support housing seal rings leaking, damaged or cut.
11. Forward sprag damaged or not holding.
12. Checkball No. 8 missing.

NO SECOND GEAR D2 OR D3

1. Second clutch plates burned or damaged.
2. Second clutch piston cracked or damaged.
3. Second clutch seals rolled, damaged or leaking.
4. Second clutch return spring broken or out of position.
5. Second sprag damaged or not holding.
6. 1-2 shift solenoid stuck On.
7. 1-2 shift valve stuck in 1st gear.

NO THIRD GEAR D3

1. 3-4 shift valve bore plug misassembled.
2. Driven sprocket support exhaust valve cup plug or valve improperly installed.
3. Third clutch plates burned or splines damaged.
4. Third clutch piston cracked, damaged or checkball damage.
5. Third clutch piston seals cut or rolled.
6. Checkballs missing or stuck.
7. 2-3 shift solenoid valve debris, wires pinched or damaged, or inoperative.
8. 1-2 shift solenoid valve debris, wires pinched or damaged, or inoperative.

NO FOURTH GEAR

1. 1-2 shift solenoid valve inoperative, debris or pinched wires.
2. Fourth band is burned, slipping or missing.
3. Fourth servo pin is broken or seized.
4. Fourth servo piston damaged.
5. Fourth servo seals rolled, cut or damaged.
6. Fourth servo cover is cracked.
7. 3-4 shift valve bore plug misassembled.

NO FIRST GEAR

1. Low roller clutch worn or damaged.
2. Forward sprag damaged or not holding.
3. Oil transfer sleeve misaligned, damaged or leaking.
4. Forward clutch plate burned or damaged.
5. Forward clutch piston seals leaking, cut or rolled.
6. Detent lever misaligned.

7. Forward and coast housing broken or spline damage.
8. Forward clutch piston cracked or damaged.
9. 1-2 and/or 2-3 shift solenoid debris, pinched or damaged wires or inoperative.
10. Manual valve misaligned.
11. Housing checkball leaking.

INCONSISTENT SHIFTS

1. 1-2 shift solenoid has O-ring damage or no compression.
2. 3-4 shift solenoid has O-ring damage or no compression.

THIRD & FOURTH GEARS ONLY

1. 2-3 shift solenoid valve stuck On.
2. 2-3 shift solenoid valve circuit pinched wire to ground.

NO ENGINE BRAKING

1. Oil transfer sleeve misaligned.
2. Drive link broken or slipping.
3. Drive & Driven sprockets damaged.
4. Drive axle splines damaged.

NO OVERRUN BRAKING IN D3

1. Coast clutch plates burned or damaged.
2. Coast clutch seal/checkball cut, scorn or nicked.
3. Forward clutch housing splines damaged or housing is cracked.
4. ATF level low or stuck in upshift position.
5. 3-4 shift valve debris or stuck.
6. 1-2 shift solenoid valve debris or stuck.

NO OVERRUN BRAKING IN D2

1. Fourth band slipping or burned.
2. Fourth band servo pin stuck or broken.
3. Fourth servo piston damaged or cracked.
4. Fourth servo seals cut, rolled or damaged.
5. Coast clutch plates burned or damaged.
6. Coast clutch seal/checkball cut, worn or nicked.
7. Transaxle fluid pressure manual valve position switch inoperative.
8. Coast clutch support seals damaged or missing.

NO ENGINE BRAKING IN D1

1. Transaxle fluid pressure manual valve position switch inoperative.
2. Coast clutch plates burned or damaged.
3. Coast clutch seal/checkball cut, worn or nicked.
4. Checkball No. 6 missing.
5. Low/reverse band slipping, burned or damaged.
6. Low/reverse servo piston damaged or seized.
7. Low/reverse servo seals leaking or rolled.

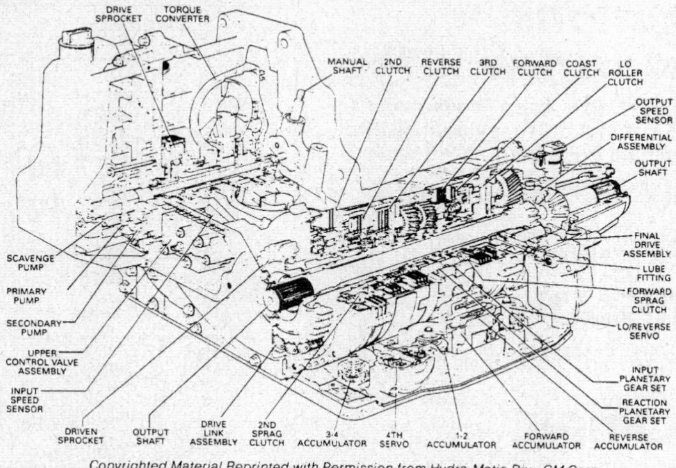

THA059300036000X

Fig. 2 Cross sectional view of 4T80-E transaxle

FORWARD MOTION IN NEUTRAL

1. Manual valve mispositioned or stuck.
2. Forward clutch springs jammed.
3. Forward clutch piston jammed.
4. Forward clutch plates seized or jammed.
5. Forward clutch housing feed hole plugged.
6. Forward and coast clutch support hub holes plugged.
7. Shift linkage mispositioned or disconnected.

ENGINE STALL

1. TCC stuck On or dragging.
2. TCC solenoid valve stuck On, pinched wire to ground or inoperative.
3. TCC solenoid circuit has.
4. Converter feed valve stuck open.
5. Turbine shaft spline damage.

LOSS OF POWER

1. ATF level low.
2. 1-2 and 2-3 shift solenoids valves 2nd gear starts.
3. TCC system stuck On or dragging.
4. Torque converter debris.
5. Turbine shaft bushing damage.

LOSS OF DRIVE

1. Inspect torque converter for the following:
   a. Broken lug or failed lug weld.
   b. Sheared lug bolts.
   c. Worn turbine shaft splines.
   d. Low ATF level.
   e. Pump hub cracked or broken.
   f. Internal failure.
   g. Closure weld failure.
   h. Cover cracked at weld.
2. Scavenger primary pump seized or broken pump gears.
3. Pump shaft broken.
4. Channel plates damaged.
5. Gaskets damaged.
6. Scavenge pipe seal damaged or mission.
7. Drive and driven sprockets broken.
8. Drive link broken.
9. Driven sprocket support damaged, porous or leaking.
10. Final drive damaged or splines worn.
11. Final drive pinions has spalled pins or pinions.
12. Final drive pinions lack lubrication.
13. Forward sprag roller worn, broken or locked.
14. Forward/coast support lacks lubricated.
15. Manual valve and link not attached to detent lever.
16. Turbine shaft dislodged or stripped splines.

ENGINE STARTS IN GEAR

1. Manual valve not engaged to detent lever or struck in wrong position.
2. Transaxle range switch inoperative or mispositioned.

NO GEAR SELECTION

1. Detent lever nut loose or missing.
2. Manual valve stuck.
3. Spacer plate or gasket holes blocked.
4. Control valve bodies, channel plate and case channels blocked.

SHIFT LEVER INDICATES WRONG GEAR

1. Manual valve not engaged to detent lever.
2. Detent roller pin missing or damaged.
3. Detent roller broken or disconnected.
4. Detent spring broken or disconnected.
5. Manual detent pivot looses or missing.
6. Manual shaft flats not parallel.
7. Indicator linkage misadjusted.

NO TORQUE CONVERTER CLUTCH (TCC) APPLY

1. Inspect TCC solenoid valve for the following:
   a. Stuck Off.
   b. O-ring failed.
   c. No voltage.
   d. Poor connection.
2. No PCM signal to TCC solenoid.
3. Inspect brake switch for the following:
   a. Contact corroded.
   b. Poor connection.
   c. Pinched wire.

d. Misadjusted.
e. No voltage.

4. TCC control valve stuck Off because of sediment or undersized bore.
5. TCC regulating valve stuck Off because of sediment or undersized bore.
6. TCC feed valve stuck Off because of sediment or undersized bore.
7. Third clutch filter screen clogged.
8. Turbine shaft to drive sprocket support O-ring seal damaged, leaking or worn.
9. Torque converter ballooning, or TCC not engaging fully or slipping.

SOFT TORQUE CONVERTER CLUTCH (TCC) APPLY

1. Turbine shaft to drive sprocket support O-ring seal worn or damaged.
2. TCC solenoid malfunction.
3. ATF level low.
4. Converter clutch limit feed valve sticking.

EARLY TORQUE CONVERTER CLUTCH (TCC) ENGAGEMENT

Transaxle temperature sensor shorted.

TORQUE CONVERTER CLUTCH (TCC) NOT DISENGAGING

1. TCC solenoid stuck On because of debris.
2. Converter feed limit valve stuck On because of debris.

CONVERTER BALLOONING

Converter feed valve stuck open because of sediment or undersized bore.

NO TORQUE MULTIPLICATION

1. Drive sprocket support broken or detached from case.
2. Drive sprocket support spline damage.

NO REVERSE

1. Reaction carrier shell missing or damaged teeth.
2. Low/reverse anchor pin broken or not positioned properly.
3. Driven sprocket support porous, broken, or feed holes blocked.
4. Driven sprocket support seals leaking.
5. Driven sprocket support bolts loose, not in grooves or mislocated.
6. Reverse band broken or worn and not anchored.
7. Reverse band apply pin too short, binding in case or broken.
8. Reverse clutch piston binding in case.
9. Reverse clutch piston seal leaking, damaged or worn.
10. Reverse clutch piston checkball missing.
11. Case cover gasket damaged or displaced.
12. Case cover damaged.
13. Fluid pressure too low.
14. Reverse clutch steel plates splines worn.

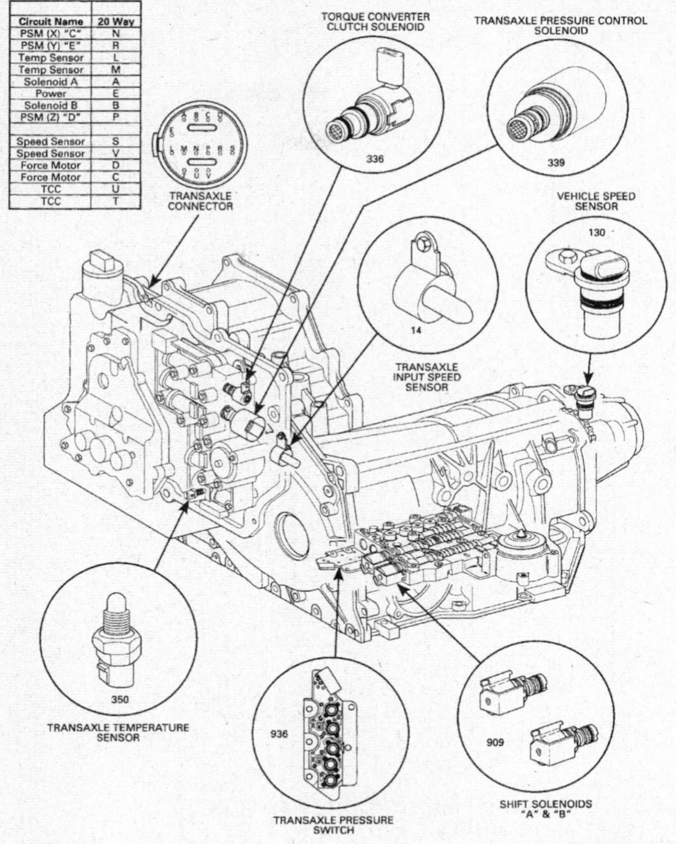

Circuit Name	20 Way
PSM (X) "C"	N
PSM (Y) "E"	R
Temp Sensor	L
Temp Sensor	M
Solenoid A	A
Power	E
Solenoid B	B
PSM (Z) "D"	P
Speed Sensor	S
Speed Sensor	V
Force Motor	D
Force Motor	C
TCC	U
TCC	T

Fig. 3 Transaxle electronic component location

15. Reverse clutch fiber plates splines or friction material worn.
16. Reverse clutch spring jammed.
17. Reverse clutch housing cracked.
18. Snap ring out.

DOES NOT STAY IN PARK

1. Detent spring weak or broken.
2. Detent lever mislocated or broken.
3. Actuator rod bent or guide damaged.
4. Park pawl pivot pin missing.
5. Parking lock gear teeth damaged.
6. Park pawl tooth damaged.
7. Manual linkage misadjusted or disconnected.

EXTENDED OR DELAYED UPSHIFTS

1. Transaxle fluid pressure manual valve position switch inoperative.
2. Pressure regulator boost valve stuck in bushing.

TRANSAXLE SEIZED

1. Cooler circuit lines blocked or leaking.
2. Cooler fittings blocked or leaking.
3. Spacer plate or gaskets' holes missing or off location.
4. Scavenger pipe damaged, clogged or poor seal.
5. Control valve bodies loose, broken or missing bolts.
6. Transaxle fluid filter sitting on side cover.
7. Filter seal cut or damaged.
8. Left and righthand scavenge screens clogged or not seated.

NOISE

1. Loose torque converter lug bolts.
2. Torque converter out of balance or internal failure.
3. Transaxle and engine misaligned.
4. Case extension axle support bushing worn.

NOISE IN ALL RANGES

Torque converter internal damage.

WHINE NOISE VARYING w/RPM OR FLUID PRESSURE

Oil pump system internal damage.

POPPING NOISE

1. Oil pump damage indicated by ATF fluid bubbles.
2. ATF strainer seam leak.
3. ATF strainer seal out of position or cut seal.

BUZZ NOISE OR HIGH FREQUENCY RATTLE SOUND

Cooler pipes binding or in contact with radiator.

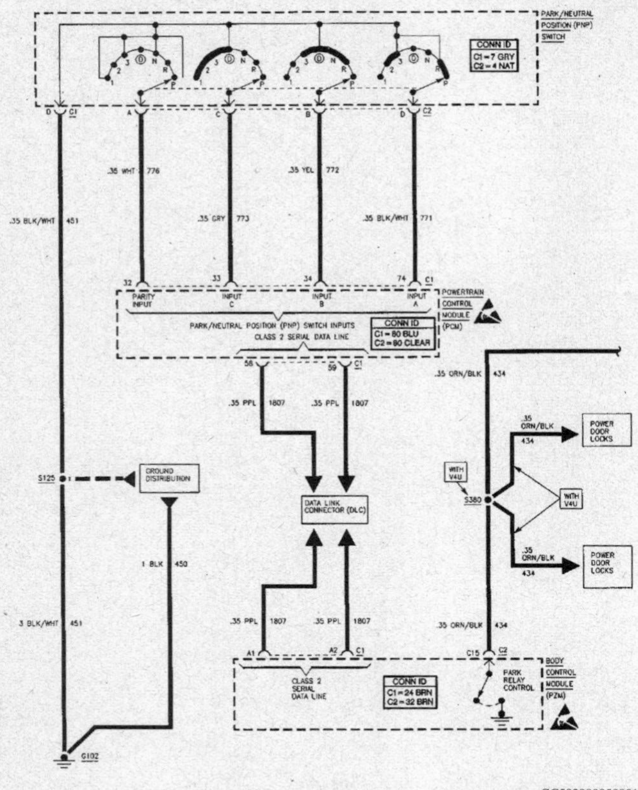

Fig. 4 BTSI system wiring circuit (Part 1 of 2). 1998–99 DeVille & Eldorado

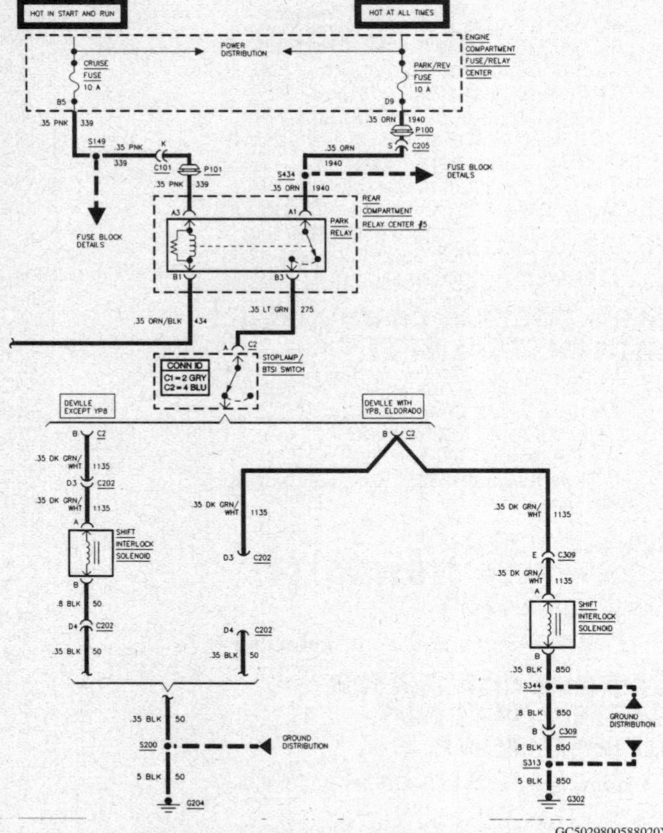

Fig. 4 BTSI system wiring circuit (Part 2 of 2). 1998–99 DeVille & Eldorado

WHINE &/OR GROWL NOISE THAT CHANGES w/VEHICLE SPEED

1. Drive link stretched.
2. Inspect drive and driven sprocket for the following:
   a. Teeth broken or sheared.
   b. Bearing surfaces nicked or scored.
   c. Gear support inner bearings race or roller bearing surfaces rough or pitted.
   d. Bearing damage.
3. Drive and driven sprocket support bearing outer race support damaged.

FINAL DRIVE NOISE OR HUM NOISE

1. Worn planet pinions or washers in final drive gear set.
2. Final drive internal gear is worn or has tooth damage.
3. Differential carrier gears worn or pitted.
4. Differential side gears thrust washer damage.

NOISE IN FIRST, SECOND, THIRD OR FOURTH

1. Worn or damaged final drive sun gears.
2. Worn or damaged final drive pinion gears.

VIBRATION DIAGNOSIS

1. Torque converter out of balance or internal failure.
2. Transaxle and engine misaligned.
3. Case extension axle support bushing worn.
4. Turbine shaft bushing worn.
5. Output shaft out of balance.

FLUID FOAMING

1. ATF contaminated with coolant.
2. Transaxle overfilled.
3. Engine overheated.
4. ATF filter cracked or not seated.
5. Filter seal damaged or not seated.
6. Vehicle overloaded.
7. Left and righthand scavenge screens clogged.

LEAK AT BOTTOM PAN

1. Bottom pan damaged or not flat.
2. Bottom pan gasket damaged or misaligned.
3. Case porous or cracked.
4. Bottom pan to case bolts flange inside out, damaged, too tight or too loose.

LEAK AT FLUID FILL INDICATOR

Indicator seal cut, nicked or missing.

LEAK AT VEHICLE SPEED SENSOR (VSS)

1. VSS bolt loose, cross-threaded or missing.
2. VSS O-ring seal cut, nicked or missing.

LEAK AT ELECTRICAL CONNECTOR

1. Electrical connector is damaged or not seated correctly.
2. O-ring seal damaged or not seated correctly.
3. Case porous or cracked.

LEAK AT COOLER CONNECTORS

1. Cooler connector threads stripped or damaged.
2. Case threads stripped or debris on threads.

LEAK AT CASE EXTENSION

1. Case extension porous or cracked.
2. Case porous or cracked.
3. Case extension to case seal cut, nicked or missing.
4. Case extension to case bolts loose or missing.
5. Front differential carrier bushing worn or damaged.
6. Output shaft bearing worn or damaged.
7. Case extension oil drain back holes plugged or missing.

LEAK AT MANUAL SHIFT

1. Manual shift seal cut, nicked or not seated.
2. Linkage misadjusted.

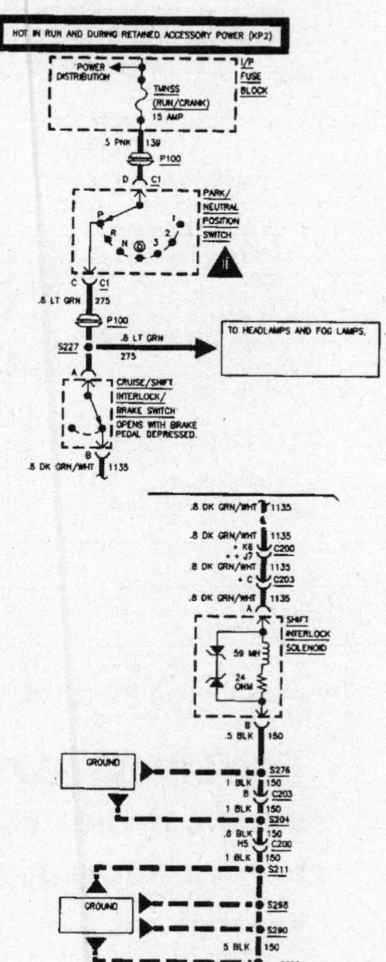

GC5029500516000X

Fig. 5 BTSI system wiring circuit. Aurora

Brake Transaxle Shift Interlock (BTSI) System Check

Step	Action	Normal Results	Abnormal Results
1	With the ignition in RUN and engine not running, attempt to shift vehicle out of PARK.	Vehicle does not shift out of PARK.	Vehicle Shifts Out Of PARK Without Brake Pedal Pressed.
2	Press brake pedal and attempt to shift vehicle out of PARK.	Vehicle shifts out of PARK.	Vehicle Does Not Shift Out Of PARK With Brake Pedal Pressed.

Vehicle Shifts Out Of PARK Without Brake Pedal Pressed

Step	Action	Value(s)	Yes	No
1	Connect a scan tool to the data link connector (DLC) and retrieve PZM DTCs. Is PZM DTC B2502 or B2503 present?	—	Body Control Module	Go to Step 2
2	1. Turn ignition switch to RUN with engine not running. 2. Remove park relay. 3. Check for voltage from park relay connector terminal A1 to ground. Is battery voltage present?	9 - 12V	Go to Step 4	Go to Step 3
3	Repair open or short to ground in CKT 1940 (ORN). Is the circuit repair complete?	—	System OK	—
4	Check for voltage from park relay connector terminal A3 to ground. Is battery voltage present?	9 - 12V	Go to Step 6	Go to Step 5
5	Repair open or short to ground in CKT 339 (PNK). Is the circuit repair complete?	—	System OK	—

GC5029800589010X

Fig. 6 BTSI troubleshooting (Part 1 of 3). 1998–99 DeVille & Eldorado

LEAK AT CONVERTER SEAL

1. Converter hub seal cut, nicked, worn or garter spring missing.
2. Torque converter bolt loose or hub damaged.

LEAK AT DRIVE AXLE SEAL

Tripot joint housing mating surface corrosion.

BRAKE TRANSAXLE SHIFT INTERLOCK (BTSI)

Refer to wiring diagrams, **Figs. 4 and 5,** and diagnosis charts, **Figs. 6 through 8,** to diagnose the BTSI system.

For the 1998–2000 Seville, Brake Transaxle Shift Interlock (BTSI) is an integral part of the Park Lock Cable and can not be serviced separately. Refer to "Park Lock Cable Replacement."

MAINTENANCE

Refer to "Lubricant Data" chart in the appropriate chassis chapter of this manual for transmission fluid specifications.

FLUID CHECK

Refer to **Fig. 9** for transaxle fluid check procedure.

FLUID CHANGE

1. Raise and support vehicle. Place suitable drain pan under transaxle fluid pan to catch fluid.
2. Loosen bottom pan bolts in sequence, **Figs. 10 and 11,** and drain fluid, noting the following:
   a. Removing fluid pan will only partially drain transaxle fluid.
   b. Remaining fluid is held in side cover and torque converter.
   c. Removing drain plug in case after fluid pan removal will drain fluid from side cover.
   d. It is not necessary to drain torque converter during most service procedures.
3. Remove fluid pan and transaxle case bolts, pan and gasket.
4. Remove left and righthand scavenger screens, **Fig. 12.**
5. Inspect fluid pan and transaxle case for dents or nicks in sealing surface, replacing if damaged.
6. Inspect bolts for thread damage, replacing if damaged.
7. Reverse procedure to install, noting the following:
   a. Install new fluid pan gasket.
   b. If complete fluid change was required, reset transaxle oil life indicator as outlined in "Resetting Transaxle Oil Life Indicator."

RESETTING TRANSAXLE OIL LIFE INDICATOR

The PCM maintains a value for transaxle oil life which indicates the percentage of oil life remaining and is calculated based on transaxle temperature and speed. When the vehicle is new, the transaxle oil life is 100%; as mileage accumulates, oil life will eventually decrease to 0%. When the value reaches 1%, the CCDIC displays the message CHANGE TRANSAXLE OIL.

The oil life indicator should be reset to 100% when transaxle oil is changed or when the transaxle is replaced. Transaxle oil life value should be recorded prior to PCM replacement and programmed into the new PCM. To reset the transaxle oil life indicator, proceed as follows:

1. Turn ignition switch to Run position.
2. Display TRANSAXLE OIL LIFE on driver information center.
3. Press and hold Reset until oil life changes to 100%.

TRANSAXLE OIL COOLER FLUSH

Refer to "Turbo Hydra-Matic 4L30-E Automatic Transmission."

RESETTING TRANSAXLE ADAPTS

The PCM maintains five transaxle adapt parameters for transaxle control. The line pressure control system has the ability to continuously adapt line pressure thereby compensating for normal wear of clutch plates, seals and springs. The five types of

Step	Action	Value(s)	Yes	No
6	1. Connect a fused jumper between park relay connector terminals A1 and B3. 2. Attempt to shift vehicle out of PARK. Is the gear shifter locked?	—	Go to Step 16	Go to Step 7
7	1. Disconnect stoplamp/BTSI switch connector 2. Check voltage at stoplamp/BTSI switch connector terminal A to ground. Is battery voltage present?	9 - 12V	Go to Step 9	Go to Step 8
8	Repair open CKT 275 (LT GRN). Is the circuit repair complete?	—	System OK	—
9	Connect a test lamp across stoplamp/BTSI switch connector C2 terminals A and B. Does the test lamp light?	—	Go to Step 11	Go to Step 10
10	Check that the stoplamp/BTSI switch is properly adjusted and that connector C2 terminals are clean and tight. If OK, replace stoplamp/BTSI switch. Is replacement complete?	—	System OK	—
11	1. Reconnect stoplamp/BTSI switch connector 2. Disconnect shift interlock solenoid connector. 3. Check for voltage at shift interlock solenoid connector terminal A to ground. Is battery voltage present?	9 - 12V	Go to Step 13	Go to Step 12
12	Repair open in CKT 1135 (DK GRN/WHT). Is the circuit repair complete?	—	System OK	—
13	Connect a test lamp across shift interlock solenoid connector terminals A and B. Does the test lamp light?	—	Go to Step 15	Go to Step 14
14	Repair open CKT 50 (BLK) or CKT 850 (BLK). Is the circuit repair complete?	—	System OK	—
15	Check that the shift interlock solenoid connector terminals are clean and tight. If OK, replace shift interlock solenoid. Is the replacement complete?	—	System OK	—
16	1. Remove fused jumper and reconnect park relay. 2. Using scan tool, enter PZM data. Does the PZM, as monitored by the scan tool, indicate that the vehicle is in PARK?	—	Go to Step 17	Engine Controls
17	1. Turn ignition OFF. 2. Disconnect body control module (PZM) connector C2. 3. Turn ignition to RUN. 4. Connect a fused jumper from PZM connector C2 terminal C16 to ground. 5. Attempt to shift the vehicle out of PARK. Is the gear shifter locked?	—	Go to Step 21	Go to Step 18

GC5029800589020X

Fig. 6 BTSI troubleshooting (Part 2 of 3). 1998–99 DeVille & Eldorado

Step	Action	Value(s)	Yes	No
18	Check CKT 434 (ORN/BLK) for an open. Is the circuit OK?	—	Go to Step 20	Go to Step 19
19	Repair open CKT 434 (ORN/BLK). Is the circuit repair complete?	—	System OK	—
20	Check park relay for poor terminal contact. If OK, replace park relay. Is the replacement complete?	—	System OK	—
21	Check body control module (PZM) connector C2 for poor terminal contact. If OK, replace PZM. Is the replacement complete?	—	System OK	—

Vehicle Does Not Shift Out Of PARK With Brake Pedal Pressed

Step	Action	Value(s)	Yes	No
1	Connect a scan tool to the data link connector (DLC) and retrieve PZM DTCs. Is PZM DTC B2502 or B2503 present?	—	Go to Body Control Module (PZM) Diagnosis	Go to Step 2
2	1. Disconnect stoplamp/BTSI switch connector C2. 2. Attempt to shift vehicle out of PARK. Is gear shifter unlocked?	—	Go to Step 3	Go to Step 4
3	Check that stoplamp/BTSI switch is properly adjusted and that connector C2 terminals are clean and tight. If OK, replace stoplamp/BTSI switch. Is the replacement complete?	—	System OK	—
4	Check for voltage at shift interlock solenoid connector terminal B. Is battery voltage present?	9 - 12V	Go to Step 5	Go to Step 6
5	Repair short to battery voltage in CKT 1135 (DK GRN/WHT). Is the circuit repair complete?	—	System OK	—
6	Check that shift interlock solenoid connector terminals are clean and tight. If OK, replace the shift interlock solenoid. Is the repair complete?	—	System OK	—

GC5029800589030X

Fig. 6 BTSI troubleshooting (Part 3 of 3). 1998–99 DeVille & Eldorado

transaxle adapts are: upshift adapt (monitors automatic transaxle input shaft speed sensor and vehicle speed sensor to monitor when shift occurs), steady state adapt (monitors speed sensor inputs after a shift to calculate amount of slippage in that gear), garage shift adapt (monitors speed sensor inputs to calculate if shift occurs too fast or too slow), WOT 1-2 adapt (monitors VSS and RPM during a 1-2 WOT shift), learn tap (accelerated PLM learn mode, technician must road test vehicle for 15 minutes, normal time 2–3 hours). The transaxle may experience harsh, soft or mushy shifts for up to two days after adapt parameters have been reset. Transaxle adapts must be reset when a transaxle overhaul or replacement has taken place. To reset PCM adapts, proceed as follows:

1. Connect suitably programmed scan tool to DLC.
2. Select miscellaneous test.
3. Select A/T outputs and clear or reset all adapts.

ADJUSTMENTS

SHIFT CONTROL CABLE

AURORA, DEVILLE & ELDORADO

1. Remove air cleaner duct and housing.
2. Pry lock button on shifter cable to unlocked position using suitable flat head screwdriver, **Fig. 13.**
3. Place transaxle shifter in Neutral and select Neutral position at lever on transaxle manual shaft.
4. Depress lock button on shifter cable into Locked position, **Fig. 13.**
5. Install air cleaner duct and housing.

SEVILLE

1. Move driver's seat to its most rearward position and remove lefthand side console trim plate.
2. Move shifter lever to N position, insert socket through hole in side of console and loosen shift control cable adjustment nut, **Fig. 14.**
3. Shift cable will set self adjust at this point. No other adjustment is required.
4. Tighten shift control cable adjustment nut and install lefthand side console trim plate.

PARK LOCK CABLE

1. Place park/lock cable adjuster into unlocked position.
2. Pull cable forward to remove slack and release cable.
3. Move cable adjuster rearward 1⁄16 inch from previous position. Hold cable in position and place park/lock cable adjuster to locked position.
4. If shift lever moves from Park with key in lock position or if key will not return to lock position, repeat adjustment procedure as required.

IN-VEHICLE REPAIRS

SHIFT CONTROL CABLE

DEVILLE, ELDORADO & SEVILLE

Removal

1. Remove air cleaner duct and housing, then disconnect shifter cable from lever on transaxle manual shaft.
2. Disconnect shifter cable from bracket on transaxle, then remove mounting bolts and bracket, if bracket replacement is required, **Fig. 15.**
3. Remove shifter knob and console trim plate, **Fig. 16.**
4. Disconnect shifter cable at shifter.
5. Loosen carpet attachments on front lefthand side of passenger compartment to access cable.
6. Remove cable grommet from cowl and cable.

Installation

1. Install cable through cowl and grommet into cowl, then route cable under carpet.
2. Attach carpet on front lefthand side of passenger compartment.
3. Connect shifter cable at shifter and install trim plate and shifter knob.
4. Install cable bracket and mounting bolts at transaxle, if bracket replacement was required.
5. Connect shifter cable at bracket on transaxle and at lever on transaxle manual shaft.
6. Pry lock button on shifter cable to unlocked position using suitable flat head screwdriver, **Fig. 13.**
7. Place transaxle shifter in Neutral and

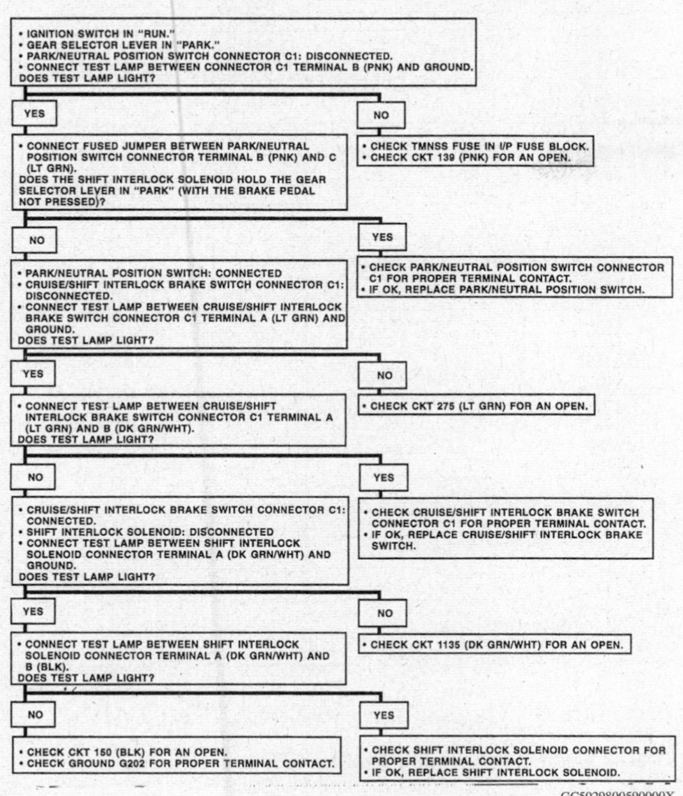

Fig. 7 Transaxle shifts out of Park w/ignition switch in Run position & brake pedal not pressed. Aurora

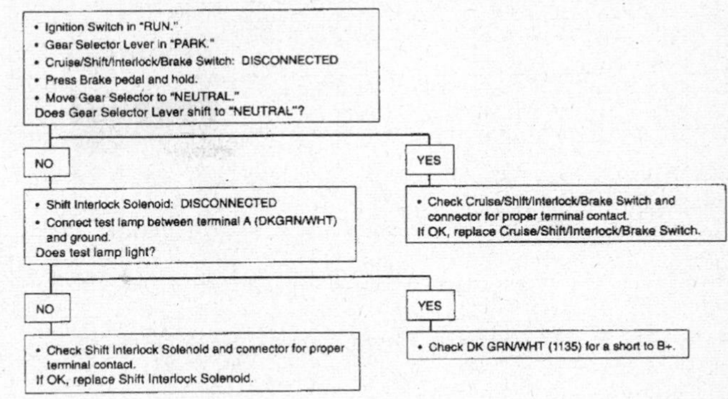

Fig. 8 Transaxle does not shift out of Park w/brake pedal depressed & ignition switch in Run position. Aurora

select Neutral position at lever on transaxle manual shaft.

8. Depress lock button on shifter cable into Locked position, **Fig. 13.**
9. Install air cleaner duct and housing.

AURORA

1. Remove cable end cap from transaxle range switch lever, **Fig. 17.**
2. Disconnect cable from bracket by prying up on lock button to unlocked position.
3. Remove lefthand I/P sound insulator.
4. Remove console center trim panel.
5. Disconnect shift control cable from floor shift.
6. Reverse procedure to install, noting the following:
   a. Pry lock button on shifter cable to unlocked position using suitable flathead screwdriver, **Fig. 13.**
   b. Place transaxle shifter in Neutral by rotating selector shaft clockwise from Park to Reverse and Neutral.
   c. Select Neutral position at lever on transaxle manual shaft.
   d. Depress lock button on shifter cable into LOCKED position, **Fig. 13.**

PARK LOCK CABLE (CONSOLE SHIFT)

Refer to **Figs. 13 through 16** when servicing park/lock (console shift) cable.

REMOVAL

1. Place shifter in Park and remove lefthand instrument panel sound insulator. Loosen lefthand front carpet to allow access to park/lock cable routing.
2. **On Seville models,** disconnect BTSI electrical connector.
3. **On DeVille and Eldorado models,** remove reinforcement plate and column mounting bolts, then lower steering column.
4. **On all models,** turn ignition key to Run position.
5. Slip suitable flat head screwdriver blade into ignition switch inhibitor slot and depress cable latch.
6. Pull park/lock cable from inhibitor. **Do not attempt with ignition key in any position other than Run.**
7. Remove radio and console trim plates, as required.
8. Disconnect park/lock cable at shifter.
9. Remove park/lock cable.

INSTALLATION

1. Pry lock button of park/lock cable into Unlocked position using suitable flat head screwdriver and connect park/lock cable at shifter.
2. With shifter in Park and ignition key in Run, snap park/lock cable into inhibitor housing.
3. **Do not with ignition key in any other position than Run.** Turn key to Lock position and snap cable end onto pin of shifter lever.
4. Push park/lock cable toward shifter lever to remove slack.
5. Push lock button on park/lock cable down into locked position.
6. With shifter in Park and ignition key in Lock position, ensure shifter cannot be moved to another position. Ignition key should not be removable from its cylinder.
7. Turn ignition key to Run position and move shifter to Neutral. Ensure ignition key cannot be turned to Lock position.
8. If previous checks are satisfactory, proceed to next step. If checks are not satisfactory, adjust park/lock cable from beginning.
9. **On DeVille and Eldorado models,** raise steering column and install bolts and reinforcement plate
10. **On Seville models,** connect BTSI electrical connector.
11. **On all models,** install console and radio trim plates and secure lefthand front carpet and lefthand instrument panel sound insulator.

BRAKE-TRANSAXLE SHIFT INTERLOCK (BTSI), REPLACE

On Seville models, BTSI is an integral part of the Park Lock Cable and can not be serviced separately.

1. Remove shifter knob and console trim plate, **Fig. 16.**
2. Disconnect electrical connector and BTSI solenoid from shifter.
3. Reverse procedure to install.

VALVE BODY, REPLACE

REMOVAL

1. Raise and support vehicle, then remove bottom pan, scavenger screens and seals, **Fig. 18.**
2. Bend back small tabs using suitable small screwdriver, to disconnect shift solenoids A, B and transaxle pressure switch connectors, **Fig. 19.**
3. Disconnect manual valve linkage clip with suitable small screwdriver.
4. Disconnect wiring harness from mounting clips on lower controls.

Step	Action	Value(s)	Yes	No
DEFINITION: Diagnose transmission fluid conditions by color.				
1	Check the fluid color. Is the fluid color red?	—	*Go to Step 2*	*Go to Step 11*
2	Is the fluid level satisfactory?	—	*Go to Step 21*	*Go to Step 3*
3	Check the fluid. Is the fluid foamy?	—	*Go to Step 8*	*Go to Step 4*
4	Check the fluid level. The proper fluid level should be in the middle of the X-hatch. Is the level high?	—	*Go to Step 9*	*Go to Step 5*
5	Fluid will be low. Add fluid to the proper fluid level. Is the fluid level satisfactory?	—	*Go to Step 6*	—
6	Check for external leaks. Did you find any leaks?	—	*Go to Step 7*	*Go to Step 21*

TH5020001288010X

Fig. 9 Transaxle Fluid Check (Part 1 of 2)

Step	Action	Value(s)	Yes	No
7	Correct the leak condition. Did you correct the leak condition?	—	*Go to Step 21*	—
8	Is the fluid level too high?	—	*Go to Step 9*	*Go to Step 10*
9	Remove excess fluid to the proper fluid level. Refer to Fluid Changing Is the fluid level satisfactory?	—	*Go to Step 21*	—
10	1. Check for contaminants in the fluid. 2. Drain the fluid to determine the source of the contamination. Did you drain the fluid?	—	*Go to Step 15*	—
11	Is the fluid color non-transparent pink?	—	*Go to Step 12*	*Go to Step 13*
12	Replace the cooler. Is the replacement complete?	—	*Go to Step 15*	—
13	**Important:** Transmission fluid may turn dark with normal use. This does not always indicate oxidation or contamination. The fluid color should be light brown. Is the fluid color light brown?	—	*Go to Step 14*	—
14	**Important:** A very small amount of material in the bottom pan is a normal condition, but large pieces of metal or other material in the bottom pan require a transmission overhaul. Drain the fluid to determine if the fluid is contaminated. Was the fluid contaminated?	—	*Go to Step 15*	*Go to Step 18*
15	Overhaul the transmission. Is the overhaul complete?	—	*Go to Step 16*	—
16	1. Clear TRANS ADAPT. 2. Reset the oil life monitor to 100%. Are the reset procedures complete?	—	*Go to Step 17*	—
17	Add new fluid. Is the procedure complete?	—	*Go to Step 20*	—
18	Change the fluid and the filter. Is this procedure complete?	—	*Go to Step 19*	—
19	Reset the oil life monitor to 100%. Are the reset procedures complete?	—	*Go to Step 20*	—
20	Check fluid level. Is the fluid level satisfactory?	—	*Go to Step 21*	—
21	Perform the *Functional Test* Is the Functional Test Procedure completed?	—	System OK	—

TH5020001288020X

Fig. 9 Transaxle Fluid Check (Part 2 of 2)

5. Remove oil transfer plate.
6. Remove bolts and two nuts. **Do not remove five bolts in lower channel plate, Fig. 20.**
7. Remove lower channel plate, valve and accumulators from case.

INSTALLATION

1. Position low reverse band using 0.02–0.03 inch shim, **Fig. 21.**
2. Place lower controls against forward support studs.
3. Hand start bolts into channel plate and remove shim stock.
4. Place oil transfer plate over open gasket area. Hand start bolts to hold plate in place, noting installation order.
5. Install forward support studs' nuts.
6. Connect manual valve to detent lever.
7. Route harness over spacer plate rib and detent lever and snap into mounting clips on lower controls.
8. Connect wiring harness to shift solenoids A and B, then transaxle pressure sensor.
9. Install scavenger screens, lip seals, bottom pan and gasket.
10. Add transaxle fluid and reset transaxle oil life indicator if complete fluid change was required.

SOLENOIDS A & B (1-2 & 2-3 SHIFT SOLENOIDS), REPLACE

1. Raise and support vehicle, then remove bottom pan, gasket, scavenger screens and seals.
2. Remove lower controls.
3. Remove mounting bolts and transaxle pressure switch manifold.
4. Remove lower control valve and gasket from lower channel plate.
5. Remove solenoids A and B mounting clips and solenoids, **Fig. 18.**
6. Reverse procedure to install. Add transaxle fluid and reset transaxle oil life indicator, if complete fluid change was required.

1-2, 3-4, FORWARD & REVERSE ACCUMULATORS, REPLACE

REMOVAL

1. Raise and support vehicle, then remove bottom pan, gasket, scavenger screens and lip seals.
2. Remove lower controls.
3. Remove nine bolts (three from channel side).
4. Remove accumulator housing from channel plate and checkballs. **Do not lose checkballs.**
5. Remove spring.
6. Remove accumulator piston top snap rings from housing side, then the 1-2 and 3-4 accumulators.
7. Remove mounting bolts, accumulator housing cover and gasket.
8. Remove forward accumulator and reverse accumulator.

INSPECTION

1. Inspect accumulator pins for straightness by rolling on flat surface.
2. Inspect accumulator seals for tearing or roll over and snap rings for overexpansion
3. Inspect accumulator bores for scratches or nicks.
4. Replace gasket and inspect springs for cracking or damage.

INSTALLATION

Lubricate all seals using light coat of ATF before installing accumulators.

1. Install forward accumulator and reverse accumulator.
2. Install new gasket and accumulator housing cover.
3. Install accumulator housing cover bolts.
4. Install 1-2 accumulator pin. Retain with two snap rings.
5. Install 1-2 accumulator spring, piston and seal.
6. Install snap ring and spring.
7. Install 3-4 accumulator pin. Retain with two snap rings.
8. Install 3-4 accumulator spring, piston and seal.
9. Install snap ring.
10. Install checkballs.
11. Install accumulator housing to lower channel plate using guide pins J-39630-2, or equivalent.
12. Remove guide pins and install remaining bolts.
13. Install lower controls.
14. Install bottom pan and gasket, scavenger screens and lip seals.
15. Add transaxle fluid as required.
16. Reset transaxle oil life indicator, if complete fluid change was required.

LOWER VALVE, SPACER PLATE & CHANNEL PLATE, REPLACE

1. Raise and support vehicle, then remove bottom pan, gasket, scavenger screens and seals
2. Remove lower controls.
3. Remove nine accumulator housing bolts (three from channel plate side).
4. Remove accumulator housing from channel plate and four checkballs.
5. Remove transaxle pressure switch manifold bolts and manifold.
6. Remove eleven bolts (two on channel plate side) and lower control valve and gasket from lower channel plate.
7. Remove four checkballs.
8. Remove manual valve link and clip and manual valve.
9. Remove low/reverse servo piston mounting ring. Push low/reverse apply pin to remove servo.
10. Remove return spring and clip and push out servo pin.
11. Remove servo cushion spring and spring washer. **Inspect check valves for movement.**
12. Remove clips and shift solenoids A and B, then solenoid screen.

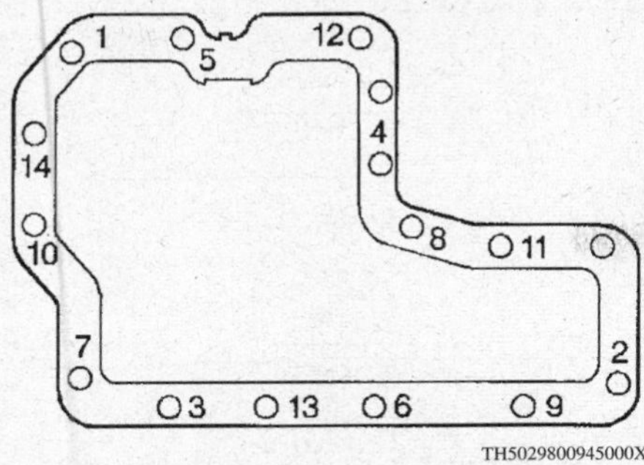

Fig. 10 Transaxle bottom pan bolt loosening & tightening sequence. Aurora

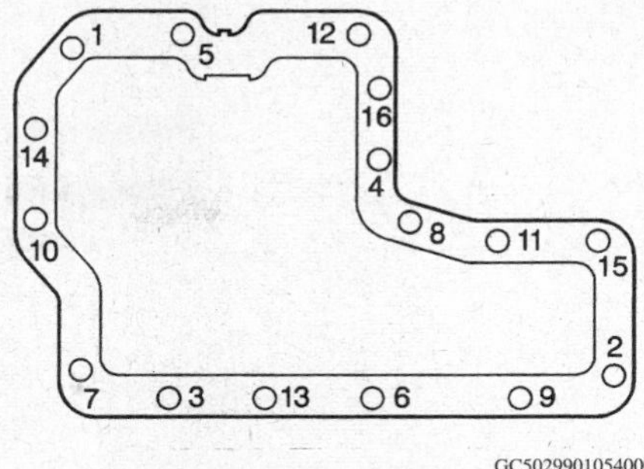

Fig. 11 Transaxle bottom pan loosening & tightening sequence. DeVille & Eldorado

13. Remove 1-2 shift valves A and B, then 1-2 shift valve spring.
14. Remove 2-3 shift valves C and D, then 2-3 shift valve spring.
15. Remove coiled spring pin.
16. Remove forward bypass valve spring and forward bypass valve.
17. Remove mounting clip and bore plug.
18. Remove 3-4 shift valve, 3-4 shift valve spring and coiled spring pin.
19. Remove reverse orifice bypass valve spring and reverse orifice bypass valve.
20. Remove mounting sleeve.
21. Remove ball check capsule and checkball.
22. Remove bolts and plate from channel plate.
23. Remove spacer plate and gasket.
24. Inspect servo seals for roll over, tearing or cuts.
25. Inspect springs for damage and mounting clips for overexpansion.
26. Inspect all valve and piston bores for nicks and wear.
27. Inspect low/reverse servo apply pin for straightness by rolling on flat surface.
28. Inspect solenoid screen for particles or damage.
29. Inspect checkball in valve body for freedom of movement.
30. Inspect valve body channel plate passages for debris.
31. Reverse procedure to install, noting the following:
    a. Install guide pins, **Figs. 22 through 25.**
    b. Remove guide pins and install mounting bolts, as required.

VEHICLE SPEED SENSOR, REPLACE

1. Raise and support vehicle, then remove righthand front wheel.
2. Disconnect electrical connector at sensor, remove mounting bolt and sensor, **Fig. 26.**
3. Reverse procedure to install.

SELECTOR SWITCH, REPLACE

REMOVAL

1. Remove air cleaner duct and housing, then disconnect shifter cable at lever on transaxle manual shaft.
2. Disconnect shifter cable from transaxle and remove shifter cable bracket, **Fig. 15.**
3. Remove mounting nut and transaxle manual shaft lever.
4. Disconnect electrical connector and hose, then remove mounting bolts and selector switch, **Fig. 27.**

INSTALLATION

1. Install transaxle range switch and mounting bolts hand tight, then rotate transaxle manual shaft to Neutral position.
2. Rotate range switch so service gauge pin can be installed, **Fig. 27.**
3. Remove service gauge pin and connect electrical connector and hose.
4. Install transaxle manual shaft lever.
5. Install shift cable bracket onto transaxle and connect cable.
6. Install shift cable at lever on transaxle manual shaft.
7. Install air cleaner duct and housing.

4TH SERVO, REPLACE

1. Raise and support vehicle.
2. Remove exhaust system as required.
3. Remove steering gear mounting bolts from lefthand side of gear.
4. Remove through bolt from righthand side of steering gear and support gear as required.
5. Remove mounting clamp from power steering lines and support transaxle with suitable jackstand.
6. Remove righthand transaxle mount bolts and support rear frame with suitable jackstand.
7. Remove rear frame bolts and lower frame to gain access to servo.
8. Remove three bolts, **Fig. 28.** Hold servo cover in place until all bolts are removed. If cover is not held in place, apply pin will damage bore in case.
9. Remove cover and servo.
10. Inspect piston for cracking, and apply pin and springs for damage.
11. Remove seal and servo cover seal.
12. Remove snap ring, pin and springs.
13. Reverse procedure to install, noting the following:
    a. Install new seal onto piston and pin, small spring, retainer, snap ring and seal to cover.
    b. Install fourth servo and large spring into cover.
    c. **On early models,** ensure piston tab is aligned with case bore notch.
    d. **On early models,** ensure flat spring is centered between bosses on cover.
    e. **On all models,** light mark may be scribed on top of piston for reference. **Do not mark side of piston or fluid leak or binding condition may result.**
    f. Install cover mounting screws. Hand start screws and tighten in star pattern.
    g. Add suitable ATF as required.

SCAVENGER SCREENS & LIP SEALS, REPLACE

1. Raise and support vehicle, then remove bottom pan.
2. Remove left and/or righthand scavenger screens and seals with suitable small screwdriver. **Do not score or damage case.**
3. Inspect screen lip seals for nicks or cuts.
4. Clean or replace scavenger screen and install.
5. Install pan.

DRIVE AXLE SEAL, REPLACE

REMOVAL

1. Raise and support vehicle, then remove wheel and tire.
2. Install suitable seal protector on outer joint.
3. Remove hub nut. Insert drift or screwdriver into caliper and rotor to prevent rotor from turning.
4. Remove ball joint cotter pin and nut, then loosen joint using suitable ball joint separator. If removing righthand axle, turn wheel to left; if removing lefthand axle, turn wheel to right.
5. Remove drive axle from hub using suitable front hub spindle remover.
6. Move strut and knuckle rearward.
7. Remove drive axle from transaxle with suitable pry bar, **Fig. 29.**
8. Pry outer seal from transaxle using suitable screwdriver and remove remaining housing of drive axle seal using suitable pliers.
9. Inspect transaxle case for damage after removing seal.
10. Clean drive axle seal mating surface on housing with crocus cloth.
11. Install drive axle seal using installer

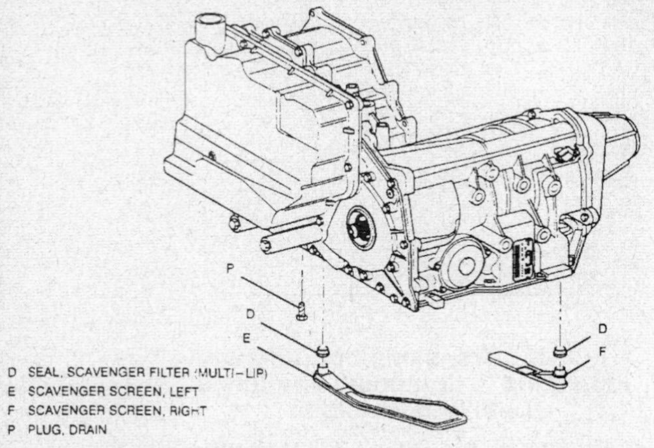

TH5029300511000X

Fig. 12 Transaxle scavenger screens & drain plug

tool No. J-39051, or equivalent, and suitable hammer.

INSTALLATION

1. If installing righthand drive axle, install suitable axle seal protector so it can be pulled out after drive axle is installed.
2. Install drive axle into transaxle. Ensure drive axle snap ring is properly seated by grasping inner joint housing and pulling outboard. **Do not pull on drive axle.** Driveshaft will remain in place when snap ring is properly seated.
3. Drive axle into hub and bearing.
4. Connect ball joint to knuckle.
5. **Torque** ball joint nut to 84 inch lbs.
6. Tighten an additional 120° (two flats).
7. When tightening nut, minimum **torque** of 37 ft. lbs. must be obtained.
8. If 37 ft. lbs. cannot be obtained, inspect for stripped threads.
9. If threads are satisfactory, replace ball joint and knuckle.
10. Turn nut up to an additional 60° (one flat) to allow for installation of cotter pin, as required.
11. Install hub nut . Prevent drive axle from turning by inserting suitable screwdriver into rotor fins.
12. Remove seal protector. If axle seal protector was installed, remove by pulling inline with handle. Ensure seal protector is completely removed and no pieces are lefthand inside of transaxle.
13. Install wheel and tire, then lower vehicle.

CASE EXTENSION & SCAVENGER PIPE, REPLACE

REMOVAL

1. Raise and support vehicle, then remove righthand front wheel assembly and splash shields.
2. Remove Real Time Damping (RTD) sensor from lower control arm.
3. Disconnect righthand stabilizer link, tie rod and ball joint from steering knuckle.
4. Remove righthand drive axle.
5. Support transaxle using suitable support fixture.

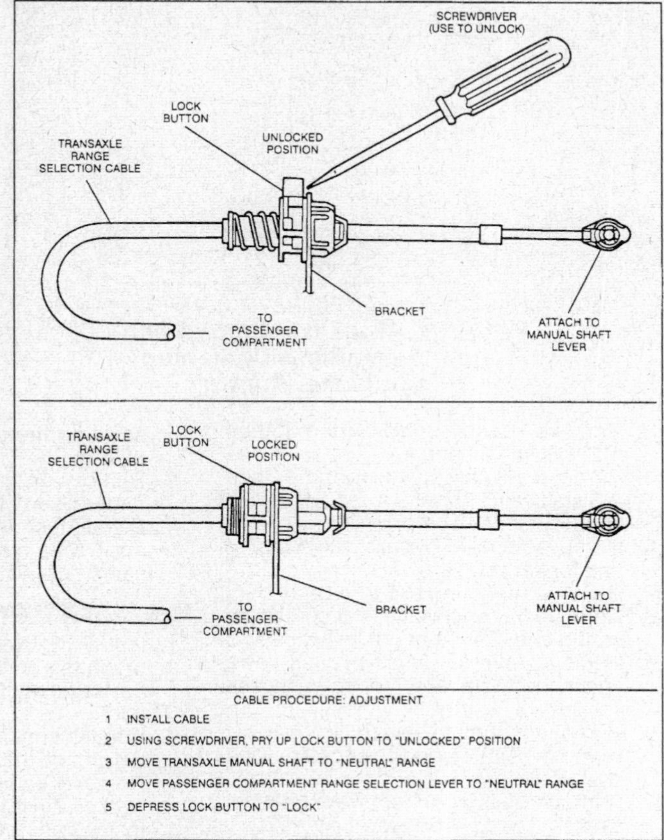

TH5029300522000X

Fig. 13 Transaxle shift control cable adjustment. Aurora, DeVille & Eldorado

6. Disconnect power steering pressure switch connector and wiring harness.
7. Disconnect righthand transaxle mount, bracket connector and wiring harness, then remove righthand transaxle to engine bracket and heat shield.
8. Disconnect VSS connector and ground from case.
9. Remove case extension bolts and stud using suitable torque wrench, case extension and seal, **Fig. 30.** Seal may remain in extension.
10. Remove roller thrust bearing and selective washer and bolt.
11. Remove scavenger pipe by prying on differential, then the seal.
12. Inspect scavenger tube for damage and clogging.
13. Inspect case extension and case mating surfaces for scoring and damage.

INSTALLATION

1. Install scavenger tube seal into case and tap scavenger tube into case using suitable plastic hammer to ensure fit, **Fig. 30.** Pipe rib will remain exposed.
2. Install scavenger bolt.
3. Install selective washer and thrust roller bearing onto differential output shaft.
4. Insert case extension seal into case extension and install case extension onto case.
5. Install bolts and stud with stud in 11 o'clock position using star pattern.
6. Connect VSS connector and ground to case.
7. Install righthand transaxle to engine bracket.
8. Install heat shield, righthand transaxle mount and bolts.
9. Install power steering pressure switch connector and wiring harness.
10. Remove transaxle support.
11. Install drive axle.
12. Connect righthand ball joint, righthand tie rod and righthand stabilizer link to steering knuckle.
13. Install RTD sensor to lower control arm.
14. Install splash shields and wheel assembly.
15. Add suitable ATF as required.

MANUAL SHAFT/PARK ACTUATOR, REPLACE

REMOVAL

1. Remove transaxle range switch.
2. Raise and support vehicle.
3. Remove bottom pan and gasket, scavenger screens and seals.
4. Remove lower controls.
5. Remove detent spring, **Fig. 31.** Grasp

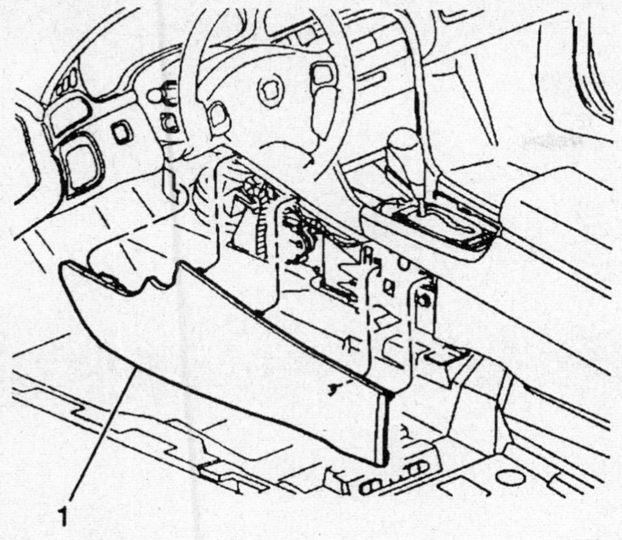

GC5029901055000X

Fig. 14 Transaxle shift control cable adjustment. Seville

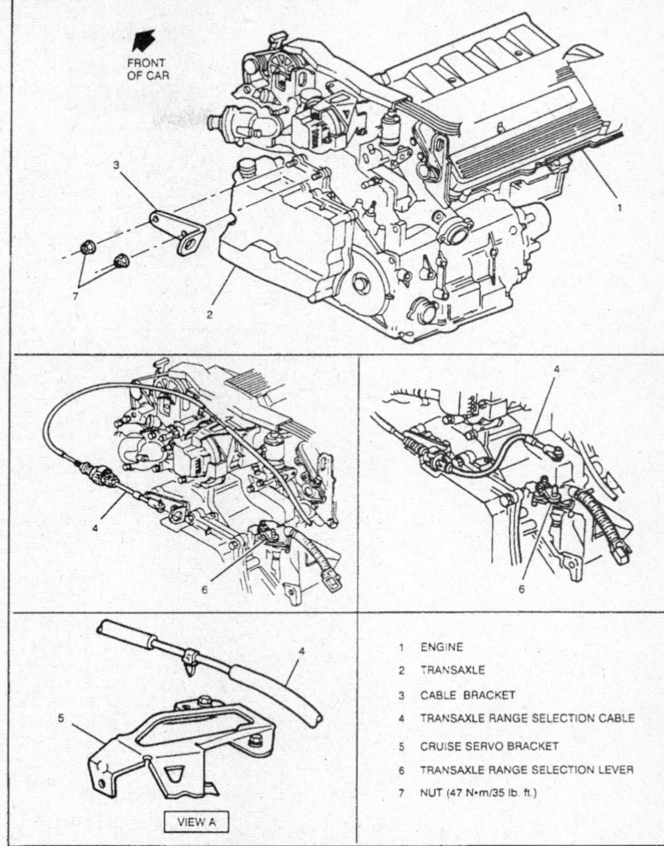

Copyrighted Material Reprinted with Permission from Hydra-Matic Div., GM Corp.

TH5029300520000X

Fig. 15 Transaxle range switch. DeVille, Eldorado & Seville

detent roller end of spring with pliers to remove.

6. Remove detent roller bolt, pivot arm, sleeve and washer.
7. Remove manual shaft nut. **Detent lever must be held in place when removing nut to prevent damage to actuator rod.**
8. Remove detent lever and actuator rod. Discard detent lever.
9. Remove manual shaft and lower vehicle.
10. Remove seal and washer.
11. Inspect actuator guide for excessive wear and actuator rod for cracked end, bent rod or broken spring.

INSTALLATION

1. Install new manual shaft seal into case.
2. Raise and support vehicle.
3. Install manual shaft and seat manual shaft (flush with case) seal with appropriate socket.
4. Attach new detent lever and actuator rod to manual shaft. Hold detent lever in place with suitable screwdriver to prevent bending of actuator rod.
5. Install manual shaft nut.
6. Install detent roller washer, pivot arm and sleeves.
7. Install detent roller bolt .
8. Install detent return spring to detent roller and manual shaft.
9. Install lower controls.
10. Install bottom pan and gasket, scavenger screens and lip seals.
11. Lower vehicle.
12. Add transaxle fluid as required.
13. If complete fluid change was required, reset transaxle oil life indicator.

PARKING PAWL, SPRING & SLEEVE, REPLACE

REMOVAL

1. Raise and support vehicle.
2. Remove bottom pan and gasket, scavenger screen and seals.
3. Remove lower controls.
4. Remove final drive.
5. Move manual shaft from Park position.
6. Drive out pivot pin mounting pin, **Fig. 32.**
7. Drive parking pawl pivot pin towards extension housing with pin punch. Push down on spring while driving shaft out.
8. Remove parking pawl and spring.
9. Remove park/lock sleeve using suitable rubber mallet. Drive out towards case extension portion of case.

INSPECTION

1. Inspect parking pawl tooth for damage.
2. Inspect parking pawl spring for over expansion
3. Inspect pivot pin for scorning and excessive wear.

INSTALLATION

1. Place pawl in case slot and attach spring to pawl.
2. Insert pivot pin through spring and pawl. Hook end of spring locates on case and square end of top of parking pawl.
3. Install mounting pin using suitable hammer and pin punch, then the actuator sleeve.
4. Install final drive.
5. Install lower controls.
6. Install bottom pan and gasket, scavenger screens and lip seals.
7. Lower vehicle.
8. Add suitable ATF and reset transaxle oil life indicator as required.

CONVERTER COVER, REPLACE

1. Raise and support vehicle.
2. Remove engine to transaxle brace bolts, mounting bolt and torque converter cover.
3. Reverse procedure to install.

FINAL DRIVE & PARKING GEAR, REPLACE

REMOVAL

Refer to **Fig. 33** when servicing the final drive gear and parking gear.

1. Remove case extension.
2. Remove differential housing bolts using suitable torque wrench. Ensure transaxle is in Park position.
3. Remove differential housing, differential gear snap ring, gear and thrust washer.
4. Remove final drive carrier, thrust bearing and sun gear.
5. Remove snap ring and final drive internal gear.

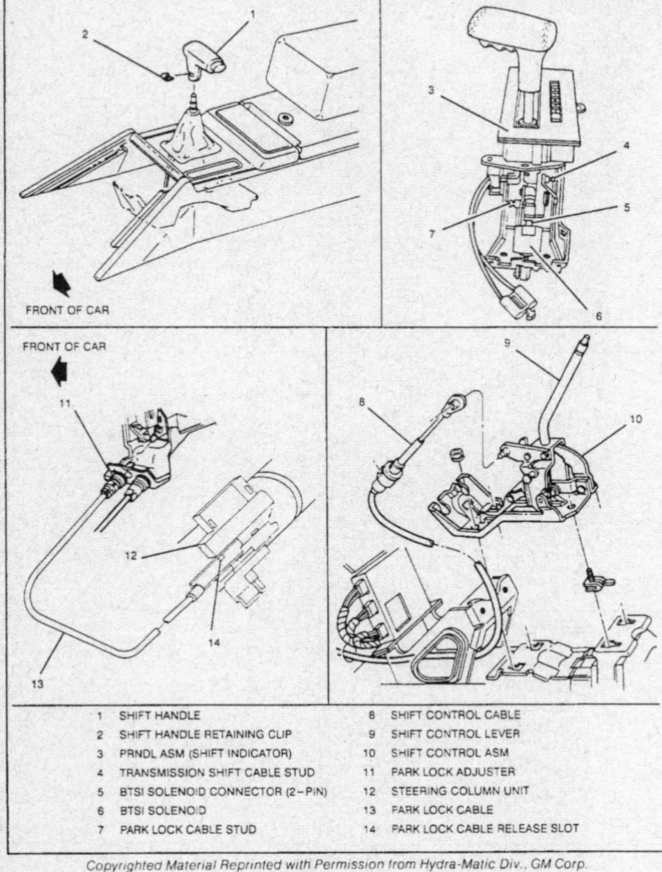

TH5029300521000X

Fig. 16 Transaxle range control system. DeVille, Eldorado & Seville

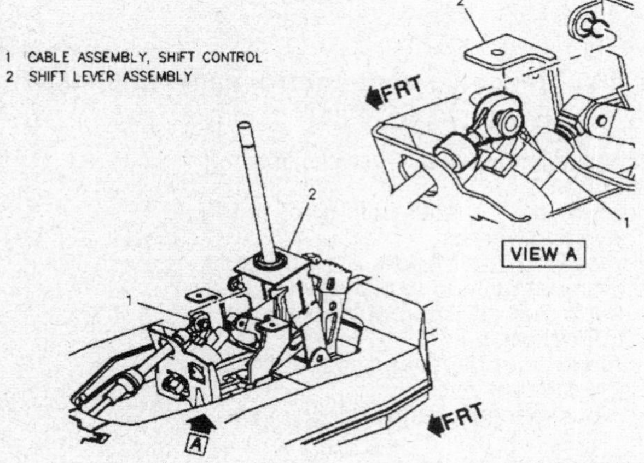

GC5029500786000X

Fig. 17 Shift control cable & shift lever. Aurora

6. Remove snap ring and parking gear with thrust bearing.

INSTALLATION

1. Install parking gear with thrust bearing.
2. Install snap ring and final drive internal gear.
3. Install sun gear with bushing and seal side facing differential.
4. Install final drive carrier, turning unit until it meshes with sun gear and internal gear teeth.
5. Install lefthand thrust washer and lefthand differential side gear.
6. Install snap ring. **Place transaxle in Park using manual shaft to lock final drive unit. Actuator rod will move up.**
7. Install differential housing and bolts. Tighten bolts in star pattern.
8. Install case extension and scavenger pipe.

OUTPUT SHAFT, REPLACE

1. Raise and support vehicle, then remove both front wheel and splash shields.
2. Disconnect both front suspension position sensors from lower control arms and position aside.
3. Disconnect both front stabilizer links from struts.
4. Separate both tie rods and ball joints from steering knuckles.
5. Remove both drive axles from transaxle.
6. Remove case extension and scavenger pipe.
7. Remove differential housing.
8. Remove snap ring and lefthand differential gear.
9. Remove output shaft through lefthand (driver's) side.
10. Reverse procedure to install, noting the following:
    a. Connect ball joint to knuckle.
    b. **Torque** ball joint nut to 84 inch lbs.
    c. Tighten an additional 120° (two flats).
    d. When tightening nut, minimum **torque** of 37 ft. lbs. must be obtained.
    e. If 37 ft. lbs. cannot be obtained, inspect for stripped threads.
    f. If threads are satisfactory, replace ball joint and knuckle.
    g. Turn nut up to an additional 60° (one flat) to allow for installation of cotter pin, as required.
    h. Connect tie rod to knuckle.
    i. **Torque** nuts to 90 inch lbs.
    j. Tighten additional ⅓ turn (two flats).
    k. When tightening tie rod end nut, minimum **torque** of 33 ft. lbs. must be obtained.
    l. If 33 ft. lbs. cannot be obtained, inspect for stripped threads.
    m. If threads are satisfactory, replace ball joint and knuckle.
    n. After tightening castellated nut, align slot in nut to cotter pin hole by tightening only.
    o. **Do not loosen nut for cotter pin installation.**

TRANSAXLE MOUNT, REPLACE

LEFTHAND SIDE

1. Install engine support fixture tool No. J-28467, or equivalent, and raise transaxle side of powertrain one inch above resting screws.
2. Raise and support vehicle, then remove front wheel assembly.
3. Disconnect RSS position sensor from lower ball stud.
4. Remove forward splash shield.
5. Remove frame to mount nuts and bracket to transaxle bolts, **Fig. 34.**
6. Reverse procedure to install.

RIGHTHAND SIDE

1. Install engine support fixture tool No. J-28467, or equivalent. Raise passenger side of powertrain 1 inch above resting position with adjusting screws.

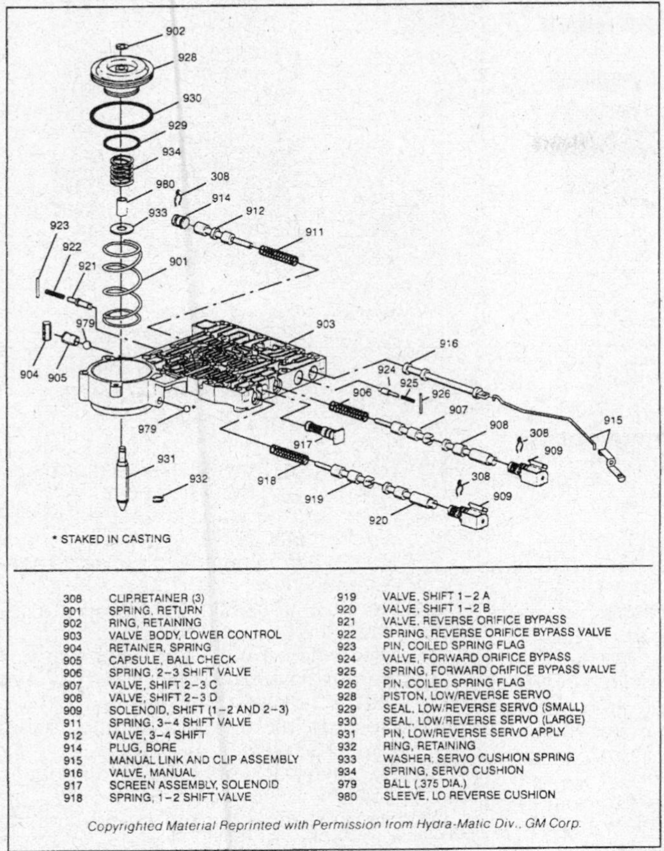

TH5029300530000X

Fig. 18 Exploded view of lower controls

2. Raise and support vehicle, then remove righthand front wheel assembly.
3. Remove frame to mount nuts. Mount should pull away from frame.
4. Remove transaxle mount, **Fig. 35.**
5. Remove bracket to transaxle bolts and bracket.
6. Reverse procedure to install.

PARK/NEUTRAL POSITION (PNP) SWITCH, REPLACE

REMOVAL

1. Place shifter in Neutral position and disconnect PNP electrical connectors.
2. Remove linkage mounting nut and disconnect shifter cable.
3. Remove manual shaft lever and PNP switch.

INSTALLATION

1. Ensure transaxle is in Neutral position and install alignment tool No. J-41545, or equivalent, onto PNP switch, **Fig. 36.**
2. Install PNP switch by aligning flats on switch with flats on manual shaft.
3. Install PNP switch mounting bolts.
4. Remove alignment tool from PNP switch and install manual shaft lever.
5. Connect shifter cable and tighten linkage mounting nut.
6. Connect electrical connectors.

OIL PAN, REPLACE

BOTTOM PAN & GASKET

1. Raise and support vehicle, then loosen bottom pan bolts to drain pan fluid into suitable container.
2. Remove pan bolts, pan and gasket.
3. Inspect pan and bolts for damage. Repair or replace as required.
4. Reverse procedure to install, noting the following:
   a. Ensure bottom pan and case sealing surfaces are clean and dry.
   b. Ensure pan bolts are dry and bolt holes free of residual fluid.
   c. Install pan mounting bolts hand tight.

SCAVENGER SCREENS & LIP SEALS

1. Raise and support vehicle, then remove bottom pan.
2. Remove left and/or righthand scavenger screens and seals with small screwdriver. **Do not score or damage case.**

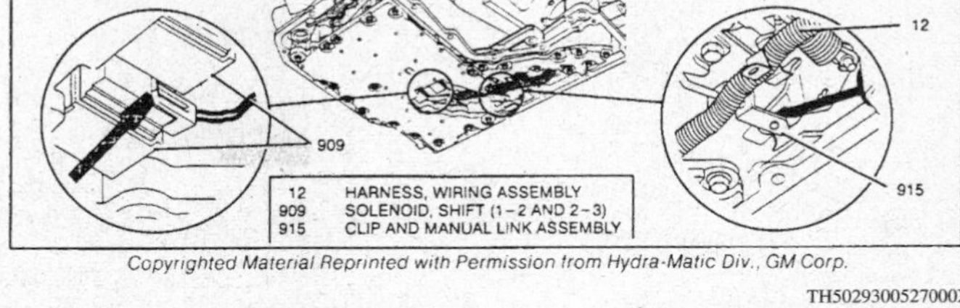

TH5029300527000X

Fig. 19 Disengaging connector tabs

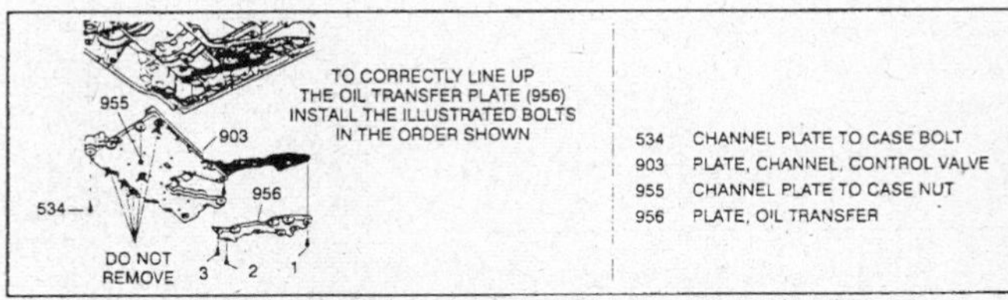

TH5029300528000X

Fig. 20 Oil transfer, channel & control valve plates

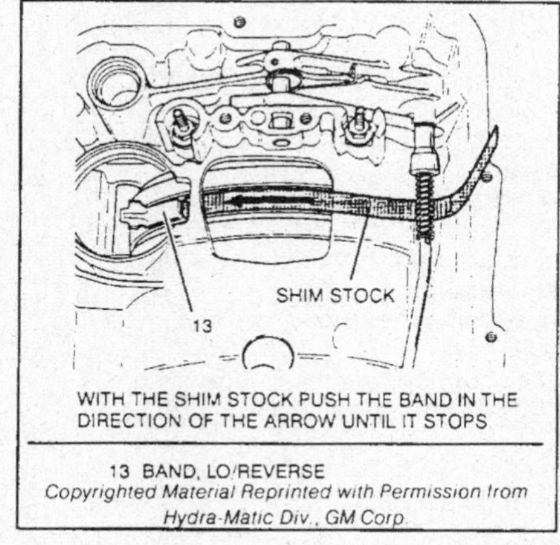

TH5029300529000X

Fig. 21 Positioning low/reverse band

3. Inspect screen lip seals for nicks or cuts.
4. Clean or replace scavenger screen and install.
5. Install pan.

TRANSAXLE

REPLACE

Refer to **Figs. 37 through 39** when removing and installing transaxle.

AURORA

1998–99

1. Remove shift control cable and bracket at transaxle.
2. Remove manual shaft lever and transaxle range selector switch.
3. Install engine support fixture tool No. J-28467, or equivalent, and raise powertrain until weight is off mounts.
4. Drain cooling system into suitable container.
5. Remove vacuum line at brake booster and transaxle vent hose.

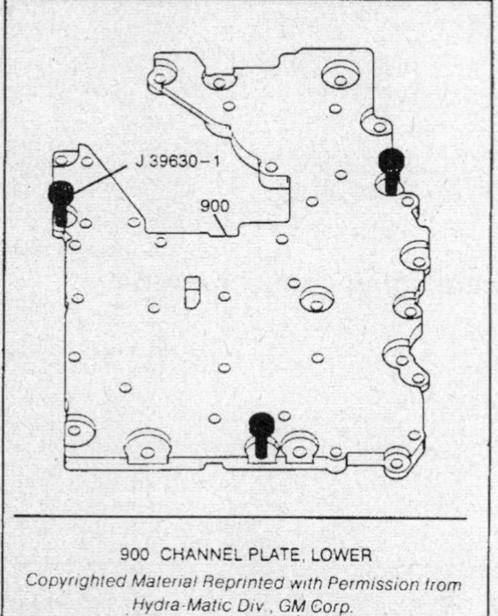

TH5029300531000X

Fig. 22 Guide pins to lower channel plate installation

6. Disconnect transaxle and power steering gear electrical connectors.
7. Disconnect upper and lower transaxle cooler lines.
8. Remove bracket mounting nut at transaxle.
9. Disconnect coolant bypass tube at thermostat housing.
10. Remove left and righthand transaxle mount bolts.
11. Raise and support vehicle, then remove both front wheel and splash shield s.
12. Remove outer tie rods and ball joints from steering knuckles.
13. Remove left and righthand drive axle nuts, then drive axles from hub.
14. Remove left and righthand drive axles from transaxle.
15. Remove oil pan to transaxle bracket.
16. Remove torque converter cover and torque converter to flywheel bolts.
17. Remove complete exhaust system as required.
18. Support transaxle using suitable jack.
19. Remove steering rack to righthand transaxle mount bolts.
20. Remove bolts and righthand transaxle mount.
21. Remove power steering lines and brackets as required.
22. Remove mounting bolt and righthand steering rack.
23. Remove support frame and knock sensor shield.
24. Remove engine to transaxle brace and transaxle mount to bracket mounting nuts.
25. Disconnect electrical connectors from neutral safety switch.
26. Remove rear transaxle mount bracket and engine to transaxle mounting bolts.
27. Remove bolts and frame.
28. Lower transaxle.
29. Reverse procedure to install.

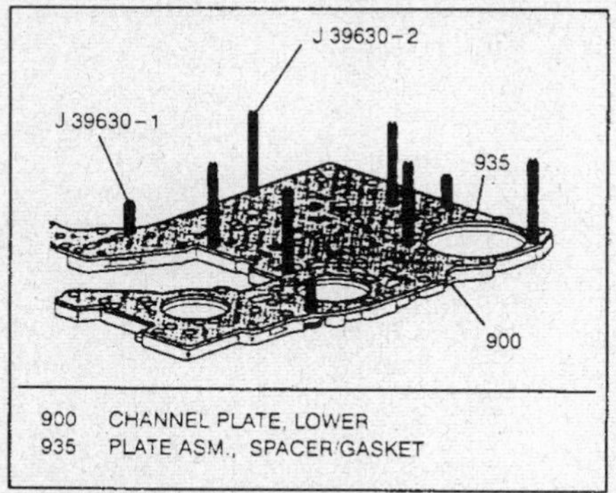

TH5029300532000X

Fig. 23 Spacer plate/gasket installation

2001-02

1. Remove air cleaner.
2. Disconnect shift control cable from shift lever.
3. Remove shift control cable from bracket and position aside.
4. Remove upper transmission line at transmission and lower line at radiator.
5. Remove both heater tube retainers from upper case side cover studs.
6. Remove coolant temperature sensor electrical connector.
7. Remove ground wire from stud near rear transaxle to engine brace.
8. Remove rear engine to transmission brace upper mounting nuts.
9. Raise and support vehicle.
10. Disconnect lefthand front wheel speed sensor and remove harness from retainer.
11. Disconnect vehicle speed sensor from transmission.
12. Disconnect power steering gear electrical connector.
13. Lower vehicle.
14. Disconnect transmission vent hose at transmission.
15. Carefully pull wiring harness up from beneath vehicle and set aside.
16. Position engine harness at transaxle top to access upper mounting bolts.
17. Remove upper transaxle mounting bolts.
18. Support engine with engine support adapters tool No. J-28467-90A, engine support adapter leg set tools No. J-36462-A and universal engine support fixture tool No. J-28467-B, or equivalents.
19. Raise and support vehicle.
20. Remove engine frame as described in "Turbo Hydra-Matic 4T60-E, 4T65-E & 4T65-E-HD Automatic Transaxles" under "Transaxle, Replace" "2001 Aurora."
21. Remove left and righthand drive axles as described in "Turbo Hydra-Matic 4T60-E, 4T65-E & 4T65-E-HD Automatic Transaxles" under "Transaxle, Replace."
22. Remove mounting nuts and exhaust heat shield at righthand side transaxle brace.

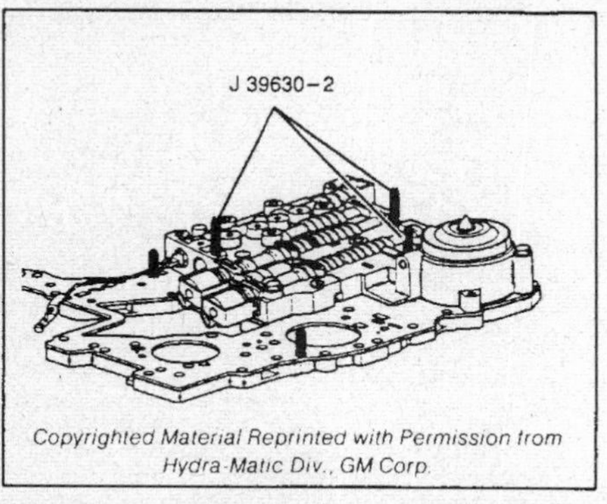

TH5029300533000X

Fig. 24 Lower valve body installation

23. Remove righthand side transaxle to engine brace mounting bolts.
24. Remove rear upper transaxle to engine mounting bolt.
25. Remove front engine to transaxle pencil brace.
26. Remove transaxle front ground connections.
27. Disconnect transaxle main harness.
28. Remove mounting bolts and engine oil pan to transaxle bracket.
29. Remove mounting bolts and torque converter cover.
30. Remove torque converter mounting bolts.
31. Remove mounting bolts and lefthand transaxle bracket from case side cover.
32. Support transaxle with suitable transmission jack.
33. Remove front lower transaxle mounting bolts.
34. Separate engine and transaxle.
35. Lower transaxle down and towards left on slight angle so case can clear starter.
36. Remove transaxle.
37. Reverse procedure to install, noting the following:
    a. Align transaxle with engine alignment dowels.
    b. **Do not use paints, lubricants, or corrosion inhibitors on mounting bolts, nuts or screw and their surfaces unless specified.**

DEVILLE & ELDORADO

1. Remove headlamp housing upper filler panel and diagonal brace.
2. Remove air cleaner and disconnect shifter cable and bracket at transaxle.
3. Remove torque struts.
4. Disconnect oil cooler lines and oil sending line at transaxle.
5. Remove two upper bellhousing bolts.
6. Disconnect power steering hose at auxiliary cooler. Plug cooler holes and return hose to prevent fluid leakage and contamination.
7. Install engine support fixture J-28467, or equivalent, and raise powertrain until weight is off mounts.
8. Raise and support vehicle, then remove both front wheel and splash shields.

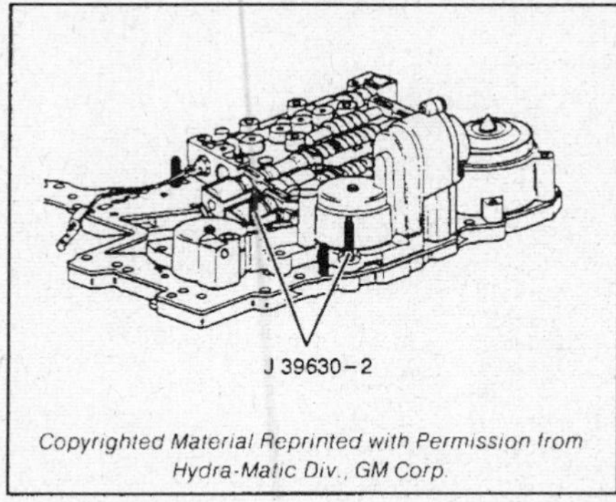

TH5029300534000X

Fig. 25 Accumulator installation

9. Disconnect both front suspension position sensors from lower control arms and position aside.
10. Separate both tie rods from steering knuckles and both ball joints from struts.
11. Remove both drive axles from hubs and transaxle.
12. Disconnect power steering filter at cradle.
13. Remove air conditioning splash shield from frame.
14. Remove ABS modulator from bracket and support.
15. Remove engine oil pan to transaxle bracket.
16. Remove torque converter cover and flywheel to converter bolts. Mark flywheel to converter position for assembly.
17. Remove powertrain mount nuts from cradle.
18. Rotate steering intermediate shaft until steering gear stub shaft clamp bolt is accessible through lefthand wheel opening.
19. Remove clamp bolt through lefthand wheel opening.
20. Remove steering intermediate shaft from steering gear. **Do not rotate steering wheel or move position of steering gear when intermediate shaft is disconnected.**
21. Disconnect electrical harness from front of cradle and support rear of cradle with suitable jackstand.
22. Remove four rear cradle bolts and lower jack stand enough to gain access to power steering gear heat shield and return line fitting.
23. Remove power steering gear heat shield and return line at gear. Plug steering gear and pressure line to avoid leakage and contamination.
24. Disconnect power steering electrical connector.
25. Raise jack stand and install one rear cradle bolt on each side to hand tightness to support cradle. Remove jack stand.
26. Support frame and remove six frame mount bolts.
27. Lower frame and/or raise vehicle with steering gear attached.
28. Disconnect transaxle, VSS, ground strap and transaxle harness from transaxle clip connectors

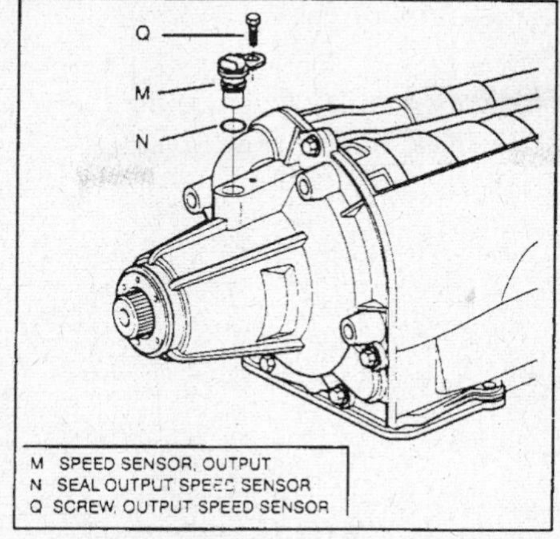

TH5029300525000X

Fig. 26 Output speed sensor replacement

29. Disconnect fuel line bundle from transaxle.
30. Remove left and righthand transaxle mount, then bracket from transaxle.
31. Install transaxle support fixture tool No. J-28664, or equivalent.
32. Remove engine to transaxle heat shield and bracket, then two engine to transaxle bolts.
33. Lower transaxle.
34. Disconnect manual shaft linkage and neutral start switch.
35. Disconnect speed sensor and oil return pipe.
36. Reverse procedure to install, noting the following:
    a. Install frame mount bolts in following order: lefthand side No. 2 mount bolt into body, lefthand side No. 1 mount bolt into body and remaining bolts in no specific order.
    b. Flush transaxle oil cooler.
    c. Adjust transaxle range switch.
    d. Adjust range control cable.
    e. Bleed power steering system.
    f. Inspect front suspension alignment. Adjust toe, as required.
    g. Reset transaxle adapts.
    h. Reset transaxle oil life indicator.

SEVILLE

1. Drain cooling system into suitable container.
2. Remove upper filler panel.
3. Remove air cleaner upper plenum and intake tube.
4. Remove surge tank inlet and outlet pipes.
5. Disconnect oil cooler lines at cooler and oil sending line at transaxle. Plug hoses to prevent leakage.
6. Disconnect shift cable from shift linkage.
7. Remove shift linkage from transaxle.
8. Remove upper transaxle to engine mounting bolts.
9. Support engine using engine support fixture tool No. J-28467-360, or equivalent.
10. Raise lefthand side of powertrain (tran-

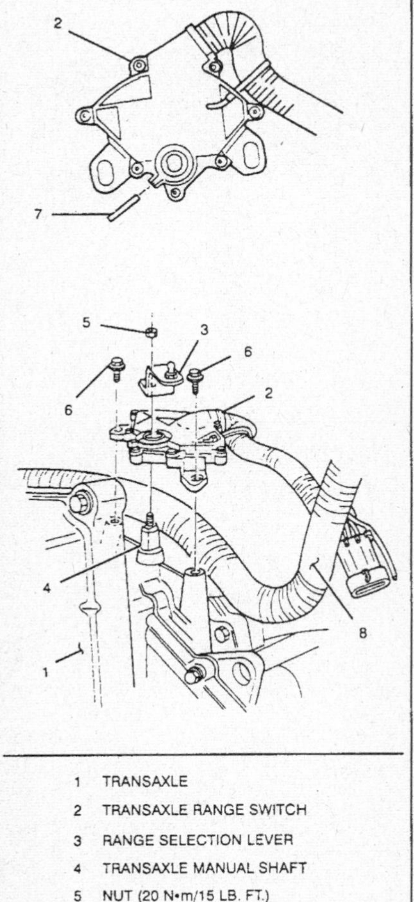

TH5029300523000X

Fig. 27 Selector switch replacement

saxle side) 1 inch above resting position.

11. Raise and support vehicle, then remove both front tires.
12. Remove lower splash shield.
13. Remove both front suspension position sensor links from lower control arms and position them aside.
14. Remove both stabilizer links from lower control arms. Allow stabilizer shaft to sit loosely on engine frame.
15. Remove both stabilizer shaft insulator brackets from engine frame.
16. Remove drive axle nuts and separate axles from hub.
17. Remove both tie rod cotter pins and nuts, then separate tie rods from steering knuckles.
18. Remove both lower ball joint cotter pins and nuts, then separate ball joints from steering knuckles.
19. Remove drive axles.

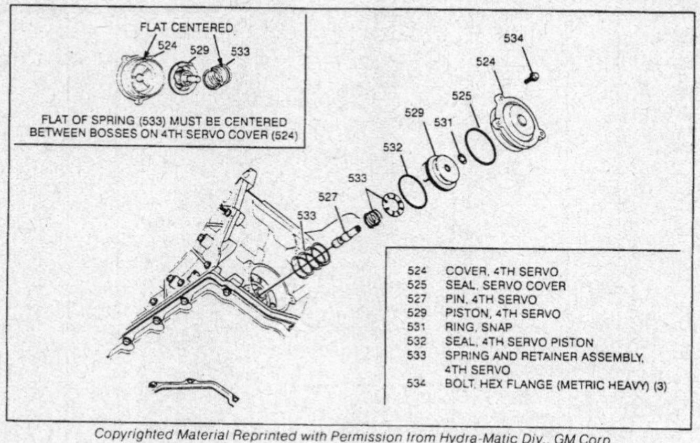

TH5029300526000X

Fig. 28 Exploded view of fourth servo

TH5029300536000X

Fig. 29 Drive axle removal

20. Remove Brake Pressure Modulator Valve (BPMV) and bracket from engine frame.
21. Remove rear transaxle mount bracket mounting bolts from lefthand frame rail.
22. Remove left and righthand engine mount mounting nuts from engine frame.
23. Remove steering rack mounting bolts from engine frame.
24. Remove brake line and power steering line retainers from engine frame.
25. Remove heat shield and disconnect post oxygen sensor.
26. Disconnect one center exhaust hanger to allow easy movement of exhaust in rearward direction.
27. Remove catalytic converter brace.
28. Lower vehicle and support engine frame using engine support table tool No. J-35580, or equivalent.
29. Remove six engine fame mount mounting bolts from engine frame.
30. Fully separate tie rod ends and lower ball joints from steering knuckles.
31. Raise vehicle slowly away from engine frame.
32. Remove engine frame and support table.
33. Remove steering rack heat shield from rack.
34. Disconnect power steering lines from steering rack.
35. Remove righthand rear engine to transaxle bracket upper mounting bolts and bracket.
36. Remove righthand transaxle mount bracket lower mounting bolts and bracket from transaxle. Support steering rack in position that allows access to bracket bolts.
37. Remove steering rack.
38. Remove righthand front engine to transaxle brace bolt, nut, brace and heat shield.
39. Remove righthand front engine to transaxle bracket.
40. Remove engine oil pan to transaxle bracket, torque converter cover brace and cover.
41. Remove flywheel to torque converter bolts. Mark flywheel to torque converter relationship for installation.
42. Disconnect all transaxle electrical connectors.
43. Remove engine to transaxle heat shield and bracket.
44. Support transaxle using suitable transaxle jack.
45. Remove engine to transaxle mounting bolts.
46. Separate transaxle from engine and lower transaxle.
47. Reverse procedure to install.

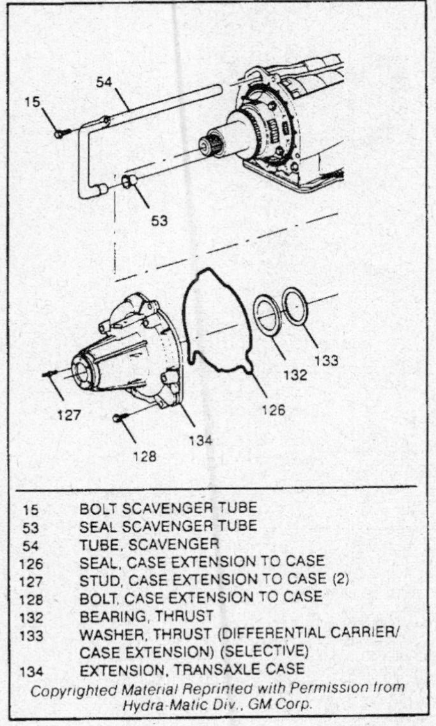

TH5029300537000X

Fig. 30 Exploded view of case extension & scavenger pipe

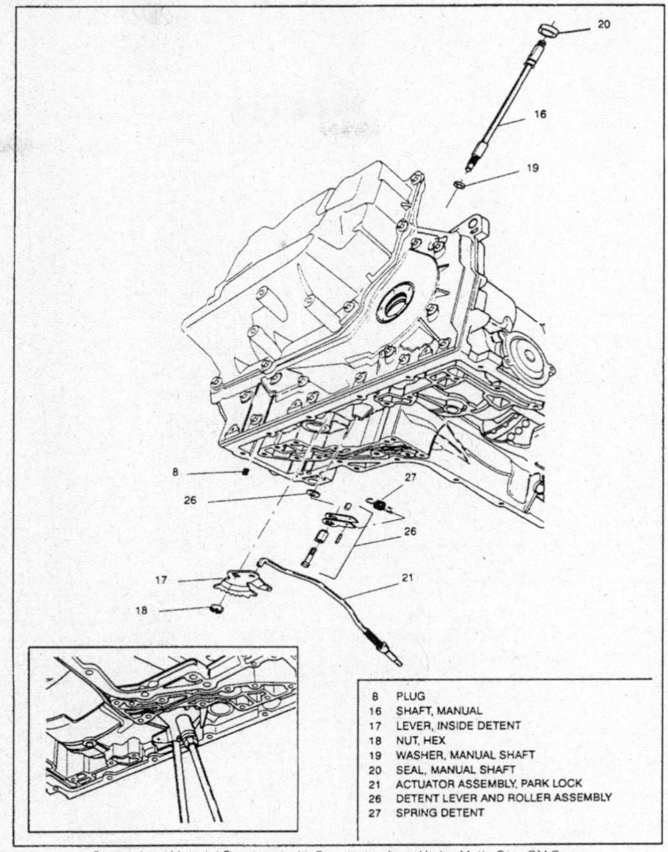

TH5029300535000X

Fig. 31 Exploded view of manual shift & detent lever

TECHNICAL SERVICE BULLETINS

SLIPPING IN 4TH GEAR OR NO 4TH GEAR

2000 DEVILLE, ELDORADO & SEVILLE & 2001 AURORA

On some of these models there may be no 4th gear or slipping in 4th gear. Diagnostic Trouble Code (DTC) P0734 may be set.

This condition may be caused by a warped lower control valve body channel plate.

To correct this condition, replace the lower control valve body channel plate and spacer plate/gasket assembly.

DELAYED REVERSE ENGAGEMENT

2001

On some of these models there may be a shift delay into reverse.

This condition may be caused by low fluid volume or pressure in the reverse accumulator, caused by internal leakage at the piston seal.

To correct this condition replace the reverse accumulator housing.

INTERMITTENT NO POWER

2000–01 DEVILLE, ELDORADO & SEVILLE & 2001 AURORA

On some of these models there may be intermittent no power during heavy acceleration or wide open throttle acceleration.

This condition may be cause by a leaking Transmission Fluid Pressure (TFP) switch.

To correct this condition replace the TFP switch.

TRANSMISSION FLUID LEAK AT LOWER TRANSMISSION COOLER LINE

2001

On some of these models there may be a small transmission fluid leak from the quick connect fitting at the case cover.

This condition may be caused by a severe cold temperature related condition. This interface will only leak for a brief moment when the vehicle is shifted into Drive and/or Reverse, and at a very low sump temperature.

To correct this condition replace the quick connect type transmission case cover cooler fitting with an inverted flare type fitting (part No. 8684086). Replace the lower cooler line with the threaded type fitting (Eldorado part No. 25658709 or Aurora, DeVille and Seville part No. 25681002.)

HARSH REVERSE ENGAGEMENT

2001

On some of these models there may be a harsh garage shift from Park to Reverse during the first shift of the day. The condition will not repeat itself after the first shift of the day, but will return the next day during the first shift of the day.

This condition may be caused by an unintended transmission fluid pressure spike occurring during the first Park to Reverse shift of the day because of air in the reverse hydraulic circuit being fed into the line pressure circuit across gasket slot.

To correct this condition replace the gasket between the spacer plate and the case cover with the new style gasket (part No. 24221401).

NO DRIVE OR NO REVERSE

1998–99 AURORA

On some of these models the transaxle has no drive or no reverse. Also, visual inspection of the transmission fluid may show a burnt appearance.

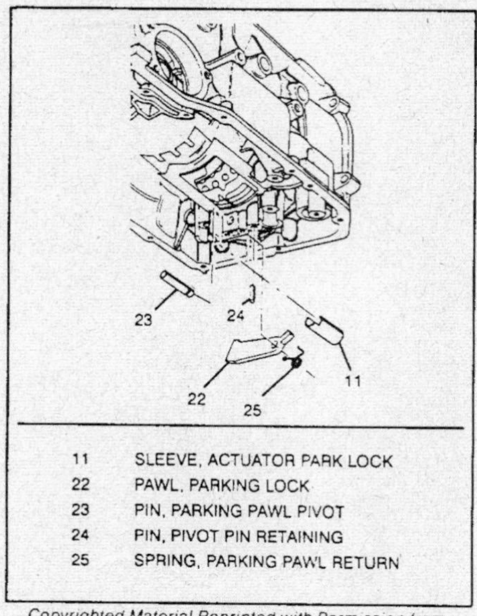

TH5029300540000X

Fig. 32 Parking pawl & actuator sleeve components

56 RING, SNAP (OUTPUT SHAFT) (3)
57 SHAFT, OUTPUT
100 CARRIER, FINAL DRIVE
102 BEARING, THRUST (SUNGEAR/CARRIER)
110 CARRIER, DIFFERENTIAL
111 WASHER, THRUST (DIFFERENTIAL) (RIGHT)
112 GEAR, DIFFERENTIAL SIDE (RIGHT)
117 WASHER, THRUST (DIFFERENTIAL) (LEFT)
118 GEAR, DIFFERENTIAL SIDE (LEFT)
119 BOLT, DIFFERENTIAL CARRIER TO FINAL DRIVE (4, 15mm)
120 GEAR, FINAL DRIVE INTERNAL
121 GEAR, FINAL DRIVE SUN
135 RING, SNAP

TH5029300538000A

Fig. 33 Exploded view of final drive & output shaft

This condition may be caused by a twist in the lower transmission cooler hose at the radiator end. The twist is caused by allowing the hose to rotate when tightening the fitting at the transmission. The twist causes the rubber hose portion of the line to kink and cut off fluid flow to the cooler.

To correct this condition replace the lower transmission oil cooler hose as follows:

1. Remove mounting bolts and upper radiator core support brace.
2. Remove lefthand cooling fan mounting bolts.
3. Disconnect electrical connector and remove lefthand cooling fan.
4. Remove air intake duct.
5. Disconnect and remove cooler hose.
6. Install lower transaxle oil cooler hose.
7. Connect oil cooler hose fitting to radiator and **torque** to 20 ft. lbs.
8. Connect oil cooler hose fitting to transaxle.
9. **Torque** hose fitting to 16 ft. lbs. **Hold hose in position to prevent twisting.**
10. Install air intake duct.
11. Install lefthand cooling fan and connect electrical connector.
12. Install lefthand cooling fan mounting bolts.
13. Install upper radiator core support brace and mounting bolts.

HARSH GARAGE SHIFT, HARSH OR DELAYED ENGAGEMENT OF PARK

1998 AURORA, DEVILLE, ELDORADO & SEVILLE

On some of these models built before Feb. 16, 1998, there may be a harsh garage shift, a delayed or harsh engagement from park to reverse or drive to reverse. It may be describe this as a metallic clunk at the end of the shift.

This condition may be caused a combination of reverse clutch configuration, accumulation and vehicle calibration of this shift maneuver.

To correct this condition install a replacement transaxle with a newer model code and calibrate the PCM.

NOISE, VIBRATION OR GROWL DURING RIGHTHAND TURNS OR HARD ACCELERATION

1998 AURORA

On some of these models there may be a noise, vibration or growl from the front of the vehicle during righthand turns or hard acceleration.

This condition may be caused by the rear transaxle mount.

To correct this condition, proceed as follows:

1. Raise and support vehicle.
2. Support transaxle with suitable screwjack.
3. Loosen rear transaxle mount nuts. **Do not remove nuts.**
4. Unload mount by lowering transaxle.
5. Remove rear transaxle mount from frame rail.
6. Adjust transaxle mount to eliminate bind or twist.
7. Raise transaxle until bracket contacts mount. Ensure mount aligns properly.
8. Position center mount studs in mount, as required.
9. Fully load mount by raising transaxle with screwjack.
10. **Torque** mounting nuts to 33 ft. lbs.
11. Remove screwjack and ensure mount alignment.

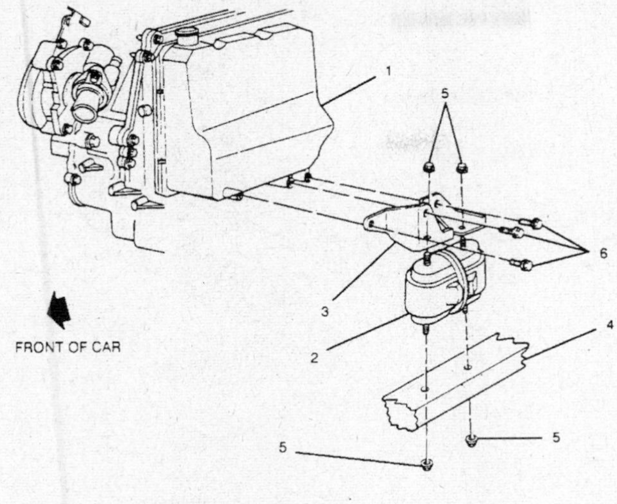

1 TRANSAXLE
2 LEFT TRANSAXLE MOUNT
3 LEFT TRANSAXLE MOUNT BRACKET
4 FRAME
5 NUT (47 N•m/35 LB. FT.)
6 BOLT (47 N•m/35 LB. FT.)

TH5029300541000X

Fig. 34 Exploded view of lefthand transaxle mount & bracket

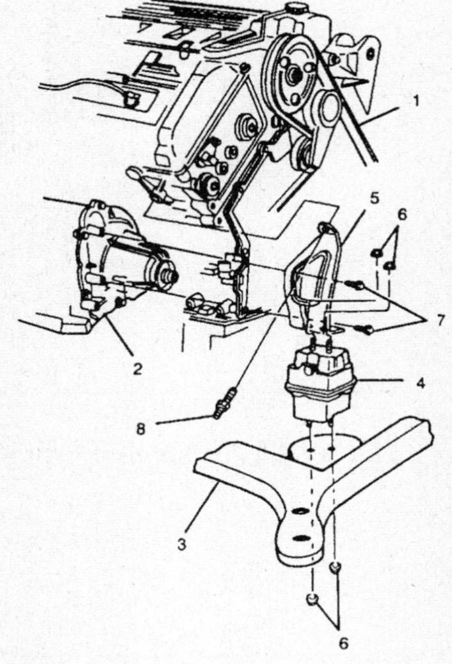

1 ENGINE
2 TRANSAXLE
3 FRAME
4 RIGHT TRANSAXLE MOUNT
5 RIGHT TRANSAXLE MOUNT BRACKET
6 NUT (N•m/35 LB. FT.)
7 BOLT (N•m/35 LB. FT.)
8 STUD (N•m/35 LB. FT.)

TH5029300542000X

Fig. 35 Exploded view of righthand transaxle mount & bracket

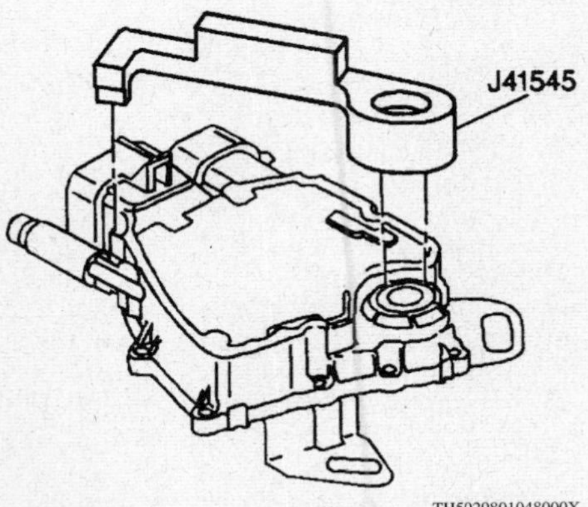

TH5029801048000X

Fig. 36 Park/Neutral position switch installation

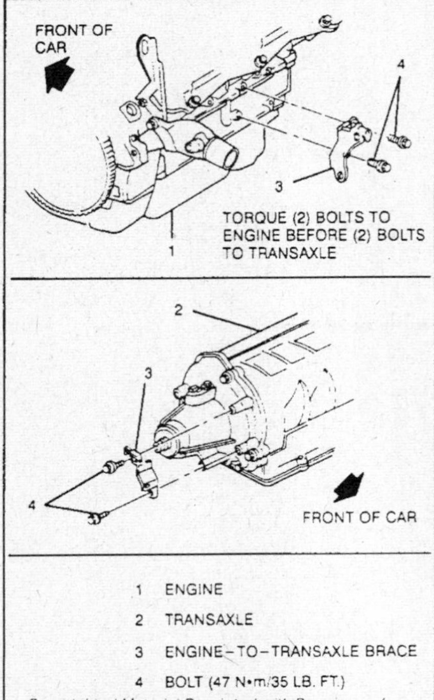

1 ENGINE
2 TRANSAXLE
3 ENGINE–TO–TRANSAXLE BRACE
4 BOLT (47 N•m/35 LB. FT.)

TH5029300543000X

Fig. 37 Engine to transaxle brace removal

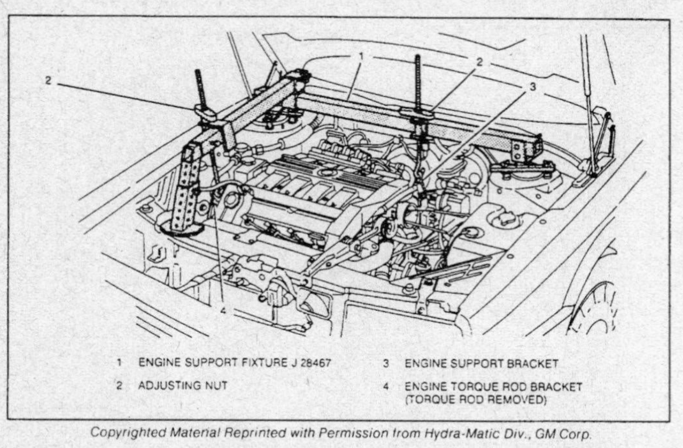

TH5029300544000X

Fig. 38 Engine support fixture installation

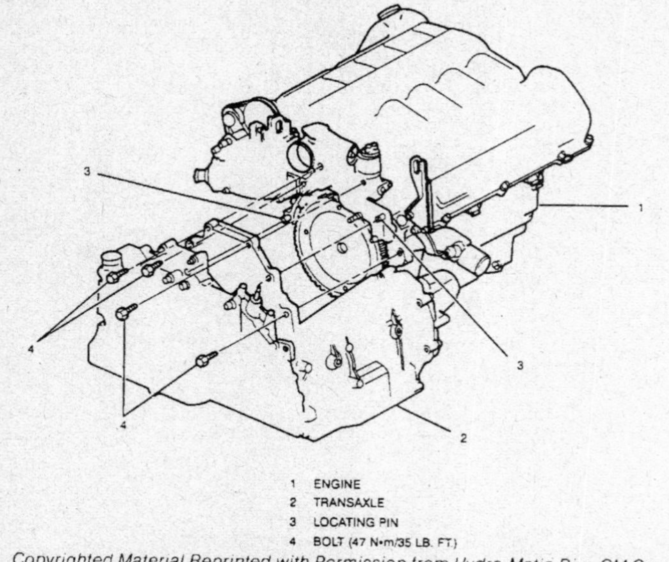

TH5029300545000X

Fig. 39 Transaxle to engine attachment locations

TIGHTENING SPECIFICATIONS

Year	Component	Torque/Ft. Lbs.
1998–2002	Accumulator Housing	72–120①
	ATF Temperature Sensor	30
	Ball Joint	②
	Bottom Pan	84–96①
	Brace To Engine	44
	Case To Engine	55
	Case Cover, Lower Center Stud	20–23
	Case Cover, Lower Lefthand Bolt	15–20
	Case Cover, Lower Righthand Bolt	20–23
	Case Cover, Lower Righthand Stud	15–20
	Case Cover, Upper Lefthand Stud	20–23
	Case Cover To Driven Sprocket Support	15–20
	Case Extension, 10mm Bolt	15–20
	Case Extension, 15mm Stud & 13mm Bolt	37–40
	Channel Plate	72–120①
	Cooler Connector, Case	19–21
	Cooler Connector, Cooler	15–20
	Detent Lever & Roller	72–120①
	Differential To Final Drive Carrier	52–56
	Drive Axle Hub	110
	Drive Sprocket Support	86–114①
	Flywheel	44
	Forward Clutch Support	19–20
	Frame Mount	74
	Input Speed Sensor	86–114①
	Manual Shaft	20–25
	Oil Pan, Bottom	84–96①
	Oil Pan Drain Plug	72–120①
	Oil Test Plug	14–19
	Oil Transfer Plate	72–120①

Continued

TIGHTENING SPECIFICATIONS—Continued

Year	Component	Torque/Ft. Lbs.
1998–2002	Pressure Control Solenoid Bracket	86–114①
	Primary Pump	86–114①
	Servo Cover	72–120①
	Scavenge Pump Cover	86–114①
	Scavenge Tube	72–120①
	Secondary Pump	86–114①
	Side Cover, Lower Bolt	15–20
	Side Cover, Upper Bolt & Stud	37–40
	Speed Sensor	72–120①
	Stabilizer Link To Strut	49
	Steering Intermediate Shaft To Steering Gear	35
	Temperature Sensor	30①
	Torque Converter	47
	Torque Converter Cover	108①
	Upper Control Valve Body	86–114①

① — Inch Lbs.
② — Refer to "Drive Axle Seal, Replace" for procedure and specifications.

FRONT WHEEL DRIVE AXLES

NOTE: On Air Bag Equipped Models, Refer To "Air Bag System Precautions" Located In The Front Of This Manual For System Disarming & Arming Procedures.

NOTE: Refer To "Computer Relearn Procedures" Located In The Front Of This Manual When Battery Power To The Computer Has Been Interrupted.

INDEX

APPLICATION CHART

Model	Year	Front Drive Axle Type
BUICK		
Century	1998–2002	Type 1
LeSabre	1998–2002	Type 1
Park Avenue	1998–2002	Type 1
Regal	1998–2002	Type 1
Riviera	1998–99	Type 1
Skylark	1998	Type 1
CADILLAC		
DeVille	1998	Type 2
	1999–2002	Type 1
Eldorado	1998	Type 2
	1999–2002	Type 1
Seville	1998–2002	Type 1
CHEVROLET		
Cavalier	1998–2002	Type 3
Impala	2000–02	Type 1
Lumina	1998–2002	Type 1
Malibu	1998–2002	Type 1
Monte Carlo	1998–2002	Type 1
Metro	1998–2002	Type 4
Prizm	1998–2002	Type 5
OLDSMOBILE		
Achieva	1998	Type 1
Alero	1999–2002	Type 1
Aurora	1998–2002	Type 1
Cutlass	1998–99	Type 1
Eighty Eight	1998–99	Type 1

Continued

APPLICATION CHART—Continued

Model	Year	Front Drive Axle Type
OLDSMOBILE		
Intrigue	1998–2002	Type 1
LSS	1998	Type 1
Regency	1998–99	Type 1
PONTIAC		
Bonneville	1998–2002	Type 1
Grand Am	1998–2002	Type 1
Grand Prix	1998–2002	Type 1
Sunfire	1998–2002	Type 3
SATURN		
L-Series	1998–2002	Type 6
S-Series	2000–2002	Type 6

PRECAUTIONS

BATTERY GROUND CABLE

Prior to service, disconnect battery ground cable and isolate as required.

JOINT PROTECTION

On models equipped with tripod joints on inboard axles, care must be taken not to overextend joints.

On models equipped with ball type constant velocity inboard joints, install inner drive joint seal protector tool No. J-34754 and install axle boot protector tool No. J-28712, or equivalents, as required.

On models equipped with tripod inboard joints, install axle boot seal protector tool No. J-28712, and tool No. J-33162, or equivalents, as required.

DESCRIPTION

Front wheel drive systems consist of an inner and outer constant velocity joint connected by an axle shaft, **Figs. 1 through 6.** The inner joint is completely flexible, and can move in and out. The outer joint is also flexible, but cannot move in and out.

TROUBLESHOOTING

CLICKING NOISE IN TURNS

Worn or damaged outboard joint, cut or damaged seals.

CLUNK WHEN ACCELERATING FROM COAST TO DRIVE

Worn or damaged constant velocity joint.

SHUDDER OR VIBRATION DURING ACCELERATION

1. Excessive CV joint angle because of incorrect toe in or incorrect trim height.
2. Worn or damaged inboard or outboard CV joints.
3. Sticking tripod joint spider assembly.

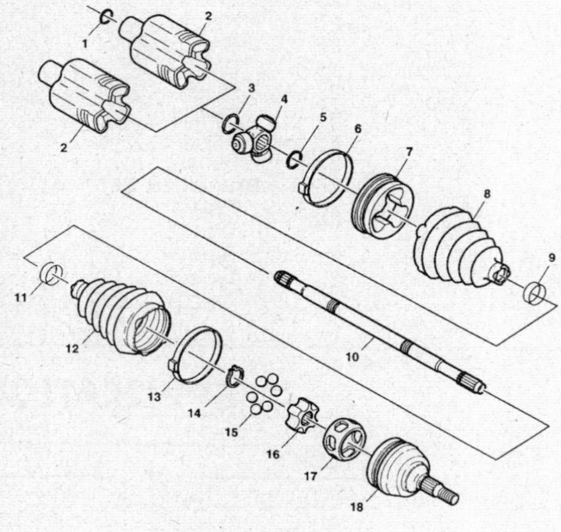

(1) Retaining Ring
(2) Retainer and Housing Assembly
(3) Shaft Retaining Ring
(4) Tripot Spider Assembly
(5) Spacer Ring
(6) Boot Retaining Clamp
(7) Tripot Trilobal Bushing
(8) Halfshaft Inboard Boot
(9) Swage Ring
(10) Halfshaft Bar
(11) Swage Ring
(12) Halfshaft Outboard Boot
(13) Boot Retaining Clamp
(14) Race Retaining Ring
(15) Chrome Alloy Ball
(16) CV Joint Inner Race
(17) CV Joint Cage
(18) CV Joint Outer Race

GC3039900339000X

Fig. 1 Exploded view of front drive axle assembly. Type 1

VIBRATION AT HIGHWAY SPEEDS

1. Out-of-balance front tires or wheels.
2. Out-of-round front tires.
3. Worn CV joint.
4. Binding or tight CV joint.

DRIVESHAFT

REPLACE

ACHIEVA

1. Cover sharp edges in drive axle area with suitable shop towels
2. Raise and support vehicle, then remove wheel and tire assembly.
3. Prevent rotor from turning by inserting suitable drift or punch into caliper and rotor.
4. Remove drive axle nut and washer.
5. Remove ball joint cotter pin and nut, then loosen joint using ball joint separator tool No. J-38892, or equivalent.
6. Disconnect ABS sensor wire.
7. Disconnect stabilizer link and separate joint using suitable ball joint separator.
8. Disconnect axle from hub and bearing using front hub spindle tool No. J-28733, or equivalent.

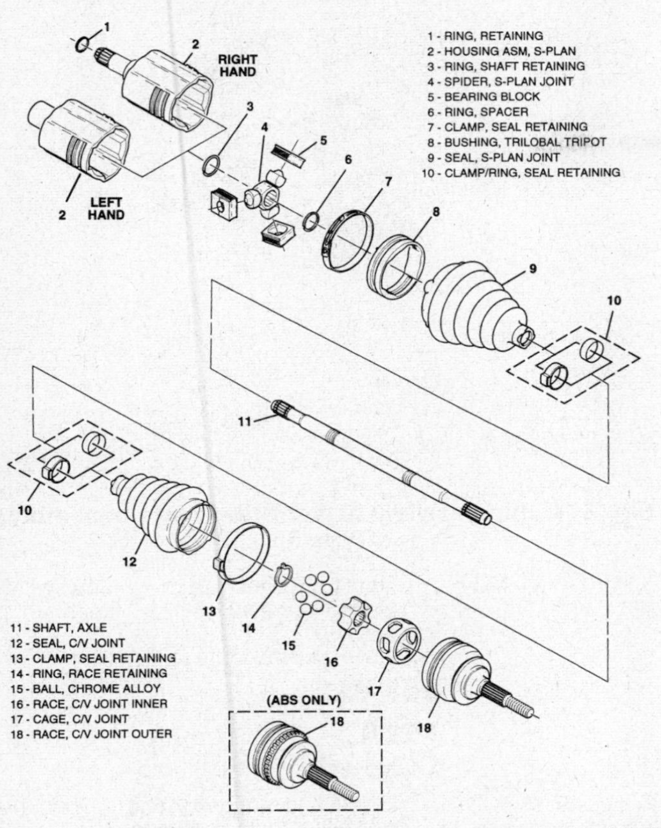

Fig. 2 Exploded view of front drive axle assembly. Type 2

GC303000033701AX

Fig. 3 Exploded view of front drive axle assembly (Part 1 of 2). Type 3

Key No.	Part Name	Key No.	Part Name
1 -	RING, RETAINING	14 -	SHAFT, AXLE (RH SHOWN, LH SIMILAR)
2 -	HOUSING ASM, RETAINER &	15 -	SEAL, DRIVE AXLE OUTBOARD
4 -	SPIDER, TRIPOT JOINT	16 -	CLAMP, SEAL RETAINING
9 -	RING, RETAINING	18 -	BALL, CHROME ALLOY
10 -	CLAMP, SEAL RETAINING	19 -	RACE, C/V JOINT INNER
11 -	BUSHING, TRILOBAL TRIPOT	20 -	CAGE, C/V JOINT
12 -	SEAL, DRIVE AXLE INBOARD	21 -	RACE, C/V JOINT OUTER
13 -	CLAMP, SEAL RETAINING		

GC303000033701BX

Fig. 3 Exploded view of front drive axle assembly (Part 2 of 2). Type 3

9. Move strut and knuckle rearward.
10. **On models equipped with intermediate shaft,** remove inner joint from transaxle using axle remover tool No. J-33088, drive axle removal extension tool No. J-29794 and slide hammer tool No. J-2619-01 or equivalents.
11. **On all models,** reverse procedure to install.

ALERO

1. Raise and support vehicle, then remove tire and wheel assembly.
2. Disconnect tie rod from the knuckle.
3. Prevent rotor from turning by inserting suitable drift into caliper and rotor, then remove axle shaft nut.
4. Disconnect stabilizer link, then separate lower control arm ball joint from steering knuckle.
5. Remove hub and bearing using front hub spindle remover tool No. J-28733-B, or equivalent.
6. Separate drive axle from transaxle using axle shaft remover tool No. J-33008 and slide hammer tool J-2619-01, or equivalents. **Do not overextend drive axle.**
7. Remove drive axle from vehicle.
8. Reverse procedure to install.

AURORA

REMOVAL

1. Raise and support vehicle, then remove tire and wheel assemblies.
2. Loosen or remove stabilizer shaft link.
3. Remove ball joint cotter pin and nut.
4. Loosen ball joint from steering knuckle using ball joint separator tool No. J-43828, or equivalent.
5. Separate ball joint from steering knuckle using a suitable pry bar between suspension support and lower control arm.
6. Prevent rotor from turning by inserting suitable drift or screwdriver into caliper and rotor, then remove hub nut.
7. Disconnect axle from hub using front hub spindle remover tool No. J-28733-B, or equivalent.
8. Position strut and knuckle rearward.
9. Remove drive axle from transaxle using axle shaft remover tool No. J-33008 and slide hammer tool No. J-2619-01, or equivalents. **Do not overextend drive axle.**

INSTALLATION

1. Inspect tripot housing at transmission seal surface for corrosion. Remove corrosion by sanding sealing surface with 320 grit emery cloth.
2. Lubricate tripot housing surface with suitable transmission fluid.
3. Push axle into transaxle, then ensure drive axle is seated by grasping inner joint housing and pulling. **Do not pull on drive axle shaft.**
4. Install drive axle into transaxle by placing suitable screwdriver into groove on joint housing and tapping until axle is seated.
5. Insert drive axle into hub and bearing, then install a new hub nut.
6. Prevent rotor from turning by inserting suitable drift or screwdriver into caliper and rotor, then tighten axle nut to specification.
7. Attach ball joint to knuckle.
8. Install stabilizer shaft link assembly.
9. Install wheels and lower vehicle.

BONNEVILLE

Refer to "Aurora" for driveshaft replacement procedure.

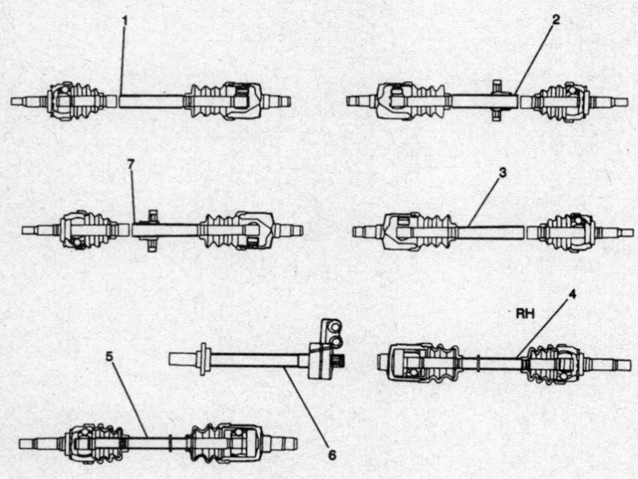

(1) Left Drive Axle Shaft (Automatic Transaxle)
(2) Right Drive Axle Shaft (Automatic Transaxle)
(3) Right Drive Axle Shaft (Manual Transaxle 1.0 L Vehicles Only)
(4) Right Drive Axle Shaft (Manual Transaxle 1.3 L Vehicles Only)
(5) Left Drive Axle Shaft (Manual Transaxle 1.3 L Vehicles Only)
(6) Right Inner Drive Axle Shaft Support Arbor (Manual Transaxle)
(7) Left Drive Axle Shaft (Manual Transaxle 1.0 L Vehicles Only)

GC3039900340000X

Fig. 4 Cutaway view of front drive axle assembly. Type 4

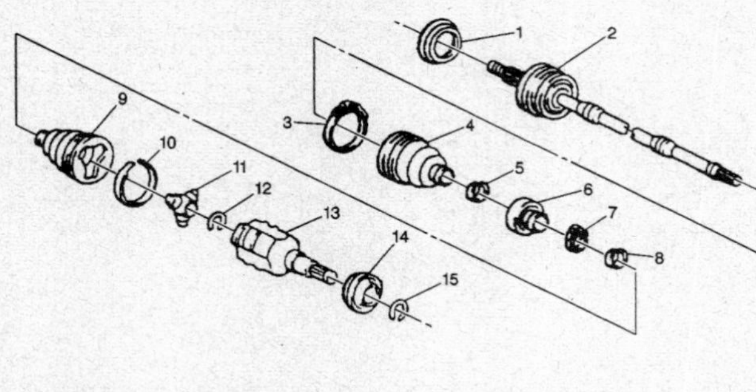

(1) Outer Joint Seal
(2) Outer Joint
(3) Outer Boot Clamp
(4) Outer Boot
(5) Outer Boot Clamp
(6) Damper (RH Shaft Only)
(7) Damper Clamp
(8) Inner Boot Clamp
(9) Inner Boot
(10) Inner Boot Clamp
(11) Tripot Joint
(12) Snap Ring
(13) Inner Joint Housing
(14) Inner Joint Seal
(15) Snap Ring

GC3039900341000X

Fig. 5 Exploded view of front drive axle assembly. Type 5

CAVALIER

1. Raise and support vehicle, then remove wheel and tire assembly.
2. Remove tie rod end to steering knuckle retaining nut, then disconnect tie rod end from steering knuckle.
3. Prevent rotor from turning by inserting suitable drift or punch into caliper and rotor, then remove drive axle nut and washer.
4. Remove ball joint cotter pin and nut, then separate joint from steering knuckle using ball joint separator tool No. J-38892, or equivalent.
5. Disconnect ABS sensor wire.
6. Disconnect stabilizer link and separate joint using suitable ball joint separator.
7. Disconnect axle from hub and bearing using front hub spindle tool No. J-28733-A, or equivalent.
8. Separate hub and bearing from axle.
9. Move strut and knuckle rearward.
10. Remove inner joint from transaxle using axle remover tool No. J-33008, drive axle removal extension tool No. J-29794 and slide hammer tool No. J-2619-01, or equivalents.
11. Reverse procedure to install.

CENTURY

1. Raise and support vehicle, then remove tire and wheel assembly.
2. Remove stabilizer link.
3. Prevent rotor from turning by inserting suitable drift or flat-bladed tool into caliper and rotor, then remove drive axle nut.
4. Disconnect tie rod from steering knuckle.
5. Disconnect ball joint from steering knuckle using ball joint/stud separator tool No. J-41820, or equivalent.
6. **On righthand drive axle,** separate drive axle from transaxle using axle shaft tool No. J-3308, extension tool No. J-29794 and puller tool No. J-2619-01, or equivalents.
7. **On lefthand side drive axle,** use frame for leverage and separate drive axle from transaxle using suitable screwdriver or pry bar in inner joint groove.
8. **On both sides,** reverse procedure to install, noting the following:
   a. Install axle seal protector tool No. J-37292-A, or equivalent, to righthand side of transaxle so it can be pulled out after drive axle is installed.
   b. Install new axle nut.

CUTLASS

1. Raise and support vehicle, then remove wheel and tire assembly.
2. Disconnect steering knuckle tie rod.
3. Prevent rotor from turning by inserting suitable drift or punch into caliper and rotor, then remove drive axle nut and washer.
4. Disconnect stabilizer link.
5. Remove ball joint cotter pin and nut, then separate ball joint from knuckle using ball joint separator tool No. J-38892, or equivalent.
6. Disconnect axle from hub and bearing using front hub spindle tool No. J-28733, or equivalent.
7. Remove righthand axle using axle shaft remover tool No. J-3308 and slide hammer tool No. J-2619-01, or equivalents.
8. Remove lefthand axle by separating shaft from transaxle using suitable flat-bladed screwdriver in tripod joint groove.
9. Reverse procedure to install.

DEVILLE

1998

Removal

1. Raise and support vehicle, then remove tire and wheel assembly.
2. Remove stabilizer shaft link.
3. Remove ball joint cotter pin and nut.
4. Loosen ball joint from steering knuckle using ball joint separator tool No. J-36226, or equivalent.
5. Separate ball joint from knuckle using suitable pry bar between suspension support and lower control arm.
6. Prevent rotor from turning by installing suitable brass drift or screwdriver, then remove axle nut and washer.
7. Remove drive axle from hub using front hub spindle remover tool No. J-28733-A, or equivalent. Position strut and knuckle rearward.
8. Remove drive axle from transaxle using axle shaft remover puller tools No. J-33008, and slide hammer tool No. J-2619-01, or equivalents.

Installation

1. **On righthand drive axle,** install drive axle seal protector tool No. J-37292-B, or equivalent. Ensure protector is installed so it can be removed after axle is installed.
2. **On lefthand and righthand drive axles,** push drive axle into transaxle. Ensure axle is properly seated by grasping inner joint and pulling. **Do not pull on shaft.**
3. Install drive axle into hub and bearing.
4. Prevent rotor from turning by inserting suitable screwdriver or drift into caliper and rotor, then install new hub nut and tighten to specifications.
5. Install ball joint to knuckle.
6. Remove axle seal protector.
7. Install wire and tire assemblies, then lower vehicle.

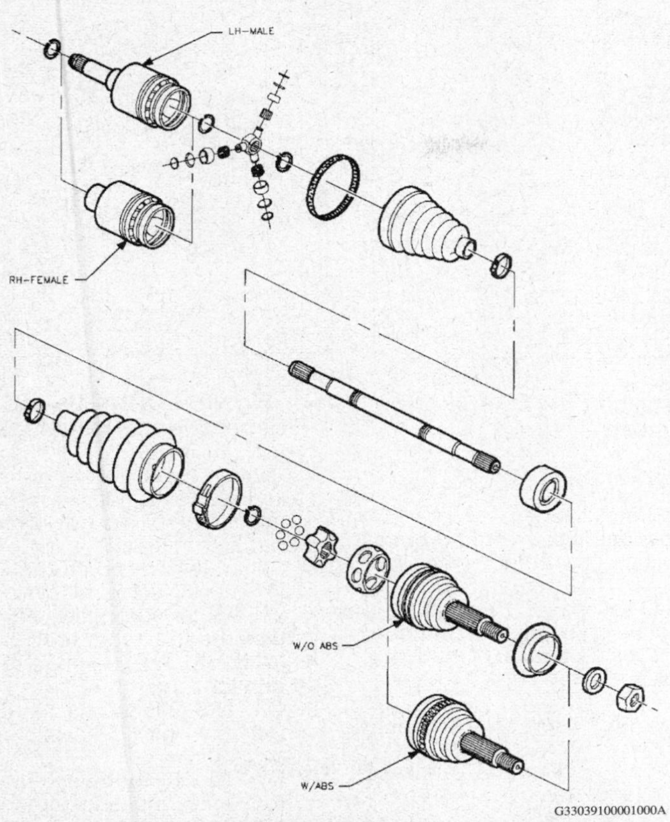

Fig. 6 Exploded view of front drive axle assembly. Type 6

1999-2002

Refer to "Aurora" for driveshaft replacement procedure.

EIGHTY-EIGHT

Refer to "Aurora" for driveshaft replacement procedure.

ELDORADO

1998

Refer to "1998" under "DeVille" for driveshaft replacement procedure.

1999-2002

Refer to "Aurora" for driveshaft replacement procedure.

GRAND AM

1998

Refer to "Achieva" for driveshaft replacement procedure.

1999-2002

Refer to "Alero" for driveshaft replacement procedure.

GRAND PRIX

Refer to "Century" for driveshaft replacement procedure.

IMPALA

Refer to "Century" for driveshaft replacement procedure.

INTRIGUE

Refer to "Century" for driveshaft replacement procedure.

LESABRE

Refer to "Aurora" for driveshaft replacement procedure.

LSS

Refer to "Aurora" for driveshaft replacement procedure.

LUMINA

Refer to "Century" for driveshaft replacement procedure.

MALIBU

Refer to "Cutlass" for driveshaft replacement procedure.

METRO

1. Raise and support vehicle, then remove tire and wheel assembly.
2. Remove mounting bolts and ABS speed sensor.
3. Unstake and remove driveshaft nut and washer.
4. Remove ball stud bolt and separate control arm from steering knuckle.
5. **On models equipped with manual transaxle,** separate righthand axle from intermediate shaft bearing by tapping gently using suitable plastic mallet.
6. **On all models,** separate lefthand driveshaft from transaxle by prying gently using suitable large screwdriver, **Fig. 7.**

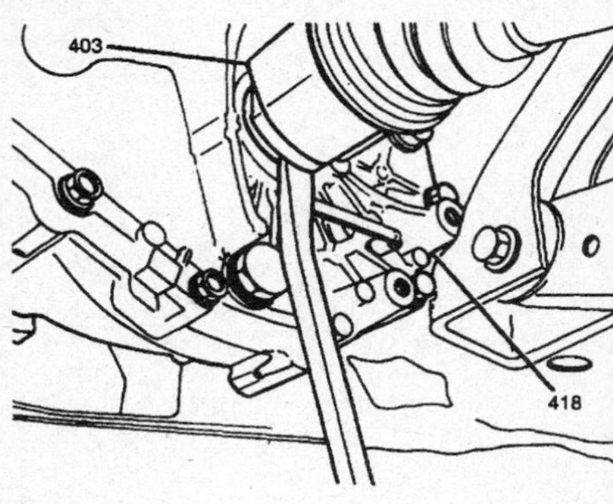

403 DIFFERENTIAL-SIDE JOINT HOUSING
418 TRANSAXLE ASSEMBLY
GC3039600278000X

Fig. 7 Inner joint removal. Metro & Prizm

7. Remove drive axle from steering knuckle.
8. Reverse procedure to install. Push drive axle into transaxle by hand until snap ring is seated in spline.

MONTE CARLO

Refer to "Century" for driveshaft replacement procedure.

PARK AVENUE

Refer to "Aurora" for driveshaft replacement procedure.

PRIZM

1. Raise and support vehicle, then remove tire and wheel assembly.
2. Remove mounting bolts and splash shield.
3. **On models equipped with ABS,** remove mounting bolt and ABS speed sensor from steering knuckle.
4. **On all models,** remove cotter pin and lock cap.
5. Prevent rotor from turning by inserting suitable drift through caliper opening into rotor, then remove wheel drive shaft hub nut and washer.
6. Remove tie rod end cotter pin and nut.
7. Separate tie rod end from steering knuckle using steering linkage and tie rod puller tool No. J-24319-B, or equivalent.
8. Remove mounting bolt, nuts and ball joint from control arm.
9. Remove drive axle outer joint from steering knuckle. **Do not overextend drive axle and do not damage ABS components.**
10. Remove drive axle inner joint by gently prying away from transaxle using suitable pry bar, **Fig. 7.**
11. Inspect boots, joints, front wheel bearing oil seals and wheel drive shaft oil seal at the transaxle for damage or wear. Replace as required.
12. Reverse procedure to install, noting the following:
    a. Lubricate wheel drive shaft splines

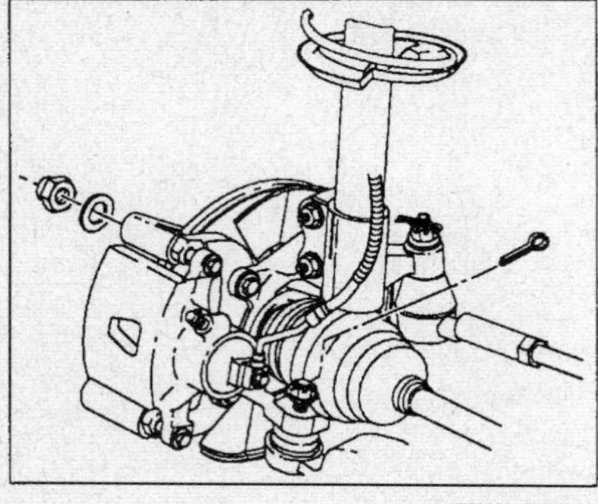
G33039100002000X

Fig. 8 Driveshaft nut & washer replacement. Saturn S Series

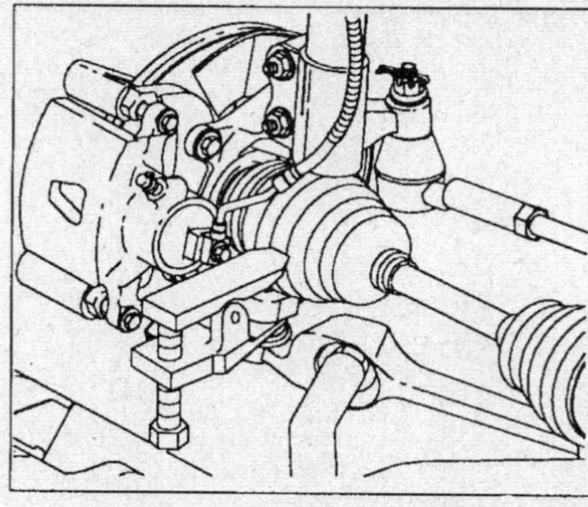
G33039100003000X

Fig. 9 Lower ball joint separation. Saturn S Series

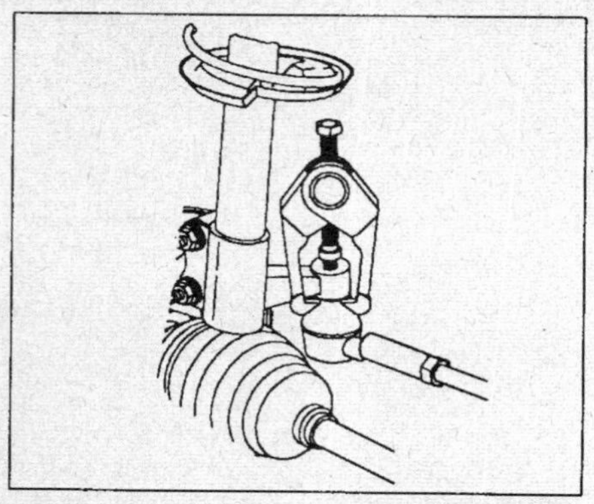
G33039100004000X

Fig. 10 Outer tie rod end separation. Saturn S Series

and seal surfaces.

b. Use only enough force to seat inner joint into transaxle.
c. Ensure joint snap ring is seated in transaxle by grasping inner joint housing and pulling outward.
d. Install new cotter pins.

REGAL

Refer to "Century" for driveshaft replacement procedure.

REGENCY

Refer to "Aurora" for driveshaft replacement procedure.

RIVIERA

Refer to "Aurora" for driveshaft replacement procedure.

SATURN

L-SERIES

Removal

1. Depress brake pedal, then remove cotter pin and drive axle nut. Discard cotter pin and nut.
2. Raise and support vehicle, then remove tire and wheel assembly.
3. Remove tie rod end torque prevailing nut, then discard nut.
4. Separate tie rod end from steering knuckle using removal tool No. SA-91100-C, or equivalent. **Do not use wedge type tool to separate joint.**
5. Remove lower control arm to steering knuckle bolt and nut, then separate lower control arm from steering knuckle.
6. Pull outer end of drive axle out of wheel hub while pulling knuckle/strut away. If it is difficult to separate axle from hub, tap on end of drive axle shaft using suitable wood block and hammer.
7. Support or suspend drive axle assembly using mechanics wire.
8. Place suitable container under transaxle to catch fluid spillage.
9. Remove drive axle by prying axle out of transaxle using suitable pry bar. **Do not contact transaxle oil seal.**
10. Remove and discard shaft retaining rings.

Installation

1. Install new retaining ring.
2. **On models equipped with automatic transaxle,** apply output shaft lubricant No. 7847638, or equivalent, to output shaft splines.
3. **On models equipped with manual transaxle,** install transaxle seal protector tool No. SA-91112-T, or equivalent.
4. **On all models,** insert drive axle into transaxle.
5. After drive axle splines have passed transaxle oil seal, remove seal protector.
6. Fully seat drive axle into transaxle. **Do not tighten at this time.**
7. Insert drive axle outer end into wheel hub, then the hub washer and new nut.
8. Install lower control arm ball stud into steering knuckle.
9. Install tie rod end into steering knuckle.
10. Fully seat tie rod end using installer tool No. J-44015, or equivalent, then install new nut.
11. **Torque** axle shaft nut to 85 ft. lbs. to seat bearing.
12. Loosen nut until it turns freely by hand.
13. **Torque** nut to 15 ft. lbs., then tighten an additional 90° and align cotter pin slot.
14. Install new cotter pin.
15. Install wheels.

S-SERIES

Removal

1. Depress brake pedal and loosen drive axle nut.
2. Raise and support vehicle, then remove wheel and tire assembly.
3. **On lefthand side drive axle,** proceed as follows:
   a. Remove front splash shield, then the rear splash shield.
   b. Drain transaxle fluid into suitable container.
4. **On righthand side drive axle,** remove rear splash shield, then the front splash shield.
5. **On lefthand and righthand drive axles,** remove drive axle nut and washer, **Fig. 8.** Discard nut.
6. Remove lower control arm to steering knuckle cotter pin. Discard cotter pin.
7. Loosen lower control arm to steering knuckle castle nut until top is even with ball stud top. **Do not remove castle nut at this time.**
8. Separate lower control arm from steering knuckle using removal tool No. SA-9132-S, or equivalent, **Fig. 9. Do not use wedge type tool to separate joint. Do not damage ABS speed sensor ring.**
9. **On 1998–99 models,** remove outer tie rod cotter pin and castle nut. Discard cotter pin.
10. **On 2000–02 models,** remove outer tie rod cotter pin and torque prevailing nut. Discard nut.
11. **On all models,** separate tie rod end from steering knuckle using removal tool No. SA-91100-C, or equivalent, **Fig. 10. Do not use wedge type tool to separate joint.**
12. Remove lower control arm to steering knuckle castle nut.
13. Separate lower control arm ball stud from steering knuckle by prying down at cradle and tension strut locations with a suitable long pry bar, **Fig. 11.**
14. Pull steering knuckle away from ball stud.
15. Pull outer end of drive axle out of wheel hub while pulling knuckle/strut away. If it is difficult to separate axle from hub, tap on end of drive axle shaft using suitable wood block and hammer, **Fig. 12.**
16. Support or suspend drive axle assembly using mechanics wire.
17. Remove righthand drive axle by tapping axle from intermediate using suitable hammer and wood block, **Fig. 13.**
18. Remove lefthand drive axle from transaxle by prying axle with a suitable large screwdriver, **Fig. 14. Do not contact transaxle oil seal.**

Installation

1. **On lefthand side drive axle,** proceed as follows:
   a. Install transaxle seal protector tool No. SA-91112-T, or equivalent, **Fig. 15.**
   b. Insert drive axle into transaxle.
   c. After drive axle splines have safely passed transaxle oil seal, remove seal protector.

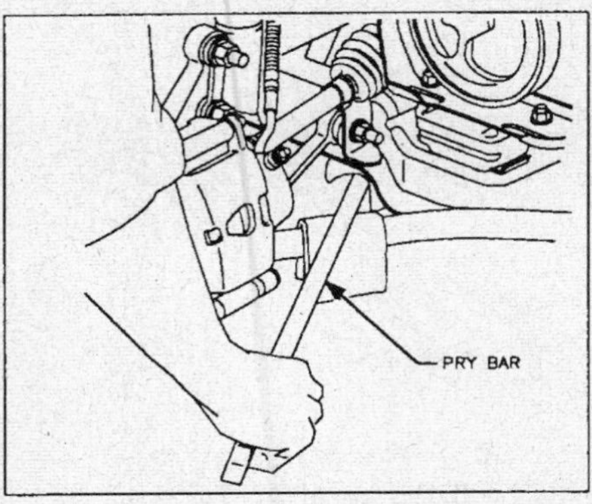

G33039100005000X

Fig. 11 Lower ball joint separation from steering knuckle. Saturn S Series

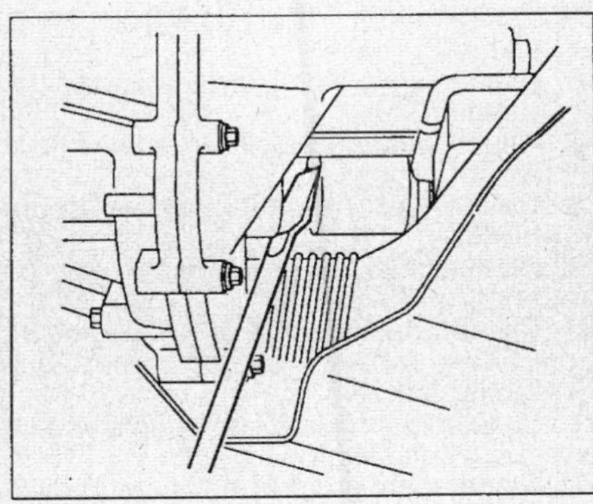

G33039100009000X

Fig. 14 Lefthand drive axle removal. Saturn S Series

d. Fully seat drive axle into transaxle.

2. **On righthand side drive axle,** insert drive axle inner end onto intermediate driveshaft outer end and push firmly to engage retaining ring.
3. **On lefthand and righthand drive axles,** insert drive axle outer end into wheel hub. **Do not install drive axle hub washer and nut at this time.**
4. Install lower control arm ball stud into steering knuckle, then the ball stud castle nut. **Do not tighten nut at this time.**
5. Install tie rod end into steering knuckle.
6. Fully seat tie rod end using installer tool No. J-44015, or equivalent, then tighten new nut to specifications.
7. Tighten ball joint stud castle nut and install new cotter pin.
8. Install axle to hub washer and new nut.
9. Install front inner fender splash shield.
10. Install wheels and lug nuts.

SEVILLE

Refer to "Aurora" for driveshaft replacement procedure.

SKYLARK

Refer to "Achieva" for driveshaft replacement procedure.

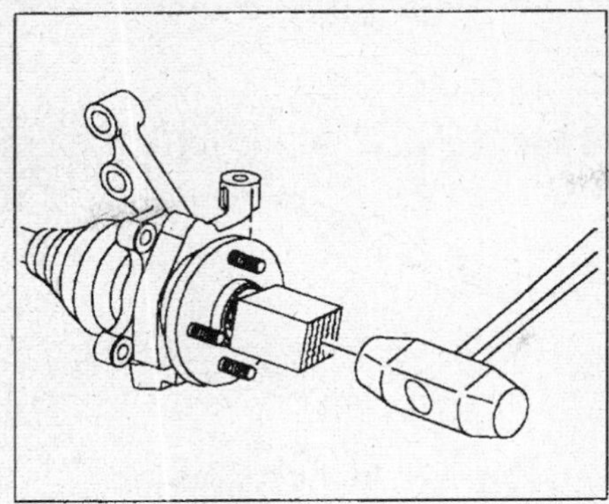

G33039100006000X

Fig. 12 Axle separation from hub. Saturn S Series

SUNFIRE

Refer to "Cavalier" for driveshaft replacement procedure.

DRIVESHAFT SERVICE

TYPE 1

INNER JOINT & BOOT

Disassemble

When the halfshaft is removed for any reason, the transmission sealing surface (tripod male/female shank of CV) should be inspected for corrosion. If corrosion is present, surface should be cleaned using crocus cloth or suitable equivalent.

1. Cut through swage ring using suitable hand grinder. **Do not damage tripod housing.**
2. Remove large boot retaining clamp from tripod joint using suitable side cutter. Discard clamp.
3. Separate inboard boot from trilobal tripod bushing at large diameter.
4. Slide boot away from joint along shaft.
5. Remove housing from tripod joint spider and shaft.
6. Remove trilobal tripod bushing from housing.
7. Spread spacer ring using snap ring pliers No. J-8059, or equivalent.
8. Slide spacer ring and tripod joint spider backward on shaft.
9. Remove retaining ring from shaft groove.
10. Slide tripod joint spider assembly off shaft.
11. Clean tripot balls and needle rollers with suitable solvent. Dry thoroughly.
12. Inspect tripot joint spider, housing, trilobal tripot bushing and needle rollers for damage or wear. Replace as required.

Assemble

1. Place new small clamp onto joint boot small end.
2. Slide boot and clamp onto shaft.
3. Position boot small end into groove.
4. Swage ring using swage tool No. J-41048, or equivalent.

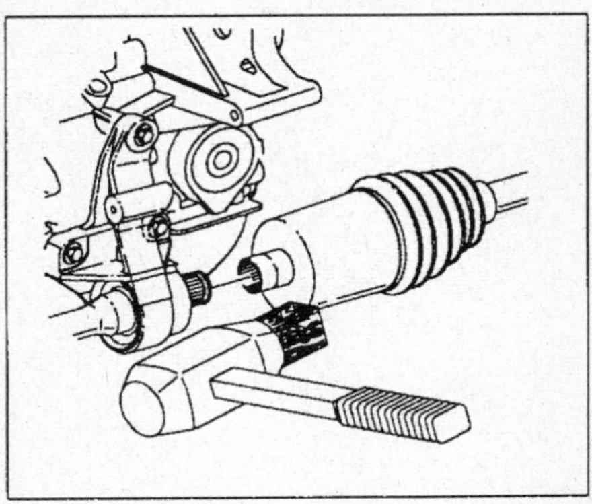

G33039100008000X

Fig. 13 Righthand drive axle removal. Saturn S Series

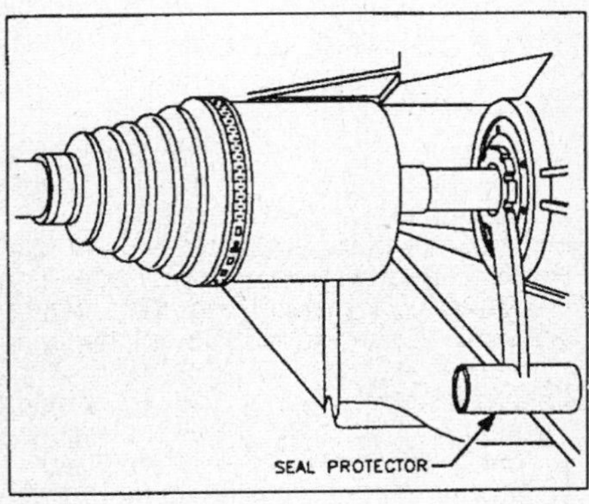

G33039100010000X

Fig. 15 Transaxle seal protector installed. Saturn S Series

5. Install retaining ring using snap ring pliers tool No. J-8059, or equivalent, **Fig. 16.**
6. Ensure counterbored face on joint spider faces toward end of shaft.
7. Slide tripot joint spider toward spacer ring as far as it will go. Ensure trilobal tripot bushing is flush with housing face.
8. Place half of kit provided grease in inboard boot. Use remaining grease to pack housing.
9. Install trilobal bushing to housing.
10. Position larger new boot retaining clamp on inboard boot and slide housing over spider.
11. Slide inboard boot large diameter with clamp in place over outside of trilobal tripod bushing and locate lip in groove.
12. Ensure shaft inboard boot is not dimpled, stretched out or out of shape. Correct using thin, flat, blunt tool between to equalize the pressure and shape by hand.
13. Align inboard boot, tripot housing and large retaining clamp.
14. Ensure boot is positioned properly.
15. Tighten clamp using eared clamp tool No. J-35910, or equivalent, suitable breaker bar and torque wrench, **Fig. 17.**

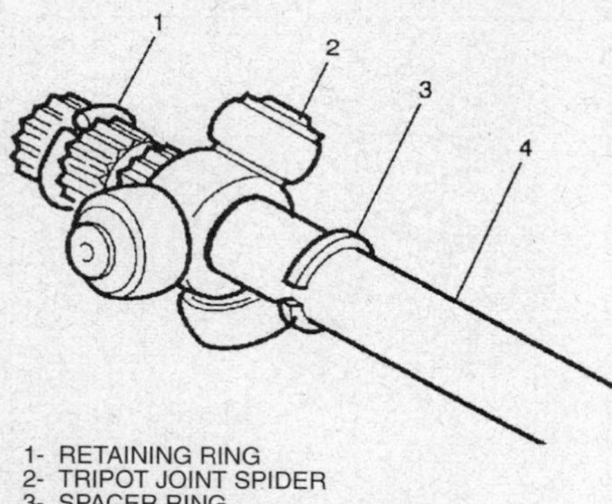

Fig. 16 Inner tripod joint assemble. Type 1

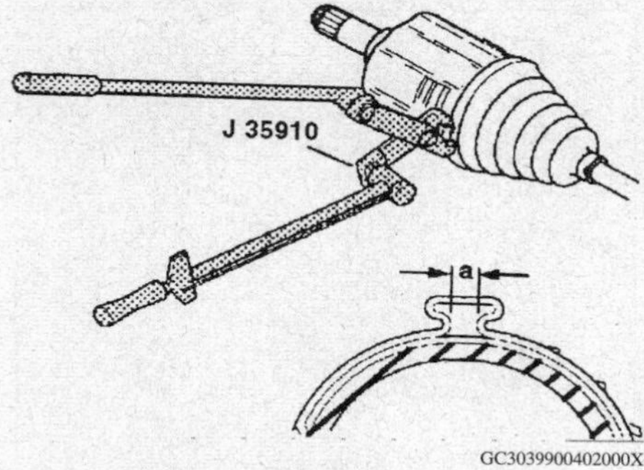

Fig. 17 Inner tripod joint alignment. Type 1

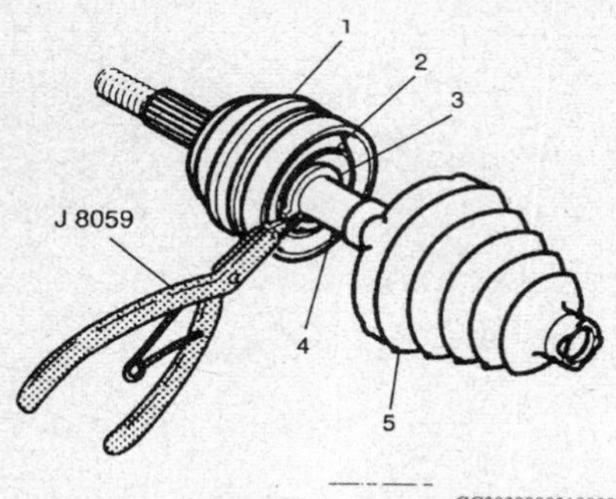

Fig. 18 Outer CV joint disassemble. Type 1

OUTER JOINT & BOOT

Disassemble

1. Remove large and small boot retaining clamps from CV joint using suitable side cutter. Discard clamps.
2. Separate outboard boot from CV joint outer race at large diameter and slide boot away form joint, **Fig. 18.**
3. Wipe grease from CV joint inner race face.
4. Spread retaining ring race ears using snap ring pliers No. J-8059, or equivalent, and remove CV joint and boot.
5. Tap CV joint cage using suitable brass drift and hammer until it is tilted enough to remove first chrome alloy ball.
6. Tilt cage in opposite direction to remove opposing ball.
7. Repeat until six balls are removed.
8. Position CV joint cage and inner race 90° to outer race centerline, and align joint cage windows with outer race lands.
9. Remove CV joint cage and inner race from outer race.
10. Rotate CV joint inner race 90° to CV joint cage centerline with inner race lands aligned with CV joint cage windows.
11. Remove inner race by pivoting into cage window.
12. Clean inner and outer races, CV joint cage and balls using suitable solvent. Dry thoroughly.

Assemble

1. Install new boot swage ring onto neck. **Do not swage at this time.**
2. Slide outboard boot onto shaft and position neck in groove.
3. Swage boot swage ring using swage tool No. J-41048, or equivalent.
4. Lightly coat inner and outer race ball grooves with kit provided grease.
5. Hold inner race at a 90° angle to cage centerline, align inner race lands with cage windows, then install inner race into cage.
6. Hold cage and inner race at a 90° angle to outer race centerline, then align cage windows with outer race lands. Ensure inner race retaining ring side faces halfshaft.
7. Install cage and inner race into outer race.
8. Install first chrome ball, then tilt cage in opposite direction and install opposing ball. Repeat until all balls are in place.
9. Place approximately half of the remaining kit provided grease inside outboard boot. Use remaining grease to pack CV joint.
10. Push CV joint onto shaft until retaining ring is seated in groove. Ensure boot is not dimpled, stretched out or out of shape. Correct by equalizing pressure and shaping by hand.
11. Slide large diameter of outboard boot with retaining clamp over outside CV joint outer race, locate lip in groove.
12. Crimp boot retaining clamp using seal clamp tool No. J-35910, or equivalent, and suitable breaker bar. Ensure gap is .012 inch.

TYPE 2

INNER JOINT & BOOT

Disassemble

1. Remove large and small boot retaining clamps using suitable side cutter. Discard clamps. **Do not cut through boot.**
2. Separate large diameter of boot from trilobal tripot bushing and slide boot away from joint along axle.
3. Separate housing from spider and shaft.
4. Wipe grease from C/V inner race face.
5. Spread spacer ring using snap ring pliers tool No. J-8059, or equivalent.
6. Slide spacer ring and spider back on axle.
7. Remove retaining ring and slide spider off shaft.
8. Remove trilobal tripot hushing from housing.
9. Remove spacer ring and boot from axle.
10. Clean bearing blocks, spider and housing thoroughly with suitable solvent. Dry thoroughly.
11. Inspect joint boot, spider, housing, trilobal tripot bushing and bearing blocks for damage or wear.

Assemble

1. Install new swage ring on neck. **Do not swage at this time.**
2. Slide boot onto axle shaft and position neck in groove.
3. Swage new swange ring using swage tool No. J-41048, or equivalent.
4. Install spacer ring onto axle shaft beyond second groove.
5. Lightly coat inside of bearing block with suitable grease.
6. Align bearing block opening and spider trunnion flats.
7. Attach bearing blocks to spider trunnion.
8. Rotate spider trunnion 90° to secure block.
9. Slide spider against spacer ring on shaft.
10. Install retaining ring in shaft groove. Ensure spider counterbored face faces shaft end.
11. Slide spider toward shaft end and seat spacer ring in groove.
12. Place approximately half of kit provided grease into boot. Use remaining grease to pack housing.
13. Maintain proper bearing block alignment by placing suitable slotted six-inch square piece of sheet metal between boot and bearing block.
14. Install trilobal tripot bushing and housing.
15. Position large clamp on boot.
16. Slide housing over spider on shaft and remove slotted sheet metal plate.
17. Slide boot large diameter with retaining clamp in place over trilobal tripot bushing and locate lip in groove.
18. Ensure boot is positioned properly.
19. Boot must not be dimpled, stretched or out of shape. Correct by equalizing pressure using suitable thin, flat, blunt tool and hand shaping.
20. Latch retaining clamp using earless seal clamp tool No. J-35566, or equivalent.

OUTER JOINT & BOOT

Disassemble

1. Remove large and small boot retaining clamps using suitable side cutter. Discard clamps.
2. Separate joint boot from C/V joint race at large diameter and slide boot away from joint along axle.
3. Wipe grease from C/V inner race face.
4. Spread race retaining ring ears using snap ring pliers tool No. J-8059, or equivalent.
5. Remove C/V joint and boot from axle shaft.

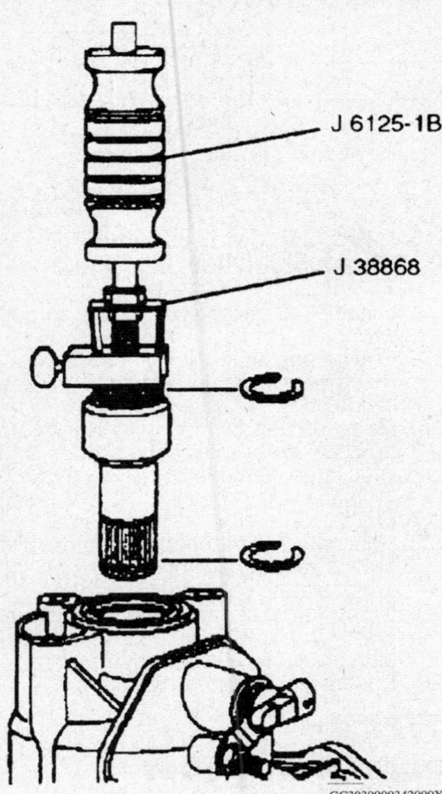

Fig. 19 Stub shaft removal. Type 3

6. Gently tap C/V joint cage using suitable brass drift and hammer until it tilts enough to remove first chrome ball.
7. Tilt cage in opposite direction and remove opposing ball.
8. Repeat procedure to remove all six balls.
9. Position cage and inner race at a 90° angle to outer race centerline, then align cage windows with outer race lands.
10. Remove cage, then the inner race from outer race.
11. Rotate inner race at a 90° angle to cage centerline, then align inner race with cage windows.
12. Remove inner race by pivoting into cage windows.
13. Clean cage, ball and the inner and outer races with suitable solvent. Dry thoroughly.

Assemble

1. Install new swage ring on neck. **Do not swage at this time.**
2. Slide boot onto axle shaft and position neck into groove.
3. Swage new swage ring using swage tool No. J-41048, or equivalent.
4. Lightly coat inner and outer race ball grooves with suitable grease.
5. Hold inner race at a 90° angle to cage centerline, then with inner race lands aligned with cage windows, insert inner race into cage.
6. Hold cage and inner race at a 90° angle to outer race centerline, then align cage windows with outer race lands.

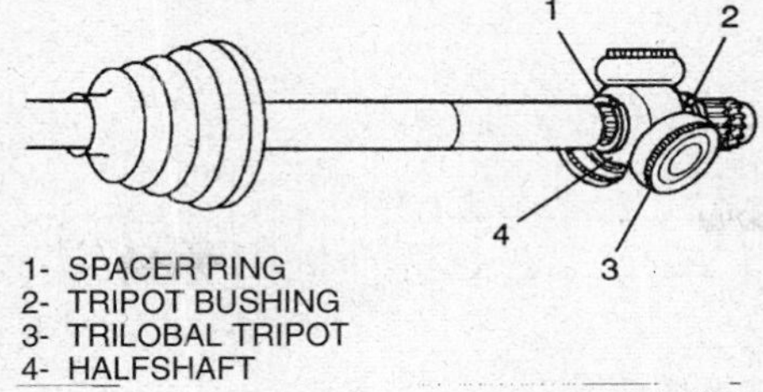

Fig. 20 Inner tripod joint replacement. Type 3

7. Install cage and inner race into outer race. Ensure inner race retaining ring side faces axle shaft.
8. Insert first chrome ball, then tilt cage and insert opposing ball. Repeat until all balls are installed.
9. Place approximately half of kit provided grease into boot. Use remaining grease to pack C/V joint.
10. Push C/V joint onto axle shaft until retaining ring is seated into groove.
11. Slide large diameter of boot with retaining clamp in place over C/V joint race and locate lip in groove.
12. Boot must not be dimpled, stretched or out of shape. Correct by equalizing pressure and hand shaping.
13. Crimp retaining clamp using seal clamp tool No. J-35910, or equivalent. Ensure gap is .102 inch.

TYPE 3

INNER JOINT & BOOT

Disassemble

1. **On models equipped with 2.4L engines,** if transaxle stub shaft disengages from transaxle during halfshaft tripot removal, separate shaft from tripod housing as follows:
   a. Remove and discard stub shaft snap ring.
   b. Remove shaft from tripot using stub shaft removal tool No. J-38868 and impact slide hammer tool No. J-6125-1B, or equivalents, **Fig. 19.**
   c. Install new snap rings onto stub shaft.
   d. Install stub axle into transaxle.
2. **On all models,** remove inboard boot small and large retaining clamps. Discard clamps.
3. Separate large diameter of inboard boot from trilobal tripot bushing.
4. Slide boot away from joint along halfshaft.
5. Remove spacer ring using snap ring pliers tool No. J-8309-A, or equivalent, **Fig. 20.** Discard spacer ring.
6. Remove tripod spider using suitable brass drift and hammer, **Fig. 21.**
7. Remove spacer ring from halfshaft shoulder using snap ring pliers tool No. J-8309-A, or equivalent.
8. Remove trilobal tripot bushing.
9. Clean tripod balls, needle rollers and housing with suitable solvent. Dry thoroughly.
10. Remove axle shaft boot.
11. Inspect inboard boot, spider, housing, trilobal tripod bushing, tripot balls, needle rollers and retaining ring for wear or damage.

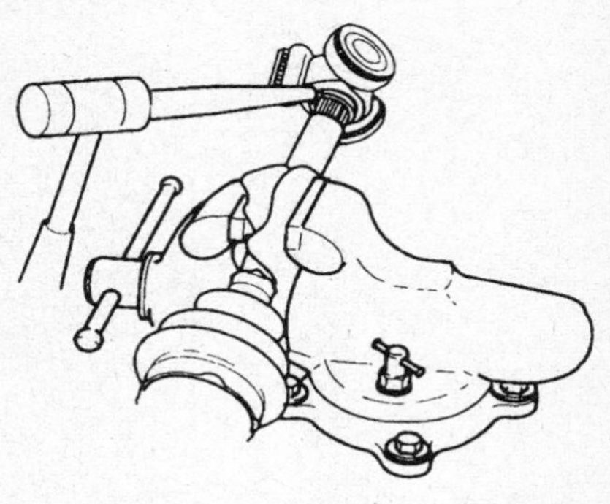

Fig. 21 Tripod spider removal. Type 3

Assemble

1. Install new small boot retaining clamp on boot neck. **Do not crimp at this time.**
2. Clean axle shaft using wire brush to remove rust from boot grooves.
3. Slide tripot boot onto halfshaft passing CV end boot grooves. Ensure spacer ring is next to halfshaft shoulder.
4. Install tripot spider.
5. Place axle assembly onto suitable arbor press with tripod spider on press plate and CV joint under press head, **Fig. 22.**
6. Lower arbor press head onto CV joint until tripod spider is next to spacer ring. **Do not exceed 4000 lbs. pressure.**
7. Remove axle assembly from arbor press.
8. Place new spacer ring in halfshaft end groove.
9. Slide tripod boot onto halfshaft groove.
10. Crimp small boot retaining clamp using seal clamp tool No. J-35910, or equivalent.
11. Place approximately one quarter of kit provided grease in boot. Use remaining grease to repack housing.
12. Install trilobal tripot bushing to housing. Ensure bushing is flush with housing face.
13. Slide housing over spider on halfshaft.
14. Position large boot retaining clamp around inboard boot.
15. Engage inboard boot.
16. Boot must not be dimpled, stretched or out of shape. Correct by equalizing pressure and shape using suitable thin, flat, blunt tool and hand.
17. Position joint properly, **Figs. 23 and 24.**
18. Ensure halfshaft inboard boot, housing and large clamp are aligned.
19. Latch boot retaining strap using seal clamp tool No. J-35566, or equivalent.

OUTER JOINT & BOOT

Disassemble

1. Remove large and small CV boot retaining clamps using suitable side cutters, discard clamps.
2. Separate large diameter of boot from

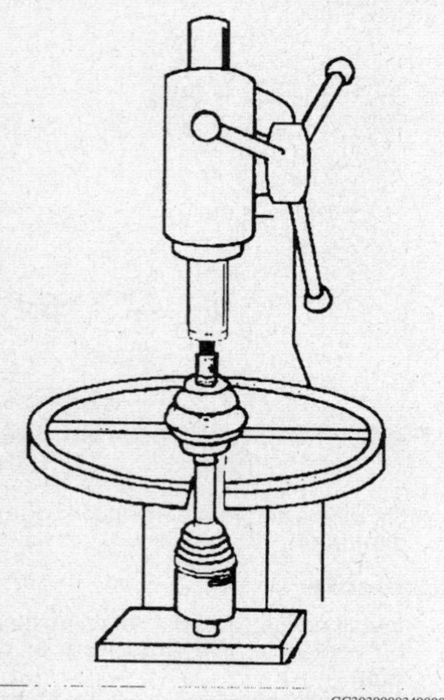

Fig. 22 Driveshaft position in arbor press. Type 3

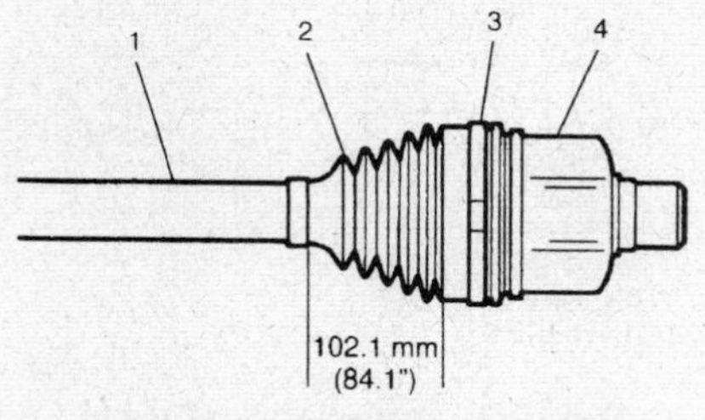

Fig. 23 Joint assembly dimension. 1998–99 Type 3

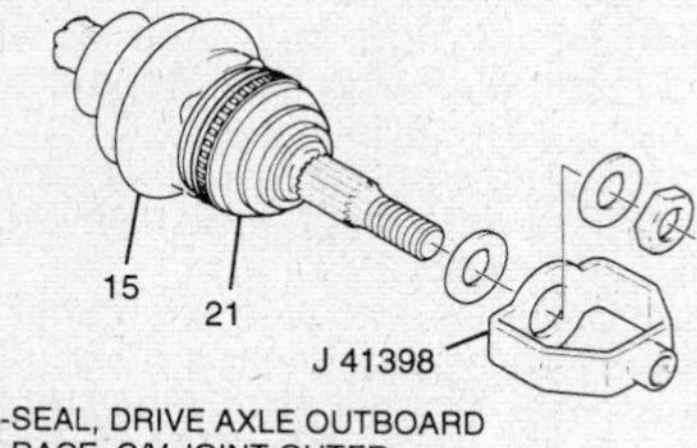

Fig. 25 Outer CV joint removal. Type 3

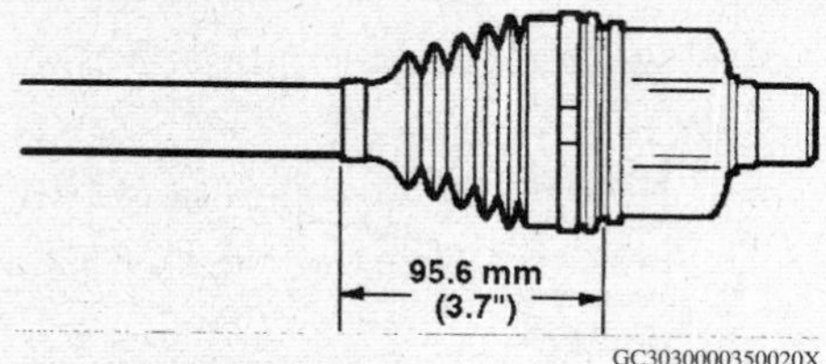

Fig. 24 Joint assembly dimension. 2000–02 Type 3

CV joint and slide away from joint along axle shaft.
3. Wipe grease away from inner CV joint race face.
4. Place reference mark on halfshaft, then measure and record distance between reference mark and CV joint inner race face for assembly reference.
5. Clamp axle into suitable vise.
6. Remove CV joint using CV puller tool No. J-41398 and slide hammer tool No. J-2619-01, or equivalents, **Fig. 25.**
7. Remove and discard retaining ring.
8. Remove CV joint boot.
9. Gently tap CV joint cage using suitable brass drift and hammer until it is tilted enough to remove first chrome ball, then tilt in the opposite direction and remove ball. Repeat until all six balls are removed.
10. Position cage and inner race at a 90° angle to outer race centerline, then align cage windows with outer race lands.
11. Remove cage and inner race from outer race.
12. Remove inner race from cage by rotating inner race upward.
13. Clean inner and outer race assemblies, cage and balls with suitable solvent. Dry thoroughly.
14. Inspect for unusual war, cracks or damage.

Assemble

1. Lightly coat inner and outer race ball grooves with kit provided grease.
2. Hold inner race at a 90° angle to cage centerline and align inner race lands with cage windows, then insert race into cage.
3. Hold cage and inner race at a 90° angle to outer race centerline, then align cage windows with outer race lands. Ensure inner race retaining ring side faces outer race.
4. Install cage and inner race into outer race.
5. Tilt cage by gently tapping with a suitable brass drift and hammer, then install first chrome ball. Repeat until all six balls are installed.
6. Pack CV joint with approximately half of kit provided grease.
7. Install new small retaining ring on CV boot neck. **Do not crimp at this time.**
8. Remove rust from CV boot mounting grooves with a suitable wire brush.
9. Slide CV joint boot onto drive axle shaft far enough to expose reference mark made during disassembly.
10. Position large retaining clamp around CV joint boot.
11. Place new retaining ring in inner race.
12. While supporting the tripot assembly, place halfshaft assembly onto suitable arbor press with CV assembly under press head.
13. Lower arbor press head onto CV joint assembly until press cannot move any further, to ensure retaining ring engages into inner race. **Do not exceed 4000 lbs. of press load.**
14. Place neck of CV joint boot into seal groove on drive axle shaft.
15. Measure distance between reference mark and CV joint inner race. If distance is not within .039 inch of distance recorded during disassembly, repeat previous steps 13 and 14.
16. Place CV joint boot neck into halfshaft boot groove. Ensure clamp is positioned correctly.
17. Crimp small retaining clamp using seal clamp tool No. J-35910, or equivalent, suitable breaker bar and torque wrench.
18. Ensure gap dimension is .085 inch.
19. Place remaining kit provided grease inside boot.
20. Measure approximately 11⁄16 inch up from CV outer joint bottom edge and slide large diameter of boot with clamp in place over outside of CV joint, **Fig. 26.**
21. Boot must not be dimpled, stretched or out of shape. Correct by equalizing pressure and shaping by hand.
22. Crimp large clamp using seal clamp tool No. J-35910, or equivalent, suitable breaker bar and torque wrench.
23. Ensure clamp gap is .102 inch.

TYPE 4

INNER JOINT & BOOT

Disassemble

1. Place index marks on inner joint and shaft for assembly reference.
2. Remove inner and outer boot bands, then slide boot back, **Fig. 27.**
3. Remove inner housing from tripod spider.
4. Place index mark on tripot joint spider and shaft for assembly reference.
5. Remove snap ring and spider.
6. Remove boot.

Inspection

1. Clean inner boot and tripot joint spider with clean, dry, solvent-free cloth. **Do not clean boots or tripot joint with solvent.**
2. Inspect boot for damage or wear.
3. Inspect tripot joint spider for excessive wear or damage.

Assemble

1. Install boot onto shaft and inner band onto boot.
2. Install tripot joint spider, align reference marks and secure with snap ring.
3. Pack inner joint housing with 2.8–3.5 oz. of kit provided grease.
4. Install inner housing onto spider.
5. Install inner band onto boot.
6. Inspect boots for distortion or dents. Correct by pulling boot outward.

OUTER JOINT & BOOT

Replace joint as an assembly. If boot is removed, pack with approximately 2.1–2.8 ounces of kit provided grease.

Disassemble

1. Place index mark on outer joint and shaft for assembly reference.

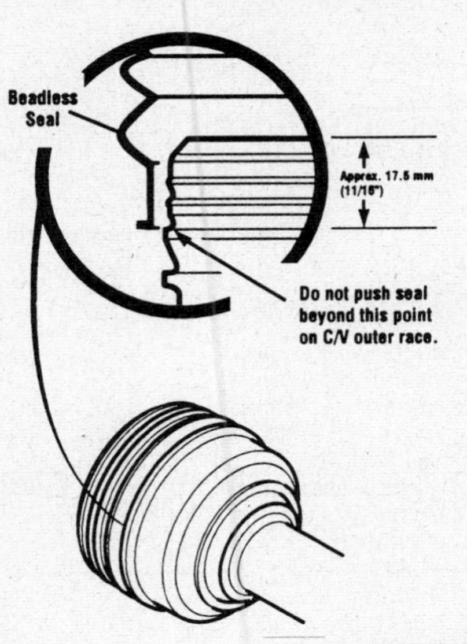

Fig. 26 CV outer joint installation measurement. Type 3

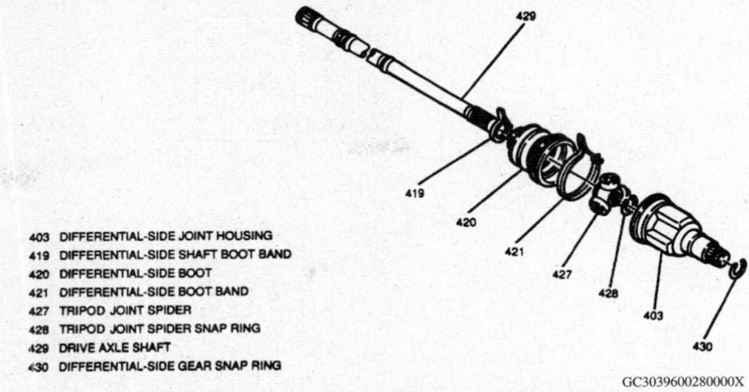

Fig. 27 Exploded view of tripod inner joint. Type 4

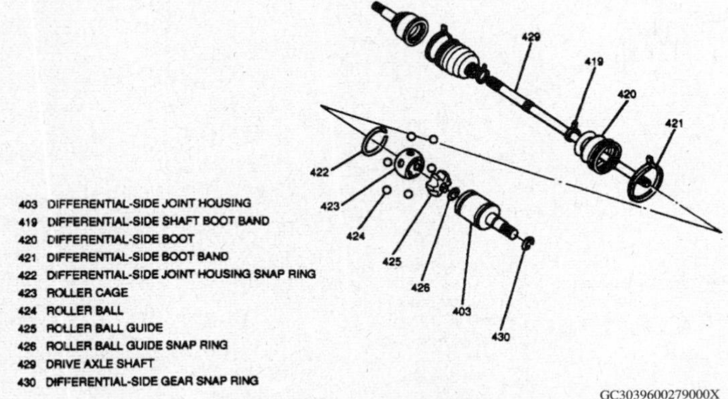

Fig. 28 Exploded view of outer joint. Type 4

2. Remove outer and inner boot bands, **Fig. 28.**
3. Remove snap ring and outer housing .
4. Remove roller ball guide snap ring.
5. Place index mark on roller ball guide and shaft for assembly reference.
6. Remove roller guide, balls and cage.
7. Remove boot.

Inspection

1. Clean boot with clean, dry, solvent-free cloth.
2. **Do not clean boots in solvent.**
3. Clean joint components with solvent and dry thoroughly.
4. Inspect boot for damage and wear.
5. Inspect joint components for excessive wear or damage.

Assemble

1. Install boot and outer band.
2. Align marks made during disassemble procedure.
3. Install roller ball guide, balls and cage with smaller diameter facing boot.
4. Install snap ring.
5. Pack joint with 1–1.4 ounces of kit provided grease.
6. Fill outer housing with remaining grease.
7. Install outer joint housing onto joint and align reference mark.
8. Install snap ring and outer boot band.
9. Inspect boots for distortion or dents. Correct by pulling boot outward.

TYPE 5

INNER JOINT & BOOT

Disassemble

1. Secure axle assembly in a suitable soft-jawed vise.
2. Remove large side inner joint boot clamp by drawing clamp hooks together using seal clamp tool No. J-35566, or equivalent, **Fig. 29.**
3. Remove small side inner joint boot clamp using suitable pliers.
4. Slide boot towards center of drive axle.
5. Place index marks on inner joint housing and drive axle shaft for assembly reference.
6. Remove inner joint housing from tripot joint spider.
7. Place index marks on tripot joint spider and drive shaft for assembly reference.
8. Remove drive axle snap ring.
9. Remove tripot joint using suitable brass drift and hammer. Place drift on tripot body, not roller.
10. Remove inner boot, then the inner joint housing seal using bearing puller tool No. J-22912-01, or equivalent, and a suitable press.

Inspection

1. Clean tripot spider and boots using clean, dry, solvent-free rag. **Do not wash tripot joint spider or boots in solvent or degreaser.**
2. Inspect tripot joint for excessive wear or damage.
3. Inspect wheel side joint for excessive wear or damage.
4. Inspect boots for excessive wear or damage.
5. Inspect righthand shaft dynamic dampener for damage or distortion.

Assemble

1. If damper was removed, proceed as follows:
   a. Install damper on righthand shaft.
   b. Position damper into shaft groove.
   c. Damper centerline should be 16.862–17.098 inches from outer joint.
   d. Crimp damper clamp using service boot clamp tool No. J-22610, or equivalent.
2. Install inner joint seal using suitable press.
3. Install inner joint housing boot and clamps. **Do not crimp clamps at this time.**
4. Align tripot joint and shaft index marks.**Ensure tripot joint beveled splines are away from transaxle.**
5. Install tripot joint and snap ring.
6. Pack inner joint housing with approximately 5.8–6.4 ounces of kit provided grease.
7. Align index marks and install outer housing onto tripot joint.
8. Install inner joint boot and clamps. **Do not crimp clamps at this time.**
9. Measure drive shaft length to ensure boots are not stretched or excessively contracted when wheel drive axle is at its standard length, **Fig. 30.** Measurements are plus or minus .197 inch.
10. Ensure boots are not distorted or dented. Correct by pulling boot out. **Do**

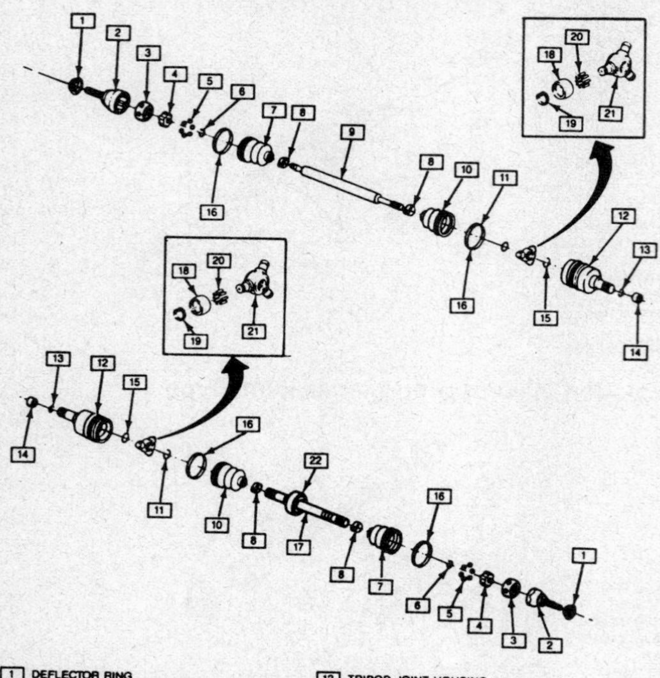

1 DEFLECTOR RING	12 TRIPOD JOINT HOUSING
2 CONSTANT VELOCITY JOINT OUTER RACE	13 AXLE SHAFT RETAINING PINS
3 CASE	14 DRIVE AXLE DUST COVER
4 CONSTANT VELOCITY JOINT INNER RACE	15 AXLE SHAFT SNAP RING
5 BALLS	16 LARGE BOOT CLAMPS
6 AXLE SHAFT SNAP RING	17 LEFT HAND DRIVE AXLE SHAFT
7 OUTBOARD BOOT	18 TRIPOD JOINT BALL
8 SMALL BOOT CLAMP	19 TRIPOD JOINT BALL AND BEARING RETAINER
9 RIGHT HAND DRIVE AXLE SHAFT	20 TRIPOD JOINT NEEDLE BEARINGS
10 TRIPOD BOOT	21 TRIPOD JOINT SPIDER
11 AXLE SHAFT RETAINING RING	22 DRIVE AXLE DAMPENER

GC3039100201000X

Fig. 29 Exploded view of front drive axle. Type 5

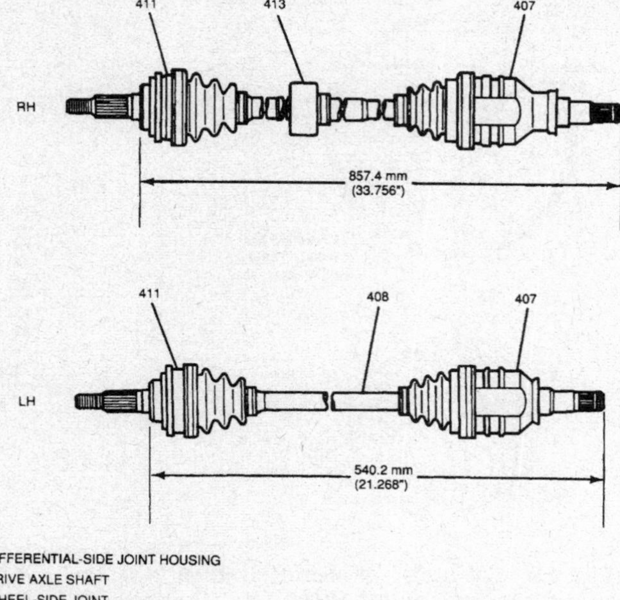

407 DIFFERENTIAL-SIDE JOINT HOUSING
408 DRIVE AXLE SHAFT
411 WHEEL-SIDE JOINT
413 DYNAMIC DAMPENER

GC3039400281000X

Fig. 30 Axle standard length. Type 5

not pull out on differential side joint.

11. Crimp clamps using seal clamp tool No. J-35566, or equivalent.

OUTER JOINT & BOOT

Disassemble

1. Remove boot retaining clamps, **Fig. 29.**
2. Slide boot toward center of shaft.
3. Place index marks on outer joint and shaft for assembly reference.
4. Remove outer joint from shaft while expanding shaft snap ring. **Do not damage ABS components.**
5. Secure axle in a suitable soft-jawed vise.
6. Remove outer joint seal.

Inspection

1. Clean boots using clean, dry, solvent-free cloth. **Do not clean boots in solvent.**
2. Inspect boot for damage or wear.
3. Inspect joint for excessive wear or damage. Replace joint as necessary. **Do not disassemble outer joint.**
4. Inspect righthand dynamic dampener for damage or distortion.

Assemble

1. Install outer joint seal using suitable sleeve and press.
2. If damper was removed, replace as described under "Inner Joint & Boot."
3. Install outer boot and clamps. **Do not crimp clamps at this time.**
4. Align outer joint and shaft index marks.
5. Slide outer joint onto shaft by expanding snap ring. Ensure snap ring is securely seated in groove.
6. Pack outer joint with approximately 5.8–6.4 ounces of kit provide green grease.
7. Measure drive axle length as described under "Inner Joint & Boot."
8. Ensure boots are not distorted or dented. Correct by pulling boot out. **Do not pull out on joint.**
9. Crimp small and large boot clamps using keystone clamp pliers tool No. J-22610, or equivalent.

TYPE 6

DISASSEMBLE

1. Clamp axle shaft in suitable soft metal or wood vise.
2. If deflector ring is damaged, remove from CV outer race using suitable brass drift and hammer, **Fig. 31.**
3. Disengage large and small boot clamps outer band from inner band at retainer peg using suitable hammer and chisel or flat-bladed screwdriver.
4. Separate large diameter of boot from CV joint race, then slide boot away from joint along axle shaft.
5. Wipe excess grease from CV inner race face.
6. Remove race retaining ring with suitable snap ring pliers, **Fig. 32.**
7. Remove CV joint from axle shaft, then the boot.
8. **On models equipped with dynamic damper,** if shaft or damper is being replaced, remove damper using suitable arbor press.
9. **On all models,** tap cage enough to remove first ball using suitable brass drift, **Fig. 33.** Remove remaining balls in similar manner.
10. Pivot cage and inner race at a 90° angle to outer race centerline, then align cage windows with outer race lands.
11. Remove cage and inner race.
12. Rotate inner race upward and out of cage.
13. Thoroughly clean and dry CV joint parts.
14. Cut tripot boot retaining clamp using suitable side cutters. Discard clamp.
15. Remove endless clamp using suitable small bladed screwdriver. Discard clamp.
16. Separate boot from large diameter of tripot housing, then slide boot along axle shaft away from joint.
17. Wipe excess grease from tripot spider face and inside tripot housing.
18. Remove tripot housing from spider and shaft, **Fig. 34.**
19. Spread spacer ring using snap ring tool No. SA-9198-C, or equivalent, then slide spacer ring and tripot spider back on axle, **Fig. 35.**
20. Remove spider retaining ring and slide spider off shaft. **Handle tripot spider with care. Tripot balls and needle rollers may separate from spider trunnions.**
21. Remove boot and thoroughly degrease housing. Allow to dry.

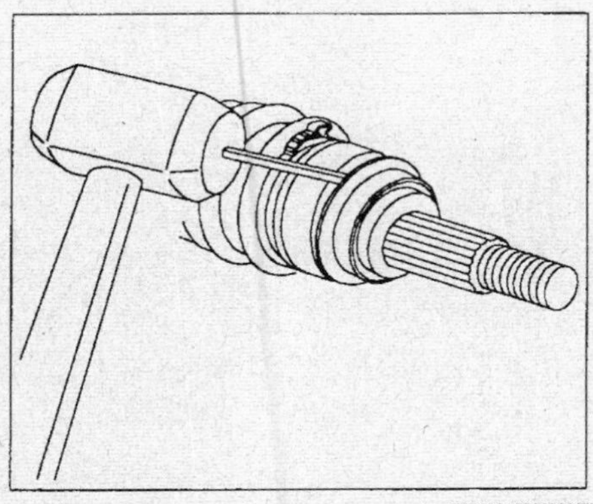

Fig. 31 Deflector ring removal. Type 6

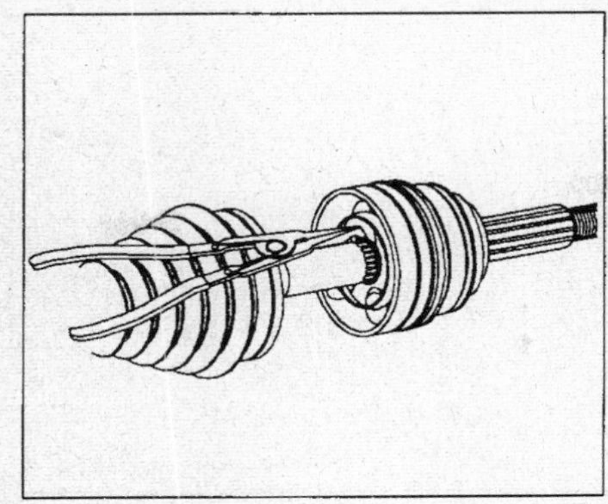

Fig. 32 Race retaining ring removal. Type 6

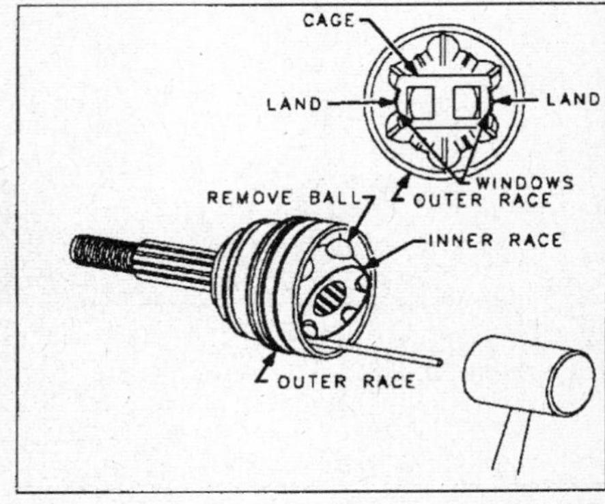

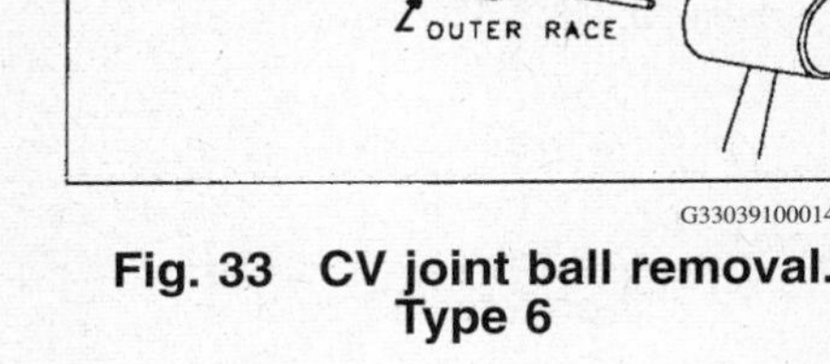

Fig. 33 CV joint ball removal. Type 6

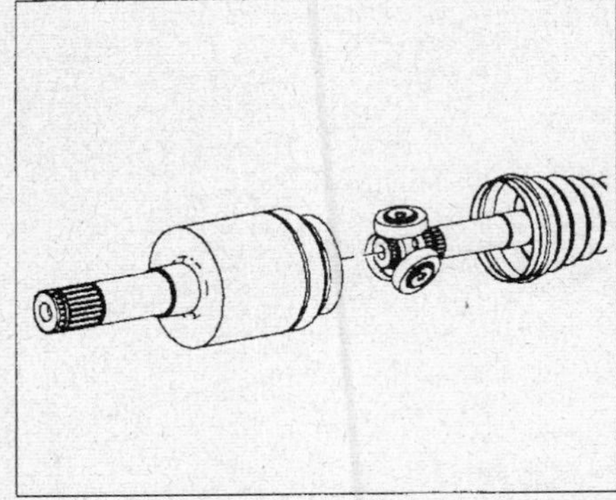

Fig. 34 Tripot housing removal. Type 6

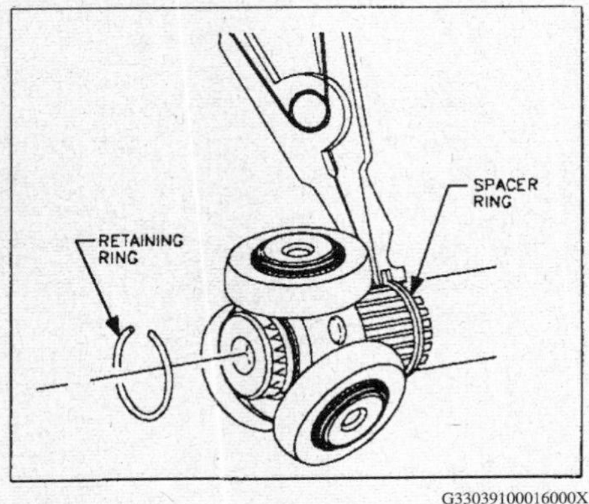

Fig. 35 Spider retaining ring removal. Type 6

Fig. 36 Small tripot retaining ring crimp. Type 6

INSPECTION

1. Inspect tripot joint components for wear, cracks and damage.
2. Clean shaft.
3. Remove rust from shaft mounting groove with a suitable wire brush.

ASSEMBLE

1. Install small retaining clamp on boot neck. **Do not crimp at this time.**
2. Slide boot onto shaft and position neck into groove.
3. Crimp boot retaining clamp using axle clamp installer tool No. SA-9203-C, or equivalent, **Fig. 36.**
4. Ensure clamp is positioned correctly.
5. Measure clamp end gap and crimp, as required.
6. Install spacer ring beyond second groove.
7. Slide tripot spider past retaining groove. Ensure tripot counterbored surface faces end of shaft.
8. Install retaining ring using C/V joint snap ring pliers tool No. SA-9198-C, or equivalent.
9. Slide tripot spider toward shaft end and seat spacer ring into groove.
10. Pack approximately half of kit provided grease inside boot. Use remaining grease to pack tripot housing.
11. Install kit provided convolute retainer over boot.
12. Position retaining clamp around large diameter of boot, then slide housing over tripot spider.
13. Slide large diameter of boot over tripot housing and position lip into housing groove.
14. Ensure boot is not dimpled, stretched or out of shape. Adjust by hand with suitable thin, flat, blunt tool.
15. Ensure tripot is installed to proper length, **Fig. 37.**
16. Install large boot retaining clamp and crimp with boot clamp installer tool No. SA9161C, or equivalent, **Fig. 38.**
17. **If replacing or installing damper,** proceed as follows:
    a. Clean shaft thoroughly.
    b. Mark damper installation point 7.95 inches from shaft outboard end with masking tape.
    c. Lubricate shaft with suitable liquid detergent (dishwashing detergent).
    d. Place shaft in suitable brass-jaw vice and start damper on by hand.
    e. Work damper onto shaft by twisting back and forth.
    f. Align damper inboard edge with tape.
    g. Remove tape.
    h. Secure damper by crimping clamp with axle boot clamp installer tool No. SA-9164-C, or equivalent, to an .085 inch gap.
18. Lightly coat inner and outer race grooves with suitable grease.
19. Insert and rotate inner race into cage.
20. Install cage and inner race into outer race, align cage windows with outer race lines.
21. Install balls, use a suitable brass drift to rotate and position cage and inner race.
22. Install inner race retaining ring.
23. Pack joint with service kit provided grease.
24. Install small retaining clamp on boot new. **Do not crimp at this time.**
25. Slide boot onto shaft, position neck into groove.
26. Crimp retaining clamp using axle clamp installer tool No. SA-9203-C, or equivalent, **Fig. 39.**
27. Ensure clamp is positioned properly around entire circumference.
28. Pack approximately half of kit provided grease inside boot. Use remaining grease to pack CV.
29. Position large retaining clamp around boot. Ensure inner race retaining ring side faces axle shaft.
30. Push CV joint onto shaft until retaining ring seats into groove.
31. Slide large diameter of boot over outside of CV joint race, position lip into housing groove.
32. Ensure boot is not dimpled, stretched or out of shape. Adjust by hand with suitable thin, flat, blunt tool.
33. Crimp retaining clamp using axle clamp installer tool No. SA-9203-C, or equivalent, **Fig. 40.**
34. Ensure clamp is positioned properly.

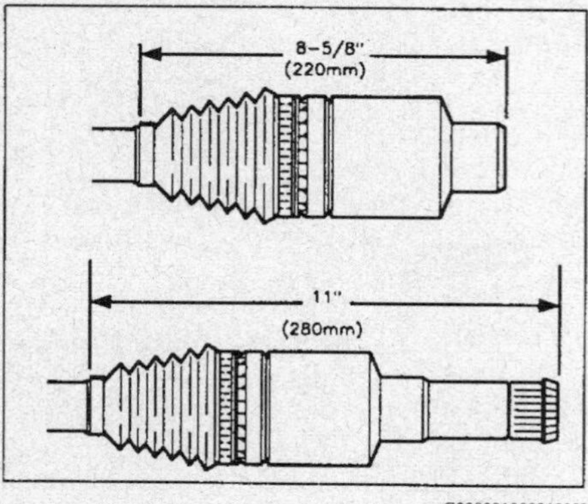

G33039100021000X

Fig. 37 Tripot assembly dimension. Type 6

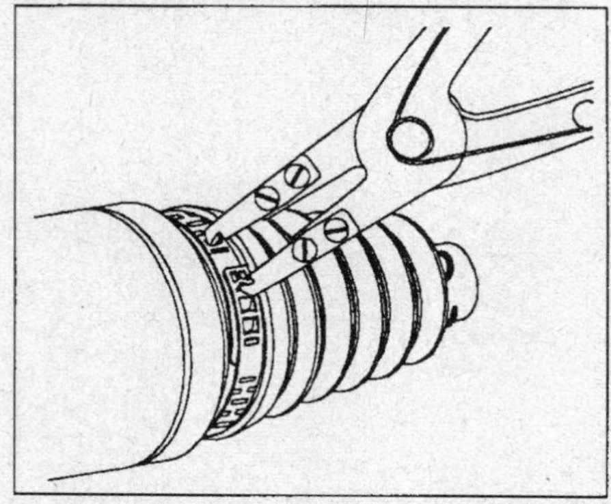

G33039100022000X

Fig. 38 Tripot large retaining clamp installation. Type 6

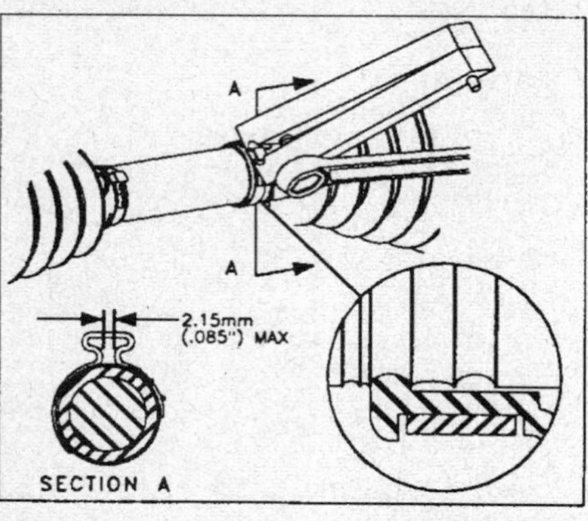

G33039100017000X

Fig. 39 Small CV joint retaining clamp installation. Type 6

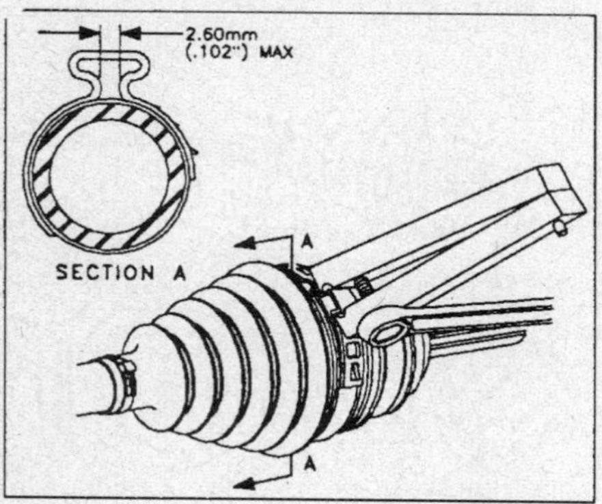

G33039100018000X

Fig. 40 Large CV joint retaining clamp crimp. Type 6

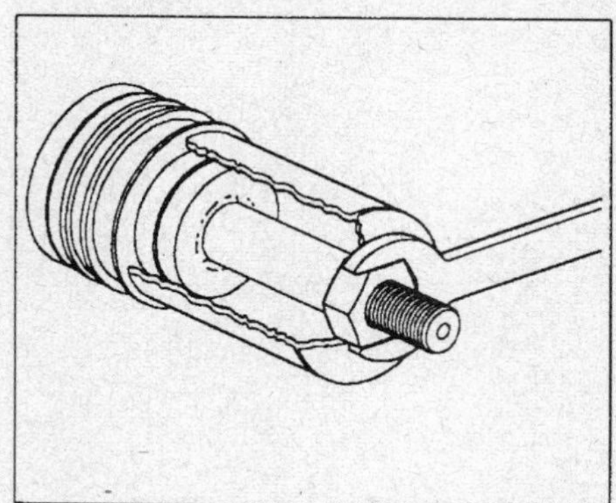

G33039100019000X

Fig. 41 Deflector ring installation. Type 6

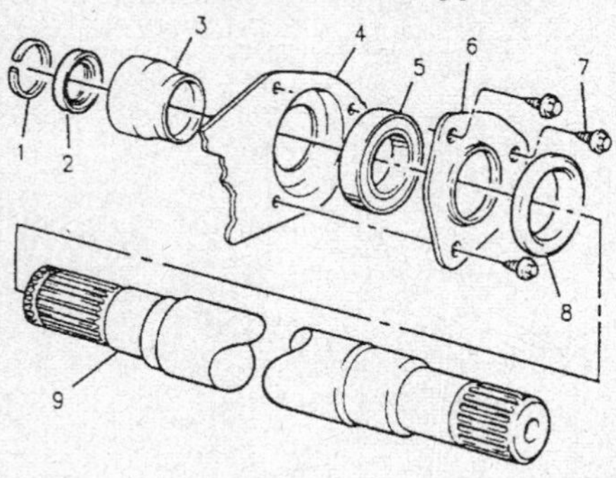

GC3039100203000X

Fig. 42 Exploded view of intermediate shaft. Types 1 & 3

35. Position deflecting ring at CV joint outer race.
36. Tighten nut until deflector bottoms against CV outer race shoulder using M20 x 1.0 mm nut and axle deflector ring installer tool No. SA-9160-C, or equivalent, **Fig. 41.**

INTERMEDIATE SHAFT

REPLACE

TYPE 1 & 3

1. Raise and support vehicle, then remove righthand tire and wheel assembly.
2. Protect outer joint from sharp edges with suitable shop towels.
3. Remove stabilizer shaft from righthand control arm.
4. Remove righthand ball joint from knuckle.
5. Remove drive axle from intermediate shaft as outlined under "Driveshaft, Replace."
6. Remove intermediate driveshaft support bracket to engine mounting bolts.
7. Remove intermediate shaft from transaxle.
8. Reverse procedure to install. Coat splines of intermediate shaft with suitable chassis grease.

TYPE 4

1. Remove righthand drive axle as outlined under "Driveshaft, Replace."
2. Remove intermediate shaft support bearing mounting bolts.
3. Remove intermediate shaft.
4. Reverse procedure to install.

TYPE 6

Removal

1. Remove righthand driveshaft as outlined under "Driveshaft, Replace."
2. **On models equipped with DOHC engine,** proceed as follows:
   a. Loosen intake manifold to intermediate axle shaft support bracket top mounting bolt. **Do not remove.**
   b. Remove intake manifold to intermediate axle shaft support bracket lower mounting bolt.
   c. Position intake manifold to intermediate axle shaft support bracket aside to provide clearance.
   d. Tighten intake manifold bracket mounting bolts to hold bracket in position.
3. **On all models,** remove support bracket to engine block mounting bolt and intermediate axle shaft.

Installation

A new inner tripot joint must be installed whenever a new intermediate axle shaft is installed.

1. Install transaxle seal protector tool No. SA-91112-T, or equivalent, **Fig. 15.**
2. Install intermediate driveshaft into transaxle. **Do not contact oil seal with shaft splines.**
3. After intermediate driveshaft splines have safely passed transaxle oil seal, remove seal protector.
4. Fully seat intermediate driveshaft into transaxle.
5. **On models equipped with SOHC engine,** install shaft support to engine block mounting bolts. **Do not tighten at this time.**
6. **On models equipped with DOHC engine,** proceed as follows:
   a. Install lower support bracket to engine block mounting bolts. **Do not tighten at this time.**
   b. Loosen support bracket to intake manifold mounting bolt and align holes.
   c. Tighten support bracket to intake manifold mounting bolts to specifications.
7. **On all models,** tighten support bracket to engine block mounting bolts to specifications.

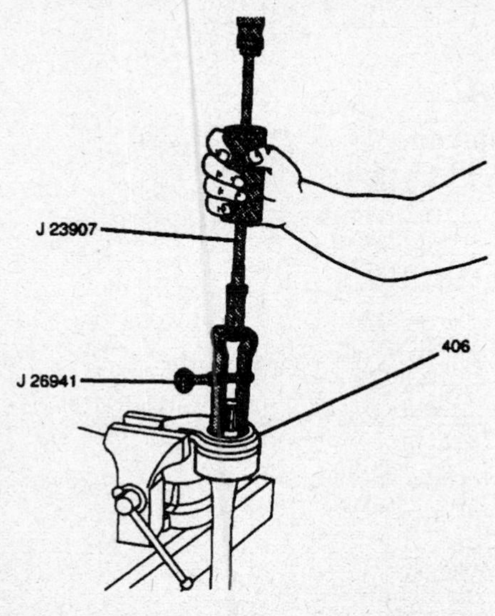

406 CENTER SUPPORT BEARING ARBOR (SEDAN MODEL)

GC3039600276000X

Fig. 43 Intermediate driveshaft support seal removal. Type 4

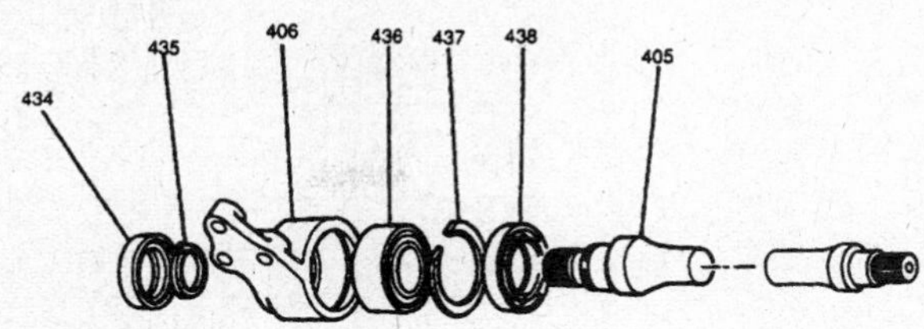

405 RIGHT INNER DRIVE AXLE (SEDAN MODEL)
406 CENTER SUPPORT BEARING ARBOR (SEDAN MODEL)
434 CENTER SUPPORT BEARING OUTER SEAL (SEDAN MODEL)
435 RIGHT INNER DRIVE AXLE SNAP RING (SEDAN MODEL)
436 CENTER SUPPORT BEARING (SEDAN MODEL)
437 CENTER SUPPORT BEARING RETAINING RING (SEDAN MODEL)
438 CENTER SUPPORT BEARING INNER SEAL (SEDAN MODEL)

GC3039600277000X

Fig. 44 Exploded view of intermediate driveshaft support. Type 4

INTERMEDIATE SHAFT SERVICE

TYPE 1 & 3

Disassemble

1. Remove retaining ring and lip seal, **Fig. 42.**
2. Press shaft from bearing by positioning split plate tool No. J-22912-1, or equivalent, behind inner slinger.
3. Remove retainer from support screws.
4. Press bearing from support using joint seal installer tool No. J-23694, or equivalent.

Assemble

1. Press bearing into support using suitable press arbor plate across bearing.
2. Press inner slinger on shaft using split plate tool No. J-22912-1, or equivalent.
3. Install retainer over shaft.
4. Place support with bearing on press arbor plate and press shaft into bearing until bearing inner race contacts shaft chamfer. **Do not press bearing beyond where chamfer begins on shaft.**
5. Press outer slinger on shaft using split plate.
6. Apply suitable RTV sealer to outer slinger and shaft joint.
7. Install lip seal using seal installer tool No. J-34115, or equivalent.
8. Install retaining ring.
9. Install retainer to support.

TYPE 4

Disassemble

1. Support intermediate shaft bearing arbor in a suitable vise.
2. Remove outer bearing seal using oil seal remover tool No. J-26941 and slide hammer tool No. J-23907, or equivalents, **Fig. 43.**
3. Remove righthand driveshaft snap ring, **Fig. 44.**
4. Press righthand driveshaft from bearing using side bearing remover tool No. J-28888-D, or equivalent.
5. Remove inner bearing seal using oil seal remover tool and slide hammer.
6. Remove retaining clip and intermediate shaft

Inspection

1. Inspect intermediate shaft bearing for excessive wear or damage.
2. Inspect intermediate shaft bearing inner and outer seal for excessive wear or damage.

Assemble

1. Apply GM No. 1051344, or suitable equivalent wheel bearing lubricant, to intermediate shaft bearing inner seal lip.
2. Install inner seal by tapping evenly using suitable plastic mallet. **Ensure seal is installed with garter spring facing out.**
3. Install righthand drive shaft into intermediate shaft into bearing using suitable hydraulic press.
4. Mount drive axle and bearing in a suitable vice.
5. Install righthand driveshaft snap ring.
6. Apply wheel bearing lubricant part No. 1051344, or equivalent, to intermediate shaft bearing outer seal lip.
7. Install outer seal using oil seal installer tool No. J-37751, or equivalent. **Ensure seal is installed with garter spring facing out.**

TIGHTENING SPECIFICATIONS

Year	Component	Torque/Ft. Lbs.
ACHIEVA & SKYLARK		
1998	Axle Nut	74②
	Ball Joint To Steering Knuckle	41–48
	CV Joint Large Boot Clamp	130
	CV Joint Small Boot Clamp	100
	Intermediate Driveshaft Support	48
	Intermediate Driveshaft Retainer To Support	89①
	Stabilizer Link	13
	Wheel Lug Nuts	100

Continued

TIGHTENING SPECIFICATIONS—Continued

Year	Component	Torque/Ft. Lbs.
ALERO		
1999–2002	Axle Nut	284
	Ball Joint To Steering Knuckle	41
	CV Joint Large Boot Clamp	130
	CV Joint Small Boot Clamp	100
	Stabilizer Link	22
	Tie Rod To Knuckle	15③
	Wheel Lug Nuts	100
AURORA		
1998–2002	Axle Nut	118
	Ball Joint To Steering Knuckle (1998–99)	84①④
	Ball Joint To Steering Knuckle (2001–02)	50
	CV Joint Boot Clamp	130
	Stabilizer Link	13
	Wheel Lug Nuts	100
BONNEVILLE, LESABRE & PARK AVENUE		
1998–2002	Axle Nut	118
	Ball Joint To Steering Knuckle	50
	CV Joint Boot Clamp	130
	Stabilizer Shaft Bracket	35
	Stabilizer Shaft Link	13
	Wheel Lug Nuts	100
CAVALIER & SUNFIRE		
1998–2002	ABS Speed Sensor	107①
	Axle Nut	144
	Ball Joint To Knuckle	50③
	CV Joint Large Boot Clamp	130
	CV Joint Small Boot Clamp	100
	Stabilizer Link	13
	Wheel Lug Nuts	100
CENTURY, IMPALA & REGAL		
1998–2002	Axle Nut	159
	Ball Joint To Steering Knuckle	15⑤
	CV Joint Large Boot Clamp	130
	CV Joint Small Boot Clamp	100
	Stabilizer Shaft Bracket	35
	Stabilizer Link Assembly Nut	17
	Wheel Lug Nuts	100
CUTLASS & MALIBU		
1998–2002	Axle Nut	284
	Ball Joint To Steering Knuckle	41
	CV Joint Large Boot Clamp	130
	CV Joint Small Boot Clamp	100
	Stabilizer Link	13
	Tie Rod To Knuckle	15③
	Wheel Lug Nuts	100
DEVILLE & ELDORADO		
1998–2002	Axle Nut	118
	Ball Joint To Steering Knuckle Nut	37
	CV Joint Boot Clamp	130
	Stabilizer Bracket To Frame	33
	Stabilizer Link	41
	Wheel Lug Nuts	100

Continued

TIGHTENING SPECIFICATIONS—Continued

Year	Component	Torque/Ft. Lbs.
EIGHTY-EIGHT, LSS & REGENCY		
1998–99	Axle Nut	118
	Ball Joint To Steering Knuckle	50
	CV Joint Boot Clamp	130
	Stabilizer Shaft Bracket	35
	Stabilizer Shaft Link	13
	Wheel Lug Nuts	100
GRAND AM		
1998	Axle Nut	74②
	Ball Joint To Steering Knuckle	41–48
	CV Joint Large Boot Clamp	130
	CV Joint Small Boot Clamp	100
	Stabilizer Link	13
	Wheel Lug Nuts	100
1999–2002	Axle Nut	284
	Ball Joint To Steering Knuckle	41
	CV Joint Large Boot Clamp	130
	CV Joint Small Boot Clamp	100
	Stabilizer Link	22
	Tie Rod To Knuckle	15③
	Wheel Lug Nuts	100
GRAND PRIX & INTRIGUE		
1998–2002	Axle Nut (1998–99)	118
	Axle Nut (2000–02)	159
	Ball Joint To Steering Knuckle	15⑤
	CV Joint Large Boot Clamp	130
	CV Joint Small Boot Clamp	100
	Stabilizer Shaft Bracket	35
	Stabilizer Link Assembly Nut	17
	Wheel Lug Nuts	100
LUMINA		
1998–2001	Axle Nut	159
	Ball Joint To Steering Knuckle	63
	CV Joint Large Boot Clamp	130
	CV Joint Small Boot Clamp	100
	Stabilizer Shaft Bracket	35
	Stabilizer Link Assembly Nut	17
	Wheel Lug Nuts	100
METRO		
1998–2001	ABS Speed Sensor	71①
	Axle Nut	129
	Ball Stud	44
	Intermediate Shaft Bearing Support	44
	Transaxle Drain	21
	Wheel Bearing Support	40
	Wheel Lug Nuts	44

Continued

TIGHTENING SPECIFICATIONS—Continued

Year	Component	Torque/Ft. Lbs.
MONTE CARLO		
1998–2002	Axle Nut	159
	Ball Joint To Steering Knuckle (1998–99)	63
	Ball Joint To Steering Knuckle (2000–02)	15⑤
	CV Joint Large Boot Clamp	130
	CV Joint Small Boot Clamp	100
	Stabilizer Shaft Bracket	35
	Stabilizer Link Assembly Nut	17
	Wheel Lug Nuts	100
PRIZM		
1998–2002	ABS Speed Sensor	71①
	Axle Nut	166
	Ball Joint-To-Lower Control Arm	105
	Splash Shield	71①
	Tie Rod End	36
	Wheel Lug Nuts	76
RIVIERA		
1998–99	Axle Nut	118
	Ball Joint To Steering Knuckle	84①④
	CV Joint Boot Clamp	130
	Stabilizer Link	13
	Wheel Lug Nuts	100
SATURN L-SERIES		
2000–02	Axle Nut	⑦
	Ball Joint Stud Castle Nut	55
	Lower Control Arm Ball Stud	75
	Tie Rod End To Steering Knuckle	45
	Wheel Lugs Nuts	92
SATURN S-SERIES		
1998–2002	Axle Nut	148
	Ball Joint Stud Castle Nut	55
	Intermediate Shaft Bracket	22
	Intermediate Shaft Support Bracket-To-Engine Block	40
	Intermediate Shaft Support Bracket-To-Intake Manifold	71①
	Tie Rod End To Steering Knuckle	33
	Wheel Lug Nuts	103
SEVILLE		
1998–2002	Axle Nut	118
	Ball Joint To Steering Knuckle Nut	88①⑥
	CV Joint Boot Clamp	130
	Stabilizer Bracket To Frame	33
	Stabilizer Link	41
	Wheel Lug Nuts	100

① — Inch lbs.
② — Tighten an additional 40.°
③ — Tighten an additional 180.°
④ — Tighten an additional 15.°
⑤ — Tighten an additional 120.°
⑥ — Tighten an additional 150.°
⑦ — Refer to “Driveshaft, Replace” for tightening procedure.

DRIVE AXLES

NOTE: On Air Bag Equipped Models, Refer To "Air Bag System Precautions" Located In The Front Of This Manual For System Disarming & Arming Procedures.

NOTE: Refer To "Computer Relearn Procedures" Located In The Front Of This Manual When Battery Power To The Computer Has Been Interrupted.

INDEX

APPLICATION CHART

Model	Gear Ratio	Ring Gear Diameter, Inch
Camaro	2.73	7.62
	3.08	7.62
	3.23	7.62
	3.42	7.62
Catera	3.90	7.40
Corvette	2.73	7.62
	3.15	7.62
	3.42	7.62
Firebird	2.73	7.62
	3.08	7.62
	3.23	7.62
	3.42	7.62

IDENTIFICATION

CAMARO & FIREBIRD

Axle identification numbers can be found stamped on the righthand front section of the axle shaft housing, **Fig. 1.** Production option codes are also located on the service parts identification label.

CORVETTE

Axle identification numbers can be found on a tag, located on the side of the differential carrier, **Fig. 2.**

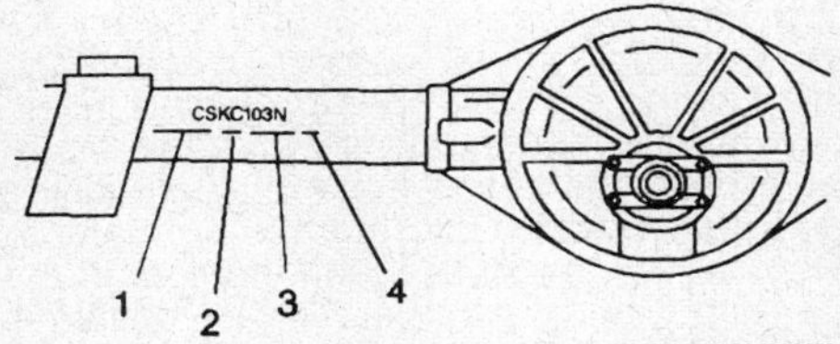

Fig. 1 Axle identification. Camaro & Firebird (1-axle code, 2-manufacturer's code, 3-build date, 4-shift)

DESCRIPTION

STANDARD SEMI-FLOATING AXLE w/HYPOID TYPE DIFFERENTIAL

The standard rear axle is a semi-floating hypoid rear axle. When the vehicle turns a corner, the differential allows the outer rear wheel to turn faster than inner wheel. The inner wheel, turning slower with respect to the outer wheel, slows its side differential pinion gear. The differential pinion gears roll around the slowed side differential pinion gear, driving the other differential pinion gear and wheel at a faster pace.

On Camaro and Firebird models equipped with the standard axle and anti-lock brakes (ABS), a single rear wheel speed sensor is located on the differential carrier behind the ring gear. A wheel speed sensor mounts on the top of the axle housing opposite the reluctor wheel.

LIMITED SLIP AXLE w/AUBURN CONE & DANA TRAC-LOK TYPE DIFFERENTIALS

Limited slip rear axles have several definitive operating characteristics. An understanding of these characteristics is required to aid in diagnosis.

The energizing force comes from the thrust side of the gears. Consequently, a free spinning wheel may not have enough resistance to driving torque to apply the clutch packs or cones. If this occurs, applying the parking brake a few notches will provide enough resistance to energize the cones.

Energizing the cones is independent of acceleration, therefore a very slow application of the throttle on starting is recommended to provide maximum traction by preventing "breakaway" of either tire.

All rear axle components of vehicles with limited slip rear axle are interchangeable with those equipped with the standard rear axle, except for the differential case. It is similar in all respects to the standard differential case with the addition of cone clutches splined to each side gear. The differential case is non-serviceable and must be replaced as a unit.

LIMITED SLIP AXLE w/ZEXEL TORSEN TYPE DIFFERENTIAL

The limited slip rear axle differential found on 1999–2002 Camaro and Firebird models is the Zexel Torsen differential. Unlike previous limited slip differentials, the Torsen assembly does not utilize cone clutches, but rather a system of close tolerance gears. With normal operation, both tires and wheels rotate at equal speeds while vehicle is being driven straight ahead. An equal driving force is delivered to each wheel during straight ahead driving. When turning a corner, the inside wheel requires extra driving force. This unequal driving force results in a compensation of inside and outside axles by differential.

All rear axle components of vehicles with limited slip rear axle are interchangeable with those equipped with the standard rear axle, except for the differential case. The differential case is non-serviceable and must be replaced as a unit.

On models equipped with limited slip axles, anti-lock brakes (ABS) and Traction Control system (TCS), rear wheel speed sensors are mounted on the axle shafts behind the axle flange. Reluctor wheels are integral with the axle shafts and are not serviced separately. The entire axle must be replaced if reluctor wheel replacement is required.

TROUBLESHOOTING

PRELIMINARY INSPECTIONS

Before the rear axle is to be serviced, ensure the source of the problem is the rear axle itself and not originating in other sources such as noise from the tires, road surface, engine, transmission, wheel bearings, muffler or body components. Perform the following procedures to inspect for other sources that could be mistaken for axle noise:

1. Ensure rear axle lubricant is at the proper level and type, then select a level asphalt road to reduce tire and body noise.
2. After vehicle has been driven far enough to warm lubricant, note at which speed the noise occurs then stop vehicle. With vehicle in neutral run engine slowly through the RPM range that the noise occurred to determine if noise was caused by the exhaust or powertrain.
3. Inspect for tire noise by temporarily inflating all tires to approximately 50 psi for test purposes only. Drive vehicle on a level asphalt road and note if a change in noise occurs compared to noise while tires are inflated at normal pressure. After test is completed ensure tires are inflated to manufacturer's specifications.
4. Inspect the front and rear wheel bearings by lightly applying the brakes while keeping vehicle speed steady. If the noise diminishes, inspect front and rear wheel bearings by jacking up the front wheels, then spinning or shaking them to determine if bearings are loose. Replace if required.
5. With vehicle jacked up, inspect for metal to metal contact between the spring and the spring opening in the frame, upper and lower control arm bushings and frame and axle housing brackets. Ensure there is no metal to metal contact between the floor of the body and the frame. Replace bushings or rubber insulators if required.

(1) GM Part Number
(2) Getrag Part Number
(3) Serial Number

Available Axle Ratios

GM P/N	Axle Ratio	Transmission
12551769	342	Manual
12554837	273 (Base)	Automatic
12556313	315 (Optional)	Automatic

GC3039700290000X

Fig. 2 Axle identification. Corvette

REAR AXLE NOISES

CAMARO & FIREBIRD

After noise has been determined to be in the axle and not from other sources, inspect for the specific type of axle noise as follows:

Rough Growl Or Grating

1. Faulty pinion or rear axle case side bearing.

Chatter On Turns

1. Wrong lubricant in axle.
2. Clutch cones worn, if applicable.

Knock At Low Speeds

1. Worn universal joint.
2. Side gear hub counterbore in the differential case worn oversize.

Clunk While Accelerating Or Decelerating

1. Worn differential case.
2. Excessive clearance between the axle shaft and side gear splines.
3. Excessive clearance between side gear hub and counterbore in case.
4. Excessive drive pinion and ring gear backlash.
5. Worn pinion and side gear teeth.
6. Worn thrust washers.

Constant Scraping Noise At Low Speeds

1. Faulty or worn pinion bearing.

Constant Whine While Driving

1. Faulty or worn ring and pinion gear.

Groan In Forward Or Reverse

1. Wrong lubricant in axle.

Whine Louder While Turning

1. Faulty or worn axle side gear and/or pinion.

CATERA

Refer to **Fig. 3** for differential noise diagnosis.

CORVETTE

Refer to **Fig. 4** for differential noise diagnosis.

LIMITED SLIP AXLE OPERATION

EXCEPT 1999–2002 CAMARO & FIREBIRD

Improper operation is often indicated by clutch slipping or grabbing which produces a whirring or chattering noise. These noises do not always indicate an axle failure but could be from lack of proper lubrication or normal noise when axle clutches are engaged during certain road conditions. Since the operational life of the limited slip unit is dependent on equal rotation of the wheels while driving straight ahead, it is important that there is no major difference in rear wheel tire size, air pressure or wear pattern, otherwise the vehicle may swerve during acceleration. If limited slip differential problems are not caused by the above, inspect for proper operation as follows:

Auburn Cone Type Differential

1. With parking brake released and automatic transmission in park or manual transmission in gear, raise both tires off the floor.
2. Remove hubcap or wheel disc and install axle shaft puller tool No. J-21579, or equivalent to either wheel with ½ ×13 adapter tool No. J-2619-01, or equivalent.
3. Using a suitable torque wrench, measure torque required to rotate one wheel, which should be 125–225 ft. lbs.
4. Place transmission in neutral position, then lower one rear tire to the ground.
5. Measure torque required to rotate the raised wheel.
6. **On 1998 Camaro and Firebird models,** torque should be 44–66 ft. lbs.
7. **On all models,** the differential case must be replaced as a unit if proper specifications are not obtained.

Dana Trac-Lok Type Differential

1. With automatic transmission in park and manual transmission in gear, raise

Condition	Cause
Noise is the same in drive or coast.	• Road noise. • Tire noise. • Front wheel bearing noise. • Rear wheel bearing noise. • Incorrect driveline angles.
Noise changes on a different type of road.	1. Road noise. 2. Tire noise.
Noise tone is lower as the vehicle speed is lowered.	Tire noise.
Noise is produced with the vehicle standing and driving.	• Engine noise. • Automatic transmission noise.
Vibration	• Unbalanced propeller shaft. • Damaged propeller shaft. • Tire unbalance. • Worn universal joint in the propeller shaft. • Incorrect driveline angles.
A knock or a click approximately every two revolutions of the rear wheel.	Rear wheel bearing.
Noise is most pronounced on turns.	• Rear wheel bearing. • Worn rear tie rod ends.
A continuous low pitch whirring or scraping noise starting at a relatively low speed.	Differential drive pinion gear inner or outer bearing noise.
Drive noise, coast noise, or float noise.	Differential ring gear and differential drive pinion gear noise.
Clunk on acceleration or deceleration	• A worn differential drive pinion gear or differential side gear hub counterbore worn oversize. • A worn universal joint on propeller shaft.
Groan in forward or reverse	• Wrong axle lubricant in axle. • Differential drive pinion gear bearing worn.
Clunk or knock on rough road operation.	Worn rear tie rod ends.

GC3039700298000A

Fig. 3 Differential noise diagnosis. Catera

Concern	Probable Cause
The noise is the same in drive or when coasting	• Road noise • Tire noise • Front wheel bearing noise
The noise changes on the different type of road surfaces	• Road noise • Tire noise
The noise tone lowers as the vehicle speed is decreased	• Tire noise • Worn bearings • Worn gear set
A similar noise is produced with the vehicle either standing or when driving	• Engine noise • Transmission noise
The noise is most pronounced on turns	Differential side gear and pinion
A continuous low pitch whirring or scraping noise starting at a relatively low speed	Pinion bearing
Drive noise, coast noise or float noise	Ring and pinion gear
A clunk on acceleration or deceleration	Worn differential shaft in case
A groan in forward or reverse	Incorrect rear axle lubricant in the differential
A chatter on turns	• Wrong rear axle lubricate in the differential • Clutch plates worn • No friction modifier in the lubricant
A clunk or knock when driving on a rough road surface	Excessive end play of yoke shafts to differential shaft

GC3039700291000A

Fig. 4 Differential noise diagnosis. Corvette

rear of vehicle until one rear tire is off the ground.

2. Remove rear wheel assembly, then attach side hammer assembly tool No. J-2619-01 and axle shaft remover tool No. J-21579, or equivalents, to axle shaft flange and a ½ inch × 13 bolt into adapter.
3. Raise other tire off the ground and attach torque wrench to side hammer assembly tool No. J-2619-01, or equivalent, then measure torque required to rotate axle shaft. If reading is less than 48 ft. lbs., remove and repair the differential unit.

DISASSEMBLE

DIFFERENTIAL

CAMARO & FIREBIRD

Drum Brakes

1. Remove axle housing drain plug or rear cover and drain fluid into an approved container, **Fig. 5.**
2. Remove rear axle assembly as outlined in "Camaro & Firebird" chapter.
3. Remove rear brake pipe assemblies from rear brake cylinders, then disconnect center hose assembly from junction block.
4. Remove rear brake assemblies from housing, then rear axle shaft bearings and seals.
5. Remove rear backing plates, then differential case and differential drive pinion gear.

Disc Brakes

A shim may be installed between the rear brake caliper mounting plate and axle shaft tube flange on housing. This shim centers the rear brake caliper and pads over the brake rotor, ensuring even brake pad assembly pressure during braking. This shim may have to be changed when the housing is replaced.

1. Remove axle housing drain plug or rear cover and drain fluid into an approved container, **Fig. 5.**
2. Remove rear axle assembly as outlined in "Camaro & Firebird" chapter.
3. Remove rear brake pipe assemblies from rear brake hose junction block, then junction block from housing.
4. Remove rear brake pipe and hose assemblies from housing.
5. Remove brake shaft bearing assemblies and seals, then caliper anchor brackets and mounting plates.
6. Remove shim, if installed.
7. Remove differential case, then differential drive pinion gear.

CATERA

1. Remove rear axle assembly as outlined in "Catera" chapter.
2. Mount differential into holding fixture tool No. J-3289-20, or equivalent.
3. Remove rear axle housing cover bolts, then rear axle housing cover.
4. Using suitable prybar, remove drive axle seals.
5. Using rear axle housing cover bolts, install side bearing preload clamp plate tool No. J-42143, or equivalent onto righthand side of rear axle housing cover, **Fig. 6.**
6. Install side bearing preload clamp plate tool No. J-42143, or equivalent onto righthand differential side bearing outer race. Tighten clamp only enough to relieve a significant amount of bearing preload from snap ring.
7. Tighten clamp onto side bearing preload clamp tool No. J-42149, or equivalent.
8. Use a hammer and a drift to rotate rear axle differential adjuster ring so that ring opening is accessible.
9. Use suitable heavy duty snap ring pliers to remove adjuster snap ring from righthand bearing cover.
10. Remove side bearing preload clamp tool and side bearing preload clamp plate tool from rear axle housing.
11. Using suitable heavy duty snap ring pliers, remove adjuster ring from lefthand side of rear axle housing.
12. Using a suitable rubber-faced mallet and a piece of wood, drive out righthand differential side bearing outer

race from cover opening of differential. Inspect differential side bearing seal on outer race for damage, replace as required.

13. Lightly tap carrier through righthand side bearing bore using a rubber mallet and a piece of wood to drive lefthand side differential bearing outer race out of housing. Inspect differential side bearing seal on outer race for damage, replace as required.
14. Remove differential carrier from rear axle housing.
15. Using a rubber mallet, remove drive pinion from differential carrier.
16. Remove drive pinion seal from differential carrier, then drive pinion outer bearing from bearing bore.
17. Remove drive pinion gear inner bearing from pinion gear.
18. Remove pinion bearing outer races from rear axle housing.

CORVETTE

1. Remove rear axle assembly as outlined in "Corvette" chapter.
2. **On models equipped with automatic transmission,** remove differential carrier seal plate from front of differential carrier housing, then O-ring. Discard O-ring.
3. **On all models,** remove differential carrier mount.
4. Remove fill plug washer and fill tag.
5. Remove drain plug, allowing fluid to drain into an approved container.
6. Remove vehicle speed sensor bolt, then speed sensor.
7. Remove righthand side differential carrier cover bolts, then the cover and O-ring seal, **Fig. 7.** Discard O-ring.
8. Install two 10 mm nuts onto righthand side transmission mounting stud and remove stud from block.
9. Remove righthand side transmission stud mount bolts, then stud mount from the differential carrier.
10. Remove righthand side output shaft snap ring.
11. Using differential housing lifting tool No. J-42155, or equivalent, remove differential case assembly from differential carrier.
12. Remove differential carrier cover bolts, then rear cover and O-ring seal. Discard O-ring.
13. Remove pinion cartridge bolts.
14. Using heat gun tool No. J-25070, or equivalent, heat differential carrier around pinion cartridge.
15. Remove pinion cartridge from differential carrier by threading two long bolts into pinion cartridge.
16. Remove pinion cartridge O-ring seal. Discard O-ring.
17. Remove pinion cartridge shim pack from differential carrier. **Tag shim pack to indicate its installation position.**
18. Remove lefthand side differential carrier cover bolts, then the cover and O-ring. Discard O-ring.

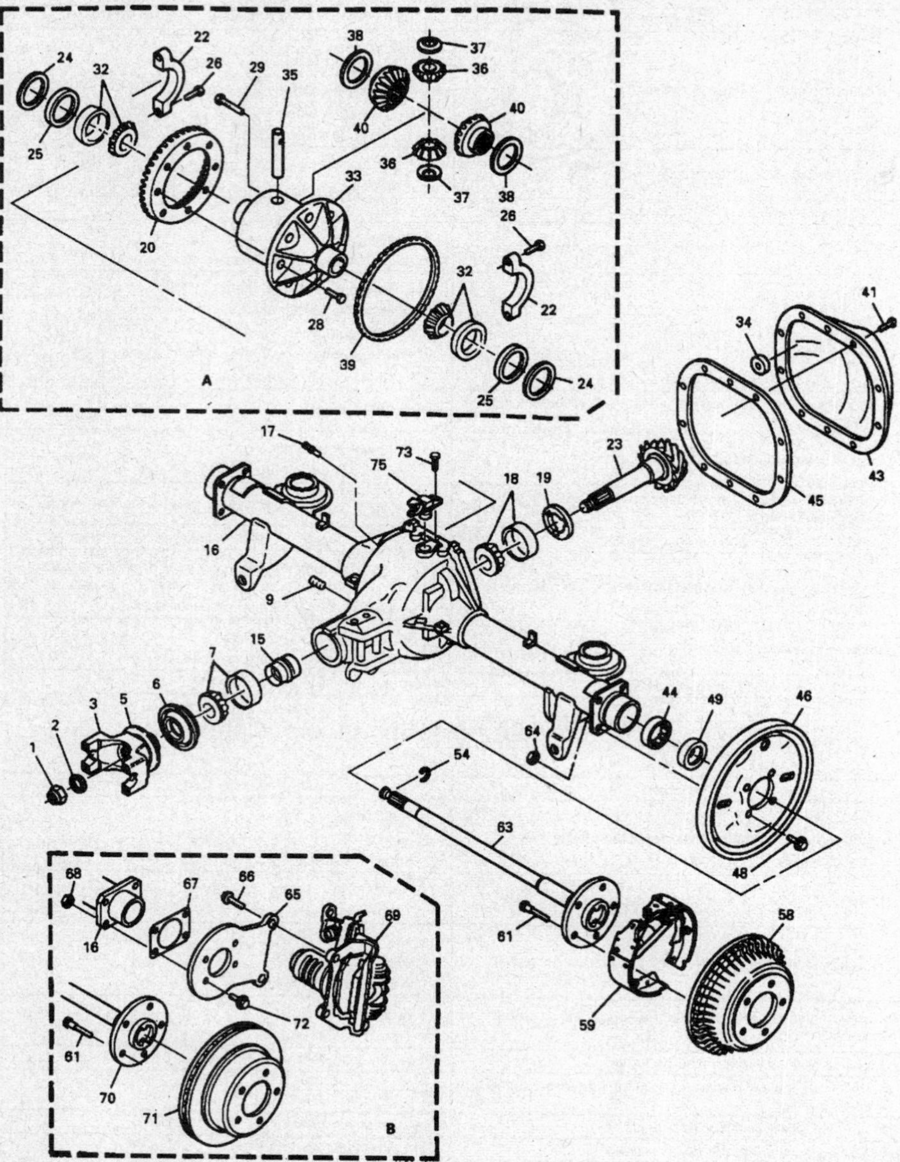

GC3039400285010X

Fig. 5 Exploded view of standard rear axle (Part 1 of 2). Camaro & Firebird

A DIFFERENTIAL
B OPTIONAL DISC BRAKE
1 NUT, DIFFERENTIAL DRIVE PINION GEAR
2 WASHER, DIFFERENTIAL DRIVE PINION GEAR
3 YOKE, DIFFERENTIAL DRIVE PINION GEAR
5 DEFLECTOR, DIFFERENTIAL DRIVE PINION GEAR DIRT
6 SEAL, DIFFERENTIAL DRIVE PINION GEAR
7 BEARING, DIFFERENTIAL DRIVE PINION GEAR OUTER
9 PLUG, REAR AXLE HOUSING DRAIN
15 SPACER, DIFFERENTIAL DRIVE PINION GEAR BEARING
16 HOUSING, REAR AXLE
17 VENT, REAR AXLE
18 BEARING, DIFFERENTIAL DRIVE PINION GEAR INNER
19 SHIM, DIFFERENTIAL DRIVE PINION GEAR
20 GEAR, DIFFERENTIAL RING
22 CAP, DIFFERENTIAL CARRIER BEARING
23 GEAR, DIFFERENTIAL DRIVE PINION
24 SHIM, DIFFERENTIAL BEARING
25 SPACER, DIFFERENTIAL BEARING
26 BOLT/SCREW, DIFFERENTIAL BEARING CAP
28 BOLT/SCREW, DIFFERENTIAL RING GEAR
29 BOLT/SCREW, DIFFERENTIAL PINION GEAR SHAFT LOCK
32 BEARING, DIFFERENTIAL
33 CASE, DIFFERENTIAL
34 MAGNET, REAR AXLE HOUSING CHIP COLLECTING
35 SHAFT, DIFFERENTIAL PINION GEAR
36 GEAR, DIFFERENTIAL PINION
37 WASHER, DIFFERENTIAL PINION GEAR THRUST
38 WASHER, DIFFERENTIAL SIDE GEAR THRUST
39 WHEEL, REAR WHEEL SPEED SENSOR RELUCTOR
40 GEAR, DIFFERENTIAL SIDE
41 BOLT/SCREW, REAR AXLE HOUSING
43 COVER, REAR AXLE HOUSING
44 BEARING, REAR AXLE SHAFT
45 GASKET, REAR AXLE HOUSING COVER
46 PLATE, REAR BRAKE BACKING
48 BOLT/SCREW, REAR BRAKE BACKING
49 SEAL, REAR AXLE SHAFT BEARING
54 LOCK, REAR AXLE SHAFT
58 DRUM, REAR BRAKE
59 BRAKE, REAR
61 BOLT/SCREW, REAR WHEEL
63 SHAFT REAR AXLE (DRUM BRAKE ASSEMBLIES)
64 NUT, REAR BRAKE BACKING PLATE
65 PLATE, REAR BRAKE CALIPER MOUNTING
66 BOLT/SCREW, CALIPER MOUNTING
67 SHIM, AXLE TUBE FLANGE
68 NUT, REAR BRAKE CALIPER MOUNTING PLATE
69 CALIPER, REAR BRAKE
70 SHAFT, REAR AXLE (DISC BRAKE ASSEMBLIES)
71 ROTOR, REAR BRAKE
72 BOLT/SCREW, REAR BRAKE BACKING PLATE
73 BOLT/SCREW, SENSOR PLUG MOUNTING
75 SENSOR, WHEEL SPEED

GC3039400285020X

Fig. 5 Exploded view of standard rear axle (Part 2 of 2). Camaro & Firebird

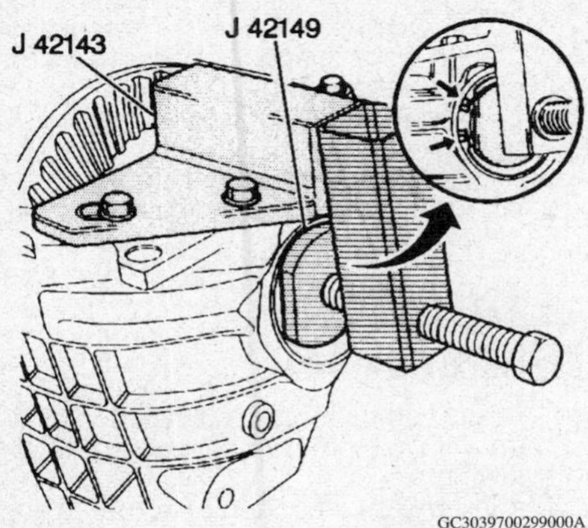

Fig. 6 Preload clamp tool installation. Catera

DRIVE PINION

CAMARO & FIREBIRD

1. Scribe reference mark between drive pinion and driveshaft yoke.
2. Hold yoke with suitable tool, then remove pinion nut and yoke. **Replace yoke if it shows wear in the seal-to-flange contacting surface.**
3. Install pinion removal tool No. J-22536, or equivalent to end of pinion shaft, then using a suitable hammer, tap pinion shaft out of pinion housing. **Apply heavy hand pressure onto tool to keep outer drive pinion gear bearing seated. Hold gear end of pinion shaft when removing to prevent it from falling from axle housing. Remove and discard pinion nut and collapsible spacer.**
4. Remove front and rear bearing races from pinion housing using drift positioned in race slots and hammer.
5. Remove rear pinion bearing using an arbor press and adapters. Measure and record thickness of shim which is found under rear bearing.

CATERA

1. Inspect differential drive pinion gear inner and outer bearing preload.
2. Shake differential drive pinion gear inner and outer bearing to inspect for drive pinion gear looseness if there is no preload reading. Defective bearings or a worn pinion flange could cause looseness.
3. Remove differential drive pinion flange.
4. Using a suitable rubber-faced dead blow hammer, drive pinion gear from differential housing.
5. Remove pinion gear bearing spacer from pinion gear.
6. Remove pinion gear inner bearing from drive pinion gear.

CORVETTE

1. Use a punch to unstake drive pinion nut from drive pinion.
2. Using spanner wrench tool No. J-42163 and pinion gear holder tool No. J-42164, or equivalents, remove drive pinion nut from drive pinion.
3. Using a hydraulic press, V-blocks and side gear compressor tool No. J-42162, or equivalent, remove drive pinion bearing, drive pinion housing and bearing spacer from drive pinion. Discard bearing and spacer. **Drive pinion bearings and spacer must be replaced as a set.**
4. Using a hydraulic press, side gear compressor tool No. J-42162 and front pinion bearing remover tool No. J-42166, or equivalents, remove front drive pinion bearing from drive pinion. Discard bearing.
5. Using a hydraulic press and bearing race remover tool No. J-42194, or equivalent, remove front drive pinion bearing inner race from drive pinion housing. Discard bearing race.
6. Using a hydraulic press and bearing race remover tool No. J-42194, or equivalent, remove rear drive pinion bearing outer race from drive pinion housing. Discard bearing race.

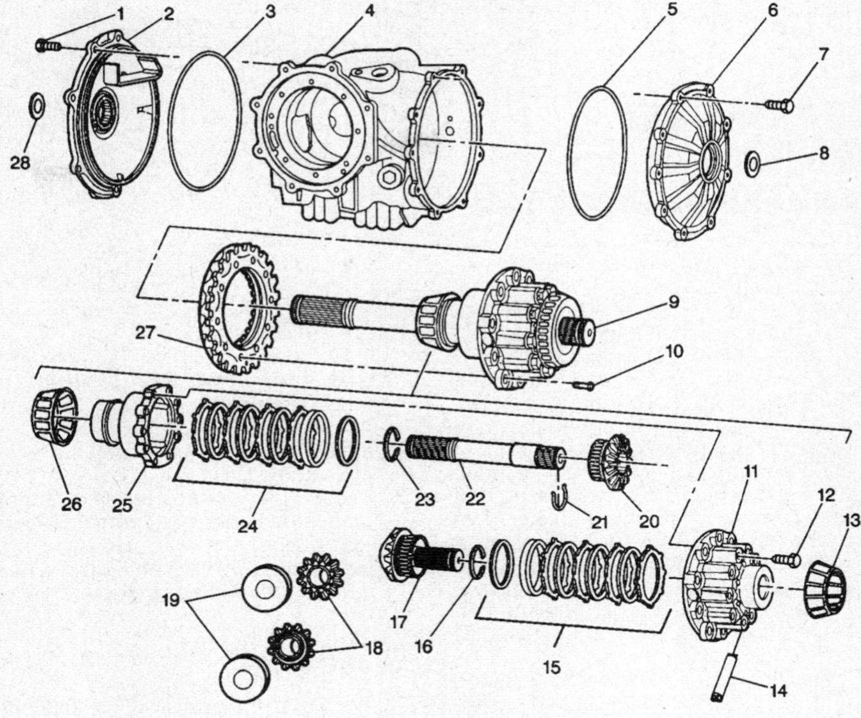

(1) Bolt
(2) Left Side Cover
(3) O-Ring Seal
(4) ifferential Carrier
(5) O-Ring Seal
(6) Right Side Cover
(7) Bolt
(8) Output Shaft Oil Seal
(9) Differential Case Assembly
(10) Bolt
(11) Right Side Differential Case
(12) Bolt
(13) Bearing
(14) Pin
(15) Clutch Pack
(16) C-Clip
(17) Right Output Gear and Shaft
(18) Side Gears
(19) Side Gear Washers
(20) Left Output Gear
(21) C-Clip
(22) Left Output Shaft
(23) C-Clip
(24) Clutch Pack

GC3039700363000X

Fig. 7 Exploded view of differential assembly. Corvette

RING GEAR & DIFFERENTIAL HOUSING

CATERA

1. Clamp differential carrier in a soft jawed vise.
2. Remove ring gear bolts.
3. Using a suitable dead blow hammer and a brass drift, separate gear from differential carrier.
4. Using a suitable drift and hammer, drive out pinion shaft from side of carrier at machined recession in shaft.
5. Remove pinion gear shaft retaining ring from differential carrier.
6. Clamp counterpiece of pinion side gear alignment tool No. J-42178, or equivalent in a vise.
7. Place carrier onto counterpiece with ring gear flange towards the bottom, facing up.
8. Attach ½ inch drive ratchet to drive shaft pinion gear (2), **Fig. 8.**
9. Use ratchet to rotate pinion gears and accompanying washer from installed

position while holding differential carrier (1), **Fig. 8.**
10. Remove shims from differential carrier.

SUBASSEMBLY SERVICE

STANDARD DIFFERENTIAL

1. If side carrier bearings are to be replaced, remove bearings using a suitable bearing puller.
2. Remove differential pinion shaft lock bolt and the pinion shaft.
3. Remove differential pinions and thrust washers, side gears and side gear thrust washers, noting installation position for assembly. Keep thrust washers with respective gears.
4. Remove ring gear bolts, then ring gear, driving ring gear from case using drift and hammer. **Ring gear bolts have lefthand hand threads. Do not pry between ring gear and case since mating surfaces will be damaged.**
5. Inspect components as outlined in "Cleaning & Inspection" and replace as required.
6. Install thrust washers on side gears and mount side gears in case. **Lubricate all components with specified gear lubricant prior to assembly.**
7. Position one differential pinion (less thrust washer) between side gears and rotate gears until pinion is directly opposite case loading opening.
8. Install other pinion with pinion shaft holes aligned, then rotate side gears and ensure pinions align with shaft openings in case.
9. When pinions are properly aligned, rotate pinions toward loading opening just enough to allow thrust washer installation and install washers.
10. Align pinions with shaft opening in case, insert pinion shaft through case, then install new lock bolt. It is not necessary to torque lock bolt at this time.
11. Ensure ring gear and case mating surfaces are clean and free from burrs, mount gear on case, install two new retaining bolts at opposite sides of gear and alternately tighten bolts to draw gear on case.
12. Install remaining ring gear bolts hand tight and ensure gear is squarely seated on case. **Always use new bolts of proper type when installing ring gear. Do not use old bolts again.**
13. Alternately **torque** ring gear bolts to 89 ft. lbs.
14. Press side bearings onto case. If old bearings are used again, ensure they are installed in their original positions.

LIMITED SLIP

Camaro & Firebird

On these models the limited slip differential cannot be serviced separately. If damaged, the differential must be replaced as a unit.

1. Remove case side bearings using tool No. J-22888-20A, or equivalent.
2. Remove all but two opposite ring gear

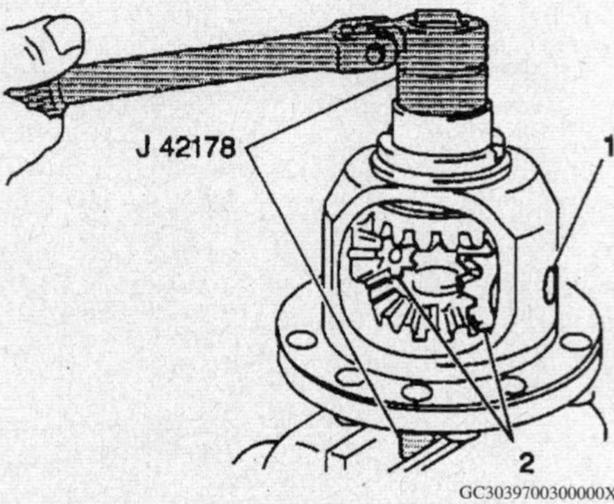

Fig. 8 Pinion & side gear removal. Catera

attaching bolts, then loosen the two remaining bolts.
3. Loosen ring gear by tapping on bolts, then remove ring gear from differential.
4. This limited slip rear axle case is not serviceable. If differential case is not satisfactory, replace complete assembly.

Corvette

1. Remove ring gear to differential case attaching bolts.
2. Using a brass punch and hammer, separate ring gear from differential case.
3. Using a hydraulic press with righthand side differential bearing remover tool No. J-42159 and side gear compressor tool No. J-42162, or equivalents, remove righthand differential case side bearing from case. Discard bearing.
4. Remove differential case bolts, then separate righthand differential case from lefthand differential case.
5. Remove lefthand output shaft from differential case.
6. Remove lefthand clutch pack from differential case, noting the following:
   a. Friction discs and plates develop specific wear patterns. Keep plates and discs in specific order in which they were removed.
   b. Inspect clutch plates and discs. If any plate or disc shows wear or scoring, replace the complete pack.
   c. Tag clutch pack to indicate its installation position.
7. Using a hydraulic press with suitable V-blocks and side gear compressor tool No. J-42162, or equivalent, remove lefthand differential case side bearing.
8. Remove C-clip from lefthand output shaft, then the output shaft from side gear.
9. Using a hydraulic press and side gear compressor tool, remove cross pin from righthand differential.
10. Note position of spider gears for installation reference, then remove them from righthand differential case.
11. Remove righthand output shaft and side gear from differential case.
12. Remove righthand clutch pack from differential case, noting the following:
    a. Friction discs and plates develop specific wear patterns. Keep plates and discs in specific order in which they were removed.
    b. Inspect clutch plates and discs. If any plate or disc shows wear or scoring, replace the complete pack.
    c. Tag clutch pack to indicate its installation position.

CLEANING & INSPECTION

1. Clean components in solvent and blow dry with compressed air, noting the following:
   a. Keep all components in order to ensure proper assembly.
   b. Do not use brush when cleaning bearings.
   c. Do not spin dry bearings since they will be damaged.
   d. Lightly lubricate components after cleaning to retard corrosion.
2. Inspect gears for cracks, chipped teeth, wear and scoring and damaged bearing or mounting surfaces. Replace gears that are damaged or excessively worn. **Ring gear and pinion must be replaced as an assembly.**
3. Inspect differential case for cracks, damage, worn side gear bores and scored bearing surfaces and replace as required.
4. Inspect housing for scored bearing mount surfaces, cracks and distortion and replace as required.
5. Inspect bearing rollers and races for pitting, scoring, overheating and damage.
6. Mate bearing with race and inspect operation.
7. Replace any bearing that is damaged, excessively worn or that fails to operate smoothly.
8. Mount differential case along with side bearings and ring gear in housing and measure runout with side bearings adjusted for zero preload and a dial indicator positioned against machined edge of ring gear.
9. If runout exceeds .003 inch and gear cannot be positioned to eliminate runout, ring gear and/or case should be replaced.

ADJUSTMENTS

DIFFERENTIAL SIDE BEARING PRELOAD

Camaro & Firebird

On these models, side bearing preload should be set before pinion is installed. If pinion is installed, remove ring gear.

1. Ensure bearing bores in housing and bearing caps are clean and free from burrs.
2. Measure production shims or service spacer and shim packs removed during disassembly to determine approximate thickness of shims required for installation. **Do not use cast iron production shims more than once as they may break during installation.**

If service spacers and shims were previously installed, they can be used again.

3. In addition to .170 inch service spacers for each side, refer to chart, **Fig. 9,** and select service shim thickness required based on measurements made in previous step.
4. Place outer races over side bearings, mount differential assembly in housing and insert service spacer between each bearing race and housing with chamfered edge against housing.
5. Install lefthand bearing cap to retain case assembly and tighten bolts hand tight so that case can be moved while inspecting adjustments. **A bearing cap bolt can be installed in lower righthand bearing cap hole to prevent case from dropping while performing shim adjustments.**
6. Select one or two shims totaling thickness calculated in step 3 and insert them between righthand bearing cap and service spacer.
7. Insert progressively larger feeler gauges between shim and service spacer until noticeable increase in drag can be felt, pushing gauge down until it contacts housing bore to obtain proper reading. **Rotate case while inserting gauges to ensure even readings.**
8. The gauge used just before additional drag is felt is proper thickness to obtain "zero preload." By starting with a thin gauge a sense of feel can be obtained for the original light drag caused by the weight of the case, allowing the drag caused by the beginning of preload to be recognized. **It will be necessary to work case in and out and to the left in order to insert feeler gauges.**
9. When the proper gauge thickness has been determined to obtain zero preload, remove bearing cap, case assembly service spacers and shim pack.
10. Select two service shims of approximate equal thickness whose total thickness is equal to the thickness of the shims installed in step 6 plus the thickness of the feeler gauge used to obtain zero preload.
11. Shims selected during this procedure allow differential assembly to be installed at zero preload, the equivalent of a "slip-fit" in case, during backlash adjustment. Final preload is not added until backlash has been adjusted.

Catera

1. Install side bearing preload clamp tool No. J-42143, or equivalent onto rear axle housing cover surfaces, **Fig. 6.** Tighten cover bolts until fully seated.
2. Install side bearing preload clamp plate tool No. J-42149, or equivalent between side bearing race and side bearing clamp tool.
3. Install dial indicator tool No. J-8001, or equivalent onto side bearing clamp tool No. J-42143, or equivalent with indicator button resting on ring gear surface.
4. Install differential carrier with bearing races into rear axle housing.

4.32 mm (0.170") SERVICE DIFFERENTIAL BEARING SPACER	
TOTAL THICKNESS OF BOTH PRODUCTION DIFFERENTIAL BEARING SHIMS REMOVED	TOTAL THICKNESS OF SERVICE DIFFERENTIAL BEARING SHIMS TO BE USED AS A STARTING POINT
10.57 mm (0.416")	1.52 mm (0.060")
10.92 mm (0.430")	1.78 mm (0.070")
11.18 mm (0.440")	2.03 mm (0.080")
11.43 mm (0.450")	2.29 mm (0.090")
11.68 mm (0.460")	2.54 mm (0.100")
11.94 mm (0.470")	2.79 mm (0.110")
12.19 mm (0.480")	3.05 mm (0.120")
12.45 mm (0.490")	3.30 mm (0.130")
12.70 mm (0.500")	3.56 mm (0.140")
12.95 mm (0.510")	3.81 mm (0.150")
13.21 mm (0.520")	4.06 mm (0.160")
13.46 mm (0.530")	4.32 mm (0.170")
13.97 mm (0.550")	4.83 mm (0.190")

GC3039100217000A

Fig. 9 Service shim thickness chart

5. Using suitable heavy duty snap ring pliers, install lefthand adjuster ring.
6. Install snap rings of various thickness until there is no movement of the differential carrier indicated by the dial indicator.
7. Add an additional .005 inch shim to each side in adjuster ring thickness. Total preload should be .010 inch.
8. If it is necessary to vary adjuster ring thickness once side bearing preload has been established, always maintain the same total thickness between the two snap rings to maintain preload. For example, if it was required that .002 inch be removed from lefthand side adjuster ring thickness to properly establish backlash, .002 inch must be added to righthand side adjuster ring thickness in order to maintain side bearing preload.
9. Using differential side bearing alignment kit tool No. J-42178, or equivalent and a suitable inch pound torque wrench, measure differential carrier rotating torque. With bearing lubricated, rotating torque should be 4.5–6.5 inch lbs.

Corvette

1. Place depth gauge tool No. J-42168-7, or equivalent onto flat of gauge block tool No. J-42168-2, or equivalent, **Fig. 10.**
2. Place depth gauge tool plunger tip against bottom of differential carrier bearing bore. Tighten setscrew to lock plunger into place.
3. Install gauge block tool No. J-42168-6, or equivalent onto gauge plate tool No. J-42168-5, or equivalent with proper gear step closest to the outer edge.
4. Install gauge plate tool into a suitable vise, **Fig. 11.**
5. Mount ring gear and case assembly onto gauge plate tool. Ensure lefthand side bearing seats in the lefthand side bearing race.
6. Place depth gauge tool No. J-42168-7, or equivalent onto back face of ring gear.
7. Measure distance between J-42168-7 and J-42168-6, **Fig. 11.**
8. Determine proper shim thickness, then tag lefthand side bearing shim pack for assembly as follows:
   a. The ring gear value stamping is in millimeters.
   b. If ring gear has a zero (0) stamping, the measured value is the shim thickness.
   c. If ring gear has a plus (+) or minus (–) value stamped on it, add or subtract that value from feeler gauge reading to calculate shim thickness.
9. Remove J-42168-2 and J-42168-12 from differential housing.
10. Using a suitable hydraulic press and race installer tool No. J-42172, or equivalent, install righthand side cover bearing race, **Fig. 12.**
11. Using a suitable hydraulic press and race installer tool, install lefthand side bearing race and shim pack into differential housing.
12. Place differential carrier onto ring gear holder tool No. J-42173, or equivalent.
13. Using differential case lifting tool No. J-42155, or equivalent, install ring gear and case into differential carrier.
14. Install righthand side differential carrier cover and bolts. **Torque** to 18 ft. lbs.
15. Position a dial indicator onto end of righthand axle shaft, **Fig. 13.**
16. Grip output shaft and move up and down to measure total travel, **Fig. 14.**
17. Add .004 inch to measurement from previous step. This is righthand side outer bearing race shim pack size.
18. Remove righthand side differential carrier cover and bolts.
19. Using hydraulic press and bearing race remover tool No. J-42194, or equivalent, remove righthand side outer bearing race.
20. Install righthand side outer bearing race and shim pack.
21. Using hydraulic press and race installer tool No. J-42172, or equivalent, install bearing race.
22. Using hydraulic press and bearing installer tool No. J-42157, or equivalent, install lefthand side output shaft bearing into cover.
23. Using seal installer tool No. J-36797, or equivalent, install lefthand side axle seal into cover.
24. Using differential case lifting tool No. J-42155, or equivalent, remove ring gear and case from differential housing.

DRIVE PINION DEPTH

Camaro & Firebird

1. Install pinion bearing races in housing using a suitable driver.
2. Lubricate pinion bearings and install bearings in races.
3. Mount depth gauging tools in housing as outlined in **Fig. 15,** noting the following:
   a. Assemble gauge plate onto preload stud.
   b. Hold pinion bearings in position, insert stud through rear bearing and pilot and front bearing and pilot, then install retaining nut and tighten nut until snug.
   c. Rotate tool to ensure bearings are properly seated.

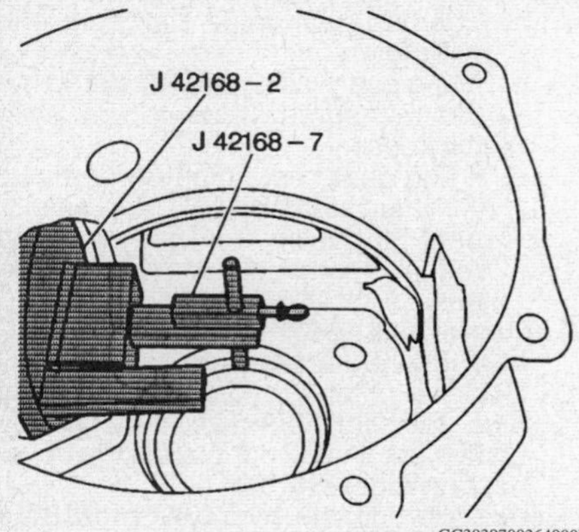

Fig. 10 Depth gauge & block setup. Corvette

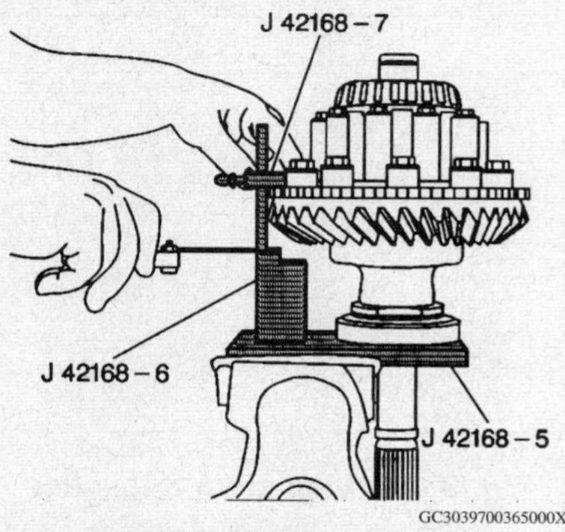

Fig. 11 Gauge plate tool installation in vise. Corvette

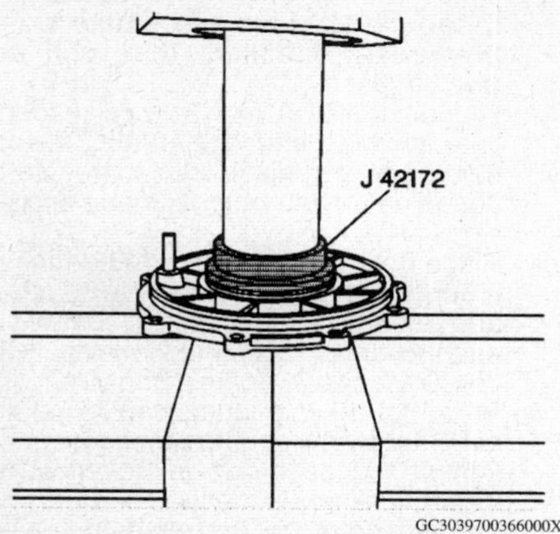

Fig. 12 Righthand side cover bearing race installation. Corvette

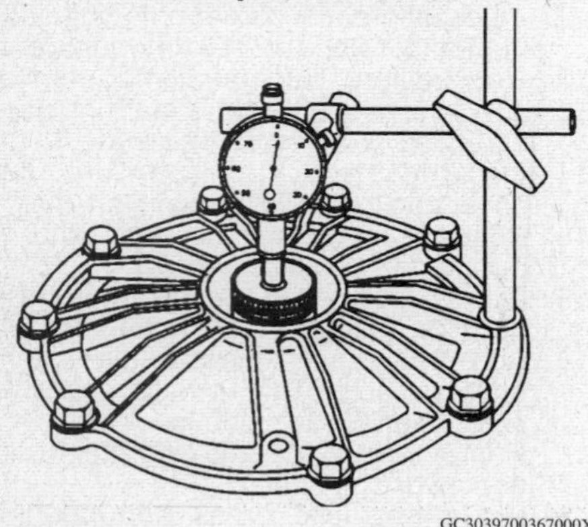

Fig. 13 Dial indicator installation onto righthand axle shaft. Corvette

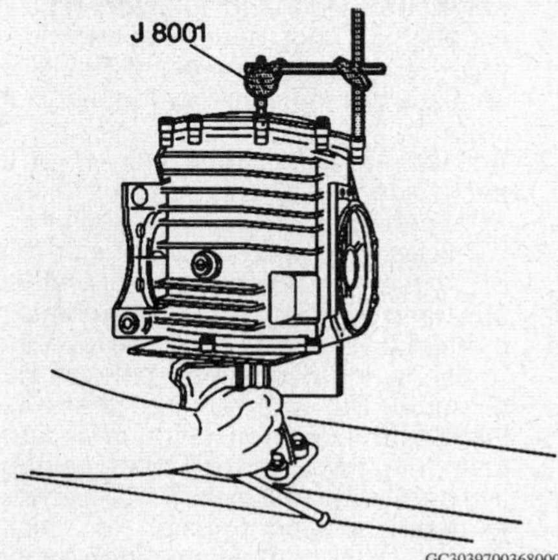

Fig. 14 Output shaft total travel measurement. Corvette

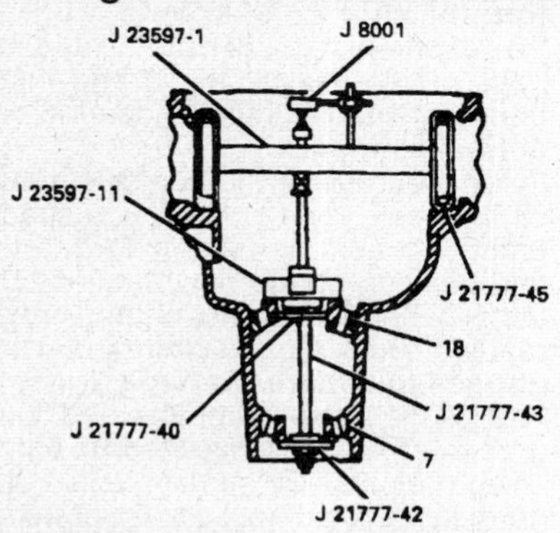

Fig. 15 Pinion gauge tool installation. Camaro & Firebird

d. Hold preload stud and tighten nut until 20 inch lbs. of torque is required to rotate stud. **To prevent damage to bearing, tighten nut in small increments, measuring rotating torque after each adjustment.**
e. Mount side bearing discs on arbor, using step for disc that corresponds to base of housing.
f. Mount arbor and plunger assembly in housing, ensuring side bearing discs are properly seated.
g. Install bearing caps, then **torque** cap bolts to 55 ft. lbs. to prevent bearing discs from moving, **Fig. 16.**

4. Mount dial indicator on arbor stud with indicator contact button bearing against top of arbor plunger.
5. Preload indicator ½ inch against plunger and secure to arbor mounting stud in this position.
6. Place arbor plunger on gauge plate, rotating plate as required so that plunger rests directly on button corresponding to ring gear size.
7. Slowly rock plunger rod back and forth across button while observing dial indicator.
8. At point on button where indicator registers greatest deflection, zero dial indicator. **Perform above two steps several times to ensure proper setting.**
9. Once verified zero reading is obtained, swing plunger aside until it is clear of gauge plate button and record dial indicator reading. **Indicator will now read required pinion depth shim thickness for a "nominal" pinion.**
10. Record dial indicator's reading at pointer position. This will indicate proper drive pinion gear shim to install. As an example, if pointer moved .067 inch counterclockwise to a reading of .033 inch, this translates to a .033 inch shim thickness.
11. Remove gauging tools and pinion bearings from housing, noting installation position of bearings.

Catera

1. When replacing differential ring and pinion set, it is important to note that the replacement drive pinion gear will have markings on the gear face, **Fig. 17.**
2. Markings indicate adjustments that need to be made to shim thickness as a result of gear production tolerances.
3. Check value, indicated in hundredths of a millimeter (+22 = .22 mm), shows how deep the drive pinion should be installed relative to the drive pinion zero line. Compare this value with the value stamped on the original pinion gear to decide which size shim should be installed.
4. Pairing value (2628) is stamped on pinion gear and ring gear. This marking identifies a matched gear set.
5. Underline value does not come into play during service.

Corvette

1. Install gauge cylinder tool No. J-42168-1 and gauge block tool No. J-42168-2, or equivalents into differential housing in the lefthand side bearing race location, **Fig. 18.**
2. Using a feeler gauge, measure distance between tip of gauge cylinder tool No. J-42168-1 and gauge block tool No. J-42168-2, or equivalents. **If the pinion gear has a plus (+) or minus (–) number (metric value) stamped on the end, the shim thickness must be adjusted by that amount.**
3. Subtract measured value from .10826 inch (2.75 mm). The value of .10826 inch is the shim thickness required if the pinion has a zero stamped on the end.
4. Refer to pinion shim selection chart, **Fig. 19,** for available shim sizes.
5. Remove gauge cylinder and gauge block tools from carrier.

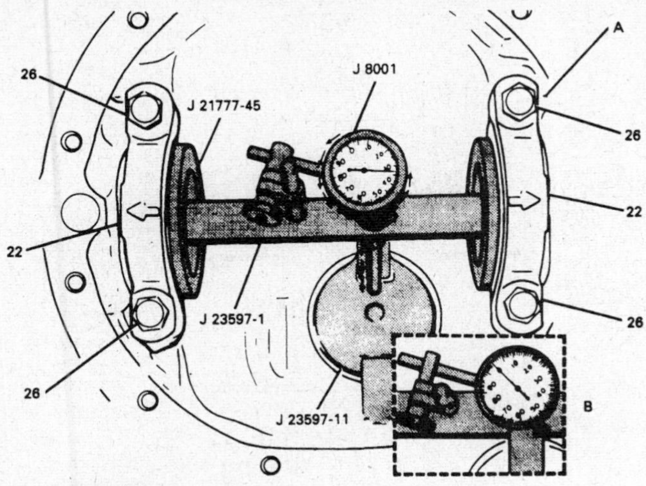

A OFF GAGE BLOCK
B ON GAGE BLOCK
22 CAP, DIFFERENTIAL CARRIER BEARING
26 BOLT/SCREW, DIFFERENTIAL CARRIER BEARING CAP

GC3039700362000X

Fig. 16 Pinion depth inspection. Camaro & Firebird

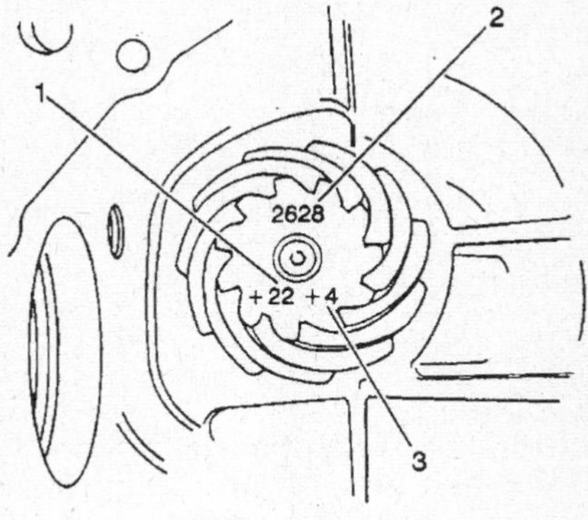

1. CHECK VALUE
2. PAIRING VALUE
3. UNDERLINE VALUE

GC3039700301000X

Fig. 17 Drive pinion gear face adjustment markings. Catera

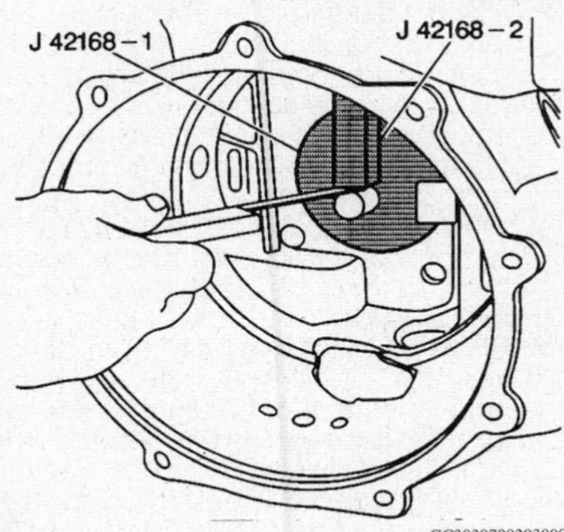

GC3039700293000A

Fig. 18 Pinion depth measurement. Corvette

ASSEMBLE

DIFFERENTIAL

Camaro & Firebird

1. Ensure pinion depth and bearing preload are properly adjusted, as described under "Adjustments."
2. Install differential case assembly and selected side bearing shims as described under "Adjustments."
3. Install bearing caps in proper position, then **torque** cap bolts to 55 ft. lbs.
4. Rotate assembly to ensure bearings are properly seated.
5. Mount dial indicator on housing with plunger bearing against tooth on ring gear, **Fig. 20.** Use small contact button on indicator plunger so that contact can be made at heel end of tooth and position dial indicator with plunger inline with gear rotation and perpendicular to gear tooth.
6. Hold pinion stationary and rock ring gear back and forth while reading backlash on indicator.
7. Measure backlash at three evenly spaced positions around ring gear and record readings. **If backlash varies by more than .002 inch at any position, inspect ring gear installation and runout and correct as required.**
8. If backlash is not within specifications, remove differential case assembly and bearing shims keeping shims in order.
9. Backlash is adjusted by increasing thickness of one shim while decreasing thickness of opposite side shim by the same amount in order to maintain proper side bearing preload. Select shims to adjust backlash as follows:
   a. If backlash is excessive, increase thickness of shim on gear tooth side and decrease thickness of shim on opposite side by the same amount.
   b. If backlash is less than specified, decrease thickness of shim on gear tooth side while increasing thickness of opposite shim by the same amount. **Each .002 inch change in shim thickness alters backlash by .001 inch.**
10. Install differential assembly, shims and bearing caps. **Torque** bearing cap bolts to 55 ft. lbs., then inspect backlash again and adjust as required.
11. If side bearing preload was set to zero during side bearing preload adjustment, proceed as follows:
    a. Remove both bearing caps and shim packs, keeping shim packs in respective lefthand or righthand positions.
    b. Select lefthand side differential preload shim from specifications chart and insert shim between lefthand bearing race and spacer, then install lefthand bearing cap with bolts hand tight.
    c. Select righthand side differential preload shim from specifications chart and insert shim between righthand bearing race and spacer using a soft faced hammer.
    d. Install righthand bearing cap, then **torque** all cap bolts to 55 ft. lbs.
12. Ensure ring gear teeth are clean and free from oil, then coat both drive and coast side of each tooth with marking compound.
13. Apply braking force to "load" ring gear, then rotate driveshaft yoke with wrench so that ring gear rotates one full revolution in each direction. **Test made without "loading" gears will not yield satisfactory pattern. Excessive gear rotation is not recommended.**
14. Compare gear tooth pattern with **Fig. 21,** and correct assembly adjustments as required.
15. When proper gear tooth contact pattern has been obtained, clean marking compound from gears.
16. Install axles and driveshaft as outlined in "Camaro & Firebird" chapter.
17. Install rear cover using RTV or new gasket and **torque** cover bolts to 22 ft. lbs.
18. Install fluid drain plug and **torque** to 26 ft. lbs., then fill rear axle with appropriate lubricant.
19. **On models equipped with limited slip differential,** add limited slip additive No. 1052358, or equivalent to rear axle lubricant.

mm	in
0.200	0.0078
0.250	0.0098
0.300	0.0118
0.500	0.0196
1.000	0.0393

GC3039700294000X

Fig. 19 Pinion adjustment shims. Corvette

Catera

1. Place differential carrier (1) on differential side and pinion alignment tool No. J-42178, or equivalent, **Fig. 22.**
2. Install counterpiece of alignment tool into opposing differential carrier bore.
3. Install new pinion gear retaining ring onto differential carrier.
4. Coat pinion gears and shims with rear axle lubricant.
5. Install thicker shim (that with notches

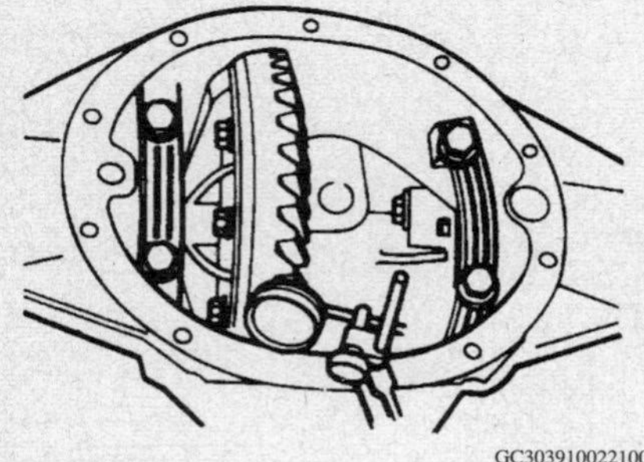

GC3039100221000X

Fig. 20 Ring gear & pinion backlash inspection. Camaro & Firebird

around outer edge) toward carrier.
6. Install thinner (conical) washer toward differential side gear.
7. Place shims on differential side gears.
8. Place differential side gears with previously installed shims into carrier and onto both pieces of alignment tool No. J-42178, or equivalent.
9. Coat pinion gears and conical washers with rear axle lubricant.
10. Engage pinion gears and conical washers with side gears. Align gears and washers so that they are exactly opposite each other in carrier window.
11. Move pinion gear conical washers forward in intended rotational direction to start or lead pinion gears into mounting position.
12. Use a ratchet to rotate alignment tool to draw pinion gears into position. **Ensure conical gears also move into position.** It may be necessary to use a small drift and hammer to assist washers into position.
13. Using a suitable dead blow hammer, drive rear axle gear shaft into carrier bore.
14. Attach a torque wrench to alignment tool No. J-42178, or equivalent and measure rotating torque, which should be 11–22 ft. lbs.
15. Heat ring gear to 212°F. **Do not overheat.**
16. Aligning bolt holes, install ring gear onto carrier.
17. Install new ring gear bolts, then using sequence outlined in **Fig. 23, torque** bolts to 85 ft. lbs.
18. Lubricate carrier side bearings and carrier bearing surface.
19. Press side bearing onto carrier using a suitable press.
20. Install inner and outer pinion bearing outer races into housing.
21. Install drive pinion gear inner bearing onto drive pinion gear.
22. Install drive pinion seal into differential.
23. Install drive pinion, then carrier into rear axle housing.
24. Using drive axle seal driver tool No. J-26234, or equivalent, drive axle seals into bearing cups.
25. Install rear axle cover, then **torque** the bolts to 44 ft. lbs.

Corvette

1. Install righthand clutch pack into differential case. Install steel plates and friction discs alternately, thicker friction washer, concave washer, then steel washer.
2. Install righthand output shaft and spider gears into differential case.
3. Using a hydraulic press and side gear compressor tool No. J-42162, or equivalent, install cross pin into differential case.
4. Install lefthand output shaft into side gear, then C-clip onto lefthand output shaft.
5. Using bearing installer tool No. J-42160, or equivalent, install lefthand differential case side bearing.
6. Install lefthand clutch pack into differential case. Install steel plates and friction discs alternately, thicker friction washer, concave washer, then steel washer.
7. Install lefthand output shaft and side gear into differential case.
8. Install lefthand differential case to righthand differential case.
9. Install differential case bolts, then **torque** to 41 ft. lbs.
10. Install ring gear onto differential case.
11. Using ring gear holder tool No. J-42173 or, equivalent, to support differential case, install ring gear bolts. **Torque** bolts to 144 ft. lbs.

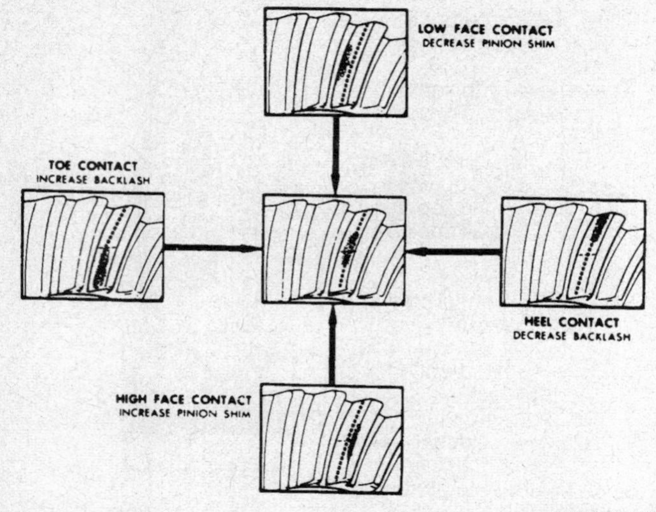

GC3039100222000X

Fig. 21 Gear tooth contact pattern inspection. Camaro & Firebird

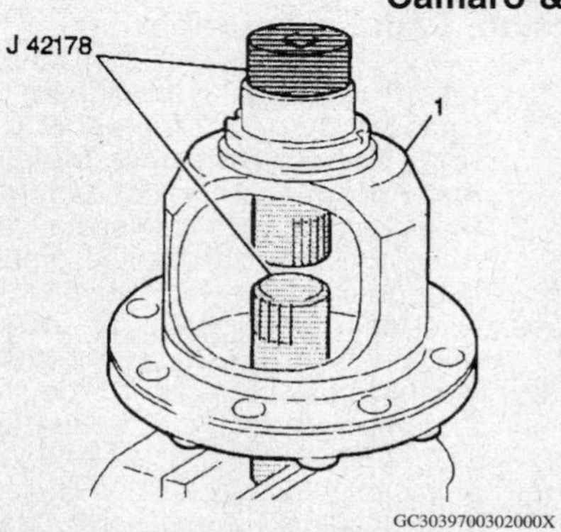

GC3039700302000X

Fig. 22 Differential carrier alignment. Catera

12. Using bearing installer tool No. J-42160, or equivalent, install righthand differential case side bearing.
13. Install gauge block tool No. J-42168-2 and plug tool No. J-42168-12, or equivalents into drive pinion location of differential carrier.
14. Place depth gauge tool No. J-42168-7, or equivalent, onto flat end of gauge block tool No. J-42168-2, or equivalent, **Fig. 10.**
15. Place tip of plunger on depth gauge tool No. J-42168-7, or equivalent against bottom of bearing bore in differential carrier. Tighten set screw to lock plunger in place.
16. Install gauge block tool No. J-42168-6, or equivalent onto gauge plate tool No. J-42168-5, or equivalent, with proper gear step closest to outer edge.
17. Place ring gear and case assembly onto gauge plate tool No. J-42168-5, or equivalent, **Fig. 11.**
18. Remove depth gauge tool No. J-42168-7, or equivalent. If ring gear has a plus (+) or minus (–) number (metric value) stamped on the side the shim thickness must be adjusted by that amount.
19. Using a feeler gauge, measure distance between plunger tip of depth gauge tool No. J-42168-7 and gauge block tool No. J-42168-6, or equivalents, **Fig. 11.** This distance is the shim thickness required if ring gear has a zero stamped on the side.
20. Remove gauge block tool No. J-42168-2 and plug tool No. J-42168-12.
21. Install lefthand side shim pack into housing.
22. Using bearing race installer tool No. J-42172, or equivalent, install lefthand side outer bearing race into carrier.
23. Using a hydraulic press and output shaft bearing installer tool No. J-42157, or equivalent, install output shaft bearing into lefthand differential carrier cover.
24. Using seal installer tool No. J-36797,

or equivalent, install new output shaft oil seal into lefthand differential carrier cover.

25. Install new O-ring seal into lefthand cover, then the cover bolts. **Torque** to 18 ft. lbs.
26. Place differential carrier on rear gear holder tool No. J-42173, or equivalent.
27. Using differential case lifting tool No. J-42155, or equivalent, install ring gear and case assembly into differential carrier.
28. Install righthand side differential carrier cover and cover bolts. **Torque** bolts to 18 ft. lbs.
29. Position measuring tool No. J-8001, or equivalent onto end of righthand axle shaft, **Fig. 13.**
30. Move output shaft up and down and measure total travel. To obtain proper size shim, add .004 inch to total travel measurement.
31. Using a hydraulic press and bearing race remover tool No. J-42194, or equivalent, remove righthand side outer bearing race.
32. Install righthand side shim pack into differential carrier cover.
33. Using a hydraulic press and bearing race installer tool No. J-42172, or equivalent, install righthand side outer bearing race.
34. Using a hydraulic press and bearing installer tool No. J-42157, or equivalent, install righthand side output shaft bearing.
35. Using seal installer tool No. J-36797, or equivalent, install righthand side output shaft oil seal into carrier cover.
36. Using differential case lifting tool No. J-42155, or equivalent, remove ring gear and case assembly from differential carrier.
37. Install lefthand side carrier cover with new O-ring, then the cover bolts. **Torque** bolts to 18 ft. lbs.
38. Install drive pinion shim pack onto pinion cartridge.
39. Lubricate new pinion cartridge O-ring seal with clean engine oil, then install O-ring into groove on pinion cartridge.
40. Using heat gun tool No. J-25070, or equivalent, heat differential carrier around drive pinion cartridge opening, then install drive pinion cartridge into differential carrier.
41. Install drive pinion cartridge bolts. **Torque** bolts to 41 ft. lbs.
42. Using a torque wrench and pinion gear holder tool No. J-42164, or equivalent, measure pinion rotating torque, which should not exceed 22 inch lbs.
43. Install rear differential cover, magnet, O-ring and rear cover bolts. **Torque** bolts to 89 inch lbs.
44. Using differential case lifting tool No. J-42155, or equivalent, install differential case assembly into carrier.
45. Install C-clip onto righthand output shaft.
46. Install righthand side transmission stud mount and bolts. **Torque** bolts to 89 inch lbs.
47. Install righthand side transmission mounting stud. **Torque** stud to 31 ft. lbs.

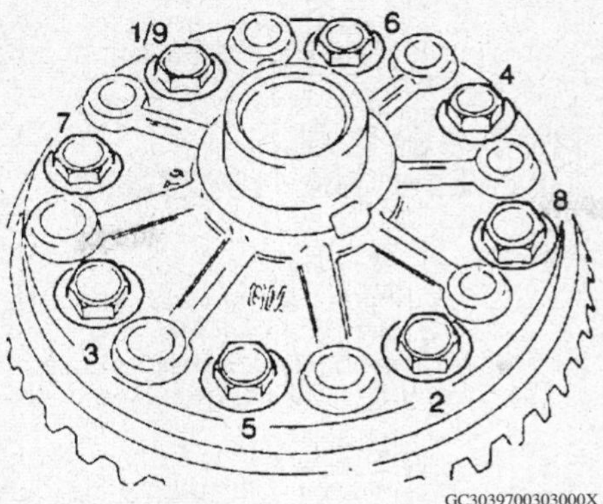

Fig. 23 Ring gear bolt tightening sequence. Catera

48. Install righthand side differential carrier cover, O-ring and cover bolts. **Torque** bolts to 18 ft. lbs.
49. Install vehicle speed sensor and bolt. **Torque** bolt to 89 inch lbs.
50. Install axle lubricant drain plug. **Torque** plug to 26 ft. lbs.
51. Fill differential with synthetic axle lubricant part No. 12378261 and limited slip additive part No. 1052358, or equivalent.
52. Install axle lubricant fill tag, washer and plug. **Torque** plug to 26 ft. lbs.

DRIVE PINION

Camaro & Firebird

1. Install selected shim onto pinion shaft, lubricate rear pinion bearing with specified axle lubricant, then press rear bearing onto pinion using suitable spacers.
2. Install new collapsible spacer onto pinion shaft, then insert pinion assembly into housing.
3. Lubricate front pinion bearing, install bearing into housing and tap bearing over pinion shaft with a drift while assistant holds pinion in place. **Old pinion nut and a large washer can be used to seat front bearing on pinion, but care must be taken not to collapse spacer if this method is used.**
4. Install new pinion seal in housing, coat seal lips with grease, then mount driveshaft yoke on pinion shaft, lightly tapping yoke until several pinion shaft threads protrude from yoke.
5. Coat rear of pinion washer with suitable sealer, then install washer and new pinion nut.
6. Hold driveshaft yoke with suitable tool, then alternately tighten pinion nut and rotate pinion until endplay is reduced to zero.
7. When endplay is reduced to zero, measure pinion bearing preload using a torque wrench.
8. Nut should be further tightened only slightly and preload should be inspected after each tightening. Exceeding preload specifications will compress the collapsible spacer too far and require installation of a new spacer. Set preload at 15–30 inch lbs. on new inner and outer bearing assemblies or 10–15 inch lbs. on used assemblies. Rotate drive pinion several times to ensure inner and outer baring assemblies have been seated, then measure preload again. If preload has been reduced by rotating drive pinion gear, reset preload to specifications.

Catera

1. Lubricate differential drive pinion gear outer bearing with suitable axle lubricant.
2. Using drive handle tool No. J-8092 and outer race installer tool No. J-42147, or equivalents, install drive pinion gear outer bearing outer race into housing.
3. Install drive pinion gear outer bearing, then the pinion seal.
4. Install pinion shim into housing.
5. Using driver handle tool No. J-8092 and pinion bearing race installer tool No. J-8608, or equivalents, install inner bearing race into housing.
6. Lubricate differential drive pinion gear inner bearing and drive pinion gear shaft with rear axle lubricant.
7. Using a suitable press, install differential drive pinion gear inner bearing onto drive pinion gear.
8. Install pinion seal, then drive pinion gear into housing.
9. Install drive pinion gear inner bearing onto drive pinion gear.
10. Install pinion gear bearing spacer onto drive pinion gear.
11. Install drive pinion gear into rear axle housing and set pinion depth.
12. Install drive pinion seal, noting the following:
    a. Preload specification is being approached when no further endplay is detected and when holder will no longer pivot freely as drive pinion gear is rotated.
    b. **Do not attempt further tightening until preload is inspected.**
    c. Tighten nut while inspecting preload after each tightening.
    d. Exceeding preload specifications will compress the collapsible spacer too far and a new spacer will be required.
13. Hold pinion flange, then tighten nut until endplay begins to disappear while intermittently rotating drive pinion gear to seat inner and outer bearings.
14. **On new bearings,** set preload to 9–15 inch lbs.
15. **On used bearings,** set preload to 8–11 inch lbs.
16. Rotate drive pinion gear several times to ensure inner and outer bearings have been seated.
17. Measure preload again and adjust as required.

Corvette

Drive pinion bearings and spacer must be replaced as a set.

1. Using a hydraulic press and bearing race installer tool No. J-42172, or equivalent, install front drive pinion bearing inner race into drive pinion housing.
2. Using a hydraulic press and bearing

race installer tool No. J-42170, or equivalent, install rear drive pinion bearing outer race into drive pinion housing.

3. Using a hydraulic press, pinion bearing installer tool No. J-42160 and pinion gear holder tool No. J-42164, or equivalents, install front pinion bearing onto drive pinion.
4. Install drive pinion and bearing into drive pinion housing.
5. Install drive pinion bearing spacer onto drive pinion.
6. Using a hydraulic press, pinion bearing installer tool No. J-42160 and pinion gear holder tool No. J-42164, or equivalents, install rear drive pinion bearing onto drive pinion.
7. Using a ¾ inch torque wrench, spanner wrench tool No. J-42163 and pinion gear holder tool No. J-42164, or equivalents, install drive pinion nut and **torque** to 392 ft. lbs.
8. Using a punch, stake areas of drive pinion nut into two notches in end of drive pinion.

RING GEAR & DIFFERENTIAL HOUSING

Catera

1. Clamp pinion alignment tool No. J-42178, or equivalent, into vise.
2. Place differential carrier onto special tool with ring gear flange facing downward.
3. Place counterpiece of pinion alignment tool into opposing differential carrier bore.
4. Install new differential pinion gear retaining ring into carrier.
5. Install shims on side gears, placing thicker shim toward carrier and thinner washer toward side gear.
6. Place side gears with shims into carrier and onto pinion alignment tool.
7. Engage pinion gears and washers, ensuring that they are opposite each other.
8. Move pinion gear washers forward in intended rotational direction, leading pinion gears into position.
9. Using ratchet, rotate pinion alignment tool to draw pinion gears into position.
10. Using deadblow hammer, drive pinion gear shaft into carrier bore and through pinion gears and washers.
11. Attach torque wrench to pinion alignment tool and inspect rotational torque. Acceptable rotational torque reading is between 11 and 22 ft. lbs.
12. Heat ring gear to 212° F, then install onto differential carrier. Ensure all bolt holes are aligned.
13. Torque ring gear bolts in sequence outlined, **Fig. 23,** to 85 ft. lbs.

DRIVE AXLE SPECIFICATIONS

CAMARO & FIREBIRD

Year	Axle Model	Ring Gear Diameter, Inch	Ring Gear Backlash, Inch	Pinion Bearing Preload, Inch Lbs.		Total Assembly Preload, Inch Lbs.		Side Bearing Preload, Inch Lbs.		Differential Bearings, Inch Lbs.	
				New	Used	New	Used	New	Used	Used	New
1998–2002	GM	7.62	.005–.009	15–30	10–15	32–55	16–28	—	—	—	—

CATERA

Year	Model	Ring Gear Back Lash, Inch	Pinion Bearing Preload, Inch Lbs.		Differential Assembly Preload, Inch Lbs.①
			New Bearings	Used Bearings	
1998–2001	All	.004–.008	9–15	8–11	4.5–6.5

① — Without pinion gear in housing.

CORVETTE

Year	Axle Model	Carrier Type	Ring Gear Backlash		Pinion Bearing Preload		Side Gear Preload	
			Method	Adjustment, Inch	Method	New Bearings Inch Lbs.	Method	Adjustment, Inch
1998–2002	Getrag	Integral	Shims	①	Shims	①	Shims	①

① — Adjustment is determined by markings on ring gear & pinion set.

VALVES

All Measurements Given In Inches Unless Otherwise Specified

Engine/VIN	Year	Stem Diameter		Valve Stem Installed Height	Valve Lash		Face Angle	Margin①
		Intake	Exhaust		Intake	Exhaust		
1.0L	1998–2000	.2148–.2157	.2142–.2148	—	⑥	⑥	45°	②
1.3L	1998–2000	.2152–.2157	.2142–.2148	—	⑥	⑥	45°	—
1.6L	1998	.2350–.2356	.2348–.2354	—	.006–.010③	.010–.014③	45°	.0200
1.8L	1998–2000	.2154–.2159	.2152–.2157	—	.006–.010③	.010–.014③	45°	—
	2001–02	.2150–.2155	.2143–.2153	—	.006–.010	.010–.014	—	—
2.2L/4	1998–99	—	—	—	.001–.003	.001–.003	45°	.0310
	2000–02	—	—	—	—	—	45	⑤
2.2L/F	2002	.2344–.2355	.2337–.2343	—	⑥	⑥	45°	—
2.4L	1998–99	.2331–.2339	.2326–.2334	.9787–1.0024	—	—	④	.0098
	2000–02	.2326–.2334	.2326–.2334	.9787–1.0024	—	—	45°	.0098
3.0L	1998–2001	.2344–.2350	.2341–.2346	—	—	—	45°	—
3.1L	1998–2002	—	—	1.7010	⑩	⑩	45°	⑪
3.4L	1999–2002	—	—	—	⑥	⑥	45°	⑪
3.5L	1999–2002	.2331–.2339	.2331–.2339	—	⑥	⑥	45°	⑨
3.8L	1998–2002	—	—	1.9305–1.9750	⑥	⑥	45°	.0250
4.0L	1998–99	.2331–.2339	.2331–.2339	⑦	⑥	⑥	45°	⑧
	2001–02	.2331–.2339	.2331–.2339	—	⑥	⑥	45°	.0421
4.6L	1998–2000	.2331–.2339	.2331–.2339	⑦	—	—	45°	⑧
	2001–02	.2331–.2339	.2331–.2339	—	—	—	45°	.0394
5.7L	1998–2002	.3130–.3140	.3130–.3140	—	⑥	⑥	45°	.050

① — Minimum.
② — Intake, .02 inch; exhaust, .027 inch.
③ — Cold.
④ — Intake valve, 46°; exhaust valve, 45.5°.
⑤ — Intake, .048–.058 inch; exhaust, .073–.083 inch.
⑥ — Hydraulic lifters, zero lash.
⑦ — Intake, 1.389–1.453 inches; Max. 1.463 inches. Exhaust, 1.332–1.392 inches; Max. 1.402 inches. Measured from top of stem to head.
⑧ — Intake, .005 inch; exhaust, .030 inch.
⑨ — Intake, .0354 inch; exhaust, .0432 inch.
⑩ — Zero lash plus 1 1/2 turns.
⑪ — Intake, .083 inch; Exhaust, .106 inch.

CAMSHAFT

All Measurements Given In Inches Unless Otherwise Specified

Engine/VIN	Year	Camshaft Journal Diameter	Maximum Journal Runout	Camshaft Bearing Clearance	Camshaft Endplay	Rocker Arm Oil Clearance	Lifter Bore Diameter	Lifter Diameter	Lifter To Bore Clearance
1.0L	1998–2000	①	.0039	.0008–.0024	—	—	1.2205–1.2214	1.2188–1.2194	.0010–.0025
1.3L	1998–2000	③	.0039	.0020–.0059⑤	—	.0005–.0035⑥	—	—	—
1.6L	1998	②	.0012	.0014–.0028	.0043	—	1.2205–1.2215	1.2191–1.2195	.0009–.0028
1.8L	1998–99	.9035–.9041	.0016	—	—	—	1.2205–1.2215	1.2191–1.2195	.0009–.0028
	2000	.9035–.9041	.0120	—	—	—	—	1.2191–1.2195	.0009–.0023
	2001–02	⑧	.0012	⑦	.0012	—	—	—	—
2.2L/4	1998–2002	1.8680–1.8690	.0010	.0005–.0035	—	—	—	—	—
2.2L/F	2002	1.0604–1.0614	—	.0016–.0034	.0016–.0057	—	—	—	—
2.4L	1998–2002	④	—	.0019–.0043	.0009–.0088	—	1.3381–1.3393	1.3369–1.3375	.0006–.0023
3.0L	1998–2001	1.0990–1.1010	—	.0015–.0020	.0016–.0057	—	—	—	—

Continued

CAMSHAFT—Continued

All Measurements Given In Inches Unless Otherwise Specified

Engine/VIN	Year	Camshaft Journal Diameter	Maximum Journal Runout	Camshaft Bearing Clearance	Camshaft Endplay	Rocker Arm Oil Clearance	Lifter Bore Diameter	Lifter Diameter	Lifter To Bore Clearance
3.1L	1998–2002	1.8680–1.8690	.0010	.0010–.0039	—	—	—	—	—
3.4L	1999–2002	1.8680–1.8690	.0010	.0010–.0039	—	—	—	—	—
3.5L	1999–2002	1.0610–1.0620	.0020	.0016–.0033	—	—	.4727–.4736	.4716–.4721	.0014–.0016
3.8L	1998–2002	1.8462–1.8448	—	.0016–.0047	—	—	—	—	—
4.0L	1998–99	1.0610–1.0620	.0009	.0020–.0030	—	—	1.2992	1.2970–1.2980	.0010–.0030
	2001–02	1.0610–1.0619	.0020	.0020–.0030	.0059	—	.4730–.4739	.4719–.4724	.0015–.0016
4.6L	1998–99	1.0610–1.0620	—	.0020–.0030	—	—	1.2992	1.2970–1.2980	.0010–.0030
	2000–02	1.0610–1.0620	.0020	.0020–.0030	—	—	.4730–.4736	.4719–.4724	.0015–.0016
5.7L	1998–2002	2.1640–2.1660	.0020	—	.0010–.0120	—	—	—	—

① — Journal No. 1, 1.0220–1.0228 inches; journal Nos. 2 & 3, 1.1795–1.1803 inches.

② — Journal No. 1, .9822–.9829 inch; journal Nos. 2, 3, 4 & 5, .9035–.9041 inch.

③ — Working from front to rear of camshaft, diameter No. 1 dual journals 1.7373–1.7381 inches; diameter No. 2 journal 1.7451–1.7640 inches; diameter No. 3 journal 1.7350–1.7539 inches; diameter No. 4 journal 1.7609–1.7618 inches; diameter No. 5 journal 1.7687–1.7697 inches.

④ — Journal No. 1, 1.5720–1.5728 inches; journal Nos. 2, 3, 4 & 5, 1.3751–1.3760 inches.

⑤ — 1998–2000, .0016–.0047 inch.

⑥ — 1998–2000, .0001–.0035 inch.

⑦ — Bearing clearance No. 1, .0014–.0030 inches; bearing clearance Nos. 2, 3, 4 & 5, .0014–.0028 inches.

⑧ — Journal No. 1, 1.3562–1.3568 inches; journal Nos. 2, 3, 4 & 5, 1.1003–1.1010 inches.

CRANKSHAFT, BEARINGS & RODS

All Measurements Given In Inches Unless Otherwise Specified

Engine/VIN	Year	Crankshaft				Bearing Clearance			Connecting Rod Side Clearance
		Standard Journal Diameter		Out of Round All①	Taper All①	Main Bearings	Connecting Rod Bearings	Thrust Bearing Clearance	
		Main Bearing	Crank Pin						
1.0L	1998–2000	②	1.6529–1.6535	.00040	.00040	.0008–.0015	.0012–.0019	.0044–.0122	.00390–.00780
1.3L	1998–2000	②	1.6529–1.6535	.00040	.00040	.0008–.0023	.0012–.0031	—	.00390–.01370
1.6L	1998	④	—	.00320	.00320	.0006–.0039	.0008–.0031	.0006–.0118	.00590–.00980
1.8L	1998–99	③	—	.00040	.00040	.0002–.0014	.0008–.0031	.0016–.0118	.00630–.01570
	2000–02	③	—	.00080	.00080	.0006–.0013	.0011–.0024	.0016–.0038	.00630–.01350
2.2L/4	1998–2002	2.4945–2.4954	1.9983–1.9994	.00019	.00019	.0006–.0019	.0010–.0031	.0020–.0070	.00390–.01490
2.2L/F	2002	2.2045–2.2040	1.9291–1.9297	—	—	.0012–.0026	.0011–.0027	—	.00280–.01460
2.4L	1998–2002	2.3622–2.3631	1.8887–1.8897	.00020	.00030	.0004–.0023	.0004–.0026	—	.00590–.01770
3.0L	1998–2001	2.6763–2.6766	1.9270–1.9280	.00120	—	.0006–.0017	.0005–.0024	—	.00270–.01100
3.1L	1998–2002	2.6473–2.6483	1.9987–1.9994	.00020	.00020	.0008–.0025	.0007–.0024	.0012–.0030	.00700–.01700
3.4L	1999–2002	2.6473–2.6483	1.9987–1.9994	.00020	.00020	.0008–.0025	.0007–.0024	.0012–.0030	.00700–.01700

Continued

CRANKSHAFT, BEARINGS & RODS—Continued

All Measurements Given In Inches Unless Otherwise Specified

Engine/VIN	Year	Crankshaft				Bearing Clearance			Connecting Rod Side Clearance
		Standard Journal Diameter		Out of Round All①	Taper All①	Main Bearings	Connecting Rod Bearings	Thrust Bearing Clearance	
		Main Bearing	Crank Pin						
3.5L	1999–2002	2.7550–2.7560	2.1829–2.1835	.00016	.00015	.0006–.0018	.0009–.0020	—	.00400–.01300
3.8L	1998–2002	2.4988–2.4998	2.2487–2.2499	.00035	.00035	⑤	.0005–.0026	—	.00400–.02000
4.0L	1998–99	2.5335–2.5337	2.1239–2.1245	.00016	.00015	.0006–.0020	.0010–.0030	—	—
	2001–02	2.5335–2.5341	2.2139–2.1245	.00020	.00020	.0006–.0021	—	—	.00790–.01970
4.6L	1998–2002	2.5335–2.5341	2.1239–2.1245	.00016	.00016	.0006–.0025	.0010–.0030	—	.00800–.02000
5.7L	1998–2002	2.5580–2.5590	2.0991–2.0999	.00031	.00078	.0007–.0021	.0006–.0025	—	.00433–.02000

① — Maximum.

② — The counter weights of No. 1 cylinder have four stamped numbers, they indicate journal diameters at bearing caps respectively. No. 1, 1.7714–1.7716 inches; No. 2, 1.7712–1.7714 inches & No. 3, 1.7710–1.7712 inches.

③ — Stamping No. 0, 1.8897–1.8898 inches; stamping No. 1, 1.8896–1.8897 inches; stamping No. 2, 1.8895–1.8896 inches; stamping No. 3, 1.8894–1.8895 inches; stamping No. 4, 1.8893–1.8894 inches; stamping No. 5, 1.8892–1.8893 inches.

④ — Stamping No. 0, 1.8895–1.8898 inches; stamping No. 1, 1.8893–1.8895 inches; stamping No. 2, 1.8891–1.8893 inches.

⑤ — No 1. bearing clearance, .0070–.0016 inch; Nos. 2, 3 and 4, .0009–.0018 inch.

PISTONS, PINS & RINGS

All Measurements Given In Inches Unless Otherwise Specified

Engine/VIN	Year	Piston Diameter (Std.)	Piston Clearance	Piston Pin Diameter①	Piston Pin To Piston Clearance	Piston Ring End Gap②		Piston Ring Side Clearance	
						Comp.	Oil	Comp.	Oil
1.0L	1998–2000	2.9122–2.9130	.00080–.00150	—	—	.0079–.0276	.0079–.0708	③	—
1.3L	1998–2000	⑧	.00080–.00150	㉑	—	.0079–.0276	.0079–.0708	.0014–.0027	.0008–.0023
1.6L	1998	⑩	.00080–.00150	—	—	.0413	.0413	⑤	—
1.8L	1998–2000	3.1073–3.1077	.00260–.00390	.7876–.7879	㉒	㉓	.0059–.0157	㉔	—
	2001–02	3.2274–3.2281	.0003–.0015	—	㉒	㉓	.0059–.0157	㉘	—
2.2L/4	1998–2002	—	.00220–.00340	.8001–.8002	.00030–.00080	㉕	.0100–.0300	㉖	.0005–.0087
2.2L/F	2002	3.3845–3.3851	.0004–.0016	.7875–.7877	.00010–.00050	④	.0100–.0300	—	—
2.4L	1998–2002	3.5404–3.5420	.00100–.00310	.8659–.8661	.00008–.00043	⑦	.0098–.0299	⑥	—
3.0L	1998–2001	⑮	.00100–.00180	.8267	.00010–.00030	.0118–.0196	0.157–.0551	.0008–.0015	.0004–.0012
3.1L	1998–2002	3.5029–3.5040	.00130–.00270	.9052–.9054	.00040–.00080	⑬	.0098–.0500	.0020–.0033	.0080
3.4L	1999–2002	3.6209–3.6216	.00130–.00270	.9052–.9054	.00040–.00080	.0060–.0140	.0098–.0500	.0020–.0033	.0080
3.5L	1999–2002	3.5210–3.5220	.00100–.00250	.8265–.8267	.00010–.00060	⑰	.0100–.0300	.0016–.0037	⑫
3.8L/K, 1	1998	—	.00040–.00200	.8659–.8661	.00030–.00090	⑪	.0100–.0300	.0013–.0031	.0009–.0079
	1999–2000	—	.00400–.00200⑲	.8659–.8661	.00008–.00051	⑳	.0100–.0300	.0013–.0031	.0009–.0079

Continued

PISTONS, PINS & RINGS—Continued

All Measurements Given In Inches Unless Otherwise Specified

Engine/VIN	Year	Piston Diameter (Std.)	Piston Clearance	Piston Pin Diameter①	Piston Pin To Piston Clearance	Piston Ring End Gap②		Piston Ring Side Clearance	
						Comp.	Oil	Comp.	Oil
3.8L/1	1999	—	.00080–.00390⑲	.9053–.9055	.00026–.00061	⑳	.0100–.0300	.0013–.0031	.0009–.0079
3.8L/K	2001–02	—	.0004–.0020⑲	.8659–.8661	.00008–.00051	⑳	.0100–.0300	.0013–.0031	.0009–.0079
3.8L/1	2001–02	—	.0008–.0017⑲	.9053–.9055	.00026–.00061	⑳	.0100–.0300	.0013–.0031	.0009–.0079
4.0L	1998	—	.00080–.00200	.8650–.8660	—	⑨	.0100–.0300	.0020–.0040	⑫
	1999	3.4230–3.4240⑱	.00080–.00200	.8650–.8660	—	⑨	.0100–.0300	.0016–.0037	⑫
	2001–02	3.4243–3.4237	—	.8266–.8268	—	⑭	.0098–.0299	.0016–.0037	⑫
4.6L	1998	3.6597–3.6603㉗	.00080–.00200	.8650–.8660	—	⑰	.0100–.0300	.0016–.0037	⑫
	1999–2000	3.6597–3.6603㉗	.00080–.00200	.8650–.8660	—	⑰	.0100–.0300	.0016–.0037	⑫
	2001–02	3.6597–3.6603㉗	.00080–.00200	.8266–.8268	—	⑰	.0100–.0300	.0016–.0037	⑫
5.7L	1998–2000	3.8962–3.8969	.00070–.00212	.9447–.9448	.00040–.00078	.0090–.0149	.0070–.0271	⑯	.0004–.0087
	2001–02	㉙	.0005–.0029	.9447–.9448	.00040–.00078	.0090–.0170	.0070–.0290	⑯	.0003–.0069

① — Pistons & pins are matched set & should be replaced as an assembly.
② — Maximum.
③ — Top ring, .0012–.0027 inch; 2nd ring, .0008–.0023 inch.
④ — Top ring, .008–.016 inch; lower ring, .014–.022 inch.
⑤ — Top ring, .0018–.0033 inch; 2nd ring, .0012–.0028 inch.
⑥ — Top ring, .0016–.0031 inch; 2nd ring, .0012–.0028 inch.
⑦ — Top ring, .006–.012 inch; 2nd ring, .0098–.0157 inch.
⑧ — There are two standard sizes of pistons marked with a No. on top. No. 1, 2.9126–2.9130 inches; No. 2, 2.9120–2.9126 inches in diameter.
⑨ — Top ring .010–.016 inch; 2nd ring .014–.020 inch.
⑩ — There are three standard sizes of pistons marked with a No. on top. No. 1, 3.1852–3.1856 inches; No. 2, 3.1856–3.1860 inches; No. 3, 3.1860–3.1864 inches.
⑪ — Top ring, .012–.022 inch; 2nd ring, .030–.040 inch.
⑫ — Zero clearance; side sealing ring.
⑬ — Top ring, .006–.014 inch; 2nd ring, .020–.028 inch.
⑭ — First compression top, .0098–.0157 inch; second compression top, .0138–.0020 inch.
⑮ — Fit designation stamped on top of piston: (8) 3.3834–3.3838 inches; (99) 3.3838–3.3842 inches; (00) 3.3842–3.3846 inches; (01) 3.3846–3.3850 inches; (02) 3.3850–3.3854 inches.
⑯ — Top ring, .0016–.0033 inch; 2nd ring, .0016–.0031 inch.
⑰ — Top ring, .010–.016 inch; 2nd ring, .014–.020 inch.
⑱ — Measured 46mm from top of piston.
⑲ — Measured 41mm from top of piston.
⑳ — Top ring, .010–.018; 2nd ring, .023–.033 inch.
㉑ — 1998–99 .7479–.7480 inch.
㉒ — Interference fit.
㉓ — Top ring, .0098–.0138 inch; lower ring, .0138–.0197 inch.
㉔ — Top ring, .0012–.0028 inch; lower ring, .0012–.0028 inch.
㉕ — Top ring, .010–.020 inch; lower ring, .0012–.0177 inch.
㉖ — Top ring, .0020–.0035 inch; lower ring, .0016–.0031 inch.
㉗ — Measured 1.58 inch from top of piston.
㉘ — Top ring, .0098–.0138 inch; lower ring, .0009–.0028 inch.
㉙ — Non-coated, 3.8964–3.8997 inch; Coated, 3.8970–3.8990 inch.

CYLINDER BLOCK

All Measurements Given In Inches Unless Otherwise Specified

Engine/VIN	Year	Cylinder Bore Diameter (Std.)	Cylinder Bore Taper Max.	Cylinder Bore Out of Round Max.
1.0L	1998–2000	①	.00390	.0039
1.3L	1998–2000	①	.0040	.0040
1.6L	1998	3.1980–3.2177	.0005	.0050
1.8L	1998–2000	3.1102–3.1107	.0039	.0039
	2001–02	3.2283–3.2289	.0039	.0039
2.2L/4	1998–2002	3.5036–3.5043	.0005	.0005
2.2L/F	2002	3.3855–3.3861	.0004	.0004
2.4L	1998–2002	3.5430–3.5435	.0003	.0004
3.0L	1998–2001	③	.0003	.0026
3.1L	1998–2002	3.5046–3.5053	.0005	.0008
3.4L	1999–2002	3.6228–3.6235	.0004	.0003
3.5L	1999–2002	3.5230④	.0004	.0004
3.8L	1998–2002	3.8000	.0010	.0010
4.0L	1998	3.4300⑤	.0040	.0040
	1999	3.4240–3.4250④	.0040	.0040
	2001–02	3.4249–3.4255②	.0039	.0039
4.6L	1998–99	3.4240–3.4250④	.0040	.0040
	2000–02	3.6611–3.6617④	.0040	.0040
5.7L	1998–2002	3.8970–3.8980	.0007	—

① — Cylinder bore diameter Nos. are stamped on top of block in sequence. No. 1, 2.9138–2.9142 inches & No. 2, 2.9134–2.9138 inches.

② — At 1.610 inch below deck surface.

③ — Fit designation stamped on block: (8) 3.3848– 3.3852 inches; (99) 3.3852–3.3856 inches; (00) 3.3856–3.3860 inches; (01) 3.3860–3.3864 inches; (02) 3.3864–3.3868 inches.

④ — At 1.610 inch below deck surface.

⑤ — At 1.970 inch below deck surface.

OIL PUMP

All Measurements Given In Inches Unless Otherwise Specified

Engine/VIN	Year	Gear Backlash	Gear To Body Clearance	Gear End-play①	Gear Pocket		Pump Gear Thickness	Pump Gear Diameter	Relief Valve To Body Clearance
					Depth	Diameter			
1.0L	1998–2000	—	.0120	.0060	—	—	—	—	—
1.3L	1998–99	—	.0120	.0060	—	—	—	—	—
1.6L	1998	.0030–.0140	.0040	.0080	—	—	—	—	—
1.8L	1998–99	.0138	.0138	.0059	—	—	—	—	—
	2000–02	.0138	.0118	.0059	—	—	—	—	—
2.2L/4	1998–2002	.0040–.0080	.0002–.0030	.0020–.0070	1.1950–1.1980	1.5030–1.5060	.6727–.6731	1.498–1.500	.0015–.0035
2.2L/F	2002	—	—	—	—	—	—	—	—
2.4L	1998	.0091–.0201	—	—	.6736–.6756	2.1273–2.1292	.6727–.6731	—	—
	1999–2002	.0029–.0055	—	—	.6023–.6043	1.7730–1.7750	.5994–.6003	—	—
3.0L②	1998–2001	—	—	—	—	—	—	—	—
3.1L	1998–2002	.0040–.0080	.0010–.0030	.0020–.0050	1.2020–1.2040	1.5030–1.5050	1.1990–1.2000	1.4980–1.5000	.0015–.0035
3.4L	1999–2002	.0037–.0077	.0010–.0030	.0020–.0050	1.2020–1.2040	1.5030–1.5050	1.1990–1.2000	1.4980–1.5000	.0015–.0035
3.5L②	1999–2002	—	—	—	—	—	—	—	—
3.8L	1998–2002	.0060	.0080–.0150	.0010–.0035	.4610–.4625	3.5080–3.5120	—	—	.0015–.0030
4.0L②	1998–99	—	—	—	—	—	—	—	—
	2001–02	—	—	—	—	—	—	—	—
4.6L②	1998–2002	—	—	—	—	—	—	—	—
5.7L②	1998–2002	—	—	—	—	—	—	—	—

① — Measured between pump cover & end of gears using straightedge & feeler gauge.

② — Pump components are not serviced separately. If any component is damaged or worn, pump should be replaced.

Saturn

INDEX

CYLINDER HEAD, VALVE GUIDE & VALVE SEATS

All Specifications Given In Inches Unless Otherwise Specified

Engine	Cylinder Head Warp-age Limit	Cylinder Head Overall Thickness	Valve Guides			Valve Seats			
			Standard I.D.	Stem To Guide Clear-ance		Seat Angle, Deg.	Seat Width		Runout
				Intake	Exhaust		Intake	Exhaust	
1.9L SOHC	①	4.4440–4.4540	.2751–.2761	.0010–.0025	.0015–.0032	44.5–45.5°	.0394–.0512	.0512–.0630	—
1.9L DOHC	①	4.4449–4.4527	.2750–.2760	.0010–.0025	.0015–.0032	44.5–45.5°	.0394–.0512	.0512–.0630	—
2.2L DOHC	.0200	—	.2362–.2367	.0012–.0022	.0016–.0026	45°	.0310	.0310	.0020
3.0L DOHC	.0020/3.9370	5.2720–5.2800	—	.0012–.0022	.0016–.0026	45°	.0394–.0551	.0551–.0709	—

SOHC — Single Overhead Cam
DOHC — Dual Overhead Cam

① — Longitudinal deck, .0040 inch; transverse deck, .0020 inch.

VALVE SPRINGS

All Specifications Given In Inches, Unless Otherwise Specified

Engine	Year	Free Length	Seated Press., Lbs. @ Inches	Comp. Press., Lbs. @ Inches	Out Of Square Limit
1.9L SOHC	1998–2002	1.8898–1.9134	76–87 @ 1.610	202–211 @ 1.280	.100
1.9L DOHC	1998–99	1.6100	55–65 @ 1.380	126–142 @ .984	.100
	2000–02	1.5600	42–48 @ 1.221	99–109 @ .874	.100

SOHC — Single Overhead Cam

DOHC — Dual Overhead Cam

VALVES

All Specifications Given In Inches, Unless Otherwise Specified

Engine	Stem Diameter		Clearance①		Face Angle	Margin Min.
	Intake	Exhaust	Intake	Exhaust		
1.9L SOHC	.2736–.2741	.2736–.2740	.0010–.0025	.0015–.0032	44.75–45.25°	②
1.9L DOHC	.2736–.2740	.2726–.2736	.0010–.0025	.0015–.0032	45.00–45.50°	②
2.2L DOHC	.2362–.2367	.2362–.2367	.0012–.0022	.0016–.0026	45°	.0310
3.0L DOHC	.2344–.2350	.2341–.2346	.0012–.0022	.0016–.0026	45°	③

SOHC — Single Overhead Cam
DOHC — Dual Overhead Cam
① — Between valve guide bushing & valve.

② — Intake width, .0350 inch; exhaust width, .0390 inch.
③ — Intake width, .0394 inch; exhaust width, .0551 inch.

CAMSHAFT

All Specifications Given In Inches, Unless Otherwise Specified

Engine	Camshaft Journal Diameter	Maximum Journal Runout	Camshaft Bearing Clearance	Camshaft Endplay	Rocker Arm Oil Clearance	Lifter Bore Diameter	Lifter Diameter	Lifter To Bore Clearance
1.9L SOHC	1.7480–1.7490	.0020–.0028	.0020–.0040	.0028–.0079	—	—	.8420–.8427	.0007–.0024
1.9L DOHC	1.1398–1.1406	.0020–.0040	.0021–.0030	.0020–.0080	—	—	1.2976–1.2982	.0010–.0026
2.2L DOHC	1.0604–1.0614	—	.0016–.0034	.0016–.0057	—	—	.8215–.8236	.0007–.0024
3.0L DOHC	1.0990–1.0100	—	.0015–.0020	.0016–.0057	—	—	1.2976–1.2982	.0010–.0026

SOHC — Single Overhead Cam

DOHC — Dual Overhead Cam

CRANKSHAFT, BEARINGS & RODS

All Specifications Given In Inches, Unless Otherwise Specified

Engine	Crankshaft				Bearing Clearance			Connecting Rod	
	Standard Journal Diameter		Out Of Round, All①	Taper, All①	Main Bearings	Connecting Rod Bearings	Thrust Bearing Clearance	Pin Bore Diameter	Side Clearance
	Main Bearing	Crank Pin							
1.9L	2.2438–2.2444	1.8500–1.8508	.0004	.0004	.0002–.0020	.0001–.0021	.0020–.0089	.7679–.7685	.0065–.0171
2.2L	2.2045–2.2050	1.9291–1.9297	.0026	.0026	.0012–.0026	.0004–.0016	.0011–.0027	.7872–.7874	.0028–.0146
3.0L	②	1.9270–1.9190	.0012	.0012	.0006–.0017	.0005–.0024	—	.7877–.7882	.0027–.0110

① — Maximum.

② — Standard size green, 2.6763–2.6766; standard size brown, 2.6766–2.6770.

PISTONS, PINS & RINGS

All Specifications Given In Inches, Unless Otherwise Specified

Engine	Piston Diameter (Std.)①	Piston Clearance	Piston Pin Diameter②③	Piston Pin To Piston Clearance	Piston Ring End Gap, Min.		Piston Ring Side Clearance	
					Comp.	Oil	Comp.	Oil
1.9L	3.2270–3.2277	④	.7676–.7677	.0001–.0004	.0098	.0197	⑤	—
2.2L	3.3845–3.3851	.0004–.0016	.7875–.7877	.0001–.0005	⑥	.0100–.0300	.0012–.0027	—
3.0L	3.3834–3.3828	.0001–.0003	.8267	.0010–.0018	.0118–.0196	.0157–.0551	.0008–.0015	.0004–.0012

① — Measured @ .20 inch from bottom of piston.

② — Pistons & pins are matched set & should be replaced as an assembly.

③ — Minimum.

④ — Bore 1, 2 & 3, .0002–.0017 inch; bore 4, .0006–.0021 inch.

⑤ — Top ring, .0016–.0035 inch; 2nd ring, .0012–.0031 inch.

⑥ — Top ring, .008–.016 inch; 2nd ring, .014–.022.

CYLINDER BLOCK

All Specifications Given In Inches, Unless Otherwise Specified

Engine	Cylinder Bore Dia. (Std.)	Cylinder Bore Taper, Max.	Cylinder Bore Out Of Round, Max.
1.9L	①	.0020	.0020
2.2L	3.3855–3.3861	.0004	.0004
3.0L	3.3848–3.3852	.0003	.0026

① — Cylinder bores 1, 2 & 3, 3.2280–3.2287 inches; cylinder bore No. 4, 3.2283–3.2291 inches.

OIL PUMP

All Specifications Given In Inches, Unless Otherwise Specified

Engine	Body To Side Clearance	Gear To Body Clearance	Tip Clearance	Gear Pocket		Pump Gear Thickness	Pump Gear Diameter	Relief Valve To Body Clearance
				Depth	Diameter			
1.9L	.0060–.0110	.0016–.0049	.0060	—	—	—	—	—
2.2L	.0120	.0030	.0060	—	—	—	—	—
3.0L	.0110	①	.0060	—	—	—	—	—

① — Inner gear to housing, .003 inch; outer gear to housing, .004 inch.

DECIMAL & MILLIMETER EQUIVALENTS

Inch	Inch	mm
1/64	.015625	.397
1/32	.03125	.794
3/64	.046875	1.191
1/16	.0625	1.587
5/64	.078125	1.984
3/32	.09375	2.381
7/64	.109375	2.778
1/8	.125	3.175
9/64	.140625	3.572
5/32	.15625	3.969
11/64	.17185	4.366
3/16	.1875	4.762
13/64	.203125	5.159
7/32	.21875	5.556
15/64	.234375	5.953
1/4	.25	6.350
17/64	.265626	6.747
9/32	.28125	7.144
19/64	.296875	7.541
5/16	.3125	7.937
21/64	.328125	8.334
11/32	.34375	8.731

Inch	Inch	mm
23/64	.359375	9.128
3/8	.375	9.525
25/64	.390625	9.922
13/32	.40625	10.319
27/64	.421875	10.716
7/16	.4375	11.113
29/64	.453125	11.509
15/32	.46875	11.906
31/64	.484375	12.303
1/2	.5	12.700
33/64	.515625	13.097
17/32	.53125	13.494
35/64	.546875	13.890
9/16	.5625	14.287
37/64	.578125	14.684
19/32	.59375	15.081
39/64	.609375	15.478
5/8	.625	15.875
41/64	.640625	16.272
21/32	.65625	16.669
43/64	.671875	17.065

Inch	Inch	mm
11/16	.6875	17.462
45/64	.703125	17.859
23/32	.71875	18.265
47/64	.734375	18.653
3/4	.75	19.505
49/64	.765625	19.447
25/32	.78125	19.884
51/64	.796875	20.240
13/16	.8125	20.637
53/64	.828125	21.034
27/32	.84375	21.431
55/64	.859375	21.828
7/8	.875	22.225
57/64	.890625	22.622
29/32	.90625	23.019
59/64	.921875	23.415
15/16	.9375	23.812
61/64	.953125	24.209
31/32	.96875	24.606
63/64	.984375	25.003
1	1	25.400

Special Service Tools

Throughout this manual references are made to and illustrations may depict the use of special tools required to perform certain jobs. These special tools can generally be ordered through the dealers of the make vehicle being serviced. It is also suggested that you check with local automotive supply firms as they also supply tools manufactured by other firms that will assist in the performance of these jobs. The vehicle manufacturers special tools are supplied by:

Chrysler Corporation........................ Miller Special Tools
OTC Division
28635 Mound Rd.
Warren, Michigan 48092-3499

Ford Motor Company .... SPX Corporation, OTC
Attn: Ford Rotunda
28635 Mound Rd.
Warren, Michigan 48092-3499

General Motors Corporation .... Kent-Moore
SPX Corporation
28635 Mound Rd.
Warren, Michigan 48092-3499

Hearst Business Publishing, Inc.
5600 Crooks Rd. Ste. 200 Troy, MI 48098
(248) 828-0000 • Fax (248) 828-0215
1 (800) 4A-MOTOR
www.motor.com

MOTOR

CUSTOMER COMMENT CARD

Dear Valued Customer:

Please use this form to advise us of any questions, comments, and/or recommendations that you have regarding this manual.

Thank you, your feedback is extremely important to us.

Service Manual Title: ______

Edition: ______

Page No.: ______ Vehicle Model & Year: ______

Comments: ______

______

______

______

Name: ______

Company: ______

Address: ______

City: ______ State: ______ Zip: ______

Phone: ______ Date: ______

Hearst Business Publishing, Inc.
5600 Crooks Rd. Ste. 200 Troy, MI 48098
(248) 828-0000 • Fax (248) 828-0215
1 (800) 4A-MOTOR
www.motor.com

MOTOR

CUSTOMER COMMENT CARD

Dear Valued Customer:

Please use this form to advise us of any questions, comments, and/or recommendations that you have regarding this manual.

Thank you, your feedback is extremely important to us.

Service Manual Title: ______

Edition: ______

Page No.: ______ Vehicle Model & Year: ______

Comments: ______

______

______

______

Name: ______

Company: ______

Address: ______

City: ______ State: ______ Zip: ______

Phone: ______ Date: ______

Hearst Business Publishing, Inc.
5600 Crooks Rd. Ste. 200 Troy, MI 48098
(248) 828-0000 • Fax (248) 828-0215
1 (800) 4A-MOTOR
www.motor.com

MOTOR

CUSTOMER COMMENT CARD

Dear Valued Customer:

Please use this form to advise us of any questions, comments, and/or recommendations that you have regarding this manual.

Thank you, your feedback is extremely important to us.

Service Manual Title: ______

Edition: ______

Page No.: ______ Vehicle Model & Year: ______

Comments: ______

______

______

______

Name: ______

Company: ______

Address: ______

City: ______ State: ______ Zip: ______

Phone: ______ Date: ______

NO POSTAGE
NECESSARY
IF MAILED
IN THE
UNITED STATES

BUSINESS REPLY MAIL

FIRST CLASS PERMIT NO. 415 TROY, MI

POSTAGE WILL BE PAID BY ADDRESSEE

ATTN: BOOK PRODUCT SUPPORT
5600 CROOKS ROAD, SUITE 200
TROY, MI 48098-9928

NO POSTAGE
NECESSARY
IF MAILED
IN THE
UNITED STATES

BUSINESS REPLY MAIL

FIRST CLASS PERMIT NO. 415 TROY, MI

POSTAGE WILL BE PAID BY ADDRESSEE

ATTN: BOOK PRODUCT SUPPORT
5600 CROOKS ROAD, SUITE 200
TROY, MI 48098-9928

NO POSTAGE
NECESSARY
IF MAILED
IN THE
UNITED STATES

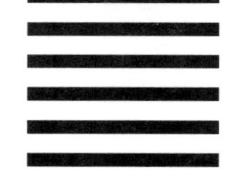

BUSINESS REPLY MAIL

FIRST CLASS PERMIT NO. 415 TROY, MI

POSTAGE WILL BE PAID BY ADDRESSEE

ATTN: BOOK PRODUCT SUPPORT
5600 CROOKS ROAD, SUITE 200
TROY, MI 48098-9928

MANUAL INFORMATION LOCATOR

Front Wheel Drive Models

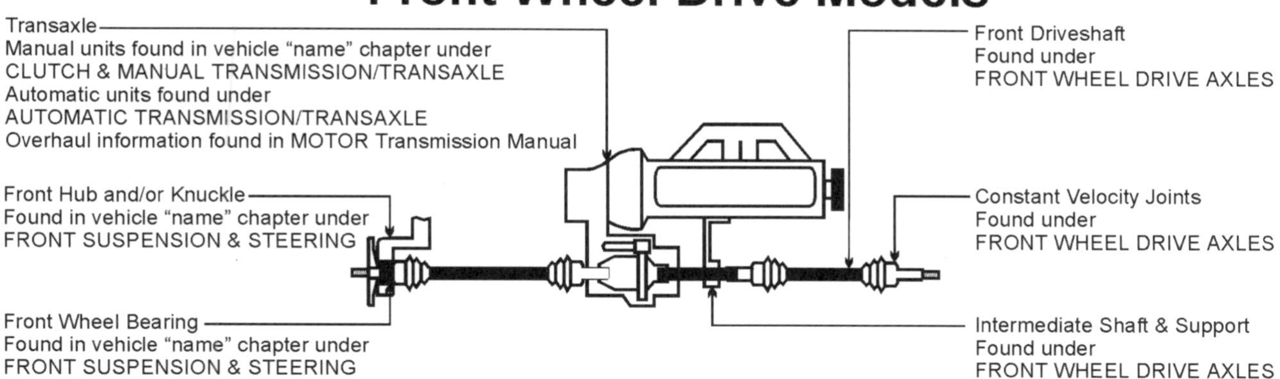

All Wheel Drive Models

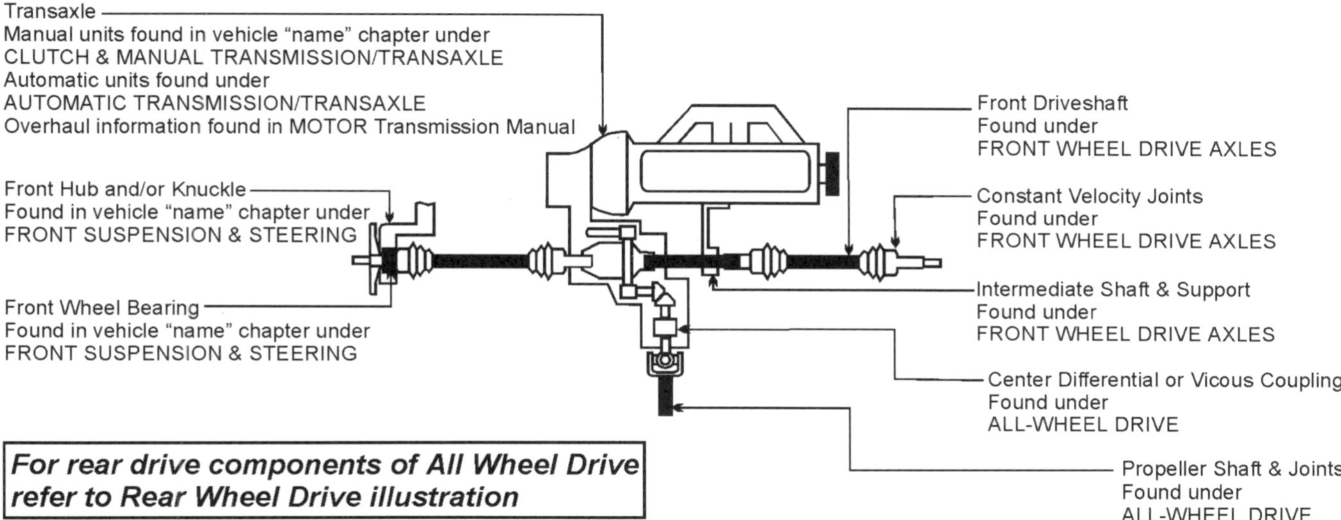

For rear drive components of All Wheel Drive refer to Rear Wheel Drive illustration

Rear Wheel Drive Models

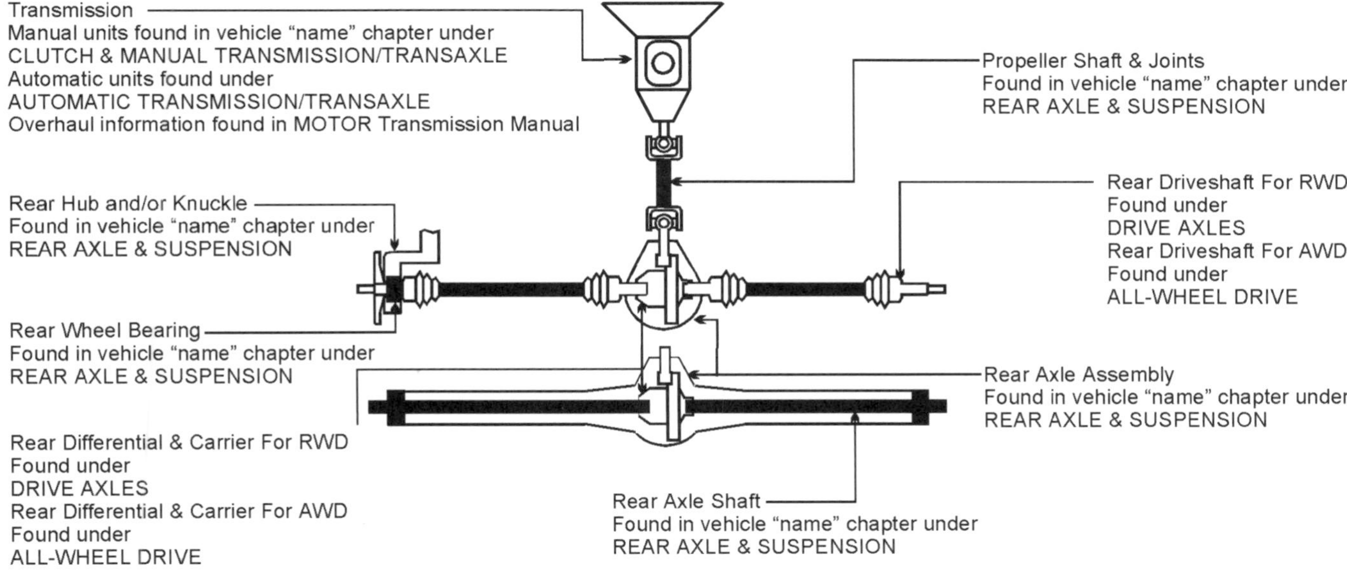

MANUAL INFORMATION LOCATOR—Continued

Operation/Subject/Topic	Auto Repair Manual, Vol. 1	Auto Repair Manual, Vol. 2	Domestic Engine Performance & Driveability Manual
Air Bags	—	X	—
Air Bag System Precautions	X	X	X
Air Conditioning	X	—	—
AIR Systems	—	—	X
All-Wheel Drive Systems	X	—	—
Alternator Specifications	X	—	—
Alternator Systems	X	—	—
Anti-Lock Brake Systems	—	X	—
Automatic Seat Belts	—	X	—
Automatic Transaxle In-Vehicle Service	X	—	—
Automatic Transmission In-Vehicle Service	X	—	—
Axle Shaft Service	X	—	—
Back-Up Light Switch, Replace	X	—	—
Balance Shaft Service	X	—	—
Ball Joint Service	X	—	—
Belt Tension Data	X	—	—
Blower Motor, Replace	X	—	—
Brake Booster Service	X	—	—
Brake Service	X	—	—
Camber Adjustment	X	—	—
Camshaft Service	X	—	—
Capacity Data	X	—	—
Caster Adjustment	X	—	—
Catalytic Converters	—	—	X
Clutch Service	X	—	—
Clutch Start Switch, Replace	X	—	—
Coil Pack, Replace	X	—	X
Coil Spring, Replace	X	—	—
Compression Check	X	—	X
Compression Pressures	X	—	X
Computer Relearn Procedures	X	X	X
Computerized Engine Control Systems	—	—	X
Control Arm Service	X	—	—
Cooling System Bleed	X	—	—
Cooling System Data	X	—	—
Crankshaft Pulley, Replace	X	—	—
Crankshaft Rear Oil Seal Service	X	—	—
Cruise Control Systems	—	X	—
Cylinder Block Specifications	X	—	—
Cylinder Head Service	X	—	—
Cylinder Head Specifications	X	—	—
Cylinder Head, Replace	X	—	—
Cylinder Liner, Replace	X	—	—
Dash Panel Service	—	X	—
Differential Service	X	—	—
Dimmer Switch, Replace	X	—	—
Disc Brake Service	X	—	—
Distributor Service	—	—	X
Distributor, Replace	X	—	X
Distributorless Ignition Systems	—	—	X
Drive Axle Service	X	—	—
Drive Belt Tension Data	X	—	—
Drum Brake Service	X	—	—
EGR System	—	—	X
Electric Engine Cooling Fans	X	—	—
Electric Fuel Pumps	X	—	X
Electrical Symbol Identification	X	X	X
Electronic Fuel Injection	—	—	X
Electronic Ignition	—	—	X
Electronic Instrumentation	—	—	X
Electronic Level Controls	—	X	—

Operation/Subject/Topic	Auto Repair Manual, Vol. 1	Auto Repair Manual, Vol. 2	Domestic Engine Performance & Driveability Manual
Emission Control Application Charts	—	—	X
Emission Controls	—	—	X
Emission Vacuum Hose Routings	—	—	X
Engine Compartment Reference Diagrams	—	—	X
Engine Cooling Fans	X	—	—
Engine Control Module, Replace	—	—	X
Engine Control Unit, Replace	—	—	X
Engine Front Cover Service	X	—	—
Engine Mounts, Replace	X	—	—
Engine Oil Seal Service	X	—	—
Engine Rebuilding Specifications	X	—	—
Engine Repairs	X	—	—
Engine Sensor Location	—	—	X
Engine Sensor Replacement	—	—	X
Engine Sensor Specifications	—	—	X
Engine System Identification Charts	—	—	X
Engine Tightening Specifications	X	—	—
Engine, Replace	X	—	—
Evaporator Core, Replace	X	—	—
Exhaust Gas Recirculation (EGR) Systems	—	—	X
Exhaust Manifold, Replace	X	—	—
Fast Idle Speed Adjustment	—	—	X
Federal Air Quality Standards	—	—	X
Flasher Location	X	—	—
Front Drive Axle Service	X	—	—
Front Wheel Alignment	X	—	—
Fuel Control System Identification	—	—	X
Fuel Filter, Replace	X	—	—
Fuel Injection Systems	—	—	X
Fuel Injector Cleaning Procedures	—	—	X
Fuel Injector, Replace	—	—	X
Fuel Pump Pressure Specifications	X	—	X
Fuel Pump Pressure Test	—	—	X
Fuel Pump Relay Location	X	—	X
Fuel Pump Replacement	X	—	X
Fuse Panel Location	X	—	—
General Engine Specifications	X	—	—
Headlight Switch, Replace	X	—	—
Heated Air Cleaners	—	—	X
Heater Core, Replace	X	—	—
Hub & Bearing Assembly Service	X	—	—
Hydraulic Brake System Service	X	—	—
Hydraulic Engine Cooling Fans	X	—	—
Hydraulic Valve LIfter Service	X	—	—
Idle Mixture Adjustments	—	—	X
Idle Speed Adjustments	—	—	X
Ignition Lock, Replace	X	—	—
Ignition Switch, Replace	X	—	—
Ignition System Application	—	—	X
Ignition Timing Procedures	—	—	X
Instrument Cluster, Replace	X	—	—
Intake Manifold, Replace	X	—	—
Intermittent Malfunction Computer Diagnosis	—	—	X
Knock Sensor, Replace	—	—	X
Leaf Spring, Replace	X	—	—
Lift Point Illustrations	X	X	—
Locking Differential Service	X	—	—
Locking Hub Service	X	—	—
Lower Ball Joint, Replace	X	—	—